Who'sWho in America®

Biographical Titles Currently Published by Marquis Who's Who

Who's Who in America
Who's Who in America Junior & Senior High School Version
Who Was Who in America
  Historical Volume (1607–1896)
  Volume I (1897–1942)
  Volume II (1943–1950)
  Volume III (1951–1960)
  Volume IV (1961–1968)
  Volume V (1969–1973)
  Volume VI (1974–1976)
  Volume VII (1977–1981)
  Volume VIII (1982–1985)
  Volume IX (1985–1989)
  Volume X (1989–1993)
  Index Volume (1607–1993)
Who's Who in the World
Who's Who in the East
Who's Who in the Midwest
Who's Who in the South and Southwest
Who's Who in the West
Who's Who in American Education
Who's Who in American Law
Who's Who in American Nursing
Who's Who of American Women
Who's Who of Emerging Leaders in America
Who's Who in Finance and Industry
Who's Who in Science and Engineering
Index to Marquis Who's Who Publications
The *Official* ABMS Directory of Board Certified Medical Specialists

Who's Who in America®

1995

49th Edition

Volume 3
Indexes

A Gift from the Estate of
Michael S. Hart

www.gutenberg.org

MARQUIS
Who's Who
A REED REFERENCE PUBLISHING COMPANY

121 Chanlon Road
New Providence, NJ 07974 U.S.A.

Marquis Who's Who
Who's Who in America®

Managing Director	Leigh C. Yuster-Freeman
Editorial Director	Paul Canning
Senior Managing Editor	Fred M. Marks

Editorial

Senior Editor	Harriet L. Tiger
Associate Editor	Kristin Anna Eckes
Assistant Editors	Hazel C. Conner
	Roger N. Generazzo
	Jacqueline M. Lewis
	Eileen McGuinness
	Stephanie A. Palenque
	Josh Samber
	Rebecca Sultzbaugh
Editorial Coordinator	Rose Marvin

Editorial Services

Manager	Nadine Hovan
Supervisors	Debra Krom
	Mary Lyn K. Sodano
Coordinator	Anne Marie C. Calcagno

Editorial Support

Manager	Kevin E. Frank
Coordinator	Sharon L. Gonzalez
Staff	J. Hector Gonzalez

Mail Processing

Manager	Kara A. Seitz
Staff	Shawn Johnston
	Cheryl A. Rodriguez
	Jill S. Terbell
	Scott Van Houten

Database Operations

Supervisor	Ren Reiner

Research

Senior Researcher	William Cherf
Researcher/Librarian	Patrick Gibbons
Researchers	Carl R. Edolo
	Connie Harbison
	Christina Moxley
Research Assistants	Lisa A. Heft
	Rosemarie Iannuzzi

Support Services

Assistant	Jeanne Danzig

Reed Reference Publishing

President, CEO Ira Siegel   **Executive Vice President** Andrew W. Meyer
Senior Vice President, Database Publishing Peter E. Simon   **Senior Vice President, Marketing** Stanley Walker
Senior Vice President, Sales Edward J. Roycroft   **Vice President & Publisher** Sandra S. Barnes

Table of Contents

Introduction

The *Who's Who in America* Geographic and Professional Indexes provide access to biographical information in the forty-ninth edition through two avenues in alphabetical form—geography and profession. Each Biographee entry contains name and occupational description. A dagger symbol (†) indicates a new name first appearing in the forty-ninth edition.

The Geographic Index lists names in the United States under state and city designations, as well as Biographees in American territories. Canadian listings include provinces and cities. Names in Mexico and other countries appear by city. Biographees whose addresses are not published in their sketches are found under Address Unpublished.

The Professional Index includes thirty-eight categories ranging alphabetically from Agriculture to Social Science. Within each area, the names appear under geographic subheadings. Names without published addresses appear at the end of each professional area listing under Address Unpublished. If the occupation does not fall within one of the specified areas, the name is listed under Unclassified.

Some Biographees have professions encompassing more than one area; each of these appears under the field best suited to the Biographee's occupation. Thus, while most bankers are listed under Finance: Banking Services, investment bankers are found in Finance: Investment Services. A Biographee with two or more diverse occupations is found under the area that best fits his or her professional profile.

The Retiree Index lists the names of those individuals whose biographical sketches last appeared in the forty-sixth, forty-seventh, or forty-eighth edition of *Who's Who in America*.

The Necrology lists Biographees of the forty-eighth edition whose deaths were reported to Marquis prior to the close of the compilation of this edition of *Who's Who in America*.

Alphabetical Practices

Names are arranged alphabetically according to the surnames, and under identical surnames according to the first given name. If both surname and first given name are identical, names are arranged alphabetically according to the second given name.

Surnames beginning with De, Des, Du, however capitalized or spaced, are recorded with the prefix preceding the surname and arranged alphabetically under the letter D.

Surnames beginning with Mac and Mc are arranged alphabetically under M.

Surnames beginning with Saint or St. appear after names that begin Sains, and are arranged according to the second part of the name, e.g. St. Clair before Saint Dennis.

Surnames beginning with Van, Von, or von are arranged alphabetically under the letter V.

Compound surnames are arranged according to the first member of the compound.

Many hyphenated Arabic names begin Al-, El-, or al-. These names are alphabetized according to each Biographee's designation of last name. Thus Al-Bahar, Mohammed may be listed either under Al- or under Bahar, depending on the preference of the listee.

Parentheses used in connection with a name indicate which part of the full name is usually deleted in common usage. Hence Abbott, W(illiam) Lewis indicates that the usual form of the given name is W. Lewis. In such a case, the parentheses are ignored in alphabetizing and the name would be arranged as Abbott, William Lewis. However, if the name is recorded Abbott, (William) Lewis, signifying that the entire name William is not commonly used, the alphabetizing would be arranged as though the name were Abbott, Lewis. If an entire middle or last name is enclosed in parentheses, that portion of the name is used in the alphabetical arrangement. Hence Abbott, William (Lewis) would be arranged as Abbott, William Lewis.

Geographic Index

†New name in *Who's Who in America*, 49th Edition

UNITED STATES

ALABAMA

Albertville
Johnson, Clark Everette, Jr. judge

Alexander City
Gade, Marvin Francis retired paper company executive
Shuler, Ellie Givan, Jr. retired air force officer

Andalusia
Fuller, William Sidney lawyer

Anniston
Andrews, Glenn farmer, former congressman
Ayers, Harry Brandt editor, publisher, columnist
Harwell, Edwin Whitley judge
Klinefelter, James Louis lawyer

Auburn
Alderman, Charles Wayne business educator
Aldridge, Melvin Dayne electrical engineering educator
Amacher, Richard Earl literature educator
Andelson, Robert Vernon social philosopher, educator
Bailey, Wilford Sherrill parisitology educator, science administrator, university president
†Ball, Donald Maury agronomist, consultant
Barker, Kenneth Neil pharmacy administration educator
Barker, Larry Lee communications educator
Barth, James Richard finance educator
Carr, Howard Earl physicist, educator
Cochran, John Euell, Jr. aerospace engineer, educator, lawyer
Crocker, Malcolm John mechanical engineer, noise control engineer, educator
†Frobish, Lowell Thomas agriculturist, researcher
Galbraith, Ruth Legg retired university dean, home economist
Irwin, John David electrical engineering educator
Jaeger, Richard Charles electrical engineer, educator, science center director
Klesius, Phillip Harry microbiologist, researcher
Lemke, Paul Arenz botany educator
Lewis, Walter David historian
†Little, Ted David lawyer
Littleton, Taylor Dowe humanities educator
Millman, Richard George architect, educator
Molz, Fred John, III hydrologist, educator
Muse, William Van university president
†Owens, John Murry dean
Perez, Joseph Dominique physics educator
Philpott, Harry Melvin former university president
Rainer, Rex Kelly civil engineer, educator
Reeve, Thomas Gilmour academic administrator
Rouse, Roy Dennis retired university dean
Samford, Thomas Drake, III university general counsel
Schafer, Robert Louis agricultural engineer, researcher
Skelton, Robert Beattie language educator
Teague, Sam Fuller association executive, educator,
Turnquist, Paul Kenneth agricultural engineer, educator
Vaughan, John Thomas veterinarian, educator, university dean
Voitle, Robert Allen college dean, physiologist

Bessemer
Allison, Robert Arthur retired professional stock car driver
Bains, Lee Edmundson lawyer, state official
Clarke, McKinley A. secondary educator

Birmingham
Acker, William Marsh, Jr. federal judge
Adams, John Powers lawyer
Alexander, James Patrick lawyer
Allen, James Madison family practice physician, lawyer, consultant
Allen, Lee Norcross historian, educator
Allen, Maryon Pittman former senator, journalist, lecturer, interior and clothing designer
Alling, Charles Calvin, III oral-maxillofacial surgeon, educator, writer
Appleton, Joseph Hayne civil engineer, educator
†Arrington, Richard, Jr. mayor
Austin, Charles John health services educator
Bailey, Charles Stanley banker
Bailey, Thomas Edward newspaper editor, book publisher
Balch, Samuel Eason lawyer
†Banton, Julian Watts banker
Barker, Samuel Booth former university dean, physiology and biology educator
Barker, Thomas Watson, Jr. energy company executive
†Barrow, Richard Edward architect
Barton, James Clyde, Jr. hematologist, medical oncologist
Bauman, Robert Poe physicist
Baxter, Arthur Pearce financial services marketing company executive
Benditt, Theodore Matthew humanities educator
†Bennett, Jim secretary of state
Bennett, Joe Claude university president
Berte, Neal Richard college president
†Birkedal-Hansen, Henning dentist, educator
Blackburn, Sharon Lovelace federal judge
Blan, Ollie Lionel, Jr. lawyer
Blount, William Houston construction materials company executive
Boomershine, Donald Eugene bureau executive, development official
Booth, Rachel Zonelle nursing educator
Bowron, Richard Anderson retired utilities executive
Bradley, John M(iller), Jr. forestry executive
Bridgers, William Frank physician, educator
Brock, Harry Blackwell, Jr. banker
†Brough, James A. airport terminal executive
Brown, Ephraim Taylor, Jr. lawyer
Brown, Jerry William cell biology and anatomy educator
Bruno, Ronald G. food service executive
Bueschen, Anton Joslyn physician, educator
Bugg, Charles Edward biochemistry educator, scientist
Caplan, Lester optometrist, educator
†Carr, William mining company executive
Carruthers, Thomas Neely, Jr. lawyer
Carter, Frances Tunnell (Fran Carter) fraternal organization administrator
Carter, John Thomas retired educational administrator, writer
Casey, Ronald Bruce journalist
Caulfield, James Benjamin pathologist, educator
Chrencik, Frank chemical company executive
†Clapp, Laurel Rebecca law librarian, law educator
Clarke, Juanita M. Waiters education educator
Clemon, U. W. federal judge
Coleman, Brittin Turner lawyer
Coleman, John James lawyer
Collier, Felton Moreland architect, planner, developer, detention, and recreation consultant, lecturer
Comer, Donald, III investment company executive
Cooper, Jerome A. lawyer
Cooper, Max Dale physician, medical educator, researcher
Copeland, Hunter Armstrong real estate executive
Cornelius, Walter Felix lawyer
Corts, Thomas Edward university president
Crichton, Douglas Bentley editor, writer
†Cullum, Mark Edward editorial cartoonist
Culp, Charles Allen financial executive
†Curtis, John J. medical educator
Dahl, Hilbert Douglas mining company executive
Daniel, Kenneth Rule former iron and steel manufacturing company executive
Davis, Julian Mason, Jr. lawyer
Dekich, Sherlie Eugene insurance company executive
Denson, William Frank, III lawyer
Dentiste, Paul George city and regional planning executive
Devane, Denis James health care company executive
de Windt, Edward Mandell manufacturing executive
Diethelm, Arnold Gillespie surgeon
Dover, James Burrell insurance executive
Durant, John Ridgeway physician
Edmonds, William Fleming retired engineering and construction company executive
Farley, Joseph McConnell lawyer
Fincher, John Albert college official, consultant
†Fine, Philip Russel medical educator
†Finebaum, Paul Alan sports columnist
Finley, Sara Crews medical geneticist, educator
Finley, Wayne House medical educator
†Floyd, John Alex, Jr. editor, marketing executive, horticulturist
Foft, John William physician, educator
Fowler, C. Thomas power equipment manufacturing executive
†Franklin, H. Allen electric company executive
Fraser, Robert Gordon diagnostic radiologist
Friedel, Robert Oliver physician
†Friedlander, Michael J. neuroscientist, animal physiologist, medical educator
Friend, Edward Malcolm, Jr. lawyer
Friend, Edward Malcolm, III lawyer
Fullmer, Harold Milton dentist, educator
Gaede, Anton Henry, Jr. lawyer
Gaffney, Michael Scully diversified manufacturing company executive
Gallups, Vivian Lylay Bess federal contracting officer
†Garcia, Julio Hernan pathology educator
Geer, Jack Charles retired pathology educator
Gerlach, Gary G. botanical garden director, columnist
Gewin, James W. lawyer
Giger, Joyce Anne Newman nursing educator, consultant
Gilbert, Rodney C. engineering executive
Gilbert, Roy W., Jr. banker
Glaze, Robert Pinckney retired university administrator
Goldman, Jay university dean, industrial engineer, educator
Goodrich, Thomas Michael engineering and construction executive
Gross, Iris Lee association executive
†Gross, Michael S. secondary school principal
Guin, Junius Foy, Jr. federal judge
Gunter, John Richmond communications executive
†Hairston, W(illiam) George, III nuclear power company executive
Hamilton, Virginia Van der Veer historian, educator
Hancock, James Hughes federal judge
Hanson, Victor Henry, II newspaper publisher
†Hanson, Victor Henry, III publishing executive
†Harbert, Raymond J. transportation executive
Hardin, Edward Lester, Jr. lawyer
Harris, Aaron management consultant
Harris, Elmer Beseler electric utility executive
Henderson, Louis Clifton, Jr. management consultant
Hendley, Dan Lunsford retired university official
†Hess, Emil Carl retail apparel company executive
†Hester, Wayne journalist
Hill, Samuel Richardson, Jr. medical educator
Hirschowitz, Basil Isaac physician
Horsley, Richard D. banker
Hull, William Edward provost, theology educator
Hutchins, William Bruce, III utility company executive
Irons, George Vernon history educator
Jackson, Harold journalist
†Johnsey, Walter F. manufacturing executive
†Johnson, Emmett Raymond hospital administrator
Johnson, Joseph H., Jr. lawyer
Jones, Arthur McDonald, Sr. consumer products company executive
Jones, D. Paul, Jr. banker, lawyer
Kelley, Everette Eugene retail company executive
†Kemp, Kathryn deVan newswriter, photographer
Kennedy, Joe David, Jr. (Joey Kennedy) editor
†Kennedy, Ted C. engineering executive
Kennedy, Theodore Clifford engineering and construction company executive, consultant
†Kirklin, John Webster surgeon
†Knox, James Lloyd bishop
Kochakian, Charles Daniel endocrinologist, educator
Koopman, William James medical educator, internist, immunologist
Krulitz, Leo Morrion manufacturing executive
Kuehn, Ronald L., Jr. natural resources company executive
Lacy, Alexander Shelton lawyer
†Lee, James A. health facility finance executive
Lee, James Michael education educator
Lewis, James Eldon health care executive
Liu, Ray Ho forensic science program director, educator
Lloyd, Lewis Keith, Jr. surgery and urology educator
Long, Thad Gladden lawyer
Longenecker, Herbert Eugene biochemist, former university president
Lynne, Seybourn Harris federal judge
Mackin, J. Stanley banker
Malone, Wallace D., Jr. bank executive
Manson-Hing, Lincoln Roy dental educator
Marks, Charles Caldwell retired investment banker, retired industrial distribution company executive
Massey, Richard Walter, Jr. investment counselor
Mays, Joseph Barber, Jr. lawyer
Mc Callum, Charles Alexander university official
McKewen, Jack Leard insurance sales executive
Mc Millan, George Duncan Hastie, Jr. lawyer, former state official
McWhorter, Hobart Amory, Jr. lawyer
Meezan, Elias pharmacologist, educator
Meriwether, Charles Minor retail and wholesale drug company executive
Miller, Dennis Edward corporate executive
Miller, Edmond Trowbridge civil engineer, educator, consultant
Mills, William Hayes lawyer
Molen, John Klauminzer lawyer
Montgomery, John Atterbury research chemist, consultant
†Moon, James E. hospital administrator
Moor, Manly Eugene, Jr. retired banker
Morgan, Hugh Jackson, Jr. bank executive
Morton, Marilyn Miller genealogy and history educator, lecturer, researcher, tour planner
Mowry, Robert Wilbur pathologist, educator
Nabers, Drayton, Jr. insurance company executive
Navia, Juan Marcelo biologist, educator
Neal, Phil Hudson, Jr. manufacturing company executive
Nelson, Dotson McGinnis, Jr. clergyman
Nelson, Edwin L. federal judge
Newfield, Mayer Ullman lawyer
†Newton, Don Allen association executive
Nichol, Victor E., Jr. banking executive
Northen, Charles Swift, III banker
Nunn, Grady Harrison political science educator emeritus
Oakes, Walter Jerry pediatric neurosurgeon
Oglesby, Sabert, Jr. retired research institute administrator
Oliver, Samuel William, Jr. lawyer
Omura, George Adolf medical oncologist
Oparil, Suzanne cardiologist, educator, researcher
Pacifico, Albert Dominick cardiovascular surgeon
Parker, Israel Frank national association consultant
Parker, John Malcolm management and financial consultant
Patzke, Richard Joseph energy company executive
Peeples, William Dewey, Jr. mathematics educator
Peters, Henry Buckland optometrist, educator
Pewitt, James Dudley academic administrator
Pfister, Roswell Robert ophthalmologist
Phillips, James Linford agricultural affairs reporter, editor
Pirkle, George Emory television and film actor, director
Pittman, James Allen, Jr. endocrinologist, dean emeritus, educator
Pizitz, Richard Alan retail and real estate group executive
Pohost, Gerald M. cardiologist, medical educator
Pointer, Sam Clyde, Jr. federal judge
Polivnick, Paul conductor, music director
†Pope, G. Phillip insurance company executive
Powell, William Arnold, Jr. retired banker
Powers, Edward Latell accountant
Propst, Robert Bruce federal judge
Putnam, Terry Michael federal judge
Quintana, Jose Booth health care executive
Redden, Lawrence Drew lawyer
†Reeves, Garland Phillip newspaper editor
Renneker, Frederick Weyman, III insurance executive
†Richards, J. Scott rehabilitation medicine professional
†Richey, Ronald Kay insurance company executive, lawyer
Riegert, Robert Adolf law educator, consultant
Roberts, David Harrill English language educator
Robin, Theodore Tydings, Jr. electric company executive, engineer
Rogers, Ernest Mabry lawyer
Rotch, James E. lawyer
Rountree, Asa lawyer
Rouse, John Wilson, Jr. research institute administrator
†Rozendale, David S. engineering and construction firm executive
Rubright, James Alfred lawyer
Rushton, William James, III insurance company executive
Russell, Richard Olney, Jr. cardiologist, educator
†Rynearson, W. John association executive
Savage, Kay Webb lawyer, health center administrator, accountant
Scarritt, Thomas Varnon newspaper editor
†Seitz, Karl Raymond editor
†Selfe, Edward Milton lawyer
Sellers, Fred Wilson banker
Shealy, David Lee physicist, educator
Sibley, William Arthur academic administrator, physics educator, consultant
Skalka, Harold Walter ophthalmologist, educator
Sklenar, Herbert Anthony industrial products manufacturing company executive
Smith, Edward Samuel federal judge
Smith, John Joseph lawyer
Smith, Peter Garthwaite energy consultant
Spence, Paul Herbert librarian
Spotswood, Robert Keeling lawyer
Stabler, Lewis Vastine, Jr. lawyer
Starr, Bart (Bryan Bartlett Starr) former professional football coach, former professional football player
Stephens, Elton Bryson bank executive, service and manufacturing company executive
Stephens, James T. publishing executive
Stephens, Jerry Wayne librarian, library director
Stewart, George Ray librarian
Stone, Edmund Crispen, III banker
Sturgeon, Charles Edwin management consultant
Styslinger, Lee Joseph, Jr. manufacturing company executive
Sutowski, Thor Brian choreographer
Tucker, Thomas James investment manager
Urry, Dan Wesley research biophysicist, educator, science facility administrator
Vinik, H(ymie) Ronald anesthesiologist, physician
Vinson, Laurence Duncan, Jr. lawyer
†Vogelsang, John Martin financial executive
Wabler, Robert Charles, II retail and distribution executive
Walker, Evelyn retired educational television executive
†Warnock, David Gene nephrologist
†Watson, William L., III banker
Weatherly, Robert Stone, Jr. banker
Weeks, Arthur Andrew lawyer, educator
†Whitehead, Lewis E, Jr. automotive consultant, management consultant
Williams, Parham Henry, Jr. lawyer
†Williamson, Edward L. retired nuclear engineer, consultant
Woodall, Norman Eugene banker
Woods, John Witherspoon banker
Wrinkle, John Newton lawyer

Brewton
Jones, Sherman J. academic administrator, management educator

Collinsville
Beasley, Mary Catherine home economics educator, administrator, researcher

Dadeville
Adair, Charles Robert, Jr. lawyer

Daphne
Jeffreys, Elystan Geoffrey geological engineer, petroleum consultant and appraiser

Dauphin Island
Porter, John Finley, Jr. physicist, conservationist, retired educator

Decatur
Caddell, John A. lawyer

Demopolis
Lloyd, Hugh Adams lawyer

Dothan
Garner, Alto Luther retired education educator
†Harrison, Thomas E. academic official
Little, Charles Lawson lawyer

Eufaula
Clayton, Preston Copeland lawyer

Fairhope
Jones, Henry Earl dermatologist, direct patient care educator

Florence
Haltom, Elbert Bertram, Jr. federal judge
Johnson, Johnny Ray mathematics educator
Potts, Robert Leslie academic administrator
†Stangel, Paul J. agronomist, soil scientist, environmentalist, consultant
Tease, James Edward judge

Fort Rucker
Adams, Ronald Emerson army officer
Robinson, John David army officer

Gadsden
†Hill, Anita Griffith principal
Sledge, James Scott federal judge
†Taylor, Fred M. school system administrator

Gulf Shores
Wallace, John Loys *aviation services executive*

Guntersville
Patterson, Harold Dean *superintendent of schools*
Sparkman, Brandon Buster *educator, writer, consultant*

Hartselle
Slate, Joe Hutson *psychologist, educator*

Harvest
Norman, Ralph Louis *physicist, consultant*

Helena
Smith, John Lee, Jr. *minister, former association administrator*

Hoover
Thompson, Wynelle Doggett *chemistry educator*

Huntsville
Anderson, Elmer Ebert *physicist, educator*
Ball, Howard Guy *education specialist educator*
Beary, Shirley Lorraine *music educator*
Boston, Edward Dale *hospital administrator*
Chappell, Charles Richard *space scientist*
Cleary, James Roy *lawyer*
Cornatzer, William Eugene *biochemist, emeritus educator*
Costes, Nicholas Constantine *aerospace technologist, government official*
†Dannenberg, Konrad K. *aeronautical engineer*
Daussman, Grover Frederick *electrical engineer, consultant*
Decher, Rudolf *physicist*
de Loach, Anthony Cortelyou *solar physicist*
Dimmock, John Oliver *university research center director*
Douillard, Paul Arthur *engineering and financial executive, consultant*
Emerson, William Kary *engineering company executive*
Franz, Frank Andrew *academic administrator*
Garriott, Owen Kay *astronaut, scientist*
Graves, Benjamin Barnes *business administration educator*
Hartman, Richard Leon *physicist*
Hettinger, Steve *mayor*
Huckaby, Gary Carlton *lawyer*
Hung, Ru J. *engineering educator*
Jones, Harvie Paul *architect*
King, Olin B. *electronics systems company executive*
Kowel, Stephen Thomas *electrical engineer, educator*
†Lee, Thomas J. *aerospace scientist*
Leslie, Lottie Lyle *retired educator*
Loshuertos, Robert Herman *clergyman*
Lundquist, Charles Arthur *university official*
Lutz, Hartwell Borden *judge*
Mc Donough, George Francis, Jr. *aerospace engineer*
McKnight, William Baldwin *physics educator*
Mc Manus, Samuel Plyler *chemist, academic administrator*
Meadlock, James W. *computer graphics company executive*
†Mercieca, Charles *philosophy and political science educator*
Moore, Fletcher Brooks *engineering company executive*
Parnell, Thomas Alfred *physicist*
Potate, John Spencer, Sr. *engineering company executive, consultant*
Potter, Ernest Luther *lawyer*
†Ramsey, V. Bruce *electronics executive*
Reaves, Benjamin F. *academic administrator*
Ritter, Alfred *aerospace consultant*
Robb, David Metheny, Jr. *art museum director, art historian*
Roberts, Frances Cabaniss *history educator*
Russell, Lynn Darnell *engineering educator*
Sapp, A. Eugene, Jr. *electronics executive*
†Schremser, Donna Barrett *library executive*
†Schroer, Bernard Jon *industrial engineering educator*
Schwinghamer, Robert John *materials scientist*
Smith, Robert Earl *space scientist*
Smith, Robert Sellers *lawyer*
Stuhlinger, Ernst *physicist*
Traylor, Orba Forest *economist, lawyer, educator*
Vaughan, William Walton *atmospheric scientist*
Vinz, Frank Louis *electrical engineer*
Watson, Sterl Arthur, Jr. *retired judge, lawyer*
Wessling, Francis Christopher *mechanical engineer, educator*
White, John Charles *historian*
Wilson, Allan Byron *graphics company executive*
Wright, John Collins *chemistry educator*
†Wu, Shi Tsan *educator, science research administrator*
Zant, Robert Franklin *computer information educator*

Jacksonville
Boswell, Rupert Dean, Jr. *academic administrator, mathematics educator*
Dunaway, William Preston *education educator emeritus*
McGee, Harold Johnston *university president*
Merrill, Martha *instructional media educator*
Reid, William James *physicist, educator*

Jasper
Rowland, David Jack *college chancellor*

Lanett
Fowler, Conrad Murphree *retired manufacturing company executive*

Lillian
Moyer, Kenneth Evan *psychologist, educator*
Shory, Naseeb Lein *dentist, retired state official*

Livingston
Green, Asa Norman *university president*

Madison
Brannan, Eulie Ross *education consultant*
Frakes, Lawrence Wright *program analyst, logistics engineer*
Hawk, Clark Wiliams *mechanical engineering educator*
Jellett, James Morgan *retired army officer, aerospace defense consultant*
†Rosenberger, Franz Ernst *physics educator*

Maplesville
Nichols, J. Hugh *education and economic development consultant*

Marshall Space Flight Center
†Johnson, Charles Leslie *aerospace physicist, consultant*

Maxwell AFB
†Johnston, Robert Michael *military officer*
Kline, John Alvin *academic administrator*
Pendley, William Tyler *naval officer, international relations educator*

Mc Calla
Gentry, Vicki Paulette *museum director*

Mentone
Herndon, Mark *musician*

Mobile
Anderson, Lewis Daniel *medical educator, orthopaedic surgeon*
Armbrecht, William Henry, III *lawyer*
Bahr, Alice Harrison *librarian*
Baker, Amanda Sirmon *academic administrator, nursing educator*
†Bedsole, Ann Smith *state senator*
Bobo, James Robert *economics educator*
Boswell, Louis Eugene *business and management educator, author*
Braswell, Louis Erskine *lawyer*
Brock, Paul Warrington *lawyer*
Brogdon, Byron Gilliam *physician, radiology educator*
Butler, Charles Randolph, Jr. *federal judge*
Byrd, Gwendolyn Pauline *school system superintendent*
Callahan, H. L. (Sonny Callahan) *congressman*
Clark, Jack *hospital company executive, accountant*
Conrad, Marcel Edward *hematologist, educator*
†Copeland, Lewis *principal*
Cox, Emmett Ripley *federal judge*
Crow, James Sylvester *retired banker, railway executive*
Damico, James Anthony *library director*
DeBakey, Ernest George *physician, surgeon*
Delaney, Thomas Caldwell, Jr. *city official*
†Dow, Michael Craig *mayor*
†Duvall, Charles Farmer *bishop*
Edwards, Jack *former congressman, lawyer*
Eichold, Samuel *medical educator, medical museum curator*
Fox, Sidney Walter *chemist, educator*
Gardner, William Albert, Jr. *pathologist, medical foundation executive*
Gottlieb, Sheldon Fred *biologist, educator*
Hamid, Michael *electrical engineering educator, consultant*
Harris, Benjamin Harte, Jr. *lawyer*
Hearin, William Jefferson *newspaper publishing company executive*
Helmsing, Frederick George *lawyer*
Holberg, Ralph Gans, Jr. *lawyer*
Holland, Lyman Faith, Jr. *lawyer*
Holmes, Broox Garrett *lawyer*
Howard, Alex T., Jr. *federal judge*
Kahn, Gordon Barry *federal bankruptcy judge*
Kimbrough, William Adams, Jr. *lawyer*
Lager, Robert John *state agency administrator*
Lipscomb, Oscar Hugh *archbishop*
Littleton, Jesse Talbot, III *radiology educator*
Lott, Kench Lee, Jr. *banker*
Lyons, Champ, Jr. *lawyer*
Lyons, George Sage *lawyer, oil industry executive, former state legislator*
McCall, Daniel Thompson, Jr. *retired justice*
McCann, Clarence David, Jr. *special events coordinator, museum curator and director, artist*
Milling, Bert William, Jr. *federal judge*
Parmley, Loren Francis, Jr. *medical educator*
Pitcock, James Kent *head and neck surgical oncologist*
Pittman, Virgil *federal judge*
†Rakich, Robert T. *insurance holding company executive*
Rewak, William John *university president, clergyman*
Richelson, Paul William *curator*
Sessions, Jefferson Beauregard, III *lawyer*
Smith, Jesse Graham, Jr. *dermatologist, educator*
†Tatum, Gordon, Jr. *fine arts editor, critic*
Taylor, Thomas Alexander, III *newspaper editor*
†Thomson, H. Bailey *editor*
Thornton, J. Edward *lawyer*
Vacik, James Paul *university administrator*
Vitulli, William Francis *psychology educator*
Whiddon, Frederick Palmer *university president*
White, Lowell E., Jr. *retired medical educator*
†Windom, Stephen Ralph *lawyer, state legislator*
Winter, Arch Reese *architect*

Monroeville
Kniskern, Maynard *editor, writer*

Montevallo
†McChesney, Robert Michael, Sr. *political science educator*

Montgomery
Albritton, William Harold, III *federal judge*
Almon, Reneau Pearson *state supreme court justice*
Amberg, Richard Hiller, Jr. *newspaper executive*
†Baggiano, Faye Stone *public health service officer*
†Baker, Clifford Cornell *state educational administrator*
Black, Robert Coleman *lawyer*
Blount, Winton Malcolm, Jr. *manufacturing company executive*
Blount, Winton Malcolm, III *investment executive*
†Bobo, Thomas *school system administrator*
†Brock, Eugene C. *landscape architect*
†Brown, William Blake *newspaper editor*
Byars, Walter Ryland, Jr. *lawyer*
Camp, Billy Joe *state official*
Cater, Douglass *former college president, former government official, writer, editor*
Clark, James S. *congressman*
Cornett, Lloyd Harvey, Jr. *retired historian*
†Dees, Morris Seligman, Jr. *lawyer*
De Ment, Ira *federal judge*
†Dixon, Larry Dean *state official*
Dubina, Joel Fredrick *federal judge*
Evans, James Harold *state attorney general*
†Findlay, R. B. *paper company executive*
Folsom, James, Jr. *governor*
Franco, Ralph Abraham *lawyer*
Frazer, Nimrod Thompson *investment banker, financial services executive*
Gainous, Fred Jerome *state agency administrator*
Godbold, John Cooper *federal judge*
Gorland, Ronald Kent *corporate executive*
Graddick, Charles Allen *lawyer*
Gribben, Alan *English language educator, research consultant*
†Gullatt, Jane *state legislator*
Harris, Patricia Lea *librarian*
Hawthorne, Frank Howard *lawyer*
Hester, Douglas Benjamin *lawyer, federal official*
Hill, Thomas Bowen, III *lawyer*
Hoffman, Richard William *banker*
†Hooper, Perry Ollie *lawyer*
Hornsby, (E.C.) Sonny *judge*
Houston, James Gorman, Jr. *state supreme court justice*
Ingram, Kenneth Frank *state supreme court justice*
Johnson, Andrew Emerson, III *educational administrator*
Johnson, Frank Minis, Jr. *federal judge*
†Langford, Charles Douglass *lawyer, state legislator*
Latham, Larry Lee *state administrator, psychologist*
Leslie, Henry Arthur *lawyer, retired banker*
Maddox, (Alva) Hugh *state supreme court justice*
McFadden, Frank Hampton *lawyer, business executive, former judge*
Myers, Ira Lee *physician*
Nachman, Merton Roland, Jr. *lawyer*
Norris, Robert Wheeler *lawyer, military officer*
Oswalt, (Eugene) Talmadge *educational administrator*
Paddock, Austin Joseph *engineering executive*
Patterson, John Malcolm *judge*
Robinson, Peter Clark *general management executive*
Rowan, John Robert *medical center director*
Salmon, Joseph Thaddeus *lawyer*
Schloss, Samuel Leopold, Jr. *food service executive*
Schwarz, Joseph Edmund *artist*
Sistrunk, William Hicks *air force officer*
Steele, Rodney Redfearn *federal judge*
Tan, Boen Hie *biochemist*
Teague, Barry Elvin *lawyer*
Teague, Larry Gene *editor*
Teague, Wayne *state education official*
Thompson, Myron H. *federal judge*
Torbert, Clement Clay, Jr. *state supreme court justice*
Van Sant, Robert William *manufacturing company executive*
Volz, Charles Harvie, Jr. *lawyer*
†Walker, Claud Ladale, Sr. *state representative*
Wallace, George Corley *former governor*
Wampold, Charles Henry, Jr. *lawyer*
Williams, James Orrin *university administrator, educator*

Mountain Brook
Haworth, Michael Elliott, Jr. *investor, former aerospace company executive*

Muscle Shoals
†Smith, Harry Delano *educational administrator*

Nauvoo
†Cagle, Johnny T. *coal miner, state legislator*

Normal
Caulfield, Henry John *physics educator*
†Henson, David B. *academic administrator*
Tan, Arjun *physics educator, researcher*

Ohatchee
Ellis, Bernice Allred *personnel executive*

Opelika
Brown, Robert Glenn *plastic surgeon*
Jenkins, Richard Lee *manufacturing company executive*
Knecht, Charles Daniel *veterinarian*
Samford, Yetta Glenn, Jr. *lawyer*

Orange Beach
Bennett, James Jefferson *higher education consultant*
Brennan, Lawrence Edward *electronics engineer*

Ozark
†Matthews, W. W. *bishop*

Pelham
Turner, Malcolm Elijah *biomathematician, educator*

Pell City
Passey, George Edward *psychology educator*

Phenix City
†Corbett, James Daniel (Danny) *state senator*

Point Clear
Elmer, William Morris *retired pipe line executive*
Englund, Gage Bush *dancer, educator*
Ferguson, Joseph Gantt *chemical engineer*

Prattville
Moorer, Frances Earline Green *vocational educator*

Rainbow City
Browning, Leslie O. *middle school educator*

Redstone Arsenal
Allan, Barry David *research chemist, government official*
Pittman, William Claude *electrical engineer*

Russellville
†Clemmons, Robert W. *school system administrator*

Selma
†Sanders, Hank *state senator, lawyer*
Stewart, Edgar Allen *lawyer*

Sheffield
†Roy, Amit H. *agricultural executive*

Shoal Creek
Ahearn, John Francis, Jr. *retired oil and gas company executive*

Sylacauga
†Felker, G. Stephen *textile company executive*

Talladega
Adams, James Wilson *physical education educator*
Johnson, Joseph Benjamin *university president*

Troy
Adams, Ralph Wyatt, Sr. *university chancellor emeritus*
Brantley, Oliver Wiley *retired lawyer*
†Flowers, Steve *state legislator*
†Hawkins, Jack, Jr. *academic administrator*
Long, John Maloy *university dean*
Marsicano, Hazel Elliott *education educator*
Thompson, Jean Tanner *retired librarian*

Tuscaloosa
Abdel-Ghany, Mohamed *family economics educator*
†Atwood, Jerry Lee *chemistry educator*
Austin, Philip Edward *university chancellor*
Baklanoff, Eric Nicholas *economist, educator*
Barban, Arnold Melvin *advertising educator*
Barfield, Robert F. *mechanical engineer, educator, university dean*
†Bell, Robert Fred *German language educator*
†Blackburn, John Leslie *small business owner*
Brown, Jack Cole *civil engineer*
Bryan, Colgan Hobson *aerospace engineering educator*
Cava, Michael Patrick *chemist, educator*
Christopher, Thomas Weldon *legal educator, administrator*
Coggins, Wilmer Jesse *physician, medical school administrator*
Cole, George David *physicist*
Cook, Camille Wright *legal educator*
Cooper, Eugene Bruce *speech-language pathologist, educator*
Coulter, Philip Wylie *physicist, educator*
Cramer, Dale Lewis *economics educator*
Darden, William Howard, Jr. *biology educator*
Davis, Anthony Michael John *mathematics educator*
Drake, Albert Estern *retired statistics educator*
†Fetner, Charles Anthony *hospital administrator*
Fish, Mary Martha *economics educator*
Flinn, David R. *federal agency research director*
Ford, James Henry, Jr. *hospital executive*
Frye, John H., Jr. *metallurgical engineering educator*
Garner, Samuel Paul *accounting educator, author*
Goossen, Jacob Frederic *composer, educator*
Griffin, Marvin Anthony *industrial engineer, educator*
Gup, Benton Eugene *banking educator*
Hocutt, Max Oliver *philosophy educator*
Hoff, Timothy *lawyer, educator, priest*
Izatt, Jerald Ray *physics educator*
Jones, Douglas Epps *natural history museum director*
LaMoreaux, Philip Elmer *geologist, hydrogeologist, consultant*
Lee, Thomas Alexander *accountant, educator*
Mac Donald, Malcolm Murdoch *editor, publisher*
Mancini, Ernest Anthony *geologist, educator, researcher*
Mayer, Morris Lehman *marketing educator*
McDonald, Forrest *historian, educator*
Mitchell, Herbert Hall *former university dean, educational consultant*
Miyagawa, Ichiro *physicist*
Morley, Lloyd Albert *mining engineering educator*
Mozley, Paul David *obstetrics and gynecology educator*
Penz, Anton Jacob *retired accounting educator*
Prigmore, Charles Samuel *social work educator*
Rafferty, James Patrick *violinist, violin educator*
Reinhart, Kellee Connely *journalist*
Rembert, Virginia Pitts *art educator, historian, critic*
†Sayers, Roger *academic administrator*
Sheeley, Eugene Charles *audiology educator*
Shellhase, Leslie John *social work educator*
Stallings, Gene Clifton *professional, university athletic coach*
Taaffe, James Griffith *university administrator, educator*
Turner, Philip Michael *university official and dean, author*
Van Artsdalen, Ervin Robert *physical chemist, educator*
Watkins, John Cumming, Jr. *law educator*
Wetzel, Robert George *botany educator*
Williams, Ernest Going *paper company executive*
Williams, Louis Gressett *biologist, educator*
Williams, Vergil Lewis *criminal justice educator*
Wu, Hsiu Kwang *economist, educator*

Tuscumbia
†Denton, Bobby E. *state senator*
Rosser, Charles D. *lawyer*

Tuskegee
Kenney, Howard Washington *physician*
Payton, Benjamin Franklin *college president*
Pryce, Edward Lyons *landscape architect*

Tuskegee Institute
Hill, Walter A. *agricultural sciences educator, researcher*
Madison, Willie Clarence *park superintendent*

ALASKA

Anchorage
Atwood, Robert Bruce *publisher*
Baily, Douglas Boyd *lawyer*
Behrend, Donald Fraser *university administrator*
†Bender, Thomas Richard *science administrator, epidemiologist*
Brady, Carl Franklin *retired aircraft charter company executive*
Branson, Albert Harold (Harry Branson) *magistrate judge, educator*
Brown, Harold MacVane *lawyer*
†Brown, Kay (Mary Kathryn Brown) *state official*
†Bunde, Con *communication educator, state legislator*
Byrd, Milton Bruce *college president, former business executive*
Cairns, John J(oseph) *retail executive*
Cuddy, Daniel Hon *bank executive*
†Davis, Bettye Jean *academic administrator, state official*
De Lisio, Stephen Scott *lawyer*

Edwards, George Kent *lawyer*
Evans, William Frederick *research chemist*
Faulkner, Sewell Ford *real estate executive*
Fink, Tom *mayor*
Groh, Clifford J., Sr. *lawyer*
Harris, Orville D. *transportation executive*
Harris, Roger J. *entrepreneur*
Henderson-Dixon, Karen Sue *psychologist*
Holland, H. Russel *federal judge*
†Holthouse, Rita J. *secondary school principal*
Hopkins, Stephen Davis *retired business executive*
Hurley, Francis T. *archbishop*
Jones, Garth Nelson *public administration educator*
†Kumin, Jonathan P. *architectural firm executive*
†Leman, Loren Dwight *civil engineer*
Lindauer, John Howard, II *newspaper publisher*
Lowe, Robert Charles *lawyer, banker*
Mala, Theodore Anthony *physician, consultant*
Mann, Lester Perry *mathematics educator*
Maynard, Kenneth Douglas *architect*
Melcher, Jerry Eugene *lawyer*
Mitchell, Michael Kiehl *elementary and secondary education educator, minister*
†Nordlund, James Robert *state legislator*
†Parsons, Donald D. *bishop*
†Pearce, Drue *state legislator*
Pearson, Larry Lester *journalism educator, communication consultant*
†Porter, Brian Stanley *police chief*
Rabinowitz, Jay Andrew *state supreme court justice*
Rasmuson, Elmer Edwin *banker, former mayor*
Risley, Todd Robert *psychologist, educator*
Roberts, John Derham *lawyer*
Robison, Paul Frederick *lawyer*
Rose, David Allan *investment manager*
Sedwick, John Weeter *judge*
Sharp, Anne Catherine *artist, educator*
Singleton, James Keith *federal judge*
Strohmeyer, John *former editor, writer*
Sullivan, George Murray *former mayor, business consultant*
Thomas, Howard Paul *civil engineer, consultant*
Thomas, Lowell, Jr. *author, lecturer, former lieutenant governor Alaska, former state senator*
†Trotter, F(rederick) Thomas *university president*
†Unruh, Leon Dale *newspaper editor*
Vandergriff, Jerry Dodson *computer store executive*
von der Heydt, James Arnold *federal judge, lawyer*
†Williams, Charles D. *bishop*
†Williams, Mark *food products executive*
Wolf, Aron S. *psychiatrist*
Young, Bettye Jeanne *secondary education educator*

Auke Bay
†Snyder, George Richard *laboratory director*

Barrow
Trainor, Jerry Allen *vocational education professional*

Chugiak
†Ondola, George *village official*

Cordova
Bugbee-Jackson, Joan *sculptor*

Eagle River
Cotten, Samuel Richard *former state legislator, fisherman*
†Willis, Edward Charles *legislator*

Fairbanks
Alexander, Vera *dean, marine science educator*
Behlke, Charles Edward *civil engineer, former university dean*
Beistline, Earl Hoover *mining consultant*
Bennett, Fred Lawrence *engineering educator*
†Brice, Tom Luther *state legislator*
†Charleston, Steve *bishop*
Cook, Donald Jean *mineral engineering educator, trade consultant*
Cutler, Howard Armstrong *economics educator, chancellor*
Doolittle, William Hotchkiss *internist*
†Doran, Timothy Patrick *principal*
†Drew, James Vandervort *university administrator*
†Eichelberger, John Charles *volcanologist, educator*
Helfferich, Merritt Randolph *geophysical research administrator*
Helmericks, Harmon *author, explorer*
Kaniecki, Michael Joseph *bishop*
Kauffman, William Ray *lawyer*
Kessel, Brina *ornithologist, educator*
Kleinfeld, Andrew Jay *federal judge*
Komisar, Jerome Bertram *university administrator*
Krauss, Michael Edward *linguist*
Ray, Charles Kendall *retired university dean*
†Reichardt, Paul Bernard *dean, chemistry educator*
Rice, Julian Casavant *lawyer*
Rice, Michael Lewis *business educator*
Roederer, Juan Gualterio *physics educator*
Smith, Robert London *commissioner, retired air force officer, political scientist, educator*
Speck, Robert Charles *geological engineer*
Tilsworth, Timothy *environmental and civil engineering educator*
Wadlow, Joan Krueger *university chancellor*
Weeks, Wilford Frank *geophysics educator, glaciologist*
Weller, Gunter Ernst *geophysics educator*
Wolting, Robert Roy *city official*
Wood, William Ransom *former university president, city official, corporate executive*
†Zarling, John Paul *mechanical engineering educator*

Fayetteville
Wilson, Charles Banks *artist*

Fort Richardson
Schnell, Roger Thomas *retired military officer, state official*

Gustavus
Jensen, Marvin O. *national park superintendent*

Haines
Haas, June F. *special education educator, consultant*

Homer
†Phillips, Gail *state legislator*

Indian
Wright, Gordon Brooks *musician, conductor, educator*

Juneau
†Albanese, Thomas *minerals company executive*
†Botelho, Bruce Manuel *state official, mayor*
†Bushre, Peter Alvin *financial executive*
Coghill, John Bruce *state official*
Deihl, Michael Allen *federal agency administrator*
†Grussendorf, Benjamin Franklin, Jr. *state house speaker*
Hickel, Walter Joseph *state governor, investment firm executive*
Kelly, Timothy Donahue *state senator*
Kenny, Michael H. *bishop*
†Kerttula, Jalmar M. *state senator*
†Lind, Marshall L. *academic administrator*
Loescher, Robert Wayne *holding company executive*
†Mackie, Jerry *state legislator, business owner*
†MacLean, Eileen Panigeo *state legislator*
†Mulder, Eldon Paul *state legislator, real estate agent*
†Nicholia, Irene Kay *organization administrator*
†Rieger, Steven Arthur *state legislator, business consultant*
Sandor, John Abraham *state agency administrator*
Schorr, Alan Edward *librarian, publisher*
†Scott, William Herbert *state agency administrator*
†Thomas, Edward K. *tribal executive, educator*
Willson, Mary F. *ecology researcher, educator*

Kodiak
Jamin, Matthew Daniel *lawyer, magistrate*
Selby, Jerome M. *mayor*

Kokhanok
†Nelson, John D., Jr. *village administrator*

Nome
†Timbers, RoseAnn S. *association executive*

North Pole
†James, Jeannette Adeline *state legislator, accountant*

Palmer
Chang, Ping-Tung *mathematics educator*

Saint Paul
†Dishman, Leland Lee *school system administrator*

Sitka
†Willman, Arthur Charles *healthcare executive*

Soldotna
Franzmann, Albert Wilhelm *wildlife veterinarian, consultant*

Tuntutuliak
Daniel, Barbara B. *secondary education educator*

Unalakleet
†Katchatag, Stanton Oswald *civic and political worker*

Valdez
†Rogers, Harry *school system administrator*

Wasilla
Butcher, Susan Howlet *dog kennel owner, sled dog racer*

ARIZONA

Apache Junction
Bothwell, Dorr *artist*

Bisbee
Eastlake, William Derry *author*
Hagstrum, Jean Howard *language professional, educator*
Holland, Robert Dale *retired magistrate, consultant*

Bullhead City
Jones, Vernon Quentin *surveyor*

Carefree
Beadle, Alfred Newman *architect*
Birkelbach, Albert Ottmar *retired oil company executive*
Byrom, Fletcher Lauman *chemical manufacturing company executive*
Craft, Robert Homan *banker, corporate executive*
Hutchison, Stanley Philip *lawyer*
Menk, Louis Wilson *retired manufacturing company executive*
Robbins, Conrad W. *naval architect*
Trimble, George Simpson *industrial executive*
Wise, Paul Schuyler *insurance company executive*

Casa Grande
Kramer, Donovan Mershon, Sr. *newspaper publisher*

Cave Creek
MacKay, John *mechanical engineer*
O'Reilly, Thomas Eugene *human resources consultant*

Chandler
Ratkowski, Donald J. *mechanical engineer, consultant*
†Stellrecht, Fritz *newspaper publishing executive*
Williams, James Eugene, Jr. *management consultant*

Coolidge
Hiller, William Clark *physics educator, engineering educator, consultant*

Flagstaff
Aurand, Charles Henry, Jr. *music educator*
Barnes, Charles Winfred *geology educator, administrator*
Cline, Platt Herrick *author*
Colbert, Edwin Harris *paleontologist, museum curator*
Hallowell, Robert Edward *French language educator*
Hammond, Howard David *retired botanist and editor*
Hooper, Henry Olcott *university dean, physicist*
Lovett, Clara Maria *university administrator, historian*
†Millis, Robert Lowell *astronomer*
Poen, Monte M. *history educator, researcher*
Putnam, William Lowell *retired travel bureau director, science association administrator*
Ririe, Craig Martin *periodontist*
Shoemaker, Eugene Merle *geologist*
Smith, Zachary Alden *political science and public administration educator*
Smyth, Joel Douglas *newspaper executive*
Somerville, Mason Harold *mechanical engineering educator, university dean*
†Verkamp, John *lawyer, state legislator*
Zoellner, Robert William *chemistry educator*

Fountain Hills
Hegyi, Julius *conductor, musician*

Glendale
†Altersitz, Janet Kinahan *principal*
†Brewer, Janice Kay *state legislator*
Joseph, Gregory Nelson *media critic*
Neff, John *recording engineer, producer*
North, Warren James *government official*
Voris, William *educational administrator*
†Wright, Patricia *state legislator*

Globe
Malott, James Raymond, Jr. *lawyer*

Goodyear
Cabaret, Joseph Ronald *electronics company executive*

Green Valley
Bates, Charles Carpenter *oceanographer*
Blickwede, Donald Johnson *retired steel company executive*
Brissman, Bernard Gustave *insurance company executive*
Carpenter, John Everett *retired principal, educational consultant*
Desjarlais, Erika Else *retired management analyst*
Dmytryshyn, Basil *historian, educator*
Egger, Roscoe L., Jr. *consultant*
Ehrenfeld, John Henry *grocery company executive*
Lasch, Robert *former journalist*
Miner, Earl Howard *retired trust banker*
Page, John Henry, Jr. *artist, educator*
Perry, Roger Lawrence *printing executive*
Peterson, Harold Albert *electrical engineer, educator*
Schirmer, Henry William *architect*
Smith, Raymond Lloyd *former university president, consultant*
Wasmuth, Carl Erwin *physician, lawyer*

Huachuca City
†Ortega, Ruben Francisco *state representative*

Lake Havasu City
Bird, Robert Wilson *lawyer*

Lake Montezuma
Burkee, Irvin *artist*

Litchfield Park
Reid, Ralph Ralston, Jr. *electronics executive, engineer*

Mesa
Allen, Merle Maeser, Jr. *lawyer*
Anderson, Herschel Vincent *librarian*
Belok, Michael Victor *education educator*
Boyd, Leona Potter *retired social worker*
DeRosa, Francis Dominic *chemical company executive*
Duecy, Charles Michael *retired lawyer*
Fairbanks, Harold Vincent *metallurgical engineer, educator*
Garwood, John Delvert *former college administrator*
Gaylor, Walter *writer, military historian*
House, Roy C. *retired hospital executive*
Johnson, Mary Elizabeth *elementary education educator*
†Mead, Tray C. *museum administrator*
†Murphy, Edward Francis *sales executive*
Rich, David Barry *city official, auditor, accountant*
Rummel, Robert Wiland *aeronautical engineer, author*
Shelley, James LaMar *lawyer*
†Shill, Victor Lamar *architect*
Stott, Brian *software company executive*
Tennison, William Ray, Jr. *financial planner, stock broker, recreational facility executive*
Thompson, Ronald MacKinnon *family physician, artist, writer*
Unser, Bobby (Robert William Unser) *professional auto racer, television commentator*

New River
Bruder, William Paul *architect*

Oracle
Rush, Andrew Wilson *artist*

Oro Valley
Rivkind, Perry Abbot *federal railroad agency administrator*

Page
Hart, Marian Griffith *retired educator*

Paradise Valley
Alcantara, Theo *conductor*
†Blumer, Harry Maynard *architect*
Carey, Ernestine Gilbreth (Mrs. Charles E. Carey) *writer, lecturer*
De Shazor, Ashley Dunn *business consultant*
Grimm, James R. (Ronald Grimm) *multi-industry executive*
Hann, J(ames) David *information systems company executive*
Heller, Jules *artist, writer*
Russell, Paul Edgar *electrical engineering educator*
Sapp, Donald Gene *minister*
Swanson, Robert Killen *management consultant*

Payson
Rich, Frances Luther *sculptor*

Peoria
Bergmann, Fredrick Louis *English language educator, theater historian*
Bernstein, Eugene Merle *physicist, retired educator*
Degnan, Thomas Leonard *lawyer*
Jones, Lillie Agnes *retired educator*
Morrison, Manley Glenn *real estate investor, former army officer*
Palmer, Alice Eugenia *retired physician, educator*
Schindler, William Stanley *retired public relations executive*

Phoenix
Adams, Gail Hayes *interior designer*
Albright, Lois *operetta company executive director*
†Allen, John Rybolt L. *chemist, biochemist*
Allen, Russell Plowman *symphony orchestra executive*
†Alston, Lela *state senator*
Anderson, Edward Frederick *biology educator*
Armstrong, Nelson William, Jr. *gaming company executive*
Arriola, David Bruce *resort and hotel marketing executive*
Aschaffenburg, Walter Eugene *composer, music educator*
Atutis, Bernard P. *manufacturing company executive*
Bachus, Benson Floyd *mechanical engineer, consultant*
Bacon, Roxana C. *lawyer*
Bain, C. Randall *lawyer*
Baker, William Dunlap *lawyer*
Bakker, Thomas Gordon *lawyer*
Ballantyne, Reginald Malcolm, III *healthcare executive*
Ballard, Ronald Lee *lawyer*
†Ballinger, James K. *art museum executive*
Bansak, Stephen A., Jr. *investment banker, financial consultant*
Barbanell, Alexander Stanley *insurance marketing company executive*
Barkley, Charles Wade *professional basketball player*
†Beezley, Linda D. *state legislator*
Begam, Robert George *lawyer*
Beltrán, Anthony Natalicio *military officer, deacon*
Benson, Stephen R. *editorial cartoonist*
Bergamo, Ron *broadcasting company executive*
Bergin, Daniel Timothy *lawyer, banker*
Bimson, Carl Alfred *bank executive*
Bishop, C. Diane *state agency administrator, educator*
Black, Joseph *marketing consultant, former corporation executive*
†Blanchard, Charles Alan *state senator*
Bower, Willis Herman *retired psychiatrist, former medical administrator*
Bradley, Gilbert Francis *retired banker*
Broomfield, Robert Cameron *federal judge*
Brown, Bart A., Jr. *consumer products company executive*
†Brunacini, Alan Vincent *fire chief*
†Bruner, James D. *trust banker*
Burchard, John Kenneth *chemical engineer*
Burg, Jerome Stuart *financial planning consultant*
Burke, Timothy John *lawyer*
Calkins, Jerry Milan *anesthesiologist, educator, administrator, biomedical engineer*
Camarillo, Richard Jon *professional football player*
Cameron, James Duke *lawyer, former state supreme court justice*
Canby, William Cameron, Jr. *federal judge*
†Caputo, Salvatore *critic*
Carman, Michael Dennis *museum director*
Carroll, Earl Hamblin *federal judge*
Carter, James Edward *judge*
Carter, Ronald Martin, Sr. *pharmaceutical company executive*
Charlton, John Kipp *pediatrician*
Chauncey, Tom Webster, II *lawyer*
Cheifetz, Lorna Gale *psychologist*
Cheshire, William Polk *newspaper columnist*
Chisholm, Tom Shepherd *environmental engineer*
Clay, Ambrose Whitlock Winston *telecommunications company executive*
Cohen, Jon Stephan *lawyer*
Cohen, Melvin Stephen *jewelry company executive*
Colangelo, Jerry John *professional basketball team executive*
Colburn, Donald D. *lawyer*
Conway, Michael J. *airline company executive*
Cooledge, Richard Calvin *lawyer*
Corbin, Robert Keith *lawyer, former state attorney general*
Cozzi, Hugo Louis *psychiatrist*
†Crews, James Cecil *hospital administrator*
Crockett, Clyll Webb *lawyer*
Daniel, James Richard *accountant, computer company financial executive*
Daughton, Donald *lawyer*
Davies, David George *lawyer*
Dawson, John Joseph *lawyer*
DeBartolo, Jack, Jr. *architect*
Deeny, Robert Joseph *lawyer*
deMatties, Nicholas Frank *artist, art educator*
†DeMenna, Kevin Bolton *lobbyist*
De Michele, O. Mark *utility company executive*
Derdenger, Patrick *lawyer*
†Dewalt, Judith K. *elementary school principal*
Diethrich, Edward Bronson *heart institute executive, cardiovascular surgeon*
Dignac, Geny (Eugenia M. Bermudez) *sculptor*
Donaldson, Wilburn Lester *property management corporation executive*
Donnelly, Charles Robert *retired college president*
Dougherty, Ronald Jary *business owner, accountant*
Drain, Albert Sterling *business management consultant*
Dunipace, Ian Douglas *lawyer*
Durrant, Dan Martin *lawyer*
Duvall, Joann *retired special education educator*
Early, Robert Joseph *magazine editor*
Eaton, Berrien Clark *lawyer, author*
†Ebert, Richard J. *principal*
Edens, Gary Denton *broadcasting executive*
Edwards, Ralph M. *librarian*
Elien, Mona Marie *air transportation professional*
Ellison, Cyril Lee *publisher*
Elmore, James Walter *architect, retired university dean*
Emerson, Frederick George *transportation company executive*
Evans, Ronald Allen *lodging chain executive*
Everroad, John D. *lawyer*
Feinstein, Allen Lewis *lawyer*
Feldman, Ira S. *accountant*
Feldman, Stanley George *state supreme court chief justice*
Fenzl, Terry Earle *lawyer*
Fine, Charles Leon *lawyer*
Fish, Barry *lawyer*
†Fitzgerald, Joan *principal*

Fitzsimmons, (Lowell) Cotton *professional basketball executive, former coach*
†Forsyth, Ben Ralph *academic administrator, medical educator*
Fournier, Donald Frederick *dentist*
Fox, Frances Juanice *retired librarian, educator, retired*
Frank, Anthony Melchior *federal official, former financial executive*
Frank, John Paul *lawyer, author*
Franke, William Augustus *corporate executive*
Freedman, Kenneth David *lawyer*
Freeman, Susan Maud *lawyer*
†Freyermuth, Clifford L. *structural engineering consultant*
Gaines, Francis Pendleton, III *lawyer*
Galvan, Elias Gabriel *bishop*
†Galvin, Elias *bishop*
Garrett, Dennis Andrew *police official*
Genrich, Mark L. *newspaper editor*
Gerard, Philip C. *lawyer*
Gibbs, William Harold *university administrator*
Giedt, Bruce Alan *paper company executive*
Gilbert, Donald R. *lawyer*
Gillis, William Freeman *telecommunications executive*
Gochnauer, Richard Wallis *consumer products company executive*
Goddard, Terry *lawyer*
Goldman, Murray Abraham *semiconductor executive*
Goldstein, Stuart Wolf *lawyer*
†Greene, John Alan *lawyer*
Greenfield, Arthur Paul *lawyer*
Grier, James Edward *lawyer, hotel executive*
Griffith, Ernest Ralph *physician, educator*
Grinell, Sheila *museum director*
†Gwozdz, Kim Elizabeth *interior designer*
Hallier, Gerard Edouard *hotel chain executive*
Halpern, Barry David *lawyer*
Harelson, Hugh *magazine publisher*
Harris, Jean E. *lawyer*
Harrison, Mark I. *lawyer*
Harte, John Joseph Meakins *bishop*
Hawkins, Jasper Stillwell, Jr. *architect*
Hawkins, Michael Daly *lawyer*
Hayden, William Robert *lawyer*
Heistand, Joseph Thomas *retired bishop*
Heller, Mitchell Thomas *hotel company executive*
Hicks, William Albert, III *lawyer*
†Hill, Edward G. *food marketing executive*
Hoecker, Thomas Ralph *lawyer*
†Hoffman, Jay Russell *mortgage investment company executive, accountant*
Hoffman, Robert B. *lawyer*
Holloway, Edgar Austin *retired diversified business executive*
Houseworth, Richard Court *banker*
Howard, William Matthew *business executive, arbitrator, lawyer, author*
Hoxie, Joel P. *lawyer*
Huck, Leonard William *banker, retired*
Hudak, Thomas Michael *plastic surgeon*
Huffman, Edgar Joseph *oil company executive*
†Hull, Jane Dee *former state legislator*
Huntwork, James R. *lawyer*
Inman, William Peter *lawyer*
Irwin, R. Neil *lawyer*
Jacobson, (Julian) Edward *lawyer*
James, Charles E., Jr. *lawyer*
Jirauch, Charles W. *lawyer*
Johnson, James Wayne *lawyer*
†Johnson, Kevin *professional basketball player*
Johnson, Paul E. *mayor*
Jorgensen, Gordon David *engineering company executive*
Katz, Lawrence Allen *lawyer*
Kaufman, Roger Wayne *county judge, lawyer*
†Keegan, John Charles *state legislator, engineer, consultant*
†Kennedy, Sandra Denise *state representative*
Kennedy, Thomas J. *lawyer*
Khan, Ahmed Mohiuddin *financial/insurance executive*
Kimball, Bruce Arnold *soil scientist*
Kinneberg, Arthur Hempton *retired copper mining company executive*
Kolbe, John William *newspaper columnist*
Kreutzberg, David W. *lawyer*
Kurn, Neal *lawyer*
Kyl, John Henry *former business executive*
†Kyle, Richard Daniel *state legislator, fundraising consultant*
Laartz, Esther Elizabeth *interior designer*
Lake, F(inley) Edward *diversified company financial executive*
†Land, George A. *philosopher, writer, educator, consultant*
†Lassen, John R. *electric utility company executive*
†Lawrence, William Doran *physician*
†Leach, John Franklin *newspaper editor, journalism educator*
LeBeau, Edward Charles *lawyer*
Lee, Stephen E. *lawyer, educator*
Lemon, Leslie Gene *consumer products and services company executive, lawyer*
Lendrum, James Thoburn *architect*
Leonard, George Edmund *finance company executive, consultant*
Lewis, Orme, Jr. *real estate company executive, land use adviser*
Lorenzen, Robert Frederick *ophthalmologist*
†Lynch, Susan H. *state legislator*
Madden, Paul Robert *lawyer, director*
Mahoney, Richard *state official*
Majerle, Daniel Lewis *professional basketball player, olympic athlete*
Mallery, Richard K. *lawyer*
Mangum, John K. *lawyer*
Manning, Danny (Daniel Ricardo Manning) *professional basketball player*
†Manning, Michael C. *lawyer*
Mardian, Daniel *construction company director*
Marks, Merton Eleazer *lawyer*
Martin, Don P. *lawyer*
Martori, Joseph Peter *lawyer*
Mason, Anthony Halstead *lawyer, environmental corporate executive*
May, Bruce Barnett *lawyer*
†McClelland, Norman P. *food products executive*
†Mc Clelland, W. Kent *food products executive*
Mc Clennen, Louis *lawyer, educator*
McGuire, Maureen A. *artist*
McNamee, Stephen M. *federal judge*
McRae, Hamilton Eugene, III *lawyer*
Melczer, Joseph T., III *lawyer*
Melner, Sinclair Lewis *insurance company executive*
Merritt, Nancy-Jo *lawyer*
Meyer, Paul Joseph *lawyer*
Miele, Anthony William *librarian*
Might, Thomas Owen *newspaper company executive*
Miller, Arthur Leonard *sales representative, retired educator*
Miller, Louis Rice *lawyer*
Mitchell, George Hall *lawyer*
Moeller, James *state supreme court justice*
†Mottek, Carl T. *hotel company executive*
Moya, Patrick Robert *lawyer*
Moyer, Alan Dean *retired newspaper editor*
Muchmore, Charles J. *lawyer*
Muecke, Charles Andrew (Carl Muecke) *federal judge*
Mullen, Daniel Robert *treasurer*
Murian, Richard Miller *book company executive*
Myers, Robert David *judge*
Nadler, Henry Louis *pediatrician, geneticist, medical educator*
Novak, Edward Frank *lawyer*
Novak, Peter John *lawyer*
O'Brien, Thomas Joseph *bishop*
Olsen, Alfred Jon *lawyer*
Olsen, Gordon *retired lawyer*
Olson, Robert Howard *lawyer*
Oppedahl, John Fredrick *newspaper editor*
Orman, Arthur Allen *English educator educator*
Pabst, Ralph Malcom *import-export, publishing and mining executive*
Parrett, Sherman O. *lawyer*
†Patti, Andrew S. *consumer products company executive*
Paul, Elias *food company consultant*
Peck, Deana S. *lawyer*
†Pena, Manuel, Jr. *state senator*
Porter, Amy R. *lawyer*
Powers, N. Thompson *lawyer*
Pulaski, Charles Alexander, Jr. *lawyer*
Quadt, Raymond Adolph *metallurgist, cement company executive*
Quinsler, William Thomson *retired investment advisor*
Radin, John William *agriculturalist, physiologist*
†Ralston, Mark David *electrical engineer*
Rathwell, Peter John *lawyer*
Rau, David Edward *real estate company executive*
Reed, Wallace Allison *physician*
Rethore, Bernard Gabriel *diversified company executive*
Robertson, Richard Curtis *credit union executive*
Rodgers, Anthony D. *hospital administrator*
Rosenblatt, Paul Gerhardt *federal judge*
Rowley, Beverley Davies *medical sociologist*
Rudolph, Gilbert Lawrence *lawyer*
Ruffner, Jay Sturgis *lawyer*
Ryan, Thomas Grady *lawyer*
St. Clair, Thomas McBryar *mining and manufacturing company executive*
†Salmon, Matthew James *state legislator, public relations specialist*
Savage, Stephen Michael *lawyer*
Schatt, Paul *newspaper editor*
Schiffner, Charles Robert *architect*
Schiller, William Richard *surgeon*
Schroeder, Mary Murphy *federal judge*
Sedares, James L. *conductor*
†Seiler, Steven Lawrence *health facility administrator*
Shane, Bob *singer*
Shaw, Lillie Marie King *vocalist*
Sherk, Kenneth John *lawyer*
Shoen, Edward Joseph *transportation and insurance companies executive*
Snell, Richard *holding company executive*
†Solomon, Ruth *state legislator, teacher*
†Spencer, John Andrew *real estate development corporation executive*
†Spitzer, Marc Lee *lawyer*
†Springer, Carol *state legislator*
Stahl, Richard G. C. *journalist, editor*
Steckler, Phyllis Betty *publishing company executive*
†Steffey, Lela *state legislator, banker*
Stern, Richard David *investment company executive*
Stine, George Harry *consulting engineer, author*
Storey, Norman C. *lawyer*
Strand, Roger Gordon *federal judge*
†Sullivan, Martin Edward *museum director*
Sutton, Samuel J. *lawyer, educator*
Symington, Fife *governor*
Tang, Thomas *federal judge*
Teel, Dale *utility company executive, consultant*
Teets, John William *diversifed company executive*
Terry, Peter Anthony *lawyer*
Thomas, Edward Francis, Jr. *synthetic fuel executive*
Traeger, Charles Henry, III *lawyer*
Trost, Eileen Bannon *lawyer*
Tubman, William Charles *lawyer*
†Turner, Warren Austin *state legislator*
Turner, William Cochrane *international management consultant*
Udall, Calvin Hunt *lawyer*
Ulrich, Paul Graham *lawyer, author, publisher, editor*
Upson, Donald V. *financial executive*
Van Arsdale, Dick *professional basketball team executive*
Wales, Harold Webster *lawyer*
Walker, Richard K. *lawyer*
Wall, Donald Arthur *lawyer*
Ward, Yvette Hennig *advertising executive*
Watson, Harold George *engineering executive, mechanical engineer*
Weil, Louis Arthur, III *newspaper publishing executive*
Weinstein, Allan M. *medical device company executive*
Westphal, Paul *professional basketball coach*
Whisler, James Steven *lawyer, mining and manufacturing executive*
Wiley, Jay D. *lawyer*
†Williams, Bill *academic administrator*
Williams, Quinn Patrick *lawyer*
Wing, David Allan *biochemistry educator*
†Winslow, Paul David *architect*
Winthrop, Lawrence Fredrick *lawyer*
Witherspoon, James Donald *biology educator*
Wolf, G. Van Velsor, Jr. *lawyer*
Woodard, George Sawyer, Jr. *surgeon, physician, retired army officer*
Woods, Bobby Joe (Bob Woods) *transportation executive*
Woods, Grant *state attorney general*
Woods, Joel Grant *state attorney general*
Woods, Richard James *lawyer*
Woolf, Michael E. *lawyer*
Yarnell, Michael Allan *lawyer*
Yearley, Douglas Cain *mining and manufacturing company executive*
Zastrow, John Thurman *judge*
Zerella, Joseph T. *pediatric surgeon*
Zine, Larry Joseph *retail executive*

Prescott
Burke, Richard Kitchens *lawyer, educator*
Chase, Loriene Eck *psychologist*
Chesson, Eugene, Jr. *civil engineering educator, consultant*
Farrar, Elaine Willardson *artist*
Harris, Earl Edward *business educator*
Kleindienst, Richard Gordon *lawyer*
Markham, Richard Glover *research executive*
Mc Cormack, Fred Allen *state social services administrator*
Russo, Joseph Frank *former college president*
Stasack, Edward Armen *artist*

Prescott Valley
Beck, John Roland *environmental consultant*

Queen Creek
Sossaman, James J. *state legislator*

Rio Verde
Jordan, Richard Charles *engineering executive*

San Simon
Zweifel, Richard George *curator*

Scottsdale
Barbee, Joe Ed *lawyer*
Blackburn, Jack Bailey *retired civil engineering educator*
Burr, Edward Benjamin *life insurance company executive, financial executive*
Carney, Richard Edgar *foundation executive*
Chase, James Keller *retired artist, museum director, educator*
Chauncey, Tom *retired radio and television executive*
Clapp, James Ford, Jr. *architect*
Cole, George Thomas *lawyer*
Cordingley, Mary Jeanette Bowles (Mrs. William Andrew Cordingley) *social worker, psychologist, artist, writer*
Curtis, Philip C. *artist*
DeHaven, Kenneth Le Moyne *retired physician*
Doede, John Henry *investment company executive*
Doglione, Arthur George *data processing executive*
Donaldson, Scott *English language educator, writer*
†Douglas, John Clifton *architect*
†Drinkwater, Herbert R. *mayor*
Evans, Tommy Nicholas *physician, educator*
Fisher, John Richard *engineering consultant, former naval officer*
Foss, Joe *association executive, speaker*
Fox, Kenneth L. *retired newspaper editor, writer*
Friedman, Shelly Arnold *cosmetic surgeon*
Furman, Robert Howard *physician, educator*
Gall, Donald Alan *data processing executive*
Garelick, Martin *transportation executive*
†Gerrity, James Robert *diversified company executive*
Golden, Libby *artist*
Goldwater, Barry Morris *former senator*
Gordon, Rena Joyce *health services researcher, educator*
Gorsuch, John Wilbert *publisher*
Grenell, James Henry *retired manufacturing company executive*
Handy, Robert Maxwell *patent lawyer*
Hansen, Donald W. *insurance and financial services executive*
Haynie, Howard Edward *lawyer*
Hill, John deKoven *architect*
Hill, Louis Allen, Jr. *former university dean, consultant*
Howard, William Gates, Jr. *electronics company executive*
Huizingh, William *former accounting educator*
Jacobson, Frank Joel *cultural organization adminsrator*
Kitchel, Denison *retired lawyer, writer*
Kizziar, Janet Wright *psychologist, author, lecturer*
Klein, Morton Joseph *chemist*
Kline, Arthur Jonathan *electronics engineer*
Krupp, Clarence William *lawyer, personnel and hospital administrator*
Lang, Margo Terzian *artist*
Lowry, Edward Francis, Jr. *lawyer*
Malsack, James Thomas *retired manufacturing company executive*
†McPhee, Malcolm Clinton *physician*
McPherson, Donald J. *metallurgist*
Messinger, Cora R. *funeral director*
Moeck, Walter F. *conductor, music director*
Newman, William Louis *geologist*
Osborn, Leslie Andrewartha *psychiatrist*
†Panks, Gary Allen *golf course architect*
Pavlik, Nancy *convention services executive*
Peterson, Louis Robert *retired consumer products company executive*
Peyton, William Maupin *transportation executive, educator*
Pomeroy, Kent Lytle *physical medicine and rehabilitation physician*
Prisbrey, Rex Prince *insurance agent, underwriter, financial consultant*
Pritzlaff, John Charles, Jr. *former state senator*
Randolph, John Maurice *financial consultant*
Rudd, Eldon *retired congressman*
Ruhlman, Terrell Louis *business executive*
Rutes, Walter Alan *architect*
†Saferite, Linda Lee *library director*
Sanderson, David R. *physician*
Scholder, Fritz *artist*
†Simon, Ernest Robert *physician, business executive*
†Smith, Harlan William *automotive parts manufacturing company executive*
†Smith, Jesse Morgan, Jr. *association executive, consultant*
Smyth, Bernard John *retired newspaper editor*
Soleri, Paolo *architect, urban planner*
Starr, Isidore *law educator*
Stuart, Derald Archie *aerospace company consultant*
Walsh, Edward Joseph *toiletries and food company executive*
Walsh, Mason *retired newspaperman*
Willoughby, Carroll Vernon *retired motel chain executive*
Wolfgang, Bonnie Arlene *musician, bassoonist*
Wright, James Corwin *international management consultant*

Sedona
Chicorel, Marietta Eva *publisher*
Eggert, Robert John, Sr. *economist*
Gregory, James *actor*
Hawkins, David Ramon *psychiatrist, writer, researcher*
Iverson, Wayne Dahl *landscape architect, consultant*
Keane, Mark Edward *public executive and educator*
Sasmor, James Cecil *publisher representative, educator*
Shors, Clayton Marion *cardiologist*
Wolfe, Al *marketing and advertising consultant*

Show Low
Collins, Copp *federal, corporate, institutional consultant*

Sierra Vista
†Lokensgard, Jon A. *school system administrator*
Meyer, William Trenholm *defense company official, real estate executive*

Sonoita
Cook, William Howard *architect*

Sun City
Brown, Robert Harold *retired geography educator*
Corcoran, Eileen Lynch *special education educator emerita*
Dapples, Edward Charles *geologist, educator*
Farwell, Albert Edmond *retired government official, consultant*
Jones, Alexander Elvin *retired foundation executive*
Lapsley, James Norvell, Jr. *minister, pastoral theology educator*
Morse, True Delbert *business and agricultural consultant, former undersecretary of agriculture*
Oppenheimer, Max, Jr. *foreign language educator, consultant, hypnotherapist*
Pallin, Irving M. *anesthesiologist*
Van Hauer, Robert *former health care company executive*

Sun City West
Anderson, Ernest Washington *manufacturing company executive*
Black, Robert Frederick *former oil company executive*
Brands, Allen Jean *pharmacist*
Cohen, Abraham J. (Al Cohen) *educational administrator*
Curtin, Richard Daniel *management consultant, retired air force officer, space pioneer*
De Layo, Leonard Joseph *former state education official*
Edwards, F(loyd) Kenneth *journalist, educator, management consultant, marketing executive*
Mariella, Raymond P. *chemistry educator, consultant*
Mc Cune, John Francis, III *retired architect*
O'Brien, Gerald James *utilities executive*
Person, Robert John *financial management consultant*
Peshkin, Samuel David *lawyer*
Randall, Claire *church executive*
Schmitz, Charles Edison *evangelist*
Schrag, Adele Frisbie *business education educator*
Smith, Virginia Dodd (Mrs. Haven Smith) *congresswoman*
Van Horssen, Arden Darrell *retired manufacturing executive*
Williams, William Harrison *retired librarian*
Woodruff, Neil Parker *agricultural engineer*

Sun Lakes
Houser, Harold Byron *epidemiologist*
Johnson, Marian Ilene *education educator*
Thompson, Loring Moore *retired college administrator, writer*

Surprise
Clark, Lloyd *historian, educator*

Tempe
†Abell, James Logan *architect*
Abraham, Willard B. *special education educator*
†Akers, Lex A. *electonics director*
Alisky, Marvin Howard *political science educator*
Anand, Suresh Chandra *physician*
Aronson, Jerome Melville *plant physiology educator*
Baker, Roland Jerald *association executive*
Balanis, Constantine Apostle *electrical engineering educator*
Beakley, George Carroll, Jr. *mechanical engineering educator*
Bennett, ElDean *mass communication educator, broadcaster*
Berman, Neil Sheldon *chemical engineering educator*
Bidwill, William V. *professional football executive*
†Borovansky, Vladimir Theodore *librarian*
Brack, O. M., Jr. *English language educator*
Burgoyne, Edward Eynon *chemistry educator*
Burke, William James *chemist, educator, consultant*
Buseck, Peter Robert *geochemistry educator*
Carpenter, Ray Warren *materials scientist and engineer, educator*
Cheatham, Glenn Wallace *leisure studies educator, consultant, researcher*
Christie, Clarence J. *insurance brokerage executive*
Clark, Gary C. *football player*
Clevenger, Jeffrey Griswold *mining company executive*
Converti, Vincenzo *computer systems company executive*
Coor, Lattie Finch *university president*
Cowley, John Maxwell *physics educator*
Dietz, Robert Sinclair *retired geology educator*
Evans, Lawrence Jack, Jr. *lawyer*
Farber, Bernard *sociologist, educator*
Farris, Martin Theodore *economist, educator*
Ferry, David Keane *electrical engineering educator*
Files, L(awrence) Burke *financial consultant*
Frischknecht, Lee Conrad *retired broadcasting executive*
Gerking, Shelby Delos, Jr. *zoologist, educator*
Goodwin, Kemper *architect, retired*
Gordon, Leonard *sociology educator*
Goronkin, Herbert *physicist*
Goyer, Robert Stanton *communication educator*
Grigsby, Jefferson Eugene, Jr. *artist, educator*
Gwinner, Robert Fred, Jr. *marketing educator*
†Hald, Alan P. *computer company executive*
Harris, Mark *English educator, author*
Harward, Naomi Markee *retired social worker and educator, volunteer*
Iverson, Peter James *historian, educator*
Joyner, Seth *professional football player*
Juvet, Richard Spalding, Jr. *chemistry educator*

Karady, George Gyorgy electrical engineering educator, consultant
Kaufman, Irving engineering educator
†Kelly, Rita Mae professor, researcher
Klett, Mark C. photographer, educator
Krus, David James statistician
Lombardi, Eugene Patsy orchestra conductor, violinist, educator, recording artist
Lounsbury, John Frederick geographer, educator
†MacKinnon, Stephen R. Asian studies administrator, educator
Marsh, Roberta Reynolds educator, consultant
Matheson, Alan Adams law educator
Mayer, James Walter materials science educator
†McKeever, Jeffrey D. computer company executive
Mc Sheffrey, Gerald Rainey architect, educator, city planner
Metcalf, Virgil Alonzo economics educator
†Metros, Mary Teresa librarian
Miller, Warren Edward political scientist
†Mitchell, Harry E. mayor, educator
Montero, Darrel Martin sociologist, social worker, educator
Ney, James Walter Edward Colby English language educator
Nigam, Bishan Perkash physics educator
Noce, Robert Henry neuropsychiatrist, educator
Overman, Glenn Delbert college dean emeritus
Pany, Kurt Joseph accounting educator, consultant
Patten, Duncan Theunissen ecologist educator
†Pettit, George Robert chemistry educator, cancer researcher
Péwé, Troy Lewis geologist, educator
Poe, Jerry B. financial educator
Raby, William Louis author
Richards, Gale Lee communications educator
Roy, Radha Raman physics educator
Ryan, James (Buddy Ryan) professional football coach
Sabine, Gordon Arthur educator, writer
Sackton, Frank Joseph university official, lecturer, retired army officer
Schroder, Dieter Karl electrical engineering educator
Shaw, Milton Clayton mechanical engineering educator
Simmons, Clyde professional football player
Simon, Sheldon Weiss political science educator
Singhal, Avinash Chandra engineering educator
Skibitzke, Herbert Ernst, Jr. hydrologist
†Smith, David John physicist, educator
Smith, Harvey Alvin mathematics educator, consultant
Starrfield, Sumner Grosby astrophysics educator, researcher
Tambs, Lewis Arthur diplomat, historian, educator
Thums, Charles William designer, consultant
Tillery, Bill W. physics educator
Treichler, Harvey Albert financial planner
Turk, Rudy Henry artist, retired museum director
Uttal, William R(eichenstein) psychology and engineering educator, research scientist
†Vandenberg, Edwin James chemist, educator
Wales, Hugh Gregory marketing educator, business executive
Walker, Theodore Delbert landscape architect
Wang, Alan Ping-I mathematics educator
Weigend, Guido Gustav geographer, educator
Whitehurst, Harry Bernard chemistry educator
Wilson, Lawrence Frank (Larry Wilson) professional football team executive
†Zeitlin, Marilyn A. museum director
†Ziurys, Lucy Marie radio astronomer, chemist

Tubac

Miller, Frederick Robeson banker

Tucson

†Abrams, Eric R. principal
Abrams, Herbert Kerman physician, educator
Acker, Robert Flint microbiologist
Alcorn, Stanley Marcus plant pathology educator
Alpert, Joseph Stephen physician, educator
Altman, Ellen librarian, educator
Anderson, Rachael Keller library administrator
Angel, James Roger Prior astronomer
Arnell, Walter James William mechanical engineering educator, consultant
Auslander, Steven Lawrence advertising executive, newspaper editor
Austin, John Norman classics educator
Barich, Dewey Frederick emeritus educational administrator
Barrett, Bruce Richard physics educator
Bartocha, Bodo scientist, educator
Barton, Stanley Faulkner management consultant
Battistelli, Joseph John electronics executive
Bayless, Charles Edward lawyer, utility executive
Beach, Lee Roy psychologist, educator
Beigel, Allan psychiatry educator
Belk, John Blanton educational and cultural organization executive
Berlat, William Leonard lawyer
†Bermingham, Peter museum director
Bernhardt, Robert music director, conductor
Beverly, Theria M. reading educator
Bilby, Richard Mansfield federal judge
Birkinbine, John, II philatelist
Block, Michael Kent economics and law educator, public policy association executive, former government official, consultant
†Bowers, William S. educator
Boyse, Edward Arthur research physician
†Brault, James William physicist
†Breckenridge, Klindt Duncan architect
Briggs, Peter Stromme art historian, curator
Broadfoot, Albert Lyle physicist
Brosin, Henry Walter psychiatrist, educator
Browning, William Docker federal judge
Bryant, Charles Austin, IV pediatrician, medical facility director
†Burg, Walter A. airport terminal executive
Burrows, Benjamin physician, educator
Capp, Michael Paul physician, educator
Carleton, Willard Tracy finance educator
Carruthers, Peter Ambler physicist, educator
†Cate, Rodney Michael academic administrator
Chafee, Judith Davidson architect
Champagne, John F., Jr. mining company executive
Chen, Chuan Fang mechanical engineering educator
Cherry, Ronald Lee law librarian, educator
Chidester, Otis Holden retired secondary education educator
Cisler, Theresa Ann osteopath
Clarke, James Weston political science educator, writer
†Clement, Nicholas I. principal
Conant, Howard Somers artist, educator
Cook, Gary Dennis music educator
Cremer, Mabelle A. obstetrician, gynecologist
Dalen, James Eugene physician, educator
Davidson, Dalwyn Robert electric utility executive
Davidson, Lacinda Susan materials engineer, chemist
Davis, James Luther retired utilities executive, lawyer
Davis, Stanley Nelson hydrologist, educator
†Day, Ann state legislator
Dessler, Alexander Jack space physics and astronomy educator, scientist
De Young, David Spencer astrophysicist
Dickinson, Donald Charles library science educator
Dickinson, Robert Earl atmospheric scientist, educator
Dinnerstein, Leonard historian, educator
Dinsmore, Philip Wade architect
Dobbs, Dan Byron lawyer
Dodd, Charles Gardner physical chemist
Dolph, Wilbert Emery lawyer
Drach, George Wisse urology educator
Dufner, Max retired German language educator
Eckdahl, Donald Edward manufacturing company executive
Eckhardt, August Gottlieb law educator
Ewy, Gordon Allen cardiologist, educator
Flint, Willis Wolfschmidt (Willi Wolfschmidt) artist
Forster, Leslie Stewart chemistry educator
†Foster, Kennith Earl life sciences educator
Franklin, John Orland lawyer
Freeh, Edward James chemical engineer
Fritts, Harold Clark dendrochronology educator, researcher
Froman, Sandra Sue lawyer
Fuller, Wallace Hamilton research scientist, educator
Galloway, Kenneth Franklin electrical engineering educator
Ganapol, Barry Douglas nuclear engineering educator, consultant
Gantz, David Alfred lawyer, university official
Gerba, Charles Peter microbiologist, educator
Gieseler, Eugene C. lawyer
Golden, Judith Greene artist, educator
Gourley, Ronald Robert architect, educator
†Grand, Marcia civic worker
Grand, Richard D. lawyer
†Green, Jerrold David political science educator, academic administrator
Green, Robert Scott biotechnology company executive
Gross, Joseph Francis retired bio-engineering educator
Guice, John Thompson retired air force officer
Guimond, John Patrick financial consultant
Hagedorn, Henry Howard entomology educator
Halonen, Marilyn Jean immunologist, pharmacologist, educator
Hampel, Alvin advertising executive
Hancocks, David Morgan museum director, architect
Harcleroad, Fred Farley education educator
Hartmann, William Kenneth astronomy scientist
Hatfield, Charles Donald newspaper executive
Haynes, Caleb Vance, Jr. geology and archaeology educator
Heins, Marilyn college dean, pediatrics educator, author
Heller, Frederick retired mining company executive
Henderson, Roger C. law educator, former dean
†Hershberger, Robert Glen dean, architect
Heurlin, Bruce R. lawyer
Hildebrand, John G(rant) neurobiologist, educator
Hill, Henry Allen physicist, educator
Hoffmann, William Frederick astronomer
Houle, Joseph Adrien orthopaedic surgeon
Howard, Robert Franklin observatory administrator, astronomer
Hubbard, William Bogel planetary sciences educator
Hucker, Charles Oscar author, former history educator
Hughes, Malcolm Kenneth dendrochronologist, educator, administrator
Hull, Herbert Mitchell plant physiologist, researcher
Humphrey, John Julius university program director, historian, writer
Hunt, Bobby Ray electrical engineering educator, consultant
Hunten, Donald Mount planetary scientist, educator
†Hurt, Charles college librarian
Hurt, Charlie Deuel, III library school director, educator
Hutchinson, Charles Smith, Jr. book publisher
Ingalls, Jeremy poet, educator
Isenhower, Eleanor Anne Hexamer state government administrator
Jackson, Kenneth Arthur physicist, researcher
Jefferies, John Trevor astronomer, astrophysicist, observatory administrator
Johnson, John Gray retired university chancellor
Jones, Frank Wyman management consultant, mechanical engineer
Jones, Roger Clyde electrical engineer, educator
Jones, Warren David landscape architect, landscape architecture educator
†Kaltenbach, C. Colin dean, educator
Kaszniak, Alfred Wayne neuropsychologist
Kececioglu, Dimitri Basil mechanical engineering educator
Kerwin, William James electrical engineering educator, consultant
Kessler, John Otto physicist, educator
Kiersch, George Alfred geological consultant, retired educator
†Kim, Yi Hwa industrial hygienist, safety engineer
Kimble, William Earl lawyer
King, Marcia management consultant
Kingery, William David ceramics and anthropology educator
Kingsolver, Barbara Ellen writer
Kinney, Robert Bruce mechanical engineering educator
Kirk, Samuel Alexander psychologist, educator
Klotz, Arthur Paul physician, educator
†Krider, E. Philip atmospheric scientist, educator
Lacagnina, Michael Anthony judge
Laird, Wilbur David, Jr. librarian
Lamb, Ursula Schaefer history educator
Lamb, Willis Eugene, Jr. physicist, educator
Langendoen, Donald Terence linguistics educator
Law, John Harold biochemistry educator
Leavitt, Jerome Edward childhood educator
Lebowitz, Michael David epidemiologist
Leibacher, John William astronomer
Lesher, Robert Overton lawyer
Levenson, Alan Ira psychiatrist, physician, educator
Levy, Eugene Howard planetary sciences educator, researcher
Lewis, Wilbur H. educational management consultant
Livermore, Joseph McMaster judge
Lohr, Mary Margaret nursing educator, university dean
Long, Austin geosciences educator
Marcus, Frank Isadore physician, educator
Marquez, Alfredo C. federal judge
Marshall, Robert Herman economics educator
Martin, Paul Edward retired insurance company executive
Maxon, Don Carlton construction company executive, mining company executive
Mc Connell, Robert Eastwood architect, educator
McCormick, Floyd Guy, Jr. agricultural educator, academic administrator
Mc Donald, John Richard lawyer
McNeill, Frederick Wallace lawyer, educator, writer, federal government consultant, former military and commercial pilot
McNulty, Michael Francis lawyer
Meeker, Robert Eldon retired manufacturing company executive
Meislin, Harvey Warren emergency healthcare physician, professional society administrator
Metcalfe, Darrel Seymour agronomist, educator
Miller, George mayor
Miller, Liz Rodriguez public library system director, librarian
Mockridge, Norton writer, editor
Momaday, Navarre Scott English educator, author
Moreno, Manuel D. bishop
†Morford, James Warren internation health care executive
Morrow, James Franklin lawyer
Mullikin, Vernon Eugene aerospace executive
Nagy, Bartholomew Stephen geochemist, educator
Nation, James Edward speech pathologist
Neal, James Madison, Jr. editor
Nelson, Edward Humphrey architect
Nelson, Lawrence Olaf administrative educator
Netting, Robert M. anthropology educator
Neuman, Shlomo P. hydrology educator
Nixon, Robert Obey, Sr. business educator
†Noland, Patricia Ann state legislator
Nordby, Gene Milo agricultural engineering educator
Nugent, Charles Arter physician
O'Leary, Thomas Michael lawyer
Olson, Lute university athletic coach
Osborne, Thomas Cramer mineral industry consultant
Osterberg, Charles Lamar marine radioecologist, oceanographer
Pace, Thomas M. lawyer
Pacheco, Manuel Trinidad university president
Parmenter, Robert Haley physics educator
Parry, Pamela Jeffcott association executive, art librarian
Pearson, Paul Brown nutritionist, educator
Peeler, Stuart Thorne petroleum industry executive and independent oil operator
Peete, Russell Fitch, Jr. aircraft appraiser
Pepper, Ian L. environmental microbiologist, research scientist, educator
Pickrell, Timothy E. lawyer
Porcello, Leonard Joseph engineering research and development executive
†Powell, Richard C. physicist, educator, researcher
Preston, Kendall, Jr. electro-optical engineer
Prince, John Luther, III engineering educator
Pronove-Irreverre, Pacita medical officer
Reid, Charles Phillip Patrick academic administrator, researcher, professor
Reinmuth, Oscar MacNaughton physician, educator
Renard, Kenneth George civil engineer
†Resnick, Cindy state legislator
Re Velle, Jack B(oyer) consulting statistician
Riggs, Frank Lewis foundation executive
†Riggs, John B. architect
Roe, Charles Richard baritone
Roemer, Elizabeth astronomer, educator
Roll, John McCarthy federal judge
Roos, Nestor Robert consultant
Rose, Hugh management consultant
Ross, Glynn opera administrator
Rountree, Janet Caryl astrophysicist
Ruggill, Solomon P. psychologist
Russ, Joanna writer, English language educator
Saul, Kenneth Louis retired utility company executive
Schaefer, John Paul chemist, corporate executive
Schannep, John Dwight brokerage firm executive
Schorr, S. L. lawyer
Schottland, Charles Irwin retired legal educator
Scott, William Coryell medical executive
Seaman, Arlene Anna musician, educator
Sears, William Rees engineering educator
Seger, Martha Romayne financial economist
Shannon, Robert Rennie optical sciences center administrator, educator
Shropshire, Donald Gray hospital executive
Shultz, Silas Harold lawyer
Sibley, William Austin neurologist, educator
Smerdon, Ernest Thomas academic administrator
Smiley, Terah Leroy geosciences educator
Smith, David Wayne psychologist
Smith, Josef Riley internist
Smith, Vernon Lomax economist, researcher
Sonett, Charles Philip physicist
Soren, David archaeology educator, administrator
Speare, Elizabeth George writer
Speas, Robert Dixon aeronautical engineer, aviation company executive
Speer, Phillip Bradford commercial business executive
Stini, William Arthur anthropologist, educator
Stoffle, Carla Joy dean university library
Strittmatter, Peter Albert astronomer, educator
Strong, John William lawyer, educator
Sundt, Harry Wilson construction company executive
Swalin, Richard Arthur scientist, company executive
Sypherd, Paul Starr microbiologist
Terlizzi, Raymond Thomas judge
Tirrell, John Albert religious organization executive, consultant
†Toppel, Alan Herman organization executive
Troup, Thomas James electronics company executive
Underwood, Jane Hainline Hammons anthropologist, educator
†Velez-Ibanez, Carlos Guillermo anthropology educator, research laboratory administrator
Vicker, Ray writer
Volgy, Thomas John mayor, political science educator
Wahlke, John Charles political science educator
Wait, James Richard electrical engineering educator, scientist
Walker, F. Ann chemistry educator, researcher
†Wallace, Terry Charles, Jr. geophysicist, educator
†Wallach, Leslie Rothaus architect
†Waterbrook, Keith Jennings hospital administrator, educator
Weaver, Albert Bruce university administrator
Weber, Charles Walter nutrition educator
Weber, Samuel editor
Weinstein, Ronald S. physician, pathologist, educator
White, Alvin Swauger aerospace scientist, consultant
Whiting, Allen Suess political science educator, writer, consultant
Wickham, John Adams, Jr. retired army officer
Williams, Ben Franklin, Jr. mayor, lawyer
Willis, Clifford Leon geologist
Willoughby, Stephen Schuyler mathematics educator
Wilson, John Lewis university official
Winfree, Arthur Taylor biologist, educator
Wolfe, William Jerome librarian, English language educator
Wolfe, William Louis optics educator
Wolff, Sidney Carne astronomer, observatory administrator
Wood, Evelyn Nielsen reading dynamics business executive
Wygnanski, Israel Jerzy aerospace engineering educator
Yassin, Robert Alan museum administrator, curator
Yocum, Harrison Gerald horticulturist, botanist, educator, researcher
Zeigler, Bernard Phillip electrical and computer engineering educator
Ziehler, Tony Joseph insurance agent
Zube, Ervin Herbert landscape architect, geographer, educator

Vail

Maierhauser, Joseph George entrepreneur

Window Rock

Zah, Peterson American Indian tribal executive

Youngtown

Gross, Al electrical engineer, consultant

Yuma

Hudson, John Irvin retired marine officer
Martin, James Franklin physician, lawyer

ARKANSAS

Arkadelphia

Dunn, Charles DeWitt academic administrator
Elrod, Ben Moody academic administrator
Grant, Daniel Ross retired university president
†Martin, Marilyn Joan library director
†Thomas, Herman L. school system administrator

Batesville

Carius, Robert Wilhelm mathematics and science educator, retired naval officer
Griffith, John Vincent academic official
Harkey, John Norman state judge

Beebe

†Owen, William Harold, Jr. academic administrator

Bella Vista

Medin, Myron James, Jr. city manager
Musacchia, X(avier) J(oseph) physiology and biophysics educator

Bentonville

Bruce, Robert Thomas retail executive
Carter, Paul R. retail executive
Glass, David D. department store company executive, professional baseball team executive
Shewmaker, Jack Clifford retired retail executive, rancher, consultant
Walton, S. Robson discount department store chain executive
†Yates, Joe Elton real estate developer, state senator

Blytheville

Fendler, Oscar lawyer

Camden

†Brown, George J. academic administrator
†Smith, Judy Seriale social services administrator

Clarksville

†Stephenson, C. Gene academic administrator

Conway

†Bartos, Phil information management technology executive
Daugherty, Billy Joe banker
Holt, Frank Ross retired aerospace engineer
Kearns, Terrance Brophy English language educator
†Kline, Rodger S. marketing professional
Mc New, Bennie Banks economics and finance educator
†Morgan, Charles Donald, Jr. manufacturing executive
†Reddin, George religious organization administrator
Stiritz, Marette McCauley English language educator, consultant
Thompson, Winfred Lee university president, lawyer
Titlow, Larry Wayne physical education and kinesiology educator

Cotter

Naylor, George LeRoy lawyer, rail transportation executive

Dermott

Kinney, Abbott Ford radio broadcasting executive

Dumas

†Schexnayder, Charlotte Tillar state legislator

El Dorado

†Barnes, Harry F. federal judge
Lee, Vernon Roy minister
McNutt, Jack Wray oil company executive
Murphy, Charles Haywood, Jr. petroleum company executive
Vaughan, Odie Frank oil company executive
Watkins, Jerry West retired oil company executive, lawyer

Eureka Springs
Dragonwagon, Crescent *writer*
Epley, Lewis Everett, Jr. *lawyer*
Sackett, Ross DeForest *publisher*

Fayetteville
†Ahlers, Glen-Peter, Sr. *library director, educator, consultant*
Andrews, John Frank *civil and environmental engineering educator*
Bassett, Woodson William, Jr. *lawyer*
†Beyrouty, Craig A. *agronomist, educator*
Brown, Connell Jean *retired animal science educator*
Burggraf, Frank Bernard, Jr. *landscape architect, educator*
Clayton, Frances Elizabeth *cytologist, scientist, educator*
Cook, Doris Marie *accountant, educator*
Davis, Wylie Herman *lawyer, educator*
Dulan, Harold Andrew *former insurance company executive, educator*
Evans, William Lee *biologist*
†Fairchild, Robert Samuel *state legislator, insurance company executive*
Farrell, Karolyn Kay McMillan *adult education educator*
Faulkner, Claude Winston *language professional*
Ferritor, Daniel E. *university official*
Gaddy, James Leoma *chemical engineer, educator*
Gatewood, Willard Badgett, Jr. *historian*
†Green, Thomas James *archaeologist*
Harrison, John Arthur *library administrator*
Hay, Robert Dean *retired management educator*
Jones, Douglas Clyde *author*
Jones, Euine Fay *architect, educator*
Jones, Fay *architect*
Kinnamon, Keneth *English language educator*
Knowles, Malcolm Shepherd *education educator*
LeFevre, Elbert Walter, Jr. *civil engineering educator*
Madison, Bernard L. *academic dean, mathematics educator*
†Malone, David Roy *university administrator, state senator*
McCartney, Allen Papin *anthropology educator*
Mc Gimsey, Charles Robert, III *anthropologist*
†Musick, Gerald Joe *entomology educator*
Niblock, Walter Raymond *lawyer*
Oxford, Charles William *university dean, chemical engineer*
Pearson, Charles Thomas, Jr. *lawyer*
Purvis, Hoyt Hughes *political scientist, academic administrator, educator*
Richardson, Nolan *university athletic coach*
Rosenberg, Leon Joseph *marketing educator*
Rutledge, Elliott Moye *soil scientist, educator*
†Scharlau, Charles Edward, III *natural gas company executive*
Schoppmeyer, Martin William *education educator*
Smart, Clifton Murray, Jr. *architect, educator*
Steele, Kenneth Franklin, Jr. *hydrology educator, resource center director, researcher*
Vorsanger, Fred S. *university administrator*
Waters, H. Franklin *federal judge*
West, Charles Patrick *agronomist, educator*
Williams, Doyle Z. *university dean, educator*
Williams, Miller *poet, translator*
Wolf, Duane Carl *microbiologist*

Flippin
Sanders, Steven Gill *utilities executive*

Foreman
†Horn, Hoye D. *state legislator, farmer*

Fort Smith
Banks, David Russell *health care executive*
Crow, Neil Edward *radiologist*
Flanders, Donald Hargis *manufacturing company executive*
Francis, Darryl Robert *former banker*
†Goins, Randall *grain company executive*
†Gooden, Benny L. *school system administrator*
Hembree, Hugh Lawson, III *diversified holding company executive*
Hendren, Jimm Larry *federal judge*
Hendrickson, Boyde W. *health products executive*
Hoge, Marlin Boyd *surgeon*
Larson, Larry *librarian*
†Marquard, William Albert *diversified manufacturing company executive*
†Pollan, Carolyn Joan *state legislator, job research administrator*
Qualls, Robert L. *manufacturing executive, banker, former state official, educator*
Snider, James Rhodes *radiologist*
Stephens, Bobby Wayne *nursing home administrator*
†Yarbrough, Jerry A. *transportation company executive*
Young, Robert A., III *freight systems executive*

Glenwood
Klopfenstein, Philip Arthur *financial development officer, historical researcher*

Greenwood
†Walters, Bill *lawyer*

Hamburg
†Murphy, N. B. (Nap Murphy) *state congressman, automobile dealer*

Harrison
Garrison, F. Sheridan *transportation executive*
Henley, J. Smith *federal judge*

Helena
†Cunningham, Ernest *state legislator*
Roscopf, Charles Buford *lawyer*

Hiwasse
Sutherland, Gail Russell *retired industrial equipment manufacturing company executive*

Hot Springs
†Farley, Roy C. *rehabilitation researcher, educator*

Hot Springs National Park
Britt, Henry Middleton *retired judge*
Tanenbaum, Bernard Jerome, Jr. *corporate executive*

Hot Springs Village
Dellow, Reginald Leonard *advertising executive*
Robinson, Donald Walter *university dean*
Schroeder, Donald Perry *retired food products company executive*

Huntsville
Carr, Gerald Paul *former astronaut, business executive, former marine officer*

Jefferson
Casciano, Daniel Anthony *biologist*
Hart, Ronald Wilson *radiobiologist, toxicologist, government research executive*

Jonesboro
Elkins, Francis Clark *history educator, university official*
Smith, Eugene Wilson *retired university president and educator*

Little Rock
Adams, Daniel Fenton *legal educator*
Ahlen, John William, III *state official, scientist, educator*
†Anderson, Joel E. *academic administrator*
Anderson, Philip Sidney *lawyer*
†Andrews, Collins Adams, III *data processing company executive*
†Argue, James B., Jr. *religious organization administrator*
Arnold, Morris Sheppard *federal judge*
Arnold, Richard Sheppard *federal judge*
Barron, Almen Leo *microbiologist*
Bethea, William C. *financial administrator, lawyer*
Bisno, Alison Peck *investment banker*
Blass, Noland, Jr. *retired architect*
Bobbitt, Max E. *telecommunications executive*
†Booth, Richard Donald *radio station executive*
Boucher, Wayne Irving *policy analyst*
Bowen, William Harvey *banker, lawyer*
†Bradbury, Curt *bank executive*
Breen, John Francis *retired banker*
Brown, Dee Alexander *author*
†Bryan, Lloyd Leon (Doc Bryan) *state legislator*
Bryant, Winston *state attorney general*
Butler, Richard Colburn *banker, lawyer*
Campbell, George Emerson *lawyer*
Campbell, Gilbert Sadler *surgery educator, surgeon*
Cave, Mac Donald *anatomy educator*
†Chaffin, Charlie Cole *senator*
†Cobb, James Richard *banker*
Compton, Susan LaNell *retired librarian*
Corbin, Donald L. *judge*
Cromwell, Edwin Boykin *architect*
Cross, J. Bruce *lawyer*
†Dillard, Dennis Alexander *department stores executive*
Dillard, William, II *department store executive*
Dillard, William T. *department store chain executive*
Diner, Wilma Canada *radiologist, educator*
Doherty, James Edward, III *physician, educator*
Donovan, Herbert Alcorn, Jr. *bishop*
Doyle, Lee Lee *research scientist, educator*
Drummond, Winslow *lawyer*
DuBois, Alan Beekman *art museum administrator, curator*
Duffey, William Simon, Jr. *lawyer*
Dumeny, Marcel Jacque *lawyer*
Dyke, James Trester *building materials distributing company executive*
Eisele, Garnett Thomas *federal judge*
Ferguson, John Lewis *state historian*
Ferris, Ernest Joseph *radiology educator*
Fiske, Robert Bishop, Jr. *lawyer*
Fogleman, John Albert *lawyer, former judge*
Ford, Joe Thomas *telephone company executive, former state senator*
†Foster, Lynn *law librarian, lawyer*
Fribourgh, James Henry *university administrator*
Friedlander, Edward Jay *journalism educator*
Garcia-Rill, Edgar Enrique *neuroscientist*
Gardner, Kathleen D. *gas company executive, lawyer*
Gates, David Allan *lawyer*
Givens, John Kenneth *manufacturing executive*
Glaze, Thomas A. *state supreme court justice*
Goss, Kenneth George *physician, educator*
Gray, John Wylie *university dean, consultant*
Greenberg, Paul *newspaperman*
Guggenheim, Frederick Gibson *psychiatry educator*
Gulley, Wilbur Paul, Jr. *former savings and loan executive*
Gunter, Russell Allen *lawyer*
Harris, Oren *retired federal judge*
†Harrison, Eric E. *journalist, entertainer*
Hatcher, Joe Branch *banker*
†Hathaway, Charles E. *academic administrator*
Haught, William Dixon *lawyer*
†Hickingbotham, Frank D. *food product executive*
†Hickingbotham, Herren C. *food products executive*
†Hinshaw, Jerrold Eldon *state legislator*
Hinson, Jack Allsbrook *research toxicologist, educator*
†Holmes, James Frederick *minister*
Holt, Jack Wilson, Jr. *state supreme court chief justice*
Hough, Aubrey Johnston, Jr. *pathologist, physician, educator*
Howard, George, Jr. *federal judge*
Jansen, G. Thomas *dermatologist*
Jennings, Alston *lawyer*
†Jones, Phillip Lindsey *librarian*
Keaton, William Thomas *academic administrator, pastor*
†Keet, Jim, III *management consultant, state legislator*
Lampkin, Stephen Bradley *hospital administrator*
Ledbetter, Calvin Reville, Jr. (Cal Ledbetter) *political science educator, university dean, former legislator*
Levy, Eugene Pfeifer *architect*
Long, Walter Edward *international trade company executive, consultant*
Lucy, Dennis Durwood, Jr. *neurologist*
Lumpkin, JimmieLou Fisher *state official*
†Lutgen, Robert R. *newspaper editor*
†Maloney, Francis Patrick *physiatrist*
May, Ronald Alan *lawyer*
McAdams, Herbert Hall, II *banker*
McCabe, Beverly Jean *nutritionist, educator*
McConnell, John Wesley *real estate-resort developer, corporate executive*
McCuen, William James (Bill) *state official*
Mc Donald, Andrew J. *bishop*
McGowan, Michael Benedict *investment banker*
McMillan, Donald Edgar *pharmacologist*
McMullin, Carleton Eugene *manufacturing executive*
†Miles, Travis Anthony *state senator*
Morris, Walter Scott *investment company executive*
Mulkey, Jack Clarendon *library director*
Murphey, Arthur Gage, Jr. *legal educator*
Nelson, Edward Sheffield *lawyer, former utility company executive*
Newbern, William David *state supreme court justice*
Patten, Gerland Paul *lawyer*
Pauly, John Edward *anatomist*
Pierson, Richard Allen *hospital administrator*
Portis, Charles McColl *reporter, writer*
Purtle, John Ingram *lawyer, former state supreme court justice*
Reasoner, Stephen M. *federal judge*
Reeves, Rosser Scott, III *investment company executive*
Roy, Elsijane Trimble *federal judge*
Shults, Robert Luther, Jr. *lawyer*
Simmons, Bill *newsman*
Smith, Charles Wilson, Jr. *university dean*
†Smith, Griffin, Jr. *lawyer*
Starr, John Robert *retired newspaper editor, political columnist*
Stead, William White *physician, educator, public health administrator*
Stephens, Jackson Thomas *investment executive*
Stephens, Warren A. *banking executive*
Suen, James Yee *otolaryngologist, educator*
Talley-Morris, Neva Bennett *lawyer*
Townsend, James Willis *computer scientist*
Truemper, John James, Jr. *architect*
Truex, Dorothy Adine *retired university administrator*
Tucker, Jim Guy, Jr. *governor*
†Walker, L. T. *bishop*
Ward, Harry Pfeffer *physician, university chancellor*
Warner, Cecil Randolph, Jr. *lawyer*
†Wassell, Irene Martin *food editor*
†Wilcox, Jerry C. *architect*
Williams, C(harles) Fred *history professor*
†Wilson, William R., Jr. *judge*
Witherspoon, Carolyn Brack *lawyer*
†Wolfe, Jonathan James *pharmacy educator*
Wolfe, Townsend Durant, III *art museum director, curator*
Woods, Henry *federal judge*
Wright, Susan Webber *federal judge*

Lowell
Bergant, Paul R. *trucking company executive, lawyer*
Thompson, James Kirk *transportation executive*

Magnolia
Brinson, Harold Thomas *university president emeritus*
†Gamble, Steven G. *academic administrator*

Malvern
†Hopkins, George *senator*

Marked Tree
†Everett, Mike *lawyer*

Monticello
Babin, Claude Hunter *history educator*
Ball, William Kenneth *lawyer*

Morrilton
Havener, Robert Dale *agricultural institute administrator*
Thompson, Robert Lee *agricultural economist, foundation administrator*

Mountain Home
Anderson, Kenneth Norman *retired magazine editor, author*
Baker, Robert Leon *naval medical officer*
†Langevin, Thomas Harvey *higher education consultant*
Saltzman, Benjamin Nathan *retired state health administrator, physician*

Newport
Boyce, Edward Wayne, Jr. *lawyer*
Thaxton, Marvin Dell *lawyer, farmer*

North Little Rock
Griffith, Jack William *medical librarian*
†Hoofman, Cliff *state senator*
Marshall, Terrell *lawyer*
Patty, Claibourne Watkins, Jr. *lawyer*

Osceola
Wilson, Ralph Edwin *lawyer, justice*

Pine Bluff
†Bradford, Jay Turner *insurance executive, state legislator*
†Davis, Lawrence A. *academic administrator*
Engle, Carole Ruth *aquaculture economics educator*
Jones, John Harris *lawyer, banker*
Long, Edward Arlo *business consultant, retired manufacturing company executive*
Ramsay, Louis Lafayette, Jr. *lawyer, banker*
Seawell, William Thomas *former airline executive*
†Wilkins, Josetta Edwards *state representative*

Rogers
Hudson, James T. *food company executive*
Hudson, Michael T. *food company executive*

Roland
Ebert, Richard Vincent *physician, educator*

Russellville
Chesnut, Franklin Gilmore *clergyman*
†Hardin, Luther *state senator*
Inch, Morris Alton *theology educator*
Jones, James Rees *retired oil company executive*
Streett, Alexander Graham *lawyer*

Scranton
Uzman, Betty Geren *pathologist, retired educator*

Searcy
†Beebe, Mike *state senator, lawyer*
†Burks, David Basil *academic administrator, educator*
†Capps, John Paul *state legislator, radio station owner*
Miller, Ken Leroy *religious studies educator, consultant, writer*
Oldham, Bill W. *mathematics educator*
Organ, Dennis Michael *English educator*
Pryor, Joseph Ehrman *chemistry educator*

Sherwood
†Wood, Marion Douglas *lawyer, state legislator*

Springdale
Cypert, Jimmy Dean *lawyer*
†Hill, Peggy Sue *principal*
Pogue, William Reid *former astronaut, foundation executive, business and aerospace consultant*
†Rogers, Jerry *principal*
†Rollins, Jimmy Don *school system administrator*
†Tollett, Leland Edward *food company executive*
Tyson, Donald John *food company executive*

State University
Fowler, Gilbert L. *dean, educator*
Hansard, James William *library director*
Jones, Charlott Ann *museum director, art educator*
Lindquist, Evan *artist, educator*
Mangieri, John Nicholas *university administrator*
Power, Mary Susan *political science educator*
Ruby, Ralph, Jr. *vocational business educator*

Stuttgart
Bell, Richard Eugene *grain and food company executive*
Jessup, Stewart E. *agricultural products executive*
†Smith, Kevin Andrew *non-profit corportation executive*

Texarkana
†Henry, James Alvin *minister, benefits executive*
Stroud, John Fred, Jr. *state supreme court justice*

West Memphis
Fogleman, Julian Barton *lawyer*
Nance, Cecil Boone, Jr. *lawyer*

CALIFORNIA

Agoura
Naylor-Jackson, Jerry *entertainer, public relations consultant, producer*

Agoura Hills
Chagall, David *journalist, author*
Chang, Chong Eun *chemical engineer*
†Cordon, Frank Joseph *insurance company executive*
deCiutiis, Alfred Charles Maria *medical oncologist, television producer*
Myers, Phillip Fenton *brokerage house executive*
Teresi, Joseph *publishing executive*

Alameda
Bartalini, C. Richard *judge*
Billings, Thomas Neal *computer and publishing executive, management consultant*
Blatt, Beverly Faye *biologist, consultant*
Klehs, Henry John Wilhelm *civil engineer*
Klein, Marc S. *editor, publishing executive*
Stonehouse, James Adam *lawyer*
Taveggia, Thomas Charles *psychology educator*
Verrill, Kathleen Wills *special education educator*
Whorton, M. Donald *occupational and environmental health physician, epidemiologist*

Alamo
Bolles, Richard Nelson *author, clergyman*
Evans, John James *management consultant*
Lee, Richard *martial arts educational executive*
Overby, Lacy Rasco *biotechnology consulting executive*
Plummer, Marcie Stern *real estate broker*
Pritchett, Thomas Ronald *retired metal and chemical company executive*
Whalen, John Sydney *management consultant*

Albany
Boris, Ruthanna *dancer, choreographer, dance therapist, educator*
Chook, Edward Kongyen *disaster medicine educator*

Albion
Martin, Bill *artist, art educator*

Alhambra
Duke, Donald Norman *publisher*
Siler, Walter Orlando, Jr. *retired business executive*

Aliso Viejo
Sanford, Sarah J. *nurse, health care executive*

Alpine
Greenberg, Byron Stanley *newspaper and business executive, consultant*
Samuelson, Derrick William *lawyer*

Alta Loma
Cooper, George Robert *electrical engineer, educator*
Wu, Seng-Chai *financial planner, life insurance agency official*

Altadena
Burden, Jean (Prussing) *poet, writer, editor*
†Gurnis, Michael Christopher *geological sciences educator*
Ikegawa, Shiro *artist*
Ziegler, Raymond Stewart *architect*

Anaheim
Arnwine, William Carrol *industrial engineer*
Balch, Glenn McClain, Jr. *academic administrator, minister, author*
Brownhill, H. Bud *canine behavior therapist*
DuBrin, Stanley *physician, hand surgeon, medical clinics director*
Frontiere, Georgia *professional football team executive*
†Griffin, Gerald D. *engineering company executive*
†Heiner, Dennis Grant *manufacturing company executive*
Herzog, Whitey (Dorrel Norman Elvert Herzog) *professional baseball team executive*
Hubbard, Charles Ronald *engineering executive*
Hughes, Allan Bebout *chamber of commerce executive*
Jackson, Bo (Vincent Edward Jackson) *professional baseball, former football player*
†Jackson, David Robert *school system administrator*

Knox, Chuck (Charles Robert Knox) *professional football coach*
†Lachemann, Marcel *professional baseball manager*
Langston, Mark *professional baseball player*
Lano, Charles Jack *management auditor*
McGarry, Eugene L. *university official*
†Nguyen, Tai Anh *minister*
Prince, Warren Victor *mechanical engineer*
Rohrer, George John *lawyer*
Sloane, Robert Malcolm *hospital administrator*
Stark, Milton Dale *sports association executive*
Waitzkin, Howard Bruce *physician, educator*

Anaheim Hills
Grose, Elinor Ruth *retired elementary education educator*

Angwin
Maxwell, D. Malcolm *college president*

Antioch
Graham, Lanier *art historian, curator, cultural planner*

Anza
Skelton, Red (Richard Skelton) *comedian, artist*

Apple Valley
Mays, George Walter, Jr. *educational administrator, educator, consultant*
Win, Khin Swe *anesthesiologist*

Aptos
Bohn, Ralph Carl *educational consultant, retired educator*
Dobey, James Kenneth *banker*
Heron, David Winston *librarian*
Mechlin, George Francis *electrical manufacturing company executive*
Woods, Gurdon Grant *sculptor*
Zischke, James Braden *entrepreneur*

Arcadia
Baillie, Charles Douglas *banker*
Broderick, Donald Leland *electronics engineer*
Eck, Dennis K. *supermarket chain executive*
Gamboa, George Charles *oral surgeon, educator*
Horner, Althea Jane *psychologist*
†Morse, Judy *science foundation administrator*
Nelson, Garrett R. *retail food company executive*
Seitz, Charles Lewis *computer scientist and engineer*
Sloane, Beverly LeBov *educational writer, consultant*
Stangeland, Roger Earl *retail chain store executive*

Arcata
Barratt, Raymond William *biologist, educator*
Bowker, Lee Harrington *academic administrator*
Emenhiser, JeDon Allen *political science educator, academic administrator*
Fox, Lawrence, III *remote sensing and natural resources educator, consultant*
Hunt, Robert Weldon *mathematics educator, consultant*
Mc Crone, Alistair William *university president*
Wayne, Lowell Grant *air pollution scientist, consultant*

Aromas
Nutzle, Futzie (Bruce John Kleinsmith) *artist, author, cartoonist*

Arrowhead
Bauer, Ralph Leroy *business executive*

Arroyo Grande
Vahsholtz, Robert John *retired manufacturing executive*

Artesia
†Ferris, Pauline *principal*
†Korsmeier, Gary *dairy products executive*
†Moffett, Kenneth Lee *superintendent schools*

Atascadero
Eggertsen, Paul Fred *psychiatrist*
Ogier, Walter Thomas *retired physics educator*

Atherton
Bales, Royal Eugene *philosophy educator*
Chetkovich, Michael N. *accountant*
Fisher, Leon Harold *physicist, emeritus educator*
Goodman, Sam Richard *electronics company executive*
Heyns, Roger William *retired foundation executive and educator*
Hogan, Clarence Lester *retired electronics executive*
Lowry, Larry Lorn *management consulting company executive*
Mc Intyre, Henry Langenberg *former business executive, lawyer*
Starr, Chauncey *research institute executive*

Auburn
Adams, Margaret Bernice *retired museum official*
Falls, Edward Joseph *lawyer, insurance executive, educator*
Hess, Patrick Henry *chemist*
Jeske, Howard Leigh *life insurance company executive, lawyer*

Avila Beach
Kamm, Herbert *journalist*

Azusa
Bonner, Patricia J. *academic dean*
†Felix, Richard E. *academic administrator*
Gray, Paul Wesley *university dean*
Kimnach, Myron William *botanist, horticulturist, consultant*

Bakersfield
Akers, Tom, Jr. *cotton broker, consultant*
Arciniega, Tomas Abel *university president*
Badgley, Theodore McBride *psychiatrist, neurologist*
Boyd, William Harland *historian*
Corder, Michael Paul *physician, educator*
Dorer, Fred Harold *chemistry educator*
†Duquette, Diane Rhea *library director*
Enriquez, Carola Rupert *museum director*
†Groefsema, Bruce *agricultural products executive*
Hart, Donald Milton *automotive and ranching executive, former mayor*
†Hefner, John *principal*
Izenstark, Joseph Louis *radiologist, physician, educator*
Lundquist, Gene Alan *cotton company executive*
Martin, George Francis *lawyer*
†McAlister, Michael Hillis *architect*
Owen, Fred Wynne *lawyer*
Owens, Buck (Alvis Edgar, Jr.) *singer, musician, songwriter*
†Price, Robert O. *police official*
Reep, Edward Arnold *artist*

Balboa Island
Daughaday, William Hamilton *retired physician*

Baldwin Park
Gregory, George G. *lawyer*
Swartz, Stephen Arthur *banker, lawyer*

Barstow
†Jones, Nathaniel *bishop*

Bayside
†Bank, Ron *principal*
Cocks, George Gosson *retired chemical microscopy educator*
Pierce, Lester Laurin *retired pilot, aviation consultant*

Bell Gardens
Hardie, George Graham *casino executive*

Belmont
Lake, David S. *publisher, lawyer*

Belvedere Tiburon
Behrman, Richard Elliot *pediatrician, neonatologist, university dean*
Caselli, Virgil P. *real estate executive*
Cook, Lyle Edwards *retired fund raising executive, consultant*
Cook, Robert Donald *financial service executive*
Crockett, Ethel Stacy *librarian*
Denton, Charles Mandaville *corporate consultant*
Elder, Rex Alfred *civil engineer*
Kramer, Lawrence Stephen *journalist*
Moffitt, Phillip William *magazine editor*
Power, Jules *television producer*

Benicia
Gomez, Edward Casimiro *physician, hospital administrator*

Berkeley
Abel, Carlos Alberto *immunologist*
Abel, Ray *graphic artist*
Adelman, Irma Glicman *economics educator*
Alhadeff, David Albert *economics educator*
Alpen, Edward Lewis *biophysicist, educator*
Alpert, Norman Joseph *merchandising executive*
Alter, Robert B. *comparative literature educator and critic*
Ames, Bruce N(athan) *biochemist, molecular biologist*
Anderson, John Richard *entomologist, educator*
Anderson, William Scovil *classics educator*
Angelakos, Diogenes James *electrical engineering educator*
†Arbegast, David Elwood *landscape architect*
Arnon, Daniel I(srael) *biochemist, educator*
Arons, Jonathan *astrophysicist, educator*
Arveson, William Barnes *mathematics educator*
Attwood, David Thomas *physicist, educator*
Baas, Jacquelynn *art historian, museum administrator*
Bagdikian, Ben Haig *journalist, emeritus university educator*
†Baletta, William *physics research administrator*
Barish, Jonas Alexander *English language educator*
Barker, Horace Albert *biochemist, microbiologist*
Barnes, Thomas G. *law educator*
Bartlett, Neil *chemist, educator*
Baumrind, Diana *research psychologist*
Bellah, Robert Neelly *sociologist, educator*
Bender, Richard *university dean, architect, educator*
Benedict, Burton *museum director, anthropology educator*
Berger, Stanley Allan *mechanical engineering educator*
Bergman, George Mark *mathematician, educator*
Bergman, Robert George *chemist, educator*
Berkner, Klaus Hans *laboratory administrator, physicist*
Berlekamp, Elwyn Ralph *former electronics company executive, mathematics educator*
Bern, Howard Alan *science educator, research biologist*
†Berring, Robert Charles, Jr. *educator, law librarian, dean*
Berry, William Benjamin Newell *geologist, educator, former museum administrator*
Bickel, Peter John *statistician, educator*
Birdsall, Charles Kennedy *electrical engineer*
Blakely, Edward James *economics educator*
Bogy, David B(eauregard) *mechanical engineering educator*
Bolt, Bruce Alan *seismologist, educator*
Bonnell, Victoria Eileen *sociologist*
Bourne, Samuel G. *mathematician, consultant, educator*
Bouwsma, William James *history educator*
Bowyer, C(harles) Stuart *astrophysicist, educator*
Bradley, Marion Zimmer *novelist, editor, educator*
Brandes, Stanley Howard *anthropology educator, writer*
Breslauer, George William *political science educator*
Brewer, Leo *physical chemist, educator*
Brillinger, David Ross *statistician, educator*
Brimhall, George H., Jr. *geologist, educator*
Bronstein, Arthur J. *former linguistics educator*
Browne, Walter Shawn *journalist, chess player*
Buckland, Michael Keeble *librarian, educator*
†Budinger, Thomas Francis *radiologist, educator*
Burger, Edmund Ganes *architect*
Burger, Robert Eugene *author, chess expert*
Burnside, Mary Beth *biology educator, researcher*
Cahill, James Francis *art history educator*
Cain, Bruce Edward *political science educator, consultant*
Cairns, Elton James *chemical engineering educator*
Calame, Alexandre Emile *emeritus French literature educator*
Callenbach, Ernest *writer, editor*
Calloway, Doris Howes *nutrition educator*
Calvin, Melvin *chemist, educator*
Cardwell, Kenneth Harvey *architect, educator*
Carmichael, Ian Stuart Edward *geologist, educator*
Casida, John Edward *entomology educator*
Castaneda, Carlos *anthropologist, author*
Castro, Joseph Ronald *physician, oncology researcher, educator*
Catlin, James C. *environmentalist, land use planner, electrical engineer*
Cerny, Joseph, III *chemistry educator, scientific laboratory administrator, university dean and official*
Chamberlain, Owen *nuclear physicist*
Chamberlin, Michael John *biochemistry educator*
Chandler, David *scientist, educator*
Chapman, G. Arnold *Romance Languages educator*
Cheit, Earl Frank *economist, educator*
Chemsak, J. A. *entomologist*
Chern, Shiing-Shen *mathematics educator*
Chew, Geoffrey Foucar *physicist*
†Chopra, Anil Kumar *civil engineering educator*
Chorin, Alexandre Joel *mathematician, educator*
Clark, James Henry *publishing company executive*
Clark, John Desmond *anthropology educator*
Clark, Thomas Willard *poet*
Clarke, John *physics educator*
Clausen, John Adam *social psychologist*
Clifford, Geraldine Joncich (Mrs. William F. Clifford) *education educator*
Cohen, Marvin Lou *physics educator*
Cole, Roger David *biochemist, educator*
Colson, Elizabeth Florence *anthropologist*
Concepción, David Alden *arbitrator, educator*
Cooper, William Secord *information science educator*
Costa, Gustavo *Italian language educator*
Craib, Ralph Grant *reporter*
Crews, Frederick Campbell *humanities educator, writer*
†Culler, David Ethan *educator*
†Curtis, Garniss Hearfield *geology educator*
Cutter, David Lee *pharmaceutical company executive*
Danton, Joseph Periam *librarian, educator*
Dauben, William Garfield *chemist, educator*
Davidson, Donald Herbert *philosophy educator*
Debreu, Gerard *economics and mathematics educator*
Denn, Morton Mace *chemical engineering educator*
DePaolo, Donald James *earth science educator*
Desoer, Charles Auguste *electrical engineer*
Diamond, Marian Cleeves *anatomy educator*
†Dornfeld, David A. *engineering educator*
Drechsel, Edwin Jared *retired magazine editor*
Dresher, Paul Joseph *composer, music educator, performer*
Dugger, Edwin Ellsworth *composer, educator*
Duhl, Leonard *psychiatrist, educator*
Dundes, Alan *anthropology, writer, educator*
Eckbo, Garrett *landscape architect, urban designer*
Eisenberg, Melvin A. *law educator*
Elberg, Sanford Samuel *university administrator*
Elliott, James Heyer *retired curator university art museum, fine arts consultant*
Ely, Robert Pollock, Jr. *physics educator, researcher*
Enoch, Jay Martin *vision scientist, educator*
Evans, James William *metallurgical educator*
Falcon, Louis Albert *entomology educator, insect pathologist*
Falicov, Leopoldo Maximo *physicist, educator*
Falkner, Frank Tardrew *physician, educator*
Fatt, Irving *optometry and bioengineering educator*
†Faulk, I. Carlton *religious organization executive*
†Faulk, Sylvia *religious organization executive*
Feller, David E. *arbitrator*
Ferrari, Domenico *computer science educator*
Finnie, Iain *mechanical engineer, educator*
Fleming, Scott *retired health services executive*
Foster, George McClelland, Jr. *anthropologist*
Fowler, Thomas Kenneth *physicist*
Freedman, David Amiel *statistics educator, consultant*
†Freedman, Sarah Warshauer *education educator*
Frisch, Joseph *mechanical engineer, educator, consultant*
Fuerstenau, Douglas Winston *mineral engineering educator*
Furman, Deane Philip *parasitologist, emeritus educator*
Gaillard, Mary Katharine *physics educator*
†Gardner, Wilford Robert *physicist, educator*
Garrison, William Louis *civil engineering educator*
Genn, Nancy *artist*
Gilbert, Neil Robin *social work educator, author, consultant*
Gilbert, Richard Joseph *economics educator*
Glaser, Donald A(rthur) *physicist*
Glaser, Harold *physicist, university administrator*
Glenny, Lyman Albert *retired education educator*
Goldhaber, Gerson *physicist, educator*
Goldsmith, Werner *mechanical engineering educator*
Graburn, Nelson Hayes Henry *anthropologist, educator*
Greenblatt, Stephen J. *English language educator*
†Greene, Albert Lawrence *hospital administrator*
Gregor, Dorothy Deborah *librarian*
Gregory, Joseph Tracy *paleontologist, educator*
Grossman, Elmer Roy *pediatrician*
Grossman, Joan Delaney *language and literature educator*
Grossman, Lawrence Morton *nuclear engineering educator*
Gruen, Erich Stephen *classics educator*
Gurgin, Vonnie Ann *social scientist*
†Hafey, Joseph Michael *health association executive*
Hahn, Erwin Louis *physicist, educator*
Haley, George Patrick *lawyer*
Hancock, Emily Stone *psychologist*
†Hanff, Peter Edward *librarian, bibliographer*
Harlan, Robert Dale *library and information studies educator, academic administrator*
Harris, Guy Hendrickson *chemical research engineer*
Harsanyi, John Charles *economics educator, researcher*
Hartman, Robert Leroy *artist, educator*
Hartsough, Walter Douglas *physicist*
Hearst, John Eugene *chemistry educator*
Heathcock, Clayton Howell *chemistry educator, researcher*
Heilbron, John L. *historian*
Heiles, Carl Eugene *astronomer, educator*
Heineman, Heinz *chemist*
†Heinemann, Heinz *chemist, researcher, consultant*
Helmholz, August Carl *physicist, educator emeritus*
Helson, Henry Berge *retired mathematics educator, publisher*
†Henkin, Leon Albert *educator, mathematician*
Herr, Richard *history educator*
Hester, Randolph Thompson, Jr. *landscape architect, educator*
Hetland, John Robert *lawyer, educator*
Hirsch, Morris William *mathematics educator*
Hitch, Charles Johnston *economist, institution executive*
Hodges, David Albert *electrical engineering educator*
Hoffman, Darleane Christian *chemistry educator*
†Holder, Harold D. *public health administrator, communications specialist, educator*
Holdren, John Paul *energy and resource educator, researcher, author, consultant*
Holton, Richard Henry *business educator*
Howell, Francis Clark *anthropologist, educator*
Hsu, Chieh Su *applied mechanics engineering educator, researcher*
Hu, Chenming *electrical engineering educator*
Hunt, Frank Bouldin *architect, water color artist*
Hurley, Morris Elmer, Jr. *management consultant*
Hutcherson, Bobby *jazz vibraphonist*
Imbrie, Andrew Welsh *composer, educator*
Jackson, J(ohn) David *physicist, educator*
Jeanloz, Raymond *geophysicist, educator*
Jeffries, Carson Dunning *physicist, educator*
Jewell, William Sylvester *engineering educator*
Johanson, Donald Carl *physical anthropologist*
Johnston, Harold S(ledge) *chemistry educator*
Jolly, William Lee *chemistry educator*
Jordan, John Emory *language professional, educator*
Jordan, June M. *poet, English language educator*
Kadish, Sanford Harold *law educator*
Kahan, William M. *mathematics educator, consultant*
Kallgren, Joyce Kislitzin *political science educator*
†Kanafani, Adib *transportation think-tank administrator/civil engineering educator*
Kaplansky, Irving *mathematician, educator, research institute director*
Karlinsky, Simon *language educator, author*
Karp, Richard Manning *computer sciences educator*
Kasten, Karl Albert *painter, printmaker*
†Kay, Herma Hill *law educator*
Kay, Paul de Young *linguist*
Keeler, Theodore Edwin *economics educator*
Kerman, Joseph Wilfred *musicologist, critic*
Kerr, Clark *university president emeritus*
Kerth, Leroy T. *physics educator*
King, Ivan Robert *astronomy educator*
Kingston, Maxine Hong *author*
Kirsch, Jack Frederick *biochemistry educator*
Kittel, Charles *physicist, educator emeritus*
Klein, Lynn E. *artist*
Klinman, Judith Pollock *biochemist, educator*
Koshland, Daniel Edward, Jr. *biochemist, educator*
Koshland, Marian Elliott *immunologist, educator*
Kretchmer, Norman *obstetrics and pediatrics educator*
Kriz, Vilem Francis *photographer, educator*
Kubler-Ross, Elisabeth *physician*
Lambert, Nadine Murphy *psychologist, educator*
Landau, Martin *political science educator*
Lane, Sylvia *economist, educator*
Lazarus, Richard Stanley *psychology educator*
Le Cam, Lucien Marie *mathematics educator*
Lee, Ronald Demos *demographer, economist, educator*
Lee, Yuan T(seh) *chemistry educator*
†Leemans, Wim Pieter *physicist*
Lehmann, Erich Leo *statistics educator*
Leitmann, George *mechanical engineering educator*
Lennette, Edwin Herman *virologist*
Leopold, Luna Bergere *geology educator*
Lesser, Wendy *literary magazine editor, writer, consultant*
Lester, William Alexander, Jr. *chemist, educator*
Letiche, John Marion *economist, educator*
Lewis, Edwin Reynolds *biomedical engineering educator*
Licht, Paul *zoologist, educator*
Lichterman, Martin *history educator*
Lidicker, William Zander, Jr. *zoologist, educator*
Linn, Stuart Michael *biochemist, educator*
Lipson, Leslie Michael *political science educator*
Littlejohn, David *journalism educator, writer*
Litwack, Leon Frank *historian, educator*
Locke, John Whiteman, III *manufacturing company executive*
Long, Anthony Arthur *classics educator*
Lyndon, Donlyn *architect, educator*
Maisel, Sherman Joseph *economist, educator*
Mandelstam, Stanley *physicist*
Maron, Melvin Earl *philosopher, educator*
†Marsden, Jerrold Eldon *mathematician, educator*
Martin, Robert Edward, Jr. *forestry educator, scientist, researcher*
Maslach, Christina *psychology educator*
Maslach, George James *former university official*
Matsumura, Kenneth N. *biomedical scientist, physician*
May, Adolf Darlington *civil engineering educator*
Mc Cullough, Helen Craig *Oriental languages educator*
Mc Evilly, Thomas Vincent *seismologist*
McFadden, Daniel Little *economics educator*
McKee, Christopher Fulton *astrophysics and astronomy educator*
McNulty, John Kent *lawyer, educator*
Meier, Richard Louis *futurist, planner, behavioral scientist*
Mel, Howard Charles *biophysics educator*
Meltzer, David *author, musician*
Merrill, Richard James *educational director*
Middlekauff, Robert Lawrence *history educator, administrator*
†Mikesell, Walter R., Jr. *mechanical engineer, engineering executive*
Miles, Raymond Edward *former university dean, organizational behavior and industrial relations educator*
Miller, William Hughes *theoretical chemist, educator*
Milosz, Czeslaw *poet, author, educator*
Minudri, Regina Ursula *library director, consultant*
Mishkin, Paul J. *lawyer, educator*
Mitchell, James Kenneth *civil engineer, educator*
Miyasaki, George Joji *artist*
Monismith, Carl Leroy *civil engineering educator*
Montgomery, Roger *dean*
Moore, C. Bradley *chemistry educator*
Moran, Rachel *lawyer, educator*
Mote, Clayton Daniel, Jr. *mechanical engineer, educator, administrator*
Muir, William Ker, Jr. *political science educator*
Muller, Richard August *physicist, author*
Muller, Richard Stephen *electrical engineer, educator*
Muscatine, Charles *English educator, author*
Nemeth, Charlan Jeanne *psychology educator*
Nero, Anthony Vincent, Jr. *physicist, environmental scientist*
Newman, Frank Cecil *legal educator, retired state supreme court justice*
Newman, John Scott *chemical engineer, educator*

Nonet, Philippe *law educator*
Ogg, Wilson Reid *poet, lyricist, curator, publisher, lawyer, educator*
Ohala, John Jerome *linguistics educator*
O'Konski, Chester Thomas *chemistry research scientist, educator*
Oldham, William George *electrical engineering and computer science educator*
Oliver, Raymond Davies *English educator*
Olsen, Donald Emmanuel *architect, educator*
Ornduff, Robert *botany educator*
Ott, David Michael *engineering company executive*
Pagni, Patrick John *mechanical and fire safety engineering science educator ,*
Park, Roderic Bruce *retired university chancellor*
Parsons, James Jerome *geographer, educator*
Pask, Joseph Adam *ceramic engineering educator*
Patterson, David Andrew *computer scientist, educator, consultant*
Paulling, John Randolph, Jr. *naval architecture educator, consultant*
†Penry, Deborah L. *biological oceanographer, educator*
Penzien, Joseph *structural engineering educator*
Penzl, Herbert *German language and linguistics educator*
Perez-Mendez, Victor *physics educator*
Perry, Dale Lynn *chemist*
Pigford, Thomas Harrington *nuclear engineering educator*
Pines, Alexander *chemistry educator, researcher*
Pitelka, Frank Alois *zoologist, educator*
Pitzer, Kenneth Sanborn *chemist, educator*
Poinar, George Orlo, Jr. *insect pathologist and paleontologist, educator*
Polak, Elijah *engineering educator, computer scientist*
Policoff, Leonard David *physician, educator*
Polsby, Nelson Woolf *political scientist, educator*
Popov, Egor Paul *engineering educator*
Potts, David Malcolm *population specialist, administrator*
Prausnitz, John Michael *chemical engineer, educator*
Quigley, John Michael *economist, educator*
Rafael, Ruth Kelson *archivist, librarian, consultant*
†Ramamoorthy, Chittor V. *computer science educator*
Ranney, (Joseph) Austin *political science educator*
Rapoport, Sonya *artist*
Rasmussen, John Oscar *chemist, scientist*
Ratner, Marina *mathematician, educator, researcher*
Rauch, Irmengard *linguist, educator*
Rausser, Gordon C(lyde) *agricultural and resource economics educator*
Raymond, Kenneth Norman *chemistry educator, research chemist*
Reginato, Robert Joseph *soil scientist*
Reynolds, John Hamilton *physicist, educator*
Rice, Edward Earl *former government official, author*
Rice, Robert Arnot *school administrator*
†Ritchie, Robert Oliver *materials science educator*
Roller, Robert Douglas, III *psychiatrist*
Rosberg, Carl Gustaf *political science educator*
†Rosen, Kenneth T. *economist*
Rosenblatt, Gerd Matthew *chemist*
Rosenzweig, Mark Richard *psychology educator*
Rowe, John Howland *anthropologist, educator*
Sarich, Vincent M. *anthropologist, educator*
Sauer, Kenneth *chemistry educator*
Saykally, Richard James *chemistry educator*
Schachman, Howard Kapnek *molecular biologist, educator*
Scheffler, Samuel *philosophy educator*
Scheiber, Harry N. *law educator*
Schmalenberger, Jerry Lew *pastor, seminary administrator*
Schoenfeld, Alan Henry *mathematics and education educator*
Schrock, Virgil Edwin *mechanical and nuclear engineer*
Schultz, Peter G. *chemistry educator*
Scordelis, Alexander Costicas *civil engineering educator*
Seaborg, Glenn Theodore *chemistry educator*
Sealey, B. Raphael *classicist, educator*
Searcy, Alan Winn *chemist, educator*
Seeba, Hinrich Claassen *foreign language educator*
Seitz, Walter Stanley *cardiovascular research consultant*
Selz, Peter Howard *art historian, educator*
Sequin, Carlo H. *computer science educator*
Sessler, Andrew Marienhoff *physicist*
Shack, William Alfred *anthropology educator, researcher, consultant*
Shank, Charles Vernon *science administrator, educator*
Shen, Hsieh Wen *civil engineer, consultant, educator*
†Shen, Yuen-Ron *physics educator*
Shugart, Howard Alan *physicist, educator*
Simpson, David William *artist, educator*
Siri, William E. *physicist*
Sloane, Thomas O. *speech educator*
Smelser, Neil Joseph *sociologist*
Smith, Alan Jay *computer science educator, consultant*
Smith, Neville Vincent *physicist*
Smolensky, Eugene *economics educator*
Somorjai, Gabor Arpad *chemist, educator*
Spear, Robert Clinton *environmental health educator, consultant*
Spinrad, Hyron *astronomer*
Staubus, George Joseph *accounting educator*
Staw, Barry Martin *business and psychology educator*
Steiner, Herbert Max *physics educator*
Stoller, Claude *architect*
Strauss, Herbert Leopold *chemistry educator*
Streitwieser, Andrew, Jr. *chemistry educator*
Stuhr, Walter M. *seminary educator, clergyman*
Susskind, Charles *engineering educator, author, publishing executive*
Symons, Timothy James McNeil *physicist*
Teeguarden, Dennis Earl *forest economist*
Teitz, Michael B. *social science educator*
Temko, Allan Bernard *writer*
Tempelis, Constantine Harry *immunologist, educator*
Thomas, Paul Emery *mathematics educator*
Thompson, Anthony Wayne *metallurgist, educator, consultant*
Tien, Chang-Lin *chancellor*
Tobias, Charles William *chemical engineer, educator*
Townes, Charles Hard *physics educator*
Tracy, Robert (Edward) *English educator, poetry translator*
Trilling, George Henry *physicist, educator*
Tsina, Richard Vasil *chemistry educator*
Twiss, Robert Hamilton, Jr. *environmental planning educator*
Tyndall, David Gordon *business educator*
Tyson, Laura D'Andrea *economist, government adviser, educator*
Valentine, James William *geology educator, author*
Van House, Nancy Anita *library educator*
Vaux, Henry James *forest economist, educator*
Vedros, Neylan Anthony *microbiologist*
Vollhardt, Kurt Peter Christian *chemistry educator*
Voulkos, Peter *artist*
Wake, David Burton *biology educator, researcher*
Wake, Marvalee Hendricks *biology educator*
Wakeman, Frederic Evans, Jr. *historian*
Wall, Brian Arthur *sculptor*
Waltz, Kenneth Neal *political science educator*
Wang, William Shi-Yuan *linguistics educator*
Washburn, Stan *artist*
†Weidman, Anna Kathryn *publishing company financial executive*
Welch, Claude (Raymond) *theology educator*
Westheimer, Gerald *optometrist, educator*
Whinnery, John Roy *electrical engineering educator*
White, Richard Manning *electrical engineering educator*
Wiegel, Robert Louis *consulting engineering executive*
Wilensky, Harold L. *political science and industrial relations educator*
Williamson, Oliver Eaton *economics and law educator*
Wolf, Joseph Albert *mathematician, educator*
Wolfinger, Raymond Edwin *political science educator*
Wood, David Kennedy Cornell *choreographer, educator*
Zadeh, Lotfi A. *engineering educator*
Zaentz, Saul *motion picture producer*
Zimring, Franklin E. *law educator*
Zumino, Bruno *physics educator, researcher*
Zwerdling, Alex *English educator*
Zwoyer, Eugene Milton *consulting engineering executive*

Bermuda Dunes
Ward, Donald Butler *minister*

Beverly Hills
Acheson, James *costume designer*
†Adams, Jane *actress*
Aguilera, Donna Conant *psychologist, researcher*
Albert, Edward *actor, photographer*
Alexander, Jason (Jay Scott Greenspan) *actor*
Alice, Mary (Mary Alice Smith) *actress*
Allen, Karen Jane *actress*
Anderson, Loni Kaye *actress*
Anderson, Richard Dean *actor*
Arquette, Rosanna *actress*
August, Bille *film director*
Avildsen, John Guilbert *film director*
Ayres, Samuel, III *physician*
Bacon, Kevin *actor*
Bailey, John *cinematographer*
Bailey, William Ralph *financial services company executive*
Baker, Anita *singer*
†Ballhaus, William Francis *retired scientific instruments company executive*
Bancroft, Anne (Mrs. Mel Brooks) *actress*
Bao, Katherine Sung *pediatric cardiologist*
Barbakow, Jeffery C. *motion picture and television company executive*
Barker, Clive *author, artist, screenwriter, director*
†Barrymore, Drew *actress*
Basinger, Kim *actress*
Bass, Ronald *screenwriter*
Bates, Kathy *actress*
†Bauer, Marty *agent*
Baxter, Meredith *actress*
Beals, Jennifer *actress*
Beck, Marilyn Mohr *columnist*
Bellisario, Donald P. *television director*
Belushi, James *actor*
Benatar, Pat (Pat Andrzejewski) *rock singer*
†Benedek, Barbara *screenwriter*
Bening, Annette *actress*
†Benjamin, Richard *actor, director*
Benson, Robby *actor, director, writer, producer*
Berenger, Tom *actor*
Bergman, Nancy Palm *real estate investment company executive*
Berle, Milton (Milton Berlinger) *actor*
Berman, Eleanore (Lazarof) *artist*
Bernhard, Harvey *producer*
Bill, Tony *actor, producer, director*
Bishop, Joey (Joseph Abraham Gottlieb) *comedian*
Bisset, Jacqueline *actress*
Black, Shirley Temple (Mrs. Charles A. Black) *ambassador, former actress*
†Bloom, Jacob A. *lawyer*
†Boam, Jeffrey David *screenwriter*
Bolton, Michael *singer, songwriter*
Brann, Alton Joseph *aerospace executive*
†Brickman, Paul *film writer, director*
Bridges, Beau (Lloyd Vernet Bridges, III) *actor*
Bridges, Jeff *actor*
Bridges, Lloyd *actor*
Brightman, Sarah *singer, actress*
Brokaw, Norman Robert *management company executive*
Bronson, Charles (Charles Buchinsky) *actor*
Brooks, Mel *producer, director, writer, actor*
Brown, Hermione Kopp *lawyer*
Bugliosi, Vincent T. *lawyer*
Burnett, Carol *actress, comedienne, singer*
Burton, Al *producer, director, writer*
Burton, Tim *film director*
Buyse, Emile Jules *film company executive*
Cage, Nicholas (Nicholas Coppola) *actor*
Caine, Michael *actor*
†Carrey, Jim *actor*
Casey, Joseph T. *corporate executive*
Channing, Carol *actress*
Chaplin, Geraldine *actress*
Cheech, (Richard Anthony Marin) *actor, writer, director*
Cher, (Cherilyn Sarkisian) *singer, actress*
Chernin, Peter *motion picture company executive*
Chong, Thomas *comedian, writer, director, musician*
Chritton, George A. *film producer*
Clayburgh, Jill *actress*
Coen, Ethan *film producer, writer*
Coen, Joel *film director, writer*
†Cohen, Larry *film director, producer, screenwriter*
Collins, Pauline *actress*
Connery, Sean (Thomas Connery) *actor*
†Coolidge, Martha *film director*
Corbin, Barry *actor, writer*
Corman, Eugene Harold *motion picture producer*
Cort, Robert W. *film company executive*
Corwin, Stanley Joel *book publisher*
Costa-Gavras, (Konstaninos Gavras) *director, writer*
Coyote, Peter (Peter Cohon) *actor*
Crenna, Richard *actor*
Crichton, (John) Michael *author, film director*
Cristofer, Michael *actor, author*
†Crowe, Cameron *screenwriter*
Culkin, Macaulay *actor*
Culp, Robert *actor, writer, director*
Curtin, Jane Therese *actress, writer*
†Curtin, Valerie *screenwriter, actress*
Curtis, Jamie Lee *actress*
Curtis, Tony (Bernard Schwartz) *actor*
Cusack, John *actor*
Cusak, Joan *actress*
Daly, Timothy *actor*
D'Angelo, Beverly *actress*
Danson, Ted *actor*
David, Clive *events planning executive*
†David, Larry *television scriptwriter*
Davis, Geena (Virginia Davis) *actress*
Davison, Bruce *actor*
Dawber, Pam *actress*
†Dearden, James *director, screenwriter*
Dekom, Peter James *lawyer*
Delany, Dana *actress*
De Laurentiis, Dino *motion picture producer*
Delevie, Harold Jacob *lawyer*
DeNiro, Robert *actor*
Dennehy, Brian *actor*
dePaolis, Potito Umberto *food company executive*
Depardieu, Gerard *actor*
Depp, Johnny *actor*
Dern, Bruce MacLeish *actor*
Dern, Laura Elizabeth *actress*
Devito, Danny Michael *actor*
Dillon, Gregory Russell *hotel executive*
Dobson, Kevin *actor*
Doherty, Shannen *actress*
Dore, Bonny Ellen *film and television production company executive*
Douglas, Kirk (Issur Danielovitch Demsky) *actor, motion picture producer*
Douglas, Michael Kirk *actor, film producer, director*
Downey, Robert, Jr. *actor*
Dunaway, (Dorothy) Faye *actress*
Eden, Barbara Jean *actress*
Eikenberry, Jill *actress*
Eisenshtat, Sidney Herbert *architect*
Elkins, Hillard *producer*
Elliott, Robert B. *comedian*
Elwes, Cary *actor*
Essex, Harry J. *screenwriter, novelist*
Eszterhas, Joseph A. *film scriptwriter*
Evans, Linda *actress*
Evans, Louise *psychologist, investor*
Evans, Robert J. *motion picture producer, actor*
Evigan, Greg *actor, musician*
Factor, Max, III *lawyer, investment adviser*
†Fahey, Jeff *actor*
Fargo, Louis James *film director*
Fein, William *ophthalmologist*
Feldshuh, Tovah S. *actress*
Finney, Albert *actor, director*
Fitzgerald, Ella *singer*
Flaum, Marshall Allen *television producer, writer, director*
Fleischer, Richard O. *film director*
Fleming, Peggy Gale *professional ice skater*
Foch, Nina *actress, creative consultant, educator*
Fonda, Bridget *actress*
Foster, Jodie (Alicia Christian Foster) *actress*
Fox, Charles Ira *composer, conductor*
Fox, Michael J. *actor*
Foxworth, Robert Heath *actor, director*
†Frank, Harriet *screenwriter*
Frankenheimer, John Michael *film and stage director*
Franklin, Aretha *singer*
†Frears, Stephen *film director*
Freberg, Stan(ley) (Victor Freberg) *satirist*
Furth, George *actor, playwright*
Garr, Teri (Ann) *actress*
Gelbart, Larry *writer, producer*
Gere, Richard *actor*
†Getchell, Robert *screenwriter*
†Geuther, Carl Frederick *financial services company executive*
Gilberg, Arnold L. *psychiatrist and psychoanalyst*
Gilbert, Melissa *actress*
Gillard, Stuart Thomas *film and television director, writer*
Giorgi, Elsie Agnes *physician*
Glenn, (Theodore) Scott *actor*
Gless, Sharon *actress*
†Goldman, Bo *screenwriter, director*
Goldman, William *writer*
Goldsmith, Bram *banker*
Gould, Elliott *actor*
†Grant, Hugh *actor*
Graves, Peter *actor*
†Grey, Jennifer *actress*
Grey, Joel *actor*
Griffin, Merv Edward *entertainer, television producer, entrepreneur*
Griffith, Andy (Andrew Samuel Griffith) *actor*
Grodin, Charles *actor, writer, director*
†Grushow, Sandy *broadcast executive*
Guardino, Harry *actor*
†Hackford, Taylor *film director, producer*
Hagman, Larry *actor*
Hamel, Veronica *actress*
†Hamilton, Linda *actress*
Hanks, Tom *actor*
Hannah, Daryl *actress*
†Hanson, Curtis *director, writer*
†Harlin, Renny (Renny Lauri Mauritz Harjola) *film director*
Harmon, Mark *actor*
Harper, Valerie *actress*
Harrelson, Woody *actor*
Harris, Jordan *record company executive*
Harris, Mel (Mary Ellen Harris) *actress*
†Harshfield, Edward Gordon *financial services company executive*
Haskell, Peter Abraham *actor*
†Hawke, Ethan *actor*
Hawn, Goldie *actress*
Headly, Glenne Aimée *actress*
Helgenberger, Marg *actress*
Heller, Paul Michael *film company executive, producer*
Helmond, Katherine *actress*
Henry, Buck *actor, writer*
Herrmann, Edward Kirk *actor*
Hershey, Barbara (Barbara Herzstein) *actress*
Hesseman, Howard *actor*
Hill, Walter *film director, writer, producer*
Hilton, Barron *hotel executive*
Hines, Gregory Oliver *actor, dancer*
Hoch, Orion Lindel *corporate executive*
Hopper, Dennis *actor, writer, photographer, film director*
†Horn, Alan *motion picture company executive*
Howard, Ron *director, actor*
Hulce, Tom *actor*
Hunt, Helen *actress*
Hunt, Linda *actress*
Hunt, Peter Huls *director, theatrical lighting designer*
†Hurd, Gale Anne *film producer*
Huston, Anjelica *actress*
Hutton, Timothy *actor*
†Jackson, Samuel L. *actor*
Jenner, Bruce *sportscaster, former Olympic athlete*
Jessup, W. Edgar, Jr. *lawyer*
Jillian, Ann (Ann Jura Nauseda) *actress, singer*
Johnson, Jimmy *sports commentator, former professional football coach*
Jones, David Hugh *theater, film and television director*
Jones, Dean Carroll *actor*
Jordan, Glenn *theater director*
Karpman, Harold Lew *cardiologist, educator, author*
Kasdan, Lawrence Edward *film director, screenwriter*
Kaufman, Philip *film director*
Keaton, Diane *actress*
Kellner, Jamie *broadcasting executive*
Kelly, Gene Curran *dancer, actor, director*
Kerkorian, Kirk *motion picture company executive, consultant*
Kilmer, Val *actor*
King, Alan *entertainer*
Kirkwood, Gene *motion picture producer*
Klausen, Raymond *sculptor, television/theatre production designer*
Klein, Arnold William *dermatologist*
†Koepp, David *screenwriter*
Kravitz, Ellen King *musicologist, educator*
†Kravitz, Lenny *singer*
Kurtz, Swoosie *actress*
Kwiker, Louis A. *business executive*
Ladd, Diane *actress*
Landis, John David *film director, writer*
Lange, Jessica *actress*
Laurie, Piper (Rosetta Jacobs) *actress*
Lawrence, Steve *entertainer*
Leachman, Cloris *actress*
Leary, Denis *comedian*
Lee, Peggy (Norma Delores Egstrom) *singer, actress*
Leibman, Ron *actor*
Leigh, Janet (Jeanette Helen Morrison) *actress*
Lemmon, Jack (John Uhler Lemmon, III) *actor*
Leonard, Robert Sean *actor*
†Leonis, John Michael *aerospace executive*
Levinson, Barry L. *film director*
Levy, David *broadcasting executive*
†Levy, Eugene *actor, director, screenwriter*
Lewine, Robert F. *broadcasting company executive*
Lewis, Juliette *actress*
Linkletter, Arthur Gordon *radio and television broadcaster*
Liotta, Ray *actor*
Lithgow, John Arthur *actor, director*
Little, Richard Caruthers (Rich Little) *comedian, impressionist, actor*
Livingston, Myra Cohn *poet, writer, educator*
†Locklear, Heather *actress*
Loeffler, Richard Harlan *retail and technology company executive*
Loggia, Robert *actor*
Loggins, Kenny (Kenneth Clarke Loggins) *singer, songwriter*
Long, Shelley *actress*
Lynch, David K. *film director, writer*
Madden, John *television sports commentator, former professional football coach*
Mann, Michael K. *producer, director, writer*
Manoff, Dinah Beth *actress*
Manulis, Martin *film producer*
†Mark, John *film company executive*
Marshall, (C.) Penny *actress, director*
Marx, Arthur (Julius) *author, playwright, director*
Mason, Marsha *actress, director, writer*
Mason, Pamela Helen *actress, producer, writer*
Masterson, Mary Stuart *actress*
Mastrantonio, Mary Elizabeth *actress*
Matlin, Marlee *actress*
Matz, Peter S. *composer, conductor, arranger*
McDonnell, Mary *actress*
McGagh, William Gilbert *financial consultant*
McGavin, Darren *actor, director, producer*
Mc Kenna, William Edward *entrepreneur*
McNaughton, John D. *director*
Mc Tiernan, John *film director*
Menges, Chris *cinematographer, film director*
Menkes, John Hans *pediatric neurologist*
Menon, Vijaya Bhaskar *recording and entertainment company executive*
Mercer, Marian *actress*
†Meyer, Nicholas *screenwriter, director*
Meyer, Ron *agent*
Meyers, Nancy Jane *screenwriter, producer*
Modine, Matthew Avery *actor*
Moloney, Jay *agent*
Moore, Demi (Demi Guynes) *actress*
Mulligan, Robert Patrick *film director, producer*
†Myers, Barton *architect*
Nabors, James Thurston *actor, singer*
†Neeson, Liam *actor*
Neill, Sam *actor*
Nelson, Judd *actor*
Neuwirth, Bebe *dancer, actress*
Newton-John, Olivia *singer, actress*
Nichols, Mike *stage and film director*
Nicholson, Jack *actor, director, producer*
Nicita, Rick *agent*
Nimoy, Leonard *actor, director*
Niven, Laurence Van Cott *author*
Noble, James Wilkes *actor*
Nykvist, Sven Vilhem *cinematographer*
Obst, Lynda Rosen *film company executive, producer, screenwriter*
O'Hara, Catherine *actress, comedienne*
Olin, Ken *actor*
Orenstein, (Ian) Michael *philatelic dealer, columnist*
Ovitz, Michael S. *artists agency executive*
†Pantoliano, Joe *actor*
†Paquin, Anna *actress*
Parker, Alan William *film director, writer*
Penderecki, Krzysztof *composer, conductor*
†Perez, Rosie *actress, choreographer*
Perkins, Elizabeth Ann *actress*

Perry, Luke (Coy Luther Perry, III) *actor*
Pesci, Joe *actor*
†Peters, Charles Victor *screenwriter*
Peters, Jon *film producer, film company executive*
†Petersen, Wolfgang *film director*
Petrie, Daniel Mannix *film, theatre and television director*
Pfeiffer, Michelle *actress*
Philon, James Leon *hotel executive*
†Pierson, Frank Romer *screenwriter, director*
Pitt, Brad *actor*
Poitier, Sidney *actor, director*
Ponty, Jean-Luc *violinist, composer, producer*
Pop, Iggy (James Newell Osterberg) *composer, singer, musician*
†Proft, Pat *screenwriter, film producer*
†Ptak, John A. *talent agent*
Quinn, Aidan *actor*
Ramis, Harold Allen *film director, screenwriter, actor*
Ransohoff, Martin *motion picture producer*
Rapke, Jack *agent*
†Ravetch, Irving *screenwriter*
Rea, Stephen *actor*
†Red, Eric *film director, screenwriter*
Reiner, Carl *actor, writer, director*
Reiner, Rob *actor, writer, director*
Reitman, Ivan *film director, producer*
Reynolds, Gene *television producer, director*
Richards, Michael *actor, comedian*
†Richardson, Patricia *actress*
Riegert, Peter *actor*
Robards, Jason Nelson, Jr. *actor*
Robbins, Tim (Timothy Francis Robbins) *actor*
Roberts, Eric *actor*
†Roberts, Norman Leslie *lawyer*
†Robinson, Phil Alden *director*
Roeg, Nicolas Jack *film director*
Rolle, Esther *actress*
Rollins, Howard Ellsworth, Jr. *actor*
Romero, George A. *film director*
†Rosenthal, Mark David *screenwriter*
Rosky, Burton Seymour *lawyer*
Ross, Stanley Ralph *writer, publisher, producer, software manufacturing executive*
†Rudnick, Paul *playwright, screenwriter*
†Rudolph, Alan *film director*
Ruehl, Mercedes *actress*
Rush, Herman E. *television executive*
Russell, Kurt Von Vogel *actor*
Ryder, Winona (Winona Laura Horowitz) *actress*
†Sadwith, James Steven *screenwriter, director*
Sager, Carole Bayer *lyricist, singer*
Salhany, Lucille S. *broadcast executive*
Schiff, Gunther Hans *lawyer*
†Schlatter, George H. *producer, director, writer*
Schulian, John (Nielsen Schulian) *screenwriter, author*
Schulman, Tom *film writer*
†Schumacher, Joel *film writer, director*
Scorsese, Martin *film director, writer*
Scott, Ridley *film director*
Seagal, Steven *actor*
Seinfeld, Jerry *comedian*
Selleck, Tom *actor*
†Shanley, John Patrick *screenwriter*
Shapell, Nathan *financial and real estate executive*
Sharif, Omar (Michael Shalhoub) *actor*
Shepard, Sam (Samuel Shepard Rogers) *playwright, actor*
†Sheridan, Jim *director, screenwriter*
Shoemaker, Bill (William Lee Shoemaker) *retired jockey*
Simmons, Jean *actress*
Simmons, Richard Milton Teagle *physical fitness specialist, television personality*
Singleton, John *director, screenwriter*
Sinise, Gary *actor*
Skerritt, Tom *actor*
Slater, Christian *actor*
Slater, Helen Rachel *actress*
Smith, Robert Harold *accountant*
Smith, Will (Fresh Prince) *actor, rap singer*
Snipes, Wesley *actor*
Spacek, Sissy (Mary Elizabeth Spacek) *actress*
Spader, James *actor*
Spheeris, Penelope *film director*
Spielberg, Steven *motion picture director, producer*
Spikings, Barry Peter *film company executive*
Stack, Robert Langford *actor*
Stallone, Sylvester Enzio *actor, writer, director*
Stamos, John *actor*
†Star, Darren *television writer*
Steel, Dawn *motion picture producer*
Steenburgen, Mary *actress*
Stefano, Joseph William *film and television producer, author*
Stein, Myron *internist, educator*
Stern, Daniel *actor*
Stewart, Patrick *actor*
Stoltz, Eric *actor*
Stone, Sharon *actress*
Strasberg, Susan *actress, writer, educator*
Strauss, Peter *actor*
Streep, Meryl (Mary Louise Streep) *actress*
Sutherland, Donald *actor*
Tambor, Jeffrey *actor, theatre director, educator*
Terry, Clark *musician*
†Thompson, Caroline Warner *film director, screenwriter*
Thompson, Larry Angelo *producer, lawyer, personal manager*
Thompson, Tina Lewis Chryar *publisher*
Toffel, Alvin Eugene *corporate executive, business and governmental consultant*
Toman, Mary Ann *federal official*
Tomei, Marisa *actress*
Torme, Mel(vin) (Howard Torme) *musician, jazz vocalist*
†Torokvei, Peter John *writer, director, actor, producer*
Towers, Bernard Leonard *medical educator*
Towne, Robert *screenwriter*
Trumbull, Douglas *film director, writer, creator special effects*
Tucker, Michael *actor*
Turner, Janine *actress*
Turturro, John *actor*
Tyre, Norman Ronald *lawyer*
Tyson, Cicely *actress*
Uggams, Leslie *entertainer*
Ullman, Tracey *actress, singer*
Urich, Robert *actor*
Van Ark, Joan *actress*
Van Dyke, Dick *actor, comedian*
†Van Sant, Gus, Jr. *director, screenwriter*
Victor, Robert Eugene *real estate corporation executive, lawyer*
Wagner, Lindsay J. *actress*
Wagner, Robert *actor*
Walken, Christopher *actor*
Walker, William Tidd, Jr. *investment banker*
Ward, David Schad *screenwriter, film director*
Wedgeworth, Ann *actress*
Weir, Peter Lindsay *film director*
Welch, Raquel *actress*
Weller, Michael *playwright, screenwriter*
Weston, Paul *composer, arranger, conductor*
White, Betty *actress, comedienne*
White, Jesse Marc *actor*
†Williams, JoBeth *actress*
Williams, Treat (Richard Williams) *actor*
†Willingham, Calder Baynard, Jr. *novelist, playwright, screenwriter*
Willson, James Douglas *aerospace executive*
†Wincer, Simon *film director*
Winkler, Henry Franklin *actor*
Winkler, Irwin *motion picture producer*
Winthrop, John *real estate executive, lawyer*
Wise, Robert *film producer, director*
†Wood, Elijah *actor*
Woodard, Alfre *actress*
Woods, James Howard *actor*
Yates, Peter *director, producer*
York, Michael (Michael York-Johnson) *actor*
Yorkin, Bud (Alan Yorkin) *producer, director*
Zanuck, Richard Darryl *motion picture company executive*
Zarem, Abe Mordecai *management consulting executive*
Zerbe, Anthony *actor*
Zimmerman, Don *film editor*

Big Bear Lake
Miles, Vera *actress*

Big Sur
Cross, Robert Louis *realtor, land use planner, writer*
†Donovan, Steven Robert *institute executive*
Owings, Margaret Wentworth *conservationist, artist*

Bishop
MacMillen, Richard Edward *biological sciences educator, researcher*

Bodega
Hedrick, Wally Bill *artist*

Bodega Bay
Hand, Cadet Hammond, Jr. *marine biologist, educator*
Jeffery, William Richard *developmental biology educator*
King, Leland W. *architect*

Bolinas
Harris, Paul *sculptor*
Murch, Walter Scott *director, writer, film editor, sound designer*

Bonita
Barnard, Arlene *secondary education educator*
Curtis, Richard Earl *former naval officer, former company executive, business consultant*
Dresser, Jesse Dale *real estate investor*
Jacobsen, Adolf M.B. *university administrator, former naval officer*
Wood, Fergus James *geophysicist, consultant*

Borrego Springs
Bowers, Bobby Eugene *metal products executive, small business owner*
Kryter, Karl David *research scientist*
Scannell, William Edward *aerospace company executive, consultant, psychologist*
Shinn, Allen Mayhew *retired naval officer, business executive*

Brawley
Jaquith, George Oakes *ophthalmologist*

Brea
Dyer, Alice Mildred *psychotherapist*
Engleman, David S. *diversified financial services executive*
†Hulsey, Neven C. *metal products executive*
Shell, Billy Joe *retired university president*

Brisbane
Anargyros, Spero *sculptor*
Orban, Kurt *foreign trade company executive*

Buena Park
†Arimoto, Masahiko *electronics company executive*
Elliott, Darrell Kenneth *minister, legal researcher*
†Raup, Ronald B. *electronics executive*

Burbank
Aaronson, Robert Jay *aviation executive*
Allen, Tim *actor, comedian*
Arkoff, Samuel Z. *motion picture executive, producer*
Berman, Bruce *entertainment company executive*
Berry, Bill *popular musician*
Brankovich, Mark J. *restaurateur*
Brogliatti, Barbara Spencer *television and motion picture executive*
Bruckheimer, Jerry *producer*
Buck, Peter *musician, guitarist*
Burke, Michele Christine *make-up artist*
†Cameron, James *film director, screenwriter, producer*
Clark, Dick *performer, producer*
Clark, Susan (Nora Goulding) *actress*
†Clements, Ronald Francis *animation director*
Cooder, Ry *recording artist, guitarist*
Coolidge, Rita *singer*
Costello, Elvis (Declan Patrick McManus) *musician, songwriter*
†Cunningham, Robert D. *lawyer*
Daly, Robert Anthony *film executive*
de Cordova, Frederick Timmins *television producer, director*
Disney, Roy Edward *broadcasting company executive*
Donner, Richard *film director, producer*
Droz, Henry *distribution company executive*
Eastwood, Clint *actor, director, former mayor*
Eisner, Michael Dammann *entertainment company executive*
Fagen, Donald *musician*
Fisher, Lucy J. *motion picture company executive*
Flanagan, Tommy (Lee) *jazz pianist*
Fleetwood, Mick *musician*
†Freeberg, Don *health care executive*
Godwin, Annabelle Palkes *retired early childhood education educator*
†Gold, Jeffrey Alan *record company executive*
Gold, Stanley P. *chemical company executive, manufacturing company executive*
†Griffith, Robert Douglas *broadcasting company executive*
Guy, Buddy *blues guitarist*
†Hartshorn, Terry O. *health facility administrator*
†Heiden, Jeri McManus *art director*
Hoberman, David *motion picture company executive*
Ingram, James *rhythm and blues songwriter, performer*
Isaak, Chris *popular musician, singer, songwriter, actor*
Karras, Alex *actor, former professional football player*
Katz, Marty *motion picture executive*
Katzenberg, Jeffrey *motion picture studio executive*
Keister, Jean Clare *lawyer*
Ketchum, Hal Michael *country music singer, songwriter*
Lanois, Daniel *record producer, musician, popular*
Lavin, Linda *actress*
Leno, Jay (James Douglas Muir Leno) *comedian, writer*
Litvack, Sanford Martin *lawyer*
Marsalis, Branford *musician*
Mathis, Johnny *singer*
†McQueen, Sherman John, Jr. *entertainment company executive*
Mc Vie, Christine Perfect *musician*
Menken, Alan *composer*
Mestres, Ricardo A., III *motion picture company executive*
Milchan, Arnon *film producer*
Miller, Clifford Albert *banker, business consultant*
Mills, Mike *popular musician*
Moonves, Leslie *television company executive*
†Mullin, Sherman N. *engineering executive*
Nardino, Gary *television and motion picture producer*
Ohlmeyer, Donald Winfred, Jr. *film and television producer*
Peterson, Ralph *financial executive*
Pryor, Richard *actor, writer*
Rauch, Paul David *television producer*
Raulinaitis, Pranas Algis *electronics executive*
†Rich, Ben Robert *aerospace executive, aero-thermodynamicist*
Rich, Lee *entertainment industry executive*
Robinson, James G. *businessman, film production executive*
Roth, Joe *motion picture company executive*
Rundgren, Todd *musician, record producer*
Sago, Paul Edward *college administrator*
Salzman, David Elliot *entertainment industry executive*
Seals, Dan Wayland *country music singer*
Semel, Terry *motion picture company executive*
Severinsen, Doc (Carl H. Severinsen) *conductor, musician*
†Shao, Shiu *financial executive*
Silver, Joel *producer*
Simpson, Don *film producer*
Steiger, Rod *actor*
Stewart, Roderick David *singer*
Stipe, Michael *musician*
Strasser, Robin *actress*
†Thomas, Betty *actress*
†Thomas, Jay *actor*
Tritt, Travis *country music singer, songwriter*
Vajna, Andy *film company executive*
Volk, Robert Harkins *aviations company executive*
Watson, Raymond Leslie *architect*
Weintraub, Jerry *motion picture producer, executive*
White, Loray Betty *writer, actress, producer*
Wolper, David Lloyd *motion picture and television executive*
Wonder, Stevie (Stevland Morris) *singer, musician, composer*

Burlingame
Bell, Herbert Aubrey Frederick *life insurance company executive*
Clover, Haworth Alfred *elementary school educator, historian*
Cotchett, Joseph Winters *lawyer, author*
Crawford, William Richard *psychologist*
†Gradinger, Gilbert P. *plastic surgeon*
Green, Robert Leonard *hospital management company executive*
Heath, Richard Raymond *business executive*
Holmes, Richard Hugh Morris *investment management executive*
Hotz, Henry Palmer *physicist*
†Kennedy, Shannon Ray *education educator*
†Loughead, Thomas A. *transportation executive*
Mc Dowell, Jack Sherman *political consultant*
Mendelson, Lee M. *film company executive, writer, producer, director*
Ocheltree, Richard Lawrence *lawyer, retired forest products company executive*
Souter, Robert Taylor *retired banker*
Truta, Marianne Patricia *oral and maxillofacial surgeon, educator, author*
Ward, William Reed *composer, educator*
Ziegler, R.W., Jr. *lawyer, consultant*

Calabasas
Bartizal, Robert George *computer systems company executive, business consultant*
Bleiweiss, Robert Morton *religious magazine editor, labor newspaper publisher*
Egan, John Frederick *electronics executive*
Ghose, Rabindra Nath *technology research company executive*
Gressak, Anthony Raymond, Jr. *sales executive*
Hawkins, Willis Moore *aerospace and astronautical consultant*
Kanaly, Steven Francis *actor*
Kitchen, Lawrence Oscar *aircraft and aerospace corporation executive*
Marafino, Vincent Norman *aerospace company executive*
Pearce, Susan Miriam *aerospace company executive*
Sargent, Ernest Douglas *retired aerospace engineer, educator*
Tellep, Daniel Michael *aerospace executive, mechanical engineer*
Young, Terence *motion picture director*

California City
Friedl, Rick *former academic administrator, lawyer*

Calistoga
Spindler, George Dearborn *anthropologist, educator, author, editor*

Camarillo
Denmark, Bernhardt *manufacturing executive*
DePatie, David Hudson *motion picture company executive*
Sime, Donald Rae *business administration educator*
Street, Dana Morris *orthopedic surgeon*

Cambria
Blundell, William Edward *journalist, consultant*
Crowther, H. David *aerospace company corporate communications executive*
DuFresne, Armand Frederick *management and engineering consultant*
Morse, Richard Jay *human resources and organizational development consultant, manufacturers' representative company executive*
Stark, Betty Andrews *corporate executive*
Villeneuve, Donald Avila *biology educator*
Wallen, Vera S. *school superintendent*

Cameron Park
Buckles, Robert Edwin *chemistry educator*

Campbell
Levy, Salomon *mechanical engineer*
Nicholson, Joseph Bruce *real estate developer*
Richards, Lisle Frederick *architect*
Ross, Hugh Courtney *electrical engineer*
Sack, Edgar Albert *electronics company executive*
Throndson, Edward Warner *residential association administrator*
Wu, William Lung-Shen (You-Ming Wu) *aerospace medical engineering design specialist*

Campo
Charles, Blanche *retired elementary education educator*

Canoga Park
†Gibbs, D.C. *materials engineer administrator*
Lederer, Marion Irvine *cultural administrator*
Taylor, Edna Jane *employment program counselor*

Capistrano Beach
Lewis, Jack (Cecil Paul Lewis) *publishing executive, editor*

Capo Beach
Roemer, Edward Pier *neurologist*

Carlsbad
Anderson, Paul Irving *management executive*
Brown, Jack *magazine editor*
†Callaway, Ely Reeves, Jr. *golf club manufacturer*
Crooke, Stanley Thomas *pharmaceutical company executive*
Dixon, William Cornelius *lawyer*
Graham, Robert Klark *lens manufacturer*
Halberg, Charles John August, Jr. *mathematics educator*
Lange, Clifford E. *librarian*
Lynn, Fredric Michael *sportscaster, former professional baseball player*
McCracken, Steven Carl *lawyer*
Pawlik, Robert Altenloh *publisher, editor*
Randall, William B. *manufacturing company executive*
Schumacher, John Christian *semiconductor materials and air pollution control equipment manufacturing company executive*
Smith, Warren James *optical scientist, consultant, lecturer*
†Vincent, John Graham *administrator*
Williams, Roger *lawyer*

Carmel
Alsberg, Dietrich Anselm *electrical engineer*
Aurner, Robert Ray *author, corporate executive*
Banathy, Bela Henrich *systems science educator, author, researcher*
Brahtz, John Frederick Peel *civil engineering educator*
Doe, Richard Philip *physician, educator*
Faul, George Johnson *former college president*
Felch, William Campbell *internist, editor*
Jordan, Edward George *business investor, former college president, former railroad executive*
Jorgensen, William Ernest *retired librarian*
Kennedy, John Edward *art dealer, appraiser, curator*
Krugman, Stanley Lee *international management consultant*
Lockhart, Brooks Javins *retired college dean*
Longman, Anne Strickland *educational consultant*
Merrill, William Dickey *architect*
Novak, Kim (Marilyn Novak) *actress*
Parker, Donald Henry *psychologist, author*
Pinkham, Frederick Oliver *foundation executive, consultant*
Robinson, John Minor *lawyer, retired business executive*
Skidmore, Howard Franklyn *public relations counsel*
Smith, Gordon Paul *management consulting company executive*
Steele, Charles Glen *retired accountant*
Stratton, Thomas Oliver *investment banker*
Weston, Theodore Brett *photographer*

Carmichael
Areen, Gordon E. *finance company executive*
Bloom, John Porter *historian, editor, administrator, archivist*
Bromberg, Walter *psychiatrist*
Givant, Philip Joachim *mathematics educator, real estate investment executive*
Hummel, Fred Ernest *architect*
McHugh, James Joseph *retired associate dean*
Probasco, Calvin Henry Charles *clergyman, college administrator*
Sahs, Majorie Jane *art educator*
Wagner, Carruth John *physician*

Carpinteria
Ehrlich, Grant C(onklin) *business consultant*
Hansen, Robert William *artist, educator*
Lessler, Richard Sigmund *advertising executive*

Schmidhauser, John Richard *political science educator*
Wheeler, John Harvey *political scientist*

Carson
Brownell, John Arnold *former university president*
Davidson, Mark *writer, educator*
Detweiler, Robert Chester *university president, historian*
Hirsch, Gilah Yelin *artist, writer*
Suchenek, Marek Andrzej *computer science educator*

Castro Valley
Dance, Maurice Eugene *college administrator*
Palmer, James Daniel *inspector*

Cathedral City
Jackman, Robert Alan *retail executive*

Cedar Ridge
Yeager, Charles Elwood (Chuck Yeager) *retired air force officer*

Central Valley
†Emmerson, A. A. *sawmill executive*

Century City
Bishop, Stephen *singer, songwriter*
Blatt, Neil A. *cinema corporation executive*
Bogdanovich, Peter *film director, writer, producer, actor*

Chatsworth
Adams, Charles Richard *manufacturing executive*
†Alagem, Beny *electronics executive*
Arnold, Stanley Richard *lawyer*
Bartling, Judd Quenton *research corporation executive*
Dart, John Seward *religion news writer*
Klein, Jeffrey S. *lawyer, newspaper executive*
Montgomery, James Fischer *savings and loan association executive*
Palko, Michael James *finance company executive*
Rawitch, Robert Joe *newspaper editor*
†Van Dine, Robert *cosmetics company executive*
Woodruff, Tom, Jr. *special effects designer*

Chico
Allen, Charles William *mechanical engineering educator*
Ediger, Robert Ike *botanist, educator*
†Esteban, Manuel Antonio *university administrator, educator*
Greb, Gordon Barry *educator, writer*
Keithley, George *writer*
Kistner, David Harold *biology educator*
Moore, Brooke Noel *philosophy educator*
Ruge, Neil Marshall *retired law educator*
Stephens, William Leonard *university provost*
Wolff, Howard Keith *computer science educator, consultant*

China Lake
†Cook, Douglas W. *weapons research administrator*

Chino
Determan, John David *lawyer*

Chula Vista
Adams, John R. *English educator*
Allen, David Russell *lawyer*
Allen, Henry Wesley *biomedical researcher*
Chapman, Laurence Arthur *finance executive*
Clement, Betty Waidlich *literacy educator, consultant*
Goldsmith, Robert Holloway *manufacturing company executive*
†Kerley, James J. *manufacturing executive*
†Schorr, Martin Mark *psychologist, educator, writer*
Wolk, Martin *electronic engineer, physicist*

Claremont
Ackerman, Gerald Martin *art historian, consultant*
Albrecht, Paul Abraham *dean*
Alexander, John David, Jr. *college administrator*
Ansell, Edward Orin *lawyer*
Barnes, Richard Gordon *English educator, poet*
Beardslee, William Armitage *religious organization administrator, educator*
Beilby, Alvin Lester *chemistry educator*
Bekavac, Nancy Yavor *academic administrator, lawyer*
Benjamin, Karl Stanley *artist, educator*
Benson, George Charles Sumner *political science educator*
Bjork, Gordon Carl *economist, educator*
Blizzard, Alan *artist*
Bond, Floyd Alden *economist, educator*
Bowman, Dean Orlando *economist, educator*
Burns, Richard Dean *history educator, publisher, author*
Casanova, Aldo John *sculptor*
Chambers, Robert Jefferson *educator, observatory administrator*
Douglass, Enid Hart *educational program director*
Dunbar, John Raine *emeritus English educator*
Dym, Clive Lionel *engineering educator*
†Fucaloro, Anthony Frank *academic dean*
Gold, Bela *educator, economist*
Goodrich, Norma Lorre (Mrs. John H. Howard) *French and comparative literature educator*
Hale, Doty Doherty *educational administrator*
Herschensohn, Bruce *film director, writer*
Hinshaw, Randall (Weston) *economist, educator*
†Kronenberg, Klaus J(ohannes) *physicist*
Kucheman, Clark Arthur *religion educator*
Liggett, Thomas Jackson *retired seminary president*
Likens, James Dean *economics educator*
Lofgren, Charles Augustin *legal and constitutional historian*
Louch, Alfred Richard *philosophy educator*
Macaulay, Ronald Kerr Steven *linguistics educator, former college dean*
Maguire, John David *university administrator, educator, writer*
Massey, Marilyn Chapin *academic administrator*
McKirahan, Richard Duncan, Jr. *classics and philosophy educator*
Mezey, Robert *poet, educator*
Molinder, John Irving *engineering educator, consultant*
Monson, James Edward *electrical engineer, educator*
Mullikin, Harry Copeland *mathematics educator*
Neal, Fred Warner *political scientist, educator*
Neumann, Harry *philosophy educator*
Olson, Richard George *historian, educator*
Palmer, Hans Christian *economics educator*
Pedersen, Richard Foote *academic administrator*
Phelps, Orme Wheelock *economics educator emeritus*
Phillips, John Richard *engineering educator*
Pinney, Thomas Clive *English language educator*
Platt, Joseph Beaven *former college president*
Purves, William Kirkwood *biologist, educator*
Rankin, Robert *retired educational foundation executive*
Reiss, Roland Martin *artist, educator*
Riggs, Henry Earle *college president, engineering management educator*
Roth, John King *philosopher, educator*
Sanders, James Alvin *minister, biblical studies educator*
Sontag, Frederick Earl *philosophy educator*
Stanley, Peter William *college president*
Stark, Jack Lee *college president*
Tanenbaum, Basil Samuel *college dean, engineering educator*
Wettack, F. Sheldon *academic administrator*
White, Kathleen Merritt *geologist*
Wrigley, Elizabeth Springer (Mrs. Oliver K. Wrigley) *foundation executive*
Wykoff, Frank Champion *economics educator*
Young, Howard Thomas *foreign language educator*

Clovis
Driscoll, Glen Robert *former university president*
Ensminger, Marion Eugene *animal science educator, author*

Coalinga
Harris, John Charles *agriculturalist*

Coarsegold
†Wyatt, Jane Ellen *tribal leader*

Coloma
Wall, Sonja Eloise *nurse, administrator*

Colton
Brown, Jack H. *supermarket company executive*

Commerce
Conover, Robert Warren *librarian*

Compton
†Allumbaugh, Byron *grocery company executive*
Bogdan, Carolyn Louetta *financial specialist*
†Briskin, Bernard *finance executive*
†Collins, Patrick W. *grocery stores company executive*
Dymally, Mervyn Malcolm *retired congressman, international business executive*

Concord
Allen, Toby *resort executive*
Anderberg, Roy Anthony *journalist*
Clooney, Rosemary *singer, popular and jazz*
Davis, Robert Leach *retired government official, consultant*
Headding, Lillian Susan (Sally Headding) *writer, forensic clairvoyant*
Jackson, Milton (Bags Jackson) *jazz musician*
†Jessup, R. Judd *managed care executive*
Lee, Low Kee *electronics engineer, consultant*
†Taylor, Barry Robert *retail executive*

Corona
†Leo, Karen Ann *library administrator*
Ohmert, Richard Allan *architect*
Tillman, Joseph Nathaniel *engineer*

Corona Del Mar
Brandt, Rexford Elson *artist*
Britten, Roy John *biophysicist*
Crump, Spencer *publisher, business executive*
Davis, Arthur David *psychology educator, musician*
Delap, Tony *artist*
Donovan, Allen Francis *aerospace company executive*
Dorius, Kermit Parrish *architect*
Helphand, Ben J. *actuary*
Hill, Melvin James *oil company executive*
Hinderaker, Ivan *political science educator*
Hobbs, Linder Charlie *computer company executive*
Jacobs, Donald Paul *architect*
Mc Guire, Joseph William *business educator*
Solberg, Ronald Louis *investment management company executive*
Tether, Anthony John *aerospace executive*
Wickman, Paul Everett *public relations executive*
Yeo, Ron *architect*

Coronado
Allen, Charles Richard *retired financial executive*
Axelson, Joseph Allen *professional athletics executive*
Brunton, Paul Edward *retired diversified industry executive*
Butcher, Bobby Gene *retired military officer*
Grant, Alan J. *business executive*
Hostler, Charles Warren *international affairs consultant*
Hudson, George Elbert *retired research physicist*
Merkin, William Leslie *lawyer*
Mock, David Clinton, Jr. *internist*
Trent-Ota, Jane Suzanne *elementary school educator*
Wagener, Hobart D. *retired architect*
Worthington, George Rhodes *naval officer*

Corte Madera
Epstein, William Louis *dermatologist, educator*
Marines, Louis Lawrence *management consultant, educator*

Costa Mesa
Anderson, Jon David *lawyer*
Crinella, Francis Michael *neuropsychologist, science foundation director*
Currie, Robert Emil *lawyer*
Damsky, Robert Philip *communications executive*
Daniels, James Walter *lawyer*
Davidson, Janet Toll *lawyer*
Frieden, Clifford E. *lawyer*
Gore, Thomas Gavin *insurance and securities broker*
Hamilton, James William *lawyer*
Hamilton, Michael Scott *accounting firm executive*
Hay, Howard Clinton *lawyer*
Jensen, Gerald Randolph *editor and graphics designer*
Jones, H(arold) Gilbert, Jr. *lawyer*
†Jordan, Lawrence Spencer *sales executive*
Lattanzio, Stephen Paul *astronomy educator*
†Mittermeier, Janice *airport terminal executive*
Muller, Jerome Kenneth *painter, editor, psychologist*
†Olson, Cal Oliver *golf architect*
Reveal, Ernest Ira, III *lawyer*
Richmond, Ronald LeRoy *aerospace engineer*
Riordan, George Nickerson *investment banker*
Savage, Sandra Hope Skeen *mathematics educator, curriculum writer*
Speers, Roland Root, II *lawyer*
Thurston, Morris Ashcroft *lawyer*
Wall, James Edward *petroleum, pharmaceutical executive*
Williams, William Corey *Old Testament educator, consultant*

Cotati
†Arminana, Ruben *university president, educator*

Covina
Fillius, Milton Franklin, Jr. *food products company executive*
†Jackson, John Jay *association administrator, minister*
Schneider, Calvin *physician*
Takei, Toshihisa *otolaryngologist*

Crockett
Somerset, Harold Richard *sugar company executive*

Cromberg
Kolb, Ken Lloyd *writer*

Culver City
Abdul, Paula (Julie) *singer, dancer, choreographer*
Berland, James Fred *business and computer management consultant*
†Bluth, Don *animator, director, screenwriter*
Boorman, John *film director, producer, screenwriter*
Brooks, James L. *writer, director, producer*
Brown, Abbott Louis *accountant*
Canton, Mark *motion picture company executive*
Clodius, Albert Howard *history educator*
Eckel, James Robert, Jr. *financial planner*
Guber, Peter *producer*
Leve, Alan Donald *electronic materials manufacturing company owner, executive*
Levine, Alan J. *entertainment company executive*
Maltzman, Irving Myron *psychology educator*
Martin, Gary O. *film company executive*
Medavoy, Mike *motion picture company executive*
Melnick, Daniel *film producer*
†Moss, Eric Owen *architect*
Nathanson, Michael *film company executive*
†Ray, Mary-Ann *architect, educator*
Reiser, Paul *actor, comedian*
Rosenfelt, Frank Edward *motion picture company executive*
Sensiper, Samuel *consulting electrical engineer*
Stark, Ray *motion picture producer*
†Tarantino, Quentin *film director, screenwriter*
Tinker, Grant A. *broadcasting executive*
von Kalinowski, Julian Onesime *lawyer*
Wayans, Damon *actor*
Williams, Kenneth Scott *entertainment company executive*
Zucker, David *director*

Cupertino
Amdahl, Gene Myron *computer company executive*
Bossen, David August *electronics company executive*
Burg, John Parker *signal processing executive*
Cheeseman, Douglas Taylor, Jr. *wildlife tour executive, photographer, educator*
Compton, Dale Leonard *retired space agency executive*
Fletcher, Homer Lee *librarian*
Gingerich, John Charles *manufacturing company executive*
Graziano, Joseph A. *computer company executive*
Horn, Christian Friedrich *venture capital company executive*
†Lindsay, Leslie *packaging engineer*
†Markkula, A. C., Jr. *entrepreneur*
Marshall, Robert Charles *computer company executive*
Mathias, Leslie Michael *electronic manufacturing company executive*
McAdams, Robert, Jr. *electronics executive*
Nelson, Richard Burton *physicist, engineer, patent consultant*
Norman, Donald Arthur *cognitive scientist*
Perkins, Thomas James *venture capital company executive*
Reed, Robert Daniel *publisher*
Sculley, John *computer company executive*
Spindler, Michael H. *computer company executive*
Wiley, Richard Haven *chemist, educator*
Zobel, Louise Purwin *author, educator, writing consultant*

Cypress
Burge, Willard, Jr. *software company executive*
Edmonds, Ivy Gordon *writer*
Hoops, Alan *health care company executive*
†Naganuma, Kazue *automotive executive*
Olschwang, Alan Paul *lawyer*
†Recchia, Richard D. *automotive sales executive*

Daly City
Hargrave, Sarah Quesenberry *marketing, public relations company executive*
Martin, Bernard Lee *former college dean*

Dana Point
Frederickson, Arman Frederick *minerals company executive*
Friedman, Barry *financial marketing consultant*
Jelinek, Robert *advertising executive, writer*
Kesselhaut, Arthur Melvyn *financial consultant*
Krogius, Tristan Ernst Gunnar *international marketing consultant, lawyer*
†Robinson, Theodore G. *golf course architect*

Danville
Amon, William Frederick, Jr. *finance company executive*
Arrol, John *corporate executive*
Behring, Kenneth E. *professional sports team owner*
†Davis, James Ivey *company president, laboratory associate*
Frederickson, John Marcus *insurance executive*
Liggett, Lawrence Melvin *vacuum equipment manufacturing company executive*
Maninger, R(alph) Carroll *engineering executive, consultant*
Mc Millan, Terry *writer, educator*
Trezek, George James *mechanical engineer*

Davis
Addicott, Fredrick Taylor *retired botany educator*
Akesson, Norman Berndt *agricultural engineer, emeritus educator*
Alder, Henry Ludwig *mathematics educator*
Allard, Robert Wayne *geneticist, educator*
Andrews, Lawrence James *chemistry educator, academic administrator*
Ardans, Alexander Andrew *veterinarian, laboratory director, educator*
Axelrod, Daniel Isaac *geology and botany educator*
Ayer, John Demeritt *law educator*
Baldwin, Ransom Leland *animal science educator*
Barbour, Michael G(eorge) *botany educator, ecological consultant*
Bartosic, Florian *lawyer, artibrator, educator*
Baskin, Ronald Joseph *zoologist, physiologist, biophysicist educator, dean*
Beadle, Charles Wilson *retired mechanical engineering educator*
Beagle, Peter Soyer *writer*
Biberstein, Ernst Ludwig *veterinary medicine educator*
Black, Arthur Leo *biochemistry educator*
Brandt, Harry *mechanical engineering educator*
Bruch, Carol Sophie *lawyer, educator*
Cahill, Thomas Andrew *physicist, educator*
Carlson, Don Marvin *biochemist*
Carman, Hoy Fred *agricultural sciences educator*
Chancellor, William Joseph *agricultural engineering educator*
Chang, Robert Shihman *virology educator*
Cheney, James Addison *civil engineering educator*
Cohen, Lawrence Edward *sociology educator, criminologist*
Colvin, Harry Walter, Jr. *physiology educator*
Conn, Eric Edward *plant biochemist*
Crane, Julian Coburn *agriculturist,retired educator*
Crowley, Daniel John *anthropologist*
Crummey, Robert Owen *history educator, university dean*
Day, Howard Wilman *geology educator*
DePaoli, Geri M. *artist, art historian*
Dorf, Richard Carl *electrical engineering and management educator*
Dykstra, Daniel James *lawyer, educator*
Elmendorf, William Welcome *anthropology educator*
Enders, Allen Coffin *anatomy educator*
Epstein, Emanuel *plant physiologist*
Forbes, Jack D. *ethnohistorian, educator, writer*
Freedland, Richard Allan *retired biologist, educator*
Fridley, Robert Bruce *agricultural engineering educator, academic administrator*
Gardner, Murray Briggs *pathologist, educator*
Gardner, William Allen *electrical engineering educator*
†Gates, Bruce Clark *chemical engineer, educator*
Ghausi, Mohammed Shuaib *electrical engineering educator, university dean*
Giedt, Warren Harding *mechanical engineer, educator*
Gifford, Ernest Milton *biologist, educator*
Grey, Robert Dean *biology educator*
†Grossman, George Stefan *library director, law eductor*
Groth, Alexander Jacob *political science educator*
Hakimi, S. Louis *electrical and computer engineering educator*
Harper, Lawrence Vernon *human development educator*
Hartmann, Hudson Thomas *agriculturist, educator*
Hawkes, Glenn Rogers *psychology educator*
Hayden, John Olin *English literature educator, author*
Hays, Peter L. *English language and literature educator*
Hedrick, Jerry Leo *biochemistry and biophysics educator*
Hess, Charles Edward *environmental horticulture educator*
Higgins, Charles Graham *geology educator*
Hoffman, Michael Jerome *humanities educator*
†Horowitz, Isaac M. *control research consultant, writer*
Horwitz, Barbara Ann *physiologist, educator, consultant*
Hrdy, Sarah Blaffer *anthropology educator*
Hsieh, Dennis P. H. *environmental toxicology educator*
†Hughes, John P. *equine research adminstrator*
Hullar, Theodore Lee *university chancellor*
Imwinkelried, Edward John *law educator*
Ives, John David (Jack Ives) *geography educator*
Jackson, William Turrentine *history educator*
Jasper, Donald Edward *clinical pathology educator*
Jett, Stephen Clinton *geography educator, researcher*
Johnston, Warren E. *agricultural economics educator, consultant*
Juenger, Friedrich Klaus *lawyer, educator*
Jungerman, John Albert *physics educator*
Kado, Clarence Isao *molecular biologist*
Keizer, Joel Edward *chemistry educator, theoretical scientist*
Kemper, John Dustin *mechanical engineering educator*
Killam, Eva King *pharmacologist*
Kofranek, Anton Miles *floriculturist, educator*
Kunkee, Ralph Edward *viticulture and enology educator*
Laidlaw, Harry Hyde, Jr. *entomology educator*
Lazarus, Gerald Sylvan *physician*
Learn, Elmer Warner *agricultural economics educator, retired*
Lipscomb, Paul Rogers *orthopaedic surgeon, educator*
Lofland, John Franklin *sociologist, educator*
Lofland, Lyn Hebert *sociology educator*
Major, Clarence Lee *novelist, poet, educator*
†Marois, Jim *plant pathologist, educator*
Martin, George Conner *pomology educator*
Mason, William A(lvin) *psychologist, educator, researcher*
McHenry, Henry Malcolm *anthropologist, educator*
McPherson, Sandra Jean *poet, educator*
Meyer, Margaret Eleanor *microbiologist, educator*
Miller, R(ussell) Bryan *chemistry educator*
Moyle, Peter Briggs *fisheries and biology educator*
Murphy, Terence Martin *botany educator*

Musolf, Lloyd Daryl *political science educator, institute administrator*
Nash, Charles Presley *chemistry educator*
Nielsen, Donald Rodney *soil and water science educator*
†Overstreet, James Wilkins *obstetrics and gynecology educator, administrator*
Owings, Donald Henry *psychology educator*
Palmer, Philip Edward Stephen *radiologist*
Pappagianis, Demosthenes *microbiology educator, physician*
Pearcy, Robert Woodwell *botany educator*
Perschbacher, Rex Robert *law educator*
Plopper, Charles George *anatomist, cell biologist*
Pritchard, William Roy *former university system administrator*
Qualset, Calvin Odell *agronomy educator*
Rappaport, Lawrence *plant physiology and horticulture educator*
Rhode, Edward Albert *veterinary medicine educator, veterinary cardiologist*
Richman, David Paul *neurologist, researcher*
Rick, Charles Madeira, Jr. *geneticist, educator*
Rocke, David Morton *statistician, educator*
Rosen, Jerome *composer, clarinetist, educator*
Rost, Thomas Lowell *botany educator*
Rothstein, Morton *historian, retired educator*
Ryu, Dewey Doo Young *biochemical engineering educator*
†Schneeman, Barbara Olds *nutrition educator, department chair*
Schoener, Thomas William *zoology educator, researcher*
Schwabe, Calvin Walter *veterinarian, medical historian, medical educator*
Shapiro, Arthur Maurice *biology educator*
Sharrow, Marilyn Jane *library administrator*
Shelton, Robert Neal *physics educator, researcher*
Sillman, Arnold Joel *physiologist, educator*
Siverson, Randolph Martin *political science educator*
Skinner, G(eorge) William *anthropologist, educator*
Smiley, Robert Herschel *university dean*
Smith, Lloyd Muir *chemist, educator*
Smith, Michael Peter *social science educator, researcher*
Sosnick, Stephen Howard *economics educator*
Stebbins, George Ledyard *research botanist, retired educator*
Steffey, Eugene Paul *veterinary medicine educator*
Stewart, James Ian *agricultural water scientist, cropping system developer, consultant*
Stowell, Robert Eugene *pathologist, retired educator*
Stumpf, Paul Karl *former biochemistry educator*
Sumner, Daniel Alan *economist, educator*
Swift, Richard G(ene) *composer, educator*
Tchobanoglous, George *civil engineering educator*
Tomlinson-Keasey, Carol Ann *university administrator*
Tupper, Charles John *physician, educator*
Vanderhoef, Larry Neil *university administrator*
Volman, David Herschel *chemistry educator*
Waddington, Raymond Bruce, Jr. *English language educator*
Wang, Shih-Ho *electrical engineer, educator*
Watt, Kenneth Edmund Ferguson *zoology educator*
Wegge, Leon Louis François *economics educator*
Werner-Jacobsen, Emmy Elisabeth *developmental psychologist*
Williams, Hibbard Earl *medical educator, physician*
Williams, William Arnold *agronomy educator*
Williamson, Alan Bacher *English literature educator, poet, writer*
Willis, Frank Roy *history educator*
Wilson, Barry William *biology educator*
Wolk, Bruce Alan *law educator*
Woodress, James Leslie, Jr. *English language educator*
Wooten, Frederick (Oliver) *applied science educator*
Wydick, Richard Crews *lawyer, educator*
Yang, Shang Fa *biochemistry educator, plant physiologist*
Youmans, Julian Ray *neurosurgeon, educator*

Del Mar
Beare, Bruce Riley *trading company and sales executive*
Comrie, Sandra Melton *human resource executive*
Cooper, Martin *electronics company executive*
†Cutrona, Louis John *engineering executive*
Farquhar, Marilyn Gist *cell biology and pathology educator*
Kaye, Peter Frederic *newspaper editor*
Reid, Joseph Lee *physical oceanographer, educator*
Sullivan, Romaine Brust *school system administrator*
Wilkinson, Eugene Parks *nuclear engineer*

Diablo
Pelandini, Thomas Francis *mmarketing executive*

Diamond Bar
Fisher, Louis Raymond *insurance executive*

Dillon Beach
Petersen, Roland *artist, printmaker*

Dinuba
Leps, Thomas MacMaster *civil engineer, consultant*

Downey
Ashton, Lillian Hazel Church *adult education educator*
Baumann, Theodore Robert *aerospace engineer, consultant, army officer*
Brofman, Woody *astronautical engineer, educator*
Demarchi, Ernest Nicholas *aerospace company executive*
†Gothold, Stuart E. *school system administrator, education educator*
Perry, Jacquelin *orthopedic surgeon*
Redeker, Allan Grant *physician, medical educator*
Sapico, Francisco Lejano *internist, educator*
Schroeder, Robert J. *veterinarian, association executive*
Shapiro, Richard Stanley *physician*
Weinberger, Frank *information systems advisor*

Duarte
Chou, Chung-Kwang *bio-engineer*
Comings, David Edward *physician, medical genetics scientist*
Greenstein, Jesse Leonard *astronomer, educator*
Levine, Rachmiel *physician*
Lundblad, Roger Lauren *research director*
Ohno, Susumu *research scientist*
†Shapero, Sanford Marvin *hospital executive, rabbi*
Smith, Hallett Darius *retired English literature educator*
Smith, Steven Sidney *molecular biologist*

Dublin
Cope, Kenneth Wayne *chain store executive*
Del Santo, Lawrence A. *retail merchandising company executive*
†Prince, Jimmie Dan *retail food chain executive*

East Los Angeles
Darby, G. Harrison *lawyer*

Edwards
Deets, Dwain Aaron *aeronautical research engineer*

El Cajon
Burnett, Lowell Jay *physicist, educator*
Donnelly, Donald Frank *mathematics educator, computer consultant*
Fike, Edward Lake *newspaper editor*
Laffoon, Carthrae Merrette *management consultant*
McClure, Donald Edwin *electrical construction executive, consultant*
McInerney, Joseph Aloysius *hotel executive*

El Centro
Flock, Robert Ashby *retired entomologist*
Lokey, Frank Marion, Jr. *broadcast executive, consultant*

El Cerrito
Conti, Isabella *psychologist, consultant*
Dillenberger, John *theology educator emeritus, minister*
Garbarino, Joseph William *labor arbitrator, economics and business educator*
Griffith, Ladd Ray *retired chemical research director*
Gwinn, William Dulaney *physical chemist, educator, consultant*
Komatsu, S. Richard *architect*
Kuo, Ping-chia *historian, educator*
Schomer, Howard *retired clergyman, educator, social policy consultant*
Wilke, Charles Robert *chemical engineer, educator*

El Macero
Raventos, Antolin *radiology educator*
Wheeler, Douglas Paul *conservationist, government official, lawyer*

El Segundo
Aldridge, Edward C., Jr. *aerospace transportation executive*
Amerman, John W. *toy company executive*
Ball, Jerry Lee *professional football player*
Barad, Jill Elikann *toy company executive*
Brill, James Lathrop *finance executive*
Brown, Timothy Donell *professional football player*
Davis, Allen *professional football team executive*
Gossett, Jeffrey Alan *professional football player*
Gupta, Madhu Sudan *electrical engineering educator*
Herrera, John *professional football team executive*
Hoover, William R(ay) *computer service company executive*
Hostetler, Jeff W. *professional football player*
Ismail, Raghib (Rocket Ismail) *professional football player*
Jaeger, Jeff Todd *professional football player*
†Level, Leon Jules *information services executive*
Mo, Roger Shih-Yah *electronics engineering manager*
Mosebar, Donald Howard *professional football player*
Paulikas, George Algis *physicist*
Pickett, Michael D. *computer hardware and software distributor*
†Plummer, James Walter *engineering company executive*
Ricardi, Leon Joseph *electrical engineer*
Sanchez-Llaca, Juan *hotel executive*
Shell, Art *professional football team coach*
Tamrat, Befecadu *aeronautical engineer*
Townsend, Greg *professional football player*
Wallace, Arthur *agricultural educator*
Wisniewski, Stephen Adam *professional football player*

Emeryville
Dezurick, Paul Anthony *lawyer*
Marcus, Frank *biochemist*
Masri, Merle Sid *biochemist, consultant*
Schwartz, David Marcus *magazine editor-in-chief*
†Winton, Charlie Bradley *publishing executive*

Encinitas
Bloomberg, Warner, Jr. *urban affairs educator emeritus*
Dennish, George William, III *cardiologist*
Goldberg, Edward Davidow *geochemist, educator*
Morrow, Charles Tabor *aerospace consulting engineer*
Wilson, Donald Grey *management consultant*

Encino
Acheson, Louis Kruzan, Jr. *aerospace engineer and systems analyst*
Bucks, Charles Alan *airline industry consultant, former executive*
Dor, Yoram *health care executive*
Erickson, Lawrence Wilhelm *education educator*
Gasich, Welko Elton *management executive*
Goodman, John *actor*
Hawthorne, Marion Frederick *chemistry educator*
Hubbard, Frederick Dewayne *trumpeter*
Karlin, Myron D. *motion picture executive*
Kaufman, Albert I. *lawyer*
Knuth, Eldon Luverne *engineering educator*
Krueger, Kenneth John *corporate executive*
†Lewitt, Maurice *health care service company executive*
Majors, Lee *actor*
Nielsen, Leslie *actor*
Roderick, Robert Lee *aerospace executive*
Singer, Gerald Michael *lawyer, educator, arbitrator and mediator*
Smith, Selma Moidel *lawyer, composer*
Stanton, Harry Dean *actor*
Webster, David Arthur *life insurance company executive*
Wood, Raymund Francis *retired librarian*
Zsigmond, Vilmos *cinematographer, director*

Escalon
Barton, Gerald Lee *food company executive*

Escondido
Allen, Donald Vail *investment executive, author, concert pianist and organist*
Barrio, Raymond *author, artist*
Briggs, Edward Samuel *naval officer*
Damsbo, Ann Marie *psychologist*
Darmstandler, Harry Max *business executive, retired air force officer*
Everton, Marta Ve *ophthalmologist*
Lux, John H. *corporate executive*
Moore, Marc Anthony *university administrator, writer, retired military officer*
Newman, Barry Ingalls *retired banker, lawyer*
O'Meara, David Collow *retired banker*
†Ortiz, Angel Vicente *church administrator*
†Packer, Russell Howard *automotive company executive*
Sternberg, Harry *artist*

Etna
Auxentios *clergyman*
Chrysostomos, (González-Alexopoulos) *bishop, clergyman, psychologist, educator*

Fair Oaks
Branch, Robert Lee *retired educational administrator*
Byrne, John James *retired manufacturing company executive*
Chernev, Melvin *retired beverages executive*
Inglis, Andrew Franklin *author, consultant*
Smiley, Robert William *industrial engineer*
Stabenau, James Raymond *research psychiatrist, educator*

Fairfax
Gores, Joseph Nicholas *novelist, scriptwriter*
Novello, Don *writer, comedian, actor*

Fairfield
Hawn, William Eugene *health care company executive*
Martin, Clyde Verne *psychiatrist*
Moore, Marianna Gay *law librarian, consultant*

Fallbrook
Burge, Henry Charles *architect*
Dennis, Ward Brainerd *retired aerospace company executive*
Freeman, Harry Lynwood *accountant*
Ragland, Jack Whitney *artist*

Felicity
Istel, Jacques Andre *mayor*

Fish Camp
Schneider, Arthur Paul *retired videotape and film editor, author*

Folsom
Aldridge, Donald O'Neal *military officer*
†Close, Gary E. *pharmaceuticals executive*
Ettlich, William F. *electrical engineer*
Whitmire, Melburn G. *pharmaceutical distribution company executive*

Fontana
†Lardieri, Anthony J. *school system administrator*

Foothill Ranch
Eckstein, Harry *political science educator*

Forestville
Benyo, Richard Stephen *magazine editor, writer*

Fortuna
Fullerton, Gail Jackson *university president*

Foster City
Baselt, Randall Clint *toxicologist*
†Dove, Millard *transportation executive*
Fisk, Edward Ray *civil engineer, author, educator*
Ham, Lee Edward *civil engineer*
MacNaughton, Angus Athole *finance company executive*
Meredith, Allen Kent *real estate developer*
Paterson, Richard Denis *financial executive*
Turner, Ross James *investment corporation executive*
Wang, Su Sun *chemical company executive, chemist*

Fountain Valley
Gittleman, Morris *metallurgist,consultant*
Gumbiner, Robert Louis *health services executive*
Patterson, Dennis Joseph *management consultant*
†Price, Westcott Wilkin, III *health care executive*
Smith, Marie Edmonds *real estate agent, property manager*
Storms, Lester (C Storms) *retired veterinarian*

Frazier Park
Nelson, Harry *journalist, medical writer*

Fremont
Ball, William *mayor*
Berry, Michael James *chemist*
Brown, David Richard *school system administrator, minister*
de Roque, Barbara Penberthy *special education educator, consultant*
Domeier, David John *food products executive*
†Evenhuis, Henk J. *research company executive*
Gill, Stephen Paschall *physicist, mathematician*
Lautzenheiser, Marvin Wendell *computer software engineer*
Ours, Marian Leah *elementary education educator*
Sanders, Adrian Lionel *gifted and talented education educator*
Urquhart, John *physician, corporation executive, medical educator*
Wang, Ying Zhe *mechanical and optical engineer*

Fresno
†Andresen, Claudia *principal*
†Barrett, Robert Daker *arts center executive*
Blum, Gerald Henry *department store executive*
Brahma, Chandra Sekhar *civil engineering educator*
Buzick, William Alonson, Jr. *investor, lawyer, educator*
Coe, William Charles *psychology educator*
Cohen, Moses Elias *mathematician, educator*
Coyle, Robert Everett *federal judge*
Crocker, Myron Donovan *federal judge*
Dackawich, S. John *sociology educator*
Dandoy, Maxima Antonio *education educator emeritus*
Darden, Edwin Speight, Sr. *architect*
Dauer, Donald Dean *investment executive*
Emrick, Terry Lamar *business consultant*
Falcone, Alfonso Benjamin *physician*
Flores, William Vincent *educator*
Gerster, Robert Gibson *composer*
Gorman, Michael Joseph *library director, educator*
Haak, Harold Howard *university president*
Halverstadt, Jonathan Scott *personal growth systems developer, consultant, lecturer*
Harvey, Raymond Curtis *conductor*
Helzer, James Dennis *hospital executive*
Holmes, Albert William, Jr. *physician*
Jamison, Oliver Morton *lawyer*
Kallenberg, John Kenneth *librarian*
Kauffman, George Bernard *chemistry educator*
Kees, Beverly *newspaper editor*
Klassen, Peter James *academic administrator, history educator*
Kouymjian, Dickran *art historian, Orientalist, educator*
Krebs, John H. *former congressman*
†Leigh, Hoyle *psychiatrist, educator*
Levine, Philip *poet, educator*
Levy, Joseph William *department stores executive*
†Maddy, Kenneth Leon *state senator, lawyer*
Mather, Allen Frederick *lawyer*
O'Brien, John Conway *economist, educator, writer*
†O'Donnell, Thomas Howard *wheelchair manufacturing executive*
Ott, Michael Duane *lawyer*
Palmer, Samuel Copeland, III *lawyer*
Patnaude, William E. *architect*
†Patterson, James *mayor*
†Pings, Anthony Claude *architect*
Pinkerton, Richard LaDoyt *management educator*
Price, Edward Dean *federal judge*
†Putman, Robert Dean *golf course architect*
Rank, Everett George *government official*
Rehart, Burton Schyler *journalism educator, freelance writer*
†Saito, Paul Makoto *landscape architect*
Schofield, John-David Mercer *bishop*
Sobey, Edwin J. C. *museum director, oceanographer, consultant*
Steinbock, John T. *bishop*
Stude, Everett Wilson, Jr. *rehabilitation counselor, educator*
Tatarian, Hrach Roger *journalist*
Tellier, Richard Davis *management educator*
Wanger, Oliver Winston *federal judge, educator*
Welty, John Donald *university president*
†Wilson, Rhea *newspaper editor*
†Wilson, Warren Samuel *clergyman, bishop*

Fullerton
Atwell, Margaret Ann *education educator*
Axelson, Charles Frederic *retired accounting educator*
Ayala, John *librarian, dean*
Begovich, Nicholas Anthony *electrical engineer, consultant*
Borst, Philip West *academic administrator*
Brattstrom, Bayard Holmes *biology educator*
†Catlin, Allen Burdett (Buck Catlin) *mayor, former naval officer*
Cole, Sherwood Orison *psychologist*
Curran, Darryl Joseph *photographer, educator*
Donoghue, Mildred Ransdorf *education educator*
Foster, Julian Francis Sherwood *political science educator*
Garrido, Augie *university athletic coach*
Goldstein, Edward David *lawyer, former glass company executive*
Gordon, Milton Andrew *academic administrator*
Hershey, Gerald Lee *psychologist*
Hollander, Gerhard Ludwig *computer company executive*
Hopping, Richard Lee *college president*
Hugstad, Paul Steven *college dean*
Jones, Claris Eugene, Jr. *botanist, educator*
Karson, Burton Lewis *musician*
McGinnis, Joán Adell *secondary school educator*
Miller, Arnold *electronics executive*
Rosso, Louis T. *scientific instrument manufacturing company executive*
Shapiro, Mark Howard *physicist, educator, academic dean, consultant*
Smith, Ephraim Philip *university dean, educator*
Smith, Joachim *artist*
Svinos, John Georgios *software consulting firm executive*
Taylor, James Walter *marketing educator*
Timm, Laurance Milo *musician, educator*
von Sadovszky, Otto Joseph *anthropology educator, linguist*

Garden Grove
Ballesteros, Juventino Ray, Jr. *minister*
Banks, Ernest (Ernie Banks) *business executive, former professional baseball player*
Ortlieb, Robert Eugene *sculptor*
†Schuller, Robert Harold *clergyman, author*
Williams, J(ohn) Tilman *insurance executive, real estate broker, city official*

Gardena
Baker, Lillian L. *author, historian, artist, lecturer*

Gardenia
Crismond, Linda Fry *association executive*

Georgetown
Lengyel, Cornel Adam (Cornel Adam) *author*

Gilroy
†Blattman, H. Eugene *foods corporation executive*
Borton, George Robert *airline captain*

Glendale
Burger, John Barclay *systems architect, computer scientist*
Colby, Barbara Diane *interior designer, consultant*
Courtney, Howard Perry *clergyman*
Cross, Richard John *banker*
†Crull, Timm F. *food company executive*
Day, John Francis *city official, former savings and loan executive, former mayor*
Dent, Ernest DuBose, Jr. *pathologist*
Duke, William Edward *petroleum company executive*
Farmer, Crofton Bernard *atmospheric physicist*
Greenwood, Richard M. *finance company executive, bank executive*
Hadley, Paul Ervin *international relations educator*

Herzer, Richard Kimball *franchising company executive*
Hoffman, Donald M. *lawyer*
Kernen, Jules Alfred *pathologist*
Knoop, Vern Thomas *civil engineer, consultant*
Marr, Luther Reese *communications executive, lawyer*
Martin, John Hugh *lawyer, retired*
Misa, Kenneth Franklin *management consultant*
†Russell, Newton Requa *state senator*
Schifrin, Lalo *composer*
†Schult, Robert W. *food products executive*
Seegman, Irvin P. *manufacturing company executive*
Trafton, Stephen J. *banking executive*
Whalen, Lucille *academic administrator*
†Zarian, Larry *mayor*

Glendora
Cahn, David Stephen *cement company executive*
Christofi, Andreas Charalambos *finance educator*
Phillips, Jill Meta *author, critic, astrologer*
Richey, Everett Eldon *religion educator*
Roland, Donald Edward *advertising executive*
†Scheller, Sanford Gregory *printing company executive*
Schiele, Paul Ellsworth, Jr. *educator, writer*
Thompson, John Reed *librarian*

Goleta
Bartlett, James Lowell, III *investment banker*
Thom, Richard David *aerospace executive*

Granada Hills
Carradine, David *actor, director*
Shoemaker, Harold Lloyd *infosystem specialist*

Granite Bay
Crossley, Frank Alphonso *former metallurgical engineer*

Grass Valley
Cartwright, Mary Lou *laboratory scientist*
Lawrence, Dean Grayson *retired lawyer*

Greenbrae
Levy, S. William *dermatologist*

Gridley
Tanimoto, George *agricultural executive, farmer*

Gualala
Gaustad, Edwin Scott *historian*

Hacienda Heights
Love, Daniel Joseph *consulting engineer*

Half Moon Bay
Bonham, George Wolfgang *magazine editor, writer, foundation executive*
Hidy, George Martel *chemical engineer, executive*
Robertson, Abel L., Jr. *pathologist*

Hanford
†Drosdick, John Girard *oil company executive*

Harbor City
†Flood, John Etchells, Jr. *software services executive*

Hawthorne
Ashkenas, Irving Louis *aerospace executive*
Kokalj, James Edward *aerospace administrator*
Testa, Gabriel *real estate broker*
Weiss, Max Tibor *aerospace company executive*

Hayward
Critzer, William Ernest *association executive*
Flora, Edward Benjamin *research and development company executive, mechanical engineer*
Glasrud, Bruce Alden *history educator*
Mayers, Eugene David *philosopher, educator*
McCune, Ellis E. *retired university system chief administrator, higher education consultant*
Morgan, Joe Leonard *former professional baseball player, investment company executive*
Ramos, Melvin John *artist, educator*
†Rees, Norma S. *university president, educator*
Resnikoff, George Joseph *university dean, mathematics and statistics educator emeritus*
Sabharwal, Ranjit Singh *mathematician*
Smith, J(ohn) Malcolm *political science educator*
†Sweeney, Michael *mayor*
Tontz, Jay Logan *university dean, educator*
Tribus, Myron *management consultant, engineer, educator*
Warnke, Detlef Andreas *geologist, educator*
Whalen, Thomas Earl *psychology educator*

Healdsburg
Canfield, Grant Wellington, Jr. *association administrator, management consultant*
Conrat, Richard Fraenkel *photographer, educator, mechanical contractor*
Eade, George James *retired air force officer, research executive, defense consultant*
Erdman, Paul Emil *author*
Kamm, Thomas Allen *lawyer, retired naval officer*
Reed, Thomas Care *business executive*

Hemet
Berger, Lev Isaac *physicist, educator*
Bible, Frances Lillian *mezzo-soprano, educator*
Kopiloff, George *psychiatrist*
Treece, Joseph Charles *insurance broker*

Hermosa Beach
McDowell, Edward R. H. *chemical engineer*

Hesperia
Butcher, Jack Robert *manufacturing executive*
Moyers, Lowell Duane *pipeline company executive*

Hidden Hills
Hodgdon, Herbert James *savings and loan executive, consultant*

Hillsborough
Blume, John August *consulting civil engineer*
Keller, John Francis *retired wine company executive, mayor*
Willoughby, Rodney Erwin *retired oil company executive*

Hollister
Parker, Patrick Johnston *entrepreneur, educator*

Hollywood
Bessman, Samuel Paul *biochemist, pediatrician*
Carter, Bennett Lester (Benny Carter) *musician, composer, conductor*
†Hovsepian, Vatche *clergyman*
Israel, David *journalist, screenwriter, producer*
Jordan, Stanley *musician*
Klingman, Lynzee *film editor*
Koch, Howard Winchel *film and television producer*
Lewis, Huey (Hugh Anthony Cregg, III) *singer, composer, bandleader*
Little Richard, (Richard Wayne Penniman) *recording artist, pianist, songwriter, minister*
Marshall, Conrad Joseph *entrepreneur*
Marshall, Frank W. *film producer, director*
Parks, Robert Myers *appliance manufacturing company executive*
Perkins, William Clinton *company executive*
Rudin, Scott *film company executive*
Salomon, Mikael *cinematographer, director*
Samuels, Cynthia Kalish *communications executive*
Schaefer, Carl George Lewis *writer, public relations and advertising executive*
Strock, Herbert Leonard *motion picture producer, director, editor, writer*
Wayans, Keenen Ivory *actor, producer*
Wilder, Billy *motion picture director, writer, producer*

Hopland
Jones, Milton Bennion *agronomist, educator*

Huntington Beach
†Allen, Doris *state legislator*
Anderson, Raymond Hartwell, Jr. *metallurgical engineer*
†Falcon, Joseph A. *mechanical engineering consultant*
Forkert, Clifford Arthur *civil engineer*
Frye, Judith Eleen Minor *editor*
†Hayden, Ron L. *library director*
†Ho, Derek *professional surfer*
Lee, Sammy *retired physician, surgeon*
Martin, Wilfred Wesley *psychologist, property manager*
Shaffer, Richard James *lawyer, former manufacturing company executive*

Huntington Park
Johnson, Patricia Hardy *early childhood specialist pre-school provider*

Indian Wells
Harris, Milton M. *distributing company executive*
Pace, Stanley Carter *retired aeronautical engineer*
Reed, A(lfred) Byron *retired apparel and textile manufacturing company*

Indio
Fischer, Craig Leland *physician*
Lloyd, Douglas George *watercolor artist, educator*

Inglewood
Abdul-Jabbar, Kareem (Lewis Ferdinand Alcindor) *former professional basketball player*
†Alaniz, Miguel José Castañeda *library director*
Beverley, Nick *hockey team executive*
Buss, Jerry Hatten *real estate executive, sports team owner*
Gretzky, Wayne *professional hockey player*
Guzy, Marguerita Linnes *educator*
†Jefferson, Bernard S. *academic administrator*
Jobe, Frank Wilson *orthopedic surgeon*
Johnson, Earvin (Magic Johnson) *professional sports team executive, former professional basketball coach*
Kimble, Bettye D. *retired educational administrator*
Kurri, Jari *professional hockey player*
Lewis, Roy Roosevelt *physicist*
McNall, Bruce *professional sports executive, numismatist*
Melrose, Barry James *professional hockey team coach*
Mlakar, Roy A. *professional hockey team executive*
Robitaille, Luc *professional hockey player*
Sharman, William *professional basketball team executive*
Turner, Norris *marketing professional*
Vachon, Rogatien Rosaire (Rogie Vachon) *professional hockey team executive*
†Vincent, Edward *mayor*
West, Jerry Alan *professional basketball team executive*
Worthy, James *professional basketball player*

Inverness
Welpott, Jack Warren *photographer, educator*

Irvine
Aigner, Dennis John *economics educator, consultant*
Alspach, Philip Halliday *manufacturing company executive*
Ang, Alfredo Hua-Sing *civil engineering educator*
Ayala, Francisco José *geneticist, educator*
Bander, Myron *physics educator, university dean*
Bartkus, Richard Anthony *magazine publisher*
Bastiaanse, Gerard C. *lawyer*
†Beckman, Arnold Orville *analytical instrument manufacturing company executive*
Bennett, Albert Farrell *biology educator*
†Berns, Michael W. *cell biologist, educator*
Bershad, Neil Jeremy *electrical engineering educator*
Boyer, Calvin James *librarian*
Bradley, Charles James, Jr. *corporate executive*
Bradshaw, Ralph Alden *biochemistry educator*
Buchanan, Lee Ann *public relations executive*
Burton, Michael Ladd *anthropology educator*
†Casey, Martin M. *food service executive*
Cho, Zang Hee *physics educator*
Chronley, James Andrew *real estate executive*
Clark, Bruce Robert *geology consultant*
Clark, Karen Heath *lawyer*
Cohen, Robert Stephen *drama educator*
Colino, Richard Ralph *communications consultant*
Connolly, John Earle *surgeon, educator*
†Cowart, Jim Cash *securities trader*
Cunningham, Dennis Dean *microbiology, molecular genetics educator*
Cushman, Robert Fairchild *political science educator, author, editor*
†Danielian, Arthur Calvin *architect*
Danziger, James Norris *political science educator*
Demetrescu, Mihai Constantin *computer company executive, scientist*
Earhart, Donald Marion *management consultant, health care company executive*
Euster, Joanne Reed *librarian*
Fan, Hung Y. *virology educator, consultant*
Feldstein, Paul Joseph *management educator*
Felton, Jean Spencer *physician*
Fitch, Walter M(onroe) *molecular biologist, educator*
Frasca, Joanne M. *lawyer*
Freeman, Linton Clarke *sociology educator*
Friedenberg, Richard Myron *radiology educator, physician*
Friou, George Jacob *immunologist, physician, educator*
Garrison, Clayton *university dean*
Geis, Gilbert Lawrence *sociology educator emeritus*
Giannini, Valerio Louis *investment banker*
Glenn, Gerald Marvin *marketing, engineering and construction executive*
Gottschalk, Louis August *neuropsychiatrist, psychoanalyst*
Greenberger, Ellen *psychologist, educator*
Gupta, Sudhir *immunologist, educator*
Guymon, Gary LeRoy *civil engineering educator, consultant*
Habermann, Norman *restaurant group executive*
†Haggerty, Charles A. *electronics executive*
†Halm, Dennis Ray *academic administrator*
Herbert, Gavin Shearer *health care products company executive*
Hilker, Walter Robert, Jr. *lawyer*
Hine, Robert Van Norden, Jr. *historian, educator*
Hoshi, Katsuo Kai *international business executive*
Jamshidipour, Yousef *bank executive, financial consultant, financial planner*
†Joliffe, James *managing partner*
Jones, Edward George *anatomy and neurobiology professor, department chairman*
Jones, Joie Pierce *acoustician, educator, writer, scientist*
†Keating, James J. *oil industry executive*
Key, Mary Ritchie (Mrs. Audley E. Patton) *linguist, author, educator*
Kingman, Dong *artist, educator*
Kluger, Ruth *German language educator, editor*
Kontny, Vincent L. *engineering and construction company executive*
Korb, Robert William *former materials and processes engineer*
Kraemer, Kenneth Leo *architect, urban planner, educator*
Krieger, Murray *English educator, author*
Lambert, Robert Lowell *scientific investigator*
Lanyi, Janos Karoly *biochemist, educator*
Lave, Charles Arthur *economics educator*
Lehnert, Herbert Hermann *foreign language educator*
Lenhoff, Howard Maer *biological sciences educator, academic administrator, activist*
Lesonsky, Rieva *editor in chief*
Lillyman, William John *German language educator*
Luce, R(obert) Duncan *psychology educator*
Lurie, Harold *engineer, lawyer*
Maestrini, Emilio *industrial projects contracts manager*
Margolis, Julius *economist, educator*
Martin, Jay Herbert *psychoanalysis and English educator*
†May, Eva Antonia *advertising agency executive*
McCann, Dean Merton *lawyer, former pharmaceutical company executive*
McCraw, Leslie G. *engineering and construction company executive*
Mc Culloch, Samuel Clyde *history educator*
Mc Gaugh, James Lafayette *psychobiologist*
McIntyre, Joel Franklyn *lawyer*
McLaughlin, Calvin Sturgis *biochemistry educator*
Miledi, Ricardo *neurobiologist*
Miller, Joseph Hillis *comparative literature educator*
Moore, David Lewis *trade association executive*
Morrison, Gilbert Caffall *psychiatrist*
Mosier, Harry David, Jr. *physician, educator*
Muller, Edward Robert *lawyer*
Nalcioglu, Orhan *physicist*
†Nelson, Robert E. *public relations executive, political consultant*
†Nishida, Atsutoshi *computer company executive*
Nomura, Masayasu *biological chemistry educator*
Otth, Edward John, Jr. *retired marine systems executive, retired naval officer*
Paul, Courtland Price *landscape architect, planner*
Pearson, William James *finance company executive*
Penrod, James Wilford *choreographer, dancer*
Power, F. William *newspaper publisher*
Qureshey, Safi U. *electronics manufacturing company executive*
Rady, Ernest S. *thrift and loan association executive*
Reines, Frederick *physicist, educator*
Rentzepis, Peter M. *chemistry educator*
Ristau, Kenneth Eugene, Jr. *lawyer*
Robinson, Rob *publishing company executive*
Rollans, James O. *service company executive*
Rowland, Frank Sherwood *chemistry educator*
Rubel, Arthur Joseph *anthropologist, educator*
Rynn, Nathan *physics educator, consultant*
Santoro, Carmelo James *electronics executive*
Saunders, Robert Mallough *engineering educator, college administrator*
Schonfeld, William Rost *political science educator, researcher*
Segal, D. Robert *publishing and broadcast company executive*
†Shepherd, William C. *pharmaceutical company executive*
Silverman, Paul Hyman *parasitologist, former university official*
Sirignano, William Alfonso *aerospace and mechanical engineer, educator*
Sklansky, Jack *electrical and computer engineering educator, researcher*
Slavich, Denis Michael *engineering and construction company executive*
Smith, Herbert Furrer *lawyer*
Smith, Lewis Dennis *biologist, college dean*
†Sonoguchi, Kazuo *automotive company executive*
Sovie, Donald E. *lawyer*
Spence, M. Anne *geneticist, medical association executive*
Sperling, George *cognitive scientist, educator*
Stack, Geoffrey Lawrence *real estate developer*
Starr, Arnold *neurologist, educator*
Stubberud, Allen Roger *electrical engineering educator*
Sutton, Dana Ferrin *classics educator*
Taagepera, Rein *social science educator*
Tennyson, Peter Joseph *lawyer*
Thomas, Joseph Allan *lawyer*
Ting, Albert Chia *bioengineering researcher*
Tobis, Jerome Sanford *physician*
Treas, Judith Kay *sociology educator*
Trolinger, James Davis *laser scientist*
van-den-Noort, Stanley *physician, educator*
Waggener, Susan Lee *lawyer*
Wallis, Richard Fisher *physicist, educator*
Wentworth, Theodore Sumner *lawyer*
†White, Douglas R. *anthropology educator*
White, Stephen Halley *biophysicist, educator*
Wiener, Jon *history educator*
Wilkening, Laurel Lynn *university official, planetary scientist*
Williams, James E. *food products manufacturing company executive*
Wintrode, Ralph Charles *lawyer*
Wolfsberg, Max *chemist, educator*
Young, Robert Anthony *association director*

Irwindale
Deihl, Richard Harry *savings and loan association executive*
Groom, John Miller *food company executive*
†Hughes, Roger K. *dairy and grocery store company executive*
Rinehart, Charles R. *savings and loan association executive*
Welch, Linda Ogden *sales executive*

Jackson
†Halvorson, William *automotive executive*

Kensington
Connick, Robert Elwell *chemistry educator*
Loran, Erle *artist*
Malkiel, Yakov *linguistics educator*
Mc Cann, Cecile Nelken *writer*
Nathan, Leonard Edward *writer, educator*
Oppenheim, Antoni Kazimierz *mechanical engineer*
Stent, Gunther Siegmund *molecular biologist, educator*
Swanson, Guy Edwin *social scientist, educator*

Kentfield
DeWolff, Maurice Konrad *lawyer, banker*
Halprin, Anna Schuman (Mrs. Lawrence Halprin) *dancer*

La Canada Flintridge
Byrne, George Melvin *physician*
Clauser, Francis H. *applied science educator*
Costello, Francis William *lawyer*
Dales, Richard Clark *history educator*
Fry, Donald Owen *broadcasting company executive*
Lamson, Robert Woodrow *retired school system administrator*
Read, William McClain *retired oil company executive*
Simmons, John Wesley *oil company executive*
Wallace, James Wendell *lawyer*

La Habra
†Burkle, Ronald W. *food service executive*
Chase, Cochrane *advertising agency executive*
†Golleher, George *food company executive*
Woyski, Margaret Skillman *retired geology educator*

La Honda
Waldhauer, Fred Donald *health care executive*

La Jolla
†Abarbanel, Henry Don Isaac *physicist, academic administrator*
Alvariño De Leira, Angeles (Angeles Alvariño) *biologist, oceanographer*
Anderson, Richard William *retired psychiatrist, educator*
†Anderson, Victor Charles *applied physics educator*
Anthony, Harry Antoniades *city planner, architect, educator*
Antin, David *poet, critic*
Antin, Eleanor *artist*
Arnold, James Richard *chemist, educator*
Arnold, Jean Ann *health science facility administrator*
Asmus, John Fredrich *physicist*
Atkinson, Richard Chatham *university chancellor, cognitive psychologist, educator*
Attiyeh, Richard Eugene *economics educator*
Backus, George Edward *theoretical geophysicist*
Baesel, Stuart Oliver *architect*
Bardwick, Judith Marcia *management consultant*
†Barnett, Tim P. *meteorologist*
Barrett, Robert John, Jr. *management consultant*
Barrett-Connor, Elizabeth Louise *epidemiologist, educator*
†Beebe, Mary Livingstone *curator*
Benson, Andrew Alm *biochemistry educator*
Bergan, John Jerome *vascular surgeon*
Bernstein, Eugene Felix *vascular surgeon, medical educator*
Bertram, H. Neal *applied physics educator, researcher*
Beutler, Ernest *physician, research scientist*
Block, Melvin August *surgeon, educator*
Bloom, Floyd Elliott *physician, research scientist*
Boger, Dale L. *chemistry educator*
Borjas, George J(esus) *economics educator*
†Bray, Nancy A. *Oceanographes Director*
Breitwieser, Charles John *engineer, educator*
Brueckner, Keith Allan *theoretical physicist, educator*
Buckingham, Michael John *oceanography educator*
Burbidge, E. Margaret *astronomer, educator*
Carmichael, David Burton *physician*
Carson, John Congleton *cardiologist, educator*
Chang, William Shen Chie *electrical engineering educator*
†Chien, Shu *physiology and bioengineering educator*
Christensen, Halvor Niels *biochemist, educator*
Conn, Robert William *engineering science educator*
Copley, David C. *newspaper publishing company executive*
Copley, Helen Kinney *newspaper publisher*
Cornette, William Magnus *scientist, research director, company executive*
Counts, Stanley Thomas *aerospace consultant, retired naval officer, retired electronics company executive*
Cox, Charles Shipley *oceanography researcher, educator*
Craig, Harmon *geochemist, oceanographer*
Cuevas, Jose Luis *painter, illustrator*
Dalessio, Donald John *physician, neurologist, educator*

Dashen, Roger Frederick physics educator, consultant
†Davies, Hugh Marlais museum director
Dixon, Frank James medical scientist, educator
Doolittle, Russell Francis biochemist, educator
Dorsey, Dolores Florence business executive, corporate treasurer
Dreilinger, Charles Lewis (Chips Dreilinger) dean
Drell, William chemical company executive
†Driscoll, Charles F. research physicist
Dulbecco, Renato biologist, educator
Dunn, David Joseph financial executive
†Early, Ames S. health facility administrator
Edelman, Gerald Maurice biochemist, educator
Farr, Richard Studley immunologist, educator, physician
Farson, Richard Evans psychologist
Feher, George physics and biophysics scientist, educator
Fisher, Frederick Hendrick oceanographer
Fishman, William Harold cancer research foundation executive, biochemist
Fosburg, Richard Garrison cardiothoracic surgeon
Freedman, David Noel religion educator
Freedman, Michael Hartley mathematician, educator
Friedman, Paul Jay radiologist, educator
Frieman, Edward Allan university administrator, educator
Fung, Yuan-Cheng Bertram bioengineering educator, author
Geiduschek, E(rnest) Peter biophysics and molecular biology educator
Gittes, Ruben Foster urological surgeon
†Goff, William James librarian
Goldman, Stanford electrical engineer, scientist
Gourevitch, Peter Alexis political science educator, dean
Granger, Clive William John economist, educator
Grier, Herbert Earl scientist, consultant
Grine, Donald Reaville geophysicist, research executive
Groves, Theodore Francis, Jr. economics educator
Guillemin, Roger C. L. physiologist
Halkin, Hubert mathematics educator, research mathematician
Harkins, Edwin L. music educator, performer
Harris, Philip Robert management and space psychologist
Harris, T George management editor
Haxo, Francis Theodore marine biologist
Helstrom, Carl Wilhelm electrical engineering educator
Hench, Philip Kahler physician
Hofmann, Alan Frederick biomedical educator, researcher
Hunter, Tony (Anthony Rex Hunter) molecular biologist, educator
Imana, Jorge Garron artist
†Ishizaka, Kimishige immunologist, educator
Itano, Harvey Akio biochemistry educator
Jeffers, Donald E. consultant
Johnson, Allen Dress cardiologist
Jones, Charlie television sports announcer
Jones, Galen Everts microbiologist, educator
†Kadonaga, James Takuro biochemist
Kaplan, Robert Malcolm health researcher, educator
Karten, Harvey Jules neurosciences educator
Katzman, Robert medical educator, neurologist
Keeling, Charles David oceanography educator
Keeney, Edmund Ludlow physician
Kent, Paula public relations, marketing and management consultant, lecturer
Kerr, Donald MacLean, Jr. physicist
Kirchheimer, Arthur E(dward) lawyer, business executive
Kitcher, Philip Stuart philosophy educator
Klein, David foreign service officer
Klinman, Norman Ralph immunologist, medical educator
Lakoff, Sanford political scientist, educator
Lal, Devendra nuclear geophysics educator
Langacker, Ronald Wayne linguistics educator
Lauer, James Lothar physicist, educator
Lele, Padmakar Pratap physician, educator
†Lerner, Richard Alan chemistry educator, scientist
Levy, Ralph engineering executive, consultant
Lewin, Ralph Arnold biologist
MacDonald, Gordon James Fraser geophysicist
MacDougall, John Douglas earth science educator
†Maher, James R. laboratory administrator
†Mandell, Arnold Joseph psychiatrist
Mandler, George psychologist
Mandler, Jean Matter psychologist, educator
Marti, Kurt chemistry educator
Mathews, Kenneth Pine physician, educator
McAnuff, Des artistic director
Mc Elroy, William David biochemist, educator
†McFadden, Lucy-Ann Adams planetary scientist
McIlwain, Carl Edwin physicist
Milstein, Laurence Bennett electrical engineering educator, researcher
Mitchell, Malcolm Stuart physician, researcher
Monaghan, Eileen artist
Monday, John Christian electronics company executive
Morse, Jack Hatton utilities consultant
Mullis, Kary Banks biochemist
Munk, Walter Heinrich geophysics educator
Nakamura, Robert Motoharu pathologist
Namias, Jerome meteorologist
Nelles, Maurice mechanical engineer, author
Newmark, Leonard Daniel linguistics educator
Nyhan, William Leo pediatrician, educator
Ogdon, Wilbur composer, music educator
Olafson, Frederick Arlan philosophy educator
†O'Neil, Thomas Michael physicist, educator
Patton, Stuart biochemist, educator
Penhune, John Paul science company executive, electrical engineer
Penner, Stanford Solomon engineering educator
Reissner, Eric (Max Erich Reissner) applied mechanics researcher
Reynolds, Roger Lee composer
Richey, Phil Horace former manufacturing executive, consultant
Ride, Sally Kristen physics educator, scientist, former astronaut
Robbins, John Michael, Jr. mortgage company executive
Rosenblatt, Murray mathematics educator
Rosenbluth, Marshall Nicholas physicist, educator
Rothschild, Michael economics educator
Rudee, Mervyn Lea engineering educator, researcher
Ruiz, Ramon Eduardo history educator
Schiller, Herbert Irving social scientist, author
†Schmid-Schoenbein, Geert Wilfried biomedical engineer, educator
Sclater, John George geophysics educator
Shakespeare, Frank ambassador
Sham, Lu Jeu physics educator
Shannahan, William Paul lawyer
Shuler, Kurt Egon chemist, educator
Siegan, Bernard Herbert lawyer, educator
Silverstone, Leon Martin pedodontist, cariologist, neuroscientist, educator, researcher
Simon, Ronald I. finance consultant
Skalak, Richard engineering mechanics educator, researcher
Spiess, Fred Noel oceanographer, educator
Spinweber, Cheryl Lynn research psychologist
Spiro, Melford Elliot anthropology educator
Spooner, Charles Edward university administrator, health educator
Starr, Ross Marc economist, educator
Steinberg, Daniel preventive medicine physician, educator
Stevens, Paul Irving manufacturing company executive
Stewart, John Lincoln university administrator
Streichler, Jerry human and technology resource development consultant
†Sung, Kuo-Li Paul bioengineering educator
Tan, Eng Meng immunologist, rheumatologist, biomedical scientist
Terry, Robert Davis neuropathologist, educator
Todd, Harry Williams aircraft propulsion system company executive
Van Lint, Victor Anton Jacobus physicist
Walker, Harold Osmonde newspaper and cable television executive
Wall, Frederick Theodore chemistry educator
Watson, Kenneth Marshall physics educator
†Wegner, Harvey E. physicist, consultant
Weigle, William Oliver immunologist, educator
Wesling, Donald Truman English literature educator
West, John Burnard physiologist, educator
Whitaker, Eileen Monaghan artist
Wilkie, Donald Walter biologist, aquarium museum director
Wilkins, Floyd, Jr. retired lawyer, consultant
Williams, Forman Arthur engineering science educator, combustion theorist
Wolf, Jack Keil electrical engineer, educator
†Wong, Chi-Huey chemistry educator
Wright, Andrew English literature educator
Wulbert, Daniel Eliot mathematician, educator
York, Herbert Frank physics educator
ZoBell, Karl lawyer

La Mesa
Bailey, Brenda Marie accountant
Burns, Kenneth Dean aerospace industry executive, retired air force major general
Douglas, Stewart publishing executive, rancher
Hansen, Grant Lewis retired aerospace and information systems executive
Schmidt, James Craig retired bank executive
Tarson, Herbert Harvey university administrator emeritus
Williams, Carlton Hinkle dentist

La Mirada
Lingenfelter, Sherwood Galen university provost, anthropology educator
Nash, Sylvia Dotseth religious organization executive, consultant

La Puente
Perret, Joseph Aloysius banker, consultant
Reddy, Nagendranath K. biochemist, researcher
†Reilly, John E. automotive executive
†Sakaino, Kozo automobile company executive
Sheridan, Christopher Frederick human resources executive

La Quinta
Boysen, Harry obstetrician, gynecologist
†Houze, William Cunningham executive recruiter, management consultant

La Selva
Brown, Alan Charlton retired aeronautical engineer

La Verne
Morgan, Stephen Charles academic administrator

Lafayette
Alexander, Kenneth Lewis editorial cartoonist
Dethero, J. Hambright banker
Dietz, Donald Arthur vocational education educator
†Harlock, Michael J. architect
Hemphill, Norma Jo special event planning and tour company executive
Kahn, Robert Irving management consultant
Kapp, Eleanor Jeanne impressionistic artist, writer, researcher
Laird, Alan Douglas Kenneth mechanical engineering educator
Lewis, Sheldon Noah technology consultant
Moore, Calvin C. mathematics educator, administrator
Sandberg, Robert Alexis former research organization administrator

Laguna Beach
†Adler, Jeffrey D. political consultant, public affairs consultant, crisis management expert
Arterburn, Stephen Forrest health care company executive
Banuelos, Betty Lou rehabilitation nurse
Bent, Alan Edward political science educator, administrator
Bezar, Gilbert Edward retired aerospace company executive, volunteer
Calderwood, James Lee English literature educator, writer
Dale, Leon Andrew economist, educator
Desmarais, Charles Joseph museum director, writer, editor
Fagin, Henry public administration consultant
Faw, Duane Leslie retired military officer, law educator, lay worker, author
Garfin, Louis actuary
Hanauer, Joe Franklin real estate executive
Iberall, Arthur Saul physicist, publisher
Smith, Leslie Roper hospital administrator
Stebbins, Elizabeth Joseph Hinton management and statistics educator, researcher
Taylor, Theodore Langhans author
Warner, Robert S. company director, former accountant
Wilson, James Newman retired laboratory executive
Wolf, Karl Everett aerospace and communications corporation executive
Youngquist, Andrew Lance construction executive

Laguna Hills
Batdorf, Samuel B(urbridge) physicist
Burns, Donald Snow registered investment advisor, financial and business consultant
Burrows, Gates Wilson retired architect
Herold, Ralph Elliott motion picture arts educator
Howard, Hildegarde (Mrs. Henry Anson Wylde) paleontologist
Hussey, William Bertrand retired foreign service officer
James, Sidney Lorraine television executive
Kaplan, Sidney Joseph sociologist, educator
Larson, Harry Thomas electronics engineer
Lederer, Jerome aerospace safety engineer, educator
Lindquist, Raymond Irving clergyman
Linton, Frederick M. strategic planning consultant
Luhring, John William former bank executive
Mc Closkey, Paul N., Jr. lawyer, former congressman
Miller, Eldon Earl consultant, retired manufacturing company executive
Rabe, David William playwright
Westover, Samuel Lee insurance company executive
Wheatley, Melvin Ernest, Jr. retired bishop

Laguna Niguel
Angelov, George Angel pediatrician, anatomist, teratologist
Carr, Bernard Francis hospital administrator
Mortensen, Arvid LeGrande lawyer, insurance company executive
Nelson, Alfred John retired pharmaceutical company executive
Pierce, Hilda (Hilda Herta Harmel) painter
York, James Orison real estate executive

Lagunitas
Holman, Arthur Stearns artist

Lake Elsinore
Wilson, Sonja Mary secondary education educator, consultant

Lake Forest
Lindsell, Harold clergyman

Lakeport
Summerill, John Frederick retired mortuary science college dean and educator

Lakewood
Bogdan, James Thomas secondary education educator, electronics researcher and developer
Fenwick, James H(enry) editor

Lancaster
Crew, Aubrey Torquil aerospace inspector
Hodges, Vernon Wray mechanical engineer

Landers
Landers, Vernette Trosper writer, educator, association executive

Larkspur
Fawcett, F(rank) Conger lawyer
Kirk, Gary Vincent investment advisor
Marker, Marc Linthacum lawyer, investment company executive
Roulac, Stephen E. real estate consultant

Lemon Grove
Whitehead, Marvin Delbert plant pathologist

Livermore
Alder, Berni Julian physicist
Bennett, Alan Jerome electronics executive, physicist
†Binkley, J. S. physical sciences research administrator
Carley, James French chemical and plastics engineer
Dyer, Richard Hutchins risk management executive
†Fortner, Richard J. physical scientist
Glass, Alexander Jacob science administrator
Hulet, Ervin Kenneth retired nuclear chemist
Johnson, Roy Ragnar electrical engineer
†Kidder, Ray Edward physicist, consultant
King, Ray John electrical engineer
Leith, Cecil Eldon, Jr. retired physicist
Max, Claire Ellen physicist
Nuckolls, John Hopkins physicist, researcher
Olsen, Clifford Wayne former physical chemist
Schock, Robert Norman geophysicist
†Shotts, Wayne J. nuclear scientist, federal agency administrator
Tarter, Curtis Bruce physicist, science administrator
†Wong, Joe physical chemist
Wood, Donald Craig marketing professional

Livingston
Fox, Robert August food company executive

Loma Linda
Adey, William Ross physician
Bailey, Leonard Lee surgeon
†Behrens, Berel Lyn physician, academic administrator
Bull, Brian Stanley pathology educator, medical consultant, business executive
Coggin, Charlotte Joan cardiologist, educator
Condon, Stanley Charles gastroenterologist
†Hinshaw, David B., Sr. hospital administrator
Hinshaw, David B., Jr. radiologist
Johns, Varner Jay, Jr. medical educator
Klooster, Judson academic administrator, dentistry educator
Kuhn, Irvin Nelson hematologist, oncologist
Llaurado, Josep G. nuclear medicine physician, scientist
Longo, Lawrence Daniel physiologist, gynecologist
Mace, John Weldon pediatrician
Maurice, Don personal care industry executive
Peterson, John Eric physician, educator
Register, Ulma Doyle nutrition educator
Rendell-Baker, Leslie anesthesiologist, educator
Roberts, Walter Herbert Beatty anatomist
Slater, James Munro radiation oncologist
Slattery, Charles Wilbur biochemistry educator
Stilson, Walter Leslie radiologist, educator
Wilcox, Ronald Bruce biochemistry educator, researcher

Lompoc
Peltekof, Stephan systems engineer

Long Beach
Alkon, Ellen Skillen physician
Anand, Rajen S. physiologist
Anatol, Karl W. E. provost
Anderson, Gerald Verne aerospace company executive
Bauer, Roger Duane chemistry educator, science consultant
Beebe, Sandra E. English language educator, artist, writer
Beljan, John Richard university administrator, medical educator
Brent, Paul Leslie mechanical engineering educator
Brisco, Valerie track and field athlete
†Christensen, Christina Marie newspaper columnist
Cynar, Sandra Jean electrical engineering educator
Dean, Charles Thomas industrial arts educator, academic administrator
de Soto, Simon mechanical engineer
†Dillon, Michael Earl engineering executive, mechanical engineer, educator
Domondon, Oscar dentist
Donald, Eric Paul aeronautical engineer, inventor
†Drosdick, John G. oil industry executive
Falletta, Jo Ann musician
Ferreira, Armando Thomas sculptor, educator
Fornia, Dorothy Louise educator
Giles, Jean Hall retired corporate executive
Hancock, John Walker, III banker
Hennessy, Thomas Anthony columnist
Hildebrant, Andy McClellan retired electrical engineer
Hu, Chi Yu physicist, educator
Kell, Ernest Eugene, Jr. mayor, contractor
Kingore, Edith Louise retired geriatrics and rehabilitation nurse
Kokaska, Charles James educational psychologist
Kurnick, Nathaniel Bertrand oncology educator, researcher
Lathrop, Ann librarian, educator
Lathrop, Irvin Tunis retired academic dean, educator
Lauda, Donald Paul university dean
Lee, Isaiah Chong-Pie social worker, educator
Lobdell, Robert Charles retired newspaper executive
Loganbill, G. Bruce logopedic pathologist
McGuire, James Charles aircraft company executive
Mills, Don Harper pathology and psychiatry educator
Muchmore, Don Moncrief museum, foundation, educational, financial fund raising and public opinion consulting firm administrator
Mullins, Ruth Gladys pediatrics nurse
Munitz, Barry chief university administrator, English literature educator, business consultant
Myers, John Wescott aviation executive
Owen, Christina L. lawyer
Polakoff, Keith Ian historian, university administrator
†Rea, William oil industry executive
Roberts, William Harrison aerospace engineer, consultant, researcher
†Ruszkiewicz, Carolyn Mae newspaper editor
Sato, Eunice Noda former mayor, consultant
†Seita, Yukifusa electronics executive
Stetler, Charles Edward English language educator
Swatek, Frank Edward microbiology educator
Taylor, Reese Hale, Jr. lawyer, former government administrator
Thompson, William Ancker intramural and recreational sports director, educator
Todd, Malcolm Clifford surgeon
†Tyrnauer, Herbert H. design educator, industrial design consultant
†Valli, Peter Constantine manufacturing company executive
Walker, Mallory Elton tenor
Weinberg, Meyer humanities educator
Williams, Donald Clyde lawyer
†Winget, Clifford oil industry executive
Wise, George Edward lawyer
†Zappe, John Paul city editor, educator

Loomis
Hartmann, Frederick Howard political science educator emeritus

Los Alamitos
†Ayling, Henry Faithful editorial director, consultant
Booth, John Nicholls minister, magician, writer, photographer
Iceland, William Frederick engineering consultant
†Myers, Edwin think-tank executive

Los Altos
Allen, Michael Graham management consultant
Barker, William Alfred physics educator
Beer, Clara Louise Johnson retired electronics executive
Bell, Chester Gordon computer engineering company executive
Drachler, Norman retired education educator
Fenn, Raymond Wolcott, Jr. retired metallurgical engineer
Fondahl, John Walker civil engineering educator
Fraknoi, Andrew astronomy educator, astronomical society executive
Fraser-Smith, Elizabeth Birdsey biologist
Frey, Christian Miller research center executive
Gray, Robert Donald mayor
Hall, Charles Frederick space scientist, government administrator
Hinckley, Gregory Keith financial executive
Johnson, Richard Damerau aerospace scientist
Jones, Robert Thomas aerospace scientist
Kazan, Benjamin research engineer
†Miller, Ronald Grant journalist
Mullaley, Robert Charles manufacturing company executive
Oder, Frederic Carl Emil retired aerospace company executive, consultant
†Peterson, Victor Lowell aerospace engineer, research center administrator
Sharpe, Roland Leonard retired engineering company executive, earthquake and structural engineering consultant
Twersky, Victor mathematical physicist, educator
Wickham, Kenneth Gregory retired army officer, institute official
†Wilbur, Colburn Sloan foundation administrator

Los Altos Hills

Ginzton, Edward Leonard engineering corporation executive
McCormac, Billy Murray physicist, research institution executive, former army officer
van Tamelen, Eugene Earle chemist, educator

Los Angeles

Aaron, Benjamin law educator, arbitrator
Aaron, Paul film and television producer and director
Abernethy, Robert John real estate developer
†Abrahamson, James Alan retired air force officer
Abrams, Norman law educator, university administrator
Abramson, Rochelle Susan violinist
Ackerman, Bettye Louise (Mrs. Sam Jaffe) actress
Ackerman, Helen Page librarian, educator
Adam, Ken production designer
Adamek, Charles Andrew lawyer
Adams, Bryan vocalist, composer
†Adams, William Wesley, III architect
Adamson, Arthur Wilson chemistry educator
Adell, Hirsch lawyer
Adler, Douglas B. lawyer
Adler, Erwin Ellery lawyer
†Afifi, Abdelmonem A. biostatistics educator, academic dean
Aiello, Danny actor
Aki, Keiiti seismologist, educator
Alarcon, Arthur Lawrence federal judge
Alexander, Herbert E. political scientist
Alkon, Paul Kent English language educator
Allen, Debbie actress, dancer, director, choreographer
Allen, Michael John Bridgman English educator
Allen, William Richard retired economist
Aller, Lawrence Hugh astronomy educator, researcher
Alley, Kirstie actress
Allman, Gregg musician
Allman-Ward, Michele Ann bank executive
Allswang, John Myers computer science educator, historian
Alpers, Edward Alter history educator
Altfeld, Sheldon Isaac communications executive
Alvarez, Rodolfo sociology educator, consultant
Amarat, Issariyaporn Chulajata diplomat
Amneus, D. A. English language educator
Amos, John actor, producer, director
Anastos, Rosemary Park retired foreign language educator
Anawalt, Patricia Rieff anthropologist
Andersen, Henning linguistics educator
Andersen, Ronald Max health services educator, researcher
Anderson, Austin Gilman economics research company consultant
Anderson, Daryl actor
†Anderson, George Edward financial services company executive
†Anderson, Jane A. scriptwriter
Anderson, Michael Joseph film director
Anderson, Richard Norman actor, film producer
Anderson, Robert retired manufacturing company executive
Anderson, W. French genticist, biochemist, physician
Angeloff, Dann V. investment banking executive
Anka, Paul singer, composer
Ansen, David B. critic, writer
Apfel, Gary lawyer
Appleby, Joyce Oldham historian
April, Rand Scott lawyer
Apt, Leonard physician
Arant, Eugene Wesley lawyer
Arbib, Michael Anthony computer scientist, educator, neuroscientist, cybernetician
Archerd, Army (Armand Archerd) columnist, television commentator
Argue, John Clifford lawyer
Armstrong, C. Michael computer business executive
Armstrong, Lloyd, Jr. physicist, educator
Armstrong, Orville judge
Arnault, Ronald J. petroleum company executive
Arnold, Dennis B. lawyer
Arnold, Tom actor, comedian, producer
†Aroesty, Sidney A. medical diagnostic manufacturing company executive
Aroni, Samuel architecture and urban planning educator
Arora, Shirley Lease Spanish language educator
Ash, Roy Lawrence business executive
Ashforth, Alden musician, educator
Ashland, Calvin Kolle federal judge
Ashley, Sharon Anita pediatric anesthesiologist
Askanas-Engel, Valerie neurologist, educator, researcher
Askin, Richard Henry, Jr. entertainment company executive
Asner, Edward actor
Astin, Alexander William education educator
Astin, John Allen actor, director, writer
Avery, Robert Dean lawyer
†Axon, Donald Carlton architect
Ayres, James Marx mechanical engineer
Bacharach, Burt composer, conductor
Badie, Ronald Peter banker
Bahr, Ehrhard Germanic languages and literature educator
Bain, Conrad Stafford actor
Baird, Lourdes G. federal judge
Baker, Kathy Whitton actress
Baker, Lawrence Colby, Jr. insurance company executive
Baker, Richard Freligh biophysicist, educator
Baker, Robert Frank molecular biologist, educator
Baker, Sheldon S. lawyer
Baker, William Garrett, Jr. investment banker
Bakshi, Ralph film and television producer, director
Baldwin, William actor
Banner, Bob television producer, director
Bao, Joseph Yue-Se orthopaedist, microsurgeon, educator
Barash, Anthony Harlan lawyer
Barber, Thomas King dentist
Barbera, Joseph motion picture and television producer, cartoonist
Bardach, Sheldon Gilbert lawyer
Barham, Patte (Mrs. Harris Peter Boyne) publisher, author, columnist
Barker, Robert William television personality
Barkin, Ellen actress
Barrall, James D. C. lawyer
Barrie, Barbara Ann actress
Barrio, Jorge Raul medical educator
Barry, Gene actor
†Barry, Julian playwright, screenwriter
Barry, Philip Semple television and film producer
Bart, Peter Benton newspaper editor, film producer, novelist
Barton, Alan Joel lawyer
Barza, Harold A. lawyer
Basil, Douglas Constantine author, educator
Basile, Paul Louis, Jr. lawyer
Bass, Saul graphic designer, filmmaker
Bassett, Angela actress
Batres, Eduardo computer model builder, animator
Battaglia, Philip Maher lawyer
Bauman, John Andrew law educator
Baumann, Richard Gordon lawyer
Bauml, Franz Heinrich German language educator
†Bayless, Raymond artist
Baylor, Elgin Gay professional basketball team executive
†Beach, Roger C. oil company executive
Beard, Ronald Stratton lawyer
Beban, Gary Joseph real estate corporation officer
Beck, John Christian physician, educator
Beckwith, Charles Emilio English educator
Bekey, George Albert computer scientist, educator, engineer
Bell, Lee Phillip television personality
Bell, Wayne Steven lawyer
Belleville, Philip Frederick lawyer
Belnap, David Foster journalist
Bender, Charles William lawyer
Bendix, Helen Irene lawyer
Bennett, Charles Franklin, Jr. biogeographer, educator
Bennett, Harve (Harve Fischman) television and film producer, writer
Bennis, Warren Gameliel business administration educator, author, consultant
Benson, Sidney William chemistry researcher
Berg, Jeffrey Spencer talent agency executive
†Berg, Philip religious denomination administrator
Bergman, Alan lyricist, writer
Bergman, (Ernst) Ingmar film director, writer
Berman, Arthur Malcolm newspaper editor
Bernacchi, Richard Lloyd lawyer
Bernhard, Herbert Ashley lawyer
Bernhard, Sandra actress, comedienne, singer
Bernheimer, Martin music critic
Bernstein, Arthur Harold venture capital executive
Bernstein, Sol cardiologist, medical services administrator
†Berry, Halle actress
Berry, Richard Douglas architectural educator, urban planner and designer
Bhaumik, Mani Lal physicist
Bice, Scott Haas lawyer, educator
Biederman, Donald Ellis lawyer
Bierstedt, Peter Richard lawyer, entertainment industry consultant
Biles, John Alexander pharmaceutical chemistry educator
Billiter, William Overton, Jr. journalist
Bird, Peter geology educator
Birnbaum, Henrik Slavic languages and literature educator
Birren, James Emmett university research center executive
Bishop, Sidney Willard lawyer
Bjork, Robert Allen psychology educator, researcher
Black, Craig Call museum administrator
Black, Donna Ruth lawyer
Blackman, Lee L. lawyer
Blackwelder, Ron Forest engineering educator, consultant, researcher
Blahd, William Henry physician
Blake, Michael writer
Blankenship, Edward G. architect
Blencowe, Paul Sherwood lawyer
Blitz, Stephen M. lawyer
Bloch, Paul public relations executive
Bloch, Robert Albert author
Blodgett, Julian Robert small business owner
Boland, Paul Anson psychology educator emeritus
Bloom, Alan lawyer
Boak, Ruth Alice physician, educator
Bobbitt, Leroy lawyer
†Bobrow, Michael Lawrence architect
Bochco, Steven screenwriter, television producer
Bodkin, Henry Grattan, Jr. lawyer
Boerlage, Frans Theodoor opera director, music educator
Bogaard, William Joseph lawyer
Bogen, Andrew E. lawyer
†Bohle, Sue public relations executive
Boime, Albert Isaac art history educator
Bok, Dean cell biologist, educator
Bomes, Stephen D. lawyer
Bondareff, William psychiatry educator
Bonner, Robert Cleve lawyer
Bono, Sonny Salvatore singer, composer, former mayor
Boone, Pat (Charles Eugene Boone) singer, actor
Boonshaft, Hope Judith public relations executive
Borko, Harold information scientist, psychologist, educator
Borsch, Frederick Houk bishop
Borsting, Jack Raymond business administration educator
Bortman, David lawyer
Bosl, Phillip L. lawyer
Bosley, Tom actor
Bost, Thomas Glen lawyer
Bostwick, Barry actor
Bottger, William Carl, Jr. lawyer
†Bouchez, L. Brent advertising agency executive
Bower, Allan Maxwell lawyer
Bower, Paul George lawyer
Boyarsky, Benjamin William journalist
Boyd, Harry Dalton lawyer, former insurance company executive
†Brach, Gérard screenwriter
Bradshaw, Carl John lawyer, consultant
Bradshaw, Murray Charles musicologist
†Braginsky, Stanislav Iosifovich physicist, geophysicist, researcher
Branca, John Gregory lawyer, consultant
Branch, Taylor writer
Brandow, George Everett civil engineer
Brandt, Frederick William lawyer
Brassell, Roselyn Strauss lawyer
Bratt, Bengt Erik academic administrator, consulting engineer
Braudy, Leo Beal English language educator, author
Braun, David A(dlai) lawyer
Braun, Zev motion picture and television producer
Breidenbach, Francis Anthony lawyer
Breslow, Lester physician, educator
Bressan, Paul Louis lawyer
Brest, Martin film director
Breuer, Melvin Allen electrical engineering educator
Bricker, Seymour (Murray) lawyer
Bridges, B. Ried lawyer
†Briley, John Richard writer
Brimley, Wilford actor
Brinegar, Claude Stout oil company executive
Brinsley, John Harrington lawyer
Broad, Eli financial services and home construction company executive
Broadhurst, Norman Neil manufacturing executive
Broccoli, Albert Romolo motion picture producer
Brockett, Peter Charles financial executive
Broderick, Carlfred Bartholomew sociology educator
Broderick, Matthew actor
Broiles, Steven Anthony lawyer
Brolin, James (James Brunderlin) actor
Bromberg, Robert aerospace company executive
†Brotman, David J. architectural firm executive
Broussard, Thomas Rollins lawyer
Brown, Edmund Gerald (Pat Brown) lawyer, former governor of California
Brown, Iona violinist, orchestra director
Brown, Louis Morris lawyer, educator
Brunner, Robert Francis composer, conductor
†Buckingham, Jerry L. hospital administrator
Buckley, Betty Lynn actress
Bucy, Richard Snowden aerospace engineering and mathematics educator, consultant
Bufford, Samuel Lawrence federal judge
Burch, Robert Dale lawyer
Burke, William M. lawyer
Burke, Yvonne Watson Brathwaite (Mrs. William A. Burke) lawyer
Burkhardt, Hans Gustav artist
Burns, Dan W. manufacturing company executive
Burns, E(dward) Bradford history educator
Burns, Marvin Gerald lawyer
Burns, Robert Ignatius historian, educator, clergyman
Burrows, James television and motion picture director, producer
Busby, Jheryl record company executive
Byers, Nina physics educator
Byrd, Christine Waterman Swent lawyer
Byrne, Jerome Camillus lawyer
Byrne, William Matthew, Jr. federal judge
Caan, James actor, director
Calder, Daniel Gillmore English language educator
Caldwell-Portenier, Patty Jean Grosskopf advocate, educator
Calhoun, Gordon James lawyer
Calhoun, Ollie Arlene elementary education educator
Callender, William Lacey savings and loan executive, lawyer
Campbell, Douglas Argyle securities broker
Campbell, Glen singer, entertainer
Campbell, Kenneth Eugene, Jr. vertebrate paleontologist
Campion, Robert Thomas manufacturing company executive
Camron, Roxanne editor
Cannell, Stephen Joseph television writer, producer, director
Cannon, Louis Simeon journalist, author
Canter, Stanley Stanton motion picture producer
Capron, Alexander Morgan lawyer, educator
Carabillo, Virginia A. (Toni Carabillo) writer, editor, graphic designer
Carden, Joy Cabbage education executive
Cardone, Bonnie Jean photojournalist
Carlin, George Denis comedian
Carlson, Robert E. lawyer
Carlson, Terrance L. lawyer
Carpenter, David Roland life insurance executive
Carpenter, John Howard screenwriter, director
Carr, Willard Zeller, Jr. lawyer
Carroll, Pat actress
Carson, Edward Mansfield banker
†Carter, Nell actress, singer
†Caruso, David actor
Castro, Leonard Edward lawyer
Cate, Benjamin Wilson Upton journalist
Cates, Gilbert film, theater, television producer and director
Cathcart, David Arthur lawyer
Catton, Ivan mechanical engineer
Cavanagh, John Edward lawyer
Cecchetti, Giovanni poet, Italian language educator, literary critic
Chacko, George Kuttickal systems science educator, consultant
Chamberlain, Wilton Norman former professional basketball player
Champlin, Charles Davenport television host, book critic, writer
Chandler, Otis publisher
Chandor, Stebbins Bryant pathologist
Chang, Henry Chung-Lien library administrator
Chapman, Orville Lamar chemist, educator
Charen, Mona syndicated columnist
Charisse, Cyd (Tula Ellice Finklea) actress, dancer
Charles, Glen television producer
Charles, Les television producer
Charles, Ray (Ray Charles Robinson) musician, singer, composer
Charwat, Andrew Franciszek engineering educator
Chase, Chevy (Cornelius Crane Chase) comedian, actor, author
Chassman, Leonard Fredric labor union administrator
Chavez, Victor Edwin judge
Cheng, Hsien Kei aeronautics educator
Cheng, Tsen-Chung electrical engineering educator
Chernick, Richard lawyer
Cherry, James Donald physician
†Chetwynd, Lionel screenwriter, producer, director
Chiate, Kenneth Reed lawyer
Chilingarian, George Varos petroleum, environmental and civil engineering educator
Ching, Anthony lawyer
Choate, Joseph lawyer
Chobotov, Vladimir Alexander aerospace engineer, educator
Chomsky, Marvin J. director
Christol, Carl Quimby lawyer, political science educator
Christopher, William actor
Chu, Morgan lawyer
Chu, Wesley Wei-Chin computer science educator, consultant
Chuang, Harold Hwa-Ming banker
Cicciarelli, James Carl immunology educator
Cimino, Michael film director, writer
Clark, Burton Robert sociologist, educator
Clark, R. Bradbury lawyer
Clark, Richard lawyer
Clarke, Peter communications and health educator
Clay, Andrew Dice (andrew clay silverstein) comedian
Clemente, Carmine Domenic anatomist, educator
Cleveland, Carl S(ervice), Jr. academic administrator, educator, physician
†Cobb, Jewel Plummer former college president, educator
†Cochran, Johnnie L., Jr. lawyer
Cochran, Sachiko Tomie radiologist
Cocker, Joe vocalist, composer
Coffey, C. Shelby, III newspaper editor
Cohan, John Robert lawyer
Cohen, Cynthia Marylyn lawyer
Cohen, Daniel Morris museum administrator, marine biology researcher
Cohen, Gary J. lawyer
Cohen, Leonard (Norman Cohen) poet, novelist, musician, songwriter
Cohen, S(tephen) Marshall philosophy educator
Cohen, William Alan marketing educator, author, consultant
Cole, Curtis Allen lawyer
Cole, Natalie Maria singer
Coleman, Charles Clyde physicist, educator
Coleman, Roger William institutional food distribution company executive
Collias, Elsie Cole zoologist
Collier, Charles Arthur, Jr. lawyer
Colton, Robert Craig lawyer
Conrad, Paul Francis editorial cartoonist
Cook, Lodwrick Monroe petroleum company executive
Coombs, John Wendell financial service executive
Coombs, Robert Holman sociologist, medical educator, author
Cooper, Edwin Lowell anatomy educator
Cooper, Jay Leslie lawyer
Cooper, Leon Melvin lawyer
Coppola, Robert E. lawyer
Corea, Chick (Armando Corea) pianist, composer
Corman, Roger William motion picture producer, director
Cornwall, John Michael physics educator, consultant, researcher
Coroniti, Ferdinand Vincent physics educator, consultant
Corum, William Thomas, III computer information systems executive
Corwin, Norman writer, director, producer
Cost, John Joseph lawyer
Cotliar, George J. newspaper editor
Cotter, George Edward former airline company executive
Coughlin, Sister Magdalen college chancellor
Counts, James Curtis management consultant
Cozen, Lewis orthopedic surgeon
†Craig, Sidney Richard theatrical agent
Cram, Donald James chemistry educator
Crandall, Edward David medical educator
†Craven, Wes film director
Crawford, Philip Stanley bank executive
Crippens, David Lee broadcast executive
Crispo, Lawrence Walter judge
Crombie, Douglass Darnill aerospace communications engineer, former government official
†Cronenberg, David film director
Crosby, Peter Alan management consultant
Cross, Glenn Laban engineering executive, development planner
Crow, John Armstrong writer, educator
Crystal, Billy comedian, actor
Cuadra, Carlos Albert information scientist, management executive
Cummings, Thomas Gerald management educator, consultant
Currie, Malcolm Roderick aerospace and automotive executive, scientist
†Curtis, Daniel M. film director
Curtis, John Joseph lawyer
Curtiss, Thomas, Jr. lawyer, educator
Cyrus, Billy Ray country music performer
D'Accone, Frank Anthony music educator
†Dahlburg, John-Thor Theodore newspaper correspondent
Dallek, Robert history educator
Dalton, Larry Raymond chemistry educator, researcher, consultant
Daly, Tyne actress
Dangerfield, Rodney (Jack Roy Dangerfield) comedian, actor, author
Daniels, Jeff actor
Daniels, John Peter lawyer
Danoff, Dudley Seth surgeon, urologist
†Dante, Joe film director
Danziger, Louis graphic designer, educator
Darby, Michael Rucker economist, educator
Daviau, Allen cinematographer
Davidson, Ezra C., Jr. physician, educator
Davidson, Gordon theatrical producer, director
Davidson, Herbert Alan Near Eastern languages and cultures educator
Davies, John G. federal judge
†Davis, Andrew film director, screenwriter
Davis, Edmond Ray lawyer
Davis, Ossie actor, author
Davis, Ronald artist, printmaker
Davis, Sybil Alicia obstetrician gynecologist
Dawson, John Myrick plasma physics educator
Day, Anthony newspaper correspondent
Dearing, Vinton Adams retired English language educator
DeBard, Roger investment executive
De Brier, Donald Paul lawyer
de Castro, Hugo Daniel lawyer
Dee, Ruby (Ruby Dee Davis) actress, writer, director
†Deemer, Candy Kaelin advertising executive
Dekmejian, Richard Hrair political science educator
De La Hoya, Oscar Olympic athlete, boxer
Del Olmo, Frank newspaper editor
DeLuce, Richard David lawyer
Delugach, Albert Lawrence journalist
De Meules, James Head lawyer
Demsetz, Harold economist, educator
Denlea, Leo Edward, Jr. insurance company executive
de Passe, Suzanne record company executive
DeQuattro, Vincent Louis physician
Deschanel, Caleb cinematographer, director
Detels, Roger epidemiologist, physician, former university dean
Deukmejian, George lawyer, former governor
Dewell, Michael theater executive, writer, producer, translator
Dewey, Donald Odell university dean
Dey, Susan actress
†Dhir, Vijay K. mechanical engineering educator
Diamond, Matthew Philip artistic director, choreographer, dancer

Diamond, Stanley Jay *lawyer*
Dickason, James Frank *land and farming company executive*
Dickerson, Jaffe Dean *lawyer*
†Didion, James J. *real estate company executive*
Dignam, William Joseph *obstetrician, gynecologist, educator*
†Dill, Donald *consumer products company executive*
†Dillingham, Charles, III *entertainment executive*
Dillman, Bradford *actor*
Dillon, Paul Sanford *artist*
†Dingwell, Everett W. *food products company executive*
Dismukes, Valena Grace Broussard *physical education educator*
Dixon, Andrew Derart *retired academic administrator*
Dixon, Wilfrid Joseph *statistics educator*
Dobson, Bridget McColl Hursley *television executive and writer*
Dockson, Robert Ray *savings and loan executive*
Dodds, Douglas Allen *lawyer*
Dolan, Peter Brown *lawyer*
Doll, Lynne Marie *public relations agency executive*
Domantay, Norlito Valdez (Lito Domantay) *communications executive*
Domino, Fats (Antoine Domino) *pianist, singer, songwriter*
Donovan, John Arthur *lawyer*
†Dooley, Paul *actor, writer*
Dorfman, Steven David *electronics company executive*
Dorman, Albert A. *consulting engineer executive, architect*
Dorn, Wanda Faye *talent agent*
Doty, George Richard *lawyer*
Dougherty, Elmer Lloyd, Jr. *chemical engineering educator, consultant*
Dows, David Alan *chemistry educator*
Drake, Hudson Billings *aerospace and electronics company executive*
Drapkin, Steven G. *lawyer*
Draznin, Jules Nathan *journalism and public relations educator, consultant*
†Dr. Dre, (Andre Young) *rapper, record producer*
Drew, Paul *entrepreneur*
Dreyfuss, Richard Stephan *actor*
Duffy, Patrick *actor*
Dummett, Clifton Orrin *dentist, educator*
Dunn, Arnold Samuel *biochemistry educator*
Dunn, Bruce Sidney *materials science educator*
Dunnahoo, Terry (Mrs. Thomas William Dunnahoo) *editor, author*
†Duritz, Adam *musician*
Dworsky, Daniel Leonard *architect*
Dwyre, William Patrick *journalist, public speaker*
Dyck, Andrew Roy *philologist*
Eamer, Richard Keith *health care company executive, lawyer*
†Earle, Timothy *anthropology educator*
Easterlin, Richard Ainley *economist, educator*
Edwards, Blake *film director*
Edwards, Howard Lee *petroleum company executive*
Edwards, Kenneth Neil *chemist, consultant*
Eichler, Peter M. *lawyer*
Einstein, Clifford Jay *advertising executive*
Eisaman, Josiah Reamer, III *advertising executive*
Eisenberg, David Samuel *molecular biologist, educator*
Eiserling, Frederick Allen *microbiologist, educator*
Elfman, Danny *composer*
Ellsworth, David G. *lawyer*
Ellsworth, Frank L. *university administrator*
Emanuel, William Joseph *lawyer*
Emmeluth, Bruce Palmer *investment banker, venture capitalist*
Engler, George Nichols *educator, financial consultant*
English, Stephen Raymond *lawyer*
Ennis, Thomas Michael *health foundation executive*
Eno, Brian (Brian Peter George St. John De La Salle Eno) *composer, musician, producer*
Enstrom, James Eugene *cancer epidemiologist*
Epstein, Julius J. *screenwriter, playwright, producer*
Erburu, Robert F. *media and information company executive*
Erickson, Ralph Ernest *lawyer*
Estevez, Emilio *actor, writer, director*
Estrich, Susan Rachel *law educator*
Estrin, Gerald *computer scientist, engineering educator, academic administrator*
Etra, Donald *lawyer*
Eule, Julian Nathan *law educator*
Ewing, Edgar Louis *artist, educator*
Fabrick, Howard David *lawyer*
†Fahey, John Leslie *immunologist*
Fairbank, Robert Harold *lawyer*
Falk, EuGene L. *publishing executive*
Falk, Peter *actor*
Farman, Richard Donald *gas company executive*
Farmer, Robert Lindsay *lawyer*
Farnsworth, Richard *actor, former stuntman*
†Farrell, Joseph *movie market analyst, producer, entertainment research company executive, writer, sculptor, designer*
Farrell, Mike *actor*
Faulwell, Gerald Edward *insurance company executive*
†Feidelson, Marc *advertising executive*
Feig, Stephen Arthur *pediatrics educator, hematologist, oncologist*
Feiman, Thomas E. *accounting company executive*
Fein, Ronald Lawrence *lawyer*
†Felker, Peter *chemistry educator*
Fenimore, George Wiley *management consultant*
Fenn, Sherilyn *actress*
Fennelly, Jane Corey *lawyer*
Fenning, Lisa Hill *federal judge*
Ferrell, Conchata Galen *actress*
Ferry, Richard Michael *executive search firm executive*
Feshbach, Seymour *psychology educator*
Fickett, Edward Hale *architect, planner, arbitrator*
Field, Richard Clark *lawyer*
Field, Ted (Frederick Field) *film and record industry executive*
Fields, Bertram Harris *lawyer*
Fields, Henry Michael *lawyer*
†Fifield, James G. *recording industry executive*
Finch, Caleb Ellicott *neurobiologist, educator*
Fine, Richard Isaac *lawyer*
Firstenberg, Jean Picker *film institute executive*
Fisch, Max Harold *educator*
Fish, Barbara *psychiatrist, educator*
Fishburne, Laurence, III *actor*
Fisher, Lawrence W. *public relations company executive*
Fisher, Raymond Corley *lawyer*
†Fitch, William C. *professional basketball coach*
Fitzgerald, Tikhon (Lee R. H. Fitzgerald) *bishop*
Flanagan, Fionnula Manon *actress, writer, producer*
Flanigan, James J(oseph) *journalist*
Fleischmann, Ernest Martin *music administrator*
Flicker, Ted *scriptwriter, director, actor*
Fogelberg, Daniel Grayling *composer, recording artist*
Fohrman, Burton H. *lawyer*
Fonkalsrud, Eric Walter *pediatric surgeon, educator*
Foote, Christopher Spencer *chemist, educator*
Ford, Donald Hainline *lawyer*
Ford, Glenn (Gwylin Samuel Newton Ford) *actor*
Forester, Bernard I. *recreational equipment company executive*
Forgnone, Robert *lawyer*
Forness, Steven Robert *educational psychologist*
Forrest, Frederic *actor*
Forsythe, John *actor*
Foster, Mary Christine *motion picture and television executive*
Frackman, Russell Jay *lawyer*
Fragner, Matthew Charles *lawyer*
Franciosa, Anthony (Anthony Papaleo) *actor*
Francis, Merrill Richard *lawyer*
Franklin, Bonnie Gail *actress*
Frazier, Joe *retired professional boxer, performer*
Freeman, Morgan *actor*
Frey, Glenn *songwriter, vocalist, guitarist*
Fried, Burton David *physicist, educator*
Friedkin, William *film director*
Friedlander, Sheldon Kay *chemical engineering educator*
Friedman, George Jerry *aerospace company executive, engineer*
Friedman, Robert Lee *film company executive*
Friedmann, Peretz Peter *aerospace engineer, educator*
Frimmer, Paul Norman *lawyer*
Frisch, Robert A. *financial planning company executive*
Fromholz, Haley James *lawyer*
Fromkin, Victoria Alexandra *linguist, phonetician, educator*
Fry, Michael Graham *historian, educator*
Fudge, Jack D. *lawyer*
Fulco, Armand John *biochemist*
Fuller, Larry *choreographer, director*
Fuller, Samuel *scriptwriter, film director*
Fybel, Richard D. *lawyer*
Gadbois, Richard A., Jr. *federal judge*
†Gal, Kenneth Maurice *advertising executive*
Galanos, James *fashion designer*
†Gale, Mary Ellen *law educator*
Gale, Robert Peter *physician, scientist, researcher*
Galef, Andrew G. *textiles executive*
Galef, Andrew Geoffrey *investment and manufacturing company executive*
Gallagher, Peter *actor*
Gambino, Jerome James *nuclear medicine educator*
Gamble, Tracy Joseph *television producer, writer, lawyer*
Gambro, Michael S. *lawyer*
Ganas, Perry Spiros *physicist*
Garcia, Andy *actor*
†Garmire, Elsa Meints *electrical engineering educator, consultant*
Garry, William James *magazine editor*
†Garza, Oscar *newspaper editor*
Gaspari, Russell Arthur *electrical engineer*
†Gates, Robert C. *health facility administrator*
Gebb, Sheldon Alexander *lawyer*
Gebhart, Carl Grant *security broker*
†Gelfand, Leonard H. *insurance comprnay executive*
Gentile, Joseph F. *lawyer, educator*
Gersh, David Lewis *lawyer*
Gest, Howard David *lawyer*
Getto, Ernest John *lawyer*
Getty, Estelle *actress*
Gibbons, Leeza *television talk show host*
Gibbs, Marla (Margaret Gibbs) *actress*
Gilbert, Judith Arlene *lawyer*
Giles, Anne Diener *flutist*
Gilman, John Joseph *research scientist*
Gilman, Nelson Jay *library director*
Ginsburg, Seymour *computer science educator*
Girard, Robert David *lawyer*
Glaser, Daniel *sociologist*
Glass, Herbert *music critic, lecturer, editor*
Glassner, Barry *sociology educator, author*
Glazer, Guilford *real estate developer*
Glick, Earl A. *lawyer*
Glitz, Dohn George *biochemistry educator*
Glover, Danny *actor*
†Glover, John *actor*
Go, Vay Liang Wong *physician, medical educator, editor*
Godbold, Wilford Darrington, Jr. *enclosure manufacturing company executive, lawyer*
Goette, Richard A. *lawyer*
Gold, Arnold Henry *judge*
Gold, Bernard *lawyer*
Gold, Richard Horace *radiologist*
Goldberg, Gary David *producer, writer*
Golden, Milton M. *paint company executive*
Goldman, Allan Bailey *lawyer*
Goldman, Benjamin Edward *lawyer*
Goldman, Donald A. *lawyer*
Goldsmith, Jerry *composer*
Goldstein, Mark A. *zoo administrator*
Goldwyn, Samuel John, Jr. *motion picture producer*
Göllner, Marie Louise *musicologist, educator*
Golomb, Solomon Wolf *mathematician, electrical engineer, educator, university official*
Gonick, Harvey Craig *nephrologist, educator*
Gooch, Lawrence Boyd *accounting executive*
Goodman, David Bryan *musician, educator*
Goodman, Max A. *lawyer, educator*
Goodwin, Willard Elmer *urologist*
Gordon, Basil *mathematics educator*
Gordon, David Eliot *lawyer*
Gordon, Lawrence *film producer*
Gordon, Malcolm Stephen *biology educator*
Gordon, Milton G. *real estate counselor, consultant*
Gordy, Berry *entrepreneur, record company executive, motion picture executive*
Gorman, Cliff *actor*
Gorman, Joseph Gregory, Jr. *lawyer*
Gorney, Roderic *psychiatry educator*
Gorski, Roger Anthony *neuroendocrinologist, educator*
Gottfried, Ira Sidney *management consulting executive*
Gottlieb, Allen Sandford *entertainment company executive*
Gould, Charles Perry *lawyer*
Gould, David *lawyer*
Gould, Harold *actor*
†Gould, Morley David *advertising agency executive*
Govier, William Charles *pharmaceutical research and development executive*
Gralnek, Donald D. *lawyer*
Grammer, Kelsey *actor*
Grant, Amy *singer, songwriter*
†Grant, David *broadcasting executive*
Grant, Lee (Lyova Haskell Rosenthal) *actress, director*
Grantham, Richard Robert *real estate company executive*
Grausam, Jeffrey Leonard *lawyer*
Gray, Jan Charles *lawyer*
Gray, Linda *actress*
Grazer, Brian *film company executive*
Green, Guy Mervin Charles *film director*
Green, William Porter *lawyer*
Greenberg, Ira Arthur *psychologist*
Greenberg, Maxwell Elfred *lawyer*
Greenberger, Martin *computer and information scientist, educator*
Greene, Alvin *service company executive, management consultant*
Greene, Donald Johnson *retired English language educator, author*
Greenstadt, Melvin *investor, retired educator*
Gregg, Lucius Perry, Jr. *aerospace executive*
Greiman, April *graphic designer*
Grinnell, Alan Dale *neurobiologist, educator, researcher*
Grobe, Charles Stephen *lawyer, accountant*
Grody, Mark Stephen *public relations executive*
Groman, Arthur *lawyer*
Grosz, Philip J. *lawyer*
†Groves, Martha *newspaper writer*
Guest, Christopher *actor, director, screenwriter*
Gumpel, Glenn J. *association executive*
Gunn, Karen Sue *psychologist*
Gurash, John Thomas *insurance company executive*
Gurfein, Peter J. *lawyer*
Guttenberg, Steve *actor*
Gutterridge, Larry G. *lawyer*
Haas, Edward Lee *business executive, consultant*
Hackman, Gene *actor*
Haden, Charles *jazz bassist, composer*
Hahn, Elliott Julius *lawyer*
Hahn, Harlan Dean *political science educator, consultant*
Haight, James Theron *lawyer, corporate executive*
Haile, Lawrence Barclay *lawyer*
Halamandaris, Harry *aerospace executive*
Halgren, Jack *lawyer*
Halkett, Alan Neilson *lawyer*
Hall, Arsenio *television talk show host, comedian*
Hall, Carlyle Washington, Jr. *lawyer*
Hall, Clarence Albert, Jr. *geologist, educator*
Hall, Jeffrey Stuart *newspaper executive*
Halstead, Harry Moore *lawyer*
†Hamblin, Richard Wallace *advertising agency executive*
Hamlin, Harry Robinson *actor*
Hammer, (Stanley Kirk Burrell) *musician*
Hammond, David Greene *engineering company executive, consultant*
Hampton, Gordon Francis *lawyer*
Hancock, Herbert Jeffrey (Herbie Hancock) *composer, pianist, publisher*
Handler, Carole Enid *lawyer, city planner*
Handschumacher, Albert Gustave *retired corporate executive*
Handy, Lyman Lee *petroleum engineer, chemist, educator*
Handzlik, Jan Lawrence *lawyer*
Hanna, William Denby *motion picture and television producer, cartoonist*
Hanrahan, Thomas P. *lawyer*
Hansell, Dean *lawyer*
Hanson, John J. *lawyer*
Harbaugh, George Milton *hotel executive*
†Harbert, Ted *broadcast executive*
Harbison, John Robert *management consultant*
Harold, John Gordon *cardiologist, internist*
Harp, Rufus William *set decorator*
Harrick, Jim *university athletic coach*
Harris, James Michael *lawyer*
Harris, Susan *television producer*
†Harris, T. C. *water transportation executive*
Harris, Theodore Edward *mathematician, educator*
Harry, Deborah Ann *singer*
Hart, John Lewis (Johnny Hart) *cartoonist*
Hart, Larry Calvin *lawyer*
Hart, Mary *television talk show host*
Hartigan, John Francis *lawyer*
†Hartke, Stephen Paul *composer, educator*
Hartman, Lisa (Lisa Hartman Black) *actress, singer*
Hastings, Robert Pusey *lawyer*
Hathaway, Harry L. *lawyer*
Hatter, Terry Julius, Jr. *federal judge*
Havel, Richard W. *lawyer*
Hawley, Philip Metschan *retail executive, consultant*
†Hay, Maureene Griffoul *advertising executive*
†Hayden, Tom *state legislator, author*
Hayes, Byron Jackson, Jr. *lawyer*
Hayes, Robert Mayo *university dean, library and information science educator*
†Haythorn, J. Denny *law librarian*
Hayutin, David Lionel *lawyer*
Hayutin, Marc I. *lawyer*
Haywood, L. Julian *physician, educator*
Hazen, Steven Kelsey *lawyer*
Headlee, Rolland Dockeray *association executive*
Hearst, George Randolph, Jr. *publishing executive, diversified ranching and real estate executive*
Heather, Fred Doenges *lawyer, educator*
Hebald, Milton Elting *sculptor*
Heer, David Macalpine *sociology educator*
Hein, Leonard William *accounting educator*
Heinisch, Robert Craig *sales and marketing executive, consultant*
Heinke, Rex S. *lawyer*
†Helms, Harold Edwin *minister*
Hemion, Dwight Arlington *television producer, director*
Hemminger, Pamela Lynn *lawyer*
Hemmings, Peter William *orchestra and opera administrator*
Henderson, Florence (Florence Henderson Bernstein) *actress, singer*
Hendrick, Hal Wilmans *human factors educator*
Hennigan, James Michael *lawyer*
†Hernandez, Antonia *lawyer*
Hershiser, Orel Leonard, IV *professional baseball player*
Hertzberg, Paul Stuart *producer, publisher, writer*
Hettler, Paul *visual effects producer*
Heyert, Martin David *lawyer*
Heyler, Grover Ross *retired lawyer*
Hibner, Don Telfer, Jr. *lawyer*
Hieronymus, Edward Whittlesey *lawyer*
†Higby, Lawrence *newspaper publishing executive*
Higgins, John Joseph *corporate lawyer*
Highberger, William Foster *lawyer*
Hight, B. Boyd *lawyer*
Highwater, Jamake *author, lecturer*
Hinerfeld, Robert Elliot *lawyer*
Hinton, Leslie Frank *media executive*
†Hirsch, Barry L. *lawyer*
Hirsch, Werner Zvi *economist, educator*
Hoang, Duc Van *theoretical pathologist, educator*
Hobelman, Carl Donald *lawyer*
Hoffenberg, Marvin *political science educator, consultant*
Hoffman, Neil James *art school executive*
Hogan, Steven L. *lawyer*
Hogarth, Burne *cartoonist, illustrator*
Holbrook, Hal (Harold Rowe Holbrook, Jr.) *actor*
Holland, John Ray *minister*
Holliday, Thomas Edgar *lawyer*
Holman, Harland Eugene *manufacturing company executive*
Holtzman, Robert Arthur *lawyer*
Hopkins, Carl Edward *public health educator*
Horn, Martin Robert *patent lawyer*
Horowitz, Ben *medical center executive*
Horowitz, David Charles *consumer commentator, newspaper columnist*
†Horwitz, David A. *medicine and microbiology educator*
Hospers, John *philosophy educator*
Houck, John Burton *retired lawyer*
Houk, Kendall Newcomb *chemistry educator*
†House, John William *otologist*
Houston, Ivan James *insurance company executive*
Hovanessian, Shahen Alexander *electrical engineer, educator*
Hovannisian, Richard G. *Armenian and Near East history educator*
Howard, Murray *manufacturing, real estate property management executive, farmer, rancher*
Howard, Sandy *motion picture producer*
Howe, John Thomas *film director, educator*
Hu, Sze-Tsen *mathematics educator*
Hubbard, John Randolph *university president emeritus, history educator, diplomat*
Hubbs, Donald Harvey *foundation president*
Huddleston, David William *actor, producer*
†Hudlin, Warrington *writer, producer, director*
Hudson, Jeffrey Reid *lawyer*
Huebner, Harlan Pierce *lawyer*
Hufstedler, Seth Martin *lawyer*
Hufstedler, Shirley Mount (Mrs. Seth M. Hufstedler) *lawyer, former federal judge*
Hughes, Barnard *actor*
Hughes, Everett Clark *otolaryngology educator*
Hummel, Joseph William *hospital administrator*
Humphreys, Robert Lee *advertising agency executive*
Hundley, Norris Cecil, Jr. *history educator*
Hunter, Larry Dean *lawyer*
Hupp, Harry L. *federal judge*
Hurt, William Holman *investment management company executive*
Hurwitz, Lawrence Neal *investment banking company executive*
Hutter, James Risque *retired lawyer*
†Hutton, Lauren (Mary Laurence Hutton) *actress, model*
Hyman, Milton Bernard *lawyer*
Iamele, Richard Thomas *law librarian*
Ice Cube, (O'Shea Jackson) *rap singer, actor*
Ice-T, (Tracy Marrow) *rap singer, actor*
Ideman, James M. *federal judge*
†Incaudo, Joseph A. *engineering company executive*
Intriligator, Michael David *economist, educator*
Irani, Ray R. *oil, gas and chemical company executive*
Ireland, Kathy *actress*
Ireland, Robert Abner, Jr. *education consultant*
Irell, Lawrence E(lliott) *lawyer*
Irving, Jack Howard *technical consultant*
Irwin, Philip Donnan *lawyer*
†Isinger, William R. *newspaper publishing executive*
†Israel, Franklin David *architect*
Itoh, Tatsuo *engineering educator*
Jackson, Isaiah *conductor*
Jackson, Janet Damita *singer, dancer*
Jackson, Kingsbury Temple *educational contract consultant*
Jackson, Mary *actress*
Jackson, Michael (Joseph) *singer*
†Jacob, Paul F., III *architectural firm executive*
Jacobs, Marilyn Susan *psychologist, author*
Jacobs, Marion Kramer *psychologist*
Jaffe, F. Filmore *judge*
Jaffe, Sigmund *educator, chemist*
James, Peter W. *lawyer*
Janofsky, Leonard S. *lawyer, association executive*
Jarmon, Lawrence *developmental communications educator*
Jarrott, Charles *film and television director*
Jarvik, Lissy F. *psychiatrist*
Jarvik, Murray Elias *psychiatry, pharmacology educator*
Jelliffe, Roger Woodham *cardiologist, clinical pharmacologist*
Jenden, Donald James *pharmacologist, educator*
Jeter, Michael *actor*
Jimirro, James P. *broadcasting and telecommunications executive*
Joffe, Charles *motion picture producer, comedy management executive*
†Johnson, Cage Saul *hematologist, educator*
Johnson, Earl, Jr. *judge, author*
Johnson, Jonathan Edwin, II *lawyer*
†Johnson, Mark Devlin *advertising executive*
Johnson, Martin Marion *lawyer*
†Johnson, Scott *architect*
†Johnston, Michael J. *brokerage house executive*
Johnston, Roy G. *consulting structural engineer*
Johnston, Ynez *artist*
Jones, Henry *actor*
Jones, James Earl *actor*
†Jones, Jerve Maldwyn *construction company executive*
†Jones, Larry Richard *advertising executive*
Jones, Quincy *producer, composer, arranger, conductor, trumpeter*
Jones, Tom *singer*
Jordan, Judd L. *lawyer*
Jordan, Robert Leon *lawyer, educator*
Jorgensen, Paul Alfred *English language educator emeritus*
Kadison, Stuart L. *lawyer*
Kagan, Jeremy Paul *director, filmmaker*
Kalaba, Robert Edwin *applied mathematician*
†Kaliski, John *architectural firm executive*
Kambara, George Kiyoshi *retired ophthalmologist, educator*

Kane, Carol *actress*
Kaneko, Mitsuru *production company executive, animation producer*
Kanemitsu, Matsumi *artist*
Kaplan, Isaac Raymond *chemistry educator, corporate executive*
Kaplan, Jonathan Stewart *film writer, director*
Kaplan, Robert B. *linguistics educator, consultant, researcher*
Kaplan, Samuel *pediatric cardiologist*
Kapur, Krishan Kishore *dental researcher, educator*
Karlin, Michael Jonathan Abraham *lawyer*
Karplus, Walter J. *engineering educator*
Karros, Eric Peter *professional baseball player*
Karst, Kenneth Leslie *legal educator*
Katleman, Harris L. *television executive*
Katz, Jason Lawrence *lawyer, insurance executive*
Katz, Ronald Lewis *physician, educator*
Kaus, Otto Michael *lawyer*
Kay, Jerome Harold *cardiac surgeon*
Keach, Stacy, Jr. *actor, director, producer, writer, musician, composer*
†Kelleher, Robert *apparel executive*
Kelleher, Robert Joseph *federal judge*
Keller, William D. *federal judge*
Kellerman, Sally Claire *actress*
Kelley, Harold Harding *psychology educator*
Kelly, Arthur Paul *physician*
Kelly, Daniel Grady, Jr. *lawyer*
Kelly, Henry Ansgar *English language educator*
Kelly, Raymond Francis *commodity company executive*
Kendall, William Denis *medical electronic equipment company executive*
Kendig, Ellsworth Harold, Jr. *lawyer*
Kennedy, George *actor*
Kennedy, Kathleen *film producer*
Kennel, Charles Frederick *physics educator, government official*
Kennelly, Sister Karen Margaret *college administrator*
Kent, William *pilot, cameraman and technical director*
Kenyon, David V. *federal judge*
Kercheval, Ken *actor*
Ketchum, Robert Glenn *photographer, print maker*
†Kiddoo, Robert James *engineering service company executive*
Kidman, Nicole *actress*
Kienholz, Lyn Shearer *international arts projects coordinator*
Kilburn, Kaye Hatch *medical educator*
Kindel, James Horace, Jr. *lawyer*
King, Joseph Paul *finance executive*
King, Robert Lucien *lawyer*
†King, Sheldon Selig *medical center administrator, educator*
Kingsley, Walter Ingalls *television executive*
Kinney, James Howard *lawyer*
Kinosian, Janet Marie *journalist*
Kinski, Nastassja (Nastassja Nakszynski) *actress*
†Kirkland, Sally *actress*
Kirschner, David *animation entertainment company executive*
Kirwan, Betty-Jane *lawyer*
Kirwan, Ralph DeWitt *lawyer*
Kivelson, Margaret Galland *physicist*
Klee, Kenneth Nathan *lawyer*
Kleiman, Joseph *engineer, consultant, retired life sciences company executive*
Klein, Benjamin *economics educator, consultant*
Klein, Joan Dempsey *judge*
Klein, Raymond Maurice *lawyer*
Kleinberg, Marvin H. *lawyer*
Kleingartner, Archie *business educator*
Kleinrock, Leonard *computer scientist*
Kleiser, John Randal *motion picture director*
Kline, Lee B. *architect*
Kline, Richard Stephen *public relations executive*
Klinger, Allen *computer science and engineering educator*
Klopf, Jeffrey A. *lawyer*
Klowden, Michael Louis *lawyer*
Knapp, Cleon Talboys *business executive*
Knight, Christopher Allen *art critic*
Knopoff, Leon *geophysics educator*
Knotts, Don *actor*
Koch, Howard W., Jr. *film producer*
Koch, Richard *pediatrician, educator*
Koelzer, George Joseph *lawyer*
Koffler, Stephen Alexander *investment banker*
Kolkey, Daniel Miles *lawyer*
Kolve, V. A. *English literature educator*
Korenman, Stanley George *medical investigator, educator*
Korman, Harvey Herschel *actor*
Korn, Lester Bernard *business executive, diplomat*
Koshalek, Richard *museum director, consultant*
Kotcheff, William Theodore (Ted Kotcheff) *director*
Kramer, Stanley E. *motion picture producer, director*
Kresa, Kent *aerospace executive*
†Krim, Mathilde *medical educator*
Kristoff, James *production company executive*
†Krouse, Diane Murray *advertising company executive*
Krueger, Robert William *management consultant*
Kruger, Lawrence *neuroscientist*
Krumm, William Frederick *insurance company executive*
Krupp, Edwin Charles *astronomer*
Kruse, Scott August *lawyer*
Kuechle, John Merrill *lawyer*
Kuehl, Hans Henry *electrical engineering educator*
Kuelbs, John Thomas *lawyer*
Kulzick, Kenneth Edmund *lawyer, writer*
Kunc, Joseph Anthony *physics and engineering educator, consultant*
Kupchick, Alan Charles *advertising executive*
Kupietzky, Moshe J. *lawyer*
Kuwayama, George *curator*
Laaly, Heshmat Ollah *research chemist, roofing consultant, author*
Laba, Marvin *management consultant*
Lachman, Morton *writer, theatrical director and producer*
Ladd, Alan Walbridge, Jr. *motion picture company executive*
Ladefoged, Peter Nielsen *phonetician*
La Force, James Clayburn, Jr. *economist, educator*
Laird, David *humanities educator emeritus*
Lambro, Phillip *composer, conductor, pianist*
Lancaster, Burt(on) *actor*
Lane, Joseph M. *orthopaedic surgeon, oncologist*
Lane, Marilyn Edith *corporate executive*
Lane, Robert Gerhart *lawyer*
Langella, Frank *actor*
†Lanni, Joseph Terrence *hotel corporation executive*
Lansing, Sherry Lee *motion picture production executive*
Lappen, Chester I. *lawyer*
Lark, Raymond *artist, art scholar*
Larroquette, John Bernard *actor*
Lasarow, William Julius *federal judge*
Lasker, Edward *lawyer*
Lasorda, Thomas Charles (Tommy Lasorda) *professional baseball team manager*
Lasswell, Marcia Lee *psychologist, educator*
Latham, Joseph Al, Jr. *lawyer*
Lauchengco, Jose Yujuico, Jr. *lawyer*
†Launer, Dale Mark *screenwriter*
Laurance, Dale R. *oil company executive*
Laventhol, David Abram *newspaper editor*
†Laverty, Roger Montgomery, III *food products executive, lawyer*
Lawrence, Barry Howard *lawyer*
Lawrence, Vicki Schultz *singer, dancer, comedienne*
Laybourne, Everett Broadstone *lawyer*
Lazzaro, Anthony Derek *university administrator*
†Leal, George D. *engineering company executive*
Lear, Norman Milton *producer, writer, director*
Leary, Timothy *psychologist, author*
Lederman, Bruce Randolph *lawyer*
Lee, Burns Wells *public relations executive*
Lee, Christopher Frank Carandini *actor, author*
†Lee, R. Marilyn *employee relations executive*
Lee, Walter William, Jr. *film writer, consultant, publishing executive*
Leener, Jack Joseph *advertising executive*
Lehan, Richard D'Aubin *English language educator, writer*
Lehman, Robert Nathan *ophthalmologist, educator*
Leibow, Ronald Louis *lawyer*
Leijonhufvud, Axel Stig Bengt *economics educator*
Lenz, Kay *actress*
Leo, Malcolm *producer, director, writer*
Leonard, Elmore John *novelist, screenwriter*
Leonard, Sheldon *television producer, director*
Leonetti, Matthew Frank *cinematographer*
†Lepape, Harry Leonard *diversified company executive*
Leritz, Lawrence *choreographer, dancer, actor*
Lesser, Henry *lawyer*
Lesser, Joan L. *lawyer*
Letts, J. Spencer *federal judge*
Letwin, Leon *legal educator*
Leung, Frankie Fook-Lun *lawyer*
Levine, Philip *classics educator*
Levine, Raphael David *chemistry educator*
Levine, Robert Arthur *economist, policy analyst*
Levine, Thomas Jeffrey Pello *lawyer*
Levy, Louis *chess master*
Levy, Norman *motion picture company executive*
Lew, Ronald S. W. *federal judge*
†Lewin, David *management educator*
Lewin, Klaus J. *pathologist, educator*
Lewis, Charles Edwin *physician, educator*
Lewis, Craig Graham David *public relations executive*
Lewis, Samella Sanders *artist, educator*
Lewis, Shari *puppeteer, entertainer*
Lewitzky, Bella *choreographer*
Leydorf, Frederick Leroy *lawyer*
Li, Gerald *architect, film producer*
Liberman, Robert Paul *psychiatry educator, researcher, writer*
Lieber, David Leo *university president*
Lien, Eric Jung-chi *pharmacist, educator*
Light, John Robert *lawyer*
Limato, Edward Frank *talent agent*
Lin, Tung Hua *civil engineering educator*
Lindholm, Dwight Henry *lawyer*
Lindsley, Donald Benjamin *physiological psychologist, educator*
Lindstedt-Siva, (Karen) June *marine biologist, oil company executive*
Link, George Hamilton *lawyer*
Linsk, Michael Stephen *real estate executive*
Lipsig, Ethan *lawyer*
Lipstone, Howard Harold *television executive*
Little, Richard Le Roy *merchant and investment banker*
Lloyd, Christopher *actor*
Lloyd, Emily (Emily Lloyd Pack) *actress*
†Loch, Robert M. *public utility company executive, civil engineer, lawyer*
Loeb, Ronald Marvin *lawyer*
Loeblich, Helen Nina Tappan *paleontologist, educator*
Löfstedt, Bengt Torkel Magnus *classics educator*
Logan, Joseph Granville, Jr. *physicist*
Long, Gregory Alan *lawyer*
Longmire, William Polk, Jr. *physician, surgeon*
Loughnane, Lee David *trumpeter*
Louis-Dreyfus, Julia *actress*
Lovelace, Jon B. *investment management company executive*
Lovitz, Jon *actor, comedian*
Lowe, Chad *actor*
Lowenthal, Abraham Frederic *international relations educator*
†Lozano, Ignacio Eugenio, Jr. *newspaper editor*
Lublinski, Michael *lawyer*
Lucero, Gene A. *lawyer*
Ludlam, James Edward *lawyer*
†Lunt, Owen Raynal *biologist, educator*
Lyman, John *psychology and engineering educator*
Lynch, Beverly Pfeifer *library science educator*
Lynch, Patrick *lawyer*
Lyne, Adrian *director*
†Lynn, Jonathan Adam *director, writer, actor*
Lyons, James Elliott *lawyer*
Macalister, Kim Porter *advertising executive*
MacGregor, Geddes *author, philosophy educator*
Mack, J. Curtis, II *civic organization administrator*
MacKenzie, John Douglas *engineering educator*
Mackerras, Sir (Alan) Charles (Mac Laurin) *conductor*
MacLaughlin, Francis Joseph *lawyer*
MacLeod, Robert Fredric *editor, publisher*
†Maddock, Brent Ritter *screenwriter*
Mager, Artur *retired aerospace company executive, consultant*
Magner, Fredric Michael *financial services executive*
Magner, Martin *theatrical producer and director*
Mahony, Roger Cardinal *archbishop*
Maki, Kazumi *physicist, educator*
Malden, Karl (Malden Sekulovich) *actor*
Malecki, Edward Stanley, Jr. *political science educator*
Malkovich, John *actor*
Mall, William John, Jr. *aerospace executive, retired air force general officer*
Maltin, Leonard *television commentator, writer*
Mancino, Douglas Michael *lawyer*
Mancuso, Frank G. *entertainment company executive*
Mandel, Babaloo *scriptwriter*
Mandel, Joseph David *university official, lawyer*
Manilow, Barry *singer, composer, arranger*
Mann, Delbert *film, theater, television director and producer*
Mann, Nancy Louise (Nancy Louise Robbins) *entrepreneur*
Manning, Donald O. *protective services official*
Manning, Sylvia *English studies educator*
Manson, Eddy Lawrence *composer, conductor, arranger, producer, clarinetist, harmonica virtuoso*
Maquet, Jacques Jerome Pierre *anthropologist, writer*
Marciniak, Thaddeus J. *lawyer*
Margol, Irving *personnel consultant*
†Margulies, Lee *newspaper editor*
Marion, Douglas Welch *magazine editor*
Markland, Francis Swaby, Jr. *biochemist, educator*
Marks, Laurence Michael *lawyer*
Marmor, Judd *psychiatrist, educator*
Maronde, Robert Francis *internist, clinical pharmacologist, educator*
Marsh, Dave Rodney *writer, publisher, editor*
Marshall, Arthur K. *lawyer, judge, arbitrator, educator, writer*
Marshall, Consuelo Bland *federal judge*
Martin, Albert Carey *architect*
Martin, Dean (Dino Crocetti) *actor, singer*
Martin, Ernest H. *theatrical and motion picture executive*
Martin, J(ohn) Edward *architectural engineer*
Martin, Ray *banker*
Martin, Steve *comedian, actor*
†Martin, Vincent Francis, Jr. *real estate investment executive*
Martin, Walter Edwin *biology educator*
Martines, Lauro *historian, educator*
Martinez, Al *journalist, screenwriter*
†Martinez, Elizabeth *librarian*
Martinez, Vilma Socorro *lawyer*
Martinez Smith, Elizabeth *librarian*
Mason, Cheryl White *lawyer*
Mason, Marshall W. *theater director*
Masri, Sami F(aiz) *civil and mechanical engineering educator, consultant*
†Matheson, Richard Burton *author, scriptwriter*
Mathias, Mildred Esther *botany educator*
Matthau, Walter *actor*
Mattson, Marcus *lawyer*
Maxwell, Donald Stanley *publishing executive*
McBurney, George William *lawyer*
Mc Callum, David *actor*
Mc Carty, Paul James, Jr. *architect*
Mc Clanahan, Rue (Eddi-Rue Mc Clanahan) *actress*
Mc Cormack, Francis Xavier *oil company executive, lawyer*
McDermott, Thomas John, Jr. *lawyer*
McDonald, Jeanne Gray (Mrs. John B. McDonald) *television producer*
Mc Donough, John Richard *lawyer*
Mc Dowall, Roddy *actor*
McGaughey, Emmett Connell *advertising agency executive*
Mc Guire, Dorothy Hackett *actress*
McIntyre, Robert Malcolm *utility company executive*
McKee, Kathryn Dian Grant *banker*
McKnight, Frederick L. *lawyer*
Mc Kuen, Rod *poet, composer, author*
McLane, Frederick Berg *lawyer*
†McLaren, Fred B. *supermarket chain executive*
McLarnan, Donald Edward *banker, corporation executive*
Mc Laughlin, Joseph Mailey *lawyer*
Mc Pherson, Rolf Kennedy *clergyman, church official*
McQueen, Justice Ellis (L. Q. Jones) *actor, director*
McSweeny, William Francis *petroleum company executive, author*
†McWilliams, Peter *poet*
†Medak, Peter *film director*
Meecham, William Coryell *engineering educator*
Melbo, Irving Robert *retired education educator*
Melkonian, Harry G. *lawyer, rancher*
Mellinkoff, David *lawyer, educator*
Mellinkoff, Sherman Mussoff *medical educator*
Meloan, Taylor Wells *marketing educator*
Mendel, Jerry Marc *electrical engineering educator*
Merchant, Roland Samuel, Sr. *hospital administrator, educator*
Merkert, George *visual effects producer*
Merrifield, Donald Paul *university chancellor*
Merritt, Bruce Gordon *lawyer*
†Mettler, Ruben Frederick *former electronics and engineering company executive*
Metzger, Robert Streicher *lawyer*
Metzner, Richard Joel *psychiatrist, psychopharmacologist, educator*
Meuli, Judith K. *communications executive, real estate developer, small business owner*
Meyer, Michael Edwin *lawyer*
Michael, George (Gergios Kyriakou Panayiotou) *musician, singer, songwriter*
Michael, William Burton *psychologist, educator*
Michel, Donald Charles *editor*
Michelson, Lillian *motion picture researcher*
Middleton, James Arthur *oil and gas company executive*
Miech, Allen C. *financial services company executive*
Mihan, Richard *dermatologist*
Miles, Jack (John Russiano) *journalist, book columnist*
Miles, Joanna *actress, playwright*
Miles, Samuel Israel *psychiatrist*
Millard, Neal Steven *lawyer*
Miller, Dennis *comedian*
Miller, Gavin *lawyer*
Miller, Jason *playwright*
Miller, Jesse D. *lawyer*
Miller, Norman *psychology educator, researcher*
Miller, Norman Charles, Jr. *newspaper editor*
Miller, Timothy Alden *plastic and reconstructive surgeon*
Milligan, Sister Mary *theology educator, religious consultant*
Mills, Donna *actress*
Mintz, Marshall G. *lawyer*
Mirels, Harold *aerospace engineer*
Mischer, Donald Leo *television director and producer*
Mishell, Daniel R., Jr. *physician, educator*
Mitchell, Briane Nelson *lawyer*
Mitchell, Joni (Roberta Joan Anderson) *singer, songwriter*
Mitchell, Joseph Nathan *real estate company executive*
Mitchell, Warren I. *utility company executive*
Mitchum, Robert Charles Durman (Charles Mitchum) *actor*
Mock, Theodore Jaye *accounting educator*
Mockary, Peter Ernest *clinical laboratory scientist, researcher*
Moe, Stanley Allen *architect, consultant*
Mohr, John Luther *biologist, environmental consultant*
†Moore, Michael *film director*
Moote, A. Lloyd *history educator*
†Moranis, Rick *actor*
Moreno, Rita *actress*
Morgan, Todd Michael *investment advisor*
Morgenstern, Leon *surgeon*
Morgner, Aurelius *economist, educator*
Mori, Jun *lawyer*
Morris, Garrett *actor, singer*
Morris, Stephen James Michael *lawyer*
Morris, William Joseph *paleontologist, educator*
Morrison, Donald Graham *business educator, consultant*
Morrison, Robert Lewin *lawyer*
Morrow, Winston Vaughan *financial executive*
Mortensen, Richard Edgar *engineering educator*
Moses, Gilbert *film and theatre director*
Mosich, Anelis Nick *accountant, author, educator, consultant*
Mosk, Richard Mitchell *lawyer*
Moskowitz, Joel Steven *lawyer*
Moss, Gary Curtis *lawyer*
Mossawir, Harve H., Jr. *lawyer*
Mossman, Thomas Mellish, Jr. *television manager*
†Mosten, Forrest S. *lawyer*
Moxley, John Howard, III *physician*
Mueller, Carl Richard *theater arts educator, author*
Mueller, John C. *lawyer*
Muldaur, Diana Charlton *actress*
Mulder, Donald Gerrit *surgeon, educator*
Mullane, Donald A. *banker*
Mulligan, Richard M. *actor, writer*
Mund, Geraldine *bankruptcy judge*
Muntz, Eric Phillip *aerospace engineering and radiology educator, consultant*
Munzer, Cynthia Brown *mezzo-soprano*
Munzer, Stephen R. *law educator*
Murphy, Eddie *comedian, actor*
Murray, James Patrick *newspaper columnist*
Nadler, Gerald *engineering educator, management consultant*
†Nakanishi, Don Toshiaki *Asian studies educator, writer*
Nanus, Burton Benjamin *management educator, researcher*
Natzler, Otto *ceramic artist*
†Neal, Joseph C., Jr. *church administrator*
Neal, Louise Kathleen *life insurance company executive, accountant*
Neely, Sally Schultz *lawyer*
Neiter, Gerald Irving *lawyer*
Nelligan, Kate (Patricia Colleen Nelligan) *actress*
Nelson, Grant Steel *lawyer, educator*
Nelson, Howard Joseph *educator, geographer*
Nelson, J. Robert *lawyer*
Nelson, Mark Bruce *interior designer*
Nesmith, Michael *film producer, video specialist*
Neufeld, Elizabeth Fondal *biochemist, educator*
Neufeld, Mace *film company executive*
†Neumann, Alfred Kurt *public health physician, educator*
†Neutra, Dion *architect*
Neville, Aaron *musician*
Neville, Art *musician*
Neville, Charles *musician*
Neville, Cyril *musician*
Nevins, Louis H. *lawyer*
Nevius, Blake Reynolds *English literature educator*
Newhart, Bob *entertainer*
Newhouse, Brian E. *lawyer*
Newman, David Wheeler *lawyer*
†Newman, Richard *engineering executive*
Nibley, Robert Ricks *retired lawyer*
Nicholas, William Richard *lawyer*
†Nicholaw, George *communications executive*
Niemeth, Charles Frederick *lawyer*
†Niese, William A. *lawyer, newspaper publishing executive*
Niles, John Gilbert *lawyer*
Nilles, John Mathias (Jack Nilles) *entrepreneur*
Nimni, Marcel Ephraim *biochemistry educator*
Nixon, John Harmon *economist*
Nobe, Ken *chemical engineering educator*
Noble, Ernest Pascal *physician, biochemist, educator*
Noble, Richard Lloyd *lawyer*
Nochimson, David *lawyer*
Nogales, Luis Guerrero *communications company executive*
Noguchi, Thomas Tsunetomi *author, forensic pathologist*
†Norian, Roger W. *glass manufacturing company executive*
Norris, Edwin L. *lawyer*
Norris, Floyd Hamilton *lawyer*
Norris, William Albert *federal judge*
Nunis, Doyce Blackman, Jr. *historian, educator*
Obrzut, Ted *lawyer*
O'Connell, Kevin *lawyer*
O'Connor, Carroll *actor, writer, producer*
O'Day, Anita Belle Colton *entertainer, singer*
Oder, Kenneth William *lawyer*
O'Donnell, Pierce Henry *lawyer*
O'Donnell, Rosie *comedienne, actress*
Ogle, Edward Proctor, Jr. *investment counseling executive*
Okrent, David *engineering educator*
Olah, George Andrew *chemist, educator*
†Olin, Lena Maria Jonna *actress*
Olmos, Edward James *actor*
Olpin, Owen *lawyer*
Olsen, Roger Milton *lawyer*
Olson, Dale C. *public relations executive*
Olson, Gary *lawyer*
Olson, Ronald Leroy *lawyer*
O'Malley, Joseph James *lawyer*
O'Malley, Peter *professional baseball club executive*
Onak, Thomas Philip *chemistry educator*
O'Neal, Tatum *actress*
O'Neill, Russell Richard *engineering educator*
Orchard, Henry John *electrical engineer*
Ordin, Andrea Sheridan *lawyer*
O'Reilly, Richard Brooks *journalist*
Orme, Antony Ronald *geography educator*
Orr, Ronald Stewart *lawyer*
Orsatti, Alfred Kendall *organization executive*
Ostroff, Peter I. *lawyer*
†Owen, Michael Lee *lawyer*
Owens, Stephen Thomas *lawyer*
Pace, Richard Randall *lawyer, educator*
Packard, Robert Charles *lawyer*

Villablanca, Jaime Rolando *medical scientist, educator*
Vogel, Charles Stimmel *lawyer*
†Vogel, William Charles *advertising executive*
Volpert, Richard Sidney *lawyer*
Von Brandenstein, Patrizia *production designer*
Vradenburg, George, III *lawyer, corporate executive*
Vredevoe, Donna Lou *research immunologist, microbiologist, educator*
Wachs, Martin *urban planning educator*
Wagner, Christian Nikolaus Johann *materials engineering educator*
Wagner, D. William *lawyer*
Wagner, William Gerard *university dean, physicist, consultant, information scientist, investment manager*
Waits, Thomas Alan *composer, actor, singer*
Walcher, Alan Ernest *lawyer*
†Walsh, John Harley *medical educator*
Ward, Fred *actor*
Ward, Leslie Allyson *journalist, editor*
†Ward, Sela *actress*
Warren, Lesley Ann *actress*
Warren, Mark Edward *travel company executive, lawyer*
Washington, Denzel *actor*
Wasserman, William Phillip *lawyer*
Waterman, Michael Spencer *mathematics educator, biology educator*
Waterman, Thomas Chadbourne *lawyer*
Waterston, Samuel Atkinson *actor*
Watring, Watson Glenn *gynecologic oncologist, educator*
†Watson, Diane Edith *state legislator*
Watson, Sharon Gitin *psychologist, executive*
Watts, Quincy *track and field athlete*
Wayte, (Paul) Alan *lawyer*
Wazzan, Ahmed R(assem) Frank *engineering educator, dean*
Weaver, Don L. *lawyer*
Wei, Jen Yu *physiologist, educator*
Weil, Jerry *animator*
Weiner, Leslie Philip *neurology educator, researcher*
Weinstein, Harvey *film company executive*
Weinstein, Irwin Marshall *internist, hematologist*
Weinstein, Robert *film company executive*
Weinstock, Harold *lawyer*
Weiss, Martin Harvey *neurosurgeon, educator*
†Weiss, Robert William (Bob) *professional basketball coach*
Weiss, Walter Stanley *lawyer*
†Weitzman, Howard L. *lawyer*
Welch, Bo (Robert W. Welch, III) *production designer*
Welch, Lloyd Richard *electrical engineering educator, communications consultant*
Welles, Melinda Fassett *artist, educator*
Werner, Gloria S. *librarian*
Wessling, Robert Bruce *lawyer*
West, Louis Jolyon *psychiatrist*
Westheimer, David Kaplan *novelist*
Weston, John Frederick *business educator, consultant*
†Wexler, Robert *university administrator*
Wheat, Francis Millspaugh *retired lawyer*
†Wheel, Lesley *design firm executive*
Wheeler, William Thornton *structural engineer, consultant*
†Whisman, Linda Anne *law librarian*
Whitaker, Forest *actor*
Whitaker, Fred Maynard *insurance agent*
White, Robert Joel *lawyer*
Whitman, Kenneth Jay *advertising executive*
Whitmore, James Allen *actor*
Whitten, Charles Alexander, Jr. *physics educator*
†Wiatt, James Anthony *theatrical agency executive*
Wiberg, Donald Martin *electrical engineering educator, consultant*
Wickes, Mary *actress*
Wigmore, John Grant *lawyer*
Wilder, Gene *actor, director, writer*
Williams, David Welford *federal judge*
Williams, Harold Marvin *foundation official*
Williams, Henry Stratton *radiologist, educator*
Williams, John Towner *composer, conductor*
Williams, Julie Ford *investment specialist*
Williams, Mark Alvin *writer, director, producer*
Williams, Paul Hamilton *composer, singer*
†Williams, Phillip L. *newspaper publishing executive*
Williams, Richard Thomas *lawyer*
Williams, Robert Martin *economist, consultant*
Williams, Robin *actor, comedian*
Williams, Russell, II *production sound mixer*
Williams, Theodore Earle *industrial distribution company executive*
Williams, Willie *protective services official*
†Willner, Alan Eli *electrical engineer, educator*
†Wills, John Elliot, Jr. *history educator, writer*
Willson, Alan Neil, Jr. *engineering educator, dean*
Wilson, Brian Douglas *recording artist, composer, record producer*
Wilson, Eugene Rolland *foundation executive*
Wilson, James Quinn *government, management educator*
Wilson, Miriam Geisendorfer *physician, educator*
Wilson, Nancy *singer*
Wilson, Stephen Victor *federal judge*
†Wilson, Steven Seth *writer, producer*
†Wilson, Thomas Henry *museum director*
Wincor, Michael Z. *psychopharmacology educator, clinician, researcher*
Winfield, Paul Edward *actor*
Winger, Debra *actress*
Winkler, Howard Leslie *investment banker, stockbroker, business consultant*
Winterowd, Walter Ross *English educator*
Winters, Barbara Jo *musician*
Winters, Ralph E. *film editor*
†Wittig, Curt *chemist, educator*
Wittrock, Merlin Carl *educational psychologist*
Wittry, David Beryle *physicist, educator*
Woelffer, Emerson Seville *artist*
Wolas, Herbert *lawyer*
Wolf, Alfred *rabbi*
Wolf, Lesley Sara *lawyer*
Wolf, Walter *chemist, pharmaceutical scientist, educator*
Wolfen, Werner F. *lawyer*
†Wolinsky, Leo C. *newspaper editor*
Wood, Karen Sue *theatre manager, stage producer, consultant*
Wood, Nancy Elizabeth *psychologist, educator*
Wood, Willis Bowne, Jr. *utility holding company executive*
Woodruff, Fay *paleoceanographer, geological researcher*
Woods, Daniel James *lawyer*
Wooten, Cecil Aaron *religious organization administrator*
Wortham, Thomas Richard *English language educator*
Wrede, Robert Kendrick *lawyer*
Wright, Donald Franklin *newspaper executive*
Wright, Ernest Marshall *physiologist, consultant*
Wright, Kenneth Brooks *lawyer*
Wurmbrand, Harry George *cosmetics company executive*
Wurtele, Morton Gaither *meteorologist, educator*
Wyatt, James Luther *drapery hardware company executive*
Wyatt, Joseph Lucian, Jr. *lawyer, educator*
Wycoff, Robert E. *petroleum company executive*
Wyman, William George *musician*
Yablans, Frank *film company executive, motion picture producer*
Yagiela, John Allen *dental educator*
Yamamoto, Joe *psychiatrist, educator*
†Yee, Stephen *airport executive*
Yeh, William Wen-Gong *civil engineering educator*
Yen, Teh Fu *civil engineering and environmental educator*
York, Gary A. *lawyer*
Young, Bless Stritar *lawyer*
Young, Charles Edward *university chancellor*
Young, Joseph Louis *artist*
Young, Loretta (gretchen young) *actress*
Young, Robert (George Young) *actor*
Yue, Alfred Shui-choh *metallurgical engineer, educator*
†Zacchino, Narda *newspaper editor*
Zarefsky, Ralph *lawyer*
Zelon, Laurie Dee *lawyer*
Zemeckis, Robert L. *film director*
†Ziering, Sigi *medical company executive*
†Ziffren, Kenneth *lawyer*
Ziffren, Lester *lawyer*
Zohn, Martin Steven *lawyer*
Zucker, Jerry *producer, director*
Zwerver, Peter John *linguistics educator*

Los Gatos
Dowdell, Dorothy Florence *novelist*
Farley, Philip Judson *former government official*
Hartinger, Patricia B. Curran *elementary school educator*
Knudsen, William Claire *geophysicist*
Leverett, Miles Corrington *retired nuclear power consultant*
Lorincz, Albert Bela *physician, educator*
Meyers, Ann Elizabeth *sports broadcaster*
†Millard, Stephens Fillmore *electronics company executive*
Naymark, Sherman *consulting nuclear engineer*
†Simonson, Ted *principal*

Los Osos
Brown, Mary Eleanor *physical therapist, educator*
Cloonan, Clifford B. *electrical engineer, educator*
Ratliff, Cecil Wayne *computer scientist*
Thomas, Robert Murray *educational psychology educator*

Lynwood
†Jorgensen, Earle M. *metal products executive*

Madera
Silk, Bertram Edward *winery executive*

Magalia
Joffre, Stephen Paul *consulting chemist*

Malibu
Aiken, Lewis Roscoe, Jr. *psychologist, educator*
Chester, Arthur Noble *physicist*
Coben, William Allen *lawyer*
Davenport, David *university president, lawyer*
Elliott, Sam *actor*
Ensign, Richard Papworth *transportation executive*
Felton, Norman Francis *motion picture producer*
Forward, Robert L(ull) *physicist, writer, consultant*
Gail, Maxwell Trowbridge, Jr. *actor, director, musician*
Hancock, John D. *film director*
Klugman, Jack *actor*
Lilly, John Cunningham *medical scientist, author*
Lindsay, Nathan James *aerospace company executive, retired career officer*
Louganis, Greg E. *former Olympic athlete, actor*
Margerum, J(ohn) David *chemist*
Mataré, Herbert F. *physicist, consultant*
Moore, John George, Jr. *medical educator*
Nolte, Nick *actor*
Pack, Walter Frank *minister, religion educator emeritus*
Pepper, David M. *physicist, educator, author, inventor*
Perlman, Rhea *actress*
Phillips, Ronald Frank *legal educator, law school dean*
Reres, Mary Epiphany *health care and administration consultant*
Smith, George Foster *retired aerospace company executive*
Widmann, Glenn Roger *electrical engineer*
Yates, Jere Eugene *business educator, management consultant*
Young, Matt Norvel, Jr. *retired university chancellor*

Manhattan Beach
†Blanton, John Arthur *architect*
Bradburn, David Denison *engineer,retired air force officer*
Brooks, Edward Howard *college administrator*
Krienke, Carol Belle Manikowske (Mrs. Oliver Kenneth Krienke) *realtor*
Stern, Daniel Alan *business management consultant*
Weinstock, Herbert Frank *public relations executive*

Manteca
Tonn, Elverne Meryl *pediatric dentist, dental insurance consultant*

Marina Del Rey
Adams, Thomas Merritt *lawyer*
Annotico, Richard Anthony *legal scholar*
Corzo, Miguelangel *institute executive*
Doebler, Paul Dickerson *publishing management executive*
Gold, Carol Sapin *international management consultant, speaker*
Patton, David Wayne *health care executive*
Smith, George Drury *publisher, editor, collagist, writer*
†Smith, Steven Warren *public relations executive*
†Tanaka, Ted Tokio *architect, educator*
Tennant, John Randall *management advisory company executive*
Valentine, De Wain *artist*
Waite, Ralph *actor*
†Zaillian, Steven *screenwriter, director*

Mariposa
Rogers, Earl Leslie *artist, educator*
Shields, Allan Edwin *writer, photographer, retired educator*

Marshall
Evans, Robert James *architect*

Martinez
Bray, Absalom Francis, Jr. *lawyer*
Burchell, Mary Cecilia *surgeon*
Meyer, Jarold Alan *oil company research executive*

Marysville
Hamilton, Richard Daniel *neurosurgeon*
Hardie, Robert C. *newspaper publishing executive*

Mendocino
Alexander, Joyce Mary *illustrator*

Menlo Park
Alexander, Theron *psychologist, writer*
Anderson, Charles Arthur *former research institute administrator*
Baez, Joan Chandos *folk singer*
Bissell, Betty Dickson *stockbroker*
Bourne, Charles Percy *information scientist, educator*
Bremser, George, Jr. *electronics company executive*
Browne, Millard Child *former newspaper editor*
Bukry, John David *geologist*
Cook, Paul M. *chemical manufacturing company executive*
Craig, Gordon Alexander *historian, educator*
Crane, Hewitt David *science advisor*
Dalrymple, Gary Brent *research geologist*
Davis, William Emrys *religious organization official*
†Denend, Leslie George *computer company executive*
Duda, Richard Oswald *electrical engineering educator, researcher*
Edson, William Alden *electrical engineer*
Elkus, Richard J. *finance and industrial company executive*
Evans, Bob Overton *electronics executive*
Fassett, Hugh Gardner *investment counselor*
Fergason, James L. *optical company executive*
Ferris, Robert Albert *lawyer, venture capitalist*
Frisco, Louis Joseph *retired materials science company executive, electrical engineer*
Fuhrman, Frederick Alexander *physiology educator*
Funkhouser, Lawrence William *retired geologist*
Gardner, David Pierpont *foundation executive*
Gilburne, Miles R. *lawyer*
Glaser, Robert Joy *physician, foundation executive*
Goldberg, Jacob *computer scientist, researcher*
Graham, Howard Holmes *manufacturing executive*
Graham, William James *packaging company executive*
Halperin, Robert Milton *electrical machinery company executive*
Hem, John David *research chemist*
†Henley, Jeffrey O. *business executive*
Hiller, Stanley, Jr. *manufacturing company executive*
Hoagland, Laurance Redington, Jr. *investment executive*
Holzer, Thomas Lequear *geologist*
Honey, Richard Churchill *retired electrical engineer*
Jorgensen, Paul J. *research company executive*
Kohne, Richard Edward *retired engineering executive*
Lachenbruch, Arthur Herold *geophysicist*
Lane, Laurence William, Jr. *retired U.S. ambassador, publisher*
Laurie, Ronald S. *lawyer*
Leadabrand, Ray L. *engineering executive, defense industry consultant*
Litfin, Richard Albert *retired news organization executive*
Lucas, Donald Leo *entrepreneur*
Lynch, Charles Allen *investment executive, corporate director*
†MacFarlane, David B. *physicist, educator*
Marken, William Riley *magazine editor*
†McCarthy, Roger Lee *mechanical engineer*
McCown, George E. *venture banking company executive*
McDonald, Warren George *accountant, former savings and loan executive*
Morrell, James Wilson *consulting company executive*
Morrison, James Ian *research institute executive*
Nichols, William Ford, Jr. *foundation executive, business executive*
O'Brien, Raymond Francis *transportation executive*
Oronsky, Arnold Lewis *scientific research company executive, medical educator*
Pallotti, Marianne Marguerite *foundation administrator*
Phipps, Allen Mayhew *management consultant*
Pooley, James Henry Anderson *lawyer, author*
Postlewait, Harry Owen *chemical company executive*
Roberts, George R. *venture capital company executive*
Salmon, Vincent *acoustical consultant*
Scandling, William Fredric *retired food service company executive*
Sidells, Arthur F. *architect*
Sladek, Ronald John *physics educator*
Sommers, William Paul *management consultant*
Sparks, Robert Dean *medical administrator, physician*
Surbeck, Leighton Homer *retired lawyer*
†Sutherland, Robert Melvin *life sciences professional, educator*
Szentirmai, George *electrical engineer, corporate executive*
Taft, David Dakin *chemical executive*
Tietjen, James *research institute administrator*
Tokheim, Robert Edward *physicist*
Turin, George Lewis *electrical engineering educator, university dean*
Vickers, Roger Spencer *physicist, program director*
†Vidale, John Emilio *geologist*
Wallace, Robert Earl *geologist*
Walsh, William Desmond *investor*
†White, Phillip E. *company executive*
Whitmore, William Francis *physicist, retired missile scientist*
Wolaner, Robin Peggy *magazine publisher*

Mentone
Stockton, David Knapp *professional golfer*

Merced
Abbott, Woodrow Acton *air force general officer*
Carroll, Paula Marie *security company executive*
Maytum, Harry Rodell *retired physician*
†Weir, Billy Louis *agricultural educator, researcher*

Mill Valley
Benezet, Louis Tomlinson *retired psychology educator, former college president*
Chilvers, Robert Merritt *lawyer*
Crews, William Odell, Jr. *seminary administrator*
D'Amico, Michael *architect, urban planner*
Dillon, Richard Hugh *librarian, author*
Fuller, Glenn R. *park ranger*
†Hair, William Bates, III *librarian*
Harner, Michael James *anthropologist, educator, author*
Ihle, John Livingston *artist, educator*
Kleiman, Harlan Philip *film company executive*
Leslie, Jacques Robert, Jr. *journalist*
Mihaly, Eugene Bramer *consultant, corporate executive, writer, educator*
Padula, Fred David *filmmaker*
†Pflueger, John Milton *architect*
Wallerstein, Robert Solomon *psychiatrist*
Winskill, Robert Wallace *manufacturing executive*

Millbrae
Li, David Wen-Chung *television company executive*
Pliska, Edward William *lawyer*

Milpitas
Berkley, Stephen Mark *computer peripherals manufacturing company executive*
†Coghlan, Paul *electronics executive*
Corrigan, Wilfred J. *data processing and computer company executive*
Huber, Paul E. *electronics industry executive*

Mission Hills
Cramer, Frank Brown *engineering executive, combustion engineer, systems consultant*
Krieg, Dorothy Linden *soprano, performing artist, educator*

Mission Viejo
Foulds, Donald Duane *aerospace executive*
†Milunas, J. Robert *health care organization executive*
Ruben, Robert Joseph *lawyer*
Sabaroff, Rose Epstein *retired education educator*
Teitelbaum, Harry *English educator*
Woodruff, Truman O(wen) *physicist, emeritus educator*

Modesto
†Bairey, Marie *principal*
Bucknam, Mary Olivia Caswell *artist*
Crawford, Charles McNeil *winery science executive*
Ferrucci, Raymond Vincent *retired food company executive*
†Gallo, Ernest *vintner*
†Kreissman, Starrett *librarian*
LaMont, Sanders Hickey *journalist*
Mayhew, William A. *lawyer*
McNickle, Michael M. *bank executive*
Mensinger, Peggy Boothe *retired mayor*
Owens, Jack Byron *lawyer*
Piccinini, Robert M. *grocery store chain executive*
†Potts, Erwin Rea *newspaper executive*
Shastid, Jon Barton *wine company executive*
Steffan, Wallace Allan *entomologist, educator*

Moffett Field
Baldwin, Betty Jo *computer specialist*
Bentley, Kenton Earl *aerospace scientist, researcher*
Cohen, Malcolm Martin *psychologist, researcher*
Dean, William Evans *aerospace agency executive*
Haines, Richard Foster *psychologist*
†Kerr, Andrew W. *aerodynamics researcher*
Lomax, Harvard *aeronautical research scientist, educator*
McCroskey, William James *aeronautical engineer*
†Park, Chul *aerospace engineer*
Ragent, Boris *physicist*
Seiff, Alvin *planetary scientist, atmosphere physics and aerodynamics consultant*
Statler, Irving Carl *aerospace engineer*

Mojave
Rutan, Elbert L. (Burt Rutan) *aircraft designer*

Monrovia
Breen, Thomas Albert *financial services executive*
Jemelian, John Nazar *merchant, financial executive*
Mac Cready, Paul Beattie *aeronautical engineer*
Moore, S. Clark *judge*
†Seiple, Robert Allen *Christian relief organization executive*
Turner, Roger Orlando *microbiologist,quality assurance director*

Montara
Gyemant, Robert Ernest *lawyer*

Montclair
Haage, Robert Mitchell *retired history educator, organization leader*

Monte Sereno
Rustagi, Jagdish Sharan *statistics educator*

Montebello
Dible, Rose Harpe McFee *special education educator*
†Shelton, Phillip Eugene *paper company executive*

Montecito
Harris, James Dexter *lawyer*
Meghreblian, Robert Vartan *manufacturing executive, physicist*
Rose, Mark Allen *humanities educator*
Wheelon, Albert Dewell *physicist*

Monterey
†Atchley, Anthony Armstrong *physicist, educator*

Benjamin, David Joel, III *radio broadcasting executive*
Black, Robert Lincoln *pediatrician*
Bomberger, Russell Branson *lawyer, educator*
Bowman, Dorothy Louise *artist*
Bradford, Howard *graphic artist, painter*
Butler, Jon Terry *computer engineering educator, researcher*
Chung, Kyung Cho *Korean language educator, author*
Collins, Curtis Allan *oceanographer*
Dedini, Eldon Lawrence *cartoonist*
Fenton, Lewis Lowry *lawyer*
†Garrett, Steven Lurie *physicist*
Gaskell, Robert Eugene *mathematician, educator*
Hamming, Richard Wesley *computer scientist*
Hernandez, Jo Farb *museum and curatorial consultant*
†Hovermale, John B. *oceanography director*
Kennedy-Minott, Rodney *international relations educator, former ambassador*
Ketcham, Henry King *cartoonist*
Malone, James L. *lawyer, diplomat*
†Marto, Paul James *mechanical engineering educator, researcher*
Miller, Susan Heilmann *publishing executive*
Newberry, Conrad Floyde *aerospace engineering educator*
Newton, Robert Eugene *mechanical engineering educator*
Packard, Julie *aquarium administrator*
†Powell, David Clark *curator, consultant*
Reneker, Maxine Hohman *librarian*
†Ryan, Sylvester D. *bishop*
Sarpkaya, Turgut *mechanical engineering educator*
Schrady, David Alan *operations research educator*
Shaw, William Vaughan *architect*
†Shimpfky, Richard Lester *bishop*
Shull, Harrison *chemist, educator*
Stern, Gerald Daniel *lawyer*
Van Der Bijl, Willem *meteorology educator*
Weaver, William Bruce *astronomer, research administrator*
†Wright, Mary R. *state park superintendent*

Monterey Park
Tucker, Marcus Othello *judge*
Waiter, Serge-Albert *retired scientist, consultant*

Moorpark
Hall, Elton A. *philosophy educator*

Moraga
Allen, Richard Garrett *health care and education consultant*
Anderson, Brother Mel *academic administrator*
Countryman, Vern *law educator*
Hollingsworth, Robert Edgar *nuclear consultant*
Sonenshein, Nathan *marine consulting company executive, retired naval officer*

Morgan Hill
Freimark, Robert (Bob Freimark) *artist*

Moss Landing
Lange, Lester Henry *mathematics educator*

Mount Shasta
Anderson, Lee Roger *landscape architect, solar, environmental, recreation and site planner*

Mountain View
Benham, James Mason *mutual fund executive*
Blachman, Nelson M(erle) *physicist*
†Bowler, James S. *educational administrator*
Braun, Michael Alan *data processing executive*
Breitmeyer, Jo Anne *sales and marketing executive*
Broadbent, Thomas Valentine *publisher*
Clark, James H. *electronics executive*
Cusumano, James Anthony *chemical company executive, former recording artist*
Di Muccio, Mary Jo *retired librarian*
Elkus, Richard J., Jr. *electronics company executive*
†Harber, M(ichael) Eric *management consultant*
Heere, Karen R. *astrophysicist*
Jarrat, Henri Aaron *semiconductor company executive*
Johnson, Noel Lars *biomedical engineer*
Kobza, Dennis Jerome *architect*
Koo, George Ping Shan *electronics executive*
Marple, Stanley Lawrence, Jr. *electrical engineer, signal processing researcher*
Mc Nealy, Scott *computer company executive*
Michalko, James Paul *library association administrator*
Pallakoff, Owen E. *retired electronics executive*
Peters, Stanley Thomas *materials engineer, consultant, educator*
Saifer, Mark Gary Pierce *pharmaceutical executive*

Murphys
Scott, Otto *writer*

Murrieta
Lewis, Donald Joseph *retired psychology educator*

Napa
Battisti, Paul Oreste *county supervisor*
Chiarella, Peter Ralph *corporate executive*
Folsom, Richard Gilman *retired mechanical engineer and academic administrator, consultant*
Francis, Marc Baruch *pediatrician*
Garnett, William *photographer*
Hill, Orion Alvah, Jr. *retired banker*
LaRocque, Marilyn Ross Onderdonk *public relations executive*
Leavitt, Dana Gibson *management consultant*
Miller, John Laurence *professional golfer*
Muedeking, George Herbert *editor*
Smith, Robert Bruce *former security consultant, retired army officer*

Newark
†Ferber, Norman Alan *retail executive*
Joyce, Stephen Francis *human resource executive*

Newbury Park
Issari, Mohammad Ali *film producer, educator, consultant*
McCune, David Franklin *publisher*
†McCune, Sara Miller *foundation executive, publisher*

Newport Beach
Adams, William Gillette *lawyer*
Albright, Archie Earl, Jr. *investment banker*
Armstrong, Robert Arnold *petroleum company executive*
Badham, Robert E. *former congressman*
Baskin, Scott David *lawyer*
†Bauer, Jay S. *architect*
Bissell, George Arthur *architect*
Botwinick, Michael *museum director*
†Brower, Edgar S. *manufacturing company executive*
Brown, Giles Tyler *history educator, lecturer*
Bryant, Thos Lee *magazine editor*
Clark, Earnest Hubert, Jr. *tool company executive*
Cox, Christopher *congressman*
Curtis, Jesse William, Jr. *retired federal judge*
Dean, Paul John *magazine editor*
Dito, John Allen *lawyer*
Dougherty, Betsey Olenick *architect*
Dovring, Karin Elsa Ingeborg *author, playwright, communication analyst*
Dykstra, David Charles *accountant, management consultant, author, educator*
Fletcher, Douglas Baden *investment company executive*
Frederick, Dolliver H. *merchant banker*
Gerken, Walter Bland *insurance company executive*
Green, Oliver Francis, Jr. *lawyer*
Guilford, Andrew John *lawyer*
Holmes, Colgate Frederick *hotel executive*
†Homan, Rich *magazine editor*
Jeffers, Michael Bogue *lawyer*
Johnson, Thomas Webber, Jr. *lawyer*
Kahn, Douglas Gerard *psychiatrist*
Katayama, Arthur Shoji *lawyer*
Kaufman, Marcus Maurice *retired judge, lawyer*
Kemper, Robert L. *savings and loan association executive*
Kenney, William John, Jr. *real estate development executive*
Klein, Maurice J. *lawyer*
Lipson, Melvin Alan *technology and business management consultant*
†Little, Lawrence Michael *publishing company executive*
Lowe, Kathlene Winn *lawyer*
Mallory, Frank Linus *lawyer*
Marcoux, Carl Henry *former insurance executive, writer*
Masotti, Louis Henry *management educator, consultant*
McAlister, Maurice L. *savings and loan association executive*
Millar, Richard William, Jr. *lawyer*
†Morgridge, Howard Henry *architect*
Phillips, Layn R. *lawyer*
Plat, Richard Vertin *corporate finance executive*
Richardson, Walter John *architect*
Rueb, Richard V., Sr. *information systems management consultant*
Schroeder, Charles Henry *corporate treasurer*
Sharbaugh, W(illiam) James *plastics engineer, consultant*
Shea, John Martin, Jr. *business executive*
Simon, John Roger *lawyer*
Singer, Gary James *lawyer*
†Soliman, Anwar S. *restaurant company executive*
Spitz, Barbara Salomon *artist*
Stephens, Michael Dean *hospital administrator*
†Strock, Arthur Van Zandt *architect*
Sutton, Thomas C. *insurance company executive*
†Tanner, R. Marshall *lawyer*
Willard, Robert Edgar *lawyer*
Wimberly, George James *architect*
Zalta, Edward *otorhinolaryngologist, utilization review physician*

Nipomo
Brantingham, Charles Ross *podiatrist, ergonomics consultant*

North Hollywood
Bishop, Kathryn Elizabeth *film company executive, writer*
Blake, Robert (Michael Gubitosi) *actor*
Boyle, Barbara Dorman *motion picture company executive*
Buffett, Jimmy *singer, songwriter*
Bull, David *fine art conservator*
Flowers, A. D. (Adlia Douglas Flowers) *retired special effects expert*
Frost, Mark *director, producer, writer*
Grasso, Mary Ann *theatre association administrator*
Gregorius, Beverly June *retired obstetrician-gynecologist*
Hulse, Jerry *journalist*
†Kaminski, Janusz Zygmuni *photographer*
†Kemp, Bernard *organizational development consultant*
Kreger, Melvin Joseph *lawyer*
Loper, James Leaders *broadcasting executive*
Milner, Howard M. *real estate developer, international real estate financier*
Mirisch, Marvin Elliot *motion picture producer*
Reynolds, Debbie (Mary Frances Reynolds) *actress*
Ribman, Ronald Burt *playwright*
Thurston, Alice Janet *former college president*

Northridge
Bassler, Robert Covey *sculptor, educator*
Bianchi, Donald Ernest *academic administrator, biology educator*
Bradshaw, Richard Rotherwood *engineering executive*
Butler, Karla *psychologist*
Chen, Joseph Tao *historian, educator*
†Curzon, Susan Carol *library administrator*
Danin, Mary Ann *artist, designer, educator*
Davidson, Sheldon Jerome *hematologist*
Devol, Kenneth Stowe *journalism educator*
Ellner, Carolyn Lipton *university dean, consultant*
Harden, Marvin *artist, educator*
Jakobsen, Jakob Knudsen *mechanical engineer*
Kuzma, George Martin *bishop*
Lehtihalme, Larry (Lauri) K. *financial planner*
†Molen, Gerald Robert *film producer*
Norris, Darell Forest *insurance company executive*
Sandoval, Rik (Charles Sandoval) *broadcasting executive*
Segalman, Ralph *sociology educator*
Stout, Thomas Melville *control system engineer*
Torgow, Eugene N. *electrical engineer*
Wilson, Blenda Jacqueline *university chancellor*

Novato
Bozdech, Marek Jiri *physician*
†Carlston, Douglas Gene *computer software executive*
Franklin, Robert Blair *cardiologist*
†Hansmeyer, Herbert *insurance company executive*
†Harding, Richard Swick *engineering executive*
†Meyer, John F. *insurance company executive*
Obninsky, Victor Peter *lawyer*
Patterson, W. Morgan *college president*
Pfeiffer, Phyllis Kramer *newspaper company executive*
Premo, Paul Mark *oil company executive*
Simon, Lee Will *astronomer*
Varney, Bernard Keith *financial executive, consultant*

Oak Park
Caldwell, Stratton Franklin *kinesiologist*

Oakdale
Thomas, William LeRoy *geography educator, cruise lecturer*

Oakhurst
Bonham, Clifford Vernon *social worker, educator*

Oakland
Adwere-Boamah, Joseph *school district administrator*
Alderson, Richard Lynn *professional baseball team executive*
Allen, Jeffrey Michael *lawyer*
Ambrose, Tommy W. *chemical engineer, executive*
Barakat, Samir F. *economic and management consulting executive*
Barlow, William Pusey, Jr. *accountant*
Beasley, Bruce Miller *sculptor*
Benham, Priscilla Carla *religion educator, college president*
Borton, Robert Ernest *lawyer*
Borum, William Donald *engineer*
Brocchini, Ronald Gene *architect*
Buckley, Mike Clifford *lawyer, electronics company executive*
Burnison, Boyd Edward *lawyer*
Burns, Catherine Elizabeth *art dealer*
Callos, Phyllis Marie *association executive*
†Caulfield, W. Harry *health care industry executive, physician*
Champlin, Malcolm McGregor *retired municipal judge*
Clancy, Thomas Gerald *newspaper company executive*
Cline, Wilson Ettason *retired administrative law judge*
Collen, Morris Frank *physician*
Cray, Robert *guitarist, singer, songwriter*
Cummins, John Stephen *bishop*
Deming, Willis Riley *lawyer*
Dempster, Lauramay Tinsley *botanist*
Dibble, David Van Vlack *educator of visually impaired, lawyer*
Dickinson, Eleanor Creekmore *artist, educator*
Dolich, Andrew Bruce *professional baseball team executive*
†Dommer, Donald Duane *architect*
Eckersley, Dennis Lee *professional baseball player*
Edwards, Robin Morse *lawyer*
†Ewell, P. Lamont *fire department chief*
†Farley, Thelma *principal*
Fink, Diane Joanne *physician*
Finnane, Daniel F. *professional basketball team executive*
Fischer, Michael Ludwig *environmental company executive*
Fogel, Paul David *lawyer*
Foley, Jack (John Wayne Harold Foley) *poet, writer, editor*
†Friedman, Gary David *epidemiologist, research facility administrator*
Goldstine, Stephen Joseph *college administrator*
†Gomez, Martin *library director*
Haas, Walter J. *professional baseball team executive*
Hardaway, Tim (Timothy Duane Hardaway) *basketball player*
Harris, Elihu Mason *mayor*
Haskell, Arthur Jacob *steamship company executive*
†Hayashi, Joji *transportation company executive*
Heafey, Edwin Austin, Jr. *lawyer*
Helvey, Julius Louis, II *finance company executive*
Henderson, Rickey Henley *professional baseball player*
Hoopes, Lorenzo Neville *former retailing executive*
Howatt, Sister Helen Clare *library director*
Isaac Nash, Eva Mae *educator*
Jukes, Thomas Hughes *biological chemist, educator*
Kennedy, Raoul Dion *lawyer*
King, Cary Judson, III *chemical engineer, educator, university official*
Kropschot, Richard H. *physicist, science laboratory administrator*
†Lanier, Bob *professional sports team executive, former basketball player*
La Russa, Tony, Jr. (Anthony La Russa, Jr.) *professional baseball manager*
Laverne, Michel Marie-Jacques *international relations consultant*
†Lawrence, David M. *health faciligy administrator*
Lee, Jong Hyuk *accountant*
Lennox, Carol *computer scientist, consultant*
Leon, Dennis *sculptor*
Lillie, John Mitchell *transportation company executive*
List, Raymond Edward *engineering and construction executive, management consultant*
Macmeeken, John Peebles *foundation executive*
Marshall, George Dwire *supermarket chain executive*
Martin, David William, Jr. *biomedical research company executive, educator*
Massey, Walter Eugene *physicist, science foundation administrator*
Matsumoto, George *architect*
McGwire, Mark *professional baseball player*
McKinney, Judson Thad *broadcast executive*
Melchert, James Frederick *artist*
Mikalow, Alfred Alexander, II *deep sea diver, marine surveyor, marine diving consultant*
†Miller, Lyle G. *bishop*
Miller, Thomas Robbins *lawyer, publisher*
†Mitrano, Joseph Charles *school principal*
†Moon, Wayne *health facility administrator*
Mullin, Chris(topher) Paul *professional basketball player*
Nelson, Donald Arvid (Nellie Nelson) *professional basketball coach*
Newsome, Randall Jackson *federal judge*
†Nicol, Robert Duncan *architect*
Okamura, Arthur *artist, educator, writer*
Patten, Bebe Harrison *minister*
Peck, Paul Arthur *lawyer, former naval officer*
Peltason, Jack Walter *university administrator*
Pierce, Ricky Charles *professional basketball player*
†Poole, Monte LaRue *sports columnist, consultant*
Potash, Stephen Jon *public relations specialist*
Power, Dennis Michael *museum director*
Quinby, William Albert *lawyer*
Rath, Alan T. *sculptor*
Reitz, Richard Elmer *physician*
†Rhein, Timothy J. *transportation company executive*
Rowlings, Donald George *international investment banker*
†Samuels, Joseph, Jr. *police chief*
Sandler, Herbert M. *savings and loan association executive*
Sandler, Marion Osher *savings and loan association executive*
Sanford, Frederic Goodman *career officer*
†Saperstein, Guy T. *lawyer*
Saunders, Ward Bishop, Jr. *retired aluminum company executive*
Schacht, Henry Mevis *writer, consultant*
Schwyn, Charles Edward *accountant*
Serenbetz, Robert *manufacturing executive*
Sierra, Ruben Angel *professional baseball player*
Silverberg, Robert *author*
Skaff, Andrew Joseph *lawyer, public utilities, energy and transportation executive*
†Skinner, Clifford *insurance company executive*
Sullivan, G. Craig *chemical executive*
Sun, Cossette Tsung-hung Wu *law librarian*
Talbert, Melvin George *bishop*
Tracy, James Jared, Jr. *law firm administrator*
Vohs, James Arthur *health care program executive*
Weinmann, Robert Lewis *neurologist*
Whitsel, Richard Harry *biologist, entomologist*
Wick, William David *lawyer*
†Wilson, James Thomas *lawyer*
Winokur, Robert M. *lawyer*
Wood, James Michael *lawyer*
Wood, Larry (Mary Laird) *journalist, author, university educator, public relations executive, environmental consultant*

Oakville
Mondavi, Robert Gerald *winery executive*

Occidental
Rumsey, Victor Henry *electrical engineering educator emeritus*

Oceanside
Erickson, Frank William *composer*
Hertweck, E. Romayne *psychology educator*
Lyon, Richard *mayor, retired naval officer*
Roberts, James McGregor *retired professional association executive*
Robinson, William Franklin *retired legal consultant*
Schuck, Carl Joseph *lawyer*

Oildale
Gallagher, Joseph Francis *marketing executive*

Ojai
Mankoff, Albert William *cultural organization administrator, consultant*
Weill, Samuel, Jr. *automobile company executive*
†Wyman, Willard G. *headmaster*

Ontario
Fatland, James R. *mayor*
†Luce, Susan Marie *library director*

Orange
Anzel, Sanford Harold *orthopaedic surgeon*
Armentrout, Steven Alexander *oncologist*
Berk, Jack Edward *physician, educator*
Braunstein, Phillip *radiologist, educator*
†Crumley, Roger Lee *surgeon, educator*
Dana, Edward Runkle *physician, educator*
†Doti, James L. *academic administrator*
Furnas, David William *plastic surgeon*
Gerhard, Nancy Lucile Dege *educator*
Hamilton, Harry Lemuel, Jr. *academic administrator*
Hofmann, Adele Dellenbaugh *pediatrician*
Levine, Howard Harris *service executive*
†Magalousis, Nicholas Michael *anthropology, archaeology educator*
†Martini, Robert Edward *wholesale pharmaceutical and medical supplies company executive*
Mc Farland, Norman Francis *bishop*
Morgan, Beverly Carver *physician, educator*
Noce, Walter William, Jr. *hospital administrator*
Quilligan, Edward James *obstetrician/gynecologist, educator*
†Reed, David Andrew *foundation executive*
Rowen, Marshall *radiologist*
Sanders, Gary Wayne *lawyer*
†Sawdei, Milan A. *lawyer*
Schoettger, Theodore Leo *city official*
†Stacho, Zoltan Aladar *construction and engineering company executive*
Starr, Richard William *retired banker*
Steffensen, Dwight A. *medical products and data processing services executive*
Thompson, William Benbow, Jr. *obstetrician/gynecologist, educator*
Toeppe, William Joseph, Jr. *retired aerospace engineer*
†Viviano, Paul Steven *medical center administrator*
Yu, Jen *medical educator*

Orinda
Bowyer, Jane Baker *life science educator*
Brookes, Valentine *retired lawyer*
Campbell-White, Annette Jane *venture capitalist*
Conran, James Michael *state government official*
Cooper, Clare Dunlap *civic worker, writer*
†Gilbert, Robert W. *secondary school principal*
†Glasser, Charles Edward *academic administrator*
†Heftmann, Erich *biochemist*
McCormick, Loyd Weldon *lawyer*
Meadowcroft, Robert Stanley *financial investment executive*
Odermatt, Robert Allen *architect*
Rosenberg, Barr Marvin *investment advisor, economist*

Oroville
Ward, Chester Lawrence *physician, county health official, retired military officer*

Oxnard
Dimitriadis, Andre C. *health care executive*
Frodsham, Olaf Milton *music educator*
Herlinger, Daniel Robert *hospital administrator*
Hill, Alice Lorraine *secondary education educator, researcher*
Lawson, William Harold *college dean, labor economist*
Lewis, Michael John *diversified financial services company executive*
O'Connell, Hugh Mellen, Jr. *architect, retired*
Parriott, James Deforis, Jr. *retired oil company executive, consultant*
Perrier, Barbara Sue *artist*
Regnier, Richard Adrian *lawyer*

Pacific Grove
†Brewer, Peter George *ocean geochemist*
Davis, Robert Edward *writer, former communication educator*
Epel, David *biologist, educator*
Fleischman, Paul *author*
Powers, Dennis Alpha *biology educator*
†Roberts, William M. *publishing executive*

Pacific Palisades
Abrams, Richard Lee *physicist*
Albert, Eddie (Edward Albert Heimberger) *actor*
Becker, Joseph *information scientist*
Cale, Charles Griffin *lawyer*
Chesney, Lee Roy, Jr. *artist*
Claes, Daniel John *physician*
†Clark, Bob H. *film director*
Crane, Richard Clement *paper manufacturing company executive*
Csendes, Ernest *chemist, corporate and financial executive*
Dignam, Robert Joseph *retired orthopaedic surgeon*
Fink, Robert Morgan *biological chemistry educator*
Flattery, Thomas Long *lawyer, legal administrator*
Fonda, Jane *actress*
Garwood, Victor Paul *retired speech communication educator*
Horner, Harry *art director, performing arts designer*
Jones, Edgar Allan, Jr. *law educator, arbitrator, lawyer*
Keaton, Michael *actor, comedian*
Klein, Joseph Mark *retired mining company executive*
Kovacs, Laszlo *cinematographer*
Kridel, James S. *banker*
Lewis, Frank Harlan *botanist, educator*
Longaker, Richard Pancoast *political science educator emeritus*
Mulryan, Henry Trist *mineral company executive, consultant*
Nash, Gary Baring *historian, educator*
Rockwell, Don Arthur *psychiatrist*
Rode, James Dean *banker*
Rothenberg, Leslie Steven *lawyer, ethicist*
Schwartz, Murray Louis *lawyer, educator, academic administrator*
Sevilla, Stanley *lawyer*
Zipper, Herbert *symphony conductor*

Pacoima
Irving, Harry Rayfield *secondary education educator*

Palisades
Diehl, Richard Kurth *retail business consultant*

Palm Desert
Brown, James Briggs *retired business forms company executive*
Budge, Hamer Harold *mutual fund company executive*
Hartman, Ashley Powell *publishing executive, journalist, educator*
Humphrey, Charles Edward, Jr. *lawyer*
Krallinger, Joseph Charles *entrepreneur, business advisor, author*
McKissock, Paul Kendrick *plastic surgeon*
Sausman, Karen *zoological park administrator*
Sicuro, Natale Anthony *academic administrator*

Palm Springs
Aikens, Donald Thomas *educational administrator, consultant*
Arnold, Stanley Norman *manufacturing consultant*
Behrmann, Joan Metzner *newspaper editor*
Browning, Norma Lee (Mrs. Russell Joyner Ogg) *journalist*
Caesar, Sid *actor, comedian*
Carter, Paul Richard *physician*
Frey, Albert *architect*
Greenbaum, James Richard *liquor distributing company executive, real estate developer*
Jones, Milton Wakefield *publisher*
Jumonville, Felix Joseph, Jr. *physical education educator, realtor*
Krick, Irving Parkhurst *meteorologist*
Kroger, William Saul *obstetrician-gynecologist*
Maree, Wendy *painter, sculptor*
Yantis, Richard William *investments executive*

Palmdale
Anderson, R(obert) Gregg *real estate company executive*
Grooms, Larry Willis *newspaper editor*

Palo Alto
Adamson, Geoffrey David *reproductive endocrinologist, surgeon*
Agras, William Stewart *psychiatry educator*
Allen, Louis Alexander *management consultant*
Amylon, Michael David *physician, educator*
Attig, John Clare *history educator, consultant*
Baldwin, Gary Lee *electronics engineer, research laboratory administrator*
Ballam, Joseph *physicist, educator*
Balzhiser, Richard Earl *research and development company executive*
Berger, Joseph *author, educator, counselor*
Bienenstock, Arthur Irwin *physicist, educator*
Bills, Robert Howard *political party executive*
Bird, Rose Elizabeth *former state chief justice, law educator*
Bohrnstedt, George William *sociology educator*
Borovoy, Roger Stuart *lawyer*
Bradley, Donald Edward *lawyer*
Briggs, Winslow Russell *plant biologist, educator*
Britton, M(elvin) C(reed), Jr. *physician, rheumatologist*
Brown, David Randolph *electrical engineer*
Brown, Robert McAfee *minister, religion educator*
Burke, Edmund Charles *retired aerospace company executive*
Buss, Claude Albert *history educator*
†Carlson, Robert Wells *physician, educator*
Chase, Robert Arthur *surgeon, educator*
Childs, Wylie Jones *metallurgical engineer*
Climan, Richard Elliot *lawyer*
Cohen, Elizabeth G. *education and sociology educator, researcher*
Cohen, Karl Paley *nuclear energy consultant*
Colin, Lawrence *aerospace scientist*
Cooper, Allen David *research scientist, educator*
Cutler, Leonard Samuel *physicist*
Dallin, Alexander *history and political science educator*
Dassoff, Christine Ellen *library administrator*
Dater, Judy Lichtenfeld *photographer*
DeLustro, Frank Anthony *biomedical company executive, research immunologist*
Dornbusch, Sanford Maurice *sociology and biology educator*
†Duggan, Susan J. *educational administrator*
Early, James Michael *electronics research consultant*
Eggers, Alfred John, Jr. *research corporation executive*
Elliott, David Duncan, III *science research company executive*
Elsen, Albert Edward *art history educator*
Eng, Lawrence Fook *biochemistry educator, neurochemist*
Eulau, Heinz *political scientist, educator*
Farquhar, John William *physician, educator*
Franson, Paul Oscar, III *public relations executive*
Friedlander, Benjamin *electrical and computer engineering educator*
Fries, James Franklin *internal medicine educator*
Furbush, David Malcolm *lawyer*
George, Alexander Lawrence *political scientist, educator*
Goff, Harry Russell *retired manufacturing company executive*
Goldstein, Avram *pharmacology educator*
Guerard, Albert Joseph *retired modern literature educator, author*
Gunderson, Robert Vernon, Jr. *lawyer*
Hammett, Benjamin Cowles *psychologist*
Hammond, Donald Leroy *computer company executive*
Haslam, Robert Thomas, III *lawyer*
Hays, Marguerite Thompson *physician*
Hecht, Lee Martin *software company executive*
†Heinemann, Klaus W. *physical sciences research administrator*
Hewlett, William (Redington) *manufacturing company executive, electrical engineer*
Hinckley, Robert Craig *lawyer*
Hodge, Philip Gibson, Jr. *mechanical and aerospace engineering educator*
Holman, Halsted Reid *medical educator*
Holmes, John Richard *physicist, educator*
Hornak, Thomas *electronics company executive*
Horngren, Charles Thomas *accounting educator*
Ivy, Benjamin Franklin, III *financial and real estate investment advisor*
†Jamison, Rex Lindsay *medical educator*
Jamplis, Robert Warren *surgeon, medical foundation executive*
Johnson, Conor Deane *mechanical engineer*
Johnson, Horace Richard *electronics company executive*
†Johnson, Noble Marshall *research scientist*
Johnston, Alan Cope *lawyer*
Jones, Robert Trent, Jr. *golf course architect*
Karp, Nathan *political activist*
Kaufman, Michael David *management executive*
Kennedy, W(ilbert) Keith, Jr. *electronics company executive*
Kino, Gordon Stanley *electrical engineering educator*
Knoles, George Harmon *history educator*
†Knott, Donald Joseph *golf course architect*
Krupp, Marcus Abraham *medical research director*
Lamport, Leslie B. *computer scientist*
Lane, William Kenneth *physician*
Latimer, Douglas Hamilton *publishing executive*
Lavendel, Giuliana Avanzini *information systems executive, writer, lecturer*
Lender, Adam *electrical engineer*
Lewis, John Wilson *political science educator*
†Lindzey, Gardner *psychologist, educator*
†Linn, Gary Dean *golf course architect*
Linna, Timo Juhani *immunologist, researcher, educator*
†Litt, Iris F. *pediatrics educator*
Loewenstein, Walter Bernard *nuclear power technologist*
Mansour, Tag Eldin *pharmacologist*
Mendelson, Alan Charles *lawyer*
Merrin, Seymour *computer marketing company executive*
Moffitt, Donald Eugene *transportation company executive*
Moll, John Lewis *electronics engineer*
Moretti, August Joseph *lawyer*
Morrison, David Fred *freight company executive*
Nanney, Herbert Boswell *musician, educator*
Nordlund, Donald Craig *corporate lawyer*
Noyes, H(enry) Pierre *physicist*
Oliver, Bernard More *electrical engineer, technical consultant*
O'Rourke, J. Tracy *manufacturing company executive*
Packard, David *manufacturing company executive, electrical engineer*
Pake, George Edward *research executive, physicist*
Panofsky, Wolfgang Kurt Hermann *physicist, educator*
Partain, Larry Dean *solar research engineer*
Patterson, Robert Edward *lawyer*
Pauling, Linus Carl *chemistry educator*
†Platt, Lewis Emmett *electronics company executive*
Quate, Calvin Forrest *engineering educator*
Rauch, Herbert Emil *electrical engineer*
Reagan, Joseph Bernard *aerospace executive*
Remington, Jack Samuel *physician*
Rivette, Gerard Bertram *manufacturing company executive*
†Robinson, Thomas Nathaniel *pediatrician, educator, researcher*
Rosenzweig, Robert Myron *educational consultant*
Saltoun, Andre Meir *lawyer*
Sandmeier, Ruedi Beat *agricultural research executive*
Sawyer, Wilbur Henderson *pharmacologist, educator*
Schonbrun, Michael Keith *health care executive*
Schrier, Stanley Leonard *physician, educator*
Scitovsky, Anne Aickelin *economist*
†Sonsini, Larry W. *lawyer*
Spinrad, Robert Joseph *computer scientist*
†Stanzler, Jordan *lawyer*
Staprans, Armand *electronics executive*
Stringer, John *materials scientist*
Strober, Samuel *immunologist, educator*
Summit, Roger Kent *retired information systems and services executive*
Taylor, John Joseph *nuclear engineer*
Taylor, Robert William *research director*
Tierney, Patrick John *information services executive*
Ullman, Edwin Fisher *research chemist*
Van Atta, David Murray *lawyer*
Warne, William Elmo *irrigationist*
Watkins, Dean Allen *electronics executive, educator*
Weiser, Mark David *computer scientist, researcher*
Weithorn, Stanley Stephen *lawyer*
Wheeler, Raymond Louis *lawyer*
Wiedmann, Tien-Wen Tao *medical scientist, educator*
Yuan, Sidney Wei Kwun *cryogenic engineer, consultant*
Zelnick, Strauss *entertainment company executive*
Zuckerkandl, Emile *molecular evolutionary biologist, scientific institute executive*

Palo Cedro
Haggard, Merle Ronald *songwriter, recording artist*

Palos Verdes Estates
Bach, Marcus *author, educator*
Christie, Hans Frederick *retired utility company subsidiaries executive, consultant*
Mennis, Edmund Addi *investment management consultant*

Palos Verdes Peninsula
Dalton, James Edward *aerospace executive, retired air force officer*
Ebsen, Buddy (Christian Ebsen, Jr.) *actor, dancer*
†Edler, Richard Bruce *advertising agency executive*
Grant, Robert Ulysses *retired manufacturing company executive*
Haynes, Moses Alfred *physician*
Leone, William Charles *retired business executive*
Raue, Jorg Emil *electrical engineer*
Ryker, Charles Edwin *consultant, former aerospace company executive*
Savage, Terry Richard *information systems executive*
Slayden, James Bragdon *retired department store executive*
Spinks, John Lee *engineering executive*
Thomas, Pearl Elizabeth *English educator*
Waaland, Irving Theodore *retired aerospace design executive*
Weaver, John Carrier *university president emeritus*
Weiss, Herbert Klemm *aeronautical engineer*
Wilson, Theodore Henry *retired electronics company executive, aerospace engineer*

Panorama City
Bass, Harold Neal *pediatrician, medical geneticist*

Paradise
Fulton, Len *publisher*

Paramount
Cook, Karla Joan *elementary education educator*
Hall, Howard Harry *lawyer*

Pasadena
Adler, Fred Peter *electronics company executive*
Albee, Arden Leroy *geologist, educator*
Allman, John Morgan *neurobiology educator*
Anderson, Don Lynn *geophysicist, educator*
Anson, Fred Colvig *chemistry educator*
Arnott, Robert Douglas *investment company executive*
Azpeitia, Lynne Marie *psychotherapist, educator*
Babcock, Horace W. *astronomer*
Bakaly, Charles George, Jr. *mediator, lawyer*
Baldeschwieler, John Dickson *chemist, educator*
Bare, Bruce *life insurance company executive*
Barnes, Charles Andrew *physicist, educator*
Barton, Jacqueline K. *chemistry educator*
Baum, Dwight Crouse *investment banking executive*
Bean, Maurice Darrow *retired diplomat*
Beer, Reinhard *atmospheric scientist*
Bejczy, Antal Károly *research scientist, research facility administrator*
Bennett, Joel Herbert *construction company executive*
Bergholz, Richard Cady *political writer*
Blandford, Roger David *astronomy educator*
Boochever, Robert *federal judge*
Boulos, Paul Fares *civil and environmental engineer*
Bourdeau, Paul Turgeon *insurance company executive*
Breckinridge, James Bernard *research physicist*
†Brennen, Christopher E. *fluid mechanics educator*
Bridges, William Bruce *electrical engineer, researcher, educator*
Brudvig, Glenn Lowell *library director*
Bush, Ronald L. *literature educator*
Caillouette, James Clyde *physician*
Caldwell, William Mackay, III *business executive*
Carroll, William Jerome *civil engineer*
Cecil, John Lamont *bank executive, lawyer*
Chahine, Moustafa Toufic *atmospheric scientist*
Chamberlain, Willard Thomas *retired metals company executive*
Chan, Sunney Ignatius *chemist*
Cohen, Marshall Harris *astronomer, educator*
Coles, Donald Earl *aeronautics educator*
Culick, Fred Ellsworth Clow *physics and engineering educator*
D'Angelo, Robert William *lawyer*
Davidson, Eric Harris *molecular and developmental biologist, educator*
Davidson, Norman Ralph *biochemistry educator*
Davis, Lance Edwin *economics educator*
Diehl, Digby Robert *journalist*
†Dougherty, Dennis A. *chemistry educator*
Dressler, Alan Michael *astronomer*
Drutchas, Gerrick Gilbert *investigator*
Elliot, David Clephan *historian, educator*
Epstein, Samuel *geologist, educator*
Everhart, Thomas Eugene *university president, engineering educator*
Fernandez, Ferdinand Francis *federal judge*
Files, Gordon Louis *judge, lawyer*
Finnell, Michael Hartman *corporate executive*
Fowler, William Alfred *retired physics educator*
Franklin, Joel Nicholas *mathematician, educator*
Frautschi, Steven Clark *physicist, educator*
Geckler, Richard Delph *metal products company executive*
Gell-Mann, Murray *theoretical physicist, educator*
Gilman, Richard Carleton *retired college president*
Goodstein, David Louis *physics educator*
Goodwin, Alfred Theodore *federal judge*
Gould, Roy Walter *engineering educator*
Gray, Harry Barkus *chemistry educator*
Grether, David Maclay *economics educator*
†Grubbs, Robert H. *chemistry educator*
Hale, Charles Russell *lawyer*
Hall, Cynthia Holcomb *federal judge*
†Hall, William E. *engineering and construction company executive*
Hammond, George Denman *physician, medical researcher, educator*
Harmsen, Tyrus George *librarian*
Harvey, Joseph Paul, Jr. *orthopedist, educator*
Hatheway, Alson Earle *mechanical engineer*
Hawkey, Philip A. *city manager*
†Heaton, Culver *architect*
Heindl, Clifford Joseph *physicist*
Hessler, Curtis Alan *newspaper publishing company executive*
Hilbert, Robert S(aul) *optical engineer*
Hitlin, David George *physicist, educator*
Hopfield, John Joseph *biophysicist, educator*
Hornung, Hans Georg *aeronautical engineering educator, science facility administrator*
Housner, George William *civil engineering educator, consultant*
Howe, Graham Lloyd *photographer, curator*
Howes, Benjamin Durward, III *mergers and acquisitions executive*
Hudson, Donald Ellis *civil engineering educator*
Hunt, Gordon *lawyer*
Iwan, Wilfred Dean *mechanical engineering educator*
Jacobs, Joseph John *engineering company executive*
Jastrow, Robert *physicist*
Jenkins, Royal Gregory *manufacturing executive*
Jennings, Paul Christian *civil engineering educator, academic administrator*
Johnson, Torrence Vaino *astronomer*
Kamb, Walter Barclay *geologist, educator*
†Kanamori, Hiroo *geophysics educator*
Kaplan, Gary *executive recruiter*
†Kent, Stephen Brian Henry *research scientist*
Kevles, Daniel Jerome *history educator, writer*
Knowles, James Kenyon *applied mechanics educator*
Konishi, Masakazu *neurobiologist*
Kousser, J(oseph) Morgan *history educator*
Kozinski, Alex *federal judge*
†Kulkarni, Shrinivas R. *astronomy educator*
Lauter, James Donald *stockbroker*
Ledyard, John Odell *economics educator, consultant*
Leonard, Nelson Jordan *chemistry educator*
Lewis, Edward B. *biology educator*
†Lewis, Nathan Saul *chemistry educator*
Liepmann, Hans Wolfgang *physicist, educator*
Loven, Andrew Witherspoon *environmental engineering company executive*
Luxemburg, Wilhelmus Anthonius Josephus *mathematics educator*
Lynch, Gerald John *management consultant*
Marcus, Rudolph Arthur *chemist, educator*
Marlen, James S. *chemical-plastics-building materials manufacturing company executive*
Mathies, Allen Wray, Jr. *physician, hospital administrator*
Mc Carthy, Frank Martin *surgical sciences educator*
Mc Duffie, Malcolm *oil company executive*
Mc Koy, Basil Vincent Charles *theoretical chemist, educator*
Mc Millan, John Robertson *energy producer*
Mead, Carver Andress *computer science educator*
†Messenger, Ron J. *health facility administrator*
Meye, Robert Paul *retired seminary administrator, writer*
Miller, Charles Daly *business executive*
Morari, Manfred *chemical engineer, educator*
Munger, Edwin Stanton *political geography educator*
†Myers, Andrew Gordon *chemistry educator*
Myers, R(alph) Chandler *lawyer*
Nackel, John George *health care consulting director*
Neal, Philip Mark *diversified manufacturing executive*
Nelson, Dorothy Wright (Mrs. James F. Nelson) *federal judge*
Neugebauer, Gerry *astrophysicist, educator*
Neugebauer, Marcia *physicist, administrator*
Newman, Joyce Kligerman *sculptor*
North, Wheeler James *marine ecologist, educator*
Nothmann, Gerhard Adolf *retired engineering executive, research engineer*
Oliver, Robert Warner *economics educator*
Ott, George William, Jr. *management consulting executive*
Owen, Ray David *biology educator*
Pickering, William Hayward *physics educator, scientist*
Pieroni, Leonard J. *construction company executive*
Plott, Charles R. *economics educator*
Politzer, Hugh David *physicist, educator*
†Presecan, Nicholas Lee *civil, environmental engineer, consultant*
Rapaport, David Alan *corporate legal executive*
Roberts, John D. *chemist, educator*
Rounds, Donald Edwin *cell biologist*
Rymer, Pamela Ann *federal judge*
Sabersky, Rolf Heinrich *mechanical engineer*
Saffman, Philip G. *mathematician*
Sandage, Allan Rex *astronomer*
Sano, Roy I. *bishop*
Sargent, Wallace Leslie William *astronomer, educator*
Schlinger, Warren Gleason *retired chemical engineer*
Schmidt, Maarten *astronomy educator*
Scott, Ronald Fraser *civil engineering educator, engineering consultant*
Scudder, Thayer *anthropologist, educator*
Searle, Eleanor Millard *history educator*
Searle, Leonard *astronomer, researcher*
Seinfeld, John Hersh *chemical engineering educator*
Sharp, Robert Phillip *geology educator, researcher*
Simon, Marvin Kenneth *electrical engineer, consultant*
Simpson, William Arthur *insurance company executive*
Slater, Richard James *engineering company executive*
Smith, Howard Russell *manufacturing company executive*
Smith, Richard Howard *banker*
Spector, Phil *record company executive*
Springer, Edwin Kent *mechanical engineer*
Steele, Gerda Govine *company president*
Stehsel, Melvin Louis *biology educator*
Stewart, Homer Joseph *engineering educator*
†Stolper, Edward Manin *geology educator*
Stone, Edward Carroll *physicist, educator*
Stone, Willard John *retired lawyer*
Sudarsky, Jerry M. *industrialist*
Tanner, Dee Boshard *lawyer*

†Terhune, Robert William *optics scientist*
Thomas, Joseph Fleshman *architect*
Thorne, Kip Stephen *physicist, educator*
Todd, John *educator, mathematician*
Tollenaere, Lawrence Robert *industrial products company executive*
Tombrello, Thomas Anthony, Jr. *physics educator, consultant*
Ulrich, Peter Henry *banker*
Van Amringe, John Howard *retired oil industry executive, geologist*
Vanoni, Vito August *hydraulic engineer*
Vaughn, John Vernon *banker, industrialist*
Vogt, Rochus Eugen *physicist, educator*
Wasserburg, Gerald Joseph *geology and geophysics educator*
Watkins, John Francis *management consultant*
Wayland, J(ames) Harold *biomedical scientist, educator*
†Wernicke, Brian Philip *geologist, educator*
Whitham, Gerald Beresford *mathematics educator*
Wood, Nathaniel Fay *editor, writer, public relations consultant*
†Wu, Theodore Yao-Tsu *engineer*
Wyllie, Peter John *geologist, educator*
†Yamarone, Charles Anthony, Jr. *aerospace engineer, consultant*
Yariv, Amnon *electrical engineering educator, scientist*
Yeh, Paul Pao *electrical and electronics engineer, educator*
Zammitt, Norman *artist*
Zewail, Ahmed Hassan *chemistry and chemical engineering educator, editor, consultant*

Paso Robles
Boxer, Jerome Harvey *computer and management consultant, vintner, accountant*
Brown, Benjamin Andrew *journalist*
Knecht, James Herbert *lawyer*

Pauma Valley
Dooley, George Elijah *manufacturing executive*

Pebble Beach
Burkett, William Andrew *banker*
Cameron, JoAnna *actress, director*
Crossley, Randolph Allin *retired corporate executive*
Dennison, David Short, Jr. *lawyer*
Fergusson, Robert George *retired army officer*
Gianelli, William Reynolds *foundation administrator, civil engineering consultant, former federal agency commissioner*
Keene, Clifford Henry *medical administrator*
Maxeiner, Clarence William *lawyer, construction company executive*
Mortensen, Gordon Louis *artist, printmaker*
Sullivan, James Francis *university administrator*

Penn Valley
Throner, Guy Charles, Jr. *engineering executive, scientist, engineer, inventor, consultant*

Petaluma
Carr, Les *psychologist, educator*
Mc Chesney, Robert Pearson *artist*
Morris, Donald James *banker*
Pronzini, Bill John (William Pronzini) *author*
Reichek, Jesse *artist*

Philo
Hill, Rolla B. *pathologist*

Pico Rivera
Mitzner, Kenneth Martin *electrical engineer*

Piedmont
Cuttle, Tracy Donald *physician, former naval officer*
Hoover, Robert Cleary *retired bank executive*
Hughes, James Paul *physician*
Knight, Jeffrey William *publishing and marketing executive*
Montgomery, Theodore Ashton *physician*
Morrison, John Gill *communications executive*
Phillips, Betty Lou (Elizabeth Louise Phillips) *author*
Putter, Irving *French educator*
Yep, Wallen Lai *international business consultant, author*

Pinole
Gerbracht, Robert Thomas (Bob Gerbracht) *painter, educator*
Grogan, Stanley Joseph, Jr. *consultant*

Pismo Beach
Saveker, David Richard *naval and marine architectural engineering executive*

Pittsburg
†Chuderewicz, Leonard H. *heavy industry executive*

Placentia
George, Julia Bever *nurse administrator, educator*
Gobar, Alfred Julian *economic consultant, educator*
Nowel, David John *marketing professional*

Placerville
Craib, Kenneth Bryden *resource development executive, physicist, economist*

Playa Del Rey
Copperman, William H *value engineer, consultant*
Waggoner, James Norman *physician*
Weir, Alexander, Jr. *utility consultant, inventor*

Pleasant Hill
Hamilton, Allen Philip *financial advisor*
Hassid, Sami *architect, educator*
Weiss, Lionel Edward *geology educator*

Pleasanton
†Cochnar, Robert John *newspaper executive*
†Dunbar, Frank Rollin *landscape architect*
Fehlberg, Robert Erick *architect*
Karn, Richard Wendall *civil engineer*
Miller, William Charles *lawyer*
†Perry, James R. *construction company executive*
Petty, George Oliver *lawyer*
Quinnan, Edward Michael *management consultant*
Stager, Donald K. *construction company executive*
†Surrence, Matthew Michael *critic, journalist*

†Tauscher, William Young *pharmaceutical and cosmetic products executive*
Vandenberghe, Ronald Gustave *accountant, real estate developer*
Weiss, Robert Stephen *medical manufacturing and services company financial executive*
†Wevurski, Peter John *newspaper editor*

Plymouth
Andreason, John Christian *lawyer*

Point Arena
Kohl, Herbert Ralph *education educator*

Point Mugu
†Newman, William E. *naval officer*

Pollock Pines
Johnson, Stanford Leland *marketing educator*

Pomona
Aurilia, Antonio *physicist, educator*
Baker, Frederick John *education educator*
Bausch, Janet Jean *lawyer*
Burrill, Melinda Jane *animal science educator*
Christensen, Allen Clare *agriculturist, educator*
Coombs, Walter Paul *retired lawyer, social science educator*
Dev, Vasu *chemistry educator*
Eagleton, Robert Don *physics educator*
Eaves, Ronald Weldon *university administrator*
Fleck, Raymond Anthony, Jr. *university administrator*
†Johnson, Richard M. *finance company executive*
Keating, Eugene Kneeland *animal scientist, educator*
Lasswell, Thomas Ely *sociology educator, author*
Lyle, John Tillman *landscape architecture educator*
†McCoy, Charles Wirth, Jr. *superior court judge*
Patten, Thomas Henry, Jr. *management, human resources educator*
Shieh, John Ting-chung *economics educator*
Smith, Donna *mayor, small business owner*
†Suzuki, Bob H. *university president*

Port Hueneme
†Chapla, P.A. *civil engineering research administrator*
Pathak, Sunit Rawly *business owner, consultant, journalist*

Portola Valley
Bach, George Leland *economist, emeritus educator*
Berghold, Joseph Philip *finance company executive*
Cooper, John Joseph *lawyer*
Creevy, Donald Charles *obstetrician-gynecologist*
†De Alessi, Ross Alan *lighting designer*
Garsh, Thomas Burton *publisher*
Hanson, Raymond Lester *retired lawyer*
Hurd, Cuthbert C. *computer company executive, mathematician*
Katz, Robert Lee *business executive*
Kuo, Franklin F. *computer scientist, electrical engineer*
Moses, Franklin Maxwell *marketing consultant*
Nycum, Susan Hubbell *lawyer*
Purl, O. Thomas *retired electronics company executive*
Ward, Robert Edward *retired political science educator and university administrator*

Poway
†Brose, Cathy *principal*
Harlan, Roma Christine *portrait painter*
Remer, Vernon Ralph *travel consultant*
†Rudolph, Charles Herman *retired computer software development executive*
Shippey, Lyn *reading center director*

Ramona
Bennett, James Chester *computer consultant, real estate developer*
Cesinger, Joan *author*
Hoffman, Wayne Melvin *retired airline official*
†Palmer, James Russworth *theoretical physicist, high energy optics researcher*
Vaughn, Robert Lockard *aerospace and astronautics company executive*

Rancho Cordova
†Alenius, John Todd *insurance executive*
Ling, Robert Malcolm *banker, publishing executive*

Rancho Cucamonga
†Ayala, Ruben Samuel *state senator*
†Christopher, Gaylaird Wiley *architect*
Hattar, Michael Mizyed *secondary education educator, mathematics educator*
Stout, Dennis Lee *lawyer, mayor*

Rancho Mirage
Buskirk, Richard Hobart *marketing educator*
Chambers, Milton Warren *architect*
Cone, Lawrence Arthur *research medicine educator*
Deiter, Newton Elliott *clinical psychologist*
Ford, Betty Bloomer (Elizabeth Ford) *health facility executive, wife of former President of United States*
Ford, Gerald Rudolph, Jr. *former President of United States*
Gardner, Donald LaVere *development company executive*
Kocen, Joel Evan *financial planner*
Kuhlmey, Walter Trowbridge *lawyer*
Rotman, Morris Bernard *public relations consultant*
Scholl, Allan Henry *retired school system administrator, education consultant*
†Stenhouse, Everett Ray *clergy administrator*
Strickman, Arthur Edwin *retired retail executive*

Rancho Palos Verdes
Fischer, Robert Blanchard *university administrator, researcher*
Lima, Luis Eduardo *tenor*
Lunden, Samuel Eugene *architect*
Marlett, De Otis Loring *retired management consultant*
McFadden, Thomas *academic administrator*

Rancho Santa Fe
Affeldt, John Ellsworth *physician*
Arms, Brewster Lee *retired corporate executive, investor*
Capen, Richard Goodwin, Jr. *ambassador*

Creutz, Edward Chester *physicist, museum consultant*
Gruenwald, George Henry *new products management consultant*
Gunness, Robert Charles *chemical engineer*
Jordan, Charles Morrell *retired automotive designer*
Kessler, A. D. *business, financial, investment and real estate advisor, consultant, lecturer, author, broadcaster, producer*
Matthews, Leonard Sarver *advertising executive, consultant*
Schirra, Walter Marty, Jr. *business consultant, former astronaut*
Stadler, Craig Robert *professional golfer*

Rancho Santa Margarita
Griffith Joyner, Florence DeLorez *track and field athlete*
Wong, Wallace *medical supplies company executive, real estate investor*

Redding
Ballew, Nellie Hester *retired secondary school educator*
Buffum, Nancy Kay *interior designer*
Treadway, Douglas Morse *academic administrator*

Redlands
Appleton, James Robert *university president, educator*
†Bricker, Neal S. *physician, educator*
Ely, Northcutt *lawyer*
Griesemer, Allan David *museum director*
Merritt, Joshua Levering, Jr. *consultant, retired engineering executive*
Rossum, Ralph Arthur *political science educator*
Skomal, Edward Nelson *aerospace company executive, consultant*
Skoog, William Arthur *retired oncologist*

Redondo Beach
Battles, Roxy Edith *novelist, consultant, educator*
†Beverly, Robert Graham *state senator, lawyer*
Buchta, Edmund *engineering executive*
Chazen, Melvin Leonard *chemical engineer*
Cohen, Clarence Budd *aerospace engineer*
Hughes, James Arthur *electrical engineer*
Ilie, Paul *foreign language educator*
Kagiwada, Reynold Shigeru *advanced technology manager*
Marsee, Stuart (Earl) *educational consultant, retired*
McWilliams, Margaret Ann *home economics educator, author*
†Sackheim, Robert Lewis *aerospace engineer, educator*
Shellhorn, Ruth Patricia *landscape architect*

Redwood City
Bentley, John Martin *lawyer*
Bonino, Mark G. *lawyer*
†Bramson, Edward J. *electronics corporation executive, financial executive*
Coddington, Clinton Hays *lawyer*
Eliassen, Rolf *environmental engineer, emeritus educator*
†Guinasso, Victor *delivery service executive*
Jobs, Steven Paul *computer corporation executive*
†Kalinske, Thomas J. *toy company executive*
Nacht, Sergio *biochemist*
Neville, Roy Gerald *chemical management and environmental consultant*
†Nosler, Peter C. *construction company executive*
Poppel, Harvey Lee *management consultant*
Seltzer, Ronald Anthony *radiologist, educator*
Speziale, A. John *organic chemist, consultant*
Swinerton, William Arthur *retired construction company executive*
Tight, Dexter Corwin *lawyer*
Tyabji, Hatim Ahmedi *computer systems company executive*
†Waller, Stephen *air transportation executive*
Wilhelm, Robert Oscar *lawyer, civil engineer, developer*

Redwood Shores
†Ellison, Lawrence J. *computer software company executive*
Jenkins, Robert Lee *management consultant*

Reedley
Dick, Henry Henry *minister*

Reseda
Aller, Wayne Kendall *psychology educator, researcher, computer education company executive, property manager*
†Anstad, Neil *director*
Roth, Leonard Jerome *financial consultant, insurance agent*

Rialto
Jackson, Betty Eileen *music and elementary school educator*

Richmond
†Anderson, Thomas Robert *scientist, entrepreneur*
†Ayers, G. W. *church adminstrator*
†Beall, Frank Carroll *science director and educator*
Bertero, Vitelmo Victorio *civil engineer*
Colvin, Lloyd Dayton *electrical engineer*
Doyle, William Thomas *retired newspaper editor*
Holmquist, Walter Richard *research chemist, molecular evolutionist, mathematics educator*
†Moehle, Jack P. *civil engineer, engineering executive*
Thomas, John Richard *chemist*
Ward, Carl Edward *research chemist*
Wessel, Henry *photographer*

Ridgecrest
Nason, Patricia Anne Woodward *museum educator, consultant*
Pearson, John *mechanical engineer*
St. Amand, Pierre *geophysicist*

Riverside
Aderton, Jane Reynolds *lawyer*
Adrian, Charles Raymond *political science educator*
Balow, Irving Henry *retired education educator*
Barnes, Martin McRae *entomologist*
Bartnicki-Garcia, Salomon *microbiologist, educator*
Beni, Gerardo *electrical and computer engineering educator, robotics scientist*
Bhanu, Bir *computer information scientist, educator, director university program*

Bovell, Carlton Rowland *biology educator, microbiologist*
Carrillo, Gilberto *engineer*
Chute, Phillip Bruce *management consultant*
Clegg, Michael Tran *genetics educator, researcher*
Cohen, Kenneth Bruce *health agency director*
Crean, John C. *housing and recreational vehicles manufacturing company executive*
Donlan, Dan M. *education educator*
Elliott, Emory Bernard *English language educator, educational adminstrator*
Embleton, Tom William *horticultural science educator*
Erwin, Donald Carroll *plant pathology educator*
Eyman, Richard Kenneth *psychologist, educator*
Fagundo, Ana Maria *creative writing and Spanish literature educator*
Fleischer, Everly Borah *academic administrator*
†Foreman, Thomas Elton *drama critic*
†Frizzel, Teresa R. *mayor*
†Garrett, John Cecil *newspaper editor*
†Geraty, Lawrence Thomas *academic administrator, archaeologist*
Green, Harry Western, II *geology educator*
Green, Jonathan William *museum administrator and educator, artist, author*
Griffin, Keith Broadwell *economics educator*
Hackwood, Susan *electrical and computer engineering educator*
†Hall, Anthony Elmitt *plant physiologist*
Hanna, Ralph, III *English educator, author*
Harrison, Ethel Mae *financial executive*
Hays, Howard H. (Tim Hays) *editor, publisher*
Hodgen, Maurice Denzil *financial development administrator, educator*
Inacker, Charles John *academic dean, business educator*
Kronenfeld, David Brian *anthropologist*
Kummer, Glenn F. *automotive executive*
Letey, John Joseph, Jr. *soil scientist, educator*
†Maas, Sally Ann *newspaper editor, journalist*
Mc Laughlin, Leighton Bates, II *journalism educator, former newspaperman*
McQuern, Marcia Alice *newspaper publishing executive*
†Mudd, John Brian *biochemist*
Norman, Anthony Westcott *biochemistry educator*
†O'Connor, June Elizabeth *religious studies educator*
Opotowsky, Maurice Leon *newspaper editor*
Orbach, Raymond Lee *physicist, educator*
Page, Albert Lee *soil science educator, researcher*
Perkins, Van L. *university administrator, educator, conservationist*
Petrinovich, Lewis F. *psychology educator*
†Pick, Arthur Joseph, Jr. *chamber of commerce executive*
Quinton, Paul Marquis *physiology educator*
Rabenstein, Dallas Leroy *chemistry educator*
Ratliff, Louis Jackson, Jr. *mathematics educator*
Ravitch, Norman *history educator*
Reuther, Walter *horticulture educator*
Reynolds, William Harold *educator, choral conductor, music critic*
Rosenberg, Alexander *philosophy educator, author*
Ross, Delmer Gerrard *historian, educator*
†Scott, Loretta Bernadette *newspaper editor*
Shapiro, Victor Lenard *mathematician*
Sherman, Irwin William *biological sciences educator, university official*
Smith, Elden Leroy *recreational vehicle company executive*
Snyder, Henry Leonard *history educator, bibliographer*
Sokolsky, Robert Lawrence *journalist, entertainment writer*
Spencer, William Franklin, Sr. *soil scientist, researcher*
Steadman, John Marcellus, III *English educator*
Steckel, Barbara Jean *city financial officer*
Talbot, Prue *biology educator*
Tuck, Russell R., Jr. *college president*
Turk, Austin Theodore *sociology educator*
Turner, Arthur Campbell *political science educator, author*
Van Gundy, Seymour Dean *nematologist, plant pathologist, educator*
Warren, David Hardy *psychology educator*
Weide, William Wolfe *housing and recreational vehicles manufacturer*
White, Robert Stephen *physics educator*
Wild, Robert Lee *physics educator*
Wilkins, Charles L. *chemistry educator*
Wilson, Jeanette Kurtz *elementary and middle school educator, behavior specialist*
Wright, John MacNair, Jr. *retired army officer*
Yacoub, Ignatius I. *university dean*
Zentmyer, George Aubrey *plant pathology educator*

Rocklin
Ha, Chong Wan *state government executive*

Rohnert Park
Babula, William *university dean*
Grivas, Theodore *retired historian, educator*
Hermans, Colin Olmsted *biology educator*
Johnston, Edward Elliott *insurance and management consultant*
Lord, Harold Wilbur *electrical engineer, electronics consultant*

Rolling Hills Estates
Bellis, Carroll Joseph *surgeon*

Rosemead
Allen, Howard Pfeiffer *electric utility executive, lawyer*
Bennett, Brian O'Leary *utilities executive*
Bryson, John E. *utilities company executive*
Bushey, Richard Kenneth *utility executive*
Hansen, Robert Dennis *educational administrator*

Roseville
Dupper, Frank Floyd *health care facility executive*
Hendricks, Ed Jerald *physician*
†Leslie, Tim *state legislator*

Ross
Godwin, Sara *writer*
Goulet, William Dawson *marketing professional*
Scott, John Walter *chemical engineer, research management executive*
Way, Walter Lee *anesthetist, pharmacologist, educator*

Rowland Heights
Perfetti, Robert Nickolas career education coordinator, educator

Running Springs
Giles, Walter Edmund alcohol and drug treatment executive

Rutherford
Eisele, Milton Douglas viticulturist
Staglin, Garen Kent finance and computer service company executive

Sacramento
Adams, Richard Maxwell English educator
Aldrich, Thomas Albert consultant, former brewing executive and air forceofficer
Andrew, John Henry lawyer, retail corporation executive
†Areias, John Rusty agriculturist, state legislator
Baccigaluppi, Roger John agricultural company executive
Baltake, Joe film critic
Benfield, John Richard surgeon
Bennett, Lawrence Allen psychologist, criminal justice researcher
†Bergeson, Marian state legislator
Betts, Bert A. former state treasurer, accountant
Bezzone, Albert Paul structural engineer
Blackwell, Frederick Wayne computer science educator
†Blum, Deborah reporter
†Boatwright, Daniel E. state legislator
Bogren, Hugo Gunnar radiology educator
Bottel, Helen Alfea columnist, writer
†Bowler, Larry Dean state legislator
Brookman, Anthony Raymond lawyer
Brown, Kathleen state treasurer, lawyer
Brown, Willie Lewis, Jr. state legislator, lawyer
Bruce, Thomas Edward thanatologist, psychology educator
Burns, John Francis archivist, state official
†Caldera, Louis Edward state legislator, lawyer
Cavigli, Henry James petroleum engineer
Chapman, Loring psychologist, educator, neuroscientist
Chapman, Michael William orthopedist, educator
†Cole, Glen David minister
Collings, Charles LeRoy supermarket executive
†Connolly, Tom M. state legislator, lawyer
†Cortese, Dominic L. state legislator, farmer
Covitz, Carl D. state official, real estate and investment executive
†Cox, David W. bank executive
Cox, Whitson William architect
Crabbe, John Crozier telecommunications consultant
Crimmins, Philip Patrick metallurgical engineer, lawyer
Cunningham, Mary Elizabeth physician
Dahl, Loren Silvester federal judge
†Dalkey, Fredric Dynan artist
Deitch, Arline Douglis Urologist
†Dexter, Peter Whittemore columnist, writer
Dorn, Robert Murray physician, psychiatrist, educator, psychoanalyst
†Eastin, Delaine Andree state legislator
Endicott, William F. journalist
†Engel, Thomas P. airport executive
Eu, March Kong Fong state official
Evrigenis, John Basil obstetrician-gynecologist
Farrell, Francine Annette psychotherapist, educator
Flournoy, Houston Irvine public administration educator
Forsyth, Raymond Arthur civil engineer
Franklin, Charles Scothern lawyer
Frey, Charles Frederick surgeon, educator
Friedman, Morton Lee lawyer
Garcia, Edward J. federal judge
Gerth, Donald Rogers university president
Gibbs, Barbara Kennedy art museum director
Gibson, Edward Fergus physicist, educator
†Glackin, William Charles arts critic, editor
Goodart, Nan L. lawyer, educator
Gray, Myles McClure insurance company executive
Greenfield, Carol Nathan psychotherapist
Hanson, Dale pension fund administrator
†Haugen, D. Peter theatre critic
Hay, John Thomas trade association executive
Hays, Patrick Gregory health care executive
Headley, Nathan Leroy laboratory executive
Herman, Irving Leonard business administration educator
Hile, Norman Carter lawyer
Holmes, Robert Eugene state legislative consultant, journalist
†Isenberg, Phillip L. state legislator
Karlton, Lawrence K. federal judge
Kemmerly, Jack Dale state official
†Killea, Lucy Lytle state legislator
†Killian, Richard M. library director
Knight, William J. (Pete Knight) state legislator, retired military officer
Knudson, Thomas Jeffery journalist
Lagarias, John Samuel engineering executive
LeBaron, Edward Wayne, Jr. lawyer
Levi, David F. federal judge
Lionakis, George architect
Loge, Frank Jean, II hospital administrator
Lukenbill, Gregg real estate developer, professional basketball team executive
†Lundstrom, Marjie newswriter
Lungren, Daniel Edward state attorney general
MacBride, Thomas Jamison federal judge
McCarthy, Leo Tarcisius state lieutenant governor
McClatchy, James B. editor, newspaper publisher
†McGrath, Daniel Bernard newspaper editor
Meier, George Karl, III pastor, lawyer
Meindl, Robert James English language educator
Merwin, Edwin Preston educator
†Mette, Joe museum director
Metzger, Bobbie Ann public relations executive
Mix, Esther federal judge
†Moore, Gwen state legislator
Muehleisen, Gene Sylvester retired law enforcement officer, state official
Nacht, Daniel Joseph architect
Nelson, Alan Curtis government official, lawyer
Newland, Chester Albert public administration educator
Nice, Carter conductor, music director
†Nussenbaum, Siegfried Fred chemistry educator
O'Brien, Kenneth R. lawyer
Plant, Forrest Albert lawyer
Post, August Alan economist, artist
†Presley, Robert Buel state senator
Quinn, Francis A. bishop
Ramirez, Raul Anthony lawyer, former federal judge
Redig, Dale Francis dentist, association executive
Reynolds, Jerry Owen professional basketball executive
Richardson, Frank Kellogg lawyer, former state justice
Riles, Wilson Camanza educational consultant
Russell, Bill professional basketball team executive
Russell, David E. federal judge
St. Jean, Garry professional basketball coach
Sawiris, Milad Youssef statistician, educator
Schaber, Gordon Duane law educator, former judge
Schmitz, Dennis Mathew English language educator
Schrag, Peter editor, writer
Schwabe, Peter Alexander, Jr. judge
Schwartz, Milton Lewis federal judge
†Serna, Joe, Jr. mayor
†Shaw, Eleanor Jane newspaper editor
†Sher, Byron D. law educator
Sherwood, Robert Petersen retired sociology educator
Shubb, William Barnet federal judge
Slater, Manning broadcasting consultant
†Smith, Freda M. minister
Stegenga, Preston Jay international education consultant
Strock, James Martin state agency administrator, lawyer, conservationist
Strong, Gary Eugene librarian
†Swatt, Stephen Benton communications executive, consultant
Takasugi, Nao state official, business developer
Thomas, Jim professional basketball team executive
†Umberg, Thomas John state legislator, lawyer
Van Camp, Brian Ralph lawyer
Walsh, Denny Jay reporter
Walston, Roderick Eugene attorney general
†Walters, Daniel Raymond political columnist
Wasserman, Barry L(ee) architect
Whiteside, Carol Gordon state official, former mayor
Wightman, Thomas Valentine rancher, researcher
Williams, Arthur Cozad broadcasting executive
Wilson, Pete governor of California
Wolfman, Earl Frank, Jr. surgeon, educator
†Zax, Stanley R. insurance company executive
†Zeff, Ophelia Hope lawyer
†Zumbrun, Ronald Arthur lawyer

Saint Helena
Amerine, Maynard Andrew enologist, educator
Kamman, Alan Bertram communications consulting company executive

Salinas
Ader, Richard Alan marketing executive
Eifler, Carl Frederick retired psychologist
Francis, Alexandria Stephanie psychologist
Martins, Evelyn Mae theatre owner
†Shaffer, Dallas Young library administrator
Shaver, Donald LaVergne research agronomist, educator
Spinks, Paul retired library director
Stevens, Wilbur Hunt accountant

San Andreas
Arkin, Michael Barry lawyer, arbitrator
Breed, Allen Forbes correctional administrator
Millsaps, Rita R. elementary school educator

San Anselmo
Goodman, Carolyn advertising executive
Keough, James Gordon publishing executive, editor
Mudge, Lewis Seymour theologian, educator, university dean
Murphy, Barry Ames lawyer
Powell, Stanley, Jr. management consultant
Waetjen, Herman Charles theologian, educator

San Bernardino
†Anderson, Barbara Louise library director
Bellis, David James public administration educator
Burgess, Mary Alice (Mary Alice Wickizer) publisher
Burgess, Michael library science educator, publisher
Evans, Anthony Howard university president
Fullerton, Robert Victor lawyer
Garson, Arnold Hugh newspaper editor
Holtz, Tobenette aerospace engineer
†Reginald, Robert publisher, university library cataloger, researcher
Straling, Phillip Francis bishop
Timmreck, Thomas C. health sciences and health administration educator
Weiny, George Azem physical education educator, consultant

San Bruno
Arthur, Greer Martin maritime container leasing firm executive
Bradley, Charles William podiatrist, educator

San Carlos
Barnard, William Calvert retired news service executive
Bellack, Daniel Willard advertising and public relations executive
Burgess, Leonard Randolph business administration and economics educator, writer
Curry, William Sims procurement manager
Glenn, Thomas Michael science and technology executive
Gutow, Bernard Sidney packing manufacturing company executive
Symons, Robert Spencer electronics engineer

San Clemente
Cederquist, John artist
Fertik, Ira J. medical laser company executive
Khachigian, Kenneth Larry lawyer
Kim, Edward William ophthalmic surgeon
Singer, Kurt Deutsch news commentator, author, publisher
Stallknecht Roberts, Clois Freda publisher, publicist
Stenzel, William A. consulting services executive
Walker, Joseph retired research executive
White, Stanley Archibald research electrical engineer
Wray, Karl newspaper broker, former newspaper owner and publisher

San Diego
Abalos, Ted Quinto electronics engineer
Adler, Louise DeCarl bankruptcy judge
Akeson, Wayne Henry orthopedic surgeon, orthopedic educator
Albritton, Robert Sanford life insurance executive
Albuquerque, Lita artist
Alpert, Michael Edward lawyer
Ames, Robert Forbes lawyer
Anderson, Paul Maurice electrical engineering educator, researcher, consultant
Anjard, Ronald Paul, Sr. business and industry executive, consultant, educator, technologist, importer
Arledge, Charles Stone former aerospace executive, entrepreneur
Atchison, Richard Calvin trade association director
Auerbach, Ernest Sigmund lawyer, company executive, writer
Bailey, David Nelson pathologist, educator
Bakko, Orville Edwin retired health care executive, consultant
Barckley, Robert Eugene economics educator
Bateman, Giles Hirst Litton finance executive
†Bell, Gene newspaper publishing executive
Benes, Andrew Charles professional baseball player
Benirschke, Kurt pathologist, educator
Bennett, Ronald Thomas photojournalist
Berger, Bennett Maurice sociology educator
Beyster, John Robert engineering company executive
Bieler, Charles Linford development director, zoo executive director emeritus
Binkley, Nicholas Burns banking executive
Blakemore, Claude Coulehan banker
Blum, John Alan urologist, educator
Blumenfeld, Alfred Morton industrial design consultant, educator
Boarman, Patrick Madigan economics and business administration educator, public official
Bolman, Pieter Simon Heinrich publishing company executive, physicist
Boyd, Robert Giddings, Jr. mental health facility administrator
Bradley, Francis Xavier aluminum company executive
Bradley, John Edmund physician, emeritus educator
Bradley, Lawrence D., Jr. lawyer
Brandes, Raymond Stewart history educator
Branson, Harley Kenneth lawyer, finance executive
Brewster, Rudi Milton federal judge
Brezzo, Steven Louis museum director
Brimble, Alan business executive
Brom, Robert H. bishop
Brooks, John White lawyer
Buncher, James Edward healthcare management executive
Burge, David Russell concert pianist, composer, piano educator
Burgin, George Hans computer scientist, educator
Burke, John science technology company executive
Campbell, Ian David opera company director
Carleson, Robert Bazil public policy consultant, corporation executive
Chandler, Floyd Copeland fine arts educator
Charles, Carol Morgan education educator
Chen, Kao consulting electrical engineer
Cobble, James Wikle chemistry educator
Cockell, William Arthur, Jr. naval officer
Colling, Kenneth Frank hospital administrator
Conly, John Franklin engineering educator, researcher
Conner, Dennis manufacturing executive, yachtsman
Coox, Alvin David history educator
Copeland, Robert Glenn lawyer
Cornett, William Forrest, Jr. local government management consultant
Cota, John Francis utility executive
Crick, Francis Harry Compton biologist, educator
†Cross, C. Michael marine museum administrator
Cunningham, Bruce Arthur biochemist
Cutright, Frances Larson marriage and family therapist
Daley, Arthur Stuart retired humanities educator
Damoose, George Lynn lawyer
Daub, Clarence Theodore, Jr. astronomer, educator
Day, Thomas Brennock university president
Deckard, Ivan Lowell pilot
Delawie, Homer Torrence architect
DeMaria, Anthony Nicholas cardiologist, educator
Derrough, Neil E. television executive
Devine, Brian Kiernan pet food and supplies company executive
†DiMattio, Terry historic site administrator
†Dolan, James Michael, Jr. zoological society executive
†Donaldson, Milford Wayne architect, educator
Duddles, Charles Weller food company executive
Eckhart, Walter molecular biologist, educator
†Edwards, Charles Cornell physician, research administrator
†Ellsworth, Peter Kennedy health care executive
Fagot, Joseph Burdell corporate executive
Feinberg, Lawrence Bernard university dean, psychologist
Feinberg, Leonard English language educator
†Fernandez, Fernando Lawrence research company executive, aeronautical engineer
Flettner, Marianne cultural organization administrator
†Fontana, J. D. naval research administration
Fox, Sheila advertising executive
Freedman, Jonathan Borwick journalist, author, lecturer
Freeman, Dick professional baseball team executive
Gastil, Russell Gordon geologist, educator
Getis, Arthur geography educator
Gigli, Irma physician, educator, academic administrator
Gill, Gail Stoorza public relations executive
Gilliam, Earl Ben federal judge
Golding, Brage former university president
Golding, Susan mayor
Goltz, Robert William physician, educator
Gonzalez, Irma E. federal judge
Goodall, Jackson Wallace, Jr. restaurant company executive
Goode, John Martin manufacturing company executive
†Greene, John M. physicist
Griffin, Herschel Emmett epidemiology educator, administrator
Grosser, T.J. administrator, developer, fundraiser
Gwynn, Anthony Keith (Tony Gwynn) professional baseball player
Halasz, Nicholas Alexis surgeon
Hales, Alfred Washington mathematics educator, consultant
Hamburg, Marian Virginia health science educator
Hargrove, John James federal judge
Harmon, Harry William architect, former university administrator
Hart, Anne author
Harwood, Ivan Richmond pediatric pulmonologist
Hawran, Paul William pharmaceutical executive
Hayes, Robert Emmet retired insurance company executive, consultant
†Hays, Garry D. academic administrator
Helinski, Donald Raymond biologist, educator
Henderson, Brian Edmond physician, educator
Henderson, John Drews architect
Heuschele, Werner Paul veterinary researcher
Higgs, DeWitt A. lawyer
Hill, Frank Whitney, Jr. insurance company executive
Hofflund, Paul lawyer
†Holl, Walter John architect, interior designer
Holman, J(ohn) Leonard retired manufacturing corporation executive
Hooper, Jere Mann consultant, retired hotel executive
Hope, Douglas Olerich newspaper editor
Hope, Frank Lewis, Jr. retired architect
Howell, Thomas Edwin manufacturing company executive
Huang, Chien Chang electrical engineer
Huff, Marilyn L. federal judge
Hughes, Author E. university president, association executive
†Hughes, Gethin B. bishop
Huston, Kenneth Dale lawyer
Hutcheson, J(ames) Sterling lawyer
Igasaki, Masao, Jr. retired utilities company executive, controller
Ingle, John Ide dental educator
Inoue, Michael Shigeru industrial engineer, electrical engineer
Isenberg, Jon Irwin gastroenterologist, educator
Ivans, William Stanley electronics company executive
Jackson, Everett Gee painter, illustrator
Jaffe, Harold writer, educator
Jensen, Michael Lee lawyer
Jeste, Dilip Vishwanath psychiatrist, researcher
Jeub, Michael Leonard financial executive
Johnson, Kenneth Owen audiologist, association executive
†Jones, Welton H., Jr. critic
Kammer, William Nolan lawyer
†Kaplan, George Willard urologist
Kaplan, Oscar Joel psychology educator
Karin, Sidney research and development executive
Kaufman, Julian Mortimer broadcasting company executive, consultant
†Kayler, Robert Samuel hospital administrator
Keep, Judith N. federal judge
Kendrick, Ronald H. banker
Kenneally, Dennis Michael government official
Kennedy, Peter Smithson personnel consultant
Kent, Theodore Charles psychologist
†Kernan, John T. education systems company executive
Klausmeier, Herbert John psychologist, educator
Klein, Herbert George newspaper editor
Kopp, Harriet Green communication specialist
Krantz, Sheldon lawyer
Krulak, Victor Harold newspaper executive
Lane, Gloria Julian foundation administrator
Lathrop, Mitchell Lee lawyer
LeBeau, Charles Paul lawyer
Lee, Jerry Carlton university administrator
Lemke, James Underwood physicist
†Lerach, William S. lawyer
†Lewis, Alan James pharmaceutical executive, pharmacologist
Linton, Roy Nathan graphic arts company executive
Litrownik, Alan Jay psychologist, educator
†Livingston, Stanley C. architect
Lomeli, Marta secondary education educator
†Lovelace, Alan Mathieson aerospace company executive
Lundin, David Erik lawyer
Lyon, Waldo Kampmeier physicist
Lyons, Earle Vaughan, Jr. minister
†Madhavan, Murugappa Chettiar economics educator, international consultant
†Madresh, Richard William bank executive
Magnuson, Harold Joseph physician
Maier, Paul Victor pharmaceutical executive
Malin, Michael Charles space scientist, former geology educator
Martin, Donald Ray chemist, educator, consultant
Martin, James John, Jr. consulting research firm executive, systems analyst
Mattingly, Thomas K. astronaut
Maurer, Lawrence Michael acting school administrator, educator
Mayer, James Hock lawyer
†McBrayer, Sandra L. educational director, homeless outreach educator
Mc Comic, Robert Barry real estate development company executive, lawyer
McGinnis, Robert E. lawyer
McGraw, Donald Jesse biologist, historian of science, writer
Mc Guigan, Frank Joseph psychologist, educator
McKee, Roger Curtis federal magistrate judge
Mc Kinnon, Clinton D. editor, former congressman
McManus, Richard Philip lawyer
Meyers, James William federal judge
Mickelson, Sig broadcasting executive, educator
Mittermiller, James Joseph lawyer
Moe, Chesney Rudolph physics educator
Moffet, Donald Pratt computer company executive
Monahan, David Emory lawyer
Monson, Forrest Truman shop owner, clergyman
Moossa, A. R. surgery educator
Morgan, Neil author, newspaper editor, lecturer, columnist
Morris, Grant Harold legal educator
Morris, Henry Madison, Jr. education educator
Morris, Richard Herbert physicist, educator
Moser, Kenneth Miles physician
Mullane, John Francis pharmaceutical company executive
Mulvaney, James Francis lawyer
Myers, Douglas George zoological society administrator
Nassif, Thomas Anthony business executive, former ambassador
Nelson, Craig Alan consultant
Netter, Irene M. secondary education educator
Noehren, Robert organist, organ builder
†Noel, Craig performing arts company executive, producer
†Norrod, James Douglas computer subsystems company executive
†Northup, T. Eugene nuclear engineer
Ohkawa, Tihiro physicist
Oliphant, Charles Romig physician
†Ollman, Arthur Lee museum director, photographer
O'Malley, Edward physician, consultant
O'Malley, James Terence lawyer
Osby, Robert Edward protective services official
Owen, Sally Ann gifted and talented education educator

Paderewski, Clarence Joseph architect
†Partida, Gilbert A. chamber of commerce executive
Pecsok, Robert Louis chemist, educator
Peters, Raymond Eugene computer systems company executive
Petersen, Martin Eugene museum curator
Peterson, Nad A. lawyer, corporate executive
Pettis, Ronald Eugene lawyer
Pfeffer, Rubin Harry publishing executive
Pfeiffer, John William publisher, management consultant
Phillips, Randall Clinger minister, university administrator
Pierson, Albert Chadwick business management educator
Pincus, Howard Jonah geologist, engineer, educator
†Pincus, Robert Lawrence art critic, cultural historian
Pray, Ralph Marble, III lawyer
Price, Robert E. manufacturing company executive
Pugh, Richard Crawford lawyer
Pulliam, Mark Stephen lawyer
Ranney, Helen Margaret physician, educator
†Ray, Gene Wells industrial executive
Rea, Amadeo Michael ethnobiologist, ornithologist
Reading, James Edward transportation executive
Reavey, William Anthony, III lawyer
Reinhard, Christopher John merchant banking company executive
Resnik, Robert medical educator
Rhoades, John Skylstead, Sr. federal judge
Rice, Clare I. electronics company executive
Riedy, Mark Joseph finance educator
Riggleman, James David professional baseball team manager
†Risser, Arthur Crane, Jr. zoo administrator
†Ristine, Jeffrey Alan reporter
Robinson, David Brooks naval officer
Roeder, Stephen Bernhard Walter chemistry and physics educator
†Rosen, Manuel Morrison architect, educator
†Rosen, Peter health facility administrator, emergency physician, educator
Ross, John, Jr. physician, educator
Rotter, Paul Talbott retired insurance executive
†Rowe, Peter A. newspaper columnist
Roy, Catherine Elizabeth physical therapist
Safa, Bahram civil engineer
†Saidman, Lawrence J. anesthesiologist
St. Clair, Hal Kay electrical engineer
St. George, William Ross lawyer, retired naval officer, consultant
Salamone, Gary P. (Pike Salamone) newspaper editor-in-chief, cartoonist
Salk, Jonas Edward physician, scientist
Sannwald, William Walter librarian
Sasaki, Tatsuo musician
Schade, Charlene Joanne adult education educator
†Scher, Valerie Jean music critic
Schmidt, Terry Lane health care executive
Schwartz, Alfred university dean
†Seau, Junior (Jr. Tiana Seau) professional football player
Sell, Robert Emerson electrical engineer
Sesonske, Alexander nuclear and chemical engineer
Shafer, Joseph Ernest economics educator emeritus, writer
Shearer, William Kennedy lawyer, publisher
Shelton, Dorothy Diehl Rees lawyer
Shneour, Elie Alexis biochemist
†Shohet, Jeffrey M. lawyer
†Silverberg, Lewis Henry business consultant
Simms, Maria Kay publishing and computer services executive
Slate, John Butler biomedical engineer
Snyder, David Richard lawyer
Spanos, Alexander Gus professional football team executive
Spanos, Dean A. business executive
Steen, Paul Joseph retired broadcasting executive
†Stepner, Michael Jay architect
Stern, Henry Louis lawyer, corporate consultant
Sterrett, James Kelley, II lawyer
Stiska, John C. lawyer
†Stoorza Gill, Gail corporate professional
Storer, Norman William sociology educator
Storms, Lowell Hanson psychologist
Sullivan, William Francis lawyer
Swoap, David Bruce children's relief administrator
Tennent, Valentine Leslie accountant
Tepedino, Francis Joseph business management company executive
Thomas, Charles Allen, Jr. molecular biologist, educator
Thompson, David Renwick federal judge
Thompson, Gordon, Jr. federal judge
Tillinghast, Charles Carpenter, III marketing company executive
Tricoles, Gus Peter electromagnetics engineer, physicist, consultant
Trout, Monroe Eugene hospital systems executive
Tuccio, Sam Anthony aerospace executive, physicist
Turrell, Eugene Snow psychiatrist
Turrentine, Howard Boyd federal judge
Vanderbilt, Kermit English language educator
Vause, Edwin Hamilton research foundation administrator
Viterbi, Andrew James electrical engineering and computer science educator, business executive
Walker, Donald Ezzell retired academic administrator
Wallace, J. Clifford federal judge
Ward-Steinman, David composer, music educator
Warner, John Hilliard, Jr. technical services, military and commercial systems and software company executive
Warren, Gerald Lee newspaper editor
Wasserman, Stephen Ira physician, educator
Weaver, Michael James lawyer
Weeks, John Robert geographer, sociology educator
Weisman, Irving social worker, educator
†Wenaas, Eric Paul electrical engineering executive
Wertheim, Robert Halley national security consultant
West, James Harold accounting company executive
White, Reggie (Reginald Howard White) professional football player
Whitmore, Sharp lawyer
Wiesler, James Ballard retired banker
Willerding, Margaret Frances mathematician
Wilson, Richard Allan landscape architect
†Winner, Karin newspaper editor
Wolff, Manfred Ernst medicinal chemist, pharmaceutical company executive
Yakan, Mohamad Zuhdi political science educator
†Yarbrough, Mary Gale hospital administrator
†Zedler, Joy Buswell ecological sciences educator
Ziegaus, Alan James public relations executive
†Zisch, William E. technical services executive

San Dimas
Cameron, Judith Lynne secondary education educator, hypnotherapist

San Fernando
Tanis, Norman Earl retired university dean, library expert

San Francisco
Abbott, Barry A. lawyer
Adams, Leon David author
Adams, Mark artist
Agabian, Nina Martha molecular biologist, biochemist, educator, parasitologist
Aird, Robert Burns neurologist, educator
Alexander, Robert C. lawyer
Allan, Walter Robert lawyer
Allemann, Sabina ballet dancer
Allen, Jose R. lawyer
Altick, Leslie L. corporate executive
Amend, William John Conrad, Jr. physician, educator
†Ammiano, Tom school system administrator
Anderson, David E. zoological park administrator
Anderson, Edward V. lawyer
Andrews, David Ralph lawyer
Ansak, Marie-Louise health care executive
Anschutz, Philip F. diversified company executive
Anthony, (Anthony Emmanuel Gergiannakis) bishop
Anthony, Elaine Margaret real estate executive, interior designer
Antipa, Gregory Alexis biology educator, researcher
Apatoff, Michael John finance executive
Arabian, Armand state supreme court justice
Archer, Richard Joseph lawyer
†Arian, David labor union official
Arieff, Allen Ives physician
†Armsby, Robert architect
Armstrong, Saundra Brown federal judge
Arnold, Kenneth James lawyer, publishing company executive
Asling, Clarence Willet anatomist, educator
Auerback, Alfred psychiatrist
†August, Katherine banker
Avery, Luther James lawyer
Bachrach, Ira Nathaniel marketing executive
Backus, John computer scientist
Bader, W. Reece lawyer
Bagdonas, Kathy Joann lawyer
Bainton, Dorothy Ford pathology educator, researcher
Baker, Cameron lawyer
Baker, Dusty (Johnnie B. Baker, Jr.) professional baseball team manager
Baker, Kenneth art critic, writer
Balin, Marty (Martyn Jerel Buchwald) musician
Bancroft, James Ramsey lawyer, business executive
†Bantock, Nick writer, illustrator
Bara, Jean Marc advertising executive
Barbagelata, Robert Dominic lawyer
Bare, Joseph Edward, Jr. retired lawyer
†Barondes, Samuel Herbert psychiatrist, educator
†Barron, Patrick Kenneth bank executive
Bashir, Naheed university administrator
Bates, John Burnham lawyer
Bates, William, III lawyer
Batlin, Robert Alfred editor
Bauch, Thomas Jay lawyer, apparel company executive
†Bauer, Michael newspaper editor
Baumhefner, Clarence Herman banker
Baxter, Marvin Ray state supreme court judge
†Baxter, Ralph H., Jr. lawyer
Beall, Dennis Ray artist, educator
Bechtel, Riley Peart engineering company executive
Bechtel, Stephen Davison, Jr. engineering company executive
Bechtle, Robert Alan artist, educator
Beck, Edward William lawyer
Beck, Rodney Roy professional baseball player
Beckmann, Jon Michael publisher
Bedford, Daniel Ross lawyer
Bedford, Lyman D. lawyer
Belli, Melvin Mouron lawyer, lecturer, writer
Benet, Leslie Zachary pharmacokineticist
Benet, Thomas Carr journalist
Bennett, James Patrick lawyer
Bennett, William oboist
Benvenutti, Peter J. lawyer
Berman, Joanna dancer
Berns, Philip Allan lawyer
Bertain, G(eorge) Joseph, Jr. lawyer
Bertelsen, Thomas Elwood, Jr. investment banker
Bibel, Debra Jan microbiologist, immunologist
Biglieri, Edward George physician
Bischof, Merriem Lanova artistic director, choreographer, educator
Bishop, John Michael biomedical research scientist, educator
Blackburn, Elizabeth Helen molecular biologist
Blackstone, George Arthur lawyer
Bloch, Julia Chang bank executive, former government official
Blomstedt, Herbert Thorson conductor, symphony director
Boles, Roger otolaryngologist
Bolin, William Harvey banker
Bonapart, Alan David lawyer
Bond, Cornelius Combs, Jr. investment advisor
Bonds, Barry Lamar professional baseball player
Bonetti, David art critic
Bonney, John Dennis oil company executive
Bookin, Daniel H. lawyer
Borne, Bonita H. ballet dancer, assistant artistic director
Borowsky, Philip lawyer
Boucher, Harold Irving lawyer
Bowers, Edgar poet, educator
Boyd, William Sprott lawyer
Boyer, Herbert Wayne biochemist
Brandel, Roland Eric lawyer
Brandin, Alf Elvin retired mining and shipping company executive
Branigan, Craig Wolfe advertising executive
Bray, Arthur Philip management science corporation executive
†Bredt, David S. neuroscience and physiology educator
Breeden, David clarinetist
Brick, Steven A. lawyer
Bridges, Robert Lysle retired lawyer
†Briebart, Jack newspaper editor
Briggs, Susan Shadinger lawyer
†Brindley, Robert E. food products executive
Bromley, Dennis Karl lawyer
Brooks, William George engineer
Broome, Burton Edward insurance company executive
Brosnahan, James Jerome lawyer
Broussard, Allen E. lawyer, former state supreme court justice
Brower, David Ross conservationist
Brown, Albert Jacob lawyer
Brown, Anthony P. lawyer
Brown, David Julian lawyer
Brown, Donald Wesley lawyer
Brown, Edmund Gerald, Jr. (Jerry Brown) former governor
†Brown, Robert L. lawyer
Browning, James Robert federal judge
Brubeck, David Warren musician
Brumbaugh, Robert Dan, Jr. economist
Bryan, Robert Russell lawyer
Buckner, John Knowles corporate executive
Budge, Hamilton Whithed lawyer
Bull, Henrik Helkand architect
Bullin, Christine Neva arts administrator
Burkett, John David professional baseball player
†Burlingame, Alma Lyman chemist, educator
Burns, Brian Patrick lawyer, business executive
†Butenhoff, Susan public relations executive
Butz, Otto William political science educator
Caen, Herb newspaper columnist, author
Cain, Leo Francis retired special education educator
Calarco, Patricia Gillam biologist, educator
Callan, Terrence A. lawyer
Calvin, Allen David psychologist, educator
Campbell, Scott Robert lawyer, former food company executive
Caniparoli, Val William choreographer, dancer
Canty, James M. lawyer
Cape, Ronald Elliot biotechnology company executive
Carlson, John Earl lawyer
Carman, John Elwin journalist
Carniglia, Stephen Davis accountant, real estate consultant, lawyer
†Carroll, Jon newspaper columnist
Carter, George Kent oil company executive
Carter, John Douglas lawyer
Cartmell, Nathaniel Madison, III lawyer
Casillas, Mark lawyer
†Castile, Rand museum administrator
†Castilla, Antonio ballet dancer
Casto, Keith Michael lawyer
Caulfield, Barbara Ann federal judge
†Chamberlain, David M. consumer products company executive
Chao, Cedric C. lawyer
Chapin, Dwight Allan columnist, writer
Cheatham, Robert William lawyer
Cheng, Wan-Lee mechanical engineer, industrial technology educator
Cherny, Robert Wallace history educator
Chesnut, Carol Fitting economist
Chiaverini, John Edward construction company executive
†Chickering, Allen Lawrence research institute executive
Chin, Sue Soone Marian (Suchin Chin) conceptual artist, portraitist, photographer, community affairs activist
Christensen, David William mathematician, engineer
Christensen, Lydell Lee telephone company executive
Chu, Kuang-Han structural engineer, educator
Cisneros, Evelyn dancer
Clanon, Thomas Lawrence hospital administrator
Clark, Edgar Sanderford insurance broker, consultant
Clark, M(ary) Margaret anthropology educator
Clarke, Richard Alan electric and gas utility company executive, lawyer
Clements, John Allen physiologist
Clever, Linda Hawes physician
Cluff, Lloyd Sterling earthquake geologist
Cobbs, Price Mashaw social psychiatrist
Coblentz, William Kraemer lawyer
Coffin, Judy Sue lawyer
Cohn, Martin advertising executive
Colbert, Lester Lum, Jr. technology products executive
Cole, Richard Charles lawyer
Coleman, Thomas Young lawyer
Collas, Juan Garduño, Jr. lawyer
Collins, Carter Compton research scientist, inventor
Collins, Dennis Arthur foundation executive
Collins, Jeremy dancer
Colwell, Kent Leigh real estate executive
Conger, Harry Milton mining company executive
Connell, William D. lawyer
Conrad, Paul Edward lawyer
Conti, Samuel federal judge
Coombe, George William, Jr. banker, lawyer
Coppola, Francis Ford film director, producer, writer
Corcoran, Maureen Elizabeth lawyer
Corrigan, Robert Anthony university president
Costello, Daniel Walter bank executive
Counelis, James Steve education educator
Cowan, Stephen A. lawyer
Cranston, Alan former senator
Cranston, Mary B. lawyer
Crawford, Roy Edgington, III lawyer
Crede, Robert Henry physician, educator
Cumming, George Anderson, Jr. lawyer
Cunningham, Arthur Francis university dean, marketing educator
Cunningham, Emmett Thomas, Jr. physician, researcher
†Curley, John Peter sports editor
Currier, Frederick Plumer market research company executive
Curry, Francis John physician
Curtis, John E., Jr. lawyer
Daggett, Robert Sherman lawyer
Dail, Joseph Garner, Jr. judge
Daniels, Alfred Harvey merchandising executive
Danoff, Eric Michael lawyer
Daugherty, Richard Bernard lawyer
David, George psychiatrist, economic theory lecturer
Davies, Paul Lewis, Jr. real estate executive
Davis, Roger Lewis lawyer
Davis, Roland Chenoweth lawyer
Dawes, Paul Harvey lawyer
†Dawson, Chandler R. ophthalmologist, educator
†Dean, Norman Emerson (Ned Dean) coffee company executive
Debas, Haile T. gastrointestinal surgeon, physiologist, educator
De Benedictis, Dario arbitrator, mediator
Delaney, Richard James investment banker
†Del Campo, Martin Bernardelli architect
Dell, Robert Michael lawyer
Dellas, Robert Dennis investment banker
De Lutis, Donald Conse investment manager, consultant
Demarest, David Franklin, Jr. banker, former government official
Derr, Kenneth T. oil company executive
Dewey, Edward Allen construction company executive
Dewey, Phelps publishing executive
deWilde, David Michael executive search consultant, financial services executive, lawyer
Dewitt, John Belton conservation executive
Diamond, Philip Ernest lawyer
Dickey, Glenn Ernest, Jr. sports columnist
Dickinson, Wade physicist, research and development company executive
Diekmann, Gilmore Frederick, Jr. lawyer
Dinkelspiel, Paul Gaines investment banking and public financial consultant
Djordjevich, Michael insurance company executive
Dodge, Peter Hampton architect
Dolby, Ray Milton engineering company executive, electrical engineer
†Donnally, Patricia Broderick newspaper fashion editor
†D'Ornellas, Robert W. food products executive
Dowlin, Kenneth Everett librarian
Doxsee, Lawrence Edward corporate lawyer
Doyle, Morris McKnight lawyer
Drayer, Cynthia dancer
Drexler, Fred insurance executive
Dryden, Robert Eugene lawyer
Du Bain, Myron diversified industry executive
Duff, James George financial services executive
Dugoni, Arthur A. orthodontics educator, university dean
Dullea, Charles W. university chancellor emeritus, priest
Dungan, Malcolm Thon lawyer
†Dunn, Richard Joseph investment counselor
Dunne, Kevin Joseph lawyer
Dupree, Stanley M. lawyer
Duscha, Julius Carl journalist
Dyer, Noel John lawyer
Eastham, Thomas foundation administrator
Eckersley, Norman Chadwick banker
Edgar, James Macmillan, Jr. management consultant
Edginton, John Arthur lawyer
†Edwards, Jack P. transportation company executive
Edwards, John Hamilton language professional
Eigner, Richard Martin lawyer
Eilenberg, Lawrence Ira theater educator, artistic director
Elderkin, E(dwin) Judge retired lawyer
Emmons, Donn architect
Enersen, Burnham lawyer
Engel, G(eorge) Larry lawyer
Engleman, Ephraim Philip physician
Epstein, Charles Joseph physician, medical geneticist, pediatrics and biochemistry educator
Epstein, John Howard dermatologist
Epstein, Leon Joseph psychiatrist
Ericson, Bruce Alan lawyer
Erskine, John Morse surgeon
Ervin, Howard Guy, III lawyer
Eschmeyer, William Neil marine scientist
Esherick, Joseph architect, educator
Estes, Carroll Lynn sociologist, educator
†Fannon, John paper company executive
Farber, Seymour Morgan physician, university administrator
Farley, Leon Alex executive search consultant
Farrell, Edward Joseph retired mathematics educator
†Feld, Michael Sperry advertising executive
Ferlinghetti, Lawrence poet
Ferris, Russell James, II freelance ghostwriter
†Festinger, Richard music educator, composer
Field, John Louis architect
†Fielder, David R. medical research administrator
Filippi, Frank Joseph lawyer
Finigan, Vincent P., Jr. lawyer
Fink, Scott Alan lawyer
Fisher, Donald G. casual apparel chain stores executive
Fisher, Robert M. foundation administrator, university administrator
Flittie, Clifford Gilliland retired petroleum company executive
Folberg, Harold Jay lawyer, mediator, educator, university dean
Foster, David Scott lawyer
Foye, Laurance Vincent physician, hospital administrator
Frantz, John Corydon librarian
Fraser, Cosmo Lyle medical educator, researcher
Fredericks, Dale E. lawyer
Freedman, Mervin Burton psychologist, educator
Freeman, Tom M. lawyer
Freund, Fredric S. real estate broker, property manager
Frick, Oscar Lionel physician, educator
Friedman, K. Bruce lawyer
Friedman, Meyer physician
Friese, Robert Charles lawyer
Fromm, Alfred distributing company executive
Fu, Karen King-Wah radiation oncologist
Fuller, Maurice DeLano, Jr. lawyer
Furst, Arthur toxicologist, educator
Furth, Frederick Paul lawyer
Gaines, Ernest J. author
Gaither, James C. lawyer
Ganong, William F(rancis) physiologist, physician
Garchik, Leah Lieberman journalist
Garoutte, Bill Charles neurophysiologist
Garvey, Joanne Marie lawyer
Gates, Milo Sedgwick construction company executive
George, Michael P. investment banker, lawyer
German, William newspaper editor
Gertler, Alfred Martin public relations executive
Gerwick, Ben Clifford, Jr. construction engineer, educator
Getty, Gordon Peter composer, philanthropist
Gill, Margaret Gaskins lawyer
Gillmar, Stanley Frank lawyer
Ginn, Sam L. telephone company executive
Ginsberg, Allen poet, photographer, musician
Glass, Laurel Ellen gerontologist, developmental biologist, physician, educator
Goldberg, Fred Sellmann advertising executive
†Goldstein, Joyce Esersky restaurant owner
Golub, Howard Victor lawyer
Gomi, Yasumasa bank executive
†Goodby, Jeffrey advertising agency executive
Gooding, Charles Arthur radiologist, physician, educator
Goodman, Joel Warren microbiologist, research scientist

Gordon, Robert Allen, Jr. *lawyer*
Gordon, Roger L. *savings and loan association executive*
Gottfried, Eugene Leslie *physician, educator*
Gowdy, Franklin Brockway *lawyer*
†Graham, Robert Arlington *newspaper entertainment editor*
Gray, Frances M. *retired college president, lecturer*
Graysmith, Robert *political cartoonist, author*
Greeley, Robert Emmett *financial analyst*
Greene, A. Crawford, Jr. *lawyer*
Greene, John Clifford *dentist, university dean*
Greenspan, Deborah *oral medicine educator*
Greenspan, Francis S. *physician*
Gregory, Michael Strietmann *English language educator*
Gresham, Zane Oliver *lawyer*
Grodsky, Gerold Morton *biochemistry educator*
†Grubb, David H. *construction company president*
Grumbach, Melvin Malcolm *physician, educator*
Guggenhime, Richard Johnson *lawyer*
Gulbenkian, Paul *inventor, conceptual civil engineer*
Gund, George, III *financier*
Gunn, Thom(son) (William) *poet*
Haas, Robert Douglas *apparel manufacturing company executive*
Haas, Walter A., Jr. *retired apparel company executive, professional baseball executive*
Haerle, Paul Raymond *lawyer*
Haire, James *theatrical producer*
Halliday, John Meech *investment company executive*
†Halsey, Milton B. *military site administrator*
Handlery, Paul Robert *hotel executive*
Hannawalt, Willis Dale *lawyer*
Hanschen, Peter Walter *lawyer*
Hardison, Donald Leigh *architect*
Hardy, David *lawyer, corporate executive*
Hargadon, Bernard Joseph, Jr. *consumer goods company executive*
Harlan, Neil Eugene *retired healthcare company executive*
†Harrington, Rex *ballet dancer*
Harris, Richard Eugene Vassau *lawyer*
Harrison, E(rnest) Frank(lin) *management educator, consultant, author, former university president and chancellor*
Harroch, Richard David *lawyer*
Hartman, John E. *lawyer*
Harvey, James Ross *finance company executive*
Hassard, Howard *lawyer*
Hasson, Kirke Michael *lawyer*
Hastings, Edward Walton *theater director*
Hatfield, Dale Charles *insurance company executive, banker*
†Hatton, Frederick L. *aircraft leasing executive*
Havel, Richard Joseph *physician, educator*
Haven, Thomas Edward *lawyer*
Hayes, Thomas Jay, III *management consultant, retired construction and engineering company executive, retired army officer*
Hazen, Paul Mandeville *banker*
Hearst, William Randolph, III *newspaper publisher*
Heaton, Jean *early childhood educator*
Heilbron, David M(ichael) *lawyer*
Heilbron, Louis Henry *lawyer*
Heller, H(einz) Robert *financial executive*
Hellman, F(rederick) Warren *investment advisor*
†Helmich, Pamela Pence *architect*
Henderson, Horace Edward *public affairs consultant, author*
Henderson, Thelton Eugene *federal judge*
Heng, Donald James, Jr. *lawyer*
Henry, Margaret Elizabeth *physician, surgeon*
Henson, Ray David *legal educator, consultant*
Herringer, Frank Casper *diversified financial services company executive*
Hershman, Lynn Lester *artist*
Herskowitz, Ira *educator, molecular geneticist*
Heyneman, Donald *parasitology educator*
Hickerson, Glenn Lindsey *leasing company executive*
High, Thomas W. *utilities company executive*
†Hill, Arthur Brian *auto insurance company executive*
Hills, Austin Edward *vineyard executive*
Hinman, Frank, Jr. *urologist, educator*
Hinman, Harvey DeForest *lawyer*
†Hitchcock, Patrick J. *investment company executive*
Hoadley, Walter Evans *economist, financial executive, lay worker*
Hobbs, Carl Fredric *artist, filmmaker, author*
Hochschild, Adam *writer, commentator, journalist*
Hoffman, Julien Ivor Ellis *pediatric cardiologist, educator*
Hofmann, John Richard, Jr. *lawyer*
Holden, Frederick Douglass, Jr. *lawyer*
Holland, Tom *artist, educator*
†Holtman, William J. *railroad company executive*
Homer, Barry Wayne *lawyer*
†Homsey, George W. *architectural firm executive*
Honig, Bill *state educational administrator*
Hooker, John Lee *singer, guitarist*
†Hooper, Roger Fellowes *architect*
Hoppe, Arthur Watterson *columnist*
Horne, Grant Nelson *corporate communications specialist*
Hotchkiss, Ralf David *engineer, educator*
†House, Steven Lindsay *architect, graphic designer*
Howard, Carl (Michael) *lawyer*
Howard, David E. *artist*
†Howley, Peter A. *communications executive*
Hoyem, Andrew Lewison *publisher*
Huddleson, Edwin Emmet, Jr. *lawyer*
Hudner, Philip *lawyer, rancher*
Hull, Cordell William *business executive*
Humenesky, Gregory *personnel and labor relations executive*
Hunter, William Dennis *lawyer*
Hurlbert, Roger William *information service industry executive*
Hurley, Mark Joseph *bishop*
Hyde, Stuart Wallace *educator, author*
†Iacono, James Michael *research center administrator*
Ikagawa, Tadaichi *banking executive*
Irwin, William Rankin *lawyer*
Jacobs, Edwin Max *oncologist, consultant*
Jacobs, John Howard *association executive*
Jacobs, Joseph Donovan *engineering firm executive*
†Jaeger, Joseph C. *insurance company executive*
†Jaffe, Robert Benton *obstetrician-gynecologist, reproductive endocrinologist*
James, George Barker, II *apparel industry executive*
Jarvis, Donald Bertram *judge*
Jenkins, Bruce *sportswriter*
Jensen, D. Lowell *federal judge, lawyer, government official*
Jewett, George Frederick, Jr. *forest products company executive*
Johnson, Herman Leonall *research nutritionist*
Johnson, Martin Wayne *lawyer*
Johnson, Reverdy *lawyer*
†Johnstone, R. C., Jr. *engineering company executive*
Jones, Pirkle *photographer, educator*
†Jordan, Frank M. *mayor*
Joseph, Allan Jay *lawyer*
†Judd, Bruce Diven *architect*
Judson, Philip Livingston *lawyer*
Jundis, Orvy Lagasca *writer, consultant*
Jurdana, Ernest J. *banker, accountant*
Kaapcke, Wallace Letcher *lawyer*
Kahn, Alice Joyce *columnist*
Kahn, Paul Markham *actuary*
Kallgren, Edward Eugene *lawyer*
Kalt, Howard Michael *public relations executive*
Kan, Yuet Wai *physician, investigator*
Kantner, Paul *musician*
Kaplan, Alvin Irving *lawyer, adjudicator, investigator*
Kasanin, Mark Owen *lawyer*
Katz, Hilliard Joel *physician*
Katz, Ronald Stanley *lawyer*
Kaufman, Christopher Lee *lawyer*
†Kavanaugh, Robert *lawyer*
Keesling, Francis Valentine, Jr. *management consultant*
Keller, Edward Lowell *electrical engineer, educator*
Keller, George Matthew *retired oil company executive*
Kelly, Thomas Brooke *accounting and consulting firm executive*
Kemp, Alson Remington, Jr. *lawyer, legal educator*
Kennard, Joyce F. *judge*
Kenny, David Culber *lawyer*
Kern, John McDougall *lawyer*
Khosla, Ved Mitter *oral and maxillofacial surgeon, educator*
Kilgore, Eugene Sterling, Jr. *surgeon*
†Kilpatrick, Rod *advertising executive*
Kingsley, Leonard Edward *financial services executive*
Kirkham, Francis Robison *lawyer*
Kirkham, James Francis *lawyer*
Klafter, Cary Ira *lawyer*
Klammer, Joseph Francis *management consultant*
Kleeman, Michael Jeffrey *telecommunications and computer consultant*
Kleinberg, David Lewis *education administrator*
Kline, John Anthony *state court justice*
Klinger, Marilyn Sydney *lawyer*
Klott, David Lee *lawyer*
Knebel, Jack Gillen *lawyer*
Kobayashi, Tom Toru *motion picture company executive*
Kobler, Raymond *concertmaster*
Koeppel, John A. *lawyer*
Kolb, Theodore Alexander *lawyer*
Korins, Leopold *stock exchange executive*
Kozloff, Lloyd M. *university dean, educator, scientist*
Krause, Lawrence Allen *financial adviser, financial planner*
Krebs, Ernst Theodor, Jr. *biochemist*
Kreitzberg, Fred Charles *construction management company executive*
Krevans, Julius Richard *university administrator, physician*
Kriken, John Lund *architect*
Krippner, Stanley Curtis *psychologist*
Kuhl, Paul Beach *lawyer*
Kuhns, Craig Shaffer *business educator*
Kuzell, William Charles *physician, instrument company executive*
Kvitash, Vadim I(ssay) *physician, scientist, inventor*
Ladar, Jerrold Morton *lawyer*
Ladd, John Curran *lawyer*
LaFollette, Charles Sanborn *business consultant*
Lai, Him Mark *writer*
Lamberson, John Roger *insurance company executive*
Landahl, Herbert Daniel *biophysicist, mathematical biologist, researcher, consultant*
Lane, Fielding H. *lawyer*
Lane, John Rodger *art museum director*
†Lara, Adair *columnist, writer*
Larson, John William *lawyer*
Lasky, Moses *lawyer*
Latcham, Franklin Chester *lawyer*
Latzer, Richard Neal *investment company executive*
Lautz, Lindsay Allan *executive search consultant*
LaVail, Jennifer Hart *neurobiologist, educator, researcher*
LeBlanc, Tina *dancer*
Lee, Brant Thomas *lawyer, federal official*
Lee, John Jin *lawyer*
†Legate, Stephen *ballet dancer*
Legge, Charles Alexander *federal judge*
Leonard, George Jay *author*
Levi, Julian Hirsch *lawyer, educator*
Levin, Alan Scott *pathologist, allergist, immunologist*
Levine, Norman Gene *insurance company executive*
Levit, Victor Bert *lawyer, foreign representative, civic worker*
Leviton, Alan Edward *museum curator*
Libbin, Anne Edna *lawyer*
Lilly, Shannon Jeanne *dancer*
Lim, Robert Cheong, Jr. *surgeon, educator*
Lin, Tung Yen *civil engineer, educator*
Lindh, Patricia Sullivan *banker, former government official*
Lindsay, George Edmund *museum director*
Lipton, Alvin E(lliot) *lawyer*
Littlefield, Edmund Wattis *mining company executive*
Livsey, Robert Callister *lawyer*
Lobdell, Frank *artist*
Lockhart, James Blakely *public affairs executive*
Loke, Kit Choy *lawyer*
London, Barry Joseph *lawyer*
Lonnquist, George Eric *lawyer*
Lo Schiavo, John Joseph *university executive*
Lotito, Michael Joseph *lawyer*
Lucas, Malcolm Millar *state supreme court chief justice*
Luckow, Lynn D. W. *publishing executive*
†Lufkin, Liz *newspaper editor*
Luft, Harold S. *health economist*
Luft, Rene Wilfred *civil engineer*
Lynch, Eugene F. *federal judge*
Lynch, Timothy Jeremiah-Mahoney *lawyer, consultant, theologian, law educator*
Lyon, David William *research executive*
MacDonald, Donald William *architect*
Mac Gowan, Mary Eugenia *lawyer*
Mach, David *artist*
†MacLeamy, Patrick *architectural firm executive*
Maddux, Parker Ahrens *lawyer*
Madison, James Raymond *lawyer*
Maffre, Muriel *ballet dancer*
Magowan, Peter Alden *professional baseball team executive, grocery chain executive*
Maibach, Howard I. *dermatologist*
Malson, Rex Richard *drug and health care corporation executive*
Malveaux, Julianne Marie *economist, writer*
Mandra, York T. *geology educator*
Maneatis, George A. *retired utility company executive*
Mann, Bruce Alan *lawyer*
Marchant, David J. *lawyer*
Marciano, Richard Alfred *research institute executive*
Marcus, Robert *aluminum company executive*
Margulis, Alexander Rafailo *physician, educator*
†Marks, Milton *state senator*
Marquis, Robert B. *architect*
Marston, Michael *urban economist, asset management executive*
Martin, Fred *artist, college administrator*
Martin, Joseph, Jr. *lawyer, former ambassador*
Martin, Joseph Boyd *neurologist, educator*
Martin, Stephen James *lawyer*
Martinson, Ida Marie *nurse, physiologist, educator*
Marvin, David Keith *international relations educator*
Mason, Dean Towle *cardiologist*
†Mathes, Stephen John *plastic and reconstructive surgeon, educator*
Mathiason, Garry George *lawyer*
Mattes, Martin Anthony *lawyer*
Maupin, Armistead Jones, Jr. *writer*
Mayer, Patricia Jayne *financial officer, management accountant*
Mays, Willie Howard, Jr. *former professional baseball player*
McAniff, Edward John *lawyer*
McCandless, Sandra Ravich *lawyer*
†McCarthy, Clement Daniel *advertising executive*
McClintock, Jessica *fashion designer*
McCorkle, Horace Jackson *physician, educator*
Mc Covey, Willie Lee *former professional baseball player*
McCrea, Peter *oil company executive*
†McDowell, David E. *pharmaceutical executive*
†McElhinny, Harold John *lawyer*
McGee, Willie *professional baseball player*
McGettigan, Charles Carroll, Jr. *investment banker*
McKee, William David *lawyer*
McKelvey, Judith Grant *lawyer, educator, university dean*
McKnight, Steven Lanier *molecular biologist*
†Mc Laughlin, Herbert E. *architect*
Mc Laughlin, Jerome Michael *lawyer, shipping company executive*
McLeod, Robert Macfarlan *lawyer, arbitrator*
McLin, Stephen T. *investment banker*
Mc Mahan, John William *real estate investment advisor*
McNally, Thomas Charles, III *lawyer*
McNamara, John Stephen *artist, educator*
McNamara, Thomas Neal *lawyer*
McQuaid, J. Dennis *lawyer*
Medwadowski, Stefan J. *consulting engineering executive, educator*
Meleis, Afaf Ibrahim *nurse sociologist, educator, clinician*
Mellor, Michael Lawton *lawyer*
Merrill, Charles Merton *federal judge*
Merrill, Harvie Martin *manufacturing executive*
Merritt, James Edward *lawyer*
Metzler, Roger James, Jr. *lawyer*
Meyer, Donald Robert *banker, lawyer*
Meyer, Thomas James *editorial cartoonist*
Mielke, Frederick William, Jr. *retired utility company executive*
Mihan, Ralph George *lawyer*
Mikuriya, Mary Jane *educational agency administrator*
†Miller, Allen Blair *public relations executive*
Miller, James Lynn *lawyer*
Miller, Paul James *coffee company executive*
†Miller, Walter Luther *scientist, physician, educator*
Miller, William Napier Cripps *lawyer*
Minnick, Malcolm David *lawyer*
Mitchell, Bruce Tyson *lawyer*
Mohan, D. Mike *transportation company executive*
Monson, Arch, Jr. *fire alarm manufacturing company executive*
Montali, Dennis *federal judge*
†Moore, Gary Heath *lawyer*
†Moris, Lamberto Giuliano *architect*
Morrin, Thomas Harvey *engineering research company executive*
Morrissey, John Carroll *lawyer*
Mosk, Stanley *state supreme court justice*
†Mostov, Keith Elliot *cell biologist, educator*
†Mulholland, Charles Bradley *transportation company executive*
†Mullenix, Travis H. *food products company executive*
Mumford, Christopher Greene *corporate financial executive*
Mundell, David Edward *leasing company executive*
Murray, Glenn Richard, Jr. *lawyer*
Murray, John Frederic *physician, educator*
Murrin, Thomas Edward *insurance company executive*
Musfelt, Duane Clark *lawyer*
Mustacchi, Piero *physician, educator*
Myers, Howard Milton *pharmacologist, educator*
Nachman, Gerald Weil *columnist, critic, author*
Naegele, Carl Joseph *university academic administrator, educator*
†Nafziger, Dean H. *special education research executive*
Needleman, Jacob *philosophy educator, writer*
†Neerhout, John, Jr. *petroleum company executive*
Nelson, David Edward *lawyer*
Nemir, Donald Philip *lawyer*
Neri, Manuel *artist, educator*
Nichols, Robert Edmund *editor, writer, journalist*
Niehans, Daniel J. *lawyer*
Noonan, John T., Jr. *federal judge, legal educator*
Noonan, William Moss *information systems executive, consultant*
Nord, Paul Elliott *accountant*
O'Connor, G(eorge) Richard *ophthalmologist*
†Odgers, Richard William *lawyer*
Offer, Stuart Jay *lawyer*
O'Flaherty, Terrence *journalist*
Oliveira, Nathan *artist, educator*
Olsen, Tillie *author*
Olson, Walter Gilbert *lawyer*
Orrick, William Horsley, Jr. *federal judge*
Osterhaus, William Eric *television executive*
†Ostler, Scott *newspaper sports columnist*
Otto, George John *investment banker*
Painter, Michael Robert *landscape architect, urban designer*
Palmer, William Joseph *accountant*
Parker, Harry S., III *art museum administrator*
Parry, Robert Troutt *bank executive, economist*
Pasahow, Lynn H(arold) *lawyer*
Pastreich, Peter *orchestra executive director*
Patel, Marilyn Hall *federal judge*
Patterson, Richard North *writer, lawyer*
Peirano, Lawrence Edward *civil engineer*
Pemberton, John de Jarnette, Jr. *lawyer, educator*
Penskar, Mark Howard *lawyer*
†Peppercorn, John Edward *chemical company executive*
Perkins, Herbert Asa *physician*
Perlman, David *science editor, journalist*
Peters, Raymond Robert *bank executive*
Peterson, Harries-Clichy *financial consultant*
Peterson, Richard Hamlin *utility executive, lawyer*
Peterson, Rudolph A. *banker*
Peterson, Wayne Turner *composer, pianist*
Petrakis, Nicholas Louis *physician, medical researcher, educator*
Pfau, George Harold, Jr. *stockbroker*
Phibbs, Roderic Henry *medical educator, pediatrician*
†Phillips, Sandra Sammataro *curator, educator*
Phillips, Theodore Locke *radiation oncologist, educator*
†Pickett, Donn Philip *lawyer*
Piel, Carolyn Forman *pediatrician, educator*
Pincus, Joseph *economist, educator*
Placier, Philip R. *lawyer*
Platt, Peter Godfrey *lawyer*
Plishner, Michael Jon *lawyer*
Poole, Cecil F. *federal judge*
Poole, Gordon Leicester *lawyer*
Popofsky, Melvin Laurence *lawyer*
Posin, Daniel Q. *physics educator, television lecturer*
Pottruck, David S. *brokerage house executive*
Powell, Sandra Theresa *timber company executive*
Preovolos, Penelope Athene *lawyer*
Pringle, Robert Bernard *lawyer*
Quiban, Estelita Cabrera *controller*
Quigley, Philip J. *telecommunications industry executive*
Quinn, John R. *archbishop*
Raciti, Cherie *artist*
†Raeber, John Arthur *architect, construction specifier consultant*
Ragan, Charles Ransom *lawyer*
Ralston, Henry James, III *neurobiologist, anatomist, educator*
Ramsey, Robert Lee *judge, lawyer*
Ransom, Edward Duane *lawyer*
Ratner, David Louis *legal educator*
Ratzlaff, James W. *investment company executive*
Rautenberg, Robert Frank *consulting statistician*
Raven, Robert Dunbar *lawyer*
Read, Gregory Charles *lawyer*
†Readmond, Ronald Warren *investment banking firm executive*
†Ream, James Terrill *architect, sculptor*
Rector, Floyd Clinton, Jr. *physiologist, physician*
Redo, David Lucien *investment company executive*
Reese, John Robert *lawyer*
Reichardt, Carl E. *banker*
Rembe, Toni *lawyer*
†Renfrew, Charles Byron *oil company executive, lawyer*
†Reynoso, Cruz *judge*
Rice, Denis Timlin *lawyer*
Rice, Dorothy Pechman (Mrs. John Donald Rice) *medical economist*
Rice, Jonathan C. *educational television executive*
Richards, Norman Blanchard *lawyer*
Riney, Hal Patrick *advertising executive*
†Rippel, Clarence W. *academic administrator*
Risse, Guenter Bernhard *physician, historian, educator*
Roberts, Gerald Jeffrey *newspaper editor, journalist*
†Roberts, Jerry *newspaper editor*
Robertson, Armand James, II *lawyer*
Robertson, David Govan *lawyer*
Robinson, Jerry H. *lawyer*
Rockrise, George Thomas *architect*
Rockwell, Alvin John *lawyer*
Rockwell, Burton Lowe *architect*
Roe, Benson Bertheau *surgeon, educator*
Roethe, James Norton *lawyer*
Rosch, John Thomas *lawyer*
Rosen, Moishe *religious organization administrator*
Rosen, Sanford Jay *lawyer*
Rosenberg, Claude Newman, Jr. *investment adviser*
Rosenberg, Richard Morris *banker*
†Rosenheim, Daniel Edward *journalist, newspaper editor*
†Rosenthal, Herbert Marshall *legal association executive*
Rosenthal, James D. *former ambassador, government and foundation executive*
Rosinski, Edwin Francis *health sciences educator*
Rosston, Edward William *lawyer*
Rowland, John Arthur *lawyer*
Rubenstein, Steven Paul *newspaper columnist*
Rudolph, Abraham Morris *physician, educator*
Runnicles, Donald *conductor*
Rusher, William Allen *writer, commentator*
Ryan, Joan *sportswriter*
Ryan, Randel Edward, Jr. *airline captain*
Ryland, David Ronald *lawyer*
Sachs, Marilyn Stickle *author, lecturer, editor*
Salomon, Darrell Joseph *lawyer*
Sanders, Charles Franklin *corporate executive*
Sanger, John Morton *lawyer, urban planner*
Santana, Carlos *guitarist*
Saras, James J. *agricultural products, grain company executive*
Satin, Joseph *language professional, university administrator*
†Saunders, Debra J. *columnist*
Saunders, Raymond Jennings *artist, educator*
Saunders, Sally Love *poet, educator*
Sax, Joseph Lawrence *lawyer, educator*
Sayre, George Edward *retired lawyer*
Scarff, Edward L. *diversified company executive*
Schachter, Julius *epidemiology educator*
Schiller, Francis *neurologist, medical historian*
Schlegel, John Peter *university president*
Schlesinger, Rudolf Berthold *lawyer, educator*
Schmid, Rudi (Rudolf Schmid) *physician, educator, academic administrator, researcher*
Schmidt, Chauncey Everett *banker*
Schmidt, Robert Milton *physician, scientist, educator*
Schmitt, George Herbert *hospital executive*
Schnacke, Robert Howard *judge*
Scholten, Paul *obstetrician-gynecologist, educator*

†Schultz, Dean M. *finance company executive*
Schwartz, Louis Brown *legal educator*
Schwarz, Glenn Vernon *editor*
Sears, George Ames *lawyer*
Seegal, John Franklin *lawyer*
Seelenfreund, Alan *distribution company executive*
†Seip, Tom Decker *securities executive*
Selman, Roland Wooten, III *lawyer*
Selover, William Charlton *corporate communications and governmental affairs executive*
Sevier, Ernest Youle *lawyer*
Shackelford, Barton Warren *retired utility executive*
Shangraw, Clarence Frank *museum official*
Shansby, John Gary *investment banker*
Shapiro, Howard Allan *gastroenterologist, medical educator*
†Shapiro, Larry Jay *pediatrician, scientist, educator*
Sheinfeld, David *composer*
Shelton, Richard Fottrell *investment executive*
Shenk, George H. *lawyer*
Shiffer, James David *utility executive*
Shimizu, Taisuke *bank executive*
Shinefield, Henry Robert *pediatrician*
Shirpser, Clara *former Democratic national committeewoman*
Shohet, Stephen Byron *medical educator*
Shor, Samuel Wendell Williston *naval engineer*
Shorenstein, Walter Herbert *commercial real estate development company executive*
Shulgasser, Barbara *writer*
Shumate, Charles Albert *retired dermatologist*
Shumway, Norman D. *former congressman*
Sias, John B. *multi-media company executive*
Siegel, Louis Pendleton *forest products executive*
†Simmons, Raymond Hedelius, Jr. *lawyer*
Simon, Cathy Jensen *architect*
Simone, Thomas B. *distribution company executive*
Singer, Allen Morris *lawyer*
†Sinton, Peter *newspaper editor*
Skinner, Harry Bryant *orthopaedic surgery educator*
Skinner, Stanley Thayer *utility company executive, lawyer*
Small, Marshall Lee *lawyer*
Smegal, Thomas Frank, Jr. *lawyer*
Smith, David Elvin *physician*
Smith, Gregory Allan *lawyer*
Smith, Kerry Clark *lawyer*
†Snedaker, Dianne *advertising agency executive*
Sneed, Joseph Tyree, III *federal judge*
Snow, Tower Charles, Jr. *lawyer*
Sokolow, Maurice *physician, educator*
Sowder, Robert Robertson *architect*
Spander, Art *sportswriter*
Sparer, Malcolm Martin *rabbi*
Sparks, John Edward *lawyer*
Sparks, Thomas E., Jr. *lawyer*
Spiegel, Hart Hunter *retired lawyer*
Sproul, John Allan *retired public utility executive*
Staring, Graydon Shaw *lawyer*
Stauffer, Thomas Michael *educational administrator*
Steer, Reginald David *lawyer*
Steinberg, Michael *music critic, educator*
Stermer, Dugald Robert *designer, illustrator, writer, consultant*
Stetler, Russell Dearnley, Jr. *private investigator*
Stewart, Samuel B. *banker, lawyer*
Stone, Michael P. W. *former federal official*
Stotter, Lawrence Henry *lawyer*
Stout, Gregory Stansbury *lawyer*
Stowell, Christopher R. *dancer*
Stratton, Richard James *lawyer*
Strawberry, Darryl *professional baseball player*
Stupski, Lawrence J. *investment company executive*
Sturdivant, Frederick David *consultant, business educator*
Sugarman, Myron George *lawyer*
Sugarman, Paul William *lawyer*
Sullivan, James N. *fuel company executive*
Sullivan, Robert Edward *lawyer*
Susa, Conrad *composer*
Susskind, Teresa Gabriel *publisher*
Sutcliffe, Eric *lawyer*
Sutton, John Paul *lawyer*
Swift, William Charles *professional baseball player, olympic athlete*
Swing, William Edwin *bishop*
Szabo, Zoltan *medical science educator, medical institute administrator*
†Taggart, Paulett Long *architect, educator*
Taylor, Glenhall E. *banker*
Taylor, John Lockhart *city official*
Taylor, Robert P. *lawyer*
Taylor, William James (Zak Taylor) *lawyer*
†Terr, Lenore Cagen *psychiatrist, writer*
†Thacher, Carter Pomeroy *diversified manufacturing company executive*
Thelen, Max, Jr. *foundation executive, lawyer*
Thieriot, Richard Tobin *publisher*
†Thistlethwaite, David Richard *architect*
Thomas, William Scott *lawyer*
†Thompson, Gary W. *public relations executive*
Thompson, Robert Charles *lawyer*
Thompson, Robert Randall (Robby Thompson) *professional baseball player*
Thornton, D. Whitney, II *lawyer*
Thornton, James Ivan, Jr. *financial executive*
†Tidball, Robert Nial *financial executive*
Tiffany, Joseph Raymond, II *lawyer*
Tingle, James O'Malley *lawyer*
Tobin, James Michael *lawyer*
Tobkin, Christine Anderson *investment banker*
Tomasson, Helgi *dancer, choreographer, dance company executive*
Trautman, William Ellsworth *lawyer*
Traynor, J. Michael *lawyer*
Trowbridge, Thomas, Jr. *mortgage banking company executive*
Tulsky, Fredric Neal *journalist*
Turnbull, William, Jr. *architect*
Turner, Marshall Chittenden, Jr. *venture capitalist*
†Turpen, Louis A. *airport terminal executive*
Tusher, Thomas William *apparel company executive*
Underwood, Patricia Ruth *clinical nursing educator, consultant*
Uri, George Wolfsohn *accountant*
†Vale, Ronald D. *biochemist, educator*
Valentine, William Edson *architect*
Van Dyck, Wendy *dancer*
Van Hoesen, Beth Marie *artist, printmaker*
Vazsonyi, Andrew *computer and management scientist*
Veitch, Stephen William *investment counselor*
Veith, Ilza *retired psychiatric history educator*
Venning, Robert Stanley *lawyer*
Volkmann, Daniel George, Jr. *architect*
Volpe, Peter Anthony *surgeon*
Vyas, Girish Narmadashankar *virologist, immunohematologist*
†Waldo, Katita *ballet dancer*
Walker, Ralph Clifford *lawyer*
Walker, Vaughn R. *federal judge*
Walkup, Bruce *lawyer*
Wallace, Arthur, Jr. *college dean*
Wallerstein, Ralph Oliver *physician*
Walsh, James Joseph *lawyer*
†Walther, Roger O. *international education estate executive*
Wang, William Kai-Sheng *legal educator*
†Ward, William T. *insurance company executive*
Warmer, Richard Craig *lawyer*
Warner, Harold Clay, Jr. *banker, investment management executive*
Watts, Malcolm S(tuart) M(cNeal) *physician, medical educator*
Way, E(dward) Leong *pharmacologist, toxicologist, educator*
†Webb, J. A. *insurance company executive*
Weihrich, Heinz *management educator*
Welborn, Caryl Bartelman *lawyer*
Welch, Thomas Andrew *lawyer*
Werson, James Byrd *lawyer*
Westberg, Robert Myers *lawyer*
Westerdahl, John Brian *nutritionist, health educator*
Westerfield, Putney *management consulting executive*
Wetzel, Cherie Lalaine Rivers *biologist*
Whalen, Philip Glenn *poet, novelist*
Whelan, John William *lawyer, educator, consultant*
Whitaker, Clem, Jr. *advertising and public relations executive*
†White, Rene *public relations executive*
Whitney, David Clay *business educator, consultant, writer*
Widman, Gary Lee *lawyer, former government official*
Wilbur, Brayton, Jr. *distribution company executive*
Wilcox, Collin M. *author*
Wilczek, John Franklin *history educator*
Wild, Nelson Hopkins *lawyer*
Wiley, Thomas Glen *retired investment company executive*
Wiley, William T. *artist*
†Wilken, Claudia Ann *judge*
Williams, Matt (Matthew Derrick Williams) *baseball player*
Williams, Morgan Lloyd *retired investment banker*
Willner, Jay R. *consulting company executive*
Willson, Prentiss, Jr. *lawyer*
Wilner, Paul Andrew *journalist*
†Wilson, Charles B. *neurosurgeon, educator*
Wilson, Ian Robert *food company executive*
Wilson, John Oliver *economist, educator, banker*
Wilson, Matthew Frederick *newspaper editor*
†Winn, Steven Jay *critic*
Wintroub, Bruce Urich *dermatologist, educator, researcher*
Wolcott, Oliver Dwight *international trading company executive*
Wolfe, Cameron Withgot, Jr. *lawyer*
Wolff, Sheldon *radiobiologist, educator*
Wood, Donald Frank *transportation educator, consultant*
Wood, George H. *investment executive*
Woodard, Clarence James *manufacturing company executive*
†Woodberry, Paul Francis *real estate executive*
Woods, James Robert *lawyer*
Woolsey, David Arthur *leasing company executive*
Wright, Rosalie Muller *newspaper and magazine editor*
Wyle, Frederick S. *lawyer*
Yamakawa, David Kiyoshi, Jr. *lawyer*
Yamaoka, Seigen Haruo *bishop*
Yost, Nicholas Churchill *lawyer*
Young, Bryant Llewellyn *lawyer, business executive*
†Yu, Eleanor Ngan-Ling *advertising company executive*
Yuan, Shao Wen *aerospace engineer, educator*
†Zaccaria, Adrian *utilities executive*
Zellerbach, William Joseph *retired paper company executive*
†Zhukov, Yuri *ballet dancer*
Ziering, William Mark *lawyer*
Zimmerman, Bernard *lawyer*
Zippin, Calvin *epidemiologist*

San Gabriel
Oestmann, Irma Emma *minister, artist, educator*

San Jose
Aguilar, Robert P. *federal judge*
†Alquist, Alfred E. *state senator*
Belluomini, Frank Stephen *accountant*
Bennett, Charles Turner *social welfare administrator*
Bentel, Dwight *emeritus journalism educator*
Beverett, Andrew Jackson *marketing executive*
†Bolger, Brenna Mercier *public relations executive*
Brewer, Richard George *physicist*
†Callan, Josi Irene *museum director*
Carey, Peter Kevin *reporter*
Ceppos, Jerome Merle *newspaper editor*
†Chen, John S. *computer company executive*
†Chen, Wen H. *engineering executive, educator*
†Chuang, Tung Jung *chemist*
†Coburn, John Wyllie *physicist, researcher*
†Collett, Jennie *principal*
Conner, Finis F. *electronics company executive*
†Cruz, B. Robert *academic administrator*
Dalis, Irene *mezzo-soprano, opera company administrator, music educator*
Dean, Burton Victor *management educator*
Dougherty, John James *computer software company executive, consultant*
Elder, Robert Laurie *newspaper editor*
Estabrook, Reed *artist, educator*
†Evans, James Handel *university president, architect, educator*
Faggin, Federico *electronics executive*
Finnigan, Robert Emmet *business owner*
Fish, James Henry *library director*
Forster, Julian *physicist, consultant*
Fowler, John Wellington *lawyer*
†Frauenfelder, Lewis *electronics executive*
Frymer, Murry *columnist, theater critic, critic-at-large*
†Gonzales, Ron *city mayor*
Granneman, Vernon Henry *lawyer*
Greenstein, Martin Richard *lawyer*
Gregory, Cynthia Kathleen *ballerina*
Grubb, William Francis X. *consumer software executive, marketing executive*
Gruber, John Balsbaugh *physics educator, university administrator*
Hall, Robert Emmett, Jr. *investment banker, realtor*
Halverson, George Clarence *business administration educator*
Hammer, Susan W. *mayor*
Hanley, Peter Ronald *corporate executive, engineer, physicist*
Harkins, Craig *management consultant*
Healey, James Stewart *library science educator*
Heiman, Frederic Paul *electronics company executive*
†Herman, Frank *research physicist*
†Hootnick, Laurence R. *electronics company executive*
Houle, Frances Anne *physical chemist*
Huang, Francis Fu-Tse *mechanical engineering educator*
Ingle, Robert D. *newspaper editor*
Ingram, William Austin *federal judge*
Johnson, Allen Halbert *surgeon*
Jordan, Thomas Vincent *advertising educator, consultant*
Kasson, James Matthews *electronics executive*
†Kramer, Richard Jay *gastroenterologist*
†Lash, Steven M. *hospital administrator*
†Lee, Sung W. *electronics executive*
Lippe, Philipp Maria *neurosurgeon, educator*
†Lovell, Glenn Michael *film critic*
Luft, Robert S. *lawyer*
McCarthy, Mary Ann Bartley *electrical engineer*
Mc Connell, John Douglas *retail corporation executive, owner*
McCoy, James M. *data processing, computer company executive*
McDowell, Jennifer *sociologist, composer, playwright, publisher*
†McGuire, Thomas Roger *distribution company executive*
Melendy, Howard Brett *historian, educator*
†Migielicz, Geralyn *photojournalist*
Mitchell, David T. *electronic computing equipment company executive*
Mitchell, David Walker *lawyer*
Montgomery, Leslie David *biomedical engineer, cardiovascular physiologist*
Moody, Frederick Jerome *mechanical engineer, consultant thermal hydraulics*
†Morgan, Rebecca Quinn *business executive*
Morgan, William Robert *lawyer*
Morimoto, Carl Noboru *computer system engineer, crystallographer*
Neptune, John Addison *chemistry educator, consultant*
†Nogawa, Kiyoshi *computer company executive*
Okerlund, Arlene Naylor *university official*
Okita, George T. *pharmacologist educator*
Pausa, Clements Edward *electronics company executive*
Pellegrini, Robert J. *psychology educator*
†Pellionisz, Andras Jeno *neurocomputer scientist*
†Rabolt, John Francis *optics scientist*
†Rha, Y. B. *electronics executive*
Ritzheimer, Robert Alan *educational publishing executive*
Rosendin, Raymond Joseph *electrical contracting company executive*
Rosenheim, Donald Edwin *electrical engineer*
Rothblatt, Donald Noah *urban and regional planner, educator*
Savage, Arthur L. *professional hockey team executive*
Schmidt, Cyril James *librarian*
Schofield, John Trevor *environmental management company executive*
Schroeder, William John *electronics executive*
Scifres, Don R. *semiconductor laser, fiber optics and electronics company executive*
Scott, Edward William, Jr. *computer company executive*
Smirni, Allan Desmond *lawyer*
†Soro, Mar Bawai *bishop*
Stacy, Richard A. *prosecutor*
Steele, Shelby *writer, educator*
Stockton, Anderson Berrian *electronics company executive, consultant, genealogist*
†Sumrall, Harry *journalist*
†Sweeny, Mary Ellen *public relations and advertising executive*
†Tanaka, Richard Koichi, Jr. *architect, planner*
Trombley, William Holden *journalist*
†Trounstine, Philip J. *editor, journalist*
Valentine, Ralph Schuyler *chemical engineer, research director*
†Vasconcellos, John *state legislator*
Ware, James W. *federal judge*
Whyte, Ronald M. *federal judge*
†Wilkins, Daniel R. *nuclear engineer, nuclear energy industry executive*
Williams, Spencer M. *federal judge*
†Winters, Harold Franklin *physicist*
Yoshizumi, Donald Tetsuro *dentist*

San Juan Capistrano
Braunstein, Herbert *pathologist, educator*
Dergarabedian, Paul *energy and environmental company executive*
Fisher, Delbert Arthur *physician, educator*
Horn, Deborah Sue *organization administrator, writer, editor*
†Huta, Henry Nicholaus *manufacturing and service company executive*
Purdy, Alan MacGregor *financial executive*
Robinson, Daniel Thomas *brokerage company executive*

San Leandro
Earle, Sylvia Alice *research biologist, oceanographer*
Leighton, Joseph *pathologist*
Odron, Edward Andrew *supermarket executive*
Pansky, Emil John *entrepreneur*
Stallings, Charles Henry *physicist*

San Lorenzo
†Glenn, Jerome T. *secondary school principal*
Lantz, Charles Alan *chiropractor, researcher*
Morrison, Martin Earl *computer systems analyst*

San Luis Obispo
Bailey, Philip Sigmon, Jr. *academic dean, chemistry educator*
Baker, Warren J(oseph) *university president*
Blattner, Ernest Willi *mechanical engineering educator*
Brown, Howard C. *horticulture educator, consultant*
Daly, John Paul *lawyer*
Deasy, Cornelius Michael *architect*
Dickerson, Colleen Bernice Patton *artist, educator*
Ericson, Jon Meyer *academic administrator, rhetoric theory educator*
†Fraser, Bruce Douglas, Jr. *architect, artist*
Grismore, Roger *physics educator, researcher*
Hasslein, George Johann *architectural engineering educator*
Holder, Elaine Edith *psychologist, educator*
Keil, David J. *biology educator, botanical consultant*
McCorkle, Robert Ellsworth *agribusiness educator*
Mc Donald, Henry Stanton *electrical engineer*
Moazzami, Sara *civil engineering educator*
Rodman, Harry Eugene *architect, educator, acoustical and illumination consultant*
†Selvaggio, John N. *airline executive*
Stream, Jay Wilson *financial consultant*
†Walch, David Bean *librarian, university official*
†Wentz, Janet *principal*

San Marcos
Barnes, Howard G. *film company executive, film and video producer*
Ciurczak, Alexis *librarian*
Knight, Edward Howden *retired hospital administrator*
†Lee, John Francis *retired international management consulting company executive, author*
Liggins, George Lawson *microbiologist-diagnostic company executive*
Lilly, Martin Stephen *university dean*
Melcher, Trini Urtuzuastegui *accounting educator*
Reed, H(orace) Curtis *insurance company executive, management consultant*
Waters, George Gary *financial service executive*

San Marino
Baldwin, James William *lawyer*
Benzer, Seymour *neurosciences educator*
Footman, Gordon Elliott *educational administrator*
Galbraith, James Marshall *lawyer, business executive*
Hull, Suzanne White *retired cultural institution administrator, writer*
Karlstrom, Paul Johnson *art historian*
Medearis, Roger Norman *artist*
Meyer, William Danielson *retired department store executive*
Moffett, William Andrew *librarian, educator*
Mortimer, Wendell Reed, Jr. *lawyer*
†Ridge, Martin *historian, educator*
Robertson, Mary Louise *archivist, historian*
Rolle, Andrew F. *historian, educator, author*
Skotheim, Robert Allen *museum administrator*
Smith, Apollo Milton Olin *retired aerodynamics engineer*
Thorpe, James *humanities scholar*
Wark, Robert Rodger *art curator*
Woodward, Daniel Holt *librarian, researcher*
Zall, Paul Maxwell *retired English language educator, consultant*
Zimmerman, William Robert *entrepreneur, engineering based manufacturing company executive*

San Mateo
Aadahl, Jorg *corporate executive*
Balles, John Joseph *banker, business consultant*
Bell, Frank Ouray, Jr. *lawyer*
Bohannon, David D. *community planner and developer*
†Briggs, Thorley D. *environmetal consultant*
Brubaker, John E. *bank executive*
Carter, Michelle Adair *editor*
Cotton, Aylett Borel *retired lawyer*
Douglass, Donald Robert *banker*
Felker, James M. *business executive*
Fenton, Noel John *venture capitalist*
Goldman, Bernard *leasing company executive*
Goldstein, Morris *publishing company executive*
†Hawkins, William (Trip), III *software executive*
Helfert, Erich Anton *management consultant, author, educator*
†Hosking, Douglas Gordon *printing company executive*
Johnson, Charles Bartlett *mutual fund executive*
Jordan, Michelle Henrietta *public relations company executive*
Kane, Robert Francis *lawyer, former ambassador, consultant*
Kidera, George Jerome *physician*
Korn, Walter *writer*
Leeder, Stuart L. *real estate financial executive*
Pappas, Costas Ernest *aeronautical engineer, consultant*
†Poulos, Gary Peter *school system administrator*
†Russell, Charles T. *bank executive*
Scott, Michael Dennis *lawyer*
Sears, William Robert *management consultant*
†Silver, William Robert *corporate finance executive*
Trabitz, Eugene Leonard *aerospace company executive*
†Van Kirk, John Ellsworth *cardiologist*

San Pablo
†Bristow, Lonnie Robert *physician*

San Pedro
Colman, Ronald William *computer science educator*
Crutchfield, William Richard *artist, educator*
Ellis, George Edwin, Jr. *chemical engineer*
McCarty, Frederick Briggs *electrical engineer*
Price, Harrison Alan *business research company executive*
Simmons, William *physicist, aerospace research executive*

San Quentin
Anderson, Douglas Sanford *vocational supervisor*

San Rafael
Brevig, Eric *special effects expert, executive*
Bruyn, Henry Bicker *physician*
Burtt, Ben *sound designer, director, editor*
Carson, Dave *special effects expert, executive*
Eekman, Thomas Adam *Slavic languages educator*
Elliott, Edward Procter *architect*
Engstrom, Eric Gustaf *interior and graphic designer, artist*
Farrar, Scott *special effects expert, executive*
Fink, Joseph Richardson *college president*
Friesecke, Raymond Francis *management consultant*
Goldman, Clint Paul *graphics expert, producer*
Gorman, Ned *film producer*
Gryson, Joseph Anthony *orthodontist*
Healy, Janet *graphics expert, producer*
Hinshaw, Horton Corwin *physician*
Holman, Tomlinson *engineer, film educator*
Jessup, Harley William *graphics expert, art director*
Joblove, George H. *graphics and special effects expert*
Kay, Douglas *graphics expert, executive*

Kennedy, James Waite *management consultant, author*
Kennedy, Thomas *executive producer*
Latno, Arthur Clement, Jr. *telephone company executive*
Lee, Robert *association executive, former theological educator, consultant, author*
Lelewer, David Kann *management consultant*
Lesh, Philip Chapman *musician, composer*
Lucas, George W., Jr. *film director, producer, screenwriter*
Mann, Jeff *special effects expert, executive*
March, Ralph Burton *retired entomology educator*
Napoles, Veronica Kleeman *graphic designer, consultant*
Nelson, James Carmer, Jr. *advertising executive, writer*
Nicholson, Bruce *graphics expert, executive*
Owens, Michael *graphics expert, executive*
Parnell, Francis William, Jr. *physician*
Ralston, Ken *graphics expert*
Roffman, Howard *motion picture company executive*
Roth, Hadden Wing *lawyer*
Scanlan, John Joseph *retired bishop*
Sheldon, Gary *conductor, music director*
Squires, Scott *special effects expert, executive*
Thompson, John William *international management consultant*
†Thompson, Peter L. H. *landscape architect, architectural firm executive*
Turner, William Weyand *author*
Wilson, Ian Holroyde *management consultant, futurist*

San Ramon
Fleming, William Sloan *energy, environmental and technology company executive*
Kahane, Dennis Spencer *lawyer*
Litman, Robert Barry *physician, author, television and radio commentator*
O'Connor, Paul Daniel *lawyer*

Santa Ana
Abbruzzese, Carlo Enrico *physician, writer, educator*
Alston, Roberta T(heresa) *medical technologist*
Blaine, Dorothea Constance Ragetté *lawyer*
Buster, Edmond Bate *metal products company executive*
†Castruita, Rudy *school system administrator*
Cheverton, Richard E. *newspaper editor*
†Dukes, David R. *computer company executive*
Ferguson, Warren John *federal judge*
Heckler, Gerard Vincent *lawyer*
Hickson, Ernest Charles *financial executive*
Holtz, Joseph Norman *marketing executive*
Humes, Edward *journalist, writer*
Jacobsen, Eric Kasner *consulting engineer*
Katz, Tonnie *newspaper editor*
Kelly, James Patrick, Jr. *retired engineering and construction executive*
†Kennedy, Donald Parker *title insurance company executive*
†Lacy, Linwood A., Jr. *computer company executive*
Lydick, Lawrence Tupper *federal judge*
†Metzler, Michael *chamber of commerce executive*
Mickelson, H(erald) Fred *electric utility executive*
Pratt, Lawrence Arthur *thoracic surgeon, foreign service officer*
Richard, Robert John *library director*
Ryan, John Edward *federal judge*
St. Clair, Carl *conductor, music director*
†Stern, Sherry Ann *journalist*
†Storer, Maryruth *law librarian*
Stotler, Alicemarie H. *federal judge*
Ware, James Edwin *retired international company executive*
Wilson, John James *federal judge*
Zabsky, John Mitchell *engineering executive*
Zaenglein, William George, Jr. *lawyer*

Santa Ana Heights
†George, Kattunilathu Oommen *homoeopathic physician, educator*
Warren, William Robinson *real estate broker*

Santa Barbara
Ackerman, Marshall *publishing company executive*
Ahlers, B. Orwin *marketing executive*
Aldisert, Ruggero John *federal judge*
Allaway, William Harris *university adminstrator*
Alldredge, Alice Louise *biological oceanography educator*
Amory, Thomas Carhart *management consultant*
Anderson, Donald Meredith *bank executive*
Atkins, Stuart (Pratt) *German language and literature educator*
Avalle-Arce, Juan Bautista *language educator*
Awramik, Stanley Michael *geology educator*
Badash, Lawrence *science history educator*
Baldwin, John David *sociologist, educator*
Bilhorn, William W. *international mining company consultant*
Blasingame, Benjamin Paul *electronics company executive*
Blum, Gerald Saul *psychologist, educator*
Bock, Russell Samuel *author*
Boehm, Eric Hartzell *information management executive*
Boisse, Joseph Adonias *library administrator*
Bongiorno, James William *electronics company executive*
Boxer, Rubin *software company owner, former research and development company executive*
Boyan, Norman J. *retired education educator*
Brant, Henry *composer*
Brantingham, Barney *journalist, writer*
Brownlee, Wilson Elliot, Jr. *history educator*
Byers, Horace Robert *former meteorology educator*
Campbell, Robert Charles *clergyman, religious organization administrator*
Campbell, William Steen *writer, magazine publisher*
Chafe, Wallace LeSeur *linguist, educator*
Childress, James J. *marine biologist, biological oceanographer*
Christman, Arthur Castner, Jr. *scientific advisor*
Clinard, Marshall Barron *sociology educator emeritus*
Collins, Robert Oakley *history educator*
Comanor, William S. *economist, educator*
Conley, Philip James, Jr. *retired air force officer*
Corman, Cid (Sidney Corman) *poet, editor*
Crawford, Donald Wesley *philosophy educator, university official*
Crowell, John C(hambers) *geology educator, researcher*
Cunningham, Julia Woolfolk *author*
Dahl, John Anton *education educator emeritus*
Dauer, Francis Watanabe *philosophy educator*
Davidson, Eugene Arthur *author*
Del Chiaro, Mario Aldo *art historian, archeologist, etruscologist, educator*
Djordjevic, Dimitrije *historian, educator*
Dougan, Robert Ormes *librarian*
Doutt, Richard Leroy *entomologist, lawyer, educator*
Dudziak, Walter Francis *physicist*
Easton, Robert (Olney) *author, environmentalist*
Eck, Robert Edwin *physicist*
Edwardsen, Kenneth Robert *administrator*
Eguchi, Yasu *artist*
Eisberg, Robert Martin *physics educator, computer software author and executive*
†Emmons, Robert John *corporate executive*
Enelow, Allen Jay *psychiatrist, educator*
Erasmus, Charles John *anthropologist, educator*
Fan, Ky *mathematician, educator*
Fingarette, Herbert *philosopher, educator*
†Fisher, Steven Kay *neurobiology eductor*
Fleming, Brice Noel *retired philosophy educator*
†Ford, Anabel *research anthropologist, archaeologist*
†Ford, Peter C. *chemistry educator*
†Fredrickson, Glenn Harold *chemical engineering and materials educator*
Frizzell, William Kenneth *architect*
Gaines, Howard Clarke *lawyer*
Gallagher, James Wes *journalist*
Gebhard, David *museum director, educator*
Gibney, Frank Bray *publisher, editor, writer, foundation executive*
Gimbel, Norman *lyricist, music publisher, television producer*
†Goodchild, Michael *geographer, educator*
Gossard, Arthur Charles *physicist*
Graham, Otis Livingston, Jr. *history educator*
Grayson, Robert Allen *marketing executive, educator*
Gunn, Giles Buckingham *English educator, religion educator*
Gutsche, Steven Lyle *physicist*
Hay, Eloise Knapp *English language educator*
Heeger, Alan Jay *physicist*
Heidenheim, Roger Stewart *automotive and electronic consultant*
Hollister, Charles Warren *history educator, author*
Hsu, Immanuel Chung Yueh *history educator*
Hubbard, David Allan *minister, educator, religious association administrator*
Iselin, Donald Grote *civil engineering and management consultant*
Jackson, Beverley Joy Jacobson *columnist, lecturer*
Jacobson, Saul P. *business consultant*
Jochim, Michael Allan *archaeologist*
Johnsen, Eugene Carlyle *mathematics educator*
†Juergensmeyer, Mark Karl *sociology educator*
Karpeles, David *museum director*
†Keator, Carol Lynne *library director*
Kendler, Howard H(arvard) *psychologist, educator*
Kennett, James Peter *geology and oceanography educator*
Kohn, Walter *educator, physicist*
Kruger, Kenneth Charles *retired architect*
Langer, James Stephen *physicist, educator*
Laub, Alan John *engineering educator*
Lawrance, Charles Holway *consulting engineer*
Leal, Leslie Gary *chemical engineering educator*
Leckie, Frederick Alexander *mechanical engineer, educator*
Lick, Wilbert James *mechanical engineering educator*
Long, Charles Houston *history of religion educator*
Louis, Barbra Schantz *dean*
Luyendyk, Bruce Peter *geophysicist, educator, institution administrator*
Lynch, Martin Andrew *retail company executive*
Mac Intyre, Donald John *college president*
†Majumdar, Arunava *mechanical engineer, educator*
Marcus, Marvin *mathematician, educator*
Markel, John Dundas *retired software company executive*
Mayer, Richard Edwin *psychology educator*
McEwen, Willard Winfield, Jr. *lawyer*
McGee, James Sears *history educator*
Mehra, Rajnish *finance educator*
Meinel, Aden Baker *optics scientist*
Merz, James Logan *electrical engineering and materials educator, researcher*
Messick, Don *actor*
Minc, Henryk *mathematics educator*
Mitchell, Maurice B. *publishing executive, educator*
Mitra, Sanjit Kumar *electrical and computer engineering educator*
Moir, Alfred Kummer *art history educator*
†Montgomery, Michael Davis *advanced technology consultant, hotelier*
Narayanamurti, Venkatesh *research administrator*
Newman, Morris *mathematician*
Norris, Robert Matheson *geologist*
Ohyama, Heiichiro *music educator, violist, conductor*
Paradise, Phil(ip Herschel) *artist*
Peale, Stanton Jerrold *physics educator*
†Perrot, Paul Norman *museum director*
Philbrick, Ralph *botanist*
†Pincus, Philip A. *chemical engineering educator*
Potter, David Samuel *former automotive company executive*
Powell, Herbert J. *architect*
Preston, Frederick Willard *surgeon*
Prindle, William Roscoe *consultant, retired glass company executive*
Pritchett, Charles Herman *political science educator*
Renehan, Robert Francis Xavier *Greek and Latin educator*
Riemenschneider, Paul Arthur *physician, radiologist*
Rosenberg, Alex *mathematician, educator*
Russell, Jeffrey Burton *historian, educator*
Scalapino, Douglas James *physics educator*
Schneider, Edward Lee *botanic garden administrator*
Sears, Joanne Lewis *retired educator, author*
Shapiro, Perry *economics educator*
Simons, Stephen *mathematics educator, researcher*
Sinsheimer, Robert Louis *former educational administrator*
Smith, Michael Townsend *author, stage director*
Smith, Robert Nathaniel *broadcasting executive, lawyer*
Sprecher, David A. *university administrator, mathematician*
Tapper, Joan Judith *magazine editor*
Taylor, Dermot Brownrigg *pharmacology researcher*
Taylor, Stuart Symington *editor, publisher*
Terry, John Timothy *insurance company executive*
Tilton, David Lloyd *savings and loan association executive*
Tilton, George Robert *geochemistry educator*
Tobler, Waldo Rudolph *geographer, cartographer*
Turner, Henry A. *political science educator, author*
Uehling, Barbara Staner *academic administrator*
Vos, Hubert Daniel *private investor*
Wade, Glen *electrical engineer, educator*
Wayland, Newton Hart *conductor*
Weaver, Sylvester Laflin, Jr. *communications consultant*
Wiemann, John Moritz *communications educator, consultant*
Wilkins, Burleigh Taylor *philosophy educator*
Wilson, Leslie *biochemist, biological sciences educator*
Winter, David Kenneth *college president*
†Witherell, Michael S. *physics educator*
Wooldridge, Dean Everett *engineering executive, scientist*
†Wudl, Fred *chemistry educator, consultant*
Yang, Henry T.Y. *university chancellor, educator*
Zelmanowitz, Julius Martin *mathematics educator, university administrator*
Zimmerman, Everett Lee *English educator, academic administrator*

Santa Clara
Alexander, George Jonathon *legal educator, former dean*
Alexanderson, Gerald Lee *mathematician, educator, writer*
Amelio, Gilbert Frank *electronics company executive*
†Anderson, Vernon Russell *technology company executive, entrepreneur*
Baird, Mellon Campbell, Jr. *electronics industry executive*
Barrett, Craig R. *computer company executive*
Carruthers, John Robert *scientist*
Chan, Shu-Park *electrical engineering educator*
Cunningham, Andrea Lee *public relations executive*
Delucchi, George Paul *accountant*
Dent, Richard Lamar *professional football player*
DuMaine, R. Pierre *bishop*
†Endo, Makoto *computer company executive*
Facione, Peter Arthur *dean, philosophy and education educator*
Greene, Frank Sullivan, Jr. *business executive*
Grove, Andrew S. *electronics company executive*
Halmos, Paul Richard *mathematician, educator*
†Hanks, Merton Edward *professional football player*
Hoagland, Albert Smiley *electrical engineer*
Hopkinson, Shirley Lois *library and information science educator*
House, David L. *electronics components company executive*
†Koffel, Martin M. *engineering company executive*
†Krause, L. William *manufacturing company executive*
Kurtzig, Sandra L. *software company executive*
†Kwock, Royal *architect*
Locatelli, Paul Leo *university administrator*
McDonald, Tim *professional football player*
McIntyre, Guy Maurice *professional football player*
McVay, John Edward *professional football club executive*
Meier, Matthias S(ebastian) *historian*
Menkin, Christopher (Kit Menkin) *leasing company executive*
Moore, Gordon E. *electronics company executive*
Morgan, James C. *electronics executive*
Oates, Bart Steven *professional football player*
Parden, Robert James *engineering educator, management consultant*
Rice, Jerry Lee *professional football player*
Seifert, George *professional football coach*
Siljak, Dragoslav D. *engineering educator*
Vincent, David Ridgely *management consulting executive*
Young, Steven *professional football player*

Santa Clarita
Deadrich, Paul Eddy *lawyer, real estate broker, retired*
DeMieri, Joseph L. *manufacturing company executive*
Fritzke, Audrey Elmere *artist*
Lavine, Steven David *college president*
Powell, Mel *composer*

Santa Cruz
Beevers, Harry *biologist*
Broadway, Nancy Ruth *landscape design and construction company executive, consultant, model and actress*
Brown, George Stephen *physicist*
Bunnett, Joseph Frederick *chemist, educator*
Child, Frank Clayton *economist, educator*
Corrick, Ann Marjorie *communications executive*
Dasmann, Raymond Fredric *ecologist*
†Dizikes, John *American studies educator*
Drake, Frank Donald *astronomy educator*
Dyson, Allan Judge *librarian*
Ellis, John Martin *German literature educator*
Faber, Sandra Moore *astronomer, educator*
Flatté, Stanley Martin *physicist, educator*
†Griggs, Gary Bruce *earth sciences educator, oceanographer, geologist, consultant*
Henderson, Ronald Wilbur *psychology educator*
†Hernquist, Lars Eric *astronomer, educator*
Heusch, Clemens August *physicist, educator*
Hill, Terrell Leslie *chemist, biophysicist*
Huskey, Harry Douglas *information and computer science educator*
Kraft, Robert Paul *astronomer, educator*
Langdon, Glen George, Jr. *electrical engineer*
Laporte, Leo Frederic *earth sciences educator*
†Lay, Thorne *geosciences educator*
Lieberman, Fredric *ethnomusicologist, educator*
Lynch, John Patrick *classics educator, university official*
Magid, Gail Avrum *neurosurgery educator*
Mc Henry, Dean Eugene *academic administrator emeritus*
Mumma, Gordon *composer, educator, author*
Musgrave, Richard Abel *economics educator*
Noller, Harry Francis, Jr. *biochemist, educator*
†Oberdorfer, Jeff *architect, firm executive*
Osterbrock, Donald E(dward) *astronomy educator*
Pettigrew, Thomas Fraser *social psychologist, educator*
Pister, Karl Stark *engineering educator*
Rydell, Amnell Roy *artist, landscape architect*
Sands, Matthew Linzee *physicist, educator*
Smith, M(ahlon) Brewster *psychologist, educator*
Suckiel, Ellen Kappy *philosophy educator*
Summers, Carol *artist*
Tharp, Roland George *psychology, education educator*
†Williams, Quentin Christopher *geophysicist*
Winston, George *keyboardist, recording company executive*
Wipke, W. Todd *chemistry educator*

Santa Fe Springs
Butterworth, Edward Livingston *retail company executive*
Popejoy, William J. *savings and loan association executive*

Santa Margarita
Thomas, John Bowman *educator, electrical engineer*

Santa Maria
Musser, C. Walton *physical scientist, consultant*
Spellman, John David *retired electrical engineer*

Santa Monica
Abrams, Irwin *historian, educator, consultant*
Alenikov, Vladimir *motion picture director and writer*
Alpert, Herb *record company executive, musician*
Anderson, Robert Helms *computer and management company executive*
Arnoldi, Charles Arthur *painter, sculptor*
Augenstein, Bruno W. *research scientist*
†Baer, Walter S. *executive*
†Barbakow, Jeffrey *health facility administrator*
Barren, Bruce Willard *merchant banker*
Bedelia, Bonnie *actress*
Bedrosian, Edward *electrical engineer*
Bedrosian, John C. *health care executive*
Black, Noel Anthony *television and film director*
Boltz, Gerald Edmund *lawyer*
Bonesteel, Michael John *lawyer*
Boyd, Malcolm *minister, religious author*
†Bronstein, Gerald Morton *holding company executive*
Brook, Robert Henry *physician, educator, health services researcher*
Cathcart, Linda *art historian*
Chartoff, Robert Irwin *film producer*
Cohen, Leonard *hospital management company executive*
†Collins, Russell Ambrose *advertising executive, creative director*
Cowan, Andrew Glenn *television writer*
Craig, Jean (Jean Craig McNeilly) *advertising executive*
Crain, Cullen Malone *electrical engineer*
Davies, Robert Abel, III *consumer products company executive*
Demond, Joan *marine biologist*
De Palma, Brian Russell *film director, writer*
Diamond, Neil Leslie *singer, composer*
Dickson, Robert Lee *lawyer*
Dreyfuss, John Alan *journalist*
†Eizenberg, Julie *architect*
Farentino, James *actor*
Feitshans, Fred Rollin (Buzz Feitshans) *film producer*
Fleischman, Albert Sidney (Sid Fleischman) *writer*
Focht, Michael Harrison *health care industry executive*
Foulkes, Llyn *artist, educator*
Garner, Donald K. *lawyer*
Gehry, Frank Owen *architect*
Gossage, James Dearl *quality department aide*
†Graff, Todd *screenwriter*
Gritton, Eugene Charles *nuclear engineer*
Gross, Sidney W. *neurosurgeon, educator*
†Gupta, Rishab Kumar *medical association administrator, educator, researcher*
Hammond, R. Philip *chemical engineer*
Holzman, D. Keith *record company executive, producer, arts consultant*
Intriligator, Devrie Shapiro *physicist*
Jacobson, Sidney *editor*
Jarreau, Alwyn Lopez *singer*
Jenkins, George *stage designer, film art director*
Jones, William Allen *lawyer, entertainment company executive*
Kahan, James Paul *psychologist*
†Karlin, Robert *automotive sales executive*
Kauffman, Robert Craig *artist, sculptor*
Kayton, Myron *engineering company executive*
Kelly, John Michael *lawyer*
King, Stephen Scott *lawyer*
†Koning, Hendrik *architect*
†Kopald, Larry S. *advertising executive*
Leaf, Paul *producer, director, writer*
Liddicoat, Richard Thomas, Jr. *association executive*
Loo, Thomas S. *lawyer*
MacLaine, Shirley *actress*
Mahal, Taj (Henry St. Clair Fredericks) *composer, musician*
Mayne, Thom *architect*
McGuire, Michael Francis *plastic and reconstructive surgeon*
Mc Intyre, James A. *diversified financial services executive*
Mc Kinney, Montgomery Nelson *advertising executive*
McMillan, M. Sean *lawyer*
Merideth, Frank E., Jr. *lawyer*
Miller, Leroy Benjamin *architect*
Morgan, Monroe *retired savings and loan executive*
Mortensen, William S. *banking executive*
†Moyer, Steven E. *lawyer, educator*
Naidorf, Louis Murray *architect*
Owens, Gary *broadcast personality, entrepreneur, author*
Pisano, A. Robert *entertainment company executive, lawyer*
Powers, Marcus Eugene *lawyer*
Prewoznik, Jerome Frank *lawyer*
Price, Frank *motion picture and television company executive*
Rand, Robert Wheeler *neurosurgeon, educator*
Rich, Michael David *research corporation executive, lawyer*
Richards, David Kimball *investor*
Risman, Michael *lawyer, business executive, securities company executive*
Roney, Robert Kenneth *retired aerospace company executive*
Salter, Robert Mundhenk, Jr. *physicist, consultant*
Salzer, John Michael *technical and management consultant*
Schlei, Norbert Anthony *lawyer*
Schultz, Michael *stage and film director, film producer*
Schwarzenegger, Arnold Alois *actor, author*
Scott, Tony *film director*
Sheller, John Willard *lawyer*
Sher, Allan L. *retired brokerage company executive*
Shubert, Gustave Harry *research executive, consultant, social scientist*

Singer, Frederick Raphael medical researcher, educator
†Smith, James Patrick economist
Sperling, George Elmer, Jr. lawyer
Stern, Jan Peter sculptor
Stone, Oliver William screenwriter, director
Thompson, Dennis Peters plastic surgeon
Thomson, James Alan research company executive
†Van Tilburg, Johannes architectural firm executive
Walker, Charles Montgomery lawyer
Walsh, John, Jr. museum director
Ware, Willis Howard computer scientist
Watrous, William Russell trombonist, composer, conductor
Watson, Doc (Arthel Lane Watson) vocalist, guitarist, banjoist, recording artist
Weatherup, Roy Garfield lawyer
†Weber, Samuel Lloyd tap dancer, choreographer
Weil, Leonard banker
Weingarten, Victor I. engineering educator
Wexler, Haskell film producer, cameraman
Williams, Albert Paine economist
Williams, George Masayasu religious organization administrator, editor
Wolf, Charles, Jr. economist, educator
Wou, Leo S. architect, planner

Santa Rosa
Aman, Reinhold Albert philologist, publisher
Barr, Roger Terry sculptor
Burton, Nanci L. professional association administrator, management consultant
Cavanagh, John Charles advertising agency executive
†Christiansen, Peggy principal
Crossland, Harriet Kent artist
de Wys, Egbert Christiaan geochemist
†Dwight, Herbert M., Jr. optical engineer, manufacturing executive
†Fream, Ronald Warren golf course architect
Frowick, Robert Holmes retired diplomat
Jaroslovsky, Alan judge
†Knight, William Hutton architectural firm executive
†Luttrell, Mary Mildred marketing management consultant
Mc Donald, David William chemist, educator
Monk, Diana Charla artist, stable owner
Person, Evert Bertil newspaper and radio executive
Pipal, George Henry journalist
Rider, Jane Louise artist, educator
Roland, Craig Williamson architect
†Sabsay, David library consultant
Schudel, Hansjoerg international business consultant
Sibley, Charles Gald biologist, educator
Swofford, Robert Lee newspaper editor, journalist

Santa Ynez
Byrne, Joseph retired oil company executive
Stern, Marvin management consultant

Santee
Vanier, Kieran Francis business forms printing company executive

Saratoga
†Araquistain, Paul A. financial professional
Cooper, George Emery aerospace consultant
Henderson, William Darryl career officer, journalist
Lynch, Milton Terrence retired advertising agency executive
Park, Joseph Chul Hui computer scientist
Syvertson, Clarence Alfred aerospace engineering consultant
Wenzel, James Gottlieb ocean engineering executive, consultant

Sausalito
Brand, Stewart editor, writer
Casals, Rosemary professional tennis player
Kuhlman, Walter Egel artist, educator
Leefe, James Morrison architect
Moody, Graham Blair lawyer
Slick, Grace Wing singer
Tift, Mary Louise artist
Treat, John Elting management consultant
Trimmer, Harold Sharp, Jr. lawyer, international telecommunications consultant
†Werner, William Arno architect

Scotts Valley
Bourret, Marjorie Ann educational advocate, consultant
Brough, Bruce Alvin public relations and communications executive
Filler, Gary B. computer company executive

Seal Beach
Bacon, Paul Caldwell training system company executive, aviation consultant, engineering test pilot
Beall, Donald Ray multi-industry high-tech company executive
Black, Kent March electronics company executive
Hirsch, David L. lawyer, corporate executive
Iacobellis, Sam Frank aerospace company executive
Merrick, George Boesch aerospace company executive
Mueth, Joseph Edward lawyer
Reynolds, Harry Lincoln physicist
Rossi, Mario Alexander architect
Thompson, Craig Snover corporate communications executive

Seaside
Wilson, Robin Scott university president, writer

Sepulveda
Costea, Nicolas Vincent physician, researcher
Solomon, George Freeman academic psychiatrist

Serl Beach
Caesar, Vance Roy newspaper executive

Shadow Hills
Cole, Roberta C. nursing educator

Shaver Lake
Lambert, Frederick William lawyer, educator

Sherman Oaks
Almeida, Laurindo guitarist, composer
Arnold, Roseanne actress, comedienne
Bower, Richard James minister
Boyd, Dawn Michele vocational expert, wage loss analyst
Buckingham, Lindsey musician
Burton, Levardis Robert Martyn (Levar Burton) actor
Champion, Marge (Marjorie Celeste Champion) actress, dancer, choreographer
†Cherones, Thomas Harry, Jr. television producer, director
Conrad, Robert (Conrad Robert Falk) actor, singer, producer, director
Cossette, Pierre agent, producer
†Dodd, Mike (M.D.) volleyball player
†Dodd, Patty Drozco volleyball player
Easton, Sheena rock vocalist
Ellison, Harlan Jay author, screenwriter
Ghent, Peer management consultant
Gilmore, Art television performer
Hamilton, Scott Scovell professional figure skater, former Olympic athlete
†Hovland, Tim (The Hov) volleyball player
Janis, Conrad actor, jazz musician, art dealer, film producer, director
Jourdan, Louis (Louis Gendre) actor
Kanter, Hal writer, producer, director
Kennedy, Burt Raphael film director
Lamas, Lorenzo actor, race car driver
Landau, Martin actor
Laney, Michael L. manufacturing executive
Light, Robert M. broadcasting association executive
Lindgren, Timothy Joseph supply company executive
Mc Kean, Michael actor
Miller, Margaret Haigh librarian
Montalban, Ricardo actor
Peplau, Hildegard Elizabeth nursing educator
†Rock, Angela volleyball player
Ross, Marion actress
Silliphant, Stirling Dale motion picture writer, producer, novelist
†Smith, Sinjin volleyball player
†Steffes, Kent volleyball player
Stevens, Andrew actor, producer, writer, director
†Stoklos, Randy (Stokey) volleyball player
Strauss, John public relations executive
†Timmons, Steve (Red) volleyball player
Williams, Billy Dee actor
Winkler, Lee B. business consultant
Zemplenyi, Tibor Karol cardiologist

Shingle Springs
Crotti, Joseph Robert aviation executive

Sierra Madre
Calleton, Theodore Edward lawyer
Dewey, Donald William magazine editor and publisher, writer
Nation, Earl F. retired urologist, educator
Whittingham, Charles Edward thoroughbred race horse owner and trainer

Signal Hill
Jarman, Donald Ray retired public relations professional, minister

Simi Valley
Beck, Mat special effects expert, photographer
Bigelow, Michael film director, visual effects expert
Deisenroth, Clinton Wilbur electrical engineer
Durst, Eric television and commercial director
Hoover, Richard special effects expert, film director
†Mow, William apparel executive
†Nesi, Vincent apparel executive
Shartle, Keith Robert producer
Stratton, Gregory Alexander computer specialist, administrator, mayor
Yeatman, Hoyt special effects expert, executive

Smith River
†Richards, William H. business owner

Soda Bay
Fletcher, Leland Vernon artist

Solana Beach
Agnew, Harold Melvin physicist
Brody, Arthur industrial executive
Engle, Harold Martin retired medical administrator
Ernst, Roger Charles former government official, natural resources consultant, association executive
Friedman, Maurice Stanley religious educator
Gildred, Theodore Edmonds ambassador
Hecker, Bruce Albert lawyer
Kempf, Paul Stuart optics company executive

Solvang
Chandler, E(dwin) Russell religious journalist, author
Hegarty, William Kevin medical center executive
Morrow, Richard Towson lawyer
Shelesnyak, Moses Chaim biodynamicist, physiologist

Somerset
Collier, Clarence Robert physician, educator

Somis
Gius, Julius retired newspaper editor

Sonoma
Allen, Rex Whitaker architect
Kizer, Carolyn Ashley poet, educator
Lackey, Lawrence Bailis, Jr. retired architect, urban designer
Markey, William Alan health care administrator
Muchmore, Robert Boyer engineering consultant executive
Stadtman, Verne August former foundation executive, editor
Woodbridge, John Marshall architect, urban planner

Sonora
Price, Joe artist, educator
Rand, John Fay retired banker
Walasek, Otto Frank chemical engineer, biochemist, photographer

South El Monte
Kay, Kenneth Jeffrey property development company executive

South Lake Tahoe
Reece, Monte Meredith lawyer, judge

South Pasadena
Askin, Walter Miller artist, educator
Girvigian, Raymond architect
Glad, Dain Sturgis retired aerospace engineer, consultant
Kopp, Eugene Howard electrical engineer
Staehle, Robert L. foundation executive
White-Thomson, Ian Leonard chemical company executive

South San Francisco
Alvarez, Robert Smyth editor, publisher
Anderson, Margaret Allyn carpet showroom manager
Crowley, Jerome Joseph, Jr. manufacturing company executive
†Henderson, Thomas James construction company executive
†Kopp, Quentin L. lawyer, state legislator
Levinson, Arthur David molecular biologist
Masover, Gerald Kenneth microbiologist
Raab, G. Kirk biotechnology company executive
Swanson, Robert A. genetic engineering company executive

Spring Valley
Gardner, Leonard Burton, II industrial automation engineer
Peterson, Donald Curtis life care executive, consultant
†Runge, Paul Edward baseball umpire, realtor

Springs
†Olofson, Roy Leonard financial executive, accountant

Stanford
Abel, Elie reporter, broadcaster, educator
Abramovitz, Moses economist, educator
Abrams, Herbert LeRoy radiologist, educator
Allen, Matthew Arnold physicist
Almond, Gabriel Abraham political science educator
Amemiya, Takeshi economist, statistician
Anderson, Annelise Graebner economist
Anderson, Martin Carl economist
Anderson, Theodore Wilbur statistics educator
Angell, James Browne electrical engineering educator
Arrow, Kenneth Joseph economist, educator
Arthur, William Brian economist, educator
Atkin, J. Myron science educator
Babcock, Barbara Allen lawyer, educator
Bagshaw, Malcolm A. radiation therapist, educator
Baker, Keith Michael history educator
Baldwin, Robert Lesh biochemist, educator
Bandura, Albert psychologist
†Banks, Peter M. aerospace science director
Barkan, Philip mechanical engineer
Barnes, Grant Alan book publisher
Barton, John Hays law educator
Basch, Paul Frederick international health educator, parasitologist
†Bauer, Eugene Andrew dermatologist, educator
Baxter, William Francis lawyer, educator
Baylor, Denis Aristide neurobiology educator
Beard, Rodney Rau physician, educator
Beaver, William Henry accounting educator
Beichman, Arnold political scientist, educator, writer
Bensch, Klaus George pathology educator
Berg, Paul biochemist, educator
Bjorkman, Olle Erik plant biologist, educator
†Bloem, Kenneth D. healthcare facility executive
Bonner, William Andrew chemistry educator
Boskin, Michael Jay economist, government official, university educator, consultant
Boudart, Michel chemist, chemical engineer, educator
Bracewell, Ronald Newbold electrical engineering and computer science educator
Bradshaw, Peter engineering educator
Brauman, John I. chemist, educator
Breitrose, Henry S. communications educator
Brest, Paul A. law educator
Bridges, Edwin Maxwell education educator
Brigham, William Everett petroleum engineering educator
Brown, Byron William, Jr. biostatistician, educator
†Brown, J. Martin oncologist, educator
†Bryson, Arthur Earl, Jr. engineering educator
Bube, Richard Howard materials scientist
Bunzel, John Harvey political science educator, researcher
Byer, Robert Louis applied physics educator, university dean
Calfee, Robert Chilton psychologist, educational researcher
Campbell, Allan McCulloch bacteriology educator
Campbell, Wesley Glenn economist, educator
Cannon, Robert Hamilton, Jr. aerospace engineering educator
Cappelletti, Mauro law educator, lawyer
Carlsmith, James Merrill psychologist, educator
Carlson, Robert Codner industrial engineering educator
Carlsson, Gunnar Erik mathematics educator
Carnochan, Walter Bliss retired English educator
Cavalli-Sforza, Luigi Luca genetics educator
Chaffee, Steven Henry communication educator
Chu, Steven physics educator
Cohen, Albert musician, educator
Cohen, Stanley Norman geneticist, educator
Cole, Wendell Gordon speech and drama educator
Coleman, Robert Griffin geology educator
Collman, James Paddock chemistry educator
Conquest, (George) Robert (Acworth) writer, historian, poet, critic, journalist
Converse, Philip Ernest social science educator
Cork, Linda Katherine veterinary pathologist, educator
Cornell, Carl Allin civil engineering educator
Cox, Donald Clyde electrical engineering educator
Cutler, Cassius Chapin physicist, educator
Dantzig, George Bernard applied mathematics educator
Davis, Kingsley sociologist, educator, researcher
Davis, Mark M. microbiologist, educator
Deal, Bruce Elmer physical chemist, educator
Degler, Carl Neumann history educator
Dekker, George Gilbert literature educator, literary scholar, writer
†Derksen, Charlotte Ruth Meynink librarian
†Dickson, Lance E. law librarian, educator
Djerassi, Carl chemist, educator, writer
Dunlop, John Barrett foreign language educator, research institution scholar
Dunn, Donald Allen engineering educator, consultant
Duus, Peter history educator
Ehrlich, Paul Ralph biology educator
Eitner, Lorenz Edwin Alfred art historian, educator
Ernst, Wallace Gary geology educator, dean
Eustis, Robert Henry mechanical engineer
Fehrenbacher, Don Edward retired history educator
Feinstein, Joseph electronics research manager
Ferguson, Charles Albert linguist, language consultant
Fernald, Russell Dawson biologist, researcher
Fetter, Alexander Lees theoretical physicist, educator
†Flavell, John Hurley psychologist, educator
Floyd, Robert W. computer scientist, educator
Follesdal, Dagfinn philosophy educator
Frank, Joseph Nathaniel comparative literature educator
Franklin, Gene Farthing electrical engineering educator, consultant
Franklin, Marc Adam law educator
Fredrickson, George Marsh history educator
French, Charles Stacy retired biology educator
Friedman, Lawrence M. law educator
Friedman, Milton economist, educator emeritus, author
Fuchs, Victor Robert economics educator
Gage, Nathaniel Lees psychologist, educator
Ganesan, Ann Katharine molecular biologist
Gardner, John William writer, educator
Geballe, Theodore Henry physics educator, communications technology consultant
Gelpi, Albert Joseph English educator, literary critic
Gelpi, Barbara Charlesworth English literature and women's studies educator
Gere, James Monroe civil engineering educator
Germane, Gayton Elwood business educator
Gibbons, James Franklin university dean, electrical engineering educator
Gibbs, James Lowell, Jr. anthropologist, researcher
Gibson, Count Dillon, Jr. physician, educator
Girard, René Noel author, educator
Giraud, Raymond Dorner retired language professional
Goldstein, Dora Benedict pharmacologist, educator
Goldstein, Paul lawyer, educator
Golub, Gene Howard computer science educator, researcher
Goodman, Joseph Wilfred electrical engineering educator
Gray, Robert Molten electrical engineering educator
Greenberg, Joseph H. anthropologist
Gross, Richard Edmund education educator
Gunther, Gerald lawyer, educator
Hall, Robert Ernest economics educator
Hanawalt, Philip Courtland biology educator, researcher
Harbaugh, John Warvelle applied earth sciences educator
Harris, Edward D., Jr. physician
Harris, Stephen Ernest electrical engineering and applied physics educator
Harvey, Van Austin religious studies educator
Heinrichs, William LeRoy obstetrician, gynecologist, educator
Henriksen, Thomas Hollinger university official
Herring, William Conyers physicist, emeritus educator
Herrmann, George mechanical engineering educator
Heyneker, Herbert Louis biochemist, biotechnology executive
Hilgard, Ernest Ropiequet psychologist
Hoff, Nicholas John mechanical and aerospace engineer
Holloway, Charles Arthur public and private management educator
†Holloway, David James political science educator
Howell, James Edwin economist, educator
Hubert, Helen Betty epidemiologist
Hughes, Thomas Joseph mechanical engineering educator, consultant
Inkeles, Alex sociology educator
Jardetzky, Oleg medical educator, scientist
Johnson, John J. historian, educator
Johnson, William Summer chemistry educator
Johnston, Bruce Foster economics educator
Kailath, Thomas electrical engineer, educator
Kane, Thomas Reif engineering educator
Karlin, Samuel mathematics educator, researcher
Kays, William Morrow university administrator, mechanical engineer
Keller, Joseph Bishop mathematician, educator
†Keller, Michael Alan librarian, educator, musicologist
Kendig, Joan Johnston neurobiology educator
Kennedy, David Michael historian, educator
Kennedy, Donald environmental science educator, former academic administrator
Kline, Stephen Jay mechanical engineer, educator
Korn, David educator, pathologist
Kornberg, Arthur biochemist
Kornberg, Roger David biochemist, structural biologist
Krauskopf, Konrad Bates geology educator
†Krensky, Alan Michael pediatrician, educator
Kreps, David Marc economist, educator
Kruger, Charles Herman, Jr. mechanical engineering educator
Krumboltz, John Dwight psychologist, educator
Kurz, Mordecai economics educator
Lau, Lawrence Juen-Yee economics educator, consultant
Lazear, Edward Paul economics and industrial relations educator, researcher
Leavitt, Harold Jack management educator
Lehman, (Israel) Robert biochemistry educator, consultant
Lepper, Mark Roger psychology educator
Levinthal, Elliott Charles physicist, educator
L'Heureux, John Clarke English language educator
Lieberman, Gerald J. statistics educator
Lindenberger, Herbert Samuel writer, literature educator
Linvill, John Grimes engineering educator
Little, William Arthur physicist, educator
Loftis, John (Clyde), Jr. English language educator
Lohnes, Walter F. W. German language and literature educator
Long, Sharon Rugel molecular biologist, plant biology educator
Luenberger, David Gilbert electrical engineer, educator
Lyman, Richard Wall foundation and university executive, historian
Lyons, Charles R. drama educator
Maccoby, Eleanor Emmons psychology educator
Macovski, Albert electrical engineering educator
Maffly, Roy Herrick medical educator
Maharidge, Dale Dimitro journalist, educator
Manley, John Frederick political scientist, educator

March, James Gardner social scientist, educator
Mark, James B. D. surgeon
Marmor, Michael Franklin ophthalmologist, educator
Massy, William Francis education educator, academic administrator
†Matisoff, Susan cultural research organization administrator
McCarthy, John computer scientist, educator
Mc Carty, Perry Lee environmental engineer, educator
McCluskey, Edward Joseph engineering educator
McConnell, Harden Marsden biophysical chemistry researcher, chemistry educator
McDevitt, Hugh O'Neill immunology educator, physician
McDonald, John Gregory financial investment educator
McDougall, Iain Ross nuclear medicine educator
Mc Lure, Charles E., Jr. economist
Mc Namara, Joseph Donald researcher, retired police chief, novelist
Melmon, Kenneth Lloyd physician, biologist, pharmacologist, consultant
Merigan, Thomas Charles, Jr. physician, medical researcher, educator
†Middlebrook, Diane Wood English language educator
Miller, William Frederick research company executive, educator, business consultant
Moffat, Robert John mechanical engineering educator, researcher
Mommsen, Katharina German language and literature educator
Montgomery, David Bruce marketing educator
Moore, Thomas Gale economist, educator
Moses, Lincoln E. statistician, educator
Nelson, Lyle Morgan communications educator
Newman-Gordon, Pauline French language and literature educator
Niederhuber, John Edward surgical oncologist and molecular immunologist, university educator and administrator
Nivison, David Shepherd Chinese and philosophy educator
Noll, Roger Gordon economist, educator
North, Robert Carver political science educator
Ornstein, Donald Samuel mathematician, educator
Ortolano, Leonard civil engineering educator, water resources planner
Osheroff, Douglas Dean physicist, researcher
Osserman, Robert mathematician, educator
Ott, Wayne Robert environmental engineer
Paffenbarger, Ralph Seal, Jr. epidemiologist
†Palm, Charles Gilman university official
Paul, Benjamin David anthropologist, educator
†Pearson, Scott Roberts economics educator
Pease, Roger Fabian Wedgwood electrical engineering educator
Pecora, Robert chemistry educator
Perkins, David D(exter) geneticist
Perloff, Marjorie Gabrielle English and comparative literature educator
Perry, John Richard philosophy educator
Pfeffer, Jeffrey business educator
Phillips, Ralph Saul mathematics educator
Pierce, John Robinson electrical engineer, educator
Porterfield, James Temple Starke business administration educator
Raffin, Thomas A. physician
Raisian, John public policy institute executive, economist
Rees, John Robert physicist
Reilly, William Kane former government official, lawyer, conservationist
Remson, Irwin retired hydrogeology educator
†Reynolds, William Craig mechanical engineer, educator
Rhode, Deborah Lynn law educator
Ricardo-Campbell, Rita economist, educator
Rice, Condoleezza academic administrator, political scientist
Richter, Burton physicist, educator
Risser, James Vaulx, Jr. journalist, educator
Roberts, Donald John economics and business educator, consultant
Robinson, Paul Arnold historian, educator, author
Rosaldo, Renato Ignacio, Jr. cultural anthropology educator
Rosenberg, Nathan economics educator
Rosenberg, Saul Allen oncologist, educator
†Ross, Alexander Duncan art librarian
Ross, John physical chemist, educator
Rosse, James Nelson economics educator, educational administrator
Roster, Michael lawyer
Roth, Bernard mechanical engineering educator, researcher
Rott, Nicholas fluid mechanics educator
Rowen, Henry Stanislaus economics educator
Rubenstein, Edward physician, educator
Schatzberg, Alan Frederic psychiatrist, researcher
Schawlow, Arthur Leonard physicist, educator
Schimke, Robert Tod biochemist, educator
Schneider, Stephen Henry climatologist, environmental policy analyst, researcher
Schoen, Richard Melvin mathematics educator, researcher
Scholes, Myron S. law and finance educator
Schroeder, John Speer cardiology educator
Scott, Kenneth Eugene lawyer, educator
Scott, W(illiam) Richard sociology educator
Seligman, Thomas Knowles museum administrator
Serbein, Oscar Nicholas business educator, consultant
Shah, Haresh C. civil engineering educator
Shapiro, Lucille molecular biology educator
Shaw, Herbert John physics educator emeritus
Sheehan, James John historian, educator
Shepard, Roger Newland psychologist, educator
Shooter, Eric Manvers neurobiology educator, consultant
Shortliffe, Edward Hance internist, medical information science educator
Shultz, George Pratt former secretary of state, economics educator
Siegman, Anthony Edward electrical engineer, educator
Silverman, Frederic Noah physician
Sorrentino, Gilbert English language educator, novelist, poet
Sowell, Thomas economist
Spence, A. Michael economics educator, academic administrator
Spicer, William Edward, III physicist, educator
Spitz, Lewis William historian, educator
Spreiter, John Robert engineering educator, space physics scientist
Springer, George Stephen mechanical engineering educator
Spudich, James A. biology educator
Staar, Richard Felix political scientist
Stansky, Peter David Lyman historian
Stinson, Edward Brad surgery educator
Stockdale, James Bond writer, research scholar, retired naval officer
Stone, William Edward association executive
Street, Robert Lynnwood civil and mechanical engineer
Strena, Robert Victor research laboratory manager
Stryer, Lubert biochemist, educator
Sturrock, Peter Andrew space science and astrophysics educator
Taube, Henry chemistry educator
Taylor, Richard Edward physicist, educator
Teller, Edward physicist
Thompson, David Alfred industrial engineer
Thompson, George Albert geophysics educator
Traugott, Elizabeth Closs linguistics educator and researcher
Triska, Jan Francis retired political science educator
Trost, Barry Martin chemist, educator
Ullman, Jeffrey David computer science educator
Van Derveer, Tara university athletic coach
Van Dyke, Milton Denman aeronautical engineering educator
Van Horne, James Carter economist, educator
Vincenti, Walter Guido aeronautical engineer, emeritus educator
Wagoner, Robert Vernon astrophysicist, educator
Walsh, William football coach
Walt, Martin physicist, consulting educator
Watt, Ian Pierre retired English literature educator
Weber, David C(arter) librarian
White, Robert Lee electrical engineer, educator
Widrow, Bernard electrical engineering educator
Williams, Howard Russell lawyer, educator
Wojcicki, Stanley George physicist, educator
Wolfson, Mark Alan accounting and finance educator
Yanofsky, Charles biology educator
Zare, Richard Neil chemistry educator
Zimbardo, Philip George psychologist, educator, writer

Stinson Beach
Metz, Mary Seawell university dean, retired college president

Stockton
†Antoci, Mario savings and loan company executive
†Atchley, Bill Lee university president
†Barnum, Robert T. bank executive
Blewett, Robert Noall lawyer
Curtis, Orlie Lindsey, Jr. lawyer
DeRicco, Lawrence Albert college president emeritus
Fish, Tom vocational school educator
Heyborne, Robert Linford electrical engineering educator
Hosie, William Carlton food products company executive
Jantzen, J(ohn) Marc retired education educator
Klinger, Wayne Julius secondary education educator
Limbaugh, Ronald Hadley history educator, history center director
McNeal, Dale William, Jr. biological sciences educator
†Meyer, Ursula library director
Montrose, Donald W. bishop
Oak, Claire Morisset artist, educator
Renson, Jean Felix psychiatry educator
Shao, Otis Hung-I corporate executive, educator
Sorby, Donald Lloyd university dean
Thompson, Thomas Sanford former college president
Whiteker, Roy Archie retired chemistry educator
Whittington, Robert Bruce retired publishing company executive

Studio City
Autry, Gene (Orvon Gene Autry) actor, radio entertainer, broadcasting executive, baseball team executive
Aykroyd, Daniel Edward writer, actor
Bloodworth-Thomason, Linda television producer, writer
Carsey, Marcia Lee Peterson television producer
Duvall, Shelley actress
English, Diane executive producer, writer television
Fisher, Joel Marshall political scientist, legal recruiter
Garver, Oliver Bailey, Jr. bishop
Gautier, Dick actor, writer
Goldthwait, Bob comedian, actor
Harrison, Gregory actor
Kenney, H(arry) Wesley, Jr. producer, director
Leider, Gerald J. motion picture and television company executive
†Malone, Nancy actor, director, producer
Metcalf, Laurie actress
Moore, Mary Tyler actress
Needham, Hal director, writer
Nieto del Rio, Juan Carlos marketing executive
Parish, James Robert author, cinema historian
Peerce, Larry film director
Pournelle, Jerry Eugene author
Reynolds, Burt actor, director
Self, William Edwin film company executive
Shavelson, Melville writer, theatrical producer and director
von Zerneck, Frank Ernest television producer
Werner, Tom television producer, professional baseball team executive
Westmore, Michael George make-up artist
Yorty, Samuel lawyer, former mayor

Summerland
Calamar, Gloria artist

Sun Valley
Kamins, Philip E. diversified manufacturing company executive

Sunnyvale
†Armistead, Robert Ashby, Jr. scientific research company executive
Bryant, Alan Willard human resources executive
Evans, Barton, Jr. analytical instrument company executive
Fialer, Philip Anthony research scientist, electronics company executive
Guastaferro, Angelo aerospace company executive
Hind, Harry William pharmaceutical company executive
Kim, Wan Hee electrical engineering educator, business executive
Leeson, David Brent electronics company executive
Lewis, John Clark, Jr. manufacturing company executive
Ma, Fengchow Clarence agricultural engineering consultant
Omura, Jimmy Kazuhiro electrical engineer
†Previte, Richard computer company executive
Quinn, Jarus William physicist, association executive
Rugge, Henry Ferdinand medical products executive
Sanders, Walter Jeremiah, III electronics company executive
Schubert, Ronald Hayward retired aerospace engineer
Schumacher, Henry Jerold former career officer, business executive
Thorington, John M., Jr. computer graphics company executive
†Tramiel, Jack computer game company executive
†Tramiel, Sam microcomputer and video game company executive
†Trimble, Charles R. electronics executive
Yep, Laurence Michael author
Zebroski, Edwin Leopold nuclear engineer consultant
Zemke, (E.) Joseph computer company executive

Sunset Beach
Faulkner, Adele Lloyd interior designer, color consultant

Susanville
Blake, Larry Jay academic administrator

Sylmar
Hoggatt, Clela Allphin English language educator

Taft
Smith, Lee L. hotel executive

Tarzana
Abbott, Philip actor
Grill, Lawrence J. lawyer, accountant, management company executive
Hansen, Robert Clinton electrical engineering consultant
Leahy, T. Liam management consultant
Lowy, Jay Stanton music industry executive
Macmillan, Robert Smith electronics engineer
Shaw, Carole editor, publisher
Shaw-Cohen, Lori Eve magazine editor
Smith, Mark Lee architect

Temecula
†Feltz, Charles Henderson former mechanical engineer, consultant
†Haynes, Raymond Neal, Jr. lawyer, state legislator
Minogue, Robert Brophy retired nuclear engineer

The Sea Ranch
Hayflick, Leonard microbiologist, cell biologist, gerontologist, educator
Resch, Joseph Anthony neurologist

Thousand Oaks
†Binder, Gordon M. health and medical products executive
†Colburn, Keith W. electronics executive
Crain, Charles Anthony telephone company executive
DeLorenzo, David A. food products executive
Fitzgerald, Janet Marie cosmetic company executive, training consultant
Gregory, Calvin insurance service executive
Hale, William Bryan, Jr. newspaper editor
Jessup, Warren T. lawyer
Kehrer, Daniel M. publishing executive, author, journalist
Krumm, Charles Ferdinand electrical engineer
†Luedtke, Luther S. academic administrator
†Malmuth, Norman David program manager
Miller, Jerry Huber university chancellor
†Pflueger, Kenneth Edgar university administrator, minister
Pitlak, Robert Thomas sales and marketing executive
Rathmann, George Blatz genetic engineering company executive
†Shankar, Vijaya V. aeronautical engineer
Sherman, Gerald nuclear physicist, financial estate planner
Sladek, Lyle Virgil mathematician, educator
Smyth, Glen Miller management consultant
Sparrow, Larry J. telecommunications executive
Van Mols, Brian publishing executive
†Weinberg, D. Mark health insurance company executive

Thousand Palms
Smith, Charles Thomas retired dentist, educator

Tiburon
Heacox, Russel Louis mechanical engineer
Macgregor, Wallace consulting mineral economist, author

Topanga
Gimbutas, Marija archaeologist, educator
Redgrave, Lynn actress

Torrance
Adelsman, (Harriette) Jean newspaper editor
Alter, Gerald L. real estate executive
†Amemiya, Koichi motor vehicle company executive
Ananth, Jambur psychiatrist, educator
†Bowen, Debra Lynn lawyer, state legislator
Brasel, Jo Anne physician
Brodsky, Robert Fox aerospace engineer
Bruinsma, Theodore August retired business executive
†Buckley, James W. librarian
Burnham, Daniel Patrick manufacturing company executive
Carey, Kathryn Ann advertising and public relations agency executive, consultant
Dankanyin, Robert John manufacturing executive
Emmanouilides, George Christos physician, educator
Everts, Connor artist
†Geissert, Katy mayor
Gurevitch, Arnold William dermatology educator
Harness, William Edward tenor
Itabashi, Hideo Henry neuropathologist, neurologist
Kaufman, Sanford Paul lawyer
Krout, Boyd Merrill psychiatrist
Kulpa, John Edward management executive, former air force officer
†Kurita, Masahiro computer company executive
Leake, Donald Lewis oral and maxillofacial surgeon, oboist
Mann, Michael Martin electronics company executive
Martin, Robert Michael prosecutor
Mason, John Latimer engineering executive
Miller, Milton Howard psychiatrist
Myhre, Byron Arnold pathologist, educator
†Niwa, Norio computer company executive
Petillon, Lee Ritchey lawyer
Prakash, Ravi physician, educator
Rogers, Howard H. chemist
†Sakai, Shinji finance company executive
Savitz, Maxine Lazarus aerospace company executive
Sheh, Robert Bardhyl environmental management company executive
Snape, William John, Jr. physician
Tanaka, Kouichi Robert physician, educator
Walti, Randal Fred management consultant
†Woodhull, John Richard electronics company executive
†Young, Scott recording tape distributor

Trabuco Canyon
Addy, Jo Alison Phears economist

Trinidad
Marshall, William Edward historical association executive

Trona
Laire, Howard George chemist

Tulare
Sickels, William Loyd secondary educator

Turlock
Ahlem, Lloyd Harold psychologist
Amrhein, John Kilian dean
Goedecke, David Stewart music educator, band educator, trumpet player
Kerschner, Lee R(onald) university president, political science educator
Kottke, Frederick Edward economics educator
Williams, Delwyn Charles telephone company executive

Tustin
†Allen, Joseph public relations executive
Bartlett, Arthur Eugene franchise executive
Charley, Philip James testing laboratory executive
Hester, Norman Eric chemical company technical executive, chemist
Krumm, John McGill bishop
London, Ray William clinical and forensic psychologist
Sognefest, Peter William manufacturing company executive
Thomas, Mitchell, Jr. aerospace company executive

Twain Harte
Kinsinger, Robert Earl property company executive, educational consultant

Twentynine Palms
Clemente, Patrocinio Ablola psychology educator

Ukiah
McAllister, (Ronald) Eric pharmaceutical executive, physician

Universal City
Baker, Richard Eugene controller, corporate executive
Boulanger, Donald Richard financial services executive
Davies, Raymond Douglas musician, songwriter
Day, Doris (Doris von Kappelhoff) singer, actress
Haas, Harold Murray motion picture company executive
Horowitz, Zachary I. entertainment company executive
†Kemp, Barry Michael writer, producer
LaBelle, Patti singer
Lansbury, Angela Brigid actress
Lindheim, Richard David television company executive
Lovett, Lyle musician
Lynn, Loretta Webb (Mrs. Oliver Lynn, Jr.) singer
Masket, Edward Seymour television executive
†Meat Loaf, (Marvin Lee Aday) popular musician, actor
Nelson, Craig T. actor
Paul, Charles S. motion picture and television company executive
Pollack, Sydney film director
Pollock, Thomas P. motion picture company executive
Sheinberg, Sidney Jay recreation and entertainment company executive
Teller, Alvin Norman music industry executive
Van Dyke, Jerry actor, comedian
Wasserman, Lew R. film, recording and publishing company executive
Yearwood, Trisha country music singer, songwriter
Young, J. Anthony entertainment company executive

Upland
Hext, Kathleen Florence regulatory compliance consultant
Jones, Nancy Langdon financial planner, investment advisor
Lewis, Goldy Sarah real estate developer, corporation executive
Lewis, Ralph Milton real estate developer

Vacaville
Coulson, Kinsell Leroy meteorologist
Emery, Rita Dorothy physical education educator
Erwin, Robert Lester biotechnology company executive
Myhre, Deanna Shirley lawyer, litigator, mediator
Wisneski, Mary Jo Elizabeth reading specialist, educator

Valencia
Davison, Arthur Lee scientific instrument manufacturing company executive, engineer

Valley Ford
Clowes, Garth Anthony *electronics executive, consultant*

Valley Village
Diller, Phyllis *actress, author*
Rosen, Alexander Carl *psychologist, consultant*

Van Nuys
Allen, Stephen Valentine Patrick William *television comedian, author, pianist, songwriter*
Blinder, Martin S. *publishing company executive*
Conway, Tim *comedian*
Cooper, Leroy Gordon, Jr. *former astronaut, business consultant*
†Fraser, Julia Diane *publishing executive*
†Gordon, Stuart *film and theater producer, director, playwright*
†Greenberg, Daniel *electronics rental company executive*
Hanlin, Russell L. *citrus products company executive*
Ivey, Judith *actress*
Kagan, Stephen Bruce (Sandy Kagan) *travel agency executive*
MacLachlan, Kyle *actor*
Mikesell, Richard Lyon *lawyer, financial counselor*
Simon, David Harold *retired public relations executive*
Sludikoff, Stanley Robert *publisher, writer*
Zucker, Alfred John *English educator, academic administrator*

Venice
Bengston, Billy Al *artist*
Berlant, Anthony *artist*
Chiat, Jay *advertising agency executive*
Clow, Lee *advertising agency executive*
Cohen, Norm *chemist*
†Ehrlich, Steven David *architect*
Eliot, Alexander *author, critic, historian*
Eversley, Frederick John *sculptor, engineer*
†Giaquinta, Gerald J. *public relations executive*
Grimshaw, Paul *producer*
†Kuperman, Robert Ian *advertising agency executive*
O'Neill, Edward *actor*
Rady, Elsa *artist*
Rosenthal, Richard Jay *real estate consultant, broker, educator*
†Shapazian, Robert Michael *publishing executive*
†Thomas, Bob *public relations executive*
Wolf, Robert Howard *advertising executive, marketing consultant*

Ventura
†Adeniran, Dixie Darlene *library administrator*
Arita, George Shiro *biology educator*
Field, A. J. *former oil drilling company executive, engineering consultant*
Gaynor, Joseph *chemical engineering consultant*
Gray, Henry David *minister, religious organization administrator*
Greenblatt, Milton *psychiatrist*
Huntsinger, Fritz Roy *former offshore equipment manufacturing company executive*
Kirman, Charles Gary *photojournalist*
Matley, Benvenuto Gilbert (Ben Matley) *computer engineer, educator, consultant*
†McElroy, Charlotte Ann *principal*
Milligan, Arthur Achille *banker*
†Milligan, Marshall *banker*
†Peck, Douglas Montgomery, Jr. *banking executive*
Wheeler, Harold Alden *retired radio engineer*

Victorville
Bascom, Earl Wesley *artist, sculptor, writer*

Villa Park
Rydell, Richard Lewis *hospital administrator, consultant*
Writer, Sharon Lisle *science educator*

Visalia
Riegel, Byron William *ophthalmologist*

Vista
Cavanaugh, Kenneth Clinton *retired housing consultant*
†Johnson, Alan *principal*
†Rader, Paul Alexander *minister, administrator*
Tiedeman, David Valentine *research education educator*

Volcano
Prout, Ralph Eugene *physician*

Walnut
Ashford, Evelyn *track and field athlete*

Walnut Creek
Acosta, Julio Bernard *obstetrician, gynecologist*
Cacho, Patrick Thomas *relocation management company executive*
Caddy, Edmund Harrington Homer, Jr. *architect*
Crandall, Ira Carlton *consulting electrical engineer*
Curtin, Daniel Joseph, Jr. *lawyer*
†Delorme, Jean *mining engineer*
Farr, Lee Edward *physician*
Garlough, William Glenn *marketing executive*
Garrett, James Joseph *lawyer, partner*
Ginsburg, Gerald J. *lawyer, business executive*
Graham, Dee McDonald *food company executive*
Grufman, Marjorie Jule *elementary art educator*
Hallock, C. Wiles, Jr. *athletic official*
Hamlin, Kenneth Eldred, Jr. *retired pharmaceutical company executive*
Haswell, T. Clayton *newspaper editor*
†Haswell, T. Clayton *newspaper editor*
Humphrey, William Albert *mining company executive*
Jackson, Dale Edward *lawyer*
Jones, Ebon Richard *retail executive*
Jones, Orlo Dow *lawyer, drug store executive*
Judah, Jay Stillson *historian, educator*
Kieffer, William Franklinn *chemistry educator*
†Lesher, Margaret Lisco *newspaper publishing, songwriter*
Long, Robert Merrill *retail drug company executive*
Madden, Palmer Brown *lawyer*
McCauley, Bruce Gordon *financial consultant*
McGrath, Don John *banker*
Merritt, Robert Edward *lawyer, educator*
Morgan, Elmo Rich *former university official*
Nelson, Elmer Kingsholm, Jr. *public administration educator, writer, mediator, consultant*
Newmark, Milton Maxwell *lawyer*
Oakeshott, Gordon B(laisdell) *geologist*
Pagter, Carl Richard *lawyer*
†Parsons, Robert Eugene *transportation consultant*
Rhody, Ronald Edward *banker, communications executive*
Roach, John D. C. *manufacturing company executive*
Santos, E(nos) Francis (Frank) *agrochemical company executive*
Satz, Louis K. *publishing executive*
Seegers, Walter Henry *hematology educator emeritus*
Skaggs, Sanford Merle *lawyer*
Smith, Robert Houston *archeologist, religious studies educator*
Woodward, Richard Joseph, Jr. *geotechnical engineer*
Zander, Alvin Frederick *social psychologist*

Watsonville
Carpenter, Philip David *laboratory administrator, environmental and organic chemist*
†Costanzo, Patrick M. *constuction executive*
Roberts, Richard Heilbron *construction company executive*

West Covina
Ebiner, Robert Maurice *lawyer*
Markham, Clarence Matthew, III *city administrator*
McHale, Edward Robertson *retired lawyer*
Saunders, Russell Joseph *utility company executive*

West Hills
Freas, Frank Kelly *illustrator*
†Jones, Dennis Edmund *film producer*
Straight, Beatrice Whitney *actress*

West Hollywood
†Bartel, Paul *film director*
Bass, Barbara DeJong *film assistant director, free-lance writer*
Beal, John *actor, director, narrator*
Benson, George *guitarist*
Black, David *writer, educator, producer*
†Black, Shane *screenwriter*
Bloom, Claire *actress*
Blumofe, Robert Fulton *motion picture producer, association executive*
Bogart, Paul *film director*
Brandauer, Klaus Maria *actor*
Brunell, Philip A. *physician*
Burns, George *actor, comedian*
Byrne, Edward Blake *broadcasting company executive*
Byrnes, James Bernard *museum director emeritus*
Carr, Allan *film and stage producer, celebrity representative*
Conniff, Ray *conductor, composer, arranger*
Conti, Bill *film composer*
Denver, John (Henry John Deutschendorf, Jr.) *singer, songwriter*
Dorsey, Helen Danner (Johna Blinn) *writer, author, educator*
Erman, John *film director*
Fein, Irving Ashley *television and motion picture executive*
Fisher, Carrie Frances *actress, writer*
Fisher, Terry Louise *television writer*
Friedman, Arthur Meeker *magazine editor, professional motorcycle racer*
Geffen, David *recording company executive, producer*
Grasshoff, Alex *writer, producer, director*
Haley, Jack, Jr. (John J. Haley) *director, producer, writer, executive*
†Hallstrom, Lasse *director*
Helin, James Dennis *advertising agency executive*
Henley, Don *singer, drummer, songwriter*
Hockney, David *artist*
Holt, Dennis F. *media buying company executive*
Ingels, Marty *theatrical agent, television and motion picture production executive*
Jackson, Joe *musician, singer, composer, songwriter*
Kassar, Mario F. *film production company executive*
†Kerr, Deborah Jane *actress*
Kidder, Margot *actress*
Kingsley, Patricia *public relations executive*
Leigh, Jennifer Jason (Jennifer Leigh Morrow) *actress*
Levine, Michael *public relations executive, author*
Lewis, Richard *actor, comedian*
Luckman, Charles *architect*
Ludwig, William *screenwriter*
Males, William James *film producer, make-up artist*
Marsalis, Wynton *musician*
May, Elaine *actress, theatre and film director*
†McKagan, Duff (Michael McKagan) *bassist*
Milius, John Frederick *film writer, director*
Moore, Dudley Stuart John *actor, musician*
Mull, Martin *comedian, singer*
Phillips, Julia Miller *film producer*
Reid, Antonio (L. A. Reid) *musician, songwriter*
Roberts, Julia Fiona *actress*
Ronstadt, Linda Marie *singer*
Rose, W. Axl (William Bruce Bailey) *singer*
Russell, Ken (Henry Kenneth Alfred Russell) *film and theatre director*
†Sargent, Joseph Daniel *motion picture and television director*
†Shaiman, Marc *composer, arranger, orchestrator*
Shaye, Robert Kenneth *cinema company executive*
Sherman, Robert B(ernard) *composer, lyricist, screenwriter*
Slash, (Saul Hudson) *guitarist*
Sloan, L. Lawrence *publishing executive*
Taylor, James Vernon *musician*
Van Buren, Abigail (Pauline Friedman Phillips) *columnist, author, writer, lecturer*
Verhoeven, Paul *film director*
von Sydow, Max (Carl Adolf von Sydow) *actor*
Wald, Donna Gene *advertising executive*
Walton, Brian *lawyer, union administrator*
Wilson, Myron Robert, Jr. *former psychiatrist*
Young, Neil *musician, songwriter*

West Los Angeles
Tamkin, S. Jerome *business executive, consultant*

Westlake Village
Blum, Fred Andrew *electronics company executive*
Caligiuri, Joseph Frank *engineering executive*
Doherty, Patrick Francis *communications executive, educator*
Easton, William Heyden *geology educator*
Fredericks, Ward Arthur *venture capitalist, food industry consultant*
Murdock, David H. *diversified company executive*
Rooney, Mickey (Joe Yule, Jr.) *actor*
Small, Richard David *research scientist*
Steadman, Lydia Duff *elementary school educator, symphony violinist*

Westminster
Armstrong, Gene Lee *systems engineering consultant, retired aerospace company executive*
Ryan, James Edwin *industrial arts educator*

Westwood
Brydon, Harold Wesley *entomologist, writer*

Whittier
Arcadi, John Albert *urologist*
Arenowitz, Albert Harold *psychiatrist*
Ash, James Lee, Jr. *academic administrator*
Bayer, William Martin *photographer, educator*
Brown, Thomas Andrew *aircraft and weaponry manufacturing executive*
Conlin, Alfred Thomas *retired food company executive, consultant*
Connick, Charles Milo *retired religion educator, clergyman*
Davidson, Alan Charles *insurance executive*
Drake, E Maylon *academic administrator*
Hurley, Eileen Beverly *school system administrator*
Lillevang, Omar Johansen *civil engineer*
Loughrin, Jay Richardson *mass communications educator, consultant*
Maxwell, Raymond Roger *accountant*
Newsom, Will Roy *former college president*
Tunison, Elizabeth Lamb *education educator*
†Zeisler, John Alfred, Jr. *clinical pharmacist, educator*

Wilmington
Smith, June Burlingame *English educator*

Windsor
Hayes, Vertis Clemon *painter, sculptor, educator*

Winters
Low, Donald Gottlob *retired veterinary medicine educator*

Woodland Hills
Abramson, Albert *television historian, consultant*
Amerine, Anne Follette *aerospace engineer*
Anaya, Richard Alfred, Jr. *accountant, investment banker*
Auger, David J. *newspaper publisher*
Caren, Robert Poston *aerospace company executive*
Chernof, David *internist*
†Crowe, Christopher *director, screenwriter*
†DeWitt, Barbara Jane *journalist*
Firestone, Morton H. *business management executive*
Fisher, Gerald Saul *publisher, financial consultant, lawyer*
Fisher, Robert James *public relations consultant, advertising executive*
Freeman, Philip Conrad, Jr. *computer systems company executive*
Fricker, John Arthur *pediatrician, educator*
Goldberg, David Charles *electrical contracting executive*
Gray, Thomas Stephen *newspaper editor*
Higginbotham, Lloyd William *mechanical engineer*
Horne, Lena *singer*
Neill, William Alexander *magazine editor*
Newman, Randy *singer, songwriter, musician*
Oltman, Henry George, Jr. *retired engineering executive*
†O'Meara, Sara *foundation administrator*
Pregerson, Harry *federal judge*
Rapoport, Ronald Jon *journalist*
Robison, Frederick Mason *financial executive*
†Rosenthal, Philip David *columnist*
†Rotenstreich, Jon W. *insurance company executive*
†Schaeffer, Leonard David *health care executive*
Scheimer, Louis *film and television producer*
Sharma, Brahama Datta *chemistry educator*
Sigholtz, Sara O'Meara *non-profit organization executive*
Strote, Joel Richard *lawyer*
Talbot, Matthew J. *oil company executive, rancher*
Taubitz, Fredricka *financial executive*
Taylor, Rowan Shaw *music educator, composer, conductor*
Vinson, William T. *lawyer, diversified corporation executive*
Weiser, Paul David *manufacturing company executive*
Wester, Keith Albert *film and television recording engineer, television executive*
Zeitlin, Herbert Zakary *retired college president*

Woodside
Ashley, Holt *aerospace scientist, educator*
Blum, Richard Hosmer Adams *foundation executive*
Kaisel, Stanley Francis *management consultant*

Yorba Linda
†Bailey, Don Matthew *aerospace and electronics company executive*
Eriksen, Otto Louis *retired manufacturing company executive*
Forth, Kevin Bernard *beverage distributing consultant*

Yountville
Goeglein, Richard John *hotel/casino chain executive*
Kay, Douglas Casey *leasing company executive*

Yreka
McFadden, Leon Lambert *artist, inventor*

Yuba City
Koury, Aleah George *retired church executive, minister*

COLORADO

Alamosa
Fulkerson, William Measey, Jr. *college president*

Arvada
Holden, George Fredric *brewing company executive, policy specialist, consultant*

Aspen
Berkó, Ferenc *photographer*
Caudill, Samuel Jefferson *architect*
Dietsch, Alfred John *real estate executive, lawyer*
†Ensign, Donald H. *landscape architect*
†Gustafson, James Arthur *architect*
Harth, Robert James *music festival executive*
Jalili, Mahir *lawyer*
McDade, James Russell *management consultant*
Soldner, Paul Edmund *artist, ceramist, educator*
Sullivan, Danny *professional race car driver*

Aurora
Bauman, Earl William *accountant, government official*
Eames, Wilmer Ballou *dental educator*
Fedak, Barbara Kingry *technical center administrator*
Fish, Ruby Mae Bertram (Mrs. Frederick Goodrich Fish) *civic worker*
†Hagedorn, Robert, Jr. *state legislator, educator*
Hickman, Grace Marguerite *artist*
Huff, Paul Emlyn *insurance executive*
†Hutchins, Charles Larry *educational association administrator, consultant*
†Jarvis, Mary G. *principal*
Motz, Kenneth Lee *former farm organization official*
†Ruddick, Stephen Richard *state legislator, lawyer, political consultant*
†Tauer, Paul E. *mayor, educator*

Basalt
Feliciano, José *entertainer*
Kazan, Lainie (Lainie Levine) *singer, actress*
Sinatra, Frank (Francis Albert Sinatra) *singer, actor*
Williams, Joe *jazz and blues singer*

Bellvue
Bennett, Jim *retired university official*
Mattson, Roy Henry *retired engineering educator*

Boulder
†Albino, Judith E. N. *university president*
†Albritton, Daniel L. *aeronomist*
Alldredge, Leroy Romney *retired geophysicist*
Anderson, Robert K. *health care company executive*
Anderson, Ronald Delaine *education educator*
Andrews, James Rowland *electronics executive, consultant*
Anthes, Richard Allen *meteorologist*
Archambeau, Charles Bruce *physics educator, geophysics research scientist*
Avery, Susan Kathryn *electrical engineering educator, researcher*
Ayad, Boulos Ayad *archaeology educator*
Bailey, Dana Kavanagh *radiophysicist, botanist*
Balog, James Dennis *photographer*
Bangs, F(rank) Kendrick *former business educator*
Barnes, Frank Stephenson *electrical engineer, educator*
Barry, Roger Graham *climatologist, educator*
†Barth, Charles Adolph *physicist, educator*
Bartlett, David Farnham *physics educator*
Barut, Asim Orhan *physicist, educator*
Baughn, William Hubert *former business educator and academic administrator*
Begelman, Mitchell C. *astrophysicist, educator*
†Bintliff, Barbara Ann *law librarian*
Birkenkamp, Dean Frederick *editor, publishing executive*
Birmingham, Bascom Wayne *retired government official*
Boss, Russel Wayne *business administration educator*
Boulding, Elise Marie *sociologist, educator*
Bourne, Lyle Eugene, Jr. *psychology educator*
Bowers, John Waite *communication educator*
Brakhage, James Stanley *filmmaker, educator*
Bright, William Oliver *linguistics educator*
Brutus, Dennis Vincent *African literature, poetry, creative writing educator*
Buchanan, Dodds Ireton *business educator, consultant*
Burghardt, Kurt Josef *marketing professional, infosystems specialist*
Burns, Daniel Hobart *management consultant*
Byerly, Radford, Jr. *science policy official*
Caine, Nelson *geomorphologist, educator*
Calvert, Jack George *atmospheric chemist, educator*
Carlson, Devon McElvin *architect, educator*
Caruthers, Marvin Harry *biochemistry educator*
Cary, John Robert *physics educator*
Cech, Thomas Robert *chemistry and biochemistry educator*
Chappell, Charles Franklin *meteorologist, consultant*
Chinnery, Michael Alistair *federal government official, geophysicist*
Choquette, Philip Wheeler *geologist, educator*
Clark, Melvin Eugene *chemical company executive*
Clifford, Steven Francis *science research director*
Codding, George Arthur, Jr. *political science educator*
Conti, Peter Selby *astronomy educator*
Corbridge, James Noel, Jr. *chancellor, educator*
Crane, Michael Patrick *art museum administrator, educator*
Cristol, Stanley Jerome *chemistry educator*
Crow, Edwin Louis *mathematical statistician, consultant*
Danilov, Victor Joseph *museum management program director, consultant, writer, educator*
†Danna, Kathleen Janet *virologist, plant molecular biologist, educator*
Darling, Frank Clayton *former political science educator, educational institute administrator*
Daughenbaugh, Randall Jay *chemical company executive*
De Fries, John Clarence *behavioral genetics educator, institute administrator*
Derr, Vernon Ellsworth *government research administrator*
Dorn, Edward Merton *poet, educator*
Dryer, Murray *physicist*
Dubin, Mark William *neuroscientist, educator*
Duckworth, Guy *musician, educator*
Echohawk, John Ernest *lawyer*
Ekstrand, Bruce Rowland *university administrator, psychology educator*
Enarson, Harold L. *emeritus university president*
†Evenson, Kenneth M. *physicist*
†Ferguson, Eldon Earl *physicist*

Fest, Thorrel Brooks former speech educator, consultant
Fiflis, Ted J. lawyer, educator
Fink, Robert Russell music theorist, university dean
Fleming, Rex James meteorologist
Folsom, Franklin Brewster author
Fuchs, Ewald Franz engineer, educator, consultant
Fukae, Kensuke infosystems specialist
Fuller, Jackson Franklin electrical engineering educator
Gabridge, Michael Gregory university administrator, science administrator
Garstang, Roy Henry astrophysicist, educator
Geers, Thomas Lange mechanical engineering educator
Gilman, Peter A. national laboratory administrator, scientist
Glover, Fred William artificial intelligence and optimization research director, educator
Goble, George G. civil engineering educator
Goeldner, Charles Raymond business educator
Gossard, Earl Everett physicist
†Gralapp, Marcelee Gayl librarian
Greenberg, Edward Seymour political science educator
Greene, David Lee physical anthropologist, educator
Griffiths, Lloyd Joseph electrical engineering educator, consultant
Gupta, Kuldip Chand electrical and computer engineering educator, researcher
Hall, John Lewis physicist, researcher
†Hanley, Howard James Mason research scientist
Hanna, William Johnson electrical engineering educator
Hanson, Robert Carl sociologist, educator
Hawkins, David Cartwright philosophy and history of science, educator
Hay, William Winn former museum director, natural history and geology educator
Healy, Alice Fenvessy psychology educator, researcher
Helburn, Nicholas geography educator
Hermann, Allen Max physics educator
Hildner, Ernest Gotthold, III solar physicist, science administrator
Hill, Boyd H., Jr. medieval history educator
Hill, David Allan electrical engineer
Hill, Harold Eugene communications educator
Hoerig, Gerald Lee chemical company executive
†Hofmann, David John atmospheric science researcher, educator
Hogg, David Clarence physicist
Holdsworth, Janet Nott women's health nurse
†Holzer, Thomas E. astronomer
Hyland, Laurie Zoe financial planner
Jerritts, Stephen G. computer company executive
†Jessor, Richard psychologist, educator
Joselyn, Jo Ann space scientist
Kanda, Motohisa electronics engineer
Kauffman, Erle Galen geologist, paleontologist
Kaye, Evelyn Patricia (Evelyn Patricia Sarson) author, publisher, travel expert
Kellogg, William Welch meteorologist
Kelso, Alec John (Jack Kelso) anthropologist, educator
King, Edward Louis retired chemistry educator
King, Helen Eileen service executive
†Kintsch, Walter psychology educator, director
Koch, Tad Harbison chemistry educator, researcher
Lanham, Urless Norton curator
Lester, Robert Carlton religious studies educator
Lineberger, William Carl chemistry educator
Little, Charles Gordon geophysicist
Lodewyk, Eric chemist, pharmaceutical executive
Low, Boon Chye physicist
Ma, Mark Tsu-han electronic engineer
Mahanthappa, Kalyana Thipperudraiah physicist, educator
Main, Jackson Turner history educator
†Malde, Harold Edwin retired federal government geologist
Maley, Samuel Wayne electrical engineering educator
Mandel, Siegfried English language educator, deceased
Mason, Leon Verne financial planner
Matthews, Eugene Edward artist
Matthews, Wanda Miller artist
Mc Intosh, J(ohn) Richard biologist, educator
Meier, Mark F. research scientist, glaciologist, educator
Melicher, Ronald William finance educator
†Mendez, Jana Wells state senator
Metzger, H(owell) Peter writer
Miller, Norman Richard diversified manufacturing company executive
Moses, Raphael Jacob lawyer
Mycielski, Jan mathematician, educator
Neinas, Charles Merrill athletic association executive
†Norcross, David Warren physicist, researcher
Oesterle, Dale Arthur law educator
Pankove, Jacques Isaac physicist
Peterson, Courtland Harry law educator
†Phelps, Arthur Van Rensselaer physicist, consultant
Pois, Robert August historian
Porzak, Glenn E. lawyer
Rich, Ben Arthur lawyer, university official
Rienner, Lynne Carol publisher
Robinson, Peter paleontology educator, consultant
Rodriguez, Juan Alfonso technology corporation executive
Rood, David S. linguistics educator
†Rotunno, Richard meteorologist
Sani, Robert LeRoy chemical engineering educator
Sarson, John Christopher television producer, director, writer
Scarritt, James Richard political science educator
Serafin, Robert Joseph science center administrator, electrical engineer
Shanahan, Eugene Miles flow measurement instrumentation company executive
Sirotkin, Phillip Leonard educational administrator
Smith, Ernest Ketcham electrical engineer
Smythe, William Rodman physicist, educator
Snow, Theodore Peck, Jr. astrophysics educator
Sodal, Ingvar Edmund electrical engineer, scientist
Spetzler, Hartmut August Werner geophysics educator
Staehelin, Lucas Andrew cell biology educator
Stanton, William John, Jr. marketing educator, author
Steuben, Norton Leslie lawyer, educator
Stone, John Helms, Jr. admiralty advisor
†Stull, Dean P. chemical company executive
†Sullivan, Donald Barrett physicist
Symons, James Martin theater and dance educator
Tatarskii, Valerian Il'ich physics researcher
Taylor, Allan Ross linguist, educator
Thomas, Daniel Foley telecommunications company executive
Timmerhaus, Klaus Dieter chemical engineering educator
Tippit, John Harlow lawyer
Tolbert, Bert Mills biochemist, educator
Trenberth, Kevin Edward atmospheric scientist
Uberoi, Mahinder Singh aerospace engineering educator
†Utlaut, William Frederick electrical engineer
†Vander Vorste, James LeRoy architect
Waldman, Anne Lesley poet, performer, editor, publisher, educational administrator
Walker, Deward Edgar, Jr. anthropologist, educator
Washington, Warren Morton meteorologist
Wedel, Waldo Rudolph archaeologist
Wheat, Joe Ben anthropologist
White, Gilbert F(owler) geographer, educator
†Wieman, Carl E. physics educator
Willam, Kaspar J. computational mechanics educator
Williams, James Franklin, II university dean, librarian
Yokell, Michael David economist

Breckenridge
†Williams, Samuel real estate executive

Brighton
†Vang, Timothy Teng church executive

Broomfield
Davis, Delmont Alvin, Jr. manufacturing company executive

Canon City
Bendell, Donald Ray writer, director, poet
Mc Bride, John Alexander retired chemical engineer

Carbondale
Cowgill, Ursula Moser biologist, educator, environmental consultant

Castle Rock
Eppler, Jerome Cannon private financial advisor
Graf, Joseph Charles retired foundation executive
Thornbury, John Rousseau radiologist, physician

Cedaredge
†Acquafresca, Steven Joseph fruitgrower, consultant, state legislator

Central City
Rodgers, Frederic Barker judge

Cherry Hills Village
Meyer, Milton Edward, Jr. lawyer, artist

Clark
Bartoe, Otto Edwin, Jr. aircraft company executive

Colorado Springs
Adams, Bernard Schroder retired college president
†Allen, J. Lamar engineering company executive, educator
Allery, Kenneth Edward air force officer
Anderson, Lawrence Keith electrical engineer
Anderson, N. Christian, III newspaper executive
Anderson, Paul Nathaniel oncologist, educator
†Armstrong, Lance professional cyclist
Austin, Timothy Olympic athlete, boxer
†Bailey, R. W. church administrator
Barrowman, Mike Olympic athlete, swimmer
Barton, Greg Olympic athlete, kayak racer
Bates, Michael Olympic athlete, track and field
Berkoff, David Olympic athlete, swimmer
Biondi, Matt Olympic athlete, swimmer
Bishop, Leo Kenneth clergyman, educator
Blanchette, Jeanne Ellene Maxant artist, educator, performer
Bowen, Clotilde Dent retired army officer, psychiatrist
Breckner, William John, Jr. retired air force officer, corporate executive, consultant
Brooks, Glenn Ellis political science educator, educational administrator
†Bubna, Paul F. church administrator
Budington, William Stone retired librarian
Buell, Bruce Temple lawyer
Burgess, Greg Olympic athlete, swimming
†Burnley, Kenneth S. school system administrator
Byrd, Chris Olympic athlete, boxer
Carmichael, Nelson skier
Conley, Mike track and field athlete
Couger, James Daniel computer scientist, writer
Cramer, Owen Carver classics educator
Cray, Seymour R. computer designer
†Davey, J. A. church administrator
Dees, Tony Olympic athlete, track and field
Dello Joio, Norman Olympic athlete, equestrian
Devers, Gail track and field athlete
Diebel, Nelson Olympic athlete, swimmer
Dimas, Trent Olympic athlete, gymnast
Doehrin, James Olympic athlete, track and field
Ehrhorn, Richard William electronics company executive
Eldredge, Todd figure skater
Engfer, Susan Marvel zoological park executive
Essick, Raymond Brooke, III amateur sports administrator
Farr, Leonard Alfred hospital administrator
Feld, Werner Joachim political scientist, educator
Flynn, James T. lawyer
Forgan, David Waller retired air force officer
Foth, Bob Olympic athlete, riflery
Fox, Douglas Allan religion educator
Goehring, Kenneth artist
Grady, Dolores Anne academic administrator, educator, consultant
Gray, Johnny Olympic athlete, track and field
Greene, Joe Olympic athlete, track and field
Groebli, Werner Fritz (Mr. Frick) professional ice skater, realtor
†Hall, Brian Howard publishing executive
Hallenbeck, Kenneth Luster numismatist
Halling, Leonard William retired pathologist, laboratory administrator
Hampton, Rex Herbert gold mining company executive, consultant
Hanifen, Richard Charles bishop
Hartwell, Erin Olympic athlete, cycling
Henrickson, Eiler Leonard geologist, educator
Hoffman, John Raleigh physicist
Isaac, Robert Michael mayor, lawyer
Jacobi, Joe Olympic athlete, canoeist
Jager, Tom Olympic athlete, swimmer
Johnson, Dave Olympic athlete, track and field
Kelsey, Floyd Lamar, Jr. architect
Kendall, Phillip Alan lawyer
†Kerrigan, Nancy professional figure skater, former Olympic athlete
Killian, George Ernest association executive
King, Peter Joseph, Jr. retired gas company executive
Kohlman, David Leslie engineering executive, consultant
Kraemer, Sandy Frederick lawyer
†Lace, Jerry E. executive
Lenzi, Mark Olympic athlete, springboard diver
Leuver, Robert Joseph former government official, association executive
Lewis, Steve Olympic athlete, track and field
MacLeod, Richard Patrick foundation administrator
Macon, Jerry Lyn software company owner, software publisher
†Mangham, R. H. church administrator
Margolis, Bernard Allen library administrator, antique book merchant and appraiser
Markert, Clement Lawrence biology educator
Marsh, Michael track and field athlete
May, Melvin Arthur computer software company executive
†May, Ronny Joe (Ron May) computer scientist, state legislator
†McIntyre, Liz Olympic athlete
Metzler, Philip Lowry, Jr. air force officer
Milton, Richard Henry retired diplomat
Mitchell, Dennis Olympic athlete, track and field
Mitchell, John Henderson retired army officer, management consultant
†Mohrman, Kathryn academic administrator
Morales, Pablo Olympic athlete, swimmer
Morris, Jason Olympic athlete
Moses, Edwin track and field athlete
Murray, Ty (The Kid) professional rodeo cowboy
†Nanfelt, P. N. church administrator
Nolan, Barry Hance publishing company executive
Noyes, Richard Hall bookseller
Olin, Kent Oliver banker
O'Rourke, Dennis lawyer
O'Shields, Richard Lee retired natural gas company executive
Payne, Billy (William A. Payne) real estate lawyer, sports association executive
†Peterson, Amy Olympic athlete
Phibbs, Harry Albert interior designer, professional speaker, lecturer
Pierce, Jack Olympic athlete, track and field
†Powers, Ray Lloyd state senator, dairy farmer, rancher
Ramsay, Robert Henry investment manager
Robinson, Robert James retired manufacturing executive
Robinson, Ronald Alan oil company executive
Rouse, Jeff Olympic athlete, swimmer
Rouss, Ruth lawyer
Sawyer, Thomas William air force officer
Schaeffer, Reiner Horst air force officer, retired librarian, foreign language professional
Schwartz, Donald chemistry educator
Shafer, Dallas Eugene psychology gerontology educator, minister
Sheridan, John Brian librarian
Sherman, Donald H. civil engineer
Simpkins, Charles Olympic athlete, track and field
Sinclair, William Donald church official, fundraising consultant, political activist
Stavig, Mark Luther English language educator
Stewart, Melvin Olympic athlete, swimmer
Stewart, Robert Lee retired army officer, astronaut
Strausbaugh, Scott David Olympic athlete, canoeist
†Street, Picabo Olympic athlete
Stulce, Mike Olympic athlete, track and field
Thomas, Darrell Denman lawyer
Todd, Harold Wade retired air force officer, consultant
Turner, Cathy Olympic athlete
Tutt, Russell Thayer investment company executive
Twardowski, Thomas John college president
Vayhinger, John Monroe psychotherapist, minister
†Wagner, David J. art center director
Watts, Oliver Edward engineering consultancy company executive
†Wells, Jeffrey M. state senator, lawyer, judge
West, Ralph Leland veterinarian
†Wheeland, D. A. church administrator
Wilcox, Rhoda Davis educator
Wilkins, Christopher Putnam conductor
Witte, Randall Erwyn publisher
†Wood, Stephen minister
Worner, Lloyd Edson retired college president
Yaffe, James author
Yamaguchi, Kristi Tsuya ice skater
Young, Kevin track and field athlete
Zapel, Arthur L. book publishing executive
Ziemer, Rodger Edmund electrical engineering educator, consultant

Colorado State University
Gillette, Edward LeRoy radiation oncology educator
†Whicker, Floyd Ward biology educator, ecologist

Columbine Valley
Wittbrodt, Edwin Stanley consultant, former bank executive, former air force officer

Conifer
Powers, Edwin Malvin consulting engineer

Crawford
Mosher, Lawrence Forsyth journalist

Denver
†Abo, Ronald Kent architect
Abram, Donald Eugene federal magistrate judge
Adler, Charles Spencer psychiatrist
†Agler, Vickie Lyn state legislator
Aikawa, Jerry Kazuo physician, educator
Albrecht, Duane Taylor veterinarian
Alfers, Stephen Douglas lawyer
†Ames, A. Gary communications company executive
Anderson, Gregg I. lawyer
Anderson, John David architect
Anderson, Robert environmental specialist, physician
Antonoff, Gary L. real estate executive
Antonoff, Steven Ross educational consultant, author
†Ashton, Rick James librarian
Atkins, Dale Morrell physician
Austin, H(arry) Gregory lawyer
Avrit, Richard Calvin defense consultant
Babcock, Lewis Thornton federal judge
Bain, Donald Knight lawyer
Ballard, Jack Stokes educator
Bard, Richard H. financial service company executive
Barkin, Roger Michael pediatrician, emergency physician, educator
Barnewall, Gordon Gouverneur news analyst, educator
†Bates, James Robert newspaper editor
Battaglia, Frederick Camillo physician
Bauder, Sister Marianna hospital administrator
Baumgart, Norbert K. government official
Baylor, Don Edward professional baseball manager
†Bearden, Thomas Howard news program producer, correspondent
Behrendt, John Charles research geophysicist
Belitz, Paul Edward lawyer
†Benavidez, Celina Garcia state legislator
Benson, Robert Eugene lawyer
Benson, Thomas Quentin lawyer
Benton, Auburn Edgar lawyer
†Berg, Karl architectural firm executive
Berland, Karen Ina psychologist
Bickerstaff, Bernard Tyrone, Sr. professional basketball team executive
†Bishop, Tilman Malcolm state senator, retired college administrator
Blager, Florence Berman voice pathology educator
Blair, Andrew Lane, Jr. lawyer, educator
Blatter, Frank Edward travel agency executive
Blunk, Forrest Stewart lawyer
Bomberg, Thomas James dental educator
Boudreau, Robert Donald meteorology educator
Bowman, Joseph Searles petroleum consultant
†Bradley, Jeff(rey) M. arts critic
Brainard, Edward Axdal academic administrator
Breck, Allen du Pont historian, educator
Brega, Charles Franklin lawyer
Brierly, Keppel retired investment executive
Brimhall, Dennis C. hospital executive
†Brock, Kathleen Kennelly advertising agency executive
Brom, Libor journalist, educator
Brown, Keith Lapham retired ambassador
Brownlee, Judith Marilyn Wiccan minister, psychotherapist
Brownson, Jacques Calmon architect
†Buechner, John C. academic administrator
†Bunn, Paul A., Jr. oncologist, educator
Burford, Anne McGill lawyer
Burke, Kenneth John lawyer
†Burrell, Calvin Archie minister
Butler, David lawyer
Butler, Owen Bradford securities advisor
Bye, James Edward lawyer
Byyny, Richard Lee academic administrator
Cain, Douglas Mylchreest lawyer
Callihan, C. Michael lieutenant governor, former state senator
Campbell, Leonard Martin lawyer
Cann, William Hopson former mining company executive
Cantwell, William Patterson lawyer
Carrigan, Jim Richard federal judge
Carver, Craig R. lawyer
Ceci, Jesse Arthur violinist
Chappell, Willard Ray physics educator, environmental scientist
Cheroutes, Michael Louis lawyer
Chidester, Alfred C. lawyer
Chinn, Peggy Lois nursing educator, editor
†Chmelir, John David engineer, consultant
Clarke, David Marshall academic administrator, priest
Clinch, Nicholas Bayard, III business executive
Clough, Nadine Doerr school psychologist, psychotherapist
Coats, Gary Lee clinical psychologist, educator
Collins, Martha Traudt lawyer
Conger, John Janeway psychologist, educator
Conover, Frederic King lawyer
Conroy, Thomas Francis insurance company executive
Cook, Albert Thomas Thornton, Jr. financial advisor
Cooper, Paul Douglas lawyer
Cope, Thomas Field lawyer
Cowee, John Widmer retired university chancellor
Cowley, Gerald Dean architect
Cox, William V. lawyer
†Craig, Lexie Ferrell career development specialist, career guidance counselor, educator
Craine, Thomas Knowlton academic administrator
Cubbison, Christopher Allen editor
Curtis, George Bartlett lawyer
†Daley, Richard Halbert foundation executive
†Dana, Richard E. oil industry executive
Darkey, Kermit Louis association executive, lawyer
Dauer, Edward Arnold law educator
Davis, Joseph Samuel retired department store executive, consultant
Davis, Marvin petroleum company executive, entrepreneur
Dean, James Benwell lawyer
†Decker, David B. architect, educator
Deering, Fred Arthur insurance company executive
†De Gette, Diana Louise lawyer, state legislator
†Deitrich, Richard Adam pharmacology educator
†DeLong, James C. air transportation executive
Dempsey, Howard Stanley lawyer, mining executive, investment banker
DeMuth, Alan Cornelius lawyer
DePew, Marie Kathryn retired secondary educator
Dobbs, Gregory Allan journalist
†Dominick, Peter Hoyt, Jr. architect
Doran, Maureen O'Keefe psychotherapist, psychiatric nursing consultant
Downey, Arthur Harold, Jr. lawyer
Drake, Sylvie (Jurras Drake) theater critic
†Dubroff, Henry Allen journalist
Ducker, Bruce novelist, lawyer
Duke, Harold Benjamin, Jr. retired holding company executive
Dunham, Stephen Sampson lawyer
Eaton, Gareth Richard chemistry educator, university dean
Ebel, David M. federal judge
Edelman, Joel medical center executive
Edwards, Phyllis Mae accountant, graphologist
Eiberger, Carl Frederick trial lawyer
Eickhoff, Theodore Carl physician
Eklund, Carl Andrew lawyer
†Engdahl, Todd Philip newspaper editor
Erickson, William Hurt state supreme court justice
Erisman, Frank lawyer
†Evans, Ginger Sunday civil engineer
†Faatz, Jeanne Ryan state legislator

Fagin, David Kyle natural resource company executive
Farley, John Michael lawyer
Faxon, Thomas Baker lawyer
Featherstone, Bruce Alan lawyer
Feder, Harold Abram lawyer
Ferguson, Lloyd Elbert manufacturing engineer
Fernandez, Tomas Isidro accountant
Finesilver, Sherman Glenn federal judge
Firminger, Harlan Irwin pathologist, educator
Fischer, James Adrian clergyman
Fisher, Louis McLane, Jr. environmental engineering firm executive
Fiske, Terry Noble lawyer
Flowers, William Harold, Jr. lawyer
Fognani, John Dennis lawyer
Fredmann, Martin artistic director ballet, educator, choreographer
Freiheit, Clayton Fredric zoo director
Friedman, H. Harold cardiologist, internist
Fugate, Ivan Dee banker, lawyer
Fulginiti, Vincent university dean
Fuller, Kenneth Roller architect
Galarraga, Andres Jose professional baseball player
†Gallagher, Dennis Joseph state senator, educator
†Garrison, T. Paul advertising executive
Gates, Charles Cassius rubber company executive
Gebhard, Bob professional baseball team executive
Gibson, Thomas Joseph diversified holding company executive
Giesen, John William advertising executive
†Giffin, Glenn Orlando, II music critic, writer, newspaper editor
Gillis, Paul Leonard accountant
Glismann, Diane Duffy health facility administrator
Golitz, Loren Eugene dermatologist, pathologist, clinical administrator, educator
†Gonzales, Richard L. fire department chief
Grant, Patrick Alexander lawyer, former state representative
Grant, William West, III banker
†Green, Charles Walter newspaper editor
Green, Jersey Michael-Lee lawyer
Green, Larry Alton physician, educator
Green, Steven J. retail executive
Greene, Leslie Speed lawyer
Grissom, Garth Clyde lawyer
Haddon, Harold Alan lawyer
†Hamblin, Kenneth Lorenzo radio talk show host, columnist
†Hamilton, Frederic Crawford oil company executive
Hamilton, Warren Bell research geologist, educator
Hamilton, William T. English educator, former academic administrator
Hardy, Wayne Russell insurance broker
Harris, Dale Ray lawyer
Harris, Ellen Gandy (Mrs. J. Ramsay Harris) civic worker
Harry, Robert Hayden lawyer
Hart, Gary W. former senator, lawyer
Hartley, James Edward lawyer
Havekost, Daniel John architect
Hawley, Robert Cross lawyer
†Hayes, Edward Lee religious organization administrator
Hendrix, Lynn Parker lawyer
†Hernandez, Tony J. computer company executive, state representative
Hesse, Stephen Max newspaper executive
†Hetzel, Fredrick William biophysicist, educator
Hill, Diane Seldon corporate psychologist
Hirschfeld, Arlene F. civic worker, homemaker
Hixon, Janet Kay Erickson nursing association administrator, educator
Hoagland, Donald Wright lawyer
Hobson, Harry Lee, Jr. lawyer
Hodson, Thane Raymond lawyer
Hoffman, Daniel Steven lawyer, legal educator
Hogan, Curtis Jule union executive, industrial relations consultant
Holleman, Paul Douglas lawyer
Holme, Richard Phillips lawyer
Holmes, Fred Gillespie sugar company executive
Holte, Debra Leah investment executive, financial analyst
Hoover, George Schweke architect
Hopfenbeck, George Martin, Jr. lawyer
Hopkins, Donald J. lawyer
Hornbein, Victor architect
Husband, John Michael lawyer
Imhoff, Walter Francis investment banker
Iona, Mario retired physics educator
Irvin, Robert D. lawyer
Iseman, Michael Dee medical educator
Issel, Daniel Paul professional basketball coach
Jackson, Richard Brooke lawyer
Jacobs, Paul Alan lawyer
Jacobson, Eugene Donald physician, administrator, educator, researcher
Jafek, Bruce William otolaryngologist, educator
†Johnson, Joan state senator
Johnston, Gwinavere Adams public relations consultant
†Kafadar, Charles Bell mechanical engineer, engineering executive
Kane, John Lawrence, Jr. federal judge
Kauvar, Abraham J. gastroenterologist, medical administrator
Keats, Donald Howard composer, educator
Keely, George Clayton lawyer
Keller, Alex Stephen lawyer
Keller, Glen Elven, Jr. lawyer
Kern, Fred, Jr. physician, educator
†Kerns, Peggy Shoup state representative
Kintzele, John Alfred lawyer
Kirgis, Frederic L. retired lawyer
Kirkpatrick, Charles Harvey physician, immunology researcher
Kirshbaum, Howard M. judge
Konrad, Peter Allen foundation administrator
Krane, Robert Alan banker
Krieger, Gary Robert environmental medicine physician
Krikos, George Alexander pathologist, educator
Krill, Arthur Melvin engineering, architectural and planning company executive
Kripke, Kenneth Norman lawyer
Kuper, Dennis Lee financial officer
†Kurz, Kelli McDonald advertising executive
†Laff, Seymour health care executive
Larsen, Gary Loy physician, researcher
†Larson, Dayl Andrew architect
Law, John Manning retired lawyer
Lee, Richard Kenneth building products company executive
Leiweke, Timothy sales executive, marketing professional
†Leprino, James G. food products executive
Lesher, Donald Miles lawyer
Levy, Mark Ray lawyer
Lewis, Jerome A. petroleum company executive, investment banker
Lilly, John Russell surgeon, educator
Livingston, Johnston R. manufacturing executive
Lohr, George E. state supreme court justice
Low, Andrew M. lawyer
Low, John Wayland lawyer
Lubeck, Marvin Jay ophthalmologist
Macey, William Blackmore oil company executive
MacGregor, George Lescher, Jr. freelance writer, brokerage house executive
Magness, Bob John telecommunications executive
Mahlman, Henry Clayton lawyer
Makowski, Edgar Leonard obstetrician and gynecologist
Malone, John C. telecommunications executive
Malone, Robert Joseph bank executive
Mandelson, Richard S. lawyer
†Markman, Howard J. psychology educator
Martin, James Russell lawyer
Martin, Richard Jay medical educator
†Martin, William Truett oral surgeon, state legislature
Martz, Clyde Ollen lawyer, educator
†Mason, Ronald Leonard architect
Matsch, Richard P. federal judge
Mauro, Richard Frank lawyer, investment manager
Maxfield, Thomas H. lawyer
†May, Clifford Daniel newspaper editor, journalist
May, Francis Hart, Jr. retired building materials manufacturing executive
McAtee, Patricia Anne Rooney medical educator
McBurney, Linda Lee health facility administrator
Mc Candless, Bruce, II engineer, former astronaut
Mc Clenney, Byron Nelson community college administrator
McClung, J(ames) David corporate executive, lawyer
McCotter, James Rawson lawyer
McGowan, Joseph Anthony, Jr. news executive
McGrath, Edward Joseph lawyer
McGraw, Jack Wilson government official
McKibben, Ryan Timothy newspaper executive
Mc Kinney, Alexis public relations consultant
McWilliams, Robert Hugh federal judge
Mead, Beverly Mirium Anderson writer, educator
Mehring, Clinton Warren engineering executive
†Meiklejohn, Alvin J., Jr. state senator, lawyer, accountant
Mendelsohn, Harold sociologist, educator
Merker, Steven Joseph lawyer
Messer, Donald Edward theological school president
Meyer, Natalie state official
†Michaud, David L. protective services official
Miller, Arlyn James oil company executive
†Miller, Donald E. rubber company executive
Miller, Gale Timothy lawyer
Miller, Robert Nolen lawyer
†Miller, Sarah Pearl librarian
Miller, Stanley Custer, Jr. physicist, retired educator
Moore, Ernest Eugene, Jr. surgeon, educator
Moore, George Eugene surgeon
Moore, John Porfilio federal judge
Moorhead, John B. lawyer
†Movshovitz, Howard Paul film critic, educator
Moye, John Edward lawyer
Muldoon, Brian lawyer
Mullarkey, Mary J. state supreme court justice
Muller, Nicholas Guthrie lawyer, business executive
Mullineaux, Donal Ray geologist
Murane, William Edward lawyer
Murdy, Wayne William mining company executive, financial officer
Musyl, Marc J. lawyer
Mutombo, DiKembe professional basketball player
Myers, Harry J., Jr. publisher
Nanda, Ved Prakash law educator
Neiser, Brent Allen professional association director
Nelson, Bernard William foundation executive, educator, physician
Nelson, Nancy Eleanor pediatrician, educator
Nelson, William Rankin surgeon
†Nessi, Dominic federal agency administrator, instructor
Neu, Carl Herbert, Jr. management consultant
Neumann, Herschel physics educator
Neville, Margaret Cobb physiologist, educator
Newton, James Quigg, Jr. lawyer
Nicholson, Will Faust, Jr. bank holding company executive
Norman, John Barstow, Jr. designer, educator
North, Phillip J. lawyer
Norton, Gale state attorney general
Notari, Paul Celestin communications executive
Nottingham, Edward Willis, Jr. federal judge
O'Keefe, Edward Franklin lawyer
Omura, James Matsumoto journalist, editor, publisher
Otten, Arthur Edward, Jr. lawyer, corporate executive
Otto, Jean Hammond journalist
†Owen, David Turner owner, operator
Owen, James Churchill, Jr. lawyer
Owens, J(ames) Cuthbert surgeon, anatomist, retired medical educator
Owens, Marvin Franklin, Jr. oil company executive
Palmer, David Gilbert lawyer
†Palmreuter, Kenneth Richard Louis principal
Parker, Catherine Susanne psychotherapist
Parry, John Robert natural resource company executive, geophysicist
†Perez, Jean-Yves engineering company executive
Petros, Raymond Louis, Jr. lawyer
Petty, Thomas Lee physician, educator
Pfenninger, Karl H. cell biology and neuroscience educator
Pfnister, Allan Orel humanities educator
†Philip, Thomas Peter mining executive
Phillips, Paul David, Jr. lawyer
Poirot, James Wesley engineering company executive
Pollard, William Sherman, Jr. civil engineer, educator
Poulson, Robert Dean lawyer
Poynter, James Morrison travel educator
Pringle, Bruce D. federal magistrate
Pringle, Edward E. legal educator, former state supreme court chief justice
Prochnow, James R. lawyer
Prosser, John Martin architect, educator, urban design consultant
Puck, Theodore Thomas geneticist, biophysicist, educator
Purcell, Kenneth psychology educator, university dean
Quiat, Gerald M. lawyer
Rael, Henry Sylvester health administrator
Rainer, William Gerald cardiac surgeon
†Ramon, David A. consumer products company executive
Ramsey, John Arthur lawyer
Randall, William Theodore state official
Ray, Bruce David lawyer
†Reidinger, Russell Frederick, Jr. fish and wildlife scientist
Reisinger, George Lambert management consultant
†Rendu, Jean-Michel Marie mining executive
†Repine, John E. pediatrician, educator
Reynolds, Collins James, III association administrator
Rich, Robert Stephen lawyer
Ris, William Krakow lawyer
Ritchie, Daniel Lee university administrator
Roberts, Neil Fletcher management consulting company executive
†Robinson, Carole Ann insurance executive
Rockwell, Bruce McKee retired banker, retired foundation executive
†Rodman, David Malcolm physician, educator
Romer, Roy R. governor
Rovira, Luis Dario state supreme court justice
Rubright, Royal Cushing lawyer
Ruge, Daniel August retired neurosurgeon, educator
Rule, Daniel Rhodes opera company executive
Rumack, Barry H. physician, toxicologist, pediatrician
Ruppert, John Lawrence lawyer
†Rutherford, Robert Barry surgeon
Sandler, Thomas R. accountant
Sasso, Cassandra Gay lawyer
Sayre, John Marshall lawyer, former government official
†Schaffer, Robert Warren state senator
Schiff, Donald Wilfred pediatrician, educator
Schneck, Stuart Austin neurologist, educator
Schneider, Gene W. cable television company executive, movie theater executive
Schrepferman, Richard Lee lawyer
Schwartz, Cherie Anne Karo storyteller
Seawell, Donald Ray lawyer, publisher, arts center executive, producer
Selbin, Joel chemistry educator
Shea, Kevin Michael lawyer
†Sheeran, Michael John Leo priest, educational administrator
Shore, James H(enry) psychiatrist
Silverman, Arnold physician
Simons, Lynn Osborn state education official
Smith, Dwight Morrell chemistry educator
Snyder, Stephen Edward lawyer
Sparr, Daniel Beattie federal judge
Spencer, Frederick Gilman newspaper editor in chief
Stafford, J. Francis archbishop
Steenhagen, Robert Lewis landscape architect, consultant
Stephens, William Thomas forest products manufacturing company executive
Stephenson, Arthur Emmet, Jr. investment company executive, banker
Stephenson, Toni Edwards publisher, investment management executive
Stewart, Lyle Bainbridge lawyer
Stockmar, Ted P. lawyer
Storey, Brit Allan historian
Sullivan, Mary Rose English educator
†Sullivan, Patrick James physician, state representative
Sutton, Raymond L., Jr. lawyer
Swenka, Arthur John food products executive
†Swenson, Mary Ann bishop
Szefler, Stanley James pediatrics and pharmacology educator
Talmage, David Wilson microbiology and medical educator, physician, former university administrator
Taylor, Edward Stewart physician, educator
†Tebedo, MaryAnne state legislator
†Teets, Peter B. aerospace executive
Thomasch, Roger Paul lawyer
Thompson, Lohren Matthew oil company executive
Timothy, Robert Keller telephone company executive
Tipton, John J. lawyer
†Todd, Donald Frederick geologist
Tomlinson, Warren Leon lawyer
Tormey, Douglass Cole medical oncologist
Tracey, Jay Walter, Jr. retired lawyer
†Traylor, Claire Guthrie state senator
Trueblood, Harry Albert, Jr. oil company executive
Udevitz, Norman publishing executive
Ulevich, Neal Hirsh photojournalist
Valot, Daniel L. oil industry executive
Vigil, Charles S. lawyer
Wagner, Judith Buck investment firm executive
Walker, Timothy Blake lawyer, educator
Wallace, Victor L., II lawyer
Washington, Reginald Louis pediatric cardiologist
Watson, William D. lawyer
Webb, Wellington E. mayor
Weihaupt, John George geosciences educator, scientist, university administrator
Weinshienk, Zita Leeson federal judge
†Weissenbuehler, Wayne bishop
†Weissmann, Paul Martin state legislator
Welles, John Galt museum director
Weston, William Lee dermatologist
†Wham, Dorothy Stonecipher state legislator
Whatley, Lisa vocational school administrator
Wheeler, Malcolm Edward lawyer, law educator
Whitlock, William Abel lawyer
Wiens, Duane Daton matrix-graphic design firm owner
Wiggs, Eugene Overbey ophthalmologist, educator
Williams, Michael Anthony lawyer
Williams, Wayne De Armond lawyer
†Winterrond, William J. bishop
Wirkler, Norman Edward architectural, engineering, construction management firm executive
Witkowski-Garcia, Phyllis Josephine early childhood specialist, headstart consultant
Wohlgenant, Richard Glen lawyer
Woods, Lucius Earle lawyer
Woodward, Lester Ray lawyer
†Yamamoto, Kaoru psychology, education educator
Yegge, Robert Bernard lawyer, college dean emeritus, educator
Zakhem, Sam Hanna diplomat
Zaranka, William F. academic administrator, author
†Zeigel, Henry Alan architect
Zimet, Carl Norman psychologist, educator

Dolores
Kreyche, Gerald Francis retired philosophy educator

Durango
Ballantine, Morley Cowles (Mrs. Arthur Atwood Ballantine) newspaper editor
Burnham, Bryson Paine retired lawyer
Jones, Joel Mackey college president
Spencer, Donald Clayton mathematician
Steinhoff, Harold William retired research institute executive

Eagle
Sullivan, Selby William lawyer, business executive

Englewood
Atwater, Stephen Dennis professional football player
†Barr, Kenneth John retired mining company executive
Beake, John professional football team executive
Beddow, David Pierce broadcasting and cable executive
†Blair, Stewart D. cable television executive, small business owner
Bryson, Gary Spath cable television and telephone company executive
Callahan, Richard J. communications company executive
Chesser, Al H. union official
†Craw, Nicholas Wesson motor sports association executive
Czartolomny, Piotr Antoni librarian
Dackow, Orest Taras insurance company executive
Elway, John Albert professional football player
English, Gerald Marion otolaryngologist
Fisher, Bob real estate broker, franchisor
Fisher, Donne Francis telecommunications executive
†Harding, W. M. cooperative financial institution executive
†Jones, Glenn Robert cable systems executive
Mahoney, Gerald Francis manufacturing company executive
Manion, Jerry R. hotel chain executive
Manley, Richard Walter insurance executive
Massey, Leon R. association executive
Mc Adams, Ronald Earl geologist
McCormick, Richard David telecommunications company executive
O'Bryan, William Hall insurance executive
Parker, Gordon Rae natural resource company executive
Pearlman, David Samuel allergist
Perry, Mervyn Francis investment company executive
Phillips, Wade professional football team coach
†Russ, Charles Paul, III lawyer, corporate executive
†Sharpe, Shannon professional football player
Shields, Marlene Sue elementary school educator
†Sims, Doug bank executive
†Strutton, Larry D. newspaper executive
Ward, Milton Hawkins mining company executive
Wilson, James Ernest geological consultant, writer
Wynar, Bohdan Stephen librarian, author and editor

Estes Park
Hillway, Tyrus author, educator
Moore, Omar Khayyam experimental sociologist
Webb, Richard C. engineering company executive

Evergreen
†Gerou, Phillip Howard architect
Haun, John Daniel petroleum geologist, educator
Jesser, Roger Franklyn former brewing company engineering executive, consultant
Link, Peter Karl geologist
Newkirk, John Burt metallurgical engineer, administrator
Phillips, Adran Abner (Abe Phillips) geologist, oil and gas exploration consultant

Fort Collins
†Abt, Steven R. civil engineering educator, laboratory director
Anderson, B(enard) Harold educational administrator
Bamburg, James Robert biochemistry educator
Bennett, Thomas LeRoy, Jr. clinical neuropsychology educator
Bernstein, Elliot Roy chemistry educator
Boyd, Landis Lee agricultural engineer, educator
Cermak, Jack Edward engineer, educator
Chambers, Joan Louise library director
Christiansen, Norman Juhl retired newspaper publisher
Collins, Royal Eugene petroleum engineering educator, physicist, consultant
Curthoys, Norman P. biochemistry educator, consultant
Eitzen, David Stanley sociologist, educator
Elkind, Mortimer Murray biophysicist, educator
Ellis, Spencer Percy landscape architect
Fields, Robert Charles retired printing company executive
Fixman, Marshall chemist, educator
Follett, Ronald Francis soil scientist
Frasier, Gary W. hydraulic engineer
†Garvey, Daniel Cyril mechanical engineer
Gilderhus, Mark Theodore historian, educator
Gubler, Duane J. research scientist, administrator
Hafford, Patricia Ann electronic company executive
Hanan, Joe John horticulture educator
Harper, Judson Morse university administrator, consultant, educator
†Heermann, Dale Frank agricultural engineer
Jaros, Dean university official
Johnson, Robert Britten geology educator
Kaufman, Harold Richard mechanical engineer and physics educator
Keim, Wayne Franklin retired agronomy educator, plant geneticist
Kennedy, George Alexander classicist, educator
Koelzer, Victor Alvin civil engineer
Maga, Joseph Andrew food science educator
†McIlwraith, Cyril Wayne veterinary surgery educator
Meyers, Albert Irving chemistry educator
†Mielke, Paul William, Jr. statistician
Mortvedt, John Jacob soil scientist
†Mosier, Arvin Ray chemist, researcher
Niehaus, Merle H. agricultural educator, international agriculture consultant
†Niswender, Gordon Dean physiologist, educator
†Norton, Jack Richard chemistry educator
Ogg, James Elvis microbiologist, educator
Patton, Carl Elliott physics educator
Peterson, Gary Andrew agronomics researcher
Quick, James S. geneticist, plant breeder
Richardson, Everett Vern hydraulic engineer, educator, administrator

Rock, Kenneth Willett *history educator*
Rogers, Garth Winfield *lawyer*
Rollin, Bernard Elliot *philosophy educator, consultant on animal ethics*
Rolston, Holmes, III *theologian, educator, philosopher*
Roos, Eric Eugene *plant physiologist*
Sandborn, Virgil Alvin *civil engineer, educator*
Schumm, Stanley Alfred *geologist, educator*
Seidel, George Elias, Jr. *animal scientist, educator*
Smith, Ralph Earl *virologist*
Sons, Raymond William *journalist*
†Stendell, Rey *ecological research director*
Suinn, Richard Michael *psychologist*
†Tweedie, Richard Lewis *statistics educator, consultant*
Voss, James Leo *veterinarian*
Walsh, Richard George *agricultural economist*
Wengert, Norman Irving *political science educator*
Wilber, Charles Grady *forensic science educator, consultant*
Woolhiser, David Arthur *hydraulic engineer*
Yates, Albert Carl *university administrator, chemistry educator*

Fort Morgan
Bond, Richard Randolph *college administrator, legislator*
Perdue, James Everett *university vice chancellor emeritus*

Frisco
Bybee, Rodger Wayne *science education administrator*

Georgetown
Stern, Mort(imer) P(hillip) *journalism and communications educator, academic administrator, consultant*

Glenwood Springs
Gallagher, David Kent *agricultural vegetation manager, consultant*
Mayer, Dennis Marlyn *academic administrator*

Golden
Ansell, George Stephen *metallurgical engineering educator, academic administrator*
Baron, Robert Charles *publishing executive*
Clagett, William H., IV *government agency administrator*
Coors, Jeffrey H. *brewery company executive*
†Coors, Joseph *brewery executive*
Coors, William K. *brewery executive*
Danzberger, Alexander Harris *chemical engineer, consultant*
Eaton, Mark Rayner *financial executive*
Eckley, Wilton Earl, Jr. *humanities educator*
Grose, Thomas Lucius Trowbridge *geologist, educator*
†Haddon, Timothy John *mining engineer*
Hager, John Patrick *metallurgy engineering educator*
†Hopper, Sally *state legislator*
Hutchinson, Richard William *geology educator, consultant*
Johnson, Marvin Donald *brewery executive*
Johnstone, James George *engineering educator*
Kaufmann, Thomas David *economist, educator*
Kazmerski, Lawrence Lee *scientist, research facility executive*
Kennedy, George Hunt *chemistry educator*
Kotch, Alex *chemistry educator*
Krauss, George *metallurgist*
Lerud, Joanne Van Ornum *library administrator*
McNeill, William *environmental scientist*
Morrison, Roger Barron *geologist, executive*
Mueller, William Martin *former academic administrator, metallurgical engineering educator*
Olson, Marian Katherine *emergency management executive, publisher*
Pegis, Anton George *English educator*
Petrick, Alfred, Jr. *mineral economics educator, consultant*
Poettmann, Frederick Heinz *retired petroleum engineering educator*
Ponder, Herman *geologist*
†Rechholtz, Robert August *brewing company executive*
Salamon, Miklos Dezso Gyorgy *mining educator*
Silverberg, Stuart Owen *obstetrician, gynecologist*
Sims, Paul Kibler *geologist*
Sneed, Joseph Donald *philosophy educator, author*
Stokes, Robert Allan *science research facility executive, physicist*
Tilton, John Elvin *mineral economics educator*
Togerson, John Dennis *computer software company executive*
Toll, Jack Benjamin *government official*
Weimer, Robert Jay *geology educator, energy consultant, civic leader*
White, James Edward *geophysicist*
Wilson, James Robert *lawyer*
Woolsey, Robert Eugene Donald *mineral economics, mathematics and business administration educator*

Grand Junction
†Agapito, J. F. T. *mining engineer, mineralogist*
Kribel, Robert Edward *academic administrator, physicist*
Moberly, Linden Emery *educational adminstrator*
Olson, Sylvester Irwin *government official*
Pantenburg, Michel *hospital administrator, health educator, holistic health coordinator*
Rutz, Richard Frederick *physicist, researcher*
Sadler, Theodore R., Jr. *thoracic and cardiovascular surgeon*
Sewell, Beverly Jean *financial executive*
Thomas, Mark Stanton *flutist*
Young, Ralph Alden *soil scientist, educator*
Zumwalt, Roger Carl *hospital administrator*

Greeley
Caffarella, Edward Philip *educational technology educator*
Cook, Donald E. *pediatrician*
Duff, William Leroy, Jr. *university dean, busiiness educator*
Hause, Jesse Gilbert *former college president*
Houtchens, Barnard *lawyer*
Jovene, Nicholas Angelo, Jr. *construction company official*
Mapelli, Roland Lawrence *food company executive*
†Monfort, Richard L. *meat packaging and distribution company executive*
†Morgensen, Jerry Lynn *construction company executive*
Mueller, Donald Dean *food company executive*
Schulze, Robert Oscar *university dean*
Seager, Daniel Albert *university librarian*
†Willis, Connie (Constance E. Willis) *author*
†Worley, Lloyd Douglas *English educator*

Greenwood Village
Barnard, Rollin Dwight *retired financial executive*
†Eccles, Matthew Alan *golf course designer, landscape architect*

Keystone
†Craig, Robert Wallace *educational administrator*

Lafayette
Short, Ray Everett *minister, sociology educator emeritus, author, lecturer*

Lakewood
†Beckman, L. David *academic administrator*
Danos, Robert McClure *oil company executive*
Elkins, Lincoln Feltch *petroleum engineering consultant*
Fox, Joseph Leland *fiduciary and business executive*
†Franta, Gregory Esser *architect, energy consultant*
Gayer, John Harrison *engineering executive, consultant*
Hall, Larry D. *energy company executive, lawyer*
Hosokawa, William K. *newspaper columnist, author*
Hurst, Leland Lyle *natural gas company executive*
†Knott, William Alan *library director, library management and building consultant*
Lu, Paul Haihsing *mining engineer, geotechnical consultant*
McAuliffe, Clayton Doyle *chemist*
Mc Bride, Guy Thornton, Jr. *college president emeritus*
Mc Hugh, Robert Clayton *lawyer, energy company executive*
Milan, Marjorie Lucille *early childhood educator*
Mueller, Raymond Jay *software development executive*
†Orullian, B. LaRae *bank executive*
Owen, Robert Roy *manufacturing company executive*
Plusk, Ronald Frank *manufacturing company executive*
Walton, Roger Alan *public relations executive, writer*
Wellisch, William Jeremiah *social psychology educator*
†West, Marjorie Edith *elementary education educator*

Larkspur
Bierbaum, J. Armin *petroleum company executive, consultant*
Bierbaum, Janith Marie *artist*

Leadville
†McCabe, James R. *school system administrator*

Littleton
Bachman, David Christian *orthopedic surgeon*
Cabell, Elizabeth Arlisse *psychologist*
Chapman, Richard LeRoy *public policy researcher*
†Chavez, Cile *school superintendent*
Clift, William Orrin *oil company executive, consultant*
Hadley, Marlin LeRoy *direct sales financial consultant*
Kazemi, Hossein *petroleum engineer*
Kearney, Joseph Laurence *athletic conference administrator*
Kleinknecht, Kenneth Samuel *retired aerospace company executive, former federal space agency official*
Kullas, Albert John *management and systems engineering consultant*
Martinen, John A. *travel company executive*
Milliken, John Gordon *research economist*
Snyder, William Harry *financial advisor*
Spelts, Richard John *lawyer*
Strang, Sandra Lee *airline official*
Ulrich, John Ross Gerald *aerospace engineer*
Vail, Charles Daniel *veterinarian, consultant*

Livermore
Evans, Howard Ensign *entomologist, educator*

Longmont
Davis, Donald Alan *author, news correspondent, lecturer*
Melendez, Joaquin *orthopedic assistant*
†Stewart, William Gene *broadcast executive*

Louisville
Day, Robert Edgar *retired artist, educator*
Poppa, Ryal Robert *manufacturing company executive*
Qualley, Charles Albert *fine arts educator*

Loveland
†Churchill, Jerry M. *environment company marketing executive*

Manassa
Garcia, Castelar Medardo *lawyer*

McCoy
Wolf, Charlotte Elizabeth *sociologist*

Middletown
MacLam, Helen *editor, periodical*

Montrose
Krumins, Girts *lawyer, management consultant*
Loesch, Harrison *lawyer, energy and natural resources consultant*

Monument
Miele, Alfonse Ralph *former government official*

Pagosa Springs
†Cassidy, Samuel H. *lawyer, state legislator*

Parker
Jankura, Donald Eugene *hotel executive, educator*
Nelson, Marvin Ray *retired life insurance company executive*

Peterson AFB
Horner, Charles Albert *air force officer*
Moorman, Thomas Samuel, Jr. *career officer*

Pueblo
Altman, Leo Sidney *lawyer*
Avery, Julia May *speech pathologist, organizational volunteer*
†Bates, Charles Emerson *library administrator*
Byrnes, Lawrence William *dean*
Casey, William Robert, Jr. *ambassador, mining engineer*
Dolsen, David Horton *mortician*
Farwell, Hermon Waldo, Jr. *parliamentarian, educator, speech communicator*
Horn, Thomas Carl *retired banker*
Occhiato, Michael Anthony *city official*
Rawlings, Robert Hoag *newspaper publisher*
†Shirley, Robert Clark *university president, strategic planning consultant, educator*
Sisson, Ray L. *dean*
Tafoya, Arthur N. *bishop*

Pueblo West
Giffin, Walter Charles *retired industrial engineer, educator, consultant*
O'Callaghan, Robert Patrick *lawyer*

Ridgway
Weaver, Dennis *actor*

Rifle
†George, Russell Lloyd *lawyer, legislator*

Sedalia
Pakiser, Louis Charles, Jr. *geophysicist*

Snowmass
Lovins, Amory Bloch *physicist, energy consultant*
†Lovins, L. Hunter *public policy institute executive*

Snowmass Village
Chase, Seymour M. *lawyer*
Diamond, Edward *gynecologist, infertility specialist, clinician*

Steamboat Springs
Langstaff, Gary Lee *food service marketing executive*

Sterling
Milander, Henry Martin *community college president*

Telluride
Smith, Samuel David *artist, educator*

Trinidad
Potter, William Bartlett *trucking company executive*

Univ Of Denver
Dance, Francis Esburn Xavier *communication educator*

Univ Of No Colo
†Lujan, Herman D. *university president*

University Of Colorado
Chamberlin, Henry Scott *artist, educator*
DePuy, Charles Herbert *chemist, educator*
†Greene, Chris H. *physicist, educator*
Leone, Stephen Robert *chemical physicist, educator*
Miller, Gifford Hubbs *geologist*

USAF Academy
Hosmer, Bradley Clark *air force officer*

Vail
†Hopkins, Pamela Withers *architect*
Knight, Constance Bracken *writer*
Searls, Melvin William, Jr. *government official*
Wilson, Brandon Laine *writer, advertising and public relations consultant, explorer*

Westcliffe
Sullivan, Whitney Brayton *municipal court judge*

Westminster
Dotson, Gerald Richard *biology educator*
Kober, Carl Leopold *exploration company executive*
Reed, John Howard *school administrator*

Wheat Ridge
Barrett, Michael Henry *civil engineer*
Gerlick, Helen J. *tax practitioner, accountant*
LaMendola, Walter Franklin *information technology consultant*
Scherich, Erwin Thomas *civil engineer, consultant*
†Willard, James Douglas *health care administrator*

Wiley
Dooley, Jennie Lee *art educator*

Winter Park
Johnson, William Potter *newspaper publisher*

CONNECTICUT

Avon
Armstrong, John Kenaston *insurance and financial services company executive*
†Jarvis, Ronald Dean *life insurance company executive*
†Johnson, Dean Adams *landscape architect*
Löe, Harald *dentist, educator, researcher*
Patricelli, Robert E. *health care company executive*
Rutland, George Patrick *banker*
Wiechmann, Eric Watt *lawyer*

Bethany
Forman, Charles William *religious studies educator*

Bethel
Ajay, Abe *artist*
Kidder, C. Robert *battery manufacturing company executive*
†Perrin, Charles R. *light manufacturing executive*

Bloomfield
Anderson, Buist Murfee *lawyer*
Desautelle, William Peter *financial executive*
†Dooley, Thomas Howard *insurance company executive*
English, Lawrence P. *insurance company executive*
Hammer, Alfred Emil *artist, educator*
Handel, Morton Emanuel *management consultation executive*
Hegeman, James Alan *corporate executive*
†Hilsenrath, Baruch M. *principal*
Houston, Howard Edwin *retired government official*
Kaman, Charles Huron *diversified technologies corporation executive*
Leonberger, Frederick John *electrical engineer, photonics manager*
Mackey, William Arthur Godfrey *computer software company executive*
Messemer, Glenn Matthew *lawyer*
Reid, Hoch *lawyer*

Branford
Blake, Peter Jost *architect*
Cohen, Myron Leslie *mechanical engineer, business executive*
†Fenn, John Bennett *chemist, educator*
Izenour, George Charles *mechanical, electrical engineering educator*
Mancheski, Frederick John *automotive company executive*
Penner, Harry Harold Hamilton, Jr. *pharmaceutical company executive, lawyer*

Bridgeport
Allen, Richard Stanley (Dick Allen) *English language educator, author*
Brunale, Vito John *aerospace engineer*
Buckley, Eugene *aircraft company executive*
Carson, David Ellis Adams *banker*
DeWerth, Gordon Henry *corporate finance executive*
Egan, Edward M. *bishop*
Eginton, Warren William *federal judge*
†Ganim, Joseph P. *mayor*
†Garcia, Edna I. *secondary education educator*
†Goodspeed, Norwick Royall Givens *banker*
Henderson, Albert *publishing company executive, dairy executive, consultant*
Hmurcik, Lawrence Vincent *electrical engineering educator*
†Johmann, Nancy *librarian*
Katz, Susan Audrey *producer, director, writer*
Kovatch, Jak Gene *artist*
Margulies, Martin B. *lawyer, educator*
McGregor, Jack Edwin *natural resource company executive*
Nevas, Alan Harris *federal judge*
†Norris, Louise *religious organization executive*
Semple, Cecil Snowdon *retired manufacturing company executive*
Shiff, Alan Howard William *federal judge*
Thomas, Dudley Breckinridge *newspaper pubisher*
van der Kroef, Justus Maria *political science educator*

Bristol
Barnes, Carlyle Fuller *manufacturing executive*
Barnes, Wallace *manufacturing executive*
Besser, John Edward *lawyer*
†Bornstein, Steven M. *broadcast executive*
†Krawiecki, Edward C., Jr. *state legislator, lawyer*
Moffitt, George, Jr. *foreign service officer*
Simms, Phillip *sports commentator, former professional football player*
Wells, Arthur Stanton *manufacturing company executive*

Brookfield
Reynolds, Jean Edwards *publishing executive*
Schetky, Laurence McDonald *metallurgist, researcher*
Westermann, Horace Clifford *sculptor*
†Whelan, Michael Raymond *artist, illustrator*

Brooklyn
Wendel, Richard Frederick *economist, educator, consultant*

Cheshire
Bozzuto, Michael Adam *wholesale grocery company executive*
Burton, Robert William *retired office products executive*
Chamberlain, John Rensselaer *columnist*
Fuller, Jack Glendon, Jr. *retired plastics engineer*
Rowland, Ralph Thomas *architect*
†Wallace, Ralph *superintendent*

Chester
Cobb, Hubbard Hanford *magazine editor, writer*
Hays, David Arthur *theater producer, stage designer*

Colebrook
Mc Neill, William Hardy *retired history educator, writer*

Collinsville
Ford, Dexter *retired insurance company executive*

Cornwall Bridge
Galazka, Jacek Michal *publishing company executive*
Pfeiffer, Werner Bernhard *artist, educator*

Cos Cob
Donahue, Barbara Lynn Sean *television producer*
Hauptman, Michael *broadcasting company executive*
Kane, Margaret Brassler *sculptor*
Ketchum, Alton Harrington *retired advertising executive*
Nolte, Richard Henry *political science researcher, consultant*
Senter, William Joseph *publishing company executive*
Woodman, Harry Andrews *retired life insurance company executive, consultant*

Danbury
Baker, Leonard Morton *manufacturing company executive*
Barth, Elmer Ernest *wire and cable company executive*
Baruch, Eduard *management consultant*
Caparn, Rhys (Mrs. Herbert Johannes Steel) *sculptor*

Cassidy, Robert Joseph consumer products company executive
Chapin, Suzanne Phillips retired psychologist
Dudley, Alfred Edward home and auto products company executive
Edelstein, David Simeon historian, educator
Finch, Carolyn-Bogart speech and language pathologist, speaker, writer
Goldstein, Joel management science educator, researcher
Hawkes, Carol Ann university dean
Holzman, Robert Stuart tax consultant
Hull, Treat Clark superior court trial referee
Kennedy, Robert Delmont petrochemical company executive
Leish, Kenneth William publishing company executive
†Lichtenberger, Horst William chemical company executive
Lisimachio, Jean Louis book publishing executive
Malino, Jerome R. rabbi
Nelson, Willie musician, songwriter
†Roach, James R. academic administrator
†Soviero, Joseph C. chemical company executive
Stewart, Albert Clifton college dean, marketing educator
Toland, John Willard historian, writer
Tolor, Alexander psychologist, educator
Weinstein, Sidney neuropsychologist

Darien
Allen, Joseph Henry retired publishing company executive
Bays, John Theophanis consulting engineering executive
Becker, Ralph Edward broadcast executive, consultant
Brooke, Avery Rogers publisher, writer
Brown, James Shelly lawyer
Buchanan, Robert Edgar retired advertising agency executive
Chevins, Anthony Charles advertising agency executive
Cowherd, Edwin Russell management consultant
de Selding, Edward Bertrand retired banker
Earle, Harry Woodward printing company executive
Forman, J(oseph) Charles chemical engineer, consultant, writer
Gammie, Anthony Petrie pulp and paper manufacturing company executive
Glenn, Roland Douglas chemical engineer
Grace, John Kenneth communications executive
Hart, Eric Mullins finance company executive
Hart, James W., Jr. manufacturing executive
Hubner, Robert Wilmore consultant, former business machines company executive
Kaynor, Sanford Bull lawyer
Kobak, Hope McEldowney publishing executive
Kutz, Kenneth John retired mining executive
Lewis, A. Duff, Jr. investment executive
Mapel, William Marlen Raines retired banking executive
McCurdy, Richard Clark engineering consultant
Mc Donough, Richard Doyle paper company executive
Moltz, James Edward brokerage company executive
Morse, Edmond Northrop investment management executive
Nava, Eloy Luis clothing executive
O'Brien, Joseph Patrick, Jr. apparel and textile company executive
Owen, Robert Vaughan financial company executive
Post, David Alan broadcast executive, producer
Schell, James Munson financial executive
Schmalzried, Marvin Eugene financial consultant
Smith, Elwin Earl mining and oil company executive
Spilman, Raymond industrial designer
Sprole, Frank Arnott retired pharmaceutical company executive, lawyer

Deep River
Healy, William Kent environmental services executive
Hieatt, Allen Kent language professional, educator
Hieatt, Constance Bartlett English language educator

Derby
Micci, Eugene D. lawyer

East Berlin
Anderson, Lawrence Leslie, Jr. manufacturing company executive, executive search company executive

East Glastonbury
Smith, David Clark research scientist

East Granby
Hostetter, Amos Barr, Jr. cable television executive
†Kimberley, John A. mechanical engineer, consultant

East Haddam
Borton, John Carter, Jr. (Terry Borton) producer, theater
Clarke, Logan, Jr. banker

East Hartford
Ahlberg, John Harold mathematician, educator
Coburn, Richard Joseph company executive, electrical engineer
†Davis, Roger L. aeronautical engineer
De Maria, Anthony John electrical engineer
Foyt, Arthur George electronics research administrator
Geckle, Robert Alan manufacturing company executive
†Hobbs, David E. mechanical engineer
†Johnson, Bruce Virgil mechanical engineer, physicist, researcher
Mordo, Jean Henri financial executive
Stephan, George Peter lawyer, international business consultant
Tanaka, Richard I. computer products company executive
Whiston, Richard Michael lawyer

East Haven
Conn, Harold O. physician, educator
Hegyi, Albert Paul association executive, lawyer
Scarf, Margaret (Maggie Scarf) author

East Windsor
Kaufmann, Sylvia Nadeau office equipment sales company executive

Ellington
Setzer, Herbert John chemical engineer

Enfield
Berger, Robert Bertram lawyer
Crocker, Frederick Greeley, Jr. financial executive
†Nirenberg, Charles convenience store executive

Essex
Curtis, Alva Marsh artist
Grover, William Herbert architect
Harper, Robert Leslie architect, educator
Kenyon, Charles Moir publishing company executive
Keppel, John writer, former diplomat
McLaughlin, David J. management executive
Russell, Thomas Wright, Jr. retired manufacturing executive
Simon, Mark architect

Fairfield
Allaby, Stanley Reynolds clergyman
Ambrosino, Ralph Thomas, Jr. retired telecommunications executive
Barone, Rose Marie Pace writer, former educator
Blau, Barry advertising agency executive
Brassil, Jean Ella psychologist
Brett, Arthur Cushman, Jr. banker
Bryan, Barbara Day librarian
Bunt, James Richard electric company executive
†Caruso, Daniel F. lawyer, state legislator
Cernera, Anthony Joseph academic administrator
Cion, Richard M. financial executive, lawyer
Clark, Eleanor author
Cole, Richard John marketing executive
Cox, Richard Joseph former broadcasting executive
Dean, George Alden advertising executive
Eigel, Edwin George, Jr. university president, mathematics educator
†Fulton, James A. automotive executive
Golub, Stephen Bruce accountant, consultant, educator
†Heineman, Benjamin Walter, Jr. lawyer
Hodgkinson, William James marketing executive
Jewitt, David Willard Pennock retired banker
Johnson, Alvin Roscoe manufacturing executive
Kantrowitz, Jonathan Daniel educational software company executive, lawyer
Kelley, Aloysius Paul university president, priest
Kenney, James Francis lawyer
†Kijanka, Dorothy M. library administrator
Lachowicz, Franciszek foreign language educator
Limpitlaw, John Donald retired publishing executive, clergyman
Lumbard, Joseph Edward, Jr. federal judge
Mc Lean, Don singer, instrumentalist, composer
Newton, Lisa Haenlein philosophy educator
O'Connell, Robert John insurance company executive
Polin, Jane Louise foundation official
Sealy, Albert Henry lawyer
Smith, Clifford Vaughn, Jr. academic administrator
Sutphen, Harold Amerman, Jr. retired paper company executive
Trager, Philip lawyer, photographer
Urquhart, John Alexander management consultant
Welch, John Francis, Jr. (Jack Welch) electrical manufacturing company executive
Wheeler, Henry Clark manufacturing company executive
Wolff, Steven Alexander arts and entertainment consultant

Falls Village
Purcell, Dale college administrator, consultant

Farmington
Bigler, Harold Edwin, Jr. investment company executive
Bronner, Felix physiologist, biophysicist, educator, painter
Cooperstein, Sherwin Jerome medical educator
Escobar, Javier Ignacio psychiatrist
Gossling, Harry Robert orthopaedic surgeon, educator
Halligan, Howard Ansel investment management company executive
†Hartley, Harry J. academic administrator
†Herbette, Leo Gerard biophysics educator
Hinz, Carl Frederick, Jr. physician, educator
Katz, Arnold Martin medical educator
Kelly, Francis J., Jr. insurance executive
Massey, Robert Unruh physician, university dean
Mayerhofer, James Thomas specialty and recycling materials company executive
Miser, Hugh Jordan systems analyst, operations researcher, consultant
Osborn, Mary Jane Merten biochemist
Paul, Christian Thomas retired insurance company executive
†Raisz, Lawrence Gideon medical educator, consultant
Rothfield, Lawrence I. microbiology educator
Rothfield, Naomi Fox physician
Schenkman, John Boris pharmacologist, educator
†Scott, David J. beverage executive
Sheeran, William James manufacturing executive, mechanical engineer
Sigman, Eugene M. retired urology educator and university dean
Spencer, Richard Paul biochemist, educator, physician
van Rooy, Jean-Pierre international executive
Walker, James Elliot Cabot physician

Georgetown
Daubenspeck, Robert Donley advertising agency executive
Roberts, Priscilla Warren artist

Glastonbury
Bruner, Robert B. hospital consultant
†Hatch, D. Patricia P. principal
Schroth, Peter W(illiam) lawyer, management and law educator

Glenbrook
Schofield, Herbert Spencer, III insurance agent

Goshen
Berleant, Arnold philosopher

Granby
†Pestka, Stanley secondary school principal

Greens Farms
Deford, Frank sportswriter, television and radio commentator, author
Fiske, Edward Bogardus newspaper editor, journalist, lecturer
McManus, John Francis, III advertising management executive
St.Marie, Satenig business consultant, writer

Greenwich
Allain, Emery Edgar retired paper company executive
Baker, Charles Ernest stockbroker
Ball, John Fleming advertising and film production executive
Bam, Foster lawyer
Bantle, Louis Francis tobacco company executive
Barber, Charles Finch retired metals company executive, financial services company executive
Barnum, William Milo architect
Bennett, Jack Franklin oil company executive
Berkley, William Robert insurance holding company executive
Bogart, Robert B. publishing company executive
Brophy, Theodore Frederick telephone company executive
Cantor, Samuel C. lawyer
Cantwell, Robert lawyer
Carmichael, William Daniel consultant, educator
Chapman, Gilbert Whipple, Jr. publishing company executive
Chase, William Howard public policy consultant, editor
Chisholm, William Hardenbergh management consultant
Clements, Robert insurance brokerage executive
Collins, Richard Lawrence magazine editor, publisher, author
Combe, Ivan DeBlois drug company executive
Coudert, Victor Raphael, Jr. marketing and sales executive
Damon, Edmund Holcombe plastics company executive
Davidson, Thomas Maxwell international management company executive
Davies, William DeAth, Jr. executive management consultant
†Davis, Ronald Vernon beverage products executive
de Mar, Leoda Miller fabric and wallcovering designer
Dianis, Walter Joseph retired banker
Donahue, Donald Jordan mining company executive
Donley, James Walton management consultant
†Dorme, Patrick John electronic company executive
Egbert, Richard Cook retired banker
†Ellsworth, Robert F. manufacturing executive
Ewald, William Bragg, Jr. author, consultant
Fisher, Everett lawyer
†Flagg, George V. business executive
Foley, Thomas C. investor
Foraste, Roland psychiatrist
Forrow, Brian Derek lawyer, corporation executive
Fuller, Theodore retired insurance executive
Gabelli, Mario J. diversified financial services company executive
Gaston, Don F. professional basketball executive
Gately, George (Gallagher Gately) cartoonist
Gierer, Vincent A., Jr. tobacco and wine holding company executive
Gillespie, Alexander Joseph, Jr. lawyer
Hanson, Maurice Francis (Maury Hanson) retired magazine publisher and editor
Heath, Gloria Whitton aerospace scientist, consultant
Heer, Edwin LeRoy insurance executive
Hicks, Paul B., Jr. retired petroleum company executive
†Holten, John V. food products executive
Horton, Jared C. retired corporation executive
Howard, John Arnold marketing educator
Ix, Robert Edward food company executive
†Jeffrey, Kim food products executive
Johnson, Herbert Michael publisher
Jones, Edwin Michael lawyer, former insurance company executive
Keegan, Richard John advertising agency executive
Keogh, James journalist
Kestnbaum, Albert S. advertising executive
Kopenhaver, Patricia Ellsworth podiatrist
Kopp, W. Brewster corporate director, advisor
Kurtz, Melvin H. lawyer, cosmetics company executive
Lanzit, Stephen Ray finance company executive, consultant
Larned, William Edmund, Jr. international development and venture capital company executive
Laudone, Anita Helene lawyer
Lawi, David Steven energy, agriservice and thermoplastic resins industries executive
Lawler, Richard Francis lawyer
Lewis, Perry Joshua investment banker
Lowenstein, Peter David lawyer
Lozyniak, Andrew manufacturing company executive
Lurie, Ranan Raymond political analyst, political cartoonist, artist, lecturer
Lynch, William Redington lawyer
MacDonald, Gordon Chalmers management consultant
†Mallardi, Joseph L. manufacturing company executive
†Mann, Marvin L. electronics executive
Marchand, Nathan electrical engineer, corporation president
Massey, James L. investment banker
McKee, Thomas J. lawyer
McLaughlin, Michael John financial executive
Mendenhall, John Ryan retired lawyer, transportation executive
Miles, Jesse Mc Lane retired accounting company executive
Mock, Robert Claude architect
Moller, William Richard, Jr. banker
Moonie, Clyde Wickliffe financial consultant
Moore, Charles Hewes, Jr. industrial and engineered products executive
More, Douglas McLochlan lawyer
Morrison, Fred Beverly real estate consultant
Nevin, Crocker investment banker
†Ordway, John Danton pension administrator, lawyer, accountant
Parrish, Thomas Kirkpatrick, III marketing consultant
Paul, Roland Arthur lawyer
Paulson, Paul Joseph advertising executive
Perless, Robert L. sculptor
Pfeiffer, Jane Cahill former broadcasting company executive, consultant
Pivirotto, Richard Roy former retail executive
Pope, Marvin Hoyle foreign language educator
Pringle, Lewis Gordon international trade and investment company executive
Randt, Clark Thorp physician, educator
Richards, Fred Tracy finance company executive
Rodenbach, Edward Francis lawyer
Rose, Richard Loomis lawyer
Rukeyser, Louis Richard economic commentator
Scheifele, Richard Paul cosmetic and chemicals manufacturing company executive
Schlafly, Hubert Joseph, Jr. communications executive
Schmidt, Herman J. former oil company executive
Schutz, Herbert Dietrich publishing executive
Scott, John Constante marketing company executive
Shaffer, David H. publishing company executive
Shepard, Thomas Rockwell, Jr. publishing consultant
Sheppard, Posy (Mrs. Jeremiah Milbank) social worker
Simonnard, Michel André manufacturing executive
Slavin, Simon social administration educator
Smith, Rodger Field financial executive
Springsteen, David Folger financial consultant
†Stern, Dennis M. lawyer
Taylor, Sir Cyril (Julian Hebden) education association administrator, consultant
Tiegs, Cheryl model, designer
Tournillon, Nicholas Brady trade finance, international investments company executive
Vance, Don Kelvin baking industry consultant
Wallach, Philip C(harles) financial, public relations consultant
Wearly, William Levi business executive
Weil, Ernst oil industry executive
Whitmore, George Merle, Jr. management consulting company executive
Willis, William Harold, Jr. management consultant, executive search specialist
†Wilson, H. Brian, Jr. public relations executive
Woelflein, Kevin Gerard banker
†Wright, Christopher J. oil company executive
Wyman, Henry Walter plastic manufacturing company executive
Wyman, Ralph Mark corporate executive

Groton
Auerbach, Michael Howard chemical company research executive
†Cooper, Richard Arthur oceanographer
English, James Fairfield, Jr. former college president
Hinman, Richard Leslie pharmaceutical company executive
Pinson, Ellis Rex, Jr. chemist, consultant
Routien, John Broderick mycologist
Sheets, Herman Ernest marine engineer
Sheets, Paulann Hosler lawyer, environmental law consultant
†Simpson, W. M. career officer administrator
Swindell, Archie Calhoun, Jr. research biochemist, statistician
†Tassinari, Melissa Sherman toxicologist

Guilford
Baillie, Priscilla Woods aquatic ecologist
†Boyle, Helen D. entrepreneur
Bryan, Courtlandt Dixon Barnes author
Engelman, Donald Max molecular biophysics and biochemistry educator
Logan, John Arthur, Jr. retired foundation executive
Morgan, Leon Alford retired utility executive
Peters, William author, producer, director
Ragan, James Thomas communications executive
Warshaw, Joseph Bennett pediatrician, educator

Hamden
Bennett, Harry Louis college educator
Cherry, Edward Earl architect
Darling, George Bapst, Jr. retired medical educator
Gay, Peter history educator, author
Gordon, Angus Neal, Jr. retired electric company executive
†Nuland, Sherwin surgeon, author
Parker, William Nelson economics educator
Resnick, Idrian Navarre foundation administrator
Roche, (Eamonn) Kevin architect
Rosenthal, Franz lanague educator
Walker, Charles Allen chemical engineer, educator
Williams, Edward Gilman retired banker
Woodward, C. Vann historian

Hartford
Addiss, Susan Silliman state government administrator
Alfano, Charles Thomas, Sr. lawyer
Anthony, J(ulian) Danford, Jr. lawyer
Baird, Zoë insurance company executive, lawyer
†Balducci, Richard Joseph state legislator
Benanav, Gary G. insurance company counsel
Berall, Frank Stewart lawyer
Berdon, Robert Irwin state supreme court justice
Bickford, Christopher Penny association executive
Bieluch, William Charles judge
Blumberg, Phillip Irvin law educator
Blumenthal, Richard state attorney general
Booth, Richard H. insurance company executive
Boyko, Gregory Andrew insurance company executive
Brauer, Rima Lois psychiatrist
Bronzino, Joseph Daniel electrical engineer
Brophy, Joseph Thomas insurance company executive
Buck, Gurdon Hall lawyer, urban planner, real estate broker
Buckingham, Harold Canute, Jr. lawyer
Budd, Edward Hey insurance company executive
Burke, Brian hockey team executive
Butterworth, Kenneth W. manufacturing company executive
Callahan, Robert J. state supreme court justice
Cantor, Donald Jerome lawyer
Cole, William Kaufman lawyer
Compton, Ronald E. insurance and financial services executive
Conard, Frederick Underwood, Jr. lawyer
Connelly, William Howard retired foundation executive
Conrad, Donald Glover insurance executive
Cooper, George Brinton historian, educator
Covello, Alfred Vincent federal judge
Crawford, Richard Bradway biologist, biochemist, educator
Crispin, Robert William investment company executive

Cronin, Daniel Anthony *bishop*
Cullina, William Michael *lawyer*
Curran, Ward Schenk *economist, educator*
Daniell, Robert F. *diversified manufacturing company executive*
Decko, Kenneth Owen *association executive*
†DePino, Chris Anthony *state legislator*
D'Eramo, David *hospital administrator*
De Rocco, Andrew Gabriel *state commissioner, educator*
†Dillon, Patricia Anne *state legislator*
Donahue, John McFall *lawyer*
Donnelly, John *psychiatrist, educator*
†Doyle, Lawrence Sawyer *insurance company executive*
†Eads, M. Adela *state senator*
Eagan, F(rancis) Owen *magistrate judge*
Elliot, Ralph Gregory *lawyer*
Ellis, William Ben *utility executive*
†Endrst, James Bryan *television critic, columnist*
†Englehart, Robert Wayne, Jr. *cartoonist*
Ewing, Robert *lawyer*
Fain, Joel Maurice *lawyer*
Farren, J. Michael *former government official, lawyer*
†Faude, Wilson Hinsdale *museum director*
†Figueroa, Juan A. *lawyer, state legislator*
Fiondella, Robert William *insurance company executive*
†Flaherty, Brian John *state legislator, editor*
†Flaherty, Patrick John *state legislator, economist*
Fox, Bernard Michael *utilities company executive, electrical engineer*
Frahm, Donald Robert *insurance company executive*
Francis, Emile Percy *professional hockey team executive*
Freeman, David *chemical company executive*
Garfield, Gerald *lawyer*
Gerson, Elliot Francis *financial services executive*
Gingold, George Norman *insurance company executive, lawyer*
†Godfrey, Robert Douglas *lawyer*
†Golden, Louis Joseph *business news editor*
Goodwin, Rodney Keith Grove *international bank and trade company executive*
Googins, Robert Reville *lawyer, insurance company executive*
Gordon, Richard H. *professional hockey team executive*
Green, Raymond Bert *lawyer*
Groark, Eunice *state official*
Guay, Edward *financial economist, investment advisor*
Guenter, Raymond Albert *lawyer, banker*
Gummere, John *insurance company executive*
Gunderson, Gerald Axel *economics educator, administrator*
†Gunther, George Lackman *state senator, natureopathic physician*
†Hajek, Thomas J. *aerospace engineer*
Hamilton, Thomas Stewart *physician, hospital administrator*
Harden, Jon Bixby *publishing executive*
Harrison, Thomas Flatley *lawyer*
Hawkanson, David Robert *theater managing director*
Heiman, Maxwell *state judge, lawyer*
Herman, Paula Lacey *lawyer*
Hermann, Robert Jay *manufacturing company engineering executive, consultant*
Hertel, Suzanne Marie *personnel administrator*
†Hess, Marilyn Ann *state representative*
Hincks, John Winslow *lawyer*
Holmgren, Paul *professional hockey coach*
Holt, Timothy Arthur *insurance company executive*
†Horgan, Denis Edward *journalist*
Irish, Leon Eugene *lawyer, educator, insurance company executive*
Jones, Richard F., III *obstetrician/gynecologist*
†Joyce, Raymond M. H. *state legislator*
†Kaimowitz, Jeffrey Hugh *librarian*
†Keating, Thomas Edward *insurance company executive*
Kelly, Peter Galbraith *lawyer*
†Kenney, John R. *insurance corporation executive, lawyer*
Kezer, Pauline Ryder *state official*
Killian, Robert Kenneth *former lieutenant governor*
King, Richard Hood *newspaper executive*
Knickerbocker, Robert Platt, Jr. *lawyer*
Korzenik, Armand Alexander *lawyer*
†Koupal, Raymond *newspaper publishing executive*
Krieble, Robert H. *corporation executive*
Lamos, Mark *artistic director, administrator, actor*
Lane-Reticker, Edward *lawyer, educator*
Lautzenheiser, Barbara Jean *insurance executive*
Loomis, Worth (Alfred Worthington Loomis) *college president, manufacturer*
Lotstein, James I. *lawyer*
Lumsden, Lynne Ann *publishing company executive*
Lyman, Peggy *dancer, choreographer, educator*
Lyon, James Burroughs *lawyer*
Mahoney, Michael Robert Taylor *art historian, educator*
†Maloney, James Henry *state senator, lawyer*
Martin, John J. *insurance company executive*
†Martin, Vernon Emil *librarian*
†Mattiello, Brian Edward *state legislator*
†McKeon, George A. *lawyer*
McLane, James Woods *insurance executive*
Mc Lean, Jackie *jazz saxophonist, educator, composer, community activist*
†Meotti, Michael Patrick *state legislator, lawyer*
Merriam, Dwight Haines *lawyer, land use planner*
Merrill, George Vanderneth *lawyer, investment executive*
Messmore, Thomas Ellison *insurance company executive*
Middlebrook, Stephen Beach *lawyer*
Miller, Jeffrey Clark *lawyer*
†Milner, Thirman L. *mayor*
Morrison, Francis Henry *lawyer*
Morrissey, Robert John *communications executive*
Mueller, Marnie Wagstaff *insurance company executive, economist*
Mullane, Denis Francis *insurance executive*
Murtha, John Stephen *lawyer*
Newman, Jon O. *federal judge*
†Nickerson, William Hoffman *state senator, real estate investor*
†Noel, Don Obert, Jr. *newspaper columnist*
Nolan, John Blanchard *lawyer*
O'Keefe, James William, Jr. *investment manager and banker*
†O'Leary, Cornelius Peter *state senator*
Osborne, George Delano *arts director*
Owen, H. Martyn *lawyer*
†Pach, Peter Barnard *newspaper columnist and editor*
Peters, Ellen Ash *state supreme court chief justice*
†Petry, Paul E. *insurance company executive*
Piehl, Donald Herbert *chemist, research and development executive*
Pinney, Sidney Dillingham, Jr. *lawyer*
Piotrowski, Richard Francis *state agency administrator, council chairman*
Psarakis, Emanuel Nicholas *lawyer*
Quinn, Andrew Peter, Jr. *lawyer, insurance executive*
Randall, Gerald J. *insurance company executive*
Reed, David Benson *bishop*
†Renner, Gerald Anthony *journalist*
†Riccio, Janet Marie *advertising executive*
Richter, Donald Paul *lawyer*
Roberts, Henry Reginald *management consultant, former life insurance company executive*
Roberts, Melville Parker, Jr. *neurosurgeon, educator*
†Robertson, Philip Scott *construction company consultant, state senator*
†Roessner, Barbara *journalist*
Rome, Donald Lee *lawyer*
Ryan, David Thomas *lawyer*
Santaniello, Angelo Gary *state supreme court justice*
Sargent, Joseph Denny *insurance executive*
Schatz, S. Michael *lawyer*
Schatzki, George *law educator*
Schweitzer, N. Tina *photojournalist, television producer, director, writer, international consultant public relations, media relations, government relations*
Scully, John Carroll *life insurance marketing research company executive*
See, Edmund M. *lawyer*
Shea, David Michael *state supreme court justice*
Siegel, Robert Gordon *lawyer*
†Simmons, Robert Ruhl *state legislator, educator*
Space, Theodore Maxwell *lawyer*
Spear, H(enry) Dyke N(ewcome), Jr. *lawyer*
Speziale, John Albert *lawyer*
Springer, John Kelley *hospital administrator*
Stephen, Michael Anthony *insurance company executive*
Stoker, Warren Cady *university president*
†Stone, Dennis J. *law librarian, educator*
Taylor, Allan Bert *lawyer*
Thomas, Calvert *lawyer*
Tingley, Floyd Warren *physician*
Totino, Louis J. *marketing executive, educator*
Trachsel, William Henry *corporate counsel*
†Upson, Thomas Fisher *state legislator, lawyer*
Vohra, Ranbir *political scientist, educator*
Voigt, Richard *lawyer*
†Wagner, Joel H. *aerospace engineer*
Weicker, Lowell Palmer, Jr. *governor*
†Weingold, Harris D. *aerospace engineer*
Westervelt, James Joseph *insurance company executive*
†White, David Oliver *museum executive*
Wilde, Wilson *insurance company executive*
Wilder, Michael Stephen *insurance company executive*
†Wilkie, Everett Cleveland, Jr. *librarian*
Wolman, Martin *lawyer*
Wright, Douglass Brownell *judge, lawyer*
Wyatt, Wilson Watkins, Jr. *finance company and public relations executive*
†Wyman, Nancy S. *state legislator*
Yoskowitz, Irving Benjamin *lawyer, manufacturing company executive*
†Young, Leslie Towner *state legislator, stockbroker*
Zakarian, Albert *lawyer*
†Zakarian, John J. *journalist*
Zikmund, Barbara Brown *minister, seminary president, church history educator*

Ivoryton
Bendig, William Charles *editor, artist, publisher*

Kent
Cronin, Robert Lawrence *sculptor, painter*
Kilham, Walter H., Jr. *architect*

Lakeville
Barnes, Robert Goodwin *publishing consultant*
Bookman, George B. *public relations consultant*
Estabrook, Robert Harley *journalist*
Lovitt, George Harold *advertising executive*
Manassero, Henri J. P. *hotel executive*

Litchfield
Booth, John Thomas *investment banker*
Shapiro, Norman Richard *Romance languages and literatures educator*
Winter, Paul Theodore *musician*

Lyme
Bloom, Barry Malcolm *pharmaceutical company executive*
Friday, John Ernest, Jr. *retired securities company executive*
Greene, Joseph Nathaniel, Jr. *former foundation executive, former diplomat*

Madison
Anderson, Roy Ryden *former insurance executive, consultant*
Azarian, Martin Vartan *publishing company executive*
Carlson, Dale Bick *writer*
Egbert, Emerson Charles *publisher*
Golembeski, Jerome John *wire and cable company executive*
Haas, Frederick Peter *lawyer*
Houghton, Alan Nourse *association executive, educator, consultant*
Keim, Robert Phillip *retired advertising executive, consultant*
Kilbourne, Edwin Dennis *virologist, educator*
Peterkin, Albert Gordon *retired education educator*
Platt, Sherman Phelps, Jr. *publishing consultant*
Purcell, Bradford Moore *publishing company executive*
Rozelle, Lee Theodore *physical chemist*
Snell, Richard Saxon *anatomist*

Manchester
Galasso, Francis Salvatore *materials scientist*
Slaiby, Theodore George *aeronautical engineer, consultant*

Mansfield Center
Aldrich, Robert Adams *agricultural engineer*
Butler, Francelia McWilliams *retired English language educator, writer*
Liberman, Alvin Meyer *psychology educator*

Meriden
Bertolli, Eugene Emil *sculptor, goldsmith, designer, consultant*
Hou, Kenneth Chaing *biochemical engineer*
†Luby, Thomas Stewart *lawyer*
†Mustone, Amelia P. *state legislator*

Middlebury
†Coleman, Robert Elliott *secondary education educator*
†Fickenscher, Gerald H. *chemicals company executive*
Galie, Louis Michael *electronics company executive*
†Mazaika, Robert J. *chemicals executive*
Todt, Malcolm S. *financial, management consultant*

Middlefield
Thermenos, Nicholas *engineering company executive*

Middletown
Adams, John Robert *librarian*
Arnold, Herbert Anton *German language educator*
Bailey, Debra Sue *psychologist, neuropsychologist*
Balay, Robert Elmore *magazine editor, reference librarian*
Briggs, Morton Winfield *Romance language educator*
Buel, Richard Van Wyck, Jr. *history educator, writer, editor*
Comfort, William Wistar *mathematics educator*
Cumming, Robert Emil *editor*
Day, William Hudson *mechanical engineer, turbomachinery company executive*
D'Oench, Russell Grace, Jr. *consultant*
Fry, Albert Joseph *chemistry educator*
Gerber, Murray A. *molding manufacturing company executive*
Gillmor, Charles Stewart *history and science educator, researcher*
Gourevitch, Victor *philosophy educator*
Greene, Nathanael *historian, university official*
Haake, Paul *chemistry and biochemistry educator*
Hoey, Edwin Anderson *editor, writer*
Horgan, Paul *writer, educator*
Kerr, Clarence William *university administrator, retired*
Loughran, Robert Hall *design-development engineering executive, physicist*
Lovell, Michael C. *economics educator*
Manchester, William *writer*
Marteka, Vincent James, Jr. *magazine editor, writer*
Miller, Richard Alan *economist, educator*
Pomper, Philip *history educator*
Reed, Joseph Wayne *American studies educator*
Reid, James Dolan *mathematics educator, researcher*
Rose, Phyllis *English language professional, author*
Rosenbaum, Robert Abraham *mathematics educator*
Scheibe, Karl Edward *psychology educator*
Sease, John W(illiam) *chemistry educator*
†Slotkin, Richard Sidney *educator, writer*
Stevens, Robert Edwin *bank executive, former insurance company executive*
Upgren, Arthur Reinhold, Jr. *astronomer, educator, outdoor lighting consultant*
Wensinger, Arthur Stevens *German language and literature educator, author*

Milford
Berchem, Robert Lee, Sr. *lawyer*
†Calabrese, Anthony *marine ecologist*
†Madigan, Michael Scott *financial executive, treasurer*
Mahoney, J. Daniel *federal judge*
†Muth, Eric Peter *optician, consultant*
Taylor, Charles Henry *psychoanalyst, educator*

Morris
Sherwood, Thorne *architect*

Mystic
Bates, Gladys Edgerly *sculptor*
Connell, Hugh P. *aquarium executive*
Johnston, Waldo Cory Melrose *museum director*
Smith, Norman Clark *fund raising consultant*
Townsend, Thomas Perkins *former mining company executive*

Naugatuck
Flannery, Joseph Patrick *manufacturing company executive*

New Britain
Adams, John Francis, Jr. *real estate executive*
Ayers, Richard H. *manufacturing company executive*
Baskerville, Charles Alexander *geologist, educator*
Beal, Dallas Knight *university president*
Dethy, Ray Charles *former university dean, management educator, consultant*
Dimmick, Charles William *geology educator*
Donahugh, Robert Hayden *library administrator*
†Eiselstein, June *library director*
Frost, James Arthur *former university president*
Gallo, Donald Robert *English educator*
Hadlow, David Moore *manufacturing executive*
Jestin, Heimwarth B. *retired university administrator*
Judd, Richard Louis *academic administrator*
Meskill, Thomas J. *federal judge*
Shumaker, John William *university president*
Weddle, Stephen Shields *manufacturing company executive*

New Canaan
Bartlett, Dede Thompson *company executive*
Bergmann, Richard Ronald *architect, photographer*
†Bosworth, Stephen Warren *foundation executive*
Burns, Ivan Alfred *grocery products and industrial company executive*
Caesar, Henry A., II *sculptor*
Coughlin, Francis Raymond, Jr. *surgeon, educator, lawyer*
Crossman, William Whittard *retired wire cable and communications executive*
Day, Castle Nason *food company executive*
Dillon, James M. *banker*
Foley, Patrick Martin *computer manufacturing company executive*
Gottlieb, Arnold *dentist*
Halan, John Paul *corporate executive*
Halverstadt, Robert Dale *mechanical engineer, metals manufacturing company executive*
Hanson, Joseph J. *publishing executive*
Hodgson, Richard *electronics company executive*
Holch, Eric Sanford *artist*
Johnston, Douglas Frederick *industrial holding company executive*
Marcus, Edward *economist, educator*
McClure, Grover Benjamin *management consultant*
McIvor, Donald Kenneth *retired petroleum company executive, university administrator*
Mc Mennamin, George Barry *advertising agency executive*
Means, David Hammond *retired advertising executive*
Mendez, Albert Orlando *industrialist, financier*
Mountcastle, Katharine Babcock *foundation executive*
O'Neill, Patrick Henry *consulting mining engineer*
Packard, Vance Oakley *writer*
Phypers, Dean Pinney *retired computer company executive*
Pike, William Edward *investment company executive*
Powers, Thomas Moore *author*
Prescott, Peter Sherwin *writer*
Richards, Walter DuBois *artist, illustrator*
Risom, Jens *furniture designer, manufacturing executive*
Rutledge, John William *former watch company executive*
Sachs, John Peter *carbon company executive*
Snyder, Nathan *entrepreneur*
Stack, J. William, Jr. *management consultant*
Thomas, Robert Dean *publisher*
Thompson, George Lee *manufacturing company executive*
Thomsen, Donald Laurence, Jr. *institute executive, mathematician*
Toumey, Hubert John (Hugh Toumey) *textile company executive*
Wallace, Kenneth Donald *lawyer*
Walsworth, Ronald Lee *consumer products executive*
Ward, Richard Vance, Jr. *management executive*
Wolfley, Alan *corporate executive*

New Hartford
Hall, Newman A. *retired mechanical engineer*

New Haven
Aaslestad, Halvor Gunerius *university official*
Abell, Millicent Demmin *university library administrator*
Adelberg, Edward Allen *genetics educator*
Aghajanian, George Kevork *medical educator*
Altman, Sidney *biology educator*
Ames, Louise Bates *child psychologist*
Apfel, Robert Edmund *mechanical engineering educator, applied physicist, research scientist*
†Appelquist, Thomas William *physicist, educator*
Apter, David Ernest *political science educator*
Bailey, William Harrison *artist, educator*
Baker, Robert Stevens *educator, organist*
Barash, Paul George *anesthesiologist, educator*
†Beals, Richard William *mathematics educator*
Behrman, Harold Richard *endocrinologist, physiologist, educator*
Bell, Wendell *sociologist, educator, futurist*
Bennett, William Ralph, Jr. *physicist, educator*
Berliner, Robert William *physician, medical educator*
Berner, Robert Arbuckle *geochemist, educator*
Berson, Jerome Abraham *chemistry educator*
†Bigland-Ritchie, Brenda R. *physiologist, neurophysiology researcher, educator*
Blatt, Sidney Jules *psychology educator, psychoanalyst*
Bloom, Harold *humanities educator*
Blum, John Morton *historian*
†Böowering, Gerhard H. *Islamic studies educator*
Boulpaep, Emile Louis J. B. *physiology educator, foundation administrator*
Boyer, James Lorenzen *physician, educator*
Brainard, Paul Henry *musicologist, music educator*
Brainard, William Crittenden *economist, educator, university official*
Braverman, Irwin Merton *dermatologist, educator*
†Brewer, Charles H., Jr. *bishop*
Brewster, Carroll Worcester *fund administrator*
Bromley, David Allan *physicist, educator*
Brooks, Peter (Preston) *French and comparative literature educator, writer*
Brown, Arvin Bragin *theater director*
Brown, Thomas Huntington *neuroscientist*
Buck, Donald Tirrell *finance educator*
†Bunney, Benjamin Stephenson *psychiatrist*
Burns, Ellen Bree *federal judge*
Burrow, Gerard Noel *physician, educator*
Burt, Robert Amsterdam *lawyer, educator*
Buss, Leo William *biologist, educator*
†Butler, David J. *newspaper editor*
Byck, Robert Samuel *psychiatrist, educator*
Cabranes, José Alberto *federal judge*
†Cappelli, Mary Antoinette *principal*
Chaet, Bernard Robert *artist, educator*
Chandler, William Knox *physiologist*
Child, Irvin Long *psychologist, educator*
Childs, Brevard Springs *religious educator*
Chupka, William Andrew *chemical physicist, educator*
†Clarke, Fred W. *architectural firm executive*
Clizbe, John Anthony *psychologist*
Coe, Michael Douglas *anthropologist, educator*
Cohen, Donald Jay *pediatrics, psychiatry and psychology educator, administrator*
Cohen, Lawrence Sorel *physician, educator*
Cohen, Morris Leo *law librarian, educator*
Collins, William F., Jr. *neurosurgery educator*
Comer, James Pierpont *psychiatrist*
Conklin, Harold Colyer *anthropologist, educator*
Cooper, Franklin Seaney *speech scientist*
Cooper, Jack Ross *pharmacology educator, researcher*
†Cosham, Don *architect*
Cottrell, Mary-Patricia Tross *banker*
Crothers, Donald Morris *biochemist, educator*
Culler, Arthur Dwight *English language educator*
Cunningham, Walter Jack *electrical engineering educator*
Damaska, Mirjan Radovan *law educator*
Dangremond, David W. *museum administrator, educator*
Davey, Lycurgus Michael *neurosurgeon*
Davis, David Brion *historian, educator*
de Bretteville, Sheila Levrant *art educator, art director, artist*
Dechant, Virgil C. *fraternal organization administrator*
Deese, James LaMotte *financial executive*
Demos, John Putnam *history educator, writer, consultant*

De Rose, Sandra Michele *psychotherapist, educator, supervisor, administrator*
DeVita, Vincent Theodore, Jr. *oncologist*
Dittes, James Edward *psychology of religion educator*
Donaldson, Robert Macartney, Jr. *physician*
Doob, Leonard William *psychology educator, academic administrator*
Dorsey, Peter Collins *federal judge*
DuBois, Arthur Brooks *physiologist, educator*
Duke, Steven Barry *law educator*
Dupré, Louis *philosopher, educator*
Ebbert, Arthur, Jr. *retired university dean*
Edelson, Marshall *psychiatry educator, psychoanalyst*
Ellickson, Robert Chester *law educator*
Elliott, Edwin Donald, Jr. *law educator, federal administrator, environmental lawyer*
Ember, Melvin Lawrence *anthropology educator*
Erikson, Kai *sociologist, educator*
Erlich, Victor *Slavic languages educator*
Evans, Alfred Spring *physician, educator*
Fassett, John D. *retired utility executive, consultant*
Feinstein, Alvan Richard *physician*
Fiss, Owen M. *law educator*
Franklin, Ralph William *library director, literary scholar*
French, Richard Frederic *emeritus music educator*
Fried, Charles A. *accountant,financial executive*
Friedlaender, Gary Elliott *orthopedist, educator*
Friedman, Erick *concert violinist, educator*
Gallup, Donald Clifford *bibliographer, educator*
Galston, Arthur William *biology educator*
†Galvin, James Norman *financial executive, investment banker*
Garner, Wendell Richard *psychology educator*
Gastwirth, Donald Edward *lawyer, literary agent*
Geanakoplos, Deno John *history educator*
Genel, Myron *pediatrician, educator*
Gewirtz, Paul D. *lawyer*
Giebisch, Gerhard Hans *physiology educator*
Gilman, Richard *author, drama educator*
Glaser, Gilbert Herbert *neuroscientist, physician, educator*
Glenn, William Wallace Lumpkin *surgeon, educator*
Glier, Ingeborg Johanna *German language and literature educator*
Goldstein, Abraham S. *lawyer, educator*
Goldstein, Joseph *law educator*
Gordon, John Charles *forestry educator*
Gordon, Robert Boyd *geophysics educator*
Greene, Liliane *French educator, editor*
Greene, Thomas McLernon *language professional, educator*
Greenfield, James Robert *lawyer*
Hallo, William Wolfgang *Assyriologist*
Hanson, Anne Coffin *art historian*
Harries, Karsten *philosophy educator, researcher*
Harrison, Henry Starin *real estate educator, appraiser, entrepreneur*
Hartman, Geoffrey H. *language professional, educator*
Hayslett, John Paul *physician, medical educator, researcher*
†Heninger, George Robert *psychiatry educator, researcher*
Herbert, Peter Noel *physician, medical educator*
Hersey, George Leonard *art history educator*
Herzenberg, Arvid *physicist, educator*
Hickey, Leo J(oseph) *museum curator, educator*
Hoffer, Paul B. *nuclear medicine physician, educator*
Hoffleit, Ellen Dorrit *astronomer*
†Hoffman, Joseph Frederick *physiology educator*
Holder, Angela Roddey *lawyer, educator*
Hollander, John *humanities educator, poet*
Holmes, Frederic Lawrence *science historian*
Holquist, James Michael *Russian and comparative literature educator*
Hoover, Roland Armitage *publisher, printer*
Horstmann, Dorothy Millicent *physician, educator*
Horváth, Csaba *chemical engineering educator, researcher*
Horwitz, Ralph Irving *internist, medical educator, epidemiologist*
†Howard, Maureen *writer*
Hsiao, James Chingnu *economics educator*
Hyman, Paula E(llen) *history educator*
†Iachello, Francesco *physicist educator*
Insler, Stanley *philologist, educator*
Jacobson, Nathan *mathematics educator*
†Jacoby, Robert Ottinger *comparative medicine educator*
Jatlow, Peter I. *pathologist, medical educator, researcher*
Jekel, James Franklin *physician, public health educator*
Johnson, Lester Fredrick *artist*
Johnson, Robert Clyde *theology educator*
Johnstone, Quintin *legal educator*
Jorgensen, William L. *chemistry educator*
Kagan, Donald *historian, educator*
Kashgarian, Michael *pathologist, physician*
Katz, Jay *psychiatry and law educator*
Kavanagh, Aidan Joseph *priest, university educator*
Kazemzadeh, Firuz *history educator*
Keck, Leander Earl *theology educator*
Kennedy, Paul Michael *history educator*
Kessen, William *psychologist, educator*
Kirchner, John Albert *retired otolaryngology educator*
Klein, Martin Jesse *physicist, educator, science historian*
Komp, Diane Marilyn *pediatric oncologist, hematologist, writer*
Krauss, Judith Belliveau *nursing educator*
Kronman, Anthony Townsend *lawyer, educator*
†Kugler, Frank J. *bank executive*
Kushlan, Samuel Daniel *physician, educator, hospital administrator*
Laderman, Ezra *composer, educator, college dean*
Lamar, Howard Roberts *educational administrator, historian*
Lang, Serge *mathematics educator*
Langbein, John Harriss *lawyer, educator*
LaPalombara, Joseph *political science educator*
Larson, Richard Bondo *astronomy educator*
Leeney, Robert Joseph *newspaper editor*
Levin, Richard Charles *economist*
Levine, Robert John *physician, educator*
Lewis, Melvin *psychiatrist, pediatrician, psychoanalyst*
Lindroth, Linda (Linda Hammer) *artist*
Logue, Frank *arbitrator, mediator, urban consultant, former mayor New Haven*
Lord, George deForest *English educator*
Lorimer, Linda Koch *college official*
MacAvoy, Paul Webster *economics educator, university dean*
MacMullen, Ramsay *retired history educator*
Malherbe, Abraham Johannes, VI *religion educator, writer*
Marcus, Ruth Barcan *philosopher, educator, writer, lecturer*
†Marmor, Theodore Richard *political science and public management educator*
Marshall, Burke *law educator*
Martz, Louis Lohr *English literature educator*
Massey, William S. *mathematician, educator*
Mayhew, David Raymond *political educator*
McClatchy, J. D. *editor, writer, educator*
McDermott, Drew Vincent *computer science educator*
Mc Guire, William James *social psychology educator*
†Meyer, Patricia Ann *veterinarian*
Miller, I. George *physician, educator, researcher*
Miller, Neal Elgar *psychologist, emeritus educator*
Miskimin, Harry Alvin *history educator*
Moore, Peter Bartlett *biochemist, educator*
Mostow, George Daniel *mathematics educator*
Mullen, Frank Albert *university official, clergyman*
Musto, David Franklin *physician, historian, consultant*
Myers, Jerome Keeley *sociology educator*
Naftolin, Frederick *physician, reproductive biologist educator*
Narendra, Kumpati Subrahmanya *electrical engineer, educator*
Natanson, Maurice Alexander *philosopher, educator*
Nelson, Lowry, Jr. *comparative literature educator*
†Newick, Craig David *architect*
Newman, Harry Rudolph *urologist, educator*
†Newman, Herbert S. *architect, educator*
Niederman, James Corson *physician*
†Nolan, Victoria Holmes *theater director*
Oliver-Warren, Mary Elizabeth *library science educator*
Ostfeld, Adrian Michael *physician*
Ostrom, John H. *vertebrate paleontologist, educator, museum curator*
Outka, Gene Harold *philosophy and Christian ethics educator*
Palisca, Claude Victor *musicologist, educator*
Papageorge, Tod *photographer, educator*
Pease, David Gordon *artist, educator*
Pelikan, Jaroslav Jan *history educator*
Pelli, Cesar *architect*
Phillips, Peter Charles Bonest *economist, educator, researcher*
Piatetski-Shapiro, Ilya *mathematics educator*
Platner, Warren *architect*
Poirion, Daniel *foreign language educator*
Polayes, Irving Marvin *plastic surgeon*
Pollitt, Jerome Jordan *art history educator*
Pospisil, Leopold Jaroslav *anthropology educator*
Priest, George L. *law educator*
Pruett, Kyle Dean *psychiatrist, writer, educator*
Prusoff, William Herman *biochemical pharmacologist, educator*
Rae, Douglas Whiting *management educator*
Rakic, Pasko *neuroscientist, educator*
Ranis, Gustav *economist, educator*
Rawson, Robert Orrin *physiologist*
Redmond, Donald Eugene, Jr. *neuroscientist, educator*
Reifsnyder, William Edward *meteorologist*
Reiser, Morton Francis *psychiatrist, educator*
Reiss, Albert John, Jr. *sociology educator*
Reynolds, Lloyd George *economist, educator*
Reynolds, Mary Trackett *political scientist*
Richards, Frederic Middlebrook *biochemist, educator*
Rickart, Charles Earl *mathematician, educator*
†Robbins, William Randolph *minister*
Robinson, (David) Duncan *museum administrator, art historian*
Robinson, Fred Colson *English language educator*
Rodgers, John *geologist, educator*
Rolland, Peter George *landscape architect*
Rose-Ackerman, Susan *law and political economy educator*
Rosenblum, M. Edgar *theater director*
Rostow, Eugene Victor *lawyer, educator, economist*
Roth, Harold *architect*
Rouse, Irving *anthropologist, emeritus educator*
Rush, William John *newspaper executive*
Ryden, John Graham *publishing executive*
Saltzman, Barry *meteorologist, educator*
Sandweiss, Jack *physicist, educator*
Sartorelli, Alan Clayton *pharmacology educator*
Sasaki, Clarence Takashi *surgeon, medical educator*
Scarf, Herbert Eli *economics educator*
Schenker, Alexander Marian *linguistics educator*
Schowalter, John Erwin *psychiatrist, educator*
Schultz, T. Paul *economics educator*
Schwartz, Peter Edward *physician, gynecologic oncology educator*
†Scully, Vincent *art historian, retired educator, writer*
†Shope, Robert Ellis *epidemiology educator*
Shubik, Martin *economics educator*
Shulman, Robert Gerson *biophysics educator*
Siggins, Jack Arthur *librarian*
Sigler, Paul Benjamin *molecular biology educator, protein crystallographer*
Silver, George Albert *physician, educator*
Simon, John Gerald *law educator*
Sims, Christopher Albert *economics educator*
Singer, Burton Herbert *statistics educator*
Slayman, Carolyn Walch *geneticist, educator*
†Smith, C. Thomas, Jr. *hospital administrator*
Smith, David Martyn *forestry educator*
†Smith, Gaddis *history professor*
Smith, John Edwin *philosophy educator*
Smith, William Hulse *forestry and environmental studies educator*
Solnit, Albert Jay *commissioner, physician, educator*
Spence, Jonathan Dermot *historian, educator*
Spiro, Howard Marget *physician, educator*
Steitz, Joan Argetsinger *biochemistry educator*
Stevens, Joseph Charles *psychology educator*
Stolberg, Irving J. *state legislator, consultant*
Stolwijk, Jan Adrianus Jozef *physiologist, biophysicist*
Stuehrenberg, Paul Frederick *librarian*
Summers, William Cofield *science educator*
Szczarba, Robert Henry *mathematics educator, mathematician*
Taylor, Kenneth John W. *physician of diognostic imagery*
Theodore, Eustace D. *alumni association executive, management consultant*
Tilson, John Quillin *lawyer*
Tirro, Frank Pascale *music educator, author, composer*
Tobin, James *economics educator*
Trinkaus, John Philip *cell and developmental biologist*
Tufte, Edward Rolf *statistics educator, publisher*
Turekian, Karl Karekin *geochemistry educator*
Underdown, David Edward *historian, educator*
Valesio, Paolo *Italian language and literature educator, writer*
Van Altena, William Foster *astronomer, educator*
Van Sinderen, Alfred White *former telephone company executive*
Vroom, Victor Harold *management consultant, educator*
Waggoner, Paul Edward *agricultural scientist*
Wagner, Allan Ray *psychology educator, experimental psychologist*
Wandycz, Piotr Stefan *history educator*
†Wasserman, Harry Hershal *chemistry educator*
Waters, Donald Joseph *information services administrator*
Waxman, Stephen George *neurologist, researcher*
†Wegener, Peter Paul *educator, author*
Weinstein, Stanley *Buddhist studies educator*
Weiss, Robert M. *urologist, educator*
Wentz, Howard Beck, Jr. *manufacturing company executive*
†Wessel, Morris Arthur *pediatrician*
Westerfield, Holt Bradford *political scientist, educator*
Whitaker, Thomas Russell *English literature educator*
†Wiberg, Kenneth Berle *chemist, educator*
Winks, Robin William *history educator*
Winter, Ralph Karl, Jr. *federal judge*
†Woerner, Peter Kurt *architect, builder*
Wolf, Werner Paul *physicist, educator*
Wright, Hastings Kemper *surgeon, educator*
Zaccagnino, Joseph Anthony *hospital administrator*
Zaret, Barry Lewis *cardiologist, medical educator*
Zeller, Michael Edward *physicist*

New London
Doro, Marion Elizabeth *political scientist, educator*
Gaudiani, Claire Lynn *academic administrator*
Goodwin, Richard Hale *botany educator*
Knowles, Elizabeth Pringle *art museum director*
MacCluggage, Reid *newspaper editor, publisher*
Owsley, Norman Lee *electrical engineer, educator*
Pinhey, Frances Louise *physical education educator*
Rogers, Brian Deane *librarian*
Wetmore, Thomas Trask, III *retired foundation administrator, retired coast guard officer*

New Milford
Altermatt, Paul Barry *lawyer*
Edmondson, John Richard *lawyer, pharmaceutical manufacturing company executive*
Fabricand, Burton Paul *physicist, educator*

New Preston
Randall, Bob *writer*

Newington
Fleeson, William *psychiatry educator*
†Sumner, David George *association executive*
Vassar, William Gerald *gifted and talented education educator*

Newtown
Cayne, Bernard Stanley *editor*
Verano, Anthony Frank *banker*

Niantic
Driskill, Clarence *publishing executive*

Norfolk
Lambros, Lambros John *lawyer, petroleum company executive*
Vagliano, Alexander Marino *banker*

North Branford
Gregan, Edmund Robert *landscape architect*

North Haven
Dahl, Robert Alan *political science educator*
Hess, Orvan W. *retired medical educator, obstetrician-gynecologist*
†Hoffmann, John J. *architect*
Mahl, George Franklin *psychoanalyst, psychologist, educator*
Peterson, George Emanuel, Jr. *lawyer, business executive*
Seton, Fenmore Roger *manufacturing company executive, civic worker*
Thorpe, James, III *publisher*
Walker, Fred Elmer *broadcasting executive*

North Stonington
Nolf, David Manstan *financial executive*

Northford
James, Virginia Stowell *elementary education educator*

Norwalk
†Balmuth, Marc I. *consumer products company executive*
Bennett, Carl *retired discount department store executive*
Bermas, Stephen *lawyer*
Bowman, Robert Gibson *publishing company executive*
Brandt, Richard Paul *communications and entertainment company executive*
Brod, Morton Shlevin *oral surgeon*
Brown, Beatrice *symphony conductor*
†Bullard, Edward Payson, IV *non-profit executive*
Caravatt, Paul Joseph, Jr. *communications company executive*
Caro, Warren *theatrical executive, lawyer*
†Clarke, Don R. *consumer products company executive*
Dresher, William Henry *research association executive*
Floch, Martin Herbert *physician*
Foster, John McNeely *accounting standards executive*
Gaertner, Christopher Wolfgang *electronics company executive*
Grace, Julianne Alice *manufacturing company executive*
Hathaway, Carl Emil *investment management company executive*
Hayashida, Ralph Francis *educational publishing company executive*
Hirsch, Leon Charles *medical company executive*
Irving, Michael Henry *architect*
Johnstone, Chauncey Olcott *pharmaceutical company executive*
Kelley, Gaynor Nathaniel *instrumentation manufacturing company executive*
Lederer, Jack Lawrence *personnel director, human resources specialist*
Maarbjerg, Mary Penzold *office equipment company executive*
Maisano, Phillip Nicholas *investment company executive*
Marnane, Joseph Peter *maritime center executive*
McDonell, Horace George, Jr. *instrument company executive*
Meredith, David Robert *personnel executive*
Mosso, David *accountant*
Needham, Charles William *neurosurgeon*
Northcutt, Robert Hull, Jr. *financial executive*
Partch, Kenneth Paul *editor, consultant*
†Payne, Paul D. *finance company executive*
Peltz, Alan Howard *manufacturing company executive*
Perry, Charles Owen *sculptor*
†Perschino, Arthur J. *secondary school principal*
Rast, Mendel Walker *manufacturing company executive*
Rawlins, Christopher John *publishing executive, director*
Sasenick, Joseph Anthony *health care company executive*
Smith, Wendell Murray *graphic arts control and equipment manufacturing executive*
Tracey, Edward John *physician, surgeon*
Vanderbilt, Hugh Bedford, Sr. *mineral and chemical company executive*
Van Norstrand, R. E. *lawyer*
†Watson, H. Mitchell, Jr. *business machines company executive*
Wiggins, Charles *educator*
†York, Theodore *electronics executive*

Norwich
Gualtieri, Joseph Peter *museum director*
Reilly, Daniel Patrick *bishop*
Sharpe, Richard Samuel *architectural company executive*

Old Greenwich
Alley, William Jack *holding company executive*
Baritz, Loren *history educator*
Bonner, Charles William, III *community services executive, newspaper writer*
Fernous, Louis Ferdinand, Jr. *corporate executive*
Hittle, Richard Howard *corporate executive, international affairs consultant*
Hume, Robert Alan *advertising agency executive, marketing consultant*
Islan, Gregory deFontaine *cable television executive*
Kenyon, Robert Edwin, Jr. *magazine journalist, magazine consultant, lecturer*
Mc Quinn, William P. *corporation executive*
Plancher, Robert Lawrence *manufacturing company executive*
Rossman, Janet Kay *architectural interior designer*
Rukeyser, Robert James *manufacturing executive*
Slack, Lewis *organization administrator*

Old Lyme
†Anderson, Theodore Robert *physicist*
†Bessie, Simon Michael *publisher*
Bond, Niles Woodbridge *cultural institute executive, former foreign service officer*
Chandler, Elisabeth Gordon (Mrs. Laci De Gerenday) *sculptor, harpist*
Cook, Charles Davenport *pediatrician, educator*
de Gerenday, Laci Anthony *sculptor*
St. George, Judith Alexander *author*

Old Saybrook
Elrod, Harold Glenn *retired engineering science educator, consultant*
Hamilton, Donald Bengtsson *author*
Jensen, Oliver Ormerod *editor, writer*
Phillips, William Eugene *advertising agency executive*
Schneider, John Arnold *business investor*
Spencer, William Courtney *foundation executive, international business executive*

Orange
Bowerman, Richard Henry *utility company executive, lawyer*
Clark, John Phelps *lawyer, automotive executive*
Miller, Henry Forster *architect*
Ratcliffe, George Jackson, Jr. *business executive, lawyer*

Plainville
Glassman, Gerald Seymour *metal finishing company executive*

Pomfret
Woodbridge, Henry Sewall *management consultant*

Ridgefield
Bye, Arthur Edwin, Jr. *landscape architect*
Couri, John A. *distribution executive*
Doran, Charles Edward *textile manufacturing executive*
Farina, Peter R. *biochemist*
†Finneran, Thomas A. *finance company executive*
Forbes, James Wendell *publishing consultant*
Julian, Alexander, II *menswear designer*
Keirns, James Jeffrey *pharmaceutical company executive, biochemist*
Kelley, Edward Allen *publisher*
Knortz, Herbert Charles *retired conglomerate company executive*
Levine, Paul Michael *paper industry executive, consultant*
Malhotra, Surin M. *aerospace manufacturing executive*
Margolis, George *pathologist, medical educator*
Mattausch, Thomas Edward *public relations consultant*
McGovern, R(ichard) Gordon *food company executive*
Norman, Richard Arthur *educator*
Phelps, Judson Hewett *marketing sales executive*
Pilbrow, Richard *theatre consultant, lighting designer*
Ruggles, Rudy Lamont, Jr. *investment banker, consultant*
Sadow, Harvey S. *health care company executive*
Wyton, Alec *composer, organist*

Riverside
Battat, Emile A. *management executive*
Coulson, Robert *retired association executive, lawyer*
Geismar, Richard Lee *communications executive*
Isaacson, Gerald Sidney *publishing company executive*
Lovejoy, Allen Fraser *retired lawyer*
McCullough, Robert Willis *former textile executive*
McSpadden, Peter Ford *retired advertising agency executive*
Otto, Charles Edward *health care administrator*
Pearson, Robert Greenlees *writing services company executive*
†Powers, Claudia McKenna *state government official*

Rocky Hill
Chuang, Frank Shiunn-Jea *engineering executive, consultant*
†Hollis, Peter B. *retail executive*
Thorner, Peter *retail executive*

Rowayton
Sills, David Lawrence *retired sociologist*

Roxbury
Anderson, Robert Woodruff *playwright, novelist, screenwriter*
Gurney, Albert Ramsdell *playwright, novelist, educator*
Miller, Arthur *playwright, author*

Salem
Diamond, Sigmund *educator, editor*

Salisbury
Bevan, Charles Albert, Jr. *minister*
Block, Zenas *management consultant, educator*
Blum, Robert Edward *business executive*

Sandy Hook
Karkut, Emil Joseph *manufacturing company executive*
Kellogg, Steven *author*

Seymour
Sims, Robert Barry *lawyer*

Sharon
Gordon, Nicholas *broadcasting executive*

Shelton
†Bowron, John B. *transportation executive*
Canosa, Albert Anthony *corporate finance officer*
Crowe, Jeffrey C. *transportation executive*
Forbes, Richard E. *retired publishing company executive*
†Greene, Richard Efraim *data processing executive*
Harvey, Michael Lee *lawyer, transportation executive*
Lobsenz, Herbert Munter *data base company executive*
McCurdy, Charles Gribbel *publishing company executive*
†Mortimer, Stanley Grafton, III *marketing company executive*
Smith, Craig Richards *manufacturing executive*
Wham, William Neil *publisher*

Sherman
Goodspeed, Barbara *artist*
Lee, Wallace Williams, Jr. *retired hotel executive*
Piel, William, Jr. *retired lawyer*
Valeriani, Richard Gerard *news broadcaster*

Simsbury
Hildebrandt, Frederick Dean, Jr. *management consultant*
Krisher, William K. *former insurance company executive*
Long, Michael Thomas *lawyer, manufacturing company executive*
Nolan, Robert Emmett *management consulting company executive*

South Norwalk
Albanese, Licia *operatic soprano*
Manning, James Forrest *computer executive*

South Windsor
†Gentile, George Michael *manufacturing company finance executive*
Gerber, Heinz Joseph *computer automation company executive*

Southbury
Atwood, Edward Charles *economist, educator*
Cassidy, James Joseph *public relations counsel*
Fabiani, Dante Carl *industrialist*
†O'Neill, Arthur Julius *lawyer, state representative*
Usher, Elizabeth Reuter (Mrs. William A. Scar) *retired librarian*
Wescott, Roger Williams *anthropologist*

Southport
Greene, Herbert Bruce *lawyer, merchant banker*
Haas, Ward John *cosmetics executive*
Hill, David Lawrence *research corporation executive*
Kingsley, John McCall, Jr. *manufacturing company executive*
McLearn, Michael Baylis *lawyer*
Miles, Leland Weber *university president*
†Parker, David Scott *architect*
Perry, Vincent Aloysius *corporate executive*
Pifer, Alan (Jay Parrish) *former foundation executive*
Roache, Edward Francis *retired manufacturing company executive*
Ruger, William Batterman *firearms manufacturing company executive*
Weller, Tom *author*
Wheeler, Wilmot Fitch, Jr. *diversified manufacturing company executive*
Wilbur, E. Packer *investment company executive*

Stafford Springs
†Guglielmo, Tony *state legislator, insurance agency executive*

Stamford
Adams, Taggart D. *lawyer*
Akers, John Fellows *information processing company executive*
Allaire, Paul Arthur *office equipment company executive*
Anderson, Susan Stuebing *business equipment company executive*
Ashton, Harris John *business executive*
Austin, Darrel *artist*
Aylesworth, Thomas Gibbons *editor, author*
Bailey, Robert William *reinsurance brokerage executive*
Barker, James Rex *corporate executive*
Barlow, Clark W. *telephone company executive*
Barton, James Miller *lawyer*
Bellows, Howard Arthur, Jr. *hardware products manufacturing company executive*
Bentley, Peter *lawyer*
Bigelow, Eugene Thayer, Jr. *media company executive*
Block, Edward Martel *consultant, former telephone company executive*
Block, Ruth *retired insurance company executive*
Bowen, Patrick Harvey *lawyer, consultant*
Brakeley, George Archibald, Jr. *fund raising counsel*
Britt, Glenn Alan *media company executive*
Britton, Robert Austin *manufacturing company executive*
Burton, Arthur Henry, Jr. *insurance company executive*
Cahill, John C. *general industry company executive*
Cain, George Harvey *lawyer, business executive*
Calarco, Vincent Anthony *specialty chemicals company executive*
Camisa, George Lincoln *beverage company executive*
Carlin, Gabriel S. *corporate executive*
Carpenter, Edmund Mogford *manufacturing executive*
Carpenter, Michael Alan *securities firm executive*
Carroll, Thomas Sylvester *business executive*
Carswell, Bruce *communications executive*
Cassetta, Sebastian Ernest *industry executive*
Cavallon, Betty Gabler *interior designer*
Chickering, Howard Allen *insurance company executive, lawyer*
Chiddix, James Alan *broadcast engineering executive*
Coleman, Ernest Albert *plastics and materials consultant*
Coleman, Joel Clifford *lawyer*
Conover, Harvey *retired publisher*
Cottle, Robert Duquemin *facial plastic surgeon, otolaryngologist*
Davison, Endicott Peabody *lawyer*
Dawson, James Ambrose *printing industry executive*
Dederick, Ronald Osburn *lawyer*
Dell, Warren Frank, II *management consultant*
De Micoli, Salvatore *metals commodity executive*
Dewing, Merlin Eugene *diversified financial services company executive*
†DiMattia, Ernest Anthony, Jr. *library administrator*
Dixon, John Morris *magazine editor*
Dolian, Robert Paul *lawyer*
Dorf, Robert L. *public relations executive, marketing and management consultant*
Drost, Marianne *lawyer*
Duke, Robert Dominick *mining executive, lawyer*
Ekernas, Sven Anders *investment company executive*
Epstein, Simon Jules *psychiatrist*
Evans, Robert Sheldon *manufacturing executive*
Farrell, Joseph Christopher *mining executive, services executive*
Ferguson, Ronald Eugene *reinsurance company executive*
Fernandez, Nino Joseph *manufacturing company executive*
Fillet, Mitchell Harris *financial services executive*
Filter, Eunice M. *business equipment manufacturing executive*
Forbes, Walter Alexander *consumer services company executive*
Fortune, Philip Robert *metal manufacturing company executive*
Frank, Charles Raphael, Jr. *financial executive*
Frese, Walter Wenzel *publisher*
Frey, Dale Franklin *financial investment company executive, manufacturing company executive*
Fuller, Mark Adin, Jr. *forest products company executive*
Garbacz, Gerald George *information services company executive*
†Gardiner, Hobart Clive *corporate executive*
Gefter, William Irvin *physician, educator*
Ginsky, Marvin H. *lawyer, corporate executive*
Gladstone, Herbert Jack *manufacturing company executive*
Griffin, Donald Wayne *defense company executive*
Griffith, F. Lee, III *lawyer*
Gross, Ronald Martin *forest products executive*
Gudger, Robert H. *retired printing company executive*
Hagner, Arthur Feodor *geologist, educator*
Hague, John William, Jr. *security company executive*
Harvey, George Burton *office equipment company executive*
Hawley, Frank Jordan, Jr. *venture capital executive*
Hedge, Arthur Joseph, Jr. *environmental executive*
Hicks, Wayland R. *electronic business equipment executive*
Higgins, Jay Francis *financial service executive*
Hoekwater, James Warren *controller*
†Hoffman, Harry Theodore *retail executive*
Hollander, Milton Bernard *electronics executive*
Hood, Edward Exum, Jr. *retired electrical manufacturing company executive*
Horrigan, D. Greg *manufacturing company executive*
†Horrigan, D. Gregory *metal products executive*
Howard, Melvin *financial executive*
Hudson, Harold Jordon, Jr. *retired insurance executive*
Hull, James Charles *industrial company executive*
Jacobson, Ishier *retired utility executive*
†Jaffe, Elliot S. *women's clothing retail chain executive*
†James, John Whitaker, Sr. *financial services executive*
Johnson, Martin Allen *publisher*
Johnstone, John William, Jr. *chemical company executive*
Kaff, Albert Ernest *journalist, author*
Kaufman, John E. *retired association executive*
Kavetas, Harry L. *finance leasing company executive*
Kellogg, Tommy Nason *reinsurance corporation executive*
Kinnear, James Wesley, III *retired petroleum company executive*
Kinsman, Robert Donald *art museum administrator, cartoonist*
Kloster, Burton John, Jr. *lawyer*
Knag, Paul Everett *lawyer*
Kobak, James Benedict *management consultant*
Kubisen, Steven Joseph, Jr. *chemical and plastics management consultant*
Landau, Michael Roy *manufacturing executive*
Lane, Hana Umlauf *editor*
Langstaff, Elliot Kennedy *management consultant*
Lee, Charles Robert *telecommunications company executive*
†Lee, Charles Tomerlin *lawyer*
†Lennard, Gerald *metal products executive*
Light, (Marvin) Lawrence *advertising agency executive*
Lowman, George Frederick *lawyer*
†Lukeman, Gerald C. *advertising executive*
MacEwen, Edward Carter *communications executive*
†Magidson, Michael D. *metals products executive*
†Margolis, Emanuel *lawyer, educator*
Marlowe, Edward *research company executive*
Marsden, Charles Joseph *financial executive*
Mata, Pedro Francisco *food products executive*
McCain, Arthur Williamson, Jr. *pension investment consultant*
McGeeney, John Stephen *lawyer*
McGrath, Richard Paul *lawyer*
Mc Kinley, John Key *retired oil company executive*
McLeod, Christopher Kevin *service company executive*
Mc Namara, Francis Joseph, Jr. *foundation executive, lawyer*
McNear, Barbara Baxter *financial communications executive, consultant*
Merritt, William Alfred, Jr. *lawyer, telecommunications company executive*
Miller, Wilbur Hobart *business diversification consultant*
†Moody, J. Roger *computer software executive*
Morgan, William J. *accounting company executive*
Murphy, Robert Blair *management consulting company executive*
Nelson, David Leonard *process management systems company executive*
Nichols, Ralph Arthur *lawyer*
Nierenberg, Roger *symphony conductor*
Norman, Geoffrey Robert *financial executive*
Nutter, Wallace Lee *paper manufacturing executive*
Oatway, Francis Carlyle *corporate executive*
Obernauer, Marne *corporate executive*
O'Connor, Frank M. *business educator, sales professional*
O'Malley, Thomas D. *diversified company executive*
O'Neill, Robert Edward *business journal editor*
Owen, Nathan Richard *manufacturing company executive*
Pacter, Paul Allan *accounting educator*
Pansini, Michael Samuel *energy company executive, consultant*
Parker, Jack Steele *retired manufacturing company executive*
Paul, Richard Stanley *lawyer*
Paul, Thomas A. *book publisher*
Perle, Eugene Gabriel *lawyer*
Peterson, Carl Eric *banker, metals company executive*
†Petrosian, Peter *food service executive*
Pollak, Edward Barry *chemical manufacturing company executive*
Porosoff, Harold *chemist, research and development director*
Quinnell, Bruce Andrew *finance executive*
Raymond, Harvey Francis *textile executive, consultant*
Reynolds, Robert Louis *financial services executive*
Rhinesmith, Stephen Headley *international management consultant*
Rickard, Norman Edward *office equipment executive*
Riggs, Douglas A. *lawyer*
Riggs, James Arthur *financial executive*
Rodriguez, J. Louis *civil engineer, land surveyor*
Rondepierre, Edmond Francois *insurance company executive*
Rosenberg, Charles Harvey *otorhinolaryngologist*
Ross, Stuart B. *corporate financial executive*
Rowe, William John *newspaper publishing executive*
Ryan, Raymond D. *retired steel company executive, insurance and marketing firm executive*
Salisbury, John Francis *distillery and chemical company executive, corporate lawyer*
Sarbin, Hershel Benjamin *management consultant, business publisher, lawyer*
†Sayers, Richard James *newspaper editor*
Schectman, Herbert A. *lawyer, corporate executive*
Schilling, Albert Henry *former government agency administrator, corporate environmental consultant*
Schmults, Edward Charles *lawyer*
Schoonmaker, Samuel Vail, III *lawyer*
Scribner, Barbara Colvin *museum administrator*
Serrani, Thom *business consultant, former mayor*
Sharp, Daniel Asher *foundation executive, corporate consultant*
Sharp, Edgar E. *diversified corporation executive*
Sigler, Andrew Clark *forest products company executive*
Silver, Charles Morton *communications company executive*
†Silver, R. Philip *metal products executive*
Sisley, G. William *lawyer*
Skidd, Thomas Patrick, Jr. *lawyer*
Smith, Edgar James, Jr. *lawyer, manufacturing company executive*
Spindler, John Frederick *lawyer*
Stapleton, James Francis *lawyer*
†Stauff, Michael Frederick *financial manager*
†Steinberg, Burt *retail executive*
Strosahl, William Austin *artist, art director*
Sveda, Michael *management and research consultant*
Teeters, Nancy Hays *economist*
Tobin, Richard J. *lawyer*
Tow, Leonard *television executive*
Toy, Arthur Dock Fon *chemist*
Tregurtha, Paul Richard *marine transportation and construction materials company executive*
Twardy, Stanley Albert, Jr. *lawyer*
Veronis, Peter *publisher*
Vest, George Graham *lawyer*
Villarreal, Homero Atenógenes *human resources executive*
Vos, Frank *advertising and marketing executive*
Wall, Stephen James *senior executive consultant*
Wallfesh, Henry Maurice *business communications company executive, editor, writer*
Walsh, Thomas Joseph *neuro ophthalmologist*
Walton, Alan George *venture capitalist*
Ware, Jennifer Peyton *communications professional*
Weitzel, William Conrad, Jr. *lawyer*
Wendt, Gary Carl *finance company executive*
Weyher, Harry Frederick, III *metals company executive*
White, Richard Booth *management consultant*
Wilensky, Julius M. *publishing company executive*
Wilhelm, Gayle Brian *lawyer*
Williams, Ernest William, Jr. *economist, educator*
Yardis, Pamela Hintz *computer consulting company executive*
Yoder, Patricia Doherty *public relations executive*
Ziegler, William, III *diversified industry executive*
Zuckert, Donald Mack *marketing executive*

Stonington
Dupont, Ralph Paul *lawyer, educator*
Van Rees, Cornelius S. *lawyer*

Storrs
Allen, George James *psychologist, educator*
Allen, John Logan *geographer*
Bartram, Ralph Herbert *physicist*
Bobbitt, James McCue *chemist*
Charters, Ann *biographer, editor, educator*
Coons, Ronald Edward *historian, educator*
Dardick, Kenneth Regen *physician, educator*
Devereux, Owen Francis *metallurgy educator*
†Di Benedetto, Anthony Thomas *chemical engineering educator*
†Galligan, James M. *material sciences educator, researcher*
Greene, John Colton *retired history educator*
Long, Richard Paul *civil engineering educator, geotechnical engineering consultant*
Marcus, Philip Irving *virology educator, researcher*
Mc Innes, William Charles *priest, campus ministry director*
Nieforth, Karl Allen *university dean, educator*
Pitkin, Edward Thaddeus *aerospace engineer, consultant*
Rosen, William *English language educator*
Shaffer, Jerome Arthur *philosophy educator*
Stwalley, William Calvin *physics and chemistry educator*
Walker, David Bradstreet *political science educator*
Wood, Wendy Deborah *filmmaker*

Storrs Mansfield
Abramson, Arthur Seymour *linguistics educator, researcher*
Anderson, Gregory Joseph *botanical sciences educator*
Azaroff, Leonid Vladimirovitch *physics educator*
Birdman, Jerome Moseley *drama educator, consultant*
Denenberg, Victor Hugo *psychology educator*
DiBenedetto, Anthony Thomas *engineering educator*
Glasser, Joseph *manufacturing and marketing executive*
Guttay, Andrew John Robert *agronomy educator, researcher*
John, Hugo Herman *natural resources educator*
Khairallah, Edward Amin *molecular biology and biochemistry professor*
Klemens, Paul Gustav *physicist, educator*
Koths, Jay Sanford *floriculture educator*
Ladd, Everett Carll *political science educator, author*
Laufer, Hans *developmental biologist, educator*
McFadden, Peter William *mechanical engineering educator*
Packard, Sheila Anne *nursing educator, researcher*
Reed, Howard Alexander *educator, historian*
Schuster, Todd Mervyn *biophysics educator, biotechnology company executive*
Schwarz, J(ames) Conrad *psychology educator*
Stevens, Norman Dennison *retired library director*
Zelanski, Paul John *art educator, author*

Stratford
†Chase, J. Vincent *state legislator, shopping center executive*
Rozarie, Vera Jean *school district administrator*
Zimmerman, Daniel D. *chemical engineer*

Suffield
†Leavitt, Joel *consumer products company executive*
Leavitt, Julian J. *wholesale food company executive*

Tariffville
Johnson, Loering M. *design engineer, historian, consultant*

Thompson
Fisher, William Thomas *business administration educator*

Tolland
Wilde, Daniel Underwood *computer engineering educator*

Torrington
†Oneglia, Raymond Robert *construction company executive*

Trumbull
Bravo, Anthony John *radiologist*
Doherty, Donna Kathryn *editor*
Ferm, David G. *magazine publisher*
FitzGerald, James W. *publishing executive*
†Galvin, Terry *magazine editor*
Gladki, Hanna Zofia *civil engineer, hydraulic mixer specialist*
†Norcel, Jacqueline Joyce Casale *educational administrator*
Seitz, Nicholas Joseph *magazine editor*
†Tarde, Gerard *magazine editor*

Uncasville
†Ryan, Kevin *optometrist, physics*

Wallingford
†Cirasuolo, Joseph J. *school system administrator*
De George, Lawrence Joseph *diversified company executive*
†Fritz, Mary G. *state legislator*
†Hay, Leroy E. *school system administrator*

Warren
Abrams, Herbert E. *artist*
Gray, Cleve *artist*

Washington
Hardee, William Covington *banker, lawyer*
Pendleton, Moses Robert Andrew *dancer, choreographer*

Washington Depot
Chase, Alison *modern dancer, choreographer, teacher*

Mandler, Susan Ruth dance company administrator
Tracy, Michael Cameron choreographer, performer

Waterbury
†Bergin, Edward Daniel mayor
Cohen, Andrew Stuart architect, landscape architect
Daly, T(homas) F(rancis) Gilroy federal judge
Glass, Robert Davis trial referee
Hamilton, John Ross financial consultant, educator
Leever, Harold chemical company executive
Narkis, Robert Joseph bank executive, lawyer
Pape, William James, II newspaper publisher
Smith, Ann Youngdahl museum administrator
Zampiello, Richard Sidney metals and trading company executive
Zeitlin, Bruce Allen superconducting material technology executive

Waterford
Commire, Anne playwright
Hinkle, Muriel Ruth Nelson naval warfare analysis company executive
Pierson, Anne Bingham physician
Sillin, Lelan Flor, Jr. retired utility executive
White, George Cooke theater director, foundation executive

West Cornwall
Klaw, Barbara Van Doren author, editor
Klaw, Spencer writer, editor, educator
Prentice, Tim sculptor, architect
Simont, Marc artist

West Granby
Conland, Stephen publishing company executive

West Hartford
Abbot, Quincy Sewall retired insurance executive
Bartels, Millard lawyer
Chiarenza, Frank John English language educator
Clear, Albert F., Jr. retired hardware manufacturing company executive
Doran, James Martin retired food products company executive
Farr, Richard Claborn private investor, corporate executive
Glasson, Lloyd sculptor, educator
Glixon, David M(orris) editor
Hickcox, Curtiss Bronson anesthesiologist
Lawson, Jonathan Nevin academic administrator
Libassi, Frank Peter lawyer, dean
Mason, George H. business educator, consultant
McCawley, Austin psychiatrist, educator
Miller, Elliott Cairns retired bank executive, lawyer
Newell, Robert Lincoln retired banker
Pustilnik, David Daniel lawyer
Pustilnik, Jean Todd elementary education educator
Raffay, Stephen Joseph manufacturing company executive
Tonkin, Humphrey Richard university president
Uccello, Vincenza Agatha artist, director, educator emerita
Welna, Cecilia mathematics educator
Whitman, Robert lawyer, educator

West Haven
Das, Rathin C. molecular and cellular biologist
†DeNardis, Lawrence J. academic administrator
Eisenman, Alvin educator, graphic designer
Ellis, Lynn Webster management educator, telecommunications consultant
Emerson, Thomas Edward, Jr. cardiovascular physiologist
†Esposito, Louis P., Jr. business owner, state legislator
Gerritsen, Mary Ellen vascular and cell biologist
Lee, Ming Cho set designer
Turner, Frank Miller historian, educator

West Redding
Benyei, Candace Reed psychotherapist
Foster, Edward John engineering physicist
Kipnis, Igor harpsichordist, fortepianist, critic
Mathews, Carmen Sylva actress
Russell, Allan David lawyer
Schramm, John Clarendon foundation executive

West Simsbury
Brinkerhoff, Peter John manufacturing company executive
Morest, Donald Kent neuroscientist

Westbrook
Hall, Jane Anna writer, model

Weston
Bleifeld, Stanley sculptor
Cadmus, Paul artist, etcher
Daniel, James business executive, writer, former editor
Fredrik, Burry theatrical producer, director
Kilty, Jerome Timothy playwright, stage director, actor
Liberatore, Nicholas Alfred business consultant
Lindsay, Charles Joseph banker
Mattoon, Henry Amasa, Jr. advertising and marketing consultant, writer
Murray, Thomas Joseph advertising executive
Offenhartz, Edward aerospace executive
Rand, Paul graphic designer, educator
Schnitzer, Robert C. theater administrator
Thompson, N(orman) David insurance company executive

Westport
Aasen, Lawrence Obert public relations executive
Albani, Suzanne Beardsley lawyer
Allen, Robert Hugh communications corporation executive
Angle, Richard Warner, Jr. not-for-profit and publishing executive
Bescherer, Edwin A., Jr. business information services company executive
Bishop, William Wade advertising executive
Blazzard, Norse Novar lawyer
Breitbarth, S. Robert manufacturing company executive
Britt, David Van Buren educational communications executive
†Bronson, Carole publishing executive
Brooks, Andrée Aelion journalist, educator, author
Brooks, Babert Vincent publisher
†Brown, Mona architect
Buchanan, William Hobart, Jr. lawyer, publishing company executive
Cederbaum, Eugene E. lawyer
Clausman, Gilbert Joseph medical librarian
Davis, Joel publisher
Daw, Harold John lawyer
De Lay, Robert Francis marketing executive, consultant
Densen-Gerber, Judianne psychiatrist, lawyer, educator
Dickson, Sally Isabelle retired public relations executive
†Dunton, James Raynor publisher
Enos, Randall cartoonist, illustrator
†Ferris, Roger Patrick architect
†Freedman, Judith Greenberg state senator, importer
Hagelstein, Robert Philip publisher
Hambleton, George Blow Elliott management consultant
Hotchner, Aaron Edward author
Joseph, Michael Thomas broadcast consultant
Kalan, George Richard venture capitalist
Kelly, Paul Knox investment banker
Knopf, Alfred, Jr. retired publisher
Kramer, Sidney B. publisher, lawyer, literary agent
Leckie, Robert Bedford lawyer
Levinger, Beryl Beth cultural organization administrator, consultant
†Malski, James Joseph airline executive, accountant
Martin, Ralph Guy writer
McCaig, Joseph J. retail food chain executive
McCormack, Donald Paul newspaper consultant
McCormack, Patricia Seger independent press service editor, journalist
McFarland, Richard M. executive recruiting consultant
McKane, David Bennett business executive
Meckler, Alan Marshall publisher, author
Murphy, Thomas John publishing executive
Nedom, H. Arthur petroleum consultant
O'Keefe, John David investment specialist
O'Leary, James John economist
Radigan, Joseph Richard human resources executive
Raikes, Charles FitzGerald lawyer
Ready, Robert James financial company executive
Rose, Reginald television writer, producer
Ross, John Michael editor, magazine publisher
Sabin, James Thomas publisher
Sacks, Herbert Simeon psychiatrist, educator, consultant
Sadler, David Gary financial institution crisis management consultant
Safran, Claire writer, editor
†Sarn, James physician, health association administrator
Satinover, Jeffrey Burke psychiatrist, health science facility administrator, lecturer, author
Savage, Robert Heath advertising executive
Scheinman, Stanley Bruce venture capital executive, lawyer
Silk, George photographer
Singer, Henry A. behavioral scientist, institute director
Stashower, Michael David retired manufacturing company executive
Tucker, Gardiner Luttrell physicist, former paper company executive
Wachsler, Robert Alan marketing consultant
Walden, Amelia Elizabeth (Mrs. John William Harmon) author
Weissman, Robert Evan publisher, financial information company executive
Wexler, Herbert Ira retail company executive

Wethersfield
†Edwards, Kenneth S. principal
Payne, Edward Carlton archbishop
Precourt, George Augustine government official

Whitneyville
Miller, Walter Richard, Jr. banker

Willimantic
†Carter, David George, Sr. university administrator
Clements, Bruce author
Philips, David Evan English language educator

Wilton
Billings, Edward Robert accountant
Brown, James Thompson, Jr. computer information scientist
Cassidy, George Thomas international business development consultant
Cook, Jay Michael accounting company executive
Cutler, Theodore John cable company executive
Farley, James Parker retired advertising agency executive
†Finlayson, John L. commodities company executive
Forger, Robert Durkin retired professional association administrator
Freiherr von Kleydorff, Ludwig Otto Alexander political scientist, consulting company executive
Fricke, Richard John lawyer
Green, John Orne lawyer
Heymann, Stephen Timothy marketing management consultant
Hoefling, Rudolf Joachim power generating company executive
†Juran, Joseph Moses engineer
Kangas, Edward A. accounting firm executive
Kopit, Arthur playwright
Lamb, Frederic Davis lawyer
†Mc Dannald, Clyde Elliott, Jr. management consultation company executive
†Morris, Michael J. book publishing executive
Nickel, Albert George advertising agency executive
Pemberton, Jeffery Kenneth publisher
†Ritter, Bruce Commodities Company executive
Rubin, Jacob Carl mechanical research engineer
Stuart, Kenneth James illustrator, art director
Willoughby, William, II retired nuclear engineer

Windsor
Auten, Arthur Herbert history educator
Clarke, Cordelia Kay Knight Mazuy management executive
†Cowen, Bruce David environmental service company executive
Kamerschen, Robert Jerome consumer products executive
Mangold, John Frederic manufacturing company executive, former naval officer
†Rocco, Vincent Anthony consulting firm executive
†Stigler, David Mack lawyer

Windsor Locks
Mc Gill, Robert Ernest, III manufacturing company executive
†Walker, K. Grahame manufacturing company executive

Wolcott
†Gerace, Robert F. secondary school principal

Woodbridge
Alvine, Robert industrialist, entrepreneur, business leader
Bondy, Philip Kramer physician, educator
Ecklund, Constance Cryer French language educator
Womer, Charles Berry retired hospital executive, management consultant

Woodbury
Farrell, Edgar Henry lawyer, building components manufacturing executive
Marsching, Ronald Lionel lawyer, former precision instrument company executive

Woodstock
Boote, Alfred Shepard marketing researcher, educator

DELAWARE

Christiana
†Neal, James Preston state senator, project engineer

Dover
†Bair, Myrna Lynn state senator
Bookhammer, Eugene Donald state government official
†Carey, V. George farmer, state legislator
Carper, Thomas Richard governor
†Cook, Nancy W. state legislator
Delauder, William B. academic administrator
delTufo, Theresa Lallana Izon state official
†Ennis, Bruce Clifford lawyer
Forgione, Pascal D., Jr. state superintendent
†George, Orlando John, Jr. state representative, college administrator
†Hauge, Richard Andrew attorney, state senator
†Holloway, Herman M., Sr. state legislator
Lowell, Howard Parsons government records administrator
†Maroney, Jane P. state legislator
Minner, Ruth Ann state official
Moran, Joseph Milbert retired banker
Ornauer, Richard Lewis retired educational association administrator
Rich, Michael Joseph lawyer
†Sorenson, Liane Beth McDowell university administrator, state legislator
†Still, John C., III insurance agent, state senator
†Vaughn, James T. former state police officer, state senator
Vawter, William Snyder computer software consultant
Wasfi, Sadiq Hassan chemistry educator

Greenville
Schroeder, Herman Elbert scientific consultant

Hockessin
Bischoff, Joyce Arlene information systems consultant, lecturer
Bischoff, Kenneth Bruce chemical engineer, educator
Sawin, Nancy Churchman educator, artist, historian
Sproesser, William David, Sr. engineering executive

Lewes
Chapman, Janet Carter Goodrich (Mrs. John William Chapman) economist, educator
†Wilson, James L. superintendent

Middletown
Jackson, Donald Richard marketing professional

Milford
†Moses, Charles E. superintendent

Millsboro
Cordrey, Richard Stephen senator
Townsend, P(reston) Coleman agricultural business executive

New Castle
Almquist, Don illustrator, artist
†Blackshear, L. T., Sr. bishop
Cansler, Leslie Ervin retired newspaper editor
Keillor, Sharon Ann computer company executive
Mac Ewen, George Dean physician, medical institute executive
Morton, Hazel Caudle elementary education educator

Newark
Allen, Herbert Ellis environmental chemistry educator
Allen, Rocelia J. retired special education educator
Bilinsky, Yaroslav political scientist
Bohner, Charles Henry English language educator
Borgaonkar, Digamber Shankarrao cytogenetecist, educator
Brams, Marvin Robert economist, mental health counselor, interfaith minister
Burmeister, John Luther chemistry educator
Byrne, John Michael energy and environmental policy educator, researcher
Campbell, Linzy Leon microbiologist, educator
Capek, Milic retired philosophy educator
Cawley, Charles M. banker
†Cochran, John R. bank executive
Colton, David Lem mathematician, educator
Cooper, Stuart Leonard chemical engineering educator, researcher, consultant
Daniels, William Burton physicist, educator
Day, Robert Androus English language educator, former library director, editor, publisher
DiRenzo, Gordon James sociologist, psychologist, educator
Doberenz, Alexander R. nutrition educator, chemist
Dow, Lois Weyman physician
Elterich, Joachim Gustav agricultural economics educator
Evans, Dennis Hyde chemist, educator
†Evenson, Paul Arthur physics educator
Graff, Harold psychiatrist, psychoanalyst, hospital administrator
Graham, David Tredway medical educator, physician
Graham, Frances Keesler (Mrs. David Tredway Graham) psychologist, educator
Gulick, Walter Lawrence psychologist, former college president
Haenlein, George Friedrich Wilhelm dairy scientist, educator
Halio, Jay Leon language professional, educator
Harkins, Roseann Hildebrandt real estate broker
Homer, William Innes art history educator, art expert, author
Hurst, Christina Marie respiratory therapist
Hutton, David Glenn environmental consultant, chemical engineer
Jones, Russel Cameron civil engineering educator
Jordan, Robert Reed geologist, educator
Keene, William Blair state education official
Kennedy, Christopher Robin ceramist
Kirch, Max Samuel modern language educator
Klein, Michael Tully chemical engineering educator, consultant
Lemole, Gerald Michael surgeon
†Lerner, Alfred bank executive
Mangone, Gerard J. international and maritime law educator
Mather, John Russell climatologist, educator
McCullough, Roy Lynn chemical engineering educator
McLaren, James Clark French educator
Merrill, James Mercer history educator, writer
Miller, Michael Barbree investment company executive
Mills, George Alexander science administrator
Mitchell, Peter Kenneth, Jr. educational consultant, association administrator
Moss, Joe Francis sculptor, painter
Murray, Richard Bennett physics educator
Ness, Norman Frederick astrophysicist, educator, administrator
†Nye, John Calvin agricultural engineer, educator
Raffel, Jeffrey Allen urban affairs educator
Roselle, David Paul university administrator, mathematician
Rowe, Charles Alfred artist, designer, educator
†Russell, Thomas William Fraser chemical engineering educator
Sandler, Stanley Irving chemical engineering educator
Scarpitti, Frank Roland sociology educator
Schiavelli, Melvyn David university provost, chemistry educator, researcher
†Schultz, Jerold Marvin materials scientist, educator
Somers, George Fredrick biology educator
South, Frank Edwin physiologist, educator
Stakgold, Ivar mathematics educator
Stark, Robert Martin mathematician, civil engineer, educator
Sten, Johannes Walter controls system engineer, consultant
Szeri, Andras Z. engineering educator
Tannian, Francis Xavier economist, educator
Tolles, Bryant Franklin, Jr. historian
Urquhart, Andrew Willard engineering and business executive
Valbuena-Briones, Angel Julian language educator, author
Venezky, Richard Lawrence English educator
Weslager, Clinton Alfred historian, writer
Wetlaufer, Donald Burton biochemist, educator
Wolters, Raymond historian, educator
Woo, S. B. (Shien-Biau Woo) former lieutenant governor, physics educator
Wright, Vernon Hugh Carroll bank executive
Wu, Jin oceanographer, educator, engineer

Newport
Kirkland, Joseph J. research chemist

Rockland
Rubin, Alan A. pharmaceutical and biotechnology consultant

Rockland Mills
Levinson, John Milton obstetrician-gynecologist

Seaford
Kittlitz, Rudolf Gottlieb, Jr. chemical engineer

Wilmington
Adams, Wayne Verdun pediatric psychologist
Aiken, Robert McCutchen retired chemical company executive, management consultant
Alles, J. A. chemical company executive
†Amick, Steven Hammond lawyer, legislator
Andersen, Donald Edward retired chemical company executive
Arrington, Charles Hammond, Jr. retired chemical director
Bader, John Merwin lawyer
Balick, Helen Shaffer federal judge
Bell, Daniel Long, Jr. lawyer, utilities executive
Benson, Barbara Ellen state agency administrator
†Blevins, Patricia M. state legislator
Boyer, David Creighton stockbroker
Bredin, J(ohn) Bruce real estate executive
Bruni, Stephen Thomas art museum director
Carson, James Elijah psychiatrist
†Cartwright, Albert Thomas association executive
Caspersen, Finn Michael Westby diversified financial services company executive
Cecala, Ted Thomas, Jr. banker, accountant
Clark, Esther Frances legal educator
†Classon, Bruce David bank executive
Connelly, Donald Preston electric and gas utility company executive
Connolly, Arthur Guild lawyer, partner emeritus
Corkran, Donald Allen bank executive
Corn, Jack W. oil company executive
Cornelison, Floyd Shovington, Jr. retired psychiatrist, former educator
Cosgrove, Howard Edward, Jr. utility executive
Crittenden, Eugene Dwight, Jr. chemical company executive
Croom, John Henry, III utility company executive
Danzeisen, John R. chemical company executive
Dayton, Richard Lee architect
DeBlieu, Ivan Knowlton plastic pipe company executive, consultant
†Desien, Mary Donna principal
†DeVivo, Sal J. newspaper executive
Dewees, Donald Charles securities company executive
†DiLiberto, Richard Anthony, Jr. lawyer
Doughty, Robert Allen medical institute director

Du Pont, Pierre Samuel, IV *lawyer, former governor of Delaware*
Durham, Davis Godfrey *ophthalmologist*
†Edelman, David Scott *arts administrator, performer*
Eichler, Thomas P. *state agency administrator*
Elliott, Richard Gibbons, Jr. *lawyer*
Farnan, Joseph James, Jr. *federal judge*
Fenton, Wendell *lawyer*
Gadsby, Robin Edward *chemical company executive*
Gebelein, Richard Stephen *judge, former state attorney general*
Gibson, Joseph Whitton, Jr. *retired chemical company executive*
Gilliam, James H., Jr. *lawyer*
Gilman, Marvin Stanley *real estate developer, educator*
Gossage, Thomas Layton *chemical company executive*
Graves, Thomas Ashley, Jr. *educational administrator*
Green, James Samuel *lawyer*
†Grenz, Linda L. *Episcopal priest*
Gunzenhauser, Stephen Charles *conductor*
Harley, Robison Dooling *physician, educator*
Harris, Robert Laird *minister, theology educator emeritus*
Hartzell, Charles R. *research administrator, biochemist, cell biologist*
Huang, Hua-Feng *electrical engineer, researcher*
Ianni, Francis Alphonse *state official, former army officer*
Inselman, Laura Sue *pediatrician*
Jaffe, Edward E(phraim) *research and development executive*
Johnson, Allen Leroy *hospital administrator*
Kane, Edward Rynex *retired chemical company executive, corporate director*
Karrh, Bruce Wakefield *industrial company executive*
Kay, Jerome *psychiatrist, educator*
Kirkpatrick, Andrew Booth, Jr. *lawyer*
Kissa, Erik *retired chemist, consultant*
Kjellmark, Eric William, Jr. *management consultant, opera company director*
†Krosser, Howard S. *aerospace company executive*
Kusheloff, David Leon *journalist*
Lange, James Braxton *chemical company executive*
Latchum, James Levin *federal judge*
Lockman, Norman Alton *newspaper editor, columnist*
Longobardi, Joseph J. *federal judge*
Lukens, Paul Bourne *financial executive*
Mackenzie, Malcolm Lewis *advertising executive*
Malloy, John Richard *lawyer, chemical company executive*
†Marshall, Robert I. *state legislator*
Mattey, John Joseph *mortgage and investment company executive, real estate analyst, appraiser*
McKelvie, Roderick R. *federal judge*
Mekler, Arlen B. *lawyer, chemist*
†Mollica, Joseph A. *pharmaceutical executive*
Molz, Robert Joseph *manufacturing company executive*
Moore, Andrew Given Tobias, II *state supreme court justice*
Moore, Carl Gordon *chemist, educator*
†Morrione, Paolo *polypropylene company executive*
Morris, Kenneth Donald *lawyer*
Mulvee, Robert Edward *bishop*
Murphy, Arthur Thomas *systems engineer*
Nottingham, Robinson Kendall *life insurance company executive*
Oberly, Charles Monroe, III *state attorney general*
†Ockun, Robert J. *manufacturing executive*
Olson, Leroy Calvin *retired educational administration educator*
Otey, Orlando *music executive, educator, pianist, theorist*
Pan, Henry Yue-Ming *clinical pharmacologist*
Parshall, George William *research chemist*
Partnoy, Ronald Allen *lawyer*
Peterson, Russell Wilbur *former association executive, former state governor*
Pew, Robert Anderson *financial corporation officer*
Porter, Glenn *museum and library administrator*
†Porter, John Francis, III *banker*
Quillen, William Tatem *lawyer, past state supreme court justice, educator*
Reeder, Charles Benton *economic consultant*
Reilley, James Clark *artist, cartoonist, small business owner*
Renshaw, John Hubert *secondary education educator*
Robinson, Sue Lewis *federal judge*
Rogoski, Patricia Diana *financial executive*
Rollins, John William, Sr. *service and transportation company executive*
Rose, Selwyn H. *chemical company executive*
Roth, Jane Richards *federal judge*
Rothschild, Steven James *lawyer*
St. Clair, Jesse Walton, Jr. *retired savings and loan executive*
Salzstein, Richard Alan *biomedical engineer, researcher*
†Schmutz, John F. *chemical company executive, corporate lawyer*
Schwartz, Murray Merle *federal judge*
Sciance, Carroll Thomas *chemical engineer*
Seitz, Collins Jacques *federal judge*
Shapiro, Irving Saul *lawyer*
Shipley, Samuel Lynn *advertising and public relations executive*
Sidell, Robert Leonard *financial planner, management consultant*
†Simmons, Howard Ensign, Jr. *chemist, research administrator*
†Skolas, John Argyle *lawyer*
Slook, George Francis *finance company executive*
Smook, Malcolm Andrew *chemist, chemical company executive*
†Smoot, Richard L(eonard) *banker*
Stapleton, Walter King *federal judge*
Steinberg, Marshall *toxicologist*
Stone, F. L. Peter *lawyer*
Sutton, Richard Lauder *lawyer*
Taylor, Bernard J., II *banker*
†Tennis, Calvin Cabell *bishop*
Trostle, Mary Pat *lawyer*
Turk, S. Maynard *lawyer*
†Wakefield, David Dean *banker*
Walsh, Joseph Thomas *state supreme court justice*
Ward, Rodman, Jr. *lawyer*
Wasserman, Edel *former chemistry educator, scientist*
Welch, Edward P. *lawyer*
Wieland, Ferdinand *hotel executive, entrepreneur*
Wier, Richard Royal, Jr. *lawyer, inventor*
Williams, Richmond Dean *library appraiser, consultant*
Willis, Franklin Knight *lawyer, environmental services company executive*
†Wodjewodzki, Catherine *reference librarian, state legislator*
Woods, Robert A. *chemical company executive*
Woolard, Edgar S., Jr. *chemical company executive*
Wright, Caleb Merrill *federal judge*
Wyer, William Clarke *management consultant, development executive*

Winterthur
Buchter, Thomas *horticulturist, garden director*
Hummel, Charles Frederick *museum official*
Lanmon, Dwight Pierson *museum director*

DISTRICT OF COLUMBIA

Bolling AFB
Gardner, Jerry Dean *brigadier general*
Jones, William Edward *air force officer*

Washington
Aaron, Henry Jacob *economics educator*
Aaronson, David Ernest *lawyer, educator*
Abbott, Rebecca Phillips *museum director*
Abeles, Charles Calvert *lawyer*
Abelson, Philip Hauge *physicist*
Abercrombie, Neil *congressman*
Ablard, Charles David *lawyer*
Able, Edward H. *association executive*
Abler, Ronald Francis *geography educator*
Abraham, George *research physicist, engineer*
†Abramowitz, Morton I. *former ambassador*
Abrams, Elliott *writer, foreign affairs consultant and analyst*
Abshire, David Manker *diplomat, research executive*
Acheson, David Campion *lawyer, author, policy analyst*
†Achtenberg, Roberta *federal official*
Acker, Lawrence G. *lawyer*
Ackerman, Gary L. *congressman*
Ackerson, Nels J(ohn) *lawyer*
Adams, A. John Bertrand *public affairs consultant*
Adams, Andrew Joseph *army officer*
Adams, Arvil Van *economist, educator*
†Adams, Gordon Merritt *federal agency administrator*
Adams, John Jillson *lawyer*
†Adams, Linette M. *principal*
†Adams, Lorraine *reporter*
Adams, Robert Edward *journalist*
Adams, Robert McCormick *anthropologist, educator*
Adams, Thomas Lynch, Jr. *lawyer*
Adamson, Terrence Burdett *lawyer*
Adelman, Roger Mark *lawyer, educator*
Adler, Howard, Jr. *lawyer*
Adler, Howard Bruce *lawyer*
Adler, Robert Martin *lawyer*
Aein, Joseph Morris *electrical engineer*
Affronti, Lewis Francis, Sr. *microbiologist, educator*
Ahmann, Mathew Hall *social action organization administrator, consultant*
Aikens, Joan Deacon *government official*
Aisenberg, Irwin Morton *lawyer*
Aiuto, Russell *science educators association executive*
Akaka, Daniel Kahikina *senator*
Akhter, Mohammad Nasir *physician, government public health administrator*
Akridge, John Edward, III *real estate management and development company executive*
Alatis, James Efstathios *university dean*
Alberger, William Relph *lawyer, government official*
†Alberts, Bruce Michael *foundation administrator, biochemist*
Albertson, Fred W(oodward) *retired lawyer, radio engineer*
Albertson, Terry L. *lawyer*
Albright, Raymond Jacob *government official*
Alexander, Benjamin Harold *professional services firm executive, past government official*
Alexander, Bettina Lawton *lawyer*
Alexander, Charles Thomas *journalism educator*
Alexander, Clifford L., Jr. *management consultant, lawyer, former secretary of army*
Alexander, Donald Crichton *lawyer*
Alexander, Jane *actress*
Allard, Dean Conrad *historian, naval history center director*
Allard, Wayne A. *congressman, veterinarian*
Allbritton, Joe Lewis *diversified holding company executive*
Allen, Frederick Warner *federal agency executive*
Allen, George Venable, Jr. *lawyer*
Allen, Richard Vincent *international business consultant, bank executive*
Allen, Toni K. *lawyer*
Allen, William Hayes *lawyer*
†Allen, William Jere *minister*
Allera, Edward John *lawyer*
Allison, Graham Tillett, Jr. *federal government official*
Allnutt, Robert Frederick *organization executive, lawyer*
†Alper, Joel Richard *satellite communications company executive*
Alpern, Robert Zellman *religious organization lobbyist/administrator*
Alperovitz, Gar *author*
Alter, Harvey *chemist, association executive*
Altman, Jeffrey Paul *lawyer*
Altman, Roger C. *U.S. Treasury deputy secretary*
Alton, Bruce Taylor *educational consultant*
Aluise, Timothy John *lawyer*
Ambach, Gordon Mac Kay *education association official*
Ambrose, Myles Joseph *lawyer*
Ames, Frank Anthony *percussionist, film producer*
Amling, Frederick *economist, educator, investment manager*
Andersen, Daniel Johannes *lawyer*
†Andersen, Per Pinstrup *think-tank executive, agricultural research administrator*
Andersen, Robert Allen *government official*
†Anderson, Bernard E. *economist*
Anderson, David Lawrence *lawyer*
Anderson, David Turpeau *government official, judge*
Anderson, Dean William *educational administrator*
Anderson, Donald Morgan *entomologist*
Anderson, Frederick Randolph, Jr. *lawyer, law educator*
Anderson, John Bayard *lawyer, educator, former congressman*
Anderson, John Weir *editor*
†Anderson, Marcus A. *career officer*
Anderson, Owen Raymond *scientific and educational organization executive*
Andewelt, Roger B. *federal judge*
†Andrews, Jessica L. *performing arts company executive*
Andrews, John Frank *editor, author, educator*
†Andrews, Laureen E. *foundation administrator*
Andrews, Mark Joseph *lawyer*
Andrews, Robert E. *congressman*
Andrews, William S. *lawyer*
†Andrews, Wyatt *news correspondent*
Andringa, Calvin Bruce *investment banker*
Angarola, Robert Thomas *lawyer*
Ansary, Cyrus A. *lawyer, investor*
Anschuetz, Norbert Lee *retired diplomat, banker*
†Anselmo, Philip Shepard *naval officer*
†Anthan, George Peter *news reporter and correspondent*
Anthony, Beryl Franklin, Jr. *congressman*
Anthony, David Vincent *lawyer*
†Anthony, Sheila F. *federal official*
Anthony, Virginia Quinn Bausch *medical association executive*
Anton, Frank A. *publishing executive*
Apfel, Kenneth S. *federal government official*
Apple, Martin Allen *high technology manufacturing executive*
Apple, Raymond Walter, Jr. *journalist*
Applebaum, Harvey Milton *lawyer*
Appleberry, James Bruce *higher education association president*
Applegarth, Paul Vollmer *investment banking and finance executive*
Applegate, Douglas *congressman*
Arcadipane, Angelo Vincent *lawyer*
Archard, Douglas Bruce *foreign service officer*
Archer, Glenn LeRoy, Jr. *federal judge*
Archer, William Reynolds, Jr. (Bill Reynolds) *congressman*
†Areen, Judith Carol *law educator*
Arent, Albert Ezra *lawyer*
Arkilic, Galip Mehmet *mechanical engineer, educator*
†Arkin, William Morris *military and political analyst*
Arlook, Ira Arthur *public interest association executive*
Armaly, Mansour F(arid) *ophthalmologist, educator*
Armstrong, Alexandra *financial advisor*
Armstrong, David Andrew *federal agency official, retired army officer*
Armstrong, Richard Burke *retired television director*
Arndt, Richard T. *writer, consultant*
Arnett, Peter *journalist*
Arnez, Nancy Levi *educational leadership educator*
Arnold, G. Dewey, Jr. *accountant*
Arnold, Gary Howard *film critic*
Arnovitz, Benton Mayer *editor*
Aronson, Arnold H. *retail company executive*
Aschheim, Joseph *economist, educator*
Aspin, Les *former U.S. secretary of defense, former congressman*
Atherton, Alfred Leroy, Jr. *foundation executive, former foreign service officer*
Atherton, Charles Henry *federal commission administrator*
Atil, Esin *Islamic art historian, researcher*
Atiyeh, George Nicholas *library administrator, educator*
Atiyeh, Naim Nicholas *psychologist, educator*
Atkeson, Timothy Breed *lawyer, former federal agency administrator*
Atkin, James Blakesley *lawyer*
Atwell, Robert Herron *association executive*
Atwood, James R. *lawyer*
Atwood, John Brian *federal official, foundation administrator*
AuCoin, Les *lobbyist, former congressman*
Aucutt, Ronald David *lawyer*
Auerbach, Stuart Charles *journalist*
Aug, Stephen M. *business journalist*
Auten, John Harold *government official*
Avery, George Allen *lawyer*
Avery, Gordon Bennett *medical educator, neonatologist*
Avil, Richard D., Jr. *lawyer*
Avram, Henriette Davidson *librarian, government official*
Axelrod, Jonathan Gans *lawyer*
Ayer, Donald Belton *lawyer*
Ayres, Mary Ellen *government official*
Ayres, Richard Edward *lawyer*
Azcuenaga, Mary Laurie *government official*
Babbin, Jed Lloyd *lawyer*
Babbitt, Bruce Edward *U.S. secretary of the interior*
Babby, Ellen Reisman *education administrator*
Bachman, Leonard *physician, retired federal official*
†Bachula, Gary R. *federal official*
Bachus, Spencer *congressman, lawyer*
Bacon, Donald Conrad *author, editor*
Bacon, Sylvia *retired judge*
Bader, Franz *retired gallery administrator*
Bader, William Banks *foundation executive, former corporate executive*
Baena Soares, João Clemente *ambassador*
Baesler, Scotty *congressman*
Bagge, Carl Elmer *association executive, lawyer, consultant*
Bahr, Morton *trade union executive*
Bailey, Charles Waldo, II *journalist, author*
†Bailey, John E. *federal agency administrator*
Bailey, Patricia Price *lawyer, government official*
Bainum, Peter Montgomery *aerospace engineer, consultant*
Bair, Sheila Colleen *commissioner*
Baird, Bruce Allen *lawyer*
†Baker, D. James *federal agency administrator*
Baker, David Harris *lawyer*
Baker, D(onald) James *federal official, oceanographer, administrator*
Baker, James Addison, III *lawyer, former government official*
Baker, John Alexander *retired foreign service officer, federal official*
Baker, Melvin C. *advertising executive*
Baker, William P. (Bill Baker) *congressman*
†Baldi, Patricia Ann *association executive*
Baldrige, Letitia *writer, management training consultant*
Baldyga, Leonard J. *diplomat, foreign service officer*
Ball, James William *army officer*
†Ball, John Wesley, III *lawyer*
Ball, (Robert) Markham *lawyer*
Ball, Robert M. *social security, welfare and health policy specialist, writer, lecturer*
Ballantyne, Robert Jadwin *former foreign service officer, consultant*
Ballenger, Thomas Cass *congressman*
Ballentine, J. Gregory *economist*
Bancroft, Elizabeth Abercrombie *publisher, analytic chemist*
†Bandow, Douglas Leighton *editor, columnist, policy consultant*
†Bane, Mary Jo *federal agency administrator*
†Banister, Judith *demographer, educator*
Banzhaf, John F., III *organization executive,lawyer*
†Baquet, Charles R., III *federal agency administrator*
Baran, Jan Witold *lawyer*
†Baranes, Shalom *architectural firm executive*
Barbash, Fred *journalist, author*
†Barbour, Haley *political organization administrator, law partner, former federal official*
Barcia, James A. *congressman*
Bardin, David J. *lawyer*
Barlow, Tom *congressman, sales executive*
Barnes, Dennis Norman *lawyer*
Barnes, Donald Michael *lawyer*
†Barnes, Frederic Wood, Jr. *journalist*
Barnes, Mark James *lawyer*
Barnes, Michael Darr *lawyer*
Barnes, Peter *laywer*
Barnes, Samuel Henry *political scientist, educator*
Barnet, Richard Jackson *author, educator*
Barnett, Arthur Doak *political scientist, educator*
Barnett, John H. *judge*
†Barnett, Robert Bruce *lawyer*
Barnett, Robert Warren *diplomat, author*
Barnum, John Wallace *lawyer*
Barone, Michael D. *journalist*
†Baroody, William Joseph, Jr. *research institute executive*
Barquin, Ramón Carlos *consulting company executive*
Barr, Michael Blanton *lawyer*
Barr, William Pelham *lawyer, former attorney general of United States*
†Barram, David J. *federal official*
Barrett, Andrew *federal agency administrator*
†Barrett, Dennis P. *ambassador to Madagascar*
†Barrett, Lake H. *energy industry executive*
Barrett, Laurence Irwin *journalist*
Barrett, Richard David *fundraising consultant*
Barrett, Thomas M. *congressman*
Barrett, William E. *congressman*
Barrett, William H. *lawyer*
Barringer, Philip E. *government official*
†Barr-Kumar, Raj *architect*
Barron, Jerome Aure *law educator*
Barrow, Robert Earl *agricultural organization administrator*
†Barshefsky, Charlene *diplomat*
Bartholomew, Reginald *diplomat*
†Bartlett, Charles J. *think-tank executive*
Bartlett, Charles Leffingwell *foundation executive, former newspaperman*
Bartlett, John Laurence *lawyer*
Bartlett, Michael John *lawyer*
Bartlett, Roscoe *congressman*
Bartnoff, Judith *lawyer*
Barton, Jean Marie *psychologist, educator*
Barton, William Blackburn *lawyer*
Barton, William Russell *government official*
Baruch, Jordan Jay *management consultant*
Barusch, Ronald Charles *lawyer*
†Baskir, Lawrence M. *lawyer*
Bass, Kenneth Carrington, III *lawyer*
Basseches, Robert Treinis *lawyer*
Bassin, Jules *foreign service officer*
Bassman, Robert Stuart *lawyer*
Bateman, Herbert Harvell *congressman*
Bateman, Paul William *government official, business executive*
Bates, John Cecil, Jr. *lawyer*
†Battin, Patricia Meyer *librarian*
Battle, Lucius Durham *former educational institution administrator, former diplomat*
Baucus, Max S. *senator*
Bauer, Gary Lee *government official*
Bauer, Robert Albert *public policy consultant*
†Baum, Ingeborg Ruth *librarian*
Baumgarten, Jon A. *lawyer*
†Baumgartner, Eileen Mary *government official*
Bayh, Birch Evans, Jr. *lawyer, former senator*
Bayly, John Henry, Jr. *judge*
Baynard, Ernest Cornish, III *lawyer*
Bayne, J. Phillip *educational association administrator*
Beach, Milo C. *art museum director*
Beach, Walter Eggert *publishing organization executive*
Beale, Betty (Mrs. George K. Graeber) *columnist, writer*
Bear, Dinah *lawyer*
Bearss, Edwin C(ole) *historian*
Beary, John Francis, III *physician, pharmaceutical executive*
Beatty, Richard Scrivener *lawyer*
Beaumont, Enid Franklin *public administration executive*
Beazley, Hamilton Scott *volunteer health organization executive*
Becerra, Xavier *congressman, lawyer*
†Becker, Brandon *lawyer*
†Becker, Daniel Frome *lawyer*
Becker, Mary Louise *political scientist*
Becker, Ralph Elihu *lawyer, diplomat*
Becker, William Watters *lawyer*
Beckett, William Wade *lawyer*
Beckler, David Zander *government official, science administrator*
Beckler, Richard William *lawyer*
Beckwith, Edward Jay *lawyer*
Bedini, Silvio A. *historian, author*
Bednarek, Jana Maria *biochemist*
Beebe, Cora Prifold *government official*
Beecher, William Manuel *government official*
Beerbower, Cynthia Gibson *lawyer*
Beghe, Renato *federal judge*
†Begleiter, Ralph J. *correspondent*
Beilenson, Anthony Charles *congressman*
Beisner, John Herbert *lawyer*
Beizer, Robert A. *lawyer*
Bell, James Frederick *lawyer*
Bell, Olin Nile *lawyer*
Bell, Robert G. *federal agency official*
Bell, Stephen Robert *lawyer*
Bell, Thomas Devereaux, Jr. *public affairs company executive*
†Bellamy, Carol *federal agency administrator*
†Bellanti, Joseph A. *microbiologist, educator*
Beller, Herbert N. *lawyer*
Bellinger, John B., Jr. *federal official*
Bello, Judith Hippler *lawyer*
Bellows, Michael Donald *foreign service officer*
Belman, A. Barry *pediatric urologist*

Belman, Murray Joel *lawyer*
Belmar, Warren *lawyer*
Belter, Leonard W. *lawyer*
Beltz, William Albert *publisher*
Bender, David Ray *library association executive*
Bendernagel, James F., Jr. *lawyer*
Benedick, Richard Elliot *diplomat*
Benjamin, Ben E. *lawyer*
Benjamin, Ernst *professional association executive*
Bennet, Douglas Joseph, Jr. *federal agency administrator*
Bennett, Alexander Elliot *lawyer*
Bennett, Betty T. *English educator, university dean, writer*
†Bennett, David Michael *naval officer*
Bennett, Gary Lee *physicist, federal agency administrator*
Bennett, John E. *diplomat*
Bennett, Marion Tinsley *federal judge*
Bennett, Robert F. *senator*
Bennett, Robert Stephen *lawyer*
†Bennitt, Brent Martin *naval officer*
Bentley, James Daniel *association executive*
Bentley, James Luther *journalist*
Ben-Veniste, Richard *lawyer*
Bercovici, Martin William *lawyer*
Berendzen, Richard *astronomer, educator, author*
Bereuter, Douglas Kent *congressman*
Berg, Norman Alf *conservation consultant*
†Berg, Olena *federal official*
†Berger, Samuel R. *federal official*
Bergmann, Barbara Rose *economics educator*
Bergmann, Fred Heinz *genetic scientist, government official*
Bergsten, C. Fred *economist*
Berkman, William Roger *lawyer, army reserve officer*
Berl, Joseph M. *lawyer*
Berlack, Evan Raden *lawyer*
Berlin, Kenneth *lawyer*
†Berlincourt, Marjorie Alkins *government official*
Berman, Howard Lawrence *congressman*
Berman, Marshall Fox *lawyer*
Berman, Paul J. *lawyer*
Berman, Sidney *psychiatrist*
Berner, Frederic George, Jr. *lawyer*
Bernhard, Berl *lawyer*
Bernius, Robert Charles *lawyer*
†Bernstein, Caryl Salomon *lawyer*
Bernstein, Edwin S. *federal judge*
Bernstein, Mitchell Harris *lawyer*
Bernthal, Frederick Michael *association executive*
†Berry, Mary Frances *history and law educator*
Berry, Max Nathan *lawyer*
Berryman, Richard Byron *lawyer*
Berube, Raymond P. *federal agency administrator*
Berz, David R. *lawyer*
Besen, Stanley Martin *economist*
Best, Judah *lawyer*
Bevan, Robert Lewis *lawyer*
Beveridge, Albert Jeremiah, III *lawyer*
Bevill, Tom *congressman, lawyer*
Bibby, Douglas Martin *mortgage association executive*
Bickart, David O. *lawyer*
Biddle, Livingston Ludlow, Jr. *former government official, author*
Biddle, Timothy Maurice *lawyer*
Biden, Joseph Robinette, Jr. *senator*
Bieber, Sander M. *lawyer*
Bierbauer, Charles *broadcast executive, cable*
Bierly, Eugene Wendell *meteorologist, science administrator*
Bierman, James Norman *lawyer*
Bigelow, Donald Nevius *educational administrator, historian, consultant*
Bilbray, James Hubert *congressman, lawyer*
Bilirakis, Michael *congressman, lawyer, business executive*
Biller, Morris (Moe Biller) *union executive*
Billings, Donald Franklin *international banking consultant*
Billington, James Hadley *historian, librarian*
†Bingaman, Anne Kovacovich *lawyer*
Bingaman, Jeff *senator*
Bishop, Barry Chapman *professional society executive, scientist*
Bishop, Sanford, Jr. *congressman*
Bishop, Wayne Staton *lawyer*
Bissell, Richard Etter *association administrator*
Bittker, David *religious organization administrator*
Bittman, William Omar *lawyer*
Black, Stephen F. *lawyer*
Blackmun, Harry Andrew *U.S. supreme court justice*
Blackwelder, Brent Francis *environmentalist*
Blackwell, Lucien E. *congressman*
Blaine, Barbara S. *lawyer*
Blair, Bonnie *professional speedskater, former Olympic athlete*
Blair, James Pease *photographer, retired*
Blair, William McCormick, Jr. *lawyer*
Blake, Jonathan Dewey *lawyer*
†Blanck, Ronald Ray *hospital administrator, internist, career officer*
Blaxall, Martha Ossoff *economist*
Blazek-White, Doris *lawyer*
Bleakley, Peter Kimberley *lawyer*
Blecher, Melvin *biochemist, educator emeritus, lawyer*
Bledsoe, Ralph Champion *archivist*
Bleicher, Samuel Abram *lawyer*
†Bleviss, Deborah Lynn *association executive*
Blinder, Alan Stuart *economist*
Bliss, Donald Tiffany, Jr. *lawyer*
Blitzer, Charles *educational administrator*
Bloch, Richard Isaac *labor arbitrator*
Block, Herbert Lawrence (Herblock) *editorial cartoonist*
Bloom, David I. *lawyer*
Bloomfield, Arthur Irving *economics educator*
Bloomfield, Maxwell Herron, III *historian, educator*
†Bloomfield, Sara *museum director*
Blum, Robert Allan *psychiatrist*
Blume, Jack Paul *retired lawyer*
Blume, Lawrence Dayton *lawyer*
Blumenfeld, Sue Deborah *lawyer*
†Blumenthal, Ronnie *lawyer*
Blute, Peter I. *congressman*
Bluth, B. J. (Elizabeth Jean Catherine Bluth) *sociologist, educator*
Boaz, David Douglas *foundation executive*
Bodde, William, Jr. *foreign service officer*
Bodner, John, Jr. *lawyer*
Boehlert, Sherwood Louis *congressman*
Boehm, Steven Bruce *lawyer*
Boehner, John A. *congressman*
Boerrigter, Glenn Charles *educational administrator*
Boese, John T. *lawyer*
Bogard, Lawrence Joseph *lawyer*
Bogdan, Victor Michael *mathematics educator, scientist*
Boggs, George Trenholm *lawyer*
Bogle, Robert W. *publishing executive, trade association administrator*
†Bohi, Douglas Ray *economist*
Boland, Christopher Thomas, II *lawyer*
Bold, Frances Ann *librarian*
Bolino, John Vincent *federal agency administrator*
Bollenbach, Stephen Frasier *hotel executive*
Bolling, Landrum Rymer *former academic administrator, writer, consultant*
Bond, Christopher Samuel (Kit Bond) *senator, lawyer*
Bond, Julian *civil rights leader*
Bond, Richard Norman *political activist*
Bonilla, Henry *congressman, broadcast executive*
Bonior, David Edward *congressman*
Bonner, Walter Joseph *lawyer*
Bono, Gaspare Joseph *lawyer*
Bonosaro, Carol Alessandra *professional association executive,former government official*
Bonvillian, William Boone *lawyer*
Book, Edward R. *association executive*
Bookbinder, Hyman H(arry) *public affairs counselor*
†Boorda, Jeremy Michael (Mike Boorda) *naval officer*
Boorstin, Daniel J. *librarian emeritus, history educator, author, editor*
Boren, David Lyle *senator*
Borg, Parker Webb *ambassador*
Borgiotti, Giorgio Vittorio *research scientist, engineering consultant*
Born, Brooksley Elizabeth *lawyer*
Borsari, George Robert, Jr. *lawyer, broadcaster*
Borski, Robert Anthony *congressman*
Borut, Donald J. *association executive*
Boskey, Bennett *lawyer*
Bostick, George Hale *lawyer*
Boucher, Frederick C. *congressman, lawyer*
Bourne, Francis Stanley *foundation administrator*
Bourne, Peter Geoffrey *physician, educator, author*
†Bowden, William P., Jr. *lawyer, banker*
†Bowie, Calvert S. *architect*
Bowker, Albert Hosmer *university dean*
Bowles, Erskine *federal agency administrator*
Bowles, Lawrence Thompson *surgeon, university dean, educator*
Bowman, Peyton Graham, III *lawyer*
Bowron, Edgar Peters *art museum curator, administrator*
Bowsher, Charles Arthur *government official*
Boxer, Barbara *senator*
Boyce, Peter Bradford *astronomer, professional association executive*
Boyd, Stephen Mather *arbitrator, mediator, lawyer*
Boyd, Thomas Marshall *federal official, lawyer*
Boyle, John Edward Whiteford *cultural organization administrator*
Boyle, Renée Kent *cultural organization executive, translator, editor*
Braden, Efrem Mark *lawyer*
Bradford, William Allen, Jr. *lawyer*
Bradford, William Hollis, Jr. *lawyer*
Bradlee, Benjamin Crowninshield *executive editor*
Bradley, Bill *senator*
Bradley, Melvin LeRoy *communications company executive*
Bradley, Mitchell Hugh *professional society administrator, retired career officer*
Brady, Nyle C. *international consultant, science educator*
Brady, Phillip Donley *lawyer*
Brady, Richard Alan *lawyer*
Braestrup, Peter *editor*
Brahms, Thomas Walter *engineering institute executive*
Bramson, Leon *social scientist, educator*
Brand, Joseph Lyon *lawyer*
†Brandt, Werner William *federal agency official*
Branigin, William Joseph *journalist*
Branson, David John *lawyer*
Branstool, Charles Eugene *farmer, federal agency administrator*
Brazaitis, Thomas Joseph *journalist*
Brazeal, Aurelia E. *ambassador*
Breathed, Berkeley *cartoonist*
Breaux, John B. *senator, former congressman*
Bredemeier, Kenneth Herbert *journalist*
Breger, Marshall J. *government official, legal educator*
Brennan, William Joseph, Jr. *former U.S. Supreme Court justice*
Bresee, James Collins *federal agency administrator*
Bretzfelder, Deborah May *museum exhibit designer, photographer*
Brewster, Bill K. *congressman*
Brewster, Robert Charles *diplomat, consultant*
†Brewster-Walker, Sandra JoAnn *public relations executive, publishing executive, genealogist, historian, consultant*
Breyer, Stephen Gerald *U.S. supreme court justice*
Briggerman, Steven Leslie *lawyer*
Briggs, Alan Leonard *lawyer*
Briggs, Harold Melvin *corporate executive*
Brinckman, Frederick Edward, Jr. *retired research chemist, consultant*
Brinkley, David *news commentator*
Briskman, Robert David *engineering executive*
†Britt, Stanford R. *architect*
Britten, Gerald Hallbeck *government official*
†Broadnax, Walter D. *federal official*
Brobeck, Stephen James *consumer advocate*
Broches, Aron *international lawyer, arbitrator*
Brockway, David Hunt *lawyer*
Broder, David Salzer *reporter*
Broderick, Anthony James *federal government administrator*
Brodie, M. J. (Jay Brodie) *architect, city planner*
Broedling, Laurie Adele *federal official, psychologist, educator*
Broering, Naomi Cordero *librarian*
†Bromwich, Michael Ray *federal official*
Bronstein, Alvin J. *lawyer*
Brooke, Edward William *lawyer, former senator*
Brooks, Daniel Townley *lawyer*
Brooks, Jack Bascom *congressman*
Broom, Richard Stuart *lawyer*
Brotzman, Donald Glenn *government official, lawyer*
Broun, Elizabeth *art historian, museum administrator*
Browder, John Glen *congressman, educator*
Brown, Barbara Berish *lawyer*
Brown, Charles Freeman *lawyer*
Brown, Corrine *congresswoman*
Brown, David Nelson *lawyer*
†Brown, David R. *think-tank executive*
Brown, David Springer *retired public administration educator*
Brown, Donald Arthur *lawyer*
Brown, Elizabeth Ann *foreign service officer*
Brown, George Edward, Jr. *congressman*
Brown, George Leslie *legislative affairs and business development consultant, former manufacturing company executive, former lieutenant governor*
Brown, Gerald Curtis *army officer, civil engineer*
Brown, Hank *senator*
Brown, Harold *corporate director, former secretary of defense*
Brown, Jeanne Pinkett *physical education educator*
†Brown, Jesse *federal official*
Brown, John Carter *art museum director emeritus*
Brown, John Patrick *newspaper executive, financial consultant*
Brown, June Gibbs *government agency official*
Brown, Kent Newville *ambassador*
†Brown, Lawrence Clifton, Jr. *foundation administrator*
Brown, Lee Patrick *federal official, law enforcement educator*
Brown, Lester Russell *research institute executive*
Brown, Michael Arthur *lawyer*
Brown, Omer Forrest, II *lawyer*
Brown, Oscar, Jr. *writer, entertainer*
Brown, Preston *lawyer*
Brown, Richard Laurence *broadcast executive*
Brown, Ronald Harmon *U.S. secretary of commerce, political organization administrator, lawyer*
Brown, Sherrod *congressman, former state official*
Brown, Thomas Philip, III *lawyer*
Brown, William Holmes *government official*
Brown, William Robert *association executive, consultant*
Browne, Ray *insurance broker*
Browne, Richard Cullen *lawyer*
Browner, Carol *federal official*
Brownlee, Paula Pimlott *association executive*
Brownstein, Philip Nathan *lawyer*
Bruce, E(stel) Edward *lawyer*
Bruce, John Foster *lawyer*
Bruce, Robert Rockwell *lawyer*
Bruder, George Frederick *lawyer*
Bruggink, Eric G. *federal judge*
Brunner, Thomas William *lawyer*
Bruno, Harold Robinson, Jr. *journalist*
Brunsvold, Brian Garrett *lawyer, educator*
Bryan, Richard H. *senator*
Bryant, Anne Lincoln *association executive*
Bryant, Arthur H. *lawyer*
Bryant, John Wiley *congressman*
†Bryant, Robert Edward *architect*
Brynn, Edward Paul *ambassador*
Brzezinski, Zbigniew *political science educator, author*
Buc, Nancy Lillian *lawyer*
Buchanan, John Donald *health physicist, radiochemist*
Buchanan, Peter McEachin *educational association executive*
Bucher, Jeffrey Martin *lawyer, banker*
Bucholtz, Harold Ronald *lawyer*
Buchwald, Art *columnist, writer*
Buckalew, Judith Adele *nurse, pharmaceutical industry executive*
Buckley, Christopher Henry, Jr. *lawyer*
Buckley, James Lane *federal judge*
Buckley, Jeremiah Stephen *lawyer*
Bucklin, Donald Thomas *lawyer*
Buente, David T. *lawyer*
Buergenthal, Thomas *lawyer, educator, international judge*
†Buffington, John Douglas *ecologist, researcher*
Buffon, Charles Edward *lawyer*
†Bulger, Roger James *academic health center executive*
Bullard, John Kilburn *federal agency administrator*
Bumpers, Dale L. *senator, former governor*
Burack, Michael Leonard *lawyer*
Burch, John Thomas, Jr. *lawyer*
Burch, Michael Ira *public relations executive, former government official*
Burcroff, Richard Tomkinson, II *economist*
Buresh, C. John *lawyer*
Burk, Francis Lewis, Jr. *lawyer, federal*
Burka, Robert Alan *lawyer*
†Burke, John *priest*
Burke, Mary *art gallery administrator*
Burnett, Arthur Louis, Sr. *judge*
Burnham, David Bright *writer*
Burnham, Sophy *writer*
Burns, Conrad Ray *senator*
Burns, David Mitchell *writer, musician, former diplomat*
Burns, Joseph M. *economist*
Burns, Stephen Gilbert *lawyer*
Burris, James Frederick *academic dean, educator*
Burt, Jeffrey Amsterdam *lawyer*
Burt, John Alan *federal agency administrator*
Burton, Danny Lee *congressman*
†Bury, Christopher Robert *journalist*
Burzynski, Norman Stephen *editor*
Busby, David *lawyer*
Buscemi, Peter *lawyer*
Busch, Richard *magazine editor*
Bush, Robert Donald *historical preservation director*
Bussard, David Andrew *federal agency administrator*
Butler, Michael Francis *lawyer*
Butterworth, Charles E. *political science educator*
Button, Kenneth Rodman *international economist, consultant*
Butynski, William *national association administrator*
Buyer, Steve E. *congressman, lawyer*
Byrd, Joann Kathleen *newswriter*
Byrd, Robert Carlyle *senator*
Byrne, Carol Susan *newspaper reporter*
Byrne, Leslie Larkin *congresswoman*
Byron, William James *management educator, former university president*
Cacciavillan, Agostino *archbishop*
Cain, Becky C. *association executive*
Calamaro, Raymond Stuart *lawyer*
Calderhead, William Dickson *former foreign service officer*
Caldwell, John L. *corporate executive*
Calhoun, John Alfred *social services administrator*
Calhoun, John Cozart *financial services marketing executive*
Calhoun, Noah Robert *oral maxillofacial surgeon, educator*
Calhoun, Robert Lathan *lawyer, state senator*
Callaway, Clifford Wayne *physician*
Callender, Clive Orville *surgeon*
Calvani, Terry *lawyer, former government official*
Calvert, Ken *congressman*
Cambel, Ali Bulent *engineering educator*
Cameron, Don R. *association director*
Cameron, Duncan Hume *lawyer*
Camp, Dave *congressman*
Camp, Donald A. *diplomat*
Campbell, Ben Nighthorse *senator*
†Campbell, Donald Alfred *government official*
Campbell, Edmund Douglas *lawyer*
Campbell, James Sargent *lawyer*
Campbell, Wallace Justin *social welfare administrator, economist*
Canady, Charles T. *congressman, lawyer*
Canapary, Herbert Carton *insurance company executive*
Canary, John Joseph *physician, educator*
Canes, Michael Edwin *trade association administrator, economist*
Canfield, Edward Francis *lawyer, business executive*
Cannon, Howard Walter *former senator*
Canter, Jerome Wolf *surgeon, educator*
Cantor, Muriel Goldsman *sociologist, educator*
†Cantu, Norma V. *federal official*
Cantwell, Maria E. *congresswoman*
Caplin, Mortimer Maxwell *lawyer, educator*
Carberry, Michael Glen *public relations executive*
Cardin, Benjamin Louis *congressman*
Cardozo, Michael Hart *lawyer*
Carey, Hugh L. *lawyer, former governor*
Carey, Ronald *labor union leader*
Carey, Sarah Collins *lawyer*
Carley, L. David *investment consultant, former college administrator*
Carliner, Michael Simon *economist, association executive*
Carlisle, Margo Duer Black *chief senatorial staff*
Carlson, Richard Warner *diplomat, journalist, federal agency administrator, broadcast executive*
Carlson, William Dwight *government agency administrator*
†Carlstrom, Robert E., Jr. *public relations executive*
Carlucci, Frank Charles, III *former secretary of defense*
†Carmody, John *newspaper columnist*
Carneal, George Upshur *lawyer*
†Carnes, Bruce M. *federal official*
Carney, David Mitchel *political party official*
Carney, Robert Thomas *lawyer*
Carns, Michael Patrick Chamberlain *air force officer*
Carpenter, Sheila Jane *lawyer*
Carpenter, Ted Galen *political scientist*
Carr, Lawrence Edward, Jr. *lawyer*
Carr, Ronald Gene *lawyer*
Carrow, Milton Michael *lawyer, educator*
Carson, Johnnie *ambassador*
†Carter, Ashton Baldwin *physicist, government agency executive*
Carter, Barry Edward *lawyer, educator, administrator*
Carto, Willis Allison *publishing executive*
Caruana, Patrick Peter *career officer*
Carwile, Stuart Frederick *lawyer*
Case, Larry D. *agricultural education specialist*
Case, Stephen H. *lawyer*
Casellas, Gilbert F. *lawyer*
Casey, Bernard J. *lawyer*
Casey, Mary Ann *diplomat*
†Cashell, Lois D. *federal agency administrator*
Cashen, Henry Christopher, II *lawyer, former government official*
Cashmore, Patsy Joy *speechwriter, editor, author, consultant, educator*
Casserly, Charley *professional football team executive*
Casserly, James Lund *lawyer*
Cassidy, Robert Charles, Jr. *lawyer*
Casson, Joseph Edward *lawyer*
†Casstevens, Kay L. *federal official*
Castle, Michael N. *congressman, former governor of Delaware, lawyer*
†Catlett, D. Mark *federal official*
Catoe, Bette Lorrina *physician, health educator*
Cavanagh, John Henry *political economist*
Cavanaugh, Gordon *lawyer*
Cavanaugh, James Michael *lawyer*
†Cavanaugh, John *think-tank executive*
Cavaney, Red *trade association administrator*
Cavnar, Samuel Melmon *author, publisher, activist*
Caws, Peter James *philosopher, educator*
†Caywood, James Alexander, III *transportation engineering company executive, civil engineer*
Cenkner, William *religion educator, academic administrator*
Cerny, Louis Thomas *civil engineer, association executive*
Chabot, Herbert L. *federal judge*
Chabot, Philip Louis, Jr. *lawyer*
Chafee, John Hubbard *senator*
Challinor, David *scientific institute administrator*
Chalmers, Franklin Stevens, Jr. *engineering consultant*
Chamberlain, Charles Ernest *lawyer, former congressman*
Chambliss, William Joseph *sociologist*
Chameides, Steven B. *lawyer*
Chandler, John Wesley *educational consultant*
†Chanin, Leah Farb *law library administrator, lawyer, consultant, law educator*
Chanin, Michael Henry *lawyer*
†Chanin, Robert Howard *lawyer*
Chapman, James L. (Jim Chapman) *congressman*
Charles, Kathleen J. *federal agency official*
Chater, Shirley Sears *university administrator*
†Chavous, Kevin Pernell *lawyer, municipal official*
Checchi, Vincent Victor *economist*
Cheek, James Edward *university president*
Chen, Ho-Hong H. H. *industrial engineering executive, educator*
Chen, Yuki Y. Kuo *industrial supplies company executive*
Cheney, Darwin Leroy *research foundation executive, medical educator*
Cheney, Dick (Richard Bruce Cheney) *former secretary of defense, former congressman*
Cheney, Lynne V. *humanities educator, writer*
Cheng, Tsung O. *cardiologist, educator*
Cherian, Joy *consulting company executive*
†Cheshes, Martin L. *ambassador*
Chester, Alexander Campbell, III *physician*
Chiazze, Leonard, Jr. *biostatistician, epidemiologist, educator*
Chierichella, John W. *lawyer*
Chilcote, Samuel Day, Jr. *association executive*
Childress, Fay Alice *university administrator*
Chilman, Catherine Earles Street *social welfare educator, author*
Chin, Cecilia Hui-Hsin *librarian*
†Chopko, Mark E. *lawyer*
Choquette, William H. *construction company executive*

Chou, Wushow information scientist, federal agency official
†Chrétien, Raymond A.J. ambassador
†Christensen, Sally Hayden government executive
Christian, Betty Jo lawyer
Christian, Ernest Silsbee, Jr. lawyer
Christopher, Warren U.S. secretary of state
Chronister, Gregory Michael newspaper editor
Chu, David S. C. economist
Chubb, Talbot Albert physicist
Church, Dale Walker lawyer
Cicconi, James William lawyer
Cikovsky, Nicolai, Jr. curator, art history educator
†Ciment, Melvyn mathematician
Cisneros, Henry G. U.S. secretary of housing and urban development
Clagett, Brice McAdoo lawyer, writer
Clapp, Charles E., II federal judge
Clark, Dick former senator, ambassador, foreign affairs specialist
Clark, Robert William, III lawyer
Clark, Roger Arthur lawyer
Clark, Wendell Mark travelers organization executive
Clarke, Richard A. federal agency administrator
Clay, Don Richard environmental consulting firm executive
Clay, William Lacy congressman
Clayton, Eva congresswoman
Clegg, Roger Burton lawyer
Clement, Bob congressman
Clemmer, Dan Orr librarian
Clevenger, Raymond C., III federal judge
Clifford, Clark McAdams lawyer
†Clift, Eleanor newspaper correspondent
Cline, Ray Steiner political scientist, historian
Cline, William Richard economist, educator
Clinger, William Floyd, Jr. congressman
Clinkscales, William Abner, Jr. government administrator
Clinton, Bill (William Jefferson Clinton) President of the United States
Clinton, Hillary Rodham First Lady of United States, lawyer
Clodius, Robert LeRoy economist, educator
Close, David Palmer lawyer
Clubb, Bruce Edwin lawyer
Clurman, Michael newspaper publishing executive
Clyburn, James E. congressman
Coady, Philip James, Jr. naval officer
Coates, Joseph Francis futurist
Coats, Daniel Ray senator
Cobb, Calvin Hayes, Jr. lawyer
Cocco, Marie Elizabeth journalist
Cochran, John Thomas professional association executive
Cocke, Erle, Jr. business consultant
Cody, Thomas Gerald management consultant, writer
Coerper, Milo George lawyer
Coffey, Timothy physicist
Coffield, Shirley A. lawyer
Coffin, Laurence Edmondston, Jr. landscape architect, urban planner
Coffin, Tristram writer, editor
Cohen, Bonnie R. government official
Cohen, Edward Barth lawyer
Cohen, Israel chain store executive
Cohen, Lewis Isaac lawyer
Cohen, Louis Richard lawyer
Cohen, Martin communications company executive
Cohen, Mary Ann federal judge
Cohen, Richard Martin journalist
Cohen, Sheldon Stanley lawyer
Cohen, William Sebastian senator
Cohn, Herbert B. lawyer
Cohn, Ronald Dennis lawyer
Cohn, Sherman Louis lawyer, educator
Cohn, Victor Edward journalist
Coia, Arthur A. labor union executive
Colby, William Egan lawyer, international consultant
Cole, Charles Glaston lawyer
Cole, John Pope, Jr. lawyer
Coleman, Bernell physiologist, educator
Coleman, Ronald D. (Ron Coleman) congressman
Coleman, Roy Melvin psychiatrist
Coleman, William Thaddeus, Jr. lawyer
Coll, Stephen Wilson journalist
†Collie, H. Cris trade association executive
Collins, Barbara-Rose congresswoman
Collins, Cardiss congresswoman
Collins, Daniel Francis lawyer
Collins, Jeremiah C. lawyer
Collins, Mac congressman
Collins, Robert Ellwood surgeon
Colman, Richard Thomas lawyer
†Colon, Gilbert federal official
Colson, Charles Wendell lay minister, writer
Colson, Earl M. lawyer
Colton, Sterling Don lawyer, business executive
†Colvin, Bill D. government official
Colvin, John O. federal judge
Combest, Larry Ed congressman
Compton, Ann Woodruff news correspondent
Conafay, Stephen Rogers lawyer
Condit, Gary A. congressman
Congel, Frank Joseph federal agency administrator, physicist
Conklin, Kenneth Edward lawyer, industry executive
Conlon, Michael William lawyer
Connell, Alastair McCrae physician
Connell, Gerald A. lawyer
Connell, Lawrence lawyer
Conrad, Kent senator
Conroy, Sarah Booth columnist, novelist, speaker, editor
Constable, Elinor Greer federal official, diplomat
Constandy, John Peter lawyer
Conti, William J. lawyer
Converse, Robert E., Jr. lawyer
Conway, John Thomas government official, lawyer, engineer
Conyers, John, Jr. congressman
†Cook, Albert George, III retired parking company executive, consultant
Cook, Frances D. diplomat
Cook, Michael Blanchard government executive
Cooke, David Ohlmer government official
Cooney, John Fontana lawyer
Cooper, Alan Samuel lawyer
Cooper, Benita Ann federal agency administrator
Cooper, James Hayes Shofner (Jim Cooper) congressman, lawyer
Cooper, Jean Saralee judge
Cooper, Josephine Smith trade association and public relations executive
Cooper, Richard Melvin lawyer
Cooper, Roger Merlin government administrator, educator
Cooper, Ronald Stephen lawyer
†Cooper-Smith, Jeffrey Paul botanic garden administrator
Cope, James Dudley association executive
Cope, John R(obert) lawyer
Coppersmith, Sam congressman, lawyer
Corcoran, Thomas Joseph retired foreign service officer, former ambassador
Corden, Warner Max economics educator
Córdova, France Anne-Dominic astrophysics educator
Corell, Robert Walden science administration educator
Coreth, Joseph Herman bank executive
Cornely, Paul Bertau physician, educator
Cornett, Richard Orin research educator, consultant
Cortese, Alfred William, Jr. lawyer, consultant
Cortright, Jane Brigid Moynahan educational administrator
Cosgrove, John Patrick editor
†Costa, Erminio pharmacologist, cell biology educator
Costello, Jerry F., Jr. congressman, former county official
Costigan, Constance Frances artist, educator
Coston, William Dean lawyer
†Cothen, Grady Coulter, Jr. lawyer
Cotruvo, Joseph Alfred federal agency administrator
Cotter, B. Paul, Jr. judge
†Coughenour, Kavin Luther career officer, military historian
Coughlin, Timothy Crathorne bank executive
Countryman, John Russell business executive, former ambassador
Couper, William banker
Courtney, William Harrison diplomat
Coverdell, Paul D. senator
†Covey-Toperoff, Janice Margaret director of publications
Cowan, Edward journalist
Cowart, Jack museum executive
Cowen, Eugene Sherman broadcasting executive
Cowen, Wilson federal judge
Cox, Chapman Beecher lawyer, corporate executive
Cox, Geraldine Vang engineering executive
Cox, Kenneth Allen lawyer, communications consultant
Cox, Walter Thompson, III federal judge
Cox, Warren Jacob architect
Coyne, William Joseph congressman
Craft, Robert Homan, Jr. lawyer
†Cragg, Nelson Randolph, Jr. architect
†Cragin, Charles Langmaid lawyer
Craig, Larry Edwin senator
Craig, Paul Max, Jr. lawyer
Cramer, James Perry association executive, publisher, educator, architectural historian
Cramer, Robert E., Jr. (Bud Cramer) congressman
Crampton, Scott Paul lawyer
Crane, Edward Harrison, III institute executive
Crane, Philip Miller congressman
Crapo, Michael Dean congressman, lawyer
Crawford, Lester Mills, Jr. veterinarian
Crawford, Susan Jean federal judge, lawyer
Crawford, William Rex, Jr. former ambassador
Crawford-Mason, Clare Wootten television producer, journalist
Cremona, Vincent Anthony federal agency administrator
Crenshaw, Albert Burford journalist
Crew, Spencer museum administrator
Crewdson, John Mark journalist, author
Crocker, Chester Arthur diplomat, scholar
Crockett, Phyllis Darlene communications executive
Cromley, Allan Wray journalist
Cromley, Raymond Avolon syndicated columnist
Croser, Mary Doreen educational association executive
Crosland, Edward Burton, Sr. lawyer, former telephone company executive
Crowell, Eldon Hubbard lawyer
†Crowley, Candy Alt news correspondent
Crowley, John Joseph, Jr. ambassador
Crum, John Kistler chemical society director
Crutcher, John William federal agency commissioner
Crutchfield, Sam Shaw, Jr. association executive, lawyer
Cua, Antonio S. philosophy educator
Cude, Reginald Hodgin architect
Cullen, Thomas Francis, Jr. lawyer
Cummings, Frank lawyer
Cummings, Martin Marc medical educator, physician, scientific administrator
Cunningham, George Woody federal official, metallurgical engineer
Cunningham, Randy congressman
Curfman, David Ralph neurological surgeon, musician
Curran, Donald Charles federal agency administrator, government librarian
Curran, R. T. foundation executive
†Curtin, Kevin Gerard lawyer
Curtin, William Joseph lawyer
Cusick, Ralph A., Jr. investment banking company executive
Custer, Benjamin Scott, Jr. lawyer
Cutler, Bernard Joseph editor in chief, writer
Cutler, Lloyd Norton lawyer, company director
Cutler, Walter Leon diplomat, foundation executive
Cylke, Frank Kurt librarian
Cymrot, Mark Alan lawyer
Cytowic, Richard Edmund neurologist
Czarra, Edgar F., Jr. lawyer
†Czinkota, Ilona Vigh architect
†Dach, Leslie Alan public relations executive
Daddario, Emilio Quincy lawyer
Daffron, MaryEllen librarian
Daileda, David Allen architect
Dalley, George Albert lawyer
Dalton, John Howard Secretary of the Navy, financial consultant
Dameron, Del Stiltner lawyer
†Dameron, William H., III ambassador
Damgard, John Michael trade association executive
†Damus, Robert George lawyer
Danaher, James William federal government executive
Dancy, John Albert news correspondent
Danforth, John Claggett senator, lawyer, clergyman
Daniel, Aubrey Marshall, III lawyer
Daniel, Leon journalist, newspaper columnist, editor
†D'Aniello, Daniel merchant banker
Daniels, Diana M. lawyer
Daniels, Michael Paul lawyer
Daniels, Stephen M. government official
Dankner, Donald K. lawyer
Danner, Patsy Ann (Mrs. C. M. Meyer) congresswoman
Danzig, Richard Jeffrey government official, lawyer
Danziger, Joan sculptor
Danziger, Martin Breitel lawyer
Dapice, Ronald R. government official
Darby, Joseph Branch, Jr. metallurgist, government official
Darden, George Washington, III (Buddy Darden) congressman, lawyer
Darman, Richard Gordon investor, former government official, former investment banker, former educator
†Darr, Carol C. lawyer
Daschle, Thomas Andrew senator
Dash, Leon DeCosta, Jr. journalist
Dash, Samuel lawyer, educator
Dausman, George Erwin federal official, aeronautical engineer
†Dauster, William Gary lawyer, economist
Davidow, Joel lawyer
Davidson, Dan Eugene language educator, educational exchange administrator
Davidson, Daniel M. tax lawyer
Davidson, Eugene Abraham biochemist, university administrator
†Davidson, Michael lawyer
Davidson, Tom William lawyer
†Davies, Tudor Thomas federal agency administrator
Davis, Carolyne Kahle health care consultant
Davis, David George federal agency executive
Davis, David Oliver radiologist, educator
Davis, Donald Ray entomologist
Davis, Evelyn Y. editor, writer, publisher, investor
Davis, Herbert Lowell utility company executive
Davis, Lance Alan research and development executive, metallurgical engineer
Davis, Lynn Etheridge political scientist, former government official
†Davis, Marilynn A. housing agency administrator
Davis, Nancy Ellen museum director
Davis, Ross Dane lawyer
Davis, S. Gareth publishing executive
Davis, Sid journalist
Davis, True corporate executive
Davison, Calvin lawyer
Davison, Roderic Hollett historian, educator
Dawson, Howard Athalone, Jr. federal judge
Dawson, Mimi (Mimi Weyforth) government affairs consultant, former government official
Dawson, Robert Kent government relations expert
Day, Daniel Edgar government information officer
Day, J(ames) Edward lawyer, former postmaster general
Day, Mary artistic director, ballet company executive
Days, Drew S., III federal official, law educator
Deal, Nathan congressman, lawyer
Dealy, John Francis management consultant, lawyer, educator, arbitrator
Dean, Alan Loren government official
†Dean, Edwin Robinson government official, economist
Dean, Leslie Alan foreign service officer
Dean, Paul Regis legal educator
Deane, James Garner magazine editor, conservationist
Dearth, Jeffrey L. magazine publisher
de Borchgrave, Arnaud editor, writer, lecturer
Deckelbaum, Nelson lawyer
De Concini, Dennis senator, lawyer
Deel, Frances Quinn librarian
Deen, Thomas Blackburn transportation research executive
†Deer, Ada E. federal agency official, social worker, educator
Dees, C. Stanley lawyer
Deets, Horace association executive
DeFazio, Peter A. congressman
DeGeorge, Francis Donald federal official
DeGiovanni-Donnelly, Rosalie Frances biology researcher, educator
DeGrandi, Joseph Anthony lawyer
DeHarde, William M. insurance company executive
DeJong, Gerben hospital research executive
deKieffer, Donald Eulette lawyer
Deland, Michael Reeves energy executive
†deLaski, Kathleen M. federal official
DeLauro, Rosa congresswoman
DeLay, Thomas D. (Tom DeLay) congressman
Del Balzo, Joseph Michael aviation consulting company executive
de Leeuw, Frank economist
Deleon, Patrick Henry lawyer
De Leon, Sylvia A. lawyer
Dellums, Ronald V. congressman
de Lugo, Ron congressman
DeMars, Bruce naval administrator
Dembling, Paul Gerald lawyer, former government official
Demetrion, James Thomas art museum director
Dempsey, David B. lawyer
DeMuth, Christopher Clay lawyer, foundation executive
Denger, Michael L. lawyer
Denlinger, John Kenneth journalist
Denney, George Covert, Jr. organization administrator
Dennin, Joseph Francis lawyer, former government official
Denniston, John Baker lawyer
Denton, Laurie R. newspaper editor
Denvir, James Peter, III lawyer
Denysyk, Bohdan marketing professional
De Pauw, Linda Grant history educator
Derrick, Butler Carson, Jr. congressman
Derrick, John Martin, Jr. electric company executive
de Saint Phalle, Thibaut investment banker, educator, lawyer, financial consultant
†DeSeve, G. Edward federal official
Detchon, Bryan Reid federal agency administrator
Determan, Sara-Ann lawyer
†Deupi, Carlos architect
Deutch, John Mark federal official, chemist, academic administrator
Deutsch, Peter congressman, lawyer
Deutsch, Stanley anesthesiologist, educator
Devaney, Dennis Martin lawyer, legal educator
De Vault, Virgil Thomas physician
de Vos, Peter Jon ambassador
Dewhurst, Stephen B. government official, lawyer
DeWitt, Charles Barbour federal government official
Diaz-Balart, Lincoln congressman
DiBona, Charles Joseph association executive
†DiCello, Francis P. lawyer
†Dickey, George Edward federal government executive
Dickey, Jay W., Jr. congressman, lawyer
Dickinson, William Boyd, Jr. editorial consultant
Dicks, Norman De Valois congressman
Dickstein, Sidney lawyer
Diercks, Walter Elmer lawyer
Dietrich, Paul George lawyer
diGenova, Joseph E. lawyer
Di Lella, Alexander Anthony biblical studies educator
Dillin, John Woodward, Jr. newspaper correspondent
Dillman, Grant journalist
†Dillon, Robert Sherwood non-profit educational organization executive
Dillon, Wilton Sterling anthropologist, foundation administrator
†DiMario, Michael F. federal agency official, lawyer
Dingell, John David, Jr. congressman
Dinneen, Gerald Paul electrical engineer, former government official
DiPerna, Frank Paul photographer, educator
Dirda, Michael book critic
†Ditlow, Clarence M. think-tank executive
Dixon, Jeane author, lecturer, realtor, columnist
Dixon, Julian Carey congressman
†Dixon, Phillip newspaper editor
Dizard, Wilson Paul, Jr. international affairs consultant, educator
Doan, Michael Frederick editor
Dobbins, James Francis, Jr. foreign service officer
Dobkin, James Allen lawyer, engineer, artist
Dobriansky, Paula Jon business and communications executive
Docter, Charles Alfred lawyer, former state legislator
Dodd, Christopher J. senator
Dodd, Thomas ambassador, educator
Dolan, Edward Charles lawyer
Dolan, Michael William lawyer
Dole, Elizabeth Hanford charitable organization administrator, former secretary of labor, former secretary of transportation
Dole, Robert J. senator
Domenici, Pete (Vichi Domenici) senator
Dommen, Arthur John agricultural economist
†Donahue, John David federal official
Donahue, Thomas Reilly trade union official
Donaldson, Jeff Richardson visual artist, educator
Donaldson, Samuel Andrew journalist
Donegan, Charles Edward lawyer, educator
†Donilon, Thomas E. federal official
Donley, Michael Bruce federal government executive, financial manager
Donley, Rosemary university official
†Donna, Roberto restaurateur, chef
Donovan, George Joseph industry executive, consultant
Dooley, Calvin Millard congressman
Doolittle, Jesse William, Jr. lawyer
Doolittle, John Taylor congressman
Dorgan, Byron Leslie senator
Dorman, Craig Emery oceanographer, academic administrator
Dorn, James Andrew editor
Dorn, Jennifer Lynn charitable organization administrator
Dornan, Robert Kenneth congressman
Dorsen, David M(ilton) lawyer
Dougherty, Jude Patrick dean
†Douglas, Bruce Colman geophysicist
Douglas, Leslie investment banker
Dowd, John Maguire lawyer
Dowd, Thomas F. lawyer
Dowley, Joseph K. lawyer, member staff U.S. House of Representatives
Downey, Arthur Thomas, III lawyer
Downey, Mortimer Leo, III transportation executive
Downie, Leonard, Jr. newspaper editor, author
Downs, Anthony urban economist, real estate consultant
Downs, Clark Evans lawyer
†Doyle, Francis Xavier religious organization administrator
Doyle, Gerard Francis lawyer
Doyle, Joyce Ann lawyer
Drabkin, Murray lawyer
Dragoumis, Paul electric utility company executive
Draper, William Henry, III former United Nations official
Dreier, David Timothy congressman
Drew, Elizabeth television commentator, journalist
Dreyer, David E. federal official
Drinan, Robert Frederick lawyer, former congressman, educator, clergyman
Droms, William George finance educator
Drouilhet, Paul Raymond, Jr. science laboratory director, electrical engineer
Du, Julie Yi-Fang Tsai toxicologist, biochemist
Dubin, Alan S. lawyer
Dublin, Thomas David physician
DuBoff, Scott M. lawyer
Duemling, Robert Werner diplomat, museum director
Duffey, Joseph Daniel federal official
Dugan, Robert Perry, Jr. minister, religious organization administrator
Duggan, Ervin S. federal agency administrator
Duke, Paul Robert lawyer
Dukert, Betty Cole television producer
Dulles, Eleanor Lansing diplomatic consultant, retired diplomat, educator
Duncan, Charles Tignor lawyer
Duncan, John Dean, Jr. lawyer
Duncan, John J., Jr. congressman
Dunkelberger, Harry Edward, Jr. lawyer
Dunn, H. Stewart, Jr. lawyer
Dunn, Jennifer Blackburn congresswoman
Dunn, Loretta Lynn lawyer
Dunne, John Richard lawyer
Dunner, Donald Robert lawyer
†Dunsmore, Barrie television news correspondent
Dur, Philip Alphonse naval officer
Durbin, Richard Joseph congressman
Durenberger, David Ferdinand senator
Durfee, Harold Allen philosophy educator
†Durham, Archer L. federal official, retired career officer
Durney, Michael Cavalier lawyer
Durnil, James B. accountant
Dutro, John Thomas, Jr. geologist, paleontologist
Dwyer, Jeffry R. lawyer
Dye, Alan Louis lawyer
Dye, Stuart S. lawyer
Dyer, Robert Francis, Jr. internist, educator
Dyk, Timothy Belcher lawyer, educator
Dyke, Charles William retired army officer
Dyvig, Peter P. ambassador
Earle, Ralph, II lawyer
Earle, Richard Alan lawyer
Earll, Jerry Miller internist, educator
Earner, William Anthony, Jr. naval officer

East, Maurice Alden *academic dean, political scientist*
Eastman, Ronald D. *lawyer*
Eastment, Thomas James *lawyer*
Eckart, Dennis Edward *lawyer, former congressman*
Eckenhoff, Edward Alvin *health care administrator*
Eddy, John Joseph *diplomat*
Edelman, Marian Wright (Mrs. Peter B. Edelman) *lawyer*
Edelman, Peter Benjamin *lawyer*
Edelson, Burton Irving *electrical engineering educator*
Edes, Nik Bruce *lawyer*
Edsall, Thomas Byrne *reporter*
Edson, Charles Louis *lawyer, educator*
Edwards, Bert Tvedt *accountant*
Edwards, Bob (Robert Alan Edwards) *radio news anchor*
Edwards, Chet *congressman*
Edwards, Don *congressman*
Edwards, Gilbert Franklin *sociologist, educator*
Edwards, Harry T. *federal judge*
Edwards, Julia Spalding *journalist*
Edwards, Otis Carl, Jr. *theology educator*
Edwards, Tony M. *lawyer*
Efron, Marc Fred *lawyer*
Efron, Samuel *lawyer*
Efros, Ellen Ann *lawyer*
†Ehlers, Vernon James *congressman*
Ehrenhaft, Peter David *lawyer*
Ehrlich, Clifford John *hotel executive*
Ein, Melvin Bennett *government official*
†Einaudi, Luigi R. *federal official*
Eisenberg, John Meyer *physician, educator*
Eisenberg, Meyer *lawyer*
Eisenberg, Milton *lawyer*
Eisenberg, Pablo Samuel *non-profit organization executive*
Eisenstat, David H. *lawyer*
Eisner, Howard *engineering educator, engineering executive*
†Eisner, Neil Robert *lawyer*
Elders, Minnie Joycelyn *public health administrator, endocrinologist*
Elfin, Mel *magazine editor*
Elgart, Mervyn L. *dermatologist*
Elias, Thomas Sam *botanist, author*
El Khadem, Hassan Saad *chemistry educator, researcher*
†Eller, Jeff *media affairs director, assistant to President*
Eller, Joseph Burton, Jr. *trade association executive*
Ellicott, John LeMoyne *lawyer*
Elliott, Emerson John *federal agency administrator, policy analyst*
Elliott, Larry Paul *cardiac radiologist, educator*
Elliott, Lee Ann *federal official*
Elliott, Robert John *lawyer*
Elliott, Thomas Michael *management services executive, educator, consultant*
Elliott, Warren G. *lawyer*
Ellis, Courtenay *lawyer*
Ellis, Lee T., Jr. *lawyer*
Ellis, Brother Patrick (H. J. Ellis) *academic administrator*
Ellis, Rudolph Lawrence *insurance company executive*
Ellsworth, Robert Fred *investment executive, former government official*
Ellwood, David T. *federal agency administrator*
Elmer, Brian Christian *lawyer*
Elrod, Eugene Richard *lawyer*
Elsey, George McKee *association executive*
Elwood, William Edward *lawyer*
Ely-Raphel, Nancy *diplomat*
Emerson, John Bonnell *lawyer, partner*
Emerson, William *congressman*
Emery, Nancy Beth *lawyer*
Emmett, Robert Addis, III *lawyer*
Emperado, Mercedes Lopez *librarian*
†Engberg, Eric Jon *news correspondent*
Engel, Elliot L. *congressman*
Engel, Ralph *manufacturers association executive*
Englert, Roy Theodore *lawyer*
English, Glenn *association executive, former congressman*
English, Karan *state representative*
English, Richard Allyn *sociologist, social work educator*
English, William deShay *lawyer*
Ennis, Bruce J. *lawyer*
†Eno, Amos S. *science foundation administrator*
Ensign, William Lloyd *architect*
Epps, Charles H., Jr. *medical educator, college dean*
†Epstein, David *lawyer, arbitrator*
Epstein, Gary Marvin *lawyer*
Epstein, Joseph *editor, writer, educator*
Epstein, Kalman Noel *newspaper publishing company executive*
Epstein, Lionel Charles *lawyer*
Epstein, Sidney *editor*
Epstien, Jay Alan *lawyer*
†Erdreich, Ben Leader *federal government agency executive*
Erlenborn, John Neal *lawyer, former congressman*
Ernstthal, Henry L. *management educator*
Erwin, Frank William *personnel research and publishing executive*
†Escudero, Stanley *ambassador*
Eshoo, Anna Georges *congresswoman*
Espy, Mike (Alphonso Michael Espy) *U.S. secretary of agriculture*
†Etters, Ronald Milton *lawyer*
Etzioni, Amitai Werner *sociologist, educator*
Eule, Norman L. *lawyer*
Evans, David C. *lawyer*
Evans, Lane *congressman*
Evans, Rowland, Jr. *newspaper columnist*
Evelyn, Douglas Everett *museum executive*
†Everett, Ralph Bernard *lawyer*
Everett, Terry *congressman, farmer, newspaper executive, bank executive*
Ewing, Ky Pepper, Jr. *lawyer*
Ewing, Samuel Daniel, Jr. *financial executive*
Ewing, Thomas W. *congressman, lawyer*
Exon, J(ohn) James *senator*
Faber, Michael Warren *lawyer*
Fahrenkopf, Frank Joseph, Jr. *lawyer*
Fairbanks, Richard Monroe, III *lawyer, former ambassador at large*
Fairchild, Samuel Wilson *professional services company executive, former federal agency administrator*
Faircloth, Duncan McLauchlin (Lauch Faircloth) *senator, businessman, farmer*
Faleomavaega, Eni F. H. *territorial diplomat*
Falk, David B. *professional athletic representative, lawyer*
Falk, James Harvey, Sr. *lawyer*
Falter, Robert Gary *correctional health care administrator*
Falter, Vincent Eugene *retired army officer, consultant*
Fant, Lester G., III *lawyer*
Farabow, Ford Franklin, Jr. *lawyer*
Farer, Tom Joel *legal educator, writer, consultant*
Farley, John Joseph, III *federal judge*
Farmer, Donald A(rthur), Jr. *lawyer*
Farmer, Thomas Laurence *lawyer*
Farr, Sam *congressman*
Farrar, Donald Eugene *capital markets advisor*
Farrell, J. Michael *lawyer*
Farrell, Joseph Michael *steamship company executive*
Farrell, June Martinick *public relations executive*
Fasman, Zachary Dean *lawyer*
Faust, Marcus G. *lawyer*
†Faux, Jeff (Geoffrey Peter Faux) *economist, writer*
Favretto, Richard J. *lawyer*
Fawcett, John Thomas *archivist*
Fawell, Harris W. *congressman*
Fay, William Michael *federal judge*
Fazio, Vic *congressman*
Fedders, John Michael *lawyer*
Fedorochko, William, Jr. *retired army officer, policy analyst*
†Feeney, Richard Joseph *trade association executive, journalist*
Feffer, Gerald Alan *lawyer*
Feighan, Edward Farrell *lawyer, former congressman*
Feinberg, Kenneth Roy *lawyer, law educator*
Feinberg, Richard E. *federal official*
Feingold, Russell Dana *senator*
Feingold, S. Norman *psychologist*
Feinstein, Martin *opera director*
Feld, Jonathan S. *lawyer*
Feld, Karen Irma *columnist, journalist, public speaker*
Feldhaus, Stephen Martin *lawyer*
Feldman, Adrienne Arsht *lawyer, broadcasting company executive, banking executive*
Feldman, Clarice Rochelle *lawyer*
Feldman, Mark B. *lawyer*
Feldman, Myer *lawyer*
Feldman, Roger David *lawyer*
Feller, Lloyd Harris *lawyer*
Fellner, Baruch Abraham *lawyer*
Fels, Nicholas Wolff *lawyer*
Felton, Gordon H. *retired publishing executive*
Felts, William Robert, Jr. *physician*
Fendrich, Roger Paul *lawyer*
†Fenton, John Henry *judge*
Fenton, Kathryn Marie *lawyer*
Ferebee, John Spencer, Jr. *corporate executive*
†Ferguson, Christine C. *lawyer*
Ferguson, Thomas Crooks *lawyer*
Ferguson, Thomas H. *newspaper executive*
Ferman, Irving *lawyer, educator*
Fern, Alan Maxwell *art historian, museum director*
Ferrara, Peter Joseph *federal official, lawyer, author, educator*
Ferrara, Ralph C. *lawyer*
Ferren, John Maxwell *federal judge*
Ferris, George Mallette, Jr. *investment banker*
Feuerstein, Donald Martin *lawyer*
Feulner, Edwin John, Jr. *research foundation executive*
Field, Andrea Bear *lawyer*
Fielding, Fred Fisher *lawyer*
Fields, Cleo *congressman*
Fields, Jack Milton, Jr. *congressman*
Fields, Suzanne Bregman *syndicated columnist*
Fields, Wendy Lynn *lawyer*
Filerman, Gary Lewis *health education executive*
Filner, Bob *congressman*
Finarelli, Margaret G. *government executive*
Finerty, Martin Joseph, Jr. *military officer, researcher*
Fingerhut, Eric D. *congressman, lawyer*
Fink, Lois Marie *art historian*
Fink, Matthew Pollack *trade association executive, lawyer*
Finkel, Eugene Jay *lawyer*
Finkelstein, James David *physician*
Finkle, Jeffrey Alan *professional association executive*
Finn, Timothy John *lawyer*
†Finney, Essex Eugene, Jr. *agricultural research administrator*
Fiorini, John E., III *lawyer*
Firestone, Charles Morton *lawyer, educator*
†Fischer, Dennis James *federal agency administrator*
Fischetti, Michael Joseph *accounting educator*
Fish, Hamilton, Jr. *congressman*
Fishbaugh, Franklin James *government intelligence officer, researcher, weapons specialist*
Fishburne, Benjamin P., III *lawyer*
Fisher, Alfred Foster *university administrator*
Fisher, Bart Steven *lawyer, lecturer*
Fisher, Benjamin Chatburn *lawyer*
Fisher, Joel Hilton *lawyer*
Fisher, Miles Mark, IV *education educator*
Fisher, Robert Dale *stockbroker, retired naval officer*
Fiske, Richard Sewell *geologist*
Fitts, C. Austin *investment banker, former federal agency administrator*
Fitzgerald, Oscar P., IV *museum administrator*
FitzGerald, William Henry G. *diplomat, corporation executive*
Fitzhugh, David Michael *lawyer*
†Fitzmyer, Joseph Augustine *theology educator, priest*
Fitzpatrick, James Franklin *lawyer*
Fitzwater, (Max) Marlin *former government official, press secretary, advertising executive*
Flagg, Ronald Simon *lawyer*
Flake, Floyd Harold *congressman*
Flanagan, Francis Dennis *retired corporate executive*
Flanigan, Alan H. *ambassador*
Flannery, Ellen Joanne *lawyer*
Flannery, Thomas Aquinas *federal judge*
Flax, Alexander Henry *aeronautical engineer, science administrator*
Fleischaker, Marc L. *lawyer*
Fleischer, Michael *chemist*
Fleit, Martin *lawyer*
Fleming, Mack Gerald *lawyer*
Fleming, Philip Andrew *lawyer*
Fleming, Robert Wright *investment banker*
Fletcher, Arthur A. *federal official*
Fletcher, James Andrew *information systems specialist*
Flint, Myles Edward *federal agency administrator, lawyer*
Florance, Colden l'Hommedieu Ruggles *architect*
Foard, Douglas W. *educational association administrator*
†Focht, Theodore Harold *lawyer, educator*
Fogt, Howard W., Jr. *lawyer*
Foley, Thomas Stephen *speaker of the U.S. House of Representatives*
Foote, Timothy Gilson *editor*
†Ford, Charles A. *federal official*
Ford, Harold Eugene *congressman*
†Ford, James David *clergyman*
†Ford, Robert Nelson *lawyer, deputy assistant attorney general U.S.*
Ford, William David *congressman, lawyer*
Foreman, Anne N. *lawyer*
Foreman, Carol Lee Tucker *corporate executive*
Foreman, Dennis I. *federal official, lawyer*
Forester, John Gordon, Jr. *lawyer*
†Forgey, Benjamin Franklin *architecture and art critic*
Forrest, Herbert Emerson *lawyer*
Forrest, Sidney *clarinetist, music educator*
†Forster, Cecil R., Jr. *lawyer*
Forster, William Hull *military officer*
Fortune, Terence John *lawyer*
†Fosler, R. Scott *academic administrator, federal agency administrator*
Fouchard, Joseph James *government agency administrator*
Foulke, Edwin Gerhart, Jr. *lawyer*
Fowler, Caleb L. *insurance company executive, lawyer*
Fowler, Earle Cabell *administrator, physicist*
Fowler, Mark Stapleton *lawyer, corporation counsel*
Fowler, Tillie Kidd *congresswoman*
†Fowler, William Edward, Jr. *lawyer*
Fowler, Wyche, Jr. *senator, former congressman*
Fox, Samuel Mickle, III *physician, educator*
†Fox-Penner, Peter Seth *economic consultant*
Francis, Samuel Todd *columnist*
Francke, Gloria Niemeyer *pharmacist, editor, publisher*
Francois, Francis Bernard *association executive, lawyer*
Frank, Barney *congressman*
Frank, Isaiah *economist, educator*
†Frank, Richard Asher *lawyer, health products executive*
Frank, Richard Sanford *magazine editor*
Frank, Theodore David *lawyer*
Frank, Victor H., Jr. *international financial consultant*
Frankel, Jeffrey Alexander *economics educator, consultant*
Frankel, Michael Henry *accountant, lawyer*
†Frankle, Edward Alan *lawyer*
Franklin, Barbara Hackman *former goverment official*
Franklin, Charles E. *career officer*
†Franklin, Hardy R. *library director*
Franks, Gary Alvin *congressman, real estate professional*
†Franzen, Byron T. (John Franzen) *media specialist*
Frasure, Robert Conway *diplomat*
Frazier, Henry Bowen, III *government official, lawyer*
Frederick, Lafayette *botanist*
Freedberg, Sydney Joseph *retired museum curator, retired fine arts educator*
Freedman, Anthony Stephen *lawyer*
Freedman, Walter *lawyer*
Freeh, Louis J. *federal agency administrator*
†Freeman, Chas. W., Jr. *ambassador*
Freeman, Milton Victor *lawyer*
†Freeman, Orville Lothrop *lawyer, former governor of Minnesota*
Freeman, Robert Turner, Jr. *insurance executive*
Freer, Robert Elliott, Jr. *lawyer*
Freitag, Robert Frederick *government official*
Freudenheim, Tom Lippmann *museum administrator*
Frey, Andrew Lewis *lawyer*
Fried, Edward R. *government official*
Friedlander, Charles *lawyer*
Friedlander, James Stuart *lawyer*
Friedlander, Michael E. *lawyer*
Friedman, Alvin *lawyer*
Friedman, Arthur Daniel *electrical engineering and computer science educator, investment management company executive*
Friedman, Daniel Mortimer *federal judge*
Friedman, Herbert *physicist*
Friedman, Miles *trade association executive, financial services company executive, university lecturer*
Friedman, Paul Lawrence *lawyer*
Fritz, Thomas Vincent *association and business executive, accountant*
Frohnmayer, John Edward *federal agency administrator*
Frost, Edmund Bowen *lawyer*
Frost, Ellen Louise *federal agency administrator*
Frost, Jonas Martin, III *congressman*
Frost, S. David *retired naval officer*
Fry, Louis Edwin, Jr. *architect*
†Fry, Tom *federal official*
Fuchs, Roland John *geography educator, university administrator*
Fugate, Wilbur Lindsay *lawyer*
Fulbright, James William *former senator*
Fuller, Edwin Daniel *hotel executive*
Fuller, Lawrence Joseph *military officer, lawyer*
Fulton, Richard Alsina *lawyer*
Funk, Sherman Maxwell *government official*
†Furash, Edward E. *management consultant*
Furgol, Edward Mackie *museum curator, historian*
Furgurson, Ernest Baker, Jr. (Pat Furgurson) *journalist*
Furse, Elizabeth *congresswoman, small business owner*
Futey, Bohdan A. *federal judge*
Futrell, Basil Lee *association executive*
Futrell, John William *institute executive, lawyer*
Futrell, Mary Alice Hatwood *education association administrator*
Gabriel, Edward Michael *public affairs executive*
Gaff, Jerry Gene *academic administrator*
†Gaffney, Susan *federal official*
Gage, Robert Jeffrey *lawyer*
Gaguine, Benito *lawyer*
†Gale, Joseph H. *lawyer*
Galioto, Frank Martin, Jr. *pediatric cardiologist, educator*
†Gall, Mary Sheila *federal agency administrator*
Gallegos, Tony Eismail *federal agency administrator*
Gallo, Dean Anderson *congressman*
Galloway, William Jefferson *former foreign service officer*
†Gallucci, Robert Louis *diplomat, federal government official*
Galston, William Arthur *political scientist, educator*
†Gannon, James Patrick *newspaper editor*
Garavelli, John Stephen *biochemistry research scientist*
Gardenier, Turkan Kumbaraci *statistical company executive, researcher*
Gardner, Alvin Frederick *oral pathologist, government official*
Gardner, William Leonard *lawyer*
†Garland, Merrick Brian *lawyer*
Garner, William Darrell *health services executive*
Garr, Lawrence David *lawyer*
Garrett, Theodore Louis *lawyer*
Garrish, Theodore John *lawyer*
Gart, Murray Joseph *journalist, newspaper editor*
Garvey, John Leo *lawyer, educator*
Gary, Marc *lawyer*
Gary, Nancy Elizabeth *nephrologist, academic administrator*
Gastwirth, Joseph Lewis *statistician, educator*
†Gati, Toby T. *federal official*
Gauldin, Michael Glen *federal agency administrator*
Gaull, Gerald Edward *nutritionist, scientist, educator, food company executive*
Gearan, Mark D. *federal official*
Gebbie, Kristine Moore *health official*
Gehrig, Leo Joseph *surgeon*
Geisel, Harold Walter *diplomat*
Gejdenson, Sam *congressman*
Gekas, George William *congressman*
Geller, Kenneth Steven *lawyer*
Gellhorn, Ernest Albert Eugene *lawyer*
Geltman, Edward A. *lawyer*
Geniesse, Robert John *lawyer*
George, Gerald William *author, administrator*
George, W. Peyton *lawyer*
Georgine, Robert Anthony *union executive*
Gephardt, Richard Andrew *congressman*
Gerber, Joel *federal judge*
Geren, Preston (Pete Geren) *congressman*
Gergen, David Richmond *federal official, magazine editor*
Gernand, Bradley Elton *archivist, manuscripts librarian*
Gerson, Stuart Michael *lawyer*
Gertig, June Munford *lawyer*
Gest, Kathryn Waters *press secretary*
Geyer, Georgie Anne *syndicated columnist, educator, author, biographer*
Giallorenzi, Thomas Gaetano *optical engineer*
Gibbons, John Howard (Jack Gibbons) *government official, physicist*
Gibbons, Samuel Melville (Sam Gibbons) *congressman*
Gibbs, Joe Jackson *former professional football coach, professional sports team executive*
Gibbs, Lawrence B. *lawyer*
Gibson, Reginald Walker *federal judge*
Gibson, Stephen Lee *lawyer*
Gibson, Thomas Fenner, III *public affairs consultant, political cartoonist*
Gideon, Kenneth Wayne *lawyer*
†Giegengack, Richard A. *architect*
Gifford, Prosser *library administrator*
Gifford, Virginia Snodgrass *cataloger, bibliographer*
Gilbert, Charles Richard Alsop *physician, medical educator*
Gilbert, Jackson B. *banker*
Gilchrest, Wayne Thomas *congressman, former high school educator*
Gildenhorn, Joseph Bernard *diplomat, lawyer*
Gilfoyle, Nathalie Floyd Preston *lawyer*
Gilliam, Dorothy Butler *columnist*
Gilliam, Sam *artist*
Gilliland, James Sevier *lawyer*
Gillingham, Robert Fenton *federal agency administrator, economist*
Gilliom, Judith Carr *government official*
Gillmor, Paul E. *congressman, lawyer*
Gilman, Benjamin Arthur *congressman*
†Gilmour, Craddock Matthew, Jr. (Sandy Gilmour) *television news correspondent*
Gingrich, Newton Leroy (Newt Gingrich) *congressman*
†Ginsberg, Mark R. *social welfare administrator*
†Ginsburg, Alan *federal agency adminstrator*
Ginsburg, Charles David *lawyer*
Ginsburg, Douglas Howard *federal judge, educator*
†Ginsburg, Gilbert J. *lawyer, law educator*
Ginsburg, Martin David *lawyer, educator*
Ginsburg, Ruth Bader *U.S. supreme court justice*
Girard, James Emery *chemistry educator*
Gitner, Geoffrey P. *lawyer*
Glanzer, Seymour *lawyer*
Glaser, Vera Romans *journalist*
Glass, Andrew James *newspaper editor*
†Glass, Elliott Michael *architect*
Glasser, Melvin Allan *health policy executive, consultant*
Glassman, James Kenneth *editor, writer, publishing executive*
Glassman, Jon David *diplomat*
Glauthier, T. James *environmental economist*
Gleason, Jean Wilbur *lawyer*
Glenn, John Herschel, Jr. *senator*
Glick, Leslie Alan *lawyer*
Glick, Warren W. *lawyer, banker*
Glickman, Daniel Robert *congressman*
Glosser, Jeffrey Mark *lawyer*
Glynn, Thomas P. *federal agency administrator*
Gober, Hershel W. *federal agency official*
Godsey, John Drew *minister, theology educator emeritus*
Goelzer, Daniel Lee *lawyer*
Goffe, William Gregory *aircraft manufacturing company executive*
Gold, George Myron *lawyer, editor, writer, consultant*
Gold, Peter Frederick *lawyer*
Goldberg, Avrum M. *lawyer*
Goldberg, Seth A. *lawyer*
†Golden, Cornelius Joseph, Jr. *lawyer*
Golden, Terence C. *realty corporation executive, former government official*
Goldfarb, Ronald Lawrence *lawyer*
Goldfield, Edwin David *statistician*
Goldhaber, Jacob Kopel *retired mathematician, educator*
Goldin, Daniel S. *government agency administrator*
†Golding, Carolyn May *government administrator*
Goldman, Aaron *foundation executive, writer*
Goldman, Eugene I. *lawyer*
Goldsmith, Willis Jay *lawyer*
†Goldson, Alfred Lloyd *oncologist, educator*
Goldstein, Allan Leonard *biochemist, educator*
Goldstein, Frank Robert *lawyer*
†Goldstein, Irving *communications company executive*
Goldstein, Michael B. *lawyer*

Goldstein, Murray health organization official
Golodner, Jack labor association official
Gonzalez, Henry Barbosa congressman
Good, Mary Lowe (Mrs. Billy Jewel Good) government official
Goode, James Moore historian
Goode, Richard Benjamin economist, educator
Goodlatte, Robert William congressman, lawyer
Goodling, William F. congressman
Goodman, Roland Alfred federal agency administrator, former military officer
Goodpaster, Andrew Jackson retired army officer
Goodrich, George Herbert judge
Goodrich, Nathaniel Herman lawyer, former government official
Gordon, Barton Jennings (Bart Gordon) congressman, lawyer
†Gordon, Harry T. architectural firm executive
Gordon, Shana trade company executive
Gore, Albert, Jr. Vice President of the United States
Gore, Tipper (Mary Elizabeth Gore) wife of Vice President of the United States
Gorelick, Jamie Shona lawyer
Gorinson, Stanley M. lawyer
Gorman, Joyce J(ohanna) lawyer
Gorn, Janet Marie government official
Gorton, Slade senator
Goslin, David Alexander research administrator, sociologist
Gossage, John Ralph photographer
†Gostin, Lawrence lawyer
Gottschalk, Thomas A. lawyer
†Gould, William Benjamin, IV federal official, lawyer, educator
Gracey, James Steele corporate director, retired coast guard officer, consultant
Graefe, Frederick H. lawyer
Graham, D. Robert (Bob Graham) senator, former governor
Graham, Donald Edward publisher
Graham, Fred Patterson journalist, lawyer
Graham, Katharine newspaper executive
Graham, Thomas, Jr. lawyer
Graham, Thomas Richard lawyer
Gramm, William Philip (Phil Gramm) senator, economist
Grams, Rodney D. congressman, construction executive, television producer and anchor
Grandy, Fred congressman, actor
Granick, Lois Wayne association administrator
Grant, Carl N. communications executive
Grant, David Alistair lawyer
Grant, Richard Evans paleontologist, museum curator
Grapin, Jacqueline G. journalist
Grassley, Charles Ernest senator
Graves, Ernest, Jr. retired army officer, engineer
Graves, Ruth Parker educational executive
Graves, William P. E. editor
Gray, Clayland Boyden lawyer
Gray, Mary Wheat statistician, lawyer
Gray, Ralph editor, writer
Gray, Robert Keith communications company executive
Gray, Sheila Hafter psychiatrist, psychoanalyst
Grayson, Lawrence Peter federal educational administrator
Green, Darrell professional football player
Green, Donald Hugh lawyer
Green, Joyce Hens federal judge
Green, June Lazenby federal judge
Green, Marshall former ambassador, consultant
†Green, Monica peace organization director
Green, Richard Alan lawyer
Green, Richard James federal agency administrator, aerospace engineer
Green, Robert Lamar, Jr. lawyer
Green, Shirley Moore political organization director
Green, Thomas Charles lawyer
Greenberg, Milton political scientist, educator
Greenberg, Robert E. lawyer
Greenberger, I. Michael lawyer
Greene, Harold H. federal judge
Greene, Timothy Geddes lawyer
Greenebaum, Leonard Charles lawyer
Greenfield, Meg journalist
Greenspan, Alan economist
Greenspan, Michael Alan lawyer
Greenstein, Robert M. non-profit organization director
Greenwald, Gerald Bernard lawyer
Greenwood, James Charles congressman
Greenwood, Janet Kae Daly psychologist, educational administrator
Greenwood, Mark A. federal agency administrator, lawyer
Greenwood, William Warren journalist
Grefé, Richard public broadcasting executive
Gregg, Judd senator, former governor
Gregory, Bettina Louise journalist
Grenier, Edward Joseph, Jr. lawyer
Gribbin, David James, III federal official
Gribbon, Daniel McNamara lawyer
Grier, Phillip Michael lawyer, association executive
Griffenhagen, George Bernard trade association executive
Griffin, James Bennett anthropologist, educator
Griffin, Joseph Parker lawyer, educator
Griffin, Robert Thomas automotive company executive
Griffith, Jerry Dice government official, nuclear engineer
†Griffith, Patricia King journalist
†Griffith, Ronald H. military career officer
Grigsby, Margaret Elizabeth physician
Grimes, Larry Bruce lawyer
Griswold, Erwin Nathaniel lawyer
Groner, Samuel Brian lawyer
†Gros, Jeffrey ecumenical theologian
†Gross, David Joseph aquarium director
Gross, Richard Alan lawyer
Grossi, Ralph Edward agricultural organization executive, farmer, rancher
Grossman, Joanne Barbara lawyer
Grossman, John Henry, III obstetrician, gynecologist, educator
Grosvenor, Gilbert Melville journalist, educator, business executive
Grow, Michael Abbott lawyer
Grub, Phillip Donald business educator
Gruenberg, Mark Jonathan correspondent
Grupe, Barbara Ann Pandzik artist, museum administrator
Guandolo, John lawyer
Guarini, Frank J. congressman
Gubser, Peter Anton political scientist, writer, educator
Guenther, Kenneth Allen business association executive, economist
Guggenheim, Charles E. film, television producer, political media consultant
Guimond, Richard Joseph federal agency executive, environmental scientist
Gulland, Eugene D. lawyer
Gumpert, Gunther artist
Gundersheimer, Werner Leonard library director
Gunderson, Steve Craig congressman
Gunther, Marc television writer
†Gustini, Raymond J. lawyer
Gutierrez, Luis V. congressman, elementary education educator
Gutierrez-Santos, Luis Emiliano economist
Gutman, Harry Largman lawyer
Gutter, Samuel I. lawyer
Guttman, Egon law educator
Gwaltney, Corbin editor, publishing executive
Haas, Ellen federal agency administrator
Haas, Warren James librarian, consultant
Haass, Richard Nathan political science educator
Hackl, Alphons J. publisher
†Hackney, Sheldon federal agency administrator, academic administrator
Hadar, Mary Ellen newspaper editor
†Hagen, Donald Floyd military officer
†Hagenstad, M. Thomas federal government administrator
Hager, Robert journalist
Haggerty, James Joseph writer
Hahn, Gilbert, Jr. lawyer
Hahn, John Stephen lawyer
Haig, Alexander Meigs, Jr. former secretary of state, former army officer, business executive
Haines, Ronald H. bishop
Hale, Marcia L. federal official
†Hales, Linda newspaper editor
Haley, George Williford Boyce lawyer
Haley, Roger Kendall librarian
†Hall, Douglas K. federal official
†Hall, Edwin King lawyer
Hall, James Henry foreign service officer
Hall, Keith R. federal official
Hall, Ralph Moody congressman
Hall, Samuel M., Jr. career educator, career development consultant
Hall, Tony P. congressman
Halle, Peter Edward lawyer
Haller, Ralph A. federal agency administrator
Hallett, Carol Boyd government official
Hallgren, Richard Edwin meteorologist
Hallinan, Joseph Thomas journalist, correspondent
Halperin, Samuel education and training policy analyst
Halpern, James Bladen lawyer
Halpern, James S. federal judge
†Halsey, Linda newspaper editor
Halstead, Dirck S. photographer, journalist
Halverson, Richard Christian minister, chaplain
Halvorson, Newman Thorbus, Jr. lawyer
Hamachek, Ross Frank media company executive
Hamarneh, Sami Khalaf historian of medicine and science, author
Hamblen, Lapsley Walker, Jr. federal judge
Hamburg, Daniel (Dan Hamburg) congressman
†Hamilton, Donald R. foreign service official
Hamilton, Donald Reed foreign service officer
Hamilton, Lee Herbert congressman
Hamilton, Milton Holmes, Sr. government executive, politico-military analyst
Hammer, Carl computer scientist, former computer company executive
Hammond, Deanna Lindberg linguist
Hammond, Jerome Jerald government program administrator, agricultural economist
Hammond, Robert Alexander, III lawyer
†Hamrick, Mark Alan radio news reporter
Hancock, Mel congressman
†Hancock, William John career officer
Hand, John Oliver museum curator
Handelsman, M. Gene association administrator
Hanft, Ruth S. Samuels (Mrs. Herbert Hanft) health care consultant, educator, economist
Hanke, Byron Reidt residential land planning and community associations consultant
†Hanley, Edward Thomas union official
Hanlon, R(obert) Timothy lawyer
Hannaford, Peter Dor public relations executive
†Hannett, Frederick James healthcare consulting company executive
Hannigan, Vera Simmons federal agency administrator
Hansell, William Howard, Jr. association executive
Hansen, Orval lawyer, former congressman
Hanson, Jean Elizabeth lawyer
Harbrant, Robert Francis labor union executive
Harden, Blaine Charles journalist
Hardesty, C. Howard, Jr. lawyer
Hardiman, Joseph Raymond investment banking executive
Hardy, Robert Gerald lawyer
Harkin, Thomas Richard senator
Harkrader, Carleton Allen lawyer
Harlem, Susan Lynn librarian
Harman, Jane congresswoman, lawyer
Harman, Sidney audio and video company executive
Harman, William Boys, Jr. lawyer
Harper, Conrad Kenneth lawyer and government official
Harper, Robert Allan consulting psychologist
Harpham, Virginia Ruth violinist
Harrington, Anthony Stephen lawyer
†Harris, David Ford federal agency administrator
Harris, Don Victor, Jr. lawyer
Harris, Jeffrey lawyer
†Harris, Judith Linda lawyer
Harris, Stanley S. federal judge
†Harris, Steven B. lawyer
Harris, Wesley L. federal agency administrator
Harrison, Donald lawyer
Harrison, Earl David lawyer, real estate executive
Harrison, Ellen Kroll lawyer
Harrison, Emmett Bruce, Jr. public relations counselor
Harrison, Jerry Calvin army officer
Harrison, Marion Edwyn lawyer
Harrison, Monika Edwards business development executive
Harrison, Patricia de Stacy consulting, public relations company executive
Harrison, Rosalie Thornton (Mrs. Porter Harmon Harrison) retired educator
Harrop, William Caldwell retired ambassador, foreign service officer
Hart, John P. federal official
Hart, Peter David opinion research firm executive
Harter, Dennis Glenn diplomat
Hartman, Arthur A. international business consultant
Hartman, (Howard) Carl newspaperman
Hartman, George Eitel architect
Hartwell, Stephen investment company executive
Harty, Sheila Therese theologian, writer, editor
†Harvey, David Michael lawyer
Harvey, John Collins physician, educator
Harwit, Martin Otto astrophysicist, educator, museum director
Harwood, Richard Lee journalist, newspaper editor
†Haseltine, John B. think-tank executive
Haskins, Caryl Parker scientist, author
Hass, Lawrence Joel lawyer
Hassett, Joseph Mark lawyer
Hastert, (J) Dennis congressman
Hastings, Alcee Lamar congressman, former federal judge
Hatfield, Mark O. senator
Hathaway, Charles Michael lawyer
Hathaway, William Dodd federal agency administrator
Hauser, Richard Alan lawyer
Havens, Charles W., III lawyer
Havlicek, Franklin J. communications executive
†Hawk, Kathleen M. federal official
Hawke, John Daniel, Jr. lawyer
Hawkins, Edward Jackson lawyer
Hawkins, Wilbur federal official
Hawley, Frederick William, III bank executive, former federal official
Hay, George Austin actor, producer, director, musician, artist
Hayes, David J. lawyer
Hayes, James Alison congressman
†Hayes, Paula Freda governmental official
Hayes, Samuel Perkins social scientist, educator
Hayes, Webb Cook, III lawyer
Haynes, R. Michael lawyer
Haynes, William J(ames), II lawyer
Hays, Donald Osborne retired government official
Hays, Michael DeWayne lawyer
Hazen, Robert Miller research scientist, musician
Healey, John G. human services organization executive
Hecht, Anthony Evan poet
Hecht, Marjorie Mazel editor
Heckman, Jerome Harold lawyer
Hedges, Harry George computer scientist, educator
Hedges, Kamla King corporate librarian
Hedrick, Floyd Dudley government official, author
Heelan, Patrick Aidan philosophy educator
Heffernan, James Vincent lawyer
Heffron, Howard A. lawyer
Hefley, Joel M. congressman
Heflin, Howell Thomas senator, lawyer, former state supreme court chief justice
Hefner, W. G. (Bill Hefner) congressman
Hefter, Laurence Roy lawyer
Heginbotham, Erland Howard international economist
Heifetz, Alan William federal judge
Heintz, John Edward lawyer
Heiss, Harry Glen archivist
Heller, Jack Isaac lawyer
Heller, John Roderick, III lawyer, business executive
†Hellmuth, George William architect
Helms, Jesse senator
Helms, Richard McGarrah international consultant
Helms, Robert Brake economist, research director
Hemley, M. Rogue lawyer
Henderson, Donald Ainslie government science administrator
Henderson, Douglas Boyd lawyer
Henderson, Karen LeCraft federal judge
Henderson, Thomas Henry, Jr. lawyer, legal association executive
Henke, Michael John lawyer
Henkin, Robert Irwin neurobiologist, internal medicine, nutrition and neurology educator, scientific products company executive
Hennemeyer, Robert Thomas diplomat
Hennessy, Ellen Anne lawyer, educator
Henry, Walter Lester, Jr. physician, educator
Herbers, Tod Arthur publisher
†Herbert, James Charles education executive
Herbst, Robert LeRoy organization executive
Herbster, William Gibson university administrator, consultant
Herger, Wally W., Jr. congressman
†Herlach, Mark Dayton lawyer
Herman, Alexis M. federal official
Herman, Andrea Maxine newspaper editor
Hermanson Ogilvie, Judith foundation executive
Hersh, Seymour M. journalist
Hervey, Homer Vaughan federal agency administrator
Herzog, Richard Barnard lawyer
Herzstein, Robert Erwin lawyer
Hess, Stephen political scientist, author
Hess, Wilmot Norton science administrator
†Heumann, Judith federal agency administrator
Hewitt, Frankie Lea theater producer
Hewitt, Paul Buck lawyer
Hey, Robert Pierpont editor association bulletin
†Heyman, Ira Michael government official, university chancellor, law educator
Hibbert, Robert George lawyer, food company executive
Hickey, Edward Joseph, Jr. lawyer, diplomatic consultant
Hickey, James Aloysius Cardinal archbishop
Hickman, R(obert) Harrison political pollster, strategist
†Hicks, Jocelyn Muriel laboratory medicine specialist
Hidalgo, Edward lawyer, former secretary of navy
Higbee, Joan Florence librarian
Higgins, James Henry, III marketing executive
Higgins, Robert (Walter) military officer, physician
†Higgins, William Robert college administrator
High, George Borman executive director, research organization
Highet, Gilbert Keith MacInnes lawyer
Hill, Bennett David history educator, Benedictine monk, priest
Hill, David Warren lawyer
Hill, Jerry C. lawyer
Hill, Jimmie Dale government official
Hill, Jonathan Booth lawyer
Hill, Stephen S. lawyer
Hillgren, Sonja Dorothy journalist
Hilliard, Earl Frederick congressman, former state senator
Hillings, E. Joseph energy company executive
Hills, Carla Anderson lawyer, former federal official
Hills, John Merrill public policy research center executive, former educational administrator
Hills, Roderick M. lawyer, business executive, former government official
Hinch, Gerald K. federal agency official
Hinchey, Maurice D., Jr. congressman
Hinden, Stanley Jay newspaper editor
Hinds, Richard De Courcy lawyer
†Hinson, Hal film critic
Hirsch, Robert Bruce lawyer
Hirsch, Robert Louis electric research company executive
Hirschhorn, Eric Leonard lawyer
Hitz, Frederick Porter federal agency administrator, lawyer
Hoagland, Jimmie Lee newspaper editor
Hoagland, Peter Jackson congressman, lawyer
Hoar, Joseph P. military officer
Hobart, Lawrence Scott service organization administrator
Hobbs, Caswell O., III lawyer
Hobbs, J. Timothy, Sr. lawyer
Hobson, David Lee congressman, lawyer
Hobson, James Richmond lawyer
Hochberg, Jerome A. lawyer
Hochbrueckner, George J. congressman
Hodges, Robert H., Jr. federal judge
Hodgson, Morgan Day lawyer
Hodson, Kenneth Joe lawyer, criminal justice consultant, retired army officer
Hoehn, William Edwin federal goverment official
Hoekstra, Peter congressman, manufacturing executive
Hoffman, E. Leslie lawyer
Hoffman, Joel Elihu lawyer
Hoffmann, Robert Shaw museum administrator, educator
Hogan, John P. federal agency official
†Hoikes, Mary Elizabeth lawyer, diplomat
Hoke, Martin Rossiter congressman
Holbrook, Douglas Cowen labor union administrator
Holdaway, Ronald M. federal judge
Holden, James Phillip lawyer
Holden, John Bernard former college president, educator
Holden, Raymond Thomas physician, educator
Holden, Tim congressman, protective official
†Holder, Eric H. prosecutor
Holland, Christie Anna biochemist, virologist
Holland, James Ricks public relations executive, association executive
Holland, Robert Carl economist
Hollander, Richard Edward real estate executive
†Holleman, Frank Sharp, III lawyer
†Holliman, John news broadcaster
Hollings, Ernest Frederick senator
Hollinshead, Ariel Cahill research oncologist
†Holloway, Harry aerospace medical doctor
Holloway, James Lemuel, III foundation executive, retired naval officer
Holloway, John Thomas physicist
Holmer, Alan Freeman lawyer
Holmes, Henry Allen government official
Holmstead, Jeffrey R. lawyer
Holtz, Edgar Wolfe lawyer
†Holum, John D. federal official
Hope, Judith Richards lawyer
Hope, William Duane zoologist, curator
Hoppe, Wolfgang lawyer
Horahan, Edward Bernard, III lawyer
Horan, Harold Eugene university administrator, former diplomat
Horlick, Gary Norman lawyer, legal educator
Horn, Charles M. lawyer
†Horn, Donald Herbert lawyer
Horn, Marian Blank federal judge
Horn, (John) Stephen congressman, political science educator
Horne, Michael Stewart lawyer
Horowitz, Herbert Eugene educator, consultant, former ambassador
Horsky, Charles Antone lawyer
Horton, Frank former congressman, lawyer
†Horyn, Cathy newspaper editor
Hosenball, S. Neil lawyer
†Hotchkin, John Francis church official, priest
Houdek, Robert G. diplomat
Hough, Lawrence A. financial organization executive
Houghton, Amory, Jr. congressman
†Houley, William Purcell federal official, career officer
Houlihan, David Paul lawyer
House, W(illiam) Michael lawyer
Hove, Andrew Christian federal agency administrator
Hovey, Justus Allan, Jr. political scientist
Hoving, John Hannes Forester consulting firm executive
Howard, Glen Scott lawyer
Howard, Jack union executive
Howard, Jeffrey Hjalmar lawyer
Howard, Kenneth Calvin, Jr. lawyer
Howard, Robert Elliott federal official
Howe, Fisher management consultant, former government official
Howerton, Helen Veronica federal agency administrator
Howrey, Edward F. lawyer
Hoyer, Steny Hamilton congressman
Hoyt, David Richard federal agency official
Hoyt, John Arthur humane society executive
Hsu, Ming Chen federal agency administrator
Huband, Frank Louis educational association executive
†Hudgins, Michael Pharr internist
Hudson, Michael Craig political science educator
†Hudson, Philip academic director
Hufbauer, Gary Clyde economist, lawyer, educator
Huffington, Michael congressman
†Hug, James Edward religious organization administrator
Hughes, Ann Hightower economist, government official
†Hughes, Arthur H. ambassador to Yemen
Hughes, James Charles lawyer
Hughes, John Vance lawyer
Hughes, Marija Matich law librarian
Hughes, Thomas Lowe foundation executive
Hughes, William John congressman
Hughitt, Jeremiah Keefe utility executive
Hulings, Joseph Simpson diplomat
Hume, Brit (Alexander Britton Hume) journalist
Hume, Paul Chandler music editor, music educator
Humphreys, Robert Russell lawyer
Hundt, Reed Eric federal official, lawyer
Hunkele, Lester Martin, III federal agency administrator
Hunnicutt, Charles Alvin lawyer
Hunt, Albert R. newspaper executive
Hunter, Kenneth James federal agency adminstrator

Hunter, Ronald V. computer administrator
Huntress, Wesley Theodore, Jr. government official
Husain, Syed Shahid bank executive
Husemann, Robert William mechanical engineer
Hushon, John Daniel lawyer
Huston, John Wilson air force officer, historian
Hutchinson, Tim congressman
Hutt, Peter Barton lawyer
Hutto, Earl congressman
Hyde, Henry John congressman
Hylden, Thomas lawyer
Hyman, Lester Samuel lawyer
Hymel, Gary Gerard lobbyist
Hynes, Terence Michael lawyer
†Iglesias, Enrique V. bank executive, former government minister
†Ignatius, David newspaper editor
Iklé, Fred Charles former federal agency administrator, policy advisor, defense expert
Imig, David Gregg educational association executive
Inglis, Robert D (Bob Inglis) congressman, lawyer
Ingoldsby, Thomas M. lawyer
Inhofe, James M. congressman
Innerst, Preston Eugene newspaper editor, journalist
Inouye, Daniel Ken senator
Inslee, Jay R. congressman, lawyer
Ireland, Patricia association executive
Irey, Nelson Sumner pathologist
Irvine, Reed John media critic, corporation executive
†Irving, Clarence L., Jr. (Larry Irving) federal official
Irving, John Stiles, Jr. lawyer
Isaac, William Michael investment firm executive, former government official
Isaacs, Amy Fay political organization executive
Isbell, David Bradford lawyer, legal educator
Isenbergh, Max lawyer, musician, educator
Isom, Harriet Winsar ambassador
Israel, Barry John lawyer
Israel, Lesley Lowe political consultant
Istook, Ernest James, Jr. (Jim Istook) congressman, lawyer
†Itteilag, Anthony L. government official
Ivers, Donald Louis federal judge
Jackson, Karl Dion government official business executive, scholar
Jackson, Neal A. lawyer
Jackson, Thomas Penfield federal judge
Jacobs, Andrew, Jr. congressman
Jacobs, Julian I. federal judge
Jacobs, Leon medical research administrator
Jacobsen, Hugh Newell architect
Jacobson, David Edward lawyer
Jacobson, Michael Faraday consumer advocate, writer
Jagoda, Barry Lionel media adviser, communications consultant
James, Frederick Calhoun bishop
Jamme, Albert Joseph archaeologist, educator
Janetatos, Jack Peter lawyer
Janis, Michael B. federal official
Jankowski, Gene F. broadcasting executive
Jankowsky, Joel lawyer
†Jansen, E. Harold bishop
†Jarrell, Jay A. health care company executive
†Jarvis, Charlene Drew councilmember
Jasinowski, Jerry Joseph economist, corporate executive
Jaskiewicz, Leonard Albert lawyer
Jaspersen, Frederick Zarr economist
Javits, Joshua Moses lawyer
Jaycox, Edward Van Kleeck bank executive
Jeelof, Gerrit electronics executive
Jefferson, William J. (Jeff Jefferson) congressman
Jeffords, James Merrill senator
†Jenifer, Franklyn Green academic administrator
Jenkins, John Smith academic dean, lawyer
Jensen, Robert Neal lawyer
Jeremiah, David Elmer naval officer
Jesseramsing, Chitmansing ambassador
Jessup, Philip Caryl, Jr. lawyer, museum executive
Jeter, Howard F. ambassador
Jetton, C. Loring, Jr. lawyer
†Joe, Thomas think-tank
Joelson, Mark Rene lawyer
Johnson, Arlene Lytle government agency official
Johnson, C. Donald, Jr. (Don Johnson) congressman
Johnson, David Raymond lawyer
Johnson, Eddie Bernice congresswoman
Johnson, Haynes Bonner journalist, author
Johnson, James A. financial organization executive
Johnson, John A. communications company executive
Johnson, John Griffith, Jr. lawyer
Johnson, Nancy Lee congresswoman
Johnson, Norma Holloway federal judge
Johnson, Oliver Thomas, Jr. lawyer
Johnson, Omotunde Evan George economist
Johnson, Philip McBride lawyer
Johnson, Ralph Raymond ambassador, federal agency administrator
Johnson, Richard Clark lawyer
Johnson, Richard Tenney lawyer
Johnson, Robert Henry political science educator
Johnson, Robert Louis cable television company executive
Johnson, Roger federal agency administrator
Johnson, Roger W. federal official, computer manufacturing company executive
Johnson, Samuel (Sam Johnson) congressman
Johnson, Stephen L. federal agency administrator
Johnson, Timothy Peter congressman
Johnson, U. Alexis diplomat
†Johnson, Willa Ann think-tank executive
Johnson, William Hall lawyer, government official
Johnston, Harry A., II congressman
Johnston, John Bennett, Jr. senator
†Johnston, Kelly Don political administrator
Johnston, Laurance Scott foundation director
Jonas, John Francis lawyer
Jones, Aidan Drexel lawyer
Jones, Alice Samuels elementary education educator, reading specialist
Jones, Boisfeuillet, Jr. lawyer, newspaper executive
Jones, Catherine Ann library administrator
†Jones, Elaine R. civil rights advocate
Jones, Howard St. Claire, Jr. electronics engineering executive
Jones, Keith Alden lawyer
Jones, Leonade Diane newspaper publishing company executive
Jones, Lois Mailou (Mrs. Vergniaud Pierre-Noel) artist, educator
Jones, Philip Howard broadcast journalist
Jones, Richard Herbert lawyer, former government official
Jones, Stanley Boyd health policy analyst, priest
Jones, Theodore Lawrence lawyer
Jones, William Bowdoin political scientist, retired diplomat, lawyer
Jones-Wilson, Faustine Clarisse education educator emeritus
Jordan, Irving King academic administrator
Jordan, John Patrick government agency executive, research scientist, educator
Jordan, Michael Jeffery baseball player, retired professional basketball player
Jordan, Robert Elijah, III lawyer
Jordan, Vernon Eulion, Jr. lawyer, former association official
Joseph, Daniel Mordecai lawyer
Josephson, Diana Hayward aerospace executive
Jost, Peter Hafner lawyer
Journey, Drexel Dahlke lawyer
Juliana, James Nicholas corporate executive
Kabel, Robert James lawyer
Kafes, William Owen lawyer
Kafka, Gerald Andrew lawyer
Kahler, Elizabeth Sartor (Mrs. Ervin Newton Chapman) physician
Kahn, Edwin Leonard lawyer
Kahn, Michael stage director
Kahn, Walter Kurt engineering and applied science educator
Kaiser, Robert Greeley newspaper editor
Kalbfeld, Brad Marshall television and radio executive, editor
Kalinger, Daniel Jay public relations and marketing executive
Kalleres, Michael Peter career officer
†Kalnay, Eugenia government official, meteorologist
Kamber, Victor Samuel political consultant
Kamm, Linda Heller lawyer
Kammerer, Kelly Christian lawyer
Kampelman, Max M. former ambassador, lawyer
Kane, Annette P. religious organization executive
Kanjorski, Paul Edmund congressman, lawyer
Kant, Gloria Jean neuroscientist, researcher
Kanter, Arnold Lee policy analyst
Kantor, Michael (Mickey Kantor) federal trade representative
Kaplan, Gilbert B. lawyer
Kaplan, Julius lawyer
Kapp, Robert Harris lawyer
Kappner, Augusta Souza government official
Kaptur, Marcia Carolyn congresswoman
Karalekas, Anne publishing executive
†Karaosmanoglu, Attila bank executive, economist
Karayn, James, Jr. broadcasting executive
Karelis, Charles Howard government official
Karklins, Vija L. librarian
Karle, Isabella chemist
Karle, Jerome physicist, researcher
Karmin, Monroe William senior editor
Kaseman, A. Carl, III lawyer
Kasich, John R. congressman
Kass, Benny Lee lawyer
Kassebaum, Donald Gene medical association administrator, physician, medical educator
Kassebaum, Nancy Landon senator
Kasten, Robert W., Jr. former senator
Katona, Peter Geza biomedical engineer, educator
Katz, Sherman E. lawyer
Katz, Sol physician
Katzen, Sally lawyer
Kaufman, John Gilbert, Jr. materials engineer
Kaufman, Paul physician, former naval officer, association executive
Kaufman, Thomas Frederick lawyer, legal educator
Kaulkin, Donna Brookman editor, writer
Kautter, David John lawyer
Kauzlarich, Richard Dale U.S. ambassador, foreign service officer
Kavanaugh, Everett Edward, Jr. trade association executive
Kay, Kenneth Robert lawyer
Kay, Thomas Oliver agricultural consultant
Keane, William K. lawyer
Kearney, Stephen Michael federal agency administrator, treasurer
†Kearns, David Todd federal agency administrator
Keating, Robert B. ambassador
Keel, Alton Gold, Jr. ambassador
Keeley, Robert Vossler academic administrator, retired ambassador
Keener, Mary Lou lawyer
Keeney, E. Andrew lawyer
Keeney, John Christopher lawyer
Keeney, John Christopher, Jr. lawyer
Keeny, Spurgeon Milton, Jr. association executive
†Kehoe, Patrick Emmett law librarian, educator
Keiner, R(obert) Bruce, Jr. lawyer
†Keith, Kenton W. ambassador to Qatar
Kelley, Edward Watson, Jr. federal agency administrator
Kelley, Wayne Plumbley, Jr. federal official
Kellison, James Bruce lawyer
Kellogg, Frederic Rogers lawyer
Kelly, Charles J., Jr. investment company executive
Kelly, Eugene Walter, Jr. counseling and human services educator, director
Kelly, Francis Joseph strategic communications company executive
Kelly, John Hubert diplomat
Kelly, Sharon Pratt mayor
Kelly, William Charles, Jr. lawyer
†Kelman, Steven Jay government official
†Kemnitzer, Susan Coady science foundation administrator
Kemp, Geoffrey Thomas Howard international affairs specialist
Kemp, Jack French association director, former U.S. secretary of housing and urban development, former congressman
Kempley, Rita A. film critic, editor
Kempner, Jonathan L. professional society administrator
Kempster, Norman Roy journalist
Kempthorne, Dirk Arthur senator
Kendall, Peter Landis television news executive
†Kendig, William L. government official, accountant
Kendrick, John Whitefield economist, educator, consultant
Kennedy, Anthony McLeod U.S. supreme court justice
Kennedy, Edward Moore senator
Kennedy, Eugene Richard microbiologist, university dean
Kennedy, Joseph Patrick, II congressman
†Kennedy, Patrick F. federal official
Kennedy, Richard Thomas government official
Kennedy, Robert Emmet, Jr. history educator
Kennedy, Roger George park services executive
Kennelly, Barbara B. congresswoman
Kenney, Richard Alec physiology educator
Kenney, Robert James, Jr. lawyer
Kent, Alan Heywood lawyer
Kent, Jill Elspeth academic administrator, lawyer, former government official
Kerber, Frank John diplomat
Kern, Harry Frederick editor
Kerrey, Bob (J. Robert Kerrey) senator
Kerry, John Forbes senator
Kerxton, Alan Smith lawyer
Kessler, Judd Lewis lawyer
Kesterman, Frank Raymond investment banker
Ketchum, James Roe curator
†Keune, Russell Victor architect, architectural association executive
Keyes, Arthur Hawkins, Jr. architect
Keys, John R., Jr. lawyer
Keyworth, George Albert, II physicist, consulting company executive
Khadduri, Majid international studies educator
Kidd, Charles Vincent former civil servant, educator
Kier, Porter Martin paleontologist
Kies, Kenneth J. lawyer
Kieve, Loren lawyer
†Kilborn, Peter Thurston journalist
Kilbourne, John Dwight museum and library director
Kildee, Dale Edward congressman
†Kilduff, Bonnie E. director of expositions
Kilgore, Edwin Carroll retired government official, consultant
Kilian, Michael David journalist, columnist, writer
Killefer, Campbell lawyer
Killgore, Andrew Ivy former ambassador
Killory, Diane Silberstein lawyer
Kim, Jay congressman
Kimball, Raymond Joel lawyer
Kimberly, William Essick investment banker
Kime, J. William career officer, engineer
Kimmitt, Robert Michael lawyer, banker, diplomat
†Kincaid, John political science educator, editor
Kindness, Thomas Norman former congressman, lawyer, consultant
King, James Cecil German educator
King, Larry (Larry Zeiger) broadcaster, radio personality
King, Nina Davis journalist
King, Peter T. congressman, lawyer
King, Rufus lawyer
†Kinghorn, Charles Morgan, Jr. federal agency administrator
Kingston, Jack congressman
Kinlow, Eugene federal agency executive
Kinsley, Michael E. magazine editor
Kiper, Ali Muhlis mechanical engineering educator, consultant
Kiplinger, Austin Huntington editor, publisher
Kiplinger, Knight A. journalist, publisher
†Kirby, Harmon E. ambassador
Kirby, Thomas Wesley lawyer
Kirk, Donald journalist
Kirkbride, Chalmer Gatlin chemical engineer
Kirkland, Joseph Lane (Lane Kirkland) labor union official
Kirkpatrick, Jeane Duane Jordan political scientist, government official
Kirtland, John C. lawyer
Kittrell, Steven Dan lawyer
Kittrie, Nicholas N(orbert Nehemiah) law educator, international consultant, author
Kitzmiller, William Michael government official
Klain, Ronald Alan lawyer
Klass, Philip Julian technical journalist, electrical engineer
Klawiter, Donald Casimir lawyer
Kleczka, Gerald D. congressman
Klein, Andrew Manning lawyer
Klein, Herbert C. congressman
Klein, Michael Roger lawyer, business executive
Kleinknecht, Christian Frederick Masonic official
†Klenk, Ann Shirley television production executive
Klepner, Jerry D. federal agency administrator
Klepper, Martin lawyer
†Kline, Jerry Robert government official, ecologist
†Kline, Norman Douglas federal judge
Kline, Raymond Adam professional organization executive
Kling, William economist, retired foreign service officer
Klink, Ron congressman, reporter, newscaster
†Klugh, James Richard military officer
Knapp, George M. lawyer
Knapp, James Ian Keith federal lawyer
Knapp, Richard Maitland association executive
†Knapp, Rosalind Ann lawyer
Knebel, John Albert lawyer, former government official
†Knebel, John Albert trade association executive
Knight, Athelia Wilhelmenia journalist
Knisely, Robert August government official, lawyer
Knoll, Jerry former government official
Knollenberg, Joseph (Joe Knollenberg) congressman
Knotts, Joseph B. lawyer
Kobrine, Arthur neurosurgeon
Koch, Bruce R. diplomat
Koch, George William lawyer
Koch, Kathleen Day lawyer
Koering, Marilyn Jean anatomy educator, researcher
Kohl, Herbert senator, professional sports team owner
Kohlhorst, Gail Lewis librarian
Kolbe, James Thomas congressman
Kolman, Mark Herbert lawyer
Komarek, Thomas Charles government official
Komer, Robert William government official, consultant
Kondratas, Skirma Anna policy analyst
†Konschnik, David Michael lawyer
Kopetski, Mike congressman
Koppel, Ted broadcast journalist
Kornberg, Warren Stanley science journalist
Kornblum, John Christian foreign service officer
Korner, Jules Gilmer, III federal judge
Kornheiser, Anthony I. journalist
Korologos, Tom Chris government affairs consultant, former federal official
Korth, Fred lawyer
Korth, Fritz-Alan lawyer
Korth, Penne Percy ambassador
Koskinen, John Andrew asset management executive
†Kossak, Shelley think-tank executive
Kostmayer, Peter Houston congressman
Kotler, Milton business executive
Kouts, Herbert John Cecil physicist
Kovach, Eugene George government official, consultant
Kovacs, William Lawrence lawyer
†Koven, Joan Follin Hughes marine biologist
Kraemer, Jay Roy lawyer
Kramer, Albert H. lawyer
Kramer, Kenneth Bentley federal judge, former congressman
Kramer, Kenneth Stephen lawyer
Kramer, Robert law school dean
Kramer, William David lawyer
Krash, Abe lawyer
Krasner, Robert Charles Jeffrey physician, military officer
Krasner, Wendy L. lawyer
Krasnow, Erwin Gilbert lawyer
†Kraus, Margery management consultant
†Krebs, Martha physicist, federal agency administrator
†Kreczko, Alan James lawyer
Kreidler, Mike congressman, optometrist
Kreuter, Gretchen V. college president
Kriesberg, Simeon M. lawyer
Kristol, Irving social sciences educator, editor
Kristol, William public policy activist
Kroener, William Frederick, III lawyer
Kroloff, George Michael public relations and advertising executive, management consultant
Krombein, Karl vonVorse entomologist
Kronstein, Werner J lawyer
Kropp, Arthur John public interest organization executive
†Kruesi, Frank E. federal agency administrator
Krulfeld, Ruth Marilyn anthropologist, educator
Krump, Gary Joseph lawyer
†Kruse, Dennis K. think-tank executive, career officer
Krys, Sheldon Jack foreign service officer
Kuchel, Roland Karl ambassador
Kuhn, Thomas R. trade association executive
Kunin, Madeleine May federal agency administrator, former governor
Kupperman, Robert Harris university official
Kurrelmeyer, Louis Hayner lawyer
Kurth, Walter Richard association executive
Kurtzke, John Francis, Sr. neurologist, epidemiologist
†Kusnet, David communications executive, speechwriter
†Kutscher, Ronald Earl federal government executive
Kyl, Jon congressman
†Lachance, Janice Rachel labor union executive, lawyer
Lachey, James Michael professional football player
Laden, Ben Ellis economist
Ladwig, Alan Michael space policy analyst, author
Laessig, Walter Bruce publishing executive
La Falce, John Joseph congressman, lawyer
Lahr, Jack Leroy lawyer
Laiou, Angeliki E. history educator
Laird, Melvin Robert former secretary of defense
Lake, Anthony federal official
Lake, Joseph Edward ambassador
Lalley, Frank Edward federal government official
Lamb, Robert Edward diplomat
†Lamb, Vincent P. industrial executive
Lambert, Blanche M. congresswoman
Lambert, Eugene Isaak lawyer
Lambert, Jeremiah Daniel lawyer
Lambert, Steven Charles lawyer
Lamberth, Royce C. federal judge
Lamm, Carolyn Beth lawyer
Lampl, Peggy Ann association administrator
Lancaster, H(arold) Martin congressman
Landau, Saul filmmaker, writer
Landfair, Stanley W. lawyer
Lane, Bruce Stuart lawyer
Lane, John Dennis lawyer
Lane, Mark lawyer, educator, author
Langan, John Patrick philosophy educator
Lanouette, William John writer, public policy analyst
†Lanpher, E. Gibson ambassador to Zimbabwe
Lantos, Thomas Peter congressman
LaPidus, Jules Benjamin association executive
LaPlante, John Baptiste naval officer
Laporte, Gerald Joseph Sylvestre lawyer
Laposata, Joseph Samuel army officer
Laqueur, Walter history educator
Lardner, George, Jr. journalist
LaRocco, Larry congressman
La Rocque, Gene Robert retired naval officer, government official, author
†LaRoe, Edward Terhune, III marine biologist, government official, educator
LaRouche, Lyndon H., Jr. economist
Larroca, Raymond G. lawyer
Larry, David Heath lawyer
Larsen, Richard Gary accounting firm executive
Larson, Charles Fred association executive
†Lash, Jonathan environmental law executive, consultant
Lash, Myles Perry hospital administrator
Lasko, Warren Anthony mortgage banker, economist
Lassman, Malcolm lawyer
Lastowka, James Anthony former federal agency executive, lawyer
Latham, Weldon Hurd lawyer
Latimer, Allie B. lawyer, government official
Lauber, John K. research psychologist
Laughlin, Felix B. lawyer
Laughlin, Gregory H. (Greg Laughlin) congressman
†Laughton, Katherine L. career officer
Lautenbacher, Conrad Charles, Jr. naval officer
Lautenberg, Frank R. senator
LaVelle, Avis federal administration official
Lavine, Henry Wolfe lawyer
†Law, David Hillis physician
LaWare, John Patrick banker, federal official
Lawrence, Glenn Robert federal administrative law judge
†Lawson, D. Dale public relations executive
Lawson, Richard Laverne trade association executive, retired military officer
Layton, John C. federal agency administrator
Lazarus, Arthur, Jr. retired lawyer
Lazarus, Kenneth Anthony lawyer
Lazio, Rick A. congressman, lawyer
Leach, James Albert Smith congressman
Leaf, Howard Westley retired air force officer, military official
Leahy, Patrick Joseph senator
Leary, Thomas Barrett lawyer
Le Baron, Joseph Evan diplomat
Lebow, Irwin Leon electronics engineering consultant
†LeBrecht, Thelma Jane Mossman reporter
Ledley, Robert Steven biophysicist
Lee, Chester Maurice government official
†Lee, Philip Randolph medical educator
Lee, Ronald Barry business executive
Leeds, Charles Alan publishing executive
Lefever, Ernest W. political philosopher, author, former institute president

Lehman, Richard Henry congressman
†Lehmberg, Robert Henry research physicist
Lehner, George Alexander, Jr. lawyer
Lehr, Dennis James lawyer
Lehrer, James Charles television journalist
Lehrman, Margaret McBride news executive, producer
Leibold, Arthur William, Jr. lawyer
Leibowitz, Jack Richard physicist, educator
Leigh, Monroe lawyer
†Leiter, Richard Allen law educator, law librarian
Lemer, Andrew Charles engineer, economist
†Le Mone, Archie religious organization administrator
Lenahan, Walter Clair retired foreign service officer
Lenhart, James Thomas lawyer
Lent, Norman Frederick, Jr. former congressman
LeoGrande, William Mark political science educator, writer
Leon, Donald Francis university dean, medical educator
Leon, Richard J. lawyer, former government official
†Leonard, Lawrence Edwards librarian
Leonard, Michael federal official
Leonard, Will Ernest, Jr. lawyer
Lepkowski, Wil (Wilbert Charles Lepkowski) journalist
†Lerner, Charles pension fund administrator, lawyer
Lescaze, Lee Adrien editor
Lesher, Richard Lee association executive
Leshy, John D. lawyer, legal educator
Leslie, John William public relations and advertising executive
Lessenco, Gilbert Barry lawyer
Lessin, Lawrence Stephen hematologist, oncologist, educator
Lessy, Roy Paul, Jr. lawyer
Lettow, Charles Frederick lawyer
Leubsdorf, Carl Philipp newspaper executive
Leva, Marx lawyer
Levalier, Dotian harpist
Leven, Ann Ruth arts administrator
Levey, Robert Frank newspaper columnist
Levin, Betsy lawyer, educator, university dean
Levin, Carl senator
Levin, Sander M. congressman
Levine, Henry David lawyer
Levine, Irving Raskin news commentator, author, lecturer
†Levine, Joseph Manney lawyer
†Levine, Theodore A. lawyer
Levinson, Daniel Ronald lawyer
Levinson, Lawrence Edward lawyer, corporation executive
Levitan, Laurence state senator, lawyer
†Levitas, Elliot Harris lawyer
Levitt, Arthur, Jr. securities and publishing executive, federal agency administrator
Levy, David A. congressman
Levy, David Corcos museum director
Levy, Mark Irving federal lawyer
†Levy, Michael B. federal official
†Lew, Ginger lawyer
Lewin, Ann White museum director
Lewin, George Forest former insurance company executive
Lewis, Ann Frank political analyst, commentator, columnist
Lewis, Charles Joseph journalist
Lewis, David Eldridge airport development executive
Lewis, David John lawyer
Lewis, Douglas art historian
Lewis, E. Grey lawyer
Lewis, Emanuel Raymond historian, librarian, psychologist
Lewis, Gregory Scott lawyer
Lewis, Jerry congressman
Lewis, John congressman
Lewis, Jordan David management consultant, author, international speaker, educator
Lewis, Thomas F., Jr. (Tom Lewis) congressman
Lewis, William Henry, Jr. lawyer
Lewis, William Walker management consultant
Liberman, Lee Sarah lawyer, educator
Libin, Jerome B. lawyer
Lichtenstein, Elissa Charlene legal association executive
Liebenson, Herbert economist, trade association executive
Lieberman, Joseph I. senator
Lieberman, Myron educational consulting firm executive
Liebman, Ronald Stanley lawyer
Liebowitz, Harold aeronautical engineering educator, dean emeritus
Liederman, David Samuel child welfare administrator
Lightfoot, James Ross congressman
Lighthizer, Robert E. lawyer
Lightner, Candace Lynne advocate, government relations consultant
Lilienfield, Lawrence Spencer physiology and biophysics educator
Lilienthal, Alfred M(orton) author, editor
Lillard, John Franklin, III lawyer
Lilley, James Roderick foreign relations expert, former federal government official
Lilley, William, III business consultant
Lilly, William Eldridge government official
Limpert, John Arthur editor
Lin, William Wen-Rong economist
Linder, John E congressman, dentist
†Lindner, Eric John parking-hospitality-hotel executive, lawyer
†Lindsey, Alfred Walter federal agency official, environmental engineer
Lindsey, Lawrence Benjamin economist
Ling, Suilin management consultant
Linowes, Harry Michael accountant
Linowitz, Sol Myron lawyer
Lipinski, William Oliver congressman
†Lippman, Marc Estes pharmacology educator
Lipstein, Robert A. lawyer
Liska, George political science educator, author
Lister, Harry Joseph financial company executive, consultant
Litan, Robert Eli lawyer, economist
Litke, Arthur Ludwig business executive
Litman, Harry Peter lawyer, educator
Litt, Nahum federal judge
Littig, Lawrence William psychologist, educator
Little, Elbert Luther, Jr. botanist, dendrologist
Little, John William plastic surgeon, educator
†Littlefield, Nick lawyer
Lively, Carol A. association executive
Livingston, Robert Linlithgow, Jr. (Bob Livingston, Jr.) congressman
Lloyd, Marilyn congresswoman
Lloyd, Timothy Charles folklorist
†Lockhart, Robert Earl lawyer
Loeffler, Robert Hugh lawyer
Loevinger, Lee lawyer
Loftus, Stephen Francis naval officer
Logue-Kinder, Joan public relations executive
Lohmiller, John M. (Chip Lohmiller) professional football player
Loker, Elizabeth St. John newspaper executive
Long, Charles Thomas lawyer
Long, Jill Lynette congresswoman
†Longanecker, David A. federal official
Longstreet, Victor Mendell government official
†Lopatin, Alan G. lawyer
Lorber, Lawrence Zel lawyer
Lord, Jerome Edmund federal education administrator, writer
Lord, Winston diplomat
Lorenz, John George librarian, consultant
Lorsung, Thomas Nicholas director, editor-in-chief
Lott, Trent senator
Lourie, Alan David federal judge
Love, Margaret Colgate lawyer
Lovejoy, Thomas Eugene tropical and conservation biologist, association executive
Lovell, Malcolm Read, Jr. public policy institute executive, educator, former government official, former trade association executive
Low, Stephen foundation executive, educator, former diplomat
Lowe, Felix Caleb publishing executive
Lowe, Harry museum director
Lowe, Mary Frances federal government official
Lowe, Randall Brian lawyer
Lowenstein, James Gordon former diplomat, international consultant
Lowey, Nita M. congresswoman
Loy, Frank Ernest foundation executive
Lubar, Jeffrey Stuart journalist
Lublin, Edward Louis lawyer
†Lucas, Frank D. congressman
Lucas, George Ramsdell, Jr. philosophy educator
Lucas, James Walter federal government official
†Lucassen, Sigurd labor union administrator
Lucchino, Lawrence lawyer, sports executive
Luce, Gregory M. lawyer
Ludwig, Eugene Allan U.S. comptroller of the currency, lawyer
Luffsey, Walter Stith business executive
Lugar, Richard Green senator
Luikart, Fordyce Whitney management consultant
Lund, Wendell Luther lawyer
Lurton, Horace VanDeventer brokerage house executive
Lutley, John H. precious metals company executive
Luttwak, Edward Nicolae political science educator, writer, consultant
†Lutz, Theodore newspaper publishing executive
Lutzker, Arnold Paul lawyer
Lybecker, Martin Earl lawyer
Lyman, Princeton Nathan foreign service officer
Lynam, Terence Joseph lawyer
Lynch, Charles Theodore, Sr. materials science engineering researcher, administrator, educator
Lynch, Thomas C. career military officer
Lynn, James Thomas investment banker, insurance company executive, government executive, lawyer
†Lynn, Larry engineering executive
Lyon, Edwin Leon lawyer
Lyons, Dennis Gerald lawyer
Lyons, Ellis lawyer
Lyons, James Robert federal official
Maas, Joe (Melvin Joseph Maas) federal agency administrator
MacBeth, Angus lawyer
Macdonald, David Robert lawyer
MacDonald, John Thomas educational administrator
MacDonald, William Lloyd architectural historian
Machtley, Ronald Keith congressman, lawyer
MacIntyre, A(lfonso) Everette lawyer
Mack, Connie, III (Cornelius Mack) senator
Mack, Julia Cooper appellate judge
Mack, Raymond Francis newspaper executive
Mackall, Laidler Bowie lawyer
MacKaye, William Ross writer
Macke, Richard Chester naval officer
Mackiewicz, Edward Robert lawyer
MacKinnon, George E. federal judge
MacLaury, Bruce King research institution executive
MacLean, Paul Donald government medical research institute official
Macleay, Donald lawyer
Mac Nelly, Jeffrey Kenneth cartoonist
Macomber, John D. industrialist
Macrory, Patrick Francis John lawyer
†Madden, Joseph Michael microbiologist
Madden, Murdaugh Stuart lawyer
Madden, William J., Jr. lawyer
†Maddock, Jerome Torrence information services specialist
Maddox, David M. career military officer
Madigan, Edward R. former secretary of agriculture
Madigan, Kimberly A. mediator, lawyer
Madigan, Michael J. lawyer
Maechling, Charles, Jr. lawyer, educator, writer
Magaw, John W. federal law enforcement official
Magazine, Alan Harrison association executive, consultant
†Magaziner, Ira federal official
Magielnicki, Robert L. lawyer
Magrath, C. Peter educational association executive
Mahan, Clarence government official, writer
Maher, Patrick Joseph utility company executive
Maisel, Herbert computer science educator
Maisto, John F. ambassador
Maiwurm, James John lawyer
Majors, Richard George psychology educator
Makris, Andreas composer
Malarkey, Martin Francis, Jr. cable television executive
Malashevich, Bruce Peter consulting executive
†Maldon, Alfonso federal official, retired military officer
Malek, Frederic Vincent finance executive
Mallory, Charles King, III lawyer
Malmgren, Harald Bernard economist
Malone, Julia Louise news reporter, White House correspondent
Maloney, Carolyn Bosher congresswoman
†Malott, Frank Stephen foreign service officer
Malott, John Raymond foreign service officer
Manatos, Andrew Emanuel policy consultant, former government official
†Manatt, Charles T. lawyer
Manbeck, Harry Frederick, Jr. lawyer
Mancher, Rhoda Ross strategic planner
Mandel, H(arold) George pharmacologist
Mandula, Jeffrey Ellis physicist
Mankiewicz, Frank F. journalist
Mankin, Hart Tiller federal judge
Manley, Audrey Forbes physician
Manley, William Tanner economist
Manly, Marc Edward lawyer
Mann, David Scott congressman, lawyer
Mann, Marion physician, educator
Mann, Oscar physician, internist, educator
Mann, Thomas Edward political scientist
Manning, George Taylor lawyer
Mansfield, Edward Patrick, Jr. advertising executive
Mansfield, Michael Joseph former ambassador, former senator
Manson, Joseph Lloyd, III lawyer
Manthei, Richard Dale lawyer, health care company executive
Manton, Thomas Joseph congressman
Manvel, Allen Dailey fiscal economist
Manzullo, Donald A congressman, lawyer
Maraniss, David reporter
Marans, J. Eugene lawyer
Marcum, Deanna Bowling library administrator
Marcuss, Stanley Joseph lawyer
†Marfiak, Thomas Fletcher career officer
Margeton, Stephen George law librarian
Margolies-Mezvinsky, Marjorie congresswoman
Margolis, Daniel Herbert lawyer
Margolis, Eugene lawyer, government official
†Margolis, James David political consulting and advertising executive
Margolis, Lawrence Stanley federal judge
Marinaccio, Charles Lindbergh lawyer
Markey, Edward John congressman
Markoski, Joseph Peter lawyer
Marks, Andrew H. lawyer
Marks, Herbert Edward lawyer
Marks, Leonard Harold lawyer
Marks, Richard Daniel lawyer
Marlowe, Howard David lobbyist, public affairs company executive
Marquez, Joaquin Alfredo lawyer
†Marquis, Christopher Holliday newspaper correspondent
Marriott, Alice Sheets (Mrs. John Willard Marriott) restaurant chain executive
Marriott, John Willard, Jr. hotel and food service chain executive
Marriott, Richard Edwin hotel and contract services executive
Marsh, Caryl Amsterdam curator, psychologist
Marsh, Quinton Neely banker
Marshall, C. Travis manufacturing executive, government relations specialist
Martin, David Briton Hadden, Jr. lawyer
Martin, Guy lawyer
Martin, Jerry L. federal agency administrator
Martin, John Joseph journalist
Martin, Keith lawyer
Martin, Susan Katherine librarian
Martin, Thomas Stephen lawyer
Martinez, Matthew Gilbert congressman
Martyak, Joseph J. lawyer
Marumoto, William Hideo management consultant
Marvin, Douglas Raymond lawyer
Marzetti, Loretta A. government agency executive, policy analyst
Marzulla, Roger Joseph lawyer
Masi, Dale A. research company executive, social work educator
Mason, Brian Harold geologist, curator
Masten, Charles C. federal agency administrator
Masters, Edward E. association executive, former foreign service officer
Matalin, Mary political consultant
Mater, Gene P. communications consultant
†Mathews, Anne Jones library director, educator
Mathews, Harlan senator
Mathews, Jessica Tuchman policy researcher, former government official
Mathias, Charles McCurdy lawyer, former senator
Mathias, Edward Joseph merchant banker
Mathias, Joseph Simon metallurgical engineer
†Mathis, William Walter career officer
Matsui, Robert Takeo congressman
†Mattar, Philip institute director, editor
Maudlin, Robert V. economics and government affairs consultant
Maxa, Rudolph Joseph, Jr. journalist
Maxwell, David E. academic administrator, educator
Maxwell, David Ogden government official, financial executive
May, Edgar former state legislator, nonprofit administrator
May, Gregory Evers lawyer
May, Randolph Joseph lawyer
May, Richard Edward lawyer
May, Stephen writer, former government official
May, Sterling Randolph health association executive
May, Timothy James lawyer
Mayer, Haldane Robert federal judge
†Mayer, Walter Georg physics educator
Mayers, Daniel Kriegsman lawyer
Mayfield, Richard Heverin lawyer
Maynes, Charles William editor, former government official
Mayo, George Washington, Jr. lawyer
†Mays, Janice Ann federal agency administrator, lawyer
Mazo, Mark Elliott lawyer
Mazzaferri, Katherine Aquino lawyer, bar association executive
Mazzoli, Romano Louis congressman
Mc Afee, Marilyn ambassador
Mc Afee, William government official
McAllister, William Howard, III newspaper reporter, columnist
McArdle, Paul Francis judge
McAvoy, John Joseph lawyer
†Mc Beath, William Henninger physician, association executive
McBride, Jonathan Evans executive search company executive
McBride, Michael Flynn lawyer
Mc Bride, Thomas Frederick lawyer, former university dean, government official
McCabe, Edward Aeneas lawyer, financial services corporation executive
McCahill, Barry Winslow federal public affairs official
McCain, John Sidney, III senator
McCallie, Marshall F. ambassador
Mc Candless, Alfred A. (Al Mc Candless) congressman
McCarthy, Abigail Quigley writer, columnist, educator
Mc Carthy, Charles Joseph lawyer, former government official
Mc Carthy, David Jerome, Jr. legal educator
†McCarthy, John B. veterinarian, veterinary association executive
McCarthy, John Thomas diplomat
Mc Carty, Robert Lee lawyer
McClain, Charles William, Jr. (Bill McClain) army officer
McClintic, Howard Gresson foundation executive
McCloskey, Frank congressman
McCloskey, J(ohn) Michael association executive
McCobb, John Bradford, Jr. lawyer
McCollam, William, Jr. utility company executive
Mc Collum, Ira William, Jr. (Bill Mc Collum) congressman
McConnell, Addison Mitchell, Jr. (Mitch McConnell, Jr.) senator, lawyer
McConnell, James Michael federal official
McConnell, John William, Jr. lawyer
†McCormack, Richard Thomas Fox government official
McCormick, Robert Junior government official
McCoy, Neal S. lawyer
McCrery, James (Jim McCrery) congressman
McCurdy, David Keith (Dave) congressman, lawyer
Mc Curdy, Patrick Pierre editor, consultant
McCurry, Michael Demaree government spokesman, press secretary
McDade, Joseph Michael congressman
†McDaniel, John Perry health care company executive
McDavid, J. Gary lawyer
McDavid, Janet Louise lawyer
Mc Dermott, Albert Leo lawyer
McDermott, Edward Aloysious lawyer
McDermott, James A. congressman, psychiatrist
McDermott, Robert Francis, Jr. lawyer
McDonald, Gail Clements government official
Mc Donald, John Warlick diplomat, global strategist
†McDowell, Charles R. columnist, news analyst
†McDuffie, Harvey Thomas, Jr. architect
McElroy, Frederick William economics educator, consultant
McElveen, Junius Carlisle, Jr. lawyer
†McEntee, Gerald W. labor union official
Mc Fee, Thomas Stuart government agency administrator
McGarry, J. Michael, III lawyer
†McGarry, John Warren government official
Mc Gaughan, Alexander Stanley architect
McGhee, George Crews petroleum producer, former government official
Mc Giffert, David Eliot lawyer, former government official
McGinley, Ronald James entomologist, researcher
McGinnies, Elliott Morse psychologist, educator
Mc Ginnis, James Michael physician
McGinty, Michael Dennis air force officer
McGlone, Denise Marie financial company executive
Mc Glothlin, James Harrison lawyer
McGlotten, Robert Miller labor union official
McGough, Duane Theodore economist, government official
McGovern, Michael Barbot lawyer
McGrath, Kathryn Bradley lawyer
McGrew, Thomas James lawyer
†Mc Grory, Mary columnist
McGrory, Mary Kathleen academic administrator
†McGue, Christie federal official
McGuire, Patricia A. lawyer, academic administrator
McGuire, Roger Alan foreign service officer
McHenry, Donald F. former diplomat, international affairs consultant, educator
McHugh, James Lenahan, Jr. lawyer
McHugh, John Michael congressman, former state senator
McInnis, Scott Steve congressman, lawyer
Mc Kay, Emily Gantz civil rights professional
McKee, Margaret Jean federal agency executive
McKee, William St. John lawyer
McKeon, Howard P. (Buck McKeon) congressman, mayor
McKinless, Kathy Jean accountant
McKinley, Brunson diplomat
McKinney, Cynthia Ann congresswoman
McKinney, James Clayton electronics executive, electrical engineer
McLarty, Thomas F., III (Mack McLarty) chief of staff
McLaughlin, John Joseph broadcast executive, television producer, journalist
†McLaughlin, Maureen A. federal agency administrator
Mc Lean, George Francis philosophy of religion educator, clergyman
McLellan, Joseph Duncan critic, journalist
McLennan, Barbara Nancy trade association executive, lawyer
McLucas, William Robert federal agency director
McMahon, Joseph Einar lawyer, consultant
†McMichael, Guy H., III federal official
McMillan, J(ohn) Alex(ander), III congressman
McMillen, (Charles) Thomas federal official
McMiller, Anita Williams army officer, transportation professional, educator
Mc Nallen, James Berl marketing executive
Mc Namara, Robert Strange corporate director
†McNamara, Thomas Edmund diplomat
McNamee, Sister Catherine educational association executive
McNeill, John Henderson government official, lawyer
McNicol, David Leon federal official
McNulty, Michael Robert congressman
McNulty, Robert Holmes civic association executive
McPeak, Merrill Anthony air force officer
Mc Phee, Henry Roemer lawyer
Mc Pherson, Harry Cummings, Jr. lawyer
McSteen, Martha Abernathy organization executive
Mead, David Edmund economist
Mead, Gilbert D(unbar) geophysicist, lawyer
Means, Marianne political columnist
Means, Thomas Cornell lawyer
Mears, Gary H. career military officer
Mears, Walter Robert journalist
Medalie, Richard James lawyer
Mederos, Carolina Luisa transportation policy consultant
Meehan, Martin Thomas congressman, lawyer
Meek, Carrie P. congresswoman
Megan, Thomas Ignatius judge
Meggers, Betty J(ane) anthropologist
Meijer, Paul Herman Ernst educator, physicist
Meikle, Philip G. government agency executive
†Meissner, Doris M. federal commissioner
Melamed, Arthur Douglas lawyer
†Melendez, Sara E. academic administrator
†Melendy, David Russell broadcast journalist
Mellon, Paul retired art gallery executive

Mellor, John Williams economist, policy consultant firm executive
Meloy, Sybil Piskur lawyer
Melton, Augustus Allen, Jr. airport executive
Meltzer, Steven Lee lawyer
Mencher, Bruce Stephan judge
Menendez, Robert congressman, lawyer
Merow, James F. federal judge
Merrill, Philip publisher
†Merry, Robert William publishing executive
Meserve, Richard Andrew lawyer
Messner, Howard Myron professional association executive
Meszar, Frank publishing executive, former army officer
Metz, Craig Huseman legislative staff
Metz, Douglas Wilber association executive, lawyer
Metzenbaum, Howard Morton senator
†Meurlin, Keith W. airport terminal executive
Meyer, Alden Merrill environmental association executive
Meyer, Armin Henry retired diplomat, author, educator
Meyer, Dennis Irwin lawyer
Meyer, Lawrence George lawyer
†Meyer, Lawrence Robert journalist
Meyers, Jan congresswoman
Meyers, Sheldon government official
Meyers, Tedson Jay lawyer
Meyers, Wayne Marvin microbiologist
Meyerson, Adam magazine editor, foundation executive
Mfume, Kweisi congressman
†Mica, Daniel A. congressman
Michaelson, Martin lawyer
Michel, James H. ambassador, lawyer
Michel, Paul Redmond federal judge
Michel, Robert Henry congressman
Michelson, Edward J. journalist
Mickey, Paul F(ogle), Jr. lawyer
Micozzi, Marc Stephen museum director, physician, educator
†Mikel, Sarah Ann librarian
†Miklaszewski, James Alan television news correspondent
Mikva, Abner Joseph federal judge
Milam, William Bryant diplomat, economist
Miles, Ellen Gross art historian, museum curator
Millar, James Robert economist, educator, university official
Miller, Andrew Pickens lawyer
Miller, Carroll Lee Liverpool educational researcher
Miller, Dan congressman
Miller, George congressman
Miller, G(eorge) William merchant banker, business executive
Miller, H. Todd lawyer
Miller, Harry Charles, Jr. physician, urologist, educator
Miller, Herbert John, Jr. lawyer
Miller, Hope Ridings author
Miller, Iris Ann landscape architectural consultant, educator
Miller, Jack Richard federal judge
Miller, James Clifford, III economist
Miller, Jeanne-Marie Anderson (Mrs. Nathan J. Miller) English educator, academic administrator
Miller, John Francis association executive, social scientist
Miller, Kenneth Gregory air force officer
Miller, Lawrence A. lawyer
Miller, Marshall Lee lawyer
Miller, Russell Loyd, Jr. physician, educator, dean
Miller, Warren Lloyd lawyer
Miller, William Lawrence government official
Millian, Kenneth Young public policy consultant
Millon, Henry Armand fine arts educator, architectural historian
†Milstein, Elliott Steven legal educator, academic administrator
Minarik, Joseph John economist, researcher
Mineta, Norman Yoshio congressman
Minge, David congressman, lawyer, law educator
Mink, Patsy Takemoto congresswoman
†Mintz, Richard I. federal official
Mintz, Seymour Stanley lawyer
Mirabelli, Mario V. lawyer
†Miranowski, John Alfred agricultural economist
Mitchell, Andrea journalist
Mitchell, George John senator, lawyer
Mitchell, Graham Richard government engineering executive
†Mitchell, Louis Livingston consortium executive
Mitchell, Roy Shaw lawyer
†Mittermeier, Russell Alan conservation executive, educator
Mizroch, John F. lawyer
Mlay, Marian government official
Moakley, John Joseph congressman
Moates, G. Paul lawyer
Mobbs, Michael Hall lawyer
Mode, Paul J., Jr. lawyer
Moe, Richard Palmer lawyer
Moffett, Charles Simonton museum director, curator, writer
Mohler, Brian Jeffery diplomat
Moler, Elizabeth Anne federal agency administrator, lawyer
Molinari, Susan K. congresswoman
Molineaux, Charles Borromeo lawyer, arbitrator
Mollohan, Alan B. congressman, lawyer
Monroe, Robert Rawson engineering and construction executive
Montelongo, Michael career officer
Montgomery, George Cranwell lawyer, former ambassador
Montgomery, G(eorge) Franklin electrical engineer, consultant
Montgomery, Gillespie V. (Sonny Montgomery) congressman
Mooney, Marilyn lawyer
Moore, Arthur Cotton architect
Moore, Bob Stahly communications executive
†Moore, Jerry religious organization administrator
Moore, John Arthur toxicologist, health science company executive
Moore, Jonathan diplomat, policy analyst, university administrator
Moore, Richard Anthony diplomat, lawyer
†Moore, Richard Thomas federal government administrator
Moore, Robert Henry insurance company executive
Moore, Robert Madison food industry executive, lawyer
Moorer, Thomas Hinman retired naval officer
Moorhead, Carlos J. congressman
Moos, Eugene federal agency administrator
Moose, George E. government official
†Moose, Richard M. federal official
Moran, James Patrick congressman, stockbroker
Morehouse, David Frank geologist
Morella, Constance Albanese congresswoman
Morgan, John Davis government official
Moring, John Frederick lawyer
Moritsugu, Kenneth Paul physician, government official
Morris, Daniel Kearns journalist
Morris, Frank Charles, Jr. lawyer, educator
Morris, William lawyer
Morse, Richard McGee historian
Moscato, Anthony Charles federal official
Moseley-Braun, Carol senator
Mosemann, Lloyd Kenneth, II government official
Moser, Donald Bruce magazine editor
Moses, Alfred Henry lawyer
Mosettig, Michael David television producer, writer
Mossinghoff, Gerald Joseph lawyer, association executive
Mostoff, Allan Samuel lawyer, consultant
Mott, William Chamberlain lawyer, retired naval officer
Mowat, Barbara Adams Shakespearian scholar
Moynihan, Daniel Patrick senator, educator
Mtewa, Mekki foundation administrator
Muckenfuss, Cantwell Faulkner, III lawyer
†Mueller, Richard Walter foreign service officer
Mueller, Robert Swan, III lawyer, former federal official
Mueller, Ronald Raymond public relations executive
Muir, J. Dapray lawyer
Muller, Scott William lawyer
Mulligan, Robert J. retail store executive, accountant
Mulvihill, James Edward periodontist, university administrator, educator, health care executive
Mundy, Carl Epting, Jr. commandant of the marine corps
Munnell, Alicia Haydock economist
Munsey, Rodney Roundy lawyer
†Munson, Richard congressional coalition policy analyst
Muntzing, L(ewis) Manning lawyer
Murchison, David Claudius lawyer
Murkowski, Frank Hughes senator
Murphy, Andrew Phillip, Jr. lawyer
Murphy, Austin John congressman
Murphy, Betty Jane Southard (Mrs. Cornelius F. Murphy) lawyer
Murphy, Caryle Marie foreign correspondent
Murphy, Gerald government official
Murphy, James Jackson actuary, association executive
Murphy, James Paul lawyer
Murphy, John Condron, Jr. lawyer
†Murphy, Kenneth Ray non-governmental organization executive
†Murphy, Patrick Vincent foundation executive
Murphy, Reg publishing executive
Murphy, Robert Earl scientist, government agency administrator
Murphy, Stephen P. lawyer
†Murphy, Terence Roche lawyer
†Murray, Christopher Charles, III architect
Murray, Fred F. lawyer
Murray, James Joseph, III association executive
Murray, John Einar lawyer, retired army officer, federal official
Murray, Patty senator
Murray, Robert Fulton, Jr. physician
Murry, Harold David, Jr. lawyer
Murtha, John Patrick congressman
Myers, Dee Dee (Margaret Jane Myers) press secretary
Myers, James R. lawyer
Myers, John Thomas congressman
Myers, Robert Manson English educator, author
Myers, Samuel Lloyd education association executive
†Nace, Barry John lawyer
Nader, Ralph consumer advocate, lawyer, author
Nadler, Jerrold Lewis congressman, lawyer
Naifeh, Steven Woodward writer
Napier, John Light lawyer
Nash, Bernard Elbert association executive
Nash, Robert R. (Bob Nash) under-secretary agriculture rural and small development
Nason, Charles Tuckey financial services executive
Natalie, Ronald Bruce lawyer
†Natter, Robert, J. federal official, military career officer
†Naughton, Paul Francis financial executive
†Naylor, Brian news correspondent
Neal, Darwina Lee government official
Neal, Richard Edmund congressman, former mayor
Neal, Stephen Lybrook congressman
Nebeker, Frank Quill federal judge
Nef, Evelyn Stefansson psychotherapist, author, editor, specialist polar regions
Nehmer, Stanley economics consultant
†Neighmond, Patricia reporter
Neill, Denis Michael government relations consulting executive
Neimark, Sheridan lawyer
Nelson, Alan Ray internist, medical assocation executive
Nelson, Charles Edward foundation/government executive
Nelson, Charles J. university administrator, international consultant, diplomat, consultant
Nelson, Gaylord Anton former senator, association executive
Nelson, John Howard (Jack Howard Nelson) journalist
Nelson, Lars-Erik newspaperman
Nelson, Richard Copeland hotel executive
Nelson, Robert Louis lawyer
Nemeroff, Michael Alan lawyer
Ness, Andrew David lawyer
Nethery, John Jay government official
Nettesheim, Christine Cook federal judge
†Neu, James Edward military officer
Neuman, Robert Henry lawyer
Neviaser, Robert Jon orthopedic surgeon, educator
Newhouse, Alan Russell federal government executive
Newman, Don Melvin federal agency administrator
Newman, Frank Neil federal official
Newman, Monroe retired economist, educator
Newman, Pauline federal judge
Newman, William Bernard, Jr. railroad executive
Newquist, Don federal agency administrator
Newton, Virginia archivist, historian
Nicholas, Robert B. lawyer
Nichols, Henry Eliot lawyer, savings and loan executive
Nichols, Kenneth David consulting engineer
Nicholson, Richard Selindh educational association administrator
Nickles, Donald (Don Nickles) senator
Nies, Helen Wilson federal judge
Nims, Arthur Lee, III federal judge
Nisbet, Robert A. historian, sociologist
Niskanen, William Arthur, Jr. economist
Nitze, William Albert lawyer, government consultant
†Noble, Ronald K. federal official
Nolan, James Lawry lawyer
Nolan, Jean federal agency official
Nolan, John Edward, Jr. lawyer
Noonberg, Lewis Allan lawyer
Norberg, Charles Robert lawyer
Norby, Ronald Brandon nurse executive
Norcross, David Frank Armstrong lawyer
Norcross, Marvin Augustus veterinarian, government agency official
†Nordhaus, Robert Riggs lawyer
Nordquist, Myron Harry lawyer
Norland, Donald Richard retired foreign service officer
Norman, William Stanley transportation company executive
†Norry, Patricia Goodwin government executive
Northrop, Carl Wooden lawyer
Norton, Eleanor Holmes lawyer, educator
Norton, Floyd Ligon, IV lawyer
Norton, Gerald Patrick lawyer
Norton, James J. union official
Norwood, Janet Lippe economist
Noshpitz, Joseph Dove child and adolescent psychiatrist
Novak, Michael (John) religion educator, author, editor
Novak, Robert David Sanders newspaper columnist, television commentator
Nover, Naomi journalist, editor, author
Nunn, Samuel (Sam Nunn) senator
Nussle, James Allen congressman
Nutter, Franklin Winston lawyer
†Oakley, Robert Louis law librarian, educator
Obee, Kent foreign service officer
Oberdorfer, Louis F. federal judge
O'Berry, Carl Gerald air force officer, electrical engineer
Oberstar, James L. congressman
Obey, David Ross congressman
O'Brien, Francis Anthony lawyer
O'Brien, Lawrence Francis, III lawyer
O'Brien, Timothy Andrew writer, journalist, lawyer
O'Brien, William James, II lawyer
†O'Bryon, James Fredrick defense executive
†Ochs, Walter J. civil engineer, drainage adviser
O'Connell, Daniel Craig psychology educator
O'Connor, Charles Aloysius, III lawyer
O'Connor, Charles P. lawyer
O'Connor, John Jay, III lawyer
O'Connor, Sandra Day U.S. supreme court justice
O'Connor, Tom corporate executive, management consultant
O'Day, Paul Thomas trade association executive
Odle, Robert Charles, Jr. lawyer
O'Doherty, Brian playwright, filmmaker
Odom, William Eldridge army officer, educator
O'Donnell, Terrence lawyer
O'Donovan, Leo Jeremiah university president, theologian, priest
†Oehme, Wolfgang Walter landscape architect
Oehrlein, Mary Lou architect
Oertel, Goetz K. H. physicist, professional association administrator
Ogilvie, Donald Gordon bankers association executive
Oh, John Kie-Chiang political science educator, university official
†O'Hagan, Malcolm Edward trade association administrator
O'Hara, James Thomas lawyer
O'Hare, Patrick K. lawyer
O'Hern, Elizabeth Moot microbiologist, writer
†Okay, John Louis information scientist
O'Keefe, William Francis association executive
†Olcott, John Whiting aviation executive
O'Leary, Hazel R. U.S. secretary of energy, former power company executive, lawyer
Oliver, Daniel foundation fellow, lawyer
†Oliver, David Rogers, Jr. naval officer
Oliver, Joseph McDonald, Jr. lawyer
Oliver, William Albert, Jr. paleontologist
Olmer, Lionel Herbert lawyer
Olmstead, Cecil Jay lawyer
Olson, Charles Eric economist
Olson, John Frederick lawyer
Olson, Theodore Bevry lawyer, government official
Olson, Walter Justus, Jr. management consultant
Olver, John Walter congressman
Ondeck, Thomas Paul lawyer
O'Neil, Joseph Francis association executive
O'Neill, Brian Dennis lawyer
O'Neill, John H., Jr. lawyer
O'Neill, William Patrick lawyer
Onek, Joseph Nathan lawyer
Ongman, John Will lawyer
†Onto, John think-tank executive
Ooms, Van Doorn economist
Oppel, Richard Alfred newspaper executive
Oppenheimer, Franz Martin lawyer
Oppenheimer, Jerry L. lawyer
Ordway, Frederick Ira, III government official, educator, consultant, researcher, author
Ornstein, Norman Jay political scientist
O'Rourke, C. Larry lawyer
†Orr, J. Scott newspaper correspondent
Ortiz, Solomon P. congressman
Orton, William H (Bill Orton) congressman, lawyer
Osnos, David Marvin lawyer
Ostar, Allan William higher education consultant
O'Sullivan, Lynda Troutman lawyer
O'Sullivan, Paul Kevin business executive, management and instructional systems consultant
Oswald, Robert Bernard science administrator, nuclear engineer
Oswald, Rudolph A. economist
O'Toole, Francis J. lawyer
†O'Toole, Tara J. federal official
Overbeck, Gene Edward retired airline executive, lawyer
Overholt, Hugh Robert lawyer, retired army officer
Overman, Dean Lee lawyer, investor, author
Oweiss, Ibrahim Mohamed economist, educator
Owen, Henry former ambassador, consultant
Owen, Roberts Bishop lawyer
Owens, Major Robert Odell congressman
Oxley, Michael Garver congressman
Oxman, Stephen A. federal official
Oyler, Gregory Kenneth lawyer
†Pace, Simone J. insurance executive
Packard, George Randolph university dean, journalist, educator
Packard, Ronald congressman
Packwood, Bob senator
Page, Harry Robert business administration educator
Page, Marcus William federal official
Page, Robert Wesley engineering and construction company executive, federal official
Page, Rodney Fred lawyer
Paige, Hilliard Wegner corporate director, consultant
Painter, William Hall law educator
Palast, Geri D. federal agency administrator
Pallone, Frank, Jr. congressman
Palmer, Alan Kenneth lawyer
Palmer, David Brent lawyer
Palmer, Ronald DeWayne Faisal retired diplomat, educator, consultant
†Palmer, Steven O. federal official
Palmeter, N. David lawyer
†Palumbo, Benjamin Lewis public affairs consulting company executive
Panetta, Leon Edward federal official, former congressman
†Pang, Frederick F. Y. federal official
Paoletta, Mark R. A. federal lawyer
Paper, Lewis J. lawyer
Papkin, Robert David lawyer
Paquin, Paul Peter mortgage finance executive
Parker, Edna G. federal judge
Parker, Gerald William physician, medical center administrator, retired air force officer
Parker, Michael (Mike Parker) congressman
Parker, Robert Allan Ridley astronaut
Parks, James Thomas financial company executive
Parr, Carolyn Miller federal judge
Parris, Robert composer
Parrish, Alvin Edward former university dean, medical educator
Parrish, Edgar Lee financial services executive
Parrott, Robert Harold pediatrician, educator
Parshall, Gerald journalist
Pasmanick, Kenneth bassoonist
Pastor, Ed congressman
Patchan, Joseph lawyer
Pate, Joan Seitz federal judge
Pate, Michael Lynn lawyer
†Patron, June Eileen federal agency administrator
Patten, Thomas Louis lawyer
Patton, Thomas Earl lawyer
Paul, Robert Dennis lawyer
Paul, William McCann lawyer
†Paulsen, Thomas Dean naval officer
Paulson, Stanley Fay association executive
Paup, Michael Lee lawyer
Pawlson, Leonard Gregory physician
Paxon, L. William congressman
†Paxson, Richard newspaper editor
Payne, Donald M. congressman
Payne, Kenneth Eugene lawyer
Payne, Lewis Franklin, Jr. (L.F. Payne) congressman
Pearlman, Ronald Alan lawyer
Pearse, Warren Harland association executive, obstetrician and gynecologist
Pearson, Roger organization executive
Peavy, Robert A. lawyer
†Peck, Robert Stephen lawyer, educator
Pedersen, Norman A. lawyer
Pedersen, Wesley Niels public relations and public affairs executive
Pedersen, William Francis, Jr. lawyer
Peele, Roger hospital administrator
Pehrson, Gordon Oscar, Jr. lawyer
Peirce, Neal R. journalist
Pell, Claiborne senator
Pellegrino, Edmund Daniel physician, educator, former university president
Pelletreau, Robert Halsey diplomat
Pelosi, Nancy congresswoman
Peña, Federico Fabian U.S. secretary of transportation, lawyer
Pendergast, William Ross lawyer
Pendleton, Mary Catherine foreign service officer
Penn, John Garrett federal judge
Penner, Rudolph Gerhard economist, educator
Penniman, W. David information scientist, foundation executive
Penny, Timothy Joseph congressman
Perella, Susanne Brennan librarian
Perez, Lillian non-profit association administrator
†Perkins, Edward J. diplomat
Perkins, Jack Edwin lawyer
Perkins, Samuel Thomas lawyer
Perle, Richard Norman government official
Perlik, William R. lawyer
Perlin, Seymour psychiatrist, educator
Perlman, Matthew Saul lawyer
Perlmutter, Jack artist, lithographer
Perros, Theodore Peter chemist, educator
Perry, B(illy) Dwight lawyer
Perry, George Lewis research economist, consultant
Perry, Seymour Monroe physician
Perry, William James mathematical scientist, government official
Persavich, Warren Dale diversified manufacturing company executive
Peter, Frances Marchbank author, editor, research agency administrator, writer, strategic planner
†Peterman, John L. economist
†Peters, Charles Given, Jr. editor
Peters, Lauralee Milberg diplomat
†Petersen, Richard Herman government executive, aeronautical engineer
Peterson, Charles Hayes trading company executive
Peterson, Collin C. congressman
Peterson, Douglas (Pete Peterson) congressman
Peterson, Esther consumer advocate
†Peterson, Malcolm Lee medical educator, administrator
†Peterson, Trudy Huskamp national archivist
Peterson, William Herbert economist
Petrash, Jeffrey Michael lawyer
Petri, Thomas Evert congressman
Pettengill, Harry Junior federal agency administrator
Pettit, John Whitney lawyer
Pettit, William Thomas broadcasting journalist
Pfeiffer, Leonard, IV executive recruiter, consultant
Pfeiffer, Margaret Kolodny lawyer
Pfeiffer, Steven Bernard lawyer
Phemister, Thomas Alexander lawyer
Philbin, Edward James federal agency commissioner, military officer, legal educator, engineer
Philion, Norman Joseph, III lawyer
Philips, Malcolm H. lawyer
Phillips, Carter Glasgow lawyer
Phillips, Cyrus Eastman, IV lawyer
Phillips, Karen Borlaug economist
Phillips, Laughlin museum president, former magazine editor
Phillips, Susan Meredith financial economist, former university administrator

Phlegar, Benjamin Focht *retired magazine editor*
Pickering, John Harold *lawyer*
Pickett, Owen B. *congressman*
Pickholtz, Raymond Lee *electrical engineering educator, consultant*
Pickle, James Jarrell (Jake Pickle) *congressman*
Pierce, Margaret Hunter *government official*
Pietrowski, Robert Frank, Jr. *lawyer*
Piez, William *government official*
Pilecki, Paul Steven *lawyer*
Pinco, Robert G. *lawyer*
†Pincus, Ann Terry *television executive*
Pincus, Walter Haskell *editor*
Pines, Burton Yale *broadcasting executive*
Pines, Wayne Lloyd *public relations counselor*
†Pinstrup-Andersen, Per *educational administrator*
†Pinstrup-Anderson, Per *food scientist director*
Pipkin, James Harold, Jr. *lawyer*
Pirie, Robert Burns, Jr. *defense analyst*
Pistor, Michael T. F. *foreign service officer*
Pitt, Harvey Lloyd *lawyer*
Pittman, Steuart Lansing *lawyer*
Pivik, Robert William *accounting executive*
Placke, James A(nthony) *foreign service officer, international affairs consultant*
Plager, S. Jay *federal judge*
Plaine, Daniel J. *lawyer*
Plaisted, Joan M. *diplomat*
Plante, William Madden *news correspondent*
Plotkin, Harry Morris *lawyer*
Plowman, R. Dean *federal agriculture agency administrator*
†Podberesky, Samuel *lawyer*
Poe, David Russell *lawyer*
Poe, Luke Harvey, Jr. *lawyer*
Pogue, Lloyd Welch *lawyer*
Polak, Jacques Jacobus *economist, foundation administrator*
Polan, Annette Lewis *artist*
Polebaum, Elliot Edward *lawyer*
Pombo, Richard *congressman, farmer, rancher*
Pomeroy, Earl R. *congressman, former state insurance commissioner*
Pomeroy, Harlan *lawyer*
†Poneman, Daniel Bruce *federal official*
†Pope, Michael Thor *chemist*
Poppler, Doris Swords *lawyer*
Porter, Elisabeth Scott (Leezee Porter) *political worker*
Porter, John Edward *congressman*
Porter, Richard Howard *lawyer*
Portman, Rob *congressman*
Portnoy, Ian Karl *lawyer*
Poshard, Glenn W. *congressman*
Post, Boyd Wallace *forester*
Postol, Lawrence Philip *lawyer*
Poteete, Robert Arthur *editor*
†Potter, Deborah Ann *news correspondent, educator*
Potter, John Francis *surgical oncologist, educator*
Potter, Trevor Alexander McClurg *lawyer*
Potts, Ramsay Douglas *lawyer, aviator*
Potts, Stephen Deaderick *lawyer*
Potvin, Raymond Herve *sociology educator, author*
Povich, David *lawyer*
Povich, Shirley Lewis *columnist, former sports editor*
Powell, Anne Elizabeth *editor*
Powell, Colin Luther *army officer*
†Powell, Joseph Lester (Jody Powell) *public relations executive*
Powell, Lewis Franklin, Jr. *retired U.S. supreme court justice*
Power, Mark *journalist, photographer, educator*
Powers, Charles Henri *federal official*
Pozen, Walter *lawyer*
Prah, Pamela Marie *journalist*
Pratt, John Helm *federal judge*
Preeg, Ernest Henry *strategic and international studies center executive*
†Preer, Jean Lyon *university administrator, educator*
Prell, Michael Jack *economist*
Press, Frank *geophysicist, educator*
Pressler, Larry *senator*
Preston, Lewis Thompson *banker*
Preston, Richard McKim *lawyer*
Prestowitz, Clyde Vincent *economist, research administrator*
Prettyman, Elijah Barrett, Jr. *lawyer*
Prewitt, Charles Thompson *geochemist*
Price, David Eugene *congressman, educator*
Price, Griffith Baley, Jr. *lawyer*
Price, Joseph Hubbard *lawyer*
†Price, Mark Michael *building development consultant*
†Price, Mary Kathleen *lawyer, law librarian, library administrator*
Pridmore, Roy Davis *government official*
Prina, L(ouis) Edgar *journalist*
Proctor, John P. *lawyer*
Proto, Neil Thomas *lawyer, educator*
Pruden, James Wesley *newspaper editor, columnist*
Pruett, James Worrell *librarian, musicologist*
Pruitt, Anne Loring *university administrator, educator*
Pryor, David Hampton *senator*
†Pucie, Charles R., Jr. *public relations executive*
Pugh, Keith E., Jr. *lawyer*
Puryear, Martin *artist*
Pusey, William Anderson *lawyer*
Pushkar, Raymond Stephen Edward *lawyer*
Putzel, Michael *journalist*
Pyke, Thomas Nicholas, Jr. *government science and engineering administrator*
Pyle, Robert Noble *public relations executive*
Pyle, Thomas Edward *oceanographer, academic director*
Quainton, Anthony Cecil Eden *diplomat*
Quale, John Carter *lawyer*
Quandt, William Bauer *political scientist*
Quarles, James Linwood, III *lawyer*
†Queenan, John Thomas *obstetrician, gynecologist, educator*
Quello, James Henry *government official*
Quigley, Thomas J. *lawyer*
Quillen, James Henry (Jimmy Quillen) *congressman*
Quinn, Jack *congressman, English language educator, sports coach*
Quinn, Sally *journalist*
Quinn-Judge, Paul Malachy *journalist*
Quint, Arnold Harris *lawyer*
Quintiere, Gary G. *lawyer*
Raaflaub, Kurt A. *classics educator*
†Rabb, Harriet Schaffer *lawyer, educator*
†Rabel, Ed *news correspondent*
†Rabin, Kenneth Hardy *public relations executive*
†Rabin, Steve Arthur *public affairs executive*
Rabinowitz, Stanley Samuel *rabbi*
Rademaker, Stephen Geoffrey *lawyer*
Rader, Randall Ray *federal judge*
Rader, Robert Michael *lawyer*
Radewagen, Fred *publisher, organization executive*
Radin, Alex *former association executive, consultant*
Rafshoon, Gerald Monroe *communications executive*
Rahall, Nick J., II (Nick Rahall) *congressman*
†Rahill, Margaret Anne *retired museum curator*
Rahn, Richard William *economist, business executive*
†Raimo, Bernard, Jr. (Bernie) *lawyer*
Raines, Franklin Delano *investment banker*
Rainey, Jean Osgood *public relations executive*
†Rales, Mitchell P. *automotive parts company executive*
Rales, Steven M. *automotive parts company executive*
Rall, David Platt *pharmacologist, environmentalist*
Ralls, Katherine *zoologist*
†Ramberg, Walter Dodd *architect*
Ramey, Carl Robert *lawyer*
Ramsay, William Charles *writer*
Ramsey, Henry, Jr. *retired judge, law school dean, lawyer*
Ramsey, William C. *ambassador*
Ramstad, Jim *congressman, lawyer*
Rand, Harry Zvi *art historian*
†Randall, Gene *news correspondent, anchor*
Randall, Robert L(ee) *ecological economist*
Randolph, Arthur Raymond *federal judge, lawyer*
Ranelli, Raymond A. *accounting firm executive*
Rangel, Charles Bernard *congressman*
Rankin, Haywood Forney *diplomat*
Rankin, Robert Arthur *journalist*
Rao, Desiraju Bhavanarayana *meteorologist, oceanographer, educator*
†Raphel, Robin *federal official*
Rasco, Carol Hampton *federal official*
Raskin, Marcus Goodman *writer, educator*
Raspberry, William James *journalist*
†Ratner, Rhoda Sue *librarian*
Rauh, Carl Stephen *lawyer*
Raul, Alan Charles *lawyer*
Raum, Arnold *federal judge*
Rausch, Howard *information service executive*
Ravenal, Earl Cedric *international relations educator, author*
Ravenel, Arthur, Jr. *congressman*
†Rawson, David P. *ambassador*
Rawson, David P. *ambassador*
†Raymond, Victor P. *federal official*
Reade, Claire Elizabeth *lawyer*
Reade, Lewis Pollock *diplomat, engineer*
†Reason, Joseph Paul *naval officer*
Reaves, John Daniel *lawyer, playwright, actor*
Reback, Joyce Ellen *lawyer*
Rechcigl, Miloslav, Jr. *government official*
Reed, Berenice Anne *art historian, artist, government official*
Reed, John Francis *congressman, lawyer*
Reed, John Hathaway *former ambassador*
Reed, Kevin Francis *lawyer*
Reed, Travis Dean *public relations consultant*
Reed, Vincent Emory *federal education official*
Reeder, Joe Robert *federal official*
Reger, Lawrence Lee *association executive*
Regnery, Alfred Scattergood *corporate executive, lawyer*
Regula, Ralph *congressman, lawyer*
Rehm, John Bartram *lawyer*
Rehnquist, William Hubbs *U.S. supreme court justice*
Reich, Alan Anderson *association executive*
Reich, Bernard *political science educator*
†Reich, David J. *lawyer*
Reich, Otto Juan *political analyst, business consultant*
Reichardt, Glenn Richard *lawyer*
Reid, George Bernard, Jr. *lawyer*
Reid, Inez Smith *lawyer, educator*
†Reid, Joseph Browning *architect*
Reid, Robert Newton *lawyer, mortgage and financial consultant*
Reidy, Gerald Patrick *federal organization executive, arbitrator, mediator, fact-finder*
Reilly, Gerard Denis *judge*
Rein, Bert Walter *lawyer*
Reingold, Nathan *historian*
†Reis, Victor H. *mechanical engineer, government official*
Remick, Forrest Jerome, Jr. *academic administrator*
Render, Arlene *ambassador*
Renninger, Mary Karen *librarian*
Reno, Janet *U.S. attorney general*
Reswick, James Bigelow *government official, rehabilitation engineer, educator*
Retsinas, Nicolas P. *federal official*
Rettig, Richard Allen *social sciences educator, policy analyst, administrator*
Reynolds, Gary Kemp *librarian*
Reynolds, Joseph Hurley *lawyer*
Reynolds, Melvin J. (Mel Reynolds) *congressman*
Reynolds, Nicholas S. *lawyer*
Reynolds, Robert Joel *economist, consultant*
Rezneck, Daniel Albert *lawyer*
Rhodes, John Jacob *lawyer, former congressman*
Ribas, Jorge Luis *research pathologist, educator*
Rice, Lois Dickson *former computer company executive*
Rich, Giles Sutherland *federal judge*
Richard, Paul *art critic*
†Richards, Cory *demographic think-tank executive*
Richards, Suzanne V. *lawyer*
Richardson, Ann Bishop *foundation executive, lawyer*
Richardson, Elliot Lee *lawyer*
Richardson, Margaret Milner *federal agency administrator, lawyer*
Richardson, William Blaine *congressman*
Richey, Charles Robert *federal judge*
Richman, Phyllis Chasanow *newspaper critic*
Richmond, David Walker *lawyer*
Richmond, Marilyn Susan *lawyer*
Riddell, Richard Anderson *naval officer*
Ridge, Thomas Joseph *congressman*
Ridgeway, James Fowler *journalist*
Ridgway, Rozanne LeJeanne *foreign policy executive*
Riecken, Henry William *psychologist, research director*
Riegle, Donald Wayne, Jr. *senator*
Rieke, Elizabeth Ann *federal agency administrator*
Rieser, Joseph A., Jr. *lawyer*
Riley, Joseph Harry *retired banker*
Riley, Richard Wilson *U.S. secretary of education*
Rill, James Franklin *lawyer*
Rimpel, Auguste Eugene, Jr. *management and technical consulting executive*
Rinzel, Daniel Francis *lawyer*
Rishe, Melvin *lawyer*
Risher, John Robert, Jr. *lawyer*
Rissetto, Harry A. *lawyer*
Ritter, Donald Lawrence *science foundation administrator, former congressman*
Rittner, Edmund Sidney *physicist*
†Rivas-Vazquez, Ana Victoria *press secretary*
Rivers, Richard Robinson *lawyer*
Rivlin, Alice Mitchell *economist*
Roach, Arvid Edward, II *lawyer*
Roach, Patrick Joseph *lawyer*
Robb, Charles Spittal *senator, lawyer*
Robb, James Willis *Romance languages educator*
Robbins, Robert B. *lawyer*
Roberts, Bert C., Jr. *telecommunications company executive*
Roberts, Charles Patrick *congressman*
Roberts, Corinne Boggs (Cokie Roberts) *correspondent, news analyst*
Roberts, Howard Richard *food scientist, association administrator*
Roberts, James Cleveland *foundation executive*
Roberts, James Harold, III *lawyer*
Roberts, Jeanne Addison *English educator*
Roberts, John Benjamin, II *public policy consultant*
Roberts, Markley *economist, educator*
Roberts, Michael James *lawyer*
Roberts, Paul Craig, III *economics educator, author, consultant*
Roberts, Steven Victor *journalist*
Roberts, Walter Ronald *political science educator, former government official*
Robinson, Aubrey Eugene, Jr. *federal judge*
Robinson, Daniel Baruch *banker*
Robinson, David B. *lawyer*
Robinson, Davis Rowland *lawyer*
Robinson, Douglas George *lawyer*
Robinson, Leonard Harrison, Jr. *international government consultant, business executive*
Robinson, Michael Hill *zoological park director, biologist*
†Robinson, Randall *think-tank executive*
Robinson, Ruth Harris *elementary education educator*
†Robinson, Sharon Porter *federal official*
†Robinson, Virginia Brown *financial services company executive*
Robinson, Wilkes Coleman *federal judge*
Rockefeller, Edwin Shaffer *lawyer*
Rockefeller, John Davison, IV (Jay Rockefeller) *senator, former governor*
Rockler, Walter James *lawyer*
Rockoff, S. David *radiologist, physician, educator*
Rocque, Vincent Joseph *lawyer*
†Rodemeyer, Michael Leonard, Jr. *lawyer*
Rodgers, Paul *lawyer, government official*
Rodman, Peter Warren *foreign policy specialist*
Rodriguez, Belgica *museum director*
Rodriguez, Rita Maria *bank executive*
Roemer, Timothy J. *congressman*
Roett, Riordan *political science educator, consultant*
Rogers, Harold Dallas (Hal Rogers) *congressman*
Rogers, James Albert *lawyer*
Rogers, James Frederick *banker, management consultant*
Rogers, Jerry L. *federal agency administrator*
Rogers, John S. *union official*
†Rogers, Kenneth Cannicott *physicist, federal agency administrator*
Rogers, Paul Grant *lawyer, former congressman*
Rogers, Raymond Jesse *federal railroad associate administrator*
Rogers, Sharon J. *university administrator*
Rogers, Warren Joseph, Jr. *journalist*
Rogers, William Dill *lawyer*
Rogovin, Mitchell *lawyer*
Rohner, Ralph John *lawyer, educator, university dean*
Rohr, David Baker *federal agency commissioner*
Rohrabacher, Dana *congressman*
Roiter, Eric D. *lawyer*
Rojas, Richard Raimond *electrical engineer*
Rokke, Ervin Jerome *career officer*
Rollins, Sherrie Sandy *publishing executive*
Romanowski, Thomas Andrew *physics educator*
Romansky, Michael A. *lawyer*
Romatowski, Peter J. *lawyer*
Romeo, Peter John *lawyer*
Romero-Barceló, Carlos Antonio *former chairman New Progressive Party, former governor, lawyer, real estate agent*
Rominger, Richard *federal agency administrator*
Rooney, Kevin Davitt *lawyer*
Rooney, William Richard *magazine editor*
Rope, William Frederick *foreign service officer*
Rosamond, John Bell *government official*
Roscher, Nina Matheny *chemistry educator*
Rose, Charles Grandison, III (Charlie Rose) *congressman*
Rose, Henry *lawyer*
Rose, James McKinley, Jr. *lawyer, government official*
Rose, Jonathan Chapman *lawyer*
†Rose, Lloyd *theatre critic*
Rosebush, James Scott *international management and public affairs consultant, former government official*
Rosen, Gerald Robert *editor*
Rosenau, James Nathan *political scientist, author*
Rosenberg, Norman Jack *agricultural meteorologist, educator*
Rosenberg, Ruth Helen Borsuk *lawyer*
Rosenberg, Sarah Zacher *institute arts administration executive, humanities administration consultant*
Rosenblatt, Peter Ronald *lawyer, former ambassador*
Rosenbloom, H. David *lawyer*
Rosenbloom, Morris Victor *author, publisher, public relations executive, government official*
Rosendhal, Jeffrey David *federal science agency administrator, astronomer*
Rosenfeld, Stephen Samuel *newspaper editor*
Rosenker, Mark Victor *trade association executive*
Rosenquist, Glenn Carl *pediatrician*
Rosensweig, Stanley Harold *retail executive*
Rosenthal, Aaron *management consultant*
Rosenthal, Alan Sayre *government official*
†Rosenthal, Andrew *newspaper editor*
Rosenthal, Douglas Eurico *lawyer, author*
Rosenthal, Steven Siegmund *lawyer*
Ros-Lehtinen, Ileana *congresswoman*
Ross, Allan Michael *physician, medical educator*
Ross, Christopher Wade Stelyan *diplomat*
Ross, Douglas *lawyer*
Ross, John Joseph *lawyer*
Ross, Robinette Davis *publisher*
Ross, Stanford Gordon *lawyer, former government official*
Ross, Thomas Bernard *federal government official*
Ross, Wendy Clucas *newspaper editor, journalist*
Rossides, Eugene Telemachus *lawyer, writer*
Rossotti, Barbara Jill Margulies *lawyer*
Rostenkowski, Dan *congressman*
Rotberg, Eugene Harvey *investment banker, lawyer*
†Roth, Alan J. *lawyer, congressional aide*
Roth, William V., Jr. *senator*
†Rothenberg, Marc *historian*
Rother, John Charles *association executive, lawyer*
†Rothkopf, David Jochanan *federal official*
Rottman, Ellis *public information officer*
Roukema, Margaret Scafati *congresswoman*
Rouvelas, Emanuel Larry *lawyer*
Rovelstad, Mathilde Verner *library science educator*
Rowan, Carl Thomas *columnist*
Rowden, Marcus Aubrey *lawyer, former government official*
Rowe, Richard Holmes *lawyer*
Rowen, Hobart *journalist*
Rowland, (James) Roy *congressman*
Rowley, William Robert *surgeon*
Rowson, Richard Cavanagh *publisher*
Roybal-Allard, Lucille *congresswoman*
Royce, Edward R. (Ed Royce) *congressman*
Roycroft, Howard Francis *lawyer*
Rubin, Kenneth Allen *lawyer*
Rubin, Robert Edward *economic advisor to President of U.S.*
Rubin, Seymour Jeffrey *lawyer, educator*
Ruby, Michael *magazine executive*
Ruckert, Edward M. *lawyer*
Rudder, Catherine E. *political science association administrator*
Ruddy, Frank S. *lawyer, former ambassador*
Rudman, Warren Bruce *former senator, lawyer*
Rudnick, Robert Alan *lawyer*
†Rugh, William Arthur *diplomat*
Rule, Charles Frederick (Rick Rule) *lawyer*
Rumford, Lewis, III *real estate company executive*
Runyon, Marvin Travis *postmaster general*
Rush, Bobby L. *congressman*
Russell, H. Diane *museum curator, educator*
Russell, Mark *comedian*
†Russell, Michael James *lawyer*
Russell, William Joseph *association executive*
†Russert, Timothy J. *broadcast executive*
Russin, Jonathan *lawyer, consultant*
Rutstein, David W. *lawyer, food products executive*
Ruttenberg, Charles Byron *lawyer*
Ruttenberg, Stanley Harvey *economist*
Ruttinger, George David *lawyer*
Ruwe, Robert P. *federal judge*
Ruyak, Robert Francis *lawyer*
Ryan, Jerry William *lawyer*
Ryan, Mary A. *diplomat*
Ryerson, Paul Sommer *lawyer*
Ryn, Claes Gösta *political science educator, author, research institute administrator*
†Ryscavage, Richard *Jesuit priest, social services administrator*
Sabo, Martin Olav *congressman*
Sabshin, Melvin *psychiatrist, educator, medical association administrator*
Sachar, Howard Morley *history educator*
Sacher, Steven Jay *lawyer*
Sachs, Stephen Howard *lawyer*
Sackler, Arthur Brian *lawyer*
Sacks, David Arnold *lawyer*
Safire, William *journalist, author*
Sagalkin, Sanford *lawyer*
Sagawa, Shirley Sachi *lawyer*
Sagett, Jan Jeffrey *lawyer, former government official*
Sahanek, Tatana *librarian, editor*
St. Germain, Fernand Joseph *congressman*
St. John, Adrian, II *retired army officer*
Salamon, Linda Bradley *university dean, English literature educator*
Salamone, Philip Joseph *federal agency administrator*
Salant, Walter S. *economist*
Salci, Larry Eugene *manufacturing executive*
Salinger, Pierre Emil George *journalist*
Salmon, William Cooper *mechanical engineer, engineering academy executive*
Saltzburg, Stephen Allan *law educator, consultant*
†Salvado, August J. *think-tank executive*
Samet, Kenneth Alan *hospital administrator*
Samman, George *obstetrician, gynecologist*
Samolis, Frank Robert *lawyer*
Sampson, Daphne Rae *library director*
Sampson, Richard Thomas *lawyer*
Sampson, Robert Neil *association executive*
Samuel, Howard David *union official*
Sandefur, James Tandy *mathematics educator*
Sanderson, Fred Hugo *economist*
Sanford, Bruce William *lawyer*
San Martin, Robert L. *federal official*
Santorum, Rick *congressman*
Santos, Leonard Ernest *lawyer*
Sapienza, John Thomas *lawyer*
Sarbanes, Paul Spyros *senator*
Sareeram, Ray Rupchand *naval officer*
Sarpalius, William C. (Bill Sarpalius) *congressman*
Sasser, James Ralph (Jim Sasser) *senator*
Sauntry, Susan Schaefer *lawyer*
Savage, Phillip Hezekiah *federal agency administrator*
Savage, Xyla Ruth *government official*
†Savarese, Ralph J. *lawyer*
Sawhill, Isabel Van Devanter *economist*
Sawyer, Thomas C. *congressman*
Saxton, H. James *congressman*
Sayler, Robert Nelson *lawyer*
Sayre, Robert Marion *ambassador*
Sazima, Henry John *oral and maxillofacial surgery educator*
Scali, John Alfred *journalist*
Scalia, Antonin *U.S. supreme court justice*
Scanlan, John Douglas *foreign service officer, former ambassador*
Scanlon, Patrick Michael *lawyer*
Scanlon, Terrence Maurice *foundation administrator*
†Scarbrough, Frank Edward *government official*
†Scassa, Eugene L. *ambassador*
Schad, Theodore MacNeeve *science research administrator, consultant*
Schaefer, Dan L. *congressman*
Schall, Alvin Anthony *judge*
Schapiro, Mary *federal agency administrator, lawyer*
Scharff, Joseph Laurent *lawyer*
†Schechter, Geraldine Poppa *hematologist*
Scheibel, Kenneth Maynard *journalist*
Schenk, Lynn *congresswoman*
Schenker, Carl Richard, Jr. *lawyer*
Scheppach, Raymond Carl, Jr. *association executive, economist*
†Schiavone, Louise L. *political correspondent, news analyst*
†Schick, Michael William *public relations executive*
†Schiff, Margaret Scott *newspaper publishing executive*

Schiff, Stefan Otto zoologist, educator
Schiff, Steven Harvey congressman, lawyer
Schifter, Richard lawyer, government official
Schlagel, Richard H. philosophy educator
Schlesinger, B. Frank architect, educator
Schlesinger, James Rodney economist
Schley, Wayne A. postal rate commissioner
Schlossberg, Stephen I. international official
Schmeltzer, Edward lawyer
Schmidt, Berlie Louis agricultural research administrator
Schmidt, John R. lawyer
Schmidt, Paul Wickham lawyer
Schmidt, Richard Marten, Jr. lawyer
Schneebaum, Steven Marc lawyer
Schneider, Keith Hilary news correspondent, journalist
Schneider, Mark Lewis government official
Schneider, Matthew Roger lawyer
Schoenbaum, Samuel English educator
Schoenberg, Mark George government agency administrator
Schoenberger, James Edwin federal agency administrator
Schosberg, Paul Alan trade association executive
Schotland, Sara Deutch lawyer
Schotta, Charles economist, government official
Schram, Martin Jay journalist
Schreiner, George E. nephrologist, educator, writer
Schriever, Bernard Adolph management consultant
Schroeder, Patricia Scott (Mrs. James White Schroeder) congresswoman
†Schroeter, Richard B. federal official
Schropp, James Howard lawyer
Schubert, Richard Francis foundation administrator
†Schulmann, Horst international economist
Schultze, Charles Louis economist, educator
Schulze, Richard Taylor congressman
†Schuman, Michael think-tank executive
Schumer, Charles Ellis congressman
Schwaab, Richard Lewis lawyer, educator
†Schwartz, Amy Elizabeth editorial writer, columnist
Schwartz, Daniel C. lawyer
Schwartz, Harry Kane lawyer
Schwartz, Marshall Zane pediatric surgeon
Schwartz, Richard Brenton English language educator, university dean, writer
Schwartz, Robert S. lawyer
Schwartz, Victor Elliot lawyer
Schwarz, Carl W. lawyer
Schwarzer, William W federal judge
Schweiker, Richard Schultz trade association executive, former senator
Schweitzer, William H. lawyer
Scofield, Richard Melbourne career officer
Scott, Catherine Dorothy librarian, consultant
Scott, Edward Philip lawyer
Scott, Irene Feagin federal judge
Scott, Joyce Alaine university official
Scott, Michael lawyer
Scott, Raymond Peter William chemistry research educator, writer
Scott, Robert Cortez congressman, lawyer
Scott, Thomas Jefferson, Jr. lawyer, electrical engineer
Scowcroft, Brent retired air force officer, government official
Sczudlo, Raymond Stanley lawyer
Seale, William Edward finance educator
Searing, Marjory Ellen government official, economist
Sears, John Patrick lawyer
Sears, Mary Helen lawyer
†Seelig, Steven Alfred government financial executive
Segal, Donald E. lawyer
†Seidel, Milton Joseph government administrator
†Seidman, Ellen Shapiro lawyer, government official
Seidman, L(ewis) William television chief commentator
Seidman, Ricki federal official
†Seignious, George Marion, II former government official, former college president, retired army officer
†Seldman, Neil Norman cultural organization administrator
Selin, Ivan federal official
Sellin, Theodore foreign service officer, consultant
Semas, Philip Wayne editor
Sender, Stanton P. lawyer
Sensenbrenner, Frank James, Jr. congressman, lawyer
Sentelle, David Bryan federal judge
†Serafin, Barry D. television news correspondent
Sernoff, Louis R. lawyer
Serrano, Jose E. congressman
†Sesno, Frank television correspondent
Sessions, William Steele former government official
Sethness, Charles Olin international financial official
†Sever, Tom labor union administrator
Sewell, John Williamson research association executive
Sexton, Ken environmental health scientist
Seymour, Jon federal government official
†Shafer, Jeffrey R. federal official
Shafer, Raymond Philip lawyer, business executive
†Shaffer, Jay Christopher lawyer
Shaheen, Michael Edmund, Jr. lawyer, government official
Shalala, Donna Edna federal official, political scientist, educator, university chancellor
Shales, Thomas William writer, journalist, television and film critic
Shalowitz, Erwin Emmanuel civil engineer
Shank, Fred Ross federal agency administrator
Shanker, Albert labor union official
Shanks, Hershel editor, writer
Shanks, Robert Bruce lawyer
Shannon, Donald Hawkins retired newspaperman
Shapiro, David Israel lawyer
Shapiro, George Howard lawyer
Shapiro, Michael Henry government executive
Sharp, Philip R. congressman
Sharpe, Rochelle Phyllis journalist
†Shattuck, John H. F. federal official
Shaw, Bernard television journalist
Shaw, E. Clay, Jr. (Clay) congressman
Shaw, Gaylord newspaper executive
Shaw, Russell Burnham association executive, author
Shaw, Sallye Brown women's health nurse
Shaw, William Frederick statistician
Shays, Christopher congressman
Shea, Donald William career officer
†Shearer, P. Scott government relations professional
†Sheehan, Michael Terrence arts administrator, historian, consultant
Sheehan, Neil reporter, scholarly writer
Sheinbaum, Gilbert Harold international consultant
Shelby, Richard Craig senator, former congressman
Shelley, Herbert Carl lawyer
Shenefield, John Hale lawyer
Shepherd, Karen congresswoman
Sherman, Charles Edwin broadcasting executive, educator
Sherman, George M. manufacturing company executive
Sherman, Wendy Ruth federal agency administrator
Sherwin, Michael Dennis government official
Sherzer, Harvey Gerald lawyer
Shestack, Alan museum administrator
Shibley, Raymond Nadeem lawyer
Shields, Perry federal judge
Shih, J. Chung-wen Chinese language educator
Shihata, Ibrahim Fahmy Ibrahim development banker, lawyer
Shine, Kenneth I. cardiologist, educator
†Shiner, Josette Sheeran editor
Shinn, David Hamilton diplomat
Shlaudeman, Harry Walter retired ambassador
Shniderman, Harry Louis lawyer
Shoemaker, Cynthia Cavenaugh Jones academic director
Shogan, Robert news correspondent
Shon, Frederick John nuclear engineer
Shook, Langley R. lawyer
Short, Elizabeth M. physician, educator, federal agency administrator
†Shribman, David M. editor
Shrier, Adam Louis investment firm executive
Shrinsky, Jason Lee lawyer
Shriver, Eunice Mary Kennedy (Mrs. Robert Sargent Shriver, Jr.) civic worker
Shriver, Robert Sargent, Jr. lawyer
Shulman, Stephen Neal lawyer
Shurtleff, Leonard Grant ambassador
Shuster, E. G. (Bud) congressman
Siciliano, Rocco Carmine institute executive
Sidey, Hugh Swanson correspondent
Sidransky, Herschel pathologist
Siegel, Allen George lawyer
Siegel, Frederic Richard geology educator
Siegel, Jack S. federal official
Siegel, Lloyd H. architect, real estate developer, consultant
Siegel, Richard David lawyer, former government official
Siegel, Robert Charles broadcast journalist
Siegfried, Richard Stephen military officer
Siemer, Deanne Clemence lawyer
Sievers, Robert H. wholesale distributing company executive
Sieverts, Frank Arne government official
Silberg, Jay Eliot lawyer
Silberman, Rosalie Gaull federal official
Silby, Donald Wayne investment executive, entrepreneur
†Sills, Hilary H. public relations executive
Silver, Brian Quayle broadcast journalist, educator, musician
Silver, Daniel B. lawyer
Silver, David financial executive, lawyer
Silver, Harry R. lawyer
Silverman, Alvin Michaels public relations consultant
Silverman, Ira Norton news producer
Simchak, Matthew Stephen lawyer
Simes, Dimitri Konstantin international affairs expert and educator
Simmons, Edwin Howard marine corps officer, historian
Simmons, Richard De Lacey mass media executive
†Simon, Jeanne Hurley federal commissioner
Simon, Justin Daniel lawyer
Simon, Kenneth Mark lawyer
Simon, Paul senator, educator, author
Simon, Rita James legal educator
Simon, Roger newspaper columnist, author
Simons, Barbara M. lawyer
Simons, Lawrence Brook lawyer
Simopoulos, Artemis Panageotis physician, educator
Simowitz, Lee H. lawyer
Simpson, Alan Kooi senator
Simpson, Carole broadcast journalist
Simpson, John W. lawyer
Simpson, Louis A. insurance company executive
Simpson, Michael Marcial science specialist, consultant
Sims, Joe lawyer
Sims, Robert Bell professional society administrator, public affairs official, newspaper publisher
Singer, Daniel Morris lawyer
Singer, Maxine Frank biochemist
Singer, Norman H. lawyer
Singer, Thomas Kenyon international business consultant
Singleton, Harry Michael lawyer
Sinkford, Jeanne Craig dentist, educator
Sisco, Joseph John management consultant, corporation director, educator, government official
Sisisky, Norman congressman, soft drink bottler
Skadden, Donald Harvey professional society executive, accounting educator
Skaggs, David E. congressman
Skeen, Joseph Richard congressman
Skelton, Isaac Newton, IV (Ike Skelton) congressman
Skene, G(eorge) Neil publisher, lawyer
Skinner, William Polk lawyer
Skog, Laurence Edgar botanist
Skol, Michael diplomat
Skolnik, Merrill I. electrical engineer
†Slagle, Larry B. federal government executive
†Slater, Rodney E. federal administrator
†Slatkin, Nora federal agency administrator
Slattery, James Charles congressman, real estate executive
Slaughter, Louise McIntosh congresswoman
Slocombe, Walter Becker government official, lawyer
Sloyan, Patrick Joseph journalist
Sly, Ridge Michael physician, educator
Small, Lawrence M. financial organization executive
Smedley, Lawrence Thomas organization executive
†Smeeton, Thomas Rooney congressional staff director
Smiley, D. E. petroleum company executive
Smilow, Michael A. mortgage company executive
†Smith, Alan W., Jr. management consultant
Smith, Anne Bowman academic administrator, editor
Smith, Barbara Jeanne library administrator
Smith, Brian William lawyer, former government official
Smith, Bruce David archaeologist
Smith, Christopher Henry congressman
Smith, Curtis Johnston government executive
†Smith, Dallas R. federal official
Smith, Daniel Clifford lawyer
Smith, Dean communications advisor, arbitrator
Smith, Delbert Dudley lawyer
Smith, Donald Kaye insurance company executive
Smith, Elaine Diana foreign service officer
Smith, Geoffrey R.W. lawyer
Smith, George Patrick, II lawyer, educator
Smith, Jack Carl foreign trade consultant
Smith, Jack Prescott journalist
Smith, Jean Kennedy ambassador
Smith, John Lewis, III lawyer
Smith, Lamar Seeligson congressman
Smith, Lee Elton surgery educator, retired military officer
Smith, Leighton Warren, Jr. naval officer
Smith, Loren Allan federal judge
Smith, Marshall Savidge government official, academic dean, education educator
Smith, Neal Edward congressman
Smith, Nick congressman, farmer
Smith, Philip Meek research organization executive
Smith, Richard Melvyn government official
Smith, Robert Clinton senator
Smith, Robert Freeman congressman
Smith, Roy Philip federal judge
Smith, Stephen Grant journalist
Smith, Stuart Seaborne writer, government official, union official
Smith, Terence Fitzgerald television news correspondent
Smith, Walter Joseph, Jr. lawyer, educator
Smith, William Dee naval officer
Smits, Helen Lida public adminstrator, physician, educator
Smuckler, Ralph Herbert university dean, political science educator
†Smyth, Paul Burton lawyer
Smythe-Haith, Mabel Murphy consultant on African economic development, speaker, writer
Sneed, James H. lawyer
Snider, Jerome Guy lawyer
Snowden, Frank Martin, Jr. classics educator
Snowe, Olympia J. congresswoman
Snyder, Allen Roger lawyer
†Snyder, Daniel James military career officer
Sockwell, Oliver R., Jr. financial services company executive
Soderberg, Nancy federal agency administrator
Sofaer, Abraham David lawyer, legal advisor, federal judge, legal educator
Sohn, Louis Bruno lawyer, educator
Solarz, Stephen Joshua congressman
Soldo, Beth Jean demography educator, researcher
Solomon, George M. newspaper editor
Solomon, Gerald Brooks Hunt congressman
Solomon, Henry university dean
Solomon, Richard Allan lawyer
Solomon, Richard Harvey political scientist
Solomon, Robert economist
Solomon, Sean Carl geophysicist, lab director
Solomons, Mark Elliott lawyer
†Somerville, Walter Raleigh, Jr. government official
Sommer, Alphonse Adam, Jr. lawyer
Sommerfelt, Soren Christian foreign affairs, international trade consultant, former Norwegian diplomat, lawyer
Sonde, Theodore Irwin lawyer
Sonnenfeldt, Helmut former government official, educator, consultant, author
†Sopher, Vicki Elaine museum director
Sorensen, John Noble mechanical and nuclear engineer
Sormani, Charles Robert insurance company executive, actuary
Southern, Hugh performing arts consultant
Spaeder, Roger Campbell lawyer
Spangler, Scott Michael private investor
†Sparrowe, Rollin D. wildlife biologist
Spears, Gregory Luttrell journalist
Specter, Arlen senator
Spector, Eleanor Ruth government executive
Speidel, John Joseph physician, foundation officer
Spence, Floyd Davidson congressman
Spence, Sandra association executive
Spencer, Samuel lawyer
Sperling, Godfrey, Jr. journalist
Spero, Joan Edelman multi-service corporation executive
Sphar, Raymond Leslie, Jr. medical administrator, researcher
†Spingler, Frank Joseph lawyer
Spiro, Benjamin Paul economist, consultant
Splete, Allen Peterjohn association executive, educator
Spoon, Alan Gary communications and publishing executive
Spooner, Mark Jordan lawyer
Sporkin, Stanley federal judge
Sprague, Edward Auchincloss association executive, economist
Spratt, John McKee, Jr. congressman, lawyer
Spreiregen, Paul David architect, planner, author
Springer, James van Roden lawyer
Sprott, John T. ambassador
Squier, Robert Dave political consultant, documentary filmmaker
Staats, Elmer Boyd foundation executive, former government official
†Stafford, Barbara Rose lawyer
Stahr, Elvis J(acob), Jr. lawyer, conservationist, educator
Stamberg, Susan Levitt radio broadcaster
Stanford, Dennis Joe archaeologist, museum curator
Stanley, Daniel Jean geological oceanographer, senior scientist
†Stanley, Thomas P. chief engineer
Stanley, Timothy Wadsworth economist
Stansbury, Philip Roger lawyer
†Stanton, Robert historic site director
Stanwick, Tad systems engineering and business management executive
†Stapleton, Jean think-tank executive
Stark, Fortney Hillman (Pete Stark) congressman
Stark, Nathan Julius insurance company executive
Stauffer, Ronald Eugene lawyer
Stavrou, Nikolaos Athanasios political science educator
Stayin, Randolph John lawyer
Steadman, Charles Walters lawyer, corporate executive, writer
Steadman, John Montague judge
Stearns, Clifford Bundy congressman, business executive
Stearns, James Gerry securities company executive
Steel, Adrian L., Jr. lawyer
Steele, Ana Mercedes government official
Steele, John Lawrence journalist
Steiger, Janet Dempsey government official
Steigman, Andrew L. academic dean
Stein, Herbert economist
Stein, Michael Henry lawyer
Steinberg, Jonathan Robert federal judge
Steinberg, Mark Robert lawyer
Steiner, Gilbert Yale political scientist
Steingold, Stuart Geoffrey lawyer
†Steinhardt, Ralph Gustav, III law educator
Stemmler, Edward Joseph physician, retired association executive, retired academic dean
Stenholm, Charles W. congressman
Stephanopoulos, George Robert federal official
Stephens, James M. federal agency administrator
Stephens, Jay B. lawyer
Stephens, Robert Louis, Jr. army officer
Stepp, Laura Sessions journalist
Stern, Carl Leonard former news correspondent, federal official
Stern, Gerald Mann lawyer
Stern, Paula international trade advisor
Stern, Samuel Alan lawyer
Sterner, Michael Edmund international affairs consultant
Steuerle, C. Eugene economist
Stevens, George, Jr. film and television producer, writer, director
Stevens, Herbert Francis lawyer, law educator
Stevens, John Paul U.S. supreme court justice
Stevens, Milton Lewis, Jr. trombonist
Stevens, Roger Lacey theatrical producer
Stevens, Theodore Fulton senator
Stevenson, A. Brockie artist
Stevenson, Eric Van Cortlandt lawyer, mortgage banker, real estate executive
Stevenson, John Reese lawyer
Stevenson, Russell B., Jr. lawyer
Stever, Horton Guyford aerospace scientist and engineer, educator, consultant
Stewart, Eugene Lawrence lawyer, trade association executive
Stewart, Frank Maurice, Jr. federal agency administrator
Stewart, George Cope, III (Scoop Stewart) lawyer
Stewart, John Daugherty publishing company executive
Stewart, John Irwin, Jr. lawyer
Stewart, Robert Gordon museum curator
Stewart, Ruth Ann public policy analyst, administrator
Stock, Stuart Chase lawyer
Stoer, Eric F. lawyer
Stokes, Arnold Paul mathematics educator
Stokes, Louis congressman
†Stoll, Louise Frankel federal official
Stoll, Richard G(iles) lawyer
Stollman, Israel city planner
Stone, Alan James lawyer, writer
Stone, Donald Raymond lawyer
Stone, Elizabeth Wenger retired dean
Stone, Jeremy Judah association executive
Stone, Marvin Lawrence journalist, government official
Stone, Russell A. sociology educator
Stonehill, Robert Michael federal agency administrator
†Stoner, Allan L. science foundation director
Stoner, John Richard federal government executive
Stookey, Laurence Hull clergyman, theology educator
Storing, Paul Edward foreign service officer
Stout, Carl Frederick finance and management executive
Strachan, David E. trade association executive
Stranahan, Robert Paul, Jr. lawyer
Strauss, Elliott Bowman economic development consultant, retired naval officer
Strauss, Stanley Robert lawyer
Streb, Alan Joseph government official, engineer
Strickland, Ted congressman, clergyman, psychology educator, psychologist
Stromberg, Clifford Douglas lawyer
Strong, Henry foundation executive
†Stuart, Sandra Kaplan federal official
Studds, Gerry Eastman congressman
Studeman, William Oliver naval officer
Stump, Bob congressman
Stumpf, Mark Howard lawyer
Stupak, Bart T. congressman, lawyer
Sturtevant, William Curtis anthropologist
Sugarman, Jule M. professional society administrator, former public administrator
†Sullivan, Brendan V., Jr. lawyer
Sullivan, Charles university dean, educator, author
Sullivan, Dennis F. transportation company executive, engineer
Sullivan, Eugene Raymond federal judge
Sullivan, Gordon R. career officer
Sullivan, John Fox publisher
†Sullivan, Kathryn D. geologist, astronaut
Sullivan, Richard John public relations executive, consultant
Sullivan, Timothy lawyer
Sultan, Terrie Frances curator
Summerford, Ben Long retired artist, educator
Summers, Lawrence under secretary treasury department
Sundquist, Donald Kenneth (Don Sundquist) congressman, sales corporation executive
Sundquist, James Lloyd political scientist
Sunley, Emil McKee economist
Suro, Dario artist, diplomat
Susman, Thomas Michael lawyer, lobbyist
Sussman, Monica Hilton lawyer
Sutherlund, David Arvid lawyer
Swankin, David Arnold lawyer, consumer advocate
Swanson, Russell Bruce federal agency administrator
Swart, Robert H. lawyer
Sweedler, Barry Martin federal agency administrator
Sweeney, Richard James economics educator
Swett, Richard Nelson (Dick Swett) congressman
Swidler, Joseph Charles lawyer
Swift, Al congressman
Swift, Evangeline Wilson lawyer
Swift, Stephen Jensen federal judge
Swing, William Lacy ambassador
Synar, Michael Lynn (Mike Lynn) congressman
Szabo, Daniel government official
Szulc, Tad journalist, commentator
Tabor, John Kaye lawyer, retired
Taishoff, Lawrence Bruce publishing company executive
Talbot, Frank Hamilton museum director, marine researcher
†Talbott, Strobe journalist
Talent, James M. congressman, lawyer
Tallent, Stephen Edison lawyer, educator
Tallent, William Hugh chemist, research administrator
Tanguy, Charles Reed foundation administrator, consultant, former foreign service officer

Tanham, George Kilpatrick *retired research company executive*
Tannen, Deborah Frances *writer, linguist*
Tannenwald, Peter *lawyer*
Tannenwald, Theodore, Jr. *federal judge*
Tanner, John S. *congressman, lawyer*
Tansill, Frederick Riker *retired judge*
Tape, Gerald Frederick *former association executive*
Taquey, Charles Henri *writer, consultant*
Tarnoff, Peter *governmental official*
Tarrant, James Richard *foreign service officer*
Tarrants, William Eugene *government official*
†Tarr-Whelan, Linda Jane *political organization administrator*
†Tarullo, Daniel K. *federal official*
†Tashjean, Catherine Richardson *librarian*
Tate, Sheila Burke *public relations executive*
Tatel, David Stephen *lawyer*
Tauber, Mark J. *lawyer*
Tauzin, Wilbert J., II (Billy Tauzin) *congressman*
Taylor, Charles H. *congressman*
Taylor, Christopher Andrew *securities industry regulation executive*
Taylor, David Kerr *international business educator, consultant*
Taylor, Estelle Wormley *English educator, college dean*
Taylor, Gene *congressman*
Taylor, Harold Allen, Jr. *federal agency administrator*
Taylor, Henry Splawn *literature educator, poet, writer*
Taylor, James, Jr. *lawyer*
Taylor, Ralph Arthur, Jr. *lawyer*
Taylor, Richard Powell *lawyer*
Taylor, Robert William *association executive*
†Taylor, William James, III *federal official*
Teague, Randal Cornell, Sr. *lawyer*
Tejeda, Frank *congressman*
Telford, Ira Rockwood *anatomist, educator*
Temko, Stanley Leonard *lawyer*
Temple, Riley Keene *lawyer*
Terry, Gary A. *lawyer, former trade association executive*
Terry, John Alfred *judge*
Terwilliger, George James, III *lawyer*
†Terzian, Philip Henry *journalist*
†Tetelman, Alice Fran *city government official*
Thayer, Edwin Cabot *musician*
Thayer, Russell, III *airlines executive*
†Thelian, Lorraine *public relations executive*
Theon, John Speridon *meteorologist*
Thomas, Charles Howard, II *federal official*
Thomas, Clarence *U.S. supreme court justice*
Thomas, Craig *congressman*
†Thomas, Fred *police chief*
Thomas, Helen A. (Mrs. Douglas B. Cornell) *newspaper bureau executive*
†Thomas, Jack Ward *wildlife biologist*
Thomas, James Bert, Jr. *government official*
†Thomas, Ralph C., III *trade association administrator, lawyer*
Thomas, Richard *civilian military employee*
Thomas, Ritchie Tucker *lawyer*
Thomas, Scott E. *federal government executive, lawyer*
Thomas, W. Dennis *paper company executive, former government official*
Thomas, William Marshall *congressman*
Thomasson, Patsy *federal official*
Thompson, Bennie G. *congressman*
Thompson, Bruce Edward, Jr. *brokerage house executive, former government official*
Thompson, Edward Kramer *editor, publisher*
†Thompson, James Robert, Jr. *federal space center executive*
Thompson, John *college basketball coach*
†Thompson, Mozelle Willmont *lawyer, federal agency administrator*
Thompson, Richard C. *magazine executive*
Thompson, Richard Leon *pharmaceutical company executive, lawyer*
Thompson, William Reid *public utility executive, lawyer*
Thornburgh, Dick (Richard L. Thornburgh) *lawyer, former United Nations official, former U.S. attorney general, former governor*
Thornton, Ray *congressman*
Thulean, Donald Myron *symphony conductor*
Thurman, Karen *congresswoman*
Thurmond, Strom *senator*
Thursz, Daniel *service organization executive*
Tidball, Charles Stanley *computer scientist, educator*
Tidwell, Moody Rudolph *federal judge*
Tiefel, William Reginald *hotel company executive*
Tierney, Susan Fallows *federal official*
Timberg, Sigmund *lawyer*
Timmer, Barbara *lawyer*
Timmons, William Evan *corporate executive*
Timperlake, Edward Thomas *public relations executive*
†Tippeconnic, John W., III *federal agency administrator*
Tipton, E. Linwood *trade association executive*
Tipton, Paul S. *former college president, association executive*
Tirana, Bardyl Rifat *lawyer*
Tisch, Ronald Irwin *lawyer*
Tobias, Robert Max *labor leader, lawyer*
Todd, David Carl *lawyer*
†Toder, Eric Jay *economist*
Tolchin, Martin *newspaper reporter, author*
Toledano, Ralph de *columnist, author, photographer*
Tolson, John J. *editor*
Tomlinson, Alexander Cooper *investment banker, consultant*
Tompkins, Daniel Reuben *horticulturist, research administrator*
Tompkins, Joseph Buford, Jr. *lawyer*
Tonkin, Leo Sampson *educational foundation administrator*
Toohey, Daniel Weaver *lawyer*
Topelius, Kathleen E. *lawyer*
Torkildsen, Peter *congressman*
Torres, Esteban Edward *congressman, business executive*
†Torres-Gil, Fernando M. *federal official*
†Torrey, Barbara Boyle *research council administrator*
Torricelli, Robert G. *congressman*
†Tortora, Robert D. *mathematician*
Totenberg, Nina *journalist*
Toth, Robert Charles *correspondent, journalist*
Tousey, Richard *physicist*
Towns, Edolphus *congressman*
Townsend, John Michael *lawyer*
Townsend, Marjorie Rhodes *aerospace engineer, business executive*

Townsend, Wardell C., Jr. *federal agency administrator*
†Toy, Charles David *lawyer*
Trachtenberg, Stephen Joel *university president*
Tracy, Thomas Miles *international health organization official*
Trafford, Abigail *editor, writer, columnist*
Traficant, James A., Jr. *congressman*
Train, Russell Errol *environmentalist*
Traister, Robert Edwin *naval officer, engineer*
Treacy, Vincent Edward *lawyer*
Trent, Darrell M. *academic and corporate executive*
Trezise, Philip Harold *government official*
†Tribett, Brenda Diane Bell *religious organization administrator*
Trilling, Donald R. *federal agency administrator*
Trisco, Robert Frederick *church historian, educator*
Trodden, Stephen Anthony *federal agency administrator*
Trooboff, Peter Dennis *lawyer*
Trosten, Leonard Morse *lawyer*
Trowbridge, Alexander Buel, Jr. *corporate director, consultant*
Troyer, Thomas Alfred *lawyer*
Truesdale, John Cushman *government executive*
Truitt, Anne Dean *artist*
Truitt, Max O'Rell, Jr. *lawyer*
Truitt, Thomas Hulen *lawyer*
Trull, Francine Sue *research foundation administrator, lobbyist*
†Truly, Richard H. *federal agency administrator*
†Trumka, Richard Louis *labor leader, lawyer*
Tuck, John Chatfield *former federal agency administrator, public policy advisor*
†Tucker, Alvin Leroy *federal government executive*
Tucker, Stefan Franklin *lawyer*
Tucker, Walter Rayford, III *congressman, lawyer, mayor*
Tufaro, Richard Chase *lawyer*
Tufty, Harold Guilford *editor, publisher*
Tuggle, Francis Douglas *management educator*
Tuohey, Mark Henry, III *lawyer*
Turaj, Frank *university dean, literature and film educator*
Ture, Norman Bernard *public policy research organization executive*
Turkus, Albert H. *lawyer*
Turnage, Fred Douglas *lawyer*
†Turnbull, Lowell D. *lawyer*
†Turner, Brenda Lorraine *social worker*
Turner, Donald Frank *retired lawyer*
Turner, James P. *lawyer*
Turner, James Thomas *federal judge*
†Turner, Leslie M. *federal official*
Turner, Norv *professional football coach*
†Turtell, Neal Timothy *librarian*
Tuthill, John Wills *former diplomat, educator*
†Tuttle, Jerry *community education and development consultant*
Tuttle, Jon F. *lawyer*
Twaddell, William Hartsthorne *diplomat*
Tydings, Joseph Davies *lawyer, former senator*
Uberall, Herbert Michael Stefan *physicist, educator*
Ucelli, Loretta Maria *communications executive*
Uehlein, E(dward) Carl, Jr. *lawyer*
Ulman, Craig Hawkins *lawyer*
Ulmer, Alfred Conrad *investment banker*
†Ulsamer, Andrew George *federal agency manager*
†Underwood, Robert A. *congressional delegate, academic administrator*
Unsell, Lloyd Neal *energy organization executive, former journalist*
Unsoeld, Jolene *congresswoman*
Upshaw, Gene *sports association executive*
Upton, Frederick Stephen *congressman*
Vacketta, Carl Lee *lawyer, educator*
Vagley, Robert Everett *insurance association executive*
Vakerics, Thomas Vincent *lawyer*
Valdez, Abelardo Lopez *lawyer*
Valenti, Jack Joseph *motion picture executive*
Valentine, I. Tim, Jr. (Tim Valentine) *congressman*
Valentine, Steven Richards *lawyer*
Van Beek, Gus Willard *archaeologist*
Van Bennekom, Pieter *news service executive*
Vance, Bernard Wayne *lawyer, government official*
Van Cleve, John Vickrey *history educator*
Van Cleve, Ruth Gill *retired lawyer, government official*
VandenBos, Gary Roger *psychologist, publisher*
Vander Clute, Norman Roland *lawyer*
Vanderstar, John *lawyer*
†Vanderveen, John E. *federal agency administrator*
Vanderver, Timothy Arthur, Jr. *lawyer*
Van Dyk, Frederick Theodore *corporate executive*
†Van Hollen, Christopher, Jr. *state legislator, lawyer*
van Horne, Jon W. *lawyer*
Van Nelson, Nicholas Lloyd *business council executive*
†Varney, Christine A. *federal official*
Vaslef, Irene *historian, librarian*
Vaslef, Nicholas P. *broadcasting executive*
Vaught, Wilma L. *foundation executive, retired air force officer*
Veatch, Robert Marlin *philosophy educator, medical ethics researcher*
Veblen, Thomas Clayton *management consultant*
Velazquez, Nydia *congresswoman*
Veliotes, Nicholas Alexander *professional association executive, former ambassador and assistant secretary of state*
Vento, Bruce Frank *congressman*
Verhalen, Robert Donald *federal agency executive*
Verheyen, Egon *art historian, educator*
Verner, James Melton *lawyer*
Vernon, Weston, III (Wes Vernon) *journalist*
Verrill, Charles Owen, Jr. *lawyer*
VerStandig, John David *broadcasting executive, investor*
Verville, Elizabeth Giavani *federal official*
Vetter, Betty McGee *commission executive*
Vickery, Ann Morgan *lawyer*
Vieth, G. Duane *lawyer*
Villforth, John Carl *health physicist*
Vince, Clinton Andrew *lawyer*
Viola, Herman Joseph *museum director*
Viorst, Judith Stahl *author*
Visclosky, Peter John *congressman, lawyer*
Vise, David Allan *journalist*
Vlcek, Jan Benes *lawyer*
Vogel, John Henry *lawyer*
Vogt, Carl William *federal official, lawyer*
Voight, Jerry D. *lawyer*
Volkmer, Harold L. *congressman*
Von Hippel, Frank Niels *public and international affairs educator*
Vosbeck, Robert Randall *architect*
Vucanovich, Barbara Farrell *congresswoman*

Wachtmeister, Count Wilhelm H. F. *diplomat*
Wade, Robert Hirsch Beard *international consultant, former government and educational association official*
Wade, Robert Paul *lawyer*
Wadlow, R. Clark *lawyer*
†Wager, Douglas Charles *artistic director*
Wagner, Curtis Lee, Jr. *federal judge*
Wagner, George Francis Adolf *naval officer*
Wait, Carol Grace Cox *organization administrator*
Waits, John A. *lawyer*
Wald, Patricia McGowan *federal judge*
Walinsky, Louis Joseph *economic consultant, writer*
Walker, Charls Edward *economist, consultant*
Walker, David A(lan) *finance educator*
Walker, John Denley *foundation director, former government official*
Walker, M. Lucius, Jr. *mechanical engineer*
Walker, Mary Ann *lawyer*
Walker, Robert Harris *historian, author, editor*
Walker, Robert Smith *congressman*
Walker, Ronald Hugh *executive search company executive*
Wallace, Don, Jr. *law educator*
Wallace, James Harold, Jr. *lawyer*
Wallace, Robert Bruce *surgeon*
Wallace, Robert Bruce lawyer, *educator*
Wallach, John Paul *newspaper editor*
Wallach, Paul Geoffry *lawyer*
Wallis, W(ilson) Allen *economist, educator, statistician*
Wallison, Frieda K. *lawyer*
Wallison, Peter J. *lawyer*
Wallman, Steven Mark Harte *lawyer*
Wallop, Malcolm *senator, rancher*
Walsh, Edward Patrick *federal agency administrator*
Walsh, James Patrick *lawyer*
Walsh, James Thomas *congressman*
Walsh, Michael J. *lawyer*
†Walsh, William H., Jr. *statistical research director*
Walters, John Linton *electronics engineer, consultant*
Walton, Kathleen Endres *librarian*
Walton, Morgan Lauck, III *lawyer*
Wand, Patricia Ann *librarian*
Wang, John Cheng Hwai *communications engineer*
Ward, Alan S. *lawyer*
Ward, Erica Anne *lawyer, educator*
Ward, George Frank, Jr. *foreign service officer*
Ward, Jennifer C. *diplomat*
Ward, Nicholas Donnell *lawyer*
Warden, Richard Dana *government labor union official*
Ware, Thaddeus Van *government official*
Waris, Michael, Jr. *lawyer*
Warner, John William *senator*
Warnke, Paul Culliton *lawyer*
Warren, Albert *publishing executive*
Warren, David Liles *educational association executive*
Warren, Edward W. *lawyer*
Washburn, Wilcomb Edward *historian, educator*
Washington, Craig A. *congressman*
Wasilewski, Vincent Thomas *retired lawyer*
Wasshausen, Dieter Carl *systematic botanist*
Waters, Jennifer Nash *lawyer*
Waters, Maxine *congresswoman*
Waters, Timothy J. *lawyer*
Watkin, Virginia Guild *lawyer*
Watkins, Birge Swift *real estate investment executive*
Watkins, David *federal official*
†Watkins, James David *government official, naval officer*
Watson, Alexander Fletcher *ambassador*
Watson, Arthur Dennis *government official*
Watson, George Henry, Jr. *broadcast executive, journalist*
Watson, Harlan L(eroy) *federal official, physicist, economist*
Watson, Jack H., Jr. *lawyer*
†Watson, Jeffrey Howard *federal official*
Watt, Melvin L. *congressman, lawyer*
Wattenmaker, Richard Joel *archive director, art scholar*
Waxman, Henry Arnold *congressman*
Waxman, Margery Hope *lawyer*
Weaver, Warren, Jr. *writer*
Webb, Robert Kiefer *history educator*
Webber, Richard John *lawyer*
Weber, Susan *research organization executive*
Weber, Thomas Andrew *federal agency executive*
Webster, George Drury *lawyer*
Webster, Robert Kenly *lawyer*
Webster, Thomas Glenn *psychiatrist*
Webster, William Hedgcock *lawyer*
Wegener, Mark Douglas *lawyer*
Wegner, Helmuth Adalbert *lawyer, retired chemical company executive*
†Weich, Ronald H. *lawyer*
Weidenfeld, Edward Lee *lawyer*
Weil, Stephen Edward *museum official*
Weinberg, Edward *lawyer*
Weinberg, Robert Lester *lawyer, educator*
†Weinberger, Daniel R. *psychiatrist*
Weiner, Robert Stephen *federal agency administrator*
Weiner, Timothy Emlyn *newspaper journalist*
Weingold, Allan B. *obstetrician, gynecologist, educator*
Weinman, Howard Mark *lawyer*
Weinmann, John Giffen *lawyer, diplomat*
Weinstein, Diane Gilbert *federal judge, lawyer*
Weinstein, Harris *lawyer*
†Weisberg, Stuart Elliot *federal official, lawyer*
†Weise, George J. *commissioner*
Weismiller, Edward Ronald *English language educator, writer*
Weiss, Ellyn Renee *lawyer*
Weiss, Gail Ellen *legislative staff director*
Weiss, James Robert *lawyer*
Weiss, Jerome Paul *lawyer*
Weiss, Leonard *mathematician, engineer, senate staff director*
Weiss, Mark Anschel *lawyer*
Weiss, Paul *philosopher, educator*
Weiss, Paul Thomas *federal agency executive*
Weiss, Stanley Alan *mining, chemicals and refractory company executive*
Weiss, Stephen Joel *lawyer*
Weissbard, Samuel Held *lawyer*
Weissman, William R. *lawyer*
Weldon, W(ayne) Curtis *congressman*
Wellen, Robert Howard *lawyer*
Weller, Janet Louise *lawyer*
†Wells, Linton, II *federal official*
Wells, Thomas B. *federal judge*
Wellstone, Paul *senator*
Wendt, E. Allan *ambassador*
Wenner, Charles Roderick *lawyer*
Werkman, Sidney Lee *psychiatry educator*

Werner, Mario *pathology educator*
Wertheim, Mitzi Mallina *business executive*
Wertheimer, Fredric Michael *association executive*
Wesberry, James Pickett, Jr. *financial management consultant, auditor, international organization executive*
West, Donald Valentine *editor, journalist*
West, Emery Joseph *financial analyst, investment portfolio manager*
West, Gail Berry *lawyer*
West, J. Robinson *petroleum finance company executive, former government official*
West, Marvin Leon *sports editor*
West, Millard Farrar, Jr. *banker*
West, Robert MacLellan *science education consultant*
West, Stephen Allan *lawyer*
West, Togo Dennis, Jr. *secretary of Army, former aerospace executive*
†West, W. Richard, Jr. *museum director*
Wetherill, George West *geophysicist, planetary scientist*
Wexler, Anne *government relations and public affairs consultant*
Weyrich, Paul Michael *political organizations executive*
Whalen, Laurence J. *federal judge*
Whalen, Richard James *author, consultant*
Wheat, Alan Dupree *congressman, economist*
Whedon, Margaret Brunssen *television and radio producer*
Wheeler, Albin Gray *career officer, educator, law firm executive*
Wheeler, Edward Kendall *lawyer*
Wheeler, Thomas Edgar *communications technology executive*
Whelan, Roger Michael *lawyer, educator*
Whitaker, A(lbert) Duncan *lawyer*
Whitaker, Meade *federal judge*
White, Byron R. *former U.S. supreme court justice*
White, Christian S. *lawyer*
†White, George *government official, physical scientist*
White, George Malcolm *architect*
White, John Arnold *physics educator, research scientist*
White, Lee Calvin *lawyer*
White, Margita Eklund *television association executive*
White, Robert M., II *newspaper executive, editor, columnist*
White, Robert Mayer *meteorologist*
White, Robert Roy *chemical engineer*
†Whitehead, John C. *think tank executive*
Whitfield, Princess D. *principal*
Whiting, Richard Albert *lawyer*
†Whitmore, Frank Clifford, Jr. *geologist*
Whitten, Jamie Lloyd *congressman*
Whyte, Martin King *sociology and Chinese studies educator*
Widnall, Sheila Evans *secretary of Air Force, aeronautical educator, university official*
Widner, Ralph Randolph *planning executive*
†Wiedemann, Kent M. *federal official*
Wiegley, Roger Douglas *lawyer*
Wiese, John Paul *federal judge*
Wilburn, Mary Nelson *lawyer, writer, educator*
†Wilcher, Shirley J. *lawyer*
Wilcox, Philip C., Jr. *foreign service officer*
Wilensky, Gail Roggin *economist*
Wiley, Richard Emerson *lawyer*
†Wilhelm, David *political organization administrator*
Wilkinson, Christopher Foster *toxicologist, educator*
Wilkinson, John Burke *former government official, novelist, biographer*
Will, George Frederick *editor, political columnist, news commentator*
Willard, Richard Kennon *lawyer*
Willenbrock, Frederick Karl *engineer, educator*
Willett, Edward Farrand, Jr. *lawyer*
Willging, Paul Raymond *trade association executive*
†Williams, Arthur E. *federal agency administrator*
Williams, B. John, Jr. *lawyer, former federal judge*
Williams, Eddie Nathan *research institution executive*
Williams, John Edward *lawyer*
Williams, Karen Hastie *lawyer*
Williams, Margaret *federal official*
Williams, Maurice Jacoutot *development organization executive*
Williams, Pat *congressman*
†Williams, Paul *federal agency administrator*
Williams, Richard Llewellyn *diplomat*
Williams, Ronald L. *pharmaceutical association executive*
Williams, S. Linn *lawyer*
Williams, Stephen Fain *federal judge*
Williams, Sylvia Hill *museum director*
Williams, T. Raymond *lawyer*
Williamson, Edwin Dargan *lawyer, former federal official*
Williamson, Richard Hall *federal official*
Williamson, Thomas Samuel, Jr. *lawyer*
Willkie, Wendell Lewis, II *lawyer*
Willmore, Robert Louis *lawyer*
Wilner, Thomas Bernard *lawyer*
Wilson, Charles (Charlie Wilson) *congressman*
Wilson, Gary Dean *lawyer*
Wilson, Glen Parten *association administrator*
Wilson, Joseph Charles, IV *ambassador*
Wilson, M(athew) Kent *chemist, researcher, educator*
Wilson, R. Merinda D. *lawyer*
Wilson, Robert Spencer *magazine editor*
Wince-Smith, Deborah L. *federal agency administrator*
Wine, L. Mark *lawyer*
Wingerter, Eugene Joseph *association executive*
Winnefeld, James Alexander *defense analyst, former naval officer, author*
Winston, Judith Ann *lawyer*
Winter, Andrew J. *ambassador*
Winter, Douglas E. *lawyer, writer*
Winter, Harvey John *government official*
Winter, Roger Paul *government official*
Winter, Sidney Graham, Jr. *economist, educator*
Winter, Thomas Swanson *editor, newspaper executive*
†Winters, J. Sam *federal official*
Wintrol, John Patrick *lawyer*
Winzenried, Jesse David *retired petroleum executive*
Wirth, Timothy Endicott *federal official, former senator*
Wirtz, William Willard *lawyer*
Wise, Robert Ellsworth, Jr. (Bob Ellsworth) *congressman*
Wiseman, Alan M(itchell) *lawyer*
Wiseman, Laurence Donald *trade association executive*

Wishart, Leonard Plumer, III *army officer*
Wisner, Frank George *federal official, foreign service officer*
Wisniewski, John William *mining engineer, bank engineering executive*
Wiss, Marcia A. *lawyer*
Witcover, Jules Joseph *newspaper columnist, author*
Witherspoon, Sharon *lawyer*
Withrow, Mary Ellen *federal government treasurer*
Witt, James Lee *federal agency administrator*
Wofford, Harris Llewellyn *senator, lawyer*
Wolanin, Barbara Ann Boese *art curator, art historian*
Wolf, Frank R. *congressman, lawyer*
Wolfe, Janice E. *business development executive*
†Wolfe, Leslie R. *think-tank executive*
Wolff, Alan William *lawyer*
Wolff, Elroy Harris *lawyer*
Wolfman, Brunetta Reid *education educator*
Wollen, W. Foster *lawyer*
Wollenberg, J. Roger *lawyer*
Wood, John Martin *lawyer*
Woodall, Samuel Roy, Jr. *trade association executive*
Woodruff, Judy Carline *broadcast journalist*
Woods, Harriett Ruth *academic administrator*
Woods, Walter Ralph *animal scientist, research administrator*
Woodward, Robert Forbes *retired government official, consultant*
Woodward, Robert Upshur *newspaper reporter, writer*
Woodward, Susan Ellen *economist, federal official*
Woolsey, Lynn *congresswoman*
Woolsey, R. James, Jr. *federal agency administrator*
†Wooten, James Terrell *journalist*
†Worden, Joan M. *public relations executive*
Work, Charles Robert *lawyer*
Woroniak, Alexander *economist, educator*
†Worsley, James Randolph, Jr. *lawyer*
Worthy, K(enneth) Martin *lawyer*
Worthy, Patricia Morris *municipal official, lawyer*
Wortley, George Cornelius *business consultant, investor*
Woteki, Catherine Ellen *nutritionist*
Wouk, Herman *writer*
Wraase, Dennis Richard *utilities company executive, accountant*
Wright, Lawrence A. *federal judge*
Wright, Thomas William Dunstan *architect*
Wruble, Bernhardt Karp *lawyer*
Wurtzel, Alan Leon *retail company executive*
Wyden, Ronald Lee *congressman*
Wynn, Albert R. *congressman*
Wyss, John Benedict *lawyer*
Yablon, Jeffery Lee *lawyer*
Yancik, Joseph John *government official*
Yang, Tony Tien Sheng *engineering educator*
Yannucci, Thomas David *lawyer*
Yardley, Jonathan *journalist, columnist*
†Yarowsky, Jonathan R. *lawyer*
Yates, Sidney Richard *congressman, lawyer*
Yeo, Edwin Harley, III *bank executive*
Yerkes, David Norton *architect*
Yochelson, Ellis L(eon) *paleontologist*
Yochelson, John *political economist*
Yock, Robert John *federal judge*
Yoder, Hatten Schuyler, Jr. *petrologist*
Yoder, Ronnie A. *federal administrative law judge*
Yost, Paul Alexander, Jr. *foundation executive, retired coast guard officer*
Young, C. W. (Bill Young) *congressman*
Young, Donald Alan *physician*
Young, Donald E. *congressman*
Young, Harrison Hurst, III *banker*
Young, Kenneth Evans *educational consultant*
Young, Patrick *editor*
Young, Peter Robert *librarian*
Young, William Fielding *lawyer*
Yulish, Charles Barry *public affairs executive*
Yurow, John Jesse *lawyer*
Yuspeh, Alan Ralph *lawyer*
†Yzaguirre, Raul Humberto *civil rights administrator*
Zausner, L. Andrew *lawyer*
Zax, Leonard A. *lawyer*
Zeifang, Donald P. *lawyer*
Zeliff, William *congressman*
Zelnick, Carl Robert *news correspondent*
Zenowitz, Allan Ralph *government official*
Zevnik, Paul A. *lawyer*
Zielinski, Charles Anthony *lawyer*
Ziglar, James W. *former federal official, lawyer, investment banker*
Zimmer, Richard Alan *congressman, lawyer*
Zimmerman, Edwin Morton *lawyer*
Zimmerman, Hyman Joseph *internist, educator*
Zimmerman, John H. *communications company executive*
Zimmerman, Richard Gayford *journalist*
Zion, Roger H. *consulting firm executive, former congressman*
Zipp, Joel Frederick *lawyer*
Zlatoper, Ronald Joseph *career officer*
Zoeller, Jack Carl *financial executive*
†Zuck, Alfred Miller *association executive*
Zuckman, Harvey Lyle *legal educator*
Zupa, Victor Joseph *lawyer*
Zweben, Murray *lawyer, consultant*
†Zwick, Charles J. *think-tank executive*
†Zwick, Kenneth Lowell *lawyer*

FLORIDA

Alachua
Brewster, Marcus Eli *pharmaceutical company executive*
Gifford, George E. *immunology and medical microbiology educator*
Marston, Robert Quarles *university president*
Schneider, Richard T(heodore) *optics research executive, engineer*
Thornton, J. Ronald *technologist*

Altamonte Springs
Rudisill, Robert Mack, Jr. *lawyer*
Wilson, George Peter *association executive*

Amelia Island
Harman, John Robert, Jr. *management consultant*

Anna Maria
Aubry, Eugene Edwards *architect*
Kaiser, Albert Farr *diversified corporation executive*

Apopka
Rufenacht, Roger Allen *accounting educator*

Arcadia
Davis, Bruce Livingston, Jr. *retired accountant*
†Turnbull, David John (Chief Piercing Eyes-Penn) *cultural association executive*

Atlantic Beach
Engelmann, Rudolph Herman *electronics consultant*
Herge, Henry Curtis, Sr. *education educator, dean emeritus*
Zechella, Alexander Philip *oil company executive, former naval officer*

Atlantis
Gough, Carolyn Harley *library director*
Newmark, Emanuel *ophthalmologist*

Aventura
Kliger, Milton Richard *financial services executive*

Avon Park
Cornelius, Catherine Petrey *college president*

Babson Park
Cloud, Linda Beal *retired secondary school educator*
Morrison, Kenneth Douglas *newspaper columnist*

Bal Harbour
Behrman, Myron M. *banker, real estate investor*
Bernay, Betti *artist*
Field, Cyrus Adams *lawyer*
Gray, Phyllis Anne *librarian*
Hastings, Lawrence Vaeth *lawyer, physician, educator*

Bay Pines
Keskiner, Ali *psychiatrist*
†Robson, Martin Cecil *surgery educator, plastic surgeon*
†Vogel, Raymond John *federal government executive*

Belleair Beach
Fuentes, Martha Ayers *playwright*

Beverly Hills
Larsen, Erik *art history educator*

Boca Grande
Baldwin, William Howard *retired foundation executive, lawyer*
Brock, Mitchell *lawyer*
Nimitz, Chester William, Jr. *manufacturing company executive*

Boca Raton
Africk, Jack *duty free company executive*
Albrecht, Arthur John *advertising agency executive*
Alvarado, Ricardo Raphael *retired corporate executive, lawyer*
Amen, Irving *artist*
Arden, Eugene *retired university provost*
Arnold, Walter Martin *vocational education educator*
Beber, Robert H. *lawyer, financial services executive*
Beck, Jan Scott *lawyer*
Bettmann, Otto Ludwig *picture archivist, graphic historian*
Blanton, Jeremy *dance company director*
Boer, F. Peter *chemical company executive*
Bolduc, J. P. *specialty chemicals and specialized health care company executive*
†Bradley, George H. *furniture company executive*
Bressler, Steven L. *cognitive neuroscientist*
Burns, Gerald Phillip *education educator*
Butler, J. Murfree *chemical company executive*
Carraher, Charles Eugene, Jr. *chemistry educator, dean*
Catanese, Anthony James *academic administrator*
Chryssafopoulos, Nicholas *civil engineer*
Cohn, Jess Victor *psychiatrist*
Deppe, Henry A. *insurance company executive*
Dorfman, Allen Bernard *international management consultant*
Dunhill, Robert W. *advertising direct mail executive*
Elliott, Robert M. *retail executive*
Epstein, Barry R. *public relations counselor*
Erdman, Joseph *lawyer*
Evert, Christine Marie (Chris Evert) *retired professional tennis player*
Fengler, John Peter *television producer, director, advertising executive*
Fetter, Richard Elwood *retired industrial company executive*
Feuerlein, Willy John Arthur *economist, educator*
Fey, Dorothy (Mrs. George Jay Fey) *former association executive*
Finegold, Ronald *computer service executive*
Finkl, Charles William, II *geologist, educator*
Goldstein, Bernard *transportation company executive*
Gordon, Marjorie *opera director, coloratura soprano, educator*
Grace, J. Peter *specialty chemicals and specialized health care company executive*
Gralla, Eugene *natural gas company executive*
Hausman, Bruce *lawyer*
Hedrick, Frederic Cleveland, Jr. *lawyer*
Herst, Herman, Jr. *writer*
Hille, Stanley James *university dean*
Ingwersen, Martin Lewis *shipyard executive*
Jaffe, Leonard Sigmund *financial executive*
Jessup, Joe Lee *business educator, management consultant*
Kelley, Eugene John *business educator*
Keyes, Daniel *author*
Kramer, Cecile E. *retired medical librarian*
Krause, Heinz Werner *computer and communications executive*
Lagin, Neil *management executive*
†Lampi, Juanita *principal*
Latané, Bibb *social psychologist*
Leahy, William F. *insurance company executive, lawyer*
Lin, Y. K. *engineer, educator*
Lipsey, John C. (Jack Lipsey) *insurance company executive*
Mandor, Leonard Stewart *real estate company executive*
Marca-Relli, Conrad *artist*
McLeod, John Wishart *architect*
Miller, Eugene *financial executive*
Miller, Kenneth Roy *management consultant*
Mirkin, Abraham Jonathan *surgeon*
†Mischler, Harland Louis *investment company executive*
Monroe, William Lewis *human resources executive*
Murray, John Ralph *former college president*
Nystrom, John Warren *geographer, educator*
Ortlip, Paul Daniel *artist*
Posner, Sidney *advertising executive*
Reid, George Kell *biology educator, researcher, author*
Reinstein, Joel *lawyer*
Richardson, R(oss) Fred(erick) *insurance executive*
Rosenthal, Myron Martin *retired electrical engineer, educator, author*
Rosner, M. Norton *business systems and financial services company executive*
Ross, Donald Edward *university administrator*
Rothbaum, Ira *advertising and marketing executive*
Russo, Kathleen Marie *art educator*
Samuels, William Mason *physiology association executive*
Selby, Roger Lowell *museum director*
Shane, Ronald *financial company executive*
Sharf, Donald Jack *speech communication educator, researcher*
Sigel, Marshall Elliot *financial consultant*
Stein, Irvin *orthopaedic surgeon, educator*
†Tennies, Robert Hunter *headmaster*
Turano, Emanuel Nicolas *architect*
Turbeville, Gus *emeritus college president*
Turner, Lisa Phillips *human resources executive*
Van Arnem, Harold Louis *capital and technology equipment leasing company executive*
†Wiener, Elliott Maxwell *construction company executive*
Wolgin, David Lewis *psychology educator*
Wright, Joseph Robert, Jr. *corporate executive*

Bonita Springs
Birky, John Edward *banker, consultant, financial planner*
Cairns, Raymond Eldon, Jr. *consultant, retired chemical company executive*
Dacey, George Clement *retired laboratory administrator, consultant*
Johnson, Franklyn Arthur *academic administrator*
†Lane, William C., Jr. *principal*
Magill, Samuel Hays *retired college administrator, higher education consultant*
Miller, Richard Dwight *professional association executive*
†Trudnak, Stephen Joseph *landscape architect*

Boynton Beach
Allison, Dwight Leonard, Jr. *investor*
Babler, Wayne E. *retired telephone company executive, lawyer*
Balis, Moses Earl *biochemist, educator*
Bartholomew, Arthur Peck, Jr. *accountant*
Bloede, Victor Gustav *retired advertising executive*
Brome, Robert Harrison *lawyer*
Bryant, Donald Loyd *insurance company executive*
Caras, Joseph Sheldon *life insurance company executive*
Crane, L(eo) Stanley *retired railroad executive*
Cross, Ralph Emerson *mechanical engineer*
Davant, James Waring *investment banker*
Eady, Carol Murphy (Mrs. Karl Ernest Eady) *medical association administrator*
Falk, Bernard Henry *trade association executive*
Fields, Theodore *consulting medical radiation physicist*
Friedman, Raymond *chemical engineer, fire protection specialist*
Heckelmann, Charles Newman (Charles Lawton) *author, publishing consultant*
Jacobs, C. Bernard *banker*
Johnson, Edward A. *manufacturing executive*
Kronman, Joseph Henry *orthodontist*
Lundgren, Robert Wayne *retired utility executive, consultant*
Miller, Emanuel *retired lawyer, banker*
Mirman, Irving R. *scientific adviser*
Peltzie, Kenneth Gerald *hospital administrator, educator*
Plossu, Bernard Pierre *photographer*
Saxbe, William Bart *lawyer, former attorney general of U.S.*
Smith, Charles Henry, Jr. *industrial executive*
Snell, Thaddeus Stevens, III *lawyer, retired building materials manufacturing company executive*
Spitz, Arnoldt John *corporate professional, consultant*
Stubbins, Hugh A(sher), Jr. *architect*
Turner, William Benjamin *electrical engineer*
Wampler, Charles Edwin *retired telephone company executive*

Bradenton
Allen, James Lovic, Jr. *humanist, writer, retired educator*
Balsley, Howard Lloyd *economist*
Beall, Robert Matthews, II *retail chain executive*
Burton, Ralph Joseph *international development consultant*
Doenecke, Carol Anne *artist*
Feeley, John Paul *retired paper company executive*
Friedrich, Robert Edmund *retired electrical engineer, corporate consultant*
Hare, John, IV *planetarium director*
Hodgell, Robert Overman *artist, art educator*
Jain, Mohinder (Mona Jain) *daycare administrator, educator*
Jones, Horace Charles *former sales company executive*
Keane, Gustave Robert *architect, consultant*
Maynard, Donald Nelson *horticulturist, educator*
McFarland, Richard Macklin *retired journalist*
Phelan, John Densmore *insurance executive, consultant*
Price, Edgar Hilleary, Jr. *business consultant*
Ridings, Dorothy Sattes *communications executive, newspaper publisher*
†Roeder, Myron A. *agricultural products company executive*
Thompson, Barbara Storck *state official*
†Waters, Will Estel *horticulturist, researcher, educator*
Wendt, Lloyd *writer*
†White, Dale Andrew *journalist*

Brandon
Williamson, Robert Charles *marketing executive*

Brooksville
Slaatte, Howard Alexander *minister, philosophy educator*

Bushnell
Hagin, T. Richard *lawyer*

Cape Canaveral
Clark, John F. *aerospace research and engineering educator*

Cape Coral
Peters, Donald Cameron *construction company executive*
Purdy, Alan Harris *biomedical engineer*
Seemann, Ernest Albright *lawyer*
Shurrager, Phil Sheridan *psychologist, educator*
West, John Merle *retired physicist, nuclear consultant*

Captiva
Fadiman, Clifton *writer, editor, radio and television entertainer*
Ronald, Peter *utility executive*

Casselberry
Medin, A. Louis *computer company executive*
Vincent, Thomas James *retired manufacturing company executive*

Cedar Key
Starnes, Earl Maxwell *urban and regional planner, architect*

Chattahoochee
Ivory, Peter B. C. B. *medical administrator*

Clearwater
Beckwith, William Hunter *clergyman*
Berman, Elihu H. *lawyer*
Bertram, Frederic Amos *architect*
Bramante, Pietro Ottavio *physiology educator, retired pathology specialist*
Carlson, Natalie Savage *author*
Caronis, George John *insurance executive*
Chamberlin, Terry McBride *sailing equipment company executive*
Darack, Arthur J. *editor*
Deadman, Leonard John *advertising executive*
Free, E. LeBron *lawyer*
Fromhagen, Carl, Jr. *obstetrician/gynecologist*
Glindeman, Henry Peter, Jr. *real estate developer*
Hoornstra, Edward H. *retail company executive*
Horton, Donna Alberg *technical writer*
Houtz, Duane Talbott *hospital administrator*
Howes, James Guerdon *airport director*
Leeds, Robert Lewis, Jr. *educator*
†Paxson, Lowell White *television station executive*
Pendleton, Sumner Alden *financial consultant*
†Pinch, John G. *radio executive*
†Raymund, Steven *computer company executive*
Smith, Marion Pafford *avionics company executive*
Turley, Stewart *retail company executive*
Whedon, George Donald *medical administrator, researcher*
Youngberg, Robert Stanley *principal, consultant*

Clermont
Chandler, Robert Flint, Jr. *international agriculture consultant*
Dyson, Raymond Clegg *building contractor, construction consultant*

Cocoa
Bacchus, James L. (Jim Bacchus) *congressman*

Coconut Grove
Denaro, Gregory *lawyer*
†Litten, H. Randall *manufacturing company executive*

Coral Gables
Baddour, Raymond Frederick *chemical engineer, educator, entrepreneur*
Bagley, Robert Waller *mathematics educator*
Blasier, Cole *political scientist*
Blumberg, David *builder, developer*
Burini, Sonia Montes de Oca *apparel manufacturing and public relations executive*
Cobb, Charles E., Jr. *corporate executive, former ambassador*
Criss, Cecil M. *chemistry educator*
Davis, Mattie Belle Edwards *retired county judge*
Einspruch, Norman Gerald *physicist, educator*
Erickson, Dennis *university football coach*
†Fung, Kee-Ying *engineer, educator, researcher*
Hertz, Arthur Herman *advertising executive*
Higginbottom, Samuel Logan *retired aerospace company executive*
Howard, Bernard Eufinger *computer science educator and mathematics*
Jacobson, Leonard I. *psychologist, educator*
Jury, Eliahu Ibraham *electrical engineer, research educator*
Kline, Jacob *biomedical engineering educator*
Kniskern, Joseph Warren *lawyer*
†Ladner, Robert Arthur, Jr. *research company executive*
Latham, Jean Lee *writer*
Leblanc, Roger Maurice *chemistry educator*
Lemos, Ramon Marcelino *philosophy educator*
McCarthy, Patrick A. *English educator*
Minahan, John *English author*
Moss, Ambler Holmes, Jr. *university dean, lawyer, former ambassador*
Murfin, Ross C *university dean, English educator*
Nunez-Portuondo, Ricardo *investment company executive*
Ramsey, John Hansberry *executive search firm executive, investment banker*
Rodgers, Frank *librarian*
Saffir, Herbert Seymour *structural engineer, consultant*
Shipley, Vergil Alan *political science educator*
†Spear, Laurinda Hope *architect*
Stewart, Harris Bates, Jr. *oceanographer*
Sumanth, David Jonnakoty *industrial engineer, educator*
Warburton, Ralph Joseph *architect, engineer, planner, educator*
Yarger, Sam Jacob *dean, educator*
Young, Tzay Y. *electrical and computer engineering educator*

Coral Springs
Elmore, Walter A. *electrical engineer, consultant*
Luing, Gary Alan *financial management educator*
†Vandiver, Frances *principal*

Crestview
Sikes, Robert L. F. *former congressman*

Crystal River
Black, Charles Alvin *consulting engineering executive*

Cypress Gardens
Gobie, Henry Macaulay *philatelic researcher, retired postal executive*

Dade City
Burdick, Glenn Arthur *physicist, engineering educator*
McBath, Donald Linus *osteopathic physician*
†Rine, Susan *principal*

Davie
Shula, Don Francis *professional football coach*

Daytona Beach
Alcott, Amy Strum *professional golfer*
†Amick, William Walker *golf course architect*
Bronson, Oswald Perry *religious organization administrator, clergyman*
Collyer, Robert B. *association executive*
Davidson, Herbert M. (Tippen), Jr. *newspaper publisher*
†Davidson, Josephine F. *newspaper editor*
Dukas, Peter *management consultant, educator*
Earnhardt, (Ralph) Dale *professional race car driver*
Elliott, Carol Harris *nutrition counselor, dietitian*
Fly, James Lawrence, Jr. *construction executive*
Gardner, Joseph Lawrence *editor, writer*
Gauch, Eugene William, Jr. *former air force officer*
Geier, George *optical engineering consultant*
Haviland, Robert Paul *engineering executive, author*
Inkster, Juli *professional golfer*
King, Betsy *professional golfer*
Libby, Gary Russell *museum director*
Locke, Edwin Allen, Jr. *investment banker*
Mallon, Meg *professional golfer*
†Marlin, Sterling *professional race car driver*
Mc Collister, John Charles *writer, clergyman, educator*
McCoy, Edward Fitzgerald *social services facility administrator*
Mechem, Charles Stanley, Jr. *former broadcasting executive, golf association executive*
Millar, Gordon Halstead *mechanical engineer, agricultural machinery manufacturing executive*
Mochrie, Dottie *professional golfer*
Osterholm, J(ohn) Roger *humanities educator*
Petty, Kyle *professional stock car driver*
†Reeves, Donna Andrews *golfer*
Sheehan, Patty *professional golfer*
†Sliwa, Steven Mark *engineering executive, academic administrator*
Whitworth, Kathrynne Ann *professional golfer*
Yarborough, William Caleb *former professional stock car race driver*

Deerfield Beach
†Assaf, Ronald G. *electronics executive*
†Bernstein, Stanley Robert *financial consultant, mortgage broker and banker*
Brown, Colin W(egand) *lawyer, diversified company executive*
Faulk, Elizabeth Hammond *psychologist*
Hochberger, Simon *communications educator*
Monteleone, Raymond R. *electronics company executive, consultant*
†Moran, James M. *automotive sales executive*
Moran, Patricia Genevieve *corporate executive*
Rung, Richard Allen *lawyer, retired air force officer, retired educator*

Deland
Brakeman, Louis Freeman *former university administrator*
Coolidge, Edwin Channing *chemistry educator*
Coulter, Borden McKee *management consultant*
Dascher, Paul Edward *academic dean, accounting educator*
Duncan, Pope Alexander *college administrator*
Fant, Clyde Edward, Jr. *religion educator*
Gill, Donald George *education educator*
Horton, Thomas R. *business advisor*
Langston, Paul T. *music educator, university dean, composer*
Lee, Howard Douglas *university president*
MacMahon, Charles Hutchins, Jr. *architect*
McCormick, Lyle Bernard, Jr. *management consultant*
Morland, Richard Boyd *retired educator*
†Renfroe, L. Edwin *bank executive*
Sorensen, Jacki Faye *choreographer, aerobic dance company executive*
Tedros, Theodore Zaki *appraiser, real estate broker, educator*

Delray Beach
Barlow, Joel *retired lawyer*
Bryan, Robert Fessler *former investment analyst*
Cary, James Donald *journalist*
Charyk, Joseph Vincent *retired satellite telecommunications executive*
Coyle, William *educator*
Draper, Line Bloom (Line B. Draper-Rubba) *artist*
Epley, Marion Jay *oil company executive*
†Fuente, D. I. *office supply manufacturing executive*
Groening, William Andrew, Jr. *lawyer, former chemical company executive*
Hegstrom, William Jean *mathematics educator*
Himmelright, Robert John, Jr. *rubber company executive*
Holmes, Walter Stephen, Jr. *retired financial executive*
Jenkins, Stanley Michael *stockbroker*
Larry, R. Heath *lawyer*
Leapman, Phyllis Lenore *retired nursing educator*
Peoples, Thomas Edward *publisher, executive, writer*
Reef, Arthur *industry business consultant*
Rippeteau, Darrel Downing *architect*
Ronk, Glenn Emery *retired executive consultant, former electronics company executive*
Ross, Beatrice Brook *artist*
Rush, Kenneth *lawyer, industrialist, government official*
Saffer, Alfred *retired chemical company executive*
Shannon, Stephen Quinby, Jr. *broadcasting human resources executive*
Shister, Joseph *labor arbitrator, law educator*
Sibigtroth, Joseph Clarence *insurance company executive*
Silver, Samuel Manuel *rabbi, author*
Smith, John Joseph *textile company executive, educator*
Stewart, Patricia Carry *foundation administrator*
Stone, Franz Theodore *retired fabricated metal products manufacturing executive*
Zarwyn, Berthold *physical scientist*

Destin
Carlton, Paul Kendall *former air force officer, consultant*
Cunningham, James Everett *retired energy services company executive*

Dover
Pearson, Walter Donald *editor, columnist*

Dundee
Johnson, Gordon Selby *consulting electrical engineer*

Dunedin
Carmichael, Mary Mulloy *foreign service officer, educator*
Espy, Charles Clifford *English educator, author, consultant, lecturer, administrator*
Geer, James Hamilton *retired broadcasting company executive*
Rosa, Raymond Ulric *retired banker*

Dunnellon
Dixon, W(illiam) Robert *retired educational psychology educator*

Eastpoint
Hoffer, Thomas William *communication educator*

Eglin A F B
†Pletcher, John Harold, Jr. *career military officer*

Englewood
Defliese, Philip Leroy *accountant, educator*
Marchand, Leslie Alexis *language educator, writer*
Schultz, Arthur Joseph, Jr. *retired trade association executive*
Simis, Theodore Luckey *investment banker, information technology executive*
Sisson, Robert F. *photographer, writer, lecturer, educator*
Suiter, John William *industrial engineer, consultant*

Eustis
Trussell, Charles Tait *columnist*

Fernandina Beach
Barlow, Anne Louise *pediatrician, medical research administrator*
†Burns, Stephen Redding *golf course architect*
D'Agnese, Helen Jean *artist*
Kurtz, Myers Richard *hospital administrator*
Rogers, Robert Burnett *naval officer*

Fisher Island
McAmis, Edwin Earl *lawyer*
Trippe, Kenneth Alvin Battershill *shipping industry executive*

Flagler Beach
Nebil, Corinne Elizabeth *artist*

Fort Lauderdale
Adams, Alfred Hugh *college president*
Adams, Daniel Lee *lawyer*
Alberg, Mildred Freed *film and television producer, writer*
†Aleff, Andrea Lee (Andy Aleff) *newspaper editor*
Anderson, Richard Edmund *city manager, management consultant*
†Andrews, John Harold *health care administrator*
Azrin, Nathan Harold *psychologist*
Barger, Carl *professional sports team executive*
Bartelstone, Rona Sue *gerontologist*
Bayles, Samuel Heagan *advertising agency executive*
Becker, Edward A. *accounting educator, consultant*
Berwig, Newton Urbano *aerospace executive*
†Bleckner, Edward, Jr. *data communication products company executive*
Buck, Thomas Randolph *lawyer*
Cannon, Herbert Seth *investment banker*
†Caporella, Nick A. *diversified company executive*
Carney, Dennis Joseph *former steel company executive, consulting company executive*
†Cicora, Kenneth Allan *public information officer*
Cryer, Eugene Edward *newspaper editor*
Csatary, Laszlo Kalman *anesthesiologist, cancer researcher*
Cumerford, William Richard *fund raising and public relations executive*
†Dawson, Muriel Amanda *legislator*
de Leon, Lidia Maria *magazine editor*
†Dickinson, Richard *landscape architect*
Dressler, Robert A. *lawyer*
Durfey, Robert Walker *sea transportation consultant*
Eisner, Will *publishing company executive*
Feldman, Stephen *university president*
Ferris, Robert Edmund *lawyer*
Fine, Howard Alan *travel industry chief executive officer*
Fischler, Abraham Saul *university president*
Fishe, Gerald Raymond Aylmer *engineering executive*
Fitzpatrick, Mark *professional hockey player*
Fox, Henry H. (Bucky Fox) *lawyer*
Fox, James Frederick *public relations counsel*
Gardner, Russell Menese *lawyer*
Gerbino, John *advertising executive*
Gilbert, Anne Wieland *journalist*
Gill, Richard Thomas *opera singer, economic analyst*
Gonzalez, Jose Alejandro, Jr. *federal judge*
†Greenberger, Sheldon Lee *newspaper advertising executive*
†Grestner, Jonathan Neil *religious studies educator*
†Gude, Nancy Carlson *publishing company executive*
Hanbury, George Lafayette, II *city manager*
Hanson, Duane Elwood *sculptor*
Hargrove, John Russell *lawyer*
Harris, Stanley Louis, Jr. *advertising executive*
†Hiaasen, Carl Andreas *lawyer*
Hirsch, Jeffrey Allan *lawyer*
Hirshson, William Roscoe *real estate consultant*
Holland, Beth *actress*
Holtzman, Gary Yale *recreational facility executive*
Huizenga, Harry Wayne *entertainment corporation executive, professional sports team executive*
Jotcham, Thomas Denis *marketing communications consultant*
Keats, Harold Alan *corporate executive*
†Keller, Larry Allan *reporter*
Kemper Littman, Marlyn *information scientist, educator*
Klein, Bernard *publishing company executive*
Kobert, Norman *asset management consultant*
Levi, Kurt *retired banker*
Lodwick, Gwilym Savage *radiologist, educator*
Lyons, Richard Chapman *urologist*
Marcus, Richard Alan *lawyer, distribution company executive*
Maucker, Earl Robert *newspaper editor*
McMahon-Dumas, Carmen Elethea *education educator*
Miller, Tanfield Charles *accountant*
†Morse, Edward J. *automotive executive*
Moss, Stephen B. *lawyer*
Murray, Bryan Clarence *professional sports team executive*
O'Bryan, William Monteith *lawyer*
Parkyn, John William *editor, writer*
Paulauskas, Edmund Walter *real estate broker*
Peterson, Colin Hampton *electronics company executive*
Pettijohn, Fred Phillips *retired newspaper executive, consultant*
Randi, James (Randall James Hamilton Zwinge) *magician, writer, educator*
Randolph, Jennings, Jr. (Jay Randolph) *sportscaster*
†Robinson, James *bank executive*
Roettger, Norman Charles, Jr. *federal judge*
Russo, Thomas Joseph *hospitality and consumer durables industry executive*
Sanders, Howard *investment company executive*
†Schulte, Frederick James *newpaper editor*
Singer, Donald Ivan *architect*
†Skiddell, Elliot Lewis *rabbi*
Sklar, Alexander *electrical company executive*
†Smith, James Edward *newspaper company executive*
†Smith, Scott Clybourn *communications company executive*
Sorensen, Allan Chresten *service company executive*
Stone, Edward Durell, Jr. *landscape architect*
Sutte, Donald T., Jr. *real estate executive*
†Tenaglia, John Franc *broadcasting executive*
†Thayer, Charles J. *investment banker*
†Thomas, Rowland Hayes, Jr. *computer services company executive*
†Torrey, William Arthur *professional hockey team executive*
Turner, Hugh Joseph, Jr. *lawyer*
†Turner, Richard Stanley *health care financial executive*
Van Alstyne, Judith Sturges *English language educator*
Vanbiesbrouck, John *professional hockey player*
Vasquez, William Leroy *marketing professional, educator*
Wallace, Joan S. *international development consultant*
Walton, Rodney Earl *lawyer*
†Weinstein, Peter M. *lawyer, state senator*
Wojcik, Cass *decorative supply company executive, former city official*
Wynne, Brian James *former association executive, consultant*
Young, Lois Catherine Williams *public administrator, consultant*
Young, William Benjamin *special education educator*
Zikakis, John P. *educator, researcher, biochemist*
†Zirkle, David H. *data processing company executive*
Zloch, William J. *federal judge*

Fort Myers
Aleo, Joseph John *pathology scientist, educator, academic research administrator*
Allen, Richard C. *retired lawyer, educator*
Ball, Robert Michael *government aviation official*
Barbour, Hugh Revell *publisher*
Barbour, William Rinehart, Jr. *retired book publisher*
Brooks, Julie Agnes *psychiatrist*
Brown, Earl Kent *historian, clergyman*
Conger, Kyril B. *urologist*
Cyphert, Frederick Ralph *academic administrator*
Ferguson, James A. *surgeon*
Fromm, Winfield Eric *retired corporate executive, engineering consultant and investor*
Gerdes, Lillian Anna *elementary education educator*
Grove, William Johnson *physician, surgery educator*
†Halgrim, Robert P. *museum director*
Hanson, Arnold Philip *retired lawyer*
Hudson, Leonard Harlow *contractor*
†Hughes, Judi E. *principal*
Kelly, William E. *psychoanalyst*
Mc Grath, William Restore *transportation planner, traffic engineer*
†McLeod, Allan L., Jr. *bank executive*
Medvecky, Robert Stephen *lawyer*
Mergler, Harry Winston *engineering educator*
Moeschl, Stanley Francis *electrical engineer, management consultant*
Morse, John Harleigh *lawyer*
Nathan, James Robert *hospital administrator*
O'Dell, William Francis *retired business executive, author*
†Ölling, Edward Henry *aerospace engineer, consulting firm executive*
Peete, Calvin *professional golfer*
Powell, Richard Pitts *writer*
Ryan, William Joseph *communications company executive*
Schwartz, Carl Edward *artist, printmaker*
Scott, Kenneth Elsner *mechanical engineering educator*
Simmons, Vaughan Pippen *medical consultant*
Solomon, Irvin D. *history educator, author*
Sypert, George Walter *neurosurgery educator, clinical neurosurgeon, research neurophysiologist*
Tyrer, John Lloyd *headmaster emeritus*
Wendeborn, Richard Donald *retired manufacturing company executive*
Zupko, Arthur George *consultant to drug industry, retired college administrator*

Fort Myers Beach
Arneson, Harold Elias Grant *manufacturing engineer, consultant*
Smyth, Joseph Vincent *manufacturing company executive*

Fort Pierce
Chapman, John Davol *communications brokerage executive*
†Garment, Robert *clergyman*
†Herman, Richard J. *marine biology administrator*
Mooney, John Bradford, Jr. *oceanographer, engineer, consultant*
Sampson, Bonita Lippard *health occupations educator*

Fort Walton Beach
Clements, Bernadette Stone *ballet director*
Gates, Philip Don *anesthesiologist*
Phillips, Loyal *newspaper executive*

Gainesville
Abbott, Thomas Benjamin *speech educator*
Abdel-Khalik, Ahmed Rashad *business educator*
Agrios, George Nicholas *plant pathology educator*
Andrew, Edward Raymond *physicist*
Anghaie, Samim *nuclear engineer, educator*
Barber, Charles Edward *newspaper executive, journalist*
Barton, Allen Hoisington *sociologist*
Baughman, George Fechtig *foundation executive*
Bedell, George Chester *retired publisher*
Bednarek, Alexander Robert *mathematician, educator*
Behnke, Marylou *neonatologist, educator*
Bennett, Thomas Peter *museum director, educator, biologist*
Bernard, H. Russell *anthropology educator, scientific editor*
Besch, Emerson Louis *physiology educator, past academic administrator*
Bishop, Budd Harris *museum administrator*
Block, Seymour Stanton *chemical engineering educator, consultant, writer*
Bodine, Willis Ramsey, Jr. *music educator, organist*
†Brown, William Samuel, Jr. *communication processes and disorders educator*
Bryan, Robert Armistead *university administrator, educator*
Canelas, Dale Brunelle *library director*
Cantliffe, Daniel James *horticulture educator*
Capaldi, Elizabeth Ann Deutsch *psychological sciences educator*
Capehart, Barney Lee *industrial and systems engineer*
Carr, Glenna Dodson *economics educator*
Challoner, David Reynolds *university official, physician*
Chang, Weilin Parrish *construction educator, administrator, researcher*
†Cheek, Jimmy Geary *university dean, agricultural education and communications educator*
†Childers, Donald Gene *electrical engineering educator, researcher*
Childers, Norman Franklin *horticulture educator*
Clark, Elmer J. *education educator*
†Clark, William Burton, IV *dentist, educator*
Cluff, Leighton Eggertsen *physician*
Copeland, Edward Meadors, III *surgery educator*
Couch, Leon Worthington *electrical engineering educator*
Couch, Margaret Wheland *research chemist*
Cousins, Robert John *nutritional biochemist, educator*
Craven, Roy Curtis, Jr. *art educator, art gallery director*
Creel, Austin Bowman *religion educator*
Davis, George Kelso *nutrition biochemist, educator*
Davis, Horance Gibbs, Jr. *retired educator, journalist*
†Delfino, Joseph John *environmental engineering sciences educator*
Der-Houssikian, Haig *linguistics educator*
DeSimone, Rory Jean *small business owner*
Detweiler, Steven Lawrence *physicist, educator*
Dewar, Michael James Steuart *chemistry educator*
Dewsbury, Donald Allen *comparative psychologist*
Dickinson, Joshua Clifton, Jr. *museum director, educator*
Dierks, Richard Ernest *veterinarian, educational administrator*
Dilcher, David Leonard *paleobotany educator*
Dinculeanu, Nicolae *mathematician*
Drago, Russell Stephen *chemist, educator*
Drucker, Daniel Charles *engineer, educator*
Drury, Kenneth Clayton *biological scientist*
Eder, George Jackson *lawyer, economist*
Eichhorn, Heinrich Karl *astronomer, educator, consultant*
Elzinga, Donald Jack *industrial engineering researcher, educator*
Emch, Gerard Gustav *mathematics and physics educator*
Emch-Dériaz, Antoinette Suzanne *historian*
Feiss, Carl Lehman *retired urban planning educator*
Finger, Kenneth Franklin *academic administrator*
Fossum, Jerry George *electrical engineering educator*
Freeland, James M. Jackson *lawyer, educator*
Gander, John Edward *biochemistry educator*
Gerberg, Eugene Jordan *entomologist*
Goggin, Margaret Knox *librarian, educator*
Goldhurst, William *retired humanities and English educator, writer*
Gravenstein, Joachim Stefan *anesthesiologist, educator*
†Green, David Marvin *psychology educator, researcher, consultant*
Greer, Melvin *medical educator*
Grundy, Betty Lou Bottoms *anesthesiology and pharmaceutics educator*
Gutekunst, Richard Ralph *microbiology educator*
†Haldeman, Joe William *novelist*
Hampton, William Wade, III *lawyer*
Hanrahan, Robert Joseph *chemist, educator*
Hanson, Harold Palmer *physicist, government official, editor, academic administrator*
Haring, Ellen Stone (Mrs. E. S. Haring) *philosophy educator*
Harrer, Gustave Adolphus *librarian, educator*
Harris, Marvin *anthropology educator*
Harrison, John Armstrong *historian, university dean*
†Harrison, Willard W. *chemist, educator*
†Hartigan, Karelisa Dorothy *classics educator*
Heflin, Martin Ganier *foreign service officer, international political economist*
Himes, James Albert *veterinary medicine educator emeritus*

Hollien, Harry Francis *speech and communications scientist, educator*
†Holloway, Paul Howard *materials science educator*
Hoy, Marjorie Ann *entomology educator, researcher*
Isaacs, Gerald William *agricultural engineer, educator*
Jacobs, Alan Martin *physicist, educator*
Jaeger, Boi Jon *health administrator educator*
Jones, Elizabeth Nordwall *county government official*
Katritzky, Alan Roy *chemistry educator, consultant*
Kenney, Thomas Frederick *broadcasting executive*
Kerslake, Kenneth Alvin *art educator, printmaker*
†Kirkpatrick, George Grier, Jr. *state legislative*
Klauder, John Rider *physics educator*
Kurzweg, Ulrich Hermann *engineering science educator*
Kushner, David Zakeri *musicologist, educator*
Legler, Donald Wayne *university dean, dentist*
Lindholm, Fredrik Arthur *electrical engineering educator, researcher*
Liquori, Martin William, Jr. *athlete, business executive, television commentator*
Locascio, Salvadore Joseph *horticulturist*
Lombardi, John V. *university administrator, historian*
Lopez, Andy *university athletic coach*
Lowenstein, Ralph Lynn *university dean*
Malvern, Lawrence Earl *engineering educator, researcher*
Mauderli, Walter *radiology educator*
Mautz, Robert Barbeau *lawyer, educator*
Medina, Jose Enrique *dentist, educator*
Merimee, Thomas Joseph *medical educator*
†Micha, David Allan *chemistry and physics educator*
Milanich, Jerald Thomas *archaeologist, museum curator*
Moberly, Robert Blakely *lawyer, educator*
Modell, Jerome Herbert *anesthesiologist, educator, dean*
Murray, Ernest Don *artist, educator*
Neims, Allen Howard *univeristy dean, medical scientist*
Neugroschel, Arnost *electrical engineering educator*
Nicoletti, Paul Lee *veterinarian, educator*
†Oberlander, Herbert *insect physiologist, educator*
†Ohanian, Mihran Jacob *engineering educator*
Ohrn, Nils Yngve *chemistry and physics educator*
Otis, Arthur Brooks *physiologist, educator*
Peebles, Peyton Zimmerman, Jr. *electrical engineer, educator*
Penland, Arnold Clifford, Jr. *college dean, educator*
Pepine, Carl John *physician, educator*
Person, Willis Bagley *chemistry educator*
Pfaff, William Wallace *physician, educator*
Phillips, Winfred Marshall *engineer, educator, university administrator*
Pierce, Robert Nash *writer*
†Pop-Stojanovic, Zoran Rista *mathematics educator*
Price, Donald Ray *agricultural engineer, university administrator*
Probert, Walter *lawyer, educator*
Proctor, Samuel *history educator*
Purcifull, Dan Elwood *plant virologist, educator*
Quarles, James Cliv *law educator*
Quesenberry, Kenneth Hays *agronomy educator*
Randall, Malcom *health care administrator*
Rhoton, Albert Loren, Jr. *neurological surgery educator*
Rosenbloom, Arlan Lee *physician, educator*
Rubin, Melvin Lynne *ophthalmologist, educator*
Schaub, James Hamilton *engineering educator*
Schiebler, Gerold Ludwig *physician, educator*
Schmeling, Gareth *classics educator*
Schmertmann, John Henry *civil engineer, educator, consultant*
†Schmidt, Peter R. *anthropology educator*
Schmidt-Nielsen, Bodil Mimi (Mrs. Roger G. Chagnon) *physiologist*
Schueller, Wolfgang Augustus *architectural educator, writer*
Severy, Lawrence James *psychologist, educator*
Sharp, Bert Lavon *retired education educator, retired university dean*
Shyy, Wei *aerospace, mechanical engineering researcher and educator*
Simmons, John Kaul *accounting educator*
Singer, Robert Norman *motor behavior educator*
Singley, John Edward, Jr. *environmental engineer, consultant*
Sisler, Harry Hall *chemist, educator*
Small, Parker Adams, Jr. *pediatrician, educator*
Smith, Alexander Goudy *physics and astronomy educator*
Smith, David Thornton *lawyer, educator*
Smith, Jo Anne *writer, retired educator*
†Smith, Stanley Kent *economics and demographics educator*
Sorensen, Andrew Aaron *provost*
Spurrier, Steve *university athletic coach*
Steadham, Charles Victor, Jr. *entertainment agent, producer*
Stehli, Francis Greenough *retired geologist, educator*
Stein, Jay M. *planning and design educator, consultant*
Stephan, Alexander F. *German language and literature educator*
Stern, William Louis *botanist, educator*
Stone, Williard Everard *accountant, educator*
Storer, Morris Brewster *emeritus philosophy educator*
Suzuki, Howard Kazuro *retired anatomist, educator*
Talbert, James Lewis *pediatric surgeon, educator*
Taylor, William Jape *physician*
Teitelbaum, Philip *psychologist*
†Teixeira, Arthur Alves *food engineer, consultant*
†Thompson, Neal Philip *food science and nutrition educator*
Thompson, Victor Alexander *political science educator*
†Tou, Julius T. *electrical and computer engineering educator*
Uelsmann, Jerry Norman *photographer*
Van Alstyne, W. Scott, Jr. *lawyer, educator*
†Vasil, Indra Kumar *botanist*
Vaughn, Rufus Mahlon *psychiatrist*
Verink, Ellis Daniel, Jr. *metallurgical engineering educator, consultant*
Vierck, Charles John, Jr. *neuroscience educator, scientist*
Viessman, Warren, Jr. *academic dean, civil engineering educator, researcher*
von Mering, Otto Oswald *anthropology educator*
Walker, Robert Dixon, III *surgeon, urologist, educator*
Wass, Hannelore Lina *educational psychology educator*
Watson, Robert Joe *hospital administrator, retired career officer*
Wethington, John Abner, Jr. *retired nuclear engineering educator*
Weyrauch, Walter Otto *legal educator*
White, Jill Carolyn *lawyer*
White, John David *composer, theorist, cellist*
Wilcox, Charles Julian *geneticist, educator*
Williams, Hiram Draper *artist, educator*
Williams, Ralph Chester, Jr. *physician, educator*
Willocks, Robert Max *retired librarian*
Wing, Elizabeth Schwarz *museum curator, educator*
Woeste, John Theodore *academic administrator*
Wood, Frank Bradshaw *retired astronomy educator*
Wyatt-Brown, Bertram *historian, educator*
Yau, Stephen Sik-sang *computer science and engineering educator, computer scientist, researcher*
York, E. Travis, Jr. *academic administrator, former university chancellor, consultant*
Young, David Michael *biochemistry and molecular biology educator, physician*
Zabel, Edward *economist, educator*
†Zerner, Michael Charles *chemistry and physics educator, consultant, researcher*

Goldenrod
Carmichael, William Jerome *publishing company executive*

Gonzalez
Plischke, Le Moyne Wilfred *research chemist*

Green Cove Springs
Watson, Thomas Campbell *economic development consulting company executive*
Yelton, Eleanor O'Dell *reading specialist*

Greenwood
Goode, Stephen Hogue *publishing company executive*

Groveland
Hamilton, Rhoda Lillian Rosen *educator, consultant*

Gulf Breeze
Lankton, Stephen Ryan *family therapist*
Mayer, Foster Lee, Jr. *toxicologist*
Menzer, Robert Everett *toxicologist, educator*
Strength, Janis Grace *management executive, educator*

Haines City
Clement, Robert William *air force officer*

Hallandale
Contney, John Joseph *association executive*
Cornblatt, Max *automotive batteries manufacturing company executive*
Haspel, Arthur Carl *podiatrist, surgeon*

Havana
Penson, Edward Martin *management consulting company executive*

Hawthorne
Fackler, Martin L(uther) *surgeon*
Ross, James Elmer *economist, administrator*

Hernando
Bell, Philip Wilkes *accounting and economics educator*

Hialeah
†Clarke, Robert Flanders *librarian, administrator, public health service officer*
Edelcup, Norman Scott *management and financial consultant*
Kennedy, Thomas Patrick *financial executive*
Shaw, Steven John *retired marketing educator, academic administrator*

Highland Beach
Frager, Albert S. *retired retail food company executive*
Gaffey, Thomas Michael, Jr. *consumer products executive*
Schor, Stanley Sidney *mathematical sciences educator*
Stimson, Frederick Sparks *Hispanist, educator*
Summers, James Irvin *retired advertising executive*
Wegman, Harold Hugh *management consultant*

Hillsboro Beach
Gibbons, Joseph John *builders supply company financial executive*

Hobe Sound
Casey, Edward Paul *manufacturing company executive*
Craig, David Jeoffrey *retired manufacturing company executive*
DeHority, Edward Havens, Jr. *retired accountant, lawyer*
Etherington, Edwin Deacon *lawyer, business executive, educator*
Fiske, Guy Wilbur *investment company executive*
Frank, Mary *sculptor, artist*
Graham, Bruce John *architect*
Havens, Oliver Hershman *lawyer, consultant*
Henley, Henry Howard, Jr. *retired manufacturing company executive*
Hotchkiss, Winchester Fitch *retired investment banker*
Markoe, Frank, Jr. *lawyer, business and hospital executive*
Matheson, William Lyon *lawyer, farmer*
Norman, Greg *professional golfer*
Simpson, Russell Gordon *lawyer*
Vanderbilt, Oliver Degray *financier*

Hollywood
Angstrom, Wayne Raymond *communications executive*
Bergman, Harry *urologist*
Cowan, Irving *real estate owner, developer*
Di Maggio, Joseph Paul *former professional baseball player*
Fell, Frederick Victor *publisher*
Goldberg, Icchok Ignacy *retired special education educator*
Graves, Walter Albert *retired association executive, editor*
Harringer, Olaf Carl *architect, museum consultant*
†Jenne, Kenneth Clarence, II *lawyer, state senator*
Korngold, Alvin Leonard *broadcasting company executive*
McQueen, Scott Robert *broadcasting company executive*
Sacco, Frank Vincent *hospital administrator*
Thomas, Thomas A. *lawyer*
Weinberg, Harry Bernard *cardiologist*

Hollywood Hills
King, Alma Jean *former health and physical education educator*

Holmes Beach
Browning, Henry Prentice *banker*
Neustadt, Barbara Mae *artist, illustrator, etcher*

Homestead
Roberts, Larry Spurgeon *zoologist*

Homosassa
Acton, Norman *international organization executive*
Clement, Howard Wheeler *lawyer*

Hudson
Sarnecki, Thomas George *special education educator*

Indialantic
Carroll, Charles Lemuel, Jr. *mathematician*
Lewis, Richard Stanley *author, former editor*
McIntyre, Joseph Charles *real estate investor*

Indian Harbour Beach
Denaburg, Charles Robert *metallurgical engineer, retired government official*

Indian Rocks Beach
Mortensen, James E. *management consultant*
Rocheleau, James Romig *academic administrator*

Interlachen
Hoffman, Edward Richard, III (Dick Hoffman) *retail and manufacturing executive*

Jacksonville
Adams, Henry *museum director*
Ade, James L. *lawyer*
Aftoora, Patricia Joan *transportation executive*
Ansbacher, Lewis *lawyer*
†Austin, Ed *mayor*
Austin, T. Edward (Ed Austin) *mayor*
†Bankhead, William Greer, Jr. *real estate administrator*
†Barley, John McKim, II *architect*
Barrett, S. Barre *academic administrator, art educator*
†Bartholomew, John Niles *church administrator*
Belin, Jacob Chapman *paper company executive*
Bennett, Charles Edward *former congressman, educator*
Black, Susan Harrell *federal judge*
Blackburn, Robert McGrady *retired bishop*
Bodkin, Lawrence Edward *inventor, research development company executive, gemologist*
Boyles, Carol Ann Patterson *career development educator*
Brady, James Joseph *academic administrator*
Brann, William Paul *retired university administrator, consultant*
†Broward, Robert C. *architect*
†Brown, Lloyd Harcourt, Jr. *newspaper editor*
Bullock, Bruce Stanley *lawyer*
Carithers, Hugh Alfred *physician*
†Carpenter, Alvin Rauso *transportation executive*
Cerveny, Frank Stanley *bishop*
Christian, Gary Irvin *lawyer*
Clarkson, Charles Andrew *real estate investment executive*
Colby, Lestina Larsen *secondary education educator*
†Commander, Charles Edward *lawyer, real estate consultant*
Coppotelli, H. Catherina *psychologist, consultant*
†Cousin, Philip R. *clergyman*
Criser, Marshall M. *lawyer*
Currie, Earl James *transportation company executive*
Davis, A. Dano *grocery store chain executive*
Davis, Jerry Ray *railroad company executive*
Dawes, Michael Francis *lawyer*
Drew, Horace Rainsford, Jr. *lawyer*
Dundon, Margo Elaine *museum director*
Ehrlich, Raymond *lawyer*
El-Ansary, Adel Ibrahim *business educator*
Elston, William Steger *food products company executive*
Ernest, Albert Devery, Jr. *banker*
Farmer, Guy Otto, II *lawyer*
Fawbush, Andrew Jackson *lawyer*
Fiorentino, Thomas Martin *transportation executive, lawyer*
Francis, James Delbert *oil company executive*
Fredrickson, Arthur Allan *retired publishing company executive*
Freeman, Judson, Jr. *lawyer*
Fruit, Melvyn Herschel *lawyer, management consultant*
Gabel, George DeSaussure, Jr. *lawyer*
Getman, Willard Etheridge *lawyer*
†Gibbons, G. Hunter *insurance executive*
†Gilson, Warren Edwin, Jr. *insurance company executive*
Godfrey, John Munro *bank economist*
Goff, Charles Wesley, Jr. *management consultant*
Graham, Cynthia Armstrong *banker*
Gregg, John Franklin *hospital administrator*
Groom, Dale *physician, educator*
Gunning, John Thaddeus *retired superintendent*
Hadley, Stanton Thomas *international manufacturing and marketing company executive, lawyer*
Hamilton, William Berry, Jr. *shipping company executive*
†Hardrick, Charles M. *airport executive*
Harmon, Gary Lee *language professional, educator*
Harriman, Constance Bastine *federal official*
Hartmann, Frederick William *newspaper editor*
†Haskell, Preston Hampton, III *construction company executive*
†Herbert, Adam William, Jr. *university president*
Hill, James Clinkscales *federal judge*
†Hill, John Steven *accountant*
Hodges, William Terrell *federal judge*
†Holzendorf, Betty Smith *state representative*
Honaman, J. Craig *health facility administrator*
Howell, John Floyd *insurance company executive*
Hrachovina, Frederick Vincent *osteopathic physician and surgeon*
Huebner, Jay Stanley *physicist, engineer, forensics consultant*
†Hulin-Salkin, Belinda *newspaper editor*
Jackson, Julian Ellis *food company executive*
†Jenkins, Leerie Thurman, Jr. *architecture engineering planning firm executive*
Joyce, Edward Rowen *chemical engineer, educator*
Kelalis, Panayotis *pediatric urologist*
†Kensey, Calvin D. *bishop*
Kent, Frederick Heber *lawyer*
Kinne, Frances Bartlett *chancellor*
Kirk, Robert Leonard *transportation company executive*
Klabosh, Charles Joseph *aerospace research and development executive*
†Koger, Ira M. *real estate executive*
†Kress, Mary Elizabeth *newspaper editor*
Kufeldt, James *retail grocery store executive*
Lane, Edward Wood, Jr. *retired banker*
Lastinger, Allen Lane, Jr. *banker*
Legler, Mitchell Wooten *lawyer*
Lestage, Daniel Barfield *retired naval officer, physician*
Lindner, Carl Henry, Jr. *financial holding company executive*
Lloyd, Raymond Grann *economist, educator*
Loomis, Henry *former broadcasting company executive, former government official*
Lyon, Sherman Orwig *rubber and chemical company executive*
Lyon, Wilford Charles, Jr. *insurance executive*
Mann, Timothy *corporate executive*
Manning, Arthur Brewster *newspaper editor*
†Mason, William Cordell, III *hospital administrator*
McCullough, Ray Daniel, Jr. *insurance company executive*
McGehee, Thomas Rives *paper company executive*
McWilliams, John Lawrence, III *lawyer*
Melton, Howell Webster, Sr. *federal judge*
Metzler, Mary Fink *elementary education educator*
Mikals, John Joseph *lawyer*
Mikulas, Joseph Frank *graphic designer, educator, painter*
Monsky, John Bertrand *investment banking executive*
Moore, David Graham *sociologist, educator*
Moore, John Henry, II *federal judge*
†Morgan, William N. *architect, educator*
Morris, William Shivers, III *newspaper executive*
Moseley, James Francis *lawyer*
Mueller, Edward Albert *transportation engineer executive*
Nicolitz, Ernst *ophthalmologist, educator*
O'Neal, Michael Scott, Sr. *lawyer*
Osborn, Marvin Griffing, Jr. *educational consultant*
Pappas, Ted Phillip *architect*
Parker, David Forster *real estate development consultant*
†Parks, Herbert Louis *insurance company executive*
Pillans, Charles Palmer, III *lawyer*
Prempree, Thongbliew *oncology radiologist*
Prom, Stephen George *lawyer*
Purcifull, Robert Otis *insurance company executive*
Reese, Dorothy Harmon *special education educator*
Reynolds, Ellis W. *chemist*
Rice, Charles Edward *banker*
Rinaman, James Curtis, Jr. *lawyer*
Rishel, Richard Clinton *banker*
Robinson, Christine Marie *mathematics educator*
Rumpel, Peter Loyd *architect, educator, artist*
Russell, David Emerson *mechanical engineer, consultant*
Sadler, Luther Fuller, Jr. *lawyer*
Schlageter, Robert William *museum administrator*
Schlesinger, Harvey Erwin *federal judge*
Scholl, Sharon Lynn *humanities educator*
Schramm, Bernard Charles, Jr. *advertising agency executive*
Schultz, Frederick Henry *investor, former government official*
Sederbaum, William *marketing executive*
†Sekely, George Frank *computer and communications executive*
Seroka, James Henry *academic program director, educator*
Shivler, James Fletcher, Jr. *retired civil engineer*
Slade, Thomas Bog, III *lawyer, investment banker*
Slaughter, Frank Gill *author, physician*
Smith, Ivan Huron *architect*
Snyder, John Joseph *bishop*
†Sparrow, William Holliday *corporate financial executive*
Stephenson, Samuel Edward, Jr. *physician*
Swenson, Courtland Sevander *retired musician*
Thornton, Winfred Lamotte *railroad executive*
Tjoflat, Gerald Bard *federal judge*
Tomlinson, William Holmes *management educator, retired army officer*
Travis, Forrest *investment firm executive*
†Verlander, William Ashley *insurance company executive*
Vincent, Norman Fuller *broadcasting executive*
Vines, Charles Jerry *minister*
Voss, Carl Hermann *clergyman, humanities educator, author*
†Walker, Robert Charles *golf course architect*
Wallis, Donald Wills *lawyer*
Walters, John Sherwood *retired newspaperman*
Webster, David A. *lawyer*
Welch, Philip Burland *electronics and office products company executive*
Williams, Judith L. *library administrator*
Wilson, C. Nick *medical educator, consultant*
Wilson, J. Tylee *business executive*
Yamane, Stanley Joel *optometrist*

Jensen Beach
Kirjassoff, Gordon Louis *consulting civil engineer*
Kraynak, Helen *special education consultant*
Sculfort, Maurice Charles *advertising agency executive*

Juno Beach
Broadhead, James Lowell *business executive*
Evanson, Paul John *utilities executive*
Migliaro, Marco William *electrical engineer*
Petillo, James Thomas *diversified utility company executive*

Jupiter
Anderson, Thomas J. *publisher, rancher, public speaker, syndicated columnist*
Ashby, Donald Wayne, Jr. *retired accountant*

Beddow, Thomas John *retired lawyer*
Biebuyck, Daniel Prosper *retired anthropologist, educator*
Danforth, Arthur Edwards *finance executive*
†Fazio, Tom *golf course designer and architect, architectural firm executive*
Marker, Robert Sydney *management consultant*
McCall, Duke Kimbrough *clergyman*
Skully, Richard Patrick *airline consultant*

Kennedy Space Center
Crippen, Robert Laurel *naval officer, former astronaut*
Young, Richard Stuart *technical services executive*

Key Biscayne
Markell, Alan William *linguistic company executive*
Palmer, Roger Farley *pharmacology educator*

Key Largo
Brown, David *retired petrochemical corporation executive*
Byrd, Mary Laager *life science researcher*
Daenzer, Bernard John *insurance company executive, legal consultant*
Daly, William Gerald *business executive*
Davidson, Thomas Noel *business executive*

Key West
Coudert, Ferdinand Wilmerding *lawyer*
Devereaux, Christian Windsor, III *computer scientist*
Ellinghaus, William Maurice *communications executive*
†Henriquez, Armando Joseph *superintendent*
†Saunders, Ron *lawyer, state legislator*
Trammell, Herbert Eugene *physicist, laboratory executive*

Lady Lake
Dore, Stephen Edward, Jr. *retired civil engineer*

Lake Alfred
†Kender, Walter John *horticulturist, educator*
Nagy, Steven *biochemist*

Lake Buena Vista
Lomonosoff, James Marc *marketing executive*
Mc Mahon, Ed *television personality*
Parke, Robert Leon *management executive*

Lake Mary
Strang, Stephen Edward *magazine editor, publisher*

Lake Placid
Layne, James Nathaniel *vertebrate biologist*

Lake Suzy
Schmidt, Harold Eugene *real estate company executive*

Lake Wales
Mumma, Albert G. *retired naval officer, retired manufacturing company executive, management consultant*
O'Connor, Robert Emmet *paper company executive*

Lake Worth
Finch, Ronald M., Jr. *savings bank executive*
Kline, Gordon Mabey *chemist, editor*
Stevens, William John *management consultant, writer, inventor, former association executive*

Lakeland
Carrier, W(illiam) David, III *geotechnical engineer*
Davis, Robert Aldine *college president*
Dufoe, William Stewart *lawyer*
Harritt, Norman L. *manufacturing company executive*
Hatten, William Seward *manufacturing company executive*
Hollis, Mark D. *federal official*
Hughes, Harold Hasbrouck, Jr. *bishop*
Jenkins, Charles H., Jr. *grocery company executive*
Jenkins, Howard M. *supermarket executive*
Kibler, David Burke, III *lawyer*
Kincart, Robert Owen *technological executive*
Kittleson, Henry Marshall *lawyer*
Koren, Edward Franz *lawyer*
Meads, Walter Frederick *executive recruitment consultant*
Miller, Robert Allen *hotel executive*
†Niswonger, Jeanne Du Chateau *biologist, writer*
†Norton, Kelly E. *ceramic flooring company executive*
Peeler, Scott Loomis, Jr. *foreign language educator*
Perez, Louis Michael *newspaper editor*
Peterson, N. Curtis, Jr. *landscape architect, former state senator*
Reich, David Lee *librarian*
Sheppard, Albert Parker, Jr. *mathematics educator*
Smith, Levie David, Jr. *real estate appraiser, consultant*
†Stephens, Jack Thomas, Jr. *hospital administrator*
Wade, Ben Frank *college administrator*

Lantana
Calder, Iain Wilson *publishing company executive*

Largo
†Benstock, Gerald Martin *uniform manufacturing executive*
Boyle, John William *retail executive*
Brown, Warren Joseph *physician*
Criqui, William Edmund *lighting company financial executive*
Dolan, John E. *consultant, retired utility executive*
Fournier, Serge Raymond-Jean *orchestra conductor*
†Gall, Keith D. *director*
Hamlin, Robert Henry *public health educator, management consultant*
†Hinesley, J. Howard *superintendent*
Loader, Jay Gordon *retired utility company executive*
†Mortham, Sandra Barringer *state legislator*
Ray, Roger Buchanan *retired communications executive, lawyer*

Lecanto
Brogan, Howard Oakley *English language educator*

Leesburg
Austin, Robert Eugene, Jr. *lawyer*
Crall, James Monroe *plant pathologist, plant breeder, educator*
Entorf, Richard Carl *management consultant*
Houston, John Coates, Jr. *consultant*
Talley, William Giles, Jr. *container manufacturing company executive*

Lehigh Acres
Moore, John Newton *retired natural science educator*

Longboat Key
Cornelius, James Alfred *advertising executive*
Goldsmith, Jack Landman *former retail company executive*
Heitler, George *lawyer*
Johnson, Carroll Frye *educational consultant*
Maha, George Edward *research facility administrator, consultant*
Prizer, Charles John *chemical company executive*
Schoenberg, Lawrence Joseph *computer services company executive*

Longwood
Blumberg, Herbert Kurt *corporate executive*
Brooker, Robert Elton *corporate executive*
Faller, Donald E. *marketing and operations executive*
Reade, Richard Sill *manufacturing executive*
Smyth, Joseph Patrick *retired naval officer, physician*
Tomasulo, Virginia Merrills *retired lawyer*

Lutz
Bedke, Ernest Alford *retired air force officer*

Mac Dill AFB
LeMoyne, Irve Charles *career officer*

Maitland
Blackburn, John Oliver *economist, consultant*
Braun, Charles Stuart *architect*
Fichthorn, Luke Eberly, III *investment banker*
Nash, Ronald Herman *philosophy educator*
St. John, John *food company executive*
Vallee, Judith Delaney *environmentalist, fundraiser*
Whitlock, Luder Gradick, Jr. *seminary president*

Manalapan
Johnstone, Edmund Frank *advertising executive*

Marathon
Janicki, Robert Stephen *retired pharmaceutical company executive*
Kolker, Roger Russell *insurance executive*
Wiecha, Joseph Augustine *linguist, educator*

Marco Island
Butler, Frederick George *retired drug company executive*
Fisher, Chester Lewis, Jr. *retired lawyer*
Guerrant, David Edward *retired food company executive*
Hurley, Patrick Mason *geology educator*
Lavin, John Halley *editor, author*
Lesser, Joseph M. *retired business executive, retail store executive*
Mollison, Richard Devol *mining company executive*
Pettersen, Kjell Will *stockbroker, consultant*
Poletti, Charles *lawyer*
Sundberg, R. Dorothy *physician, educator*
Thorson, Oswald Hagen *architect*
Wheeler, Warren G(age), Jr. *retired publishing executive*

Marianna
Flowers, Virginia Anne *academic administrator emerita*

Mayo
Durham, Guinevere McCabe *educational administrator, writer, consultant*

Melbourne
Abbott, Robert Tucker *zoologist, author*
Babich, Michael Wayne *chemistry educator, educational administrator*
Baney, Richard Neil *physician, internist*
Boan, Bobby Jack *chemist*
Boyd, Joseph Aubrey *communications company executive*
Cacciatore, S. Sammy, Jr. *lawyer*
Cockriel, Russell George, Sr. *crime investigation official*
Edwards, David Northrop *university administrator*
†Ehrig, John Paul *architect*
Gabriel, Roger Eugene *management consulting executive*
Hartley, John T., Jr. *electronic systems, semiconductor, communications and office equipment executive*
Helmstetter, Charles Edward *microbiologist*
†Henson, Llewellyn Lafayette, III *library director*
†Hollingsworth, Abner Thomas *university dean*
Krieger, Robert Edward *publisher*
Lakshmikantham, Vangipuram *mathematics educator*
Lewis, Bernard Leroy *electronic scientist, consultant*
Means, Michael David *hospital administrator*
Michalski, Thomas Joseph *city planner, developer*
Nelson, Gordon Leigh *chemist, educator*
Noonan, Norine Elizabeth *academic administrator, researcher*
Roub, Bryan R(oger) *financial executive*
Sottile, James *financier*
Spezzano, Vincent Edward *newspaper publisher*
Stark, Bruce Gunsten *artist*
Storrs, Eleanor Emerett *research institute executive*
Swalm, Thomas Sterling *aerospace executive, retired military officer*
von Ohain, Hans Joachim P. *aerospace scientist*
Weaver, Lynn Edward *academic administrator, consultant, editor*

Melrose
Burt, Alvin Victor, Jr. *journalist*
Meyer, Harvey Kessler, II *retired academic administrator*

Miami
†Ajamil, Luis *civil engineer*
Alexenberg, Mel *art educator*
Alonso, Antonio Enrique *lawyer*
Anderson, Douglas Richard *ophthalmologist, educator, scientist, researcher*
†Anger, Paul *newspaper Sports Editor*
Arango, Jorge Sanin *architect*
†Arison, Micky *cruise line company executive*
Armstrong, James Louden, III *lawyer*
Astigarraga, Jose I(gnacio) *lawyer*
†Atlas, Randall I. *architect, criminologist*
Atwood, Donald Keith *oceanographer, chemist*
Baena, Scott Louis *lawyer*
Balmaseda, Liz *columnist*
Barnes, Donald Winfree *banker*
Barritt, Evelyn Ruth Berryman *nurse, educator, university dean*
Barry, Dave *columnist, author*
Basile, Michael *lawyer*
Bastian, James Harold *air transport company executive, lawyer*
Batten, James Knox *newspaper executive*
Bellero, Chiaffredo John *civil engineer*
Benford, Norman J. *lawyer*
Berkman, Harold William *marketing educator*
Berley, David Richard *lawyer*
Berman, Bruce Judson *lawyer*
Bezdek, Hugo Frank *scientific laboratory administrator*
†Birger, Larry *newspaper editor, columnist*
Bishopric, Karl *investment banker, real estate executive, advertising executive*
Bitter, John *university dean emeritus, musician, businessman, diplomat*
Black, Creed Carter *newspaper executive*
Blackburn, James Ross, Jr. *business executive, retired airline pilot*
Blanco, Luciano-Nilo *physicist*
Bolooki, Hooshang *cardiac surgeon*
Bradley, Ronald Calvin *investment company executive*
Brady, Alexander Childs *dancer*
Brinkman, Paul Del(bert) *foundation executive*
Brock, James Daniel *retired airline executive, consultant*
Brown, Stephen Thomas *U.S. magistrate judge*
Brownell, Edwin Rowland *banker, civil engineer*
†Bubnow, Vic *newspaper publishing executive*
Buchanan, Edna *journalist*
Bufman, Zev *stage producer, theater chain executive*
†Bunge, Richard Paul *cell biologist, educator*
Burkett, Marjorie Theresa *nursing educator, gerontology nurse*
Burnett, Henry *lawyer*
Burns, Mitchel Anthony *transportation services company executive*
Butson, Alton Thomas *mathematics educator*
†Carr, Chuck (Charles Lee Glenn Carr, Jr.) *baseball player*
Casariego, Jorge Isaac *psychiatrist, psychoanalyst, educator*
Catanzaro, Tony *dancer*
Cesarano, Gregory Morgen *lawyer*
Chapman, Alvah Herman, Jr. *newspaper executive*
Chavin, Walter *biological science educator and researcher*
Clark, Ira C. *hospital association administrator, educator*
Clark, John Russell *ecologist*
Clark, Stephen P. *mayor*
Clarke, Mercer Kaye *lawyer*
Clarkson, Kenneth Wright *economics educator*
†Clifton, Douglas C. *newspaper editor*
Cohen, Alex *retired publisher*
Cohen, Eugene Erwin *university health institute administrator, accounting educator emeritus*
†Cohen, Jacob *bishop*
Cohen, Sanford Irwin *physician, educator*
Cole, Robert Bates *lawyer*
Colwin, Arthur Lentz *biologist, educator*
Comras, Rema *library director*
Connor, Terence Gregory *lawyer*
†Conrad, Barry L. *food service executice*
Cooper, Thomas Astley *banking executive*
†Coords, Robert H. *bank executive*
Corcoran, Eugene Francis *chemist, educator*
Correll, Helen Butts *botanist, researcher*
†Cosgrove, John Francis *lawyer, state legislator*
Coton, Carlos David *finance manager*
Courshon, Arthur Howard *banker, lawyer*
Courshon, Carol Biel *civic worker*
Cristol, A. Jay *federal judge*
Critchlow, Richard H. *lawyer*
†Cubas, Jose M(anuel) *advertising agency executive*
Cullom, William Otis *trade association executive*
Dady, Robert Edward *lawyer*
Daughtry, DeWitt Cornell *surgeon, physician*
Davis, Edward Bertrand *federal judge*
Deaktor, Darryl Barnett *lawyer*
Dean, Stanley Rochelle *psychiatrist*
de la Guardia, Mario Francisco *electrical engineer*
†Dellapa, Gary J. *airport terminal executive*
Denison, Floyd Gene *insurance executive*
Dickason, John Hamilton *foundation executive*
†Dickey, Arden *newspaper publishing executive*
†Dickinson, Robert H. *water transportation executive*
†Dolen, Christine Arnold *theater critic*
Dorion, Robert Charles *entrepreneur, investor*
†Dubocq, Tom *newspaper reporter*
Duffy, Earl Gavin *hotel executive*
DuFresne, Elizabeth Jamison *lawyer*
†Dye, H. Michael *engineering executive*
Dyer, David William *federal judge*
Dyer, John Martin *lawyer, marketing educator*
Eaglstein, William Howard *dermatologist, educator*
Ehrlich, Morton *international finance executive*
England, Arthur Jay, Jr. *lawyer, former state justice*
Estefan, Gloria Maria *singer, songwriter*
Etling, Russell Hull *museum director, production company executive*
Evans, Peter Kenneth *advertising executive*
Fain, Richard David *cruise line executive*
Fascell, Dante B. *lawyer, congressman*
Fay, Peter Thorp *federal judge*
Feito, Jose *architect*
†Ferguson, Wilkie D., Jr. *federal judge*
Ferrer, Esteban A. *lawyer*
†Fichtner, Margaria *newspaper editor*
Fine, Rana Arnold *chemical,physical oceanographer*
Fletcher, John Sheidley *lawyer*
†Flynn, John T. *ophthalmologist*
†Fontaine, John C. *newspaper company executive*
†Fort-Brescia, Bernardo *architect*
Freshwater, Michael Felix *hand surgeon*
†Garcia-Serra, Alberto J. *advertising executive*
Garner, John Michael *investment company executive*
Gassen, Joseph Albert *lawyer, former judge*
Gelband, Henry *pediatric cardiologist*
Gerber, Seymour *publishing company executive*
Getz, Morton Ernest *internist, gastroenterologist*
Gibb, Maurice *vocalist, songwriter*
Gibb, Robin *vocalist, songwriter*
Gibbons, Barry J. *food service executive*
Gibby, Mabel Enid Kunce *psychologist*
Giller, Norman Myer *banker, architect, author*
Ginsberg, Myron David *neurologist*
Gittess, Ronald Marvin *dentist*
Gittlin, Arthur Sam *industrialist, banker*
Glaser, Luis *biochemistry educator*
Godofsky, Lawrence *lawyer*
Gold, Alan Stephen *lawyer, educator, judge*
Gong, Edmond Joseph *lawyer*
Gonzalez-Pita, J. Alberto *lawyer*
Gordon, Jack David *senator, foundation executive*
Graboski, Thomas Walter *designer, artist*
Gragg, Karl Lawrence *lawyer*
Graham, Donald Lynn *federal judge*
Greenberg, Melvin Nathaniel *lawyer*
Hall, Andrew Clifford *lawyer*
Hall, Miles Lewis, Jr. *lawyer*
†Hampton, Jim *newspaper editor*
Hampton, John Lewis *newspaper editor*
Hampton, Mark Garrison *architect*
Harless, Byron Brittingham *newspaper executive*
Harris, Douglas Clay *newspaper executive*
Harvey, Bryan Stanley *professional baseball player*
†Hayashi, Teru *zoologist, educator*
Hector, Louis Julius *lawyer*
Henson, John Denver *international management consulting firm executive*
Herron, James Michael *lawyer*
Hertz, David Bendel *management consultant, educator, lawyer*
Heuer, Robert Maynard, II *opera company executive*
Highsmith, Shelby *federal judge*
Higley, Bruce Wadsworth *orthodontist*
Hills, Lee *foundation administrator, newspaper executive, consultant*
Hoeveler, William M. *federal judge*
Hoffman, Larry J. *lawyer*
Houlihan, Gerald John *lawyer*
Howell, Ralph Rodney *pediatrician, educator*
Hoy, William Ivan *minister, religion educator*
Hoyt, Clark Freeland *journalist, newspaper editor*
Hudson, Robert Franklin, Jr. *lawyer*
Hurtgen, Peter Joseph *lawyer*
Huston, Edwin Allen *transportation company executive*
Huysman, Arlene Weiss *psychologist, educator*
†Johnson, Glendon E. *insurance company executive*
Jones, Eddie J. *professional football team executive*
Jones y Diez Arguelles, Gastón Roberto *language educator*
Jude, James Roderick *cardiac surgeon*
Kanter, Joseph Hyman *banker, community developer*
Keeley, Brian E. *hospital administrator*
Kehoe, James W. *federal judge*
Kenin, David S. *lawyer, shareholder*
Kepner, Woody *public relations executive*
Ketcham, Alfred Schutt *surgeon, educator*
Khalil, Tarek Mohamed *industrial engineering educator*
King, James Lawrence *federal judge*
Kirsner, Robert *language educator*
Kleinberg, Howard J. *newspaper columnist*
Kline, Charles C. *lawyer*
Klock, Joseph Peter, Jr. *lawyer*
Knight, Charles Frasuer *architect*
Korchin, Judith Miriam *lawyer*
Kozlowski, Ronald Stephan *librarian*
Kraft, C. William, Jr. *federal judge*
Kram, Michael Arnold *magazine publisher*
Kreutzer, Franklin David *lawyer*
Lachemann, Rene George *professional sports manager*
Lampen, Richard Jay *lawyer, investment banker*
Landon, Robert Kirkwood *insurance company executive*
Landy, Burton Aaron *lawyer*
Lapidus, Morris *retired architect, interior designer*
Lasseter, Kenneth Carlyle *pharmacologist*
Lataif, Lawrence P. *lawyer*
Lawrence, David, Jr. *newspaper editor, publisher*
†Le Duc, Albert Louis, Jr. *college official*
Lehrman, Irving *rabbi*
Lemberg, Louis *cardiologist, educator*
Le Mehaute, Bernard Jean *marine physics educator*
Lewis, John Milton *cable television company executive*
†Lieff, Ann Spector *music company executive*
Lindquist, Claude S. *electrical and computer engineering educator*
Louis, Paul Adolph *lawyer*
†Maidique, Modesto Alex *academic administrator*
Man, Eugene Herbert *chemist, educator, business executive*
Mandine, Salvador G. *insurance executive*
Marcus, Stanley *federal judge*
Martínez, Luis Osvaldo *radiologist, educator*
Mathews, Byron B., Jr. *lawyer*
McCarthy, Edward Anthony *archbishop*
Mc Kenzie, John Maxwell *physician*
Meller, George Mieczyslaw Jerzy *international trade consulting company executive*
†Mentzer, Carl Forrest *banker*
†Milian, Emilio M. *broadcasting executive*
Millard, David Ralph, Jr. *plastic surgeon, educator*
Miller, Gene Edward *newspaper reporter and editor*
†Miller, Leonard *construction company executive*
Mitchell, Mitch *business owner*
Mooers, Christopher Northrup Kennard *physical oceanographer, educator*
Moore, Kevin Michael *federal judge*
Moore, Michael T. *lawyer*
Moreno, Federico Antonio *federal judge*
Morgan, Andrew Wesley *artist, educator*
Morgan, Marabel *author*
Mozian, Gerard Paul *real estate company executive, business consultant*
Mudd, John Philip *lawyer*
Myerburg, Robert Jerome *physician, scientist, educator*
Myers, Kenneth M. *lawyer*
Myrberg, Arthur August, Jr. *marine biological sciences educator*
Nagel, Joachim Hans *biomedical engineer, educator*
†Natoli, Joe *newspaper publishing executive*
Navarro, Antonio (Luis) *public relations executive*
Nesbitt, Lenore Carrero *federal judge*
Nicholson, William Mac *naval architect, marine engineer, consultant*
O'Brien, William Andrew *information management executive*
O'Donnell, Edward Thomas *lawyer*
O'Farrill, Francisca Josefina *early childhood educator*

Ostlund, H. Gote *atmospheric and marine scientist, educator*
†O'Sullivan, Mary J. *physician, maternal fetal medicine educator*
Page, Larry Keith *neurosurgeon, educator*
Pallot, E. Albert *lawyer, savings and loan executive*
†Pancake, John *newspaper editor*
Papper, Emanuel Martin *anesthesiologist*
Papy, Charles C., III *lawyer*
Parker, Alfred Browning *architect*
Paul, Robert *lawyer*
Pearson, Daniel S. *lawyer*
†Pitts, Leonard Garvey, Jr. *columnist, writer*
†Plater-Zyberk, Elizabeth Maria *architectural educator*
Plungis, Barbara Marie *health facility nursing administrator*
Politano, Victor Anthony *urology educator, physician*
Pomeranz, Felix *accounting educator*
Pope, John Edwin, III *newspaper sports editor*
†Porter, Charles King *advertising executive*
†Posner, Steven *diversified business executive*
Posner, Victor *diversified business executive*
Potter, James Douglas *pharmacology educator*
†Powers, Joseph Edward *marine biologist*
Prineas, Ronald James *epidemiologist, educator*
Quentel, Albert Drew *lawyer*
†Quintana, Mack *newspaper publishing executive*
Raffel, Leroy B. *real estate development company executive*
Raines, Jeff *biomedical scientist, medical research director*
Rebozo, Charles Gregory *banker*
Reed, Alfred *retired composer, conductor*
Reed, George Francis *architect*
Reid, R(alph) Benjamine *lawyer*
Reigrod, Robert Hull *manufacturing executive*
†Reisinger, Sandra Sue *journalist, lawyer*
Ripstein, Charles Benjamin *surgeon*
Robbie, Timothy John *professional football team executive*
†Roberts, Brian L. *cable company executive*
Rockstein, Morris *science writer, editor, consultant*
Roedema, Charles E(dward) *advertising agency executive*
Roemer, Elaine Sloane *real estate broker*
†Rosenberg, Mark B. *think-tank executive*
Rosenn, Keith Samuel *lawyer, educator*
Rosenthal, Stanley Lawrence *meteorologist*
†Ross, David Lee *lawyer*
Rothchild, Howard Leslie *advertising executive*
Routh, Donald K(ent) *psychology educator*
Russell, Elbert Winslow *neuropsychologist*
Russell, James Webster, Jr. *newspaper editor, columnist*
†Russell, Terence Lee *transportation company executive*
Ryan, James Walter *physician, medical researcher*
Sackner, Marvin Arthur *physician*
Salazar-Carrillo, Jorge *economics educator*
Salvaneschi, Luigi *real estate and development executive, business educator*
Sanchez, Robert Francis *journalist*
Sandoval, Arturo *jazz musician*
Santiago, Benito Rivera *professional baseball player*
Sapp, Neil Carleton *international airline pilot, industrial consultant*
†Saunders, Norman Thomas *military officer*
Savage, James Francis *editor*
Scheinberg, Peritz *neurologist*
Scheinberg, Steven Eliot *investment banker*
Schiff, Eugene Roger *medical educator, hepatologist*
†Schofield, Calvin Onderdonk, Jr. *bishop*
Schuetzenduebel, Wolfram Gerhard *engineering executive*
Schulman, Clifford A. *lawyer*
Schwartz, Kessel *modern language educator*
Seitz, Patricia Ann *lawyer*
†Seline, Rex *reporter*
Shaklan, Allen Yale *broadcast executive*
†Sheets, Robert Chester *meteorologist*
Sheffield, Gary Antonian *professional baseball player*
Shepherd, Frank Andrew *lawyer*
Shevin, Robert Lewis *lawyer*
Shoemaker, Don (Donald Cleavenger Shoemaker) *columnist*
Short, Eugene Maurice, Jr. *lawyer, accountant*
†Shroder, Tom *newspaper editor*
Silber, Norman Jules *lawyer*
Silva, Felipe *former tobacco company executive*
Simkins, Leon Jack *paper company executive*
Sims, James Larry *hospital administrator, healthcare consultant*
†Sims, Keith *professional football player*
Smathers, Frank, Jr. *banker, horticulturist*
†Smith, Samuel Stuart *lawyer*
†Smith, Steven Delano *professional basketball player*
†Sonnett, Neal Russell *lawyer*
†Sonsky, Steve *newspaper editor*
†Steinback, Robert Lamont *newspaper columnist*
Stephan, Egon, Sr. *cinematographer, film equipment company executive*
Stickler, Daniel Lee *health care management consultant*
Stiehm, Judith Hicks *university official, political science educator*
Stokes, Paul Mason *lawyer*
Stover, James Howard *real estate executive*
†Stratos, Kimarie Rose *lawyer, sports agent*
Strauss, José *pediatric nephrologist*
Strickland, Thomas Joseph *artist*
Stuzin, Charles Bryan *savings and loan association executive*
Suarez, Roberto *newspaper publishing executive*
Suarez, Xavier Louis *lawyer, mayor*
Sussex, James Neil *psychiatrist, educator*
Tarkoff, Michael Harris *lawyer*
Taylor, Stephen Dewitt *savings and loan association executive*
Teicher, Morton Irving *social worker, educator*
Telesca, Francis Eugene *architect*
†Terilli, Samuel A., Jr. *newspaper publishing executive*
Tew, Jeffrey Allen *lawyer*
Thornton, Sandi Tokoa *secondary education educator*
Traurig, Robert Henry *lawyer*
Treyz, Joseph Henry *librarian*
Ungaro-Benages, Ursula *federal judge*
†Valdes, Carlos Leonardo *realtor, mortgage broker, state legislator*
Valdes-Dapena, Marie Agnes *pediatric pathologist, educator*
VanBrode, Derrick Brent, IV *association executive*
Van Wyck, George Richard *insurance company executive*
†Verdeja, Sam *newspaper publishing executive*

Veziroglu, Turhan Nejat *mechanical engineering educator, energy researcher*
Vila, Adis Maria *former government official, lawyer*
von Clemm, Michael *financial executive*
Wackenhut, George Russell *security services executive*
Wackenhut, Richard Russell *security company executive*
†Wallace, Milton Jay *lawyer*
Walters, David McLean *lawyer*
Waters, Willie Anthony *opera and orchestra conductor*
Webb, Richmond Jewel *professional football player*
Weber, Nancy Walker *charitable trust administrator*
Weigel, Rainer R. *lawyer*
Weiner, Morton David *banker, insurance agent*
Weinstein, Alan Edward *lawyer*
Weinstein, Andrew H. *lawyer*
Weiser, Ralph Raphael *recovery company executive*
Weiser, Sherwood Manuel *hotel and corporation executive, lawyer*
†Weitzel, Peter Andre *editor, newspaper*
Weldon, Norman Ross *manufacturing company executive*
†Weller, John Albert, Jr. *landscape architect*
Wells, Daniel Ruth *physics educator*
Werth, Susan *lawyer*
Whelan, William Joseph *biochemistry educator*
Whisenand, James Dudley *lawyer*
Wickstrom, Karl Youngert *publishing company executive*
†Williams, James A. *principal*
Williamson, William Paul, Jr. *journalist*
Wilson, Milner Bradley, III *banker*
Wilson, Robert Gordon *investment banker, waste management manager*
Wolf, Clarence, Jr. *stockbroker*
Wolfson, Richard Frederick *lawyer*
Wolper, Marshall *insurance and financial consultant*
Wood, William McBrayer *lawyer*
Yee, Albert Hoy *psychologist, educator*
Young, John Hendricks *lawyer*
†Zack, Stephen Neil *lawyer*
Zanakis, Steve H. *information systems educator*
Zeigler, Cynthia Walker *zoological association executive*
Zeiller, Warren *former aquarium executive, consultant*

Miami Beach
†Abraham, William Michael *physiologist*
Chirovsky, Nicholas Ludomir *economics educator, historian, author*
Cunningham, Billy (William John Cunningham) *professional basketball team executive, television sportscaster*
Filosa, Gary Fairmont Randolph V., II *film company executive, financier*
Gitlow, Abraham Leo *retired university dean*
Goldstein, Burton Jack *psychiatrist*
Meyer, Sylvan Hugh *editor, magazine executive, author*
Michaels, Willard A. *retired broadcasting executive*
Schaffel, Lewis *professional basketball team executive*
Shapiro, Samuel Bernard *management consultant*
Wax, William Edward *photojournalist*

Miami Lakes
Dominik, Jack Edward *lawyer*
Ringo, James Joseph *mortgage company executive*
Wolter, Duane Roland *retail executive*

Miami Shores
O'Laughlin, Sister Jeanne *university administrator*
Trustman, Benjamin Arthur *lawyer*

Micanopy
Cripe, Wyland Snyder *veterinary medicine educator, consultant*

Micco
Muller, Henry John *real estate developer*

Monticello
Hooks, Mary Linda *adult education educator*

Mount Dora
Adams, Carl Morgan, Jr. *real estate appraiser, mortgage banker*
Goodwin, Harry Eugene *journalist, educator*
Hensinger, Margaret Elizabeth *horticultural and agricultural advertising and marketing executive*
Hoag, Arthur Howard, Jr. *retired architect*
Myren, Richard Albert *criminal justice consultant*
Santini, John Amedeo *educational consultant*

Murdock
Cross, George R. *insurance consultant*

Naples
Abbott, John Sheldon *law school dean and chancellor emeritus*
Arthur, William Bolling *retired editor*
†Baldwin, Ralph Belknap *retired manufacturing company executive, astronomer*
Barth-Wehrenalp, Gerhard *chemical company executive*
Beam, Robert Thompson *retired lawyer*
Benedict, Manson *chemical engineer, educator*
Berman, Robert S. *marketing consultant*
Biondo, Michael Thomas *retired paper company executive*
Buccello, Henry Louis *advertising executive*
Budd, David Glenn *lawyer*
Bush, John William *business executive, federal official*
Card, Orson Scott (Byron Walley) *writer*
Carter, Jaine M(arie) *human resources development company executive*
Chartrand, Robert Lee *information scientist*
Clapp, Roger Howland *retired newspaper executive*
Clark, Kenneth Edwin *psychologist, former university dean*
Clay, W(illiam) Robert *retired chemical company executive*
Colbert, Lester Lum *investor, lawyer, former automobile executive*
Conant, Colleen Christner *newspaper editor*
Craighead, Rodkey *banker*
Crehan, Joseph Edward *lawyer*
Crone, William Gerald *hospital administrator*
Daniels, Myra Janco (Mrs. Draper Daniels) *advertising agency executive*
Dickie, Brian *opera director*

Dion, Nancy Logan *health care administrator, management consultant*
†Dover, Clarence Joseph *entrepreneur, public and employee relations executive, educator, consultant, communication director*
Duff, Daniel Vincent *former insurance company executive, former mayor*
Eldridge, David Carlton *art appraiser*
Elliott, Edward *investment executive, financial planner*
Emerson, John Williams, II *lawyer*
Farese, Lawrence Anthony *lawyer*
Fess, Philip Eugene *accountant, educator*
Frazer, John Howard *tennis association executive*
Freedman, Stanley Marvin *manufacturing company executive*
Gebhardt, Robert Charles *lawyer*
George, Charles William *retired aerospace equipment executive*
Gordon, Martin *publisher, print dealer*
Gresham, Robert Coleman *transportation consultant*
Gross, Paul *pathologist, educator*
Guarino, Roger Charles *consulting company executive*
Gushman, John Louis *former corporation executive, lawyer*
Harvey, Curran Whitthorne, Jr. *investment management executive*
Hennessy, Brother Paul Kevin *religion educator*
Hobbs, Ranald Purcell *publisher*
Hochschwender, Herman Karl *international consultant*
Hooper, John Allen *retired banker*
Ivancevic, Walter Charles *former gas distribution company executive*
Jackson, Daniel Francis *engineering scientist, educator*
Johnson, Walter L. *corporate executive*
Johnson, Zane Quentin *retired petroleum company executive*
Jones, Edward Magruder *television producer and writer, correspondent*
Kapnick, Harvey Edward, Jr. *retired corporate executive*
Kay, Herbert *retired natural resources company executive*
Kennedy, Robert Emmet *retired newspaperman*
Kley, John Arthur *banker*
Leitner, Alfred *mathematical physicist, educator, educational film producer*
Levitt, LeRoy Paul *psychiatrist, psychoanalyst*
†Lewis, Gordon Gilmer *golf course architect*
Maloon, James Harold *business executive, economist*
Martinuzzi, Leo Sergio, Jr. *banker*
Mc Combs, G. B. *publishing company executive*
McCowen, Max Creager *research scientist*
McMackin, F. Joseph, III *lawyer*
Mc Queen, Robert Charles *retired insurance executive*
Montgomery, Ruth Shick *author*
Myers, Charles Andrew *retired economist*
Oliver, Robert Bruce *retired investment company executive*
Parish, John Cook *insurance executive*
Peck, Bernard Sidney *lawyer*
Price, Thomas Benjamin *former textile company executive*
Putzell, Edwin Joseph, Jr. *lawyer, mayor*
Quigley, Jack Allen *service company executive*
Reed, John Franklin *instrument manufacturing company executive*
Richmond, Robert Linn *management consultant*
Roberts, William B. *lawyer, business executive*
Rowe, Herbert Joseph *retired trade association executive*
Rowe, Jack Field *retired electric utility executive*
Scarlett, Harold O. *retired retail executive, consultant*
Schauer, Wilbert Edward, Jr. *lawyer, manufacturing company executive*
Searle, Philip Ford *banker*
Sharpe, Robert Francis *equipment manufacturing company executive*
Smith, Willis Allen *retired consultant, former food company executive*
Snyder, Marion Gene *lawyer, former congressman*
Starnes, James Wright *lawyer*
Stevens, William Kenneth *lawyer*
Sullivan, Haywood Cooper *professional baseball team executive*
Suziedelis, Vytautas A. *engineering corporation executive*
†Tanner, Robert Hugh *engineer, consultant*
Terenzio, Peter Bernard *hospital administrator*
Van der Eb, Henry Gerard *retired packaging company executive*
Vickrey, Robert Remsen *artist*
von Arx, Dolph William *food products executive*
Waller, George Macgregor *historian, educator*
Weeks, Richard Ralph *marketing educator*
Westman, Carl Edward *lawyer*
White, Roy Bernard *theater executive*
Widman, Richard Gustave *engineering and construction company executive*
Williams, George Earnest *engineer, retired business executive*
Wodlinger, Mark Louis *broadcast executive*
Wyant, Corbin A. *newspaper publisher*

New Port Richey
Oliveto, Frank Louis *recreation consultant*
Rhodes, Eric Foster *real estate and insurance executive, consultant*
Robichaud, Phyllis Ivy Isabel *artist, educator*

New Smyrna Beach
Makela, Benjamin R. *editor, research director*
Skove, Thomas Malcolm *retired manufacturing company financial executive*

Niceville
Burns, John Joseph *consultant, retired aerospace executive, retired air force officer*
Phillips, Richard Wendell, Jr. *air force officer*

Nokomis
Cather, Donald Warren *civil engineer*
Halladay, Laurie Ann *public relations consultant, former franchise executive*
Lesch, George Henry *household products company executive*
Meyerhoff, Jack Fulton *financial executive*
Peters, Farnsley Lewellyn *retired association executive*

North Fort Myers
DiCarlo, Louis Michael *speech pathology educator*
Rogliano, Aldo Thomas *publishing executive*

North Miami
Anscher, Bernard *plastics manufacturing executive, consultant*
Cliff, Jimmy (James Chambers) *vocalist, composer*
Polley, Richard Donald *microbiologist, polymer chemist*

North Miami Beach
Averch, Harvey Allan *economist, educator, academic administrator*
Beckley, Donald K. *fundraiser*
†Birnbaum, Joel M. *health care company executive*
Fishel, Peter Livingston *accounting business executive*
Rosenbluth, Morton *periodontist, educator*
Tenzel, Richard Ruvin *ophthalmologist*
†Terry, Morton *academic administrator, physician*
Wolfenson, Azi U. *electrical engineer*

North Palm Beach
Chane, George Warren *management consultant*
Connor, John Thomas *retired bank and corporate executive, lawyer*
Edwards, William James *broadcasting executive*
Fauver, John William *mayor, retired business executive*
Gray, Harry Jack *investment executive*
Hayman, Richard Warren Joseph *conductor*
Hushing, William Collins *retired corporate executive*
Kenna, Edgar Douglas *manufacturing company executive*
Nicklaus, Jack William *professional golfer*
Oleksiw, Daniel Philip *former foreign service officer, consultant*
Rimmer, Jack *retired chemical company executive*
Staub, W. Arthur *health care products executive*

Ocala
Booth, George Warren *artist, advertising executive*
Forgue, Stanley Vincent *physics educator*
†Harris, Charles Edison *banker, lawyer*
Johnson, Winston Conrad *mathematics educator*
Killian, Ruth Selvey *home economist*
Parker, Harry Lee *retired military officer, counselor*

Ocoee
Rose, Peter Edward *former professional baseball player and manager*

Odessa
Lister, Thomas Mosie *composer, lyricist, publishing company executive, minister*

Oldsmar
Brunner, George Matthew *management consultant, former business executive*
Burrows, William Claude *aerospace executive, retired air force officer*
Hirschman, Sherman Joseph *lawyer, educator*
Ligett, Waldo Buford *chemist*
Sloane, Thomas Charles *lawyer*

Ona
†Rechcigl, Jack Edward *soil and environmental sciences educator*

Opa Locka
Greene, Joe (Charles Edward Greene) *former professional football player*
†Hopton, Janice *elementary school principal*
Jackson, Keith Jerome *football player*
Kosar, Bernie, Jr. *professional football player*
Marino, Daniel Constantine, Jr. *professional football player*

Orange City
Gorman, Burton William *retired education educator*

Orange Park
Enney, James Crowe *former air force officer, business executive*
Kirkwood, Maurice Richard *banker*
Ratzlaff, Judith L. *secondary school educator*
Rice, Ronald James *hospital administrator*
Webb, Robert Lee *chemical company executive*

Orlando
Abbott, Edward Leroy *finance executive*
Andrews, Brad Francis *zoological park administrator*
Argirion, Michael *editor*
Arnett, Warren Grant *interior designer*
Aronow, Neil Arthur *publishing company executive*
Baker, David A. *federal judge*
Baker, Peter Mitchell *laser scientist and executive, educator*
Ball, G. Thomas *lawyer*
†Ball, Joseph E. *association executive*
Berry, Stephen Joseph *reporter*
Blackford, Robert Newton *lawyer*
Blair, Mardian John *hospital management executive*
†Blue, Joseph Edward *physicist*
Boehle, William Randall *music educator emeritus*
Bollen, Roger *cartoonist*
Brownlee, Thomas Marshall *lighting manufacturing company executive*
Buchanan, Walter Woolwine *engineering educator, electrical engineer*
Canan, Michael J. *lawyer, author*
Cary, Freeman Hamilton *physician*
Cohen, Jules Simon *lawyer*
Conti, Louis Thomas Moore *lawyer*
Conway, Anne Callaghan *federal judge*
Davis, William Albert *theme park director*
Deo, Narsingh *computer science educator*
Dorsey, Norbert M. *bishop*
†Dunn, William Bruna, III *journalist*
DuRose, Richard Arthur *lawyer*
†Dyer, John Hugh *lawyer, state senator*
Eagan, William Leon *lawyer*
Fawsett, Patricia Combs *federal judge*
Fulton, Richard T. *lawyer*
Grady, Thomas J. *bishop*
Grant, Raymond Thomas *arts administrator*
Gray, Anthony Rollin *capital management company executive*
†Guest, Larry Samuel *newspaper columnist*
Haile, L. John, Jr. *journalist, newspaper executive*
Hall, Richard C. Winton *psychiatrist*
Handley, Leon Hunter *lawyer*

Harris, Martin Harvey aerospace company executive
Healy, Jane Elizabeth newspaper editor
Henry, William Oscar Eugene lawyer
Hill, Brian professional basketball team coach
†Hitt, John Charles university president
Hollis, Reginald archbishop
Horan, John Patrick lawyer
Hornick, Richard Bernard physician
†Howe, John Wadsworth bishop
Ispass, Alan Benjamin utilities executive
Ivey, James Burnett political cartoonist
†Jennings, Toni state senator, construction company executive
Jones, Joseph Wayne food and beverage company executive, entrepreneur
Jontz, Jeffry Robert lawyer
Leonhardt, Frederick Wayne lawyer
†Le Tellier, Gary airport terminal executive
Linscott, Jerry R. lawyer
Llewellyn, Ralph Alvin physics educator
†Maupin, Elizabeth Thatcher theater critic
McNulty, Chester Howard bank holding company executive
Medin, Julia Adele educator, researcher
Meunier, Paul Dennis aviation company executive
Miller, Charles Edward, Jr. financial executive
Mock, Frank Mackenzie lawyer
Moltzon, Richard Francis computer manufacturing executive
†Morgan, Richard T. publishing executive
Morris, Max F. lawyer
†Morrisey, Marena Grant art museum administrator
Norris, Franklin Gray thoracic and cardiovascular surgeon
O'Neal, Shaquille Rashaun professional basketball player
Pantuso, Vincent Joseph food service consultant
Pauley, Bruce Frederick history educator
Pope, Theodore Campbell, Jr. utilities executive, consultant
Reed, John Alton lawyer
†Reese, Charles Edgar columnist
Rice, Stephen Landon engineering educator
Roesner, Larry August civil engineer
Rolle, Christopher Davies lawyer
Rosenthal, Paul Edmond lawyer
Rush, Fletcher Grey, Jr. lawyer
†Santiago, Carlos minister
Sasseen, George Thiery aerospace engineering executive
Sathre, Leroy educator, consultant
†Sconiers, M. L. bishop
Sharp, George Kendall federal judge
Sharp, Joel H., Jr. lawyer
Silfvast, William T. laser physics educator, consultant
Simon, James Lowell lawyer
Skambis, Christopher Charles, Jr. lawyer
Smith, Paul Frederick plant physiologist, consultant
Soileau, Marion Joseph engineering and physics educator
Stephenson, Jan Lynn professional golfer
†Strack, J. Gary hospital administrator
Swedberg, Robert Mitchell opera company director
Tillotson, Frank Lee naval officer
Urban, James Arthur lawyer
Werner, Thomas Lee hospital administrator
Williamson, Thomas Arnold publishing company executive
Wolski, Patrick Edward newspaper executive
Yesawich, Peter Charles advertising executive
Young, George Cressler federal judge

Ormond Beach
Coke, C(hauncey) Eugene consulting company executive, scientist, educator, author
Riley, Daniel Edward air force officer
Wendelstedt, Harry Hunter, Jr. umpire

Osprey
Allen, George Howard publishing management consultant
Coates, Clarence Leroy, Jr. research engineer, educator
Cort, Winifred Mitchell microbiologist, biochemist
Crispin, Mildred Swift (Mrs. Frederick Eaton Crispin) civic worker, writer
Gross, James Dehnert pathologist
Maddocks, Robert Allen lawyer, manufacturing company executive
Strongin, Theodore journalist
Woodall, William Leon retired insurance executive

Oviedo
Martin, Judson Phillips retired education educator
Whitworth, Hall Baker forest products company executive

Palm Bay
Bachmann, Albert Edward engineering educator

Palm Beach
Adduci, Vincent James business executive
Adler, Frederick Richard lawyer, financier
Alimanestianu, Calin retired hotel consultant
Alpert, Seymour anesthesiologist, educator
Artinian, Artine French literature scholar, collector
Asencio, Diego C. state agency administrator, former federal commission administrator, consultant, business executive
Bagby, Joseph Rigsby financial investor
Bane, Charles Arthur lawyer
Barness, Amnon Shemaya financial service executive
Beasley, James W., Jr. lawyer
Bishop, Warner Bader finance company executive
Black, Leonard J. retail store consultant
Bonan, Seon Pierre real estate developer
Chittick, Elizabeth Lancaster association executive, women's rights activist
Chopin, L. Frank lawyer
Cook, Edward Willingham diversified industry executive
Curry, Bernard Francis former banker, consultant
Donnell, John Randolph petroleum executive
Druck, Kalman Breschel public relations counselor
Ferrin, Allan Wheeler association executive
Fogelson, David retired lawyer
Ford, Thomas Patrick lawyer
Graubard, Seymour lawyer
Gundlach, Heinz Ludwig investment banker, lawyer
Habicht, Frank Henry industrial executive
Hall, Kathryn Evangeline writer, lecturer
Halmos, Peter investment company executive
Isenberg, Abraham Charles shoe manufacturing company executive
Jackson, John Tillson corporate executive
Kaplan, Muriel Sheerr sculptor
Korn, David investor
Levine, Laurence Brandt investment banker
Pryor, Hubert editor, writer
Riefler, Donald Brown financial consultant
Rinker, Ruby Stewart foundation administrator
†Robb, David Buzby, Jr. financial services company executive, lawyer
Roberts, Margaret Harold editor, publisher
Rudolph, Malcolm Rome investment banker
Rumbough, Stanley Maddox, Jr. industrialist
Scott, Harold Bartlett manufacturing executive
Stoneman, Samuel Sidney cinema company executive
Tiecke, Richard William pathologist, educator, association executive
Walsh, Cornelius Stephen leasing company executive
Wheelock, Morgan Dix, Jr. landscape architect
Winkler, Joseph Conrad former recreational products manufacturing executive
Wirtz, Willem Kindler garden and lighting designer, public relations consultant

Palm Beach Gardens
Awtrey, Jim L. sports association executive
Baker, Jean Mary cable television executive
Bubrick, George Joseph corporate executive
Calcevecchia, Mark professional golfer
Christian, Robert Henry architect
Collado, Emilio Gabriel energy company executive, consultant
Daly, John professional golfer
Emiliani, Cesare geology educator, author
Harnett, Joseph Durham oil company executive
Herrick, John Dennis consultant, former law firm executive, retired food products executive
Howse, Robert Davis business executive
Lebed, Hartzel Zangwill insurance company executive
Mendelson, Richard Donald former communications company executive
Mergler, H. Kent investment counselor
Mize, Larry professional golfer
Player, Gary Jim professional golfer
Rodriguez, Chi Chi (Juan Rodriguez) professional golfer
Sabatini, Gabriela tennis player
Symons, J. Keith bishop

Palm City
Ammarell, John Samuel retired college president, former security services executive
Burton, John Routh lawyer
Henry, David Howe, II former diplomat and international organization official
Huntington, Earl Lloyd lawyer, retired natural resources company executive
Pepitone, Byron Vincent former government official
Senter, William Oscar retired air force officer
White, Eugene James retired technology company executive
Wirsig, Woodrow magazine editor, trade organization executive, business executive
Wishart, Ronald Sinclair retired chemical company executive

Palm Coast
Dickson, David Watson Daly retired college president
Franco, Annemarie Woletz editor
Godfrey, Eutha Marek elementary education educator, consultant

Palmetto
Compton, Charles Daniel chemistry educator

Panama City
D'Arcy, Gerald Paul engineering executive, consultant
Dykes, James Edgar advertising educator, consultant
Green, Hubert professional golfer

Panama City Beach
Miller, Robert William personal property appraiser, writer

Pembroke Pines
Ladin, Eugene communications company executive
Sigel, M(ola) Michael scientist, medical educator

Penney Farms
Kimbrough, Ralph Bradley educational administration educator emeritus

Pensacola
Adams, Joseph Peter retired lawyer, consultant
Arnow, Winston Eugene federal judge
†Bear, Lewis, Jr. food and electronics company executive
Bowden, Jesse Earle newspaper editor, author, cartoonist, journalism educator
Bozeman, Frank Carmack lawyer
Bullock, Ellis Way, Jr. architect
Caton, Betty Ann health science administrator
Collier, Lacey Alexander federal judge
DeBardeleben, John Thomas, Jr. retired insurance company executive
Dixon, James Andrew, Jr. protective services official
Frye, John William, III retired senior judge
Furlong, George Morgan, Jr. retired naval officer, museum foundation executive
Geeker, Nicholas Peter lawyer, judge
Gregory, Flaudie Stewart special education educator
Groner, Pat Neff health care executive
Hass, Charles John William probation officer
Jones, Walter Harrison chemist
†Kahn, Robert H., Jr. retail executive
Killian, Lewis Martin sociology educator
Love, Robert William, Jr. retired physician, government administrator
†Marx, Morris Leon academic administrator
McSwain, Richard Horace materials engineer, consultant
Moulton, Wilbur Wright, Jr. lawyer
Mountcastle, William Wallace, Jr. philosophy and religion educator
†Rasmussen, Robert museum director
Ray, Donald Hensley biologist
Usry, Milton Franklin accounting educator
VanSlyke, Robert Emmett health care executive
Vinson, C. Roger federal judge
Watt, Stuart George engineering contracting company executive
Weisner, Maurice Franklin former naval officer
†Woolf, Kenneth Howard architect

Pineland
Doherty, Michel George alcohol and drug treatment facility administrator

Pinellas Park
†Athanson, Mary Catheryne elementary school principal
†Brennan, Mary M. state legislator
Hall, Charles Allen aerospace and energy company executive
Perry, Paul Alverson utility executive

Placida
Grissom, Joseph Carol retired leasing and investments business executive
Schwarting, Arthur Ernest university dean

Plant City
Bruton, James DeWitt, Jr. retired judge
Holland, Gene Grigsby (Scottie Holland) artist
†Patronelli, Raymond church administrator
Tully, Darrow newspaper publisher

Plantation
Baez, Manuel health care executive
Hicks, Ele Wyatte management consultant
Shoemaker, William Edward financial executive

Plymouth
Voelker, Charles Robert archbishop, academic dean

Pompano Beach
Ayres, John Cecil retired public health executive
Bliznakov, Emile George biomedical research scientist
Calatchi, Ralph Franklin economist
Crandell, K(enneth) James management and strategic planning consultant, entrepreneur
Elder, Robert Lee professional golfer
Freimark, Jeffrey Philip retail supermarket executive
Kester, Stewart Randolph banker
Mulvey, John Thomas, Jr. financial consultant
Patterson, Alan Bruce obstetrician-gynecologist
Rifenburgh, Richard Philip investment company executive
Roen, Sheldon R. publisher, psychologist
Schwartz, Joseph retired container company executive
Slovin, Bruce diversified holding company executive
Trenery, Mary Ellen librarian
Zinman, Jacques former insurance agency executive

Ponce Inlet
†Connor, Edward Hollis, III golf course architect

Ponte Vedra Beach
Agassi, Andre Kirk tennis player
Azinger, Paul professional golfer
Beman, Deane Randolph association executive
Chang, Michael tennis player
Cook, John professional golfer
Couples, Fred golfer
Edberg, Stefan professional tennis player
Faxon, Brad professional golfer
Floyd, Raymond professional golfer
Forsman, Dan professional golfer
Green, Norman Kenneth retired oil industry executive, former naval officer
Hanigan, Marvin Frank investment company executive, consultant
Hartzell, Karl Drew retired dean
Janzen, Lee professional golfer
Kite, Thomas O., Jr. professional golfer
Klacsmann, John Anthony retired chemical company executive
Krusen, Henry Stanley investment banker
Kuhn, Bowie K. lawyer, former professional baseball commissioner, consultant
Love, Davis, III professional golfer
McMullan, William Patrick, Jr. banker
Milbrath, Robert Henry retired petroleum executive
Moore, Philip Walsh appraisal company executive
O'Brien, Raymond Vincent, Jr. banker
Pavin, Corey professional golfer
Phelan, Martin DuPont retired film company executive
Price, Nick professional golfer
ReMine, William Hervey, Jr. surgeon
Schultz, Andrew Schultz, Jr. industrial engineering educator
Spence, Richard Dee paper products company executive, former railroad executive
Stewart, (William) Payne (Payne Stewart) professional golfer
Thorndike, Richard King former brokerage company executive
Wadkins, Lanny professional golfer
Zoeller, Fuzzy professional golfer

Port Charlotte
†Flanders, Jefferson publishing executive
Munger, Elmer Lewis civil engineer, educator
Norris, Dolores June elementary educator

Port Manatee
Falls, William Wayne aquaculturist

Port Richey
Baiardi, John Charles retired scientific laboratory director
Radomski, Jack London pharmacologist, consultant

Port Saint Lucie
Clark, Harold Steve architect
Rhodes, Alfred William former insurance company executive
Sommers, Robert Thomas editor, publisher, author

Punta Gorda
Bulzacchelli, John G. financial executive
Harrington, John Vincent retired communications company executive, engineer, educator
Hepfer, John William, Jr. consultant, retired air force officer
Hill, Richard Earl academic administrator
†Kavanaugh, Frank James film producer, educator
Wilson, Dwight Liston former military officer, investment advisor

Quincy
Lindquist, Mark Alvin artist
Teare, Iwan Dale agronomy educator, research scientist

Ridge Manor
Widmer, Raymond Arthur financial holding company executive

River Ranch
Swett, Albert Hersey retired lawyer, business executive, consultant

Rockledge
†Posey, William J. realtor
Sutton, Betty Sheriff elementary education educator

Royal Palm Beach
Graham, Carl Francis consultant, former chemical products company executive, chemist

Ruskin
Nissen, Carl Andrew, Jr. minister, retired procurement analyst

Saint Augustine
Adams, William Roger historian
Armstrong, John Alexander emeritus political science educator
Baker, Norman Henderson association executive
Davis, Bertram George association executive, lawyer
Edwards, Page Lawrence, Jr. author, archivist, historical society administrator
Greenberg, Michael John biologist, research director
LeBeau, Hector Alton, Jr. management consultant, former confectionary company executive
Nolan, Joseph Thomas journalism educator, communications consultant
Oliver, Elizabeth Kimball writer, historian
Proctor, William Lee college president
Russell, Josiah Cox historian, educator
Shortlidge, Richard Lynn, Jr. foreign affairs consultant, retired foreign service officer, human resource economist
Theil, Henri economist, educator
Zellers, Carl Fredrick, Jr. railway executive

Saint Cloud
Everett, Woodrow Wilson electrical engineer, educator

Saint Leo
Mouch, Frank Messman college president, priest

Saint Petersburg
Armacost, Peter Hayden college president
Barnes, Andrew Earl newspaper editor
Battaglia, Anthony Sylvester lawyer
Belich, John Patrick, Sr. journalist
Benbow, Charles Clarence retired writer, critic
Blumenthal, Herman Bertram accountant
Byrd, Isaac Burlin fishery biologist, fisheries administrator
Cane, Paula P. speech and language pathologist, scriptwriter, actor
Carlson, Jeannie Ann writer
Carroll, Charles Michael music educator
Castle, Raymond Nielson chemist, educator
Collins, Carl Russell, Jr. architectural and engineering company executive
Cook, Marian Alice musician
Critchfield, Jack Barron utilities company executive
DiFilippo, Fernando, Jr. lawyer
Donaldson, Merle Richard electrical engineering educator, consultant
Emerson, William Allen retired investment company executive
Favalora, John Clement bishop
†Fischer, David J. mayor
Foley, Michael Francis newspaper executive
Freeman, Corinne financial services, former mayor
Galbraith, John William securities company executive
Ginn, Ronn architect, urban planner, general contractor
Godbold, Francis Stanley investment banker, real estate, oil and gas executive
Good, Robert Alan physician, educator
Grube, Karl Bertram judge
Haiman, Robert James newspaper editor, journalism educator
Hansel, Paul George physicist, consultant
Hargrave, Victoria Elizabeth librarian
Harris, Roger S. bishop
Hines, Andrew Hampton, Jr. utilities executive
†Hull, Anne Victoria journalist
Jacob, Bruce Robert dean, academic administrator, law educator
Kazor, Walter Robert statistical process control and quality assurance consultant
Kuttler, Carl Martin, Jr. college president
Layton, William George management consultant, human resources executive
Mann, Sam Henry, Jr. lawyer
Martin, Susan Taylor newspaper editor
Mc Connell, Robert Chalmers former city official
McIntyre, Deborah psychotherapist, author
Mc Lean, Thomas Edwin retired manufacturing company executive
McMurray, Joseph Patrick Brendan financial consultant
Meinke, Peter writer, retired educator
Mills, William Harold, Jr. construction company executive
Mosby, John Davenport, III investment banking executive
Nussbaum, Leo Lester retired college president, consultant
†O'Hearn, John Howard publishing company executive
Oleck, Howard Leoner legal educator, writer
Papa, Anthony Emil retired army officer
Patterson, Eugene Corbett retired editor, publisher
Peterson, Arthur Laverne former college president
Pittman, Robert Turner retired newspaper editor
Remke, Richard Edwin lumber company executive
Rester, Alfred Carl, Jr. physicist
Roney, Paul H(itch) federal judge
Root, Allen William pediatrician, educator
Runge, De Lyle Paul retired library director, consultant
Schuck, Marjorie Massey publisher, editor, consultant
Schultz, G. Robert lawyer
Scott, Lee Hansen holding company executive
Sembler, Mel company executive, former ambassador
Serrie, Hendrick anthropology and international business educator
Shank, Clare Brown Williams political leader

Sheen, Robert Tilton manufacturing company executive
Sibley, Mark Anderson ophthalmologist
Silver, Lawrence Alan marketing executive
†Snider, Eric Ross music critic
Southworth, William Dixon retired education educator
Stewart, Joseph Lester rubber company executive
†Tash, Paul C. editor-in-chief
†Wallace, Peter Rudy state senator
Wedding, Charles Randolph architect
Wisler, Willard Eugene health care management executive
Wittner, Ted Philip insurance company executive
†Woodard, Joseph Lamar law librarian, law educator

Saint Petersburg Beach
Hurley, Frank Thomas, Jr. realtor

Sanibel
Adair, Charles Valloyd retired physician
Ball, Armand Baer former association executive, consultant
Courtney, James Edmond real estate development
Crown, David Allan criminologist, educator
Herriott, Donald Richard optical physicist
Kiernan, Edwin A., Jr. lawyer, corporation executive

Sanibel Island
Horecker, Bernard Leonard retired biochemistry educator

Santa Rosa Beach
Wright, John Peale retired banker

Sarasota
Abbott, J. Carl architect, planner, inventor, educator
Adams, Richard Towsley university president, educational consultant
Albrecht, Robert Downing retail executive
Altabe, Joan Augusta Berg artist, writer, art and architecture critic
Arreola, John Bradley diversified financial service company executive, financial planner
Augsburger, Aaron Donald clergyman
Bailey, Robert Elliott financial executive
Beck, George William retired industrial engineer
Beck, Robert Alfred hotel administration educator
Bewley, David Charles financial planner
†Booker, Margaret Elizabeth theater director, artistic director, performing arts educator
Browdy, Alvin lawyer
Burket, Harriet (Mrs. Francis B. Taussig) editor
Chamberlain, John Angus sculptor
Christ-Janer, Arland Frederick college president
Connor, Robert T. former government official
Cottone, Benedict Peter retired lawyer
Covert, Michael Henri healthcare facility administrator
Deere, Cyril Thomas retired computer company executive
Dlesk, George retired pulp and paper industry consultant
Downey, John Charles university dean, zoology educator
Eachus, Joseph J(ackson) computer scientist, consultant
Eliscu, Frank sculptor
Estrin, Richard William newspaper editor
Fabrycy, Mark Zdzislaw retired economist
Feder, Allan Appel management executive, consultant
Fendrick, Alan Burton retired advertising executive
Friedberg, Harold David cardiologist
Gilbert, Perry Webster emeritus educator
Gittelson, Bernard public relations consultant, author, lecturer
Glasser, Otto John former business executive, former air force officer
†Gordon, Sanford Daniel economics educator
Graham, Otto Everett, Jr. retired athletic director
Gray, Hope Diffenderfer industrial specialist
Greenfield, Robert Kauffman lawyer
Grubbs, Elven Judson retired newspaper publisher
Gurvitz, Milton Solomon psychologist
Hagen, George Leon business consultant
Hamberg, Daniel economist, educator
†Handelman, Jay Harold theater critic
Hansen, Elisa Marie art historian
Harmon, (Loren) Foster art dealer
†Hayes, Joseph author
Herbert, James Paul advertising executive
†Highland, Marilyn M. principal
Hoffman, Oscar Allen retired forest products company executive
Hoover, Dwight Wesley history educator
Hrones, John Anthony mechanical engineering educator
Irwin, Theodore writer
Ives, George Skinner arbitrator, former government official
Jaeger, Leonard Henry former public utility executive
Jones, Tracey Kirk, Jr. minister, educator
Kelley, Susan Curtin writer
Kerker, Milton chemistry educator
Kimbrough, Robert Averyt lawyer
Kiplinger, Glenn Francis pharmacologist, consultant
Lambert, John Phillip financial executive, consultant
Levitt, Irving Francis investment company executive
Lewis, Brian Kreglow computer consultant
Lindsay, David Breed, Jr. aircraft company executive, former editor and publisher
Loomis, Wesley Horace, III former publishing company executive
Loving, George Gilmer, Jr. retired air force officer
MacDonald, Robert Taylor newspaper executive
Mackey, Leonard Bruce lawyer, former diversified manufacturing corporation executive
Mahadevan, Kumar marine laboratory director, researcher
Marino, Eugene Louis publishing company executive
Mattran, Donald Albert management consultant, educator
McCollum, John Morris tenor
McFarlin, Diane H. newspaper editor
Miles, Arthur J. financial planner, consultant
Myerson, Albert Leon physical chemist
Noether, Emiliana Pasca historian, educator
†North, Marjorie Mary columnist
Page, George Keith banker
Palermo, Joseph language educator
Powers, Dudley musician
Proffitt, Waldo, Jr. newspaper editor
Radnay, Paul Andrew physician
Raimi, Burton Louis lawyer
Roberts, Merrill Joseph economist, educator
Ross, Gerald Fred engineering executive, researcher
Roth, James Frank manufacturing company executive, chemist
Sawyer, Helen Alton artist
Schersten, H. Donald management consultant, realtor, mortgage broker
Schwartz, Norman L. lawyer
Seibert, Russell Jacob botanist, research associate
Simon, Joseph Patrick food services executive
†Smith, Mark Hallard architect
Smith, Richard Emerson (Dick Smith) make-up artist
Solomon, Syd artist
Taplin, Winn Lowell historian, retired senior intelligence operations officer
Tatum, Joan Glennalyn John business, vocational educator
Tolley, James Little corporate public relations consultant
Turner, Eugene Andrew manufacturing executive
Veinott, Cyril George electrical engineer, consultant
Vestal, Lucian LaRoe financier
Weeks, Albert Loren author, educator, journalist
Weeks, Walter LeRoy electrical engineering educator
†Welch, John Dana urologist, performing arts association executive
White, Will Walter, III public relations consultant, writer
Wigton, Paul Norton steel company consultant, former executive
Wilson, Kenneth Jay writer
Yordan, Carlos Manuel foreign service officer

Satellite Beach
Button, Kenneth John physicist
Hogan, Henry Leon, III business executive, retired air force officer
†St John, Constance R. school system administrator
Van Arsdall, Robert Armes engineer, retired air force officer
Vilardebo, Angie Marie management consultant, parochial school educator

Sebastian
Breman, Joseph Eliot lawyer
Mauke, Otto Russell retired college president
Pieper, Patricia Rita artist, photographer

Sebring
Sherrick, Daniel Noah real estate broker

Seminole
Haile, James Francis hospital administrator
McGinn, Donald Joseph English educator
Nesbitt, Robert Edward Lee, Jr. physician, educator
Silver, Paul Robert marketing executive, consultant

Shalimar
Humphreys, James W. surgeon, former air force officer, medical board executive

Siesta
Held, Philip artist

Sorrento
†Welch, Jerry oil company executive

South Miami
Benbow, John Robert banker
Bruel, Iris Barbara psychologist

South Pasadena
Minton, Joseph Paul retired safety organization executive

Spring Hill
Finney, Roy Pelham, Jr. urologist, surgeon, inventor
Rojas, Victor Hugo retired vocational education educator
Youngman, Henny comedian

Starke
Loper, George Wilson, Jr. physical education educator

Stuart
†Ankrom, Charles Franklin golf course architect, consultant
Conklin, George Melville retired food company executive
Derrickson, William Borden manufacturing executive
Haserick, John Roger retired dermatologist
Jefferson, Peter Augustus architect
Leibson, Irving industrial executive
Mc Kenna, Sidney F. technical company executive
McQuillan, William Hugh building company executive
Morena, John Joseph manufacturing engineer, executive
Murchake, John publishing executive
†Myers, William George physician, state senator
Pisani, Joseph Michael physician
Shurick, Edward Palmes television executive, rancher
Slade, Gerald Jack publishing company executive
Snider, Harlan Tanner former manufacturing company executive
Wasiele, Harry W., Jr. diversified electrical manufacturing company executive
Westlake, Robert Elmer, Sr. physician
Wood, Harleston Read retired manufacturing executive

Sun City Center
Fields, Ralph Raymond education educator
†Fleischman, Sol Joseph, Sr. retired television broadcasting executive
Hall, John Fry psychologist, educator
Jeffries, Robert Joseph retired engineering educator, business executive
McGrath, John Francis utility executive
Parsons, George Williams retired medical center administrator, cattle rancher
Sevold, Gordon James savings and loan executive

Sunrise
Hayes, Peter John retail executive

Surfside
Albert, Calvin sculptor
Prystowsky, Harry physician, educator

Tallahassee
Adams, Perry Ronald former college administrator
Albright, John Rupp physics educator
Anthony, William Philip management educator
Ashler, Philip Frederic international trade and development advisor
Aurell, John Karl lawyer
Avant, David Alonzo, Jr. realty company executive, photographer
Barnett, Martha Walters lawyer
Baum, Werner A. former academic administrator, meteorologist
Beck, Earl Ray historian, educator
Bowden, Bobby university athletic coach
Boyd, Joseph Arthur, Jr. lawyer
Braswell, Robert Neil scientist, engineer, educator
Brueckheimer, William Rogers social science educator
†Burnette, Ada M. Puryear educational administrator
Burroway, Janet G. English language educator, novelist
Butterworth, Robert A. state attorney general
Carson, Leonard Allen lawyer
†Chen, Ching Jen mechanical engineering educator, research scientist
Chiles, Lawton Mainor governor, former senator
Choppin, Gregory Robert chemistry educator
Clarke, Allan J. oceanography educator, consultant
Clarkson, Julian Derieux lawyer
Colberg, Marshall Rudolph economist
Coloney, Wayne Herndon civil engineer
Crider, Irene Perritt educator, consultant
†Crow, Jack E. physics administrator
Dadisman, Joseph Carrol newspaper executive
D'Alemberte, Talbot (Sandy D'Alemberte) lawyer, educator
Davis, Bertram Hylton retired English educator
De Forest, Sherwood Searle agricultural engineer, agribusiness services executive
Dillingham, Marjorie Carter foreign language educator
Dorn, Charles Meeker art education educator
Durrence, James Larry state executive, history educator
Dye, Thomas Roy political science educator
Earhart, Eileen Magie retired home and family life educator
Early, Johnnie L., II pharmacy educator
Ervin, Robert Marvin lawyer
Fox, John David educator, physicist
Frechette, Ernest Albert foreign language educator emeritus
Friedmann, E(merich) Imre biologist, educator
Gil, Lazier university dean
Glenn, Rogers psychologist, student advisor, consultant
Golden, Leon classicist, educator
Goodner, Dwight Benjamin mathematician, emeritus educator
Gould, Bruce Allan state agency administrator, educator, consultant
Griffith, Elwin Jabez lawyer, university administrator
Grimes, Stephen Henry state supreme court chief justice
Gunter, William Dawson, Jr. (Bill Gunter) insurance company executive
Hafner, Lawrence Erhardt education educator
Hall, Houghton Alexander engineering professional
Harding, Major Best state supreme court justice
Harper, George Mills English language educator
Harper, William C. artist, educator
Harrison, Thomas James electrical engineer, educator
Harsanyi, Janice soprano, educator
Hatchett, Joseph Woodrow federal judge
†Hawkins, Mary Ellen Higgins (Mary Ellen Higgins) state legislator, public relations consultant
Heldman, Louis Marc newspaper editor
†Herndon, Roy Clifford physicist
Holcombe, Randall Gregory economics educator
Housewright, Wiley Lee music educator
†Humphries, Frederick S. university president
Hunt, John Edwin insurance company executive, consultant
Johnsen, Russell Harold chemist, educator
Johnson, Benjamin F., VI real estate developer, consulting economist
Kaelin, Eugene Francis philosophy educator
†Kemper, Kirby Wayne physics educator
Kenshalo, Daniel Ralph psychologist, educator
Kirk, Colleen Jean conductor, educator
Kogan, Gerald state supreme court justice
Laird, William Everette, Jr. economics educator, administrator
†Lannutti, Joseph Edward physics educator
Lewis, Gerald A. state comptroller
Lick, Dale Wesley mathematician, university president, educator
Light, Robley Jasper chemistry educator
Lipner, Harry physiologist, educator
Macesich, George econmomics professor
MacKay, Kenneth "Buddy" Hood state official, former congressman
Maguire, Charlotte Edwards retired physician
†Makowski, Lee science administrator, biology and chemistry educator
Mandelkern, Leo biophysics and chemistry educator
Marshall, Stanley former educator, business executive
McCrimmon, James McNab language educator
McDonald, Parker Lee state supreme court justice
McTarnaghan, Roy E. acadamic administrator
†Meredith, Michael science educator
Moore, Duncan healthcare executive
Moore, John Hebron history educator
Morgan, Lucy W. journalist
Morgan, Robert Marion educational research educator
Mustian, Middleton Truett hospital administrator
Nam, Charles Benjamin sociologist, demographer, educator
Navon, Ionel Michael mathematics educator
Newell, Barbara Warne economist, educator
Nichols, Eugene Douglas mathematics educator
Nimmons, Ralph Wilson, Jr. federal judge
O'Brien, James Joseph meteorology and oceanography educator
Oldson, William Orville history educator
Overton, Benjamin Frederick state supreme court justice
Palladino-Craig, Allys museum director
Paredes, James Anthony anthropologist, educator
Paul, Maurice M. federal judge
Pelham, Thomas Gerald lawyer
Penrod, Kenneth Earl medical education consultant
†Pestle, Ruth Ellen home economics educator
Peterson, Rodney Delos mediator, forensic economist
Pfeffer, Richard Lawrence geophysics educator
Reed, Charles Bass university system chancellor
Robbins, Jane Borsch library science educator, information science educator
Roberts, B. K. lawyer, former judge
†Robson, Donald physics educator
Rockwood, Ruth H. former library science educator
Rubenstein, Richard Lowell theologian, educator
Ryll, Frank Maynard, Jr. association executive
Schrieffer, John Robert physics educator, science administrator
†Schroeder, Edwin Maher law educator
†Serow, William John economics educator
Shaw, Leander Jerry, Jr. state supreme court justice
†Shaw, Robert D., Jr. newspaper editor
†Sheline, Raymond K. nuclear chemistry educator
†Sindler, Robert Brian state legislator, veterinarian
Smith, Eric Alan meteorology educator
Smith, James C. secretary of state, former state attorney general
Stafford, William Henry, Jr. federal judge
Stiff, Robert Martin newspaper editor
Sturges, Wilton, III oceanography educator
Summers, Frank William librarian
Summers, Lorraine Dey Schaeffer librarian
Sundberg, Alan Carl former state supreme court justice, lawyer
Taylor, J(ames) Herbert cell biology educator
Trezza, Alphonse Fiore librarian, educator
Tuckman, Bruce Wayne educational psychologist, educator, researcher
†Voran, James F. principal
Walborsky, Harry M. chemistry educator, consultant
†Wetherell, Virginia Bacon state legislator, engineering company executive
Wilkins, (George) Barratt librarian
†Williams, Theodore P. biophysicist, biology educator
Zachert, Martha Jane retired librarian
Zaiser, Kent Ames lawyer

Tamarac
Fish, Robert Jay dental surgeon, lawyer, medico-legal consultant, diversified entrepreneur

Tampa
†Abell, Jan Mary architect
†Adams, Henry Lee, Jr. federal judge
Adkins, Edward Cleland lawyer
Afield, Walter Edward psychiatrist, service executive
Aitken, Thomas Dean lawyer
Alexander, William Olin finance company executive
Allen, Timothy Andrew law enforcement officer
Anderson, Robert Henry education educator
†Anton, John Peter philosophy educator
Ashley, James Robert electrical engineer, inventor, educator
Baker, Carleton Harold physiology educator
Barford, George, IV lawyer
Barkin, Marvin E. lawyer
Barness, Lewis Abraham physician
Barton, Bernard Alan, Jr. lawyer
Battle, Jean Allen writer, educator
Baynes, Thomas Edward, Jr. judge, lawyer, educator
Behnke, Roy Herbert physician, educator
Benjamin, Robert Spiers foreign correspondent, writer, publicist
Beytin, Kenneth Alan lawyer
†Bice, Michael O. health science association administrator
†Biebel, John health care administrator
Bierley, John Charles lawyer
Binford, Jesse Stone, Jr. chemistry educator
Bondi, Joseph Charles, Jr. education educator, consultant
Bowen, Thomas Edwin cardiothoracic surgeon, retired army officer
Brown, John Lott retired university president, educator
Brown, Troy Anderson, Jr. electrical distributing company executive
†Bucklew, Susan Cawthon federal judge
Bujones, Fernando Calleiro ballet dancer
Bukantz, Samuel Charles physician, educator
Bussone, David Eben hospital administrator
Campbell, David Ned retired electric utility executive, business consultant
Campbell, Richard Bruce lawyer
Carey, Larry Campbell surgeon
Casey, Phillip Earle steel company executive
Castagna, William John federal judge
Cavanagh, Denis physician, educator
Christopher, Wilford Scott public relations consultant
Corcoran, C. Timothy, III judge
†Creed, Thomas G. steel company executive
†Crisp, Terry Arthur professional hockey coach
Crowe, Eugene Bertrand retired investment counselor
Culverhouse, Hugh Franklin lawyer, professional sports team executive
Cundiff, Paul Arthur English language educator
Cutler, Edward I. lawyer
Davis, Richard Earl lawyer
†Davis, W. E. clergyman, bishop
del Regato, Juan Angel radio-therapeutist and oncologist, educator
DeMontier, Paulette LaPointe chemist
Dempster, Richard Vreeland environmental company executive
†Dent, Sharon Pierce transportation executive
Deutsch, Sid bioengineer, educator
DeVine, B. Mack corporate executive
Doliner, Nathaniel Lee lawyer
Dunn, Henry Hampton television commentator, former editor
Ellwanger, Thomas John lawyer
Farrior, Joseph Brown otologist
Flom, Edward Leonard retired steel company executive
†Floto, Ronald John supermarket executive
Frankowiak, James Raymond public relations executive
Franzen, Lavern Gerhard bishop
Freedman, Sandra Warshaw mayor
Frias, Jaime Luis pediatrician, educator
Gassler, Frank Henry lawyer
Gilbert, Leonard Harold lawyer
Gilbert-Barness, Enid F. pathologist, pathology and pediatrics educator
Gillen, William Albert lawyer
Givens, Paul Edward industrial engineer, educator
Givens, Paul Ronald former university chancellor
Glasser, Stephen Paul cardiologist
†Glickman, Ronnie Carl state official, lawyer
Gonzalez, Joe Manuel lawyer
†Grant, John Audley, Jr. state senator, lawyer
Greenfield, George B. radiologist
†Gregg, Charles W. engineering executive

Hankenson, E(dward) Craig, Jr. *performing arts executive*
Harkness, Mary Lou *librarian*
†Harrell, Cecil Stanford *pharmacy management service company executive*
Hartmann, William Herman *pathologist, educator*
Harvill, H. Doyle *newspaper publisher*
†Hayes, Don A. *data processing commpany executive*
Heck, James Baker *university official*
Hegarty, Thomas Joseph *academic administrator*
Henning, Rudolf Ernst *electrical engineer, educator, consultant*
Hernandez, Gilberto Juan *accountant, auditor*
Holder, Harold Douglas, Sr. *investor, industrialist*
Holmes, Dwight Ellis *architect*
Homan, Paul M. *financial consultant*
Howey, John Richard *architect*
Hoyt, Brooks Pettingill *lawyer*
Hyatt, Kenneth E(rnest) *building materials company executive*
Jacobson, Howard Newman *obstetrics/gynecology educator, researcher*
Jennewein, James Joseph *architect*
Johnson, Ewell Calvin *research and engineering executive*
Jones, Gregory Gilman *lawyer*
Jones, John Arthur *lawyer*
†Karl, Frederick Brennan *lawyer, former state justice*
Kaufman, Ronald Paul *physician, school official*
Kelly, Thomas Paine, Jr. *lawyer*
†Kemp, Thomas Jay *librarian*
Kiernan, William Joseph, Jr. *lawyer, real estate investor*
Koehn, George Waldemar *bank executive*
Kovachevich, Elizabeth Anne *federal judge*
Krizek, Thomas Joseph *plastic surgeon*
Krzanowski, Joseph John, Jr. *pharmacology educator*
Leavengood, Victor Price *telephone company executive*
Levine, Jack Anton *lawyer*
†Lim, Daniel Van *microbiology educator*
Litschgi, A. Byrne *lawyer*
†Locker, Raymond Duncan *editor*
Lockey, Richard Funk *allergist, educator*
†Loft, Kurt *science writer, music critic*
Maass, R. Andrew *museum director*
MacDonald, Thomas Cook, Jr. *lawyer*
MacManus, Susan Ann *political science educator, researcher*
†Martens, Ernesto *glass products company executive*
Martin, Gary Wayne *lawyer*
Matlock, Kenneth Jerome *building materials company executive*
McAdams, John P. *lawyer*
McCook, Kathleen de la Peña *university educator*
McMillan, Donald Ernest *internal medicine educator, state program director*
Meisels, Gerhard George *academic administrator, chemist, educator*
Menendez, Manuel, Jr. *judge*
Merryday, Steven D. *federal judge*
Miller, Charles Leslie *civil engineer, planner, consultant*
†Miller, Lesley James, Jr. *congressman*
Miller, William Jones *lawyer*
†Mirro, Richard Allen *bank executive*
†Molnar, Lewis K. *health facility administrator*
Munoz, Michael Anthony *professional football player*
Muroff, Lawrence Ross *nuclear medicine physician*
Nagera, Humberto *psychiatrist, psychoanalyst, educator, author*
Naimoli, Vincent Joseph *diversified operating and holding company executive*
Nakamura, Yoshio *professional sports team executive*
Neusner, Jacob *humanities and religious studies educator*
Nevins, Albert J. *publisher, editor, author*
Nord, Walter Robert *business administration educator, researcher, consultant*
O'Neill, Albert Clarence, Jr. *lawyer*
O'Sullivan, Brendan Patrick *lawyer*
Perry, James Frederic *philosophy educator, author*
Pfeiffer, Eric Armin *psychiatrist, gerontologist*
Poe, William Frederick *insurance agency executive, former mayor*
Pollara, Bernard *immunologist, pediatrician*
Preto-Rodas, Richard Anthony *foreign language educator*
Read, Peter Kip *health care administrator*
Reading, Anthony John *physician*
Richardson, Edward James *federal government agency official*
Richardson, Sylvia Onesti *physician*
Roberson, Bruce H. *lawyer*
Roberts, Edwin Albert, Jr. *newspaper editor, journalist*
Rosenkranz, Stanley William *lawyer*
Rothenberg, Frederick M. *lawyer*
Rowlands, David Thomas *pathology educator*
Ruffer, David Gray *college president*
†Rush, Brian Paul *state legislator, lawyer*
Sada, Federico G. *glass manufacturing executive*
Saff, Edward Barry *mathematics educator*
Sams, Robert Alan *lawyer*
Sanchez, Mary Anne *secondary school educator*
Savard, Denis *professional hockey player*
†Schmidt, Paul Joseph *physician, educator*
Schnitzlein, Harold Norman *anatomy educator*
†Schonwetter, Ronald Scott *physician, educator*
Schwenke, Roger Dean *lawyer*
Shively, John Adrian *pathologist*
†Silver, Richard Abraham *hospital administrator*
Smith, Donn L. *university dean*
Sparkman, Steven Leonard *lawyer*
†Spellacy, William Nelson *obstetrician-gynecologist, educator*
Stafford, Josephine Howard *lawyer*
Stallings, (Charles) Norman *lawyer*
Studer, William Allen *county official*
Tabor, Curtis Harold, Jr. *library director*
Taub, Theodore Calvin *lawyer*
Thomas, Wayne Lee *lawyer*
Troxell, Raymond Robert, Jr. *college administrator*
Velez, Francisco S. *financial planner*
Wade, Thomas Edward *university research administrator, electrical engineering educator*
Wagner, Frederick William (Bill Wagner) *lawyer*
Walker, H(erbert) Leslie, Jr. *architect*
Weiner, Irving Bernard *university administrator, psychologist, educator*
†Whipple, Thomas A. *food marketing professional*
Wilson, Wallace *art educator, artist*
Wyche, Samuel David *professional football coach*
Zeno, Phyllis Wolfe *association executive, editor*

Tarpon Springs
Byrne, Richard Hill *counselor, educator*
Thompson, Mack Eugene *history educator*
Vajk, Hugo *manufacturing executive*

Tavernier
Mabbs, Edward Carl *management consultant*
Zim, Herbert Spencer *author, educator*

Temple Terrace
Rink, Wesley Winfred *banker*

Tequesta
Hart, Frederick Donald *retired heating equipment executive*
Holmes, Melvin Almont *insurance company executive*
Luster, George Orchard *professional society administrator*
Milton, Robert Mitchell *chemical company executive*
Peterson, James Robert *retired writing instrument manufacturing executive*
Ruoff, Andrew Christian, III *orthopedic surgeon, educator, consultant*
Stanger, John William *finance company executive*
Turrell, Richard Horton, Sr. *retired banker*
Vollmer, James *consulting company executive*

Thonotosassa
Grant, Pauline Larry *owner and director daycare center, consultant*

Tierra Verde
Gaffney, Thomas Francis *investment company executive*
Kubiet, Leo Lawrence *newspaper advertising and marketing executive*

Titusville
†Haise, Fred Wallace, Jr. *aerospace company executive, former astronaut*

University Of Miami
Foote, Edward Thaddeus, II *university president, lawyer*

Valrico
†Nelson, Norman Daniel *career officer*

Venice
Appel, Wallace Henry *retired industrial designer*
Bluhm, Barbara Jean *communications agency executive*
Concordia, Charles *consulting engineer*
Corrigan, William Thomas *retired broadcast news executive*
Dodderidge, Richard William *retired marketing executive*
Hardenburg, Robert Earle *horticulturist*
Jamrich, John Xavier *retired university administrator*
Leidheiser, Henry, Jr. *retired chemistry educator, consultant*
Miller, Allan John *lawyer*
Nevins, John J. *bishop*
Ogan, Russell Griffith *business executive, retired air force officer*
O'Keefe, Robert James *retired banker*
Shaw, Bryce Robert *author*
Thomas, David Ansell *retired university dean*
Torrey, Richard Frank *utility executive*

Vero Beach
Allik, Michael *diversified industry executive*
Berkovitch, Boris S. *bank executive, lawyer*
Bradford, Charles Lobdell *management consultant*
Brim, Orville Gilbert, Jr. *former foundation administrator, author*
Cartwright, Alton Stuart *electrical manufacturing company executive*
Christy, Nicholas Pierson *physician*
Conway, Earl Cranston *manufacturing company executive, educator*
†Corr, Thomas L. *oil industry executive*
Dillard, Rodney Jefferson *real estate company executive*
Dragone, Allan R. *manufacturing company executive*
Feagles, Robert West *insurance company executive*
Fisher, Andrew *management consultant*
Furrer, John Rudolf *retired manufacturing business executive*
Glassmeyer, Edward *investment banker*
Grobman, Hulda Gross (Mrs. Arnold B. Grobman) *horticulturist, retired public health educator*
†Grove, Thomas Keith *periodontist, veterinarian, consultant*
Hancock, Thomas *machinery manufacturing executive*
Haywood, Oliver Garfield *engineer*
Hill, Henry Parker *accountant*
Kinard, Hargett Yingling *financial consultant*
Lawrence, Merle *medical educator*
Leonsis, Theodore John *publishing company executive*
MacTaggart, Barry *corporate executive*
Mc Afee, Jerry *retired oil company executive, chemical engineer*
Mc Namara, John J(oseph) *advertising executive, writer*
Mills, Harlan Duncan *software engineer, mathematician, educator*
Nichols, Carl Wheeler *retired advertising agency executive*
Petersmeyer, C(harles) Wrede *retired broadcasting executive, venture capitalist*
Reed, Sherman Kennedy *chemical consultant*
Riley, Randy James *banker*
Ritterhoff, C(harles) William *retired steel company executive*
Schulman, Harold *obstetrician, gynecologist, perinatologist*
Sheehan, Charles Vincent *investment banker*
Slater, George Richard *retired banker*
Thompson, William David *investment banking executive*
Ward, William Binnington *agriculturist*
Youngman, William Sterling *lawyer*

Village Of Golf
Bates, Edward Brill *retired insurance company executive*

Wellington
Flagler, Robert Loomis *global export company executive, consultant*

Wesley Chapel
Holloway, Marvin Lawrence *retired automobile club executive, rancher, vintager*

West Palm Beach
Aaron, M. Robert *electrical engineer*
Beelner, Ken Phillip *investigator, legal assistant*
Bower, Ruth Lawther *retired mathematics educator*
Brown, Paul A. *physician, business executive*
Brumback, Clarence Landen *physician*
Burck, Arthur Albert *lawyer, corporate merger expert*
Coar, Richard John *mechanical engineer, aerospace consultant*
Corts, Paul Richard *academic administrator*
Davis, Robert Edwin *manufacturing executive*
Diener, Bert *former food broker, artist*
Elder, Stewart Taylor *dentist, retired naval officer*
Eppley, Roland Raymond, Jr. *retired financial services executive*
Eschbach, Jesse Ernest *federal judge*
Fairbanks, Richard Monroe *broadcasting company executive*
Flanagan, L. Martin *lawyer*
Giacco, Alexander Fortunatus *chemical industry executive*
†Gillette, Frank C., Jr. *aeronautical engineer*
Giuffrida, Tom A. *publisher*
Gowan, Joseph Patrick, Jr. *entertainment and food services company executive*
Gowing, Delmer Charles, III *lawyer*
†Greene, Addie Lue *English educator, mayor, state legislator*
Hall, E. Eugene *communication arts educator*
Hamilton, Neil Alfred *financial executive*
Hill, Thomas William, Jr. *lawyer, educator*
Hoewing, Mark Wesley *real estate association executive*
Hudson, Alice Peterson *chemistry consulting laboratory executive*
Kaslow, Florence W. *psychologist*
Katz, William David *psychologist, psychoanalytic psychotherapist, educator, mental health consultant*
Knott, James Robert *state judge, retired lawyer*
Knudsen, Raymond Barnett *clergyman, association executive, author*
Koff, Bernard L. *engineering executive*
Lively, Edwin Lowe *sociology educator*
Livingstone, John Leslie *accountant, management consultant, business economist, educator*
Lynch, William Walker *savings and loan association executive*
MacDonald, Richard Annis *pathologist, physician, educator*
McBride, Nancy Allyson *child resource center administrator*
McGinnes, Paul R. *environmental chemist*
Montgomery, Robert Morel, Jr. *lawyer*
Moore, George Crawford Jackson *lawyer*
Mora, Abraham Martin *lawyer*
Nelson, Richard Henry *manufacturing company executive*
O'Brien, Robert Brownell, Jr. *investment banker, savings bank executive, yacht broker*
O'Brien, Thomas George, III *lawyer*
O'Flarity, James P. *lawyer*
O'Hara, Thomas Patrick *managing editor*
Olsak, Ivan Karel *civil engineer*
Orr-Cahall, Christina *art gallery director, art historian*
Paine, James Carriger *federal judge*
†Passy, Charles *arts critic*
Petersen, David L. *lawyer*
Pottash, A. Carter *psychiatrist, hospital executive*
Price, William James, IV *investment banker*
†Pritchard Schoch, Teresa Noreen *lawyer, law librarian*
Rinker, Marshall Edison, Sr. *cement company executive*
Rivers, Marie Bie *broadcasting executive*
Roberts, Hyman Jacob *internist, researcher, author, publisher*
Robinson, Raymond Edwin *musician, music educator, writer*
Ronan, William John *corporate executive*
Royce, Raymond Watson *lawyer, rancher, citrus grower*
Ryskamp, Kenneth Lee *federal judge*
Sammond, John Stowell *lawyer*
Scheckner, Sy *former greeting card company executive*
Sears, Edward Milner, Jr. *newspaper editor*
Smith, David Shiverick *lawyer, former ambassador*
Sokmensuer, Adil *physician, educator*
Sturrock, Thomas Tracy *botany educator, horticulturist*
Turner, Arthur Edward *college administrator*
Turner, David Reuben *publisher, author*
Vecellio, Leo Arthur, Jr. *construction company executive*
Wagner, Arthur Ward, Jr. *lawyer*
Wilensky, Alvin *real estate investment trust executive*
Wright, Donald Conway *editorial cartoonist*

Windermere
Alexander, Judd Harris *retired paper company executive*
Blackstone, Sandra Lee *lawyer, educator, former government official*
Graese, Clifford Ernest *retired accountant*
Hylton, Hannelore Menke *retired manufacturing executive*

Winter Garden
Clifford, Margaret Louise *psychologist*

Winter Haven
Burns, Arthur Lee *architect*
Chase, Lucius Peter *lawyer, retired corporate executive*
Grierson, William *retired agricultural educator*
Kerner, Howard Alex *English and communications educator, writer, literary manager*
†Lansdale, Daryl L. *retail executive*
Love, John Wesley, Jr. *English language and reading educator*
O'Connor, R. D. *health care executive*
Peck, Maryly VanLeer *college president, chemical engineer*

Winter Park
Armstrong, (Arthur) James *minister, religion educator, religious organization executive, consultant*
Balliett, Gene (Howard Eugene Balliett) *writer, lecturer*
Bornstein, Rita *academic administrator*
Britton, Erwin Adelbert *clergyman, college administrator*
Brooten, Kenneth Edward, Jr. *lawyer*
Costa, Linda Alice *marketing and public relations executive*
Dawson, Ray Fields *research scientist, educator, consultant, tropical agriculturist*
Edge, Findley Bartow *clergyman, religious education educator*
Fernandez, Joseph Anthony *educational administrator*
Flick, Carl *electrical engineer, consultant, free-lance author*
Hawkins, Paula *federal official, former senator*
Hoche, Philip Anthony *life insurance company executive*
Holt, Georgina L. *ceramic artist*
Kost, Wayne L. *business executive*
MacKenzie, Ralph Sidney *aerospace executive*
Mc Kean, Hugh Ferguson *college president, painter, writer*
Mc Kean, Keith Ferguson *former education educator*
McKean, Thomas Wayne *dentist, retired naval officer*
Mica, John L. *congressman*
Olsson, Nils William *former association executive*
Patterson, Robert Youngman, Jr. *retired lawyer, utility executive*
Perkins, James Patrick *advertising executive*
Plane, Donald Ray *management science educator*
Richards, Max De Voe *management educator, consultant, researcher, author*
Rogers, Donald Patrick *business administration educator*
Rogers, Rutherford David *librarian*
Sedwick, (Benjamin) Frank *language educator*
Seymour, Thaddeus *English educator*
Spake, Ned Bernarr *energy company executive*
Weir, William C., III *lighting manufacturing company executive*

Zephyrhills
Jernstrom, Joan *secondary education educator*

GEORGIA

Ailey
Windsor, James Thomas, Jr. *printing company executive, newspaper publisher*

Albany
Greene, William Joshua, III *investment executive and consultant*

Alpharetta
Balows, Albert *microbiologist, educator*
Barr, John Baldwin *chemist, reserach scientist*
Beringer, William Ernst *retired electrical equipment executive, lawyer*
Byrd, Bette Jean *artist, author*
†Kingrea, Ann B. *principal*
†Malott, Thomas J. *manufacturing company executive, mechanical engineer*

Americus
Capitan, William Harry *college president*
Counts, Wayne Boyd *chemistry educator*
Fuller, Millard Dean *charitable organization executive, lawyer*
Gray, Margaret Edna *nursing educator*
†Hooks, George Bardin *state senator, insurance and real estate company executive*
†McGrady, Clyde A. *secondary school principal*
Stanford, Henry King *college president*

Andersonville
†Boyles, Frederick Holdren *historian*

Athens
Adomian, George *applied mathematician, physicist*
Agee, Warren Kendall *journalism educator*
Agosin, Moises Kankolsky *zoology educator*
Albersheim, Peter *biology educator*
Allinger, Norman Louis *chemistry educator*
Ansel, Howard Carl *pharmacist, educator*
Avise, John Charles *geneticist, educator*
Barry, John Reagan *psychology educator*
Beaird, James Ralph *legal educator*
Black, Clanton Candler, Jr. *biochemistry educator, researcher*
Bowen, John Metcalf *pharmacologist, toxicologist, educator*
Boyd, George Edward *physical chemist*
Boyd, Louis Jefferson *agricultural scientist, educator*
Bruce, David Lionel *anesthesiologist, educator*
Buccino, Alphonse *university dean*
Bullock, Charles Spencer, III *political science educator, author, consultant*
Carlson, Ronald Lee *lawyer, educator*
Carter, Mary Eddie *government administrator*
Clute, Robert Eugene *political and social science educator*
Cutlip, Scott Munson *university dean*
†Darvill, Alan G. *biochemist, botanist, educator*
Dickie, Margaret McKenzie *English language educator*
Dooley, Vincent Joseph *college athletics administrator*
Douglas, Dwight Oliver *university administrator*
Dunn, Delmer Delano *political science educator*
Ellington, Charles Ronald *lawyer, educator*
Eriksson, Karl-Erik Lennart *biochemist, educator*
Feldman, Edmund Burke *art critic*
Fincher, Cameron Lane *educator*
Fink, Conrad Charles *journalism educator, communications consultant*
Freer, Coburn *English language educator*
Fuller, Melvin Stuart *botany educator*
Garbin, Albeno Patrick *sociology educator*
Giles, Norman Henry *educator, geneticist*
†Green, Frank C. *agricultural administrator*
Herbert, James Arthur *artist, filmmaker*
Hester, Albert Lee *journalism educator*
Hillenbrand, Martin Joseph *diplomat, educator*

Hilton, James L. *plant physiologist, agricultural research administrator*
Holder, Howard Randolph, Sr. *broadcasting company executive*
Holland, Thomas Powell *social work educator*
Horton, Gerald Talmadge *public relations executive, educator*
Hunt, Jacob Tate *special education educator emeritus*
†Johnson, Michael Kenneth *chemistry educator*
Kamerschen, David Roy *economist, educator*
Kent, Robert B. *artist, educator*
King, Robert Bruce *chemistry educator*
Knapp, Charles Boynton *economist, educator, academic administrator*
Kraszewski, Andrzej Wojciech *electrical engineer, researcher*
Kretzschmar, William Addison, Jr. *English language educator*
†Landau, David Paul *physics educator*
Levine, David Lawrence *social work educator*
Lindberg, Stanley William *English language educator, editor*
Mamatey, Victor Samuel *history educator*
Mc Feely, William Shield *historian, writer*
McGuire, John Murray *chemist, researcher*
Mc Whorter, Hezzie Boyd *former collegiate athletic commissioner, English language educator*
Melton, Charles Estel *physicist, educator*
Miller, Herbert Elmer *accountant*
Moore, Rayburn Sabatzky *American literature educator*
Morrison, Darrel Gene *landscape architecture educator*
Nelson, Stuart Owen *agricultural engineer, researcher, educator*
Neter, John *statistician*
Newsome, George Lane, Jr. *education educator*
†Norred, William Preston, Jr. *pharmacologist, educator*
†Nute, Donald E., Jr. *philosophy educator*
Odum, Eugene Pleasants *ecologist, educator*
Pavlik, William Bruce *psychologist, educator*
Payne, William Jackson *microbiologist, educator*
Peacock, Lelon James *psychologist, educator*
Pelletier, S. William *chemistry educator*
Perkins, Edward A. *management educator*
Phillips, Walter Ray *lawyer, educator*
Plummer, Gayther L(ynn) *climatologist, ecologist, researcher*
Potter, William Gray, Jr. *library director*
†Puckett, Elizabeth Ann *law librarian, law educator*
Pulliam, Howard Ronald *ecology educator*
Rusk, Dean *educator, former secretary of state*
Schaefer, Henry Frederick, III *chemistry educator*
Smith, Howard Ross *economics educator, academic administrator, researcher, consultant*
Speering, Robin *educator, computer specialist*
Spurgeon, Edward Dutcher *law educator*
Staub, August William *drama educator, theatrical producer*
Steer, Alfred Gilbert, Jr. *foreign language educator*
Stovall, Allen D. *landscape architect, educator*
Summers, Anne O'Neill *microbiology educator*
†Surrency, Erwin Campbell *librarian, educator*
†Tesser, Abraham *social psychologist*
Tillman, Murray Howell *instructional technology educator*
Torrance, Ellis Paul *psychologist, educator*
Trim, Cynthia Mary *veterinarian, educator*
Tyler, David Earl *veterinary medical educator*
Van Eseltine, William Parker *microbiologist, educator*
†Verma, Brahm Prakash *agricultural engineer*
Wall, Bennett Harrison *history educator*
Watson, William A. J. *law educator*
Wellman, Richard Vance *legal educator*
Wood, Betty A. *utilities executive*
†Yen, William Mao-Shung *physicist*
Younts, Sanford Eugene *university administrator*

Atlanta
Aaron, Hank (Henry L. Aaron) *professional baseball team executive*
Abdel-Khalik, Said Ibrahim *nuclear and mechanical engineering educator*
Abrams, Bernard William *construction manufacturing and property development executive*
Abrams, Edward Marvin *construction company executive*
Abrams, Harold Eugene *lawyer*
†Ackerman, F. Duane *utility company executive*
Addison, Edward L. *utility holding company executive*
Alexander, Cecil Abraham *retired architect, consultant, educational director*
Alexander, Miles Jordan *lawyer*
Alford, Walter Helion *telecommunications executive, lawyer*
Allan, Frank Kellog *bishop*
Allen, Ivan, Jr. *shop owner*
Allen, Ronald W. *airline company executive*
Allio, Robert John *management consultant, educator*
Ambrose, Samuel Sheridan, Jr. *urologist*
Ames, William Francis *mathematician, educator*
†Amisano, Joseph *architect*
Anderson, Gloria Long *chemistry educator*
Anderson, Peter Joseph *lawyer*
Andrews, Gary Blaylock *state judge, lawyer*
†Antolovich, Stephen Dale *engineering educator*
†Arani, Ardy A. *professional sports marketing executive, lawyer*
Ashe, Robert Lawrence, Jr. *lawyer*
Attridge, Richard Byron *lawyer*
Aulbach, George Louis *property investment company executive*
Avery, Steven Thomas *professional baseball player*
Babcock, Peter Heartz *professional sports executive*
†Babyface, (Kenny Edmunds) *songwriter*
Bacon, Louis Albert *retired consulting civil engineer*
Bainbridge, Frederick Freeman, III *architect*
Bakay, Roy Arpad Earle *neurosurgeon, educator*
Baker, David S. *lawyer*
Bakewell, Peter John *history educator*
Baldi, Angelo C. *lawyer*
†Balke, Robert Roy *architect*
Banks, Bettie Sheppard *psychologist*
Baran, William Lee *food service company executive*
Baranowski, Tom *public health educator, researcher*
Barker, William Daniel *hospital administrator*
Barkett, Rosemary *federal judge*
Barkoff, Rupert Mitchell *lawyer*
Barksdale, Richard Dillon *civil engineer, educator*
Barnard, Susan Muller *zookeeper*
Barnett, Crawford Fannin, Jr. *internist, educator, cardiologist*
Barnett, Elizabeth Hale *organizational consultant*
Barnwell, Thomas Pinkney, III *electrical engineering educator, business executive*
Barry, Rick (Richard Francis Dennis Barry, III) *former professional basketball player, broadcaster*
Bassett, Peter Q. *lawyer*
Batson, Richard Neal *lawyer*
Baxter, Harry Stevens *lawyer*
Baxter, Robert Hampton, III *insurance executive*
†Beard, Rick *cultural organization administrator*
Beattie, George *artist*
Beckman, Gail McKnight *law educator*
†Bell, Eldrin *protective services official*
Bell, Griffin B. *lawyer, former attorney general*
Benario, Herbert William *classics educator*
Benatar, Leo *packaging company executive*
Benham, Robert *state supreme court justice*
Bennett, Jay D. *lawyer*
Benson, Ronald Edward *state humanities program executive, clergyman, educator*
Benston, George James *accountant, economist*
†Berry, Dennis *newspaper publishing executive*
Bevington, E(dmund) Milton *electrical machinery manufacturing company executive*
Biggers, William Joseph *retired manufacturing company executive*
Birch, Stanley Francis, Jr. *federal judge*
Bird, Wendell Raleigh *lawyer*
Bisher, James Furman *journalist, author*
Black, Kenneth, Jr. *insurance executive, educator, author*
Blackstock, Jerry Byron *lawyer*
Blank, Arthur M. *home and lumber retail chain executive*
Blauser, Jeffrey Michael *professional baseball player*
Bleser, Joseph G. *financial executive*
Bloodworth, A(lbert) W(illiam) Franklin *lawyer*
†Blount, Ben B., Jr. *apparel executive*
Boeke, Eugene H., Jr. *construction executive*
Boisseau, Richard Robert *lawyer*
Boland, Thomas Edwin *banker*
Bolch, Carl Edward, Jr. *corporation executive, lawyer*
Boman, John Harris, Jr. *retired lawyer*
Bonds, John Wilfred, Jr. *lawyer*
Bondurant, Emmet Jopling, II *lawyer*
Boone, J. William *lawyer*
Booth, Gordon Dean, Jr. *lawyer*
Bourne, Henry Clark, Jr. *electrical engineering educator, former academic official*
Bowden, Henry Lumpkin *lawyer*
Bowden, Henry Lumpkin, Jr. *lawyer*
Bowers, Michael Joseph *state attorney general*
†Bradfield, Richard H. *architectural firm executive*
Bragg, John Mackie *actuarial consultant*
Branch, Thomas Broughton, III *lawyer*
Brands, James Edwin *medical products executive*
Brannon, Lester Travis, Jr. *lawyer*
Bratton, James Henry, Jr. *lawyer*
Brecher, Armin G. *lawyer*
Bridgewater, Herbert Jeremiah, Jr. *radio host*
Bright, David Forbes *academic administrator, classics and comparative literature educator*
Brinkley, Donald R. *oil industry executive*
Brinton, Margo Ann *virology educator, researcher*
Brittain, James Edward *science and technology educator, researcher*
Brooks, David William *farmer cooperative executive*
Brooks, Wilbur Clinton *lawyer*
Broome, Claire Veronica *epidemiologist, researcher*
†Brown, John Robert *lawyer, priest*
Brown, Lorene B(yron) *library educator, educational administrator*
†Brown-Olmstead, Amanda *public relations executive*
Buck, Lee Albert *retired insurance company executive, evangelist*
Buker, Robert Hutchinson, Sr. *army officer, thoracic surgeon*
Buoch, William Thomas *corporate executive*
Burge, William Lee *retired business information executive*
Burns, Carroll Dean *insurance company executive*
Burns, Thomas Samuel *history educator*
Byrd, Larry Donald *behavioral pharmacologist*
Cadenhead, Alfred Paul *lawyer*
Callison, James W. *former airline executive, lawyer*
Cameron, Rondo *economic history educator*
Camp, Jack Tarpley, Jr. *federal judge*
†Campbell, Bill *mayor, broadcasting executive*
Candler, John Slaughter, II *retired lawyer*
Cann, Sharon Lee *librarian*
Cannon, William Ragsdale *bishop*
Cantrell, Wesley Eugene, Sr. *office equipment company executive*
Caprio, Anthony S. *university official*
Carey, Gerald John, Jr. *former air force officer, research institute director*
†Carl, Robert Delroy, III *health care company executive, lawyer*
Carlson, Robert Lee *engineering educator*
Carnes, Julie E. *federal judge*
Carter, Dan T. *history educator*
Carter, Jimmy (James Earl Carter, Jr.) *former President of United States*
†Casarella, William Joseph *physician*
Casey, Charles Francis *diversified company executive*
Chace, William Murdough *university administrator*
Chaiet, Alan Howard *advertising agency executive*
†Chalmers, Alan Knight *financial corporation executive*
Chambers, Anne Cox *newspaper executive*
Chapman, Hugh McMaster *banker*
Charania, Barkat *real estate consultant*
Chasen, Sylvan Herbert *computer applications consultant, investment advisor*
Cheatham, Richard Reed *lawyer*
Chilivis, Nickolas Peter *lawyer*
Chilton, Horace Thomas *pipeline company executive*
Chisholm, Tommy *lawyer, utility company executive*
Chitwood, Harold Otis *food company executive*
Churchwell, Charles Darrett *librarian*
Circeo, Louis Joseph, Jr. *research center director, civil engineer*
Clark, Thomas Alonzo *federal judge*
Clark, William Franklin *lawyer*
Clarke, Clifford Montreville *health foundation executive*
Clarke, Thomas Hal *lawyer*
Cleland, Joseph Maxwell (Max) *state official*
Clements, James David *psychiatry educator, physician*
Clendenin, John L. *telecommunications company executive*
†Clifton, David Samuel, Jr. *research executive, economist*
†Clough, Gerald Wayne *academic administrator*
†Coan, Gaylord O. *agribusiness executive*
Cohen, Ezra Harry *lawyer*
Cohen, George Leon *lawyer*
Cohen, N. Jerold *lawyer*
Cole, David Andrew *management consultant executive*
Cole, Johnnetta Betsch *academic administrator*
†Cole, Thomas Winston, Jr. *chancellor, college president, chemist*
Collins, Marcus E., Sr. *state agency administrator*
Collins, Steven M. *lawyer*
Connell-Tatum, Elizabeth Bishop *physician*
Connor, Charles William *airline pilot*
Cooper, Frederick Eansor *lawyer*
Cooper, Jerome Maurice *architect*
Cooper, Thomas Luther *retired printing company executive*
Copeland, Floyd Dean *lawyer*
Copeland, John Alexander, III *physicist*
Corr, James Vanis *furniture manufacturing executive, investor, lawyer, accountant*
Correll, Alston Dayton, Jr. *forest products company executive*
Cotton, James Perry, Jr. *holding company executive*
Cox, Bobby (Robert Joe) *professional baseball manager*
Coxe, Tench Charles *lawyer*
Cramer, Howard Ross *geologist, environmental consultant*
Cross, Joyce Annette Oscar *newscaster*
Cumming, David Robert, Jr. *lawyer*
†Cupp, Robert Erhard *golf course designer, land use planner*
Cutshaw, Kenneth Andrew *lawyer*
Dahlberg, Alfred William *electric company executive*
Dahlke, Wayne Theodore *civil engineer, corporate executive*
Dalrymple, Gordon Bennett *former engineering company executive*
Dalton, John J. *lawyer*
†Daniels, Stanley L. *architect*
Davis, Eleanor Kay *museum administrator*
Davis, Frank Tradewell, Jr. *lawyer*
†Davis, Lawrence William *radiation oncologist*
Dees, Julian Worth *academic administrator*
†Dell, J. Howard *bishop*
Dennison, Stanley Scott *retired lumber company executive, consultant*
Denny, Richard Alden, Jr. *lawyer*
†Diedrich, Richard Joseph *architect*
Dillingham, William Byron *literature educator, author*
Dillon, John Robert, III *communications executive*
Dodge, William Douglas *risk management, insurance, benefits consultant*
Dolive, Earl *retired business executive*
†Dollar, Steve *music critic*
Dotson, Robert Charles *news correspondent*
Dougherty, John Ernest *federal judge*
Douglas, John Lewis *lawyer*
Dowling, Roderick Anthony *investment banker*
Downs, Harry *retired legal corporate executive*
Doyle, Michael Anthony *lawyer*
Drake, Miriam Anna *librarian, educator*
Drucker, Melvin Bruce *psychology educator*
†Dubberly, Ronald Alvah *library director*
DuBose, Charles Wilson *lawyer*
†Dunahoo, Charles *religious publisher, religious organization administrator*
Durbetaki, Pandeli *mechanical engineer, educator, researcher*
Durrett, James Frazer, Jr. *lawyer*
Dykes, John Henry, Jr. *finance executive*
Dysart, Benjamin Clay, III *environmental management consultant, conservationist, engineer*
†Dyson, Brian G. *beverage company executive*
Eason, William Everette, Jr. *lawyer*
Easterly, David Eugene *newspaper executive*
†Easton, Loretta J. *real estate executive*
Eber, Herbert Wolfgang *psychologist*
Ebneter, Stewart Dwight *federal agency administrator*
Eckert, Charles Alan *chemical engineering educator*
Eckert, Michael Joseph *cable and broadcast television executive*
†Edelhauser, Henry F. *physiologist, ophthalmic researcher, educator*
Edge, J(ulian) Dexter, Jr. *lawyer*
Edmondson, James Larry *federal judge*
Edwards, Howard Dawson *business executive, physicist, academic administrator*
Edwards, Louis Ward, Jr. *diversified manufacturing company executive*
Egan, Michael Joseph *lawyer*
Ehrlichman, John Daniel *company executive, author, former assistant to President of United States*
†Elam, Merrill L. *architectural firm executive*
Ellis, Elmo Israel *broadcast executive, consultant, newspaper columnist*
†Ellis, Richard Lee *physical chemistry educator, researcher*
Elsas, Louis Jacob, II *medical educator*
Epstein, David Gustav *lawyer*
Erck, Theodore Augustus, Jr. *lawyer*
Etheridge, Jack Paul *arbitrator, mediator, former judge*
Evans, Edwin Curtis *internist, educator, geriatrician*
Evans, Orinda D. *federal judge*
†Ezell, Reva Gross *radio station manager, writer*
Fajardo, Katharine Lynn *public relations and marketing executive*
†Farley, Charles P. *public relations executive*
†Farrington, Frank *architect*
Fash, William Leonard *retired architecture educator, college dean*
Felton, Jule Wimberly, Jr. *lawyer*
Finkelstein, David *physicist, educator, consultant*
†Fitzgerald, David Patrick *advertising agency executive*
Fitzgerald, John Edmund *civil engineering educator, dean*
Fleming, Julian Denver, Jr. *lawyer*
†Flemming, David Paul *biologist*
Fletcher, Norman S. *state supreme court justice*
Flinn, Patrick L. *bank executive*
Foley, James David *computer science educator, consultant*
Forbes, Theodore McCoy, Jr. *lawyer, arbitrator, mediator*
Foreman, Edward Rawson *lawyer*
Forrestal, Robert Patrick *banker, lawyer*
Forrester, J. Owen *federal judge*
Foster, Roger Sherman, Jr. *surgeon, educator, health facility administrator*
†Fowler, Andrea *teachers academy administrator*
†Fox, James Harold, Jr. *superintendent of schools*
Fox, Ronald Forrest *physics educator*
Foxen, Gene Louis *insurance executive*
Fox-Genovese, Elizabeth Ann *humanities educator*
Frank, Ronald Edward *marketing educator*
Frank, William Pendleton *sales and marketing executive*
Frost, Norman Cooper *retired telephone company executive*
Frye, Billy Eugene *university administrator, biologist*
Fuqua, John Brooks *retired consumer products and services company executive*
Gable, Carl Irwin *business consultant, private investor, lawyer*
Galambos, John Thomas *medical educator, internist*
Gallagher, Thomas C. *diversified manufacturing executive*
Gambrell, David Henry *lawyer*
Garner, Robert Edward Lee *lawyer*
Gayer, Alan J. *hospital administrator*
Gayles, Joseph Nathan, Jr. *medical educator, administrator*
Gearon, John Michael *professional basketball team executive*
Genovese, Eugene Dominick *historian, educator*
†Giffin, Gordon D. *lawyer*
†Gilchrist, Paul R. *religious organization administrator*
Gilmer, Harry Wesley *publishing executive, educator*
Girth, Marjorie Louisa *lawyer, educator*
Glassick, Charles Etzweiler *cultural organization administrator*
Glavine, Tom (Thomas Michael Glavine) *baseball player*
Gleason, James Marne *manufacturing company executive*
Godard, James McFate *retired educational consultant*
Goizueta, Roberto Crispulo *food and beverage company executive*
Goldman, Joel Stanley *lawyer*
†Goldstein, Burton Benjamin, Jr. *communications executive*
Goldstein, Elliott *lawyer*
Goldstein, Jacob Herman *retired physical chemist*
Goodwin, George Evans *public relations executive*
†Gowland, Douglas R. *service industry executive*
†Grace, Donald J. *engineering researcher*
Grant, Walter Matthews *lawyer, diversified consumer products executive*
†Green, Holcombe Tucker, Jr. *investment executive*
Greenberg, Raymond Seth *dean, educator*
†Greene, Milton Anthony *investment securities executive*
Greer, Bernard Lewis, Jr. *lawyer*
Gregory, Mel Hyatt, Jr. *retired insurance company executive*
Griffin, Clayton Houstoun *retired power company engineer, lecturer*
Groton, James Purnell *lawyer*
Grumet, Priscilla Hecht *fashion specialist, consultant, writer*
†Guberman, Sidney Thomas *painter, writer*
†Guest, Rita Carson *interior designer*
Guinan, Mary Elizabeth *physician, research scientist*
†Gyger, Terrell Lee *minister*
Haas, George Aaron *lawyer*
Hackett, Stanley Hailey *lawyer*
Hahn, Thomas Marshall, Jr. *forest products corporation executive*
Hale, Jack K. *mathematics educator, research center administrator*
Hall, Robert Howell *federal judge*
Hall, Wilbur Dallas, Jr. *medical educator*
Harkey, Robert Shelton *lawyer*
Harlin, Robert Ray *lawyer*
Harris, Henry Wood *cable television executive*
Harrison, John Raymond *retired newspaper executive, foundation executive*
Hartle, Robert Wyman *retired foreign language and literature educator*
Hasson, James Keith, Jr. *lawyer*
Hatch, Henry J. *engineering executive*
Hatcher, Charles Ross, Jr. *cardiothoracic surgeon, medical center executive*
Haverty, John Rhodes *physician, former university dean*
Hawkins, Robert Garvin *management educator, consultant*
Hawks, Barrett Kingsbury *lawyer*
†Hay, Peter *law educator*
Hayes, Sarah Hall *magazine editor, educator*
Henderson, Albert John *federal judge*
Henry, John Dunklin *hospital administrator*
Henry, William Ray *business administration educator*
†Hiers, Mary A. *museum director*
†Hill, Craig Livingston *chemistry educator, consultant*
Hill, Paul Drennen *lawyer, banker*
Hilliard, Robert Glenn *insurance company executive, lawyer*
†Hinman, Alan Richard *public health administrator, epidemiologist*
Hodges, Dewey Harper *aerospace engineer, educator*
Hoff, Gerhardt Michael *lawyer, insurance company executive*
Hogan, John Donald *college dean, finance educator*
†Hogan, Ronald P. *forest products company executive*
Hollis, Charles Eugene, Jr. *savings and loan association executive*
Holzel, David Benjamin *newspaper editor*
†Hoover, Ray C., III *architect*
Hopkins, Donald Roswell *public health physician*
Hopkins, George Mathews Marks *lawyer, business executive*
Horsman, David A. Elliott *author, financial services executive, educator*
Houk, Vernon Neal *retired public health administrator*
Houpt, Jeffrey Lyle *psychiatrist, educator*
House, Donald Lee, Sr. *software executive, private investor, management consultant*
Howard, Harry Clay *lawyer*
†Hubbard, Richard Buell, III *hospital administrator*
†Hubbell, Richard A. *manufacturing executive*
Hubble, Don Wayne *business executive*
Hug, Carl Casmir, Jr. *pharmacology and anesthesiology educator*
†Hughes, James Mitchell *epidemiologist*
†Hughes, Rufus R., II *architectural firm executive, architectural educator*
†Hulbert, Daniel J. *theater critic, entertainment writer*
Humphrey, Charles Durham *microbiologist, biomedical researcher*
Hunter, Forrest Walker *lawyer*
†Husband, J. D. *bishop*
†Hutchins, Ralph Edwin, Jr. *banker*
Ide, Roy William, III *lawyer*
Iodice, Joanna DiMeno (Jody Iodice) *psychotherapist*

Isdell, Edward Neville *food products executive*
Israili, Zafar Hasan *scientist, clinical pharmacologist, educator*
Ivester, Melvin Douglas *beverage company executive*
Izard, John *lawyer*
Izlar, William Henry, Jr. *lawyer, banker*
Jackson, Richard Delyn *bank executive*
Janney, Donald Wayne *lawyer*
Jeffery, Geoffrey Marron *medical parasitologist*
Jeffries, McChesney Hill *retired lawyer*
Jenkins, Albert Felton, Jr. *lawyer*
Jeschke, Channing Renwick *librarian*
Johnson, Barry Lee *public health research administrator*
Johnson, Ronald Carl *chemistry educator*
†Johnson, William B. *hotel executive*
Johnson, Wyatt Thomas, Jr. (Tom Johnson) *cable news executive*
†Johnston, Lynn Henry *insurance company executive*
Jones, Christine Massey *furniture company executive*
Jones, Frank Cater *lawyer*
Jones, George Henry *university dean, research administrator, biology educator*
Jones, J. Kenley *journalist*
Jordan, Elizabeth Clark *elementary education educator*
Jova, Henri Vatable *architect*
Joy, Edward Bennett *electrical engineer, educator*
Jurkiewicz, Maurice John *surgeon, educator*
Justice, David Christopher *baseball player*
Kahn, Bernd *radiochemist, educator*
Kaiser, Fred *computer leasing company executive*
Kalafut, George Wendell *distribution company executive, retired naval officer*
Karp, Herbert Rubin *neurologist, educator*
Kasten, Stanley Harvey *sports association executive*
Keiller, James Bruce *college dean, clergyman*
Keith, Leroy, Jr. *college president*
Kelley, James Francis *lawyer*
†Kelley, James P. *delivery service executive*
Kelley, Jeffrey Wendell *lawyer*
Kelly, William Watkins *educational association executive*
Kennedy, Alfred Doby *performing arts administrator*
Kennedy, James C. *publishing and media executive*
Keough, Donald Raymond *investment banking executive*
King, Coretta Scott (Mrs. Martin Luther King, Jr.) *educational association administrator, lecturer, writer, concert singer*
King, Frederick Alexander *neuroscientist, educator*
Kinzer, William Luther *lawyer*
Klamon, Lawrence Paine *lawyer*
†Klein, Luella Voogd *obstetrics-gynecology educator*
†Kloer, Philip Baldwin *television critic*
Kneisel, Edmund M. *lawyer*
Knobloch, Carl William, Jr. *oil and gas services executive*
Knowles, Marjorie Fine *lawyer, educator, dean*
Kokko, Juha Pekka *physician, educator*
†Kolb, David L. *carpet company executive*
Koplan, Jeffrey Powell *physician*
†Korn, Steven W. *broadcasting company executive, corporate lawyer*
Kraft, Arthur *academic dean*
Kranzberg, Melvin *history educator*
Kravitch, Phyllis A. *federal judge*
Kuntz, Marion Lucile Leathers *classicist, historian, educator*
Kuse, James Russell *chemical company executive*
Kyle, John Emery *mission executive*
Lackland, Theodore Howard *lawyer*
La Farge, Timothy *plant geneticist*
Lamkin, William Pierce *editor*
Lamon, Harry Vincent, Jr. *lawyer*
Lane, Louis *musician, conductor*
Langdale, Noah Noel, Jr. *research educator, former university president*
Langway, Richard Merritt *lawyer*
†Lanier, John Hicks *apparel company executive*
Lawson, A(bram) Venable *librarian, educational administrator*
Lee, R(aymond) William, Jr. *apparel company executive*
Lemen, Richard Alan *epidemiologist*
Leonard, David Morse *lawyer*
Lester, Charles Turner, Jr. *lawyer*
Letton, Alva Hamblin *surgeon, educator*
Levi, Yoel *orchestra conductor*
Lewcock, Ronald Bentley *architect, educator*
†Lewis, Larry Lynn *college official, minister, denominational official*
†Lin, Ming-Chang *physical chemistry educator, researcher*
Linkous, William Joseph, Jr. *lawyer*
Lipman, Bernard *internist, cardiologist*
Lipshutz, Robert Jerome *lawyer, former government official*
Lobb, William Atkinson *financial services executive*
Loewy, Robert Gustav *engineering educator, aeronautical engineering executive*
Lokey, Hamilton *lawyer*
Long, Maurice Wayne *physicist, electrical engineer, radar consultant*
Loory, Stuart Hugh *journalist*
†Loudermilk, R. Charles *sales executive*
Lower, Robert Cassel *lawyer, educator*
Lowery, Joseph E. *clergyman*
Lubin, Michael Frederick *physician*
Lucchesi, John C. *biology educator*
Lunsford, Julius R(odgers), Jr. *lawyer*
Lurey, Alfred Saul *lawyer*
†Lybarger, Jeffrey A. *epidemiology research administrator*
Maddux, Greg (Gregory Alan Maddux) *baseball player*
Mafico, Temba Levi Jackson *Old Testament and Semitic languages educator, clergy*
Malaspina, Alex *soft drink company executive*
Manley, Frank *English language educator*
Manners, George Emanuel *business educator, emeritus dean*
Marcus, Bernard *retail executive*
†Margolis, Harold Stephen *epidemiologist*
Marsh, Carole *author, photographer, publisher*
Marshall, John Treutlen *lawyer*
Marshall, Thomas Oliver, Jr. *lawyer*
Martin, David Edward *health sciences educator*
†Martin, James Francis *state legislator, lawyer*
Martin, Kenneth Douglas *consumer products company executive*
†Martin, Ron *newspaper editor in chief*
†Martindale, Larry *hotel executive*
†Marzilli, Luigi Gaetano *chemistry educator, consultant*
Massey, Charles Knox, Jr. *advertising agency executive*
†Mathews, George W., Jr. *manufacturing company executive*
Matula, Richard A(llan) *academic administrator*
†McBee, Mary Louise *state legislator, former academic administrator*
McClellan, James Harold *electrical engineering educator*
McCormick, Donald Bruce *biochemist, educator*
†McDonagh, Kathryn Joyce *hospital administrator*
McDonald, John C. *telecommunications company executive*
McDuffie, Frederic Clement *physician*
McGowan, John Edward, Jr. *microbiology educator*
McGriff, Fred (Frederick Stanley McGriff) *baseball player*
Mc Intosh, James Eugene, Jr. *interior designer*
Mc Kenzie, Harold Cantrell, Jr. *retired manufacturing executive*
McLean, James Albert *artist, educator*
McMahon, Donald Aylward *investor, corporate director*
†McMaster, Belle Miller *religious organization administrator*
McNeill, Thomas Ray *lawyer*
Merdek, Andrew Austin *publishing executive, lawyer*
Merritt, Lynn Garnard *trade association executive*
Mersereau, Russell Manning *electrical engineering educator, consultant*
Miles, John Karl *marketing executive*
Millar, John Donald *occupational and environmental health consultant, educator*
Miller, James Hugh, Jr. *retired public utility executive*
†Miller, Neal Louis *software company executive*
†Miller, Robert James *architect, educator*
Miller, Rosalind Elaine *librarian, educator*
Miller, Thomas Marshall *marketing consultant*
Miller, Zell Bryan *governor*
†Mills, Robin Kate *law librarian*
Mobley, John Homer, II *lawyer*
Moderow, Joseph Robert *package distribution company executive*
Moeling, Walter Goos, IV *lawyer*
Monroe, Melrose *retired banker*
Montgomery, James Morton *public relations, marketing executive, association executive*
Moore, Henry Rogers *civil engineer, railroad operating officer*
Moore, John W. *lawyer*
Moran, Thomas Francis *chemistry educator*
†Mortensen, Davis K. *building products company executive*
Moulthrop, Edward Allen *architect, artist*
Mulaik, Stanley Allen *psychology educator*
Murphy, Gerald Patrick *urologist, educator*
Murphy, Margaret H. *federal bankruptcy judge*
Murphy, Thomas Bailey *state legislator*
Muth, Richard Ferris *economics educator*
Nahmias, André Joseph *physician, educator, scientist*
Navalkar, Ramchandra Govindrao *microbiologist, immunologist*
Neely, Edgar Adams, Jr. *lawyer*
Neisser, Ulric *psychology educator*
Nelson, Kent C. *delivery service executive*
Nelson, Robert Earl, Jr. *financial services company executive*
Nemhauser, George L. *industrial, systems engineer, operations research educator*
Nerem, Robert Michael *engineering educator, consultant*
Nethercut, Philip Edwin *honorary consul*
†Newbill, Sallie Puller *state senator*
Newman, James Michael *communications company executive*
Newman, Stuart *lawyer*
Nichols, Horace Elmo *state justice*
Nichols, William Curtis *psychologist, family therapist, consultant*
†Norris, T. H. *oil industry executive*
O'Brien, Mark Stephen *pediatric neurosurgeon*
O'Kelley, William Clark *federal judge*
Oliker, Vladimir *mathematician, educator*
†Olson, Frank L. *electrical power industry executive*
O'Neil, Daniel Joseph *research executive*
Oppenlander, Robert *retired airline executive*
Ordover, Abraham Philip *corporate executive*
†Ottinger, Richard Estes *public broadcasting executive*
†Overstreet, Jim *public relations executive*
Owen, Robert Hubert *lawyer, real estate broker*
Owings, Francis Barre *surgeon*
Pantel, Stan Roy *newspaper publishing executive*
Parker, John Garrett *lawyer*
Parks, R(obert) Keith *missionary, religious organization administrator*
Parsons, Leonard Jon *marketing educator, consultant*
Partain, Eugene Gartly *lawyer*
Patterson, William Robert *lawyer*
Patti, Sister Josephine Marie *health science facility administrator*
Pattillo, Manning Mason, Jr. *academic administrator*
Patton, Carl Vernon *academic administrator, educator*
Payne, Maxwell Carr, Jr. *retired psychology educator*
Peacock, George Rowatt *retired life insurance company executive*
Peacock, Lamar Batts *physician*
Pendleton, Terry Lee *baseball player*
Perdue, Garland Day *surgeon, educator, hospital director*
Perkowitz, Sidney *physicist, educator, author*
Perry, Timothy Sewell *lawyer*
Persons, J. Robert *lawyer*
Persons, Oscar N. *lawyer*
Phillips, Barry *lawyer*
Phillips, Herbert Alvin, Jr. *retired financial executive*
Phillips, James D. *diplomat*
Piassick, Joel Bernard *lawyer*
Pierotti, Robert Amedeo *chemistry educator*
Pike, Larry Samuel *lawyer*
Poe, H. Sadler *lawyer*
Portman, John C., Jr. *architect, developer*
Poythress, David Bryan *lawyer, state commissioner*
Pratt, John Sherman *lawyer*
Prince, Larry L. *automotive parts and supplies company executive*
†Pucket, Susan *newspaper editor*
Pulgram, William Leopold *architect, space designer*
†Purcell, Ann Rushing *state legislator, office manager medical business*
†Ragan, Harold James *retired educator, senator*
Raines, Mary Elizabeth *airline executive*
Ramsay, Ernest Canaday *lawyer*
Ramsey, Ira Clayton *pipeline company executive*
Raper, Charles Albert *management consultant*
Rasnake, James Hamilton, Jr. *portfolio manager*
†Rathburn, Robert Richard *museum director*
†Rauh, Richard Paul *architect*
Reed, Glen Alfred *lawyer*
Reed, James Whitfield *physician, educator*
†Reedy, Edward K. *system engineer administrator*
Reeves, Alexis Scott *journalist*
Regenstein, Lewis Graham *conservationist, author, lecturer, speech writer*
Regenstein, Louis *lawyer*
Reichardt, Delbert Dale *financial executive*
Reith, Carl Joseph *apparel industry executive*
Richards, Robert Wadsworth *civil engineer, consultant*
†Riddle, Dennis Raymond *banker*
Ridley, Clarence Haverty *lawyer*
Rierson, Robert Leak *broadcasting executive, television writer*
†Ringel, Eleanor *film critic*
Roberts, Edward Graham *librarian*
Robinson, Florence Claire Crim *composer, conductor, educator*
Rock, John Aubrey *gynecologist and obstetrician, educator*
Rodrigue, George Pierre *electrical engineering educator, consultant*
Roeck, Thomas J., Jr. *airline financial executive*
Rogers, C. B. *lawyer*
†Rogers, C. B., Jr. *information services executive*
Rogers, Werner *state education official*
Rojas, Carlos *Spanish literature educator*
†Rollins, Gary Wayne *service company executive*
†Rollins, R. Randall *diversified services company executive*
Rosenberg, George A. *public relations company executive*
Rosenfeld, Arnold Solomon *newspaper editor*
Rousseau, Ronald William *chemical engineering educator, researcher*
Rucker, Charles Thomas *science facility administrator*
Russell, Harold Louis *lawyer*
Saidman, Gary K. *lawyer*
†Salter, Sally *reporter*
Sands, Don William *agricultural products company executive retired*
†Satcher, David *public health service officer, federal official*
Satrum, Jerry R. *chemicals company executive*
Savell, Edward Lupo *lawyer*
Schafer, Ronald William *electrical engineering educator*
†Schewe, Donald Bruce *archivist, library director*
Schimberg, Henry Aaron *soft drink company executive*
Schlant, Robert Carl *cardiologist, educator*
Schroder, Jack Spalding, Jr. *lawyer*
†Schrutt, Norman *broadcast company executive*
Schulte, Jeffrey Lewis *lawyer*
Schulze, Horst H. *hotel company executive*
Schwartz, Dale Marvin *lawyer*
Schwartz, Herbert Marshall *business executive*
Schwartz, William A(llen) *broadcasting and cable executive*
Schwartz, William B., Jr. *ambassador*
†Scott, David Albert *state senator, advertising agency executive*
Scott, William Fred *cultural organization administrator*
Scovil, Roger Morris *engineering company executive*
†Seabrook, Charles *reporter*
Sears, Curtis Thornton, Jr. *educational administrator*
Seffrin, John Reese *medical society executive*
Sessoms, Walter Woodrow *telecommunications executive*
Seto, William Roderick *public accounting company executive*
Shaw, Robert Lawson *symphony orchestra conductor*
Shelton, Robert Warren *marketing executive*
Sherman, Roger Talbot *surgeon, educator*
Sherry, Henry Ivan *marketing consultant*
Sheth, Jagdish Nanchand *business administration educator*
†Shirk, Richard D. *insurance company executive*
Shoob, Marvin H. *federal judge*
†Shutze, Virgil Cox *advertising executive*
Sibley, Celestine (Mrs. John C. Strong) *columnist, reporter*
Sibley, Horace Holden *lawyer*
Sibley, James Malcolm *retired lawyer*
†Siegel, Randy *public relations executive*
Simms, Arthur Benjamin *management consultant, financier*
Sink, John Davis *leadership consultant, scientist*
Sitter, John Edward *English literature educator*
†Skillrud, Harold Clayton *Lutheran bishop*
Skinner, B. Franklin *retired telecommunications executive*
Skipper, Harold Dallas, Jr. *insurance educator*
Slappey, Sterling Greene *writer, journalist, researcher*
Sloan, Stanley *management consultant*
†Slotin, Ronald David *state legislator*
Smith, Alexander Wyly, Jr. *lawyer*
Smith, Glenn Stanley *electrical engineering educator*
Smith, James Louis, III *lawyer*
Smith, Jeffrey Michael *lawyer*
Smith, Joseph Newton, III *retired architect, educator*
Smith, Peter John *professional baseball player*
Smith, Robert Boulware, III *vascular surgeon, educator*
Smith, Sidney Oslin, Jr. *lawyer*
Smith, W. P., Jr. *food products executive*
Smith, Walton Napier *lawyer*
Smoltz, John Andrew *professional baseball player*
Snelling, George Arthur *banker*
Spann, George William *management consultant*
Spiegel, John William *bank executive*
Spitznagel, John Keith *microbiologist, immunologist*
Spivey, Ted Ray *English educator*
†Stacey, Weston Monroe, Jr. *nuclear engineer, educator*
Stanhope, William Henry *lawyer*
†Stanley, LaNett Lorraine *state legislator*
Stanton, Donald Sheldon *university administrator*
Steed, Robert Lee *lawyer, columnist*
Steinhaus, John Edward *physician, medical educator*
Stimpert, Michael Alan *agricultural products company executive*
Stokes, James Sewell *lawyer*
Stokes, Mack (Marion) Boyd *bishop*
Stormont, Richard Mansfield *hotel executive*
Strauss, Robert David *lawyer*
Streeb, Gordon Lee *diplomat, economist*
†Stubbs, Thomas Hubert *company executive*
Su, Kendall Ling-Chiao *engineering educator*
Sullivan, Louis Wade *former secretary health and human services, physician*
Summerlin, Glenn Wood *advertising executive*
Suojanen, Waino W. *management educator*
†Surber, Eugene Lynn *architect*
Sutherland, Raymond Carter *clergyman, English educator emeritus*
Suttles, William Maurrelle *university administrator, clergyman*
Sutton, Berrien Daniel *beverage company executive*
Swan, James Robert Duncan *hotel executive*
Swann, Jerre Bailey *lawyer*
Swift, Frank Meador *lawyer*
Tanner, W(alter) Rhett *lawyer*
Tarkenton, Francis Asbury *computer comany executive, sports commentator, management consultant, former professional football player*
Tarr, Curtis W. *business executive*
Tarver, Jackson Williams *newspaper executive*
Taylor, George Kimbrough, Jr. *lawyer*
†Taylor, Maria Centofanti *marketing professional*
Taylor, Virginia S. *lawyer*
Teepen, Thomas Henry *newspaper editor, journalist*
†Teja, Amyn S. *chemical engineering educator, consultant*
Thakker, Ashok *aerospace engineering company executive*
Tharpe, Frazier Eugene *journalist*
†Thomas, Nadine *nurse, legislator, state official*
Thomas, Patrick Herbert *information services company executive*
Thompson, Larry Dean *lawyer*
Thuesen, Gerald Jorgen *industrial engineer, educator*
Thumann, Albert *association executive, engineer*
Tidwell, George Ernest *federal judge*
Tierney, Michael Stewart *newspaper editor*
Tindall, George Taylor *neurosurgeon, educator*
Tipping, William Malcolm *social services administrator*
†Toler, James C. *electrical engineer*
Tolsma, Dennis Dwayne *federal agency administrator*
Toner, Mike *journalist*
Tornabene, Thomas Guy *microbiologist, researcher, administrator*
Tracy, Thomas Kit *investment company executive*
Tschinkel, Sheila Lerner *banker, economist*
Tucker, Cynthia Anne *journalist*
Tucker, Robert Dennard *health care products executive*
Tummala, Rao Ramamohana *engineering educator*
†Turner, Ed Sims *broadcast executive, writer*
Turner, John Sidney, Jr. *otolaryngologist, educator*
Turner, Michael Griswold *advertising executive*
Turner, Ted (Robert Edward Turner) *television executive*
Tuttle, Elbert Parr *federal judge*
Tyler, Carl Walter, Jr. *physician, health research administrator*
Underwood, Arthur Louis, Jr. *chemistry educator, researcher*
Vaishnavi, Vijay Kumar *computer science educator, researcher*
Van Horn, Lecia Joseph *television newswriter*
†VanLandingham, William Jennings *banker*
†Van Meter, James Combs *forest products company executive*
Varner, Chilton Davis *lawyer*
†Ventulett, Thomas Walker, III *architect*
Verrill, F. Glenn *advertising executive*
Vickery, Trammell Eugene *lawyer*
Vigtel, Gudmund *museum director emeritus*
Vining, Robert Luke, Jr. *federal judge*
Voss, William Charles *retired oil company executive*
Walker, David Michael *compensation and benefits consultant, accountant*
Waller, John Louis *anesthesiology educator*
Walsh, W. Terence *lawyer*
†Walter, John W., Jr. *newspaper editor*
Ward, Horace Taliaferro *federal judge*
Ward, Richard Storer *child psychiatrist, educator emeritus*
Webb, Brainard Troutman, Jr. *lawyer, distribution company executive*
Webb, Roger Paul *electrical engineer, educator*
Weber, Owen *broadcast executive*
Weiss, Jay M(ichael) *psychologist, educator*
Wells, Donald Eugene *hospital administrator*
Wells, Everett Clayton, Jr. *economic development executive*
West, Ruth Tinsley *lawyer*
Westerhoff, John Henry, III *clergyman, theologian, educator*
†White, Gayle Colquitt *religion writer, journalist*
White, John Austin, Jr. *engineering educator, dean, consultant*
White, Perry Merrill, Jr. *orthopedic surgeon*
White, Ronald Leon *financial management consultant*
Whitehead, John Jed *computer systems company executive*
Whitley, Joe Dally *lawyer*
Whitt, Richard Ernest *reporter*
Wiedeman, John Herman *civil engineer*
Wilkins, J. Ernest, Jr. *mathematician*
Williams, Charles Murray *computer information systems educator, consultant*
Williams, David Howard *lawyer*
†Williams, Ervin Eugene *religious organization administrator*
Williams, James Bryan *banker*
Williams, Lyman Neil, Jr. *lawyer*
Williams, Ralph Watson, Jr. *retired securities company executive*
†Williams, Thomas Franklin *architect*
Willis, Kevin Alvin *professional basketball player*
Wilson, Alexander Erwin, Jr. *lawyer, management consultant*
Wilson, James Hargrove, Jr. *lawyer*
Winer, Ward Otis *mechanical engineer, educator*
Winship, Wadleigh Chichester *holding company executive*
†Winter, Wilburn Jackson, Jr. *financial executive*
Wolbrink, James Francis *real estate investor*
Wolensky, Michael K. *lawyer*
Woodard, John Roger *urologist*
Wright, Peter Meldrim *lawyer*
Wu, James Chen-Yuan *aerospace engineering educator*
Wylly, Barbara Bentley *performing arts association administrator*
Yates, Ella Gaines *library consultant*
Yates, Mary Mitchell *lawyer*
†Yoganathan, Ajit Prithiviraj *biomedical engineer, educator*
†Yother, Michele *publisher*
Young, Andrew *clergyman, civil rights leader, former mayor, former ambassador, former congressman*
Young, Robert Alan *physicist, educator*

Zaban, Erwin diversified manufacturing company executive
†Zalkow, Leon H. organic chemistry educator
Zimmermann, John financial consultant
Zink, Charles Talbott lawyer

Augusta
Barnard, Druie Douglas, Jr. former congressman
Bloodworth, William Andrew, Jr. academic administrator
Bowen, Dudley Hollingsworth, Jr. federal judge
Bray, Donald Claude hospital administrator
Cashin, Edward Joseph history educator
Chandler, Arthur Bleakley pathologist, educator
Colborn, Gene Louis anatomy educator, researcher
Davison, Frederick Corbet foundation executive
Feldman, Elaine Bossak medical nutritionist, educator
†Folker, James Edward, Jr. newspaper editor
Gambrell, Richard Donald, Jr. endocrinologist, educator
Gillespie, Edward Malcolm hospital administrator
Given, Kenna Sidney surgeon, educator
Greenbaum, Lowell Marvin pharmacologist, educator
Hammer, Wade Burke oral and maxillofacial surgeon, educator
†Howell, Robert Edward hospital administrator
Luxenberg, Malcolm Neuwahl ophthalmologist, educator
Mahesh, Virendra Bhushan endocrinologist
Mallette, Alfred John army officer
Mansberger, Arlie Roland, Jr. surgeon
Martin, Willie Pauline secondary education educator, illustrator
Parrish, Robert Alton retired pediatric surgeon, educator
†Peloquin, Garry Wayne hospital executive
Puryear, James Burton college administrator
Rosen, James Mahlon artist, art historian, educator
Rowland, Arthur Ray librarian
Taylor, Janelle Diane Williams writer
Tedesco, Francis Joseph medical college president, educator
†Woodhurst, Robert Stanford, Jr. architect
Woods, Gerald Wayne lawyer
Zachert, Virginia psychologist, educator

Bainbridge
Frieling, Thomas Jerome library director

Blairsville
†Colwell, Carlton H. state legislator, construction executive

Bolingbroke
Geary, David Leslie communications executive, educator, consultant

Brunswick
Alaimo, Anthony A. federal judge
Brubaker, Robert Paul food products executive
Harper, Janet Sutherlin Lane educational administrator, writer
Iannicelli, Joseph chemical company executive, consultant

Buford
Carswell, Virginia Colby primary school educator, special education educator
Ziegler, Delores mezzo-soprano

Canton
Hasty, William Grady, Jr. lawyer

Carrollton
Harrison, Earle former county official
Johnson, Harris Tucker educational institution administrator
Morris, Robert Christian education educator
Richards, Roy, Jr. wire and cable manufacturing company executive

Cartersville
Harris, Joe Frank former governor

Cleveland
Raznoff, Beverly Shultz education educator

Cochran
Welch, Joe Ben academic administrator

Cohutta
†Little, Thomas Michael architect

Columbus
Amos, Daniel Paul insurance executive
Amos, Paul Shelby insurance company executive
Blanchard, James Hubert finance company executive
Brabson, Max LaFayette health care executive
Brinkley, Jack Thomas lawyer, former congressman
Bugg, William Joseph, Jr. insurance executive
Cloninger, Kriss, III insurance company executive
Diaz-Verson, Salvador, Jr. investment advisor
Elliott, James Robert federal judge
†Harbison, Ed state senator, broadcast journalist
Harper, Henry H. military officer
Laney, John Thomas, III federal judge
†Leebern, Donald M. distilled beverage executive
Martin, Frank Kieffer mayor, lawyer
McGlamry, Max Reginald lawyer
Page, William Marion lawyer
Patrick, Carl Lloyd theatre executive
Riggsby, Ernest Duward science educator
†Robinson, Pete lawyer, state senator
†Slay, Ken sales executive
†Swift, George P., Jr. corporate professional
Watson, Billy publishing executive, newspaper
Zallen, Harold corporate executive, scientist, former university official

Conyers
Mc Clung, Jim Hill light manufacturing company executive

Covington
Penland, John Thomas import/export and development companies executive

Dacula
Bascom, Perry Bagnall retired marketing sales executive

Dahlonega
Allen, Delmas James anatomist, educator, university administrator
Jones, William Benjamin, Jr. electrical engineering educator

Dallas
Friedrich, Stephen Miro credit bureau company executive

Dalton
Clark, Winston Craig neurosurgeon
†Kinnamon, Gregory Harold lawyer
Shaw, Julius C. carpet manufacturing company executive
†Shaw, Robert E. carpeting company executive
†Thomason, Frank W. superintendent

Decatur
Alderete, Joseph Frank psychiatrist, medical service adminstrator
Bain, James Arthur pharmacologist, educator
Carey, John Jesse academic administrator, religion educator
†Cassity, (Allen) Turner poet
Gay, Robert Derril county official
Hill, Thomas Glenn, III dermatologist
Howard, Pierre lieutenant governor, president senate
Knight, Walker Leigh editor, publisher, clergyman
Loehle, Betty Barnes artist, painter
Martinez-Maldonado, Manuel medical service administrator, physician
Middleton, James Boland lawyer
Myers, Clark Everett retired business administration educator
Myers, Orie Eugene, Jr. university official
Pepperdene, Margaret Williams English educator
Poole, Albert Mitchell, Jr. trucking company executive
Robb, Felix Compton association executive, consultant
Shulman, Arnold judge, lawyer
Strawn-Hamilton, Frank jazz musician, folksinger, composer and arranger, educator
Wilkinson, Ben chancellor, evangelist, ministry organizer, writer
Winn, Albert Curry clergyman
Young, James Harvey historian, educator

Dillard
Wilkinson, Albert Mims, Jr. lawyer

Dobbins AFB
McIntosh, Robert Alan military career officer

Doraville
†Wempner, Gerald Arthur engineering educator
Yancey, Eleanor Margaret Garrett crisis intervention clinician

Douglas
King, Ruby Thompson secondary education educator, civic worker
†Palmer, Timothy bank executive
Purvis, Mary Ruth Moore special education educator

Dublin
Greene, Jule Blounte lawyer

Duluth
†Neuman, Ted R. principal
Tennant, Thomas Michael lawyer
†Torian, Merville Russell, Sr. construction company executive

Dunwoody
Bartolo, Donna M. hospital administrator, nurse
Cox, Albert Harrington, Jr. economist

East Point
†Gloster, Hugh Morris retired college president, college association consultant

Evans
Beaudreau, David Eugene dentist, educator
Hartlage, Lawrence Clifton neuropsychologist, educator
Little, Robert Colby physiologist, educator

Fairburn
Montague, Mary Ellen social studies educator

Fayetteville
Burch, Robert Joseph writer
Harris, Dorothy Clark interior architect, designer, design instructor

Folkston
Crumbley, Esther Helen Kendrick educator, realtor

Forsyth
Clarke, Harold Gravely retired state supreme court chief justice

Fort Benning
Grube, Dick DeWayne museum director
Ramsey, Russell Wilcox national security affairs educator

Fort Gordon
Xenakis, Stephen Nicholas psychiatrist, physician, military officer

Fort Lewis
Cavezza, Carmen James career officer

Fort McPherson
Reimer, Dennis J. career military officer

Fort Valley
Marchman, Robert L., III lawyer, pecan farmer

Gainesville
Burd, John Stephen academic administrator, music educator
Duffy, Thomas Edward publisher
†Hemmer, Jane Reynolds state senator, real estate executive
Kartzinel, Ronald pharmaceutical company executive, neuroscientist
Leet, Richard Hale oil company executive
†McNeece, Richard A. bank executive
†Wagner, Clarence historian

Glynco
Rinkevich, Charles Francis federal official

Greenville
Johnson, Hardwick Smith, Jr. school psychologist

Griffin
†Arkin, Gerald Franklin agricultural research administrator, educator
†Doyle, Michael Patrick food microbiologist, educator, researcher
Duncan, Ronny Rush agriculturist, reseacher
Shuman, Larry Myers soil chemist
Wilkinson, Robert Eugene plant physiologist

Hinesville
Gennrich, Robert Paul, II radiologic technologist

Jasper
Parrish, Carmelita secondary school educator

Jersey
Batchelor, Joseph Brooklyn, Jr. electronics engineer, consultant

Kennesaw
Sowers, George Frederick civil engineer

Kings Bay
Ellis, Winford Gerald military career officer, federal agency administrator

La Grange
Anderson, Ray C. carpet company executive
Ault, Ethyl Lorita academic administrator
Copeland, Robert Bodine internist, cardiologist
Gordon, Robert Edward university administrator
Murphy, Walter Young college president, clergyman
West, John Thomas surgeon

Lawrenceville
Fetner, Robert Henry radiation biologist
Gericke, Paul William minister, educator
†Wall, Clarence Vinson congressman

Lilburn
Forsee, Joe Brown library director
Graham, Richard container company executive

Lookout Mountain
Hitching, Harry James retired lawyer

Mableton
Day, Afton J. elementary school educator and administrator

Macon
†Alexander, David Lee clergyman
Anderson, Robert Lanier, III federal judge
†Bayliss, Mary Rosina principal
†Bundy, John Franklin, Jr. national monument administrator
Cockfield, Jamie Hartwell history educator
Crawford, Edwin Mack health facilities executive
†Drinkard, Lawrence W. service executive
Dunwody, Eugene Cox architect
Ennis, Edgar William, Jr. lawyer
Faulk, Alfred Donald, Jr. hospital administrator
Fickling, William Arthur, Jr. health care administrator
Fitzpatrick, Duross federal judge
Gerson, Robert Walthall judge, retired lawyer
†Godsey, R(aleigh) Kirby university president
Hails, Robert Emmet aerospace consultant, business executive, former air force officer
†Haynes-Hooks, Ella Mae journalist
Hershner, Robert Franklin, Jr. federal judge
†Hicks, C. J. bishop
Innes, David Lyn university official, educator
Jones, John Ellis real estate broker
†Looney, Richard Carl bishop
†Mac Crawford, Edwin health facility administrator
Marshall, Howard Lowen music educator, musicologist
Murdoch, Bernard Constantine psychology educator
Owens, Garland Chester accounting educator
Owens, Wilbur Dawson, Jr. federal judge
Rich, Arthur Lowndes music educator
Rutledge, Ivan Cate retired legal educator, arbitrator
Savage, Randall Ernest journalist
†Schmidt, Charles J. library administrator
Sell, Edward Scott, Jr. lawyer
Smith, Constance Lewis educator
†Snow, Cubbedge, Jr. lawyer
Steeples, Douglas Wayne university vice president, consultant, researcher
Swartwout, Joseph Rodolph obstetrics and gynecology educator, university administrator
Volpe, Erminio Peter biologist, educator
Yancy, Cecil Henton, Jr. editor

Marietta
Aronoff, Craig Ellis management educator, consultant
†Barnes, Roy Eugene lawyer
Blackwell, James Augusta, Jr. aerospace executive
†Bonn, Edward Joseph hospital executive
Breese, John Allen chemical industry executive
Bridges, Alan Lynn physicist, researcher, information systems specialist
Burkey, J(acob) Brent lawyer, company executive
†Cauthorn, Thomas Edward, III judge
Cheshier, Stephen Robert university president, electrical engineer
Cooper, Keith Harvey insurance consultant
Diercks, Chester William, Jr. capital goods manufacturing company executive
Dunwoody, Kenneth Reed magazine editor
†Foster, Finley B. engineering company executive
Hall, George Ralph school system administrator
†Hammond, John William lawyer
Hayes, Robert Deming electrical engineer, consultant
Ingram, George Conley lawyer
Johnson, Herbert Frederick sales executive, former university administrator, librarian
†Klein, Edward W., III (Kip Klein) state legislator, lawyer
Overton, Bruce personnel executive, consultant
Petit, Parker Holmes health care corporation executive
Rainey, Kenneth Tyler English language educator
Rocker, Peggy Bland retired home economics educator
Siegel, Betty Lentz college president
Smith, Baker Armstrong management executive, lawyer
Smith, George Thornewell retired state supreme court justice
†Toal, Desmond James manufacturing company executive
†Vaughan, Jack Dixon, Jr. state legislator, insurance agent

Metter
Doremus, Ogden lawyer

Midway
Cobb, John Anthony retired state veterinarian

Milledgeville
Engerrand, Doris Dieskow business educator

Millwood
McCarthy, William Daniel retired banking educator

Monroe
†Felker, George Stephen textiles executive
Lynch, Lillian educator

Moultrie
Vereen, William Coachman, Jr. textile company executive
Vereen, William Jerome uniform manufacturing company executive

Mount Berry
Mathis, Luster Doyle college administrator, political scientist
Mew, Thomas Joseph, III (Tommy Mew) artist, educator
Shatto, Gloria McDermith college administrator, economist

Newnan
Cowles, Milly education educator
Harvey, Edwin Malcolm retired manufacturing company executive
Morgan, Lewis Render federal judge

Norcross
Adams, Kenneth Francis automobile executive
Born, Allen mining executive
Conway, Hobart McKinley, Jr. geo-economist
Crymes, Ronald Jack draftsman,structural steel detailer
†Cullison, William Lester association executive
†Currey, Bradley, Jr. paper company executive
†Darst, Bobby Charles soil chemist, administrator
Dibb, David Walter research association administrator
Esher, Brian Richard environmental company executive
Francisco, Edgar Wiggin, III management consultant
Harris, William North consulting company executive
Harrison, Gordon Ray engineering executive, consultant, research scientist
Helander, Robert Charles lawyer
†Kelly, William S. automotive executive
Nardelli-Olkowska, Krystyna Maria ophthalmologist, educator
†Pippin, John Eldon electronics engineer, electronics company executive
Rouse, William Bradford systems engineering executive, researcher, educator
†Sage, Gordon metal products executive

Oxford
Sitton, Claude Fox newspaper editor

Peachtree City
Eichelberger, Charles Bell retired career officer
Roobol, Norman Richard chemistry educator, industrial painting consultant
Yeosock, John John army officer

Perry
†Hinnant, Tony superintendent

Pine Mountain
Callaway, Howard Hollis business executive

Quitman
Baum, Joseph Herman retired biomedical educator

Ringgold
†Poston, McCracken King, Jr. lawyer, state representative

Robins A F B
Gillis, Richard Fred career officer

Rockmart
†Dean, Nathan D. state senator

Rome
Janowski, Thaddeus Marian architect
Johnson, Mary nursing administrator
Murphy, Harold Loyd federal judge
†Overbeck, James A. library director, educator

Roswell
Bristow, Preston Abner, Jr. civil engineer, environmental engineer
Burgess, John Frank management consultant, former utility executive, former army officer
†DeVictor, D. J. landscape architect
Forbes, John Ripley museum executive, educator
Graham, Charles Passmore retired army officer
†Hill, Dennis James trade show exhibition manager, consultant
Jordan, DuPree, Jr. management consultant, educator, journalist, publisher, business executive
Peterson, Donald Robert magazine editor, vintage automobile consultant
Siepi, Cesare opera singer
Topliss, Harry, Jr. financial consultant, former corporation executive

Saint Simons Island
Douglas, William Ernest *retired government official*
Riedeburg, Theodore *management consultant*
†Tomberlin, William G. *principal*

Sandersville
Thiele, Paul Frederick *mining company executive*

Sapelo Island
Alberts, James Joseph *scientist, researcher*

Sautee Nacoochee
Miller, Wilbur Randolph *retired university administrator*

Savannah
Albert, Theodore Merton *computer scientist*
Alley, James Pinckney, Jr. *computer art and graphic design educator*
Ball, Ardella Patricia *library science educator*
Barnes, Benjamin Shields, Jr. *retired banker*
Beals, L(oren) Alan *association executive*
Bell, William Henry, Jr. *banker*
†Breidenbach, Fred A. *aerospace company executive*
Burnett, Robert Adair *university administrator, history educator*
†Cave, Kent R. *national park ranger*
Coffey, Thomas Francis, Jr. *editor*
Dickey, David Herschel *lawyer, accountant*
Edenfield, Berry Avant *federal judge*
Forbes, Morton Gerald *lawyer*
Gay, Lee Anderson *financial consultant*
Gillespie, Daniel Curtis, Sr. *retired non-profit company executive, consultant*
†Glenn, Albert H. *aerospace company executive*
Granger, Harvey, Jr. *manufacturing company executive*
Hale, Charlotte *author, publishing executive*
Horan, Leo Gallaspy *physician, educator*
Hsu, Ming-Yu *engineer, educator*
†Ives, John Elway *hospital administrator*
†Johnson, Victor L. *trucking executive*
Krahl, Enzo *retired surgeon*
Lessard, Raymond W. *bishop*
McAlpin, Kirk Martin *lawyer*
†Menzel, David Washington *oceanographer*
Rawson, William Robert *lawyer, retired manufacturing company executive*
Rousakis, John Paul *former mayor*
Schafer, Thomas Wilson *advertising agency executive*
Scott, Walter Coke *retired sugar company executive, lawyer*
Smith, Gregory Allgire *art museum director*
Sortor, Harold Edward *financial executive*
Spitz, Seymour James, Jr. *retired fragrance company executive*
Sprague, William Wallace, Jr. *food company executive*
Su, Helen Chien-fan *research chemist*
Theis, Francis William *business executive*
Tobey, Carl Wadsworth *retired publisher*
Warlick, Roger Kinney *history educator, assistant dean*
†Weiner, Susan S. *mayor*
Wheeler, Ed Ray *mathematics educator*
Windsor, Patricia Frances (Katonah Summertree) *author, educator, lecturer*

Sea Island
Brown, Ann Catherine *investment company executive*
Brown, George Hay *investment counselor*
Carter, Don Earl *newspaper editor, publisher*

Smyrna
†Atkins, William A. (Bill) *state legislator*
Head, John Francis, Jr. *distributing company executive*
†Lenker, Max V. *consumer products company executive*
†Ragan, Hugh Adams *electric utility executive, state senator*
Wallace, Clifford Noble, III *public assembly facility management executive*
Wilding, Diane *marketing, financial and information systems executive*

Statesboro
Black, Charlene Rushton *university official, sociology educator*
Henry, Nicholas Llewellyn *political science educator, university administrator*
Talmadge, Mary Christine *nursing educator*

Stockbridge
†Davis, Raymond Gilbert *retired career officer, real estate developer*

Stone Mountain
Le Roy, L. David *journalist*
Rogers, James Virgil, Jr. *retired radiologist and educator*
Speed, Billie Cheney (Mrs. Thomas S. Speed) *retired editor, journalist*
Wagner, Robert Earl *agronomist*
Wingate, Henry Taylor, Jr. *foundation administrator, fundraiser*

Suwanee
†Hebert, Bobby Joseph, Jr. *professional football player*
†Jones, June *professional football coach*
Rison, Andre *football player*
Sanders, Deion Luwynn *baseball and football player*
†Sanders, Ricky Wayne *professional football player*
†Shelley, Elbert Vernell *professional football player*
Smith, Taylor *professional football team executive*

Thomaston
Hightower, Neil Hamilton *textile manufacturing company executive*

Thomasville
Flowers, Langdon Strong *foods company executive*
Flowers, William Howard, Jr. *food company executive*
Mc Mullian, Amos Ryals *food company executive*
Stepanek, David Leslie *financial services company executive*

Thomson
†Smith, Robert L. *principal*

Tifton
Austin, Max Eugene *horticulture educator*
Douglas, Charles Francis *agronomist*
Miller, John David *retired agronomist*
†Rogers, Charlie Ellic *entomologist*
†Thomas, Adrian Wesley *laboratory director*

Toccoa
Maypole, John Floyd *real estate holding company executive*

Toccoa Falls
Alford, Paul Legare *college and religious foundation administrator*

Townsend
Collins, David Browning *religious institution administrator*

Tucker
Kilgore, Tom D. *electric power company executive*
†Ordway, Ronald Dale *video display company executive*
Rogers, Richard Hilton *service executive*
Valk, Henry Snowden *physicist, educator*

Valdosta
Bailey, Hugh Coleman *university president*
Bowling, John Selby *hospital administrator*
Branan, John Maury *psychology educator, counselor*
Peace, Barbara Lou Jean *education educator*
Scruggs, Betty Joyce Clenney *public school administrator*

Warner Robins
Nugteren, Cornelius *air force officer*
Scott, Robert Lee, Jr. *career military officer, writer, lecturer*

Washington
Wills, Olive Boline *elementary education educator*

Watkinsville
Box, James Ellis, Jr. *research soil scientist*
†Langdale, George Wilfred *research soil scientist*
Wright, Robert Joseph *lawyer*

West Point
Glover, Clifford Clarke *retired construction company executive*
Jennings, Joseph Leslie, Jr. *textile executive*
†Monk, Richard Hunley, Jr. *textile company executive*
Terry, Richmond Bohler *textiles executive*

Winterville
Anderson, David Prewitt *university dean*
Shockley, W. Ray *travel trade association executive*

Woodstock
Austin, John David *financial executive*

Young Harris
Yow, Thomas Sidney, III *college administrator*

HAWAII

Aiea
Heinz, Don J. *agronomist*

Captain Cook
Gilliam, Jackson Earle *bishop*

Eleele
Takanishi, Lillian K. *elementary school educator*

Ewa Beach
Williamson, J(ohn) Craig *professional golfer*

Haiku
Cost, James Peter *artist*

Haleiwa
Woolliams, Keith Richard *arboretum and botanical garden director*

Hanalei
Ching, Lawrence Lin Tai *retail executive*

Hilo
Dixon, Paul William *psychology educator*
Evans, Franklin Bachelder *marketing educator emeritus*
†Nagao, Mike Akira *horticulturist, county administrator*
†Perrin, Kenneth Lynn *university chancellor*
Taniguchi, Tokuso *surgeon*
Ushijima, John Takeji *state senator, lawyer*
Wang, James Chia-Fang *political science educator*
Werner, Marlin Spike *speech pathologist and audiologist*

Honolulu
Abbott, Isabella Aiona *biology educator*
Abramson, Norman *electronics executive*
Akinaka, Asa Masayoshi *lawyer*
Alicata, Joseph Everett *microbiology researcher, parasitologist*
Alm, Richard Sanford *education educator*
Amor, Simeon, Jr. *photographer, historian*
Andrasick, James Stephen *agribusiness company executive*
Antal, Michael Jerry, Jr. *mechanical engineering educator*
Ashford, Clinton Rutledge *judge*
Ashton, Geoffrey Cyril *geneticist, educator*
†Ayer, David Clay *architect*
Barbieri, David Arthur *company executive*
Barr, Jon Michael *naval officer, federal official*
Behnke, Richard Frederick *investment banking executive*
Bender, Byron Wilbur *linguistics educator*
Bess, Henry David *dean*
Betts, Barbara Stoke *artist, educator*
Bitterman, Morton Edward *psychologist, educator*
Bloede, Victor Carl *lawyer, academic executive*
Botsai, Elmer Eugene *architect, educator, former university dean*
Brantley, Lee Reed *chemistry educator*
Bruce, Nadine Cecile *internist, educator*
Buchman, Mark Edward *banker*
Buyers, John William Amerman *agribusiness and specialty foods company executive*
†Cachola, Romy Munoz *state representative*
Cades, Julius Russell *lawyer*
Cain, Raymond Frederick *landscape architect, planning company executive*
Callies, David Lee *lawyer, educator*
Case, James Hebard *lawyer*
Cayetano, Benjamin Jerome *lieutenant governor, former state senator and representative*
†Chang, Anthony Kai Ung *state legislator*
†Chang, Donald S. M. *fire department chief*
Chaplin, George *newspaper editor*
Char, Vernon Fook Leong *lawyer*
Chee, Percival Hon Yin *ophthalmologist*
Ching, Chauncey Tai Kin *agricultural economics educator*
Ching, Larry Fong Chow *construction company executive*
Chiozzi, Richard Emilio *bank executive*
Cho, Lee-Jay *social scientist, demographer*
Choy, Herbert Young Cho *federal judge*
Chuck, Walter G(oonsun) *lawyer*
Chung, Kea Sung *television broadcasting executive*
Clark, Henry Benjamin, Jr. *retired food company executive, community service volunteer*
Copi, Irving Marmer *philosophy educator*
Cornuelle, Herbert Cumming *retired corporate executive*
Corsini, Raymond Joseph *psychologist*
Cotlar, Morton *organizational scientist, educator*
Couch, John Charles *diversified company executive*
Cowie, Lennox Lauchlan *astrophysicist*
Cox, Richard Horton *civil engineering executive*
†Cruthers, Evan Douglas *architect*
Day, Arthur Grove *author, educator*
Devens, Paul *lawyer*
Dods, Walter Arthur, Jr. *bank executive*
Dolly, John Patrick *university dean, educational psychologist*
†Driskill, Thomas Malcolm, Jr. *military officer*
†Duckworth, Walter Donald *museum executive, entomologist*
Dyen, Isidore *linguistic scientist, educator*
Edel, (Joseph) Leon *biographer, educator*
Ellis, George Richard *museum administrator*
Enoki, Donald Yukio *curriculum specialist*
Ezra, David A. *federal judge*
Fasi, Frank Francis *mayor*
†Fernandes Salling, Lehua *lawyer, state senator*
Ferrario, Joseph A. *bishop*
Fischer, Joel *social work educator*
Flanagan, John Michael *editor, publisher*
Fong, Bernard W. D. *physician, educator*
Fong, Harold Michael *federal judge*
Fong, Hiram L. *former senator*
Fong, Peter C. K. *lawyer, judge*
Force, Roland Wynfield *anthropologist, museum executive*
Fullmer, Daniel Warren *psychologist, educator*
Gary, James Frederick *business and energy advising company executive*
Gay, E(mil) Laurence *lawyer*
Gelber, Don Jeffrey *lawyer*
†George, Mary Shannon *state senator*
George, Peter T. *orthodontist*
Gialanella, Philip Thomas *newspaper publisher*
Greenfield, David W. *academic dean, ichthyologist*
Greer, Howard Earl *former naval officer*
†Hagino, Gerald Takao *state senator*
†Hale, Nathan Robert *architect*
Hall, Donald Norman Blake *astronomer*
†Hall, Marvin B. *hospital administrator*
Halloran, Richard Colby *communications research executive, former news correspondent*
†Hamada, Duane Takumi *architect*
Hanson, Dennis Michael *medical imaging executive*
Hara, Ernest Hideo *architect*
Harrison, Jeremy Thomas *dean*
Hart, Donald Purple *bishop*
Hatfield, Elaine Catherine *psychology educator*
Hawke, Bernard Ray *planetary scientist*
Hays, Ronald Jackson *naval officer*
Heller, Ronald Ian *lawyer*
Herbig, George Howard *astronomer, educator*
†Hirono, Mazie Keiko *state legislator*
Ho, Donald Tai Loy *entertainer, singer*
†Ho, Reginald Chi Shing *medical educator*
Ho, Stuart Tse Kong *investment company executive*
Hoag, John Arthur *bank executive*
Holland, Charles Malcolm, Jr. *retired health care executive, development corporation executive, retired banker*
Hong, Norman G. Y. *architect*
Hook, Ralph Clifford, Jr. *business educator*
Hufschmidt, Maynard Michael *resources planning educator*
Hughes, Robert Harrison *former agricultural products executive*
Ihrig, Judson La Moure *chemist*
†Ikeda, Donna Rika *state legislator*
Ikeda, Moss Marcus Masanobu *educational administrator, lecturer, consultant*
Inaba, Lawrence Akio *educational director*
†Isbell, Virginia *state legislator*
†Iwase, Randall Yoshio *state senator*
Jackson, Miles Merrill *university dean*
Jellinek, Roger *editor*
Johanos, Donald *orchestra conductor*
Johnson, Lawrence M. *banker*
Jongeward, George Ronald *systems analyst*
Jordan, Amos Azariah, Jr. *foreign affairs educator, retired army officer*
Kamemoto, Fred Isamu *zoologist*
Kamemoto, Haruyuki *horticulture educator*
Kane, Bartholomew Aloysius *state librarian*
Kanehiro, Kenneth Kenji *insurance educator, risk analyst, consultant*
Katayama, Robert Nobuichi *lawyer*
Kay, Alan Cooke *federal judge*
Keil, Klaus *geology educator, consultant*
Keir, Gerald Janes *newspaper editor*
Keith, Kent Marsteller *academic administrator, corporate executive, government official, lawyer*
Kelley, Richard Roy *hotel executive*
Kelly, James Andrew *policy reseach executive, former government official*
Kenda, Juanita Echeverria *artist, educator*
Keogh, Richard John *management consultant*
Khan, Mohammad Asad *geophysicist, educator, former energy minister and senator of Pakistan*
†Kiessling, Ralph J. *health insurance company executive*
†King, Arthur R., Jr. *education educator, researcher*
Knowlton, Edgar Colby, Jr. *linguist, educator*
†Kobayashi, Ann H. *state legislator*
Kohloss, Frederick Henry *consulting engineer*
Koide, Frank Takayuki *electrical engineer*
Kolonel, Laurence Norman *epidemiologist, public health educator*
†Krauss, Robert *newspaper columnist, author*
†Lamoureux, Charles Harrington *botanist, arboretum administrator*
Langhans, Edward Allen *drama and theater educator*
†Lau, Charles Kwok-Chiu *architect, architectural firm executive*
Lee, Beverly Ing *educational administrator*
Levine, Aaron *city planner*
Lewin, John Calvert *public health administrator*
Lilly, Michael Alexander *lawyer*
Linman, James William *retired physician, educator*
Loui, Patricia M. L. *marketing company executive*
Lum, Jean Loui Jin *nurse educator*
Mark, Shelley Muin *economist, educator*
Marks, Michael J. *lawyer, corporate executive*
†Marumoto, Barbara Chizuko *state legislator*
Marvit, Robert Charles *psychiatrist*
Matsuda, Fujio *director academic research*
†Matsunaga, Matthew Masao *lawyer, accountant*
Mau, William Koon-Hee *financier*
Mc Dermott, John Francis, Jr. *psychiatrist, physician*
McGinn, Susan Frances *musician*
Miccio, Joseph V. *business educator, consultant*
Michael, Jerrold Mark *public health specialist, former university dean, educator*
Midkiff, Robert Richards *consultant*
Miller, Richard Sherwin *legal educator*
Minhas, Faqir Ullah *aerospace engineer*
†Miyamoto, Owen *state agency administrator*
Moore, Willson Carr, Jr. *lawyer*
Moreno, Rose Lani *secondary schools administrator*
†Morita, James Masami *banker, lawyer*
Morse, Richard *social scientist*
Murabayashi, Harris Nozomu *management analyst*
Myers, A(nthony) Maurice *airline executive*
Nakagawa, Jean Harue *diversified corporation executive*
†Nakakura, Wilfred Satoru *construction company executive*
†Nakamura, Michael S. *protective services official*
Niles, Geddes Leroy *private investigator*
Nishimura, Pete Hideo *oral surgeon*
Oda, Yoshio *physician, internist*
Ogburn, Hugh Bell *chemical engineer, consultant*
Okinaga, Lawrence Shoji *lawyer*
Oksenberg, Michel Charles *political scientist, educator*
Olmsted, Ronald David *foundation executive, consultant*
Omori, Morio *lawyer*
O'Neill, Charles Kelly *marketing executive, former advertising agency executive*
†Onishi, Patrick Tomeo *architect*
Paige, Glenn Durland *political scientist, educator*
Pang, Herbert George *ophthalmologist*
Person, Donald Ames, Sr. *pediatrician, rheumatologist*
†Peters, Henry H. *state legislator*
Peterson, Barbara Ann Bennett *history educator*
Pfeiffer, Robert John *water transportation executive*
Pickens, Alexander Legrand *education educator*
Porter, Michael Pell *lawyer*
Quinn, William Francis *lawyer*
Raleigh, Cecil Baring *geophysicist*
†Rambo, A. Terry *anthropologist, research program director*
Ramler, Siegfried *school administrator*
Rapson, Richard L. *history educator*
Reed, Robert George, III *petroleum company executive*
†Retz, William Andrew *naval officer*
Roberti, Mario Andrew *lawyer, former energy company executive*
Robertson, Gregg Westland *diversified company executive*
Robinson, Robert Blacque *association executive*
Rutherford, Robert L. *career military officer*
Safford, Florence Viray Sunga *travel agent and consultant*
Sagawa, Yoneo *horticulturist, educator*
Saiki, Patricia (Mrs. Stanley Mitsuo Saiki) *former federal agency administrator, former congresswoman*
Salmon, Charles B., Jr. *diplomat*
Satoh, Yoshiharu *banker*
Schatz, Irwin Jacob *cardiologist*
Scheuer, Paul Josef *chemistry educator*
Schnack, Gayle Hemingway Jepson (Mrs. Harold Clifford Schnack) *corporate executive*
Schubert, Glendon *political scientist, educator*
Seymour, Richard Kellogg *linguist, educator*
Sherman, Martin *entomologist*
Simonds, John Edward *newspaper editor*
Simpson, Andrea Lynn *energy communication executive*
Smith, Albert Charles *biologist, educator*
Smith, Barbara Barnard *music educator*
Smyser, Adam Albert *newspaper editor*
Solheim, Wilhelm Gerhard, II *anthropologist, educator*
Sparks, Robert William *publishing executive*
Stahl, Margo Schneebalg *marine biologist*
Starn, Peter *lawyer*
Statler, Oliver Hadley *writer*
†Stebbins, Dennis Robert *international business and environmental management consultant*
Stephan, John Jason *historian, educator*
Stephenson, Herman Howard *banker*
Stevens, Robert David *librarian, educator*
†Suh, Dae-Sook *political science educator*
Sutton, Charles Richard *architect, designer*
Swanson, Richard William *statistician*
†Takumi, Roy Mitsuo *state representative*
†Tam, Rod *state legislator*
Tatibouet, André Stephan *condominium and resort management firm executive*
†Thielen, Cynthia Henry *lawyer, state legislator*
Toyomura, Dennis Takeshi *architect*
Tuan, San Fu *theoretical physics, political science educator*
†Tungpalan, Eloise Yamashita *state legislator*
Tuttle, Daniel Webster *retired political science educator*
Twigg-Smith, Thurston *newspaper publisher*
Ueberroth, John A. *air transportation executive*
†Ushijima, Arthur Akira *health facility administrator*
Varley, Herbert Paul *Japanese language and cultural history educator*
Waihee, John David, III *governor, lawyer*

Wainwright, Paul Edward Blech *construction company executive*
Wang, Jaw-Kai *agricultural engineering educator*
Weyand, Frederick Carlton *retired military officer*
Williams, Carl Harwell *utilities executive*
†Williamson, Harwood Danford *utility company executive*
Wolff, Herbert Eric *banker, former army officer*
Wright, Chatt Grandison *academic administrator*
Wyrtki, Klaus *oceanography educator*
Yamato, Kei C. *international business consultant*
Yee, Alfred Alphonse *structural engineer, consultant*
Yeh, Raymond Wei-Hwa *architect, educator*
†Young, Jacqueline Eurn Hai *state legislator*
Yount, David Eugene *physicist, university official*

Kahului
Riecke, Hans Heinrich *architect*

Kailua
Engelbardt, Robert Miles *telecommunications executive*
†Tam, William *secondary school principal*
†Tokumaru, Roberta *principal*

Kailua Kona
Ashley, Darlene Joy *psychologist*
Clewett, Kenneth Vaughn *college official*
Feaver, Douglas David *university dean, classics educator*

Kaneohe
Baker, Paul Thornell *anthropology educator*
†Fisette, Scott Michael *golf course designer*
Hanson, Richard Edwin *civil engineer*
†Kamiyama, Linda *elementary school principal*
Lagoria, Georgianna Marie *curator, writer, editor, visual art consultant*
McGlaughlin, Thomas Howard *publisher, retired naval officer*
Smales, Fred Benson *corporate executive*

Kapaau
McFee, Richard *electrical engineer, physicist*

Koloa
Blair, Samuel Ray *lawyer*
Gustafson, Charles Ivan *hospital administrator*

Kula
Becker, Walter *guitarist, record producer*
Rohlfing, Frederick William *lawyer, judge*

Lahaina
Sato, Tadashi *artist*

Laie
Bradshaw, James R. *business educator*

Lihue
Cobb, Rowena Noelani Blake *real estate broker*

Makawao
Mascho, George Leroy *education educator emeritus*

Mililani
Kiley, Thomas *rehabilitation counselor*

Pearl City
Sue, Alan Kwai Keong *dentist*

Pearl Harbor
Fitzgerald, James Richard *naval officer*
Larson, Charles Robert *naval officer*

Princeville
Kaye, Wilbur Irving *chemist, researcher, consultant*

Waialua
Singlehurst, Dona Geisenheyner *horse farm owner*

Waianae
Pinckney, Neal Theodore *psychologist, educator*

Waikoloa
Copman, Louis *radiologist*

Wailuku
Kinaka, William Tatsuo *lawyer*

Waipahu
Matsui, Jiro *importer, wholesaler, small business owner*

IDAHO

Aberdeen
Sparks, Walter Chappel *horticulturist, educator*

Boise
Agee, William J. *transportation, engineering and construction company executive*
Andrus, Cecil Dale *governor*
Bakes, Robert Eldon *retired state supreme court justice*
Barr, Robert Dale *university dean, educator*
Beaumont, Pamela Jo *marketing professional*
Bistline, Stephen *state supreme court justice*
†Black, Max C. *insurance agent*
†Black, Pete *state legislator, educator*
†Bolles, Charles Avery *librarian*
Brown, Tod David *bishop*
Burnell, Bates Cavanaugh *engineering and construction company executive*
Callister, Marion Jones *federal judge*
Cenarrusa, Pete T. *secretary of state*
Cleary, Edward William *retired diversified forest products company executive*
Cline, Glen Edwin *architect, planner*
Crane, Charles Arthur *college president*
†Curran, James J. *banker*
†Darrington, Denton *state senator*
EchoHawk, Larry *state attorney general*
†Ellis, Ted Ellsworth *banker*
Evans, Jerry Lee *school system administrator*
Ferguson, E. Robert *construction and engineering company executive*
Fery, John Bruce *forest products company executive*
Griffin, Sylvia Gail *reading specialist*
Guarino, John Ralph *physician, scientist, educator*
†Gurnsey, Kathleen Wallace *state legislator*
Hibbs, Robert Andrews *analytical chemistry educator*
†Hunsucker, (Carl) Wayne *architectural firm executive, educator*
†Ingram, Cecil D. *accountant, state legislator*
Johnson, Byron Jerald *state supreme court judge*
Jones, D. Michael *banker*
Kayser, Donald Robert *financial executive*
Kemp, J. Robert *beef industry consultant, food company executive*
Klein, Edith Miller *lawyer, former state senator*
Leroy, David Henry *lawyer, state and federal official*
Littman, Irving *forest products company executive*
Lodge, Edward J. *federal judge*
†Long, William D. *grocery store executive*
Lowder, Robert Jackson *insurance agent*
†Madsen, Roger Bryan *lawyer*
Maloof, Giles Wilson *academic administrator, educator*
Marcus, Craig Brian *lawyer*
McClary, James Daly *retired contractor*
McDevitt, Charles Francis *state supreme court justice*
McKee, Joseph Fulton *engineering and construction executive*
†McLaughlin, Marguerite P. *state senator, logging company executive*
McNutt, Suzzanne Marie *legal assistant*
Mc Quade, Henry Ford *state justice*
Michael, Gary G. *supermarket and drug chain executive*
Minnick, Walter Clifford *building materials company executive*
Nelson, Thomas G. *federal judge*
Nguyen, King Xuan *historian*
Nyborg, Lester Phil *physician*
Olson, Richard Dean *researcher, pharmacology educator*
O'Riordan, William Hugh *lawyer*
Otter, Clement Leroy *lieutenant governor*
Overgaard, Willard Michele *political scientist, jurisprudent*
†Pomeroy, Horace Burton, III *accountant, corporate executive*
†Reents, Sue *state legislator*
†Ricks, Mark G. *state senator, farmer*
Risch, James E. *lawyer*
†Ruch, Charles P. *university official*
Ryan, Harold L. *federal judge*
Schwartz, Theodore B. *physician, educator*
Scudder, David Benjamin *economist, foundation administrator*
Shurtliff, Marvin Karl *lawyer*
†Silak, Cathy R. *judge*
Simplot, John R. *agribusiness executive*
Speer, William Thomas, Jr. *banker, rancher*
Steinfort, James Richard *university program director*
†Stone, Ruby R. *state legislator*
Sullivan, James Kirk *forest products company executive*
†Taylor, W.O. (Bill) *state legislator, business consultant*
†Thornton, John S., IV *bishop*
Trott, Stephen Spangler *federal judge, musician*
True, Leland Beyer *civil engineer, consultant*
VanHole, William Remi *lawyer*
Wasserlein, John Henry *paper manufacturing company executive*
Wells, Merle William *historian, state archivist*
Wilbur, Lyman Dwight *consulting engineering executive*
Wilson, Jack Fredrick *retired federal government official*
Woodard, Larry L. *Bible college official*

Bonners Ferry
McClintock, William Thomas *health care administrator*

Calder
Rechard, Ottis William *mathematics and computer science educator*

Caldwell
Attebery, Louie Wayne *English language educator, folklorist*
Gipson, Gordon *publishing company executive*
Hendren, Robert Lee, Jr. *academic administrator*
†Kerrick, David Ellsworth *senator lawyer*
Lonergan, Wallace Gunn *economics educator, management consultant*

Challis
†Barrett, Lenore Hardy *mining and investment consultant, state legislator*

Coeur D Alene
Ayers, Stephen M. *lawyer*
Duke, Patty (Anna Marie Duke) *actress*
Griffith, William Alexander *former mining company executive*
†Jenkins, Janet E. *state legislator, lawyer*
†Reed, Mary Lou *state legislator*
Rolphe, Ben Richard, Jr. *publishing company executive*
†Wheeler, Dennis Earl *mining company executive, lawyer*

Craigmont
†McPherson, James L. *school system administrator*

Eagle
†Carlson, Herb *state legislator*

Emmett
Farnham, Wallace Dean *historian*
Holverson, Harmon E. *family practice physician*

Idaho Falls
Harris, Darryl Wayne *publishing executive*
Newman, Stanley Ray *oil refining company executive*
Reich, Charles William *nuclear physicist*
Riemke, Richard Allan *mechanical engineer*
Stosich, Davidjohn *company executive*
Williams, Phyllis Cutforth *retired realtor*
†Woodall, David Monroe *research engineer*

Island Park
Stratford, Ray Paul *electrical engineer, consultant*

Jerome
†Bell, Maxine Toolson *librarian, state legislator*

Ketchum
Earle, Arthur Scott *plastic surgeon*
Hogue, Terry Glynn *lawyer*

Kimberly
†Carter, David LaVere *soil scientist, researcher, consultant*

Lewiston
Chinchinian, Harry *pathologist, educator*
McCann, William Vern, Jr. *lawyer*
†Morgan, Glen D. *superintendent*
Peterson, Philip Everett *legal educator*
Ware, Marcus John *lawyer*

Mc Call
Evans, Darrell J. *art educator*

Meridian
†Lance, Alan George *lawyer, legislator*

Moscow
Bartlett, Robert Watkins *academic dean, metallurgist*
Bobisud, Larry Eugene *mathematics educator*
Bray, R(obert) Bruce *music educator*
Butterfield, Samuel Hale *former government official and educator*
Crawford, Don Lee *microbiologist*
†DeShazer, James Arthur *agricultural engineer, educator, administrator*
Force, Ronald Wayne *librarian*
†Hendee, John Clare *college dean, natural resources educator*
Jackson, Melbourne Leslie *chemical engineering educator and administrator, consultant*
Jacobsen, Richard T. *mechanical engineering educator*
LeTourneau, Duane John *biochemist, educator*
Martin, Boyd Archer *political science educator emeritus*
Miller, Maynard Malcolm *geologist, educator, research foundation director, explorer, state legislator*
Peterson, Charles Loren *agricultural engineer, educator*
Renfrew, Malcolm MacKenzie *chemist, educator*
Roberts, Lorin Watson *botanist, educator*
†Schroeder, Gary Joseph *business owner, state legislator, writer*
†Seeger, Leinaala Robinson *law librarian, educator*
Shreeve, Jean'ne Marie *chemist, educator*
Zinser, Elisabeth Ann *university president*

Mountain Home
†Wetherell, Claire *state legislator*

Payette
†Hartung, Mary *state legislator*
Ilett, Frank, Jr. *trucking company executive*
Jones, Donna Marilyn *real estate broker, legislator*

Pocatello
Bowen, Richard Lee *academic administrator, political science educator*
Hillyard, Ira William *pharmacologist, educator*
†Hofman, Elaine D. *state legislator*
Jackson, Allen Keith *museum administrator*
†Lloyd, Mary Ellen *state legislator*
Nelson, Arthur Alexander, Jr. *university dean, pharmacist*
Nye, W. Marcus W. *lawyer*
Sagness, Richard Lee *education educator, former academic dean*
Seeley, Rod Ralph *physiology educator*
Stanek, Alan Edward *music educator*
Wilson, Albert Eugene *nuclear engineering educator*

Post Falls
†Chamberlain, Barbara Kaye *state legislator*

Rigby
Peterson, Erle Vidaillet *retired metallurgical engineer*

Rupert
†Antone, Steve *state legislator, farmer*
Bellwood, Sherman Jean *arbitrator, consultant, retired judge*

Saint Maries
Carlson, George Arthur *artist*

Sandpoint
Glock, Charles Young *sociologist*
Murray, James Michael *law librarian*

Sun Valley
†Bryant, Woodrow Wesley *architect*
Janss, William Cluff *resort development executive*
†McMillen, Darryl Charles *architect*
†Nickelson, Donald Eugene *brokerage house executive*

Twin Falls
†Jones, Douglas Raymond *farming executive, state legislator*
†Stubbs, Mark Darwin *lawyer*

ILLINOIS

Abbott Park
Burnham, Duane Lee *pharmaceutical company executive*
Coughlan, Gary Patrick *pharmaceutical company executive*
Hodgson, Thomas Richard *health care company executive*
Lussen, John Frederick *pharmaceutical laboratory executive*
Sasahara, Arthur Asao *cardiologist, educator, researcher*

Addison
Brunken, Gerald Walter, Sr. *manufacturing company executive*

Alton
Heuertz, Sarah Jane *dentist*
Hoagland, Karl King, Jr. *lawyer*
King, Ordie Herbert, Jr. *oral pathologist*
Minsker, Robert Stanley *consultant, former industrial relations executive*
Schlafly, Phyllis Stewart *author*
Schnabel, John Henry *music educator*
Struif, Leo James *lawyer*

AMF Ohare
Fisher, Patricia Sweeney *business executive, lawyer*
Pope, John Charles *airline company executive*

Antioch
Strang, Charles Daniel *marine engine manufacturing company executive*

Argonne
Appelman, Evan Hugh *chemist*
Berger, Edmond Louis *theoretical physicist*
†Berkowitz, Joseph *physicist, physical chemist, researcher*
†Blander, Milton *chemist*
Carpenter, John Marland *engineer, physicist*
†Chang, Yoon Il *nuclear engineer*
Derrick, Malcolm *physicist*
Ferraro, John Ralph *chemist*
Fields, Paul Robert *research nuclear chemist, consultant*
†Green, David William *chemist, educator*
Herzenberg, Caroline Stuart Littlejohn *physicist*
Jorgensen, James Douglas *research physicist*
Krauss, Alan Robert *physicist*
Kumar, Romesh *chemical engineer*
Martin, Ronald Lavern *physicist*
†Morss, Lester Robert *chemist*
Nolen, Jerry Aften, Jr. *physicist*
†Perlow, Gilbert J(erome) *physicist, editor*
Peshkin, Murray *physicist*
Schiffer, John Paul *physicist*
Schriesheim, Alan *research administrator*
†Steindler, Martin Joseph *chemist*
†Zeidman, Benjamin *nuclear physicist*

Arlington Heights
Baumann, Daniel E. *newspaper executive*
Church, Herbert Stephen, Jr. *retired construction company executive*
†Dickau, John C. *religious organization executive*
†Di Corcia, Edward Thomas *oil company executive*
Fellers, James Davison, Jr. (Dave Fellers) *professional association executive*
†Hughes, John *chemical company executive*
†Jenny, Daniel P. *retired engineer*
Johnson, Clifford R. *retired retail executive, consultant*
†Lampinen, John A. *newspaper editor*
Lewin, Seymour Zalman *chemistry educator, consultant*
Nerlinger, John William *association executive*
Ness, James McCullie, Jr. *sales and marketing executive*
†Paddock, Robert Young *publisher*
†Paddock, Stuart R., Jr. *publishing executive*
Pochyly, Donald Frederick *physician, university administrator*
†Ray, Douglas *newspaper editor*
Roderick, William Rodney *academic administrator*
Stratman, Frank Herman *travel company executive*
†terHorst, Cheryl Ann *journalist*
Wine-Banks, Jill Susan *lawyer*

Aurora
Alschuler, Sam *lawyer*
Ball, William James *pediatrician*
†Deuchler, Suzanne Louise *state legislator*
Etheredge, Forest DeRoyce *former state senator, university administrator*
Halloran, Kathleen L. *financial executive, accountant*
†Lindner, Patricia Reid *state representative, lawyer*
Lowe, Ralph Edward *lawyer*
Tyler, Lloyd John *lawyer*
†Zarle, Thomas H. *university president*

Bannockburn
Vuckovich, Dragomir Michael *neurologist, educator*
Zorio, John William *financial services executive*

Barrington
Andler, Donald Andrew *marketing executive*
Bash, Philip Edwin *publishing executive*
Bassett, Robert Cochem *lawyer, publisher*
Baxter, Reginald Robert *investment company executive*
Edwards, Wilbur Shields *communications company executive*
†Farina, Nick Charles *investor relations consultant*
Kartalia, Mitchell P. *electrical equipment manufacturing executive*
Koelling, Herbert Lee *printing company executive*
Kroha, Bradford King *electronics manufacturing corporation executive*
Ligare, Kathleen Meredith *sales and marketing executive*
Marshall, Gordon Bruce *construction company executive*
Mathis, Jack David *advertising executive*
Rey, Carmen Rosello *food product researcher*
†Victor, Michael Gary *lawyer, physician*
Woltz, Kenneth Allen *consulting executive*
Wyatt, James Frank, Jr. *lawyer*
†Zeller, Joseph Paul *advertising executive*

Barrington Hills
Spak, Lorin Mitchell *retired office products industry executive*

Batavia
†Bardeen, William Allan *research physicist*
Chrisman, Bruce Lowell *physicist, administrator*
Jonckheere, Alan Mathew *physicist*
Lach, Joseph Theodore *physicist*
Nash, E(dward) Thomas *physicist*
Pewitt, Edward Gale *laboratory administrator, research physicist*
Tollestrup, Alvin Virgil *physicist*

Bedford Park
Herbert, Victor James *association executive*
†Hough, Richard T. *chemical company executive*
†Wenstrup, H. Daniel *chemical executive*

Belleville
Bauman, John Duane *lawyer*
Berkley, Gary L. *newspaper publisher*
Boyle, Richard Edward *lawyer*
Coghill, William Thomas, Jr. *lawyer*
Connors, Jimmy (James Scott Connors) *professional tennis player*
Ferguson, John Marshall *retired federal magistrate judge*
Fietsam, Robert Charles *accountant*
Heiligenstein, Christian E. *lawyer*
Hess, Frederick J. *lawyer*
Keleher, James P. *bishop*
†Kirchoff, Virgil L. *oil company executive, consultant*
Parham, James Robert *lawyer*
Stevens, C. Glenn *judge*

Belvidere
Keller, Harold William *chemical company executive*

Bensenville
Greanias, Stanley Louis *coffee company executive*
Lewis, Darrell L. *retail executive*
Matera, Richard Ernest *minister*

Benton
Foreman, James Louis *retired judge*
Gilbert, J. Phil *federal judge*

Berwyn
Misurec, Rudolf *physician, surgeon*

Bloomingdale
Pedicini, Louis James *manufacturing company executive*

Bloomington
Baer, Kenneth Peter *farmer cooperative executive*
Bower, Marvin D. *insurance company executive*
Bragg, Michael Ellis *lawyer*
Bray, Robert C. *literature educator*
Brown, Jared *theater director, educator, writer*
Callis, Bruce *insurance company executive*
Curry, Alan Chester *insurance company executive*
Edmondson, James William (Jay Edmondson) *insurance company executive*
Engelkes, Donald John *insurance company executive*
Goebel, William Mathers *lawyer*
Gregor, Marlene Pierce *primary educator, elementary science consultant*
Johnson, Earle Bertrand *insurance executive*
Jones, Norman Thomas *service executive*
Jordan, Leo John *lawyer*
Joslin, Roger Scott *insurance company executive*
Merwin, Davis Underwood *newspaper executive*
Miller, Duane Leon *insurance company executive*
Montgomery, William Adam *lawyer*
Myers, Minor, Jr. *college administrator, political science educator*
Nelson, Walter Gerald *insurance company executive*
Prescott, Richard Paul, Jr. *computer company consultant*
Rust, Edward Barry, Jr. *insurance company executive, lawyer*
Shelley, Edward Herman, Jr. *retired insurance company executive*
Stevenson, Ernest Vail *retired farmer cooperative executive*
Sullivan, Laura Patricia *lawyer, insurance company executive*
Trosino, Vincent Joseph *insurance company executive*
Vayo, David Joseph *composer, music educator*
Vincent, Norman L. *insurance company executive*
Wamboldt, Donald George *insurance executive*
Watkins, Lloyd Irion *university president*
Webb, O. Glenn *farm supplies company executive*
†White, John, Jr. *insurance company executive, farm organization executive*
†Wills, Edgar W. (Bill) *newspaper editor*
Wright, Charles Richard *insurance executive*

Blue Island
Kollmann, Hilda Hanna *banker*

Bolingbrook
†Meyer, James Henry *state representative, insurance broker*
Price, Theodora Hadzisteliou *social worker*

Breese
†Granberg, Kurt Michael *lawyer*

Brimfield
Kress, Ralph Herman *manufacturing company executive*

Broadview
Hohage, Frederick William *automotive parts company executive*

Brookfield
Pawley, Ray Lynn *zoological park herpetology curator*
Rabb, George Bernard *zoologist*

Buffalo Grove
†Clayton, Verna Lewis *state legislator*
Denov, Sam *musician*
Jette, Lorraine Doris *letter shop services executive*
Kaplan, Mitchell Philip *consulting engineer, marketing executive*
Siegel, Sid *composer, lyricist*

Burr Ridge
Danly, Donald Robert *retired manufacturing company executive*
Peterson, Carl Roy *lawyer*
Sund, Jeffrey Owen *publishing company executive*

Cairo
†Cobb, J. *bishop*

Calumet City
Edwards, James Clifford *finance company executive*
Self, Madison Allen *chemical company executive*

Carbondale
Ammon, Harry *history educator*
†Bauner, Ruth Elizabeth *library administrator, reference librarian*
Best, Joel Gordon *sociology educator*
†Brown, James Montgomery *English language and literature educator emeritus, academic administrator*
Buckley, John Joseph, Jr. *health care executive*
Burr, Brooks Milo *zoology educator*
Casey, John P. *special education educator*
†Chugh, Yoginder Paul *mining engineering educator*
Clemons, John Robert *lawyer*
Covington, Patricia Ann *university administrator*
Derge, David Richard *political science educator*
Dixon, Billy Gene *academic administrator*
Elkins, Donald Marcum *associate dean, agronomy educator*
†Eynon, Thomas Grant *sociology educator*
Fladeland, Betty *historian, educator*
Gilbert, Glenn Gordon *linguistics educator*
Guyon, John Carl *university administrator*
Habiger, Richard J. *lawyer*
Hahn, Lewis Edwin *philosopher, retired educator*
Handler, Jerome Sidney *anthropology educator*
Harper, Robert Alexander *geography educator*
Hart, James Warren *athletic director, restaurant owner, former professional football player*
Haynsworth, Harry Jay, IV *lawyer, educator*
†Houdek, Frank George *law librarian*
Kionka, Edward James *lawyer*
Lesar, Hiram Henry *lawyer, educator*
†Mead, John Stanley *university administrator*
Mohlenbrock, Robert Herman, Jr. *botanist, educator*
Orthwein, William Coe *mechanical engineer*
Rubin, Harris B. *psychology educator*
Schilpp, Paul Arthur *philosopher, editor, clergyman*
Smith, James Gilbert *electrical engineer*
Snyder, Carolyn Ann *university dean, librarian*
Snyder, Charles Royce *sociologist, educator*
Somit, Albert *political educator*
Spees, Emil Ray *philosophy educator*
Takayama, Akira *economics educator*
Tao, Rongjia *physicist, educator*
Verduin, Jacob *botany educator*
†Webb, Howard William, Jr. *humanities educator, university official*
Whitlock, John Joseph *museum director*
Wills, Walter Joe *agricultural marketing educator*
Woodbridge, Hensley Charles *retired librarian, foreign languages educator*
Wotiz, John Henry *chemist, educator*

Carlinville
Mc Conagha, Glenn Lowery *chancellor emeritus*
Schweizer, Melvin *food products executive*
Southwell, Leonard J. *dairy corporation executive*

Carmi
Edwards, Judith Elizabeth *advertising executive*

Carol Stream
Berkley, James Donald *editor*
†Catone, Lucio *manufacturing executive*
Coffman, Roy Walter, III *publishing company executive*
Franzen, Janice Marguerite Gosnell *magazine editor*
Fricke, H. Walter *minister*
Myra, Harold Lawrence *publisher*
†Pond, Byron O. *manufacturing company executive*
Schmerold, Wilfried Lothar *dermatologist*
Shorney, George Herbert *publishing executive*
Taylor, Kenneth Nathaniel *publishing executive, author*
Yancey, Philip David *editor, author*

Carpentersville
Wilson, Delbert Ray *publisher, author*

Carrollton
Strickland, Hugh Alfred *lawyer*

Carthage
Glidden, John Redmond *lawyer*

Cary
Bowen, John Richard *former chemical company executive*
Schultz, Theodore Edward *retail executive*

Centralia
Wargo, Tom *professional golfer*

Champaign
Arnould, Richard Julius *economist, educator, consultant*
Bailey, Andrew Dewey, Jr. *accounting educator*
Baker, Jack Sherman *architect, designer, educator*
Batzli, George Oliver *ecology educator*
Bender, Paul Edward *lawyer*
Birdzell, Samuel Henry *hospital administrator*
Brems, Hans Julius *economist, educator*
Brighton, Gerald David *accounting educator*
Bryan, William Royal *finance educator*
Buschbach, Thomas Charles *geologist, consultant*
Cammack, Trank Emerson *retired university dean*
Cartwright, Keros *hydrogeologist, researcher*
†Changnon, Stanley A., Jr. *research executive*
Clark, Roger Gordon *educational administrator*
Cohen, Jozef *psychophysicist, educator*
Cribbet, John Edward *legal educator, former university chancellor*
†Crummey, Donald Edward *history educator*
Davis, James Henry *psychology educator*
Due, John Fitzgerald *economist, educator emeritus*
Dulany, Elizabeth Gjelsness *university press administrator*
Easley, John Allen (Jack Easley) *science educator*
Eilbracht, Lee Paul *retired association executive*
Eriksen, Charles Walter *psychologist, educator*
Estabrook, Leigh Stewart *dean, library science educator*
Flanders, Dwight Prescott *economist*
Foreman, John Richard *journalist*
Frampton, George Thomas *legal educator*
Frankel, Marvin *economist, educator*
Fredrickson, L(awrence) Thomas *composer*
Friedberg, Maurice *Russian literature educator*
Friedman, Joan M. *computer consultant*
Froom, William Watkins *banker*
Garvey, John Charles *violist, conductor, retired music educator*
Gross, David Lee *geologist*
Herzog, Beverly Leah *hydrogeologist*
Humphreys, Lloyd Girton *research psychologist, educator*
Jackson, Billy Morrow *artist, retired art educator*
Kanet, Roger Edward *political science educator, university administrator*
Kanfer, Frederick H. *psychologist, educator*
Kindt, John Warren, Sr. *lawyer, educator, consultant*
Knox, Charles Milton *purchasing agent, consultant*
†Koenker, Diana P. *history educator*
Kotoske, Roger Allen *artist, educator*
Krause, Harry Dieter *lawyer, educator*
Kruger, William Arnold *consulting civil engineer*
Krummel, Donald William *librarian, educator*
Kuck, David Jerome *computer system researcher, administrator*
Levin, Geoffrey Arthur *botanist*
†Love, Joseph L. *history educator, cultural studies center administrator*
Maggs, Peter Blount *lawyer, educator*
Mamer, Stuart Mies *lawyer*
Mapother, Dillon Edward *physicist, university official*
†McCulloh, Judith Marie *editor*
Meyer, August Christopher, Jr. *broadcasting company executive, lawyer*
Miller, Harold Arthur *lawyer*
Neumann, Frederick Loomis *accounting educator, academic administrator, consultant*
Nowak, John E. *law educator*
O'Neill, John Joseph *speech educator*
†Orr, Daniel *educator, economist*
Perry, Kenneth Wilbur *accounting educator*
Peshkin, Alan *education educator*
Peterson, Roger Lyman *insurance company executive*
Philipp, Walter Viktor *mathematician, educator*
Replinger, John Gordon *architect*
Ridlen, Samuel Franklin *agriculture educator*
Rotunda, Ronald Daniel *law educator, consultant*
Schoenfeld, Hanns-Martin Walter *accounting educator*
Schowalter, William Raymond *college dean, educator*
Sechrist, Chalmers F., Jr. *electrical engineering educator*
Semonin, Richard Gerard *state official*
Shupp, Franklin Richard *economist*
Slichter, Charles Pence *physicist, educator*
†Smarr, Larry Lee *science administrator, educator, astrophysicist*
Smith, Ralph Alexander *cultural and educational policy educator*
Smith, Robert Lee *agriculturalist*
Spence, Clark Christian *history educator*
Spodek, Bernard *curriculum educator*
Sprenkle, Case Middleton *economics educator*
Sprugel, George, Jr. *ecologist*
Stapleton, Harvey James *physics educator*
†Surles, Richard Hurlbut, Jr. *law librarian*
Vedder, Byron Charles *newspaper executive*
Wajenberg, Arnold Sherman *retired librarian, educator*
Wert, Lucille Mathena *librarian, educator*
Wolfram, Stephen *physicist, computer company executive*

Charleston
Buckellew, William Franklin *education educator*
Jorns, David Lee *university president*
Laible, Jon Morse *college dean, former mathematics educator*
Price, Dalias Adolph *geography educator*
Rives, Stanley Gene *university president emeritus*

Chester
Welge, Donald Edward *food manufacturing executive*

Chicago
Abcarian, Herand *surgeon, educator*
Abrams, Lee Norman *lawyer*
Abrams, Susan Elizabeth *book editor, publisher*
Abularach, Gloria Nancy *education specialist*
Acker, Frederick George *lawyer*
Acs, Joseph Steven *transportation engineering consultant*
Adair, Wendell Hinton, Jr. *lawyer*
Adams, Hall, Jr. (Cap Adams) *advertising agency executive*
Adams, John Richard *psychiatrist, educator*
Adams, Roy M. *lawyer, writer*
Addy, Frederick Seale *oil company executive*
Adelman, Stanley Joseph *lawyer*
Adelman, Steven Herbert *lawyer*
Adkins, Arthur William Hope *humanities educator*
Adler, Mortimer Jerome *philosopher, author*
Africano, Nicholas *artist*
Agarwal, Gyan Chand *engineering educator*
Agnew, David M. *lawyer*
Aitay, Victor *violinist, music educator*
Akerson, Daniel Francis *telecommunications industry executive*
Akos, Francis *violinist*
Aland, Robert H. *lawyer*
Albrecht, Ronald Frank *anesthesiologist*
Aldrich, Thomas Lawrence *lawyer*
Alesia, James H(enry) *federal judge*
Alexander, William Henry *lawyer*
Alexandroff, Mirron (Mike Alexandroff) *academic administrator*
Alexis, Geraldine M. *lawyer*
Aliber, Robert Z. *economist, educator*
Allan, Stanley Nance *architect*
Allard, Jean *lawyer, urban planner*
Allen, Belle *management consulting firm executive, communications company executive*
Allen, Richard Blose *legal editor, lawyer*
Allen, Thomas Draper *lawyer*
Allgyer, Robert Earl *accounting company executive*
†Almeida, Richard J. *finance company executive*
Almen, Lowell Gordon *church official*
Alschuler, Albert W. *law educator*
Altheimer, Alan J. *lawyer*
Altman, Louis *lawyer, author, educator*
†Altmann, Jeanne *zoologist, educator*
Altmann, Stuart Allen *biologist, educator*
Amato, Isabella Antonia *real estate executive*
Amberg, Thomas Law *public relations executive*
Ambrose, Gerald A. *lawyer*
Amstadter, Laurence *retired architect*
Anagnost, Themis John *lawyer*
Andersen, Burton Robert *physician, educator*
Andersen, Wayne R. *federal judge*
Anderson, David A. *lawyer*
Anderson, Donald W. *lawyer*
Anderson, Douglas Charles *juvenile probation administrator*
Anderson, J. Trent *lawyer*
Anderson, John Thomas *lawyer*
Anderson, Jon Stephen *newswriter*
Anderson, Kimball Richard *lawyer*
Anderson, Louise Eleanor *biochemistry educator*
Anderson, William Cornelius, III *lawyer*
Andreoli, Kathleen Gainor *nurse, educator, administrator*
Angelo, Percy L. *lawyer*
Angle, John Edwin *lawyer*
Angst, Gerald L. *lawyer*
†Annable, James Edward *economist*
Anshaw, Carol *writer*
Anthony, Michael Francis *lawyer*
Anvaripour, M. A. *lawyer*
Apcel, Melissa Anne *lawyer*
Appel, Nina S. *law educator, dean*
Appelson, Wallace Bertrand *academic administrator*
Applebaum, Edward Leon *otolaryngologist, educator*
Appleton, Arthur Ivar *retired electric products manufacturing company executive, horse breeder*
Archambault, Bennett *corporate executive*
Archer, James G. *lawyer*
Arditti, Fred D. *economist, educator*
Arlow, Allan Joseph *lawyer*
Armstrong, Edwin Richard *lawyer, publisher, editor*
†Arnason, Barry Gilbert Wyatt *neurologist, educator*
Arnsdorf, Morton Frank *cardiologist, educator*
Aronson, Howard Isaac *linguist, educator*
Aronson, Simon H. *lawyer*
Aronson, Virginia L. *lawyer*
Arrington, Michael Browne *travel management company executive*
Arroyo, Robert Edward *lawyer*
Artner, Alan Gustav *art critic, journalist*
Artwick, Frederic *lawyer*
Arzbaecher, Robert C(harles) *research institute executive, electrical engineer, researcher*
Ash, J. Marshall *mathematician, educator*
Ashley, James Wheeler *lawyer*
†Ashwill, Terry M. *advertising executive*
Aspen, Marvin Edward *federal judge*
Athas, Gus James *lawyer*
Athens, Andrew A. *steel company executive*
Auerbach, Marshall Jay *lawyer*
Austen, Ralph A. *historian, educator*
Austin, Richard William *lawyer*
Austin, Robert B. *lawyer*
Auwarter, Franklin Paul *lawyer*
Avedisian, Armen George *industrialist, financier*
Avery, Cameron Scott *lawyer*
Avison, David *photographer*
†Axelrod, David Alan *lawyer*
Axley, Frederick William *lawyer*
Babcock, Lyndon Ross, Jr. *environmental engineer, educator*
Badel, Julie *lawyer*
Badger, Charles H. *manufacturing company executive*
Baer, John Richard Frederick *lawyer*
Baetz, W. Timothy *lawyer*
Baffes, Thomas Gus *cardiac surgeon, lawyer*
Bahadur, Chance *retail executive*
Bailey, Orville Taylor *neuropathologist*
Bailey, Robert, Jr. *advertising executive*
Bailey, Robert Short *lawyer*
Baird, Douglas Gordon *law educator*
Baird, Russell Miller *lawyer*
Baker, Donald *lawyer*
Baker, James Edward Sproul *retired lawyer*
†Baker, James Nettleton *railroad association executive*
Baker, Pamela *lawyer*
Bakwin, Edward Morris *banker*
†Balasi, Mark Geoffrey *architect*
Baloun, John Charles *wholesale grocery company executive*
Balousek, John B. *advertising executive*
Balz, Douglas Charles *journalist*
Balzekas, Stanley, Jr. *museum director*
Ban, Stephen Dennis *natural gas industry research institute executive*
†Banik, Douglas Heil *advertising executive*
†Banks, Deirdre Margaret *church organization administrator*
Banoff, Sheldon Irwin *lawyer*
Banta, Merle Henry *graphics equipment and service company executive*
Baptist, Allwyn J. *health care consultant*
Barany, Kate *biophysics educator*
Barbour, Claude Marie *minister*
Bard, John Franklin *consumer products executive*
Barenberg, Sumner *polymer physicist, business executive*
Barker, Emmett Wilson, Jr. *trade association executive*
Barker, Walter Lee *thoracic surgeon*
Barker, William Thomas *lawyer*
Barliant, Ronald *federal judge*
Barnard, Morton John *lawyer*
Barnard, Robert N. *lawyer*
†Barnard, Susan C. *church administrator*
Barnes, James Garland, Jr. *lawyer*
Barnett, Robert L. *utilities executive*
Barnette, Dennis Arthur *management consultant*
†Barney, Carol Ross *architect*
Barr, John Robert *lawyer*
Barrett, Roger Watson *lawyer*
Barron, Howard Robert *lawyer*
Barrow, Charles Herbert *investment banker*
Barry, Norman J., Jr. *lawyer*
Bartholomay, William C. *insurance brokerage company executive, professional baseball team executive*
Bartlit, Fred Holcomb, Jr. *lawyer, educator*
Bartoletti, Bruno *conductor*
Barton, Evan Mansfield *physician*
Bartter, Brit Jeffrey *investment banker*
Baruch, Hurd *lawyer*
Bashwiner, Steven Lacelle *lawyer*
Batlle, Daniel Campi *nephrologist*
Bauer, William Joseph *federal judge*
Baugher, Peter V. *lawyer*
Baum, Bernard Helmut *sociologist, educator*
†Bauman, Stephen P. *minister, church administrator*
Baumgartner, William Hans, Jr. *lawyer*
Baumhart, Raymond Charles *church administrator*
Bayer, Gary Richard *advertising executive*
Bearden, Patricia Ann *education educator*
Beattie, Janet Holtzman *accounting firm executive*
Beatty, William Kaye *medical bibliography educator*
Beaty, Harry Nelson *internist, educator, university dean*
Beck, Joan Wagner *journalist*
Beck, Philip S. *lawyer*
†Beck, Robert N. *nuclear medicine educator*
Becker, Gary Stanley *economist, educator*
Becker, Theodore Michaelson *lawyer*
Beeby, Thomas H. *architect*
Beecher, William John *zoologist, museum director*
Beem, Jack Darrel *lawyer*
Begando, Joseph Sheridan *former university chancellor, educator*
Beggan, John Francis *lawyer*

Beigl, William *physician, naturopath, hypnotist, acupuncturist, consultant*
Beitler, J. Paul *real estate developer*
Belfour, Ed *professional hockey player*
Bell, Clark Wayne *business editor, educator*
Bell, George Antonio *professional baseball player*
†Bellas, Jean *architect*
Bellow, Saul C. *writer*
Bellows, Randall Trueblood *ophthalmologist, educator*
†Belluschi, Anthony C. *architect*
Belmore, F. Martin *lawyer*
Bender, Janet Pines *artist*
†Bennett, Beverly *newspaper editor*
Bennett, Lerone, Jr. *magazine editor, author*
Bennett, M(ary) Elizabeth *lawyer*
Bennett, Russell Odbert *lawyer*
Bensinger, Peter Benjamin *consulting firm executive*
Bentley, Peter John Hilton *lawyer*
Berens, Mark Harry *lawyer*
†Berg, Mildred M. *church administrator*
Berger, Robert Michael *lawyer*
Berghoff, John C., Jr. *lawyer*
Bergonia, Raymond David *venture capitalist*
Bergstrom, Robert William *lawyer*
†Berk, Harlan Joseph *numismatist, writer, antiquarian*
Berkery, Michael John *management consultant*
Berland, Abel Edward *lawyer, realtor*
Berlin, Stanton Henry *lawyer*
†Berman, Arthur Leonard *state senator*
Berman, Bennett I. *lawyer*
Berman, Howard Allen *rabbi*
Bernadetta, Sister Maria *special education educator*
Bernard, Frank Charles *lawyer*
Bernardin, Joseph Louis Cardinal *archbishop, university chancellor*
Bernatowicz, Frank Allen *management consultant, expert witness*
Berner, Robert Lee, Jr. *lawyer*
Bernick, David M. *lawyer*
Berning, Larry D. *lawyer*
Bernstein, H. Bruce *lawyer*
Bernstein, Howard L. *lawyer*
Berolzheimer, Karl *lawyer*
Berry, Alan M. *lawyer*
Berry, John Willard *librarian, consultant*
Berry, Leonidas Harris *gastroenterologist, internist*
†Bess, Ronald W. *sales executive*
Betke, James E. *lawyer*
Betts, Henry Brognard *physician, health facility administrator, educator*
Betz, Hans Dieter *theology educator*
Bevington, David Martin *English literature educator*
Bezman, Victor H. *lawyer*
Bidwell, Charles Edward *sociologist, educator*
Biebel, Paul Philip, Jr. *lawyer*
Bielawski, Alan P. *lawyer*
Bierig, Jack R. *lawyer*
Biggles, Richard Robert *marketing executive*
Biggs, Robert Dale *Near Eastern studies educator*
Bilandic, Michael A. *state supreme court chief justice, former mayor*
Bishop, Oliver Richard *state official*
Bitner, John Howard *lawyer*
Bixby, Frank Lyman *lawyer*
Bjorneberg, Paul Grant *public relations executive*
Blair, Bowen *investment banker*
Blair, Edward McCormick *investment banker*
Blakely, Robert John *retired journalist, educator*
Blakemore, Thomas F. *lawyer*
Blanco, Jim L. *lawyer*
Blatt, Richard Lee *lawyer*
Bleveans, John *lawyer*
Bliwas, Ronald Lee *advertising agency executive*
Block, George Edward *surgeon, educator*
Block, Neal Jay *lawyer*
Block, Philip Dee, III *investment counselor*
Bloom, Christopher Arthur *lawyer*
Blount, Michael Eugene *lawyer*
†Bluhm, Neil Gary *real estate company executive*
Blum, Michael Stephen *financial services executive*
Blum, Walter J. *lawyer, educator*
Blumberg, Avrom Aaron *physical chemistry educator*
Blutter, Joan Wernick *interior designer*
Boberg, Wayne D. *lawyer*
Bockelman, John Richard *lawyer*
Bodine, Laurence *lawyer, editor, marketer*
Boers, Terry John *sportswriter, radio and television personality*
Boggess, Thomas Phillip, III *graphic arts company executive*
Boggs, Joseph Dodridge *pediatric pathologist, educator*
Bohne, Carl John, Jr. *accountant*
Boies, Wilber H. *lawyer*
Boley, John N. *lawyer*
Bolnick, Howard Jeffrey *insurance company executive*
Bomchill, Fern Cheryl *lawyer*
Bonser, Sidney Henry *diversified manufacturing company executive*
Boodell, Thomas Joseph, Jr. *lawyer*
Booth, Wayne Clayson *English literature and rhetoric educator, author*
Borders, Thomas C. *lawyer*
Boris, William O. *advertising agency executive*
Borleis, Melvin William *management consultant*
Bornholdt, Laura Anna *university administrator*
Bornstein, Deborah H. *lawyer*
Boshes, Louis D. *physician, scientist, educator*
Bosselman, Fred Paul *law educator*
Botica, Matthew J. *lawyer*
Bott, Harold Sheldon *accountant, management consultant*
Bottom, Dale Coyle *association executive*
Bouchard, Craig Thomas *international banker*
Bouma, Robert Edwin *lawyer, diversified company executive*
Bowe, William John *lawyer*
Bowen, Stephen Stewart *lawyer, educator*
Bowen, William Joseph *management consultant*
Bower, Bruce Lester *lawyer*
Bower, Glen Landis *lawyer*
Bowman, Barbara Taylor *academic administrator*
Bowman, George Arthur, Jr. *federal judge*
Bowman, James Edward *physician, educator*
†Bowman, John *architectural firm executive*
Bowman, Leah *fashion designer, consultant, photographer, educator*
Bowytz, Robert B. *lawyer*
Boyce, David Edward *transportation and regional science educator*
Boyd, David J. *lawyer*
Boyd, Willard Lee *museum administrator, educator, lawyer*
Boyer, John William *history educator, dean*
Bradburn, Norman M. *behavioral science educator*
Braidwood, Linda Schreiber *archaeologist*
Braidwood, Robert J. *archaeologist, educator*
Brake, Cecil Clifford *diversified manufacturing executive*
Bramnik, Robert Paul *lawyer*
†Brashears, Donald Robert *advertising agency executive*
Brashler, William *author*
Braun, W(illiam) David *lawyer*
Breakstone, Donald S. *lawyer*
Brennan, Bernard Francis *retail chain store executive*
Brennan, Edward A. *merchandising, insurance and real estate executive*
†Brennan, James Joseph *lawyer*
Brennan, Richard J. *lawyer*
Brennan, Richard Snyder *lawyer, bank executive*
†Breslin, Michael Edward *advertising agency executive, lawyer*
Bresnahan, James Francis *medical ethics educator*
Breyer, Norman Nathan *metallurgical engineering educator, consultant*
Brice, James John *retired accounting firm executive*
Brice, Roger Thomas *lawyer*
Brickhouse, John B. (Jack Brickhouse) *sports broadcaster*
Bridewell, David Alexander *lawyer*
Bridgman, Thomas Francis *lawyer*
Brinkman, John Anthony *historian, educator*
Brissie, Eugene Field, Jr. *publisher*
Britton, Dennis A. *newspaper editor*
Brizzolara, Charles Anthony *lawyer*
Brodsky, William J. *futures options exchange executive*
Brooker, Thomas Kimball *oil company executive*
Brooks, Gwendolyn *writer, poet*
Brooks, Robert Liss *lawyer*
Brophy, Joan Edmonds *lawyer*
Brotman, Barbara Louise *columnist, writer*
Broutman, Lawrence Jay *materials engineering educator*
Brown, Donald James, Jr. *lawyer*
Brown, Gregory K. *lawyer*
Brown, Richard Harris *telecommunications industry executive*
Brown, Richard Holbrook *library administrator, historian*
Brown, Rowine Hayes *physician, former medical administrator*
Browning, Don Spencer *religion educator*
Brubaker, Charles William *architect*
†Bruckman, Carol Jeannette *advertising executive*
Brueschke, Erich Edward *physician, researcher, educator*
Brumback, Charles Tiedtke *newspaper executive*
Brummel, Mark Joseph *magazine editor*
Bruner, Stephen C. *lawyer*
Brutlag, Rodney Sheldon *management consultant*
Bryan, John Henry *food and consumer products company executive*
Bryson, Cheryl Blackwell *lawyer*
Bua, Nicholas John *retired federal judge*
Buchholz, Edward J. *lawyer*
†Buck, Genevieve Carol *fashion journalist*
Buckle, Frederick Tarifero *international holding company executive, political and business intelligence analyst*
Buckley, Joseph Paul, III *polygraph specialist*
Buckner, James Lowell *dentist*
Budenholzer, Roland Anthony *mechanical engineering educator*
Buenz, John Buechler *architect*
Bueschel, David Alan *management consultant*
†Bugielski, Robert Joseph *state legislator*
Bulger, Brian Wegg *lawyer*
Bumsted, Robert Milton *physician*
Bunge, Jonathan Gunn *lawyer*
Burack, Elmer Howard *management educator*
Burdelik, Thomas Louis *lawyer*
Burditt, George Miller, Jr. *lawyer*
Burger, Mary Louise *psychologist, educator*
Burgess, Robert Kyle *lawyer*
Burgett, George L. *lawyer*
Burhoe, Brian W. *automotive service executive*
Burhoe, Ralph Wendell *religion and science educator*
Burke, Thomas Joseph, Jr. *lawyer*
Burkey, Lee Melville *lawyer*
†Burrus, Clark *banker*
Burt, Robert Norcross *diversified manufacturing company executive*
Burton, Erlie P. *academic administrator*
Burton, Raymond Charles, Jr. *transportation company executive*
Busey, Roxane C. *lawyer*
Buss, Daniel Frank *environmental scientist*
Butler, Richard Dean *interior designer*
Butler, Robert Allan *psychologist, educator*
Butt, Edward Thomas, Jr. *lawyer*
Byman, Robert Leslie *lawyer*
Bynoe, Peter Charles Bernard *real estate developer, legal consultant*
Caccamo, Nicholas James *financial executive*
Cahan, James N. *lawyer*
Calderon, Alberto P. *mathematician, educator*
Caldwell, Ethel Louise Lynch *academic administrator*
Calenoff, Leonid *radiologist*
Callaway, Karen A(lice) *journalist*
Campbell, Bruce Crichton *hospital administrator*
Campbell, Calvin Arthur, Jr. *mining and plastics molding equipment manufacturing company executive*
Campbell, Edward Fay, Jr. *religion educator*
Campbell, Wendell Jerome *architect*
Camper, John Jacob *writer, university administrator*
Camras, Marvin *electrical and computer engineering educator, inventor*
†Canning, John Anthony, Jr. *venture capital company executive*
Caplis, Kevin J. *lawyer*
†Capparelli, R. Cary *marketing executive*
Cappo, Joseph C. *publisher*
Caray, Harry Christopher *sports announcer*
Carlin, Dennis J. *lawyer*
†Carlson, Marjorie J. *church administrator*
Carlson, Stephen Curtis *lawyer*
Carlson, Walter Carl *lawyer*
Carlton, Dennis William *economics educator*
Carney, Jean Kathryn *psychologist*
Carnow, Bertram Warren *occupational and environmental health consultant*
Caro, William Allan *physician*
Carone, Frank *medical educator, pathologist*
Carpenter, Allan *author, editor, publisher*
Carpenter, David William *lawyer*
Carren, Jeffrey P. *lawyer*
Carrier, Mark Anthony *professional football player*
†Carroll, Howard William *state senator, lawyer*
Carroll, James J. *lawyer*
Carroll, John M. *lawyer*
Carroll, William Kenneth *law educator, psychologist, theologian*
Carton, Laurence Alfred *lawyer*
Cassel, Christine Karen *physician*
Cassling, Donald Roger *lawyer*
†Cavalier, Frank N. *construction company executive, civil engineer*
Center, Robert A. *accounting firm executive*
Chabraja, Nicholas D. *lawyer*
Chacko, Samuel *association official*
†Chadwick, Joanne *church administrator*
Chaffetz, Hammond Edward *lawyer*
†Chaitin, Anthony *management services executive*
Chakrabarty, Ananda Mohan *microbiologist*
Chaleff, Carl Thomas *brokerage house executive*
Chambers, Donald Arthur *biochemistry educator*
Champagne, Ronald Oscar *academic administrator, mathematics educator*
†Champion, Charles F. *newspaper publishing executive*
†Chandler, John W. *biochemistry educator, ophthalmology educator*
†Chandler, John William *ophthalmologist, educator*
Chandler, Kent, Jr. *lawyer*
Chandrasekhar, Subrahmanyan *astrophysicist, educator*
Chanen, Franklin Allen *lawyer*
Chapman, Alger Baldwin *finance executive, lawyer*
Chapman, Howard Stuart *lawyer*
Chapman, Stephen James *columnist*
Charles, Allan G. *physician, educator*
Charlesworth, Brian *biologist, genetics and evolution educator*
Charlier, Roger Henri *oceanographer, geographer, educator*
Chartier, Janellen Olsen *airline service coordinator*
Chatterton, Robert Treat, Jr. *reproductive endocrinology educator*
Cheely, Daniel Joseph *lawyer*
Chefitz, Joel Gerald *lawyer*
Chelios, Christos K *professional hockey player*
Chen, Wai-Kai *electrical engineering and computer science educator, consultant*
Cherney, James Alan *lawyer*
Chiles, Stephen Michael *lawyer*
Chilstrom, Herbert Walfred *bishop*
Chlebowski, John Francis, Jr. *financial executive*
Chookaszian, Dennis Haig *financial executive*
Chorengel, Bernd *international hotel corporation executive*
Choyke, Phyllis May Ford (Mrs. Arthur Davis Choyke, Jr.) *management executive, editor, poet*
Christensen, George B. *lawyer*
Christiansen, Richard Dean *newspaper editor*
Chung, Joseph Sang-hoon *economics educator*
Chung, Paul Myungha *mechanical engineer, educator*
Ciccarone, Richard Anthony *financial executive*
†Ciccone, Richard *newspaper editor*
†Ciotola, Nicholas Anthony *financial executive*
Citrin, Phillip Marshall *retired lawyer*
Citron, Diane *lawyer*
†Claeys, Jerome Joseph, III *real estate company executive*
Clark, James Allen *lawyer, educator*
Clark, James E. *lawyer*
Clark, John Whitcomb *diagnostic radiologist*
Clarke, Philip Ream, Jr. *investment banker*
Clarke, Richard Stewart *security company executive*
Clay, John Ernest *lawyer*
Clayton, Robert Norman *chemist, educator*
Clemenceau, Paul B. *lawyer*
Clemens, Richard Glenn *lawyer*
Cloonan, James Brian *investment executive*
Closen, Michael Lee *law educator*
Coar, David H. *federal judge*
Coase, Ronald Harry *economics educator*
Coe, Donald Kirk *university official*
Coe, Fredric L. *physician, educator, researcher*
Coffey, Raymond Richard *newspaper editor, journalist*
Cohan, George Sheldon *advertising and public relations executive*
Cohen, Christopher B. *lawyer*
Cohen, Edward Philip *microbiology and immunology educator, physician*
Cohen, Jerome *psychology educator*
Cohen, Maynard Manuel *neurologist, neurochemist, educator*
Cohen, Melanie Rovner *lawyer*
Cohen, Melvin R. *physician, educator*
Cohen, Ted *philosophy educator*
Cohler, Bertram Joseph *social sciences educator, clinical psychologist*
Cohodes, Eli Aaron *publisher*
Cole, Franklin Alan *investment company executive*
Cole, Thomas Amor *lawyer*
Coleman, James Samuel *sociologist, educator*
Collen, Sheldon Orrin *lawyer*
Collens, Lewis Morton *university president, legal educator*
†Collins, Earlean *state legislator*
Colman, Jeffrey D. *lawyer*
Colter, Cyrus *novelist, lawyer*
Comiskey, Michael Peter *lawyer*
Conant, Howard Rosset *steel company executive*
Cone, Joseph Jay *investment banking officer*
Congalton, Susan Tichenor *lawyer*
Conibear, Shirley Ann *occupational health consultant, physician*
Conidi, Daniel Joseph *private investigation agency executive*
Conklin, Thomas William *lawyer*
Conlon, Suzanne B. *federal judge*
Conlon, William F. *lawyer*
Connelly, Vincent J. *lawyer*
Connolly, Eugene B., Jr. *building materials company executive*
Connors, Dorsey *television and radio commentator, newspaper columnist*
Connors, Mary Eileen *psychologist*
Consey, Kevin Edward *museum administrator*
Considine, Frank William *container corporation executive*
Constant, Anita Aurelia *publisher*
†Conte, Lou *artistic director, choreographer*
Conte, Richard Nicholas *architect*
Conti, Lee Ann *lawyer*
Conviser, Richard James *law educator, lawyer, publications company executive*
†Conway, James Joseph *physician*
Conway, Michael Anthony *insurance executive*
Conway, Michael Maurice *lawyer*
Cook, Richard Borreson *architect*
†Cooke, Robert Phillip *architect*
Cooney, Robert John *lawyer*
Cooper, Charles Gilbert *toiletries and cosmetics company executive*
Cooper, Ilene Linda *magazine editor, author*
Copeland, Edward Jerome *lawyer*
Copley, Stephen Michael *materials science and engineering educator*
Corbett, Frank Joseph *advertising executive*
Corboy, Philip Harnett *lawyer*
Corcoran, James Martin, Jr. *lawyer, writer, lecturer*
Corwin, Sherman Phillip *lawyer*
Costello, John William *lawyer*
Cotner, C(arol) Beth *financial services company executive*
Cotsonas, Nicholas John, Jr. *physician, medical educator*
†Cotter, Daniel A. *diversified company executive*
Cotting, James Charles *manufacturing company executive*
Cotton, Eugene *lawyer*
Coughlan, Kenneth Lewis *lawyer*
Coughlin, Joseph E. *lawyer*
Coulson, John Selden *retired marketing executive*
Covalt, Robert Byron *chemicals executive*
Covey, Frank Michael, Jr. *lawyer, educator*
Covington, George Morse *lawyer*
Cox, Allan James *management consultant*
Cox, Charles C. *economist*
Crain, Gertrude Ramsay *publishing company executive*
Crain, Rance *publishing company executive*
Crane, Barbara Bachmann *photographer, educator*
Crane, Mark *lawyer*
Craven, George W. *lawyer*
Crawford, Dewey Byers *lawyer*
Crawford, William Basil, Jr. *journalist*
Crawford, William F. *corporate executive, consultant*
Creamer, Robert Allan *lawyer*
Creighton, Neal *foundation administrator, retired military officer*
Cremin, Susan Elizabeth *lawyer*
Crihfield, Philip J. *lawyer*
Crisham, Thomas Michael *lawyer*
Cronin, James Watson *physicist, educator*
Cronin, Robert E. *lawyer*
Cropsey, Joseph *political science educator*
Cross, Dolores Evelyn *university administrator, educator*
Cross, Robert Clark *journalist*
Crossan, John Robert *lawyer*
Crowe, Robert William *lawyer, mediator*
Crown, Lester *manufacturing company executive*
Crumbaugh, David Gordon *lawyer*
Crusto, Mitchell Ferdinand *lawyer, environmental consultant*
Cudahy, Richard D. *federal judge*
Cullen, Charles Thomas *historian, librarian*
†Cullerton, John James *state senator, lawyer*
Cummings, Walter J. *federal judge*
Cunningham, Robert James *lawyer*
Curatolo, Alphonse Frank *architect*
Curley, Robert E. *lawyer*
Curran, Barbara Adell *law foundation administrator, writer*
†Currie, James Barker *lawyer, corporate secretary*
Curwen, Randall William *journalist, editor*
†Cusack, John Thomas *lawyer*
Cushman, Aaron D. *public relations executive*
Custer, Charles Francis *lawyer*
Cyr, Arthur *association executive*
D'Alexander, William Joseph *publishing company executive*
Daley, Richard Michael *mayor*
†Daley, Rosie *cook, writer*
Dam, Kenneth W. *lawyer, law educator*
D'Amato, Anthony *law educator*
Dammeyer, Rodney Foster *distribution company executive*
Dancewicz, John Edward *investment banker*
Daniel, David Logan *retired state welfare agency administrator*
Darby, Edwin Wheeler *newspaper financial columnist*
Darnall, Robert J. *steel company executive*
Darr, Milton Freeman, Jr. *banker*
Davidson, Stanley J. *lawyer*
†Davies, Peter Francis *pathology educator, medical educator*
†Davis, Andrew Bashaw *publishing executive*
Davis, J. Steve *advertising agency executive*
Davis, Michael W. *lawyer*
†Davis, Monique D. (Deon Davis) *state legislator*
Davis, Muller *lawyer*
Davis, Ralph E. *lawyer*
Davis, Scott Jonathan *lawyer*
Davison, Richard *physician, educator*
Dawson, Suzanne Stockus *lawyer*
DeBat, Donald Joseph *newspaper editor*
Debus, Allen George *history educator*
DeCarlo, William S. *lawyer*
Dechene, James Charles *lawyer*
Decker, Richard Knore *lawyer*
De Costa, Edwin J. *physician, surgeon*
Dederick, Robert Gogan *economist*
De Francesco, John Blaze, Jr. *public relations company executive*
Degroot, Leslie Jacob *medical educator*
Dehmlow, Louis Henry Theodore, III *wholesale and distribution company executive*
de Hoyos, Debora M. *lawyer*
Deignan, Robert E. *lawyer*
Deitrick, William Edgar *lawyer*
del Greco, Francesco *physician, educator*
Delony, Patty Litton *management consultant*
DeLorey, John Alfred *printing company executive*
Delp, Wilbur Charles, Jr. *lawyer*
Dembowski, Peter Florian *foreign language educator*
Denvir, Robert F. *lawyer*
†De Paoli, Alexander M. *veterinary pathologist, researcher*
†Depoy, Phil E. *spcial studies think-tank executive*
Derlacki, Eugene L(ubin) *otolaryngologist, physician*
Desch, Theodore Edward *health insurance company executive, lawyer*
D'Esposito, Julian C., Jr. *lawyer*
Despres, Leon Mathis *lawyer, former city official*
Detmer, Lawrence McCormick *professional society administrator*
Detuno, Joseph Edward *lawyer*
DeWolfe, John Chauncey, Jr. *lawyer*
De Yoe, David P. *lawyer*
Diamond, Seymour *physician*
Diefenbach, Viron Leroy *dental, public health educator, university dean*
Dilling, Kirkpatrick Wallwick *lawyer*
Dilworth, Robert Holden *lawyer*
Dimond, Robert Edward *publisher*
Dix, Rollin C(umming) *mechanical engineering educator, consultant*

Dixon, Stewart Strawn lawyer
Dobbs, Frank Wilbur chemistry educator
Dockterman, Michael lawyer
Dodds, Claudette La Vonn radio executive and consultant
Dolan, Thomas Christopher association executive
†Dold, Robert Bruce journalist
Dondanville, John Wallace lawyer
Donenfeld, J. Douglas lawyer
Doniger, Wendy history of religions educator
Donlevy, John Dearden lawyer
Donnell, Harold Eugene, Jr. association executive
Donnelley, James Russell printing company executive
Donohoe, Jerome Francis lawyer
†Donovan, Dianne Francys journalist, literary editor
Donovan, Thomas B. lawyer
Donovan, Thomas Roy futures exchange executive
Doolittle, Sidney Newing retail executive
Dorman, Jeffrey Lawrence lawyer
Dorr, Williams Peter lawyer
Doty, Carl K. retired printing company executive
Douglas, Charles W. lawyer
Douglass, Andrew Ian lawyer, financial executive
Downing, Joan Forman editor
Downing, Robert Allan lawyer
†Doyle, Daniel M. bank executive
Doyle, John Robert lawyer
Drexler, Richard Allan manufacturing company executive
Driskell, Claude Evans dentist
Dropkin, Allen Hodes lawyer
Druick, Douglas Wesley museum administrator
Drymalski, Raymond Hibner lawyer, banker
D'Souza, Anthony Frank mechanical engineering educator, consultant, researcher
Dubin, Arthur Detmers architect
Dubin, Martin David architect
Duecker, Robert Sheldon bishop
Duell, Daniel Paul artistic director, choreographer, lecturer
Duez, David Joseph lawyer
Duff, Brian Barnett federal judge
Duhl, Michael Foster lawyer
Duncan, John Patrick Cavanaugh lawyer
Duncan, Starkey Davis, Jr. behavioral sciences educator
Dunea, George nephrologist, educator
†Dunphy, Thomas insurance company executive
Dupont, Todd F. mathematics and computer science educator
Durchslag, Stephen P. lawyer
Durso, John J. lawyer
Dyer, Robert Campbell printing ink company executive
Dykla, Edward George social services administrator
Dykstra, Paul Hopkins lawyer
Dyrud, Jarl Edvard psychiatrist
Early, Bert Hylton lawyer, legal search consultant
Early, Patrick Joseph oil and gas company executive
Easterbrook, Frank Hoover federal judge
†Eastham, Dennis Michael advertising executive
Eaton, John C. composer, educator
Eaton, Larry Ralph lawyer
Ebert, Paul Allen surgeon, educator
Ebert, Roger Joseph film critic
Echlin, Bernard Joseph lawyer
Echols, M(ary) Evelyn travel consultant
Eckel, John M. lawyer
Economou, Steve George surgery educator
Eddy, David Latimer banker
Edelman, Alvin lawyer
Edelman, Daniel Joseph public relations executive
Edelstein, Teri J. museum administrator, educator
Egan, Kevin James lawyer
Eggert, Russell Raymond lawyer
Egloff, Fred Robert manufacturers representative, writer, historian
Ehrman, Joseph S. lawyer
Eidell, Ronald George financial executive
Eimer, Nathan Philip lawyer
Einhorn, Edward Martin (Eddie Einhorn) professional baseball team executive
Eisenman, Trudy Fox dermatologist
†Eisner, Michael C. electric power industry executive
Ejiogu, Lem Onyeaduzim software engineer
Ekdahl, Jon Nels lawyer, corporate secretary
Ekstrom, Robert Carl musician, music educator, choral director, singer
Elbaz, Sohair Wastawy library director, consultant
Elden, Gary Michael lawyer
Elleman, Barbara editor
Elliot, Willard Somers musician, composer
Ellwood, Scott lawyer
Elson, Alex lawyer, legal educator
Emerson, Carter Whitney lawyer
Ender, John T. investment management executive, banker
Engebretson, Milton Benjamin clergyman
Engel, Joel Stanley telecommunications executive
Engling, Robert John lawyer
†Engman, John Daniel non-profit foundation administrator
Ephraim, Donald Morley lawyer
Eppen, Gary Dean business educator
Epstein, Laura social work educator, consultant
Epstein, Raymond engineering and architectural executive
Epstein, Richard A. law educator
Epstein, Sidney architectural engineer
Epstein, Wolfgang biochemist, educator
Erber, Thomas physics educator
Erdos, Ervin George pharmacology and biochemistry educator
Erens, Jay Allan lawyer
Ergas, Jean-Pierre Maurice packaging company executive
Ericson, Robert W. lawyer
Erlebacher, Albert history educator
Erlebacher, Arlene Cernik lawyer
†Esmond, Truman H., Jr. health facility administrator
Esrick, Jerald Paul lawyer
Essex, Joseph Michael visual communication planner
Ettinger, Joseph Alan lawyer
Eubanks-Pope, Sharon G. real estate entrepreneur
Evans, Earl Alison, Jr. biochemist
Even, Francis Alphonse lawyer
Everson, Leonard Charles lawyer
Ewers, R. Darrell food products company executive
Eyerman, Thomas Jude architect
Fahner, Tyrone C. lawyer, former state attorney general
Fairchild, Gary Lee lawyer
Fairchild, Thomas E. federal judge
†Falls, Robert Arthur artistic director
Fano, Ugo physicist, educator
Fanta, Paul Edward chemist, educator
Farley, William F. corporation executive
†Farrakhan, Louis religious leader
Favors, Malachi jazz musician, bassist
Fayhee, Michael R. lawyer
Fazio, Peter Victor, Jr. lawyer
Feagley, Michael Rowe lawyer
Feder, Robert television and radio columnist
Feeley, Henry Joseph, Jr. (Hank Feeley) artist, former advertising agency executive
Fein, Roger Gary lawyer
Feinstein, Fred Ira lawyer
Feldman, Burton Gordon printing company executive
Feldman, Scott M. lawyer
Feldstein, Charles Robert fund raising consultant
Feldstein, Joel Robert public relations executive
Fellows, Jerry Kenneth lawyer
†Felton, Cynthia principal
Fennessy, John James radiologist, educator
Fenton, Clifton Lucien investment banker
Ferencz, Robert Arnold lawyer
Ferguson, Bradford Lee lawyer
Ferguson, Donald John surgeon, educator
Ferrara, Stephen Arthur publishing company executive, editor
Ferrini, James Thomas lawyer
Fetridge, Bonnie-Jean Clark (Mrs. William Harrison Fetridge) civic volunteer
Fetridge, Clark Worthington publisher
Fickinger, Wayne Joseph advertising executive
†Fiechter, Charlotte E. church administrator
Field, Henry Frederick lawyer
Field, Marshall business executive
Field, Robert Edward lawyer
Fieldman, Leon lawyer
Fierer, Joshua Allan pathology educator
Fifer, Samuel lawyer
Fifield, William O. lawyer
Figge, Frederick Henry, Jr. retired publishing executive
Finch, Herman Manuel academic administrator
Fink, John editor, newspaper
Finke, Robert Forge lawyer
Finley, Harold Marshall investment banker
Fiorentino, Leon Francis holding company executive
Fischel, Daniel R. law educator
Fischer, Fredric H. lawyer
†Fisher, John James advertising executive
Fisher, Lester Emil zoo administrator
Fisher, Wendy Astley-Bell marketing executive
Fishman, Irving S. lawyer
Fisk, Carlton Ernest retired professional baseball player
Fitch, Frank Wesley pathologist, immunologist, educator, university dean
Fitch, Morgan Lewis, Jr. patent lawyer
†Fitzgerald, Peter Gosselin lawyer
Fitzgerald, Robert Maurice financial executive
Fitzpatrick, Peter lawyer
Fix, John Neilson banker
Fizdale, Richard advertising agency executive
Flaherty, John Joseph quality assurance company executive
Flanagan, Joseph Patrick advertising executive
Flanagan, Thomas Patrick accountant
Flanagin, Neil lawyer
Flaum, Joel Martin federal judge
Fleischer, Cornell Hugh history educator
Fleming, Graham Richard chemistry educator
Fletcher, James L. lawyer
Flynn, Peter Anthony lawyer
Flynn-Franklin, Gertrude Elizabeth elementary education educator, social worker
Fogel, Henry orchestra administrator
Fogel, Robert William economist, educator, historian
Fogelson, Raymond David anthropology educator
Foldi, Andrew Harry singer, educator
Foley, Joseph Lawrence sales executive
Foley, L(ewis) Michael real estate executive
Foote, Edward L. lawyer
Foran, Thomas Aquinas lawyer
Ford, L. H. bishop
†Ford, Larry John computer company executive
Ford, Michael W. lawyer
Forrester, J(ohn) Paul lawyer
Fort, Jeffrey C. lawyer
Fortune, Michael Joseph religion educator
Foster, Hugh Warren transportation company executive
Foster, Irene Parks special projects administrator
Foudree, Bruce William lawyer
Fox, David Wayne banker
Fox, Jacob Logan lawyer
Fox, Paul T. lawyer
Franch, Richard Thomas lawyer
Francois, William Armand packaging company executive, lawyer
Frank, Stanley Donald publishing company executive
Franke, Richard James investment banker
Franklin, Richard Mark lawyer
Fraumann, Willard George lawyer
†Frazee, John Powell, Jr. telecommunications executive
Frazier, A. D., Jr. banker
Frederiksen, Marilynn Elizabeth Conners physician
Freed, Karl Frederick chemistry educator
Freedman, Philip physician, educator
Freehling, Paul Edward lawyer
Freehling, Stanley Maxwell investment banker
Freehling, Willard Maxwell stockbroker
Freeman, Lee Allen, Jr. lawyer
Freeman, Leslie Gordon anthropologist, educator
Freeman, Louis S. lawyer
Freeman, Susan Tax anthropologist, educator
Freidheim, Cyrus F., Jr. management consultant
French, Kenneth Ronald finance educator
Fried, Josef chemist, educator
Friedland, Richard Stewart electronics company executive
†Friedman, Lawrence Milton lawyer
Friedman, Roselyn L. lawyer
Friedrich, Paul anthropologist, linguist, poet
Frings, Manfred Servatius philosophy educator
Frisch, Henry Jonathan physics educator
Fritzsche, Hellmut physics educator
Frohman, Lawrence Asher endocrinology educator, scientist
Fromm, Erika (Mrs. Paul Fromm) clinical psychologist
Frommelt, Jeffrey James management consulting firm executive
Fross, Roger Raymond lawyer
Fuchs, Elaine V. molecular biologist, educator
Fujita, Tetsuya Theodore educator, meteorologist
Fukui, Yoshio biology educator
Fulgoni, Gian Marc market research company executive
Fullagar, William Watts lawyer
Fuller, Harry Laurance oil company executive
Fuller, Jack William writer, newspaper executive
Fuller, Perry Lucian lawyer
Fullmer, Paul public relations counselor
Fultz, Dave meteorology educator
Furda, Gregory H. lawyer
Furlane, Mark Elliott lawyer
Furman, James Merle foundation executive
Fuson, Douglas Finley lawyer
Gaggini, John Edmund lawyer
Gaines, Kenneth R. lawyer
Gaines, William Chester journalist
Gallagher, John Pirie corporation executive
Gancer, Donald Charles lawyer
Gandhi, Bharat R. construction company executive
Gangemi, Columbus Rudolph, Jr. lawyer, educator
Gannon, Sister Ann Ida retired philosophy educator, former college administrator
Garber, Daniel Elliot philosophy educator
Garber, Samuel Baugh lawyer, retail company executive
Garbutt, Eugene James lawyer
Gardner, Edward G. manufacturing company executive
Gardner, Howard Alan travel marketing executive, travel writer and editor
Gardner, James Harkins educational organization executive
Gareis, Robert J. lawyer
Garland, James Wilson, Jr. physics educator, researcher, consultant
Garnett, Marion Winston judge
Garrett, Shirley Gene nuclear medicine technologist
Garrigan, Richard Thomas finance educator, consultant, editor
Garth, Bryant Geoffrey law educator, foundation executive
Gartner, Lawrence Mitchel pediatrician, medical college educator
Garvey, Michael J. lawyer
Garvey, Richard J. lawyer
Gates, Stephen Frye lawyer
Gavin, John Neal lawyer
Gaynor, James M., Jr. lawyer
Geannopulos, Nicholas George publisher
Gearen, John J. lawyer
Gecht, Martin Louis physician, bank executive
Gehr, Mary illustrator, painter, printmaker
Geiman, J. Robert lawyer
Geis, Norman Winer lawyer
Genetski, Robert James economist
George, John Martin, Jr. lawyer
Geraldson, Raymond I. lawyer
Geraldson, Raymond I., Jr. lawyer
Gerber, Lawrence lawyer
Gerbie, Albert Bernard obstetrician, gynecologist, educator
Gerdes, Neil Wayne library director
Gerek, William Michael lawyer
Gerlits, Francis Joseph lawyer
Gerrish, Brian Albert theologian, educator
Gershbein, Leon Lee chemist, educator
Gerson, Jerome Howard lawyer
†Gerst, C(ornelius) Gary real estate executive
Gerstner, Robert William structural engineering educator, consultant
Gertz, Elmer lawyer, author, educator
Getzels, Jacob Warren psychologist, educator
Getzendanner, Susan lawyer, former federal judge
Gewertz, Bruce Labe surgeon, educator
Giampietro, Wayne Bruce lawyer
Gibbons, William John lawyer
Gibson, McGuire archaeologist, educator
Gidwitz, Gerald cosmetics company executive
Gidwitz, Ronald J. personal care products company executive
Gies, Thomas Anthony publishing company executive
Giesen, Richard Allyn business executive
Gilbert, Howard N(orman) lawyer
Gilford, Steven Ross lawyer
Gill, Michael J. lawyer
Gill, William Haywood insurance broker
Gillette, Susan Downs advertising executive
Gilson, Jerome lawyer, writer
Gingiss, Benjamin Jack retired formal clothing stores executive
Ginley, Thomas J. banker
Ginsberg, Lewis Robbins lawyer
Ginsburg, Norton Sydney geography educator
Giovacchini, Peter Louis psychoanalyst
Gislason, Eric Arni chemistry educator
Given, Ronald B. lawyer
Gladden, James Walter, Jr. lawyer
Gladstone, Lee psychiatrist, addictionist
†Glasner, LeRoy A. public relations executive
Glass, Ronald Lee real estate executive
Glass, Stanford Lee lawyer
Glasser, James J. leasing company executive
Gleeson, Paul Francis lawyer
Glieberman, Herbert Allen lawyer
Glovka, Richard Paul lawyer
Goeke, Joseph R. lawyer
Goepp, Robert August dental educator, oral pathologist
Goetz, John Bullock graphic designer
Goggin, Joseph Robert financial consultant
Golan, Stephen Leonard lawyer
Gold, Norman Myron lawyer
Goldberg, Arthur M. gaming and fitness company executive
†Goldberg, Sherman I. banking company executive
Goldberg, Stephanie Benson editor, writer, lawyer
Goldblatt, Stanford Jay lawyer
Golden, Bruce Paul lawyer
Golden, William C. lawyer
Goldiamond, Israel experimental psychologist, educator
Goldman, Louis Budwig lawyer
Goldring, Norman Max advertising executive
Goldsborough, Robert Gerald publishing executive, author
Goldschmidt, Lynn Harvey lawyer
Goldsmith, John Anton linguist, educator
Goldsmith, Julian Royce geochemist, educator
Goldstein, Alfred George retail executive
Goldstein, Fern fine artist, custom designer, design consultant
Goldstein, Norman R. alcoholic beverage company executive
Goldwasser, Eugene biochemist, educator
Golin, Alvin public relations company executive
Golomb, Harvey Morris oncologist, educator
Golomski, William Arthur consulting company executive
Gomer, Robert chemistry educator
Gonzalez, Ruben professional musician
Goodman, Elliott I(rvin) lawyer
Goodman, Gary Alan lawyer
Goodman, Stuart Lauren lawyer
Gordon, Ellen Rubin candy company executive
Gordon, Ezra architect, educator
Gordon, Phillip lawyer
Gordon, William A. lawyer
Gorter, James Polk investment banker
Goschi, Nicholas Peter lawyer
Goss, Howard S(imon) manufacturing executive
Goss, Richard Henry lawyer
Gossett, Philip musicologist
Gottlieb, Gidon Alain Guy law educator
Gould, Arthur Irwin lawyer
Gould, John Philip, Jr. economist, educator
Graber, Doris Appel political scientist, editor, author
Grabowski, Roger J. business, intangible assets, real estate appraiser
Grace, Mark Eugene professional baseball player
Gradowski, Stanley Joseph, Jr. publishing company executive
Grady, John F. federal judge
Graettinger, John Sells physician, educator
Graham, David F. lawyer
Graham, Jarlath John publishing executive
Graham, Patricia Albjerg education educator, foundation executive
Graham, Robert L. lawyer
Gralen, Donald John lawyer
Granger, Bill columnist
Grant, Dennis newspaper publishing executive
Grant, Paul Bernard industrial relations educator
Grant, Robert McQueen humanities educator
Grant, Robert Nathan lawyer
Graupe, Daniel electrical and computer engineering educator, systems and biomedical engineer
Graves, Robert Lawrence mathematician, educator
Gray, Hanna Holborn history educator
Gray, James S. lawyer
Gray, Milton Hefter lawyer
Gray, Richard art dealer, consultant, holding company executive
Grayck, Marcus Daniel lawyer
Grayhack, John Thomas urologist, educator
Greenbaum, Kenneth lawyer
Greenberg, Arthur A. diversified real estate and financial services executive, manufacturing company executive
Greenberg, Bernard entomologist, educator
Greenberger, Ernest lawyer
Greenblatt, Ray Harris lawyer
Greenblatt, Russell Edward lawyer, consultant
Greene, Charles Cassius advertising agency executive
Greene, Robert Bernard, Jr. (Bob Greene) broadcast television correspondent, columnist, author
Gregg, Jon Mann lawyer
Gregory, Byron L. lawyer
†Grenesko, Donald C. publishing company executive
†Griffin, Howard newspaper publishing executive
Griffin, Hugh C. lawyer
Griffin, Jean Latz newspaper reporter
Griffin, Mary English language educator
Griffith, B(ezaleel) Herold physician, educator, plastic surgeon
Griffith, Donald Kendall lawyer
Grimes, Hugh Gavin physician
Grimm, Terry M. lawyer
Grimm, Victor E. lawyer
Griswold, Frank Tracy, III bishop
†Gross, Dorothy-Ellen library director, dean
Gross, Theodore Lawrence university administrator, author
Grossi, Francis Xavier, Jr. lawyer, educator
Grossweiner, Leonard Irwin physicist, educator
Grove, Helen Harriet historian, artist
Gruber, William Paul journalist
Grunsfeld, Ernest Alton, III architect
Guenzel, Paul Walter corporate executive
Guillen, Ozzie (Oswaldo Jose Barrios Guillen) baseball player
Gunn, Robert Murray lawyer, farmer
Gupta, Krishna Chandra mechanical engineering educator
Guralnick, Sidney Aaron civil engineering educator
Gutek, Gerald Lee education and history educator
Guthman, Jack lawyer
Gutmann, David Leo psychology educator
Guyette, James M. airline executive
Gwinn, Robert P. publishing executive
Haarlow, John B. lawyer
Haas, Howard Green bedding manufacturing company executive
†Haas, Jonathan museum research organization executive
Haber, Meryl Harold physician, educator, author
Hackl, Donald John architect
Haddix, Carol Ann Mighton journalist
Haderlein, Thomas M. lawyer
Haffner, Charles Christian, III retired printing company executive
Hagan, Robert K. lawyer
Haggerty, Lawrence George business executive
Hahn, Frederic Louis lawyer
Haines, Martha Mahan lawyer
Hales, Daniel B. lawyer
†Haley, Clifton Edward car rental company executive
Haley, George Romance languages educator
Hall, Joan M. lawyer
Hall, Lee Boaz publishing company consultant, author
Hall, Tom T. songwriter, performer
Hall, W. Reginald manufacturing company executive
Hall, William King manufacturing company executive
Hallagan, Robert E. management consultant
Halpern, Jack chemist, educator
Halprin, Rick lawyer
Hamada, Robert S(eiji) economist, educator
Hamilton, Thomas Mackin, Jr. lawyer
Hamister, Donald Bruce electronics company executive
Hammesfahr, Robert Winter lawyer
Hamp, Eric Pratt linguist
Hanbury, Marshall E. lawyer
Hand, Elbert O. clothing manufacturing and retailing company executive
Hand, Roger physician, educator
Handler, Steven P. lawyer
Hannah, Wayne Robertson, Jr. lawyer
Hannay, William Mouat, III lawyer
Hansen, Carl R. management consultant
Hansen, Claire V. financial executive
Hanson, Floyd Bliss applied mathematician, computational scientist, mathematical biologist
Hanson, Heidi Elizabeth lawyer
Hanson, Richard A. lawyer
Hanson, Ronald William lawyer
Hanzlik, Paul F. lawyer

Hardgrove, James Alan lawyer
Harding, James Warren finance company executive
Hardy, John Edward English language educator, author
Haring, Olga Munk medical educator, physician
Harmon, Robert Lon lawyer
Harrington, Carol A. lawyer
Harrington, James Timothy lawyer
Harris, Chauncy Dennison geographer, educator
Harris, Donald Ray lawyer
Harris, Irving Brooks cosmetics executive
Harris, Jules Eli medical educator, physician, clinical scientist, administrator
Harris, Neil history educator
Harrold, Bernard lawyer
Hart, Cecil William Joseph otolaryngologist, head and neck surgeon
Hart, David Churchill lawyer
Hart, William Thomas federal judge
Hartigan, Neil F. lawyer, former state attorney general, lieutenant governor
Hartley-Leonard, Darryl hotel company executive
Hartnett, James Patrick engineering educator
Hartz, Renee Semo cardiothoracic surgeon
Harvanek, Robert Francis philosophy educator, clergyman
Harvey, Paul news commentator, author, columnist
Harvey, Ronald Gilbert research chemist
Haselkorn, Robert virology educator
Hassan, M. Zia management educator
Hast, Malcolm Howard medical educator, scientist
Hasten, Michael V. lawyer
Haubold, Samuel Allen lawyer
†Haupt, Roger A. advertising executive
Hausman, William Ray fund raising and management consultant
Havdala, Henri Salomon anesthesiologist, educator, consultant
†Hawkinson, John former investment management company executive
Hay, Howard newspaper publishing executive
†Hayden, Carla Diane librarian, educator
†Hayden, Thomas H. advertising executive
Hayes, David John Arthur, Jr. legal association executive
Hayes, Richard Johnson association executive, lawyer
Hayes, William Aloysius economics educator
†Haymes, David Allen architect
Hayward, Thomas Zander, Jr. lawyer
Head, Patrick James lawyer
Heagy, Thomas Charles banker
Heatwole, Mark M. lawyer
Hecht, Frank Thomas lawyer
Heckman, James Joseph economist, econometrician, educator
Heckmann, Irvin Lee former college dean, educator
Hefner, Christie Ann international media and marketing executive
Hefner, Hugh Marston editor in chief
Hefner, Philip James theologian
Heidrick, Gardner Wilson management consultant
Heidrick, Robert Lindsay management consultant
Heindl, Warren Anton law educator, retired
Heine, Spencer H. corporate lawyer, real estate executive
Heinecken, Robert Friedli art educator, artist
Heineman, Ben Walter corporation executive
Heineman, Natalie (Mrs. Ben W. Heineman) civic worker
Heinz, John Peter lawyer, educator
Heinz, William Denby lawyer
Heisler, Quentin George, Jr. lawyer
Heiss, Robin lawyer
Heitland, Ann Rae lawyer
Heller, Paul medical educator
Heller, Reinhold August art educator, consultant
Heller, Stanley J. lawyer, physician
Hellie, Richard Russian history educator, researcher
Hellman, Samuel radiologist, physician, educator
Helman, Robert Alan lawyer
Helmbold, Nancy Pearce classical languages educator
Helmholz, R(ichard) H(enry) law educator
Heltne, Paul Gregory museum executive
Hengstler, Gary Ardell publisher, editor, lawyer
Henikoff, Leo M., Jr. academic administrator, medical educator
Henning, Joel Frank lawyer, author, publisher, consultant
Henning, Mark G. lawyer
Henry, Frederick Edward lawyer
Henry, Robert John lawyer
Hensel, Paul H. lawyer
Herbst, Arthur Lee obstetrician-gynecologist
Herguth, Robert John columnist
Herman, Sidney N. lawyer
Hermann, Donald Harold James lawyer, educator
Hermann, Edward Robert occupational and environmental health consultant
Herpe, David A. lawyer
Herzel, Leo lawyer
Herzog, Fred F. legal educator
Hess, Peter A. lawyer
Hess, Sidney J., Jr. lawyer
Hester, Thomas Patrick lawyer
Heuer, Michael Alexander dentist, educator
Hewitt, Brian journalist
Hickey, John Thomas, Jr. lawyer
Hickey, Kevin Francis insurance company executive
Hickman, Frederic W. lawyer
†Hicks, Sherman Gregory bishop
Higgins, Jack editorial cartoonist
Hilborn, Michael G. lawyer, real estate development executive
Hildebrand, Roger Henry astrophysicist, physicist
†Hill, Arthur J. real estate company executive
Hill, Raymond Joseph packaging company executive
†Hiller, David D. lawyer
Hilliard, David Craig lawyer
Hillis, Margaret conductor, musician
Himes, Laurence Austin professional baseball executive
Himmelfarb, John David artist
Hines, James Rodger surgeon
Hinojosa, Raul physician, ear pathology researcher
Hirshman, Harold Carl lawyer
Hitch, James T., III lawyer
Hlavacek, Roy George publishing executive, magazine editor
Hoban, George Savre lawyer
Hobbs, Marvin engineering executive
Hodes, Scott lawyer
Hodgman, David Renwick lawyer
Hoeft, Steven H. lawyer
Hoey, Rita Marie public relations executive
Hofer, Roy Ellis lawyer
Hoff, William Bruce, Jr. lawyer
Hoffman, Douglas W. lawyer
Hoffman, Philip Andrew property tax consultant
Hoffman, Richard Bruce lawyer
Hoffman, Valerie Jane lawyer
Hoffmann, Howard M. lawyer
†Hoffmann, Philip pharmacology educator
Holabird, John Augur, Jr. retired architect
Holderman, James F., Jr. federal judge
Holland, Eugene, Jr. lumber company executive
Hollins, Mitchell Leslie lawyer
Hollis, Donald Roger banker
Holmen, Neil E. lawyer
†Holton, Lisa newspaper editor
Holzer, Edwin advertising executive
Homans, Peter psychology and religious studies educator
Honig, George Raymond pediatrician
Horn, Milton sculptor
Horne, John R. farm equipment company executive
†Hornung, Mark newspaper editor
Horwath, Leslie Kathleen lawyer
Horwich, Allan lawyer
Horwitz, Irwin Daniel otolaryngologist, educator
Hoskins, Richard Jerold lawyer
†Hotz, V. Joseph economics educator
Houston, Simpson Pete secondary education educator
Howe, Jonathan Thomas lawyer
Howe, Lawrence lawyer, business executive
Howell, R(obert) Thomas, Jr. lawyer, food company executive
Hron, Michael G. lawyer
Huber, Richard Leslie banker
Hucker, Brian S. lawyer
Huckman, Michael Saul neuroradiologist, educator
†Hudson, Dawn Emily advertising executive
Huebsch, Robert P. lawyer
Huggins, Charles Brenton surgical educator
Huggins, Rollin Charles, Jr. lawyer
Hughes, John Russell physician, educator
Hummel, Gregory William lawyer
Hunt, Donald Samuel banker
Hunt, Lawrence Halley, Jr. lawyer
Hunt, Roger Schermerhorn hospital administrator
†Hunt, Steven J. media and advertising executive
Hunter, James Alexander surgeon, educator
Hunter, J(ames) Paul English language educator, literary critic, historian
†Huntley, Robert Stephen newspaper editor
Hurlbert, Robert P. lawyer
Hurley, William James, Jr. English language educator
Hurst, Charles Jackson newspaper columnist
Husar, John Paul newspaper columnist, television panelist
Hussey, Charles E., II lawyer
Huston, DeVerille Anne lawyer
†Huston, John Leo trade association executive
Huston, John Lewis chemistry educator
Hutchins, Harley lawyer
Hutchinson, Leland E. lawyer
Hutchison, Clyde Allen, Jr. chemistry educator
Hynes, Mary Ann publishing executive, lawyer
Iakovos, (Iakovos Garmatis) bishop
†Inskeep, Kenneth W. church administrator
Isaacs, Roger David public relations executive
Ivan, Thomas Nathaniel professional hockey team executive
Jachna, Joseph D. photographer, educator
Jackson, David Munro association executive
Jackson, Jesse Louis civic and political leader, clergyman
Jackson, Philip Douglas professional basketball coach
Jacobson, David Cary lawyer
Jacobson, Harold LeLand lawyer
Jacobson, Marian Slutz lawyer
Jacobson, Richard Joseph lawyer
Jacoby, John Primm lawyer
Jacover, Jerold Alan lawyer
Jager, Melvin Francis lawyer
Jahn, Helmut architect
Jahns, Adam A. banking executive
Jahns, Jeffrey lawyer
Jakstas, Alfred John museum conservator, consultant
Jakubik, Jerome W. lawyer
Jambor, Robert Vernon lawyer
†James, A. Lincoln, Sr. minister, religious organization executive
Janson, Patrick singer, actor, conductor, educator
Jarc, Frank Robert printing company executive
Jean, Kenneth conductor
Jeffay, Henry biochemistry educator
Jerome, Jerrold V. insurance company executive
Jerrick, Ronald M. lawyer
Jersild, Thomas Nielsen lawyer
Jibben, Laura Ann state agency administrator
Jock, Paul F., II lawyer
Johnson, Beverly June librarian, educator
Johnson, C. Richard lawyer
†Johnson, Chauncey Paul banker
Johnson, Daniel Leroy lawyer
Johnson, David Gale economist, educator
Johnson, Elmer William lawyer
Johnson, Gary Thomas lawyer
Johnson, Glenn Thompson judge
Johnson, H. Arvid lawyer
Johnson, Janet Helen Egyptology educator
Johnson, Joan B. cosmetics company executive
Johnson, John H. publisher, consumer products executive, chairman
Johnson, Richard Fred lawyer
Johnson, Robert Bruce public relations executive
Johnston, Alan Rogers lawyer
Johnston, Thomas Watts lawyer
Jonas, Harry S. professional society administrator
†Jonasson, Olga surgeon, educator
†Jones, Emil, Jr. state legislator
Jones, Mark Elmer, Jr. lawyer, former judge
Jones, Peter d'Alroy history educator, author
Jones, Philip Newton physician, medical educator
Jones, Richard Cyrus lawyer
Jones, Richard Melvin bank executive, former retail executive
Jones, Robert Doyne oil and chemical executive
Jones, Thomas M. lawyer
Jordan, Michelle Denise lawyer
Jordan, V. Craig endocrine pharmacologist, educator
Joseph, Robert Thomas lawyer
Josephson, Kenneth Bradley artist, educator
Joslin, Rodney Dean lawyer
Joyce, Robert Hyland lawyer
Juhl, Loren Earl lawyer
Junewicz, James J. lawyer
Jurek, Kenneth J. lawyer
Kadanoff, Leo Philip physicist
Kahan, Samuel D. economist
†Kahn, Harold retail executive
Kahn, Herta Hess (Mrs. Howard Kahn) retired stockbroker
Kahn, James Steven museum director
Kaiserlian, Penelope Jane publishing company executive
Kamin, Chester Thomas lawyer
Kamyszew, Christopher D. museum curator, executive educator, art consultant
Kanne, Michael Stephen federal judge, educator
Kanwit, Glen Harris lawyer
Kaplan, Harold L. lawyer
Kaplan, Jared lawyer
Kaplan, Morton A. political science educator
Kaplan, Sidney Mountbatten lawyer
Kaplan, Wayne S. lawyer
Karaba, Frank Andrew lawyer
Karanikas, Alexander English language educator, author, actor
Karge, Stewart W. lawyer
Kark, Robert M. physician, educator
Karl, Barry Dean historian, educator
Karlin, Bernard Richard principal
Karp, Robert surgeon, educator
Kasbeer, Stephen Frederick university official
Kass, Leon Richard life sciences educator
Kastel, Howard L. lawyer
Katten, Melvin L. lawyer
Katz, Adrian Izhack physician, educator
Katz, Harold Ambrose lawyer, former state legislator
Katz, Stuart Charles lawyer, concert jazz musician
Kaufman, Andrew Michael lawyer
Kaufman, Ira Jeffrey investment banker
Kazazis, Kostas linguist, educator
Kazik, John Stanley newspaper executive
Kearney, John Walter sculptor, painter
Keck, Robert Clifton lawyer
Keck, William architect
Keehn, Silas banker
Keenan, James George classics educator
†Keierleber, Stephen James advertising executive
Kelley, Duane Matthew lawyer
Kelley, Michael John newspaper editor
Kelliher, Peter Maurice lawyer, arbitrator
Kelly, Arthur Lloyd management and investment company executive
Kelly, Charles Arthur lawyer
Kelly, Richard Smith judge
Kelly, Robert Donald consultant
Kelman, Robert Andrew lawyer
Kempf, Donald G., Jr. lawyer
Kennedy, Eugene Cullen psychology educator, writer
Kennett, Robert L. publisher
Kenney, Frank Deming lawyer
Kenny, Edmund Joyce lawyer
†Kent, Conrad S. chemicals executive
Kent, Geoffrey pathology educator, physician
Kerbis, Gertrude Lempp architect
Kessler, Stanton A. lawyer
†Kestnbaum, Robert Dana management consultant
Kiani, Reza endocrinology, metabolism, medical physician nsm
Kickler, James Arnold insurance company executive
Kiel, William Frederick architectural specifications consultant
Kiley, Roger J. lawyer
Kim, H. J. (Shaun Kim) engineer
King, Andre Richardson architectural graphic designer
King, Billie Jean Moffitt professional tennis player
King, Clark Chapman, Jr. lawyer
King, David Edgar librarian, editor
King, Michael Howard lawyer
King, Sharon L. lawyer
Kins, Juris lawyer
Kinsinger, Jack Burl chemist, educator
Kinzie, Raymond Wyant banker, lawyer
Kipnis, Mark S. lawyer
Kipperman, Lawrence I. lawyer
Kirby, William Joseph corporation executive
Kirkland, John Leonard lawyer
Kirschner, Barbara Starrels pediatric gastroenterologist
Kirsner, Joseph Barnett physician, educator
Kisor, Henry Du Bois newspaper editor, critic, columnist
Kissel, Richard John lawyer
Kite, Steven B. lawyer
Kittle, Charles Frederick surgeon
Klapperich, Frank Lawrence, Jr. investment banker
Klarich, Nina Marie economic development executive
Klaviter, Helen Lothrop magazine editor
Klement, Vera artist
Klenk, James Andrew lawyer
Kloc, Emily Alvina elementary principal
†Klutz, C. H. church administrator
Knapp, Donald Roy musician, educator
Knight, Christopher Nichols lawyer
Knight, Robert Milton independent journalist, educator
Knoblauch, Mark George librarian
Knospe, William Herbert medical educator
Knox, James Edwin lawyer
Knox, Lance Lethbridge venture capital executive
Knuti, Robert A. lawyer
Kobs, James Fred advertising agency executive
Kocoras, Charles Petros federal judge
Koenig, Bonnie non-profit organization administrator
Koester, Robert Gregg record company executive
Koga, Mary artist, photographer, social worker
Kohn, Shalom L. lawyer
Kohrman, Arthur Fisher pediatric educator
Kolb, Gwin Jackson language professional, educator
Kolek, Robert Edward lawyer
Koltin, Allan David accountant
Kopel, David psychologist, educator
Koran, Janet M. lawyer
Kornel, Ludwig medical educator, physician, scientist
Kortright, Richard T. lawyer
Koten, John A. retired communications executive
Kotlowitz, Alex writer, journalist
Kotulak, Ronald newspaper science writer
Kouvel, James Spyros physicist, educator
Koven, Howard Richard lawyer
Kowitt, Arthur Jay lawyer
Kozitka, Richard Eugene consumer products company executive
Kraft, Sumner Charles physician, educator
Krainik, Ardis opera company executive
Kramer, Ferdinand mortgage banker
Kraus, Herbert Myron public relations executive
Krause, Jerry (Jerome Richard Krause) professional basketball team executive
Kravitt, Jason Harris Paperno lawyer
Krawetz, Arthur Altshuler chemist, science administrator
Kriss, Robert J. lawyer
Krivkovich, Peter George advertising executive
Kroch, Carl Adolph retail executive
Kroll, Barry Lewis lawyer
Krueger, Bonnie Lee editor, writer
Krueger, Herbert William lawyer
Krupka, Robert George lawyer
Krupnik, Vee M. financial company executive
Kruskal, William Henry statistician, educator
Kubida, Judith Ann museum administrator
Kucera, Daniel Jerome lawyer
Kudish, David J. financial executive
Kullberg, Duane Reuben accounting firm executive
†Kunkle, William Joseph, Jr. lawyer
Kupcinet, Irv columnist
†Kupperman, Melvin civil engineer, construction and development company executive
Kurland, Philip B. lawyer, educator
Kurtich, John William architect, film-maker, educator
Kuta, Jeffrey Theodore lawyer
Kyle, Robert Campbell, II publishing executive
Lach, Alma Elizabeth food and cooking writer, consultant
Lafontant-Mankarious, Jewel (Mrs. Naguib S. Mankarious) diplomat, lawyer
Laitin, David Dennis political science educator
Lamb, Gordon Howard academic administrator
Lamont, Gene professional baseball team manager
Landan, Henry Sinclair lawyer
Landau, Richard L. physician, educator
Landes, William M. law educator
Landow-Esser, Janine Marise lawyer
Landsman, Stephen A. lawyer
Lane, Kenneth Edwin retired advertising agency executive
Lane, Robert G. lawyer
Lane, Ronald Alan lawyer
Laner, Richard Warren lawyer
Lang, Richard A. lawyer
Langhenry, John Godfred, Jr. lawyer
Langsley, Donald Gene psychiatrist, medical board executive
Lanzl, Lawrence Herman medical physicist
Lapidus, Allan E. lawyer
Lappin, Richard C. corporate executive
Larsen, Paul Emanuel religious organization administrator
Larson, Allan Louis political scientist, educator, lay church worker
Larson, Roy journalist, publisher
LaRue, Paul Hubert lawyer
LaRue, Paul Hubert, Jr. lawyer
†LaSage, John David public relations firm executive
Lasky, Laurence D. lawyer
Lassar, Scott R. lawyer
Lassers, Willard J. judge
Latimer, Kenneth Alan lawyer
Lauder, Norma J. corporate finance executive
Lauer, Robert Lee consumer products executive
Laumann, Edward Otto sociology educator
LaVelle, Arthur anatomy educator
Lawler, James Ronald French language educator
†Lawrie, Henry DeVos, Jr. lawyer
Lazarus, George Milton newspaper columnist
Leahigh, Alan Kent public relations executive
Lebedow, Aaron Louis consulting company executive
Lecker, Abraham former banker
Leckey, Andrew A. financial columnist
Lederman, Leon Max physicist, educator
LeDuc, John Andre lawyer
Lee, Bernard Shing-Shu research company executive
Lee, William Marshall lawyer
LeFevre, Perry Deyo minister, theology educator
Leff, Alan Richard medical educator
Legge Kemp, Diane architect, landscape architect
Lehman, George Morgan food sales executive
Lehrman, Nat magazine editor
Leigh, Sherren communications executive, editor, publisher
Leighton, George Neves retired federal judge
Leinenweber, Harry D. federal judge
Leiseca, Sergio A. Jr. lawyer
Leisten, Arthur Gaynor lawyer
Lemein, Gregg D. lawyer
†Lenneberg, Hans music librarian, educator
Lennes, Gregory manufacturing and financing company executive
Lerner, Nathan Bernard artist
Lesly, Philip public relations counsel
Lev, Allen P. lawyer
Levenfeld, Milton Arthur lawyer
Levi, Edward Hirsch former attorney general, university president emeritus
Levi, John G. lawyer
Levin, Charles Edward lawyer
Levin, Jack S. lawyer
Levin, Michael David lawyer
Levine, Donald Nathan sociologist, educator
Levine, Laurence Harvey lawyer
Levinson, Irving Bert lawyer
Levi-Setti, Riccardo physicist, director
Levit, Louis W. lawyer
Levy, Arnold S(tuart) real estate company executive
Levy, Donald Harris chemistry educator
Levy, Jerre Marie psychobiology educator
Levy, Richard Herbert lawyer
Lewis, Charles A. investment company executive
Lewis, John D. financial services company executive
Lewis, Julius lawyer
Lewis, Philip educational and technical consultant
Lewis, Phillip Harold museum curator
Lewis, Ramsey Emanuel, Jr. pianist, composer
Lewis, Sylvia Gail journalist
Lewy, Ralph I. hotel executive
Liao, Shutsung biochemist
Lichter, Edward Arthur physician, educator
Lieb, Michael English educator, humanities educator
Lieberman, Myron lawyer
Light, John Caldwell chemistry educator
Light, Kenneth B. manufacturing company executive
Lin, Chin-Chu physician, educator, researcher
Lin, James Chih-I biomedical and electrical engineer, educator
†Lincicome, Bernard Wesley journalist
†Lincoln, Sandy investment management executive
Lind, Jon Robert lawyer
Lindberg, George W. federal judge
Lindblom, Marjorie Press lawyer
Linde, Ronald Keith corporate executive, private investor
Linden, Henry Robert chemical engineering research executive
Link, Carl Dean insurance company executive
Linklater, William Joseph lawyer
Lipinski, Ann Marie newspaper editor
Lippe, Melvin Karl lawyer

Lipton, Richard M. lawyer
List, David Patton lawyer
Listrom, Linda L. lawyer
Litow, Merrill advertising executive
Little, George Daniel clergyman
Litweiler, John Berkey writer, editor
Litwin, Burton Howard lawyer
Litwin, Michael Joseph finance company executive
Litzsinger, Paul Richard publishing company executive
Liu, Ben-chieh economist
Livingston, Homer J., Jr. stock exchange executive
Livingston, Theodore A., Jr. lawyer
Lloyd, William F. lawyer
Locher, Richard Earl editorial cartoonist
Locke, Charles Stanley manufacturing company executive, director
Lockwood, Gary Lee lawyer
Lohan, Dirk architect
Lohman, Gordon R. manufacturing executive
Longman, Gary Lee accountant
Longworth, Richard Cole journalist
Looman, James R. lawyer
Lopata, Helena Znaniecka sociologist, researcher, educator
Lorand, Laszlo biochemist, educator
Lorch, Kenneth F. lawyer
Lorenz, Hugo Albert insurance executive
Lorenz, Richard Theodore, Jr. lawyer
Lorie, James Hirsch business administration educator
Lorincz, Allan Levente physician, educator
Lotocky, Innocent H. bishop
Lott, David Stuart lawyer
Loucks, Ralph Bruce, Jr. investment company executive
Lowrie, William G. oil company executive
Lowry, James Hamilton management consultant
†Lubawski, James Lawrence health care administrator
Lubin, Donald G. lawyer
Lucas, John Kenneth lawyer
Lumpkin, John Robert public health physician, state official
Lundberg, George David, II medical editor, pathologist
Lundergan, Barbara Keough lawyer
Lundy, Joseph R. lawyer
Lurie, Paul Michael lawyer
Luscombe, George A. II lawyer
Lutter, Paul Allen lawyer
Lutz, Karl Evan lawyer
Lykos, Peter George educator, scientist
Lyman, Arthur Joseph financial executive
Lyman, John Root oil company executive
Lynch, John Peter lawyer
Lynch, William Thomas, Jr. advertising agency executive
Lynn, Laurence Edwin, Jr. university administrator, educator
Lynnes, R. Milton advertising executive
Lyon, Jeffrey journalist, author
Lyons, Jeffrey film critic
†Lythcott, Marsha S. newspaper editor
MacCarthy, Terence Francis lawyer
MacDougal, Gary Edward foundation trustee, director, arts manager
†Mackiewicz, Laura advertising agency executive
MacLane, Saunders mathematician, educator
Macsai, John architect
Madansky, Albert statistics educator
Madigan, John William publishing executive
Maggio, Michael John artistic director
Maguire, David Edward personnel executive, consultant
Maher, David Willard lawyer
Mahoney, John actor
Mahowald, Anthony Peter geneticist, cell biologist, educator
Makinen, Marvin William biophysicist, educator
Malato, Stephen H. lawyer
Malik, Raymond Howard economist, scientist, corporate executive, multi-lingual, inventor, educator
Malkin, Cary Jay lawyer
†Malkin, Judd D. diversified corporation executive
Mallory, Robert Mark controller, finance executive
Malone, James Laurence, III lawyer
Malott, Robert Harvey manufacturing company executive
Malovance, Gregory J. lawyer
Malstrom, Robert A. lawyer
Maltz, J. Herbert physician, hospital director
Mancoff, Neal Alan lawyer
Mandell, Floyd A. lawyer
Manelli, Donald Dean screenwriter, film producer
Mann, H. George lawyer
Manny, Carter Hugh, Jr. architect, foundation administrator
Maram, Barry S. lawyer
Marcus, Joseph child psychiatrist
Marcus, Stephen A. lawyer
Marcuse, Manfred Joachim paper products executive
Margoliash, Emanuel biochemist, educator
Margolis, Jeremy lawyer
Marineau, Philip Albert food company executive
Mariotti, Jay Anthony journalist
Marks, Dennis A. lawyer
Marks, Jerome lawyer
Markus, Fred H. engineering and architectural company executive
Markus, Robert Michael journalist
†Marotta, Sabath Fred physiology educator
Marovich, George M. federal judge
Marovitz, James Lee lawyer
Marsh, Jeanne Cay social welfare educator, researcher
†Marshall, Cody bishop
Marshall, Donald Glenn English language and literature educator
Marshall, Eric C. lawyer
Marshall, John David lawyer
Marshall, Prentice H., Jr. lawyer
Marston-Scott, Mary Vesta nurse, educator
Martin, Arthur Mead lawyer
Martin, R. Eden lawyer
Martin, Siva lawyer
Martinez, Miguel Angel Spanish language educator
Marty, Martin Emil religion educator, editor
Marwedel, Warren John lawyer
Marx, David, Jr. lawyer
†Marziano, Fredric G. insurance company executive
Mason, Bruce advertising agency executive
Mason, Henry Lowell, III lawyer
Masserman, Jules Homan neuropsychiatrist, psychoanalyst
Massolo, Arthur James banker
Matasar, Ann B. former dean, business and political science educator
Mateles, Richard Isaac biotechnologist
Matis, Nina B. lawyer
Matthei, Edward Hodge architect
Mattos Neto, Sebastiao De Souza lawyer
Mattson, Stephen Joseph lawyer
Maxson, M. Finley lawyer
May, J. Peter mathematics educator
Mayer, Frank D., Jr. lawyer
Mayer, Raymond Richard business administration educator
Mayers, Barbara W. lawyer
†Mayo, J. Haskell, Jr. bishop
McBreen, Maura Ann lawyer
McCaleb, Malcolm, Jr. lawyer
McCarron, John Francis columnist
Mc Carter, John Wilbur, Jr. corporation executive
McCarthy, Charles Justin lawyer
McCarthy, Paul lawyer
McCarville, Mark John food company executive
McCaskey, Edward W. professional football team executive
†Mc Caskey, Raymond F. insurance company executive
McCausland, Thomas James, Jr. brokerage house executive
McClung, James Allen chemical and machinery manufacturing company executive
Mc Clure, James J., Jr. lawyer, former municipal executive
McCombs, Hugh R., Jr. lawyer
†McConahey, Stephen George securities company executive
McConnell, E. Hoy, II advertising executive
McCormack, Robert Cornelius investment banker
McCormick, Steven D. lawyer
McCoy, Wayne A. lawyer
†McCracken, Thomas James, Jr. lawyer
McCrone, Walter Cox research institute executive
McCue, Howard McDowell, III lawyer, educator
McCue, Judith W. lawyer
†McCullagh, Grant Gibson architect
McCullough, Henry G(lenn) L(uther) nuclear engineer
McCullough, Michael William, Jr. minister, educator, researcher, writer, missionary, gospel singer, consultant
McCullough, Richard Lawrence advertising agency executive
McCurry, Margaret Irene architect, educator
McDaniel, Charles-Gene journalism educator, writer
McDermott, John H(enry) lawyer
McDermott, Robert B. lawyer
McDonald, Thomas Alexander lawyer
McDonough, John Michael lawyer
Mc Dougall, Dugald Stewart retired lawyer
McDowell, Jack Burns professional baseball player
McDowell, William S. lawyer
McGarr, Frank James retired federal judge, dispute resolution consultant
McGinn, Bernard John religious educator
†McGivern, Arthur J. corporate lawyer, food products company executive
McGrath, William Joseph lawyer
McGuigan, John V. lawyer
Mc Guirt, Wayne Robert publishing company executive
McIntyre, Kathryn Joan publisher, editorial director
Mc Kay, Neil banker
McKee, Keith Earl manufacturing technology executive
Mc Keel, Sam Stewart newspaper executive
Mc Kenna, Thomas Joseph advertising executive
McKittrick, William Wood lawyer
McLaughlin, T. Mark lawyer
McLean, Robert David lawyer
McMahon, Thomas Michael lawyer
McMenamin, John Robert lawyer
†McNeely, Stephen Allen company executive
McNeill, G. David psychologist, educator
McNeill, Robert Patrick investment counselor
McNeill, Thomas B. lawyer
McQueen, Thomas K. lawyer
McVisk, William Kilburn lawyer
McWhirter, Bruce J. lawyer
Measelle, Richard L. accountant
Mecklenburg, Gary Alan hospital executive
Medved, Michael film critic, author
Medvin, Harvey Norman financial executive, treasurer
Meers, Henry W. investment banker
Mehlman, Mark Franklin lawyer
Melamed, Leo investment company executive
Meleney, John Alexander lawyer
Melton, David Reuben lawyer
Meltzer, Bernard David legal educator
Menchin, Robert Stanley marketing executive
Menson, Richard L. lawyer
Mercer, David Robinson association executive
Merlin, Peter Helmuth lawyer
Metz, Charles Edgar radiology educator
Metz, Lawrence Anthony lawyer
Meyer, Charles Appleton former retailing executive
Meyer, Donald Gordon college dean, educator
†Meyer, Edward Paul advertising executive
Meyer, J. Theodore lawyer
Meyer, Michael Louis lawyer
Meyer, Paul Reims, Jr. orthopedic surgeon
Meyer, Peter physicist, educator
Meyer, Raymond Joseph former college basketball coach
Meyers, Dorothy educator, writer
Michalak, Edward Francis lawyer
Michelson, Irving aerospace engineer
Migala, Lucyna Jozefa broadcast journalist, arts administrator, radio station executive
Migdal, Sheldon Paul lawyer
Mikesell, Marvin Wray geography educator
Miletich, Ivo library and information scientist, bibliographer, educator, linguist, literature research specialist
Millard, Richard Steven lawyer
Miller, Bernard Joseph, Jr. advertising executive
†Miller, Charles S. clergy member, church administrator
Miller, Frederick Staten music educator, academic administrator
Miller, Irving Franklin chemical engineering educator, academic administrator
Miller, James Edwin, Jr. English language educator
Miller, Mark newspaper editor
Miller, Maurice James lawyer
Miller, Merton Howard finance educator
Miller, Michael I. lawyer
Miller, Patrick William research administrator, educator
Miller, Paul J. lawyer
Miller, Stephen Ralph lawyer
Miller, Theodore Norman lawyer
Miller, William H. public relations executive
Millichap, Joseph Gordon neurologist, educator
Millner, Robert B. lawyer
Milnikel, Robert Saxon lawyer
Milstein, Albert lawyer
Miner, Thomas Hawley international entrepreneur
Minichello, Dennis lawyer
Minkowycz, W. J. mechanical engineering educator
†Minnick, Malcolm L. clergy member, church administrator
†Minogue, John P. academic administrator, priest, educator
Minow, Josephine Baskin civic worker
Minow, Newton Norman lawyer
Mintz, Harry artist, educator
Mirkin, Bernard Leo clinical pharmacologist, pediatrician
Mirza, David Brown economist, educator
Mitchell, Douglas Farrell trust company executive, lawyer
Mitchell, Lee Mark communications executive, investment fund manager, lawyer
Mitchell, W. J. T. English language, literature and visual arts educator, editor
Mlsna, Timothy Martin lawyer
Moawad, Atef obstetrician-gynecologist, educator
Moelmann, Lawrence R. lawyer
†Moller-Gunderson, Mark Robert minister, administrator
†Moller-Gunderson, Mary Ann clergy member, church administrator
Molloy, James B. corrugated packaging executive
Moltz, Marshall Jerome lawyer
Mone, Peter John lawyer
Montgomery, Charles Howard retired bank executive
Moor, Roy Edward finance educator
Moore, John Ronald manufacturing executive
†Moore, Sister Marie nun, hospital executive
Moran, James Byron federal judge
Moravy, L. Joe accountant, financial consultant
Morgan, Howard Campbell banker
Morris, Ralph William chronopharmacologist
Morrison, John Horton lawyer
Morrison, Michael P. lawyer
Morrison, Portia Owen lawyer
†Morrison, Samuel F. library administrator, chief librarian
Morrissey, Francis Daniel lawyer
†Morrow, Charles Gay, III state legislator, utility company representative
Morrow, John Ellsworth lawyer
Morrow, Richard Martin retired oil company executive
Morsch, Thomas Harvey lawyer
†Mortensen, Audrey R. church administrator
†Mosena, David R. aviation commissioner
Moses, Irving Byron architect
†Mosley, Elaine Christian Savage principal, chief education officer, consultant
Mourek, Joseph Edward musician
Moutoussamy, John Warren architect
Mowder, Gary Leroy lawyer
Mrozek, Donald L. lawyer
Muchin, Allan B. lawyer
Mueller, Gregory M. museum curator, botanist, researcher
Mueller, Richard Edward lawyer
Muench, John E. lawyer
Mukoyama, James Hidefumi, Jr. securities executive
Mullan, John Francis (Sean Mullan) neurosurgeon, educator
Mullen, J. Thomas lawyer
Muller, Dietrich Alfred Helmut physicist, educator
†Muller, Ralph W. hospital administrator
Mullin, Leo Francis banker
Mulvihill, Terence Joseph investment banking executive
Mumford, Manly Whitman lawyer
Mundlak, Yair agriculture and economics educator
Munitz, Gerald F. lawyer
Munson, James Calfee lawyer
Murata, Tadao engineering and computer science educator
Murdock, Charles William lawyer, educator
†Murphy, Barth T. insurance company executive
Murphy, Ellis association management executive
Murphy, Michael Emmett food company executive
Murray, Daniel Richard lawyer
Murray, Gregory S. lawyer
Murray, James Cunningham, Jr. lawyer
Murtaugh, Christopher David lawyer
Murtaugh, Michael K. lawyer
Musa, Mahmoud Nimir psychiatry educator
†Myers, Jim church administrator
Myers, Lonn William lawyer
Myers, Randall Kirk professional baseball player
Nachman, James L. lawyer
Nachman, Norman Harry lawyer
Nadherny, Ferdinand executive recruiting company executive
Nadler, Mark B. executive editor
Nagel, Sidney Robert physics educator
Nahrwold, David Lange surgeon, educator
Najita, Tetsuo history educator
Nambu, Yoichiro physics educator
Narahashi, Toshio pharmacology educator
Nash, Donald Gene commodities specialist
Nason, Robert E. accountant
Nault, William Henry publishing executive
Neal, Stephen C. lawyer
Neal, Steven George journalist
Nebel, Kai Allen lawyer
Nechin, Herbert Benjamin lawyer
Neis, James M. lawyer
Nekritz, Barry B. lawyer
Nelsen, Timothy Alan lawyer
Nelson, H(arry) Donald communications executive
Nelson, Kenneth Edward consulting engineer
Nelson, Richard David lawyer
Nelson, Thomas R. lawyer
†Nelson, William Bruce newspaper company executive
Nemerovski, Steven H. lawyer
Nero, Ellie Theresa elementary education educator
Nesburg, Alan D. lawyer
Neubauer, Charles Frederick investigative reporter
Neugarten, Bernice Levin social scientist
Neuhausen, Benjamin Simon auditor, accountant
†Nevling, Lorin Ives, Jr. museum administrator
Newell, Frank William ophthalmologist, educator
Newey, Paul Davis lawyer
Newlin, Charles Fremont lawyer
Newman, Dennis Nathan lawyer
†Newman, Gordon Harold lawyer, food company executive
Newman, Ralph Geoffrey literary scholar historian
Newman, Robert William lawyer
Newman, Terry E. lawyer
†Nicastro, Neil David business executive, lawyer
Nichol, Norman J. manufacturing executive
Nicholas, Arthur Soterios manufacturing company executive
Nicholas, Ralph Wallace anthropologist, educator
Nicholls, David G. editor
Nickel, Melvin Edwin metallurgical engineer
Nicklin, Emily lawyer
Niefeld, Jaye Sutter advertising executive
Nims, John Frederick writer, educator
Nissen, William John lawyer
Nitikman, Franklin W. lawyer
Nixon, Harvey lawyer
Noha, Edward J. insurance company executive
Nolan, Robert D. advertising company executive
Noll, Kenneth Eugene air resources engineering educator
Nord, Henry J. transportation executive
Nord, Robert Eamor lawyer
Nordberg, John Albert federal judge
Nordland, Gerald art museum administrator, historian, consultant
Nordstrand, Raymond William broadcasting company executive
Norgle, Charles Ronald, Sr. federal judge
†Norris, James Rufus, Jr. chemist, educator, consultant
Norton, Peter Bowes publishing company executive
Notebaert, Richard C. telecommunications industry executive
Notz, John Kranz, Jr. lawyer
Novick, David civil engineer, educator
Novick, Peter historian, educator
Novotny, David Joseph lawyer
Nowacki, James Nelson lawyer
Nussbaum, Bernard J. lawyer
Nutt, Jim artist
Nyhus, Lloyd Milton surgeon, educator
Oates, James G. advertising executive
Obenhaus, Victor theology educator, clergyman
O'Brien, James Phillip lawyer
O'Brien, Patrick William lawyer
†O'Connell, Dennis A. advertising executive
O'Connell, Harold Patrick, Jr. banker
O'Connor, Daniel J. lawyer
O'Connor, James John utility company executive
O'Connor, John Killeen lawyer
O'Connor, Joseph William reinsurance company executive
O'Dell, James E. newspaper publishing executive
Odorizzi, Michele L. lawyer
Oehme, Reinhard physicist, educator
Oesterle, Eric Adam lawyer
Offer, Daniel psychiatrist
Offutt, Gerald M. lawyer
O'Flaherty, Paul Benedict lawyer
O'Hagan, James Joseph lawyer
O'Hare, John Mitchell lawyer
O'Hare, Linda Parsons management consultant
Oka, Takeshi physicist, chemist, astronomer, educator
O'Leary, Daniel Vincent, Jr. lawyer
O'Leary, Frank J. lawyer
Olian, Robert Martin lawyer
Olins, Robert Abbot communications research executive
Oliver, Harry Maynard, Jr. retired brokerage house executive
Olsen, Edward John geologist, educator
Olsen, Rex Norman trade association executive
†O'Malley, Jack state's attorney
Orbon, Margaret J. lawyer
O'Reilly, Charles Terrance university dean
Organ, Joseph B. lawyer
Orozco, Raymond E. protective services official
Orr, Richard Tuttle journalist
Oryshkevich, Roman Sviatoslav physician, physiatrist, dentist, educator
O'Shea, Lynne Edeen advertising and media company executive, educator
Osiyoye, Adekunle obstetrician/gynecologist, educator
†Ostrow, Jay Donald gastroenterology educator, researcher
Ott, James Forgan finance company executive
†Oulvey, David E. accountant, brokerage house executive
Overgaard, Mitchell Jersild lawyer
Overton, George Washington lawyer
Overton, Jane Vincent Harper biology educator
Oxtoby, David William chemistry educator
Ozog, Edward J. lawyer
Pachman, Daniel J. physician, educator
Page, Clarence E. newspaper columnist
Page, Ernest medical educator
Pallasch, B. Michael lawyer
Pallmeyer, Rebecca Ruth federal judge
Palm, Gary Howard lawyer, educator
†Palmer, Alice J. state legislator
Palmer, John Bernard, III lawyer
Palmer, Patrick Edward radio astronomer, educator
Palmer, Robert Erwin association executive
Palmer, Robert Towne lawyer
Palmore, Roderick Alan lawyer
Panich, Danuta Bembenista lawyer
Pape, Arthur Edward lawyer
†Pappageorge, George C. architect
Pappas, George Demetrios anatomy and cell biology educator, scientist
Parisi, Joseph (Anthony) magazine editor, writer-consultant, educator
Park, Chung Il librarian
Park, Dale, Jr. lawyer
Parker, Eugene Newman physicist, educator
Parkhurst, Todd Sheldon lawyer
Parrish, Overton Burgin, Jr. pharmaceutical corporation executive
Parsons, Keith I. lawyer
Parzen, Stanley Julius lawyer
Pascal, Roger lawyer
Pascale, Daniel Richard judge
Paschke, Edward F. artist, illustrator
Patel, Homi Burjor apparel company executive
Patterson, James William environmental engineering educator, consultant
Patterson, Roy physician, educator
Pattishall, Beverly Wyckliffe lawyer
Patton, Stephen Ray lawyer
Paul, Arthur artist, graphic designer, illustrator, art and design consultant
Paul, Ronald Neale management consultant
Paulson, Glenn environmental scientist
Pavalon, Eugene Irving lawyer
Pearl, Melvin E. lawyer, film producer
Peck, Donald Vincent musician
Peerman, Dean Gordon magazine editor
Pekow, Eugene hotel company executive
Pell, Wilbur Frank, Jr. federal judge

Pelton, Russell Meredith, Jr. lawyer
Peltzman, Sam economics educator
Pemberton, Scott Bender editor, publishing executive
Peres, Judith May journalist
Perkins, James L. lawyer
Perlberg, Jules Martin lawyer
Perlis, Michael Steven magazine publisher
Perlman, Judy Platt lawyer
Perlstadt, Sidney Morris lawyer
Pesmen, Sandra (Mrs. Harold William Pesmen) editor
Pestureau, Pierre Gilbert literature educator, literary critic, editor
Petacque, Arthur M. journalist
Peters, Gordon Benes musician
Petersen, Donald Sondergaard lawyer
Petersen, William Otto lawyer
Peterson, Gerald C. lawyer
†Peterson, Marybeth A. church administrator
Peterson, Mildred Othmer (Mrs. Howard R. Peterson) lecturer, writer, librarian, civic leader
Petrakis, Peter lawyer
Petrie, James Stanton lawyer
Pezzella, Jerry James, Jr. investment and real estate corporation executive
Phelan, Richard John county administrator, lawyer
Phelps, Paul Michael lawyer
Philipps, Louis Edward data systems manufacturing company executive
†Philipson, Morris university press director
†Phillips, Donald W. investment company executive
†Phillips, Frederick Falley architect
Pick, Ruth research scientist, physician, educator
†Piderit, John J. academic administrator
Piekarski, Victor J. lawyer
Pierce, Daniel Marshall lawyer, mayor
†Pierson, Don sports columnist
Pikler, Charles musician
Pilkington, Alan Ralph advertising executive
Pincus, Theodore Henry public relations executive
Pippen, Scottie professional basketball player
Pitt, George lawyer
Pitts, Robert Eugene, Jr. marketing educator, consultant
Pizer, Howard Charles professional baseball team executive, lawyer
Pizzi, Pier Luigi costume and scenic designer, film director
Plank, Betsy Ann (Mrs. Sherman V. Rosenfield) public relations counsel
Platz, George Arthur, III lawyer
Platzman, George William geophysicist, educator
Plotkin, Manuel D. management consultant, educator, former corporate executive and government official
Plotnick, Harvey Barry publishing executive
Plotnik, Arthur publishing executive
†Plummer, Roger Lawrence information systems executive
Plunkett, Paul Edward federal judge
Podesta, Robert Angelo investment banker
Poe, Douglas Allan lawyer
Polley, Edward Herman anatomist, educator
Pollick, G. David academic administrator
Pollock, Alexander John banker
Pollock, Earl Edward lawyer
Pollock, George Howard psychiatrist, psychoanalyst
Pollock, Sheldon Ivan language professional, educator
Pope, Daniel James lawyer
Pope, Jerome W. lawyer
Pope, Kerig Rodgers magazine executive
Pope, Lena Elizabeth human resources specialist
†Pope, Richard M. rheumatologist
Posner, Richard Allen federal judge
†Powell, Allen Royal bishop
Powles, Peter B. lawyer
Poznanski, Andrew Karol pediatric radiologist
Pratt, Robert Windsor lawyer
Preschlack, John Edward management consultant
Presser, Stephen Bruce lawyer, educator
Prior, Gary L. lawyer
Pritikin, David T. lawyer
Pritikin, James B. lawyer, employee benefits consultant
Pritzker, Jay Arthur lawyer
Pritzker, Nicholas J. diversified services corporation executive
Pritzker, Robert Alan manufacturing company executive
†Pritzker, Thomas Jay lawyer, business executive
Prochnow, Douglas Lee lawyer
Prochnow, Herbert Victor former government official, banker, author
Prochnow, Herbert Victor, Jr. lawyer
Proctor, Barbara Gardner advertising agency executive
Proctor, Edward George lawyer
†Proops, Jay D. agricultural products executive
Prosperi, David Philip public relations executive
Provus, Barbara Lee executive search consultant
Puerner, John newspaper publishing executive
Pugh, Roderick Wellington psychologist, educator
Pugliese, Robert J. lawyer
Pumper, Robert William microbiologist
Quaal, Ward Louis broadcast executive
Quade, Victoria Catherine editor, writer
Quanstrom, Walter Roy oil executive, educator
Quebe, Jerry Lee architect
Quinlan, William Joseph, Jr. lawyer
Rachwalski, Frank Joseph, Jr. financial executive
Radell, Nicholas John management consultant
Radler, Warren S. lawyer
Rafelson, Max Emanuel, Jr. biochemist, medical school administrator
Rafferty, Nancy Schwarz anatomy educator
Rahe, Maribeth Sembach bank executive
Rahl, James Andrew lawyer, educator
Raines, Tim professional baseball player
†Rajan, Fred E. N. clergy member, church administrator
Ralph, William J. lawyer
Ramberg, Christina artist, educator
Ran, Shulamit composer
Rank, John Thomas lawyer
Rankin, James Winton lawyer
Ranney, George A., Jr. lawyer
Raphaelson, Joel advertising agency executive
Rasin, Rudolph Stephen investment banker
Rasor, Robert D. lawyer
Ratner, Gerald lawyer
Rauch, George Washington lawyer
Raup, David Malcolm paleontology educator
†Raven, Corinne principal
Raymond, Spencer Henry lawyer
Redfield, James Michael humanities and classics educator
Reed, Charles Allen anthropologist
Reed, Janet Lynn lawyer
Reed, John Shedd former railway executive
Reed, Keith Allen lawyer
Reedy, Jerry Edward editor, writer
Reeves, Michael Stanley public utility executive
Regensteiner, Else Friedsam (Mrs. Bertold Regensteiner) textile designer, educator
Reggio, Vito Anthony management consultant
Reich, Allan J. lawyer
Reichelt, Fred (Ferdinand Herbert Reichelt) insurance and finance company executive
Reicin, Ronald Ian lawyer
Reiffel, Leonard physicist, scientific consultant
Reilly, Robert Frederick valuation consultant
Reingold, Haim mathematics educator
Reinsdorf, Jerry Michael professional baseball team executive, real estate executive, lawyer
Reiss, Dale Anne accounting executive
Reiter, Michael A. lawyer
Reitman, Jerry Irving advertising agency executive
Relias, John Alexis lawyer
Remini, Robert Vincent historian, educator
Renshaw, Charles Clark, Jr. retired publishing executive
Reschke, Michael W. real estate executive
Resnick, Donald Ira lawyer
Reum, James Michael lawyer
Reynolds, Frank Everett religious studies educator
Reynolds, Thomas A., Jr. lawyer
Reynolds, Thomas A., III lawyer
Rhea, Edward Buford, Jr. brokerage house executive
Rhind, James Thomas lawyer
Rhoads, Paul Kelly lawyer
Rhodes, Charles Harker, Jr. lawyer
Rhone, Douglas Pierce pathologist, educator
Rice, Linda Johnson publishing executive
Rice, William Edward newspaper columnist
Rich, S. Judith public relations executive
Richardson, Jerome Johnson food service company executive
Richardson, John Thomas university chancellor, clergyman
Richardson, William F. lawyer
Richman, Harold Alan social welfare policy educator
Richman, John Marshall lawyer, business executive
Richman, William Sheldon furniture company executive
Richmond, William Patrick lawyer
Riddell, Matthew Donald Rutherford consulting environmental engineer
Rieger, Mitchell Sheridan lawyer
Rielly, John Edward association executive
Rikoski, Richard Anthony engineering executive, electrical engineer
Rissman, Burton Richard lawyer
Ritchie, Albert lawyer
Ritchie, William Paul lawyer
Rizzo, Ronald Stephen lawyer
Robbins, Henry Zane public relations and marketing executive
Roberts, Harry Vivian statistics educator
Roberts, Theodore Harris banker
Robertson, Sara Stewart investment company executive
Robinson, Martin F. lawyer
Robinson, Theodore Curtis, Jr. lawyer
Rocek, Jan chemist, educator
Roche, James McMillan lawyer
Rodgers, James Foster association executive, economist
Rodgers, Johnathan broadcast executive
Rodriguez, Matt L. protective services professional
Roebuck, John Clifford lawyer
Roenick, Jeremy professional hockey player
Roeper, Richard columnist
Rogers, Eddy J. lawyer
Rogers, John W., Jr. brokerage house executive
Rogers, Lee Frank radiologist
†Rohlin, Diane Elizabeth financial public relations executive
Roin, Howard James lawyer
Roizman, Bernard virologist, educator
Rollhaus, Philip Edward, Jr. diversified manufacturing company executive
Rooney, Matthew A. lawyer
Ropski, Gary Melchior lawyer
Roque, Roberto Dizon city official
†Rose, Merrill public relations counselor
Rosemarin, Carey Stephen lawyer
Rosen, George economist, educator
Rosen, Sherwin economist, educator
†Rosen, Steven Terry oncologist, hematologist
Rosenbaum, Michael A. investor relations consultant
Rosenberg, Gary Aron business executive, lawyer
Rosenberg, Milton J. social psychologist, educator
Rosenberg, Richard M. lawyer
Rosenberg, Robert Brinkmann research organization executive
Rosenbloom, Lewis Stanley lawyer
†Rosenbloom, Steve sportswriter
Rosenblum, Michael F. lawyer
Rosenblum, Victor Gregory political science and law educator
Rosenfield, Robert Lee pediatric endocrinologist, educator
Rosenheim, Edward Weil English educator
Rosenheim, Margaret Keeney social welfare policy education educator
Rosenthal, Albert Jay advertising agency executive
Rosenthal, Earl Edgar art history educator
Rosenthal, Ira Maurice pediatrician, educator
Rosenthal, Samuel Robert lawyer
Rosner, Jonathan Lincoln physicist, educator
Rosner, Robert astrophysicist
Ross, Jeffrey Kenneth lawyer
Ross, John Thompson, Jr. (Tom Ross) advertising executive
Roston, David C. lawyer
Roth, Sanford Irwin pathologist, educator
Rothschild, Edwin Alfred lawyer
Rothschild, George William judge, lawyer
†Rothstein, Ruth M. hospital adminstrator
Rovner, Ilana Kara Diamond federal judge
Rowder, William Louis lawyer
Rowen, Robert G. savings and loan executive
Rowley, Janet Davison physician
Roy, David Tod Chinese literature educator
Royko, Mike newspaper columnist
Rubenstein, Arthur Harold physician, educator
Rubin, Bonnie Miller journalist
Rubin, E(rwin) Leonard lawyer
Rubin, Robert J. lawyer
Ruder, David Sturtevant lawyer, educator, government official
Rudnick, Paul David lawyer
Rudolph, Lloyd Irving political science educator
Rudolph, Susanne Hoeber political and social science educator
Rudstein, David Stewart law educator
Rudy, Lester Howard psychiatrist
Rumsfeld, Donald Henry former government official, corporate executive
Rundio, Louis Michael, Jr. lawyer
Runkle, Martin Davey library director
Rupert, Donald William lawyer
Rusch, William Graham religious organization administrator
Russell, James H. lawyer
Russell, Lillian medical, surgical nurse
Russell, Paul Frederick lawyer
†Rutherford, Jack Dow manufacturing executive
Rutigliano, Louis J. telecommunications industry executive
Rutkoff, Alan Stuart lawyer
Ryan, Howard Chris state supreme court justice
Ryan, Leo Vincent business educator
Ryan, Patrick G. insurance company executive
Ryan, Thomas F. lawyer
Rychlak, Joseph Frank psychology educator, theoretician
Rycroft, Donald Cahill insurance executive
Ryder, David R. lawyer
Rydholm, Ralph Williams advertising agency executive
†Rymer, William Zev research scientist, administrator
†Rynkiewicz, Stephen Michael journalist
Sabl, John J. lawyer
†Sachs, Lloyd Robert entertainment critic, writer
Sachs, Robert Green physicist, educator, laboratory administrator
Sager, William F. retired chemistry educator
Saller, Richard Paul classics educator
Salomon, Richard Adley lawyer
Salpeter, Alan N. lawyer
†Samuels, Joel L. librarian, clergyman
Samuels, Lawrence Robert lawyer
Sanders, David P. lawyer
Sanders, Richard Henry lawyer
†Sanderson, Richard Burr advertising agency executive
Sandner, John Francis commodity futures broker, lawyer
Sandquist, Elroy Charles, Jr. lawyer
Sangerman, Harry M. lawyer
Santangelo, Mario Vincent dental association executive, educator
†Sauer, Kenneth H. bishop
Saul, Peter artist
Saunders, David Alan lawyer
Saunders, George Lawton, Jr. lawyer
Savner, David A. lawyer
Sawdey, Richard Marshall lawyer
Sawinski, Vincent John chemistry educator
Sawyier, Calvin P. lawyer
Sawyier, David R. lawyer
Scalish, Frank Anthony labor union administrator
Scanlan, Thomas Cleary publishing executive, editor
Scarpelli, Dante Giovanni pathologist, educator
Schafer, Michael Frederick orthopedic surgeon
†Schap, Evelyn K. advertising executive
Schauer, Louis Frank lawyer
Schechter, Allen E(dward) retired publishing company executive
Scheinkman, José Alexandre economics educator
Scherer, Ross Paul retired sociology educator
Schieser, Hans Alois education educator
Schiffman, David M. lawyer
Schiller, Donald Charles lawyer
Schiller, Eric M. lawyer
Schillinger, Edwin Joseph physics educator
Schilsky, Richard Lewis oncologist, researcher
Schimberg, A(rmand) Bruce lawyer
Schindel, Donald Marvin lawyer
Schink, James Harvey lawyer
Schippers, David Philip lawyer
Schirn, Janet Sugerman interior designer
Schlickman, J. Andrew lawyer
Schlitter, Stanley Allen lawyer
Schloss, Nathan economist
Schlossman, John Isaac architect
Schmetterer, Jack Baer federal judge
Schmiege, Robert railroad executive
Schneider, Dan W. lawyer, consultant
Schneider, Robert Jerome lawyer
Scholle, Roger Hal dentist
†Schommer, Carol Marie principal
Schoonhoven, Ray James retired lawyer
Schorer, Joseph U. lawyer
Schornack, John James accountant
Schoumacher, Bruce Herbert lawyer
Schramm, David Norman astrophysicist, educator
Schreck, Robert A., Jr. lawyer
Schriver, John T., III lawyer
Schroeder, Charles Edgar banker, investment management executive
Schroeder, Douglas Fredrick architect
Schroeder, W(illiam) Widick educator
Schubert, William Henry curriculum studies educator
Schuerman, John Richard social work educator
Schuette, Michael lawyer
Schug, Kenneth Robert chemistry educator
†Schulfer, Roche Edward theater director
Schulhofer, Stephen Joseph law educator
Schulman, Sidney neurologist, educator
Schulte, David Michael investment banker
Schulte, Stephen Charles lawyer
Schultz, Arthur Warren communications company executive
Schultz, Kurt Lee lawyer
Schultz, Theodore William retired educator, economist
Schulz, Keith Donald corporate lawyer
Schumer, William surgeon, educator
Schupp, Ronald Irving civil rights leader, clergyman
Schuyler, Daniel Merrick lawyer, educator
Schwartz, Charles Phineas, Jr. replacement auto parts company executive, lawyer
Schwartz, Donald Lee lawyer
Schwartz, John Norman health care executive
Schweikert, Norman Carl musician
Scogland, William Lee lawyer
Scott, Alice H. librarian
Scott, John Brooks research institute executive
Scott, Louis Edward advertising agency executive
Scott, Theodore R. lawyer
Scully, Joseph C. bank executive
Seaman, Irving, Jr. public relations consultant
Sedelmaier, John Josef film director, cinematographer
Seely, Robert Fleming lawyer
Seidenfeld, Glenn Kenneth lawyer
Seidner, Frederic Jay public relations executive
†Seitz, Tim church administrator
Seki, Hoken S. lawyer
Selander, Larry lawyer
Seligman, Richard Michael lawyer
Sen, Ashish Kumar urban planner, educator
Sengstacke, John Herman Henry publishing company executive
Sereno, Paul C. paleontologist, educator
Serritella, James Anthony lawyer
Serritella, William David lawyer
Serwer, Alan Michael lawyer
Sfikas, Peter Michael lawyer, educator
Shadur, Milton I. judge
Shadur, Robert H. lawyer
†Shafer, Eric Christopher minister
Shambaugh, George Elmer, III internist
†Shanahan, Edmond Michael savings and loan executive
Shanas, Ethel sociology educator
Shank, William O. lawyer
Shanks, Gerald Robert insurance company executive
Shannon, Peter Michael, Jr. lawyer
Shapey, Ralph composer, conductor, educator
Shapiro, Harold David lawyer, educator
Shapiro, Stanley materials scientist
Shapiro, Stephen Michael lawyer
Shapo, Marshall Schambelan lawyer, educator
†Shelby, David T. manufacturing executive
Sheldon, Harvey M. lawyer
Shepherd, Stewart Robert lawyer
Shepro, Richard W. lawyer
Sherck, Timothy C. lawyer
Shere, Dennis publishing executive
†Sherman, Robert Frank banker
Shields, Thomas Charles lawyer
Shields, Thomas William surgeon, educator
Shindler, Donald A. lawyer
Shirley, Virginia Lee advertising executive
Shuman, Nicholas Roman journalist, educator
†Shute, David retail executive, lawyer
Sibbald, John Ristow management consultant
Sido, Kevin Richard lawyer
Siegel, Arthur corporate executive
Siegel, Howard Jerome lawyer
Siegler, Mark internist, educator
Sigal, Michael Stephen lawyer
Sigmon, Joyce Elizabeth association executive
Silberman, Alan Harvey lawyer
Silets, Harvey Marvin lawyer
Simmons, Adele Smith foundation president, former educator
Simon, Bernece Kern social work educator
Simon, John Bern lawyer
Simon, John P. lawyer
Simon, Mordecai religious association administrator, clergyman
Simon, Ralph rabbi
Simon, Seymour lawyer, former state supreme court justice
Simons, Helen school psychologist, psychotherapist
Simonson, Margaret newspaper publishing executive
†Simpson, Donald Bruce library director
Simpson, John Alexander physicist
Singer, Emel staffing industry executive
Siske, Roger Charles lawyer
Siskel, Gene (Eugene Kal Siskel) film critic
Sive, Rebecca Anne public affairs company executive
Skinner, Samuel Knox utilities executive, lawyer
Sklarsky, Charles B. lawyer
Skrebneski, Victor photographer
Slansky, Jerry William investment company executive
Slavitt, Earl Benton lawyer
Slocomb, Paul D. lawyer
Slomka, Sister Stella Louise hospital administrator
Smart, Allen Rich, II lawyer
Smith, Adrian Devaun architect
Smith, Arthur B(everly), Jr. lawyer
Smith, David Waldo Edward pathology educator, physician
Smith, Freddye L(ee) financial planner
Smith, Gordon Howell lawyer
Smith, John Gelston lawyer
Smith, John J. (Jack Smith) advertising agency executive
Smith, Kenneth Bryant seminary administrator
Smith, Lawrence R. lawyer
Smith, Raymond Thomas anthropology educator
Smith, Robert Drake railroad executive
Smith, Spencer Bailey engineering and business educator
Smith, Stan Vladimir economist, financial service company executive
Smith, Tefft W. lawyer
Smithburg, William Dean food manufacturing company executive
†Sneed, Michael (Michele) columnist
Snider, Lawrence K. lawyer
Snyder, John Lindsey lawyer
Sobel, Walter Howard architect
Sochen, June historian
Socolofsky, Jon Edward banker
Soeteber, Ellen journalist, newspaper editor
Solomon, Jack Avrum lawyer, automotive distributor, art dealer
Solomonson, Charles D. corporate executive
Solotorovsky, Julian lawyer
Solovy, Jerold Sherwin lawyer
Solti, Sir Georg conductor
Somers, Antoinette Nadezhda telecommunications executive
Sonderby, Peter R. lawyer
Sonderby, Susan Pierson federal bankruptcy judge
Sopranos, Orpheus Javaras manufacturing company executive
Sorensen, Leif Boge physician, educator
†Sorensen, W. Robert clergy member, church administrator
Soto, Ramona training specialist
Sparberg, Marshall Stuart gastroenterologist, educator
Spector, David M. lawyer
Spector, Harold Norman physics educator
Speidel, Richard Eli lawyer, educator
Spellmire, George W. lawyer
Spencer, Lewis Douglas lawyer
Spencer, Rozelle Jeffery moving and storage company executive
Sperling, Robert Y. lawyer
†Spindler, George S. lawyer, oil industry executive
Spiotto, James Ernest lawyer
Spivey, Bruce E. health care executive
Springer, David Edward lawyer
Sproger, Charles Edmund lawyer
Sprowl, Charles Riggs lawyer
Squires, John Henry federal bankruptcy judge
Stack, John Wallace lawyer
Stack, Stephen S. manufacturing company executive
Stahl, Charles Eugene lawyer
Stahl, David M. lawyer
Staley, Augustus Eugene, III advertising executive

Staley, Charles Ralls *lawyer*
Stanley, Justin Armstrong *lawyer*
Staples, James G. *lawyer*
Starkman, Gary Lee *lawyer*
Stassen, John Henry *lawyer*
Stead, James Joseph, Jr. *securities company executive*
Stearns, Neele Edward, Jr. *diversified holding company executive*
Steck, Theodore Lyle *biochemistry and molecular biology educator, physician*
†Stegemoeller, Harvey A. *clergy member, church administrator*
†Stein, A. C. *clergy member, church administrator*
Stein, Jay Wobith *legal research and education consultant*
Stein, Paula Jean Anne Barton *real estate company executive*
Steinberg, Morton M. *lawyer*
Steiner, Barbara S. *lawyer*
Steiner, Donald Frederick *biochemist, physician, educator*
Steinfeld, Manfred *furniture manufacturing executive*
Steingraber, Frederick George *management consultant*
Stelmack, Gloria Joy *elementary education educator*
†Stelzel, Walter Tell, Jr. *accountant, financial company executive*
Stephan, Edmund Anton *lawyer*
Stepto, Robert Charles *physician, educator*
Steptoe, Philip P., III *lawyer*
Stern, Richard Gustave *author, educator*
Stern, Robert Louis *lawyer*
Sternberg, Paul *retired ophthalmologist*
Sternstein, Allan J. *lawyer*
Stetler, David J. *lawyer*
Stevens, Thomas Lee *lawyer*
Stevenson, Adlai Ewing, III *lawyer, former senator*
Stevenson, George Franklin *pathologist, association executive*
Stickler, K. Bruce *lawyer*
Stigler, Stephen Mack *statistician, educator*
Stillman, Nina Gidden *lawyer*
Stinson, James R. *lawyer*
Stirling, James Paulman *investment banker*
Stitt, Frederick Hesse *insurance broker*
Stock, Leon Milo *chemist, educator*
Stocking, George Ward, Jr. *anthropology educator*
Stoll, John Robert *lawyer, educator*
Stone, Alan *container company executive*
†Stone, Daniel Hunter *metallurgical engineer, researcher*
Stone, Geoffrey Richard *law educator, lawyer*
†Stone, Howard Lawrence *lawyer*
Stone, James Howard *management consultant*
Stone, Randolph Noel *law educator*
Stone, Roger Warren *container company executive*
Stone, Steven Michael *sports announcer, former baseball player*
Stotter, David W. *marketing executive*
Stover, Leon (Eugene) *anthropology educator, writer, critic*
Strasburger, Joseph Julius *retired lawyer*
Strauch, Gerald Otto *surgeon*
Streff, William Albert, Jr. *lawyer*
Strenski, James B. *communications executive*
Strobel, Pamela B. *lawyer*
Strobel, Russ M. *lawyer*
Strubel, Richard Perry *manufacturing company executive*
Struggles, John Edward *management consultant*
Stuart, Robert *container manufacturing executive*
Studwell, Thomas W. *lawyer*
Stukel, James Joseph *university official, mechanical engineering educator*
Sulkin, Howard Allen *college president*
Sullivan, Bernard James *accountant*
Sullivan, Cornelius J. *lawyer*
Sullivan, Marcia Waite *lawyer*
Sullivan, Peggy (Anne) *association executive*
Sullivan, Thomas Patrick *lawyer*
Sumner, William Marvin *anthropology and archaeology educator*
†Sunstein, Cass R. *law educator*
Sutherland, Joe Allen *lawyer*
Sutter, Darryl *professional hockey coach*
Sutter, William Paul *lawyer*
Swan, Richard Gordon *mathematics educator*
Swaney, Thomas Edward *lawyer*
Swanson, Bernet Steven *consulting engineer, former educator*
Swanson, Don Richard *university dean*
Swanson, Patricia K. *university administrator, librarian*
Swartz, William John *transportation resources company executive/retired*
Sweeney, James Patrick *management consultant*
Sweeney, James Raymond *lawyer*
Sweeney, Michael J. *lawyer*
Sweet, Charles Wheeler *executive recruiter*
Swerdlow, Martin Abraham *physician, pathologist*
Swett, Daniel Robert *lawyer*
Swibel, Steven Warren *lawyer*
Swift, Dolores Monica Marcinkevich *public relations executive*
Swift, Edward Foster, III *investment banker*
Szala, Scott J. *lawyer*
Szczepanski, Slawomir Zbigniew Steven *lawyer*
Tabin, Julius *patent lawyer, physicist*
Tadlock, R. Jerry *manufacturing and logistics consultant*
Talbot, Pamela *public relations executive*
Tallant, David, Jr. *lawyer*
Tannenberg, Dieter E. A. *manufacturing company executive*
Tanner, Helen Hornbeck *historian*
†Tardy, Medney Eugene, Jr. *otolaryngologist*
Tarun, Robert Walter *lawyer*
Taswell, Howard Filmore *pathologist, blood bank specialist, educator*
Tatooles, Constantine John *cardiovascular and thoracic surgeon*
Taub, Richard Paul *social sciences educator*
Taylor, George Allen *advertising agency executive*
Taylor, John Wilkinson *education educator*
Taylor, Roger Lee *lawyer*
Teichner, Lester *management consulting executive*
Telling, Edward Riggs *former retail, insurance, real estate and financial services executive*
Terkel, Studs (Louis) (Louis Terkel) *author, interviewer*
Terp, Dana George *architect*
Terry, Clifford Lewis *journalist*
Terry, Richard Edward *public utility holding company executive*
Thaden, Edward Carl *history educator*
Theobald, Edward Robert *lawyer*
Theobald, Thomas Charles *banker*
Thies, Richard Brian *lawyer*
Thomas, Dale E. *lawyer*
Thomas, Frank Edward *baseball player*
Thomas, Frederick Bradley *lawyer*
Thomas, John Thieme *management consultant*
Thomas, Marion May *educational program coordinator*
Thomas, Richard Lee *banker*
Thomas, Stephen Paul *lawyer*
Thompson, James Robert, Jr. *lawyer, former governor*
†Thomsen, Mark William *religious organization administrator*
Thomson, George Ronald *lawyer, educator*
Thorne-Thomsen, Thomas *lawyer*
Thornton, Theodore Kean *investment advisor*
Tibble, Douglas Clair *lawyer*
Tigerman, Stanley *architect, educator*
Tillett, Samuel Raymond *lawyer*
†Tingleff, Thomas Alan *transportation company executive*
Tippins, Bedell A. *lawyer*
Tobin, Calvin Jay *architect*
Tobin, Thomas F. *lawyer*
†Todd, James S. *surgeon, educator, medical association administrator*
Todd, James Stiles *surgeon, professional executive association*
Todd Copley, Judith Ann *materials and metallurgical engineering educator*
Toles, Edward Bernard *retired judge*
Toll, Daniel Roger *corporate executive, civic leader*
Tompsett, William C. *lawyer*
Tone, Jeffrey R. *lawyer*
Tone, Philip Willis *lawyer, former federal judge*
Tongue, William Walter *economics and business consultant, educator emeritus*
Toohey, James Kevin *lawyer*
Topol, Clive M. *lawyer*
Torbert, Preston M. *lawyer*
Torgersen, Torwald Harold *architect, designer*
Torshen, Jerome Harold *lawyer*
Towne, L. Stanton *lawyer*
Tozer, Forrest Leigh *lawyer*
Trapp, James M. *lawyer*
Trauscht, Donald C. *security services executive*
Travis, Dempsey Jerome *real estate executive, mortgage banker*
†Trebelhorn, Thomas Lynn *professional baseball team manager*
Treece, John W. *lawyer*
Tresnowski, Bernard Richard *health insurance company executive*
Trexler, Edgar Ray *minister, editor*
Trienens, Howard Joseph *lawyer*
†Trotter, Donne E. *hospital administrator*
Trukenbrod, William Sellery *banker*
Truran, James Wellington, Jr. *astrophysicist*
Truskowski, John Budd *lawyer*
Tsou, Tang *political science educator, researcher*
Tucker, Watson Billopp *lawyer*
Tulsky, Alex Sol *physician*
Turkevich, Anthony Leonid *chemist, educator*
†Turner, Jack Henry *can manufacturing company executive*
Turner, Lynne Alison (Mrs. Paul H. Singer) *harpist*
†Turner, Michael Stanley *physics educator*
Turner, Sadie Lee *elementary educator*
Turow, Scott F. *lawyer, author*
Tyler, W(illiam) Ed *printing company executive*
Tymm, William E. *lawyer*
†Tyner, Howard A. *newspaper editor, journalist*
†Ulbricht, Robert E. *lawyer, savings and loan executive*
Ultmann, John Ernest *physician, educator*
Uvena, Frank John *printing company executive, lawyer*
Vaillancourt, Daniel Gilbert *philosophy educator*
Valdes, Miguel A. *lawyer*
†Valerio, Joseph M. *architectural firm executive, educator*
Valukas, Anton Ronald *lawyer, former federal official*
Van Demark, Ruth Elaine *lawyer*
†VanderBeke, Patricia K. *architect*
Vander Wilt, Carl Eugene *banker*
Vanecko, Robert Michael *surgeon, educator*
Van Valen, Leigh Maiorana *biologist, educator*
Varro, Barbara Joan *health journal editor*
†Varsbergs, Vilis *minister, former religious organization administrator*
Veit, Fritz *librarian*
†Veitch, Michael J. *newspaper publishing executive*
Ventura, Robin Mark *professional baseball player*
†Verdi, Robert William *sports columnist*
Verschoor, Curtis Carl *business educator, consultant*
Vie, Richard Carl *insurance company executive*
Vieregg, Robert Todd *lawyer*
Vinci, John Nicholas *architect, educator*
Vittum, Daniel Weeks, Jr. *lawyer*
Vogler, James R. *lawyer*
von Ferstel, Marilou McCarthy *public relations executive*
von Rhein, John Richard *music critic, editor*
Voortman, John J. *lawyer*
Vrablik, Edward Robert *import/export company executive*
†Vrechek, George G. *architectural firm executive*
Vree, Roger Allen *lawyer*
Wackerle, Frederick William *management consultant*
Wadden, Richard Albert *environmental science educator, consultant, researcher*
Wade, Edwin Lee *lawyer*
†Wagner, Joseph M. *church administrator*
Wahlen, Edwin Alfred *lawyer*
Waintroob, Andrea Ruth *lawyer*
Waite, Dennis Vernon *investor relations consultant*
Waite, Ellen Jane *library director*
Waite, Norman, Jr. *lawyer*
Walberg, Herbert John *psychologist, educator, consultant*
Waldstein, Sheldon Saul *physician, educator*
Walker, Ronald Edward *psychologist, educator*
Wall, James McKendree *minister, editor*
Wall, Robert F. *lawyer*
†Wallace, Julia Diane *newspaper editor*
Walsh, Joseph A., Jr. *lawyer*
Walter, Douglas Hanson *lawyer*
Walter, Priscilla Anne *lawyer*
Walton, Stanley Anthony, III *lawyer*
Waltz, Jon Richard *lawyer, educator, author*
Wander, Herbert Stanton *lawyer*
†Wang, Albert James *violinist, educator*
Wanke, Ronald Lee *lawyer*
Ward, Daniel Patrick *lawyer*
Wardropper, Ian Bruce *museum curator, educator*
Ware, Mitchell *lawyer*
Warnecke, Michael O. *lawyer*
†Warnecke, Richard Basley *sociologist, educational administrator*
Wasan, Darsh Tilakchand *university official, chemical engineer educator*
Wasik, John Francis *editor, writer, publisher*
Wasiolek, Edward *literary critic, language and literature educator*
Watkins, Cheryl Denise *special education educator*
Watson, Ben Charles *financial services company executive*
Watson, Lee Ann *lawyer*
Watson, Robert R. *lawyer*
Watts, Dey Wadsworth *retired lawyer*
Weaver, William Townsend *laywer*
Webb, Dan K. *lawyer*
Weber, Arthur *publisher*
Weber, Daniel E. *marketing professional*
†Weber, Donald B. *advertising and marketing executive*
Weber, Frederic *lawyer*
†Weber, Hanno *architect*
Webster, Albert Knickerbocker *consultant in performing arts*
Webster, James Randolph, Jr. *physician*
Weclew, Victor T. *dentist*
Weese, Benjamin Horace *architect*
Weese, Cynthia Rogers *architect, educator*
Weil, John David *envelope company executive*
Weil, Roman Lee *accounting educator*
Weinberg, David B. *lawyer*
Weinberg, Harvey A. *apparel company executive*
Weinberg, Lila Shaffer *writer, editor*
Weinkopf, Friedrich J. *lawyer*
Weinsheimer, William Cyrus *lawyer*
Weintraub, Joseph Barton *publishing executive*
Weissman, Michael Lewis *lawyer*
Weitzman, Robert Harold *investment company executive*
Wellington, Robert Hall *manufacturing company executive*
Wells, Joel Freeman *editor, author*
West, Byron Kenneth *banker*
Westbrooks, Alphonso *public relations executive*
Wexler, Raymond P. *lawyer*
Wexler, Richard Lewis *lawyer*
Whalen, Wayne W. *lawyer*
White, Barry A. *lawyer*
White, Craig Mitchell *lawyer*
White, H. Blair *lawyer*
White, John Abiathar *pilot, consultant*
White, Linda Diane *lawyer*
White, R. Quincy *lawyer*
White, Thomas Stuart *lawyer*
Whitehead, James S. *lawyer*
Whiteley, Sandra Marie *librarian, editor*
Whitney, Patrick Foster *design educator*
Wied, George Ludwig *physician*
Wiener, Stanley Lewis *medical educator*
Wier, Patricia Ann *publishing executive*
Wiggins, Charles Henry, Jr. *lawyer*
Wilcox, Mark Dean *lawyer*
Wilczek, Robert Joseph *lawyer*
Wilder, Ronald *lawyer*
Wildermuth, Gordon Lee *architect*
Wildman, Max Edward *lawyer*
Wilkes, Delano Angus *architect*
Williams, Ann Claire *federal judge*
Williams, Billy Leo *professional baseball coach*
Williams, Carl Chanson *publishing company executive*
Williams, Douglas H. *lawyer*
Williams, Edward Joseph *banker*
Williams, George Howard *lawyer, association executive*
Williams, H. Randolph *lawyer*
Williams, Harold Milton *trade association executive*
Williams, John Cobb *lawyer*
†Williams, Mark H. *advertising agency executive*
Williams, Richard Lucas, III *electronics company executive, lawyer*
Williams, Robert Jene *lawyer, rail car company executive*
Williams-Ashman, Howard Guy *biochemistry educator*
Williamson, Joel V. *lawyer*
Williamson, Richard Salisbury *lawyer*
Willian, Clyde Franklin *lawyer*
Willoughby, William Franklin, II *physician, researcher*
Wilmouth, Robert K. *commodities executive*
Wilson, Bruce G. *lawyer*
Wilson, Gahan *cartoonist, author*
Wilson, Harry L. *lawyer*
Wilson, Karen Lee *museum curator*
Wilson, Richard Harold *government official*
Wilson, Roger Goodwin *lawyer*
Wilson, William Julius *sociologist, educator*
Winfrey, Oprah *television talk show host, actress, producer*
Winger, Howard Woodrow *library educator*
Winnie, Alon Palm *anesthesiologist, educator*
Winninghoff, Albert C. M. *advertising company executive*
Winston, Roland *physicist, educator*
Wirsching, Charles Philipp, Jr. *brokerage house executive, investor*
Wirszup, Izaak *mathematician, educator*
Wirtz, Arthur Michael, Jr. *professional hockey team executive*
Wise, William Jerrard *lawyer*
Wiser, James Louis *political science educator*
Wishner, Maynard Ira *finance company executive, lawyer*
Witcoff, Sheldon William *lawyer*
Witwer, Samuel Weiler, Sr. *lawyer*
Witwer, Samuel Weiler, Jr. *lawyer*
Wojcik, Lawrence A. *lawyer*
Wolf, Charles Benno *lawyer*
Wolf, Neal Lloyd *lawyer*
Wolf, Stephen M. *airline executive*
Wolfe, David Louis *lawyer*
Wolfe, Sheila A. *journalist*
Wolfson, Larry M. *lawyer*
Wolpert, Edward Alan *psychiatrist*
Wood, Arthur MacDougall *retired retail executive*
Wood, James Clarence *lawyer*
Wood, James Nowell *museum director and executive*
Wood, Timothy McDonald *diversified security company executive, controller*
Woods, Robert Archer *investment counsel*
Worley, Gordon Roger *retail chain financial executive*
Wright, Benjamin Drake *psychology educator*
†Wright, Judith Margaret *law librarian, educator*
Wright, Patricia Donovan *communications executive*
Wrigley, William *corporation executive*
Wycliff, Noel Don *journalist, newspaper editor*
Wynn, Thomas Joseph *county judge, educator*
Yacktman, Donald Arthur *financial executive, investment counselor*
Yale, Seymour Hershel *dental radiologist, educator, university dean, gerontologist*
Yamakawa, Allan Hitoshi *university administrator*
Yarkony, Gary Michael *physician, researcher*
†Yee, Edmond *church administrator*
York, Donald Gilbert *astronomy educator, researcher*
Young, Ronald Faris *commodity trader*
Youngman, Owen Ralph *newspaper editor*
Yu, Anthony C. *religion and literature educator*
Yuenger, James Laury *newspaper editor*
Zabel, Sheldon Alter *lawyer, educator*
Zabrosky, Alex Walter *lawyer*
Zagel, James Block *federal judge*
Zajicek, Jeronym *music educator*
Zaki, Abdelmoneim Emam *dental educator*
Zaremski, Miles Jay *lawyer*
Zarnowitz, Victor *economist, educator*
Zaslow, Jeffrey Lloyd *syndicated columnist*
Zatuchni, Gerald Irving *physician, educator*
Zavis, Michael William *lawyer*
Zeffren, Eugene *toiletries company executive*
Zekman, Pamela Lois (Mrs. Fredric Soll) *reporter*
Zell, Samuel *transportation leasing company executive*
Zemans, Frances Kahn *legal association executive*
Zemm, Sandra Phyllis *lawyer*
Zenner, Sheldon Toby *lawyer*
Ziebarth, Robert Charles *management consultant*
†Zimmer, Robert J. *mathematician*
†Zimmerman, Martin E. *financial executive*
Zito, James Anthony *retired railroad company executive*
Zlatoff-Mirsky, Everett Igor *violinist*
Zmuda, Sharon Louise *construction executive*
Zolno, Mark S. *lawyer*
Zonis, Marvin *political scientist, educator*
Zorn, Eric J. *newspaper columnist*
Zucaro, Aldo Charles *insurance company executive*
Zukowsky, John Robert *curator*
Zulkey, Edward John *lawyer, author*
Zwiren, Jan Marie *advertising executive*

Chicago Heights
Cifelli, John Louis *lawyer*
Hurd, Byron Thomas *newspaper executive*

Christopher
†Severns, Penny L. *state legislator*

Clarendon Hills
Gorski, Nancy Anne *elementary education educator*
Moritz, Donald Brooks *mechanical engineer, consultant*

Crete
Langer, Steven *human resources management consultant and industrial psychologist*

Crystal Lake
Althoff, J(ames) L. *construction company executive*
Anderson, Lyle Arthur *manufacturing company executive*
Chamberlain, Charles James *railroad labor union executive*
Keller, William Francis *publishing consultant*
Knox, Susan Marie *paralegal*
Linklater, Isabelle Stanislawa Yarosh-Galazka (Lee Linklater) *secondary education educator*

Danville
Baker, Harold Albert *federal judge*
Braun, Harry Jean *college president*

De Kalb
Ashmann, Jon *art professor, designer*
†Aung-Thwin, Michael *history educator*
Bach, Jan Morris *composer, educator*
Bickner, Bruce Pierce *agriculture executive*
Even, Robert Lawrence *art educator*
Hagelman, Charles William, Jr. *language professional, educator*
Hanna, Nessim *marketing educator*
Kevill, Dennis Neil *chemistry educator*
Kies, Cosette Nell *library science educator, consultant*
Kimball, Clyde William *physicist, educator*
†Kleppner, Paul *social studies think-tank administrator*
La Tourette, John Ernest *academic administrator*
Monat, William Robert *university official*
†Rossing, Thomas D. *physics educator*
Troyer, Alvah Forrest *seed corn company executive, plant breeder*
Vance Siebrasse, Kathy Ann *newspaper publishing executive*
Wit, Daniel *international consultant*
Witmer, John Harper, Jr. *lawyer*
Zar, Jerrold H(oward) *biology educator, statistician*

Decatur
Andreas, Michael Dwayne *agricultural business executive*
Blake, William Henry *credit and public relations consultant*
Braun, William Joseph *underwriter*
Cain, Richard Duane *small business owner*
Decker, Charles Richard *business educator*
†Dunn, John Francis *lawyer, state representative*
Erickson, Roy Lydeen *lawyer*
Graf, Karl Rockwell *nuclear engineer*
Haab, Larry David *utility company executive*
Harris, Donald Wayne *research scientist*
Kelley, Wendell J. *retired utilities executive*
Koucky, John Richard *metallurgical engineer, manufacturing executive*
Kraft, Burnell D. *agricultural products company executive*
†McCray, Curtis Lee *university president*
Mohan, J. Patrick *lawyer*
†Moorman, John A. *librarian*
†Morgan, E. A. *church administrator*
Perry, Anthony John *retired hospital executive*
Randall, James R. *manufacturing company executive*
Requarth, William Henry *surgeon*
Staley, Henry Mueller *manufacturing company executive*
Strong, John David *insurance company executive*
Wells, Charles William *utility executive*
Womeldorff, Porter John *utilities executive*

Deerfield
Abbey, G(eorge) Marshall *lawyer, former health care company executive, general counsel*
Ames, Craig L. *lawyer*
Barth, David Keck *industrial distribution industry consultant*
Batts, Warren Leighton *diversified industry executive*
Boyd, Joseph Don *financial services*
Charlson, David Harvey *executive search company professional*
Cruikshank, John W., III *life insurance underwriter*
†Donovan, Nancy S. *financial services executive*
Fodrea, Carolyn Wrobel *educational researcher, publisher*
Foght, James Loren *banker*
Gaples, Harry Seraphim *computer service company executive*
†Gash, Lauren Beth *lawyer, state legislator*
Graham, William B. *pharmaceutical company executive*
Halaska, Robert H. *insurance company executive*
Helpap, John Frederick *retired health care executive*
Hersher, Richard Donald *management consultant*
Howell, George Bedell *equity investing and managing executive*
Hunter, Charles David *retail company executive*
Jorndt, Louis Daniel *drug store chain executive*
Kinzelberg, Harvey *leasing company executive*
Kotsonis, Frank Nick *toxicologist, scientist, food company research executive*
Kushner, Jeffrey L. *manufacturing company executive*
Larrimore, Randall Walter *manufacturing company executive*
Loucks, Vernon R., Jr. *health care products and services company executive*
Massie, Edward Lindsey, Jr. *publishing company executive*
Meyer, Kenneth Marven *academic administrator*
†O'Donnell, Lawrence James *architect*
†Oettinger, Julian Alan *lawyer, pharmacy company executive*
Pigozzi, Raymond Anthony *architect*
Sanford, Roy Leon *hospital supply company executive*
Scheiber, Stephen Carl *psychiatrist*
Staubitz, Arthur Frederick *lawyer, healthcare products company executive*
Thorne, Oakleigh Blakeman *publishing company executive*
Vollen, Robert Jay *lawyer*
Walgreen, Charles Rudolph, III *retail store executive*
White, Tony L. *health and medical products executive*
Young, Arthur Price *librarian, educator*
Zywicki, Robert Albert *electrical distribution company executive*

Des Moines
†Kelley, Bruce Gunn *insurance company executive, lawyer*

Des Plaines
Altschul, Alfred Samuel *airline executive*
Babb, Michael Paul *engineering magazine editor*
Brodl, Raymond Frank *lawyer, former lumber company executive*
†Butler, Marty *state legislator*
Carroll, Barry Joseph *manufacturing and real estate executive*
Clapper, Lyle Nielsen *magazine publisher*
Clapper, Marie Anne *magazine publisher*
†Coburn, James LeRoy *educational administrator*
Demouth, Robin Madison *lawyer, corporate executive*
Dlouhy, Phillip Edward *engineering, construction executive*
Farley, James Newton *manufacturing executive, engineer*
†Frank, James S. *automotive executive*
Gillette, Halbert Scranton *publisher*
Henrikson, Lois Elizabeth *photojournalist*
Jacobs, William Russell, II *lawyer*
Kelly, Timothy Michael *magazine publisher*
Klemens, Thomas Lloyd *editor*
†Koffman, Morley *trucking executive*
†Kubalanza, Ronald J. *bank executive*
Kudenholdt, Sharon Sue *freelance author*
Kuennen, Thomas Gerard *magazine editor*
Li, Norman N. *chemicals executive*
†Malchow, Dennis *food products executive*
Meinert, John Raymond *clothing manufacturing and retailing executive, investment banker*
†Mulligan, Rosemary Elizabeth *paralegal*
Munden, Robin Ghezzi *lawyer*
Neel, Judy Murphy *association executive*
Newman, Wade Davis *trade association executive*
Saporta, Jack *psychologist, educator*
†Schmidt, Robert L. *export company executive*
†Shoults, Harold E. *social services administrator*
Shoup, Wesley Dale *publishing company executive*
Sisson, George Allen, Sr. *physician, educator*
Tory, John A. *newspaper publishing executive*
Wallace, Jane Young (Mrs. Donald H. Wallace) *editor*
†Wilkie, Michael Leighton *manufacturing company executive*
Yarnell, Jeffrey Alan *regional credit executive*
Young, Richard Alan *publishing company executive*

Dixon
Shaw, Thomas Douglas *newspaper executive*

Downers Grove
Boese, Robert Alan *forensic chemist*
Colbert, Marvin Jay *retired internist, educator*
Erickson, Robert Daniel *management services company executive*
Fruin, Robert Cornelius *physician, hospital administrator*
Gioioso, Joseph Vincent *psychologist*
Hegenderfer, Jonita Susan *public relations executive*
Katai, Andrew Andras *chemical company executive*
Kirkegaard, R. Lawrence *architectural acoustician*
Lulay, Gail C. *human resources executive, consultant*
Pollard, Charles William *diversified services company executive*
Pollock, John Glennon *contract management services company executive*
†Ryan, John Michael *landscape architect*

Dunlap
Bailey, John Maxwell *mechanical engineer, consultant*

Dwight
Oughton, James Henry, Jr. *corporate executive, farmer*

East Moline
Bosworth, Douglas LeRoy *farm implement company executive*
Puffer, Richard Judson *retired college chancellor*
Silliman, Richard George *retired lawyer, retired farm machinery company executive*

East Peoria
Grisham, George Robert *mathematics educator*
Walker, Philip Chamberlain, II *health care executive*

East Saint Louis
Beatty, William Louis *federal judge*
Dunham, Katherine *choreographer, dancer, anthropologist*
Lindsley, James Bruce *sales and marketing executive*
Randolph, Robert Lee *economist, educator*
†Reilly, Michael K. *mining executive*
Stiehl, William D. *federal judge*

Edwardsville
Cameron, Colleen Irene *alcoholism counselor*
Going, William Thornbury *language professional, educator*
Kovarik, M. Leora *elementary principal*
Lazerson, Earl Edwin *university president emeritus*
Malone, Robert Roy *artist, art educator*
Ottwein, Merrill William George *real estate company executive, veterinarian*
Potthast, Ray Joseph *secondary education educator*
Virgo, John Michael *economist, researcher, educator*

Elburn
Etter, David Pearson *poet, editor*

Elgin
Brinckman, Donald Wesley *industrial company executive*
Burian, Robert J *human resources executive*
†Deeter, Joan G. *church administrator*
†Furst, Warren Arthur *retired holding company executive*
Gwillim, Russell Adams *manufacturing company executive*
Hamlet, Joseph Frank *service and liquid hazardous waste industry executive*
Hoeft, Elizabeth Bayless *speech and language pathologist*
Juister, Barbara Joyce *mathematics educator*
Kelly, Matthew Edward *association executive*
Kirkland, Alfred Younges, Sr. *federal judge*
†Mehlis, David Lee *publishing executive*
†Minnich, Dale E. *religious administrator*
†Murphy, William Holland *financial executive*
†Myers, Anne M. *church administrator*
Nelson, John Thilgen *hospital administrator, physician*
†Nolen, Wilfred E. *church administrator*
†Ratthahao, Sisouphanh *minister*
†Saliba, Jacob *manufacturing executive*
†Steiner, Duane *religious administrator*
†Timmons, Glenn F. *church administrator*
Transue, Brooke Mullen *occupational assessment and career specialist*
Weber, Harm Allen *former college president*
†Zack, Daniel Gerard *library director*
†Ziegler, Earl Keller *minister*

Elk Grove Village
Best, Willis D. *retired international union official*
Edwardson, John Albert, Jr. *telecomunications company executive*
Halloran, James Joseph *editor*
McLain, Roger Sette *electronics company executive*
Nadig, Gerald George *manufacturing executive*

Elmhurst
Burton, Darrell Irvin *engineering executive*
Cureton, Bryant Lewis *political science educator, academic administrator*
Ephland, John Russell *magazine editor*
Fornatto, Elio Joseph *otolaryngologist, educator*
†Gerber, C. Allen *food products executive*
Hildreth, R(oland) James *foundation executive, economist*
Klatt, Melvin John *library administrator*
Townsend, Merton LeRoy *metal products executive*
†Wyman, Thomas H. *food products executive*

Elmwood Park
Spina, Anthony Ferdinand *lawyer*

Elsah
Hodgson, Peter John *music educator*

Eureka
Hearne, George Archer *academic administrator*

Evanston
Abnee, A. Victor *trade association executive*
Achenbach, Jan Drewes *engineer and scientist*
Adelson, Bernard Henry *physician*
Balachandran, Bala Venkataraman *accounting systems educator*
Bankoff, Seymour George *chemical engineer, educator*
Bareiss, Erwin Hans *computer scientist, mathematician, nuclear engineer, educator*
Bashook, Philip G. *medical association executive, educator*
Basolo, Fred *chemistry educator*
Belytschko, Ted Bohdan *civil, mechanical engineering educator*
Bernstein, Susan Powell *development and fundraising consultant*
Bishop, David Fulton *library administrator*
†Borcover, Alfred Seymour *journalist*
Bowman, Monroe Bengt *architect*
Brazelton, William Thomas *chemical engineering educator*
Brown, Laurie Mark *physicist, educator*
†Bufe, Noel Carl *program director*
Burwell, Robert Lemmon, Jr. *chemist, educator*
Butt, John Baecher *chemical engineering educator*
Carlin, Donald Walter *retired food products executive, consultant*
Carr, Stephen Howard *materials engineer, educator*
Cassell, Frank Hyde *business educator*
†Cates, Jo Ann *librarian, management consultant*
Catlett, George Roudebush *accountant*
†Chang, R. P. H. *materials science educator*
Cheng, Herbert Su-Yuen *mechanical engineering educator*
Christian, Richard Carlton *university dean, former advertising agency executive*
Cohen, David Harris *neurobiology educator, university official*
Cohen, Jerome Bernard *materials science educator*
Cole, Douglas *English literature educator*
Colton, Frank Benjamin *retired chemist*
Condit, Carl Wilbur *history educator*
Conger, William Frame *artist, educator*
Corey, Gordon Richard *financial advisor, former utilities executive*
Crawford, James Weldon *psychiatrist, educator, administrator*
†Crawford, Susan Y. Young *library director, educator*
Crotty, William *political science educator*
Dallos, Peter John *neurobiologist, educator*
Daniels, Arlene Kaplan *sociology educator*
Davis, Stephen Howard *applied mathematics educator*
De Coster, Cyrus Cole *Spanish language and literature educator*
Devinatz, Allen *mathematics educator*
Dockery, J. Lee *medical school administrator*
Duncan, Robert Bannerman *strategy and organizations educator*
Dwass, Meyer *mathematician, educator*
Eberley, Helen-Kay *opera singer, classical record company executive, poet*
Eisner, Robert *economics educator*
Enroth-Cugell, Christina Alma Elisabeth *neurophysiologist, educator*
Epstein, Max *electrical engineering educator*
Fine, Arthur I. *philosopher*
Fine, Morris Eugene *materials engineer, educator*
Fisher, Neal Floyd *minister*
Fisher, Walter Dummer *economist, educator*
Fox, Edward Inman *education administrator and Spanish educator*
Frey, Donald Nelson *industrial engineer, educator, manufacturing company executive*
Friedman, Hans Adolf *architect*
Fryburger, Vernon Ray, Jr. *advertising and marketing educator*
Galati, Frank Joseph *stage and opera director, educator, screen writer, actor*
†Garbarino, James *psychologist*
†Gellman, Aaron Jacob *transportation center administrator, engineering educator*
Gibbons, William Reginald, Jr. *poet, editor*
Giordano, August Thomas (Gus Giordano) *choreographer, dancer*
Goldstick, Thomas Karl *biomedical engineering educator*
Gordon, Julie Peyton *foundation administrator*
Gordon, Robert James *economics educator*
Gormley, R(obert) James *retired lawyer*
Graber, Thomas M. *orthodontist*
Greenbaum, Stuart I. *economist, educator*
Haberman, Shelby Joel *statistician, educator*
Haddad, Abraham Herzl *electrical engineering educator, researcher*
Haiman, Franklyn Saul *author, communications educator*
†Harlow, Robert Dean *packaging company executive*
Herron, Orley R. *college president*
Huff, Stanley Eugene *dermatologist*
Hurter, Arthur Patrick *economist, educator*
Ibers, James Arthur *chemist, educator*
Ihlanfeldt, William *university administrator, consultant*
Ionescu Tulcea, Cassius *research mathematician, educator*
Irons, William George *anthropology educator*
Jacob, Herbert *political science educator*
Jacobs, Norman Joseph *publishing company executive*
Janda, Kenneth Frank *political science educator*
Janeway, Michael Charles *journalism educator, school dean*
Jencks, Christopher Sandys *sociology educator*
Jerome, Joseph Walter *mathematics educator*
Johnson, David Lynn *materials scientist, educator*
Johnson, Lael Frederic *lawyer*
Jones, Robert Russell *magazine editor*
Kaatz, Ronald B. *advertising educator, consultant*
Kalai, Ehud *decision sciences educator, researcher in economics and decision sciences*
Karlins, M(artin) William *composer, educator*
Keer, Leon Morris *engineering educator*
Kern, Charles William *university official, chemistry educator*
Kerr, Thomas Jefferson, IV *academic official*
†Khandekar, Janardan Dinkar *oncologist, educator*
King, Robert Charles *biologist, educator*
Kistler, Alan Lee *engineering educator*
Kliphardt, Raymond A. *engineering educator*
Klotz, Irving Myron *chemist, educator*
Kotler, Philip *marketing educator, consultant, educator*
Kreml, Franklin Martin *educational administrator, association executive*
Krizek, Raymond John *civil engineering educator, consultant*
Kuenster, John Joseph *magazine editor*
Kujala, Walfrid Eugene *musician, educator*
Lambert, Joseph Buckley *chemistry educator*
Lavengood, Lawrence Gene *management educator, historian*
Lavine, John M. *journalism educator, newspaper publisher*
Letsinger, Robert Lewis *chemistry educator*
Lippincott, James Andrew *biochemistry, biological sciences educator, administrator*
Lyles, Jean Elizabeth Caffey *journalist*
Mack, Raymond Wright *university provost*
Magee, Robert Paul *accounting and information systems educator*
Mah, Richard Sze Hao *chemical engineering educator*
Mahowald, Mark Edward *mathematics educator*
Marhic, Michel Edmond *engineering educator, entrepreneur, consultant*
Marks, Tobin Jay *chemistry educator*
Matkowsky, Bernard Judah *applied mathematician, educator*
McDougal, Alfred Leroy *publisher*
†McGee, Julia Ann *publishing company executive*
Mc Nerney, Walter James *health policy educator, consultant*
Miller, Thomas Williams *former university dean*
Mintzer, David *physics educator*
Mitchell, Kendall *writer, literary critic*
Moskos, Charles C. *sociology educator*
Moskow, Michael H. *federal official*
Murphy, Gordon John *engineering educator*
Myerson, Roger Bruce *game theorist, economist, educator*
Neaman, Mark Robert *hospital administrator*
Neuschel, Robert Percy *educator, former management consultant*
Novales, Ronald Richards *zoologist, educator*
Oakes, Robert James *physics educator*
Offner, Franklin Faller *biophysics educator*
Olmstead, William Edward *mathematics educator*
Ottino, Julio Mario *chemical engineering educator, scientist*
Otwell, Ralph Maurice *retired newspaper editor*
Pabst, Edmund G. *retired insurance company executive, lawyer*
Page, Benjamin Ingrim *political science educator, researcher*
†Panzar, John C. *economist, educator, consultant*
Paynter, John Philip *conductor*
Peck, Abraham *editor, writer, educator, magazine consultant*
Pines, Herman *chemistry educator, consultant*
Plaut, Eric Alfred *psychiatrist, educator*
Polzin, John Theodore *lawyer*
Pople, John Anthony *chemistry educator*
Prince, Thomas Richard *accountant, educator*
Ratner, Mark Alan *chemistry educator*
Reeder, Robert Harry *retired lawyer*
Reimer, Bennett *music educator, writer*
Reiter, Stanley *economist, educator*
Revsine, Lawrence *accounting educator, consultant*
Rolfe, Michael N. *management consulting firm executive*
Saari, Donald Gene *mathematician*
Sachtler, Wolfgang Max Hugo *chemistry educator*
Sade, Donald Stone *anthropology educator*
Salzman, Arthur George *architect*
Samter, Max *physician, educator*
Samuels, Ernest *author, educator*
†Schakowsky, Janice *state legislator*
Schank, Roger Carl *computer science and psychology educator*
Schnaiberg, Allan *sociology educator*
Schwartz, Neena Betty *endocrinologist, educator*
Scott, Walter Dill *education educator*
Shah, Surendra Poonamchand *engineering educator, researcher*
Shanafield, Harold Arthur *educator*
Sheridan, James Edward *history educator*
Shriver, Duward Felix *chemistry educator, researcher, consultant*
Silverman, Richard Bruce *chemist, educator, biochemist*
Sobel, Alan *electrical engineer, physicist*
Sprang, Milton LeRoy *obstetrician, gynecologist, educator*
Stern, Louis William *marketing educator, consultant*
Swanton, Virginia Lee *publishing company administrator, editor*
Taam, Ronald Everett *physics and astronomy educator*
Taflove, Allen *electrical engineer, educator, researcher, consultant*
Tankin, Richard Samuel *fluid dynamics educator*
Taronji, Jaime, Jr. *lawyer*
Thompson, Tyler *minister, philosophy educator*
Thrash, Patricia Ann *association executive*
Tornabene, Russell C. *communications executive*
Traisman, Howard Sevin *pediatrician*
Trutter, John Thomas *consulting company executive*
Ulmer, Melville Paul *physics and astronomy educator*
Vanderstappen, Harrie Albert *Far Eastern art educator*
Vanneman, Edgar, Jr. *lawyer*
Van Ness, James Edward *electrical engineering educator*
Ver Steeg, Clarence Lester *historian, educator*
Wagner, Durrett *former publisher, picture service executive*
Walker, Harold Blake *minister*
Weber, Arnold R. *university president*
Weertman, Johannes *materials science educator*
Weertman, Julia Randall *materials science and engineering educator*
Weil, Irwin *Slavic languages and literature educator*
Weisbrod, Burton Allen *economist, educator*
Werckmeister, Otto Karl *philosopher educator*
†Wessels, Bruce W. *materials scientist, educator*
White, Willmon Lee *magazine editor*
Wilber, Laura Ann *audiologist*
Wilks, Ivor Gordon Hughes *historian, educator*
Wills, Garry *journalist, educator*
Worthy, James Carson *educator*
Wright, Donald Eugene *retired librarian*
Wright, John *classics educator*
Wu, Tai Te *biological sciences and engineering educator*
Yoder, Frederick Floyd *fraternity executive*
Zarefsky, David Harris *academic administrator, communication studies educator*
†Zolomij, Robert William *landscape architect, consultant*

Evergreen Park
Ephraim, Max, Jr. *mechanical engineer*
Lucas, Shirley Agnes Hoyt *management executive*
†Smith, Lawrence J. *bishop*

Fairview Heights
Barkofske, Francis Lee *lawyer, coal company executive*
Cunningham, Joseph Francis, Jr. *retired state supreme court justice*
†Hughes, John W. *mining executive*
Sullivan, Joseph Patrick *agricultural product company executive*
†Vyas, Chand Bhaourbhai *coal company executive*

Flossmoor
Garrison, Ray Harlan *lawyer*
Lis, Edward Francis *pediatrician, consultant*
Vogt, John Henry *corporate executive*
Wagner, Alvin Louis, Jr. *real estate appraiser, consultant*
†Walker, George W. *bishop*

Forest Park
Orland, Frank Jay *oral microbiologist, educator*

Fox River Grove
Abboud, Alfred Robert *banker, consultant, investor*

Frankfort
Dennis, Peter Ray *environmental corporate executive*

†Pearson, Gerald P. *hospital administrator*

Franklin Park
Dean, Howard M., Jr. *food company executive*
Simpson, Michael *metals service center executive*
Tompson, Marian Leonard *association executive*
Wagner, Betty Valiree *medical organization executive*
Watts, Ernest Francis *manufacturing company executive*

Freeport
Ferguson, Daniel C. *diversified company executive*
Kleindl, James Nicholas *business educator, consultant*
Knecht, Roland Edward *household goods manufacturing company executive*

Galena
Hermann, Paul David *retired association executive*
Rauner, Vincent Joseph *lawyer, electronics company executive, retired*

Galesburg
Hane, Mikiso *history educator*
Kirk, Sherwood *librarian*
Kowalski, Richard Sheldon *hospital administrator*
Tourlentes, Thomas Theodore *psychiatrist*

Garden Prairie
Channick, Herbert S. *lawyer, arbitrator, retired real estate and broadcasting corporation executive*

Geneseo
Cherry, Robert Earl Patrick *retired food company executive*

Geneva
Barney, Charles Richard *transportation company executive*
Conterato, Bruno Paul *architect*
Goulet, Charles Ryan *retired insurance company executive*
Pershing, Robert George *retired telecommunications company executive*
Young, Jack Allison *financial executive*

Genoa
Cromley, Jon Lowell *lawyer*

Gilman
Ireland, Herbert Orin *engineering educator*

Glen Ellyn
Clark, Samuel Smith *urologist*
Crumbaugh, Lee Forrest *publisher, consultant*
Dieter, Raymond Andrew, Jr. *physician, surgeon*
Egan, Richard Leo *medical association administrator, medical educator*
Frateschi, Lawrence Jan *economist, statistician, educator*
Kirkpatrick, Clayton *former newspaper executive*
Larson, Ward Jerome *lawyer, retired banker*
Lischer, Ludwig Frederick *consultant, former utility company executive*
Logan, Henry Vincent *transportation executive*
McAninch, Harold D. *college president*
Patten, Ronald James *dean*
Sigalos, George Peter *company executive*
Temple, Donald *allergist, dermatologist*

Glencoe
Baer, Joseph Winslow *retired lawyer, mediator, arbitrator*
†Bernstein, Myron *veterinarian*
Fenninger, Leonard Davis *medical educator, consultant*
Friederici, Hartmann H.R. *physician, educator*
Gordon, Bernard *management and communications consultant*
Grabow, Beverly *learning disability therapist*
Rubin, David Robert *corporate executive*
Silver, Ralph David *distilling company director*
Stewart, Charles Leslie *lawyer*
Taylor, Roy Lewis *botanist*

Glenview
Adler, Robert *electronics engineer*
Ampel, Leon Louis *anesthesiologist*
Berkman, Michael G. *lawyer, chemical consultant*
†Bible, Geoffrey Cyril *tobacco company executive*
Borst, John, Jr. *lawyer, electronics corporation executive*
†Bradtke, Philip Joseph *architect*
Corley, Jenny Lynd Wertheim *educator*
Cozad, James William *retired oil company executive*
Hafner, Arthur Wayne *author, information scientist, medical librarian*
Harris, Ronald David *chemical engineer*
Lacy, Herman Edgar *management consultant*
Levine, Edwin Burton *retired classics educator*
Mabley, Jack *newspaper columnist, communications consultant*
McCarthy, Gerald Michael *electronics engineer*
Mc Cormick, James Charles *leasing and financial services company executive*
†McGrew, Jean B. *superintendent*
Miller, Edward Boone *lawyer*
Nichols, John Doane *diversified manufacturing corporation executive*
†Nyquist, Kathleen A. *publishing executive*
Pearlman, Jerry Kent *electronics company executive*
Ptak, Frank S. *manufacturing executive*
Rorig, Kurt Joachim *chemist, research director*
Russell, Henry George *structural engineer*
Sherman, Elaine C. *gourmet foods company executive, educator*
Smith, Harold *manufacturing executive*
Stern, Gerald Joseph *advertising executive*
Taylor, D(arl) Coder *architect*
Traudt, Mary B. *elementary education educator*
Van Zelst, Theodore William *civil engineer, natural resource exploration company executive*
White, John Francis *retired corporate executive*
Winett, Samuel Joseph *manufacturing company executive*
Wright, Arthur McIntosh *lawyer, industrial products executive*

Godfrey
McDaniels, John Louis *mathematics educator*

Goreville
Fosse, E(rwin) Ray *insurance company executive*

Grayslake
Brown, Sandra Lee *educational consultant*

Great Lakes
Andrews, Carolyn Fraser *psychologist*
Gaston, Mack Charles *naval officer*

Greenville
Stephens, William Richard *college president emeritus*

Hartford
Christian, Nelson Frederick *chemical engineer*

Harvey
Jensen, Harold Leroy *physician*
†Shotts, David Allison *manufacturing executive*

Hawthorn Woods
Schmitz, Shirley Gertrude *marketing and sales executive*

Hennepin
Bumgarner, James McNabb *judge*

Hickory Hills
Johnson, (Mary) Anita *physician, medical service administrator*

Highland
†Baumer, Martha Ann *minister*

Highland Park
Asher, Frederick *former mail order company executive*
Bluefarb, Samuel Mitchell *physician*
Boruszak, James Martin *insurance company executive*
Dobkin, Irving Bern *entomologist, sculptor*
Dolin, Albert Harry *lawyer*
Friend, Peter Michael *hospital executive*
Gordon, Edward *music association executive*
Grimmer, Margot *dancer, choreographer, director*
Haber, Ralph Norman *psychology educator*
Haight, Edward Allen *lawyer*
Harris, Thomas L. *public relations executive*
Hirsch, Jay G. *psychiatrist, educator*
Johnson, Curtis Lee *publisher, editor, writer*
Karol, Nathaniel H. *lawyer, consultant*
Maas, Duane Harris *distilling company executive*
Markman, Raymond Jerome *marketing executive*
Mehta, Zarin *music association administrator*
Mordini, Marilyn Heuer *physical education educator*
Rudo, Milton *retired manufacturing company executive, consultant*
Rutenberg-Rosenberg, Sharon Leslie *journalist*
Smith, Malcolm Norman *manufacturing company executive*
Uhlmann, Frederick Godfrey *commodity and securities broker*
Weinberg, Michael, Jr. *commodities broker*

Highwood
Brown, Lawrence Haas *banker*

Hillside
†Kloster, Carol Good *marketing executive*

Hines
†Cummings, Joan E. *health facility administrator*
Mason, George Robert *surgeon, educator*
Paloyan, Edward *physician, educator, reseacher*
Zvetina, James Raymond *pulmonary physician*

Hinsdale
†Aldinger, Thomas Lee *manufacturing executive*
Anderson, Harry Frederick, Jr. *architect*
†Bergerson, J. Steven *lawyer*
Berry, Virgil Jennings, Jr. *management consultant*
†Biggert, Judith Borg *lawyer*
Birnholz, Jason Cordell *radiologist, consultant, educator*
Bloom, Stephen Joel *distribution company executive*
Burrows, Donald Albert *college dean*
Butler, Margaret Kampschaefer *retired computer scientist*
Cannon, Patrick Francis *public relations executive*
Christian, Joseph Ralph *physician*
Cohen, Burton David *franchising executive, lawyer*
Dyer, Goudyloch Erwin *state legislator*
†Gustafson, F. Edward *plastics company executive*
†Hodnik, David F. *retail company executive*
Kaminsky, Manfred Stephan *physicist*
Kelly, Donald Philip *entrepreneur*
Kinney, Kenneth Parrish *banker, retired*
Lowenstine, Maurice Richard, Jr. *retired steel executive*
†Lynch, Charles J. *secondary school principal*
Merrion, James M. *real estate company officer*
†Mikos, David Edward *architect*
Ochiltree, Ned A., Jr. *retired metals manufacturing executive*
Rinder, George Greer *retired retail company executive*
Sheehan, Dennis William *lawyer, business executive*
†Wheeler, Paul James *real estate executive*
Whitney, William Elliot, Jr. *advertising agency executive*

Hodgkins
†Winn, Elwood F. *consumer product company executive*

Hoffman Estates
Costello, John H., III *business and marketing executive*
Dennis, Steven Pellowe *retail executive*
Laubenstein, Vernon Alfred *state agency administrator*
Martinez, Arthur C. *retail company executive*
Pagonis, William Gus *retired army officer*
Rooney, John Edward, Jr. *communications company executive*
Weston, Roger Lance *banker*

Homewood
Dietch, Henry Xerxes *judge*
Grunwald, Arnold Paul *communications executive, engineer*
MacMaster, Daniel Miller *museum official emeritus*
Manson, Bruce Malcolm *construction company executive*
†McClellan, Larry Allen *minister, writer*

Schumacher, Gebhard Friederich Bernhard *obstetrician-gynecologist*

Hudson
Mills, Lois Jean *legislative aide, former education educator*

Huntley
Glickman, Louis *industrial sewing equipment executive*
†Suzuki, Mikio *machine manufacturing executive*

Indian Head Park
Frisque, Alvin Joseph *retired chemical company executive*

Ingleside
Propst, Catherine Lamb *biotechnology company executive*

Inverness
Hetzel, William Gelal *executive search consultant*
Schwab, Susan Carol *electronics company executive*

Island Lake
Benson, John Earl *construction executive*

Itasca
†Fowler, Jack W. *printing company executive*
Gilchrest, Thornton Charles *association executive*
Grue, Howard Wood *former insurance company executive*
Kendrick, William Monroe *pension manager*
†Rowsey, Michael *printing company executive*
Sheridan, James Leslie *real estate developer*

Jacksonville
Findley, Paul *former congressman, author, educator*
Gallas, Martin Hans *librarian*
Hack, Carole Mae *media generalist*
Olinger, Glenn Slocum *entrepreneur, consultant, investor*
Pfau, Richard Anthony *college president*

Joliet
Barber, Andrew Bollons *bank executive*
Benfer, David William *hospital administrator*
†Brown, Keith Jeffery *banker*
†Dunn, Thomas Aquinas *lawyer, state legislator*
Imesch, Joseph Leopold *bishop*
†Johnston, James Robert *library director*
Kaffer, Roger Louis *bishop*
Marion, Marjorie Anne *English educator*
Ring, Alvin Manuel *pathologist*

Kankakee
Berkenkamp, Fred Julius *management consultant*
†Bowling, John C. *academic administrator*
Sayes, James Ottis *religion educator, minister*
Schroeder, David Harold *health care facility executive*

Kenilworth
Clary, Rosalie Brandon Stanton *timber farm executive*
Corrigan, John Edward, Jr. *banker, lawyer*
Frederick, Earl James *healthcare consultant*
Guelich, Robert Vernon *retired management consultant*
Hodson, Thomas William *health care company executive*
Weiner, Joel David *retired food products executive*

Kewanee
Damron, Marvin Arthur *principal*

La Grange
Carroll, Thomas John *advertising executive*
Norby, William Charles *financial consultant*

La Grange Park
Webster, Lois Shand *association executive*

Lafox
Seils, William George *lawyer*

Lake Bluff
Albrecht, Edward Daniel *metals manufacturing company executive*
Anderson, Roger E. *bank executive*
Felknor, Bruce Lester *editorial consultant*
Fromm, Henry Gordon *retired manufacturing and marketing executive*
Grant, John Robert *management consultant*
Schreiber, George Richard *association executive, writer*
Stetson, John Charles *corporate executive*
Stevens, George Richard *business consultant, public policy commentator*
Wacker, Frederick Glade, Jr. *manufacturing company executive*

Lake Forest
†Anderluh, John Russell *business forms and information management company executive*
Bennett, Edward Herbert, Jr. *architect*
Bernthal, Harold George *health care company executive*
†Bransfield, Joan *principal*
Brown, Cameron *insurance company consultant*
Carter, Donald Patton *advertising executive*
Christopherson, Weston Robert *retired bank executive*
Coutts, John Wallace *chemist, educator*
Deters, James Raymond *retired manufacturing and services company executive*
Ditka, Michael Keller *restaurateur, former professional football coach*
†Eckert, Ralph John *insurance company executive*
Emerson, William Harry *lawyer, oil company executive*
Ford, Donald James *retired insurance company executive, consultant, lawyer*
†Frederick, Virginia Fiester *state legislator*
Fuhs-Smith, Wendy L. *foundation executive*
Hammar, Lester Everett *health care manufacturing company executive*
Hanlon, James Allison *confectionery company executive*
Heslop, Terence Murray *business executive*
Hillman, Stanley Eric Gordon *former corporate executive*

Hotchkiss, Eugene, III *college president emeritus*
Hughes, John W. *film producer, screenwriter, film director*
†Jones, Dante Delaneo *professional football player*
Kenly, Granger Farwell *marketing consultant, college official*
Kenton, James Alan *pharmaceutical company financial executive*
†Kreischer, Gary C. *secondary school principal*
Krouse, Ann Wolk *publishing executive*
Lambert, John Boyd *chemical engineer, consultant*
Leatham, John Tonkin *business executive*
Levy, Nelson Louis *physician, scientist, corporate executive*
McCaskey, Michael B. *professional football team executive*
†McClean, Graham J. *business forms company executive*
Miller, Arthur Hawks, Jr. *librarian, consultant*
Mohr, Roger John *advertising agency executive*
Morgan, Richard Thomas *publishing executive*
Murad, Ferid *physician*
O'Loughlin, John Kirby *retired insurance executive*
O'Mara, Thomas Patrick *manufacturing company executive*
†Peterson, Donald Matthew *insurance company executive*
Rand, Kathy Sue *public relations executive*
Reichert, Jack Frank *manufacturing company executive*
Reichert, Norman Vernon *financial services consultant*
Salter, Edwin Carroll *physician*
Schulze, Franz, Jr. *art critic, educator*
Sikorovsky, Eugene Frank *retired lawyer*
Singletary, Michael *retired professional football player*
†Stirling, Ellen Adair *retail executive*
†Stone, W. Clement *insurance company executive, civic leader*
Van Gorkom, Jerome William *financial executive*
†Vastardis, Anthony George *finance executive*
Waehner, Ralph Livingston *business forms company executive, consultant*
Walter, Robert Irving *chemistry educator, chemist*
Wannstedt, David Raymond *professional football team coach*
Weston, Arthur Walter *chemist, scientific and business executive*
Wilbur, Richard Sloan *physician, foundation executive*
†Woolford, Donnell *professional football player*
Yaconetti, Dianne Mary *business executive*

Lake Zurich
Harrod, Scott *consulting manufacturing executive*
Luecke, Joseph E. *insurance company executive*
Schultz, Carl Herbert *real estate management and development company executive*
Timbers, Stephen Bryan *financial services company executive*

Lawrenceville
†Whelan, John M. *insurance company executive*
†Wright, John D. R. *oil industry executive*

Lemont
Chen, Shoei-Sheng *mechanical engineer*
Herriford, Robert Levi, Sr. *army officer*
Katz, Joseph Jacob *chemist, educator*
†Mitchell, Wanda Gayle *chemist*
Tomkins, Frank Sargent *physicist*
Williams, Jack Marvin *chemist*

Lewistown
Novak, Martha Lois *elementary education educator*

Libertyville
Burrows, Brian William *research and development manufacturing executive*
†Kremkau, Paul *principal*
Krolopp, Rudolph William *industrial designer, consultant*
Kummer, Daniel William *insurance executive*
†Mraz, Alana L. *elementary school principal*
Ranney, George Alfred *lawyer, former steel company executive*
Ransom, Margaret Palmquist *public relations executive*
Thominet, Maurice J. *architect*
Thompson, David Jerome *chemical company executive, biochemist, nutritionist*

Lincoln
Wilson, Robert Allen *religion educator*

Lincolnshire
†DuFour, Richard P. *school system administrator*
†Ellen, Martin M. *financial services executive*
Freund, Charles Gibson *retired holding company executive*
Guist, Fredric Michael *minerals, chemicals and waste services corporation executive*
Hughes, William Franklin, Jr. *ophthalmologist, emeritus educator*
Iosue, Carmine A. *company executive*
Macmillan, Douglas Hathaway *financial executive*
O'Connell, Edward Joseph, III *financial executive, accountant*
†Tucker, Arlie G. *manufacturing executive*
Woods, John Lucius *management consultant*

Lincolnwood
Astrin, Marvin H. *broadcasting company executive*
Pattis, S. William *publisher*

Lisle
†Aprati, Robert L. *lawyer, car rental company executive*
Batory, Ronald Louis *transportation executive*
Becker, Richard Charles *college president*
Birck, Michael John *manufacturing company executive, electrical engineer*
Krehbiel, Frederick August, II *electronics company executive*
Krehbiel, John H. *electronics company executive*
Krehbiel, John H., Jr. *electronics company executive*
Long, Charles Franklin *corporate communications executive*
Melsa, James Louis *electrical engineer*
Psaltis, John Costas *manufacturing company executive*
Reum, W. Robert *manufacturing executive*
Sandrok, Richard William *lawyer*

Schwemm, John Butler *printing company executive, lawyer*
Tyson, Kirk W. M. *business consultant*

Litchfield
Jackson, David A. *retired newspaper editor*

Lombard
†Ahlberg, James E. *technical services company executive*
Ahlstrom, Ronald Gustin *artist*
Branum, William Howell *engineering company executive*
†Grubb, Daniel B. *oil company executive*
Johnson, Dennis Lester *marketing consultant*
†Lapp, James Merrill *clergyman, marriage and family therapist*
Poppe, Wassily *chemist*
Royster, Darryl *computer programmer and analyst*
Velardo, Joseph Thomas *molecular biology and endocrinology educator*
Williams, Ronald Boal, Jr. *financial training company executive*
†Yeager, David P. *management consultant*
†Yeager, Phillip Charles *transportation company executive*

Long Grove
Ausman, Robert K. *surgeon, research executive*
Connor, James Richard *foundation administrator*
Fitzpatrick, John Henry *insurance company executive*
Liuzzi, Robert C. *chemical company executive*
Maatman, Gerald Leonard *insurance company executive*
Mathis, David B. *financial services and insurance company executive*
Obert, Paul Richard *manufacturing company executive, lawyer*
Standbridge, Peter Thomas *insurance company executive*
Tarjan, Robert Wegg *information services executive*

Lynwood
Dyer-Dawson, Diane Faye *educational administrator*

Macomb
†Anderson, Richard Vernon *ecology educator, researcher*
Ballew, David Wayne *mathematics and computer science educator*
Brown, Spencer Hunter *historian*
Dexter, Donald Harvey *surgeon*
Hopper, Stephen Rodger *hospital administrator*
Malpass, Leslie Frederick *retired university president*
Spencer, Donald Spurgeon *historian, academic administrator*
Vos, Morris *foreign languages educator, language services consultant*
Wagoner, Ralph Howard *academic administrator, educator*
Witthuhn, Burton Orrin *university official*

Madison
Pope, Sarah Ann *elementary education educator*

Marengo
†Franks, Herbert Hoover *lawyer*

Marion
Lincoln, Lucian Abraham *coal company executive*
Livengood, Richard Vaughn *healthcare executive*

Maryville
Hurteau, William James *hospital administrator consultant*

Matteson
Leak, Alberta Hedgley *newspaper editor*
Yager, Vincent Cook *banker*

Mattoon
Horsley, Jack Everett *lawyer, author*
Phipps, John Randolph *retired army officer*
Sherline, Harold Albert *adult education professional*

Maywood
Blumenthal, Harold Jay *microbiologist, educator*
Canning, John Rafton *urologist*
Celesia, Gastone Guglielmo *neurologist, neurophysiologist, researcher*
Cera, Lee Marie *veterinarian*
Ellington, Mildred L. *librarian*
Freeark, Robert James *surgeon, educator*
†Gamelli, Richard L. *surgeon, educator*
Greenlee, Herbert Breckenridge *surgeon, educator*
Hanin, Israel *pharmacologist, educator*
Slogoff, Stephen *anesthesiologist, educator*

Mc Henry
Duel, Ward Calvin *health care consultant*

Melrose Park
Bernick, Howard Barry *manufacturing company executive*
Cernugel, William John *personal/food products company financial executive*
†Di Matteo, Dominick, Jr. *supermarket chain executive*
Lavin, Bernice E. *cosmetics executive*
Lavin, Leonard H. *personal care products company executive*
Umans, Alvin Robert *manufacturing company executive*

Mendota
†Du Bois, Clarence Hazel, Jr. *clergy member*
Hume, Horace Delbert *manufacturing company executive*

Metamora
Crow, Mary Jo Ann *elementary education educator*

Minooka
Flatness, Mary Linda *educational administrator*

Mokena
†Janssen, Sister Norma *hospital administrator*
Sangmeister, George Edward *congressman, lawyer*

Moline
Arnell, Richard Anthony *radiologist*
Becherer, Hans Walter *agricultural equipment manufacturing executive*
Cottrell, Frank Stewart *lawyer, manufacturing executive*
England, Joseph Walker *heavy equipment manufacturing company executive*
Hallene, Alan Montgomery *elevator and escalator company executive*
Hank, Bernard J., Jr. *elevator manufacturing company executive*
Hanson, Robert Arthur *retired agricultural equipment executive*
†Harrington, Roy Edwards *agricultural engineer, author*
Leroy, Pierre Elie *manufacturing executive*
Schaeffer, Robert Ollie *elevator company executive*
Stowe, David Henry, Jr. *agricultural and industrial equipment company executive*

Monmouth
Haywood, Bruce *college president*
Johnson, John Prescott *philosophy educator*

Mooseheart
O'Hollaren, Paul Joseph *former international fraternity administrator*

Morrison
French, Raymond Douglas *insurance agent, realtor,*

Morton Grove
Farber, Isadore E. *psychologist, educator*
McKenna, Andrew James *paper distribution and printing company executive, baseball club executive*
†Shaw, Jeffrey A. *commodities trader*

Mount Prospect
†Alexy, R. James *manufacturing company executive*
Cucco, Ulisse P. *obstetrician, gynecologist*
Flagg, Michael James *communications and graphics company executive*
Hansen, H. Jack *management consultant*
†Krakowiak, Edward T. *manufacturing company executive*
Rible, Morton *manufacturing executive, lawyer*
Rogers, Richard F. *construction company executive, architect, engineer*
†Scott, Norman Laurence *engineering consultant*
Singer, Norman Sol *food products executive, inventor*
Sissors, Jack Zanville *marketing educator*
Stamper, James M. *retired English language educator*
Sweet, Cody *performing artist, non-verbal communication expert*

Mount Vernon
Withers, W. Russell, Jr. *broadcast executive*

Mundelein
Burns, Kenneth Jones, Jr. *lawyer, consultant*
Kennedy, George D. *chemical company executive*
Mills, James Stephen *medical supply company executive*

Murphysboro
Brewer, Donald Louis *school superintendent*
Jacobs, Robert *education educator emeritus*
Miller, Donald Morton *physiology educator*

Naperville
Arzoumanidis, Gregory G. *chemist*
Burnham, Robert Danner *electronics executive, scientist*
Clark, Worley H., Jr. *specialty chemical company executive*
Cline, Richard Gordon *health medical products executive*
†Cowlishaw, Mary Lou *state legislator*
Crawford, Raymond Maxwell, Jr. *nuclear engineer*
Dranias, Dean Anthony *financial corporation consultant*
Fields, Ellis Kirby *research chemist*
†Fleisher, Robert E. R. *trucking executive*
Frank, Dieter *technical consultant, retired chemical company executive*
Fritz, Roger Jay *management consultant*
Grimley, Jeffrey Michael *dentist*
Harreld, James Bruce *food company executive*
Hensley, Albert Lloyd, Jr. *research chemist, technical consultant*
Karayannis, Nicholas Marios *chemist*
Landwehr, Arthur John *minister*
Mooney, Edward Joseph, Jr. *chemical company executive*
†Oberwortmann, C. D. *banker*
†Olliver, Denis G. *transportation company executive*
†Olson, Donald W. *transportation executive*
†O'Meara, Robert P. *banker*
Oxenreiter, Maurice Frank *chemical engineer*
Reuss, Robert Pershing *telecommunications executive, consultant*
Rovner, Jack Alan *lawyer*
Sadowski, Anthony James *chemical company executive, physical chemist*
Schaack, Philip Anthony *retired beverage company executive*
Schilling, Arlo Leonard *bank executive*
Schwab, Paul Josiah *psychiatrist educator*
†Scullen, Thomas G. *superintendent*
Shaw, Michael Allan *lawyer, mail order company executive*
Spiotta, Raymond Herman *consulting editor*
Triggiani, Leonard Vincent *corporate executive*
Ulrich, Werner *patent lawyer*
Wharton, Lennard *engineering company executive*
Wilde, Harold Richard *college president*
Wolfram, Thomas *physicist*

Nashville
†Deering, Terry William *state legislator*

Niles
Chertack, Melvin M. *internist*
†Herb, Marvin J. *food products executive*
Isenberg, Howard Lee *manufacturing company executive*
†Powell, David *manufacturing company executive*
Salamoun, Peter V. *retired manufacturing executive*
Schreiber, Jeffrey Lee *computer sales executive*

Normal
Bolen, Charles Warren *university dean*
Brown, Francis Robert *mathematics educator*
Jelks, Edward Baker *archaeologist, educator*
Jones, Graham Alfred *mathematics educator*
Matsler, Franklin Giles *higher education educator*
Mc Knight, William Warren, Jr. *publisher*
†Ohinouye, Tsuneo *automobile manufacturing executive*
Peterson, Fred McCrae *librarian*
Strand, David Axel *university executive*
Wallace, Thomas Patrick *university administrator*
Williams, Michael Roy *marketing research, management educator*
Young, Robert Donald *physicist, educator*

North Barrington
Bergstrom, Richard Norman *civil engineer*

North Chicago
Beer, Alan Earl *physician, medical educator*
Ehrenpreis, Seymour *pharmacology educator*
Freese, Uwe Ernest *physician, educator*
Gall, Eric Papineau *physician educator*
†Garrity, Keith R. *metal products company executive*
†Hawkins, Richard Albert *life sciences educator, administrator*
Hindo, Walid Afram *radiology educator, researcher*
Johnson, Lucille Merle Brown *elementary school principal*
Kim, Yoon Berm *immunologist, educator*
Kringel, John G. *health products company executive*
Loga, Sanda *physicist, educator*
†Metcoff, Jack *pediatrician*
Morris, Charles Elliot *neurologist*
Nair, Velayudhan *pharmacologist, medical educator*
Rogers, Eugene Jack *medical educator*
Rudy, David Robert *physician, educator*
Schneider, Arthur Sanford *physician, educator*
Sierles, Frederick Stephen *psychiatrist, educator*
Sladek, Celia Davis *neuroscientist, educator*
Taylor, Michael Alan *psychiatrist*
Weil, Max Harry *physician, medical educator, medical scientist*

Northbrook
Boyce, Donald Nelson *diversified industry executive*
Clarey, John Robert *executive search consultant*
Cohen, Seymour *lawyer*
Crowell, Edward Prince *retired association executive*
Day, Emerson *physician*
Degen, Bernard John, II *association executive*
Demaree, David Harry *utilities executive*
Flieder, John Joseph *insurance executive, marketing professional*
†Freedman, Walter G. *corporate services executive*
Gangware, Edgar Brand, Jr. *retired music educator*
Harris, Neison *manufacturing company executive*
Hartman, Robert S. *retired paper company executive*
Hedien, Wayne Evans *insurance company executive*
Heitmann, Frederick William *bank executive, lecturer*
Hirsch, Lawrence Leonard *physician, retired educator*
Jacobs, Richard Alan *management consultant*
Kasperson, Richard Willet *retired pharmaceutical company executive*
Kubek, Ralph A. *management consultant, accountant*
Kuby, Edward Raymond *insurance company executive*
Lapin, Harvey I. *lawyer*
Lenon, Richard Allen *chemical corporation executive*
†Lever, Alvin *health science association administrator*
Lower, Louis Gordon, II *insurance company executive*
Lucas, Lawrence Newton *sales and marketing consultant*
Magad, Samuel *orchestra concertmaster, conductor*
Marshall, Irl Houston, Jr. *company executive*
McFadden, Joseph Patrick *insurance company executive*
Mc Laren, John Alexander *retired physician*
Nordman, Richard Dennis *chemical company executive*
Piccolo, C. A. Lance *healthcare company executive*
Pinsof, Nathan *retired advertising executive*
Resnick, Myron J. *insurance company executive, lawyer*
Rodriguez-Erdmann, Franz *physician*
Ross, Bernard Harris *fitness company executive, certified public accountant, consultant*
Rudnick, Ellen Ava *health care executive*
Russell, William Steven *finance executive*
Saunders, Kenneth D. *insurance company executive, consultant, arbitrator*
Sayatovic, Wayne Peter *manufacturing company executive*
Scanlon, Edward F. *surgeon, educator*
Segal, Gordon I. *retail executive*
Slattery, James Joseph (Joe Slattery) *actor*
Snader, Jack Ross *publishing company executive*
†Soffer, Alfred *physician*
Terra, Daniel James *chemical company executive*
Tolan, James Francis *corporate and financial communications executive, marketing consultant, financial analyst*
Tucker, Frederick Thomas *electronics company executive*
Turner, Billie B. *chemical company executive*
†Turner, Lee *travel company executive*
Wajer, Ronald Edward *management consultant*
Weinstein, Ira Phillip *advertising executive*

Northfield
Bruns, Nicolaus, Jr. *retired agricultural chemicals company executive, lawyer*
Cartwright, Howard E(ugene) *retired association executive*
Cutler, Robert Porter *psychiatrist, psychoanalyst*
Edelson, Ira J. *venture banker*
Fraenkel, Stephen Joseph *engineering and research executive*
Glass, Henry Peter *industrial designer, interior architect, educator*
Hotze, Charles Wayne *publisher, printer*
Leslie, John Hampton *mnufacturing executive*
Louis, John (Jeffry), Jr. *former ambassador*
O'Brien, Maurice James *business executive*
Otis, James, Jr. *architect*
Parry, Rawdon Moira Crozier *marketing executive*
Porter, Helen Viney (Mrs. Lewis M. Porter, Jr.) *lawyer*
Sernett, Richard Patrick *lawyer*

Smart, Jackson Wyman, Jr. *business executive*
Smeds, Edward William *food company executive*
Stepan, Frank Quinn *chemical company executive*
†Stern, Grace Mary *state legislator*

Northlake
†Di Matteo, James *food products executive*
†Jasper, Paul Tucker *food company executive*

O'Fallon
Jenner, William Alexander *meteorologist, educator*

Oak Brook
†Baker, Robert J(ohn) *hospital administrator*
Brown, Dale Weaver *clergyman, theologian, educator*
Buntrock, Dean Lewis *waste management company executive*
Cooper, Richard Harris *investment company executive*
†Cosenza, G. Joseph *real estate executive*
Degerstrom, James Marvin *engineering manager*
Duerinck, Louis T. *retired railroad executive, attorney*
†Getz, Herbert A. *lawyer*
Gibson, James Thomas, Jr. *lawyer, consultant, antique dealer*
†Goodwin, Daniel L. *real estate company executive*
Greenberg, Jack M. *food products executive*
Holsinger, Wayne Townsend *apparel manufacturing executive*
Honeywell, Larry Gene *publishing company executive, travel company executive*
Iorgulescu, Jorge *international executive, chemical engineer*
Johnson, Grant Lester *lawyer, retired manufacturing company executive*
Jones, John Earl *construction company executive*
Kearney, Michael John *operations executive*
Peterson, Roger Eric *hardware wholesale company executive*
Quinlan, Michael Robert *fast food franchise company executive*
†Risk, Richard R. *health facility administrator*
Schueppert, George Louis *financial executive*
Stauffer, Delmar J. *professional association executive*
Stonich, Timothy Whitman *financial executive*
†Turner, Fred L. *fast food franchise executive*

Oak Forest
Hull, Charles William *special education educator*
†Lawler, Edmund G. *hospital administrator*

Oak Lawn
Massura, Eileen Kathleen *family therapist*
Rathi, Manohar Lal *pediatrician, neonatologist*

Oak Park
Adelman, William John *university labor and industrial relations educator*
†Bell, Robert Alan *architect*
Bowman, James Henry *writer*
Brackett, Edward Boone, III *orthopedic surgeon*
Cary, William Sterling *church executive*
Clark, John Peter, III *engineering consultant*
Davis, Christine Eurich *elementary education educator*
Denne, Joan Mallery *educator*
Devereux, Timothy Edward *advertising agency executive*
Douglas, Kenneth Jay *food products executive*
Kramer, Charles Henry *psychiatrist*
Neil, William *composer*
Notaro, Michael R. *data processing and computer service executive*
Robinson, Charlie Davis *food company executive*
Schultz, Bryan Christopher *dermatologist, educator*
Sengpiehl, Paul Marvin *lawyer, former state official*
Valinsky, Mark Steven *podiatrist*
Varchmin, Thomas Edward *environmental health administrator*
Worley, Marvin George, Jr. *architect*

Oakbrook Terrace
†Effa, Herman *clergy member, religious organization administrator*

Okawville
Schmale, Allen Lee *financial services company executive*

Olney
Edwards, Ian Keith *obstetrician, gynecologist*
Potter, David Lynn *retail executive*

Olympia Fields
Purdy, Charles Robert *corporate executive*
Sprinkel, Beryl Wayne *economist, consultant*

Oregon
Abbott, David Henry *manufacturing company executive*

Orland Park
Denys, Edward Paul *education educator*
Dyott, Richard Burnaby *research engineering executive*
English, Floyd Leroy *telecommunications company executive*
Gittelman, Marc Jeffrey *manufacturing and financial executive*
Leonard, Robert Dougherty *communications company executive*
Schultz, Barbara Marie *insurance company executive*

Ottawa
Willet, Shirley Hill *geriatrics and maternal-women's health nurse*

Palatine
Butler, John Musgrave *business financial consultant*
Fitzgerald, Gerald Francis *banker*
†Flavin, Patrick Brian *investment company executive, securities analyst*
Francis, Philip Hamilton *technology executive*
Hull, Elizabeth Anne *English language educator*
Kasten, Richard John *accountant*
Kern, Byron Mehl *retired chemical company executive*
Makowski, M. Paul *electronics research executive*
Medin, Lowell Ansgard *management executive*
Nagatoshi, Konrad R. *anthropology educator, information systems specialist*

Novak, Robert Louis *civil engineer, pavement management consultant*
Pohl, Frederik *writer*
Roe, Richard C. *industry consultant, former home furnishings manufacturing executive*
Zandier, Fred F. *special education educator*

Palos Heights
Hofeldt, John W. *lawyer*
†Nederhood, Joel H. *church organization executive, minister*

Palos Park
Crewe, Albert Victor *physicist, business executive, former research administrator*
Nelson, Lawrence Evan *business consultant*

Paris
Russell, Turner Alan *financial executive*

Park Forest
†Billig, Etel Jewel *theater director, actress*
Goodrich, John Bernard *lawyer*
Putnam, Robert E. *writer, editor*

Park Ridge
Adkins, Howard Eugene *aluminum company executive*
Boe, Gerard Patrick *health science association administrator*
Bridges, Jack Edgar *electronics engineer*
Carr, Gilbert Randle *retired railroad executive*
Curtis, Philip James *lawyer*
Ellis, Robert Griswold *engineering executive*
Howlett, Phyllis Lou *athletics conference administrator*
Kukla, Robert John *association executive*
Mack, Clifford Glenn *investment banker, management consultant*
Margolies, Raymond *management consulting company executive*
†McCarthy, Michael Shawn *health care company executive, lawyer*
Peterson, Richard Elton *publisher*
Raffel, Louis B. *association executive*
Rosenheim, Howard Harris *corporate executive*
Ryan, Judith Andre *health care executive, hospital administrator, nurse*
Schultz, Richard Carlton *plastic surgeon*
Tosh, Nancy Peckham *magazine editor*
†Ummel, Stephen L. *health facility administrator*
†Wardell, Kevin Stuart *hospital administrator*
Weber, Philip Joseph *retired manufacturing company executive*
Weinberg, Milton, Jr. *cardiovascular-thoracic surgeon*

Pecatonica
Smith, Janet Faye *special education educator*

Pekin
Clevenger, Robert Vincent *lawyer*
Heiple, James Dee *state supreme court justice*
Herbstreith, Yvonne Mae *primary education educator*
Wherry, Nancy Jeanne *elementary education educator*

Peoria
Allen, Lyle Wallace *lawyer*
Ballowe, James *English educator, author*
Brazil, John Russell *academic administrator*
Chamberlain, Joseph Miles *astronomer, educator*
Christison, William Henry, III *lawyer*
†Crawford, John Wickham *architect*
Cunningham, Raymond Leo *research chemist*
Dabney, Seth Mason, III *lawyer*
Dancey, Charles Lohman *newspaper executive*
†Doyle, Richard Lee *architect, engineer*
Dryden, Robert Charles *construction company executive*
†Dunkle, Richard L. *agriculturalist, researcher*
Eissfeldt, Theodore L. *lawyer*
Fites, Donald Vester *tractor company executive*
Grundbacher, Frederick John *geneticist, educator*
Hackler, John Byron, III *architect*
†Herring, Susan Kay *library director*
Kauffman, Robert Joseph *magistrate judge*
†Kenyon, Leslie Harrison *architect*
Lindgren, William Dale *librarian*
MacBurney, Edward Harding *bishop*
†Maloof, James A(loysius) *mayor, real estate company executive*
†Masching, Sister Frances Marie *healthcare system executive*
McCollum, Jean Hubble *medical assistant*
McConnell, John Thomas *newspaper executive, publisher*
McDade, Joe Billy *federal judge*
Meriden, Terry *physician*
†Michael, Jonathan Edward *insurance company executive*
Mihm, Michael Martin *federal judge*
Morgan, Robert Dale *federal judge*
Murphy, Sharon Margaret *university official, educator*
Myers, John Joseph *bishop*
Nielsen, Harald Christian *retired chemist*
Osborn, Terry Wayne *biochemist*
Parsons, Donald James *retired bishop*
†Peak, William Roy *newspaper editor*
Poupard, James J. *controller*
†Rainson, Ronald Lee *engineering executive, consultant*
Rothfus, John Arden *chemist*
Ryan, Michael Beecher *lawyer, former government official*
†Slane, Henry Pindell *broadcasting executive*
Slone, R. Wayne *utility company executive*
Smith, Clyde R. *counselor educator*
†Stephens, Gerald D. *insurance company executive*
Strodel, Robert Carl *lawyer*
Sullivan, Paul John *legal administrator*
Traicoff, Sandra M. *lawyer*
Viets, Robert O. *utilities executive*
Watson, Ellen I. *library director*
Wogsland, James Willard *heavy machinery manufacturing executive*

Peru
Carus, André Wolfgang *educational publishing firm executive*
Carus, Marianne *magazine editor*
Carus, Milton Blouke *chemical company executive, publisher*

†Weaver, Stanley B. *state senator*

Plainfield
Chakrabarti, Subrata Kumar *marine research engineer*
Schinderle, Robert Frank *hospital administrator*

Poplar Grove
Hullah, Ann Marie *elementary education educator*

Princeton
Johnson, Watts Carey *lawyer*

Prophetstown
Thompson, George Howard *livestock transportation company executive*

Prospect Heights
Clark, Donald Cameron *financial services company executive*
Clark, Donald Robert *retired insurance company executive*
Hull, J(ames) Richard *lawyer, business executive*
Larson, Gaylen Nevoy *financial executive*
†Osborne, Richard Cogswell *manufacturing company executive*

Quincy
†Cain, Richard Evan *radio station executive*
†Donahue, Laura Kent *state senator*
†Dorsey, Jeffrey Alan *broadcaster*
Liebig, Richard Arthur *retired manufacturing company executive*
Points, Roy Wilson *municipal official*
†Shade, Thomas L. *agricultural products executive*
Toal, James Francis *academic administrator*
Tyer, Travis Earl *librarian*

Rantoul
†Kosick, Howard Allen *accountant, finance executive*

River Forest
Brace, William *information science educator*
†Columbus, Chris Joseph *film director, screenwriter*
Hamper, Robert Joseph *marketing executive*
Koenig, Michael Edward Davison *information science educator*
Krentz, Eugene Leo *university president, educator, minister*
Li, Tze-chung *lawyer, educator*
Lund, Sister Candida *college chancellor*
Marco, Guy Anthony *librarian*
McCusker, Mary Lauretta *library science educator*
Murray, Sister Jean Carolyn *college president*
Rimbach, Evangeline Lois *music educator*
Sloan, Jeanette Pasin *artist*
Tomek, Laura Lindemann *marketing executive*
Wanamaker, Robert Joseph *advertising company executive*
White, Philip Butler *artist*

River Grove
Follett, Robert John Richard *publisher*
Hillert, Gloria Bonnin *anatomist, educator*

Riverdale
Saulsbury, Ruth Eva *retired special education educator*

Riverside
Fleck, Gordon Pierce *accounting firm executive*
Howlett, Carolyn Svrluga *art educator*
Perkins, William H., Jr. *finance company executive*
†Potokar, Richard Albert *architect*

Riverwoods
Bartlett, Robert William *lawyer, publishing executive*
Douglas, Bruce Lee *oral and maxillofacial surgeon, educator, health consultant, gerontology consultant*
Ferkenhoff, Robert J. *retail executive*
Kirby, Emily Baruch *psychologist, writer*

Rock Island
Bergendoff, Conrad John Immanuel *clergyman*
Brauch, Merry Ruth Moore *gifted education consultant*
Cheney, Thomas Ward *insurance company executive*
Horstmann, James Douglas *college official*
Lardner, Henry Petersen (Peter Lardner) *insurance company executive*
Lousberg, Peter Herman *lawyer*
Sundelius, Harold W. *geology educator*
Telleen, John Martin *judge*
Tredway, John Thomas *college president*
Wallace, Franklin Sherwood *lawyer*
Whitmore, Charles Horace *utility executive, lawyer, management consultant*

Rockford
Anderson, LaVerne Eric *lawyer*
Barrick, William Henry *lawyer*
Block, Stanley Marlin *engineering educator, arbitrator*
†Bradley, Charles MacArthur *architect*
Chitwood, Julius Richard *librarian*
†DeLuca, August Frank, Jr. *financial executive*
Donovan, Paul *aerospace executive*
Duck, Vaughn Michael *software company executive*
Eliason, Jon Tate *electrical engineer*
†Giolitto, Barbara *state representative*
Gloyd, Lawrence Eugene *diversified manufacturing company executive*
†Hasley, Ronald K. *bishop*
Heerens, Robert Edward *physician*
Hendershott Love, Arles June *television news director*
Horst, Bruce Everett *manufacturing company executive*
Howard, John Addison *former college president, institute executive*
Lynn, Janet (Janet Lynn Nowicki Salomon) *professional figure skater*
†Marelli, Sister M. Anthony *secondary school principal*
Maysent, Harold Wayne *hospital administrator*
O'Donnell, William David *construction firm executive*
Olson, Stanley William *physician, educator, medical school dean*
O'Neill, Arthur J. *bishop*

Pritikin, Roland I. *opthalmologic surgeon, writer, lecturer*
Reinhard, Philip G. *federal judge*
Reno, Roger *lawyer*
Schilling, Richard M. *lawyer, corporate executive*
Steele, Carl Lavern *academic administrator*
Stonecipher, Harry C. *manufacturing company executive*
Van Vleet, William Benjamin *lawyer, life insurance company executive*
Ward, Sylvan Donald *music conductor, educator*
Weissbard, David Raymond *minister*
Whitsell, Doris Benner *retired educator*

Rolling Meadows
Bongiorno, John Jacques *financial corporation executive*
Brennan, Charles Martin, III *construction company executive*
Grogan, Kenneth Augustine *publishing company executive*
Johnson, Robert Lawrence, Jr. *bank executive*

Romeoville
Mills, Jon K. *psychologist, educator*

Roselle
Poth, Edward Cornelius *construction company executive*

Rosemont
Baron, Richard Albert *sales executive*
†Burkhardt, Edward Arnold *transportation company executive*
Good, William Allen *professional society executive*
Trznadel, Frank Dwight, Jr. *leasing company executive*

Round Lake
Johnston, William David *health care company executive*
Kingdon, Henry Shannon *physician, biochemist, educator, executive*

Round Lake Park
Corcoran, Gregory Michael *corporate real estate executive*

Saint Charles
McCartney, Charles Price *retired obstetrician-gynecologist*
Mc Kay, Thomas, Jr. *lawyer*
Schultz, Robert Vernon *entrepreneur*
Stone, John McWilliams, Jr. *electronics executive*
Urhausen, James Nicholas *real estate developer, construction executive*

Savanna
Foulk, David Wingerd *civilian military executive*

Scales Mound
Lieberman, Archie *photographer, writer*

Schaumburg
†Bauchiero, James *transportation executive*
†Bolinder, William Howard *insurance company executive*
Boston, Leona *organization executive*
Chitwood, Lera Catherine *information professional, manufacturing company manager*
Collins, James Francis *lawyer*
Edmunds, Jane Clara *communications consultant*
Galvin, Christopher B. *electronics company executive*
Galvin, Robert W. *electronics executive*
Geiger, Joseph Francis *financial planner*
Greenwell, Ronald Everett *communications executive*
Halloran, Daniel Edward *personnel executive*
†Heaton, Syd N. *computer company executive*
Hickey, John Thomas *electronics company executive*
†Kadish, Steven A. *retail executive*
Keil, M. David *international association executive*
Krebs, Robert Duncan *transportation company executive*
Langsdorf, Alexander, Jr. *physicist*
Meltzer, Brian *lawyer*
†Miller, Vernon Dallace *minister*
Milne, Garth LeRoy *electronics executive*
Morgan, David Ernest *computer and communications research executive*
Nauert, Peter William *insurance company executive*
Nettleton, David *religious administrator*
Payton, Walter (Sweetness) *professional race car driver, former professional football player*
Rashkow, Ronald *home improvement company executive*
Roach, William Russell *training and education executive*
†Schulmeyer, Gerhard *manufacturing executive*
Splitt, Frank George *telecommunications company executive*
Stephens, Norval Blair, Jr. *marketing consultant*
Sundry, Arthur P. *business executive*
Tooker, Gary Lamarr *electronics company executive*
†Walker, Robert Giles, Jr. *architect*
Weise, Richard Henry *lawyer, corporate executive*
Weisz, William Julius *electronics company executive*
†Wojcik, Kathleen Louise *state representative*

Schiller Park
†Ring, Alice Ruth Bishop *physician*

Scott AFB
Fogleman, Ronald Robert *military officer*
Landers, Paul E., Jr. *military career officer*

Shelbyville
†Gloede, Richard *management consulting executive*

Skokie
Alexander, John Charles *pharmaceutical company executive, physician*
Bakalar, John Stephen *printing and publishing company executive*
Bendix, William Emanuel *equipment manufacturing company executive*
Bogomolny, Robert Lee *lawyer*
Boxer, Robert William *allergist*
Breen, Thomas John *form publishing company executive*
Childers, John Henry *talent company executive, personality representative*
Corley, William Gene *engineering research executive*
Cunningham, R. John *financial consultant*

Dishman, Leonard I. *accountant*
Filler, Robert *chemistry educator*
Fluno, Jere David *business executive*
Gleason, John Patrick, Jr. *trade association executive*
†Goeckel, Werner Frederick *plastics company executive*
Goldberg, Arthur Lewis *manufacturing company executive*
Goldmann, Morton Aaron *cardiologist*
Grainger, David William *distribution company executive*
Herting, Robert Leslie *pharmaceutical executive*
Hognestad, Eivind *retired civil engineer*
†Johansson, Nils A. *manufacturing executive*
Kranz, Norman *advertising executive*
Krucks, William *electronics manufacturing executive*
Mayes, Frank Gorr *food company executive*
McNally, Andrew, III *printer, publisher*
McNally, Andrew, IV *publishing executive*
Olwin, John Hurst *surgeon*
Panarese, William C. *civil engineer*
Pappano, Robert Daniel *corporate treasurer*
†Rubow, W. Steven *food company executive*
Searle, William Louis *investment company executive*
Siegal, Burton Lee *product designer, consultant, inventor*
Siegal, Rita Goran *engineering company executive*
White, William James *information management and services company executive;*
Wildermuth, Roger Gregory *publishing company executive*

South Barrington
Smith, William Lewis *hotel executive*

South Elgin
Burdett, George Craig *plastics industry executive*

South Holland
†Mulder, Dennis Marlin *religious organization executive*
Poprick, Mary Ann *psychologist*
Schaap, Marcia *special education educator*

Springfield
Blackman, Jeanne A. *lobbyist*
Budinger, Charles Jude *state agency insurance analyst*
Burris, Roland Wallace *state attorney general*
Cadigan, Patrick Joseph *lawyer*
Clarke, John Patrick *newspaper publisher*
†Clarke, Robert Thorburn *medical center executive*
†Currie, Barbara Flynn *state legislator*
†DeAngelis, Aldo A. *state senator*
DeMoss, Jon W. *legal association administrator, lawyer*
Dodd, Robert Bruce *physician, educator*
Edgar, Jim *governor*
†Ferguson, Mark Harmon *banker, lawyer*
Fischoff, Ephraim *humanities educator, sociologist, social worker*
Frank, Stuart *cardiologist*
Gallina, Charles Onofrio *nuclear regulatory official*
Giesecke, G(ustav) Ernst *education educator emeritus*
Gucker, Jane Gleason *architect*
†Hahn, Ralph Crane *structural engineer, consultant*
†Hallmark, Donald Parker *museum director*
Hanson, Walter Edmund *consulting civil engineer*
Heintz, Jack *publishing company executive*
Holland, John Madison *family practice physician*
†Homer, Thomas J. *state legislator*
Hudson, Claude Earl *banker*
Humphrey, Howard C. *insurance company executive*
Jackson, Robert William *utility company executive*
†Kaitschuk, John Paul *bishop*
†Karpiel, Doris Catherine *state legislator*
Laabs, Allison C. *hospital administrator*
†Lamont, Bridget Later *librarian, consultant*
†Layzell, Thomas D. *academic administrator*
Lessen, Larry Lee *federal judge*
Lohman, Walter Rearick *banker*
Lynn, Naomi B. *university president, public administration educator*
Lyons, J. Rolland *civil engineer*
Madigan, Michael Joseph *state legislator*
Mc Millan, R(obert) Bruce *museum executive, anthropologist*
†Mervis, Louis *school system administrator*
Miller, Benjamin K. *state supreme court justice*
Mills, Richard Henry *federal judge*
†Mogerman, Susan *state agency administrator*
Moy, Richard Henry *academic dean, educator*
Munyer, Edward A. *zoologist, museum adminstrator*
Myers, Phillip Ward *otolaryngologist*
Oxtoby, Robert Boynton *lawyer*
†Petterchak, Janice A. *library director*
†Philip, James (Pate Philip) *state senator*
Poorman, Robert Lewis *higher education consultant, academic administrator*
Rabinovich, Sergio *physician, educator*
Reed, John Charles *chemical engineer*
Resnick, Joel H. *motion picture distributing executive*
†Rose, T. T. *bishop*
Rowe, Max L. *lawyer, corporate executive, management consultant, judge*
Ryan, Daniel Leo *bishop*
Segatto, Bernard Gordon *lawyer*
Shim, Sang Koo *state mental health official*
†Shotwell, Malcolm Green *minister*
†Smith, Margaret *state legislator*
Stooksbury, Walter Elbert *insurance company executive*
Stroh, Raymond Eugene *personnel executive*
†Tarr, Paul Cresson, III *insurance company executive*
Taylor, Mary Kathleen *school system administrator*
Temple, Wayne Calhoun *historian*
Thomas, Payne Edward Lloyd *publisher*
Travis, Lawrence Allan *accountant*
†Trstensky, Sister Jomary *hospital administrator*
Van Meter, Abram DeBois *lawyer, retired banker*
Wehrle, Leroy Snyder *economist, educator*
†Welch, Patrick Daniel *state senator*
Wood, Harlington, Jr. *federal judge*
Zook, Elvin Glenn *plastic surgeon, educator*

Sterling
Albrecht, Beverly Jean *special education educator*
Gurnitz, Robert Ned *steel industry company executive*
Knight, Herbert Borwell *manufacturing company executive*
†von Bergen Wessels, Pennie Lea *state legislator*

Streator
Harrison, Frank Joseph *lawyer*

Summit
Abramowicz, Alfred L. *bishop*

Summit Argo
Urban, Patricia A. *elementary school educator*

Sumner
Trent, Wendell Campbell *business owner*

Sycamore
Grace, John Eugene *business forms company executive*
Johnson, Yvonne Amalia *elementary education educator, science consultant*

University Park
Lingamneni, Jaganmohan Rao *criminology educator*
Strukoff, Rudolf Stephen *music educator*
Wentz, Walter John *health administration educator*

Urbana
Addy, Alva Leroy *mechanical engineer*
Aiken, Michael Thomas *academic administrator*
Albrecht, Felix Robert *mathematics educator*
Aldridge, Alfred Owen *English language educator*
†Alkire, Richard Collin *chemical engineering educator*
Andersen, Kenneth Eldon *speech communication educator*
Antonsen, Elmer Harold *Germanic languages and literature educator*
Arnstein, Walter Leonard *historian, educator*
Assanis, Dennis N. (Dionissios Assanis) *mechanical engineering educator*
Axford, Roy Arthur *nuclear engineering educator*
Baer, Werner *economist, educator*
Baker, David Hiram *nutritional biochemist*
Balbach, Stanley Byron *lawyer*
Banwart, Wayne Lee *agronomy, environmental science educator*
Basar, Tamer *electrical engineering educator*
Bateman, John Jay *classics educator*
Bateman, Paul Trevier *mathematician, educator*
Bates, James Leonard *historian*
Baym, Nina *English educator*
Bayne, James Wilmer *mechanical engineering educator*
Beak, Peter Andrew *chemistry educator*
Beavers, Alvin Herman *soil science educator*
Beck, Paul Adams *metallurgist, educator*
Becker, Donald Eugene *animal science educator*
Bedford, Norton Moore *accounting educator*
Bentley, Orville George *retired agricultural educator, dean emeritus*
Bergeron, Clifton George *ceramic engineer, educator*
Birnbaum, Howard Kent *materials science educator*
Blair, Lachlan Ferguson *urban planner, educator*
Bloomfield, Daniel Kermit *college dean, physician*
Boardman, Eunice *music educator*
Brichford, Maynard Jay *archivist*
Broudy, Harry Samuel *retired philosophy educator*
Brown, Theodore Lawrence *chemistry educator*
Browne, Gerald Michael *classics educator*
Brün, Herbert *composer*
Bruner, Edward M. *anthropology educator*
Bryant, Marvin Pierce *bacteriologist, microbiologist, educator*
Buck, William Boyd *toxicology educator*
Buetow, Dennis Edward *physiology educator*
Burdge, Rabel James *sociology educator*
Burger, Ambrose William *agronomy educator*
Burkholder, Donald Lyman *mathematician, educator*
Carey, James William *university dean, educator, researcher*
Carmen, Ira Harris *political scientist, educator*
Carroll, Robert Wayne *mathematics educator*
Chao, Bei Tse *mechanical engineering educator*
Chato, John Clark *mechanical engineering educator*
Chow, Poo *wood technologist, scientist*
Clausing, Arthur M. *mechanical engineering educator*
Cohen, Stephen Philip *political science and history educator*
Conry, Thomas Francis *mechanical engineering educator, consultant*
Courson, Roger Lee *agricultural educator*
Crang, Richard Francis Earl *plant and cell biologist, research center administrator*
Crofts, Antony Richard *biophysics educator*
Cunningham, Clark Edward *anthropology educator*
Cusano, Cristino *mechanical engineer, educator*
Davis, Lloyd Edward *veterinary medicine educator*
Dawn, Clarence Ernest *history educator*
Debrunner, Peter George *physics educator*
Dickinson, David Budd, Jr. *horticulture educator*
Dobrovolny, Jerry Stanley *engineering educator*
Doob, Joseph Leo *mathematician, educator*
Dovring, Folke *land economics educator, consultant*
Drickamer, Harry George *retired chemistry educator*
Due, Jean Margaret *agricultural economist, educator*
Dunn, Floyd *biophysicist, bioengineer, educator*
Economy, James *polymer researcher, consultant*
†Edelsbrunner, Herbert *computer scientist, mathematician*
Eden, James Gary *electrical engineering and physics educator, researcher*
Elyn, Mark *opera singer, educator*
Engelbrecht, Richard Stevens *environmental engineering educator*
Faulkner, Larry Ray *chemistry educator, academic officer*
Feinberg, Walter *cultural values and ethics director*
Fitz-Gerald, Roger Miller *lawyer*
Forbes, Richard Mather *biochemistry educator*
Ford, Richard Earl *plant virologist, educator, academic administrator*
Fossum, Robert Merle *mathematician, educator*
Frazzetta, Thomas H. *evolutionary biologist, functional morphologist, educator*
Friedman, Stanley *insect physiologist, educator*
Gabriel, Michael *psychology educator*
Gaddy, Oscar Lee *electrical engineering educator*
Gaeng, Paul Ami *foreign language educator*
Garrigus, Upson Stanley *animal science and international agriculture educator*
George, William Leo, Jr. *plant geneticist, educator*
Giertz, J. Fred *economics educator*
Giles, Eugene *anthropology educator*
Goering, Carroll E. *agricultural engineering educator*
Goldberg, Samuel Irving *mathematics educator*
Goldwasser, Edwin Leo *physicist*
Gomes, Wayne Reginald *college dean*
Goodman, William I. *urban planner, educator*
Gorecki, Jan *sociologist, educator*
Gove, Samuel Kimball *political science educator*
Govindjee *biophysics and biology educator*
Gray, John Walker *mathematician, educator*
†Greene, Laura Helen *physicist*
Greenough, William Tallant *psychobiologist, educator*
Greenwold, Warren Eldon *retired physician, medical educator*
Gunsalus, Irwin C. *biochemistry educator, consultant*
Gutowsky, Herbert Sander *chemistry educator*
Guttenberg, Albert Ziskind *planning educator*
Hager, Lowell Paul *biochemistry educator*
Haile, H. G. *German language and literature educator*
Hajj, Ibrahim Nasri *electrical and computer engineering educator*
Hall, William Joel *civil engineer, educator*
Hannon, Bruce Michael *engineer, educator*
Hanratty, Thomas Joseph *chemical engineer, educator*
Harlan, Jack Rodney *geneticist, emeritus educator*
Harper, James Eugene *plant physiologist*
Hawkins, Neil Middleton *civil engineer, educator*
Hay, Richard Le Roy *geology educator*
Heichel, Gary Harold *agronomy educator*
Hendrick, George *English language educator*
Henson, C. Ward *mathematician, educator*
Herrin, Moreland *civil engineering educator, consultant*
Hess, Karl *electrical and computer engineering educator*
Hill, Lowell Dean *agricultural marketing educator*
Hixon, James Edward *physiology educator*
Hoeft, Robert Gene *agriculture educator*
Hoffmeister, Donald Frederick *zoology educator*
Holonyak, Nick, Jr. *electrical engineering educator*
Holt, Donald A. *university administrator, agronomist, consultant, researcher*
Horwitz, Alan Fredrick *cell and molecular biology educator*
Huang, Thomas Shi-Tao *electrical engineering educator, researcher*
Hunt, Donnell Ray *agricultural engineering educator*
Hurt, James Riggins *English language educator*
Hymowitz, Theodore *plant geneticist, educator*
Iben, Icko, Jr. *astrophysicist, educator*
Ikenberry, Stanley Oliver *university president*
Jacobson, Howard *classics educator*
Jerrard, Richard Patterson *mathematics educator*
Jockusch, Carl Groos, Jr. *mathematics educator*
Jonas, Jiri *chemistry educator*
Kachru, Braj Behari *linguist*
Kachru, Yamuna *linguist*
Kang, Sung-Mo (Steve Kang) *electrical engineering educator*
Kesler, Clyde Ervin *engineering educator*
Kim, Chin-Woo *linguist, educator*
Kirkpatrick, R(obert) James *geology educator*
Klein, Miles Vincent *physics educator*
†Klemperer, Walter George *chemistry educator, researcher*
Knake, Ellery Louis *weed science educator*
Knight, Frank Bardsley *mathematics educator*
Kolodziej, Edward Albert *political scientist, educator*
Konisky, Jordan *microbiology educator*
Kumar, Panganamala Ramana *electrical and computer engineering educator*
Langenheim, Ralph Louis, Jr. *geology educator*
†Lauffenburger, Douglas Alan *chemical engineering educator*
Lauterbur, Paul C(hristian) *chemistry educator*
Lawrie, Duncan H. *computer science educator, consultant*
Lazarus, David *physicist, educator*
Leuthold, Raymond Martin *agricultural economics educator*
Lieberman, Laurence *poet, educator*
Linowes, David Francis *political economist, educator, corporate executive*
Littlewood, Thomas Benjamin *journalism educator*
Lodge, James Robert *dairy science educator*
Mainous, Bruce Hale *foreign language educator*
†Makri, Nancy *chemistry educator*
†Marcovich, Miroslav *educator*
May, Walter Grant *chemical engineer*
Mayer, Robert Wallace *emeritus finance educator*
Mayes, Paul Eugene *engineering educator, technical consultant*
Mazumder, Jyotirmoy *mechanical and industrial engineering educator*
Mc Clellan, William Monson *library administrator*
McColley, Robert McNair *history educator*
Mc Conkie, George Wilson *education educator*
Mc Glamery, Marshal Dean *agronomy, weed science educator*
Melby, John B. *composer, educator*
Merkelo, Henri *electronics scientist*
Meyer, Richard Charles *microbiologist*
Mihalas, Dimitri Manuel *astronomer, educator*
Miley, George Hunter *nuclear engineering educator*
Miller, Robert Earl *engineer, educator*
†Minear, Roger Allan *chemist, educator*
Nanney, David Ledbetter *genetics educator*
Nelson, Ralph Alfred *physician*
Nettl, Bruno *anthropology and musicology educator*
Newman, John Kevin *classics educator*
Ogren, William Lewis *physiologist, educator*
O'Morchoe, Charles Christopher Creagh *administrator, anatomical sciences educator*
Ormsbee, Allen Ives *aeronautical and astronautical engineering educator, researcher, consultant*
Pai, Anantha Mangalore *electrical engineering educator, consultant*
Parker, Alan John *veterinary neurologist, educator, researcher*
Parrish, John Bishop *economics educator*
Perkins, William Randolph *electrical engineer, educator*
Peterson, Theodore Bernard *retired journalism educator*
Pethick, Christopher John *physicist*
†Poss, Jeffrey Scott *architect, educator*
Prosser, C. Ladd *physiology educator, researcher*
†Prussing, Laurel Lunt *state official, economist*
Queller, Donald Edward *historian, educator*
Ramirez, Domingo Victor *physiologist, educator*
Rao, Nannapaneni Narayana *electrical engineer*
Rebeiz, Constantin Anis *plant physiology educator*
Resek, Robert William *university administrator*
Rich, Robert F. *political sciences educator, academic administrator*
Ricketts, Gary Eugene *animal scientist*
Riley, Robert Bartlett *landscape architect*
Rotzoll, Kim Brewer *advertising and communications educator*
Rowland, Theodore Justin *physicist, educator*
Salamon, Myron Ben *physicist, educator*
†Sameh, Ahmed Hamdy *computer science educator*
Sandage, Charles Harold *advertising educator*
Scanlan, Richard Thomas *classics educator*
Schacht, Richard Lawrence *philosopher, educator*
Schmidt, Stephen Christopher *agricultural economist, educator*
†Schweizer, Kenneth Steven *physics educator*
Seigler, David Stanley *botanist, chemist, educator*
Seitz, Wesley Donald *agricultural economics educator*
Shtohryn, Dmytro Michael *librarian, educator*
Shuman, R(obert) Baird *academic program director, writer, english educator, educational consultant*
Shurtleff, Malcolm C. *plant pathologist, consultant, educator, extension specialist*
Siedler, Arthur James *nutrition and food science educator*
Siess, Chester Paul *civil engineering educator*
Simon, Jack Aaron *geologist, former state official*
Small, Erwin *veterinarian, educator*
Snyder, Lewis Emil *astrophysicist*
Socie, Darrell Frederick *mechanical engineering educator*
Solberg, Winton Udell *history educator*
Soo, Shao Lee *mechanical engineer, educator*
Spitze, Robert George Frederick *agricultural economics educator*
Splittstoesser, Walter Emil *plant physiologist*
Stallmeyer, James Edward *engineer, educator*
Stein, Arnold *English educator*
Stillinger, Jack Clifford *English educator*
Stout, Glenn Emanuel *water resources center administrator*
Suzuki, Michio *mathematics educator*
Swenson, George Warner, Jr. *electronics engineer, radio astronomer, educator*
Switzer, Robert Lee *biochemistry educator*
Talbot, Emile Joseph *French educator*
Tang, Wilson Hon-chung *engineering educator*
Thompson, Margaret M. *physical education educator*
Todd, Kenneth S., Jr. *parasitologist, educator*
Tondeur, Philippe Maurice *mathematician, educator*
Trick, Timothy Noel *electrical and computer engineering educator, researcher*
†Trigger, Kenneth James *manufacturing engineering educator*
Van Arsdell, Paul Marion *economics and finance educator*
Van Valkenburg, Mac Elwyn *electrical engineering educator*
Visek, Willard James *nutritionist, animal scientist, physician, educator*
Voss, Edward William, Jr. *immunologist, educator*
Waldbauer, Gilbert Peter *entomologist, educator*
Warfield, William Caesar *singer, actor, educator*
Watson, Paula D. *library administrator*
Wattenberg, Albert *physicist, educator*
Watts, Emily Stipes *English educator*
Wedgeworth, Robert *university librarian, dean, former association exe*
Weir, Morton Webster *retired university chancellor and educator*
Wert, Charles Allen *metallurgical and mining engineering educator*
Westwater, James William *chemical engineering educator*
White, Robert Allan *mechanical engineering educator*
White, W(illiam) Arthur *geologist*
Whitt, Gregory Sidney *molecular phylogenetics, evolution educator*
Williams, Benjamin Tallifaro *pathologist, educator*
Williams, Martha Ethelyn *information science educator*
Wilson, Winnie Ruth *elementary education educator, reading specialist*
Wirt, Frederick Marshall *political scientist*
Wisniewski, Thomas Joseph *music educator*
Wolfe, Ralph Stoner *microbiology educator*
Wolynes, Peter Guy *chemistry researcher, educator*
Yoerger, Roger Raymond *agricultural engineer, educator*
Yu, George Tzuchiao *political science educator*

Venice
Purdes, Alice Marie *secondary education educator*

Vernon Hills
Claassen, W(alter) Marshall *employment company executive*
†Mignano, Richard Alan *marketing professional*
†Wilson, J. Steven *lumber company executive*

Villa Park
Becker, Robert Jerome *allergist, health care consultant*
†Binder, John *minister, religious organization executive*
†Devlin, Barbara Jo *school district administrator*
Evans, Austin James *hospital administrator*
Fenech, Joseph C. *lawyer*
Grant, Charles Truman *business recapitalization and health care management executive*
Kohlstedt, James August *lawyer*
Leston, Patrick John *lawyer*
McDonnell, Dennis J. *securities industry executive*
O'Leary, Dennis Sophian *medical organization executive*
†Rogers, Peter Norman *food company executive*
†Russell, Richard *religious organization adminstrator*
Treat, Thomas Frank *health care executive*
Webb, James Okrum, Jr. *insurance company executive*
Williams, David Arthur *marketing professional*
Willis, John Fristoe *concertmaster*
†Wozniak, Edward F. *manufacturing company executive*

Washington
McKinney-Keller, Margaret Frances *retired special education educator*

Wauconda
†Bolchazy, Ladislaus J. *publishing company executive*

Waukegan
Bleck, Virginia Eleanore *illustrator*
Chapman, James Claude *marine equipment manufacturing executive*
Cherry, Peter Ballard *electrical products corporation executive*
Cherry, Walter Lorain *engineer, electronics executive*
Crutcher, Harold Trabue, Jr. *chemical company executive*
Hall, Albert Leander *lawyer*
Henrick, Michael Francis *lawyer*
†Petropoulos, Gust A. *retail company executive*

West Chicago
Ball, G(eorge) Carl *seed company executive*

Westchester
Clarke, Richard Lewis *health science association administrator*
Masterson, John Patrick *retired English language educator*
†Walsh, Thomas J. *state representative*

Western Springs
Carroll, Jeanne *public relations executive*
Darrell, George Albert *architect*
†Swiatek, Kenneth Robert *neuroscientist*

Westmont
Wesbury, Stuart Arnold, Jr. *health care consultant*

Wheaton
Beers, V(ictor) Gilbert *publishing executive*
Bogdonoff, Maurice Lambert *physician*
†Botti, Aldo E. *lawyer*
†Estep, John Hayes *religious denomination executive, clergyman*
†Fawell, Beverly Jean *state legislator*
Flynn, James Rourke *retired insurance company executive*
Haenszel, William Manning *epidemiologist, educator*
Jack, Nancy Rayford *supplemental resource company executive, consultant*
Jett, Charles Cranston *management consultant*
Kelly, Robert Thomas *publisher*
Loebig, Wilfred F. *health care executive*
Maibenco, Helen Craig *anatomist, educator*
Mellott, Robert Vernon *advertising executive*
Melvin, Billy Alfred *clergyman*
Pint, Sister Rose Mary *nun, religious order administrator, health care executive*
Reszka, Alfons *computer systems architect*
Roberts, Keith Edward, Sr. *lawyer*
†Roskam, Peter James *lawyer, state legislator*
Sweeney, Mark Owen *publisher*
Taylor, Mark Douglas *publishing executive*
Thompson, Bert Allen *retired librarian*

Wheeling
Hammer, Donald Price *librarian*
Koch, Peter F. *management consultant*
Mc Clarren, Robert Royce *librarian*
Smith, Justine Townsend *recreational association executive*

Wilmette
Albright, Townsend Shaul *investment banker, government benefits consultant*
Barnett, Ralph Lipsey *engineering educator*
Biedron, Theodore John *newspaper executive*
Brink, Marion Francis *association executive*
Espenshade, Edward Bowman, Jr. *geographer, educator*
Fries, Robert Francis *historian, educator*
Hansen, Andrew Marius *retired library association executive*
Henry, Alan Pemberton *newspaper editor, journalist*
Ingersoll, Robert Stephen *former diplomat, federal agency administrator*
Kurtzman, Allan Roger *advertising executive*
Mc Nitt, Willard Charles *business executive*
Merrier, Helen *actress, director*
Muhlenbruch, Carl W. *civil engineer*
Nash, Jay Robert, III *author, playwright, publisher*
Nelson, James F. *judge, religious organization administrator*
Randolph, Lillian Larson *medical association executive*
Smutny, Joan Franklin *academic director, educator*
Stipp, John Edgar *financial consultant, lawyer*
Williams, Emory *former retail company executive, banker*

Wilmington
Anderson, Mary Jane *public library director*

Winnetka
Abell, David Robert *lawyer*
Andersen, Kenneth Benjamin *retired association executive*
Bartlett, William McGillivray *hospital and scientific products company executive*
Bogart, Homer Gordon *marketing executive*
Carrow, Leon Albert *physician*
Curtin, John William *retired plastic surgeon, educator*
Davis, Britton Anthony *lawyer*
Davis, Chester R., Jr. *lawyer*
dePeyster, Frederic Augustus *surgeon*
Earle, David Prince, Jr. *physician, educator*
Folds, Charles Weston *merchandising consultant*
Fulk, Roscoe Neal *retired accountant*
Gavin, James John, Jr. *diversified company executive*
Gray, Sheldon *metal products executive*
Greeley, Joseph May *retired advertising executive*
Hudnut, Robert Kilborne *clergyman, author*
Kahn, Paul Frederick *executive search company executive*
Kapnick, Richard Bradshaw *lawyer*
†Lindsay, Dianna Marie *educational administrator*
Mancuso, James Vincent *automobile columnist*
Mathers, Thomas Nesbit *financial consultant*
†Mayer, Richard Philip *food executive*
Mc Millen, Thomas Roberts *lawyer, arbitrator, mediator, retired judge*
Menke, Allen Carl *industrial corporation executive*
O'Malley, John Daniel *legal educator, banker*
Owens, Luvie Moore *association executive*
Pattison, Abbott Lawrence *sculptor*
Piper, Robert Johnston *architect, urban planner*
Plowden, David *photographer*
Puth, John Wells *consulting company executive*
Sharboneau, Lorna Rosina *artist, educator, writer*
Sick, William Norman, Jr. *investment company executive*
Sommers, Herbert Myron *pathology educator, retired physician*
Teninga, Walter Henry *retail executive*
VanBremen, Lee *medical association executive*
Weber, John Bertram *architect*
Weldon, Theodore Tefft, Jr. *retail company executive*

Winthrop Harbor
Fuhrman, Kenneth Wayne *pilot, aviation consultant*

Wood Dale
Kearns, Janet Catherine *corporate secretary*
Thompson, John Henry *consulting executive*
Ward, Katheryn Hope *marketing educator and administrator, consultant*

Woodridge
Allen, Charles Joseph, II *advertising agency executive*
Emerson, Edward James *computer software executive*

Woodstock
Hale, Hamilton Orin *retired lawyer*
Kuhajek, Eugene James *chemical research executive*

Zion
†Geo-Karis, Adeline Jay *state senator*

INDIANA

Anderson
†Conrad, Harold August *retired pension board executive*
Contos, Larry D *food products executive*
†Dale, Doris *religious organization executive*
†Dye, Dwight Latimer *minister*
†Edwards, James L. *university president*
Foggs, Edward L. *church administrator*
†Grubbs, J. Perry *church administrator*
†Hayes, Sherill D. *religious organization administrator*
King, Charles Ross *physician*
†Lutz, L. Jack *retail executive, congressman*
Nicholson, Robert Arthur *college president*
†Patton, Norman S. *church administrator*
†Rist, Robert G. *religious publishing executive*

Angola
Elliott, Carl Hartley *former university president*

Attica
†Harrison, Joseph William *state senator*

Auburn
Kempf, Jane Elmira *marketing executive*

Batesville
Hillenbrand, Daniel A. *manufacturing company executive*
Smith, Lonnie Max *diversified industries executive*

Bedford
Schurz, Scott Clark *journalist, publisher*
†Skillman, Becky Sue *state legislator*

Beech Grove
Clapper, George Raymond *accountant, computer consultant*

Berne
†Lehman, Doyle *superintendent*

Beverly Shores
Ruzic, Neil Pierce *author, publisher, scientist*

Bloomington
Adams, William Richard *archaeologist, lecturer, curator*
Aman, Alfred Charles, Jr. *law educator*
Anderson, Judith Helena *English language educator*
Arnove, Robert Frederick *education educator*
Bain, Wilfred Conwell *former university dean, music educator, opera theater director*
Bair, Edward Jay *chemistry educator*
Barnes, A. James *academic dean*
Barnes, Robert Merton *artist, educator*
Barnstone, Willis (Robert Barnstone) *language literature educator, poet, scholar*
Battenhouse, Roy Wesley *English educator*
Bauman, Richard *anthropologist, educator*
Baxter, Maurice Glen *historian, educator*
Beckwith, Christopher Irving *social sciences educator, writer, composer*
Belth, Joseph Morton *retired business educator*
Bent, Robert Demo *physicist, educator*
Bishop, Michael Daryl *emergency physician*
Boerner, Peter *language and literature educator*
Brown, Keith *musician, educator*
Buelow, George John *musicologist, educator*
Burgan, Mary Alice *English language educator*
Burton, Philip Ward *advertising executive, educator*
Byrnes, Robert Francis *history educator*
Cagle, William Rea *librarian*
Caldwell, Lynton Keith *social scientist, educator*
Calinescu, Adriana Gabriela *museum curator, art historian*
Campaigne, Ernest Edward *chemistry educator*
Chisholm, Malcolm Harold *chemistry educator*
Clevenger, Sarah *botanist, computer consultant*
Cohen, William Benjamin *historian, educator*
Cole, Bruce Milan *art historian*
Counsilman, James Edward *physical education educator*
†Davidson, Ernest Roy *chemist, educator*
Davis, Charles Hargis *information scientist, educator*
DeHayes, Daniel Wesley *management executive, educator*
Diamant, Alfred *political science educator*
Dieterle, Donald Lyle *accountant, educator*
Dinsmoor, James Arthur *psychology educator*
Dodd, James Robert *geologist, educator*
Dunn, Jon Michael *philosophy educator*
Edgerton, William B. *foreign language educator*
Edmondson, Frank Kelley *astronomer*
Ehrlich, Thomas *university administrator, law educator*
†Escobar, Jose Fernando *mathematician, educator*
Ferrell, Robert Hugh *historian, educator*
Foster, Kathleen Adair *art historian, museum curator*
Gealt, Adelheid Maria *museum director*
Gest, Howard *microbiologist, educator*
Gordon, Paul John *business management educator*
Gough, Pauline Bjerke *magazine editor*
Gousha, Richard Paul *education educator*
Grieco, Paul Anthony *chemistry educator*
Gros Louis, Kenneth Richard Russell *university chancellor*
Guth, Sherman Leon (S. Lee Guth) *psychologist, educator*
Hagen, Charles William, Jr. *botany educator*
Hanson, Karen *philosopher, educator*
Harder, John E. *electrical engineer*
Hattin, Donald Edward *geologist, educator*
Hegeman, George Downing *microbiology educator*
Heise, George Armstrong *psychologist, educator*
Heiser, Charles Bixler, Jr. *botany educator*
Hess-Lüttich, Ernest Walter Bernhard *Germanic studies educator*
†Hieftje, Gary Martin *analytical chemist, educator*
Hites, Ronald Atlee *environmental science educator, chemist*
Hodge, Carleton Taylor *linguist, educator*
Hofstadter, Douglas Richard *cognitive, computer scientist, educator*
Hopkins, Jack Walker *former university administrator, environmental educator*
Jacobi, Peter Paul *journalism educator, author*
Johnson, Hollis Ralph *astronomy educator*
†Johnson, Owen Verne *program director*
Juergens, George Ivar *history educator*
Klotman, Robert Howard *music educator*
Knight, Bobby *college basketball coach*
Kohr, Roland Ellsworth *hospital administrator*
†Komunyakaa, Yusef (James Willie Brown, Jr.) *poet*
Kudryk, Oleg *librarian*
Lee, Don Yoon *publisher, academic researcher and writer*
Leftwich, Richard Henry *economist, educator*
Long, John D. *retired insurance educator*
Lowe, Marvin *artist*
Mac Watters, Virginia Elizabeth *singer, music educator, actress*
†Magnus, Philip Douglas *chemistry educator*
Markman, Ronald *artist, educator*
Martins, Heitor Miranda *foreign language educator*
Mc Clung, Leland Swint *microbiologist, educator*
†McDowell, John Holmes *folklore educator, institute director*
Mehlinger, Howard Dean *education educator*
Mitchell, Bert Breon *literary translator*
Mobley, Tony Allen *university dean, recreation educator*
Moore, Ward Wilfred *medical educator*
Murray, Haydn Herbert *geology educator*
Muth, John Fraser *economics educator*
Nolan, Val, Jr. *biologist, lawyer*
†Novotny, Milos V. *chemistry educator*
O'Hearn, Robert Raymond *stage designer*
Oinas, Felix Johannes *foreign language educator*
O'Meara, Patrick O. *political science educator*
Orrego-Salas, Juan Antonio *composer, retired music educator*
Ostrom, Elinor *political science educator, researcher*
Ostrom, Vincent A(lfred) *political science educator*
Otteson, Schuyler Franklin *former university dean, educator*
Pagels, Jürgen Heinrich *balletmaster, dance educator, dancer, choreographer, author*
Parmenter, Charles Stedman *chemistry educator*
Patrick, John Joseph *social sciences educator*
Patterson, James Milton *marketing specialist, educator*
Peters, Dennis Gail *chemist*
Phillips, Harvey *musician, music educator*
Pletcher, David Mitchell *history educator*
Pollock, Robert Elwood *nuclear physicist*
Pozzatti, Rudy Otto *artist*
Preer, John Randolph, Jr. *biology educator*
Prosser, Franklin Pierce *computer scientist*
Purdom, Paul Walton, Jr. *computer scientist*
Puri, Madan Lal *mathematics educator*
Putnam, Frank William *biochemistry and immunology educator*
Rebec, George Vincent *neuroscience researcher, educator, administrator*
Rink, Lawrence Donald *cardiologist*
Rosenberg, Samuel Nathan *French and Italian language educator*
Rousseau, Eugene Ellsworth *musician, music educator, consultant*
Rudolph, Lavere Christian *library director*
Ruesink, Albert William *biologist, plant sciences educator*
Ryan, John William *retired university president*
Samuelsen, Roy *bass-baritone*
Schaich, William L. *physics educator*
Schmidt, Nancy J. *anthropologist, educator*
†Schroeder, Henry J. *health science organization administrator*
Schuessler, Karl Frederick *sociologist, educator*
Sebeok, Thomas Albert *linguistics educator*
Sebok, Gyorgy *pianist, educator*
Simmons, Merle Edwin *foreign language educator*
†Simpson, Vi *state senator*
Sinor, Denis *Orientalist, educator*
Smith, Frederick Robert, Jr. *social studies educator*
†Sperling, Elliot Harris *history educator*
Spulber, Nicolas *economics educator emeritus*
Stolnitz, George Joseph *economist, educator, demographer*
Strohm, Paul Holzworth, Jr. *English language educator, educational administrator*
†Sullivan, Michael Francis, III *executive*
Svetlova, Marina *ballerina, choreographer, educator*
Swanson, Robert Mclean *retired business educator*
Thiagarajan, Sivasailam *educational association administrator, educator*
Vitaliano, Charles J(oseph) *geologist, educator*
von Furstenberg, George Michael *economics educator, researcher*
Warren, Donald *university dean, education educator*
Weaver, David Hugh *journalism educator, communications researcher*
Webb, Charles Haizlip, Jr. *university dean*
Weinberg, Eugene David *microbiologist, educator*
Wells, Herman B *university chancellor*
Wentworth, Jack Roberts *business educator, consultant*
Westfall, Richard Samuel *historian*
White, Herbert Spencer *research library educator, university dean*
Williams, Camilla *soprano, voice educator*
Williams, Edgar Gene *university administrator*
†Wilson, George Macklin *history educator, cultural studies center administrator*
Wittlich, Gary Eugene *music theory educator*
Young, Frank Nelson, Jr. *biology educator, entomologist*

Bluffton
Brockmann, William Frank *medical facility administrator*
Lawson, William Hogan, III *electrical motor manufacturing executive*
Nixon, Robert Pleasants *former electric motor manufacturing company executive*
Pfister, Dean William *motor manufacturing company financial executive*

Boggstown
Gray, Carlos Gibson *restaurateur, seedsman, entertainer*

Boonville
†Phillips, Michael Keith *lawyer, state legislator*

Burns Harbor
Brown, Gene W. *steel company executive*

Butler
Ford, Lee Ellen (Leola Ford) *scientist, educator, retired lawyer*

Camby
Hay, John Franklin *church administrator*

Carmel
†Chittenden, Michael Dennis *hospital administrator*
†Dick, Rollin Merle *insurance company executive*
Eden, Barbara Janiece *commercial and residential interior designer*
Ferrero, Louis Peter *computer services company executive*
†Gongaware, Donald Francis *insurance company executive*
†Hartman, Robert D. *superintendent*
†Hilbert, Stephen C. *insurance company executive*
Mc Laughlin, Harry Roll *architect*
Pickens, Robert Bruce *accountant*
Roche, James Richard *pediatric dentist, university dean*
Shoup, Charles Samuel, Jr. *chemicals and materials executive*

Charlestown
Schmidt, Jakob Edward *medical and medicolegal lexicographer, physician, author, inventor*

Chesterfield
Fry, Meredith Warren *civil engineer, consultant*

Chesterton
Martino, Robert Salvatore *orthopedic surgeon*
Petrakis, Harry Mark *author*

Clarksville
Hoehn, Elmer L. *lawyer*

Columbus
Abts, Henry William *banker*
Baker, James Kendrick *specialty metals manufacturing company executive*
Berman, Lewis Paul *financial executive*
Boll, Charles Raymond *engine company executive*
Draeger, Wayne Harold *manufacturing company executive*
Durham, James Michael, Sr. *diesel engine company executive*
†Garton, Robert Dean *state senator*
Hackett, John Thomas *economist*
Hamilton, Peter Bannerman *lawyer, manufacturing company executive*
Hartley, James Michaelis *aerospace systems, printing and hardwood products manufacturing executive*
Henderson, James Alan *engine company executive*
Higgins, Harold Bailey *executive search company executive*
Jolly, Bruce Dwight *manufacturing company executive*
Kamo, Roy *engineering company executive*
†McGinty, John C., Jr. *healthcare executive*
Miller, Joseph Irwin *automotive manufacturing company executive*
Nash, John Arthur *bank executive*
Sales, A. R. *financial executive*
Schacht, Henry Brewer *diesel engine manufacturing company executive*
Stoner, R(ichard) B(urkett) *manufacturing company executive, member of Democratic national committee*

Crawfordsville
Barnes, James John *history educator*
Ford, Andrew Thomas *university dean, educational administrator*
Michal, Philip Quentin *veterinarian, mayor*

Crown Point
Bartolome, Joseph S. *bank executive*
Haines, Robert Earl *retired industrial construction executive*
Snearly, Sandra Jo *accountant*

Culver
Holaday, Allan Gibson *English educator*
Kammerer, William Henry *physician*
Manuel, Ralph Nixon *private school executive*

De Motte
†Roorda, Walter John *small business owner, state legislator*

Dubois
†Heeke, Dennis Henry *state legislator*

Dyer
Teuscher, George William *dental educator*

East Chicago
Blaskovich, Thomas Robert *automobile dealer*
Crum, James Francis *waste recycling company executive*
Psaltis, Helen *medical and surgical nurse*
†Randolph, Lonnie Marcus *lawyer, state senator*
Vis, Mary A. Murga *elementary education educator*

Elkhart
Bender, Ross Thomas *minister*
Bowers, Richard Stewart, Jr. *lawyer*
Bryant, Donald Loudon *pharmaceutical company executive*
Chism, James Arthur *information systems executive*
Corson, Thomas Harold *manufacturing company executive*
Decio, Arthur Julius *manufacturing company executive*
Dille, John Flint, Jr. *newspaper and broadcasting executive*
Ellis, Joseph Newlin *distribution company executive*
Free, Helen M. *chemist, consultant*
Gassere, Eugene Arthur *lawyer, business executive*
Groom, Gary Lee *recreational vehicle manufacturing executive*
Harman, John Royden *lawyer*
Hill, Thomas Stewart *electronics executive, consultant, engineer*
Holtz, Glenn Edward *bank instrument manufacturing executive*
Kerich, James Patrick *manufacturing company executive*
Kloska, Ronald Frank *manufacturing company executive*
†Kovach, John Michael *museum director, historian*
Mischke, Frederick Charles *manufacturing company executive*
†O'Hagan, William D. *metal products executive*
Oltz, Richard John *publishing executive, minister*
Rand, Phillip Gordon *chemist*
Robinson, Joseph Albert *corporate executive*
Tatum, Rita *communications executive*
Treckelo, Richard M. *lawyer*
Vite, Frank Anthony *realtor*

Elwood
Vance, Joan Emily Jackson (Mrs. Norval E. Vance) *elementary school educator*

Evansville
Able, Warren Walter *natural resource company executive, physician*
Anderson, Milton Henry *psychiatrist*
Barber, Charles Turner *political science educator*
Brill, Alan Richard *financial executive*
Brooks, Gene Edward *federal judge*
Capshaw, Tommie Dean *federal judge*
Clouse, John Daniel *lawyer*
Dailey, Donald Earl *industrial design consultant*
Denner, Melvin Walter *life sciences educator*
Faw, Melvin Lee *retired physician*
Gaither, John Francis *accountant, consultant*
†Gerhart, Philip Mark *mechanical engineering educator*
Gettelfinger, Gerald Andrew *bishop*
Graves, Wallace Billingsley *retired university executive*
Guthrie, Catherine S. Nicholson (Catherine S. Nicholson-Guthrie) *research scientist*
Hampel, Robert Edward *advertising executive*
Hargrave, Robert Webb *banker*
Hartsaw, William O. *mechanical engineering educator*
†Howard, Edward Allen *library administrator, consultant*
Jackson, Bill D. *newspaper editor*
Kiechlin, Robert Jerome *retired coal company executive, financial consultant*
Kitch, Frederick David *advertising executive*
Koch, Robert Louis, II *manufacturing company executive, mechanical engineer*
†McDonald, Frank F., II *mayor*
Muehlbauer, James Herman *manufacturing executive*
Penkava, Robert Ray *radiologist, educator*
Prybil, Lawrence Dewey *health system executive*
Riechmann, Fred B. *retired newspaper publisher*
Ryder, Thomas Michael *newspaper editor*
†Server, Gregory Dale *state legislator, guidance counselor*
Shaw, Margery Wayne Schlamp *geneticist, physician, lawyer*
Streetman, John William, III *museum official*
Vinson, James Spangler *university president*

Fishers
Gatto, Louis Constantine *retired college president*

Fort Wayne
Andorfer, Donald Joseph *academic administrator, educator*
Anker, Robert Alvin *insurance company executive*
Baker, Carl Leroy *lawyer*
†Beals, Duane *church administrator*
Beineke, Lowell Wayne *mathematics educator*
†Bunkowske, Eugene Walter *religious studies educator*
Burns, Thagrus Asher *manufacturing company executive, former life insurance company executive*
†Carpenter, Charles *religious organization administrator*
Clarke, Kenneth Stevens *insurance company executive*
Cole, Kenneth Duane *architect*
Cox, David Jackson *biochemistry educator*
Curtis, Douglas Homer *small business owner*
D'Arcy, John Michael *bishop*
Donesa, Antonio Braganza *neurosurgeon*
†Dorman, Barry *waste management executive*
Dunsire, P(eter) Kenneth *insurance company executive*
Edris, Charles Lawrence *insurance company executive*
Faeth, Paul Alfred *physical chemist*
Fairchild, David Lawrence *philosophy educator*
Flynn, Pauline T. *speech pathologist, educator*
Gerberding, Miles Carston *lawyer*
†Goeglein, Gloria J. *state legislator*
†Helmke, (Walter) Paul, Jr. *mayor, lawyer*
†Henschen, Bob *church administrator*
Hirschy, Gordon Harold *insurance agent, auctioneer*
Hunter, Jack Duval *lawyer*
†Jackson, Paul Howard *librarian*
Keefer, J(ames) Michael *lawyer*
Kerr, Frederick H. *hospital administrator, college president*
Klugman, Stephan Craig *newspaper editor*
Krull, Jeffrey Robert *library director*
Kruse, Edgar Christ *former hospital administrator*
Latz, G. Irving, II *manufacturing company executive*
Lee, Shuishih Sage *pathologist*
Lee, William Charles *federal judge*
Lewark, Carol Ann *special education educator*
†Liechty, Eric *church administrator*
Lockwood, Robert Philip *publishing executive*
Lupke, Duane Eugene *insurance company executive*
Lyons, Jerry Lee *mechanical engineer*
Mahmoud, Aly Ahmed *electrical engineering educator*
Mallers, George Peter *lawyer*
Mann, David William *minister*

Mansfield, Maynard Joseph computer science educator, academic dean
Marine, Clyde Lockwood agribusiness consultant
McClelland, Michael wholesale distribution executive
†McFarlane, Neil church administrator
Menge, Richard Cramer electric utility executive
†Moran, John religious organization administrator
Morehart, Donald Hadley food products executive
†Moses, Winfield C., Jr. state legislator
Niewyk, Anthony lawyer
Pease, Ella Louise elementary education educator
Peebles, Carter David lawyer
†Pellegrene, Thomas James, Jr. editor, researcher
Quinby, Charles Edward, Jr. manufacturing company executive
Quinn, C. Jack mechanical engineering educator, consultant
Ratliff, Gerald Lee speech and theatre educator
Richardson, Joseph Hill physician, educator
Ridderheim, David Sigfrid hospital administrator
†Rifkin, Leonard metals company executive
Robertson, Richard Stuart insurance holding company executive
Rolland, Ian McKenzie insurance executive
Sack, James McDonald, Jr. radio and television producer, marketing executive
Sandeson, William Seymour cartoonist
Scheetz, Sister Mary JoEllen English language educator
Shaffer, Paul E. banker
Shoaff, Thomas Mitchell lawyer
†Speicher, Opal church administrator
Steinbronn, Richard Eugene lawyer
Stevenson, Kenneth Lee chemist, educator
†Stucky, Ken clergy member, religious publication editor, church organization administrator
Swanson, David Heath agricultural company executive
Vachon, Marilyn Ann retired insurance company executive
†von Gunten, David church administrator
Weatherford, George Edward civil engineer
West, Thomas Meade insurance company executive
Williams, Leamon Dale feed and grain company executive, consultant
Williams, Walter Jackson, Jr. electrical engineer, consultant
†Wyss, Thomas John state senator

Fowler
Brouillette, Donald G. grain company executive

Frankfort
Borland, Kathryn Kilby author

Franklin
Jacobs, Harvey Collins newspaper editor, writer

Gary
†Barnes, Thomas Vernon mayor, lawyer
Gaughan, Norbert F. bishop
†Meyerson, Seymour retired chemist
Richards, Hilda university administrator
Roberts, Samuel Alden secondary education educator
†Smith, Vernon G. education educator, state representative

Goshen
Lehman, Karl Franklyn accountant
Morris, Robert Julian, Jr. manufacturing company executive
†Newberry, Richard Alan corporate executive
Schrock, Harold Arthur manufacturing company executive
Stoltzfus, Victor Ezra academic administrator

Grabill
Gerig, Abner F. small business owner

Granger
Brissey, Ruben Marion retired container company executive

Greencastle
Anderson, John Robert retired mathematics educator
Bingham, Jinsie Scott broadcast company executive
Bottoms, Robert Garvin academic administrator
DiLillo, Leonard Michael Spanish educator, researcher, academic administrator
Gass, Clinton Burke mathematics educator
Phillips, Clifton J. history educator
Weiss, Robert Orr speech educator

Greenfield
Bettler, Janet Louise Bell foreign language educator

Greensburg
Ricke, David Louis agricultural and environmental consultant
Small, Ralph Milton publisher, clergyman

Greentown
†Healy, Stephen C. seconadry school principal

Greenwood
Means, George Robert organization executive

Hammond
Adik, Stephen Peter energy company executive
Ammeraal, Robert Neal biochemist
†Ash, Frederick Melvin manufacturing company executive
Bahls, Gene Charles agricultural products company executive
†Burton, Charles Wesley gas and electric company coordinator
Delph, Donna Jean (Maroc) education educator, consultant, university administrator
†Diamond, Eugene Christopher lawyer, hospital administrator
Eichhorn, Frederick Foltz, Jr. lawyer
Lozano, Rudolpho federal judge
Moody, James T(yne) federal judge
Neale, Gary Lee utilities executive
Neff, Gregory Pall manufacturing engineering educator, consultant
Pierson, Edward Samuel engineering educator, consultant
Schroer, Edmund Armin utility company executive
Steen, Lowell Harrison physician
Yackel, James William mathematician, academic administrator

Yovich, Daniel John marketing professional educator

Highland
Gregory, Marian Frances educator, counselor

Hope
Golden, Eloise Elizabeth community health nurse

Huntingburg
Matthews, William Edmund newspaper and travel magazine publisher

Huntington
Doermann, Paul Edmund retired surgeon
†Kopp, Clarence Adam, Jr. clergyman

Indianapolis
Albright, Terrill D. lawyer
Aldo-Benson, Marlene Ann medical educator, researcher, physician
†Alexander, Gary Lee architect
†Allan, Marc D. music critic
Allen, David James lawyer
Allen, Stephen D(ean) pathologist, microbiologist
†Allerheiligen, Sandra Renee pharmacokineticist
†Altemeyer, Donald Blaine architect
Andretti, John professional race car driver
†Antich, Rose Ann state legislator
Applegate, Malcolm W. newspaper executive
Aprison, Morris Herman biochemist, neurobiologist, educator
Aschleman, James Allan lawyer
Austin, Spencer Peter minister
Badger, David Harry lawyer
Baetzhold, Howard George English language educator
†Banks, Lloyd J. insurance company executive
Bannister, Geoffrey university president, geographer
Barcus, Mary Evelyn primary school educator
Barcus, Robert Gene educational association administrator
Barker, Sarah Evans federal judge
Bash, James Francis insurance company executive
Bates, Gerald Earl bishop
Bayh, Evan governor
†Beaty, James Ralph minister
Beckwith, Lewis Daniel lawyer
Beeler, Virgil L. lawyer
†Behar, Lucien E. church administrator
†Bellamy, Robert K. lawyer
Bennett, Bruce W. construction company executive, civil engineer
Bennett, Claire Richardson landscape architect
Bepko, Gerald Lewis academic administrator, law educator, lecturer, consultant, lawyer
†Besch, Henry Roland, Jr. pharmacologist, educator
Bessey, William Higgins physicist, educator
Betley, Leonard John lawyer
Bindley, William Edward pharmaceutical executive
†Birky, Nathan Dale publishing company executive
Blackwell, Henry Barlow, II lawyer
Blankenbaker, Ronald Gail physician
Blanton, W. C. lawyer
Block, Amanda Roth artist
Boldt, Michael Herbert lawyer
Bonifield, William C. economist, educator
†Bonney, M. Doane religious organization director
Born, Emily Marie editor, association executive
Born, Samuel Roydon, II lawyer
Bower, Sandra Irwin communications executive
Brandt, Ira Kive pediatrician, medical geneticist
†Brannon, Ronald Roy minister
Brannon-Peppas, Lisa chemical engineer, researcher
Brashear, Diane Lee marital and sex therapist
Brickley, Richard Agar retired surgeon
Brinkerhoff, Tom J. financial services executive
†Brinkman, Joyce Elaine state legislator
Brown, Edwin Wilson, Jr. physician, educator
Brown, Lawrence Harvey (Larry Brown) basketball coach
†Browne, William Albert, Jr. architectural firm executive
†Broxmeyer, Hal Edward medical educator
Bruess, Charles Edward lawyer
Buechlein, Daniel Mark bishop
†Bundy, David Dale librarian, educator
Butler, Wilford Arthur association executive
Buttrey, Donald Wayne lawyer
Campbell, Judith Lowe child psychiatrist
Capehart, Homer Earl, Jr. lawyer
Caperton, Albert Franklin newspaper editor
Carey, Edward Marshel, Jr. accounting company executive
Carney, Joseph Buckingham lawyer
Carpenter, Susan Karen lawyer
Carr, James Michael lawyer
Carr, William H(enry) A. public relations executive, author
Carter, Pamela Lynn state attorney general
Casebeer, Edwin Frank, Jr. English language educator
Cassel, Herbert William religion educator
†Castle, Howard Blaine religious organization administrator
Chernish, Stanley Michael physician
Choplin, John M., II lawyer
Christenson, Le Roy Howard insurance company officer
Christian, Joe Clark medical genetics researcher, educator
Claffey, Stephen Allen lawyer
†Clark, Charles M., Jr. educational institution administrator, researcher
Cliff, Johnnie Marie mathematics and chemistry educator
Cofield, Howard John lawyer
Cohen, Gabriel Murrel editor, publisher
Cohen, Marlene Lois pharmacologist
Cones, Van Buren electronics engineer, consultant
Conley, James Daniel retired foundation executive
Cramer, Betty F. life insurance company executive
†Crosby, Susan state legislator, mental health services executive
Cross, Leland Briggs, Jr. lawyer
Crow, Paul Abernathy, Jr. clergyman, religious council executive, educator
Daly, Walter Joseph physician, educator
†Davis, F. Benjamin academic administrator
DeBruler, Roger O. state supreme court justice
Deer, Richard Elliott lawyer
DeLaney, Edward O'Donnell lawyer
Dickinson, Richard Donald Nye clergyman, educator, theological seminary administrator
Dietz, William Ronald financial services executive, consultant
Dillin, S. Hugh federal judge

Dortch, Carl Raymond former association executive
Dougherty, Douglas Wayne retail executive
†Drawbaugh, Kevin Alan newspaper editor
Durbin, Robert Cain hotel executive
Dutton, Clarence Benjamin lawyer
Dykstra, Craig Richard theologian, educator, foundation administrator
Eigen, Howard pediatrician, educator
Einhorn, Lawrence Henry medical educator
Ellerbrook, Niel Cochran gas company executive
†Ellis, Carollyn religious organization administrator
†Ellis, Raymond W. religious organization executive, consultant
Elrod, Robert Grant lawyer
Emerson, Andrew Craig lawyer, insurance executive
Emtman, Steven Charles professional football player
Engledow, Jack Lee college administrator, consultant, researcher
Evans, Daniel Fraley college administrator, banker, retail executive
Evans, Daniel Fraley, Jr. lawyer
Ewick, Charles Ray librarian
Farris, Bain Joseph health care executive
Faulk, Ward Page immunologist
Feigenbaum, Harvey cardiologist, educator
Felicetti, Daniel A. academic administrator, educator
Ferger, Lawrence A. gas distribution utility executive
Fisch, Charles physician
Fischler, Barbara Brand librarian
Fisher, Gene Lawrence financial executive
Fisher, James R. lawyer
FitzGibbon, Daniel Harvey lawyer
†Fleming, Marcella journalist
Fortune, William Lemcke journalist
Foster, David Mark bishop
†Foulkes, John R. minister
French, Philip Franks agricultural cooperative corporate executive
Frenzel, Otto N., III banker
Fritz, Cecil Morgan investment company executive
Fruehwald, Kristin G. lawyer
Fuller, Samuel Ashby lawyer, mining company executive
Funk, David Albert law educator
Furlow, Mack Vernon, Jr. financial executive, treasurer
†Fuson, Wayne Edward sports editor
Gantz, Richard Alan museum administrator
†Gard, Beverly J. state legislator
†Garmel, Marion Bess Simon journalist
Gehring, Perry James toxicologist, chemical company executive
Geib, George Winthrop history educator
Geisler, Hans Emanuel gynecologic oncologist
Ghetti, Bernardino Francesco neuropathologist, neurobiology researcher
Gibson, David Mark biochemist, educator
Gibson, James Edwin toxicologist
Gilman, Alan B. restaurant company executive
Gilmore, H. William college dean, dentistry educator
Givan, Richard Martin state supreme court justice
Givens, David W. banker
Glazner, Raymond Charles technical services manager
Gnat, Raymond Earl librarian
Goldsmith, Stephen mayor
Goodwin, William Maxwell financial executive
†Gould, Karen J. elementary school principal
†Grant, Claudia Ewing minister
Grayson, John Allan lawyer
Green, Morris physician, educator
Greenwald, John Edward magazine executive
Greist, Mary Coffey dermatologist
Griffiths, David Neil utility executive
Grosfeld, Jay Lazar pediatric surgeon, educator
Grossman, Elizabeth Korn nursing administrator, retired college dean
Haines, Lee Mark, Jr. religious denomination administrator
Hamburger, Richard James physician, educator
Handel, David Jonathan health care administrator
Harden, Mary Louise human resources management specialist
†Hardin, Boniface academic administrator
Harris, Robert Allison biochemistry educator
†Haslam, Robert B. religious publication editor
†Hathaway, David Roger physician, medical educator, scientist
Hayford, John Sargent retail executive
†Haynes, Thomas Joseph marketing executive
†Headden, Susan M. reporter
Heard, William Robert insurance company executive
Hegel, Carolyn Marie farmer, farm bureau executive
†Heger, Martin L. bank executive
Helmkamp, John G. accounting educator, consultant
Helveston, Eugene McGillis pediatric ophthalmologist, educator
Henderson, Eugene Leroy lawyer
Herman, Barbara F. psychologist
†Higgins, William Robert, III journalist
Highfield, Robert Edward lawyer
Hingtgen, Joseph Nicholas psychologist, neuroscientist, educator
Hodes, Marion Edward genetics educator, physician
Hogsett, Joseph H. state official
Holt, Worthe Seymour pharmaceutical company executive
Hubbard, Jesse Donald pathology educator
†Huber, Richard C. insurance company executive
Hudnut, William Herbert, III political scientist, fellow
Huffman-Hine, Ruth Carson adult education administrator, educator
Husman, Catherine Bigot insurance company executive, actuary
Husted, Ralph Waldo former utility executive
Huston, Michael Joe lawyer
Ilangyi, Bya'ene Akulu bishop
Ilchman, Warren Frederick university administrator, political science educator
Irsay, James Steven professional football team executive
Irvine, George professional basketball coach
Irwin, Glenn Ward, Jr. medical educator, physician, university official
Irwin, H. William lawyer
†Janis, F. Timothy technology company executive
Jegen, Lawrence A., III law educator
Jewett, John Rhodes real estate executive
Johnson, David Allen singer, songwriter, investor
†Johnson, James P. religious organization executive
Johnston, Cyrus Conrad, Jr. internist, educator
Johnstone, Robert Philip lawyer
Jones, Robert C. symphony orchestra administrator
Jontz, Polly museum director
Joyner, John Erwin medical educator, neurological surgeon

Justice, Brady Richmond, Jr. medical services executive
Kacek, Don J. management consultant, business owner
Kahlenbeck, Howard, Jr. lawyer
Kappes, Philip Spangler lawyer
Kaufman, Barton Lowell financial services company executive
Kaufman, Karl Lincoln consultant, former state agency administrator
Kemper, James Dee lawyer
Kempski, Ralph Aloisius bishop
Kerr, William Andrew lawyer, educator
Khalil, Michael O. actuary
†Kilgore, Gary M. church administrator
†King, J. B. pharmaceutical company executive, lawyer
Kitchen, John Milton lawyer
Klaper, Martin Jay lawyer
Kleiman, David Harold lawyer
†Kline, Bruce L. church administrator
†Klinker, Sheila Ann J. middle school educator, state legislator
Knebel, Donald Earl lawyer
Knight, Margarett Lee lawyer, editor
Knoebel, Suzanne Buckner cardiologist, medical educator
Koppel, Gary Allen chemist, immunologist
Krasean, Thomas Karl historian
Kreegar, Phillip Keith educational administrator
Kreuscher, Wayne Charles lawyer
Krueger, Alan Douglas communications company executive
Krueger, Betty Jane telecommunications company executive
Lanford, Luke Dean electronics company executive
Lantz, George Benjamin, Jr. business executive, college executive, consultant
Lee, Stephen W. lawyer
Lefstein, Norman lawyer, educator
Lemberger, Louis pharmacologist, physician
†Lent, James A. analytical equipment company executive
Lewis, Dale Kenton lawyer
Lindemann, Donald Lee utility executive
Lindseth, Richard Emil orthopedic surgeon
Lobley, Alan Haigh lawyer
Long, Clarence William accountant
Long, William Allan retired forest products company executive
Loveday, William John hospital administrator
†Lubbers, Teresa S. state senator, public relations executive
†Lugar, Thomas R. manufacturing executive
†Lyst, John Henry journalist
†Lytle, L(arry) Ben insurance company executive, lawyer
†MacVittie, Paula Rae advertising executive
Maginn, M. Joseph insurance agent
Maine, Michael Roland lawyer
Mallon, David Joseph, Jr. lawyer
Manders, Karl Lee neurosurgeon
†Mannweiler, Paul S. state legislator
†Manworren, Donald B. church administrator
Marchibroda, Ted (Theodore Joseph Marchibroda) professional football coach
Marsolais, Harold Raymond association executive
Massey, James D. bank holding company executive
Mc Carthy, Harold Charles retired insurance company executive
†McCarty, William Dennis state senator, lawyer
McDermott, James Alexander lawyer
Mc Farland, H. Richard food company executive
McKinney, E. Kirk, Jr. retired insurance company executive
McKinney, Larry J. federal judge
†Mc Kinney, Robert Hurley lawyer, business executive
Melton, Owen B., Jr. banking company executive
Merrill, William H., Jr. lawyer, corporate professional
Merritt, Doris Honig pediatrics educator
†Merritt, James W. real estate developer
Miller, David W. lawyer
†Miller, Patricia Louise state legislator, nurse
†Miller, Reginald Wayne professional basketball player
†Mills, Morris Hadley state senator, farmer
Mirsky, Arthur geologist, educator
Miyamoto, Richard Takashi otolaryngologist
Monical, Robert Duane consulting structural engineer
Morris, James Thomas utilities executive
Mullen, Thomas Edgar real estate consultant
Mutz, Oscar Ulysses manufacturing and distribution executive
Myers, Woodrow Augustus, Jr. physician, corporate medical director
Nolan, Alan Tucker retired lawyer
Norins, Arthur Leonard physician, educator
Norman, LaLander Stadig insurance company executive
†Nugent, Johnny tractor company executive, state senator
Nugent, Thomas D. food products executive
†Nurnberger, John I., Jr. psychiatrist, educator
Nyhart, Eldon Howard employee benefits consultant, lawyer
O'Bannon, Frank Lewis state official, lawyer
O'Brien, Frank B. accounting firm executive
Ochs, Sidney neurophysiology educator
†Orcutt, Daniel C. airport terminal executive
†Paine, Andrew J., Jr. banker
†Palmer, Lester Davis minister
Pantzer, Kurt Friedrich, Jr. lawyer
Pattyn, Remi Ceasar management consultant
†Paul, Allen E. state senator
†Paul, Gerald retail company executive
Paul, Stephen Howard lawyer
†Pearlstein, Robert M. physics educator
Perelman, Melvin pharmaceutical company executive
Petersen, James L. lawyer
Pettinga, Cornelius Wesley pharmaceutical company executive
Phillippi, Wendell Crane editor
Plater, William Marmaduke English language educator, academic administrator
Pless, John Edward forensic pathologist, educator
Polizotto, Bruce Alan lawyer
†Polston, Mark Franklin minister
Ponder, Lester McConnico lawyer, educator
Powlen, David Michael lawyer
Pulliam, Eugene Smith newspaper publisher
†Pulliam, Russell Bleecker editor, elder
Quayle, J(ames) Danforth former vice president of United States, investment company executive
Quayle, Marilyn Tucker lawyer, wife of former vice president of U.S.

Ralph, Roger Paul *arbitrator*
Rasper, Deborah Young *hospital administrator*
Read, Frank Thompson *lawyer, legal association consultant*
Reeve, Ronald Cropper, Jr. *manufacturing executive*
Reich, Jack Egan *insurance company executive*
Reid, William Hill *mathematics educator*
Reilly, Peter C. *chemical company executive*
Reynolds, Alan Anthony *economist, writer, consultant*
Reynolds, Robert Hugh *lawyer*
Richmond, James Ellis *restaurant company executive*
Richter, Judith Anne *pharmacology educator*
†Riegsecker, Marvin Dean *pharmacist, state senator*
†Riemenschneider, Dan LaVerne *religious organization administrator*
Risk, John Fred *banker, investment banker*
Roberts, William Everett *lawyer*
Robinson, Larry Robert *insurance company executive*
†Rogers, Earline S. *state legislator*
Rogers, Robert Ernest *medical educator*
Ross, Edward *cardiologist*
Roth, Lawrence Max *pathologist, educator*
Ruben, Gary A. *marketing and communications consultant*
Russell, Frank Eli *newspaper publishing executive*
Rusthoven, Peter James *lawyer*
Ryan, Earl M. *public affairs analyst*
Ryder, Henry C(lay) *lawyer*
Salentine, Thomas James *pharmaceutical company executive*
†Sayre, Larry D. *religious organization executive*
Scaletta, Phillip Ralph, III *lawyer*
Scanlon, Thomas Michael *lawyer*
Schlegel, Fred Eugene *lawyer*
Schmidt, William C. *chemical company executive*
†Scholer, Sue Wyant *state legislator*
†Schwindt, Robert F. *diagnostic medical products executive*
Scism, Daniel Reed *lawyer*
Segar, Geoffrey *retired lawyer*
†Seitz, Melvin Christian, Jr. *distributing company executive*
Semler, Jerry D. *insurance company executive*
Seneff, Smiley Howard *business owner*
†SerVaas, Beurt Richard *corporate executive*
Shepard, Randall Terry *judge*
Shideler, Shirley Ann Williams *lawyer*
Shula, Robert Joseph *lawyer*
Silver, David Mayer *former university official*
Simon, Herbert *professional basketball team executive*
†Sindlinger, Verne E. *bishop*
Slaymaker, Gene Arthur *public relations executive*
†Smith, Keith *protective services official*
Smith, Stephen Kendall *lawyer*
Snyder, Jack Ralph *lawyer*
†Sobieray, Richard Joseph *architect*
Soper, Quentin Francis *chemist*
Speth, Gerald Lennus *education educator, business programs director*
†Staff, Charles Bancroft, Jr. *music and theater critic*
Standish, Samuel Miles *oral pathologist, college dean*
Stark, Rohn Taylor *professional football player*
Stayton, Thomas George *lawyer*
Steckler, William Elwood *federal judge*
Steger, Evan Evans, III *lawyer*
Stein, Carole Ruth *social services administrator, researcher*
Stein, Richard Paul *lawyer*
Steinrauf, Jean Hamilton *biochemistry professor*
Step, Eugene Lee *retired pharmaceutical company executive*
†Stern, Raymond *principal*
Stoelting, Robert K. *anesthesiologist, medical association executive*
Stone, Donald Crawford *public administrator, educator*
Stookey, George Kenneth *research institute administrator, dental educator*
Stout, William Jewell *department store executive*
Strauss, Jerome Manfred *lawyer, banker*
Stroble, Larry James *lawyer*
Sutherland, Donald Gray *lawyer*
Suzuki, Hidetaro *violinist*
Sweezy, John William *political party official*
Swhier, Claudia Versfelt *lawyer*
Tabler, Bryan G. *lawyer*
Tabler, Norman Gardner, Jr. *lawyer*
Thomas, Beth Eileen Wood (Mrs. Raymond O. Thomas) *editor*
†Thompson, Stanley B. *church administrator*
Thompson, W(ilmer) Leigh *pharmaceutical company executive, physician, pharmacologist*
Tinder, John Daniel *federal judge*
Tobias, Randall L. *pharmaceuticals company executive*
Todd, Zane Grey *utility executive*
Tomlinson, Joseph Ernest *manufacturing company executive*
†Ton, L. Eugene *church official*
Townsend, Earl Cunningham, Jr. *lawyer, writer*
†Updegraff Spleth, Ann L. *church executive, pastor*
†Van Valin, John E. *publisher*
Vereen, Robert Charles *retired trade association executive*
Voos, William John *university administrator, artist, art educator*
Walker, Frank Dilling *market research executive*
Walker-Smith, Angelique Keturah *minister, religious organization administrator*
†Wallace, F. Blake *aerospace executive, mechanical engineer*
Waller, Aaron Bret, III *museum director*
Walsh, Donnie *sports club executive*
Walsh, John Charles *metallurgical company executive*
Walther, Joseph Edward *health facility administrator, retired physician*
Wampler, Lloyd Charles *retired lawyer*
Watanabe, August Masaru *physician, scientist, medical educator, corporate executive*
†Watkins, Harold Robert *minister*
Weber, George *oncology and pharmacology researcher, educator*
Webster, Daniel Robert *lawyer*
Weinberger, Myron Hilmar *medical educator*
†Welsh, Robert K. *religious organization executive*
Werner, Charles George *cartoonist*
Whale, Arthur Richard *lawyer*
Wheeler, Daniel Scott *publishing executive, editor*
†Wheeler, Harold H. *state senator, utility contractor*
†Whelan, John Martin *insurance executive*
White, Arthur Clinton *physician*
White, James Patrick *law educator*
Whitehead, James Ray *medical association executive, management consultant*
Wilson, Charles Edward *lawyer*
†Wilson, Earle Lawrence *church administrator*
Wilson, Harry Cochrane *clergyman*
Wishard, Gordon Davis *lawyer*
Wolsiffer, Patricia Rae *insurance company executive*
†Wong, David T. *biochemist*
Wood, Richard Donald *pharmaceutical company executive*
Wood, William Jerome *lawyer*
Woodard, Harold Raymond *lawyer*
Wooden, Reba Faye Boyd *guidance counselor*
Woodring, DeWayne Stanley *religion association executive*
Woollen, Evans *architectural firm executive*
Worrell, David Charles *lawyer*
Wright, David Burton *retired newspaper publishing company executive*
†Yan, Sau-Chi Betty *biochemist*
†Young, Richard *religious organization executive*
Yovits, Marshall Clinton *computer and information science educator, university dean*
Zapapas, James Richard *pharmaceutical company executive*
Zipes, Douglas Peter *cardiologist, researcher*

Jasper
Fleck, Albert Henry, Jr. *insurance agency executive*
Geiger, Victor Alan *international sales executive*
†Habig, Douglas Arnold *manufacturing company executive*
Habig, Thomas Louis *manufacturing executive*
Kohler, Jeffrey Martin *office furniture manufacturing executive*
†Thyen, James C. *furniture company executive*

Jeffersonville
†Deming, Frank *religious organization administrator*
Reisert, Charles Edward, Jr. *real estate executive*

Kokomo
†Hall, Milton L. *bishop*
†Hill, Emita Brady *academic administrator*
Schraut, Kenneth Charles *mathematician, educator*
Wilhelm, Ralph Vincent, Jr. *electronics company executive, ceramics engineer*

La Porte
Grott, Geraldine *librarian*
Hiler, John Patrick *former government official, former congressman, business executive*
Morris, Leigh Edward *hospital executive officer*

Lafayette
Andrews, Frederick Newcomb *emeritus university administrator*
Brewster, James Henry *retired chemistry educator*
Christensen, Nikolas Ivan *geophysicist, educator*
Claflin, Robert Malden *veterinary educator, university dean*
Coburn, Patricia Ellen *oncological nurse*
de Branges de Bourcia, Louis *mathematics educator*
Emery, Alden Hayes, Jr. *chemical engineer, educator*
Etzel, James Edward *environmental engineering educator*
Feuer, Henry *chemist, educator*
Fox, Robert William *mechanical engineering educator*
Gartenhaus, Solomon *physicist*
Gautschi, Walter *mathematics educator*
Geddes, LaNelle Evelyn *nursing educator, physiologist*
Geddes, Leslie Alexander *bioengineer, physiologist, educator*
Gustafson, Winthrop Adolph *aeronautical and astronautical engineering educator*
Higi, William L. *bishop*
Howarth, David H. *retired bank executive*
Judd, William Robert *engineering geologist, educator*
Loeffler, Frank Joseph *physicist, educator*
Maickel, Roger Philip *pharmacologist, educator*
Mc Laughlin, John Francis *civil engineer, educator*
Melhorn, Wilton Newton *geosciences educator*
Meyer, Brud Richard *pharmaceutical company executive*
Ott, Karl Otto *nuclear engineering educator, consultant*
Porile, Norbert Thomas *chemistry educator*
†Posey, Edwin Dalfield *librarian*
Rubin, Jean Estelle *mathematics educator*
Sperandio, Glen Joseph *pharmacy educator*
Stob, Martin *physiology educator*
Truce, William Everett *chemist, educator*
VanHandel, Ralph Anthony *librarian*
Veenker, Claude Harold *health education educator*

Lake Bluff
Gage, Calvin William *retired*

Lakeville
†Mangus, Richard W. *farmer*

Lanesville
Cleveland, Peggy Rose Richey *cytotechnologist*

Lawrenceburg
†Bischoff, Robert John *state representative*
Dautel, Charles Shreve *retired mining company executive*

Lebanon
Ohmart, Sally Jo *elementary education educator*

Leo
†Worman, Richard W. *insurance company executive, state senator*

Lowell
Boller, Carole Ann *visual artist*

Madison
Gunter, Frank Elliott *artist*
Hall, Marion Trufant *botany educator, arboretum director*

Marion
†Barnes, James Byron *university president*
Dixon, Ruth Ann Storey *education educator*
East, Frank Howard *paper company executive*
Fisher, Pierre James, Jr. *physician*
McIntyre, Robert Walter *church official*

Martinsville
†Foley, Ralph Morton *lawyer*

Kendall, Robert Stanton *newspaper editor, journalist*

Merrillville
Crawford, Mary B. *small business owner*
Magry, Martha J. *elementary education educator*

Michigan City
†Alevizos, Thomas James *state representative, lawyer*
†Bowser, Anita Olga *state legislator, education educator*
†Brockway, Lee J. *architect*
Higgins, William Henry Clay, III *retired telecommunications consultant*
Musgrave, Charles Edward *music director, correctional facility official*
†Ruby, Burton Bennett *men's apparel manufacturer*

Middlebury
†Guequierre, John Phillip *manufacturing company executive*

Mishawaka
Goebel, Richard Alan *veterinarian*
Hagiwara, Kokichi *steel company executive*
†Kapson, Jordan *automotive executive*
†Ponko, William Reuben *architect*
Scott, Darrel Joseph *healthcare executive*
†Troyer, LeRoy Seth *architect*

Monrovia
Bennett, James Edward *retired plastic surgeon, educator*

Monticello
Hardin, Lowell Stewart *retired economics educator*
Haskins, Perry Glen *insurance company executive*
†Wolf, Katie Louise *state legislator*

Montpelier
Neff, Kenneth D. *realtor, mayor*

Morgantown
Boyce, Gerald G. *artist, educator*

Mount Vernon
Bach, Steve Crawford *lawyer*

Muncie
Anderson, Stefan Stolen *bank executive*
Barber, Earl Eugene *consulting firm executive*
Bell, Stephen Scott (Steve Bell) *journalist, educator*
Bennon, Saul *electrical engineer, transformer consultant*
Carmin, Robert Leighton *retired geography educator*
Connally, Sandra Jane Oppy *art educator*
Eddy, Darlene Mathis *poet, educator*
Fisher, John Wesley *manufacturing company executive*
Harris, Joseph McAllister *chemist*
Hendrix, Jon Richard *biology educator*
Henzlik, Raymond Eugene *zoophysiologist, educator*
Joyaux, Alain Georges *art museum director*
Kumbula, Tendayi Sengerwe *journalism educator*
†Looney, H. Ray *manufacturing company executive*
Marsh, Helen Unger *retired educational administrator*
Mertens, Thomas Robert *biology educator*
Neiman, Lionel Joseph *sociologist, educator*
Owsley, Alvin *manufacturing executive, lawyer*
Park, Sung Jae *physical education educator*
Radcliff, William Franklin *lawyer*
Robold, Alice Ilene *mathematician, educator*
Sappenfield, Charles Madison *architect, educator*
Sargent, Thomas Andrew *political science educator, university program director*
Shondell, Donald Stuart *physical education educator*
Sissel, George Allen *lawyer, manufacturing executive*
Swartz, B(enjamin) K(insell), Jr. *archaeologist, educator*
Thomas, Harvey Gantenbein *dentist*
Wheeler, David Laurie *university dean*

Munster
†Corsiglia, Robert Joseph *electrical construction company executive*
Luerssen, Frank Wonson *retired steel company executive*
Purcell, James Francis *consultant, former utility executive*
Sherman, Mona Diane *school system administrator*

Nappanee
Borger, Michael Hinton Ivers *osteopathic physician*

Nashville
McDermott, Renée R(assler) *lawyer*

New Albany
Braden, Samuel Edward *economics educator*
Conway, William Frederick, Sr. *business founder*
Crooks, Edwin William *former academic administrator*
Rand, Leon *university administrator*

New Castle
Dudley, Harry Bruce *oil company executive*

New Haven
Chapman, Reid Gillis *former broadcasting company executive*

Newburgh
Tierney, Gordon Paul *real estate broker, genealogist*

Newport
Weeks, Catherine Claire *elementary education educator*

Noblesville
Almquist, Donald John *retired electronics company executive*
†Wechter, Larry Scot *retail food executive*
†Wilson, Norman Glenn *church administrator, writer*

North Manchester
Harshbarger, Richard B. *economics educator*

Notre Dame
Alcock, Charles Benjamin *materials science educator*
Aldous, Joan *sociology educator*
Arnold, Peri Ethan *political scientist*
Bella, Salvatore Joseph *management educator*
Browne, Cornelius Payne *physics educator*
Bruns, Gerald L. *English literature educator*
Cason, Neal Martin *physics educator*
Castellino, Francis Joseph *university dean*
Craig, George Brownlee, Jr. *entomologist*
Craypo, Charles *labor economics educator*
Crosson, Frederick James *former university dean, humanities educator*
Delaney, Cornelius Francis *philosophy educator*
De Santis, Vincent Paul *educator, historian*
Despres, Leo Arthur *sociology and anthropology educator, academic administrator*
Faccenda, Philip John *lawyer*
Fehlner, Thomas Patrick *chemistry educator*
Feigl, Dorothy Marie *chemistry educator, university official*
Gabriel, Astrik Ladislas *educator, scholar*
Goulet, Denis André *political science educator, writer, development ethicist*
Gray, William Guerin *civil engineering educator*
Grazin, Igor Nikolai *law educator, former state official*
Gunn, Alan *law educator*
Gurulé, Jimmy *legal educator*
Gutting, Gary Michael *philosophy educator*
Hallinan, Maureen Theresa *sociologist*
Hatch, Nathan Orr *university administrator*
Helquist, Paul M. *chemistry educator, researcher*
†Hesburgh, Theodore Martin *clergyman, former university president*
Holtz, Louis Leo *college football coach*
†Jacobs, Roger Francis *librarian, educator, lawyer*
Jensen, Richard Jorg *biology educator*
Jerger, Edward William *mechanical engineer, university dean*
Kennedy, John Joseph *political science educator*
Kerrigan, (Thomas) Anthony *writer, translator*
Kmiec, Douglas William *government official, law educator*
Kogge, Peter Michael *computer and electronics executive*
Kohn, James Paul *engineering educator*
Langford, James Rouleau *university press administrator*
Lauck, Anthony Joseph *artist, retired art educator, priest*
Leege, David Calhoun *political scientist, educator*
MacIntyre, Alasdair *philosophy educator*
Malloy, Edward Aloysius *priest, university administrator, educator*
Marshalek, Eugene Richard *physics educator*
McBrien, Richard Peter *theology educator*
McCormick, Richard Arthur *priest, religion educator, writer*
McInerny, Ralph Matthew *philosophy educator, author*
Mc Mullin, Ernan Vincent *philosophy educator*
Michel, Anthony Nikolaus *electrical engineering educator, researcher*
Miller, Robert Carl *library director*
Mirowski, Philip Edward *economics educator*
Nugent, Walter Terry King *historian*
O'Meara, Onorato Timothy *academic administrator, mathematician*
O'Meara, Thomas Franklin *priest, educator*
O'Rourke, William Andrew *English language educator, author*
Pollard, Morris *microbiologist, educator*
Quinn, Philip Lawrence *philosophy educator*
Reilly, Frank Kelly *business educator*
Rice, (Ethel) Ann *publishing executive, editor*
Rosenberg, Charles Michael *art historian, educator*
Sain, Michael Kent *electrical engineering educator*
Sayre, Kenneth Malcolm *philosophy educator*
Scheidt, W. Robert *chemistry educator, researcher*
Schmitz, Roger Anthony *chemical engineering educator, academic administrator*
Schuler, Robert Hugo *chemist, educator*
Shaffer, Thomas Lindsay *lawyer, educator*
Shannon, William Norman, III *marketing and international business educator, food service executive*
Sommese, Andrew John *mathematics educator*
Stoll, Wilhelm *mathematics educator*
Szewczyk, Albin Anthony *engineering educator*
Thomas, John Kerry *chemistry educator*
Trozzolo, Anthony Marion *chemistry educator*
Valenzuela, Julio Samuel *sociologist, educator*
Varma, Arvind *chemical engineering educator, researcher*
Vecchio, Robert Peter *business management educator*
†Wadsworth, Michael A. *ambassador, director of athletics, former professional football player*
Walicki, Andrzej Stanislaw *history educator*

Ogden Dunes
Mulvaney, Mary Jean *physical education educator*

Oldenburg
†Leising, Jean *state legislator*

Orleans
Keys, Steven Franklin *chemical engineer*

Pendleton
Kischuk, Richard Karl *insurance company executive*
†Phenis, Nancy Sue *educational administrator*

Peru
Bronson, Kenneth Caldean *newspaper company executive*
Stackhouse, John Wesley *publishing executive*

Plainfield
Rogers, James Eugene *electric utility executive*

Portage
Gasser, Wilbert (Warner), Jr. *retired banker*
Katsahnias, Thomas George *steel company executive*

Princeton
Fair, Robert James *lawyer*
Mullins, Richard Austin *chemical engineer*

Rensselaer
Banet, Charles Henry *college president, clergyman*

Richmond
Farber, Evan Ira *librarian*
Kirk, Thomas Garrett, Jr. *librarian*

†Maurer, Johan Fredrik religious denomination administrator
†Nelms, Charlie academic administrator
Passmore, Jan William investment company executive
†Talbot, Ann editor
Wood, Richard J. college president

Rockville
Davis, William Eugene architect

Saint Mary Of The Woods
Doherty, Sister Barbara (Ann Doherty) academic administrator

Saint Meinrad
Daly, Simeon Philip John librarian

Sandborn
†Gregg, John Richard lawyer, state legislator

Santa Claus
Platthy, Jeno cultural association executive

Seymour
Bollinger, Don Mills grocery company executive
Orben, Robert Allen engine company executive
Terkhorn, Henry K. food company executive

Shelbyville
†Linder, Jeffrey Mark lawyer, farmer

South Bend
Altman, Arnold David business executive
†Armour, James Author military vehicle manufacturing company executive
Bancroft, Bruce Richard lawyer
Black, Virginia Morrow writer
Burkhart, Charles Barclay outdoor advertising executive
Carey, John Leo lawyer
Charles, Isabel university administrator
†Cohen, Ronald S. accountant
Ebey, Carl Finley priest, religious order superior
Ecker, Carol Adele veterinarian
Ford, George Burt lawyer
Grant, Robert Allen federal judge
Gray, Francis Campbell bishop
†Gray, Frank C. bishop
Harriman, Gerald Eugene retired business educator, former university dean
Horsbrugh, Patrick architect, educator
†Jones, Wellington Downing, III banker
Kalamaros, Edward Nicholas lawyer
Kohn, William Irwin lawyer
Lake, Brian James lawyer
MacLeod, John college basketball coach
Manion, Daniel Anthony federal judge
McGill, Warren Everett lawyer, consultant
McKernan, Leo Joseph manufacturing company executive
Miller, Robert L., Jr. federal judge
Mills, Nancy Anne elementary education educator
†Murphy, Christopher Joseph, III financial executive
†Napoli, Donald J. library director
Niemeyer, Gerhart political science educator
Pfeil, Richard John electric company executive
Raclin, Ernestine Morris banker
Reinke, William John lawyer
Ripple, Kenneth Francis federal judge
Rodibaugh, Robert Kurtz federal judge
Schurz, Franklin Dunn, Jr. media executive
Seall, Stephen Albert lawyer
Sharp, Allen chief federal judge
Szarwark, Ernest John lawyer
†Vandenberg, Sister Patricia Clasina health system executive
Vogel, Nelson J., Jr. lawyer
Wiegand, George Frederick, Sr. financial services executive
Wurzburg, Richard Joseph health insurance executive

Speedway
Unser, Alfred, Jr. professional race car driver

Terre Haute
Ashbrook, William Sinclair, Jr. music educator, musicologist
Baker, Ronald Lee English educator
Campbell, Judith May physical education educator
Carmony, Marvin Dale linguist, educator
Cowden, Robert Laughlin music educator
De Marr, Mary Jean English language educator
Frantz, Welby Marion business executive
Gilman, David Alan education educator, editor
†Gray, Robert Linwood manufacturing executive
Grimley, Liam Kelly special education educator
Guthrie, Frank Albert chemistry educator
Hulbert, Samuel Foster college president
Hunt, Effie Neva former college dean, former English educator
Jerry, Robert Howard education educator
Johnson, Jack Thomas political science educator
Kicklighter, Clois Earl academic administrator
Kunkler, Arnold William surgeon
Lamis, Leroy artist, retired educator
Landini, Richard George university president, emeritus English educator
Leach, Ronald George university dean, librarian
Little, Robert David library science educator
Mausel, Paul Warner geography educator
Meany, John Joseph newspaper publisher
†Moore, John W. academic administrator
Moore, John William university administrator
Perry, Eston Lee real estate and equipment leasing company executive
Puckett, Robert Hugh political scientist, educator
Quick, Edward Raymond museum director
†Smith, Charles Oliver engineer
Smith, Donald Eugene banker
Steinbaugh, Robert P. management and finance educator
Van Til, William education educator, writer
Wheelock, Larry Arthur engineer, consultant

Unionville
Franklin, Frederick Russell retired legal association executive

Upland
Kesler, Jay Lewis university administrator
Shulze, Frederick Bennett music educator

Valparaiso
Carr, Wiley Nelson hospital administrator
Cook, Addison Gilbert chemistry educator
Ehren, Charles Alexander, Jr. lawyer, educator
Harre, Alan Frederick university president
Hillila, Bernhard Hugo Paul education educator
Hires, Jack Merle law educator
Miller, John Albert university administrator, marketing consultant
Mundinger, Donald Charles college president retired
†Persyn, Mary Geraldine law librarian, law educator
Peters, Howard Nevin foreign language educator
Schlender, William Elmer management sciences educator
Schnabel, Robert Victor retired academic administrator

Veedersburg
Marshall, Carolyn Ann M. church official, consultant

Vincennes
†Doll, Maurice Edward, Jr. lawyer, state senator
Rose, Robert Carlisle banker

Wabash
†Cooke, Danny Frank apparel company owner, consultant
Curless, Larry Dean tax consultant, farm manager
Flott, Leslie William quality control professional
Scales, Richard Lewis manufacturer's representative

Walton
Chu, Johnson Chin Sheng physician

Warsaw
Dalton, William Matthews foundry executive

West Lafayette
Abhyankar, Shreeram S. mathematics and industrial engineering educator
Adelman, Steven Allen theoretical physical chemistry educator
Albright, Jack Lawrence animal science and veterinary educator
Albright, Lyle Frederick chemical engineering educator
Allen, Durward Leon biologist, educator
Altman, Joseph biological sciences educator
Altschaeffl, Adolph George civil engineer
Amstutz, Harold Emerson veterinarian, educator
Amy, Jonathan Weekes scientist, educator
Anderson, James George sociologist, educator
Andres, Ronald Paul chemical engineer, educator
Axtell, John David genetics educator, researcher
Baird, William McKenzie chemical carcinogenesis researcher, biochemistry educator
Barany, James Walter industrial engineering educator
Barber, Stanley Arthur agronomy educator
Barnes, Virgil Everett, II physics educator
Baumgardt, Billy Ray university official, agriculturist
Beering, Steven Claus university president, medical educator
Belcastro, Patrick Frank pharmaceutical scientist
Bement, Arden Lee, Jr. engineering educator
Bogdanoff, John Lee aeronautical engineering educator
Borowitz, Joseph Leo pharmacologist
Brown, Donald Ray psychologist, university administrator
Brown, Herbert Charles chemistry educator
Butler, Larry Gene biochemistry educator, researcher
Byrn, Stephen R. medical educator
Caputo, David Armand political scientist educator
Carmony, D(onald) Duane physicist
Christian, John Edward health science educator
Cicirelli, Victor George psychologist
Cochrane, Thomas Thurston tropical soil scientist, agronomist
Cohen, Raymond mechanical engineer, educator
Conte, Samuel Daniel computer scientist, educator
Contreni, John Joseph, Jr. humanities educator
Coolbaugh, Ronald Charles botany educator
Cooper, James Albert, Jr. electrical engineering educator
Cramer, William Anthony biochemistry and biophysics researcher, educator
Curtis, Kenneth Stewart land surveyor
Dayananda, Mysore Ananthamurthy materials engineering educator
Delleur, Jacques William civil engineering educator
Diamond, Sidney chemist, educator
Dolch, William Lee retired engineering materials educator
Drake, John Warren aviation consultant
†Drnevich, Vincent Paul civil engineering educator
Eagly, Alice Hendrickson social psychologist
Eckert, Roger E(arl) chemical engineering educator
Farris, Paul Leonard agricultural economist
†Farris, Thomas N. engineering educator, researcher
Feldhusen, John Frederick educational psychology educator
Ferris, Virginia Rogers nematologist, educator
Fischbach, Ephraim physicist
Franzmeier, Donald Paul agronomy educator, soil scientist
Frick, Gene Armin university administrator
Friedlaender, Fritz Josef electrical engineering educator
Fukunaga, Keinosuke engineering educator
Gentry, Don Kenneth academic dean
Gottfried, Leon Albert English language educator
Grace, Richard Edward engineering educator
Grimley, Robert Thomas chemistry educator
Gruen, Gerald Elmer psychologist, educator
Haas, Felix former mathematics educator, university administrator
Haelterman, Edward Omer veterinary microbiologist, educator
Hanks, Alan R. chemistry educator
Haring, Marilyn Joan academic dean
Harmon, Bud Gene animal sciences educator, consultant
Hem, Stanley Lawrence pharmacy educator, researcher
Hillberry, Ben(ny) M(ax) mechanical engineering educator
Hinkle, Charles Nelson retired agricultural engineering educator
Hodges, Thomas Kent plant physiologist
Hoover, William Leichliter forestry and natural resources educator, financial consultant
Horwich, George economist, educator
Ichiyama, Dennis Yoshihide design educator, consultant
Incropera, Frank Paul mechanical engineering educator
Jacko, Robert Bertram environmental engineering educator
Janick, Jules horticultural scientist, educator
Johannsen, Chris Jakob agronomist, educator, administrator
Johnson, Robert Willard management educator
Kampen, Emerson chemical company executive
Kashyap, Rangasami Lakshmi Narayan electrical engineering educator
King, Donald C. psychologist, educator
Kirksey, Avanelle nutrition educator
Knevel, Adelbert Michael pharmacy educator
Knudson, Douglas Marvin forestry educator
Landgrebe, David Allen electrical engineer
Laskowski, Michael, Jr. chemist, educator
Leap, Darrell Ivan hydrogeologist
†Lechtenberg, Victor L. university administrator
Leimkuhler, Ferdinand Francis industrial engineering educator
Leitch, Vincent Barry literary studies educator
Le Master, Dennis Clyde forest economics and policy educator
Levandowski, Donald William geologist
Lewellen, Wilbur Garrett management educator, consultant
Liley, Peter Edward mechanical engineering educator
Lin, Pen-Min electrical engineer, educator
Lipschutz, Michael Elazar chemistry educator, consultant, researcher
Low, Philip Funk soil chemistry educator, consultant, researcher
Lynch, Robert Emmett mathematics educator
Mannering, Jerry Vincent agronomist, educator
Margerum, Dale William chemistry educator
Markee, Katherine Madigan librarian, educator
Marshall, Francis Joseph aerospace engineer
Mc Bride, William Leon philosopher, educator
McDonald, Robert Bond chemical company executive
McFee, William Warren soil scientist
McGee, Reece Jerome sociology educator, researcher
Mc Gillem, Clare Duane electrical engineering educator
McMillin, David Robert chemistry educator
Mengel, David Bruce agronomy educator
Michael, Harold Louis civil engineering educator
Michaud, Howard Henry conservation educator
Mobley, Emily Ruth library dean, educator
†Molnar, Donald Joseph landscape architecture educator
Morre, D. James biochemist, educator
Morrison, Harry chemistry educator, university dean
Moskowitz, Herbert management educator
Mullen, James Gentry physics educator
Neudeck, Gerold Walter electrical engineering educator
†Newby, Timothy James education educator, researcher
Ohm, Herbert Willis agronomy educator
Ong, Chee-Mun engineering educator
Ortman, Eldon E. entomologist, educator
Overhauser, Albert Warner physicist
Peck, Garnet Edward pharmacist, educator
Peppas, Nikolaos Athanassiou chemical engineering educator, consultant
Perrucci, Robert sociologist, educator
Pratt, Dan Edwin chemistry educator
Pritsker, A. Alan B. engineering executive, educator
Reichard, Hugo Manley English literature educator
Rice, John Rischard computer scientist, researcher, educator
Ringel, Robert Lewis university administrator
Robinson, Farrel Richard pathologist, toxicologist
Rossmann, Michael George biochemist, educator
Rothenberg, Gunther Erich history educator
Rutledge, Charles Ozwin pharmacologist, educator
†Sadeghi, Farshid engineering educator
Salvendy, Gavriel industrial engineer
Sato, Hiroshi materials science educator
Schendel, Dan Eldon management consultant, business educator
Schönemann, Peter Hans psychology educator
Schrader, Lee Frederick agricultural economist
Schreiber, Marvin Mandel agronomist, educator
Schuhmann, Reinhardt, Jr. metallurgical engineering educator, consultant
†Schwartz, Richard John electrical engineering educator, researcher
Shaw, Stanley Miner nuclear pharmacy scientist
Sherman, Louis Allen biologist, researcher
Shertzer, Bruce Eldon education educator
Solberg, James Joseph industrial engineering educator
Sozen, Mete Avni civil engineering educator
Stevenson, Warren Howard mechanical engineering educator
Stone, Marguerite Beverley former university dean, former dean of students
Stump, John Edward veterinary anatomy educator, ethologist
Swensen, Clifford Henrik, Jr. psychologist, educator
Taber, Margaret Ruth electrical engineering technology educator, electrical engineer
Theen, Rolf Heinz-Wilhelm political science educator
Tyner, Wallace Edward economics educator
Van Sickle, David Clark veterinary anatomy educator, researcher
Vest, Robert Wilson ceramic engineering educator
Viskanta, Raymond mechanical engineering educator
Wankat, Phillip Charles chemical engineering educator
Weaver, Connie Marie foods and nutrition educator
Weidenaar, Dennis Jay college dean
Weinstein, Michael Alan political science educator
White, Joe Lloyd soil scientist, educator
Williams, Theodore Joseph engineering educator
Wilson, Franklin Leondus, III political science educator
Wilson, Olin Chaddock astronomer
Woodman, Harold David historian
Wright, Alfred George James band symphony orchestra conductor, educator
Wright, Gordon Pribyl management, operations research educator

Westville
Alspaugh, Dale William university administrator, aeronautics and astronautics educator

Winona Lake
†Ashman, Charles Henry retired minister
Davis, John James religion educator
†Julien, Thomas Theodore religious denomination administrator
†Lewis, Edward Alan religious organization adminstrator

Zionsville
Hansen, Arthur Gene former academic administrator, consultant

IOWA

Adel
†Garst, Elizabeth bank executive

Amana
†Setzer, Kirk religious leader

Ames
Ahmann, John Stanley psychology educator
Ahrens, Franklin Alfred veterinary pharmacology educator
Anderson, Lloyd Lee animal science educator
Anderson, Robert Morris, Jr. electrical engineer
Angelici, Robert J. chemistry educator
Barnes, Richard George physicist, educator
Basart, John Philip electrical engineering and radio astronomy researcher, educator
Baumann, Edward Robert sanitary engineering educator
Benbow, Camilla Persson psychology educator, researcher
†Beran, George Wesley veterinary microbiology educator
Berger, P(hilip) Jeffrey animal science educator, quantitative geneticist
Black, Charles Allen soil scientist, educator
Bowen, George Hamilton, Jr. astrophysicist, educator
Boylan, David Ray retired chemical engineer, educator
Bremner, John McColl agronomy and biochemistry educator
Brown, Frederick Gramm psychology educator
Brown, Robert Grover engineering educator
Bruner, Charlotte Hughes French language educator
Buchele, Wesley Fisher agricultural engineering educator, consultant
Burnet, George, Jr. engineering educator
Burris, Joseph Stephen agronomy educator
†Cantrell, Ronald Paul agronomy educator, plant breeder
Carithers, Jeanine Rutherford veterinary educator
Christensen, George Curtis university official
Cleasby, John LeRoy civil engineer, educator
Clem, John Richard physicist, educator
†Colvin, Thomas Stuart agricultural engineer, farmer
Corbett, John Dudley chemistry educator
Crabtree, Beverly June college dean
Curry, Norval Herbert retired agricultural engineer
David, Herbert Aron statistics educator
Dobson, John McCullough historian
Eaton, Nancy L. librarian, dean
Ebbers, Larry Harold education educator
Edwards, David Charles psychology educator
Ekberg, Carl Edwin, Jr. civil engineering educator
Fehr, Walter Ronald agronomist, researcher, educator
Finnemore, Douglas Kirby physics educator
Fox, Karl August economist, eco-behavioral scientist
Freeman, Albert E. agricultural science educator
†Frey, Kenneth John plant breeder, researcher
Fritz, James Sherwood chemist, educator
Fuller, Wayne Arthur statistics educator
Gaertner, Richard Francis manufacturing research center executive
Gartner, Michael Gay editor, television executive
Geiger, Randall L. electrical engineering educator, design engineer
Ghoshal, Nani Gopal veterinary anatomist, educator
Greve, John Henry veterinary parasitologist, educator
Gschneidner, Karl Albert, Jr. metallurgist, educator, editor, consultant
Hadwiger, Don Frank political science educator, researcher
Hallauer, Arnel Roy geneticist
Handy, Charles Brooks accountant, educator
Hansen, Robert Suttle chemist, educator
Harl, Neil Eugene economist, lawyer, educator
Hatfield, Jerry Lee plant physiologist, biometeorologist
Herrnstadt, Richard Lawrence American literature educator
Horowitz, Jack biochemistry educator
†Houk, Robert Samuel chemistry educator
Isely, Duane biology and botany educator
Iversen, James Delano aerospace engineering educator, consultant
Jacobson, Norman L. retired agricultural educator, researcher
Jacobson, Robert Andrew chemistry educator
Jischke, Martin C. academic administrator
Johnson, Lawrence Alan cereal technologist, educator, researcher, administrator
†Johnson, Stanley R. economist, educator
Jones, Edwin Channing, Jr. electrical engineering educator
Kainlauri, Eino Olavi architect
Kalton, Robert Rankin crop scientist
Karlen, Douglas Lawrence soil scientist
Keeney, Dennis Raymond soil science educator
Kelly, William Harold physicist, physics educator
Kempthorne, Oscar statistics educator emeritus
Kirkham, Don soil physicist, educator
Klonglan, Gerald Edward sociology educator
Larsen, William Lawrence materials science and engineering educator
Larson, Maurice Allen chemical engineer, educator
Lynch, David William physicist, educator
Manatt, Richard education educator
Mengeling, William Lloyd veterinarian, virologist, researcher
†Mischke, Charles Russell mechanical engineering educator
Moon, Harley William veterinarian
†Mullen, Russell E. agricultural studies educator
O'Berry, Phillip Aaron veterinarian
Okiishi, Theodore Hisao mechanical engineering educator
†Owen, Michael agronomist, educator
Palermo, Gregory Sebastian architect
Papadakis, Emmanuel Philippos physicist, university research director, consultant
Pearson, Phillip Theodore veterinary clinical sciences and biomedical engineering educator
Redmond, James Ronald zoology educator, researcher

†Rice, Ronald Max superintendent
Riley, William Franklin mechanical engineering educator
†Rosenberg, Ralph state senator, lawyer, consultant, educator
Ross, Richard Francis veterinarian, microbiologist, educator
Ruedenberg, Klaus theoretical chemist, educator
Russell, Glen Allan chemist, educator
Sanders, Wallace Wolfred, Jr. civil engineer
†Seaton, Vaughn Allen veterinary pathology educator
Smiley, Jane Graves author, educator
Smith, John Francis materials science educator
†Starleaf, Dennis Roy economics educator
Svec, Harry John chemist, educator
Tannehill, John C. aerospace engineer, educator
Thompson, Louis Milton agronomy educator, scientist
Topel, David Glen college dean, animal science educator
Voss, Regis Dale agronomist, educator
Wallin, Jack Robb research plant pathology educator
Wass, Wallace Milton veterinarian, clinical science educator
Wilder, David Randolph materials engineer, consultant
†Wilhelm, Harley A. metallurgist, chemist
Willham, Richard Lewis animal science educator
Wilson, Lennox Norwood aeronautical engineering educator
Wilt, Alan Freese history educator
Yeung, Edward Szeshing chemist
Young, Donald Fredrick engineering educator
†Young, Jerry Wesley animal nutrition educator

Ankeny
Hartog, John, II theology educator, librarian

Bettendorf
Edgerton, Winfield Dow gynecologist
Shenk, John Christian, Jr. retired savings bank executive

Burlington
Hoth, Steven Sergey lawyer

Camanche
Rittmer, Elaine Heneke library media specialist

Cambridge
Frederick, Lloyd Randall soil microbiologist

Cedar Falls
Carlson, Jerry Alan editor
Curris, Constantine William university president
Hanson, Roger James physics educator
Maier, Donna Jane-Ellen history educator
Oster, Merrill James entrepreneur, publisher, author, lecturer
†Slife, Harry Gene broadcast executive, former state senator
Thompson, Thomas Henry philosophy educator
Wilson, Robley Conant, Jr. English educator, editor, author

Cedar Rapids
Albright, Justin W. lawyer
†Anderson, Gerald Lee advertising executive
†Armitage, Thomas Edward library director
Boettcher, Norbe Birosel chemist
Brown, John Edward college president
†Damrow, Richard G. advertising executive
Faches, William George lawyer
†Falconio, Patrick E. insurance company executive
Feld, Thomas Robert college president
Hansen, David Rasmussen federal judge
Healey, Edward Hopkins architect
†Hladky, Joseph F., Jr. newspaper publisher, broadcasting executive
Hladky, Joseph F., III publishing executive
Huber, Rita Norma civic worker
Kucharski, Robert Joseph finance executive
†Ledford, Sandra principal
Lisio, Donald John historian, educator
Malès, René Henri utility executive
Mc Manus, Edward Joseph federal judge
Nazette, Richard Follett lawyer
Norris, Albert Stanley psychiatrist, educator
Novetzke, Sally Johnson former ambassador
†Plagman, Ralph principal
Quarton, William Barlow broadcasting company executive
†Running, Richard V. state legislator, college official
Schrimper, Vernon L. manufacturing, marketing executive
†Stadlen, Diane Elizabeth marketing professional
†Stone, Herbert Marshall architect
Wallace, Samuel Taylor hospital administrator
†Wieck, Paul H. fraternal organization executive
Wilson, Robert Foster lawyer

Center Point
Neenan, Thomas Francis association executive, consultant

Centerville
†Liu, Lee utility company executive

Chariton
†Pearson, Ronald Dale retail food stores corporation executive
†Pickens, Earl consumer products company executive

Charles City
Mc Cartney, Ralph Farnham lawyer, federal judge

Clinton
†Ollie, C(lifford) Arthur history educator, state representative
Weil, Myron retired banker

Coon Rapids
Shirbroun, Richard Elmer veterinarian, cattleman

Council Bluffs
†Gibson, Richard Charles insurance company executive
†Nelson, H. H. Red insurance company executive
Peterson, Richard William lawyer, magistrate judge

Dallas Center
McDonald, John Cecil lawyer

Davenport
Bhatti, Iftikhar Hamid chiropractic educator
Bright, Stanley J. utilities executive
Burgess, Janet Helen interior designer
Copes, Marvin Lee college dean
Gottlieb, Richard Douglas media executive
Jecklin, Lois Underwood art corporation executive, consultant
Juckem, Wilfred Philip manufacturing company executive
Le Grand, Clay former state justice
Luzkow, Jack Lawrence history educator, writer, consultant
Moeller, Donald Joseph academic administrator, educator
O'Keefe, Gerald Francis bishop, retired
Rogalski, Edward J. university administrator
Rohlf, Paul Leon urologist
†Runge, Kay Kretschmar library director
Schermer, Lloyd G. publishing and broadcasting company executive
Shaw, Donald Hardy lawyer
Sulg, Madis corporation executive
†Tinsman, Margaret Neir state senator
†Wenz, Richard L. school system and church administrator
Wittenmeyer, Charles E. lawyer

Davis City
†Boswell, Leonard L. state senator

Decorah
Erdman, Lowell Paul civil engineer, land surveyor
Farwell, Elwin D. minister, educational consultant
Vigen, Kathryn L. Voss nursing administrator, educator

Des Moines
Baxter, Elaine state government official
Belin, David William lawyer
Boyle, Bruce James publisher
Branstad, Terry Edward governor, lawyer
†Brinkman, Richard J. financial services company executive
Bucksbaum, Martin real estate developer
Bucksbaum, Matthew real estate development company president
†Buhr, Florence D. state senator
Burnett, Robert A. publisher
†Cambridge, Daniel Arthur creative director
Campbell, Bonnie Jean state attorney general
Canfield, Earle Lloyd university dean, mathematics educator
Cash, Paul Thalbert retired physician
Christiansen, Russell utility company executive
Claypool, David L. lawyer
Conlin, Roxanne Barton lawyer
Cordes, Donald Wesley health care consultant
Corning, Joy Cole state official
†Crosson, David Earl historical agency administrator
†Cruger, F. Christopher corporate executive
†Daggett, Horace Clinton state legislator
Dahl, Harry Waldemar lawyer
Davis, A. Arthur lawyer
de Gravelles, William Decatur, Jr. physician
†Deluhery, Patrick John state senator
†Dieleman, William Wilbur state senator
†Drake, Richard Francis state senator
Duncan, Hearst Randolph lawyer
†Dunlap, Paul D. bank holding company executive
Durrenberger, William John retired army general, educator, investor
Edwards, Charles C., Jr. newspaper publisher
†Edwards, John Duncan law educator, librarian
Ehrle, Roy W. insurance company executive
Ellis, Mary Louise Helgeson insurance company executive
Elmets, Harry Barnard osteopath, dermatologist
Epting, C. Christopher bishop
Estes, Elaine Rose Graham librarian
Fagg, George Gardner federal judge
Ferrari, Michael Richard, Jr. university administrator
Finley, Gary Roger financial company executive
Fisher, Thomas George lawyer, media company executive
Fitzgerald, Michael Lee state official
Flansburg, James Sherman editor, columnist
Frohock, Joan (Joan Walton) industrial supply company executive
†Gall, Donald Arthur minister
†Garman, Teresa Agnes state legislator
Glomset, Daniel Anders physician
Goldsmith, Janet Jane pediatric nurse practitioner
Grefe, Rolland Eugene lawyer
†Grubbs, Steven Eric state representative
†Grundberg, Betty state legislator, property manager
Hansell, Edgar Frank lawyer
Harris, Charles Elmer lawyer
Harris, K. David state supreme court justice
Hartsook, Larry D. financial executive
†Hennesy, Craig insurance company executive
†Herbert, Charles Emmet architect
Hill, Luther Lyons, Jr. lawyer
Hockenberg, Harlan David lawyer
Hubbell, James Windsor, Jr. retired insurance company executive
Hurd, G. David insurance company executive
Hutchison, Theodore Murtagh insurance company executive
Jensen, Dick Leroy lawyer
Jordan, Charles Wesley bishop
Jordan, David Loran editor
Josten, Robert E. lawyer
Kalainov, Sam Charles insurance company executive
Kelley, Robb Beardsley insurance company executive
Kerr, William T. publishing company executive
Kruidenier, David newspaper executive
Langdon, Herschel Garrett lawyer
Larson, Jerry L. state supreme court justice
Larson, Paul Edward insurance company executive
†Lawless, James L. editor, columnist
Leighton, Paul Joe lawyer
LemMon, Jean Marie editor in chief periodical
Lepley, William state education official
†Lewis, Calvin Fred architect, educator
Little, Christopher Mark publishing company executive, lawyer
Longstaff, Ronald E. federal judge
Lund, Doris Hibbs dietitian
MacDonald, Kenneth journalist, former editor
Marker, David George university president
McGiverin, Arthur A. state supreme court justice
Meredith, Edwin Thomas, III media executive
Miller, Kenneth Edward sociologist, educator
Mitchell, Orlan E. clergyman, former college president
†Murphy, Patrick Joseph state representative
†Myers, M. Kathleen publishing executive
Neiman, John Hammond lawyer
Neis, Arthur Veral healthcare and development company executive
†Newsome, Jon P. insurance company executive
Nyemaster, Ray lawyer
†Pate, Paul Danny state senator, business executive, entrepreneur
Peddicord, Roland Dale lawyer
Peterson, David Charles photojournalist
Plambeck, Herbert Henry agricultural consultant, retired government official
Powell, Sharon Lee social welfare organization administrator
Power, Joseph Edward lawyer
Proctor, William Zinsmaster lawyer
Puotinen, Arthur Edwin college president, clergyman
Putney, Mark William lawyer, utility executive
†Ramsey, David Selmer hospital executive
†Ray, Robert D. health insurance company executive
Reece, Maynard Fred artist, author
Rehm, Jack Daniel publishing executive
Richards, Riley Harry insurance company executive
†Rittmer, Sheldon farmer, senator
Rogers, Rodney Albert biologist, educator
Rohm, Charles Edward insurance company executive
Rosen, Matthew Stephen botanist, consultant
†Runger, Donald R. bank executive
Schneider, William George former life insurance company executive
†Schrader, David F. congressman
Shoff, Patricia Ann lawyer
†Simbro, William Charles journalist
Slade, Llewellyn Eugene lawyer, engineer
Smith, Mary Louise politics and public affairs consultant
Speas, Raymond Aaron retired insurance company executive
Stauffer, William Albert insurance company executive
†Stoffer, Terry James advertising executive
Stuart, William Corwin federal judge
†Sullivan, Sister Patricia Clare hospital administrator
†Szymoniak, Elaine Eisfelder state senator
Thoman, Mark Edward pediatrician
Urban, Thomas N. agricultural products company executive
†Vande Krol, Jerry Lee architect
Van Zante, Shirley Mae magazine editor
†Varn, Richard James state legislator, lawyer, consultant
Vietor, Harold Duane federal judge
Vorbrich, Lynn Karl lawyer, utility executive
Wine, Donald Arthur lawyer
†Winick, Alfred Zell data services corporation executive
Witke, David Rodney newspaper editor
Wolle, Charles Robert federal judge
Young, Dennis Eugene financial services executive

Dubuque
Agria, John Joseph college official
Barta, James Omer priest, psychology educator, academic administrator
Bertsch, Frank Henry furniture manufacturing company executive
Brown, William Clifford publishing company executive
Crahan, Jack Bertsch manufacturing company executive
Drummond, Richard Henry religion educator
Dunn, M. Catherine college administrator, educator
Hemmer, Paul Edward musician, broadcasting executive
Herzberger, Eugene E. neurosurgeon
Husfloen, Kyle Douglas editor
McDonald, Robert Delos manufacturing company executive
Peterson, Walter Fritiof academic administrator
Toale, Thomas Edward school system administrator, priest
Tully, Thomas Alois building materials executive, consultant, educator
†Wahlert, Robert Henry food company executive

Fairfield
†Hawthorne, Timothy Robert direct response advertising and communications company executive
Schaefer, Jimmie Wayne, Jr. agricultural company executive

Fayette
Wenger, Eugene Edward insurance agent

Fonda
Kuhl, Margaret Helen Clayton (Mrs. Alexius M. Kuhl) banker

Forest City
Beebe, Raymond Mark lawyer
Hanson, John K. recreational vehicle manufacturing company executive
Vammen, James Oliver human services administrator

Fort Dodge
†Kersten, James Burke state senator, financial investment officer
Pratt, Diane Adele elementary education educator

Glenwood
Campbell, William Edward state hospital school administrator

Grinnell
Christiansen, Kenneth Allen biologist, educator
Erickson, Luther Eugene chemist, educator
Ferguson, Pamela Anderson mathematics educator, educational administrator
†Fitzgerald, Michael J. secondary school principal
Kissane, James Donald English literature educator
Leggett, Glenn former English language educator, academic administrator
McKee, Christopher Fulton librarian, naval historian, educator
Walker, Waldo Sylvester academic administrator
Wall, Joseph Frazier historian, educator

Hartley
Pearson, Gerald Leon food company executive

Indianola
Jennings, Stephen Grant academic administrator
Larsen, Robert LeRoy artistic director

Iowa City
Abboud, Francois Mitry physician, educator
Addis, Laird Clark, Jr. philosopher, educator, musician
Afifi, Adel Kassim physician
Albrecht, William Price economist, educator, government official
Andreasen, Nancy Coover psychiatrist, educator
Andrews, Clarence Adelbert historian, educator, writer, publisher
Arora, Jasbir Singh engineering educator
Aydelotte, Myrtle Kitchell nursing administrator, educator, consultant
Baird, Robert Dahlen religious educator
Baker, Richard Graves geology educator, palynologist
Balukas, Jean professional pocket billiard player
Banker, Gilbert Stephen industrial and physical pharmacy educator, administrator
†Bar, Robert S. endocrinologist
Barkan, Joel David political science educator
Baron, Jeffrey pharmacologist, educator
Bayne, David Cowan priest, lawyer, law educator
Bedell, George Noble physician, educator
Bentz, Dale Monroe librarian
Bishara, Samir Edward orthodontist
Bonfield, Arthur Earl lawyer, educator
Bonfiglio, Michael surgeon, educator
Branson, Dan Earle civil engineer, educator
Brennan, Robert Lawrence psychometrician
Bruch, Delores Ruth education educator, musician
Burns, C(harles) Patrick hematologist-oncologist
Burton, Donald Joseph chemistry educator
Butchvarov, Panayot Krustev philosophy educator
Clifton, James Albert physician
Coffman, William Eugene educational psychologist
Collins, Daniel W. accountant, educator
Colloton, John William university health care executive
Cooper, Reginald Rudyard orthopedic surgeon, educator
Damasio, Antonio R. physician, neurologist
Deligiorgis, Stavros G. literature educator
Dickeson, Robert Celmer retired university president, corporation president, political science educator
Donelson, John Everett biochemistry educator, molecular biologist
Downer, Robert Nelson lawyer
Eckhardt, Richard Dale physician, educator
Eckstein, John William physician, educator
Ehrenhaft, Johann Leo surgeon
Eyman, Earl Duane electrical science educator, consultant
Fellows, Robert Ellis medical educator, medical scientist
†Ferguson, Richard L. educational administrator
Filer, Lloyd Jackson, Jr. pediatric educator, clinical investigator
Fitz, Annette Elaine physician, educator
Forell, George Wolfgang religion educator
†Forsythe, Robert Elliott economics educator
Franken, Edmund Anthony, Jr. radiologist, educator
Froeschle, Robert Edward professional association administrator
Fry, Hayden university athletic coach
Galask, Rudolph Peter obstetrician-gynecologist
Gantz, Bruce Jay otolaryngologist, educator
Gerber, John Christian English language educator
Gergis, Samir Danial anesthesiologist, educator
Goldstein, Jonathan Amos ancient history and classics educator
Goodridge, Alan Gardner research biochemist, educator
†Green, William archaeologist
Gurnett, Donald Alfred physics educator
Hammond, Harold Logan pathology educator, oral pathologist
Hardt, Hanno Richard Eduard communications educator
Hardy, James Chester speech pathologist, educator
Haug, Edward Joseph, Jr. mechanical engineering educator, simulation research engineer
Hausler, William John, Jr. microbiologist, educator, public health laboratory administrator
Hawley, Ellis Wayne historian, educator
Helm, June anthropologist, educator
Hering, Robert Gustave mechanical engineer, educator, university administrator
Hines, N. William law educator, administrator
Hoffmann, Louis Gerhard immunologist, educator, sex therapist
Hogg, Robert Vincent, Jr. mathematical statistician, educator
Holstein, Jay Allen Judaic studies educator
Hornsby, Roger Allen classics educator
Jacobs, Richard Matthew dentist, orthodontics educator
January, Lewis Edward physician, educator
Johnson, Eugene Walter mathematician
Justice, Donald Rodney poet, educator
Keller, Eliot Aaron broadcasting executive
Kelley, Robert E. English language educator
Kerber, Linda Kaufman historian, educator
Kessel, Richard Glen zoology educator
†Kirchner, Peter T. physician nuclear medicine, educator, consultant
Klaus, Carl Hanna English language educator
Kleinfeld, Erwin mathematician, educator
Knutson, John Franklin psychology educator, clinical psychologist
Kottick, Edward Leon music educator, harpsichord maker
Krause, Walter retired economics educator, consultant
Kurtz, Sheldon Francis lawyer, educator
Lance, George Milward mechanical engineering educator
Levey, Samuel health care administration educator
Loewenberg, Gerhard political science educator
Long, John Paul pharmacologist, educator
Lonngren, Karl Erik electrical and computer engineering educator
Lopes, Lola Lynn psychologist, educator
Madsen, Donald Howard engineering educator, consultant
Manasse, Henri Richard, Jr. health services administrator
†Marshall, Jeffrey Scott mechanical engineer, educator
Mason, Edward Eaton surgeon
Mather, Betty Bang musician, educator

Mather, Roger Frederick *music educator, freelance technical writer*
Mc Leran, James Herbert *university dean, oral surgeon*
Milkman, Roger Dawson *genetics educator, molecular evolution researcher*
Montgomery, Rex *biochemist, educator*
Morriss, Frank Howard, Jr. *pediatrics educator*
Nathan, Peter E. *psychologist, educator*
Nelson, Herbert Leroy *psychiatrist*
Neumann, Roy Covert *architect*
Nicewander, Walter Alan *psychology educator*
Obermann, C. Esco *psychologist, rehabilitation consultant*
Olin, William Harold *orthodontist, educator*
Osborne, James William *radiation biologist*
Patel, Virendra Chaturbhai *mechanical engineering educator*
Percas de Ponseti, Helena *foreign language and literature educator*
Persons, Stow Spaulding *historian, educator*
Pietrzyk, Donald John *chemistry educator*
Plapp, Bryce Vernon *biochemistry educator*
Ponseti, Ignacio Vives *orthopaedic surgery educator*
Potra, Florian Alexander *mathematics educator*
Prokopoff, Stephen Stephen *art museum director, educator*
Raeburn, John Hay *English language educator*
Rawlings, Hunter Ripley, III *university administrator*
Richerson, Hal Bates *physician, internist, allergist, immunologist, educator*
Riesz, Peter Charles *marketing educator, consultant*
Ringen, Catherine Oleson *linguistics educator*
Robertson, Timothy Joel *statistician, educator*
Ross, Russell Marion *political science educator*
Saks, Michael Jay *law educator*
Sayre, Robert Freeman *English educator*
Schmidt, Julius *sculptor*
Schoenbaum, David Leon *historian*
Schultz, Louis William *judge*
Schulz, Rudolph Walter *university dean*
Shannon, Lyle William *sociology educator*
Siebert, Calvin D. *economist, educator*
Skorton, David Jan *university official, physician, educator*
Solbrig, Ingeborg Hildegard *German literature educator*
Steele, Oliver *English educator*
Strauss, John Steinert *dermatologist, educator*
Tephly, Thomas Robert *pharmacologist, toxicologist, educator*
Thompson, Herbert Stanley *neuro-ophthalmologist*
Titze, Ingo Roland *physics educator*
Tomasini, Wallace J(ohn) *art historian, educator, university official*
Trank, Douglas Monty *rhetoric and speech communications educator*
Van Allen, James Alfred *physicist, educator*
Van Gilder, John Corley *neurosurgeon, educator*
Vaughan, Emmett John *academic dean, insurance educator*
Wachal, Robert Stanley *linguistics educator, consultant*
Wasserman, Edward Arnold *psychology educator*
Weinberger, Miles M. *physician, pediatric educator*
Weingeist, Thomas Alan *ophthalmology educator*
†Werger, Paul Myron *bishop*
Widiss, Alan I. *lawyer, educator*
Wiley, Robert Allen *pharmaceutical educator*
Williams, Richard Dwayne *physician, educator*
Winokur, George *psychiatrist, educator*
Wunder, Charles C(ooper) *physiology and biophysics educator, gravitational biologist*
Ziegler, Ekhard Erich *pediatrics educator*
Zimmer, Paul Jerome *editor, poet*

Johnston
†Churchill, Steven Wayne *fund-raising consultant*
Duvick, Donald Nelson *plant breeder*
Steele, Betty Louise *retired banker*

Knoxville
Chang, Theodore Chien-Hsin *psychologist*
Joslyn, Wallace Danforth *psychologist*

Lamoni
Higdon, Barbara J. *college president*

Larchwood
Onet, Virginia C(onstantinescu) *research scientist, educator, writer*
Zangger, Russell George *organization executive, flying school executive*

Madrid
Handy, Richard Lincoln *civil engineer, educator*

Marion
Starr, David Evan *corporate executive*

Marshalltown
Brennecke, Allen Eugene *lawyer*

Mason City
MacNider, Jack *retired cement company executive*
Rosenberg, Dale Norman *psychology educator*
Wallace, Ralph Howes *retired engineering company executive*

McCallsburg
Lounsberry, Robert Horace *former state government administrator*

Mount Pleasant
Haselmayer, Louis August *college president emeritus*

Muscatine
Carver, Martin Gregory *tire manufacturing company executive*
Coulter, Charles Roy *lawyer*
Dahl, Arthur Ernest *former manufacturing executive, consultant*
Dvorchak, Thomas Edward *financial executive*
Fosholt, Sanford Kenneth *consulting engineer*
Howe, Stanley Merrill *manufacturing company executive*
Johnson, Donald Lee *agricultural materials processing company executive*
Kautz, Richard Carl *chemical and feed company executive*
Koll, Richard Leroy *retired chemical company executive*

Lewis, Charles John *feed, grain and chemicals company executive*
McMains, Melvin L(ee) *controller*
Stanley, Richard Holt *consulting engineer*
Thomopulos, Gregs G. *consulting engineering company executive*

Nevada
Countryman, Dayton Wendell *lawyer*

Newton
Bennett, Edward James *lawyer*
Hadley, Leonard Anson *appliance manufacturing corporation executive*
Schiller, Jerry A. *retired manufacturing company executive*

Oakdale
Spriestersbach, Duane Caryl *university administrator, speech pathology educator*

Orange City
Scorza, Sylvio Joseph *religion educator*

Osage
†Koenigs, Deo A. *state representative*

Osceola
Reynoldson, Walter Ward *state supreme court chief justice*

Oskaloosa
Porter, David Lindsey *history and political science educator, author*

Ottumwa
†Moreland, Michael Joseph *state representative, associate*
†Roseberry, Donald G. *chief administrator*

Pella
Bevis, James Wayne *manufacturing company executive*
Farver, Mary Joan *building products company executive*

Plainfield
Lynes, James William, Sr. *communications company executive*

Schaller
Currie, James Morton *bank executive*

Sioux Center
Hulst, John B. *academic administrator*

Sioux City
Deck, Paul Wayne, Jr. *federal judge*
Engle, Richard Carlyle *utilities executive*
†Foster, Paul David, Jr. *agri-business executive*
Hagen, R. E. *bank executive*
Johnson, Marlys Dianne *utility company executive*
Juon, Lester Allen *utility executive*
Krenz, Dean Albert *newspaper publisher*
Madsen, George Frank *lawyer*
Marks, Bernard Bailin *lawyer*
Nymann, P. L. *lawyer*
O'Brien, Donald Eugene *federal judge*
†Olsen, Janus Frederick, III *library director*
Silverberg, David S. *financial consultant*
Soens, Lawrence D. *bishop*
Spellman, George Geneser, Sr. *internist*
Tommeraasen, Miles *college president*
Wharton, Beverly Ann *utility company executive*
Wick, Sister Margaret *college administrator*

Spirit Lake
Brett, George Wendell *retired geologist, philatelist*
Hedberg, Paul Clifford *broadcasting executive*

Springville
Nyquist, John Davis *retired radio manufacturing company executive*

Steamboat Rock
†Taylor, Ray *state senator*

Storm Lake
Briscoe, Keith G. *college president*
†Miller, Curtis Herman *bishop*
Shafer, Everett Earl *business administration educator*

Waterloo
Broshar, Robert Clare *architect*
Kimm, Robert George *animal science educator*
Kober, Arletta Refshauge (Mrs. Kay L. Kober) *educational administrator*
Mast, Frederick William *construction company executive*
Taylor, Lyle Dewey *economic development company executive*

Waverly
Brown, Laurence David *retired bishop*
†Brunkhorst, Bob John *computer programmer, state representative*
Vogel, Robert Lee *college administrator, clergyman*

West Branch
Mather, Mildred Eunice *retired archivist*
†Smith, Richard Norton *library director*

West Des Moines
Alberts, Marion Edward *physician*
Alumbaugh, JoAnn McCalla *magazine editor*
Brooks, Roger Kay *insurance company executive*
Bump, Wilbur Neil *lawyer*
Davis, Ronald Arthur *life insurance brokerage executive*
Dooley, Donald John *publishing executive*
Kimm, Dorothy Allene *elementary education educator*
Marshall, Russell Frank *research company executive*
Pomerantz, Marvin Alvin *container corporation executive*
Sather, Everett Norman *accountant*
Starr, V. Hale *communications executive*
Westerbeck, Kenneth Edward *retired insurance company executive*

Zimmerman, Jo Ann *health services and educational consultant, former lieutenant governor*

West Union
†Vettrus, Richard James *minister*

Windsor Heights
Ansorge, Iona Marie *retired real estate agent, musician*
Demorest, Allan Frederick *psychologist, consultant*
Ferrone, Patrick Francis *consultant*

KANSAS

Atchison
Cray, Cloud Lanor, Jr. *grain products company executive*

Atwood
†Gatlin, Fred *seed and feed business owner, state legislator*

Baldwin City
Keeling, Joe Keith *academic administrator, provost*
Lambert, Daniel Michael *academic administrator*

Bonner Springs
Elliott-Watson, Doris Jean *psychiatric, mental health and gerontological nurse educator*

Clay Center
Braden, James Dale *former state legislator*

Coffeyville
†Garner, Jim David *lawyer, state legislator*
Seaton, Richard Melvin *newspaper and broadcasting executive*

Colby
†Frahm, Sheila *state legislator*
†Morrison, James Frank *optometrist, state legislator*

Concordia
Buechel, William Benjamin *lawyer*
Casado, Antonio Francisco *retired real estate executive*

Derby
Barker, Gary Leland *mining company executive*

Dighton
Stanley, Ellen May *historian, consultant*

Dodge City
Chaffin, Gary Roger *business executive*
Clifton-Smith, Rhonda Darleen *museum curator*
Schlarman, Stanley Gerard *bishop*

Downs
La Barge, William Joseph *tutor, researcher*

El Dorado
Edwards, James Lynn *educational administrator*
Flaming, Iretha Mae *elementary education educator*

Emporia
Christiansen, David K. *hospital administrator*
Glennen, Robert Eugene, Jr. *university president*
Hashmi, Sajjad Ahmad *business educator, university dean*

Enterprise
Wickman, John Edward *librarian, historian*

Fairway
Marquardt, Christel Elisabeth *lawyer*

Fort Leavenworth
Miller, John Edward *army officer*
Oliver, Thornal Goodloe *health care executive*

Fort Riley
†Van Meter, Terry *museum director*

Fort Scott
Emery, Frank Eugene *publishing executive*
†McCurley, F. C. *insurance company executive*

Goodland
Sharp, Glenn (Skip Sharp) *vocational education administrator*

Great Bend
Jones, Edward *physician, pathologist*

Hamilton
Lockard, Walter Junior *petroleum company executive*

Haven
Schlickau, George Hans *cattle breeder, professional association executive*

Hays
Budke, Charles Henry *secondary education educator*
Coyne, Patrick Ivan *physiological ecologist*
Hammond, Edward H. *university president*
Lee, Carla Ann Bouska *nursing educator*

Hesston
†Samuelson, Ellen Banman *state legislator*
Yost, Lyle Edgar *farm equipment manufacturing company executive*

Hiawatha
Pennel, Marie Lucille Hunziger *elementary education educator*

Hugoton
Nordling, Bernard Erick *lawyer*

Hutchinson
Baumer, Beverly Belle *journalist*
Buzbee, Richard Edgar *newspaper editor*
Dick, Harold L. *manufacturing executive*

Dillon, David Brian *retail grocery executive*
†Hanes, John T. *food products executive*
Hayes, John Francis *lawyer*
†Kerr, David Mills *state legislator*
†O'Neal, Michael Ralph *lawyer, state representative*
Schmidt, Gene Earl *hospital administrator*

Independence
†Empson, Cynthia Sue *retail executive, nurse*
Swearingen, Harold Lyndon *oil company executive*

Industrial Airport
†Mendelson, Lewis A. *manufacturing company executive*

Iola
Talkington, Robert Van *state senator*

Kansas City
Anderson, Harrison Clarke *pathology educator, biomedical researcher*
Arakawa, Kasumi *physician, educator*
Baska, James Louis *wholesale grocery company executive*
Bechtholdt, Henry Wilbert *international union executive*
Behbehani, Abbas M. *clinical virologist, educator*
†Bond, Richard Lee *banker, state senator*
†Bruns, G(erald) Thomas *state representative, pharmacist*
†Cade, Walter *church administrator*
Campbell, Joseph Leonard *trade association executive*
†Carolan, Douglas *wholesale company executive*
Cho, Cheng Tsung *pediatrician, educator*
Clifford, James Michael *clinical research administrator*
Coles, Anna Louise Bailey *nursing administrator, college dean*
†DeFabis, Mike *food products company executive*
Dunn, Marvin Irvin *physician*
Ebner, Kurt Ewald *biochemistry educator*
Elkin, Irvin J. *milk marketing cooperative executive*
Forst, Marion Francis *bishop*
Godfrey, Robert Gordon *physician*
Godwin, Harold Norman *pharmacist, educator*
Goldberg, Ivan D. *microbiologist, educator*
Goodwin, Donald William *psychiatrist, educator*
†Grantham, Jared James *nephrologist, educator*
Greenberger, Norton Jerald *physician*
Greenwald, Gilbert Saul *physiologist*
Hall, R. Vance *psychology researcher, educator, administrator, consultant, business executive*
Hassanein, Khatab M. *biostatistics educator, consultant*
Hollander, Daniel *gastroenterologist, medical educator*
Hollenbeck, Marynell *municipal government official*
Hudson, Robert Paul *medical educator*
Jerome, Norge Winifred *nutritionist, anthropologist*
†Jones, Sherman J. *state senator*
Krantz, Kermit Edward *physician, educator*
Lungstrum, John W. *federal judge*
Mathewson, Hugh Spalding *anesthesiologist, educator*
Mohn, Melvin Paul *anatomist, educator*
Morrison, David Campbell *immunology educator*
O'Connor, Earl Eugene *federal judge*
Olofson, Tom William *private investor, business executive*
Potter, Glenn Edward *hospital administrator*
Robinson, David Weaver *surgeon, educator*
Rushfelt, Gerald Lloyd *magistrate judge*
Ruth, William Edward *physician, educator*
Samson, Frederick Eugene, Jr. *neuroscientist, educator*
Schloerb, Paul Richard *surgeon, educator*
Stoskopf, William Howard *retired music educator*
Strecker, Ignatius J. *archbishop*
Van Bebber, George Thomas *federal judge*
Vratil, Kathryn Hoefer *federal judge*
Walaszek, Edward Joseph *pharmacology educator*
Waxman, David *physician, university consultant*
Whelan, Richard J. *director special education and pediatrics programs, academic administrator*
Ziegler, Dewey Kiper *neurologist*

Kingman
Burket, George Edward, Jr. *family physician*

Lawrence
Alexander, John Thorndike *historian, educator*
Ammar, Raymond George *physicist, educator*
Andrews, William Leake *English educator*
Angino, Ernest Edward *geology educator*
Armitage, Kenneth Barclay *biology educator, ecologist*
Augelli, John Pat *geography educator, author, consultant, rancher*
Baumgartel, Howard J., Jr. *psychology educator, academic administrator*
Beedles, William LeRoy *finance educator, financial consultant*
Benjamin, Bezaleel Solomon *architecture and architectural engineering educator*
Borchardt, Ronald Terrance *biochemistry and pharmaceutical chemistry educator, consultant*
Bovee, Eugene Cleveland *protozoologist, emeritus educator*
Bowman, Laird Price *retired foundation administrator*
Brawley, Robert Julius *artist, art educator*
Budig, Gene Arthur *university chancellor*
Bulgren, William Gerald *computer science educator, researcher*
Burroughs, William Seward *writer*
Byers, George William *retired entomology educator*
Carlson, Robert Gideon *chemistry educator*
Casad, Robert Clair *legal educator*
Cherniss, Michael David *English educator*
Crowe, William Joseph *dean of libraries, educator*
Davidson, John Pirnie *theoretical physicist, educator*
Davis, John Clements *geomathematician, natural resources and computer science consultant*
Dean, Thomas Scott *architect, educator*
De George, Richard Thomas *philosophy educator*
Dreschhoff, Gisela Auguste Marie *physicist, educator*
Duerksen, George Louis *music educator, music therapist*
Eblen, George Thomas (Tom Eblen) *journalist*
Eldredge, Charles Child, III *art history educator*
Enos, Paul *geologist, educator*
Forman, George Whiteman *mechanical design consultant*
Frederickson, Horace George *former college president, public administration educator*

Genova, Anthony Charles *philosophy educator*
Gerhard, Lee Clarence *geologist, educator*
Ginn, John Charles *journalism educator, former newspaper publisher*
Grabow, Stephen Harris *architecture educator*
Green, Don Wesley *chemical and petroleum engineering educator*
Harmony, Marlin Dale *chemistry educator, researcher*
Heller, Francis H(oward) *law and political science educator emeritus*
Himmelberg, Charles John, III *mathematics educator, researcher*
†Holtzman, Julian Charles *electrical engineer*
†Hurst, George Cameron, III *history educator*
Johnston, Richard Fourness *biologist*
Kleinberg, Jacob *chemist, educator*
†Koepp, Donna Pauline Petersen *librarian*
Laird, Roy Dean *political science educator*
Landgrebe, John Allan *chemistry educator*
Leonard, Roy Junior *civil engineering educator*
Levine, Stuart George *editor, English literature educator, author*
Li, Chu-Tsing *art history educator*
Locke, Carl Edwin, Jr. *academic administrator, engineering educator*
Lucas, William Max, Jr. *structural engineer, university dean*
Lundsgaarde, Henry Peder *anthropology educator, researcher*
Mackenzie, Kenneth Donald *management consultant, educator*
Martin, Edwin J(ohn) *psychologist*
Mc Coy, Donald Richard *historian*
Mc Kinney, Ross Erwin *civil engineering educator*
Michener, Charles Duncan *entomologist, biologist, educator*
Miller, Don Robert *surgeon*
Mitscher, Lester Allen *chemist, educator*
Moore, Richard Kerr *electrical engineering educator*
Muirhead, Vincent Uriel *aerospace engineer*
Norris, Andrea Spaulding *art museum director*
Orel, Harold *literary critic, educator*
Papanek, Victor *designer, educator, writer*
Paretsky, David *microbiology educator*
Phillips, Oliver Clyde, Jr. *classics educator*
Pickett, Calder Marcus *retired journalism educator*
Pinet, Frank Samuel *former university dean*
Pozdro, John Walter *music educator, composer*
Quinn, Dennis B. *English language and literature educator*
Robinson, Walter Stitt, Jr. *historian*
Rolfe, Stanley Theodore *civil engineer, educator*
Roskam, Jan *aerospace engineer*
Ross, Jack Lewis *psychiatrist*
Rowland, James Richard *electrical engineering educator*
Saul, Norman Eugene *history educator*
Schiefelbusch, Richard L. *research administrator*
Schilling, John Michael *golf course executive*
Schoeck, Richard Joseph *English and humanities scholar*
†Schroeder, Stephen Robert *psychology researcher*
Seaver, James Everett *historian, educator*
Sheridan, Richard Bert *economics educator*
Simons, Dolph Collins, Jr. *newspaper publisher*
Smith, Glee Sidney, Jr. *lawyer*
Smith, Howard Wesley *engineering educator*
Smith, Robert Lee *retired civil engineering educator*
Spires, Robert Cecil *foreign language educator*
Stokstad, Marilyn Jane *art history educator, curator*
Tacha, Deanell Reece *federal judge*
Tsubaki, Andrew Takahisa *theater director, educator*
Turnbull, Ann Patterson *special education educator, consultant*
Tuttle, William McCullough, Jr. *history educator*
Vanatta, Chester B. *business executive, educator*
Williams, Roy *university athletic coach*
Willner, Ann Ruth *political scientist, educator*
Wilson, Paul Edwin *lawyer, educator*
†Winter, Winton Allen, Jr. *lawyer, state senator*
Woelfel, James Warren *philosophy educator*
Woodward, Frederick Miller *publisher*
Worth, George John *English literature educator*
Young, J(ohn) Michael *philosophy educator*
Zeller, Edward Jacob *physics, astronomy and geology educator, consultant*
Zerwekh, Robert Paul *engineering administrator, engineering management educator, researcher, consultant, artist*

Leavenworth
Clifford, Brother Peter *academic administrator, religious educator*
†Glatt, Sister Marie Damian *healthcare corporation executive*
McGilley, Sister Mary Janet *nun, educator, writer, academic administrator*
Mengel, Charles Edmund *physician, medical educator*
Stanley, Arthur Jehu, Jr. *federal judge*

Leawood
Ballard, John William, Jr. *banker*
†Carmody, Timothy James *lawyer, educator*

Lebanon
Colwell, John Edwin *retired aerospace scientist*

Lecompton
Conard, John Joseph *financial official*

Lee's Summit
Puglisi, Philip James *electrical engineer*

Lenexa
Ascher, James John *pharmaceutical executive*
†Parkinson, Mark Vincent *lawyer, state senator*
Rayburn, George Marvin *business executive, investment executive*

Liberal
†Holmes, Carl Dean *landowner, state legislator*

Manhattan
Appl, Fredric Carl *mechanical engineering educator*
Babcock, Michael Ward *economics educator*
Barkley, Theodore Mitchell *biology educator*
Chang, Amos Ih-Tiao *retired educator*
Coffman, James Richard *academic administrator, veterinarian*
Davis, Kenneth Sidney *writer*
Durkee, William Robert *retired physician*
†Ealy, Robert Phillip *horticulture and landscape architecture educator*
†Erickson, Howard Hugh *veterinarian*
Fateley, William Gene *scientist, educator, inventor, administrator*
†Fenton, Donald Lee *mechanical engineering educator, consultant*
Foerster, Bernd *architecture educator*
Higham, Robin *historian, editor, publisher*
Howe, H(ugh) Philip *banker*
Hoyt, Kenneth Boyd *educational psychology educator*
†Johnson, Marc Anton *agricultural economics educator*
Johnson, Terry Charles *biologist, researcher*
Johnson, William Howard *agricultural engineer, educator*
Kirkham, M. B. *plant physiologist, educator*
Kirmser, Philip George *engineering educator*
Kremer, Eugene R. *architecture educator*
Kruh, Robert F. *university administrator*
Lee, E(ugene) Stanley *industrial engineer, mathematician, educator*
†Lorenz, Michael Duane *veterinary medicine educator*
Marsh, Harry Dean *journalism educator*
McCulloh, John Marshall *historian*
†McKee, Richard Miles *animal studies educator*
Mosier, Jacob Eugene *veterinarian, consultant*
Murray, John Patrick *psychologist, educator, researcher*
Nafziger, Estel Wayne *economics educator*
Oehme, Frederick Wolfgang *medical researcher and educator*
†Oleen, Lana *state legislator*
Paulsen, Gary Melvin *agronomy educator*
Phares, E. Jerry *psychology educator*
Sears, Rollin George *wheat geneticist, small grains researcher*
Seaton, Edward Lee *newspaper editor and publisher*
Setser, Carole Sue *food science educator*
Setser, Donald Wayne *chemistry educator*
Simons, Gale Gene *nuclear engineering educator, university administrator*
Spears, Marian Caddy *dietetics and institutional management educator*
Stolzer, Leo William *bank executive*
Twiss, Page Charles *geology educator*
Vetter, James L. *food research association administrator*
Vorhies, Mahlon Wesley *veterinary pathologist, educator*

Marion
Meyer, Bill *newspaper publisher, editor*

Mc Pherson
Hull, Robert Glenn *retired financial administrator*
Mason, Stephen Olin *academic administrator*
Nichols, Richard Dale *former congressman, banker*
Shriver, Garner Edward *lawyer, former congressman*
†Steffes, Don C. *state senator*
Williams, Larry Emmett *oil company executive*

Merriam
Mealman, Glenn *corporate marketing executive*
†Snowbarger, Vincent Keith *lawyer, state representative*

Mission
†Downing, David Charles *minister*
Novak, Alfred *retired biology educator*
Thomas, Christopher Yancey, III *surgeon, educator*

Neosho Falls
Bader, Robert Smith *biology, zoology educator and researcher*

Newton
†Barrett, Lois Yvonne *minister*
†Preheim, Vern Quincy *religious organization administrator, minister*

North Newton
†Fast, Darrell W. *minister*

Olathe
Burke, Paul E., Jr. *state senator, investment banker*
Chipman, Marion Walter *judge*
Lowe, Roy Goins *lawyer*
Williams, Eleanor Joyce *air traffic control specialist*

Ottawa
Howe, William Hugh *artist*

Overland Park
†Baker, Charles H. *engineering company executive*
Balloun, Joseph Eugene *lawyer*
Burger, Henry G. *anthropologist, vocabulary scientist, publisher*
Byrne, Catherine *swimmer*
Dore, James Francis *financial services executive*
Gaar, Norman Edward *lawyer, former state senator*
Green, John Lafayette, Jr. *education executive*
†Kline, Phillip D. *lawyer*
Krauss, Carl F. *lawyer*
Linn, James Herbert *retired banker*
Longan, George Baker, III *real estate executive*
Oldham, Dale Ralph *life insurance company executive, actuary*
†Powell, George Everett, Jr. *motor freight company executive*
Powell, George Everett, III *trucking company executive*
Ruse, Steven Douglas *lawyer*
Sampson, William Roth *lawyer*
Short, Joel Bradley *lawyer, consultant*
Stanton, Roger D. *lawyer*
†Vancrum, Robert James *state senator, partner*
Van Dyke, Thomas Wesley *lawyer*
Waxse, David John *lawyer*
Webb, William Duncan *lawyer, investment executive*

Paola
Cleary, William Richard *superintendent of schools*

Pittsburg
Behlar, Patricia Ann *political science educator*
Nettels, George Edward, Jr. *mining company executive*
Sullivan, Frank Victor *academic dean, industrial arts educator*
Wilson, Donald Wallin *university president, educator*

Prairie Village
Hannah, Hamner, III *surgeon*
Souders, James P. *professional association executive*
Stock, Gregg Francis *retired association executive*

Pratt
Loomis, Howard Krey *banker*

Russell
Anschutz, Mary Anna *special education educator*

Saint Marys
Latham, Dudley Eugene, III (Del Latham) *printing and paper converting executive*

Salina
Ashby, John Forsythe *bishop*
Cosco, John Anthony *health care executive, educator*
Crawford, Lewis Cleaver *engineering executive*
Fitzsimons, George K. *bishop*
Ryan, Stephen Collister *funeral director*
†Tompkins, John Andrew *school system administrator*

Shawnee Mission
†Adkins, David Jay *lawyer*
Arneson, George Stephen *manufacturing company executive, management consultant*
Asher, Donna Thompson *psychiatric-mental health nurse*
Barton, C. Robert *insurance company executive*
Bennett, Robert Frederick *lawyer, former governor*
Bigger, John P. *motor carrier executive*
Biggs, J. O. *lawyer, general industry company executive*
†Bogina, August, Jr. *state senator*
Boyd, John Kent *advertising executive*
Byers, Walter *athletic association executive*
Cahal, Mac Fullerton *lawyer, publisher*
Callahan, Harry Leslie *civil engineer*
Clay, George Harry *lawyer*
Connelly, John Matthew *lawyer, insurance company executive*
Deaver, Darwin Holloway *former utility executive*
Dockhorn, Robert John *physician*
Dougherty, Robert Anthony *manufacturing company executive*
Fairchild, Robert Charles *pediatrician*
Findlay, Theodore Bernard *management consultant*
Gamet, Donald Max *appliance company executive*
†Goetz, Kenneth Lee *cardiovascular physiologist*
Haggard, Forrest Deloss *minister*
Hechler, Robert Lee *financial services company executive*
Heineman, Paul Lowe *consulting civil engineer*
Herring, Raymond Mark *marketing and planning executive*
†Hershman, Mark Steven *lighting designer*
Holliday, John Moffitt *insurance company executive*
Holter, Don Wendell *retired bishop*
Howard, Theodore Walter *mutual fund corporation executive*
†Kaplan, Marjorie Ann Pashkow *school district administrator*
Keach, Margaret Sally *writer, lecturer*
†Lakin, Scott Bradley *insurance agent*
†Langworthy, Audrey Hansen *state legislator*
McEachen, Richard Edward *banker, lawyer*
Miller, Stanford *insurance consultant*
Mindlin, Richard Barnett *marketing executive*
†Mischler, Paul *grain company executive*
†Myhre, Roger L. *agricultural products executive*
Pierson, John Theodore, Jr. *manufacturer*
Price, James Gordon *physician*
Putman, Dale Cornelius *management consultant, lawyer*
Robinson, Thomas Bullene *retired civil engineer*
Rubin, Charles Elliott *lawyer, sports agent*
Shipman, David Norval *healthcare consultant*
†Smith, Robert Hugh *engineering construction company executive*
Snyder, Willard Breidenthal *lawyer*
Steele, Dorothy Pauline *retired elementary education educator*
Strubbe, Thomas R. *diagnostic testing industry executive*
Sunderland, Robert *cement company executive*
†Watanabe, Hirosuko *grain merchandising company executive*
Watson, Thomas Sturges *professional golfer*
Wenner, Herbert Allan *pediatrician*
Widder, Willard Graves *retired banker*

Silver Lake
Rueck, Jon Michael *manufacturing executive*

Stanley
†Brown, Nancy J. *state representative*

Strawn
†Lawrence, Douglass Ray *radio station executive, state legislator*

Topeka
Abbott, Bob *state supreme court justice*
Abrahams, John Hambleton *life insurance company executive*
Allegrucci, Donald Lee *state supreme court justice*
Angermeier, Ingo *hospital administrator, educator*
Ayres, Ted Dean *lawyer, academic counsel*
Carlin, John William *former governor*
Clarke, Gary Kendrick *zoologist*
Cogswell, Glenn Dale *lawyer*
Cohen, Sheldon Hersh *chemistry educator*
Comstock, Glen David *civil engineer*
Crow, Sam Alfred *federal judge*
Dicus, John Carmack *savings and loan association executive*
Droegmueller, Lee *state education official*
†Eisenbarth, Gary *insurance company executive*
Fink, H. Bernerd *corporate professional*
Fink, Ruth Garvey *diversified company executive*
Finney, Joan McInroy *governor*
Francisco, James L. *lieutenant governor*
Franklin, Benjamin Barnum *dinner club executive*
Frazier, John Warren *civil engineer*
†Fricke, Howard R. *insurance company executive*
Gabbard, Glen Owens *psychiatrist, psychoanalyst*
Graves, William Preston *state official*
Hayes, John Edward, Jr. *electric power industry executive*
Heitz, Mark V. *insurance company executive*
†Hilpert, Dale W. *retail shoe company executive*
Holmes, Richard Winn *state supreme court justice*
Johnson, Arnold William *mortgage company executive*
†Karr, Gerald Lee *agricultural economist, state senator*
†Karst, Gary Gene *architect*
Laster, Ralph William, Jr. *insurance company executive, accountant*
†Lee, Janis K. *state legislator*
Marshall, Herbert A. *lawyer*
Marvin, James Conway *librarian, consultant*
†Mays, M. Douglas *state legislator, financial consultant*
McCandless, Barbara J. *auditor*
McFarland, Kay Eleanor *state supreme court justice*
Menninger, Roy Wright *medical foundation executive, psychiatrist*
Menninger, William Walter *psychiatrist*
Metzler, Dwight Fox *civil engineer, retired state official*
Miller, Robert Haskins *retired state chief justice*
†Miller, Thomas L. *insurance company executive*
Peavler, Nancy Jean *editor*
†Petty, Marge *state senator*
Powers, Harris Pat *broadcasting executive*
Powers, Ramon Sidney *historical society administrator, historian*
Pusateri, James Anthony *federal bankruptcy judge*
Randall, Elizabeth Ellen *personnel manager*
Rogers, Richard Dean *federal judge*
Rosenberg, John K. *lawyer*
Sader, Carol Hope *state representative, legal editor*
Saffels, Dale Emerson *federal judge*
†Salisbury, Alicia Laing *state legislator*
Samuelson, Marvin Lee *veterinarian*
Schneider, Raymond Clinton *architect, educator*
Sheffel, Irving Eugene *psychiatric institution executive*
†Shuler, Howard L. *superintendent*
Simpson, William Stewart *retired psychiatrist, sex therapist*
Six, Fred N. *state supreme court justice*
Skoog, Ralph Edward *lawyer*
Smalley, William Edward *bishop*
Spohn, Herbert Emil *psychologist*
Spring, Raymond Lewis *legal educator*
Stauffer, John H. *newspaper and broadcast executive*
†Stauffer, Peter Wallace *newspaper executive*
Stauffer, Stanley Howard *newspaper and broadcasting executive*
Stephan, Robert Taft *state attorney general*
Thompson, Hugh Lee *university president*
Thompson, Sally Engstrom *state official*
Varner, Charleen LaVerne McClanahan (Mrs. Robert B. Varner) *nutritionist, educator, administrator, dietitian*
†Vidricksen, Ben Eugene *food service executive, state legislator*
†Wagnon, Joan *state legislator, association executive*
Wagnon, William Odell, Jr. *university professor*
†Wells, Elaine Louise *state legislator, health care administrator*

University Of Kansas
Humphrey, Philip Strong *university museum director*
Kraft, David Christian *civil engineering educator*
†Kuznesof, Elizabeth Anne *history educator*

Vassar
Visser, John Evert *university president emeritus, historian*

Wellington
Ferguson, William McDonald *retired lawyer, rancher, author, banker, former state official*

Westwood
Buckner, William Claiborne *real estate broker*
Esrey, William Todd *telecommunications company executive*
Schultz, Richard Dale *national athletic organizations executive*

Wichita
Andrew, Kenneth L. *research physicist, physics educator*
Barents, Brian Edward *marketing executive*
†Bell, Baillis F. *airport terminal executive*
Bell, Charles Robert, Jr. *lawyer*
Brown, Wesley Ernest *federal judge*
Bunten, William Daniel *banker*
Cadman, Wilson Kennedy *retired utility company executive*
Cheesman, John Michael *aeronautics company executive, community activist*
Chen, Zuohuang *conductor*
†Claassen, Sherida Dill *newspaper editor*
Clark, Susan Matthews *psychologist*
Curfman, Lawrence Everett *lawyer*
†Curtright, Robert Eugene *newspaper critic and columnist*
Davis, Robert Louis *lawyer*
Docking, Thomas Robert *lawyer, former state lieutenant governor*
Dyck, George *psychiatry educator*
Eastburn, Jeannette Rose *religious publishing executive*
Eby, Martin Keller, Jr. *construction company executive*
Egan, Sister M. Sylvia *hospital administrator*
Egbert, Robert Iman *electrical engineering educator, academic administrator*
Ellington, Howard Wesley *architect*
†Ellis, David R. *aeronautical researcher*
Farha, William Farah *food company executive*
Frazier, John Lionel Devin *food products executive*
†Gates, Walter Edward *rental company executive, business owner*
Gerber, Eugene J. *bishop*
†Getz, Robert Lee *newspaper columnist*
†Goebel, Christopher J. *lumber company executive*
Gosman, Albert Louis *mechanical engineering educator*
†Grotewiel, Ken *state representative*
Gurney, Hugh Douglas *historic site administrator*
Guthrie, Richard Alan *physician*
Hanna, William W. *chemical company executive*
†Harris, Michael Terry *state senator, partner*
Hatteberg, Larry Merle *photojournalist*
Hicks, M. Elizabeth *pharmacist*
Jabara, Francis Dwight *merchant banker, educator, entrepreneur*
Kelly, Patrick F. *federal judge*
Knudsen, Darrell G. *diversified financial services company executive*
Koch, Charles de Ganahl *corporation executive*
†Lahti, Richard *quality improvement administrator*

Lair, Robert Louis catering company executive
Lorelli, Michael Kevin corporate executive
Lusk, William Edward real estate, oil company executive
Manning, Robert Thomas physician, educator
Mc Kee, George Moffitt, Jr. civil engineer, consultant
Meyer, Russel William, Jr. aircraft company executive
Myers, Jesse Jerome lawyer, construction company executive
Pearson, John King federal judge
Peterman, Bruce Edgar aircraft company executive
Pohlman, Randolph Allen business administration educator, dean
†Pottorff, Jo Ann state legislator
Rademacher, Richard Joseph librarian
Rainey, William Joel lawyer
Reals, William Joseph pathologist, academic administrator, educator
Redman, Peter finance company executive
Reed, Darwin Cramer health care consultant
Reinemund, Steven S. restaurant chain executive
†Rutledge, Joel R. state legislator, small business owner
Sills, Milton D. engineer, air transportation executive
Skubitz, Dan Joseph lawyer
Sowers, Wesley Hoyt lawyer, management consultant
Theis, Frank Gordon federal judge
Thompson, M(orris) Lee lawyer
†Tiahrt, W. Todd state senator
†Tiffany, Charles Ferguson aerospace executive
Varner, Sterling Verl retired oil company executive
†Welshimer, Gwen R. state legislator, real estate broker, appraiser, tax consultant
Welton, Robert Breen aircraft manufacturing company executive
†Wentz, William H., Jr. aerospace engineer, educator
Wilhelm, William Jean civil engineering educator
Williams, Ronald Paul lawyer
†Witsman, Forest Tim association executive
Wooden, Howard Edmund museum director, art researcher
†Zehr, Clyde James church administrator
Zytkow, Jan Mikolaj computer science educator

Winfield
Crowley, Marilyn critical care nurse, educator
Miller, Franklin Rush retired internist, educator
Willoughby, John Wallace former college dean, provost

KENTUCKY

Ashland
Boyd, James Robert oil company executive
†Carter, David Edward communications executive
Chellgren, Paul Wilbur petroleum company executive
Dansby, John Walter oil company executive
Hall, John Richard oil company executive
Justice, Franklin Pierce, Jr. oil company executive
Lacy, James Daniel oil company executive
Weaver, Carlton Davis retired oil company executive
Wilhoit, Henry Rupert, Jr. federal judge
Yancey, Robert Earl, Jr. oil company executive

Benton
†Lewis, Richard Hayes lawyer, state representative

Berea
Hager, Paul Calvin college administrator, educator

Beulah Heights
†Barthel, F. Ernest insurance company executive

Bowling Green
Cangemi, Joseph Peter psychologist, consultant, educator
Constans, Henry Philip, Jr. philosopher, educator
Cravens, Raymond Lewis political science educator
Haynes, Robert Vaughn university administrator, historian
Holland, John Ben clothing manufacturing company executive
Kalab, Kathleen Alice sociology educator
Meredith, Thomas C. academic administrator
Minton, John Dean historian, educator
Murrell, Estelle C. elementary school educator
†Richards, Jody art educator, artist
Slocum, Donald Warren chemist

Burkesville
Smith, Paul Traylor mayor, former business executive, former army officer

Corbin
Barton-Collings, Nelda Ann political activist, newspaper, bank and nursing home executive

Covington
Gross, Joseph Wallace hospital administrator
†Harper, Kenneth Franklin state legislator, real estate broker
†Head, Joseph Henry, Jr. lawyer
†Kerr, Thomas Robert lawyer
Trimble, Vance Henry retired newspaper editor

Crestwood
†Upchurch, Paul principal

Danville
Adams, Michael F. academic administrator, political communications specialist
Breeze, William Hancock college administrator
Campbell, Stanley Richard library services director
Lively, Pierce federal judge
Newhall, David Sowle history educator
†Rowland, Robert E. secondary school principal
Spragens, Thomas Arthur educational consultant

Elizabethtown
Modderman, Melvin Earl health administrator

Elkton
Manthey, Frank Anthony physician, director

Erlanger
Hughes, William Anthony bishop

Fort Thomas
Scott, Ralph Mason physician, radiology educator

Frankfort
Adams, Robert Waugh, Jr. bank executive
Babbage, Robert A. state official
†Blandford, Donald Joseph state legislator, speaker of the house
Carroll, Julian Morton lawyer, former governor
Gale, Steven Hershel humanities educator
Geddes, LaDonna McMurray speech educator
Gorman, Chris state attorney general
†Johns, Susan D. state senator
Jones, Brereton C. governor
Leibson, Charles M. state supreme court justice
McDonald, Alice Coig state education official
Mills, Frances Jones state official
Nelson, James Albert librarian, state official
†Northup, Anne Meagher state legislator
Palmore, John Stanley, Jr. lawyer
†Palumbo, Ruth Ann state legislator
Patton, Paul E. state official
†Rogers, John D. state senator
Stephens, Robert F. state supreme court chief justice
†Stumbo, Gregory D. state legislator
†Ward, Michael Delavan former state legislator
Wintersheimer, Donald Carl state supreme court justice

Franklin
Clark, James Benton railroad industry consultant, former executive

Georgetown
†Warren, Alex McLean, Jr. automotive executive

Gilbertsville
Mathues, Thomas Oliver retired automobile company executive

Goshen
Mc Clinton, Donald G. diversified holding company executive
Strode, William Hall, III photojournalist, publisher

Grayson
Waite, Lemuel Warren library director

Harrods Creek
Chandler, James Williams retired securities company executive

Harrodsburg
Cummins, Bonnie Norvell gifted and talented education educator
Lunger, Irvin Eugene university president emeritus, clergyman

Hebron
†Holscher, Robert F. county official

Highland Heights
Boothe, Leon Estel university president
Carr, George Francis, Jr. lawyer
Hopgood, James F. anthropologist
Jones, William Rex lawyer, educator
Street, David Hargett manufacturing company executive
Wallace, Harold Lew historian, educator

Hindman
†Bailey, Benny Ray health care administrator, state senator

Hopkinsville
Freer, John Herschel psychiatrist
Riley, Thomas Leslie retired college president

Leitchfield
†Moore, Virgil C. state senator, retired army officer

Lexington
Allison, James Claybrooke, II broadcasting executive
Anderson, Richard L(oree) mathematician, educator
Avant, Robert Frank physician, educator
Barnhart, Charles Elmer animal sciences educator
Baumann, Robert Jay child neurology educator
Beshear, Steven L. lawyer
Bhattacharya-Chatterjee, Malaya cancer research scientist
Blanton, Jack Christopher academic administrator
Bosomworth, Peter Palliser university medical administrator
Boyer, Lillian Buckley artist, educator
Breathitt, Edward Thompson, Jr. lawyer, railroad executive
Brown, William Randall geology educator
Bryant, Joseph Allen, Jr. English language educator
Butler, Frank Anthony hospital administrator
†Caroland, William Bourne structural engineer
Cheniae, George Maurice plant biochemist
Clawson, David Kay orthopedic surgeon
Cochran, Lewis W. physicist, university official
†Cole, Henry Philip educational psychologist
Cone, Carl Bruce history educator
Cremers, Clifford John mechanical engineering educator
Davenport, Guy Mattison, Jr. author, retired educator
David, Miriam Lang physician
Davis, Vincent political science educator
DeLong, Lance Eric physics educator, researcher
DeLuca, Patrick Phillip pharmaceutical scientist, educator, administrator
Diana, John Nicholas physiologist
†Diedrich, Donald Frank pharmacology educator
Dittert, Lewis William pharmacy educator
Drudge, Harold J. veterinary educator
Eberle, Todd Bailey lawyer, educator
Ehmann, William Donald chemistry educator
†Eller, Ronald D historian, educator
Ettensohn, Frank Robert geologist, educator
Forester, Karl S. federal judge
Frazier, Donald Tha, Sr. medical educator, scientist, researcher
Friedell, Gilbert Hugo pathologist, hospital administrator, educator, cancer center director
Frye, Wilbur Wayne soil science educator, researcher, administrator
Gable, Robert Elledy real estate investment company executive
Gilliam, M(elvin) Randolph urologist, educator
Girone, Vito Anthony architect, city planner, educator emeritus, artist
Glenn, James Francis urologist, educator
Goldman, Alvin Lee lawyer, educator
Grabau, Larry J. physiologist, educator
Hagan, Wallace Woodrow geologist
†Hagen, Michael Dale medical educator, family practice researcher
Hamburg, Joseph physician, educator
†Hanson, Mark Todt engineering mechanics educator
Heffelbower, Dwight Earl engineering services company executive
Heitzman, Robert Edward retired materials handling equipment manufacturing company executive
Hemenway, Robert E. university administrator, language educator
Henderson, Hubert Platt fine arts association executive
Henson, Glenda Maria newspaper writer
Hochstrasser, Donald Lee cultural anthropologist, community health and public administration educator
Holsinger, James Wilson, Jr. physician
†Houlihan, Ed association executive
Hultman, Charles William economics educator
Jewell, Robert Burnett engineering company executive
Jokl, Ernst F. retired physician
Kasperbauer, Michael John plant physiology educator, researcher
Keeling, Larry Dale journalist
Kelly, Timothy Michael newspaper editor
Kern, Bernard Donald retired educator, physicist
†Knapp, Frederick Whiton entomologist, educator
†Kuc, Joseph A. educator, consultant
Landon, John William minister, social worker, educator
Lewis, Thomas Proctor legal educator
†Liu, Keh-Fei Frank physicist, educator
†Lodder, Robert Andrew chemistry and pharmaceutics educator
Logan, Joyce Polley education educator
Madden, Edward Harry philosopher, educator
Manley, Margaret Edwards primary education educator
Markesbery, William R. neurology and pathology educator, physician
Mason, Ellsworth Goodwin librarian
Mercer, Leonard Preston, II biochemistry educator
Miller, Harry B(enjamin) lawyer
†Miller, Pamela Gundersen mayor
Mink, John Robert dental educator
Mitchell, George Ernest, Jr. animal scientist, educator
Mostert, Paul Stallings mathematician, educator
Nasar, Syed Abu electrical engineering educator
†Newton, John Thomas utility company executive
Nyere, Robert Alan banker
Oberst, Paul law educator
Owens, Lewis E. newspaper executive
Parks, Harold Francis anatomist, educator
Pass, Bobby Clifton entomology educator
Perdue, Theda history educator, author
Perreiah, Alan Richard philosophy educator
Phillips, Henry Alan communications executive
Philpott, James Alvin, Jr. lawyer
Pirone, Thomas Pascal plant pathology educator
Pitino, Richard college basketball coach
Robinson, Thomas Christopher academic administrator, educator
Rodriguez, Juan Guadalupe entomologist
Romanowitz, Byron Foster architect, engineer
Sands, Donald Edgar chemistry educator
Schaeffer, Edwin Frank, Jr. lawyer
Schneider, George William horticulturist, educator, researcher
Scruggs, John Dudley landscape architect
Sendlein, Lyle V. A. geology educator
Shepherd, Robert James plant pathology researcher, educator
Shipley, David Elliott university dean, lawyer
Sineath, Timothy Wayne librarian, educator, university administrator
Singletary, Otis Arnold, Jr. university president emeritus
Steele, Earl Larsen electrical engineering educator
Stober, William John, II economics educator
Straus, Robert behavioral sciences educator
Tauchert, Theodore Richmond mechanical engineer, educator
Tietz, Norbert Wolfgang clinical chemistry educator, administrator
Timoney, Peter Joseph veterinarian, virologist, educator, consultant
Traynor, Harry Sheehy engineering consultant
†Turner, Larry William educator
Ulmer, Shirley Sidney political science educator, researcher, consultant
Varellas, Sandra Motte judge
Walker, John Neal agricultural engineering educator
Wallace, Donald Querk architect, civil engineer
Warth, Robert Douglas history educator
Wethington, Charles T., Jr. academic administrator
†Whitley, Michael R. utilities executive
Williams, James Kendrick bishop
Willis, Paul Allen librarian
Worell, Judith P. psychologist, educator
Young, Paul Ray medical board executive, physician
Zechman, Fred William, Jr. physiologist, educator, administrator

London
†Coffman, Jennifer B. federal judge
Early, Jack Jones college administrator
Siler, Eugene Edward, Jr. federal judge
Unthank, G. Wix federal judge

Louisville
Aberson, Leslie Donald lawyer
†Abramson, Jerry mayor
†Ackerson, Jon W. lawyer, state senator
Allen, Charles Mengel federal judge
Andrews, Billy Franklin pediatrician, educator
Andrews, James Edgar church official, minister
Ardery, Joseph Lord lawyer
Ardery, Philip Pendleton lawyer
Aronoff, George Rodger medicine and pharmacology educator
†Ayotte, Robert C. metal products executive
Bailey, Irving Widmer, II insurance holding company executive
Baron, Martin Raymond psychology educator
Baxter, James William, III insurance and investment executive
Becker, Gail Roselyn museum director
Belanger, William Joseph chemist, polymer applications consultant
†Benfield, Ann Kolb lawyer
Berman, Edward Henry education educator
Bingham, George Barry, Jr. publishing and broadcasting executive
Bingham, Walter D. retired minister
Boggs, Danny Julian federal judge
†Bow, Stephen Tyler, Jr. insurance company executive
Brennan, William Bernard, Jr. small business owner
Brockwell, Charles Wilbur, Jr. history educator
Brown, Owsley, II diversified consumer products company executive
†Brown, Timothy Charles manufacturing company executive, accountant
Brown, William Lee Lyons, Jr. consumer products company executive
Bryant, Oscar Sims, Jr. investment advisor
Bujake, John Edward, Jr. beverage company executive
Bullard, Claude Earl newspaper, commercial printing and radio and television executive
Burse, Raymond Malcolm lawyer
Callen, Jeffrey Phillip dermatologist, educator
Carpenter, Marj Collier news director
Chancey, Malcolm B., Jr. bank executive
Clark, John Hallett, III consulting engineering executive
†Clements, Kerry religious organization administrator
†Coffin, John religious organization administrator
Coggins, Homer Dale retired hospital administrator
Cohn, David V(alor) biochemistry educator
Conner, Stewart Edmund lawyer
Cornelius, Wayne Anderson engineering technology educator, consultant
Cowan, Frederic Joseph lawyer
Cranor, John food service executive
Crum, Denny Edwin (Denzel Crum) nonprofessional basketball coach
Cybulski, Joanne Karen nutritionist, diabetes educator
†Dale, Judy Ries religious organization administrator
†Danzl, Daniel Frank emergency physician
Daulton, David Coleman actuary
Davenport, Gwen (Mrs. John Davenport) author
Davidson, Gordon Byron lawyer
Davidson, Michael Walker energy company executive
Davis, Finis E. business executive
Davis, Harry Scott, Jr. banker
†Deering, Ronald Franklin librarian, minister
DeVries, William Castle surgeon, educator
†Drury, Ralph Leon newspaper executive
Dudley, George Ellsworth lawyer
Early, Glen Alan biology educator
Edwards, Grace Coleman librarian
Eighmey, Douglas Joseph, Jr. hospital administrator
Ekstrom, William Ferdinand college administrator
†Ellison, William Louie, Jr. newspaper editor, journalist
†Ensign, David James law librarian
Ewald, Robert Charles lawyer
†Ferguson, Duncan Sheldon education administrator
Ferguson, Jo McCown lawyer
Fitch, Howard Mercer lawyer, labor arbitrator, travelogue exhibitor and producer
Ford, Gordon Buell, Jr. English language and linguistics educator, author, hospital industry financial management executive
Frazier, Owsley B. beverage company executive
Garcia, Rafael Jorge chemical engineer
Garfinkel, Herbert university official
Garretson, Henry David neurosurgeon
†Gillis, Frank Lauren insurance executive
†Granady, Juanita H. religious organization administrator
Gray, Laman A., Jr. thoracic surgeon, educator
Gummere, Walter Cooper educator, consultant
†Hale, Hershel David bank executive
†Hale, Roger W. utilities company executive
Hanley, Thomas Richard engineering educator
Hawpe, David Vaughn newspaper editor, journalist
Haynes, Douglas Martin physician, educator
Hazen, Elizabeth Frances special education educator
Heiden, Charles Kenneth former army officer, metals company executive
†Henderson, Harriet librarian
Hendricks, William Lawrence theology educator
Heyburn, John G., II federal judge
†Higgins, Walter M., III electric power industry executive
Hower, Frank Beard, Jr. retired banker
†Hoye, Robert Earl higher education educator, health care consultant
Huang, Kee Chang pharmacology educator, physician
Hull, John Thomas, Jr. life insurance company executive
Hunter, William Jay, Jr. lawyer
†Jenkins, C(arle) Frederick religious organization executive, minister, lawyer
Johnson, Alan Arthur physicist, educator
Jones, David Allen health facility executive
Keeney, Arthur Hail physician, educator
Kelley, Noble Henry former psychologist, educator
Kelly, Thomas Cajetan archbishop
Kinsey, William Charles building materials company executive
†Kirkpatrick, Clifton minister, church administrator
Kleinert, Harold Earl plastic surgery educator
Klotter, John Charles retired legal educator
Kmetz, Donald R. academic administrator
Lansing, Allan Meredith cardiovascular surgeon, educator
Lay, Norvie Lee legal educator
Lomicka, William Henry investor
Lonergan, Jeanette Nancy nurse
Luber, Thomas J(ulian) lawyer
†Lundy, Mary Ann religious organization administrator
Luvisi, Lee concert pianist
MacKinnon, Cyrus Leland retired newspaper executive
Maddox, Robert Lytton lawyer
Martin, Boyce Ficklen, Jr. federal judge
McCormick, Steven Thomas insurance company executive
†McIntyre, Robert Donald publishing executive, consultant
Melnykovych, Andrew O. journalist
Meredith, Ronald Edward federal judge
Miller, John Ulman minister, author
Miller, Robert Henry English educator
Monroe, Burt Leavelle, Jr. biology educator
Morrin, Peter Patrick museum director
Mountz, Wade retired health service management executive
†Mueller, James E. agricultural products executive
†Neely, J. Randall public relations executive
Neustadt, David Harold physician
Nystrand, Raphael Owens university dean, educator

Parkins, Frederick Milton *dental educator, university dean*
Peden, Katherine Graham *industrial consultant*
Peebles, Robert Alvin *horse breed registry executive*
Pettyjohn, Shirley Ellis *lawyer, real estate executive*
†Pickle, James C. *hospital administrator*
Polk, Hiram Carey, Jr. *surgeon, educator*
Porter, Henry Homes, Jr. *investor*
Prough, Russell Allen *biochemistry educator*
Quinn, Joseph Michael *coatings industry executive*
Ratterman, David Burger *lawyer*
Ray, Randy Wayne *museum director*
†Rice, Jerry W. *insurance company executive*
Roberts, J. Wendell *federal judge*
Rollo, F. David *hospital management company executive, radiology educator*
Rosky, Theodore Samuel *insurance company executive*
Royer, Robert Lewis *retired utility company executive*
†Runyon, Keith Leslie *lawyer, newspaper editor*
St. Clair, Robert Neal *English language and linguistics educator*
Sandefur, Thomas Edwin, Jr. *tobacco company executive*
†Schaefer, J. Scott *religious organization administrator*
Schmidt, Stephen Robert *lawyer*
Schwab, John Joseph *psychiatrist, educator*
Shaver, Jesse Milton, Jr. *manufacturing company executive*
Shoemaker, Gradus Lawrence *chemist, educator*
Silverthorn, Robert Sterner, Jr. *lawyer*
Simpson, Charles R., III *federal judge*
Skees, William Leonard, Jr. *lawyer*
Smillie, Thomson John *opera producer*
†Smith, Jeffrey Coursen *architect*
Smith, Lawrence Leighton *conductor*
†Smith, Wayne T. *healthcare company executive*
Speed, John Sackett *insurance company executive*
Stosberg, David Thomas *bankruptcy judge*
†Strachan, Gladys *executive director*
Straus, R(obert) James *lawyer*
Swain, Donald Christie *university president, history educator*
Talbott, Ben Johnson, Jr. *lawyer*
Tallichet, Leon Edgar *retired publishing executive, financial administrator*
Taylor, Kenneth Grant *chemistry educator*
Taylor, Robert Lewis *academic administrator*
Teller, David Norton *neurochemist*
†Thompson, James *distilleries and importing company executive*
†Tinsley, Tuck, III *book publishing executive*
Towles, Donald Blackburn *retired newspaper publishing executive*
†Turner, Gene *religious organization administrator*
Uhde, George Irvin *physician*
†Vandewater, David *hospital administrator*
VanMeter, Vandelia L. *library director*
Volz, Marlin Milton *legal educator*
Waddell, William Joseph *pharmacologist, toxicologist*
Ward, Jasper Dudley, III *architect*
Ward, Thomas Leon *engineering educator*
Weisskopf, Bernard *pediatrician, child behavior, development and genetics specialist, educator*
†Wenz, Rodney E. *public relations executive*
Wingenbach, Gregory Charles *minister, religious-ecumenical agency director*
Woolsey, Frederick William *retired journalist, music critic*
Wyatt, Wilson Watkins *lawyer*
Zimmerman, Gideon K. *minister*
Zimmerman, Thom Jay *ophthalmologist, educator*

Mayfield
Harris, Isaac Henson *university dean*

Midway
Clay, Robert N. *thoroughbred breeder*

Morehead
Besant, Larry Xon *librarian, administrator, consultant*
Herron, James Dudley *chemist, educator*

Murray
Hunt, Charles Brownlow, Jr. *university dean, musician*
Hunt, Mark Alan *museum director*
Kurth, Ronald James *university president, retired naval officer*
Pogue, Forrest Carlisle *retired historian*

Nazareth
†Dundon, Mark Walden *hospital administrator*

Newport
Siverd, Robert Joseph *lawyer*

Owensboro
Best, Robert Wayne *gas transmission company executive, lawyer*
Carneal, James William *former natural gas corporation executive*
Cocklin, Kim Roland *lawyer*
Eaton, Clara Barbour *librarian*
Hood, Mary Bryan *museum director, painter*
Hulse, George Althouse *steel company executive*
McRaith, John Jeremiah *bishop*
†Wright, Patrick E. *grain company executive*

Paducah
Broady, Fannie Marie *vocational school educator*
Johnstone, Edward H. *federal judge*
Walden, Robert Thomas *physicist, consultant*
Westberry, Billy Murry *lawyer*

Pewee Valley
Gill, George Norman *newspaper publishing company executive*

Pikeville
Hood, Joseph M. *federal judge*

Pineville
Whittaker, Bill Douglas *minister*

Port Royal
Berry, Wendell *author, English educator*

Prospect
Dunbar, Wallace Huntington *manufacturing company executive*
Helm, Hugh Barnett *retired judge*

Richmond
Branson, Branley Allan *biology educator*
Burkhart, Robert Edward *English language educator*
Franke, Charles H(enry) *mathematics educator, department chair*
Funderburk, H(enry) Hanly, Jr. *college president*
Kirkpatrick, Dorothy Louise *education educator, program coordinator*
Martin, Robert Richard *emeritus college president, former senator*
Shearon, Forrest Bedford *humanities educator*
Witt, Robert Wayne *English educator*

Russell
Crimmins, Sean T(homas) *oil company executive*

Saint Catherine
Collins, Martha Layne *college president, former governor*

Scottsville
Wilcher, Larry Keith *lawyer*

Somerset
Jasper, Patrick Lee *pediatrician, medical association executive*

Trappist
Hart, Patrick Joseph *editor*

Versailles
Freehling, William Wilhartz *historian, educator*

West Liberty
†Blevins, Walter, Jr. *dentist, state legislator*

Wilmore
†Faupel, David William *minister, theological librarian*
Kinlaw, Dennis Franklin *clergyman, society executive*
McKenna, David Loren *seminary president, clergyman*

LOUISIANA

Alexandria
Bolton, Robert Harvey *banker*
†Brady, James Joseph *lawyer*
Brocato, Joseph Myron *architect*
Gist, Howard Battle, Jr. *lawyer*
†Hargrove, Robert Jefferson, Jr. *bishop*
Keller, Christoph, Jr. *bishop*
Little, F. A., Jr. *federal judge*
Scott, Nauman S. *federal judge*
Smith, Joe Dorsey, Jr. *newspaper executive*

Arnaudville
LaGrange, Claire Mae *special education educator*

Baker
Moody, Lamon Lamar, Jr. *civil engineer*
Roberson, Patt Foster *mass communications educator*

Baton Rouge
Acar, Yalcin Bekir *civil engineer, soil remediation technology executive, educator*
Aghazadeh, Fereydoun *industrial engineer, educator*
Arceneaux, William *historian, educator, association official*
Arman, Ara *civil engineering educator*
†Arveson, Raymond G. *state superintendent*
Bayard, Alton Ernest, III *lawyer*
Beckner, Donald Lee *lawyer*
Bedeian, Arthur George *business educator*
Berg, Irwin August *psychology educator*
Besch, Everett Dickman *veterinarian, university dean emeritus*
Blackman, John Calhoun, IV *lawyer*
Booth, George Geoffrey *finance educator*
Boyce, Bert Roy *university dean, library and information science educator*
Bray, George August *physician, scientist, educator*
†Brickman, Kenneth Alan *state lottery executive*
Brockway, William Robert *architect*
Brown, Dale Duward *basketball coach*
Brown, James H., Jr. *state official, lawyer*
†Brun, Judith *principal*
Bybee, Jay Scott *lawyer, educator*
Byrd, Warren Edgar, II *lawyer*
Caffey, H(orace) Rouse *academic administrator, consultant*
Campbell, Lyle Richard *linguistics educator*
Chen, Peter Pin-Shan *electrical engineering and computer science educator, data processing executive*
Cherry, William Ashley *surgeon, state health officer*
†Christian, Frederick Ade *entomologist, physiologist, biology educator*
Clausen, Sally Ilene *state official*
Coates, Jesse *retired chemical engineer*
Cole, Luther Francis *state supreme court associate justice*
Coleman, James Malcolm *marine geology educator*
Constantinides, Dinos Demetrios (Constantine Constantinides) *music educator, composer, conductor*
Cooper, William James, Jr. *history educator*
Copping, Allen Anthony *university president*
Cox, Hollis Utah *veterinarian*
Cundy, Vic Arnold *mechanical engineer, educator*
Dalrymple, Margaret Fisher *university press editor, writer*
†Dardenne, John Leigh, Jr. *lawyer*
†Davidge, Robert Cunninghame, Jr. *hospital administrator*
Davis, William Eugene *university administrator*
Desbrandes, Robert *petroleum engineering educator, consultant*
Desmond, John Jacob *architect*
†Dimos, Jimmy *state representative*
Duffy, John *history educator*
Edgeworth, Robert Joseph *classical languages educator*
Edwards, Edwin Washington *governor*
†Flournoy, Melissa *state legislator*
French, Dennis Donald *veterinary medicine educator, researcher*
†Fussell, Bonnie Gene *lottery corporation executive*
Geiselman, Paula Jeanne *psychologist*
Giles, William Elmer *journalism educator, former newspaper editor*
Gilmore, Clarence Percy *writer, magazine editor*
Glissant, Edouard Mathieu *French language educator, writer*
Goldstein, Jerome Arthur *mathematics educator*
Gopu, Vijaya K.A. *engineer, consultant*
†Greer, Robert Stephenson *insurance company executive*
Griffin, G. Lee *banker*
Guedry, Leo J. *agricultural economics educator*
†Hancock, Paul Byron *headmaster*
Hansel, William *biology educator*
†Hatfield, Jack Daniel *newspaper editor*
Hawkland, William Dennis *law educator*
Haynes, Leonard L., Jr. *philosophy educator, clergyman*
Hazel, Joseph Ernest *geology educator, stratigrapher*
Hughes, Alfred Clifton *bishop*
Ieyoub, Richard Phillip *state attorney general*
Jay, James Albert *insurance company executive*
†Jenkins, Louis (Woody) *television executive, state legislator*
Lambremont, Edward Nelson, Jr. *nuclear science educator*
Lamonica, P(aul) Raymond *lawyer, academic administrator, educator*
Landolt, Arlo Udell *astronomer, educator*
Larkin, John Montague *microbiology educator, researcher*
Lee, Betty Redding *architect*
Leonard, Paul Haralson *retired lawyer*
Liuzzo, Joseph Anthony *food science educator*
Lucas, Fred Vance *pathology educator, university administrator*
Madden, David *author*
Manship, Charles Phelps, Jr. *newspaper executive, retired association executive*
Manship, Douglas *broadcast and newspaper executive*
Marshak, Alan Howard *electrical engineer, educator*
Mathews, Sharon Walker *ballet educator, artistic director*
Mayfield, William Stephen *law educator*
Mc Cameron, Fritz Allen *university administrator*
Mc Clendon, William Hutchinson, III *lawyer*
Mc Glynn, Sean Patrick *physical chemist, educator*
McKeithen, Walter Fox *secretary of state*
McLaughlin, Edward *chemical engineering educator, dean*
McLindon, Gerald Joseph *planning and environmental design consultant, university dean emeritus*
Moody, Gene Byron *engineering executive, small business owner*
Moyse, Hermann, Jr. *banker*
Norem, Richard Frederick, Sr. *musician, music educator*
O'Connell, Robert Francis *physics educator*
Oden, William Bryant *bishop, educator*
Olney, James *English language educator*
Parker, John Victor *federal judge*
Patrick, William Hardy, Jr. *wetland biogeochemist, educator, laboratory director*
Patterson, Charles Darold *librarian, educator*
Phillabaum, Leslie Ervin *publisher*
†Phills, Bobby Ray *dean, agricultural research director*
†Pike, Ralph Webster *chemical engineer, educator, university official*
Polozola, Frank Joseph *federal judge*
Pope, David E. *geologist, micropaleontologist*
Prestage, James Jordan *university chancellor*
Pryor, William Austin *chemistry educator*
†Pugh, George Willard *legal educator*
Rabideau, Peter Wayne *university dean, chemistry educator*
†Rayburn, B. B. *state senator, farmer*
Reich, Robert Sigmund *retired landscape architect*
†Reilly, Sean E. *cable company executive*
†Richard, John Benard *library director*
Riopelle, Arthur Jean *psychologist*
Robertson, George Leven *retired association executive*
Robinson, Bert Kris *lawyer*
Roider, Karl Andrew, Jr. *history educator, university dean*
Schwegmann, Melinda *state official*
Schwing, Charles E. *architect*
†Shaw, Richard Francis *fisheries administrator, oceanography educator*
Shih, Jason Cheng *architecture and engineering educator and consultant, university director*
Siegel, Laurence *human resources executive, former psychology educator*
Simmons, Dolores Brown *finance officer, accountant*
Smith, David Jeddie *American literature educator*
Smyth, David John *economist*
Soderbergh, Peter Andrew *educator*
Stanford, Donald Elwin *English educator, editor, poet, critic*
†Stopher, Peter Robert *civil and transportation engineering educator, consultant*
†Swaggart, Jimmy Lee *evangelist, gospel singer*
Timmons, Edwin O'Neal *psychologist*
Traynham, James Gibson *chemist, educator*
Tucker, Shirley Lois Cotter *botany educator, researcher*
†Turner, Bert S. *construction executive*
Urban, Gilbert William *banker*
West, Philip William *chemistry educator*
West, Robert Cooper *geography educator*
Wheeler, Otis Bullard *academic administrator, educator emeritus*
Williams, Hulen Brown *former university dean*
Williamson, William Floyd, Jr. *architect*
Witcher, Robert Campbell *bishop*
Woodin, Martin Dwight *retired university system president*
Yiannopoulos, Athanassios Nicholas *legal educator*

Belle Chasse
†Arimura, Akira *biomedical research laboratory administrator, educator*

Benton
Dunnihoo, Dale Russell *physician, medical educator*

Boyce
Chilton, St. John Poindexter *former plant pathology educator, farm owner*

Carencro
Clark, George Bryan *geophysicist*

Covington
†Bankston, Terry *school system administrator*
Blossman, Alfred Rhody, Jr. *banker*
Files, Mark Willard *business and financial consultant*
†Gerone, Peter John *microbiologist, research institute administrator*
Roberts, James Allen *urologist*
†Stroup, Sheila Tierney *columnist*

Deridder
Coquilla, Beatriz Hordista *dermatologist, army officer*

Eunice
Rogers, Donald Onis *language educator*

Franklin
Fairchild, Phyllis Elaine *counselor*

Geismar
Coombs, Douglas A. L. *chemical company executive*

Grambling
Robinson, Eddie Gay *college football coach*
†Wilkerson, Pinkie Carolyn *state legislator, lawyer*

Gretna
Calhoun, Milburn *publishing executive, rare book dealer, physician*
Lupin, Ellis Ralph *physician, lawyer, coroner*

Hammond
Cook, Myrtle *special education educator*
Hejtmancik, Milton Rudolph *medical educator*
Kemp, John Randolph *journalist, author*
Matheny, Tom Harrell *lawyer*
Parker, Clea Edward *university president*
Smith, Grant Warren, II *university administrator, physical sciences educator*
Thorburn, James Alexander *humanities educator*

Harahan
†Bowler, Shirley *state legislator*

Harvey
Romagosa, Elmo Lawrence *clergyman, retired editor*

Houma
Boudreaux, Warren Louis *retired bishop*
†Saia, Louis P., III *transportation executive*

Kenner
Cook, Willie Chunn *elementary education educator*
Scherich, Edward Baptiste *retired diversified company executive*
Siebel, Mathias Paul *mechanical engineer*

La Place
†Landry, Ronald Jude *lawyer, state senator*

Lacombe
Hendricks, Donald Duane *librarian*

Lafayette
Andrew, Catherine Vige *elementary education educator*
Burnam, Paul Wayne *accountant, educator*
Carstens, Jane Ellen *library science educator*
Chieri, Pericle Adriano Carlo *educator, consulting mechanical and aeronautical engineer, naval architect*
†Clement, James Barney *oil company executive*
Davis, William Eugene *federal judge*
Doherty, Rebecca Feeney *federal judge*
Domingue, Emery *consulting engineering company executive*
Duhe, John Malcolm, Jr. *federal judge*
Dur, Philip Francis *political science educator emeritus, retired foreign service officer*
Haik, Richard T., Sr. *federal judge*
Heatherly, Henry Edward *mathematics educator*
Lenox, Charles N(ewton), Jr. *newspaper editor*
Leon, Benjamin Joseph *electrical engineering educator, consultant*
Mickel, Joseph Thomas *lawyer*
Nolan, Paul Thomas *retired English and humanities educator*
Poe, (Lydia) Virginia *reading educator*
Shaw, John Malach *federal judge*
†Small, George M. *oil company executive*
†Stewart, Robert E. *ecological research director*
Stuart, Walter Bynum, III *banker*

Lake Charles
Aranow, Peter Jones *service company executive*
Beam, James C. (Jim Beam) *editor, newspaper*
Butler, Robert Olen *writer, educator*
†Cox, James Joseph *lawyer, state senator*
†Drez, David Jacob, Jr. *orthopaedic surgeon, educator*
Everett, John Prentis, Jr. *lawyer*
Hebert, Robert D. *academic administrator*
Hunter, Edwin Ford, Jr. *federal judge*
McHale, Robert Michael *lawyer*
Shaddock, William Edward, Jr. *lawyer*
Speyrer, Jude *bishop*
Trimble, James T., Jr. *federal judge*

Leesville
Boren, Lynda Sue *small business owner, educator*

Luling
Smith, Raymond Kermit *former educational administrator*

Mandeville
Christian, John Catlett, Jr. *lawyer*
†Deano, Edward Joseph, Jr. *lawyer, state legislator*

Mansfield
Smelley, Joyce Marie *special education supervisor*

Marksville
†Riddle, Charles Addison, III *state legislator, lawyer*

Metairie
Andersen, Morten football player
†Benson, Jerome automotive sales executive
Benson, Tom professional football executive
Best, Eugene Crawford, Jr. musician
Brisolara, Ashton substance abuse and employee assistance programs consultant
Colbert, Charles Ralph architect
Costello, Joseph Mark, III broadcasting and motion picture executive
Falco, Maria Josephine political scientist, academic administrator
Finks, James Edward professional football club executive, consultant
Flake, Leone Elizabeth special education educator
†Gauthier, Wendell Haynes lawyer
†Jackson, Rickey professional football player
†Johnson, Beth Michael principal
Johnson, Vaughan football player
Krauss, Steven James clothing executive
†McShan, Clyde Griffin, II financial executive
Mills, Samuel Davis, Jr. professional football player
Mora, James Ernest professional football coach
Murphy, Alvin Leo educational administrator
†Roaf, William professional football player
†Turnbull, Renaldo professional football player
Walsh, Maurice David, Jr. former librarian, business executive

Minden
†Doerge, Everett Gail retired school system administrator, congressman

Monroe
Curry, Robert Lee, III lawyer
Jones, Emma Jean principal
†Post, Glen Fleming, III telecommunications executive
Sartor, Daniel Ryan, Jr. lawyer

Napoleonville
†Gunnell, William N. school system administrator

Natchitoches
Alost, Robert Allen university executive
Brittain, Jack Oliver lawyer
Egan, Shirley Anne retired nursing educator

New Iberia
†Cavalier, David J. school system administrator
Henton, Willis Ryan bishop
†Romero, Craig F. state senator, cattle farmer

New Orleans
Abad, Rosario Dalida elementary educator
Acomb, Robert Bailey, Jr. lawyer, educator
Agrawal, Krishna Chandra pharmacology educator
Allen, F(rank) C(linton), Jr. manufacturing executive, lawyer
Allen, Gary Curtiss geology educator
Alsobrook, Henry Bernis, Jr. lawyer
Ambrose, Stephen Edward history educator, author
†Amoss, W. James, Jr. shipping company executive
†Amoss, Walter James, III editor
†Andrews, Bethlehem Kottes research chemist
Andrus, Gerald Louis utilities holding company consultant
Arnof, Ian banker
Ates, J. Robert lawyer
Azaceta, Luis Cruz artist
Bachmann, Richard Arthur oil company executive
†Bajoie, Diana E. state legislator
†Ball, Millie (Mildred Porteous Ball) editor, journalist
Barham, Mack Elwin lawyer, educator
†Barkate, John Albert microbiologist, food scientist
Barnett, Walter Michael lawyer
Baron, John Herschel music educator, musicologist
Barry, Francis Julian, Jr. lawyer
Barthelemy, Sidney John mayor
Beard, Elizabeth Letitia physiologist, educator
Beason, Amos Theodore banker
Beer, Peter Hill federal judge
Benerito, Ruth Rogan (Mrs. Frank H. Benerito) chemist
Benjamin, Edward Bernard, Jr. lawyer
Bennett, Joan Wennstrom biology educator
Berenson, Gerald Sanders physician
†Berlin, Charles I. audiologist, scientist
Bernstein, David Howard lawyer
Bernstein, Joseph lawyer
Bieck, Robert Barton, Jr. lawyer
Birtel, Frank Thomas mathematician, philosopher, educator
Blitch, James Buchanan architect
†Blitch, Ronald Buchanan architect
Boudreaux, Kenneth Justin finance and economics educator, consultant
Brannan, William urologist, educator
Brian, A(lexis) Morgan, Jr. lawyer
Bricker, Harvey Miller anthropology educator
Bricker, Victoria Reifler anthropology educator
Brown, James Barrow bishop
Buccino, Salvatore George physics educator
Bullard, Edgar John, III museum director
†Butler, Edward Scannell organization executive
Calogero, Pascal Frank, Jr. state supreme court chief justice
Campbell, Margaret M. academic dean
Carr, Patrick E. judge
Carter, James Clarence university administrator
Carter, Rebecca Davilene surgical oncology educator
Cassibry, Fred James lawyer, retired federal court judge
Cheatwood, Roy Clifton lawyer
Christman, John Francis science administrator, former university administrator
Claverie, Philip deVilliers lawyer
Clement, Edith Brown federal judge
Cody, Wilmer St. Clair educational administrator
Cohen, Joseph English literature educator, writer, business owner
Cohn, Isidore, Jr. surgeon, educator
Coleman, James Julian lawyer
Combe, David Alfred law librarian, educator
Combe, John Clifford, Jr. lawyer
†Connolly, Edward S. neurologist
Cook, Samuel DuBois university president, political scientist
Cook, Victor Joseph, Jr. marketing educator, consultant
†Copelin, Sherman Nathaniel, Jr. entrepreneur, business executive
Corey, Orlin Russell publisher, editor
Correro, Anthony James, III lawyer
Corrigan, James John, Jr. pediatrician
Corrigan, Robert Emmett psychologist
Cosenza, Arthur George opera director
Couch, Harvey Crowley, III law educator
Couhig, Robert Emmet lawyer
D'Ambrosia, Robert Dominick orthopaedic educator
Daniels, Robert Sanford psychiatrist, medical school dean
Davis, Verda Merlyn nursing educator
Deasy, William John construction, marine dredging, engineering and mining company executive
Defenbaugh, Richard Eugene marine ecologist
Denegre, George lawyer
Dennery, Moise Waldhorn lawyer, educator
Dennis, James Leon state supreme court justice
Dickinson, Catherine Schatz microbiologist
Dittmann, Albert Stephen, Jr. lawyer
Dixon, Irma Muse state commissioner, former state legislator, social worker
†Dodds, Richard Crofton theater critic
Doley, Harold Emanuel, Jr. securities company executive
Domer, Floyd Ray pharmacologist, educator
Domingue, Gerald James microbiology, immunology and urology educator, researcher, clinical bacteriologist
Duffy, John Charles psychiatrist, physician
Duncan, Margaret Caroline physician
Duplantier, Adrian Guy federal judge
Dyment, Paul George adolescent medicine educator
Easson, William McAlpine psychiatrist
Edmonson, Munro Sterling anthropologist, educator
Edwards, James Kennedy quality assurance director, safety-fire protection engineer
Epstein, Arthur William physician, educator
Ewing, Channing Lester biomechanics researcher, corporate executive
Fagaly, William Arthur curator
Fantaci, James Michael lawyer
Feldman, Martin L. C. federal judge
Ferguson, Charles Austin retired newspaper editor
Filson, Ronald Coulter architect, educator, college dean
Fine, David Jeffrey hospital executive, educator, consultant, lecturer
Fingerman, Milton biologist, educator
Fisher, James William medical educator, pharmacologist
Force, Robert legal educator
†Forman, L. Ronald park and zoological garden administrator
Fountain, Peter Dewey, Jr. (Pete Fountain) clarinetist
Franco, Philip Anthony lawyer
†Frantz, Phares Albert architect
Freeman, Montine McDaniel museum trustee
Freudenberger, Herman retired economics educator
Friedlander, Miles Herbert ophthalmologist
Friedman, Joel William law educator
Frohlich, Edward David physician
García Oller, José Luis neurosurgeon
Gathright, John Byron, Jr. colon and rectal surgeon, educator
Gelfand, M. David lawyer, educator
Gelpi, C. James (Jim Gelpi) lawyer
Gerber, Michael Albert pathologist, researcher
Glasgow, Vaughn Leslie museum curator and administrator
Goins, Richard Anthony lawyer, educator
Gonzales, Brother Alexis (Joseph M. Gonzales) theater and communications educator
Gordon, Joseph Elwell university official, educator
Gottlieb, A(braham) Arthur medical educator, biotechnology corporate executive
Grau, Shirley Ann (Mrs. James Kern Feibleman) writer
†Greene, John Frederick oil company executive, geologist
Greenleaf, Richard Edward Latin American history educator
Hall, Luther Egbert, Jr. lawyer
Hamlin, James Turner, III university dean, physician
Hansel, Stephen Arthur holding company executive
†Harper, Robert John, Jr. chemist, researcher
†Hassenboehler, Donalyn principal
Healy, George William, III lawyer
Heebe, Frederick Jacob Regan federal judge
Hewitt, Robert Lee surgeon, educator
Hinton, James Forrest, Jr. lawyer
Howson, Robert E. construction company executive
Huot, Rachel Irene cell biologist
Hyman, Albert Lewis cardiologist
Ivens, Mary Sue microbiologist, mycologist
Jacobsen, Thomas Warren archaeologist, educator
Jaffe, Bernard Michael surgeon
Johnsen, Erik Frithjof transportation executive
Johnson, Lee Harnie dean, educator
Jung, Rodney C. internist, academic administrator
Kastin, Abba Jeremiah endocrinologist, researcher
Keller, Thomas Clements lawyer
Kelly, Eamon Michael university president
Kilanowski, Michael Charles, Jr. oil, natural gas, minerals exploration company executive, lawyer
Kline, David Gellinger neurosurgery educator
Krementz, Edward Thomas surgeon
Laborde, Alden James oil company executive
Laborde, John Peter international energy company executive
Lambert, Olaf Cecil hotel executive
Lang, Erich Karl physician, radiologist
Lannes, William Joseph, III electrical engineer
Latorre, Robert George naval architecture and engineering educator
LaValle, Irving Howard decision analysis educator
Lavelle, Paul Michael lawyer
†Lee, Frank W. transportation company executive
Lee, Griff Calicutt civil engineer
Leger, Walter John, Jr. lawyer
Leinbach, Philip Eaton librarian
Le Jeune, Francis Ernest, Jr. otolaryngologist
Lemann, Thomas Berthelot lawyer
†Levell, Edward, Jr. city official
Levert, John Bertels, Jr. investment executive
†Levy, Sam consumer products company executive
Lewis, Floyd Wallace former electric utility executive
Lewy, John Edwin pediatric nephrologist
Lind, Thomas Otto utility company executive
Litwin, Martin Stanley surgeon
Livaudais, Marcel, Jr. federal judge
Lovejoy, Barbara Campbell sculptor, architectural designer
Lovett, William Anthony law and economics educator
Low, Frank Norman anatomist, educator
Lowe, Robert Charles lawyer
Luza, Radomir Vaclav historian, educator
Lykes, Joseph T., III shipping company executive
Mackin, Cooper Richerson university chancellor
Madera, Carmen Soria lawyer
Makielski, Stanislaw John, Jr. political science educator
Marcus, Bernard lawyer
Marcus, Walter F., Jr. state supreme court justice
Martin, Edward Fontaine lawyer
Martinez, Andrew Tredway lawyer
Mason, Henry Lloyd political science educator
†McCormick, Eugene F., Jr. transportation company executive
McDougal, Luther Love, III law educator
McFarland, James W. academic administrator
†McMahon, Maeve principal
McMillan, Lee Richards, II lawyer
McNamara, A. J. federal judge
†McNaughton, Eugene Eean architect, educator
Mealey, George Allan mining executive
Mentz, Henry Alvan, Jr. federal judge
Messerli, Franz Hannes cardiologist
Mickal, Abe physician
Milling, R(oswell) King bank executive, lawyer
Mintz, Albert lawyer
Mirzai, Pirooz (Victor Mirzai) architect, educator, consultant
Mitchell, Lansing Leroy federal judge
Mitchell, Michael Stuart lawyer
Moffett, James Robert oil and gas company executive
Mogabgab, William Joseph epidemiologist, educator
Molony, Michael Janssens, Jr. lawyer
Monachino, Francis Leonard music educator
Monroe, James Walter organization executive
†Morial, Marc H. mayor
†Morial, Marc Haydel lawyer, educator
†Morrell, Arthur Anthony lawyer, state legislator
Murrish, Charles Howard oil and gas exploration company executive, geologist
Navar, Luis Gabriel physiology educator, researcher
†Nelson, James Smith pathologist, educator
Nice, Charles Monroe, Jr. physician, educator
Nichols, Ronald Lee surgeon, educator
Norwood, Colvin Gamble, Jr. lawyer
Nuzum, Robert Weston lawyer
Ochsner, John Lockwood thoracic-cardiovascular surgeon
Olson, Richard David psychology educator
O'Meallie, Kitty artist
O'Neal, Edgar Carl psychology educator
Orihel, Thomas Charles parasitology educator, research scientist
Ortique, Revius Oliver, Jr. judge
Osakwe, Christopher lawyer, educator
Pankey, George Atkinson physician, educator
Paolini, Gilbert literature and science educator
Phelps, Ashton, Jr. newspaper publisher
Pickering, Thomas Clifford retailing executive
Pittman, Jacquelyn mental health nurse, nursing educator
Pizer, Donald author, educator
Plaeger, Frederick Joseph, II lawyer
Platou, Joanne (Dode) museum director
Poesch, Jessie Jean art historian
Poitevent, Edward Butts, II lawyer
†Pope, John M. journalist
Purtell, Lawrence Robert lawyer
Purvis, George Frank, Jr. life insurance company executive
Puyau, Francis Albert physician, radiology educator
Quirk, Peter Richard engineering company executive
Rayson, Jack Henry dentist, educator, retired
Read, William Edgar army officer, engineer
Reck, Andrew Joseph philosophy educator
Reddix, Rowena Pinkie retired elementary school principal
Redmon, Harry Smith, Jr. lawyer
Remley, Theodore Phant, Jr. counselor, educator and lawyer
Richardson, Donald Edward neurosurgery educator
†Riedlinger, Brian A. principal
Rigby, Perry Gardner medical center administrator, educator, former university dean, physician
Roberts, Elliott C., Sr. hospital administrator
Roberts, John Kenneth, Jr. life insurance company executive
Roberts, Louise Nisbet philosopher
Robins, Robert Sidwar political science educator, administrator
Robinson, Phillip Dean hospital executive
Robinson, Susan Shelton human resources specialist
Rodriguez, Myrtle Mary protective service official
Roesler, Robert Harry newspaper editor
Rosen, Charles, II lawyer
Rosen, William Warren lawyer
Rosenberg, Dennis Melville Leo retired surgeon
Rosensteel, George T. physics educator, nuclear physicist
Roskoski, Robert, Jr. biochemist, educator
Salvaggio, John Edmond physician, educator
Sarpy, Leon lawyer
Schally, Andrew Victor endocrine oncologist, researcher
Schneider, George T. obstetrician-gynecologist
Schulte, Francis B. archbishop
Schwartz, Charles, Jr. federal judge
†Schwegmann, John F. consumer products comprany executive
Sear, Morey Leonard federal judge, educator
Sefcik, James Francis museum director
Sellin, Eric linguist, poet, educator
Sharma, Bhu Dev mathematics educator, researcher
Sher, Leopold Zangwill lawyer
Shinn, Clinton Wesley lawyer
Simon, H(uey) Paul lawyer
Sims, John William lawyer
Sinor, Howard Earl, Jr. lawyer
Smith, John Webster retired naval officer, company executive
Smith, Margaret Hamilton Donald physician
Snyder, Charles Aubrey lawyer
Spitzer, John J. physiologist
Stapp, Dan Ernest retired lawyer, utility executive
Steg, J(ames) L(ouis) artist
†Steinmetz, Deborah Susan interior designer
†Steinmetz, Robert Charles architect
Stephens, Richard Bernard natural resource company executive
Straumanis, John Janis, Jr. psychiatry educator
†Suggs, Carroll W. aerospace transportation executive
Sumrell, Gene research chemist
Surprenant, Mark Christopher lawyer
Tarver, Michael Keith lawyer
†Taylor, Kenneth Byron, Jr. librarian, minister, religion educator
Tewell, Joseph Robert, Jr. electrical engineer
Thompson, Annie Laura foreign language educator
Thornell, Jack Randolph photographer
Toussaint, Allen Richard recording studio executive, composer, pianist
Trapolin, Frank Winter retired insurance executive
Trostorff, Alexander Peter lawyer
Tusa, Joseph, Jr. energy company financial executive
Usdin, Gene Leonard physician, psychiatrist
Vance, Robert Patrick lawyer
Vanselow, Neal Arthur university administrator, physician
Villavaso, Stephen Donald urban planner, lawyer
Waechter, Arthur Joseph, Jr. lawyer
†Waggonner, Joseph David, III architect
Wakefield, Benton McMillin, Jr. banker
†Walk, Frank Humphrey consulting engineer
Walsh, John Joseph medical school administrator, physician
Waring, William Winburn pediatric pulmonologist, educator
Washington, Robert Orlanda university administrator, former university dean
Watson, Jack Crozier state supreme court justice
Webb, Watts Rankin surgeon
Weigel, John J. lawyer
Weill, Hans physician, educator
Weiss, Kenneth Andrew lawyer, law educator
Weiss, Thomas Edward physician
Welden, Arthur Luna biology educator
Welsh, Ronald Arthur physician, educator
White, Charles Albert, Jr. medical educator, obstetrician-gynecologist
Wicker, Veronica DiCarlo federal judge
Wilford, Walton Terry economics educator
Willenzik, David S. lawyer
Williamson, Ernest Lavone petroleum company executive
Wilson, C. Daniel, Jr. library director
Wilson, Samuel, Jr. architect
Wisdom, John Minor federal judge
Wohleber, Robert Michael treasurer
Womack, Edgar Allen, Jr. technology executive
Woodward, Ralph Lee, Jr. historian, educator
Wootan, Guy lawyer
Wright, Thomas Joe electric utility executive
Yates, Robert Doyle anatomy educator
Zimny, Marilyn Lucile anatomist, educator

New Roads
Haag, William George anthropologist, educator

Pineville
†Boswell, Bill Reeser religious organization executive
Howell, Thomas history educator
Martin, W. Terry librarian
Matthews, Betty Parker special education educator

Ruston
Barron, Randall Franklin mechanical engineer, educator, consultant
Freasier, Aileen W. special education educator
Halliburton, Lloyd Romance philology educator
Hudnall, Jarrett, Jr. management and marketing educator
Maxfield, John Edward retired university dean
Painter, Jack Timberlake civil engineer
Reneau, Daniel D. university administrator
Sale, Tom S., III financial economist, educator
Taylor, Foster Jay retired university president
†Warrington, Robert O'Neil, Jr. mechanical engineering educator and administrator, researcher
Wicker, William Walter librarian

Saint Bernard
Gilbert, Norman Sutcliffe research physician

Saint Martinville
†Durand, Sydnie Mae state legislator

Shreveport
Achee, Roland Joseph lawyer
Beaird, Charles T. publishing executive
Boyd, Clarence Elmo surgeon
Bradley, Ronald James neuroscientist
Breffeilh, Louis Andrew ophthalmologist, educator
Crissinger, Karen Denise pediatric gastroenterologist, physiologist
Darling, John Rothburn, Jr. university administrator, educator
Demopulos, Chris engineering company executive
Dilworth, Edwin Earle obstetrician, gynecologist
†Elberson, Edwin Wallace architect
Fort, Arthur Tomlinson, III physician
Friend, William Benedict bishop
Ganley, James Powell ophthalmology educator
George, Ronald Baylis physician
Greene, Dallas Whorton, Jr. fire chief
Haas, Lester Carl architect
Hall, John Whitling geography educator
Jamison, Richard Melvin virologist, educator
Jones, Ernest Edward minister, religious organization administrator
Lazarus, Allan Matthew retired newspaper editor
McDonald, John Clifton surgeon
Misra, Raghunath Prasad physician, educator
Payne, Roy Steven judge
Pederson, William David political scientist, educator
Pelton, James Rodger librarian
Politz, Henry Anthony federal judge
Ramey, Cecil Edward, Jr. lawyer
Reddy, Pratap Chandupatla cardiologist, educator, researcher
Roddey, John B(arber) (Bob Roddey) gas and oil company executive, consultant
Schober, Charles Coleman, III psychiatrist, psychoanalyst
Shelby, James Stanford cardiovascular surgeon
†Simpkins, C.O. dentist, state legislator
Snow, William Hayden retired utility company executive
Stagg, Tom federal judge
Thurmon, Theodore Francis medical educator
†Tiner, Stanley Ray business communications executive, former editor
Tullis, John Ledbetter retired wholesale distributing company executive
Walter, Donald Ellsworth federal judge
Wiener, Jacques Loeb, Jr. federal judge
Zadeck, Donald Julian oil and gas exploration company executive

Slaughter
Gremillion, Curtis Lionel, Jr. psychologist, hospital administrator, musician

Slidell
†Faust, Marilyn B. elementary school principal
Hall, Ogden Henderson allied health educator

Springhill
†Schoenrock, James V. *religious organization administrator*

Sunset
†Brinkhaus, Armand J. *lawyer, state senator*

Thibodaux
Chotigeat, Tosporn *economist, educator*
Fairchild, Joseph Virgil, Jr. *accounting educator*
Swetman, Glenn Robert *English language educator, poet*
Worthington, Janet Evans *academic director, English language educator*

West Monroe
Rentfro, Larry Dean *hospital administrator*

MAINE

Andover
Ellis, George Hathaway *retired banker and utility company executive*

Auburn
Clifford, Robert William *judge*
Farwell, Margaret Wheeler *elementary education educator*
Phillips, Charles Franklin *economic consultant*

Augusta
Adelberg, Arthur William *lawyer*
†Amero, Jane Adams *state official*
†Barth, Alvin Ludwig *state legislator*
†Berube, Georgette B. *state legislator*
Billings, Richard Whitten *association executive*
†Bustin, Beverly Miner *state legislator*
†Cahill, Pamela Lee *state legislator*
Carpenter, Michael E. *state attorney general*
Cohen, Richard Stockman *lawyer*
†Daggett, Beverly Clark *state legislator*
Diamond, G. William *secretary of state*
†Foster, Ruth Sullivan *state senator*
Gervais, Paul Nelson *foundation administrator, psychologist, public relations executive*
Hunter, Matthew *public utility executive*
†Kilkelly, Marjorie Lee *state legislator*
†Ludwig, Margaret G. *state legislator*
Martin, John L. *state legislator*
McKernan, John Rettie, Jr. *governor*
Nickerson, John Mitchell *political science educator*
†Phillips, Joseph Robert *museum director*
Roberts, Donald Albert *advertising, public relations, marketing and media consultant*
Sewell, Dwight A. *state government official*
†Simonds, Stephen Paige *state legislator, former university official*
Sotir, Thomas Alfred *healthcare executive, retired shipbuilder*
†Titcomb, Bonnie L. *state legislator*
†Tracy, Richard H.C. *state legislator*

Bailey Island
Carter, William Caswell *computer scientist*

Bangor
Brody, Morton Aaron *federal judge*
Hunt, Walter L. *real estate and petroleum company executive*
Mills, David Harlow *psychologist, association executive*
Roderick, Richard Michael *petroleum distribution and real estate company financial executive*
†Saxl, Jane Wilhelm *state legislator*
Turner, Marta Dawn *youth program specialist*
Warford, Malcolm Lyle *seminary president, theology educator*
Warren, Richard Jordan *newspaper publisher*
Warren, Richard Kearney *newspaper publisher*
†Winn, Julie *state representative*

Bar Harbor
Green, Earl Leroy *retired biomedical research administrator, geneticist*
Hoppe, Peter Christian *biologist, geneticist*
Paigen, Kenneth *geneticist, educator*
Snell, George Davis *geneticist*
Swazey, Judith Pound *institute president, sociomedical science educator*

Bath
Ipcar, Dahlov *illustrator, painter, author*
†O'Keefe, Patrick *transportation executive*
Webb, Todd (Charles Clayton Webb) *photographer, writer*
Weber, Jean MacPhail *museum director*
Weiss, David Raymond *lawyer*

Biddeford
Ford, Charles Willard *university administrator, educator*
Lefebvre, Albert Paul Conrad *lawyer*

Blue Hill
Kherdian, David *author*
Lowry, James David *author, consultant*

Blue Hill Falls
Stookey, Noel Paul *folksinger, composer*

Boothbay Harbor
Cavanaugh, Tom Richard *artist, antiques dealer, retired art educator*
Eames, John Heagan *etcher*
Grossman, Morton S. *artist*
Lenthall, Franklyn *theatre historian*

Brewer
†Campbell, Richard H. *hardware industry executive*

Bridgton
†Thompson, Larry A. *principal*

Bristol
Schmidt, Thomas Carson *international development banker*

Brooksville
Kleiner, Richard Arthur *writer, editor*

Brunswick
Brown, James Monroe, III *museum administrator*
Chandler, John, Jr. *retired educational consultant*
Dixon, Thomas Francis *aviation company executive*
Edwards, Robert Hazard *college president*
Fuchs, Alfred Herman *psychologist, college dean, educator*
Geoghegan, William Davidson *religion educator, minister*
Greason, Arthur LeRoy, Jr. *university administrator*
Hodge, James Lee *German language educator*
Huntington, Charles Ellsworth *biologist, educator*
Morgan, Richard Ernest *political scientist, educator*
†Pfeiffer, Sophia Douglass *state legislator, lawyer*
Porter, Richard Sterling *retired metal processing company executive, lawyer*
Schwartz, Elliott Shelling *composer, author, music educator*
Tucker, Allen Brown, Jr. *computer science educator*
Watson, Katharine Johnson *art museum director, art historian*

Camden
Anderson, George Harding *broadcasting company executive*
Lavenson, James H. *corporation executive*
Lavenson, Susan Barker *corporate executive, consultant*
Shuman, Samuel Irving *lawyer, law educator*
Spock, Benjamin McLane *physician, educator*
Thomas, (Charles) Davis *editor*
Weidman, Hazel Hitson *anthropologist, educator*

Canaan
Walker, Willard Brewer *anthropology educator, linguist*
†Zikorus, Albert M. *landscape architect*

Cape Elizabeth
Emerson, Paul Carlton *retired publishing executive*

Caribou
†Donnelly, James Owen *state legislator, bank executive*
†McElwain, Franklin Roy *educational administrator*

Castine
Booth, Philip *poet, educator*
Davis, Peter Frank *filmmaker, author*
Hall, David *sound archivist, writer*
Hartmann, William Edward *architect*
Wiswall, Frank Lawrence, Jr. *lawyer*
Zehring, Karen *information executive*

Center Lovell
Adams, Herbert Ryan *retired clergyman, educator, publishing executive*

Cumberland Foreside
Dill, William Rankin *college president*
Harper, Ralph Champlin *retired banker*

Cushing
Magee, A. Alan *artist*

Damariscotta
Blake, Bud (Julian Watson) *cartoonist*
Hauschka, Theodore Spaeth *biologist, researcher, educator*
Johnson, Arthur Menzies *retired college president, historian, educator*
Robinson, Walter George *arts management and funding consultant*

Dover-Foxcroft
†Cross, Ruel P. *state representative*

East Blue Hill
Taylor, Samuel Albert *playwright*

East Boothbay
Eldred, Kenneth McKechnie *acoustical consultant*
Smith, Merlin Gale *engineering executive, researcher*

Ellsworth
Dudman, Richard Beebe *communications company executive, journalist*
Eustice, Russell Clifford *consulting company executive*
Goodyear, Austin *electronics and retail company executive*
Wiggins, James Russell *newspaper editor*

Fairfield
†Gwadosky, Dan A. *state legislator*

Falmouth
Oates, Maureen Katherine *environmental educator*
Sadik, Marvin Sherwood *art consultant, former museum director*

Farmington
Kalikow, Theodora J. *academic administrator*

Freeport
†Gorman, Leon A. *mail order company executive*
Lea, Lola Stendig *lawyer*
†Poole, Norman A. *retail executive*

Friendship
MacIlvaine, Chalmers Acheson *retired financial executive, former association executive*

Gorham
Bearce, Jeana Dale *artist, educator*

Gouldsboro
Wexler, Ginia Davis *singer, association executive*

Hallowell
†Treat, Sharon Anglin *state legislator*

Hampden
Brown, Robert Horatio *retired orthopedic surgeon*

Hartland
†Larochelle, Richard Clement *tanning company executive*

Jefferson
Fiore, Joseph Albert *artist*

Kennebunk
Alling, Charles Booth, Jr. *management consultant*
Betts, Edward *artist*
Escalet, Frank Diaz *art gallery owner, artist, educator*
†McConnell, David M. *secondary school principal*

Kittery Point
Howells, William White *anthropology educator*

Leeds
Lynn, Robert Wood *theologian, educator, dean*

Lewiston
Baxter, William MacNeil *priest*
Chute, Robert Maurice *retired biologist, educator, poet*
Dufresne, Armand Alphee, Jr. *state justice*
Harward, Donald *academic official*
Murray, Michael Peter *educator, economist*
Stauffer, Charles Henry *retired chemistry educator*
Tighe, Thomas James Gasson, Jr. *healthcare executive*
†Young, William Wade, Jr. *health care executive*

Lincoln
Kneeland, Douglas Eugene *retired newspaper editor*

Lincolnville
Nichols, David Arthur *mediator, retired state justice*
Williams, Robert Luther *city planning consultant*

Little Deer Isle
Mc Closkey, Robert *artist*

Manset
Delehanty, Edward John *investment company executive*

Milbridge
Enslin, Theodore Vernon *poet*

Monhegan Island
Hudson, Jacqueline *artist*

Monmouth
†McCormick, Dale *state legislator*

New Harbor
Fradley, Frederick Macdonell *architect*
Lyford, Cabot *sculptor*

New Vineyard
West, Arthur James, II *biologist*

North Brooklin
Schmidt, Klaus Dieter *management consultant, university administrator, marketing and management educator*
Yglesias, Helen Bassine *author, educator*

North Fryeburg
Bolomey, Roger Henry *sculptor*

North Windham
Hart, Loring Edward *academic administrator*
†Libby, James Delmas *educator, marketing consultant*

Oakland
†Albanese, J. Duke *school system administrator*
Koons, Donaldson *geologist, educator*
†Poulin, Thomas Edward *marine engineer, state legislator, retail business owner*

Old Orchard Beach
†Bartner, Jay B. *school system administrator*
Holmes, Reed M. *clergyman, former religious organization administrator*

Orient
Chenevert, Edward Valmore, Jr. *retired librarian, real estate broker*

Orono
Borns, Harold William, Jr. *geologist, educator*
Campana, Richard John *retired plant pathology educator, writer, consultant*
Coupe, John Donald *university official, economics educator*
Csavinszky, Peter John *physicist, educator*
Devino, William Stanley *economist, educator*
Fort, Raymond Cornelius, Jr. *chemistry educator*
Goldstone, Sanford *psychology educator*
Hartgen, Vincent Andrew *museum director, educator, artist*
Hatlen, Burton Norval *English educator*
Hutchinson, Frederick Edward *university president*
Ives, Edward Dawson *folklore educator*
Knight, Fred Barrows *forester, entomologist, educator*
Norton, Stephen Allen *geological sciences educator*
Rauch, Charles Frederick, Jr. *academic official*
Rivard, William Charles *mechanical engineering educator*
Tarr, Charles Edwin *physicist, educator*
†Wiersma, G. Bruce *dean, forest resources educator*
Wilson, Dorothy Clarke *author*

Pemaquid Beach
Brown, Donald Vaughn *technical educator, engineering consultant*

Phippsburg
Mc Lanathan, Richard (Barton Kennedy) *author, consultant*

Port Clyde
Thon, William *artist*

Portland
Allen, Charles William *lawyer*
Andrews, Thomas H. *congressman*
Bonney, Weston Leonard *bank executive*
Bradford, Carl O. *judge*
Carter, Gene *federal judge*
Chalfant, Edward Cole *bishop*
†Chisholm, Colin Alexander Joseph, III *media professional*
Coffin, Frank Morey *federal judge*
Cohen, David Michael *federal magistrate judge*
†Conley, Gerard P. *state senator, railroad clerk*
Coughlan, Patrick Campbell *lawyer*
Durgin, Frank Albert, Jr. *economics educator*
Freilinger, James Edward *insurance and investments company executive*
Gerry, Joseph John *bishop*
Gilmore, Roger *academic administrator*
Glassman, Caroline Duby *state supreme court justice*
Goodman, James A. *federal judge*
Graffam, Ward Irving *lawyer*
Grosset, Alexander Donald, Jr. *banker*
Harte, Christopher McCutcheon *newspaper executive*
†Haynes, Peter Lancaster *utility holding company executive*
Hirshon, Robert Edward *lawyer*
Hornby, David Brock *federal judge*
Kendrick, Peter Murray *communications executive, investor*
Lancaster, Ralph Ivan, Jr. *lawyer*
Loper, Merle William *law educator*
MacKinnon, Bernard Leo *writer*
McDowell, Donald L. *hospital administrator*
McGorrill, Bruce Courtney *broadcasting executive*
McKusick, Vincent Lee *former state supreme judicial court chief justice, lawyer*
†Miller, Elizabeth Jane *historian*
Murray, Peter Loos *lawyer, educator*
†Neavoll, George Franklin *newspaper editor*
O'Leary, Edward Cornelius *bishop*
Orr, James F., III *insurance company executive*
Parks, George Richard *librarian*
Philbrick, Donald Lockey *lawyer*
Potter, Lillian Florence *business executive secretary*
Powell, Larson Merrill *investment advisory service executive*
Raisbeck, Gordon *systems engineer*
Roberts, David Glendenning *state supreme court justice*
Ryan, William J. *bank executive*
Saufley, William Edward *banker, lawyer*
Shaffer, James Burgess *communications executive*
Shimada, Toshiyuki *orchestra conductor, music director*
Silverman, George Alan *broadcasting executive*
Skolnik, Barnet David *lawyer*
Smith, William Charles *lawyer*
Tierney, Kevin Joseph *lawyer*
Ureneck, Louis Adam *newspaper editor*
Wathen, Daniel Everett *state supreme court chief justice*
†Wells, William Woodrow, Jr. *lawyer, educator, librarian*
Wroth, L(awrence) Kinvin *lawyer, educator*
Zarr, Melvyn *lawyer, educator*

Presque Isle
†Gallagher, John *church administrator*
McGrath, Anna Fields *library director*

Prospect Harbor
Shipman, Charles William *chemical engineer*

Readfield
†Metzler, Glenn Elam *minister*

Rockland
Collins, Samuel W., Jr. *judge*
†Crosman, Christopher Byron *art museum administrator*
Taylor, Roger Conant *writer*

Rockport
Duarte, Patricia M. *real estate and insurance broker*
Fernald, Harold Allen *publishing executive*
Jackson, David Pingree *publishing executive*
Swenson, Orvar *surgeon*

Salsbury Cove
†Dawson, David C. *marine biology administrator*

Scarborough
Brackett, Norman E. *retail company executive*
Farrington, Hugh G. *wholesale food and retail drug company executive*
Moody, James L., Jr. *retail food distribution company executive*

Sebago Lake
Murray, Wallace Shordon *publisher, educator*

Sedgwick
Mc Millan, Brockway *former communications executive*
Schroth, Thomas Nolan *editor*

South Berwick
Carroll, Gladys Hasty *author*

South Harpswell
Barnes, George William *architecture and engineering company executive*

South Portland
Birk, John R. *marketing/financial services executive*
Dalbeck, Richard Bruce *insurance executive*
Katz, Steven Edward *psychiatrist, state health official*
†Martin, Joseph Robert *financial executive*

Southwest Harbor
Rabineau, Louis *academic administrator, former state official*

Springvale
Eastman, Harland Horace *former foreign service officer*

Spruce Head
Bird, John Adams *educational consultant*

Surry
Kilgore, John Edward, Jr. *former petroleum company executive*
Pickett, Betty Horenstein *psychologist*
Sopkin, George *cellist, music educator*
Whitcomb, Benjamin Bradford, Jr. *neurosurgeon*

Thorndike
Treleaven, Phillips Albert retired publishing company executive

Topsham
Tierney, James Edward attorney general

Town
†Attean, Priscilla Ann state legislator

Trenton
Kates, Robert William geographer, educator, scholar

Union
Buchan, Ronald Forbes preventive medicine physician

Vinalhaven
Indiana, Robert artist

Waterville
Bassett, Charles Walker English language educator
Bennett, Miriam Frances biologist, educator
Cotter, William Reckling college president
Ezhaya, Joseph Bernard brokerage house executive
Gemery, Henry Albert economics educator
Hudson, Yeager philosophy educator, minister
Muehlner, Suanne Wilson library director
Reid, Evans Burton chemist, artist, educator
Rohrman, Nicholas Leroy psychologist, educator, consultant
Zukowski, Walter Henry administrative science educator

Wells
†Carleton, Joseph G., Jr. lawyer, state legislator
Grimes, William Alvan retired state supreme court chief justice
Neilson, Elizabeth Anastasia health sciences educator, association executive, author, editor

West Brownfield
Kloskowski, Vincent John, Jr. educational consultant, writer

Winthrop
Skeete, F. Herbert bishop

Wiscasset
†Leslie, Seaver artist

Yarmouth
Hertz, Willard Joel foundations and nonprofit organizations consultant

York Beach
Davison, Nancy Reynolds artist

York Harbor
Curtis, Edward Joseph, Jr. gas industry executive, management consultant

MARYLAND

Aberdeen
†Bonsack, Rose Mary Hatem state legislator, physician

Aberdeen Proving Ground
Atwater, William Felix museum director
Coburn, John G. career officer
†Frasier, John T. ballistic research administrator
†Paules, Palmer L. engineering director

Adamstown
Ohlke, Clarence Carl public affairs consultant

Adelphi
†DeMonte, Vito J. physical sciences research administrator
Langenberg, Donald Newton academic administrator, physicist
Lyons, John W(inship) government agency administrator, chemist
Miller, Raymond Jarvis agronomy educator

Annapolis
Aery, Shaila Rosalie state educational administrator
Allen, John Loyd technical engineering consultant
†Amoss, William Hamilton state senator
Anderson, William Carl association executive, environmental engineer, consultant
Asbell, Fred Thomas campaign director
Baldwin, John Ashby, Jr. retired naval officer
Barber, James Alden military officer
†Boergers, Mary H. senator
Bontoyan, Warren Roberts chemist, state laboratories administrator
Brady, Frank Benton retired technical society executive
†Brewster, Gerry Leiper lawyer
Brock, William Emerson former secretary of labor
Brunk, William Edward astronomer
Cabral, Judith Ann telecommunications executive
†Cade, John A. state senator
Calvin, Teresa Ann B. secondary education educator
Casey, Edward Dennis newspaper editor
Chambers, Ronald D. book publishing executive
Clotworthy, John Harris oceanographic consultant
Colussy, Dan Alfred aviation executive
Coogle, Joseph Moore, Jr. management consultant
Coulter, James Bennett state official
†Cullen, John Wesley, IV hotel company executive
†Dembrow, Dana Lee lawyer
DiAiso, Robert Joseph civil engineer
†Doory, Ann Marie lawyer, legislator
Elder, Samuel Adams physics educator
Eldridge, John Cole state appeals judge
Ellis, George Fitzallen, Jr. energy services company executive
†Forehand, Jennie Meador state legislator
†Garrott, Idamae T. state senator
Goldstein, Louis Lazarus state official
†Granger, Robert Alan aerospace engineer
Groves, George L., Jr. air freight service company executive
Henderson, William Boyd engineering consulting company executive
†Hixson, Sheila Ellis state legislator
†Hollinger, Paula Colodny state senator
Hospodor, Andrew Thomas electronics executive
Howard, Joseph Harvey retired librarian
Howell, Barbara Fennema research chemist
Hyde, Lawrence Henry, Jr. industrial company executive
Jackson, Elmer Martin, Jr. newspaper executive
Johnson, Bruce engineering educator
Johnson, David Simonds meteorologist
Kapland, Mitchell Arthur engineering firm executive
†Kelley, Delores Goodwin state legislator
†Klima, Martha Scanlan state legislator
†Kopp, Nancy Kornblith state legislator
†Lapides, Julian Lee state senator, lawyer
†Lee, T. Girard architect
Long, Robert Lyman John naval officer
†Madden, Martin G. state legislator, insurance agent
†Maloney, Timothy Francis lawyer, state legislator
†Masters, Kenneth Halls state legislator
Maurer, Lucille Darvin state treasurer
McAfee, Lawrance Wiley finance executive
McDonough, Joseph Corbett former army officer, aviation consultant
Meima, Ralph Chester, Jr. corporate execuitve, former foreign service officer
†Menes, Pauline H. state legislator
†Mitchell, R. Clayton, Jr. state legislator
Moellering, John Henry aviation maintenance company executive
Montague, Brian John consulting company executive
†Morgan, John Stephen state representative, materials science researcher
Muller, Richard W. (Wilhelm Gustav Muller) retired textile importer
Murphy, Robert C(harles) judge
Ness, Frederic William former academic administrator, educator, consultant
Nuesse, Celestine Joseph educational administrator
Papenfuse, Edward Carl, Jr. archivist, state official
†Perry, Marsha Gratz legislator, professional skating coach
†Piccinini, Janice state legislator
†Roesser, Jean Wolberg state legislator
Rowell, Charles Frederick chemistry educator
†Ruben, Ida Gass state senator
†Sauerbrey, Ellen Elaine Richmond state legislator
Schaefer, William Donald governor, former mayor
†Shea, Walter James labor union executive
Steinberg, Melvin Allen lieutenant governor, lawyer
†Stup, Janet Anita delegate state general assembly
Taussig, Joseph Knefler, Jr. retired government official, lawyer
Werking, Richard Hume librarian, historian, academic administrator
Wilkes, Joseph Allen architect
†Winegrad, Gerald William lawyer, state senator, educator

Arnold
Green, John Cawley lawyer
Smith, Clifford Lee clergyman

Baltimore
†Abeloff, Martin David medical administrator, educator, researcher
Abramson, William Edward psychiatrist
Achinstein, Asher economist
Achinstein, Peter Jacob philosopher, educator
Adams, Harold Lynn architect
Adkins, Edward James lawyer
Ahearn, John Stephen research physicist
Aisner, Joseph oncologist, physician
Albert, Charles Thompson lawyer
Albinak, Marvin Joseph chemistry educator
Allen, Donald Clinton lawyer
Allen, Ronald John astrophysics educator, researcher
Alliker, Stanford Arnold hospital administrator
†Ambler, Bruce Melville finance company executive
Anderson, Gary Dean architect, educator
Andres, Reubin gerontologist
Anfinsen, Christian Boehmer biochemist
†Angelos, Peter G. lawyer
Apgar, Mahlon, IV real estate management counselor
Archibald, James Kenway lawyer
Arey, Patrick Kane lawyer
Astrachan, James Barry lawyer
Ayers, Richard Winston architect
Ayres, Jeffrey Peabody lawyer
Bachur, Nicholas Robert, Sr. research physician
Bacigalupo, Charles Anthony brokerage company executive
Backas, James Jacob foundation administrator
Baines, Harold Douglass professional baseball player
Bair, Robert Rippel lawyer
Baker, R. Robinson surgeon
Baker, Susan P. public health educator
Baker, Timothy Danforth physician, educator
Baker, William Parr lawyer
Baldwin, Henry Furlong banker
Baldwin, John Chandler lawyer
Baldwin, John Wesley history educator
Barber, John Merrell banker
†Barnhouse, Robert Bolon lawyer
Barrett, John Anthony printing company financial executive
Bart, Polly Turner commercial real estate developer
Barth, John Simmons writer, educator
Bartlett, James Wilson, III lawyer
Bastedo, Ralph W(alter) museum administrator, educator
Battle, Mark Garvey social services executive
Bayless, Theodore M(orris) gastroenterologist, educator, researcher
Beall, George lawyer
Beasley, Robert Scott aerospace company executive
Beckenstein, Myron journalist
†Becker, Lewis Charles cardiology educator
Beer, Michael biophysicist, educator
Bell, James Frederick physicist, educator
Benedict, Linda Sherk insurance company executive
Bennett, Scott Boyce librarian
Bentley, Helen Delich (Mrs. William Roy Bentley) congresswoman
Benton, George Stock meteorologist, educator
Bereston, Eugene Sydney dermatologist
†Berg, Jeremy M. chemistry educator
Berlin, Fred Saul psychiatrist
Berman, Barnett internist, educator
Berman, Barry David lawyer
Bernhardt, Herbert Nelson lawyer, educator
†Bigelow, George E. pharmacology administrator
Black, Walter Evan, Jr. federal judge
Blake, Norman Perkins, Jr. finance company executive
Blanton, Edward Lee, Jr. lawyer
Block, James A. hospital administrator, pediatrician
Boardman, John Michael mathematician, educator
Boone, Harold Thomas retired lawyer
Bor, Jonathan Steven journalist
Borden, Ernest Carleton physician, educator
Bowen, Lowell Reed lawyer
Bowser, Geneva Beatrice secondary school educator, principal
Bradley, Thomas Andrew insurance company executive
Brady, Joseph Vincent behavioral biologist, educator
Bramble, Frank P. bank executive
Breitenecker, Rudiger pathologist
Bridges, Leon architect
Brieger, Gert Henry medical historian, educator
Bright, Margaret sociologist
Brinkley, James Wellons investment company executive
Brock, Mary Anne research biologist, consultant
Brody, Eugene B. psychiatrist, educator
Brotman, Phyllis Block advertising and public relations executive
Brown, Donald David biology educator
Brown, John Walter vocational education supervisor
Brown, Nicholas aquarium administrator
Brumbaugh, John Maynard lawyer, educator
Brunson, Dorothy Edwards broadcasting executive
Brusilow, Saul pediatrics educator
Burch, Francis Boucher, Jr. lawyer
Burgess, R. William, Jr. investment banking executive
Cacossa, Anthony Alexander Romance languages educator
Cahill, William Walsh, Jr. lawyer
Carbine, James Edmond lawyer
Carey, Anthony Morris lawyer
Carey, Jana Howard lawyer
Carlin, Paul Victor legal association executive
Carlton, Sara Boehlke rehabilitation services administrator
Carney, Bradford George Yost lawyer, educator
Carper, Gertrude Esther artist, marina owner
Carroll, John Sawyer newspaper editor
Cashman, Edmund Joseph, Jr. investment banker
Catania, A(nthony) Charles psychology educator
Chapanis, Alphonse human factors engineer, ergonomist
Chaplin, Peggy Fannon lawyer
Charache, Samuel hematologist
Charles, Allan Frederick advertising agency executive
Chartrand, Mark Ray astronomer, telecommunications consultant
†Chasanow, Deborah K. federal judge
Chavis, Benjamin Franklin, Jr. civil rights advocate, minister
Chiarello, Donald Frederick lawyer
Childs, Barton physician, educator
Chiu, Hungdah lawyer, legal educator
Chylinski-Polubinski, Roger academic administrator
Civiletti, Benjamin R. lawyer, former U.S. attorney general
Clapp, Roger Alvin lawyer
Clark, Gilbert Michael association executive, lawyer
†Clark, John Baker, II architect
Clark, Raymond Skinner retired transportation and distribution company executive
Clarke, Edward Owen, Jr. lawyer
†Clements, Mary Lou epidemiologist, educator
Coe, Ward Baldwin, Jr. retired lawyer
Cohen, Marc Kami lawyer
Cohen, Warren I. history educator
Cohn, Marvin consulting engineering executive
Cole, Charles W., Jr. bank holding company executive
Colhoun, Howard Post financial executive
Collins, George Joseph investment counselor
Conley, Carroll Lockard physician, emeritus educator
Connor, Thomas Byrne physician, educator
Cook, Bryson Leitch lawyer
Cooper, Jerrold Stephen historian, educator
Cooper, Joseph political scientist, educator
Corn, Morton environmental engineer, educator
Cornblath, Marvin pediatrician, educator
Corotis, Ross Barry civil engineering educator, academic administrator
†Couchoud, B. Carlton federal agency administrator
†Cowan, Dwaine Oliver chemist, educator
†Creagh, David Michael public radio executive
Crenshaw, Marion Carlyle, Jr. obstetrician, educator
Crooke, Edward A. utility company executive
Crowe, Thomas Leonard lawyer
Cruz, Bobby professional boxer
Cullen, James Patrick international trading company executive
Cummings, Charles William physician, educator
Cunningham, M(urray) Hunt, Jr. aerospace company executive, mechanical engineer, author
Curley, John Francis, Jr. securities company executive
Curran, J. Joseph, Jr. state attorney general
Curran, Robert Bruce lawyer
†Dagdigian, Paul Joseph chemistry educator
†Dailey, George R., Jr. insurance company executive
†Dale, James Michael advertising executive, writer
Daly, Warren B., Jr. lawyer
Dannenberg, Arthur Milton, Jr. experimental pathologist, immunologist, educator
Davidson, Frederic McShan electrical engineering educator
Davis, Curtis Carroll writer, reviewer, critic
Davison, Warren Malcolm lawyer
†DeAngelis, Catherine D. pediatrics educator
Degenford, James Edward electrical engineer, educator
†Della, George Washington, IV state senator
Deoul, Neal electronics company executive
Derby, Ernest Stephen federal judge
Dietze, Gottfried political science educator
Digges, Dudley Perkins retired editor
Dilloff, Neil Joel lawyer
DiPentima, Renato Anthony government agency official
Dodge, Calvert Renaul education and training executive, author, educator
Domokos, Gabor research physicist
Donahoo, Melvin Lawrence aerospace management consultant, industrial engineer
Donkervoet, Richard Cornelius architect
Donohue, Marc David chemical engineering educator
Doory, Robert Leonard, Jr. lawyer
Dorsey, John Russell art critic, journalist
Dorst, John Phillips physician, radiology and pediatrics educator
†Dunn, Edward K., Jr. banker
Dunne, Richard Edwin, III lawyer
Eanes, Joseph Cabel, Jr. surety company executive
Eastman, Albert Theodore bishop
Eckerman, Jerome physicist
Edidin, Michael Aaron biologist
Eichhorn, Gunther Louis chemist
†Eisenberg, Howard Michael neurosurgeon
Eisner, Henry Wolfgang advertising executive
Ellin, Marvin lawyer
Ellingwood, Bruce Russell structural engineering researcher
Engel, Bernard Theodore psychologist, educator
Engel, Paul Bernard lawyer
Englund, Paul Theodore biochemist, educator
Entwisle, Doris Roberts sociology educator
Epstein, Daniel Mark poet, dramatist
Epstein, Selma pianist, musicologist, author, artist, critic
Fedoroff, Nina Vsevolod research scientist, consultant
Feldman, Gordon physics educator
†Felsenthal, Gerald physiatrist, educator
Fenselau, Catherine Clarke chemistry educator
Fergenson, Arthur Friend lawyer
†Ferrara, Steven educational administrator, researcher, consultant
Finch, Walter Goss Gilchrist lawyer, engineer, accountant, retired army officer
Finnegan, Sara Anne publisher
Finnerty, Joseph G., Jr. lawyer
Finney, Jervis Spencer lawyer
Fisher, George Wescott geology educator
Fisher, Jack Carrington environmental engineering educator
Fisher, Morton Poe, Jr. lawyer
†Fishman, Bernard Philip museum director
Fishman, Jacob Robert psychiatrist, educator, corporate executive, investor
Fitzgerald, Thomas Rollins university administrator
Fleishman, Avrom Hirsch English educator
Ford, John Gilmore interior designer
Fowler, Bruce Andrew toxicologist, marine biologist
Frank, Jerome David psychiatrist, educator
Frank, Robert Allen real estate investment analyst
Freeman, John Mark pediatric neurologist
Fried, Herbert Daniel advertising executive
Friedman, Louis Frank lawyer
Fuentealba, Victor William professional society administrator
Furst, Norma Fields academic administrator
Gaber, Robert psychologist
Gall, Joseph Grafton biologist, researcher
Garbis, Marvin Joseph federal judge
Gardner, R. H. (Rufus Hallette Gardner, III) retired drama and film critic
Gately, Mark Donohue lawyer
Gauvey, Susan K. lawyer
Gibbons, Thomas Michael communications executive
Giddens, Don Peyton engineering educator, researcher
Gillece, James Patrick, Jr. lawyer
Ginsberg, Benjamin political science educator
Glasgow, Jesse Edward newspaper editor
Glassgold, Israel Leon construction company executive, engineer, consultant
Glynn, Edward college administrator
Godenne, Ghislaine Dudley physician, psychoanalyst
Goedicke, Hans archeology educator
Goellner, Jack Gordon publishing executive
Goetz, Clarence Edward magistrate
Goldberg, Alan Marvin toxicologist, educator
Goldberg, Morton Falk ophthalmologist, educator
Goldman, Brian Arthur lawyer, accountant
Goldscheider, Sidney lawyer
Goldstein, Franklin lawyer
†Goldstein, Gary W. rehabilitation research administrator
Gordis, Leon physician
Graham, George Gordon physician
Graham, John Stuart, III lawyer
†Grant, Albert internist
Grasmick, Nancy S. superintendent
Graves, Pirkko Maija-Leena clinical psychologist, psychoanalyst
Gray, Carol Joyce nurse, educator
Gray, Frank Truan lawyer
Gray, Oscar Shalom lawyer
†Green, Benjamin Louis wholesale food distribution executive
Green, Bernard food products executive
Green, Robert Edward, Jr. physicist, educator
†Green, Warren Arthur health facility administrator
Greene, Jack Phillip historian, educator
Greenough, William Bates, III medical educator
Greenspan, Arnold Michael computer company executive
Grieb, Elizabeth lawyer
Griffith, John Earl, Jr. lawyer, educator
Griffith, Lawrence Stacey Cameron cardiologist
Griswold, Benjamin Howell, IV investment banker
Grossman, Lawrence biochemist, educator
Guest, James Alfred public service official
Habermann, Helen Margaret plant physiologist, educator
Hafets, Richard Jay lawyer
Haig, Frank Rawle physics educator, clergyman
Haines, Thomas W. W. lawyer
Hall, Richard Leland food processing company consultant
Hankin, Robert Michael lawyer
Hanks, James Judge, Jr. lawyer
Hanle, Paul Arthur museum administrator
Hansen, Barbara Caleen physiology educator, scientist
Hargrove, John R. federal judge
†Harp, Solomon airport executive
Harrison, Michael opera company executive
Hartigan, Grace artist
Hartman, Charles Henry association executive, educator
Harvey, Abner McGehee physician, educator
Harvey, Alexander, II federal judge
Harvey, F. Barton, Jr. investment banker
Harvey, Robert Dixon Hopkins banker
Hayes, Charles Lawton insurance company executive, holding company executive
Hecht, Alan Dannenberg insurance executive
Helrich, Martin anesthesiologist, educator
Henderson, Lenneal Joseph, Jr. political science educator
Henry, Richard Conn astrophysicist, educator
Heptinstall, Robert Hodgson physician
Hess, Stanford Donald lawyer
Higham, John history educator
Hilgenberg, Eve Brantly Handy government official
Hillers, Delbert Roy Near East language educator
Hillman, Robert Sandor lawyer
Himelfarb, Richard Jay securities firm executive
†Hirsh, Allan T., III book publisher
Hirsh, Allan Thurman, Jr. publishing executive
Hirsh, Theodore William lawyer
Hochberg, Bayard Zabdial lawyer

†Hoffman, Barbara A. state legislator
Holley, Lauren Allana psychologist
Honemann, Daniel Henry lawyer
Hopkins, Samuel retired investment banker
†Hord, Edward Marshall architect
Houck, James I. newspaper editor
Howard, J. Woodford, Jr. political science educator
Howard, Joseph Clemens federal judge
Huang, Pien Chien biochemistry educator, scientist
Hubbard, Herbert Hendrix lawyer
Hug, Richard Ernest environmental company executive
Huggins, William Herbert electrical engineering educator
Hughes, Harry Roe lawyer
Hulse, Stewart Harding, Jr. educator, experimental psychologist
Hungerford, David Samuel orthopaedic surgeon, educator
†Hutchinson, Leslie E fiscal programs manager, consultant
†Hyman, Harris, IV investment banker
Igusa, Jun-Ichi mathematician, educator
Ihrie, Robert oil, gas and real estate company executive
Immelt, Stephen J. lawyer
Irwin, John Thomas humanities educator
Ivey, Jean Eichelberger composer
Jacobs, Richard James banker, educator
Jacox, Ada Kathryn nurse, educator
Janney, Stuart Symington, III investment company executive
Jelinek, Frederick electrical engineer, educator
Jenkins, Benjamin Larry insurance company executive
†Jenkins, Carrell Ray newspaper editor
Jensen, Arthur Seigfried consulting engineering physicist
Jernigan, Kenneth association executive
†Johns, Michael Marieb Edward otolaryngologist, university dean
Johns, Richard James physician
†Johnson, Kenneth Peter neurologist, medical researcher
Johnson, Michael Paul history educator
Johnson, Richard T. neurology, microbiology and neuroscience educator, research virologist
Johnston, George W. lawyer
Jones, John Martin, Jr. lawyer
Jones, Raymond Moylan strategy and public policy educator
Judd, Brian Raymond physicist, educator
Judson, Horace Freeland history of science, writer, educator
Junghans, Paula Marie lawyer
Karni, Edi economics educator
Kastor, John Alfred cardiologist, educator
Katz, Joseph Louis chemical engineer, educator
Kaufman, Frank Albert federal judge
Keill, Stuart Langdon psychiatrist
Kelly, Thomas Jesse, Jr. molecular biologist
Kent, Edgar Robert, Jr. investment banker
Kessler, Herbert Leon art historian, educator
Kidd, Langford pediatrician, cardiologist, educator
King, Ora Sterling education educator
Kingsbury, David T. microbiologist, science administrator
Kinnard, William James, Jr. pharmacy educator
†Kirk, Robert L. rail transportation executive
Klarman, Herbert Elias economist, educator
Klinefelter, Stanard T. lawyer
Klitzke, Theodore Elmer former college dean, arts consultant
†Knapp, David Allan pharmaceutical educator, researcher
Knoedler, Elmer L. retired chemical engineer
Knott, Henry Joseph construction company executive
Kohn, Melvin L. sociologist
Kosaraju, S. Rao computer science researcher
Kowal, Charles Thomas astronomer
Kowal, Robert Paul hospital administrator
Kowarski, Allen Avinoam endocrinologist, educator
Kramer, Morton biostatistician, epidemiologist
Kruger, Jerome materials science educator, consultant
Kues, Irvin William health care system financial executive
Kurth, Lieselotte foreign language educator
Kwiterovich, Peter Oscar, Jr. medical science educator, researcher, physician
Lafferty, Joyce G. Zvonar retired educator
Lamy, Peter Paul gerontologist, educator
Lane, Malcolm Daniel biological chemistry educator
Laric, Michael Victor academic administrator
Larrabee, Martin Glover biophysics educator
Lazarus, Fred, IV college president
Lebowitz, Harvey M. lawyer
Lee, Yung-Keun physicist, educator
Legg, Benson Everett federal judge
Legum, Jeffrey Alfred automobile company executive
Lehman, Arnold Lester museum official, art historian
Levasseur, William Ryan lawyer
Levin, Edward Jesse lawyer
Levin, Marshall Abbott judge, educator
†Levine, Jerome psychiatrist, educator
Levine, Richard E. lawyer
Lewis, Alexander Ingersoll, III lawyer
Liberto, Joseph Salvatore banker
Lichtenstein, Lawrence Mark allergy, immunology educator, physician
Lidtke, Vernon LeRoy history educator
Liebmann, George William lawyer
Lin, Shin biophysics educator
Littlefield, John Walley physiology educator, geneticist, cell biologist, pediatrician
Lohr, Walter George, Jr. lawyer
Loker, F(rank) Ford, Jr. lawyer
Long, Donlin Martin surgeon, educator
Long, Robert Radcliffe fluid mechanics educator
Lucas, Barbara B. electrical equipment manufacturing executive
Luck, Georg Hans Bhawani classics educator
Machen, Arthur Webster, Jr. lawyer
Macleod, Donald clergyman, educator
Madansky, Leon particle physicist, educator
Magida, Arthur Jay newspaper editor, writer
Magnuson, Nancy librarian
Majev, Howard Rudolph lawyer
Maletz, Herbert Naaman federal judge
Maloney, John Alexander hospital administrator
†Manson, Paul Nellis plastic surgeon
Marimow, William Kalmon journalist
†Marsh, Bruce David geologist, educator
†Martin, George Reilly federal agency administrator
Mason, Raymond Adams brokerage company executive
McCarter, P(ete) Kyle, Jr. Near Eastern studies educator
McCarthy, Carol M. health care association executive, lawyer
McCarty, Harry Downman tool manufacturing company executive
McCarty, Richard Earl biochemist, biochemistry educator
†McClung, A(lexander) Keith, Jr. lawyer
Mc Cord, Kenneth Armstrong consulting engineer
McDowell, Elizabeth Mary pathology educator
McGowan, George Vincent public utility executive
McGuire, Charles Carroll, Jr. banking executive
McGuirk, Ronald Charles banker
Mc Hugh, Paul R. psychiatrist, neurologist, educator
Mc Kenney, Walter Gibbs, Jr. lawyer, publishing company executive
McKhann, Guy Mead physician, educator
Mc Kusick, Victor Almon geneticist, educator
McManus, Walter Leonard investment executive
†McPartland, James Michael university official
McPherson, Donald Paxton, III lawyer
McWilliams, John Michael lawyer
Medani, Charles Richard pediatric nephrology educator
Melvin, Norman Cecil lawyer
†Messitte, Peter Jo judge
Meyer, Jean-Pierre Gustave mathematician, educator
Migeon, Claude Jean pediatricics educator
Miller, Decatur Howard lawyer
Milnor, William Robert physician
Mintz, Sidney Wilfred anthropologist
Mitchell, Geoffrey Sewell lawyer
†Mocko, George Paul minister
†Moeller, Philip Theodore newspaper business editor
Mogol, Alan Jay lawyer
Money, John William psychologist
Monroe, Russell Ronald psychiatrist, educator
Montgomery, Paula Kay school editor, publishing executive
Morris, Edwin Thaddeus construction consultant
Moser, Hugo Wolfgang physician
Moser, M(artin) Peter lawyer
Moszkowski, Lena Iggers educator
Motz, John Frederick federal judge
†Mross, Charles Dennis health facility administrator
†Muffolett, Joseph Robert lawyer, government official
Mulligan, Joseph Francis physics educator
Munster, Andrew Michael surgeon, educator
Murnaghan, Francis Dominic, Jr. federal judge
†Murphy, Nancy L. state legislator
†Murphy, Philip Francis bishop
Murray, Joseph William banker
Mussina, Michael Cole professional baseball player
Nägele, Rainer German and comparative literary educator
Nathans, Daniel biologist
†Nathanson, Constance A. health science organization administrator, sociology educator
Natividad, Evangelia de Hitta Spanish educator, court interpreter, translator
Newhall, Charles Watson, III venture capitalist
†Newman, William C. bishop
Nichols, Stephen George romance languages educator
Nickerson, William Milnor federal judge
Nickon, Alex chemist, educator
Niemeyer, Paul Victor federal judge
Nilson, George Albert lawyer
Norman, Colin Arthur astrophysics educator
Norman, Philip Sidney physician
Northrop, Edward Skottowe federal judge
Nuckolls, Robert Theodore cemetery executive
Nwagbaraocha, Joel Onukwugha college president, educator
Oates, Johnny professional baseball team manager
Ober, Douglas Gary investment company executive
O'Connell, Kevin Michael lawyer
†O'Hare, Thomas J(ames), Jr. federal commissioner
Ohly, D. Christopher lawyer
O'Melia, Charles Richard environmental engineering educator
Orman, Leonard Arnold lawyer
†Osborn, Thomas Ray physics and oceanography educator
Oski, Frank Aram physician, educator
Ott, John Harlow museum administrator
Owen, Stephen Lee lawyer
Pappas, George Frank lawyer
†Passano, E. Magruder, Jr. publishing executive
Passano, Edward Magruder printing company executive
Patz, Arnall physician
Patz, Edward Frank lawyer
Paulson, Ronald Howard English and humanities educator
Peck, James Stevenson banker
Peirce, Carol Marshall English educator
Permutt, Solbert physiologist, physician
Pettijohn, Francis John geology educator
Pevsner, Aihud physicist, educator
Phillips, Owen Martin oceanographer, geophysicist, educator
Pittman, Carolyn artist
Plant, Albin MacDonough lawyer
Platt, William Rady pathology educator
Plummer, Risque Wilson lawyer
†Pocock, John Greville Agard historian, educator
Poindexter, Christian Herndon utility company executive
Pokempner, Joseph Kres lawyer
Pollak, Mark lawyer
Pollard, Thomas Dean biologist, educator
Popel, Aleksander S. engineering educator
Posner, Gary Herbert chemist, educator
Preston, Mark I. investment company executive
Price, Thomas Ransone neurologist, educator
†Prince, Charles O., III lawyer
†Prince, Jerry Ladd engineering educator
Proctor, Donald Frederick otolaryngology educator, physician
Proctor, Kenneth Donald lawyer
Provorny, Frederick Alan lawyer
Putzel, Constance Kellner lawyer
Quinn, Michael Desmond diversified financial services executive
Rabb, Bernard Paul book publisher, consultant
Rafferty, William Bernard lawyer
Rank, Larry Gene executive director
Ranum, Orest Allen historian, educator
†Rapoport, Morton I. medical educator, university administrator
Ray, Robert Franklin banker
Rayson, Glendon Ennes internist, preventive medicine specialist, writer
Redden, Roger Duffey lawyer
Redman, Barbara Klug nursing educator
Reeder, Oliver Howard paint products manufacturing executive
Reese, Errol Lynn university administrator, dentist
Reid, Lauretta Glasper retired principal
Rembski, Stanislav artist, portrait painter
Rennels, Marshall Leigh neuroanatomist, biomedical scientist, educator
Reno, Russell Ronald, Jr. lawyer
ReVelle, Charles S. environmental engineer, geophysicist, systems analysis and economics educator
Reynolds, William Leroy lawyer, educator
†Ricard, John H. bishop, educator
Richardson, William Chase university administrator
Riepe, James Sellers investment company executive
Ripken, Calvin Edwin, Jr. (Cal Ripken) professional baseball player
Robinson, Florine Samantha marketing executive
Robinson, Frank former professional baseball manager
Rodowsky, Lawrence Francis judge
†Rodricks, Daniel John columnist, television commentator
Rogers, Archibald Coleman architect
Rose, Noel Richard immunologist, microbiologist, educator
Roseman, Saul biochemist, educator
Rosenberg, Henry A., Jr. petroleum executive
Rosenstein, Beryl Joel physician
Rosenthal, William J. lawyer
Ross, Richard Starr medical school dean emeritus, physician, cardiologist
Roth, George Stanley research biochemist, physiologist
Rothschild, Amalie Rosenfeld artist
†Rousuck, J. Wynn theater critic
Russell-Wood, Anthony John R. history educator
Sack, Sylvan Hanan lawyer
†Salamon, Lester Milton political science educator
Scaggs, Howard Irwin savings and loan association executive, lawyer
Schaefer, Robert Wayne banker
Schatzow, Michael lawyer
Scheeler, Charles construction company executive
Schimpff, Stephen Callender internist, oncologist
Schmoke, Kurt L. mayor
Schneewind, Jerome Borges philosophy educator
Schneider, James Frederick federal judge
Schuster, Charles Roberts federal government scientist
Scott, Frederick Isadore, Jr. editor, business executive
Scott, Robert Edward, Jr. lawyer
Scriggins, Larry Palmer lawyer
Seaman, Tony university athletic coach
Semans, Truman Thomas investment company executive
Sfekas, Stephen James lawyer
Shaeffer, Charles Wayne investment counselor
Shamoo, Adil Elias biochemist, biophysicist, educator
Shapiro, Harry Dean lawyer
Shapiro, Ronald Maurice lawyer
Shapiro, Sam health care analyst, biostatistician
Sharfstein, Steven Samuel psychiatrist, government research institute administrator, association executive, hospital executive
Sharpe, Donald Edward lawyer
Sharpe, William Norman, Jr. mechanical engineer, educator
Shattuck, Mayo Adams, III investment banking executive
Shiffman, Bernard mathematician, educator
Short, Alexander Campbell lawyer
†Sibeck, David G. geophysicist
Silbergeld, Ellen Kovner environmental epidemiologist and toxicologist
Silverstein, Arthur Matthew ophthalmic immunologist, educator, historian
†Simon, David principal
Slatkin, Murray paint sundry distribution executive
Slepian, Paul mathematician, educator
Smalkin, Frederic N. federal judge
Smith, Gardner Watkins physician
Smith, Hamilton Othanel molecular biologist, educator
Smith, Hoke LaFollette university president
Smith, Julian Payne gynecological oncologist, educator
Smouse, H(ervey) Russell lawyer
†Snead, James Arrington architect
Snyder, Solomon Halbert psychiatrist, pharmacologist
Somerville, Romaine Stec arts consultant
Sommer, Alfred public health professional, ophthalmologist, epidemiologist
Sorkin, Alan Lowell economist, educator
Stalfort, John Arthur lawyer
Stanley, Julian Cecil, Jr. psychology educator
†Stanley, Steven Mitchell paleobiologist, educator
Starfield, Barbara Helen physician, educator
Steiner, Robert Frank biochemist
†Steinwachs, Donald Michael public health educator
Sternberger, Ludwig Amadeus neurologist, educator
Sterne, Joseph Robert Livingston newspaper editor
Stevens, Elisabeth Goss (Mrs. Robert Schleussner, Jr.) writer, journalist
Stewart, C(ornelius) Van Leuven lawyer
Stifler, William Curtis, III lawyer
†Stobo, John David physician, educator
Stolley, Paul David medical educator, researcher
†Stone, Norman R., Jr. state legislator
Strickland, George Thomas, Jr. physician, researcher, educator
†Strickland, Marshall Hayward bishop
Strull, Gene technology consultant, retired electrical manufacturing company executive
Suskind, Sigmund Richard microbiology educator
Sykes, Melvin Julius lawyer
Tabatznik, Bernard physician, educator
Talalay, Paul pharmacologist, physician
Talbot, Donald Roy consulting services executive
Taylor, Carl Ernest physician, educator
Taylor, Lindsay David, Jr. health care executive
Taylor, Meldrick professional boxer, Olympic athlete
Tepper, Michael Howard publishing company executive
Teret, Stephen Paul health law educator
Thomas, Gary Lynn financial executive
Thompson, Lawrence Hyde federal agency official
†Topping, Brian Barclay trust banker
Trimble, William Cattell, Jr. lawyer
Trostel, Michael Frederick architect
Trpis, Milan vector biologist, scientist, educator
Truesdell, Clifford Ambrose, III author, editor
Ts'o, Paul On-Pong biophysical chemist, educator
Tyler, Anne (Mrs. Taghi M. Modarressi) author
Tyler, George Thomas lawyer
†Tyler, John W. historic site administrator
Vasile, Gennaro James health care executive
†Vogelstein, Bert oncology educator
Wagner, Henry Nicholas, Jr. physician
Walker, Irving Edward lawyer
†Walker, Mack historian, educator
Wallach, Edward Eliot physician, educator
Walser, Mackenzie physician, educator
Wasserman, Richard Leo lawyer
Welch, Robert Bond ophthalmologist, educator
West, Christopher Read lawyer
Westerhout, Gart retired astronomer
Westheimer, Julius Milton investment executive, media financial commentator
White, Pamela Janice lawyer
Whitman, Marland Hamilton, Jr. lawyer
Wierman, John Charles mathematician, educator
Wilke, Robert Thomas advertising executive
Williams, G(eorge) Melville surgeon, medical educator
Williams, Harold Anthony retired newspaper editor
Wilson, Donald Edward physician, educator
Wilson, Robert James Montgomery investment company executive
Winn, James Julius, Jr. lawyer
Wintriss, Lynn lawyer
Wolf, Fred, III lawyer
Wolman, M. Gordon geography educator
Wood, Howard Graham banker
Woodward, Theodore Englar medical educator, internist
Yannuzzi, William A(nthony) conductor
Yarmolinsky, Adam lawyer, educator, university administrator
Young, Barbara psychiatrist, psychoanalyst, psychiatry educator, photographer
Young, Joseph H. federal judge
Zaiman, Joel Hirsh rabbi
Zassenhaus, Hiltgunt Margret physician
Ziff, Larzer English language educator
†Ziger, Steven G. architectural firm executive
Zinman, David Joel conductor

Bel Air
Crocker, Michael Pue lawyer
Eichelberger, Robert John retired government research and development administrator, consultant
Miller, Max Dunham, Jr. lawyer
Powers, Doris Hurt engineering company executive

Beltsville
Adams, Jean Ruth entomologist
Andre, Pamela Q. J. library director
Carroll, Stephen John, Jr. business educator
Diener, Theodor Otto plant pathologist
Duke, James Alan botanist, author, consultant
Dupont, Jacqueline food and nutrition educator, education and research administrator, scientist
Faust, Robert McNeer science research administrator
Foy, Charles Daley research soil scientist
Guttman, Helene Nathan research executive
Kasprick, Lyle Clinton medical products company executive
†Levin, Gilbert Victor bioengineering and environmental control company executive
Lincicome, David Richard biomedical and animal scientist
Marten, Gordon Cornelius research agronomist, educator, federal agency administrator
Murphy, Charles Franklin agriculturist
†Norris, Karl Howard optics scientist, agricultural engineer
†Parker, Stephen L. architectural firm executive
Quirk, Frank Joseph management consulting company executive
Shands, Henry Lee plant geneticist, administrator
Terrill, Clair Elman animal scientist, geneticist, consultant
Thomas, Stuart Denis textile company executive
Tso, Tien Chioh federal agency official, plant physiologist
Vanderslice, Joseph Thomas chemist
van Schilfgaarde, Jan agricultural engineer, government agricultural service administrator

Berlin
Crawford, Norman Crane, Jr. academic administrator, consultant
Horner, William Harry biochemist
Howarth, Thomas tax consultant
Passwater, Richard Albert biochemist, writer

Bethesda
Abbrecht, Peter Herman medical educator
Abrams, Samuel K. lawyer
Alexander, Duane Frederick pediatrician, research administrator
Alper, Jerome Milton lawyer
Altobello, Daniel Joseph service executive
Amende, Lynn Meridith government health scientist
Atlas, David meteorologist, research scientist
Atwell, Constance Woodruff health services executive, researcher
Auerbach, Seymour architect
Augustine, Norman Ralph industrial executive
Axelrod, Julius pharmacologist, biochemist
Baird, Charles Fitz minings and metals company executive
Baldwin, Wendy Harmer social demographer
Banik, Sambhu Nath psychologist
Banks, Henry Stephen systems software company executive
Barber, Arthur Whiting communications company executive
Barter, Robert Henry physician, retired educator
Bauersfeld, Carl Frederick lawyer
Beall, Robert Joseph foundation executive
Becker, Edwin Demuth chemist, laboratory director
Bennett, Lawrence Herman physicist
†Benson, Elizabeth Polk Pre-Columbian art specialist
Berendes, Heinz Werner medical epidemiologist, pediatrician
Berger, Robert Lewis biophysicist, researcher
Bernardini, Isa biochemist
Berns, Walter Fred political scientist, educator
Bick, Katherine Livingstone scientist, international liaison consultant
Blair, William Draper, Jr. conservationist
†Borsos, Tibor pathology educator
†Bosnak, Robert J. mechanical engineer, federal agency administrator
Bowles, Walter Donald economist, educator
Brady, Roscoe Owen neurogeneticist, educator
Breggin, Peter Roger psychiatrist, author

Bregman, Jacob Israel *environmental consulting company executive*
Breslow, Jerome Wilfred *communications company executive*
Brickfield, Cyril Francis *lawyer, association executive*
Briggs, Shirley Ann *organization executive*
Brodine, Charles Edward *physician*
Brouha, Paul *association executive, fishery-wildlife biologist*
†Brown, Ann *federal agency administrator*
Brown, Dudley Earl, Jr. *psychiatrist, educator, health executive, former federal agency administrator, former naval officer*
Brown, Earle Palmer *advertising agency executive*
Brown, Jeremy Earle *advertising executive*
Bryan, Billie Marie (Mrs. James A. Mackey) *biologist*
Bryant, Bertha Estelle *retired nurse*
Bucherre, Veronique *environmental company executive*
Burg, Maurice Benjamin *renal physiologist, physician*
Burton, Benjamin Theodore *government official*
Burton, Charles Henning *lawyer*
Butler, Sydney J. *zoological and aquarium association administrator*
Callmer, James Peter *architect*
Calvert, Gordon Lee *retired legal association executive*
Campbell, Arthur Andrews *government official*
Carpenter, Malcolm Breckenridge *retired neuroanatomist, educator*
Casey, Thomas J. *lawyer*
Cass, Millard *lawyer, arbitrator*
Cassman, Marvin *biochemist*
Castelli, Alexander Gerard *accountant*
Cath, Stanley Howard *psychiatrist, psychoanalyst*
Catravas, George Nicholas *biologist*
†Chabner, Bruce A. *oncologist, researcher*
Chase, Thomas Newell *neurologist, researcher, educator*
Chen, Philip S., Jr. *government official*
Clancy, Joseph Patrick *lawyer*
Clark, Blake *author, business executive*
†Clark, William Doran *government official*
Clay, Jasper R. *federal government official*
Cohen, Allan Yale *social science research administrator*
†Cohen, Gene David *psychiatrist*
Cohen, Max Harry *surgeon*
Cohen, Sheldon Gilbert *physician*
Coleman, Joseph Michael *transportation consultant*
Collins, Francis S. *medical research scientist*
Comings, William Daniel, Jr. *mortgage banker, housing development executive*
Cooney, David Martin *organization administrator, retired naval officer*
Cooper, Merri-Ann *psychologist*
Cooper, William Ewing, Jr. *retired army officer*
Corbett, Jack Elliott *mutual fund officer, clergyman, author*
Corn, Milton *academic dean, physician*
Cornish, Edward Seymour *magazine editor*
Cottony, Herman Vladimir *electronic engineer, consultant*
Cowie, Catherine Christine *epidemiologist*
Crout, J(ohn) Richard *physician, pharmaceutical researcher*
Cummings, Nancy Boucot *nephrologist*
Curtis, Mark Hubert *historian, former educational association executive*
†Daly, John W. *chemistry research administrator*
Daniel, Charles Dwelle, Jr. *consultant, retired army officer*
Dawid, Igor Bert *biologist*
Dawson, John Frederick *architect*
Day, Robert Dwain, Jr. *foundation executive, lawyer*
Decker, John Laws *physician*
Delappe, Irving Pierce *scientist, government official*
de Vries, Margaret Garritsen *economist*
Dietrich, Robert Anthony *pathologist, medical administrator, consultant*
Dogoloff, Lee Israel *clinical social worker, psychotherapist, consultant*
†Dresing, Robert K. *health care executive*
Drucker, William Richard *surgeon*
Dubner, Ronald *neurobiologist*
Duma, Richard Joseph *microbiologist, physician, pathologist, researcher, educator*
Duncan, Francis *historian, government official*
Dunning, Herbert Neal *government official, physical chemist*
Dyer, Frederick Charles *writer, consultant*
Dykstra, Vergil Homer *retired academic administrator*
Eaves, George Newton *research administrator*
Eden, Murray *electrical engineer, emeritus educator*
Elin, Ronald John *pathologist*
Ellis, Sydney *pharmacological scientist, former pharmacology educator*
Elman, Philip *lawyer*
Epps, Roselyn Elizabeth Payne *pediatrician, educator*
Ernst, Roger *development consultant*
Evans, Charles Hawes, Jr. *immunologist, medical researcher*
Farmer, Richard Gilbert *physician, foundation administrator, medical advisor*
Fauci, Anthony Stephen *health facility administrator, physician*
Faulders, C. Thomas, III *communications company executive*
Ferris, Frederick Joseph *gerontologist, social worker*
Frank, Martin *physiology educator, health scientist, association executive*
Fraumeni, Joseph F., Jr. *scientific researcher, medical educator, physician, military officer*
Free, Ann Cottrell *writer*
Freedman, Joseph *sanitary and public health engineering consultant*
Fri, Robert Wheeler *non-profit research executive*
Frommer, Peter Leslie *physician, medical institute administrator*
†Frosh, Brian Esten *lawyer, state legislator*
Gaarder, Marie *speech pathologist*
Gallagher, Hubert R. *governmental consultant*
†Gallin, John J. *medical research administrator*
Gallo, Robert Charles *research scientist*
Garges, Susan *microbiologist*
Gartland, William Joseph, Jr. *research institute administrator*
Gates, Theodore Ross *economic consultant*
Gerwin, Brenda Isen *research biochemist*
Gibson, Sam Thompson *internist, educator*
Gilbert, Daniel Lee *physiologist*
Ginsburg, Ann *biochemist, researcher*
Gleazer, Edmund John, Jr. *retired education educator*
Gluckstein, Fritz Paul *veterinarian, biomedical information specialist*
Gold, Philip William *neurobiologist*
Goldberg, Herman Raphael *government agency official, educator*
Goldstein, Robert Arnold *physician*
Grau, John Michael *trade association executive*
†Green, Jerome George *federal government official*
Greenwald, Alan Frank *real estate company finance executive, lawyer*
Greenwald, Peter *physician, government medical research director*
Groner, Beverly Anne *lawyer*
Gude, Gilbert *former state and federal legislator, nurseryman, writer*
Gutheim, Robert Julius *government official*
Hall, Arthur Raymond, Jr. *minister*
Hall, John Allen *international nuclear consultant*
Hall, William Darlington *lawyer*
Hallett, Mark *physician, neurologist, health research institute administrator*
Hancock, Charles Cavanaugh, Jr. *scientific association administrator*
Hanley, (Charles) Robert, Jr. *computer systems executive, real estate developer*
Hannah, Norman Britton *former foreign service officer*
Harding, Fann *health scientist, administrator*
Harlan, William Robert, Jr. *physician, educator, researcher*
Harney, Kenneth Robert *editor, columnist*
Hart, Betty Miller *artist*
Hartmann, Robert Trowbridge *author, consultant*
Haseltine, Florence Pat *research administrator, obstetrician, gynecologist*
Hauck, Frederick Hamilton *retired naval officer, astronaut, business executive*
†Hausman, Steven Jack *health science administrator*
†Hearing, Vincent Joseph, Jr. *cell biologist, researcher*
Helm, Lewis Marshall *public affairs executive*
Hempstone, Smith, Jr. *diplomat, journalist*
Henze, Paul Bernard *author, former government official*
Herman, Edith Carol *journalist*
Herman, Stephen Allen *lawyer*
Hersh, Stephen Peter *psychiatrist, educator*
Higgins, Robert Louis *trade association executive*
Highfill, Philip Henry, Jr. *retired language educator*
Hodgdon, Harry Edward *association executive, wildlife biologist*
Hoenack, August Frederick *architect*
Holmes, Randall Kent *microbiology educator, physician, university administrator*
Holt, Helen Keil *physicist*
Horakova, Zdenka Zahutova *retired toxicologist, pharmacologist*
Hughes, Carl Wilson *physician*
Hurd, Suzanne Sheldon *federal agency health science director*
Hutchinson, Everett *lawyer*
Hutton, John Evans, Jr. *surgery educator, retired military officer*
Hyson, Charles David *economist, consultant*
Iglehart, John K. *journalist*
Ingraham, Edward Clarke, Jr. *foreign service officer*
Jackson, Michael John *physiologist, association executive*
Jayson, Lester Samuel *lawyer, educator*
Jonas, Gary Fred *health care center executive*
Jones-Smith, Jacqueline *federal commission administrator, lawyer*
Jordan, Elke *molecular biologist, government medical research institute executive*
Joy, Robert John Thomas *medical history educator*
Kamenske, Bernard Harold *journalist, communications specialist*
†Kamerow, Martin Laurence *accountant*
Kapikian, Albert Zaven *physician, epidemiologist*
Keiser, Harry Robert *physician*
Kelly, William Clark *science administrator*
Kety, Seymour S(olomon) *physiologist, neuroscientist*
King, Charles McDonald, Jr. *association foundation executive*
Kingsley, Thomas Drowne *economist*
Kirschstein, Ruth Lillian *physician*
Kleine, Herman *economist*
Knachel, Philip Atherton *librarian*
Kohlmeier, Louis Martin, Jr. *newspaper reporter*
Kolbye, Albert Christian, Jr. *epidemiologist, toxicologist, lawyer*
Koltnow, Peter Gregory *engineering consultant*
†Kopin, Irwin Jerome *physician, pharmacologist*
Korn, Edward David *biochemist*
Krause, Richard Michael *medical scientist, government official, educator*
Kruger, Gustav Otto, Jr. *oral surgeon, educator*
Kupfer, Carl *ophthalmologist, science administrator*
Laingen, Lowell Bruce *diplomat*
Lally, Richard Francis *aviation security consultant, former association executive, former government official*
Larrabee, Donald Richard *publishing company executive*
Larson, Clarence Edward *association executive*
Lauret, Curtis Bernard, Jr. *marketing professional*
Law, Lloyd William *geneticist*
Lee, Edward Brooke, Jr. *real estate executive, fund raiser*
Lee, John Chonghoon, Sr. *financial executive, lawyer, consultant*
Lee, Young Jack *federal agency administrator*
Lenfant, Claude Jean-Marie *physician*
Leonard, James Joseph *physician, educator*
Leonard, Sugar Ray (Ray Charles Leonard) *professional boxer*
Leventhal, Carl M. *neurologist*
Levine, Arthur Samuel *physician, scientist*
Lewis, David *association executive*
Lewis, James Histed *retired foreign service officer*
Lindberg, Donald Allan Bror *library administrator, pathologist, educator*
†Liotta, Lance Allen *pathologist*
†Liu, Darrell Teh Yung *biochemist, researcher*
Lo, Ronald Ping Wong *banker*
†Lugt, Hans Josef *physicist*
Lukens, Alan Wood *retired ambassador and foreign service officer*
Lystad, Mary Hanemann (Mrs. Robert Lystad) *sociologist, author, consultant*
Lystad, Robert Arthur Lunde *retired university dean, educator*
Macnamara, Thomas Edward *physician, educator*
Malouff, Frank Joseph *health care association executive*
Massa, Paul Peter *publisher*
†Masys, Daniel Rochard *library director*
McAfee, John Gilmour *nuclear medicine physician*
McClure, Brooks *management consultant*
McCurdy, Harry Ward *otolaryngologist*
Mc Gurn, Barrett *communications executive, writer*
Mc Kenna, James Aloysius *broadcasting executive, former lawyer*
McKenna, Stephen James *lawyer, corporate executive*
McManus, Edward Hubbard *government official*
McMurphy, Michael Allen *energy company executive, lawyer*
McNamara, Francis John *writer*
Meier, Louis Leonard, Jr. *lawyer*
Meltzer, Jack *consultant, retired college dean*
Menaker, Frank H., Jr. *lawyer*
Meredith, Ellis Edson *association and business executive*
Meredith, William (Morris Meredith) *poet, English language educator*
†Metcalfe, Dean Darrel *medical research physician*
Metzger, Henry *federal research institution administrator*
Miller, Bennett *physicist, former government official*
Mishkin, Mortimer *neuropsychologist*
Morgan, William Bruce *naval architect*
Morton, Herbert Charles *editor, economist*
Moseley, Chris Rosser *marketing executive*
Moshman, Jack *statistical consultant*
Moskowitz, Jay *health sciences administrator*
Moss, Bernard *virologist, researcher*
Murayama, Makio *biochemist*
Nash, Howard Allen *biochemist, researcher*
Navarro, Bruce Charles *federal government official, lawyer*
Navarro, Joseph Anthony *statistician, consultant*
Naylor, Phyllis Reynolds *author*
Nelligan, William David *association executive*
Nessen, Ronald Harold *public affairs executive*
Neumann, Robert Gerhard *ambassador, consultant*
Neva, Franklin Allen *physician, educator*
Nirenberg, Marshall Warren *biochemist*
North, William Haven *foreign service officer*
Nyirjesy, Istvan *obstetrician, gynecologist*
O'Callaghan, Jerry Alexander *government official*
O'Connell, Quinn *lawyer*
O'Donnell, James Francis *health science administrator*
Oler, Wesley Marion, III *physician, educator*
Olmsted, Jerauld Lockwood *telephone company executive*
Ommaya, Ayub Khan *neurosurgeon*
Onufrock, Richard Shade *pharmacist, researcher*
O'Shaughnessy, Gary William *military officer*
Otte, Ruth L. *cable television executive*
†Oudens, Gerald Francis *architect, architectural firm executive*
Owen, Thomas Barron *retired naval officer, space company executive*
Packard, Barbara Baugh *science institute administrator, physician, physiologist*
Pankopf, Arthur, Jr. *lawyer*
Paro, Tom Edward *broadcasting company executive*
Parry, Hugh Jones (James Cross) *social scientist, educator, author*
†Paul, Steven M. *psychiatrist*
Paul, William Erwin *immunologist, researcher*
Peck, Edward Lionel *retired foreign service officer, corporate executive*
Pemberton, Melissie Collins *retired elementary education educator*
Peterson, Eric Christian *federal agency administrator*
Petralia, Ronald Sebastian *entomologist, neurobiologist, educator*
Pfister, Cloyd Harry *consultant, former career officer*
Phillips, Kevin Price *columnist, author*
Pickerell, James Howard *photojournalist*
†Pollard, Harvey B. *physician, neuroscientist*
Pompa, James Robert *computer industry executive*
Pospisil, George Curtis *biomedical research administrator*
Pras, Robert Thomas *hotel executive*
Pratt, Dana Joseph *publishing consultant*
Pritchard, Wilbur Louis *telecommunications engineering executive*
Purcell, Robert Harry *virologist*
Quinnan, Gerald Vincent, Jr. *medical educator*
Quraishi, Mohammed Sayeed *health scientist, administrator*
Rall, Joseph Edward *physician*
†Rapoport, Judith *psychiatrist*
Raullerson, Calvin Henry *political scientist, consultant*
Reichard, John Francis *association executive*
Reighard, Homer Leroy *physician*
Resnik, Harvey Lewis Paul *psychiatrist*
Richards, Merlon Foss *retired diversified technical services company executive*
Richardson, John *retired international relations executive*
Riley, Matilda White (Mrs. John W. Riley, Jr.) *sociology educator*
Roberts, Chalmers McGeagh *reporter*
Roberts, Doris Emma *epidemiologist, consultant*
Robinson, David Mason *physiologist*
Robinson, Lynn P. *association executive*
†Rodbard, David *endocrinologist, biophysicist*
Rogers, Alan Victor *former career officer*
†Rosen, Saul Woolf *research scientist, health facility administrator*
Rosenberg, Steven Aaron *surgeon, medical researcher*
Ross, William Warfield *lawyer*
Roth, Harold Philmore *physician*
Rowell, Edward Morgan *foreign service officer, lecturer*
Rubin, William *editor*
Ruppe, Loret Miller *former ambassador*
†Saffiotti, Umberto *pathologist*
Salisbury, Franklin Cary *foundation executive, lawyer*
Salisbury, Tamara Paula *foundation executive*
Sammet, Jean E. *computer scientist*
Saunders, Charles Baskerville, Jr. *retired association executive*
Saville, Thorndike, Jr. *coastal engineer, consultant*
Schambra, Philip Ellis *federal agency administrator, radiobiologist*
Schiavo, A. Mary Fackler *federal official, lawyer*
Schmeltzer, David *lawyer*
Schneider, John Hoke *health science administrator*
Schoch, Claude Martin *computer scientist, publishing company executive*
Schurman, Joseph Rathborne *lawyer*
Schwartz, Charles Frederick *economist, consultant*
Schwinn, Robert James *architect*
Sevik, Maurice *engineer*
†Shapiro, Irving S. *medical think-tank executive*
Shellow, Robert *management service company executive, consultant*
Sheridan, Philp Henry *pediatrician, neurologist*
†Sherman, Kenneth *oceanographer*
Shipler, David Karr *journalist, correspondent, author*
Shulman, Lawrence Edward *biomedical research administrator, rheumatologist*
Sinclair, Warren Keith *radiation biophysicist, organization executive, consultant*
Sindelar, William Francis *surgeon, researcher*
Small, William Edwin, Jr. *association executive*
Smith, Ruth Lillian Schluchter *librarian*
Snow, James Byron, Jr. *physician, research administrator*
Sokoloff, Louis *physiologist, neurochemist*
Sontag, James Mitchell *cancer researcher*
†Sorensen, Kurt *biomedical research administrator*
Southwick, Paul *retired public relations executive*
Spangler, Miller Brant *science and technology analyst, planner, consultant*
Spector, Melbourne Louis *management consultant*
Spivak, Alvin A. *public relations executive*
Sponsler, George Curtis, III *research administrator, lawyer*
Sprott, Richard Lawrence *government official, researcher*
Spurling, Everett Gordon, Jr. *architect, construction specifications consultant*
Stadtman, Earl Reece *biochemist*
Stadtman, Thressa Campbell *biochemist*
Steers, Newton Ivan, Jr. *former congressman*
Stewart, Harold Leroy *physician, educator*
Stolz, Walter Sargent *health scientist administrator*
Striner, Herbert Edward *economics educator*
Sturtz, Donald Lee *physician, naval officer*
Sulkin, Sidney *editor, writer*
Talbot, Bernard *government medical research facility official, physician*
Taylor, Jimmie Wilkes *naval officer*
Teitel, Simon *economist*
Tilley, Carolyn Bittner *information manager, technical information specialist*
Toomey, Thomas Murray *lawyer*
Trumbull, Richard *psychologist*
Tuttle, William G(ilbert) T(ownsend), Jr. *management consultant, retired army officer*
Vaitukaitis, Judith Louise *medical research administrator*
Varmus, Harold Eliot *microbiologist, educator*
Vaughan, Martha *biochemist*
Vest, George Southall *diplomat*
Vickers, James Hudson *veterinarian, research pathologist*
von Kann, Clifton Ferdinand *aviation and space executive, financial consultant*
Vosburgh, Frederick George *writer, editor*
Wagner, Henry George *medical research scientist, naval officer*
Waldmann, Thomas Alexander *medical research scientist, physician*
Walker, Lannon *foreign service officer*
Walker, Mallory *real estate executive*
Walleigh, Robert Shuler *consultant*
†Walter, Robert *think-tank executive, career officer*
Walter, William Arnold, Jr. *physician*
Walters, Judith Richmond *neuropharmacologist*
Webster, Henry deForest *experimental neuropathologist*
Weinberger, Alan David *corporate executive*
Wertheimer, Franc *retired corporate executive*
Whaley, Storm Hammond *retired government official, consultant*
Williams, Charles Laval, Jr. *physician, international organization official*
Willner, Dorothy *anthropologist, educator*
Witkop, Bernhard *chemist*
†Wong, Ma-Li *psychiatrist*
Woolley, George Walter *biologist, geneticist, educator*
Wright, Helen Patton *association executive*
Wright, James Roscoe *chemist*
Wurtz, Robert Henry *physiologist, scientist*
Yaffe, Sumner Jason *pediatrician, research center administrator, educator*
†Yamada, Kenneth Manao *cell biologist*
Young, A. Thomas *defense, aerospace, energy and information systems company executive*
Zimble, James Allen *naval officer, physician*
†Zinn, Dale W. *think-tank executive*
Zurkowski, Paul George *information company executive*
Zwanzig, Robert Walter *chemist, physical science educator*

Bowie
†Green, Leo Edward *state legislator*
Kepley, Thomas Alvin *management consultant*
Mc Manus, Charles Anthony, Jr. *retired federal official, political and public relations executive*
Purcell, Steven Richard *international management consultant, engineer, economist*
Stone, Edward Harris, II *landscape architect*
Sullivan, Francis Edward *research administrator*
Towle, Laird Charles *book publisher*

Braddock Heights
Wirths, Theodore William *public policy consultant*

Bradshaw
Chisholm, Carol Lee *research psychologist*

Brentwood
†Kaskey, Raymond John *sculptor*

Brookeville
Wilson, Vincent Joseph, Jr. *writer, historian, publisher*

Brooklandville
Darcy, George Robert *public relations executive*
Miller, Paul George *computer company executive*

Burtonsville
†Yang, Jackson *aerospace engineering company executive*

Cabin John
Gallagher, Hugh Gregory *government affairs author, consultant*
Sewell, Winifred *pharmaceutical librarian*
Shropshire, Walter, Jr. *biophysicist emeritus, pastor*

Calverton
Appell, Louise Sophia *consulting company executive*

Kotler, Martin *corporate executive*

Canton
Grable, Edward E. *obstetrician, gynecologist*

Catonsville
Cadman, Theodore Wesley *chemical engineering educator*
Loerke, William Carl *art history educator*
Stowe, David Henry *arbitrator*
Vanderlinde, Raymond Edward *clinical chemist*
Wynn, John Charles *clergyman, retired religion educator*

Centreville
Amos, James Lysle *photographer*

Chester
Dabich, Eli, Jr. *insurance company executive*
Pelczar, Michael Joseph, Jr. *microbiologist, educator*

Chestertown
Clarke, Garry Evans *composer, educator, musician, administrator*
Gordon, James Braund *management consultant*
†Newlin, Peter Caverly *architect*
Sener, Joseph Ward, Jr. *securities company executive*
Trout, Charles Hathaway *historian, educator*
Williams, Henry Thomas *retired banker, real estate agent*

Cheverly
Lockyer, Charles Warren, Jr. *corporate executive*

Chevy Chase
Adler, James Barron *publisher*
Asher, Lila Oliver *artist*
Baily, Nathan Ariel *business executive, consultant, association official, former government official, educator*
Bissinger, Frederick Lewis *retired manufacturing executive, consultant*
Bush, Frederick Morris *federal official*
Calfee, William Howard *sculptor, painter*
Chase, Nicholas Joseph *lawyer, educator*
Chaseman, Joel *media executive*
Choppin, Purnell Whittington *research administrator, virology researcher, educator*
Corrigan, Robert Foster *business consultant, retired diplomat*
Cowan, William Maxwell *neurobiologist*
Crawford, Meredith Pullen *research psychologist*
Cross, Christopher T. *association executive*
Delano, Victor *retired naval officer*
Emery, Robert Firestone *economist, educator*
Faulkner, Winthrop Waldron *architect*
Ferguson, James Joseph, Jr. *researcher, educator*
Freeman, Harry Louis *financial services company executive*
Freeman, Raymond Lee *landscape architect, planning consultant*
Geber, Anthony *economist, retired foreign service officer*
Ginzburg, Yankel *artist*
Goodwin, Ralph Roger *historian, editor*
Greenberg, Robert Milton *retired psychiatrist*
Harr, Karl Gottlieb, Jr. *lawyer*
Harter, Donald Harry *research administrator, medical educator*
Hudson, Anthony Webster *retired federal agency administrator*
Hudson, Ralph P. *physicist*
Ikenberry, Henry Cephas, Jr. *lawyer*
Kainen, Jacob *artist, former museum curator*
Ketcham, Orman Weston *lawyer, former judge*
Key, Kerim Kami *historian, educator*
Mayers, Jean *aeronautical engineering educator*
Mc Closkey, Robert James *former diplomat*
Michaelis, Michael *management and technical consultant*
Mulligan, James Kenneth *government official*
Pancoast, Edwin C. *retired foreign service officer, writer, researcher*
Promisel, Nathan E. *materials scientist, metallurgical engineer*
Riley, John Winchell, Jr. *consulting sociologist*
Ritchie, Royal Daniel *economic development executive*
Rockwell, Theodore *nuclear engineer*
Romansky, Monroe James *physician, educator*
Rose, John Charles *physician, educator*
Sauer, Richard John *association executive*
Saul, B. Francis, II *bank executive*
Scammon, Richard Montgomery *political scientist*
Schlegel, John Frederick *management consultant, speaker, trainer*
Stetler, C. Joseph *lawyer*
Vance, Sheldon Baird *lawyer, former diplomat*
Vanderryn, Jack *philanthropic foundation administrator*
Walk, Richard David *retired psychology educator*
Wallerstein, Leibert Benet *economist*
Weisman, John *author*
Welch, Arnold D(emerritt) *pharmacologist, biochemist*

Chevy Chase Village
Durant, Frederick Clark, III *aerospace history and space art consultant*

Claiborne
Moorhead, Paul Sidney *geneticist*

Clarksburg
Bargellini, Pier Luigi *electrical engineer*
Evans, John Vaughan *satellite laboratory executive, physicist*
Mahle, Christoph Erhard *electrical engineer*
Townsend, John William, Jr. *physicist, retired federal aerospace agency executive*

Clarksville
Brancato, Emanuel Leonard *electrical engineering consultant*

Clinton
Averett-Short, Geneva Evelyn *college administrator*

Cockeysville Hunt Valley
Brown, Adrienne Jean *microbiology diagnostic testing company official*
Edgett, William Maloy *lawyer, labor arbitrator*
Hirsch, Richard Arthur *mechanical engineer*
Jacobsen, Josephine Winder Boylan *author*
Kunisch, Robert Dietrich *business services company executive*
Peirce, Brooke *English language educator*
Whitehurst, William Wilfred, Jr. *management consultant*

College Park
†Aloimonos, Yiannis John *computer sciences educator*
Anderson, John David, Jr. *aerospace engineer*
Antman, Stuart Sheldon *mathematician, educator*
Aylward, Thomas James, Jr. *communication arts and theatre educator*
Barbe, David Franklin *electrical engineer, educator*
Benesch, William Milton *molecular physicist, atmospheric researcher, educator*
Berman, Louise Marguerite *education educator*
Birnbaum, Robert *higher education educator*
Blankenship, Gilmer Leroy *electrical engineering educator, engineering company executive*
Blewett, John Paul *physicist*
†Brill, Dieter Rudolf *physicist*
Brodsky, Marc Herbert *physicist, research and publishing executive*
Brown, Peter Gilbert *philosopher, educator*
Burke, Frank Gerard *archivist*
Castellan, Gilbert William *chemistry educator*
Clark, Eugenie *zoologist, educator*
Cleghorn, Reese *journalist, educator*
Colwell, Rita Rossi *microbiologist, molecular biologist*
Coughlin, Peter Joseph *economics educator, researcher*
Cunniff, Patrick Francis *mechanical engineer*
Dally, James William *mechanical engineering educator, consultant*
Davidson, Roger H(arry) *political scientist, educator*
DeMonte, Claudia Ann *artist, educator*
†DeSilva, Alan W. *physics educator, researcher*
Destler, I. M(ac) *political scientist, foreign policy writer*
Dieter, George Elwood, Jr. *university dean*
Dietrich, Martha Jane (Martha Jane Shultz) *genealogist*
Dorsey, John Wesley, Jr. *university administrator, economist*
Dragt, Alexander James *physicist*
†Efrat, Isaac *mathematician, educator*
Ehrlich, Gertrude *retired mathematics educator*
Embody, Daniel Robert *biometrician*
Ephremides, Anthony *electrical engineering educator*
Fallon, Daniel *university administrator*
Fanning, Delvin Seymour *soil science educator*
Finkelstein, Barbara *education educator*
Fisher, Michael Ellis *mathematical physicist, chemist*
Fuegi, John *comparative literature educator, author, filmmaker*
Gaylin, Ned L. *psychology educator*
Gessow, Alfred *aerospace engineer, educator*
Gluckstern, Robert Leonard *physics educator*
Gouin, Francis R. *physiologist*
Granatstein, Victor Lawrence *electrical engineer, educator*
Greenberg, Jerrold Selig *health education educator*
Greenberg, Oscar Wallace *physicist, educator*
Greer, Thomas Vernon *business consultant and educator*
Griem, Hans Rudolf *physicist, educator*
†Griffin, James Joseph *physics educator*
Grim, Samuel Oram *chemistry educator*
Grunig, James Elmer *communications educator, researcher, public relations consultant*
Gupta, Ashwani Kumar *mechanical engineering educator*
Gurr, Ted Robert *political science educator, author*
†Hardy, Robert Charles *human development educator*
Harlan, Louis Rudolph *history educator, writer*
Heath, James Lee *food science educator, researcher*
Hey, Nancy Henson *educational administrator*
Hiebert, Ray Eldon *journalism educator, author, consultant*
Holder, Sallie Lou *training and meeting management consultant*
Holton, William Milne *English language and literature educator*
Irwin, George Rankin *physicist, mechanical engineering educator*
Jaquith, Richard Herbert *chemistry educator, retired university official*
Just, Richard Eugene *agricultural and resource economics educator*
Keller, Samuel William *aerospace administrator*
Kerr, Frank John *astronomer, educator*
Kirwan, William English, II *mathematics educator, university official*
Kolodny, Richard *finance educator*
Kotz, Samuel *statistician, educator, translator*
Kramer, Irvin Raymond *metallurgist, researcher*
†Kundu, Mukul Ranjan *physics and astronomy educator*
Lamone, Rudolph Philip *business educator*
Lapinski, Tadeusz Andrew *artist, educator*
Levine, William Silver *electrical engineering educator*
Lewis, Roger Kutnow *architect, educator, author*
Lightfoot, David William *linguistics educator*
Ligomenides, Panos Aristides *electrical and computer engineering educator, consultant*
Locke, Edwin Allen, III *psychologist, educator*
Lubkin, Gloria Becker *physicist*
Marcus, Steven Irl *electrical engineering educator*
Massey, Thomas Benjamin *academic administrator*
Mayer, William Emilio *dean*
Mc Donald, Frank Bethune *physicist*
Michels, Eugene *physical therapist*
Mikulski, Piotr Witold *mathematics educator*
Miller, Raymond Edward *computer science educator*
Minker, Jack *computer scientist, educator*
Misner, Charles William *physics educator*
Moss, Lawrence Kenneth *composer, educator*
Nerlove, Marc Leon *economics educator*
Newcomb, Robert Wayne *electrical engineer*
Olson, Keith Waldemar *history educator*
Olson, Mancur Lloyd *economics educator*
Olver, Frank William John *retired research educator*
Oster, Rose Marie Gunhild *foreign language professional, educator*
†Pai, Shih I. *aeronautical engineer*
†Panichas, George Andrew *English language educator, critic, editor*
Pasch, Alan *philosophy educator*
Patterson, Glenn Wayne *botany educator*
Peterson, David Frederick *government agency executive*
Piper, Don Courtney *political science educator*
Polakoff, Murray Emanuel *university dean, economics and finance educator*
Popper, Arthur N. *zoology educator*
Prentice, Ann Ethelynd *academic adminstrator*
Presser, Harriet Betty *sociology educator*
Quebedeaux, Bruno *horticulture educator*
Quester, George Herman *political science educator*
Rabin, Herbert *physicist, university administrator*
Rosen, Steven *lawyer*
Rosenfeld, Azriel *computer science educator, consultant*
Russell, John David *English literature educator*
†Sagdeev, Roald Zinnurovi *physicist educator*
†Sagoff, Mark *philosopher, educator, academic administrator*
Scannell, Dale Paul *dean, university educator*
Schelling, Thomas Crombie *economist, educator*
Schneider, Benjamin *psychology educator*
Seefeldt, Carol *education educator*
Sigall, Harold Fred *psychology educator*
Silverman, Joseph *chemistry educator, scientist*
Simon, Julian Lincoln *economics educator*
Singh, Amarjit *engineering executive, scientist, management consultant*
Smith, Betty Faye *textile chemist*
Smith, Theodore Goodwin *chemical engineering educator*
Snow, George Abraham *physicist*
Sorter, Bruce Wilbur *federal program administrator, educator, consultant*
Stark, Francis C., Jr. *horticulturist, educator*
Stephens, John Frank *association executive, researcher*
Stewart, Gilbert Wright *computer science educator*
Stover, Carl Frederick *foundation executive*
Taylor, Leonard Stuart *engineering educator, consultant*
Toll, John Sampson *association administrator, former university administrator, physics educator*
Ulmer, Melville Jack *economist, educator*
Vandersall, John Henry *dairy science educator*
Wasserman, Paul *library and information science educator*
†Webb, Richard A. *physicist*
Weeks, John David *chemistry and physical science educator*
Weil, Raymond Richard *soil scientist*
Whittemore, Edward Reed, II *poet, retired educator*
Williams, Aubrey Willis *anthropology educator*
Winik, Jay B. *political scientist, writer, consultant*
Yaney, George *history educator*
Zen, E-an *research geologist*

Columbia
Alexander, Bruce Donald *real estate executive*
†Askew, Laurin Barker, Jr. *architect*
Baker, Russell Tremaine, Jr. *lawyer*
Barrow, Lionel Ceon, Jr. *communications and marketing consultant*
†Bitonti, James Anthony *business machinery company executive*
Bruley, Duane Frederick *academic administrator, consultant, engineer*
Butcher, (Charles) Philip *English language educator, author*
Carr, Charles Jelleff *pharmacologist, educator, toxicology consultant*
Clark, Billy Pat *physicist*
Cook, Stephen Bernard *homebuilding company executive*
Deutsch, Robert William *physicist*
DeVito, Mathias Joseph *real estate executive*
Fisher, Dale John *chemist, instrumentation and medical diagnostic device investigator*
Hart, Robert Gordon *federal agency administrator*
Hegedus, L. Louis *chemical engineer, research and development executive*
Hilderbrandt, Donald Franklin, II *urban designer, landscape architect, artist*
Hotchkies, Barry *financial executive*
Keeton, Morris Teuton *research institute director*
Khare, Mohan *chemist*
Lapides, Jeffrey Rolf *corporate executive*
Lorton, Lewis *dentist, researcher, computer scientist*
†Luskin, Jack *manufacturing company executive*
McCauley, Richard Gray *real estate developer, lawyer*
McCuan, William Patrick *real estate company executive*
Millspaugh, Martin Laurence *real estate developer, urban development consultant*
Morgan, Walter Edward *management consultant*
Peck, Charles Edward *retired construction and mortgage executive*
Slater, John Blackwell *landscape architect*
Steele, Richard J. *management consultant*
Trohan, Walter *newspaperman*
Ulman, Louis Jay *lawyer*
van Remoortere, Francois Petrus *chemical company research and development executive*
Whiting, Albert Nathaniel *former university chancellor*
Wolter, John Amadeus *librarian, government official*

Crofton
Gongwer, Carolyn Jane *technical training consultant*
Kelley, Albert Benjamin *consulting company executive*
Watson, Robert Tanner *physical scientist*

Crownsville
Lawrence, William Porter *former naval officer, academic administrator*
Wright, Harry Forrest, Jr. *retired banker*

Cumberland
Fiedler, Lee N. *automotive products executive*

Darnestown
Knox, Bernard MacGregor Walker *retired classics educator*

Davidsonville
Mahaffey, Redge Allan *movie producer, director, writer*

Dayton
Fischell, Robert Ellentuch *physicist*

Denton
†Thornton, Robert Alan, Jr. *lawyer, state legislator*

Dundalk
†Arnick, John Stephen *lawyer, legislator*

Dunkirk
Ewing, Richard Tucker *diplomat, educator, publisher*

Easton
Belmont, August *investment banker*
Burns, Michael Joseph *operations and sales-marketing executive*
Engle, Mary Allen English *physician*
Engle, Ralph Landis, Jr. *internist, educator*
Goldner, Sheldon Herbert *export-import company executive*
Hayes, James Edward *retired insurance executive*
Jacobs, Michael Joseph *lawyer*
Lockwood, Willard Atkinson *publisher*
Maffitt, James Strawbridge *lawyer*
Peterson, James Kenneth *manufacturing company executive*
Quinn, William Wilson *manufacturing executive*
Read, William Lawrence *business executive, former naval officer*
Woods, William Ellis *lawyer, pharmacist, association executive*

Edgewater
Holm, Jeanne Marjorie *author, consultant, government official, former air force officer*

Elkton
Harrington, Benjamin Franklin, III *business consultant*
Scherf, Christopher N. *association executive*
Zebley, Joseph Wildman, Jr. *management consultant*

Ellicott City
Faulstich, Albert Joseph *banking consultant*
†Hickey, Michael E. *school system administrator*
Hoffberger, Jerold Charles *corporation executive*
Lakhani, Dilawar *accountant, financial planner*
†Phelps, Catherine *elementary school principal*
Weingarten, Murray *manufacturing executive*

Emmitsburg
Nakhleh, Emile A. *governmental sciences educator*

Faulkner
Freeze, James Donald *administrator, clergyman*

Forest Hill
Hartenstine, Warren Richard *apparel industry equipment distribution company executive*

Forestville
Povey, Thomas George *office systems company executive*

Fort George G Meade
†McConnell, John Michael *federal agency administrator*
Runyon, Floyd Lawrence *army officer*

Fort Howard
Alexander, C. Alex *physician*

Fort Washington
Cameron, Rita Giovannetti *writer, publisher*
Coffey, Matthew B. *association executive*
Kelley, Bennett Wallace *manufacturing company executive, consultant*
McKenzie, Ruth Bates Harris *diversity human relations consultant, writer*

Frederick
Anderson, William Bert *import company executive*
Beran, Denis Carl *publisher*
Brown, Frederick James *education educator*
Bryan, John Leland *retired engineering educator*
Byron, Beverly Butcher *congresswoman*
Church, Martha Eleanor *college president*
Delaplaine, George Birely, Jr. *newspaper editor, cable television executive*
†Farmer, Noel T., Jr. *school system administrator*
Garver, Robert Vernon *research physicist*
Hoff, Charles Worthington, III *banker*
Hogan, Ilona Modly *lawyer*
Housewright, Riley Dee *microbiologist, former society executive*
Kappe, David Syme *environmental chemist*
Lewis, Robert Alan *biologist, environmental scientist, researcher, educator, administrator, author*
Lijinsky, William *biochemist*
†Papas, Takis S. *oncology research administrator*
†Rice, Jerry Mercer *medical research center administrator*
Tidball, M. Elizabeth Peters *retired physiology educator, author*
†Triebe, John Roger *oil company executive*

Frostburg
Gira, Catherine Russell *university president*
Heckert, Paul Charles *sociologist, educator*
Root, Edward Lakin *university dean, educator*
Tam, Francis Man Kei *physics educator*

Gaithersburg
Ambler, Ernest *government official*
Berger, Harold *physicist*
Bochicchio-Ausura, Jill Arden *photographer*
Boddiger, George Cyrus *corporate consultant*
†Buckley, Gerard Duke *science facility administrator*
†Burrows, James H. *computer scientist*
Cahn, John Werner *metallurgist, educator*
Casella, Russell Carl *physicist*
†Caswell, Randall Smith *physicist*
Clark, Alan Fred *physicist*
Colvin, Burton Houston *mathematician, government official*
Cookson, Alan Howard *electrical engineer, researcher*
Costrell, Louis *physicist*
Crisp, Elizabeth Amanda *physician*
†Danos, Michael *physicist*
Dean, Stephen Odell *physicist*
Deprit, Andre Albert *mathematician, consultant*
†Deslattes, Richard Day, Jr. *physicist*
Deutsch, Judith Sloan *journalist, newspaper editor*
Ewing, Frank Marion *lumber company executive, industrial land developer*

Flickinger, Harry Harner *organization and business executive, management consultant*
French, Judson Cull *government official*
Fuhrman, Ralph Edward *civil and environmental engineer*
†Gebbie, Katharine Blodgett *astrophysicist*
Harman, George Gibson *physicist, consultant*
Hertz, Harry Steven *government official*
Hoppes, Harrison Neil *corporate executive, chemical engineer*
Hougen, Jon Torger *physical chemist, researcher*
†Hsu, Stephen M. *materials scientist, chemical engineer*
Hubbell, John Howard *radiation physicist*
Isbister, James David *business executive*
†Jefferson, David *scientist*
Kammer, Raymond Gerard, Jr. *government official*
†Karch, Karen Brooke *principal*
Katz, Martin Howard *lawyer*
Kessler, Karl Gunther *physicist*
Klein, Sami Weiner *librarian*
Kushner, Lawrence Maurice *physical chemist*
Kuyatt, Chris E(rnie) (Earl) *physicist, radiation measurement services administrator*
Levelt Sengers, Johanna Maria Henrica *research physicist*
Levine, Robert Sidney *chemical engineer*
Marozsan, John Robert *publishing company executive*
McGarrity, Gerard John *microbiologist*
McShefferty, John *research company executive*
†Mills, Kevin Lee *government executive*
Nemecek, Albert Duncan, Jr. *retail company executive, investment banker, management consultant*
Oettinger, Frank Frederic *electronics executive, researcher*
Pande, Krishna Prasad *electrical engineer, physicist*
Prabhakar, Arati *federal administration research director, electrical engineer*
†Pugh, Edison Neville *metallurgist*
Rabinow, Jacob *electrical engineer, consultant*
†Reader, Joseph *physicist*
†Rollow, Thomas A. *federal official*
Rosenblatt, Joan Raup *mathematical statistician*
Ross, Sherman *psychologist, educator*
Rupert, (Lynn) Hoover *minister*
Sayer, John Samuel *information systems consultant*
Schaefer, William G. *lawyer*
Schrenk, W(illi) Juergen *chemicals executive*
Schwartz, Lyle H. *materials scientist, government official*
Schwartzberg, Allan Zelig *psychiatrist, educator*
Semerjian, Hratch Gregory *research and development executive*
†Smith, Leslie E. *physical chemist*
Snell, Jack Eastlake *federal agency administrator*
Taylor, Barry Norman *physicist*
†Thompson, J. Stark *chemical company executive*
Ulbrecht, Jaromir Josef *chemical engineer*
Warshaw, Stanley Irving *federal agency official*
†Watkins, Michael Dean *town planner*
Weber, Alfons *physicist*
Whallon, Evan Arthur, Jr. *orchestra conductor*
Wicklein, John Frederick *journalist, educator*
Wiederhorn, Sheldon Martin *materials scientist, ceramic engineer*
†Wiese, Wolfgang Lothar *physicist*
†Wineland, David J. *physicist*
Witzgall, Christoph Johann *mathematician*
Wright, Richard Newport, III *civil engineer, government official*

Garrett Park
Baldwin, Calvin Benham, Jr. *retired medical research administrator*
Friedman, Edward David *lawyer, arbitrator*
Melville, Robert Seaman *chemist*

Germantown
Christian, John Kenton *organization executive, publisher, writer, marketing consultant*
Price, William James *organization executive*
Shaw, Jack Allen *communications company executive*

Glen Arm
Jackson, Theodore Marshall *retired oil company executive*
Mc Cord, Marshal *civil engineer*

Glen Echo
Simpson, Robert Edward *economist, consultant*

Glenelg
Williams, Donald John *research physicist*

Glenwood
Simms, Charles Averill *environmental management company executive*

Grantsville
Ruddell, Gary Ronald *publisher*

Grasonville
Andrews, Archie Moulton *government official*
Prout, George Russell, Jr. *medical educator, urologist*

Greenbelt
Alexander, Joseph Kunkle, Jr. *physicist*
Blackwell, Camellia Ann *art educator*
†Boarman, Gerald L. *principal*
Cooper, Robert Shanklin *engineering executive, former government official*
Day, John H. *physicist*
Fichtel, Carl Edwin *physicist*
Fitzmaurice, Michael William *electrical and mechanical engineer*
†Gehrels, Neil *astrophysicist*
Hauser, Michael George *astrophysicist*
Holt, Stephen S. *astrophysicist*
Kenkel, James Edward *judge*
Langel, Robert Allan, III *geophysicist*
Maran, Stephen Paul *astronomer*
Mather, John Cromwell *astrophysicist*
Mumma, Michael Jon *physicist*
†O'Mara, Arthur James *civil engineer*
†O'Sullivan, Judith Roberta *legal association administrator*
Pratt, Terrence Wendall *information research scientist*
†Ramaty, Reuven Robert *physicist, researcher*
†Rothenberg, Joseph Howard *federal agency administrator*
Simpson, Joanne Malkus *meteorologist*
Smith, David Edmund *geophysicist*
Stief, Louis John *chemist*
Work, Henry Harcus *physician, educator*

Hagerstown
†Coles, Robert Nelson *religious organization administrator*
Corderman, John Printz *lawyer, judge*
Fisher, Charles Worley *editor*
Harrison, Lois Smith *hospital executive, educator*
Palmisano, Sister Maria Goretti *principal*
†Poole, D. Bruce *lawyer*
Tuckwell, Barry Emmanuel *musician, music educator*
†Warner, Harry Backer, Jr. *retired journalist, freelance writer*

Hampstead
Staub, Martha Lou *elementary school educator*

Hancock
Popenoe, John *horticultural consultant, retired botanical garden administrator*

Hanover
Dibos, Dennis Robert *electronics industry executive*
†Hay, Lewis *food marketing executive*
†Miller, James L. *food products executive*

Havre De Grace
Wetter, Edward *broadcasting executive*

Hollywood
Hertz, Roy *physician, educator, researcher*

Hunt Valley
DiCamillo, Gary Thomas *manufacturing executive*
Kinstlinger, Jack *engineer executive, consultant*
McKay, Jack Alexander *electronics engineer, physicist*
Mulligan, Martin Frederick *clothing executive, professional tennis player*

Huntingtown
†Haller, Harlan Thomas *federal agency administrator*
Mitchell, Robert Greene *industrial manufacturing executive, consultant*

Hyattsville
Ahl, Alwynelle Self *zoology, ecology and veterinary medical executive*
†Feinleib, Manning *public health physician, educator*
Herrmann, Douglas J. *psychology educator, researcher*
Israel, Robert Allan *statistician*
Lovick, Norman *accountant*
Manos, Pete Lazaros *supermarket executive*
McLin, William Merriman *foundation administrator*
†Moylan, John L. *secondary school principal*
Rodgers, Mary Columbro *university chancellor, English educator, author*
†Schoenfeld, Jim *professional hockey coach*

Ijansville
Calton, Gary Jim *chemical company executive, medical educator*

Kensington
Attix, Frank Herbert *medical physics educator, researcher*
Braden, Joan Kay *mental health counselor*
Clarke, Frederic B., III *risk analysis consultant*
Daisley, William Prescott *lawyer*
Jackson, Mary Jane McHale *principal*
Jackson, William David *research executive*
LaGasse, Alfred Bazil, III *association executive*
Marienthal, George *telecommunications company executive*
May, G. Lynwood *aerospace executive, engineering consultant*
Rather, Lucia Porcher Johnson *library administrator*
Revoile, Charles Patrick *lawyer*
Rogers, Kenneth Norman *retired foreign service officer, lawyer, international political and commercial consultant*
Root, William Alden *export control consultant*
Schmerling, Erwin Robert *retired government official*

Kingsville
Pullen, Keats A., Jr. *electronics engineer*

La Plata
†Braun, Stephen John *prosecutor*
Merrick, Barbara Barnhart *school administrator*

Landover
Colyer, Sheryl Lynn *psychologist*
Drahmann, Brother Theodore *academic administrator*
Freeman, Ernest Robert *engineering executive*
Hechinger, John Walter *hardware chain executive*
Huggins, David *custom software development executive*
Lynam, Jim *professional basketball coach*
Nash, John N. *professional basketball team executive*
O'Malley, Susan *professional basketball team executive*
Poile, David Robert *professional hockey team executive*
Pollin, Abe *professional basketball executive, builder*
Sachs, Jerry *professional basketball team executive*
Unseld, Westley Sissel *former professional basketball coach*

Lanham
Cannon, Charles C. *footwear company executive*
Lucido, Chester Charles, Jr. *marketing executive*
McCarthy, Kevin John *lawyer*
Nagan, Peter Seymour *publisher*

Lanham Seabrook
Blanchard, David Lawrence *aerospace executive, real estate developer*
Fellers, Raymond *publisher*
Fischel, David *astrophysicist, remote sensing specialist*
†Herman, Kenneth *food marketing executive*

Laurel
Abbagnaro, Louis Anthony *corporate executive*
Apel, John Ralph *physicist*
Avery, William Hinckley *physicist, chemist*
†Billig, Frederick Stucky *mechanical engineer*
Bostrom, Carl Otto *physicist, laboratory director*
Dallman, Paul Jerald *engineer, writer*
Eaton, Alvin Ralph *aeronautical and systems engineer, research and development administrator*
†Fristrom, Robert Maurice *chemist*
Gottsman, Earl Eugene *academic administrator*
Halushynsky, George Dobroslav *systems engineer*
Hutcheson, Janet Reid *radiologist*
Kossiakoff, Alexander *chemist*
Krimigis, Stamatios Mike *physicist, researcher, space science/engineering manager, consultant*
Lavin, Charles Blaise, Jr. *realtor, association executive*
†O'Connor, Harold J. *wildlife research administrator*
Perrone, Nicholas *mechanical engineer, business executive*
Robbins, Chandler S(eymour) *research biologist*
Sherwood, Aaron Wiley *aerodynamics educator*
Wales, Sister Patrice *school system administrator*

Leonardtown
Briscoe, John Hanson *judge, lawyer, former state legislator*

Linthicum
Skillman, William Alfred *consulting engineering executive*

Lusby
†Eshelman, Ralph Ellsworth *historian, consultant*
Howell, James Theodore *medical consultant, internist*
Radcliffe, Redonia Wheeler (Donnie Radcliffe) *journalist, author*
Simpich, William Morris *public affairs consultant*

Lutherville
Barton, Meta Packard *business executive, medical science research executive*
Morgan, James Gilmor *insurance executive*
Sanders, Roger Cobban *radiologist*
Tebay, James Elwood *retired foundation executive*

Lutherville Timonium
Barnes, Wilson King *lawyer, former judge*
Bond, Calhoun *lawyer, retired*
Bundick, William Ross *dermatologist*
Cappiello, Frank Anthony, Jr. *investment advisor*
Cedrone, Louis Robert, Jr. *critic*
Chapman, Robert Breckenridge, III *management consulting company executive*
Hambleton, Thomas Edward *theatrical producer*
Kerr, Patrick Corbitt *real estate appraiser, consultant*
†Parker, Lewis E. S. *research company executive, commercial vineyard operator*
Shriver, Pamela Howard *professional tennis player*

Mardela Springs
Harcum, Louise Mary Davis *retired elementary education educator*

Marriottsville
†Fitzgerald, John L. *hospital administrator*

Mays Chapel
Sagerholm, James Alvin *retired naval officer*

Mechanicsville
Henderson, Madeline Mary (Berry) *chemist, researcher, consultant*

Mitchellville
Bever, Christopher Theodore *psychiatrist*
Blough, Roy *retired economist*
Kendall, Katherine Anne *social worker*
Phelps, Flora L(ouise) Lewis *editor, anthropologist, photographer*

Monkton
Mountcastle, Vernon Benjamin *neurophysiologist*
Ryker, Norman J., Jr. *retired manufacturing company executive*
Weller, Frank Harlow, Jr. *lawyer, consultant*

Monrovia
Atanasoff, John Vincent *physicist*

Mount Airy
Collins, Henry James, III *insurance company executive*

Mount Rainier
Steinbach, Donald Ervin *middle school educator*

Myersville
Blake, John Ballard *retired historian*

New Windsor
Culver, Charles George *federal agency administrator, civil engineer*

North Bethesda
Foa, Joseph Victor *aeronautical engineer, educator*
Levin, Carl *public and government relations consultant*
†Stansfield, Charles W. *educational administrator*

North Potomac
†Bavier, Robert Newton, III *architect*
†Passantino, Richard J. *architect*

Oakland
Farrar, Richard Bartlett, Jr. *secondary education educator, wildlife biology consultant*

Olney
Delmar, Eugene Anthony *architect*

Owings Mills
Disharoon, Leslie Benjamin *retired insurance executive*
†Gloth, Fred M., Jr. *insurance company executive*
Holdridge, Barbara *book publisher*
Kershaw, Robert Alan *corporate treasurer*
†Montague, Kenneth C. *congressman*
Walsh, Semmes Guest *retired insurance company executive*
Wieczynski, Frank Robert *insurance brokerage executive*

Oxford
Mc Kee, Kinnaird Rowe *retired naval officer*
Radcliffe, George Grove *retired life insurance company executive*
Stanley, Edmund Allport, Jr. *foundation administrator, philanthropist*
Waetjen, Walter Bernhard *university president emeritus*

Oxon Hill
†Crudup, W. *bishop*
†Lawlah, Gloria Gary *state legislator, educator*

Parkville
Munson, Paul Lewis *pharmacologist*

Pasadena
Kreps, Robert Wilson *research chemist*
†Young, Russell Dawson *physics consultant*

Perry Hall
Houck, John Roland *clergyman*

Perry Point
Peszke, Michael Alfred *psychiatrist, educator*

Poolesville
†Newman, John Dennis *neuroethologist, biomedical researcher*

Port Republic
Hughes, Phillip Samuel *government official, social scientist*
Miller, Ewing Harry *architect*

Potomac
Antoniou, Lucy D. *internist, nephrologist*
Bollum, Frederick James *biotechnology executive*
Bradley, Mark Edmund *physician, consultant*
Brewer, Nathan Ronald *veterinarian, consultant*
Broderick, John Caruthers *retired librarian, educator*
Conner, Troy Blaine, Jr. *lawyer, writer*
Cotton, William Robert *dentist*
Engelmann, Rudolf Jacob *meteorologist*
Epstein, Edward S. *meteorologist*
Fink, Daniel Julien *management consultant*
Fox, Arthur Joseph, Jr. *editor*
Frey, James McKnight *government official*
Haddy, Francis John *physician, educator*
Hammond, Harold Francis *former association executive*
Jones, Sidney Lewis *economist, government official*
Karson, Emile *international business executive*
Kessler, Ronald Borek *journalist*
Mc Bryde, Felix Webster *geographer, ecologist, consultant*
Munroe, Pat *retired newsman*
Nichol, Henry Ferris *former government official, environment consultant*
Noonan, Patrick Francis *conservation executive*
Peter, Phillips Smith *lawyer*
Peters, Frank Albert *retired chemical engineer*
Proffitt, John Richard *investment banking executive*
Reynolds, Frank Miller *retired government administrator*
Rhode, Alfred Shimon *business consultant, educator*
Schonholtz, Joan Sondra Hirsch *banker, civic worker*
Shapiro, Richard Gerald *retired department store executive, consultant*
Shepard, William Seth *government official, diplomat*
Terragno, Paul James *information industry executive*
Whang, Yun Chow *space science educator*

Preston
Suggs, Leo H. *transportation executive*

Princess Anne
Adams, James Alfred *natural science educator*
Hytche, William Percy *university president*

Queenstown
Bancroft, Paul, III *investment company executive, venture capitalist*
Mc Laughlin, David Thomas *academic administrator, business executive*
O'Toole, James Joseph *business educator*

Riverdale
Guetzkow, Daniel Steere *technology company entrepreneur*
†Hedgepeth, Leroy J. *park director*
Love, Richard Harvey *lawyer*
†O'Reilly, Thomas Patrick *state senator, lawyer*

Rockville
Aamodt, Roger Louis *federal agency administrator*
Anderson, Walter Dixon *trade association management consultant*
Arnstein, Sherry Phyllis *health care executive*
Au, Mary Lee *school system administrator*
Barkley, Brian Evan *lawyer, political consultant*
Beattie, Donald A. *energy scientist, consultant*
Beckjord, Eric Stephen *energy researcher, nuclear engineering educator*
Birns, Mark Theodore *physician*
Blankenheimer, Bernard *economics consultant*
Brandhorst, Wesley Theodore *information manager*
Bruck, Stephen Desiderius *biochemist*
Brumback, Gary Bruce *industrial and organizational psychologist*
Bryant, Edward Clark *statistician*
†Carey, John Edward *information services executive*
Chapin, James Chris *lawyer*
Christie, R(obert) Brent *real estate and hotel executive*
Cohen, Robert Abraham *retired physician*
Cowart, Elgin Courtland, Jr. *naval medical officer*
Day, LeRoy Edward *aerospace scientist, consultant*
Dockser, William Barnet *real estate, finance and development company executive*
Doub, William Offutt *lawyer*
Drzewiecki, Tadeusz Maria *corporate executive, defense consultant*
Dubey, Satya Deva *statistical scientist, researcher, executive*
Dunn, Bonnie Brill *chemist*
DuPont, Robert Louis *psychiatrist, physician*
Elliott, Benjamin Paul *architect*
†Finlayson, John Sylvester *biochemist*

Fischetti, Michael *public administration educator, arbitrator*
Forbes, Allan Louis *physician, foods and nutrition consultant*
Fthenakis, Emanuel John *diversified aerospace company executive*
Geier, Mark Robin *obstetrical genetics and infertility physician*
†Gordon, Michael Robert *lawyer*
Gougé, Susan Cornelia Jones *microbiologist*
Grady, Lee Timothy *pharmaceutical chemist*
Graff, Stuart Leslie *accounting executive*
Grist, Clarence Richard *chemist, precious metals investor*
†Guest, Gerald Bentley *veterinarian*
Haffner, Marlene Elisabeth *internist, health care administrator*
Halperin, Jerome Arthur *pharmacopeial convention executive*
Hanna, Michael George, Jr. *immunologist, institute administrator*
Harvey, Donald Phillips *retired naval officer*
Haudenschild, Christian Charles *pathologist, educator*
Hawkins, James Alexander, II *mental health fund executive*
Henderson, Edward Shelton *oncologist*
Hewlett, Richard Greening *historian*
†Hoffman, C. Michael *federal agency administrator*
†Hoobler, James Ferguson *federal executive*
Horowitz, Harold *architect*
†Hoth, Daniel *infectious diseases administrator*
Howard, Lee Milton *international health consultant*
†Hoyer, Leon William *physician, educator*
Huber, John Michael *director non-profit organization*
Jamieson, Graham A. *biochemist, organization official*
†Jochum, George T. *management company executive*
Johnson, Elaine McDowell *federal government administrator*
Johnson, Emery Allen *physician*
Josephs, Melvin Jay *professional society administrator*
Kadish, Richard L. *lawyer*
Kalton, Graham *survey statistics, research scientist*
Karnow, Stanley *journalist, writer*
Kelso, John Hodgson *government official*
Kessler, David A. *health services commissioner*
Kindt, Thomas James *chemist*
Knox, C. Neal *political and governmental affairs consultant, writer*
Koslow, Stephen Hugh *science administrator, pharmacologist*
Landon, John Campbell *medical research company executive*
†Leshner, Alan Irvin *science foundation administrator*
Leslie, John Walter *development consultant*
Ley, Herbert Leonard, Jr. *retired epidemiologist*
Lim, David Jong Jai *otolaryngology educator, researcher*
Lindblad, Richard Arthur *health services administrator, drug abuse epidemiologist*
Lloyd, Douglas Seward *physician, public health administrator*
Lutwak, Leo *physician, educator*
Mannes, Paul *federal judge*
Matthews, Daniel George *editorial consultant*
†McCormick, Kathleen Ann Krym *geriatrics nurse, federal agency administrator*
McDonald, Capers Walter *biomedical engineer, corporate executive*
McMahon, Edward Peter *systems engineer, consultant*
Mertz, Walter *retired government research executive*
Meyer, F. Weller *bank executive*
Milan, Thomas Lawrence *accountant*
Miller, Kenneth Michael *electronics executive*
Milner, Max *food and nutrition consultant*
Missar, Charles Donald *librarian*
Molitor, Graham Thomas Tate *lawyer*
Munson, John Christian *acoustician*
Murray, Peter *metallurgist, manufacturing company executive*
†Naft, Barry Niel *waste management administrator, chemical engineer*
Nash, Jonathon Michael *program manager, mechanical engineer*
Naunton, Ralph Frederick *surgeon, educator*
Nelson, Joseph Conrad *lawyer, business executive, educator*
†Nora, Audrey Hart *physician*
Nora, James Jackson *physician, author, educator*
Nystrom, Harold Charles *lawyer, labor consultant*
†O'Keefe, Kevin *public relations executive*
Parler, William Carlos *lawyer*
†Petzold, Carol Stoker *state legislator*
†Poljak, Roberto Juan *research director, biotechnology educator*
Pollack, Louis *telecommunications company executive*
Pollard, George Marvin *economist*
Porter, John Robert, Jr. *space technology company executive, geochemist*
Rafajko, Robert Richard *medical research company executive*
Ramsey, William Edward *retired naval officer, space systems executive*
Regeimbal, Neil Robert, Sr. *journalist*
Rheinstein, Peter Howard *government official, physician, lawyer*
Ruth, James Perry *financial planning executive*
Sacchet, Edward M. *foreign service officer*
Sanks, Charles Randolph, Jr. *minister, psychotherapist*
Schindler, Albert Isadore *physicist, educator*
Seltser, Raymond *epidemiologist, educator*
Shadoan, George Woodson *lawyer*
Shaw, Robert William, Jr. *management consultant, venture capitalist*
Shelton, Wayne Vernon *professional services and systems integration company executive*
Shepherd, Alan J. *construction executive, management consultant*
Snyder, Marvin *neuropsychologist*
Spahr, Frederick Thomas *association executive*
Sparks, David Stanley *university administrator*
Springer, Michael Louis *federal agency administrator*
Sumaya, Ciro Valent *pediatrician, educator*
Temple, Robert *physician, federal agency administrator*
Teske, Richard Henry *veterinarian*
Titus, Roger Warren *lawyer*
Towle, Leland Hill *government official*
Tripp, Frederick Gerald *investment advisor*
Trost, Carlisle Albert Herman *retired naval officer*
Weinberger, Leon Walter *sanitary engineer*
Willoughby, Harvey William *lawyer, financial and real estate executive*
Wonnacott, (Gordon) Paul *economics educator*
Zoon, Kathryn Egloff *biochemist*

Saint Leonard
Andrews, John Stewart *management consultant*

Saint Michaels
Jones, Raymond Edward, Jr. *brewing executive*
Marshall, Robert Gerald *language educator*

Salisbury
†Becker, Thomas McKean *architect*
Houlihan, Hilda Imelio *physician*
Khazeh, Khashayar (Kashi Khazeh) *finance educator*
Kleiman, Gary Howard *broadcast, advertising and cellular communications consultant*
†May, Everette Lee, Jr. *pharmacologist, educator*
Moultrie, Fred *geneticist*
Perdue, Franklin P. *poultry products company executive*
†Perdue, James *food products executive*

Sandy Spring
Cope, Harold Cary *former university president, higher education association executive*
Gibian, Thomas George *chemical company executive*
Kanarowski, Stanley Martin *chemist, chemical engineer, government official*

Savage
Filby, Percy William *library consultant*

Seabrook
Brugger, George Albert *lawyer*
Durrani, Sajjad Haidar *space communications engineer*
Laurenson, Robert Mark *mechanical engineer*

Severna Park
Greulich, Richard Curtice *retired anatomist, gerontologist*
Retterer, Bernard Lee *electronic engineering consultant*
Schick, Edgar Brehob *German literature educator*

Silver Spring
Bailey, John Martin *transportation planner*
†Bainum, Stewart *health care and lodging company executive*
†Bainum, Stewart William, Jr. *health care and lodging company executive*
Ball, Anne H. *writer, editor, public relations consultant*
Barber, Ben Bernard Andrew *journalist*
Bardack, Paul Roitman *lawyer, nonprofit administrator*
Barkin, Robert Allan *graphic designer, newspaper executive, consultant*
†Beach, Bert Beverly *clergyman*
Berger, Allan Sidney *psychiatrist*
Blake, Lamont Vincent *electronics consultant*
†Briscoe, Melbourne G. *oceanographer, administrator*
Brog, David *consultant, former air force officer*
Brooks, Bruce Delos *writer*
Butler, Broadus Nathaniel *retired university administrator*
Cain, David Lee *corporate executive*
Calinger, Ronald Steve *historian*
Carnell, Paul Herbert *federal education official*
Coates, Robert Jay *retired electronic scientist*
Cole, Wayne Stanley *historian, educator*
Cooke, Joseph Peter *construction contracting company executive*
Dale, Charles *trade association executive*
Dalton, Robert Edgar *mathematician, computer scientist*
Dame, William Page, III *banker, school administrator*
Dimino, Joseph T. *archbishop*
Doherty, William Thomas, Jr. *historian, retired educator*
†Dorman, Arthur *state legislator*
Douglass, Carl Dean *biochemistry consultant, former government official*
Douglis, Avron *mathematician*
Eades, James Beverly, Jr. *aeronautical engineer*
Edwards, Kamala Doris *humanities educator*
Eiserer, Leonard Albert Carl *publishing executive*
Fanelli, Joseph James *retired public affairs executive, consultant*
Flieger, Howard Wentworth *editor*
Fockler, Herbert Hill *foundation executive*
†Folkenberg, Robert S. *religious organization administrator*
Foresti, Roy, Jr. *chemical engineer*
Friday, Elbert Walter, Jr. *federal agency administrator, meteorologist*
Gaunaurd, Guillermo C. *physicist, engineer, researcher*
Geiger, Anne Ellis *secondary educator*
Gilbert, Arthur Charles Francis *psychologist*
†Gilbert, Donald F. *church administrator*
Glenn, Robert Edward *industrial hygienist, trade association executive, former government research administrator*
Goott, Daniel *government official, consultant*
Grubbs, Donald Shaw, Jr. *actuary*
Hackett, John Francis *archivist*
Hamill, James Paul *hospital administrator*
Hannan, Myles *lawyer, banker*
Hanson, Angus Alexander *geneticist*
Hayman, Harry *association executive, electrical engineer*
Haynes, Leonard L., III *government official, consultant*
Hegstad, Roland Rex *magazine editor*
Hermach, Francis Lewis *consulting engineer*
Hersey, David Floyd *information resources management consultant, government official;*
Holloway, William Jimmerson *retired educator*
Howze, Karen Aileen *newspaper editor, lawyer, multi-cultural communications consultant*
Hsueh, Chun-tu *political science educator, foundation executive*
Humphries, Weldon R. *real estate executive*
Jacobs, George *telecommunications engineering consulting company executive*
Jaskot, John Joseph *insurance company executive*
†Kabela, Frank, Jr. *broadcast executive*
Kendrick, James Earl *business consultant*
Kohler, Max Adam *consulting hydrologist, weather service administrator*
Kronstadt, Arnold Mayo *community and architectural planner*
Leedy, Daniel Loney *ecologist*
Lynch, Sonia *data processing consultant*
Menkello, Frederick Vincent *computer scientist*
Milligan, Glenn Ellis *psychologist*
Mitchell, Milton *lawyer*
Mooney, James Hugh *newspaper editor*
Mundel, Marvin Everett *industrial engineer*
Myers, Evelyn Stephenson *editor, writer*
Odland, Gerald Clark *association executive*
Orkand, Donald Saul *management consultant*
†Ostenso, Ned Allen *oceanographer, government official*
Papas, Irene Kalandros *English educator, author, poet*
Pearman, Reginald James *educational administrator*
Peipel, Adam *kinetic and video sculptor*
Pellerzi, Leo Maurice *lawyer*
Perlmutter, Jerome Herbert *communications specialist*
Petitt, Gerald William *hotel executive*
Phillips, Craig *aquarium administrator*
Podgorny, Richard Joseph *government official*
Popkin, Roy Sandor *emergency management consultant, writer, researcher*
Porter, Dwight Johnson *former electric company executive, foreign affairs consultant*
Raphael, Coleman *business school dean*
Rasi, Humberto Mario *religious education director, editor, clergyman*
Rayburn, Carole (Mary Aida) Ann *psychologist, researcher, writer*
Rueger, Lauren John *retired physicist*
†Sampugnaro, Trudy M. *principal*
Schaaf, C(arl) Hart *economic consultant, writer, former international organization official*
Scheer, Milton David *physical chemist*
†Schmitten, Rolland Arthur *government official*
Schneider, William Charles *aerospace consultant*
Scipio, L(ouis) Albert, II *aerospace science engineering educator, architect, military historian*
Senseman, Ronald Sylvester *architect*
Shames, Irving Herman *engineering educator*
†Sher, Patricia Ruth *state legislator*
Shih Carducci, Joan Chia-mo *cooking educator, biochemist, medical technologist*
†Thompson, George Ralph *church denomination administrator*
†von Hake, Margaret Joan *librarian*
Waldrop, Francis Neil *physician*
Whitten, Leslie Hunter, Jr. *author, newspaper reporter*
Wilson, William Stanley *oceanographer*
Winston, Michael Russell *foundation executive, historian*
Yeakel, Joseph Hughes *clergyman*
Young, Kenneth *union official*

Solomons
Samuels, Sheldon Wilfred *philosophy educator*

Sparks
Barr, Irwin Robert *retired aeronautical engineer*
Felton, John Walter *spice company executive*
Harrison, James Joshua, Jr. *food products executive*
McCormick, Charles Perry, Jr. *food products company executive*
Nelson, John Howard *food company research executive*
Single, Richard Wayne, Sr. *lawyer*
Suarez-Murias, Marguerite C. *retired language and literature educator*

Springfield
Delaney, Jean M. *art educator*

Stevenson
†Hendler, Nelson Howard *physician, medical clinic director*
Jacobs, Bradford McElderry *newspaper editor*
Schnering, Philip Blessed *investment banker*

Stevensville
Kent, James A. *university dean, author, consultant*

Suitland
Cary, Boyd Balford, Jr. *physicist*
†Green, Gordon Woodrow, Jr. *economist, federal agency administrator*

Sykesville
Buck, John Bonner *retired biologist*
Enoff, Louis D. *international consultant*

Takoma Park
McLain, Sandra Brignole *art educator*

Tantallon
Dickens, Doris Lee *psychiatrist*

Temple Hills
†Bishop, Cecil *bishop*
Day, Mary Jane Thomas *cartographer*
Miller, John Richard *interior designer*
Whidden, Stanley John *physiologist, physician*
Wilcox, Richard Hoag *information scientist*

Thurmont
Lucey, Charles Timothy *journalist, author*

Timonium
Morrel, William Griffin, Jr. *banker*

Towson
Baker, Jean Harvey *history educator*
Caret, Robert Laurent *university administrator, author*
Chappell, Annette M. *university dean*
Hildebrand, Joan Martin *education educator*
Howell, Harley Thomas *lawyer*
Irwin, Sister Marie Cecilia *hospital administrator*
Johnston, Edward Allan *lawyer*
Lerch, Richard Heaphy *lawyer*
Mark, Michael Laurence *academic administrator*
Mc Indoe, Darrell Winfred *nuclear medicine physician, former air force officer*
Muuss, Rolf Eduard *psychologist, educator*
Peacock, James Daniel *lawyer*
Spodak, Michael Kenneth *forensic psychiatrist*
Udvarhelyi, George Bela *neurosurgery educator emeritus, cultural affairs administrator*

Trappe
Anderson, Andrew Herbert *retired army officer*

Union Bridge
Laughlin, Henry Prather *physician, psychiatrist, educator, author, editor*

Upper Marlboro
†Bowles, Liza K. *construction executive*
Chasanow, Howard Stuart *judge, lecturer*
†Elwood, Patricia *educator, political consultant*
Parker, Ellis Jackson, III *lawyer, broadcaster*
Smith, Ralph Lee *author, musician*

Waldorf
†Simpson, James Carroll *state senator*

Walkersville
†Buterbaugh, Noel Lee *biotechnologist, health products executive*

Westminster
Bryson, Brady Oliver *lawyer*
Chambers, Robert Hunter, III *college president, American studies educator*
Dulany, William Bevard *lawyer*

Woodbine
Brush, Peter Norman *federal agency administrator, lawyer*

Woodstock
†Fitzgerald, John *health facility executive*
Price, John Roy, Jr. *financial executive*

Wye Mills
Schnaitman, William Kenneth *finance company executive*

MASSACHUSETTS

Acton
Anderson, Bob *environmental company executive, consultant*
†Barrett, James *computer software company executive*
Golden, John Joseph, Jr. *manufacturing company executive*
Kittross, John Michael *retired communications educator*
Lee, Shih-Ying *mechanical engineering educator*
†Moir, Ronald Brown, Jr. *museum director*
Tod, G. Robert *consumer marketing executive*

Allston
Becton, Henry Prentiss, Jr. *broadcasting company executive*
Bley, Carla Borg *jazz composer*
Katayama, Toshihiro *artist, educator*
Metheny, Patrick Bruce *musician*
Mills, Daniel Quinn *business educator, consultant, author*
Sanders, Pharoah *saxophonist, composer*
Silk, Alvin John *business educator*

Amherst
Abbott, Douglas Eugene *engineering educator*
†Adrion, William Richards *academic administrator, computer and information sciences educator, author*
Akers, Sheldon Buckingham, Jr. *electrical and computer engineering educator*
Alfange, Dean, Jr. *political science educator*
Anderson, Ronald Trent *art educator*
Archer, Ronald Dean *chemist, educator*
Arkes, Hadley P. *political science and jurisprudence educator*
Averill, James Reed *psychology educator*
Babb, Lawrence Alan *anthropology educator*
Bagg, Robert Ely *English educator, poet*
Baker, Lynne Rudder *philosophy educator*
Beals, Ralph Everett *economist, educator*
Belt, Edward Scudder *sedimentologist, educator*
Benson, Lucy Peters Wilson *political and diplomatic consultant*
Bentley, Richard Norcross *regional planner, consultant*
Berger, Bernard Ben *environmental and civil engineer, former educator and public health officer*
Berger, Seymour Maurice *social psychologist*
Bestor, Charles Lemon *composer, educator*
Bezucha, Robert Joseph *history educator*
Bischoff, David Canby *university dean*
Bozone, Billie Rae *librarian, consultant*
Brandon, Liane *filmmaker, educator*
Bridegam, Willis Edward, Jr. *librarian*
Bromery, Randolph Wilson *geologist, educator*
Buell, Victor Paul *marketing educator, author, editor*
Byron, Frederick William, Jr. *physicist, educator, university dean*
Carpino, Louis A. *chemist, educator*
Catlin, Donald Edward *mathematics educator*
Chappell, Vere Claiborne *philosophy educator*
Clayton, Joe Todd *agricultural and food engineering educator*
Coppinger, Raymond Parke *biologist, educator*
Cornish, Geoffrey St. John *golf course architect*
Creed, Robert Payson, Sr. *literature educator*
Demerath, Nicholas Jay, III *sociology educator*
Ehrlich, Paul *chemist, educator*
Fink, Richard David *chemist, educator*
†Fleischman, Paul R. *psychiatrist, writer*
Fox, Thomas Walton *veterinary science educator*
Franks, Lewis E. *electrical and computer engineering educator, researcher*
Gerety, Tom *college administrator, educator*
†Godfrey, Paul Joseph *science foundation director*
Goldman, Sheldon *political science educator*
Goldstein, Joseph Irwin *materials scientist, educator*
Gordon, Joel Ethan *physics educator*
Grose, Robert Freeman *psychology educator*
Haensel, Vladimir *chemical engineering educator*
Harrison, Edward Robert *physicist, educator*
Hendricks, James Powell *artist*
Hernon, Joseph Martin, Jr. *history educator*
Hewlett, Horace Wilson *former educational administrator, association executive*
Hillel, Daniel *soil physics and hydrology educator, researcher, consultant*
Holmes, Francis William *plant pathologist*
Holmes, Helen Bequaert *researcher*
Inglis, David Rittenhouse *physicist*

Jenkins, Paul Randall *poet, editor*
Kantor, Simon William *chemistry educator*
Kinney, Arthur Frederick *literary history educator, author, editor*
Klare, Michael Thomas *social science educator, program director*
Langland, Joseph Thomas *author, emeritus educator*
Larson, Joseph Stanley *environmentalist, educator, researcher*
Laurence, Robert Lionel *chemical engineering educator*
†Lenz, Robert William *polymer chemistry educator*
Liebling, Jerome *photographer, educator*
MacKnight, William John *chemist, educator*
Marcum, James Benton *college dean*
Mc Garrah, Robert Eynon *business administration educator*
McIntosh, Robert Edward, Jr. *electrical engineering educator, consultant, electronics executive*
Menon, Premachandran Rama *electrical engineering educator*
Motherway, Joseph Edward *mechanical engineer, educator*
Nash, William Arthur *civil engineer, educator*
Nicholson, Walter *economist, educator*
Oates, Stephen Baery *history educator*
O'Brien, Richard Desmond *university administrator, neurobiologist*
Palser, Barbara F. *botany researcher, retired educator*
Parkhurst, Charles *museum official*
Partee, Barbara Hall *linguist, educator*
Peterson, Gerald Alvin *physicist*
Porter, Dennis Dudley *foreign language educator*
Porter, Roger Stephen *chemistry educator*
Pouncey, Peter Richard *college president, classics educator*
Prince, Gregory Smith, Jr. *academic administrator*
Quin, Louis DuBose *chemist, educator*
†Ragle, John Linn *chemistry educator*
†Rohde, Richard A. *plant pathologist educator*
Rosbottom, Ronald Carlisle *academic administrator, French culture and literature educator*
Rossi, Alice S. *sociology educator, author*
Rupp, William John *architect*
Sandweiss, Martha A. *museum director, author, American studies educator*
Sarat, Austin D. *jurisprudence and political science educator*
Schaubert, Daniel Harold *electrical engineering educator*
Schmalz, Carl Nelson, Jr. *artist, educator, printmaker*
Scott, David Knight *physicist, university administrator*
Singleton, Philip Arthur *corporate executive*
Slakey, Linda Louise *biochemistry educator*
Stein, Otto Ludwig *botany educator*
Stein, Richard Stephen *chemistry educator*
Strickland, Bonnie Ruth *psychologist, educator*
Swift, Calvin Thomas *electrical and computer engineering educator*
Tager, Jack *historian, educator*
Talbot, Richard Joseph *library administrator*
Tate, James Vincent *poet, English educator*
Taubman, William Chase *political science educator*
Tippo, Oswald *botanist, educator, university administrator*
White, Merit Penniman *engineering educator*
Wideman, John Edgar *English literature educator, novelist*
Wilcox, Bruce Gordon *publisher*
Wills, David Wood *minister, educator*
Wolff, Robert Paul *philosophy educator*
Woodbury, Richard Benjamin *anthropologist, educator*
Wyman, David Sword *historian, educator*
Zimmerman, William Frederick *biology educator*

Andover
Cook, Christopher Capen *artist, educator, museum director*
Ellis, Elliot Frederic *physician*
Fitzgerald, Michael Anthony *insurance company executive*
Jakes, William Chester *electrical engineer*
Lloyd, Robert Andrew *art educator*
Mac Neish, Richard Stockton *archaeologist, educator*
Wise, Kelly *private school educator, photographer, critic*

Arlington
†Fletcher, Norman Collings *architect*
Fulmer, Vincent Anthony *retired college president*
Gumpertz, Werner Herbert *structural engineering company executive*
LaFauci, Horatio Michael *education educator emeritus*

Ashfield
Nye, Edwin Packard *mechanical engineering educator*
Pepyne, Edward Walter *lawyer, former educator*

Ashland
Borgeson, Earl Charles *law librarian, educator*
Gohlke, Frank William *photographer*

Attleboro
†Buckley, Charles E. *engineering executive*
Griffin, Edwin H., Jr. (Hank Griffin) *chemist*

Auburn
Baker, David Arthur *small business owner, manufacturer*

Babson Park
Genovese, Francis Charles (Frank Genovese) *economist, consultant, editor*
Glavin, William Francis *academic administrator*

Bedford
Alarcon, Rogelio Alfonso *physician, researcher*
†Aronstein, Laurence W. *middle school principal*
Brady, Upton Birnie *editor*
Carr, Paul Henry *physicist*
Cronson, Harry Marvin *electronics engineer*
Dill, Melville Reese, Jr. *industrial engineering consultant*
Dulchinos, Peter *lawyer*
Fante, Ronald Louis *engineering scientist*
Furumoto, Horace Wataru *medical products company executive*
Gilmartin, John A. *medical products company executive*
Goodman, William Beehler *editor, literary agent*
Griffin, Donald R(edfield) *zoology educator*
Hicks, Walter Joseph *electrical engineer, consultant*
Horowitz, Barry Martin *systems research and engineering company executive*
Jelalian, Albert V. *electrical engineer*
Kennedy, X. J. (Joseph Kennedy) *writer*
Kouyoumjian, Charles H. *diversified financial services company executive*
Kovaly, John Joseph *consulting engineering executive, educator*
†Landry, John Bernard, III *data processing executive*
Mailloux, Robert Joseph *physicist*
Ren, Chung-Li *engineer*
Stollerman, Gene Howard *physician, educator*
Volicer, Ladislav *physician, educator*
†Wagner, Harvey Alan *finance executive*
Wallace, John Edwin *retired meteorologist, consultant*
Zraket, Charles Anthony *systems research and engineering company executive*

Belmont
Allison, Elisabeth Kovacs *information company executive*
Bergson, Abram *economist, educator*
Bird, Edward Dennis *physician*
Buckley, Jerome Hamilton *English language educator*
Cohen, Bruce Michael *psychiatrist, educator, scientist*
†Frey, John Ward *landscape architect*
Gui, James Edmund *architect*
Haralampu, George Stelios *electric power engineer, former engineering executive electric utility company*
Keil, Alfred Adolf Heinrich *marine engineering educator*
†Klein, Martin Samuel *management consulting executive*
Levendusky, Philip George *clinical psychologist, administrator*
Luick, Robert Burns *lawyer*
†Merrill, Edward Wilson *chemical engineering educator*
Onesti, Silvio Joseph *psychiatrist*
Pope, Harrison Graham, Jr. *psychiatrist, educator*
Rowe, Richard R. *on-line information and management services company executive*
Seifert, William Walther *electrical engineering educator*
Sifneos, Peter Emanuel *psychiatrist*
Weiss, Roger Douglas *psychiatrist*

Beverly
Barger, Richard Wilson *hotel executive*
†Roberts, Richard John *molecular biologist*

Billerica
Gray, Charles Agustus *chemical company research executive*
Kolb, Charles Eugene *research corporation executive*
†Leblois, Axel *computer company executive*
LeCompte, Malcolm Aaron *research scientist*
†Mackenzie, Ward D. *computer company executive*
McCaffrey, Robert Henry, Jr. *retired manufacturing company executive*
Schmidt, James Robert *facilities engineer*

Boston
Ablow, Joseph *artist, educator*
Aborn, Foster Litchfield *insurance company executive*
Abraham, Nicholas Albert *lawyer, real estate developer*
Abrams, Ruth Ida *state supreme court justice*
Abt, Clark C. *social scientist, executive, engineer, publisher, educator*
Achatz, John *lawyer*
†Acton, Lloyd Phelps, Jr. *architect*
Adams, Douglass Franklin *radiologist, educator*
Adams, Phoebe-Lou *journalist*
Adelstein, S(tanley) James *physician, educator*
Adler, David Avram *psychiatrist*
Akin, Steven Paul *financial company executive*
Alden, Vernon Roger *corporate director, trustee*
Aldrich, Bailey *federal judge*
†Alexander, James Garth *architect*
Allard, David Henry *judge*
Allen, Nancy Schuster *librarian*
Alpert, Joel Jacobs *medical educator, pediatrician*
Ames, Adelbert, III *neurophysiologist, educator*
Ames, Damaris *publishing executive*
Ames, James Barr *lawyer*
†Amirault, Richard B. *career officer*
†Amorello, Matthew John *state senator*
Amy-Moreno de Toro, Angel Alberto *social sciences educator, writer, oral historian*
Anderson, Arthur Irvin *lawyer*
Anderson, John Edward *mechanical engineering educator*
Anderson, Timothy Christopher *consulting company executive*
Andre, Rae *writer, organizational behavior educator*
Andrews, Kenneth Richmond *business administration educator*
Angelou, Maya *author*
Anselme, Jean-Pierre Louis Marie *chemist*
Antoniades, Harry Nicholas *educator, research biochemist*
†Appelbaum, Diana Karter *author*
Argyris, Chris *organizational behavior educator*
Arias, Irwin Monroe *physician, educator*
Arkuss, Neil Philip *lawyer*
Arky, Ronald Alfred *medical educator*
Armand, Patrick *dancer*
Armstrong, Rodney *librarian*
Arnold, John David *management counselor, consultant*
Aronow, Saul *physicist*
Astrue, Michael James *lawyer*
†Atherton, William *insurance company executive*
Auerbach, Joseph *lawyer, educator*
Auerbach, Red (Arnold Jacob Auerbach) *professional basketball team executive*
Austen, K(arl) Frank *physician*
Austen, W(illiam) Gerald *surgeon, educator*
Avery, Mary Ellen *pediatrician, educator*
†Bae, Frank S. H. *law educator, law librarian*
Baer, Michael Alan *political scientist, educator*
Bailey, Richard Briggs *investment company executive*
†Bailey, Stephen *newspaper reporter*
Baker, Charles Duane *business administration educator, former management executive*
Bangs, Will Johnston *lawyer*
Banks, Henry H. *academic dean, physician*
Barger, A(braham) Clifford *physiology educator*
†Bargmann, Joel David *architect*
Barker, Edwin Bogue *musician*
Barlow, Charles Franklin *physician, educator*
†Barlow, John Sutton *neurophysiologist, electroencephalographer*
Barry, Patricia Pound *physician, educator*
Batchelder, Samuel Lawrence, Jr. *corporate lawyer*
Bates, Jeffrey C. *lawyer*
Batista, Duane R. *lawyer*
Bauer, Elaine Louise *ballet dancer*
Beal, Ilene *bank executive*
Beal, Robert Lawrence *real estate executive*
Beard, Charles Julian *lawyer*
Beatty, Jack J. *magazine editor*
Beck, William Samson *physician, educator, biochemist*
Becker, Fred Ronald *lawyer*
Beinhocker, Gilbert David *investment banker*
Belin, Gaspard d'Andelot *lawyer*
†Bellefontaine, Edgar John *law librarian, lawyer*
Benacerraf, Baruj *pathologist, educator*
Benjamin, William Chase *lawyer*
Bennett, George Frederick *investment manager*
Bennett, Rhona *bank administrator, consultant*
Berenberg, William *physician, educator*
†Berenson, Paul Stewart *advertising executive*
Berg, Norman Asplund *management educator*
Berg, Warren Stanley *retired banker*
Bergen, Kenneth William *lawyer*
Berger, Francine Ellis *radio executive, educator*
Berlew, Frank Kingston *lawyer*
Berman, William H. *publishing company executive*
Bernfield, Merton Ronald *pediatrician, scientist, educator*
Bernhard, Alexander Alfred *lawyer*
Bernhard, William Francis *thoracic and cardiovascular surgeon*
†Berry, Frederick E. *state legislator*
†Bertman, Richard Jay *architect*
†Bertonazzi, Louis Peter *state senator*
Bettenhausen, Elizabeth Ann *theology educator*
Bines, Harvey Ernest *lawyer, educator, writer*
Bird, Larry Joe *professional basketball player*
Blampied, Peter J. *banker*
Blau, Monte *radiology educator*
Blendon, Robert Jay *public health educator*
Bloch, Kurt Julius *physician*
Bloom, Howard Martin *lawyer*
Blout, Elkan Rogers *biological chemistry educator, university dean*
†Boch, William Joseph *advertising agency executive*
Bodman, Samuel Wright, III *specialty chemicals and materials company executive*
Bohnen, Michael J. *lawyer*
Bok, John Fairfield *lawyer*
Borenstein, Milton Conrad *lawyer, manufacturing company executive*
Bornheimer, Allen Millard *lawyer*
Borod, Ronald Sam *lawyer*
Boudin, Michael *federal judge*
†Bourque, Michael H. *interior designer*
Bourque, Ray *professional hockey player*
Bower, Joseph Lyon *business administration educator*
Bowler, Marianne Bianca *judge*
†Boyan, William L., Jr. *insurance company executive*
Boyden, W(alter) Lincoln *lawyer*
Brain, Joseph David *biomedical scientist*
†Brandt, Allan M. *medical history educator*
Braunwald, Eugene *physician, educator*
†Braver, Barbara Leix *religious organization communications administrator*
Brazelton, Thomas Berry *pediatrician, educator*
Brecher, Kenneth *astrophysicist*
Brenner, Barry Morton *physician*
†Brenton, Marianne Webber *state legislator, technical librarian*
†Britton, Richard Lindsay *advertising executive*
Brody, Richard Eric *lawyer*
Broitman, Selwyn Arthur *microbiologist, educator*
Bromsen, Maury Austin *historian, bibliographer, antiquarian bookseller*
Brountas, Paul Peter *lawyer*
Brovarski, Edward Joseph *curator, Egyptologist*
†Brown, David A.B. *strategy consultant*
Brown, Judith Olans *lawyer, educator*
Brown, Matthew *lawyer*
Brown, Michael *information technology executive*
Brown, Michael Robert *lawyer*
Brown, Stephen Lee *insurance company executive*
Brown, William L. *banker*
Browne, Kingsbury *lawyer*
Brownell, Gordon Lee *physicist, educator*
Bruns, William John, Jr. *business administration educator*
Buchanan, John Robert *physician, educator*
Buchanan, Robert McLeod *lawyer*
Buchin, Stanley Ira *management consultant, educator*
Buckley, Joseph W. *insurance company executive*
†Buckley, Mortimer Joseph *physician*
†Bulger, William Michael *state senator*
Burack, Sylvia Kamerman *editor, publisher*
Burakoff, Steven James *immunologist, educator*
Burgess, John Allen *lawyer*
Burleigh, Lewis Albert *lawyer*
Burnes, Kennett Farrar *chemical company executive*
Burns, Padraic *physician, psychiatrist, psychoanalyst, educator*
Burns, Richard Michael *public utility company executive*
Burns, Thomas David *lawyer*
Burr, Francis Hardon *lawyer*
Bustin, Edouard Jean *political scientist, educator*
Butterworth, George William, III *lawyer*
Cabot, Charles Codman, Jr. *lawyer*
Cabot, John G. L. *chemical manufacturing company executive*
Cabot, Louis Wellington *chemical manufacturing company executive*
Cabot, Thomas Dudley *chemical company executive*
Calderwood, Stanford Matson *investment management executive*
Caldwell, Gail *book critic*
Callow, Allan Dana *surgeon*
Campbell, Levin Hicks *federal judge*
Campbell, Richard P. *lawyer*
Canellos, George P. *physician educator*
Caner, George Colket, Jr. *lawyer*
Cantella, Vincent Michele *stockbroker*
Cantor, Charles Robert *biochemistry educator*
Caplan, Louis Robert *neurology educator*
†Carboni, Edwin Peters *advertising executive*
Cardona, Rodolfo *Spanish language and literature educator*
Carpenter, Charles Bernard *medical educator*
Carr, Jay Phillip *critic*
Carroll, James *author*
†Carroll, Matthew Shaun *reporter*
Carty, John Lydon *financial services executive*
†Casey, Paul C. *state legislator*
Cashel, Thomas William *lawyer, educator*
Casner, Truman Snell *lawyer*
Caso, Gasper *librarian, lawyer*
Cass, Ronald Andrew *lawyer, educator*
Cassidy, Carl Eugene *physician*
Cassilly, Richard *tenor*
Cellucci, Argeo Paul *state official*
Cervieri, John Anthony, Jr. *real estate company officer*
†Cevoli, Victor *graphic designer*
Chalmers, Thomas Clark *physician, educational and research administrator*
Chandler, Louis *lawyer*
Chapin, Melville *lawyer*
Cheever, Daniel Sargent *international affairs educator, editor*
†Chen, Ching-chih *information science educator, consultant*
Chen, Lincoln Chin-ho *medical educator*
†Child, Julia McWilliams (Mrs. Paul Child) *cooking expert, television personality, author*
Childress, Alice *playwright*
Chilvers, Derek *insurance company executive*
†Chinlund, Christine *newspaper editor*
Chobanian, Aram Van *medical school dean, cardiologist*
Christensen, Carl Roland *business administration educator*
Christenson, Charles John *business educator*
†Clancy, John M. *architectural firm executive*
Clapp, Eugene Howard, II *financial executive*
Clarke, Terence Michael *public relations and advertising executive*
†Clay, Landon Thomas *investment company executive*
Clemens, (William) Roger *professional baseball player*
Cleveland, Richard Joseph *surgeon*
†Cleven, Carol Chapman *state legislator*
Coffman, Jay Denton *physician, educator*
Cogan, John Francis, Jr. *lawyer*
Cogan, Robert David *composer, school official*
Cohen, Alan Seymour *internist*
Cohen, Jonathan Brewer *molecular neurobiologist, biochemist*
Cohen, Rachelle Sharon *journalist*
Cohen, Robert Sonné *physicist, philosopher, educator*
Cohn, Andrew Howard *lawyer*
Cohn, Robert Mark *publishing executive*
Colburn, Kenneth Hersey *investment banker*
Coleman, C. Norman *radiologist, oncologist, researcher, educator*
Coleman, John Joseph *telephone company executive*
Collings, Robert Biddlecombe *federal judge*
Collins, John Joseph, Jr. *cardiac and thoracic surgeon*
Collins, Monica Ann *journalist*
†Colloredo-Mansfeld, Ferdinand *real estate company executive*
Comegys, Walker Brockton *lawyer*
†Cone, Carol Lynn *public relations executive*
Connell, William Francis *diversified company executive*
Conners, John Brendan *insurance company executive*
Connolly, Michael Joseph *state official*
Connolly, Paul K., Jr. *lawyer*
Connors, Donald Louis *lawyer, land use planner*
Connors, John Michael, Jr. *advertising agency executive*
Conroy, Pat (Donald Patrick Conroy) *writer*
†Cook, David *editor*
Coolidge, Francis Lowell *lawyer*
Cooper, Scott Kendrick *professional baseball player*
Copeland, Anne Pitcairn *psychologist*
Corcoran, Paul John *physician*
Cornwall, Deborah Joyce *consulting firm executive, management consultant*
†Cotran, Ramzi S. *pathologist, educator*
Cotter, Joseph Francis *bank officer*
Coughlin, William Brendan *corporate executive*
Countryman, Gary Lee *insurance company executive*
Cousy, Bob Joseph *sports commentator*
Cox, Howard Ellis, Jr. *venture capitalist*
Crane, Andrew B. *state official*
Craver, James Bernard *lawyer*
Cronin, Bonnie Kathryn Lamb *legislative staff executive*
Cronin, Philip Mark *lawyer*
Crook, Robert Wayne *mutual funds executive*
Crowley, William Francis, Jr. *medical educator*
Crozier, William Marshall, Jr. *bank holding company executive*
Curley, Arthur *library director*
†Curran, Emily Katherine *museum director*
Curry, John Anthony, Jr. *university administrator*
Curry, John Michael *investment banker*
Curtin, John Joseph, Jr. *lawyer*
Curtin, Phyllis *music educator, former dean, operatic singer*
Curtis, Christopher Michael *magazine editor*
Cushing, Steven *educator, researcher, consultant*
Cutler, Arnold Robert *lawyer*
Dacey, Kathleen Ryan *judge*
D'Agostino, Ralph Benedict *mathematician, statistician, educator, consultant*
D'Alessandro, David Francis *financial services company executive*
Daley, Paul Patrick *lawyer*
Danziger, Jeff *political cartoonist, writer*
Darehshori, Nader Farhang *publishing sales executive*
Dassori, Frederic Davis, Jr. *lawyer*
†Davies, Don *educator*
Davis, George Wilmot *electric utility executive*
Davis, Harold Truscott *retired lawyer*
†Davis, Michael Richard *architect*
Davis, Robert Jocelyn *engineering executive*
Davis, William Arthur *writer, editor*
Davison, Peter *editor, poet*
Davison, Peter Fitzgerald *retired science administrator, consultant*
Dawson, Andre Fernando *professional baseball player*
Dean, Robert Charles *architect*
de Burlo, Comegys Russell, Jr. *investment advisor, educator*
De Cherney, Alan Hersh *obstetrics and gynecology educator*
Dederer, William Bowne *music educator, dean*
Deissler, Mary A. *foundation executive*
Delaney, John White *lawyer*

Delbanco, Thomas Lewis *medical educator, researcher*
Delinsky, Stephen R. *lawyer*
De Luca, Carlo John *biomedical engineer*
Denniston, Brackett Badger, III *lawyer*
Dentler, Robert Arnold *sociologist, educator*
de Rham, Casimir, Jr. *lawyer*
DeSanctis, Roman William *cardiologist*
Desforges, Jane Fay *medical educator, physician*
Deutsch, Stephen B. *lawyer*
Di Domenica, Robert Anthony *musician, composer*
Diener, Betty Jane *marketing educator, university administrator*
Dignan, Thomas Gregory, Jr. *lawyer*
Dillon, James Joseph *lawyer*
Dineen, John K. *lawyer*
DiStasio, James Shannon *accountant*
Dixon, Andrew Lee, Jr. *cable television company executive, lawyer*
Donahue, Douglas Aidan, Jr. *business executive*
Donaldson, David Marbury *lawyer*
†Donovan, Carol Ann *state legislator*
†Donovan, Helen W. *newspaper editor*
Dooley, Arch Richard *business administration educator*
Doorley, Thomas Lawrence, III *management consulting firm executive*
†Doran, Stephen William *state legislator, mortgage banker*
Dreben, Raya Spiegel *judge*
†Driscoll, John S. *newspaper editor*
Driver, William Raymond, Jr. *banker*
Drohan, Thomas H. *investment management executive*
†Duffy, Kenneth J. *insurance company executive*
†Durand, Robert Alan *state senator*
Dusseault, C. Dean *lawyer*
Dvorak, Harold F. *pathologist, educator, scientist*
Eastman, Thomas George *investment management executive*
Eckstein, Marlene R. *vascular radiologist*
Eder, Richard Gray *newspaper critic*
Egdahl, Richard Harrison *surgeon, medical educator, health science administrator*
Ehrlich, M. Gordon *lawyer*
Eichorn, John Frederick Gerard, Jr. *utility executive*
Eisenberg, Leon *psychiatrist, educator*
†Eisner, Alan S. *newspaper editor*
Eisner, Sister Janet Margaret *college president*
El-Baz, Farouk *program director, educator*
Eldridge, Larry (William Lawrence Eldridge) *journalist*
Elfers, William *retired investment company director*
Elfner, Albert Henry, III *mutual fund management company executive*
Elkus, Howard Felix *architect*
Elliott, Byron Kauffman *lawyer, business executive*
Ellis, David Wertz *museum director*
Ellis, Franklin Henry, Jr. *surgeon, educator*
Elsbree, John Francis *banker*
Engel, David Lewis *lawyer*
Epstein, Franklin Harold *physician, educator*
Erickson, Kenneth W. *lawyer*
Eskandarian, Edward *advertising agency executive*
Essex, Myron Elmer *microbiology educator*
Estabrooks, Gordon Charles *secondary education educator*
Estin, Hans Howard *investment executive*
Evans, Donald John *lawyer*
†Everitt, Charles Bell *publishing executive*
†Fagan, Thomas Maurice *trade show management executive*
Fairbanks, Jonathan Leo *museum curator*
Falb, Peter Lawrence *mathematician, educator, investment company executive*
†Faller, Douglas V. *cancer research administrator*
Fanning, Katherine Woodruff *editor, journalism educator*
Farrah, Elias George *lawyer*
Fausch, David Arthur *public relations executive*
Fay, Michael Leo *lawyer*
Fazzone, David A. *lawyer*
†Feder, Donald Albert *syndicated columnist*
Feeney, Mark *newspaper editor*
†Feldman, Gerald *advertising executive*
Feldman, Robert George *neurologist, medical educator*
Felter, John Kenneth *lawyer*
Ferris, Benjamin Greeley, Jr. *retired physician, environmental researcher, educator*
Field, James Bernard *internist, educator*
Fields, Bernard Nathan *microbiologist, physician*
Fieleke, Norman Siegfried *economist*
Fine, Samuel *biomedical engineering educator, consultant*
Fineberg, Harvey Vernon *physician, educator*
Finegold, Maurice Nathan *architect*
Fink, Joanna Elizabeth *art dealer*
Finnegan, Neal Francis *banker*
Fischer, Eric Robert *lawyer, educator*
Fischer, Thomas Covell *law educator, consultant, writer, lawyer*
Fish, David Earl *insurance company executive*
Fisher, Champe Andrews *lawyer*
†Fitzgibbons, James M. *diversified company executive*
Fitzpatrick, Thomas Bernard *dermatologist, educator*
Flaherty, Charles Francis *state speaker of the house*
Flansburgh, Earl Robert *architect*
Fletcher, Robert Hillman *medical educator*
Fletcher, Suzanne Wright *physician, educator*
†Flint, Anthony Evans *journalist*
Floor, Richard Earl *lawyer*
Folkman, Moses Judah *surgeon*
Fonvielle, William Harold *management consultant*
Forbes, Peter *architect*
Ford, Chris *professional basketball coach*
†Forman, Peter *state legislator*
Foss, Clive Frank Wilson *history educator*
Fox, Bernard Hayman *cancer epidemiologist, educator*
Fox, Francis Haney *lawyer*
Frankenheim, Samuel *lawyer*
Frankl, Spencer Nelson *dentist, university dean*
Fraser, Robert Burchmore *lawyer*
Freed, Rita Evelyn *curator, Egyptologist*
Freedberg, A. Stone *physician*
Freehling, Daniel Joseph *law educator, law library director*
†Freeman, Lisa M. *veterinarian*
Frei, Emil, III *physician, medical researcher, educator*
Freiman, David Galland *pathologist, educator*
Freishtat, Harvey W. *lawyer*
Fremont-Smith, Marion R. *lawyer*
Frigoletto, Fredric David, Jr. *physician*
Fruitt, Paul N. *manufacturing executive*
Gabel, Creighton *anthropologist, educator*

Galaburda, Albert Mark *neurologist, researcher, educator*
†Gallary, Peter Hayden *financial services company executive*
†Gallaudet, Denison *bank executive*
Galvani, Paul B. *lawyer*
Gamson, Zelda *sociologist, researcher*
†Gamst, Frederick Charles *anthropology educator*
Gang, Stephen R. *motion picture executive, consultant*
Garai, Gabor *lawyer*
Garcia, Adolfo Ramon *lawyer*
Gardner, Dorsey Robertson *finance company executive*
Gardner, George Peabody *investment banker*
Garrison, Althea *health center executive, civic worker, former goverment official*
Gaudreau, Russell A., Jr. *lawyer*
Gault, Robert Mellor *lawyer*
†Gavitt, Dave *professional sports team executive*
Gellis, Sydney Saul *physician*
†Gendron, George *magazine editor*
Gens, Peter David *lawyer*
†Gergely, John *biochemistry educator*
Gerstmayr, John Wolfgang *lawyer*
Gesmer, Henry *lawyer*
Gianino, John Joseph *insurance executive*
Gibbons, Ronald John *microbiologist, educator*
Gibran, Kahlil *sculptor*
Gibson, Barry Joseph *magazine editor*
Gifford, Charles Kilvert *banker*
Gifford, Nelson Sage *financial company executive*
Gimbrone, Michael Anthony, Jr. *pathologist, educator*
Giso, Frank, III *lawyer*
Glass, Milton Louis *retired manufacturing company executive*
Glassman, Herbert Haskel *architect*
Glazer, Donald Wayne *business executive, lawyer, educator*
Glazer, Michael H. *lawyer*
Gleason, Jean Berko *psychology educator*
Glimcher, Melvin Jacob *orthopedic surgeon*
Glosband, Daniel Martin *lawyer*
Godine, David Richard *publishing company executive*
Goldberg, Avram Jacob *consulting and investing company executive, arbitrator*
Goldberg, Irving Hyman *molecular pharmacology and biochemistry educator*
Goldsmith, Harry Sawyer *surgeon, educator*
†Goodglass, Harold *psychologist, neurology educator*
Goodman, Louis Allan *lawyer*
†Goodman, Sherri Wasserman *lawyer*
Goody, Joan *architect*
Gorham, William Hartshorne *lawyer*
Gorman, James Lou *professional baseball team executive*
Gottlieb, Leonard Solomon *pathology educator*
Goyal, Raj Kumar *medical educator*
†Graham, Gary L. *architect*
†Graham, John David *public health educator*
Graham, Patrick Francis *management consulting company executive*
Greco, Michael S. *lawyer*
Greeley, Walter Franklin *management and acquisition corporation executive, lawyer*
Green, Gareth Montraville *physician, educator, scientist*
Green, Howard *cellular physiologist, educator, administrator*
Greenblatt, David J. *pharmacologist, educator*
†Greene, Leonard J. *newspaper columnist*
Greene, Robert Allan *former university administrator*
Greenwald, Sheila Ellen *writer, illustrator*
Greer, Gordon Bruce *lawyer*
Grillo, Hermes Conrad *surgeon*
Gross, Ira Kenneth *lawyer*
Grossfeld, Stan *newspaper photography executive, author*
Grossman, Frances Kaplan *psychologist*
Grossman, Jerome Harvey *medical educator, administrator*
Gruhl, Robert Herbert *insurance company executive*
Gulley, Joan Long *banker*
Haas, Kenneth Gregg *orchestra executive*
Haber, Edgar *physician, educator*
Haber, Robert J. *mutual fund manager*
Haddad, Ernest Mudarri *lawyer*
Hagler, Jon Lewis *investment executive*
Hailey, Arthur *writer*
Haley, Joseph William *lawyer*
†Haley, Paul Richard *lawyer, state legislator*
Hall, Henry Lyon, Jr. *lawyer*
Hall, John Emmett *orthopedic surgeon, educator*
Hamill, John P. *bank executive*
Hamilton, John Dayton, Jr. *lawyer*
†Hamilton, Kerry Lee *advertising executive*
Hammer, Roy Armand *lawyer*
Hammock, John Calvin *international economic developer, consultant*
Hammond, Norman David Curle *archaeology educator, researcher*
Hampton, Henry Eugene, Jr. *film and television producer*
Hand, John *lawyer*
Handford, Martin John *illustrator, author*
†Harkins, Lida E. *state legislator, educator*
Harrington, Edward F. *federal judge*
Harrington, John Leo *baseball company executive, foundation administrator*
Harrington, John Michael, Jr. *lawyer*
Harris, Barbara C(lementine) *bishop*
Harris, Burton Henry *surgeon*
Harris, William Hamilton *orthopedic surgeon*
Harshbarger, Scott *state attorney general*
Harter, Richard Morton *lawyer*
Hartmann, Edward George *historian, educator*
Harvey, Leslie Leo (Les Harvey) *composer, production company executive*
Harvey, William Burnett *law educator emeritus*
Hassan, William Ephriam, Jr. *lawyer*
Haussermann, Oscar William, Jr. *lawyer*
†Hawke, Robert Douglas *state legislator*
Hawkey, G. Michael *lawyer*
Hawley, Anne *museum director*
Hay, Elizabeth Dexter *embryology researcher, educator*
Hayes, Andrew Wallace, II *consumer products company executive*
Hayes, Robert Francis *lawyer*
Hayes, Robert Herrick *technology management educator*
Hayes, Samuel Linton, III *business educator*
Hayward, Charles E. *publishing company executive*
†Hayward, Jeffrey J. *state legislator*

†Healy, Gerald Burke *otolaryngologist*
Hedley-Whyte, Elizabeth Tessa *neuropathologist*
Heigham, James Crichton *lawyer*
Hein, John William *dentist, educator*
†Heineman, Robert M. *architectural firm executive*
Hemnes, Thomas Michael Sheridan *lawyer*
Henry, DeWitt Pawling, II *creative writing educator, writer, arts administrator*
Henry, Joseph Louis *university dean*
Herwitz, Carla Barron *lawyer*
Hiatt, Howard H. *physician, educator*
†Hicks, Lucile P. *state legislator*
Higgins, George Vincent *journalist, lawyer, author*
Hill, George Jackson, III *advertising agency executive*
Hill, Richard Devereux *retired banker*
Hillman, William Chernick *federal bankruptcy judge*
Hills, Patricia Gorton Schulze *curator*
Hines, Marion Ernest *electronic engineering consultant*
Hingson, Ralph W. *medical educator*
Hintikka, Jaakko *philosopher, educator*
†Hirtle, Richard C. *insurance company executive*
Hjerpe, Edward Alfred, III *finance and banking executive*
Hobbs, Matthew Hallock *investment banker*
Hobson, Butch *major league baseball team manager*
Hobson, John Allan *psychiatrist, researcher, educator*
Hoffman, Christian Matthew *lawyer*
Hoffman, S. Joseph *advertising agency executive*
Hohler, G. Robert *marketing consultant*
†Holey, Ronald Loren *retired construction company executive*
Holland, Hubert Brian *lawyer*
Holloway, Bruce Keener *former air force officer*
Hooker, Michael Kenneth *college president*
Hoort, Steven Thomas *lawyer*
†Hornblower, Augusta *state legislator*
Hornig, Donald Frederick *scientist*
Horowitz, Morris A. *economist*
Hotchkiss, Andra Ruth *lawyer*
Houtchens, Robert Austin, Jr. *biochemist*
Howe, Jas. Murray *lawyer*
Hoyt, Herbert Austin Aikins *television producer*
Hsiung, Robert Yuan Chun *architect*
Hubel, David Hunter *physiologist, educator*
Hughes, George Michael *lawyer*
Hurd, J. Nicholas *executive recruiting consultant, former banker*
†Hutchinson, Bernard Thomas *ophthalmologist*
Hutter, Adolph Matthew, Jr. *cardiologist, educator*
Iafrate, Al Anthony *professional hockey player*
Isaacs, Helen Coolidge Adams (Mrs. Kenneth L. Isaacs) *artist*
Isaacson, John Magyar *executive search firm executive*
†Isham, Carolynn Clough *advertising executive*
Jandl, James Harriman *physician, educator*
Jaroch, Timothy D. *lawyer*
†Jehlen, Patricia D. *state legislator*
Jenks, Homer Simeon *newspaper editor, free-lance writer*
Jochum, Veronica *pianist*
Johannsen, Peter George *lawyer*
Johnson, David Elliot *bishop*
Johnson, Edward Crosby, III *financial company executive*
Johnston, Richard Alan *lawyer*
†Jones, Donald Wayne *publisher*
Jones, Hugh Richard, Jr. *lawyer*
Jones, Jeffrey Foster *lawyer*
Jones, Rodney G. *poet, English educator*
Jones, Sheldon Atwell *lawyer*
Jordan, Alexander Joseph, Jr. *lawyer*
†Julian, Sheryl *newspaper writer*
Kahn, Carl Ronald *research laboratory administrator*
Kamer, Joel Victor *insurance company executive, actuary*
Kames, Kenneth F. *manufacturing company executive*
Kane, E(dward) Leonard *electronics company executive, lawyer, association executive*
Kane, Louis Isaac *merchant*
Kanin, Dennis Roy *lawyer*
Kannel, William Bernard *cardiovascular epidemiologist*
Kanter, Rosabeth Moss *management educator, consultant, writer*
Kapioltas, John *hotel company executive*
Kaplan, Lawrence Edward *lawyer*
Karelitz, Robert N(elson) *lawyer*
Karnovsky, Manfred L. *biochemistry educator*
Karnovsky, Morris John *pathologist, biologist*
†Kassirer, Jerome Paul *editor-in-chief*
†Katz, Larry *writer*
Katz, Peter *lawyer*
†Kauffman, Godfrey *newspaper publishing executive*
Kazemi, Homayoun *physician, medical educator*
Keating, Michael Burns *lawyer*
Keeton, Robert Ernest *federal judge*
Kehoe, William Francis *lawyer*
Keller, Stanley *lawyer*
†Kelly, Edmund F. *insurance company executive*
Kelly, Thomas J. *lawyer*
Kennedy, Eugene Patrick *biochemist, educator*
Kenner, Brian T. *lawyer*
Kenney, Raymond Joseph, Jr. *lawyer*
†Kerry, Cameron F. *lawyer*
Kiang, Nelson Yuan-sheng *medical educator*
Kieff, Elliott Dan *medical educator*
Kimball, George E., III *sports columnist*
Kimura, Robert Shigetsugu *otologic researcher*
King, Kernan Francis *insurance company executive, lawyer*
†King, Nick *Newspaper editor*
King, Robert David *insurance company executive*
King, William Bruce *lawyer*
Kingman, William Lockwood *financial consultant*
Kirchick, William Dean *lawyer*
Kirk, Paul Grattan, Jr. *lawyer, former political organization official*
Kirkpatrick, Edward Thomson *college administrator, mechanical engineer*
Kitz, Richard John *anesthesiologist, educator*
Klarfeld, Jonathan Michael *journalism educator*
Kleiner, Fred Scott *art history and archaeology educator, editor*
Klem, Christopher A. *lawyer*
†Klempner, Mark Steven Joel *physician, research scientist, educator*
Klotz, Charles Rodger *shipping company executive*
Knight, Norman *broadcast executive*
†Knox, Richard Albert *journalist*
†Koetter, Fred *architectural firm executive, educator, dean*
Koffel, William Barry *lawyer*

†Kolodner, Richard David *biochemist, educator*
Kopelman, Leonard *lawyer*
Korb, Kenneth Allan *lawyer*
Korff, Ira A. *rabbi*
Kotter, John Paul *organizational behavior educator, management consultant*
Krakow, Barbara Levy *art gallery executive*
Krane, Stephen Martin *physician, educator*
Kretschmer, Keith Hughes *stockbroker*
Kubzansky, Philip Eugene *environmental and organizational psychologist*
Kunkel, Louis Martens *research scientist, educator*
Kurzweil, Edith *sociology educator, editor*
Kwasnick, Paul Jack *retail executive*
†La Fontaine, Raymond M. *insurance company executive*
Laine, Richard R. *banking executive*
Lampert, James B. *lawyer*
Lane, Harold Edwin *retired management educator, consultant*
Lane, Newton Alexander *lawyer*
Langer, Lawrence Lee *English educator, writer*
Langermann, John W.R. *institutional equity salesperson*
Larkin, Michael John *newspaper editor, journalist*
LaRow, Sister DeChantal *hospital administrator, health councillor*
Lasagna, Louis Cesare *medical educator*
Last, Michael P. *lawyer*
Latham, James David *lawyer*
Lawrence, Merloyd Ludington *editor*
Lawrence, Paul Roger *retired organizational behavior educator*
Leaf, Alexander *physician, educator*
Lee, David Stoddart *investment counselor*
†Lee, Donald Young (Don Lee) *publishing executive, editor, writer*
Lee, Jonathan Owen *financial services company executive, lawyer*
†Lee, Robin S. *surgeon, researcher*
Lees, Sidney *research facility administrator, bioengineering educator*
Leibler, Kenneth Robert *financial service executive*
Leland, Warren Hanan *engineering-construction company executive*
Leone, Peter R. *lawyer*
Le Quesne, Philip William *chemistry educator, researcher*
Lesser, Laurence *music conservatory president, cellist, educator*
Lettieri, Richard Joseph *lawyer*
Levine, Ruth Rothenberg *biomedical science educator*
Levine, Sol *sociologist*
Levinsky, Norman George *physician, educator*
Lewis, Anthony *newspaper columnist*
Ley, Andrew James *lawyer*
Liacos, Paul Julian *state supreme judicial court chief justice*
Libby, Peter *cardiologist, medical researcher*
Lichtenberg, Margaret Klee *publishing company executive*
Lichtin, Norman Nahum *chemistry educator*
Lindsay, Stephen Prout *lawyer*
Lipton, Stuart Arthur *neuroscientist*
Little, Arthur Dehon *investment banker*
Little, John Bertram *physician, radiobiology educator, researcher*
Livingston, David Morse *biomedical scientist, physician, internist*
Locke, Steven Elliot *psychiatrist*
Lockwood, Rhodes Greene *retired lawyer*
Lodge, George C(abot) *business administration educator*
Loeser, Hans Ferdinand *lawyer*
Logue, Edward Joseph *development company executive*
Looney, William Francis, Jr. *lawyer*
Loring, Arthur *lawyer, financial services company executive*
Loring, Caleb, Jr. *investment company executive*
Loughlin, Kevin Raymond *urologic surgeon, researcher*
Lowry, Bates *art historian, museum director*
Lowry, Lois (Hammersberg) *author*
Luongo, C. Paul *public relations executive*
Lykins, Marshall Herbert *insurance company executive*
Lyman, Henry *retired publisher, marine fisheries consultant*
Lynch, Francis Charles *lawyer*
Lynch, Peter S. *retired portfolio manager*
Lynch, Sandra Lea *lawyer*
Lynton, Ernest Albert *physicist, educator, former university official*
Lyons, Paul Vincent *lawyer*
MacCombie, Bruce Franklin *composer, college administrator*
MacDougall, Peter *lawyer*
Macera, Salvatore *industrial executive*
†Macomber, John D. *construction executive*
Malamy, Michael Howard *molecular biology educator*
Malenka, Bertram Julian *physicist, educator*
Malone, Joseph P. *state treasurer*
Maloney, Therese Adele *insurance company executive*
†Mandell, Samuel W. W. *corporate lawyer*
†Manfredi, David Peter *architect*
Mankin, Henry Jay *physician, educator*
Mannick, John Anthony *surgeon*
Manning, Robert Joseph *editor*
†Manning, Thomas Allen *publishing company executive*
Manning, William Frederick *wire service photographer*
Marcellino, James J. *lawyer*
Markham, Jesse William *economist*
Marks, Bruce *artistic director, choreographer*
Marshall, Martin Vivan *business administration educator, business consultant*
Mason, Herbert Warren, Jr. *religion and history educator, author*
Matthews, Roger Hardin *lawyer*
May, James Warren, Jr. *plastic surgeon, medical association executive*
Mazzone, A. David *federal judge*
McArdle, John *publishing company executive*
Mc Arthur, Janet Ward *endocrinologist, educator*
†Mc Carthy, Denis Michael *investment executive*
Mc Carthy, Joseph Michael *historian*
Mc Carthy, Patrick Edward *institute president*
McChesney, S. Elaine *lawyer*
McCluskey, Jean Louise *civil and consulting engineer*
McCluskey, Robert Timmons *physician*
McCraw, Thomas Kincaid *author, educator*
McDaniels, John Francis *investment banker*

Mc Dermott, William Vincent, Jr. physician, educator
†Mc Donough, William corporate lawyer
McDougal, William Scott urology educator
McFarlan, Franklin Warren business administration educator
McGovern, A. Lane lawyer
McHale, Kevin Edward former professional basketball player
McHugh, Edward Francis, Jr. lawyer
McKibben, Gordon Charles journalist, correspondent
McKinley, William Thomas composer, performer, educator
†McKinnell, Noel Michael architect, educator
†McMahon, Lillian Elizabeth hematologist
McMullin, Ruth Roney retired publishing company executive
Mc Neice, John Ambrose, Jr. investment company executive
McPhee, Jonathan music director, conductor
Medearis, Donald Norman, Jr. physician, educator
Meister, Mark Jay museum director, professional society administrator
Melbin, Murray sociologist
†Melconian, Linda Jean state senator, lawyer
Mellins, Harry Zachary radiologist, educator
Mendler, Edward Charles lawyer
Menino, Thomas M. mayor
Menoyo, Eric Felix lawyer
Menyuk, Paula developmental psycholinguistics educator
Menzies, Ian Stuart newspaper editor
Mercer, Douglas lawyer
Merton, Robert C. economist, educator
Meserve, Robert William lawyer
Meserve, William George lawyer
Messerle, Judith Rose medical librarian, public relations director
Messing, Arnold Philip lawyer
Metcalf, Arthur George Bradford electronics company executive
Metzer, Patricia Ann lawyer
Mikels, Richard Eliot lawyer
Miliora, Maria Teresa chemist, psychotherapist, psychoanalyst, educator
Millar, Sally Gray nurse
Miller, Alan Gershon lawyer
Miller, Alan Robert lawyer
Miller, J. Philip television producer, director, educator
†Miller, John A., Jr. public relations executive
Miller, Keith Wyatt pharmacology educator
Miller, Naomi art historian
Milley, Jane Elizabeth academic administrator
Mitchell, Peter McQuilkin educational administrator
Mitchell, W. Randle, Jr. textile company executive
†Modugno, Maria publishing executive
Moellering, Robert Charles, Jr. internist, educator
Monaco, Anthony Peter surgery educator, medical institute administrator
†Monaghan, William Henry advertising executive
Moncreiff, Robert P. lawyer
Monrad, Ernest Ejner trust company executive
Montgomery, William Wayne surgeon
Mooney, Michael Edward lawyer
Moore, Francis Daniels retired surgeon, educator, consultant, editor
Moore, Richard Lawrence structural engineer, consultant
Moran, James J., Jr. lawyer
Morby, Jacqueline venture capitalist
Morgan, Frank Brown Webb, Jr. journalist, consultant
†Morgentaler, Abraham urologist, researcher
Moriarty, George Marshall lawyer
Moriarty, John opera administrator, artistic director
†Morris, Gerald Douglas newspaper editor
Morrison, Gordon Mackay, Jr. investment company executive
Morse, Garlan, Jr. real estate investment counseling officer
Morton, Edward James insurance company executive
Morton, John Hall lawyer
Morton, William Gilbert, Jr. stock exchange executive
Moseley, Frederick Strong, III investment banker
†Moskowitz, Michael Arthur neuroscientist, neurologist
Moss, Guy B. lawyer
Muldoon, Robert Joseph, Jr. lawyer
Mullaney, Joseph E. lawyer
Mulvoy, Thomas F., Jr. newspaper editor, journalist
Munro, Hamish Nisbet biochemist, educator
Munsat, Theodore L. neurologist, researcher
Murchie, Guy author
†Murphy, Dennis Michael state legislator
Murphy, Evelyn Frances healthcare administrator, former lieutenant governor
Mygatt, Susan Hall lawyer
Nadas, Alexander Sandor pediatric cardiologist
Naimi, Shapur cardiologist, educator
Nashe, Carol insurance executive, consultant
Nathan, David Gordon physician, educator
Neely, Cam professional hockey player
Neely, Thomas Emerson lawyer
Nelson, David S. federal judge
Nesmith, Richard Duey clergyman, theology educator
Nesson, H. Richard medical administrator, physician
Neville, Robert Cummings philosophy and religion educator
Newberg, Joseph H. lawyer
Newhouse, Joseph Paul economics educator
Newman, Richard Alan publisher, editor and consultant
Nichols, David Harry gynecologic surgeon, obstetrics and gynecology educator, author
Nichols, William Deming lawyer
Norris, Melvin lawyer
Norton, Augustus Richard political science educator
Notopoulos, Alexander Anastasios, Jr. lawyer
†Notter, George Madison, Jr. architect
Novack, Kenneth Joseph lawyer
Nutt, Robert L. lawyer
Nutt, William James investment, management and mutual funds company executive
Nylander, Jane Louise museum director
Oates, Adam R. professional hockey player
Oates, William Armstrong, Jr. investment company executive
O'Block, Robert Paul management consultant
O'Connell, Kevin George priest, fundraiser, former college president
O'Dell, Edward Thomas, Jr. lawyer
O'Donnell, Thomas Lawrence Patrick lawyer
O'Hern, Jane Susan psychologist, educator
Ojemann, Robert Gerdes neurosurgeon
O'Leary, Joseph Evans lawyer
O'Neil, William Francis academic administrator
O'Neill, Philip Daniel, Jr. lawyer, educator
O'Neill, Timothy P. lawyer
Orr, Bobby (Robert Gordon Orr) former hockey player
Osteen, Carolyn McCue lawyer
Packer, Rekha Desai lawyer
Papagiannis, Michael Dimitrios astronomer, educator
Pardee, Arthur Beck biochemist, educator
Pardus, Donald Gene utility executive
Paris, Stephen J. lawyer
Park, James Theodore microbiologist, educator
†Park, William H(erron) financial executive
Park, William Wynnewood law educator
Parker, Christopher William lawyer
Parker, Everett Hoitt lawyer
Partan, Daniel Gordon lawyer, educator
Patterson, John de la Roche, Jr. lawyer
Patterson, Robert Logan librarian, country and western dance promoter
Paul, Oglesby physician
†Payette, Thomas Martin architect
Pechilis, William John lawyer
Peckham, John Munroe, III investment executive, author
Penney, Sherry Hood university chancellor, educator
Perera, Lawrence Thacher lawyer
Perkins, James Wood lawyer
Perkins, John Allen lawyer
Perkins, Malcolm Donald lawyer
Perkins, Samuel lawyer
Perocchi, Paul Patrick lawyer
Peterson, Roger Tory ornithologist, artist
Pettit, John W. hospital administrator
Peyton, Malcolm C. composer
Phillips, Daniel Anthony trust company executive
Phillips, William English language educator, editor, author
Pierce, Allan Dale engineering educator, researcher
Pierce, Daniel investment company executive
Pierce, Joel Farwell lawyer
Pierce, Martin E., Jr. fire commissioner
Pineda, Marianna sculptor, educator
†Pines, Lois G. state legislator
Pinsky, Robert Neal poet, educator
Piret, Marguerite Alice investment banker
Ploszaj, Stephen Charles lawyer
Pochi, Peter Ernest physician
Pomeroy, Robert Corttis lawyer
†Popeo, R. Robert lawyer
Poser, Charles Marcel neurology educator
Poussaint, Alvin Francis psychiatrist, educator
Pratt, Albert financial consultant, trustee
Pratt, John Winsor statistics educator
Prescott, John Hernage aquarium executive
Preston, Malcolm artist, art critic
†Prior, Ronald L. animal scientist, nutritionist
Prout, Curtis physician
†Provost, David Emile financial services executive
Psathas, George sociologist, educator
Purcell, Patrick Joseph newspaper publisher
Pynchon, Thomas author
Quelle, Frederick William, Jr. physicist
Rabkin, Mitchell Thornton physician, hospital administrator, educator
Rabstejnek, George John management consultant
Radloff, Robert Albert real estate executive
Raemer, Harold Roy electrical engineering educator
Raish, David Langdon lawyer
†Raskin, Paul D. resoure management and environmental research administrator
Raviola, Elio anatomist, neurobiologist
†Rawn, William Leete, III architect
Ray, William F. banker
Reck, Joel M(arvin) lawyer
Reichlin, Seymour physician, educator
Reid, Lynne McArthur pathologist
Reiling, Henry Bernard business educator
Reinherz, Helen Zarsky social services educator
Relman, Arnold Seymour physician, educator
Reppert, Steven Marion pediatrician, educator
Resnik, Peter L. lawyer
Reynolds, Hanson Shallcross lawyer
†Richie, Jerome Paul surgeon, educator
Riley, Robert Edward financial services company executive
Riley, Stephen Thomas historian, librarian
†Riordan, James Francis biochemistry educator
Ritt, Roger Merrill lawyer
Rittner, Carl Frederick educational administrator
Rizzo, William Ober lawyer
Robinson, Sumner Martin college administrator
†Robinson, Walter newspaper editor
Rodgers, William Henry professional runner
†Rodman, Oliver newspaper publishing executive
Roehrig, C(harles) Burns internist, health policy consultant, editor
†Roffey, Robert C., Jr. insurance company executive
†Rogeness, Mary Speer state legislator
†Rogers, John Healy congressman
Rohda, Rodney Raymond insurance company executive
Roman, William Edward investment banker
Romney, W Mitt investment company executive
Ronayne, Michael Richard, Jr. academic dean
Rose, Alan Douglas lawyer
Rosen, Fred Saul pediatrics educator
†Rosenberg, Irwin Harold physician, educator
†Rosenberg, James William marketing executive
Rosenberg, Manuel retail company executive
Rosenblatt, Michael medical researcher, educator
Rosensteel, John William insurance company executive
Ross, Carolyn Thayer lawyer
Rossell, Christine Hamilton political science educator
Rotenberg, Sheldon violinist
Row, Peter L. musician, educator
Rush, David medical investigator, epidemiologist
†Rushing, Byron state legislator
Russell, Paul Snowden surgeon, educator
Rutstein, Stanley Harold apparel retailing company executive
Ryan, Kenneth John physician, educator
Sager, Ruth geneticist
St. Clair, James Draper lawyer
Saleh, Bahaa E. A. electrical engineering educator
†Sales, Robert Julian newspaper editor
Sanders, Irwin Taylor sociology educator
Sandson, John I. physician, educator, retired university dean
Saparoff, Peter M. lawyer
Saper, Clifford Baird neurobiology and neurology educator
Sargeant, Ernest James lawyer
Sargent, David Jasper university executive, lawyer
†Saris, Patti B. federal judge
Sasson, Michel conductor
Sauer, David Andrew librarian
Saunders, Donald Leslie hotel executive, commercial real estate company executive
Saunders, Roger Alfred hotel group executive
Savrann, Richard Allen lawyer
Saxe, Edward A. lawyer
†Say, Allen children's writer, illustrator
Schaechter, Moselio microbiology educator
Schaeneman, Lewis G., Jr. retail company executive
Schaller, Jane Green pediatrician
Schildkraut, Joseph Jacob psychiatrist, educator
Schlossman, Stuart Franklin physician, educator, researcher
Schmelzer, Henry Louis Phillip lawyer, financial company executive
Schram, Ronald Byard lawyer
Schuknecht, Harold Frederick physician, educator
Schwartz, Bernard physician
Schwartz, Jules Jacob management educator
†Schwartz, Lloyd music critic, poet
Scipione, Richard Stephen insurance company executive, lawyer
Scott, A. Hugh lawyer
†Scott, Arnold Duane lawyer
Scrimshaw, Nevin Stewart physician, nutrition and health educator
Sears, John Winthrop lawyer
Seddon, Johanna Margaret ophthalmologist, epidemiologist
Segal, Robert Mandal lawyer
Selkoe, Dennis Jesse neurologist, researcher, educator
†Sellars, Peter theater director
Sessoms, Allen Lee academic administrator, former diplomat, physicist
Shader, Richard Irwin psychiatrist, educator
Shafto, Robert Austin insurance company executive
Shapiro, Eli business consultant, educator, economist
Shapiro, Jerome Herbert radiologist, educator
Shapiro, Sandra lawyer
Shattuck, Roger Whitney author, educator
Shaw, James Headon nutritionist, educator
Shemin, Barry L. insurance company executive
Shepley, Hugh architect
Sherman, Elliot Mark lawyer
Shields, Lawrence Thornton orthopedic surgeon, educator
Shira, Robert Bruce university administrator, oral surgery educator
Shklar, Gerald oral pathologist, periodontist, educator
†Shucart, William Arthur neurosurgeon
Silber, John Robert university president
Silberman, Robert A. S. lawyer
Silvey, Anita Lynne editor
Simons, Steven J(ay) lawyer
Sinai, Allen Leo economist, educator
Sinden, Harry professional hockey team executive
Sinex, Francis Marott biochemist, educator
Singer, Thomas Eric industrial company executive
Sirkin, Joel H. lawyer
†Siskind, Paul M. holding company executive
Skinner, Walter Jay federal judge
Skinner, Wickham business administration educator
Skwar, Donald R. newspaper editor
Slechta, Robert Frank biologist, educator
†Slinger, Michael Jeffery law library director
Sloane, Carl Stuart management consultant, educator
Slosberg, Mike advertising executive
Smith, Edwin Eric lawyer
Smith, Keith A. artist
Smith, Philip Jones lawyer
Smith, Thomas Woodward cardiologist, educator
Smyth, Peter Hayes radio executive
Snyder, Richard Joseph lawyer
Sobin, Julian Melvin international consultant
Soden, Richard Allan lawyer
Solet, Maxwell David lawyer
Solomon, Arthur Kaskel biophysics educator
Sommerfeld, Nicholas Ulrich lawyer
Sonnabend, Roger Philip hotel company executive
Sonnenschein, Adam lawyer
Southard, William G. lawyer
Southgate, Richard W. lawyer
Spackman, David Glendinning lawyer
†Spengler, Kenneth C. meteorologist, professional society administrator
Spilhaus, Karl Henry textiles executive, lawyer
Stanley, H(arry) Eugene physicist, educator
Stare, Fredrick John nutritionist, biochemist, physician
†Stearns, Richard Gaylore judge
Stebbins, Theodore Ellis, Jr. museum curator
†Steele, Glenn Daniel, Jr. surgical oncologist
Steere, Allen Caruthers, Jr. physician, educator
Steig, William author, artist
Stepanian, Ira banker
Stern, Ernest science research executive, electrical engineer
Stevenson, Howard Higginbotham business educator
Stevenson, Philip Davis lawyer
Stobaugh, Robert Blair business educator, business executive
Stokes, James Christopher lawyer
Stone, Arthur Harold mathematics educator
Stone, David Barnes investment advisor
Stone, James J. photographer
Storin, Matthew Victor newspaper editor
Streeter, Henry Schofield lawyer
Strothman, Wendy Jo book publisher
Stull, Donald LeRoy architect
Sugarman, Paul Ronald lawyer, educator, academic administrator
Sullivan, James Leo organization executive
Sullivan, John Louis, Jr. search company executive
Surkin, Elliot Mark lawyer
Sutter, Brian professional hockey coach
Sutton, Peter Campbell museum curator
Swaim, Charles Hall lawyer
Swartz, Morton Norman medical educator
Swope, Jeffrey Peyton lawyer
Szep, Paul Michael editorial cartoonist
Tangney, Eugene Michael banker
Tappé, Albert Anthony architect
Taqqu, Murad Salman mathematics educator
Tarlov, Alvin Richard former philanthropic foundation administrator, physician, educator, researcher
†Tarr, Bruce Edward lawyer, state legislator
Tauber, Alfred Imre hematologist, immunologist, philosopher of science
Taubman, Martin Arnold immunologist
Tauro, Joseph Louis federal judge
Taveras, Juan Manuel physician, educator
Taylor, Benjamin B. newspaper publishing executive
†Taylor, Stephen Emlyn publishing executive
Taylor, Thomas William lawyer
†Teixeira, Joseph advertising executive
Temkin, Robert Harvey accountant
Tempel, Jean C. bank executive
Terrill, Ross Gladwin author, educator
†Thomas, Peter biochemistry educator
Thomas, Roger Meriwether lawyer
Thorn, George Widmer physician, educator
Thorndike, John Lowell investment executive
Tooker, Carl E. department store executive
Toran, Daniel James insurance executive
†Torto, Raymond Gerald economist
Totenberg, Roman violinist, music educator
Towles, Stokley Porter commercial and investment banking executive
Trier, Jerry Steven gastroenterologist, educator
Trimmier, Roscoe, Jr. lawyer
Tsongas, Paul Efthemios lawyer, former senator
Tuchmann, Robert lawyer
Tucker, Louis Leonard historical society administrator
Tucker, Richard Lee financial executive
†Turek, Sonia Fay journalist
Turillo, Michael Joseph, Jr. management consultant
†Turkington, Eric Thornton state legislator, lawyer
Utiger, Robert David medical editor
Uyterhoeven, Hugo Emil Robert business educator and consultant
†Vaillant, George Eman psychiatrist
Van, Peter lawyer
Vance, Verne Widney, Jr. lawyer
Van Domelen, John Francis academic administrator
van Gestel, Allan lawyer
Vatter, Paul August business administration educator, dean
Vaughan, Herbert Wiley lawyer
†Vaughn, Maurice Samuel baseball player
Vermeule, Cornelius Clarkson, III museum curator
Vermilye, Peter Hoagland banker
Vershbow, Arthur Emmanuel mechanical engineer
Villee, Claude Alvin, Jr. biochemistry educator
Vineburgh, James Hollander banking executive
Vinik, Jeffrey investment portfolio manager
Viola, Frank John, Jr. professional baseball player
Volk, Jan professional basketball team manager
Volpe, Joseph John pediatric neurologist, educator
Wainberg, Alan footwear company executive
Wakefield, Dan author, screenwriter
Walcott, Derek Alton poet, playwright
Walker, Gordon T. lawyer
†Wallace, David Dunsmore architect
Wallraff, Barbara Jean magazine editor, writer
†Walrath, Patricia A. state legislator
Walton, Bill (William Theodore Walton, III) sportscaster
Walton, Richard Eugene business educator
Wangler, William Clarence insurance company executive
Ward, Richard Paul lawyer
Warga, Jack mathematician, educator
Warshaw, Andrew Louis surgeon, researcher
Washburn, H. Bradford, Jr. museum administrator, cartographer, photographer
Watts, Charles Henry, II university administrator
†Waxlax, Lorne R. manufacturing company executive
†Webb, Alexander, III portfolio manager
Webster, Edward William medical physicist
Wechsler, Henry research psychologist
Weiner, Howard Lee physician, immunologist, educator, researcher
Weiner, Stephen Mark lawyer
Weinstein, Milton Charles health policy educator
Weiss, Earle Burton physician
Weitzel, John Patterson lawyer
Weitzman, Arthur Joshua English educator
Welch, Claude Emerson surgeon
Weld, William Floyd governor, lawyer
Weltman, David Lee lawyer
Wermuth, Paul Charles retired educator
Westcott, John McMahon, Jr. lawyer
Westling, Jon university administrator
†Wetmore, Robert Delvey state senator
Wheatland, Richard, II fiduciary services executive, museum executive
Wheelwright, Steven C. religious organization administrator, business educator
White, Barry Bennett lawyer
Whitlock, John L. lawyer
Whitters, James Payton, III lawyer
Whitworth, William A. magazine editor
Wieckowski, Zdislaw Wladyslaw lawyer
Wiesel, Elie writer, educator
†Wiesner, David illustrator, children's writer
Wilkes, Brent Ames management consultant
Wilkins, (Jacques) Dominique professional basketball player
Wilkins, Herbert Putnam judge
Williams, Charles Marvin commercial banking educator
Williams, John Taylor lawyer
Williams, Rhys minister
Williams, Robert Dana lawyer
Willock, Marcelle Monica medical educator
Wilson, Robert Gould management consultant
Winkelman, James Warren hospital administrator, pathology educator
Winter, Donald Francis lawyer
Wirth, Peter lawyer
†Wiseman, James Richard classicist, archaeologist, educator
Wodlinger, Eric W. lawyer
Wolbach, William Wellington, Sr. retired business executive
Wolf, David lawyer
Wolf, Mark Lawrence federal judge
Wolf, William Martin computer company executive, consultant
†Wood, Henry Austin architect
Woodburn, Ralph Robert, Jr. lawyer
Woodlock, Douglas Preston federal judge
Woolsey, John Munro, Jr. lawyer
†Worthley, Harold Field minister, educator
Wortzel, Lawrence Herbert marketing educator
Wu, Tung curator, art historian, art educator
Wyman, Stanley Moore radiologist
†Yamamoto, Tamotsu art educator
Yastrzemski, Carl Michael former baseball player, public relations executive
†Yemma, John newspaper editor
Young, David William accounting educator
Young, Laura dance educator, choreographer
Young, Raymond Henry lawyer
Young, William Glover federal judge
Zack, Arnold Marshall lawyer, mediator, arbitrator
Zahn, Carl Frederick museum publications director, designer, photographer
Zaleznik, Abraham psychoanalyst, management specialist, educator
Zannieri, Nina museum director

Zarins, Bertram orthopaedic surgeon
Zeien, Alfred M. consumer products company executive
Zellman, Ande editor
Zervas, Nicholas Themistocles neurosurgeon
Zimmerman, George Ogurek physicist, educator
†Zinner, Michael Jeffrey surgeon, educator
Zobel, Hiller Bellin judge
Zobel, Rya W. federal judge
Zoll, Paul Maurice cardiologist
Zupcofska, Peter F. lawyer

Bourne
Roper, Burns Worthington retired opinion research company executive

Boxboro
Demmer, William Roy engineering executive
Gary, Benjamin Walter, Jr. landscape architect
†Nitta, Kenjiro Computer company executive

Braintree
Foster, Arthur Rowe mechanical engineering educator
Harris, Jeffrey Sherman direct marketing company executive
Latham, Allen, Jr. manufacturing company consultant

Brewster
Coburn, John Bowen retired bishop
Hay, John writer
Hemsing, Albert E. public affairs adviser
Lindquist, Susan Pratzner museum executive

Bridgewater
Anderson, Marcia Kay physical education educator
Bardo, John William university administrator
Neubauer, Richard A. library science educator, consultant
Rondileau, Adrian college president
Tinsley, Adrian college president

Brighton
Bernstein, Emil Steven financial executive
Law, Bernard Francis Cardinal archbishop

Brockton
Clark, Carleton Earl tax consultant
Droukas, Ann Hantis management executive
Hart, Daniel Anthony bishop

Brookfield
Kring, Walter Donald minister

Brookline
Barron, Ros artist
†Biederman, Joseph psychiatrist
Blake, Ran jazz pianist, composer
Blom, Gaston Eugene psychiatrist
Brooks, Joae Graham psychiatrist, educator
Cooney, Charles Leland chemical and biochemical engineering educator
Cromwell, Adelaide M. sociology educator
Dukakis, Michael Stanley former governor
Epstein, Alvin actor, director, singer, mime
Feinberg, Robert I(ra) lawyer
Frankel, Ernst Gabriel shipping and aviation business executive, educator
Gray, Seymour medical educator, author
Jakab, Irene psychiatrist
Kadin, Marshall Edward hematopathologist, educator
Katz, Israel engineering educator, retired
Kibrick, Anne nursing educator, university dean
Krasner, Louis concert violinist
Litschgi, Richard John computer manufacturing company executive
Mc Cormick, Thomas Julian art history educator
Mesch, Barry academic administrator
Nadelson, Carol Cooperman psychiatrist, educator
†Papademetriou, George Constantine priest, director, educator
Shaw, Samuel Ervine, II retired insurance company executive, consultant
Spring, Bernard Polmer architect
Swan, Barbara artist
Tournas, Methodios (Methodios of Boston) bishop, academic administrator
Tuchman, Maurice Simon library director
Tyler, H. Richard physician
Vallee, Bert Lester biochemist, physician, educator
Wax, Bernard historian, research consultant, lecturer
Wilson, John artist

Burlington
Barlas, Julie Sandall computer scientist, former librarian
Bright, Willard Mead manufacturing company executive
Clerkin, Eugene Patrick physician
†Connors, Richard J. principal
Fager, Charles Anthony physician, neurosurgeon
Freeman, Donald Chester, Jr. health care company executive
†Groman, John Edward marketing executive
Kern, Fred Robert, Jr. engineer
Moschella, Samuel L. dermatology educator
Reno, John Findley corporate executive
†Schoetz, David John, Jr. colon and rectal surgeon
Veidenheimer, Malcolm Charles surgeon
Wise, Robert Edward radiologist

Byfield
Kozol, Jonathan author

Cambridge
Abernathy, Frederick H. mechanical engineering educator
Ackerman, James Sloss fine arts educator
Alberty, Robert Arnold chemistry educator
Alcalay, Albert S. artist, educator
Alevizos, Susan Bamberger lawyer, santouri player, author
Alevizos, Theodore G. lawyer, singer, author
Alexiou, Margaret Beatrice Greek studies educator
Alfred, William author, educator
Alker, Hayward Rose political science educator
Allen, Lew, Jr. laboratory executive, former air force officer
Allen, Thomas John management educator
Alonso, William population studies educator, demographer
Alt, James Edward political science educator
Anderson, Donald Gordon Marcus mathematics educator
Anderson, Stanford Owen architect, architectural historian, educator
Anderson, William Henry psychobiologist, educator
Anderson-Imbert, Enrique retired Hispanic literature educator, author
†Appiah, Kwame Anthony philosophy educator
Appley, Mortimer Herbert psychologist, university president emeritus
Areeda, Phillip lawyer, educator
Argon, Ali Suphi mechanical engineering educator
Aronson, Michael Andrew editor
Athans, Michael electrical engineering educator, consultant
Babson, David Leveau retired investment counsel
Badian, Ernst history educator
Bailyn, Bernard historian, educator
Baker, James Gilbert optics scientist
Bales, Robert Freed social psychologist, educator
Baltimore, David microbiologist, educator
Banfield, Edward Christie political science educator
Barger, James Edwin physicist
Barnet, Sylvan educator
Baron, Judson Richard aerospace educator
Baron, Sheldon research and development company executive
Barro, Robert Joseph economics educator, consultant
Bartee, Thomas Creson computer scientist, educator
Bartholet, Elizabeth law educator
Bartus, Raymond Thomas neuroscientist, pharmaceutical executive, writer
Bate, Walter Jackson English literature educator
Bator, Francis Michel economist, educator
Battin, Richard Horace astronautical engineer
Bazzaz, Fakhri A. plant biology educator, administrator
Bedrosian, Edward Robert investment management company executive
Beér, János Miklós engineering educator
Bekefi, George physics educator
Bell, Daniel sociologist
Beranek, Leo Leroy scientific foundation executive, engineering consultant
Berg, Howard C. biology educator
Berger, Harvey James pharmaceutical company executive, physician, educator
Berliner, Joseph Scholom economics educator
†Bernard, Michael Mark city planning consultant, lawyer
Bernays, Anne Fleischman writer, educator
Bernays, Edward L. public relations counsel
†Berndt, Ernst Rudolf economist, educator
Berndt, Jerry W. photographer, film producer
Berstein, Irving Aaron biotechnology and medical technology executive
Biemann, Klaus chemistry educator
Billings, Marland Pratt geologist, educator
Birgeneau, Robert Joseph physicist, educator
Bishop, Robert Lyle economist, educator
Bizzi, Emilio neurophysiologist, educator
Blackmer, Donald Laurence Morton political scientist
Bloch, Konrad Emil biochemist
Block, Ned philosophy educator
Bloembergen, Nicolaas physicist, educator
Bloomfield, Lincoln Palmer political scientist
Bloomfield, Richard J. international relations executive
Bluestone, Hugh Lawrence architect
Bogorad, Lawrence biologist
Bok, Derek law educator, former university president
Bolster, Arthur Stanley, Jr. history educator
Bond, William Henry librarian, educator
Boolos, George Stephen philosophy educator
Booth, I(srael) MacAllister photography products company executive
Bott, Raoul mathematician, educator
Bottiglia, William Filbert humanities educator
Bowes, Frederick, III publishing executive
Bradt, Hale Van Dorn physicist, x-ray astronomer, educator
Branscomb, Lewis McAdory physicist
Bras, Rafael Luis engineering educator
Breneman, David Worthy former university president, economics educator
Brenner, Howard chemical engineering educator
Brockett, Roger Ware engineering and computer science educator
Brooks, John Robinson surgeon, educator
Brown, Edgar Cary retired economics educator
Brown, Robert Arthur chemical engineering educator
Brown, Roger William psychologist, educator
Bruce, James Donald electrical engineering educator
Bruck, Ferdinand Frederick architect
Bruck, Phoebe Ann Mason landscape architect
Brusch, John Lynch physician
Brustein, Robert Sanford English language educator, theatre director, author
Buckler, Sheldon A. photographic company executive
Budiansky, Bernard engineering educator
Buell, Lawrence Ingalls English language educator
Bullock, Francis Jeremiah pharmaceutical research executive
Burchfiel, Burrell Clark geology educator
Burke, Bernard Flood physicist, educator
Burnham, Charles Wilson mineralogy educator
Burns, Carol J. architect, educator
Butler, Fred Jay, Jr. manufacturing company executive
Butler, James Newton chemist, educator
Cameron, Alastair Graham Walter astrophysicist, educator
Campbell, Robert architect, writer
Canizares, Claude Roger astrophysicist, educator
†Carliner, Geoffrey Owen economist, director
Carpenter, Kenneth E. librarian, bibliographer
Carrier, George Francis applied mathematics educator
Castaldi, David Lawrence health care company executive
Cavanagh, Richard Edward academic administrator, consultant, writer
Cavell, Stanley philosophy educator, writer
Cazden, Courtney B(orden) education educator
Chall, Jeanne Sternlicht psychologist, educator
Champion, (Charles) Hale political science educator, former public official
Chang, Kwang-Chih anthropologist, educator
Chapin, Richard arbitrator, consultant
Charren, Peggy consumer activist
Chayes, Abram law educator, lawyer
†Cheatham, Thomas Edward, Jr. computer scientist, educator
†Chen, Peter chemistry educator
Chen, Sow-Hsin nuclear engineering educator, researcher
Chernoff, Herman statistics educator
Chomsky, Avram Noam linguistics and philosophy educator
Chubb, Stephen Darrow medical corporation executive
†Clark, Robert Charles lawyer, educator, dean
Clark, William Cummin academic director, educator
Clausen, Wendell Vernon classics educator
Clifton, Anne Rutenber psychotherapist
Cohen, Morris engineering educator
Cohen, Robert Edward chemical engineering educator, consultant
Cohn, Marjorie Benedict curator, art historian, educator
Colby, Anne psychologist
Cole, Heather E. librarian
Coleman, Sidney Richard physicist, educator
Coles, Robert child psychiatrist, educator, author
Colton, Clark Kenneth chemical engineering educator
Conway, Jill Kathryn Ker former college president
Cooper, Richard Newell economist, educator
Corbato, Fernando Jose electrical engineer and computer science educator
Corey, Elias James chemistry educator
Coser, Lewis Alfred sociology educator
Covert, Eugene Edzards aerophysics educator
Cox, Archibald lawyer, educator
Craig, Albert Morton Asian studies educator
Crandall, Stephen Harry engineering educator
Cross, Frank Moore, Jr. foreign language educator
Cumings, Edwin Harlan biology educator
†Cuno, James art museum director
Curtiss, Trumbull Cary banker
Dalby, Alan James biotechnology company executive
Daley, Royston Tuttle architect
Dalgarno, Alexander astronomy educator
Davidson, Charles Sprecher physician
Davie, Joseph Myrten physician, pathology and immunology educator, science administrator
Davis, Edgar Glenn science and health policy executive
De Gennaro, Richard library director
†Demain, Arnold Lester microbiologist, educator
de Neufville, Richard Lawrence engineering educator
Dennis, Jack Bonnell computer consultant
Dershowitz, Alan Morton lawyer, educator
Dertouzos, Michael Leonidas computer scientist, electrical engineer, educator
de Varon, Lorna Cooke choral conductor
Diaconis, Persi W. mathematical statistician, educator
Doering, William von Eggers organic chemist, educator
Domar, Evsey David economics educator
Dominguez, Jorge Ignacio government educator
Donald, Aida DiPace publishing executive
†Donnelly, Thomas William physicist
Dorfman, Robert economics educator
Dornbusch, Rudiger economics educator
Dowling, John Elliott biology educator
Downey, Richard Ralph lawyer, consultant
Drake, Elisabeth Mertz chemical engineer
Dreben, Burton Spencer philosopher,educator
Dresselhaus, Mildred Spiewak physics and engineering educator
Dubowsky, Steven mechanical engineering educator
Dudley, Richard Mansfield mathematician, educator
Duecker, Heyman Clarke chemical executive, researcher
Duffy, Robert Aloysius aeronautical engineer
Dugundji, John aeronautical engineer
Dunlop, John Thomas economics educator, former secretary of labor
Dunn, Charles William educator, author
Dupree, Anderson Hunter historian, educator
Durant, Graham John medicinal chemist, drug researcher
Dyck, Arthur James ethicist, educator
†Eagar, Thomas Waddy metallurgist, educator
Eagleson, Peter Sturges hydrologist, educator
Eckaus, Richard Samuel economist, educator
Edgerly, William Skelton banker
Edsall, John Tileston biological chemistry educator
Ehrenreich, Henry physicist, educator
Einsweiler, Robert Charles research director
Eisen, Herman Nathaniel immunology educator, medical researcher
†Eisenberg, Carola university academic director, psychiatrist
Elias, Peter electrical engineering educator
Emanuel, Kerry Andrew earth sciences educator
Emerson, Anne Devereux university administrator
Emmons, Howard Wilson engineer, educator, consultant, researcher
Epstein, David Mayer composer, conductor
Epstein, Henry David electronics company executive
Erdely, Stephen Lajos music educator
Erikson, Raymond Leo biology educator
Estes, William Kaye psychologist, educator
Eurich, Nell P. educational consultant
Evans, Lawrence Boyd business executive
Evans, Robley Dunglison physicist
Fagans, Karl Preston real estate facilities executive
Fanger, Donald Lee Slavic language and literature educator
Fano, Robert Mario electrical engineering educator
Fay, James Alan mechanical engineering educator
Feininger, Theodore Lux artist
Feld, Michael Stephen physics educator
Feldman, Gary Jay physicist, educator
Feldstein, Martin Stuart economist, educator
Feshbach, Herman physicist, educator
Field, George Brooks theoretical astrophysicist
Field, Robert Warren chemistry educator
†Fink, Gerald Ralph geneticist, biochemist
Fiorenza, Francis P. religion educator
Fischer, Kurt Walter education educator
Fischer, Stanley economics educator
Fisher, Franklin Marvin economist
Fisher, Roger Dummer lawyer, educator, negotiation expert
†FitzGerald, Maura public relations executive
Fleischer, Dorothy Ann administrative assistant
Fleming, Donald Harnish educator, historian
Fleming, Ronald Lee urban designer, administrator, preservation planner, environmental educator
Flier, Michael Stephen Slavic languages educator
Foner, Simon research physicist
Ford, Franklin Lewis history educator, historian
Ford, Patrick Kildea Celtic studies educator
Forman, Richard T. T. ecology educator
Forrester, Jay Wright management specialist, educator
Fortmann, Thomas Edward research and development company executive
Fox, John Bayley, Jr. university dean
Fox, Maurice Sanford molecular biologist, educator
French, Anthony Philip physicist, educator
Frey, Frederick August geochemistry researcher, educator
Fried, Charles lawyer, educator
Friedman, Benjamin Morton economics educator
Friedman, Jerome Isaac physics educator, researcher
Frisch, Rose Epstein population sciences researcher
Frosch, Robert Alan retired automobile manufacturing executive, physicist
Frug, Gerald E. law educator
Frye, Richard Nelson historian, educator
Fujimoto, James G. electrical engineering educator
Gage, (Leonard) Patrick corporate research executive
Gagliardi, Ugo Oscar systems software architect, educator
Galbraith, John Kenneth retired economist
Gallager, Robert Gray electrical engineering educator
Ganley, Oswald Harold university official
Gardner, Howard Earl psychologist, author
Garland, Carl Wesley chemist, educator
†Gaskell, Ivan George Alexander De Wend art museum curator
Gates, Henry Louis, Jr. English language educator
Gatos, Harry Constantine engineering educator
Gerrish, Hollis G. confectionery company executive
Gilbert, Walter molecular biologist, educator
Gilligan, Carol psychologist, writer
Gingerich, Owen Jay astronomer, educator
Glaser, Peter Edward mechanical engineer, consultant
†Glauber, Roy Jay theoretical physics educator
Glauner, Alfred William lawyer, engineering company executive
Glazer, Nathan sociologist, educator
Gleason, Andrew Mattei mathematician, educator
Goldberg, Ray Allan agribusiness educator
Goldblith, Samuel Abraham food science educator
Goldfarb, Warren (David) philosophy educator
Goldin, Claudia Dale economics educator
Goldman, Ralph Frederick research physiologist, educator
Goldstone, Jeffrey physicist
Gomes, Peter John clergyman, educator
Gonson, S. Donald lawyer
Gordon, Roy Gerald chemistry educator
Gould, Stephen Jay paleontologist, educator
†Grabowicz, George Gregory Slavic studies educator
Graham, Loren Raymond historian, educator
Grant, Nicholas John metallurgy educator
Graubard, Stephen Richards history educator, editor
Gray, Paul Edward academic official
Green, Jerry Richard economist, educator
Green, Richard John architect
Greene, Frederick D., II chemistry educator
Greeno, J(ohn) Ladd consulting company executive
Greenspan, Harvey Philip applied mathematician, educator
Greitzer, Edward Marc aeronautical engineering educator, consultant
Greytak, Thomas John physics educator
†Griffin, Robert G. physics administrator
Griffith, Peter mechanical engineering educator, researcher
Griliches, Zvi educator, economist
Grindlay, Jonathan Ellis astrophysics educator
Grosz, Barbara Jean computer science educator
†Grove, Timothy L. geology educator
Guth, Alan Harvey physicist, educator
Guthke, Karl Siegfried foreign language educator
Gyftopoulos, Elias Panayiotis mechanical and nuclear engineering educator
Halle, Morris linguist, educator
Halperin, Bertrand Israel physics educator
Hamilton, Malcolm Cowan librarian, editor, indexer, personnel educator
†Hamner, W. Easley architect
Hanan, Patrick Dewes foreign language professional, educator
Handlin, Oscar historian, educator
Hansen, Kent Forrest nuclear engineering educator
†Hansman, Robert John, Jr. aeronautics and astronautics educator
Hanson, Paul David religion educator
Harbison, John composer
Harkness, John Cheesman architect
Harleman, Donald Robert Fergusson environmental engineering educator
†Harrington, Joseph, Jr. consulting mechanical engineer
Harris, Charles Ward landscape architect and educator, land development consultant, editor
Harrison, Stephen Coplan biochemist
Hart, Oliver D'Arcy economics educator
Hartl, Daniel Lee genetics educator
†Hass, Michael Shepherdson architect
Hastings, John Woodland biologist, educator
Haus, Hermann Anton electrical engineering educator
Hausman, Jerry Allen economics educator, consultant
Havens, Leston Laycock psychiatrist, educator
Hax, Arnoldo Cubillos management educator, industrial engineer
Heaney, Seamus Justin poet, educator
Heimert, Alan Edward humanities educator
Helgason, Sigurdur mathematician, educator
Heney, Joseph Edward environmental engineer
Henrichs, Albert Maximinus classicist, educator
Herrnstein, Richard Julius psychology educator
Herschbach, Dudley Robert chemistry educator
Heywood, John Benjamin mechanical engineering educator
Hibbett, Howard Scott foreign language professional, educator
Ho, Yu-Chi electrical engineering educator
Hoag, David Garratt aerospace engineer
†Hobbs, Linn Walker materials science educator
Hoffman, Paul Felix geologist, educator
Holberton, Philip Vaughan biotechnology company executive
Holbik, Karel economics educator
Holton, Gerald physicist, science historian
Holzman, Philip Seidman psychologist, educator
Homburger, Freddy physician, scientist, artist
†Horrell, Jeffrey Lanier library administrator
Horvitz, Howard Robert biology educator, researcher
Horwitz, Paul physicist
Houthakker, Hendrik S(amuel) economics educator, consultant
Hsiao, William C. economist, actuary, educator
Huang, Kerson physics educator
Hubbard, Ruth biology educator
Huchra, John Peter astronomer, educator

Huntington, Samuel Phillips political science educator
Hynes, Richard Olding biology educator
Iriye, Akira historian, educator
Jackiw, Roman physicist, educator
Jackson, Francis Joseph research and development company executive
†Jacob, Daniel James atmospheric chemistry educator
Jacobson, Ralph Henry laboratory executive, former air force officer
Jacoby, Henry Donnan economist, educator
Jaffe, Arthur Michael physicist, mathematician, educator
John, Richard Rodda transportation executive
†Johnson, Carol Roxane landscape architect
Johnson, Howard Wesley former university president, business executive
Johnson, Willard Raymond political science educator, consultant
Jones, Robert Emmet French language educator
Jordan, Thomas Hillman geophysicist, educator
Jorgenson, Dale Weldeau economist, educator
Joskow, Paul Lewis economist, educator
Joss, Paul Christopher astrophysicist, educator
Judson, Arnold Sidney management consultant
Kac, Victor G. mathematician, educator
Kagan, Jerome psychologist, educator
Kalb, Marvin public policy and government educator
Kalelkar, Ashok Satish consulting company executive
Kamentsky, Louis Aaron biophysicist
Kaplan, Benjamin judge
Kaplan, Justin author
Karplus, Martin chemistry educator
Kassman, Herbert Seymour lawyer, management consultant
Katz, Milton legal educator, public official
Kaufman, Andrew Lee law educator
Kaufman, Gordon Dester theology educator
Kaysen, Carl economics educator
Kazhdan, David mathematician, educator
Keenan, Edward Louis history educator
Kelley, Albert Joseph management educator, executive consultant
†Kemp, Daniel Schaeffer chemistry educator, consultant
Kendall, Henry Way physicist
Kennedy, Robert Spayde electrical engineering educator
Kennedy, Stephen Dandridge economist, researcher
Kerpelman, Larry Cyril consulting firm executive
Kerrebrock, Jack Leo aeronautics and astronautics engineering educator
Keyfitz, Nathan educator, sociologist, demographer
Keyser, Samuel Jay linguistics educator, university official
Khorana, Har Gobind chemist, educator
Kilson, Martin Luther, Jr. government educator
Kim, Earl composer
†Kim, Peter Sungbai biochemistry educator
King, Patricia Miller library administrator, historian
King, Ronold Wyeth Percival physics educator
Kirchner, Leon composer, pianist, conductor
Kirkpatrick, Francis H(ubbard), Jr. biophysicist, consultant
Kistiakowsky, Vera physics researcher, educator
Kleiman, Steven Lawrence mathematics educator
Kleinman, Arthur Michael medical anthropologist, psychiatrist, educator
Klemperer, William chemistry educator
Kleppner, Daniel physicist, educator
Klibanov, Alexander Maxim chemistry educator
Kliem, Peter Otto imaging company executive
Knoll, Andrew Herbert biology educator
Knowles, Jeremy Randall chemist, educator
†Kobus, Richard Lawrence architectural company executive
Koester, Helmut Heinrich theologian, educator
Kostant, Bertram mathematician, educator
Kovach, Bill educational foundation administrator
†Krieger, Alex architecture and design educator
†Kruger, Kenneth architect
Krugman, Paul Robin economics educator
Kung, Patrick Chung-Shu biotechnology executive
Kyhl, Robert Louis electrical engineering educator
Ladd, Charles Cushing, III civil engineering educator
La Mantia, Charles Robert management consulting company executive
Lamberg-Karlovsky, Clifford Charles anthropologist, archaeologist
Lamport, Felicia (Mrs. Benjamin Kaplan) writer
Langer, Ellen Jane psychologist, educator, writer
†Langer, Robert Martin retired chemical engineering company executive, consultant
Langer, Robert Samuel chemical, biochemical engineering educator
Langstaff, John Meredith musician
Larson, Richard Charles electrical engineer, educator, operations researcher
Latanision, Ronald Michael materials science and engineering educator, consultant
LaTores, Santo Joseph federal transportation executive
Layzer, David astrophysicist, educator
Lee, Leo Ou-fan Far Eastern languages educator
Lee, Thomas Henry electrical engineer, educator
Leehey, Patrick mechanical and ocean engineering educator
Leonard, Herman Beukema (Dutch Leonard) public finance and management educator
Lerman, Leonard Solomon science educator, scientist
Levi, Herbert Walter biologist, educator
LeVine, Robert Alan anthropology educator, researcher
Levinson, Harry psychologist, educator
Levy, Stephen Raymond diversified high technology company executive
†Lewin, Walter H. G. physics educator
Lewis, Henry Rafalsky manufacturing company executive
Lieberson, Stanley sociologist, educator
Light, Richard Jay statistician, education educator
Lindzen, Richard Siegmund meteorologist, educator
Lippard, Stephen James chemist, educator
Lipscomb, William Nunn, Jr. retired physical chemistry educator
Little, John Dutton Conant management scientist, educator
Littlefield, Paul Damon management consultant
†Livingston, James Duane physicist, educator
Lloyd, Boardman investment executive
Lockwood, Lewis Henry musicologist, educator
Lodish, Harvey Franklin biologist, educator
Lomon, Earle Leonard physicist, educator, consultant
Longwell, John Ploeger chemical engineering educator
Lorenz, Edward Norton meteorologist, educator
Loss, Louis lawyer, educator emeritus
Low, Francis Eugene physics educator
†Luchetti, Robert James architect, industrial designer
Lucker, Jay K. library administrator, consultant
Lunt, Horace Gray linguist, educator
Lynch, Harry James biologist
Lynch, Nancy Ann computer scientist, educator
Lyon, Richard Harold educator, physicist
Maass, Arthur political science and environmental studies educator
†Mackey, George Whitelaw educator, mathematician
MacMaster, Robert Ellsworth historian, educator
MacPherson, Robert Duncan mathematician, educator
Madsen, Peter Eric architecture and real estate development firms executive
Magee, John Francis research company executive
†Magnanti, Thomas L. management and engineering educator
Maher, Brendan Arnold psychology educator, editor
Mahoney, Thomas Henry Donald historian, educator, government official
Maier, Charles Steven history educator
Makhoul, John Ibrahim electrical engineer, researcher
†Malmstad, John Earl Slavic languages and literature educator
†Man, Lawrence Kong architect, entrepreneur
Maniatis, Thomas Peter molecular biology educator
Mann, Robert Wellesley biomedical engineer, educator
Manzi, Jim computer software company executive
Marini, Robert Charles environmental engineering executive
Markey, Winston Roscoe aeronautical engineering educator
Marks, David Hunter civil engineering educator
Marolda, Anthony Joseph management consulting company executive
Marsden, Brian Geoffrey astronomer
Marshall, Margaret Hilary lawyer
†Martin, Harry Stratton, III law librarian
Martin, Paul Cecil physicist, educator
Martino, Donald James composer, educator
Marx, Leo retired American cultural history educator
Masamune, Satoru chemistry educator, consultant
Maybank, Joseph architect, architectural resources company executive
Mayr, Ernst emeritus zoology educator, author
Mazlish, Bruce educator, historian
Mazur, Michael artist
McArthur, John Hector university dean, business educator
McCarthy, James Joseph oceanography educator
McCue, Gerald Mallon architect
McElroy, Michael physicist, researcher
McGarry, Frederick Jerome civil engineering educator
McKenna, Margaret Anne college president
Mc Kie, Todd Stoddard artist
McMahon, Thomas Arthur biology and applied mechanics educator
Medoff, James Lawrence economics educator
Meissner, William Walter psychiatrist, clergyman
Mendelsohn, Everett Irwin science educator
Meselson, Matthew Stanley biochemist, educator
Meyer, John Edward nuclear engineering educator
Meyer, John Robert economist, educator
Miles, Margaret Ruth theology educator
Milgram, Jerome H. marine and ocean engineer, educator
Miller, Arthur Raphael legal educator
Miller, Rene Harcourt aerospace engineer, educator
Miller, S(eymour) M(ichael) sociology educator
†Minsky, Marvin Lee mathematician, educator
Mitten, David Gordon classical archaeologist
†Mitter, Sanjoy K. electrical engineering educator
Mnookin, Robert Harris lawyer, educator
†Modigliani, Lazzaro G. chemicals executive
Molina, Mario Jose physical chemist, educator
†Moneo, José Rafael architecture educator
Mongan, Agnes museum curator, art historian, educator
†Moniz, Ernest Jeffrey physics educator
Montgomery, John Dickey political science educator
Moore, Mark Harrison criminal justice, public policy educator
Moore, Sally Falk anthropology educator
†Moran, James Michael, Jr. astronomer
†Morel, François Marie Michel civil and environmental engineering educator
Moses, Joel computer scientist, educator
Mosteller, Frederick mathematical statistician, educator
Mowry, Robert Dean art museum curator, educator
Mueller, Robert Kirk consultant
†Mulligan, Richard C. molecular biology educator
Mumford, David Bryant mathematics educator
Negele, John William physics educator, consultant
Nelson, David Robert physics educator
Nelson, William George, IV software company executive
Neustadt, Richard Elliott political scientist, educator
Newell, Reginald Edward physics educator
Newman, John Nicholas naval architect educator
Nordell, Hans Roderick journalist, editor
Norkus, Michael management consultant
Notkin, Leonard Sheldon architect
Nozick, Robert philosophy educator, author
Nykrog, Per French literature educator
Oettinger, Anthony Gervin mathematician, educator
Ogilvie, T(homas) Francis engineer, educator
O'Neil, Wayne linguist, educator
Oommen, George architect
Oppenheim, Alan Victor electrical engineering educator
Orchard, Robert John theater producer, educator
Orlen, Joel association executive
Owen, Walter Shepherd materials science and engineering educator
†Oye, Kenneth A. political scientist, educator
Ozment, Steven historian, educator
Pappenheimer, Alwin M(ax), Jr. biochemist, immunologist
Pardue, Mary Lou biology educator
Parker, Harry Lambert university rowing coach
†Parker, Sam finance company executive
Parthum, Charles Albert civil engineer
Patterson, Orlando sociologist
Paul, William physicist, educator
Payne, Harry Morse, Jr. architect
Peattie, Lisa Redfield urban anthropology educator
Penfield, Paul Livingstone, Jr. electrical engineering educator
Perkins, Dwight Heald economics educator
Petersen, Ulrich geology educator
Pfister, Donald Henry biology educator
Pian, Rulan Chao musicologist, scholar
Pian, Theodore Hsueh-Huang engineering educator, consultant
Piene, Otto artist, educator
Pierce, Naomi Ellen biology educator, researcher
Pilbeam, David Roger paleoanthropology educator
Pinkham, Daniel composer
Pipes, Richard (Edgar) historian, educator
Polenske, Karen Rosel economics educator
†Pollock, Wilson F. architectural firm executive
†Porkolab, Miklos physics educator, researcher
Porter, Roger Blaine government official, educator
Porter, William Lyman architect, educator
†Postol, Theodore A. physicist, nuclear engineer, educator
Potter, Ralph Benajah, Jr. theology and social ethics educator
Pounds, William Frank management educator
Powers, Michael Kevin architectural and engineering executive
Press, William Henry astrophysicist, computer scientist
Preyer, Robert Otto English literature educator
Price, Don K. political science educator
Pritchard, David Edward physics educator
Probstein, Ronald Filmore mechanical engineering educator
Purcell, Edward Mills physics educator
Pye, Lucian Wilmot political science educator
Quine, Willard Van Orman philosophy educator
Rabinowicz, Ernest mechanical engineer, tribologist, educator
Ragone, David Vincent former university president
Ramsey, Norman F. physicist, educator
Rands, Bernard composer, educator
Rasmussen, Norman Carl nuclear engineer
Rathbone, Perry Townsend art museum director
Rathjens, George William political scientist, educator
†Rebek, Julius, Jr. chemistry educator, consultant
Rediker, Robert Harmon physicist
†Redwine, Robert Page physicist, educator
Reid, Robert Clark chemical engineering educator
Reimann, William Page artist, educator
Rey, Margret Elizabeth retired writer, prose, juvenile
Rha, ChoKyun biomaterials scientist and engineer, researcher, educator, inventor
Rice, James Robert engineering scientist, geophysicist
Rich, Alexander molecular biologist, educator
Riesman, David lawyer, social scientist
Robbins, Phillips Wesley biology educator
Roberts, Edward Baer technology management educator
Roberts, Nancy computer educator
Robinson, Allan Richard oceanography educator
Robinson, Marguerite Stern anthropologist, educator, consultant
Roche, John Jefferson lawyer
Roedder, Edwin Woods geologist
Rogers, Peter Philips environmental engineering educator, city planner
Rohsenow, Warren Max retired mechanical engineer, educator
Roos, Daniel civil engineering educator
Rose, Robert Michael materials science and engineering educator
Rosenblith, Walter Alter scientist, educator
Rosenbloom, Richard Selig business administration educator
Rosenfeld, Walter David, Jr. architect, writer
Rosenfield, John Max art educator
Rosenthal, Robert psychology educator
Rosovsky, Henry economist, educator
Rota, Gian-Carlo mathematician, educator
Rothenberg, Albert psychiatrist, educator
Rowe, Peter Grimmond architecture educator, researcher
Rubin, Jeffrey Zachary psychologist, educator
Rubin, Jerome Sanford publishing company executive, lawyer
Rubin, Lawrence Gilbert physicist, laboratory manager
Rudenstine, Neil Leon academic administrator, educator
Ruina, Jack Philip electrical engineer, educator
Russell, George Allen composer, musicologist
Russell, Kenneth Calvin metallurgical engineer, educator
Ryan, Allan Andrew, Jr. lawyer, author, lecturer
Safran, Edward Myron financial service company executive
Saltzer, Jerome Howard computer science educator
Samuelson, Paul Anthony economics educator
Sapolsky, Harvey Morton political scientist, educator
Saponaro, Joseph A. company executive
Satterfield, Charles Nelson chemical engineer, educator
Schacter, Daniel Lawrence psychology educator
Schama, Simon historian, educator, author
Schauer, Frederick Franklin legal educator
Scheffler, Israel philosopher, educator
Scherer, Frederic Michael economics educator
Schimmel, Paul Reinhard biochemist, biophysicist, educator
Schmalensee, Richard Lee economist, former government official, educator
Schmid, Wilfried mathematician
Schmitt, Francis Otto neuroscientist, emeritus educator
Schneider, Gerald Edward neuroscience and animal behavior educator
†Schreiber, Stuart L. chemist, educator
Schreiber, William Francis electrical engineering educator
Schuessler Fiorenza, Elisabeth theology educator
Schultes, Richard Evans ethnobotanist, museum executive, educator, conservationist
Schwartz, Martha landscape architect, educator, artist
Seamans, Robert Channing, Jr. astronautical engineering educator
Seamans, Warren Arthur museum director
Segal, Charles Paul classics educator, author
Segal, Irving Ezra mathematics educator
Sekler, Eduard Franz architect, educator
†Sen, Amartya Kumar economist
Sevcenko, Ihor history and literature educator
Seyferth, Dietmar chemist, educator
Shapiro, David Louis lawyer, educator
Shapiro, Irwin Ira physicist, educator
Sharp, Phillip Allen academic administrator, biologist, educator
Shinagel, Michael English literature educator
Shore, Miles Frederick psychiatrist, educator
Siebert, William McConway electrical engineering educator
Siever, Raymond geology educator
Silbey, Robert James chemistry educator, researcher
Simon, Eckehard (Peter) foreign language educator
Sims, Ezra composer
Singer, Isadore Manuel mathematician, educator
Sisler, William Philip publishing executive
Sizer, Irwin Whiting biochemistry educator
Skolnikoff, Eugene B. political science educator
†Slater, Jonathan E. director
Slive, Seymour museum director, fine arts educator
Smith, Joseph LeConte, Jr. engineering educator, science laboratory administrator
Smith, Kenneth Alan chemical engineer, educator
Smith, Merritt Roe history educator
Smith, Ronald Lee academic administrator, public policy educator
Solow, Robert Merton economist, educator
Southern, Eileen (Mrs. Joseph Southern) music educator
Spaepen, Frans August applied physics researcher, educator
Spunt, Shepard Armin real estate executive, management and financial consultant
Squire, James Robert retired publisher, consultant
Staelin, David Hudson electrical engineering educator, consultant
Stager, Lawrence E. archeologist, educator
Steiner, Henry Jacob law and human rights educator
Steinfeld, Jeffrey Irwin chemistry educator, consultant, author
Stephanopoulos, Gregory chemical engineering educator, consultant, researcher
Stevens, Kenneth Noble electrical engineering educator
Stoddard, Roger Eliot librarian
Stone, Andrew Grover lawyer
Strandberg, Malcom Woodrow Pershing physicist
Strang, William Gilbert mathematician, educator
Strauch, Karl physicist, educator
Stroock, Daniel Wyler mathematician, educator
Stubbe, JoAnne chemistry educator
Suh, Nam Pyo mechanical engineering educator
Sulloway, Frank Jones historian
Susskind, Lawrence Elliott urban and environmental planner, educator, mediator
Swets, John Arthur psychologist, scientist
Szabo, Albert architect, educator
†Szekely, Julian materials engineering educator
Ta, Tai Van lawyer, researcher
Tambiah, Stanley Jeyarajah anthropologist
Tannenbaum, Steven Robert toxicologist, chemist
Tarrant, R(ichard) J(ohn) classicist, educator
Teeter, Karl van Duyn retired linguistic scientist, educator
Tema-Lyn, Laurie management consultant
†Termeer, Henricus Adrianus biotechnology company executive
Thaddeus, Patrick physicist, educator
Thernstrom, Stephan Albert historian, educator
Thiemann, Ronald Frank dean, religion educator
†Thomas, Edwin L. materials engineering educator
Thomas, Harold Allen, Jr. civil engineer, educator
Thomas, Owen Clark clergyman, educator
Thompson, Dennis Frank political science and ethics educator, consultant
Thompson, James Burleigh, Jr. geologist, educator
Thorburn, David literature educator
Thurow, Lester Carl economics educator
Timmer, Charles Peter agricultural economist
Ting, Samuel Chao Chung physicist, educator
Tinkham, Michael physicist, educator
Tobin, James Robert biotechnology company executive
Tonegawa, Susumu biology educator
Torriani-Gorini, Annamaria microbiologist
†Torroella, Mario Jaime architect, artist
Trainor, Bernard Edmund journalist, educator, retired marine corps officer
Tribe, Laurence Henry lawyer, educator
Trilling, Leon aeronautical engineering educator
Tsipis, Kosta Michael science educator
†Tsoi, Edward Tze Ming architect, interior designer, urban planner
Tu, Wei-Ming historian, philosopher, writer
Turnbull, David physical chemist, educator
Tyler, Lewis Adair not-for-profit organization executive
Ulam, Adam B. history and political science educator
Ungar, Eric Edward mechanical engineer
Urbanowski, Frank publishing company executive
Vagts, Detlev Frederick lawyer, educator
Valiant, Leslie Gabriel computer scientist
van der Merwe, Nikolaas Johannes archaeologist
Vander Velde, Wallace Earl aeronautical and astronautical educator
Vanger, Milton Isadore history educator
Vendler, Helen Hennessy literature educator, poetry critic
Verba, Sidney political scientist, educator
Vermeule, Emily Townsend (Mrs. Cornelius C. Vermeule, III) classicist, educator
Vernon, Raymond economist, educator
Vessot, Robert Frederick Charles physicist
Vest, Charles Marstiller university administrator
Vigier, François Claude Denis city planning educator
Villars, Felix Marc Hermann physicist, educator
Vincent, James Louis biotechnology company executive
Vivian, Johnson Edward retired chemical engineering educator
Vogel, Ezra F. sociology educator
Vogt, Evon Zartman, Jr. anthropologist
von Mehren, Arthur Taylor lawyer, educator
Vorenberg, James lawyer, educator, university dean
Voss, John retired association executive
Wachman, Harold Yehuda space environmental sciences educator
Wacker, Warren Ernest Clyde physician, educator
Wald, George biochemist, educator
Walters, Alan Stanley consulting firm executive
†Wang, Daniel I-Chyau biochemical engineering educator
Wang, James Chuo biochemistry and molecular biology educator
Ward, John Milton music educator
Ward, Robertson, Jr. architect
†Wardell, William Michael drug development executive
Warren, Alvin Clifford, Jr. lawyer
Waugh, John Stewart chemist, educator
†Weber, Larry public relations executive
Wechsler, Alfred Elliot consulting company executive, chemical engineer

†Weiler, Paul Cronin *law educator*
Weinberg, Robert Allan *biochemist, educator*
Weiner, Myron *political science educator*
Weiss, Thomas Fischer *electrical engineering educator, biophysicist*
Wendorf, Richard Harold *library director, educator*
Wenger, Luke Huber *educational association executive, editor*
†West, Cornel *philosopher, writer*
Westheimer, Frank Henry *chemist, educator*
Wheeler, Leonard *lawyer*
Whipple, Fred Lawrence *astronomer*
White, David Calvin *electrical engineer, energy educator, consultant*
Whitesides, George McClelland *chemistry educator*
Whitlock, Charles Preston *former university dean*
Whitman, Robert Van Duyne *civil engineer, educator*
Whitney, Charles Allen *astronomer, writer*
Wiesner, Jerome Bert *engineering educator, researcher*
Wilcox, Maud *editor*
Wiley, Don Craig *biochemistry and biophysics educator*
Willard, Louis Charles *librarian*
Williams, George Huntston *church historian, educator*
Williams, Preston Noah *theology educator*
Willie, Charles Vert *sociology educator*
Wilson, Edward Osborne *biologist, educator*
Wilson, Linda Smith *university administrator*
†Wilson, Richard *physicist, educator*
Winner, Thomas G. *foreign literature educator*
Wiseman, Frederick *filmmaker*
†Witt, August Ferdinand *aerospace scientist, educator*
Wogan, Gerald Norman *toxicology educator*
Wolff, Cynthia Griffin *humanities educator, author*
Wolfman, Bernard *lawyer, educator*
Wood, John Armstead *planetary scientist, geological sciences educator*
Wrangham, Richard Walter *anthropology educator*
Wrighton, Mark Stephen *chemistry educator*
Wu, Tai Tsun *physicist, educator*
Wuensch, Bernhardt John *ceramic engineering educator*
†Wunderlich, Renner *film producer, cinematographer*
Wunsch, Carl Isaac *oceanographer, educator*
Wurtman, Richard Jay *physician, educator*
Yannas, Ioannis Vassilios *polymer science and engineering educator*
Yau, Shing-Tung *mathematics educator*
Yergin, Daniel Howard *writer, consultant*
†Yip, Sidney *nuclear engineering educator*
Young, Laurence Retman *biomedical engineer, educator*
Zeidenstein, George *population educator*
Zinberg, Dorothy Shore *science policy educator*

Canton
Bihldorff, John Pearson *hospital director*
†Burr, George S. *manufacturing company executive*
Ferrera, Arthur Rodney *food distribution company executive*
Ferrera, Kenneth Grant *food distribution company executive*
Holt, Donald Edward, Jr. *retail executive*
Lyman, Charles Peirson *comparative physiologist*
Pitts, Virginia M. *human resources executive*

Carlisle
Fohl, Timothy *consulting and investment company executive*

Centerville
Anderson, Gerald Edwin *utilities executive*
Kiernan, Owen Burns *educational consultant*
Scherer, Harold Nicholas, Jr. *electric utility company executive, engineer*

Charlestown
†Argov, Gideon *engineering company executive*
Armstrong, Nancy L. *soprano, voice coach*
Bonventre, Joseph Vincent *physician, scientist, medical educator*
Isselbacher, Kurt Julius *physician, educator*
Lamont-Havers, Ronald William *physician, research administrator*
McLennan, Bernice Claire *human resources professional*
Waldfogel, Morton Sumner *prefabricated housing/plywood company executive*

Chatham
Hester, William Francis *engineering executive*
Leighten, Edward Henry *publisher, consultant*
Pacun, Norman *lawyer*

Chelmsford
Fulks, Robert Grady *engineering computer executive*
Grossman, Debra A. *lawyer, real estate manager*

Chelsea
†Birmingham, Thomas *state legislator*
Dunn, Norman Samuel *plastics and textiles company executive*

Chestnut Hill
Altbach, Philip *comparative education director, educator*
Barth, John Robert *English educator, priest*
Baum, Jules Leonard *ophthalmologist, educator*
Belsley, David Alan *economics educator, consultant*
Blanchette, Oliva *philosophy educator*
†Bresky, H. Harry *diversified manufacturing company executive*
Bushnell, Clarence William *hospital consultant*
Casper, Leonard Ralph *American literature educator*
Courtiss, Eugene Howard *plastic surgeon, educator*
Daly, Robert J. *theology educator*
Duhamel, Pierre Albert *English language professional*
Fouraker, Lawrence Edward *social and business organizations director, former business administration educator*
Glynn, Arthur Lawrence *business administration and accounting educator*
Hunt-Clerici, Carol Elizabeth *academic personnel assistant*
Kane, Edward James *economics educator*
Knapp, Robert Charles *retired obstetrics and gynecology educator*
Levy, James Peter *publishing company executive*
Lowell, Juliet *author*
Mahoney, John L. *English literature educator*

Monan, James Donald *college president*
Plaut, James Sachs *foundation executive*
Rodrigues, Joseph E. *grain company executive*
Smith, Richard Alan *movie theater and specialty retailing executive*
Stanbury, John Bruton *physician, educator*
Tarr, Robert Joseph, Jr. *publishing executive, retail executive*
Valette, Rebecca Marianne *Romance languages educator*

Chilmark
Geyer, Harold Carl *artist, writer*
Low, Joseph *artist*

Cohasset
Campbell, John Coert *political scientist, author*
Lyne, Austin Francis *sporting goods business executive*
Sewall, Tingey Haig *banker*

Concord
Baldwin, Everett Newton *food company executive*
Berger, Raoul *lawyer, educator, violinist*
Bloom, Edwin John, Jr. *human resources consultant*
Cavazos, Lauro Fred *former U.S. secretary of education, former university president*
Cutting, Heyward *designer, planner*
Daltas, Arthur John *management consultant*
Drew, Philip Garfield *consultant engineering company executive*
Edmonds, Walter Dumaux *author*
Hogan, Daniel Bolten *management consultant*
Ihara, Michio *sculptor*
Kasputys, Joseph Edward *corporate executive, economist*
Link, David M. *medical products consultant*
Lombardo, Gaetano (Guy Lombardo) *venture capitalist*
Moore, Robert Lowell, Jr. (Robin Moore) *author*
Morgan, Charles Sumner *retired association executive*
Palay, Sanford Louis *retired scientist, educator*
Schiller, Pieter Jon *venture capital executive*
Smith, Peter Walker *finance executive*
Valley, George Edward, Jr. *physicist, educator*
Villers, Philippe *mechanical engineer*
White, James Barr *lawyer, real estate investor, consultant*
Woll, Harry J. *electrical engineer*

Conway
Mallary, Robert *sculptor*

Cotuit
Miller, Robert Charles *retired physicist*

Cummington
Wilbur, Richard Purdy *writer, educator*

Danvers
Langford, Dean Ted *lighting and precision materials company executive*
†St. Onge, Vincent A. *electronics executive*
Traicoff, George *college president*
Waite, Charles Morrison *food company executive*

Dedham
Culver, Edward Holland *marketing executive*
Firth, Everett Joseph *timpanist*
†Krivsky, William A. *building materials executive, researcher*
Lake, Ann Winslow *lawyer*
†Lynch, David B. *financial executive*
Magner, Jerome Allen *entertainment company executive*
Redstone, Sumner Murray *entertainment company executive*
Russo, Peter Francis *financial executive, accountant*
Schork, Rudolph Joseph, Jr. *philologist*
†Spoolstra, Linda Carol *minister, educator, religious organization administrator*

Dennis
Weilbacher, William Manning *advertising and marketing consultant*

Dorchester
Brelis, Matthew Dean Burns *journalist*
Bruzelius, Nils Johan Axel *journalist*
Daly, Charles Ulick *foundation executive, investor*
Goodman, Ellen Holtz *journalist*
Greenway, Hugh Davids Scott *journalist*
Hatfield, Julie Stockwell *journalist, newspaper editor*
Huff, William Braid *publication company executive*
Kaufman, Jonathan Reed *journalist*
Kingsbury, Arthur French, III *newspaper publishing executive*
Larkin, Alfred Sinnott, Jr. *newspaper editor*
Leland, Timothy *newspaper executive*
Ockerbloom, Richard C. *newspaper executive*
Stanger, David N. *newspaper publishing executive*
Steller, Arthur Wayne *educational administrator*
Taylor, William Osgood *newspaper executive*
Washington, Mary Louise *retired elementary and special education educator*

Dover
Aldrich, Frank Nathan *bank executive*
Borel, Richard Wilson *communications executive, consultant*
Chattoraj, Sati Charan *biochemistry educator, researcher*
Crittenden, Gazaway Lamar *retired banker*
Fulchino, Paul Edward *management consultant*
Roberts, Francis Donald *manufacturing company executive*
Ryburn, Samuel McChesney *corporate executive*
†Scott, Ronald Bruce *business executive, writer*
Smith, William Henry Preston *writer, editor, former corporate executive*
Stockwell, Ernest Farnham, Jr. *banker*

Duxbury
Albritton, William Hoyle *training and consulting executive, lecturer, writer*
Mc Carthy, D. Justin *college president*
Vose, Robert Churchill, Jr. *former art gallery executive*

East Falmouth
George, M(erton) Baron T(isdale) *aerospace researcher, aviation artist*

East Orleans
Hallowell, Burton Crosby *economist, educator*
MacMillan, Douglas Clark *naval architect*
Nenneman, Richard Arthur *retired publishing executive*
Rath, George Edward *bishop*

East Wareham
Dormitzer, Henry, II *retired manufacturing company executive*

Eastham
McLaughlin, Richard Warren *retired insurance company executive*

Easthampton
†Grubbs, Dennis H. *secondary school principal*
Perkins, Homer Guy *manufacturing company executive*

Edgartown
Piper, George Earle *retailing design and service company executive*
Treat, Lawrence *author*
Walsh, Philip Cornelius *mining consultant*

Essex
McMillen, Louis Albert *architect*

Everett
Jenkins, Alexander, III *business executive*

Fall River
†Correia, Robert *state legislator*
Ingles, James H. *learning resources academic director*
Liebenow, Larry Albert *textile company executive*
†O'Malley, Sean *bishop*

Falmouth
Bonn, Theodore Hertz *computer scientist, consultant*
Brewer, William Dodd *former ambassador, political science educator emeritus*
Gilmour, Edward Ellis *psychiatrist*
Goody, Richard Mead *geophysicist*
Hollister, Charles Davis *oceanographer*
Mitchell, Charles Archie *financial planning consultant, engineer*

Fitchburg
Bogdasarian, John Robert *otolaryngologist*
Mara, Vincent Joseph *college president*
Timms, Peter Rowland *art museum administrator*
Wiegersma, Nan *economics educator*

Foxboro
Armstrong, Bruce Charles *professional football player*
Bowditch, Hoel Lawrence *design engineer inventor, consultant*
†Bush, Raymond T. *accountant, corporate professional*
Ghosh, Asish *control engineer, consultant*
Orthwein, James B. *professional football team executive*
Parcells, Bill (Duane Charles Parcells) *professional football coach*
Pierce, Francis Casimir *civil engineer*
Sullivan, William Hallisey, Jr. *professional football team executive*

Framingham
Atsumi, Ikuko *management school administrator, educator*
Ballou, Kenneth Walter *retired transportation executive, university dean*
Bogard, Carole Christine *lyric soprano*
Bose, Amar Gopal *electrical engineering educator*
†Cammarata, Bernard *retail company executive*
Feldberg, Sumner Lee *retail company executive*
Gaffin, Gerald Eliot *lawyer*
†Holmes, Jack E. *insurance company executive*
†Kuklinski, Joan Lindsey *librarian*
Meltzer, Jay H. *lawyer, retail company executive*
Merser, Francis Gerard *manufacturing company executive, consultant*
Oleskiewicz, Francis Stanley *retired insurance executive*
Preve, Roberta Jean *librarian, researcher*
†Reeves, Anthony Henry *healthcare executive*
Waters, James Logan *analytical instrument manufacturing executive*
Wilson, John Benedict *office supplies company executive*
Wishner, Steven R. *retail executive*

Framington
Scherr, Allan Lee *computer scientist, executive*

Franklin
Bonin, Paul Joseph *real estate and banking executive*

Gardner
Wagenknecht, Edward *author*

Gloucester
Baird, Gordon Prentiss *publisher*
Curtis, Roger William *artist, educator*
Duca, Alfred Milton *artist*
Hancock, Walker Kirtland *sculptor*
Lauenstein, Milton Charles *management consultant*
Socolow, Arthur Abraham *geologist*

Grafton
Haggerty, John Edward *former army officer, research center administrator*

Granby
Edmonds, Anne Carey *librarian*

Great Barrington
Aigner, Lucien L. *writer, photographer*
Gilmour, Robert Arthur *foundation executive, educator*
Schenck, Benjamin Robinson *insurance consultant*
Syer, Warren Bertram *publisher*

Greenfield
†Curtiss, Carol Perry *registered nurse, consultant*
Lee, Marilyn (Irma) Modarelli *law librarian*

Groton
Silvestro, Clement Mario *museum director, historian*
Smith, Alan Harvey *former editor*

Halifax
Fanning, Margaret Beverly *psychotherapist*

Hanover
Fantozzi, Peggy Ryone *environmental planner*
Hart, Richard Nevel, Jr. *finance company executive, financial consultant*
Lonborg, James Reynold *dentist, former professional baseball player*

Hanscom AFB
†Kirkwood, Robert Keith *applied physicist*

Hanson
Norris, John Anthony *health sciences executive, lawyer, educator*

Harvard
Oyler, James Russell, Jr. *manufacturing executive*
Sutherland, Malcolm Read, Jr. *clergyman, educator*

Harwich
Bush, Richard James *engineering executive, lay church worker*
Thorndike, Joseph Jacobs, Jr. *editor*

Harwich Port
Staszesky, Francis Myron *electric company consultant*

Hatfield
Yolen, Jane Hyatt *author*

Haverhill
Dimitry, John Randolph *college president*

Heath
Kades, Charles Louis *retired lawyer*

Hingham
Ford, Joseph *retired superior court judge*
†Hinkley, Clark J. *retail executive*
Lane, Frederick Stanley *lawyer*
Replogle, David Robert *publishing company executive*
†Zetcher, Arnold B. *apparel executive*

Holden
Botty, Kenneth John *editor, newspaper executive*

Holyoke
Dwight, William, Jr. *former newspaper executive, restaurateur*

Hopkinton
Preston, William Hubbard *consultant to specialty businesses*

Housatonic
Levy, Sy *advertising and direct marketing executive*

Hull
Burgess, David Lowry *artist*
Chase, David Marion *applied physicist, mathematical modeler*

Hyannis
Himstead, Scott *newspaper publisher*
Kennedy, Rose Fitzgerald (Mrs. Joseph P. Kennedy) *philanthropist*
MacIntyre, R. Douglas *information technology executive*
White, Timothy Oliver *newspaper editor*

Hyannis Port
Ludtke, James Buren *business and finance educator*

Hyde Park
Riley, Lawrence Joseph *bishop*

Ipswich
Berggren, Dick *editor*
†Getchell, Charles Willard, Jr. *lawyer, publisher*

Jamaica Plain
Cook, Robert Edward *plant ecology researcher, educator*
Pierce, Chester Middlebrook *psychiatrist, educator*
Shapiro, Ascher Herman *mechanical engineer, educator, consultant*
Snider, Gordon Lloyd *physician*

Kingston
†Squarcia, Paul Andrew *school superintendent*
Stair, Gobin *publishing executive, painter, graphic designer*

Lanham
Horowitz, David Joel *author*

Lawrence
Gowdy, Curtis *sportscaster*

Lee
†Miller, Samuel Aaron *dance association executive*

Leeds
Baskin, Leonard *sculptor, graphic artist*

Lenox
Curtis, William Edgar *conductor, composer*
LiMarzi, Joseph *artist*
Novak, William Arnold *author, lecturer*
Pierson, John Herman Groesbeck *economist, writer*
Shammas, Nazih Kheirallah *environmental engineering educator*
Stonier, Tom *educator, author*

Leominster
Cormier, Robert Edmund *writer*

Leverett
Barkin, Solomon *economist*

Lexington
Aldrich, Ralph Edward *physicist*
Alloway, Robert Malcombe *computer consulting executive*
Bailey, Fred Coolidge *retired engineering consulting company executive*
Bainbridge, Kenneth Tompkins *physicist, educator*
Bartlett, Paul Doughty *chemist, educator*
Barton, David Knox *engineering executive, radar engineer*
Bell, Carolyn Shaw *economist, educator*
Bernardi, John Lawrence, Jr. *economic historian, educator, consultant*
Bishop, Robert Calvin *pharmaceutical company executive*
Bleck, Max Emil *aircraft company executive*
Brick, Donald Bernard *consulting company executive*
Brookner, Eli *electrical engineer*
Buchanan, John Machlin *biochemistry educator*
Bursma, Albert, Jr. *publishing company executive*
Cathou, Renata Egone *chemist, consultant*
Chaskelson, Marsha Ina *neuropsychologist*
Ciampa, Dan *management consultant*
Cooper, William Eugene *consultant engineer*
Deitcher, Herbert *financial executive*
Duboff, Robert Samuel *marketing professional*
Eaton, Allen Ober *lawyer*
Eberle, William Denman *corporate executive*
Fallon, John Golden *banker*
Fillios, Louis Charles *nutritional scientist*
Fray, Lionel Louis *management consultant*
Freed, Charles *engineering consultant, researcher*
Freitag, Wolfgang Martin *librarian, educator*
Garing, John Seymour *retired physicist, research executive*
Gibbs, Martin *biologist, educator*
†Hardy, John W. *optics scientist*
Harkness, Sarah Pillsbury *architect*
Hoffmann, Christoph Ludwig *lawyer*
Holzman, Franklyn Dunn *economics educator*
Hoopes, Walter Ronald *chemical company executive*
Kanter, Irving *mathematical physicist*
Kindleberger, Charles P., II *economist, educator*
Kingston, Robert Hildreth *engineering educator*
Korte, Loren A. *publishing company executive*
Kotelly, George Vincent *editor, writer*
Lawton, Eugene Alfred *banking executive*
Mack, Jane Louise *early childhood educator, administrator*
McWhorter, Alan Louis *electronics research executive, electrical engineering educator*
Melngailis, Ivars *solid state research executive*
Mollo-Christensen, Erik Leonard *oceanographer*
Morrow, Walter Edwin, Jr. *electrical engineer, university laboratory administrator*
Nash, Leonard Kollender *chemistry educator*
O'Donnell, Robert Michael *electrical engineering executive*
Osepchuk, John Moses *engineering physicist, consultant*
Papanek, Gustav Fritz *economist, educator*
Parl, Steen Allan *corporate executive*
Phillips, Thomas L. *corporate executive*
Picard, Dennis J. *electronics company executive*
Pierce, Walter S. *architect*
Price, Robert *electronics consultant*
Risch, Martin Donald *marketing-management consulting company executive*
Schloemann, Ernst Fritz (Rudolf August) *physicist, engineer*
Schultz, Samuel Jacob *clergyman, educator*
Shull, Clifford G. *physicist, educator*
Smith, Edgar Eugene *biochemist, university administrator*
Smith, Robert Louis *construction company executive*
Wathne, Carl Norman *hospital administrator*
Williamson, Richard Cardinal *physicist*
Winter, David Louis *systems engineer,human factors scientist*
Wood, Elwood Steven III *chemical company executive*
Wyss, David Alen *financial service executive*

Leyden
Garston, Gerald Drexler *artist*

Lincoln
Adams, Thomas Boylston *writer*
Barrett, Beatrice Helene *psychologist*
Bolt, Richard Henry *science educator, business executive*
Donald, David Herbert *author, history educator*
Eschenroeder, Alan Quade *environmental scientist*
Fernald, George Herbert, Jr. *retired photographic company executive*
Green, David Henry *manufacturing company executive*
Kalba, Kas *international consultant*
LeGates, John Crews Boulton *information scientist*
Master-Karnik, Paul Joseph *art museum director*
Merrill, Vincent Nichols *landscape architect*
Schwann, William Joseph *publisher, musician, discographer*
Schwartz, Edward Arthur *lawyer, foundation executive*
Sprague, John Louis *management consultant*

Lincoln Center
Cannon, Bradford *surgeon*

Littleton
Fuller, Samuel Henry, III *computer engineer*

Longmeadow
Blake, Stewart Prestley *retired ice cream company executive*
Keady, George Cregan, Jr. *judge*
Lo Bello, Joseph David *banking executive*
Locklin, Wilbert Edwin *management consultant*
Skelton, Don Richard *consulting actuary, retired insurance company executive*
Stewart, Alexander Doig *bishop*
Wright, Jeanette Tornow *college president*

Lowell
Baker, Adolph *physicist*
Belle Isle, Albert Pierre *electronics company executive*
Carr, George Leroy *physicist, educator*
Coleman, Robert Marshall *biology educator*
Hoffman, Paul Roger *aerospace executive*
Kahalas, Harvey *manufacturing educator*
Natsios, Nicholas Andrew *retired foreign service officer*
Osenton, Thomas George *publisher*
Rayfield, Allan Laverne *electronics company executive*
Salamone, Joseph Charles *polymer chemistry educator*
Sheldon, Eric *physics educator*
Shirvani, Hamid *philosophy educator, university dean, critic*
†Story, Robert P., Jr. *financial executive*
†Tripathy, Sukant Kishore *chemistry educator*
†Tucci, Joseph M. *computer products manufacturing executive*
Vanderslice, Thomas Aquinas *electronics executive*

Ludlow
Koeninger, Edward Calvin *chemical engineer*

Lynn
Sisk, Philip Laurence *lawyer*
Stark, Dennis Edwin *banker*

Manchester
Bundy, Harvey Hollister *retired bank executive*
Lothrop, Kristin Curtis *sculptor*

Mansfield
Forney, G(eorge) David, Jr. *electronics company executive*
Meelia, Richard J. *healthcare products executive*
†Rosa, Edward A. *principal*

Marblehead
Dolan, John Ralph *retired corporation executive*
Ehrich, Fredric F. *aeronautical engineer*
Kemelman, Harry *author*
†Krebs, James Norton *retired electric power industry executive*
Pruyn, William J. *energy industry executive*
Rogow, Bruce Joel *industry research consultant*
Sanders, Frederick *meteorologist*

Marion
Schmidek, Henry Hans-Heinz *neurosurgeon, educator*

Marlborough
Axline, Robert Paul *electronics executive*
Bennett, C. Leonard *consulting engineering executive*
†Lawrence, Peter Gordon *design management executive*
Lohr, Harold Russell *bishop*
†Morley, Thomas Mark *computer company executive*
Pittack, Uwe Jens *engineer, physicist*
Shepp, Allan *physicist, scientist*
Stiffler, Jack Justin *electrical engineer*

Marshfield
Mc Carthy, Thomas Patrick *magazine publisher*

Marshfield Hills
Stacey, Kathleen Mary *advertising executive*

Marstons Mills
Martin, Vincent George *management consultant*
Vila, Robert Joseph *television host, designer, real estate developer*
Wheeler, Richard Warren *banker*

Mashpee
Stauffer, Robert Allen *former research company executive*

Maynard
Palmer, Robert B. *computer company executive*
†Siekman, Thomas Clement *lawyer*
Smith, John F. *computer company executive*

Medford
Anderson, Thomas Jefferson, Jr. *composer, educator*
Astill, Kenneth Norman *mechanical engineering educator*
Balabanian, Norman *electrical engineering educator*
Bedau, Hugo Adam *philosophy educator*
Berman, David *lawyer, poet*
Bernstein, I(rving) Melvin *university official and dean, materials scientist*
Burke, Edward Newell *radiologist*
Burnim, Kalman Aaron *theatre educator emeritus*
Caviness, Madeline Harrison *art history educator, researcher*
Ch'en, Li-li *Chinese language and literature educator, writer*
Conklin, John Evan *sociology educator*
Cormack, Allan MacLeod *physicist, educator*
Dennett, Daniel Clement *philosopher, author, educator*
DiBiaggio, John A. *university administrator*
Elkind, David *psychology educator*
Gittleman, Sol *university official, humanities educator*
Goldstein, Charles Henry *architect, consultant*
Greif, Robert *mechanical engineering educator*
Guertin, Robert Powell *physics educator, university dean*
Gunther, Leon *physicist*
Hecht, Norman Bernard *biology educator*
Howell, Alvin Harold *engineer*
Junger, Miguel Chapero *acoustics researcher*
Klema, Ernest Donald *nuclear physicist, educator*
Laurent, Pierre-Henri *history educator*
Luria, Zella Hurwitz *psychology educator*
Mancke, Richard Bell *university dean, economics educator*
Mc Carthy, Kathryn A. *physicist*
Miczek, Klaus Alexander *psychology educator*
Milburn, Richard Henry *physics educator*
Mumford, George Saltonstall, Jr. *former university dean, astronomy educator*
Nelson, Frederick Carl *mechanical engineering educator, university dean*
Reynolds, William Francis *mathematics educator*
Salacuse, Jeswald William *lawyer, educator*
Schneps, Jack *physics educator*
Simches, Seymour Oliver *language educator*
Sloane, Marshall M. *banker*
Sung, Nak-Ho *science educator*
Sussman, Martin Victor *chemical engineering educator, inventor, consultant*
Swap, Walter Charles *academic dean, psychology educator*
Uhlir, Arthur, Jr. *electrical engineer, university administrator*
Urry, Grant Wayne *chemistry educator*
Wechsler, Judith Glatzer *art historian, filmmaker, educator*

Medway
Yonda, Alfred William *mathematician*

Melrose
Fremont-Smith, Thayer *associate justice*

Middleboro
Beeby, Kenneth Jack *lawyer, food products executive*
Llewellyn, John Schofield, Jr. *food company executive*

Middleton
Stover, Matthew Joseph *communications company executive*

Milford
Desmarais, Maurice *trade association administrator*

Millbury
Pan, Coda H. T. *mechanical engineering educator, consultant, researcher*

Milton
Dinneen, James Francis *lawyer, business executive*
Dunn, Martin Joseph *dentist*
†Giuliano, Frank J., Jr. *school system administrator*
Ingold, Catherine White *academic administrator*
Kennedy, Thomas Leo *investment management company executive*
Place, David Elliott *lawyer*

Minneapolis
Garton, Thomas William *lawyer*

Montague
Coughlin, Jack *printmaker, sculptor, art educator*

Nantucket
Jesser, Benn Wainwright *chemical engineering and construction company executive*
Lethbridge, Francis Donald *architect*
Murray, Caroline Fish *psychologist*
Rorem, Ned *composer, author*

Natick
Bensel, Carolyn Kirkbride *psychologist*
Cukor, Peter *chemical research and development executive, consultant*
Current, Richard Nelson *historian, educator*
†Denniston, J. *environmental medical research administrator*
Deutsch, Marshall E(manuel) *medical products company executive, inventor*
Donovan, R. Michael *management consultant*
Geller, Esther (Bailey Geller) *artist*
†Gionfriddo, Maurice Paul *research and development manager, aeronautical engineer*
Gomberg, Sydelle *dancer educator*
Milius, Richard A. *organic chemist*
Planitzer, Russell E. *computer company executive*
Strayton, Robert Gerard *public communications executive*
Wang, Chia Ping *physicist, educator*

Needham
Burrell, Sidney Alexander *history educator*
Cantor, Pamela Corliss *psychologist*
Carey, Robert Williams *retired insurance company executive*
Cogswell, John Heyland *retired telecommunications executive, financial consultant*
Cohen, Lewis Cobrain *security products firm executive*
Cowens, David William (Dave Cowens) *former professional basketball player, basketball school executive, insurance executive*
Hunter, Elizabeth Ives-Valsam *fashion consultant*
†Kilburn, Donald C. *publishing company executive*
Lebowitz, Marshall *publishing company executive*
Pucel, Robert Albin *electronics research engineer*
Tarsky, Eugene Stanley *accountant, management and systems consultant*
Toner, Walter Joseph, Jr. *transportation engineer, financial consultant*
Vermette, Raymond Edward *clinical laboratories administrator*
Walworth, Arthur *author*
Weller, Thomas Huckle *physician, emeritus educator*

New Bedford
Chang, Robin *engineering executive*
Hodgson, James Stanley *antiquarian bookseller*
McCarter, Robert *banking executive*
Merolla, Michele Edward *chiropractor*
Ragsdale, James Marcus *editor*
†Shapiro, Gilbert Lawrence *orthopedist*
†Straus, William Marc *lawyer, state legislator*

New Salem
Lenherr, Frederick Keith *neurophysiologist, computer scientist*

Newburyport
Howard, John Tasker *city planner*

Newton
Baron, Charles Hillel *lawyer, educator*
Bewick, John Arters *consulting firm executive*
Blacher, Richard Stanley *psychiatrist*
Caldwell, Sarah *opera producer, conductor, stage director and administrator*
Coleman, Gerald Christopher *management consultant*
Coquillette, Daniel Robert *lawyer, educator*
Deats, Paul Kindred, Jr. *religion educator, clergyman*
Dunlap, William Crawford *physicist*
Forsberg, Roy Walter *publishing company executive*
Frieden, Bernard Joel *urban studies educator*
Gerrity, (James) Frank, II *building materials company executive*
Gill, Benjamin Franklin *physician*
Hauser, Harry Raymond *lawyer*
Heins, Ethel L. *children's literature consultant, critic*
Heyn, Arno Harry Albert *retired chemistry educator*
Kaplan, Steven F. *business management executive*
Katz, Sanford Noah *lawyer, educator*
Kosowsky, David I. *retired biotechnical company executive*
Krakoff, Robert Leonard *publishing executive*
Manners, Robert Alan *anthropologist*
Mason, Charles Ellis, III *magazine editor*
Mautner, Henry George *chemist*
Myerson, Paul Graves *psychiatrist, educator*
Oles, Paul Stevenson (Steve Oles) *architect, perspectivist, educator*
Porter, Jack Nusan *writer, sociologist, historian, Jewish activist*
Price, Roland John Stuart *dancer*
Ranalli, Daniel *artist, writer*
Rodman, Sumner *insurance executive*
Rogoff, Jerome Howard *psychiatrist, psychoanalyst, forensic expert*
Saffran, Kalman *engineering consulting company executive, entrepreneur*
Sarna, Nahum Mattathias *biblical studies educator*
Sbordon, William G. *publisher*
Simon, Harold *radiologist*
Stein, Seymour *electronic scientist*
Stundza, Thomas John *journalist*
Tannenwald, Leslie Keiter *educational administrator*
Thompson, Stephen Arthur *publishing executive*
Weisskopf, Victor Frederick *physicist*
White, Burton Leonard *educational psychologist, author*
Young, James Morningstar *physician, naval officer*

Newton Center
Ault, Hugh Joseph *legal educator*
Mark, Melvin *consulting mechanical engineer, educator*
Schuller, Gunther Alexander *composer*
Shannon, David Thomas *theological seminary executive*
†Walker, Bradford C. *architect*

Newtonville
Polonsky, Arthur *artist, educator*

North Adams
Markou, Peter John *business educator, business and tax consultant*
Thurston, Donald Allen *broadcasting executive*

North Amherst
Andersen, Richard Arnold *author, writing consultant*
Lester, Julius B. *author*

North Andover
Buchanan, Ellery Rives *sales executive*
McGovern, Barbara Elizabeth Ann *elementary educator*
Olney, Peter Butler, Jr. *retired management consulting firm executive*

North Billerica
Coco, Samuel Barbin *venture consultant*
Fink, David A. *rail transportation executive*
†Sodini, Peter J. *food service executive*

North Brookfield
Neal, Avon *artist, author*
Parker, Ann (Ann Parker Neal) *photographer, graphic artist*

North Chatham
McCarthy, Joseph Harold *consultant, former retail food company executive*
Rowlands, Marvin Lloyd, Jr. *publishing and communications consultant*

North Dartmouth
Andersen, Laird Bryce *university administrator*
Cressy, Peter Hollon *naval officer, academic administrator*
Dace, Tish *drama educator*
Law, Frederick Masom *engineering educator, structural engineering firm executive*
†Tuttle, Clifford Horace, Jr. *marketing executive*
Waxler, Robert Phillip *university educator, consultant*
†Yoken, Mel B. *foreign language educator, author*

North Dighton
Cserr, Robert *psychiatrist, physician, hospital administrator*

North Eastham
Simmel, Marianne Lenore *graphic designer*

North Egremont
Le Comte, Edward Semple *author, educator*

North Falmouth
Morse, Robert Warren *research administrator*

North Grafton
Loew, Franklin Martin *veterinary medical and biological scientist, university dean*
Nelson, John Martin *corporate executive*
Ross, James Neil, Jr. *veterinary educator*
Schwartz, Anthony *veterinary surgeon, educator*

North Quincy
Allinson, A. Edward *banking executive*
Porter, John Stephen *television executive*

North Reading
Dolan, Edward Corcoran *real estate developer and investor*
Green, Jack Allen *lawyer*
O'Neil, John P(atrick) *athletic footwear company executive*

Northampton
†Blomberg, Marcia Christine *newspaper editor*
Burk, Carl John *biological sciences educator*
Crosby, Faye Jacqueline *psychology educator, author*
Dashef, Stephen Sewell *psychiatrist*
Derr, Thomas Sieger *religion educator*
Donfried, Karl Paul *minister, theology educator*
Dunn, Mary Maples *college president*
Elkins, Stanley Maurice *historian, educator*
Ellis, Frank Hale *English literature professional*
Fleck, George Morrison *chemistry educator*
Flesher, Hubert Louis *religion educator*
Hoyt, Nelly Schargo (Mrs. N. Deming Hoyt) *history educator*
Lehmann, Phyllis Williams *archaeologist, educator*
Little, Lester Knox *historian, educator*

MacLachlan, Patricia *author*
Munson, Richard Howard *horticulturist*
Murdock, Mary-Elizabeth *history educator*
Naegele, Philipp Otto *violinist, violist, music educator*
Olivo, Margaret Ellen Anderson (Margaret Ellen Anderson) *physiologist, educator*
†Piccinino, Rocco Michael *librarian*
Pickrel, Paul *English educator*
Robinson, Donald Leonard *social scientist, educator*
Rose, Peter Isaac *sociologist, writer*
Rupp, Sheron Adeline *photographer, educator*
Smith, Malcolm Barry Estes *philosophy educator, lawyer*
Vaget, Hans Rudolf *language professional, educator*
Vesely, Alexander *civil engineer*
Volkmann, Frances Cooper *psychologist, educator*
von Klemperer, Klemens *historian, educator*

Northborough
Fulmer, Hugh Scott *physician, educator*
Jeas, William C. *electronics and aerospace engineering executive*

Norton
Dahl, Curtis *English literature educator*
Norris, Curtis Bird *writer, journalist*
Olson, Roberta Jeanne Marie *art historian, author, educator*
Taylor, Robert Sundling *English educator, art critic*

Norwell
Brett, Jan Churchill *illustrator, author*
Mullare, T(homas) Kenwood, Jr. *lawyer*
†Rolnik, Zachary Jacob *senior editor, publisher*
†Smith, Jeffrey K. *publishing executive*
Wentworth, Murray Jackson *artist, educator*

Norwood
Berliner, Allen Irwin *dermatologist*
†Freni, Anthony *church administrator*
Imbault, James Joseph *engineering executive*
Pence, Robert Dudley *biomedical research administrator, hospital administrator*
Sheingold, Daniel H. *electrical engineer*
Tracy, Allen Wayne *manufacturing company executive*

Orange
Bate, Judith Ellen *artist*
Preece, Warren Eversleigh *editor*

Palmer
Dupuis, Robert Simeon *sales executive*

Pittsfield
Anderson, John Gaston *electrical engineer*
Cornelio, Albert Carmen *insurance executive*
Feigenbaum, Armand Vallin *systems engineer, systems equipment executive*
Gregware, James Murray *financial planner*

Plymouth
Gregory, Dick *comedian, civil rights activist*

Provincetown
Brock, Alice May *restaurateur, author*
Oliver, Mary *poet*

Quincy
Bierman, George William *technical consulting executive, food technologist*
Levin, Robert Joseph *retail grocery chain store executive*
†Lippincott, Joseph P. *photojournalist, educator*
Lydon, Mary C. *physical education educator*
Mancini, Rocco Anthony *civil engineer*
†McGlinchey, Joseph Dennis *retail corporation executive*
Miller, George David *retired air force officer, marketing consultant*
Pitts, James Atwater *financial executive*
Shuster, Herbert Victor *corporate executive, consultant*
†Watson, Warren Edward *retired library administrator*
Young, Richard William *corporate consultant*

Randolph
Doulton, Charles William *business executive*
†Lee, M. David *architect*
Morrissey, Edmond Joseph *classical philologist*
Rosenberg, Robert Michael *restaurant franchise company executive*
Ross, Edward Joseph *architect*

Reading
Burbank, Nelson Stone *investment banker*
Gelb, Arthur *science association executive, electrical and systems engineer*
†Stone, Warren R. *book publishing executive*

Richmond
Sexton, William Cottrell *journalist*

Rockport
Bakrow, William John *college president emeritus*
Bissell, Phil (Charles P. Bissell) *cartoonist*
Deedy, John Gerard, Jr. *writer*
Delakas, Daniel Liudviko *retired foreign language educator*
Nicholas, Thomas Andrew *artist*
Strisik, Paul *artist*
Walen, Harry Leonard *historian, lecturer, author*

Roxbury
Adamec, Joseph Victor Otto *bishop*
Berman, Marlene Oscar *neuropsychologist, educator*
Franzblau, Carl *biochemist, consultant, researcher*
†Jacobs, Annette *health facilities administrator*
MacNichol, Edward Ford, Jr. *biophysicist, educator*
Peters, Alan *anatomy educator*
Short, Janet Marie *principal*
Simons, Elizabeth R(eiman) *biochemist, educator*

Rutland
Cormick, Albina *foreign language educator*

Salem
Cavallaro, Mary Caroline *physics educator*
Ettinger, Mort *marketing educator*
†Goss, Kenneth David *museum director*
Griffin, Thomas McLean *retired lawyer*
Harrington, Nancy D. *college president*
Hope, Lawrence Latimer *physicist*
†La Moy, William Thomas *library director, editor*
Miaskiewicz, Theresa Elizabeth *secondary educator*
O'Brien, Robert Kenneth *insurance company executive*
Piro, Anthony John *radiologist*

Sandwich
Terrill, Robert Carl *hospital administrator*

Saugus
Austill, Allen *dean emeritus*

Sharon
Honikman, Larry Howard *pediatrician*
Olum, Paul *mathematician, former university president*
Segersten, Robert Hagy *lawyer, investment banker*

Sheffield
†Haworth, Donald Robert *educator, retired association executive*
Unsworth, Richard Preston *minister, school administrator*
Velmans, Loet Abraham *retired public relations executive*

Sherborn
Kennedy, Chester Ralph, Jr. *former state official, art director*
Pickhardt, Carl Emile, Jr. *artist*

Shirley
Field, Hermann Haviland *architect, educator*

Shrewsbury
†Pederson, Thoru Judd *biologist, research institute director*
Piggford, Roland Rayburn *library and information services consultant*
Zamecnik, Paul Charles *oncologist, medical research scientist*

Somerville
†Bakanowsky, Louis Joseph *visual arts educator, architect, artist*
†Korobkin, Barry Jay *architect*
Safdie, Moshe *architect*
Verderber, Joseph Anthony *capital equipment company executive*
†Wheeler, Katherine Frazier (Kate Wheeler) *writer*

South Attleboro
Glenn, James *sales executive*

South Dartmouth
Stern, T. Noel *political scientist, educator*
Ward, Richard Joseph *university official, educator, author*

South Easton
†Clarke, Cornelius Wilder *superintendent, minister*

South Hadley
Bennett, Jean Louise McPherson *physicist, research scientist*
Berek, Peter *English educator*
Brodsky, Joseph (Alexandrovich) *poet, educator*
Brownlow, Frank Walsh *English language educator*
Campbell, Mary Kathryn *chemistry educator*
Ciruti, Joan Estelle *Spanish language and literature educator*
†Desai, Anita *writer*
Farnham, Anthony Edward *English language educator*
Hall, Lee *artist, educator*
Harrison, Anna Jane *chemist, educator*
Herbert, Robert Louis *art history educator*
Johnson, Richard August *English language educator*
Kennan, Elizabeth Topham *college president*
Kraske, Karl Vincent *paper company executive*
†Lansky, Aaron Jonathan *non-profit organization executive*
Mazzocco, Angelo *language educator*
Quinn, Betty Nye *former classics educator*
Robin, Richard Shale *philosophy educator*
Viereck, Peter *poet, historian, educator*

South Hamilton
Kalland, Lloyd Austin *minister*
Patton, George Smith *military officer*

South Harwich
Micciche, Salvatore Joseph *journalist, lawyer*

South Orleans
Fleck, Gustav Peter *former banker, former securities firm executive, clergyman*
Hickok, Richard Sanford *accountant*

South Wellfleet
Macauley, Robie Mayhew *retired editor*

South Yarmouth
Arthur, George Roland *accountant,engineer, mathematician*
Benoit, Leroy James *language educator*
McIlveen, Edward E. *electrical engineer, association executive*

Southborough
Dews, P(eter) B(ooth) *medical scientist, educator*

Southbridge
†Ghiglione, Loren Frank *newspaper editor*
Mangion, Richard Michael *health care executive*

Southwick
MacEwan, Barbara Ann *middle school educator*

Springfield
Bixby, Allan Barton *insurance company executive*
Brennen, Patrick Wayne *library director*
Canavan, John James, Jr. *employment services executive*
Clark, William J. *life insurance company executive*
Clark, William James *insurance company executive*
†Costello, Thomas Murray *library and museums executive*
†Daly, Michael Joseph *hospital administrator*
†Dunn, Donald Jack *law librarian, law educator, lawyer*
Esposito, Joseph John *publishing company executive*
Finnegan, Thomas Joseph, Jr. *insurance executive, lawyer*
Frankel, Kenneth Mark *thoracic surgeon*
Friedman, Arnold S. *newspaper editor*
Gallup, John Gardiner *retired paper company executive*
†Garvey, Richard Conrad *journalist*
†Gordon, Ronni Anne *journalist*
Haggerty, Thomas Francis *newspaper editor*
†Hinterhaeuser, Hermann *metal manufacturing company executive*
Johnson, Robert Allison *life insurance company executive*
Keough, Francis Paul *librarian*
Kerr, Tim *professional hockey player*
†Lees, Brian Paul *state senator*
Liptzin, Benjamin *psychiatrist*
†Long, Brian Joseph *newspaper publishing executive*
†Markel, Robert Thomas *mayor*
Marshall, John Aloysius *bishop*
†McGee, William Tobin *internist*
Miller, Beverly White *college president*
Miller, J(ohn) Wesley, III *lawyer, writer*
Milstein, Richard Sherman *lawyer*
Mish, Frederick Crittenden *editor*
†Morse, John M. *book publishing executive*
Muhlberger, Richard Charles *former museum administrator, writer*
Naughton, John M. *insurance company executive*
†Norton, Peter J. *publishing executive*
Oldershaw, Louis Frederick *lawyer*
Ponsor, Michael A. *federal judge*
Porter, Burton Frederick *philosophy educator, author*
Riddle, James Douglass *college administrator*
†Stack, May E. *library director*
†Stanley, Thomas E. *publishing company executive*
Sturges, Hollister, III *museum director*
Utley, F. Knowlton *library director, educator*
Wheeler, Thomas Beardsley *insurance company executive*
†Woods, David Fitzwilliam *business, estate and financial planner*

Stockbridge
Gibson, William *author*
Rich, Philip Dewey *publishing executive*
Shapiro, Edward Robert *psychiatrist, educator, psychoanalyst*

Stoneham
†Mc Donald, Andrew Jewett *securities firm executive*

Stoughton
Fireman, Paul B. *footwear/apparel company executive*

Stow
Olsen, Kenneth Harry *manufacturing company executive*

Sturbridge
Flynn, Richard Jerome *manufacturing company executive*
McMahon, Maribeth Lovette *physicist*

Sudbury
Aronson, David *artist, retired art educator*
Blackey, Edwin Arthur, Jr. *geologist*
Blum, Seymour L. *ceramic engineer*
Fowler, Charles Albert *electronics engineer*
Henderson, Ernest, III *health care executive*
Hillery, Mary Jane Larato *editor, producer, television host, columnist, reserve army officer*
Meltzer, Donald Richard *treasurer*
Read, Philip Lloyd *computer design and manufacturing executive*

Swampscott
†Mulcahy, John J. *bishop*
†Neumann, Gerhard *mechanical engineer*
Truog, Dean-Daniel Wesley *educator, consultant*

Taunton
†Donly, Michael J. *headmaster*
Dykstra, William Henry *corporate treasurer*

Tewksbury
†DeMoulas, Telemachus A. *retail grocery company executive*
†Miamis, James D. *retail grocery chain executive*

Topsfield
Peirce, John Wentworth *architect*
Webster, Larry Russell *artist*

Truro
Falk, Lee Harrison *performing arts executive, cartoonist*
Woolley, Catherine (Jane Thayer) *author*

Uxbridge
†Silva, Brian Maurice *landscape architect*

Vineyard Haven
Billingham, Rupert Everett *zoologist, educator*

Wakefield
Bartl, Frederick J. *marketing professional*
Goldberg, Harold Seymour *electrical engineer, academic administrator*
Hunt, Samuel Pancoast, III *lawyer, corporate executive*
Kelley, John Dennis *librarian*
Roberts, Louis Wright *transportation executive*
Zeo, Frank James *technology company executive*

Walpole
Dexter, Lewis *physician*
Warthin, Thomas Angell *physician, educator*

Waltham
Abeles, Robert Heinz *biochemistry educator*
Adamian, Gregory Harry *academic administrator*
Altman, Stuart Harold *economist*
Arena, Albert A. *museum director*
Berger, Arthur Victor *music educator, composer, critic*
Bernstein, Stanley Joseph *manufacturing executive*
Black, Eugene Charlton *historian, educator*
Bohlen, Nina *artist*
Boykan, Martin *composer, music educator*
Bradstreet, Bernard Francis *computer company executive*
Brown, Edgar Henry, Jr. *mathematician, educator*
Brown, Seyom *international relations educator, government consultant*
Bumpus, Frederick Joseph *insurance executive*
Caspar, Donald Louis Dvorak *physics and structural biology educator*
Cohen, Saul G. *chemist, educator*
†Curnan, Susan Patricia Anne *human resource development executive, educator, consultant*
Decker, C(harles) David *research and development executive*
De Rosier, David John *biophysicist, educator*
Deser, Stanley *educator, physicist*
Ellenbogen, George *poet, educator*
Epstein, Irving Robert *chemistry educator*
Evans, Robert, Jr. *economics educator*
Fasman, Gerald David *biochemistry educator*
Feldman, Mark Russel *architect, policy consultant*
Floyd, John Taylor *electronics executive*
Foxman, Bruce Mayer *chemist, educator*
Fuchs, Lawrence Howard *government official, educator*
Fulton, Chandler Montgomery *cell biologist*
Ganong, William Francis, III *speech sciences research executive*
Gerety, Robert John *microbiologist, pharmaceutical company executive, pediatrician, vaccinologist*
Gilbert, David *computer company executive*
Grunwald, Ernest Max *chemistry educator*
Hahn, Bessie King *library administrator, lecturer*
†Halas, Paul J. *lawyer, corporate secretary*
Harth, Erica *French language and comparative literature educator*
Hatsopoulos, George Nicholas *mechanical engineer, thermodynamicist, educator*
Hatsopoulos, John Nicholas *high-technology company executive*
†Hayes, Sherman L. *library director*
Hennessey, Robert John *pharmaceutical company executive*
Hindus, Milton *writer, literature educator*
Huxley, Hugh Esmor *molecular biologist, educator*
Jackendoff, Ray Saul *linguistics educator*
Jeanloz, Roger William *biochemist, educator*
Jencks, William Platt *biochemist, educator*
Jewett, John Persinger *electronics executive, lawyer*
Johnson, William Alexander *clergyman, philosophy educator*
Kunkel, Barbara *psychologist, consultant, educator*
Kustin, Kenneth *chemist*
Lackner, James Robert *aerospace medicine educator*
Leach, Robert Ellis *physician, educator*
Lees, Marjorie Berman *biochemist, neuroscientist*
†Levine, Jerome Paul *mathematician, educator*
Marshall, Robert Lewis *musicologist, educator*
McCulloch, Rachel *economics educator*
†McManmon, Thomas Arthur, Jr. *oil industry executive*
†Mitchell, Janet Brew *health services researcher*
Morant, Ricardo Bernardino *psychology educator*
Nelson, Arthur Hunt *corporate executive*
Nisonoff, Alfred *biochemist, educator*
Nogelo, Anthony Miles *health care company executive*
Pantazelos, Peter George *financial executive*
Petri, Peter Alexander *economist, educator, director*
†Petsko, Gregory Anthony *chemistry and biochemistry educator*
Poduska, John William, Sr. *computer company executive*
†Reilly, Philip *medical research administrator*
Reinharz, Jehuda *university president, history educator*
Riley, Henry Charles *banker*
Rosenblum, Myron *chemist, educator*
Ross, Douglas Taylor *software company executive*
Ross, George William *social scientist, educator*
Schiff, Jerome Arnold *biologist, educator*
Schweber, Silvan Samuel *physics and history educator*
Sekuler, Robert William *psychology educator, scientist*
Slifka, Alfred A. *oil corporation executive*
Stambaugh, Armstrong A., Jr. *restaurant and hotel executive*
Staves, Susan *English educator*
Thier, Samuel Osiah *physician, educator*
Titcomb, Caldwell *music and theatre historian*
Touster, Saul *legal educator*
Wasserstein, Bernard Mano Julius *historian*
Weaver, William Charles *manufacturing executive*
Weckstein, Richard Selig *economics consultant*
Weinert, Henry M. *biomedical company executive*
Wyner, Yehudi *composer, pianist, conductor, educator*
Yancey, Wallace Glenn *insurance company executive*
Young, Dwight Wayne *ancient civilization educator, rancher*
Zohn, Harry *author, educator*

Ware
Shirtcliff, Christine Fay *healthcare facility executive*

Watertown
Crissman, James Hudson *architect*
Dawson, Stuart Owen *landscape architect, urban designer*
†El-Bisi, Hamed Mohamed *scientist*
Goodheart, Eugene *English language educator*
Katz, William Emanuel *chemical engineer*
†Lampkin, M. Martha *architect, city planner*
†Pellegrom, Daniel Earl *international health and development executive*
Rivers, Wilga Marie *foreign language educator*
Savage, James Cathey, III *lawyer, military officer, educator*
True, Edward Keene *architectural engineer*
†Ward, Alan L. *architectural landscape designer*
†Wright, Edward S. *materials technology administrator*

Wayland
Blair, John *electronics company executive*
Bullard, Robert Oliver, Jr. *lawyer*
Clark, Melville, Jr. *physicist, electrical engineer, consultant*
Davis, Luther, Jr. *physicist*

Ebert, Robert Higgins *physician, educator, foundation consultant*
Freed, Murray Monroe *physician, medical educator*
Hagenstein, Perry Reginald *economist*
Hoffmann, Martin Richard *lawyer*
Huygens, Remmert William *architect*
O'Connell, Paul Edmund *publisher*
Shrader, William Whitney *radar consulting scientist*
Weil, Thomas Alexander *electronics engineer*
Williams, James P., Jr. (Jay Williams) *broadcasting executive*
Wolf, Irving *clinical psychologist*

Wellesley
Aldrich, Richard Orth *lawyer*
Allen, Michael W *management consultant*
†Anathan, James Mone, III *retail executive*
Anthony, Edward Lovell, II *retired investments executive*
Beckedorff, David Lawrence *investment manager, computer scientist*
Coyne, Mary Downey *biologist, endocrinologist, educator*
Doku, Hristo Chris *dental educator*
Eilts, Hermann Frederick *international relations educator, former diplomat*
Farnham, Sherman Brett *retired electrical engineer*
Gailius, Gilbert Keistutis *manufacturing company executive*
†Gerson, Samuel J. *apparel executive*
Gladstone, Richard Bennett *retired publishing company executive*
Goglia, Charles A., Jr. *lawyer*
†Goldman, James Warren *advertising agency executive*
Hildebrand, Francis Begnaud *mathematics educator*
Horn, David Dinsmore *insurance company executive*
Jacobs, Ruth Harriet *poet, playwright, sociologist, gerontologist*
Kobayashi, Yutaka *biochemist, consultant*
Kucharski, John Michael *scientific instruments manufacturing company executive*
Levin, Burton *diplomat*
Marcus, William Michael *rubber and vinyl products manufacturing company executive*
Miller, Linda B. *political scientist*
Murray, Joseph Edward *plastic surgeon*
Myers, Arthur M. *journalist, author*
Nagler, Leon Gregory *management consultant*
Papageorgiou, John Constantine *management science educator*
Parker, William H., III *federal official*
Reiss, Martin Harold *engineering executive*
Ritt, Paul Edward *communications and electronics company executive*
Rubinovitz, Samuel *diversified manufacturing company executive*
Ruiz-de-Conde, Justina *retired foreign language educator*
Shea, Robert McConnell *lawyer*
Valente, Louis Patrick (Dan Valente) *technical corporation executive*

Wellfleet
Dugger, Ronnie E. *writer, publisher*
Hopkins, Budd *artist, writer*
Jentz, John Macdonald *engineer, travel executive*
Piercy, Marge *poet, novelist, essayist*

West Barnstable
Corsa, Helen Storm *language professional*

West Boylston
Moorefield, James Lee *retired insurance executive, lawyer*

West Chatham
McHale, Thomas Anthony *sales and marketing consultant*

West Falmouth
Vaccaro, Ralph Francis *marine biologist*

West Hyannisport
Corry, Andrew Francis *consulting engineering executive*

West Newbury
Coit, Margaret Louise *writer*
Dooley, Ann Elizabeth *freelance writers cooperative executive, editor*

West Newton
Elya, John Adel *bishop*

West Roxbury
Hedley-Whyte, John *anesthesiologist, educator*
Wiegner, Allen Walter *biomedical engineering educator, researcher*

West Springfield
Butterfield, Jack Arlington *hockey league executive*
Engebretson, Douglas Kenneth *architect*
Krach, Mitchell Peter *retired financial services executive*

West Tisbury
Smith, Henry Clay *retired psychology educator*

Westborough
Bok, Joan Toland *utility executive*
Greenman, Frederic Edward *utility executive*
Houston, Alfred Dearborn *energy company executive*
Jackson, Frederick Herbert *educational administrator*
Nichols, Guy W. *institute executive, former utilities executive*
†Nichols, Guy Warren *science administrator*
Rowe, John William *utility executive*
Skates, Ronald Louis *computer manufacturing executive*
Young, Roger Austin *natural gas distribution company executive*

Westfield
Applbaum, Ronald Lee *academic administrator*
Buckmore, Alvah Clarence, Jr. *computer scientist, ballistician*
Tower, Horace Linwood, III *consumer products company executive*

Westford
Bowman, George Leo *artist*
Dennison, Byron Lee *electrical engineering educator, consultant*
Salah, Joseph Elias *research scientist, educator*
Stansberry, James Wesley *air force officer*

Weston
Aquilino, Daniel *banker*
Clayton, Richard Reese *holding company executive*
DeVito, Richard A(nthony) *publisher*
Fine, Bernard J. *retired psychologist, consultant*
Haas, Jacqueline Crawford *lawyer*
Higgins, Sister Therese *English educator, former college president*
Ives, J. Atwood *financial executive*
Kendall, Julius *consulting engineer*
Kraft, Gerald *economist*
Mc Elwee, John Gerard *retired life insurance company executive*
Megley, Sheila *university executive, administrator, English educator*
Oelgeschlager, Guenther Karl *publisher*
Press, Aida Kabatznick *writer*
Rockwell, George Barcus *financial consultant*
Rogers, Howard Gardner *consultant, photographic company research director emeritus*
Saad, Theodore Shafick *retired microwave company executive*
Sack, Burton Marshall *business executive*
Sturgis, Robert Shaw *architect*
Sullivan, Barbara Boyle *management consultant*
†Wacker, John Lee *landscape architect*
Whitehouse, David Rempfer *physicist*
Wind, Herbert Warren *writer*

Westport
Howard, James Merriam, Jr. *education writer*

Westwood
Bernfeld, Peter Harry William *biochemist*
Borgman, George Allan *journalist*
Funkhouser, Elmer Newton, Jr. *retired academic official*
Gillette, Hyde *investment banker*
Goodman, Bruce Gerald *lawyer*
Philbrick, Margaret Elder *artist*

Weymouth
Parsons, Edwin Spencer *clergyman, educator*

Wianno
Old, Bruce Scott *chemical and metallurgical engineer*

Wilbraham
Anderson, Eric William *retired food service company executive*
Gale, William Henry *artist*
†O'Shaughnessy, Joseph A. *restaurant company executive*
Wise, Warren Roberts *lawyer*

Williamsburg
Healy, Robert Danforth *manufacturing executive*
Snow, Elizabeth Jean *poet, inventor, farmer, small business owner*

Williamstown
†Art, Henry Warren *biology educator*
Bahlman, Dudley Ward Rhodes *history educator*
Bolton, Roger Edwin *economist, educator*
Brooke, David Stopford *art gallery official*
Conklin, Susan Joan *psychotherapist*
Crider, Andrew Blake *psychologist*
Dalzell, Robert Fenton, Jr. *historian*
Dew, Charles Burgess *historian, educator*
Eusden, John Dykstra *theology educator, minister*
Fox, William Templeton *geologist, educator*
†Gibson, Sarah Ann Scott *art librarian*
Goethals, George R., II *psychology educator*
Graver, Lawrence Stanley *English language professional*
Hamilton, George Heard *curator*
Hastings, Philip Kay *psychology educator*
Hill, Victor Ernst, IV *mathematics educator, musician*
Hyde, John Michael *history educator*
Lee, Arthur Virgil, III *corporate executive*
Markgraf, J(ohn) Hodge *chemist, educator*
McGill, Thomas Emerson *psychology educator*
Oakley, Francis Christopher *history educator, former college president*
Park, David Allen *physicist, educator*
Pasachoff, Jay Myron *astronomer, educator*
Payne, Harry Charles *historian, educator*
Petersen, Norman Richard, Jr. *religious studies educator*
Pistorius, George *language educator*
†Raab, Lawrence Edward *English educator*
Rudolph, Frederick *history educator*
Shainman, Irwin *music educator, musician*
Sheahan, John Bernard *economist, educator*
Stamelman, Richard Howard *French and humanities educator*
Taylor, Alfred Hendricks, Jr. *former foundation executive*
Waite, Robert George Leeson *history educator*
Welch, Neal William *retired electric company executive*
Wikander, Lawrence Einar *librarian*
Wilkins, Earle Wayne, Jr. *surgery educator emeritus*
Winston, Gordon Chester *economic educator, former academic administrator*
Wobus, Reinhard Arthur *geologist, educator*

Wilmington
Bartlett, John Bruen *financial executive*
Buckley, Robert Paul *aerospace company executive*
DiFillippo, Anthony Francis *service company executive*
Faccini, Ernest Carlo *mechanical engineer*
Foster, Henry Louis *veterinarian, laboratory executive*
Reeves, Barry Lucas *aerophysics research engineer*
Sabosik, Patricia Elizabeth *publisher, editor*

Winchester
Bigelow, Robert P. *arbitrator, writer*
Brennan, Francis Patrick *banker*
Cecich, Donald Edward *manufacturing executive*
Cowgill, F(rank) Brooks *retired insurance company executive*
Ewing, David Walkley *magazine editor*
Hansen, Robert Joseph *civil engineer*
Hirschfeld, Ronald Colman *retired consulting engineering executive*
Hottel, Hoyt Clarke *consulting chemical engineer*
Neuman, Robert Sterling *art educator, artist*
Shannon, Claude Elwood *mathematician, educator*
Smith, Robert Moors *anesthesiologist*
Smith, Whitney *vexillologist*
Taggart, Ganson Powers *management consultant*

Winthrop
†Costantino, Frank Mathew *architectural illustrator*
Moses, Ronald Elliot *retired toiletries products executive*

Woburn
†Breazeale, Kelly Wade *health care association executive, consultant*
Eddison, Elizabeth Bole *entrepreneur, information specialist*
†Flummerfelt, J. Kent *electronics executive*
Freund, Mitchell David *cable television executive, producer, director*
†Klein, Michael James *broadcast executive, engineer*
Mehra, Raman Kumar *data processing executive, automation and control engineering researcher*
†Tomaszewski, James M. *electronics executive*
Tritter, Richard Paul *information systems consulting executive*

Woods Hole
Ballard, Robert Duane *marine scientist*
Berggren, William Alfred *geologist, research micropaleontologist, educator*
†Broadus, James Matthew *research center administrator*
Burris, John Edward *biologist*
†Butman, Bradford *oceanographer*
†Carlton, Winslow *health association administrator*
Cohen, Seymour Stanley *biochemist, educator*
Copeland, Donald Eugene *research marine biologist*
Ebert, James David *research biologist, educator*
Emery, Kenneth Orris *marine geologist*
Fofonoff, Nicholas Paul *oceanographer, educator*
Gagosian, Robert B. *chemist, educator*
Grice, George Daniel *marine biologist, science administrator*
Hart, Stanley Robert *geochemist, educator*
Inoué, Shinya *microscopy and cell biology scientist, educator*
Steele, John Hyslop *marine scientist, oceanographic institute administrator*
Von Herzen, Richard Pierre *research scientist, consultant*
Woodwell, George Masters *ecologist, educator, author, lecturer*

Worcester
Alie, Arthur Henry *financial services company executive*
Apelian, Diran *materials scientist, provost*
Appelbaum, Paul Stuart *psychiatrist, educator*
Bagshaw, Joseph Charles *molecular biologist, educator*
Baughman, Susan S. *library director*
Bell, Peter Mayo *geophysicist*
Berth, Donald Frank *university official, consultant*
Biederman, Ronald R. *mechanical engineer, educator*
Billias, George Athan *history educator*
Bonkovsky, Herbert Lloyd *gastroenterologist, educator*
Brazelton, Roy Dale *real estate executive*
Brill, A. Bertrand *nuclear medicine educator*
Brooks, John Edward *college president*
Cabot, Harold *banker*
Candib, Murray A. *business executive, retail management consultant*
Carlson, Suzanne Olive *architect*
Charney, Evan *pediatrician, educator*
Clarke, Edward Nielsen *engineering science educator*
Clements, Kevin Anthony *dean, electrical engineering educator, consultant*
Cowan, Fairman Chaffee *lawyer*
DeFalco, Frank Damian *civil engineering educator*
Densmore, William Phillips *management consultant*
Dewey, Henry Bowen *lawyer*
Dorman, Harry Gaylord, III *hospital administrator*
Drachman, David Alexander *neurologist*
Dunlap, Ellen S. *library administrator*
Dunlop, George Rodgers *surgeon*
Fries, Donald Eugene *lawyer, insurance executive*
Gorton, Nathaniel Matheson *federal judge, lawyer*
Graf, Robert Arlan *financial services executive*
Greenberg, Nathan *accountant*
Grogan, William Robert *university dean*
Hagan, Joseph Henry *college president*
Hanshaw, James Barry *physician, educator*
Hanson, Susan Easton *geography educator*
Harrington, Timothy J. *bishop*
Hohenemser, Christoph *physics educator, researcher*
Hunt, John David *retired banker*
Hunter, Richard Edward *physician*
†Isaksen, Robert L. *bishop*
†Janensch, Paul *newspaper editor*
Jareckie, Stephen Barlow *museum curator*
†Johnson, Penelope B. *librarian*
Kaplan, Melvin Hyman *immunology, rheumatology, medical educator*
†Kelly, John Francis *lawyer*
King, Anthony Gabriel *museum administrator*
Klein, Michael William *physics educator*
Laster, Leonard *physician, academic administrator*
Levine, Peter Hughes *physician, health facility administrator*
Ludlum, David Blodgett *pharmacologist, educator*
Lutz, Francis Charles *university dean, civil engineering educator*
†Magiera, Frank Edward *journalist, critic*
Majno, Guido *pathologist, educator*
Malone, Joseph James *mathematics educator, researcher*
Mc Corison, Marcus Allen *librarian, cultural organization administrator*
†McManus, William Joseph, II *state legislature, lawyer*
McQuarrie, Bruce Cale *mathematics educator*
Menon, Mani *urological surgeon, educator*
Morton, Donald John *librarian*
O'Brien, John F., Jr. *insurance company executive*
Olson, Robert Leonard *retired insurance company executive*
Onorato, Nicholas Louis *program director, economist*
Pavlik, James William *chemistry educator*
Sioui, Richard Henry *chemical engineer*
Smith, Edward Herbert *radiologist, educator*
†Soule, Charles Everett *insurance executive*
Spencer, Harry Irving, Jr. *retired banker*
Strauss, Jon Calvert *university president*
Titcomb, Woodbury Cole *bank executive, consultant*
Townes, Philip Leonard *pediatrician, educator*
Traina, Richard Paul *university president*
Ullrich, Robert Albert *business management educator*
Von Laue, Theodore Herman *historian, educator*
Wapner, Seymour *psychologist, educator, administrator*
Weiss, Alvin Harvey *chemical engineering educator, catalysis researcher and consultant*
Welu, James A. *art museum director*
Wheeler, Hewitt Brownell *surgeon, educator*
Wilbur, Leslie Clifford *mechanical engineering educator*
Wilkinson, Harold Arthur *neurosurgeon*
Zeugner, John Finn *history educator, writer*
Zurier, Robert Burton *medical educator, clinical investigator*
Zwiep, Donald Nelson *mechanical engineering educator, administrator*

Worthington
Hastings, Wilmot Reed *lawyer*

Wrentham
Teplow, Theodore Herzl *valve company executive*

Yarmouth Port
Gorey, Edward St. John *author, artist*
Hall, James Frederick *retired college president*
Hesse, William R. *marketing and advertising executive*
Stott, Thomas Edward, Jr. *engineering company executive*
†Teague, Edward B., III *insurance and investment broker*

MICHIGAN

Ada
Beutner, Roger Earl *manufacturing executive*
DeVos, Richard Marvin *network marketing company executive*
DeVos, Richard Marvin, Jr. (Dick DeVos) *direct sales company exexutive*
Van Andel, Jay *home and personal products company executive*
Whitney, William Chowning *retired banker, financial consultant*

Addison
Knight, V. C. *manufacturing executive*

Adrian
Caine, Stanley Paul *college administrator*
Dombrowski, Mark Anthony *librarian*
Kralick, Richard Louis *lawyer*
Weathers, Milledge Wright *retired economics educator*

Albion
Vulgamore, Melvin L. *college president*

Allen Park
Manov, Leslie Joan Boyle *radiologist, medical administrator*
Simpson, Bruce Howard *training company executive*

Allendale
Murray, Diane Elizabeth *librarian*
Niemeyer, Glenn Alan *academic administrator, history educator*

Alma
Sanders, Jack Ford *physician*
Stone, Alan Jay *college administrator*
Swanson, Robert Draper *college president*

Alpena
†Bodem, Dennis Richard *museum director*
Henry, DeLysle Leon *lawyer*

Ann Arbor
Abrams, Gerald David *physician, educator*
Adamson, Thomas Charles, Jr. *aerospace engineering educator, consultant*
Agno, John G. *management consultant*
Agranoff, Bernard William *biochemist, educator*
Akcasu, Ahmet Ziyaeddin *nuclear engineer, educator*
Akerlof, Carl William *physics educator*
Aldridge, John Watson *English language educator, author*
Allen, Sally Lyman *biologist*
Aller, Margo Friedel *astronomer*
Alpern, Mathew *physiological optics educator*
Amann, Peter Henry *historian, educator*
Anderson, Austin Gothard *university administrator, lawyer*
†Anderson, Barbara A. *sociologist, educator*
†Anderson, William R. *biologist, educator, curator, director*
Ansbacher, Rudi *physician*
Apperson, Jean *psychologist*
†Armstrong, William Floyd *medical educator*
Arthos, John *English language educator*
Ash, Major McKinley, Jr. *dentist, educator*
Ashe, Arthur James, III *chemistry educator*
Atreya, Sushil Kumar *space science educator, researcher*
†Aupperle, Eric Max *data network center administrator, research scientist, engineering educator*
Avery, James Knuckey *dental educator*
Bailey, David Roy Shackleton *classics educator*
Bailey, Reeve Maclaren *museum curator*
Bailey, Richard Weld *English educator*
Baker, Sheridan *English educator, author*
Banks, Peter Morgan *electrical engineering educator*
†Barbarin, Oscar Anthony *psychologist*
Bartell, Lawrence Sims *chemist, educator*
Bartle, Robert Gardner *mathematics educator*
Bassett, Leslie Raymond *composer, educator*
Beaubien, Anne Kathleen *librarian*
Beaver, Frank Eugene *communication educator, film critic and historian*
Becher, William Don *electrical engineering educator, engineering consultant*
Becker, Marvin Burton *historian*
Bedard, Patrick Joseph *editor, writer, consultant*
Beeton, Alfred Merle *laboratory director, limnologist, educator*
Belcher, Louis David *marketing and operations executive, former mayor*

Benford, Harry Bell naval architect
Bernstein, Isadore Abraham biochemistry educator, researcher
Beutler, Frederick Joseph information scientist
†Bhattacharya, Pallab Kumar electrical engineering educator, researcher
Bidlack, Russell Eugene librarian, educator and dean emeritus
Bilello, John Charles materials science and engineering educator
Bitondo, Domenic engineering executive
Blinder, Seymour Michael chemistry educator
Blotner, Joseph Leo English language educator
Bolcom, William Elden musician, composer, educator, pianist
Bole, Giles G. physician, researcher, medical educator
Bornstein, George Jay literary educator
Bornstein, Morris economist, educator
Boylan, Paul Charles music educator, academic administrator
Brandt, Richard Booker former philosophy educator
†Bressler, Philip Jack food products executive, consultant
Britton, Clarold Lawrence lawyer, consultant
Brown, Deming Bronson Slavic languages and literature educator
Brown, Morton B. biostatistics educator
†Brown, William Milton electrical engineering educator
Bryant, Barbara Everitt academic researcher, market research consultant, former federal agency administrator
Buchanan, Robert Alexander pharmaceutical company executive, physician
†Burbank, Jane Richardson Russian and European studies educator
Burdi, Alphonse Rocco anatomist
Burling, Robbins anthropologist, educator
Buyse, Leone Karena orchestral musician, educator
Cain, Charles Alan electrical engineering educator, researcher
Calahan, Donald Albert electrical engineering educator
Cannell, Charles Frederick psychologist, educator
Cantrall, Irving J(ames) entomologist, educator
Carlen, Sister Claudia librarian
Casey, Kenneth Lyman neurologist
Cassara, Frank artist, printmaker
Castor, C. William, Jr. physician, educator
†Chaffin, Donald B. industrial engineer, researcher
Chambers, Leigh Ross French language educator
Chen, Michael Ming mechanical engineering educator
Christensen, A(lbert) Kent anatomy educator
Christiansen, Richard Louis orthodontics educator, research director, former dean
Christman, James Edward landscape architect
†Chupp, Timothy E. physicist, educator, nuclear scientist, academic administrator
Clark, John Alden mechanical engineering educator
Clark, Noreen Morrison behavioral science educator, researcher
Clark, Thomas Bertram, Sr. real estate broker
†Cohen, Malcolm Stuart economist, research institute director
†Cole, Juan R.I. cultural organization administrator
Conway, Lynn Ann computer scientist, educator
Cooper, Edward Hayes lawyer, educator
Coran, Arnold Gerald pediatric surgeon, educator
Cornelius, Kenneth Cremer, Jr. finance executive
Counsell, Raymond Ernest pharmacology educator
Cowen, Roy Chadwell, Jr. German language educator
†Cox, John William architect, educator
Craig, Robert George dental science educator
Crane, Horace Richard educator, physicist
Crawford, Charles Merle business administration educator
Crawford, Richard musicology educator
†Csere, Csaba magazine editor
Curley, Edwin Munson philosophy educator
Curtis, George Clifton psychiatry educator, clinical research investigator
†Danly, Robert Lyons Japanese studies educator, author, translator
D'Arms, John Haughton classics educator, university dean
Davenport, Horace Willard physiologist
†Davis, Wayne Kay university dean, educator
Dawson, William Ryan zoology educator
Day, Colin Leslie publisher
Decker, Raymond Frank scientist, technology executive
Dekker, Eugene Earl biochemistry educator
De La Iglesia, Felix Alberto pathologist, toxicologist
Delonis, Robert J. bank executive
DeVine, Edmond Francis lawyer
DeWeese, Marion Spencer educator, surgeon
Diana, Joseph A. retired foundation executive
†Dirks, Nicholas B. cultural research organization administrator/history educator
Dolph, Charles Laurie theoretical physics educator
Domino, Edward Felix pharmacologist, educator
Donabedian, Avedis physician
Donahue, Thomas Michael physics educator
Dougherty, Richard Martin library and information science educator
Douvan, Elizabeth social psychologist, educator
Dow, William Gould electrical engineer, educator
Drach, John Charles researcher, dental basic science educator
Dubin, Howard Victor dermatologist
Duderstadt, James Johnson university president
Dunlap, Connie librarian
Duquette, Donald Norman law educator
Duren, Peter Larkin mathematician, educator
Easter, Stephen Sherman, Jr. biology educator
Eby, Cecil DeGrotte English language educator, writer
Eggertsen, Claude Andrew education educator
Eisenberg, Marvin art history educator
Eisendrath, Charles Rice journalism educator, manufacturer, farmer, consultant
Eisenstein, Elizabeth Lewisohn historian, educator
Ellmann, William Marshall lawyer, mediator, arbitrator, researcher
England, Anthony Wayne electrical engineering and computer science educator, astronaut, geophysicist
Enns, Mark Kynaston electrical engineer
Eron, Leonard David psychology educator
Evans, Francis Cope ecologist
Fader, Daniel Nelson English language educator
Faeth, Gerard Michael aerospace engineering educator, researcher
Fajans, Stefan Stanislaus internist, retired educator
†Farrand, William Richard geology educator
Faulkner, John Arthur physiologist, educator
Feng, Hsien Wen biochemistry educator, researcher
Feuerwerker, Albert history educator
Fifield, Russell Hunt political science educator
Filisko, Frank Edward physicist, educator
Finney, Ross Lee composer
Fitzsimmons, Joseph John publishing executive
Fleming, Suzanne Marie university official, chemistry educator
Foley, Daniel Ronald business and personnel executive
Forsyth, Ilene Haering art historian
Forsyth, John D. hospital administrator
Foster, Alan Herbert financial consultant
Fox, James Carroll aerospace engineer, program manager
Fraser, Russell Alfred author, educator
Freedman, Ronald sociology educator
Freeth, Douglas Duncan banker
†Fry, Richard E. architectural firm executive
Fusfeld, Daniel Roland economist
Gans, Carl zoologist, educator
Gehring, Frederick William mathematician, educator
Gelehrter, Thomas David medical and genetics educator, physician
†Gelman, Charles medical manufacturing executive
Gibala, Ronald metallurgical engineering educator
Gikas, Paul William medical educator
†Gilbert, Elmer Grant aerospace engineering educator, control theorist
Gilbert, Robert Edward lawyer
Gilman, Sid neurologist
Gingerich, Philip Derstine paleontologist, evolutionary biologist, educator
Ginsburg, David human genetics educator, researcher
Goad, Linda May research scientist
†Goldstein, Irwin Joseph medical research executive
Gomberg, Edith S. Lisansky psychologist, educator
Gomberg, Henry Jacob nuclear engineer
Gomez, Luis Oscar Asian and religious studies educator
†Gramlich, Edward Martin public policy, economics educator
Grant, Michael Peter electrical engineer
Grassmuck, George Ludwig political science educator
†Greden, John Francis psychiatrist, educator
†Greene, Douglas A. internist, educator
Griffin, Carleton Hadlock accountant, educator
Griffith, John Randall health services administrator, educator
†Grisham, Rita Miller automotive executive
Guardo, Carol J. association executive
Guthrie, Harvey Henry, Jr. clergyman
Guy, Ralph B., Jr. federal judge
Hackett, Roger Fleming history educator
Haddad, George Ilyas engineering educator, research scientist
Haddock, Fred T. astronomer, educator
Haddox, Mark electronic engineer
Hagen, John William psychology educator
Hanson, Robert Duane civil engineering educator
Hawkins, Joseph Elmer, Jr. otolaryngologist, educator, acoustic physiologist
Hawthorne, Victor Morrison epidemiologist, educator
Hayes, John Patrick electrical engineering and computer science educator, consultant
Heidelberger, Kathleen Patricia physician
Henderson, John Woodworth ophthalmologist, educator
Hennessey, William John museum director
†Hernandez, Ramon Robert public library director
Hess, Bartlett Leonard clergyman
Hessler, David William information management educator, information systems consultant
Hill, Bruce Marvin statistician, scientist, educator
Hiss, Roland Graham physician, medical educator
Hochster, Melvin mathematician, educator
Hoff, Julian Theodore physician, educator
Holbrook, Robert Sumner economist, educator
Horowitz, Samuel Boris biomedical researcher, educational consultant
†House, James Stephen social psychologist, educator
Howell, Joel DuBose physician, educator
Howrey, Eugene Philip economics educator, consultant
Huelke, Donald Fred anatomy and cell biology educator, research scientist
Huetteman, Raymond Theodore, Jr. lawyer
Huntington, Curtis Edward actuary
†Islam, Mohammed N. optics scientist
Israel, Jerold Harvey law educator
Jackson, James Sidney psychology educator
Jackson, John Howard lawyer, educator
Jacobson, Harold Karan political science educator, researcher
†Jelinek, Fran school system administrator
Johnson, Harold R. social work and gerontology educator, academic administrator
Johnston, Lloyd Douglas social scientist
Jones, Lawrence William educator, physicist
Jones, Phillip Sanford mathematics educator emeritus
Joscelyn, Kent Buckley lawyer, criminologist, research scientist
Kahn, Douglas Allen legal educator
Kalisch, Beatrice Jean nursing educator, consultant
Kalisch, Philip A. social science educator
Kamisar, Yale lawyer, educator
Kamrowski, Gerome artist
Kaufman, Peter Bishop biological sciences educator
Kauper, Thomas Eugene lawyer, educator
Kelch, Robert Paul pediatric endocrinologist
Kelly, Raymond Case anthropology educator
Kempe, Lloyd Lute chemical engineering educator
Kennedy, David Boyd foundation executive, lawyer
Kennedy, Frank Robert lawyer
Kerr, William nuclear engineering educator
Kesler, Stephen Edward economic geology educator
Kim, E. Han finance and business administration educator
Kimbrough, William Walter, III psychiatrist
Kingdon, John Wells political science educator
Kirkpatrick, Dorothy Ann early childhood education educator
Kish, Leslie research statistician, educator
Kister, James Milton mathematician, educator
Kleinsmith, Lewis Joel cell biologist, educator
Knoll, Glenn Frederick nuclear engineering educator
Knott, John Ray, Jr. language professional, educator
†Knox, Eric botanist, educator
Koenen, Ludwig classical studies educator
Konigsberg, Ira film and literature educator, writer
Kostyo, Jack Lawrence physiology educator
Kozma, Adam electrical engineer
Krause, Charles Joseph otolaryngologist
Krier, James Edward law educator, author
†Krimm, Samuel physicist, educator
Krisch, Alan David physics educator
Kuhl, David Edmund physician, radiology educator
La Du, Bert Nichols, Jr. pharmacology educator, physician
Lapides, Jack urologist, medical educator
La Plata, George federal judge
Leith, Emmett Norman electrical engineer, educator
Lempert, Richard Owen lawyer, educator
Leonard, Joanne photographer, educator
†Lewis, Donald John mathematics educator
Lewis, Robert Enzer lexicographer, educator
Lichter, Paul Richard ophthalmology educator
Lillya, Clifford Peter musician, educator
Liu, Vi-Cheng aerospace engineering educator
Livingstone, Frank Brown anthropologist, educator
Long, Patrick Brien advanced technology company executive
Longone, Daniel Thomas chemistry educator
†MacKinnon, Catharine A. law educator, legal scholar, writer
Macnee, Alan Breck electrical engineer, educator
Manis, Melvin psychologist, educator
Margolis, Philip Marcus psychiatrist, educator
Martel, William radiologist, educator
Martin, Claude Raymond, Jr. marketing consultant, educator
McCarus, Ernest Nasseph language educator
McClamroch, N. Harris aerospace engineering educator, consultant, researcher
Mc Cracken, Paul Winston economist, business educator
McCuen, John Francis, Jr. lawyer
McDougal, Stuart Yeatman comparative literature educator, author
†Mc Gibbon, William landscape architect
Mc Keachie, Wilbert James psychologist, educator
Mersereau, John, Jr. Slavic languages and literatures educator
Metcalf, Robert Clarence architect, educator
Meyer, Alfred George political science educator
Meyer, John Frederick engineering and computer science educator, researcher, consultant
Midgley, A(lvin) Rees, Jr. reproductive endocrinology educator, researcher
†Miller, Josef M. otolaryngologist, educator
Mitchell, Edward John economist, retired educator
Moeller, Gary university athletic coach
†Moll, Russell Addison aquatic ecologist, science administrator
Monaghan, Thomas Stephen restaurant chain executive
Moore, Thomas E. biology educator, museum director
Morgan, James Newton research economist, educator
Morgan, Raleigh, Jr. linguistics educator
Morley, George William gynecologist
Morris, Phyllis Sutton philosophy educator
Moss, Cruse Watson automobile company executive
Munro, Donald Jacques philosopher, educator
Murphey, Rhoads history educator
Nagy, Andrew Francis engineering educator
Neal, Homer Alfred physics educator, researcher, university administrator
Neidhardt, Frederick Carl microbiologist
Ning, Xue-Han (Hsueh-Han Ning) physiologist, researcher
Nisbett, Richard Eugene psychology educator
Nordman, Christer Eric chemistry educator
Nugent, Theodore Anthony musician
Oliver, William John pediatrician, educator
Oncley, John Lawrence biophysics educator, consultant
Organski, Abramo Fimo Kenneth political scientist, educator
Orringer, Mark B. thoracic surgeon
Osborn, June Elaine pediatrician, microbiologist, educator
Packard, Peter Kim diversified products company executive
†Paige, Jeffery Mayland sociologist, educator
Parkinson, William Charles physicist, educator
Parsons, Jeffrey Robinson anthropologist, educator
Paul, Ara Garo university dean
Paulsen, Serenus Glen architect, educator
Pedley, John Griffiths archaeologist, educator
Pehlke, Robert Donald materials and metallurgical engineering educator
Petrick, Ernest Nicholas mechanical engineer
Pierce, Roy political science educator
Pierce, William James law educator
Pierpont, Wilbur K. retired acounting educator
Pitt, Bertram cardiologist, consultant
Ploger, Robert Riis retired military officer, engineer
Pollack, Henry Nathan geophysics educator
†Pollack, Lana state senator
Pollock, Stephen Michael industrial engineering educator, consultant
Porter, John Wilson education executive
Pulgram, Ernst linguist, philologist, Romance and classical linguistics educator, writer
Radock, Michael foundation executive
Reck, J. David lawyer
Reed, John Wesley lawyer, educator
Regan, Donald H. lawyer, educator
Richardson, Rudy James toxicology and neurosciences educator
Richart, Frank Edwin, Jr. civil engineer, educator
Riggs, Donald Eugene librarian, university dean
Robbins, Jerry Hal educational administration educator
Robertson, Richard Earl physical chemist, educator
Roe, Byron Paul physics educator
Romani, John Henry health administration educator
Root, William Lucas electrical engineering educator
Rosenthal, Amnon pediatric cardiologist
†Rosseels, Gustave Alois music educator
Rumman, Wadi (Saliba Rumman) civil engineer
Rupp, Ralph Russell audiologist, educator, author
Ryan, William Frank management consultant
Rycus, Mitchell Julian urban planning educator, urban security and energy planning consultant
St. Antoine, Theodore Joseph legal educator
Sandalow, Terrance law educator
†Sargent, Charles Lee recreation vehicle and pollution control systems manufacturing company executive
Saussele, Charles William marking systems company executive
Savageau, Michael Antonio microbiology and immunology educator
Schacht, Jochen Heinrich biochemistry educator
Schottenfeld, David epidemiologist, educator
Schriber, Thomas Jude computer and information systems educator, researcher
Schultz, Albert Barry engineering educator
Schuman, Howard sociologist, educator
Senior, Thomas Bryan A. electrical engineering educator, researcher, consultant
Shappirio, David Gordon biologist, educator
†Shayman, James Alan nephrologist, educator
†Sheldon, Ingrid Kristina mayor
Silverman, Albert Jack psychiatrist, educator
Singer, Joel David political science educator
Slavens, Thomas Paul information and library studies educator
Sloan, Herbert Elias physician, surgeon
†Smith, David John, Jr. plastic surgeon
Smith, Gary Allen portfolio manager
Smith, J(ames) E(verett) Keith psychologist, educator
Snyder, Jeanne Anne interior designer, educator
Solomon, David Eugene engineering company executive
Southwick, Arthur Frederick legal educator
Sparling, Peter David dancer, dance educator
Stafford, Frank Peter, Jr. economics educator, consultant
Stark, Joan Scism education educator
Starr, Chester G. history educator
Stein, Eric retired law educator
Steiner, Erich Ernst botany educator
Steiner, Peter Otto economics educator, dean
Steinhoff, William Richard English literature educator
Stevenson, Harold William psychology educator
Stolper, Wolfgang Friedrich retired economist, educator
Stolz, Benjamin Armond foreign language educator
Stowe, Leland journalist, writer
Strang, Ruth Hancock pediatrician, educator, pediatric cardiologist
Striffler, David Frank dental public health educator
Stross, Jeoffrey Knight physician, educator
Sullivan, Donald John health care corporation executive
Super, Robert Henry English educator
Surovell, Edward David real estate company executive
Tai, Chen-To electrical engineering educator
Tamres, Milton chemistry educator
†Tandon, Rajiv psychiatrist, educator
Taren, James Arthur neurosurgeon, educator
Taylor, William Brooks, II retired dermatologist
Terpstra, Vern marketing educator
Thompson, Norman Winslow surgeon, educator
Townsend, LeRoy B. chemistry educator, university administrator, researcher
Trautmann, Thomas Roger history and anthropology educator
Turcotte, Jeremiah George physician, surgery educator
Ulaby, Fawwaz Tayssir electrical engineering and computer science educator, research center administrator
Upatnieks, Juris optical engineer, researcher, educator
Van der Voo, Rob geophysicist
Van Houweling, Douglas Edward university administrator, educator
Varian, Hal Ronald economics educator
†Veit, Werner newspaper executive
†Veltman, Martinus J. physics educator
†Vesecky, John F. aerospace science educator, electrical engineering educator, researcher
Vining, (George) Joseph law educator
Waggoner, Lawrence William law educator
Waggoner, Raymond Walter neuropsychiatrist
Wagman, Frederick Herbert librarian, educator, deceased
Wagner, Warren Herbert, Jr. botanist, educator
†Wahl, Richard Leo radiology educator, nuclear medicine cancer researcher
Wall, Carroll Edward librarian, publisher
†Waller, Patricia Fossum transportation executive, researcher, psychologist
Ward, Peter Allan pathologist, educator
Ware, Richard Anderson foundation executive
Warner, Kenneth E. public health educator, consultant
Warner, Robert Mark archivist, historian, university dean
Warshaw, Martin Richard marketing educator
Watson, Andrew Samuel psychiatry and law educator
Weber, Walter Jacob, Jr. engineering educator
Weber, Wendell William pharmacologist
Weg, John Gerard physician
Wegman, Myron Ezra physician, educator
Weinreich, Gabriel physicist, minister, educator
Weisbuch, Robert Alan English educator
Whitaker, Gilbert Riley, Jr. academic administrator, business economist
White, James Boyd law educator
†Wicha, Max S. oncologist, educator
†Wiggins, Roger C. internist, educator, researcher
Williams, John Andrew physiology educator, consultant
Williams, John Troy librarian, educator
Willmarth, William Walter aerospace engineering educator
Wilson, Richard Christian engineering firm executive
Wineman, Alan Stuart mechanical engineering and applied mechanics educator
Woodcock, Leonard humanities educator, former ambassador
Wylie, Evan Benjamin civil engineering educator, consultant, researcher
Yates, Brock Wendel editor, journal
Yeh, Chai electrical engineer, educator
Yih, Chia-Shun fluid mechanics educator
Young, Edwin Harold chemical and metallurgical engineering educator
†Zajonc, Robert B(oleslaw) psychology educator
Zarafonetis, Chris John Dimiter physician, emeritus educator
Zimmerman, William political science educator
Zucker, Robert A(lpert) psychologist

Auburn
Schram, Geraldine Moore security administrator

Auburn Hills
Chaney, Don professional basketball coach
Donald, Larry Watson sports journalist
Dumars, Joe, III professional basketball player
†Grava, Alfred H. automotive and business equipment manufacturing company executive
Iorio, Ralph Arthur automotive company executive
†Kerr, John E. automotive executive
Neumann, Charles Henry mathematics educator
Robertson, Alvin Cyrrale professional basketball player
†Schuler, V. Edmund light manufacturing executive

Thomas, Isiah Lord, III *former professional basketball player, basketball executive*

Bad Axe
†Rosenfeld, Joel *ophthalmologist, lawyer*

Battle Creek
Brown, Norman A. *foundation executive*
Bruce, Thomas Allen *physician, philanthropic administrator*
Clark, Richard McCourt *lawyer, food company executive*
Cline, Charles William *poet, rhetoric and literature educator*
Costley, Gary Edward *food company executive*
Davis, Laura Arlene *foundation administrator*
DeVries, Robert Allen *foundation administrator*
Fritz, William Warren *accountant, foundation executive*
Grace, Helen Kennedy *foundation administrator*
†Hutson, Don D. *insurance company executive*
Langbo, Arnold Gordon *food company executive*
Mawby, Russell George *foundation executive*
McKay, Eugene Henry, Jr. *food company executive*
Nichols, Robert Lee *food company executive*
Olin, Thomas Franklin *food products executive*
Pattullo, Andrew *former foundation executive*
Schaller, Daryl Richard *cereal company executive*
Thar, Ferdinand August (Bud Thar) *trade company executive*

Bay City
Churchill, James Paul *federal judge*
Cleland, Robert Hardy *federal judge*
†McDermott, Larry Arnold *newspaper publisher*
Spector, Arthur Jay *federal judge*
Van Dyke, Clifford Craig *banker*
Zuraw, Kathleen Ann *special education and physical education educator*

Belding
Mason, Donald Roger *protective services official, city official*

Belleville
Carlson, James Ellsworth *wholesale distribution executive*

Benton Harbor
Callahan, Michael J. *manufacturing company executive*
Goldin, Sol *marketing consultant*
Hopp, Daniel Frederick *manufacturing company executive, lawyer*
Samartini, James Rogers *appliance company executive*
Whitwam, David Ray *appliance manufacturing company executive*

Berrien Springs
Ali, Muhammad (Cassius Marcellus Clay) *former professional boxer*
Lesher, William Richard *university president*
Schwarz, Richard William *historian, educator*
Stokes, Charles Junius *economist, educator*
Waller, John Oscar *English language educator*

Beulah
Auch, Walter Edward *securities company executive*

Beverly Hills
Landuyt, Bernard Francis *economist, educator*

Big Rapids
Barnes, Isabel Janet *microbiology educator, college dean*
Mathison, Ian William *chemistry educator, academic dean*
Santer, Richard Arthur *geography educator*
Thapa, Khagendra *survey engineering educator*
Weinlander, Max Martin *retired psychologist*

Bingham Farms
Berline, James H. *advertising executive, public relations agency executive*
Garpow, James Edward *financial executive*
Williams, Edson Poe *retired automotive company executive*

Birmingham
Birkerts, Gunnar *architect*
Bromberg, Stephen Aaron *lawyer*
Bublys, Algimantas Vladas *architect*
Catallo, Clarence Guerrino, Jr. *financial services company executive*
Chodorkoff, Bernard *psychoanalyst, psychiatrist*
Dirks, Lee Edward *newspaper executive*
Elsman, James Leonard, Jr. *lawyer*
Gold, Edward David *lawyer*
Hirschhorn, Austin *lawyer*
McCuen, John Joachim *defense contracting company executive*
Ortman, George Earl *artist*
†Powell, Robert Barrows *architectural firm executive*
VanDeusen, Bruce Dudley *defense contractor company executive*
Ziegelman, Robert Lee *architect*

Bloomfield
Brown, Lynette Ralya *journalist, publicist*

Bloomfield Hills
Adams, Charles Francis *advertising and real estate executive*
Adams, Thomas Brooks *advertising consultant*
Allen, Maurice Bartelle, Jr. *architect*
Andrews, Frank Lewis *lawyer*
Baker, Robert Edward *lawyer, retired financial corporation executive*
Bates, Baron Kent *automobile company executive*
Benton, Robert Austin, Jr. *investment banker, broker*
Benton, William Pettigrew *advertising agency executive*
Bianco, Joseph Paul, Jr. *foundation and art museum executive*
Bissell, John Howard *marketing executive*
Bonner, Thomas Neville *history and higher education educator*
Brewer, George Eugene Francis *chemical consultant*
Brown, Jack Wyman *architect*
Bruegel, David Robert *lawyer*
Burgess, Robert K. *construction company executive*
Caldwell, Will M. *former automobile company executive*
Cannon, John Kemper *lawyer*
Caplan, John David *retired automotive company executive, research director*
†Carr, Robin *advertising executive*
Casey, John Patrick (Jack Casey) *public relations executive, political analyst*
Chason, Jacob (Leon Chason) *neuropathologist*
Clippert, Charles Frederick *lawyer*
Colladay, Robert S. *trust company executive, consultant*
Cooper, John Arnold *financial analyst*
Dawson, Stephen Everette *lawyer*
†Doyle, Jill J. *elementary school principal*
Forrester, Alan McKay *capital company executive*
Googasian, George Ara *lawyer*
Gornick, Alan Lewis *lawyer*
†Heinen, Charles M. *retired chemical and materials engineer*
Hertz, Richard Cornell *rabbi*
†Hillman, Donald M. *middle school principal*
Houston, E. James, Jr. *bank officer*
Hsu, John J. *psychiatrist*
Jacobowitz, Ellen Sue *museum administrator*
James, William Ramsay *cable television executive*
†Johnson, John K. *advertising executive*
Kasischke, Louis Walter *lawyer*
Klingler, Eugene Herman *consulting engineer, educator*
Knights, Edwin Munroe *pathologist*
Knudsen, Semon Emil *manufacturing company executive*
Lehman, Richard Leroy *lawyer*
LoPrete, James Hugh *lawyer*
Marko, Harold Meyron *diversified industry executive*
Marks, Craig *management educator, consultant, engineer*
Marxer, John A. *lawyer, real estate developer*
Maxwell, Jack Erwin *manufacturing company executive*
McCoy, Katherine Braden *designer, educator*
McCoy, Michael Dale *designer, educator*
Mc Donald, Patrick Allen *lawyer, arbitrator, educator*
Meyer, George Herbert *lawyer*
Mills, Peter Richard *advertising executive*
†Morton, Alexander A., III *advertising agency executive*
Nolte, Henry R., Jr. *lawyer, former automobile company executive*
Norris, John Hart *lawyer*
Pappas, Edward Harvey *lawyer*
Pingel, John Spencer *advertising executive*
Plaut, Jonathan Victor *rabbi*
Poth, Stefan Michael *retired sales financing company executive*
Preston, David Michael *lawyer*
Rader, Ralph Terrance *lawyer*
Rom, (Melvin) Martin *securities executive*
Roth, James Seymour *retired manufacturing executive*
Rusin, Edward A. *bank executive*
Sillman, Herbert Phillip *accounting firm executive*
Slade, Roy *artist, college president, museum director*
†Smith, Richard Allen *manufacturing company executive*
Snyder, George Edward *lawyer*
Stivender, Donald Lewis *mechanical engineering consultant*
Sullivan, Brian *lawyer*
Suter, Kenneth Harris *personal investments consultant*
Thurber, John Alexander *lawyer*
†Tunstall, Sharon Sue *advertising executive*
Vlasic, Robert Joseph *food company executive*
Wagner, Bruce Stanley *advertising agency executive*
†Ward, Richard C. *advertising executive*
Weil, John William *technology management consultant*
Williams, Walter Joseph *lawyer*
†Winograd, Bernard *financial adviser*
†Zimmer, David Rodney *manufacturing executive*

Brighton
†Jensen, Baiba *principal*

Buchanan
French, Robert Warren *economics educator emeritus, writer, consultant*

Carsonville
†Kummerow, Arnold A. *superintendent of schools*

Cass City
Althaver, Lambert Ewing *manufacturing company executive*

Chelsea
†Holmes, Howard Sumner *association executive*

Clarkston
Erkfritz, Donald Spencer *mechanical engineer*

Clinton Township
†Gire, Sharon Lee *state legislator*
Hollerman, Charles Edward *pediatrician*

Coldwater
†Spittle, James Pratt *theatre administrator*

Coloma
Tallman, Clifford Wayne *school system administrator, consultant*

Colon
Walsh, Loren Melford *retired journal editor*

Copemish
Wells, Herschel James *physician, former hospital administrator*

Cross Village
Stowe, Robert Allen *catalytic and chemical technology consultant*

Dearborn
Bixby, Harold Glenn *manufacturing company executive*
Brennan, Leo Joseph, Jr. *foundation executive*
Brown, James Ward *mathematician, educator, author*
Brucker, Eric *academic administrator*
Cairns, James Robert *mechanical engineering educator*
Caldwell, John Thomas, Jr. *communications executive*
Chou, Clifford Chi Fong *research engineering executive*
Christy, Perry Thomas *lawyer, air transport company executive*
†Coady, Reginald Patrick *library director*
Coburn, Ronald Murray *ophthalmic surgeon, researcher*
Czarnecki, Richard Edward *business educator*
Darin, Frank Victor John *automotive company executive*
Fair, Jean Everhard *education educator*
†Fitzgerald, Gerald Dennis *hospital administrator*
Ford, William Clay *automotive company executive*
Gilmour, Allan Dana *automotive company executive*
Jelinek, John Joseph *public relations executive*
Joseph, Ramon Rafael *physician, educator*
Libertiny, George Zoltan *automotive company research engineer*
Little, Robert Eugene *mechanical engineering educator, materials behavior researcher, consultant*
Lundy, J(oseph) Edward *retired automobile company executive*
Marquis, Rollin Park *retired librarian*
Martin, John William, Jr. *lawyer, automotive industry executive*
Mc Cammon, David Noel *automobile company executive*
McTague, John Paul *automobile manufacturing company executive, chemist*
Meitzler, Allen Henry *electrical engineering educator, automotive scientist*
Morshead, Richard Williams *philosophy of education educator*
Odom, William E. *automobile finance company executive*
Poling, Harold Arthur *retired automobile company executive*
Powers, William Francis *automobile manufacturing company executive*
Sagan, John *former automobile company executive*
Schneider, Michael Joseph *biologist*
Seneker, Stanley A. *automobile manufacturing company executive*
Simon, Evelyn *lawyer*
Skramstad, Harold Kenneth *museum administrator, consultant*
Smith, Stanton Kinnie, Jr. *utility executive*
Taub, Robert Allan *lawyer*
†Trotman, Alexander James *automobile manufacturing company executive*

Detroit
Abramson, Hanley Norman *pharmacy educator*
Abt, Jeffrey *art and art history educator*
Adamany, David Walter *university administrator*
Adams, William Johnston *financial and tax consultant*
†Albom, Mitch David *sports columnist*
Allen, James Lee *lawyer*
Amerman, John Ellis *lawyer*
Amsden, Ted Thomas *lawyer*
Anderson, Sparky (George Lee Anderson) *professional baseball team manager*
†Anstett, Pat *newspaper editor*
Archer, Dennis Wayne *mayor*
Ashenfelter, David Louis *editor and former newspaper reportor*
Audia, Christina *librarian*
Avant, Grady, Jr. *lawyer*
Baba, Marietta Lynn *business anthropologist*
Babcock, Charles Witten, Jr. *lawyer*
†Bainbridge, Leesa *newspaper editor*
Banas, Christine Leslie *lawyer*
Barden, Don H. *communications executive*
Barr, Martin *health care administrator*
Barringer, Leland David *lawyer*
Bassett, Tina *communications executive*
Battista, Robert James *lawyer*
Baumann, Gary Joseph *accountant*
Beaufait, Frederick W(illiam) *civil engineering educator*
Beltaire, Beverly Ann *public relations executive*
Bennett, Margaret Ethel Booker *psychotherapist*
Bergeron, Jeffrey David *accountant*
Bieber, Owen F. *labor union official*
Blain, Alexander, III *surgeon, educator*
Blevins, William Edward *management consultant*
Bohm, Henry Victor *physicist*
Bostic, Florine *nursing administrator*
Boyle, Patricia Jean *judge*
Bradford, Christina *newspaper editor*
Brady, Edmund Matthew, Jr. *lawyer*
Brammer, Forest Evert *electrical engineering educator*
Brand, George Edward, Jr. *lawyer*
Braun, Richard Lane, II *lawyer*
†Braun, Robert B. *airport executive*
Bray, Thomas Joseph *journalist, editor*
Brodhead, William McNulty *lawyer, former congressman*
Brown, Eli Matthew *anesthesiologist*
Brown, Ray Kent *biochemist, physician, educator*
Brown, Stratton Shartel *lawyer*
Brown, William Paul *investment executive*
Brustad, Orin Daniel *lawyer*
†Bullard, George *newspaper editor*
Burstein, Richard Joel *lawyer*
Burzynski, Susan Marie *newspaper editor*
Busbey, Douglas Earle *lawyer*
Buselmeier, Bernard Joseph *insurance company executive*
†Bushnell, George Edward, Jr. *lawyer*
Calarco, N. Joseph *theatre educator*
Callaway, David Henry, Jr. *investment banker*
†Campbell, David James *hospital administrator*
Candler, James Nall, Jr. *lawyer*
Cantoni, Louis Joseph *psychologist, poet, sculptor*
Cantor, George Nathan *journalist*
†Casstevens, Bill J. *labor union administrator*
Cerny, Joseph Charles *urologist, educator*
Chapin, Roy Dikeman, Jr. *automobile company executive*
Charfoos, Lawrence Selig *lawyer*
Charla, Leonard Francis *lawyer*
Cheveldae, Tim *professional hockey player*
Choate, Robert Alden *lawyer*
Christopher, William Garth *lawyer*
†Clark, Dennis J. *lawyer*
Coffey, Paul *professional hockey player*
Cohan, Leon Sumner *lawyer, retired electric company executive*
Cohen, Sanford Ned *pediatrics educator, academic administrator*
Colby, Joy Hakanson *art critic*
Coleman, David Manley *chemistry educator*
Collier, James Warren *lawyer*
Connor, Laurence Davis *lawyer*
†Cooper, Byron Daugherty *legal educator, law librarian*
Cortada, Rafael Leon *university president*
Cothorn, John Arthur *lawyer*
Cox, Clifford Ernest *deputy superintendent, chief information officer*
Cummings, Roger Holt *lawyer*
Curtis, Jean Trawick *library director*
†Czarnecki, Walter P. *trucj rental company executive*
Darlow, Julia Donovan *lawyer*
Darr, Alan Phipps *curator*
Dart, Judith C(andelor) Lalka *lawyer*
Davis, Eric Keith *professional baseball player*
DeRamus, Betty Jean *columnist*
†Desmet, Kathleen Marie (Kate Desmet) *journalist*
Devellano, James Charles *professional hockey manager*
DeVine, (Joseph) Lawrence *drama critic*
Di Chiera, David *performing arts impresario*
Dickerson, Brian *editor, periodical*
Diebolt, Judy *managing editor, newspaper*
Diehl, Gerald George *architect*
Dobranski, Bernard *law educator*
Dortch, Heyward *utility company executive*
Draper, James Wilson *lawyer*
Driker, Eugene *lawyer*
Dudley, Arthur, II *lawyer*
Dudley, John Henry, Jr. *lawyer*
Duggan, Patrick James *federal judge*
Dunham, Frank L. *accounting company executive*
Dunn, William Bradley *lawyer*
Dykema, John Russel *retired lawyer*
Dziuba, Henry Frank *dental school administrator*
Eads, George Curtis *economics executive*
Earley, Anthony Francis, Jr. *utilities company executive, lawyer*
Easlick, David Kenneth *telephone company executive*
Eaton, Robert James *automotive company executive*
Ebbing, Darrell Delmar *chemist, educator*
Edmunds, Nancy Garlock *federal judge*
Eggertsen, John Hale *lawyer*
Elsila, David August *editor*
Ernst, Calvin Bradley *vascular surgeon, surgery educator*
Ethridge, James Merritt *writer, former publishing company executive*
Falls, Joseph Francis *sportswriter, editor*
Fay, Sister Maureen A. *university president*
Feikens, John *federal judge*
Fielder, Cecil Grant *professional baseball player*
Fisher, Charles Thomas, III *banker*
Fisher, Max Martin *diversified company executive*
Fitzgerald, Robert Hannon, Jr. *orthopedic surgeon*
†Flint, Robert H. *printing ink company executive*
Frade, Peter Daniel *chemist*
Fradkin, David Milton *physicist, educator*
†Francis, Edward D. *architect*
Franco, Anthony M. *public relations executive*
†Freedman, Eric *journalist*
†Frenette, Geraldine Gloria *librarian*
Friedman, Bernard Alvin *federal judge*
Fromm, David *surgeon*
Fryman, David Travis *professional baseball player*
Gadola, Paul V. *federal judge*
†Gans, Bruce Merrill *physiatrist, physician, hospital executive*
Garberding, Larry Gilbert *utilities companies executive*
Garzia, Samuel Angelo *lawyer*
Gelder, John William *lawyer*
†Gerstel, Judith Ross *film critic*
Getz, Ernest John *lawyer*
Giles, Robert Hartmann *newspaper editor*
Gilmore, Horace Weldon *federal judge*
†Givhan, Robin Deneen *journalist*
Glancy, Alfred Robinson, III *public utility company executive*
Goodman, Allen Charles *economics educator*
Gormley, Dennis James *manufacturing and distribution company executive*
Gould, Wesley Larson *political science educator*
Graves, Ray Reynolds *federal judge*
Green, Jerome Frederic *sportswriter, journalist*
Grow, Richard Dennis *lawyer*
Guinn, John Rockne *music critic*
Gumbleton, Thomas J. *bishop*
Gupta, Suraj Narayan *physicist, educator*
Gushee, Richard Bordley *lawyer*
Haass, Erwin Herman *lawyer*
Hackett, Barbara (Kloka) *federal judge*
Halperin, Jerome Yale *accountant*
Hampton, Verne Churchill, II *lawyer*
Hanson, David Bigelow *construction company executive, engineer*
Hardon, John Anthony *priest, research educator*
Harling, Carlos Gene *savings and loan executive*
Hatie, George Daniel *lawyer*
Hay, Frederick Dale *automotive supply company executive*
Heaphy, John Merrill *lawyer*
Hearns, Thomas *professional boxer*
Herstein, Carl William *lawyer*
Hill, Draper *editorial cartoonist*
Hoglund, William Elis *automotive company executive*
Holmes, Peter Douglas *lawyer*
†Holness, Gordon Victor Rix *engineering executive, mechanical engineer*
†Honet, Joseph C. *rehabilitation medicine physician*
†Hough, Leslie Seldon *educational administrator*
Housley, Charles Edward *hospital system executive*
Howbert, Edgar Charles *lawyer*
Hughes, Robert Edwin *banking executive*
†Hutton, Carole Leigh *newspaper editor*
Iacobell, Frank Peter *hospital administrator*
Ilitch, Marian *professional hockey team executive*
Ilitch, Michael *professional hockey team executive*
Istock, Verne George *banker*
Jackson, Robert Lee, II *university administrator*
†Jampel, Robert Steven *ophthalmologist, educator*
Jarvi, Neeme *conductor*
Jeffries, Charles Dean *microbiology educator, scientist*
Jeffs, Thomas Hamilton, II *banker*
†Johnson, Carl Randolph *chemist, educator*
Johnson, Robert Bertram *hospital administrator*
Kachadoorian, Zubel *artist, educator*
Kalman, Andrew *manufacturing company executive*
Kantrowitz, Adrian *surgeon, educator*
Kaplan, Bernice Antoville *anthropologist, educator*
Keith, Damon Jerome *federal judge*
Kelleher, Timothy John *publishing company executive*
†Kelly, John Francis *state senator*

Kennedy, Cornelia Groefsema *federal judge*
Kessler, Philip Joel *lawyer*
Kessler, William Henry *architect*
Kienbaum, Thomas Gerd *lawyer*
King, John Lane *lawyer*
Kinnaird, Charles Roemler *lawyer*
Kirschner, Stanley *chemist*
Kiska, Timothy Olin *newspaper columnist*
Kline, Kenneth Alan *mechanical engineering educator*
†Klont, Barbara Anne *librarian*
Kowalczyk, Richard Leon *English language educator, technical writing consultant*
Krauss, Charles A(nthony), Jr. *finance company executive*
†Krawetz, Stephen Andrew *molecular biology and genetics educator*
†Krsul, John Aloysius, Jr. *lawyer*
Krull, Edward Alexander *dermatologist*
Kuehn, George E. *lawyer, beverage company executive*
Kummler, Ralph H. *chemical engineering educator*
†Kushma, David William *journalist*
†Laitner, Bill *reporter*
Lamborn, LeRoy Leslie *legal educator*
Lane, James McConkey *investment executive*
†Lannon, Linnea *newspaper editor*
Lasker, Gabriel Ward *anthropologist, educator*
†Laughlin, Nancy *newspaper editor*
Lawrence, John Kidder *lawyer*
Ledwidge, Patrick Joseph *lawyer*
Lee, James Edward, Jr. *educational administrator*
Leininger, Madeleine Monica *nursing educator, administrator, consultant, editor*
Lenga, J. Thomas *lawyer*
Lerner, Stephen Alexander *microbiologist, physician, educator*
Lesch, Michael *cardiologist*
Levy, Edward Charles, Jr. *manufacturing company executive*
Lindow, Donald August *insurance company executive*
Livingood, Clarence S. *dermatologist*
Lobbia, John E. *utility company executive*
Lockman, Stuart M. *lawyer*
Longhofer, Ronald Stephen *lawyer*
Lucow, Milton *lawyer*
†Lupulescu, Aurel Peter *medical educator, researcher, physician*
†Lusher, Jeanne Marie *pediatric hematologist, educator*
Lyon, Maud Margaret *museum director*
Mack, Robert Emmet *hospital administrator*
Madgett, Naomi Long *educator, editor, poet*
Maibach, Ben C., III *construction company executive*
Maida, Adam J. *bishop*
Majzoub, Mona Kathryne *lawyer*
Mallett, Conrad LeRoy, Jr. *state supreme court justice*
Malone, Daniel Patrick *lawyer*
Mamat, Frank Trustick *lawyer*
Mandel, Leon, III *author*
†Margerum, Roger Williams, Jr. *architect*
Martin, Fred *municipal official*
Martin, John Gustin *investment banker*
Martin, J(oseph) Patrick *lawyer, educator*
Marx, Thomas George *economist*
Massie, Noel David *lawyer*
Massura, Edward Anthony *accountant*
Maurer, David L. *lawyer*
Maycock, Joseph Farwell, Jr. *lawyer*
McCracken, Caron Francis *data processing consultant*
†McCracken, Thomas Charles *retail executive*
†McCrackin, William K. *gas company executive*
Mc Gehee, H(arry) Coleman, Jr. *bishop*
McGriff, Deborah *school system administrator*
†McGruder, Robert *newspaper publishing executive*
McIntyre, Ronald Llewellyn *electric utility executive*
McKim, Samuel John, III *lawyer*
†McKinnon, Isaiah *police chief*
Mc Millan, James *manufacturing executive*
McNair, Russell Arthur, Jr. *lawyer*
†McNamara, Edward Howard *mayor*
McWilliams, Michael G. *writer, television critic*
Meilgaard, Morten Christian *food products executive, international consultant*
Meisel, Jerome *electrical engineer*
Mengden, Joseph Michael *investment banker*
Meriwether, Heath J. *newspaper editor*
Mika, Joseph John *library director, consultant*
†Mikon, Arnold *architect*
Miller, Eugene Albert *banker*
Miller, George DeWitt, Jr. *lawyer*
Miller, Orlando Jack *physician, educator*
Mitseff, Carl *lawyer*
†Mitzelfeld, Jim *newspaper reporter*
Moldenhauer, Judith A. *graphic design educator*
Moss, Leslie Otha *court administrator*
Murphy, Thomas Aquinas *former automobile manufacturing company executive*
Musone, Fred James *manufacturing and logistic executive*
Negrepontis, Michael (Timothy) *bishop*
†Newcomb, Martin Eugene, Jr. *chemistry educator*
Nicholson, George Albert, Jr. *financial analyst*
Novak, Raymond Francis *research institute director, pharmacology educator*
†O'Gorman, Kathy *newspaper editor*
Oliver, John Preston *chemistry educator, academic administrator*
†Olmstead, Laurence Daniel *journalist*
O'Meara, John Corbett *lawyer*
Orton, Colin George *medical physicist*
†Ownby, Dennis Randall *pediatrician, allergist, educator, researcher*
Parker, George Edward, III *lawyer*
†Parry, Dale D. *newspaper editor*
Paul, Richard Wright *lawyer*
†Pearce, Harry Jonathan *lawyer*
Peck, William Henry *museum curator, art historian, archaeologist, author, lecturer*
†Penske, Roger S. *manufacturing and transportation executive*
Pepper, Jonathon Lester *newspaper columnist*
Pero, Joseph John *insurance company executive*
Phillips, Elliott Hunter *lawyer*
Phillis, John Whitfield *physiologist, educator*
Ponitz, John Allan *lawyer*
†Porter, Arthur T. *oncologist, educator*
Prasad, Ananda Shiva *medical educator*
Raden, Louis *tape and label corporation executive*
Rajlich, Vaclav Thomas *computer science educator, researcher, consultant*
Rakolta, John *construction company executive*
Rassel, Richard Edward *lawyer*
Rezabek, Christina JoAnn *adult education educator*
Richards, Frederick Edward Maxwell *school system administrator*
†Richardson, Joan *reporter*
Rines, John Randolph *automotive company executive*
Rintelmann, William Fred *audiology educator*
Roberts, Seymour M. (Skip Roberts) *advertising executive*
Robinson, James Kenneth *lawyer*
Roche, Douglas David *lawyer, bar examiner*
†Roehling, Carl *architect*
Ronca, Luciano Bruno *geologist, educator*
Rosen, Gerald Ellis *federal judge*
†Ross, Mary O. *religious organization administrator*
Rossen, Jordan *lawyer*
†Ross-Flanigan, Nancy *reporter*
Rossman, Richard Alan *lawyer*
Rozof, Phyllis Claire *lawyer*
Ruffner, Frederick G., Jr. *book publisher*
Russell, Robert Gilmore *lawyer*
Ruwart, David Peter *lawyer*
Ryan, James Leo *federal judge*
Sachs, Samuel, II *museum director*
Santo, Ronald Joseph *lawyer*
Saurbier, Scott Alan *lawyer*
Sax, Stanley Paul *manufacturing company executive*
Saxton, William Marvin *lawyer*
Saylor, Larry James *lawyer*
Scherer, Karla *foundation executive, venture capitalist*
Schiffer, Daniel L. *gas company executive*
Schindler, Marvin Samuel *foreign language educator*
Schmidt, Robert *mechanical and civil engineering educator*
Schreiber, Bertram Manuel *mathematics educator*
Schultz, Dennis Bernard *lawyer*
Schuster, Elaine *civil rights professional, state official*
Schwartz, Alan E. *lawyer*
Schwartz, Jerome Merrill *lawyer*
Schweitzer, Peter *advertising agency executive*
Scott, John Edward Smith *lawyer*
Semple, Lloyd Ashby *lawyer*
Sengupta, Dipak Lal *electrical engineering and physics educator, researcher*
Seppala, Katherine Seaman (Mrs. Leslie W. Seppala) *retail company executive*
Shaevsky, Mark *lawyer*
Shannon, Margaret Anne *lawyer*
Shaw, Nancy Rivard *museum curator, art historian*
Shay, John E., Jr. *college president*
Sheffield, Horace Lindsey, Jr. *union official*
Shine, Neal James *newspaper editor*
Simpkin, Lawrence James *utilities executive*
Small, Melvin *history educator*
Smith, Frank Earl *association executive*
Smith, John Francis, Jr. *automobile company executive*
Smyntek, John Eugene, Jr. *newspaper editor*
†Snead, David L. *assistant education superintendent*
Sott, Herbert *lawyer*
Sparrow, Herbert George, III *lawyer*
Spencer, Milton Harry *economics and finance educator*
Spina, Anthony *photojournalist*
Spyers-Duran, Peter *librarian, educator*
†Stark, Susan R. *Film Critic*
Stein, Paul David *cardiologist*
Stella, Daniel Francis *lawyer*
Stella, Frank Dante *food service and dining equipment executive*
Stewart, Melbourne George, Jr. *physicist, educator*
†Stroh, Peter Wetherill *brewery executive*
Stroud, Joe Hinton *newspaper editor*
Stynes, Stanley Kenneth *retired chemical engineer, educator*
Sullivan, Joseph B. *retired judge*
Surdam, Robert McClellan *retired banker*
†Sylvain, Rick *newspaper editor*
Szary, Richard M. *manufacturing company executive*
Szilagyi, D(esiderius) Emerick *surgeon, researcher, educator*
†Talbert, Bob *newspaper columnist*
Taylor, Anna Diggs *federal judge*
Teagan, John Gerard *newspaper executive*
Thelen, Bruce Cyril *lawyer*
Thomas, Edward St. Clair *hospital administrator*
†Thomas, Jacqueline Marie *journalist, editor*
Thurber, Peter Palms *lawyer*
Toll, Sheldon Samuel *lawyer*
†Tong, James *librarian, consultant*
Turnley, David Carl *photojournalist*
Uicker, James Leo *mechanical engineer*
†Uicker, Joseph Bernard *engineering company executive*
Ursache, Victorin (His Eminence The Most Reverend Archbishop Victorin) *archbishop*
†Vaitkevicius, Vainutis K. *foundation administrator, medical educator*
van der Marck, Jan *art historian*
†Vega, Frank J. *newspaper publishing executive*
Vincent, Charles Eagar, Jr. *sports columnist*
Volz, William Harry *legal educator, administrator*
Wagner, Harvey Arthur *nuclear engineer*
Waldmeir, Peter Nielsen *journalist*
Waldmeir, Peter William *lawyer*
Walker, Joseph Vincent *lawyer*
Walt, Alexander Jeffrey *surgeon, educator*
Warden, Gail Lee *health care executive*
Warren, William Gerald *lawyer*
†Watson, Susan *newspaper columnist*
Weiss, Mark Lawrence *anthropology educator*
Weiss, Robert Benjamin *lawyer*
Werba, Gabriel *public relations consultant*
†Wesselmann, Glenn Allen *hospital executive*
White, Joseph B. *reporter*
Whitehouse, Fred Waite *endocrinologist, researcher*
Wiener, Joseph *pathologist*
Williams, J. Bryan *lawyer*
Williamson, Marilyn Lammert *English educator, university adminstrator*
Willingham, Edward Bacon, Jr. *ecumenical minister, administrator*
Winsten, I. W. *lawyer, law educator*
Wise, John Augustus *lawyer*
Wittlinger, Timothy David *lawyer*
Wittrup, Richard Derald *health care executive*
†Wood, R. Stewart *bishop*
Woods, George E. *federal judge*
Worden, William Michael *city agency administrator, preservation consultant*
Wynne, James Earl *lawyer*
Young, Donald Soutar *lawyer*
Young, Gordon Ellsworth *composer, organist*
Youngren, Ralph Park *architect*
Yzerman, Steve *professional hockey player*
Zatkoff, Lawrence P. *federal judge*
Ziegler, John Augustus, Jr. *lawyer*

Dundee
Byland, Peter *construction materials company executive*

East Grand Rapids
Bolinder, Scott W. *publishing company executive*

East Lansing
Abeles, Norman *psychologist, educator*
Abolins, Maris Arvids *physics researcher and educator*
Abramson, Paul Robert *political scientist, educator*
Allen, Bruce Templeton *economics educator*
Andersland, Orlando Baldwin *civil engineering educator*
Anderson, David Daniel *retired humanities educator, writer, editor*
Andrew, Gwen *university dean, retired*
Appel, John J. *history educator*
Asmussen, Jes, Jr. *electrical engineer*
Austin, Sam M. *physics educator*
Axinn, George Harold *rural sociology educator*
Bandes, Susan Jane *museum director, educator*
Benenson, Walter *nuclear physics educator*
Bergen, Werner Gerhard *animal science educator, nutritionist*
Bettinghaus, Erwin Paul *university dean*
Bickart, Theodore Albert *electrical and computer engineering educator, university dean*
Blosser, Henry Gabriel *physicist*
Brody, Theodore Meyer *pharmacologist, educator*
†Brophy, Jere Edward *education educator, researcher*
Bukovac, Martin John *horticulturist, educator*
Butcher, James Walter *biologist*
Byerrum, Richard Uglow *college dean*
Carr, M. Robert (Bob Carr) *congressman*
Chapin, Richard Earl *librarian*
Chen, Kun-Mu *electrical engineering educator*
Courtney, Gladys (Atkins) *nursing educator, former dean*
Cross, Aureal Theophilus *geology and botany educator*
Cutts, Charles Eugene *civil engineering educator*
De Benko, Eugene *educator, librarian*
Dennis, Frank George, Jr. *horticulture educator*
Dewhurst, Charles Kurt *museum director, curator, folklorist, English educator*
D'Itri, Frank Michael *environmental research chemist*
Dulai, Surjit Singh *English literature educator, literary critic, editor*
Dye, James Louis *chemistry educator*
Eadie, John William *history educator*
†Enzer, Norbert Beverley *psychiatry educator*
Falk, Julia S. *linguistics educator*
Fischer, Lawrence Joseph *toxicologist, educator*
Fisher, Alan Washburn *historian, educator*
Fisher, Ronald C. *economics educator*
Foss, John Frank *mechanical engineering educator*
†Frame, James Sutherland *retired mathematics educator*
Fromm, Paul Oliver *physiology educator*
Gast, Robert Gale *agriculture educator, experiment station administrator*
†Gelbke, Claus-Konrad *nuclear physics educator*
Gerhardt, Philipp *microbiologist, educator*
Goodman, Erik David *engineering educator*
Gottschalk, Alexander *radiologist, diagnostic radiology educator*
Grant, Rhoda *biomedical researcher, educator, medical physiologist*
Greenberg, Bradley Sander *communications educator*
Greer, Thomas Hoag *historian, educator*
Grimes, Margaret Whitehurst *medievalist, educator*
Hackel, Emanuel *science educator*
Hamlin, Roger Eugene *urban planning educator, economic and financial analyst*
Harrison, Michael Jay *physicist, educator*
Hickey, Howard Wesley *education educator*
Hildebrand, Verna Lee *human ecology educator*
Hocking, John Gilbert *mathematics educator*
Hollander, Stanley Charles *marketing educator*
Hoppensteadt, Frank Charles *mathematician, university dean*
Huzar, Eleanor Goltz *history educator*
Ilgen, Daniel Richard *psychology educator*
†Johnson, J. David *communication educator*
Johnson, John Irwin, Jr. *neuroscientist*
Johnson, Theodore Oliver, Jr. *musician, educator*
Johnson, Tom Milroy *academic dean, medical educator, physician*
Jones, Kensinger *advertising executive*
Jones, Margaret Eileen Zee *pathologist, educator, scientist*
Kay, Bernard Melvin *osteopathic pediatrician, educational administrator*
†Keegstra, Kenneth G. *botany administrator*
Kende, Hans Janos *plant physiology educator*
Kirk, Edgar Lee *musician, educator*
Krecke, Charles Francis *radiologist, educator*
Kreer, John Belshaw *retired electrical engineering educator*
Kreinin, Mordechai Eliahu *economics educator*
Kronegger, Maria Elisabeth *French and comparative literature educator*
Larrowe, Charles Patrick *economist, educator*
Lashbrooke, Elvin Carroll, Jr. *legal educator, consultant*
Leader, Robert Wardell *pathologist*
Leepa, Allen *artist, educator*
Lloyd, John Raymond *mechanical engineering educator*
Lockwood, John LeBaron *plant pathologist*
Lowe, Kenneth Stephen *magazine editor*
Lowry, Sheldon Gaylon *sociology educator, marriage and family counselor*
Lucas, Robert Elmer *soil scientist*
Luecke, Richard William *biochemist*
Lund, Lois Ann *food science and human nutrition educator*
Mackey, Maurice Cecil *university president, economist, lawyer*
Manderscheid, Lester Vincent *agricultural economics educator*
Manning, Peter Kirby *sociology educator*
Mansour, George P. *Spanish language and literature educator*
McConnell, David Graham *research biochemist, educator*
McMeekin, Dorothy *botany, plant pathology educator*
Merva, George Ellis *agricultural engineer, educator, researcher*
Miracle, Gordon Eldon *advertising educator*
Montgomery, Donald Joseph *physicist, educator*
Moore, Kenneth Edwin *pharmacology educator*
Moran, Daniel Austin *mathematician*
Mukherjee, Kalinath *materials science and engineering educator, researcher*
Munger, Benson Scott *association executive*
Murray, Raymond Harold *physician*
Nelson, Ronald Harvey *animal science educator, researcher*
Netzloff, Michael Lawrence *pediatric educator, endocrinologist*
Paananen, Victor Niles *English educator*
Papsidero, Joseph Anthony *social scientist, educator*
Paul, Eldor Alvin *agriculture, ecology educator*
Platt, Franklin Dewitt *history educator*
Poland, Robert Paul *business educator, consultant*
Pollack, Gerald Leslie *physicist, educator*
Pollack, Norman *history educator*
Potchen, E. James *radiology educator*
Preiss, Jack *biochemistry educator*
Press, Charles *retired political science educator*
Ralph, David Clinton *communications educator*
Rasche, Robert Harold *economics educator*
Reinhart, Mary Ann *medical board executive*
Ricks, Donald Jay *agricultural economist*
Ries, Stanley K. *plant physiologist, university educator*
Ristow, George Edward *neurologist, educator*
Robbins, Lawrence Harry *anthropologist*
Root-Bernstein, Robert Scott *biologist, educator*
Rovner, David Richard *endocrinology educator*
Rudman, Herbert Charles *education educator*
Saul, William Edward *academic administrator, civil engineering educator*
†Sawyer, Donald Craig *veterinary anesthesia and pharmacology educator*
Schlesinger, Joseph Abraham *political scientist*
†Shaw, Robert Eugene *minister, administrator*
Silverman, Henry Jacob *history educator*
Smith, Victor Earle *economist, educator*
Snell, John Raymond *civil engineer*
Snoddy, James Ernest *education educator*
Sollenberger, Harold Myers *accounting educator*
Sommers, Lawrence Melvin *geographer, educator*
Soutas-Little, Robert William *mechanical engineer, educator*
Sparks, Harvey Vise, Jr. *physiologist*
Spence, Robert Dean *physics educator*
Stapleton, James Hall *statistician, educator*
Strassmann, W. Paul *economics educator*
Suits, Daniel Burbidge *economist*
Summitt, (William) Robert *chemist, educator*
Tasker, John Baker *veterinary medical educator, college dean*
Telewski, Frank William *botanical garden administrator, researcher*
Tesar, Milo Benjamin *agricultural researcher and educator*
Tien, H. Ti *biophysics and physiology educator, scientist*
Tolbert, Nathan Edward *biochemistry educator, plant science researcher*
Useem, John Hearld *sociologist, anthropologist*
Useem, Ruth Hill *sociology educator*
Velicer, Leland Frank *veterinarian, microbiologist, virologist, educator*
Von Tersch, Lawrence Wayne *electrical engineering educator, university dean*
Wakoski, Diane *poet*
Walker, Bruce Edward *anatomy educator*
Whallon, William *literature educator*
Williams, Donald Herbert *psychiatric education administrator*
†Wilson, Deborah Valanne *veterinary anesthesiology educator*
Wilson, R. Dale *marketing educator, consultant*
Winder, Clarence Leland *psychologist, educator*
Witter, Richard Lawrence *veterinarian, educator*
Wojcik, Anthony Stephen *computer science educator*
Wolterink, Lester Floyd *biophysicist, educator*
Wronski, Stanley Paul *education educator*
Yussouff, Mohammed *physicist, educator*

Eastpointe
Humita, Tiberius Ted *languages educator*
Sturman, Robert Harries *neurological surgeon, consultant neurologist*

Elk Rapids
Briggs, Robert Peter *banker*

Escanaba
Reid, Duane Lee *government official*

Farmington
Baker, Edward Martin *engineering and industrial psychologist*
Burns, Sister Elizabeth Mary *hospital administrator*
Elder, Jean Katherine *education administrator*
Headlee, Richard Harold *insurance company executive*
Lakritz, Isaac *fundraising organization executive*
Mylod, Robert Joseph *banker*
†Shapiro, Mickey *real estate developer, financier*
Weber, Leo L. *electrical engineer*
Wine, Sherwin Theodore *rabbi*

Farmington Hills
Abrams, Roberta Busky *hospital administrator, nurse*
Fox, Dean Frederick *coporate executive*
Gladchun, Lawrence L. *banker, lawyer*
Haliw, Andrew Jerome, III *lawyer, engineer*
Harwell, William Earnest (Ernie Harwell) *broadcaster*
†Heid, Sister Mary Corita *hospital administrator*
Heiss, Richard Walter *banker, consultant*
Kinsey, Charles John *industrial auctioneer, consultant, cattle breeder, farmer*
Landry, Thomas Henry *construction executive*
Leonard, Michael A. *automotive executive*
Pelham, Judith *hospital administrator*
Prady, Norman *advertising executive, writer, marketing consultant*
Schwartz, Michael Robinson *health administrator*
Webb, George Henry *material handling company executive*

Ferndale
Braude, Edwin S. *manufacturing company executive*
Dunn, Elwood *minister*

Flint
Davis, Stephen Robert *power engineering educator, former academic dean, automotive engineer*
Diemecke, Enrique Arturo *conductor*
Duckett, Bernadine Johnal *elementary principal*
†Dutcher, Phillip Charles *health care administrator*
Farrehi, Cyrus *cardiologist, educator*

Germann, Steven James *museum director*
Gratch, Serge *mechanical engineering educator*
Hackworth, Donald E. *automotive manufacturing company executive*
Hamady, Jack Ameen *retail food company executive*
Heywood, Robert Wales *history educator*
Himes, George Elliott *pathologist*
Jayabalan, Vemblaserry *nuclear medicine physician, radiologist*
†Johnson, Donald E., Jr. *bank executive*
Kugler, Lawrence Dean *mathematics educator*
Lorenz, John Douglas *college official*
Lovejoy, William Joseph *automotive company executive*
Mahey, John Andrew *museum director*
†McKesson, Michael Alan *journal editor*
Newblatt, Stewart Albert *federal judge*
Piper, Mark Harry *retired banker*
Rappleye, Richard Kent *financial executive, consultant, educator*
Simmons, Robert Randolph *principal*
Stanley, Woodrow *mayor*
Tauscher, John Walter *pediatrician, educator*
Tomblinson, James Edmond *architect*
†Weeks, Charles R. *bank executive*
White, William Samuel *foundation executive*
Wong, Victor Kenneth *physics educator, academic administrator*

Flushing
Schriner, Jon Leslie *sports medicine physician*

Frankfort
Acker, Nathaniel Hull *retired educational administrator*
Foster, Robert Carmichael *banker*

Franklin
Adler, Philip *osteopathic physician*
Buesser, Frederick Gustavus, III *lawyer*

Fraser
Kirjas, Zoran Nikola *economist*

Gaylord
Cooney, Patrick Ronald *bishop*

Glenn
Rizzolo, Louis B. M. *artist, educator*

Grand Blanc
Tomlinson, James Lawrence *mechanical engineer*

Grand Haven
Anderson, Cynthia Finkbeiner Sjoberg *speech and language pathologist*

Grand Rapids
†Anderson, Roger Gordon *minister*
Auwers, Stanley John *motor carrier executive*
Babcock, Wendell Keith *religion educator*
Baker, Hollis MacLure *furniture manufacturing company executive*
Baker, Richard Lee *book publishing company executive*
Barnes, Thomas John *lawyer*
Beeke, Joel Robert *minister, theology educator, writer*
Bell, Robert Holmes *federal judge*
Blovits, Larry John *retired art educator*
Bolt, Eunice Mildred DeVries *artist*
†Borgdorff, Peter *church adminstrator*
Boyden, Joel Michael *lawyer*
Bradshaw, Conrad Allan *lawyer*
Brady, James S. *lawyer*
Bransdorfer, Stephen Christie *lawyer*
Brenneman, Hugh Warren, Jr. *federal magistrate judge*
Brink, William P. *clergyman*
Calkins, Richard W. *college president*
Canepa, John Charles *banking executive*
Comet, Catherine *conductor*
Curtin, Timothy John *lawyer*
Curtiss, Robert Louis *osteopathic physician*
Daniels, Joseph *neuropsychiatrist*
Deems, Nyal David *lawyer, mayor*
†DeHaan, John *religious organization administrator*
Deihl, Charles L. *college president*
Delnick, Martha Joyce *elementary education educator*
DeVries, Robert K. *religious book publisher*
DeWitt, Jon Francis *lawyer*
Diekema, Anthony J. *college president*
Emery, Marcia Rose *parapsychologist, psychologist, consultant*
Engel, Albert Joseph *federal judge*
Frankforter, Weldon DeLoss *retired museum administrator*
†Gantos, LeRoy Douglas *retail clothing executive*
Gibson, Benjamin F. *chief federal judge*
Gundry, Stanley N. *publishing company executive*
Hardy, Michael C. *performing arts administrator*
Heiden, Thomas John *lawyer*
Heynen, A. James *organizational consultant*
Hillman, Douglas Woodruff *federal judge*
Hoekema, David Andrew *philosophy educator, academic administrator*
Hoffius, Dirk Cornelius *lawyer*
Hofman, Leonard John *minister*
Holton, Earl D. *retail company executive*
†Jacobsen, Arnold *archivist*
Kara, Paul Mark *lawyer*
Kay, Richard Allan *lawyer*
Lloyd, Michael Stuart *newspaper editor*
Logie, John Hoult *mayor, lawyer*
†MacKeigan, John Malcolm *surgeon*
Mc Callum, Charles Edward *lawyer*
McGarry, John Everett *lawyer*
Mears, Patrick Edward *lawyer*
Meijer, Douglas *retail company executive*
†Meijer, Frederik *retail company executive*
Meijer, Hendrik *retail company executive*
†Meijer, Mark *retail executive*
Miles, Wendell A. *federal judge*
†Monsma, Marvin Eugene *library director*
Morin, William Raymond *bookstore chain executive*
†Mulder, Gary *religious publisher*
†Myers, Jerry K. *medal products executive*
Perez, Peter Manuel *woodworking products company executive*
Pestle, John William *lawyer*
Peterson, Edward Nohl *physician, medical educator*
Pew, Robert Cunningham, II *office equipment manufacturing company executive*
†Quinn, Patrick Michael *wholesale food executive*
Quist, Gordon Jay *federal judge*
Rougier-Chapman, Alwyn Spencer Douglas *furniture manufacturing company executive*
†Rozeboom, John A. *religious organization administrator*
Ryskamp, Bruce E. *publishing executive*
Sadler, Robert Livingston *banker*
Smith, Peter Wilson *symphony orchestra administrator*
Sobol, Judith Ellen *museum director, art historian*
†Stevenson, William Alexander *architect*
Sytsma, Fredric Alan *lawyer*
Titley, Larry J. *lawyer*
VanderLaan, Robert D. *lawyer*
†Vander Meer, Harry *church administrator*
†Vander Weele, Ray *religious organization administrator*
VanHarn, Gordon Lee *college provost*
Van't Hof, William Keith *lawyer*
†Van Tol, William *religious organization administrator*
†Vinton, Samuel R., Jr. *academic administrator*
Vrancken, Robert Danloy *facilities management educator*
Wege, Peter M. *office furniture manufacturing company executive*
Wold, Robert Lee *architect, engineer*

Greenbush
Paulson, James Marvin *engineering educator*

Grosse Ile
Smith, Veronica Latta *real estate corporation officer*

Grosse Pointe
Allen, Lee Harrison *wholesale company executive, industrial consultant*
Beierwaltes, William Henry *physician, educator*
Beltz, Charles Robert *engineering executive*
Brucker, Wilber Marion *lawyer*
Canfield, Francis Xavier *priest, English language educator*
Christian, Edward Kieren *radio station executive*
Droll, Marian Clarke *energy company public affairs executive*
French, John Henry, Jr. *banker*
Gilbert, Ronald Rhea *organization executive, lawyer*
Gilbride, William Donald *lawyer*
McWhirter, Glenna Suzanne (Nickie McWhirter) *newspaper columnist*
Mogk, John Edward *legal educator, association executive*
Peters, Thomas Robert *writer, educator*
Pytell, Robert Henry *lawyer, former judge*
Richardson, Dean Eugene *retired banker*
†Robie, Joan *elementary school principal*
Smith, Leonard Bingley *musician*
Sphire, Raymond Daniel *anesthesiologist*
Thurber, Cleveland, Jr. *trust banker*
Thurber, Donald MacDonald Dickinson *public relations counsel*
Trebilcott, James Joseph *former utility executive*
Valk, Robert Earl *corporate executive*
Whittaker, Jeanne Evans *newspaper columnist*
Wilkinson, Warren Scripps *manufacturing company executive*
Wilson, Henry Arthur, Jr. *management consultant*

Grosse Pointe Farms
Axe, John Randolph *lawyer, financial executive*
Cartmill, George Edwin, Jr. *retired hospital administrator*
Gofrank, Frank Louis *retired machine tool company executive*
Mc Bride, Robert Dana *steel company executive*
Mecke, Theodore Hart McCalla, Jr. *management consultant*

Gwinn
Lasich, Vivian Esther Layne *secondary education educator*

Hamtramck
Weinert, Carl Robert *retired banker*

Hancock
Dresch, Stephen Paul *economist, state legislator*

Harbert
Morrissette, Bruce Archer *Romance languages educator*

Harbor Springs
Graham, Robert C. *management consultant*

Harper Woods
DeGiusti, Dominic Lawrence *medical science educator, academic administrator*

Haslett
Hotaling, Robert Bachman *community planner, educator*

Hastings
Adrounie, V. Harry *dean, environmental scientist, educator*

Hickory Corners
Bristol, Norman *lawyer, arbitrator, former food company executive*
Hubbard, William Neill, Jr. *pharmaceutical company executive*
Lauff, George Howard *biologist*

Highland
†Doyle, James H. *school system administrator*

Highland Park
†Gale, Thomas Charles *automotive design executive*
Lutz, Robert Anthony *automotive company executive*
Omar, Ameenah E.P. *college dean*

Hillsdale
Castel, Albert Edward *history educator*
Roche, George Charles, III *college administrator*

Holland
Cook, James Ivan *clergyman, religion educator*
†Haworth, Gerrard Wendell *office systems manufacturing company executive*
†Haworth, Richard G. *office furniture mamufacturer*
Hill, JoAnne Francis *elementary education educator*
Hoddy, Raymond Arthur *industrial consultant*
Hountras, Peter Timothy *psychologist, educator*
Inghram, Mark Gordon *physicist, educator*
Jacobson, John Howard, Jr. *college president*
†Johanneson, Gerald B. *office products company executive*
†Miglore, Joseph James *financial executive*
Nyenhuis, Jacob Eugene *college official*
Quimby, Robert Sherman *retired humanities educator*
Van Wylen, Gordon John *former college president*

Houghton
Heckel, Richard Wayne *metallurgical engineering educator*
Huang, Eugene Yuching *civil engineer, educator*
Krenitsky, Michael V. *librarian*
Lumsdaine, Edward *mechanical engineering educator, university dean*
Pelc, Karol I. *engineering management educator, researcher*
Smith, Darrell Wayne *metallurgical engineering educator, consultant*
Tompkins, Curtis Johnston *university president*

Huntington Woods
Gutmann, Joseph *art history educator*

Jackson
†Buckman, Frederick W. *gas utility executive*
Demcoe, Lloyd Robert *social worker*
Feldmann, Judith G. *language professional, educator*
Fowler, John Russell *retail executive*
Genyk, Ruth Bel *psychotherapist*
Henderson, John William *chemistry educator*
Kelly, Robert Vincent, Jr. *metal company executive*
Marcoux, William Joseph *lawyer*
McCormick, William Thomas, Jr. *electric and gas company executive*
Patrick, Ueal Eugene *oil company executive*
Popp, Nathaniel (William George) (His Grace Bishop Nathaniel) *bishop*
Rosenfeld, Mark Kenneth *retail store executive*
Vischer, Harold Harry *manufacturing company executive*
Weaver, Franklin Thomas *newspaper executive*
†Wright, Gordon Lee *oil company executive*

Kalamazoo
Aladjem, Silvio *obstetrician, gynecologist, educator*
Barrett, Nancy Smith *university administrator*
Breisach, Ernst A. *historian, educator*
†Bridenstine, James Aloysius *museum director*
Brown, Eric Vandyke, Jr. *lawyer*
Bryan, Lawrence Dow *college administrator*
Calloway, Jean Mitchener *mathematician, educator*
Carlson, Andrew Raymond *archivist*
Carver, Norman Francis, Jr. *architect, photographer*
Chodos, Dale David Jerome *physician, consumer advocate*
Clarke, Allen Bruce *mathematics educator, retired academic administrator*
Connable, Alfred Barnes *business director*
Cyrus, Kenneth M. *pharmaceutical company executive, lawyer*
Donovan, Paul V. *bishop*
Dykstra, David Allen *corporate executive*
Edmondson, Keith Henry *chemical company executive*
Enslen, Richard Alan *federal judge*
Fitch, W. Chester *industrial engineer*
†Freed, Karl Francis *professional planner*
Gilmore, James Stanley, Jr. *broadcast executive*
Gladstone, William Sheldon, Jr. *radiologist*
Gordon, Jaimy *English educator*
Greenfield, John Charles *bio-organic chemist*
Gregory, Ross *history educator, author*
Griffeth, Paul Lyman *retired educator*
Grotzinger, Laurel Ann *library science educator*
Haenicke, Diether Hans *university president*
Hite, Judson Cary *pharmaceutical company executive*
Holland, Harold Herbert *banker*
Hooker, Richard Alfred *lawyer*
Kayser, Thomas Arthur *art consultant*
Klein, Richard Dean *banker*
Lawrence, William Joseph, Jr. *corporate executive*
†Lee, Edward L. *bishop*
Lewis, Dean Sumter *lawyer*
Light, Christopher Upjohn *writer, computer musician*
Light, Timothy *linguistics, religious and Asian studies educator, academic administrator*
Lowrie, Jean Elizabeth *librarian, educator*
Maier, Paul Luther *history educator, author, chaplain*
†Markin, David Robert *motor company executive*
Marshall, Vincent de Paul *industrial microbiologist, researcher*
McCarty, Theodore Frederick *banker*
Moritz, Edward *educator, historian*
Norris, Richard Patrick *museum director, history educator*
Novitch, Mark *physician, retired pharmaceutical executive*
O'Boyle, Robert L. *landscape architect*
Ritter, Charles Edward *lawyer*
Smith, Daniel R. *bank holding company executive*
Smith, Robert James *immunopharmacologist*
†Stufflebeam, Daniel LeRoy *education educator*
Taborn, Jeannette Ann *real estate investor*
†Tessler, Allan R. *trucking company executive*
Thomas, Philip Stanley *economics educator*
Waring, Walter Weyler *English language educator*
Zupko, Ramon *composer, music professor*

Kincheloe
Light, Kenneth Freeman *college administrator*

Lake Angelus
Kresge, Bruce Anderson *retired physician*

Lake Leelanau
Shannahan, John Henry Kelly *energy consultant*

Lakeside
Nicholson, Thomas Laurence *lawyer*

Lansing
Anderton, James Franklin, IV *holdings company executive*
†Arends, Herman J. *insurance company executive*
Austin, Richard H. *state official*
Baker, Frederick Milton, Jr. *lawyer*
Ballbach, Philip Thornton *political consultant*
†Bankes, Lyn R. *state legislator*
Beardmore, Dorothy *state education administrator*
Binsfeld, Connie Berube *lieutenant governor*
Brennan, Thomas Emmett *law school president*
†Brown, Mary C. *state representative*
†Bryant, William Robert, Jr. *lawyer*
Bullard, Willis Clare, Jr. *state legislator*
Cavanagh, Michael Francis *state supreme court chief justice*
†Cisky, Jon Ayres *state senator*
†Demlow, Daniel J. *lawyer*
†Dobronski, Agnes Marie *state legislator*
†Dolan, Jan Clark *state legislator*
Dykhouse, David Jay *commissioner, lawyer*
†Emmons, Joanne *state senator*
Engler, John *governor*
Ernst, Albert *lawyer*
Fink, Joseph Allen *lawyer*
Fitzgerald, John Warner *legal educator*
Foster, Joe C., Jr. *lawyer*
Franck, Michael *lawyer, association executive*
Fry, James Wilson *state librarian*
†Geake, Raymond Robert *state senator*
Griffin, Robert Paul *state supreme court justice, former U.S. senator*
Hales, David Foster *natural resources educator*
†Hammerstrom, Beverly Swoish *state representative*
†Harder, Clark Andrew *state representative*
†Harrison, Charlie J., Jr. *state representative*
Harvey, Joanne H. *genealogist*
Hines, Marshall *construction engineering company executive*
†Hoffman, Philip Edward *state legislator*
†Holle, Reginald Henry *bishop*
†Kaza, Greg John *state representative, economist*
Kelley, Frank Joseph *state attorney general*
†Kilpatrick, Carolyn Cheeks *state representative, educator*
Kluge, Len H. *director, actor, theater educator*
Lindemer, Lawrence Boyd *lawyer, former utility executive, former state justice*
McKeague, David William *federal judge*
McLellan, Richard Douglas *lawyer*
†McManus, Michelle Ann *state representative, cherry farmer*
Moody, G. William *retired aerospace manufacturing company executive*
†Munsell, Susan Grimes *state legislator, accountant*
†Pitoniak, Gregory Edward *state representative*
†Posthumus, Richard Earl *state senator, farmer*
Povish, Kenneth Joseph *bishop*
†Rhead, Kim Alan *state representative*
Rooney, John Philip *law educator*
Saltzman, Robert Paul *insurance company executive*
†Schroer, Mary Bernadette *state representative*
†Schwarz, John J.H. *state senator, surgeon*
†Smith, Virgil Clark *state legislator*
†Stabenow, Deborah Ann *state legislator*
†Stallworth, Alma Grace *state legislator*
Stevens, J. Paul *entrepreneur*
Suhrheinrich, Richard Fred *federal judge*
Valade, Alan Michael *lawyer*
†Vaughn, Jackie, III *state legislator*
†Welborn, John Alva *state senator*
Wiegenstein, John Gerald *physician*
Wilkinson, William Sherwood *lawyer*

Lapeer
†Galas, Thomas A. *financial executive*

Leland
†Small, Hamish *chemist*

Livonia
†Baker, Ronald Seymour *construction executive*
Brandon, David A. *marketing and publishing executive*
Hanket, Mark John *lawyer*
Holtzman, Roberta Lee *foreign language educator*
Larson, Karen Elaine *business owner*
Sobel, Howard Bernard *osteopath*
Utley, John Eddy *automotive supplies executive*
Van de Vyver, Sister Mary Francilene *academic administrator*

Madison Heights
Chapman, Gilbert Bryant *physicist*
Jeffe, Sidney David *automotive engineer*
Kafarski, Mitchell I. *chemical processing company executive*
O'Hara, Thomas Edwin *association executive*
Pricer, Wayne Francis *counseling administrator*

Mancelona
Whelan, Joseph L(eo) *neurologist*

Maple City
Morris, Donald Arthur Adams *college president*

Marine City
Cronenworth, Charles Douglas *manufacturing company executive*

Marquette
Burt, John Harris *bishop*
Camerius, James Walter *marketing educator, corporate researcher*
Carlson, David Leroy *political science educator*
Heldreth, Leonard Guy *university administrator*
Manning, Robert Hendrick *development director*
†Ray, Thomas Kreider *bishop*
†Skogman, Dale R. *bishop*
Vandament, William Eugene *academic administrator, educator*

Metamora
Blass, Gerhard Alois *physics educator*

Midland
Barker, Nancy Lepard *college official*
Boulanger, Rodney Edmund *energy company executive*
†Byers, Rosemarie *library director*
Carson, Gordon Bloom *engineering executive*
Chao, Marshall S. *chemist*
Dorman, Linneaus Cuthbert *retired chemist*
Dow, Herbert Henry, II *foundation executive*
Falla, Enrique Crabb *chemical company executive*
Gant, George Arlington Lee *chemist*
Hampton, Leroy *retired chemical company executive*
Hanes, James Henry *consulting business executive, lawyer*
†Hazleton, Richard A. *chemicals executive*

Hyde, Geraldine Veola *secondary education educator, retired*
Ludington, John Samuel *manufacturing company executive*
Maneri, Remo R. *management consultant*
Mansfield, Marc Lewis *chemist, research scientist*
McKennon, Keith Robert *chemical company executive*
Meister, Bernard John *chemical engineer*
Nowak, Robert Michael *chemist*
Popoff, Frank Peter *chemical company executive*
Speier, John Leo, Jr. *chemist*
Stull, Daniel Richard *research thermochemist, educator, consultant*
Weyenberg, Donald Richard *chemist*

Monroe
Halthon, John Louis *quality engineer*
Heselton, Patricia Ann *clinical psychologist*
Keck, Merel Fogg *bank executive*
Knabusch, Charles Thair *manufacturing company executive*
Lipford, Rocque Edward *lawyer, corporate executive*
†Mlocek, Sister Frances Angeline *finance director*
Sewell, Robert Terrell, Jr. *executive search company owner*
Siciliano, Elizabeth Marie *secondary art educator*
White, Gary L. *trucking executive*

Mount Clemens
Darby, Lewis Randal *special education educator*
†Fraser, Blanche E. *school system administrator*

Mount Pleasant
Dietrich, Richard Vincent *geologist, educator*
Grabinski, Carol Joanne *gerontologist, educator*
Lippert, Robert J. *administrator and culinary arts educator, consultant*
†McBryde, James Edward *sales representative, county commissioner*
Meltzer, Bernard N(athan) *sociologist, educator*
Orlik, Peter Blythe *media educator, author, musician*

Muskegon
Austin, William Lamont *educational consultant, former superintendent of schools*
†Florjancic, Frederick Joseph, Jr. *manufacturing executive*
Johnson, Dale A. *manufacturing company executive*
Stevenson, James Lyall *academic administrator*
Van Leuven, Robert Joseph *lawyer*
Werner, R(ichard) Budd *business executive*

Negaunee
Friggens, Thomas George *state official, historian*

New Buffalo
Laird, Evalyn Walsh *lawyer*

Newaygo
†Grodus, Edward T. *secondary school principal*

North Muskegon
Mason, Robert Joseph *automotive parts company executive*

Northville
†Fletcher, Richard *health facility administrator*
Gerson, Ralph Joseph *corporate executive*
Jensen, Reuben Rolland *former automotive company executive*
Opre, Thomas Edward *magazine editor, film company executive, corporate travel company executive*

Novi
Chow, Chi-Ming *retired mathematics educator*

Oak Park
McManus, Martin Joseph *lawyer, priest*
Novick, Marvin *investment company executive, former automotive supplier executive, accountant*

Okemos
Giacoletto, Lawrence Joseph *electronics engineering educator, researcher, consultant*
Huddleston, Eugene Lee *retired American studies educator*
Killingsworth, Charles Clinton *economist*
Oberg, Roger Winston *management educator*
Ochberg, Frank Martin *psychiatrist, health science facility administrator, author*
Solo, Robert Alexander *economist, educator*

Olivet
Bassis, Michael Steven *academic administrator*

Orchard Lake
Haven, Thomas Kenneth *financial consultant*
Ingram, Robert John *business education educator*

Oscoda
Stone, William Lyndon *retired minister*

Owosso
Hoddy, George Warren *electric company executive, electrical engineer*

Paw Paw
Warner, James John *small business owner*

Pinckney
Roach, Thomas Adair *lawyer*

Plymouth
Bates, J(ohn) Bertram *retired chemical company executive*
Grannan, William Stephen *safety engineer, consultant*
McClendon, Edwin James *health science educator*
Merrill, Kenneth Coleman *retired automobile credit company executive*
Mondry, Ira *electronic appliance company executive*
Moore, Joan Elizabeth *human resources executive, lawyer*
Morgan, Donald Crane *lawyer*
†Petrie, Milton J. *retail company executive*
Ramamurthy, Subramanian *management consultant*
Scott, George Ernest *publisher, writer*
†Vlcek, Donald Joseph, Jr. *food distribution company executive*

Pontiac
Berlow, Robert Alan *lawyer*
Blades, Horatio Benedict (Bennie Blades) *professional football player*
Brown, Lomas, Jr. *professional football player*
†Cullen, John Patrick *hospital administrator*
Decker, Peter William *academic administrator*
Fontes, Wayne *professional football team head coach*
Grant, Barry M(arvin) *judge*
Gray, Mel *professional football player*
Mahone, Barbara Jean *automotive company executive*
McIntyre, Bruce Herbert *publishing company executive*
Robinson, Jack Albert *retail drug stores executive*
Sanders, Barry *football player*
Schmidt, Chuck *professional football team executive*
Smith, Roger Bonham *automotive manufacturing executive*
Spielman, Chris *professional football player*
Stryker, James William *automotive executive, former military officer*
Swilling, Pat *professional football player*

Port Huron
Coury, John, Jr. *surgeon*
DeMascio, Robert Edward *federal judge*
Haynes, Marcia Margaret *insurance agent*
Kirby, Ward Nelson *gas company executive*
Rowark, Maureen *fine arts photographer*
Thomson, Robert James *natural gas distribution company executive*
Wu, Harry Pao-Tung *librarian*

Portland
†Adams, Bill *principal*

Redford
†Flint, H. Howard, II *printing company executive*
Koci, Ludvik Frank *automotive manufacturing company executive*

Riverdale
Kirby, Kent Bruce *artist, educator*

Rochester
Callewaert, Denis Marc *biochemistry educator*
Horwitz, Ronald M. *business administration educator*
Hovanesian, Joseph Der *mechanical engineering educator*
Packard, Sandra Podolin *university president*
Polis, Michael Philip *academic administrator, electrical engineering educator*
Thomas, S. Bernard *history educator*
Unakar, Nalin Jayantilal *biological sciences educator*

Rochester Hills
Cook, Leonard Clarence *manufacturing company executive*
Farrar, Stephen Prescott *federal official*
Matthews, George Tennyson *history educator*

Rockford
Duzan, Dee *elementary school principal*
Gleason, Thomas Daues *shoe company executive*

Romulus
Archer, Hugh Morris *consulting engineer, manufacturing professional*
Girardin, Burton Lee *retired protective services official*
Gulda, Edward James *automotive executive*

Roseville
Baden, Robert Charles *manufacturing executive*

Royal Oak
Bernstein, Jay *pathologist, researcher, educator*
Dworkin, Howard Jerry *nuclear physician, educator*
Fredericks, Marshall Maynard *sculptor*
Karavite, Carlene Marie *psychologist, real estate property manager*
LaBan, Myron Miles *physician, administrator*
Matzick, Kenneth John *hospital administrator*
Myers, Kenneth Ellis *hospital administrator*
Stephens, Martha Foster *advertising executive*
Walker, Richard Harold *pathologist, educator*

Saginaw
Chaffee, Paul Charles *newspaper editor*
Cline, Thomas William *real estate leasing company executive, management consultant*
Doud, Kenneth Eugene, Jr. *accountant*
Evans, Harold Edward *banker*
†Flegenheimer, Ernest *sugar company executive*
†Jersevic, Roland Joseph *lawyer*
Kern, Franklin Lorenz *auditor*
Najar, Leo Michael *conductor, arranger, educator*
Thatcher, Rex Howard *newspaper publisher*
Untener, Kenneth E. *bishop*
†Williams, Herbert J. *bishop*
†Wilson, J. Parrish *religious organization administrator*

Saint Clair Shores
Gordon, Steven Stanley *automotive parts company executive*
Shehan, Wayne Charles *lawyer*
Walker, Frank Banghart *pathologist*

Saint Joseph
†Michelotti, Carl Anthony *electronics company executive*

Saline
Cornell, Richard Garth *biostatistics educator*
Frank, Richard Calhoun *architect*

Sault Sainte Marie
Johnson, Gary Robert *political scientist, editor*

South Haven
Nequist, John Leonard *retired food company executive*

Southfield
†Andrus, Leonard Carl *marketing executive*
Borden, John Anthony *manufacturing company executive*
Brown, June *journalist*
Cantwell, Dennis Michael *finance company executive*
†Caponigro, Jeffrey Ralph *public relations counselor*
Chamasrour, Joseph Albert *automotive executive*
Chambers, Charles MacKay *university president*
†Connolly, Brian Michael *hospital administrator*
Considine, John Joseph *advertising executive*
Dawson, Dennis Ray *lawyer, manufacturing company executive*
Doctoroff, Martin Myles *judge*
Dorfman, Henry S. *meat products company executive*
Dorfman, Joel Marvin *meat products company executive*
Doyle, James Thomas *marketing and communications executive*
Ellis, Robert William *engineering educator*
Fleming, Mac Arthur *labor union administrator*
†Graham, Michael Alan *advertising executive*
Hammel, Ernest Martin *medical educator, academic administrator*
†Hammond, John B., Jr. *advertising executive*
Harlan, John Marshall *construction company executive*
Hotelling, Harold *law and economics educator*
Jacobs, John Patrick *lawyer*
Jeffrey, Walter Leslie *corporation executive*
Johnson, Richard Alan *advertising executive*
Kalter, Alan *advertising agency executive*
Link, Robert Allen *lawyer, financial company executive*
Maibach, Ben C., Jr. *service executive*
Mathog, Robert Henry *otolaryngologist, educator*
†Matthes, Gerald Stephen *advertising agency executive*
Mikelberg, Arnold *meat packing company executive*
†Minghine, Rocco Raymond *meat packing company executive*
Morganroth, Fred *lawyer*
†Neman, Thomas Edward *advertising and marketing executive*
†Olsen, Douglas H. *superintendent*
Papazian, Dennis Richard *history educator, political commentator*
Peiser, Robert Alan *financial executive*
†Redstone, Daniel Aaron *architect*
Redstone, Louis Gordon *architect*
Reins, Ralph Erich *automotive products company executive*
Rosenzweig, Norman *psychiatry educator*
†Rossiter, Robert E. *diversified corporation executive*
†Runk, Lee Hammond *automotive company executive*
Satovsky, Abraham *lawyer*
Smith, Nancy Hohendorf *sales and marketing executive*
Stern, Guy *educator, writer*
†Symons, Douglas Michael *advertising executive*
Tauber, Joel David *manufacturing company executive*
Tierney, John Patrick *financial services executive*
Turnquist, Gary Edward *systems consultant, educator*
Tyler, David Malcolm *lawyer*
Van Dine, Harold Forster, Jr. *architect*
Weisenburger, Randall *manufacturing executive*
Welch, Martin E., III *manufacturing company executive*

Southgate
†Peacock, Lowell *bank executive*
Torok, Margaret Louise *insurance company executive*

Spring Arbor
Cherem, Barbara Frances *educational program director, professor*

Stanwood
Cawthorne, Kenneth Clifford *financial planner*

Sterling Heights
Dea, David Young Fong *electrical engineer, consultant*
Ice, Orva Lee, Jr. *history educator*
Koski, Deanna Eleanor *city official, real estate broker, closing officer*

Suttons Bay
Skinner, Thomas *broadcasting and film executive*

Taylor
Bright, Gerald *lawyer, manufacturing company executive*
Leekley, John Robert *lawyer*
Lyon, Wayne Barton *corporate executive*
Manoogian, Alex *manufacturing company executive*
Manoogian, Richard Alexander *manufacturing company executive*
Rosowski, Robert Bernard *manufacturing company executive*
Ullrich, John Frederick *diversified manufacturing company executive*
Wilkinson, E. G., Jr. *bank executive*

Tecumseh
Herrick, Kenneth Gilbert *manufacturing company executive*
Herrick, Todd W. *manufacturing company executive*
Taylor, Robert Lee *financial services and sales executive, information systems account executive, educator*

Thompsonville
Perry, Margaret *librarian, writer*

Three Rivers
Allen, Janet Louise *school system administrator*

Traverse City
†Bourdo, G. F. *principal*
Brown, Paul Bradley *architect*
Howe, Gordon *former professional hockey player, sports association executive*
LeJeune, Dennis Edward *investment counsel*
Rosser, Richard Franklin *education consultant*
Taylor, Donald Arthur *marketing educator*
Warrington, Willard Glade *former university official*
Wolfe, Richard Ratcliffe *lawyer*
Zimmerman, Paul Albert *retired college president, minister*

Trenton
Crooks, Archibald Muir, Jr. *engineer, licensed builder*

Troy
Adderley, Terence E. *corporate executive*
Alterman, Irwin Michael *lawyer*
Antonini, Joseph E. *discount department store executive*
Baker, Ernest Waldo, Jr. *advertising executive*
Buschmann, Siegfried *manufacturing executive*
Cantor, Bernard Jack *patent lawyer*
Carlson, David Martin *retail executive*
Corace, Joseph Russell *automotive parts company executive*
Crane, Louis Arthur *labor arbitrator*
Drakos, Irene Sasso *chemist*
Fellingham, David Andrew *mortgage banker*
Ferguson, Harley Robert *service company executive*
Hartwig, Eugene Lawrence *lawyer*
Inatome, Rick *retail computer company executive*
Kelly, William R. *employment agency executive*
Koch, Albert Acheson *manufacturing executive*
Krabbenhoft, Kenneth Lester *radiologist, educator*
Kruse, John Alphonse *lawyer*
Leach, Ralph F. *banker*
Marshall, John Elbert, III *foundation executive*
McAllister, Robert Cowden *retail company executive*
McDonald, Alonzo Lowry, Jr. *manufacturing executive*
Mrkonic, George Ralph, Jr. *retail executive*
Ovshinsky, Stanford Robert *physicist, inventor, energy and information company executive*
Ricketts, Thomas Roland *savings bank executive*
Sandy, William Haskell *training and communications systems executive*
Sharf, Stephan *automotive company executive*
Simons, Leonard Norman Rashall *advertising executive*
Sloan, Hugh Walter, Jr. *automotive industry executive*
Smith, Glen B. *consumer products company executive*
Strome, Stephen *distribution company executive*
†Weinhardt, W. John *manufacturing company executive*
Wetstein, Gary M. *accountant, company executive*
Williams, David Perry *manufacturing company executive*

University Center
Gilbertson, Eric Raymond *academic administrator, lawyer*
Miller, Roberta Balstad *science administrator*

Warren
†Agley, Randolph J. *pharmaceutical company executive*
Bell, Bradley J. *household appliance manufacturing company executive*
Bonkowski, Ronald Lawrence *mayor*
Dow, Peter Anthony *advertising agency executive*
Foxworth, John Edwin, Jr. *automotive executive, philatelist*
Fredericks, Wesley Charles, Jr. *automotive executive, lawyer*
Gallopoulos, Nicholas Efstratios *chemical engineer*
†Gilbert, Suzanne Harris *advertising executive*
Gothard, Donald Lee *auto company executive*
Herbst, Jan Francis *physicist, researcher*
Hopp, Anthony James *advertising agency executive*
Horton, William David, Jr. *army officer*
Jacovides, Linos Jacovou *electrical engineering research manager*
†Kassab, Sir Charles Shaw *banker*
Lau, Ian Van *safety research engineer, biomechanics expert*
Lett, Philip Wood, Jr. *defense consultant*
Morelli, William Annibale, Sr. *aerospace manufacturing company executive*
Nagy, Louis Leonard *engineering executive, researcher*
Reickert, Erick Arthur *automotive executive*
Ryan, Jack *physician, hospital corporation executive*
Schultz, Louis Michael *advertising agency executive*
Schwartz, Shirley E. *chemist*
Smith, George Wolfram *physicist, educator*
†Smith, John Robert *materials scientist*
Valerio, Michael Anthony *financial executive*
Viano, David Charles *automotive safety research scientist*
Wallace, Jack Harold *employee development specialist, educator*

Washington
Frey, Stuart Macklin *automobile manufacturing company executive*

Waterford
Edwards, Wallace Winfield *retired automotive company executive*
Hampton, Phillip Michael *consulting engineering company executive*

West Bloomfield
†Childress, Carl T. *principal*
Colton, Victor Robert *real estate developer, manufacturing executive*
†Dobb, Barbara Jeane *accountant*
Meyers, Gerald Carl *management consultant, author, educator, lecturer, former automobile company executive*
†Peterson, Esther *secondary school principal*
Sarwer-Foner, Gerald Jacob *physician, educator*
Sawyer, Howard Jerome *physician*

West Branch
Pattullo, Douglas Ernest *hospital administrator*

Whitehall
Youngquist, Alvin Menvid, Jr. *publisher, editor*

Williamsburg
Goodell, Warren Franklin *retired university administrator*

Williamston
Landis, Elwood Winton *retired newspaper editor*

Wixom
Boynton, Irvin Parker *educational administrator*

Wyandotte
†Strube, J. F. *agricultural products executive*

Ypsilanti
Barnes, James Milton physics and astronomy educator
†Beck, Mary Clare librarian
Boone, Morell Douglas academic administrator, information and instructional technology educator
Cantrell, Linda Maxine counselor
Caswell, Herbert Hall, Jr. retired biology educator
Corriveau, Arlene Josephine educational specialist
Duncan, Charles Howard business education educator
Evans, Gary Lee communications educator and consultant
Goldenberg, Ronald Edwin university dean
Gwaltney, Thomas Marion education educator, researcher
Krajewski-Jaime, Elvia Rosa social worker
McNutt, Kristen Wallwork consumer affairs executive
Perkins, Bradford history educator
Ritter, Frank Nicholas otolaryngologist, educator
Robek, Mary Frances business education educator
Sullivan, Thomas Patrick college president
Weinstein, Jay A. social science educator, researcher
Wilson, Lorraine M. medical, surgical nurse, nursing educator

Zeeland
Campbell, J. Kermit office products company executive
Ruch, Richard Hurley manufacturing company executive

MINNESOTA

Alexandria
Hultstrand, Donald Maynard bishop
Templin, Kenneth Elwood paper company executive

Annandale
Johnson, Jon E. editor, periodical

Arden Hills
Jones, Samuel Vadakedath ministries executive
†Lindmark, Ronald Dorance retired federal agency administrator

Austin
Hodapp, Don Joseph food company executive
Holman, Ralph Theodore biochemistry and nutrition educator
Knowlton, Richard L. food and meat processing company executive
†Piper, Pat Kathryn state senator
†Schmid, Harald Heinrich Otto biochemistry educator, academic director

Bayport
†Johnson, Alan lumber company executive

Bemidji
Bridston, Paul Joseph strategy consultant
Kief, Paul Allan lawyer
Paul, Sherman retired English language educator

Bloomington
Allen, Mary Louise Hook physical education educator
†Cuthill, Robert T. church administrator
Jodsaas, Larry Elvin computer components company executive
Krueger, Eugene Rex academic program director
Kuntz, Lila Elaine secondary education educator
McDill, Thomas Allison minister
McGrath, Dennis Britton public relations executive
Meyer, Scott D. public relations firm executive
Mona, David L. public relations executive
Smith, Henry Charles, III symphony orchestra conductor

Blue Earth
Haertel, Charles Wayne minister

Brooklyn Park
Peterson, Donn Neal forensic engineer

Burnsville
†Gardner, Dennis (Den) public relations executive
†Knutson, David Lee lawyer
†Morrison, Constance Faith state legislator, realtor

Cass Lake
†Wadena, Darrell Eugene indian tribe executive

Chanhassen
Rose, Elizabeth (Patricia H. Burke) author, environmental poisoning specialist, satirist
Thorson, John Martin, Jr. electrical engineer, consultant

Chisago City
Bergstrand, Wilton Everet minister

Chisholm
†Tomassoni, David Joseph insurance agent, state representative

Circle Pines
†McClellan, John R. school system administrator

Cokato
†Thomas, Paul S. principal

Collegeville
Haile, Getatchew archivist, educator
Henry, Patrick G. religious research administrator
Reinhart, Dietrich Thomas university president, history educator

Crookston
Balke, Victor H. bishop

Dassel
†Kay, Craig principal

Detroit Lakes
Eginton, Charles Theodore surgeon, educator

Dresbach
Saline, Lindon Edgar industrial company executive

Duluth
†Aadland, Thomas Vernon minister
†Aufderheide, Arthur Carl pathologist
Balmer, James Walter lawyer
Billig, Thomas Clifford publishing and marketing executive
Bowman, Roger Manwaring real estate executive
Chee, Cheng-Khee artist
Coffman, Phillip Hudson music educator, arts administrator
Eisenberg, Richard M. pharmacology educator
Fischer, Roger Adrian history educator
Franks, Ronald Dwyer university dean, psychiatrist, educator
Gallinger, Lois Mae medical technologist
Heaney, Gerald William federal judge
Jankofsky, Klaus Peter medieval studies educator
Johnson, Arthur Gilbert microbiology educator
Latto, Lewis M., Jr. broadcasting company executive
Lease, Martin Harry, Jr. political science educator
Leland, Paula Susan educational administrator, educator
Pearce, Donald Joslin librarian
Rapp, George Robert, Jr. (Rip) geology and archeology educator
†Salmela, David Daniel architect
Schroeder, Fred Erich Harald humanities educator
Schwietz, Roger L. bishop
Whiteman, Richard Frank architect
Wood, Douglas author, composer, musician

Eagan
Opperman, Dwight Darwin publishing company executive
Scott, Andrew corporate executive

Eden Prairie
Carter, Anthony football player
Doleman, Christopher John professional football player
†Dunwiddie, Foster Wilfred architect, educator
Emison, James W. petroleum company executive
Green, Dennis professional football coach
Hanson, Dale S. banker
Headrick, Roger Lewis professional sports executive
Hinton, Christopher Jerrod professional football player
Jordan, Steven Russell professional football player
Lau, Michele Denise advertising consultant, sales trainer, television personality
McCoy, Gerald Leo superintendent of schools
McDaniel, Randall Cornell professional football player
Moon, Warren professional football player
Skoglund, John C. former professional football team executive
Thomas, Henry Lee, Jr. professional football player

Edina
Burdick, Lou Brum public relations executive
Johnson, Paul Owen lawyer
Saltzman, William painter, sculptor, designer
Thorndyke, Lloyd Milton computer company executive

Elysian
Nickerson, James Findley education consultant

Excelsior
Bilka, Paul Joseph physician
French, Lyle Albert surgeon
Rich, Willis Frank, Jr. banker

Faribault
Turnbull, Charles Vincent real estate broker

Fergus Falls
†Egge, Joel clergy member, academic administrator
Emmen, Dennis R. electric utility executive
Hartl, Albert Victor utility executive
†Olson, Jarle clergy member, Church administrator
Overgaard, Robert Milton religious organization administrator
†Rinden, David Lee editor
Smedsrud, Milton E. health association executive, consultant
†Westby, John clergy member, church administrator

Forest Lake
Marchese, Ronald Thomas ancient history and archaeology educator

Golden Valley
†Estergren, Eric DeWayne corporate executive
Hagglund, Clarance Edward lawyer, publishing company owner

Grand Rapids
King, Sheryl Jayne secondary education educator, counselor
Radecki, Anthony Eugene paper company executive

Hastings
Bzoskie, James Steven minister

Hopkins
Beeler, Donald Daryl retail executive
Burke, Steven Francis organization executive
Eugster, Jack Wilson retail executive
Haugen, Gerald Alan financial consultant
†Haworth, Charles Dale advertising executive
Mayeron, Carol Ann Cantor
†Passi, Beth school administrator
Rappaport, Gary Burton defense equipment and computer company executive

Hutchinson
Graf, Laurance James communications executive

Inver Grove
Webster, Elroy diversified supplies and machinery executive

Ivanhoe
Hoversten, Ellsworth Gary insurance executive, producer

Lake Elmo
Shervheim, Lloyd Oliver insurance company executive, lawyer

Lakeville
Phinney, William Charles retired geologist

Litchfield
Johnson, Richard Warren civil engineer

Little Falls
†Eichten, Sister Beatrice Mary pastoral psychotherapist

Lutsen
Napadensky, Hyla Sarane engineering consultant

Luverne
Manfred, Frederick Feikema (Feike Feikema) writer

Madison
Husby, Donald Evans engineering company executive

Mankato
Daly, Denis Jon agricultural business executive
Gage, Fred Kelton lawyer
†Hottinger, John Creighton lawyer, state legislator
Hustoles, Paul John theater educator
Larson, Michael Len newspaper editor
†Orvick, George Myron church denomination executive, minister
†Taylor, Glen professional sports team executive, printing and graphics company executive

Maple Grove
St. Mary, Edward Sylvester direct mail marketing company executive

Maple Plain
Larson, Mark Allan financial executive

Marcell
Aldrich, Richard John agronomist, educator

Marshall
Libby, Ronald Theodore political science educator, consultant, researcher
†Schwan, Alfred food products executive

Minneapolis
Aaron, Allen Harold lawyer
Abrams, Richard Brill lawyer
Ackerman, Eugene biophysics educator
Ackman, Lauress V. lawyer
Adams, John Stephen geography educator
Adams, Thomas Lewis lawyer
Adamson, Oscar Charles, II lawyer
Aguilera, Richard Warren (Rick Aguilera) professional baseball player
†Albright, Susan Newspaper editor
Alcott, James Arthur communications executive
Alton, Ann Leslie judge, lawyer, educator
Amdahl, Byrdelle John security products company executive
Amdahl, Douglas Kenneth retired state supreme court justice
Anderson, Albert Esten publisher
Anderson, Charles S. college president, clergyman
Anderson, Chester Grant English educator
Anderson, Clyde Bailey musician, educator
Anderson, Eric Scott lawyer
Anderson, Geraldine Louise laboratory scientist
Anderson, Laurence Alexis lawyer
†Anderson, Lowell Carlton insurance company executive
†Anderson, Robert Marshall bishop
Anderson, Thomas Willman lawyer
Andrews, Albert O'Beirne, Jr. lawyer
Appel, William Frank pharmacist
Aris, Rutherford applied mathematician, educator
Armstrong, Elizabeth Neilson curator
Arndt, Roger Edward Anthony hydraulic engineer, educator
Asp, William George librarian
Asplin, Edward William retired packaging company executive
Atwater, Horace Brewster, Jr. food company executive
Baillie, James Leonard lawyer
Baker, John Stevenson (Michael Dyregrov) writer
Baker, Michael Harry chemical engineer
Bakken, Earl Elmer electrical engineer, bioengineering company executive
Bales, Kent Roslyn English language educator
Balfour, Henry Hallowell, Jr. medical educator, researcher, physician, writer
Barnhill, Howard Eugene insurance company executive
†Bartkowski, William Patrick finance company executive
Bartle, Emery W(arness) lawyer
Baum, David Roy research psychologist
†Beardsley, John Ray public relations firm executive
Bell, Jerry professional sports team executive
†Belton, Sharon Sayles mayor
Benson, Donald Erick holding company executive
Bentz, Frederick Jacob architect
Berens, William Joseph lawyer
Berg, Stanton Oneal firearms and ballistics consultant
Berg, Thomas Kenneth lawyer
Bergerson, David Raymond lawyer
Bergerson, Stephen Richard lawyer
Berry, David J. financial services company executive
†Berryman, Robert Glen accounting educator, consultant
Berscheid, Ellen S. psychology educator, author, researcher
Beukema, John Frederick lawyer
Bileydi, Sumer advertising agency executive
Biller, Leslie Stuart banker
Bisping, Bruce Henry photojournalist
Blackburn, Henry Webster, Jr. physician
Bleck, Michael John lawyer
Blomquist, Robert Oscar insurance company executive
Blood, Edward Linford consumer products company executive
Bly, Robert poet
Boelter, Philip Floyd lawyer
Bolan, Richard Stuart urban planner, educator, researcher
†Bonsignore, Michael Robert electronics company executive
Borger, John Philip lawyer
Boubelik, Henry Fredrick, Jr. car rental company executive
Bouchard, Thomas Joseph, Jr. psychology educator, researcher
Bowie, Norman Ernest university official, educator
Brand, Steve Aaron lawyer
Brasket, Curt Justin systems analyst, chess player
Breimayer, Joseph Frederick patent lawyer
Bress, Michael E. lawyer
Brings, Lawrence Martin publisher
Brink, David Ryrie lawyer
Brosnahan, Roger Paul lawyer
Brown, David M. physician, educator, dean
Browne, Donald Roger speech communication educator
Browne, Michael Dennis poet, educator
Bruner, Philip Lane lawyer
Buchwald, Henry surgeon, educator, researcher
†Buoen, Roger newspaper editor
Buratti, Dennis P. lawyer
Burk, Robert S. lawyer
Burke, Martin Nicholas lawyer
†Burke, Paul Bradford lawyer, manufacturing executive
Burns, Neal Murray advertising agency executive
Burns, Robert A. lawyer
Burton, Charles Victor physician, surgeon, inventor
Busdicker, Gordon G. lawyer
Byrd, Richard Edward minister, psychologist
Cadogan, William J. (Bill Cadogan) telecommunications company executive
Caldwell, Michael DeFoix surgeon, educator
Campbell, James Robert banker
Campbell, Karlyn Kohrs speech and communication educator
Cantelon, John Edward academic administrator
Cardozo, Richard Nunez marketing, entrepreneurship and business educator
Carlson, Curtis LeRoy business executive
Carlson, Don D. lawyer
Carlson, Norman A. government official
Carlson, Thomas David lawyer
Carlton, Steven Norman former professional baseball player
†Carmody, John architectural educator
†Carpenter, Marshall Le Roy corporation financial executive
Carpenter, Norman Roblee lawyer
Carr, Charles William biochemist, emeritus educator
Carr, Robert Wilson, Jr. chemistry educator
†Carruthers, Philip Charles lawyer
Carter, Roy Ernest, Jr. journalist, educator
Cavert, Henry Mead physician, retired educator
Cavin, William Brooks architect
Cedar, Paul Arnold church executive, minister
Champlin, Steven Kirk lawyer
Chipman, John Somerset economist, educator
Chisholm, Tague Clement pediatric surgeon, educator
Chou, Shelley Nien-chun neurosurgeon, university official, educator
Christiansen, Jay David lawyer
Ciresi, Michael Vincent lawyer
Clarke, Robert Earle (Bobby Clarke) hockey executive
†Clayton, Paula Jean psychiatry educator
†Clemence, Roger Davidson landscape architect, educator
Cleveland, (James) Harlan political scientist, public affairs executive
Clinton, Joseph Edward emergency physician
Cohen, Arnold A. electrical engineer
Comstock, Rebecca Ann lawyer
Conforti, Michael Peter museum curator, art historian
Conley, Tom Clark literature educator
Conn, Gordon Brainard, Jr. lawyer
Cook, Jay F. lawyer
Coonrod, Richard Allen agricultural products company executive
Cooper, William Allen banking executive
Cope, Lewis newspaper reporter
Corcoran, Mary Elizabeth educational psychology educator emeritus
Corrigan, Fredric H. retired corporate executive
†Cowles, John, III newspaper publishing executive
Cox, David Carson media company executive
Craig, James Lynn physician, consumer products company executive
Crosby, Jacqueline Garton journalist
Crosby, Thomas Manville, Jr. lawyer
†Crouch, Steven L. mining engineer
Cummings, Larry Lee psychologist, educator
Cutler, Kenneth Lance lawyer
Dabill, Phillip Alvin wholesale foods executive
Dahlberg, Burton Francis real estate corporation executive
Dahler, John Spillers chemist, educator
Davies, R. Scott lawyer
Davis, Howard Ted chemical engineering educator
Davis, Julia McBroom college dean, speech pathology and audiology educator
Dawis, René V. psychology educator, research consultant
Degenhardt, Robert Allan architectural and engineering firm executive
Degnan, Joseph magazine editor
Deming, Frederick Lewis banker
DeNero, Henry T. department store chain executive
DiGangi, Frank Edward academic administrator
Diracles, John Michael, Jr. financial executive
Dittrich, Raymond Joseph lawyer
Dorsey, Peter lawyer
Doty, David Singleton federal judge
Drawz, John Englund lawyer
Dubes, Michael J. insurance company executive
DuFour, R(ichard) W(illiam), Jr. lawyer
Dugmore, Edward artist
Dunlap, William DeWayne, Jr. advertising agency executive
Dworkin, Martin microbiologist, educator
Eastwood, J. Marquis lawyer
Eck, George Gregory lawyer
Eckert, Ernst R. G. mechanical engineering educator
Egekvist, W. Soren corporate consultant, educator
†Eidelman, Terry philosophy educator, publisher
Elzay, Richard Paul dental school administrator
Emmerich, Karol Denise former retail company executive, consultant
Endorf, Verlane L. lawyer
†Engebrecht, Julie newspaper sports editor
Erickson, Gerald Meyer classical studies educator
Erickson, W(alter) Bruce business and economics educator, entrepreneur

Etzwiler, Donnell Dencil *pediatrician*
Eyberg, Donald Theodore, Jr. *architect*
Fairhurst, Charles *civil and mining engineering educator*
Falker, John Richard *investor relations counsel*
Farah, Caesar Elie *Middle Eastern and Islamic studies educator*
Ferner, David Charles *non-profit management and development consultant*
Ferrera, Robert James *superintendent of schools*
Ferris, Thomas Francis *physician*
Fetler, Paul *composer*
Finch, Harold Bertram, Jr. *wholesale grocery company executive*
Finzen, Bruce Arthur *lawyer*
Firchow, Evelyn Scherabon *German educator, author*
Firchow, Peter Edgerly *language professional, educator, author*
†Firestone, Jon *advertising executive*
Fisch, Robert Otto *medical educator*
Fischer, Robert William *financial executive*
Fisher, Michael Bruce *lawyer*
Flanagan, Barbara *journalist*
Flaskamp, William Davidson *lawyer*
Fleezanis, Jorja Kay *violinist, educator*
†Fleischer, Daniel *minister, religious organization administrator*
Fletcher, Edward Abraham *engineering educator*
Flom, Gerald Trossen *lawyer*
Fogg, Richard Lloyd *food products company executive*
Foley, Thomas *brokerage house executive*
Fox, Howard Tall, Jr. *professional baseball team executive*
Franklin, Robert Brewer *journalist*
Frechette, Peter Loren *dental products executive*
Frecon, Alain *lawyer*
French, John Dwyer *lawyer*
Friedman, Avner *mathematician, educator*
Froehlke, Robert Frederick *financial services executive*
Fronek, David N. *lawyer*
Fulton, Robert Lester *sociology educator*
Gage, Edwin C., III (Skip Gage) *travel, marketing services executive*
Gagnon, Craig William *lawyer*
Gainor, Thomas Edward *banker*
Galambos, Theodore Victor *civil engineer, educator*
Gallagher, Gerald Raphael *venture capitalist*
†Gandrud, Robert P. *insurance company executive*
Gannon, Mary Carol *nutritional biochemist*
Gardner, William Earl *university dean*
Garmezy, Norman *psychology educator*
Garon, Philip Stephen *lawyer*
Garry, Vincent Ferrer *environmental toxicology researcher, educator*
Gasiorowicz, Stephen George *physics educator*
Gault, N. L., Jr. *physician, educator*
Gearty, Edward Joseph *lawyer*
Gedgaudas, Eugene *radiologist, educator*
Geistfeld, Ronald Elwood *dental educator*
George, Melvin Douglas *university official*
Gerberich, William Warren *engineering educator*
Gerlach, Luther Paul *anthropologist*
Geweke, John Frederick *economics educator*
Gherty, John E. *food products and agricultural products company executive*
†Giere, Ronald Nelson *research director, philosophy educator*
Gill, Richard Lawrence *lawyer*
Gilpin, Larry Vincent *retail executive*
Goldberg, Luella Gross *investment company executive*
Goldberg Kent, Susan *library director*
Goldfus, Donald Wayne *glass company executive*
Goldman, Allen Marshall *physics educator*
Goldstein, Mark David *advertising agency executive*
Goldstein, Richard Jay *mechanical engineer, educator*
Goodman, Elizabeth Ann *lawyer*
Gordon, John Bennett *lawyer*
Gorham, Eville *science educator*
Gorlin, Robert James *medical educator*
Gottier, Richard Chalmers *computer company executive*
Gottschalk, Stephen Elmer *lawyer*
Graham, William Franklin (Billy Graham) *evangelist*
Grant, David James William *pharmacy educator*
Gray, Virginia Hickman *political science educator*
Grayson, Edward Davis *lawyer, manufacturing company executive*
Greene, Clifford M. *lawyer*
Greener, Ralph Bertram *lawyer*
Grieman, John Joseph *communications executive*
Griffin, Edward Michael *language professional, educator*
Griffith, G. Larry *lawyer*
Grim, Eugene Donald *physiology educator*
Groves, Franklin Nelson *business executive*
Grundhofer, John F. *banker*
Gudeman, Stephen Frederick *anthropology educator*
Gudorf, Kenneth Francis *business executive*
Guillaume, Marnix Leo Karl *insurance company executive*
Gullickson, Glenn, Jr. *physician, educator*
Gustafson, Richard Charles *rental and leasing company executive*
Haase, Ashley Thomson *microbiology educator, scientist*
Halbreich, Kathy *museum director*
Hale, Roger Loucks *manufacturing company executive*
Halley, James Woods, Jr. *physicist*
Hallman, Gary L. *photographer, educator*
Hamermesh, Morton *physicist, educator*
†Hanson, A. Stuart *physician*
Hanson, Samuel Lee *lawyer*
Hargens, William Garman *architect*
Harper, Donald Victor *transportation and logistics educator*
Harper, Michael Henry, Jr. *lawyer*
Harris, John Edward *lawyer*
Hasselquist, Maynard Burton *retired lawyer*
Haugen, Rolf Eugene *leasing company executive*
Hayward, Edward Joseph *lawyer*
Heiberg, Robert Alan *lawyer*
Hemphill, Stuart R. *lawyer*
Hendrixson, Peter S. *lawyer*
Henson, Robert Frank *lawyer*
†Hertogs, Mary Helen *educational administrator*
Hetland, James Lyman, Jr. *banker, lawyer, educator*
Hibbs, John Stanley *lawyer*
Hibbs, William R. *lawyer*
Hinderaker, John Hadley *lawyer*
Hippee, William H., Jr. *lawyer*
Hitch, Horace *lawyer*
Hoard, Heidi Marie *lawyer*
Hobbie, Russell Klyver *physicist*
Hobbins, Robert Leo *lawyer*
Hodder, William Alan *fabricated metal products company executive*
Hoffmann, Thomas Russell *business management educator*
Hogenkamp, Henricus Petrus Cornelis *biochemistry researcher, biochemistry educator*
Holt, Robert Theodore *political scientist, dean, educator*
Holter, Arlen Rolf *cardiothoracic surgeon*
Hooke, Roger LeBaron *geomorphology and glaciology educator*
Horns, Howard Lowell *physician, educator*
Horsch, Lawrence Leonard *corporate revitalization executive, venture capitalist*
†Houlton, Loyce J. *artistic director, choreographer*
†Howland, Joan Sidney *law librarian, law educator*
Hoyer, Harvey Conrad *retired college president, clergyman*
Hudec, Robert Emil *lawyer, educator*
†Hull, Bill *clergy member, church administrator*
Hull, William Henry *publishing company executive*
Humphrey, Edward William *surgeon, medical educator*
Hurwicz, Leonid *economist, educator*
Huston, Beatrice Louise *banker*
Huttner, Marian Alice *library administrator*
Infante, Ettore Ferrari *mathematician, educator, university administrator*
Isbin, Herbert Stanford *chemical engineering educator*
†Ison, Christopher John *investigative reporter*
Jackson, J. David *lawyer*
Jacob, Bernard Michel *architect*
Jarboe, Mark Alan *lawyer*
Jensen, Roland Jens *utility company executive*
†Johnson, Cheryl *newspaper columnist*
Johnson, Clark Eugene, Jr. *electronics and computer company executive, magnetics physicist*
Johnson, David Wolcott *psychologist, educator*
Johnson, Eugene Laurence *lawyer*
Johnson, Gary M. *lawyer*
Johnson, John Warren *association executive*
Johnson, Larry Walter *lawyer*
Johnson, Lloyd Peter *banker*
Johnson, Sankey Anton *manufacturing company executive*
Johnson, Scott William *lawyer, manufacturing company executive*
Johnson, Walter Kline *civil engineer*
Jones, Norman M. *finance executive*
Jones, Thomas Walter *astrophysics educator, researcher*
Jones, William Arnold *writer, former newspaper columnist*
Joseph, Burton M. *grain merchant*
Joseph, Daniel Donald *aeronautical engineer, educator*
Joseph, Geri Mack (Geraldine Joseph) *former ambassador, educator*
Kain, Richard Yerkes *electrical engineer, researcher, educator*
Kallok, Michael John *physiologist, research administrator*
Kampf, William Ira *lawyer*
Kane, Robert Lewis *public health educator*
†Kapanke, John *church administator*
Kaplan, Manuel E. *physician, educator*
Kaplan, Sheldon *lawyer*
Karan, Bradlee *lawyer, educator*
Karigan, James Andrew *lawyer*
Keane, William Francis *nephrology educator, research foundation executive*
Kelly, A. David *lawyer*
Kelly, Tom (Jay Thomas Kelly) *major league baseball club manager*
Kennedy, B(yrl) J(ames) *medicine and oncology educator*
Keppel, William James *lawyer*
Keyes, Jeffrey J. *lawyer*
Kidwell, David Stephen *academic administrator*
Kilzer, Louis Charles *journalist*
Kinderwater, Joseph C. (Jack Kinderwater) *publishing company executive*
King, Lyndel Irene Saunders *art museum director*
King, Richard Harding *financial consultant, retired food processing company executive*
King, Robert Cotton *association consultant*
Kinney, Earl Robert *mutual funds company executive*
Kirby, John D. *lawyer*
Kitchak, Peter Ramon *lawyer*
Klaas, Paul Barry *lawyer*
†Kleinglass, Steven Peter *health care administrator*
Kletschka, Harold Dale *cardiovascular surgeon, biomedical company executive*
Kling, Richard William *insurance executive*
†Klobuchar, James John *columnist*
Knoke, David Harmon *sociology educator*
Knopman, David S. *neurologist*
Kohlstedt, Sally Gregory *history educator*
Kolehmainen, Jan Waldroy *association executive*
Koneck, John M. *lawyer*
Konopka, Gisela Peiper (Mrs. Erhardt Paul Konopka) *social worker, author, lecturer, educator*
Korotkin, Fred *writer, philatelist*
Koutsky, Dean Roger *advertising executive*
Kovacevich, Richard M. *banker*
Kramer, Joel Roy *journalist, newspaper executive*
Kramp, Richard William *biotechnology executive*
Kraut, Gerald Anthony *data processing services company executive, investment banker*
Kressel, Robert J. *federal judge*
Krislov, Samuel *political science educator*
Krohnke, Duane W. *lawyer*
Kruse, Paul Walters, Jr. *physicist, consultant*
Kudrle, Robert Thomas *economist, educator*
Kuhi, Leonard Vello *astronomer, university administrator*
Kvalseth, Tarald Oddvar *mechanical engineer, educator*
Laettner, Christian Donald *professional basketball player*
Laing, Karel Ann *magazine publishing executive*
Lakin, James Dennis *allergist, immunologist*
Lambert, Robert Frank *electrical engineer, educator*
Landry, Paul Leonard *lawyer*
Langer, Leonard O., Jr. *radiologist, educator*
Lareau, Richard George *lawyer*
Larkin, Eugene David *artist, educator*
Larson, Dale Irving *lawyer*
Larson, Earl Richard *federal judge*
Layton, Edwin Thomas, Jr. *science and technology history educator, writer*
Lazar, Raymond Michael *lawyer, educator*
Lebedoff, David M. *lawyer, author*
Lebedoff, Randy Miller *lawyer*
Lee, E. Bruce *electrical engineering educator*
Lee, Joe R. *food products company executive*
Lehmberg, Stanford Eugene *historian, educator*
LeMond, Gregory James *professional bicycle racer*
Leon, Arthur Sol *research cardiologist, exercise physiologist*
Leppert, Richard David *humanities educator*
Lerner, Harry Jonas *publishing company executive*
Levine, John David *lawyer*
Levitt, Seymour Herbert *physician, radiology educator*
Lindell, Edward Albert *former college president, religious organization administrator*
Lindgren, D(erbin) Kenneth, Jr. *lawyer*
†Liszt, Howard Paul *advertising executive*
Liu, Benjamin Young-hwai *engineering educator*
Loud, Warren Simms *mathematician*
Lowe, Sidney *professional basketball coach*
Lubben, David J. *lawyer*
†Luepker, Russell Vincent *epidemiology educator*
Luiso, Anthony *international food company executive*
Lumry, Rufus Worth, II *chemist, educator*
Lurton, H. William *retail executive*
Luthringshauser, Daniel Rene *manufacturing company executive*
Lynch, Peter John *dermatologist*
Lyon, James McDonald *lawyer, banker*
Mack, Shane Lee *professional baseball player, olympic athlete*
Macke, Kenneth A. *retail executive*
MacLaughlin, Harry Hunter *federal judge*
†MacMillan, Whitney *food products and import/export company executive*
MacPhail, Andy *professional baseball team executive*
Magnuson, Roger James *lawyer*
†Mahaffey, Gary John *architect*
Mahoney, Jerry C. D. *lawyer*
Malfeld, Diane D. *lawyer*
Mammel, Russell Norman *retired food distribution company executive*
Manning, William Henry *lawyer*
Manthey, Thomas Richard *lawyer*
Marks, Florence C. Elliott *nursing administrator*
Markus, Lawrence *retired mathematics educator*
Marshak, Marvin Lloyd *physicist, educator*
†Marshall, Sherrie *newspaper editor*
Martens, Keith Otto *investment company executive*
Martenson, Edward Allen *theater manager*
Martin, Phillip Hammond *lawyer*
Martin, Roger Bond *landscape architect, educator*
Mason, John Milton (Jack Mason) *lawyer*
Matson, Wesley Jennings *educational administrator*
Matthews, James Shadley *lawyer*
Maurer, Evan Maclyn *art museum director*
Mazze, Roger Steven *medical educator, researcher*
McClintock, George Dunlap *lawyer*
McCullough, John Jeffrey *pathologist, research scientist, medical center administrator, educator*
McDonald, William Andrew *classics educator*
Mc Elrath, Gayle William *management consultant, educator*
†McEnroe, Paul *reporter*
McErlane, Joseph James *insurance company executive*
McGehee, Richard Paul *mathematics educator*
McGuire, Timothy James *newspaper editor, lawyer*
†McKenna, Robert J. *car rental company executive*
McQuarrie, Donald Gray *surgeon, educator*
Meador, Ron *newspaper editor, writer*
Meehl, Paul Everett *psychologist, educator*
Mellum, Gale Robert *lawyer*
Melrose, Kendrick Bascom *manufacturing company executive*
Merkle, John Hallock *lawyer*
Merwin, Jack Clifford *retired education educator*
Meshbesher, Ronald I. *lawyer*
Meyer, Maurice Wesley *physiologist, dentist, neurologist*
Michael, Alfred Frederick, Jr. *physician, medical educator*
Miller, Donald Muxlow *accountant, administrator*
Miller, John William, Jr. *bassoonist*
Miller, Willard, Jr. *mathematician, educator*
Miller, William Alvin *clergyman, author*
Minish, Robert Arthur *lawyer*
Mitau, Lee R. *lawyer*
Mitchell, James Austin *insurance company executive*
Moe, Thomas O. *lawyer*
Montgomery, Henry Irving *financial planner*
Mooty, John William *lawyer*
Moraczewski, Robert Leo *publisher*
Morgan, Arthur Edward *management executive*
Morgan, Carol Marie *marketing executive*
Morris, David Hugh *manufacturing and marketing executive*
Morrison, Clinton *banker*
†Mortenson, M. A., Jr. *construction executive*
Moscowitz, Albert Joseph *chemist, educator*
†Mulfinger, Dale *architect*
Mulich, Steve Francis *safety engineer*
Murphy, Diana E. *federal judge*
Murphy, Joseph Edward, Jr. *broadcast executive*
Murray, Kenneth Richard *banking executive*
Myers, Malcolm Haynie *artist, art educator*
Najarian, John Sarkis *surgeon, educator*
Nanne, Louis Vincent *professional hockey team executive*
Nathan, Marshall Ira *electrical engineering educator*
Nelson, Glen David *medical products executive, physician*
Nelson, Richard Arthur *lawyer*
Nelson, Steven Craig *lawyer*
Nelson, Susan Richard *lawyer*
†Neumann, L. N. *grain company executive*
Newhall, David Gillette *lawyer*
†Nicholson, Bruce J. *insurance company executive*
†Nilles, John Michael *lawyer*
Nitsche, Johannes Carl Christian *mathematics educator*
Nixon, Raymond Blalock *journalist, educator*
Noonan, Thomas Schaub *history educator, Russian studies educator*
†Norberg, Arthur Lawrence, Jr. *historian, physicist educator*
Nordbye, Rodger Lincoln *lawyer*
†Norling, Richard Arthur *health care executive*
Nyrop, Donald William *airline executive*
Ogata, Katsuhiko *engineering educator*
O'Keefe, Daniel P. *lawyer*
O'Keefe, Thomas Michael *foundation executive*
†Oliver, Edward Carl *state senator, retired investment executive*
Olson, Clifford Larry *management consultant, entrepreneur*
Olson, Ronald Dale *grain company executive*
Olson, Theodore Alexander *former environmental biology educator*
O'Neill, Brian Boru *lawyer*
Oriani, Richard Anthony *metallurgical engineering educator*
Ovitsky, Steven Alan *musician, symphony orchestra executive*
Palmer, Brian Eugene *lawyer*
Palmer, Deborah Jean *lawyer*
Palms, Roger Curtis *religious magazine editor, clergyman*
Paparella, Michael M. *otolaryngologist*
†Parker, Leonard Sam *architect, educator*
†Patankar, Suhas V. *engineering educator*
Payne, William Bruce *lawyer*
Pedoe, Daniel *mathematician, writer, artist*
†Penrod, Steven David *law educator*
Perlman, Lawrence *business executive*
Persson, Erland Karl *electrical engineer*
Petersen, Anne Cheryl *university official and dean, educator*
Pfender, Emil *mechanical engineering educator*
Pflug, Irving John *food scientist, engineer, educator*
Phibbs, Clifford Matthew *surgeon, educator*
Philipson, Willard Dale *curriculum and instructional educator*
Pihlstrom, Bruce *periodontist, dental educator*
Pile, Robert Bennett *advertising executive, writer, consultant*
Pillsbury, George Sturgis *investment adviser*
Piper, Addison Lewis *securities executive*
Pluimer, Edward J. *lawyer*
Pohlad, Carl R. *professional baseball team executive, bottling company executive*
Polesky, Herbert Fred *physician*
Popham, Wayne Gordon *lawyer*
Porter, Philip Wayland *geography educator*
Porter, William L. *electrical engineer*
Portoghese, Philip Salvatore *medicinal chemist, educator*
Potuznik, Charles Laddy *lawyer*
Pour-El, Marian Boykan *mathematician, educator*
Prager, Stephen *chemistry educator*
Pratte, Robert John *lawyer*
Prem, Konald Arthur *physician, educator*
Preuss, Roger E(mil) *artist*
Price, Joseph Michael *lawyer*
Prince, Robb Lincoln *manufacturing company executive*
Puckett, Kirby *professional baseball player*
Putnam, Frederick Warren, Jr. *bishop*
Quie, Paul Gerhardt *physician, educator*
Rachie, Cyrus *lawyer*
Radmer, Michael John *lawyer, educator*
Rahman, Yueh-Erh *biologist*
Rahn, Alvin Albert *former banker*
†Rand, Peter Anders *architect*
Rand, Sidney Anders *retired college administrator*
Ranheim, David A. *lawyer*
†Ranum, Jane Barnhardt *lawyer*
†Rapson, Ralph *architect, educator*
Rath, R. John *historian, educator*
Ratner, Harvey *professional basketball team owner*
Rauenhorst, Gerald *design and construction company executive*
Read, John Conyers *filtration company executive*
Reichgott Junge, Ember D. *lawyer, state senator*
Reidenberg, Louis Morton *lawyer*
Reilly, George *lawyer*
Rein, Stanley M. *lawyer*
Reinhart, Robert Rountree, Jr. *lawyer*
Reiss, Ira Leonard *sociology educator, writer*
Reister, Raymond Alex *lawyer*
Renier, James J. *diversified electronic equipment manufacturing company executive*
Retzler, Kurt Egon *diversified management company executive, hospitality, travel and marketing company executive*
Reuter, James William *lawyer*
Reynolds, David G(eorge) *physiologist, educator*
Rockenstein, Walter Harrison, II *lawyer*
Rockwell, Winthrop Adams *lawyer*
Roe, John H. *manufacturing company executive*
†Rogers, David *apparel executive*
Rogers, William Cecil *political science educator*
Rohr, Daniel C. *banker*
Rose, Thomas Albert *artist, art educator*
Rosen, Judah Ben *computer scientist*
Rosenbaum, James Michael *federal judge*
Ross, Donald, Jr. *English language educator, university administrator*
Ross, Percy Nathan *business executive, newspaper columnist*
Rubens, Sidney Michel *physicist, technical advisor*
Rudelius, William *marketing educator*
Sabath, Leon David *internist, educator*
Sackett, William Tecumseh, Jr. *electrical engineer*
Saeks, Allen Irving *lawyer*
Safley, James Robert *lawyer*
Salyer, Stephen Lee *broadcast executive*
Sampson, John Eugene *food company executive*
Sanger, Stephen W. *consumer products company executive*
Sanner, Royce Norman *lawyer*
Satorius, John Arthur *lawyer*
†Saunders, R. Reed *financial services company executive*
Savelkoul, Donald Charles *lawyer*
Sawchuk, Ronald John *pharmaceutical scientist, educator*
Scallen, Thomas Kaine *broadcasting executive*
Scheerer, Paul J. *lawyer*
Schnell, Robert Lee, Jr. *lawyer*
Schnobrich, Roger William *lawyer*
†Schoenke, Richard Warren *banker*
Schofield, William *psychologist, educator*
Schreiner, John Christian *economics consultant, software publisher*
Schuh, G(eorge) Edward *university dean, agricultural economist*
Schultz, Louis Edwin *management executive*
Schwartzbauer, Robert Alan *lawyer*
Scott, Robert Lee *speech educator*
Scoville, James Griffin *economics educator*
Scriven, L. E(dward), II *chemical engineering educator, scientist*
Seaman, William Casper *news photographer*
Serrin, James Burton *mathematics educator*
Shapiro, Burton Leonard *experimental pathologist, geneticist, educator*
Shapiro, Fred Louis *physician, educator*
Shaughnessy, Thomas William *librarian, consultant*
Sheehy, Lee Edward *lawyer*
†Shipp, Roger Lee *finance company executive*
Shively, William Phillips *political scientist, educator*
Shnider, Bruce Jay *lawyer*
Silverman, Robert Joseph *lawyer*
Skrowaczewski, Stanislaw *conductor, composer*
Slagle, James Robert *computer science educator*
Slorp, John S. *academic administrator*

†Slovut, Gordon *reporter*
†Smetanka, Mary Jane *reporter*
Smith, Eldred Reid *library educator*
†Smyrl, William H. *chemistry educator*
Sonkowsky, Robert Paul *classicist, educator, actor*
Sorbo, Allen Jon *actuary, consultant*
Sowada, Alphonse Augustus *bishop*
Sparrow, Ephraim Maurice *mechanical engineering scientist, educator*
Speer, David James *public relations executive*
Spencer, David James *lawyer*
†Spinner, Robert Keith *hospital administrator*
Spoor, William Howard *food company executive*
†Sprenger, Gordon M. *hospital administrator*
Staba, Emil John *pharmacognosy and medicinal chemistry educator*
Steilen, James R. *lawyer*
Stein, Bob *professional basketball team executive*
Sterling, Raymond Leslie *civil engineering educator, researcher, consultant*
Stern, Leo G. *lawyer*
†Strickler, Jeff *newspaper movie critic*
Stroup, Stanley Stephenson *lawyer, educator*
Struyk, Robert John *lawyer*
Stubbs, Jan Didra *travel industry executive*
Stuebner, James Cloyd *real estate developer, contractor*
Sullivan, Austin P(adraig), Jr. *diversified food company executive*
Sullivan, Michael Patrick *food service executive*
†Susanka, Sarah Hills *architect*
Sveinson, Pamela J. *human resources executive*
Swaiman, Kenneth Fred *pediatric neurologist, educator*
Swanson, Lloyd Oscar *former savings and loan association executive*
Swartz, Donald Everett *television executive*
†Swatsky, Ben *church administrator*
Swenson, Donald Craig *lawyer*
Symchych, Janice M. *lawyer*
Szalapski, Judith Raines *nursing administrator*
Tagatz, George Elmo *obstetrician, gynecologist, educator*
Teachout, Noreen Ruth *writer*
Thomas, Margaret Jean *clergywoman, religious research consultant*
Thompson, Clarence Miles, Jr. *advertising executive*
Thompson, Theodore Robert *pediatric educator*
Thompson, William Moreau *radiologist, educator*
Thornton, John T. *corporate financial executive*
Tinkham, Thomas W. *lawyer*
Todd, John Joseph *lawyer*
†Tompkins, Richard Weller, Jr. *advertising executive*
Tordoff, Harrison Bruce *retired zoologist, educator*
Torres, Fernando *physician, educator*
Toscano, James Vincent *medical foundation administrator*
Toupin, Harold Ovid *chemical company executive*
Tracy, James Donald *historian*
Tree, David L. *advertising agency executive*
Trestman, Frank D. *distribution company executive*
Trucano, Michael *lawyer*
Truhlar, Donald Gene *chemist, educator*
Tufte, Obert Norman *retired research executive*
Turner, John Gosney *insurance company executive*
Ueland, Sigurd, Jr. *lawyer*
Vander Molen, Thomas Dale *lawyer*
†Van Housen, Thomas Corwin, III *architect, designer, builder*
†Vaughan, Peter H. *theater critic*
Vecoli, Rudolph John *history educator*
†Vernier, Robert Lawrence *physician, educator*
Viera, James Joseph *financial executive*
†Wade, Lewis V. *mineral research director*
Wahoske, Michael James *lawyer*
†Wainwright, Charles Anthony *advertising company executive*
Waldera, Wayne Eugene *crisis management specialist*
†Waller, Joel N. *consumer products executive*
Wallin, Winston Roger *manufacturing company executive*
†Walsh, Paul S. *food products executive*
Walter, Frank Sherman *retired health care corporation executive*
Walters, Glen Robert *banker*
Wang, L. Edwin *church official*
Ward, David Allen *sociology educator*
Ward, Wallace Dixon *medical educator*
Ware, D. Clifton *singer, educator*
Warner, William Hamer *applied mathematician*
Watson, Catherine Elaine *journalist*
Watson, Dennis Wallace *microbiology educator, scientist*
†Watson, Stephen E. *department store executive*
Weisberg, Leonard R. *research and engineering executive*
Weiss, Gerhard Hans *German language educator*
Weiss, James Michael *financial analyst, portfolio manager*
Wescoe, W(illiam) Clarke *physician*
White, James George *pediatrician, hematologist, pathologist, educator*
White, Robert James *newspaper editor, columnist*
Whitehill, Clifford Lane *lawyer*
Wickesberg, Albert Klumb *retired management educator*
Wiener, Daniel Norman *psychologist*
Wild, John Julian *physician, director medical research institute*
Wille, Karin L. *lawyer*
Willes, Mark Hinckley *food industry executive*
Willis, Bruce Donald *lawyer*
Willis, Raymond Edson *strategic management and organization educator*
Wilson, Leonard Gilchrist *history of medicine educator*
Wilson, Theodore Alexander *engineering educator, respiratory physiologist*
Windhorst, John William, Jr. *lawyer*
Wine, Mark Philip *lawyer*
Winfield, David Mark *professional baseball player*
Winter, Robert Bruce *orthopaedic surgeon, educator*
Wirtschafter, Jonathan Dine *neuro-ophthalmology educator, scientist*
Wolfenson, Marv *professional basketball team executive*
†Wolff, Larry F. *dental educator, researcher*
Wollenberg, Bruce Frederick *electrical engineering educator, consultant*
Wood, Joseph George *neurobiologist, educator*
Woods, Robert Edward *lawyer*
Wright, Frank Gardner *newspaper editor*
Wright, (James) Garland *artistic director*
Wright, Herbert E(dgar), Jr. *geologist*
Wright, Michael William *wholesale food company executive*
Wurtele, Christopher Angus *paint and coatings company executive*
Wyman, James Thomas *petroleum company executive*
Youngblood, Richard Neil *columnist*
Younger, Judith Tess *lawyer, educator*
Yourzak, Robert Joseph *management consultant, engineer, educator*
Ysseldyke, James Edward *psychology educator, research center administrator*
Zaidi, Mahmood A. *economics educator*
Zalk, Robert H. *lawyer*
Ziebarth, E. William *news analyst, educator*

Minnetonka
Anderson, H(arry) Robert *insurance agent*
Carey, Gregory Brian *magazine publisher*
Ehlert, John Ambrose *publisher*
Gillies, Donald Richard *advertising agency and marketing consultant*
Henningsen, Peter, Jr. *diversified industry executive*
Johnson, Kay Durbahn *real estate manager, consultant*
List, Charles Edward *management and organization development consultant*
†Maxwell, Robert Oliver *insurance company executive*
Mc Guire, William W. *health maintenance organization executive*
Nagel, Paul Chester *historian, writer, lecturer*
Palmer, John Marshall *lawyer*
Randall, Dean Bowman *retired electronics manufacturing company executive*
†Robbins, Orem Olford *insurance company executive*
Rogers, James Devitt *judge*
†Sorensen, Stuart L. *actuary*
Vanstrom, Marilyn June *elementary education educator*

Moorhead
Anderson, Jerry Maynard *speech educator*
Cahill, James David *lawyer*
Coomber, James Elwood *English language educator*
Dille, Roland Paul *college president*
Gee, Robert LeRoy *agriculturist, dairy farmer*
Heuer, Gerald Arthur *mathematician, educator*
Noblitt, Harding Coolidge *political scientist, educator*
†Rimmereid, Arthur V. *bishop*
Sinner, George Albert *former state governor, farmer, corporate executive*
Sun, Li-Teh *economics educator*
Trainor, John Felix *economics educator*
Treumann, William Borgen *university dean*
Wai, Samuel Siu Ming *food product company financial executive*

Morris
Johnson, David Chester *university chancellor, sociology educator*
Kemble, Ernest Dell *psychology educator*

Mound
†Olson, Gen *state legislator*

New Brighton
Shier, Gloria Bulan *mathematics educator*

New Ulm
Lucker, Raymond Alphonse *bishop*

Nisswa
Marmas, James Gust *retired businees educator, retired college dean*

North Oaks
†Asch, Marc *state legislator, consultant*

Northfield
Appleyard, David Frank *mathematics, computer science educator*
Berwald, Helen Dorothy *education educator*
Buchwald, Caryl Edward *geology educator, environmental consultant, educational consultant*
Burton, Alice Jean *biology educator*
Casper, Barry Michael *physics educator*
Clark, Clifford Edward, Jr. *history educator*
Clark, William Hartley *political science educator*
Crouter, Richard Earl *religion educator*
Dittmann, Reidar *art educator*
Flaten, Robert Arnold *ambassador, retired*
Foss, Harlan Funston *religious education educator, academic administrator*
Haworth, Dale Keith *art history educator, gallery director*
Hong, Howard Vincent *library administrator, philosophy educator, editor, translator*
Hvistendahl, Joyce Kilmer *journalism and communications educator*
Lamson, George Herbert *economics educator*
Mason, Perry Carter *philosophy educator*
Metz, T(heodore) John *librarian, consultant*
†Neuville, Thomas M. *lawyer*
Noer, Richard J. *physics educator, researcher*
Ramette, Richard Wales *chemistry educator*
Schuster, Seymour *mathematician, educator*
Soule, George Alan *literature educator*
Sovik, Edward Anders *architect*
Will, Robert Erwin *economics educator*

Osseo
Haun, James William *chemical engineer, retired food company executive, consultant*
Hersch, Russell LeRoy *secondary education educator*
†Ramsey, Mark *school system administrator*

Owatonna
†Buxton, Charles Ingraham, II *insurance company executive*
†Nelson, Kirk N. *insurance company executive*

Paynesville
†Bertram, Jeff Nickolas *farmer, state legislator*

Pipestone
Scott, William Paul *lawyer*

Plymouth
Fowler, James D., Jr. *manufacturing company financial executive*
Friswold, Fred Ravndahl *manufacturing executive*
Froemming, Herbert Dean *retail executive*
Kahler, Herbert Frederick *diversified business executive*

Red Wing
Biederman, Charles Joseph *artist*
Seymour, Arthur Hallock *retired newspaper editor*
Vonch, David Lee *insurance agent, writer, financial consultant*

Redlake
Ceterski, Dorothy *nutritionist*

Redwood Falls
†Anderson, Charles D. *bishop*

Robbinsdale
Anderson, Scott Robbins *hospital administrator*

Rochester
Anderson, James Gerard *hospital administrator*
Bartholomew, Lloyd Gibson *physician*
Beahrs, Oliver Howard *surgeon*
Berge, Kenneth George *retired internist, educator*
Bisel, Harry Ferree *oncologist*
Boldan, Kelton John (Kelly Boldan) *editor, journalist*
†Brimijoin, William Stephen *pharmacology educator, neuroscience researcher*
Bulbulian, Arthur H. *biomedical scientist, medical graphics and facial prosthetics specialist*
Butt, Hugh Roland *gastroenterologist, educator*
Carlson, Roger Allan *manufacturing company executive, accountant*
Corbin, Kendall Brooks *physician, scientist*
Danielson, Gordon Kenneth, Jr. *cardiovascular surgeon, educator*
DeRemee, Richard Arthur *physician, educator, researcher*
Douglass, Bruce E. *physician*
Du Shane, James William *physician, educator*
Engel, Andrew George *neurologist*
Feldt, Robert Hewitt *pediatric cardiologist, educator*
Gastineau, Clifford Felix *retired physician*
Gervais, Sister Generose *hospital consultant*
Gilchrist, Gerald Seymour *pediatric hematologist, oncologist, educator*
Gleich, Gerald Joseph *immunologist, medical scientist*
Gomez, Manuel Rodriguez *physician*
Gracey, Douglas Robert *physician, physiologist, educator*
Hattery, Robert R. *radiologist, educator*
†Hinckley, Michael Richards *marketing professional*
Hudson, Winthrop Still *minister, history educator*
Huffine, Coy Lee *retired chemical engineer, consultant*
Husband, Richard Lorin, Sr. *consulting company executive*
Kao, Pai Chih *clinical chemist*
Kempers, Roger Dyke *obstetrics and gynecology educator*
Key, Jack Dayton *librarian*
Keys, Thomas Edward *medical library consultant*
Kovach, John Stephen *oncologist, research center administrator*
Krom, Ruud Arne Finco *surgeon*
Kurland, Leonard Terry *epidemiologist educator*
Kyle, Robert Arthur *medical educator, oncologist*
Lantz, William Charles *lawyer*
†Larson, April U. *bishop*
Leachman, Roger Mack *librarian*
Leonard, David Arthur *hospital executive emeritus*
Lofgren, Karl Adolph *surgeon*
Lucas, Alexander Ralph *child psychiatrist, educator*
Malkasian, George Durand, Jr. *physician, educator*
Martin, Gordon Mather *physician, educator, administrator*
Martin, Maurice John *psychiatrist*
Mc Goon, Dwight Charles *retired surgeon, educator*
Michenfelder, John Donahue *anesthesiology educator*
Milner, Harold William *hotel executive*
Morlock, Carl Grismore *physician, medical educator*
Mulder, Donald William *physician, educator*
Muller, Sigfrid Augustine *dermatologist, educator*
Neel, Harry Bryan, III *surgeon, scientist, educator*
Nichols, Donald Richardson *medical educator*
†Nycklemoe, Glenn Winston *bishop*
Olsen, Arthur Martin *physician, educator*
Orwoll, Gregg S. K. *lawyer*
Payne, W(illiam) Spencer *retired surgeon*
Perry, Harold Otto *dermatologist*
Phillips, Sidney Frederick *gastroenterologist*
Pittelkow, Mark Robert *dermatology educator, researcher*
Polley, Howard Freeman *physician*
Pratt, Joseph Hyde, Jr. *surgeon*
Reed, Charles Emmett *internist, educator*
Reitemeier, Richard Joseph *physician*
Rosenow, Edward Carl, III *medical educator*
†Seeger, Ronald L. *lawyer*
Shepherd, John Thompson *physiologist*
Siekert, Robert George *neurologist*
†Spencer, Edson White *computer systems company executive*
Stillwell, G(eorge) Keith *physician*
Symmonds, Richard Earl *gynecologist*
Szurszewski, Joseph Henry *physiologist*
Tyce, Francis Anthony *hospital administrator, psychiatrist*
Waller, Robert Rex *ophthalmologist, educator, foundation executive*
Whisnant, Jack Page *neurologist*
Wicks, John R. *lawyer*
Wojcik, Martin Henry *foundation development official*
†Wood, Earl Howard *physiologist, educator*
Woods, John Elmer *plastic surgeon*

Roseville
Berry, James Frederick *biochemistry educator*

Saginaw
Stauber, Marilyn Jean *educator, consultant*

Saint Cloud
Berling, John George *academic dean*
Conroy, Robert Warren *psychiatrist*
†Frobenius, John Renan *hospital administrator*
Hanus, Jerome *bishop*
Henry, Edward LeRoy *former foundation executive, consultant, college president, public official*
Higgins, Robert Arthur *electrical engineer, educator, consultant*

Saint Joseph
O'Connell, Sister Colman *nun, college administrator, consultant*
Rowland, Howard Ray *mass communications educator*

Saint Louis Park
Dahl, Christopher T. *broadcasting executive*
†Dooley, David J. *elementary school principal*
Gerike, Ann Elizabeth *psychologist*
Knighton, David Reed *vascular surgeon, educator*
Rothenberg, Elliot Calvin *lawyer, writer*
Svendsbye, Lloyd August *college president, clergyman, educator*

Saint Paul
†Adkins, Betty A. *state legislator*
Alm, John Richard *beverage company executive*
Alsop, Donald Douglas *federal judge*
Andersen, Anthony L. *chemical company executive*
Andersen, Elmer Lee *manufacturing and publishing executive, former governor of Minnesota*
†Anderson, Ellen Ruth *state senator*
†Anderson, Tim *airport terminal executive*
Appelhof, Ruth Stevens *museum director, curator, art historian*
Archabal, Nina M(archetti) *historical society director*
Ashton, Sister Mary Madonna *healthcare administrator*
Assink, Brent E. *performing arts executive*
Baker, Donald Gardner *soil science educator*
†Baker, Thomas F. *agricultural grain company executive*
Barnwell, Franklin Hershel *zoology educator*
Baukol, Ronald Oliver *manufacturing company executive*
Benforado, David M. *environmental engineer*
†Benson, Joanne *state legislator*
†Berglin, Linda *state senator*
Betz, Charles W. *manufacturing company executive*
†Betzold, Donald Richard *state senator*
Bingham, Christopher *statistics educator*
Bjorklund, Frederick *savings and loan association executive*
†Blatz, Kathleen Ann *state legislator*
Bloomfield, Coleman *insurance company executive*
Bloomfield, Victor Alfred *biochemistry educator*
Boehnen, David Leo *grocery company executive, lawyer*
†Bothun, Donald Dean *controller*
Boudreau, James Lawton *insurance company executive*
†Boxmeyer, Donald Harold *columnist*
†Brushaber, George Karl *academic president, minister*
Burchell, Howard Bertram *retired physician, educator*
Burnside, Orvin Charles *agronomy educator, researcher*
Caldwell, Elwood Fleming *food science educator, researcher, editor*
Carlson, Arne Helge *governor*
†Carlson, Lyndon Richard *state legislator, educator*
Checchi, Alfred A. *airline company executive*
Cheng, H(wei) H(sien) *agriculture and environmental science educator*
Chiang, Huai Chang *entomologist, educator*
†Christison, Richard James *advertising company executive*
Clapp, C(harles) Edward *research chemist, soil biochemistry educator*
Clary, Bradley Grayson *lawyer, educator*
Close, Elizabeth Scheu *architect*
Close, Winston Arthur *retired architect*
Collins, Theodore Joseph *lawyer, educator*
Corn, Joseph Edward, Jr. *arts management consultant*
Crippin, Byron Miles, Jr. *lawyer, religious organization professional, consultant*
Crookston, Robert Kent *agronomy educator*
Czarnecki, Caroline MaryAnne *veterinary anatomy educator*
Czarniecki, Myron James, III *art museum director, cultural planner*
Dahl, Reynold Paul *agricultural economics educator*
Dalton, Howard Edward *accounting executive*
Daly, Joseph Leo *law educator*
Davis, Margaret Bryan *paleoecology researcher, educator*
†Dawkins, Andrew John *lawyer*
Dennis, Clarence *surgeon, educator*
†Desimone, Livio Diego *diversified manufacturing company executive*
Devney, John Leo *lawyer*
Diesch, Stanley La Verne *veterinarian, educator*
Dietz, Charlton Henry *lawyer*
†Dille, Stephen Everett *farmer, state legislator, veterinarian*
Doctor, Kenneth Jay *editor*
Doermann, Humphrey *foundation administrator*
Doyle, Terence Nicholas *lawyer*
Dunlop, Robert Hugh *veterinary medicine educator*
Dyrstad, Joanell M. *lieutenant governor*
Ebert, Robert Alvin *retired lawyer, retired airline executive*
Edwards, Jesse Efrem *physician, educator*
Ek, Alan Ryan *forestry educator*
†Elrod, Bernett Richard (Sam Elrod) *newspaper editor*
Emeagwali, Philip Chukwurak *computer scientist, educator, mathematician, researcher*
Enfield, Franklin D. *geneticist*
Engle, Donald Edward *retired railway executive, lawyer*
Estenson, Noel K. *gas, oil industry executive*
Faricy, Richard Thomas *architect*
Farnum, Sylvia Arlyce *physical chemist*
Feinberg, David Erwin *publishing company executive*
Fesler, David Richard *foundation director*
Fingerson, Leroy Malvin *corporate executive, engineer*
Finnegan, John Robert, Sr. *retired newspaper executive*
†Flynn, Carol *state legislator*
Flynn, Harry Joseph *bishop*
†Fogg, James W. *printing company executive*
Frame, Clarence George *retired oil and gas refining company executive*
†Frederickson, Dennis Russel *state legislator, farmer*
Friel, Bernard Preston *lawyer*
Fryxell, David Allen *publishing executive, newspaper editor*
Fuller, Benjamin Franklin *physician, educator*
Galvin, Michael John, Jr. *lawyer*
†Garcia, Astrid J. *personnel director*
Garretson, Donald Everett *retired manufacturing company executive*
Gavin, Robert Michael, Jr. *college president*
Gehrz, Robert Gustave *retired railroad executive*

Geis, Jerome Arthur lawyer, legal educator
Goff, Lila Johnson historical society administrator
Goodman, Lawrence Eugene structural analyst, educator
Goodrich, Leon Raymond lawyer
Graham, Charles John university educator, former university president
Green, Philip Bevington publishing company executive
†Greiling, Marion Gail (Mindy Greiling) state legislator
Grieve, Pierson MacDonald specialty chemicals and services company executive
Griffin, Judith Ann strategic planning and operating executive
Growe, Joan Anderson state official
†Gutknecht, Gilbert William, Jr. state legislator, auctioneer
Halverson, Richard Paul investment management company executive
Hammond, Frank Joseph lawyer
†Hansen, L(eslie) B. agricultural studies educator
Hansen, Robyn L. lawyer
Hanson, Allen Dennis grain marketing and processing cooperative executive
Hardman, James Charles lawyer, motor carrier executive
†Haukoos, Melvin Robert state representative
Haverty, Harold V. forms and check printing company executive
Heidenreich, Douglas Robert lawyer
Henry, John Thomas retired newspaper executive
Herman, William Sparkes zoology educator
Hill, James Stanley computer consulting company executive
Holbert, Sue Elisabeth archivist, writer, consultant
Hopper, David Henry religion educator
Hubbard, Stanley Stub broadcast executive
Huber, Sister Alberta college president
Hughes, Jerome Michael state senator, educator
Humphrey, Hubert Horatio, III state attorney general
Hunstad, Robert Edward insurance company executive
Ivey, Elizabeth S. acoustician, physicist
Jensen, James Robert dentist, educator
Jessup, Paul Frederick financial economist, educator
†Johnson, Janet B. state legislator
Johnson, Kenneth Harvey veterinary pathologist
Johnson, Paul Oren lawyer
Jones, C. Paul lawyer, educator
Jones, Richard Lamar entomology educator
Jones, Thomas Neal manufacturing executive, mechanical engineer
Kane, Lucile Marie archivist, historian
Kane, Patricia Lanegran language professional, educator
Kane, Stanley Phillip insurance company executive
Kane, Thomas Patrick lawyer
Kaner, Harvey Sheldon lawyer, executive
Keffer, Charles Joseph academic administrator
Keillor, Garrison Edward writer, radio host, storyteller
Keith, Alexander MacDonald state supreme court chief justice
Kenyon, Jane Jennifer poet, writer
Kirwin, Kenneth F. law educator
Kishel, Gregory Francis federal judge
Kling, William Hugh broadcasting executive
Kommedahl, Thor plant pathology educator
†Krueger, Richard Arnold state legislator
Kyle, Richard H(ouse) federal judge
Lay, Donald Pomeroy federal judge
Leatherdale, Douglas West insurance company executive
Lebedoff, Jonathan Galanter federal judge
Lehr, Lewis Wylie diversified manufacturing company executive
Lein, Malcolm Emil architect
†Leppik, Margaret W. legislator
Levi, Arlo Dane lawyer
Lillehei, Clarence Walton surgeon
Ling, Joseph Tso-Ti manufacturing company executive, environmental engineer
Loken, James Burton federal judge
†Long, Dee state legislator
Luis, Juanita Bolland lawyer, insurance company executive
Lund, Bert Oscar, Jr. publisher
Lundy, Walker newspaper editor
†Lynch, Teresa Ann state legislator
MacDonald, Roderick library director
Maclin, Alan Hall lawyer
MacTaggart, Terrence Joseph academic administrator
Magee, Paul Terry geneticist and molecular biologist, college dean
†Magnuson, Norris Alden librarian, history educator
Magnuson, Paul Arthur federal judge
Markwardt, Kenneth Marvin former chemical company executive
†Marty, John state senator, writer
Mather, Richard Burroughs retired Chinese language and literature educator
Matteson, Robert Eliot former college administrator
McGrath, Michael Alan state government officer
McKinnell, Robert Gilmore zoology, genetics and cell biology educator
McLaughlin, David Jordan botanist
McMillan, Mary Bigelow retired minister, volunteer
McNeely, John J. lawyer
Merrill, Arthur Lewis theology educator
†Mondale, Theodore Adams state senator
†Murphy, Mary C. state legislator
†Murphy, Steven Leslie state senator, utilities company official
Murray, Peter Bryant English language educator
Nash, Nicholas David retailing executive
Nicholson, Morris Emmons, Jr. metallurgist, educator
Noel, Franklin Linwood federal magistrate judge
Nugent, Daniel Eugene business executive
Nugent, G. Eugene manufacturing company executive
Oppenheimer, James Richard lawyer
†Orfield, Myron Willard, Jr. state legislator, educator
†Osman, Stephen Eugene historic site administrator
Osnes, Larry G. academic administrator
Ostby, Ronald dairy and food products company executive
†Ostman, Eleanor A. food writer
†Ousley, James E. computer company executive
Palmer, Roger Raymond accounting educator
Pampusch, Anita Marie academic administrator
†Pappas, Sandra L. state legislator
†Pariseau, Patricia state senator
Parisi, Franklin Joseph communications executive
Paulus, Stephen Harrison composer
Pendergast, Edward Gaylord insurance company executive
Peterson, James Lincoln museum executive
Peterson, Robert Austin manufacturing company executive retired
Peterson, Willis Lester economics educator
Phillips, Ronald Lewis plant geneticist, educator
Popovich, Peter Stephen lawyer, former state supreme court chief justice
Powell, Linda state education official
Powers, David Richard educational administrator
Preus, David Walter bishop, minister
†Rafferty, Craig Elliot architect, educator
Rastogi, Anil Kumar medical device manufacturer executive
Reardon, Robert Joseph financial corporation executive
Rebane, John T. lawyer
Ridder, Bernard Herman, Jr. newspaper publisher
Roach, John Robert archbishop
Robertson, Jerry Earl retired mining and manufacturing company executive
†Robertson, Martha Rappaport state senator, consultant
Rogosheske, Walter Frederick former state justice
Rosengren, William R. lawyer, corporation executive
Rossmann, Jack Eugene psychology educator
Rothmeier, Steven George merchant banker
Rowe, Clarence John psychiatrist
Rusch, Thomas William manufacturing executive
Ruttan, Vernon Wesley agricultural economist
Ryan, Lehan Jerome lawyer
Schafer, John Francis plant pathologist
†Schmitt, Michael A. agronomist, educator
Schultz, Alvin Leroy internist, endocrinologist, health science facility administrator
†Segal, Gloria May retired state legislator
Seymour, McNeil Vernam lawyer
Shannon, Michael Edward specialty chemical company executive
Sippel, William Leroy lawyer
†Smith, Steve C. lawyer, state legislator
†Solberg, Loren Albin state legislator, secondary education educator
Spear, Allan Henry state senator, historian, educator
Stewart, James Brewer historian, author, college administrator
Stewart, Melville Yorke philosophy educator
†Sullivan, William E. public relations executive
†Sviggum, Steven A. farmer, state representative
Tecco, Romuald Gilbert Louis Joseph violinist, concertmaster
Titus, Jack L. pathologist, educator
Troske, L. A. insurance executive
†Ursu, John Joseph lawyer
Vaughn, John Rolland auditor
†Vellenga, Kathleen Osborne state legislator
†Wagenius, Jean state representative
Wagner, Mary Margaret library and information science educator
Wahl, Rosalie E. state supreme court justice
†Walker, Charles Thomas physicist, educator
Walton, Matt Savage geologist, educator
Washburn, Donald Arthur lawyer, travel industry executive
Weiner, Carl Dorian historian
Wendt, Hans Werner life scientist
Whelpley, Dennis Porter lawyer
Williams, Chester Arthur, Jr. insurance educator
Williams, Phillip Stephen banker
Wilson, Gary L. air transportation executive
Wollner, Thomas Edward manufacturing company executive
†Wyse, Donald L. agronomist, educator
Zammit, John P. financial planner
Zirbes, Mary Kenneth social justice ministry coordinator
Zylstra, Stanley James farmer, food company executive

Saint Peter
Haeuser, Michael John library administrator
Mc Rostie, Clair Neil economics educator
Nelsen, William Cameron foundation president, former college president
†Ostrom, Don state legislator, political science educator

Scandia
Borchert, John Robert geography educator

Shoreview
Briggs, Rodney Arthur agronomist, consultant

Slayton
Anderson, Merlyn Dean lawyer

South Saint Paul
†Pugh, Thomas Wilfred lawyer

Spring Grove
Hellyer, Clement David writer

Stillwater
†Anderson, Burnell principal
O'Brien, Daniel William lawyer, corporation executive
Pollack, Joseph diversified company executive
Sowman, Harold Gene ceramic engineer, researcher

Victoria
Courtney, Eugene Whitmal computer company executive

Virginia
†Damberg, John Paul architect
Knabe, George William, Jr. pathologist, educator

Waseca
Frederick, Edward Charles university official

Waubun
Christensen, Marvin Nelson venture capitalist

Wayzata
Alton, Howard Robert, Jr. lawyer, real estate and food company executive
Blodgett, Frank Caleb food company executive, retired
Detlefsen, Guy-Robert management consultant
Fish, James Stuart college dean, advertising consultant
Hoffman, Gene food company executive, consultant
Judkins, Donald Ward retired banker, art historian
Mithun, Raymond O. advertising agency executive, banker, real estate and insurance executive
Shannon, James Patrick foundation consultant, retired food company executive
Swanson, Donald Frederick retired food company executive

White Bear Lake
Gutchë, Gene composer
Holmen, Reynold Emanuel chemist
Williams, Julie Belle psychiatric social worker

Willmar
Zitterkopf, Irvin Leroy sugar manufacturing company executive

Winona
DeThomasis, Brother Louis college president
Finucan, J(ohn) Thomas priest, religious institution administrator
Krueger, Darrell William academic administrator
Preska, Margaret Louise Robinson institute executive
Towers, James Mc education educator
Vlazny, John George bishop

Woodybury
†Clancy, Robert J. insurances company executive

MISSISSIPPI

Aberdeen
Davidson, Glen Harris federal judge
Davis, Jerry Arnold judge
Senter, Lyonel Thomas, Jr. federal judge

Amory
Brown, James Leaman, Jr. vocational education educator
†Bryan, Hob lawyer, state senator

Bay Saint Louis
Sidders, Patrick Michael financial executive
Skramstad, Robert Allen oceanographer

Biloxi
Bramlette, David C., III federal judge
Gex, Walter Joseph, III federal judge
Hagood, Annabel Dunham speech communication educator, communication consultant
Hash, John Frank broadcasting executive
Howze, Joseph Lawson Edward bishop
Weeks, Roland, Jr. newspaper publisher

Brandon
Buckley, Frank Wilson newspaper executive
Samsel, Maebell Scroggins (Midge Samsel) paralegal

Canton
Hill, Ronald Guy craft school director

Carriere
Wilson, Raymond Clark former hospital executive

Carrollton
McConnell, David Stuart retired federal executive

Clarksdale
Curtis, Chester Harris lawyer, retired bank executive

Cleveland
Alexander, William Brooks lawyer, former state senator
Cash, William McKinley history educator
Howorth, Lucy Somerville lawyer
Thornton, Larry Lee psychotherapist, educator
Wyatt, Forest Kent university president

Clinton
Bigelow, Martha Mitchell retired historian
†Montgomery, Keith Norris, Sr. insurance executive, state legislator
Nobles, Lewis college president

Columbia
†Simmons, Miriam Quinn state legislator

Columbus
Fant, Joseph Lewis, III retired junior college president
†Ivy, Robert Adams, Jr. architect, writer
†Kaye, Samuel Harvey architect, educator
Rent, Clyda Stokes university president
Stringer, Mary Evelyn art historian, educator

Diamond Head
Jaumot, Frank Edward, Jr. automobile parts manufacturing company executive

Fayette
La Salle, Arthur Edward historic foundation executive

Fulton
†Mills, Michael Paul lawyer, state legislator

Greenville
†Cameron, Thomas F., III advertising and realty company executive

Greenwood Springs
†Huskey, William Jerome state legislaator, farmer, retired army officer

Gulfport
Allen, Harry Roger lawyer
Daffron, Martha retired education educator
†Diaz, Oliver E., Jr. lawyer, state representative
†Guice, Daniel Dicks, Jr. state legislator
Harral, John Menteith lawyer
†Hewes, William Gardner, III insurance executive, real estate agent, legislator
Holleman, Boyce lawyer
Jones, Carol Ann psychology educator
Pickering, Shelbie Jean mortgage loan executive
Russell, Dan M., Jr. federal judge
Schloegel, George Anthony banker
Thatcher, George Robert banker
Walker, Harry Grey retired state supreme court justice
Yeager, Andrea Wheaton editor

Hattiesburg
Barr, Jacob Dexter banker
Burrus, John N(ewell) sociology educator
Gonzales, John Edmond history educator
†Gordon, Granville Hollis church official
Lucas, Aubrey Keith university president
Noblin, Charles Donald clinical psychologist, educator
Noonkester, James Ralph retired college president
Odom, Janet Lynn postanesthesia nurse
Pickering, Charles W. federal judge
Rawlings, Paul C. retired government official
Riley, Thomas Jackson lawyer
Saucier Lundy, Karen college dean, educator
Sims, James Hylbert English educator, former university administrator
Traylor, Joan Sadler interior design educator
Woodall, Lowery A. hospital administrator

Holly Springs
Beckley, David Lenard academic administrator

Indianola
Matthews, David clergyman
Powell, Anice Carpenter librarian

Itta Bena
Henderson, Robbye Robinson library director
Ware, William Levi physical education educator, researcher

Jackson
Achord, James Lee gastroenterologist, educator
Allin, John Maury bishop
Ball, Carroll Raybourne anatomist, medical educator, researcher
†Ballard, Thomas Hickok library director
Baltz, Richard Jay health care company executive
Barbour, William H., Jr. federal judge
Barksdale, Rhesa Hawkins federal judge
Barnett, Robert Glenn lawyer
Batson, Blair Everett pediatrician, educator
Biggs, Thomas Jones architect
Bloom, Sherman pathologist, educator
†Bourdeaux, Norma Sanders state legislator
†Bray, Donald Lawrence minister
Briggs, Eddie J. state official
Brooks, Thomas Joseph, Jr. preventive medicine educator
Burnham, Tom state school system administrator
Burns, Robert, Jr. architect, freelance writer, artist
Burwell, Dudley Sale retired investment executive and food executive
Butler, George Harrison lawyer
Capers, Charlotte state archives director emeritus
†Carter, David Ray banker
Clark, Charles lawyer
Cruse, Julius Major, Jr. pathologist
Currier, Robert David neurologist
Dallas, Thomas Abraham retired utility company executive
Dean, Jack Pearce retired insurance company executive
Ditto, (John) Kane mayor
†Dodson, William H. school system administrator
Downing, Margaret Mary newspaper editor
Draper, Edgar psychiatrist
Dubbert, Patricia Marie psychologist
†Ford, Timothy Alan state representative
Fordice, Daniel Kirkwood, Jr. (Kirk Fordice) governor, construction company executive, engineer
†Fordice, Kirk governor
Forks, Thomas Paul osteopathic physician
Fuselier, Louis Alfred lawyer
Galloway, Patricia Kay systems analyst, ethnohistorian
Gray, Duncan Montgomery, Jr. retired bishop
†Green, Tomie Turner lawyer, state legislator
†Gunn, F. Michael direct marketing professional
Guyton, Arthur Clifton physician, educator
Halaris, Angelos psychiatrist, educator
†Hall, Dick state legislator
†Harden, Alice V. state legislator
Harmon, George Marion college president
Harrison, Robert Vernon McElroy architect
Hawkins, Armis Eugene state supreme court chief justice
Henderson, W. Guy editor, minister
Hodge, Elbert Clifton, Jr. lawyer
†Holman, William Henry, Jr. retail executive
Hosemann, C. Delbert, Jr. lawyer
Houck, William Russell bishop
Hutchison, William Forrest parasitologist, educator
Irby, Stuart Charles, Jr. construction company executive
Jolly, E. Grady federal judge
†Kingsley, Oliver Dowling, Jr. energy company executive
†Lampton, Leslie B., Sr. oil industry executive
Langford, James Jerry lawyer
Lee, Tom Stewart federal judge
Lewis, Robert Edwin, Jr. pathology immunology educator, researcher
†Liles, William Jackson, Jr. transportation executive
Lilly, Thomas Gerald lawyer
Mabus, Raymond Edwin, Jr. ambassador, former governor
Malloy, James Matthew health care consultant
McCarty, William Bonner, Jr. retail grocery executive
Mc Gregor, Donald Thornton newspaper editor, journalist
†McKnight, William Edwin minister
McMillan, Howard Lamar, Jr. banker
†Miller, Hainon Alfred lawyer, investor
Moize, Jerry Dee lawyer
Molpus, Dick state official
Moore, Mike state attorney general
Morrison, Francis Secrest physician
Nelson, Norman Crooks surgeon, academic administrator, educator
Parks, James Franklin, Jr. librarian
Pearce, David Harry biomedical engineer
Penick, George Dial, Jr. foundation executive
Phillips, George L. prosecutor
Pittman, Edwin Lloyd state supreme court justice
†Powell, Amy Tuck state senator, lawyer
Prather, Lenore Loving state supreme court presiding justice
Ray, H. M. lawyer
†Rayborn, William Lee state senator

†Reeves, John Raymond *lawyer, state legislator*
Robinson, E. B., Jr. *bank executive*
Saunders, Doris Evans *editor, educator, business executive*
Seltzer, Ada May *librarian, medical library director*
Sewell, Charles Haslett *banker*
Stampley, Norris Lochlen *former electric utility executive*
Stovall, Jerry (Coleman Stovall) *insurance company executive*
†Strum, Marvin Kent *medical center executive*
Stubbs, James Carlton *retired hospital administrator*
Sugg, Robert Perkins *former state supreme court justice*
Sullivan, Michael David *state supreme court justice*
Thrash, Edsel E. *educational administrator*
†Timmer, Wayne F. *architectural firm executive*
†Todd, Chris *photojournalist*
Tullos, John Baxter *banker*
Wall, Oscar Edward *chemical company executive*
Watts, John McCleave *financial services executive*
Welty, Eudora *author*
Williams, James Kelley *diversified resources company executive*
Williams, William Lane *university administrator, anatomist*
Wingate, Henry Travillion *federal judge*
Winter, William Forrest *former governor, lawyer*
Wise, Sherwood Willing *lawyer*
†Woodfield, Clyde V. *senator*
Woodrell, Frederick Dale *health care executive*

Kosciusko
Kearley, F. Furman *minister, religious educator, magazine editor*

Laurel
†Howell, Stephen Wayne *church organization administrator, clergyman*

Mc Comb
†Bancroft, Joseph C. *metal products company executive*

Meridian
Blackwell, Cecil *science association executive*
Church, George Millord *real estate executive*
†Drawdy, Larry A. *school system administrator*
Marshall, John Steven *artist, educator, museum administrator*
Phillips, Patricia Jeanne *retired educational administrator, consultant*

Mississippi State
Bishop, Calvin Thomas *landscape architect, educator*
Cliett, Charles Buren *aeronautical engineer, educator, academic administrator*
Clynch, Edward John *political science educator, researcher*
Donaghy, Henry James *English literature educator, academic administrator*
Dorough, H. Wyman *toxicologist, educator, consultant*
Hawkins, Merrill Morris *college administrator*
Hodges, Harry F. *agronomist educator, plant physiologist*
Howell, Everette Irl *physicist, educator*
Jacob, Paul Bernard, Jr. *electrical engineering educator*
Lee, John Edward, Jr. *university administrator*
Leyden, Dennis Roger *economics educator*
Lowery, Charles Douglas *history educator, academic administrator*
†Mabry, Donald Joseph *university administrator, history educator*
†Man, Cameron Robert James *landscape architect*
Martin, Edward Curtis, Jr. *landscape architect, educator*
McRae, John Malcolm *college dean, architect*
Nash, Henry Warren *marketing educator*
Parrish, William Earl *history educator*
†Parsons, George William *city planner, educator*
Powe, Ralph Elward *university administrator*
Shillingsburg, Peter LeRoy *English language educator*
Stennis, John Cornelius *former senator*
†Taylor, Clayborne Dudley *engineering educator*
†Thompson, Joe Floyd *aerospace engineer, researcher*
†Thompson, Warren S. *dean, academic administrator*
Vasek, Richard Jim *academic dean*
Wiltrout, Ann Elizabeth *foreign language educator*
Zacharias, Donald Wayne *university president*

Mize
†Thames, Billy Howard *state senator*

Monticello
Allen, Frank Carroll *retired banker*

Natchez
Parker, Mary Evelyn *former state treasurer*

New Albany
†Graham, Walter A. *state legislator, agricultural products executive*

Ocean Springs
Bates, Mable Johnson *business technology educator*
McIlwain, Thomas David *laboratory director, marine biologist, educator*
McNulty, Matthew Francis, Jr. *health sciences and health services administrator, educator, university administrator, consultant, horse and cattle breeder*

Oxford
Biggers, Neal Brooks, Jr. *federal judge*
†Foster, George Rainey *soil erosion research scientist*
Moorhead, Sylvester Andrew *education educator retired*
†Mutchler, Calvin Kendal *hydraulic research engineer*

Pascagoula
Carlson, John Henry *lawyer*
Colingo, Joe Ross *lawyer*
Corben, Herbert Charles *physicist, educator*

Pass Christian
Clark, John Walter, Jr. *shipping company executive*
McCardell, James Elton *retired naval officer*

Perkinston
Parker, Ora Dean Simmons *elementary school educator*

Ridgeland
Dye, Bradford Johnson, Jr. *former lieutenant governor of Mississippi, lawyer, partner*
Morgan, Madel Jacobs *retired archives and library administrator*

Ripley
Clawson, John Addison *financier, investor*

Rose Hill
Young, Thomas Daniel *retired humanities educator, author*

Shelby
Campany, Sarah Wilson *special education educator*

Southaven
†Ready, George Banks *lawyer*
Utroska, William Robert *veterinarian*

Starkville
Carley, Charles Team, Jr. *mechanical engineer*
Emerich, Donald Warren *retired chemistry educator*
†Ford, Robert MacDonald, III *architect, educator*
Loftin, Marion Theo *sociologist, educator*
Martin, Theodore Krinn *former university administrator*
Mercer, H. Dwight *university dean, veterinarian*
Priest, Melville Stanton *consulting hydraulic engineer*
Wolverton, Robert Earl *classics educator*
Yancey, Jimmie Isaac *marketing professional*

Stennis Space Center
Baker, Robert Andrew *environmental research scientist*
Gaffney, Paul Golden, II *military officer*
Mc Call, Jerry Chalmers *government official*
†Royestess, Roy *aerospace science administrator*

Stoneville
†Hardee, D. D. *laboratory administrator*
†Putnam, Paul Adin *government agency official*
†Ranney, Carleton David *plant pathology researcher, administrator*

Tupelo
Bush, Fred Marshall, Jr. *lawyer*
†Jarvis, Morris O. *fabric company executive*
†Neelly, Edwin Clyde, III *banker*
†Patterson, Aubrey Burns, Jr. *banker*
Radojcsics, Anne Parsons *librarian*
Smith, John Willis *banker*

University
Cooker, Philip George *psychology educator*
†Ferris, William Reynolds *folklore educator*
Hannah, Barry *educator, writer*
Horton, Thomas Edward, Jr. *mechanical engineering educator*
Jordan, Winthrop Donaldson *historian, educator*
Keiser, Edmund Davis, Jr. *biologist, educator*
Kiger, Joseph Charles *history educator*
Leary, William James *educational administrator*
Meador, John Milward, Jr. *university dean*
Paterson, Alan Leonard Tuke *mathematics educator*
Sam, Joseph *retired university dean*
Smith, Allie Maitland *university dean*
Turner, Robert Gerald *university chancellor*
Walton, Gerald Wayne *university administrator*

Vicksburg
Albritton, Gayle Edward *structural engineer*
Gunnison, Douglas *microbiologist, researcher*
†Herrmann, Frank A., Jr. *hydraulics laboratory director, researcher*
Mather, Bryant *research administrator*

West Point
†Turner, Bennie L. *lawyer*

Whitfield
Morton, James Irwin *hospital administrator*

Yazoo City
Arnold, David Walker *chemical company executive, engineer*
Breese, Frank Chandler, III *newsprint company executive, lawyer*
Brown, Marion Lipscomb, Jr. *publisher, retired chemical company executive*
Hawkins, William F. *chemical company executive*

MISSOURI

Ballwin
†Banton, Stephen Chandler *lawyer*
Bodner, Herbert *engineering and construction executive*
Cornell, William Daniel *mechanical engineer*
†Kern, Gary L. *golf course architect*
Tyler, William Howard, Jr. *advertising executive*

Blue Springs
†Foudree, Charles M. *financial executive*
Nelson, Freda Nell Hein *librarian*
†Olsson, Björn Eskil *railroad supply company executive*
Reed, Tony Norman *aviation company executive*

Bolivar
Jackson, James Larry *recreation educator*

Boonville
Cline, Dorothy May Stammerjohn (Mrs. Edward Wilburn Cline) *educator*

Branson
Williams, Andy *entertainer*

Bridgeton
Brock, Louis Clark *business executive, former professional baseball player*
Davis, Stephen John *public relations executive, automotive executive*
Joyner-Kersee, Jacqueline *track and field athlete*
McSweeney, Michael Terrence *manufacturing executive*
†Myers, William Killeen *marketing executive*

California
Wood, Mary Marie *business educator*

Camdenton
Mullens, William Reese *retired insurance company executive*

Cameron
Griffin, Bob Franklin *state legislator, lawyer*

Cape Girardeau
Blackwelder, Richard E(liot) *entomologist, zoology educator, archivist*
†Dahiya, Jai Narain *physics educator, researcher*

Carthage
Cornell, Harry M., Jr. *home furnishings company executive*
Jefferies, Robert Aaron, Jr. *furniture company executive, lawyer*
Wright, Felix E. *manufacturing company executive*

Cassville
†Melton, Emory Leon *state legislator, lawyer, publisher*

Centralia
Harmon, Robert Wayne *electrical engineering executive*
Lomo, Leif *electrical manufacturing company executive*

Chamois
†Townley, Merrill Moses *veterinarian, state legislator*

Chesterfield
Armstrong, Theodore Morelock *corporate executive*
Bowling, William Glasgow *language professional, educator*
Bradshaw, Stanley J. *financial holding company executive*
Carpenter, Will Dockery *chemical company executive*
Harbison, Earle Harrison, Jr. *chemical company executive*
Henry, Roy Monroe *financial planner*
Hunter, Harlen Charles *orthopedic surgeon*
†Jacobsen, James Conrad *apparel manufacturing executive*
†Klarich, David John *lawyer, state representative*
Liggett, Hiram Shaw, Jr. *retired diversified industry financial executive*
Malvern, Donald *retired aircraft manufacturing company executive*
Neiner, A(ndrew) Joseph *corporate executive*
Palazzi, Joseph L(azarro) *manufacturing executive*
†Plunkett, Larry Neil *electrical engineer*
Smith, Lawrence Abner *aeronautical engineer*
†Turley, Clarence M. *finance company executive*
Unterreiner, C. Martin *financial advisor*
Upbin, Hal Jay *consumer products executive*
Willis, Frank Edward *retired air force officer*
Yardley, John Finley *aerospace engineer*

Chillicothe
Hamilton, Max Chester *farmer, writer*

Clarkson Valley
McCarthy, Paul Fenton *aerospace executive, former naval officer*

Clayton
Belz, Mark *lawyer*
Buechler, Bradley Bruce *plastic processing company executive, accountant*
†Christner, Theodore Carroll *architect*
†Kohm, Barbara *principal*
Osterloh, Everett William *county official*
Turner, Terry Madison *architect*
Zimmerman, Harold Seymour *elementary school educator*

Clinton
†Deskins, Gary *school system administrator*
†Schemenauer, Robert George *accountant, state representative*

Columbia
Adams, Algalee Pool *college dean, art educator*
Alexander, Martha Sue *librarian*
Alexander, Thomas Benjamin *history educator*
Allen, William Cecil *physician, educator*
Almony, Robert Allen, Jr. *librarian, businessman*
Anderson, Donald Kennedy, Jr. *English educator*
Archer, Stephen Murphy *theater educator*
Atwater, James David *journalist, educator*
†Barbero, Giulio John *physician, educator*
Basu, Asit Prakas *statistician*
Bauman, John E., Jr. *chemistry educator*
Beem, John Kelly *mathematician, educator*
Biddle, Bruce Jesse *social psychologist, educator*
Bien, Joseph Julius *philosophy educator*
†Blaine, Edward H. *health science association administrator*
Blevins, Dale Glenn *agronomy educator*
Blount, Don H. *physiology educator*
Breimyer, Harold Frederick *agricultural economist*
Brown, Olen Ray *medical microbiology research educator*
Bryant, Lester R. *surgeon, educator*
Bunn, Ronald Freeze *political science educator, lawyer*
Burchett, Betty Martela *science education educator*
Burdick, Allan Bernard *geneticist*
Calabrese, Diane Marie *entomologist, writer*
Carroll, Carmal Edward *librarian, educator, clergyman*
†Coe, Edward Harold, Jr. *agronomist, educator, geneticist*
Colwill, Jack Marshall *physician, educator*
Darrah, Larry Lynn *plant breeder*
Davis, James O(thello) *physician, educator*
Day, Cecil LeRoy *agricultural engineering educator*
Decker, Wayne Leroy *meteorologist, educator*
Denney, Arthur Hugh *consultant*
Dolliver, Robert Henry *psychology educator*
Duncan, Donald Pendleton *retired forestry educator*
Eggers, George William Nordholtz, Jr. *anesthesiologist, educator*
Ethington, Raymond Lindsay *geology educator, researcher*
Finkelstein, Richard Alan *microbiologist*
Fisch, William Bales *lawyer*
Frisby, James Curtis *agricultural engineering educator*
Fulweiler, Howard Wells *language professional*
Gavan, James Anderson *anthropologist, educator*
Gehrke, Charles William *biochemistry educator*
Geiger, Louis George *historian*
Geiger, Mark Watson *management consultant*
Goodrich, James William *historian, association executive*
Gysbers, Norman Charles *education educator*
Hatley, Richard V(on) *education educator*
Heldman, Dennis Ray *engineering educator*
Hensley, Elizabeth Catherine *nutritionist, educator*
Hillman, Richard Ephraim *pediatrician, educator*
Ignoffo, Carlo Michael *insect pathologist-virologist*
Johns, William Davis, Jr. *geologist, educator*
Jones, William McKendrey *language professional, educator*
Kashani, Javad Hassan-Nejad *physician*
Kausler, Donald Harvey *psychology educator*
Kiesler, Charles Adolphus *psychologist, academic administrator*
Lago, Mary McClelland *English language educator, author*
Lambeth, Victor Neal *horticulturist, researcher*
Larson, Sidney *art educator, artist, writer, painting conservator*
Lenox, Mary Frances *academic dean*
LoPiccolo, Joseph *psychologist, educator, author*
†Martin, Mark Edward *molecular biologist, biochemist*
Mayer, Dennis Thomas *biochemist, educator*
McCollum, Clifford Glenn *college dean emeritus*
Mc Ginnes, Edgar Allen, Jr. *forestry educator*
Merilan, Charles Preston *dairy husbandry scientist*
Miller, Paul Ausborn *adult education educator*
†Mitchell, Roger Lowry *agronomy educator*
Monroe, Haskell M., Jr. *university professor*
Morehouse, Lawrence Glen *veterinarian, educational administrator*
†Moseley, Joe Lynn *lawyer, state legislator*
Mullen, Edward John, Jr. *Spanish language educator*
Nelson, Curtis Jerome *agronomist, educator*
Nikolai, Loren Alfred *accounting educator, author*
Overby, Osmund Rudolf *art historian, educator*
Palo, Nicholas Edwin *professional society administrator*
Parrigin, Elizabeth Ellington *lawyer*
Perkoff, Gerald Thomas *physician, educator*
Perry, Michael Clinton *physician, medical educator, academic administrator*
†Poehlmann, Carl John *agronomist, researcher*
Pringle, Oran Allan *mechanical and aerospace engineering educator*
†Puckett, C. Lin *plastic surgeon, educator*
Rabjohn, Norman *chemistry educator emeritus*
Ratti, Ronald Andrew *economics educator*
Reid, Loren Dudley *speech educator*
Rothwell, Robert Clark *agricultural products executive*
Rowlett, Ralph Morgan *archaeologist, educator*
Russell, George Albert *university president*
Sampson, Patsy Hallock *college president*
Schrader, Keith William *mathematician*
Silver, Donald *surgeon, educator*
Silvoso, Joseph Anton *accounting educator*
Sprinsteel, Frederick Neil *computer science educator*
Stephenson, Hugh Edward, Jr. *retired physician, educator*
Strickland, Arvarh Eunice *history educator*
Taft, William Howard *journalism educator*
†Thompson, Warren A. *mental health services educator, director*
Timberlake, Charles Edward *history educator*
Twaddle, Andrew Christian *sociology educator*
Unklesbay, Athel Glyde *geologist, educator*
Viswanath, Dabir Srikantiah *chemical engineer*
Wagner, Joseph Edward *veterinarian, educator*
Wagner, William Burdette *business educator*
Warder, Richard Currey, Jr. *mechanical aerospace engineering educator*
Weiss, James Moses Aaron *psychiatrist, educator*
Welliver, Warren Dee *lawyer, retired state supreme court justice*
Westbrook, James Edwin *lawyer, educator*
Wheeler, Otis V., Jr. *public school principal*
Williams, Frederick *statistics educator*
Witt, Ruth Elizabeth *retired museum administrator*
Witten, David Melvin *radiology educator*
Yanders, Armon Frederick *biological sciences educator, research administrator*
Yarwood, Dean Lesley *political science educator*
Yasuda, Hirotsugu Koge *chemical engineering professor*
Zemmer, Joseph Lawrence, Jr. *mathematics educator*

Crestwood
Reitter, Charles Andrew *personal financial planner*

Creve Coeur
Dodge, Paul Cecil *academic administrator*

Cuba
Work, Bruce Van Syoc *business consultant*

Eagle Rock
Rowan, Gerald Burdette *insurance company executive, lawyer*

Earth City
Anderhalter, Oliver Frank *educational organization executive*

Eminence
†Staples, Danny Lew *state senator*

Fairfax
Cleveland, Edna Charlotte *writer, typist*

Fenton
Baer, Robert J. *transportation company executive*
Korn, Irene Elizabeth *elementary education educator, consultant*
Maritz, William E. *communications company executive*
Stolar, Henry Samuel *corporate lawyer*

Florissant
†Bartlett, Robert James *principal*
Kelly, James Joseph *printing company executive*
Martin, Edward Brian *electrical engineer*

Ordinachev, Joann Lee *special education counselor and administrator*

Fort Leonard Wood
†Combs, Robert Kimbal *museum director*

Fortuna
Ramer, James LeRoy *civil engineer*

Fulton
Barnett, Jahnae Harper *academic administrator*
Davidson, Robert Laurenson Dashiell *college president emeritus, philatelist*

Gallatin
Wilsted, Joy *elementary education educator, reading specialist, consultant*

Grandview
Dietrich, William Gale *lawyer, real estate developer, consultant*
Justesen, Don Robert *psychologist*

Gravois Mills
Jones, Charles Edward *advertising executive*

Hale
†Danner, Steve *senator*

Hannibal
Dothager, Julie Ann *librarian*
Sweets, Henry Hayes, III *museum director*

Harrisonville
White, Ray William, Jr. *county official*

Hattiesburg
†Saucier, Gene Duane *state legislator, import/export company executive*

Hazelwood
†Bellar, Willis Franklin *bakery products company executive*
†McClintock, Eugene Jerome *minister*
Mohrmann, Robert E. *wholesale distribution executive*
†Rose, Joseph Hugh *clergyman*
†Seitz, Harold A. *supermarket executive*
Urshan, Nathaniel Andrew *minister, church administrator*

Highlandville
Pruter, Karl Hugo *bishop*

Hillsboro
Adkins, Gregory D. *academic administrator*

Independence
†Booth, Paul Wayne *minister*
Ferguson, John Wayne *library director*
†Ferguson, John Wayne, Sr. *librarian*
Hansen, Francis Eugene *minister*
†Henley, Robert Lee *school system administrator*
†Mack, Ronald J. *park superintendent*
†Mitchell, Earl Wesley *clergyman*
Potts, Barbara Joyce *historical society executive*
Sheehy, Howard Sherman, Jr. *minister*
Smith, Wallace Bunnell *physician, church official*
Strang, Marian Boundy *librarian*
Tyree, Alan Dean *clergyman*
Vaughan, Luva D. *motion picture theatre executive*
Walsh, Rodger John *lawyer*
Zobrist, Benedict Karl *library director, historian*

Jefferson City
Bartlett, Alex *lawyer*
Bartman, Robert E. *state education official*
Benton, W. Duane *judge*
Carnahan, Mel *governor, lawyer*
†Caskey, Harold Leroy *state senator*
†Clay, William Lacy, Jr. *state legislator*
Cook, Sam B. *banker*
Covington, Ann K. *lawyer, judge*
Deck, Robert Alan *state government official*
Deutsch, James Bernard *lawyer*
Donnelly, Robert True *retired state supreme court justice*
Ganey, Terry Joseph *journalist, author*
†Gaw, Robert Steven *lawyer, state representative*
†Griesheimer, John Elmer *state representative*
†Hale, David Clovis *state representative*
Holden, Bob *state official*
Holstein, John Charles *state supreme court justice*
†Karll, Jo Ann *state agency administrator, lawyer*
†Kauffman, Sandra Daley *state legislator*
†Kelley, Pat *minister, state legislator*
†Linton, William Carl *state legislator*
†Maxwell, Joe *state representative, lawyer*
Mc Auliffe, Michael F. *bishop*
†McCarthy, Karen P. *state representative*
†McCarthy, Thomas William, III *state senator*
McClain, Charles James *state educational administrator*
†McGee, Jacqueline T. *state legislator*
Moriarty, Judith Kay Spry *state official*
Nixon, Jeremiah W. (Jay Nixon) *state attorney general*
†Olson, Lawrence E. (Gene) *state representative*
Parr, Lloyd Byron *state official*
Robertson, Edward D., Jr. *state supreme court chief justice*
Rockelman, Georgia F(owler) Benz *retail furniture executive*
Scott, Gary Kuper *academic administrator*
†Smith, Todd Patrick *state legislator, marketing professional*
Tettlebaum, Harvey M. *lawyer*
†Treppler, Irene Esther *state senator*
†Waters, Stephen Russell *state legislator*
†Wible, Connie *state legislator*
†Wiggins, Harry *state senator, lawyer*
Wilson, Roger B. *lieutenant governor, school administrator*
Winn, Kenneth Hugh *archivist, historian*
†Witt, Gary Dean *state legislator*

Joplin
†Burke, Charles Don *church administrator, minister*
Fancher, Robert Burney *electric utility executive*
Gee, James David *minister*
Haley, David Alan *preferred provider organization executive*

Harris, Robert A. *music educator*
Hughes, Fred George *retired newspaper publisher*
Lamb, Robert Lewis *electric utility executive*
Malzahn, Ray Andrew *chemistry educator, university dean*
Pulliam, Frederick Cameron *educational administrator*
†Singleton, Marvin Ayers *otolaryngologist, senator*
†Vansell, Robert Edward *religious organization director*
Williams, Rex Enoch *international union representative*
†Wilson, Aaron Martin *religious studies educator, college executive*

Kahoka
Huffman, Robert Merle *insurance company executive*

Kansas City
Abdou, Nabih I. *physician, educator*
†Abend, Stephen Neil *architect*
Acheson, Allen Morrow *retired engineering executive*
Adam, Paul James *engineering company executive, mechanical engineer*
Allen, Marcus *professional football player*
Alt, John *football player*
Anderson, Christopher James *lawyer*
†Anderson, David *church administrator*
†Anderson, David Charles *media specialist*
Anderson, James Keith *retired magazine editor*
†Andrews, Kathleen W. *book publishing executive*
Appier, (Robert) Kevin *professional baseball player*
Aslin, M. M. *banker*
Ayres, John Samuel *chemical engineer*
Baker, John Russell *utilities executive*
Baker, Robert Thomas *interior designer*
Barnes, Donald Gayle *management consultant*
Barnes, Peter Crain *stockbroker*
Bartlett, D. Brook *federal judge*
Bartlett, Paul Dana, Jr. *agribusiness executive*
Bates, William Hubert *lawyer*
Batiuk, Thomas Martin *cartoonist*
Becker, Thomas Bain *lawyer*
Beckett, Theodore Charles *lawyer*
Beihl, Frederick *lawyer*
Benner, Richard Edward, Jr. *management and marketing consultant, investor*
†Berard, Dennis *church administrator*
†Berardi, J. F. *food products executive*
Berg, W. Robert *agricultural products company executive*
Berkley, Eugene Bertram (Bert Berkley) *envelope company executive*
Berkowitz, Lawrence M. *lawyer*
Berrey, Robert Wilson, III *lawyer, judge*
Bianchino, Bernard Anthony *lawyer*
†Bishop, Steven C. *protective services official*
Bixby, Walter E. *insurance company executive*
Black, John Sheldon *lawyer*
Blackwell, Menefee Davis *lawyer*
Blim, Richard Don *pediatrician*
Bloch, Henry Wollman *tax preparation company executive*
Bloch, Thomas Morton *tax company executive*
Boland, Raymond James *bishop*
Bolender, Todd *choreographer*
Bombeck, Erma Louise (Mrs. William Bombeck) *author, columnist*
†Bowers, Curtis Ray, Jr. *chaplain*
Bowman, Pasco Middleton, II *federal judge*
Boyd, John Addison, Jr. *civil engineer*
Bradbury, Daniel Joseph *library administrator*
Bradshaw, Jean Paul, II *prosecutor*
Bradshaw, William David *insurance company executive*
Brandt, William Perry *lawyer*
†Brannon, Wilbur *church administrator*
Bransby, Eric James *muralist, educator*
Braude, Michael *commodity exchange executive*
Brenner, Daniel Leon *lawyer*
Brett, George Howard *baseball executive, former professional baseball player*
†Brisbane, Arthur Seward *newspaper editor*
Britt, James Thomas *lawyer*
Brouillette, Gary Joseph *lawyer*
Brown, Bob Oliver *manufacturing company executive*
Brown, John O. *banker*
Brown, Peter W. *lawyer*
Bruening, Richard P(atrick) *lawyer*
†Buchanan, John Clark *bishop*
Bugher, Robert Dean *association executive*
Burg, George Roscoe *journalist*
Burk, Norman *oral surgeon*
Busby, Marjorie Jean (Marjean Busby) *journalist*
†Butler, Martin *church administrator*
Bywaters, David R. *management consultant*
Campbell, Newton Allen *consulting engineering company executive, consulting electrical engineer*
†Canfield, Robert Cleo *lawyer*
†Cantrell, (Thomas) Scott *newspaper editor, music critic*
Cappon, Alexander Patterson *English language educator*
Carr, Jack Richard *candy company executive*
Chastain, Larry Kent *insurance company executive*
Ching, Wai Yim *physics educator, researcher*
Chisholm, Donald Herbert *lawyer*
Clarke, Milton Charles *lawyer*
†Clarkson, William Edwin *construction company executive*
†Cleberg, Harry C. *food products company executive*
†Cloud, Randy *church administrator*
Collins, Mark *professional football player*
†Comment, Jeffrey W. *jewelry retail executive*
Cone, David Brian *professional baseball player*
Conrad, William Merrill *architect*
Conway, Thomas James *lawyer*
Cook, Mary Rozella *psychophysiologist*
†Costin, James D. *performing company executive*
Couch, Daniel Michael *healthcare executive*
Courson, Marna B. P. *public relations executive*
Crawford, Howard Allen *lawyer*
Crider, Stephen Wayne *banker, lawyer*
Cross, William Dennis *lawyer*
Davis, F(rancis) Keith *civil engineer*
Davis, James Robert *cartoonist*
Davis, John Charles *lawyer*
Davis, John Edward *banking executive*
Davis, Richard Francis *city government official*
Deacy, Thomas Edward, Jr. *lawyer*
†Dees, Stephen Phillip *petroleum, farm and food products company executive, lawyer*
Devlin, James Richard *lawyer*
Dillingham, John Allen *marketing professional*
Dimond, Edmunds Grey *medical educator*
†Dozois, Gardner *editor, writer*

Driscoll, Robert Louis *lawyer*
Dumovich, Loretta *real estate and transportation company executive*
†Durig, James Robert *college dean*
Durwood, Edward D. *motion picture corporation executive*
Edgar, John M. *lawyer*
Edwards, George W., Jr. *railway company executive*
Edwards, Horace Burton *former state official, former oil pipeline company executive, management consultant*
Egan, Charles Joseph, Jr. *greeting card company executive, lawyer*
Eldridge, Truman Kermit, Jr. *lawyer*
Ellfeldt, Howard James *orthopedic surgeon*
†Estep, Mike *church administrator*
Eubanks, Eugene Emerson *education educator, consultant*
Farris, Jefferson Davis *university administrator*
Feldmiller, George E. *lawyer*
Field, Lyman *lawyer*
†Fisher, Charles *protective services official*
Flora, Jairus Dale, Jr. *statistician*
Foland, William James *lawyer*
Fonne, Hiram A. *dean*
Foster, Mark Stephen *lawyer*
Fox, Thomas Charles *editor, writer*
Frank, Eugene Maxwell *bishop*
Frauens, Marie *editor, researcher*
French, Linda Jean *lawyer*
Freund, Ronald S. *management consultant, marketing company executive*
Fries, James Lawrence *trade association executive*
Frost, Earle Wesley *lawyer, retired judge*
†Frost, James E. *agricultural organization executive*
†Fullerton, Fred *church administrator*
Gaitan, Fernando J., Jr. *federal judge*
Gardner, Brian E. *lawyer*
Getty, Carol Pavilack *government official*
Gibson, Floyd Robert *federal judge*
Gibson, John Robert *federal judge*
Gier, Audra May Calhoon *environmental chemist*
Giffin, Reggie Craig *lawyer*
†Gile, Herbert R., Jr. *airport terminal executive*
Gorman, Gerald Warner *lawyer*
Graham, James Robert, III *physician, medical society administrator*
†Gray, Helen Theresa Gott *religion editor*
Grider, Joseph Kenneth *theology educator, writer*
Grosskreutz, Joseph Charles *physicist, engineering researcher, educator*
Grossman, Jerome Barnett *retired service firm executive*
Grunt, Jerome Alvin *pediatric endocrinologist*
Guisewite, Cathy Lee *cartoonist*
†Gunter, Moody *church administrator*
Gusewelle, Charles Wesley *journalist*
Hagans, Robert Frank *industrial clothing cleaning company executive*
†Hall, Beth Shand *holding company executive*
Hall, Donald Joyce *greeting card company executive*
†Hall, Miriam *church administrator*
Hartzler, Geoffrey Oliver *cardiologist*
Hazlett, James Arthur *insurance administrator*
Hendrickson, Marshall David *banker*
†Hendrix, Ray *church administrator*
Henson, Paul Harry *corporate executive*
Hicks, Lawrence Wayne *manufacturing company executive*
Hockaday, Irvine O., Jr. *greeting card company executive*
†Hoenig, Thomas M. *bank executive*
Hoffman, Alfred John *mutual fund executive*
Hoffman, John Raymond *lawyer*
Hoffmann, Donald *architectural historian*
Hogan, Thomas John *insurance company executive*
Holder, Thomas Martin *physician*
Hoskins, William Keller *lawyer, pharmaceutical company executive*
Hubbell, Ernest *lawyer*
Hunt, Lamar *professional football team executive*
Hunter, Elmo Bolton *federal judge*
Hunzicker, Warren John *research consultant, physician, cardiologist*
Ingram, Robert Palmer *magazine publisher*
†Isler, Mamie *secondary school principal*
Jackson, Don Merrill *lawyer*
Jenkins, Orville Wesley *retired religious administrator*
Johnson, Dora Myrtle Knudtson *principal*
†Johnson, Jerald D. *religious organization administrator*
Johnson, Mark Eugene *lawyer*
†Julian, Lanny *printing company executive*
Karmeier, Delbert Fred *consulting engineer*
†Keathley, George *performing arts executive*
Keith, Alan George *lawyer*
Kemper, David Woods, II *banker*
Kemper, James Madison, Jr. *banker*
†Kemper, Jonathan McBride *banker*
Kemper, Rufus Crosby, Jr. *banker*
Kilroy, John Muir *lawyer*
Kilroy, William Terrence *lawyer*
King, Richard Allen *lawyer*
Kingsley, James Gordon *health care executive*
Kipp, Robert Almy *greeting card company executive*
†Kittoe, Larry *grain company executive*
Koger, Frank Williams *federal judge*
Kramer, Lawrence John *college president*
Kroenert, Robert Morgan *lawyer*
Kronschnabel, Robert James *manufacturing company executive*
La Budde, Kenneth James *librarian*
Langworthy, Robert Burton *lawyer*
Larsen, Robert Emmett *federal judge*
Larson, Gary *cartoonist*
Latshaw, John *entrepreneur*
Lee, Margaret Norma *artist*
†Levi, Peter Steven *chamber of commerce executive, lawyer*
Lindsey, David Hosford *lawyer*
Logan, James C. *lawyer*
Lombardi, Cornelius Ennis, Jr. *lawyer*
Loudon, Donald Hoover *lawyer*
Lubin, Bernard *psychologist, educator*
†Lyons, Frederick William, Jr. *pharmaceutical company executive*
Lysaught, Patrick *lawyer*
Malacarne, C. John *insurance company executive, lawyer*
Manka, Ronald Eugene *lawyer*
Martin, Donna Lee *publishing company executive*
Martin-Bowen, (Carole) Lindsey *freelance writer*
Martinez-Carrion, Marino *biochemist, educator*
Matheny, Edward Taylor, Jr. *lawyer*
Mc Coy, Frederick John *retired plastic surgeon*
Mc Gee, Joseph John, Jr. *former insurance company executive*

Mc Kelvey, John Clifford *research institute executive*
McKenna, George LaVerne *art museum curator*
†McKinley, James C. *English educator, editor*
McLarney, Charles Patrick *lawyer*
McManus, James William *lawyer*
Mc Meel, John Paul *newspaper syndicate and publishing executive*
†McMindes, Carl Lee *religious organization, church administrator*
McRae, Hal (Harold Abraham McRae) *major league baseball team manager*
McSweeney, William Lincoln, Jr. *publishing executive*
Mebust, Winston Keith *surgeon, educator*
Merriman, Joe Jack *insurance company executive*
Mick, Howard Harold *lawyer*
Miller, Patricia Elizabeth Cleary *American and British literature educator*
Moffatt, David John *anatomy educator*
Molz, Otis *oil industry executive*
Mongan, James John *physician*
Monica, John C. *lawyer*
Montana, Joseph C., Jr. *professional football player*
Montgomery, Jeffrey Thomas *professional baseball player*
Moore, David Lowell *dentist*
Moore, Dorsey Jerome *dentistry educator, maxillofacial prosthetist*
†Moore, E. Harris *bishop*
Mordy, James Calvin *lawyer*
Morefield, Richard Watts *lawyer*
†Moseley, Furman C. *timber company executive*
Murdock, Stuart Laird *retired banker, investment adviser*
†Mutti, Albert Frederick *minister*
Nease, Stephen Wesley *college president*
Newsom, James T. *lawyer*
Noback, Richardson Kilbourne *medical educator*
Northrip, Robert Earl *lawyer*
†Nottberg, Henry, III *construction company executive*
Nulton, William Clements *lawyer*
O'Hearne, John Joseph *psychiatrist*
Oliphant, Patrick *editorial cartoonist*
Olson, Kay Melchisedech *magazine editor*
Palmer, Cruise *newspaper editor*
Palmer, Dennis Dale *lawyer*
Parizek, Eldon Joseph *geologist, college dean*
Patterson, Russell *conductor, opera executive*
Payne, James Leroy *newspaper publishing executive*
Pedram, Marilyn Beth *reference librarian*
Pelofsky, Joel *lawyer*
Pendleton, Barbara Jean *retired banker*
Perrin, John Paul *medical school president*
Peterson, Carl *professional football team executive*
Petosa, Jason Joseph *publisher*
Piepho, Robert Walter *pharmacy educator, researcher*
Pike, George Harold, Jr. *religious organization executive, clergyman*
Pistilli, Philip *hotel executive*
†Polsky, Norman *furniture company executive*
Popham, Arthur Cobb, Jr. *lawyer*
Popper, Robert *law educator, former dean*
Presson, Ellis Wynn *health services executive*
Price, Charles H., II *former ambassador*
Prugh, William Byron *lawyer*
†Ramsey, Craig Ray *financial officer*
Reaves, Charles William *insurance company executive, writer, educator, investment advisor*
Reiter, Robert Edward *banker*
†Rheinfrank, Lamson, Jr. *manufacturing company executive*
Rice, H. Wayne *food products executive*
Robertson, Leon H. *management consultant, educator*
Robinson, John Hamilton *civil engineer*
Robinson, Spencer T. (Herk Robinson) *professional baseball team executive*
Rosenberg, Morton Yale *lawyer*
Rost, William Joseph *chemist*
Rowland, Landon Hill *diversified holding company executive*
Sachs, Howard F(rederic) *federal judge*
Sanchez, Beatrice Rivas *art institute executive, artist*
Sauer, Gordon Chenoweth *physician, educator*
Savage, Thomas Joseph *college president, governance and planning consultant, educator, priest*
†Sayler, J. W., Jr. *insurance company executive*
Schmitt, Edward E. *lawyer*
Schoolman, Arnold *neurological surgeon*
Schottenheimer, Martin Edward *professional football coach*
Scott, Deborah Emont *curator*
Scott, James White *newspaper editor*
†Scott, Robert Hal *minister*
See, Andrew Bruce *lawyer*
Seligson, Theodore H. *architect, interior designer, art consultant*
Semegen, Patrick William *lawyer*
Setzler, Edward Allan *lawyer*
Sexton, Donald Lee *business administration educator*
Shabbir, Mahnaz Mehdi *healthcare marketing manager*
Shaw, John W. *lawyer*
Shutz, Byron Christopher *real estate executive*
Skahan, Paul L(aurence) *bank executive, lawyer*
Skidmore, Max Joseph *political science educator*
†Skiles, Paul *church administrator*
†Skinner, Willis Dean *consulting engineering company executive*
†Smee, John *church administrator*
Smith, Neil *professional football player*
Solberg, Elizabeth Transou *public relations executive*
†Solomon, John Davis *aviation executive*
Spalty, Edward Robert *lawyer*
Stanley, David *retail company executive*
Steadman, Jack W. *professional football team executive*
†Steele, Kathleen Frances *federal official*
Stevens, Joseph Edward, Jr. *federal judge*
Stewart, Albert Elisha *safety engineer, industrial hygienist*
Stites, C. Thomas *journalist, publisher*
Stone, Jack *religious organization administrator*
Stowers, James Evans, Jr. *investment company executive*
†Sullivan, Bill *church administrator*
Sullivan, Charles A. *food products executive*
Sullivan, John Joseph *bishop*
Svadlenak, Jean Hayden *museum administrator, consultant*
Tammeus, William David *journalist, columnist*
†Taylor, Jeff *reporter*
Temple, Joseph George, Jr. *pharmaceutical company executive*
Thomas, Larry Wayne *secondary school educator*
Thompson, Bennie *professional football player*

Thornton, Thomas Noel *publishing executive*
†Titens, Sherman Jay *strategic planning consulting company executive, lawyer*
Toll, Perry Mark *lawyer*
Townsend, Harold Guyon, Jr. *publishing company executive*
Tripp, David Richard *lawyer*
Ucko, David Alan *museum director*
Ulrich, Robert Gene *judge*
Van Ackeren, Maurice Edward *college administrator*
Vander Clute, Howard Edmund, Jr. *association executive*
Vandever, William Dirk *lawyer*
Varner, Barton Douglas *lawyer*
Vaughan, Kirk William *banker*
Vering, John Albert *lawyer*
Viani, James L. *lawyer*
Vogel, Arthur Anton *clergyman*
†Walker, John Ernst *insurance company executive*
Ward, John Orson *economics educator, consultant*
Ward, Louis Larrick *candy company executive*
Watterson, Bill *cartoonist*
Wheeler, Charles Bertan *pathologist*
Whipple, Dean *federal judge*
Wiggins, Kip Acker *lawyer*
Williams, Wade Hampton, III *motion picture producer, director, distributor*
Wilson, Marc Fraser *art museum administrator and curator*
Wilson, Tom *cartoonist, greeting card company executive*
Wolf, Dale Joseph *utilities company executive*
Woods, Richard Dale *lawyer*
Wright, Scott Olin *federal judge*
Wrobley, Ralph Gene *lawyer*
Wyrsch, James Robert *lawyer*
Zeller, Marilynn Kay *librarian*
Zimmerman, William Gene *lawyer*

Kirksville
Festa, Roger Reginald *chemist, educator*
Knight, Ronald Allen *mathematics educator, researcher*
Warren, Russell Glen *academic administrator*

Kirkwood
Holsen, James Noble, Jr. *retired chemical engineer*

Laddonia
Scheffler, Lewis Francis *pastor, educator, research scientist*

Lake Lotawana
Hinkle, B. J. *retired food company executive, consultant*

Lake Saint Louis
Czarnik, Marvin Ray *retired aerospace engineer*
German, John George *transportation consultant*
Royal, William Henry *real estate developer, architect*

Lambert Airport
Griggs, Leonard LeRoy, Jr. *fedearl agency administrator*

Lebanon
Dryden, Martin Francis, Jr. *retired gas company executive*
Hutson, Don *lawyer*
†Plaster, Stephen Robert *gas company executive*

Lees Summit
†Hall, Glenn Allen *lawyer, state representative*
Korschot, Benjamin Calvin *investment executive*
Timmons, Joseph Dean *insurance company executive*
Waite, Daniel Elmer *retired oral surgeon*

Liberty
†Ferrell, James Edwin *energy company executive*
Harriman, Richard Lee *English language educator*
Tanner, Jimmie Eugene *college dean*

Liguori
O'Connor, Francine Marie *magazine editor*

Manchester
†Warner, Vinnie *principal*

Marshall
Gruber, Loren Charles *English language educator, writer*
Tweito, Eleanor Marie *social services administrator*

Maryland Heights
Beumer, Richard Eugene *engineer, architect, construction firm executive*
Doheny, Donald Aloysius *lawyer, business executive*
Dokoudovsky, Nina Ludmila *dance educator*
Hampton, Margaret Josephine *secondary education educator, decorating consultant*
†Schwartz, Henry Gerard, Jr. *consulting engineering company executive*
Smith, Brice Reynolds, Jr. *engineering company executive*
Sobol, Lawrence Raymond *lawyer*
Uselton, James Clayton *engineering executive*
†Whitfield, J. D. *engineering executive*

Maryville
Hubbard, Dean Leon *university president*
†Jonagan, Glenn E. *principal*

Maysville
Bram, Isabelle Mary Rickey McDonough (Mrs. John Bram) *civic worker*

Mexico
Hummer, Paul F., II *manufacturing company executive*
Stover, Harry M. *corporate executive*

Moberly
Blackmar, Charles Blakey *state supreme court justice*
Pelfrey, Lloyd Marvin *college president*

Neosho
Hargis, Billy James *minister*
Wilson, Alice Hornbuckle *retired physician*

Nevada
Ewing, Lynn Moore, Jr. *lawyer*
Hizer, Marlene Brown *library director*
Hornback, Joseph Hope *mathematics educator*
Morton, John, III *banker*

Normandy
†Goode, Wayne *state senator*

North Kansas City
Hagan, John Charles, III *ophthalmologist*
Hartley, Richard Glendale *association executive*

Parkville
Breckon, Donald John *academic administrator*

Poplar Bluff
Black, Ronnie Delane *religious organization administrator, mayor*
†Carr, Charles Louis *religious organization administrator*
†Duncan, Leland Ray *administrator*

Raytown
†Barnes, James Richard *county official*

Rolla
Adawi, Ibrahim Hasan *physics educator*
Alexander, Ralph William, Jr. *physics educator*
Armstrong, Daniel Wayne *chemist, educator*
Babcock, Daniel Lawrence *chemical engineer, educator*
Barr, David John *civil, geological engineering educator*
Cheng, Franklin Yih *civil engineering educator*
Crosbie, Alfred Linden *mechanical engineering educator*
Datz, Israel Mortimer *information systems specialist*
Day, Delbert Edwin *ceramic engineering educator*
French, Eunice Pelafigue *university international programs administrator*
Grimm, Louis John *mathematician, educator*
Hagni, Richard Davis *geology and geophysics educator*
Irion, Arthur Lloyd *psychologist, educator*
James, William Joseph *chemistry educator*
Johnson, James Winston *chemical engineering educator*
Mc Farland, Robert Harold *physicist, educator*
Minor, Joseph Edward *civil engineer, educator*
†Mullin, Lenore Marie Restifo *computer scientist, researcher*
Munger, Paul R. *civil engineering educator*
O'Keefe, Thomas Joseph *metallurgical engineer*
Omurtag, Yildirim (Bill) *engineering educator*
Saperstein, Lee Waldo *mining engineering educator*
Sauer, Harry John, Jr. *mechanical engineering educator, university administrator*
Tsoulfanidis, Nicholas *nuclear engineering educator*
Warner, Don Lee *dean emeritus*
Zobrist, George Winston *computer scientist, educator*

Saint Charles
Barnett, Howard Albert *English language educator*
Castro, Jan Garden *author, arts consultant, educator*
Dauphinais, George Arthur *import company executive*
Dieterich, Russell Burks *obstetrician/gynecologist*
†Gross, Charles Robert *personnel executive, legislator, appraiser*
Radke, Rodney Owen *agricultural research executive*

Saint Joseph
†Chilcote, Gary M. *museum director, reporter*
Head, J. Michael *transportation executive*
Johnson, Marvin Melrose *consulting industrial engineer*
Kranitz, Theodore Mitchell *lawyer*
Lockwood, George J. *newspaper editor*
Miller, Lloyd Daniel *real estate agent*

Saint Louis
Abelov, Stephen Lawrence *uniform clothing company executive*
Abrahamson, Barry *chemical company executive*
Ackerman, Joseph J. H. *chemistry educator*
Ackers, Gary Keith *biophysical chemistry educator, researcher*
Adams, Albert Willie, Jr. *lubrication company executive*
Adorjan, J(ulius) Joe *electric company executive*
Agrawal, Harish Chandra *neurobiologist, researcher, educator*
Akerson, Alan W. *public relations company executive*
†Alberici, Gabriel J. *construction company executive*
Allen, Garland Edward *biology educator, science historian*
†Allen, Renee *principal*
Allen, Robert Smith *lawyer*
Alpers, David Hershel *physician, educator*
Anderson, Charles Bernard *surgeon, educator*
Anderson, James Donald *chemical company executive*
Andes, G. Thomas *banker*
Appleton, R. O., Jr. *lawyer*
Arnold, John Fox *lawyer*
Arvidson, Raymond Ernst *planetary geology educator*
Asa, Cheryl Suzanne *research biologist*
Atwood, Hollye Stolz *lawyer*
Avis, Robert Grier *investment company executive, civil engineer*
Aylward, Ronald Lee *lawyer*
Babb, Ralph Wheeler, Jr. *banker*
Babington, Charles Martin, III *lawyer*
Bachmann, John William *securities firm executive*
Backer, Matthias Henry, Jr. *obstetrician-gynecologist*
Badgley, William S. *multi-bank holding company executive*
Baernstein, Albert, II *mathematician*
Bagley, Mary Carol *educator, writer, broadcaster*
Baldwin, Edwin Steedman *lawyer*
Ball, William Ernest *computer science educator*
Ballinger, Walter Francis *surgeon, educator*
Baloff, Nicholas *business educator, consultant*
Barken, Bernard Allen *lawyer*
Barksdale, Clarence Caulfield *banker*
Barmann, Lawrence Francis *history educator*
†Barnes, Harper Henderson *movie critic*
Barnes, Zane Edison *communications company executive*
Barnett, William Arnold *economics educator*
Barney, Steven Matthew *human resources executive*
Barrie, John Paul *lawyer, educator*
Barta, James Joseph *federal judge*
†Barth, Karl Luther *retired seminary president*
Bartlett, Walter E. *communications company executive*
Bascom, C. Perry *lawyer*
Battram, Richard L. *retail executive*
Baue, Arthur Edward *surgeon, educator, administrator*
Bauman, George Duncan *former newspaper publisher*
Bealke, Linn Hemingway *bank executive*
Bean, Bourne *lawyer*
Beare, Gene Kerwin *electric company executive*
Beck, Lois Grant *anthropologist, educator*
Becker, David Mandel *legal educator, author, consultant*
Becker, Rex Louis *architect*
Benberry, Cuesta Ray *historian*
Bender, Carl Martin *physics educator, consultant*
Bensinger, David August *dentist, university dean*
Bentele, Raymond F. *retired minerals corporate executive*
Beracha, Barry Harris *brewery executive*
Berg, Leonard *neurologist, educator*
Berger, John Torrey, Jr. *lawyer*
Bernstein, Donald Chester *brokerage company executive, lawyer*
†Bernstein, Mark D. *theater director*
Bernstein, Merton Clay *lawyer, educator, arbitrator*
Berthoff, Rowland Tappan *historian, educator*
Betts, Warren R. *health facilty administrator*
Biondi, Lawrence *university administrator, priest*
Bird, Harrie Waldo, Jr. *psychiatrist, educator*
Bloemer, Rosemary Celeste *bookkeeper*
Bloomberg, Terry *early childhood education administrator*
Bock, Edward John *chemical manufacturing company executive*
Bohle, Bruce William *editor*
Bohne, Jeanette Kathryn *mathematics and science educator*
†Boldt, H. James *church administrator*
Boothby, William Munger *mathematics educator*
†Bosley, Freeman Robertson, Jr. *mayor*
Bottini, Thomas H. *lawyer*
Bourke, Vernon Joseph *philosophy educator*
Bowen, James Ronald *banker*
Bowen, Stephen Francis, Jr. *ophthalmic surgeon*
Boyd, Robert Cotton *English educator*
Bracken, Robert W. *food products executive*
Brasunas, Anton de Sales *metallurgical engineering educator*
Breece, Robert William, Jr. *lawyer*
Breihan, Erwin Robert *civil engineer, consultant*
Brennan, John Merritt *banker*
Brickey, Kathleen Fitzgerald *law educator*
Brickson, Richard Alan *lawyer*
†Bridgewater, Bernard Adolphus, Jr. *footwear and specialty retailing company executive*
Briggs, William Benajah *aeronautical engineer*
Brodeur, Armand Edward *pediatric radiologist*
Brodsky, Philip Hyman *chemical executive, research director*
Brody, Lawrence *lawyer, educator*
Broeg, Bob (Robert William Broeg) *writer*
Browde, Anatole *electronics company executive, consultant*
Browman, David L(udvig) *archaeologist*
Brown, Jay Wright *food manufacturing company executive*
Brown, Melvin F. *telecommunications industry executive*
Brown, Virginia Suggs *language arts educator, consultant*
Brownlee, Robert Hammel *lawyer*
Brunstrom, Gerald Ray *engineering executive, consultant*
Bryan, Henry C(lark), Jr. *lawyer*
Bryant, Ruth Alyne *banker*
Buck, Jack *sportscaster*
Buesinger, Ronald Ernest *security and commodity brokerage executive*
Burgess, James Harland *physics educator, researcher*
Burke, James Donald *museum administrator*
†Burkett, Randy James *lighting designer*
Burks, Verner Irwin *architect*
†Burnett, Roger H. *construction executive*
Busch, August Adolphus, III *brewery executive*
Butler, James Lawrence *financial planner*
Byrnes, Christopher Ian *academic dean, researcher*
Cahill, Clyde S. *federal judge*
Cain, James Nelson *arts school administrator*
Cairns, Donald Fredrick *engineering educator, management consultant*
Callis, Clayton Fowler *research chemist*
Cameron, Paul Scott *architect*
Capellupo, John P. *air transportation executive*
Carmody, Gerard Timothy *lawyer*
Caron, Ronald Jacques *professional sports team executive*
Carp, Richard Lawrence (Larry Carp) *lawyer*
Carr, Gary Thomas *lawyer*
†Cejka, Susan Ann *executive search company executive*
Chandler, James Barton *international education consultant*
Chaplin, Hugh, Jr. *physician, educator*
†Chivetta, Anthony Joseph *architect*
†Chomeau, David Douglass *insurance company executive*
†Christie, Carole Sullivan *advertising agency executive*
Christopher, Glenn A. *publishing company executive*
Clear, John Michael *lawyer*
†Cleary, Thomas John *aluminum products company executive*
Clement, Richard Francis *retired investment company executive*
Cloninger, Claude Robert *psychiatric researcher, educator, genetic epdemiologist*
Cobb, Donna Deanne Hill *physical therapist*
Coco, Charles Edward *food products company executive*
Coerver, Elizabeth Ann *data base consultant*
Coffin, Richard Keith *lawyer*
Cole, Barbara Ruth *pediatrician, nephrologist*
Collins, Margaret Elizabeth *librarian*
Colten, Harvey Radin *pediatrician, educator*
Conaway, Mary Ann *professional counselor, educator*
Conerly, Richard Pugh *retired corporation executive*
Conran, Joseph Palmer *lawyer*
Cori, Carl Tom *chemicals executive*
Cornelius, William Edward *utilities company executive*
Cornfeld, Dave Louis *lawyer*
Costigan, Edward John *investment banker*
†Cotton, W(illiam) Philip, Jr. *architect*
Cox, Jerome Rockhold, Jr. *electrical engineer*
Craig, Andrew Billings, III *bank holding company executive*
Crampton, William DeVer *tax lawyer*
Crutsinger, Robert Keane *diversified food wholesale company executive*
Cunningham, Charles Baker, III *manufacturing company executive*
Curran, Michael Walter *management scientist*
Curtiss, Roy, III *biology educator*
Dames, Joan Foster (Mrs. Urban L. Dames) *magazine editor, columnist*
Danforth, William Henry *university chancellor, physician*
Davis, Richard Whitlock *history educator, writer*
Davis, Steven L. *lawyer*
Deal, Joseph Maurice *university dean, art educator, photographer*
Delaney, Robert Vernon *logistics and transportation executive*
Demoff, Samuel Louis *retired retail chain executive*
Denneen, John Paul *lawyer*
DesRosiers, Roger I. *artist, educator*
†Deuel, Thomas Franklin *physician*
Devantier, Paul W. *communications executive, broadcaster*
Dewald, Paul Adolph *psychiatrist*
Dezort, Jacquelyn Louise Link *bank executive*
†Di Cera, Enrico *biophysicist*
Dierdorf, Daniel Lee (Dan Dierdorf) *football analyst, sports commentator, former professional football player*
Dill, Charles Anthony *manufacturing and computer company executive*
Dill, John Francis *publishing company executive*
Dill, Virginia S. *accountant*
Dodge, Philip Rogers *physician, educator*
Domjan, Laszlo Karoly *newspaper executive*
Dommermuth, William P. *marketing consultant, educator*
Donohue, Carroll John *lawyer*
Dorsey, Gray Lankford *law educator emeritus*
Dorwart, Donald Bruce *lawyer*
Dougherty, Charles Joseph *retired utility executive*
Douglas, Mary Younge Riley *secondary education educator*
†Dowd, Edward L. *prosecutor*
Dreifke, Gerald Edmond *electrical engineering educator*
Dressel, Roy Robert *insurance company executive*
Drews, Robert Carrel *physician*
Du Bois, Philip Hunter *psychologist, educator*
†Duesenberg, Richard William *lawyer*
Duhme, H(erman) Richard, Jr. *sculptor, educator*
Eagleton, Thomas Francis *former senator*
Edison, Bernard Alan *retired retail apparel company executive*
Elkin, Stanley Lawrence *author, literature educator*
Elkins, Ken Joe *broadcasting executive*
Elliott, Howard, Jr. *gas distribution company executive*
Ellis, Dorsey Daniel, Jr. *dean*
†Ellis, James D. *communications executive, corporate lawyer*
Engelhardt, Thomas Alexander *editorial cartoonist*
Epner, Steven Arthur *computer consultant*
Erwin, James Walter *lawyer*
†Essman, Alyn V. *photographic studios company executive*
Etzkorn, K. Peter *sociologist, educator, author*
Evens, Ronald Gene *radiologist, medical center administrator*
Ewan, Joseph (Andorfer) *botanist, biohistorian, research bibliographer*
Falk, William James *lawyer*
Farrell, David Coakley *department store executive*
Farrell, John Timothy *hospital administrator*
Farris, Charles Lowell *city official*
Fascia, Remo Mario *aviation consultant, airplane manufacturing company executive*
Faught, Harold Franklin *electrical equipment manufacturing company executive*
Feir, Dorothy Jean *entomologist, physiologist, educator*
Ferguson, Gary Warren *public relations executive*
Ferrendelli, James Anthony *neurologist, educator*
†Filenwarth, Albert Floyd *advertising agency financial executive*
Filippine, Edward Louis *federal judge*
†Finan, John Joseph *hospital administrator*
Finkel, Donald *poet*
Finnigan, Joseph Townsend *public relations executive*
Fischer, Harry William *radiologist, educator*
Fitch, Coy Dean *physician, educator*
Fletcher, James Warren *physician*
Flye, M. Wayne *surgeon, immunologist, educator*
Fogarty, William Martin, Jr. *physician*
Folk, Roger Maurice *laboratory director*
†Forrestal, Patrick George *sales promotion agency executive*
Fournie, Robert G. *retired boiler works executive*
Fox, John Reid *advertising executive*
Frager, Norman *stockbroker*
Frawley, Thomas Francis *physician*
Frederick, William Sherrad *manufacturing and retailing company executive*
†Fredrickson, John Murray *otolaryngologist*
†Freeland, A. Jerome *publishing executive*
Fricke, Thomas Freeland *lawyer*
Frieden, Carl *biochemist, educator*
Friedlander, Michael Wulf *physicist, educator*
Friedman, William Hersh *otolaryngologist, educator*
Fryer, Edwin Samuel *lawyer*
Gaddes, Richard *performing arts administrator*
Garr, Louis Joseph, Jr. *lawyer, retail company executive*
Gaspar, Peter Paul *chemistry educator*
Gauen, Patrick Emil *newspaper correspondent*
Gazzoli, John Joseph, Jr. *lawyer*
†Gelman, Warren Jay *metals trading company executive*
Gerard, Jules Bernard *law educator*
Gerdine, Leigh *retired academic administrator*
Gershenson, Harry *lawyer*
†Gibbons, Michael Randolph *lawyer*
Gibbons, Patrick Chandler *physicist, educator*
Gibson, Robert *broadcaster, former baseball player*
Gilbert, Allan Arthur *utilities executive*
†Gilligan, Sandra Kaye *private school director*
Gladding, Nicholas C. *lawyer*
Godiner, Donald Leonard *lawyer*
Goebel, John J. *lawyer*
†Goff, Raymond Ellis *brewery executive*
Goldberg, Norman Albert *music publisher, writer*
Goldstein, Michael Gerald *lawyer*
Goldstein, Samuel R. *oil company executive*
Goldstein, Steven *lawyer*

†Gomes, Edward Clayton, Jr. *construction company executive*
Goodman, Harold S. *lawyer*
Gordon, Larry Dean *elementary education educator*
Gould, Phillip L. *civil engineering educator, consultant*
Graff, George Stephen *aerospace company executive*
Graham, Colin *stage director*
Graham, John Dalby *public relations executive*
Gray, Charles Elmer *lawyer, rancher, investor*
Gray, Walter Franklin *banker*
Green, Dennis Joseph *lawyer*
Green, Maurice *molecular biologist, virologist, educator*
Griffin, W(illiam) L(ester) Hadley *shoe company executive*
†Grisham, Richard *health facility administrator*
Groennert, Charles Willis *electric company executive*
Gross, Michael Lawrence *chemistry educator*
Guenther, Charles John *librarian, writer*
Guerri, William Grant *lawyer*
Gunn, George F., Jr. *federal judge*
†Gunn, Russell C. *financial services company executive*
Gupta, Surendra Kumar *chemical firm executive*
Guze, Samuel Barry *psychiatrist, educator, university official*
†Haake, Arthur C. *church administrator*
†Haake, Earle E. *church administrator*
Haberstroh, Richard David *insurance agent*
Haimo, Deborah Tepper *mathematics educator*
Hakkinen, Raimo Jaakko *aeronautical engineer, scientist*
Hamburger, Viktor *retired biology educator*
Hamilton, Jean Constance *federal judge*
Handel, Peter H. *physics educator*
Hansen, Charles *lawyer*
Harmon, Robert Lee *corporate executive*
Harper, Roy W. *federal judge*
Harris, Whitney Robson *lawyer*
†Hastings, Bryce *architect*
Hayes, Alice Bourke *university official, biology educator*
Hayes, Samuel Banks, III *banking company executive*
Hays, Ruth *lawyer*
Hecker, George Sprake *lawyer*
Hedlund, James Lane *retired psychologist, educator*
Heininger, S(amuel) Allen *retired chemical company executive*
Heinrich, Ross Raymond *geophysicist, educator*
Heisler, John Columbus *investment banker*
Hellmuth, George Francis *architect*
Hellmuth, Theodore Henning *lawyer*
Henle, Robert John *former university president*
Herbert, Kevin Barry John *classics educator*
†Hermann, Robert R. *zoological park administrator*
Hermann, Robert Ringen *conglomerate company executive*
Hershey, Falls Bacon *surgeon, educator*
Herzfeld-Kimbrough, Ciby *mental health educator*
Hewitt, Thomas Edward *financial executive*
Hexter, Jack H. *historian, educator*
Higgins, Edward Aloysius *newspaper editor*
Hilgert, Raymond Lewis *management and industrial relations educator, consultant, arbitrator*
Hillard, Robert Ellsworth *public relations consultant*
Hillis, Mark B. *lawyer*
Hirsch, Raymond Robert *chemical company executive, lawyer*
Hirsh, Ira Jean *pyschology educator, researcher*
Hoblitzelle, George Knapp *former state legislator*
Hoessle, Charles Herman *zoo director*
Hofstatter, Leopold *psychiatrist, researcher*
Hohenberg, Charles Morris *physics educator*
Holt, Glen Edward *library administrator*
Holten, James Joseph *meat processing company executive*
Holtzer, Alfred Melvin *chemistry educator*
Horwitt, Max Kenneth *biochemist, educator*
Howard, Walter Burke *chemical engineer*
Hull, Brett A. *professional hockey player*
Humphreys, James Burnham *hospital administrator*
Hungate, William Leonard *retired federal judge, former congressman*
†Hunt, Carlton Cuyler, Jr. *physiologist, educator*
Hunter, Earle Leslie, III *professional association executive*
Hunter, Thom Hugh *seminary administrator*
Ihde, Daniel C. *health science executive*
Immel, Vincent Clare *retired law educator*
Inkley, John James, Jr. *lawyer*
Irwin, Hale S. *professional golfer*
Israel, Martin Henry *astrophysicist, educator, academic administrator*
Isselhard, Donald Edward *dentist*
Ittner, H. Curtis *architect*
Jackson, Rebecca R. *lawyer*
Jacobsen, Thomas H(erbert) *banker*
†Jamboretz, Glennon Donald *advertising agency executive*
James, William W. *banker*
Janecke, Ronald Brian *newspaper editor, journalist, sports columnist*
Jefferies, Gregory Scott *professional baseball player*
Jenkins, James Allister *mathematician, educator*
Jenks, Downing Bland *railroad executive*
Jennings, Michael Eugene *banker*
Jobe, Muriel Ida *medical technologist*
Johnson, E. Perry *lawyer*
Johnson, Kennett Conrad *advertising agency executive*
Johnston, Gerald Andrew *aerospace company executive*
Joist, Johann Heinrich *hematologist, medical researcher, educator*
Jones, Ronald Woodbridge *human resources specialist, small business owner*
Jones, Wilbur Boardman, Jr. *trust company executive*
Jones, William Catron *legal educator*
Kagan, Sioma *economics educator*
Kanne, Marvin George *newspaper publishing executive*
Kaplan, Henry Jerrold *ophthalmologist, educator*
Keller, Juan Dane *lawyer*
Kelley, Richard Alan *electric utility executive*
Keltner, Raymond Marion, Jr. *surgeon, educator*
†Kerwin, Richard G. *grain company executive*
Kessler, Nathan *technology consultant*
Keyes, Marion Alvah, IV *manufacturing company executive*
Killenberg, George Andrew *newspaper consultant, former newspaper editor*
Kimmey, James Richard, Jr. *medical educator, consultant*
King, Morris Kenton *medical school dean*
†King, Robert Henry *minister, church denomination executive, former educator*
King, William Terry *manufacturing company executive*
Kinsella, Ralph Aloysius, Jr. *physician*
Kipnis, David Morris *physician, educator*
†Kirberg, Leonard Carl *engineering executive*
Klahr, Saulo *physician, educator*
Kleban, Kenneth A. *lawyer*
Kling, Merle *political scientist, university official*
Kling, S(tephen) Lee *banker*
Klobasa, John Anthony *lawyer*
Kniffen, Jan Rogers *finance executive*
Knight, Charles Field *electrical equipment manufacturing company executive*
†Kodner, Ira J. *surgeon, educator*
Koff, Robert Hess *academic program director*
Kolker, Allan Erwin *ophthalmologist*
Korando, Donna Kay *journalist*
Kornblet, Donald Ross *communications company executive*
Kouchoukos, Nicholas Thomas *surgeon*
†Krenzke, Richard *church administrator*
Krukowski, Lucian *philosophy educator, artist*
†Kugelman, Irwin Jay *civil engineering educator*
Kuhlmann, Fred L. *brewery consultant, lawyer, baseball executive*
Kultermann, Udo *architectural and art historian*
†Kummer, Fred S. *construction company executive*
Kurz, Joseph Louis *chemistry educator*
Lacy, Norris Joiner *French language and literature educator*
Lacy, Paul Eston *pathologist*
Lagunoff, David *physician, educator*
Lambright, Stephen Kirk *brewing company executive*
Lamoreux, Frederick Holmes *financial executive*
Landau, William Milton *neurologist*
Lander, David Allan *lawyer*
Laskowski, Leonard Francis, Jr. *microbiologist*
Lause, Michael Francis *lawyer*
†Lazorko, Anthony, Jr. *art director*
Lebowitz, Albert *lawyer, author*
†Leer, Steven F. *mining executive*
Lemon, Eric V. *lawyer*
Lents, Don Glaude *lawyer*
Leonard, Eugene Albert *banker*
Leven, Charles Louis *economics educator*
Levin, Marvin Edgar *physician*
Le Vine, Victor Theodore *political science educator*
Liberman, Lee Marvin *utility executive*
†Lickhalter, Merlin Eugene *architect*
Liddy, Richard A. *insurance company executive*
†Liddy, Steven Thomas *career military officer, educator*
Lieberman, Edward Jay *lawyer*
†Liese, Christopher A. *benefits and financial consulting company owner, state legislator*
Limbaugh, Stephen Nathaniel *federal judge*
Lindner, Kurt Julius *fund management company executive*
Lipeles, Maxine Ina *lawyer*
Lipkin, David *chemist*
Lipman, David *multimedia company executive*
Loeb, Jerome Thomas *retail executive*
Loeb, Virgil, Jr. *oncologist, hematologist*
†Loftin, Sister Mary Frances *health facility administrator*
Logan, Joseph Prescott *lawyer*
Long, Helen Halter *author, publishing executive, educator*
†Lorenzini, Paul G. *manufacturing executive*
Lovelace, Eldridge Hirst *retired landscape architect, city planner*
Lovin, Keith Harold *university administrator, philosophy educator*
Loynd, Richard Birkett *consumer products company executive*
Lucking, Peter Stephen *marketing consultant, industrial engineering consultant*
Lucy, Robert Meredith *lawyer*
Luedde, Charles Edwin Howell *lawyer, corporation executive*
Luepke, Henry Francis, Jr. *lawyer*
Luther, George Aubrey *orthopedic surgeon*
MacCarthy, John Peters *banker*
Macias, Edward S. *chemistry educator, university official*
Maguire, John Patrick *investment company executive*
Mahan, David James *school superintendent*
Mahoney, Richard John *manufacturing company executive*
†Mahsman, David Lawrence *religious publications editor*
Majerus, Philip Warren *physician*
†Mall, Ida *church administrator*
Malloy, James B. *packaging company executive*
Mandelker, Daniel Robert *law educator*
Mandelstamm, Jerome Robert *lawyer*
Manske, Paul Robert *orthopedic hand surgeon, educator*
†Marsh, James C., Jr. *secondary school principal*
Marsh, Miles L. *holding company executive*
Marshall, Garland Ross *biochemist, biophysicist, medical educator*
Massey, Raymond Lee *lawyer*
Masters, William Howell *physician, educator*
Mattson, William Royce, Jr. *health care consulting company executive*
Maxvill, Dal *professional baseball team executive*
McCarter, Charles Chase *lawyer*
†Mc Carthy, Francis F. *construction executive*
McCarty, Philip Norman *bank holding company executive*
Mc Daniel, James Edwin *lawyer*
McDonald, David P. *federal judge*
McDonnell, John Finney *aerospace and aircraft manufacturing company executive*
McDonnell, Sanford Noyes *aircraft company executive*
McFadden, James Frederick, Jr. *surgeon*
McFarland, Mary A. *elementary/secondary school educator/administrator*
McGarrell, James *artist, educator*
McGinty, John *marketing consultant*
†McGrath, Edward A. *electronic equipment company executive*
McKelvey, James Morgan *chemical engineering educator*
McKenna, William John *textile products executive*
McKinney, John Benjamin *steel company executive*
McKinnis, Michael B. *lawyer*
†McKissack, Patricia Carwell *children's book author*
McMillian, Theodore *federal judge*
Meisel, George Vincent *lawyer*
Meissner, Edwin Benjamin, Jr. *real estate broker*
Merbaum, Michael *psychology educator, clinical psychologist*
Merrell, James Lee *religious editor, clergyman*
Merrill, Charles Eugene *lawyer*
Mertz, Stuart Moulton *landscape architect*
Metcalfe, Walter Lee, Jr. *lawyer*
†Mette, Virgil Louis *publishing executive, biology educator*
†Meyer, John *church administrator*
†Meyer, William F. *church administrator*
Michaelides, Constantine Evangelos *architect, educator*
Micheletto, Joe Raymond *food products executive, controller*
Middelkamp, John Neal *pediatrician, educator*
Miller, Frank William *legal educator*
Miller, Gary J. *political economist*
Miller, James Gegan *research scientist, physics educator*
Miller, Michael Everett *chemical company executive*
Miller, Theresa Ann *management consultant*
Mills, Linda S. *public relations executive*
Mink, Eric P. *newspaper columnist*
Minnich, Virginia *retired medical researcher, educator*
Mitchell, Carol *daycare administrator*
Mohan, John J. *lawyer*
Monroe, Thomas Edward *industrial corporation executive*
Moore, McPherson Dorsett *lawyer*
Morgan, Robert Peter *engineering educator*
†Morice, James L. *public relations executive*
Morley, Harry Thomas, Jr. *real estate executive*
Morrow, Ralph Ernest *historian, educator*
Moulder, James Edwin *civil engineer*
Mueller, Charles William *electric utility executive*
†Mueller, David Brian *accountant, chief financial officer*
Mueller, John Alfred *church executive*
†Muller, Lyle Dean *religious organization administrator*
Muller, Marcel W(ettstein) *electrical engineering educator*
Mulligan, Michael Dennis *lawyer*
Mulligan, Robert William *university official, clergyman*
†Munk, Peter *oil industry executive*
Murray, Robert Wallace *chemistry educator*
Musial, Stan(ley) (Frank Musial) *baseball executive, hotel and restaurant executive*
Nelson, Michael Underhill *aerospace company executive, association executive*
Nemanick, Richard Charles *business executive*
Neufeind, Wilhelm *economics educator, university administrator*
Neville, James Morton *food company executive, lawyer*
Newman, Andrew Edison *retail executive*
Newman, Charles A. *lawyer*
Newman, Eric Pfeiffer *retail chain store executive*
Newman, Joan Meskiel *lawyer*
Newton, George Addison *investment banker, lawyer*
Noel, Edwin Lawrence *lawyer*
Noonan, Ray John *retired newspaper editor*
Normile, Michael T. *treasurer*
North, Douglass Cecil *economist, educator*
†Novelly, Paul A. *petrochemical and refining company executive*
Nussbaum, A(dolf) Edward *mathematician, educator*
†Obata, Gyo *architect*
O'Brien, Albert James *management consultant*
O'Brien, Thomas Francis *manufacturing company executive*
O'Connell, Dennis E. *lawyer*
O'Donnell, Edward Joseph *bishop, former editor*
Oetter, Bruce Christian *lawyer*
O'Keefe, Michael Daniel *lawyer*
Olson, Clarence Elmer, Jr. *newspaper editor*
Olson, Robert Grant *lawyer*
O'Malley, Kevin Francis *lawyer, writer, educator*
O'Neill, Eugene Milton *consumer products executive consultant*
†O'Neill, Sheila *principal*
Ong, Walter Jackson *priest, English educator, author*
Orton, George Frederick *aerospace engineer*
†O'Shoney, Glenn *church administrator*
O'Toole, Terrence J. *lawyer*
Owens, William Don *anesthesiology educator*
Owyoung, Steven David *curator*
Ozawa, Martha Naoko *social work educator*
Palans, Lloyd Alex *lawyer*
Paris, Paul Croce *mechanics educator, engineering consultant, researcher*
Peck, William Arno *physician*
Pellett, Thomas Rowand *retired food company executive*
Penniman, Nicholas Griffith, IV *newspaper publisher*
Peper, Christian Baird *lawyer*
Perez, Carlos A. *radiation oncologist, educator*
Peters, David Allen *mechanical engineering educator, consultant*
Peters, Frank Lewis, Jr. *retired arts editor*
Petrie, Roy H. *obstetrician, gynecologist, educator*
†Pfautch, Roy *minister, public affairs consultant*
Pfefferkorn, Michael Gene, Sr. *secondary education educator, writer*
Pflueger, M(elba) Lee *academic administrator*
Pickens, Buford Lindsay *architectural educator, historian*
Pickle, Robert Douglas *lawyer, diversified industry executive*
Pittman, David Joshua *sociologist, educator, researcher, consultant*
Plager, Bob *professional hockey coach*
Podosek, Frank Anthony *geochemistry, geology educator*
†Polizzi, Jan Crandall *community and maternal-women's health nurse*
Pollack, Joe *newspaper critic and columnist, free-lance writer*
Pollack, Seymour Victor *computer science educator*
Poscover, Maury B. *lawyer*
Prensky, Arthur Lawrence *pediatric neurologist, educator*
Preus, Jacob Aall Ottesen *former seminary president and church executive*
Price, Joseph Levering *neuroscientist, educator*
Prickett, Gordon Odin *mining, mineral and energy engineer*
Pulitzer, Emily S Rauh (Mrs. Joseph Pulitzer, Jr.) *art consultant*
Pulitzer, Michael Edgar *publishing executive*
Purnell, John H. *beverage company executive*
Pylipow, Stanley Ross *retired manufacturing company executive, advisor*
†Quenon, Robert H. *bank executive*
Quenon, Robert Hagerty *consultant, retired holding company executive*
Quinn, Jack J. *professional hockey team executive*
†Ractliffe, Robert Edward George *management executive*
Ramming, Michael Alexander *school system administrator*
Randolph, Joe Wayne *machine manufacturing executive*
†Raskas, Heschel Joshua *food company executive, educator*
Rataj, Edward William *lawyer*
Raven, Peter Hamilton *botanical garden director, botany educator*
Reams, Bernard Dinsmore, Jr. *lawyer, educator*
†Redmond, Donald Paul *insurance company executive*
Reinert, Paul Clare *university chancellor emeritus*
†Reinhard, James Richard *judge*
Reynolds, James E. *lawyer*
Rich, Harry E. *footwear and specialty retailing financial executive*
Richmond, Richard Thomas *journalist*
Riddle, Veryl Lee *lawyer*
Ritter, Robert Forcier *lawyer*
Ritterskamp, Douglas Dolvin *lawyer*
Roberts, Hugh Evan *business investment services company executive*
Robins, Lee Nelken *medical educator*
†Rocklage, Sister Mary Roch *health system executive*
†Rockwell, Hays Hamilton *bishop*
†Rodgers, Timothy Francis *advertising executive*
Rodin, Ervin Yechiel Lászlo *mathematician*
Rosenthal, Harold Leslie *biochemistry educator*
Rosenzweig, Saul *psychologist, educator, administrator*
Ross, Donald Kenneth *consulting engineering executive*
Ross, Monte *electrical engineer*
Rubenstein, Jerome Max *lawyer*
Ruland, Richard Eugene *English and American literature educator, critic, literary historian*
Ryckman, DeVere Wellington *consulting environmental engineer*
Sachs, Alan Arthur *lawyer, corporate executive*
Sale, Llewellyn, III *lawyer*
Sale, William Merritt *classicist, educator*
Saligman, Harvey *consumer products and services company executive*
Salisbury, Robert Holt *political science educator*
†Samples, Ronald Eugene *coal company executive*
Sanders, Fred Joseph *aerospace company executive*
Sanders, Steven Paul *lawyer*
Sant, John Talbot *lawyer*
†Santiago, Julio V. *medical educator, medical association administrator*
Saperstein, Marc Eli *religious history educator, rabbi*
Sathe, Sharad Somnath *chemical company executive*
†Sauer, Georgia Booras *newspaper writer*
†Sauer, Robert C. *religious organization administrator*
Scherrer, Richard Bennington *lawyer*
Schierholz, William Francis, Jr. *real estate developer*
Schmidt, Robert Charles, Jr. *finance company executive*
†Schneller, George Charles *chiropractor*
Schnuck, Craig *grocery stores company executive*
Schoendienst, Albert Fred (Red Schoendienst) *professional baseball coach, former baseball player*
Schoenhard, William Charles, Jr. *health care executive*
†Schonfeld, Gustav *medical educator*
Schroeder, Paul J., Jr. *lawyer*
Schumacher, Frederick Carl *former insurance company executive*
Schwartz, Alan Leigh *pediatrician, educator*
Schwartz, Henry Gerard *surgeon, educator*
Schwarz, Egon *humanities and German language educator, author, literary critic*
†Searls, Eileen Haughey *lawyer, librarian, educator*
Selfridge, George Dever *dentist, retired naval officer*
Sestric, Anthony James *lawyer*
Sexton, Owen James *vertebrate ecology educator, conservationist*
Shanahan, Michael Francis *manufacturing executive, hockey team executive*
Shands, Courtney, Jr. *lawyer*
Shank, Robert Ely *physician, preventive medicine educator emeritus*
Shapiro, Harold Benjamin *accountant*
†Shaw, Charles Alexander *judge*
†Shaw, James *church administrator*
Shaw, John Arthur *lawyer*
Shea, Daniel Bartholomew, Jr. *English language educator, actor*
†Shelton, O. L. *state legislator*
Shepperd, Thomas Eugene *accountant*
Shipton, Harold William *biomedical engineering educator, researcher*
Shrauner, Barbara Wayne Abraham *electrical engineering educator*
Siemer, Paul Jennings *public relations executive*
†Sigurdson, Erik D. *oil industry executive*
Siteman, Alvin Jerome *banker*
Slatkin, Leonard Edward *conductor, music director, pianist*
Slavin, Raymond Granam *allergist, immunologist*
†Smith, Jeffrey E. *library director*
Smith, Ozzie (Osborne Earl Smith) *professional baseball player*
Smurfit, Michael William Joseph *manufacturing company executive*
†Sneider, Martin Karl *retail company executive*
Snyder, Peter Larsen *public relations executive*
Sonnino, Carlo Benvenuto *electrical manufacturing company executive*
†Spainhower, James Ivan *retired college president*
Spector, Gershon Jerry *physician, educator, researcher*
Spector, Stanley *foreign language educator*
Stahl, Philip Damien *physiology and cell biology educator*
Staley, Robert W. *mechanical engineer, electric company executive*
Stalnaker, Armand Carl *former insurance company executive, retired educator*
Stauder, William Vincent *geophysics educator*
Stearley, Robert Jay *retired packaging company executive*
Stein, Elliot H. *investment broker*
†Stewart, Ernest William *market research executive*
Stewart, John Harger *voice educator*
Stiritz, William P. *food company executive*
Stith, Richard Taylor, Jr. *insurance company executive*
Stoecker, David Thomas *banker*
Stohr, Donald J. *federal judge*
Stokes, Patrick T. *brewery company executive*
Storandt, Martha *psychologist*
Stork, Donald Arthur *advertising executive*
Stretch, John Joseph *social work educator, management and evaluation consultant*

†Strunk, Robert C. *physician*
†Stuhl, Harold Maxwell *manufacturing executive*
Suba, Antonio Ronquillo *surgeon*
Suelflow, August Robert *historical institute administrator, educator*
†Suggs, James C. *religious publishing executive*
Suhre, Walter Anthony, Jr. *lawyer, brewery executive*
Suter, Albert Edward *manufacturing company executive*
Sutera, Salvatore Philip *mechanical engineering educator*
Sutter, Richard Anthony *physician*
†Svetanics, Neil *fire chief*
Szabo, Barna Aladar *mechanical engineering educator, mining engineer*
Takano, Masaharu *physical chemist*
Tarn, Tzyh-Jong *electrical engineering educator, researcher*
†Taylor, Jack C. *automobile company executive*
Teasdale, Kenneth Fulbright *lawyer*
Teasdale, Thomas Hennings *architect*
Teitelbaum, Steven Lazarus *pathology educator*
Templeton, Alan Robert *biology educator*
Ternberg, Jessie Lamoin *pediatric surgeon*
Tewksbury, Robert Alan *professional baseball player*
Thach, William Thomas, Jr. *neurobiology and neurology educator*
Thalden, Barry R. *architect*
Thayer, Gerald Campbell *beer company executive*
Thomas, Lewis Jones, Jr. *anesthesiology educator, biomedical researcher*
Thomas, Rhonda Churchill *lawyer*
Thompson, James Clark *utilities executive*
Thompson, James David *financial services company executive, lawyer*
Throdahl, Monte Corden *former chemical company executive*
Tober, Lester Victor *shoe company executive*
Torre, Joseph Paul (Joe Torre) *professional baseball team manager*
Touhill, Blanche Marie *university chancellor, history-education educator*
Tremayne, Bertram William, Jr. *lawyer*
Trova, Ernest Tino *artist, sculptor*
†Trusheim, H. Edwin *insurance executive*
Tulloch, George Sherlock, Jr. *electrical equipment distribution company executive, lawyer*
Turley, Michael Roy *lawyer*
Turner, Harold Edward *education educator*
†Ulett, George Andrew *psychiatrist*
Ullian, Joseph Silbert *philosophy educator*
Van Bokkelen, William Requa *health facility administrator*
Van Cleve, William Moore *lawyer*
Vandover, Samuel Taylor *lawyer*
Varner, Joseph Elmer *biology educator, researcher*
Ver Hagen, Jan Karol *electrical manufacturing company executive*
†Virgil, Robert L. *dean*
Wack, Thomas E. *lawyer*
Walker, Dale Rush *banker*
Walker, Earl E. *manufacturing executive*
Walker, George Herbert, III *investment banking company executive, lawyer*
Walker, Robert Mowbray *physicist, educator*
Walsh, John E., Jr. *business educator, consultant*
Walsh, Thomas Charles *lawyer*
Walz, Bruce James *radiation oncologist*
Wandling, Marilyn Elizabeth Branson *art educator*
†Ward, R. J. *bishop*
Waters, Richard *retired publishing company executive*
Watkins, Hortense Catherine *middle school educator*
Watson, Patty Jo *anthropology educator*
Watson, Richard Allan *philosophy educator, writer*
Weaver, William Clair, Jr. (Mike Weaver) *human resources development executive*
†Weber, Gloria Richie *minister, retired, state representative*
Weber, Morton M. *microbial biochemist, educator*
Weeks, Paul Martin *plastic surgeon, educator*
Weidenbaum, Murray Lew *economics educator*
Weil, Paul P. *lawyer*
Weiss, Charles Andrew *lawyer*
Weiss, Robert Francis *former academic administrator, religious organization administrator, consultant*
Wellman, Carl Pierce *philosophy educator*
Wells, Ben Harris *retired beverage company executive*
Wells, Samuel Alonzo, Jr. *surgeon, educator*
Wenzel, Fred William *apparel manufacturing executive*
Wheeler, Burton M. *literature educator, higher education consultant, college dean*
†Wickline, Samuel Alan *cardiologist, educator*
Wiley, Gregory Robert *publisher*
†Wilke, LeRoy *church administrator*
Will, Clifford Martin *physicist, educator*
Williams, Frank James, Jr. *department store chain executive, lawyer*
Williams, Thom Albert *insurance company executive*
Williamson, Donald Ray *retired career officer*
Willman, John Norman *management consultant*
Willman, Vallee Louis *physician, surgery educator*
Wilson, Betty May *finance company executive*
Wilson, Edward Nathan *mathematician, educator*
Wilson, Harry Burgoyme *retired public relations company executive*
Wilson, Margaret Bush *lawyer, civil rights leader*
†Winer, Warren James *insurance executive*
Wint, Dennis Michael *museum director*
Winter, David Ferdinand *electrical engineering educator, consultant*
Winter, William Earl *retired beverage company executive*
Wirth, Arthur George *education educator*
Wissner, Seth Ernst *gynecologist, educator*
Withers, W. Wayne *lawyer*
Witherspoon, William *investment economist*
†Wittich, Brenda June *religious organization executive, minister*
Wolfe, Charles Morgan *electrical engineering educator*
Wolff, Frank Pierce, Jr. *lawyer*
Woo, William Franklin *newspaper editor*
Woodruff, Bruce Emery *lawyer*
†Woolf, Steven Michael *artistic director*
Worseck, Raymond Adams *economist*
Wright, Tamela Jean (T.J. Wright) *disc jockey, entertainer*
Wu, Nelson Ikon *art history educator, author, artist*
†Yates, Michael Zane *lawyer*
Young, Marvin Oscar *lawyer*
Young, Paul Andrew *anatomist*
†Zavaglia, Greg J. *management consultant*
Zuker, Michael *biomathematician*
Zurheide, Charles Henry *consulting electrical engineer*

Saint Peters
Krey, Mary Ann Reynolds *beer wholesaler executive*

Sibley
Morrow, Elizabeth *sculptress, educator, museum association administrator, business owner*

Sparta
Madore, Joyce Louise *gerontology nurse*

Springfield
Abraham, Yohannan *management educator*
Ames, Jimmy Ray *education educator*
Berger, Jerry Allen *museum director*
Boehm, Robert Kenneth *telecommunications consultant*
Carlson, Thomas Joseph *lawyer, mayor*
†Champion, Norma Jean *communications educator, state legislator*
Champion, Richard Gordon *editor, journalism educator*
Clark, Russell Gentry *federal judge*
Cox, Lester Lee *broadcasting executive*
Criswell, Charles Harrison *analytical chemist, environmental and forensic consultant, executive*
Cunningham, Robert Cyril *clergyman, editor*
†Dailey, Parker Stokes *minister*
Dearmore, Thomas Lee *retired journalist*
Denton, D. Keith *management educator*
†Flower, Joseph Reynolds *administrative executive*
Glazier, Robert Carl *publishing executive*
Gruhn, Robert Stephen *parole officer*
Hackett, Earl Randolph *neurologist*
†Hanman, Gary Edwin *dairy company executive*
Hansen, John Paul *metallurgical engineer*
H'Doubler, Francis Todd, Jr. *surgeon*
Himstedt, Ronald Eugene *union official*
Hulston, John Kenton *lawyer*
†Jacobi, Fredrick Thomas *newspaper publisher*
Jura, James J. *electric utility executive*
King, (Jack) Weldon *photographer*
Leibrecht, John Joseph *bishop*
†Linnemeyer, Annie *library director*
Liu, Yuan Hsiung *drafting and design educator*
Lowther, Gerald Halbert *lawyer*
†McCartney, N. L. *investment banker*
Moore, John Edwin, Jr. *college president*
Nuccitelli, Saul Arnold *civil engineer, consultant*
Orms, Howard Raymond *dramatics educator*
†Ostergren, Gregory Victor *insurance company executive*
Ownby, Jerry Steve *landscape architect, educator*
Shealy, Clyde Norman *neurosurgeon*
Spicer, Holt Vandercook *speech and theater educator*
Stone, Allan David *economics educator*
Stovall, Richard L. *academic administrator*
Strickler, Ivan K. *dairy farmer*
†Swift, James William *health care executive*
†Sylvester, Ronald Charles *newspaper writer*
Thompson, Clifton C. *chemistry educator, university administrator*
†Trask, Thomas E. *religious organization administrator*
†Triplett, Loren O. *religious organization administrator*
Van Cleave, William Robert *international relations educator*
Westphal, Leonard Wyrick *health care executive, consultant*

Sweet Springs
Long, Edwin Tutt *surgeon*

University City
Shen, Jerome Tseng Yung *pediatrician*

Viburnum
West, Roberta Bertha *writer*

Warrensburg
Elliott, Eddie Mayes *college president*
Harmon, Lynn Adrian *banker*
Smith, Dolores Maxine Plunk *dancer, educator*

Warrenton
Dapron, Elmer Joseph, Jr. *communications executive*

Washington
Carroll, John Howard *sales executive*

Webb City
Blanset, Robert James *newspaper editor*

Webster Groves
Kramer, Gerhardt Theodore *architect*
Osver, Arthur *artist*
†Schenkenberg, Mary Martin *principal*

Wentzville
Berry, Chuck (Charles Edward Anderson Berry) *singer, composer*

West Plains
Gunter, DeVona Elizabeth *special education educator*

Willow Springs
Evins, Marylou *special education educator*

MONTANA

Anaconda
†McCarthy, Bea *state legislator*

Antelope
Olson, Betty-Jean *elementary education educator*

Arlee
Gregory, Russell Arthur *education and training consultant*

Big Fork
Blumberg, Nathan(iel) Bernard *journalist, educator, writer and publisher*

Big Timber
Yuzeitis, James Richard *information specialist*

Bigfork
Shennum, Robert Herman *retired telephone company executive*

Billings
Battin, James Franklin *judge, former congressman*
Carpenter, Bruce H. *academic administrator*
†Cochran, William Michael *librarian*
DeRosier, Arthur Henry, Jr. *college president*
Evans, Judith Christien Lunbeck *elementary school principal*
†Fagg, Russell *lawyer, state legislator*
Haughey, James McCrea *lawyer, artist*
Heiny, Robert Wayne *special education educator*
Jones, James Leonard *lawyer*
†Keating, Thomas Francis *state senator*
Larsen, Richard Lee *former city manager, business, municipal and labor relations consultant, arbitrator*
Marcovitz, Leonard Edward *retail executive*
†McCracken, Joe C. *school system administrator*
Murphy, Gregory Gerard *lawyer*
Reed, Kenneth G. *petroleum company executive*
Rehberg, Dennis R. *state official*
†Russell, Angela Veta *state legislator, social worker*
†Rye, David Blake *television news anchor*
Sample, Joseph Scanlon *foundation executive*
Shanstrom, Jack D. *federal judge*
Sites, James Philip *lawyer, consul*
Small, Lawrence Farnsworth *history educator*
Surwill, Benedict Joseph, Jr. *college dean, educator*
Thompson, James William *lawyer*
†Towe, Thomas Edward *lawyer*
†Vogel, Randy Charles *state legislator, police officer*

Bozeman
Berg, Lloyd *chemical engineering educator*
Caughlan, Georgeanne Robertson *retired physics educator*
Davis, Nicholas Homans Clark *finance company executive*
DeHaas, John Neff, Jr. *retired architecture educator*
Dunkel, Florence Vaccarello *entomologist*
Goering, Kenneth Justin *college administrator*
Gray, Philip Howard *psychologist, educator*
Harris, Christopher Kirk *lawyer*
Hovin, Arne William *agronomist, educator*
Knox, James Lester *electrical engineer*
†Mattson, George Arthur *architect*
Mertz, Edwin Theodore *biochemist, emeritus educator*
†Pittendrigh, Colin Stephenson *retired biologist, educator*
Refsland, Gary Arlan *retired sociology educator*
Sanks, Robert Leland *environmental engineer, emeritus educator*
Spencer, Robert C. *political science educator*
Stanislao, Joseph *consulting engineer, educator*
Stroup, Richard Lyndell *economics educator, writer*
†Swenson, Robert J. *physics educator*

Browning
Scriver, Robert Macfie *sculptor*

Butte
Beuerman, Donald Roy *chemistry educator*
Burke, John James *utility executive*
Mc Elwain, Joseph Arthur *retired power company executive*
†Ruppel, Edward Thompson *geologist*
†Sherick, John Matthew (Jack Sherick) *technical services company executive*
Studebaker, Irving Glen *engineering educator, researcher*

Cascade
†Mesaros, Kenneth Lee *rancher, state senator*

Columbia Falls
Ruder, Melvin Harvey *retired newspaper editor*

Corvallis
Koch, Peter *wood scientist*

Darby
Brandborg, Stewart Monroe *conservationist, government official*

Dayton
Catalfomo, Philip *university dean*

Galata
†Aklestad, Gary C. *state legislater*

Great Falls
†Christiaens, Bernard F. *state legislator, innkeeper*
Christiaens, Chris (Bernard F. Christiaens) *financial analyst, senator*
Davidson, David Scott *architect*
†Doherty, Steve *lawyer, state legislator*
Downer, William John, Jr. *hospital administrator*
Hatfield, Paul Gerhart *federal judge, lawyer*
Hoiland, Andrew Calvin *architect*
Manning, John Willard *lawyer*
Milone, Anthony M. *bishop*
Overfelt, Clarence Lahugh *lawyer*
Sletten, John Robert *construction company executive*
Stevens, George Alexander *realtor*
Walker, Leland Jasper *civil engineer*

Hamilton
Munoz, John Joaquin *research microbiologist*

Harrison
Jackson, Peter Vorious, III *retired association executive*

Havre
Thompson, Theodore Kvale *lawyer*

Helena
†Barnhart, Beverly Homyak *management consultant*
Blair, Gary Charles *military officer*
Curtiss, Elden F. *bishop*
†Ewer, David *state legislator, bond program officer*
†Fitzpatrick, Lois Ann *library administrator*
Gray, Karla Marie *state supreme court justice*
Harrison, John Conway *state supreme court justice*
Hunt, William E., Sr. *state supreme court justice*
†Jacobson, Judith Helen *state senator*
Johnson, David Sellie *civil engineer*
Jones, Charles Irving *bishop*
Lindgren, Robert Kemper *securities investor, county tax collector*
Lovell, Charles C. *federal judge*
Malcolm, Andrew Hogarth *journalist, writer*
Marks, Robert L. (Bob Marks) *treasurer ex-officio, rancher*
Mazurek, Joseph P. *state attorney general*
McDonough, Russell Charles *retired state supreme court justice*
Opitz, John Marius *clinical geneticist, pediatrician*
Racicot, Marc F. *governor*
Trieweiler, Terry Nicholas *state supreme court justice*
Turnage, Jean A. *state supreme court chief justice*
†Vaughn, Eleanor *state legislator*
†Waterman, Mignon Redfield *public relations executive, state legislator*
Weber, Fred J. *state supreme court justice*

Hot Springs
Erickson, James Gardner *retired artist, cartoonist*

Hungry Horse
†Wagner, Douglas T. *state legislator, millwright*

Kalispell
†Dowell, Timothy John *educator*
James, Marion Ray *magazine founder, publisher and editor*
Ormiston, Patricia Jane *educator*

Laurel
†Blaylock, Chet *state legislator*

Livingston
Feldstein, Albert B. *retired editor, artist, writer*
Harrison, James Thomas (Jim Harrison) *author*

Mc Leod
Hjortsberg, William Reinhold *author*
Mc Guane, Thomas Francis, III *author, screenwriter*

Miles City
†Bergman, Ellen Marie *state legislator*

Missoula
Ammons, Robert Bruce *psychologist, behavior consultant*
Banaugh, Robert Peter *computer science educator*
†Brown, Robert Munro *museum director*
Dennison, George Marshel *academic administrator*
Fawcett, Don Wayne *anatomist*
Fisher, William Henry *education educator*
Haddon, Sam Ellis *lawyer*
Jakobson, Mark John *physics educator*
Jenni, Donald Alison *zoology educator*
Kemmis, Daniel Orra *mayor, author*
Kindrick, Robert LeRoy *academic administrator, English educator*
Knowles, William Leroy (Bill) *television news producer, journalism educator*
†Kraft, Dennis *school system administrator*
Lopach, James Joseph *political science educator*
†Millin, Laura J. *museum director*
Murray, Raymond Carl *forensic geologist, educator*
Nakamura, Mitsuru James *microbiologist, educator*
Osterheld, R(obert) Keith *chemistry educator*
Peterson, James Algert *geologist, educator*
Power, Thomas Michael *economist, educator*
Rippon, Thomas Michael *art educator, artist*
Sogard, Jeffrey W. *lawyer*
†Toole, Howard *lawyer*
†Van Valkenburg, Frederick Robert, II *lawyer*
Watkins, John Goodrich *psychologist, educator*
Weber, Brom *literature educator*
†Winston, Bente *academic administrator*

Polson
†Harding, Ethel M. *state legislator*
†Stanford, Jack Arthur *biological station administrator*

Red Lodge
Kauffman, Marvin Earl *geoscience consultant*

Seeley Lake
†Larson, Donald Edward *state legislator*

Troy
Sherman, Signe Lidfeldt *former research chemist, securities analyst*

West Glacier
Lusk, Harlan Gilbert *national park superintendent*
Mihalic, David Anthony *national park administrator*

Whitefish
Miller, Ronald Alfred *family physician*

Wolf Point
Listerud, Mark Boyd *retired surgeon*

NEBRASKA

Alliance
Haefele, Edwin Theodore *political theorist, consultant*
Knight, Robert Edward *banker*

Auburn
Winegardner, Rose Mary *special education educator*

Bellevue
†Hinz, Calvin L. *architectural firm executive*
Muller, John Bartlett *college president*
†Raynor, Dennis L. *architect, firm executive*

Boys Town
†Peter, Val Joseph *social service administrator, educator, priest*

Chadron
Scott, Jerry Don *management and marketing educator*
Winkle, William Allan *music educator*

Clay Center
Hahn, George LeRoy *agricultural engineer, biometeorologist*
†Laster, Danny Bruce *animal scientist*

Columbus
†Bellum, Fred Lewis *school system administrator*
Whitehead, John C. *state judge*

Crete
Brakke, Myron Kendall *retired research chemist and educator*

Dakota City
†Andriessen, Roel *management consulting company executive*
Broyhill, Roy Franklin *manufacturing executive*
Grigsby, Lonnie Oscar *food company executive*
Haines, Perry Vansant *cattle company executive*
Peterson, Robert L. *meat processing executive*
Tinstman, Dale Clinton *investment company executive*

Daykin
Rife, Ronald Eugene *elementary education educator*

Ewing
†Dierks, Merton Lyle *veterinarian*

Fremont
Dunklau, Rupert Louis *personal investments consultant*
Gill, Lyle Bennett *lawyer*

Gibbon
Wiley, Ronald LeRoy *financial executive*

Grand Island
Dobesh, Ernest Leonard *farmer, mayor*
Etheridge, Margaret Dwyer *medical center director*
Mason, Doris Ann *county official*
Mc Namara, Lawrence J. *bishop*

Gretna
†Riley, Kevin M. *principal*

Hastings
†Larsen, Glen L. *school system administrator*
McEwen, Larry Burdette *retired English language arts and theatre arts educator*

Holdrege
Hendrickson, Bruce Carl *life insurance company executive*

Humboldt
Rumbaugh, Melvin Dale *geneticist, agronomist*

Kearney
Lund, Virginia Llego *museum director, curator, chemistry educator*

Las Vegas
Haas, Robert John *aerospace engineer*

Lincoln
Ackerman, James Nils *lawyer*
Adams, Charles Henry *retired animal scientist, educator*
Arth, Lawrence Joseph *insurance executive*
Babchuk, Nicholas *sociology educator, researcher*
Bahar, Ezekiel *electrical engineering educator*
Bailey, Dudley *English educator*
Beam, Clarence Arlen *federal judge*
Beermann, Allen J. *state official*
Blad, Blaine L. *agricultural meteorology educator, consultant*
Boslaugh, Leslie *judge*
Bradley, Richard Edwin *retired university president*
Broman, Keith Leroy *finance educator, financial planner*
Caporale, D. Nick *state supreme court justice*
Cederberg, John Edwin *accountant*
Childs, Gayle B(ernard) *retired education educator*
Crompton, Louis William *English literature educator*
†Crosby, LaVon Kehoe Stuart *civic leader*
Curtis, Carl Thomas *former senator*
Day, Richard Putnam *insurance executive*
Diffendal, Anne P. *archivist, consulting historian*
Digman, Lester Aloysius *management educator*
Dyer, William Earl, Jr. *retired newspaper editor*
Eckhardt, Craig Jon *chemistry educator*
Edison, Allen Ray *electrical engineer, educator*
Edwards, Donald Mervin *biological systems engineering educator, university dean*
Elias, Samy E. G. *engineering executive*
Fahrnbruch, Dale E. *state supreme court justice*
Fisher, Calvin David *food manufacturing company executive*
†Fisher, Dan *state legislator, bank executive*
Francis, Charles Andrew *agronomy educator, consultant*
Fuenning, Samuel Isaiah *sports medicine research director*
Gardner, Charles Olda *plant geneticist and breeder, design consultant, analyst*
†Geist, James E. *telecommunication company executive*
Genoways, Hugh Howard *museum director*
Grew, Priscilla Croswell *university official, geology educator*
†Haberman, Rex Stanley *state senator*
Haire, James Robert *insurance company individual administration and strategic development executive*
Hamilton, David Wendell *medical services executive*
†Hanna, Milford A. *agricultural engineering educator*
Hanway, Donald Grant *retired agronomist, educator*
Hastings, William Charles *state supreme court chief justice*
Hendrickson, Kent Herman *dean, librarian*
Heng, Stanley Mark *military officer*
Hermance, Lyle Herbert *education educator*
Hewitt, James Watt *lawyer*
Hillegass, Clifton Keith *publisher*
†Hillman, Joyce *state legislator*
Hirai, Denitsu *surgeon*
Hodges, Clarence Eugene *charitable organization executive, former government official*
Hoffman, Peter Toll *law educator, judge*
Holdt, Leland LaMar Stark *insurance company executive*
Janzow, Walter Theophilus *retired college administrator*
†Johanns, Michael O. *mayor*
Johnson, Margaret Kathleen *business educator*
Johnson, Virgil Allen *retired agronomist*
Jolliff, Carl R. *clinical biochemist, immunologist, laboratory administrator*
Jones, Alice J. *soil scientist, educator, federal agency administrator*
Jones, Lee Bennett *chemist, educator*
Kopf, Richard G. *federal judge*
Koszewski, Bohdan Julius *internist, medical educator*
†Landis, David Morrison *state legislator*
Laursen, Paul Herbert *retired university educator*
Lee, Sang Moon *management educator, author, consultant*
Leinieks, Valdis *classicist, educator*
Liggett, Twila Marie Christensen *public television company executive, academic administrator*
Louis, Kenneth Clair *insurance company executive*
Luedtke, Roland Alfred *lawyer*
†Luetchens, Melvin Harvey *minister, religious organization administrator*
Lutjeharms, Joseph Earl *commissioner*
MacPhee, Craig Robert *economist, educator*
Marsh, Frank (Irving) *former state official*
Massengale, Martin Andrew *agronomist, university president*
McClurg, James Edward *research laboratory executive*
Morrow, Andrew Nesbit *interior designer, business owner*
Moul, Maxine Burnett *state official*
Nelson, Darrell Wayne *university administrator*
Nelson, E. Benjamin *governor*
Nolte, Walter Eduard *retired retirement home executive, foundation counsel, former banker*
Oldfather, Charles Eugene *lawyer*
O'Leary, Marion Hugh *chemistry educator*
Osborne, Tom *college football coach*
Ottoson, Howard Warren *agricultural economist, former university administrator*
Peterson, Wallace Carroll, Sr. *economics educator*
Piester, David L(ee) *magistrate judge*
†Pirsch, Carol McBride *state senator, community relations manager*
†Preister, Donald George *greeting card manufacturer, state senator*
†Rasmussen, Jessie K. *state legislator*
Rawley, Ann Keyser *small business owner, picture framer*
Rawley, James Albert *history educator*
Raz, Hilda *editor-in-chief periodical, educator*
Robson, John Merritt *library and media administrator*
Rogers, Vance Donald *former university president*
Rosenow, John Edward *foundation executive*
Sander, Donald Henry *soil scientist, researcher*
Sawyer, Robert McLaran *history educator*
†Schimek, DiAnna R. *state legislator*
Schmidt, John Wesley *agronomy educator*
Schmitz, John Albert *veterinary pathologist*
Schwendiman, Gary *business administration educator*
†Sellmyer, David Julian *physicist, educator*
†Shanahan, Thomas M. *state supreme court justice*
Sheffield, Leslie Floyd *agricultural educator*
Sonderegger, Theo Brown *psychology educator*
Spanier, Graham Basil *university administrator, family sociologist*
†Spellman, J. R. *book publishing executive*
Splinter, William Eldon *agricultural engineering educator*
†Stange, James Henry *architect*
Stenberg, Donald B. *state attorney general*
Steward, Weldon Cecil *architecture educator, architect, consultant*
Stover, John Ford *railroad historian, educator*
Stuart, James *banker, broadcaster*
Swartz, Jack *association executive*
Swartzendruber, Dale *soil physicist, educator*
Swihart, Fred Jacob *lawyer*
†Tavlin, Michael John *telecommunications company executive*
Thorson, Thomas Bertel *zoologist, educator*
Treves, Samuel Blain *geologist, educator, administrator*
Tyner, Neal Edward *insurance company executive*
Ullman, Frank Gordon *electrical engineering educator*
Urbom, Warren Keith *federal judge*
Wagner, Rod *library director*
†Wesely, Donald Raymond *state senator*
White, John Wesley, Jr. *university president*
†Wiegand, Sylvia Margaret *mathematician, educator*
Wiersbe, Warren Wendell *clergyman, author, lecturer*
†Will, Eric John *state senator*
†Woollam, John Arthur *electrical engineering educator*
Wright, Flavel Allen *lawyer*
Young, Dale Lee *banker*

Lindsay
†Parker, Gary Dean *manufacturing company executive*

Madison
Say, Marlys Mortensen (Mrs. John Theodore Say) *school system administrator*

Norfolk
†Day, Connie Jo *moving company executive, consultant*
Wehrer, Charles Siecke *business educator*
Wozniak, Richard Michael, Sr. *city and regional planner*

Offult
Curtin, Gary Lee *air force officer*

Offutt A F B
Tindal, Ralph Lawrence *career officer*
Torma, Michael Joseph *career officer, surgeon*

Omaha
†Abboud, Christopher William *state senator*
Ames, George Ronald *insurance marketing executive*
Andersen, Harold Wayne *director, contributing editor, newspaper executive*
Andrews, Richard Vincent *physiologist, educator*
Badeer, Henry Sarkis *physiology educator*
Barmettler, Joseph John *lawyer*
Barrett, Frank Joseph *insurance company executive*
Batchelder, Anne Stuart *former publisher, political party official*
Bauer, Otto Frank *university official, communication educator*
Beal, Graham William John *museum director*
Bechtel, James M. *retired civil servant*
Bell, C(lyde) R(oberts) (Bob Bell) *association executive*
Bergquist, Gordon Neil *English educator*
†Bookout, John G. *insurance company executive*
†Bowen, Gary Roger *architect*
Brody, Alfred Walter *pulmonologist*
Buffett, Warren Edward *corporate executive*
Burke, Denis Patrick *lawyer*
Cambridge, William G. *federal judge*
†Campbell, Charles H. *construction company executive*
Casey, Murray Joseph *Obstetrician Gynecologist*
Christensen, Curtis Lee *lawyer*
†Cochran, John R. *bank executive*
Conley, Eugene Allen *retired insurance company executive*
Cox, Robert Sayre, Jr. *pathologist, researcher, educator*
Coy, William Raymond *civil engineer*
Cunningham, Glenn Clarence *government official*
Cunningham, William Francis, Jr. *English language educator, university administrator*
Davidson, Richard K. *railroad company executive*
Davis, Chip *record producer, arranger*
Davis, John Byron *surgeon*
Davis, Richard Bradley *internal medicine, pathology educator, physician*
Dolan, James Vincent *lawyer*
Dougherty, Charles John *philosophy and medical ethics educator*
Dubes, George Richard *geneticist*
Eggers, James Wesley *personnel consultant*
Erickson, James Paul *financial service company executive*
Ferer, Harvey Dean *metals company executive*
Fitzgerald, William Allingham *savings and loan association executive*
†Fjell, Mick *principal*
†Fletcher, Philip B. *food products company executive*
Flickinger, Thomas Leslie *hospital alliance executive*
Forbes, Franklin Sim *lawyer, educator*
Fowler, Stephen Eugene *retired military officer*
Frazier, Chet June *advertising agency executive*
Frederickson, Keith Alvin *advertising agency executive*
Fusaro, Ramon Michael *dermatologist, researcher*
Gambal, David *biochemistry educator*
Gardner, Paul Jay *anatomist, educator*
Gordon, John Leo *anesthesiologist*
†Graham, Wayne *insurance company executive*
Grant, John Thomas *retired state supreme court justice*
†Grauer, Allan L. *lawyer*
Greer, Randall Dewey *investment company executive*
Grewcock, William L. *mining company executive*
Gugas, Chris, Sr. *criminologist, polygraphist, author*
Hamann, Deryl Frederick *lawyer, bank executive*
Haney, J. Terrence *insurance consultant*
Hangen, Bruce Boyer *conductor, music director*
Harned, Roger Kent *radiology educator*
Harr, Lawrence Francis *lawyer*
Haselwood, Eldon LaVerne *education educator*
Heaney, Robert Proulx *physician, educator*
Hodgson, Paul Edmund *surgeon*
Horning, Jerome Kay *artist, educator*
Horning, Ross Charles, Jr. *historian, educator*
Howe, G(ary) Woodson *newspaper editor*
Hruska, Roman Lee *lawyer, retired senator*
Hultquist, Paul Fredrick *electrical engineer, educator*
Imray, Thomas John *radiologist, educator*
Jay, Burton Dean *insurance actuary*
Jelensperger, Francis J. *engineering and architectural executive*
Jensen, Sam *lawyer*
Jugel, Richard Dennis *corporate executive, management consultant*
†Klassen, Lynell W. *rheumatologist, transplant immunologist*
Knobbe, Urban *food products executive*
Korbitz, Bernard Carl *oncologist, hematologist, educator, consultant*
Krogstad, Jack Lynn *accounting educator*
†Krohn, Robert Finley *bank executive*
†Krotz, James Edward *bishop*
Lauritzen, John Ronnow *banker*
Lemon, Henry Martyn *physician, educator*
Lenz, Charles Eldon *electrical engineering consultant, author*
Lindsay, James Wiley *agricultural company executive*
Lynch, Benjamin Leo *oral surgeon educator*
Mackenzie, Charles Westlake, III *software developer*
Maginn, John Leo *insurance company executive*
Martin, Elaine M. *lawyer*
Matthies, Frederick John *architectural engineer*
Maurer, Harold Maurice *pediatrician*
†McDaniels, B. T. *bishop*
McEniry, Robert Francis *education educator*
Miller, Morris Folsom *banker*
†Moeller, A. Diane *health facility administrator*
Mohiuddin, Syed Maqdoom *cardiologist, educator*
†Monaghan, Thomas Justin *prosecutor*
Monasee, Charles Arthur *healthcare foundation executive*
Morgan, P. J. *mayor*
Morrison, Michael Gordon *university president, clergyman, history educator*
†Myers, Herman E., Jr. *life insurance company executive*
Newton, John Milton *acadmeic administrator, psychology educator*
O'Brien, Richard L(ee) *academic administrator, physician, cell biologist*
O'Donohue, Walter John, Jr. *medical educator*
Omer, Robert Wendell *hospital administrator*
Pearson, Paul Hammond *physician*
Phares, Lynn Levisay *public communications executive*
†Polsky, Donald Perry *architect*
†Rikkers, Layton F. *surgeon*
†Rismiller, David A. *banking company executive*
†Rock, Harold L. *lawyer*
Roskens, Ronald William *association administrator*
Ruddon, Raymond Walter, Jr. *pharmacology educator*
†Rupp, Mark Edmund *medical educator*
Sanders, W(illiam) Eugene, Jr. *physician, educator*
Sawtell, Stephen M. *private investor, lawyer*
†Schellpeper, Gene Harold *insurance executive*
Schlessinger, Bernard S. *retired university dean*
Schwartz, C. Edward *hospital administrator*
†Scott, Robert Michael *data processing executive*
†Scott, Walter, Jr. *construction company executive*
Sheehan, Daniel Eugene *bishop*
Sheehan, John Francis *cytopathologist, educator*
Simmons, Lee Guyton, Jr. *zoological park director*
Skoog, Donald Paul *retired physician, educator*
Skutt, Thomas James *insurance company executive*
Slusky, Jerry Marvin *lawyer*
Sokolof, Phil *industrialist, consumer advocate*
Soshnik, Joseph *investment banking consultant*
Strom, Lyle Elmer *federal judge*
Tollman, Thomas Andrew *librarian*
Truhlsen, Stanley Marshall *physician, educator*
†Tucker, Michael *elementary school principal*
Tunnicliff, David George *civil engineer*
Velde, John Ernest, Jr. *business executive*
Waggener, Ronald Edgar *radiologist*
Wagner, John Julius *lawyer*
Watt, Dean Day *retired biochemistry educator*
Weekly, John William *insurance company executive*
Werner, Clarence L. *transportation executive*
Wright, Norman Harold *lawyer*
Wunsch, James Stevenson *political science educator*
Zepf, Thomas Herman *physics educator, researcher*

Papillion
Dvorak, Allen Dale *radiologist*

Plattsmouth
†Wehrbein, Roger Ralph *state senator*

Scottsbluff
Fisher, J. R. *marketing executive*
†Fritschen, Robert David *educational administrator, animal science educator, researcher*
†Scovil, Larry Emery *minister*
†Weichenthal, Burton A. *educational administrator, beef specialist*

Seward
Vrana, Verlon Kenneth *professional society administrator, conservationist*

South Sioux City
†Hohenstein, Kurt Alan *lawyer*

Wayne
Mash, Donald J. *college president*

West Point
Paschang, John Linus *retired bishop*

Wood River
Bish, Milan David *former ambassador, consultant*

Wymore
Meyer, Melvin A. *lumber and hardware executive, freelance designer*

NEVADA

Battle Mountain
†Hensley, E. Leon *school system administrator*

Boulder City
West, Arleigh Burton *retired water resources consultant*

Carson City
Ayres, Janice Ruth *social service executive*
Crawford, John Edward *geologist, scientist*
Del Papa, Frankie Sue *state attorney general*
†Glomb, Diana *state legislator*
Gunderson, Elmer Millard *state supreme court justice, law educator*
Larson, Gerald Lee *auditor*
Lau, Cheryl *state official*
Miller, Robert Joseph *governor, lawyer*
†Nevin, Leonard Verne *state legislator, retired police officer*
Noland, Robert LeRoy *retired manufacturing company executive*
Paslov, Eugene T. *state education official*
Rocha, Guy Louis *archivist, historian*
Rose, Robert E. *state supreme court justice*
Seale, Robert L. *state treasurer*
Springer, Charles Edward *state supreme court justice*
Wagner, Sue Ellen *state official*
Young, C. Clifton *judge*

East Ely
Alderman, Minnis Amelia *psychologist, educator, small business owner*

Gardnerville
Manoukian, Noel Edwin *lawyer, former state supreme court chief justice*

Glenbrook
Buscaglia, (Felice) Leo(nardo) *special education educator, author*
Jabara, Michael Dean *investment banker*

Hawthorne
Graham, Lois Charlotte *retired educator*

Henderson
Benson, James DeWayne *university administrator*
Carter, Thomas Smith, Jr. *retired railroad executive*
Creech, Wilbur Lyman *air force officer*
Freyd, William Pattinson *fund raising executive, consultant*
Turner, Florence Frances *ceramist*

Incline Village
Anderson, Arthur George *former computer company executive, consultant*
Dale, Martin Albert *investment banking executive*
Diederich, J(ohn) William *financial consultant*
Eastin, Keith E. *lawyer*
Henderson, Paul Bargas, Jr. *economic development consultant*
Hiatt, Robert Worth *former university president*
Johnson, James Arnold *business consultant, venture capitalist*
Merdinger, Charles John *civil engineer, naval officer, academic administrator*
Strack, Harold Arthur *retired electronics company executive, retired air force officer, planner, analyst, musician*

Wahl, Howard Wayne *retired construction company executive, engineer*
White, Richard Hugh *dean student affairs*

Jean
Schaeffer, Glenn William *casino corporate financial executive*

Las Vegas
Adams, Charles Lynford *English language educator*
Ann-Margret, (Ann-Margret Olsson) *actress, performer*
Arce, Phillip William *hotel and casino executive*
Atkins, Cholly (Charles Atkinson) *choreographer, consultant*
†Augustine, Kathy Marie *state legislator, primary school educator*
Bandt, Paul Douglas *physician*
Barber, Jerry Randel *medical device company executive*
Barger, James Daniel *physician*
Basile, Richard Emanuel *retired management consultant, educator*
Bishop, William Peter *research scientist*
Boehm, Robert Foty *mechanical engineer, educator, researcher*
Bradshaw, Ira Webb *accountant*
Brebbia, John Henry *lawyer*
Bretthauer, Erich Walter *chemist*
†Broadbent, Robert N. *government official, pharmacist*
Brown, Brice Norman *surgeon, educator*
†Brown, Lori Lipman *secondary school educator*
Capelle, Madelene Carole *international opera singer, educator, soprano*
†Cheever, Dan J. *bank executive*
†Colston, Bill W. *engineering executive*
Curley, Elmer Frank *librarian*
Cwerenz-Maxime, Virginia Margaret *secondary education educator*
DeFelice, Eugene Anthony *physician, medical educator, consultant, magician*
Di Palma, Joseph Alphonse *company executive, lawyer*
Earl, Boyd L. *chemistry educator*
Eastwood, DeLyle *chemist*
†Flippin, Perry Welch *newspaper editor*
Galane, Morton Robert *lawyer*
Geihs, Frederick Siegfried *lawyer*
George, Lloyd D. *federal judge*
†Giovenco, John V. *hotel corporation executive*
Goodall, Leonard Edwin *public administration educator*
Goodwin, Nancy Lee *corporate executive*
Goulet, Robert Gerard *singer, actor*
†Gregory, William David (Bill Gregory) *former state legislator, marketing executive*
†Guinn, Kenny C. *utility company executive*
Hamilton, Richard Lee *surgeon*
Hardbeck, George William *economics educator*
Harpster, Robert Eugene *engineering geologist*
Healy, Mary (Mrs. Peter Lind Hayes) *singer, actress*
Herch, Frank Alan *lawyer, law librarian*
Herte, Mary Charlotte *plastic surgeon*
Herzlich, Harold J. *chemical engineer*
†Hess, John Warren *scientific institute administrator, educator*
Hilbrecht, Norman Ty *state legislator, lawyer*
†Hill, Michael John *newspaper editor*
Hunsberger, Charles Wesley *library director*
Iorio, John Emil *retired education educator*
Johns, Albert Cameron *political scientist*
Johnston, Robert Jake *federal magistrate judge*
†Jones, Jan Laverty *mayor*
Kaiser, Glen David *construction company executive*
†Kenny, Erin Leigh *advertising executive, state legislator*
Knight, Gladys (Maria) *singer*
Koho, Clarence Herbert *agriculture laboratory executive, biologist, researcher*
Landau, Ellis *gaming company executive*
Laub, William Murray *retired utility executive*
Law, Flora Elizabeth (Libby Law) *community health and pediatrics nurse*
Lazerson, Jack *pediatrician, educator*
Levin, Bruce Alan *lawyer, real estate developer*
Lewis, Jerry (Joseph Levitch) *comedian*
Lovell, Carl Erwin, Jr. *lawyer*
Malek, James Stanley *language professional*
†Marnell, Anthony Austin, II *architect*
Martin, Thomas E. *motel chain executive*
Massimino, Roland V. *university basketball coach*
McDonald, Malcolm Gideon *education educator*
Mc Kenzie, Jeremy Alec *food service and baking company executive*
Messenger, George Clement *engineering executive, consultant*
Michel, Mary Ann Kedzuf *nursing educator*
†O'Donnell, William Russell *state senator*
Ogren, Carroll Woodrow *retired hospital administrator*
Polk-Matthews, Josephine Elsey *school psychologist*
Popeil, Ron *consumer products company executive*
†Pridham, Thomas Grenville *research microbiologist*
Pro, Philip Martin *federal judge*
†Rawson, Raymond D. *dentist*
†Reichartz, W. Dan *hotel executive*
Rogers, David Hughes *banker*
Rogich, Sig *advertising executive*
Rossin, Herbert Yale *television broadcaster*
Sabanas-Wells, Alvina Olga *orthopedic surgeon*
†Sandvick, Frederick *gaming company executive, accountant*
†Sawyer, Grant *lawyer*
Shettles, Landrum Brewer *obstetrician-gynecologist*
Shutler, Kenneth Eugene *lawyer*
Stevens, Arthur Wilber, Jr. *English language educator, writer, editor*
Thomas, Peter M. *bank executive*
Thomas-Orr, Betty Jo *retired public relations specialist*
†Toomin, Louis Allen *small business owner, state legislator*
Trimble, Thomas James *utility company executive, lawyer*
Troidl, Richard John *banker*
†Turner, Clyde T. *service executive*
Wada, Harry Nobuyoshi *training company executive*
†Webb, E. N. *bishop*
Wiemer, Robert Ernest *film and television producer, writer, director*
Wiener, Valerie *communications company owner*
Wilson, Warner Rushing *psychology educator*
Wyman, Richard Vaughn *engineering educator, exploration company executive*
Wynn, Kenneth Richard *design and furnishings company executive*
Wynn, Stephen A. *hotel, entertainment facility executive*
Zehm, Stanley James *education educator*

Laughlin
†Bennett, William Gordon *casino executive*

Logandale
Smiley, Robert William, Jr. *investment banker*

Lovelock
†Kiley, James P. *retired school system administrator*

Mercury
Schwichtenberg, Daryl Robert *drilling engineer*

North Las Vegas
Gowdy, Miriam Betts *nutritionist*
†Regan, John Bernard (Jack Regan) *community relations executive, assemblyman*

Pahrump
Hersman, Marion Frank *professional administrator, lawyer*

Reno
Barnet, Robert Joseph *cardiologist*
Becker, Patricia Winifred *hotel and casino company executive*
Bijou, Sidney William *psychology educator*
Binns, James Edward *banker*
Bohmont, Dale Wendell *agricultural consultant*
Broili, Robert Howard *lawyer*
Brunetti, Melvin T. *federal judge*
Cain, Edmund Joseph *education educator, emeritus dean*
†Casazza, Ralph Anthony *architect*
Clarke, Janice Cessna *educational administrator*
Crowley, Joseph Neil *academic administrator*
Cummings, Nicholas Andrew *psychologist*
Daugherty, Robert Melvin, Jr. *university dean, medical educator*
Di Salvo, Arthur Francis *physician, public health official*
Evans, Larry Melvyn *newspaper columnist, chess expert*
†Fox, Carl Alan *research institute executive*
†Freeman, Vivian Lois *state legislator, retired nurse*
†Gibbons, James Arthur *lawyer, pilot*
†Gifford, Gerald Frederic *environmental program director*
Gould, Martha Bernice *librarian*
Guild, Clark Joseph, Jr. *lawyer*
†Hagen, David W. *judge*
Helm, Donald Cairney *hydrogeologist*
Hibbs, Loyal Robert *lawyer*
Hill, Earl McColl *lawyer*
Horton, Gary Bruce *transportation company executive*
Horton, Robert Carlton *geologist*
Hug, Procter Ralph, Jr. *federal judge*
Humphrey, Neil Darwin *university president, retired*
Johnson, Arthur William, Jr. *planetarium executive*
Jordan, Joseph Rembert *airline pilot*
Krenkel, Peter Ashton *engineer, educator*
Leipper, Dale Frederick *physical oceanographer, educator*
Leland, Joy Hanson *anthropologist, alcohol research specialist*
Loveless, Edward Eugene *education educator, musician*
Marshall, Robert William *lawyer, rancher*
Martz, John Roger *lawyer*
Mathewson, Charles Norman *manufacturing company executive*
May, Jerry Russell *psychologist*
McHardy, Louis William *professional association executive, educator*
McKibben, Howard D. *federal judge*
Middlebrooks, Eddie Joe *environmental engineer*
Miller, Newton Edd, Jr. *communications educator*
Neidert, Kalo Edward *accountant, educator*
Newberg, Dorothy Beck (Mrs. William C. Newberg) *portrait artist*
†Pierson, William Roy *chemist*
Pough, Frederick Harvey *mineralogist*
†Raggio, William John *state senator*
Reed, Edward Cornelius, Jr. *federal judge*
Ritter, Dale Franklin *geologist, research association administrator*
†Sader, Robert Mayo *lawyer, state assemblyman*
Savoy, Douglas Eugene *bishop, religion educator, explorer, writer*
†Sferrazza, Peter Joseph *mayor, lawyer*
†Smith, Aaron *research director, clinical psychologist*
Taranik, James Vladimir *geologist, educator*
Tuxon, Linda Louise *banking officer*
Walsh, Daniel Francis *bishop*
Weems, Robert Cicero *economist, educator*
Weinberg, Leonard Burton *political scientist*
Wells, Richard H. *casino consultant, business broker*
Wheeler, Sessions Samuel *former foundation executive, author*
Wiggins, Charles Edward *federal judge*

Smith
Weaver, William Merritt, Jr. *investment banker*

Sparks
Chapman, Samuel Greeley *political science educator, criminologist*
Kleppe, John Arthur *electrical engineering educator, business executive*

Tuscarora
†Rhoads, Dean Allan *state senator, cattle rancher*

Yerington
Dini, Joseph Edward, Jr. *state legislator*
†Stahl, Stacy L. *tribal chairman*

Zephyr Cove
Proctor, Robert Swope *retired petroleum company executive*

NEW HAMPSHIRE

Alstead
Hanson, George Fulford *geologist*
Lyon, Bryce Dale *historian, educator*

Alton
†Ziegra, Alice Stevenson *state legislator*

Amherst
†Collins, Paul D. *principal*
†Lalley, Richard A. *school system administrator*
Mason, Phillip Howard *corporate executive, retired army officer*

Bedford
Collins, Diana Josephine *psychologist*
Cronin, Timothy Cornelius, III *computer manufacturing executive*
Hall, Pamela S. *environmental consulting firm executive*

Bow
†Johnson, C. William *retired federal agent, state representative*

Bridgewater
†Larson, Nils H. *state legislator, resort owner*

Bristol
Fisher, Robert George *neurological surgeon, educator*

Center Sandwich
Booty, John Everitt *historiographer*
Shoup, Carl Sumner *retired economist*
Simmons, Alan Jay *electrical engineer, consultant*

Chester
Preston, Faith *college president*

Concord
†Arnold, Thomas Ivan, Jr. *retired legislator*
Barbadoro, Paul J. *federal judge*
Batchelder, William F. *state supreme court justice*
Bownes, Hugh Henry *federal judge*
Brock, David Allen *state supreme court chief justice*
Brunelle, Robert L. *retired state education director*
Burns, Harold W. *state representative, insurance company executive*
Cann, William Francis *judge*
†Conroy, Janet M. *former state legislator*
†Cote, David Edward *state legislator*
Crosier, John David *association administrator*
Currie, Glenn Kenneth *financial consultant*
Day, Russell Clover *federal agency administrator*
†Delahunty, Joseph Lawrence *state senator, business investor*
Devine, Shane *federal judge*
†Dunn, Miriam D. *research firm executive, state legislator*
Dupuis, Sylvio Louis *optometrist, educator, administrator*
†Durham, Susan B. *state legislator*
†Flanagan, Natalie Smith *state representative*
Gardner, William Michael *state official*
†Hazelton, Robert G., III *state legislator*
†Hollingworth, Beverly A. *state senator*
Horton, Sherman D., Jr. *state supreme court justice*
Hosmer, Bradley Edwin *corporate executive*
†Hurst, Sharleene Page *state legislator*
Johnson, William R. *state supreme court justice*
Kalipolites, June E. Turner *rehabilitation professional*
†Kane, Cecelia Drapeau *state legislator, registered nurse*
Lederer, Richard Henry *writer, educator, columnist*
Levins, John Raymond *investment advisor, management consultant, educator*
Marston, Charles *state education official*
McAuliffe, Steven James *federal judge*
†McLane, Susan Neidlinger *state legislator*
Merrill, Stephen *governor*
Mevers, Frank Clement *state archivist, historian*
†Newland, Matthew John *state legislator*
†Packard, Bonnie Bennett *state legislator*
†Pignatelli, Debora Becker *state legislator*
†Podles, Eleanor Pauline *state senator*
Rath, Thomas David *lawyer, former state attorney general*
Rines, Robert Harvey *lawyer, inventor, law center executive, educator*
Roberts, George Bernard, Jr. *business and government affairs consultant, former state legislator*
†Rogers, Katherine D. *political consultant, state legislator*
†Schotanus, Merle William *fruit grower, state legislator*
†Shaw, Randall Francis *state legislator*
†Skinner, Patricia Morag *state legislator*
Stahl, Norman H. *federal judge*
Swope, John Franklin *insurance company executive*
†Teschner, Douglass Paul *state legislator*
Thayer, W(alter) Stephen, III *state supreme court justice*
†Theuner, Douglas Edwin *bishop*
†Wallner, Mary Jane *state legislator, director child care organization*
Wiggin, Kendall French *state librarian*

Conway
Solomon, Richard Lester *retired psychology educator*

Derry
†Aranda, Mary Kathryn *state legislator*
†Katsakiores, George N. *state legislator, retired restauranteur*
†Katsakiores, Phyllis *small business owner, city councilor*

Dover
†Burr, Peter Haskell *publisher, political consultant*
Catalfo, Alfred, Jr. (Alfio Catalfo) *lawyer*
†Pelletier, Arthur Joseph *state legislator, industrial arts and computer programming educator*
†Pelletier, Marsha Lynn *state legislator, secondary school educator*

Dublin
†Avery, Stephen Goodrich *publishing company sales executive*
Biklen, Paul *retired advertising executive*
Hale, Judson Drake, Sr. *editor*
Wolfe, Albert Blakeslee *lawyer*

Durham
†Aber, John David *global ecosystem research adminstrator*
Appel, Kenneth I. *mathematician, educator*
Beckett, John Angus *management educator, consultant*
Berrill, Norman John *developmental biologist, writer, former educator*
Faiman, Robert Neil *academic administrator*
Farrell, William Joseph *university chancellor*
Flynn, Paul Bartholomew *marketing executive*
Hapgood, Robert Derry *English educator*
Harter, Robert Duane *soil scientist, educator*
Lawson, John H. *university official*
†Merritt, Deborah Foote *state legislator, small business owner*
Nitzschke, Dale Frederick *university president*
Palmer, Stuart Hunter *academic dean, sociology educator*
Pistole, Thomas Gordon *microbiology educator, researcher*
†Powers, John H. *school system administrator*
Ritvo, Roger Alan *university dean, health management-policy educator*
Romoser, George Kenneth *political science educator*
Rosen, Sam *economics educator emeritus*
†Rouman, John Christ *Classics educator*
Sproul, Otis Jennings *dean*
Tischler, Herbert *geologist, educator*
Ulrich, Laurel Thatcher *historian, educator*
Voll, John Obert *history educator*
Wheeler, Katherine Wells *state legislator*

Etna
†Copenhaver, Marion Lamson *state legislator*
Ferm, Vergil Harkness *anatomist, embryologist*

Exeter
Beck, Albert *manufacturing company executive*
Boggess, Jerry Reid *protective services official*
Brownell, David Paul *business executive*
Dailey, Daniel Owen *artist, educator, designer*
Erickson, Raymond Leroy *dean, psychologist*
Kozlowski, L. Dennis *manufacturing company executive*
Thomas, Jacquelyn May *librarian*

Francestown
Milton, Peter Winslow *artist*
White, Ruth O'Brien (Mrs. Wallace B. White) *civic worker*

Franconia
Merwin, John David *lawyer, former governor*

Franklin
Meader, Ralph Gibson *medical administrator*
Santolucito, Joseph Anthony *laminate company executive*
Wiehl, John Jack *foundry executive*

Fremont
Richardson, Artemas P(artridge) *landscape architect*

Gilmanton
Osler, Howard Lloyd *controller*

Goffstown
Gillmore, Robert *syndicated columnist, author, editor, publisher*

Grantham
Boothroyd, Herbert J. *insurance company executive*
Feldman, Roger Bruce *government official*
Hansen, Herbert W. *management consultant*
†MacNeill, Arthur Edson *physician, science consultant*

Greenfield
Caverly, Gardner A. *foundation executive*

Groveton
Kegeles, Gerson *chemistry educator*

Hampton
†Canas, Jon *hotel executive*
Clarizio, Josephine Delores *corporate services executive, former manufacturing and engineering company executive, foundation executive*
Coviello, Robert Frank *retail executive*
Dingman, Michael David *industrial company executive*
Montrone, Paul Michael *scientific instruments company executive*
Ranelli, John Raymond *footwear and apparel company executive*
Rice, Frederick Colton *environmental managment consultant*
Rizzo, Richard David *financial service company executive*
†Vogel, Phillip T. *manufacturing executive*

Hancock
Herman, George Edward *radio and television correspondent*

Hanover
Almy, Thomas Pattison *physician, educator*
Anthony, Robert Newton *emeritus management educator*
Arkowitz, Martin Arthur *mathematician, educator*
Arndt, Walter Werner *Slavic scholar, linguist, writer, translator*
Baumgartner, James Earl *mathematics educator*
Bien, Peter Adolph *English language educator, author*
Blaydon, Colin Campbell *university professor*
Boghosian, Varujan Yegan *sculptor*
Bollinger, Lee Carroll *law educator*
Bower, Richard Stuart *economist, educator*
Braun, Charles Louis *chemistry educator, researcher*
Brooks, H. Allen *architectural educator, author, lecturer*
Browning, James Alexander *engineering company executive,inventor*
Cahill, George Francis, Jr. *physician, educator*
Campbell, Colin Dearborn *economist, educator*
Chapman, Carleton Burke *physician*
Clement, Meredith Owen *economist, educator*
†Crory, Elizabeth L. *state legislator*
Crowell, Richard Henry *mathematician, educator*
Daniell, Jere Rogers, II *history educator, consultant*

Dean, Robert Charles, Jr. *mechanical engineer, entrepreneur, innovator*
Deshpandé, Rohit *marketing educator*
Doenges, Norman Arthur *classics educator*
Doney, Willis Frederick *philosophy educator*
Doyle, William Thomas *physicist, educator*
Eberhart, Richard *poet*
Ermenc, Joseph John *mechanical engineering educator*
Flaccus, Edward *retired biology educator*
Fox, Edward A. *college dean*
Freedman, James Oliver *university president, lawyer*
Gert, Bernard *philosopher, educator*
Gilbert, John Jouett *aquatic ecologist, educator*
Green, Ronald Michael *ethics and religious studies educator*
Guest, Robert Henry *state legislator, management educator*
Gustman, Alan Leslie *economics educator*
Harbury, Henry Alexander *biochemist, educator*
Hennessey, John William, Jr. *academic administrator*
Hill, Errol Gaston *drama educator, director, author*
Hutchinson, Charles Edgar *engineering school dean*
Kantrowitz, Arthur *physicist, educator*
Kleck, Robert Eldon *psychology educator*
Koop, Charles Everett *surgeon, government official*
Lamperti, John Williams *mathematician, educator*
Lathem, Edward Connery *librarian, editor, educator*
Logue, Dennis Emhardt *financial economics educator, consultant*
Long, Carl Ferdinand *engineering educator*
Lubin, Martin *cell physiologist educator*
Lyons, Gene Martin *political scientist, educator*
Mansell, Darrel Lee, Jr. *English educator*
†Marvin, Eugene L. *civil engineer*
Masters, Roger Davis *government educator*
McCollum, Robert Wayne *physician, educator*
Mc Farland, Thomas L. *book publishing executive*
Montgomery, David Campbell *physicist, educator*
Montgomery, William J. *finance company executive*
†Morain, William D. *surgeon, educator*
Otto, Margaret Amelia *librarian*
Oxenhandler, Neal *language educator, writer*
Paganucci, Paul Donnelly *banker, lawyer, former college official*
Parton, James *historian*
Penner, Hans Henry *historian*
Perrin, Noel *environmental studies educator*
Queneau, Paul Etienne *metallurgical engineer, educator*
Rieser, Leonard Moos *college administrator, physics educator*
Riggs, Lorrin Andrews *psychologist, educator*
Roos, Thomas Bloom *biological scientist, educator*
Russell, Robert Hilton *romance languages and literature educator*
Rutter, Frances Tompson *publisher*
Scher, Steven Paul *literature educator*
Sheldon, Richard Robert *Russian language and literature educator*
Slesnick, William Ellis *mathematician, educator*
Snell, James Laurie *educator, mathematician*
Spiegel, Melvin *retired biology educator*
Staples, O. Sherwin *orthopaedic surgeon*
Starzinger, Vincent Evans *political science educator*
Stearns, Stephen Russell *civil engineer, forensic engineer, educator*
Stockmayer, Walter H(ugo) *chemistry educator*
Sturge, Michael Dudley *physicist*
Wallace, Andrew Grover *physician*
Wallis, Graham Blair *engineer, educator*
Webster, Frederick Elmer, Jr. *marketing educator, consultant*
Wegner, Gary Alan *astronomer*
Weiss, Ira Francis *retired banker*
†White, Cleveland Stuart, Jr. *architect*
Wood, Charles Tuttle *history educator*
Young, Oran Reed *political scientist, educator*
Zubkoff, Michael *medical educator*

Henniker
†Braiterman, Thea Gilda *economics educator, state legislator*
Cowan, Stuart DuBois *publisher, consultant, writer*
Cummiskey, J. Kenneth *former college president*
O'Connell, William Raymond, Jr. *college president*

Hill
Thierry, John Adams *heavy machinery manufacturing company executive, lawyer*

Hillsboro
Gibson, Raymond Eugene *clergyman*
Marsh, Richard J. *strategic management consultant*
†Walmsley, Arthur Edward *bishop*

Hinsdale
†Smith, Edwin O. *real estate executive, state legislator*

Holderness
Cutler, Laurence Stephan *architect, urban designer, advertising executive, educator*

Hollis
Dyer, Travis Neal *army officer*
Lerner, Arnold Stanley *radio station executive*
Merritt, Thomas Butler *lawyer*
†Wright, George Walter *aeronautical engineer, state legislator*

Hooksett
†Bagan, Merwyn *neurological surgeon*

Hudson
Hargreaves, David William *communications company executive*
†Weergang, Alida *cosmetology educator and administrator, consultant*

Jackson
Johnson, Ned (Edward Christopher Johnson) *publishing company executive*
Synnott, William Raymond *retired management consultant*

Jaffrey
Alderman, Bissell *architect*
Hillsmith, Fannie L. *artist*
Schott, John (Robert) *international consultant, educator*
Von Eckardt, Wolf *design critic, educator*
Walling, Cheves Thomson *chemistry educator*

Keene
Baldwin, Peter Arthur *psychologist, educator, minister*
Bell, Ernest Lorne, III *lawyer*
Burkart, Walter Mark *manufacturing company executive*
Colby, Kenneth Poole *insurance company executive*
Lyon, Ronald Edward *management consultant*
Plaut, Nathan Michael *retired lawyer*
Scranton, William Maxwell *manufacturing company executive, consultant*

Kingston
Curtis, Staton Russell *university dean*

Laconia
Heald, Bruce Day *English and music educator, historian*

Lancaster
Drapeau, Phillip David *banking executive*
†Pratt, Leighton C. *state legislator*

Lebanon
Clendenning, William Edmund *dermatologist*
Cornwell, Gibbons Gray, III *physician, medical educator*
Emery, Virginia Olga Beattie *psychologist, researcher*
Galton, Valerie Anne *endocrinology educator*
Kelley, Maurice Leslie, Jr. *gastroenterologist, educator*
Mc Cann, Frances Veronica *physiologist, educator*
McIntyre, Oswald Ross *physician*
Munck, Allan Ulf *physiologist, educator*
Myers, Warren Powers Laird *physician, educator*
Rawnsley, Howard Melody *physician, educator*
Rolett, Ellis Lawrence *medical educator, cardiologist*
Rous, Stephen Norman *urologist, educator*
Smith, Barry David *obstetrician-gynecologist, educator*
Sox, Harold Carleton, Jr. *physician, educator*
Varnum, James William *hospital administrator*
Wallace, Harold James, Jr. *physician*

Londonderry
†Dean, Richard T. *pharmaceutical company executive*
Nelson, Lloyd Steadman *manufacturing company executive, consultant*

Loudon
†Moore, Bea *religious organization executive*

Lyme
Darion, Joe *librettist, lyricist*
Dwight, Donald Rathbun *newspaper publisher, corporate communications executive*
Swan, Henry *forester, consultant*

Lyndeborough
Morison, John Hopkins *casting manufacturing company executive*

Madbury
Bruce, Robert Vance *historian, educator*

Manchester
†Adams, James W. *journalist*
†Arnold, Barbara Eileen *state legislator*
†Brensinger, Barry L. *architectural firm executive*
Comeau, Reginald Alfred *academic administrator, consultant*
Constance, Joseph William, Jr. *library director*
Craig, William Francis *banker*
DeFelice, Jonathan Peter *college president, priest*
Dobbins, James Joseph *artist*
Emery, Paul Emile *psychiatrist*
Epstein, William Stuart *financial executive, trust company executive*
Goodspeed, Scott Winans *hospital administration executive*
Gustafson, Richard Alrick *college president*
Hoffman, Marilyn Friedman *museum director*
Loeb, Nackey Scripps *publisher*
Mc Lane, John Roy, Jr. *lawyer*
McQuaid, Joseph Woodbury *newspaper executive*
Middleton, Jack Baer *lawyer*
Millimet, Joseph Allen *retired lawyer*
†Mires, Dennis Burnard *architect*
Nixon, David Lee *lawyer*
O'Neil, Leo E. *bishop*
†Pantano, Richard Thomas *library director*
Perkins, Charles, III *newspaper editor*
Thurber, Davis Peabody *banker*
Zachos, Kimon Stephen *lawyer*

Meredith
†Williams, Christopher P. *architect*

Merrimack
Hower, Philip Leland *semiconductor device engineer*

Nashua
Barton, Carl P. *retired insurance company executive*
Bickford, Andrew Thomas *newspaper publisher*
Carter, John Avery *architect*
†Clemons, Jane Andrea *state legislator*
Clough, Charles Elmer *consumer products company executive*
Gregg, Hugh *former cabinet manufacturing company executive, former governor New Hampshire*
Hemming, Walter William *business financial consultant*
Holton, Robert Page *publishing executive*
†Jean, Claudette R. *retired elementary educator*
Light, James Forest *English educator*
Mitchell, William Edmund *electronics executive*
Perkins, George William, II *financial services executive, film producer*
†Rudolph, John W. *architectural firm executive*
Stein, Robert *consumer products company executive*
Taeuber, Conrad *demography educator, former government statistician*
Webber, Howard Rodney *computer company executive*
Weinstein, Jeffrey Allen *consumer products company executive, lawyer*
Woodruff, Thomas Ellis *electronics consulting executive*

New Castle
Silva, Joseph Donald *English language educator*

New London
Cleveland, James Colgate *lawyer, former congressman*
Condict, Edgar Rhodes *medical electronics, aviation instrument manufacturing and medical health care executive, inventor, mediator*
Nye, Thomas Russell *retired drafting, reproduction and surveying company executive*
Pearson, Roy Messer, Jr. *clergyman*
Phillips, Roscoe Wendell, Jr. *architect*
†Sheerr, Deirdre McCrystal *architectural firm executive*
Wheaton, Perry Lee *management consultant*

Newport
†Stamatakis, Carol Marie *state legislator, lawyer*

North Hampton
Goldberger, Stephen A. *retail stores executive*
White, Ralph Paul *manufacturing executive, consultant*

Pelham
†Borsa, Andrew John *electronics engineering consultant*

Pembroke
†Mears, Edgar Harry *state legislator*

Plaistow
†Senter, Merilyn P(atricia) *state legislator, retired freelance reporter*

Plymouth
†Driscoll, William J. *state legislator, retired postmaster*
Swift, Robert Frederic *music educator*

Portsmouth
†Brage, Carl Willis *genealogist*
†Bulmer, Edward E. *oil industry executive*
Clee, Jan Evert *educator, consultant, executive*
Doleac, Charles Bartholomew *lawyer*
Friese, George Ralph *retail executive*
Harden, Acheson Adair, Jr. *retired military officer, retired mathematics educator*
Hopkins, Jeannette E. *book publisher, editor*
Lyman, William W., Jr. *retired architect*
Morin, Carlton Paul *private investments executive*
†O'Toole, Dennis Allen *museum director*
Powers, Henry Martin, Jr. *oil company executive*
†Somes, James Hamilton, Jr. *architect*
Thornhill, Arthur Horace, Jr. *retired book publisher*
Tillinghast, John Avery *technology company executive*
Tober, Stephen Lloyd *lawyer*
Volk, Kenneth H. *lawyer*
†Warner, James M. *architect*

Raymond
†Warburton, (Nathaniel) Calvin, Jr. *state legislator, retired clergyman*

Rindge
†Riley, William Allen *history educator, state legislator*
Sandback, Frederick Lane *artist*

Rochester
†Hambrick, Patricia *state legislator*

Rumney
†King, Wayne Douglas *state senator*

Rye
†Grandmaison, J. Joseph *political consultant*
MacRury, King *management counselor*

Salem
†Irvine, Horace Hills, II *manufacturing company executive*
Simmons, Marvin Gene *geophysics educator*
Sununu, John H. *former chief of staff President of U.S., former governor*

Sanbornton
Andrews, Henry Nathaniel, Jr. *botanist, scientist, educator*

Sandown
Densen, Paul Maximillian *former health administrator, educator*

Silver Lake
Pallone, Adrian Joseph *research scientist*

Strafford
Simic, Charles *English language educator, poet*

Sunapee
Cary, Charles Oswald *aviation executive*
Chait, Lawrence G. *marketing consultant*
MacKinnon, Malcolm D(avid) *retired insurance company executive*
Rauh, John David *manufacturing company executive*

Walpole
Burns, Kenneth Lauren *filmmaker, historian*
Gooding, Judson *writer*

Warner
Hunt, Everett Clair *engineering educator, researcher, consultant*

Washington
Halverson, Wendell Quelprud *former educational association executive, clergyman, educator*

Waterville Valley
Grimes, Howard Ray *management consultant*

West Lebanon
MacAdam, Walter Kavanagh *consulting engineering executive*

West Peterborough
†Dyer, Merton S. *pharmacist, state legislator*

Winchester
MacKay, Neil Duncan *plastic company executive*

Wolfeboro
Murray, Roger Franklin *economist, educator*
Steadman, David Rosslyn Ayton *business executive, corporate director*

NEW JERSEY

Absecon
Steinruck, Charles Francis, Jr. *management consultant, lawyer*

Allaire
†Smith, Sibley Judson, Jr. *historic site administrator*

Allendale
Birdsall, Blair *consulting engineering executive*
Castor, William Stuart, Jr. *chemist, consultant, laboratory executive, educator*
Hollands, John Henry *electronics consultant*

Allenhurst
Delaney, William Francis, Jr. *reinsurance broker*
Hinson, Robert William *advertising executive, consultant*

Allenwood
Shortess, Edwin Steevin *marketing consultant*

Alpine
Yuelys, Alexander *former cosmetics company executive*

Andover
†Gioseffi, Daniela *poet, author, educator*
Klein, Joseph Michelman *musical director*

Annandale
Cohen, Morrel Herman *physicist, biologist, educator*
†Gorbaty, Martin Leo *chemist, researcher*
Lohse, David John *physicist*
Rosensweig, Ronald Ellis *research scientist*
Sinfelt, John Henry *chemist*

Asbury
Konrad, Adolf Ferdinand *artist*

Asbury Park
Holm, Audrey Christine *health care organization administrator*
Jobson, Thomas Wootten *retired editor*

Atlantic City
Gillman, Richard *hotel, casino company executive*
Knight, Edward R. *judge, law educator, psychologist*
Perry, James Benn *casino and hotel executive*
†Pratt, Jack E., Jr. *hotel and casino executive*
Tucci, Mark A. *state agency administrator*

Atlantic Highlands
Crowley, Cynthia Johnson *secondary education educator*
Fink, Dolores Hesse *special education educator*
Kevenides, Herve Arnaud *economic and real estate consultant*

Avalon
Yochum, Philip Theodore *retired motel and cafeteria chain executive*

Avon By The Sea
Bruno, Grace Angelia *accountant, educator*

Barnegat
Schmoll, Harry F., Jr. *lawyer, educator*

Barnegat Light
Gibbs, Frederick Winfield *lawyer, communications company executive*

Barrington
Florio, Maryanne J. *state health research scientist*

Basking Ridge
Allen, Robert Eugene *communications company executive*
Bodman, Richard Stockwell *telecommunications executive*
Chittick, David Rupert *telecommunications executive*
Collis, Sidney Robert *retired telephone company executive*
Condon, Verner Holmes, Jr. *retired utility executive*
†Ferguson, Forest D. *marketing executive*
Heckendorf, Glenn *sales and marketing executive*
Hoyt, Monty *communications executive*
McCall, David W. *chemist, administrator, materials consultant*
Miller, Richard Wesley *electronics company executive*
Munch, Douglas Francis *pharmaceutical and health industry consultant*
Peterson, John Douglas *museum administrator*

Bay Head
Benning, Joseph Francis, Jr. *portfolio manager, financial analyst*
McCormick, John Crimmins *consumer products company executive*

Bayonne
Gorman, William David *artist, graphic artist*
Sullivan, George Edmund *editorial and marketing company executive*

Beach Haven
Brunt, Harry Herman, Jr. *psychiatrist*

Bedminster
Becker, Ivan Endre *retired plastics company executive*
David, Edward Emil, Jr. *electrical engineer, business executive*
Kean, John *utility company executive*
Luke, James Phillip *manufacturing executive*

Belle Mead
†Evans, Frederick John *psychologist*
Hansen, Ralph Holm *chemist*
Singley, Mark Eldridge *agricultural engineering educator*
Stampfl, Rudolf Alois *government official*

Belleville
Pincus, George *university dean, engineering educator*

Bellmawr
Hughes, James Sinclair *electronic engineer and executive*

Bergenfield
Pei, Ming L. *civil engineering educator*

Berkeley Heights
Gottheimer, George Malcolm, Jr. *insurance executive, educator*
Kestler, Jeffrey Lewis *lawyer*
Rabiner, Lawrence Richard *electrical engineer*
Thomsen, Thomas Richard *communications company executive*

Bernardsville
Abeles, James David *manufacturing company executive*
Coheleach, Guy Joseph *artist*
Cooperman, Saul *foundation administrator*
DiDomenico, Mauro, Jr. *communication executive*
Dixon, Richard Wayne *retired communications company executive*
†Ewing, John H. *senator*
Vairo, Robert John *insurance company executive*

Blairstown
Bean, Bennett *artist*

Bloomfield
Becker, Robert Clarence *clergyman*
Solomon, Stephen Michael *chemical engineer, company executive*
Stella, John Anthony *investment company executive*
Vincent, Tony *cable television/radio executive and personality*

Bloomingdale
Baeder, Donald Lee *petroleum and chemical company executive, financial consultant*

Bogota
Condon, Francis Edward *foundation administrator, retired chemistry educator*

Bordentown
†Walther, John Henry *banker*

Bound Brook
Chandler, Marguerite Nella *real estate corporation executive*
Furst, E(rrol) Kenneth *transportation executive, accountant*
Gould, Donald Everett *chemical company executive*
Karol, Frederick John *industrial chemist*

Bradley Beach
Unger, Irwin *historian, educator*

Branchville
Hallowell, Walter Henry *insurance company executive*

Bridgeton
Vogel, Charles A., Jr. *banker*

Bridgewater
Allen, Randy Lee *management consulting executive*
Cohen, Walter Stanley *accountant, financial consultant*
Freeman, Henry McCall *newspaper publisher*
Grubman, Wallace Karl *chemical company executive*
Harrigan, Laura G. *newspaper editor*
Healey, Lynne Kover *editor, broadcaster, writer, educator*
Kennedy, James Andrew *chemical company executive*
Lewis, Donald Emerson *banker*
Patton, Diana Lee Wilkoc *artist*
Pickett, Doyle Clay *employment and training counselor, consultant*
Skidmore, James Albert, Jr. *management, computer technology and engineering services company executive*

Brigantine
Birdwhistell, Ray L. *retired folklore and communication educator*

Butler
†Carelli, Gloria A. *advertising executive*
Davis, Dorinne Sue Taylor Lovas *audiologist*
Klaas, Nicholas Paul *management and technical consultant*
Ward, Robert Allen, Jr. *advertising executive*

Caldwell
Chatlos, William Edward *management consultant*
Kapusinski, Albert Thomas *economist, educator*

Califon
Hannigan, Frank *sportswriter, television writer and commentator, golf course design consultant*
Rosen, Carol Mendes *artist*

Camden
Ances, I. G(eorge) *obstetrician/gynecologist, educator*
†Beck, David Paul *biochemist*
Brotman, Stanley Seymour *federal judge*
Coleman, John Michael *lawyer, food products executive*
Eshbach, William Wallace *architect*
Fairbanks, Russell Norman *law educator, university dean*
Ford, Joseph Raymond *manufacturing company executive*
Gerry, John Francis *federal judge*
Gordon, Walter Kelly *provost, English language educator*
†Holman, Joseph S. *automotive sales executive*
Irenas, Joseph Eron *federal judge*
Johnson, David Willis *food products executive*
Kirk, James Robert *research development and quality assurance executive*
McHugh, James T. *bishop*
Morrison, Ashton Byrom *pathologist, medical school official*
Polin, Claire *musician*
Pomorski, Stanislaw *lawyer, educator*
Rapaport, Robert M. *financial executive*
Rodriguez, Joseph H. *federal judge*
Showalter, English, Jr. *French educator*
Sigler, Jay Adrian *political scientist, educator*
Simandle, Jerome B. *federal judge*
Weise, Frank Earl, III *food products company executive*
Wellington, Judith Lynn *cultural organization administrator*

Cape May
Cadge, William Fleming *gallery owner, photographer*
Cunningham, Robert Morton *communications company executive*
Janosik, Edward Gabriel *retired political science educator*
Lassner, Franz George *educator*
Wilson, H(arold) Fred(erick) *chemist, research scientist*

Cape May Court House
Cohen, Daniel Edward *writer*
Cohen, Susan Lois *author*
†Kurtz, James Eugene *freelance writer, minister*
Poel, Robert Walter *career officer, physician*

Carlstadt
Daniels, Robert Alan *marketing executive*

Carteret
†Corliss, Robert *sporting goods company executive*

Cedar Grove
Brownstein, Alan P. *health foundation executive, consultant*
Nash, Annamarie *secondary education educator*
Spagnardi, Ronald Lee *publishing executive*
Thiel, Thelma King *foundation executive*

Cedar Knolls
†Lingnau, Lutz *pharmaceutical executive*

Chatham
Barnes, William Oliver, Jr. *lawyer*
Bast, Ray Roger *retired utility company executive*
Feeney, John Robert *banker*
Gonzalez, Efren William *science information services administrator*
Hinderliter, Richard Glenn *electrical engineer*
Kaulakis, Arnold Francis *management consultant*
Lenz, Henry Paul *management consultant*
Little, James Stuart *lawyer, corporate executive*
Manning, Frederick William *retired retail executive*
Sayles, Thomas Dyke, Jr. *banker*
Woods, Reginald Foster *management consulting executive*

Cherry Hill
Adams, Raymond Edward *ophthalmologist*
Beebe, Leo Clair *industrial equipment executive, former educator*
†Belin, Henry A., Jr. *bishop*
Biddle, Daniel R. *reporter*
Boyer, Peter Jay *lawyer*
Callaway, Ben Anderson *journalist*
Cazes, Jack *chemist, marketing consultant, editor*
Dunfee, Thomas Wylie *law educator*
†Higurashi, Takeshi *automotive executive*
Iglewicz, Raja *state agency administrator, researcher, industrial hygienist*
†Ignarri, Robert Joseph *architect*
Israelsky, Roberta Schwartz *speech pathologist, audiologist*
Margolis, Gerald Joseph *psychiatrist, educator*
†Muller, George T. *automotive executive*
Myers, Daniel William, II *lawyer*
Newell, Eric James *financial planner, tax consultant, former insurance executive*
Norton, George Dawson *retired banker*
Olearchyk, Andrew S. *cardiothoracic surgeon, educator*
Parker, Jack Royal *engineering executive*
Rabil, Mitchell Joseph *lawyer*
†Radey, Frank Herbert, Jr. *architect*
Rudman, Solomon Kal *magazine publisher*
Sax, Robert Edward *corporate officer*
†Schad, James L. *bishop*
Schelm, Roger Leonard *information systems specialist*
Weinstein, Steven David *lawyer*

Chester
Gurian, Mal *telecommunications executive*
Maddalena, Lucille Ann *management executive*

Cinnaminson
Johnson, Victor Lawrence *banker*

Clark
†Augeri, Joseph *personal care industry executive*

Cliffside Park
Heimbaugh, James Ross *hotel executive*
Jaspen, Nathan *educational statistics educator*
Pushkarev, Boris S. *research foundation director, writer*

Clifton
Adelsberg, Harvey *hospital administrator*
†Bubba, Joseph L. *financial advisor, state senator*
Fein, Seymour Howard *pharmaceutical executive*
Feinstein, Miles Roger *lawyer*
Magnus, Frederick Samuel *investment banker*
Olson, Bob Moody *marketing executive*
†Rigolo, Arthur Emil *architect*
Rodimer, Frank Joseph *bishop*
Srinivasachari, Samavedam *chemical engineer*
Swystun-Rives, Bohdana Alexandra *dentist*

Clinton
Acerra, Michele (Mike Acerra) *engineering and construction company executive*
†Atwater, N. William *engineering and construction executive*
Boyland, Joseph Francis *corporate controller*
Daman, Ernest Ludwig *mechanical engineer*
DeGhetto, Kenneth Anselm *engineering and construction company executive*
Deones, Jack E. *corporate executive*
Kennedy, Harold Edward *lawyer*
Newman, Stephen Alexander *chemical engineer, thermodynamicist*
Winkin, Justin Philip *engineering executive*
Wolsky, Murray *corporation executive*

Collingswood
Mohrfeld, Richard Gentel *heating oil distributing company executive*

Colts Neck
French, Charles Ferris, Jr. *banker*
Rode, Leif *real estate agent*

Convent Station
Weber, Joseph H. *communications company executive*
Wright, Robert Burroughs *financial consultant*

Cranbury
Cuthbert, Robert Allen *pet products company executive*
Daoust, Donald Roger *pharmaceutical and toiletries company executive, microbiologist*
Koras, William *concessions, restaurants and publishing company executive*
Lee-Smith, Hughie *artist, educator*
Rector, Milton Gage *social work educator, former association executive*
Reichek, Morton Arthur *retired magazine editor, writer*
Wang, Chih Chun *material scientist, business executive*
Yoseloff, Julien David *publishing company executive*
Yoseloff, Thomas *publisher*

Cranford
Bardwil, Joseph Anthony *investments consultant*
Bodian, Nat G. *publishing, marketing consultant, author, lecturer, lexicographer*
Cleaver, William Pennington *consultant, retired sugar refining company executive*
Eisenberg, R. Neal *restoration company executive*
Schink, Frank Edward *electrical engineer*
Sommerlad, Robert Edward *environmental research engineer*

Cresskill
Gardner, Richard Alan *psychiatrist, writer*
Smyth, Craig Hugh *fine arts educator*

Deal
Becker, Richard Stanley *music publisher*

Denville
Breed, Ria *anthropologist*
†Kimmel, Betty *chief executive officer*
Minter, Jerry Burnett *electronic component company executive, engineer*

Dover
Kajor, Michael Steven *electrical engineer*
Mc Donald, John Joseph *electronics executive*
Tatyrek, Alfred Frank *materials engineer, research chemist, consultant*

East Brunswick
Avallone, Michael Angelo *author*
Chang, Stephen S. *food scientist, educator, researcher, inventor*
†Fisher, Lucille *principal*
Georgantas, Aristides William *banking executive*
Haupin, Elizabeth C. *retired secondary school educator*
Johnson, Edward Elemuel *psychologist, educator*
†King, Charles M. *principal*
Mooney, William Piatt *actor*
Nemser, Robert Solomon *visual communications consultant, art director, designer, educator*
Rosenberg, Norman *surgeon*
Thompson, Robert McBroom *publishing executive*
Wagman, Gerald Howard *library administrator*

East Hanover
Anderson, Gary William *physician*
Finkel, Marion Judith *physician*
†Hassan, Frederich *pharmaceutical executive*
Leveille, Gilbert Antonio *food products executive*
Nemecek, Georgina Marie *molecular pharmacologist*
†Rejeange, Jacques F. *pharmaceutical executive*

East Orange
Bowe, Riddick Lamont *professional boxer*
Brown, Paulette *lawyer*
Gibson, Althea *professional tennis player, golfer, state official*
Green, David *insurance company executive*
Holyfield, Evander *boxer*
Howe, James Everett *investment company executive*
†Medley, Alex Roy *ministry executive*
†Moorer, Michael *professional boxer*
Simmons, Jean Elizabeth Margaret (Mrs. Glen R. Simmons) *chemistry educator*
†Talmadge, Quilla Esther *county management specialist*
†Wolff, Derish Michael *economist, company executive*

East Rutherford
Aufzien, Alan L. *professional sports team executive*
†Beard, Butch *professional basketball coach*
†Coleman, Derrick D. *professional basketball player*
Daly, Chuck (Charles Jerome) *former professional basketball coach*
Gerstein, David Brown *hardware manufacturing company executive, professional basketball team executive*
Lamoriello, Louis Anthony *professional hockey team executive*
Lemaire, Jacques *professional hockey coach*
Mann, Bernie *professional basketball team executive*
Mara, Wellington T. *professional football team executive*
Reed, Willis *professional basketball team executive, former head coach*
Reeves, Daniel Edward *professional football coach*
Taylor, Lawrence *sports commentator, former professional football player*
Wadler, Arnold L. *lawyer*
Young, George Bernard, Jr. *professional football team executive*

Eatontown
Van Winkle, William *financial planner*

Edison
Behr, Marion Ray *artist, author*
Behr, Omri M. *lawyer*
Carretta, Richard Louis *beverage company executive*
Cavanaugh, James Henry *former government official, corporate executive*
Comstock, Robert Ray *journalism educator, newspaper editor*
†Corman, Randy *lawyer*
Danzis, Rose Marie *emeritus college president*
†Francis, Peter T. *gas and oil industry executive*
Holt, Jonathan Turner *public relations executive*
†Huber, Michael W. *petroleum company executive*
Hunter, Michael *publishing executive*
Lo Surdo, Antonio *physical chemist, educator*
Maeroff, Gene I. *educational association administrator, journalist*
Marash, Stanley Albert *consulting company executive*
Mount, Karl A. *manufacturing executive*
Renzulli, Mary Ann *parochial education educator*
†Romano, Dominick V. *food products executive*
†Ross, Stephen Bruce *public affairs consultant*
Schenk, George *oil industry executive*
Scheuring, Garry Joseph *banker*
Schwalje, Joseph Louis *mechanical engineering consultant*
†Shulman, Hyman *food service executive*
Silberstein, Alan Mark *banker*
†Sullivan, Cornelius Francis, Jr. *banking executive*
†Warsh, Jeffrey A. *lawyer, state legislator*

Egg Harbor City
Dittenhafer, Brian Douglas *banker, economist*
Hamilton, Thomas Herman *savings and loan association executive*
Melick, George Fleury *mechanical engineer, educator*

Elizabeth
Buonanni, Brian Francis *health care facility administrator, consultant*
Chard, Roland Turner *retired banker*
†Clare, Thomas J. *consumer products company executive*
Gellert, George Geza *food importing company executive*
†Infusino, Thomas P. *food distribution company executive*
†Karlberg, John *transportation company executive*
†Keenan, Joseph James, Jr. *library director*
Klein, Peter Martin *lawyer, transportation company executive*
Leonett, Anthony Arthur *banker*
Tolan, David Joseph *transportation executive*

Elizabethtown
Taylor, David Wyatt Aiken *retired clergyman*

Elmer
Slavoff, Harriet Emonds *learning disabilities teacher, consultant*

Elmwood Park
†Hazama, Hajime *electronics executive*
Kerr, James Joseph *construction company executive, engineer*
Scudder, Richard B. *newspaper executive*

Emerson
†Rooney, John Edward *state legislator, electrical company executive*

Englewood
Anuszkiewicz, Richard Joseph *artist*
Beer, Jeanette Mary Scott *foreign language educator*
Bullough, John Frank *organist, music educator*
Casarella, Edmond *sculptor, printmaker*
†Caulo, Ralph Daniel *publishing executive*
Deresiewicz, Herbert *mechanical engineering educator*
Downes, John *writer, editor*
†Essey, Basil *bishop*
Friedman, Emanuel *publishing company executive*
Gambee, Eleanor Brown *writer, lecturer, civic worker*
Hertzberg, Arthur *rabbi, educator*
†Hess, Blaine R. *manufacturing company executive*
Kane, Daniel A. *hospital administrator*
†Khouri, Antoun *church administrator*
Lapidus, Arnold *mathematician*
Mc Mullan, Dorothy *nurse educator*
Miles, Virginia (Mrs. Fred C. Miles) *marketing consultant*
Morgenstein, William *shoe company executive*
Neis, Arnold Hayward *pharmaceutical company executive*
Orlando, George (Joseph) *union executive*
Saliba, Philip E. *archbishop*
†Wilcha, John Samuel *food products company executive*
Zwilich, Ellen Taaffe *composer*

Englewood Cliffs
Bogert, Ivan Lathrop *sanitary engineer*
Bradler, James Edward *publishing company executive*
Butterfield, Bruce Scott *publishing company executive*
Cantwell, John Walsh *advertising executive*
†Glasser, Lynn Schreiber *publisher*
†Glasser, Stephen Andrew *publishing executive, lawyer*
Green, Alvin *lawyer, corporate executive*
Guiher, James Morford, Jr. *publisher*
Haltiwanger, Robert Sidney, Jr. *book publishing executive*
Hurst, Kenneth Thurston *publisher*
Meendsen, Fred Charles *food company executive*
Schlatter, Konrad *corporate executive*
Scott, John William *food processing executive*
Shoemate, Charles Richard *agricultural products executive*
Shrem, Charles Joseph *metals corporation executive*
Storms, Clifford Beekman *lawyer*

Englishtown
Chung, Douglas Chu *pharmacist, consultant*

Fair Haven
Gagnebin, Albert Paul *retired mining executive*
Labrecque, Theodore Joseph *lawyer*

Fair Lawn
Hayden, Neil Steven *communications company executive*
†Panella, Elizabeth M. *secondary school principal*
Parker, Adrienne Natalie *art educator, art historian, lecturer*
†Wygod, Martin J. *pharmaceuticals executive*

Fairfield
Boccone, Andrew Albert *chemical company executive*
Finn, James Francis *consulting engineering executive*
Giambalvo, Vincent *manufacturing company executive*
Mackin, Scott George *environmental and energy company executive*
MacKinnon, Walter Allan *employee benefits administration company executive*
Mehta, Narinder Kumar *marketing executive*
Meilan, Celia *food products executive*
Oolie, Sam *investment company executive*
Stein, Robert Alan *electronics company executive*

Fairview
Anton, Harvey *textile company executive*

Fanwood
Peeney, James Doyle *executive search consultant*

Far Hills
Ellsworth, Duncan Steuart, Jr. *retired utility company executive*
Fay, David B. *sports association executive*

Farmingdale
Schluter, Peter Mueller *electronics company executive*

Flemington
Accettola, Albert Bernard *orthopedic surgeon, educator*
Foti, Margaret Mai *education consultant*
Griffin, Bryant Wade *judge*
Katcher, Avrum L. *pediatrician*
Kettler, Carl Frederick *airline executive*
Kozikowski, Mitchell *public relations executive*
†Lance, Leonard *assemblyman*
McGregor, Walter *medical products company designer, inventor, consultant, educator*
Russo, Wenona Berrie *business educator*
Umbreit, Wayne William *bacteriologist, educator*

Florham Park
Bossen, Wendell John *insurance company executive*
Bottelli, Richard *architect*
†Brown, Leanna *state senator*
Eidt, Clarence Martin, Jr. *research and development executive*
Erickson, Charles Edward *insurance company executive*
Fischer, Pamela Shadel *public relations executive*
Griffo, James Vincent, Jr. *resource development consultant, retired biology educator, educational administrator*
Hardin, William Downer *lawyer*
Jameson, J(ames) Larry *cable company executive*
Kluge, J. Hans *company executive*
Laulicht, Murray Jack *lawyer*
Lieberman, Lester Zane *engineering company executive*
†Lovell, Robert Marlow, Jr. *investment company executive*
Luker, Jeffrey Paul *management information consultant*
McDonagh, Thomas Joseph *physician*
Mott, Vincent Valmon *publisher, author*
Naimark, George Modell *marketing and management consultant*
Perham, Roy Gates, III *industrial psychologist*
Smith, Robert William *former insurance company executive, lawyer*
Whitley, Arthur Francis *retired international consulting company executive, engineer, lawyer*

Folsom
Levitt, Gerald Steven *natural gas company executive*

Fords
Brown, James *singer, broadcasting executive*
Kaufman, Alex *chemicals executive*

Fort Hancock
Klein, George D. *geologist, science executive*

Fort Lee
Abut, Charles C. *lawyer*
†Barr, Edward Evan *chemical company executive*
Fischel, Daniel Norman *publishing consultant*
†Gharib, Susie *television newscaster*
Goldberg, Harry Finck *lawyer*
†Insana, Ronald Gerard *newscaster*
†Kim, Gil *minister*
Lippman, William Jennings *investment company executive*
†Lynaugh, Joseph T. *health care executive*
Manniello, John Baptiste Louis *research scientist*
†Ramsey, Douglas Kenneth *television anchor, journalist*
Schiessler, Robert Walter *retired chemical and oil company executive*
Seitel, Fraser Paul *public relations executive*
†Sturtevant, Peter Mann, Jr. *television news executive*
Sugarman, Alan William *educational administrator*
Vignolo, Biagio Nickolas, Jr. *chemical company executive*
Weitzer, Bernard *telecommunications executive*
Williams, Edwin William *publisher*

Fort Monmouth
†Campi, Anthony V. *engineering research administrator*
Kalwinsky, Charles Knowlton *government official*
Perlman, Barry Stuart *electrical engineer, researcher*
Schwering, Felix Karl *electronics engineer, researcher*
Thornton, Clarence Gould *electronics engineering executive*

Franklin
Kline, Donald *food company executive*

Franklin Lakes
Andrews, Willard Douglas *retired medical products manufacturer, consultant*
Appert, Richard Henry *health products manufacturing executive*
Berger, Murry P. *food company executive*
Friedman, Martin Burton *chemical company executive*
Galiardo, John William *lawyer*
Ginsberg, Barry Howard *physician, researcher*
Hegelmann, Julius *retired pharmacy educator*
†Hetzel, Donald Stanford *chemist*
Howe, Wesley Jackson *medical supplies company executive*
Lovell, Theodore *electrical engineer, consultant*
Natale, Samuel Michael *psychotherapist, educator, priest*

Freehold
Fisher, Clarkson Sherman, Jr. *judge*
Foster, Eric H., Jr. *retail executive*
Hillegass, Christine Ann *psychologist*
Laden, Karl *toiletries company executive*

Frenchtown
Scaglione, Aldo Domenico *language educator*

Garfield
Kodaka, Kunio *plastics company executive*

Gibbsboro
Censits, Richard John *health care company executive*

Gladstone
Detwiler, Peter Mead *investment banker*

Glassboro
Gephardt, Donald Louis *college official*
James, Herman Delano *college administrator*

Glen Ridge
Agnew, Peter Tomlin *employee benefit consultant*
Bracken, Eddie (Edward Vincent) *actor, director, writer, singer, artist*
Clemente, Celestino *physician, surgeon*
Szamek, Pierre Ervin *research anthropologist*

Glen Rock
Feeks, J. Michael *bank executive*
Fine, Seymour Howard *marketing educator, lecturer, author, consultant*

Green Village
Castenschiold, Rene *engineering company executive, author, consultant*

Hackensack
Ahearn, James *newspaper columnist*
†Araki, K. *electronics company executive*
Baker, Andrew Hartill *clinical laboratory executive*
†Benfield, Richard Ernest *journalist*
†Blomquist, David Wels *journalist*
Borg, Malcolm Austin *communications company executive*
Delaney, Patrick James *investment company executive*
Ferguson, John Patrick *medical center executive*
Gross, Peter Alan *epidemiologist, researcher*
Kestin, Howard H. *judge*
Layman, William Arthur *psychiatrist, educator*
†Mack, Patricia Johnson *newspaper editor*
Margulies, James Howard *editorial cartoonist*
Massler, Howard Arnold *lawyer, corporate executive*
Mavrovic, Ivo *chemical engineer*
Mehta, Jay *financial executive*
Michel, Robert Charles *retired engineering company executive*
†Pennington, William Mark *sportswriter*
†Schmidt, Ronald Hans *architect*
†Schuber, William Patrick *lawyer*
Spackman, Thomas James *radiologist*
†Waixel, Vivian *journalist*
Walsh, Joseph Michael *magazine distribution executive*

Haddon Heights
Gwiazda, Stanley John *university dean*
Romer, Jeanne Geraldine *delivery service executive, consultant*

Haddonfield
†Adler, John Herbert *lawyer, state legislator*
†Aglialoro, John Joseph *business executive*
Capelli, John Placido *nephrologist*
Cheney, Daniel Lavern *retired magazine publisher*
Iavicoli, Mario Anthony *lawyer*
LaBarge, Richard Allen *financial analyst, educator*
Shaub, Harold Arthur *food products executive*
Siskin, Edward Joseph *engineering and construction company executive*

Hamburg
Buist, Richardson *corporate executive, retired banker*

Hanover
Salans, Lester Barry *physician, scientist, educator*

Harrison
Winnerman, Robert Henry *home building company executive*

Harvey Cedars
Elliott, Joseph Gordon, Jr. *retired newspaper executive*

Haworth
Shields, Brooke Christa Camille *actress, model*
Stokvis, Jack Raphael *urban planner and developer, government agency administrator*

Hawthorne
Cole, Leonard Aaron *political scientist, dentist*
†Fry, Ronald William *publishing executive*

Hazlet
Leibow, Lois May *educator*
Miller, Duane King *health and beauty care company executive*

Morrison, James Frederick *flavor and fragrance company administrator*

Hewitt
Selwyn, Donald *engineering administrator, researcher, inventor, educator*

Highland Lakes
Ansorge, Helen J. *retired elementary school educator*

Highland Park
Brudner, Harvey Jerome *physicist*
Green, James Weston *educator, physiologist*
Pane, Remigio Ugo *Romance languages educator*

Hightstown
Arnold, Matthew Charles *real estate corporation officer*
Brodman, Estelle *librarian, retired educator*
Howard, Barbara Sue Mesner *artist*
Kilborne, William Skinner *retired business consultant*
†O'Connor, Eugene Francis *architect*
Phelan, Richard Paul *trust company executive*

Hillsdale
Bey, Gwendolyn *legal administrator*

Hillside
Enslow, Ridley Madison, Jr. *book publisher*
Patell, Mahesh *pharmacist, researcher*

Ho Ho Kus
Tobin, John Everard *lawyer*

Hoboken
Abel, Robert Berger *science administrator*
†Bernstein, Jeremy *physicist, educator*
Boesch, Francis Theodore *electrical engineer, educator*
Bonsal, Richard Irving *textile marketing executive*
†Bruno, Michael Stephen *ocean engineering educator, researcher*
Fajans, Jack *physics educator*
†Gans, Manfred *chemical engineer*
Griskey, Richard George *chemical engineering educator*
Johnson, James Myron *psychologist, educator*
Jurkat, Martin Peter *management educator*
Kunhardt, Erich Enrique *physicist, educator*
Raveché, Harold Joseph *university administrator, physical chemist*
Regazzi, John James, III *publishing executive*
Savitsky, Daniel *engineer, educator*
Schmidt, George *physicist*
Sisto, Fernando *mechanical engineering educator*
Widdicombe, Richard Palmer *librarian*

Holmdel
Abate, John E. *electrical and electronic engineer, communications consultant*
Bjorkholm, John Ernst *physicist*
Boyd, Gary Delane *electro-optical engineer, researcher*
Burrus, Charles Andrew, Jr. *research physicist*
†Frenkiel, Richard Henry *electronics company research and development executive*
†Gordon, James Power *optics scientist*
Haskell, Barry Geoffry *communications company research administrator*
Heirman, Donald Nestor *telecommunications engineering company manager*
Johannes, Virgil Ivancich *electrical engineer*
Kaminow, Ivan Paul *physicist*
Kogelnik, Herwig Werner *electronics company executive*
Li, Tingye *electrical engineer*
Mac Rae, Alfred Urquhart *physicist, electrical engineer*
Marcuse, Dietrich *physicist*
Meadors, Howard Clarence, Jr. *electrical engineer*
Miller, David Andrew Barclay *physicist*
Mollenauer, Linn Frederick *physicist*
Netravali, Arun N. *communications executive*
Opie, William Robert *retired metallurgical engineer*
Ross, Ian Munro *electrical engineer*
†Shah, Jagdeep *physicist, researcher*
Tien, Ping King *electronics engineer*
Wilson, Robert Woodrow *radio astronomer*
Wyndrum, Ralph W., Jr. *communications company executive*

Hopatcong
†Harsanyi, Andrew *bishop*
Reese, Harry Edwin, Jr. *electronics executive*

Hope
Laine, Cleo (Clementina Dinah Dankworth) *singer*

Hopewell
Halpern, Daniel *poet, editor, educator*

Imlaystown
†Richardson, Donald Campbell *land planner, landscape architect*

Iselin
Clarke, David H. *industrial products executive*
Dornbusch, Arthur A., II *lawyer*
Garfinkel, Harmon Mark *specialty chemicals company executive*
Hecht, William David *accountant*
Kracht, Richard William *lawyer*
†Mackinnon, Robert *medical products executive*
†Raos, John G. *manufacturing executive*
Shaw, Alan John *manufacturing and financial corporation executive*
Smith, Orin Robert *chemical company executive*
Tice, George A(ndrew) *photographer*
Vitt, David Aaron *medical manufacturing company executive*
White, Sir (Vincent) Gordon Lindsay *textile company executive*

Jackson
Hagberg, Carl Thomas *financial executive*

Jamesburg
Chase, Aurin Moody, Jr. *biology educator*
Denton, John Joseph *retired pharmaceutical company executive*
Gross, Leroy *sugar company executive*

Maxwell, Bryce *engineer,educator*
Miller, Theodore Robert *surgeon, educator*

Jersey City
Alfano, Michael Charles *pharmaceutical company executive*
Bavasi, Peter Joseph *professional baseball team executive*
Block, Leonard Nathan *drug company executive*
D'Amico, Thomas F. *economist, educator*
Dreman, David Nasaniel *investment counselor, security analyst*
Dubin, Michael *financial services executive*
Fortune, Robert Russell *financial consultant*
Foster, Delores Jackson *elementary school principal*
Fox, Thomas George *academic adminstrator, healthscience educator*
†Gurevich, Grigory *visual artist, educator*
Howard, Stanley Louis *investment banker*
Ingrassia, Paul Joseph *publishing executive*
Katz, Colleen *editor in chief*
†Luthi, Wilfried T. *manufacturing executive*
Manischewitz, Bernard *food products company executive*
Marshall, Philips Williamson *insurance agency executive*
McGhee, Elaine Simmons *school director, consultant*
Melnick, Gilbert Stanley *radiologist, educator*
†Metsch, Jonathan M. *health facility executive*
Meyer, Howard Robert *lawyer*
Mortensen, Eugene Phillips *hospital administrator*
†Myers, Walter Dean *young adult's book author*
Nash, Lee J. *banker*
Niemiec, Edward Walter *professional association executive*
Reynolds, Scott Walton *academic administrator*
†Roma, Patrick James *lawyer, state legislator*
Sanders, Franklin D. *insurance company executive*
Serra-Badue, Daniel Francisco *artist, educator*
Shildneck, Barbara Jean *accounting magazine editor*
Tognino, John Nicholas *financial services executive*
Tugwell, John *bank executive*
Tymon, Leo F., Jr. *banker*
Wagner, Douglas Walker Ellyson *journal editor*
Williams, Alan Davison *publishing company executive*
†Wilzig, Siggi Bert *banker*
Zuckerberg, David Alan *pharmaceutical company executive*

Kendall Park
Goldberg, Bertram J. *social agency admininistrator*
Hershenov, Bernard Zion *electronics research and development company executive*

Kenilworth
Conklin, Donald Ransford *pharmaceutical company executive*
Darrow, William Richard *pharmaceutical company executive*
Ganguly, Ashit Kumar *organic chemist*

Keyport
Warren, Craig Bishop *flavor and fragrance company executive, researcher*

Kinnelon
Haller, Charles Edward *engineering consultant*
Preston, Andrew Joseph *pharmacist, drug company executive*
Richardson, Irene M. *nursing educator*
Schafer, John Stephen *foundation administrator*

Lake Hopatcong
Dowling, Robert Murray *oil company executive*

Lakehurst
Case, Elizabeth *artist, writer*
Millar, John Francis *industrial products company executive*
†Raffetto, David J. *engineering administrator*

Lakewood
Bowers, John Zimmerman *physician, historian, educator*
Levovitz, Pesach Zechariah *rabbi*
Quinn, Evelyn Saul *social work educator*
Williams, Barbara Anne *college president*

Laurel Springs
Cleveland, Susan Elizabeth *library administrator, researcher*

Lawrenceville
Bly, Herbert Arthur *pharmaceutical company executive*
†Bunting, Josiah, III *college president*
Coleman, Wade Hampton, III *management consultant, mechanical engineer, former banker*
Holcombe, William Jones *manufacturing company executive*
Iversen, David Stewart *librarian*
Kihn, Harry *electronics engineer, manufacturing company executive*
Norback, Craig Thomas *author*
Terracciano, Anthony Patrick *banker*
Tharney, Leonard John *education educator, consultant*

Lebanon
Kone, Russell Joseph *advertising agency executive, film producer*
†Pollazzi, Roger G. *transportation executive*

Liberty Corner
Apruzzese, Vincent John *lawyer*
Miller, Walter Neal *insurance company executive*
Rajani, Prem Rajaram *transportation company financial executive*
†Stoll, Roger G. *health insurance company executive*

Lincroft
Keenan, Robert Anthony *financial services company executive, educator, consultant*
Sullivan, Brother Jeremiah Stephen *former college president*

Linden
Covino, Charles Peter *metal products company executive*
Hansen, Christian Andreas, Jr. *chemical company executive*
Tamarelli, Alan Wayne *chemical company executive*

Linwood
†Gaffney, John Francis *state congressman*

Little Falls
Dohr, Donald R. *metallurgical engineer, researcher*
Nash, James John *superintendent*

Little Silver
Finch, Rogers Burton *association management consultant*
Labbett, John Edgar *corporate executive*

Livingston
Caballes, Romeo Lopez *pathologist, bone tumor researcher*
†Del Mauro, Ronald *hospital administrator*
Heilmeier, George Harry *electrical engineer, researcher*
Krieger, Abbott Joel *neurosurgeon*
†Lager, Henry S. *transporation executive*
Lucky, Robert Wendell *electrical engineer*
Mandelbaum, Howard Arnold *advertising executive*
Oishi, Satoshi *architectural and engineering executive*
Pantages, Louis James *lawyer*

Lodi
Karetzky, Stephen *library director, educator, researcher*
†Meno, John Peter *chorepiscopus*
Pivinski, Sister Mary Lorene *academic administrator*
Samuel, Athanasius Yeshue *archbishop*

Long Branch
Arvanitis, Cyril Steven *surgeon, educator*
Barnett, Lester Alfred *surgeon*
Lagowski, Barbara Jean *writer, book editor*
Nahavandi, Amir Nezameddin *retired engineering firm executive*
Royce, Paul Chadwick *medical administrator*

Long Valley
†Goldstein, Eliot Warren *architect, planner*

Lyndhurst
†Albosta, Richard Francis *engineering and construction company executive*
Lasky, David *lawyer, corporate executive*
†Mosher, Howard Ira *automotive executive*
Sieger, Charles *librarian*
†Tinggren, Carl Jurgen *manufacturing executive*

Lyons
Kidd, A. Paul *hospital administrator, government official*

Madison
Byrd, Stephen Fred *human resource consultant*
Calligan, William Dennis *retired life insurance company executive*
Campbell, William Cecil *biologist*
Comey, J. Martin *pharmaceutical company executive*
Coughlin, Caroline Mary *library director, educator*
D'Andrade, Hugh A(lfred) *pharmaceutical company executive, lawyer*
deStevens, George *chemist, educator*
Emerling, Carol G(reenbaum) *consumer products company executive*
Fogarty, John Thomas *lawyer*
Gibson, William Ford *author*
Gnichtel, William Van Orden *lawyer*
Hays, Thomas R. *electronics executive*
Hoynes, Louis LeNoir, Jr. *lawyer*
Irons, Neil L. *bishop*
Johnson, William Joseph *stockbroker*
Kean, Thomas H. *academic administrator, former governor*
Knox, John, Jr. *philosopher, educator*
Kogan, Richard Jay *pharmaceutical company executive*
Kushen, Allan Stanford *lawyer*
Leak, Margaret Elizabeth *insurance company executive*
Luciano, Robert Peter *pharmaceutical company executive*
McCulloch, James Callahan *manufacturing company executive*
Mc Mullen, Edwin Wallace, Jr. *English language educator*
†Monte, Bonnie J. *performing company executive*
Siegel, George Henry *international business development consultant*

Mahwah
Borowitz, Grace Burchman *chemistry educator, researcher*
Bram, Leon Leonard *publishing company executive*
Bryan, Thomas Lynn *lawyer, educator*
Carey, William Joseph *retired controller*
Eiger, Richard William *publisher*
†Hirooka, Sueyuki *electronics company executive*
Hollerith, Richard, Jr. *industrial designer, consultant*
†Lynch, Kevin A. *book publishing executive*
Padovano, Anthony Thomas *theologian, educator*
†Schecter, M. *book publishing executive*
Scott, Robert Allyn *college administrator*

Manalapan
Harrison-Johnson, Yvonne Elois *pharmacologist*
Stone, Fred Michael *lawyer*

Mantoloking
Fragomen, Austin Thomas *capital goods company executive*
Morris, Robert *lawyer, writer*

Maplewood
†Hammond, Caleb Dean, Jr. *cartographer, publisher*
†Hammond, Caleb Dean, III *publishing executive*
†Hammond, Kathleen Doorish *publishing executive*
MacWhorter, Robert Bruce *retired lawyer*
Palisi, Anthony Thomas *psychologist, educator*
Weston, Randy (Randolph Edward Weston) *pianist, composer*

Margate City
Kennedy, Berenice Connor (Mrs. Jefferson Kennedy, Jr.) *magazine executive, writer, consultant*
†Weiss, Mordechai *principal*

Marlboro
Leveson, Irving Frederick *economist*
Schwartz, Perry Lester *information systems engineer, consultant*

Marlton
Byerly, LeRoy James *psychiatrist, educator*
Forbes, Gordon Maxwell *sports journalist, commentator*
Luchak, Frank Alexander *lawyer*

Matawan
Kesselman, Bruce Alan *marketing executive, consultant*

Medford
Dunn, Roy J. *landscape architect*
Hogan, Thomas Harlan *publisher*
Katzell, Raymond A. *psychologist, educator*
Kesty, Robert Edward *chemical manufacturing company executive*
†Konstantinos, K. Kiki *school system administrator*
Wallis, Robert Ray *psychologist, entrepreneur*

Mendham
Desjardins, Raoul *medical association administrator, financial consultant*
Fenner, Peter David *communications executive, management consultant*
Kaprelian, Edward K. *mechanical engineer, physicist*
Kirby, Allan Price, Jr. *investment company executive*
Mercer, Richard Joseph *retired advertising executive, freelance writer*
Posunko, Barbara *elementary education educator*

Merchantville
†Shreiber, Gerald B. *food products executive*

Metuchen
Cangemi, Michael Paul *accountant, financial executive*
Daub, Albert Walter *publishing executive*
Horrocks, Norman *publisher*
Hughes, Edward T. *bishop*
Jacobey, John Arthur, III *surgeon, educator*
Stapley, Edward Olley *retired microbiologist, research administrator*

Middletown
Cooper, Charles Gerson *computer company executive*
Levi, Ilan Mosche *computer and communications company executive*
O'Neill, Eugene Francis *communications engineer*
Roesner, Peter Lowell *manufacturing company executive*

Midland Park
Koster, John Peter, Jr. *journalist, author*

Milford
Carter, Clarence Holbrook *artist*

Millburn
†Cohen, Geoffrey Merrill *theater executive*
Echikson, Richard *retail consultant*
Liben, Michael Paul *magazine publisher*
†Ogden, Maureen Black *state legislator*
Raff, Gilbert *publishing company executive*

Millington
Donaldson, John Cecil, Jr. *consumer products company executive*

Milltown
Bradley, Edward William *sports foundation executive*

Monmouth Beach
Herbert, LeRoy James *retired accounting firm executive*

Monmouth Junction
†Neff, Peter John *chemicals, mining and metal processing executive*
Summerfield, Martin *physicist*

Montclair
Alexander, Fernande Gardner *writer, photographer*
Beerman, Miriam *artist, educator*
Behrle, Franklin Charles *physician*
Bolden, Theodore Edward *dentist, educator*
†Boyd, Hugh Alan *architect*
Brightman, Robert Lloyd *importer, textile company executive, consultant*
Brown, Geraldine Reed *lawyer, consulting executive*
Brownrigg, Walter Grant *cartoonist, corporate executive*
Campbell, Stewart Fred *foundation executive*
Draper, Daniel Clay *lawyer*
†Dubrow, Marsha Ann *high technology company executive, composer*
Fleming, Thomas Crawley *physician, medical director, former editor*
Gogick, Kathleen Christine *magazine editor, publisher*
Hardin, John Alexander *retired broadcasting consultant*
Jacoby, Tamar *journalist, author*
†Jones, Rees Lee *golf course architect*
Kidde, John Lyon *investment manager*
Mc Carthy, Daniel Christopher, Jr. *manufacturing company executive*
Pierson, Robert David *banker*
Richart, John Douglas *investment banker*
Sabin, William Albert *editor*
Schlesinger, Stephen Lyons *foundation executive, nurseryman*
†Strobert, Barbara *principal*
Walker, George Theophilus, Jr. *composer, pianist, music educator*
Ward, Roger Coursen *lawyer*

Montvale
†Bassermann, Michael N. *automotive executive*
Beattie, James Raymond *lawyer*
Borman, Earle Kirkpatrick, Jr. *chemical company executive*
Brecht, Warren Frederick *business executive*
Corrado, Fred *food company executive*
Gallagher, Michael Robert *consumer products company executive*
Kanter, Carl Irwin *lawyer*
Kennedy, John Raymond *pulp and paper company executive*
Kennedy, Quentin J., Sr. *lawyer, paper company executive*
Larkin, Michael Joseph *retail food executive*
Mundt, Barry Maynard *management consultant*
Pfister, James Joseph *publishing company executive*
†Pitkowsky, Murray *financial executive*
Rourke, Michael James *retail company executive*
Rowe, James W. *food chain executive*
†Saper, Lawrence *data processing company executive*
Sbarbaro, Robert Arthur *banker*
Scopes, Gary Martin *professional association executive*
Sifton, David Whittier *magazine editor*
Smernoff, Richard Louis *oil company executive*
†Steinberg, Charles Allan *electronics manufacturing company executive*
Stillwell, James Paul *food company exective*
Ulrich, Robert Gardner *retail food chain executive, lawyer*
Wood, James *supermarket executive*

Montville
Galella, Ronald Edward *photojournalist*
Klapper, Byron D. *financial company executive*

Moorestown
Bennington, William Jay *public relations executive*
†Colburn, Harold L. *dermatologist, state legislator*
†Hassinger, Herman A. *architect*
†Korth, James Scott *minister*
Schwerin, Horace S. *marketing research executive*
Springer, Douglas Hyde *retired food company executive, lawyer*

Morris Plains
Bruggink, Herman *publishing executive*
Chin-Kee-Fatt, Hollis Romauld *marketing professional*
de Vink, Lodewijk J. R. *consumer pharmaceutical products company executive*
Goodes, Melvin Russell *manufacturing company executive*
Picozzi, Anthony *dentistry educator, educational administrator*
Rakay, William R. *publishing company executive*
†Shanley, Kevin *medical supply company executive*
Williams, Joseph Dalton *pharmaceutical company executive*

Morristown
Ahl, David Howard *writer, editor*
Arnow, Leslie Earle *scientist*
Aspero, Benedict Vincent *lawyer*
Barpal, Isaac Ruben *technology and operations executive*
Barter, John William, III *corporate executive*
†Bauhs, David J. *manufacturing executive*
Belzer, Alan *diversified manufacturing company executive*
Berkley, Peter Lee *lawyer*
Bickerton, John Thorburn *retired pharmaceutical executive*
Bossidy, Lawrence Arthur *industrial manufacturing executive*
Bromberg, Myron James *lawyer*
Callahan, Edward William *chemical engineer, manufacturing company executive*
Cameron, Nicholas Allen *diversified corporation executive*
Campion, Thomas Francis *lawyer*
Clemen, John Douglas *lawyer*
Clifford, Robert L. *state supreme court justice*
Day, John W. *international corporation executive*
†Dayson, Diane Harris *superintendent, park ranger*
DeHope, Edward Kim *lawyer*
DeLury, Bernard E. *vice president labor relations*
Fredericks, Robert Joseph *chemical company executive*
Graham, Paul E(ugene) *lawyer*
Granet, Roger B. *psychiatrist, educator*
Herman, Robert Lewis *cork company executive*
Herzberg, Peter Jay *lawyer*
Hesselink, Ann Patrice *financial executive, lawyer*
Hyland, William Francis *lawyer*
Isko, Irving David *corporate executive*
Kandravy, John *lawyer*
Katzenbach, Nicholas deBelleville *lawyer*
Kearns, William Michael, Jr. *investment banker*
Kirby, Fred Morgan, II *corporation executive*
†Klindt, Steven *art museum director*
†Kreindler, Peter Michael *lawyer*
Krumholz, Dennis Jonathan *lawyer*
Kurtz, Bruce Edward *chemical engineer, research and development executive*
Lavey, Stewart Evan *lawyer*
Lindner, Joseph, Jr. *physician, medical administrator*
Lunin, Joseph *lawyer*
Martin, Alvin Charles *lawyer*
McCarthy, G. Daniel *lawyer*
Mc Elroy, William Theodore *lawyer*
Miller, Hasbrouck Bailey *financial and travel services company executive*
Moore, Milo Anderson *banking executive*
Munson, William Leslie *insurance company executive*
Murphy, Joseph F. *lawyer*
†Nadaskay, Raymond *architect*
Newhouse, Robert J., Jr. *insurance executive*
Nittoly, Paul Gerard *lawyer*
O'Grady, Dennis Joseph *lawyer*
Pantel, Glenn Steven *lawyer*
Parr, Grant Van Siclen *surgeon*
Perretti, Peter Nicholas, Jr. *lawyer*
Personick, Stewart David *electrical engineer*
Powell, David Greatorex *public affairs executive*
Puffer, Leonard Bruce, Jr. *lawyer*
Reed, Rex Raymond *retired telephone company executive*
Reid, Charles Adams, III *lawyer*
Rose, Robert Gordon *lawyer*
Salisbury, Kevin Mahon *lawyer*
Samet, Andrew Benjamin *lawyer*
Scott, Susan *lawyer*
Sharkey, Vincent Joseph *lawyer*
Shumate, Paul William, Jr. *communications executive*
†Simon, William Edward *investment banker, former secretary of treasury*
Stanton, Patrick Michael *lawyer*
Suchodolski, Ronald Eugene *publishing company executive*
Szuch, Clyde Andrew *lawyer*
Teiger, David *management consultant*
Tesch, Lorraine Barbara *medical technology assessment writer*
Tierney, Raymond Moran, Jr. *lawyer*
Tokar, Edward Thomas *manufacturing company executive*
Van Uitert, LeGrand Gerard *chemist*
Wajnert, Thomas C. *leasing company executive*
Warlick, Robert Patterson *investment management company executive*
Weinstein, Stephen Brant *communications executive, researcher, writer*
†Weinstein, Stephen Saul *lawyer*
Whitmer, Frederick Lee *lawyer*
†Wilks, Alan Delbert *chemical research and technology executive, researcher*
†Yrigoyen, Charles, Jr. *church denomination executive*

Mount Laurel
Buchan, Alan Bradley *land planner, consultant, civil engineer*
Calzolano, John Joseph *engineering and construction company executive*
Grey, Richard E. *toy company executive*
Hart, Larry Edward *communications company executive*
Instone, John Clifford *manufacturing company executive*
Klein, Anne Sceia *public relations executive*
Laubach, Roger Alvin *accountant*

Mount Tabor
Lender, Herman Joseph *reinsurance company executive*

Mountain Lakes
Case, Manning Eugene, Jr. *corporate executive*
Cook, Charles Francis *insurance executive*
†Hubert, Bernhard *computer company financial executive*
Mattes, Hans George *communications system design scientist, researcher*
Turnheim, Palmer *financial consultant, banker*
Williams, Edward David *data processing executive*
Wolff, Ivan Lawrence *venture capitalist*

Mountainside
Cardoni, Horace Robert *retired lawyer*
DiPietro, Ralph Anthony *marketing and management consultant, educator*
Good, Allen Hovey *acquisitions broker, real estate broker*
Gordon, Eugene Irving *electrical and computer engineering educator*
Lipton, Bronna Jane *marketing communications executive*

Mullica Hill
†Demola, James *church administrator*

Murray Hill
Atal, Bishnu Saroop *speech research executive*
Baker, William Oliver *research chemist, educator*
Bonnes, Charles Andrew *lawyer*
Brinkman, William Frank *physicist, research executive*
Capasso, Federico *physicist, research administrator*
Cho, Alfred Yi *electrical engineer*
Cohen, Melvin Irwin *telephone company executive*
Dyer, Alexander Patrick *industrial gas manufacturing company executive*
†Fleury, Paul Aimé *physicist*
†Geusic, Joseph Edward *physicist*
Glass, Alastair Malcolm *physicist, research director*
Graham, Ronald Lewis *mathematician*
Helfand, Eugene *chemist*
Hohenberg, Pierre Claude *research physicist*
Johnson, David W., Jr. *ceramic scientist, researcher*
Logan, Ralph Andre *physicist*
Mayo, John Sullivan *telecommunications company executive*
Morgan, Samuel P(ope) *physicist, applied mathematician*
Murthy, Srinivasa K. *engineering corporation executive*
Musa, John Davis *computer and infosystems executive, software reliability engineering researcher and expert*
†Pinczuk, Aron *physicist*
Radner, Roy *economist, educator, researcher*
†Rayner, Robert Martin *financial executive*
Sloane, Neil James Alexander *mathematician, researcher*
Stillinger, Frank Henry *chemist, educator*
Wagner, Edward Kurt *publishing company executive*
Wernick, Jack Harry *chemist*
†White, Alice Elizabeth *physicist, researcher*

Neptune
Aguiar, Adam Martin *chemist, educator*
†Clurfeld, Andrea *editor, food critic*
†Colantoni, Alfred Daniel *newspaper executive*
Harrigan, John Thomas, Jr. *physician, obstetrician-gynecologist*
Lass, E(rnest) Donald *communications company executive*
Lloyd, John Koons *hospital administrator*
Ollwerther, William Raymond *newspaper editor*
†Plangere, Jules L., III *newpaper company executive*
†Strauss, Robert Seth *critic*
Suozzo, Frank Vincent *insurance company executive*

Neshanic Station
Muckenhoupt, Benjamin *retired mathematics educator*

New Brunswick
Alexander, Robert Jackson *economist, educator*
Amarel, Saul *computer scientist, educator*
Anderson, James Doig *library and information science educator*
†Becker, Ronald Leonard *archivist*
Boehm, Werner William *social work educator*
Bolden, Frank A. *lawyer*
Boocock, Sarane Spence *sociologist*
Budd, Richard Wade *communications scientist, educator, lecturer, consultant, university dean*
Burke, James Edward *consumer products company executive*
Campbell, Robert E. *healthcare products company executive*
Carman, John Herbert *elementary education educator*
Cate, Phillip Dennis *art museum director*
Chelius, James Robert *economics educator*
†Chou, Nelson Lingsun *librarian*
Cohen, Amy *mathematics educator*
†Day, Peter Rodney *geneticist, educator*
Dill, Ellis Harold *university dean*
†Duell, Robert William *agronomist*
Eager, George Sidney, Jr. *electrical engineer, business executive*

Edelman, Hendrik *library and information science educator*
Ehrenfeld, David William *biology educator, author*
Elinson, Jack *sociology educator*
Ettinger, Lawrence Jay *pediatric hematologist-oncologist, educator*
Fine, Roger Seth *pharmaceutical executive, lawyer*
Funk, Cyril Reed, Jr. *agronomist, educator*
Gardner, Lloyd Calvin, Jr. *history educator*
Garner, Charles William *educational administration educator, consultant*
Gillette, William *historian, educator*
Glasser, Paul Harold *sociologist, educator, university administrator, social worker*
Gocke, David Joseph *immunology educator, physician, medical scientist*
Goffen, Rona *art educator*
†Grassle, John Fredrick *oceanographer, marine sciences educator*
Grob, Gerald N. *historian, educator*
Gussin, Robert Zalmon *health care company executive*
Hartman, Mary S. *historian*
Hayakawa, Kan-Ichi *food science educator*
Holzberg, Harvey Alan *hospital administrator*
Horowitz, Irving Louis *publisher, educator*
Hurst, Gregory Squire *artistic director, director, producer*
Jacob, Charles Elmer *political scientist, educator*
Karel, Marcus *food science educator*
Katz, Carlos *electrical engineer*
Kelley, Donald Reed *historian*
Kovach, Barbara Ellen *management and psychology educator*
Kruskal, Martin David *mathematical physicist, educator*
†Kulikowski, Casimir Alexander *computer science educator, research program director*
Lachance, Paul Albert *food science educator, clergyman*
Larsen, Ralph S(tanley) *health care company executive*
Lebowitz, Joel Louis *mathematical physicist, educator*
Lee, Cheng-few *finance educator*
Leggett, John Carl *sociology educator*
Lettvin, Theodore *concert pianist*
Levine, George Lewis *English language educator, literature critic*
†Lewis, David Levering *history educator*
Liao, Mei-June *biopharmaceutical company administrator*
†Lynch, John A. *lawyer, state senator*
Maramorosch, Karl *virologist, educator*
Matuska, John E. *hospital administrator*
Mc Cormick, Richard Patrick *history educator*
McGuire, John Lawrence *pharmaceuticals research executive*
Mc Laren, Malcolm Grant, IV *ceramic engineering educator*
Mechanic, David *social sciences educator*
Merrill, Leland Gilbert, Jr. *retired environmental science educator*
Midlarsky, Manus Issachar *political scientist, educator*
Morrison, Karl Frederick *history educator*
Moynahan, Julian Lane *English language educator, author*
Nawy, Edward George *civil engineer, educator*
Nelson, Jack Lee *education educator*
O'Neill, William Lawrence *history educator*
Peterson, Donald Robert *psychologist, educator, university administrator*
Plano, Richard James *physicist, educator*
Poirier, Richard *English educator, literary critic*
Potenza, Joseph A(nthony) *chemistry educator, academic administrator*
Psuty, Norbert Phillip *marine sciences educator*
Reed, James Wesley *social historian, educator*
†Richards, Pamela Spence *library and information studies educator*
Roberts, Albert Roy *social work educator*
Rosenberg, Seymour *psychologist, educator*
Roth, Herbert, Jr. *corporate executive*
Roussakis, Nicolas *composer, music educator*
Ruben, Brent David *communication educator*
Russell, Louise Bennett *economist, educator*
Scanlon, Jane Cronin *mathematics educator*
Scully, John Thomas *obstetrician, gynecologist, educator*
†Seibold, James Richard *physician, researcher*
Shanno, David Francis *mathematics educator*
Snyderman, Reuven Kenneth *plastic surgeon, educator*
Solberg, Myron *food scientist, educator*
Stimpson, Catharine Roslyn *English language educator, writer*
Strauss, Ulrich Paul *educator, chemist*
†Strawderman, William E. *statistics educator*
Stuart, Robert Crampton *economics educator*
Taft, Earl Jay *mathematics educator*
Tanner, Daniel *curriculum theory educator*
Tedrow, John Charles Fremont *soils educator*
†Temmer, Georges Maxime *physicist*
Tiger, Lionel *social scientist, anthropology consultant*
Toby, Jackson *sociologist, educator*
Turock, Betty Jane *library and information science educator*
Vieth, Wolf Randolph *chemical engineering educator*
Wilkinson, Louise Cherry *psychology educator, dean*
Wolfe, Robert Richard *bioresource engineer, educator*
Yttrehus, Rolv Berger *composer, educator*

New Monmouth
Donnelly, Gerard Kevin *retail executive*

New Providence
Andrews, Gordon Clark *lawyer*
Barnes, Sandra Henley *publishing company executive*
Chatterji, Debajyoti *manufacturing company executive*
Cooper, Carol Diane *publishing company executive*
†Coppersmith, Susan Nan *physicist*
Fishburn, Peter Clingerman *research mathematician, economist*
Gall, Martin *chemist, research and development manager*
Gaylord, Norman Grant *chemical and polymer consultant*
†Grinfeder, Claude *construction materials executive*
Kotynek, George Roy *mechanical engineer, educator, marketing executive*
Lanzerotti, Louis John *physicist*
Laudise, Robert Alfred *research chemist*

Longfield, William Herman *health care company executive*
Maloney, George Thomas *health industry executive*
Mitchell, James Winfield *science administrator*
Shepp, Lawrence Alan *mathematician, educator*
Siegel, Ira Theodore *publishing executive*
†Sinto, Otavio *marketing executive*
Stormer, Horst Ludwig *physicist*
Sundberg, Carl-Erik Wilhelm *telecommunications executive, researcher*
Symanski, Robert Anthony *treasurer*
Thompson, Larry Flack *chemical company executive*
†Walker, Stanley P. *publishing executive*
†Wertheim, Gunther Klaus *physicist*
Wyner, Aaron Daniel *mathematician*

New Vernon
Dugan, John Leslie, Jr. *foundation executive*
Huck, John Lloyd *pharmaceutical company executive*
Margetts, W. Thomas *automobile parts company executive, lawyer*

Newark
Abeles, Theodore Lillien *lawyer*
†Abrams, Roger I. *academic dean, labor arbitrator*
Ackerman, Harold A. *federal judge*
Alito, Samuel Anthony, Jr. *federal judge*
†Allen, David *newspaper editor*
Allen, Michael Lewis *lawyer*
Arabie, Phipps *marketing educator, researcher*
†Askin, Frank *law educator*
Baker, Herman *vitaminologist*
Bar-Ness, Yeheskel *electrical engineer, educator*
Barry, Maryanne Trump *federal judge*
†Bartner, Martin *newspaper executive*
Bassler, William G. *federal judge*
Beck, Robert Arthur *insurance company executive*
Ben-Menachem, Yoram *radiologist*
Bergen, Stanley Silvers, Jr. *university president, physician*
Beyer-Mears, Annette *physiologist*
Bhavaraju, Murty Parabrahma *electric utility executive*
Bigley, William Joseph, Jr. *control engineer*
Bishop, Gordon Bruce *journalist*
Bissell, John W. *federal judge*
†Bonaventura, Vincent E. *transportation executive*
Bornstein, Lester Milton *medical center executive*
Boyd, Alex *library director*
†Braun, Robert *newspaper editor*
†Buck, Anne Marie *library director, consultant*
Cahn, Jeffrey Barton *lawyer*
Caldwell, Wesley Stuart, III *lawyer, lobbyist*
Canfield, William Newton *editorial cartoonist*
Carroll, John Douglas *mathematical-statistical psychologist*
Chagnon, Joseph V. *school system administrator*
Cheng, Mei-Fang *psychobiology educator, neuroethology researcher*
Chesler, Stanley Richard *federal judge*
Chinard, Francis Pierre *physiologist, physician*
Christakos, Sylvia *biochemist, educator, researcher*
Christodoulou, Aris Peter *pharmaceutical executive, investment banker*
Cinotti, Alfonse Anthony *ophthalmologist, educator*
†Clark, Dewey P. *insurance company executive*
†Cocchia, Neal *newspaper editor*
Codey, Lawrence R. *electric power company executive*
Colli, Bart Joseph *lawyer*
Connor, John Thomas, Jr. *lawyer*
Cook, Stuart Donald *physician, educator*
Crew, Louie (Li Min Hua) *language professional, educator*
Day, Edward Francis, Jr. *lawyer*
Debevoise, Dickinson Richards *federal judge*
†De Lisa, Joel Alan *rehabilitation physician*
Del Tufo, Robert J. *lawyer, former state attorney general*
Dickson, Jim *playwright, stage director*
†Dwane, James E. *insurance company executive*
Eittreim, Richard MacNutt *lawyer*
English, Nicholas Conover *lawyer*
English, Woodruff Jones *lawyer*
Eslami, Hossein Hojatol *surgeon, educator*
Estrin, Herman Albert *English language educator*
Evans, Hugh E. *pediatrician*
†Everett, Richard G. *newspaper editor*
Fenster, Saul K. *university president*
†Ferland, E. James *electric utility executive*
Fink, Aaron Herman *box manufacturing executive*
Flaherty, John Edmund *lawyer*
Friedland, Bernard *engineer, educator*
Gardner, Bernard *surgeon, educator*
Garth, Leonard I. *federal judge*
Genzer, Stephen Bruce *lawyer, educator*
Gerathy, E. Carroll *former insurance executive, real estate developer*
†Gilboy, Thomas V. *financial executive*
Gillen, James Robert *insurance company executive, lawyer*
Gillett, Jonathan Newell *publishing executive*
Goldenberg, David Milton *experimental pathologist, oncologist*
†Gossett, George Boyd *human service executive*
Gottfredson, Don Martin *criminal justice educator*
Greenbaum, Jeffrey J. *lawyer*
†Greendorfer, Terese Grosman *fashion editor*
Greenfield, Sanford Raymond *architect*
Griffinger, Michael R. *lawyer*
Guenzel, Frank Bernhard *chemical engineer*
Guido, Joseph Matthew *air transport company executive*
†Hadas, Rachel *poet, educator*
Hanesian, Deran *chemical engineer, chemistry and environmental science educator, consultant*
Hannon, John Robert *investment company executive*
Haring, Eugene Miller *lawyer*
†Harrison, Charles *newspaper editor*
Harrison, Roslyn Siman *lawyer*
Hart, Paul *dean, poet, educator*
Henderson, Dorland John *retired electrical engineer*
Hermann, Steven Istvan *textile executive*
Hill, George James *surgeon, educator*
†Hiltz, Starr Roxanne *sociologist, educator, computer scientist, writer, lecturer, consultant*
Hobson, Robert Wayne, II *surgeon*
Hollander, Toby Edward *education educator*
†Horii, Howard Nobuo *architect, educator*
Horton, William Harrison *lawyer*
Howe, Carroll Victor *construction equipment company executive*
Hrycak, Peter *mechanical engineer, educator*
Hsieh, Jui Sheng *mechanical engineer, educator*
Hsu, Cheng-Tzu Thomas *civil engineering educator*
Hutcheon, Duncan Elliot *physician, educator*

Iffy, Leslie *medical educator*
James, Sharpe *mayor*
Jones, Etta *singer*
†Kanzler, George *journalist, critic*
Karp, Donald Mathew *lawyer, banker*
Keith, Garnett Lee, Jr. *insurance company investment executive*
†Klein, Willie *newspaper editor*
Knee, Stephen H. *lawyer*
†Koeppe, Alfred C. *telecommunications company executive*
Kott, David Russell *lawyer*
Lanzoni, Vincent *medical school dean*
Latini, Anthony A. *insurance company financial executive*
Lawatsch, Frank Emil, Jr. *lawyer*
Lechner, Alfred James, Jr. *federal judge*
Ledeen, Robert Wagner *neurochemist, educator*
Lederman, Peter (Bernd) *environmental services executive, consultant, educator*
Leevy, Carroll Moton *medical educator, hepatology researcher*
†Lenehan, Art *newspaper editor*
Levin, Simon *lawyer*
Lieberman, Leonard *retired supermarket executive*
Lifland, John C. *federal judge*
Light, Dorothy Kaplan *insurance executive, lawyer*
†Link, William P. *insurance company executive*
Lory, Marc H. *hospital administrator*
Mahler, Harry Bez *architect, planner*
†Marano, Rocco John *telephone company executive*
†Martinez, Arturo *newspaper editor*
†Maske, Monica *newspaper editor*
Mattson, Leroy Harry *lawyer*
Mc Carrick, Theodore Edgar *archbishop*
McGlynn, Richard Bruce *lawyer*
†McGuire, William B(enedict) *lawyer*
†McKelvey, Jack M. *bishop*
McKinney, John Adams, Jr. *lawyer*
Mitchell, James Lowry *lawyer, former government official*
Morgenstern, Dan Michael *jazz historian, educator, editor*
Moskowitz, Sam (Sam Martin) *author, editor, publisher*
†Murnick, Daniel Ely *physicist, educator*
Murray, Constance Ann *college dean*
†Murray, John Peter *insurance company executive*
Muscato, Andrew *lawyer*
†Newhouse, Mark William *publishing executive*
Newman, Samuel *trust company executive*
O'Leary, Paul Gerard *investment executive*
Panson, Gilbert Stephen *chemistry educator*
Paul, James Caverly Newlin *law educator, former university dean*
Pfeffer, Edward Israel *educational administrator*
Pfeffer, Robert *chemical engineer, academic administrator, educator*
Pignataro, Louis James *engineering educator*
Pisano, Joel A. *federal judge*
Politan, Nicholas H. *federal judge*
Pye, Mort *newspaper editor*
Reichman, Lee Brodersohn *physician*
Reilly, William Thomas *lawyer*
Robertson, William Withers *lawyer*
Rosenberg, Jerry Martin *business administration educator*
Roth, Allan Robert *lawyer, educator*
Sarokin, H. Lee *federal judge*
Scally, John Joseph, Jr. *lawyer*
†Schoon, Richard G. *association executive*
†Schweizer, Karl Wolfgang *author, historian*
Silipigni, Alfredo *opera conductor*
Simmons, Peter *urban planning educator*
†Sleed, Joel *newspaper editor*
Spillers, William Russell *civil engineering educator*
Spong, John Shelby *bishop*
Starks, Florence Elizabeth *special education educator*
Stein, Donald Gerald *psychology educator*
Strum, Brian J. *real estate executive*
†Tallal, Paula *psychologist*
Thomas, Gary L. *academic administrator*
Tischman, Michael Bernard *lawyer*
Vevier, Charles *historian, educator, consultant, university administrator*
Von Glahn, Keith G. *lawyer*
Wachenfeld, William Thomas *lawyer, foundation executive*
Weiss, Gerson *physician, educator*
Winters, Robert Cushing *insurance company executive*
Wolfe, Lilyan *special education educator, clinician*
Wolin, Alfred M. *federal judge*
Wolper, Allan L. *journalist, educator*
Wyer, James Ingersoll *lawyer*
Yamner, Morris *lawyer*
Yu, Yi-Yuan *mechanical engineering educator*
Zinbarg, Edward Donald *insurance company executive*

Newfield
McKee, Mary Elizabeth *producer*

Newton
Carstens, Harold Henry *publisher*

North Bergen
†Allen, Gordon Erwin *apparel company executive*
Chazen, Jerome A. *apparel company executive*
†Goodman, Lawrence Baron *retail executive*
Lanier, Thomas *chemical and export company executive*
Miller, Samuel Martin *apparel company finance executive*
Scarne, John *game company executive*

North Branch
†Gartlan, Philip M. *secondary school director*

North Brunswick
Bern, Ronald Lawrence *consulting company executive*

North Caldwell
Stevens, William Dollard *consulting mechanical engineer*

North Haledon
Brown, James Joseph *manufacturing company executive*

North Plainfield
Johnson, Lowell Ferris *consumer products executive, consultant*

Northvale
Aronson, Jason *publisher*
Founds, Henry William *pharmaceutical executive, microbiologist*
Goodman, Stanley Leonard *advertising executive*
†Kurzweil, Arthur *publisher, writer, educator*
Peer, George Joseph *metals company executive*

Nutley
Behl, Charanjit R. *pharmaceutical scientist*
Boardman, Harold Frederick, Jr. *lawyer, corporate executive*
Burns, John Joseph *pharmacology educator*
Connor, John Arthur *neuroscientist*
†Conrad, Herbert J. *pharmaceutical executive*
Douvan-Kulesha, Irina *chemist*
Drews, Jürgen *pharmaceutical researcher*
English, Robert Joseph *electronic corporation executive*
Kuntzman, Ronald *pharmacology research executive*
†Lerner, Irwin *pharmaceutical company executive*
Machlin, Lawrence J. *nutritionist, biochemist, educator*
Mallard, Stephen Anthony *retired utility company executive*
Mostillo, Ralph *medical association executive*
Udenfriend, Sidney *biochemist*
Wasserman, Martin Allan *pharmaceutical company executive*
Weissbach, Herbert *biochemist*

Oakhurst
Konvitz, Milton Ridbaz *legal educator*
Wilentz, Robert Nathan *state supreme court justice*

Oakland
Bacaloglu, Radu *chemical engineer*
Bloom, Arnold Sanford *lawyer*

Ocean
Abrams, Robert Allen *lawyer*

Ocean City
Brown, Frederick Harold *insurance company executive*
Speitel, Gerald Eugene *consulting environmental engineer*

Oceanport
Paley, Alfred Irving *value engineering and consulting company executive, lecturer*

Old Bridge
Engel, John Jacob *communications executive*
Swett, Stephen Frederick, Jr. *principal*

Old Tappan
Ferriter, Warren Joseph *information systems executive*

Oldwick
Blewitt, George Augustine *physician, pharmaceutical company executive*
Hitchcock, Ethan Allen *lawyer*
Snyder, Arthur *publishing company executive*

Oradell
Dinsmore, Gordon Griffith *management consultant*
Regazzi, John Henry *retired corporate executive*
Roe, Kenneth Keith *power and industrial engineering/construction company executive*
†Wells, Peter Raymond *architect*

Orange
Chlopak, Donna Gayle *marketing and management consultant*

Palmyra
Kroeger, Lin J. *management consultant*
Overholt, Miles Harvard, III *management consultant, family therapist*

Paramus
Baczko, Joseph R. *consumer products executive*
Bagli, Vincent Joseph *plastic surgeon*
Birchby, Kenneth Lee *banker*
†DiGeronimo, Suzanne Kay *architect*
Fader, Shirley Sloan *writer*
†Gingras, Paul Joseph *real estate management company executive*
Goldstein, Michael *retail executive*
†Kosco, Louis F. *senator*
Lazarus, Charles *retail toy company executive*
Maclin, Ernest *biomedical diagnostics company executive*
Nakasone, Robert C. *retail toy and game company executive*
Plucinsky, Constance Marie *school counselor, supervisor*
Ross, William *financial planner*
Smith, Donald Gene *investment management company executive*
Underwood, Steven Clark *publishing executive*
†Yegen, Christian Conrad, Jr. *business executive, lawyer*

Park Ridge
De Pol, John *artist*
Kaplan, Daniel I. *service executive*
Kennedy, Brian James *marketing executive*
†Koch, Craig R. *automobile rental and leasing company executive*
Noyes, Robert Edwin *publisher, writer*
Olson, Frank Albert *car rental company executive*
Takashima, Hideo *lawyer*

Parsippany
Ajmera, Pravin V. *engineer, business and technical consultant*
Bean, Bruce Winfield *investment banker, lawyer*
Bernthal, Frederick W. *chemical company executive*
Bridwell, Robert Kennedy *lawyer*
†Brualdi, Ulysses J., Jr. *electrical company executive*
Clark, Philip Raymond *nuclear utility executive, engineer*
†Cochran, Larry B. *amusement park executive*
Florio, Jim *lawyer, former governor*
Geyer, Thomas Powick *newspaper publisher*
Gorman, Thomas Francis *tax manager, computer systems developer*
Graham, John Gourlay *utility company executive*

Greeniaus, H. John food products company executive
†Harber, Joseph F. food marketing executive
Haselmann, John Philip marketing executive
†Jenkins, Katherine Erskine advertising executive
Jolles, Ira Hervey lawyer
Kallmann, Stanley Walter lawyer
†Kirkman, James A. food products executive
Kleinberg, Lawrence H. food industry executive
Laskowski, Robert Anthony financial executive
Leva, James Robert electric utility company executive
Lutz, William Andrew sales and marketing executive
Maness, Mildred reading specialist
Miller, Harold Joseph metals manufacturing company executive
Muratore, Robert Peter advertising executive
Nalewako, Mary Anne corporate secretary
Olsen, Robert John savings and loan association executive
Parrish, Barry Jay marketing executive
Purdum, Robert L. steel manufacturing company executive
Raber, Marvin utility company executive
†Secula, Elena advertising executive
Shaw, Alan lawyer, corporate executive
Singleterry, Gary Lee investment banker
Sommer, Joseph William educator
Stein, J. Dieter chemical company executive
Visocki, Nancy Gayle infosystems design consultant
Waggoner, Leland Tate insurance company executive

Passaic
Haddad, Jamil Raouf physician
Levine, David M. newspaper editor
Reiss, Sidney H. judge, lawyer

Paterson
Brady, Sister Jane Frances hospital executive
Danziger, Glenn Norman chemical sales company executive
†Pascrell, William J., Jr. mayor, assemblyman
Pulhamus, Marlene Louise elementary school educator

Peapack
Brennan, William Joseph manufacturing company executive
†Giordano, Salvatore manufacturing company executive
†Giordano, Salvatore, Jr. air conditioner manufacturing company executive
Weiss, Allan Joseph transport company executive, lawyer

Pennington
†Calvo, Roque John association executive
Halasi-Kun, George Joseph hydrologist, educator
Harris, Frederick George publishing company executive
Wallace, John Duncan banker
Widmer, Kemble geologist

Pennsauken
Alday, Paul Stackhouse, Jr. mechanical engineer
Connor, Wilda government health agency administrator
Gans, Samuel Myer temporary employment service executive
O'Brien, James Jerome construction management consultant

Perrineville
Hoffman, Maryhelen H. Paulick communications company executive

Perth Amboy
Gemmell, Joseph Paul banker

Phillipsburg
†Cooper, Paul mechanical engineer, research director
Paige, Richard Bruce financial information executive
Stull, Frank Walter educator

Piscataway
Alderfer, Clayton Paul organizational psychologist, educator, author, administrator
Alekman, Stanley Lawrence chemical company executive
Bretschneider, Ann Margery histotechnologist
Burke, Jacqueline Yvonne telecommunications executive
Cagan, Robert H. manufacturing company research executive, biochemist
Chien, Yie W. pharmaceutics educator
Colaizzi, John Louis college dean
Conney, Allan Howard pharmacologist
Denhardt, David Tilton molecular and cell biology educator
Edelman, Norman H. medical educator
Flanagan, James Loton electrical engineer, educator
†Fogiel, Max publishing executive
Freeman, Herbert computer engineering educator
†Glickman, Norman Jay economist, urban policy analyst
Goldstein, Bernard David physician, educator
Goodwin, Douglas Ira steel distribution company executive
Goodyear, John Lake artist, educator
Gotsch, Audrey Rose environmental health sciences educator, researcher
Hulse, Robert Douglas high technology executive
Julesz, Bela experimental psychologist, educator, electrical engineer
Kear, Bernard Henry materials scientist
Lazarus, Arnold Allan psychologist, educator
Lindenfeld, Peter physics educator
†Liotta, Raymond C. landscape architect, golf course design consultant
Messing, Joachim Wilhelm molecular biology educator
Murphree, Henry Bernard Scott psychiatry educator, consultant
Ortiz, Raphael Montañez performance artist, educator
†Pandina, Robert John neuropsychologist
Passmore, Howard Clinton, Jr. geneticist, biological sciences educator
Pollack, Irwin William psychiatrist, educator
Pond, Thomas Alexander physics educator
Pramer, David microbiologist, educator, research administrator
Robbins, Allen Bishop physics educator
Sannuti, Peddapullaiah electrical engineering educator
Schlesinger, Robert Walter microbiologist, microbiology educator emeritus
Schwebel, Milton psychologist, educator
Shapiro, Michael sportswear license corporate officer
Shatkin, Aaron Jeffrey biochemistry educator
Shea, Stephen Michael physician, educator
†Smith, Robert G. lawyer, assemblyman, educator
Snitzer, Elias physicist
Welkowitz, Walter biomedical engineer, educator
Williams, James Richard human factors engineering psychologist
Witkin, Evelyn Maisel geneticist
Yacowitz, Harold biochemist, nutritionist
Young, James Earl ceramics educator, educational administrator

Pittstown
Jacob, Harry Myles mining executive
Link, Fred Motter communications consultant

Plainfield
Granstrom, Marvin Leroy civil and sanitary engineering educator
Kopicki, John R. hospital administrator

Plainsboro
†Hewitt, N. J. investment company executive
Jones, Allen N. insurance company executive
Schreyer, William Allen retired investment firm executive
†Talkington, William Ale publishing company executive
Urciuoli, J. Arthur investment executive
Yun, Samuel minister, educator

Pleasantville
†Briant, Maryjane newspaper editor
Fabietti, Victor Armando accountant
Hopson, James Warren newspaper publisher
†Linz, Carla Jean newspaper editor

Point Pleasant Beach
Motley, John Paul psychiatrist, consultant

Pomona
Bukowski, Elaine Louise physical therapist
Farris, Vera King college president

Pompton Lakes
Brolsma, Catherine secondary education educator, educational administrator

Port Murray
Kunzler, John Eugene physicist

Pottersville
Lynch, James Henry, Jr. lawyer

Princeton
Aarsleff, Hans linguistics educator
Ackourey, Peter Paul lawyer
Adler, Stephen Louis physicist
†Aizenman, Michael mathematics and physics educator, researcher
Allen, Diogenes clergyman, philosophy educator
Anderson, Ellis Bernard retired lawyer, pharmaceutical company executive
Anderson, Philip Warren physicist
Appelbaum, Michael Arthur finance company executive
Armstrong, James Franklin religion educator
Armstrong, Richard Stoll minister, ministry and evangelism educator
Ashenfelter, Orley Clark economics educator
†Austin, Danforth Whitley newspaper executive
Axtmann, Robert Clark nuclear and chemical engineering educator
Ayers, William McLean electrochemical engineering company executive
Babbitt, Milton Byron composer
Bahcall, John Norris astrophysicist
Baker, Richard Wheeler, Jr. real estate executive
Ball, George Wildman lawyer, investment banker, author, diplomat
Banse, Robert Lee lawyer
Barker, Richard Gordon corporate research and development executive
Barlow, Walter Greenwood public opinion analyst, management consultant
Bartolini, Robert Alfred electrical engineer, researcher
Baumol, William Jack economist, educator
Beeners, Wilbert John speech professional, minister
Beidler, Marsha Wolf lawyer
Benacerraf, Paul Joseph Salomon philosophy educator
Bergman, Richard Isaac consulting company executive
Billington, David Perkins civil engineering educator
Bogan, Elizabeth Chapin economist, educator
Bogdonoff, Seymour Moses aeronautical engineer
Borel, Armand mathematics educator
Bowersock, Glen Warren historian
Boyer, Ernest LeRoy foundation executive
Bradford, David Frantz economist
Brennan, William Joseph, III lawyer
Brombert, Victor Henri literature educator, author
Brown, Leon Carl history educator
Bunn, William Bernice, III physician, lawyer, epidemiologist
Bunnell, Peter Curtis photography and art educator, museum curator
Buttenheim, Edgar Marion publishing executive
Caffarelli, Luis Angel mathematician, educator
Cakmak, Ahmet Sefik civil engineering educator
Canright, Sarah Anne artist, educator
Carlson, Charlotte Booth book illustrator
Carnes, James Edward electronics executive
Carver, David Harold physician, educator
†Cassidy, Brendan Francis art educator and director
Chamberlin, John Stephen investor, former cosmetics company executive
Champlin, Edward James classics educator
Chandler, James John surgeon
Chang, Clarence Dayton chemist
Chow, Gregory Chi-Chong economist, educator
Cinlar, Erhan engineering educator
Clagett, Marshall historian, educator
Coale, Ansley Johnson economics educator
Coffey, Joseph Irving international affairs educator
Coffin, David Robbins art historian, educator
Cohen, Alan Barry foundation executive
Cole, Nancy Stooksberry educational research executive
†Colquhoun, Alan H. architectural educator
Conn, Hadley Lewis, Jr. physician, educator
Connor, Geoffrey Michael lawyer
Cook, Michael Allan social sciences educator
Cooke, Theodore Frederic, Jr. chemist
Corngold, Stanley Alan German and comparative literature educator, writer
Cox, Edward Charles biology educator
Crespi, Irving public opinion and market research consultant
Curschmann, Michael Johann Hendrik German language and literature educator
Curtiss, Howard Crosby, Jr. mechanical engineer, educator
†D'Augusta, Alfred M. human resources executive
Davidson, Ronald Crosby physicist, educator
Davies, Horton Marlais clergyman, religion educator
Davis, Richard K. management consultant executive
Deaton, Angus Stewart economist, educator
de Grazia, Sebastian political philosopher, author
Deligné, Pierre R. mathematician
Denlinger, Edgar Jacob electronics engineering research executive
Diamond, Malcolm Luria retired religion educator, therapist
Dickinson, Bradley William electrical engineering educator
Dilworth, Joseph Richardson investment banker
Doherty, Leonard Edward financial publishing company executive
Doig, Jameson Wallace political science educator
Dornburgh, William Walter banker
Douglass, Jane Dempsey theology educator
Dovey, Brian Hugh health care products company executive, venture capitalist
Drakeman, Donald Lee corporate executive, lawyer
Draper, Theodore author
Durbin, Enoch Job aeronautical engineering educator
Dyson, Freeman John physicist
Ehrenberg, Edward executive, investor
Ekstrom, Ruth Burt psychologist
Emmerich, Walter psychologist
Estey, Audree Phipps artistic director
Faltings, Gerd mathematician, educator
Farley, Edward Raymond, Jr. mining and manufacturing company executive
Fenichel, Richard Lee biochemist
Ferguson, Stephen librarian
†Fernandes, Prabhavathi Bhat molecular biologist
File, Joseph research physics engineer
Finch, Jeremiah Stanton English language educator
†Fisch, Nathaniel Joseph physicist
Fitch, Val Logsdon physics educator
Fleming, John Vincent humanities educator
Florey, Klaus Georg chemist, pharmaceutical consultant
†Ford, Jeremiah, III architect
Fouss, James H. marketing executive
Fox, Mary Ann Williams librarian
Fresco, Jacques Robert biochemist, educator
Funk, Peter V. K. writer, scholarly, lexical semanticist
Gale, Paula Jane chemist
Gear, Charles William computer scientist
Geertz, Clifford James anthropology educator
George, Emery Edward foreign language and studies educator
George, Thomas artist
Gibson, James John electronics engineer, consultant
†Gillespie, Richard Joseph advertising agency executive
Gillespie, Thomas William theological seminary administrator, religion educator
Gillham, John Kinsey chemical engineering educator
Gips, Walter Fuld, Jr. manufacturing company executive
Girgus, Joan Stern psychologist, university administrator
Glassman, Irvin mechanical and aeronautical engineering educator, consultant
Goheen, Robert Francis classicist, educator, former ambassador
Goldfeld, Stephen Michael economics educator, university official
Goldman, Clifford Alan financial advisor
Gordenker, Leon political sciences educator
Gordon, Ernest clergyman
Gott, J. Richard, III astrophysicist
Grabar, Oleg art educator
Graessley, William Walter chemical engineering educator
†Gramlich, James Vandle chemical products company executive
Grasselli, Robert Karl physical chemist, research scientist
Graves, Michael architect, educator
†Green, Jack W. biostatistician
Green, Joseph chemist
Greenberg, Herbert M(arvin) psychologist, corporate executive
Greenberg, Joel S. management consultant, engineer
Greenstein, Fred Irwin political science educator
Griffiths, Phillip A. mathematician, academic administrator
Gross, Charles Gordon psychology educator, neuroscientist
Groves, John Taylor, III chemist, educator
Gunn, James Edward astrophysicist
Gunning, Robert Clifford mathematician, educator
Habicht, Christian Herbert history educator
Haggerty, John Richard banker
†Haldane, Frederick Duncan Michael physics educator
Halpern, Manfred political science educator
Happer, William, Jr. physicist, educator
Hardy, Daniel Wayne theological center director, theologian, educator
Harford, James Joseph retired aerospace association executive
Harman, Gilbert Helms philosophy educator
Harris, Robert lawyer, investment company executive
Harvey, Norman Ronald finance company executive
†Hawryluk, Richard Janusz physicist
Hayes, Edwin Junius, Jr. business executive
Hearn, Ruby Puryear foundation executive
Hendrickson, Robert Frederick pharmaceutical company executive
Henkel, William financial services executive
Henneman, John Bell, Jr. library bibliographer
Hill, James Scott lawyer
Hillier, James communications executive, researcher
Hillier, J(ames) Robert architect
Hirschman, Albert Otto political economist, educator
Hoebel, Bartley Gore psychology educator
Hollander, Robert B., Jr. Romance languages educator
Holst, Willem oil company executive
Holt, Philetus Havens, III architect
Horovitz, Zola Philip pharmaceutical company executive
†Hulse, Russell Alan physicist
Hunter, John Stuart statistician, consultant
Hunter, Sam art historian, educator
Hynes, Samuel English language educator, author
†Inderbitzin, Paul Herold reinsurance company executive
Issawi, Charles Philip economist, educator
Itzkowitz, Norman history educator
Jacobson, Herbert Leonard electronics company executive
Jahn, Robert George university dean, engineering educator
Jeffery, Peter Grant musicologist, fine arts educator
Jellinek, Paul S. foundation executive, health economist
†Jenkins, Edward Beynon research astronomer
†Jobe, Edward B. insurance company executive
Johnson, Ernest Frederick chemical engineer, educator
Johnson, Walter Curtis electrical engineering educator
Johnston, Robert Chapman lawyer
Johnston, Robert Fowler venture capitalist
Jordan, William Chester history educator
Joyce, William Leonard librarian
Judge, Marty M. lawyer
Judson, Sheldon geology educator
Kahng, Dawon physicist, research and development executive
Karol, Reuben Hirsh civil engineer, sculptor
Kateb, George Anthony political science educator
Kaufman, Nancy J. health foundation executive
Kauzmann, Walter Joseph chemistry educator
Keeley, Edmund LeRoy English, creative writing and modern Greek studies educator, author
†Kehrt, Allan W. architectural firm executive
Kemmerer, Peter Ream financial executive
Kenen, Peter Bain economist, educator
Kennan, George Frost historian, educator, former ambassador,
Khachadurian, Avedis physician
Knight, Walter Early association executive
Knoepflmacher, Ulrich Camillus literature educator
Kobayashi, Hisashi computer scientist, communication theorist, educator
Koepp, Donald William librarian
Kohn, Joseph John mathematician, educator
†Kuh, Charlotte Virginia economist
Labalme, Patricia Hochschild educational administrator
Lam, Sau-Hai aeronautical engineering educator
Lange, Victor language educator, author
Langlands, Robert Phelan mathematician
†Law, Chung King aerospace engineering educator, researcher
Lechner, Bernard Joseph consulting electrical engineer
†LeGrange, Jane Deborah industrial physicist
Lemelson, Jerome H. inventor
Lemonick, Aaron physicist, educator
Lerner, Ralph architect, university dean
Lester, Richard Allen economist, educator
Levine, Arnold Jay molecular biology educator, researcher
Levy, Kenneth music educator
Lewis, Bernard Near Eastern studies educator
Lewis, David Kellogg philosopher, educator
Libchaber, Albert Joseph physics educator
Lieb, Elliott Hershel physicist, mathematician, educator
Lieberman, David Ira mathematician, administrator
Lippincott, Walter Heulings, Jr. publishing executive
Litz, Arthur Walton, Jr. English language educator
Lopresti, Philip Vincent electrical engineer, researcher, consultant
Ludwig, Richard Milton English literature educator, librarian
MacPherson, Frank Becker, III advanced technology executive
Mahlman, Jerry David research meteorologist
Mahoney, Michael Sean history educator
Majda, Andrew J. mathematician, educator
Malkiel, Burton Gordon economics educator
Malkiel, Nancy Weiss college dean, history educator
Manabe, Syukuro climatologist
Manning, Winton Howard psychologist, educational administrator
Marks, John Henry Near Eastern studies educator
Massa, Conrad Harry seminary dean
Mc Clure, Donald Stuart physical chemist, educator
Mc Cullough, John Price retired oil company executive
McKearn, Thomas Joseph immunology and pathology educator, scientist
Mc Pherson, James Munro history educator
Metzger, Bruce Manning clergyman, educator
Miller, George Armitage psychologist, educator
Miller, Patrick Dwight, Jr. religion educator, minister
Mills, Bradford merchant banker
†Mills, Michael James architect
Mills, Robert Gail retired physicist
Miner, Earl Roy English educator
Minton, Dwight Church manufacturing company executive
Miyakoda, Kikuro meteorologist, lecturer
Montagu, Ashley anthropologist, social biologist
Montgomery, Ronald Eugene chemist, research and development director
Morrill, William Ashley research executive
Morris, Mac Glenn advertising bureau executive
Morrison, Toni (Chloe Anthony Morrison) novelist
Mueller, Peter Sterling psychiatrist, educator
Murphy, Walter Francis political science educator, author
Napoliello, Michael John psychiatrist
Navrotsky, Alexandra geophysics educator
Nehamas, Alexander philosophy educator
Nucciarone, A. Patrick lawyer
Oates, Joyce Carol author
O'Connor, Neal William former advertising agency executive
O'Donnell, Laurence Gerard newspaper editor
Ondetti, Miguel Angel chemist, consultant
Oort, Abraham Hans meteorologist, researcher, educator
Ostriker, Jeremiah Paul astrophysicist, educator
Palmer, Robert Roswell historian, educator
†Palsho, Dorothea Coccoli information services executive
Paneyko, Stephen Hobbs banker
Paret, Peter historian
Paris, Peter Junior religion educator, minister
Peebles, Phillip James E. physicist, educator

Penick, Joe Edward *petroleum consultant*
Perhach, James Lawrence *pharmaceutical company executive*
Peterson, Willard James *Chinese history educator*
Phillips, Daniel Miller *lawyer*
Poor, Harold Vincent *electrical engineering educator*
Popper, Robert David *computer and management consultant*
Putnam, Peter Brock *author, lecturer*
Quandt, Richard Emeric *economics educator*
Rabb, Theodore K. *historian, educator*
Ragno, Nancy Nickell *educational writer*
†Rampersad, Arnold *writer, literature educator*
Rebenfeld, Ludwig *chemist*
Reinhardt, Uwe Ernst *economist, educator*
Reynolds, George Thomas *physics educator, researcher, consultant*
Reynolds, Richard Clyde *physician, foundation administrator*
Rhett, Haskell Emery Smith *foundation executive, educator*
Rich, Jude T. *management consulting firm executive*
Rigolot, François *French literature educator, literary critic*
Roberts, Peter A. *banker*
Robertson, Nat Clifton *chemist*
Rodgers, Daniel Tracy *history educator*
Rodwell, John Dennis *biochemist*
Rosen, Harvey Sheldon *economics educator*
Rosen, Norman Edward *lawyer*
†Rosenbaum, Allen *art museum administrator*
Rosenberg, Leon E. *medical educator, geneticist, university dean*
Rosenthal, Howard Lewis *political science educator*
Roth, William Matson *former corporate executive*
Royce, Barrie Saunders Hart *physicist*
Rozman, Gilbert Friedell *sociologist, educator*
Rutherford, Paul Harding *physicist*
Savage, Naomi *photographer*
Saville, Dudley Albert *chemical engineering educator*
Schafer, Carl Walter *investment executive*
Schofield, Robert E(dwin) *history educator, academic administrator*
Schorske, Carl Emil *historian, educator*
Schroeder, Alfred Christian *electronics research engineer*
Schroeder, Steven Alfred *medical educator, researcher, foundation executive*
Scibetta, Louis Paul *health care company executive*
Seawright, James L., Jr. *sculptor, educator*
Seizinger, Bernd Robert *molecular geneticist, physician, researcher*
Semrod, T. Joseph *banker*
Sethi, Shyam Sunder *management consutant*
Setton, Kenneth M. *historian, educator*
Shapiro, Harold Tafler *university president, economist*
Shear, Theodore Leslie, Jr. *archaeologist, educator*
Shenk, Thomas Eugene *molecular biology educator*
Shimizu, Yoshiaki *art historian, educator*
Shoemaker, Frank Crawford *physicist, educator*
Showalter, Elaine *humanities educator*
Sigmund, Paul Eugene *political science educator*
Silhavy, Thomas Joseph *molecular biology educator*
†Sinai, Yakov G. *theoretical mathematician, educator*
Smagorinsky, Joseph *meteorologist*
Smith, Arthur John Stewart *physicist, educator*
Smith, Hayden, Jr. *lawyer*
Socolow, Robert Harry *mechanical and aerospace engineering educator, scientist*
†Spencer, Thomas C. *mathmatician*
Spies, Claudio *composer, educator*
Spiro, Thomas George *chemistry educator*
Starr, Paul Elliot *sociologist, writer, editor, educator*
†Stein, Elias M. *mathematician, educator*
Steiner, Robert Lisle *language consultant*
Stengel, Robert Frank *mechanical and aerospace engineering educator*
Stern, Gail Frieda *historical association director*
Sterzer, Fred *research physicist*
Stix, Thomas Howard *physicist, educator*
Stokes, Donald Elkinton *political science educator*
Stone, Lawrence *historian*
Sugerman, Abraham Arthur *psychiatrist*
†Sussna, Robert Earl *architect*
Tabell, Anthony *financial analyst*
†Tarbox, Dick *communications engineering executive*
Tarjan, Robert Endre *computer scientist, educator*
Taylor, Edward Curtis *chemistry educator*
Taylor, Howard Francis *sociology educator, researcher, consultant*
Taylor, Joseph Hooton, Jr. *radio astronomer, physicist*
Tierney, Bill *university athletic coach*
Tilghman, Shirley Marie *biology educator*
Townsend, Charles Edward *Slavic languages educator*
Treiman, Sam Bard *physics educator*
Twitchett, Denis Crispin *historian*
Uitti, Karl David *language educator*
Ullman, Richard Henry *political science educator*
Umscheid, Ludwig Joseph *computer specialist*
Vahaviolos, Sotirios John *electrical engineer, scientist, corporate executive*
Van Houten, Franklyn Bosworth *geologist, educator*
Vanmarcke, Erik Hector *civil engineering educator*
Vann, Joseph McAlpin *nuclear engineer*
Wallace, Walter L. *sociologist, educator*
Walzer, Michael Laban *political science educator*
Wei, James *chemical engineering educator, academic dean*
†Weigmann, Hans-Dietrich H. *chemist*
Weimer, Paul K(essler) *electrical engineer*
Weiss, Renée Karol *editor, writer, musician*
Weiss, Robert Jerome *psychiatrist, educator*
Weiss, Theodore Russell *poet, editor*
Wentz, Sidney Frederick *insurance company executive, foundation executive*
West, Charles Converse *theologian, educator*
Westergaard, Peter Talbot *composer, music educator*
Westoff, Charles Francis *demographer, educator*
Wheeler, John Archibald *physicist, educator*
White, Morton Gabriel *philosopher, author*
Wightman, Arthur Strong *physicist, educator*
Wigner, Eugene Paul *physicist, educator*
Wilczek, Frank Anthony *physics educator*
Wilkinson, David Todd *physics educator*
Willig, Robert Daniel *economics educator*
Willingham, Warren Willcox *psychologist, testing service executive*
Wilmerding, John *art history educator, museum curator*
Wilson, Donald Malcolm *publishing executive*
Wilson, Margaret Dauler *philosophy educator*
Wise, John James *oil company executive*
Witten, Edward *mathematical physicist*
Wolpert, Julian *geographer, educator*
Wong, Ching-Ping *chemist*
Wood, Eric Franklin *earth and environmental sciences educator*
Woolf, Harry *historian, educator*
Zierler, Neal *mathematician*
Ziolkowski, Theodore Joseph *comparative literature educator*
†Zissman, Lorin *marketing research, consulting company executive*

Princeton Junction
Haddad, James Henry *chemical engineering consultant*

Rahway
Horan, John J. *pharmaceutical company executive*
Kaczorowski, Gregory John *biochemist, researcher, science administrator*
Linemeyer, David Lee *molecular biologist*
†Reynolds, Glenn Franklin *medicinal research scientist*
Shapiro, Bennett Michaels *biochemist, educator*

Ramsey
Eklund, Donald Arthur *trade association executive*
†Kusumoto, Sadahei *light manufacturing executive*
†Markowitz, Arthur Walter *food brokerage executive*
†Oliver, Joseph J. *consumer products company executive*

Rancocas
Burke, James Joseph *banker*

Red Bank
Auerbach, Philip Gary *lawyer*
Chynoweth, Alan Gerald *telecommunications research executive*
Dale, Madeline Houston McWhinney *banker*
Fleischer, Paul E. *electrical engineer*
Hertz, Daniel Leroy, Jr. *entrepreneur*
Hollywood, John Matthew *electronics consultant*
†Hovnanian, Kevork S. *real estate developer*
†Koch, Udo *oil industry executive*
Liao, Paul Foo-Hung *communications research company executive, physicist*
McCann, John Francis *financial services company executive*
McWhinney, Madeline H. (Mrs. John Denny Dale) *economist*
Meredith, George (Marlor) *association executive, writer*
Reinhart, Peter Sargent *corporate executive, lawyer*
Rogers, Lee Jasper *lawyer*
Schimpf, John Joseph *real estate developer*
Schneider, Sol *electronic engineer, consultant, researcher*
Silverman, Herbert R. *corporate financial executive*
Sorsby, James Larry *home building company executive*
Weiant, William Morrow *investment banking executive*

Ridgefield Park
Case, Gerard Ramon *drafting technician*
†Kim, Ok-Nyun *manufacturing executive*

Ridgewood
Abplanalp, Glen Harold *civil engineer*
Anderson, Thomas Kemp, Jr. *editor*
†Azzara, Michael William *hospital administration executive*
Catania, Lorraine Laura *psychologist*
Economaki, Chris Constantine (Christopher Economaki) *publisher, editor*
Healey, Frank Henry *retired research executive*
Hetsko, Cyril Francis *retired lawyer, corporation executive*
Kiernan, Richard Francis *publisher*
Knies, Paul Henry *former life insurance company executive*
Lucca, John James *retired dental educator*
McBride, William Bernard *treasurer*
Molnar, Thomas *educator, author*

River Edge
Gass, Manus M. *accountant, business executive*
†Kempner, Michael W. *public relations executive*
†Seymour, Harry Duane *marketing executive*
Sommer, Robert George *public relations executive*

River Vale
Meyer, Grace Tomanelli *lawyer*
Moderacki, Edmund Anthony *music educator, conductor*

Riverside
Gouda, Moustafa Abdel-Hamid *geotechnical engineer consultant*

Robbinsville
Goldstein, Norman Robert *safety engineer*

Rochelle Park
Laskey, Richard Anthony *medical device company executive*
Mack, Earle Irving *real estate company executive*
Schapiro, Jerome Bentley *chemical company executive*

Rockaway
Allen, Dorothea *secondary school educator*
Ruch, William Vaughn *author, consultant, educator*

Rockleigh
†Heslin, Cathleen Jane *artist, designer, entrepreneur*
Heslin, John Thomas *entrepreneur, historic preservationist*

Roosevelt
Landau, Jacob *artist*

Roseland
Berkowitz, Bernard Solomon *lawyer*
†Casale, Robert J. *communications executive*
Costanzo, Hilda Alba *retired banker*
D'Avella, Bernard Johnson, Jr. *lawyer*
Dore, Michael *lawyer, educator*
Eakeley, Douglas Scott *lawyer*
Fleischman, Joseph Jacob *lawyer*
Greenberg, Stephen Michael *lawyer, businesss executive*
Kemph, Carleton Richard *lawyer*
Kohl, Benedict M. *lawyer*
Korf, Gene Robert *lawyer*
Lafer, Fred Seymour *data processing company executive*
Lowenstein, Alan Victor *lawyer*
MacKay, John Robert, II *lawyer*
Malafronte, Donald *health executive*
Margolis, Theodore *lawyer*
†McElwee, Andrew Allison *finance executive, lawyer*
Rodburg, Michael Lee *lawyer*
Shoulson, Bruce Dove *lawyer*
Slutsky, Kenneth Joel *lawyer*
Steinhart, Ashley *lawyer*
Stern, Herbert Jay *lawyer*
Sturtz, Ronald M. *lawyer*
Taub, Henry *retired computer services company executive*
†Turner, William J. *data processing company executive*
†Weinbach, Arthur Frederic *computing services company executive*
†Wells, Theodore V., Jr. *lawyer*
Weston, Josh S. *data processing company executive*
Wovsaniker, Alan *lawyer*

Rumson
Alexander, Nicholas Anthony *accounting executive*
†Brenner, Theodore Engelbert *retired trade association executive*
Christianson, Lloyd Fenton *management consultant*
Cocker, Barbara Joan *marine artist, interior designer*
Creamer, William Henry, III *insurance company executive*
Feiner, Alexander *retired communications company executive*
Freeman, David Forgan *foundation executive*
Robinson, William Wheeler *editor*
Rosen, Bernard H. *chemical engineer*

Rutherford
Gerety, Peter Leo *archbishop*
Law, Janet Mary *music educator*
Liptak, Irene Frances *retired business executive*
†Marchitto, Alfred J. *furniture company executive*
Mertz, Francis James *academic administrator*
Petrie, Ferdinand Ralph *illustrator, artist*
Sarsfield, Luke Aloysius *school system administrator*

Saddle Brook
†Anderson, David J. *metals company executive*

Saddle River
Buckler, Beatrice *editor*
Dowden, Carroll Vincent *publishing company executive*
Lehmann, Doris Elizabeth *elementary education educator*
Warrington, Clayton Linwood, Jr. *advertising executive*

Salem
Foster, Paul *playwright*
Petrin, Helen Fite *lawyer, consultant*
Seabrook, John Martin *retired food products executive, chemical engineer*

Scotch Plains
Abramson, Clarence Allen *pharmaceutical company executive, lawyer*
Avery, James Stephen *oil company executive*
Bishop, Robert Milton *former stock exchange official*
Cleminshaw, Frank Foster *electronic company executive*
Edwards, Thomas Robert, Jr. *language professional, investment company executive*
Klock, John Henry *lawyer*
Ungar, Manya Shayon *volunteer, consultant*

Sea Bright
Plummer, Dirk Arnold *electrical engineer*

Secaucus
Bender, Bruce F. *book publishing executive*
†Bidermann, Maurice *textiles executive*
†Bolt, J. Andrew *textiles executive*
Brown, Ira Bernard *data processing executive*
Feaster, S. Edward *insurance agent*
†Gerstein, Hilda Kirschbaum *clothing company executive*
Heller, Fred *illumination manufacturing company executive*
Kilburn, Edwin Allen *lawyer*
†Kraft, Richard A. *electronics executive*
†Marcus, Alan C. *public relations consultant*
Pinsker, Penny Collias (Pangeota Pinsker) *television producer*
Ryan, Daniel Nolan *financial corporation executive*
Saltz, Ralph *corporate lawyer*
Schenck, Frederick A. *business executive*
Thomas, Ian Leslie Maurice *publisher*
Unanue, Joseph *food products executive*

Short Hills
Aviado, Domingo M. *pharmacologist, toxicologist*
Bartels, Stanley Leonard *investment banker*
Broder, Patricia Janis *art historian, writer*
Brous, Philip *retail consultant*
Gitner, Deanne *writer*
Good, Joan Duffey *artist*
Greenberg, Carl *lawyer*
Harwood, Jerry *market research executive*
Hazlehurst, Robert Purviance, Jr. *lawyer*
Jackson, William Ward *chemical company executive*
Kaye, Jerome R. *retired engineering and construction company executive*
Klemme, Carl William *banker*
Lax, Philip *land developer, space planner*
Mebane, William Black *controller, financial consultant*
Meredith, George Davis *advertising executive, publisher*
Moore, Robert Condit *civil engineer*
Perez, Bertin John *investment banker*
Pilchik, Ely Emanuel *rabbi, writer*
Schaefer, Charles James, III *advertising agency executive, consultant*
Schaffer, Edmund John *management consultant, retired engineering executive*
Siegfried, David Charles *lawyer*
Soderlind, Sterling Eugene *newspaper industry consultant*
Winter, Ruth Grosman (Mrs. Arthur Winter) *journalist*

Shrewsbury
Duff, Thomas M. *textiles executive*
Hopkins, Charles Peter, II *lawyer*
Jones, Charles Hill, Jr. *banker*
Reich, Bernard *telecommunications engineer*

Skillman
Brill, Yvonne Claeys *engineer, consultant*
Kral, Frank *biophysical chemist*

Somerset
Aronson, Louis Vincent, II *manufacturing executive*
DeVaris, Jeannette Mary *psychologist*
†Goldberg, Arthur M. *food products executive, lawyer*
Kozlowski, Thomas Joseph, Jr. *lawyer, trust company executive*
†Neff, Richard B. *consumer products company executive*
Noonan, William Francis *public relations company executive*
Plenty, Royal Homer *writer*

Somerville
†Beck, Eckardt C. *engineering executive*
Benz, Harry R. *business executive*
Cirello, John *environmental management and engineering company executive*
Deieso, Donald Allan *air pollution control company executive, scientist*
†Dormann, Juergen *chemical company executive*
Drew, Ernest Harold *chemical company executive*
†Glenn, Arthur L. *engineering company executive*
Hildebrandt, Bradford Walter *consulting company executive*
Hyde, Mary Morley Crapo (Viscountess Eccles) *author*
Johnson, Nicholas *writer, lawyer, lecturer*
McCoy, Eileen Carey *academic dean*
†Shive, Richard Byron *architect*

South Hackensack
Kiselik, Paul Howard *manufacturing company executive*

South Orange
De Varis, Panayotis Eric *architect*
Fleming, Edward J. *priest, educator*
Green, Donald Webb *economist*
†Harahan, Robert E. *rector*
Houle, Joseph E. *mathematics educator*
Reilly, George Love Anthony *history educator*
Sontag, Frederick H. *public affairs and research consultant*

South Plainfield
Borah, Kripanath *pharmacist*
Ferry, Bryan *singer, songwriter*

Southampton
Knortz, Walter Robert *accountant, former insurance company executive*

Sparta
Buist, Jean Mackerley *veterinarian*
Granieri, Michael Nicholas *electronics executive, educator*
Harrison, Alice Kathleen *elementary educator*
Spence, Robert Leroy *publishing executive*

Spring Lake
Connor, Frances Partridge *education educator*
Ernst, John Louis *management consultant*

Springfield
Adams, James Mills *chemicals executive*
†Merachnik, Donald *superintendent of schools*
Panish, Morton B. *physical chemist, consultant*
Shilling, A. Gary *economic consultant, investment advisor*

Stillwater
Finkelstein, Louis *retired art educator*

Stockholm
dePaolo, Ronald Francis *editor, publisher*

Stockton
Kent, George Cantine, Jr. *zoology educator*
Mahon, Robert *photographer*
Schoenherr, John (Carl) *artist, illustrator*
Tunley, Roul *author*

Stratford
†Humphrey, Frederick James, II *educator, child psychiatrist, psychoanalyst*

Summit
Batzer, R. Kirk *accountant*
Bostwick, Randell A. *retired retail food company executive*
Brown, John Hampton *pharmaceutical company executive*
Fuess, Billings Sibley, Jr. *advertising executive*
Fukui, Hatsuaki *electrical engineer, art historian*
Geiger, Richard Lawrence *entrepreneur*
Gonnella, Nina Celeste *biophysical chemist*
Hagstrum, Homer Dupre *physicist*
Hittinger, William Charles *electronics company executive*
Kenyon, Edward Tipton *lawyer*
LeDuc, J. Adrien M. *publishing company executive, consultant*
Mathis, James Forrest *retired petroleum company executive*
May, Ernest Max *charitable organization official*
Mueller, Paul Henry *retired banker*
Natkin, Alvin Martin *environmental company executive*
Nessen, Ward Henry *typographer, lawyer*
Pace, Leonard *retired management consultant*
Parsons, Judson Aspinwall, Jr. *lawyer*
Phillips, James Charles *physicist, educator*
†Pollak, Henry Otto *retired utility research executive, educator*
Rossey, Paul William *superintendent of schools*
Rousseau, Irene Victoria *sculptor*
Scudder, Edward Wallace, Jr. *newspaper and broadcasting executive*
Slepian, David *mathematician, communications engineer*
Sniffen, Michael Joseph *hospital administrator*

†Tannenbaum, Sanford *lawyer*
Vogel, Julius *consulting actuary, former insurance company executive*
†Wissbrun, Kurt F. *chemist, consultant*

Surf City
Aurner, Robert Ray, II *oil company, auto diagnostic, restaurant franchise and company development executive*

Sussex
Holbert, Theodore Frank *banker*
Sekula, Edward Joseph, Jr. *financial executive*

Teaneck
Borg, Sidney Fred *mechanical engineer, educator*
Browne, Robert Span *economist*
Brudner, Helen Gross *social sciences educator*
Cassimatis, Peter John *economics educator*
Churg, Jacob *pathologist*
†Downing, Robert Franklin *lawyer*
Ehrlich, Ira Robert *mechanical engineering consultant*
Fairfield, Betty Elaine Smith *psychologist*
Fanshel, David *social worker*
Feinberg, Robert S. *plastics manufacturing company executive, marketing consultant*
Forson, Norman Ray *controller*
Gordon, Jonathan David *psychologist*
Gordon, Lois Goldfein *English language educator*
Gordon, Maxwell *pharmaceutical company executive*
Herman, Kenneth *psychologist*
Jugenheimer, Donald Wayne *advertising and communications educator, university administrator*
Kay, Ulysses Simpson *composer, educator*
Kramer, Bernard *physicist, educator*
Margolis, Sidney O. *textile and apparel company executive*
Ngai, Shih Hsun *physician*
Oser, Bernard Levussove *food and drug consultant*
Palitz, Clarence Yale, Jr. *commercial finance executive*
Pischl, Adolph John *school administrator*
Roth, June Doris Spiewak *author*
Rudy, Willis *historian*
Walsh, Peter Joseph *physics educator*
Williams, John A. *English educator, author*
Zwass, Vladimir *computer scientist, educator*

Tenafly
Cosgriff, Stuart Worcester *internist, consultant*
Gerst, Elizabeth Carlsen (Mrs. Paul H. Gerst) *university dean, researcher, educator*
Gibbons, Robert Philip *management consultant*
Hartung, Walter Magnus *retired aeronautical college executive*
Koons, Irvin Louis *design executive, graphic artist, consultant*
Kullberg, John Francis *association executive*
Lang, Hans Joachim *engineering company executive*
Levy, Norman Jay *investment banker, financial consultant*
Lilley, Theodore Robert *financial executive*
Rosenberger, Walter Emerson *percussionist, educator*
Stowe, David Metz *clergyman*
Vinocur, M. Richard *publisher*

Teterboro
Gambino, S(alvatore) Raymond *medical laboratory executive, educator*
Young, John Morgan *aviation executive*
Zomick, David Alan *engineering executive*

Three Bridges
Lawrence, Gerald Graham *management consultant*

Tinton Falls
Furman, Samuel Elliott *dentist*
Orlando, Carl *medical research and development executive*
Priesand, Sally Jane *rabbi*

Titusville
Marden, Kenneth Allen *advertising executive*

Toms River
Curreri, John Robert *mechanical engineer, consultant*
Fanuele, Michael Anthony *electronics engineer, research engineer*
Gottesman, Roy Tully *chemical company executive*
Kanarkowski, Edward Joseph *data processing company executive*
Pilla, Mark Domenick *hospital administrator*
Unger, Howard Albert *artist, photographer, educator*
Whitman, Russell Wilson *lawyer*

Totowa
Barbarow, Thomas Steven *public school system administrator*
Jelliffe, Charles Gordon *banker*

Trenton
†Bandish, Dennis Michael *insurance company executive*
Belshaw, George Phelps Mellick *bishop*
Bigham, William J. *lawyer*
†Bilotti, Richard *newspaper publisher*
Brandinger, Jay Jerome *electronics executive, state official*
Brown, Dorothea Williams *technology consulting company executive*
Brown, Garrett Edward, Jr. *federal judge*
Chavooshian, Marge *artist, educator*
Clymer, Brian William *federal agency administrator*
†Courtney, Esau *bishop*
Cowen, Robert E. *federal judge*
Crane, Samuel *treasurer*
Cushman, David Wayne *research biochemist*
Dalton, Daniel J. *secretary of state*
†DiFrancesco, Donald T. *state senator*
Domm, Alice *lawyer*
Eickhoff, Harold Walter *college president, humanities educator*
†Farina, David *church administrator*
Fisher, Clarkson Sherman *federal judge*
Gindin, William Howard *federal judge*
Greenberg, Morton Ira *federal judge*
Haberle, Joan Baker *state official*
Handler, Alan B. *state supreme court justice*
Jester, Roberts Charles, Jr. *engineering services company executive*
Kelly, Thomas Joseph, III *photojournalist*

†Lipman, Wynona M. *state legislator*
†Minervino, Louise *librarian*
O'Hern, Daniel Joseph *state supreme court justice*
Parell, Mary Little *federal judge, former banking commissioner*
†Park, Carl S. *atmospheric research administrator*
Pollock, John Crothers, III *opinion research executive, educator*
Pollock, Stewart Glasson *state supreme court justice*
Pruitt, George Albert *college president*
Reiss, John C. *bishop*
Roebling, Mary Gindhart *banker*
Russell, Joyce Anne Rogers *librarian*
Sterns, Joel Henry *lawyer*
Stewart, Barbara Elizabeth *free-lance magazine editor, artist*
Thompson, Anne Elise *federal judge*
Tucker, Robert Keith *environmental scientist, research administrator*
Weinberg, Martin Herbert *psychiatrist*
†Weissman, Daniel *journalist*
†Whitman, Christine Todd *governor*
Wolfe, Deborah Cannon Partridge *government education consultant*

Tuckerton
Egan, Roger Edward *publishing executive*

Union
Bahniuk, Frank Theodore *utility company executive*
†Bassano, C. Louis *state senator, fuel oil company executive*
Hochstadt, Joy *biomedical research scientist, scientific and research director*
Lapidus, Norman Israel *food broker*
Pasvolsky, Richard Lloyd *parks, recreation, and environment educator*
Schiffman, Robert S. *environmental test equipment manufacturing executive*
Zois, Constantine Nicholas Athanasios *meteorology educator*

Union City
Conklin, Anna Immaculata G. *mathematics and language arts educator*
Neilson, Kenneth Thomas *bank executive*

Upper Montclair
Aronson, David *chemical and mechanical engineer*
Coes, Kent Day *artist*
Cordasco, Francesco *sociologist, educator, author*
Kowalski, Stephen Wesley *chemistry educator*
Stevens, John Galen *mathematics and computer science educator*

Upper Saddle River
Farley, Edward John *advertising executive*
Wallace, William, III *engineering executive*

Ventnor City
Bolton, Kenneth Albert *corporate professional*
Frudakis, Evangelos William *sculptor*
Robbins, Hulda Dornblatt *artist, printmaker*
Zuckerman, Stuart *psychiatrist, educator*

Verona
Ayaso, Manuel *artist*
Greenwald, Robert *public relations executive*
Meyer, Helen (Mrs. Abraham J. Meyer) *retired editorial consultant*
Root, Alan Charles *diversified manufacturing company executive*

Vineland
Hunt, Howard Francis *psychologist, educator*

Voorhees
Barone, Donald Anthony *neurologist, educator*
Cohen, Mark N. *business executive*
Lewis, Marilyn Ware *water company executive*
†Myslowka, Myron William (Ron Myslowka) *labor union executive*

Waldwick
Surdoval, Donald James *accounting and management consulting company executive*

Wall
Colford, Francis Xavier *gas industry executive*

Warren
Blass, Walter Paul *consultant, management educator*
Chubb, Percy, III *insurance company executive*
Cohen, Bertram David *psychologist, educator*
Georgieff, Gregory *insurance executive*
Hartman, David Gardiner *actuary*
Jackson, John Wyant *business executive*
Lennon, Marilyn Ellen *environmentalist*
Maull, George Marriner *music director, conductor*
†Norton, Donn H. *insurance company executive*
O'Hare, Dean Raymond *insurance company executive*
Parker, Henry Griffith, III *insurance executive*
Sartor, Anthony Joseph *environmental engineer*
Smith, Dudley Renwick *insurance company executive*
Smith, Richard D. *insurance holding company executive*
Werner, Richard Vincent *insurance company executive*

Watchung
Knudson, Harry Edward, Jr. *retired electrical manufacturing company executive*
Schaefer, Jacob Wernli *military systems consultant*

Wayne
Benedict, Theresa Marie *mathematics educator*
Blauvelt, John Clifford *diversified consumer products company executive*
Boekenheide, Russell William *forest products company executive*
Bridges, Beryl Clarke *marketing executive*
Buckstein, Mark Aaron *lawyer, educator*
Burlant, William Jack *chemical company executive*
Cartledge, Raymond Eugene *retired paper company executive*
Cheng, David Hong *mechanical engineering educator*
Coslow, Richard David *electronics company executive*
Costello, Albert Joseph *diversified consumer products executive*
†Crane, Thomas R., Jr. *oil industry executive*

Donald, Robert Graham *retail food chain personnel executive*
Drossman, Jay Lewis *aerospace executive*
†Eckardt, Carl R. *chemical and building materials executive*
Ellenbogen, Leon *nutritionist, pharmaceutical company executive*
Fleisher, Seymour *manufacturing company executive*
Goetz, William Walter *education and history educator*
Haswell, Carleton Radley *banker*
Haxton, David *computer animator, artist, director, computer graphics educator*
Heyman, Samuel J. *chemicals and building materials manufacturing company executive*
Hirsch, Gary D. *supermarket executive*
Jeffrey, Robert George, Jr. *industrial company executive*
Jones, Deborah *architect*
Katz, Leandro *artist*
Nicastro, Francis Efisio *defense electronics and retailing executive*
O'Connor, John Morris, III *philosophy educator*
†Pinyuh, Sam P. *banker*
Sanok, Gloria *mathematics educator, author*
Sergey, John Michael, Jr. *manufacturing company executive*
Soutendijk, Dirk Rutger *lawyer, corporate executive*
Speert, Arnold *college president, chemistry educator*
Trice, William Henry *paper company executive*
White, Doris Gnauck *science educator, biochemical and biophysics researcher*
Wolynic, Edward Thomas *specialty chemicals technology executive*

West Caldwell
Fascetta, Salvatore Charles *pharmaceutical company executive*
McEntee, Robert Edward *management consultant*
Page, Frederick West *business consultant*
Sostilio, Robert Francis *office equipment marketing executive*

West Long Branch
Rouse, Robert Sumner *former college official*
Stafford, Rebecca *college president, sociologist*

West Milford
Kinney, Dorothy Jean *elementary educator*

West New York
Aquino, Felix John *college administrator*
Carluccio, Charles Goldhammer *physician*
Gruenberg, Elliot Lewis *electronics company executive*
Kelly, Lucie Stirm Young *nursing educator*

West Orange
Berman, Mona S. *actress, playwright, theatrical director and producer*
Brodkin, Roger Harrison *dermatologist, educator*
Mandelbaum, Barry Richard *lawyer*
Osborne, John Walter *historian, educator, author*
Rayfield, Gordon Elliott *playwright, political risk consultant*
Richmond, Harold Nicholas *lawyer*
Sosnow, Lawrence Ira *health care company executive*

West Paterson
Dickinson, Fairleigh Stanton, Jr. *former manufacturing company executive*
Kaufman, Allan M. *actuary, consultant*
Metz, Philip John *mathematics educator*
Vandervoort, Peter *lawyer*

West Trenton
†LaRossa, Richard Joseph *state legislator, computer consultant*
Roman, Cecelia Florence *cardiologist*
Roshon, George Kenneth *manufacturing company executive*

Westfield
Bartok, William *environmental technologies consultant*
Boutillier, Robert John *accountant*
Connell, Grover *food company executive*
†Connell, Ted *food products company executive*
Connolly, Ronald Cavanagh *financial services executive*
Cushman, Helen Merle Baker *management consultant*
Feret, Adam Edward, Jr. *dentist*
Florian, Frank Lee *planning executive*
McLean, Vincent Ronald *former manufacturing company financial executive*
Miller, Gabriel Lorimer *physicist, researcher*
O'Connor, James Joseph *lawyer, consultant, engineering-construction firm executive*
Purcell, Richard Fick *lawyer, food company executive*
Simon, Martin Stanley *commodity marketing company executive, economist*
Stoudt, Thomas Henry *research microbiologist*

Westville
†Doughty, A. Glenn *minister*

Westwood
Cullen, Ruth Enck *reading specialist, elementary education educator*
Dubnick, Bernard *retired pharmaceutical company administrator*
Folley, Clyde H. *diversified manufacturing executive*
†Gerlinger, Karl *automotive executive*
Mastroserio, Joe *association consultant*
Mulligan, William G(oeckel) *machinery manufacturing company executive*
Nachtigal, Patricia *equipment manufacturing company executive, general counsel*
Schutz, Donald Frank *geochemist, corporate executive*

Wharton
Rodzianko, Paul *corporate executive*

Whippany
Golden, John F. *packaging company executive*
Michaelis, Paul Charles *engineering physicist executive*
Pinkin, James Edward *sales and marketing executive*
†Spina, Dennis J. *gas industry executive*

White House Station
Atieh, Michael Gerard *accountant*
Darien, Steven Martin *pharmaceuticals executive*
Douglas, Robert Gordon, Jr. *physician*
Gilmartin, Raymond V. *health care products company executive*
Levey, Gerald Saul *physician, educator*
Lewent, Judy C. *pharmaceutical executive*
†McDonald, Mary M. *lawyer*
Nusim, Stanley Herbert *chemical engineer, executive director*
Vagelos, Pindaros Roy *pharmaceutical company executive*

Whiting
Williams, Roger Wright *public health educator*

Willingboro
Schnapf, Abraham *aerospace engineer, consultant*

Wood Ridge
Castagnetta, Grace Sharp *pianist, piano educator*

Woodbridge
Amato, Vincent Vito *business executive*
Babineau, Anne Serzan *lawyer*
Becker, Frederic Kenneth *lawyer*
Brauth, Marvin Jeffrey *lawyer*
Brown, Morris *lawyer*
Buchsbaum, Peter A. *lawyer*
Cirafesi, Robert J. *lawyer*
†Cuti, Anthony J. *consumer products company executive*
D'Amico, Andrew John *oil company executive*
Fee, Geraldine Julia *psychophysiologist*
Futterman, Jack *supermarket chain executive*
Greenbaum, Robert S. *lawyer*
Hoberman, Stuart A. *lawyer*
Jaffe, Sheldon Eugene *lawyer*
Mills, George Marshall *state official, insurance executive*
Molloy, Brian Joseph *lawyer*
†Murray, Arthur G. *food products executive*
†Nies, Judy Ann *advertising agency executive*
Wildstein, David M. *lawyer*

Woodbury
Wallace, Jesse Wyatt *pharmaceutical company executive*
White, John Lindsey *lawyer*
†Zane, Raymond J. *lawyer, state senator*

Woodcliff Lake
Black, Theodore Halsey *retired manufacturing company executive*

Woodstown
Crouse, Farrell Rondall *psychiatrist, physician*
Koehler, George Applegate *broadcasting company executive*

Wyckoff
Abdelrahman, Talaat Ahmad Mohammad *financial executive*
Anstatt, Peter Jan *marketing services executive*
Bauer, Theodore James *physician*
Cropper, Susan Peggy *veterinarian*
Lavery, Daniel P. *management consultant*

NEW MEXICO

Alameda
Hooker, Van Dorn *architect, artist*

Alamogordo
Stapp, John Paul *surgeon, former air force officer*
Way, Jacob Edson, III *museum director*

Albuquerque
Adams, Clinton *artist, historian*
†Anaya, Rudolfo *educator, writer*
Anderson, Darrell Edward *psychologist, educator*
†Anspach, Judith Ford *law librarian, law educator*
Antreasian, Garo Zareh *artist, lithographer, art educator*
Armstrong, Glenn Garnett *artist, retired postal executive*
Bacon, Phillip *geographer, author, consultant*
Bahm, Archie John *philosophy educator*
Ballard, David Eugene *anesthesiologist*
Barbo, Dorothy Marie *obstetrician-gynecologist, educator*
Bardacke, Paul Gregory *lawyer, former attorney general*
Barrow, Thomas Francis *artist, educator*
Basso, Keith Hamilton *cultural anthropologist, linguist, educator*
Bawden, Garth Lawry *museum director*
Beckel, Charles Leroy *physics educator*
†Beeler, Gary *materials science administrator*
Bell, Stoughton *computer scientist, mathematician, educator*
†Benavides, Tom R. *state senator, realtor*
Beusch, Gladys Jeanette *optician*
†Bleiweis, Paul Benjamin *environmental services executive*
Bolie, Victor Wayne *electrical and computer engineering educator*
Burciaga, Juan Guerrero *federal judge*
†Burton, Johanna King *journalist*
Buss, William Charles *research pharmacology educator*
†Campbell, C. Robert *architect*
Caplan, Edwin Harvey *university dean, accounting educator*
Cargo, David Francis *lawyer*
†Carraro, Joseph John *senator, small business owner, consultant*
Carrick, David Stanley *electrical engineer*
Caruso, Mark John *lawyer*
†Chavez, Martin Joseph *mayor, attorney*
Clark, Alan Barthwell *city administrator*
Cofer, Charles Norval *psychologist, educator*
Condie, Carol Joy *anthropologist, research facility administrator*
Conway, John E. *federal judge*
Corliss, John Ozro *zoology educator*
Danziger, Jerry *broadcasting executive*
Dixon, George Lane, Jr. *orthopaedic surgeon*
Doberneck, Raymond C. *surgical educator*
Dorato, Peter *electrical and computer engineering educator*

Dressel, Diane Lisette *dancer, choreographer, electrical designer*
Drummond, Harold Dean *education educator*
Easley, Mack *retired state supreme court chief justice*
Eaton, George Wesley, Jr. *oil company executive*
Edwards, William Sterling, III *cardiovascular surgeon*
Evans, Bill (James William Evans) *dancer, choreographer, educator, arts administrator*
Evans, Max Allen *writer, artist*
Garcia, F. Chris *academic administrator, political science educator, public opinion researcher*
Goldston, Barbara M. Harral *editor*
Gordon, Larry Jean *public health administrator and educator*
Gorham, Frank DeVore, Jr. *petroleum company executive*
†Grady, William G. (Bing Grady) *banker*
†Graham, Robert Albert *research physicist*
†Griffin, W. C. *bishop*
Guthrie, Patricia Sue *newspaper reporter, free-lance writer*
Hadas, Elizabeth Chamberlayne *publisher*
Haddad, Edward Raouf *civil engineer, consultant*
Hahn, Betty *artist, photographer, educator*
Hale, Bruce Donald *marketing professional*
Hall, Jerome William *research engineering educator*
Hamilton, Jerald *musician*
Hanna, Robert Cecil *lawyer, lecturer, hotelier*
Hansen, Curtis LeRoy *federal judge*
Harris, Fred R. *political science educator, former senator*
Harrison, Charles Wagner, Jr. *applied physicist*
Hart, Frederick Michael *law educator*
Heady, Ferrel *retired political science educator*
Howard, William Jack *mechanical engineer, retired*
Hsi, David Ching Heng *plant pathologist and geneticist, educator*
Johnson, Robert Hersel *journalist*
Johnson, Stewart Willard *civil engineer*
Johnson, William Hugh, Jr. *hospital administrator*
Jones, Donald L. *lawyer*
Karni, Shlomo *electrical engineering educator*
Kelley, Robert Otis *medical science educator*
Kellshaw, Terence *bishop*
†Kelshaw, Terence *bishop*
Kepler, Raymond Glen *physicist*
King, James Claude *physicist*
King, James Nedwed *construction company executive, lawyer*
Korman, Nathaniel Irving *research and development company executive*
Kramarsic, Roman Joseph *engineering consultant*
Kutvirt, Duda Chytilova (Ruzena) *scientific translator*
Lang, Thompson Hughes *publishing company executive*
Lattman, Laurence Harold *retired academic administrator*
Liberman, Ira L. *real estate broker*
Loftfield, Robert Berner *biochemistry educator*
Looney, Ralph Edwin *journalist, editor, author, photographer*
Lujan, Manuel, Jr. *former U.S. secretary of the interior, former congressman*
MacCurdy, Raymond Ralph, Jr. *modern language educator*
†Malina, Robert S. *investment company executive*
Mauderly, Joe Lloyd *veterinary respiratory physiologist*
May, Gerald William *university administrator, educator, civil engineering consultant*
McCarty, W(illard) Duane *obstetrician-gynecologist, physician executive*
McKiernan, John William *mechanical engineer*
Mc Million, John Macon *retired newspaper publisher*
Mitovich, John *association executive*
Molzen, Dayton Frank *consulting engineering executive*
Napolitano, Leonard Michael *anatomist, university administrator*
Narath, Albert *laboratory administrator*
Nash, Gerald David *historian*
Neidhart, James Allen *physician, educator*
Newsom, Melvin Max *research company executive*
Norman, Ralph David *consulting psychologist, former university administrator*
Omer, George Elbert, Jr. *orthopaedic surgeon, hand surgeon, educator*
Ottensmeyer, David Joseph *neurosurgeon, health care executive*
Paler, Peggy Louise D'Arcy *elementary education educator, education educator*
Parker, James Aubrey *federal judge*
†Paster, Janice D. *state legislator*
Pasternak, Derick Peter *physician, medical center executive*
Pearl, George Clayton *architect*
Peck, Ralph Brazelton *civil engineering educator, consultant*
Peck, Richard Earl *academic administrator, playwright, novelist*
Phillips, Ronald Edward (Ron) *sales executive*
†Ramo, Roberta Cooper *lawyer*
Riordan, William F. *lawyer*
Robinson, Charles Paul *nuclear physicist, diplomat, business executive*
†Roehl, Jerrald J(oseph) *lawyer*
Roehl, Joseph E. *lawyer*
Romo, Gene David *municipal official*
Rosenberg, Arthur James *business executive*
†Rutherford, Thomas Truxtun, II *state senator, lawyer*
†Sabatini, William Q. *architect*
Sanchez, Victoria Wagner *science educator*
Schmitt, Harrison Hagan *former senator, geologist, astronaut, consultant*
Schoen, Stevan Jay *lawyer*
Schwerin, Karl Henry *anthropology educator, researcher*
†Scully, Marlan Orvil *physics educator*
Shedd, Ben Alvin *film producer, director, production company executive*
Sheehan, Michael Jarboe *archbishop*
Sickels, Robert Judd *political science educator*
Sisk, Daniel Arthur *lawyer*
Solomon, Arthur Charles *pharmacist*
Sparks, Morgan *physicist*
Stahl, Jack Leland *real estate company executive*
Stamm, Robert Jenne *building contractor, construction company executive*
Stephenson, Barbera Wertz *lawyer*
†Stieber, Tamar *newswriter*
Sturm, Fred Gillette *philosopher, educator*
Tatum, Ronald Winston *physician, endocrinologist*
Thompson, Rufus E. *lawyer*
Tope, Dwight Harold *retired management consultant*
Travelstead, Chester Coleman *former educational administrator*
Uhlenhuth, Eberhard Henry *psychiatrist, educator*
Unser, Al *professional auto racer*
†Vazquez, Martha Alicia *lawyer*
Vook, Frederick Ludwig *physicist*
Ward, Charles Richard *extension and research entomologist, educator*
Wellborn, Charles Ivey *lawyer*
†Welsome, Eileen *journalist*
Wengerd, Sherman Alexander *geologist, educator*
Westwood, Albert Ronald Clifton *metallurgical engineer*
Whiddon, Carol Price *writer, editor, consultant*
Wildin, Maurice Wilbert *mechanical engineering educator*
Winslow, Walter William *psychiatrist*
Witkin, Joel-Peter *photographer*
Wollman, Nathaniel *economist, educator*
Woodbridge, Ruth I. *elementary education educator*
†Wray, Tom Charles *state senator, electrical engineering consultant*
†Wright, James Burnell *music librarian*
Youngdahl, James Edward *lawyer*
†Zink, Lee B. *academic administrator, economist, educator*

Angel Fire
Dillon, Robert Morton *retired association executive, architectural consultant*

Artesia
Sarwar, Barbara Duce *school system administrator*

Belen
†Gutjahr, Allan Leo *mathematics educator, researcher*
Toliver, Lee *mechanical engineer*

Bloomfield
†Donisthorpe, Christine Ann *state legislator*

Carlsbad
†Cooper, Richard *zoological park administrator*
†Kidd, Melvin Don *banker*
Markle, George Bushar, IV *surgeon*
Reif, Laurie Louise *psychotherapist*
†Stell, Joe M., Jr. *state legislator*

Cebolla
Berryman, Donald Carroll *cattle rancher*

Cedar Crest
Sheppard, Jack W. *retired air force officer*

Chama
Moser, Robert Harlan *physician, educator*

Cimarron
†Lopez, Joe A. *school system administrator*

Clovis
Rehorn, Lois Marie Smith *nursing administrator*

Corrales
Adams, James Frederick *psychologist, educational administrator*
Eaton, Pauline *artist*
Martin, Harold Clark *humanities educator*
Page, Jake (James K. Page, Jr.) *writer, editor*

Farmington
Garretson, Owen Loren *engineer*
†Plummer, Steven Tsosie *bishop*
Risley, Larry L. *air transportation executive*
Swetnam, Monte Newton *petroleum exploration executive*

Gallup
Boucher, Raymond Joseph *educator*
Crouch, Altha Marie *health educator, consultant*
Hastrich, Jerome Joseph *bishop*
†Pederson, Robert David *lawyer*

Glorieta
Mc Coy, Robert Baker *publisher*

Hobbs
Garey, Donald Lee *pipeline and oil company executive*
†Reagan, Gary Don *lawyer*

Kirtland A F B
Baum, Carl Edward *electromagnetic theorist*
Harrison, George Brooks *career officer*

Las Cruces
Borman, Frank *former astronaut, laser patent company executive*
Coburn, Horace Hunter *retired physics educator*
Cochrun, John Wesley *insurance agent*
Cowden, Louis Fredrick *electronics executive, engineer*
Dickinson, James Gordon *editor*
†Easterling, Kathy *elementary school principal*
Ford, Clarence Quentin *mechanical engineer, educator*
Gale, Thomas Martin *university dean*
Hall, Larry Bruce *minister*
Halligan, James Edmund *university administrator, chemical engineer*
Harary, Frank *mathematician, computer scientist, educator*
Jacobs, Kent Frederick *dermatologist*
Kemp, John Daniel *biochemist, educator*
Lease, Richard Jay *police science educator, former police officer*
Lutz, William Lan *lawyer*
Matthews, Larryl Kent *mechanical engineering educator*
McCaslin, Bobby D. *soil scientist, educator*
Medoff, Mark Howard *playwright, screenwriter, novelist*
Morgan, John Derald *electrical engineer*
Peterson, Robin Tucker *marketing educator*
†Porter, William Emme *state legislator, small business owner*
Ramirez, Ricardo *bishop*
Reeves, Billy Dean *obstetrics/gynecology educator emeritus*
Reinfelds, Juris *computer science educator*
Roscoe, Stanley Nelson *psychologist, aeronautical engineer*
Sandenaw, Thomas Arthur, Jr. *lawyer*
Schemnitz, Sanford David *wildlife biology educator*
Southward, Glen Morris *statistician, educator*
Thode, Edward Frederick *chemical engineer, educator*

Las Vegas
Riley, Carroll Lavern *anthropology educator*
Sanchez, Gilbert *university president, microbiologist, researcher*

Los Alamos
†Alexander, John Bradfield *weaponry manager, retired army officer*
Allred, John Caldwell *physicist*
Bame, Samuel Jarvis, Jr. *research scientist*
Bell, George Irving *biophysics researcher*
Bradbury, Norris Edwin *physicist*
Colgate, Stirling Auchincloss *physicist*
Engel, Emily Flachmeier *school administrator*
Engelhardt, Albert George *physicist*
†Fisk, Zachary *physical scientist*
†Flynn, Edward Robert *physicist*
†Friar, James Lewis *physicist*
Garvey, Gerald Thomas *physicist, researcher*
†Gibson, Benjamin Franklin *physicist*
†Ginocchio, Joseph Natale *theoretical physicist*
Gregg, Charles Thornton *research company executive*
Grilly, Edward Rogers *physicist*
Hecker, Siegfried Stephen *metallurgist*
Jackson, James F. *nuclear engineer*
Jarmie, Nelson *physicist*
†Johnson, Mikkel Borlaug *physicist*
Judd, O'Dean P. *physicist*
Keepin, George Robert, Jr. *physicist*
Kelly, Robert Emmett *physicist, educator*
†Kubas, Gregory Joseph *research chemist*
†Linford, Rulon Kesler *physicist, program director*
Maraman, William Joseph *nuclear engineering company executive*
Matlack, George Miller *radiochemist*
McNally, James Henry *physicist*
Mendius, Patricia Dodd Winter *editor, educator, writer*
Metropolis, Nicholas Constantine *mathematical physicist*
Mitchell, Terence Edward *materials scientist*
†Nix, James Rayford *nuclear physicist, consultant*
Nunz, Gregory Joseph *aerospace engineer and educator*
Onstott, Edward Irvin *research chemist*
†Pack, Russell T *theoretical chemist*
Penneman, Robert Allen *retired chemist*
Rosen, Louis *physicist*
†Schneider, Barry Irwin *theoretical atomic and molecular physicist*
Selden, Robert Wentworth *physicist, science advisor*
Smith, James Lawrence *research physicist*
Stoddard, Stephen Davidson *ceramic engineer, former state senator*
†Strottman, Daniel David *physicist*
Terrell, (Nelson) James *physicist*
Thompson, Lois Jean Heidke Ore *industrial psychologist*
†Wahl, Arthur Charles *retired chemistry educator*
†Wallace, Jeannette Owens *state legislator*
Whetten, John Theodore *geologist*
Zurek, Wojciech Hubert *physicist*
Zweig, George *physicist, neurobiologist*

Los Lunas
Mateju, Joseph Frank *hospital administrator*

Mesilla
Box, Thadis Wayne *university dean emeritus, educator*
Willey, Darrell S. *education educator*

Mesilla Park
Shutt, Frances Barton *special education educator*
Tombaugh, Clyde William *astronomer, educator*

Montezuma
†Geier, Philip O., III *academic adminstrator*

New Mexico State Capitol
†Watkins, Karen J. *librarian*

Pecos
Price, Thomas Munro *computer consultant*

Placitas
Dunmire, William Werden *author, photographer*
Forrest, Suzanne Sims *research historian*
Pirkl, James Joseph *industrial designer, educator*

Portales
Agogino, George Allen *anthropologist, educator*
Matheny, Robert Lavesco *history educator, former university president*
Paschke, Donald Vernon *music educator*
Williamson, Jack (John Stewart Williamson) *writer*

Questa
†Cisneros, Carlos R. *state senator*

Rancho de Taos
Brown, David Warfield *former academic administrator*

Reserve
Tackman, Arthur Lester *newspaper publisher, management consultant*

Roswell
Anderson, Donald Bernard *oil company executive*
Anderson, Robert Orville *oil and gas company executive*
Baldock, Bobby Ray *federal judge*
†Casey, Barbara A. Perea *state representative, educator*
Ebie, William D. *museum director*
†Jennings, Emmit M. *surgeon*
†Jennings, Timothy Zeph *rancher, state senator*
†Knowles, Richard Thomas *state legislator, retired army officer*
Lewis, George Raymond *clinical social worker*
†Olson, Richard Earl *lawyer, state legislator*
Pretti, Bradford Joseph *lay worker, insurance company executive*

Ruidoso Downs
Knapp, Thomas Edwin *sculptor, painter*

Santa Fe
Agresto, John *college president*
Ancona, George Ephraim *photographer, film producer, author*
†Baca, Edward Dionicio *national guard officer*
Baca, Joseph Francis *state supreme court judge*
Baerwald, John Edward *traffic and transportation engineer, educator*
Ballard, Louis Wayne *composer*
Barnes, John Fayette *research scientist, educator*
Baustian, Robert Frederick *conductor*
Becker, Stephen Arnold *museum director*
†Bejnar, Thaddeus Putnam *lawyer, law librarian*
Bergé, Carol *author*
Bond, Thomas Alden *university president*
Buckley, Richard Edward *conductor*
†Calloway, Larry *columnist*
Campos, Santiago E. *federal judge*
Cannon, Helen Leighton *retired geologist, government official*
†Cerny, Charlene Ann *museum director*
Chatfield, Cheryl Ann *non profit organization executive, educator*
Chicago, Judy *artist*
Clift, William Brooks, III *photographer*
Connell, Evan Shelby, Jr. *author*
Conron, John Phelan *architect*
Cowan, George Arthur *chemist, bank executive, director*
Crosby, John O'Hea *conductor, opera manager*
Cuming, George Scott *retired lawyer, retired gas company official*
Davis, Shelby M. C. *investment executive, consultant*
Denman, William Foster *retired academic administrator, educator*
Dennison, Charles Stuart *institutional executive*
Dodds, Robert James, III *lawyer*
Drabanski, Emily Ann *editor*
Dreisbach, John Gustave *investment banker*
Duval, Michael Raoul *investment banker*
Erdman, Barbara *visual artist*
Ettinger, Richard Prentice *publishing company executive*
Fisher, Robert Alan *laser physicist*
Forsdale, (Chalmers) Louis *education and communication educator*
Franchini, Gene Edward *state supreme court justice*
†Garcia, Mary Jane Madrid *state legislator*
†Giovanielli, Damon Vincent *physicist, consulting company executive*
Gonzales, Stephanie *state official*
Grover, Phyllis Bradman *artist, consultant*
Hall, Edward Twitchell *anthropologist, educator, author*
Hatch, John Davis *design consultant, art historian*
†Howes, Gloria *state legislator*
Jaramillo, Arthur Lewis *lawyer*
Kelly, Paul Joseph, Jr. *federal judge*
King, Bruce *governor*
King, David W. *state treasurer*
Knapp, Edward Alan *scientist, government administrator*
Koessel, Donald Ray *retired banker*
Leon, Bruno *architect, educator*
Lewis, James Beliven *state government official*
Livesay, Thomas Andrew *museum administrator*
Longley, Bernique *artist, sculptor*
Loriaux, Maurice Lucien *artist, ecclesiologist*
Maes, Petra Jimenez *judge*
Mann, Herbie *flutist*
Martin, George Raymond Richard *author*
Mc Kinney, Robert Moody *newspaper editor and publisher*
McLaughlin, Ted John *speech educator*
Miller, Edmund Kenneth *retired electrical engineer*
Moellenbeck, Albert John, Jr. *engineering executive*
Morgan, Alan D. *state education official*
Noble, Merrill Emmett *retired psychology educator, psychologist*
Nuckolls, Leonard Arnold *retired hospital administrator*
Nurock, Robert Jay *investment analysis company executive*
Phister, Montgomery, Jr. *computer engineering consultant, writer*
Pickrell, Thomas Richard *retired oil company executive*
Pollock, Marvin Erwin *lawyer*
Ransom, Richard E. *state supreme court chief justice*
Ratliff, Floyd *biophysics educator, scientist*
Robertson, Stewart *conductor*
†Robinson, Shannon *state legislator*
†Sanchez, Raymond G. *state legislator*
Scheinbaum, David *photography educator*
Schwartz, George R. *physician*
Schwarz, Michael *lawyer*
Seth, Oliver *federal judge*
Shubart, Dorothy Louise *artist, educator*
Smith, Richard Bowen *national park superintendent*
Stephenson, Donnan *lawyer, former state supreme court justice*
Stevens, Ron A. *lawyer, public interest organization administrator*
Stevenson, Robert Edwin *microbiologist, culture collection executive*
Subotnick, Morton *composer, clarinetist*
Tarn, Nathaniel *poet, translator, educator*
Udall, Thomas *state attorney general*
Upton, Arthur Canfield *experimental pathologist, educator*
†Ward, John William *physical chemist*
Watkins, Stephen Edward *accountant*
White, David Hywel *physics educator*
Whiteford, Andrew Hunter *anthropologist*
Williams, Stephen *anthropologist, educator*
Wolf, Cynthia Tribelhorn *librarian, library educator*
Yalman, Ann *lawyer*

Sante Fe
†Frenkel, Jacob Karl *physician, consultant, researcher*

Silver City
†Altamirano, Ben D. *merchant, state senator*
†Foy, Thomas Paul *lawyer, state legislator*
Gilbert, Kathie Simon *economist, educator*
Snedeker, John Haggner *university president*
Sturgen, Winston *photographer, printmaker, artist*

Socorro
Kottlowski, Frank Edward *geologist*
Lancaster, John Howard *civil engineer*

Petschek, Albert George *physics educator*

Sunspot
Altrock, Richard Charles *astrophysicist*

Taos
Bacon, Wallace Alger *speech communications educator, author*
Bell, Larry Stuart *artist*
Crespin, Leslie Ann *artist*
Dickey, Robert Preston *author, educator, poet*
Murphey, Michael Martin *country western singer, songwriter*
Witt, David L. *curator, writer*
Young, Jon Nathan *archeologist*

Tesuque
Poedtke, Carl Henry George, Jr. *management consultant*

Tijeras
Vizcaino, Henry P. *mining engineer, consultant*

Univ Of New Mexico
Ellis, Willis Hill *lawyer, educator*
Hull, McAllister Hobart, Jr. *retired university administrator*
Sarto, Gloria Elizabeth *obstetrician/gynecologist, educator*
Snell, Patricia Poldervaart *librarian, consultant*
Thorson, James Llewellyn *English language educator*

Wagon Mound
†Abeyta, Jose Reynato *retired pharmacist, state legislator, cattle rancher*

White Sands Missle Range
Arthur, Paul Keith *electronic engineer*
†Evans, Ronald L. *atmospheric science research administrator*
Niles, Franklin Elvie *physicist*

NEW YORK

Albany
Aceto, Vincent John *librarian, educator*
†Alexander, Fritz W., II *judge*
Ashe, Bernard Flemming *lawyer*
†Ball, David Standish *bishop*
Beach, John Arthur *lawyer*
Beebe, Richard Townsend *physician*
†Begg, Robert Thomas *law library adminstrator, law librarian, lawyer*
Beharriell, Frederick John *German and comparative literature educator*
Bellacosa, Joseph W. *judge*
Belsky, Martin Henry *law educator, lawyer*
Biggs, Donald Anthony *psychologist, educator*
Blount, Stanley Freeman *marketing educator*
Bosart, Lance F. *meteorology educator*
Bradford, Peter Amory *state official*
Bradley, Wesley Holmes *physician*
Brown, Albert Joseph, Jr. *banker*
†Brown, Judith Anne *law librarian*
†Bruno, Joseph L. *state legislator*
Burke, Joseph C. *university interim chancellor*
Carovano, John Martin *not-for-profit adminstrator, conservationist*
Carpenter, Howard Grant, Jr. *lawyer, savings and loan association executive*
Case, Forrest N., Jr. *lawyer*
Chassin, Mark Russell *state official*
Cholakis, Constantine George *federal judge*
Chorbajian, Herbert G. *bank executive*
†Connelly, Elizabeth Ann *state legislator*
Cornell, David Roger *hospital administrator*
Cotter, William Donald *state commissioner, former newspaper editor*
Creegan, Robert Francis *philosophy educator*
Csiza, Charles Karoly *veterinarian, microbiologist*
Cuomo, Mario Matthew *governor*
Davis, Paul Joseph *endocrinologist*
†Demerjian, Kenneth L. *atmospheric science educator, research center director*
DeNuzzo, Rinaldo Vincent *pharmacy educator*
Donovan, Robert Alan *English educator*
Dougherty, James *orthopedic surgeon, educator*
Doyle, Joseph Theobald *physician, educator*
Dunn, James Robert *geologist*
†Eastman, William Don *publishing executive*
Eckstein, Jerome *philosopher, educator*
Engel, David Anthony *lawyer*
Everett, James William, Jr. *lawyer*
†Farley, Hugh T. *state senator, law educator*
Ferguson, Henry *international management consultant*
Frisch, Harry Lloyd *chemist, educator*
Frost, Robert Edwin *chemistry educator*
†Furlong, Patrick Louis *health science association administrator*
†Galiber, Joseph Lionel *state senator*
Galvin, Thomas John *information science policy educator, librarian, information scientist*
†Gay, Charles *church administrator*
Gellhorn, Alfred *physician, educator*
†Gottfried, Richard Norman *state legislator*
Grove, William Boyd *bishop*
†Gruber, Scott Alan *medical educator*
Hagoort, Thomas Henry *lawyer*
Halsey, Richard Sweeney *information scientist, educator*
Han, Jaok *cardiologist, researcher, educator*
Happ, Harvey Heinz *electrical engineer, educator*
†Harenberg, Paul E. *state legislator*
Herman, Robert S. *former state official, economist, educator*
Hitchcock, Karen Ruth *biology educator, university dean, academic administrator*
Hof, Liselotte Bertha *biochemist*
†Hoffmann, Nancy Larraine *state legislator*
Hoffmeister, Jana Marie *cardiologist*
†Holland, Joseph R. *state senator*
Holstein, William Kurt *business administration educator*
Hubbard, Howard James *bishop*
Hughs, Richard Earl *business school dean*
†Johnson, Owen H. *state senator*
Katz, William Armstrong *library science educator*
Kaye, Gordon Israel *pathologist, anatomist, educator*
Kaye, Judith Smith *judge*
Kekes, John *philosopher, educator*
Kennedy, William Joseph *novelist, educator*
Kiepper, James Julius *education educator*
Kim, Jai Soo *physics educator*
†Kinney, Thomas J. *adult education educator*
Knoll, Bruce Evans *state agency administrator*
Kuivila, Henry Gabriel *chemist, educator, consultant*
†Lack, James J. *state senator, lawyer*
†Langlitz, Harold N. *pension fund administrator*
†Leichter, Franz S. *state senator*
Lenardon, Robert Joseph *classics educator*
Levine, Louis David *museum director, archaeologist*
Ley, Ronald *psychologist, educator*
Lumpkin, Lee Roy *dermatologist, educator*
Lundine, Stanley Nelson *state government official, former congressman, lawyer*
†Luster, Martin A. *state legislator*
Lynch, Daniel *newspaper editor, writer*
Macario, Alberto Juan Lorenzo *physician*
Mahoney, Justin J. *federal judge*
†Marchi, John Joseph *lawyer, state legislator*
†Marino, Ralph J. *state legislator*
McCarthy, Mary Lynn *social work educator*
†Mendez, Olga A. *state legislator*
Mihm, Martin Charles, Jr. *pathologist, educator*
Miles, Christine Marie *museum director*
Miner, Roger Jeffrey *federal judge*
Moelleken, Wolfgang Wilfried *Germanic languages and literature educator*
Morga Bellizzi, Celeste *editor*
Morgan, George Jefferson *interior designer*
Murphy, Thomas Joseph *communications consultant*
Murray, David *journalist, author*
Nathan, Richard P(erle) *political scientist, educator*
Naumann, Hans Juergen *manufacturing company executive*
†Nolan, Howard Charles, Jr. *state senator, lawyer*
†Padavan, Frank *state legislator*
†Papiernik, Richard Lawrence *editor, business columnist*
†Paterson, David Alexander *state senator*
Paulson, Peter John *librarian, publishing company executive*
Picotte, Michael Bernard *real estate developer*
Pohlsander, Hans Achim *classics educator*
Purves, Alan Carroll *English language educator, education educator*
Quellmalz, Henry *printing company executive*
†Ray, Alan *museum director*
Reese, William Lewis *philosophy educator*
Reichert, Leo Edmund, Jr. *biochemist, endocrinologist*
Reid, William James *social work educator*
†Reynolds, Joseph P. *publishing executive, educational consultant*
Riley, Victor J., Jr. *financial services company executive*
Robbins, Cornelius (Van Vorse) *education administration educator*
Roberts, Warren Errol *history educator*
Robinson, John Bowers, Jr. *bank holding company executive*
Rosenfeld, Harry Morris *editor*
Rosenkrantz, Daniel J. *computer science educator*
Roth, Laura Maurer *physics educator, researcher*
Sacklow, Stewart Irwin *advertising executive*
†Santiago, Nellie *state legislator*
Schneider, Allan Stanford *biochemistry and pharmacology educator, biomedical research scientist*
Shaffer, Gail S. *state government official*
Shubert, Joseph Francis *librarian*
Siegel, David Donald *law educator*
Simons, Richard Duncan *judge*
Singer, Cecile D. *state legislator*
†Skelos, Dean G. *senator*
Smith, Ralph Wesley, Jr. *federal judge*
Sobol, Thomas *state education commissioner*
†Solomon, Martin M. *state senator*
Sprow, Howard Thomas *lawyer, educator*
†Stachowski, William T. *state senator*
†Stafford, Ronald B. *state legislator*
Standish, John Spencer *textile manufacturing company executive*
Stewart, Margaret McBride *biology educator, researcher*
Swartz, Donald Percy *physician*
Swygert, H. Patrick *lawyer, educational administrator*
Tedeschi, James Theodore, Jr. *psychologist educator*
Teevan, Richard Collier *psychology educator*
Thompson, Frank Joseph *political science educator*
Thornberry, Terence Patrick *criminologist, educator*
Thornton, Maurice *university administrator*
Titone, Vito Joseph *judge*
Tuttle, Frank James *bank executive*
Vaccaro, Louis Charles *college president*
Vachon, Russell Bertrand *transportation executive*
†Vitaliano, Eric N. *state legislator, lawyer*
†Volker, Dale Martin *state senator, lawyer*
Wallender, Michael Todd *lawyer*
†Ward, Frank Jay *banker*
Wetzler, James Warren *economist, state official*
Wright, Theodore Paul, Jr. *political science educator*
Zacek, Joseph Frederick *history educator, international studies consultant, East European affairs specialist*
Zimmerman, Joseph Francis *political scientist, educator*

Alfred
Billeci, Andre George *art educator, sculptor*
Coll, Edward Girard, Jr. *university president*
Frechette, Van Derck *ceramic engineer*
Higby, (Donald) Wayne *artist, educator*
Keith, Timothy Zook *psychology educator*
Ott, Walter Richard *academic administrator*
Potter, Barrett George *historian, educator*
Rossington, David Ralph *physical chemistry educator*
Spriggs, Richard Moore *ceramic engineer, research center administrator*

Alfred Station
Love, Robert Lyman *educational consulting company executive*

Amagansett
Lustig, Harry *physicist, educator, administrator*
†Opper, John *painter, retired educator*

Amherst
Alfiero, Salvatore Harry *manufacturing company executive*
Arrison, Clement R. *manufacturing company executive*
Brown, Stephen Ira *mathematics educator*
Clark, Donald Malin *association executive*
Coover, James Burrell *music educator*
Cramer, Stanley Howard *psychology educator, author*
Eberlein, Patricia James *mathematician, computer scientist, educator*
Fujita, Shigeji *physicist, educator*
Gracia, Jorge Jesus Emiliano *philosopher, educator*
Henderson, Donald *biophysics educator*
Howland, Murray Shipley, Jr. *gastroenterologist*
Jen, Frank Chifeng *finance and management educator*
Lee, George C. *civil engineer, university administrator*
Lewis, Lionel Stanley *sociology educator*
Mills, Theodore Mason *sociologist, educator*
Ralston, Anthony *computer scientist, mathematician, educator*
Reinhorn, Andrei M. *civil engineering educator, consultant*
Rossberg, Robert Howard *psychology educator, former university dean*

Amityville
Brennan, Patrick Thomas *meteorology company executive*

Annandale
†Achebe, Chinua *humanist, educator*

Annandale On Hudson
Ashbery, John Lawrence *language educator, poet, playwright*
Frank, Elizabeth *English literature educator, author*
Kelly, Robert *poet, educator*
†Manea, Norman *writer, educator*
Sullivan, Jim *artist*

Ardsley
Barth, Richard *pharmaceutical executive*
Benjamin, Jeff *lawyer*
Ricklin, Arthur H. *hospital administrator*
Sanders, Robert Martin *commodity trader*
†Sullivan, Joseph Thomas *chemical executive, chemical engineer*

Armonk
Bailey, William O. *retired insurance company executive*
Behr, Richard Henry *architect, educator*
Bergson, Henry Paul *association executive*
Bolduc, Ernest Joseph *management consultant*
Bolton, John Roger *public relations executive*
Eastman, Dean Eric *science research executive*
Elliot, David H. *insurance company executive*
Elson, Charles *stage designer, educator*
Evangelista, Donato A. *lawyer, computer and infosystems manufacturing company executive*
Gerstner, Louis Vincent, Jr. *diversified company executive*
Godfrey, Robert R. *financial services executive*
Grove, David Lawrence *economist*
Karvelis, Leon J., Jr. *investment company executive*
Levy, Kenneth James *advertising executive*
Lynett, Lawrence Wilson *electronics company executive*
Mellors, Robert Charles *physician scientist*
Quinn, James W. *lawyer*
Sharpe, Myron Emanuel *publisher, editor, writer*
York, Jerome B. *financial executive*
Zuckerman, Frederick William *electronics company executive*

Astoria
Douglas, Eileen *news broadcaster*
Koszarski, Richard *film historian, writer*
†McCormick, Douglas Walter *cable, broadcast executive*

Athens
Lew, Roger Alan *manufacturing company executive*

Auburn
Eldred, Thomas Gilbert *secondary education educator, historian*

Aurora
Shilepsky, Arnold Charles *mathematics educator, computer consultant*

Averill Park
Haines, Walter Wells *retired economics educator*

Babylon
Collis, Charles *aircraft company executive*
Haley, Priscilla Jane *artist, printmaker*
Hennelly, Edmund Paul *lawyer, oil company executive*
Keane, Daniel J. *banker*
Lopez, Joseph Jack *oil company executive, consultant*
Meirowitz, Claire Cecile *public relations executive*

Baldwin
Lister, Bruce Alcott *food scientist, consultant*

Baldwin Place
Kurian, George Thomas *publisher*
Mc Kay, Dean Raymond *computer company executive*

Ballston Lake
Fiedler, Harold Joseph *electrical engineer, consultant*

Ballston Spa
Barba, Harry *publisher, editor, author, educator*

Barrytown
Higgins, Dick (Richard Carter Higgins) *writer, publisher, composer, artist*

Batavia
Steiner, Stuart *college president*

Bath
Huang, Edwin I-Chuen *physician, environmental researcher*
Sandt, John Joseph *psychiatrist, educator*

Bay Shore
Cohen, Lawrence N. *health care company executive*
De Pasquale, John Anthony *direct marketing agency executive*

Bayport
Courant, Ernest David *physicist*
Poli, Kenneth Joseph *editor*

Bayside
Bernstein, Louis *clergyman*
D'Amato, Domenico Donald *lawyer*
Goldstein, Milton *art educator, printmaker, painter*
Zinn, William *violinist, composer, business executive*

Beacon
Flagello, Ezio Domenico *basso*
Pollart, Dale F(lavian) *petroleum company research executive*
Witte, Lawrence Mark *hospital administrator*

Bearsville
Wickiser, Ralph Lewanda *painter, educator, author*

Bedford
Atkins, Ronald Raymond *lawyer*
†Benedek, Armand *landscape architect*
Bowman, James Kinsey *publishing company executive, rare book specialist*
Damora, Robert Matthew *architect*
†Jalkut, Richard Alan *telecommunications executive*
Philip, Peter Van Ness *former trust company executive*
Root, Oren *lawyer*
Ruppel, George Robert *accountant*
Weinman, Robert Alexander *sculptor*

Bedford Hills
Diebold, John *management consultant*
Fissell, William Henry *investment advisor*
Ludlum, Robert *author*
Marshall, William Emmett *biotechnology company executive, biochemistry researcher*
Schwartz, Edward Malcolm *management consultant*
Waller, Wilhelmine Kirby (Mrs. Thomas Mercer Waller) *civic worker, organization official*

Bellport
Barton, Mark Quayle *physicist*
Hughes, Elinor Lambert *drama and film critic*

Berlin
Stephens, Donald Joseph *retired architect*

Bethpage
Anderson, John Robert *defense and aerospace executive*
Brown, James Kenneth *computer engineer*
Caporali, Renso L. *aerospace executive*
Dely, Steven *aerospace company executive*
Genovese, Thomas Leonardo *lawyer*
Melnik, Robert Edward *aeronautical engineer*
Myers, Robert Jay *aerospace company executive*
Reinertsen, Norman *aircraft systems corporate executive*
Rockensies, John William *mechanical engineer*

Binghamton
Anderson, Warren Mattice *lawyer*
Babb, Harold *psychology educator*
Banks, Arthur Sparrow *political scientist, educator*
†Bearsch, Lee Palmer *architect, city planner*
Best, Robert Mulvane *insurance company executive*
Block, Haskell Mayer *humanities educator*
Brehm, Sharon Stephens *psychology educator, university administrator*
Carrigg, James A. *utility company executive*
Coates, Donald Robert *geology educator, scientist*
Cornacchio, Joseph Vincent *engineering educator, computer researcher, consultant*
Defleur, Lois B. *university president, sociology educator*
Dunn, Melvin Bernard *insurance company executive*
Eisch, John Joseph *chemist, educator*
Feisel, Lyle Dean *university dean, electrical engineering educator*
Fleming, Russell, Jr. *utility company executive, lawyer*
Gaddis Rose, Marilyn *comparative literature educator, translator*
Gerhart, Eugene Clifton *lawyer*
Hilton, Peter John *mathematician, educator*
Hinman, George Lyon *lawyer*
Ippolito, Angelo *artist, educator*
Isaacson, Robert Lee *psychology educator, researcher*
Jennings, Frank Louis *engineering company executive, engineer*
Kessler, Milton *English language educator, poet*
Klir, George Jiri *systems science educator*
†Koffman, Burton I. *manufacturing company executive*
Levis, Donald James *psychologist, educator*
†Libous, Thomas W. *state senator*
Lowen, Walter *mechanical engineering educator*
Mazrui, Ali Al'Amin *political science educator, researcher*
McAvoy, Thomas James *federal judge*
Pearson, Paul Holding *insurance company executive*
Piaker, Philip Martin *accountant, educator*
†Salem-Murdock, Muneera *anthropologist*
Schwartz, Aubrey Earl *artist*
Schwartz, Richard Frederick *electrical engineering educator*
Shillestad, John Gardner *financial services company executive*
Sklar, Kathryn Kish *historian, educator*
Stein, George Henry *historian, educator, administrator*
†Su, Stephen Y. H. *computer science and engineering educator, consultant*

Bloomington
Ruffing, Anne Elizabeth *artist*

Bohemia
Manley, Gertrude Ella *librarian, media specialist*

Brewster
Huckabee, Carol Brooks *psychologist*
Melsheimer, Mel P(owell) *consumer products business executive*

Briarcliff Manor
Bhargava, Rameshwar Nath *physicist*
Bornmann, Carl M(alcolm) *lawyer*
Callahan, Daniel John *institute director*
Carey, James Henry *banker*

Dolmatch, Theodore Bieley management consultant
Gaylin, Willard physician, educator
Glassman, Jerome Martin clinical pharmacologist, educator
Haddad, Jerrier Abdo engineering management consultant
Leiser, Burton Myron philosophy and law educator
Luck, Edward Carmichael association executive
Radandt, Friedhelm K. college president
Weintraub, Michael Ira neurologist
Zimmar, George Peter publishing executive, psychology educator

Briarwood
Danna, Jo J. publisher, author, anthropologist

Bridgehampton
Jackson, Lee artist
Needham, James Joseph consultant
Phillips, Warren Henry publisher

Brockport
Bretton, Henry L. political scientist, educator
Fagan, Garth choreographer, artistic director, educator
Harter, Michael Thomas college dean, health sciences consultant
Marcus, Robert D. historian, educator
Stack, George Joseph philosophy educator
Studer, Ginny college dean
Van de Wetering, John E(dward) college president

Bronx
Abbott, Jim (James Anthony Abbott) baseball player
Adams, Alice sculptor
Ansbro, John Joseph philosophy educator
Auerbach, Paul Ira lawyer
Balka, Sigmund Ronell lawyer
Berger, Frederick Jerome electrical engineer, educator
Bhalodkar, Narendra Chandrakant cardiologist
Blank, Benjamin retail executive, consultant
Blaufox, Morton Donald physician, educator
Boggs, Wade Anthony professional baseball player
Bowers, Francis Robert literature educator
Brescia, Michael Joseph physician
Bruenn, Howard Gerald physician
Brush, Craig Balcombe French language and computer educator
†Bryant, Roy, Sr. bishop
Burde, Ronald Marshall neuro-ophthalmologist
Buschke, Herman neurologist
Carrick, Bruce Robert publishing company executive
Cherkasky, Martin physician
Cimino, James Ernest physician
Cohen, Herbert Jesse physician, educator
Conway, William Gaylord zoologist, zoo director
Corinaldi, Austin former hospital administrator
Cornfield, Melvin lawyer, university institute director
DeMartino, Anthony Gabriel cardiologist, internist
Dulles, Avery priest, theologian
Duncalf, Deryck anesthesiologist
Edelmann, Chester Monroe, Jr. pediatrician, medical school dean
Eder, Howard Abram physician
Elkin, Milton radiologist, physician, educator
†Espada, Pedro, Jr. state senator
Fernandez, Ricardo R. university administrator
Fishman, Joshua Aaron sociolinguist, educator
†Fleischer, Norman director of endocrinology, medical educator
†Foreman, Spencer pulmonary specialist, hospital executive
†Forero, Enrique botanical garden research director
Frater, Robert William Mayo surgeon, educator
Freeman, Leonard Murray radiologist, nuclear medicine physician, educator
Friedman, Joel Matthew oral and maxillofacial surgeon, educator
Fulop, Milford physician
Gerst, Paul Howard physician
Gliedman, Marvin L. surgeon, educator
Gootzeit, Jack Michael rehabilitation institute executive
Greenberg, Blu author
†Greene, Aurelia state legislator
Gross, Ludwik physician
Hait, Gershon pediatric cardiologist
Hallett, Charles Arthur, Jr. English and humanities educator
Hankin, Leonard J. merchant
Heilbrun, James economist, educator
†Hein, Karen K. pediatrician, epidemiologist
Hennessy, Thomas Christopher clergyman, educator, retired university dean
Himmelberg, Robert Franklin historian, educator
Hirano, Asao neuropathologist
Hovnanian, H. Philip biomedical engineer
Howell, Alfred Hunt former banker
Humphry, James, III librarian
†Iazetti, Anthony M. school system administrator
Jacobson, Harold Gordon radiologist, educator
Jaffé, Ernst Richard medical educator and administrator
Kahn, Thomas medical educator
Karasu, T(oksoz) Byram psychiatry educator
Karmen, Arthur physician, science administrator, educator
Karp, Abraham Joseph historian, rabbi, educator
†Kassoy, Hortense (Honey Kassoy) artist
Keane, John Patrick secondary education educator
Key, Jimmy (James Edward Key) professional baseball player
Kitzie, John, Jr. retail electronic products executive
Koranyi, Adam mathematics educator
Koss, Leopold G. pathologist, educator, physician
Kucic, Joseph management consultant, industrial engineer
Lattis, Richard Lynn zoo director
Lawn, John C. professional baseball team executive, former federal government official
Lieber, Charles Saul physician, educator
Lilly, Frank oncogenetic biomedical researcher
†Long, Gregory R. botanic garden administrator
Macklin, Ruth bioethics educator
Marx, Gertie Florentine anesthesiologist
Mattingly, Donald Arthur professional baseball player
Messing, Janet Agnes Kapelsohn economist, educator
Moritz, Charles Fredric book editor
Muschel, Louis Henry immunologist, educator
Nagler, Arnold Leon pathologist, scientist, educator
Nathanson, Melvyn Bernard university provost, mathematician
Nathenson, Stanley Gail immunology educator
O'Keefe, Vincent Thomas clergyman, educational administrator
Orkin, Louis Richard physician, educator
Ottenberg, James Simon hospital executive
Parker, Everett Carlton clergyman
Pellowski, Anne Rose author, consultant, educator, former librarian
Pitchumoni, Capecomorin Sankar gastroenterologist, educator
†Potkin, Harvey food company executive
Purpura, Dominick P. neuroscientist, university dean
Rapin, Isabelle physician
Revelle, Donald Gene manufacturing and health care company executive, consultant
Reynolds, Benedict Michael surgeon
†Rizzuto, Phillip Francis (Scooter) former sports broadcaster, former professional baseball player
Roberts, Burton Bennett administrative judge
Romney, Seymour Leonard physician, educator
Rose, Israel Harold mathematics educator
Rothstein, Anne Louise education educator, college official
Ruben, Robert Joel physician, educator
Scanlan, Thomas Joseph college president, educator
Schaller, George Beals zoologist
Scharff, Matthew Daniel immunologist, cell biologist, educator
Scharrer, Berta Vogel anatomy and neuroscience educator
Schaumburg, Herbert Howard neurology educator
Schwam, Marvin Albert graphic design company executive
Shafritz, David Andrew physician, research scientist
Shamos, Morris Herbert physicist educator
†Sherman, Judith Dorothy producer, recording company owner, recording engineer
Showalter, Buck (William Nathaniel Showalter, III) major league baseball team manager
Smith, Lee Arthur professional baseball player
Spitzer, Adrian pediatrician, medical educator
Stein, Milton Michael lawyer
†Stein, Ruth Elizabeth Klein physician
Steinbrenner, George Michael, III professional baseball team executive, shipbuilding company executive
Sterling, Kenneth research physician, educator
Stuhr, David Paul business educator, consultant
Surks, Martin I. medical educator, endocrinologist
Tong, Hing mathematician, educator
Tregde, Lorraine C. hospital administrator
†Tusiani, Joseph foreign language educator, author
Ultan, Lloyd historian
†Velella, Guy J. state legislator
Waltz, Joseph McKendree neurosurgeon, educator
Weins, Leo Matthew publishing company executive
Wiernik, Peter Harris oncologist, educator
Williams, Marshall Henry, Jr. physician, educator
Wolf, Robert Thomas lawyer
Yalow, Rosalyn Sussman medical physicist
Zalaznick, Sheldon editor, journalist
Zeichner, Oscar historian, educator

Bronxville
Armstrong, John Kremer lawyer, artist
Arndt, Kenneth Eugene banker
Barkhuus, Arne physician
Barnhart, Clarence Lewis lexicographer, editor
Biscardi, Chester composer, educator
†Blank, Richard Mark advertising licensing and product development executive
Bozeman, Adda Bruemmer international relations scholar, educator, consultant, author
Conant, Miriam Bernheim political scientist, educator
Cook, Charles David international lawyer, arbitrator, consultant
†Doty, Mark poet
Dvorak, Roger Gran health facility executive
Farber, Viola Anna dancer, choreographer
Forester, Erica Simms decorative arts historian, consultant, educator
Franklin, Margery Bodansky psychology educator, researcher
Hutchison, Dorris Jeannette retired microbiologist, educator
Ilchman, Alice Stone college president, former government official
Jordan, Louis Hampton retired accounting educator
Kirk, Grayson Louis retired political science educator, retired universtiy president, trustee
Knapp, George Griff Prather insurance consultant, arbitrator
Krupat, Arnold English educator, writer
L'Huillier, Peter (Peter) archbishop
Lombardo, Philip Joseph broadcasting company executive
Martin, R. Keith business and information systems educator, consultant
Noble, James Kendrick, Jr. media industry consultant
Penisten, Gary Dean entrepreneur
Peters, Sarah Whitaker art historian, writer, lecturer
Prakapas, Eugene Joseph art gallery director
Pratt, John Adams, Jr. bank executive
Randall, Francis Ballard historian, educator, writer
Root, Stuart Dowling lawyer, former banker and government official
†Schönberg, Bessie dance educator
Swerdlow, Amy historian, educator, writer
Wilson, John Donald banker, economist

Brooklyn
Abrahamsen, Samuel Judaic studies educator emeritus
Adams, George Harold hospital and health executive
Adasko, Mary speech pathologist
Agard, Emma Estornel psychotherapist
Ahrens, Thomas H. production company executive
Alfonso, Antonio Escolar surgeon
Al-Hafeez, Humza minister, editor
Allen, Percy, II hospital administrator
Alley, Frederick Don hospital executive
Altura, Burton Myron physiologist, educator
Amon, Carol Bagley federal judge
Anderson, Lennart artist
Artschwager, Richard Ernst artist
Ashley, Leonard Raymond Nelligan English language educator
Bachman, George mathematics educator
Bartels, John Ries federal judge
Battle, Turner Charles, III art educator, educational association administrator
Bergeron, R. Thomas radiologist, educator
Bertoni, Henry Louis electrical engineering educator
Bianco, Anthony Joseph, III newswriter
Birenbaum, William M. former university president
Biro, Laszlo dermatologist
Blackman, Robert Irwin real estate developer and investor, lawyer, accountant
Blasi, Alberto Romance languages educator, writer
Bode, Walter Albert editor
Bowers, Patricia Eleanor Fritz economist
Bramwell, Henry federal judge
Brandwein, Larry library administrator
Brownstone, Paul Lotan emeritus speech communications and drama educator
Buck, Robert Treat, Jr. museum director, educator
Bugliarello, George university president
Carlile, Janet Louise artist, educator
Carlson, Ralph Lawrence book publisher
Carruthers, Walter Edward Royden (Roy Carruthers) graphic designer, artist
Carswell, Lois Malakoff botanical gardens executive, consultant
Carter, Betty (Lillie Mae Jones) jazz singer, songwriter
Castleman, Louis Samuel metallurgist, educator
†Castro, Nikki Marie dancer
Charton, Marvin chemist, educator
Chernow, Ron writer, columnist
Clark, Peggy theatrical lighting designer
Clune, John Richard library administrator
†Comer, John F. superintendent
Contino, Rosalie Helene English educator, costume designer
Cornell, Thomas Browne artist, educator
Corry, Emmett Brother librarian, educator, researcher, archivist
Cracco, Roger Quinlan medical educator, neurologist
Daily, Thomas V. bishop
Dearie, Raymond Joseph federal judge
DeBock, Florent Alphonse controller
DeCarava, Roy R. photographer, educator
Dellomo, Frank A. banker
Delson, Elizabeth artist
Delson, Sidney Leon architect
Dinnerstein, Harvey artist
Dinnerstein, Simon Abraham artist, educator
Dodge, Charles Malcolm composer, music educator
†Eirich, Frederick Roland chemist, educator
Enquist, Irving Fridtjof surgeon
Ettrick, Marco Antonio theoretical physicist
Everdell, William Romeyn humanities educator
Faison, Seth Shepard retired insurance broker
Farsetta, James Joseph medical center director
Federici, William Vito newspaper reporter
Felsen, Leopold B. engineer, educator
Ferber, Linda S. museum curator
Finberg, Laurence pediatrician, educator, college dean
Fischman, Myrna Leah accountant, educator
Flam, Jack Donald art historian, educator
Franco, Victor theoretical physics educator
Friedman, Eli A. nephrologist
Friedman, Howard Samuel cardiologist, educator
Friedman, Paul chemistry educator
Friis, Erik Johan editor, publisher
Gabriel, Mordecai Lionel biologist, educator
Garcia, Marc Anthony diplomat
†Garibaldi, Louis aquarium administrator
Gaston, Oland P. music educator
†Geller, Sheldon comsumer products company executive
Gintautas, Jonas physician, scientist, administrator
Giordano, Anthony Bruno electrical engineering educator, retired college dean
Glasser, Israel Leo federal judge
Glickman, Franklin Sheldon dermatologist, educator
Goodman, Alvin S. engineering educator, consultant
Gordon, Conrad J. financial executive
Gotta, Alexander Walter anesthesiologist, educator
Grado, Angelo John artist
Graham, Arnold Harold lawyer, educator
†Grayson, D. W. bishop
Grayson, Gerald Herbert economics and labor-management relations educator, publisher
†Gresser, Carol A. school system administrator
Gross, Stephen Mark pharmacist, academic dean
†Halperin, Donald Marc state senator, lawyer
Halpern, Alvin Michael physicist, educator
Hamm, Charles John banker
Harris, James Arthur, Sr. economics educator
Harvey, Edmund Huxley, Jr. (Tad Harvey) editor
Helly, Walter Sigmund engineering educator
†Herman, Susan N. legal educator
Hochstadt, Harry mathematician, educator
Hohenrath, William Edward retired banker
Holden, David Morgan medical educator
Hoogenboom, Ari Arthur historian, educator
†Hopkins, Karen art administrator
Horowitz, Carl chemical company president
Imperato, Pascal James physician, health administrator, author, editor, medical educator
†Ireys, Alice Recknagel landscape architect
Jackson, Sarah Jeanette sculptor, graphic artist, copier artist, bookmaker
Jacobson, Leslie Sari biologist, educator
Jarman, Joseph jazz musician
Jofen, Jean foreign language educator
Johnson, Sterling, Jr. federal judge
Jones, Susan Emily fashion educator, administrator, educator
Kamholz, Stephan L. physician
Kempner, Joseph aerospace engineering educator
Kimmich, Christoph Martin academic administrator, educator
King, Margaret Leah history educator
Kippel, Gary M. psychologist
Kjeldaas, Terje, Jr. physics educator emeritus
Korman, Edward R. federal judge
†Kraemer, Richard A. bank executive
Kunjukunju, Pappy insurance company financial executive
Kuskin, Karla writer, illustrator
Langer, Arthur Mark mineralogist
†Lawrence, Deirdre Elizabeth librarian
Lederman, Stephanie Brody artist
Lee, Spike (Shelton Jackson Lee) filmmaker
Lee, Stanley physician, educator
Leeman, Cavin Philip psychiatrist, educator
Leiman, Sid Zalman Judaic studies educator
Levere, Richard David physician, academic administrator, educator
Lewis, Felice Flanery lawyer, educator
Leyh, Richard Edmund, Sr. retired investment executive
Lichtenstein, Harvey performing arts executive
†Lipski, Donald G. sculptor
Lobron, Barbara L. writer, editor
†Loran, Carlos Anthony hospital administrator
†Maddalena, Frank Joseph health care executive
Malach, Monte physician
Margolin, Harold metallurgical educator
Masterson, Charles Francis retired social scientist
Matthews, Craig Gerard gas company executive
Mendelson, Sol physical science educator, consultant
Milhorat, Thomas Herrick neurosurgeon
Minkoff, Jack economics educator
†Montgomery, Velmanette state legislator
Moore, Arthur James editor
Morawetz, Herbert chemistry educator
Mundy, Mark James hospital administrator
Murillo-Rohde, Ildaura Maria marriage and family therapist, consultant, educator, dean
Murphy, Edward Patrick, Jr. gas utility company executive
Namba, Tatsuji physician, researcher
Nickerson, Eugene H. federal judge
Norstrand, Iris Fletcher psychiatrist, neurologist, educator
O'Connor, Sister George Aquin (Margaret M. O'Connor) college president, sociology educator
Olson, Harry Andrew, Jr. communications consultant
Olson, Robert Goodwin philosophy educator
Onken, George Marcellus lawyer
Othmer, Donald Frederick chemical engineer, educator
Oussani, James John stapling company executive
Pan, Huo-Hsi mechanical engineer, educator
†Pearce, Eli M. chemistry educator, administrator
Pearlstein, Seymour artist
Pennell, William Brooke lawyer
Pennisten, John William computer scientist, linguist, actuary
Pfaffman, William Scott sculptor
Plotz, Charles Mindell physician
Pollack, Bruce banker, real estate consultant
Poser, Norman Stanley law educator
Purdy, James writer
†Quick, Norman bishop
Raggi, Reena federal judge
†Raphael, Carol health care administrator
Raskind, Leo Joseph legal educator
Ravitz, Leonard J., Jr. physician, scientist, consultant
Reich, Nathaniel Edwin physician, artist, educator
Reinisch, June Machover psychologist, educator
†Reissman, Maurice L. bank executive
Rice, John Thomas mechanical engineering and architecture educator
Ries, Martin artist, educator
†Robbins, Sara Ellen law librarian, educator, lawyer
Rocco, Ron artist
Roess, Roger Peter university vice president and dean
†Safir, Howard fire commissioner
Sands, Edith Sylvia Abeloff (Mrs. Abraham M. Sands) finance educator, author
Sanford, David Boyer writer, editor
Schaefer, Marilyn Louise artist, writer, educator
Schiffman, Gerald microbiologist, educator
Schmidt, Fred (Orval Frederick Schmidt) editor
Schussler, Theodore lawyer, physician, educator
Schwarz, Richard Howard obstetrician/gynecologist, educator
†Seybert, Joanna judge
Shalita, Alan Remi dermatologist
Sharify, Nasser librarian, educator, author
Shaw, Doris creative marketing consultant
Shaw, Leonard Glazer electrical engineering educator, consultant
Shaw, Maurice Kenneth utility company executive
Shechter, Ben-Zion artist, illustrator
Shechter, Laura Judith artist
Shooman, Martin Lawrence electrical engineer, computer scientist, educator
Shulman, Max L. corporate executive
Sifton, Charles Proctor federal judge
Silver, Horace Ward Martin Tavares composer, pianist
†Smith, Ada L. state legislator
Snyder, Joan artist
Sonenberg, Jack artist
†Spector, Robert Donald language professional, educator
Spero, Barry Melvin medical center executive
Sternlight, Peter Donn economist, retired banker
†Stevenson, Gale librarian
Stracher, Alfred biochemistry educator
Sullivan, Donald college president
†Sullivan, Joseph M. bishop
Sultzer, Barnet Martin microbiology and immunology researcher, educator
Swenson, Karen poet, journalist
Swirsky, Judith Perlman arts administrator, consultant
Szenberg, Michael economics educator, editor, consultant
Tamir, Theodor electrophysics researcher, educator
†Trager, David G. judge, lawyer, educator
Twining, Lynne Dianne psychotherapist, researcher, writer
†Valero, René Arnold clergyman
Vogl, Otto polymer science and engineering educator
Walsh, George William publishing company executive, editor
Wasserman, Arnold Saul academic dean, industrial design executive
Weill, Georges Gustave mathematics educator
Weiner, Irwin M. medical educator, college dean, researcher
Weinstein, Jack B. federal judge
†Weston, I. Donald architect
Williams, Ethel Coger elementary education educator
Wolf, Edward Lincoln physics educator
Wolfe, Ethyle Renee (Mrs. Coleman Hamilton Benedict) college administrator
Wolintz, Arthur Harry physician, neuro-ophthalmologist
Wollman, Leo physician
Zayek, Francis Mansour bishop
Zelin, Jerome retail executive
†Zuk, Judith botanic garden administrator

Brookville
Huber, Don Lawrence publisher
Woodsworth, Anne university dean, librarian

Buffalo
Abrahams, Athol Denis geography researcher, educator
Ackerman, Philip Charles utility executive, lawyer
Allen, William Sheridan history educator
Ambrus, Clara Maria physician
Ambrus, Julian L. physician, medical educator
Ament, Richard anesthesiologist, educator
Anbar, Michael biophysics educator
Anderson, Wayne Arthur electrical engineering educator
Arcara, Richard Joseph federal judge

Ashgriz, Nasser *mechanical and aerospace engineer, educator*
Aurbach, Herbert Alexander *sociology educator*
Bakay, Louis *neurosurgeon*
Bardos, Thomas Joseph *chemist, educator*
Barney, Thomas McNamee *lawyer*
Basu, Rajat Subhra *physicist, researcher*
Batty, J. Michael *geographer, educator*
Bean, Edwin Temple, Jr. *lawyer*
Behling, Charles Frederick *psychology educator*
Benenson, David Maurice *engineering educator*
Berlin, Lorna Chumley *artist*
Berner, Robert Frank *statistics educator*
Birch, David William *business manager*
Birmingham, Richard Gregory *lawyer*
Bishop, Beverly Petterson *physiologist*
Blaine, Charles Gillespie *lawyer*
†Blane, Howard Thomas *institute administrator*
Bobinski, George Sylvan *librarian, educator*
Borst, Lyle Benjamin *physicist, educator*
†Brady-Borland, Karen *reporter*
†Brandt, Barbara Berryman *cultural organization administrator*
Brody, Harold *neuroanatomist, gerontologist*
Brooks, John Samuel Joseph *pathologist, researcher*
Bross, Irwin Dudley Jackson *biostatistician*
Brott, Irving Deerin, Jr. *lawyer, judge*
Bruckenstein, Stanley *chemistry educator*
Calkins, Evan *physician, educator*
Carmichael, Donald Scott *lawyer, business executive*
Chapman, Frederick John *manufacturing executive*
Chrisman, Diane J. *librarian*
Chryssa *sculptor*
Chu, Tsann Ming *immunochemist, educator*
Chutkow, Jerry Grant *neurologist, educator*
Ciancio, Sebastian Gene *periodontist, educator*
Clark, Randall Livingston *manufacturing company executive*
Cleave, James H. *bank executive*
Clemens, David Allen *lawyer*
Cloudsley, Donald Hugh *library administrator*
Coburn, Lewis Alan *mathematics educator*
Coles, Robert Traynham *architect*
Collins, J. Michael *public broadcasting executive*
Coppens, Philip *chemist*
Cordes, Alexander Charles *lawyer*
Creaven, Patrick Joseph *physician, research oncologist*
Creeley, Robert White *author, English educator*
†Curran, Robert *columnist*
Day, Donald Sheldon *lawyer*
Draper, Verden Rolland *accountant*
Drew, Fraser Bragg Robert *English language educator*
Drinnan, Alan John *oral pathologist*
Duax, William Leo *biological researcher*
Duke, Emanuel *lawyer*
Durand, Henry J., Jr. *academic administrator*
†Farhi, Leon Elie *physiology educator, researcher*
Fay, Albert Hill *building materials executive*
Federman, Raymond *novelist, English and comparative literature educator*
Feldman, Irving *poet*
Fiedler, Leslie Aaron *English educator, actor, author*
Flint, Mark Addison *financial executive*
Floyd, David Kenneth *lawyer, judge*
Frake, Charles Oliver *anthropology educator*
Friedlander, John Eastburn *health facility administrator*
Fuhr, Grant *professional hockey player*
Fung, Ho-Leung *pharmacy educator, researcher, consultant*
Fuzak, Victor Thaddeus *lawyer*
Gardner, Arnold Burton *lawyer*
Garvey, James Anthony *lawyer*
Gemmett, Robert James *university dean, English language educator*
†Givi, Peyman *science and engineering educator*
Glanville, Robert Edward *lawyer*
Glasauer, Franz Ernst *neurosurgeon*
Glickman, Marlene *social organization administrator*
Goldberg, Neil A. *lawyer*
Goldhaber, Gerald Martin *communication educator, author, consultant*
Gort, Michael *economics educator*
Graham, (Lloyd) Saxon *epidemiology educator*
Grasser, George Robert *lawyer*
Gray, F(rederick) William, III *lawyer*
Greene, Robert Michael *lawyer*
Greiner, William Robert *university administrator, educator, lawyer*
Gresham, Glen Edward *physician*
Gruen, David Henry *financial executive, consultant*
Hall, David Edward *lawyer*
Halpern, Ralph Lawrence *lawyer*
Halpert, Leonard Walter *retired editor*
Hare, Peter Hewitt *philosophy educator*
Hauptman, Herbert Aaron *mathematician, educator, researcher*
Hawerchuk, Dale *professional hockey player*
Hayes, Waldron Stanley, Jr. *lawyer*
Head, Edward Dennis *bishop*
Headrick, Thomas Edward *lawyer, educator*
Heilman, Pamela Davis *lawyer*
Helm, Frederick *dermatology educator*
Hetzner, Donald Raymund *social studies educator*
Horoszewicz, Juliusz Stanislaw *oncologist, cancer researcher, laboratory administrator*
Iggers, Georg Gerson *history educator*
†Ireland, Barbara Hennig *newspaper editor*
Irwin, Robert James Armstrong *investment company executive*
Jackson, Hermoine Prestine *psychologist*
Jacobs, Jeremy M. *diversified holding company executive, hockey team owner*
Jain, Piyare Lal *physics educator*
Jasen, Matthew Joseph *state justice*
Johnstone, D. Bruce *university administrator*
Kaeser, Clifford Richard *lawyer, food service industry executive*
†Kailbourne, Erland E. *banker*
Katz, Jack *audiology educator*
†Kelley, Sister Helen *hospital executive*
Kenzie, Ross Bruce *retired banker*
Kieffer, James Marshall *lawyer*
Kinzly, Robert Edward *engineering company executive*
Kiser, Kenneth M(aynard) *academic dean, chemical engineering educator*
Knox, Northrup Rand *banker*
Koontz, Eldon Ray *financial consultant*
Kurlan, Marvin Zeft *surgeon*
Kurtz, Paul *philosopher, educator, publisher*
Lafontaine, Pat *professional hockey player*
†Lamb, Charles F. *minister*
†Lammert, Richard Alan *corporate lawyer*
Landi, Dale Michael *industrial engineer, academic administrator*
Larson, Wilfred Joseph *chemical company executive*
Laurenzo, Vincent Dennis *industrial management company executive*
†Layton, Rodney Eugene *controller, newspaper executive*
Lee, Richard Vaille *physician, educator*
†Leland, Harold Robert *research and development corporation executive, electronics engineer*
Levine, George Richard *English language educator*
Levy, Kenneth Jay *psychology educator, academic administrator*
Liew, Fah Pow *mechanical engineer*
Light, Murray Benjamin *newspaper editor*
Linnen, Thomas Francis *international strategic management consulting firm executive*
Lippes, Gerald Sanford *lawyer, business executive*
Littlewood, Douglas Burden *business brokerage executive*
Loew, Ralph William *clergyman, columnist*
Lubick, Donald Cyril *lawyer*
MacLeod, Gordon Albert *lawyer*
Maloney, Milford Charles *internal medicine educator*
Manes, Stephen Gabriel *concert pianist, educator*
†Markwart, Paul Martin *architect*
McGuire, Beryl Edward *retired federal judge*
Meehan, Gerry *professional hockey team executive*
Meredith, Dale Dean *civil engineering educator*
Metzger, Ernest Hugh *aerospace engineer, scientist*
Middleton, Elliott, Jr. *physician*
Milgrom, Felix *immunologist, educator*
Millane, Lynn *town official*
Milligan, John Drane *historian, educator*
Mindell, Eugene Robert *surgeon, educator*
Miner, John Burnham *industrial relations educator, writer*
Mirand, Edwin Albert *medical scientist*
Morgan, James Durward *computer company executive*
Muckler, John *professional hockey coach*
Naughton, John Patrick *cardiologist, medical school administrator*
†Newman, George Charles *library administrator*
Newman, Stephen Michael *lawyer*
†Okun, Janice *food editor*
Ortolani, Minot Henry *zoo director*
†Ottenbacher, Kenneth J. *dean, educator*
Panaro, Victor Anthony *radiologist*
Payne, Frances Anne *literature educator, researcher*
Pearson, Paul David *lawyer*
Pegels, C. Carl *management science and systems educator*
Peradotto, John Joseph *classics educator, editor*
†Pett, John Lyman *banker*
†Phillips, Stanley F *restaurant company executive*
Piccillo, Joseph *artist*
Priore, Roger L. *biostatistics educator, consultant*
Pruitt, Dean Garner *psychologist, educator*
†Rappolt, William Carl *banker*
Regan, Peter Francis, III *physician, psychiatry educator*
Reif, Louis Raymond *lawyer, utilities executive*
Reismann, Herbert *engineer, educator*
Reitan, Paul Hartman *geologist, educator*
Rekate, Albert C. *physician*
Rice, Victor Albert *global industrial company executive*
†Rich, Robert E., Sr. *frozen foods company executive*
†Rich, Robert E., Jr. *food products company executive*
Richards, David Gleyre *German educator*
Richardson, F. C. *academic administrator*
Richmond, Allen Martin *speech pathologist, educator*
Riepe, Dale Maurice *philosopher, writer, educator, Asian art dealer*
†Robinson, David Clinton *reporter*
Rochwarger, Leonard *former ambassador*
Rogovin, Milton *photographer, retired optometrist*
Rooney, Paul Monroe *former library administrator*
Rosenthal, Donald B. *political scientist, educator*
Ruckenstein, Eli *chemical engineering educator*
†Sahlem, James Robert *law librarian*
Salisbury, Eugene W. *lawyer, justice*
Saperston, Howard Truman, Sr. *lawyer*
Sarjeant, Walter James *electrical and computer engineering educator*
Saveth, Edward Norman *history educator*
Schieder, Joseph Eugene *clergyman*
Schroeder, Harold Kenneth, Jr. *lawyer*
Schultz, Douglas George *art museum director*
Seidl, Fredrick William *dean, social work educator*
Seller, Robert Herman *cardiologist, family physician*
Shanahan, Robert B. *banker*
Shapiro, Stuart Charles *computer scientist, educator*
Sharma, Sushil Chandra *hospital administrator*
Sharpe, Daniel Roger *lawyer*
Shaw, David Tai-Ko *electrical and computer engineering educator, university administrator*
Shedd, Donald Pomroy *surgeon*
Sherwood, Arthur Morley *lawyer*
Siener, William Harold *museum director, historian, consultant*
Skretny, William Marion *federal judge*
Small, S(aul) Mouchly *psychiatrist, educator*
Solo, Alan Jere *medicinal chemistry educator, consultant*
Spaulding, Robert Mark *lawyer*
†Spencer, Foster Lewis *newspaper editor*
Stainrook, Harry Richard *banker*
Starks, Fred William *chemical company executive*
Steegmann, Albert Theodore, Jr. *anthropology educator*
Stein, William Warner *anthropology educator*
Stoll, Howard Lester, Jr. *dermatologist*
Stull, G. Alan *university dean, health professions educator*
Tedlock, Dennis *anthropology and literature educator*
†Thompson, Michael F. *food service executive*
Toles, Thomas Gregory *editorial cartoonist*
Tomasi, Thomas B. *cell biologist, administrator*
Treanor, Charles Edward *physicist*
Triggle, David John *university dean, consultant*
†Trotter, Herman Eager, Jr. *music critic*
Tufariello, Joseph James *chemistry educator*
Urban, Henry Zeller *newspaperman*
Valdes, Maximiano *orchestra director*
Vardon, James Lewes *bank executive*
†Vogel, Michael N. *journalist, writer, historian*
Wadsworth, James Marshall *lawyer*
Wang, Jui Hsin *biochemistry educator*
Weber, Thomas William *chemical engineering educator*
Weller, Sol William *chemical engineering educator*
Wickser, John Philip *lawyer*
Wiesen, Richard A. *academic administrator, educator*
Wilmers, Robert George *banker*
Wisbaum, Wayne David *lawyer*
Wolck, Wolfgang Hans-Joachim *linguist, educator*
Wolf, Richard Lloyd *automotive company executive, lawyer*
Wright, John Robert *pathologist*
Zaleski, Marek Bohdan *immunologist*
Zarembka, Paul *economics educator*

Buskirk
Johanson, Patricia Maureen *artist, architect, park designer*

Cambridge
Guma, Greg William *producer, writer*

Campbell Hall
Greenly, Colin *artist*
Ottaway, James Haller, Jr. *newspaper publisher*
Stone, Peter George *lawyer, publishing company executive*

Canaan
Bell, James Milton *psychiatrist*

Canton
Goldberg, Rita Maria *foreign language educator*
O'Connor, Daniel William *retired religious studies and classical languages educator*
Peterson, Patti McGill *college president*
Pollard, Fred Don *finance company executive*
Romey, William Dowden *geologist, educator*

Carle Place
Kahn, Leonard Richard *communications and electronics company executive*
Linchitz, Richard Michael *psychiatrist, physician*

Carmel
Carruth, David Barrow *landscape architect*
Lowe, E(dwin) Nobles *lawyer*
Shen, Chia Theng *former steamship company executive, religious institute official*

Castle Point
Greene, Jerry George *physician*

Castleton On Hudson
Lanford, Oscar Erasmus, Jr. *retired university vice chancellor*

Catskill
Kingsley, John Piersall *lawyer*

Centerport
Fischel, Edward Elliot *physician*
Mallett, Helene Gettler *elementary education educator*

Central Islip
Gillespie, Eileen Rose *elementary education educator*
McGowan, Harold *real estate developer, investor, scientist, author, philanthropist*

Chappaqua
Brockway, George Pond *economist*
Cronin, Raymond Valentine *financial executive*
†Demuth, Joseph E. *physicist, research administrator*
George, Jean Craighead *author, illustrator*
Gstalder, Herbert William *publisher*
Harris, David Henry *retired life insurance company executive*
Laun, Louis Frederick *government official*
Lundberg, Ferdinand Edgar *author*
Maloney, John Frederick *marketing specialist*
O'Neill, Robert Charles *consultant, inventor*
Pomerene, James Herbert *retired computer engineer*
Stralem, Pierre *retired stockbroker*
Whittingham, Charles Arthur *library administrator, publisher*

Chestnut Ridge
Bickel, Henry Joseph *electronics company executive*
Day, Stacey Biswas *physician, educator*

Chittenango
Cassell, William Walter *retired accounting operations consultant*

Circleville
Hazan, Marcella Maddalena *author, educator, consultant*

Clarence
Greatbatch, Wilson *biomedical engineer*
Hubler, Julius *artist*
Mehaffy, Thomas N. *retired tire company executive*

Clearwater
Torell, John Raymond, III *banker*

Clifton Park
Farley, John Joseph *library science educator emeritus*
Favreau, Donald Francis *corporate executive*
Kleinschrod, Walter Andrew *publishing company executive, author, journalist*
Schmitt, Roland Walter *retired academic administrator*
Sharbaugh, Amandus Harry *electric company executive*

Climax
Adler, Lee *artist, educator, marketing executive*

Clinton
Anthony, Donald Charles *librarian, educator*
Blackwood, Russell Thorn, III *philosophy educator*
Couper, Richard Watrous *foundation executive, educator*
†Fuller, Ruthann *principal*
Ring, James Walter *physics educator*
Wagner, Frederick Reese *language professional*
Wertimer, Sidney *economics educator*

Cobleskill
Ingels, Jack Edward *horticulture educator*

Cold Spring
Brill, Ralph David *architect, real estate developer, venture capitalist*
Sherman, Suzette *interior design consultant*

Cold Spring Harbor
Freeman, Ira Henry *author, journalist*
Hargraves, Gordon Sellers *banker*
Huffman, Carol Koster *middle school educator*
Nightingale, Geoffrey Joseph *communications company executive, consultant*
Roberts, Francis Joy *educator, journalist*
Watson, James Dewey *molecular biologist, educator*
Wigler, Michael H. *molecular biologist*

Colton
Bulger, Dennis Bernard *military officer, engineer*

Commack
Nelson, Marvin Bernard *financial executive*
Seymour, John Herbert *computer technology analyst*

Conesus
Dadrian, Vahakn Norair *sociology educator*

Congers
Gussow, Alan *artist, sculptor*

Coopers Plains
Wilson, Louise Astell Morse *educator, home economist*

Cooperstown
Blumenstock, David Albert *retired surgeon*
Carew, Rodney Cline *batting coach, former professional baseball player*
Harman, Willard Nelson *malacologist, educator*
Hermann, William Henry *retired hospital administrator, consultant*
Jenkins, Ferguson Arthur, Jr. (Fergie Jenkins) *former baseball player*
MacLeish, Archibald Bruce *museum director*
†Pearson, Thomas Arthur *epidemiologist, educator*

Corning
Ahrens, Kent *museum director, art historian*
Behm, Forrest Edwin *glass manufacturing company executive*
Booth, Chesley Peter Washburn *glass products manufacturing company executive*
Buechner, Thomas Scharman *artist, retired glass manufacturing company executive, museum director*
Duke, David Allen *glass company executive*
Dulude, Richard *glass manufacturing company executive*
Ecklin, Robert Luther *glass company executive*
Flynn, James Leonard *manufacturing executive*
Houghton, James Richardson *glass manufacturing company executive*
Josbeno, Larry Joseph *physics educator*
Keck, Donald Bruce *physicist*
Maurer, Robert Distler *retired industrial physicist*
Meiling, Gerald Stewart *materials scientist*
Peck, Arthur John, Jr. *consumer products executive*
Spillman, Jane Shadel *curator, researcher, writer*
Stuart, Ben R. *manufacturing company executive*
Swindells, David W. *manufacturing executive*
Ughetta, William C. *glass works executive, lawyer*
Ughetta, William Casper *lawyer, manufacturing company executive*

Cornwall On Hudson
Weiss, Egon Arthur *retired library administrator*

Corona
†Jackson, Andrew Preston *library director*

Cortland
Anderson, Donna Kay *musicologist, educator*
Clark, James Milford *college president*
Kaminsky, Alice Richkin *English language educator*
Miller, John David *manufacturing company executive*
Zipp, Arden Peter *chemistry educator*

Cranberry Lake
Glavin, James Edward *landscape architect*

Cross River
Baxter, Bruce Osborne *hotel executive*
Smith, Lawrence Beall *artist*

Croton On Hudson
Adelson, Alexander M. *physicist*
Coleman, Earl Maxwell *publishing company executive*
Henderson, Harry Brinton, Jr. *author, editor*
Kahn, Roger *author*
Karales, James Harry *photojournalist*
Miranda, Robert Nicholas *publishing company executive*
Nelson, Charles Arthur *publisher, consultant*
Plotch, Walter *management consultant, fund raising counselor*
†Rubinfien, Leo H. *photographer, filmmaker*
Straka, Laszlo Richard *publishing consultant*

Cutchogue
Dank, Leonard Dewey *medical illustrator, audio-visual consultant*
O'Connell, Francis Joseph *lawyer, arbitrator*

Deer Park
Caputi, William James, Jr. *engineering company consultant*
Taub, Jesse J. *electrical engineering researcher*

Delhi
MacDonald, Robert Bruce *county official*

Delmar
Birdsey, Anna Campas *civil engineer, architect*
Button, Rena Pritsker *public relations company executive*
Mangouni, Norman *publisher*
Nitecki, Joseph Zbigniew *librarian*
Odenkirchen, Carl Josef *educator Romance languages and literatures*

Dix Hills
Fisher, Fenimore *business development consultant*
†Murphy, Edward J. *school system administrator*

Dobbs Ferry
Adler, Stephen Fred *chemical company executive*
Cohen, Philip Francis *publishing company executive*
Fritz, Jean Guttery *writer*
Grunebaum, Ernest Michael *investment banker*
Holtz, Sidney *publishing company executive*
Juettner, Diana D'Amico *lawyer, educator*
Kapp, Richard P. *conductor, arts administrator*
Levy, Alan Joseph *editor, journalist, writer*
Perelle, Ira B. *psychologist, educator*
Simon, Lothar *publishing company executive*
Sutton, Francis Xavier *social scientist, consultant*
†Triplett, Kelly B. *chemist*
Whiting, John Randolph *publisher, writer, editor*
†Wilcauskas, Eugene *chemicals executive*

Douglaston
Costa, Ernest Fiorenzo *graphic designer*

Dundee
Pfendt, Henry George *retired information systems executive, management consultant*

East Amherst
Bauer, Paul David *retired food service executive*
†Soong, Tsu-Teh *engineering science educator*

East Aurora
†Bingham, William *toy executive*
Hawk, George Wayne *electronics company executive*
†Hayes, Bonaventure Francis *priest*
Spahn, Mary Attea *retired education educator*
Weidemann, Julia Clark *principal, educator*
Woodard, Carol Jane *educational consultant*

East Berne
Grenander, M. E. *English language educator, critic*

East Garden City
Baker, J. A., II *pension architect and plan engineer*

East Hampton
Dalzell, Fred Briggs *consultant*
Damaz, Paul F. *architect*
De Bruhl, Arthur Marshall *writer, editor, publishing consultant*
Dello Joio, Norman *composer*
Garrett, Charles Geoffrey Blythe *physicist*
Ignatow, David *poet*
Jacobs, Helen Hull *writer*
Karp, Harvey Lawrence *electrical and metal products manufacturing company executive*
Lassaw, Ibram *sculptor, painter*
Munson, Lawrence Shipley *management consultant*
Paxton, Tom *songwriter, entertainer, author*
Praetorius, William Albert, Sr. *artist, former advertising and real estate executive*
Richenburg, Robert Bartlett *artist, retired art educator*
Stein, Ronald Jay *artist, airline transport pilot*

East Islip
Fleishman, Philip Robert *internist*

East Meadow
Adler, Ira Jay *lawyer*
Albert, Gerald *clinical psychologist*
Beyer, Norma Warren *educator*
†Freeman, Clifford Lee *advertising executive*
Rachlin, Stephen Leonard *psychiatrist*

East Northport
Hayo, George Edward *management consultant*
Reed, Robert Monroe *publishing executive*

East Patchogue
Metz, Donald Joseph *scientist*

East Rochester
Murray, James Doyle *accountant*

East Setauket
Duff, Ronald G. *research scientist*
†Englebright, Steven Cale *assemblyman*
Layton, Billy Jim *composer*
Thom, Joseph M. *librarian*

Eastchester
Keeffe, John Arthur *lawyer, director*

Eatons Neck
Altner, Peter Christian *orthopedic surgeon, medical educator*

Edmeston
Price, James Melford *physician*

Elizabethtown
Lawrence, Richard Wesley, Jr. *mining executive*

Ellenville
Baer, Albert Max *metal products executive*
Straus, R. Peter *communications company executive, broadcasting executive*

Elmhurst
†Wachsteter, George *illustrator*

Elmira
Burke, Rita Hoffmann *educational administrator*
Meier, Thomas Keith *college president, English educator*
Orsillo, James Edward *computer systems engineer, company executive*

Elmont
Cusack, Thomas Joseph *banker*
Pilkington, Frances Jean *secondary school educator*
Stephens, Woodford Cefis (Woody Stephens) *horse trainer, breeder*

Elmsford
Bostin, Marvin Jay *hospital and health services consultant*
Shaviv, Eddie *marketing and sales executive*

Endwell
Wagner, Peter Ewing *physics and electrical engineering educator*

Erieville
Snodgrass, W. D. *writer, educator*

Esopus
Tetlow, Edwin *author*

Fairport
Haylett, Margaret Wendy *television director, engineer*
Oldshue, James Y. *chemical engineering consultant*

Farmingdale
†Blum, Melvin *chemical company executive, researcher*
Bolle, Donald Martin *engineering educator*
Bongiorno, Joseph John, Jr. *electrical engineering educator*
Cipriani, Frank Anthony *college president*
Dordelman, William Forsyth *food company executive*
Engelhardt, Dean Lee *biotechnology company executive*
Guggenheimer, Heinrich Walter *mathematician, educator*
Horowitz, Sidney *corporation executive*
Klosner, Jerome Martin *applied mechanics educator*
Lamberg, Stanley Lawrence *medical technologist, educator*
LaTourrette, James Thomas *retired electrical engineering and computer science educator*
Lieu, Hou-Shun *economist, educator*
Marcuvitz, Nathan *electrophysics educator*
Marshall, Clifford Wallace *mathematics educator*
Nolan, Peter John *physics educator*
Shmoys, Jerry *electrical engineering educator*
Smith, Joseph Seton *electronics company executive, consultant*
Steckler, Larry *publisher, editor*

Fayetteville
Cantwell, John Dalzell, Jr. *management consultant*
Carlson, Russell Charles *banker*
Dosanjh, Darshan S(ingh) *aeronautical engineer, educator*
Evans, Nolly Seymour *lawyer*
Pachter, Irwin Jacob *pharmaceutical consultant*
Pulos, Arthur Jon *industrial design executive*
Sager, Roderick Cooper *retired life insurance company executive*
Sears, Bradford George *landscape architect*
Wallace, Spencer Miller, Jr. *hotel executive*

Feura Bush
Byrne, Donn Erwin *psychologist, educator*

Floral Park
Chatoff, Michael Alan *legal editor*
Corbett, William John *public relations consultant, lawyer*
†Moskowitz, Stanley Alan *financial executive*
†Scricca, Diane Bernadette *principal*
Weinrib, Sidney *retired optometric and optical products and services executive*

Florida
†Bronstein, David G. *food products executive*
†Koppele, Gary S. *food service executive*
Mench, John William *retail store executive, electrical engineer*

Flushing
†Albert, Gerald *sonar manufacturing company executive*
Allen, Ralph Gilmore *dramatist, producer, drama educator*
Birnstiel, Charles *consulting engineer*
Bonilla, Bobby (Roberto Martin Antonio Bonilla) *baseball player*
Boylan, Elizabeth Shippee *biology educator, academic administrator*
Bruder, Harold Jacob *artist, educator*
Brush, George W. *college president*
Carlson, Cynthia Joanne *artist, educator*
Carlton, Doreen Charlotte *special education supervisor and administrator*
Cashen, J. Frank *professional baseball team executive*
Cathcart, Robert Stephen *mass media consultant*
Commoner, Barry *biologist, educator*
Diehl, Stephen Anthony *banker*
Doubleday, Nelson *professional baseball team executive*
Dumaresq, John Edward *lawyer*
Fichtel, Rudolph Robert *retired association executive*
Finks, Robert Melvin *paleontologist, educator*
Friedman, Alan Jacob *museum director*
Gafney, Harry D. *chemistry educator*
Goldman, Norman Lewis *chemistry educator*
Goldsmith, Howard *writer, consultant*
Gooden, Dwight Eugene *professional baseball player*
Green, Dallas (George Dallas Green) *professional baseball team manager*
Hacker, Andrew *political science educator*
Hatcher, Robert Douglas *physicist, educator*
Henshel, Harry Bulova *watch manufacturer*
Hirshson, Stanley Philip *history educator*
Hoffman, Merle Holly *political activist, social psychologist, author*
Hyman, Milton *dental educator*
Johnson, Howard Michael *baseball player*
Johnson, Thomas Stephen *banker*
Kaplan, Stephen *parapsychologist*
Kenny, Shirley Strum *college administrator*
Kiner, Ralph McPherran *sports commentator, former baseball player*
Laderman, Gabriel *artist*
Lamont, Rosette Clementine *Romance languages educator, theatre journalist, translator*
Madden, Joseph Daniel *trade association executive*
Mendelson, Elliott *mathematician, educator*
Moriarty, Michael *actor*
Nelson, Ralph Lowell *economics educator*
Parmet, Herbert Samuel *historian, educator*
Patai, Raphael *former anthropology educator*
Peirce, George Leighton *airport administrator*
Psomiades, Harry John *political science educator*
Rabassa, Gregory *Romance languages educator, translator*
Rafanelli, Kenneth Robert *physics educator*
†Ryan, William R. *mechanical engineer*
Saberhagen, Bret *professional baseball player*
Schere, Jonathan Lawrence *aerospace and electronics company executive*
Schnall, Edith Lea (Mrs. Herbert Schnall) *microbiologist, educator*
Silver, Jonathan *lawyer*
†Smaldone, Edward Michael *composer*
Speidel, David Harold *geology educator*
†Strevey, Tracy Elmer, Jr. *army officer, surgeon*
Sutherland, Alan Roy *association executive*
Tytell, John *English educator, writer*
†Vasilachi, Vasile *priest, vicar*
Wolz, Henry George *philosophy educator*

Fly Creek
Dusenbery, Walter Condit *sculptor*

Forest Hills
Callo, Joseph Francis *marketing and corporate communications consultant*
Crystal, Boris *artist*
Gayner, Esther K. *artist*
LeFrak, Richard Stone *real estate developer*
Levine, Charles Michael *publishing company executive, consultant*
Lipkin, Seymour *pianist, conductor, educator*
Miller, Donald Ross *management consultant*
Phelan, Arthur Joseph *financial executive*
Polakoff, Abe *baritone*
Prager, Alice Heinecke *music company executive*
Silver, Sheila Jane *composer, music educator*
Stinson, Richard James *editor*
Tewi, Thea *sculptor*

Fort Covington
Dunwich, Gerina *magazine editor, author*

Franklin Square
Indiviglia, Salvatore Joseph *artist, retired naval officer*

Fredonia
Barnard, Walther M. *geosciences educator*
Benton, Allen Haydon *biology educator*
Dowd, Morgan Daniel *political science educator*
Fries, Maureen Holmberg *English literature educator*
Jordan, Robert *concert pianist, educator*
MacPhee, Donald Albert *academic administrator*
Mac Vittie, Robert William *retired college administrator*
Sonnenfeld, Marion *linguist, educator*

Freeport
Antoine, Yvetot Marc *university director*
Landsberg, Jerry *management and investment consultant, optical laboratory executive*
Pullman, Maynard Edward *biochemist*

Fresh Meadows
Ganz, Samuel *human resource and management professional*

Friendship
Kingdon, Mary Oneida Grace *elementary education educator*

Fulton
Long, Robert Emmet *author*

Garden City
Accordino, Frank Joseph *architect, car rental company executive*
Conlon, Thomas James *marketing executive*
Cook, George Valentine *lawyer*
Corsi, Philip Donald *lawyer*
Crom, James Oliver *professional training company executive*
Desch, Carl William *banker, consultant*
Diamandopoulos, Peter *philosopher, educator*
Doucette, Mary-Alyce *computer company executive*
Fishberg, Gerard *lawyer*
Fleisig, Ross *aeronautical engineer, engineering manager*
†Fristedt, Hans *manufacturing company executive*
†Glass, Arthur *mining company executive*
Golden, Christopher Anthony *lawyer*
Gordon, Barry Joel *investment advisor*
Gordon, Jay F(isher) *lawyer*
Guttenplan, Harold Esau *food company executive*
Harr, Alma Elizabeth Tagliabue *nursing educator*
Jenkins, Kenneth Vincent *literature educator, writer*
Larocca, James Lawrence *lawyer*
†Larsson, Hans Lennart *match company executive*
Lioz, Lawrence Stephen *lawyer, accountant*
Lovely, Thomas Dixon *banker*
McNicholas, David Paul *automobile rental company executive*
Minicucci, Richard Francis *lawyer, former hospital administrator*
Nicklin, George Leslie, Jr. *psychoanalyst, educator, physician*
Ohrenstein, Roman Abraham *economics educator, economist, rabbi*
Olcott, William Alfred *magazine editor*
Roche, John Edward *human resources management consultant*
Schenck, Andrew Craig *conductor, music director*
Shneidman, J. Lee *historian, educator*
Tucker, William Philip *lawyer, writer*
Vigilante, Joseph Louis *social worker, social policy educator*
Vittoria, Joseph V. *car rental company executive*
Webb, Igor Michael *university administrator*
Westermann, David *lawyer, educator, electronics industry executive*
Williams, Irving Laurence *physics educator*
Zirkel, Gene *computer science educator and mathematics*

Gardiner
Mabee, Carleton *historian, educator*

Garrison
Chasins, Edward A. *communications company executive*
Egan, Daniel Francis *priest*
†Grossman, Allen *educational administrator*
Pierpont, Robert *fund raising executive, consultant*

Geneseo
Battersby, Harold Ronald *anthropologist, archaeologist, linguist*
Edgar, William John *philosophy educator*
Fausold, Martin Luther *history educator*
Forest, Herman Silva *biology educator*
Harter, Carol Clancey *university president, English language educator*
Hickman, John Hampton, III *entrepreneurial investment banker, industrialist, educator*
Small, William Andrew *mathematics educator*

Geneva
Berta, Joseph Michel *music educator, musician*
Caponegro, Mary *English language educator*
Hersh, Richard H. *academic administrator*
Roelofs, Wendell Lee *biochemistry educator, consultant*
Siebert, Karl Joseph *food science educator, consultant*
†Wilcox, Wayne F. *plant pathologist, educator, researcher*

Germantown
Rollins, (Theodore) Sonny *composer, musician*

Gilbertsville
Roos, Casper *actor*

Glen Cove
Conti, James Joseph *chemical engineer, educator*
Dehn, Joseph William, Jr. *chemist*
Deming, Donald Livingston *lawyer*
Greenberg, Allan *advertising and marketing research consultant*
Maxwell, J. Douglas, Jr. *chemical service company executive*
Mills, Charles Gardner *lawyer*

Glen Head
†Boyrer, Elaine M. *principal*
Sutherland, Donald James *investment company executive*

Glendale
Hess, Karsten *trading company executive*

Glenham
Douglas, Fred Robert *cost engineering consultant*

Glenmont
Block, Murray Harold *educational consultant*
Kolb, Lawrence Coleman *psychiatrist*
†Robillard, Donald J. *elementary school principal*

Glens Falls
Bartlett, Richard James *lawyer, former university dean*
Bitner, William Lawrence, III *banker, educator*
†Malkki, Olli *paper company executive*

Glenville
Anderson, Roy Everett *electrical engineering consultant*

Goshen
Goodreds, John Stanton *newspaper publisher*

Grand Island
†Fujita, Peter Kozo *tire manufacturing executive*
Rader, Charles George *chemical company executive*
White, Ralph David *retired editor and writer*

Great Neck
Arlow, Jacob A. *psychiatrist, educator*
Brand, Oscar *folksinger, author, educator*
Busner, Philip H. *lawyer, arbitrator, judge*
Donenfeld, Kenneth Jay *management consultant*
Elkowitz, Lloyd Kent *dental anesthesiologist, dentist, pharmacist*
Fialkov, Herman *investment banker*
Fiel, Maxine Lucille *journalist, behavioral analyst, lecturer*
Friedland, Louis N. *retired communications executive*
Gellman, Yale H. *lawyer*
Glushien, Morris P. *lawyer, arbitrator*
Goldberg, Melvin Arthur *communications executive*
Hamovitch, William *economist, educator, university official*
Hampton, Benjamin Bertram *brokerage house executive*
Hurwitz, Johanna (Frank) *author, librarian*
Joskow, Jules *economic research company executive*
Katz, Edward Morris *banker*
Kraft, Leo Abraham *composer*
Lampel, Ronald B. *human resources executive*
Lees, Benjamin *composer*
Longobardo, Anna Kazanjian *mechanical engineer*
Machiz, Leon *electronic equipment manufacturing executive*
Mc Quade, Walter *author*
Panes, Jack Samuel *publishing company executive*
Pohl, Gunther Erich *retired library administrator*
Pollack, Paul Robert *airline service company executive*
Reich, Pauline Carole *international business consultant, author*
Roth, Harvey Paul *publisher*
Rubin, Irving *editor*
†Rubin, Michael *accountant, finance company executive*
Satinskas, Henry Anthony *airline services company executive*
Seidler, Doris *artist*
Shaffer, Bernard William *mechanical and aerospace engineering educator*
Simon, Arthur *pharmacologist, research laboratory executive*
†Spielman, Harold M. *marketing professional*
Velie, Lester *journalist*
Wachsman, Harvey Frederick *lawyer, neurosurgeon*
Wank, Gerald Sidney *periodontist*

Greece
†Ryan-Johnson, Deborah *principal*

Greene
Raymond, George Gamble, Jr. *material handling equipment company executive*
Sternberg, Paul J. *lawyer*

Greenfield Center
Conant, Robert Scott *harpsichordist, music educator*
Templin, John Leon, Jr. *healthcare consulting executive*

Greenlawn
Bachman, Henry Lee *electrical engineer, engineering executive*
Stevens, John Richard *architectural historian*

Greenport
†Breeze, Roger Gerrard *federal agency administrator*
Mebus, Charles Albert *veterinarian*

Greenvale
Araoz, Daniel Leon *psychologist, educator*
Cook, Edward Joseph *college president*
Gillespie, John Thomas *university administrator*
Halper, Emanuel B(arry) *real estate lawyer, developer, consultant, author*
Leipzig, Arthur *photographer, educator emeritus*
Pall, David B. *manufacturing company executive, chemist*
Soreff, Stephen Mayer *artist*
Steinberg, David Joel *academic administrator, historian, educator*
†Webel, Richard Karl *landscape architect*

Greenwood
Rollins, June Elizabeth *elementary education educator*

Griffiss A F B
Diamond, Fred I. *electronic engineer*

Guilderland
Gordon, Leonard Victor *psychologist, educator emeritus*
†Nordley, Gerald David *writer, investor*
Persico, Joseph Edward *author*

Hadley
Gray-Aldrich, Gretchen Elise *state agency administrator, nursing educator*

Hamburg
Killeen, Henry Walter *lawyer*

Hamilton
Bergen, Daniel Patrick *librarian, retired educator*
Berlind, Bruce Peter *poet, educator*
Blackton, Charles S(tuart) *history educator*
Busch, Briton Cooper *historian*
Busch, Frederick Matthew *writer, literature educator*
Cochran, John Charles *chemistry educator*
Edmonston, William Edward, Jr. *publisher*
Farnsworth, Frank Albert *economics educator*
Hathaway, Robert Lawton *Romance languages educator*
Holbrow, Charles Howard *physicist, educator*
Jones, Frank William *language educator*
Jones, Howard Langworthy *educational administrator, consultant*
Kessler, Dietrich *biology educator*
Linsley, Robert Martin *geology educator*
Noyes, Judith Gibson *library director*
Pownall, Malcolm Wilmor *mathematics educator*
Van Schaack, Eric *art historian, educator*

Hammond
Musselman, Francis Haas *lawyer*

Hampton Bays
Yavitz, Boris *business educator and dean emeritus*

Hancock
DeLuca, Ronald *consultant, former advertising agency executive*

Harrison
Fuchs, Hanno *communications consultant*
McCaffrey, Neil *publishing executive*
Serenbetz, Warren Lewis *financial management company executive*
Wadsworth, Frank Whittemore *educator*

Hartsdale
Carroll, Albert *corporate executive*
Katz, John *investment banker, business consultant, lawyer*

Hastings On Hudson
Clark, Kenneth Bancroft *psychologist, educator*
Shillinglaw, Gordon *accounting educator, consultant, writer*
†Weinstein, Edward Michael *architect, consultant*
Wolfe, Stanley *composer, educator*

Hauppauge
Arams, Frank Robert *electronics company executive*
Cohen, Martin Gilbert *physicist*
Hausman, Howard *electronics executive*
†Hershberg, David E. *communications corporation executive*
Hurley, Denis R. *federal judge*
Jordan, David Francis, Jr. *retired lawyer*
†Miller, Kenneth Allen *electrical engineer*
Miller, Ronald M. *manufacturing executive*
Oschmann, Joan Edythe *gifted and elementary education educator*
Reis, Don *publishing executive*
†Shalam, John Joseph *car stereo and cellular telephone company executive*
†Stoehr, Charles Michael *financial executive*
Wang, Charles B. *computer software company executive*
Wexler, Leonard D. *federal judge*
†Wheatley, George Milholland *medical administrator*

Hawthorne
Kane, James Golden *banker*
†Koffler, Richard Max *publishing company executive, author, translator*
McConnell, John Edward *electrical engineer, company executive*
†Olson, William Furman *bank executive, lawyer*
Press, Jeffery Bruce *chemist*
Sandbank, Henry *photographer, film director*
†Scheffler, Eckart Arthur *publisher*
Swift, Michael Ronald *physician, scientist, educator*

Hempstead
Adams, Robert Hugo *business news publisher, English teacher*
Agata, Burton C. *lawyer, educator*
Altimari, Frank X. *federal judge*
Andrews, Charles Rolland *library administrator*
Berliner, Herman Albert *university provost and dean, economics educator*
Block, Jules Richard *psychologist, educator, university official*
†Carroll, Pete *professional football coach*
Chapman, Lenora Rosamond *social service organization director*
Chapman, Ronald Thomas *musician, educator*
Coslet, Bruce N. *professional football coach*
Esiason, Boomer (Norman Julius Esiason) *professional football player*
Freedman, Monroe Henry *lawyer, educator*
Goldstein, Stanley Philip *engineering educator*
Gutman, Steve *professional football team executive*
Hassett, Carol Alice *psychologist*
Haynes, Ulric St. Clair, Jr. *academic dean*
Hijuelos, Oscar *novelist*
Laano, Archie Bienvenido Maaño *cardiologist*
†Lewis, Mo *professional football player*
Lott, Ronnie (Ronald Mandel Lott) *professional football player*
†Lowery, Dominic Gerald (Nick) *professional football player*
Mahon, Malachy Thomas *lawyer, educator*
Maier, Henry B. *environmental engineer*
Masheck, Joseph Daniel *art critic, educator*
Mayer, Carl Joseph *law educator*
†Meola, Tony *professional football player, former professional soccer player*
Monk, Art *football player*
Montana, Patrick Joseph *management educator*
Pell, Arthur Robert *human resources development consultant, author*
Regan, John J. *law educator*
Shuart, James Martin *university president*
Sparberg, Esther B. *chemist, educator*
Steinberg, Dick *professional football team executive*
Turgeon, Edgar Lynn *economics educator*
Wattel, Harold Louis *economics educator*

Henrietta
Carmel, Simon J(acob) *anthropologist*
Snyder, Donald Edward *corporate lawyer*

Herkimer
Mitchell, Donald J. *former congressman*

Hewlett
Dalrymple, Richard William *banker*
Kislik, Louis A. *marketing company executive*
Large, James Mifflin, Jr. *banker*
Sickle, Cody T. *banker*

Hicksville
Kneitel, Thomas Stephen *writer, consultant, editor*
Salsberg, Arthur Philip *publishing company executive*
Tinghitella, Stephen *publishing company executive*
Walsh, Charles Richard *banker*

Hillsdale
Richards, Joseph Edward *artist*

Holbrook
Lissman, Barry Alan *veterinarian*

Holland
Blair, Robert Noel *artist*

Holland Patent
Giacobbe, Anna Gretchen Steinhauer *elementary education educator*

Hollis
†Vai, Steve *guitarist*

Homer
Gustafson, John Alfred *biology educator*

Hoosick Falls
Dodge, Cleveland Earl, Jr. *manufacturing executive*
Hatfield, David Underhill *artist*

Hopewell Junction
Walden, Stanley Eugene *composer, clarinetist*

Horseheads
Cusimano, Adeline Mary *educational administrator*
Slade, Paul Graham *physicist*

Houghton
Chamberlain, Daniel Robert *college president*
Luckey, Robert Reuel Raphael *retired academic administrator*

Howard Beach
Berliner, Patricia Mary *psychologist*

Hudson
Avedisian, Edward *artist*

Hudson Falls
Bronk, William *writer, retail businessman*

Huntington
Augello, William Joseph *lawyer*
Bendiner, Robert *writer, editor*
Christiansen, Donald David *editor, publisher, electrical engineer*
Connor, J. Robert *editor*
Coraor, John Edward *museum director*
D'Addario, Alice Marie *school administrator*
Hayden, Ralph Frederick *accountant, financial consultant*
Holahan, Richard Vincent *former magazine and book publisher*
Jackson, Richard Montgomery *former airline executive*
†Jordan, Daniel Patrick, Jr. *law librarian*
†Mara, John Lawrence *veterinarian, consultant*
Mead, Lawrence Myers, Jr. *retired aerospace executive*
Munson, Nancy Kay *lawyer*
Noll, Anna Cecilia *curator*
Papoulis, Athanasios *electrical engineering educator*
Ponton, Richard Edward *business consultant*
Twardowicz, Stanley Jan *artist, photographer*

Huntington Bay
Schulz, William Frederick *human rights association executive*

Huntington Station
Agosta, Vito *mechanical/aerospace engineering educator*
Barron, Barbara Marilyn *fibre artist*
Braun, Ludwig *educational technology consultant*
Herz, Leonard *financial consultant*
Lanzano, Ralph Eugene *civil engineer*
†Liguori, Frank Nickolas *temporary personnel company executive*
Pierce, Charles R. *electric company consultant*
†Schell, Jonathan Edward *writer*
Schoenfeld, Michael P. *lawyer*
†Tollerson, Ernest *newspaper editor*

Hyde Park
Newton, Verne Wester *library director*

Interlaken
Bleiler, Everett Franklin *writer, publishing company executive*

Irvington
Devons, Samuel *educator, physicist*
Holden, Donald *author, artist*
Lugenbeel, Edward Elmer *publisher*
Marshall, J(ulian) Howard, Jr. *lawyer*
Massie, Robert Kinloch *author*
Stimpson, John Hallowell *insurance company executive*
Turk, Stanley Martin *advertising agency executive*
Wolf, Eric Robert *anthropologist, educator*

Ithaca
Abrams, Meyer Howard *English language educator*
Adler, Kraig (Kerr) *biology educator*
Alexander, Gregory Stewart *law educator*
Alexander, Martin *microbiology educator, researcher*
Allee, David Jepson *economics educator*
Ammons, Archie Randolph *poet, English educator*
Ascher, Robert *anthropologist, archaeologist, educator, filmmaker*
Ashcroft, Neil William *physics educator, researcher*
Bail, Joe Paul *agricultural educator emeritus*
Ballantyne, Joseph Merrill *science educator, program administrator, researcher*
Barcelo, John James, III *law educator*
Barney, John Charles *lawyer*
Bassett, William Akers *geologist, educator*
Bates, David Martin *botanist, educator*
Batterman, Boris William *physicist, educator, academic director*
†Bauer, Simon Harvey *chemistry educator*
Bauman, Dale Elton *nutritional biochemistry educator*
Ben Daniel, David Jacob *entrepreneurship educator, consultant*
Berger, Toby *electrical engineer*
Berkelman, Karl *physics educator*
Bethe, Hans Albrecht *physicist, educator*
Bird, John Malcolm *geologist*
Blackler, Antonie William Charles *biologist*
Blau, Francine Dee *economics educator*
Booker, John Franklin *mechanical engineer, educator*
Bourne, Russell *publisher, author*
Bramble, James Henry *mathematician, educator*
Brazell, Karen Woodard *Japanese literature educator*
Briggs, Vernon Mason, Jr. *economics educator*
Bronfenbrenner, Urie *psychologist*
Brown, Theodore Morey *art history educator*
Brunk, Max Edwin *marketing educator emeritus*
Burns, Joseph Arthur *planetary science educator*
Call, David Lincoln *agricultural economics educator, administrator*
Caputi, Anthony *comparative literature educator*
Carlin, Herbert J. *electrical engineering educator, researcher*
†Carpenter, Barry Keith *chemistry educator, researcher*
Clark, David Delano *physicist, educator*
Clermont, Kevin Michael *law educator*
†Coffman, William Ronnie *plant breeding educator*
Colby-Hall, Alice Mary *Romance studies educator*
Conklin, Gordon Leroy *retired editor*
Conway, Richard Walter *computer scientist, educator*
Cooke, William Donald *university administrator, chemistry educator*
Corson, Dale Raymond *retired university president, physicist*
Cotton, Dorothy Foreman *former director student activities, consultant*
Craft, Harold Dumont, Jr. *university official, radio astronomer*
†Craighead, Harold G. *physics educator*
Cramton, Roger Conant *lawyer, legal educator*
†Crepet, William Louis *botanist, educator*
Culler, Jonathan Dwight *English language educator*
Dalman, Gisli Conrad *electrical engineering educator*
Darlington, Richard Benjamin *psychology educator*
Davies, Peter John *plant physiology educator, researcher*
De Boer, Pieter Cornelis Tobias *mechanical and aerospace engineering educator*
Dick, Richard Irwin *environmental engineer, educator*
†Di Salvo, Francis Joseph, Jr. *chemistry educator*
Dobson, Alan *veterinary physiology educator*
Dodd, Jack Gordon, Jr. *physicist, educator*
Dworsky, Leonard B. *civil and environmental engineer, educator*
Dyckman, Thomas Richard *accounting educator*
Earle, Clifford John, Jr. *mathematician*
Easley, David *economics educator*
Eastman, Lester Fuess *electrical engineer, educator*
Eddy, Donald Davis *English language educator*
Eisenberg, Theodore *law educator*
Eisner, Thomas *biologist, educator*
Elledge, Scott Bowen *language professional, educator*
Farley, Daniel W. *lawyer, utility company executive*
Fay, Robert Clinton *chemist, educator*
Fick, Gary Warren *agronomy educator, forage crops researcher*
Finch, C. Herbert *archivist, library administrator, historian*
Fine, Terrence Leon *electrical engineering and statistics educator*
Firebaugh, Francille Maloch *university official*
Fireside, Harvey Francis *political scientist, educator*
Fitchen, Douglas Beach *physicist, educator*
Fleischmann, Hans Hermann Paul *physics educator*
Foote, Robert Hutchinson *animal physiology educator*
Forker, Olan Dean *agricultural economics educator*
Fox, Francis Henry *veterinarian*
†Fréchet, Jean Marie Joseph *chemistry educator*
Freed, Jack Herschel *chemist, educator*
†Fuchs, Wolfgang Heinrich *mathematics educator*
Geller, A. Neal *business educator, financial consultant*
George, Albert Richard *aerospace and mechanical engineering educator*
Gibian, George *Russian and comparative literature educator*
Gibson, Quentin Howieson *biochemist*
†Gierasch, Peter Jay *astronomy educator*
†Gilbert, Robert Owen *veterinary educator, researcher*
Gillespie, James Howard *veterinary microbiologist, educator*
Gilman, Sander Lawrence *German educator*
Giovanelli, Riccardo *astronomer*
Glock, Marvin David *retired psychology educator*
†Gold, Daniel *religious studies educator*
Gold, Thomas *astronomer, educator*
Goldsmith, Paul Felix *physics and astronomy educator*
Gottfried, Kurt *physicist, educator*
Greisen, Kenneth Ingvard *physicist, emeritus educator*
Gries, David Joseph *computer science researcher, educator*
Grippi, Salvatore William *artist*
Groos, Arthur Bernhard, Jr. *German literature educator*
Grunes, David Leon *research soil scientist, educator, editor*
Gubbins, Keith Edmund *chemical engineering educator*
Habicht, Jean-Pierre *public health researcher, educator, consultant*
Halpern, Bruce Peter *physiologist, consultant*
Hammond, Jane Laura *retired law librarian, lawyer*
Hardy, Ralph W. F. *biochemist, biotechnology executive*
†Hardy, W. F. *botary administrator*
†Hart, Edward Walter *physicist*
Hartmanis, Juris *computer scientist, educator*
Hatcher, Allen Edward *mathematician, educator*
Haynes, Martha Patricia *astronomer*
Hess, George Paul *biochemist, educator*
Hockett, Charles Francis *anthropology educator*
†Hoffman, Lawrence *architect*
Hoffmann, Roald *chemist, educator*
Hohendahl, Peter Uwe *German language and literature educator*
Holcomb, Donald Frank *physicist, academic administrator*
†Hopcroft, John Edward *dean, computer science educator*
Hsu, John Tseng Hsin *music educator, cellist, gambist, barytonist, conductor*
†Hubbard, John Hamal *mathematician, educator*
Husa, Karel Jaroslav *composer, conductor, educator*
†Isaacson, Michael Saul *physics educator, researcher*
†Isard, Walter *economics educator*
Isen, Alice M. *experimental social psychologist, behavioral science educator*
Jagendorf, Andre Tridon *plant physiologist*
Jarrow, Robert Alan *finance and economics educator, consultant*
Jones, Barclay Gibbs *regional economics researcher*
Kahin, George McTurnan *political science and history educator*
Kahn, Alfred Edward *economist, educator, government official*
Kallfelz, Francis A. *veterinary medicine educator*
†Kalos, Malvin Howard *university researcher, educator, and administrator*
Kammen, Michael *historian, educator*
Katz, Steven Theodore *religious educator*
Kendler, Bernhard *editor*
Kennedy, Kenneth Adrian Raine *biological anthropologist, forensic anthropologist*
Kennedy, Wilbert Keith, Sr. *agronomy educator, retired university official*
Kent, Robert Brydon *law educator*
Kingsbury, John Merriam *botanist, educator*
Kirsch, A(nthony) Thomas *anthropology and Asian studies educator, researcher*
Kollias, George Van, Jr. *veterinary educator, researcher, clinician*
Kosikowski, Frank Vincent *food scientist, educator*
Kramer, Edward John *materials science and engineering educator*
Kramer, John Paul *entomologist, educator*
Kramnick, Isaac *government educator*
Kronik, John William *Romance studies educator*
Kubota, Joe *soil scientist*
LaCapra, Dominick Charles *historian*
LaFeber, Walter Frederick *history educator, author*
Lambert, William Wilson *psychology educator*
Ledford, Richard Allison *food science educator, food microbiologist*
Lee, David Morris *physics educator*
Leibovich, Sidney *engineering educator*
Lengemann, Frederick William *physiology educator, scientist*
Liboff, Richard Lawrence *physicist, educator*
Longin, Thomas Charles *academic administrator*
Loucks, Daniel Peter *environmental systems engineer*
Lowi, Theodore J(ay) *political science educator*
Lumley, John Leask *physicist, educator*
Lurie, Alison *author*
Lynn, Walter Royal *civil engineering educator, university administrator*
Lyons, David Barry *philosophy and law educator*
†Lyons, Thomas Patrick *economics educator*
Maas, James Beryl *psychology educator, lecturer, filmmaker*
Martin, Peter William *lawyer, educator*
Maxwell, William Laughlin *industrial engineering educator*
McConkey, James Rodney *English educator, writer*
McDaniel, Boyce Dawkins *physicist, educator*
†Mc Guire, William *civil engineer, educator*
McIsaac, Paul Rowley *electrical engineer, educator*
McLafferty, Fred Warren *chemist, educator*
†McMurry, John Edward *chemistry educator*
Meinwald, Jerrold *chemist, educator*
Mermin, N. David *physicist, educator, essayist*
Merten, Alan Gilbert *university dean*
Meyburg, Arnim Hans *transportation engineer, educator, consultant*
Mikus, Eleanore Ann *artist*
Miller, J(ames) Gormly *retired librarian, educator*
Moore, Norman Slawson *physician*
Morrison, George Harold *chemist, educator*
Mortlock, Robert Paul *microbiologist, educator*
Mueller, Betty Jeanne *social work educator*
Murra, John Victor *anthropologist, educator*
Nation, John Arthur *electrical engineering educator, researcher*
Nerode, Anil *mathematician, educator*
†Nesheim, Malden C. *university administrator*

Norton, Mary Beth history educator, author
Novak, Joseph Donald science educator, knowlege studies specialist
Oblak, John Byron academic administrator
Oglesby, Ray Thurmond aquatic science educator
Oliver, Jack Ertle geophysicist
Orear, Jay physics educator, researcher
O'Rourke, Thomas Denis civil engineer, educator
Osgood, Russell King law educator
†Park, Roy Hampton, Jr. advertising media executive
†Parks, Thomas W. electrical engineering educator, consultant
Parsons, Kermit Carlyle urban planning educator, former university dean
Payne, Lawrence Edward mathematics educator
Pearson, Oscar Harris plant breeder, geneticist
Phelan, Richard Magruder mechanical engineer
Phemister, Robert David college dean
Pimentel, David entomologist, educator
Plaisted, Robert Leroy plant breeder, educator
Pohl, Robert Otto physics educator
Polenberg, Richard history educator
Poleskie, Stephen Francis artist, educator
Pope, Stephen Bailey engineering educator
Poppensiek, George Charles veterinary scientist, educator
Porte, Joel Miles English educator
Radzinowicz, Mary Ann language educator
Rehkugler, Gerald Edwin agricultural engineering educator, consultant
Reppy, John David, Jr. physicist
Rhodes, Frank Harold Trevor university president, geologist
†Rhodin, Thor Nathaniel educational administrator
Roberts, E. F. lawyer, educator
Robinson, Franklin Westcott museum director, art historian
Rodríguez, Ferdinand chemical engineer, educator
Rosenberg, Edgar English and comparative literature educator
Rossi, Faust F. lawyer, educator
Rossiter, Margaret Walsh history of science educator
Ruoff, Arthur Louis physicist, educator
Sagan, Carl Edward astronomer, educator, author
Salpeter, Edwin Ernest physical sciences educator
Salton, Gerard computer science educator
Saltzman, Sidney city and regional planning educator
Scheraga, Harold Abraham physical chemistry educator
Schlafer, Donald Hughes veterinary pathologist
Schwartz, Donald Franklin communication educator
†Scott, Fredric Winthrop veterinarian
Scott, Norman Roy academic administrator, agricultural engineering educator
Seeley, Harry Wilbur, Jr. microbiology educator
Seibert, Mary Lee college official
Shell, Karl economics educator
†Shen, Shan-Fu aeronautical engineering educator, consultant
Shoemaker, Sydney S. philosophy educator
Shore, Richard Arnold mathematics educator
Shuler, Michael Louis biochemical engineering educator, consultant
†Sievers, Albert John, III physics educator
Silbey, Joel Henry history educator
Sims, William Riley, Jr. design and facility management educator, consultant
Simson, Gary Joseph law educator
Skipper, James Everett librarian
Slate, Floyd Owen chemist, materials scientist, civil engineer, educator, researcher
Smith, Julian Cleveland, Jr. chemical engineering educator
Smith, Robert John anthropology educator
Smith, Robert Samuel banker, former agricultural finance educator
Squier, Jack Leslie sculptor, educator
Stamp, Neal Roger lawyer
†Staples, Richard Cromwell microbiologist, researcher
Streett, William Bernard university dean, engineering educator
Strout, Sewall Cushing, Jr. humanities educator
Stycos, Joseph Mayone demographer, educator
Sudan, Ravindra Nath electrical engineer, physicist, educator
Terzian, Yervant astronomy and astrophysics educator
Thaler, Richard H. economics educator
Thomas, J. Earl physicist
†Thomas, Wright Moore communications executive
Thorbecke, Erik economics educator
Thorp, James Shelby electrical engineering educator
†Tigner, Maurice physicist, educator
Tomek, William Goodrich agricultural economist
†Trautmann, Charles Home museum director, civil engineer
†Trotter, Leslie Earl operations research educator, consultant
Turcotte, Donald Lawson geophysical sciences educator
Tynes, Theodore Archibald school administrator
†Van Campen, Darrell Robert chemist
Vanek, Jaroslav economist, educator
Van Houtte, Raymond A. financial executive
Walcott, Charles ornithology laboratory administrator
†Wang, Kuo-King manufacturing engineer, educator
Wasserman, Robert Harold biology educator
Webb, Watt Wetmore physicist, educator
Welch, Ross Maynard plant physiologist, researcher, educator
Whalen, James Joseph college president
Whitaker, Susanne Kanis veterinary medical librarian
White, Richard Norman civil and environmental engineering educator
Whyte, William Foote industrial relations educator, author
Widom, Benjamin chemistry educator
Wiesenfeld, John Richard chemistry educator
Williams, Leslie Pearce history educator
Williams, Robin Murphy, Jr. sociology educator
Wilson, Robert Rathbun retired physicist
Windmuller, John Philip industrial relations educator, consultant
Wolf, Edward Dean electrical engineering educator
Wolfram, Charles William law educator
Wu, Ray Jui biochemistry educator
Wyatt, David Kent history educator
Zall, Robert Rouben food scientist, educator
Zilversmit, Donald Berthold nutritional biochemist, educator

Jackson Heights
Kanidinc, Salahattin graphic artist, consultant art director
Schiavina, Laura Margaret artist
Sklar, Morty E. publisher, editor

Jamaica
Aiken, William accountant
Angione, Howard Francis lawyer, editor
Bartilucci, Andrew Joseph university administrator
Beard, Joseph James law educator
Cade, Walter, III artist, musician, singer, actor
†Clemmons, Ithiel bishop
Conway, Alvin James hospital administrator
Cooke, Constance Blandy librarian
Crivelli, Joseph Louis security specialist
Desser, Maxwell Milton art director, filmstrip producer
Fay, Thomas A. philosopher, educator
Geffner, Donna Sue speech pathologist, audiologist
Greenberg, Jacob biochemist, educator, consultant
†Hammer, Deborah Marie librarian
Harmond, Richard Peter educator
Harrington, Donald James university president
Hoppe, Charles W. railroad company executive
†Lengyel, István chemist, educator
Mc Kinnon, Clinton Dan aerospace transportation executive
Paolucci, Anne Attura playwright, poet, English and comparative literature educator
Re, Edward D. law educator, retired federal judge
Rosner, Fred physician, educator
Rowe, Richard Lloyd aviation executive, management consultant
Seltzer, Vicki Lynn obstetrician-gynecologist
†Tschinkel, Andrew Joseph, Jr. law librarian
Vasilopoulos, Athanasios V. engineering educator

Jamestown
Anderson, R. Quintus diversified company executive
Bargar, Robert Sellstrom investor
Benke, Paul Arthur college president
Bush, Paul Stanley furniture company executive
Goldman, Simon broadcasting executive
†Hauck, Donald F. business executive
Idzik, Martin Francis lawyer
Okwumabua, Benjamin Nkem corporate executive

Jamesville
DeCrow, Karen lawyer, author, lecturer
George, Earl composer, conductor, critic
Levy, George Charles chemistry educator, corporate executive
Mazer, Norma Fox writer

Jeffersonville
Craft, Douglas Durwood artist
Harms, Elizabeth Louise artist

Jericho
Astuto, Philip Louis retired Spanish educator
Axinn, Donald Everett real estate investor, developer
Berger, Charles Martin food company executive
Blau, Harvey Ronald lawyer
Fitteron, John Joseph petroleum products company executive
†Mandery, Mathew M. secondary school principal
Rosen, Robert Arnold management company executive
Salzman, Stephen Philip petroleum company executive
Shinners, Stanley Marvin electrical engineer
Spivack, Henry Archer life insurance company executive

Johnson City
Aswad, Betsy (Betsy Becker) writer
Sargent, Pamela writer

Katonah
Baker, John Milnes architect
Bashkow, Theodore Robert electrical engineering consultant, former educator
Fry, John magazine editor
Giobbi, Edward Giacchino artist
Krefting, Robert J(ohn) publishing company executive
Raymond, Jack journalist, public relations executive, foundation executive
Shanaphy, Edward John publishing executive
Simpson, William Kelly curator, Egyptologist, educator
Toney, Anthony artist
White, Harold Tredway, III management consultant

Kenmore
†Vienne, Dorothy Titus school principal

Kew Gardens
Schnakenberg, Donald G. financial administrator

Kinderhook
†Benamati, Dennis Charles law librarian, consultant
Lankhof, Frederik Jan publishing executive

Kings Park
Calviello, Joseph Anthony research electrophysicist, consultant
Greene, Robert William media consultant

Kings Point
Billy, George John library director
Bloom, Murray Teigh author
Matteson, Thomas T. academic administrator
Mazek, Warren F(elix) academic administrator, economics educator

Kingston
Agerwala, Tilak Krishna Mahesh computer company executive
Arnold, William Edwin foundation administrator
Lanitis, Tony Andrew market researcher
Tsirpanlis, Constantine N. theology and history educator

Lagrangeville
LaMont, Barbara Gibson librarian

Lake Success
Chafitz, Alan Herbert financial services company executive
Lee, Brian Edward lawyer
†Parsont, Robert Edward chemical company executive
Stevens, Gary professional jockey

Lancaster
Neumaier, Gerhard John environment consulting company executive
Weinberg, Norman Louis electrochemist

Larchmont
Aburdene, Odeh Felix banker
Bauer, George marketing consultant
Bellak, Leopold psychiatrist, psychoanalyst, psychologist
Berridge, George Bradford retired lawyer
Bloom, Lee Hurley lawyer, public affairs consultant, retired household products manufacturing executive
Diforio, Robert G. literary agent
Engel, Ralph Manuel lawyer
Fletcher, Denise Koen strategic and financial consultant
Gallaher, Carolyn Combs secondary education educator
Gillman, Arthur Emanuel psychiatrist
Greenwald, Carol Schiro professional services marketing research executive
Hinerfeld, Ruth J. civic organization executive
Holleb, Arthur Irving surgeon
†Josevie, Arnold management consultant
Kaufmann, Henry Mark mortgage banker
Kerr, Jean writer
Kerr, Walter F. retired drama critic, author
Levi, James Harry real estate executive, investment banker
Pelton, Russell Gilbert lawyer
Plumez, Jean Paul advertising agency executive, consultant
Rosenberg, Paul physicist, consultant
Sandell, Richard Arnold international trade executive, economist
Schwatka, Mark Andrew advertising agency executive
Seton, Charles B. lawyer
Silverstone, David advertising executive
Sonneborn, Henry, III former chemical company executive, business consultant
Tobey, Alton Stanley artist
Wielgus, Charles Joseph information services company executive

Lawrence
Sklarin, Burton S. endocrinologist
Wurzburger, Walter Samuel rabbi, philosophy educator

Levittown
Rubin, Arnold Jesse aeronautical engineer

Lewiston
Dexter, Theodore Henry chemist
Kennedy, G. Alfred federal agency administrator
Newlin, Lyman Wilbur bookseller, consultant

Lido Beach
Billauer, Barbara Pfeffer lawyer, educator

Lily Dale
†Merrill, Joseph Hartwell religious association executive

Lima
†Reynolds, Lewis Dayton administrator
Spencer, Ivan Carlton clergyman

Lindenhurst
Boltz, Mary Ann aerospace materials company executive, travel agency executive
Farrell-Logan, Vivian actress
Hamilton, Daniel Stephen clergyman

Liverpool
Kogut, John Anthony retail executive, pharmacist
Morabito, Bruno Paul machinery manufacturing executive
Winahradsky, Michael Francis drug company executive
Wolfson, Warren David lawyer, specialty retail store executive

Lloyd Harbor
Deavers, Karl Alan investment banker

Lockport
Carr, Edward Albert, Jr. pharmacology educator, physician
Hoyme, Chad Earl packaging company executive
Penney, Charles Rand lawyer, civic worker
Shah, Ramesh Keshavlal automotive company executive

Locust Valley
Benson, Robert Elliott investment banker, consultant
Bentel, Frederick Richard architect, educator
Bentel, Maria-Luise Ramona Azzarone (Mrs. Frederick R. Bentel) architect, educator
Lippold, Richard sculptor
McGee, Dorothy Horton writer, historian
Schaffner, Charles Etzel consulting engineering executive
Schor, Joseph Martin pharmaceutical executive, biochemist
Sunderland, Ray, Jr. retired insurance company executive
Van Rensselaer, Stephen banker
Zulch, Joan Carolyn retired medical publishing company executive

Long Beach
Robbins, Jeffrey Howard media consultant, research writer, educator
Siegel, Herbert Bernard business executive, consultant
Thompson, Dorothy Barnard elementary school educator

Long Eddy
Hoiby, Lee composer, concert pianist
Van Swol, Noel Warren secondary education educator

Long Island
Ulrich, Werner Richard union education administrator

Long Island City
Brustein, Lawrence financial executive
Carey, Edward John utility executive
Cushing, Robert Hunter lawyer, real estate investment executive
Di Suvero, Mark sculptor
Donneson, Seena Sand artist
Fife, Bernard automobile products manufacturing company executive
Gussow, Roy sculptor, educator
Lang, William Charles retail executive
Modell, Michael Steven lawyer, business executive
†Sadao, Shoji architect

Loudonville
McConville, William academic administrator

Lowville
Becker, Robert Otto orthopedic surgery educator

Mahopac
†Gould, Sandra M. elementary school principal
Richards, Edgar Lester psychologist, educator

Mahopac Falls
†Karimi, Reza artist

Malone
Quesnel, Elizabeth Dimick secondary school educator

Malverne
Engoren, Sampson Seymour interior designer
Freund, Richard L. communications company executive, consultant, lawyer
Knight, John Francis insurance company executive
Ryan, Suzanne Irene nursing educator

Mamaroneck
Allensworth, Dorothy Alice education foundation administrator
Halpern, Abraham Leon psychiatrist
Hettich, Arthur Matthias editor
Holz, Harold A. chemical and plastics manufacturing company executive
Mazzola, Claude Joseph physicist, small business owner
Mizrahi, Abraham Mordechay cosmetics and health care company executive, physician

Manhasset
Arnold, Charles Burle, Jr. psychiatrist, epidemiologist, writer
Barrett, James P. lawyer
Carucci, Samuel Anthony lawyer
Cerami, Anthony biochemistry educator
Fenton, Arnold N. obstetrician, gynecologist, educator
Frankum, James Edward airlines company executive
Gallagher, John S. T. (Jack Gallagher) hospital administrator
Grossi, Olindo architect, educator
Hayes, Arthur Michael lawyer
Kreis, Willi physician
Leeds, Lilo J. publishing executive
Lindow, John Wesley banker, corporate executive
Meilman, Edward physician
Rostky, George Harold editor
Scherr, Lawrence physician, educator
Schiller, Arthur A. architect, educator
Spitz, Charles Thomas, Jr. clergyman
Wallace, Richard editor, writer
Wallace, Richard K. editor, journalist
Warren, Kenneth S. medical educator, physician

Marcellus
Lafferty, Richard Thomas architect

Maryknoll
Gormley, Robert John book publisher

Massapequa
Aiello-Contessa, Angela Marie physician
Hughes, Spencer Edward, Jr. financial executive, consultant

Massapequa Park
Plotkin, Martin retired electrical engineer
Zizzo, Alicia concert pianist

Mattituck
†Kanas, John Adam banker
†Paulsen, Joanna publishing executive

Melville
Asimov, Stanley newspaper executive
†Bass, Elizabeth editor
†Bengelsdorf, Peter newspaper editor
Brandt, Robert Frederic, III newspaper editor, journalist
Colen, B. D. journalist
Cooke, Robert William science journalist
Dixon, Lawrence Paul insurance company executive
†Dooley, James C. newspaper editor
Fox, Douglas Brian newspaper publishing company executive
Green, Carol H. lawyer, educator, journalist
Hall, Charlotte Hauch newspaper editor
Hildebrand, John Frederick newspaper columnist
Isenberg, Steven Lawrence newspaper executive
Jagoda, Donald Robert sales promotion agency executive
Kahn, David editor, author
Kaufman, Stephen P. electronics company executive
Kett, Herbert Joseph drug store chain executive
Klatell, Robert Edward lawyer, electronics company executive
Klurfeld, James Michael journalist
Large, G. Gordon M. data processing company executive
†Lengel, David Lee electronics manufacturing executive
Lynn, James Dougal newspaper editor, journalist
Maller, Robert Russell certified management consultant, banker
Marro, Anthony James newspaper editor
McMillan, Robert Ralph lawyer
Moran, Paul James journalist, columnist
†Nassberg, Edward chemicals executive

Payne, Leslie newspaper editor, columnist, journalist, author
Ray, Gordon Thompson communications executive
Redder, Thomas H. newspaper publishing executive
†Robins, Marjorie Kaplan newspaper editor
†Roel, Ron newspaper editor
Schneider, Howard Stewart newspaper editor, educator
†Sommer, Jeff journalist
Toedtman, James Smith newspaper editor, journalist
Viklund, William Edwin banker
Woldt, Harold Frederick, Jr. newspaper publishing executive

Mendon
Krause, Richard William manufacturing executive, consultant

Merrick
Beckman, Judith Kalb financial counselor and planner, educator, writer
Cariola, Robert Joseph artist
Cherry, Harold insurance company executive
Copperman, Stuart Morton pediatrician
Doyle, James Aloysius retired association executive
Dubov, Spencer Floyd podiatrist, educator
O'Brien, Kenneth Robert life insurance company executive
Paul, Martin Ambrose physical chemist

Middle Island
†Mastrion, Guy secondary school principal

Middle Village
Farb, Edith Himel chemist
Kolatch, Alfred Jacob publisher
Meyers, Edward photographer, writer, publisher

Middletown
†Bedell, Barbara Lee newspaperwoman
Blumenthal, Fritz printmaker
Byrne, Mary Margaret (Meg Byrne) elementary education educator
†Gaydos, Robert John newspaper editor
†Kennedy, William Townsend newspaper executive
†Sprick, Dennis Michael critic, copy editor

Mill Neck
Grieve, William Roy education educator, educational association administrator
Phelan, John J., Jr. former stock exchange executive, corporate director

Millbrook
Johnston, Robert Cossin consulting engineer executive
Likens, Gene Elden ecologist

Mineola
Bartlett, Clifford Adams, Jr. lawyer
Cirker, Hayward publisher
Delaney, Martin Joseph hospital administrator
†English, John F. lawyer
Hankin, Errol Patrick hospital administrator
Hendler, Samuel I. corporate lawyer
Maulik, Dev obstetrician-gynecologist, educator
McGonigle, James Gregory consultant
Meyer, Bernard Stern lawyer, former judge
Mogil, Bernard Marc judge
Paterson, Basil Alexander lawyer
Rains, Harry Hano lawyer, arbitrator, mediator
Rushmore, Stephen hotel consulting and appraisal specialist
Salten, David George university administrator, educator
Schaffer, David Irving lawyer
Wurzel, Leonard candy manufacturing company executive

Monroe
Werzberger, Alan pediatrician

Montauk
Duryea, Perry Belmont, Jr. corporate executive
First, Wesley publishing company executive
Garvey, Richard Anthony lawyer
Lavenas, Suzanne editor

Monticello
Cooke, Lawrence Henry lawyer, former state chief judge
Lauterstein, Joseph cardiologist

Moriches
†Casciano, Paul principal

Morrisville
Rouse, Robert Moorefield mathematician, educator

Mount Kisco
Couture, Ronald David art administrator, design consultant
Crowe, John Carl airline company executive
Eckhoff, Carl D. manufacturing executive
Goodhue, Mary Brier former state senator, lawyer
Icahn, Carl C. arbitrator, options specialist, corporation executive
Keesee, Thomas Woodfin, Jr. financial consultant
King, Robert John real estate executive
Laster, Richard biotechnology executive
O'Neill, John Robert airline executive
Pastorelle, Peter John film company executive, radiological services and waste management company executive
Schwarz, Wolfgang psychologist
Senkier, Robert Joseph foundation administrator, educator
Singer, Craig investor, consultant
Wood, James broker

Mount Vernon
Leonard, John Harry advertising executive
Mc Neill, Charles James publishing executive
†Richardson, W. Franklyn religious organization administrator
Rossini, Joseph contracting and development corporate executive

Munnsville
Carruth, Hayden poet

Nanuet
Burden, Ordway Partridge investment banker
†Gold, Arline elementary school principal

Naples
Beal, Myron Clarence osteopathic physician

New City
Elberg, Darryl Gerald publisher, educator
Feld, Joseph construction executive
†Gromack, Alexander Joseph state legislator
Prestegaard, Peter systems company executive

New Hartford
Jones, Hugh Richard lawyer
Maurer, Gernant Elmer metallurgical executive, consultant
Muzyka, Donald Richard specialty metals executive, metallurgist

New Hyde Park
†Fanning, John Charles service company executive
†Fink, Martin Neil hospital administrator
†Fujii, Kenji medical equipment executive
Isenberg, Henry David microbiology educator
Jacob, Gary Steven real estate developer
Koplewicz, Harold Samuel child and adolescent psychiatrist
Lanzkowsky, Philip physician
Offner, Eric Delmonte lawyer
Reddan, Harold Jerome sociologist, educator
Rich, Eric plastics company executive
Richards, Bernard investment company executive
Wolf, Julius medical educator

New Kingston
†Maffei, Dorothy Jean theatre manager

New Paltz
Fleisher, Harold computer scientist
†Hasbrouck, Kenneth Edward professional society administrator
Hathaway, Richard Dean language professional, educator
Nyquist, Thomas Eugene academic administrator
Ryan, Marleigh Grayer Japanese language educator
Schnell, George Adam geographer, educator

New Rochelle
Beardsley, Robert Eugene microbiologist, educator
Berlage, Gai Ingham sociologist, educator
Blotner, Norman David lawyer, real estate broker, corporate executive
Branch, William Blackwell playwright, producer
Brodie, Norman retired financial actuary
Burns, Joseph William lawyer
Frenkel, Michael lawyer
Gallagher, John Francis academic administrator, education educator
Gunning, Francis Patrick lawyer, insurance association executive
†Hayes, Arthur Hull, Jr. physician, clinical pharmacology educator, medical school dean, business executive, consultant
Kelly, Sister Dorothy Ann college president
Klein, Arthur Luce theatrical company executive
Markinson, Martin theatre owner, producer
Merrill, Robert baritone
Murphy, Austin de la Salle economist, educator, banker
Nienburg, George Frank photographer
Nolte, Judith Ann magazine editor
Palihnich, Nicholas Joseph, Jr. retail chain executive
Petrucelli, R(occo) Joseph, II nephrologist
Primus, Pearl dancer, choreographer
Rovinsky, Joseph Judah obstetrician, gynecologist
Saperstein, David Allan novelist, screenwriter, film director
Saunders, Rubie Agnes former magazine editor, author
Slotnick, Mortimer H. artist
Vernon, Lillian mail order company executive
Wolotsky, Hyman retired college dean

New Windsor
†Calhoun, Nancy P. state legislator

New York
Aaron, Chloe Wellingham association executive
†Aaron, Lynn dancer
Abbe, Colman investment banker
Abberley, John J. lawyer
Abbey, Scott Gerson computer information scientist
Abbott, George playwright, director, producer
Abboud, Joseph M. fashion designer
Abel, Reuben educator
Abeles, Sigmund M. artist, printmaker
Abelson, Alan columnist
Abercrombie, Stanley magazine editor
Abernathy, James Logan public relations executive
Abish, Cecile artist
Ablon, R. Richard service company executive
†Ablon, Ralph E. manufacturing company executive
Abraham, F(ahrid) Murray actor, educator
Abrahams, William Miller editor, author
Abrahamsen, David psychiatrist, psychoanalyst, author
Abram, Prudence Beatty federal judge
Abramovitz, Max architect
Abrams, Bertram Alan lawyer
†Abrams, Floyd lawyer
Abrams, Marc R. lawyer
Abrams, Muhal Richard pianist, composer
Abrams, Robert former state attorney general
Abrams, Vivien artist
Abramson, Sara Jane radiologist, educator
Abularach, Rodolfo Marco Antonio artist
Abu-Lughod, Janet Lippman sociologist, educator
Acampora, Anthony Salvator electrical engineer, educator
Acampora, Ralph Joseph brokerage firm executive
Acconci, Vito (Hannibal) conceptual artist
Achenbaum, Alvin Allen marketing and management consultant
Achtert, Walter Scott publisher
Ackman, Milton Roy lawyer
†Acrivos, Andreas chemical engineering educator
Adams, Alice writer
Adams, Dennis Paul artist
Adams, Douglas Noel writer
Adams, Edward Thomas (Eddie Adams) photographer
Adams, Joey comedian, author
Adams, John Hamilton lawyer
†Adams, Jonathan L. advertising agency executive
†Adams, Seibert Gruber, Jr. publisher
Adamson, John William hematologist
Addison, Herbert John publishing executive
Adler, Freda Schaffer (Mrs. G. O. W. Mueller) criminologist, educator
Adler, Joel A. lawyer
Adler, Renata writer
Adler, Richard composer, lyricist
Adolfo, (Adolfo F. Sardiña) fashion designer
Adri, (Adrienne Steckling) fashion designer
Adrian, Barbara (Mrs. Franklin C. Tramutola) artist
†Agha, Mahmoud F. architectural firm executive
Agisim, Philip advertising and marketing company executive
Agosta, William Carleton chemist, educator
Agostinelli, Robert Francesco investment banker
Ahern, Patrick V. bishop
†Ahmad, Jameel civil engineer, researcher, educator
Ahrens, Edward Hamblin, Jr. physician
Aibel, Howard lawyer
Aidinoff, M(erton) Bernard lawyer
†Aiello, Stephen public relations executive
Ailes, Roger Eugene television producer, consultant
Ainslie, Michael Lewis art-related holding company executive
Aisenbrey, Stuart Keith trust company official
Akalaitis, JoAnne theater director, writer, actress
†Akins, Ellen writer
Akiyoshi, Toshiko jazz composer, pianist
Aksen, Gerald lawyer, educator
Alazraki, Jaime Romance languages educator
Albee, Edward Franklin author, playwright
Albers, Charles Edgar investment manager, insurance executive
Albert, Marv sportscaster, program director
Albert, Neale Malcolm lawyer
Albert, Rory Judd lawyer
Albright, Harry Wesley, Jr. banking executive, former government official, lawyer
Albright, Madeleine federal official, political scientist
Albright, Warren Edward advertising executive
Alcott, Mark Howard lawyer
Aldea, Patricia architect
Alden, Steven Michael lawyer
†Alderson, Philip Otis radiologist, educator
Aldredge, Theoni Vachliotis costume designer
Alessandroni, Venan Joseph lawyer
Alexander, Barbara Toll investment banker
Alexander, Frank Lyon corporate executive
Alexander, Harold bioengineer, educator
Alexander, Norman E. diversified manufacturing company executive
Alexander, Roy public relations executive, editor, author
Alexander, Shana journalist, author, lecturer
Alexopoulos, Helene ballet dancer
Alford, Robert Ross sociologist
†Alicea-Baez, Johnny religious organization administrator
Allard, Linda Marie fashion designer
Allen, Alice Catherine Towsley public relations professional, writer, consultant
Allen, Betty (Mrs. Ritten Edward Lee, III) mezzo-soprano
Allen, Herbert investment banker
Allen, Jay Presson writer, producer
Allen, Leon Arthur, Jr. lawyer
†Allen, Nancy musician, educator
Allen, Ralph Dean telecommunications corporate executive
Allen, Richard Marlow lawyer
Allen, Roberta L. fiction and nonfiction writer, conceptual artist
Allen, William Frederick, Jr. mechanical engineer
Allers, Franz orchestra conductor
†Allison, David Bradley psychologist
Allison, Herbert Monroe, Jr. investment firm executive
Allison, Wick publishing executive
Allmendinger, Paul Florin retired engineering association executive
Allner, Walter Heinz designer, painter, art director
†Almodóvar, Pedro filmmaker
Alonzo, Martin Vincent mining and aluminum company executive, investor, financial consultant
Alper, Merlin Lionel financial executive
Alpern, Andrew architect, lawyer
†Alpern, David Mark magazine editor, broadcast journalist and producer
Alpert, Gordon Myles lawyer
Alpert, Warren oil company executive, philanthropist
Alprin, William Samuel women's accessory company executive
Alter, David lawyer
Alter, Eleanor Breitel lawyer
Alter, Jonathan Hammerman journalist
†Altfest, Lewis Jay financial and investment advisor
Altman, Edward Ira finance educator, consultant, editor
Altman, Lawrence Kimball physician, journalist
Altman, Robert B. film director, writer, producer
Altman, Roy Peter pediatric surgeon
Altschul, Arthur Goodhart investment banker
†Alvarez, Mercedes advertising executive
Alvarez-Recio, Emilio De La Torre personal care products company executive
Alvary, Lorenzo bass
Alworth, Sandra Ann municipal bond salesperson, brokerage house executive
Amabile, John Louis lawyer
Amara, Lucine opera and concert singer
†Ambasz, Emilio architect, industrial designer, graphic designer
Amberg, Stanley Louis lawyer
Ambrose, Daniel Michael publishing executive
Amdur, Martin Bennett lawyer
†Amdur, Neil sports editor, writer
Ameling, Elly soprano
Ames, George Joseph investment banker
Amhowitz, Harris J. lawyer, educator
Ammirati, Ralph advertising agency executive
Amonte, Anthony Lewis professional hockey player
Amory, Cleveland writer
†Amos, Tori singer, musician
Amram, David Werner composer, conductor, musician
Amster, Linda Evelyn newspaper executive, consultant
Amsterdam, Anthony Guy law educator
Anchlia, Than Mal distribution company executive
Ancona, Barry publishing and marketing consultant
Anderegg, George Francis, Jr. lawyer
Andersen, K(ent) Tucker investment executive
†Andersen, Kurt Byars magazine editor, critic, writer
Anderson, Arthur Allan management consultant
Anderson, Arthur N. retired utility company executive
Anderson, Bradley Jay cartoonist
Anderson, David Poole sportswriter
Anderson, Eugene Robert lawyer
†Anderson, Gavin public relations consultant
Anderson, Jack Northman newspaper columnist
Anderson, Laurie performance artist
Anderson, O(rvil) Roger biology educator, researcher marine biology
Anderson, Poul William author
Anderson, Quentin English language educator, critic
Anderson, Ron advertising executive
Anderson, Ross Sherwood architect
Anderson, Sydney biologist, museum curator
Anderson, Theodore Wellington portfolio strategist
Anderson, Walter Herman magazine editor
Andolsen, Alan Anthony management consultant
Andre, Carl sculptor
†Andren, Karl Goesta transportation executive
Andrews, Frederick Franck newspaper editor
Andrews, Gerald Bruce textile executive
Andrus, Roger Douglas lawyer
†Andruskevich, Thomas A(nthony) corporate executive
†Anfield, Frank A. advertising executive
Angell, Roger writer, magazine editor
Angier, Natalie Marie science journalist
†Anneken, William B. apparel company executive
Annese, Domenico landscape architect
Anshen, Melvin business educator
Anspach, Ernst economist, lawyer
Anthoine, Robert lawyer, educator
Anthony, William Graham artist
Antilla, Susan journalist
Antonakos, Stephen sculptor
Antonell, Walter John publishing executive
Antonuccio, Joseph Albert hospitality industry executive
Antupit, Samuel Nathaniel art director
Apostolakis, James John shipping company executive
Appel, Alfred lawyer
Appel, Karel artist, illustrator
Apple, Max Isaac English educator
Applebaum, Stuart S. public relations executive
Appleton, Myra magazine editor, writer
Aquilino, Thomas Joseph, Jr. federal judge, law educator
Araskog, Rand Vincent diversified telecommunications multinational company executive
Arcara, James Amadeus broadcasting company executive
Arcaro, Eddie (George Edward) sports broadcasting journalist, former jockey
Archibald, Reginald Mac Gregor physician, chemist, educator
Arcilesi, Vincent Jasper artist
Arenson, Gregory K. lawyer
Arenson, Karen Wattel journalist
Arias, Jimmy professional tennis player
Arkin, Alan Wolf actor
Arledge, Roone television executive
Arlow, Arnold Jack advertising agency executive
Arman, Armand Pierre sculptor
Armani, Giorgio fashion designer
Armitage, Karole dancer, choreographer
Armour, Lawrence A. communications executive
Armstrong, James Sinclair lawyer, banker
Armstrong, Michael Francis lawyer
Arning, John Fredrick lawyer
Arnold, Eddy singer
Arnold, Kenneth Lloyd publisher, playwright
Arnold, Martin journalist
†Arnot, Bob physician, medical correspondent
Aron, Alan Milford pediatric neurology educator
Aronoff, Michael Stephen psychiatrist
Arons, Michael Eugene physicist, academic administrator
Aronson, Donald Eric consultant to professional services firms
Aronson, Edgar David venture capitalist
Aronson, Esther Leah association administrator, psychotherapist
Aronstam, Neil Lee media marketing firm executive
Arouh, Jeffrey Alan lawyer
Arpino, Gerald Peter performing company executive
Arquit, Kevin James lawyer
Arron, Judith Hagerty concert hall executive
†Arsene, Vladimir architect
Arther, Richard Oberlin polygraphist, educator
Arvystas, Michael Geciauskas orthodontist, educator
Asahina, Robert James editor, publishing company executive
Asakawa, Takako choreograper, dance teacher
Asanuma, Hiroshi physician, educator
Asch, Arthur Louis apparel company executive
†Ascher, Michael transportation executive
Asen, Shel F. publishing company executive
†Ashdown, Marie Matranga (Mrs. Cecil Spanton Ashdown, Jr.) writer, lecturer
Asher, Aaron editor, publisher
Ashinoff, Reid L. lawyer
Ashjian, Mesrob archbishop
Ashkinazy, Larry Robert dentist
Ashley, Elizabeth actress
Ashley, Merrill ballerina
†Ashrafi, Dariush apparel company executive
Ashton, Dore author, educator
†Ashton, Jean Willoughby library director
Ashton, Robert W. lawyer, foundation administrator
Ashworth, Richard Goodspeed lawyer
Assael, Henry marketing educator
Astor, Brooke foundation executive, civic worker
Athanassiades, Ted insurance company executive
Atkins, Peter Allan lawyer
Atkinson, Holly Gail physician, journalist, author, lecturer
†Atkinson, Paul C. newspaper publishing executive
Atlas, James Robert writer
†Attkisson, Sharyl T. news correspondent, writer
Atwater, Verne Stafford finance educator
Auchincloss, Kenneth magazine editor
Auchincloss, Louis Stanton writer
Auel, Jean Marie author
Auerbach, William lawyer
Aufses, Arthur H(arold), Jr. surgeon, medical educator
†Augeri, Joseph Leonard packaging engineer
Auriemmo, Frank Joseph, Jr. financial holding company executive
Austad, Vigdis computer software company executive
Auster, Paul writer
Austin, Gabriel Christopher publisher
Austrian, Neil R. football league executive
Autera, Michael Edward health care products company executive
†Aved, Barry retail executive
Avedon, Richard photographer

Avi, (Avi Wortis) *author*
†Avni, Ran *artistic director*
Avrett, John Glenn *advertising executive*
Ax, Emanuel *pianist*
Axelrod, Charles Paul *lawyer*
Axelrod, Norman N(athan) *technology and strategic technical planning consultant*
Axinn, Stephen Mark *lawyer*
Aycock, Alice *artist*
Ayers, Emory Daniel *management consultant*
Azuma, Norio *artist, art dealer*
Babson, Irving K. *publishing company executive*
Bacall, Lauren *actress*
Bach, Arthur James *investment banker*
Bache, Theodore Stephen *recording company executive*
Bachelder, Joseph Elmer, III *lawyer*
Bacher, Judith St. George *executive search consultant*
Bachrach, Nancy *advertising executive*
Backer, William Montague *advertising agency executive*
Backman, Gerald Stephen *lawyer*
Bacon, James Edmund *corporate director*
Bacot, John Carter *banker*
Baden, Michael M. *pathologist, educator*
Badertscher, David Glen *law librarian, consultant*
Baechle, James Joseph *lawyer, banker*
†Baer, Harold, Jr. *judge*
Baer, Norbert Sebastian *art conservation educator, chemist*
Baer, Rudolf Lewis *dermatologist, educator*
Baer, Thomas James *lawyer*
Baeza, Mario Leon *lawyer*
†Bagger, Richard Hartvig *lawyer*
Bagnall, Roger Shaler *history educator*
Bagnoli, Vincent James, Jr. *engineer, construction company executive*
Bahash, Robert J. *publishing executive*
Bahr, Lauren S. *publishing company executive*
Bahrenburg, D. Claeys *publishing executive*
Bailey, Glenn Waldemar *manufacturing company executive*
Bailey, James Martin *minister, ecumenical executive, public relations consultant*
Bailey, Janet Dee *publishing company executive*
Bailey, Lawrence Randolph, Sr. *lawyer*
Bains, Harrison MacKellar, Jr. *financial executive*
Bains, Leslie Elizabeth *banker*
Bainton, J(ohn) Joseph *lawyer*
Baird, Dugald Euan *oil field service company executive*
Baity, John Cooley *lawyer*
†Baitz, Jon Robin *playwright*
Bakal, Carl *writer, public relations counsel, photojournalist*
Baker, David Remember *lawyer*
Baker, Edwin Herbert *lawyer*
Baker, Elizabeth Calhoun *magazine editor*
Baker, Elmer Elias, Jr. *speech pathology and communication educator*
Baker, James Barnes *architect*
Baker, James Estes *foreign service officer*
Baker, Paul Raymond *history educator*
Baker, Russell Wayne *columnist, author*
Baker, Stephen *advertising executive, author*
Baker, Stuart David *lawyer*
Baker, William Franklin *public broadcasting company executive*
Baker, William George *publishing company financial executive*
Baker-Riker, Margery *television executive*
†Balaban, Bob *actor, director*
Balakian, Anna *foreign language educator, scholar, critic, writer*
Baldasaro, P. Michael *tax consultant*
Baldassano, Corinne Leslie *radio executive*
†Baldwin, David Allen *political science educator*
Baldwin, David Shepard *physician*
Ball, John H(anstein) *lawyer*
Ball, John Paul *publishing company executive*
Ballantine, Ian *publisher*
Ballard, Charles Alan *investment banker*
Balliett, Whitney *writer, critic*
†Ballon, Charles *lawyer*
Balson, John Bruce *advertising agency executive*
Bamberger, Michael Albert *lawyer*
Bancroft, Alexander Clerihew *lawyer*
Bancroft, Margaret Armstrong *lawyer*
Bandier, Martin *music publisher*
Bandy, Mary Lea *museum official*
Banerjee, (Bimal) *artist, educator*
Banker, Stephen M. *lawyer*
†Banks, Jeffrey *fashion designer*
Banks, Russell *chemical company executive*
Bankston, Archie Moore, Jr. *lawyer*
Banner, Stephen Edward *company executive, lawyer*
†Baquero, José Maria *architect, artist*
†Baquet, Dean Paul *investigative reporter*
Baragwanath, Albert Kingsmill *curator*
Baraka, Amiri (LeRoi Jones) *author*
Barandes, Robert *lawyer*
Baranik, Rudolf *artist*
Baranski, Joan Sullivan *publisher*
Barasch, Clarence Sylvan *lawyer*
Barasch, Mal Livingston *lawyer*
Barbash, Joseph *lawyer, arbitrator*
Barbee, Victor *ballet dancer*
Barber, Russell Brooks Butler *television producer*
Bardach, Joan Lucile *clinical psychologist*
Bardin, Clyde Wayne *biomedical researcher and developer of contraceptives*
Barist, Jeffrey A. *lawyer*
Barker, Barbara Ann *ophthalmologist*
Barker, Charles *conductor*
Barkhorn, Henry Charles, III *investment banker*
Barnard, Kurt *retail marketing forecaster, publisher*
Barnard, Scott *artist consultant*
Barnes, Clive Alexander *drama and dance critic*
Barnes, Duncan *magazine editor, writer*
Barnes, Edward Larrabee *architect*
Barnes, Jack Whittier *political party official*
Barnes, Jhane Elizabeth *fashion design company executive, designer*
Barnet, Will *artist, educator*
Barnett, Bernard *accountant*
Barnett, Henry Lewis *medical educator, pediatrician*
Barnett, Jonathan *architect, city planner*
Barnett, Richard Blair *lawyer*
Barnett, Vivian Endicott *curator*
Baron, Carolyn *editor, author, publishing executive*
Baron, Melvin Leon *civil engineer, consultant*
Baron, Mitchell Neal *lawyer*
Baron, Theodore *public relations executive*
Barondess, Jeremiah Abraham *physician*
Barondess, Linda Hiddemen *professional society executive*
Barr, Michael Charles *securities analyst, lawyer, investment banker*
Barr, Thomas D. *lawyer*
†Barratt, Michael Scott *architect*
Barrett, Bill *sculptor*
Barrett, Herbert *artists management executive*
Barrett, Loretta Anne *publishing executive*
Barrett, Robert James, III *investment banker*
Barrett, William L. D. *lawyer*
Barron, Francis Patrick *lawyer*
Barron, James Turman *journalist*
Barron, Susan *clinical psychologist*
Barry, David Earl *lawyer*
Barry, Desmond Thomas, Jr. *lawyer*
Barry, Edward William *publisher*
Barry, Lynda *cartoonist, playwright, author*
Barry, Mary Alice *retired financial executive*
Barry, Thomas Corcoran *investment counsellor*
Barry, Thomas M. *banker*
Barry, William Garrett, III *publishing company executive*
Barsalona, Frank Samuel *theatrical agent*
Barsamian, Khajag Sarkis *primate*
Barth, Mark Harold *lawyer*
Bartle, Annette Gruber (Mrs. Thomas R. Bartle) *artist, writer, photographer*
Bartlett, Jennifer Losch *artist*
†Bartlett, John *fashion designer*
Bartlett, Joseph Warren *lawyer*
Bartley, Robert LeRoy *newspaper editor*
Bartoli, Cecilia *coloratura soprano, mezzo soprano*
Baruch, Ralph M. *communications executive*
Baryshnikov, Mikhail *ballet dancer*
Barzilay, Isaac Eisenstein *historian*
Barzun, Jacques *author, literary consultant*
Basden, Cameron *assistant ballet mistress, dancer*
Baskin, Stuart Jay *lawyer*
Bass, Hyman *mathematician, educator*
Bass, Joel Leonard *artist*
Bassen, Ned H. *lawyer*
Bateman, Robert McLellan *artist*
Bates, Don *public relations and marketing executive*
Batscha, Robert Michael *museum executive*
Battle, Kathleen Deanna *soprano*
Baudendistel, Daniel *dancer*
Bauer, Douglas F. *lawyer*
Bauer, Marion Dane *writer*
Bauer, Ralph Glenn *lawyer, maritime arbitrator*
Baum, Eleanor *electrical engineering educator, academic administrator*
Bauman, Martin Harold *executive search firm executive*
Baumann, Karl H. *health, medical products executive*
Baumgardner, John Ellwood, Jr. *lawyer*
Baumgarten, Paul Anthony *lawyer*
Baumgarten, Sidney *lawyer*
Baumrin, Bernard Stefan Herbert *lawyer, educator*
Bausch, James John *foundation executive*
†Baxter, John Hanley *consultant company executive*
Baylis, Robert Montague *investment banker*
†Bazell, Robert Joseph *science correspondent*
Bazerman, Steven Howard *lawyer*
Beal, Jack *artist*
Beale, Christopher William *investment banker*
Bear, Larry Alan *lawyer, educator*
Beard, Eugene P. *advertising agency executive*
Beardsley, Charles William *engineering publisher, editor, writer*
Beardsley, Theodore S(terling), Jr. *association executive*
Bearn, Alexander Gordon *physician scientist, former pharmaceutical company executive*
Beattie, Ann *author*
Beattie, Edward James *surgeon, educator*
Beatty, John Lee *scenic designer*
†Beatty, Talley *choreographer*
Beaumont, Richard Austin *management consultant*
Beck, Adrian Robert *surgeon, educator*
Beck, Rosemarie *artist, educator*
Becker, Don Crandall *newspaper executive*
Becker, Herbert P. *mechanical engineer*
Becker, Isidore A. *business executive*
†Becker, Ivan *advertising executive*
Becker, Michael Lewis *advertising executive*
Becker, Robert A. *advertising executive*
Beckham, Edgar Frederick *foundation administrator*
Beckhard, Herbert *architect*
Beckwith, Rodney Fisk *management consulting firm executive*
Becofsky, Arthur Luke *arts administrator, writer*
Bederson, Benjamin *physicist, educator*
Bedford, Brian *actor*
Bedi, Rahul *import company executive*
Bednar, Rudy Gerard *television producer, director*
Beene, Geoffrey *fashion designer*
Beers, Charlotte Lenore *advertising agency executive*
Beeson, Jack Hamilton *composer, educator, writer*
Begell, William *publisher*
Begley, Louis *lawyer, writer*
Beha, James Joseph *lawyer*
Behrendt, John Thomas *lawyer*
Behrens, Hildegard *soprano*
Beim, David Odell *investment banker, educator*
Beim, Norman *playwright, actor, director*
Beinecke, Candace Krugman *lawyer*
Beinecke, Frederick William *lawyer, corporation executive*
Beinecke, William S. *corporate executive*
Bekesi, Julis George *medical researcher*
Belden, David Leigh *professional association executive, engineering educator*
Belford, Richard David *lawyer*
Bel Geddes, Joan *author*
Belkin, Boris David *violinist*
Belknap, Norton *petroleum company consultant*
Belknap, Robert Ernest, III *investment counselor*
Belknap, Robert Lamont *Slavic language educator*
Belkov, Meredith Ann *landmark administrator*
Bell, David Arthur *advertising agency executive*
Bell, Derrick Albert *legal educator*
Bell, James Halsey *lawyer*
Bell, Jonathan Robert *lawyer*
Bell, Martin Allen *corporate executive*
†Bell, Richard *arts education executive*
Bellanger, Serge René *banker*
Bellas, Albert Constantine *investment banker, advisor*
Belle, John Leighton *architect, planner*
†Belle, Regina *popular musician*
Beller, Gary A. *financial services company executive, lawyer*
Bellin, Milton Rockwell *artist*
Bellson, Louis Paul *drummer*
Belnick, Mark Alan *lawyer*
Bemis, Mary *editor-in-chief, magazine*
Benchley, Peter Bradford *author*
Bendelius, Arthur George *engineering firm executive*
Bender, Thomas *history and humanities educator, writer*
Bendixen, Henrik Holt *physician, educator, dean*
Benedetto, M. William *investment banker*
Benedict, James Nelson *lawyer*
Benedikt, Michael *poet, educator, author, editor, free-lance consultant*
Ben-Eli, Michael Uri *management consultant*
Benenson, Edward Hartley *realty company executive*
Benenson, Mark Keith *lawyer*
Benesch, Ruth Erica *chemistry educator*
Benglis, Lynda *artist, sculptor*
Ben-Haim, Zigi *artist*
Benham, Isabel Hamilton *think tank company executive*
Benichou, Pascal *dancer*
†Benjamin, Alan *children's book author and editor*
Benjamin, George David *insurance company executive*
Benjamin, Harvey E. *lawyer, sports executive*
Benkard, James W. B. *lawyer*
Benn, T(heodore) Alexander (Alec Benn) *writer*
Bennack, Frank Anthony, Jr. *publishing company executive*
†Bennett, Edward A. *broadcast company executive*
Bennett, Georgette *communications and planning consultant*
Bennett, Reynold *lawyer*
Bennett, Saul *public relations agency executive*
Bennett, Tony (Anthony Dominick Benedetto) *entertainer*
†Benshoof, Janet L. *lawyer, association executive*
Benson, Lenore J. *association executive*
Bentley, Eric *author, playwright, comparative literature educator*
Benton, Nicholas *theater producer*
Benton, Robert *film director, screenwriter*
Benway, Joseph Calise *advertising agency financial executive*
†Ben-Yishay, Yehuda *medical educator*
Bercovitch, Hanna Margareta *editor*
Berens, Rodney Bristol *investment banker*
Berenson, Robert Leonard *advertising agency executive*
Berenstain, Janice *author, illustrator*
Berenstain, Stanley *author, illustrator*
Berezin, Tanya *artistic director, actress*
Berg, David *author, artist*
†Berg, Wayne *architect, educator*
Bergan, Philip James *lawyer*
Bergen, D. Thomas *business executive*
Bergen, G. S. Peter *lawyer*
Bergen, John Donald *communications, public affairs executive*
Berger, Andrew L. *investment banker, lawyer*
†Berger, Arnold R. *advertising executive*
Berger, Bruce *finance and information services consultant*
Berger, Curtis Jay *law educator*
Berger, Eric *magazine editor*
Berger, Frank Milan *biomedical researcher, scientist, former pharmaceutical company executive*
Berger, George *lawyer*
Berger, Oscar *artist*
Berger, Pearl *library director*
Berger, Stephen *financial services company executive*
†Berger, Vivian Olivia *lawyer, educator*
Bergin, John Francis *advertising agency executive*
†Bergman, Andrew *motion picture director*
Bergman, Marilyn Keith *writer, lyricist*
Bergonzi, Carlo *tenor*
Bergson, Maria *designer*
Bergstein, Daniel Gerard *lawyer*
Beringer, Stuart Marshall *investment banker*
Berk, Alan S. *law firm executive*
Berk, Paul David *physician, scientist, educator*
Berkman, Jack Neville *lawyer, corporate executive*
Berkman, Lillian *foundation executive, corporation executive, art collector*
Berkow, Ira Harvey *author, journalist*
Berkwitt, George Joseph *editor*
Berle, Peter Adolf Augustus *lawyer, association executive*
Berlin, Andrew Mark *advertising agency executive*
Berlin, Emily *lawyer*
Berlin, Howard Richard *investment advisory company executive*
Berlin, Jordan Stuart *investment company executive*
Berlind, Robert Elliot *artist*
Berlind, Roger Stuart *stage and film producer*
†Berliner, Barbara *librarian, consultant*
Berliner, Ruth Shirley *real estate company executive*
Berliner, William Michael *business educator*
Berman, Ariane R. *artist*
Berman, Joshua Mordecai *lawyer, manufacturing company executive*
Berman, Julius *lawyer*
Berman, Lazar *pianist*
†Berman, Martin M. *television producer*
Berman, Mira *advertising agency executive*
Berman, Richard Angel *health science facility administrator*
Berman, Richard Miles *lawyer*
Berman, Simeon Moses *mathematician, educator*
Bermann, George Alan *law educator, lawyer*
Bernard, David George *management consultant*
Bernard, Kenneth (Otis Bernard) *poet, author, playwright*
Bernard, Lewis W. *foundation executive*
Bernard, Richard Phillip *lawyer*
Bernard, Viola Wertheim *psychiatrist*
Bernard, Walter *art director*
Bernardi, Mario *conductor*
Bernbach, John Lincoln *advertising executive*
Berne, Bruce J. *chemistry educator*
Bernstein, Alan Arthur *oil company executive*
Bernstein, Anne Elayne *psychoanalyst*
Bernstein, Bernard *lawyer, corporate executive*
Bernstein, Carl *author, journalist*
Bernstein, Daniel Lewis *lawyer*
Bernstein, Elliot Louis *television executive*
Bernstein, Richard Allen *publishing company executive*
Bernstein, Robert Louis *book publishing company executive*
Bernstein, Theresa *artist*
Berresford, Susan Vail *philanthropic foundation executive*
Berrien, James Stuart *magazine publisher*
Berry, Charles Gordon *lawyer*
Berry, Edna Janet *lawyer, chemist*
Berry, Joyce Charlotte *university press editor*
Berry, Nancy Michaels *nonprofit development executive*
Berry, Walter *baritone*
†Berstein, Richard A. *insurance company executive*
Berthot, Jake *artist*
Bertino, Joseph Rocco *physician, educator*
Bertles, John Francis *physician, educator*
Berton, Lee *writer*
Beshar, Christine *lawyer*
Beshar, Robert Peter *lawyer*
Bessey, Edward Cushing *health care company executive*
Best, Geoffry D. C. *lawyer*
Betanzos, Amalia V. *social services administrator*
Betcher, Albert Maxwell *anesthesiologist*
†Betley, John R. *accountant*
Bettman, Gary Bruce *lawyer*
Betts, Dicky (Richard Forrest Betts) *guitarist, songwriter, vocalist*
Beuchert, Edward William *lawyer*
Bewkes, Eugene Garrett, Jr. *investment company executive, consultant*
Bewkes, Jeff *television broadcasting company executive*
Beyman, Jonathan Eric *investment banker*
Bezahler, Donald Jay *lawyer*
Bezanson, Thomas Edward *lawyer*
Bhavsar, Natvar Prahladji *artist*
Bialer, Seweryn *political science educator, author, consultant*
Bialkin, Kenneth Jules *lawyer*
Bialo, Kenneth Marc *lawyer*
Bickers, David Rinsey *physician, educator*
Bickford, Jewelle Wooten *investment banker*
Bicks, David Peter *lawyer*
Biddle, Flora Miller *art museum administrator*
Bidwell, James Truman, Jr. *lawyer*
†Biebelberg, David Mark *marketing professional*
Biederman, Barron Zachary (Barry Biederman) *advertising agency executive*
†Biedler, June L. *oncologist*
Bielenstein, Hans Henrik August *Oriental studies educator*
Bienenstock, Martin J. *lawyer*
Bierman, Steven M. *lawyer*
Biewen, Robert L. *publishing executive*
Biggar, Barry P. *lawyer*
Bigger, John Thomas, Jr. *physician, educator*
Biggs, Barton Michael *investment company executive*
Biggs, Jeremy Hunt *trust company executive*
Biggs, John Herron *insurance company executive*
†Bijur, Arthur William *advertising executive*
Bikel, Theodore *actor, singer*
Biller, Hugh Frederick *medical educator*
Billian, Cathey R. *sculptor, educator*
Binger, Wilson Valentine *civil engineer*
Bingham, Bruce Bryan *real estate developer*
Binkerd, Gordon Ware *composer*
Binkert, Alvin John *hospital administrator*
Binkowski, Edward Stephan *research analysis director, lawyer, educator*
Binns, Walter Gordon, Jr. *automobile manufacturing company executive*
Biondi, Frank J., Jr. *entertainment company executive*
Birch, William Dunham, Jr. *asset manager*
Bird, Mary Lynne Miller *association executive*
Birkelund, John Peter *investment banking executive*
Birkenhead, Thomas Bruce *theatrical producer and manager, educator*
Birman, Joseph Leon *physics educator*
Birmingham, Stephen *writer*
Birnbaum, Edward Lester *lawyer*
Birnbaum, Henry *librarian*
Birnbaum, Irwin Morton *lawyer*
Birnbaum, Robert Jack *lawyer*
Birnbaum, Sheila L. *lawyer, educator*
Bishop, André *artistic director, producer*
†Bishop, Susan Katharine *executive search company executive*
†Bite-Dickson, Guna *newspaper editor*
Bizar, Irving *lawyer*
Black, Barbara Aronstein *legal history educator*
Black, Hillel Moses *publisher*
Black, James Isaac, III *lawyer*
Black, Jerry Bernard *lawyer*
Black, Neil Spencer *magazine publishing executive*
†Black, Rosemary *newspaper editor*
†Black, Shawn Morgado, . *dancer*
Blackford, Leo Price *investment banker*
Blackiston, Henry Curtis, III *lawyer*
Blackman, Kenneth Robert *lawyer*
Blackwell, John Wesley *securities industry executive, consultant*
Blackwell, Richard Manning *lawyer*
Blades, Ruben *singer, songwriter, composer*
Blaine, Nell *artist, printmaker*
Blair, William Granger *retired newspaperman*
Blake, Richard Charles *lawyer*
Blakeslee, Edward Eaton *lawyer, insurance executive*
Blalock, Sherrill *investment advisor*
Blanc, Peter (William Peters Blanc) *sculptor, painter*
Blanc, Roger David *lawyer*
†Bland, Frederick Aves *architect*
Blaney, John *advertising executive*
Blank, Blanche Davis *political science educator*
Blank, Marion Sue *psychologist*
Blass, Bill (William Ralph Blass) *designer apparel, home furnishings*
Blattmachr, Jonathan George *lawyer*
Blatty, William Peter *writer*
Blechman, R. O. *artist, filmmaker*
Bleiberg, Robert Marvin *retired financial editor*
Bleich, David Lloyd *lawyer*
Blind, William Charles *lawyer*
Blinder, Richard Lewis *architect*
Blinken, Robert James *manufacturing and communications company executive*
Blitzer, Andrew *otolaryngologist, educator*
Bliven, Bruce, Jr. *writer*
Bliven, Naomi *book reviewer*
Bliwise, Lester Martin *lawyer*
Blobel, Gunter *cell biologist, educator*
Block, Dennis Jeffery *lawyer*
Block, John Douglas *auction house executive*
Block, Lawrence *author*
†Block, Paul J. *cosmetic company executive*
Bloom, Robert Avrum *lawyer*
Bloomer, Harold Franklin, Jr. *lawyer*
Bloomgarden, Kathy Finn *public relations executive*
Blos, Joan W. *author, critic, lecturer*
Blount, Robert Grier *pharmaceutical company executive*
Blumberg, Gerald *lawyer*
Blume, Judy Sussman *author*
Blumenthal, W(erner) Michael *manufacturing company executive, former secretary of treasury, investment banker*
Blumkin, Linda Ruth *lawyer*
Blumstein, Allan *lawyer*
Blumstein, Reneé J. *research and statistical consultant*
Blumstein, William A. *insurance company executive*

Blyth, Myrna Greenstein *publishing executive, editor, author*
Blythe, William LeGette, II *editor, writer*
Boal, Peter Cadbury *dancer*
Boardman, Seymour *artist*
Bocca, Julio *dancer*
Bochner, Mel *artist*
Bock, Walter Joseph *zoology educator*
Bockstein, Herbert *lawyer*
Boehm, David Alfred *publisher, producer*
†Boehm, Lincoln A. *publishing company executive*
Boelzner, Gordon *orchestral conductor*
Boes, Lawrence William *lawyer*
Bogdonoff, Morton David *physician, educator*
Boggs, Gil *principal ballet dancer*
Bohn, John Augustus, Jr. *banker, lawyer*
Boice, Craig Kendall *management consultant*
Bolan, Thomas Anthony *lawyer*
Boley, Bruno Adrian *engineering educator*
Boley Bolaffio, Rita *artist*
Bollman, Mark Brooks, Jr. *communications executive*
†Bolt, Thomas *writer, artist*
Bona, Frederick Emil *public relations executive*
Bonazzi, Elaine Claire *mezzo-soprano*
Bond, J. Max, Jr. *architect, educational administrator*
Bond, Jonathan Holbert *advertising executive*
Bonfante, Larissa *classics educator*
Bonforte, Richard James *pediatrician, educator*
Bonino, Fernanda *art dealer*
Bon Jovi, Jon *rock singer, composer*
Bonniwell, Katherine *magazine executive*
Bono, (Paul Hewson) *singer, songwriter*
Bonomi, John Gurnee *lawyer*
Boodey, Cecil Webster, Jr. *political science educator*
Bookhardt, Fred Barringer, Jr. *architect*
Booth, Albert Edward, II *real estate executive*
Booth, Edgar Hirsch *lawyer*
†Booth, Margaret A(nn) *communications company executive*
Booth, Mitchell B. *lawyer*
Boothby, Willard Sands, III *bank executive*
Boothe, Power *visual artist, educator, filmmaker, set designer*
Borda, Deborah *symphony orchestra executive*
†Borden, Elizabeth B. *publishing executive*
Borders, William Alexander *journalist*
Bordiga, Benno *automotive parts manufacturing company executive*
Borelli, Francis J(oseph) (Frank Borelli) *insurance brokerage and consulting firm financial executive*
Borenstein, Abe Isaac *securities industry executive*
Borer, Jeffrey Stephen *cardiologist*
Borge, Victor *entertainer, comedian, pianist*
Borisoff, Richard Stuart *lawyer*
Bornet, Stephen Folwell *public relations and marketing communications executive*
Borofsky, Jonathan *artist*
Boros, Jerome S. *lawyer*
Borowitz, Sidney *retired physics educator*
Borsody, Robert Peter *lawyer*
Bosco, Philip Michael *actor*
Boshkov, Stefan Hristov *mining engineer, educator*
Boshkov, Stefan Robert *lawyer*
Bosley, John Scott *editor*
Bosniak, Morton Arthur *physician, educator*
Bostock, Roy Jackson *advertising agency executive*
Botero, Fernando *artist*
Bothmer, Dietrich Felix von *museum curator, archaeologist*
Boucher, Henry Joseph (Bud Boucher) *management consultant*
†Bouloukos, Don P. *broadcast company executive*
Boultinghouse, Marion Craig Bettinger *editor*
Boundas, Louise Gooch *editor*
Bourdon, David *art critic, writer, editor*
Bourgeois, Louise *sculptor*
Bourjaily, Vance *novelist*
Boutros-Ghali, Boutros *United Nations official*
Bove, John Louis *chemistry and environmental engineering educator, researcher*
Bovin, Denis Alan *finance company executive*
Bowden, Sally Ann *choreographer, teacher, dancer*
†Bowen, Jean *music librarian, consultant*
†Bowen, John Sheets *advertising agency executive*
Bowen, William Gordon *economist, educator, foundation administrator*
Bower, John Joseph *lawyer*
Bower, Marvin *management consultant*
Bowie, Jonathan Munford *lawyer*
Bowling, James Chandler *food products company consultant*
Bowman, Robert A. *hotel company executive*
Bown, Patti (Ann Bown) *musician, composer*
Boxer, Leonard *lawyer*
†Boyarski, Joel I. *financial executive*
Boyce, Joseph Nelson *journalist*
Boyd, Michael Alan *investment banking company executive, lawyer*
Bozorth, Squire Newland *lawyer*
Brack, Reginald Kufeld, Jr. *publisher*
Bradbury, Ray Douglas *author*
Brademas, John *former university president, former congressman*
Bradford, Barbara Taylor *writer, journalist, novelist*
Bradford, John Carroll *retired magazine executive*
Bradford, Richard Roark *writer*
Bradford, Robert Ernest *motion picture producer*
Bradley, E. Michael *lawyer*
Bradley, Edward R. *news correspondent*
Bradley, Lisa M. *artist*
Bradstock, John *advertising executive*
Brady, Adelaide Burks *public relations agency executive, giftware catalog executive*
Brady, James Winston *writer, television commentator*
Braham, Randolph Lewis *political science educator*
Brams, Steven John *political scientist, educator, game theorist*
Brancato, Carolyn Kay *economist, consultant*
Brand, Leonard *physician, educator*
Brandt, Grace Borgenicht *art dealer*
Brandt, Warren *artist*
Brant, Sandra *magazine publisher*
Braude, Robert Michael *medical library administrator*
Braun, Craig Allen *producer*
Braun, Jeffrey Louis *lawyer*
Braun, Lilian Jackson *writer*
Braverman, Robert Jay *international consultant, public policy educator*
Bravo, Rose Marie *retail executive*
†Braxton, Toni *popular musician*
Braziller, George *publisher*
Brazinsky, Irving *chemical engineering educator*
†Brecher, John *newspaper editor*
†Brechner, Stanley *artistic director*
Brecker, Manfred *retail company executive*
Breglio, John F. *lawyer*
Bregman, Martin *film producer*
†Breindel, Eric Marc *editor, columnist, educator*
Breines, Simon *architect*
Breinin, Goodwin M. *physician*
Brendel, Alfred *concert pianist*
Brennan, Daniel L. *accounting, consulting firm executive*
Brennan, Donald P. *aircraft parts manufacturing executive*
Brennan, Henry Higginson *architect*
Brennan, Murray Frederick *surgeon, oncologist*
Brennan, Timothy William *entertainment company executive*
Brenner, Egon *university official, education consultant*
Brenner, Erma *author*
Brenner, Frank *lawyer*
Brenner, Gita Kedar Voivodas *small business owner, research and editing consultant*
Brenner, Howard Martin *banker*
Bresani, Federico Fernando *business executive*
Bresler, Martin I. *lawyer*
Breslin, Jimmy *columnist, author*
†Breslow, Jan Leslie *scientist, educator, physician*
Breslow, Ronald Charles *chemist, educator*
Bressler, Bernard *lawyer*
Breuer, Lee *writer, theatrical director, producer, actor*
Brewer, John Charles *journalist*
†Brewer, Karen *librarian*
Brewster, Robert Gene *concert singer, educator*
Brezenoff, Stanley *bi-state agency administrator*
Brice, John R. *publishing sales manager*
Bricken, Barry Irwin *fashion designer*
Brickman, Marshall *screenwriter, director*
Brief, Henry *association executive*
†Brier, Pamela Sara *health facility administrator*
Briess, Roger Charles *brewing and food industry executive*
Briggs, Jean Audrey *publishing company executive*
Briggs, Philip *insurance company executive*
Briggs, Taylor Rastrick *lawyer*
†Brill, Steven *magazine editor*
Brilliant, Richard *art history educator*
Briloff, Abraham Jacob *accountant, educator*
Brimelow, Peter *journalist*
†Bring, Murray H. *lawyer*
†Brinker, Robert J. *investment company executive, radio talk show host*
†Brinkley, Christie *model*
Bristah, Pamela Jean *librarian*
Britell, Peter Stuart *lawyer*
Brittenham, Raymond Lee *investment company executive*
Broadwater, Douglas Dwight *lawyer*
Broadwin, Joseph Louis *lawyer*
†Broches, Paul Elias *architect*
Brocksmith, James G., Jr. *accounting, management consulting firm executive*
Brockway, Merrill LaMonte *television producer and director*
Broder, Douglas Fisher *lawyer*
Brodkey, Harold Roy *writer*
Brodsky, Samuel *lawyer*
Brodsky, Stanley Martin *engineering technology educator, researcher*
Brody, Alan Jeffrey *business executive*
Brody, Alexander *advertising executive*
†Brody, Edward Isaac *marketing professional*
Brody, Eugene David *investment company executive*
Brody, Jacqueline *editor*
Brody, Jane Ellen *journalist*
Brody, Kenneth David *investment banker*
Brody, Saul Nathaniel *English literature educator*
†Broecker, Wallace S. *geophysics educator*
Brofman, Lance Mark *portfolio manager, mutual fund executive*
Brokaw, Clifford Vail, III *investment banker, business executive*
Brokaw, Thomas John *television broadcast executive, correspondent*
Brome, Thomas Reed *lawyer*
†Bronfman, Edgar M., Jr. *food products executive*
Bronfman, Edgar Miles *distillery executive*
Bronkema, Frederick Hollander *minister, church official*
Bronstein, Richard J. *lawyer*
Brook, David William *psychiatrist*
Brooke, Paul Alan *finance company executive*
Brooks, Diana D. *auction house executive*
Brooks, Gary *management consultant*
Brooks, Geraldine *reporter, correspondent*
Brooks, Jerome Bernard *English and Afro-American literature educator*
Brooks, Lorimer Page *patent lawyer*
Brooks, Russell Edwin *lawyer*
Brooks, Timothy H. *media executive*
Brooks, Tyrone *dancer*
Brooksbank, Randolph Wood *broadcasting executive*
Bross, Steward Richard, Jr. *lawyer*
Brothers, Joyce Diane *television personality, psychologist*
Broude, Richard Frederick *lawyer, educator*
Broughton, Phillip Charles *lawyer*
Broun, Heywood Hale *author, broadcaster, actor*
Browdy, Joseph Eugene *lawyer*
Brown, Carroll *diplomat, association executive*
Brown, Charles Dodgson *lawyer*
Brown, David *motion picture producer, writer*
†Brown, Edward Glenn *chef, restauranteur*
Brown, Francis Cabell, Jr. *lawyer*
Brown, Fred Elmore *investment executive*
Brown, G(lenn) William, Jr. *investment banker*
Brown, Helen Gurley *writer, editor*
Brown, Hobson, Jr. *executive search firm consultant and executive*
Brown, Jason Walter *neurologist, educator, researcher*
Brown, Jonathan *art historian, fine arts educator*
Brown, Les (Lester Louis) *journalist*
Brown, Marvin S. *publisher*
Brown, Meredith M. *lawyer*
Brown, Milton Wolf *art historian, educator*
Brown, Paul M. *lawyer*
Brown, Peter Megargee *lawyer, writer, lecturer*
Brown, Ralph Sawyer, Jr. *lawyer, business executive*
†Brown, Raymond Edward *educator, priest*
Brown, Robert Delford *artist*
Brown, Robert William *baseball league executive, physician*
Brown, Ronald *stockbroker*
Brown, Seymour William *engineering executive, consultant*
Brown, Terrence Charles *art association executive, researcher, lecturer*
Brown, Tina *magazine editor*
Brown, Trisha *dancer*
†Browne, Arthur *newspaper editor*
Browne, Jeffrey Francis *lawyer*
Browne, Leslie *dancer, actress*
Browne, Malcolm Wilde *journalist*
Browne, Morgan Trew *editor*
Browning, Edmond Lee *bishop*
Browning, John *pianist*
Brownwood, David Owen *lawyer*
Bruckmann, Donald John *investment banker*
Bruckmann, Mark F. *lawyer*
Bruggeman, Terrance John *corporate executive*
Brumback-Henry, Sarah Elizabeth *industrial psychologist, management and corporate consultant*
Brumm, James Earl *trading company executive*
Brundage, Susan *art dealer, gallery director*
Brundige, Robert W., Jr. *lawyer*
Brunie, Charles Henry *investment manager*
Brush, Charles Francis *anthropologist*
Bruzs, Boris Olgerd *management consultant*
Bryan, Barry Richard *lawyer*
Bryant, Gay *magazine editor, writer*
Brydon, Donald James *media consultant, former news service executive*
Brzustowicz, Stanislaw Henry *clinical dentistry educator*
Bschorr, Paul Joseph *lawyer*
†Buatta, Mario *interior designer*
Buchwald, Elias *public relations executive*
Buchwald, Naomi Reice *federal magistrate judge*
Buck, Louise Zierdt *psychologist*
Buckles, Robert Howard *investment company executive*
Buckley, Priscilla Langford *magazine editor*
Buckley, Virginia Laura *editor*
Buckley, William Frank, Jr. *magazine editor, writer*
Buckman, Thomas Richard *foundation executive, educator*
Bucko, John Joseph *investment corporation executive*
Buhagiar, Marion *editor, author*
†Bujold, Lois McMaster *science fiction writer*
Bullen, Richard Hatch *former corporation executive*
Bulliet, Richard Williams *history educator, novelist*
Bullock, H. Ridgely *management and investment executive, lawyer*
Bullock, Hugh *investment banker*
Bumbry, Grace *soprano*
Bundschuh, George August William *insurance company executive*
Bundy, McGeorge *former government official, history educator*
†Bungey, Michael *advertising executive*
Bunts, Frank Emory *artist*
†Burandt, Gary Edward *advertising agency executive*
Burback, Steven Brent *military administrator*
Burenga, Kenneth L. *publishing executive*
Burg, Mitchell Marc *advertising executive*
Burgee, John Henry *architect*
Burger, Chester *retired management consultant*
Burgheim, Richard Allan *magazine editor*
Burgweger, Francis Joseph Dewes, Jr. *lawyer*
Burke, Chris *actor*
Burke, Daniel Barnett *retired communications corporation executive*
Burke, James Joseph, Jr. *investment banker*
Burke, Thomas Edmund *lawyer*
Burkhardt, Ronald Robert *advertising executive*
Burland, Brian Berkeley *novelist, poet, artist, scenarist, playwright*
Burlingame, Lloyd Lamson *design instructor*
Burns, Arnold Irwin *lawyer*
Burns, John F. *reporter*
Burns, John Joseph, Jr. *business executive*
Burns, Robin *cosmetics company executive*
Burns, Ronald S. *advertising company executive*
Burns, Ward *textile company executive*
Burnshaw, Stanley *writer*
Burrell, Kenneth Earl *guitarist, composer*
Burrill, Kathleen R. F. (Kathleen R. F. Griffin-Burrill) *Turkologist, educator*
Burrows, Michael Donald *lawyer*
Burrows, Selig Saul *industrialist*
Bursky, Herman Aaron *lawyer*
Burson, Harold *public relations executive*
Burton, John Campbell *university dean, educator, consultant*
Burton, Robert Gene *printing and publishing executive*
†Burton, Steven Bryant *advertising agency executive*
†Bush, Gage *ballet mistress*
Bush, Kate (Catherine Bush) *singer, songwriter*
Bushey, Alan Scott *insurance holding company executive*
Bushnell, John Alden *diplomat, economist*
Bussell, Mark Stephen *newspaper picture editor*
Butcher, Willard Carlisle *banker*
Butler, Jonathan Putnam *architect*
Butler, Robert Neil *gerontologist, psychiatrist, writer, educator*
Butler, Samuel Coles *lawyer*
Butler, Vincent Paul, Jr. *physician, educator*
Butler, William Joseph *lawyer*
Butowsky, David Martin *lawyer*
Buttenwieser, Lawrence Benjamin *lawyer*
Butterfield, R. Keith *financial company executive*
Button, Richard Totten *television and stage producer, former figure skating champion*
†Buttrick, Harold *architect*
Buxton, Jorge Norman *ophthalmologist*
Byington, Homer Morrison, III *financial consultant*
Bylinsky, Gene Michael *magazine editor*
Byrne, Gerard Anthony *publishing company executive, marketing consultant*
Byrne, James Thomas, Jr. *banker, lawyer*
Bystryn, Jean-Claude *dermatologist, educator*
Cable, Paul Andrew *lawyer*
Cadwell, Franchellie Margaret *advertising agency executive, writer*
Cafiero, Eugene Anthony *manufacturing company executive*
Caggiano, Joseph *advertising executive*
Cahan, William George *surgeon, educator*
Cahn, Joshua Binion *lawyer*
Cahn, Steven M. *philosopher, educator*
Cajigal, Joseph A. *financial services executive*
Cajori, Charles Florian *artist, educator*
Calabrese, Rosalie Sue *professional arts administrator, writer*
Calder, Kenneth Thomas *psychiatrist, psychoanalyst, educator*
†Caldwell, Earl *newspaper columnist*
Caldwell, Philip *financial services company executive, retired automobile manufacturing company executive*
Caldwell, Susan Hanes *art dealer*
Caldwell, Zoe *actress, director*
Calegari, Maria *ballerina*
Calise, Ronald Jan *investment banking executive*
Calise, William Joseph, Jr. *lawyer*
Calisher, Hortense (Mrs. Curtis Harnack) *author*
Call, Neil Judson *corporate executive*
†Callagy, John M. *lawyer*
Callahan, Joseph Patrick *lawyer*
Callen, John Holmes, Jr. *executive search consultant*
Callum, Myles *magazine editor, writer*
Calvey, Brian J. *lawyer*
Calvillo, Ricardo C. *advertising agency executive*
Cameron, Eleanor *author*
†Campbell, Colin (Soupy) *professional hockey coach*
Campbell, Colin Goetze *foundation president*
Campbell, Douglass *banker*
†Campbell, George, Jr. *physicist, administrator*
Campbell, Joan Brown *religious organization executive*
Campbell, Mary Schmidt *dean art school*
†Campbell, Naomi *model*
†Campbell, Robert Chambers *critic, playwright*
Campbell, Ronald Neil *magazine designer*
Campbell, Scott G. *lawyer*
Campbell, William Foley *public relations executive*
Campbell, William I. *cigarette company executive*
Campbell, Woodrow Wilson, Jr. *lawyer*
†Campi, John G. *newspaper publishing executive*
Canby, Vincent *film critic*
Cancro, Robert *psychiatrist*
Candia, Oscar A. *ophthalmologist, physiology educator*
†Canin, Ethan *writer*
Cannaliato, Vincent, Jr. *investment banker, mathematician*
Cannell, John Redferne *lawyer*
Cannella, John Matthew *federal judge*
Cannon, James Anthony *advertising executive*
†Cannon, John Haile *retail executive*
Canoni, John David *lawyer*
Canter, Stanley D. *retired marketing consulting company executive*
Cantilli, Edmund Joseph *safety engineering educator, writer*
Cantor, Alexandra S. E. *professional society administrator*
Cantor, Bernard Gerald *financial executive*
Cantor, Melvyn Leon *lawyer*
Cantor, Norman Frank *history educator, writer*
Cantor, Richard Ira *physician, corporate health executive*
Cantrell, Lana *actress, singer*
Cantwell, Mary *journalist*
Caouette, John Bernard *insurance company executive*
Capalbo, Carmen Charles *director, producer*
Caplan, Richard V. *lawyer*
Caples, Richard James *dance company executive, lawyer*
Cappon, Andre Alfred *management consultant*
Cappon, Rene Jacques *news editor*
Capriati, Jennifer Maria *professional tennis player*
Caputo, Philip Joseph *author, journalist, screenwriter*
Caraley, Demetrios *political scientist, educator, author*
Caras, Roger Andrew *author, motion picture company executive, television correspondent, radio commentator*
Carb, Stephen Ames *lawyer*
Carberry, Charles Michael *lawyer*
Cardenes, Andres Jorge *violinist, music educator*
Cardew, William Joseph *bank executive*
Cardinale, Kathleen Carmel *medical center administrator*
Cardinali, Albert John *lawyer*
Cardozo, Benjamin Mordecai *lawyer*
Cardozo, Michael A. *lawyer*
Carelli, Gabor Paul *opera singer*
Carey, J. Edwin *lawyer*
Carey, Mariah *vocalist, songwriter*
Carey, Thomas Hilton *advertising agency executive*
Carey, William Polk *investment banker*
Cariou, Len Joseph *actor, director*
Carley, John Halliday *lawyer*
Carling, Francis *lawyer*
Carlson, David Bret *lawyer, consultant*
Carlson, Marian Bille *geneticist, researcher, educator*
Carlson, Marvin Albert *theater educator*
†Carlson, P(atricia) M(cElroy) *writer*
Carlson, Theodore Joshua *lawyer, retired utility company executive*
Carman, Gregory Wright *federal judge*
Carnase, Thomas Paul *graphic designer, typographic consultant*
Carnella, Frank Thomas *information executive*
Caro, Robert Allan *author*
Caroff, Phyllis M. *social work educator*
Carpenter, Mary-Chapin *country music singer*
Carpenter, Patricia *music educator*
Carr, Arthur Charles *psychologist, educator*
Carr, Gladys Justin *publishing company executive*
Carr, Ronald Edward *ophthalmologist, educator*
Carra, Andrew Joseph *advertising executive*
Carreras, José *tenor*
Carret, Philip Lord *corporate executive*
†Carrey, Bernard S. *lawyer*
Carroll, J. Speed *lawyer*
Carroll, Joseph J(ohn) *lawyer*
†Carroll, Kent *book publishing executive*
Carroll, Raoul Lord *lawyer, investment banker*
Carroll, Thomas Joseph *investment services company executive*
†Carter, Carolyn Houchin *advertising agency executive*
†Carter, Graydon *editor*
Carter, James Hal, Jr. *lawyer*
Carter, John Mack *publishing company executive*
†Carter, Kevin *photographer*
Carter, Marshall Nichols *banker*
Carter, Robert Lee *federal judge*
†Carter, Sylvia *journalist*
Carthaus, James Arthur *financial service company executive*
Cartland, Barbara *author*
Caruso, Victor Guy *investment banker*
Carver, Brent *actor*
Carvey, Dana *actor, stand up comedian*
Casals-Ariet, Jordi *physician*
Case, Eugene Lawrence *advertising agency executive*
Case, Hadley *oil company executive*
Casebere, James Edward *artist*
Casei, Nedda *mezzo-soprano*
Cash, Rosanne *country singer, songwriter*
Cashin, Richard Marshall *international aid official*
Caso, Ronald George *lawyer, accountant*
Cassell, Eric Jonathan *physician*
Cassell, Kay Ann *librarian*
Cassella, William Nathan, Jr. *organization executive*
Castel, P. Kevin *lawyer*
Castelli, Leo *art dealer*
Castellino, Ronald Augustus Dietrich *radiologist*

Castle, John Krob merchant banker
Castleberry, May Lewis librarian,curator,editor
Castleman, (Esther) Riva museum curator
Castronovo, David English language educator
Catlett, Elizabeth sculptor, printmaker, educator
Catley-Carlson, Margaret association executive
†Cato, John David religious organization administrator
Catsimatidis, John Andreas retail chain executive, airline executive
Catuzzi, J. P., Jr. lawyer
Cauthen, Steve jockey
Cavaglieri, Giorgio architect
Cavior, Warren Joseph communications executive
Caws, Mary Ann French language and comparative literature educator, critic
Cayne, James E. investment banker
Cazeaux, Isabelle Anne Marie retired musicology educator
Cedarbaum, Miriam Goldman federal judge
Ceresney, Ian lawyer
Cesarani, Sal fashion designer
Chajet, Clive communications consultant
Chalif, Seymour H. lawyer
Chalk, Howard Wolfe advertising agency executive
Chalsty, John Steele investment banker
Chamson, Sandra Potkorony psychologist
Chan, Lo-Yi Cheung Yuen architect
Chan, W. Y. pharmacologist, educator
Chancellor, John William former news correspondent
Chandler, Kenneth A. newspaper editor
Chandler, Robert Leslie public relations executive
Chaney, Verne Edward, Jr. surgeon, foundation executive, educator
Chang, Robert Timothy fixed-income researcher, consultant
Channing, Alan Harold hospital administrator
†Chao, James S. C. maritime executive
Chapin, Hugh A. lawyer
Chapin, Schuyler Garrison cultural affairs executive, university dean
Chapman, Peter Herbert investment company executive
Chapnick, David B. lawyer, partner
Chappell, John Charles lawyer
Chargaff, Erwin biochemistry educator emeritus, writer
Charlesworth, Sarah E. photographer, conceptual artist
Charnin, Martin theatrical director, lyricist, producer
Charrier, Michael Edward investment banker
Charron, Paul Richard apparel company executive
Chase, Merrill Wallace immunologist, educator
Chase, Oscar G(ottfried) law educator, consultant, author
Chase, Sylvia B. journalist
Chaves, Jose Maria diplomat, foundation administrator, lawyer, educator
Chazen, Hartley James lawyer
†Checker, Chubby (Ernest Evans) popular musician
Checketts, David Wayne professional basketball team executive
Chefitz, Harold Neal investment banker
Cheh, Huk Yuk engineering educator, electrochemist
Chell, Beverly C. lawyer
Chen, Chi (Chen Chi) artist
Chenault, Kenneth Irvine financial services company executive
Cheney, Richard Eugene public relations executive
Cheng, Chuen Yan biochemist, educator
Chereskin, Alvin advertising executive
Chermayeff, Ivan graphic designer
Chernin, Fredric David advertising agency executive
†Chernoff, Allan correspondent
Chernow, David A. former distillery executive, consultant
Cherovsky, Erwin Louis lawyer, writer
Cherry, Rona Beatrice magazine editor, writer
Chervokas, John Vincent advertising executive
†Chesnutt, Jane publishing executive
Chester, Giraud television executive
Chester, John Geoffrey lawyer
†Cheung, Ambrose Lin-Yau microbiologist, researcher
Chevalier, Samuel Fletcher banker
Chevray, Rene physics educator
Chiarchiaro, Frank John lawyer
Chiarelli, Joseph accountant, banker
Childs, John Farnsworth investment banker
†Chiles, Nick newspaper reporter
Chilstrom, Robert Meade lawyer
Chimsky, Mark Evan editorial executive
Chin, Sylvia Fung lawyer
Chinnis, Pamela P. religion organization administrator
Chitty, Arthur Ben historiographer, consultant
Chook, Paul Howard publishing executive
†Chopra, Deepak writer
Chou, Wen-chung composer
Chow, Yuan Shih mathematician, educator
Chrisanthopoulos, Peter advertising executive
Christaldi, Brian lawyer
Christensen, Dieter ethnomusicologist, educator
Christensen, Henry, III lawyer
Christian, Darrell L. journalist
Christo, (Christo Vladimirov Javacheff) artist
Christopher, Maurine Brooks foundation administrator, writer, editor
Christy, Arthur Hill lawyer
Chromow, Sheri P. lawyer
Chryst, Gary ballet dancer
Chu, C. K. applied mathematician, educator
Chu, Roderick Gong-Wah management consultant
Chua, Nam-Hai molecular biologist, educator
Chudnovsky, Gregory Volfovich mathematician, educator
Chung, Constance Yu-hwa (Connie Chung) broadcast journalist
Church, Frank Forrester minister, author, columnist
Chwast, Seymour graphic artist
Ciechanover, Joseph banker, lawyer
Citron, Richard Ira management consultant
Clabby, William Robert editor
Claiborne, Liz (Elisabeth Claiborne Ortenberg) fashion designer
Claire, Thomas Andrew treasurer
Clamar, Aphrodite J. psychologist
Clancy, Thomas L. novelist
Clapman, Peter Carlyle insurance company executive, lawyer
Clapton, Eric musician
Clarens, John Gaston investment executive
Clark, Cameron lawyer
Clark, Carolyn Cochran lawyer
Clark, Howard Longstreth lawyer, business executive
Clark, Howard Longstreth, Jr. finance company executive
Clark, J. Thomas advertising agency executive
Clark, Jonathan Montgomery lawyer
†Clark, Leonard J., Jr. personnel service executive
Clark, Matt science writer
Clark, Merrell Edward, Jr. lawyer
Clark, Ramsey lawyer
Clark, Robert Henry, Jr. holding company executive
Clark, Thomas Carlyle banker
Clark, William Stratton physician
†Clarke, Frank William advertising agency executive
Clarke, Garvey Elliott educational association administrator, lawyer
Clarke, Hope choreographer
Clarke, John Clem artist
Clarke, Kenneth Kingsley electrical equipment company executive
†Clarke, Richard M. chemicals executive
Claro, Jaime metal trading company executive
Clary, Richard Wayland lawyer
†Claster, Jill Nadell university administrator, history educator
†Clausen, Ned Carl advertising executive
Clauson, James Wilson accountant
Clavell, James author, screenwriter, producer, director, playwright
Clayton, Joe Don lawyer
†Clayton, Jon Kerry holding company executive
Clayton, William L. investment banking executive
Cleary, Beverly Atlee (Mrs. Clarence T. Cleary) author
Cliff, Walter Conway lawyer
Clifford, Stewart Burnett banker
Close, Charles Thomas (Chuck Close) artist
Close, Michael John lawyer
Cloward, Richard Andrew social work educator
Clurman, Richard Michael journalist
Cobb, Henry Nichols architect
Cochrane, James Louis economist
Coelho, Tony former congressman
Coen, Robert Joseph advertising agency executive
Cogan, James Richard lawyer
Cogan, Marshall S. entrepreneur
Cohen, Alan Norman business executive
†Cohen, Arnold apparel executive
Cohen, Arthur Morris artist
Cohen, Burton Jerome financial service executive
Cohen, Cora artist
Cohen, Edmund Stephen lawyer
Cohen, Edward civil engineer
Cohen, Edward Herschel lawyer
Cohen, Eli Edward sociology educator
Cohen, Ezechiel Godert David physicist, educator
Cohen, Fred Howard lawyer
Cohen, Henry Rodgin lawyer
Cohen, Herman Nathan private investigator
Cohen, Hollace T. lawyer
Cohen, Irving Elias real estate executive
Cohen, Irving I. financial executive
Cohen, Isidore Leonard violinist, educator
Cohen, Jeff media critic, columnist
Cohen, Joel Ephraim scientist, educator
Cohen, Joel J. lawyer, investment banker
Cohen, Jonathan Little investment banker
Cohen, Lawrence Alan real estate executive
Cohen, Mildred Thaler art gallery director
Cohen, Miriam writer, educator
Cohen, Myron lawyer
Cohen, Noel Lee otolaryngologist, educator
Cohen, Richard Gerard lawyer
Cohen, Samuel Israel clergyman, organization executive
Cohen, Saul Bernard former college president, geographer
Cohen, Selma Jeanne dance historian
Cohen, Stephen Frand political scientist, historian, educator, author
Cohn, Bertram Josiah investment banker
†Cohn, Bob public relations executive
Cohn, David Herc retired foreign service officer
Cohn, Harvey mathematician
Cohn, Sam motion picture and theatrical agent
Cohn, Theodore management consultant
Colasuonno, Louis Christopher newspaper editor
Colbourn, Frank Edwin communications educator
Colby, Marvelle Seitman business management educator, administrator
Colby, Robert Alan retired library science educator
Cole, Carolyn Jo brokerage house executive
Cole, Elma Phillipson (Mrs. John Strickler Cole) social welfare executive
Cole, Jonathan Richard sociologist, academic administrator
Cole, Lewis George lawyer
Cole, Max artist
Cole, Sylvan, Jr. art dealer
Cole, Vinson tenor
Coleman, Cy pianist, composer, producer
Coleman, D. Jackson ophthalmologist, educator
Coleman, Denis Patrick, Jr. investment banker
Coleman, George Edward tenor, alto and soprano saxophonist
†Coleman, Leonard S., Jr. sports association executive
Coleman, Lester Laudy otolaryngologist
Coleman, Martin Stone office furniture company executive
Coleman, Morton oncologist, hematologist, educator
Coleman, Ornette composer, instrumentalist
Coler, Myron A(braham) chemical engineer, educator
†Coles, Michael H. investment banker
Colin, Georgia Talmey interior designer
Colker, Edward artist, educator
Coll, John Peter, Jr. lawyer
Collamore, Thomas Jones corporate executive
Collins, Adrian Anthony lawyer, accountant, educator
Collins, Bud sports commentator
Collins, Judy Marjorie singer, composer
Collins, Wayne Dale lawyer
Collins, William T. lawyer
Collinson, Dale Stanley lawyer
Collyer, Michael lawyer
Colombo, Frank V. securities company executive
Colombo, Furio Marco corporate executive
Colonel, Sheri Lynn advertising agency executive
Comden, Betty writer, dramatist, lyricist, performer
Comey, Dale Raymond insurance company executive
Comfort, William Twyman, Jr. banker
Comfrey, Kathleen Marie lawyer
Comissiona, Sergiu conductor
Comitas, Lambros anthropologist
Como, Perry singer
Conarroe, Joel Osborne foundation administrator, educator, editor
Conboy, Kenneth lawyer, former federal judge
Concannon, Richard James lawyer
Cone, James Hal theologian, educator, author
Conklin, Thomas J. insurance company executive
Conlon, James Joseph conductor
Connelly, Albert R. lawyer
Conner, William Curtis judge
Connick, Harry, Jr. jazz musician, actor, singer
Connolly, John Joseph health care company executive
Connolly, William Gerard newspaper editor
Connor, Joseph E. accountant
Connor, Martin Edward state senator, lawyer
Connor, Robert Patrick investment company executive
Conover, Robert Fremont artist, educator
Conrad, Winthrop Brown, Jr. lawyer
Consagra, Sophie Chandler academy administrator
Constance, Thomas Ernest lawyer
Constantine, Jan Friedman lawyer
Conston, Henry Siegismund lawyer
Conway, David Antony corporate executive
Conway, Kevin actor, director
Cook, Bart R. dancer
Cook, Blanche Wiesen history educator, journalist
Cook, James magazine editor
Cook, Michael Lewis lawyer
Cook, Robert Stansfield, Jr. lawyer
Cook, Robin author
Cooke, Alfred Alistair correspondent, broadcaster
Cooke, Gordon Richard retail executive
Cooke, Mary A. hospice director
Cookson, Albert Ernest telephone and telegraph company executive
Cooney, Joan Ganz broadcasting executive
Cooney, John Patrick, Jr. lawyer
†Cooper, Andrew public relations executive
Cooper, Arnold Michael psychiatrist
Cooper, Arthur Martin magazine editor
Cooper, Guy editor periodical
Cooper, Irving Ben federal judge
Cooper, Marilyn actress
Cooper, Mario artist, educator
Cooper, Michael Anthony lawyer
Cooper, Norman Streich pathologist, medical educator
Cooper, Paula art dealer
Cooper, Paulette Marcia writer
Cooper, R. John, III advertising agency executive, lawyer
Cooper, Stephen Herbert lawyer
Coplan, Norman Allan lawyer
Coppel, Alfred author
Corbin, Herbert Leonard public relations executive
Corbin, Sol Neil lawyer
Corcoran, David newspaper editor
Corcoran, Robert Lee, Jr. banker
Cordero, Angel T., Jr. jockey
Core, Mary Carolyn W. Parsons radiologic technologist
Corigliano, John Paul composer
Corley, Leslie M. investment banker
Corliss, Richard Nelson critic, magazine editor
Corman, Avery author
Cornell, George W. journalist
Cornez, Gerald H. association executive
†Cornstein, David B. finance executive
Corporon, John Robert broadcasting executive
Corr, Gary Alan finance company executive
Corrigan, E. Gerald investment banker
†Corrigan, Timothy Patrick Pennington Blake advertising executive
Corry, Carl dancer
Corry, John Adams lawyer
Corsaro, Frank Andrew theater, musical and opera director
Corso, Gregory Nunzio poet
Cortor, Eldzier artist, printmaker
Cory, Charles Robinson media investment banker
Corzine, Jon Stevens investment banker
†Cose, Ellis magazine editor
Cosell, Howard (Howard William Cohen) sports journalist
Cossotto, Fiorenza mezzo-soprano
†Costa, Max health facility administrator, pharmacology educator, environmental medicine educator
Costello, Gerald Michael editor
Costello, John Robert linguistics educator
Costello, Richard Neumann advertising agency executive
Costikyan, Edward N(azar) lawyer
†Cotler, Joanna children's book editor, artist
Cotter, Ernest Robert, III finance company executive
Cotter, James Michael lawyer
Cotton, Richard lawyer
†Coulter, Catherine writer
†Coupland, Douglas C. writer
Couric, Katherine broadcast journalist
Court, Kathryn Diana editor
Cowan, Martin B. lawyer
Cowan, Richard vocalist
Cowan, Wallace Edgar lawyer
Cowen, Edward S. lawyer
Cowen, Robert Nathan lawyer
Cowin, Stephen Corteen biomedical engineering educator, consultant
Cowles, Charles art dealer
Cowles, Frederick Oliver lawyer
Cox, Archibald, Jr. investment banker
Cox, Marshall lawyer
Cox, Robert Gene management consultant
†Cox, Winston H. television executive
Craft, Randal Robert, Jr. lawyer
Craig, Charles Samuel marketing educator
Craig, George publishing executive
Crain, Irving Jay psychiatrist, educator
Cramer, Edward Morton lawyer, music company executive
Cramer, Marjorie plastic surgeon
Crames, Michael J. lawyer
Crane, Benjamin Field lawyer
Crane, Stephen Andrew insurance company executive
Cranefield, Paul Frederic pharmacology educator, physician, scientist
Crary, Miner Dunham, Jr. lawyer
Crawford, Bruce Edgar advertising executive
Crawford, Cindy model
Crawford, Harold Bernard publisher
Crawley, John Boevey publisher
Creedon, John J. insurance company executive
Creel, Thomas Leonard lawyer
Crespin, Regine soprano
Crews, Harry Eugene author
†Crier, Catherine television news correspondent
Crile, Susan artist
Crisci, Mathew G. marketing executive
Crisona, James Joseph lawyer
Crist, Judith film and drama critic
†Critchell, Simon James corporate executive
Critchlow, Charles Howard lawyer
Crivello, Anthony actor
Croce, Arlene Louise critic
Crohn, Max Henry, Jr. lawyer
Cromwell, Oliver Dean investment banker
Cronholm, Lois S. biology educator
Cronkite, Walter radio and television news correspondent
Crosby, John Griffith investment banker
Crosland, Philip Crawford advertising company executive
Cross, George Alan Martin biochemistry educator, researcher
Cross, Peter A. lawyer
Cross, Samuel S. lawyer
Cross, Theodore Lamont publisher, author
Cross, William Redmond, Jr. corporate director, foundation executive
†Crow, Elizabeth publishing company executive
Crow, Elizabeth Smith publishing company executive
Crowdus, Gary Alan film company executive
Cryer, Gretchen playwright, lyricist, actress
Crystal, James William insurance company executive
Crystal, Lester Martin television producer
Cubitto, Robert J. lawyer
Culhane, John William journalist, author, film historian
Culhane, Shamus producer, author
Cullen, Patrick Colborn English educator
Culligan, John William retired corporate executive
Cullman, Edgar Meyer diversified consumer products company executive
Cullman, Hugh retired tobacco company executive
Culp, Michael securities company executive, research director
Cumming, Ian M. holding company executive
Cummins, Herman Zachary physicist
Cuneo, Donald Lane lawyer, educator
†Cunningham, Bill photographer
†Cunningham, Jeffrey Milton publishing executive
Cunningham, Merce dancer
Cunningham, Patrick Joseph advertising agency executive
Cuozzo, Steven David newspaper editor
Curley, Walter Joseph Patrick, Jr. diplomat, investment banker
Currie, Bruce artist
†Curry, Ann broadcast journalist
Curry, Jack magazine editor
Curry, Jane Louise writer
Curtin, Brian Joseph ophthalmologist
Curtis, Frank R. lawyer
Curtis, Paul James mime
Curtis, Robert Joseph financial advisor
Curtis, Sheldon lawyer
Curtis, Susan Grace lawyer
Cushing, Harry Cooke, IV investment banker
†Cutie, James A. newspaper publishing executive
Cutler, Kenneth Burnett lawyer, investment company executive
†Cutler, Laurel advertising agency executive
Cutler, Rhoda psychologist
†Cutler, Richard J. metal products executive
Czerwinski, Edward Joseph foreign language educator
Dabah, Haim apparel executive
Dacey, Eileen M. lawyer
Dacey, Michael F. bank executive
Dadakis, John D. lawyer
Dailey, Benjamin Peter chemistry educator
†Daily, John Charles software company executive
Daitz, Ronald Frederick lawyer
Dajani, Virginia arts administrator
Dakin, Christine Whitney dancer, educator
†Daldry, Stephen theatrical director
Dale, Harvey Philip law educator
Dale, Jim actor
†D'Alessio, Catherine Anne fragrance company executive
Daley, James E. accounting firm executive
Dallas, William Moffit, Jr. lawyer
Dallmann, Daniel F. artist, educator
Dalrymple, Jean Van Kirk theatrical producer, publicist, author
Dalton, Dennis Gilmore political science educator
Daly, Charles Patrick publishing company executive
Daly, George Garman college dean, educator
Daly, Joe Ann Godown publishing company executive
Daly, John Neal investment company executive
†Daly, Margaret V. magazine editor
†Daly, Michael newspaper columnist
d'Amboise, Christopher ballet dancer, artistic director, choreographer
d'Amboise, Jacques Joseph dancer, choreographer
Damson, Barrie Morton oil and gas exploration company executive
Dana, F(rank) Mitchell theatrical lighting designer
Danaher, Frank Erwin transportation technologist
Dane, Maxwell former advertising executive
D'Angelo, Joseph Francis publishing company executive
Dangler, Richard Reiss corporate service companies executive, entrepreneur
Daniel, David Ronald management consultant
Daniel, Gerard Lucian physician, pharmaceutical company executive
Daniel, Richard Nicholas fabricated metals manufacturing company executive
†Daniels, Aaron Martin broadcasting executive
Daniels, Faith newscaster
†Daniels, Joanne D. publisher
Danilek, Donald J. lawyer
Danilova, Alexandra ballet dancer, choreographer
Danish, Roy Bertram communications consultant
Danitz, Marilynn Patricia choreographer
Dannhauser, Stephen J. lawyer
Danson, Stephen Michael brokerage firm executive
Danto, Arthur Coleman author, philosophy educator
Danzig, Aaron Leon lawyer
Danzig, Frederick Paul newspaper editor
Danzig, Jerome Alan (Jerry) management consultant
†Danzig, Robert James newspaper executive
Danzig, Sarah H. Palfrey retired advertising agency executive, writer
†Danziger, Bruce Edward structural engineer
†Danziger, Paula author
Daphnis, Nassos artist
†DaPuzzo, Peter James investment banker, trader, financial consultant
Darling, Robert Edward designer, stage director
Darlington, Henry, Jr. investment broker
†Darnell, James Edwin, Jr. molecular biologist, educator
Darrell, Norris, Jr. lawyer
Darrow, Jill E(llen) lawyer
†Darrow, Katherine Prager lawyer, publishing executive

Darst, David Martin investment banking company executive, writer, educator
Darvarova, Elmira violinist, concertmaster
†Dattner, Richard architect, educator
Dauben, Joseph Warren history educator
D'Auria, Anthony J. lawyer
David, Hal lyricist
David, Miles association and marketing executive
†David, Theoharis Lambros architect, educator
Davidovich, Bella pianist
Davidovich, Jaime video artist, researcher
Davidson, Donald William advertising executive
Davidson, George Allan lawyer
Davidson, Joy Elaine mezzo-soprano
Davidson, Mark Edward lawyer
Davidson, Nancy Brachman artist, educator
Davidson, Robert Bruce lawyer
David-Weill, Michel Alexandre investment banker
Davies, Dennis Russell conductor, music director, pianist
Davies, Jane B(adger) (Mrs. Lyn Davies) architectural historian
†Davies, Martha Hill dance educator
Davis, Andrew Frank conductor
Davis, Clive Jay record company executive
Davis, Douglas Matthew artist, educator, author
Davis, Edward Shippen lawyer
Davis, Evan Anderson lawyer
Davis, Frederick Townsend lawyer
Davis, George Linn banker
†Davis, J. Morton investment company executive, economist
†Davis, Jerry Albert architect
Davis, Karen Padgett fund executive
Davis, Kathryn Wasserman foundation executive, writer, lecturer
†Davis, Kenneth A. retail executive
†Davis, Kenneth Leon psychiatrist, pharmacologist, medical educator
Davis, Leonard violist
Davis, Lorraine Jensen writer, editor
Davis, Martin S. investment company executive
Davis, Orlin Ray publisher, consultant
Davis, Perry John computer executive
Davis, Richard Bruce investment banker
Davis, Richard Joel lawyer, former government official
Davis, Richard Ralph lawyer
Davis, Samuel hospital administrator, educator, consultant
Davis, Steven Howard lawyer
Davis, Wendell, Jr. lawyer
Davison, Daniel Pomeroy fine arts auction executive
†Davoe, David publishing executive
Dawn, Deborah dancer
Dawson, Thomas Cleland, II financial executive
Dayan, Rodney S. lawyer
Deak, Istvan historian, educator
Dean, Sidney Walter, Jr. business and marketing executive
Deane, James Richard lawyer
Deare, Jennifer Laurie marketing professional
de Bary, William Theodore Asian studies educator
De Blasio, Michael Peter electronics company executive
Debo, Vincent Joseph lawyer
DeBow, Jay Howard Camden public relations company executive
Debs, Richard A. investment banker, government official
DeBusschere, David Albert former professional basketball player and team executive, brokerage firm executive
Decaminada, Joseph Pio insurance company executive, educator
†DeCarlo, Donald Thomas lawyer, insurance company executive
de Champlain, Vera Chopak artist, painter
†Decker, Bob newspaper editor
de Cou, Emil conductor
Decter, Midge writer
De Deo, Joseph E. advertising executive
Dedman, Bill journalist
de Duve, Christian René chemist, biologist, educator
Deem, George artist
Deems, Richard Emmet magazine publisher
De Ferrari, Gabriella curator, writer
Deffenbaugh, Ralston H., Jr. immigration agency executive, lawyer
De Gaster, Zachary engineering company executive
DeGroff, Ralph Lynn, Jr. investment banker
†De Harak, Rudolph painter, graphic designer
de Hartog, Jan writer
Deitz, Paula magazine editor
De Johnette, Jack musician
Dekker, Marcel publishing company executive
de Kooning, Willem artist
†de la Falaise, Lucie model
de la Gueronniere, Raphael securities firm executive
Delaney, Robert Vincent former gas company executive, economic development consultant
Delano, Lester Almy, Jr. advertising executive
de la Renta, Oscar fashion designer
DeLay, Dorothy (Mrs. Edward Newhouse) violinist, educator
Delikat, Michael lawyer
DeLillo, Don author
Dell, Ralph Bishop pediatrician, researcher
†Della Femina, Jerry advertising agency executive
Delman, Stephen Bennett lawyer
Delson, Robert lawyer
Delz, William Ronald petroleum company executive
DeMarco, Robert Thomas investment company executive
Demarest, Daniel Anthony retired lawyer
Demaria, Walter sculptor
Demaris, Ovid (Ovid Desmarais) author
DeMartini, Richard Michael financial services company executive
deMause, Lloyd psychohistorian
Dembo, Joseph T. communications educator
Demme, Jonathan director, producer, writer
de Montebello, Philippe Lannes museum administrator
Dempsey, Louis F(rancis), III banker
De Natale, Andrew Peter lawyer
Denes, Agnes C. environmental artist
Denham, Robert Edwin lawyer, investment company executive
Denhof, Miki graphic designer
Denker, Henry playwright, author, director
Dennis, Donna Frances sculptor, art educator
Dennis, Everette Eugene, Jr. foundation executive, journalism educator, media critic, author
Dennis, Robert (Arthur) (Arthur Dennis) composer, educator
Dennis, Walter Decoster suffragan bishop
Dent, V. Edward former advertising and communications company executive
DeNunzio, Ralph Dwight investment banker
†dePaola, Thomas Anthony illustrator, children's author
de Planque, E. Gail physicist
Derchin, Michael Wayne research director, investment banker, financial analyst
Derman, Cyrus mathematical statistician
DeRoma, Leonard James securities firm executive
Derow, Peter Alfred publishing company executive
Derryck, Vivian Lowery executive non-profit organization
Desai, Vishakha N. gallery director
de Saint Phalle, Pierre Claude lawyer
†De Santo, Samuel J. architectural firm executive, educator
†DeScherer, Richard K. lawyer
De Sear, Edward Marshall lawyer
Desnick, Robert John human geneticist
Despommier, Dickson Donald microbiology educator, parasitologist, researcher
des Rioux, Deena Victoria Coty artist, graphics designer
Dessi, Adrian Frank marketing, communications executive
†Destino, Ralph, Jr. retail executive
Deupree, Marvin Mattox business consultant, accountant
Deuss, Jean librarian
Deutsch, Martin Bernard Joseph editor, publisher
deVeer, Robert Kipp, Jr. investment banker
Deveraux, Jude (Jude Gilliam White) writer
Devers, Peter Dix lawyer
De Vido, Alfredo Eduardo architect
DeVito, Francis Joseph advertising agency executive
De Vivo, Darryl Claude pediatric neurologist
de Vries, Rimmer economist
Dewar, James McEwen marketing, aerospace and defense executive, consultant
De Witt, Eugene A. advertising agency executive
Diamant, Anita literary agent
Diamant, Aviva F. lawyer
Diamond, David Howard lawyer
Diamond, Freda designer, home furnishings consultant, lecturer
†Diamond, Harris corporate communications executive, lawyer
Diamond, Irene foundation administrator
Diamond, Robert Stephen publishing company executive
Diamondstone, Lawrence paper company executive
Diamonstein-Spielvogel, Barbaralee writer, television interviewer/ producer
DiBenedetto, Joseph A. lawyer
diBuono, Anthony Joseph lawyer, business executive
DiCarlo, Dominick L. federal judge
Dichter, Barry Joel lawyer
Dichter, Misha concert pianist
Dicker, Marvin lawyer
Dicterow, Glenn Eugene violinist
Didion, Joan author
†Diekmann, Nancy Kassak stage producer
Di Franco, Loretta Elizabeth lyric coloratura soprano
Diggins, Peter Sheehan ballet company administrator
Dilenschneider, Robert Louis public relations company executive
Dillard, Annie author
Dillingham, Robert Bulger publishing executive
Dillon, Clarence Douglas retired investment company executive
Dillon, Matt actor
DiMaggio, Frank Louis civil engineering educator
†Di Maria, Valerie Theresa public relations executive
†DiMartino, Joseph Salvatore investment company executive
Dimen, Muriel Vera psychoanalyst
Di Meo, Dominick artist, sculptor, painter
Di Mitri, Piero fashion designer
Dimling, John Arthur marketing executive
Dimon, James financial services executive
Dinaburg, Mary Ellen art education and curatorial consultant
Dine, Jim artist
Dintenfass, Terry art dealer
Dionne, Joseph Lewis publishing company executive
Di Paola, Robert Arnold mathematics and computer science educator
†Di Paolo, Nicholas P. corporate executive, real estate investor
†Dirks, Dennis John financial services executive
Di Salvo, Nicholas Armand dental educator, orthodontist
Diskant, Gregory L. lawyer
Disney, Anthea editor
Dispeker, Thea artists' representative
†DiTolla, Alfred W. international union executive
Diver, William linguistics educator
Dobbs, John Barnes artist, educator
Dobell, Byron Maxwell magazine consultant
Doctorow, Edgar Lawrence novelist, English educator
Dodd, Lois artist, art professor
Dodson, Daryl Theodore ballet administrator, arts consultant
Doel, Kenneth John textile executive
Doerr, Harriet writer
Doherty, Thomas publisher
Dohrenwend, Bruce Philip psychiatric epidemiologist, social psychologist, educator
Dojny, Richard Francis publishing company executive
Dolan, James Francis lawyer
Dolan, Michael G. lawyer
Dolan, Raymond Bernard insurance executive
Dole, Vincent Paul medical research executive, educator
Dolgen, Jonathan L. motion picture company executive
Dolger, Jonathan editor, literary agent
Dolgin, Martin cardiologist
Dolman, John Phillips, Jr. (Tim Dolman) communications company executive
Doman, Nicholas R. lawyer
Domingo, Placido tenor
Dominianni, Emilio Anthony (Mike Dominianni) lawyer, accountant
Donahue, Phil television personality
Donald, Norman Henderson, III lawyer
†Donald, Roger Thomas publishing executive
Donaldson, Stephen Reeder author
Donaldson, William Henry financial executive
Donati, Enrico artist
Doner, Frederick Nathan advertising and communications executive
Dooner, John Joseph, Jr. advertising executive
Dooskin, Herbert P. manufacturing company executive
Dormann, Henry O. magazine publisher
Dormire, Corwin Brooke lawyer
†Dornemann, Michael book publishing executive
†Dorsen, Harriette K. lawyer
Dorsen, Norman lawyer, educator
Douglas, Gordon Watkins medical educator
Douglas, Philip Le Breton lawyer
Douglass, Robert Royal banker, lawyer
Dowell, Anthony James ballet dancer
Dowling, Edward Thomas economics educator
Downes, Edward Olin Davenport musicologist, critic, radio broadcaster
Downey, John Alexander physician, educator
Downs, Hugh Malcolm radio and television broadcaster
Doyle, Eugenie Fleri pediatric cardiologist, educator
Doyle, Joseph Anthony lawyer
Doyle, L. F. Boker trust company executive
Doyle, Paul Francis lawyer
Doyle, William Stowell venture capitalist
Drakos, Charles Peter investment banker
Draper, James David art museum curator
Draper, William Franklin artist, portrait and landscape painter
Drapkin, Arnold Howard consulting picture editor, journalist, program director
Drasner, Fred newspaper publishing executive
Drebsky, Dennis Jay lawyer
Dreizen, Alison M. lawyer
Dressner, Howard Roy foundation executive, lawyer
†Drewry, Elizabeth newspaper publishing executive
Dreyfus, Alfred Stanley rabbi
Driver, Tom Faw theology educator, writer
Drobis, David R. public relations company executive
Druck, Mark director, producer, writer
†Druckenmiller, Robert T. public relations executive
Drucker, Mort commercial artist
Druckman, Jacob Raphael composer
Druker, Henry Leo investment banker
Druker, Isaac E. lawyer
Drury, Allen Stuart writer
Dubin, James Michael lawyer
Dubin, Morton Donald management consultant, film producer
Dubin, Seth Harris lawyer
DuBois, Jonathan Delafield lawyer
Dubroff, Charles Mark lawyer
Duchin, Peter Oelrichs musician
Dudack, Gail Marie brokerage house executive
†Duddy, Joan Frances performing arts administrator, dancer
Dueves, Henry C. computer company executive
Duff, John Ewing sculptor
†Duff, John Richard book publisher
†Duffy, David L. public relations executive
Duffy, Edmund Charles lawyer
Duffy, Kevin Thomas federal judge
Duffy, Nicole dancer
Duffy, W. Leslie lawyer
Dufour, Val (Albert Valery Dufour) actor
Dugan, Edward Francis investment banker
DuGan, Gordon F. investment banker
Dugan, Michael J. former air force officer, health agency executive
Duggan, Dennis Michael newspaper editor
†Duggan, Rosemary H. vocational administrator
Dukakis, Olympia actress
Duke, Angier Biddle retired university chancellor, retired diplomat
Duke, Anthony Drexel sociologist, educator, philanthropist
Dulaine, Pierre ballroom dancer
Duncan, Joseph Wayman business economist
Duncan, Richard magazine editor
Dundas, Philip Blair, Jr. lawyer
Dune, Steve Charles lawyer
Dunham, Christine dancer
Dunham, Corydon Busnell lawyer, broadcasting executive
Dunham, Donald Carl diplomat
Dunham, Wolcott Balestier, Jr. lawyer
Dunleavy, Rosemary ballet dancer
Dunn, James Joseph magazine publisher
†Dunn, Martin newspaper editor-in-chief
Dunn, M(orris) Douglas lawyer
Dunn, Susan singer
Dunne, Dominick writer
Dunne, John Gregory author
Dunne, Thomas Leo editor, author, publisher
Dunst, Laurence David advertising executive
Dupuy, Frank Russell, Jr. magazine publisher
Dusenberry, Philip Bernard advertising executive
Duva, Philip publishing executive
Dwek, Cyril S. banker
Dworetzky, Murray physician, educator
†Dworin, Steven advertising executive
†Dworkin, David Lee retail executive
Dworkin, Ronald Myles legal educator
Dykhouse, David Wayne lawyer
Dylan, Bob (Robert Allen Zimmerman) singer, composer
†Dyson, Robert R. investment company executive
Dystel, Jane Dee literary agent
Dyyon, Frazier (LeRoy Frazier) artist
Dzodin, Harvey Cary communications executive
†Earle, Gordon W. public relations executive
Earle, Victor Montagne, III lawyer
Ebbitt, Kenneth Cooper, Jr. investment company executive
Ebersol, Dick television broadcasting executive
Eberstein, Arthur biomedical engineering educator, researcher
Ebin, Robert Felix lawyer
Eckert, Allan W. author
Eckhaus, Jay Elliot lawyer
Eckman, Fern Marja journalist
Eckstut, Michael Kauder management consultant
Edelbaum, Philip R. lawyer
†Edelman, Asher Barry financier
Edelman, Harold architect
Edelman, Herbert Stephen lawyer
Edelman, Isidore Samuel biochemist and medical educator
Edelman, Judith Hochberg architect
Edelman, Paul Sterling lawyer
Edelman, Richard Winston public relations executive
Edelman, Thomas Jeffery oil company executive
Edelson, Gilbert Seymour lawyer
Edelstein, David Northon federal judge
Edelstein, Haskell banker, tax lawyer
Edgar, Harold Simmons Hull law educator
Edinger, Lewis Joachim political science educator
Edlow, Kenneth Lewis securities brokerage executive
Edmiston, Mark Morton publishing company executive
Edmonds, Robert Scott lawyer
Edmunds, Robert Thomas retired surgeon
†Edson, Andrew Stephen public relations executive
Edwards, Franklin R. economist, educator, consultant
Edwards, Harold Mortimer mathematics educator
Edwards, James Cook investment counselor
Edwards, James D. accounting company executive
Edwards, James Malone lawyer
Eforo, John Francis financial officer
Eger, Joseph conductor, music director
Eggers, Ernest Russell management consultant
†Egielski, Richard illustrator
Egle, Jack educational association executive
Ego-Aguirre, Ernesto surgeon
Ehinger, Albert Louis, Jr. securities trader
Ehlers, Kathryn Hawes (Mrs. James D. Gabler) physician
Ehrenbard, Robert lawyer
Ehrenkranz, Joel S. lawyer
Ehrenkranz, Shirley Malakoff university dean, social work educator
Eidson, Thomas E. public relations firm executive
Eig, Norman investment company executive
Einarson, Baldvin Oliver lawyer
Einbender, Alvin H. securities dealer
Einiger, Carol Blum foundation executive
Einiger, Roger W. brokerage house executive
Eisen, Mark fashion designer
Eisenberg, Alan association executive
Eisenberg, Sonja Miriam artist
Eisenman, Peter David architect, educator
Eisenstadt, G. Michael diplomat, author, lecturer, research scholar
Eisenstaedt, Alfred photojournalist
Eisenthal, Kenneth B. physical chemistry educator
Eisert, Edward Gaver lawyer
Eisler, Colin Tobias art historian, curator
Eisler, Susan Krawetz advertising executive
†Eisner, Richard Alan accountant
Ekern, George Patrick lawyer
Ekman, Richard foundation executive, educator
Elam, Leslie Albert association executive
Elder, Eldon stage designer, theatre consultant
Elderfield, John art historian, museum curator
†El-Erian, Tahani library administrator
†Elia, Claudio manufacturing executive
Elias, Rosalind mezzo-soprano
Elicker, Gordon Leonard lawyer
Eliot, Lucy Carter artist
Elkes, Terrence Allen communications executive
Elkin, Jeffrey H. lawyer
Ellenberger, Jack Stuart law librarian
Ellerbee, Linda broadcast journalist
Elliman, Donald magazine company executive
Ellington, Mercer Kennedy trumpeter, conductor, composer
Elliott, A. Wright banker
Elliott, Chris actor
Elliott, Eleanor Thomas foundation executive, civic leader
Elliott, John, Jr. advertising agency executive
Elliott, Osborn journalist, educator, former university dean
Elliott, Tim advertising agency executive
Elliott-Smith, Paul Henry marketing and economics consultant
Ellis, Albert clinical psychologist, educator, author
Ellis, Bret Easton author
Ellis, Carolyn Terry lawyer
Ellis, Charles Richard publishing executive
Ellis, John Taylor pathologist, educator
Ellis, Kent radiologist, consultant
Ellison, Solon Arthur microbiology and dentistry educator
Ellsworth, Arthur Whitney publishing consultant
Ellsworth, Robert Malcolm ophthalmologist, educator
Elman, Naomi Geist artist, producer
Elsen, Sheldon Howard lawyer
Elster, Samuel Kase college dean, medical educator, physician
Embree, Ainslie Thomas history educator
Emerson, Alice Frey political scientist, educator emerita
†Emerson, Ken newspaper editor
†Emerson, Robert Monroe advertising executive
†Emick, Jarrod actor
Emmerich, Andre art gallery executive, author
Emmerman, Michael N financial analyst
Emmert, Richard Eugene professional association executive
Enberg, Dick sportscaster
Enders, Elizabeth McGuire artist
Engelhardt, Sara Lawrence organization executive
Englander, Roger Leslie television producer, director
Engler, Robert political science educator, author
Entremont, Philippe conductor, pianist
Ephron, Nora writer
Epling, Richard Louis lawyer
Eppner, Gerald Allen lawyer
Epstein, Barbara editor
Epstein, Cynthia Fuchs sociology educator, writer
Epstein, Jason publishing company executive
Epstein, Jeremy G. lawyer
Epstein, Melvin lawyer
Epstein, Michael Alan lawyer
Erbsen, Claude Ernest journalist
Ercklentz, Alexander Tonio banker
Ercklentz, Enno Wilhelm, Jr. lawyer
Ergas, Enrique orthopedic surgeon
Erhardt, Edward Richard advertising company executive
Erlanger, Bernard Ferdinand biochemist, educator
Erlanger, Steven Jay journalist
Erosh, William Daniel financial services company executive
Ertegun, Ahmet Munir record company executive
Erwitt, Elliott Romano photographer, cinematographer
Eschenbach, Christoph conductor, pianist
Esman, Aaron H. physician, psychiatrist
Esperian, Kallen Rose soprano
†Esposito, Richard Joseph journalist
Espy, Willard Richardson author
†Esquivel, Laura writer
Essandoh, Hilda Brathwaite kindergarten educator
Esterow, Milton magazine editor, publisher
Estes, Richard artist
Estes, Simon Lamont opera singer, bass-baritone
Eswein, Bruce James, II human resources executive
Etheridge, Melissa singer, songwriter
Eustice, James Samuel lawyer, educator
†Evangelista, Linda model
†Evans, Abigail Winifred theatrical executive
Evans, Alfred Lee, Jr. advertising executive
Evans, Edward Parker former publishing company executive
†Evans, Harold M. publishing executive, writer

Garrison-Jackson, Zina tennis player
Garrow, David Jeffries historian, author
Gartner, Alan P. university official, author
Gartner, Murray lawyer
Garver, Robert S. banker
Garvin, Andrew Paul information company executive, author, consultant
Garzarelli, Elaine Marie brokerage house executive, economist
Gassel, Philip Michael lawyer
Gatch, Milton McCormick, Jr. library administrator, clergyman, educator
Gates, Jodie dancer
Gatje, Robert Frederick architect
†Gatti, Frank R. publishing executive
Gattie, Erma Charlotte opera singer
Gaudieri, Alexander V. J. museum administrator
Gaudieri, Millicent Hall association executive
Gaughan, Eugene Francis accountant
Gavrity, John Decker insurance company executive
Gazouleas, Panagiotis J. journalist
Gazzara, Ben actor
Gechtoff, Sonia artist
†Geddie, William Fredrick television producer
Geduldig, Alfred communications executive
†Geen, William John lawyer
Geer, John Farr religious organization administrator
Geier, Philip Henry, Jr. advertising executive
†Geiger, H. Jack medical educator
Geis, Bernard book publisher
Geisenheimer, Emile J. electronics industry executive, venture capitalist
Geiser, Elizabeth Able publishing company executive
Geismar, Thomas H. graphic designer
Geissbuhler, Stephan graphic designer
Gelb, Arthur newspaper editor
Gelb, Harold Seymour investor
Gelb, Joseph W. lawyer
Gelb, Judith Anne lawyer
Gelb, Leslie Howard organization president, lecturer
Gelb, Richard Lee pharmaceutical corporation executive
Gelbart, Abe mathematician, educator
Gelber, Jack playwright, director
Gelfand, Neal oil company executive
Gelfman, Robert William lawyer
Geller, Robert James advertising agency executive
Gellermann, Henry journalist, cultural organization administrator
Gellert, Michael Erwin investment banker
Gellhorn, Walter law and political science educator, author
†Gellman, Isaiah science foundation
Geltzer, Sheila Simon public relations executive
Genin, Roland energy executive
Genkins, Gabriel physician
Genova, Joseph Steven lawyer
Geoghegan, Patricia lawyer
George, Beauford James, Jr. lawyer, educator
George, David Alan investment banker
†George, Gladys hospital administrator
Georges, Paul Gordon artist
Georgescu, Peter Andrew advertising executive
Georgopoulos, Maria architect
Geraci, F. Phillip advertising executive, lawyer, entrepreneur
Geraghty, Kenneth George financial services company executive
Gerard, Emanuel investment banking executive
Gerard, Whitney Ian lawyer
Gerber, Robert Evan lawyer
Gerber, Roger Alan lawyer, business executive
Gerdts, William Henry art history educator
Gerhardt, Lillian Noreen magazine editor
Germano, William Paul publisher
Gerra, Ralph A., Jr. lawyer
Gerry, Elbridge Thomas, Jr. banker
Gershengorn, Marvin Carl physician, scientist, educator
Gershon, Nina federal judge
†Gershuny, Donald Nevin lawyer
Gerson, Irwin Conrad advertising executive
Gersony, Welton Mark physician, pediatric cardiologist, educator
†Gersten, Bernard theatrical producer
Gertler, Menard M. physician, educator
Gessner, Charles Herman apparel company executive
Gewirtz, Elliot lawyer
Gewirtz, Gerry editor
Gianinno, Susan McManama marketing executive, advertising agency executive
Giannetti, Thomas Leonard lawyer
Giannini, Cynthia dancer
Gibb, Barry vocalist, songwriter
Gibbs, L(ippman) Martin lawyer
Gibbs, Richard Leslie public relations executive
Giblin, James Cross author, editor
Gibson, Charles DeWolf broadcast journalist
Gibson, Ralph H(olmes) photographer
Gibson, William B. advertising, marketing executive
Gibson, William Francis investment banking executive
Gibson, William Shepard insurance executive
Giddins, Gary Mitchell music critic, columnist
†Giddon, Donald B(ernard) psychologist, educator
Gideon, Miriam composer
Gifford, Frank Newton sportscaster, commentator
Gifford, Kathie Lee television personality
Gilbert, Bradley professional tennis player, Olympic athlete
Gilbert, Phil Edward, Jr. lawyer
Gilbert, Pia S. musical educator, composer
Gilinsky, Stanley Ellis department store executive
Gill, Ardian C. actuary
Gill, Brendan writer
Gill, E. Ann lawyer
Gill, John Joseph, Jr. construction executive
Gill, Vince country musician, singer
Gillespie, George Joseph, III lawyer
Gillespie, Sarah Ashman newspaper syndicate executive
Gillett, Charles travel executive
Gillham, Robert bank executive
Gilliatt, Neal advertising executive, consultant
Gilman, Charles Alan lawyer
†Gilman, Richard H. newspaper publishing executive
Gilmont, Ernest Rich chemist
Gilmore, Robert Gordon insurance company executive
Gilpatric, Roswell Leavitt lawyer
Giniger, Kenneth Seeman publisher
Ginsberg, David Lawrence architect
Ginsberg, Ernest lawyer, banker
Ginsberg, Frank Charles advertising executive
Ginsberg, Harold Samuel virologist, educator
Ginsberg, Hersh Meier rabbi, religious organization executive
Ginsberg-Fellner, Fredda pediatric endocrinologist, researcher
Ginsburg, Ellin Louis public relations executive
Ginsburg, Sigmund G. academic administrator
Ginzberg, Eli economist, emeritus educator, government consultant, author
Ginzburg, Ralph editor, writer
†Giral, Angela librarian
Giraldi, Robert Nicholas film director
Girden, Eugene Lawrence lawyer
Giroux, Robert editor, book publisher, author
Gitner, Gerald L. aviation executive
Gitter, Max lawyer
Gitterman, Alex social work educator
Giuliani, Rudolph W. mayor, former lawyer
Giusti, Gino Paul natural resources company executive
Gladis, Jay lawyer
Gladstone, William Louis accountant
Glasberg, Paula Drillman advertising executive
Glasco, Joseph Milton artist
Glaser, Joseph Bernard association executive
Glaser, Milton interior designer
Glaser, Robert Leonard television executive
Glass, Daniel S. record company executive
Glass, Philip composer, musician
Glasser, Ira Saul civil liberties organization executive
Glassgold, Alfred Emanuel physicist, educator
Glassman, Alexander Howard psychiatrist, researcher
Glassman, Steven J. lawyer
Glazer, Esther violinist
†Gleason, Edward L. manufacturing executive
Gleason, Joanna actress
Gleason, John James theatrical lighting designer
Gleick, James writer, software designer
Glekel, Jeffrey Ives lawyer
Glickstein, Steven lawyer
Glidden, Allan Hartwell insurance company executive
Glos, Margaret Beach management company executive, real estate developer
Glynn, Gary Allen pension fund executive
Gochberg, Thomas Joel real estate investor, financial executive
Goddess, Lynn Barbara commercial real estate broker
Godman, Gabriel Charles pathology educator
Godson, Godfrey Nigel molecular geneticist, educator
Godunov, Alexander Boris ballet dancer, actor
Goelet, Robert G. corporate executive
Goertz, Augustus Frederick, III artist
Goetz, Cecelia Helen lawyer, retired judge
Goetz, Maurice Harold lawyer
Gold, Albert artist
†Gold, Emanuel R. lawyer, state senator
Gold, Jay D. broadcasting company executive
Gold, Jeffrey Mark investment banker, financial adviser
Gold, Leonard Singer librarian, translator
Gold, Martin Elliot lawyer, educator
Gold, Simeon lawyer
Gold, Stuart Walter lawyer
Gold, Sylviane entertainment editor, writer, critic
Goldberg, Arthur Abba merchant banker, financial advisor
†Goldberg, Bernard R. news correspondent
Goldberg, David Alan investment banker, lawyer
Goldberg, Edward L. financial services executive
Goldberg, Michael artist
Goldberg, Richard W. federal judge
Goldberg, Sidney editor
†Goldberg, Steven M. architect
Goldberger, Paul Jesse architecture critic, writer, educator, editor
Goldblatt, David Ira lawyer
Golde, David William physician, educator
Golden, Arthur F. lawyer
Golden, Robert Charles brokerage executive
†Golden, Soma newspaper editor
†Golden, Stephen publishing executive, forest products company executive
Golden, William Robert, Jr. lawyer
Golden, William Theodore corporate executive
Goldenberg, Charles Lawrence real estate company executive
Goldfield, Alfred Sherman lawyer
Goldin, Alan Gary advertising executive
Goldin, Leon artist, educator
Goldman, Charles Norton lawyer, corporation executive
Goldman, Donald Howard lawyer
†Goldman, Francisco writer
Goldman, George David psychologist, psychoanalyst
Goldman, James playwright, screenwriter, novelist
Goldman, Lawrence Saul lawyer
Goldman, Leo psychologist, educator
†Goldman, Marvin Gerald lawyer
Goldman, Robert Irving financial services company executive
Goldmark, Peter Carl, Jr. foundation executive
Goldschmid, Harvey Jerome law educator
Goldschmidt, Charles advertising agency executive
Goldschmidt, Robert Alphonse financial executive
Goldsmith, Arthur Austin magazine editor
Goldsmith, Barbara author, social historian, journalist
Goldsmith, Clifford Henry former tobacco company executive
Goldsmith, Donald Alan lawyer
†Goldsmith, Gary L. advertising executive
Goldsmith, Lee Selig lawyer, physician
Goldsmith, Mark L. international trade marketing consulting company executive
Goldsmith, Robert Lewis youth association magazine executive
Goldsmith, Stanley Joseph nuclear medicine physician, educator
Goldstein, Alvin lawyer
Goldstein, Bernard Herbert lawyer
Goldstein, Charles Arthur lawyer
Goldstein, Fred accountant
†Goldstein, Gary Alan creative director
Goldstein, Howard Warren lawyer
Goldstein, Jack transportation executive
Goldstein, Jonathan lawyer
Goldstein, Marcia Landweber lawyer
Goldstein, Menek neurochemistry educator
Goldstein, Norm editor, writer
Goldstein, Richard A. consumer products company executive
Goldstone, Steven F. lawyer
Gollin, Albert Edwin media research executive, sociologist
Gollin, Stuart Allen accountant
Gollob, Herman Cohen publishing company executive, editor
Golomb, Frederick Martin surgeon, educator
Golson, George Barry editor
Golub, Alan clothing company executive
Golub, Harvey financial services company executive
Golub, Leon Albert artist
†Goluboff, Hal advertising executive
Gomory, Ralph Edward mathematician, manufacturing company executive, foundation executive
Gonzalez, Eugene Robert investment banker
Gooch, Anthony Cushing lawyer
†Goodacre, Jill model
Goodale, James Campbell lawyer
Goodale, Toni Krissel development consultant
Goodchild, Robert Marshall trust company executive
Goode, Richard Stephen pianist, educator
Goodfriend, Herbert Jay lawyer
Goodhartz, Gerald law librarian
†Gooding, Richard newspaper editor
Goodkind, Louis William lawyer
Goodman, Gary A. lawyer
Goodman, George Jerome Waldo (Adam Smith) author, television journalist, editor
Goodman, Jordan Elliot journalist
Goodman, Thomas Andrew public relations executive
Goodridge, Allan D. lawyer
†Goodstein, Les newspaper publishing executive
Goodstone, Edward Harold insurance company executive
Goodwillie, Eugene William, Jr. lawyer
Goodwin, Bernard lawyer, executive, educator
Goodwin, Todd banker
Gopnik, Adam editor, writer
Gordimer, Nadine author
Gordon, Albert Hamilton investment banker
Gordon, David playwright, director, choreographer
Gordon, Diana Russell political science educator
†Gordon, Elizabeth Jane publisher
Gordon, Jacques Nicholas real estate economist
Gordon, Mary Catherine author
Gordon, Michael Mackin lawyer
Gordon, Nicole Ann lawyer
Gordon, Ronnie Roslyn pediatrics educator, consultant
Goren, Alexander Mircea investment company executive
Goren, Arnold Louis educator, former university official
Gorham, David L. newspaper executive
Gorlin, Richard physician, educator
Goss, Mary E. Weber sociology educator
†Gossage, Wayne library director, management consultant, executive recruiter
Gossett, Oscar Milton advertising executive
Gossett, Robert Francis, Jr. merchant banker
Gotlieb, Irwin I. broadcast executive
Gotschlich, Emil Claus physician, educator
Gottesman, David Sanford investment executive
Gottlieb, Jane Ellen librarian
Gottlieb, Jerrold Howard advertising executive
Gottlieb, Morton Edgar theatrical and film producer
Gottlieb, Paul publishing company executive
Gottlieb, Robert Adams publisher
Gottschall, Edward Maurice graphic arts company executive
Goulazian, Peter Robert broadcasting executive
Gould, Harry Edward, Jr. industrialist
Gould, Jay Martin economist, consultant
Gould, Milton Samuel lawyer, business executive
Goulden, Joseph Chesley author
Goulianos, Konstantin physics educator
Gourdine, Simon Peter professional basketball executive
Graber, Edward Alex obstetrician, gynecologist, educator
†Grace, E. engineering executive
Grace, H. David economist, international finance consultant
Grace, Jason Roy advertising agency executive
Grad, Frank Paul lawyer
Graf, Peter Gustav accountant, lawyer
Graff, George L. lawyer
Graff, Randy actress
Graffin, Guillaume ballet dancer
Grafstein, Bernice physiology and neuroscience educator, researcher
Graham, Alma Eleanor magazine editor, writer, educational consultant
Graham, Howard Barrett publishing company executive
Graham, Jesse Japhet, II lawyer
Gralla, Lawrence publishing company executive
Gralla, Milton publisher
†Gralnick, Jeff broadcasting company executive
Granger, David investment banker
†Grann, Phyllis publisher, editor
Grano, Joseph J., Jr. securities industry executive
Grant, Alfred D. orthopaedic surgeon, educator
†Grant, Cynthia D. writer
Grant, Dale B. consulting company executive
Grant, James Deneale health care company executive
Grant, James Pineo international organization executive
Grant, Leonard Tydings educational association president
Grant, Merrill Theodore producer
Grant, Stephen Allen lawyer
Grant, Virginia Annette newspaper editor, journalist
Grant, William Robert investment banker
Grappelli, Stephane jazz violinist
Grashof, August Edward lawyer
Grasso, Richard A. stock exchange executive
†Graves, Adam professional hockey player
Graves, Earl Gilbert publisher
Graves, Fred Hill librarian
Graves, Lorraine Elizabeth dancer, educator, coach
Graves, Nancy Stevenson artist
Gray, Arthur, Jr. investment counselor
Gray, Barry Sherman radio commentator
Gray, C(harles) Jackson retail executive
Gray, Diane dancer, choreographer
Gray, George mural painter
†Gray, Robert Loren association executive
Gray, Spalding actor, writer, performance artist
Gray, William H., III association executive, former congressman
Greaney, Patrick Joseph electronics executive
Grebow, Edward television executive, banker
Greco, Jose choreographer
Green, Adolph playwright, lyricist
Green, Al singer, clergyman
Green, Ashbel publishing executive, book editor
Green, Dan publishing company executive
†Green, David Edward librarian, priest, translator
Green, David O. accounting educator, educational administrator
Green, George Joseph publishing executive
Green, Gerald author
Green, Jack Peter pharmacology educator, medical scientist
Green, Maurice Richard neuropsychiatrist
Green, Paula advertising agency executive
Green, Robert S. lawyer
Green, Saul biochemist
Greenawalt, Peggy Freed Tomarkin advertising executive
Greenawalt, Robert Kent lawyer
Greenawalt, William Sloan lawyer
Greenbaum, Maurice C. lawyer
Greenberg, Alan Courtney (Ace Greenberg) stockbroker
Greenberg, Freddi Jane editor-in-chief, magazine
Greenberg, Ira George lawyer
Greenberg, Jack lawyer
Greenberg, Jerome advertising executive
Greenberg, Joshua F. lawyer, educator
Greenberg, Maurice Raymond insurance company executive
Greenberg, Ronald David law educator
†Greenberg, Scott Neil patent development company executive
†Greenberger, Daniel Mordecai physics educator
Greenberger, Howard Leroy lawyer, educator
Greene, A(lvin) C(arl) author
Greene, Bernard Harold lawyer
Greene, Carl William utility company executive
Greene, David Elsworth advertising agency executive, accountant
Greene, Howard Paul communications executive
Greene, Shecky entertainer
Greenfield, Gordon Kraus software company executive
Greenfield, Jay lawyer
Greenfield, (Henry) Jeff news analyst
Greenfield, Seymour Stephen mechanical engineer
Greengard, Paul neuroscientist
Greenhill, Robert Foster investment banker
Greenhouse, Bernard cellist, educator
Greenland, Leo advertising executive
Greenman, Jane Friedlieb lawyer
Greenstein, Abraham Jacob mortgage company executive, accountant
Greenwald, Martin publishing company executive
Greer, Allen Curtis, II lawyer
Greer, James Alexander, II lawyer
Gregorio, Luis Justino Lopes transportation executive
Greif, Edward Louis public relations executive
Greig, Robert Thomson lawyer
Greilsheimer, James Gans lawyer
Grein, Richard Frank bishop, pastoral theology educator
Grenquist, Peter Carl publishing executive
Gresov, Boris (Vladimir) economist
Grey, Linda book publisher
Griefen, John Adams artist, educator
Griesa, Thomas Poole federal judge
Griffiths, Daniel Edward dean emeritus
Griffiths, Sylvia Preston physician
Grigsby, Henry Jefferson, Jr. editor
Grillo, Joann Danielle mezzo-soprano
Grimaldi, Nicholas Lawrence social services administrator
Grimes, Charles B., Jr. bank executive
Grimes, Martha author
Grimsley, Will Henry author
Grindea, Daniel international economist
Grisanti, Eugene Philip flavors and fragrances company executive
Grisham, John writer
Grisi, Jeanmarie Conte finance executive
Grizzard, George actor
Groban, Robert Sidney, Jr. lawyer
Groberg, James Jay information sciences company executive
Grody, Donald judge, lawyer, arbitrator, actor
Grooms, Red artist
Gropp, Louis Oliver editor in chief
Gropper, Allan Louis lawyer
†Grose, Molly Pickering performing company executive
Grose, William Rush publishing executive
Groseclose, Everett Harrison editor
Gross, Abraham rabbi, educator
Gross, Ernest Arnold lawyer
Gross, Jonathan Light computer scientist, mathematician, educator
Gross, Steven Ross lawyer
†Grossman, Barbara Susanne publisher
Grossman, Dan S. lawyer
Grossman, Jack advertising agency executive
Grossman, Jacob S. structural engineer
Grossman, Janice publisher
Grossman, Nancy artist
Grossman, Sanford lawyer
†Grove, Barry theater executive
Groves, Ray John accountant
Gruber, Alan Richard insurance company executive
†Grubin, Sharon E. federal judge
†Grubman, Allen J. lawyer
Gruenberger, Peter lawyer
Grumbach, Doris novelist, editor, critic, educator, bookseller
Grumbach, George Jacques, Jr. lawyer
Grunberger, Dezider biochemist, researcher
Grunes, Robert Lewis engineering consulting firm executive
Grunewald, Raymond Bernhard lawyer
Grusin, Dave film composer, record producer, performer
Gruskin, Mary J. (Mrs. Alan D. Gruskin) art gallery director emeritus
Gruson, Michael lawyer
Gruver, William Rolfe investment banker
Guare, John playwright
Guccione, Anthony Joseph, II media entrepreneur, cable television executive
Guccione, Robert Charles Joseph Edward Sabatini publisher
Gudenberg, Harry Richard business consultant
Guenther, Jack Donald banker
Guenther, Paul Bernard securities company executive
Guest, Barbara author, poet
Guest, Judith Ann author
Guettel, Henry Arthur retired arts executive
Gugel, Craig Thomas advertising executive
Guida, Peter Matthew surgeon, educator
†Guillen, Michael Arthur mathematical physicist, educator, writer, television journalist
Guimaraes, George Gomes advertising agency executive
Guise, David Earl architect, educator
Guldimann, Till M. banker
Gumbel, Bryant Charles broadcaster

Gumbinner, Paul S. advertising and executive recruitment agency executive
Gunther, Jane Perry (Mrs. John Gunther) editor, writer
Gurfein, Stuart James jewelry manufacturing company executive
Gurin, Meg dancer
Gurnee, Hal television director
Gurwitch, Arnold Andrew communications executive
Gusberg, Saul Bernard physician, educator
Guth, Paul C. lawyer
Guthrie, Randolph Hobson, Jr. plastic surgeon
†Gutman, Jeremiah Sheldon lawyer
Gutman, Robert William retired fine arts educator
Guttman, Zoltan Lou exchange executive
Gwathmey, Charles architect
†Gwertzman, Bernard newspaper editor
†Gyulassy, Miklos physics educator
†Haacke, Hans Christoph Carl artist, educator
Haas, Frederick Carl paper and chemical company executive
Habecker, Eugene Brubaker association executive
Habeeb, Virginia Thabet magazine editor
Haber, Ira Joel artist, art educator
Hackett, Kevin R. lawyer
Haddad, Heskel Marshall ophthalmologist
Haddock, Robert Lynn information services entrepreneur, writer
Hadley, Jerry opera singer
Haerer, Carol artist
Haessle, Jean-Marie Georges artist
Haffner, Alden Norman university official
Haffner, Alfred Loveland, Jr. lawyer
Haft, Marilyn Geisler lawyer
Hagen, Uta Thyra actress
Hagendorn, William lawyer
Hager, Charles Read lawyer
Hager, Larry Stanley book editor, publishing executive
Haggerty, Robert Henry lawyer
Haig, Robert Leighton lawyer
Haiken, Leatrice Brown periodical editor
Haims, Bruce David lawyer
Haire, John Russell corporate executive, lawyer
Haje, Peter Robert lawyer
†Hajim, Edmund A. financial services executive
Halberg, G. Peter ophthalmologist
Halberstam, David journalist, author
Halberstam, Malvina legal educator, lawyer
Hall, Anthony Robert pharmaceuticals and consumer products company executive
Hall, Daryl musician
Hall, Gus (Arvo Kusta Halberg) political party official
Hall, John Herbert lawyer
Hall, Nancy Christensen publishing company executive, author, editor
Hall, Susan author, film producer
Hallam, Beverly (Beverly Linney) artist
†Halle, Lisa Ellen advertising executive
Halliday, Joseph William lawyer
Hallingby, Paul, Jr. investment banker
Halloran, Leo Augustine retired financial executive
Halper, Harlan Richard executive recruiter
Halper, Thomas political science educator
Halperin, Richard E. lawyer, holding company executive
Halpern, Charles Robert foundation executive, educator, lawyer
Halpern, Nathan Loren communications company executive
Halpin, Anna Marie architect
Halsband, Frances architect
Hamblen, L. Jane lawyer
Hambrick, George Walter, Jr. dermatologist, educator
Hamburg, Beatrix Ann medical educator, researcher
Hamburg, Charles Bruce lawyer
Hamburg, David A. psychiatrist, foundation executive
Hamburger, Philip (Paul) writer
Hamel, Rodolphe lawyer, pharmaceutical company executive
Hamilton, Bill advertising executive
Hamilton, Thomas Michael marketing executive
Hamm, David Bernard lawyer
Hammer, Emanuel Frederick clinical psychologist, psychoanalyst
Hammerling, Robert Charles lawyer
Hammerman, Stephen Lawrence lawyer, financial services company executive
Hammett, William M. H. foundation executive
Hammond, Lou Rena Charlotte public relations executive
Hammond, Steven Alan lawyer
Hampton, Philip McCune banker
Hanafusa, Hidesaburo virologist
Hancock, Gerre Edward musician
Handberg, Irene Deak educational executive
Handelsman, Lawrence Marc lawyer
Handler, Arthur M. lawyer
Handler, Mark S. retail executive
Handler, Milton lawyer
†Hansen, James E. physicist, meteorologist, federal agency administrator
Hansen, Richard Arthur insurance company executive, psychologist
Hansmann, Ralph Emil investment executive
Happel, John chemical engineer, researcher
Harbison, James Wesley, Jr. lawyer
Harder, Lewis Bradley ore bodies development company executive
Hardesty, Egbert Railey retired engineering firm executive
Hardin, Adlai Stevenson, Jr. lawyer
Hardison, Ruth Inge sculptor
Hardwick, Charles Leighton pharmaceutical company executive, state legislator
Hardwick, Elizabeth author
Hardy, Gordon Alfred music educator, music school president
Hardy, Hugh architect
Hardy, Thomas Austin sculptor
†Harfst, Jeffrey Loren accountant
†Hariri, Gisue architect, educator
†Harkarvy, Benjamin dance director
Harkna, Eric advertising executive
Harkrader, Milton Keene, Jr. academic administrator
Harlan, Leonard Morton merchant banker
Harleston, Bernard Warren college president
Harley, Colin Emile lawyer
Harley, Naomi Hallden radiation specialist, environmental medicine educator
Harlow, George Eugene mineralogist, curator
Harmon, Lily artist, author
Harnett, Thomas Aquinas lawyer
Harnick, Sheldon Mayer lyricist
Harper, Charles Michel food company executive
Harper, Emery Walter lawyer
Harrell, Lynn Morris cellist
Harris, Allen lawyer, educator
Harris, Ann S. editor
Harris, Arlene lawyer
Harris, Aurand playwright
Harris, Charles Frederick book publishing executive
Harris, Colin Cyril mineral engineer, educator
Harris, Cyril Manton physicist, engineering and architecture educator, consulting acoustical engineer
Harris, David Alan not-for-profit organization executive
Harris, Ed(ward Allen) actor
Harris, Ellen W. lawyer
Harris, Henry William physician
Harris, Joel B(ruce) lawyer
Harris, Julie (Ann) actress
Harris, Louis public opinion analyst, columnist
Harris, Richard Max corporate executive
Harris, Thomas author
Harris, William Vernon history educator
Harrison, Gerald publisher
Harrison, Gilbert Warner investment banker
Harrison, John Alexander financial executive
Harrison, S. David lawyer
Harrison, William Neal author, educator
Harrod, B(illy) J(oe) professional association executive
Harrow, Nancy (Mrs. Jan Krukowski) jazz singer, songwriter, editor
Hart, Gurnee Fellows investment counselor
Hart, Kenneth Nelson lawyer
Hart, Kitty Carlisle arts administrator
Hart, Robert M. lawyer
Harter, Hugh Anthony foreign language educator
Hartford, Huntington financier, art patron
Hartford, William H. magazine editor, writer, lecturer
Harth, Sidney musician, educator
Hartley, Duncan fund raising executive
Hartman, Stephen Jennings, Jr. banker
†Hartwig, Myron Arthur public relations executive
Hartzell, Andrew Cornelius, Jr. lawyer
Harvey, Cynthia ballet dancer
Harvey, Donald Joseph history educator
Harwood, Stanley retired judge, lawyer
Hasen, Burton Stanley artist
Haskell, Barbara curator
Haskell, John Henry Farrell, Jr. investment banking company executive
Hassell, Gerald L. banker
†Hassler, Howard E. retail stores executive
Hasso, Signe Eleonora Cecilia actress
Hastings, Baird conductor, music educator, writer
Hastings, Donald Francis actor, writer
Hatfield, Robert Sherman former packaging company executive
Hatheway, John Harris advertising agency executive
†Haubert, Alaine ballet dancer
Hauck, Marguerite Hall broadcasting executive, antique dealer
Hauptman, William playwright
Hauser, Fred P. insurance company executive
Hauser, Gustave M. cable and electronic communications company executive
Hauser, Rita Eleanore Abrams lawyer
Hawes, Douglas Wesson lawyer
Hawke, Roger Jewett lawyer
†Hawkey, Penelope J. advertising agency executive
Hawkins, Ashton museum executive, lawyer
Hawkins, Erick dancer, choreographer
Hawkins, Katherine Ann hematologist
†Hawley, John Stratton religious studies educator
Hawver, Dennis Arthur psychological consultant
Hayden, Raymond Paul lawyer
Hayes, Gerald Joseph lawyer
Hayes, Isaac composer, singer
Haynes, Jean Reed lawyer
Haynes, Todd film writer, producer, director
†Hayon, Jack publishing executive
Hays, Kathryn actress
Hayward, Jane museum curator
Haywood, H(erbert) Carl(ton) psychologist, educator
Hazard, John Newbold retired law educator
Hazen, William Harris finance executive
†Hazlitt, Donald Robert artist
Hazzard, Shirley author
Heal, Geoffrey Martin economics educator
Healy, Harold Harris, Jr. lawyer
Healy, Nicholas Joseph lawyer, educator
Heard, Edwin Anthony banker
Hearle, Douglas Geoffrey public relations consultant
Hearn, George Henry lawyer, steamship corporate executive
Hearst, Randolph Apperson publishing executive
Hebert, Bliss Edmund opera director
Hechinger, Fred Michael newspaper editor, columnist, foundation executive
Heckart, Robert Lee lawyer
Heckscher, August journalist, author, foundation executive
Heckscher, Morrison Harris museum curator, architectural historian
Hedley, David Van Houten investment banker
Hedlund, Ronald baritone
Hedstrom, Mitchell Warren banker
Heekin, James Robson, III advertising executive
Heffner, Richard Douglas educator, historian, communications consultant, television producer
Heilbroner, Robert L. economist, author
Heile, Leo James information technology executive
Heiloms, May (Mrs. Samuel Heiloms) artist
Heimann, John Gaines investment banker
†Heimbold, Charles Andreas, Jr. pharmaceutical company executive
Heine, Edward Joseph, Jr. lawyer
Heineman, Andrew David lawyer
Heinzerling, Larry Edward communications executive
Heisel, Ralph Arthur architect
Heisler, Stanley Dean lawyer
Hejduk, John Quentin dean, architect
Held, Al artist, educator
Held, Virginia philosophy educator
†Helferich, Gerard Marion book editor
Heliker, John artist
Hellawell, Robert law educator
Hellenbrand, Samuel Henry lawyer, diversified industry executive
Heller, Arthur advertising agency executive
Heller, Edwin lawyer
Heller, Joseph writer
Heller, Robert Martin lawyer
Hellerstein, Alvin Kenneth lawyer
Hellerstein, Jerome Robert lawyer
Hellmold, Ralph O. investment banker
Helman, Joseph Arthur art dealer
Helmreich, William Benno sociology educator, consultant
Heloise columnist, lecturer, broadcaster, author
Helpern, David Moses shoe corporation executive
Heming, Charles E. lawyer
Hemingway, Mariel actress
Hemmerdinger, H. Dale real estate executive
Hemming, Roy G. writer, magazine editor, broadcaster
†Hemsley, Maarten D. business financial executive
Henderson, Donald Bernard, Jr. lawyer
Henderson, Harold Richard, Jr. lawyer, labor relations executive
Henderson, Joe jazz tenor saxophonist
Henderson, Skitch (Lyle Russell Cedric) pianist, conductor
Hendricks, Edward David association executive
Hendrickson, Charles John bank executive
Hendrickson, Robert Augustus lawyer
Hendry, Andrew Delaney consumer products company executive
Henkin, Louis lawyer, law educator
Henley, Arthur author, editor, television consultant
Henley, Beth playwright, actress
†Henley, Deborah newspaper editor
Hennes, Robert Taft former management consultant, investment executive
†Hennesey, John M. diversified financial servies company executive
Hennessy, John M. brokerage house executive
Hennig, Frederick E. retail company executive
†Henning, Alyson Balfour advertising executive
Henninger, Daniel Paul editor
Henry, Marguerite author
Henry, Paul James lawyer, health care administrator
Hensler, Guenter Manfred record company executive
Hentoff, Margot columnist
Hentoff, Nathan Irving writer
Herbert, Bob newspaper columnist
Herbits, Stephen Edward alcoholic beverage company executive
Herkness, Lindsay Coates, III securities broker
†Herman, Carol Korngut advertising agency executive
Herman, Jerry composer-lyricist
†Herman, John Joseph publisher
Herman, Kenneth Beaumont lawyer
Hernstadt, Judith Filenbaum city planner, real estate executive, broadcasting executive
Herold, Karl Guenter lawyer
Herregat, Guy-Georges Jacques banker
Herrera, Carolina fashion designer
†Herrera, Paloma dancer
Herrera, Paul Fredrick accountant
Herrmann, Lacy Bunnell investment company executive, financial entrepreneur, venture capitalist
Hersch, Dennis Steven lawyer
†Hershfield, Allan F. academic administrator
Hertz, Leon publishing executive
Hertz, Rudolf Heinrich banker
†Hertzberg, Daniel journalist
Hertzberg, Hendrik magazine editor, writer
Herzog, Arthur, III author
Herzog, John E. securities executive
Heslin, James J. association executive
Hess, Dennis John investment banker
Hess, Leon oil company executive
†Hess, Robert B. producer
Hesselbein, Frances Richards foundation executive, consultant
Hester, James McNaughton foundation administrator
Hester, Melvyn Francis labor union executive
†Hetfield, James singer
Hetherington, John Warner lawyer
Heuer, Kenneth John publishing company executive
Hewes, Henry drama critic
Hewitt, Carl Herbert lawyer
Hewitt, Dennis Edwin financial executive
Hewitt, Don S. television news producer
Hewitt, Vivian Ann Davidson (Mrs. John Hamilton Hewitt, Jr.) librarian
Heyde, Martha Bennett (Mrs. Ernest R. Heyde) psychologist
Heydebrand, Wolf Von sociology educator
Heyer, Paul Otto college president, architect
Heyman, George Harrison, Jr. securities company executive
Heyman, William Herbert securities firm executive
Heyward, Andrew John television producer
Heyworth, James O. communications company executive
Hiatt, John musician, country, popular
Hibel, Bernard financial consultant, former apparel company executive
Hickman, J. Kenneth accounting company executive
Hicks, Tyler Gregory publishing company executive, writer
Hiden, Robert Battaile, Jr. lawyer
Higginbotham, A. Leon, Jr. lawyer, educator
†Higgins, Harrison Scott investment company executive
Higginson, James Jackson lawyer
Higgs, John H. lawyer
Highleyman, Samuel Locke, III lawyer
Hilfiger, Tommy fashion designer
Hilgartner, Margaret Wehr pediatric hematologist, educator
Hill, Alfred lawyer, educator
Hill, Clinton artist
†Hill, Elizabeth Starr writer
Hill, George Roy film director
Hill, J(ames) Tomilson investment banker
Hill, Norman Julius publisher, author, editor, playwright
Hill, Pamela television executive
Hill, Robert Arthur ballet dancer
Hilliard, Landon banker
†Hillman, Howard Budrow author, editor, publisher, consultant
Hills, Frederic Wheeler editor, publishing company executive
Hilton, Alice Mary cybernetics and computing systems consultant, author, mathematician, art historian
Hilton, Andrew Carson management consultant, former manufacturing company executive
Hinds, Thomas Sheldon publisher, organization executive
Hinerfeld, Norman Martin manufacturing company executive
Hines, Anna Grossnickle author, illustrator
†Hinrichs, Horst manufactoring executive
Hinton, S(usan) E(loise) author
Hinz, Dorothy Elizabeth writer, editor, international corporate communications and public affairs specialist
†Hinz, Theodore Vincent architect
†Hios, Theodore painter, graphic artist
†Hirata, H. grain company executive
†Hirota, Yutaro metal products executive
Hirsch, Barry lawyer
Hirsch, George Aaron publisher
Hirsch, Jerome Seth lawyer
Hirsch, Judd actor
†Hirsch, Jules physician, scientist
Hirsch, Roseann Conte publisher
†Hirsch, Steven Richard broadcast executive
Hirschfeld, Albert artist
Hirschfeld, Michael lawyer
Hirschfield, Robert S. political science educator
Hirschhorn, Kurt pediatrics educator
†Hirschhorn, Rochelle genetics educator
Hirschman, Shalom Zarach physician
Hirshfield, Stuart lawyer
Hirshon, Sheldon Ira lawyer
Hirshowitz, Melvin Stephen lawyer
Hiss, Tony writer
Hlinka, Nichol dancer
Hoagland, Edward author
Hobbs, Franklin Warren, IV investment banker
Hoblin, Philip J., Jr. securities lawyer
†Hochberg, Irving audiologist, educator
Hochberg, Julian psychologist
†Hockenberry, John television journalist
†Hodapp, Siegfried petroleum industry executive
Hodes, Robert Bernard lawyer
Hoeflin, Ronald Kent philosopher, test designer, journal publisher
Hoeft, Julius Albert publishing company executive
†Hoelterhoff, Manuela Vali newspaper editor, critic
Hofer, Myron A(rms) psychiatrist, researcher
Hoff, Jonathan M(orind) lawyer
Hoff, Margo artist, printmaker, muralist
Hoff, Syd(ney) cartoonist, author
Hoffenberg, Harvey advertising executive
Hoffert, Martin Irving applied science educator
†Hoffman, Alice writer
Hoffman, Dustin Lee actor
Hoffman, John Ernest, Jr. retired lawyer
Hoffman, John Fletcher lawyer
Hoffman, Martin Leon psychology educator
Hoffman, Mathew lawyer
Hoffman, Michael Eugene editor, publisher, museum curator
Hoffman, William M. playwright, editor
Hoffmann, Malcolm Arthur lawyer
Hoge, Warren M. newspaper and magazine editor
Hohn, Harry George insurance company executive, lawyer
†Holabird, Katherine children's book author
Holder, Geoffrey dancer, actor, choreographer, director
Holderness, Algernon Sidney, Jr. lawyer
Holderness, G(eorge) Malcolm lawyer
Holl, Steven Myron architect
Holland, Bradford Wayne artist
Holland, Isabelle Christian author
Holland, Michael Francis investment company executive
Hollander, Edwin Paul psychologist, educator
Hollander, Lorin pianist
Hollenbeck, Ralph Anthony retired editor, book reviewer
Holliday, Jennifer Yvette singer, actress
Holliday, Polly Dean actress
Hollinshead, Byron Sharpe, Jr. publishing company executive
Holloway, David baritone
Holman, Bud George lawyer
Holman, Margaret Mezoff fund raising consultant
Holmes, Miriam H. publisher
Holmgren, Laton Earle clergyman
Holroyd, Michael author
Holstein, Marilyn Anne publishing company executive
Holt, Donald Dale magazine editor
Holt, Nancy Louise artist
Holt, Peter Rolf physician, educator
Holtzman, Alexander lawyer, consultant
Holtzman, Ellen A. foundation executive
Holtzmann, Howard Marshall lawyer, judge
Holtzschue, Karl Bressem lawyer, author, educator
Holub, Martin architect
Holzer, Hans author
†Holzer, Jenny artist
Holzman, Malcolm architect
Hommes, Frits Aukustinus biology educator
Honan, William Holmes journalist, writer
Honig, Barry Hirsh biophysics educator
Hooper, Ian (John Derek Glass) advertising agency executive
Hootkin, Pamela Nan apparel company executive
†Hoover, James Lloyd law librarian, educator
Hope, Michael S. entertainment and communications company executive
†Hopkins, Harold Anthony, Jr. bishop
Hopper, Walter Everett lawyer
Hopple, Richard Van Tromp, Jr. advertising agency executive
Horiuchi, Gen professional dancer
Hormats, Robert David economist, investment banker
Horn, Charles G. textile executive
Horn, Shirley vocalist, pianist
†Hornby, Geoffrey oil industry executive
Horne, Marilyn mezzo-soprano
Horner, Larry Dean retired accounting firm executive, brokerage firm executive
Hornick, Robert Newton lawyer
Horovitz, Israel Arthur playwright
Horowitz, David H. communications industry executive, lawyer, consultant
Horowitz, Frances Degen academic administrator, psychology educator
Horowitz, Gedale Bob investment banker
Horowitz, Raymond J. lawyer
†Hoser, Albert electronics executive
Hoskins, William John obstetrician/gynecologist, educator
†Hosokawa, David advertising executive
Host, Stig oil company executive
Houghton, Charles Norris stage director, author, educator
†Hould-Ward, Ann theatrical costume designer
House, Karen Elliott company executive, former editor, reporter
Houston, James Archibald designer, author, artist
Houston, Whitney vocalist, recording artist
Hovde, Carl Frederick language professional, educator
Hovdesven, Arne lawyer
Hover, John Calvin, II banker
Hovhaness, Alan composer
Hoving, Thomas museum and cultural affairs consultant, author

Howard, David ballet school administrator
Howard, Elizabeth corporate communications and marketing executive
Howard, M(oses) William, Jr. minister, seminary president
Howard, Nathan Southard investment banker, lawyer
Howat, John Keith museum executive
Howatson, Marianne publisher
Howe, Florence English educator, writer, publisher
Howe, Richard Rives lawyer
†Howe, Tina playwright
Howell, Wesley Grant, Jr. lawyer
Howes, Alfred S. business and insurance consultant
Hoxie, Ralph Gordon educational administrator, author
Hoxter, Curtis Joseph international economic adviser, public relations and affairs counselor
†Hoyt, Charles King architect, editor
Hoyt, Henry Hamilton, Jr. pharmaceutical and toiletry company executive
Hoyt, Seth publisher
Hruska, Alan J. lawyer
Hsu, Charles Jui-cheng manufacturing company executive, advertising agent
Hu, Joseph Chi-Ping mortgage securities analyst
Hubbe, Nikolaj dancer
Hudspeth, Stephen Mason lawyer
Huettner, Richard Alfred lawyer
†Hufham, Barbara Frances publishing executive, lawyer
Hughes, Allen music critic
Hughes, Kevin Peter lawyer
Hughes, Robert Studley Forrest art critic
Hugo, Norman Eliot plastic surgeon, medical educator
Huhs, John I. lawyer
Hulbert, Richard Woodward lawyer
Hull, Cathy artist, illustrator
Hull, Philip Glasgow lawyer
†Hultberg, John artist
Hultquist, Timothy Allen investment banker
Humperdinck, Engelbert (Arnold George Dorsey) singer
†Humphreys, Richard advertising executive
†Hunnewell, Francis O. bank executive
Hunt, Franklin Griggs lawyer
Hunt, Richard sculptor
Hunte, Beryl Eleanor mathematics educator, consultant
Hunter, Evan (Ed Mc Bain) author
†Hunter, Rachel model
†Hunter-Gault, Charlayne journalist
Hunter-Stiebel, Penelope art historian, art dealer
†Huntington, Lawrence Smith investment banker
Hupper, John Roscoe lawyer
Hurewitz, J(acob) C(oleman) international relations educator emeritus, author, consultant
Hurford, John Boyce investment counselor
Hurley, Cheryl Joyce publishing company executive
Hurley, Geoffrey Kevin lawyer
Hurlock, James Bickford lawyer
Hurst, Robert Jay securities company executive
Hurvitz, Arthur Isaac pathologist, researcher
Hurwitz, Sol business policy organization executive
Hussein, Ahmed Dia investment banker
Hutchens, John Kennedy journalist, editor
Hutchings, Peter Lounsbery insurance company executive
Hutner, Seymour Herbert microbiologist, protozoologist
Hutter, Rudolf Gustav Emil physics educator
Huxtable, Ada Louise architecture critic
Huyssen, Andreas German literature educator
Hwang, David Henry playwright, screenwriter
Hyams, Joe writer
†Hyatt, Jim newspaper editor
Hyde, David Rowley lawyer
Hyman, Alan Barry lawyer
Hyman, Bruce Malcolm ophthalmologist
Hyman, Earle actor, educator
Hyman, Jerome Elliot lawyer
Hyman, Morton Peter shipping company executive
Hyman, Seymour capital and product development company executive
†Hytner, Nicholas theatrical director
Iakovos, (Demetrios A. Coucouzis) archbishop
Ianni, Francis Anthony James anthropologist, psychoanalyst, educator
Iannuzzi, John Nicholas lawyer, author, educator
Ibarguen, Alberto newspaper executive
Idzik, Daniel Ronald lawyer
Iger, Robert A. broadcast executive
Iglesias, Julio (Julio Jose Iglesias De La Cueva) singer, songwriter
†Iman, (Iman Abudulmajid) model
Imparato, Anthony Michael vascular surgeon, medical educator, researcher
Incandela, Gerald Jean-Marie artist
Inez, Colette poet
†Ingraham, David Wood broadcast executive
Ingraham, John Wright banker
Ingram, Samuel William, Jr. lawyer
Ink, Dwight A. government agency administrator
Innaurato, Albert Francis playwright
Innis, Roy Emile Alfredo organization official
†Inoue, Minoru manufacturing executive
Insel, Michael S. lawyer
Iovenko, Michael lawyer
Ireland, Patrick artist
Irvin, Tinsley Hoyt insurance broker
Isaacson, Allen Ira lawyer
†Isaacson, Melvin Stuart library director
Isaacson, Walter Seff editor
Isay, Jane Franzblau publisher
Isay, Richard Alexander psychiatrist
Iselin, John Jay university president
Isley, Alexander Max graphic designer, lecturer
†Isogai, Masaharu women's apparel executive
Isquith, Fred Taylor lawyer
Israel, Margie Olanoff psychotherapist
Issler, Harry lawyer
Ittleson, H(enry) Anthony bicycle vacation company executive
†Itzkowitz, Murray health facility administrator
Ivanick, Carol W. Trencher lawyer
Ives, Colta Feller museum curator, educator
Ivory, James Francis film director
Jacey, Charles Frederick, Jr. accounting company executive, consultant
Jackel, Lawrence publishing company executive
Jacker, Corinne Litvin playwright
Jackson, Anne (Anne Jackson Wallach) actress
†Jackson, David Parker radio news anchor
Jackson, Glenda actress
Jackson, Keith MacKenzie television commentator, writer, producer
Jackson, Kenneth Terry historian, educator
Jackson, Reginald Martinez former professional baseball player
Jackson, Richard George advertising agency executive
Jackson, Thomas Gene lawyer
Jackson, Ward artist
Jackson, William Eldred lawyer
Jacob, Edwin J. lawyer
Jacob, Jerry Rowland airline executive
Jacob, John Edward social service agency executive
Jacob, Marvin Eugene lawyer
Jacobs, Albert Lionel, Jr. lawyer
Jacobs, Arnold Stephen lawyer
Jacobs, Bernard B. theater executive
Jacobs, Dennis G. federal judge
Jacobs, Jane Brand lawyer
Jacobs, Jim actor, playwright, composer, lyricist
Jacobs, Marc fashion designer
Jacobs, Mark Neil financial services corporation executive, lawyer
Jacobs, Robert Alan lawyer
Jacobs, Sherry Raphael retail executive, lawyer
Jacobs, Stephen Benjamin architect, planner, developer
Jacobson, Gary Steven lawyer
Jacobson, Gaynor I. retired association executive
Jacobson, Jerold Dennis lawyer
Jacoby, A. James securities brokerage firm executive
Jacoby, Jacob consumer psychology educator
Jacoby, Robert Harold management consulting executive
Jacquette, Yvonne Helene artist
Jaffe, Alan Steven lawyer
Jaffe, Leo motion picture executive
Jaffe, Nora artist
Jaffe, Rona author
Jaffe, Susan ballerina
Jaffee, Sandra Schuyler financial executive
Jaffin, Charles Leonard lawyer
Jagger, Mick (Michael Philip Jagger) singer, musician
†Jagiello, Georgiana M. geneticist, educator
Jakes, John author
Jakes, Peter H. lawyer
James, Hamilton Evans investment banking firm executive
James, Robert Leo advertising agency executive
Jameson, Richard magazine editor, film critic
Jamieson, Edward Leo magazine editor
†Jamieson, Robert John television journalist
Jamin, Gerald Alan petroleum company executive
Jamison, Judith dancer
Jampolis, Neil Peter designer
Jander, Klaus Heinrich lawyer
Janeway, Elizabeth Hall author
Janiak, Anthony Richard, Jr. investment banker
Janklow, Linda LeRoy civic worker, volunteer
Janklow, Morton Lloyd lawyer, literary agent
Janowitz, Henry David physician, researcher, medical educator
Janson, Joseph Bror, II editor, publishing executive
Janssen, Peter Anton magazine editor and publisher
Jánszky, Andrew Béla lawyer
Jarblum, William lawyer
Jarecki, Henry George physician, financial executive
Jaroff, Leon Morton magazine editor
Jarriel, Thomas Edwin correspondent
Jassy, Everett Lewis lawyer
Jaudon, Valerie artist
Javits, Eric Moses lawyer
Jedlicka, Judith Ann organization executive
Jefferies, Jack P. lawyer
†Jefferson, Denise dance school director
Jelinek, Josef Emil dermatologist
Jellinek, George broadcast executive, writer, music educator
Jenkins, Leroy violinist, composer
Jenkins, Paul artist
Jenkins, Robert Nesbit real estate executive
Jennings, Frank Gerard editor
Jennings, Peter Charles television anchorman
Jenrette, Richard Hampton investment and insurance company executive
Jensen, Michael Charles journalist, lecturer, author
Jepson, Hans Godfrey investment company executive
†Jerome, Albert David broadcasting company executive
Jerome, Fred Louis science organization executive
Jervis, Robert political science educator
Jessup, John Baker lawyer
Jeydel, Richard K. lawyer
Jeynes, Mary Kay college dean
Jhabvala, Ruth Prawer author
Jibaja, Gilbert insurance company executive
Jinnett, Robert Jefferson lawyer
Joel, Billy (William Martin Joel) musician
Joffe, Robert David lawyer
Johansen, David (Buster Poindexter) popular musician, actor
†John, Fritz mathematician, educator
Johns, Jasper artist
Johnsen, Niels Winchester ocean shipping company executive
†Johnson, Angela children's book author
Johnson, Betsey Lee fashion designer
Johnson, Charles writer, teacher
Johnson, Clarke Courtney finance educator
†Johnson, Denis poet, writer
Johnson, Freda S. public finance consultant
Johnson, Harold Earl personnel executive
Johnson, Horton Anton pathologist
Johnson, J. Chester financial executive, poet
Johnson, James Gann, Jr. lawyer
Johnson, James M. orchestra executive
Johnson, John William, Jr. executive recruiter
†Johnson, Kate dancer
Johnson, Philip Cortelyou architect
Johnson, Virginia Alma Fairfax ballerina
Jonas, Joan artist
Jonas, Ruth Haber psychologist
Jonas, Saran neurologist, educator
Jones, Abbott C. advertising agency executive
Jones, Alex S. reporter
Jones, Barclay Gibbs, III investment banker
Jones, Bill T. dancer, choreographer
†Jones, Caroline Robinson advertising executive
†Jones, Colin Howard publishing company executive
Jones, David Milton economist, educator
Jones, David Rhodes newspaper editor
Jones, Diana Wynne writer
Jones, Edward Powis artist
†Jones, Elaine civil rights advocate
Jones, Gwenyth Ellen director information systems
Jones, Gwyneth soprano
Jones, Julie art museum curator
Jones, Landon Y., Jr. magazine editor
Jones, Laurie Lynn magazine editor
Jones, Lucian Cox lawyer
†Jones, Rickie Lee singer, songwriter
Jones, Ronald David lawyer
†Jones, Thomas W. insurance company executive
Jones, William Kenneth law educator
Jones, William Randall publisher
Jong, Erica Mann author, poet
Jordan, Jerry Neville advertising executive
†Jordan, John W., II holding company executive
†Jordan, Susan newspaper editor
Jordan, Thomas Richard public relations executive
Jordan, Wilma Elizabeth Hacker publishing executive
Joseph, Frederick Harold investment banker
Joseph, Gregory Paul lawyer
Joseph, L. Anthony, Jr. lawyer
Joseph, Leonard lawyer
Joseph, Michael Sarkies accountant
Josephs, Ray public relations and advertising executive, writer, international relations consultant
Josephson, Marvin corporation executive
Josephson, William Howard lawyer
Juceam, Robert E. lawyer
Judson, Jeannette Alexander artist
Julia, Raul actor
Jung, Doris dramatic soprano
Juviler, Peter Henry political scientist, educator
Kabat, Elvin Abraham immunochemist, biochemist, educator
†Kaden, Ellen Oran lawyer, broadcasting corporation executive
Kaden, Lewis B. law educator
Kadet, Samuel lawyer
Kael, Pauline film critic, author
Kafin, Robert Joseph lawyer
Kagan, Julia Lee magazine editor
Kahan, Marlene professional association executive
Kahana, Aron bank executive
Kahen, Harold I. lawyer
Kahn, Alfred Joseph social worker and planner, educator
Kahn, Jenette Sarah publishing company executive
Kahn, Joseph Gabriel newspaperman
Kahn, Norman pharmacology and dentistry educator
Kahn, Richard Dreyfus lawyer
Kahn, Robert Theodore photojournalist
Kahn, Wolf artist
Kailas, Leo George lawyer
Kaish, Luise Clayborn sculptor
Kaish, Morton artist, educator
Kalamotousakis, George John economist
Kalat, Peter Anthony lawyer
†Kalech, Marc newspaper editor
Kalikow, Peter Stephen real estate developer, former newspaper owner, publisher
Kalish, Arthur lawyer
Kalish, Myron lawyer
Kallir, Jane Katherine art gallery director, author
Kalmanoff, Martin composer
Kalmus, Allan Henry public relations executive
Kals, Stephen A. lawyer
Kalsner, Stanley pharmacologist, physiologist, educator
Kamali, Norma fashion designer
Kamen, Harry Paul life insurance company executive, lawyer
Kamerman, Sheila Brody social worker, educator
†Kamiel, Jerald apparel executive
†Kamihara, Takashi electronics firm executive
Kamin, Sherwin lawyer
Kaminer, Peter H. lawyer
Kaminsky, Arthur Charles lawyer
Kaminsky, Howard publisher
Kamlot, Robert performing arts executive
Kamm, Laurence Richard television producer, director
Kampouris, Emmanuel Andrew corporate executive
Kamsky, Leonard economist, retired manufacturing executive, financial advisor
Kan, Diana Artemis Mann Shu artist
†Kanade, I. manufacturing executive
Kander, John Harold composer
Kane, Daniel Hipwell lawyer
Kane, Herman William research company executive, political scientist
Kane, Jay Brassler banker
Kanin, Garson writer, theatrical director
Kann, Peter Robert journalist, business reporting and services company executive
Kanovitz, Howard artist
Kanuk, Leslie Lazar management consultant, educator
Kaplan, Carl Eliot lawyer
Kaplan, Harold Irwin psychiatrist, psychoanalyst, educator
Kaplan, Joseph Solte lawyer
†Kaplan, Larry public relations executive
Kaplan, Leo Sylvan social scientist, former college administrator
Kaplan, Lewis A. lawyer
Kaplan, Lloyd Arthur public relations executive
Kaplan, Mark Norman lawyer
Kaplan, Peter James lawyer
Kaplan, Philip Thomas lawyer
†Kaplan, Richard James producer, director, writer, educator, consultant
Kaplan, Robert Arthur association executive
Kappas, Attallah physician, medical scientist
Karalekas, George Steven advertising agency executive, political consultant
Karan, Donna (Donna Faske) fashion designer
Karasz, Peter lawyer
Karatz, William Warren lawyer
Karchin, Louis Samuel composer
Kardon, Janet museum director, curator
Karmel, Roberta S. lawyer, educator
Karotkin, Stephen K. lawyer
Karp, Marshall Warren creative director, writer
Karp, Martin Everett management consultant
Karp, Richard M. advertising executive
Karpel, Craig S. journalist, editor
Karpen, Marian Joan financial executive
Karr, Norman association executive
Karsen, Sonja Petra Spanish educator emeritus
†Karten, Terry book editor
†Karter, Jerome insurance company executive
Kartiganer, Joseph lawyer
Kasa, Pamela Dorothy lawyer
Kasinec, Edward Joseph library administrator
Kaskell, Peter Howard association executive, lawyer
Kasowitz, Marc Elliot lawyer
Kassel, Virginia Weltmer television producer, writer
Kata, Edward John industrial products manufacturing company executive
†Katalinich, Peggy newspaper editor
Katsh, Abraham Isaac university president emeritus, educator
Katsh, Salem Michael lawyer
Katz, Abraham retired foreign service officer
Katz, Alex artist
Katz, Gregory lawyer
Katz, Hilda artist
Katz, Jerome Charles lawyer
Katz, Marcia public relations company executive
Katz, Norman manufacturing company executive
Katz, Phyllis Pollak magazine publisher and editor
Katz, Ronald S. lawyer
Katz, Stanley Nider law history educator, association executive
Katz, William Loren author
Katzen, Lila Pell sculptor
Katzman, Herbert Henry artist
Kauffmann, Stanley Jules author
Kaufman, Arthur Stephen lawyer
Kaufman, Bel author, educator
Kaufman, Martin N. metal processing company executive
Kaufman, Robert Max lawyer
†Kaufman, Victor A. film company executive
Kaufmann, Jack lawyer
Kaufmann, Mark Steiner banker
Kavaler, Thomas J. lawyer
Kavee, Robert Charles insurance company executive
Kavesh, Robert A. economist, educator
†Kay, Michelle Suzanne advertising executive
Kaye, Judy actress
Kaye, Stephen Rackow lawyer
Kaye, Walter financial executive
Kaz, Nathaniel sculptor
Kazanjian, John Harold lawyer
†Kazanjian, Shant religious organization administrator
Kazemi, Farhad political science educator
Kazin, Alfred writer
Kean, Hamilton Fish lawyer
Keane, Bil cartoonist
Keany, Sutton lawyer
Kearse, Amalya Lyle federal judge
Keating, Cornelius Francis record company executive
Keating, Karen Rupert commercial banker
Keating, Robert Edward public relations executive
Keegan, Gerard C. bank executive
Keenan, John Fontaine federal judge
Keenan, Michael Edgar advertising executive
Keene, Christopher conductor, author, librettist, musician
Keeshan, Bob television producer, actor
Keeshan, Michael advertising agency executive
Keeshan, William Francis, Jr. advertising executive
Keevil, Philip Clement investment banker
†Kehr, David film critic
Kehret, Peg writer
Keilin, Eugene Jacob investment banker, lawyer
†Keller, Bill journalist
Keller, Kenneth Harrison engineering educator, science policy analyst
Kellerman, Jonathan Seth pediatric psychologist, writer
Kelley, Sheila Seymour public relations executive, crisis consultant
Kellman, Barnet Kramer film, stage and television director
Kellner, Irwin L. economist
Kellogg, Cal Stewart, II conductor, composer
Kellogg, David publisher
Kellogg, Herbert Humphrey metallurgist, educator
Kellogg, Peter R. securities dealer
Kelly, David Austin food and chemical products executive
Kelly, James artist
Kelly, L. Thomas magazine publisher, museum director
Kelly, Robert J. accounting firm executive
Kelman, Charles D. ophthalmologist, educator
Kelmenson, Leo-Arthur advertising executive
Kelne, Nathan editorial and public relations consultant
Kempa, Gerald manufacturing company executive
Kemper, Randolph E. fashion designer
Kennedy, Ian Glen art appraiser
Kennedy, Moorhead foundation administrator
Kenney, Jerome P. finance company executive
Kenney, John Joseph lawyer
†Kenney, Martin Edward, Jr. publishing company executive
†Kenney, Matthew chef
Kenny, Roger Michael executive search consultant
†Kent, Julie Ann ballet dancer, actress, model
Kent, Linda Gail dancer
Keogh, Kevin lawyer
Kepets, Hugh Michael artist
Keppler, Herbert publishing company executive
†Kern, Ellis corporate professional
Kern, George Calvin, Jr. lawyer
Kern, Jerome H. lawyer
Kern, Martin H(arold) supermarket chain executive
Kernochan, John Marshall lawyer, educator
†Kerrison, Ray newspaper columnist
†Kessel, Barry Lee advertising and marketing executive
Kessel, Mark lawyer
Kessler, Jeffrey L. lawyer
Kessler, Ralph Kenneth lawyer, manufacturing company executive
Kesting, Theodore magazine editor
Kezsbom, Allen lawyer
Khan, Chaka (Yvette Marie Stevens) singer
Khanzadian, Vahan tenor
Khayatt, Shaker Albert investment banker
Kheel, Theodore Woodrow lawyer, labor arbitrator and mediator
Khuri, Nicola Najib physicist, educator
Kidd, John Edward lawyer, corporate executive
Kidd, Michael (Milton Greenwald) choreographer, director
Kidder, (John) Tracy writer
Kideckel, Arnold lawyer
†Kiechel, Walter, III magazine editor
Kieren, Thomas Henry management consultant
Kifner, John William journalist, newspaper correspondent
Kilburn, H(enry) T(homas), Jr. investment banker
Kill, Lawrence lawyer
Killefer, Tom banker
†Killeffer, Louis MacMillan advertising executive
Kim, Willa costume designer
Kimball, Richard Arthur, Jr. lawyer
Kinberg, Judy television producer, director
King, B. B. (Riley B. King) singer, guitarist
King, Don boxing promoter
King, Douglas Lohr insurance executive, lawyer
King, Henry Lawrence lawyer
King, Lawrence Philip lawyer, educator
King, Thomas Creighton thoracic surgeon, educator
King, Woodie, Jr. producer, actor, director
Kingsberg, Harold Joseph investment management company executive

†Kingsland, James Arthur *architect*
Kingsley, Sidney *playwright*
Kinney, Stephen Hoyt, Jr. *lawyer*
Kinsolving, Charles McIlvaine, Jr. *marketing executive*
Kinstler, Everett Raymond *artist*
Kinzey, Warren Glenford *anthropology educator*
Kinzler, Thomas Benjamin *lawyer*
Kirby, John Joseph, Jr. *lawyer*
Kirk, Alexis Vemian *designer*
Kirk, Donald James *consultant, accounting educator*
Kirkland, Gelsey *dancer*
Kirsch, Arthur William *investment banker*
Kirschbaum, Myron *lawyer*
†Kirschen, Robert Steven *music director*
Kirschner, Marc Steven *lawyer*
†Kirshbaum, Laurence J. *book publishing executive*
†Kirshenbaum, Richard Warren *creative director*
Kirstein, Lincoln *ballet promoter*
Kish, Joseph Laurence, Jr. *management consultant*
Kismaric, Carole Lee *editor, writer, book packaging company executive*
Kisner, Jacob *poet, editor*
Kissel, Howard William *drama critic*
Kissiloff, William *industrial designer*
Kissinger, Henry Alfred *former secretary of state, international consulting company executive*
Kistler, Darci Anna *ballet dancer*
Kitt, Eartha Mae *actress, singer*
Kivette, Ruth Montgomery *English language educator*
Kiwitt, Sidney *motion picture production consultant*
Klaperman, Joel Simcha *lawyer*
Klass, Morton *anthropology educator, consultant*
Klatell, Jack *dentist*
†Klatsky, Bruce J. *apparel company executive*
Kleemann, Ronald Allen *artist*
Klein, Arnold Spencer *lawyer*
Klein, Calvin Richard *fashion designer*
Klein, Donald Franklin *scientist, psychiatrist, educator*
†Klein, John E. *agricultural products company executive*
Klein, Morton *industrial engineer, educator*
Klein, Paul E. *insurance company executive, lawyer*
Klein, Robert *comedian, actor*
Klein, Robert Majer *bank executive*
Klein, T(heodore) E(ibon) D(onald) *writer*
Klein, William, II *lawyer*
Kleinbard, Edward D. *lawyer*
Kleinberg, Norman Charles *lawyer*
Klemm, Richard Henry *investment company executive*
Kligfield, Paul David *physician, medicine educator*
Kliment, Robert Michael *architect*
Kliment, Stephen Alexander *architect, editor*
Kline, Eugene Monroe *lawyer*
Kline, Milton Vance *psychologist, educator*
Klingenstein, Frederick Adler *investment banking executive*
Klingsberg, David *lawyer*
Klink, Fredric J. *lawyer*
†Klipper, Mitchell S. *book publishing executive*
Kloos, Edward John Michael, Jr. *minister*
Klopf, Gordon John *college dean, educational consultant*
Klotz, Florence *costume designer*
Kluberdanz, Wallace *publishing executive*
Knapp, Whitman *federal judge*
Knell, Gary Evan *media executive, lawyer*
Kneller, John William *French language educator*
Kner, Andrew Peter *art director*
Kness, Richard Maynard *tenor*
Knickerbocker, Daniel Candee, Jr. *legal educator*
Knight, Robert Huntington *lawyer, bank executive*
Knight, Townsend Jones *lawyer*
†Knisley, Patrick Allen *advertising company executive*
Knobler, Alfred Everett *ceramic engineer, manufacturing company executive, publisher*
Knobler, Peter Stephen *magazine editor, writer*
Knowles, Edward F(rank) *architect*
Knox, George L(evi), III *corporate executive*
Knudsen, Rudolph Edgar, Jr. *insurance company executive*
Knutson, David Harry *lawyer, banker*
Kobak, James Benedict, Jr. *lawyer, educator*
†Kobayashi, Hisao *financial company executive*
Kober, Jane *lawyer*
Kobler, John *writer*
Kobrin, Lawrence Alan *lawyer*
Koch, Edward I. *former mayor, lawyer*
Koch, Kenneth *poet, playwright*
Koch, Sidney *investment banker*
Koegel, William Fisher *lawyer*
Koeltl, John George *lawyer*
†Koenig, Marvin *heavy manufacturing executive*
Koeppel, Noel Immanuel *financial planner, securities and real estate broker*
Koerner, James David *author, foundation executive, consultant*
†Kogstad, Rolf Egil *sales company executive*
Kohlenberg, Stanley *marketing executive*
Kohn, A. Eugene *architect*
Kohut, John Walter *corporate executive*
Koke, Richard Joseph *author, exhibit designer, museum curator*
Kolatch, Myron *magazine editor*
Kolb, Daniel Francis *lawyer*
Kolb, Jerry Wilbert *accountant*
Kolbe, Karl William, Jr. *lawyer*
†Kolbert, Kathryn *lawyer, educator*
Kolesar, Peter John *business and engineering educator*
Kolodny, Edwin Hillel *neurologist, geneticist, medical administrator*
Kolpakova, Irina *dancer, educator, coach*
Komar, Arthur B. *physicist, educator*
Komaroff, Stanley *lawyer*
Komarovsky, Mirra (Mrs. Marcus A. Heyman) *sociology educator*
Komisar, Arnold *otolaryngologist, educator*
Kondas, Nicholas Frank *shipping company executive*
†Kondylis, Costas Andrew *architect*
Konner, Joan Weiner *university administrator, educator, broadcasting executive, television producer*
Konzal, Joseph Charles *sculptor*
Koob, Charles Edward *lawyer*
†Koons, Linda Gleitsman *editor*
Koontz, Dean Ray *writer*
Koontz, Richard Harvey *financial printing company executive*
Kopelman, Richard Eric *management educator*
†Koplik, Michael R. *durable goods company executive*
†Koplik, Perry H. *durable goods company executive*
Koplovitz, Kay *communication network executive*
†Kopp, Wendy *volunteer program administrator*
Koppelman, Chaim *artist*
Koppelman, Charles *record company executive*
Koppelman, Dorothy Myers *artist, consultant*
Koppenaal, Richard John *psychology educator*
Korach, William Mark *marketing executive*
Koral, Alan M. *lawyer*
Koren, Edward Benjamin *cartoonist, educator*
Korman, Barbara *artist, educator*
Korman, Jess J. *advertising executive*
Korman, Lewis J. *film company executive, consultant, lawyer*
Kornberg, Alan William *lawyer*
Korner, Anthony David *publisher*
Kornreich, Edward Scott *lawyer*
†Kornreich, Morton Alan *insurance brokerage company executive*
Kornstein, Don Robert *investment banker*
Korotkin, Michael Paul *lawyer*
Kors, Michael (Karl Anderson, Jr.) *fashion designer*
Kortepeter, Carl Max *history educator, columnist*
Koshar, Louis David *civil engineer*
Kosner, Edward A(lan) *magazine editor and publisher*
Kosovich, Dushan Radovan *psychiatrist*
†Kosstrin, Jane Edith *designer*
Kostelanetz, Boris *lawyer*
Kostelanetz, Richard *writer, artist*
Koster, Elaine Landis *publishing executive*
Kotcher, Raymond Lowell *public relations executive*
Kotecha, Mahesh Kanjibhai *financial guarantee insurance company executive*
Kotlowitz, Robert *writer,editor*
Kotzwinkle, William *author*
Kourides, Peter Theologos *lawyer*
†Kovak, Ellen B. *public relations firm executive*
Kovalcik, Kenneth John *accountant*
Kozlov, Leonid *ballet dancer*
Kozlova, Valentina *ballerina*
Kozodoy, Neal *magazine editor*
Kraemer, Lillian Elizabeth *lawyer*
Krakow, Amy Ginzig *author, advertising and marketing executive, consultant*
Kram, Shirley Wohl *federal judge*
Kramer, Alan Sharfsin *lawyer*
Kramer, Fred Russell *molecular biologist*
Kramer, George P. *lawyer*
Kramer, Jane *author*
Kramer, Joyce L. *lawyer*
Kramer, Marc B. *forensic audiologist*
Kramer, Morris Joseph *lawyer*
Kramer, Philip *retired petroleum refining executive*
Kranwinkle, Conrad Douglas *lawyer*
Krasna, Alvin Isaac *biochemist, educator*
Krasner, Daniel Walter *lawyer*
†Krasno, Richard Michael *educational organization executive, educator*
†Krat, Gary Walden *financial services company executive*
Kraus, Alfredo (Alfredo Kraus Trujillo) *tenor*
Kraus, Douglas M. *lawyer*
Kraus, Norma Jean *industrial relations executive*
Kraushar, Jonathan Pollack *communications and media consultant*
Krauss, Herbert Harris *psychologist*
Kravis, Henry R. *venture financier*
Krawitz, Herman Everett *television producer*
Kreh, Kent Q. *magazine publishing executive*
Kreisberg, Neil Ivan *advertising executive*
Kreitman, Benjamin Zvi *rabbi, Judaic studies educator*
Kreitzman, Ralph J. *lawyer*
Krementz, Jill *photographer, author*
Krenek, Debby *newspaper editor*
Krens, Thomas *museum director*
Krensky, Harold *retired retail store executive, investor*
Krents, Milton Ellis *broadcast executive*
Kressel, Henry *venture capitalist*
Kreston, Martin Howard *advertising, marketing, public relations, and publishing executive*
Kretschmer, Paul Robert *investment banker*
Krickstein, Aaron *professional tennis player*
Krieger, Sanford *lawyer*
Krimendahl, Herbert Frederick, II *investment banker*
†Kriney, Marilyn Walker *publishing executive*
Krinsky, Carol Herselle *art history educator*
Krinsky, Robert Daniel *consulting firm executive*
Krinsly, Stuart Z. *lawyer, manufacturing company executive*
Kristeller, Paul Oskar *former philosophy educator*
Kristof, Nicholas Donabet *journalist*
†Kroeber, C. Kent *human resources executive*
Kroeber, Karl *English language educator*
Kroft, Steve *news correspondent, editor*
Kroll, Alexander S. *advertising agency executive*
Kroll, Arthur Herbert *lawyer, law educator*
Krominga, Lynn *cosmetic and health care company executive, lawyer*
Krone, Gerald Sidney *theatrical and television producer*
Krone, Helmut *consultant, former advertising executive*
Krone, Julie *jockey*
Krosnick, Joel *cellist*
Krouse, George Raymond, Jr. *lawyer*
†Kruech, Paul C. *bank executive*
Krueger, Harvey Mark *investment banker, lawyer*
Krugman, Saul *physician, educator, researcher*
Krulik, Barbara S. *museum director, curator*
Krupman, William Allan *lawyer*
Krupp, Fred *lawyer, environmental agency executive*
Krupska, Danya (Mrs. Ted Thurston) *theater director, choreographer*
Krushenick, Nicholas *artist*
Krzyzanowski, Eve *broadcasting executive*
Kubek, Anthony Christopher (Tony Kubek) *sports announcer*
Kubilus, Norbert John *information technology executive*
Kubin, Michael Ernest *advertising and marketing executive*
Kubly, Herbert *author, educator*
Kufeld, William Manuel *lawyer*
Kuh, Richard Henry *lawyer*
†Kuhn, Denis Glen *architectural firm executive*
Kuhn, Michael *motion picture company executive*
Kuklin, Anthony Bennett *lawyer*
†Kull, F. Thomas, Jr. *newspaper publishing executive*
Kullberg, Gary Walter *advertising agency executive*
Kumble, Steven Jay *lawyer*
Kumin, Maxine Winokur *author, poet*
Kummel, Eugene H. *advertising agency executive*
Kunitz, Stanley Jasspon *poet, editor, educator*
Kunstler, William Moses *lawyer, educator, lecturer, author*
Kuntz, Lee Allan *lawyer*
Kuntz, William Francis, II *lawyer, educator*
†Kuo, John Tsungfen *geophysicist, educator, researcher*
Kupfer, Sherman *physician, educator, researcher*
Kupferman, Theodore R. *state justice*
Kuralt, Charles Bishop *writer, former television news correspondent*
Kurnit, Paul David *advertising executive*
Kurnit, Shepard *advertising agency executive*
Kurnow, Ernest *statistician, educator*
Kurtis, William Horton (Bill Kurtis) *broadcast journalist*
Kurtyka, Ruthanne *lawyer*
Kurtz, Jerome *lawyer, educator*
†Kurtz, Michael J. *newspaper publishing executive*
Kury, Bernard Edward *lawyer*
Kurz, Mitchell Howard *marketing communications executive*
Kurzweil, Harvey *lawyer*
Kushner, Tony *playwright*
Kvint, Vladimir Lev *economist, mining engineer, educator*
†Kvint, Vladimir Lev *business educator, economist*
Kwa, Raymond Pain-Boon *cardiologist*
LaBarre, Dennis W. *lawyer*
Labrecque, Thomas G. *banker*
Labunski, Stephen Bronislaw *association executive*
Lacey, Frederick Bernard *lawyer, former federal judge*
Lachenbruch, David *editor, writer*
Lachman, Lawrence *business consultant, former department store executive*
Lachman, Marguerite Leanne *real estate investment advisor*
Lackritz, Marc E. *securities trade association executive*
Lacovara, Philip Allen *lawyer*
Lacy, Robinson Burrell *lawyer*
Lacy, Steve *jazz musician*
Ladau, Robert Francis *architect, planner*
Lader, Lawrence *writer*
Ladjevardi, Hamid *fund manager*
LaForce, William Leonard, Jr. *photojournalist*
La Fosse, Robert *ballet dancer*
Lahr, John *author*
Lai, W(ei) Michael *mechanical engineer, educator*
Laidlaw, William Samuel Hugh *oil company executive*
Laird, Robert Winslow *journalist*
Lakah, Jacqueline Rabbat *political scientist, educator*
Lala, Dominick J. *manufacturing company executive*
†Lalli, Cele Goldsmith *editor*
†Lalli, Frank *magazine editor*
Lamb, George Richard *foundation executive*
Lambert, Eleanor (Mrs. Seymour Berkson) *public relations executive, fashion authority, journalist*
Lambert, Paul Christopher *lawyer, former ambassador*
Lamel, Linda Helen *insurance company executive, college president, lawyer*
Lamia, Thomas Roger *lawyer*
Lamirande, Arthur Gordon *editor*
Lamm, Donald Stephen *publishing company executive*
Lamm, Norman *academic administrator, rabbi*
Lamont, Lansing *journalist, public affairs executive, author*
Lamont, Lee *art management executive*
Lamport, Anthony Matthew *investments and venture capitalist*
Lancaster, Kelvin John *economics educator*
Lanchner, Bertrand Martin *lawyer, advertising executive*
Land, David Potts *lawyer*
Landa, Howard Martin *lawyer, business executive*
Landau, Peter Edward *editor*
Landau, Ralph *chemical engineer*
Landau, Sidney I. *publishing executive, lexicographer*
Landau, Walter Loeber *lawyer*
Landes, George Miller *biblical studies educator*
Landes, Robert Nathan *lawyer*
Landesman, Heidi *set designer*
Landrigan, Philip John *epidemiologist*
Lane, Alvin S. *lawyer*
Lane, Arthur Alan *lawyer*
Lane, Frederick Carpenter *investment banker*
Lane, Jeffrey Bruce *financial services company executive*
Lane, Kenneth Jay *jewelry designer*
Lane, Lois N. *artist*
Lane, Nancy *editor*
Lane, Nathan (Joseph Lane) *actor*
Lane, William W. *electronics executive*
Lang, Daniel S. *artist*
Lang, Eugene M. *technology development company executive*
Lang, George *restaurateur*
lang, k. d. (Katherine Dawn Lang) *country music singer, composer*
Lang, Pearl *dancer, choreographer*
Lang, Robert Todd *lawyer*
Lang, Theresa *investment banker*
Lange, Marvin Robert *lawyer*
Lange, Phil C. *education educator*
Langer, Andrew J. *advertising agency executive*
Langer, Horst *financial corporate executive*
Langham, Michael *theatrical director*
Langton, Cleve Swanson *advertising executive*
Lannamann, Richard Stuart *executive recruiting consultant*
La Noue, Terence David *artist, educator*
Lansbury, Edgar George *theatrical producer*
Lansing, Robert Howell *actor, director*
Lansner, Kermit Irvin *editor, consultant*
Lantay, George Charles (Wagner) *psychologist, psychotherapist, consultant*
Lanyon, Ellen (Mrs. Roland Ginzel) *artist, educator*
Lanza, Frank C. *electronics executive*
Lapham, Lewis Henry *editor, author, television host*
Lapierre, Dominique *author, historian*
Lapine, James Elliot *playwright, director*
Laporte, Cloyd, Jr. *retired manufacturing executive, lawyer*
†Laragh, John Henry *physician, scientist, educator*
Laren, Kuno *investment banker*
Larkin, June Noble *foundation executive*
Larkin, Leo Paul, Jr. *lawyer*
Larkins, Gary Thomas *accountant*
La Rossa, James M(ichael) *lawyer*
Larr, Peter *banker*
†Larsen, Anne *editor*
Larsen, Robert Dhu *lawyer*
La Rue, (Adrian) Jan (Pieters) *musicologist, educator, author*
Lascher, Alan Alfred *lawyer*
Lash, Stephen Sycle *auction company executive*
Lasker, Jonathan Lewis *artist*
Lasker, Joseph L. *artist, illustrator*
Lasser, Joseph Robert *investment company executive*
Lasser, Louise *actress*
Lassiter, Phillip B. *insurance company executive*
Lattes, Raffaele *physician, educator*
Lattimer, John Kingsley *physician, educator*
Lattin, Albert Floyd *banker*
Lauder, Estee *cosmetics company executive*
Lauder, Leonard Alan *cosmetic and fragrance company executive*
Lauer, Eliot *lawyer*
Lauersen, Niels Helth *physician, educator*
Laufer, Donald L. *lawyer*
Laufman, Harold *surgeon*
Laughlin, James *publishing company executive, writer, lecturer*
Laughlin, John Seth *physicist, educator*
Laughren, Terry *advertising executive*
Lauren, Ralph *fashion designer*
†Laurence, Jeffrey Conrad *immunologist*
Laurus, (Laurus Skurla) *archbishop*
Lavey, Kenneth Henry *advertising agency executive, designer*
Lavin, William Kane *retail executive*
Lavine, Lawrence Neal *investment banker*
Lavinsky, Larry Monroe *lawyer, consultant*
Lavitt, Mel S. *investment company executive*
Lawrence, Barbara *information manager*
Lawrence, Henry Sherwood *physician, educator*
Lawrence, James Bland *advertising executive*
Lawrence, Robert Swan *physician, educator, foundation executive*
Lawrence, Ruddick Carpenter *public relations executive*
Lawry, Sylvia (Mrs. Stanley Englander) *association executive*
Lawson-Johnston, Peter Orman *foundation executive*
Lax, Melvin *theoretical physicist*
Lax, Peter David *mathematics educator*
†Laybourne, Geraldine *broadcasting executive*
Layer, Meredith Mitchum *financial services company executive, public responsibility professional*
Layton, Donald Harvey *banker*
Lazarus, Mell *cartoonist*
Lazarus, Rochelle Braff *advertising executive*
Lazarus-Franklin, Paula Guillermina *vocational services administrator*
Leach, Michael Glen *publisher*
Leach, Robin *producer, writer, television host*
Leaf, Roger Warren *business consultant*
Leahy, Michael Joseph *newspaper editor*
Lear, Evelyn *soprano*
Lear, Robert William *holding company executive*
Leavitt, Charles Loyal *English language educator, administrator*
Leavitt, David Adam *writer*
Lebbad, John A. *advertising, marketing, communications executive*
Lebec, Alain *investment banker*
Lebensfeld, Harry *manufacturing company executive*
Leber, Lester *advertising agency executive*
Leber, Steven Edward *film producer, corporate executive*
LeBlond, Richard Knight, II *banker*
Lebouitz, Martin Frederick *financial services industry executive, consultant*
LeBow, Bennett S. *communications executive*
Lebow, Mark Denis *lawyer*
Le Buhn, Robert *investment company executive*
Lechay, James *artist, emeritus art educator*
LeClerc, Paul *library director*
Lederberg, Joshua *geneticist, educator*
Lederer, Edith Madelon *journalist*
Lederer, Peter David *lawyer*
Lederman, Lawrence *lawyer, writer, educator*
Ledger, William Joe *physician, educator*
LeDoux, Harold Anthony *cartoonist, painter*
Lee, Barbara A. *federal magistrate judge*
Lee, Catherine *sculptor, painter*
†Lee, Clement William Khan *association administrator*
Lee, Dai-Keong *composer*
Lee, David James *lawyer*
Lee, J. Daniel, Jr. *insurance company executive*
Lee, Jerome G. *lawyer*
Lee, Martin Yongho *mechanical engineer*
†Lee, Mathew Hung Mun *physiatrist*
Lee, Paul L. *lawyer*
Lee, Robert Sanford *psychologist*
Lee, Sarah Tomerlin *design executive*
Lee, Stan (Stanley Martin Lieber) *cartoon publisher, writer*
Lee, Tsung-Dao *physicist, educator*
†Leeds, Candace *public relations executive*
Leeds, Douglas Brecker *advertising agency executive, theatre producer*
†Leeds, Laurence Carroll, Jr. *apparel manufacturing company executive*
Leet, Mildred Robbins *corporate executive, consultant*
Leetch, Brian *hockey player*
LeFevre, David E. *lawyer, professional sports team executive*
Le Fevre, William Mathias, Jr. *brokerage company executive*
Lefferts, Gillet, Jr. *architect*
Lefkowitz, Howard N. *lawyer*
Lefkowitz, Lawrence *lawyer*
LeFrak, Francine *theatre and film producer*
Lefrak, Joseph Saul *lawyer, accountant*
Lehman, Edward William *sociology educator, researcher*
Lehman, Orin *retired state official*
Lehmann, Frederick Gliessmann *university administrator*
Lehmann-Haupt, Christopher Charles Herbert *book reviewer*
Lehr, Janet *art dealer*
Lehrer, Leonard *artist, educator*
Lehrer, Sander *lawyer*
Leiber, Gerson August *artist*
Leiber, Judith Maria *designer, manufacturer*
Leibovitz, Annie *photographer*
Leibowitz, Herbert Akiba *English language educator, author*
Leichtling, Michael Alfred *lawyer*
Leigh, Stephen *industrial designer*
Leighton, Lawrence Ward *investment banker*
Leisure, George Stanley, Jr. *lawyer*
Leisure, Peter Keeton *federal judge*
Leiter, Elliot *urologist*
Leland, Richard G. *lawyer*
Leland, Sara *ballet master*
Lelchuk, Alan *author, educator*
Lelyveld, Joseph Salem *newspaper editor, correspondent*
†Le Mener, Georges Philippe *hotel executive*
Lemesh, Nicholas Thomas *designer, filmmaker*

Lencek, Rado L. *Slavic languages educator*
Leness, George Crawford *lawyer*
L'Engle, Madeleine (Mrs. Hugh Franklin) *author*
Lennox, Annie *rock musician*
Leo, Jacqueline *magazine editor-in-chief*
Leonard, Edward F. *chemical engineer, educator*
Leonard, Edwin Deane *lawyer*
Leontief, Wassily *economist, educator*
Lepore, Michael Joseph *gastroenterologist, educator*
Leppard, Raymond John *conductor, harpsichordist*
†Lepri, Daniel B. *light manufacturing executive*
Lerner, Martin *museum curator*
Lerner, Ralph E. *lawyer*
Lesch, Michael Oscar *lawyer*
Leser, Bernard H. *publishing executive*
Leslie, John Webster, Jr. *communications company executive*
Leslie, Seymour Marvin *communications executive*
Lesser, Edward Arnold *banker*
Lesser, Lawrence J. *advertising agency executive*
Letterman, David *television personality, comedian, writer*
Leubert, Alfred Otto Paul *international business consultant*
†Levai, Pierre Alexandre *art gallery executive*
Leval, Pierre Nelson *federal judge*
†Levenson, Richard Neil *advertising executive*
Levenstein, Alan Peter *advertising executive*
†Leventhal, Kathy Neisloss *magazine publisher*
Levertov, Denise *poet*
Levie, Joseph Henry *lawyer*
Levien, Joy *corporate lawyer*
Levin, Aaron Reuben *pediatrician, educator*
Levin, Alan M. *television journalist*
Levin, Ezra Gurion *lawyer*
Levin, Gerald Manuel *publishing company executive*
Levin, Ira *author, playwright*
Levin, Jerry Wayne *business executive*
Levin, Martin P. *publishing executive, lawyer*
†Levin, Michael Stuart *steel company executive*
†Levin, Neil D. *bank executive*
Levin, Robert Daniel *lawyer*
Levine, Arthur Elliott *academic administrator, educator*
Levine, Carl Morton *motion picture exhibition, real estate executive*
Levine, David *artist*
Levine, Edward Leslie *lawyer*
†Levine, Ellen R. *magazine editor*
Levine, Gerald Richard *investment banker, finanical advisor, estate planning and philanthropy specialist, commercial real estate broker*
Levine, Harry *public relations executive*
Levine, Israel E. *writer*
Levine, James *conductor, pianist, artistic director*
Levine, Laurence William *lawyer*
Levine, Lawrence Steven *lawyer*
Levine, Mark Leonard *lawyer*
Levine, Naomi Bronheim *university administrator*
Levine, Richard James *publishing executive*
Levine, Robert Jay *lawyer*
Levine, Ronald Jay *lawyer*
†Levine, Sol *cosmetics company executive*
Levine, Suzanne Braun *magazine editor*
Levinson, Robert Alan *textile company executive*
†Levinson, Warren Mitchell *broadcast journalist*
Levison, Harold George *lawyer*
Levitan, Dan *investment banker*
Levitan, David M(aurice) *lawyer, educator*
Levitan, James A. *lawyer*
Levitas, Mitchel Ramsey *editor*
Levitt, Daniel Philip *lawyer*
Levitt, Mitchell Alan *management consultant*
Levitz, Paul Elliot *publishing executive*
Levoy, Myron *author*
Levy, Alain M. *record company executive*
Levy, Benjamin *artist*
Levy, Herbert Monte *lawyer*
†Levy, Joel Martin *health facility administrator*
Levy, Joseph *lawyer*
Levy, Leon *investment company executive*
Levy, Marvin David *composer*
Levy, Norma Berta *lawyer*
Levy, Stanley Herbert *lawyer*
Levy, Walter James *oil consultant*
Levy, Walter Kahn *management consultant executive*
†Lewinton, Christopher *business executive*
Lewis, Albert B. *lawyer*
Lewis, Allan *conductor, ballet company music director*
Lewis, Flora *journalist*
Lewis, George Ralph *consumer goods company executive*
Lewis, Grant Stephen *lawyer*
Lewis, James Berton *law educator*
Lewis, Jerry Lee *country-rock singer, musician*
Lewis, John Leeman, Jr. *obstetrician, gynecologist*
Lewis, Richard Warren *advertising executive*
Lewis, Robert Charles *lawyer*
Lewis, Russell T. *newspaper publishing executive*
Lewis, Sherman Richard, Jr. *investment banker*
Lewis, W. Walker *cosmetics executive*
Lewis, William Scheer *electrical engineer*
LeWitt, Sol *artist*
Lewyn, Thomas Mark *lawyer*
Libby, John Kelway *financial services company executive*
Liberman, Alexander *artist, editor*
Libin, Paul *theatre executive, producer*
†Licari, Joseph *real estate company executive*
Lichtblau, John H. *economist*
†Lichtenstein, Seymour *clothing manufacturing company executive*
Lieberman, Charles *economist*
Lieberman, Gail Forman *finance executive*
Lieberman, Seymour *biochemistry educator emeritus*
Liebermann, Lowell *composer, pianist, conductor*
Liebman, Lance Malcolm *dean, lawyer*
Liebman, Milton *publisher, journalist*
Liebman, Theodore *architect*
Lifland, Burton R. *federal judge*
Lifland, William Thomas *lawyer*
Liftin, John Matthew *lawyer*
Lifton, Robert Jay *psychiatrist, author*
Lifton, Robert Kenneth *diversified companies executive*
Liggio, Carl Donald *lawyer*
Lightfoot, Gordon Meredith *singer, songwriter*
Lilien, Mark Ira *publishing, retailing and systems executive*
Lilley, Albert Frederick *lawyer*
Lillie, James Woodruff, Jr. *lawyer*
Liman, Arthur L. *lawyer*
Limbaugh, Rush Hudson *radio and talk show host*
Lin, Joseph Pen-Tze *neuroradiologist, clinical administrator, educator*
Lin, Wuu-Long *economist*
Lincoln, Abbey (Anna Marie Woolridge, Gaby Lee, Aminata Moseka) *jazz singer*
Lincoln, Edmond Lynch *investment banker*
Linden, Hal *actor, singer*
Lindenbaum, Sandford Richard *lawyer*
Lindley, David Morrison *lawyer*
Lindsay, George Nelson *lawyer*
Lindsay, George Peter *lawyer*
Lindsay, Robert Van Cleef *trust company executive*
Lindskog, David Richard *lawyer*
Lingeman, Richard Roberts *editor, writer*
Linney, Romulus *author, educator*
Linsenmeyer, John Michael *lawyer*
Linz, Werner Mark *publishing executive*
Lionni, Leonard *author, artist*
Lipkin, Mack, Jr. *psychiatrist, researcher, educator*
Lipkin, Martin *physician, scientist*
Lipman, Samuel *musician, music critic*
Lipp, Robert I. *bank holding company executive*
Lipper, Kenneth *investment banker*
Lipsey, Robert Edward *economist, educator*
Lipton, Charles *public relations executive*
Lipton, Joan Elaine *advertising executive*
Lipton, Lester *ophthalmologist, entrepreneur*
Lipton, Martin *lawyer*
Lipton, Robert Steven *lawyer*
†Lipton, William James *accountant, lawyer*
Lish, Gordon *author, educator, editor*
Lissack, Michael Robert *investment banker*
†Litewka, Albert Bernard *communications and publishing company executive*
Littlefield, Martin (Martin Kleinwald) *book publishing executive*
†Litwin, Alisa Gabriel *advertising executive*
†Liu, Brian Cheong-Seng *urology and oncology educator, researcher*
Livengood, Victoria Ann *opera singer*
Livingston, Jay Harold *composer, lyricist*
†Livnat, Joshua *accounting educator, consultant*
LL Cool J, (James Todd Smith) *rap singer, actor*
Lloyd-Jones, Donald J. *transportation executive*
Localio, S. Arthur *retired surgeon, educator*
Lochner, Philip Raymond, Jr. *lawyer*
Lockett, Pierre *dancer*
Lockhart, James Bicknell, III *investment banker*
Lockwood, Molly Ann *communications company executive*
Loeb, John Langeloth *banker, broker*
Loeb, John Langeloth, Jr. *investment counselor*
Loeb, Marshall Robert *journalist, magazine editor*
Loeb, Peter Kenneth *money manager*
Loengard, John Borg *photographer; editor*
Loengard, Richard Otto, Jr. *lawyer*
LoFrisco, Anthony F. *lawyer*
Logan, Francis Dummer *lawyer*
Logan, J. Murray *investment manager*
Logan, Kenneth R. *lawyer*
†Logan, Vicki *advertising executive*
Logsdon, Richard Henry *retired librarian and educator*
Lohf, Kenneth A. *librarian, writer*
Lohse, Austin Webb *banker*
†Loman, Michael *scriptwriter, television producer*
London, Herbert Ira *humanities educator*
London, Martin *lawyer*
Londoner, David Jay *investment banker, analyst*
Loney, Glenn Meredith *drama educator*
Long, Melvin Durward *university president*
Longley, Marjorie Watters *newspaper executive*
Longstreth, Bevis *lawyer*
†Loomis, Carol J. *journalist*
Loomis, Philip Clark *investment executive*
Loomis, Robert Duane *publishing company executive, author*
Lopez, Lourdes *ballerina*
Lorch, Ernest Henry *lawyer*
Lorch, Maristella De Panizza (Mrs. Inama von Brunnenwald) *Romance languages educator, writer, lecturer*
Lord, Herbert Mayhew *lawyer*
Lord, M. G. *writer*
Lore, Martin Maxwell *lawyer*
Loren, Pamela *telecommunications executive*
Lorenz, Lee Sharp *cartoonist*
Loring, John Robbins *artist*
Lortel, Lucille *theatrical producer*
LoSchiavo, Linda Bosco *library director*
Losee, Thomas Penny, Jr. *publisher*
Loss, Margaret Ruth *lawyer*
Loss, Stuart Harold *financial executive*
Lotas, Judith Patton *advertising executive*
Lotwin, Stanford Gerald *lawyer*
Loudon, Dorothy *actress*
Louis, Murray *dancer, choreographer, dance teacher*
Love, Kenneth Del *design company director, consultant*
Love, Richard Emerson *equipment manufacturing company executive*
Loveless, Patty (Patty Ramey) *country music singer*
Loving, Alvin Demar, Jr. *artist, educator*
Low, Anthony *English language educator*
Low, Barbara Wharton *biochemist, biophysicist*
†Low, Dana Evarts *consulting engineer*
Low, Richard H. *broadcasting executive, producer*
Lowe, Mary Johnson *federal judge*
Lowen, Gerard Gunther *mechanical engineering educator*
Lowenfeld, Andreas Frank *legal educator, arbitrator*
Lowenfels, Fred M. *lawyer*
†Lowenfels, Lewis David *lawyer*
Lowenstein, Louis *legal educator*
Lowenthal, Constance *art historian*
Lowenthal, Jacob *finance executive*
Lowry, William Ketchin, Jr. *insurance company executive*
Lowy, George Theodore *lawyer*
†Loynes, John Hamilton *insurance company executive*
Lubalin, Peter *advertising agency executive*
†Lubetski, Edith Esther *librarian*
Lubic, Ruth Watson *association executive, nurse-midwife*
Lubkin, Virginia Leila *ophthalmologist*
Lubovitch, Lar *dancer, choreographer*
Lucas, Craig *playwright, screenwriter*
Lucas, Henry Cameron, Jr. *information systems educator, writer, consultant*
Lucas, James E(vans) *operatic director*
Lucchesi, Bruno *sculptor*
Lucci, Susan *actress*
Luce, Charles Franklin *former utilities executive, lawyer*
Luce, Henry, III *foundation executive*
Lucht, John Charles *management consultant, executive recruiter*
Lucido, Louis Charles *finance company executive*
Luck, David Jonathan Lewis *biologist, educator*
Luders, Adam *ballet dancer*
Ludgin, Chester Hall *baritone, actor*
Ludovici, Anthony *security investment executive*
Luening, Otto *composer, conductor, flutist, educator*
Luers, William Henry *art museum administrator*
Luftglass, Murray Arnold *manufacturing company executive*
Luke, John A., Jr. *paper, packaging and chemical company executive*
Luke, John Anderson *paper company executive*
Lumet, Sidney *film director*
Lund, Peter Anthony *broadcast executive*
Lunden, Joan *television personality*
Lunding, Christopher Hanna *lawyer*
Lundquist, James Harold *lawyer*
†Lundquist, John Milton *librarian, author, lecturer*
†Luo, Gangming M. *mechanical engineer*
Lupkin, Stanley Neil *lawyer*
†Lupo, Frank Michael *architect*
LuPone, Patti *actress*
Lupton, Ellen *curator, graphic designer*
Luria, Mary Mercer *lawyer*
Lurie, Alvin David *lawyer*
Lurie, William L. *lawyer, association executive*
Lusky, Louis *legal educator*
Lustenberger, Louis Charles, Jr. *lawyer*
Lustgarten, Ira Howard *lawyer*
Luther, James Howard *lawyer, retired pharmaceutical company executive*
Lutringer, Richard Emil *lawyer*
†Lynch, Frank Joseph *insurance company executive*
Lynch, Gerald Weldon *college president, psychologist*
†Lynch, James C. *newspaper editor*
†Lynch, John T. *management consultant*
Lynch, Owen Martin *anthropologist, educator*
Lynch, William Dennis, Jr. *broadcast journalist*
†Lyne, Susan *magazine editor*
Lynn, Theodore Stanley *lawyer*
Lynton, Harold Stephen *lawyer*
Lyon, Carl Francis, Jr. *lawyer*
Lyons, Laurence *securities executive*
Ma, Yo Yo *cellist*
Maas, Peter *writer*
Maas, Werner Karl *microbiology educator*
†Macaluso, Michael Joseph, Sr. *architect*
Macan, William Alexander, IV *lawyer*
MacArthur, John Roderick C. G. (Rick MacArthur) *magazine publisher, journalist*
Macchiarola, Frank Joseph *political science, business and law educator*
MacCrate, Robert *lawyer*
Macdonald, Clifford Palmer *editor, writer*
†Macdonald, R. Fulton *venture developer, business educator*
Macdonald, Robert Rigg, Jr. *museum director*
†MacDougall, Malcolm D. *advertising agency executive*
MacEwan, Nigel Savage *merchant banker*
MacGrath, C. Richard *retired business executive*
MacHale, Joseph P. *financial executive*
Machlin, Eugene Solomon *metallurgy educator, consultant*
Machlin, Milton Robert *magazine editor, writer*
Macioce, Frank Michael, Jr. *lawyer, financial services company executive*
MacIver, Loren *artist*
Mack, Daniel Richard *furniture designer*
Mack, Dennis Wayne *lawyer, textile company executive*
Mack, Joseph P. *advertising agency executive*
†Mackall, Robert Wain *advertising agency executive*
MacKay, Malcolm *executive search consultant*
MacKenzie, John Pettibone *journalist*
Mackerodt, Fred *public relations specialist*
Mackie, Robert Gordon *costume and fashion designer*
MacKinnon, John Alexander *lawyer*
MacKinnon, Roger Alan *psychiatrist*
Mackler, Tina *artist*
Mac Namara, Donal Eoin Joseph *criminologist*
MacNeil, Robert Breckenridge Ware *broadcast journalist*
†Macpherson, Elle *model*
MacRae, Cameron Farquhar, III *lawyer*
Macri, Theodore William *book publisher*
Macro, Lucia Ann *editor*
Macurdy, John Edward *basso*
Madden, Donald Paul *lawyer*
Madden, John Joseph *lawyer*
Madden, John Kevin *publishing executive*
Madden, Michael Daniel *finance company executive*
Madonia, Valerie *dancer*
Madonna, (Madonna Louise Veronica Ciccone) *singer, actress*
Madonna, Jon C. *accounting firm executive*
Madsen, Loren Wakefield *sculptor*
Madsen, Stephen Stewart *lawyer*
Magdol, Michael Orin *bank executive*
Mager, Ezra Pascal *automobile dealership group executive*
Maguire, Robert Alan *Slavic languages and literatures educator*
Maher, Stephen Albert *investment banker*
Mahon, Arthur J. *lawyer*
Mahoney, Margaret Ellerbe *foundation executive*
Maidman, Richard Harvey Mortimer *lawyer*
Mailer, Norman *author*
Makin, Edward *food products executive*
†Makovsky, Kenneth Dale *public relations executive*
Makrianes, James Konstantin, Jr. *management consultant*
Malabre, Alfred Leopold, Jr. *journalist, author*
Malamed, Seymour H. *motion picture company executive*
Maldonado-Bear, Rita Marinita *economist, educator*
Malefakis, Edward E. *history educator*
Maleska, Martin Edmund *investment banker*
†Malgieri, Nick *chef, author*
Malin, Irving *English educator, literary critic*
Malin, Robert Abernethy *investment management executive*
Malina, Judith *actress, director, producer, writer*
Malina, Michael *lawyer*
Malino, John Gray *real estate executive*
Malis, Leonard Irving *neurosurgeon*
Malitz, Sidney *psychiatrist, educator, researcher*
Malkin, Peter Laurence *lawyer*
Malkin, Stanley Lee *neurologist*
Mallardi, Michael Patrick *broadcasting company executive*
Malle, Louis *film director*
†Mallory, Kenneth W. *religious organization administrator*
Mallozzi, Cos M. *public relations executive*
Malm, James Royal *surgeon*
Malone, Joseph Lawrence *linguistics educator*
Maloney, Michael Patrick *lawyer, corporate executive*
Maloney, William Gerard *retired investment company executive*
Malozemoff, Plato *mining executive*
Maltby, Richard Eldridge, Jr. *theater director, lyricist*
†Maltese, Serphin Ralph *state senator, lawyer*
Mamlok, Ursula *composer, educator*
Mamorsky, Jeffrey Dean *lawyer*
Mandel, Irwin Daniel *dentist*
Mandelsberg-Weiss, Rose Gail *editor in chief*
Mandelstam, Charles Lawrence *lawyer*
Maneker, Morton M. *lawyer*
Maneker, Roberta S(ue) *public relations executive*
Maney, Michael Mason *lawyer*
Mangan, Mona *association executive, lawyer*
Manger, William Muir *internist*
Manges, James Horace *investment banker*
†Mangino, Robert *insurance company executive*
Mango, Wilfred Gilbert, Jr. *construction company executive*
†Mangold, Glenn E. *securities industry executive*
Mangold, Robert Peter *artist*
Mankin, Robert Stephen *financial executive*
Mann, Robert Nathaniel *violinist*
Mann, Theodore *theatrical producer and artistic director*
Manning, Burt *advertising executive*
Manning, Jack *photographer, columnist, author*
Manning, Jerome Alan *lawyer*
Manning, William Joseph *lawyer*
Manoff, Richard Kalman *advertising executive, nutrition policy consultant*
Mansi, Joseph Anneillo *public relations company executive*
Manski, Wladyslaw Julian *microbiology educator, medical scientist*
Mantegna, Joe Anthony *actor, playwright*
Mantell, Lester J. *business executive*
Mantell, Suzanne *editor*
Mantle, Raymond Allan *lawyer*
Manton, Edwin Alfred Grenville *insurance company executive*
Mapes, Glynn Dempsey *newspaper editor*
Mapes, Lynn Calvin *publishing executive*
Maraldo, Pamela Jean *nursing association executive, lecturer, consultant*
Maraynes, Allan Lawrence *filmmaker, television producer*
Marbury, Benjamin Edward *anesthesiologist*
Marceau, Marcel *pantomimist, actor, director, painter, poet*
Marceau, Yvonne *ballroom dancer*
Marchioni, Allen *publishing company executive*
Marcosson, Thomas I. *service company executive*
Marcus, Barry Philip *lawyer*
†Marcus, Beth E. *religious organization administrator*
Marcus, Eric Peter *lawyer*
Marcus, Hyman *business executive*
Marcus, James Stewart *investment banker*
Marcus, Leon Charles *lawyer*
Marcus, Norman *lawyer*
Marcus, Steven *dean, English educator*
Marcusa, Fred Haye *lawyer*
Marcuse, Adrian Gregory *college administrator*
Marden, John Newcomb *lawyer*
Mardenborough, Leslie A. *newspaper publishing company executive*
Marder, John G. *real estate investor, marketing consultant, corporate director*
Marder, Michael Zachary *dentist, researcher, educator*
Marella, Philip Daniel *broadcasting company executive*
Margaritis, John Paul *public relations executive*
Margolis, David I(srael) *corporate executive*
†Margolis, Jay M. *clothing executive*
Margolis, Milton Joseph *marketing executive*
†Margulis, Les *advertising executive*
Marion, John Louis *fine arts auctioneer and appraiser*
Marisol, (Marisol Escobar) *sculptor*
†Mariucci, John Ubaldo *advertising agency executive*
Mark, Jonathan I. *lawyer*
Mark, Reuben *consumer products company executive*
Marke, Julius Jay *law librarian, educator*
Markle, Cheri Virginia Cummins *nurse*
Markowitz, Harry M. *finance and economics educator*
†Marks, Andrew Robert *molecular biologist*
Marks, Edward B. *international social service administrator*
Marks, Edwin S. *merchant banker*
Marks, Paul Alan *oncologist, cell biologist, educator*
Marks, Theodore Lee *lawyer*
Marlas, James Constantine *holding company executive*
Marlette, Douglas Nigel *editorial cartoonist, comic strip creator*
Marlin, Richard *lawyer*
Marron, Donald Baird *investment banker*
Marsee, Susanne Irene *lyric mezzo-soprano*
Marsh, Jean Lyndsey Torren *actress, writer*
Marsh, William Laurence *retired research pathology executive*
Marshall, Alton Garwood *real estate counselor*
Marshall, Daniel Stuart *advertising executive*
Marshall, Geoffrey *university administrator*
Marshall, John Patrick *lawyer*
Marshall, Sheila Hermes *lawyer*
Marshall, Thomas Carlisle *applied physics educator*
Marston, Robert Andrew *public relations executive*
Martin, Agnes *artist*
Martin, Andrea Louise *actress, comedienne, writer*
Martin, Ann Matthews *writer, juvenile*
†Martin, Donald *advertising agency executive*
Martin, Elliot Edwards *theatrical producer*
Martin, George J., Jr. *lawyer*
Martin, James Smith *insurance executive*
Martin, John S., Jr. *federal judge*
Martin, Judith Sylvia *journalist, author*
Martin, Malcolm Elliot *lawyer*
Martin, Mary-Anne *art gallery owner*
Martin, Richard Harrison *curator, art historian*
Martinez, Roman, IV *financial executive*
Martins, Nilas *dancer*
Martins, Peter *ballet master, choreographer, dancer*
Martone, Patricia Ann *lawyer*
Marx, Owen Cox *lawyer*
Marzulli, John Anthony, Jr. *lawyer*
Masey, Jack *exhibition designer*
Mashberg, Gregg M. *lawyer*
Masin, Michael Terry *lawyer*
Masinter, Edgar Martin *lawyer*
Maskin, Arvin *lawyer*
†Maslin, Janet *film critic*
Maslow, Will *lawyer, association executive*

Mason, Bobbie Ann novelist, short story writer
Mason, Jackie comedian, actor
Massey, Stephen Charles auctioneer
Masters, Jon Joseph lawyer
Masterson, James Francis psychiatrist
Mastromonaco-Adler, Ellen G. publishing company executive
Masur, Kurt conductor
Mata, Eduardo conductor
Matalon, Vivian theatrical director
Mathers, William Harris lawyer
Mathes, Sorrell Mark investment banker
Mathews, Jack Wayne journalist, film critic
Mathews, Linda McVeigh newspaper editor
Matlock, Jack Foust, Jr. diplomat
†Matloff, Robert Leonard publisher
Matteson, William Bleecker lawyer
Matthews, Edward E. insurance company executive
Matthews, Edwin Spencer, Jr. lawyer
Matthews, Gilbert Elliott investment banker
Matthews, Norman Stuart department store executive
Matthews, Westina L. finance and banking executive
Matthews, William Procter English educator
Mattis, Louis Price pharmaceutical and consumer products company executive
Mattone, Vincent J. investment banker
Mattson, Francis Oscar librarian, rare books curator
Mattson, Walter Edward retired publishing company executive
Matz, Robert physician, educator
Maubert, Jacques Claude headmaster
Maughan, Deryck C. investment banker
Mauldin, William H. (Bill Mauldin) cartoonist
Maulsby, Allen Farish lawyer
Maurer, Gilbert Charles media company executive
Maurer, Jeffrey Stuart finance executive
Mauzerall, David Charles biophysics educator, research scientist
Max, Herbert B. lawyer
Max, Peter artist
Maxwell, Anders John brokerage house executive
Maxwell, Carla Lena dancer, choreographer, educator
†Maxwell, Charles Thoburn petroleum securities analyst
Maxwell, Hamish diversified consumer products company executive
Maxwell, William writer
May, William Frederick manufacturing executive
Mayden, Barbara Mendel lawyer
Mayer, Margery Weil publishing executive
Mayer, Theodore V.H. lawyer
Mayerson, Philip classics educator
Mayerson, Sandra Elaine lawyer
Mayfield, Curtis Lee musician
†Mayle, Peter writer
Maynard, John Rogers English educator
†Maynard, Parrish ballet dancer
Mayne, William writer
Mayotte, Timothy Spencer professional tennis player
†Mazur, Jay J. trade union official
Mazza, Thomas Carmen lawyer
Mazzia, Valentino Don Bosco physician, educator, lawyer
Mazzilli, Paul John investment banker
Mazzo, Kay ballet dancer, educator
Mazzola, Anthony Thomas editor, art consultant, designer
Mazzola, John William former performing arts center executive, consultant
McAward, Patrick Joseph, Jr. architectural and engineering company executive
McBaine, John Neylan lawyer
McBride, Rodney Lester investment counselor
McCabe, David Allen lawyer
McCaffrey, Carlyn Sundberg lawyer
McCaffrey, William Thomas financial services company executive
McCall, David Bruce advertising executive
McCandless, Carolyn Keller entertainment, media company executive
McCandless, Stephen Porter financial executive
McCann, Edward investment banker
Mc Cann, John Joseph lawyer
Mc Carter, Thomas N., III investment counseling company executive
McCarthy, Bernard William lawyer
McCarthy, Bryant accounting firm executive
McCarthy, Cormac writer
McCarthy, Denis artist, educator
†McCarthy, James sociology researcher, educator
McCarthy, Joseph Gerald plastic surgeon, educator
†McCarthy, Michael Anthony architecture executive
McCarty, Maclyn medical scientist
McCarver, James Timothy sportscaster
McCleary, Benjamin Ward investment banker
†McClellan, Anne Starr environmentalist
†McClelland, Timothy Reid baseball umpire
McClimon, Timothy John lawyer
McClung, Richard Goehring lawyer
Mc Clure, Michael Thomas poet, playwright, educator
McConnell, Charles Warren marketing management executive
McCord, Alice Bird association executive
McCormack, John Joseph, Jr. insurance executive
Mc Cormack, Thomas Joseph publishing company executive
McCormick, Donald E. librarian, archivist
Mc Cormick, Edward Allen foreign language educator
McCormick, Hugh Thomas lawyer
McCormick, James Michael management consultant
Mc Cormick, Kenneth Dale retired editor
McCoy, Millington F. corporation executive
McCracken, A. Michael marketing executive
Mc Cracken, Daniel Delbert computer science educator, author
Mc Crie, Robert Delbert editor, publisher, educator
Mc Crory, Wallace Willard pediatrician, educator
McCulloch, Kenneth John lawyer
McCullough, David author
McCully, Emily Arnold illustrator,writer
McDarrah, Fred William photographer, editor, writer, photography reviewer
McDavid, William Henry lawyer
McDermott, Richard T. lawyer, educator
†McDonald, Audra Ann actress
Mcdonald, Gregory Christopher author
McDonald, James L. accounting firm executive
McDonald, Willis, IV lawyer
McDonell, Robert Terry magazine editor, novelist
McDormand, Frances actress
McDowell, Jay Hortenstine lawyer
Mc Elrath, Richard Elsworth insurance company executive
†McElroy, Edmund G., Jr. investment company executive
McEnroe, John Patrick lawyer
Mc Enroe, John Patrick, Jr. professional tennis player
McEnroe, Patrick professional tennis player
McFadden, David Revere museum director and curator
Mc Fadden, G. Bruce hospital administrator
Mc Fadden, James Patrick publisher
Mc Fadden, Mary Josephine fashion industry executive
†Mc Fadden, Robert Dennis reporter
McFarland, Alan Roberts investment banker
McFerrin, Bobby singer, musician, composer and conductor
McGahren, Richard George lawyer
McGanney, Thomas lawyer
McGarry, John Patrick, Jr. advertising agency executive
McGeady, Sister Mary Rose religious organization administrator, psychologist
Mc Gillicuddy, John Francis banker
Mc Ginnis, Arthur Joseph publisher
McGinnis, Arthur Joseph, Jr. public relations executive
McGinnis, John Oldham lawyer, educator
Mc Ginniss, Joe writer
McGirr, David William John investment banker
Mc Goldrick, John Gardiner lawyer
McGonigal, Richard M. lawyer
McGovern, John Hugh urologist, educator
McGovern, Joseph W. lawyer
Mc Gowin, William Edward artist
McGrath, Eugene R. utility company executive
†McGrath, Patrick J. advertising agency executive
McGrath, Thomas J. lawyer, writer, film producer
McGraw, Harold Whittlesey, Jr. publisher
†McGraw, Harold Whittlesey, III (Terry McGraw) financial services company executive
McGraw, Robert Pierce publishing executive
Mc Gruder, Stephen Jones portfolio manager
Mc Guire, Alfred James former basketball coach, sports equipment company executive, basketball commentator
McGunigle, Brian Edward lawyer
McHenry, Barnabas lawyer
McInerney, Jay author
†McInnis, Helen Louise publishing company executive
McIntyre, Douglas Alexander magazine publisher
Mc Kay, Jim television sports commentator
McKay, Kenneth Gardiner physicist, electronics company executive
†McKean, Henry P. mathematics institute administrator
†McKelvey, Andrew J. advertising executive
McKenna, Lawrence M. federal judge
Mc Kenna, Malcolm Carnegie vertebrate paleontologist, curator, educator
McKenzie, Herbert A(lonza) pharmaceutical company executive
McKenzie, Kevin Patrick ballet dancer
McKenzie, Mary Beth artist
Mc Keown, William Taylor magazine editor, author
McKerrow, Amanda ballet dancer
McKessy, Stephen W. accounting firm executive
McKillop, Daniel James insurance company real estate executive
McKinley, (Jennifer Carolyn) Robin writer
McKinnon, Floyd Wingfield textile executive
†Mc Kitrick, Eric Louis historian, educator
†McLaughlin, Joseph lawyer
McLaughlin, Joseph Michael federal judge, law educator
McLaughlin, Joseph Thomas lawyer
†Mclaughlin, Mark John media director
McLaughlin, Mary Rittling magazine editor
McLaughlin, Michael John insurance company executive
McLean, Edward Cochrane, Jr. lawyer
McLean, Edward Peter executive search consultant
Mc Lendon, Heath Brian securities investment company executive
McMahon, Colleen lawyer
McManus, Jason Donald editor
McMeen, Albert Ralph, III writer, lecturer
McMeen, Elmer Ellsworth, III lawyer
†McMenamy, Kristen model
McMullan, William Patrick, III investment banker
Mc Murtry, James Gilmer, III neurosurgeon
McMurtry, Larry author
McNally, John Joseph lawyer
McNally, Terrence playwright
Mc Namara, J(ohn) Donald lawyer, business executive
McNamee, Daniel Vincent, III management consultant
McNamee, Louise advertising agency executive
McNeill, Alfred Thomas, Jr. construction executive
Mc Nicol, Donald Edward lawyer
Mc Pherson, Paul Francis publishing company executive
Mc Quade, Lawrence Carroll lawyer, corporate executive
Mc Queeney, Henry Martin, Sr. publisher
McQuillen, Harry A. publishing company executive
McRae, Carmen singer
Meachin, David James Percy investment banker, import-export executive
Meaders, Paul Le Sourd lawyer
Meadow, Lynne (Carolyn Meadow) theatrical producer and director
†Meadow, Phyllis Whitcomb psychoanalyst
Meadows, Sharon Marie investment banker
Meagher, Mark Joseph publishing company executive
†Medenica, Gordon corporate planner
Medina, Standish Forde, Jr. lawyer
†Medley, Clayton Edward apparel executive
Medwick, Craig Steven lawyer
Mee, Charles L., Jr. playwright, historian, editor
Meehan, John Joseph brokerage house executive
Mehta, A. Sonny publishing company executive
Mehta, Ved (Parkash) writer, literature and history educator
Meier, August historian, educator
Meier, Paul statistician, mathematics educator
Meier, Richard Alan architect
Meigher, S. Christopher, III communications and media investor
Meikle, Thomas Harry, Jr. foundation administrator, neuroscientist, educator
Meisel, Louis Koenig art dealer, art historian, writer
Meisel, Martin English and comparative literature educator
Meisel, Perry English educator
Meisel, Steven advertising photographer
Meiselas, Susan Clay photographer
Meislich, Herbert chemistry educator emeritus
Meister, Alton biochemist, educator
Meister, Doris Powers auction house executive
†Melamede, Ada Karmi architectural firm executive
†Melamid, Alexander economics educator, consultant
Mellencamp, John (John Cougar) singer, songwriter
Mellins, Robert B. pediatrician, educator
Mello, H. Joseph lawyer
Melone, Joseph James insurance company executive
Meltzer, Milton author
Melvin, Russell Johnston magazine publishing consultant
Mencher, Melvin journalist, retired educator
Mendell, Oliver M. banking executive
Mendelsohn, John oncologist, hematologist, educator
Mendelsohn, Walter lawyer
Mendelson, Edward James English literature educator
Mendelson, Haim artist, educator, art gallery director
Menges, Carl Braun investment banker
Menk, Carl William executive search company executive
Menninger, Edward Joseph public relations executive
Menschel, Robert Benjamin investment banker
Menses, Jan artist, draftsman, etcher, lithographer, muralist
Menton, Francis James, Jr. lawyer
†Menuez, D. Barry religious organization administrator
Menuhin, Yehudi violinist
Meranus, Arthur Richard advertising agency executive
Merchant, Ismail Noormohamed film producer
Mercorella, Anthony J. lawyer, former state supreme court justice
Merow, John Edward lawyer
Merrifield, Robert Bruce biochemist, educator
Merriss, Philip Ramsay, Jr. banker
Mertens, Joan R. museum curator, art historian
Merton, Robert K. sociologist, educator
Merwin, William Stanley poet
Mescon, Richard Alan lawyer
Mesnikoff, Alvin Murray psychiatry educator
Messer, Thomas Maria museum director
Messier, Mark professional hockey player
†Messineo, Karen newspaper publishing executive
Messing, Mark P. advertising executive
Messinger, Scott James advertising executive
Messner, Thomas G. advertising executive, copywriter
Mestres, Ricardo Angelo, Jr. lawyer
Mesznik, Joel R. investment banker
Metcalf, William Edwards coin museum curator
Metz, Emmanuel Michael investment company executive, lawyer
Metz, Robert Roy publisher, editor
Metzner, Charles Miller federal judge
Meyaart, Paul Jan distilling company executive
Meyer, Edward Henry advertising agency executive
Meyer, Edward N. lawyer
Meyer, Fred Josef advertising executive
Meyer, Karl Ernest journalist
Meyer, Kerstin mezzo-soprano, music educator
Meyer, Pearl executive compensation consultant
Meyer, Pucci newspaper editor
†Meyer, Richard E. insurance agent
Meyer, Sandra W(asserstein) management consultant
Meyer, Susan E. publisher
Meyer-Bahlburg, Heino F. L. psychologist
Meyerhoff, Erich librarian, administrator
†Meyers, Bruce A. advertising executive
Meyers, Dale (Mrs. Mario Cooper) artist
Meyers, John Allen magazine publisher
Miano, Louis Stephen advertising executive
Michaels, Alan Richard sports commentator
Michaels, James Walker magazine editor
Michaels, Joseph Eugene television director
Michaels, Lorne television writer, producer
Michaelson, Arthur M. lawyer
Michals, Duane photographer
Michanowsky, George research foundation executive, author
Michas, Athanassios N. investment company executive
Michel, Clifford Lloyd lawyer, investment executive
†Michel, Harriet R. association executive
Michel, Henry Ludwig civil engineer
Michels, Robert psychiatrist
Michelson, Gertrude Geraldine retired retail company executive
Michenfelder, Joseph Francis public relations executive
Middendorf, John Harlan English literature educator
Middleton, David physicist, applied mathematician, educator
Midler, Bette singer, entertainer, actress
Midori, (Midori Goto) classical violinist
†Miele, Joel Arthur, Sr. civil engineer
Mikita, Joseph Karl broadcasting executive
Milbank, Jeremiah foundation executive
Mildvan, Donna infectious diseases physician
Miles, Michael Arnold tobacco, food and beer company executive
Milgrim, Roger Michael lawyer
Millard, John Alden lawyer
†Millard, Wenda Harris magazine publisher
Miller, B. Jack investment company executive
Miller, Charles Hampton lawyer
Miller, David lawyer, advertising executive
Miller, Donald Baldwin advertising executive
Miller, Donald Keith asset management executive
Miller, Donald LeSessne publishing executive
Miller, Edward Daniel banker
Miller, Edward Doring, Jr. anesthesiologist
Miller, Ernest Charles management consultant
Miller, Gerri magazine editor, writer
†Miller, Glenn Alan advertising executive
Miller, Harvey R. bankruptcy reorganization lawyer
Miller, Harvey S. Shipley foundation trustee
Miller, Israel rabbi, university administrator
Miller, Laurence Glenn art gallery owner and director
Miller, Lawrence Edward lawyer
Miller, Lee Anne artist, educator
Miller, Lenore labor union official
Miller, Mildred opera singer, recitalist
Miller, Morgan Lincoln textile manufacturing company executive
Miller, Neil S. financial officer, advertising executive
Miller, Nicole Jacqueline fashion designer
Miller, Paul Lukens investment banker
Miller, Phebe Condict lawyer, financial executive
Miller, Philip Boyd retail executive
†Miller, Philip Efrem librarian
Miller, Richard Jerome bank executive
Miller, Richard Kidwell artist, actor, educator
Miller, Richard McDermott sculptor
Miller, Richard Steven lawyer
Miller, Robert advertising executive
†Miller, Robert A. finance company executive
Miller, Robert L. publishing company executive
Miller, Roberta Davis editor
Miller, Sam Scott lawyer
Millett, Katherine Murray (Kate Millett) political activist, sculptor, artist, writer
Millman, Robert Barnet psychiatry and public health educator
Millo, Aprile Elizabeth opera singer
Millson, Rory Oliver lawyer
Millstein, Ira M. lawyer, lecturer
Milnes, Sherrill Eustace baritone
Minahan, Daniel F. manufacturing company executive, lawyer
Minard, Everett Lawrence, III journalist, magazine editor
Minard, Frank Pell Lawrence investment manager
Mincer, Jacob economics educator
†Mines, Herbert Thomas executive recruiter
Minick, Michael publishing executive
Minicucci, Robert A. business executive
Minkel, Herbert Philip, Jr. lawyer
Minkowitz, Martin lawyer, former state government official
Minnelli, Liza singer, actress
Minor, Raleigh Colston management consultant
Mintz, Donald Edward psychologist, educator
Mintz, Norman Nelson investment banker, educator
Mintz, Shlomo conductor, violist, violinist
Mintz, Stephen Allan real estate company executive, lawyer
Mintz, Walter investment company executive
†Mirabella, Grace magazine publishing executive
Mirsky, Sonya Wohl librarian, curator
Mishkin, Edwin B. lawyer
Mishkin, Jeffrey Alan lawyer
Miss, Mary artist
Missan, Richard Sherman lawyer
Mitchell, Arthur dancer, choreographer
Mitchell, John Dietrich theatre arts institute executive
Mitchell, Joseph (Quincy) writer
Mitchell, Leona Pearl soprano
†Mitchell, Martin Morgan, Jr. advertising executive, educator
Mitchell, Richard Boyle advertising executive
Mitgang, Herbert author, journalist
Mittelstadt, Charles Anthony advertising executive
Miyake, Issey fashion designer
†Miyaoka, K. grain company executive
Mizrahi, Isaac fashion designer
†Mizuno, Masaru retail executive
Moak-Mazur, Connie J. investment consultant, marketing professional
†Mobius, Michael chemicals executive
†Model, Iris cosmetics executive
Model, Peter molecular biologist
Modell, Frank cartoonist, writer
Modlin, Howard S. lawyer
Moerdler, Charles Gerard lawyer
Mohler, Mary Gail magazine editor
Mohr, Jay Preston neurologist
Moise, Edwin Evariste mathematician, educator
Molho, Emanuel publisher
Molholt, Pat university official
Moloney, Thomas Joseph lawyer
Moloney, Thomas Walter consulting firm executive
Molz, Redmond Kathleen public administration educator
Monaco, Michael P. finance company executive
Mondlin, Marvin antiquarian book dealer
Monge, Jay Parry lawyer
Monk, Debra actress
Monk, Meredith Jane artistic director, composer, choreographer, film maker, director
Monroe, Kendyl Kurth lawyer
Monroe, Vernon Earl, Jr. former professional basketball player
Montgomerie, Bruce Mitchell lawyer
Montgomery, Robert Humphrey, Jr. lawyer
Montgomery, Walter George communications executive, consultant
†Montorio, John Angelo magazine editor
Mooney, Richard E. editorial writer
Mooney, Ted (Edward Comstock Mooney) writer
Moore, Brian writer
Moore, Donald Francis lawyer
Moore, Franklin Hall, Jr. lawyer
Moore, Geoffrey Hoyt economist
Moore, Jane Ross librarian
Moore, John Dennis publisher
Moore, John Joseph lawyer
Moore, Kathleen dancer
Moore, Malcolm Andrew Stephen cancer researcher
Moore, Oliver Semon, III publishing executive, consultant
Moore, Paul, Jr. bishop
Moore, Sonia theatre administrator, researcher
†Moore, Susanna writer
Moore, Thomas R. lawyer
Moorhead, Thomas Burch lawyer, pharmaceutical company executive
Morales, Pablo A. urologist
Moran, Charles A. securities executive
Moran, John A. investment company executive
Moran, Juliette M. management consultant
Moran, Martin Joseph fund raising company executive
Morath, Inge photographer
Morawetz, Cathleen Synge mathematician
Moreira, Marcio Martins advertising executive
Morgado, Robert music company executive
Morgan, Frank Edward, II lawyer
Morgan, (George) Frederick poet, editor
Morgan, Jacqui illustrator, painter, educator
Morgan, Robin Evonne poet, author, journalist, activist, editor
Morgan, Thomas Bruce media and public affairs executive, author
†Morgen, Lynn public relations executive
Morgenthau, Robert Morris lawyer
Mori, Hanae fashion designer
Morley, Michael B. public relations executive
†Morris, Clayton Leslie priest
†Morris, Douglas Peter recording company executive
Morris, Eugene Jerome lawyer
Morris, James Peppler bass-baritone
Morris, Kenneth Baker mergers, acquisition and real estate executive
Morris, Mark choreographer
Morris, Mark Ronald advertising agency executive
Morris, Michael Howard public relations executive
Morris, Robert artist
Morris, Robert C. historian, archivist, educator

Morris, Robert Lee gallery administrator, jewelry designer
Morris, Stephen Burritt marketing information executive
Morris, Thomas Quinlan hospital administrator, physician
Morris, William Charles investor
Morris, Wright novelist, critic
Morrissey, Dolores Josephine insurance executive
Morrissey, Thomas Jerome investment banker
Morrow, E. Frederic consultant, retired banker
Morrow, Lance writer
Morse, Robert Alan actor
Mortimer, Henry Tilford, Jr. financial assurance executive
Mortimer, Peter Michael lawyer
Morton, Frederic author
Mosbacher, Martin Bruce public relations executive
Moseley, Carlos DuPre former music executive, musician
Moskin, John Robert editor, writer
Moskin, Morton lawyer
Moskowitz, Arnold X. strategist, economist, educator
Moss, Charles advertising agency executive
†Moss, Kate model
Moss, William John lawyer
Mossbrucker, Tom dancer
Mosse, Peter John Charles financial services executive
Mosser, Thomas Joseph public relations agency executive
Most, Jack Lawrence lawyer, consultant
Most, Nathan securities exchange executive
Motley, Constance Baker (Mrs. Joel Wilson Motley) federal judge, former city official
Mottola, Gary F. lawyer
Mountcastle, Kenneth Franklin, Jr. stockbroker
Mow, Van C. engineering educator, researcher
Moyers, Bill D. journalist
Moynahan, John Daniel, Jr. insurance executive
Moyne, John Abel computer scientist, linguist, educator
†Mroz, John Edwin political scientist
†Muenzen, Lee John commodity trading company executive
Mukasey, Michael B. federal judge
†Mulder, Edwin George minister, church official
Mullen, Peter P. lawyer
Muller, Charlotte Feldman economist, educator
Muller, Frank B. advertising executive
Muller, Henry James journalist, magazine editor
Muller, Jennifer choreographer, dancer
Muller, Peter lawyer, entertainment company executive, retail company executive, consultant
Muller, Robert Henry securities research company executive
Mulligan, Gerald Joseph (Gerry Mulligan) composer, arranger, musician, songwriter
Mulligan, Hugh Augustine journalist
Mulreany, Robert Henry lawyer
Mulvihill, Roger Denis lawyer
Mulvoy, Mark journalist
Mundheim, Robert Harry law educator
Mundy, John Hine history educator
Munera, Gerard Emmanuel manufacturing company executive
Munhall, Edgar curator, art history educator
Muñoz, Carlos Ramón bank executive
Munro, Alice author
Munro, J. Richard publishing company executive
Munroe, George Barber former metals company executive
Muradian, Vazgen composer, viola d'amore player
Murase, Jiro lawyer
Muratore, Peter Frederick securities executive
†Murchie, Edward Michael accountant
Murdock, Robert Mead art consultant, curator
Muro, Roy Alfred independent media service corporation executive
†Murphy, Ann Pleshette magazine editor-in-chief
Murphy, Arthur William lawyer, educator
Murphy, Barry John publishing executive
Murphy, Catherine painter
Murphy, Charles Joseph investment banker
Murphy, Daniel Hayes, II lawyer
†Murphy, Donna actress
Murphy, Eugene Francis consultant, retired government official
†Murphy, James E. public relations executive
†Murphy, Jill public relations executive
Murphy, John Arthur tobacco, food and brewing company executive
Murphy, John Cullen illustrator
Murphy, Joseph Samson political science educator
Murphy, Richard William retired foreign service officer, Middle East specialist, consultant
Murphy, Rosemary actress
Murphy, Thomas S. media company executive
Murray, Anita Jean data processing executive, consultant
Murray, Elizabeth artist
Murray, Paul Brady lawyer, banker
Murray, Richard Maximilian insurance executive
Murray, Thomas Francis real estate executive
Murray, William food products executive
Muse, Martha Twitchell foundation executive
Musgrave, R. Kenton federal judge
Musser, Tharon theatrical lighting designer, theatre consultant
Muth, John Francis newspaper editor, columnist
Myerberg, Marcia investment banker
Myers, Gerald E. humanities educator
Myers, Wayne Alan psychiatrist, educator
Myers, William S. magazine publishing executive
Myerson, Toby Salter lawyer
Nabi, Stanley Andrew investment executive
Nadel, Elliott investment firm executive
Nadich, Judah rabbi
Nadiri, M. Ishaq economics educator, researcher, lecturer, consultant
Naftalis, Gary Philip lawyer, educator
Nagler, Stewart Gordon insurance company executive
Nagourney, Herbert publishing company executive
Nahas, Gabriel Georges pharmacologist, educator
Naiburg, Irving B., Jr. publisher
†Najarian, Haigazoun church administrator
Nakamura, James I. economics educator
Nakanishi, Koji chemistry educator, research institute administrator
Namath, Joseph William entertainer, former professional football player
Nance, Allan Taylor lawyer
†Nardin, Theodore Celeste publisher
Nash, Edward L. advertising agency executive
Nash, Graham William singer, composer
Nash, Paul LeNoir lawyer
Nassau, Michael Jay lawyer
†Nathan, Andrew James political science educator
Nathan, Carl Francis medical educator
Nathan, Frederic Solis lawyer
Nathan, Paul S. editor, writer
Natori, Josie Cruz apparel executive
Nauert, Roger Charles health care executive
Navasky, Victor Saul magazine editor
Nayden, Denis J. diversified financial services company executive
Nazem, Fereydoun F. venture capitalist, financier
Neal, Philip dancer
†Nebb, Edward Alan investor relations executive
Neblett, Carol soprano
Necarsulmer, Henry investment banker
Nederlander, James Morton theater executive
Nederlander, Robert E. entertainment and television executive, lawyer
Nee, Owen D., Jr. lawyer
†Neeck, Bernard J. insurance company executive
Needham, George Austin investment banker
Needham, Richard Lee magazine editor
Neely, Mark E., Jr. writer
Neff, Craig periodical editor
Neff, Robert Arthur business and financial executive
Neff, Thomas Joseph executive search firm executive
Neft, David Samuel marketing professional
Neidell, Martin H. lawyer
Neier, Aryeh author, human rights organization administrator
Neilly, Andrew Hutchinson, Jr. publisher
†Neilson, Roger professional hockey coach
Neiman, LeRoy artist
Nelkin, Dorothy sociology and science policy educator, researcher
Nell, Edward John economist, educator
Nelson, Bruce Sherman advertising agency executive
Nelson, Joni Lysett lawyer, business executive
Nelson, Lindsey sportscaster
Nelson, Merlin Edward international business consultant, company director
Nelson, Richard lighting designer, consultant
†Nelson, Richard John playwright
Nemser, Earl Harold lawyer
Nero, Peter pianist, conductor, composer, arranger
Nesbit, Robert Grover consultant
Netzer, Dick economics educator
Neu, Harold Conrad physician, educator
Neubauer, Peter Bela psychoanalyst
Neuberger, Roy R. investment counselor
†Neufeld, Victor television executive
Neuhaus, Max artist, composer
†Neuhaus, Sydney Ann public relations executive
Neuthaler, Paul David publisher
Neuwirth, Alan James lawyer
Neuwirth, Robert Samuel obstetrician, gynecologist
Neveloff, Jay A. lawyer
Nevling, J. Kelley, Jr. lawyer
New, Maria Iandolo physician, educator
Newbauer, John Arthur editor
Newbold, Herbert Leon, Jr. psychiatrist, writer
Newborn, Jud cultural anthropologist, writer
Newcomb, Danforth lawyer
†Newcomb, Jonathan publishing executive
Newcombe, George Michael lawyer
Newell, Norman Dennis paleontologist, geologist, museum curator, educator
†Newfield, Jack columnist
†Newhouse, Nancy R. newspaper editor
Newhouse, Samuel I., Jr. publishing executive
Newman, Arnold photographer
Newman, Elias artist
Newman, Fredric Samuel lawyer, business executive
Newman, Geraldine Anne advertising executive
Newman, Howard Neal lawyer, educator
Newman, Jane advertising agency executive
Newman, Lawrence lawyer
Newman, Lawrence Walker lawyer
Newman, Norman lawyer
Newman, Rachel magazine editor
Newman, Robert Gabriel physician
Newman, Thomas Rubin lawyer
Newman, William real estate executive
Newton, Blake Tyler, III lawyer
Ney, Edward N. ambassador, advertising and public relations company executive
Nibley, Andrew Mathews editorial executive
Nicholls, Richard H. lawyer
Nichols, C. Walter, III trust company executive
Nichols, Carol D. real estate professional, association executive
Nichols, Kyra ballerina
Nichols, Rodney Wayson science and technology executive, policy analyst, former university administrator
Nida, Eugene Albert linguist, minister and author
Nied, Thomas H. publishing company executive
Niehoff, Karl Richard Besuden financial executive
†Nielsen, Nancy publishing executive
Nieman, John Francis advertising executive
Niemiec, David Wallace investment company executive
Nightingale, Elena Ottolenghi geneticist, physician, administrator
Niles, Nicholas Hemelright publisher
Nimetz, Matthew lawyer
Nimkin, Bernard William retired lawyer
Nirenberg, Louis mathematician, educator
Nisenholtz, Martin Abram advertising executive, educator
Nixon, Joan Lowery writer
Noback, Charles Robert anatomist, educator
Nodelman, Jared Robert investment advisor
Nolan, Richard Edward lawyer
Nolan, Terrance Joseph, Jr. lawyer
Nolan, William Joseph, III banker
†Noonan, Susan Abert public relations counselor
Norcia, Stephen William advertising executive
†Nord, Peter Robert advertising executive
Norfolk, William Ray lawyer
†Norgren, William Andrew religious denomination administrator
Norman, Jessye soprano
Norman, Marsha playwright
Norman, Stephen Peckham financial services company executive
Norton, Paul Allen insurance executive
Norville, Deborah news correspondent
Notarbartolo, Albert artist
†Novacek, Michael John curator, museum administrator
Novak, Barbara art history educator
Novak, Eugene Francis advertising executive
Novello, Antonia Coello U.S. surgeon general
Novick, Nelson Lee dermatologist, internist, writer
Novick, Robert physicist, educator
Novitz, Charles Richard television executive
Novogrod, Nancy Ellen editor
Nowick, Arthur Stanley metallurgy, materials science educator
Nucci, Leo baritone
Nugent, Nelle theater, film and television producer
Nusbacher, Gloria W. lawyer, partner
Nusbaum, Jack Henry lawyer
Nuzum, John M., Jr. banker
Nyren, Neil Sebastian publisher, editor
Oakes, John Bertram writer, editor
Ober, Eric W. broadcasting executive
Oberman, Michael Stewart lawyer
Obernauer, Marne, Jr. corporate executive
Obolensky, Ivan investment banker, foundation consultant, writer, publisher
O'Brian, Jack journalist
O'Brien, Conan writer, performer, talk show host
O'Brien, Donal Clare, Jr. lawyer
O'Brien, Edward Ignatius lawyer, trade association executive
†O'Brien, Geoffrey Paul editor
O'Brien, John M. newspaper publishing company executive
O'Brien, Kevin J. lawyer
O'Brien, Orin Ynez musician, educator
O'Brien, Richard Francis advertising agency executive
O'Brien, Timothy James lawyer
O'Brien, William K. accounting firm executive
Ochiltree, Stuart A. cosmetics company executive
Ochs, Michael editor, librarian, music educator
O'Connell, Christopher Patrick lawyer
O'Connor, Francis X. securities corporation executive
O'Connor, John Joseph Cardinal archbishop, former naval officer
O'Connor, Sinead singer, songwriter
O'Dea, Dennis Michael lawyer
Odell, Stuart Irwin lawyer
Odenweller, Robert Paul philatelist association executive, airline pilot
O'Donnell, John Logan lawyer
†O'Donnell, Richard Walter lawyer, accountant, brokerage company executive
†O'Donoghue, Michael producer, director, writer, actor
Oechler, Henry John, Jr. lawyer
Oettgen, Herbert Friedrich physician
Offensend, David Glenn investment executive
Offit, Morris Wolf investment management executive
Offit, Sidney writer, educator
O'Flinn, Peter Russell lawyer
Ogden, Alfred lawyer
Ogden, Dayton executive search consultant
O'Grady, John Joseph, III lawyer
†O'Grady, William M. manufacturing executive
†Ohannessian, Griselda Jackson publishing executive
O'Hara, Alfred Peck lawyer
O'Hare, Joseph Aloysius university president, priest
†O'Healy, Quill insurance company executive
Ohlson, Douglas Dean artist
O'Horgan, Thomas Foster composer, director
†Ohrenstein, Manfred state senator, lawyer
†Ohtake, Yoshito metal products executive
Ohtsu, Masakazu electronics executive
Okun, Herbert Stuart ambassador, international executive
Olafsson, Olafur J. publishing company executive
Old, Lloyd John cancer biologist
Oldenburg, Claes Thure artist
Oldenburg, Richard Erik museum director
Oldham, John Michael physician, psychiatrist, educator
Oldham, Todd fashion designer
Olds, John Theodore banker
Olick, Arthur Seymour lawyer
Olick, Philip Stewart lawyer
Oliensis, Sheldon lawyer
Oliva, Lawrence Jay university official, history educator
Oliveira, Elmar violinist
Oliver, Alexander R. management consultant
Oliver, Stephanie Stokes magazine editor
Olmstead, Clarence Walter, Jr. lawyer
Olsen, David Alexander insurance executive
Olsen, Richard W. advertising executive
†Olshan, Karen advertising agency executive
Olshan, Kenneth S. advertising agency executive
Olsinski, Peter Kevin international outplacement executive
Olson, Thomas Francis, II communications company executive
Olsson, Carl Alfred urologist
Olyphant, David cultural, educational association executive
O'Malley, Shaun F. accounting firm executive
O'Neil, James Peter financial printing company executive
O'Neil, John Joseph lawyer
O'Neil, Stephen Edward lawyer, investor
O'Neill, Daniel J. lawyer
O'Neill, Francis Xavier, III marketing executive
O'Neill, Harry William survey research company executive
O'Neill Bidwell, Katharine Thomas fine arts association executive, performing arts executive
Onufrak, Joseph J. lawyer
Opel, John R. business machines company executive
Opotowsky, Stuart Berger holding company executive
†Oppenheim, Ellen W. media director, advertising executive
Oppenheimer, Martin J. lawyer
Oppenheimer, Michael physicist
Orben, Jack Richard investment company executive
Orce, Kenneth W. lawyer
Oreskes, Irwin biochemistry educator
Oresman, Donald entertainment and publishing company executive, corporate lawyer
Orkin, Leonard lawyer
Ornitz, Richard Martin lawyer, business executive
O'Rorke, James Francis, Jr. lawyer
O'Rourke, P. J. (Patrick Jake O'Rourke) writer, humorist
Orr, Terrence S. dancer
Osborn, Donald Robert lawyer
Osborne, Richard de Jongh mining and metals company executive
Osborne, Stanley de Jongh investment banker
†Osbourn, Gordon Cecil materials scientist
Osgood, Charles news broadcaster, journalist
Osgood, Richard M., Jr. applied physics and electrical engineering educator, research administrator
Osgood, Robert Mansfield lawyer
Osmond, Gordon Condie lawyer, playwright
Osnos, Gilbert Charles management consultant
Osnos, Peter Lionel Winston publishing executive
Ostergard, Paul Michael bank executive
Osterhout, Dan Roderick insurance executive
Ostling, Paul James lawyer
Ostling, Richard Neil journalist, author, broadcaster
Ostrager, Barry R. lawyer
Ostrander, Thomas William investment banker
Ostrow, Joseph W. advertising executive
†Ostrow, Samuel David public relations executive
Ostrum, Dean Gardner actor, calligrapher
O'Sullivan, Eugene Henry retired advertising executive
O'Sullivan, Thomas J. lawyer
O'Toole, John E. advertising executive
Ott, Gilbert Russell, Jr. lawyer
Otter, John Martin, III television advertising consultant
Owen, Lynn Rasmussen soprano, voice educator
Owen, Michael ballet dancer
Owen, Richard federal judge
†Owen, Sylvia interior design executive
Owen, Thomas Llewellyn, Sr. investment executive
Owsley, David Thomas art consultant, appraiser, lecturer, author
Oxley, Geraldine Motta insurance company executive
Oxman, David Craig lawyer
Ozawa, Seiji conductor, music director
Ozero, Brian John chemical engineer
Ozick, Cynthia author
Oznowicz, Frank Richard (Frank Oz) puppeteer, film director
Paalz, Anthony L. beverage company executive
Paaswell, Robert Emil civil engineer, educator
Pace, Eric Dwight journalist
Pace, Richard Alan bank data processing executive
Pace, Stephen Shell artist, educator
Pacella, Bernard Leonardo psychiatrist
Pacino, Al (Alfredo James Pacino) actor
Pack, Leonard Brecher lawyer
†Padberg, Manfred Wilhelm mathematics educator
Paddock, Anthony Conaway management consultant
Padilla, James Earl lawyer
Pados, Frank John, Jr. trust company executive
†Pagnozzi, Amy columnist
Pais, Abraham physicist, educator
Paisner, Bruce Lawrence lawyer, television and film executive
Pakula, Alan J. producer, director
Paladino, Daniel R. lawyer, beverage corporation executive
Palladino, Vincent Neil lawyer
Palmer, Edward Lewis banker
Palmer, James Alvin baseball commentator
Palmer, Robert Baylis librarian
Palmer, Robert J(oseph) advertising executive, winery owner
Palmieri, Victor Henry lawyer, business executive
Paluszek, John L. public relations firm executive
Pampel, Joseph Philip Stevenson investment executive
Pandolfi, Francis P. publishing executive
Paneth, Donald J. editor, writer
Panitch, Michael B. brokerage house executive
Panken, Peter Michael lawyer
Papa, Vincent T. insurance company executive
Papalia, Diane Ellen human development educator
Papernik, Joel Ira lawyer
Pappas, Alceste Thetis consulting company executive, educator
Paradise, Robert Richard publishing executive
Pardee, Scott Edward securities dealer
Pardes, Herbert psychiatrist, educator
Pardo, Dominick George (Don Pardo) broadcasting announcer
†Parent, Louise Marie lawyer
Parfit, Gavin J. international executive
Parish, J. Michael lawyer, writer
Parker, Charles A. insurance company executive
Parker, Douglas Martin lawyer
Parker, James retired curator
Parker, Maceo jazz musician, alto saxophone
Parker, Maynard Michael journalist, magazine executive
Parker, Mel editor
Parker, Nancy Winslow artist, writer
Parker, Olivia photographer
Parker, Robert Andrew artist
Parker, Susan Brooks rehabilitation administrator
†Parkin, Gerard Francis Ralph chemistry educator, researcher
Parkinson, Georgina ballet mistress
Parkinson, Thomas Ignatius, Jr. lawyer
Parks, Gordon Roger Alexander Buchanan film director, author, photographer, composer
Parks, Robert Henry consulting economist, educator
Parr, Ferdinand Van Siclen, Jr. lawyer
Parsons, Andrew John management consultant
Parsons, David artistic director, choreographer
Parsons, Estelle actress
Parsons, Richard Dean banker, lawyer
Parver, Jane W. lawyer
†Pasanella, Giovanni architect, architectural educator
Pasanella, Marco furniture designer
Pascal, David artist
Pasquarelli, Joseph J. real estate, engineering and construction executive
Passow, Aaron Harry education educator
Pastorek, Norman Joseph facial plastic surgeon
Paterson, Katherine Womeldorf writer
Paton, Leland B. investment banker
†Patrell, Oliver Lincoln insurance company executive
†Patrick, Hugh Talbot economist, educator
†Patrick, Thomas H. brokerage house executive
Patrikis, Ernest T. lawyer
Patten, John W. magazine publisher
Patterson, Edward investment banker
Patterson, Ellmore Clark banker
Patterson, James Brendan, Jr. advertising agency executive
Patterson, Jerry Eugene author
Patterson, Robert Porter, Jr. federal judge
Patterson, Russel Hugo, Jr. neurosurgeon, educator
Patton, Joanna advertising executive
Patton, Joëlle Delbourgo publishing executive
Paugh, Thomas Francis magazine editor, writer, photographer
Paul, Douglas Allan insurance executive
Paul, Eve W. lawyer
Paul, James William lawyer
Paul, Robert David management consultant
Pauley, Jane television journalist
†Paulsen, Diana religious organization administrator
Pavarotti, Luciano lyric tenor
Pavis, Jesse Andrew sociology educator
†Pavlika, Holly Ann art director
Paxton, Robert Owen historian, educator
Payson, Martin David entertainment company executive, lawyer
Pearlstine, Norman media company executive
Pearsall, Otis Pratt lawyer

Pearson, Clarence Edward management consultant
Pearson, Henry Charles artist
Pearson, John Edward lawyer
Peasback, David R. recruiting company executive
Peaslee, James M. lawyer
Pechukas, Philip chemistry educator
Peck, Fred Neil economist, educator
Peck, M(organ) Scott psychiatrist, writer
Peck, Richard Wayne novelist
Pecker, David J. magazine publishing company executive, financial executive
Peckolick, Alan graphic designer
Peebler, Charles David, Jr. advertising executive
Peerce, Stuart Bernard lawyer
Peet, Charles D., Jr. lawyer
Pegram, John Braxton lawyer
Pei, Ieoh Ming architect
Pelé, (Edson Arantes do Nascimento) professional soccer player
Pellegrini, Anna Maria soprano
Peloso, John Francis Xavier lawyer
Pelster, William C. lawyer
Pelz, Robert Leon lawyer
Penglase, Frank Dennis publishing company executive
Penn, Arthur Hiller film and theatre producer
Penn, Stanley William journalist,columnist
Pennario, Leonard concert pianist, composer
†Penney, Alexandra magazine editor-in-chief, writer
Pennoyer, Paul Geddes, Jr. lawyer
Pennoyer, Robert M. lawyer
†Pennoyer, Russell Parsons oil company executive
Peper, George Frederick editor
Pepper, Allan Michael lawyer
Pepper, Beverly artist, sculptor
Peppers, Jerry P. lawyer
Perahia, Murray pianist
†Perales, Cesar Augusto government official
Percus, Jerome Kenneth physicist, educator
Perdunn, Richard Francis management professional
Perell, Edward Andrew lawyer
Perelman, Ronald Owen diversified holding company executive
Peress, Gilles photographer
Peress, Maurice symphony conductor, musicologist
Peritz, Abraham Daniel business executive
Perkiel, Mitchel H. lawyer
†Perkins, Lawrence Bradford, Jr. architect
Perkins, Roswell Burchard lawyer
Perless, Ellen advertising executive
Perlis, Donald M. artist
†Perlman, Gilbert E. publishing executive
Perlmuth, William Alan lawyer
Perlmutter, Alvin Howard television and film producer
Perlmutter, Diane F. communications executive
Perlmutter, Louis investment banker, lawyer
Perls, Klaus Gunther art dealer
Perrotta, Fioravante Gerald lawyer
†Perry, David priest
Perry, Douglas opera singer
Perry, Frank motion picture executive, director, producer, writer
Perry, Ronald dancer
Perschetz, Martin L. lawyer
Persell, Caroline Hodges sociologist, educator, author, researcher, consultant
Pershan, Richard Henry lawyer
Pesner, Carole Manishin art gallery owner
Peterkin, DeWitt, Jr. banker
Peters, Alton Emil lawyer
Peters, Arthur King international trade executive, author, consultant
Peters, Bernadette (Bernadette Lazzara) actress
Peters, Roberta soprano
Petersen, Raymond Joseph publishing company executive
Peterson, Charles Gordon retired lawyer
Peterson, Kirk Charles ballet dancer
Peterson, Kristina publishing company executive
Peterson, Nadeen advertising agency executive
Peterson, Peter G. banker
Peterson, Ralph Edward clergyman
Petrie, Donald Joseph banker
Pettibone, Peter John lawyer
Pettus, Barbara Wyper bank executive
Petty, John Robert banker
Petz, Edwin V. real estate executive, lawyer
Petzal, David Elias editor, writer
Peyronnin, Joseph Felix, III network news executive
Pfaff, Donald W. neurobiology and behavior educator
Pfeffer, David H. lawyer
Pflaum, Susanna Whitney college dean
Phelps, Edmund Strother economics educator
Philbin, Regis television personality
†Philips, George publishing company executive
Phillips, Anthony Francis lawyer
Phillips, Anthony Mark auction house executive
Phillips, Barnet, IV lawyer
Phillips, Charles Gorham lawyer
Phillips, Elizabeth Joan marketing executive
Phillips, Ethel C. (Mrs. Lloyd J. Phillips) writer
Phillips, Gerald Baer internal medicine educator, scientist
†Phillips, Graham Holmes advertising executive
Phillips, Howard William investment banker
Phillips, John David corporate executive
Phillips, Lawrence S. apparel company executive
Phillips, Russell Alexander, Jr. foundation executive
†Phillips, William Dodd book publishing executive
Phillpot, Clive James art librarian
Philp, Richard Nilson writer, editor
Pickholz, Jerome Walter advertising agency executive
Pickholz, Marvin G. lawyer
Picower, Warren Michael magazine editor
Piel, Gerard editor, publisher
Pierce, Charles Eliot, Jr. library director, educator
Pierce, Lawrence Warren federal judge
Pierce, Morton Allen lawyer
Piereson, James Eugene foundation administrator
Pierpoint, Powell lawyer
Pierson, Richard Norris, Jr. medical educator
Pietersen, William Gerard pharmaceutical company executive
†Pietrini, Andrew Gabriel automotive aftermarket executive
Pietruski, John Michael, Jr. biotechnology company executive, pharmaceuticals executive
Pietrzak, Alfred Robert lawyer
Pike, Laurence Bruce retired lawyer
Pilgrim, Dianne Hauserman art museum director
†Piliguian, Tro advertising executive
Pimsler, Alvin J. artist
Pincay, Laffit, Jr. jockey
Pincus, Lionel Irwin venture banker
Pine, Granville Martin lawyer
Pinsker, Essie Levine sculptor, former advertising and public relations executive
Piore, Emanuel Ruben physicist
Piper, Thomas Laurence, III investment banker
Pirani, Conrad Levi pathologist, educator
Pirie, Robert S. investment banker, lawyer
†Pirner, David musician, songwriter
Pirsig, Robert Maynard author
Pisano, Ronald George art consultant
†Piser, Donald Harris construction company executive
Pisetzner, Emanuel structural engineer
†Pi-Sunyer, F. Xavier medical educator, medical investigator
Pittaway, David Bruce investment banker, lawyer
Pitti, Donald Robert financial service company executive
Pittman, Robert Warren entertainment executive
Pitts, Thomas E. lawyer
Piven, Frances Fox political scientist, educator
Placzek, Adolf Kurt librarian
†Plain, Belva writer
Plant, David William lawyer
Platnick, Norman I. curator, arachnologist
Platt, Charles Adams architect, planner
Platt, Nicholas Asian affairs specialist, ambassador
Plavoukos, Spencer advertising executive
Plimpton, George Ames writer, editor, television host
Plunkett, Maryann actress
Podd, Ann newspaper publishing executive
Podhoretz, Norman magazine editor, writer
Pogo, Beatriz Teresa Garcia-Tunon cell biologist, virologist, educator
Pogrebin, Letty Cottin writer, lecturer
Pokorny, Jan Hird architect
Polak, Vivian Louise lawyer
Polak, Werner L. lawyer
Polisi, Joseph W(illiam) college administrator
Poll, Robert Eugene, Jr. bank executive
Pollack, Milton federal judge
Pollack, Robert Elliot biological sciences educator, writer, scientist
†Pollack, Stanley P. lawyer
Pollack, Stephen J. stockbroker
Pollak, Martin Marshall patent development company executive, lawyer
Pollak, Richard writer, editor
Pollak, Tim advertising agency executive
†Pollak, William L. newspaper publishing executive
Pollicino, Joseph Anthony investment company executive
Pollock, M. Duncan advertising executive
Pollock-O'Brien, Louise Mary public relations executive
†Polshek, James Stewart architect
Pomerance, Norman publishing company executive
Pomerance, Ralph retired architect
†Pomerantz, Charlotte writer
Pomerantz, John J. manufacturing executive
†Pomerantz, Saul W. corporate executive
Pomeroy, Lee Harris architect
Pompadur, I. Martin communications executive
Pool, Mary Jane design consultant, author, lecturer
Poons, Larry artist
Poor, Anne artist
Poor, Peter Varnum producer, director
Pope, Leavitt Joseph broadcast company executive
Poppe, Fred Christoph advertising agency executive
Poppel, Seth Raphael corporate executive
†Poppen, Alvin J. religious organization administrator
Porizkova, Paulina model, actress
Porretta, Emanuele Peter bank executive
Porter, Karl Hampton orchestra musical director, conductor
Porter, Liliana Alicia artist, printmaker
Porter, Stephen Winthrop stage director
Portnoy, Sara S. lawyer
Posamentier, Alfred Steven mathematics educator, university administrator
Posen, Susan Orzack lawyer
Posner, Donald art historian
Posner, Jerome Beebe neurologist, educator
Posner, Roy Edward finance executive
Post, Emily (Elizabeth Lindley Post) author
Post, Joseph physician, researcher, consultant
Potoker, Edward Martin English language educator, author
Potter, Cary Nicholas banker
Potter, Guy Dill radiologist, educator
Potter, Hamilton Fish, Jr. lawyer, consultant, author
Potter, William James investment banker
Pounder, Richard A. advertising executive
†Poussaint, Renee Francine journalist
Povich, (Maurice) Maury Richard broadcast journalist, talk show host, television producer
†Powell, Harold Fryburg food products executive
Powell, James Henry lawyer
Powell, Lillian Marie music educator
Powell, Mike olympic athlete, track and field
Powell, Richard Gordon retired lawyer
Powers, Edward Alton minister, educator
Powers, Elizabeth Whitmel lawyer
Powers, Richard F., III finance company executive
Pratt, Michael Theodore book publishing company executive, marketing, sales and publishing specialist
Pratt, Richardson, Jr. retired college president
Preble, Laurence George lawyer
Preiskel, Barbara Scott lawyer, association executive
Preiss, David Lee publishing company executive
†Prelutsky, Jack author
Prem, F. Herbert, Jr. lawyer
Prentice, Eugene Miles, III lawyer
Preska, Loretta A. federal judge
†Presley, Janet Passidomo advertising executive
Prestbo, John Andrew newspaper editor, journalist, author
Preston, Frances W. performing rights organization executive
Preston, James E. cosmetics company executive
Prewitt, Kenneth political science educator, foundation executive
Price, Hugh B. foundation executive, lawyer
Price, Leontyne concert and opera singer
Price, Reynolds novelist, poet, playwright, essayist, educator
Price, Robert lawyer, media executive, investment banker
Prieto, Robert manufacturing executive
Primis, Lance Roy newspaper executive
Primps, William Guthrie lawyer
Prince, Carl E. historian, educator
Prince, Harold theatrical producer
Prince, Kenneth Stephen lawyer
Princz, Judith publishing executive
Prizzi, Jack Anthony investment banking executive
†Procope, Ernesta Gertrude insurance broker
Prosky, Robert Joseph actor
Protas, Ron dance company executive
Proulx, Edna Annie writer
Prouty, Norman R. investment banker
Provine, John C. lawyer
Pryce, Jonathan actor
Puente, Tito Anthony orchestra leader, composer, arranger
Puleo, Frank Charles lawyer
Pulling, Thomas Leffingwell investment advisor
Purcell, James Lawrence lawyer
Purcell, Philip James financial services company executive
Puris, Martin Ford advertising agency executive
Purse, Charles Roe real estate company executive
Putney, John Alden, Jr. insurance company executive
Putney, Paul William lawyer
Pye, Gordon Bruce economist
Pye, Lenwood David materials science educator, researcher, consultant
Pyle, Robert Milner, Jr. financial services company executive
Pyne, Eben Wright banker
Quackenbush, Robert Mead artist, author, psychoanalyst
Quain, Mitchell I. investment executive
Quaintance, Robert Forsyth, Jr. lawyer
Quale, Andrew Christopher, Jr. lawyer
Quaytman, Harvey painter
Queler, Eve conductor
Quennell, Nicholas landscape architect, educator
Quest, James Howard advertising executive
Questel, Mae actress
Quick, Thomas Clarkson brokerage house executive
Quigley, Austin Edmund literature and language educator
Quigley, Martin Schofield publishing company executive, educator
Quilico, Louis baritone
Quindlen, Anna journalist, author
Quinlan, Guy Christian lawyer
Quinn, Anthony Rudolph Oaxaca actor, writer, artist
Quinn, Jane Bryant journalist, writer
Quinn, Yvonne Susan lawyer
Quinson, Bruno Andre publishing executive
Quint, Ira retail executive
Quintero, Jose theatrical director
Quintero, Ronald Gary management consultant
Quirk, John James investment company executive
Quisgard, Liz Whitney artist, sculptor
Raab, Selwyn journalist
Raab, Sheldon lawyer
Rabb, Bruce lawyer
Rabb, Maxwell M. lawyer, former ambassador
Rabin, Jack lawyer
Rabiner, Susan editor
Rabinowitch, David George sculptor
Rabinowitz, Jack Grant radiologist, educator
Rabinowitz, Mayer Elya librarian, educator
Rachleff, Owen Spencer (Owen Spencer Rackleff) actor, author
Rachow, Louis A(ugust) librarian
Racz, Andre artist, engraver, educator
Radovic, Mildred Hope Fisher Witkin psychotherapist, educator
Raffael, Joseph artist
Rafferty, Brian Joseph investor relations consultant
Raffo, Steve artist
Ragan, David publishing company executive
Ragusa, Olga Maria Italian language educator
Rahm, David Alan lawyer
Rahm, Susan Berkman lawyer
Raimondi, Ruggero opera singer
Rainer, John David psychiatrist
Raines, Howell Hiram newspaper editor, journalist
†Raines, Joan Binder literary agent
Rainier, Robert Paul publisher
Raisler, Kenneth Mark lawyer
Rakoff, Jed Saul lawyer, author
Ralli, Constantine Pandia lawyer
†Ramat, Charles S. apparel executive
Ramey, Samuel Edward bass soloist
Ramirez, Maria Fiorini economist, investment advisor
Ramond, Charles Knight, II financial forecaster, publisher
Ramsay, Gustavus Remak actor
Ramsey, Peter Christie bank executive
Rand, Calvin Gordon arts and education producer and consultant
Rand, Harry Israel lawyer
Rand, Lawrence Anthony investor and financial relations executive
Rand, William lawyer, former state justice
Randall, Tony (Leonard Rosenberg) actor
†Randazzo, Anthony dancer
Randinelli, Tracey Anne magazine editor
Randolph, David conductor
Rankin, Clyde Evan, III lawyer
Ransom, Jeremy ballet dancer
†Raphael, Frank Lewis broadcast executive
Raphael, Sally Jessy talk-show host
Rapoport, Bernard Robert lawyer
Rappaport, Charles Owen lawyer
Rashad, Ahmad (Bobby Moore) sports broadcaster, former professional football player
Rasmus, John A. magazine executive
Rather, Dan broadcast journalist
Rattazzi, Serena art museum and association administrator
Rattner, Steven Lawrence investment banker
Rauch, Arthur Irving management consultant
Rauch, Rudolph Stewart, III periodical editor, journalist
Rauschenberg, Robert artist
Ravitch, Diane Silvers historian, educator, author, government official
Ravitz, Robert Allan advertising agency executive
Rawl, Arthur Julian retail executive, accountant, consultant, author
Rawls, Eugenia actress
Rawn, Stanley Ryle, Jr. oil company executive
Rawson, Eleanor S. publishing company executive
Raylesberg, Alan Ira lawyer
Raynolds, John F., III executive search consultant
Raynor, Richard Benjamin neurosurgeon, educator
Read, David Haxton Carswell clergyman
Rebay, Luciano Italian literature educator, literary critic
Rechy, John Francisco author
Redden, David Normand auction house executive
Reddy, Krishna Narayana artist, educator
Redlich, Norman lawyer
Redo, S(averio) Frank surgeon
Reed, Ishmael Scott writer
Reed, James Donald journalist, author
Reed, John Shepard banker
†Reed, John W. religious organization administrator
Reed, Pamela actress
Reed, Rex author, critic
Reeve, Christopher actor
Reff, Theodore art historian
†Regan, Judith T. editor
Regan, Sylvia playwright
†Regenbogen, Leslie Alan textile company executive
Reges, Marianna Alice marketing executive
Reibstein, Richard Jay lawyer
Reich, Larry Sam lawyer
Reich, Seymour David lawyer, former fraternal organization executive
Reich, Steve composer
Reich, Yaron Z. lawyer
Reichel, Walter Emil advertising executive
Reichl, Ruth Molly restaurant critic
Reichman, Walter psychologist, educator
Reid, John Phillip law educator
Reid, Robert Dennis artist, educator
Reid, Sarah Layfield lawyer
Reid-Crisp, Wendy publishing executive
Reidenberg, Marcus Milton physician, educator
Reidy, Carolyn Kroll publisher
Reig, June Wilson writer, director, producer
Reilly, Edward Arthur lawyer
†Reilly, Edward T., Jr. publisher
Reilly, William Francis publishing company executive
Reiman, Donald Henry English educator
Rein, Catherine Amelia financial services executive, lawyer
Reinhard, Keith Leon advertising executive
Reinhold, Richard Lawrence lawyer
Reininghaus, Ruth artist
Reinstein, Paul Michael lawyer
Reinthaler, Richard Walter lawyer
Reis, Arthur Robert, Jr. men's furnishings manufacturer
Reis, Donald Jeffery neurologist, neurobiologist, educator
Reis, Judson Patterson investment banker
Reisberg, Barry geropsychiatrist, neuropsychopharmacologist
Reisner, Milton psychoanalyst, psychiatrist
Reiss, Alvin writer
Reiss, Steven Alan lawyer, law educator
Reiss, Timothy James comparative literature educator, writer
Relson, Morris patent lawyer
Rembar, Charles (Isaiah) lawyer, writer
Remington, Deborah Williams artist
†Remnick, David J. magazine writer
Reneberg, Richard (Richey Reneberg) professional tennis player
†Renick, Kyle artistic director
†Rennie, Milbrey Tower television news producer
Renvall, Johan ballet dancer
Repko, William Clarke banker
Resika, Paul artist
Resnick, Marcia Aylene photographic artist, educator
Resnick, Milton artist
Resnik, Frank Edward tobacco company executive
Resnik, Regina operatic singer
Resor, Stanley Rogers lawyer
Restani, Jane A. federal judge
Reuben, Alvin Bernard entertainment executive
Reuter, Carol Joan insurance company executive
Reuther, David Louis children's book publisher, writer
Reutter, Eberhard Edmund, Jr. education and law educator
†Reverand, Diane publisher, editor
Reverdin, Bernard J. lawyer
Reyes, Andre ballet dancer
Reynolds, Warren Jay retired publisher
Reynolds, W(ynetka) Ann university system administrator, educator
Rhoads, Geraldine Emeline editor
Rhodes, James Whitfield architect
Rhodes, John Bower management consultant
†Rhodes, Milton arts association administrator
Rhodes, Richard Lee writer
Rhodes, Samuel violist
†Rhodes, Yorke E(dward) chemist
Ribicoff, Abraham A. lawyer, former senator
†Ricci, Kenneth architect
Ricciardi, Lawrence R. food products company executive, lawyer
Ricciarelli, Katia soprano
Rice, Anne author
Rice, Charles Duncan academic dean, history educator, writer
Rice, Donald Sands lawyer
Rice, James A. investment company executive
Rice, Joseph Lee, III lawyer
Rich, Adrienne writer
Rich, Frank Hart critic
Rich, Kenneth Malcolm executive search and management consultant
Rich, R(obert) Bruce lawyer
†Richard, Ellen theater executive
Richards, David Alan lawyer
Richards, Keith musician
Richards, Lloyd George theatrical director, university administrator
Richards, Reuben Francis natural resource company executive
Richardson, David John ballet dancer, educator
Richardson, John Carroll lawyer
Richardson, Midge Turk magazine editor
Richardson, Miranda actress
Richman, Martin Franklin lawyer
Richter, Barry brokerage firm executive
†Richter, Georg book publishing executive
†Richter, Michael Thomas professional hockey player
†Richter, Richard William television producer
Ricker, John Boykin, Jr. insurance counselor
Ridder, Eric newspaper publisher
Riddle, Sturgis Lee minister
Rideout, Philip Munroe publishing company executive
Riffaterre, Michael educator, writer
Rifkin, Harold physician, educator
Rifkind, Robert S(inger) lawyer
Rifkind, Simon Hirsch lawyer
Rigby, Paul Crispin artist, cartoonist
†Riggio, Leonard book publishing executive
Riggio, Stephen book store chain executive
†Riggs, Andy J., Jr. newspaper publishing executive
Riggs, Michael David magazine editor, writer
Riker, Walter F., Jr. pharmacologist, physician
†Riklis, Meshulam manufacturing and retail executive
Riley, Ivers Whitman stock exchange executive

Riley, Patrick James *professional basketball coach*
Riley, William *corporate executive, writer*
Rimerman, Ira Stephen *banker*
Rinaldini, Luis Emilio *investment banker*
Rindlaub, John Wade *advertising agency executive*
Rinehart, Jonathan *public relations executive*
Rines, S. Melvin *investment banker*
Ring, Renee E. *lawyer*
Ringel, Dean *lawyer*
Ringer, James Milton *lawyer*
Ringler, Lenore *educational psychology educator*
Rinsland, Roland DeLano *university official*
Riordan, James Quentin *retired company executive*
Riordan, John Thomas *trade association executive*
Riss, Eric *psychologist*
Ritch, Herald LaVern *finance company executive*
Ritch, Kathleen *diversified company executive*
Ritter, Robert Joseph *lawyer*
Rivera, Chita (Conchita del Rivero) *actress, singer, dancer*
Rivera, Geraldo *television personality, journalist*
Rivers, Kenneth Jay *judicial administrator, consultant*
Rivlin, Benjamin *political science educator*
Rizzo, Francis *arts administrator, writer, stage director*
Roach, John Hendee, Jr. *bank executive, investment banker*
Roach, Maxwell Lemuel *musician*
Robbins, Edith Schultz *microscopy educator*
Robbins, Harold *author*
Robbins, Jerome *choreographer, director*
Robbins, John Clapp *corporate executive*
Robbins, Kenneth L. *advertising agency executive*
Roberts, Donald Munier *banker, trust company executive*
Roberts, Francis Stone *advertising executive*
†Roberts, James Lewis *medical sciences educator*
Roberts, John J. *accounting firm executive*
Roberts, John Joseph *insurance company executive*
Roberts, Sidney I. *lawyer*
Roberts, Tony (David Anthony Roberts) *actor*
Robertson, Edwin David *lawyer*
Robertson, Jaquelin Taylor *architect, educator*
Robertson, Leslie Earl *structural engineer*
Robinowitz, Stuart *lawyer*
Robinson, Barbara Paul *lawyer*
Robinson, David Zav *foundation administrator*
Robinson, Enders Anthony *geophysics educator, writer*
Robinson, Irwin Jay *lawyer*
Robinson, James Dixon, III *corporate executive*
Robinson, James LeRoy *architect, educator, developer*
Robinson, Lee Harris *lawyer*
Robinson, Marvin Stuart *lawyer*
Robinson, Maurice Richard, Jr. *publishing executive*
Robinson, Richard *publishing company executive*
Robinson, Robert Armstrong *pension fund executive*
Robinson, Stanley Daniel *lawyer*
Robison, Paula Judith *flutist*
Robock, Stefan Hyman *economics educator emeritus*
†Roche, John J. *banking company executive, corporate lawyer*
†Roche, Kevin Joseph *finance executive*
Rockefeller, David *banker*
Rockwell, John Sargent *music critic, journalist*
Rodgers, Nile *musician, record producer*
Rodman, Leroy Eli *lawyer*
Rodriguez, Beatriz *ballerina*
Rodriguez, Geno (Eugene Rodriguez) *artist, arts administrator*
Rodriguez, Vincent Angel *lawyer*
Roeder, Robert Gayle *biochemist, educator*
Roehm, Carolyne Jane *fashion designer*
Roehm, MacDonell, Jr. *investment firm executive*
Roellig, Leonard Oscar *physics educator*
Roerick, William (George) (William Roehrick) *actor, author*
Roessler, Ronald James *lawyer*
Roethenmund, Otto Emil *financial and banking executive*
Rogalin, Roger Richard *publishing executive*
Rogers, Arthur Merriam, Jr. *banker*
Rogers, David Elliott *physician, educator, author*
Rogers, Elizabeth Barlow *municipal park administrator*
Rogers, Eugene Charles *investment firm executive*
Rogers, Kenneth R. *advertising executive*
Rogers, Mary Martin *publishing company executive*
Rogers, Theodore Courtney *investment company executive*
Rogin, Gilbert Leslie *editor, author*
Rohatyn, Felix George *investment company executive*
†Rohrbasser, Markus *securities broker executive*
Rolfe, Robin Ann *trade association executive, lawyer*
Rolfe, Ronald Stuart *lawyer*
Rollin, Betty *author, television journalist*
Rollins, Jack *motion picture producer*
Rolontz, Robert *recording company executive*
†Rom, William N. *physician*
Roman, Kenneth, Jr. *consultant*
†Roman, Stanford Augustus, Jr. *medical educator, dean*
Romans, John Niebrugge *lawyer*
Romney, Richard Bruce *lawyer*
Roney, Wallace *musician*
Ronson, Raoul R. *publishing executive*
Rooney, Andrew Aitken *writer, columnist*
Rooney, Paul C., Jr. *lawyer*
†Rooney, Terence *public relations executive*
Roosevelt, Theodore, IV *investment banker*
Root, Nina J. *librarian*
Root, William Pitt *poet, educator*
†Rosado, David *city official*
Rosdeitcher, Sidney S. *lawyer*
Rose, Charles *television journalist*
Rose, Elihu *real estate executive*
Rose, Herman *artist*
Rose, Leatrice *artist, educator*
Rose, Milton Curtiss *lawyer*
Rose, Robert Neal *brokerage house executive*
Rose, Zeldon E. *public relations company executive*
Rosen, Benjamin Maurice *venture capitalist*
Rosen, David Michael *university administrator, public affairs consultant*
†Rosen, Hy *advertising executive*
Rosen, Nathaniel Kent *cellist*
Rosen, Richard Lewis *lawyer, real estate developer*
†Rosenbaum, Joan Hannah *museum director*
Rosenbaum, Steven Ira *public relations and publishing executive, photographer*
Rosenberg, Alan Stewart *lawyer*
†Rosenberg, Burton M. *apparel company executive*
Rosenberg, Jerome I. *lawyer*
Rosenberg, John David *English educator, literary critic*
Rosenberg, Maurice *lawyer, educator*
Rosenberg, Michael Joseph *financial executive*
Rosenberger, Carol *concert pianist*
Rosenberger, Ernst Hey *judge*
Rosenblatt, Arthur Isaac *architect, former museum director*
Rosenblatt, Lester *naval architect*
Rosenbloom, Daniel *investment banker, lawyer*
†Rosenblum, Constance *newspaper editor*
Rosenblum, Robert *art historian, educator*
†Rosenbluth, Lucille M. *health research facility administrator*
Rosenfeld, Arthur H. *lawyer, publisher*
Rosenfeld, Herb *educational consultant*
Rosenfeld, Steven B. *lawyer*
Rosenfield, Allan *physician*
Rosenfield, Jay Gary *publisher*
Rosenhouse, Irwin J. *artist, designer*
Rosensaft, Menachem Zwi *lawyer, author, community activist*
Rosenshine, Allen Gilbert *advertising agency executive*
Rosenthal, Albert Joseph *university dean, law educator, lawyer*
†Rosenthal, Imre *financial company executive*
Rosenthal, Jacob (Jack Rosenthal) *newspaper editor*
Rosenthal, Lucy Gabrielle *writer, editor, educator*
Rosenthal, Macha Louis *author, educator*
Rosenthal, Milton Frederick *minerals and chemical company executive*
Rosenthal, Nan *curator, author*
Rosenthal, Peter *public relations executive*
Rosenthal, Tony (Bernard) *sculptor*
Rosenthal, William Forshaw *advertising executive*
Rosenwald, E. John, Jr. *brokerage house executive, investment banker*
Rosenwald, William *investment executive, philanthropist*
Roskind, E. Robert *real estate company executive*
Rosner, Lydia S. *sociology educator, author*
†Rosoff, Jeannie I. *association administrator*
Rosow, Stuart L. *lawyer*
Ross, Brian Elliott *news correspondent*
Ross, Charles *artist*
Ross, Coleman DeVane *accountant, insurance company consultant*
Ross, David A. *art museum director*
Ross, Diana *singer, actress, entertainer, fashion designer*
Ross, Donald Edward *engineering company executive*
Ross, Donald Keith *retired insurance company executive*
Ross, Elise Jane *newspaper executive*
Ross, Jeffrey Allan *political scientist, educator*
Ross, Michael Aaron *lawyer*
Ross, Norman Alan *publisher*
Rossant, James Stephane *architect*
Rossellini, Isabella *model, actress*
Rosset, Barnet Lee, Jr. *publisher*
Rossi, Dominick F., Jr. *advertising agency executive*
Rossner, Judith *novelist*
Rossoff, Mack Fredric *investment banker*
Rostagno, Derrick *professional tennis player*
Rosten, Leo Calvin (Leonard Q. Ross) *author, political scientist*
Rostropovich, Mstislav Leopoldovich *musician*
Roth, Ann *costume designer*
Roth, Henry *writer*
Roth, Judith Shulman *lawyer*
Roth, Michael I. *lawyer, financial executive*
Roth, Paul Norman *lawyer*
Roth, Philip *writer*
Roth, Richard, Jr. *architect*
Roth, Sol *rabbi*
Rothberg, Gerald *editor, publisher*
Rothenberg, Jerome *author*
Rothenberg, Peter Jay *lawyer*
Rothenberg, Robert Edward *physician, surgeon, author*
Rothenberg, Robert Philip *public relations counselor*
Rothenberg, Susan *artist*
Rothholz, Peter Lutz *public relations executive*
Rothman, Bernard *lawyer*
Rothman, Henry Isaac *lawyer*
Rothman, Howard Joel *lawyer*
Rothman, James Edward *cell biologist, educator*
Rothstein, Fred H. *clothing executive*
Rothstein, Gerald Alan *investment company executive*
†Rothstein, Richard *public relations executive*
Roubos, Gary Lynn *diversified manufacturing company executive*
†Rousset, Alain *advertising agency executive*
Rover, Edward Frank *lawyer*
Rovine, Arthur William *lawyer*
Rowe, John Wallis *academic administrator, hospital administrator*
†Rowen, Harold Charles *shoe company executive*
Rowen, Ruth Halle *musicologist, educator*
Rowland, Esther E(delman) *college dean*
Rowland, Herbert Leslie *public relations executive*
Rowland, Lewis Phillip *neurologist, medical editor, educator*
Roy, Melinda *dancer*
Rozel, Samuel Joseph *lawyer*
Rozelle, Pete (Alvin Ray Rozelle) *former commissioner National Football League*
Rozen, Jerome George, Jr. *research entomologist, museum curator and research administrator*
Ruben, Lawrence *real estate developer, building company executive, lawyer*
Ruben, Richards *artist, educator*
Ruben, William Samuel *marketing consultant*
Rubenfeld, Stanley Irwin *lawyer*
Rubenstein, Howard Joseph *public relations executive*
Rubenstein, Joshua Seth *lawyer*
Rubenstein, Stanley Ellis *public relations consultant*
†Rubin, Albert L. *physician, educator*
Rubin, Edwin Manning *advertising executive*
Rubin, Gustav *orthopedic surgeon, consultant, researcher*
Rubin, Harry Meyer *entertainment industry executive*
Rubin, Herbert *lawyer*
Rubin, Joel Edward *consulting company executive*
Rubin, Lawrence Edward *art dealer*
Rubin, Norman Julius *columnist*
Rubin, Richard Allan *lawyer*
Rubin, Robert Samuel *investment banker*
Rubin, Stephen Edward *editor, journalist*
Rubin, Stephen Wayne *lawyer*
Rubin, Theodore Isaac *psychiatrist*
Rubino, Victor Joseph *law institute executive*
Rubinstein, Aaron *lawyer*
Rubinstein, Frederic Armand *lawyer*
Rubinstein, Laurence Henry *university administrator, fund raiser*
Rudd, Nicholas *marketing communications company executive*
Rudel, Julius *conductor*
Ruder, William *public relations executive*
Ruding, Herman Onno *banker, former Dutch minister of finance*
Rudoff, Sheldon *lawyer, administrator religious organization*
Ruebhausen, Oscar Melick *lawyer*
Ruegger, Philip Theophil, III *lawyer*
Ruello, Samuel Angus *management consultant*
Ruffle, John Frederick *banker*
Ruggiero, Thomas William *lawyer*
†Ruinsky, Sam *newspaper publishing executive*
Rukeyser, M. S., Jr. *television consultant, writer*
Rupp, George Erik *university president*
Ruscha, Edward *artist*
Rush, Peter *public relations executive*
Rushnell, Squire Derrick *television executive*
Rusmisel, Stephen R. *lawyer*
†Russell, Charles F. *newspaper publishing executive*
Russell, John St. Clair, Jr. *lawyer*
†Russo, Anthony Joseph *public relations professional*
†Russo, Barbara Gans *advertising agency executive*
Russo, Gregory Thomas *lawyer*
Russo, Thomas Anthony *lawyer*
Ruth, Carol A. *public relations executive*
Ruthchild, Geraldine Quietlake *training and development consultant, writer, poet*
Rutkin, Seymour *architect*
Rutman, Mark Charles *public relations executive*
Ruvane, John Austin *pharmaceutical industry consultant*
Ryan, J. Richard *lawyer*
Ryan, Michael Clifford *lawyer*
Ryan, Michael E. *newspaper publishing executive*
Ryan, Michael Edmond *communications company executive, lawyer*
Ryan, Regina Claire (Mrs. Paul Deutschman) *editor, book packager, literary agent*
Ryan, Thomas Timothy, Jr. *banker, lawyer, government official*
Ryle, Joseph Donald *public relations executive*
Ryman, Robert Tracy *artist*
Rysanek, Leonie *soprano*
Ryskamp, Charles Andrew *museum executive, educator*
Saal, Hubert Daniel *journalist*
Sabel, Bradley Kent *lawyer*
Sabetta, John Carl *lawyer*
Sabinson, Harvey Barnett *cultural organiztion administrator*
Sacerdote, Peter M. *investment banker*
Sachar, David Bernard *gastroenterologist, medical educator*
Sachdev, Ved Parkash *neurosurgeon*
Sachs, David *lawyer*
Sachs, Susan F. *publishing executive*
Sack, Robert David *lawyer*
Sackeim, Harold *psychologist, educator*
†Sackman, Ruth *foundation executive*
Sacks, David G. *retired distilling company executive, lawyer*
Sacks, Ira Stephen *lawyer*
Sacks, Oliver Wolf *neurologist, writer*
Sacks, Temi J. *public relations executive*
Saddler, Donald Edward *choreographer, dancer*
Sade, (Helen Folasade Adu) *singer, songwriter*
†Sadegh, Ali M. *mechanical engineering educator, researcher, consultant*
Sadler, Eric *recording industry executive*
Sadock, Benjamin James *psychiatrist, educator*
Safer, Jay Gerald *lawyer*
Safer, Morley *journalist*
Sagami, Kim *dancer*
Sagendorf, Bud (Forrest Cowles Sagendorf) *cartoonist*
Sager, Clifford J(ulius) *psychiatrist, educator*
Sahid, Joseph Robert *lawyer*
Said, Edward W. *English language and literature educator*
Saiman, Martin S. *lawyer*
Sainer, Arthur *writer, theater educator*
St. Clair, Michael *art dealer*
Sainty, Guy Stair *art dealer*
Sakita, Bunji *physicist, educator*
Saks, Arnold *graphic designer*
†Saladino, John F. *architect, interior decorator, furniture designer*
†Salberg, Melvin *lawyer*
Sale, (John) Kirkpatrick *writer*
Salembier, Valerie Birnbaum *publishing executive*
Salgado, Lissette *dancer*
Salinger, Jerome David *author*
†Salisbury, Nancy *convent director*
Salle, David *artist*
Salmans, Charles Gardiner *banker*
Salomon, Richard *investor*
Salomon, Robert S., Jr. *portfolio manager*
Salonga, Lea *actress, singer*
Saltz, Carole Pogrebin *publisher*
Salvador, Sal *jazz musician, guitarist, music educator, composer*
†Salvadori, Mario *mathematical engineer*
Salzman, Robert Jay *accountant*
†Samers, Bernard Norman *fund raising organization executive*
†Samuels, Leslie B. *federal agency administrator, lawyer*
Samuels, Nathaniel *business executive, government administrator*
†Sanborn, Robert B. *insurance company executive*
Sand, Leonard B. *federal judge*
Sandalls, William Thomas, Jr. *financial services company executive*
Sander, Volkmar *foreign language educator*
Sanders, Fredric M. *lawyer*
Sanders, Lawrence *author*
Sanders, Richard Louis *assistant managing editor*
Sandler, Jenny *dancer*
Sandler, Lucy Freeman *art historian*
Sandler, Richard Jay *lawyer*
Sandler, Robert Michael *insurance company executive, actuary*
Sandler, Ross *law educator*
Sanford, Charles Steadman, Jr. *banker*
Sanger, Gail *lawyer*
Sansaverino, Joseph F. *human resources executive*
Santulli, Thomas Vincent *surgeon*
Sapinsky, Joseph Charles *magazine executive, photographer*
†Sarachik, Myriam Paula *physics educator*
Sarazen, Richard Allen *media company executive*
Sard, George *public relations company executive*
†Sardanis, Andrew S. *investment company executive*
Sargent, James Cunningham *lawyer*
Sargent, Joseph Dudley *insurance executive*
Sarnelle, Joseph R. *electronic publishing specialist, magazine and newspaper editor*
Sarnoff, Albert *communications executive*
Sarnoff, William *publishing company executive*
Sartori, Giovanni *political scientist*
Sarver, Eugene *finance educator*
†Sasaki, Mikio *import/export company executive*
Satine, Barry Roy *lawyer*
Sauerhaft, Stan *public relations executive, consultant*
Saul, John Woodruff, III *writer*
Saunders, Arlene *opera singer*
Saunders, Dero Ames *writer, editor*
Saunders, Paul Christopher *lawyer*
†Saunders, Thomas A., III *investment company executive*
Savas, Emanuel S. *public management educator*
Savelli, Angelo *artist*
†Savich, René *broadway theater executive, producer*
Savrin, Louis *lawyer*
Sawabini, Nabil George *banker*
Sawyer, (L.) Diane *television journalist*
Sawyer, Forrest *newscaster*
Sawyer, John Edward *foundation officer*
Sawyer, William Dale *physician, educator, university dean, foundation administrator*
Saxe, Leonard *social psychologist, educator*
Saxena, Brij B. *biochemist, endocrinologist, educator*
Saylor, Steven Warren *writer, prose, fiction*
Scanlon, Peter Redmond *accountant*
Scanlon, Rosemary *economist*
Scarborough, Charles Bishop, III *broadcast journalist, writer*
Scardino, Don *artistic director*
Scardino, Marjorie Morris *publishing company executive*
Scardino, Michael Christopher *advertising executive*
Scaturro, Philip David *investment banker*
Scavullo, Francesco *photographer*
†Scelsa, Joseph Vincent *sociologist*
Schaap, Richard Jay *journalist*
Schacht, Ronald Stuart *lawyer*
Schachter, Oscar *lawyer, educator, arbitrator*
Schade, Malcolm Robert *lawyer*
Schaller, Christopher L. *apparel products company executive*
Schanberg, Sydney Hillel *newspaper editor, columnist*
Schapiro, Donald *lawyer*
Schapiro, Herb *playwright, educator*
Schapiro, Meyer *retired art history educator*
Schapiro, Miriam *artist*
Schapiro, Morris A. *investment banker*
Schaub, Sherwood Anhder, Jr. *management consultant*
Schechner, Richard *theater director, author, educator*
Schechter, Daniel Philip *lawyer*
Schechter, Stephen Lloyd *investment banker*
Scheeder, Louis *theater producer, director, educator*
†Scheinberg, Labe Charles *physician, educator*
Scheindlin, Raymond Paul *Hebrew literature educator, translator*
Scheler, Brad Eric *lawyer*
Scher, Irving *lawyer*
Scher, Paula Joan *graphic designer*
Scher, Stanley Jules *lawyer*
Schewel, Stanford *lawyer*
Schiavi, Raul Constante *psychiatrist, educator, researcher*
Schick, Harry Leon *investment company executive*
Schickele, Peter *composer*
Schieffer, Bob *broadcast journalist*
Schiff, David Tevele *investment banker*
†Schiffer, Claudia *model*
Schiffrin, Andre *publisher*
†Schilling, Maris *associate creative director*
Schindler, Alexander Moshe *rabbi, organization executive*
Schirmeister, Charles F. *lawyer*
Schisgal, Murray Joseph *playwright*
Schizer, Zevie Baruch *lawyer*
Schlaifer, Charles *advertising executive*
Schlesinger, Arthur (Meier), Jr. *writer, educator*
Schlesinger, David Harvey *medical educator, researcher*
Schlesinger, Edward Bruce *neurological surgeon*
Schlesinger, Sanford Joel *lawyer*
Schless, Phyllis Ross *investment banker*
†Schlessinger, Joseph *pharmacology educator*
Schlosser, Herbert S. *broadcasting company executive*
Schmemann, Serge *journalist*
Schmertz, Eric Joseph *lawyer, educator*
Schmertz, Herbert *public relations and advertising executive*
Schmertz, Mildred Floyd *editor, writer*
Schmetterer, Robert Allen *advertising executive*
Schmidt, Stanley Albert *editor, writer*
Schmitter, Charles Harry *electronics manufacturing company executive, lawyer*
Schmitz, Robert Allen *publishing executive, investor*
Schmolka, Leo Louis *law educator*
Schnabel, Julian *artist*
Schnabel, Karl Ulrich *pianist*
†Schnackenberg, Gjertrud Cecelia *poet*
Schneck, Jerome M. *psychiatrist, medical historian, educator*
†Schneider, Bernard *industrial machinery executive*
Schneider, Donald Frederic *banker*
Schneider, Howard *lawyer*
Schneider, JoAnne *artist*
†Schneider, Martin Aaron *photojournalist, ecologist, engineer, writer, artist, television director, public intervenor, educator, university instructor, lecturer*
Schneider, Norman M. *food manufacturing company executive*
Schneider, Willys Hope *lawyer*
Schneiderman, David Abbott *publisher, journalist*
Schneiderman, Irwin *lawyer*
Schneier, Arthur *rabbi*
Schnell, Joseph *dancer*
Schonberg, Harold Charles *music critic, columnist*
Schoonover, Jean Way *public relations consultant*
Schorer, Suki *ballet educator*
Schorsch, Ismar *clergyman, Jewish history educator*
Schotter, Andrew Roye *economics educator, consultant*
Schrag, Karl *artist*
†Schragis, Steven M. *publisher, lawyer*
Schramm, Texas E. *football league executive*
Schreiber, Alfred Lawrence *marketing executive, special events consultant*
Schreiber, Paul Solomon *lawyer*
Schreyer, Leslie John *lawyer*
Schriever, Fred Martin *energy, environmental and information technology executive*
Schroeder, Aaron Harold *songwriter*

Schroeder, Edmund R. lawyer
Schubart, Mark Allen arts and education executive
†Schuchert, Joseph light manufacturing executive
Schueller, Thomas George lawyer
Schulberg, Budd author
Schulberg, Jay William advertising agency executive
Schulhof, Michael Peter entertainment, electronics company executive
Schulman, Grace poet, English language educator
Schulman, Paul Martin advertising executive
Schulte, Stephen John lawyer, educator
Schulz, Charles Monroe cartoonist
Schumacher, Harry Richard lawyer
Schumacher, Robert Denison banker
Schupak, Leslie Allen public relations company executive
Schur, Jeffrey advertising executive
Schuur, Robert George lawyer
Schwab, Frank, Jr. management consultant
Schwab, George David social science educator
Schwab, Terrance Walter lawyer
Schwarcz, Steven Lance lawyer
Schwartz, Allen G. judge, lawyer
Schwartz, Anna Jacobson economic historian
Schwartz, Bernard L. electronics company executive
Schwartz, Daniel Bennett artist
Schwartz, Eugene M. art collector, patron
Schwartz, Felice N. social activist, educator
Schwartz, Herbert Frederick lawyer
Schwartz, Irving Leon physician, scientist, educator
Schwartz, Jack Theodore retired publisher
Schwartz, Jacob T. computer scientist
Schwartz, Marvin lawyer
Schwartz, Mischa electrical engineering educator
Schwartz, Paul advertising creative director
Schwartz, R. Malcolm management consultant
Schwartz, Renee Gerstler lawyer
Schwartz, Robert George retired insurance company executive
Schwartz, Roselind Shirley Grant podiatrist
Schwartz, Stephen Lawrence composer, lyricist
Schwartz, William lawyer
Schwartzman, David economist, educator
Schwarz, Gerard Ralph conductor, musician
Schwarz, H. Marshall trust company executive
Schwarz, Melvin A. lawyer
Schwarz, Ralph Jacques university dean
Schwarzkopf, H. Norman retired army officer, engineer
Schwarzman, Stephen Allen investment banker
Schwed, Peter author, retired editor and publisher
Schwerin, Warren Lyons real estate developer
Schwimmer, David physician, educator
Schwind, Michael Angelo law educator
†Scieszka, Jon children's author
†Sciulli, Frank physicist, educator
Scofield, John jazz guitarist
Scopaz, John Matthew banker
Scott, Mimi Koblenz psychotherapist
Scott, Willard Herman radio and television performer
Scott, William Clement, III entertainment industry executive
Scotto, Renata soprano
†Scowcroft, John Arthur portfolio manager
Scribner, Charles, III publisher, art historian, lecturer
Scribner, Richard Orestes lawyer, securities firm executive
Scullion, Tsugiko Yamagami non-profit organization executive
Scully, Sean Paul artist
†Scutt, Der architect
Seadler, Stephen Edward business and computer consultant, social scientist
Seaman, Alfred Barrett journalist
Seaman, Alfred Jarvis retired advertising agency executive
Seaman, Barbara (Ann Rosner) author
Seaman, Robert Lee lawyer
Seaman, William Bernard physician, radiology educator
Searle, Ronald artist
Seaver, Tom (George Thomas Seaver) former professional baseball player
Secunda, Arthur (Holland Secunda) artist
Secunda, Don Elliott lawyer, realtor
Secunda, Eugene marketing communications executive, educator
Sedaka, Neil singer, songwriter
Sederbaum, Arthur David lawyer
Sedlin, Elias David physician, orthopedic researcher, educator
Seegal, Herbert Leonard department store executive
Seeger, Pete songwriter
Seely, Robert Daniel physician, medical educator
Seessel, Thomas Vining civic organization executive
Seevers, Gary Leonard investment banker
Seff, Leslie S. securities trader
Segal, George actor
Segal, George sculptor
Segal, Joel Michael advertising executive
Segal, Jonathan Bruce editor
Segal, Lore writer
Segal, Martin Eli retired actuarial and consulting company executive
Segal, Sheldon Jerome biologist, educator, foundation administrator
Segalas, Hercules Anthony investment banker
Segall, Harold Abraham lawyer
Seidelman, Susan film director
Seiden, Henry (Hank Seiden) advertising executive
Seiden, Steven Arnold executive search consultant
†Seidler, Lee J. investment banker
Seidler, Norman Howard lawyer
Seidman, Herta Lande international trade and information company executive
Seidman, Samuel Nathan investment banker, economist
Seifert, Thomas Lloyd lawyer
Seigel, Jerrold Edward historian, writer
Seigel, Stuart Evan lawyer
Seitz, Frederick university president emeritus
Selby, Cecily Cannan dean, educator, scientist
Selig, Karl-Ludwig language and literature educator
Seliger, Charles artist
†Seliger, Mark Alan photographer
Seligman, Daniel editor
Seligson, Carl H. investment banker
Selkowitz, Arthur advertising agency executive
Sellers, Peter Hoadley mathematician
Sells, Harold E. retail company executive
Seltzer, Leo filmmaker, educator, lecturer
Seltzer, Richard C. lawyer
Seltzer, William statistician, international organization director
Selver, Paul Darryl lawyer
Semmel, Bernard historian, educator
Sendak, Maurice Bernard writer, illustrator
Sendax, Victor Irven dentist, educator, dental implant researcher
Sendrovic, Israel bank executive
Senior, Enrique Francisco investment banker
Senn, Laurence Vaughn, Jr. lawyer
Sennett, Richard sociology educator
Senzel, Martin Lee lawyer
Seraphine, Danny Peter drummer
Serbaroli, Francis J. lawyer, educator, writer
Serkin, Peter pianist
Serota, Susan Perlstadt lawyer
Serra, Richard sculptor
Seth, Vikram writer
Setrakian, Berge lawyer
†Settipani, Frank G. news correspondent
Settle, Mary Lee author
Settle, William Sydnor lawyer
Severs, Charles A., III lawyer
Seward, George Chester lawyer
Sexton, John Edward lawyer, educator
Sexton, Richard lawyer, diversified manufacturing company executive
†Seymore, James W., Jr. magazine editor
Shaffer, David psychiatrist
Shaffer, Paul musician, bandleader
Shaffer, Peter Levin playwright
Shaffer, Russell K. advertising agency executive
†Shaine, Theodore Harris advertising executive
Shair, David Ira human resources executive
Shamask, Ronaldus fashion designer
Shane, Harold David mathematics educator, consultant
Shane, Rita opera singer
Shange, Ntozake playwright, poet
Shanks, Eugene B., Jr. banker
Shanman, James Alan lawyer
Shapiro, Babe artist
Shapiro, George M. lawyer
Shapiro, Harvey poet
Shapiro, Howard Alan lawyer
Shapiro, Isaac lawyer
Shapiro, Ivan lawyer
Shapiro, Jerome Gerson lawyer
Shapiro, Joel Elias artist
Shapiro, Judith R. anthropology educator, academic administrator
Shapiro, Mark Lawrence investment banker
Shapiro, Marvin Lincoln communications company executive
Shapiro, Murray structural engineer
Shapiro, Robert Frank investment banking company executive
Shapiro, Theodore psychiatrist, educator
Shapley, Robert Martin neurophysiology educator
Shapoff, Stephen H. financial executive
Sharbel, Jean M. editor
Sharpe, Jean Elizabeth lawyer
Shatzkin, Leonard publishing consultant
Shaughnessy, James Michael lawyer
Shaw, Alan Roger financial executive, educator
Shaw, (Francis) Harold performing arts administrator
Shaw, (George) Kendall artist, educator
†Shaw, L. Edward, Jr. lawyer
†Shaw, Ray financial publishing company executive
Shawn, Wallace playwright, actor
†Shaykin, Leonard P. investor
Shays, Rona Joyce lawyer
Shea, Dion Warren Joseph educational association executive, physicist
Shea, Edward Emmett lawyer, educator, author
Shea, James William lawyer
†Shear, Matthew Joel publishing executive
Sheehan, Robert W. lawyer
Sheehan, Susan writer
Sheehy, Eugene Paul retired librarian, author
Sheets, Michael Jay consumer products company executive
Shelanski, Michael L. cell biologist, educator
Shelby, Jerome lawyer
Sheldon, Eleanor Harriet Bernert sociologist
Sheldon, Sidney author
Shelley, Carole Augusta actress
Shellman, Eddie J. ballet dancer, teacher, choreographer
Shen, Theodore Ping investment banker
Shenker, Joseph college administrator
Shepard, Elaine Elizabeth writer, lecturer
Shepard, Robert M. lawyer, investment banker, engineer
Shepard, Stephen Benjamin journalist, magazine editor
Sheppard, William Stevens investment banker
Sherak, Thomas Mitchell motion picture company executive
Sherman, Cindy artist
Sherman, Eugene Jay marketing executive, economist
Sherman, Jeffrey Barry retail executive
Sherman, Norman Mark advertising agency executive
Sherman, Randolph S. lawyer
Sherman, Saul Lawrence lawyer, government official
Shern, Stephanie Marie accountant
†Sherr, Lynn Beth TV news correspondent
Sherry, George Leon political science educator
Sherva, Dennis G. investment company executive
Shestack, Melvin Bernard editor, author, filmmaker, television producer
Shields, James Joseph, Jr. educator, educational administrator, author
Shields, Virginia advertising executive
Shientag, Florence Perlow lawyer
Shikler, Aaron artist
Shimer, Zachary lawyer
Shineman, Edward William, Jr. retired pharmaceutical executive
Shinn, George Latimer investment banker, consultant, educator
Shinn, Richard Randolph former insurance executive, former stock exchange executive
Shinnar, Reuel chemical engineering educator, industrial consultant
Shipley, Walter Vincent banker
Shnayerson, Robert Beahan editor
Shore, Stephen photographer
Short, Robert Waltrip (Bobby Short) entertainer, author
Shorter, James Russell, Jr. lawyer
Shortz, Will puzzle editor
Shoss, Cynthia Renée lawyer
Shostakovich, Maxim Dmitriyevich symphonic conductor
Shriver, Donald Woods, Jr. theology educator
†Shriver, Maria Owings news correspondent
Shuff, Lily artist, wood engraver
Shuker, Gregory Brown publishing and production company executive
Shulevitz, Uri author, illustrator
Shull, Richard Bruce actor
Shuman, Stanley S. investment banker
Shupack, Paul Martin law educator
Shur, Walter retired insurance company executive
Sidamon-Eristoff, Anne Phipps museum official
Sidamon-Eristoff, Constantine lawyer
Sidney, Sylvia (Sophia Kossow) actress
†Sidrane, Michelle Diana publishing executive
Siebert, Muriel brokerage house executive,former state banking official
Siegal, Allan Marshall newspaper editor
Siegel, Alan Michael communications and design consultant
Siegel, Charles lawyer, investment banking and brokerage executive
Siegel, Jeffrey Norton lawyer
Siegel, Joel Steven television news correspondent
Siegel, Marc Monroe television and film producer, writer, director
Siegel, Martin Jay lawyer, investment advisor
Siegel, Marvin newspaper editor
Siegel, Morton Kallos religious organization administrator, educational administrator
Siegel, Stanley lawyer, educator
Siegler, Thomas Edmund investment banking executive
Siekevitz, Philip biology educator
Siemer, Fred Harold securities analyst
Siffert, Robert Spencer orthopedic surgeon
†Sifton, Elisabeth book publisher
Siguler, George William financial services executive
Silberberg, Richard Howard lawyer
Silberman, Charles Eliot magazine editor, author
Silberman, H. Lee public relations executive
Silberman, James Henry editor, publisher
Silberman, John Alan lawyer
Silk, Leonard Solomon economist, columnist, editor
Silkenat, James Robert lawyer
Silleck, Harry Garrison lawyer
Sills, Beverly (Mrs. Peter B. Greenough) opera company director, coloratura soprano
Silver, Joan Micklin film director, screenwriter
Silver, Morris economist, educator
Silver, Paul architect
Silver, Richard Tobias physician, educator
Silver, Ron actor, director
†Silver, Sheldon lawyer, state legislator
Silverberg, Michael Joel lawyer
Silverman, Arthur Charles lawyer
Silverman, Burton Philip artist
Silverman, Henry Richard diversified business executive, lawyer
Silverman, Jeffrey Stuart manufacturing executive
Silverman, Kenneth Eugene English educator, writer
Silverman, Marylin A. advertising agency executive
Silverman, Moses lawyer
Silverman, Samuel Joshua lawyer
Silverman, Stephen M. journalist, author, television scriptwriter
Silvers, Eileen S. lawyer
Silvers, Robert Benjamin editor
†Silvers, Sally choreographer, performing company executive
Silverstein, Howard Alan investment banker
Silverstein, Samuel Charles cellular biology and physiology educator, researcher
Silverstein, Shelby (Shel Silverstein) author, cartoonist, composer, folksinger
Sim, Craig Stephen investment banker
Simmons, Charles author
†Simmons, Dan science fiction writer
Simmons, Gene musician
Simmons, Hardwick investment banker
Simmons, J. Gerald management consultant
Simmons, John Derek investment banker
Simmons, Russell recording industry executive
Simon, Eric Jacob neurochemist, educator
Simon, Jacqueline Albert political scientist, writer
Simon, Joanna singer
Simon, John Ivan film and drama critic
Simon, Neil playwright, television writer
Simon, Robert G. lawyer
Simon, Ronald Charles curator
Simone, Joseph R. lawyer
Simons, Albert, III lawyer
Simonson, Lee Stuart broadcast company executive
Simpson, Adele costume designer
Sinclair, Daisy advertising executive, casting director
Singer, Arthur Louis, Jr. foundation executive
Singer, Eleanor sociologist, editor
Singer-Magdoff, Laura Joan Silver (Mrs. Samuel Magdoff) psychotherapist
†Singerman, Martin newspaper publishing executive
Singleton, Donald Edward journalist
Sinsheimer, Warren Jack lawyer
Siphron, Joseph Rider lawyer
Sirna, Anthony Alfred, III investment company executive
Sirowitz, Leonard advertising agency executive
†Sis, Peter illustrator, children's book author, artist, filmmaker
Sischy, Ingrid Barbara magazine editor, art critic
Sisk, Robert Joseph lawyer
†Siskind, Arthur lawyer, director
Siskind, Donald Henry lawyer
Sitrick, James Baker lawyer
Sive, David lawyer
Skigen, Patricia Sue lawyer
Skillin, Edward Simeon magazine publisher
†Skinner, Peter Graeme publishing executive, lawyer
Skirnick, Robert Andrew lawyer
Sklaren, Cary Stewart lawyer
†Sklaver, David R. advertising executive
†Skollar, Robert Alan advertising executive
Skupinski, Bogdan Kazimierz artist
Skwiersky, Paul accountant
†Sky, Alison artist, designer
Slade, Bernard playwright
Slain, John Joseph legal educator
†Slater, Don advertising executive, creative director
Slater, Joseph Elliott educational institute administrator
Slavin, Arlene artist
Slavin, Neal photographer
Sleigh, Sylvia artist, educator
†Slomanson, Lloyd H. architect, musician
Slonaker, Norman Dale lawyer
Sloves, Marvin advertising agency executive
Slusser, William Peter investment banker
Slutsky, Lorie Ann foundation executive
Small, George LeRoy geographer, educator
Small, Jeffrey lawyer, law educator
Small, Jonathan Andrew lawyer
Smalley, David Vincent lawyer
Smart, L(ouis) Edwin, Jr. lawyer, business executive
Smethurst, E(dward) William, Jr. brokerage house executive
Smit, Jacobus Wilhelmus history educator
Smith, Alexander John Court insurance executive
Smith, Anna Deavere actress, playwright
†Smith, Anna Nicole model
Smith, Bradley Youle lawyer
Smith, Charles Buchanan lawyer
Smith, Clarence O'Farrell publishing company executive
Smith, Corlies Morgan publishing executive
Smith, Datus Clifford, Jr. former foundation executive
†Smith, Derek Armand publishing company executive
Smith, Edward Paul, Jr. lawyer
Smith, G. E. Kidder architect, author
Smith, George S., Jr. communications financial executive
†Smith, Gordon H. civil engineer
Smith, Guy Lincoln, IV strategic communications company executive
†Smith, H. C. Bowen investment banker
Smith, J. Kellum, Jr. foundation executive, lawyer
Smith, James Oscar (Jimmy Smith) jazz organist
Smith, John Matthew insurance company executive
Smith, Joseph Phelan film company executive
Smith, Kathleen Tener bank executive
Smith, Leon Polk artist
Smith, Lewis Motter, Jr. advertising and direct marketing executive
Smith, Liz (Mary Elizabeth Smith) newspaper columnist, broadcast journalist
Smith, Lowell dancer
Smith, Malcolm Bernard investment company executive
Smith, Malcolm Sommerville bass
Smith, Martin Jay advertising and marketing executive
†Smith, Murray Livingstone advertising executive
Smith, Norman Obed physical chemist, educator
Smith, Paul Thomas financial services company executive
Smith, Peter Bennett banker
Smith, Peter Lawrence investment banker, lawyer
Smith, Phillips Guy banker
Smith, Pierce Reiland stock brokerage, investment banking executive
Smith, R. Evan lawyer
†Smith, R. Jeffery grain company executive
Smith, Richard Anthony investment banker
Smith, Richard Mills editor in chief, magazine executive
Smith, Robert Everett lawyer
Smith, Robert Kimmel author
Smith, Shirley artist
†Smith, Steven James insurance company executive
Smith, Stuart A. lawyer
Smith, Vincent DaCosta artist
Smith, Vincent Milton lawyer
Smith, William Jay author
Smith, Winthrop Hiram, Jr. financial services executive
†Smith-Miller, Henry Houck architect
Smolinski, Edward Albert holding company executive, lawyer, accountant, deacon
Smotrich, David Isadore architect
Smuin, Michael choreographer, director, dancer
Snibbe, Richard W. architect
Snitow, Charles lawyer
Snoddon, Larry E. public relations executive
Snyder, Richard Elliott publishing company executive
†Sobel, Shepard Michael artistic director
Soden, Paul Anthony lawyer
Soffer, Sasson artist, sculptor
Softness, John public relations executive
Sohmer, Bernard mathematics educator, administrator
Soika, Helmut Emil retirement plan administrator
Solar, Richard Leon banker
†Soldatos, Paul W. holding company executive
†Solem, Karen Lynn publishing executive
Solender, Sanford social worker
†Solender, Stephen David philanthropic organization executive
†Solheim, James Edward church executive, journalist
Solinger, David Morris lawyer
Solman, Joseph artist
Solomon, Howard pharmaceutical company executive
Solomon, Joseph lawyer
Solomon, Maynard Elliott music historian, former recording company executive
Solomon, Zachary Leon apparel manufacturing company executive
Solomons, Gus, Jr. (Gustave Martinez) choreographer, dancer, writer
Solov, Zachary choreographer, ballet artist
Solzhenitsyn, Aleksandr Isayevich author
Somasundaran, Ponisseril surface and colloid engineering, applied science educator
Somers, John Arthur insurance company executive
Sonenberg, Martin biochemistry educator, physician
Songster, John Hugh legal administrator
Sonneman, Eve artist
Sonnenberg, Ben playwright, poet, editor
Sontag, Susan film and theatre director
Sorel, Claudette Marguerite pianist
Soren, Tabitha L. television newscaster, writer
Sorensen, Burton Erhard investment banker
Sorensen, Gillian Martin United Nations official
Sorensen, Robert C. marketing executive, educator
Sorensen, Theodore Chaikin lawyer, former special counsel to President of U.S.
Sorkin, Laurence Truman lawyer
Soros, George fund management executive
Sorrel, William Edwin psychiatrist, educator, psychoanalyst
Sorter, George Hans accounting and law educator, consultant
Soter, George Nicholas advertising executive
Soto, Jock dancer
Sotomayor, Sonia federal judge
Souham, Gérard communications executive
Soule, Gardner Bosworth author
Southall, Ivan Francis author
Sovern, Michael Ira law educator
Soviero, Diana Barbara soprano
Soyer, David cellist, music educator
Soyster, Margaret Blair lawyer
Spacey, Kevin actor
Spaeh, Winfried Heinrich banker
Spangler, Arnold Eugene investment banker
Spar, Edward Joel demographer
Sparano, Vincent Thomas editor
Spatt, Robert Edward lawyer
Spear, Harvey M. lawyer
Speciale, Richard bank executive
Spector, Abraham ophthalmic biochemist, educator, laboratory administrator

Spector, Johanna Lichtenberg ethnomusicologist, former educator
Speiran, Edward Patrick lawyer
Spelker, Arnold William banker
Spence, James Robert, Jr. television sports executive
Spencer, Henry Benning insurance industry investment advisor
†Spencer, LaVyrle writer
Spencer, Scott novelist
Sperakis, Nicholas George artist
Sperling, Allan George lawyer
Speth, James Gustave United Nations executive, lawyer
Spiegel, Arthur Henry, III managing director, president
Spiegel, Herbert psychiatrist, educator
Spiegelman, Art author, cartoonist
Spielvogel, Carl international marketing executive
Spielvogel, Sidney Meyer investment banker
Spinella, Stephen actor
Spinks, Michael professional boxer
Spirn, Michele Sobel communications professional, writer
Spivack, Gordon Bernard lawyer, lecturer
†Spivak, Helayne advertising agency executive
Spizzirri, Richard Dominic lawyer
Spoto, Donald writer, educator
Sprague, Peter Julian semiconductor company executive, lecturer
Sprecher, Baron William Gunther pianist, composer, conductor, diplomat
Spring, Michael editor, writer
Springer, John Shipman public relations executive
Springsteen, Bruce singer, songwriter, guitarist
Sprinson, David Benjamin biochemistry educator
Sprizzo, John Emilio federal judge
†Spruch, Larry physicist, educator
†Squire, Walter Charles lawyer
†Srere, Linda Jean advertising executive
Stack, Edward William business management and foundation executive
Stade, George Gustav humanities educator
Stafford, John Rogers pharmaceutical and household products company executive
†Staheli, Donald L. grain company executive
Stahl, Frank Ludwig civil engineer
Stahl, Lesley R. journalist
Staley, Delbert C. telecommunications executive
Stamas, Stephen investment executive
Stamos, Theodoros artist
Stanger, Abraham M. lawyer
Stanger, Ila writer, editor
Staniar, Burton B. entertainment company executive
Stanley, Bob artist
Stanton, Alexander public relations executive
Stanton, Edward M. public relations company executive
Stanton, Frank communications executive
Stanton, Ronald P. export company executive
Stapp, Olivia Brewer opera singer
Stark, Richard Boies surgeon
Starn, Douglas artist, photographer
Starn, Mike P. artist, photographer
Starr, Martin Kenneth management educator
†Stasior, William F. engineering company executive
Steedman, Doria Lynne Silberberg advertising agency executive
Steegmuller, Francis author
Steel, Danielle Fernande author
Steere, William Campbell, Jr. pharmaceutical company executive
Stefanelli, Joseph James (Joe Stefanelli) artist
Steffen, Christopher J. bank executive
Steffens, John Laundon brokerage house executive
Steiger, Paul Ernest newspaper editor, journalist
Stein, Bennett Mueller neurosurgeon
Stein, Bernard stockbroker
Stein, Carl architect
Stein, David Fred investment executive
Stein, Gilbert professional hockey executive
Stein, Howard mutual fund executive
Stein, Howard S. banker
Stein, Joseph playwright
†Stein, Martin Donald architect
Stein, Marvin psychiatrist, educator
Stein, Stephen William lawyer
Steinberg, Howard E. lawyer, holding company executive
Steinberg, Joseph Saul investment company executive
Steinberg, Leo art historian, educator
Steinberg, Robert M. holding company executive
Steinberg, Saul artist
Steinberg, Saul Phillip holding company executive
Steinem, Gloria writer, editor, lecturer
Steiner, Jeffrey Josef industrial manufacturing company executive
Steiner, Lee Nathan lawyer
Steinfeld, Thomas Albert publisher
Steinfels, Margaret O'Brien editor
Steinmetz, Richard Bird, Jr. holding company executive, lawyer
Steir, Pat Iris artist
Stella, Frank Philip artist
Stenzel, Kurt Hodgson physician, nephrologist, educator
Stephens, Gary Ralph American literature and journalism educator
Stephens, Lester John, Jr. corporate controller
Stephens, Olin James, II naval architect, yacht designer
Stephenson, Alan Clements lawyer
Stergios, Peter Doe lawyer
†Sterling, David M. graphic designer
Sterling, Robert Lee, Jr. investment company executive
Stern, David Joel basketball association executive
Stern, Fritz Richard historian, educator
Stern, Geoffrey Adlai investment banker
Stern, Howard Allan radio disc jockey, television show host
Stern, Isaac violinist
Stern, James Andrew investment banker
Stern, Joseph A. lawyer
†Stern, Leonard Norman pet supply manufacturing company executive
Stern, Leslie Warren management consultant
Stern, Lewis Arthur lawyer
Stern, Madeleine Bettina rare books dealer, author
Stern, Marvin psychiatrist, educator
†Stern, Robert Arthur Morton architect, educator
Stern, Robert D. publishing executive
Stern, Roslyne Paige magazine publisher
Sternglass, Lila M. advertising agency executive
Sternman, Joel W. lawyer
Steuer, Richard Marc lawyer
Stevens, Art public relations executive
Stevens, Martin English educator
Stevens, Shane novelist
Stevenson, Justin Jason, III lawyer
Stevenson, William Henri author
Stever, Donald Winfred lawyer
Stewart, Charles Edward, Jr. federal judge
Stewart, Charles Evan lawyer
Stewart, Duncan James lawyer
Stewart, Gordon Curran insurance information association executive
Stewart, James B. journalist
Stewart, James M. merchant banker
Stewart, James Montgomery banker
Stewart, Jeff advertising agency executive
Stewart, Kirk T. public relations executive
Stewart, Richard Burleson lawyer, educator
Steyer, Roy Henry retired lawyer
Stiebel, Gerald Gustave art dealer
Stiefler, Jeffrey E. financial services executive
Stiles, Thomas Beveridge, II investment banking executive
Still, William Clark, Jr. chemistry educator
Stillman, Calvin Whitney agricultural and environment educator
Stills, Stephen musician, vocalist, composer
Stilwell, Richard Dale baritone
Stimmel, Barry cardiologist, internist, educator, university dean
†Stine, R(obert) L(awrence) children's book author
Stocker, Jule E(lias) lawyer
Stockman, David Allen former federal official, congressman, financier
Stoddard, George Earl investment company financial executive
Stoddard, Laurence Ralph, Jr. advertising executive
Stoddart, George Anderson oil service company executive
Stoll, Neal Richard lawyer
†Stolper, Pinchas Aryeh religious organization executive, rabbi
Stoltzman, Richard Leslie clarinetist
Stone, David Kendall financial executive
Stone, David Philip lawyer
Stone, Joseph advertising agency executive
Stone, Merrill Brent lawyer
Stone, Peter playwright, scenarist
Stone, Robert Anthony author
Stookey, John Hoyt chemical company executive
Storette, Ronald Frank lawyer
Stork, Gilbert (Josse) chemistry educator, investigator
Storke, William Frederick Joseph film producer
Storr, Robert curator painting and sculpture, artist, writer
†Stossel, John news analyst
Stovall, Robert H(enry) money management company executive
Stowers, Carlton Eugene writer
†Strachan, William Bruce publisher, editor
Stram, Hank Louis former professional football coach, television and radio commentator
Strand, Curt Robert hotel executive
Strand, Mark poet
Strasfogel, Ian opera company director
Stratas, Teresa (Anastasia Strataki) opera singer
Straton, John Charles, Jr. investment banker
Stratton, Walter Love lawyer
Straub, Chester John lawyer
Strauber, Donald I. lawyer
Straus, Alan Gordon lawyer
Straus, Donald Blun retired company executive
Straus, Irving Lehman public relations executive
Straus, Kenneth Hollister former retail store executive
Straus, Oscar S., II foundation executive
Straus, Roger W., Jr. publishing company executive
Straus, Roger W, III book publishing executive, photographer
Strauss, Audrey lawyer
†Strauss, Harold L. advertising executive
Strauss, Peter L(ester) law educator
Strear, Joseph D. public relations executive
Strelzer, Martin religious organization administrator
Stretton, Ross ballet dancer
Strickon, Harvey Alan lawyer
Stringer, Howard television executive
Stroke, Hinko Henry physicist, educator
Strom, Milton Gary lawyer
Strong, Robert S. banker
Strong, William L., III investment executive
Stroock, Mark Edwin, II public relations company executive
Strossen, Nadine law educator, human rights activist
Strum, Jay Gerson lawyer
Struminger, Laura Sharon academic administrator
Strupp, David John lawyer
Struve, Guy Miller lawyer
Stuart, Carole publishing executive
Stuart, John McHugh, Jr. public relations consultant, retired foreign service officer
Stuart, Lyle publishing company executive
Sturges, John Siebrand management consultant
Styne, Jule composer, producer
Subak-Sharpe, Gerald Emil electrical engineer, educator
Sugarman, George artist
Sugarman, Irwin J. lawyer
Sugarman, Robert Gary lawyer
Sugihara, Kenzi publishing executive
†Sugimoto, Yoshihisa import/export company executive
Sui, Anna fashion designer
Sulcer, Frederick Durham advertising executive
Sulger, Francis Xavier lawyer
Sulimirski, Witold Stanislaw banker
Sullivan, Anne Elizabeth publishing executive
Sullivan, Eugene John Joseph manufacturing company executive
Sullivan, Joseph Peter insurance broker
Sullivan, Thomas John communications company executive
Sullivan, Walter Seager editor, author
Sultan, Donald Keith artist, printmaker
Sulzberger, Arthur Ochs newspaper executive
Sulzberger, Arthur Ochs, Jr. newspaper publisher
Summerall, Pat (George Allan Summerall) sportscaster
Summers, Andy (Andrew James Somers) popular musician
Surrey, Milt artist
Suskind, Dennis A. investment banker
Susser, Mervyn Wilfred epidemiologist, educator
Sussman, Alexander Ralph lawyer
Sussman, Gerald publishing company executive
†Sussman, Judith Helen public relations company executive
Sussman, Leonard Richard foundation executive
Sutherland, William Paul advertising executive
Sutton, Kelso Furbush publishing executive
Sutton, Pat Lipsky artist, educator
Sutton-Straus, Joan M. journalist
†Suzuki, Ryosuke securities firm executive
Svenson, Charles Oscar investment banker
Swados, Elizabeth A. composer, director, writer
Swain, Robert artist
Swanke, Albert Homer architect
Swann, Brian writer, humanities educator
Swanzey, Robert Joseph data processing executive
Sweeney, Thomas Joseph, Jr. lawyer
Sweet, Robert Workman federal judge
Sweezy, Paul Marlor editor, publisher
Swenson, Eric Pierson publishing company executive
Swid, Stephen Claar business executive
Swift, Isabel Davidson editorial director
Swift, John Francis health care advertising company executive
Swing, John Temple lawyer, association executive
Symmers, William Garth international maritime lawyer
Syron, Richard Francis financial services executive, economist
Szabad, George Michael lawyer, former mayor
Szer, Wlodzimierz biochemist, educator
Taber, Carol A. magazine publisher
Tabler, William Benjamin architect
Taddei, Giuseppe baritone
Tafel, Edgar architect
Tagliabue, Paul John national football league commissioner
Tagliaferri, Lee Gene investment banker
Tagliaferro, John Anthony broadcasting company executive
†Taguchi, Tadao electronics company executive
Talbot, Phillips Asian affairs specialist
†Talcott, Jane Victoria advertising executive
Talese, Gay writer
Talese, Nan Ahearn publishing company executive
Tallackson, Jeffrey Stephen lawyer
Talley, Truman Macdonald publisher
Tallmer, Margot psychologist, psychoanalyst, gerontologist
Talmi, Yoav conductor, composer
Tamm, Igor biomedical scientist, educator
Taney, J. Charles advertising agency executive
Tannenbaum, Bernice Salpeter religious organization executive
Tanner, Harold investment banker
Tanselle, George Thomas English language educator, foundation executive
†Tansky, Burton department store executive
Tapella, Gary Louis manufacturing company executive
Tapley, Donald Fraser university official, physician, educator
Taran, Leonardo classicist, educator
Tarantino, Dominic A. accounting firm executive
Targ, William editor, writer
Tarnopol, Michael L. bank executive
Tarter, Fred Barry advertising executive
†Taschetti, Vincent S. advertising executive
Tash, Martin Elias publishing company executive
Tauber, Ronald Steven investment banker
Tavel, Mark Kivey money management company executive, economist
†Tavon, Mary E. public relations executive
Taylor, Cecil Percival pianist, composer, educator
Taylor, Clyde Calvin, Jr. literary agent
Taylor, Elizabeth Rosemond actress
Taylor, Humphrey John Fausitt information services executive
Taylor, John Chestnut, III lawyer
Taylor, Lance Jerome economics educator
†Taylor, Nicole Renée model
Taylor, Paul choreographer
Taylor, Regina actress
Taylor, Richard Trelore retired lawyer
Taylor, Richard William investment banker, securities broker
Taylor, Sherril Wightman broadcasting company executive
Taylor, Telford lawyer, educator
Tcherkassky, Marianna Alexsavena ballerina
Teclaff, Ludwik Andrzej law educator, consultant, author, lawyer
Tehan, John Bashir lawyer
Teich, Malvin Carl electrical engineering educator
Teiman, Richard B. lawyer
†Teitelbaum, William Allen investment banker
Te Kanawa, Kiri opera and concert singer
Tellefsen, Gerald management consultant
Temple, Wick journalist
Tendler, David international trade company executive
Tengi, Frank R. lawyer, insurance company executive
Tenney, Charles Henry federal judge
Tenney, Dudley Bradstreet lawyer
Tepper, Lynn Marsha gerontology educator
Teran, Timothy Eric Alba marketing professional
Terborgh, Bert dancer
Ternes, Alan Paul editor
Terrell, J. Anthony lawyer
Terry, F. Davis, Jr. investment company executive
Terry, Frederick Arthur, Jr. lawyer
Terry, James Joseph, Jr. lawyer
Terry, Megan playwright, performer , photographer
Tesich, Steve author
Testa, Michael Harold lawyer
Tetley, Glen choreographer
Tetzeli, Frederick Edward banker
Teubner, Ferdinand Cary, Jr. publishing company executive
Thackeray, Jonathan E. lawyer
Thal, Steven Henry lawyer
Thalacker, Arbie Robert lawyer
Tharp, Twyla dancer, choreographer
Themelis, Nickolas John metallurgical engineering educator
Thoman, Mark lawyer
Thomas, Brooks publishing company executive
Thomas, David Hurst archaeologist
Thomas, Debi (Debra J. Thomas) ice skater
Thomas, John Cox, Jr. publisher
Thomas, Michael Tilson symphony conductor
Thomas, Richard actor
Thomas, Robert Morton, Jr. lawyer
Thomas, Roger Warren lawyer
Thompson, David Duvall physician
Thompson, Hunter Stockton author, political analyst, journalist
Thompson, Martin Christian news service executive
Thompson, Robert L., Jr. lawyer
Thompson, William Cannon, Jr. advertising agency executive
Thompson, William Irwin humanities educator, author
Thomson, Gerald Edmund physician, educator
Thomson, William Barry retail company executive
Thorne, Francis composer
Thornton, John Vincent lawyer, educator
Thoyer, Judith Reinhardt lawyer
Thrall, Donald Stuart artist
Thurman, Ralph Holloway health care company executive
Tierney, Paul E., Jr. food service executive
Tietjen, John Henry biology and oceanography educator, consultant
Tigay, Alan Merrill editor
Tilberis, Elizabeth editor in chief
Tillinghast, David Rollhaus lawyer
Tillis, Pam country singer, songwriter
Tilson, Dorothy Ruth word processing executive
Tilton, James Floyd theatrical designer, art director
Timbers, William Homer federal judge
Timothy, Raymond Joseph television executive
Timpane, Philip Michael college administrator
Tipton, Jennifer lighting designer
Tirakis, Judith Angelina financial company executive
Tisch, Laurence Alan broadcast corporation executive
Tisch, Preston Robert finance executive
Tishman, Robert V. real estate and construction company executive
Tison-Braun, Micheline Lucie French language educator
Tizzio, Thomas Ralph brokerage executive
†Tober, Barbara D. (Mrs. Donald Gibbs Tober) editor
Tobias, Julius sculptor
Tocklin, Adrian Martha insurance company executive, lawyer
Todd, David Fenton Michie architect
Todd, Ronald Gary lawyer
Toepke, Utz Peter lawyer
†Toff, Nancy Ellen book editor
Toffler, Alvin author
Toller, William Robert chemical and oil company executive
Tomkins, Calvin writer
Tomlinson, James Francis retired news agency executive
Tondel, Lawrence Chapman lawyer
Toote, Gloria E. A. developer, lawyer, columnist
Topol, Robert Martin financial services executive, securities trader
†Torello, Judy S. corporate communications executive
Torre, Douglas Paul dermatologist
Torrence, (John) Richard administrator, special events producer
†Torres, Edwin state judge, writer
Tortorella, Albert James public relations executive, consultant
Tortoriello, Robert Laurence lawyer
Towbin, A(braham) Robert investment banker
Townley, Preston association executive, former dean
†Townsend, Charles H. publishing executive
Townsend, M. Wilbur manufacturing company executive
Townshend, Peter musician, composer, singer
Tozer, W. James, Jr. investment company executive
Tracey, Margaret dancer
Trachtenberg, Matthew J. bank holding company executive
†Tracy, David M. textile manufacturing company executive
†Tracy, Janet Ruth legal educator, librarian
Trager, William biology educator
Train, John investment counselor, writer, government official
Traina, Albert Salvatore publishing executive
Tramontine, John O. lawyer
Traub, J(oseph) F(rederick) computer scientist, educator
†Traub, Marvin Stuart department store executive
Traub, Richard Kenneth lawyer
Traum, Jerome S. lawyer
Treadway, James Curran investment company executive, lawyer, former government official
Tree, Michael violinist, violist, educator
†Treitler, Leo musicologist, educator
Trigere, Pauline fashion designer
Trillin, Calvin Marshall columnist
Tripodi, Louis Anthony advertising agency executive
Trost, J. Ronald lawyer
†Troubetzkoy, Alexis S. foundation administrator, educator
Trubin, John lawyer
Trueheart, Harry Parker, III lawyer
Trueman, Walter retired advertising agency executive
Truesdell, Wesley Edwin public relations and investor relations consultant
Truitt, Richard Hunt public relations agency executive
†Trygg, Steve Lennart advertising executive
†Tryhane, Gerald newspaper publishing executive
Trzetrzelewska, Basia musician, vocalist
Tscherny, George graphic designer
Tse, Stephen Yung Nien insurance executive
Tsoucalas, Nicholas federal judge
Tuck, Edward Hallam lawyer
Tucker, Alan David publisher
†Tucker, Marcia museum director, curator
†Tucker, Paul Thomas information systems executive
Tudryn, Joyce Marie professional society administrator
Tufts, David Albert, Jr. securities company executive
Tulchin, David Bruce lawyer
†Tulin, John Alexander mens accessory company executive
Tully, Daniel Patrick investment company executive
Tumminello, Stephen Charles consumer electronics manufacturing executive
Tune, Tommy (Thomas James Tune) musical theater director, dancer, choreographer, actor
Tung, Ko-Yung lawyer
Turino, Gerard Michael physician, medical scientist, educator
Turkel, Stanley hotel consultant, management executive
†Turlington, Christy model
Turnbaugh, Douglas Blair arts administration executive, author
Turner, Almon Richard art historian, educator
Turner, E. Deane lawyer
Turner, Hester Hill management consultant
Turner, Roderick L. retired consumer packaged products manufacturing company executive
†Turner, Stuart paper company executive
Turrentine, Stanley William musician
Turro, Nicholas John chemistry educator
Tuttleton, James Wesley English educator
Tutun, Edward H. retired retail executive
Twiname, John Dean minister, health care executive
†Tyler, David A. auction house executive

Tyler, Harold Russell, Jr. lawyer, former government official
†Tyler, Richard fashion designer
Tyson, Harry James investment banker
Tzimas, Nicholas Achilles orthopedic surgeon, educator
Ubell, Robert Neil editor, publisher, consultant, literary agent
Uchitelle, Louis journalist
Udcoff, George Joseph financial executive
Udell, Richard lawyer
Ufford, Charles Wilbur, Jr. lawyer
Uhry, Alfred Fox playwright
Ulanov, Barry author, educator
Ullman, Myron Edward, III retail executive
Ullmann, Liv actress
†Ullmark, Hans advertising agency executive
†Ulrich, Lars drummer
Ulrich, Max Marsh executive search consultant
Ulrich, Theodore Albert lawyer
Underberg, Mark Alan lawyer
Underhill, Jacob Berry, III retired insurance company executive
Underweiser, Irwin Philip mining company executive, lawyer
†Underwood, Joanna DeHaven environmental research and education organizations president
†Ungaro, Susan Kelliher magazine editor
Unger, Peter Kenneth philosophy educator
Unger, Ronald Lawrence lawyer
Updike, Helen Hill economist, investment manager, financial planner
Uppman, Theodor concert and opera singer, voice educator
Upright, Diane Warner auction house executive
Upshaw, Dawn soprano
Upson, Stuart Barnard advertising agency executive
Urdang, Alexandra book publishing executive
Uris, Leon author
Urkowitz, Michael banker
Urowsky, Richard J. lawyer
Urstadt, Charles Jordan real estate executive
Vai, Marjorie Theresa language educator, university administrator, author
Vale, Norman advertising executive
Valenstein, Suzanne Gebhart art historian
Valenti, Carl M. newspaper publisher
Valk, Elizabeth magazine publisher
†Valletta, Amber model
Van Brunt, Albert Daniel advertising agency executive
Van Campen, Stephen Bernard executive recruiter, consultant
Vance, Andrew Peter lawyer
Vance, Cyrus Roberts lawyer, former government official
van den Akker, Koos fashion designer
Van Dine, Vance investment banker
Vandross, Luther singer
Van Eysinga, Frans W. publisher
Van Gundy, Gregory Frank lawyer
Van Halen, Eddie guitarist, rock musician
van Hengel, Maarten banker
VanItallie, Theodore Bertus physician
Van Nostrand, Morris Abbott, Jr. publisher
†Van Sant, Peter Richard news correspondent
van Vogt, Alfred Elton author
Varet, Michael A. lawyer
†Vargas, Eduardo advertising executive
Varnedoe, John Kirk Train museum curator
Varney, Carleton Bates, Jr. interior designer, columnist, educator, author
Vascellaro, Frank John insurance company executive
Vass, Joan fashion designer
Vaughan, Edwin Darracott, Jr. urologist, surgeon
Vaughan, Samuel Snell editor, author
Vázquez, José Antonio education educator
Vecsey, George Spencer sports columnist
†Vedder, Eddie singer
Vega, Marylois Purdy journalist
Vega, Matias Alfonso lawyer
Velasquez, Jorge Luis, Jr. jockey
†Vendela model
Ventres, Romeo John manufacturing company executive
Venza, Jac broadcast executive
†Verbridge, Gerald religious organization administrator
Verdi, David Joseph broadcast news executive
Verdon, Gwen (Gwyneth Evelyn) actress, dancer, choreographer
Versace, Gianni fashion designer
Versfelt, David Scott lawyer
†Vestal, Jeanne Marie Goodspeed book publishing company executive
Vick, James Albert publishing executive, consultant
Vickrey, William Spencer economist, emeritus educator
Victor, A. Paul lawyer
Viener, John D. lawyer
Viermetz, Kurt F. banker
Vig, Vernon Edward lawyer
Vignelli, Massimo architecture and design executive
Vignone, Ronald John advertising agency executive
Vilcek, Jan Tomas medical educator
Violenus, Agnes A. school system administrator
Vitale, Alberto Aldo publishing company executive
†Vitale, Dick color commentator, sports writer
Vitt, Sam B. communications media services executive
Vittadini, Adrienne fashion designer
Vittorini, Carlo publishing company executive
Viviano, Sam Joseph illustrator
Vizard, Frank Joseph journalist
Voell, Richard Allen real estate services company executive
Vogel, Eugene L. lawyer
Vogel, Henry James biochemist, educator
Vogelman, Joseph Herbert scientific engineering company executive
Volckhausen, William Alexander lawyer, banker
Volk, Norman Hans financial executive
Volk, Stephen Richard lawyer
Volpe, Joseph opera company administrator
Volpe, Thomas J. advertising executive
Volpi, Walter Mark lawyer, diversified company executive
von der Heyden, Karl Ingolf Mueller manufacturing company executive
Von Fraunhofer-Kosinski, Katherina bank executive
von Furstenberg, Betsy actress, writer
Von Furstenberg, Diane Simone Michelle fashion designer
von Knorring, Henrik Johan publisher
von Mehren, Robert Brandt lawyer
Vonnegut, Kurt, Jr. writer
Von Ringelheim, Paul Helmut sculptor
Von Stade, Frederica mezzo-soprano
Voorsanger, Bartholomew architect
Vora, Ashok financial economist
Voultsos-Vourtzis, Pericles Count composer, conductor, educator, author, former honorary consul to Grenada
Vuilleumier, Francois curator
Wachner, Linda Joy apparel marketing and manufacturing executive
†Wachsman, Phyllis Geri advertising executive
Wachtel, David Edward magazine publisher
Wachtel, Eli investment banking executive
Wachtel, Harry H. lawyer, chain store executive
Wachtel, Norman Jay lawyer
Wada, Sadami (Chris) manufacturing executive
Waddell, Harry Lee editor, publisher
Wade, George Joseph lawyer
Wade, James O'Shea publisher
Wade, Nicholas Michael Landon journalist
Wadsworth, Charles William pianist
Wadsworth, Dyer Seymour lawyer
Wadsworth, Robert David advertising agency executive
Wager, Walter Herman author, communications director
Wagner, Alan Cyril television and film producer
Wagner, Christina Breuer publishing company executive
Wagner, Robin Samuel Anton stage and set designer
Wahlberg, Allen Henry construction executive
Wailand, George lawyer
Wainwright, Carroll Livingston, Jr. lawyer
Waks, Jay Warren lawyer
Waksman, Byron Halsted neuroimmunologist, experimental pathologist, educator, medical association administrator
Waksman, Ted Stewart lawyer
Wald, Bernard Joseph lawyer
Wald, Sylvia artist
†Waldon, Alton Ronald, Jr. state commissioner
Wales, Gwynne Huntington lawyer
Walke, David Michael public relations executive
Walker, Alice Malsenior author
Walker, Charles R., III lawyer
†Walker, Douglas Craig publisher
Walker, Edward S., Jr. diplomat
†Walker, Joan H. public relations executive
Walker, John Lockwood lawyer
Walker, John Mercer, Jr. federal judge
Walker, Kenneth Henry architect
Walker, Mark A. lawyer
Walker, Mort cartoonist
Walker, Sally Barbara retired glass company executive
Walker, Sandra mezzo-soprano
Walker, Wendy Joy ballet mistress
Walker, William Bond retired librarian
Walkowitz, Daniel J. historian, filmmaker, educator
Wallace, Christopher broadcast television correspondent
†Wallace, Edward Corbett lawyer
Wallace, Mike television interviewer and reporter
†Wallace, Robert F. dancer
†Wallace, Robert Fergus banker
Wallace, Robert James mathematics and science educator
Wallace, Thomas C(hristopher) editor, literary agent
†Wallace, Thomas J. magazine editor-in-chief
Wallace, Thomas Robert public relations executive
Wallace, Walter C. lawyer, government official
Wallach, Allan Henry former senior critic
Wallach, Eric Jean lawyer
Wallach, Ira writer
Wallance, Gregory J. lawyer
†Waller, Robert James writer
Walman, Jerome psychotherapist, publisher, consultant, critic
Walpin, Gerald lawyer
Walsh, Annmarie Hauck research firm executive
Walsh, Kevin A. lawyer
Walsh, Thomas Gerard actuary
Walter, Ingo economics educator
Walters, Barbara television journalist
Walters, Milton James investment banker
Walters, Raymond, Jr. newspaper editor, author
Walton, Anthony John (Tony Walton) theater and film designer, book illustrator
Walzer, Judith Borodovko university administrator, educator
Wanek, William Charles public relations executive
Wang, Arthur Woods publisher
†Wang, Charles Pei social service administrator
†Wang, Julie Caroline public relations executive
†Wang, Vera fashion designer
†Ward, Charlie professional basketball player
Ward, Geoffrey Champion author, editor
Ward, Robert Joseph federal judge
Warden, Jack actor
Warden, John L. lawyer
Wardwell, Allen art historian
Wareham, Raymond Noble investment banker
Waren, Stanley A. university administrator, theatre and arts center administrator, director
Warfield, Gerald Alexander composer, writer
Warhaftig, Solomon L. lawyer
Warner, Douglas Alexander, III banker
Warner, Edward Waide, Jr. lawyer
Warner, John Edward advertising executive
Warner, Peter David publishing executive
Warner, Rawleigh, Jr. oil company executive
Warren, Irwin Howard lawyer
Warren, William Bradford lawyer
Warren, William Clements lawyer, educator
Warsawer, Harold Newton real estate appraiser and consultant
Warshauer, Irene Conrad lawyer
Warshaw, Leon J(oseph) physician
Warwick, Dionne singer
Washburn, David Thacher lawyer
Washington, MaliVai professional tennis player
Washington, Shelley Lynne dancer
Wasser, Henry English educator, university administrator
Wasserman, Albert writer, director
Wasserman, Bert W. communications and publishing company executive
Wasserman, Dale playwright
Wasserman, Louis Robert physician, educator
†Wasserman, Marlie P(arker) publisher
Wasserstein, Bruce investment banker
Waters, Sylvia dance company artistic director
Watkins, Charles Booker, Jr. mechanical engineering educator
†Watkins, Stanley academic director
Watson, Albert MacKenzie photographer
†Watson, Anthony L. health facility executive
Watson, James Lopez federal judge
Watson, John King, Jr. lawyer
Watson, John Lawrence, III trade association executive
Watson, Solomon Brown, IV lawyer, business executive
Watt, Douglas (Benjamin Watt) writer, critic
Wattleton, Alyce Faye association executive
Wattman, Malcolm Peter lawyer
Watts, André concert pianist
Watts, David Eide lawyer
Watts, Harold Wesley economist, educator
Watts, Heather ballerina
Watts, Henry Miller, Jr. stockbroker
Waugh, Theodore Rogers orthopedic surgeon
Wax, Edward L. advertising executive
Waxenberg, Alan M. publisher
Way, Kenneth L. seat company executive
†Waydo, George J. food products company executive
Waylett, Thomas Robert management consultant executive
Weathersby, George Byron investment management executive
Weatherstone, Dennis trust company executive
Weaver, Fritz William actor
Weaver, Sigourney (Susan Alexandra Weaver) actress
†Webb, Veronica fashion model, journalist
Weber, Karl William book publisher
Weber, Robert Maxwell cartoonist
Weberman, Ben journalist, editor
Webster, John Kimball investment executive
Wechsler, Arnold L. marketing executive
Wechsler, Herbert emeritus legal educator
Wechsler, Raymond Henry management company executive
Weeks, Brigitte publishing executive
Weeks, David Frank foundation administrator
Wegman, William George artist
Weida, Lewis Dixon marketing analyst, consultant
Weidlinger, Paul civil engineer
Weidman, Jerome author
Weil, Frank A. investment banker, lawyer
Weil, Gilbert Harry lawyer
Weil, Leon Jerome diplomat
Weil, Peter Henry lawyer
†Weil-Garris Brandt, Kathleen art historian
†Weill, Gus, Jr. communications consultant
Weill, Sanford I. banker
Weinbach, Lawrence Allen accounting executive
Weinberg, H. Barbara art historian, educator, curator paintings and sculpture
Weinberg, Herschel Mayer lawyer
Weinberg, Jeffrey J. lawyer
Weinberg, John Livingston investment banker
Weinberger, Caspar Willard publishing executive, former secretary of defense
Weinberger, Harold Paul lawyer
Weiner, Annette B. university dean, anthropology educator
Weiner, Earl David lawyer
Weiner, Max educational psychology educator
Weiner, Richard public relations executive
Weiner, Stephen Arthur lawyer
Weiner, Walter Herman banker, lawyer
Weingrow, Howard L. financial executive, investor
Weinschel, Alan Jay lawyer
Weinstein, Herbert chemical engineer, educator
Weinstein, I. Bernard physician
Weinstein, Mark Michael lawyer
Weinstein, Martin aerospace manufacturing executive, materials scientist
Weinstein, Ruth Joseph lawyer
Weinstein, Sidney university program director
Weinstock, Leonard lawyer
†Weintraub, Daniel Ralph social welfare administrator
Weintraub, Ruth G. political science educator
Weintz, Walter Louis book publishing company executive
Weir, Peter Frank lawyer
Weisberg, Jonathan Mark public relations executive
Weisfeldt, Myron Lee physician, educator
Weisgall, Hugo David composer, conductor
Weiss, Charles Stanard investment banker
Weiss, David religion educator
Weiss, Donald L(ogan) sports association executive
Weiss, George C. lawyer
†Weiss, Mark public relations executive
Weiss, Marvin lawyer
†Weiss, Melvyn I. lawyer
Weiss, Myrna Grace investment banker, consultant
Weiss, Ronald Whitman real estate executive, lawyer
Weissman, Norman public relations executive
Weissman, Paul Marshall investment company executive
Weissmann, Gerald medical educator, researcher, writer, editor
Weiswasser, Stephen Anthony lawyer, broadcast executive
Weithas, William Vincent advertising agency executive
Weitz, John fashion designer, writer
Weitzner, Harold mathematics educator
Weld, Jonathan Minot lawyer
Welikson, Jeffrey Alan lawyer
Welkowitz, Joan psychology educator
Weller, Peter actor
Weller, Ralph Albert retired elevator company manufacturing executive
Welles, James Bell, Jr. lawyer
Wellington, Harry Hillel lawyer, educator
Wellington, Sheila Wacks foundation administrator, psychiatry educator
Wells, Linda Ann editor-in-chief
Wells, Melissa Foelsch foreign service officer
Wells, Victor Hugh, Jr. advertising agency executive
Welsh, Donald Emory publisher
Wemple, William lawyer
Wendel, Martin lawyer
Wendel, Thomas Michael financial services company executive
Wender, Ira Tensard lawyer
Wender, Phyllis Bellows literary agent
†Wenders, Wim film director
Wenglowski, Gary Martin economist
Wenner, Jann Simon editor, publisher
Werner, Robert L. lawyer
Wertkin, Gerard Charles museum director, lawyer
Wertsman, Vladimir Filip librarian, information specialist, author
Weschler, Anita sculptor, painter
Weschler, Lawrence Michael writer, journalist
Wesely, Edwin Joseph lawyer
Wesley, John Mercer artist
Wessinger, W. David management consultant
West, Bernard investor
West, Richard Rollin business educator
West, Stephen Kingsbury lawyer
Westerman, Sylvia Hewitt journalist
Westheimer, Ruth Siegel (Karola Ruth Siegel Westheimer) psychologist, television personality
Westin, Alan Furman political science educator
†Westin, David Lawrence lawyer
Westlake, Donald Edwin author
Weston, M. Moran, II educator, real estate developer, banker, clergyman
Wetzler, Monte Edwin lawyer
Wexler, Peter John producer, director, set designer
Weyher, Harry Frederick lawyer
Wham, George Sims publishing executive
Wharton, Clifton Reginald, Jr. former university president, former government official, former insurance executive
Wheeler, Wesley Dreer marine engineer, naval architect, consultant
Whelan, Elizabeth Ann Murphy epidemiologist
Whelan, Stephen Thomas lawyer
Whelan, Wendy ballet dancer
†Whipple, Judith Roy book editor
Whitcraft, Edward C. R. investment banker
White, Edmund Valentine author
White, Harry Edward, Jr. lawyer
White, John Simon opera director
White, Kate magazine editor in chief
White, Kerr Lachlan physician, foundation director
White, Lawrence J. economics educator
†White, Leonard motion picture company executive
White, Norval Crawford architect
†White, Samuel Giltinan architect
White, Thomas Edward lawyer
White, Timothy Thomas Anthony writer, editor, broadcaster
White, William Dekova (Bill White) baseball league executive
Whitehead, E. Douglas urology educator
Whitehead, John Cunningham investment executive
Whitehead, Robert theatrical producer
Whiteman, Douglas E. publisher
Whiteman, H(orace) Clifton banker
Whitener, William Garnett dancer, choreographer
Whiting, Richard Brooke investment banker
Whitman, Bruce Nairn flight safety executive
†Whitmer, Kevin newspaper sports editor
Whitmore, John Rogers banker
Whitmyer, Russell Eliot retired electric company executive
Whitney, Edward Bonner investment banker
Whitney, Ruth Reinke magazine editor
Whittemore, Laurence Frederick private banker
Whitworth, John Harvey, Jr. lawyer
Whoriskey, Robert Donald lawyer
Wickes, R(ichard) Paul lawyer
Widlund, Olof Bertil computer science educator
†Widmann, Nancy C. broadcast executive
Wiedemann, George Stanhope advertising executive
Wiegers, George Anthony investment banker
Wiener, Malcolm Hewitt investment management company executive
Wiener, Marvin S. rabbi, editor, executive
Wiener, Robert Alvin accountant
Wiesel, Torsten Nils neurobiologist, educator
Wieser, Charles Edward financial consultant
Wiest, Dianne actress
Wigmore, Barrie Atherton investment banker
Wilcox, John Caven lawyer, corporate consultant
Wilde, Donald Raymond advertising company executive
Wildes, Leon lawyer, educator
Wiley, Deborah E. publishing executive
Wilford, John Noble, Jr. news correspondent
Wilhite, Clayton Edward advertising executive
†Wilkerson, Isabel journalist
Wilkinson, John Hart lawyer
Williams, Anthony lawyer
Williams, Dave Harrell investment executive
Williams, David Benton advertising agency executive
Williams, Donald Maxey dancer, singer, actor
Williams, Garth Montgomery illustrator
Williams, Lowell Craig lawyer, employee relations executive
†Williams, Lucinda country musician
Williams, Milton Lawrence judge, educator
Williams, Omer S. J. lawyer
Williams, Peter Whitridge lawyer
Williams, Stanley ballet dancer and teacher
Williams, Thomas Allison lawyer
†Williams, Tod Culpan architect
Williams, Tony jazz drummer
Williams, Vanessa recording artist, actress
Williams, Vaughn Charles lawyer
Williams, William Thomas artist, educator
Williamson, Douglas Franklin, Jr. lawyer
Williamson, Liz (Elizabeth Anne Ray Williamson) choreographer, dancer, educator
Willis, Everett Irving lawyer
Willis, Gordon cinematographer
Willis, John Alvin editor
Willis, Thornton Wilson painter
Willis, William Ervin lawyer
Wilmerding, Harold Pratt banker, investment counselor
Wilson, August playwright
Wilson, F(rancis) Paul novelist
Wilson, Judy Vantrease publishing executive
Wilson, Paul Holliday, Jr. lawyer
Wilson, Robert M. theatrical artist
Wilson, Thomas William lawyer
Winawer, Sidney Jerome physician, clinical investigator, educator
†Wincenc, Carol concertizing flutist, educator
Windels, Paul, Jr. lawyer
Windhager, Erich Ernst physiologist, educator
Windsor, Laurence Charles, Jr. publishing executive
Winfield, Richard Neill lawyer
Winfrey, Carey Wells journalist, magazine editor
Wing, John Russell lawyer
Winger, Ralph O. lawyer
Winick, Charles sociologist, educator
Winick, Myron educator, physician
†Winokur, Herbert Simon, Jr. diversified company executive
Winship, Frederick Moery journalist
Winsor, Jackie artist
Winsor, Kathleen writer
Winterer, Philip Steele lawyer
Wintour, Anna editor
Wirz, Pascal Francois trust company executive
Wise, David author, journalist
Wise, Robert F., Jr. lawyer
Wisehart, Arthur McKee lawyer
Wit, Harold Maurice investment banker, lawyer, investor
Wittmer, James Frederick preventive medicine physician, educator
Wittreich, Joseph Anthony, Jr. English language educator, author

Wittstein, Edwin Frank stage and film production designer
Wixom, William David art historian, museum administrator, educator
Woetzel, Damian Abdo ballet dancer, educator
Wogan, Robert broadcasting company executive
Woglom, Eric Cooke lawyer
Wohl, Ronald Gene lawyer
Wohlgelernter, Beth organization executive
Wohlstetter, Charles telephone company executive
Woit, Erik Peter corporate executive, lawyer
Woitach, Richard conductor, pianist
Wojnilower, Albert Martin economist
Wolcott, John Winthrop, III corporate executive
Wolcott, Samuel H., III investment banker
Wolf, Gary Wickert lawyer
Wolf, James Anthony insurance company executive
†Wolf, Naomi writer
Wolf, Peter Michael investment and land planning consultant, educator, author
Wolfe, George C. theater director, producer, playwright
Wolfe, James Ronald lawyer
Wolfe, Thomas Kennerly, Jr. writer, journalist
Wolfensohn, James David bank executive
Wolff, Jesse David lawyer
Wolff, Kurt Jakob lawyer
Wolff, Sanford Irving lawyer
†Wolff, Virginia Euwer writer, secondary education educator
Wolff, William F., III investment banker
Wolfson, Michael George lawyer
Wolins, Joseph artist
Wolitzer, Steven Barry investment banker
Wolkoff, Eugene Arnold lawyer
Wolman, William economist, journalist, broadcaster
Wolowitz, Steven lawyer
Wolson, Craig Alan lawyer
Wong, Kwan Shut art appraiser, artist
Wonham, Frederick Stapley trust bank executive
Wood, Christopher L. J. real estate consulting firm executive
Wood, Kimba M. federal judge
Wood, Paul F. national health agency executive
†Wood, Robert Elkington, II financial services company executive
Wood, Ronald musician
Woodbury, Marion A. insurance company executive
Woodbury, Thomas Bowring, II lawyer, public utility executive
Wooden, Ruth A. public service advertising executive
Woodman, Timothy artist
Woodman, William E. theater, opera and television director
Woodrum, Robert Lee executive search consultant
Woods, Rodney Ian banker
Woodside, William Stewart service company executive, museum official
Woodward, M. Cabell, Jr. financial executive
Woolfenden, William Edward art administrator and historian
Worenklein, Jacob Joshua lawyer
Worley, Robert William, Jr. lawyer
†Worman, Howard Jay physician, educator
Worth, Irene actress
Wortman, Richard S. historian, educator
Wragg, Laishley Palmer, Jr. lawyer
Wray, Cecil, Jr. lawyer
Wright, Gwendolyn art center director, writer, educator
Wright, Hugh Elliott, Jr. association executive, writer
Wright, Irving Sherwood physician, emeritus educator
Wright, Jane Cooke physician, educator, consultant
Wright, Jeanne Elizabeth Jason advertising executive
†Wright, Jeffrey actor
Wright, Laurali R. (Bunny Wright) writer
Wright, P(aul) Bruce lawyer
Wright, Richard John business executive
Wright, Robert C. broadcasting executive
Wright, Robert F. petroleum products company executive
Wriston, Walter Bigelow retired banker
Wrong, Dennis Hume sociologist, educator
†WuDunn, Sheryl journalist, correspondent
Wulf, Melvin Lawrence lawyer
Wunderman, Jan Darcourt artist
Wunderman, Lester advertising agency executive
Wuorinen, Charles Peter composer
Wurmfeld, Sanford artist, educator
†Wyatt, Mary Jean (M.J. Wyatt) public relations executive
Wyckoff, Edward Lisk, Jr. lawyer
Wynder, Ernst Ludwig science foundation director, epidemiologist
Wynette, Tammy singer
Wyse, Lois advertising executive, author
Wyser-Pratte, John Michael lawyer
Yablon, Leonard Harold publishing company executive
Yahr, Melvin David physician
Yalen, Gary N. insurance company executive
Yancey, Richard Charles investment banker
Yang, Edward S. electrical engineering educator
Yankelovich, Daniel social researcher, public opinion analyst
Yanowitch, Michael H. lawyer
Yassky, Lester lawyer, bank executive
Yeager, Cheryl Lynn ballet dancer
Yelle, Richard Wilfred artist, product designer
Yellin, Thomas Gilmer broadcast executive
Yellin, Victor Fell composer, music educator
Yerman, Fredric Warren lawyer
Yerushalmi, Yosef Hayim historian, educator
Yeston, Maury composer, lyricist, educator
Yetman, Leith Eleanor administrator, educator
†Yorinks, Arthur children's author
York, Richard Travis art dealer
York, Stephen Stanier lawyer
†Young, Ed (Tse-chun) illustrator, children's author
Young, Genevieve Leman publishing executive, editor
Young, John Edward lawyer
Young, Michael Warren geneticist, educator
Young, Nancy lawyer
Young, Robert Francis publisher
†Young, Vivian advertising executive
Youngerman, Jack artist, sculptor
Youngwood, Alfred Donald lawyer
Yuncker, Barbara science writer
Yunich, David Lawrence consumer goods consultant
†Yunich, Peter B. publishing executive
Yurchenco, Henrietta Weiss ethnomusicologist, writer
Zabel, William David lawyer
Zabriskie, Virginia M. art dealer
Zacharius, Walter publishing company executive
Zackheim, Adrian Walter editor
Zahn, Paula newscaster
Zahn, Timothy writer
Zahnd, Richard Hugo professional sports team executive, lawyer
Zakanitch, Robert Rahway artist
Zakim, David biochemist
Zakkay, Victor aeronautical engineering educator, scientist
†Zaks, Jerry theatrical director, actor
Zand, Dale Ezra business management educator
Zapf, Hermann book and type designer
Zara, Louis author, editor
Zarb, Frank Gustave investment company executive
Zawinul, Josef bandleader, composer, keyboardist, synthesist
†Zawistowski, Stephen Louis psychologist, educator
Zeckendorf, William, Jr. real estate developer
Zedrosser, Joseph John lawyer
Zeikel, Arthur investment company executive
Zeisler, Richard Spiro investor
Zeldin, Richard Packer publisher
Zerin, Steven David lawyer
Zeuschner, Erwin Arnold investment advisory company executive
Zhu, Ai-Lan opera singer
Ziegler, Henry Steinway lawyer
Ziegler, Michael Lewis lawyer
Ziegler, Richard Ferdinand lawyer
Ziegler, William Alexander lawyer
Zifchak, William C. lawyer
Ziff, William Bernard, Jr. publishing executive
Zimand, Harvey Folks lawyer
Zimmerman, James M. retail company executive
Zimmerman, William Edwin newspaper editor and publisher
Zimmett, Mark Paul lawyer
Zindel, Paul author
Zinder, Norton David genetics educator, university dean
Zinn, Keith Marshall ophthalmologist, educator
Zinsser, William Knowlton editor, writer, educator
†Zipko, Raymond Edward advertising executive
Zipprodt, Patricia costume designer
Zirin, James David lawyer
Zitrin, Arthur physician
Zlowe, Florence Markowitz artist
Zoeller, Donald J. lawyer
Zofnass, Paul Jesse investment banker
Zolberg, Aristide Rodolphe political science educator, researcher
Zolotow, Charlotte Shapiro author, editor
Zoogman, Nicholas Jay lawyer
Zox, Larry artist
Zuccotti, John Eugene construction company executive
Zuck, Alfred Christian consulting mechanical engineer
Zuckerberg, Roy J. investment banking executive
Zuckerman, Harriet sociologist, educator
Zuckerman, Mitchell lawyer, art auction firm executive
Zuckerman, Mortimer Benjamin real estate developer, publisher, editor
Zukerman, Morris E. investment banker
Zukerman, Pinchas concert violinist, violist, conductor
Zweibel, Joel Burton lawyer
Zweig, Michael Philip lawyer
Zwerling, Gary Leslie investment bank executive
Zylberberg, Abraham Lieb lawyer
Zylis-Gara, Teresa Gerarda soprano

Newburgh
Apuzzo, Gloria Isabel accountant
Cloudman, Francis Harold, III computer company executive
†Joyce, Mary Ann principal
Saturnelli, Annette Miele school system administrator
Severo, Richard writer
Turkenkopf, Iris Jane biology educator
Wilcox, David Eric consultant

Newton Falls
Hunter, William Schmidt engineering executive, environmental engineer

Newtonville
Apostle, Christos Nicholas social psychologist

Niagara Falls
Albanese, Jay Samuel criminologist educator
Anton, Ronald David lawyer
Collins, Christopher Carl manufacturing executive
Dojka, Edwin Sigmund civil engineer
Kirchner, Bruce McHarg manufacturing company executive
†Pillittere, Joseph T. congressman
Powers, Bruce Raymond academic administrator, writer
Sheeran, Thomas Joseph education educator, consultant, judge

Niagara University
O'Connell, Brian James academic administrator, priest
O'Leary, Daniel Francis university dean
Osberg, Timothy M. psychologist, educator, researcher, clinician

Niagra Falls
King, George Gerard chemical company executive

Niskayuna
Fitzroy, Nancy deLoye technology executive, engineer
Johnson, Ingolf Birger retired electrical engineer
Katz, Samuel geophysics educator
Lafferty, James Martin physicist
Mangan, John Leo retired electrical manufacturing company executive, international trade and trade policy specialist
Mihran, Theodore Gregory retired physicist
Whittingham, Harry Edward, Jr. retired banker

North Hills
Wingate, David Aaron manufacturing company executive

North Salem
Larsen, Jonathan Zerbe journalist

North Tarrytown
Schmidt, Klaus Franz advertising executive
Zegarelli, Edward Victor retired dental educator, researcher

North Tonawanda
Nadler, Sigmond Harold physician, surgeon

North White Plains
Erla, Karen artist, painter, collagist, printmaker
Hearon, Shelby writer, lecturer, educator

Northport
Brown, John Edward textile company executive
Gebhard, David Fairchild aeronautical engineer, consultant
Tsapogas, Makis J. surgeon

Norwich
Hanna, Eduardo Zacarias pharmaceutical company executive

Nyack
Esser, Aristide Henri psychiatrist
Hendin, David Bruce literary agent, author, consultant, numismatist
Karp, Peter Simon marketing executive
Keil, John Mullan advertising agency executive
†Lehman, Paul V. minister
Leiser, Ernest Stern journalist
Loeffel, Bruce software company executive, consultant
Mann, Kenneth Walker retired minister, psychologist
Rossi, Harald Hermann retired radiation biophysicist, educator, administrator
†Ryan, William B. F. geologist

Oakdale
Kramer, Aaron English educator emeritus, poet, author
Meskill, Victor Peter college president, educator
Tompkins, Daniel D. landscape architect, horticulturist

Oceanside
Mills, James Spencer author

Ogdensburg
Brzana, Stanislaus Joseph bishop
Rusaw, Sally Ellen librarian

Old Brookville
Fairman, Joel Martin broadcasting executive
Feinberg, Irwin L. retired manufacturing company executive

Old Westbury
Cheek, King Virgil, Jr. lawyer, educational administrator
Ozelli, Tunch economics educator, consultant
Pettigrew, L. Eudora university president
Rabil, Albert, Jr. humanities educator
Ranu, Harcharan Singh biomedical scientist, administrator, orthopaedic biomechanics educator
Schure, Alexander university chancellor
Schure, Matthew college president

Oneida
Matthews, William D(oty) lawyer, consumer products manufacturing company executive
Muschenheim, Frederick pathologist

Oneonta
Bergstein, Harry Benjamin psychology educator
Diehl, Lesley Ann psychologist
Donovan, Alan Barton college president
Johnson, Richard David librarian
Smith, Geoffrey Adams special purpose mobile unit manufacturing executive

Orangeburg
Hennessy, James Ernest college official, educator
†Lajtha, Abel biochemist
Weinig, Sheldon materials company executive, metallurgist, educator

Orchard Park
Bennett, Cornelius professional football player
Franklin, Murray Joseph retired steel foundry executive
Hull, Kent football player
Kelly, Jim (James Edward Kelly) professional football player
Levy, Marvin Daniel professional football coach
Reed, Andre Darnell professional football player
Reid, Thomas Fenton minister
Smith, Bruce professional football player
Sullivan, Mortimer Allen, Jr. lawyer
Talley, Darryl Victor professional football player
Tasker, Steven Jay professional football player
Thomas, Thurman professional football player

Orient
Hanson, Thor retired health agency executive and naval officer

Ossining
Beard, Janet Marie health care administrator
Carter, Richard publisher, writer
Cober, Alan Edwin artist, illustrator, printmaker, educator
Daly, William Joseph lawyer
Frisch, Harry David lawyer, consultant
†Galef, Sandra Risk state legislator
Ravis, Howard Shepard conference planner and publishing consultant
Reynolds, Calvin management consultant, business educator
Stein, Sol publisher, writer, editor in chief

Oswego
Fox, Michael David art educator, visual imagist artist
Geisinger, Kurt Francis academic dean, psychometrician, educator
Gerber, Barbara Ann Witter university dean, educator
Gooding, Charles Thomas psychology educator, college dean
Gordon, Norman Botnick psychology educator
Moody, Florence Elizabeth education educator, retired college dean
Nesbitt, Rosemary Sinnett theatre educator
Silveira, Augustine, Jr. chemistry educator
Smiley, Marilynn Jean musicologist
Turco, Lewis Putnam language professional, educator
Weber, Stephen Lewis academic administrator

Owego
Blahut, Richard Edward electrical engineer
Nolis, William M. aerospace engineer, consultant

Oyster Bay
Robinson, Edward T., III lawyer
Schwab, Hermann Caspar banker
Trevor, Bronson economist

Ozone Park
†Taylor, Joyce religious organization executive

Painted Post
Hammond, George Simms chemist
Sands, John W. nursing home administrator

Palisades
Berger, Thomas Louis author
†Bracco, Lorraine actress
Cane, Mark Alan oceanography and climate researcher
Cavett, Dick entertainer
Davis, Dorothy Salisbury author
Hayes, Dennis Edward geophysicist, educator
Keitel, Harvey actor
Kent, Dennis Vladimir geophysicist, researcher
Knowlton, Grace Farrar sculptor, photographer
Krainin, Julian Arthur film director, producer, writer, cinematographer
Murray, Bill actor, writer
Richards, Paul Granston geophysics educator, seismologist
Sykes, Lynn Ray geologist, educator

Palmyra
Blazey, Mark Lee management consultant

Patchogue
Shore, Ferdinand John physicist, educator

Pawling
Peale, Ruth Stafford (Mrs. Norman Vincent Peale) religious leader

Pearl River
Barik, Sudhakar microbiologist, researcher
†Colman, Samuel assemblyman
Danforth, Elliot, Jr. medical educator
Davis, Harold veterinary pathologist
Fischer, Frank Ernest utility executive
McBennett, Robert Joseph utility executive
Meyer, Irwin Stephan lawyer, accountant
Smith, James Francis utilities executive

Peekskill
Manthey, Robert Wendelin educator
Rosenberg, Marilyn R. artist, visual poet

Pelham
Bornand, Ruth Chaloux antique music box specialist
Calamari, John Daniel retired law educator
Freidberg, Sidney lawyer, real estate development company executive, author
Moore, Ellis Oglesby retired public affairs consultant
Srere, Benson M. communications company executive, consultant
Weintz, Caroline Giles advertising executive, travel writer

Penfield
Amish, Keith Warren retired utility executive
Battaglini, Frank Paul engineering company executive

Piermont
Der Harootian, Khoren sculptor
Fox, Matthew Ignatius publishing company executive

Pittsford
Benson, Warren Frank composer, educator
Dorsey, Eugene Carroll former foundation and communications executive
Faloon, William Wassell physician, educator
†Gates, Martha Meyer architect
†Herge, Henry Curtis, Jr. consulting firm executive
Hess, Donald K. university administrator
Kieffer, James Milton lawyer
Lyttle, Douglas Alfred photographer, educator
Marticelli, Joseph John lawyer, editor
Ouellette, Bernard Charles pharmaceutical company executive
Palermo, Peter M., Jr. photography equipment company executive
Schubert, John Edward former banker
Woodhull, Nancy Jane publishing executive

Plainview
Bornstein, Robert Joseph hospital administrator
Brill, Steven Charles financial advisor, lawyer
Fulton, Richard lecture bureau executive
Linn, Edward Allen writer
Newman, Edwin Harold news commentator

Plattsburgh
Myers, John Lytle historian
Smith, Noel Wilson psychology educator

Pleasantville
Ahrensfeld, Thomas Frederick lawyer
†Antonecchia, Donald A. principal
†Barnett, Charles E. lawyer
Black, Percy psychology educator
†Glotzer, Marilyn principal
Grune, George Vincent publishing company executive
Hormozi, Farrokh Zad economist, educator, consultant, business forecaster
†Murdock, William John librarian
Oursler, Fulton, Jr. editor-in-chief, writer
Pastore, Joseph Michael, Jr. university administrator, business educator
Pike, John Nazarian optical engineering consultant
Reps, David Nathan finance educator
Robak, Rostyslaw Wsewolod psychologist, educator

Robinson, Jay (Thurston Robinson) artist
Ruggiero, Anthony William direct mail company executive
†Schadt, James P. publishing executive
†Tomlinson, Kenneth Y. periodical editor in chief
Willis, William Henry marketing executive

Poestenkill
Radley, Virginia Louise humanities educator

Point Lookout
Stack, Maurice Daniel retired insurance company executive

Port Chester
Ailloni-Charas, Dan marketing executive
Beach, Lani Leroy food products company executive
Blumenfeld, Seth David communications company executive
Schwartz, Arthur Leonard pulp company executive, lawyer

Port Kent
Mc Kee, James, Jr. retired banker

Port Washington
Blakeslee, Alton Lauren scientific writer
Bogen, Samuel Adams electrical engineer, consultant
Brownstein, Martin Herbert dermatopathologist, educator
†Donohue, Peter Joseph publishing executive
Hackett, John Byron advertising agency executive, lawyer
Jay, Frank Peter educator, writer
Johnson, Tod Stuart market research company executive
Keen, Constantine retired manufacturing company executive
McGreal, Joseph A., Jr. publishing company executive
Navajas-Mogro, Hugo diplomat
Read, Frederick Wilson, Jr. lawyer, educator
Simmons, Lee Howard book publishing company executive
Sonnenfeldt, Richard Wolfgang business educator
†Williams, George Leo retired educator

Potsdam
Cotellessa, Robert Francis retired electrical engineering educator, academic administrator
Demerdash, Nabeel Aly Omar electrical engineer
Dicello, John Francis, Jr. physicist, educator
Gallagher, Richard Hugo university official, engineer
Hammam, M. Shawky electrical engineer, educator
Harder, Kelsie Brown retired language professional, educator
†Mackay, Raymond Arthur chemist
Matijevic, Egon chemistry educator, researcher, consultant
Washburn, Robert Brooks university dean, composer
Whelehan, Patricia Elizabeth anthropology educator
†Wilcox, William Ross chemical engineering educator, researcher

Poughkeepsie
Ahern, John Joseph Italian studies educator
Bartlett, Lynn Conant English literature educator
Beck, Curt Werner chemist, educator
Bird, Caroline author
Brenner, Marshall Leib lawyer
Chu, Richard Chao-Fan mechanical engineer
Conklin, D(onald) David college president
Daniels, Elizabeth Adams English language educator
Deiters, Sister Joan Adele chemistry educator, nun
Dolan, Thomas Joseph lawyer
Emerson, William R. retired library executive, historian
Fergusson, Frances Daly college president, educator
Glasse, John Howell retired philosophy and theology educator
Griffen, Clyde Chesterman retired history educator
Heller, William Russell physicist, computer scientist
Henley, Richard James healthcare institution administrative and financial officer
Henry, Charles Jay library director
Hytier, Adrienne Doris French language educator
Johnson, Lucille Lewis anthropology educator, archaeologist
Johnson, M(aurice) Glen political science educator
Kim, David Sang Chul seminary president, publishing executive
Lang, William Warner physicist
Lipschutz, Ilse Hempel French and Franco-Spanish relations, painting and literature educator
Logue, Joseph Carl electronics engineer, consultant
Mack, John Edward, III utility company executive
Maling, George Croswell, Jr. physicist
Marshall, Natalie Junemann university official
McEnroe, Caroline Ann legal assistant
Millman, Jode Susan lawyer
O'Shea, John P. insurance executive
Ostertag, Robert Louis lawyer
Pliskin, William Aaron physicist
Rosenblatt, Albert Martin state supreme court justice
Tavel, Morton Allen physics educator, researcher
Van Zanten, Frank Veldhuyzen library system director
†Wager, Richard Kenneth newspaper executive
Willard, Nancy Margaret writer, educator
Wilson, Richard Edward composer, pianist, music educator
Winn, Otis Howard English educator

Pound Ridge
Bright, Craig Bartley lawyer
Ferro, Walter artist
Ostrow, Stuart theatrical producer
Throckmorton, Joan Helen advertising agency executive
Webb, Richard Gilbert financial executive

Princeton
Karel, Frank, III foundation executive

Purchase
Butler, Robert Clifton forest products industry executive
Calloway, D. Wayne food and beverage products company executive
Clark, Mary Twibill philosopher, educator
Deering, Allan Brooks beverage company executive
Dettmer, Robert Gerhart beverage company executive
Dwyer, Andrew T. utility and utility service company executive
Ehrman, Lee geneticist
†Gedeon, Lucinda Heyel museum director
Georges, John A. paper company executive
Grebstein, Sheldon Norman university administrator
Guedry, James Walter lawyer, paper corporation executive
Hunziker, Robert McKee paper company executive
Joyce, Joseph James lawyer, food products executive
Kelly, Edmund Joseph lawyer, investment banker
Lacy, Bill college president
Lamagra, Anthony James concert pianist, television host, music educator
Lessin, Andrew Richard accounting executive
†MacInnis, Frank T. construction company executive, holding company executive
McKenna, Matthew Morgan lawyer
Melican, James Patrick, Jr. lawyer
Myers, Catherine R. academic administrator
Noonan, Frank R. business executive
Ryan, Edward W. economics educator
Sandler, Irving Harry art critic, art historian
Siegel, Nathaniel Harold sociology educator
Suwyn, Mark A. paper company executive
Wallach, Ira David lawyer, business executive
Wilderotter, James Arthur lawyer
Wright, David L. food and beverage company executive

Purdys
Burlingame, Edward Livermore publishing company executive

Putnam Valley
Bracken, Harry McFarland philosophy educator

Queens
Curzio, Francis Xavier finance company executive
Farkas, Edward Barrister airport administrator, electrical engineer

Queensbury
Borgos, Stephen John business educator, consultant, municipal administrator, real estate broker
Lake, William Thomas financial consultant
Mead, John Milton banker
Winsten, Archer retired newspaper and movie critic

Quogue
Cooke, Robert John history and law educator
Laurents, Arthur playwright
Macero, Teo composer, conductor
Moss, Ronald Jay lawyer, former state official, former advertising executive

Ransomville
Mayer, George Merton elementary education educator

Rego Park
Cronyn, Hume actor, writer, director
LeFrak, Samuel J. housing and building corporation executive
Tandy, Jessica actress

Remsenburg
Billman, Irwin Edward publishing company executive
Edwards, Arthur Anderson retired mechanical engineer

Rensselaerville
Dudley, George Austin architect, planning consultant, educator

Rexford
Kirchmayer, Leon Kenneth retired electrical engineer

Rhinebeck
Clutz, William (Hartman Clutz) artist, educator
Ethan, Carol Baehr psychotherapist
Kohn, Henry lawyer
Rabinovich, Raquel artist, sculptor

Rhinecliff
Dierdorff, John Ainsworth retired editor

Richfield Springs
Mc Kelvey, John Jay, Jr. retired foundation executive

Richmond Hill
Scheich, John F. lawyer

Ridge
Adams, Peter David physicist, editor

Ridgewood
Jones, Harold Antony banker

Riverdale
Friedman, Ronald Marvin cellular biologist
Hubley, Faith Elliott filmmaker, painter, animator
Moss, Stanley poet
Phocas, George John international lawyer, business executive

Rochester
Abood, Leo George biochemistry educator
Adams, G. Rollie museum executive
Adler, Samuel Hans conductor, composer
Alling, Norman Larrabee mathematics educator
Annunziata, Frank history educator
Arden, Bruce Wesley computer science and electrical engineering educator
Balderston, William, III retired banker
Barton, Russell William psychiatrist, author
Basu, Asish Ranjan geological sciences educator, researcher
Baum, John physician
Bennett, John Morrison medical oncologist
Berg, Robert Lewis physician, educator
Berman, Howard James medical association administrator
Berman, Milton history educator
Bernstein, Paul retired academic dean
Beston, Rose Marie college president
Bluhm, William Theodore political scientist, educator
†Boeckman, Robert Kenneth, Jr. chemistry educator, organic chemistry researcher
Borch, Richard Frederic pharmacology and chemistry educator
Borgstedt, Harold Heinrich pharmacologist, toxicologist
Bouyoucos, John Vinton research and development company executive
Bowen, William Henry dental researcher, dental educator
Braunsdorf, Paul Raymond lawyer
Brennan, John Edward manufacturing company executive
Brody, Bernard B. physician, educator
Brown, John Robert advertising executive, writer
Brzustowicz, Richard John neurosurgeon, educator
Buckley, Michael Francis lawyer
Buff, Frank Paul chemist, educator
Burgener, Francis André radiology educator
Burns, Stephen James engineering educator, materials science researcher
†Burrill, William George bishop
Burton, Richard Irving orthopedist, educator
Carlton, Charles Merritt linguistics educator
Carstensen, Edwin Lorenz biomedical engineer, biophysicist
Castle, William Eugene academic administrator
Chang, Jack Che-man photoscience research laboratory director
†Chapin, Louis William, III architect
Chey, William Yoon physician
Chiarenza, Carl art historian, critic, artist, educator
Ciccone, J. Richard psychiatrist
Clark, Matthew Harvey bishop
Clarkson, Thomas William toxicologist, educator
Clement, Thomas Earl lawyer
Coburn, Theodore James retired physicist
Cockett, Abraham T. K. urologist
Cohen, Jules academic dean, physician, educator
Cohen, Nicholas immunologist, educator
Cokelet, Giles Roy biomedical engineering educator
Coleman, Paul David neurobiology researcher, educator
Cowen, Emory L. psychology educator
Crane, Irving Donald pocket billiards player
Crino, Marjanne Helen anesthesiologist
Crumb, Owen Joseph public relations executive
D'Agostino, Anthony Carmen anthropologist, educator
†Deavenport, Earnest W., Jr. chemical executive
Deci, Edward Lewis psychologist, educator
DeMarco, Roland R. foundation executive
de Papp, Elise Wachenfeld pathologist
Diamond, David Leo composer
Dohanian, Diran Kavork art historian, educator
Donovan, Kreag lawyer
Doty, Robert William neurophysiologist, educator
Doyle, Justin P lawyer
DuBrin, Andrew John behavioral sciences, management educator, author
Eaves, Morris Emery English language educator
Eisenberg, Richard S. chemistry educator
Elder, Fred Kingsley, Jr. physicist, educator
Engel, George Libman psychiatrist, internist, educator
Engelmann, Lothar Klaus photographic science educator
Engerman, Stanley Lewis economist, educator, historian
Enyeart, James L. museum director
Everett, Claudia Kellam special education educator
Featherstone, John Douglas Bernard biochemistry educator
Feinberg, Martin Robert chemical engineering educator
Fenno, Richard Francis, Jr. political science educator
Ferbel, Thomas physics educator, physicist
Fischer, Richard Samuel lawyer
Fisher, George Myles Cordell electronics equipment company executive, mathematician, engineer
Forbes, Gilbert Burnett physician, educator
Fox, Edward Hanton lawyer
Frank, Irwin Norman urologist, educator
Frazer, John Paul surgeon
Freckleton, Jon Edward engineering educator, consultant, retired military officer
Freeman, Robert Schofield musicologist, educator, pianist
Frisina, Robert Dana sensory neuroscientist
Gans, Roger Frederick mechanical engineering educator
Gates, Marshall DeMotte, Jr. chemistry educator
Gaudion, Donald Alfred former diversified manufacturing executive
Geertsma, Robert Henry psychologist, educator
George, Nicholas optics educator, researcher
George, Richard Neill lawyer
Giles, Peter photographic equipment manufacturing executive
Gill, Daniel E. optical manufacturing company executive
Gitler, Samuel Carlos mathematics educator, researcher
Glazer, Laurence Charles mail order executive, real estate developer
†Gleason, James S. machinery parts manufacturing company executive
Goldman, Joel J. lawyer
Goldsmith, Lowell Alan medical educator
Goldstein, David Arthur biophysicist, educator
†Gootnick, Margery Fischbein lawyer
Gordon, Dane Rex philosophy educator, minister
Griner, Paul Francis hospital administrator, physician
Gumaer, Elliott Wilder, Jr. lawyer
Hai, Carol Sue interior designer
†Hall, Donald S. planetarium administrator
Hampson, Thomas Meredith lawyer
Hanushek, Eric Alan economics educator
Hargrave, Alexander Davidson banker, lawyer
Harris, Alfred social anthropologist, educator
Harris, Diane Carol health care and optics products executive
†Harris, Richard M., Jr. paper company executive
Harris, Wayne Manley lawyer
Harvey, Douglass Coate retired photographic company executive
Hauser, William Barry history educator, historian
Heidke, Ronald Lawrence photographic products company executive
Herminghouse, Patricia Anne foreign language educator
Herz, Marvin Ira psychiatrist
Hilf, Russell biochemist
Hoch, Edward Dentinger author
Hodkinson, Sydney Phillip composer, educator
Hoffberg, David Lawrence lawyer
Holcomb, Grant, III museum director
Hollingsworth, Jack Waring mathematics and computer science educator
Holmes, Jay Thorpe lawyer
Holmes, Robert Lawrence philosophy educator
†Hood, John B. lawyer
Hood, William Boyd, Jr. cardiologist
Hoot, William John retired brewery executive
Hopkins, Thomas Duvall economics educator
Horak, Jan-Christopher film studies educator, curator
Horsford, Howard Clarke English language educator
Howard, Hubert Wendell English language educator, academic administrator, choral conductor
Hoy, Cyrus Henry language professional, educator
Hughey, Richard Kohlman lawyer, legal publisher
Hutchins, Frank McAllister advertising executive
Hyman, Ralph Alan journalist, consultant
†Iglewski, Barbara Hotham microbiologist, educator
†Insel, Richard medical facility administrator/pediatrics educator
Jackson, Thomas Humphrey university president
†Jacobs, Bruce political science educator
Jacobs, Laurence Stanton physician, educator
Johnson, Bruce Marvin English language educator
Johnson, James William English educator, author
Johnson, Jean Elaine nursing educator
Jones, Ronald Winthrop economics educator
Jorne, Jacob chemical engineer, educator
Joyce, John Joseph English educator
Joynt, Robert James academic administrator
Kampmeier, Jack August Carlos chemist, educator
Kende, Andrew Steven chemistry educator
Khosla, Rajinder Paul physicist
Kingslake, Rudolf retired optical designer
Kinnen, Edwin electrical engineer, educator
Klimas, Antanas linguist, educator
†Knauer, James P. physicist
Knox, Robert Seiple physicist, educator
Kohrt, Carl Fredrick manufacturing executive, scientist
Kowalke, Kim H. music educator, musicologist, conductor, foundation executive
Kreilick, Robert W. chemist, educator
Kunkel, David Nelson lawyer
Kurland, Harold Arthur lawyer
Kyburg, Henry Guy Ely, Jr. philosophy and computer science educator
La Celle, Paul Louis biophysics educator
Laires, Fernando concert piano educator
Laniak, David Konstantyn utility company executive
Larimer, David George federal judge
Latella, Robert Natale brewing company executive, lawyer
Laties, Victor Gregory psychology educator
Law, Michael R. lawyer
Lessen, Martin engineering educator, consulting engineer
Liebert, Arthur Edgar. hospital administrator
Long, John Broaddus, Jr. economist, educator
Lundback, Staffan Bengt Gunnar lawyer
Makous, Walter Leon visual scientist, educator
Mandel, Leonard physics and optics educator
†Mandt, John F. religious organization executive
Maniloff, Jack biophysicist, educator
Mann, Alfred musicology educator, choral conductor
Marcellus, John Robert, III trombonist, educator
Margolis, Richard Martin photographer, educator
Marinetti, Guido V. biochemistry educator
Marsh, David O. neurology and toxicology educator
†Matzek, Richard Allan library director
McCrory, John Brooks retired lawyer
McCrory, Robert Lee physicist, mechanical engineering educator
McCurdy, Gilbert Geier retailer
Mc Donald, Joseph Valentine neurosurgeon
Mc Isaac, George Scott business policy educator, past business executive
Mc Kelvey, Jean Trepp industrial relations educator
Mc Kenzie, Lionel Wilfred economist, educator
McKie, W. Gilmore human resources executive
McLendon, George Leland chemistry educator, researcher
McWilliams, C. Paul, Jr. engineering executive
Melissinos, Adrian Constantin physicist, educator
Menguy, Rene surgeon, educator
Merritt, Howard Sutermeister retired art educator
Mertin, Roger photographer
†Moore, Duncan Thomas optics educator
Morey, James Newman advertising executive
Morgan, William Lionel, Jr. physician, educator
†Morrison, Patrice B. lawyer
Morrow, Paul Edward toxicology educator
Morton, John H. surgeon, educator
Muchmore, William Breuleux zoologist, educator
Mueller, John E. political science educator, dance critic and historian
Munson, Harold Lewis education educator
Niemi, Richard Gene political science educator
Oberlies, John William construction company executive
Olson, Russell L. pension fund administrator
O'Mara, Robert Edmund George radiologist, educator
†Orr, Jim (James D. Orr) columnist, writer
Pacala, Leon retired assocation executive
Palermo, Anthony Robert lawyer
Paley, Albert Raymond art educator, sculptor
Paley, Gerald Larry lawyer
Palmer, Harvey John chemical engineering educator, consultant
Palvino, Jack Anthony broadcasting executive
Panner, Bernard J. pathologist, educator
†Parker, Kevin James electrical engineer educator
Parsons, George Raymond, Jr. lawyer
Pearce, William Joseph public broadcasting executive
Pearse, Robert Francis psychologist, educator
Pease, Donald E. dairy farmer, food products company executive
Pettee, Daniel Starr neurologist
Pickett, William Lee academic administrator
Pitkin, Patricia Albanese library administrator
Plosser, Charles Irving dean, economics educator
Prezzano, Wilbur John photographic products company executive
Ramsey, Jarold William English language educator, author
Rauscher, Tomlinson Gene electronics company executive, management consultant
Reed, James Alexander, Jr. lawyer
Regenstreif, S(amuel) Peter political scientist, educator
Reifler, Clifford Bruce psychiatrist, educator
Reveal, Ernest Ira food company executive
Robfogel, Susan Salitan lawyer
Rosenbaum, Richard Merrill lawyer
Rosett, Richard Nathaniel economist, educator
Rothberg, Abraham author, educator, editor
Rouse, Christopher Chapman, III composer
Rowley, Peter Templeton physician, educator
Saisselin, Remy Gilbert fine arts educator

Sangree, Walter Hinchman *social anthropologist, educator*
Sapos, Mary Ann *advertising agency executive*
Saunders, William Hundley, Jr. *chemist, educator*
Scalise, Francis Allen *adminstrator, consultant*
Schumacher, Jon Lee *lawyer*
Schwantner, Joseph *composer, educator*
Schwartz, Seymour Ira *surgeon, educator*
Scutt, Robert Carl *lawyer*
Seessel, Adam H. *writer, journalist*
Segal, Sanford Leonard *mathematics educator*
Shapiro, Sidney *physicist, educator*
Sherman, Charles Daniel, Jr. *surgeon*
Sieg, Albert Louis *photographic company executive*
Silkett, Robert Tillson *food business consultant*
Simon, Albert *physicist, engineer, educator*
Simon, Leonard Samuel *banker*
Simon, William *biomathematician, educator*
Simone, Albert Joseph *academic administrator*
Slattery, Paul Francis *physicist, educator*
Smith, John Stuart *lawyer*
†Soures, John M. *physicist, researcher*
Sproull, Robert Lamb *retired university president, physicist*
Steamer, Robert Julius *political science educator*
Stewart, Sue Stern *lawyer*
Stonehill, Eric *lawyer*
Swanton, Susan Irene *library director*
Teichert, Curt *geologist, educator*
Telesca, Michael Anthony *federal judge*
Thaler, Otto Felix *psychiatrist*
Thomas, Garth Johnson *psychology educator emeritus*
Thomas, John Howard *astrophysicist, engineer, educator*
Thomas, Leo J. *manufacturing company executive*
Thompson, Brian John *university provost, optics educator*
Thorndike, Edward Harmon *physicist*
Tomaino, Michael Thomas *lawyer*
Toribara, Taft Yutaka *radiation biologist, biophysicist, chemist, toxicologist*
Trubek, Josephine Susan *lawyer*
†Turri, Joseph A. *lawyer*
Tyler, John Randolph, Jr. *lawyer*
Underberg, Alan J. *lawyer*
Van Bortel, Howard Martin *automarketing consultant*
Van Graafeiland, Ellsworth Alfred *federal judge*
†Van Graafeiland, Gary P. *lawyer*
Von Holden, Martin Harvey *psychologist*
†Wager, Barbara *principal*
Waite, Stephen Holden *lawyer*
Walker, Michael Charles, Sr. *retirement services executive*
Watanabe, Ruth Taiko *music historian, library science educator*
Wayland-Smith, Robert Dean *banker*
†Wegman, Robert B. *food service executive*
Weiss, Howard A. *violinist, concertmaster, conductor, music educator*
Wheeler, Ladd *psychology educator*
Whitmore, Kay Rex *retired photographic company executive*
Whitten, David George *chemistry educator, researcher*
Wild, Robert Warren *lawyer*
Wiley, Jason LaRue, Jr. *neurosurgeon*
Wilkens, Beth Ela *lawyer*
Willett, Thomas Edward *lawyer*
Williams, Thomas Franklin *physician, educator*
Witmer, George Robert, Jr. *lawyer*
Wolf, Emil *physics educator*
Woods, John Joseph *executive director*
Wyatt, James Franklin *librarian*
Wynne, Lyman Carroll *psychiatrist*
Young, Mary Elizabeth *history educator*
Zagorin, Perez *historian, educator*
Zax, Melvin *psychologist, educator*

Rock Hill
Schary, Emanuel *artist*

Rockaway Beach
Kelly, George Anthony *clergyman, author, educator*

Rockville
Burton, Daniel G. *insurance executive*

Rockville Centre
Conrad, Pam *author*
Fitzgerald, Sister Janet Anne *college president*
Friedman, Neil Stuart *insurance company executive*
Halliday, Walter John *lawyer*
McGann, John Raymond *bishop*
Mc Grath, John Joseph *management consultant*

Rocky Point
Kretschmer, Ingrid Butler *elementary education educator*

Rome
Coppola, Anthony *electrical engineer*
Gabelman, Irving Jacob *consulting engineering executive, retired government official*
Griffith, Emlyn Irving *lawyer*
Waters, George Bausch *newspaper publisher*

Roosevelt
Wisner, Roscoe William, Jr. *human resources executive*

Roosevelt Island
Kaslick, Ralph Sidney *dentist, educator*

Roslyn
Cooper, Milton *real estate development executive*
Gelfand, Morris Arthur *librarian, publisher*
Risom, Ole Christian *publishing company executive*
Scollard, Patrick John *hospital executive*
Verdi, Philip Paul *credit card company executive*

Roslyn Heights
Faber, Adele *author, educator*
Jaffe, Melvin *securities company executive*
Lord, Marvin *apparel company executive*
Rogatz, Peter *physician*
†Tully, Michael J., Jr. *state senator*

Rouses Point
†Casey, William Rossiter *international transport executive*
Weierstall, Richard Paul *pharmaceutical chemist*

Rye
†Anderson, Allan *architectural firm executive*
Barker, Harold Grant *surgeon*
Beldock, Donald Travis *financial executive*
Dyche, David Bennett, Jr. *management consultant*
Erlick, Everett Howard *broadcasting company executive*
Flanagan, Eugene John Thomas *retired lawyer*
Goldstein, Stanley P. *retail company executive*
Huth, Robert D. *retail company executive*
Lehman, Lawrence Herbert *consulting engineering executive*
Lobl, Herbert Max *lawyer*
Metzger, Frank *management consulting*
Netter, Kurt Fred *building products company executive*
Newburger, Howard Martin *psychoanalyst*
Reader, George Gordon *physician, educator*
Ross, Charles Worthington, IV *metals company executive*
Stoller, Ezra *photojournalist*
Troller, Fred *graphic designer, painter, visual consultant, educator*
Tung, David Hsi Hsin *consulting civil engineer, emeritus engineering educator*
Wagner, Edward Frederick, Jr. *investment management company executive*
Wessler, Stanford *physician, educator*
Wilmot, Irvin Gorsage *former hospital administrator, educator, consultant*

Rye Brook
Cammaker, Sheldon Ira *lawyer*
Dangoor, David Ezra Ramsi *consumer goods company executive*
Masson, Robert Henry *paper company executive*

Sag Harbor
Sheed, Wilfrid John Joseph *author*

Sagaponack
Appleman, Marjorie (M. H. Appleman) *playwright, educator, poet*
Appleman, Philip *educator, writer, poet*
Butchkes, Sydney *artist*
Francke, Linda Bird *journalist*
Isham, Sheila Eaton *artist*

Saint Bonaventure
Dooley, Patrick Kiaran *philosopher, educator*
Doyle, Mathias Francis *university president, political scientist, educator*
Khairullah, Zahid Yahya *management sciences and marketing educator, consultant*
O'Connell, Neil James *priest, academic administrator*
Wallace, Malcolm Vincent Timothy *classics educator*

Saint James
Bigeleisen, Jacob *chemist, educator*
Irvine, Thomas Francis, Jr. *mechanical engineering educator*

Sands Point
Bollet, Alfred Jay *internist, educator*
Lear, Erwin *anesthesiologist, educator*

Saranac Lake
North, Robert John *biologist*

Saratoga Springs
Aldrich, Alexander *lawyer*
Boyers, Margarita Anne (Peggy Boyers) *editor, periodical, writer, translator*
Boyers, Robert *English language educator*
Hall, James William *college president*
Porter, David Hugh *pianist, classicist, academic administrator, liberal arts educator*
Upton, Richard Thomas *artist*
Walter, Paul Hermann Lawrence *chemistry educator*

Scarborough
Hopkins, Lee Bennett *writer, educator*
Wittcoff, Harold Aaron *chemist*

Scarsdale
Bernstein, Irving *international organization executive*
Blinder, Abe Lionel *management consultant*
Blitman, Howard Norton *construction company executive*
Breinin, Raymond *painter, sculptor*
Buttinger, Catharine Sarina Caroline *psychiatrist*
Clark, Merrell Mays *management consultant*
Cohen, Irwin *economist*
Cooper, Daniel *management consultant*
Cox, Robert Hames *chemist, scientific consultant*
Duncan, George Harold *broadcasting company executive*
Fendelman, Helaine *art appraiser*
Ferry, Wilbur Hugh *foundation consultant*
Frankel, Stanley Arthur *columnist, educator, business executive*
Gialleonardo, Victor *graphic designer*
Glickenhaus, Sarah Brody *speech therapist*
Graff, Henry Franklin *historian, educator*
Hayman, Seymour *former food company executive*
Hines, William Eugene *banker*
Hoffman, Richard M. *lawyer*
Howard, John Brigham *lawyer, foundation executive*
Johnson, Boine Theodore *instruments company executive, mayor*
Kaufman, Robert Jules *communications consultant, lawyer*
Lee, Robert Earl *physician*
Liston, Mary Frances *retired nursing educator*
O'Neill, Michael James *editor, author*
Oswald, George Charles *advertising executive, management and marketing consultant*
Rosow, Jerome Morris *institute executive*
Schwartz, Harry *journalist*
Sullivan, Adèle Woodhouse *organization official*
Topping, Seymour *publishing executive, newspaper*
Wertheimer, Sydney Bernard *lawyer*
Wile, Julius *former corporate executive, educator*

Schenectady
Adler, Michael S. *control systems and electronic technologies*
Alpher, Ralph Asher *physicist*
Anthony, Thomas Richard *research physicist*
Barthold, Lionel Olav *engineering executive*
Board, Joseph Breckinridge, Jr. *political scientist, educator*
Briant, Clyde Leonard *metallurgist, researcher*
Bulloff, Jack John *physical chemist, consultant*
Chestnut, Harold *foundation administrator, engineering executive*
Coffin, Louis Fussell, Jr. *mechanical engineer*
†Feibes, Werner Louis *architect*
Golub, Lewis *supermarket company executive*
†Golub, Neil *supermarket chain executive*
Grant, Ian Stanley *engineering company executive*
Hart, Howard Roscoe, Jr. *physicist*
Hebb, Malcolm Hayden *physicist*
Hedman, Dale Eugene *consulting electrical engineer*
Huening, Walter Carl, Jr. *retired consulting application engineer*
Hull, Roger Harold *college president*
Huntley, Charles William *psychology educator*
Kambour, Roger Peabody *polymer physical chemist, researcher*
LaForest, James John *retired electrical engineer*
Lawrence, Albert Weaver *insurance company executive*
Linville, Thomas Merriam *engineer*
Luborsky, Fred Everett *research physicist*
Mafi, Mohammad *civil engineer, educator*
Matta, Ram Kumar *aeronautical engineer*
McMurray, William *consultant, retired electrical engineer*
Morris, John Selwyn *philosophy educator, college president emeritus*
Murphy, William Michael *literature educator, biographer*
Panek, Jan *electrical power engineer, consultant*
Pasamanick, Benjamin *psychiatrist, educator*
Petersen, Kenneth Clarence *chemical company executive*
Philip, A. G. Davis *astronomer, editor, educator*
Redington, Rowland Wells *physicist, researcher*
Ringlee, Robert James *consulting engineering executive*
Robb, Walter Lee *retired electric company executive, management company executive*
Robbins, Daniel *author, art history educator*
Rycheck, Jayne Bogus (Mrs. Roy Richard Rycheck) *retired educational administrator*
Taub, Eli Irwin *lawyer, arbitrator*
Terry, Richard Allan *consulting psychologist, former college president*
Walsh, George William *engineering executive*
Wilson, Delano Dee *consulting company executive*

Schoharie
Duncombe, Raynor Bailey *lawyer*

Schroon Lake
Swanson, Norma Frances *federal agency administrator*

Scottsville
Dwyer, Ann Elizabeth *equine veterinarian*

Sea Cliff
Popova, Nina *dancer, choreographer, director*

Seaford
Setzler, William Edward *chemical company executive*

Searingtown
Entmacher, Paul Sidney *insurance company executive, physician, educator*

Seneca Falls
Ardia, Stephen Vincent *pump manufacturing company executive*
Butler, Susan Lowell *association executive, writer*
Morphy, John *manufacturing company executive*
Tarnow, Robert L. *manufacturing corporation executive*

Setauket
Irving, A. Marshall *marine engineer*
Levine, Sumner Norton *industrial engineer, educator, editor, author, financial consultant*
Simpson, Louis Aston Marantz *English educator, author*
Vetog, Edwin Joseph *retired gas utility executive*
Werner, Joseph *retired secondary education educator, administrator*

Shady
Ruellan, Andree *artist*

Shelter Island
Culbertson, Janet Lynn *artist*
Dowd, David Joseph *banker, builder*

Shoreham
Reynolds, Carolyn Mary *elementary educator*
Spier, Peter Edward *artist, author*

Shrub Oak
Roston, Arnold *information specialist, educator, advertising executive, artist, editor*

Sidney
Haller, Irma Tognola *secondary social studies educator*

Silver Bay
Parlin, Charles C., Jr. *retired lawyer*

Silver Creek
Schenk, Worthington George, Jr. *surgeon, educator*

Skaneateles
Allyn, William Finch *manufacturing executive*
Pickett, Lawrence Kimball *physician, educator*
†Sullivan, Walter J. *school system administrator*

Slingerlands
Ellis, David Maldwyn *history educator*
Fenton, William Nelson *anthropologist, anthropology educator emeritus*
Wilcock, Donald Frederick *mechanical engineer*

Smithtown
Pruzansky, Joshua Murdock *lawyer*
Sporn, Stanley Robert *electronic company executive*

Snyder
Breverman, Harvey *artist*

Somers
Abu Zayyad, Ray S. *electronics executive*
Case, Richard Paul *electronics executive*
Finnerty, Louise Hoppe *beverage and food company executive*
Lane, David Oliver *retired librarian*
Rubin, Samuel Harold *physician, consultant*
†Thoman, G. Richard *computer company executive*

South Nyack
†Degenshein, Jan *architect, planner*

South Salem
Howard, Joan Alice *artist*

Southampton
Atkins, Victor Kennicott, Jr. *investment banker*
Brophy, James David, Jr. *humanities educator*
Fuller, Sue *artist*
Knowles, John *author*
Lerner, Abram *retired museum director, artist*
Lichtenstein, Roy *artist*
Lieberman, Carol Cooper *healthcare marketing communications consultant*
Louchheim, Donald Harry *journalist*
Silverstein, Louis *art director, designer, editor*
Sims, Everett Martin *publishing company executive*
Smith, Dennis (Edward) *publisher, author*

Southold
Bachrach, Howard L. *biochemist*
Callis, Jerry Jackson *veterinarian*
Knight, Harold Edwin Holm, Jr. *utility company executive*
Mitchell, Robert Everitt *lawyer*

Sparkill
Dahl, Arlene *actress, author, designer, cosmetic executive*

Spencertown
Lieber, Charles Donald *publisher*

Staatsburg
Gury, Jeremy *writer, advertising executive, artist*

Stafford
Moran, John Henry, Jr. *electrical engineer, consultant*

Stamford
Bergleitner, George Charles, Jr. *investment banker*

Stanley
Jones, Gordon Edwin *horticulturist*

Staten Island
Aiken, William Eric *securities research executive*
Auh, Yang John *librarian, academic administrator*
Barton, Jerry O'Donnell *telecommunications executive*
Berger, Herbert *retired internist, educator*
Chapin, Elliott Lowell *retired bank executive*
Diamond, Richard Edward *publisher*
Fafian, Joseph, Jr. *management consultant*
Greene, Bradford Marson *landscape architect*
Greenfield, Val Shea *ophthalmologist*
Johnson, Frank Corliss *psychologist*
Mencher, Stuart Alan *sales and marketing executive*
†Newhouse, Donald E. *newspaper publishing executive*
Porter, Darwin Fred *writer*
Smith, Norman Raymond *college president*
†Stanzione, Dominick Michael *hospital administrator*
†Wisniewski, Henryk Miroslaw *pathology and neuropathology educator, research facility administrator, research scientist*

Sterling
Seawell, Thomas Robert *artist, retired educator*

Stillwater
†Lindsay, W. Douglas, Jr. *historic site administrator*

Stony Brook
Alexander, John Macmillan, Jr. *chemistry educator*
Aronoff, Mark H. *linguistics educator, author, consultant*
Baron, Samuel *flutist*
Bonner, Francis Truesdale *chemist, educator, university dean*
Booth, George *cartoonist*
Boucher, Louis Jack *dentist, educator*
Briggs, Philip Terry *biologist*
†Brown, Gerald Edward *physicist, educator*
Burnham, Harold Arthur *pharmaceutical company executive, physician*
Carlson, Elof Axel *genetics educator*
Cess, Robert Donald *atmospheric sciences educator*
Chang, Sheldon Shou Lien *electrical engineer*
Chen, Chi-Tsong *electrical engineering educator*
Cope, Randolph Howard, Jr. *electronic research and development executive, educator*
Davis, James Norman *neurologist, pharmacology researcher*
Douglas, Ronald George *mathematician*
Edelstein, Tilden Gerald *academic administrator, history educator*
Feinberg, Eugene Alexander *mathematics educator*
†Fine, Richard Nisan *pediatrician, educator*
Fleagle, John Gwynn *anthropology and paleontology educator*
Fritts, Harry Washington, Jr. *physician, educator*
Glass, David Carter *psychology educator*
Glimm, James Gilbert *mathematician*
Goldberg, Homer Beryl *English language educator*
Goodman, Norman *sociologist, researcher*
Hanson, Gilbert Nikolai *geochemistry educator*
Henn, Fritz Albert *psychiatrist*
Herman, Herbert *materials science educator*
Hill, C(lyde) Denson *mathematician, educator*
Ihde, Don *philosophy educator, university administrator*
Jonas, Steven *public health physician, medical educator, writer*
Kahn, Peter B. *physics educator*
†Kaplan, Allen P. *physician, educator, academic administrator*
Katkin, Edward Samuel *psychology educator*
Kim, Charles Wesley *microbiology educator*
†Koch, Peter MacWilliams *physics educator, researcher*
Koppelman, Lee Edward *regional planner, educator*
Kott, Jan K. *writer, scholar*

Kuspit, Donald Burton art historian, art critic, educator
†Lane, Dorothy Spiegel physician
†Lawson, H(erbert) Blaine, Jr. mathematician, educator
Lennarz, William Joseph research biologist, educator
Levin, Richard Louis English language educator
Levinton, Jeffrey S. biology educator, oceanographer
Marburger, John Harmen, III university president, physics educator
Mc Hugh, John Laurence marine biologist, educator
Meyers, Morton Allen physician, radiology educator
Mignone, Mario B. Italian studies educator
Miller, Frederick pathologist
Neuberger, Egon economics educator
Newell, William Talman, Jr. hospital administrator
Olson, Robert Eugene physician, biochemist, educator
Pekarsky, Melvin Hirsch artist
Pindell, Howardena Doreen artist
Poppers, Paul Jules anesthesiologist, educator
Pritchard, Donald William oceanographer
Rapaport, Felix Theodosius surgeon, researcher, educator
†Rohlf, F. James biometrician, educator
Schneider, Mark political science educator
Schubel, Jerry Robert marine science educator, scientist, university dean and official
†Shamash, Yacov dean, electrical engineering educator
Silverman, Hugh J. philosophy educator
Smith, John Brewster dean library sciences, director
†Solomon, Philip M. astronomer, atmospheric scientist
Spector, Marshall philosophy educator
Sreebny, Leo M. dentist, educator
Steigbigel, Roy Theodore infectious disease physician and scientist, educator
Travis, Martin Bice political scientist, educator
Tucker, Alan Curtiss mathematics educator
Visich, Marian, Jr. engineering educator, university dean
†Weidner, Donald J. geophysicist educator
Williams, George Christopher biologist, ecology and evolution educator
Wurster, Charles Frederick environmental scientist, educator
Yahil, Amos astrophysicist, educator
Yang, Chen Ning physicist, educator
Zemanian, Armen Humpartsoum electrical engineer, mathematician

Stony Point
Miller, Leonard Martin manufacturing executive

Suffern
Marchetti, Peter Louis real estate executive
Sutherland, George Leslie retired chemical company executive
Walsh, James Jerome philosophy educator
Ward, William Francis, Jr. real estate investment banker
Zecca, John Andrew retired association executive

Syosset
Bainton, Donald J. diversified manufacturing company executive
Barry, Richard Francis retired life insurance company executive
†Guthart, Leo A. electronics executive
Hershey, Alfred Day geneticist
Kantor, Edwin investment company executive
Lazor, Theodosius (His Beatitude Metropolitan Theodosius) archbishop
Nydick, David schools superintendent
Puglisi, Anthony Joseph service company executive
Rudman, Michael P. publishing executive
Vermylen, Paul Anthony, Jr. oil company executive

Syracuse
†Abbott, George Lindell librarian
Akiyama, Kazuyoshi conductor
Alston, William Payne philosophy educator
†Baldwin, John Edwin chemistry educator
Baldwin, Robert Frederick, Jr. lawyer
Balk, Alfred William journalist
Barclay, H(ugh) Douglas lawyer, former state senator
Beeching, Charles Train, Jr. lawyer
Bennett, Robert John banker
Berra, P. Bruce computer educator
Birge, Robert Richards chemistry educator
Birkhead, Guthrie Sweeney, Jr. political scientist, university dean
Black, Lois Mae clinical psychologist, educator
Braungart, Richard Gottfried sociology and international relations educator
Brennan, Paul Joseph civil engineer, educator
Bunn, Timothy David newspaper editor
Burgess, Robert Lewis ecologist, educator
Burstyn, Joan Netta educator
Burtt, Benjamin Pickering retired chemistry educator
Butler, Katharine Gorrell speech-language pathologist, educator
Cargo, Gerald Thomas mathematics educator
Charters, Alexander Nathaniel education educator emeritus
Church, Philip Throop mathematician, educator
Cirando, John Anthony lawyer
Clausen, Jerry Lee psychiatrist
Cohen, William Nathan radiologist
Conan, Robert James, Jr. chemistry educator, consultant
Cooke, Goodwin international relations educator
Coplin, William David policy studies educator
Costello, Thomas Joseph bishop
Crowley, John W(illiam) English language educator
Daly, Robert W. psychiatrist, medical educator
Darrone, Donald William retired tool corporation executive
Davis, William E. utility executive
†DeFrancisco, John A. state senator, lawyer
†Delmar, Mario cardiac physiology educator
Denise, Theodore Cullom philosophy educator
DiLorenzo, Louis Patrick lawyer
Driver, Robert Baylor, Jr. opera administrator
Dudewicz, Edward John statistician
Dunham, Philip Bigelow biology educator, physiologist
†Eisenberg, Michael Bruce information studies educator
Endries, John Michael utility executive
Eveleigh, Virgil William electrical and computer engineering educator
Fendler, Janos Hugo chemistry educator
Ferguson, Tracy Heiman lawyer, educational administrator
Fitzgerald, Harold Kenneth social work educator, consultant
Fitzpatrick, James David lawyer
Fox, Geoffrey Charles computer science and physics educator
Fraser, Henry S. lawyer
Frohock, Fred Manuel political science educator
Gaal, John lawyer
Goetzmann, Harry Edward, Jr. leasing company executive
Gold, Joseph medical researcher
Goodman, Donald C. university administrator
Graver, Jack Edward mathematics educator
Hansen, Per Brinch computer scientist
Harrington, Roger Fuller electrical engineering educator, consultant
Hayes, David Michael lawyer
Heberlig, Harold Dean, Jr. lawyer
Heffner, Ralph H. agricultural products company executive
Herzog, Peter Emilius legal educator
Hiemstra, Roger adult education educator, writer
Hoffman, Arthur Wolf English language educator
Hole, Richard Douglas lawyer
Holm, Robert Arthur environmental scientist
Honig, Arnold physics educator, researcher
Incaudo, Claude J. food products company executive
Jefferies, Michael John electrical engineer
Jensen, Robert Granville geography educator, university dean
Jump, Bernard, Jr. economics educator
Kenna, E. Douglas retired plastics company executive
Ketcham, Ralph history and political science educator
Kieffer, Stephen Aaron radiologist, educator
King, Chester Harding, Jr. lawyer
King, Robert Bainton neurosurgeon
Konski, James Louis civil engineer
Kopp, Robert Walter lawyer
Krathwohl, David Reading education educator emeritus
†Kriebel, Mahlon Edward physiology educator, inventor
†Kriesberg, Louis sociologist, educator
Kuchta, Ronald Andrew art museum director, educator
Landaw, Stephen Arthur physician, educator
†Lanzafame, Samuel James manufacturing company executive
Lawton, Joseph J., Jr. lawyer
Lee, Kermit James, Jr. architect, educator
Lemanski, Larry Fredrick medical educator
LePage, Wilbur Reed electrical engineering educator
Libove, Charles mechanical and aerospace engineering educator
Lichtblau, Myron Ivor language educator
Lillestol, Jane Marie academic administrator
Liu, Hao-wen mechanical and aerospace engineering educator, consultant
Lyman, Frederic A. mechanical and aerospace engineering educator, researcher
Mannion, John Francis Xavier insurance company executive
Marcoccia, Louis Gary accountant, university administrator
Marge, Michael disability prevention specialist
Martonosi, Anthony Nicholas biochemistry educator, researcher
Mazur, Allan Carl sociologist, educator
McCurn, Neal Peters federal judge
McGraw, James L. retired ophthalmologist, educator
McNaughton, Samuel Joseph botany educator
Meinig, Donald William geography educator
Mesrobian, Arpena Sachaklian publisher, editor, consultant
Meyers, Peter L. banker
Miron, Murray Samuel psychologist, educator
Monmonier, Mark graphics educator, geographer
Morton, William Gilbert banker
Moses, Robert Edward lawyer
Muller, Ernest H. geology educator
Munson, Howard G. federal judge
Murray, David George orthopaedic surgeon, educator
Murray, Raymond William, Jr. lawyer
Nafie, Laurence Allen chemistry educator
Nelli, D. James school administrator, accountant
Nelson, Douglas A. pathologist, educator
†Nicoletti, Joseph New York state assemblyman
O'Day, Royal Lewis former banker
O'Keefe, Joseph Thomas bishop
Palmer, John L. social sciences researcher, educator
Pardee, Otway O'Meara computer science educator
Pellow, David Matthew lawyer
Pennock, Donald William retired mechanical engineer
Peterfreund, Sheldon Paul educator
Phillips, Arthur William, Jr. biology educator
Phillips, Richard Hart psychiatrist
Powell, James Matthew history educator
Prucha, John James geologist, educator
Ranalli, Michael Patrick utility company executive
Reed, George Farrell physician
†Roberts, Robert engineering organization executive, think-tank executive
Robinson, John Alan logic and computer science educator
Robinson, Joseph Edward geology educator, consulting petroleum geologist
Rogers, Stephen newspaper publisher
Rosenbaum, Arthur Elihu radiologist, educator
Russell-Hunter, W(illiam) D(evigne) zoology educator, research biologist, writer
Samuels, Marwyn Stewart geography educator
Sargent, Robert George engineering educator
Schulte, Henry Frank journalism educator
Schwartz, Richard Derecktor sociologist, educator
Scullin, Frederick James, Jr. federal judge
Shattuck, George Clement lawyer
Shaw, Kenneth Alan university president
Simmons, Roy, Jr. university athletic coach
Skoler, Louis architect, educator
Smith, Kenneth Judson, Jr. chemist, theoretician, educator
Stam, David Harry librarian
Stephens, Edward Carl communications educator, writer
Sternlicht, Sanford English and theater arts educator, writer
Strait, Bradley Justus electrical engineering educator
Sutton, Walter English educator
Szasz, Thomas Stephen psychiatrist, educator, writer
Tatham, David Frederic art historian, educator
Taylor, Richard Fred, Jr. lawyer
Terry, John Hart lawyer, former utility company executive, former congressman
Thomas, Sidney fine arts educator, researcher
†Thompson, Tazewell Alfred artistic director, writer
Thorson, Stuart J. political science educator
Tolley, William Pearson former university chancellor, former airline executive
Tully, William P. civil engineer, academic administrator
van Inwagen, Peter Jan philosophy educator
†Verrillo, Ronald Thomas neuroscientist
†Wadley, Susan Snow anthropologist
Wali, Kameshwar physicist, educator
Waterman, Daniel mathematician, educator
Weiss, Volker university administrator, educator
Wellner, Marcel Nahum physics educator, researcher
Whittle, John Joseph insurance company executive
Wiecek, William Michael law educator
Wiggins, James Bryan religion educator
Wiley, Richard Gordon electrical engineer
Williams, William Joseph physician, educator
Wolff, Tobias (Jonathan Ansell Wolff) author

Tappan
Dell, Robert Christopher geothermal sculptor, scenic artist
Fox, Muriel public relations executive
Nickford, Juan sculptor, educator

Tarrytown
Anderson, John Erling chemical engineer
Ashburn, Anderson magazine editor
Bartoo, Richard Kieth chemical engineer, consultant
Chu, Foo physician
Dobkin, John Howard art administrator
†Dorland, Byrl Brown civic worker
Ferrari, Robert Joseph business educator, former banker
†Flanigen, Edith Marie materials scientist
Goldin, Milton fund raising counsel, author
†Gsand, William L. computer company executive
Hurley, William Joseph information systems executive
Jarrett, Eugene Lawrence chemical company executive
Kane, Stanley Bruce food products executive
Kaplan, Richard magazine editor
Kroll, Nathan film producer, director
Marcus, Sheldon social sciences educator
Neill, Richard Robert retired publishing company executive
Oelbaum, Harold lawyer, corporate executive
Rath, Bernard Emil trade association executive
Raymond, George Marc city planner, educator
Savage, Whitney Lee artist, filmmaker
Shaw, Bryan P. H. retired investment company executive
†Toda, K. electronics executive
†Welsh, Dennie M. data processing executive

Thornwood
Bassett, Lawrence C management consultant
Chin, Carolyn Sue business executive
Douglas, Patricia Jeanne systems designer

Ticonderoga
†Westbrook, Nicholas Kilmer museum administrator, historian

Tonawanda
Browning, James Franklin professional society executive
Haller, Calvin John banker
Hettrick, John Lord banker, manufacturer

Troy
Abetti, Pier Antonio consulting electrical engineer, technology management and entrepreneurship educator
Ahlers, Rolf Willi philosopher, theologian
Anderson, John Bailey electrical engineering educator
Archer, Sydney chemistry educator
Baron, Robert Alan psychology and business educator, author
Bean, Charles Palmer biophysicist
Berg, Daniel science and technology educator
Bergles, Arthur Edward mechanical engineering educator
Block, Robert Charles nuclear engineering and engineering physics educator
Bonney, William Lawless data processing and telecommunications educator
Brazil, Harold Edmund political science educator
Breed, Helen Illick ichthyologist, educator
Brunelle, Eugene John, Jr. mechanical engineering educator
Buckley, J. Stephen newspaper publisher
Bunce, Stanley Chalmers chemist, educator
Chapman, Sara Simmons academic administrator, English educator
†Cole, Julian D. mathematician, educator
Corelli, John Charles physicist, educator
Daves, Glenn Doyle, Jr. science educator, chemist, researcher
†Desrochers, Alan Alfred electrical engineer
Diwan, Romesh Kumar economics educator
Doremus, Robert Heward glass and ceramics processing educator
Drew, Donald Allen mathematical sciences educator
†Duquette, David Joseph materials science and engineering educator
Dutton, Robert Edward, Jr. medical educator
Evans, Edwin Charles consultant, former manufacturing executive
Feeser, Larry James civil engineering educator, researcher
Ferris, James Peter chemist, educator
Fleischer, Robert Louis physics educator
Giaever, Ivar physicist
Gill, William Nelson chemical engineering educator
Glicksman, Martin Eden materials engineering educator
Gorenstein, Shirley Slotkin anthropologist, educator
Greenwood, Allan N. engineering educator, researcher
Haviland, David Sands architectural educator, researcher, administrator
Hickok, Robert Lyman, Jr. electrophysics educator
Horton, John Tod engineering company executive
Jacobson, Melvin Joseph applied mathematician, acoustician, educator
Jones, E. Stewart, Jr. lawyer
Jones, Owen Craven, Jr. nuclear and mechanical engineer, educator
Jordan, Mark Henry consulting civil engineer
Judd, Gary university administrator
Kahl, William Frederick retired college president
Krause, Sonja chemistry educator, researcher
Krempl, Erhard mechanics educator, consultant
†Le Maistre, Christopher William educational director
Levinger, Joseph Solomon physicist, educator
Littman, Howard chemical engineer, educator
Lockett, Barbara Ann librarian
McDonald, John Francis Patrick electrical engineering educator
McKinley, William A. educator, physicist
McNaughton, Robert Forbes, Jr. computer science educator
Medicus, Heinrich Adolf physicist, educator
Miller, Donald Spencer geologist, educator
Modestino, James William electrical engineering educator
Nelson, John Keith electrical engineer
O'Neil, Mary Agnes health science facility administrator
Pfau, Charles Julius biology educator, researcher
Phelan, Thomas clergyman, academic administrator, educator
Pipes, Robert Byron academic administrator, mechanical engineer
Potts, Kevin T. chemistry educator
Resnick, Robert physicist, educator
Richtol, Herbert Harold academic dean
†Romond, James principal
Saridis, George Nicholas electrical engineer
Smith, Rex William journalist
Sperber, Daniel physicist
Wait, Samuel Charles, Jr. academic administrator, educator
Watson, Donald Ralph academic dean, architect, author
†Wentorf, Robert Henry physical chemist
Whitburn, Merrill Duane English literature educator
White, Frederick Andrew physics educator, physicist
Wiberley, Stephen Edward chemistry educator, consultant
Wilson, Jack Martin university administrator, scientific association executive, physics educator
Woods, John William electrical, computer and systems engineering educator, consultant

Trumansburg
Billings, Peggy Marie religious organization administrator, educator
Mc Connell, John Wilkinson labor relations educator, labor arbitrator, former socio-economics educator
Taylor, Richard philosopher, educator

Tuckahoe
Silk, Eleana S. librarian

Tupper Lake
Welsh, Peter Corbett museum consultant, historian

Tuxedo Park
Brown, Walston Shepard lawyer
Domjan, Joseph (Spiri Domjan) artist
Hall, Frederick Keith chemist
Heusser, Calvin John biology educator, researcher
Shore, Howard Leslie composer

Unadilla
Compton, John Robinson printing company executive

Union
Franks, Robert D. (Bob Franks) congressman

Uniondale
Bossy, Michael professional hockey player
Brown, Kenneth Lloyd lawyer
†Corva, Angelo Francis architect
†Frashier, Gary Even corporation executive
†Guenzel, Rudolf Paul banker
†Henning, Lorne Edward professional hockey coach
Kress, Heather Gabrielle lawyer
Mishler, Jacob federal judge
Pierce, Stanley lawyer
Platt, Thomas Collier, Jr. federal judge
Pratt, George Cheney federal judge
Savino, William M. lawyer
Shapiro, Barry Robert lawyer
Spatt, Arthur Donald federal judge
Tempest, Harrison F. bank executive
Wright, Franklin Leatherbury, Jr. lawyer, banker

Unionville
Kemnitz, Thomas Milton publisher

Upton
Baron, Seymour engineering and research executive
Blume, Martin physicist
Bond, Peter Danford physicist
†Casten, Richard Francis physicist
Chrien, Robert Edward physicist
†Chung, Suh-Urk physicist
Cronkite, Eugene Pitcher physician
†Dover, Carl Bellman physicist, consultant
Friedlander, Gerhart nuclear chemist
Goldhaber, Gertrude Scharff physicist
Goldhaber, Maurice physicist
Hamilton, Leonard Derwent physician, molecular biologist
Hendrie, Joseph Mallam physicist, nuclear engineer, government official
Higinbotham, William Alfred physicist
†Holroyd, Richard Allan researcher
Kato, Walter Yoneo physicist
Lindenbaum, S(eymour) J(oseph) physicist
Lowenstein, Derek Irving physicist
Marr, Robert Bruce physicist, educator
McWhan, Denis Bayman physicist
Petrakis, Leonidas research scientist, administrator
Radeka, Veljko electronics engineer
Rau, Ralph Ronald physicist
Samios, Nicholas Peter physicist
Schwartz, Melvin physics educator, laboratory administrator
Setlow, Jane Kellock biophysicist
Setlow, Richard Burton biophysicist
†Shirane, Gen science administrator
Steinberg, Meyer chemical engineer
Studier, Frederick William biophysicist
Susskind, Herbert biomedical engineer, educator
Sutin, Norman chemistry educator, scientist
Wolf, Alfred Peter chemist, educator

Utica
†Antzelevitch, Charles research center executive

Boyle, William Leo, Jr. *educational consultant, retired college president*
Cardamone, Richard J. *federal judge*
Donovan, Donna Mae *newspaper publisher*
Ehre, Victor Tyndall *insurance company executive*
Harney, Patrick Joseph Dwyer *meteorologist, consultant*
Pribble, Easton *artist*
Raymonda, James Earl *banker*
Schrauth, William Lawrence *banker, lawyer*
Schweizer, Paul Douglas *museum director*
Simpson, Michael Kevin *college president, political science educator*
Trojan, Penelope Ann *physical education educator*

Vails Gate
Fife, Betty H. *librarian*

Valhalla
Adler, Karl Paul *medical educator, academic administrator*
Camerano, Franklin *medical center administrator*
Carter, Anne Cohen *physician*
Christenson, William Newcome *physician*
Cimino, Joseph Anthony *physician, educator*
Danishefsky, Isidore *biochemist*
Del Guercio, Louis Richard Maurice *surgeon, educator, company executive*
Ferrone, Soldano *microbiology and immunology educator, physician*
†Fink, Raymond *medical educator*
Hodgson, W(alter) John B(arry) *surgeon*
Itskovitz, Harold David *physician*
Jones, James Robert *obstetrician, gynecologist, educator*
Levy, Norman B. *psychiatrist, educator*
McGiff, John C(harles) *pharmacologist*
Niguidula, Faustino Nazario *pediatric cardiothoracic surgeon*
Weisburger, John Hans *medical researcher*
Williams, Gary Murray *medical researcher, pathology educator*

Valley Cottage
Atha, Stuart Kimball, Jr. *retired banker*

Valley Stream
Blakeman, Royal Edwin *lawyer*
†Golden, Hyman *beverage products company executive*
Lehrer, Stanley *magazine publisher, editorial director, corporate executive*
Natow, Annette Baum *nutritionist, author, consultant*
Rachlin, Harvey Brant *author, music publishing company executive*

Van Hornesville
Case, Everett Needham *former university president, educator*
Young, Richard *lawyer*

Waccabuc
Hall, Elizabeth *writer*
Kislik, Richard William *publishing executive*
Thompson, Edward Thorwald *magazine editor*

Wainscott
Dubow, Arthur Myron *investor, lawyer*
Henderson, William Charles *editor*
Russo, Alexander Peter *artist, educator*
Wainwright, Stuyvesant, II *lawyer*

Walden
Hanau, Kenneth John, Jr. *packaging company executive*

Wallkill
Koch, Edwin Ernest *artist, interior decorator*

Wantagh
Dawson, George Glenn *economics educator emeritus*
†DeNapoli, Anthony *middle school principal*
Litman, Bernard *electrical engineer, consultant*
Mur, Raphael *lawyer, retired aerospace manufacturing executive*
Ross, Sheldon Jules *dentist*
Smits, Edward John *museum consultant*
Torrenzano, Richard *public affairs executive*
Zinder, Newton Donald *stock market analyst, consultant*

Wappingers Falls
Engelman, Melvin Alkon *retired dentist, business executive, scientist*
Hogan, Edward Robert *financial services executive*
Johnson, Jeh Vincent *architect*
Maissel, Leon Israel *physicist, engineer*

Warwick
Franck, Frederick Sigfred *artist, author, dental surgeon*

Washingtonville
Castel, Nico *tenor, educator*

Water Mill
Mac Whinnie, John Vincent *artist*
Rosenberg, Alex Jacob *art dealer, curator, fine arts appraiser, educator*

Waterford
Gold, James Paul *museum director*

Watermill
D'Urso, Joseph Paul *designer*

Watertown
Coe, Benjamin Plaisted *state official*
Johnson, John Brayton *editor, publisher*

Watervliet
Kitchens, Clarence Wesley, Jr. *physical science administrator*

Webster
Conwell, Esther Marly *physicist*
Duke, Charles Bryan *research and development manufacturing executive, physics educator*
Garg, Devendra *financial executive*
Johnson, Ray Clifford *mechanical engineering educator, consultant, writer*
†Machell, Arthur R. *retired mechanical engineer, association board member*
Nicholson, Douglas Robert *accountant*
Witmer, G. Robert *retired state supreme court justice*

Weedsport
†Cichello, Samuel Joseph *architect*

Wellsville
Taylor, Theodore Brewster *physicist, business executive*

West Brentwood
†O'Neill, Peggy *health care executive*

West Hempstead
Brodsky, Irwin Abel *retired stockbroker*
Klebanoff, Stanley Milton *lawyer*
Pollio, Ralph Thomas *editor, writer, magazine consultant*
Rothberg, June Simmonds *nursing educator emerita, psychotherapist, psychoanalyst*

West Islip
Softness, Donald Gabriel *marketing and manufacturing executive*

West Nyack
Gillespie, John Fagan *mining executive*
Hornik, Joseph William *civil engineer*
†Michaelson, Martin J. *textile company executive, computer consultant*
Painter, Carl Eric *manufacturing company executive*
Pringle, Laurence Patrick *writer*

West Point
Barr, Donald Roy *statistics and operations research educator, statistician*
Galloway, Gerald Edward, Jr. *dean*
Galvin, John Rogers *educator, retired army officer*
Graves, Howard Dwayne *army officer, academic administrator, educator*
Johnson, A(lyn) William *chemistry educator, consultant*
Watson, Georgianna *librarian*

West Stockholm
O'Brien, Neal Ray *geology educator*

Westbury
Barboza, Anthony *photographer, artist*
Cannizzaro, Paul Peter *food products executive*
†Cullen, John B. *food products company executive*
De Pauw, Gommar Albert *priest, educator*
Eisenberg, Dorothy *federal judge*
Fogg, Joseph Graham, III *investment banking executive*
†Fortunoff, Alan Meyer *retail company executive*
†Kennedy, Bernard D. *food products executive*
†Martin, Daniel Richard *pharmaceutical company executive*
†Sandler, Gerald Howard *aerospace executive*
Sherbell, Rhoda *artist, sculptor*
Tulchin, Stanley *banker, lecturer, author, business reorganization consultant*

Westfield
Brown, Kent Louis, Sr. *surgeon*

Westhampton Beach
Maas, Jane Brown *advertising executive*

Westport
Davis, George Donald *land use policy consultant*

White Plains
†Alin, Robert David *lawyer*
Bagwill, John Williams, Jr. *retired pension fund company executive*
Benjamin, Theodore Simon *publishing company executive*
Berlin, Alan Daniel *lawyer, international energy and legal consultant*
Bijur, Peter I. *petroleum company executive*
Blank, H. Robert *psychiatrist*
Blass, John Paul *medical educator, physician*
Bober, Lawrence Harold *retired banker*
Boudreaux, John *public relations specialist*
Brazell, James Ervin *oil company executive, lawyer*
Brieant, Charles La Monte *federal judge*
Broderick, Vincent Lyons *federal judge*
†Burke, Raymond F. *lawyer*
†Busch, Paul Louis *engineering company executive, consultant*
Carey, John *lawyer, judge*
Cohen, Richard Norman *insurance executive*
Cohn, Howard *retired magazine editor*
Colwell, Howard Otis *advertising executive*
Cooke, Lloyd Miller *former organization executive*
Davidson, Carl B. *oil company executive*
DeCrane, Alfred Charles, Jr. *petroleum company executive*
Dickinson, Richard Raymond *oil company executive*
Dowd, Peter Jerome *public relations executive*
Ellenbogen, Milton Joseph *publishing executive, editor, writer*
†Ellenbogen, Rudolph Solomon *library curator*
†Endresen, Jan Ralph *export company executive*
Feldman, Jay Newman *lawyer, telecommunications executive*
†Fjelde, Rolf Gerhard *translator, writer*
Foster, John Horace *consulting environmental engineer*
Friedman, Ralph *airplane instrument manufacturing company executive*
Fudge, Ann Marie *marketing executive*
Gjertsen, O. Gerard *lawyer*
Godofsky, Stanley *lawyer*
Goettel, Gerard Louis *federal judge*
†Graham, Lawrence Otis *lawyer, writer, television personality*
†Grayson, Richard Steven (Lord Eynsford) *international legal and political management consultant, foreign correspondent*
Greene, Leonard Michael *aerospace manufacturing executive, institute executive*
†Gurahian, Vincent *church official, former judge*
Henningsen, Victor William, Jr. *food company executive*
Howse, Jennifer Louise *foundation administrator*
Jensen, Eric Finn *lawyer*
Jensen, Grady Edmonds *association executive*
Johnson, Daniel Robert *lawyer*
†Johnston, Richard Boles, Jr. *pediatrician, educator, biomedical researcher*
Katz, Michael *pediatrician, educator*
Kisseberth, Paul Barto *publishing executive*
Krantz, Melissa Marianne *public relations company executive*
Krowe, Allen Julian *oil company executive*
LaBant, Robert James *information processing executive*
Machover, Carl *computer graphics consultant*
Magaziner, Elliot Albert *musician, conductor, educator*
Marano, Anthony Joseph *cardiologist*
Marci-Mariani, Anita *designer, illustrator*
Massey, Charles L. *health organization executive*
McDowell, Fletcher Hughes *physician, educator*
McQuaid, John G. *lawyer*
Mitchell, Robert Dale *consulting engineer*
Morrison, Robert Scheck *food processing company executive*
Moser, Marvin *physician, educator, author*
Nickerson, Ruth *sculptor*
Older, Jack Stanley *lawyer*
O'Rourke, Andrew Patrick *lawyer, county official*
Papp, Laszlo George *architect*
Payson, Martin Fred *lawyer*
Peck, Alexander Norman *physical education educator, day camp administrator*
Peyton, Donald Leon *retired standards association executive*
Pirnie, Malcolm, Jr. *consulting engineer*
Rapp, Richard Tilden *economist, consultant*
Roll, Irwin Clifford (Win Roll) *advertising and marketing executive*
Rose, William Allen, Jr. *architect*
Rosenberg, Michael *lawyer*
Samii, Abdol Hossein *physician, educator*
†Sherlock, Gary Fuller *newspaper publisher*
Smith, Elizabeth Patience *oil industry executive, lawyer*
Smith, Gerard Peter *neuroscientist*
Stein, Ralph Michael *lawyer, educator*
†Stith, Forrest Christopher *bishop*
Teitell, Conrad Laurence *lawyer, author*
Tell, William Kirn, Jr. *oil company executive, lawyer*
Theisz, Erwin Jan *scientist*
†Tobin, Steven Michael *insurance company executive*
Triffin, Nicholas *law librarian, law educator*
Turley, James Anthony, Jr. *lawyer*
†Westerhoff, Garret Peter *environmental engineer, executive*
Westerman, Gayl Shaw *law educator*
Wheaton, David *professional tennis player*
Wilson, Malcolm *banker, lawyer, former governor*

Whitestone
Catapano, Joseph John *construction company executive*

Williamsville
Danni, F. Robert *municipal official*
Harnack, Robert Spencer *retired education educator*
Paladino, Joseph Anthony *clinical pharmacist*
Reisman, Robert E. *physician, educator*

Wolcott
Bartlett, Cody Blake *lawyer, educator*

Woodbury
Bell, William Joseph *cable television company executive*
Bleicher, Sheldon Joseph *endocrinologist, medical educator*
†Dolan, Charles Francis *cable systems company executive*
Lemle, Robert Spencer *lawyer*
Randolph, Francis Fitz, Jr. *cable television executive*
Sweeney, Daniel Thomas *cable television company executive*
Tatta, John Louis *cable television executive*
†Zirkel, Don *public information official*

Woodmere
Abramson, Martin *author, journalist*
Bobroff, Harold *lawyer*
Raab, Ira Jerry *lawyer*
†Weiss, Stephen Ira *advertising executive*

Woodside
Burchell, Jeanne Kathleen *primary school educator*

Woodstock
Banks, Rela *sculptor*
Cox, James David *art gallery executive*
Fortess, Karl Eugene *artist, lithographer*
Godwin, Gail Kathleen *author*
Hoyt, Earl Edward, Jr. *industrial designer*
Ober, Stuart Alan *investment consultant, book publisher*
Smith, Albert Aloysius, Jr. *electrical engineer, consultant*

Wyandanch
Barnett, Peter John *property development executive, educator*

Yonkers
Atkins, Leola Mae *special education educator*
Augustine, John *accountant*
Baumel, Herbert *violinist, conductor*
Denver, Eileen Ann *magazine editor*
Drisko, Elliot Hillman *marriage and family therapist*
Eimicke, Victor W(illiam) *publishing company executive*
†Foy, James E. *hospital administrator*
Holtz, Gilbert Joseph *steel company executive*
Karpatkin, Rhoda Hendrick *consumer information organization executive, lawyer*
Kresh, Paul *author, editor*
Landau, Irwin *magazine publishing company executive*
Liggio, Jean Vincenza *artist, educator*
Miller, Jacqueline Winslow *library director*
Philipps, Edward William *banker, real estate appraiser*
Robinson, Chester Hersey *retired dean*
Rosch, Paul John *physician, educator*
Varma, Baidya Nath *sociologist, broadcaster*

York
Coleman, David Cecil *financial executive*

Yorktown Heights
Agarwal, Ramesh Chandra *applied mathematician, researcher*
Allen, Frances Elizabeth *computer scientist*
Almasi, George Stanley *electrical engineer, computer scientist*
Dennard, Robert Heath *engineering executive, scientist*
d'Heurle, François Max *research scientist, engineering educator*
Fowler, Alan Bicksler *retired physicist*
Green, Paul Eliot, Jr. *communications scientist*
†Gutzwiller, Martin Charles *theoretical physicist, research scientist*
Hoffman, Alan Jerome *mathematician, educator*
†Holtzberg, Frederic *chemist, solid state researcher*
Hong, Se June *computer engineer*
Hsieh, Hazel Tseng *elementary education educator*
Jaffe, Jeffrey Martin *computer scientist*
†Johnson, Ellis Lane *mathematician*
Jones, Lauretta Marie *artist, graphic designer, computer interface designer*
Keyes, Robert William *physicist*
Kirkpatrick, Edward Scott *physicist*
Klein, Richard Stephen *internist*
Landauer, Rolf William *physicist*
Lang, Norton David *physicist*
LaRussa, Joseph Anthony *optical company executive*
Laventhol, Henry L(ee) (Hank Laventhol) *artist, etcher*
Mandelbrot, Benoit B. *mathematician, scientist, educator*
Ning, Tak Hung *physicist, microelectronic technologist*
Pugh, Emerson William *electrical engineer*
†Romankiw, Lubomyr Taras *materials engineer*
Rosenblatt, Stephen Paul *marketing and sales promotion company executive*
Rosenfeld, Steven Ira *artistic director, music publisher*
Samalin, Edwin *lawyer, educator*
Sorokin, Peter Pitirimovich *physicist*
Spiller, Eberhard Adolf *physicist*
Terman, Lewis Madison *electrical engineer, researcher*
Troutman, Ronald R. *electrical engineer*
Winograd, Shmuel *mathematician*
Wong, Chak-Kuen *computer scientist*

Youngstown
Alpert, Norman *chemical company executive*
†Dunnigan, Brian Leigh *historic site administrator*

NORTH CAROLINA

Advance
†Cochrane, Betsy Lane *state senator*
Huber, Thomas Martin *container company executive*
Legere, Laurence Joseph *government official*

Albemarle
Bramlett, Christopher Lewis *academic administrator*

Apex
Knapp, Richard Bruce *anesthesiologist*

Asheville
Armstrong, Robert Baker *textile company executive*
Baker, Robert Hart *conductor*
Baldwin, Garza, Jr. *lawyer, manufacturing company executive*
Banks, James Barber *publishing executive*
Becker, Quinn Henderson *orthopaedic surgeon, army officer*
Bissette, Winston Louis, Jr. *lawyer, mayor*
†Burgin, Robert F. *medical center administrator*
Cecil, William A. V., Sr. *landmark director*
Coli, Guido John *chemical company executive*
Conroy, David James *retired chemical, diversified manufacturing executive*
Damtoft, Walter Atkinson *editor, publisher*
†Davenport, L. B. *bishop*
Davis, Roy Walton, Jr. *lawyer*
Etter, Robert Miller *retired consumer products executive, chemist*
Everett, Durward R., Jr. *retired banker*
Gabriel, Robert *art association administrator*
Gaffney, Thomas Edward *retired physician*
Haggard, William Henry *meteorologist*
Hall, Francoise Puvrez *psychiatrist*
†Hyde, Herbert Lee *lawyer*
Johnston, John Devereaux, Jr. *law educator*
Jones, J. Kenneth *art dealer, former museum administrator*
King, Joseph Bertram *architect*
Merrill, Edward Clifton, Jr. *emeritus university president*
Powell, Norborne Berkeley *urologist*
Pulleyn, S(amuel) Robert *publishing company executive*
†Reed, Patsy Bostick *university administrator*
Rufa, Robert Henry *artist, writer, editor*
Smith, Norman Cutler *geologist, business executive, educator*
Squibb, Samuel Dexter *chemistry educator*
Vander Voort, Dale Gilbert *textile company executive*
Voorhees, Richard Lesley *federal judge*
Weed, Maurice James *composer, retired music educator*
Weil, Thomas P. *health services consultant*
Wilson, Lauren Ross *academic administrator*

Atlantic Beach
Barnes, James Thomas, Jr. *aquarium administrator*

Banner Elk
Isbell, Robert *writer*
Speer, Allen Paul, III *political science educator*

Barnardsville
Acito, Daniel Joseph *interior designer*

Beaufort
Bonaventura, Joseph *biochemist, educator, research center director*
Hayman, Carol Bessent *poet, author*

Biscoe
McIlvaine, William L. *educational director, computer science educator*

Black Mountain
Holden, Reuben Andrus *retired college president*
Kennedy, William Bean *theology educator*
Lathrop, Gertrude Adams *chemist, consultant*
Pinkerton, Linda F. *lawyer*
Weatherford, Willis Duke, Jr. *college president emeritus*
Weinhauer, William Gillette *retired bishop*

Bladenboro
Walters, Cathryne Brunson *primary school educator*

Blowing Rock
Haley, Gail E(inhart) *author*

Boiling Springs
Lamb, Robert Lee *religion educator*
White, Martin Christopher *academic administrator*

Boone
Auten, Janet Sue *business education educator*
Borkowski, Francis Thomas *university administrator*
Bowden, Elbert Victor *banking, finance and economics author and educator*

Boonville
Reece, Joe Wilson *engineering company executive*

Brevard
Phillips, Euan Hywel *publishing executive*
Wall, Robert Wilson, Jr. *former utility executive*

Buies Creek
Davis, Ferd Leary, Jr. *law educator, lawyer, consultant*
Funderburk, David B. *history educator, former ambassador*
Wiggins, Norman Adrian *university administrator, legal educator*

Burlington
Kee, Walter Andrew *former government official*
Powell, James Bobbitt *biomedical laboratories executive, pathologist*
Tolley, Jerry Russell *clinical laboratory executive*
Weavil, David Carlton *clinical laboratory services executive*
Wilson, William Preston *psychiatrist, emeritus educator*

Burnsville
†Bernstein, William Joseph *glass artist, educator*
Doyle, John Lawrence *artist*

Calabash
Strunk, Orlo Christopher, Jr. *psychology educator*

Camden
Hammond, Roy Joseph *reinsurance company executive*

Carrboro
Greenslade, Forrest Charles *international health care executive*

Carthage
Benade, Leo Edward *lawyer, retired army officer*

Cary
†Andrews, John Woodhouse *newspaper publisher*
†Conrad, Hans *materials engineering educator*
Garrison, Jane Gayle *astrologer*
Gehringer, Richard George *publishing executive*
Jones, James Arthur *retired utilities executive*
McCarty, Thomas Joseph *publishing company executive*
Miranda, Constancio Fernandes *civil engineering educator*
Mochrie, Richard D. *physiology educator*
Reynolds, Edward *book publisher*
Sussenguth, Edward Henry *computer company executive, computer network designer*
Talbert, Luther Marcus *physician*

Cashiers
O'Connell, Edward James, Jr. *psychology educator, computer applications and data analysis consultant*

Chapel Hill
Andrews, Richard Nigel Lyon *environmental policy educator, environmental studies administrator*
Azar, Henry Amin *pathologist, medical historian*
Baerg, Richard Henry *podiatrist, surgeon, educator*
Bain, Robert Addison *English literature educator*
Baker, Charles Ray *engineering and mathematics educator, researcher*
Baker, Ronald Dale *dental educator, surgeon, university administrator*
Barnett, Thomas Buchanan *physician, medical educator*
Baroff, George Stanley *psychologist, educator*
Baron, Samuel Haskell *historian*
Bauer, Frederick Christian *motor carrier executive*
Bawden, James Wyatt *dental educator, dental scientist*
Beal, John M. *surgeon, medical educator*
Behrman, Jack Newton *economist*
Best, Winfield Judson *writer, television producer, public relations consultant*
Betts, Doris June Waugh *author, English language educator*
Black, Stanley Warren, III *economics educator*
Blau, Peter Michael *sociologist, educator*
Boggs, Robert Newell *editor*
Bolas, Gerald Douglas *art museum administrator, art history educator*
Bondurant, Stuart *physician, educational administrator*
Boone, Franklin Delanor Roosevelt, Sr. *cardiovascular perfusionist, realtor*
Bowers, Thomas Arnold *journalism educator*
Brinkhous, Kenneth Merle *pathologist, educator*
Brockington, Donald Leslie *anthropologist, archaeologist, educator*
Brooks, Frederick Phillips, Jr. *computer scientist*
Broun, Kenneth Stanley *lawyer, educator*
Brown, Frank *social science educator*
Brownlee, Robert Calvin *pediatrician, educator*
Brummet, Richard Lee *accounting educator*
†Buck, Richard Pierson *chemistry educator, researcher*

Bursey, Maurice M. *chemistry educator*
Butler, James Robert *geology educator*
†Campbell, B. (Obby) Jack *university official*
Campbell, Jerry Dean *librarian*
Carpenter, Raymond Leonard *information science educator*
Carroll, John Bissell *psychologist, educator*
†Carroll, Roy *academic administrator*
Clark, Richard Lee *radiologist*
Clifford, Donald Francis, Jr. *law educator*
Clyde, Wallace Alexander, Jr. *pediatrics and microbiology educator*
Cobb, Henry Van Zandt *psychologist*
Cole, Richard Ray *university dean*
Colen, Donald Jerome *public affairs specialist, writer*
Coulter, Elizabeth Jackson *biostatistician, educator*
Coulter, Norman Arthur, Jr. *biomedical engineering educator emeritus*
Crane, Julia Gorham *anthropology educator*
Cromartie, William James *medical educator, researcher*
Dahlstrom, William Grant *psychologist, educator*
†Daniel, Evelyn Hope *library science educator, university dean*
Dareff, Hal *author, editor, publisher*
Davis, Morris Schuyler *astronomer*
Dearman, Henry Hursell *chemistry educator, administrator*
Debreczeny, Paul *Slavic language educator, author*
Dennison, John Manley *geologist, educator*
Denny, Floyd Wolfe, Jr. *pediatrician*
†Dixon, Frederick Dail *architect*
Dixon, John Wesley, Jr. *retired religion and art educator*
Dolan, Louise Ann *physicist*
Droegemueller, William *gynecologist, obstetrician, medical educator*
Easterling, William Ewart, Jr. *obstetrician, gynecologist*
Eaton, Charles Edward *English language educator, author*
Edwards, Richard LeRoy *academic dean, social work educator, non-profit management consultant*
Eifrig, David Eric *ophthalmologist, educator*
Eisenbeis, Robert A. *business educator*
Eisenbud, Merril *environmental engineer*
Eliel, Ernest Ludwig *chemist, educator*
Ellis, Fred Wilson *pharmacology educator*
Ellis, Michael *theatrical producer*
Falk, Eugene Hannes *foreign language educator emeritus*
Farmer, Thomas Wohlsen *neurologist, educator*
Fischer, Janet Jordan *retired physician, educator, researcher*
Fischer, Newton Duchan *otolaryngologist, educator*
Flora, Joseph M(artin) *English language educator*
Fordham, Christopher Columbus, III *university dean and chancellor, medical educator*
Forman, Donald T. *biochemist*
Fox, Ronald Ernest *psychologist*
Frampton, Paul Howard *physics researcher, educator*
†Frankenberg, Dirk *marine scientist*
Frelinger, Jeffrey Allen *immunologist, educator*
Friday, William Clyde *university president emeritus*
Friedman, James Winstein *economist, educator*
Fullagar, Paul David *geology educator, geochemical consultant*
Furst, Lilian Renee *language professional, educator*
Gallman, Robert Emil *economics and history educator*
†Gasaway, Laura Nell *law librarian, educator*
Gil, Federico Guillermo *political science educator*
Gilbert, Lawrence Irwin *biologist, educator*
Glassman, Edward *management consultant, columnist, educator*
Godschalk, David Robinson *architect, urban development planner, educator*
Goldman, Leonard Manuel *physicist, engineering educator*
Gottschalk, Carl William *physician, educator*
Goyer, Robert Andrew *pathology educator*
Graham, George Adams *political scientist, emeritus educator*
Graham, John Borden *pathologist, educator*
Gray-Little, Bernadette *psychologist*
Greganti, Mac Andrew *physician, medical educator*
Gressman, Eugene *lawyer*
Grisham, Joe Wheeler *pathologist, educator*
Gulick, John *anthropology educator*
†Guthridge, Richard Clay *designer*
Hairston, Nelson George *animal ecologist*
Hammond, David Alan *stage director, educator*
Haskell, Paul Gershon *law educator*
Hatfield, William Emerson *chemist, educator*
Hawkins, David Rollo, Sr. *psychiatrist, educator*
Hendricks, Charles Henning *retired obstetrics and gynecology educator*
Heninger, Simeon Kahn, Jr. *English language educator*
†Henson, O'Dell Williams, Jr. *anatomy educator*
Hershey, H(oward) Garland, Jr. *university administrator, orthodontist*
Hirsch, Philip Francis *pharmacologist, educator*
Hochbaum, Godfrey Martin *retired behavioral scientist*
Holcomb, George Ruhle *anthropology educator*
Holley, Edward Gailon *library science educator, former university dean*
Hollister, William Gray *psychiatrist*
Hubbard, Paul Stancyl, Jr. *physics educator*
Hulka, Barbara Sorenson *epidemiology educator*
Hulka, Jaroslav Fabian *obstetrician, gynecologist*
Irene, Eugene Arthur *physical chemistry educator, researcher*
Jackson, Blyden *English language educator*
Jerdee, Thomas Harlan *business administration educator, organization psychology researcher and consultant*
Johnson, George, Jr. *physician, educator*
Jones, Houston Gwynne *history educator*
Jones, Mary Ellen *biochemist*
Joyner, Leon Felix *university administrator*
Kasarda, John Dale *business educator, researcher, administrator, consultant*
Kettelkamp, Donald Benjamin *surgeon, educator*
Kilgour, Frederick Gridley *librarian, educator*
Kittredge, John Kendall *retired insurance company executive*
Klarmann, Dave *university athletic coach*
Kohn, Richard H. *historian, educator*
Kuenzler, Edward Julian *ecologist and environmental biologist*
Kusy, Robert Peter *biomedical engineering and orthodontics educator*
Landsberger, Henry A. *sociology educator*
Langdell, Robert Dana *medical educator*
Langenderfer, Harold Quentin *accountant, educator*
Lauder, Valarie Anne *editor, educator*

Lauterborn, Robert F. *advertising educator*
Lawrence, David Michael *lawyer, educator*
Lee, Sherman Emery *art historian, curator*
Levine, Madeline Geltman *Slavic literatures educator, translator*
Loeb, Ben Fohl, Jr. *lawyer, educator*
Long, Douglas Clark *philosophy educator*
Lucas, Carol Lee *biomedical engineer*
Ludington, Charles Townsend, Jr. *English and American studies educator*
Macdonald, James Ross *physicist, educator*
MacGillivray, Lois Ann *academic administrator*
MacRae, Duncan, Jr. *social scientist, educator*
Manire, George Philip *bacteriologist, educator*
Markham, Jordan J. *physicist, retired educator*
Martin, Harry Corpening *state supreme court justice, retired*
Mayer, Eugene Stephen *physician, university administrator*
McBay, Arthur John *toxicologist, consultant*
Mc Curdy, Harold Grier *psychologist*
McMillan, Campbell White *pediatric hematologist*
Memory, Jasper Durham *academic administrator, physics educator*
†Merzbacher, Eugen *physicist, educator*
Meyer, Philip Edward *journalism educator*
Meyer, Thomas J. *chemistry educator*
Miller, C. Arden *physician, educator*
Miller, Daniel Newton, Jr. *geologist, consultant*
Mitchell, Earl Nelson *physicist, educator*
Miya, Tom Saburo *retired pharmacologist, educator*
Moran, Barbara Burns *librarian, educator*
Munsat, Stanley Morris *philosopher, educator*
Munson, Eric Bruce *hospital administrator*
Murphy, James Lee *college dean, economics educator*
Murray, Royce Wilton *chemistry educator*
Nelson, Philip Francis *musicology educator, consultant, choral conductor*
Ness, Albert Kenneth *artist, educator*
Neumann, Andrew Conrad *geological oceanography educator*
Newman, William Stein *music educator, author, pianist, composer*
Norwood, George Joseph *pharmacy educator*
Okun, Daniel Alexander *environmental engineering educator, consulting engineer*
Oliver, Mary Wilhelmina *law librarian, educator*
Ontjes, David Ainsworth *medicine and pharmacology educator*
†Pagano, Joseph Stephen *physician, researcher, educator*
Palmer, Jeffress Gary *hematologist, educator*
Parr, Robert Ghormley *chemistry educator*
Pavão, Leonel Maia (Lee Pavão) *advertising executive*
Perreault, William Daniel, Jr. *business administration educator*
Pfouts, Ralph William *economist, consultant*
Pollitzer, William Sprott *anatomy educator*
Powell, Burnele Venable *law educator*
Powell, Carolyn Wilkerson *music educator*
Prange, Arthur Jergen, Jr. *psychiatrist, neurobiologist, educator*
Proffit, William Robert *orthodontics educator*
Richardson, Richard Judson *political science educator*
†Riggs, Timothy Allan *museum curator*
†Rindfuss, Ronald Richard *sociology educator*
Roberts, Louis Douglas *physics educator, researcher*
Rogers, John James William *geology educator*
Rosen, Benson *business administration educator*
Rubin, Louis Decimus, Jr. *English language and literature educator, writer, publisher*
St. Jean, Joseph, Jr. *micropaleontologist, educator*
Schier, Donald Stephen *language educator*
Schopler, John Henry *psychologist, educator*
†Schoultz, Lars *political scientist, educator*
Scott, Tom Keck *biologist, botanist, educator*
Shapiro, Lee Tobey *planetarium administrator, astronomer*
Sharpless, Richard Kennedy *lawyer*
Sheldon, George F. *medical educator*
Shuman, Mark Samuel *environmental and electroanalytical chemistry educator*
Simons, Gordon Donald, Jr. *statistician*
Simpson, Richard Lee *sociologist, educator*
Slifkin, Lawrence Myer *physics educator*
Smith, Dean Edwards *university basketball coach*
Smith, James Finley *economist, educator*
Smith, Sidney Rufus, Jr. *linguist, educator*
Spangler, Clemmie Dixon, Jr. *academic administrator*
Spencer, Elizabeth *author*
Stadter, Philip Austin *classicist, educator*
Stanat, Donald F. *computer science educator*
Stasheff, James Dillon *mathematics educator*
Steponaitis, Vincas Petras *archaeologist, anthropologist, educator*
Stewart, Richard Edwin *insurance consulting company executive*
Stidham, Shaler, Jr. *operations research educator*
Stipe, Robert Edwin *design educator*
Stiven, Alan Ernest *population biologist, ecologist*
Strauss, Albrecht Benno *English educator, editor*
†Stumpf, Walter Erich *cell biology educator, researcher*
Sugioka, Kenneth *anesthesiologist educator*
Suzuki, Kunihiko *biomedical educator, researcher*
Thakor, Haren Bhaskerrao *manufacturing company executive*
Thomas, Colin Gordon, Jr. *surgeon, medical educator*
Tillman, Rollie, Jr. *university official*
Tindall, George Brown *historian, educator*
Tolley, Aubrey Granville *hospital administrator*
Treml, Vladimir Guy *economist, educator*
Tsiapera, Maria *linguistics educator*
Upshaw, Harry Stephan *psychology educator*
Van Seters, John *biblical literature educator*
Van Wyk, Judson John *endocrinologist, pediatric educator*
Vogler, Frederick Wright *French educator*
Wahl, Jonathan Michael *mathematics educator*
Warren, Donald William *physiology educator, dentistry educator*
Waud, Roger Neil *economics educator*
Weinberg, Gerhard Ludwig *history educator*
Weiss, Charles Manuel *environmental biologist*
Weiss, Shirley F. *urban and regional planner, economist, educator*
Wheeler, Clayton Eugene, Jr. *dermatologist, educator*
White, Raymond Petrie, Jr. *dentist, educator*
Wilcox, Benson Reid *cardiothoracic surgeon, educator*
Wilson, Glenn *economist, educator*
Wilson, John Eric *biochemist*

Wilson, Robert Neal *sociologist, educator*
Winfield, John Buckner *rheumatologist, educator*
Wogen, Warren Ronald *mathematics educator*
Wolfenden, Richard Vance *biochemistry educator*
Wright, Deil Spencer *political science educator*
York, James Wesley, Jr. *theoretical physicist, educator*
Ziff, Paul *philosophy educator*

Charlotte
†Abbott, James A. *mortgage company executive*
Abernathy, Joseph Duncan *data processing executive*
Anderson, Gerald Leslie *financial executive*
Ayscue, Edwin Osborne, Jr. *lawyer*
†Barrows, Frank Clemence *newspaper editor*
†Battle, George Edward, Jr. *minister*
Begley, Michael Joseph *bishop*
†Belk, John M. *retail company executive*
Belk, Thomas Milburn *apparal executive*
Betzold, Paul Frederick, Jr. *hospital administrator*
Birle, James Robb *investment banker*
Blaschke, Robert Carvel *education coordinator*
†Bost, Walter Lee *architect, printing company executive*
Bowden, James Alvin *construction company financial executive*
Boyd, Edward Lee *financial executive*
Bradshaw, Howard Holt *management consulting company executive*
Brazeal, Donna Smith *psychologist*
Brigden, Richard Nevius *financial executive*
Bristow, Allan Mercer *professional basketball coach*
†Brown, Tony *theater and dance critic*
Buchan, Jonathan Edward, Jr. *lawyer*
Burke, Mary Thomas *university administrator, educator*
Cannon, Robert Eugene *librarian, public administrator, fund raiser*
Citron, David Sanford *physician*
†Clark, Ann Blakeney *educational administrator*
Clodfelter, Daniel Gray *lawyer*
†Cochrane, Luther Parks *construction executive, contractor*
Cogdell, Joe Bennett, Jr. *lawyer*
Colvard, Dean Wallace *emeritus university chancellor*
†Cotton, James *construction company executive*
Covington, William Clyde, Jr. *banker*
Crosland, John, Jr. *real estate developer*
Crutchfield, Edward Elliott, Jr. *banker*
Dagenhart, Larry Jones *lawyer*
Daniels, William Carlton, Jr. *construction executive*
Davenport, Dona Lee *telecommunications consultant*
†Davidson, Charles Tompkins *construction company executive*
Davis, William Maxie, Jr. *lawyer*
Dickson, Rush Stuart *holding company executive*
Donoghue, John F. *bishop*
Edwards, Harold Mills *government official, lawyer*
†Eppes, Thomas Evans *public relations executive*
Ethridge, Mark Foster, III *writer, publisher, newspaper consultant*
†Evans, Bruce Haselton *art museum director*
†Ferebee, Stephen Scott, Jr. *architect*
†Ferguson, James Elliot, II *lawyer*
Figge, Fredric J., II *bank executive*
Fretwell, Elbert Kirtley, Jr. *university chancellor emeritus, consultant*
Georgius, John R. *bank executive*
Greene, William Henry L'Vel *academic administrator*
Grier, Joseph Williamson, Jr. *lawyer*
Griffith, Steve Campbell, Jr. *lawyer*
Grigg, William Humphrey *utility executive*
†Gunn, Robert T. *architectural firm executive*
Hall, Peter Michael *physics educator, electronics researcher*
Hanna, George Verner, III *lawyer*
†Hannah, Thomas E. *textiles executive*
Hannon, William Evans *manufacturing executive, consultant*
Harrison, J. Frank, Jr. *soft drink company executive*
Helms, Fred Bryan *lawyer*
Henson, Reid M. *wholesale company executive*
Hill, Ruth Foell *language consultant*
†Holland, William Ray *diversified company executive*
†Huberman, Jeffrey Allen *architect*
Hudgins, Catherine Harding *business executive*
Iverson, Francis Kenneth *metals company executive*
Johnson, Larry Demetric *professional basketball player*
Johnson, Phillip Eugene *mathematics educator*
Jones, Johnie H. *construction company executive*
Jones, Lewis Bevel, III *bishop*
Kelly, Luther Wrentmore, Jr. *physician, educator*
Kim, Rhyn Hyun *engineering educator*
King, L. Ellis *civil engineer, educator and administrator*
†Koch, Richard Joseph *lawyer, publishing company executive*
Lee, William States *utility executive*
Love, Franklin Sadler *retired trade association executive*
Martin, James Grubbs *governor*
Mazze, Edward Mark *marketing consultant, business educator*
McBryde, Neill Gregory *lawyer*
McCall, Billy Gene *charitable trust executive*
McColl, Hugh Leon, Jr. *banker*
McConnell, David Moffatt *lawyer*
†McKeon, Robert B. *textiles executive*
McMillan, James Bryan *federal judge, retired*
McVerry, Thomas Leo *manufacturing company executive*
Mendelsohn, Robert Victor *insurance company executive*
Moore, James L., Jr. *beverage company executive*
†Mourning, Alonzo *professional basketball player*
Mullen, Graham C. *federal judge*
†Murata, Junichi *electronics company executive*
Myrick, Sue *advertising agency executive, former mayor*
Naumoff, Philip *physician*
Neal, William Weaver *systems integration and software executive*
Neel, Richard Eugene *economics educator*
Neill, Rolfe *newspaper executive*
†Nicholson, Freda Hyams *museum executive, medical educator*
†Norwood, Philip Weltner *lawyer*
†Nurkin, Harry Abraham *hospital administrator*
†Orr, T. J. (Jerry Orr) *airport terminal executive*
Orsbon, Richard Anthony *lawyer*
Osborne, Richard Jay *electric utility company executive*
Owen, Warren Herbert *utility executive*
†Parish, Robert L. *professional basketball player*

Phillips, Howard Mitchell real estate developer
Potter, Robert Daniel federal judge
†Powell, Charles Roland financial services company executive
Preyer, Norris Watson history educator
Raper, William Cranford lawyer
Redden, Forrest Richard, Jr. management executive
Regelbrugge, Roger Rafael steel company executive
Rodite, Robert R.R. engineering scientist, technology strategist
†Ross, David E. church official
†Schmidt, Peter construction company executive
†Sherman, Joseph Howard clergyman
Shinn, George professional basketball executive
Shive, Philip Augustus architect
Siegel, Samuel metals company executive
Sintz, Edward Francis librarian
Smith, Arthur radio and television producer, composer
Smith, James Copeland controller
Stair, Frederick Rogers retired foundation executive, former seminary president
Stephens, Louis Cornelius, Jr. insurance executive
Stolpen, Spencer professional sports team executive
Taylor, David Brooke lawyer, banker
Thies, Austin Cole retired utility company executive
Thigpen, Richard Elton, Jr. lawyer
Thomas, Joe Carroll human resources director
Thompson, James William banker
†Turner, Thomas Patrick architect
Twisdale, Harold Winfred dentist
Ubell, Donald Paul lawyer
Van Allen, William Kent lawyer
Vane, Terence G., Jr. finance and insurance company executive, lawyer
Vinroot, Richard Allen lawyer, mayor of Charlotte, North Carolina
Walker, Clarence Wesley lawyer
†Walker, James Marion construction company executive
Walls, George Rodney lawyer
Ward, Marion Haggard retired air force officer, museum president
Watkins, Carlton Gunter retired pediatrician
Wenner, Gene Charles arts foundation executive
Wentz, Billy Melvin, Jr. finance executive
†White, David Lee journalist
†Williams, Edwin Neel newspaper editor
Williford, Donald Bratton bank executive
†Wilson, Constance Kramer bank officer
†Winner, Leslie Jane lawyer
Witherspoon, Jere Warthen foundation executive
Woodward, James Hoyt university chancellor, engineer
Woolard, William Leon lawyer, electrical distributing company executive

Cherryville
Huffstetler, Palmer Eugene lawyer, transportation executive
Mayhew, Kenneth Edwin, Jr. transportation company executive
Younger, Kenneth G. freight carrier corporation executive

China Grove
Baker, Ira Lee journalist, former educator

Columbus
Weber, Ernst engineering consultant

Corolla
Schrote, John Ellis retired government executive

Creedmoor
Cross, June Crews music educator

Cullowhee
Blethen, Harold Tyler, III history educator
Coulter, Myron Lee retired academic administrator
Reed, Alfred Douglas university official

Dallas
Blanton, Robert D'Alden anthropology and history educator

Davidson
Abernethy, George Lawrence philosophy educator
Burnett, John Nicholas chemistry educator
Cole, Richard Cargill English educator
Jackson, Herb artist, educator
Jones, Arthur Edwin, Jr. library administrator, English and American literature educator
Kuykendall, John Wells academic administrator, educator
Lester, Malcolm historian, educator
†McKelway, Alexander Jeffrey religion studies educator
Park, Leland Madison librarian
Proctor, Jesse Harris, Jr. political science educator
Ratliff, Charles Edward, Jr. economics educator
Spencer, Samuel Reid, Jr. educational consultant, former university president
Williams, Robert Chadwell history educator
Zimmermann, T. C. Price historian, educator

Drexel
†Richetta, Fred J. manufacturing executive

Dunn
†Davis, Dolly religious organization administrator
†Ellis, W. L. religious arganization administrator
†Hammond, James Thurman educator, clergyman
†Hardison, Chuch religious organization administrator
†Heath, Preston clergy member, religious organization administrator
†Sauls, Don religious organization administrator, clergyman
†Taylor, David clergy member, religious administrator

Durham
Agusta, Benjamin J. computer company executive
Aldrich, John Herbert political science educator
Allard, William Kenneth mathematician
Amos, Dennis B. immunologist
Anderson, William Banks, Jr. ophthalmology educator
Anlyan, William George surgeon, university administrator
Baker, Lenox Dial orthopaedist, genealogist
Barber, James David political scientist, educator
Beckum, Leonard Charles academic administrator
†Bejan, Adrian mechanical engineering educator
Bell, Robert Maurice biochemistry educator, consultant
Bennett, Peter Brian researcher, anesthesiology educator
Bettman, James Ross management educator
Bevan, William retired foundation executive
Billings, William Dwight ecology educator
Blum, Jacob Joseph physiologist, educator
Bradford, William Dalton pathologist, educator
Braibanti, Ralph John political scientist, educator
Brodie, Harlow Keith Hammond psychiatry educator, former university president
Bryan, Paul Robey, Jr. musician, educator
Buckley, Rebecca Hatcher physician
Budd, Louis John English language educator
Burger, Robert Mercer semiconductor device research executive
Burmeister, Edwin economics educator
Bursey, Joan Tesarek chemist
Busse, Ewald William psychiatrist, educator
†Butters, Ronald Richard English language educator
Cady, Edwin Harrison English language educator, author
†Caesar, Shirley gospel singer, evangelist
Campbell, Dennis Marion theology dean, educator, university administrator
Canada, Mary Whitfield librarian
Cartmill, Matt anthropologist, anatomy educator
Casey, H(orace) Craig, Jr. electrical engineering educator
Chaddock, Jack Bartley mechanical engineering educator
Chafe, William Henry history educator
Chambers, Julius LeVonne lawyer
Chesnut, Donald Blair chemistry educator
Christie, George Custis lawyer, educator, author
Christmas, William Anthony internist, educator
Clark, Arthur Watts insurance company executive
Clement, William Alexander insurance compnay executive
Cocks, Franklin Hadley materials scientist
Cohen, Harvey Jay physician, educator
Coleman, Ralph Edward nuclear medicine physician
Collins, Bert insurance executive
Colton, Joel historian, educator
Cook, Clarence Edgar research facility executive
Cooper, Charles Howard photojournalist, newspaper publishing company executive
Counce-Nicklas, Sheila Jean cell biology educator
Crumbliss, Alvin Lee chemistry educator, consultant
Cruze, Alvin M. research institute executive
Culberson, William Louis botany educator
†Cusson, Ronald Yvon theoretical physicist
Danner, Richard Allen law educator, dean
Davidson, Cathy Notari English language educator, writer
Davis, Calvin De Armond historian, educator
Davis, James Evans general and thoracic surgeon, parliamentarian, author
Day, Eugene Davis, Sr. immunology educator, researcher
Demott, Deborah Ann lawyer, educator
†Dorfman, Ariel writer, educator
Dowell, Earl Hugh university dean, aerospace and mechanical engineering educator
Dunbar, Leslie Wallace writer, consultant
Dunteman, George Henry organizational psychologist
Durden, Robert Franklin history educator
Elliot, Jeffrey M. political science educator, author
Estes, Edward Harvey, Jr. medical educator
Evans, Ralph Aiken physicist, consultant
Everett, Robinson Oscar federal judge, law educator
Fair, Richard Barton electronics executive, educator
Falletta, John Matthew pediatrician
Feldman, Jerome Myron physician
Ferguson, David Robert energy research manager
Fish, Stanley Eugene English language and literature educator
Fisher, Charles Page, Jr. consulting geotechnical engineer
Fleishman, Joel Lawrence university administrator, journalist, law educator
Fouts, James Ralph pharmacologist, educator, clergyman
Frank, Michael M. physician
Fraser-Reid, Bertram Oliver chemistry educator
Fridovich, Irwin biochemistry educator
Frothingham, Thomas Eliot pediatrician
Fulton, Katherine Nelson journalist
†Gaddis, Dale library director
Garg, Devendra Prakash mechanical engineer, educator
Georgiade, Nicholas George physician
Gillham, Nicholas Wright geneticist, educator
Gittler, Joseph Bertram sociology educator
Gleckner, Robert Francis English language professional, educator
Golding, Martin Philip law and philosophy educator
Gratz, Pauline former nursing science educator
Greenfield, Joseph Cholmondeley, Jr. physician, educator
†Gulley, Wilbur Paul lawyer, mayor
Hammes, Gordon G. chemistry educator
Hammond, Charles Bessellieu obstetrician-gynecologist, educator
Han, Moo-Young physicist
Handy, Rollo Leroy economics educator, research executive
Harman, Charles Morgan mechanical engineer
Harmel, Merel Hilber anesthesiologist, educator
Harris, Jerome Sylvan pediatrician, pediatrics and biochemistry educator
Havighurst, Clark Canfield law educator
Hawkins, William E. N. newspaper editor
Hayes, Brian Paul editor, writer
Hill, Robert Lee biochemistry educator
Hillerbrand, Hans Joachim historian, university administrator
Hobbs, Marcus Edwin chemistry educator
Hochmuth, Robert Milo mechanical and biomedical engineer, educator
Holley, Irving Brinton, Jr. historian, educator
Holsti, Ole Rudolf political scientist, educator
Hopkins, Everett Harold education educator
Horowitz, Donald Leonard lawyer, educator, researcher, political scientist, arbitrator
Jaszczak, Ronald Jack physicist, researcher, consultant
Jennings, Robert Burgess experimental pathologist, medical educator
Johnston, William Webb pathologist, educator
Joklik, Wolfgang Karl biochemist, virologist, educator
Katz, Samuel Lawrence pediatrician, scientist
Keller, Thomas Franklin dean, management science educator
Kelley, Allen Charles economist, educator
Kempner, Walter physician
Keohane, Nannerl Overholser college president, political scientist
Keohane, Robert Owen political scientist, educator
King, Lowell Restell pediatric urologist
Kirk-Duggan, Michael Allan law and computer sciences educator emeritus
Kirshner, Norman pharmacologist, researcher, educator
Koepke, John Arthur hematologist, clinical pathologist
Krakauer, Thomas Henry museum director
Kramer, Paul Jackson plant physiologist, educator, writer, editor
Kreps, Juanita Morris former secretary of commerce
Krzyzewski, Mike university athletic coach
†Kuniholm, Bruce Robellet public policy studies institute director, history educator
Kylstra, Johannes Arnold physician
Lack, Leon pharmacology and biochemistry educator
Land, Kenneth Carl sociology educator, demographer, statistician, consultant
Lange, David L. law educator
Leach, Richard Heald political scientist, educator
Lefkowitz, Robert Joseph physician, educator
†Lejdemalm, Ronny communications executive
Lerner, Warren historian
Lieberman, Melvyn biology educator
Lifton, Walter M. psychology and education consultant
Lincoln, C(harles) Eric sociologist, educator, author
Little, Larry Chatmon head football coach
Livingstone, Daniel Archibald zoology educator
Lockhead, Gregory Roger psychology educator
Loveland, Donald William computer science educator
Madey, John M. J. physics educator
Markham, Charles Buchanan lawyer
Mauskopf, Seymour Harold history educator
Maxwell, Richard Callender lawyer, educator
McClellan, Roger Orville toxicologist
McElhaney, James Harry biomedical engineer
McMahon, John Alexander lawyer, educator
Mc Phail, Andrew Tennent chemist, educator
Meyer, Horst physics educator
Mickiewicz, Ellen Propper political science educator
Miller, David Edmond physician
Moore, John Wilson neurophysiologist, educator
Myers, George Carleton sociology and demographics educator
Naylor, Aubrey Willard botany educator
Nicklas, Robert Bruce cell biologist
Niedel, James E. pharmaceuticals executive
Nygard, Holger Olof English and folklore educator
Oates, John Francis classics educator
O'Barr, William McAlston anthropologist, educator
†Opara, Emmanuel Chukwuemeka biochemistry educator
Osterhout, Suydam physician, educator
Otterbourg, Robert Kenneth public relations consultant
Page, Ellis Batten behavioral scientist, educator
Palmer, Richard Alan chemistry educator
Parker, Joseph B., Jr. psychiatrist, educator
Parker, Roy Turnage obstetrician-gynecologist, educator
Pearsall, George Wilbur materials scientist, mechanical engineer, educator, consultant
Peete, William Pettway Jones surgeon
Perkins, Ronald Dee geologist, educator
Peters, William P. oncologist, science administrator, educator
†Philyaw, A. Roger insurance company executive
Piatt, William McKinney, III consulting engineering executive
Pilkey, Orrin H. geology educator
Plonsey, Robert electrical and biomedical engineer
Pratt, Philip Chase pathologist, educator
Preston, Richard Arthur historian
Richardson, Lawrence, Jr. Latin educator, archeologist
Roberson, Nathan Russell physicist, educator
Robertson, Horace Bascomb, Jr. law educator
Robertson, James David neurobiologist educator
Rogers, Mark Charles physician, educator
Rollins, Edward Tyler, Jr. newspaper executive
Rose, Donald James computer science educator
Rosenthal, Julian Bernard lawyer, association executive
Rossiter, Alexander, Jr. news service executive, editor
Rouse, Doris Jane physiologist, research administrator
Rowe, Thomas Dudley, Jr. legal educator
Ryals, Clyde de Loache humanities educator
Ryan, Gerard Spencer inn executive
Sabiston, David Coston, Jr. surgeon, educator
†Sanders, Charles Addison pharmaceutical company executive, physician
Sanford, David Hawley philosophy educator
Sassaman, Anne Phillips science administrator
Schanberg, Saul Murray pharmacology educator
Schmalbeck, Richard Louis university dean, lawyer
Schmidt-Nielsen, Knut physiologist, educator
Scott, Anne Byrd Firor history educator
Searles, Richard Brownlee botany educator, marine biology researcher
Selkirk, James Kirkwood biochemist
Serafin, Donald plastic surgeon
Sessoms, Stuart McGuire physician, educator, retired insurance company executive
Shimm, Melvin Gerald law educator
Simons, Elwyn LaVerne physical anthropologist, primatologist, paleontologist, educator
Smith, Grover Cleveland English language educator
Smith, Harmon Lee, Jr. clergyman, moral theology educator
Smith, Peter chemist, educator, consultant
Snyderman, Ralph medical educator, physician
Somjen, George Gustav physiologist
Spach, Madison Stockton cardiologist
Spencer, John Richard art historian
Squire, Alexander management consultant
Staddon, John Eric Rayner psychology, zoology, neurobiology educator
Staelin, Richard business administration educator
Stead, Eugene Anson, Jr. physician
Steinmetz, David Curtis religion educator, publisher, minister
†Straub, Karl David biochemist, researcher
Strohbehn, John Walter engineering science educator
Stroscio, Michael Anthony physicist, educator
Tebbel, John writer, educator
Thomas, Jean-Jacques Robert romance languages educator
Thorn, Rosemary Kost librarian
Tiryakian, Edward Ashod sociology educator
†Tracy, Philip R. computer company executive
Urbaniak, James Randolph orthopaedic surgeon
Utku, Senol civil engineer, computer science educator
Van Alstyne, William Warner law educator
Vitter, Jeffrey Scott computer science educator, consultant
Wainwright, Stephen A. zoology educator, design consultant
Walter, Richard Lawrence physicist, educator
Ward, Robert composer, conductor, educator
Wardropper, Bruce Wear language educator
Warner, Seth L. mathematician, educator
Warren, David Grant lawyer, educator
Watts, Charles DeWitt surgeon, corporate medical director
Werman, David Sanford psychiatrist, psychoanalyst, educator
†Westbrook, Don Arlen minister
Wilbur, Karl Milton zoologist, educator
Wilder, Pelham, Jr. chemist, pharmacologist, educator
Wilkins, Robert Henry neurosurgeon, editor
Williams, George Walton English educator
Williams, Redford Brown medical educator
Wilson, Ruby Leila nurse, educator
Winkler, Robert Lewis statistics educator, researcher, author, consultant
Woodbury, Max Atkin polymath, educator
Wright, Paul, Jr. banker

Eden
Staab, Thomas Robert textile company financial executive

Edenton
Walklet, John James, Jr. publishing executive

Efland
Efland, Simpson Lindsay entrepreneur

Elizabeth City
Boyle, Terrence W. federal judge
Griffin, Gladys Bogues critical care nurse, educator
†Twiford, Travis W. school system administrator

Elm City
Parker, Josephus Derward horticulturist

Elon College
Knesel, Ernest Arthur, Jr. clinical laboratory executive
Young, James Fred college president

Farmville
†Monk, Albert C., III manufacturing executive

Fayetteville
Bowman, Charles Harwood, Jr. historian, educator
Hackley, Lloyd Vincent university administrator, retired air force officer
†Hendrick, J. R., III automotive executive
†Thrasher, Jerry Arthur library director

Fearrington Village
Abrahamson, James Leonard history educator
Bailey, Herbert Smith, Jr. retired publisher
Doenges, Byron Frederick economist, educator, former government official
Hauser, Charles Newland McCorkle newspaper consultant
Schwinn-Jordan, Barbara (Barbara Schwinn) painter

Flat Rock
Demartini, Robert John textile company executive

Fort Bragg
Davis, Harley Cleo career officer
†Palmer, Gary Stephen career officer, healthcare administrator
Younger, Kenneth Maurice military officer

Foxfire Village
Krebs, Max Vance retired foreign service officer, educator

Fremont
Ackerman, Lennis Campbell management consultant

Fuquay Varina
Hairston, William Michael manufacturing engineer

Garner
Dobyns, Lloyd (Allen) free-lance journalist

Gastonia
Alala, Joseph Basil, Jr. lawyer, accountant
Kimbrell, Willard Duke textile executive
Kiser, Clyde Vernon retired demographer
Lawson, William David, III cotton company executive
Stott, Grady Bernell lawyer
Stout, Richard Alan museum director
Teem, Paul Lloyd, Jr. savings and loan executive
†Williams, Raymond F. regigious organization executive

Gibsonville
Foster, C(harles) Allen lawyer

Gloucester
Price, Marion Woodrow journalist

Granite Falls
Humphreys, Kenneth King engineer, educator, association executive

Greensboro
Allen, Jesse Owen, III management development and organizational
Bardolph, Richard historian, educator
Barker, Walter William, Jr. artist, educator
Blackwell, William Ernest insurance company executive, financial analyst
Bryan, Joseph McKinley insurance company executive
Bullock, Frank William, Jr. federal judge
Cardwell, Jessie Womack elementary education educator
Carr, Howard Ernest retired insurance agency executive
Carter, Wilbur Lee, Jr. retired insurance executive

Chappell, Fred Davis English language educator, poet
Clark, Clifton Bob physicist
†Clark, Joanne school system administrator
Cline, Ned Aubrey newspaper editor
Compton, John Carroll accountant
Danahy, James Patrick textile executive
Davis, Herbert Owen lawyer
Davis-Seaver, Elizabeth Jane elementary school educator
†DuBuisson, Charles David newspaper editor
Eason, Robert Gaston psychology educator
Edinger, Lois Virginia education educator emeritus
Elam, Harper Johnston, III textile company executive, lawyer
Floyd, Jack William lawyer
Goldman, Bert Arthur psychologist, educator
Gordon, Eugene Andrew judge
Greenberg, Frank S. textile company executive
Greenberg, George mill company executive
Gumbiner, Kenneth Jay lawyer
Gutter, Robert Harold conductor, music educator
Harllee, JoAnn Towery lawyer, educator
Hayes, Charles A. mill company executive
†Henderson, George, III textiles executive
Hidore, John Junior geographer, educator
Hopkins, John David lawyer
Howard, Paul Noble, Jr. retired construction company executive
Howard, Richard Turner construction company executive
Hughes, Donald R. textile executive
Hull, James Ernest religion and philosophy educator
Hunter, Bynum Merritt lawyer
Jellicorse, John Lee communications and theatre educator
Johnson, Andrew Myron pediatric immunologist, educator
Kennedy, Charles G. wholesale distribution executive
Koonce, Neil Wright lawyer
Korb, William Brown, Jr. manufacturing company executive
Kornegay, Horace Robinson trade association executive, former congressman, lawyer
Kretzer, William T. textile company executive
Lolley, William Randall minister
Macon, Seth Craven retired insurance company executive
Mann, Lowell Kimsey retired manufacturing executive
†Martin, William Nelson lawyer
McGinn, Max Daniel lawyer
Mebane, George Allen corporate executive, rancher
Mecimore, Charles Douglas accounting educator
Melvin, Charles Edward, Jr. lawyer
Middleton, Herman David, Sr. theater educator
Miller, Marilyn Lea library science educator
Miller, Robert Louis university dean, chemistry educator
Moore, Beverly Cooper lawyer
Morris, Edwin Alexander retired apparel manufacturing company executive
†Nussbaum, V. M., Jr. former mayor
Osteen, William L., Sr. federal judge
Posey, Eldon Eugene mathematician, educator
Poteet, Daniel P(owell), II college provost
Reed, William Edward government official, educator
Rogers, William Raymond college president, psychology educator
†Rowlenson, Richard Charles lawyer
St. George, Nicholas James lawyer, manufactured housing company executive
Schell, Braxton lawyer
Schwenn, Lee William retired medical center executive
Scott, Gloria Dean Randle academic administrator
Sewell, Elizabeth author, English educator
†Seymour, Mary Powell state senator
Shelton, David Howard economics educator
Smink, Mary Jane graphic communications technology educator
Smith, John McNeill, Jr. lawyer
Smith, Lanty L(loyd) lawyer, business executive
Soles, William Roger insurance company executive
Spears, Alexander White, III tobacco company executive
Speight, Velma Ruth academic director
Thompson, James Howard historian, library administrator
Tilley, Norwood Carlton, Jr. federal judge
Trogdon, Dewey Leonard, Jr. textile executive
Ulmer, Walter F., Jr. leadership development executive, former army officer
†Vetack, Richard S. textiles executive
Viele, George Brookins library executive
†von der Lippe, Edward Joseph museum director
Watson, Robert Winthrop poet, English language educator
Wright, Kieth Carter librarian, educator
Zopf, Paul Edward sociologist

Greenville
Bearden, James Hudson university official
Bolande, Robert Paul pathologist, scientist, educator
Chauncey, Beatrice Arlene music educator
Clemens, Donald Faull chemistry educator
Cramer, Robert Eli geography educator
Eakin, Richard Ronald academic administrator, mathematics educator
Frisell, Wilhelm Richard biochemist, educator
Hallock, James Anthony pediatrician, school dean
Hines, Danny Ray accountant, educator
Holt, Robert LeRoi philosophy educator
Howard, Malcolm Jones federal judge
Howell, John McDade retired university chancellor, political science educator
Hudgins, Herbert Cornelius, Jr. education educator
Jackson, Bobby Rand minister
Jones, Billy Ernest dermatology educator
Laupus, William Edward physician, educator
Lee, Kenneth Stuart neurosurgeon
Leggett, Donald Yates university program director
†Lennon, Donald Ray archivist, historian
Maier, Robert Hawthorne biology educator
Mattsson, Ake psychiatrist, physician
McRae, David Carroll hospital administrator
Norris, H. Thomas pathologist, academic administrator
Pories, Walter Julius surgeon, educator
Sanchez, Rafael Camilo physician
Sayetta, Thomas Charles physics educator
Schellenberger, Robert Earl management educator and department chairman
Snyder, Scott William geology educator
Thomas, Francis Thornton surgeon, immunologist, consultant
Thurber, Robert Eugene physiologist, researcher
Tingelstad, Jon Bunde physician
Waugh, William Howard biomedical educator
Williams, Melvin John sociologist, educator

Hampstead
Solomon, Robert Douglas pathology educator

Henderson
Church, John Trammell retail stores company executive
Jones, George L. retail executive

Hendersonville
†Byrd, Charles L. school system administrator
Haynes, John Mabin retired utilities executive
Jones, J(ohn) Charles education educator
Moore, John Travers poet, author
Payne, Gerald Oliver elementary education educator
Peckham, Howard Henry librarian, educator
Saby, John Sanford physicist
Schooley, Charles Earl consultant
Sims, Bennett Jones minister, educator

Hickory
†George, Boyd Lee consumer products company executive
Gingrich-Petersen, Carolyn Ashcraft psychologist
Ingle, John David lawyer
†Knedlik, Ronald W. food wholesale and retail executive
McDaniel, Michael Conway Dixon bishop, theology educator
Nash, Robert Fred grocery company executive
Shuford, Harley Ferguson, Jr. furniture manufacturing executive

High Point
Brackett, Douglas Lane trade association executive
Coggins, George Miller, Jr. strategic planning and finance educator
Fenn, Ormon William, Jr. furniture company executive
†Grubbs, Gerald Reid furniture manufacturing company executive
Howard, Lou Dean Graham elementary education educator
Huston, Fred John automotive engineer
Johnson, Richard Arthur factoring credit executive
Jones, Ronald Lee furniture manufacturing executive
Kleeman, Walter Benton, Jr. interior and furniture designer, consultant, author
Marsden, Lawrence Albert retired textile company executive
Martinson, Jacob Christian, Jr. university president
Phillips, Earl Norfleet, Jr. financial services executive
Sheahan, Robert Emmett lawyer, management employment and environment law consultant
†Wood, Stephen Wray religious studies educator, state legislator

Highland
Sandor, George Nason mechanical engineer, educator

Hillsborough
Goodwin, Craufurd David economics educator

Horse Shoe
Howell, George Washington lawyer, consultant

Jacksonville
Daugherty, Robert Michael music educator, composer
Hutto, James Calhoun retired financial executive

Jefferson
Franklin, Robert McFarland book publisher

Kannapolis
Ridenhour, Joseph Conrad textile company executive
Thigpen, Alton Hill motor transportation company executive

Kinston
†Fuchs, David clothing manufacturing company executive
Matthis, Eva Mildred Boney college official
Petteway, Samuel Bruce college president
Sanders, Brice Sidney bishop
†Schechter, Sol clothes company executive
Sutton, Frederick Isler, Jr. realtor

Kure Beach
Funk, Frank E. retired university dean

Lake Junaluska
Bryan, Monk retired bishop
Hale, Joseph Rice church organization executive
Tullis, Edward Lewis retired bishop

Lake Lure
Newbrough, Edgar Truett retired management consultant

Lake Sunaluska
Stokes, John Lemacks, II clergyman, university administrator

Laurinburg
Nance, Tony Max-Perry designer, illustrator

Lenoir
Carswell, Jane Triplett family physician

Liberty
Garner, Mildred Maxine religion educator emeritus

Lincolnton
†Gaither, Ann Heafner sales executive
†Gamble, John Reeves, Jr. surgeon
Saine, Betty Boston elementary education educator

Locust
†Barbee, Bobby Harold state legislator, insurance agency executive

Lumberton
Byrne, James Frederick banker
Lee, Elizabeth Bobbitt architect
Orr, L. Glenn, Jr. banker

Manteo
†Basnight, Marc state senator
†Hartman, Thomas historical site adminstrator
†Miller, William Lee, Jr. minister

Mars Hill
Bentley, Fred Blake academic administrator
Jolley, Betty Cornette history educator

Matthews
†Rivenbark, Jan Meredith food service products corporate executive

Monroe
†Griffin, Bobby F. entrepreneur
†Griffin, Gwyn secondary school principal

Montreat
De Jong, Arthur Jay education consultant, former university president

Morganton
Ervin, Samuel James, III federal judge
Simpson, Daniel Reid lawyer

Mount Airy
Woltz, Howard Osler, Jr. steel and wire products company executive

Mount Holly
Copeland, John Wesley textile company executive

Mount Olive
Raper, William Burkette college president

Mount Ulla
†Kluttz, Henry G. principal

Murfreesboro
Whitaker, Bruce Ezell college president

New Bern
Baughman, Fred Hubbard aeronautical engineer, former naval officer
Degnan, Herbert Raymond financial executive, lawyer, accountant
Kellum, Norman Bryant, Jr. lawyer
Moeller, Dade William environmental engineer, educator
†Nichols, John M. bank executive
†Perdue, Beverly M. state legislator, geriatric consultant
Skipper, Nathan Richard, Jr. lawyer

Newport
Little, Loyd Harry, Jr. author

North Wilkesboro
Herring, Leonard Gray marketing company executive
Pardue, Dwight Edward venture capitalist
Underwood, Harry Burnham, II financial executive, accountant

Oxford
†Pruitt, Dorothy J. Gooch educational administrator

Pilot Mountain
Ross, Norman Alexander retired banker

Pine Knoll Shores
Benson, Kenneth Victor manufacturing company executive, lawyer
Lynn, Otis Clyde former army officer

Pinehurst
Amspoker, James Mack retired gas company executive
Blake, Joan Johnston Wallman playwright, lyricist
Carroll, Kent Jean retired naval officer
Ellis, William Harold former naval officer
Garman, Willard Hershel former government official, scientist
Gilmore, Voit travel executive
Henderson, Paul Audine banker, consultant
Huizenga, John Robert nuclear chemist, educator
Lebeck, Warren Wells commodities consultant
†Maples, Dan golf course designer
†Morgan, Richard Timothy insurance executive
Nuzzo, Salvatore Joseph defense, nuclear executive
O'Neill, John Joseph, Jr. business consultant, former chemical company executive
Owings, Malcolm William retired management consultant
Roberts, Francis Joseph retired army officer, retired educational administrator, global economic advisor
Stingel, Donald Eugene management consultant
Stroud, Richard Hamilton aquatic biologist, scientist, consultant
Twitty, James Watson artist

Pisgah Forest
Albyn, Richard Keith retired architect

Pittsboro
Gustafson, Sarah elementary school educator
Lewis, Henry Wilkins university administrator, lawyer, educator
Robinson, Ormsbee Wright educational consultant

Point Harbor
Heffernan, Phillip Thomas, Jr. retired publisher

Raleigh
Agrawal, Dharma Prakash engineering educator
Anderson, Glenn Elwood investment banker
Andrews, William Parker, Jr. lawyer
Aronson, Arthur Lawrence veterinary pharmacology and toxicology educator
Aspnes, David Erik physicist, educator
Atchley, William Reid geneticist, evolutionary biologist, educator
Baliga, Bantval Jayant electrical engineering educator, consultant
Barham, Charles Dewey, Jr. electric utility executive, lawyer
Barmore, Gregory Terhune capital mortgage company executive
Beatty, Kenneth Orion, Jr. chemical engineer
Bell, Richard Chevalier landscape architect
Bergsma, Daniel retired medical foundation executive, consultant
Bishop, Paul Edward microbiologist
Bitzer, Donald Lester electrical engineering educator, retired research laboratory administrator
†Blackmon, John (Jerry) state senator
Bloomfield, Peter statistics educator
Boyles, Harlan Edward state official
Breytspraak, John, Jr. management consultant
Britt, W. Earl federal judge
†Buchanan, David Royal associate dean
†Burns, Norma DeCamp architect
Burns, Robert Paschal architect, educator
Caldwell, John Tyler political science educator, former university administrator
Cameron, John Lansing retired government official
Carlton, Alfred Pershing, Jr. lawyer
Case, Charles Dixon lawyer
Casey, Ethel Laughlin concert and opera singer
Champ, Raymond Lester hospital administrator
Church, Kern Everidge engineer, consultant
Clarke, Lewis James landscape architect
Cockerham, Columbus Clark retired geneticist, educator
Collins, Thomas Asa minister
Cook, Maurice Gayle soil science educator, consultant
Cooper, Arthur Wells ecologist, educator
Cox, Herbert Bartle natural gas company executive
†Cummings, Frances McArthur state official, retired educational administrator
Cummings, Ralph Waldo soil scientist, educator, researcher
Dameron, Thomas Barker, Jr. orthopaedic surgeon, educator
Daniels, Frank Arthur, Jr. newspaper publisher
Daniels, Frank Arthur, III publishing executive
Dannelly, William D. lawyer
†Daub, Margaret E. plant pathologist, educator
Davey, Charles Bingham soil science educator
Davis, Egbert Lawrence, III lawyer
Davis, William Robert physicist
Denson, Alexander Bunn federal magistrate judge
Doherty, Robert Cunningham advertising executive
Dolce, Carl John education administration educator
†Dudziak, Donald John nuclear engineer, educator
Dunphy, Edward James crop science extension specialist
Dupree, Franklin Taylor, Jr. federal judge
Eagles, Sidney Smith, Jr. judge
Easley, Michael F. state attorney general
Eason, Joseph W. lawyer
Eberly, Harry Landis retired communications company executive
Edmisten, Rufus Ligh state official
Edwards, Charles Archibald lawyer
†Ellington, John David state official
Ellis, Lester Neal, Jr. lawyer
Estill, Robert Whitridge retired bishop
Exum, James Gooden, Jr. state supreme court chief justice
Fadum, Ralph Eigil university dean
†Ferrell, James K. chemical engineering educator, dean
Fletcher, Oscar Jasper, Jr. college dean
†Flournoy, William Louis, Jr. landscape architect
Foley, Peter Michael lawyer
Frye, Henry E. state supreme court justice
Gardner, Robin Pierce engineering educator
†Gilbert, Charles Gorman civil engineering educator
Glass, Margaret Smyllie corporate treasurer, lawyer
Godwin, James Beckham retired landscape architect
Goldstein, Irving Solomon chemistry educator, consultant
Goodman, Major Merlin botanical sciences educator
Gossman, Francis Joseph bishop
†Gottovi, Karen Elizabeth state legislator, political consultant, researcher
Graham, William Edgar, Jr. utility company executive, lawyer
Grayson, Susan Cubillas environmental health administrator
Grubb, Donald Hartman paper industry supplies company executive
Hanson, John M. civil engineering and construction educator
Hardin, Eugene Brooks, Jr. banker
Hardin, James W. botanist, herbarium curator, educator
Hauser, John Reid electrical engineering educator
Hodgson, Ernest toxicology educator
†Holding, Frank B. bank executive
Holding, Lewis R. banker
Horton, Horace Robert biochemistry educator
Hugus, Z Zimmerman, Jr. chemistry educator
Hunt, James Baxter, Jr. governor, lawyer
Hunter, Edgar Hayes architect
Hunter, Margaret King architect
Jennings, Burgess Hill mechanical engineering educator
Jessen, David Wayne accountant
Jividen, Loretta Ann Harper secondary education educator
†Johnson, Joseph Edward state senator
Johnson, Marvin Richard Alois architect
Jordan, John Richard, Jr. lawyer
Joyner, Walton Kitchin lawyer
Kelman, Arthur plant pathologist, educator
†Kessel, John Joseph English language educator, writer
Kimbrell, Odell Culp, Jr. physician
†King, George Edward insurance executive
Klein, Verle Wesley corporate executive, retired naval officer
Kriz, George James agricultural research administrator, educator
Leak, Robert E. management consultant
Leddicotte, George Comer business executive, consultant
†Lemmond, Joseph Shawn state legislator, insurance agent
Levine, Ronald H. physician, state official
Lewis, Richard Jay marketing educator, university dean
Littleton, Isaac Thomas, III retired university library administrator, consultant
MacLeod, John Daniel, Jr. religious organization administrator
Maidon, Carolyn Howser academic program administrator
†Malecha, Marvin John architect, academic administrator
Malone, Thomas Francis university administrator, meteorologist
Mason, David Dickenson statistics educator
Maupin, Armistead Jones lawyer

McKinney, Charles Cecil *investment company executive*
Menius, Arthur Clayton, Jr. *former university dean*
Meyer, Louis B. *state supreme court justice*
Michael, Patricia Ann *physician, clinical systems research director*
†Miller, John Henry *clergyman*
†Miller, R. Bradley *lawyer, state legislator*
Miller, Robert James *lawyer*
†Miner, David Morris *state representative*
Minnick, Carlton Printess, Jr. *bishop*
Mitchell, Burley Bayard, Jr. *state supreme court justice*
Mitchell, Gary Earl *physicist, educator*
Monteith, Larry King *university chancellor*
Moore, Thomas Lloyd *librarian*
Murray, Elizabeth Davis Reid *writer, lecturer*
Murray, Raymond Le Roy *nuclear engineering educator*
Nagle, Hubert Troy, Jr. *electrical engineering educator*
Newman, Slater Edmund *psychologist, educator*
Nickel, Donald Lloyd *engineering executive*
Ofner, J(ames) Alan *management consultant*
Page, Anne Ruth *gifted education educator, education specialist*
Parker, Charles Brand, Jr. *training company executive*
Parker, Joseph Mayon *printing and publishing executive*
Patterson, William S. *lawyer*
Peacock, Erle Ewart, Jr. *surgeon, lawyer, educator*
Pendleton, Gary H(erman) *life insurance agent*
Peterson, Elmor Lee *mathematical scientist, educator*
Poulton, Bruce Robert *former university chancellor*
Powell, Drexel Dwane, Jr. *editorial cartoonist*
Powell, Durwood Royce *lawyer*
Poyner, James Marion *lawyer*
Ragsdale, George Robinson *lawyer*
†Ramsey, Liston Bryan *state legislator*
Rawlings, John Oren *statistician, researcher*
Reeves, Ralph B., III *publisher, editor*
Rhodes, Donald Robert *electrical engineer, educator*
Roach, Wesley Linville *lawyer, insurance executive*
Robinson, Prezell Russell *college administrator*
Rochelle, Lugenia *academic administrator*
†Rogers, Dennis Stanley *columnist, actor, author*
†Rohrbach, Roger Phillip *agricultural engineer, educator*
Royster, Vermont (Connecticut) *journalist*
Sagan, Hans *mathematician, educator, author*
Sanford, Terry *lawyer, former U.S. senator, former governor, former university president*
Scandalios, John George *geneticist, educator*
Schneiderman, Richard Steven *museum official*
†Shaw, Robert Gilbert *restaurant executive, senator*
Shaw, Talbert O. *university president*
Shih, Jason Chia-Hsing *biotechnology educator*
Skaggs, Richard Wayne *agricultural engineering educator*
†Skube, Michael *journalist, critic*
Sloan, O. Temple, Jr. *automotive equipment executive*
Small, Alden Thomas *federal judge*
Smith, Macon Strother *architect*
Smith, Sherwood Hubbard, Jr. *utilities executive*
Sorrell, Furman Yates *mechanical engineering educator*
Speck, Marvin Luther *microbiologist, educator*
Sprinthall, Norman Arthur *psychology educator*
Stiles, Phillip John *physicist, educator*
†Stoskopf, Michael Kerry *educator*
Stuber, Charles William *genetics educator, researcher*
Suhr, Paul Augustine *lawyer*
†Sutton, Ronnie Neal *lawyer, state legislator*
Swaisgood, Harold Everett *biochemist, educator*
†Tally, Lura Self *state legislator*
Timothy, David H. *biology educator*
Tompkins, James Arthur *consulting firm executive, industrial engineer*
Turinsky, Paul Josef *nuclear engineer, educator*
†Ward, Marvin *state senator, former superintendent of schools*
Webb, John *state supreme court justice*
Wesler, Oscar *mathematician, educator*
Whichard, Willis Padgett *state supreme court justice*
Whitten, Jerry Lynn *chemistry educator*
Wicker, Dennis A. *lieutenant governor*
Williams, Hugh Alexander, Jr. *retired mechanical engineer, consultant*
Willis, John Randolph *hospital administrator*
†Wilson, Richard Ferrol *plant physiologist, educator*
Winstead, Nash Nicks *university administrator, phytopathologist*
Wollum, Arthur George, II *microbiologist, researcher, educator*
Woodson, Richard Peyton, III *entrepreneur*
†Wright, Thomas James *chemical company executive*
†Wynne, Johnny Calvin *university official, plant breeding researcher*
Zimmermann, Gerhardt *conductor*
Zorowski, Carl Frank *engineering educator, university administrator*

Randleman
Petty, Richard *professional race car driver*

Research Triangle Park
†Barrett, J. Carl *cancer researcher, molecular biologist*
Bursiek, Ralph David *information systems company executive*
†Cipau, Gabriel *pharmaceutical executive*
Connor, Walter Robert *classics educator, humanities center administrator*
de Serres, Frederick Joseph *genetic toxicologist*
Drake, John Walter *geneticist*
Elion, Gertrude Belle *research scientist, pharmacology educator*
Gaither, John Stokes *chemical company executive*
Griesemer, Richard Allen *veterinary pathologist*
Hagan, John Aubrey *financial executive*
†Hagan, Joseph Lawrence *communications executive*
†Heck, Henry Darcy *toxicologist*
Herbert, George Richard *research executive*
Hitchings, George Herbert *retired pharmaceutical company executive, educator*
Holton, William Coffeen *electrical engineering executive*
Karr, Alan Francis *statistics educator, academic administrator*
†King, Theodore M. *obstetrician, gynecologist, educator*
Krenitsky, Thomas Anthony *biochemist, research director*
Kuhn, Matthew *engineering company executive*
Larsen, Ralph Irving *environmental research engineer*
Maroni, Donna Farolino *science administrator*
Martin, William Royall, Jr. *association executive*
May, Michael Lee *magazine editor*
Olden, Kenneth *public health service administrator, researcher*
Rodbell, Martin *biochemist*
Tilson, Hugh Hanna *epidemiologist*
†Wilsnack, Roger E. *medical association administrator*
Wooten, Frank Thomas *research facility executive*

Rockingham
†Robertson, Ralph S. *secondary school principal*

Rocky Mount
Autry, Robert F. *restaurant chain executive*
†Cooper, Roy Asberry, III *lawyer*
Laughery, Jack Arnold *restaurant chain executive*
Mauldin, Robert Ray *banker*
Pitt, Theophilus Harper, Jr. *insurance and real estate company executive*
Powers, James Bascom *banker*
Wilkerson, William Holton *banker*
†Wilson, Richard P. *human resources executive*

Salemburg
Baugh, Charles Milton *biochemistry educator, college dean*

Salisbury
Kelly, Brendan William *engineering executive*
Ketner, Ralph Wright *retail food company executive*
Shalkop, Robert Leroy *retired museum consultant*
Smith, Tom Eugene *retail food company executive*
†Speaks, Ruben Lee *bishop*
Tlalka, Jacek *mathematics educator*
Trexler, Wynn Ridenhour *paralegal*

Saluda
Mowery, Bob Lee *librarian*

Sanford
Higgins, George Edward *sculptor*
Raisig, Paul Jones, Jr. *lawyer*

Saxapahaw
Bulla, Ben F. *treasurer*

Shelby
Edgar, Ruth R. *educator*

Southern Pines
Lowry, Charles Wesley *clergyman, lecturer*
Mataxis, Theodore Christopher *consultant, lecturer, writer, retired army officer, educator*
Ragan, Samuel Talmadge *newspaper editor, publisher, educator, poet laureate*
Toon, Malcolm *former ambassador*
Towell, William Earnest *forester, former association executive*
Vanderwoude, J. Stephen *communications company executive*
Yarborough, William Pelham *writer, lecturer, retired army officer, consultant*

Southport
Harrelson, Walter Joseph *minister, religion educator emeritus*
Worzel, John Lamar *geophysicist, educator*

Sparta
Adams, Marion Ruth Allison *special education educator*

Spring Hope
Hildreth, James Robert *air force officer*
Lavatelli, Leo Silvio *retired physicist, educator*

Swansboro
Mullikin, Thomas Wilson *mathematics educator*

Tabor City
Jorgensen, Ralph Gubler *lawyer*

Tarboro
Hopkins, Grover Prevatte *lawyer*

Thomasville
Starr, Frederick Brown *furniture manufacturing executive*

Tryon
Claud, Joseph Gillette *banker*
Stinson, George Arthur *lawyer, former steel company executive*
Thayer, Lee *educator, author, consultant*

Wadesboro
†Hightower, Foyle Robert, Jr. *state legislator, ice and fuel company executive*

Wake Forest
Binkley, Olin Trivette *clergyman, seminary president emeritus*

Warrenton
†Ballance, Frank W., Jr. *state senator, lawyer*

Washington
†Edwards, Zeno L., Jr. *state legislator, retired dentist*
Hackney, James Acra, III *industrial engineer, manufacturing company executive*
Timour, John Arnold *retired librarian, medical bibliography and library science educator*

Waxhaw
Lamparter, William C. *printing and publishing consultant, digital printing and information systems specialist*

Waynesville
Matlock, Clifford Charles *retired foreign service officer*

Weaverville
Boyce, Emily Stewart *retired library and information science educator*
Parsons, Vinson Adair *retired computer software company executive*
Wallin, Franklin Whittelsey *educational consultant, former college president*

Weldon
Barringer, Paul Brandon, II *lumber company executive*
Conger, Stephen Halsey *lumber company executive*

West End
Cartwright, William Holman *education educator emeritus*
Moncure, James Ashby *historian*

Whispering Pines
Blanchard, George Samuel *retired military officer, consultant*
Enlow, Donald Hugh *anatomist, educator, university dean*

Whiteville
†Sasser, Edward Rhone *bank executive*

Williamston
Cowen, Robert Henry *lawyer*

Wilmington
Brauer, Ralph Werner *physiologist, educator*
Cahill, Charles L. *university administrator, chemistry educator*
Crigler, T. P. *foreign products and investments executive*
Dixon, N(orman) Rex *speech and hearing scientist, educator*
Fox, James Carroll *federal judge*
Haselden, Clyde LeRoy *librarian*
Janson, Anthony Frederick *art educator, former museum curator*
Leutze, James Richard *academic administrator, television producer and host*
Martin, Ned Harold *chemistry educator*
†McManus, Hugh F. *principal*
Meyer, John *newspaper editor*
Morrison, William Fowler, Jr. *health care consultant*
Roer, Robert David *physiologist, educator*
Scheu, David Robert, Sr. *historic site director*
Silloway, Benton, Jr. *food products executive*
Thompson, Donald Charles *electronics company executive, former coast guard officer*
Wade, James Michael *treasurer*
Wagoner, William Hampton *university chancellor*
Wright, Thomas Henry *bishop*
†Zimmer, Alan Mark *retail jewelry chain executive*

Wilson
Allison, John Andrew, IV *bank executive*
Durrer, Christopher Thomas *hospital executive*
Hemby, James B., Jr. *college president*
Herring, Jerone Carson *lawyer, bank executive*
Kehaya, Ery W. *tobacco holding company executive*
Murray, J. Alec G. *manufacturing executive*
Ross, Guy Matthews, Jr. *corporate executive*
Stewart, Burton Gloyden, Jr. *banker*
Williamson, Henry Gaston, Jr. *banker*

Winston Salem
Alderson, William Thomas *historian, consultant*
Alexander, Eben, Jr. *neurological surgeon*
Atkinson, G. Douglas, Sr. *marketing executive, consultant*
Austell, Edward Callaway *banker*
Barnett, Richard Chambers *historian, educator*

Winston-Salem
Barnhardt, Zeb Elonzo, Jr. *lawyer*

Winston Salem
Benfield, Marion Wilson, Jr. *lawyer, educator*
Blynn, Guy Marc *lawyer*
†Bowman, Marjorie Ann *physician, academic administrator*
Butner, Fred Washington, Jr. *architect*
Carter, Henry Moore, Jr. *foundation executive*
Cawood, Hobart Guy *historic site administrator*
†Clarkson, Thomas Boston *comparative medicine educator*
Copenhaver, W. Andrew *lawyer*
Corbett, Leon H., Jr. *lawyer, educator, university official*
Cotterill, David Lee *banker*
Covey, Cyclone *history educator*
Cowan, Robert Jenkins *radiologist, educator*
Cramer, John Scott *retired banker*
Davis, Courtland Harwell, Jr. *neurosurgeon*
Davis, John Wesley, III *investment banker*
Davis, Linwood Layfield *lawyer*
Davis, Thomas Henry *airline executive*
Davis, William Allison, II *lawyer*
†Dean, Richard Henry *surgeon, educator*
Dodd, Virginia Marilyn *veterinarian*
Doggett, Aubrey Clayton, Jr. *real estate executive, consultant*
Doster, Joseph C. *newspaper publisher*
Ehle, John Marsden, Jr. *writer*
Ehmann, Carl William *consumer products executive, researcher*
Eliason, Russell Allen *federal judge*
Emken, Robert Allan *diversified company executive*
Erwin, Richard Cannon *federal judge*
Ewing, Alexander Cochran *chancellor*
Faccinto, Victor Paul *artist, gallery administrator*
Farr, Henry Bartow, Jr. *lawyer*
Fitzgerald, Ernest Abner *retired bishop*
Flory, Walter S., Jr. *geneticist, botanist, educator*
†Ford, Yancey William, Jr. *tobacco company executive*
Foy, Herbert Miles, III *lawyer, educator*
Gitter, Allan Reinhold *lawyer*
Gleason, Norman Dale *association executive*
Goodman, Joseph Champion *editor*
Gray, James Alexander *historic preservation official*
Greason, Murray Crossley, Jr. *lawyer*
Griscom, Thomas Cecil *presidential assistant, public relations executive*
Gunzenhauser, Gerard Ralph, Jr. *management consultant, investor*
Hanes, Frank Borden *author, farmer, former business executive*
Hanes, Ralph Philip, Jr. *textile company executive*
Hazzard, William Russell *geriatrician, educator*
Healy, Joseph Francis, Jr. *lawyer, arbitrator, retired airline executive*
Helm, Robert Meredith *philosophy educator*
Hendricks, J(ames) Edwin *historian, educator, consultant, author*
Hendrix, Rufus Sam, Jr. *sales executive*
Herndon, Claude Nash *retired geneticist, physician*
Hopkins, Judith Owen *oncologist*
Howell, Charles Maitland *dermatologist*
Janeway, Richard *university executive*
Johnson, Norman *music director, opera producer, educator*
Johnston, James Wesley *tobacco company executive*
Kaufman, William *internist*
Kerr, Sandria Neidus *mathematics and computer science educator*
†Kohut, Robert Irwin *otolaryngologist, educator*
Leonard, R. Michael *lawyer*
Lorentz, William Beall *pediatrician*
Mackey, Dallas L. *financial consultant, development officer*
MacKinnon, Sally Anne *retired fast food company executive*
†Mandelbaum, Allen *poet, English language and literature educator*
Martin, James Alfred, Jr. *religious studies educator*
Maselli, John Anthony *food products company executive*
Maynard, Charles Douglas *radiologist*
†McCullough, David L. *urologist*
McNair, John Franklin, III *banker*
Medlin, John Grimes, Jr. *banker*
Mokrasch, Lewis Carl *neurochemist, educator*
Mueller-Heubach, Eberhard August *medical educator, obstetrician-gynecologist*
Newton, George Durfee, Jr. *lawyer*
†Oppermann, Joseph Kay *architect*
O'Steen, Wendall Keith *neurobiology and anatomy educator*
Penry, James Kiffin *physician, neurology educator*
Perret, Peter James *symphony conductor*
Podgorny, George *emergency physician*
Preslar, Len Broughton, Jr. *hospital administrator*
Prichard, Robert Williams *pathologist, educator*
Ray, Michael Edwin *lawyer*
†Rights, Graham Henry *minister*
Riley, Leslie Walter, Jr. *corporate executive*
Roberts, William Hugh, III *library director, consultant*
Rodgman, Alan *chemist, consultant*
Roth, Marjory Joan Jarboe *special education educator*
Rudel, Lawrence Lee *biochemist*
Runnion, Howard J., Jr. *banker*
Sandridge, William Pendleton, Jr. *lawyer*
Scales, James Ralph *history educator, former university president*
Schollander, Wendell Leslie, Jr. *lawyer*
Shapere, Dudley *philosophy educator*
Sharpe, Keith Yount *lawyer*
†Shils, Maurice Edward *physician, educator*
Simon, Jimmy Louis *pediatrician, educator*
Smith, Zachary Taylor, II *retired tobacco company executive*
Spach, Jule Christian *church executive*
†Sparber, Gordon Mark *music journalist*
Sperry, Michael Winton *banker*
Spurr, Charles Lewis *medical educator, cancer chemotherapy clinical researcher*
†Steele, Thomas McKnight *law librarian, law educator*
Sticht, J. Paul *retired food products and tobacco company executive*
Strickland, Robert Louis *business executive*
Stroupe, Henry Smith *university dean*
Theros, Elias George *radiology educator and author*
Thompson, Cleon F., Jr. *university administrator*
Toole, James Francis *medical educator*
Trautwein, George William *conductor*
Vance, Charles Fogle, Jr. *lawyer*
Vincent, Clark Edward *sociologist*
Walker, George Kontz *law educator*
†Walter, Lloyd Guy, Jr. *architect*
Wanders, Hans Walter *banker*
Ward, Hiram Hamilton *federal judge*
Watlington, John Francis, Jr. *banker*
Wells, Dewey Wallace *lawyer*
Wiles, Paul Martin *hospital administration executive*
Williams, John Edwin *psychology educator*
Wilson, Edwin Graves *university official*
Womble, William Fletcher *lawyer*
†Wood, Martha Swain *mayor*
Woods, James Watson, Jr. *cardiologist*
Worley, Bland Wallace *banker*
Zagoria, Sam D(avid) *arbitrator, author, educator*

Winterville
Myers, Robert Durant *biologist, research director, medical educator*

Wrightsville Beach
Mc Ilwain, William Franklin *newspaper editor, writer*

Zebulon
†Marshall, Michael P. *computer company sales executive*

NORTH DAKOTA

Ashley
†Kretschmar, William Edward *lawyer, state legislator*

Bismarck
†Carlisle, Ronald Dwight *nursery owner*
Carmichael, Virgil Wesly *mining, civil and geological engineer, former coal company executive*
†Cleary, Audrey *state legislator, nurse volunteer*
Conmy, Patrick A. *federal judge*
Erickstad, Ralph John *judge, retired state supreme court chief justice*
†Evanson, Barbara Jean *middle school education educator*
Gilmore, Kathi *state treasurer*
†Heinrich, Bonnie *state legislator*
Heitkamp, Heidi *state attorney general*
Hook, William Franklin *radiologist*
Jaeger, Alvin A. (Al Jaeger) *secretary of state*
Kinney, John Francis *bishop*
†Lips, Evan E. *state senator, insurance company executive*
Maichel, Joseph Raymond *lawyer, business executive*
Malmberg, John Andrew *bank executive*

Meschke, Herbert Leonard *state supreme court justice*
†Montz, Florence Stolte *church official*
Murry, Charles Emerson *lawyer, national guard official*
Myrdal, Rosemarie Caryle *state official, former state legislator*
Nelson, Keithe Eugene *lawyer, state court administrator*
Newborg, Gerald Gordon *historical agency administrator*
†Olsen, Dagne B. *state legislator*
Pederson, Vernon R. *judge*
Sanstead, Wayne Godfrey *state superintendent, former lieutenant governor*
Schafer, Edward T. *governor of North Dakota*
Schuchart, John Albert, Jr. *utility executive*
Smith, Richard Ernest *retired insurance company executive*
Solberg, Nellie Florence Coad *artist*
†Sperry, James Edward *anthropologist*
Stastney, Agnes Florence *principal*
Strutz, William A. *lawyer*
VandeWalle, Gerald Wayne *state supreme court chief justice*
Van Sickle, Bruce Marion *federal judge*

Cando
†Nicholas, Eugene Joseph *farmer, state representative*

Crosby
†Andrist, John M. *state senator*

Devils Lake
†Traynor, John Thomas, Jr. *lawyer*

Dickinson
Conn, Philip Wesley *university president*
†Morud, Rollie D. *school system administrator*

Dunseith
Gorder, Steven F. *association administrator*

Fargo
Bright, Myron H. *federal judge, educator*
Dill, William Joseph *newspaper editor*
†Fairfield, Andrew H. *biship*
†Foss, Richard John *bishop*
Hill, William A(lexander) *bankruptcy judge*
Lohman, John Frederick *editor*
Magill, Frank John *federal judge*
Marcil, William Christ, Sr. *publisher, broadcast executive*
†Mathern, Tim *state senator, social worker*
Mengedoth, Donald Roy *commercial banker*
†Nalewaja, Donna *state legislator*
Nickel, Janet Marlene Milton *geriatrics nurse*
Ommodt, Donald Henry *dairy company executive*
†Orr, Steven R. *health facility administrator*
Ozbun, Jim L. *academic administrator*
Paulson, John Doran *newspaper editor, retired*
†Payne, Douglas G. *retired insurance company executive*
Query, Joy Marves Neale *medical sociology educator*
†Scherber, Catherine A. (Kit Scherber) *state legislator, trainer persons with disabilities*
Schmidt, Claude Henri *retired research administrator*
Spaeth, Nicholas John *lawyer, former state attorney general*
Sullivan, James Stephen *bishop*
Swedback, James M. *insurance company executive*
Tallman, Robert Hall *investment company executive*
†Wallwork, William Wilson, III *corporate executive*
Webb, Rodney Scott *federal judge, lawyer*
Williams, Norman Dale *geneticist, researcher*
†Zimmerman, Don Charles *plant physiologist, biochemist*

Garrison
†Schlieve, Hy C. J. *superintendent*

Grafton
†Tallackson, Harvey D. *real estate and insurance salesman*

Grand Forks
Baker, Kendall L. *academic administrator*
Carlson, Edward C. *anatomy educator*
Carroll, Jack Adien *hospital administrator*
Clifford, Thomas John *university president*
†DeMers, Judy Lee *state legislator, dean*
Duerre, John Arden *biochemist*
Gjovig, Bruce Quentin *manufacturing consultant*
†Glassheim, Eliot *museum director, state legislator*
†Gott, Gary Dean *law library director, educator*
Jacobs, Francis Albin *biochemist, educator*
Lindquist, Mary Louise *special education educator*
†Nielsen, Forrest Harold *research nutritionist*
Nordlie, Robert Conrad *biochemistry educator*
O'Kelly, Bernard *university dean*
†Poolman, Jim *state legislator*
Sand, Phyllis Sue Newnam *retired special education educator*
Senechal, Alice R. *lawyer*
†Stenehjem, Wayne Kevin *lawyer, state senator*
Vogel, Robert *lawyer, educator*
Widdel, John Earl, Jr. *lawyer*
Wold, Richard Otto *banker*

Hannaford
†Wogsland, Dan *state senator*

Jamestown
Hjellum, John *retired lawyer*
Walker, James Silas *college official*

Lefor
†Martin, Clarence *farmer, state legislator*

Mandan
Halvorson, Ardell David *research leader, soil scientist*
Kautzmann, Dwight C(larence) H(arry) *lawyer, magistrate*
†Mushik, Corliss *state legislator*

Mayville
Karaim, Betty June *librarian*

Minot
Armstrong, Phillip Dale *lawyer*
Haugland, Brynhild *retired state legislator, farmer*
†Krebsbach, Karen K. *state legislator*
Shaar, H. Erik *academic administrator*
†Tollefson, Ben C. *sales manager, retired, financial consultant*

Regent
†Krauter, Aaron Joseph *farmer, state senator*

Saint Anthony
†Tomac, Steven W. *state senator, farmer*

Sanborn
†Gerntholz, Gereld Felix *farmer, state representative*

Turtle Lake
†Grosz, Albert Mick *sales executive*

Watford City
Stenehjem, Leland Manford *banker*

Williston
Adducci, Joseph Edward *obstetrician, gynecologist*
Burdick, Eugene Allan *retired judge, lawyer, surrogate judge*
†Rennerfeldt, Earl Ronald *farmer, rancher*

OHIO

Ada
Cooper, Ken Errol *management educator*
Freed, DeBow *college president*
Hanson, Eugene Nelson *judge*
†Leonard, James *law librarian, educator*
Quick, Albert Thomas *academic law administrator, educator*

Akron
Aggarwal, Sundar Lal *technology management consultant*
Albrecht, Frederick Steven *grocery company executive, lawyer*
Allen, William Dale *newspaper editor*
Altenau, Alan Giles *tire and rubber company executive*
Arnett, James Edward *retired insurance company executive, retired secondary school educator*
Auburn, Norman Paul *university president*
Barker, Harold Kenneth *former university dean*
Barnett, James Wallace *manufacturing executive*
Bartlo, Sam D. *lawyer*
Bell, Samuel H. *federal judge*
Bonsky, Jack Alan *chemical company executive, lawyer*
Brock, James Robert *manufacturing company executive*
Brown, David Rupert *engineering executive*
Bryant, Keith Lynn, Jr. *history educator*
Calise, Nicholas James *lawyer*
Castronovo, Thomas Paul *architect, consultant*
Childs, James William *lawyer, legal educator*
Clapp, Joseph Mark *motor carrier company executive*
Considine, William Howard *health care administrator*
Contie, Leroy John, Jr. *federal judge*
†Cooper, David Booth *newspaper editor*
Coyne, Thomas Joseph *economist, finance educator*
Crawford, Robert John *credit company executive*
Dotson, John Louis, Jr. *newspaper executive*
Dowd, David D., Jr. *federal judge*
Elliott, Peggy Gordon *university president*
Evans, Douglas McCullough *surgeon, educator*
Fisher, James Lee *lawyer*
Frank, John V. *foundation executive*
Friedman, Richard Everett *librarian*
Gault, Stanley Carleton *manufacturing company executive*
Gent, Alan Neville *physicist, educator*
Gilbert, Albert Francis *hospital administrator*
Greenman, John Frederick *newspaper executive*
Heckel, John Louis (Jack Heckel) *aerospace company executive*
Heider, Jon Vinton *lawyer, corporate executive*
Hodge, James Robert *psychiatrist*
Holland, Willard Raymond, Jr. *electric utility executive*
Holloway, Donald Phillip *lawyer*
Isles, Marvin Lee *manufacturing executive*
Jones, Robert Huhn *history educator*
Kahan, Mitchell Douglas *art museum director*
Kaufman, Donald Leroy *aluminum products company executive*
†Kelley, Frank Nicholas *dean*
Kelley, John Paul *communications consultant*
†Kelley, Robert W. *bishop*
Kennedy, Joseph Paul *polymer scientist, researcher*
†Kirksey, Charles Ron *journalist*
Knepper, George W. *history educator*
Kodish, Arline Betty *principal*
Krause, David James *accountant, transportation company executive*
Levy, Richard Philip *physician, educator*
LoIudice, Thomas Anthony *gastroenterologist, researcher*
Lombardi, Frederick McKean *lawyer, judge*
Marini, Frank Nicholas *public administration and political science educator*
†Martino, Frank Dominic *union executive*
McCormick, William Edward *environmental consultant*
†Mehlfeldt, Horst K. *tire manufacturing company*
Monacelli, Amieto *professional bowler*
†Ockene, Alan L. *tire manufacturing executive*
Ong, John Doyle *lawyer*
Ozio, David *professional bowler*
Pengilly, Brian William *manufacturing company executive*
Phillipson, John Samuel *retired English educator*
Plusquellic, Donald L. *mayor*
Poll, Heinz *choreographer, artistic director*
†Ray, Roy Lee *public finance consultant, state legislator*
Rebenack, John Henry *retired librarian*
Reynolds, A. William *manufacturing company executive*
†Richert, Paul *law educator*
Rogers, Justin Towner, Jr. *retired utility company executive*
Schrader, Helen Maye *retired municipal worker*
Schubert, Barbara Schuele *performing company executive*
Seiberling, John Frederick *former congressman, law educator, lawyer*
Skakun, Mark John, III *lawyer*
Sonnecken, Edwin Herbert *management consultant*
Spetrino, Russell John *retired utility company executive, lawyer*
Stroll, Beverly Marie *elementary school principal*
Timmons, Gerald Dean *pediatric neurologist*
Tobler, D. Lee *chemical and aerospace company executive*
Trotter, Thomas Robert *lawyer*
Uscheek, David Petrovich *chemist*
Wells, Hoyt Mellor *manufacturing executive*
White, Harold F. *federal judge*
†Wickham, Michael W. *transportation executive*

Alexandria
Palmer, Melville Louis *retired agricultural engineering educator*

Alliance
Rockhill, Jack Kerrigan *collections company executive*
Rodman, James Purcell *astrophysicist, educator*
Weber, Ronald Gilbert *retired college president*
Woods, Rose Mary *consultant, former presidential assistant*

Alpha
James, Francis Edward, Jr. *investment counselor*

Andover
Mathay, John Preston *elementary education educator*

Ashland
Cox, Harry Seymour *financial executive*
Ford, Lucille Garber *economist, educator, college official*

Ashtabula
Bonner, David Calhoun *chemical company executive*
Taylor, Norman Floyd *computer educator, administrator*

Ashville
Beckman, Judith *art educator*

Athens
Borchert, Donald Marvin *philosopher, educator*
Bruning, James Leon *university official, educator*
Cohn, Norman Stanley *botany educator, university dean*
Crowl, Samuel Renninger *English language educator*
Dinos, Nicholas *engineering educator, administrator*
Eckelmann, Frank Donald *geology educator, retired*
Eckes, Alfred Edward, Jr. *historian, international trade analyst*
Gaddis, John Lewis *history educator*
Gallaway, Gladys McGhee *elementary education educator*
Glidden, Robert Burr *musician, educator, academic administrator*
Gustavson, Carl Gustav *historian, educator*
Hamby, Alonzo Lee *historian, educator*
Klare, George Roger *psychology educator*
Lee, Hwa-Wei *librarian, educator*
Matthews, Jack (John Harold Matthews) *English educator, writer*
Miller, Peggy McLaren *management educator*
Miller, Richard Irwin *education educator, university administrator*
Patriquin, David Ashley *osteopath, educator*
Patterson, Harlan Ray *finance educator*
Ping, Charles Jackson *university administrator, educator*
Rakes, Ganas Kaye *finance and banking educator*
Robe, Thurlow Richard *engineering educator, university dean*
Russell, David L(awson) *psychology educator*
Schneider, Duane Bernard *English literature educator, publisher*
Scott, Charles Lewis *photojournalist*
Stempel, Guido Hermann, III *journalism educator*
Ungar, Irwin Allan *botany educator*
Wen, Shih-Liang *mathematics educator*
Whealey, Lois Deimel *humanities scholar*

Aurora
Lawton, Florian Kenneth *artist, educator*
Wiegner, Edward Alex *multi-industry executive*

Avon Lake
†McLaughlin, Ronald Paul *labor union administrator*

Barberton
Moss, Robert Drexler *lawyer*

Batavia
Rosenhoffer, Chris *lawyer*

Bay Village
Hiller, Deborah Lewis *long term care and retirement facility executive*

Beachwood
Ellett, Alan Sidney *real estate development company executive*
Lerner, Alfred *real estate and financial executive*
†Seelbach, William Robert *corporate executive*
Swank, Emory Coblentz *world affairs consultant, lecturer*
Zelikow, Howard Monroe *management and financial consultant*

Beavercreek
McCormick, Jack Edward *retired military officer, educator*
Rodin, Alvin Eli *pathalogist, medical educator, author*

Bedford
Parch, Grace Dolores *librarian*

Bedford Heights
Moore, Dianne J. Hall *insurance claims administrator*

Beechwood
Donnem, Roland William *real estate manager, lawyer*

Bellaire
Hahn, David Bennett *hospital administrator, marketing professional*

Bellefontaine
Johnson, Renie *real estate executive, publisher*

Berea
Belichick, Bill *professional football coach*
Blumer, Frederick Elwin *philosophy educator*
Byner, Earnest Alexander *professional football player*
Irwin, Richard Loren *systems management association executive*
Jensen, Adolph Robert *former chemistry educator*
Malicky, Neal *college president*
Modell, Arthur B. *professional football team executive*
Pattison, Robert Maynicke *architect*
Perry, Michael Dean *professional football player*
Rypien, Mark Robert *football player*
Strew, Suzanne Claflin *choreographer, dance educator*

Bluffton
Smucker, Barbara Claassen *former librarian, writer*

Boardman
Walton, Ralph Gerald *psychiatrist, educator*

Bowling Green
Baird, James Abington *judge*
Brecher, Arthur Seymour *biochemistry educator*
Browne, Ray Broadus *popular culture educator*
Clark, Eloise Elizabeth *biologist, university official*
Clark, Robert King *communications educator emeritus, lecturer, consultant, actor, model*
Denisoff, R. Serge *sociologist, writer*
Guthrie, Mearl Raymond, Jr. *business administration educator*
Hakel, Milton Daniel, Jr. *psychology educator, consultant, publisher*
Hanna, Martin Shad *lawyer*
Holmes, Robert Allen *lawyer, educator, consultant, lecturer*
Lavezzi, John Charles *art history educator, archaeologist*
Lunde, Harold Irving *management educator*
McCaghy, Charles Henry *sociology educator*
Ocvirk, Otto George *artist*
Rockett, Carlton Lee *biological sciences educator*
Scott, John Paul *psychologist, educator, author*
Smith, Stan Lee *biology educator*
Weaver, Richard L., II *speech communication educator*

Bratenahl
Jones, Trevor Owen *automobile supply company executive, management consultant*

Brecksville
Chatman, Rosie A. *nursing administrator*
Galloway, Ethan Charles *technology development executive, former chemicals executive*
Johnson, L. Neil *school system administrator*
Worden, Alfred Merrill *former astronaut, research company executive*

Brook Park
Bluford, Guion Stewart, Jr. *engineering company executive*
Wilson, Jack *aeronautical engineer*

Brooklyn
Conomy, John Paul *neurologist, lawyer, corporate executive*

Brookpark
Kosmahl, Henry G. *electron physicist*

Brookville
Juhl, Daniel Leo *manufacturing and marketing firm executive*

Bucyrus
Moore, Thomas Paul *broadcast executive*

Canal Winchester
Burrier, Gail Warren *physician*

Canfield
Bachmeyer, Robert Wesley *retired hospital administration consultant*
Itts, Elizabeth Ann Dunham *psychotherapist, consultant, designer*

Canton
Arora, Sardari Lal *chemistry educator*
Bennington, Ronald Kent *lawyer*
Boulton, Edwin Charles *bishop*
Carpenter, Noble Olds *banker*
Dettinger, Warren Walter *lawyer*
†Dorsett, Anthony Drew (Tony Dorsett) *former professional football player*
Duncan, Joyce Louise *real estate broker*
Elliott, Peter R. *athletic organization executive*
Elsaesser, Robert James *retired manufacturing executive*
Fouts, Daniel Francis *sports announcer, former professional football player*
†Grant, Bud (Harold Peter Grant) *retired professional football coach*
Hoecker, David *engineering executive*
Howland, Willard J. *radiologist, educator*
†Johnson, Jimmy *former professional football player*
†Kelly, Leroy *former professional football player*
Koniecko, Edward S(tanley) *biochemist*
Koontz, Raymond *security equipment company executive*
Lindamood, John Beyer *lawyer*
Mokodean, Michael John *lawyer, accountant*
Ognibene, Andre J(ohn) *physician, army officer, educator*
†Pryce, Richard James *hospital administrator*
†Smith, Jackie *former professional football player*
Timken, W. Robert, Jr. *manufacturing company executive*
Toot, Joseph F., Jr. *bearing manufacturing company executive*
Warner, E. John *manufacturing financial executive*

Cedarville
Gordin, Dean Lackey *retired agricultural products executive*

Centerville
Fulk, Paul Frederick *chiropractor*
Keating, Tristan Jack *retired aeronautical engineer*
Kelso, Harold Glen *family practice physician*
†Mattia, Frank J. *secondary school principal*
Perrich, Jerry Robert *environmental consulting company executive*

Chagrin Falls
Cadou, Peter Brosius *mechanical engineer*
Church, Irene Zaboly *personnel services company executive*
Cordes, Loverne Christian *interior designer*
Daniel, Clarence Huber *former manufacturing company executive, consultant*
Dunning, Ann Marie *architect*
Eastburn, Richard A. *consulting firm executive*
Fisher, Will Stratton *illumination consultant*
Frohring, Paul Robert *former business executive*
Gelb, Victor *business executive*
Gillam, James Kennedy *publishing company executive*
Grasselli, Jeanette Gecsy *university official*
Groeger, Joseph Herman *retired metal company executive*
Lingl, Friedrich Albert *psychiatrist*
Nyberg, Donald Arvid *oil company executive*
Pauly, Bruce Henry *engineering consultant*
Phillips, Dorothy Ormes *elementary education educator*
Rawski, Conrad H(enry) *humanities educator, medievalist*
Strachan, Donald M. *accountant*
Streicher, James Franklin *lawyer*

Chardon
Dietrich, Joseph Jacob *chemist, research executive*
Nara, Harry Raymond *engineering educator*
Reinhard, Sister Mary Marthe *educational organization administrator*

Chesapeake
Harris, Bob L(ee) *principal*

Chesterland
Driggs, Charles Mulford *lawyer*
Durn, Raymond Joseph *lawyer*
Kancelbaum, Joshua Jacob *lawyer*

Cincinnati
Adams, Edmund John *lawyer*
Adams, James Louis *newspaper editor, retired*
Addison, Harry Metcalf *insurance executive*
Adolph, Robert J. *physician, medical educator*
Alexander, James Marshall, Jr. *architect, retired educator*
Alexander, James Wesley *surgeon, educator*
Alexander, John J. *chemistry educator*
Anderson, James Milton *lawyer*
Anderson, William Hopple *lawyer*
Aniskovich, Paul Peter, Jr. *insurance company executive*
Anno, James Nelson *nuclear engineering scientist, educator*
Anthony, Thomas Dale *lawyer*
Arnold, Lynn Ellis *metallurgist, consultant*
Artzt, Edwin Lewis *consumer products company executive*
Ashley, Lynn *educational coordinator*
Atteberry, William Duane *diversified manufacturing company executive*
Aug, Jonathan Vincent *federal bankruptcy judge*
Baas, Robert Miller *school administrator*
Bahlman, William Thorne, Jr. *lawyer*
Bahr, Donald Walter *chemical engineer*
Baker, Norman Robert *education educator*
Beard, Thomas Lee *magazine editor*
Beckwith, Barbara Jean *journalist*
†Beekman, Philip E. *retail company executive*
Belew, Adrian *guitarist, singer, songwriter, producer*
Bench, Johnny Lee *former professional baseball player*
Bernstein, I. Leonard *physician, educator*
Bestehorn, Ute Wiltrud *retired librarian*
Biddinger, Paul Williams *pathologist, educator*
Bieliauskas, Vytautas Joseph *clinical psychologist, educator*
Bingham, Eula *environmental health educator*
Bishop, George Franklin *political social psychologist, educator*
Black, David deLaine *investment consultant*
Blake, George Rowell *newspaper editor, journalist*
Blank, Cynthia Fisher *lawyer*
Blanken, Sarah S. *retired foundation administrator*
Bleznick, Donald William *Romance languages educator*
Bluestein, Paul Harold *management engineer*
Bluestein, Venus Weller *retired psychology educator*
Blum, William Lee *lawyer*
Boat, Thomas Frederick *physician, educator, researcher*
†Borgman, James Mark *editorial cartoonist*
Bostian, Harry Edward *chemical engineer*
Bradley, Sister Myra James *health science facility executive*
†Breth, James Raymond *scrap metals company executive*
Bridenbaugh, Phillip Owen *anesthesiologist, physician*
Bridgeland, James Ralph, Jr. *lawyer, mayor*
Brinkman, Herbert Charles *lawyer*
Brod, Stanford *graphic designer, educator*
Bromberg, Barbara Schwartz *lawyer*
Bromberg, Robert Sheldon *lawyer*
†Bronson, Peter William *newspaper editor*
Brown, Dale Patrick *advertising executive*
Brown, Mike *professional sports team executive*
†Brown, William J. *architect, consultant*
Brumm, Paul Michael *banker*
Brunner, Gordon F(rancis) *household products company executive*
Buchman, Elwood *physician, pharmaceutical company medical director*
†Buenger, Clement Lawrence *banker*
Bullock, John McDonell *banker*
Burleigh, William Robert *newspaper executive*
†Burt, DeVere *museum administrator*
Byers, Kenneth Vernon *insurance company executive*
†Cantu, John Maurice *insurance company executive*
Carney, Robert Alfred *health care administrator*
Carothers, Charles Omsted *orthopedic surgeon*
†Carr, Albert Anthony *organic chemist*
Carro, Jorge Luis *law librarian, educator*
Carroll, Robert Henry *accountant*
Carson, Nolan Wendell *lawyer*
Chase, William Rowell *manufacturing executive*
†Chatterjee, Jayanta *educator, urban designer*
Chesley, Stanley Morris *lawyer*
Christensen, Paul Walter, Jr. *gear manufacturing company executive*
Christenson, Gordon A. *law educator*
Church, John Franklin, Jr. *paper company executive*
†Ciani, Alfred Joseph *language professional, dean*
Cissell, James Charles *lawyer*
Clark, James Norman *insurance executive*
Cody, Thomas Gerald *lawyer*
Cohen, Hirsh Joel *health care administrator*
Collins, Larry Wayne *health facility administrator*
Conaton, Michael Joseph *financial service executive*
†Conley, Robert T. *educational administrator*
Cook, Bruce Alan *air conditioning sales and service executive*
Cook, Jack McPherson *hospital administrator*
Coombe, V. Anderson *valve manufacturing company executive*
Cowan, Jerry Louis *lawyer*
Craig, L. Clifford *lawyer*
Crowe, James Joseph *shoe company executive, lawyer*
Crumes, William Edward *bishop*
Curtin, Leah Louise *nurse, consultant, editor, author*
de Blasis, James Michael *artistic director, producer, stage director*
DeBrunner, Gerald Joseph *accounting firm executive*
Dehner, Joseph Julnes *lawyer*
DeLeone, Carmon *conductor, musician, educator*
DeLong, Deborah *lawyer*
Dember, William Norton *psychologist, educator*
Derstadt, Ronald Theodore *health care administrator*
Devitt, John William *physicist*
Dewar, Norman Ellison *chemical company executive*
Dickey, John Miller *health care facility executive*
Diller, Edward Dietrich *lawyer*
†Dinicola, Robert *consumer products company executive*
Dornette, W(illiam) Stuart *lawyer, educator*
Dubuc, Kenneth E *management consultant*
Dunning, Thomas E. *newspaper editor*
Durbrow, Brian Richard *management consultant*
Eager, William Earl *information systems corporation executive*
Edelstein, Chaim Y. *retail executive*
Elleman, Lawrence Robert *lawyer*
Erickson, Richard J. *lawyer*
Fagin, Richard *litigation consultant*
Faller, Susan Grogan *lawyer*
Ferriss, David Platt *advertising consultant*
Fine, Lawrence Jay *internist, occupational preventive medicine*
Fingerhut, Marilyn Ann *federal agency administrator*
Fink, Jerold Albert *lawyer*
Finkelmeier, Philip Renner *law librarian, lawyer*
Flanagan, Martha Lang *corporate secretary*
Flick, Thomas Michael *mathematics educator, educational administrator*
†Fokker, J. P. *waste management executive*
Ford, Emory A. *chemist, researcher*
Fowler, Noble Owen *physician, university administrator*
Francis, Marion David *consulting chemist*
Freedman, William Mark *lawyer*
Freshwater, Paul Ross *consumer goods company executive*
Gant, Ron (Ronald Edwin Gant) *baseball player*
Geier, James Aylward Develin *manufacturing company executive*
†Gemunder, Joel Frank *medical association adminstrator*
Gesteland, Robert Charles *neurophysiologist*
Gettler, Benjamin *lawyer, manufacturing company executive*
Glendening, Everett Austin *architect*
Glenn, Jerry Hosmer, Jr. *foreign language educator*
†Goetzman, Bruce Edgar *architecture educator*
Goodman, Bernard *physics educator*
Goodman, Stanley *lawyer*
Gosling, David *university administrator*
†Gossman, Craig Eugene *architect*
Gottschalk, Alfred *college president*
Graham, Scharleen Walker *counselor*
Gray, John Augustus *physical chemist*
Greenberg, David Bernard *chemical engineering educator*
Greenberg, Gerald Stephen *lawyer*
Greengus, Samuel *academic administrator, religion educator*
Greenwalt, Tibor Jack *physician, educator*
†Griffin, William Ralph *business executive*
Groth, Jon Quentin *management consultant*
Guggenheim, Richard E. *lawyer, shoe company executive*
Haag, Walter M(onroe), Jr. *research institute executive, industrial engineer*
Hall, Ernest L. *electrical engineer, robotics educator*
Hardy, William Robinson *lawyer*
Harmon, Patrick *newspaperman*
Harrell, Samuel Macy *grain company executive*
Harrington, Jeremy Thomas *clergyman, publisher*
Harris, Irving *lawyer*
Harrison, Donald Carey *academic administrator, cardiologist*
†Harrison, Robert Sattler *piano and organ manufacturing executive*
Harshman, Morton Leonard *physician, business executive*
Hartleb, David Frederick *academic administrator, legal educator*
†Harville, Thomas T. *consumer goods company executive*
Hayden, Joseph Page, Jr. *finance company executive*
Heimlich, Henry Jay *physician, surgeon*
Heinlen, Ronald Eugene *lawyer*
†Heldman, Gary W. *manufacturing and distributing company executive*
†Hendricks, Harry *church administrator*
Henry, J(ohn) Porter, Jr. *sales consultant*
Hermanies, John Hans *lawyer*
†Herring, Milton S. *church administrator*
Hess, Donald C. *lawyer*
Hess, Evelyn Victorine (Mrs. Michael Howett) *medical educator*
Hiatt, Marjorie McCullough *service organization executive*
Hicks, Irle Raymond *retail food chain executive*
Hill, Thomas Clark *lawyer*
Hoermann, Edward Richard *urban planning educator*
Hoff, James Edwin *university president*
Hoffheimer, Daniel Joseph *lawyer*
Hoffman, Joel Harvey *composer*
Hornbaker, Alice Joy *author*
Horwitz, Harry *radiologist, physician, educator*
†Houser, Dwane Russell *insurance company executive*
Hubbard, Arthur Thornton *chemistry educator, electro-surface chemist*
Hubschman, Henry Allan *lawyer*
Hudson, Bannus B. *footwear manufacturing and apparel retail executive*
Hummel, Robert Paul *surgeon*
Huron, Roderick Eugene *religious organization administrator*
†Hutton, Edward Luke *diversified public corporation executive*
Huvos, Kornel *linguistics educator*
†Hyre, James G. *educational administrator*
Jackobs, Miriam Ann *dietitian*
Jaffe, Murray Sherwood *surgeon*
Johnson, C. Scott *management consultant*
Johnson, Davey (David Allen Johnson) *baseball team manager*
†Johnson, James J. *lawyer*
Johnson, K(enneth) O(dell) *aerospace engineer*
Jones, Nathaniel Raphael *federal judge*
Joseph, David J., Jr. *trading company executive*
Kaplan, Stanley Meisel *psychoanalyst*
Katz, Robert Langdon *human relations educator, rabbi*
Katzen, Raphael *consulting chemical engineer*
Kawahara, Fred Katsumi *research chemist*
Keener, C(harles) Richard *food company information systems executive*
Kehew, William James *environmental, quality assurance engineering manager*
Kelley, John Joseph, Jr. *lawyer*
Kelly, Roberto Conrado (Bobby Kelly) *professional baseball player*
Kenrich, John Lewis *lawyer*
Kiel, Frederick Orin *lawyer*
King, Elaine A. *curator, art historian, critic*
King, James Calvin *university radio director, educator*
Kite, William McDougall *lawyer*
Klinedinst, Thomas John, Jr. *insurance agency executive*
Knipschild, Robert *artist, educator*
Knowlton, Austin E. (Dutch Knowlton) *professional football team executive*
Knue, Paul Frederick *newspaper editor*
†Koebel, Sister Celestia *hospital administrator*
Kohl, David *dean, librarian*
Kordons, Uldis *lawyer*
Koster, William Pfeiffer *materials engineering executive*
Krohn, Claus Dankertsen *insurance company executive*
Kroll, Robert James *aerospace engineering educator*
Kunzel, Erich, Jr. *conductor, arranger, educator*
Larkin, Barry Louis *professional baseball player*
Lawrence, James Kaufman Lebensburger *lawyer*
Lawson, Randall Clayton, II *financial executive*
Le Blond, Patricia Morrison *real estate company executive*
†Leser, Lawrence A. *broadcasting company executive*
Lewis, Gene Dale *historian, educator*
†Leylek, James H. *aerospace engineer*
Lichtin, (Judah) Leon *pharmacist*
Lienhart, David Arthur *geologist, laboratory director*
Lindberg, Charles David *lawyer*
Lindner, Keith E. *food company executive*
Lindner, Robert David *finance company executive*
Lindsey, Sanford Chapdu *priest*
†Linsey, Nathaniel L. *bishop*
Lintz, Robert Carroll *financial holding company executive*
Liss, Herbert Myron *newspaper publisher, communications company executive*
Lloyd, David Livingstone, Jr. *lawyer*
Lockhart, John Mallery *management consultant*
Lockhart, Michael D. *electric company executive*
Loggie, Jennifer Mary Hildreth *medical educator, physician*
Long, Phillip Clifford *museum director*
Longenecker, Mark Hershey, Jr. *lawyer*
Lopez-Cobos, Jesus *conductor*
Lucas, Stanley Jerome *radiologist, physician*
Lucke, Robert Vito *merger and acquisition executive*
Luckner, Herman Richard, III *interior designer*
Lutz, James Gurney *lawyer*
Macpherson, Colin R(obertson) *pathologist, educator*
Magnusson, M(arylin) Sue Shirey *real estate executive*
Maier, Craig Frisch *restaurant executive*
†Maier, Jack C. *food products company executive*
Maisel, Michael *clothing executive*
Manley, Robert Edward *lawyer, economist*
Mantel, Samuel Joseph, Jr. *management educator, consultant*
Marcus, Jacob Rader *history educator*
Marcus, Leonard *retail company executive*
Marmer, Melvin E. *lawyer*
Martin, Daniel William *acoustical physicist*
Martin, John Bruce *chemical engineer*
Maruska, Edward Joseph *zoo administrator*
Mattingly, Paul R. *lawyer*
Maxwell, Robert Wallace, II *lawyer*
Mayer, James Joseph *corporate lawyer*
McClain, William Andrew *lawyer*
McCoy, John Joseph *lawyer*
McDonough, James Francis *civil engineer, educator*
McDowell, John Eugene *lawyer*
McGavran, Frederick Jaeger *lawyer*
Mc Henry, Powell *lawyer*
McNulty, John William *retired public relations executive, automobile company executive*
Meal, Larie *chemistry educator, consultant*
Meisner, Gary Wayne *landscape architect*
Meranus, Leonard Stanley *lawyer*
Merchant, Mylon Eugene *physicist, engineer*
Meyer, Daniel Joseph *machinery company executive*
Middendorf, William Henry *electrical engineering educator*
Milligan, Lawrence Drake, Jr. *consumer products executive*
†Milnes, William Robert, Jr. *insurance company executive*
Mitchell, Kevin Darrell *baseball player*
Mitchell, Otis Clinton, Jr. *history educator*
Molitor, Sister Margaret Anne *nun, former college president*
Monroe, Murray Shipley *lawyer*
Mooney, Donald James, Jr. *lawyer*
†Mooney, Timothy M. *retail executive*
Moore, Alfred Anson *corporate executive*
†Moore, Michael C. *retail executive*
Morgan, John Bruce *hospital care consultant*
Morgan, Robert B. *insurance company executive*
Munn, Stephen P. *manufacturing company executive*
Muntz, Ernest Gordon *historian, educator*
Murphy, Dennis Joseph *lawyer*
Murphy, Eugene F. *aerospace, communications and electronics executive*
Naylor, Paul Donald *lawyer*
Nebert, Daniel Walter *molecular geneticist, research administrator*
Nechemias, Stephen Murray *lawyer*
Nelson, David Aldrich *federal judge*
Nelson, Frederick Dickson *lawyer*
Nester, William Raymond, Jr. *university administrator*
Neumark, Michael Harry *lawyer*
Nielsen, George Lee *architect*
Niemoller, Arthur B. *electrical engineer*
Nordlund, James John *dermatologist*
Olson, Robert Wyrick *lawyer*
Papadakis, Constantine N. *dean, civil engineering educator*
Parker, R. Joseph *lawyer*
†Peck, Abraham Joseph *historian*
†Pennacchio, Joseph *apparel executive*
Pepper, John Ennis, Jr. *consumer products company executive*
Perlman, Burton *federal judge*
Perry, Norman Robert *priest, magazine editor*
Peterson, Gale Eugene *historian*
Petry, Thomas Edwin *manufacturing company executive*
Pettengill, Kroger *investment counselor*
Phillips, T. Stephen *lawyer*
Pichler, Joseph Anton *food products executive*
†Pike, Larry Ross *insurance executive*
Pilarczyk, Daniel Edward *archbishop*
Preiser, Wolfgang Friedrich Ernst *architect, educator, consultant, researcher*
Price, Thomas Emile *export and investment company executive*
†Proffitt, H. Kevin *archivist*
Puchta, Charles George *lawyer*
†Qualls, Roxanne *mayor of Cincinnati*
Raskin, Fred Charles *transportation and utility holding company executive*
Rebar, Robert William *obstetrician, gynecologist, educator*
Reichert, David *lawyer*
Rexroth, Nancy Louise *photographer*
Rich, Robert Edward *lawyer*
Roberts, Richard Stewart *lawyer*
Rockwell, R(onald) James, Jr. *laser and electro-optics consultant*
Roe, Clifford Ashley, Jr. *lawyer*
Rogers, Lawrence H., II *retired television executive, investor, writer*
Rogers, Millard Foster, Jr. *art museum director*
Roomann, Hugo *architect*
Rose, Donald McGregor *lawyer*
Rubin, Carl Bernard *federal judge*
Rubin, Stanley Gerald *aerospace engineering educator*
Rubinstein, Jack Herbert *health center administrator, pediatrics educator*
Rudney, Harry *biochemist, educator*
Saenger, Eugene Lange *radiology educator, laboratory director*
Safferman, Robert Samuel *microbiologist*
Samuel, Gerhard *orchestra conductor, composer*
Sanford, Wilbur Lee *elementary education educator*
Sawyer, John *professional football team executive*
Scarpino, Pasquale Valentine *environmental microbiologist*
Schaeter, George A., Jr. *banking executive*
†Schiff, Gilbert Martin *virologist, microbiologist, medical educator*
Schiff, John Jefferson *insurance company executive*
Schneider, Harold Joel *radiologist*
Schott, Marge *professional baseball team executive*
Schottelkotte, Albert Joseph *broadcasting executive*
Schreiner, Albert William *physician, educator*
Schrier, Arnold *historian, educator*
Schubert, William Kuenneth *hospital medical center executive*
Schuck, Thomas Robert *lawyer*
†Schuler, Robert Leo *appraiser, consultant*
Schwartz, Arnold (Arnie Shayne) *pharmacologist, biophysicist, biochemist, educator, actor, director, producer*
Scoggins, Samuel McWhirter *lawyer*
Scott, Ralph C. *physician, educator*
Scripps, Charles Edward *newspaper publisher*
Sedgwick-Hirsch, Carol Elizabeth *financial executive*
Semon, Warren Lloyd *retired computer sciences educator*
†Senhauser, John Crater *architect*
Servodidio, Pat Anthony *broadcast executive*
†Sherman, Jeffrey *retail executive*
Shore, Thomas Spencer, Jr. *lawyer*
Shula, David D. *professional football team coach*
†Siebenburgen, David A. *airline company financial executive*
Siekmann, Donald Charles *accountant*
Silbersack, Mark Louis *lawyer*
†Silvers, Gerald Thomas *publishing executive*
Sjoerdsma, Albert *research institute executive*
Slater, John Greenleaf *manufacturing company executive*
Smale, John Gray *diversified industry executive*
Smith, C. LeMoyne *publishing company executive*
Smith, Leroy Harrington, Jr. *mechanical engineer, aerodynamics consultant*
Smith, Roger Dean *pathologist*
Smittle, Nelson Dean *electronics executive*
†Socol, Howard *department store executive*
Sodd, Vincent Joseph *nuclear medicine researcher, educator*
Sperelakis, Nicholas *physiology and biophysics educator, researcher*
Spiegel, S. Arthur *federal judge*
Steger, Joseph A. *university president*
Stein, Jacob K. *lawyer*
Stern, Joseph Smith, Jr. *former footwear manufacturing company executive*
Stolley, Alexander *advertising executive*
Stone, Andrew Logan *corporate executive*
†Stonestreet, Robert *library director*
†Strange, Peter Stanton *construction company executive*
Strubbe, John Lewis *retired food chain store executive*
Sullivan, Connie Castleberry *artist, photographer*
Suskind, Raymond Robert *physician, educator*
Swigert, James Mack *lawyer*
Taft, Robert, Jr. *state official, lawyer, former senator*
Tatgenhorst, (Charles) Robert *lawyer*
†Terhar, Louis F. *waste management administrator*
Terp, Thomas Thomsen *lawyer*

Thiemann, Charles Lee *banker*
Thompson, Herbert, Jr. *bishop*
Thompson, Morley Punshon *textile company executive*
†Thrun, Robert Read *architect*
Tihany, Leslie Charles *retired foreign service officer, educator*
†Timpano, Anne *museum director, art historian*
Tobias, Charles Harrison, Jr. *lawyer*
Tobias, Paul Henry *lawyer*
Tocco, James *pianist*
Toftner, Richard Orville *engineering executive*
Totlis, Gust John *title insurance company executive*
Townsend, Robert J. *lawyer*
Ullman, Louis Jay *financial executive*
Vander Laan, Mark Alan *lawyer*
Victor, William Weir *retired telephone company executive, consultant*
Vilter, Richard William *physician, educator*
Voet, Paul C. *specialty chemical company executive*
Voluse, Charles Rodger, III *education educator*
Vorholt, Jeffrey Joseph *lawyer, telecommunications company executive*
Waddell, Oliver W. *banker*
Wales, Ross Elliot *lawyer*
Walker, Michael Claude *finance educator*
Walker, Ronald F. *corporate executive*
†Warden, Glenn Donald *burn surgeon*
Warnemunde, Bradley Lee *insurance company executive*
Warrington, John Wesley *lawyer*
Watts, Barbara Gayle *law academic administrator*
Weber, Herman Jacob *federal judge*
Weed, Ithamar Dryden *life insurance company executive*
Weeks, Steven Wiley *lawyer*
Wehling, Robert Louis *household products company executive*
Weiskittel, Ralph Joseph *real estate executive*
Weisman, Joel *nuclear engineering educator, engineering consultant*
Werner, Robert Joseph *college dean, music educator*
Weseli, Roger William *health care executive*
West, Clark Darwin *pediatric nephrologist, educator*
†West, John A. *lawyer*
Westheimer, Ruth Welling *retired management consultant*
†Whipple, Harry *newspaper publishing executive*
White, Terry R. *hospital administrator*
Wigginton, Eugene H. *publishing executive*
Williams, James Case *metallurgist*
†Williams, William Joseph *insurance company executive*
Wilson, Lucy Jean *librarian*
Winkler, Henry Ralph *retired university president, historian*
Wiot, Jerome Francis *radiologist*
†Wisler, David Charles *aerospace engineer, educator*
Witten, Louis *physics educator*
Wood, Daniel G. *health care financial executive*
Woods, Bruce Walter *editor, poet*
Woods, Donald DeWayne *advertising materials designer/manufacturer*
Wygant, Foster Laurance *art educator*
Yund, George Edward *lawyer*
Yurchuck, Roger Alexander *lawyer*
Zafren, Herbert Cecil *librarian, educator*

Circleville

†Norman, Jack Lee *church administrator, consultant*
Scherer, Robert Davisson *retired association executive*
†Tipton, Daniel L. *religious organization executive*

Cleveland

†Abid, Ann B. *art librarian*
Adams, Albert T. *lawyer*
Adubato, Richard Adam (Richie Adubato) *professional basketball coach*
Aikawa, Masamichi *pathologist*
Aldrich, Ann *federal judge*
Alfidi, Ralph Joseph *radiologist, educator*
Alfieri, Lisa Gwyneth *ballet dancer, teacher*
Alfred, Karl Sverre *orthopedic surgeon*
Alfred, Stephen Jay *lawyer*
Alomar, Sandy, Jr. (Santos Velazquez Alomar) *baseball player*
Alspaugh, Robert Odo *industrial management consultant*
Anderson, Harold Albert *engineering and building executive*
†Anderson, James R. *engineering executive*
Andorka, Frank Henry *lawyer*
Andrews, Oakley V. *lawyer*
Angus, John Cotton *chemical engineering educator*
Arison, Barbara J. *lawyer*
Ashmus, Keith Allen *lawyer*
Atherton, James Dale *publishing executive*
Atkinson, William Edward *lawyer*
Austin, Arthur Donald, II *lawyer, educator*
Awais, George Musa *obstetrician, gynecologist*
Azoff, Elliot Stephen *lawyer*
Babin, Mara L. *lawyer*
Bacon, Brett Kermit *lawyer*
Badal, Daniel Walter *psychiatrist, educator*
Baer, Eric *engineering and science educator*
Baerga, Carlos Obed Ortiz *professional baseball player*
Bahniuk, Eugene *mechanical engineering educator*
Bailey, John Turner *public relations executive*
Baker, Saul Phillip *geriatrician, cardiologist, internist*
†Ball, Robert L. *metal products company executive*
Bamberger, David *opera company executive*
Bamberger, Richard H. *lawyer*
Bank, Malvin E. *lawyer*
Barnard, Thomas Harvie *lawyer*
Barnes, Geoffrey K. *lawyer*
Barr, Douglas N. *lawyer*
Bartunek, Robert Richard *retired physician*
Bates, Walter Alan *lawyer*
Batt, John Paul *lawyer*
Battisti, Frank Joseph *federal judge*
Baughman, R(obert) Patrick *lawyer*
Baumgartner, Bruce O. *lawyer*
Baxter, Howard H. *lawyer*
Beall, Cynthia *anthropologist, educator*
†Beggs, Lyman M. *manufacturing executive*
Beggs, Lyman M., III *manufacturing company executive*
Begun, Semi Joseph *management consultant*
Behnke, William Alfred *landscape architect, planner*
Beling, Helen *sculptor*
Belle, Albert Jojuan *professional baseball player*
†Bennett, Michael *newspaper editor*
Bennett, Paul Edward *lawyer*
†Benseler, David Price *foreign language educator*
Berger, Sanford Jason *lawyer, securities dealer, real estate broker*
Bergholz, David *foundation administrator*
Bergman, Robert Paul *museum administrator, art historian, educator, lecturer*
Berick, James Herschel *lawyer*
Bernard, Lowell Francis *academic administrator, educator, consultant*
Berry, Dean Lester *lawyer*
Bersticker, Albert Charles *chemical company executive*
Besse, Ralph Moore *lawyer*
Bidelman, William Pendry *astronomer, educator*
Bilchik, Gary B. *lawyer*
Binford, Gregory Glenn *lawyer*
Bingham, Richard Donnelly *journal editor, director, educator*
Binstock, Robert Henry *public policy educator, writer, lecturer*
Blackwell, John *polymer scientist, educator*
Blasius, Donald Charles *appliance company executive*
Blattner, Robert A. *lawyer*
Blodgett, Omer William *electric company design consultant*
Blum, Arthur *social work educator*
Bockhoff, Frank James *chemistry educator*
Bodurtha, James H. *lawyer*
Bogomolny, Richard Joseph *retail food chain executive*
Borowitz, Albert Ira *lawyer, author*
Bowen, Richard Lee *architect*
Bowerfind, Edgar Sihler, Jr. *physician, medical administrator*
Boyd, Richard Alfred *foundation administrator*
Boyle, Kammer *management psychologist*
Branagan, James Joseph *lawyer*
Brandon, Edward Bermetz *banker*
Braverman, Herbert Leslie *lawyer*
Bravo, Kenneth A. *lawyer*
Breen, John Gerald *manufacturing company executive*
Brennan, Maureen A. *lawyer*
Brentlinger, Paul Smith *venture capital executive*
Brooks, Arthur V. N. *lawyer*
Brophy, Jere Hall *manufacturing company executive*
Brosilow, Coleman Bernard *chemical engineering educator*
Brown, Helen Bennett *biochemist*
Brown, Seymour R. *lawyer*
Brown, Troy R. *lawyer*
Brucken, Robert Matthew *lawyer*
Bryenton, Gary L. *lawyer*
†Bucchieri, Stephen Joseph *architect*
Buchanan, D(aniel) Harvey *art history educator*
Buchmann, Alan Paul *lawyer*
Budd, John Henry *physician*
Buescher, Stephen L. *lawyer*
Buhrow, William Carl *religious organization administrator*
Bumpass, T. Merritt, Jr. *lawyer*
Burghart, James Henry *electrical engineer, educator*
Burke, John Francis, Jr. *economist*
Burke, Kathleen B. *lawyer*
Burke, Lillian Walker *retired judge*
Burlingame, John Hunter *lawyer*
†Burnside, Pershing Elliott *trucking company executive*
Butler, William E. *manufacturing company executive*
Cairns, James Donald *lawyer*
Calfee, John Beverly, Sr. *lawyer*
Calfee, William Lewis *lawyer*
†Calfee, William Rushton *mining company executive*
Calkins, Hugh *elementary school educator*
Campbell, Paul Barton *lawyer*
Canary, Nancy Halliday *lawyer*
Cannon, Norman Lawrence *treasurer*
Cardwell, James William *business strategy consultant*
Carlson, James R. *lawyer*
Carlsson, Bo A. V. *economics educator*
†Carrick, Kathleen Michele *law librarian*
Carter, James Rose, Jr. *medical educator*
Carter, John Dale *organizational development executive*
Cascorbi, Helmut Freimund *anesthesiologist, educator*
Case, Betsey Brewster *lawyer*
Cassill, Herbert Carroll *artist*
Caston, J(esse) Douglas *medical educator*
†Cerone, David *academic administrator*
Chapman, Diane P. *lawyer*
†Chapman, Robert L. *bishop*
Charnas, Michael (Mannie Charnas) *packaging company executive*
†Chase, R. F. *oil industry executive*
Chatterjee, Pranab *social sciences educator*
Chema, Thomas V. *government official, lawyer*
Cherniack, Neil Stanley *physician, medical educator*
Cieslak, Arthur Kazimer *surgeon*
Clark, Gary R. *newspaper editor*
Clark, Robert Arthur *mathematician, educator*
Clarke, Charles Fenton *lawyer*
Cleary, Martin Joseph *real estate company executive*
Cligrow, Edward Thomas, Jr. *manufacturing executive*
Cline, Cathie B. *hospital administrator*
Clutter, Bertley Allen, III *management company executive*
Cochran, Earl Vernon *manufacturing executive*
†Cole, Jeffrey A. *retail stores executive*
Cole, Monroe *neurologist, educator*
†Cole, Stephan William *manufacturing executive*
Collin, Robert Emanuel *electrical engineering educator*
Collin, Thomas James *lawyer*
Collins, Susan B. *lawyer*
Colombo, Louis A. *lawyer*
Commes, Thomas A. *manufacturing company executive*
Conaway, Orrin Bryte *political scientist, educator*
Connelly, John James *oil company technical specialist*
†Connors, Joanna *film critic*
Cooper, Hal Dean *lawyer*
Coquillette, William Hollis *lawyer*
Cornell, John Robert *lawyer*
Coscarelli, Dianne Smith *lawyer*
Coughlin, Barring *lawyer*
Coulman, George Albert *chemical engineer, educator*
Courier, Jim (James Spencer Courier, Jr.) *tennis player*
Coyle, Martin Adolphus, Jr. *lawyer*
Crist, Paul Grant *lawyer*
Crosby, Fred McClellan *retail home and office furnishings executive*
Cullis, Christopher Ashley *dean, biology educator*
Currivan, John Daniel *lawyer*
Cutler, Alexander MacDonald *manufacturing company executive*
Daberko, David A. *banker*
Dadley, Arlene Jeanne *sleep therapist*
Dakin, Carol F. *lawyer*
Dampeer, John Lyell *lawyer*
†Damsel, Richard A. *transportation company executive*
Danco, Léon Antoine *management consultant, educator*
†Dannemiller, John C. *transportation company executive*
Daroff, Robert Barry *neurologist*
Davis, David Aaron *journalist*
†Davis, Pamela Bowes *pediatric pulmonologist*
Day, Charles Roger, Jr. *editor in chief*
de Acosta, Alejandro Daniel *mathematician, educator*
Deissler, Robert George *fluid dynamicist, researcher*
Dell'Osso, Louis Frank *neuroscience educator*
De Marco, Thomas Joseph *periodontist, educator*
Dempsey, James Howard, Jr. *lawyer*
Denko, Joanne D. *psychiatrist, writer*
†Dewald, Ernest Leroy *landscape architect*
†Dipko, Thomas E. *minister, national church executive*
Donaldson, Richard Miesse *retired oil company executive, lawyer*
Doris, Alan S(anford) *lawyer*
Dossey, Richard L. *accountant*
Dowell, Michael Brendan *chemist*
Downie, John Francis *lawyer*
Downing, George *lawyer*
Drane, Walter Harding *publishing executive, business consultant*
Drinko, John Deaver *lawyer*
Drotning, John Evan *industrial relations specialist*
Duffy, John C., Jr. *lawyer*
Duncan, Ed Eugene *lawyer*
Dunn, John P. *lawyer*
Dunn, Leslie D. *lawyer*
†Dupuy, William L. *public relations executive*
Durham, Mary Lynn *lawyer*
Duvin, Robert Phillip *lawyer*
Dye, Sherman *lawyer*
Dy Liacco, Tomas Enciso *engineering consulting executive*
Easton, John Edward *accountant, financial executive*
Eastwood, Douglas William *anesthesiologist*
Eaton, Henry Felix *public relations executive*
†Eberhard, William Thomas *architect*
Edelman, Murray R. *utility company executive*
Edwards, John Wesley, II *lawyer*
Eiben, Robert Michael *pediatric neurologist, educator*
Ekelman, Daniel Louis *lawyer*
†Ellis, Stephen C. *lawyer*
Epp, Eldon Jay *religion educator*
†Epstein, Marvin Morris *construction executive*
Erb, Donald *composer*
Eyre, Paul P. *lawyer*
Fabens, Andrew Lawrie, III *lawyer*
Fabris, James A. *journalist*
Fairweather, John C. *lawyer*
Falsgraf, William Wendell *lawyer*
Farling, Robert J. *utility company executive*
Fay, Regan Joseph *lawyer*
Fay, Robert Jesse *lawyer*
Fazio, Victor Warren *physician, colon and rectal surgeon*
Feinberg, Paul H. *lawyer*
Feliciano, José Celso *lawyer*
Fenton, Alan *artist*
Ferguson, Suzanne Carol *English educator*
Finn, Robert *music critic, educator*
Finneburgh, Morris Lewis *electronic manufacturing executive*
†Fleischman, Richard *architect*
Fletcher, Robert *lawyer, horologist*
Foltz, Clinton Henry *advertising executive*
Ford, Robert Barney *lawyer*
Fountain, Ronald Glenn *management consultant*
Frantz, Michael Jennings *lawyer*
Fratello, Michael Robert *professional basketball coach*
Friedman, Barton Robert *English educator*
Friedman, Harold Edward *lawyer*
Friedman, James Moss *lawyer*
Fruchtenbaum, Edward *greeting card company executive*
†Fufuka, Natika Njeri Yaa *retail executive*
Fullmer, David R. *lawyer*
Garda, Robert Allen *management consultant*
Garner, James Parent *lawyer*
Garver, Theodore Meyer *lawyer*
Geha, Alexander Salim *cardiothoracic surgeon, educator*
Gelfand, Ivan *investment advisor*
Gerhart, Peter Milton *law educator*
Gherlein, John Harlan *retired lawyer*
Giannetti, Louis Daniel *film educator, film critic*
Gibans, James David *architect*
Gibson, Walter Samuel *humanities educator*
Gifford, Ray Wallace, Jr. *physician, educator*
Gillespie, Robert Wayne *banker*
Ginn, Robert Martin *retired utility company executive*
Ginsberg, Edward *lawyer*
Ginsburg, Edward S. *lawyer*
Glaser, Robert Edward *lawyer*
Gleisser, Marcus David *author, lawyer, journalist*
Glenn, Peter G. *lawyer*
Glickman, Carl David *banker*
†Goehler, James Lawrence *finance company executive*
Goffman, William *mathematician, educator*
Goins, Frances Floriano *lawyer*
Gold, Gerald Seymour *lawyer*
Goldfarb, Bernard Sanford *lawyer*
Goldstein, Marvin Emanuel *aerospace scientist, research center administrator*
Goldstein, Melvyn C. *anthropologist, educator*
Goodger, John Verne *electronics and computer systems executive*
Gorman, Joseph Tolle *corporate executive*
Grabner, George John *manufacturing executive*
Graham, Robert William *areospace research engineer*
Greer, Thomas H. *newspaper executive*
Greppin, John Aird Coutts *philologist, editor, educator*
Griswold, James B. *lawyer*
Groetzinger, Jon, Jr. *lawyer, consumer products executive*
Gronick, Patricia Ann Jacobsen *school system administrator*
Grossman, Theodore Martin *lawyer*
Gruber, Sheldon *electrical engineering educator*
Gruettner, Donald W. *lawyer*
Grundstein, Nathan David *lawyer, management science educator, management consultant*
Grundy, Kenneth William *political science educator*
Gutfeld, Norman E. *lawyer*
Hackbirth, David William *aluminum company executive*
Haiman, Irwin Sanford *lawyer*
Hajek, Otomar *mathematics educator*
Hall, David *newspaper editor*
Hamilton, J. Richard *lawyer*
Hamilton, William Milton *retired industrial company executive*
Hammer, Daniel William *lawyer*
Hanna, Harry Adolphus *lawyer*
Hanson, Richard Winfield *biochemist, educator*
†Harayda, Janice *newspaper book editor, author*
Hardesty, Hiram Haines *ophthalmologist, educator*
Harding, Frank I., III *trust banker*
Hardis, Stephen Roger *manufacturing company executive*
Hardy, Michael Lynn *lawyer*
†Hardy, Richard Allen *mechanical engineer, diesel fuel engine specialist*
Hargrove, Mike (Dudley Michael Hargrove) *professional baseball team manager*
Harris, John William *physician, educator*
Hart, Alvin Leroy *electric manufacturing company executive*
Hartley, Robert Frank *education educator, author*
Hastings, Donald F. *electric company executive*
Hatchadorian, Matthew J. *lawyer*
Hauserman, William Foley *manufacturing company executive*
Hayes, Scott Birchard *raw materials company executive*
Heald, Morrell *humanities educator*
Healy, Bernadine P. *physician, educator, federal agency administrator*
Heddesheimer, Walter Jacob *lawyer*
Heffern, Gordon Emory *banker*
Hellman, Peter Stuart *technical manufacturing executive*
Henes, Samuel Ernst *lawyer*
†Henry, Edward Frank *computer accounting service executive*
Hermann, Philip J. *lawyer*
Herndon, Charles Harbison *retired orthopaedic surgeon*
Heuer, Arthur Harold *material science and engineering educator*
Hoag, David H. *steel company executive*
Hochman, Kenneth George *lawyer*
Hoerner, Robert Jack *lawyer*
Hokenstad, Merl Clifford, Jr. *social work educator*
Holck, Frederick H. George *priest, educator, counselor*
Holderfield, Marilyn Ida *jazz vocalist*
†Holland, Darrell Wendell *newspaper religion editor*
Holland, Patricia Marcus *lawyer*
Hollington, Richard Rings, Jr. *lawyer*
Holzbach, Raymond Thomas *gastroenterologist, author, educator*
Hook, John Burney *investment company executive*
Hooker, David Joseph *lawyer*
Hopkins, John S., III *lawyer*
Hopps, Sidney Bryce *lawyer*
†Horn, Karen Nicholson *banker*
Horvitz, Michael John *lawyer*
Hottois, Lawrence Daniel *banking executive*
Hruby, Frank M. *musician, critic, educator*
Hushen, John W. *manufacturing company executive*
Hyde, Alan Litchfield *lawyer*
Ivy, Conway Gayle *paint company executive*
Izant, Robert James, Jr. *pediatric surgeon*
Jacobs, Leslie William *lawyer*
Jacobs, Richard E. *real estate executive, sports team owner*
Janke, Ronald Robert *lawyer*
Jeavons, Norman Stone *lawyer*
Jenkins, Thomas Llewellyn *physics educator*
Jenson, Jon Eberdt *association executive*
Johnson, John Frank *professional recruitment executive*
Jones, Theodore William *banker, lawyer*
Jordan, Howard Emerson *retired engineering executive*
Jordan, Jerry Lee *economist, banker*
Jorgenson, Mary Ann *lawyer*
Kacir, Barbara Brattin *lawyer*
Kahana, Eva Frost *sociology educator*
Kahrl, Robert Conley *lawyer*
Kaiser, Gordon S., Jr. *lawyer*
Kallock, Roger William *marketing professional, logistics consultant*
Kamm, Jacob Oswald *manufacturing executive, economist*
Karch, George Frederick, Jr. *lawyer*
Karch, Sargent *lawyer*
Katcher, Richard *lawyer*
Katz, Lewis Robert *legal educator*
Keegan, Jane *opera and music theatre producer*
Kellermeyer, Robert William *physician, educator*
Kelly, Dennis Michael *lawyer*
Kelly, J. Peter *steel company executive*
†Kelly, John Terence *architect*
Kerr, Thomas Adolphus *retired construction company executive*
Kilbane, Thomas Stanton *lawyer*
Kirchick, Calvin B. *lawyer*
Kiser, William Sites *physician executive, urologic surgeon*
Klaus, Charles *lawyer*
Klopman, Gilles *chemistry educator*
Knopp, Albert J. *lawyer*
Ko, Wen-Hsiung *electrical engineering educator*
Koch, Charles John *credit agency executive*
Koch, Charles Joseph *banker*
Kola, Arthur Anthony *lawyer*
Kolb, David Allen *psychology educator*
Korb, Donald Lee *lawyer*
Kordalski, Anthony Tadausz *retail department store executive*
†Kovacic, Edward P. *protective services official*
†Kovacs, Rosemary *newspaper editor*
Kovel, Ralph M. *author, authority on antiques*
Kovel, Terry Horvitz (Mrs. Ralph Kovel) *author, antiques authority*
Kowalski, Kenneth Lawrence *physicist, educator*
Kramer, Andrew Michael *lawyer*
Kramer, Eugene Leo *lawyer*
Krasney, Samuel Joseph *multi-industry company executive*
Krieger, Irvin Mitchell *chemistry educator, consultant*
Krupansky, Blanche *judge*
Krupansky, Robert Bazil *federal judge*
Kuhn, David Alan *lawyer*
Kundtz, John Andrew *lawyer*

Kurit, Neil *lawyer*
Lambros, Thomas Demetrios *federal judge*
Lamm, Michael Emanuel *pathologist, immunologist, educator*
Lampl, Jack Willard, Jr. *retired finance company executive*
Landau, Bernard Robert *biochemistry educator, physician*
Landefeld, Charles Willis *lawyer*
Lando, Jerome Burton *macromolecular science educator*
Lang, H. Jack *advertising executive, author*
Lavelle, Michael Joseph *economist, academic administrator*
Lawniczak, James Michael *lawyer*
Lease, Robert K. *lawyer*
Leavitt, Jeffrey Stuart *lawyer*
Lebovitz, Harold Paul (Hal Lebovitz) *journalist*
Leech, John Dale *lawyer*
Lefebvre, Gabriel Felicien *retired chemical company executive*
Lefferts, William Geoffrey *physician, educator*
Leidner, Harold Edward *lawyer*
Leiken, Earl Murray *lawyer*
Lelyveld, Arthur Joseph *rabbi*
Lemke, Judith A. *lawyer*
Lenkoski, Leo Douglas *psychiatrist, educator*
Lenn, Stephen Andrew *lawyer*
Leonard, Irvin Alan *lawyer*
Leukart, Richard Henry, II *lawyer*
Lewis, John Bruce *lawyer*
Lewis, John Francis *lawyer*
Lewis, Robert Lawrence *lawyer*
Liegl, Joseph Leslie *lawyer*
Lindberg, Lawrence V. *lawyer*
Litt, Morton Herbert *macromolecular science educator, researcher*
Little, Robert Andrews *architect, designer, painter*
Liu, Chung-Chiun *chemical engineering educator*
Lofton, Kenneth *professional baseball player*
Long, Kenneth Robert *natural gas company executive, lawyer*
†Long, Robert M. *newspaper publishing executive*
Lopez, Nancy *professional golfer*
Lowenthal, Henry *greeting card company executive*
Lucier, P. Jeffrey *publishing executive*
†Ludenia, Krista *psychologist, health facility administrator*
Luke, Randall Dan *retired tire and rubber company executive, lawyer*
Luttner, Edward F. *career management consultant*
Lynch, John Edward, Jr. *lawyer*
†Lynch, Maxine *newspaper publishing executive*
Machaskee, Alex *newspaper publishing company executive*
Mac Laren, David Sergeant *pollution control company executive*
Madden, James Desmond *forensic engineer*
Madison, Robert Prince *architect*
Madsen, H(enry) Stephen *retired lawyer*
Mahmoud, Adel A. F. *physician, educator, investigator*
Mandel, Jack N. *manufacturing company executive*
Mandel, Morton Leon *industrial corporation executive*
†Manning, Henry Eugene *hospital administrator*
Manning, William Dudley, Jr. *retired specialty chemical company executive*
Manos, John M. *federal judge*
Marcus, Donald Howard *advertising agency executive*
Margulies, Jeffrey J. *lawyer*
†Marino, Sal F. *publisher*
Markey, Robert Guy *lawyer*
Markos, Chris *real estate company executive*
Markus, Richard M. *lawyer*
Martin, Paul Joseph *biomedical engineer, cardiology researcher, educator, consultant*
Marting, Michael G. *lawyer*
Mason, Marilyn Gell *library administrator, writer, consultant*
Mason, Thomas Albert *lawyer*
Matia, Paul Ramon *federal judge*
Mawardi, Osman Kamel *plasma physicist*
Mayer, Robert Anthony *art institute executive*
Mayland, Kenneth Theodore *economist*
Mayne, Lucille Stringer *finance educator*
McAndrews, James Patrick *lawyer*
McArdle, Richard Joseph *academic administrator*
Mc Cartan, Patrick Francis *lawyer*
McCarthy, Mark Francis *lawyer*
Mc Clelland, James Craig *lawyer*
McConnell, Michael *opera company director*
†McCormick, William Charles *manufacturing company executive*
†McCormick, William Charles *manufacturing company executive*
McCreary, Robert Grosvenor, Jr. *lawyer*
McCullough, Joseph *college president emeritus*
Mc Elhaney, James Wilson *lawyer, educator*
Mc Fadden, John Volney *retired manufacturing company executive*
Mc Farlane, Karen Elizabeth *concert artists manager*
McGervey, John Donald *physics educator, researcher*
McGinty, Thomas Edward *management consultant*
McHale, Vincent Edward *political science educator*
Mc Innes, Robert Malcolm *lawyer*
McKee, Thomas Frederick *lawyer*
McLaughlin, Patrick Michael *lawyer*
Mc Murrin, Lee Ray *educational administrator*
McVey, William Mozart *sculptor*
Meaney, Michael Joseph *lawyer*
†Mecredy, James R. *management consultant*
Meisel, George Ira *lawyer*
Melsher, Gary W. *lawyer*
†Melsop, James William *architect*
Meltzer, Herbert Yale *psychiatry educator*
Mendelson, Ralph Richard *water heater manufacturing executive*
Messinger, Donald Hathaway *lawyer*
Meyer, G. Christopher *lawyer*
Meyer, Gerald Justin *energy company executive*
Milgrim, Franklin Marshall *merchant*
Milic, Louis Tonko *English educator*
Miller, Carl George *manufacturing executive*
Miller, Genevieve *medical historian*
Miller, Ivan Lawrence *lawyer*
Miller, John Robert *environmental recycling company executive*
Miller, Richard Hamilton *lawyer, broadcasting company executive*
†Miller, Warren *bishop*
Millstone, David J. *lawyer*
Milner, Irvin Myron *lawyer*
Miyares, Benjamin David *editor, publisher, consultant*
Modic, Stanley John *business editor, publisher*
†Molyneaux, David Glenn *newspaper travel editor*
Moore, Anthony R. *lawyer*
Moore, Kenneth Cameron *lawyer*
Morin, Patrick Joyce *advertising executive*
Morley, John C. *electronic equipment company executive*
Morris, Thomas William *symphony orchestra administrator*
Morrison, Donald William *lawyer, utility executive*
Mortimer, J. Thomas *biomedical engineering educator*
†Morway, Richard A. *newspaper publishing executive*
Moscarino, George J. *lawyer*
Moss, Thomas Henry *university dean, physicist*
†Mottl, Ronald M. *lawyer, state legislator*
†Muller, Claudya Barbara *librarian*
Murfin, Donald Leon *investment company executive*
Murray, Eddie Clarence *professional baseball player*
†Murray, Thomas Henry *bioethics educator, writer*
Myers, David N. *construction executive*
Nahat, Dennis F. *artistic director, choreographer*
Nance, Larry Donnell *professional basketball player*
Naparstek, Arthur J. *social work educator*
Navratilova, Martina *professional tennis player*
Naylor, John Lewis, Jr. *lawyer*
Nelson, Raymond John *mathematics and philosophy educator*
Nelson, Robert Bruce *lawyer*
Neuhauser, Duncan von Briesen *health services educator*
Newborn, Karen B. *lawyer*
Newell, Sterling, Jr. *lawyer*
Newman, John M., Jr. *lawyer*
Newman, Joseph H. *advertising executive*
Nims, Michael A. *lawyer*
Noall, Roger *bank executive*
†Nolan, Cary J. *medical products manufacturer*
†Noneman, Edward E. *engineering executive*
†Norris, Dennis E. *religious organization executive*
Novatney, John F., Jr. *lawyer*
Novick, Andrew Carl *urologist*
Oakar, Mary Rose *former congresswoman*
Oberdank, Lawrence Mark *lawyer, arbitrator*
Obert, Charles Frank *banker*
O'Brien, John Feighan *investment banker*
O'Donnell, Kevin *retired metal working company executive*
O'Donnell, Thomas Michael *brokerage firm executive*
Oesterling, Thomas Ovid *pharmaceutical company executive*
Ollinger, W. James *lawyer*
Olson, Walter Theodore *research scientist, consultant*
Olszewski, Edward John *art history educator*
Ornstein, Robert *humanities educator*
Orr, Parker Murray *lawyer*
Ostrach, Simon *engineering educator*
Pallam, John James *lawyer*
Pao, Yoh-Han *engineering educator*
Paris, Zachary T. *lawyer*
Parker, Patrick Streeter *manufacturing executive*
Parker, Robert Frederic *university dean emeritus*
Pascarella, Perry James *magazine editor*
Pataki, Andrew *bishop*
†Peckham, P. Hunter *biomedical engineer, educator*
†Percy, S. W. *oil industry executive*
Perkinson, Diana Agnes Zouzelka *import company executive*
Perkovic, Robert Branko *international consultant*
Perks, Roger Ian *minister*
Perris, Terrence George *lawyer*
Perry, George Williamson *lawyer*
Phipps, Wilma J. *nursing educator, author*
†Pianalto, Sandra *bank executive*
Pike, Kermit Jerome *library director*
Pilla, Anthony Michael *bishop*
Plesec, William Thomas *lawyer*
Podboy, Alvin Michael, Jr. *lawyer, law library director*
Pogue, Richard Welch *lawyer*
Porter, James Morris *state judge*
Preston, Robert Bruce *lawyer*
Price, Charles T. *lawyer*
†Pringle, Barbara Carroll *state legislator*
Ptaszek, Edward Gerald, Jr. *lawyer*
Pursell, Carroll Wirth *history educator*
Putka, Andrew Charles *lawyer*
Pyke, John Secrest, Jr. *lawyer, polymers company executive*
Pytte, Agnar *academic administrator, theoretical physicist*
†Quagliata, John *restaurant company executive*
Rader, Hannelore *library director, consultant*
Rains, Merritt Neal *lawyer*
Rakita, Louis *cardiologist, educator*
Ramig, Alexander, Jr. *paint company executive, chemist*
Ransom, William Harrison *lawyer*
Rapp, Robert Neil *lawyer*
Rasmussen, Frank Morris *lawyer*
Ratnoff, Oscar Davis *physician, educator*
Rawson, Robert H., Jr. *lawyer*
Reale, William A. *lawyer*
Reeves, Charles Howell *classics educator*
Reid, James Sims, Jr. *automobile parts manufacturer*
Reisman, Arnold *management science educator*
Reitman, Robert Stanley *manufacturing and marketing executive*
Rekstis, Walter J., III *lawyer*
Remington, Charles Bradford *professional services firm executive*
Reppert, Richard Levi *lawyer*
Reshotko, Eli *aerospace engineer, educator*
Ritchey, William Michael *chemistry educator*
Robbins, Frederick Chapman *physician, medical school dean emeritus*
Roberts, Clyde Francis *business executive*
Roberts, James Owen *financial planning executive*
Robertson, William Richard *banker, holding company executive*
Robiner, Donald Maxwell *lawyer*
Robinson, Donald Keith *physicist, educator*
Rodewig, John Stuart *manufacturing company executive*
Rogers, Charles Edwin *physical chemistry educator*
Roj, William Henry *lawyer*
Romei, Lura Knachel *magazine editor*
Roop, James John *public relations executive*
Rorimer, Louis *lawyer*
Rosegger, Gerhard *economist, educator*
Rosenbaum, Jacob I. *lawyer*
Rosenthal, Leighton A. *aviation company executive*
Ross, Lawrence John *federal agency administrator*
†Ross, Ronald Jay *radiologist*
Roth, Jack Joseph *historian, educator*
Rothstein, Ronald *professional basketball coach*
Rotolo, Joseph Anthony *lawyer*
Roulston, Thomas Henry *investment adviser*
Ruben, Alan Miles *lawyer, educator*
Rupert, John Edward *retired savings and loan executive, business and civic affairs consultant*
†Russell, Valerie Eileen *social service executive*
Ruxin, Paul Theodore *lawyer*
Rydzel, James A. *lawyer*
Saada, Adel Selim *civil engineer, educator*
Sabo, Richard Steven *electrical company executive*
Sager, John William *lawyer*
Salazar, Alberto *Olympic professional runner*
Salomon, Roger Blaine *English language educator*
Sandburg, Helga *author*
Sande, Theodore Anton *architect, educator, foundation executive*
Savin, Samuel Marvin *geologist*
†Savinell, Robert Francis *engineering educator*
Sawyer, Raymond Terry *lawyer*
Sayler, Richard H. *lawyer*
Scarpa, Antonio *medicine educator, biomedical scientist*
Schaefer, David Arnold *lawyer*
Scharp, Anders *manufacturing company executive*
Schaut, Joseph William *banker*
Schiller, James Joseph *lawyer*
Schlotfeldt, Rozella May *nursing educator*
Schneider, David Miller *lawyer*
Schnell, Carlton Bryce *lawyer*
Schorr, Alvin Louis *social worker, educator*
Schuele, Donald Edward *physics educator*
Schulze, John B. *manufacturing executive*
Schurmeier, L. Jon *health care executive*
Scovil, Samuel Kingston *mining company executive*
Seger, Thomas M. *lawyer*
Seikel, Oliver Edward *lawyer*
Seles, Monica *tennis player*
†Selhorst, Lawrence O'Hare *manufacturing executive*
Seltzer, Phyllis Estelle *painter, printmaker*
Serra, Anthony Michael *nursing home administrator*
Shakno, Robert Julian *hospital administrator*
Shanker, Morris Gerald *lawyer, educator*
Shapiro, Fred David *lawyer*
Sharp, Robert Weimer *lawyer*
Shaw, Russell Clyde *lawyer*
Shea-Stonum, Marilyn *lawyer*
Shelley, John Fletcher *lawyer*
Sherrill, H. Virgil *securities company executive, manufacturing company executive*
Sherry, Paul Henry *minister, religious organization administrator*
Shuck, Jerry Mark *surgeon, educator*
Sibley, Willis Elbridge *anthropology educator, consultant*
Sicherman, Marvin Allen *lawyer*
Siefers, Robert George *banker*
†Siegel, Robert *heat transfer engineer*
Sigalow, Steven E. *lawyer*
†Silverman, William A. *public relations executive*
Simonson, John Alexander *banking executive*
Skinner, Charles Scofield *technology management service executive, consultant, mechanical engineer*
Skulina, Thomas Raymond *lawyer*
Sloan, David W. *lawyer*
Smercina, Charles Joseph *mayor, accountant*
Smith, Barbara Jean *lawyer*
Smith, Charles Kent *family medicine physician*
Smith, James A. *lawyer*
Snyder, Kenneth F. *lawyer*
Sogg, Wilton Sherman *lawyer*
Solomon, Randall L. *lawyer*
Springel, Barry L. *lawyer*
Stadtler, Beatrice Horwitz *author*
Stanley, Hugh Monroe, Jr. *lawyer*
Stanton-Hicks, Michael D'Arcy *anesthesiologist, educator*
Stavitsky, Abram Benjamin *immunologist, educator*
Stein, Herman David *academic administrator, social sciences and social work educator*
Steinberg, Arthur G(erald) *geneticist*
Steinbrink, William H. *lawyer*
Steindler, Howard Allen *lawyer*
Steinhouse, Carl Lewis *lawyer*
†Stevens, Edward *public relations executive*
Stevens, Thomas Charles *lawyer*
Stinchcomb, Robert G. *lawyer*
Stinson, Robert Charles *lawyer*
Stokes, Carl Burton *judge, former mayor, former state legislator*
Stone, Harry H. *business executive*
Stone, Irving I. *greeting card company executive*
Straffon, Ralph Atwood *urologist*
Strang, James Dennis *editor*
Strange, Curtis Northrop *professional golfer*
Strassmeyer, Mary *newspaper columnist*
Stratton-Crooke, Thomas Edward *financial consultant*
Strauch, John L. *lawyer*
Strauss, David J. *lawyer*
Strauss, Walter Adolf *foreign languages educator*
Streeter, Richard Edward *lawyer*
Striefsky, Linda A(nn) *lawyer*
Strimbu, Victor, Jr. *lawyer*
Stuhan, Richard George *lawyer*
Swartzbaugh, Marc L. *lawyer*
Swift, David L. *manufacturing company executive*
Szarek, Stanislaw Jerzy *mathematics educator*
Taft, Seth Chase *retired lawyer*
Taw, Dudley Joseph *sales executive*
Taylor, J(ocelyn) Mary *museum administrator, zoologist, educator*
Taylor, Philip Liddon *physics educator*
Taylor, Steve Henry *zoologist*
Taylor, Thomas Hewitt, Jr. *construction equipment company executive*
Thomas, William Kernahan *federal judge*
Thompson, Renold Durant *mining and shipping executive*
Thomson, Maynard F. *lawyer*
Tinker, H(arold) Burnham *chemical company executive*
†Tipton-Martin, Toni *newspaper editor*
Toohey, Brian Frederick *lawyer*
Toomajian, William Martin *lawyer*
Traci, Donald Philip *lawyer*
Trawick, Leonard Moses *English educator*
Trevor, Leigh Barry *lawyer*
†Trudell, Thomas Jeffrey *hospital administrator, educator*
True, William Herndon *healthcare administrator*
Tung, Theodore Hschum *banker, economist*
Turner, Evan Hopkins *retired art museum director*
Ulchaker, Stanley Louis *public relations consultant*
Unger, Paul A. *packaging executive*
Updegraft, Kenneth E., Jr. *lawyer*
Urbach, Frederick Lewis *chemistry educator*
†Urban, Richard *newspaper editor*
Van Ummersen, Claire A(nn) *university president, biologist, educator*
von Dohnányi, Christoph *musician, conductor*
von Mehren, George M. *lawyer*
Wadsworth, Homer Clark *foundation consultant*
Waldeck, John Walter, Jr. *lawyer*
Walker, Martin Dean *specialty chemical company executive*
Wallace, R. Byron *lawyer*
Wallach, Mark Irwin *lawyer*
Walters, Farah M. *hospital administrator*
Wamsley, James Lawrence, III *lawyer*
Watson, Richard Thomas *lawyer*
Watt, Ronald William *public relations executive*
Weaver, Robin Geoffrey *lawyer, educator*
Weber, Robert Carl *lawyer*
Webster, Leslie Tillotson, Jr. *pharmacologist, educator*
Weible, Robert A. *lawyer*
Weidenthal, Maurice David (Bud Weidenthal) *educational administrator, journalist*
Weiler, Jeffry Louis *lawyer*
Weinberg, Helen Arnstein *American art and literature educator*
Weiss, Morry *greeting card company executive*
Werber, Stephen Jay *lawyer, educator*
Wert, James William *banker*
Wertheim, Sally Harris *academic administrator, dean, education educator*
Whelan, Richard Vincent, Jr. *lawyer*
White, Fred Rollin, Jr. *mining and shipping company executive*
White, George W. *federal judge*
White, Michael Reed *mayor*
White, Paul Dunbar *lawyer*
White, Robert J. *neurosurgeon, neuroscientist, educator*
Whiteman, Joseph David *lawyer, manufacturing company executive*
Whiting, Hugh Richard *lawyer*
Whitney, Richard Buckner *lawyer*
Wilharm, John H., Jr. *lawyer*
†Williams, Arthur Benjamin, Jr. *bishop*
Williams, Clyde E., Jr. *lawyer*
Williams, Gordon Bretnell *construction company executive*
†Wise, Michael W. *lawyer*
Wolff, Gunther Arthur *physical chemist*
Wolinsky, Emanuel *physician, educator*
Woodring, James H. *lawyer*
Wotman, Stephen *dentistry educator, academic administrator*
Woyczynski, Wojbor Andrzej *mathematician, educator*
Wright, Marshall *retired manufacturing executive, former diplomat*
Yeager, Ernest Bill *physical chemist, electrochemist, educator*
Yosowitz, Sanford *lawyer, metal sales and fabricating executive*
†Young, Davis *public relations executive*
Young, James Edward *lawyer*
Young, Jess R. *physician*
Zambie, Allan John *manufacturing company executive*
Zangerle, John A. *lawyer*
Zdanis, Richard Albert *academic administrator*
†Zung, Thomas Tse-Kwai *architect*

Columbus

Ackerman, John Henry *health services consultant, physician*
Ackerman, Kenneth Benjamin *management consultant, writer*
Adams, John Marshall *lawyer*
Adams, Lee Stephen *lawyer, banker*
Alexander, Carl Albert *ceramic engineer*
Alger, Chadwick Fairfax *educator, political scientist*
Allen, Larry Rollar *management consultant*
Alutto, Joseph Anthony *university dean, management educator*
Anderson, Carole Ann *nursing educator*
Anderson, Jon Mac *lawyer*
Anderson, Sandra Jo *lawyer*
Antler, Morton *consulting engineering executive, author, educator*
Armes, Walter Scott *vocational school administrator*
Arthur, William Edgar *lawyer*
Ayers, James Cordon *lawyer*
Ayers, Randy *university athletic coach*
Babcock, Charles Luther *classics educator*
Bagby, Frederick Lair, Jr. *research institute executive*
Bailey, Cecil Dewitt *aerospace engineer, educator*
Bailey, Daniel Allen *lawyer*
Banasik, Robert Casmer *nursing home administrator, educator*
Banwart, George Junior *food microbiology educator*
Baranowski, Edwin Michael *lawyer, writer*
Barker, Judy *foundation executive*
Barker, Llyle James, Jr. *journalism educator, public relations executive, former military officer*
Barner, Bruce Monroe *state agency administrator*
Barnes, Wallace Ray *lawyer*
Barry, James P(otvin) *writer, editor, association executive*
Barth, Rolf Frederick *pathologist, educator*
Barthelmas, Ned Kelton *investment and commercial real estate banker*
Battersby, James Lyons, Jr. *English language educator*
Baughman, George Washington, III *retired university official, financial consultant*
Becher, Paul Ronald *health benefits executive*
†Bechtel, Stephen E. *mechanical engineer, educator*
Beck, Kenneth David *lawyer*
Beck, Paul Allen *political science educator*
Beckwith, Sandra Shank *federal judge*
Bedford, Keith Wilson *civil engineering and atmospheric science educator*
Behrman, Edward Joseph *biochemistry educator*
Beja, Morris *English literature educator*
Bell, George Edwin *retired physician, insurance company executive*
Bentz, William Frederick *accounting educator*
Berggren, Ronald Bernard *surgeon, emeritus educator*
Bergstrom, Stig Magnus *geology educator*
Berry, William Lee *business administration educator*
Beverley, Jane Taylor *artist*
Beytagh, Francis Xavier, Jr. *college dean, lawyer*
†Bhushan, Bharat *mechanical engineer*
Bianchine, Joseph Raymond *pharmacologist*
Bibart, Richard L. *lawyer*
Billings, Charles Edgar *physician*
Bishop, James Joseph *dean*
Black, Larry David *library director*
Blackmore, Josiah H. *university president, lawyer, educator*
Blair, William Travis (Bud Blair) *retired organization executive*
Boardman, William Penniman *lawyer, banker*

Boh, Ivan *philosophy educator*
†Böhm, Friedrich (Friedl) K.M. *architectural firm executive*
†Bope, Edward Tharp *family practitioner*
Boudoulas, Harisios *physician*
Boulger, Francis William *metallurgical engineer*
Bourguignon, Erika Eichhorn *anthropologist, educator*
Brandes, Norman Scott *psychiatrist*
Branscomb, Lewis Capers, Jr. *librarian, educator*
Bridgman, G(eorge) Ross *lawyer*
Briggs, Marjorie Crowder *lawyer*
Brodkey, Robert Stanley *chemical engineering educator*
Brooks, Keith *educator*
Brooks, Richard Dickinson *lawyer*
Brown, Firman Hewitt, Jr. *drama educator, theatrical director*
Brown, Herbert Russell *lawyer, writer*
Brown, Paul W. *retired lawyer, retired state supreme court justice*
Brown, Philip Albert *lawyer*
Brown, Rowland Chauncey Widrig *information systems, strategic planning and ethics consultant*
Brubaker, Robert Loring *lawyer*
Buchenroth, Stephen Richard *lawyer*
Buchsieb, Walter Charles *orthodontist*
Burke, Kenneth Andrew *advertising executive*
Burnham, John Chynoweth *historian, educator*
Burtch, John Hamrick *lawyer*
Byrd, Richard Hays *food company executive*
Cacioppo, John Terrance *psychology educator*
†Cain, Madeline Ann *state representative*
Calhoun, Donald Eugene, Jr. *federal judge*
Callander, Kay Eileen Paisley *business owner, retired gifted talented education educator, writer*
†Campbell, Jane Louise *state representative*
Campbell, Richard Rice *retired newspaper editor*
Capen, Charles Chabert *veterinary pathology educator, researcher*
Carlson, Larry Vernon *insurance company executive*
Carnahan, John Anderson *lawyer*
Carpenter, Jot David *landscape architect, educator*
Carpenter, Michael H. *lawyer*
Case, William R. *lawyer*
Casey, Raymond Richard *agricultural business executive*
Cearlock, Dennis Bill *research executive*
Celebrezze, Anthony J., Jr. *lawyer*
Chandrasekaran, Balakrishnan *computer and information science educator*
Chapman, Erie, III *hospital administrator*
Charles, Bertram *radio broadcasting executive*
Chester, John Jonas *lawyer*
Christensen, John William *lawyer*
Christoforidis, A. John *radiologist, educator*
Clark, Christine May *editor, author*
Clovis, Albert Lee *lawyer, educator*
Cogan, J. Kevin *lawyer*
Cole, Charles Chester, Jr. *educational administrator*
Cole, Clarence Russell *college dean*
Cole, Ransey Guy, Jr. *lawyer*
Collier, David Alan *management educator*
Cook, Samuel Ronald, Jr. *lawyer*
Copeland, William Edgar, Sr. *physician*
Corbato, Charles Edward *geology educator*
Cornwell, David George *biochemist, educator*
†Cottrell, David Alton *school system administrator*
Covault, Lloyd R., Jr. *hospital administrator, psychiatrist*
Cox, Mitchel Neal *editor*
Craig, Judith *bishop*
Cramblett, Henry Gaylord *pediatrician, virologist, educator*
Crane, Jameson *plastics manufacturing company executive*
Cruz, Jose Bejar, Jr. *engineering educator*
Cunnyngham, Jon *economist, information systems educator*
Cushman, James Butler *lawyer*
Cvetanovich, Danny L. *lawyer*
Daehn, Glenn Steven *materials scientist*
Daub, Berger Ellis *real estate agent*
†Dawson, Virginia Sue *newspaper editor*
Day, Roger F. *lawyer*
Deckrosh, Hazen Douglas *state agency administrator, educator*
Deep, Ira Washington *plant pathology educator*
De Lucia, Frank Charles *physicist, educator*
DeMaria, Peter James *utility company executive*
DeRousie, Charles Stuart *lawyer*
Dervin, Brenda Louise *communications educator*
DeWine, R. Michael *lieutenant governor, lawyer*
Dickinson, David Walter *welding engineer, educator*
Dillon, Merton Lynn *historian, educator*
Di Lorenzo, John Florio, Jr. *lawyer*
Disbrow, Richard Edwin *retired utility executive*
Disinger, John Franklin *natural resources educator*
Douglas, Andrew *state supreme court justice*
Dowd, Andrew Joseph *lawyer, utility company executive*
Dowling, Thomas Allan *mathematics educator*
Doyle, Patrick Lee *insurance company executive*
Draper, E(rnest) Linn, Jr. *electric utility executive*
Dreher, Darrell L. *lawyer*
Druen, William Sidney *lawyer*
Drvota, Mojmir *cinema educator, author*
Duckworth, Winston Howard *ceramic engineer*
Dugan, Charles Francis, II *lawyer*
Duryee, Harold Taylor *insurance executive*
Dwon, Larry *retired electrical engineer, educator, consultant*
Edwards, John White *lawyer*
Eickleberg, John Edwin *process control company executive*
Elam, John Carlton *lawyer*
Elliot, David Hawksley *geologist*
Emanuelson, James Robert *retired insurance company executive*
Engdahl, Richard Bott *mechanical engineer*
Ensminger, Dale *mechanical engineer, electrical engineer*
Epstein, Arthur Joseph *physics and chemistry educator*
Fahey, Richard Paul *lawyer*
†Fass, Robert J. *epidemiologist, academic administrator*
Faure, Gunter *geology educator*
Fawcett, Sherwood Luther *research laboratory executive*
Feck, Luke Matthew *utility executive*
Fenton, Robert Earl *electrical engineering educator*
Firestone, Richard Francis *chemistry educator*
Fisher, John Edwin *insurance company executive*
Fisher, Lee I. *state attorney general*
Fisher, Lloyd Edison, Jr. *lawyer*
†Flinn, William Loren *sociology educator, agricultural economics educator*
†Foland, Kenneth A. *geological sciences educator*
Fornshell, Dave Lee *educational broadcasting executive*
Fraley, Ralph Reed *hospital administrator*
†Franks, Richard Matthew *newspaper executive*
Frenzer, Peter Frederick *insurance company executive*
Fried, Samuel *lawyer*
Fry, Donald Lewis *physiologist, educator*
Fullerton, Charles William *retired insurance company executive*
Funk, John William *emergency vehicle manufacturing executive, packaging company executive, lawyer*
†Gaeth, Matthew Ben *state senator*
Gall, Maryann Baker *lawyer*
Galloway, Harvey Scott, Jr. *insurance company executive*
Gee, Elwood Gordon *university administrator*
Gerber, William Kenton *financial executive*
Gibson, Rankin MacDougal *lawyer*
†Gillmor, Karen Lako *state legislator, strategic planner*
Ginter, James Lee *business educator, researcher, consultant*
Glaser, Ronald *microbiology educator, scientist*
Goodman, Norton Victor *lawyer*
Goorey, Nancy Jane *dentist*
Gotherman, John E. *lawyer*
Gouke, Cecil Granville *economist, educator*
Gozon, Jozsef Stephan *engineering educator*
Graham, James Lowell *federal judge*
Grant, Dennis Duane *lawyer*
Grapski, Ladd Raymond *accountant*
Greek, Darold I. *lawyer*
Gross, James Howard *lawyer*
†Grossberg, Michael Lee *theater critic, writer*
Gunnels, Lee O. *retired finance and management educator*
Gunsett, Daniel J. *lawyer*
†Guthrie, Marc D. *congressman*
Habash, Stephen J. *lawyer*
Haddad, George Richard *musician, educator*
Hahm, David Edgar *classics educator*
Hairston, George W. *lawyer*
Hamilton, Harold Philip *fund raising executive*
Haque, Malika Hakim *pediatrician*
Hardymon, David Wayne *lawyer*
Hare, Robert Yates *music history educator*
Harris, Donald *composer*
Havens, John Franklin *retired banker*
†Hedrick, Larry Willis *airport executive*
Heffner, Grover Chester *retired corporate executive, retired naval officer*
Helgerson, John Walter *lawyer*
Henning, Harry Leonard *lawyer*
†Hermann, Charles F. *academic director, political science educator*
Hetzel, Joseph Adam *manufacturing executive*
†Hildebrand, Richard Allen *bishop*
Hinshaw, Virgil Goodman, Jr. *philosopher, emeritus educator*
Hire, Charles H. *lawyer*
Hoberg, John William *lawyer*
Hoffmann, Charles Wesley *retired foreign language educator*
†Holmes, Robert G. *agricultural studies educator*
Holschuh, John David *federal judge*
Hopkins, Thomas Gene *retail company executive*
Horton, John Edward *periodontist, educator*
Hoskins, W. Lee *banker*
Howarth, Robert F., Jr. *lawyer*
Howe, Robert Wilson *education educator*
Hsu, Hsiung *engineering educator*
Huber, Joan Althaus *sociology educator*
Huff, C(larence) Ronald *public administration and criminology educator*
†Hughes, Donald Allen, Jr. *law librarian and educator*
Hunt, William Edward *neurosurgeon, educator*
Ichiishi, Tatsuro *economics and mathematics educator*
Jackson, Curtis Maitland *metallurgical engineer*
Jarvis, Gilbert Andrew *humanities educator*
Jenkins, George L. *lawyer*
Jenkins, John Anthony *lawyer*
Jennings, Edward Harrington *business educator*
Jezek, Kenneth Charles *geophysicist, educator, researcher*
Johnson, Mark Alan *lawyer*
Johnston, Philip Crater *lawyer*
Kampmeier, Curtis Neil *management consultant*
Kapral, Frank Albert *medical microbiology and immunology educator*
Keaney, William Regis *engineering and construction services executive, consultant*
†Kearns, Merle Grace *state senator*
Kefauver, Weldon Addison *publisher*
Keller, John Kistler *lawyer*
Kendrick, Ronald Edward *orthopaedic surgeon*
Kennedy, James Patrick *lawyer*
Kennedy, Lawrence Allan *mechanical engineering educator*
Kessel, John Howard *political scientist, educator*
Kilman, James William *surgeon, educator*
Kim, Moon Hyun *physician, educator*
Kincaid, Robert M., Jr. *lawyer*
Kindig, Fred Eugene *statistics educator, arbitrator*
King, G. Roger *lawyer*
King, James R. *lawyer*
King, Norah M. *federal judge*
Kinneary, Joseph Peter *federal judge*
†Kirk, Ballard Harry Thurston *architect*
Knepper, William Edward *lawyer*
Knilans, Michael Jerome *supermarkets executive*
Ko, Hsien Ching *electrical engineer, educator*
Koenigsknecht, Roy A. *university dean*
†Kolattukudy, Pappachan Ettoop *biochemist, educator*
Koncelik, Joseph Arthur *industrial design educator*
Kozyris, Phaedon John *law educator, consultant*
†Krebs, Eugene Kehm, II *state legislator*
Ksienski, Aharon Arthur *electrical engineer*
Kuehn, Edmund Karl *artist*
Kuehnle, Kenton Lee *lawyer*
Kuhn, Albert Joseph *English educator*
Kurtz, Charles Jewett, III *lawyer*
†Kyees, John Edward *apparel company executive*
Ladman, Jerry R. *economist, educator*
Lahey, John H. *lawyer*
Lal, Rattan *soil scientist, researcher*
Lashutka, Gregory S. *mayor, lawyer*
Leach, Russell *judge*
Lehiste, Ilse *language educator*
Lehman, Harry Jac *lawyer*
Leissa, Arthur William *mechanical engineering educator*
Leiter, William C. *banking executive, controller*
Leland, Henry *psychology educator*
Lewis, Richard Phelps *physician, educator*
Lince, John Alan *pharmacist*
Lipinsky, Edward Solomon *chemist*
Logan, Terry James *agronomist educator*
†Long, Jan Michael *state legislator*
Long, Thomas Leslie *lawyer*
Lowe, Clayton Kent *visual imagery, cinema, and video educator*
Luck, James I. *foundation executive*
Lundman, Richard Jack *sociology educator*
Lundstedt, Sven Bertil *behavioral and social scientist, educator*
Lynn, Arthur Dellert, Jr. *economist, educator*
Madia, William Juul *chemist*
Magliocca, Larry Anthony *education educator*
†Maier, Johnnie A., Jr. *state legislator*
Malenick, Donald H. *metals manufacturing company executive*
Maloney, Gerald P. *utility executive*
Maloon, Jerry L. *lawyer, physician, medicolegal consultant*
Marble, Duane Francis *geography educator, researcher*
Marcus, Lola Eleanor *elementary and secondary education educator*
Martin, William Giese *lawyer*
Marzluf, George Austin *biochemistry educator*
Massie, Robert Joseph *publishing company executive*
Masterson, Michael Rue *journalist, educator, editor*
Mathews, Robert Edward *banker*
Mayer, Victor James *geological science educator*
Maynard, Robert Howell *lawyer*
Mayo, Elizabeth Broom *lawyer*
Mazzaferri, Ernest Louis *physician, educator*
McAlister, Robert Beaton *lawyer*
Mc Caffrey, Thomas R. *utilities company executive*
McClain, Thomas E. *communications executive*
McConnaughey, George Carlton, Jr. *lawyer*
McConnell, John Henderson *metal and plastic products manufacturing executive*
Mc Cormac, John Waverly *judge*
Mc Coy, John Bonnet *banker*
McCoy, John Gardner *banker*
McCutchan, Gordon Eugene *lawyer, insurance company executive*
Mc Donagh, Edward Charles *sociologist, university administrator*
McFerson, D. Richard *insurance company executive*
McKenna, Alvin James *lawyer*
†McLin, Rhine Lana *state representative, funeral service executive, educator*
McMahon, John Patrick *lawyer*
McMaster, Robert Raymond *accountant*
McMorrow, Richard Mark *research company executive*
McNealey, J. Jeffrey *lawyer, corporate executive*
McWhorter, Donald L. *bank executive*
Meider, Elmer Charles, Jr. *publishing company executive*
Meiling, George Robert Lucas *bank holding company executive*
†Meshel, Harry *state senator*
Meuser, Fredrick William *retired seminary president, church historian*
Meyer, Donald Ray *psychologist, brain researcher*
Meyer, Patricia Morgan *neuropsychologist, educator*
Milford, Frederick John *retired research company executive*
Miller, Dixon Fullerton *lawyer*
Miller, Don Wilson *nuclear engineering educator*
Miller, Frederick Powell *agronomy educator*
Miller, Malcolm Lee *retired lawyer*
†Miller, Terry Alan *chemistry educator*
Miller, Terry Morrow *lawyer*
Mills, Robert Laurence *physicist, educator*
Minister, Michael E. *lawyer*
Minor, Charles Daniel *lawyer*
Minor, Robert Allen *lawyer*
Minor, Robert Walter *lawyer*
Mirman, Joel Harvey *lawyer*
Moloney, Thomas E. *lawyer*
Mone, Robert Paul *lawyer*
†Montgomery, Betty D. *state legislator*
†Moody, Curtis Jerome *architect*
Moore, Donald Paul *retired electrical engineer*
Moritz, Michael Everett *lawyer*
†Morrow, Grant, III *genetecist*
†Mottley, J. Donald *state legislator, lawyer*
Moul, William Charles *lawyer*
Moulton, Edward Quentin *civil engineer, educator*
Moyer, Thomas J. *state supreme court chief justice*
Muller, Mervin Edgar *information systems educator, consultant*
†Murphy, Andrew J., Jr. *newspaper editor*
Mussey, Joseph Arthur *health and medical product executive*
Namboodiri, Krishnan *sociology educator*
Naylor, James Charles *psychologist, educator*
Neckermann, Peter Josef *insurance company executive*
†Ness, Gary Clifford *historical society administrator*
†Nettle, Robert Dale *state legislator, former insurance and real estate broker*
Newcomb, Lawrence Howard *agricultural educator*
†Newland, Ron *airport executive*
Newman, Diana S. *community foundation executive*
Newsom, Gerald Higley *astronomy educator*
Newton, William Allen, Jr. *pediatric pathologist*
Norris, Alan Eugene *federal judge*
†O'Brien, Jacquelyn Kirtley *state legislator*
O'Dorisio, Thomas Michael *internal medicine educator, researcher*
Ojalvo, Morris *civil engineer, educator*
Olesen, Douglas Eugene *research institute executive*
Oliphant, James S. *lawyer*
Oman, Richard Heer *lawyer*
†Opfer, Darrell Williams *state representative, educator*
Osipow, Samuel Herman *psychology educator*
Osmer, Patrick Stewart *astronomer*
Otte, Paul John *college administrator, consultant, trainer*
Page, Linda Kay *banking executive*
Parks, Darrell Lee *vocational education administrator*
Patterson, Samuel Charles *political science educator*
Pavony, William H. *retail executive*
Penn, Gerald Melville *pathologist*
Perkins, Robert Louis *physician, educator*
Peterle, Tony John *zoologist, educator*
Peters, Leon, Jr. *electrical engineering educator, research administ*
Petricoff, M. Howard *lawyer, educator*
Pfening, Frederic Denver, III *manufacturing company executive*
Phillips, James Edgar *lawyer*
Pieper, Heinz Paul *physiology educator*
Pigman, Jack Richard *lawyer*
Plagenz, George Richard *minister, journalist, columnist*
Pliskin, Marvin Robert *lawyer*
Pohlman, James Erwin *lawyer*
Pointer, Peter Leon *investment executive*
Poirier, Frank Eugene *physical anthropology educator*
Porter, Samuel Hamilton *lawyer*
†Porterfield, Hubert William *healthcare executive*
†Prentiss, C.J. *state legislator*
Pressley, Fred G., Jr. *lawyer*
Pyatt, Leo Anthony *real estate broker*
Quigley, John Bernard *law educator*
Radnor, Alan T. *lawyer*
Ramey, Denny L. *bar association executive director*
Rapp, Robert Anthony *metallurgical engineering educator, consultant*
Ray, Edward John *economics educator, administrator*
Ray, Frank David *government agency official*
Reasoner, Willis Irl, III *lawyer*
Reece, Robert William *zoological park administrator*
Reeve, John Newton *molecular biology and microbiology educator*
Reibel, Kurt *physicist, educator*
Relle, Ferenc Matyas *chemist*
Resnick, Alice Robie *state supreme court justice*
Richardson, Laurel Walum *sociology educator*
Ridgley, Thomas Brennan *lawyer*
†Riffe, Vernal G., Jr. *state representative*
Robinson, Barry R. *lawyer*
Rogers, Sarah Jeanne *curator*
Rose, Michael Dean *lawyer, educator*
Roth, Robert Earl *environmental educator*
Rowland, Ronald Lee *lawyer*
Royalty, Kenneth Marvin *lawyer*
†Ruberg, Robert Lionel *surgery educator*
Rubin, Alan J. *environmental engineer, chemist*
†Rudmann, Sally Anne *medical technology educator*
Rule, John Corwin *history educator*
†Rund, Douglas Andrew *emergency physician, educator*
Russell, William Fletcher, III *opera company director*
Ryan, Joseph W., Jr. *lawyer*
Ryan, Robert Seibert *consulting company executive*
†Sahai, Yogeshwar *engineering educator*
St. Arnold, Dale S. *hospital administrator*
St. Pierre, George Roland, Jr. *materials science and engineering administrator, educator*
St. Pierre, Ronald Leslie *anatomy educator, university administrator*
Salgia, Tansukh Jawaharlal *academic administrator*
Satyapriya, Combatore Keshavamurthy *geotechnical engineering executive*
Sawyers, Elizabeth Joan *librarian, administrator*
Sayers, Martin Peter *pediatric neurosurgeon*
Scanlan, James Patrick *philosophy and Slavic studies educator*
Schafer, William Harry *electric power industry executive*
†Schlichting, Nancy Margaret *hospital administrator*
†Schottenstein, Saul *retail company executive*
Schrag, Edward A., Jr. *lawyer*
†Schuller, David Edward *cancer center administrator, otolaryngology*
Schwab, Glenn Orville *retired agricultural engineering educator, consultant*
Schwebel, Andrew I. *psychology educator*
Scott, Thomas Clevenger *lawyer*
Selcer, David Mark *lawyer*
Sellers, Barbara Jackson *federal judge*
Seltzer, Martin Stanley *lawyer*
Senff, Mark D. *lawyer*
Senhauser, Donald A(lbert) *pathologist, educator*
Shamansky, Robert Norton *lawyer, partner*
Sharp, Paul David *institute administrator*
Shayne, Stanley H. *lawyer*
Sherrill, Thomas Boykin, III *newspaper publishing executive*
Shook, Robert Louis *business writer*
Sidman, Robert John *lawyer*
Siehl, Richard W. *lawyer*
Silbajoris, Frank Rimvydas *Slavic languages educator*
†Silcott, James *principal*
†Simonetta, Richard James *public transportation executive*
Sims, August Charles *lawyer, policeman*
Sims, Richard Lee *hospital administrator*
Skiest, Eugene Norman *food company executive*
Skillman, Thomas Grant *endocrinology consultant, former educator*
Slettebak, Arne *astronomer, educator*
Slonim, Arnold Robert *biochemist, physiologist*
Smith, George Curtis *federal judge*
Smith, George Leonard, Jr. *industrial engineering educator*
Smith, Norman T. *lawyer*
Smith, Robert Burns *newspaper magazine executive*
†Sofranko, Joel E. *pension fund administrator*
Sokol, Saul *insurance agency executive*
Soloway, Albert Herman *medicinal chemist*
Stearns, Robert Leland *curator*
Stedman, Richard Ralph *lawyer*
Stephens, Thomas M(aron) *education educator*
Stern, Geoffrey *lawyer, disciplinary counsel*
Stinehart, Roger Ray *lawyer*
†Stinziano, Michael Peter *state representative, real estate broker*
String, John F. *financial executive*
†Strode, George K. *sports editor*
Studer, William Joseph *library director*
†Suhadolnik, Gary C. *state senator*
Sweeney, Asher William *state supreme court justice*
Taft, Bob *state official*
Taft, Sheldon Ashley *lawyer*
Taggart, Thomas Michael *lawyer*
Tait, Robert Ed *lawyer*
Tarpy, Thomas Michael *lawyer*
Taylor, Celianna I. *information systems specialist*
Taylor, Joel Sanford *lawyer*
Tell, A. Charles *lawyer*
Thomas, Duke Winston *lawyer*
Thomas, Stephen Clair *software publisher, writer, editor, consultant*
Tiefel, Virginia May *librarian*
†Tilley, C. Ronald *gas company executive*
Tipton, Clyde Raymond, Jr. *communications and resources development consultant*
Todd, William Michael *lawyer*
Tomassini, Lawrence Anthony *accounting educator, consultant*
Trevor, Alexander Bruen *computer company executive*
Trimble, Marian Alice Eddy *mutual fund executive*

Triplehorn, Charles A. entomology educator, insects curator
Tully, Richard Lowden architect
Turano, David A. lawyer
Tway, Stephen Edward marketing communications executive, consultant
Tzagournis, Manuel physician, educator, university dean and official
Uotila, Urho Antti Kalevi geodesist, educator
Van Heyde, J. Stephen lawyer
Vassell, Gregory S. electric utility consultant
Voelker, Larry retired retail corporation executive
Voinovich, George V. governor
Vorys, Arthur Isaiah lawyer
Voss, Jerrold Richard city planner, educator, university official
Waldron, Acie Chandler agronomy and entomology educator
Wali, Mohan Kishen environmental science and natural resources educator
Ware, Brendan John electrical engineer, electric utility company executive
Warmbrod, James Robert agriculture educator, university administrator
Warner, Charles Collins lawyer
Webb, Thomas Evan biochemistry educator
Weinhold, Virginia Beamer interior designer
Weisberg, Herbert Frank political science educator
Weisgerber, David Wendelin editor, chemist
Wentworth, Andrew Stowell lawyer
Wexner, Leslie Herbert retail executive
Wheeler, George Charles quality assurance professional
Whipps, Edward Franklin lawyer
Wightman, Alec lawyer
Wigington, Ronald Lee retired chemical information services executive
Wilhelmy, Odin, Jr. insurance agent
Wilkins, John Warren physics educator
Williams, David Fulton industrial distribution company executive
Williams, Gregory Howard lawyer, educator
Wobst, Frank Georg banker
Wojcicki, Andrew Adalbert chemist, educator
†Wolfe, J. W. newspaper publishing executive
Wolfe, John F. publishing executive
Wolfe, John Walton investment banker
Wright, Harry, III lawyer
Wright, J. Craig state supreme court associate justice
Yashon, David neurosurgeon, educator
†Yenkin, Bernard Kalman paint company executive
Yohn, David Stewart virologist, science administrator
Zakin, Jacques Louis chemical engineering educator
†Zaleski, Alan Joseph state legislator
Zartman, David Lester dairy science educator, researcher
Zuspan, Frederick Paul obstetrician/gynecologist, educator

Concord
Watterson, Joyce Grande academy director
Whedon, Ralph Gibbs manufacturing executive

Curtice
Cashen, Elizabeth Anne elementary school educator

Cuyahoga Falls
Haag, Everett Keith architect
Hooper, Blake Howard manufacturing executive
†Jones, Wayne M. lawyer, state representative
Moses, Abe Joseph international financial consultant

Cuyahoga Heights
Tyrrell, Thomas Neil metal processing executive

Dayton
Arn, Kenneth Dale physician, city official
Barnes, Herman Verdain internist, educator
Bartlett, Robert Perry, Jr. lawyer
Battino, Rubin chemistry educator
Bedell, Kenneth Berkley computer specialist, educator
Benedict, Samuel S. paper company executive
Berrey, Robert Forrest lawyer
†Berry, John William investment company executive, retired telephone directory advertising company executive
Betz, Eugene William architect
Bigley, Nancy Jane microbiology educator
Birkholz, Raymond James metal products manufacturing company executive
Boren, Arthur Rodney sales management executive
†Bowman, Ed principal
Brand, Vance Devoe astronaut, government official
Bridges, Roy Dubard, Jr. career officer
Burick, Lawrence T. lawyer
†Cawood, Albert McLaurin (Hap Cawood) newspaper editor
Chait, William librarian, consultant
Chattoraj, Shib Charan chemical engineer
Chernesky, Richard John lawyer
Christensen, Julien Martin psychologist, educator
Clark, William Alfred federal judge
Crowe, Shelby educational specialist, consultant
Daley, Robert Emmett foundation executive
Darragh, John K. printing company executive
D'Azzo, John Joachim electrical engineer, educator
†Deardorff, Darryl K. business consultant, accountant
DeWall, Richard Allison retired surgeon
Diggs, Matthew O'Brien, Jr. air conditioning and refrigeration manufacturing executive
Duval, Daniel Webster manufacturing company executive
Elliott, Daniel Whitacre surgeon, retired educator
Emrick, Donald Day chemist, consultant
Enouen, William Albert paper corporation executive
Fang, Zhaoqiang research physicist
Faruki, Mahmud Taji psychiatrist, hospital administrator
Finn, Chester Evans lawyer
Freedman, Stanley Arnold lawyer
Frydman, Paul real estate broker and developer
Gies, Frederick John education educator, university dean
†Glaser, Herbert Otto retail executive
Goesch, William Holbrook aeronautical engineer
Gottschlich, Gary William lawyer
Granzow, Paul H. printing company executive
Gray, Edman Lowell metal distribution company executive
Gregor, Clunie Bryan geology educator
Hadley, Robert James lawyer
Haigh, Peter Leslie software company executive, consultant
Halki, John Joseph retired military officer, physician
Harden, Oleta Elizabeth English educator, university administrator
Harkness, Laurence Patrick health facility administrator
Harlan, Norman Ralph construction executive
Harrington, Thomas Joseph lawyer
†Hartley, Milton E. retail executive
Hastler, Russell Clifford, Jr. research and development company executive
Hawthorne, Douglas Lawson banker
Hayman, Jeffrey Lloyd corporate lawyer
Heft, James Lewis academic administrator, theology educator
Helling, James T. library director
Heyman, Ralph Edmond lawyer
Hoge, Franz Joseph accounting firm executive
Holiga, Ludomil Andrew metallurgical engineer
Holmes, David Richard computer and business forms company executive
†Horn, Charles F. lawyer, electrical engineer, state legislator
Houpis, Constantine Harry electrical engineering educator
Humbert, James Ronald pediatrician, educator
Hutchings, Brian LaMar biochemist, college administrator
Isaacson, Milton Stanley research and development company executive, engineer
James, Robert Charles business equipment manufacturing company executive
Janning, John Louis high technology scientist, consultant
Jenks, Thomas Edward lawyer
Johnson, C. Terry lawyer
Johnston, George Gustin automotive executive
Kazimierczuk, Marian Kazimierz electrical engineer, educator
Kegerreis, Robert James management consultant, marketing educator
Keto, John Edwin consulting electrical engineer
Khalimsky, Efim mathematics and computer science educator
Kinlin, Donald James lawyer
†Klinck, Cynthia Anne library director
Klink, Robert Michael consulting engineer, management consultant
Kogut, Maurice David pediatric endocrinologist
†Krug, Maurice F. engineering company executive
Ladehoff, Leo William metal products manufacturing executive
Lewis, Welbourne Walker, Jr. lawyer
Love, Rodney Marvin retired judge, former congressman
Lowry, Bruce Roy lawyer
Macklin, Crofford Johnson, Jr. lawyer
Maly, George Joseph, Jr. lawyer
Martin, James Gilbert university provost emeritus
Martino, Joseph Paul research scientist
Mason, Steven Charles forest products company executive
Matheny, Ruth Ann editor
Mathews, David foundation executive
McSwiney, Charles Ronald lawyer
Mc Swiney, James Wilmer retired pulp and paper manufacturing company executive
Merz, Michael federal judge
Mohler, Stanley Ross physician, educator
Morse, Kenneth Pratt manufacturing executive
Nam, Sang Boo physicist
Nevin, Robert Charles information systems executive
Nyerges, Alexander Lee museum director
O'Brien, Elmer John librarian, educator
†Peterson, Skip (Orley R. Peterson, III) newspaper photographer
Philips, Jesse retired manufacturing company executive
Ponitz, David H. academic administrator
Porter, Walter Arthur judge
Price, Harry Steele, Jr. construction materials company executive
Przemieniecki, Janusz Stanislaw college dean, engineer
Rapp, Gerald Duane lawyer, manufacturing company executive
Reese, Richard Bruce customer service executive
†Reid, Marilyn Joanne lawyer
Rinzler, Allan consulting company executive
Rogers, Richard Hunter lawyer, business executive
Romaguera, Enrique foreign language educator, corporate interpreter
Rowe, Joseph Everett electrical engineering educator, administrator
Schell, Allan Carter electrical engineer
Schmitt, George Frederick, Jr. materials engineer
Schorgl, Thomas Barry arts administrator
Schwartz, Irving Lloyd history educator emeritus
Schwartzhoff, James Paul foundation executive
Schwarz, Josephine Lindeman retired ballet company director, choreographer
Shaw, Harry Alexander, III manufacturing company executive
Shuey, John Henry diversified products company executive
Spicer, John Austin physicist
Stander, Joseph William former university administrator, mathematics educator
†Stewart, D. L. newspaper columnist
Stout, Donald Everett real estate developer, environmental preservationist
Thomas, Donald Charles microbiology educator, former university dean and administrator
†Thorsland, Edgar, Jr. health facility administrator
Tillson, John Bradford, Jr. newspaper publisher
Torley, John Frederic iron and steel company executive
Twyman, Jack wholesale grocery company executive, management services company executive
Uphoff, James Kent education educator
Vander Wiel, Kenneth Carlton computer services company executive
Von Gierke, Henning Edgar biomedical science educator, former government official, researcher
Walden, James William accountant, educator
Wallach, John S(idney) library administrator
Walters, Jefferson Brooks musician, retired real estate broker
Weinberg, Sylvan Lee cardiologist, educator, author, editor
Wertz, Kenneth Dean real estate executive
Whitlock, David C. retired military officer
Yates, Ronald Wilburn air force officer

Defiance
Hodapp, Shirley Jeaniene curriculum administrator
Mirchandaney, Arjan Sobhraj mathematics educator

Delaware
Burns, George Washington retired botany educator
Courtice, Thomas Barr college president
Dempsey, John Cornelius manufacturing company executive
Eells, William Hastings retired automobile company executive
Mendenhall, Robert Vernon mathematics educator

Delphos
Clark, Edward Ferdnand lawyer

Dresden
Reidy, Thomas Anthony lawyer

Dublin
Casey, John K. restaurant chain executive
Clement, Henry Joseph, Jr. diversified building products executive
Felger, Ralph William retired military officer, educator
Freytag, Donald Ashe management consultant
Gores, Gary Gene credit union executive
Graham, Bruce Douglas pediatrician
†Lamp, Benson J. tractor company executive
Madigan, Joseph Edward financial executive, consultant, director
Major, Coleman Joseph chemical engineer
Near, James W. restaurant and franchise executive
Rakestraw, Warren Vincent lawyer
Schinagl, Erich Friedrich health care company executive, physician
Smith, K(ermit) Wayne computer company executive
Teter, Gordon F. fast food chain company executive
Thomas, R. David food services company executive
Walter, Robert D. wholesale pharmaceutical distribution executive
†Wyatt, Glenn Thomas chemical company executive

Duncan Falls
Cooper, April Helen nurse

East Liverpool
Lang, Francis Harover lawyer

Elyria
Beckett, John Douglas manufacturing company executive
Kreighbaum, John Scott banker

Englewood
Shearer, Velma Miller clergywoman

Euclid
Giegerich, Thomas Anthony orthodontist

Fairborn
Leffler, Carole Elizabeth mental health nurse, women's health nurse
Martin, Donald William psychiatrist

Fairfield
Dizney, Robert Edward secondary education educator
Goodman, Myrna Marcia school nurse
Murphy, Dennis F. retail executive
Nichols, David L. retail executive
Robertson, Oscar Palmer former professional basketball player, chemical company executive

Fairlawn
Gibson, Charles Colmery former rubber manufacturing executive
Herman, Roger Eliot professional speaker, consultant, futurist, writer

Findlay
Draper, David Eugene seminary president
Frank, J. Louis oil company executive
Gorr, Ivan William rubber company executive
Jetton, Girard Reuel, Jr. lawyer, retired oil company executive
Kremer, Fred, Jr. manufacturing company executive
†Martin, Jim G. church renewal consultant
†Perry, Travis Calvin religious organization administrator
†Rave, James A. bishop
Reinhardt, James Alec rubber industry executive
Wilkin, Richard Edwin clergyman, religious organization executive
Yammine, Riad Nassif oil company executive

Franklin
Smith, Lynn Howard manufacturing company executive

Fremont
†Bridges, Roger Dean historical agency administrator

Galion
Cobey, Ralph industrialist

Gallipolis
Clarke, Oscar Withers physician
Niehm, Bernard Frank mental health center administrator

Gambier
Browning, Reed S. college official
Jordan, Philip Harding, Jr. academic administrator
Sharp, Ronald Alan English literature educator, author

Gates Mills
Doolittle, Robert Frederick lawyer
Enyedy, Gustav, Jr. chemical engineer
Schanfarber, Richard Carl real estate broker
Veale, Tinkham, II former chemical company executive, engineer

Germantown
Lansaw, Charles Ray rendering industry consultant

Girard
Wolanin, Sophie Mae civic worker, tutor, scholar, lecturer

Granville
†Fisher, Robert Allison minister, church administrator
Jacobs, Richard Allen industrial engineer
Morris, Charles Joseph, Jr. university provost
Myers, Michele Tolela academic administrator

Green Springs
Copeland, Terrilyn Denise speech pathologist

Grover Hill
†Harr, Joseph religious organization administrator

Hamilton
Battaglia, Michael Salvatore security company executive
Belew, David Lee retired paper manufacturing company executive
Johnson, Pauline Benge nurse, anesthetist
Linsenmann, William Michael lawyer, former insurance company executive
Marcum, Joseph LaRue insurance company executive
Marzano, Angelo Mario company executive
Patch, Lauren Nelson insurance company executive
Rorer, Leonard George psychology educator

Harrison
Kocher, Juanita Fay auditor
†Stoll, Robert W. principal

Hilliard
Cupp, David Foster photographer, journalist
Keyes, James Lyman, Jr. diesel engines distributor company owner

Hillsboro
†Snyder, Harry Cooper state senator

Hiram
Jagow, Elmer retired college administrator
Oliver, G(eorge) Benjamin academic administrator, philosophy educator

Holland
Kennedy, James L. accountant
†Marsden, Brian William Hugh steel company executive
Stewart, Daniel Robert glass company executive

Holmesville
Bolender, James Henry tire and rubber manufacturing executive

Hubbard
Rose, Ernst dentist

Hudson
Kirchner, James William electrical engineer
Stec, John Zygmunt real estate company executive
Wooldredge, William Dunbar investment banker

Huron
Clark, Thomas Garis rubber products manufacturer

Independence
Callsen, Christian Edward retail company executive
Hawkinson, Gary Michael utility holding company executive

Ironton
Mitchell, Maurice McClellan, Jr. chemist

Jackson
Clark, M. Juanita vocational education evaluator

Jackson Center
Thompson, Wade Francis Bruce manufacturing company executive

Jamestown
Liem, Darlene Marie secondary education educator

Kent
Beer, Barrett Lynn historian, educator
Buttlar, Rudolph Otto college dean
Byrne, Frank Loyola history educator
Cooperrider, Tom Smith botanist
Cummins, Kenneth Burdette emeritus science and mathematics educator
Dante, Harris Loy history educator
Du Mont, Rosemary Ruhig university dean
Georgopoulos, Nenos Aristides philosophy educator
Giffen, Daniel Harris lawyer, educator
Gould, Edwin Sheldon chemist, educator
Hall, Bernard retired economics educator and university official
Harkness, Bruce English language educator
Hassler, Donald Mackey, II English language educator, writer
Heimlich, Richard Allen geologist, educator
James, Patricia Ann philosophy educator
Koller, Marvin Robert sociology educator, writer
Poorman, Paul Arthur educator, media consultant
Powell, Robert Ellis mathematics educator, former college dean
Rylant, Cynthia author
Schwartz, Michael university president, sociology educator
Stackelberg, Olaf Patrick Von mathematician
†Varga, Richard Steven mathematics educator
Vars, Gordon Forrest education educator
Williams, Harold Roger economist, educator
Zornow, William Frank historian, educator

Kingston
Mathew, Martha Sue Cryder retired education educator

Lakewood
†Berman, Phillip L. author, institute administrator
Bradley, J.F., Jr. retired manufacturing company executive
Condon, George Edward journalist
†Gordon, Anne Kathleen editor
Seaton, Robert Finlayson planned giving consultant

Lancaster
Fox, Robert Kriegbaum manufacturing company executive

Hurley, Samuel Clay, III *investment company executive*
Katlic, John Edward *management consultant*
Libert, Donald Joseph *lawyer*
Phillips, Edward John *consulting firm executive*
Voss, Jack Donald *international business consultant, lawyer*
Wagonseller, James Myrl *real estate executive*

Lebanon
Holtkamp, Dorsey Emil *medical research scientist*
Maves, Paul Benjamin *clergyman, gerontologist*

Lima
†Bassett, James H. *landscape architect*
Becker, Dwight Lowell *physician*
Collins, William Thomas *pathologist*
†Cupp, Robert Richard *state senator, attorney*
Dicke, Candice Edwards *library educator*
Pranses, Anthony Louis *retired electric company executive, organization executive*
Robenalt, John Alton *lawyer*

Logan
Carmean, Jerry Richard *broadcast engineer*
Dillon, Neal Winfield *lawyer*

London
†Hughes, Clyde Matthew *religious denomination executive*

Lorain
†Szucs, Zoltan Daniel *religious organization executive, minister, psychologist, educator*

Loudonville
Battison, John Henry *broadcasting executive, consulting engineer*

Louisville
Sinclair, Virgil Lee, Jr. *lawyer, writer*

Lyndhurst Mayfield
Sevin, Eugene *engineer, consultant, educator*

Macedonia
Roth, Edwin Morton *manufacturing executive*

Mansfield
Baker, James Allan *banker*
Ellison, Lorin Bruce *management consultant*
Gorman, James Carvill *pump manufacturing company executive*
Houston, William Robert Montgomery *ophthalmic surgeon*

Maple Heights
Sargent, Liz Elaine (Elizabeth Sargent) *safety consulting executive*

Marblehead
Haering, Edwin Raymond *chemical engineering educator, consultant*

Marietta
Broughton, Carl L(ouis) *food company executive*
Fields, William Albert *lawyer*
Hausser, Robert Louis *lawyer*
Ling, Dwight L. *college administrator, history educator*
McDonough, Patrick Dennis *university executive*
Tipton, Jon Paul *allergist*
Wilbanks, Jan Joseph *philosopher*

Marion
Ashworth, John Lawrence *lawyer*
Tozzer, Jack Carl *civil engineer, surveyor*

Martins Ferry
Gracey, Robert William *account executive, minister*

Marysville
Hines, Anthony Loring *automotive executive*

Mason
Clarke, W. Hall *engineer*

Massillon
Dawson, Robert Earle *utilities executive*

Materials Park
Langer, Edward L. *association executive*

Maumee
Allen, Darryl Frank *industrial company executive*
Gosline, Robert Bradley *lawyer*
Huffman, (Bernard) Leslie, Jr. *physician*
†Iott, Wallace D. *supermarket chain executive*
Kline, James Edward *lawyer*
Marsh, Benjamin Franklin *lawyer*
Selland, Howard M. *manufacturing executive*
Tigges, Kenneth Edwin *retired financial executive*
Walrod, David James *retail grocery chain executive*

Mayfield Heights
Lewis, Peter Benjamin *insurance company executive*
O'Brien, Frank B. *manufacturing executive*
Rankin, Alfred Marshall, Jr. *business executive*
Smith, Ward *manufacturing company executive, lawyer*

Mechanicsburg
Maynard, Joan *education educator*

Medina
Ballard, John Stuart *law educator, former mayor*
Batchelder, Alice M. *federal judge*
†Batchelder, William George, III *attorney general, lawyer, professional society administrator*
Gossett, Robert M. *rubber industry executive*
Morris, John Hite *chemical industry executive*
Smith, Richey *chemical company executive*
Sullivan, Thomas Christopher *coatings company executive*

Mentor
Andrassy, Timothy Francis *trade association executive*
†Davis, Barbara Snell *principal*
†Miller, Frances Suzanne *historic site curator*
Richter, Hans *real estate broker and developer*
Skerry, Philip John *English educator*

Miamisburg
Northrop, Stuart Johnston *manufacturing company executive*
Wieland, Robert Richard *lawyer*

Middleburg Heights
Hartman, Lenore Anne *physical therapist*
Maciuszko, Kathleen Lynn *librarian, educator*

Middletown
Clinton, Mariann Hancock *association executive*
†Gilby, Steve *metallurgical engineering researcher*
Gilmore, June Ellen *psychologist*
Graham, Thomas Carlisle *steel company executive*
Jones, Fred E. *state judge*
Rathman, William Ernest *lawyer, minister*
Redding, Barbara J. *nursing administrator, occupational health nurse*

Milford
Fischer, Robert Andrew *computer executive*
Klosterman, Albert Leonard *technical development business executive, mechanical engineer*
†Morley, Bradford Charles *software company executive*

Millersburg
Childers, Lawrence Jeffrey *superintendent of schools*

Mount Saint Joseph
Roach, Sister Jeanne *hospital administrator*

Mount Vernon
†Schaub, Fred S. *mechanical engineer*
Turner, Harry Edward *lawyer*

Napoleon
†Walker, Frank Houston, Jr. *minister*

Navarre
Gardner, David Edward *baking company executive*

New Albany
Kessler, John Whitaker *real estate developer*

New Bremen
Dicke, James Frederick, II *manufacturing company executive*
Poppe, Beverly Reed *special education educator*

New Concord
Speck, Samuel Wallace, Jr. *academic administrator*

New Philadelphia
Doughten, Mary Katherine (Molly Doughten) *retired secondary education educator*
Goforth, Mary Elaine Davey *secondary education educator*

Newark
Fortaleza, Judith Ann *school system administrator*
Greenstein, Julius Sidney *academic administrator*
Mantonya, John Butcher *lawyer*
McConnell, William Thompson *commercial banker*

Niles
Darlington, Oscar Gilpin *historian, educator*
Travaglini, Raymond Dominic *corporate executive*

North Canton
George, Donald James *architecture educator, administrator*
Lynham, C(harles) Richard *foundry company executive*

North Olmsted
Lundin, Bruce Theodore *engineering and management consultant*
Zilli, Harry Angelo, Jr. *business executive*

North Ridgeville
Haddox, Arden Ruth Stewart *automotive aftermarket manufacturing executive*
Nagy, Robert David *tenor*

Northfield
Baltazzi, Evan Serge *engineering research consulting company executive*

Norwalk
Carpenter, Paul Leonard *lawyer*
French, Marcus Emmett *manufacturing company executive*
Germann, Richard P(aul) *chemist, chemical company executive*

Novelty
Miller, Dwight Richard *hair design executive*

Oberlin
Arnold, Paul Beaver *artist, educator*
Boe, David Stephen *musician, educator, college dean*
Carlton, Terry Scott *chemist, educator*
Carrier, Samuel Crowe, III *college official*
Colish, Marcia Lillian *history educator*
Distelhorst, Garis Fred *association executive*
†Dye, Nancy Schrom *academic administrator, history educator*
English, Ray *library administrator*
Gladieux, Bernard Louis *management consultant*
Greenberg, Nathan Abraham *classics educator*
Layman, Emma McCloy (Mrs. James W. Layman) *psychologist, educator*
Long, Herbert Strainge *classics educator*
Moore, Anne Frances *museum director*
Pease, Donald James *former congressman, political educator*
Reinoehl, Richard Louis *social work consultant, writer, artist*
Spear, Richard Edmund *art history educator*
Startup, Charles Harry *airline executive*
Young, David Pollock *humanities educator, author*
Zinn, Grover Alfonso, Jr. *religion educator*

Olmsted Township
Laessig, Robert H. *artist*

Oregon
Culver, Robert Elroy *osteopathic physician*
St. Clair, Donald David *lawyer*

Oxford
Baldwin, Arthur Dwight, Jr. *geology educator*
Brown, Edward Maurice *retired lawyer, business executive*
Eshbaugh, W(illiam) Hardy *botanist, educator*
Goodell, George Sidney *finance educator*
Gordon, Gilbert *chemist, educator*
Heimsch, Charles *retired botany educator*
Henry, Ronald James Whyte *university official*
Katon, John Edward *chemist, educator*
Kelm, Bonnie G. *art museum director, educator*
Lehmkuhl, Lois D. *music educator*
Macklin, Philip Alan *physics educator*
Miller, Harvey Alfred *botanist, educator*
Miller, Robert James *association executive*
Paulin, Henry Sylvester *antiques dealer, emeritus educator*
Pearson, Paul Guy *university president emeritus*
Pont, John *football coach, educator*
Pratt, William Crouch, Jr. *English language educator*
Rejai, Mostafa *political science educator*
Risser, Paul Gillan *botanist, academic administrator*
Sanders, Gerald Hollie *communications educator*
Seltzer, Mildred M. *gerontologist, educator*
Sessions, Judith Ann *librarian, university library dean*
Shriver, Phillip Raymond *university president*
Thompson, Bertha Boya *retired educator*
Ward, Roscoe Fredrick *engineering educator*
Williamson, Clarence Kelly *microbiologist, educator*
Winkler, Allan Michael *history educator*
Zwirn, Robert *architect,architecture educator*

Painesville
Clement, Daniel Roy, III *accountant, assistant nurse, small business owner*
Humphrey, George Magoffin, II *plastic molding company executive*
Jayne, Theodore Douglas *technical research and development company executive*

Parma
Moskal, Robert M. *bishop*

Paulding
Hitchcock, J. Gareth *retired judge*

Peninsula
Ludwig, Richard Joseph *ski resort executive*

Pepper Pike
Bray, Pierce *business consultant*
Froelich, Wolfgang Andreas *neurologist*
Mc Call, Julien Lachicotte *banker*
Stroesenreuther, George Dale *financial executive*

Perrysburg
Autry, Carolyn *artist, art history educator*
Barbe, Betty Catherine *financial analyst*
Danford, Ardath Anne *retired librarian*
Eastman, John Richard *retired manufacturing company executive*
McMaster, Harold Ashley *manufacturing company executive, inventor*
Williamson, John Pritchard *utility executive*
Yager, John Warren *retired banker, lawyer*

Pickerington
†Burrell, Richard Lee *footware company executive*
†Zacks, Gordon Benjamin *manufacturing company executive*

Piketon
†Patton, Finis S., Jr. *nuclear chemist*

Port Clinton
Subler, Edward Pierre *advertising executive*

Portsmouth
Davis, Donald W. *government official*
Horr, William Henry *lawyer*

Powell
Adeli, Hojjat *civil engineering educator, computer scientist*
Hanna, Jack Bushnell *zoo director*
†Kriegel, David L. *retail executive*
†Lombardi, Celeste *zoological park administrator*

Randolph
Pecano, Donald Carl *truck, trailer and railcar manufacturing executive*

Reynoldsburg
Goostree, Robert Edward *political science and law educator*
Lynch, Rose Peabody *art gallery executive*
Woodward, Greta Charmaine *construction company executive*

Richfield
†Berkey, Timothy B. *principal*
Daugherty, Brad(ley) (Lee) *professional basketball player*
Embry, Wayne Richard *basketball executive*
Price, (William) Mark *professional basketball player*

Richmond Heights
†Marino, Michael *church administrator*

Riverside
Willardson, Kimberly Ann Carey *editor, writer, publisher*

Rocky Ridge
†Cruft, Edgar Frank *mining company executive*

Rocky River
Castele, Theodore John *radiologist*
De Long, Erika Venta *psychiatrist*

Rootstown
Blacklow, Robert Stanley *physician, medical college administrator*
Campbell, Colin *obstetrician, gynecologist, school dean*
Hutterer, Ferenc *biochemistry educator, researcher*
Saltzman, Glenn Alan *behavioral sciences educator*
Sayre, Jean Williams *librarian, educator*

Saint Clairsville
Dankworth, Margaret Anne *management consultant*

Salem
†Durfee, John B. *religious organization administrator*
Fehr, Kenneth Manbeck *computer systems company executive*

Sandusky
Link, Frank Albert *retired city manager*
Round, Alice Faye Bruce *school psychologist*
Tone, Kenneth Edward *lawyer*

Seven Hills
Stanczak, Julian *artist, educator*

Shaker Heights
Adler, Naomi Samuel *real estate counselor*
Eakin, Thomas Capper *sports promotion executive*
Held, Lila M. *art appraiser*
Wolf, Milton Albert *economist, former U.S. ambassador, business executive*

Sharonville
Ehrnschwender, Arthur Robert *former utility company executive*

Shelby
Moore, Florian Howard *electronics engineer*

Sidney
Laurence, Michael Marshall *magazine publisher, writer*
Lawrence, Wayne Allen *publisher*
Stevens, Robert Jay *magazine editor*

Silver Lake
Chrobak, Dennis Steven *chemical engineer*

Solon
Richard, Edward H. *manufacturing company executive, former municipal government official*
Stauffer, Thomas George *hotel executive*
Weiss, Joseph Joel *consulting company executive*

South Euclid
Loehr, Marla *college president*

Spring Valley
Singhvi, Surendra Singh *finance and strategy consultant*

Springboro
Saxer, Richard Karl *metallurgical engineer, retired air force officer*

Springfield
Browne, William Bitner *lawyer*
Dominick, Charles Alva *college official*
Kinnison, William Andrew *university president*
Maddex, Myron Brown (Mike Maddex) *broadcasting executive*
Maki, Jerrold Alan *medical center administrator*
Martin, Oscar Thaddeus *retired lawyer*
Montag, John Joseph, II *librarian*
Pearson, Norman Ralston *librarian*
Reck, W(aldo) Emerson *retired university administrator, public relations consultant, writer*

Steubenville
Johnson, Micah William *television newscaster, director*
Kasprzak, Lucian Alexander *physics educator, researcher*

Streetsboro
Kearns, Warren Kenneth *business executive*

Strongsville
Oltman, C. Dwight *conductor, educator*
Opplt, Jan Jiri *clinical pathologist, educator*

Sugar Grove
Bonner, Herbert Dwight *construction management educator*
Young, Nancy Henrietta Moe *elementary education educator*

Sylvania
Kneller, William Arthur *geologist, educator*
Kurek, Dolores Bodnar *physical science and mathematics educator*
Lock, Richard William *packaging company executive*
Sampson, Earldine Robison *education educator*
Verhesen, Anna Maria Hubertina *counselor*

Tiffin
Cassell, William Comyn *college president*
Davison, Kenneth Edwin *American studies educator*
Kramer, Frank Raymond *classicist, educator*
Porter, Arthur Reno *economist, arbitrator*

Tipp City
Taylor, Robert Homer *quality assurance professional, pilot*

Toledo
Anderson, Dale Kenneth *retired lawyer*
Bagley, Brian G. *materials science educator, researcher*
Baker, Bernard Robert, II *lawyer*
Baker, Richard Southworth *lawyer*
Bardis, Panos Demetrios *sociologist, social philosopher, historian, author, editor, poet, educator*
Batt, Nick *property and investment executive*
Bergsmark, Edwin Martin *trust company executive*
Bick, David Greer *health care marketing executive*
Billups, Norman Fredrick *college dean, pharmacist*
Block, Allan James *communications executive*
Block, John Robinson *newspaper publisher*
Block, William Karl, Jr. *newspaper executive*
Boeschenstein, William Wade *glass products manufacturing executive*
Boesel, Milton Charles, Jr. *lawyer, business executive*
Boggs, Ralph Stuart *lawyer*
Boller, Ronald Cecil *glass company executive*

Brown, Charles Earl *lawyer*
Carson, Samuel Goodman *retired banker, company director*
Chakraborty, Joana *physiology educator, research center administrator*
Christiansen, Eric George *marketing specialist*
Colasurd, Richard Michael *lawyer*
Craig, Harald Franklin *lawyer*
Dalrymple, Thomas Lawrence *lawyer*
Depew, Charles Gardner *research company executive*
DiDio, Liberato John Alphonse *anatomist, educator*
Farison, James Blair *electrical engineer, educator*
†Finkbeiner, Carleton S. (Carty) *mayor*
Fisher, Donald Wiener *lawyer*
Fuhrman, Charles Andrew *country club proprietor, real estate management executive, lawyer*
†Furney, Linda Jeanne *state legislator*
Gearhart, Thomas Lee *newspaper editor*
Glowacki, Richard Chester *real estate, brokerage house executive*
Hartmann, Ann Wilson *financial planner*
Hauenstein, Henry William *civil engineer*
Hawkins, Donald Merton *lawyer*
Hiett, Edward Emerson *retired lawyer, glass company executive*
†Hills, Arthur W. *architectural firm executive*
Hiner, Glen Harold, Jr. *materials company executive*
Hirsch, Carl Herbert *manufacturing company executive*
†Hoffman, James Al *banker*
Hoffman, James R. *bishop*
Hood, Douglas Crary *electronics educator*
Horton, Frank Elba *university official, geography educator*
James, Harold Arthur *lawyer*
†James, William *bishop*
Kunze, Ralph Carl *savings and loan executive*
Lanigan, Robert J. *packaging company executive*
La Rue, Carl Forman *lawyer*
Leech, Charles Russell, Jr. *lawyer*
Lemieux, Joseph Henry *manufacturing company executive*
Mabry, Guy O. *manufacturing company executive*
†Mac Guidwin, Mark J. *manufacturing executive*
†Martin, Robert Edward *architect*
Massey, Andrew John *conductor, composer*
Mayhew, Harry Eugene *physician, educator*
McCormick, Edward James, Jr. *lawyer*
McGlauchlin, Tom *artist*
Morcott, Southwood J. *automotive parts manufacturing company executive*
Mulrow, Patrick Joseph *medical educator*
Northup, John David *management consultant, inventor*
O'Connell, Maurice Daniel *lawyer*
Paquette, Jack Kenneth *management consultant, antiques dealer*
Potter, John William *federal judge*
Proefrock, Carl Kenneth *academic medical administrator*
Rissing, Daniel Joseph *hospital administrator*
†Robb, A. M. *glass manufacturing executive*
Romanoff, Milford Martin *building contractor*
†Rosenbaum, Kenneth E. *journalist, editor*
†Royhab, Ronald *journalist, newspaper editor*
Rubin, Allan Maier *physician, surgeon*
Saffran, Murray *biochemist*
Saunders, Donald Herbert *utility company executive*
Shelley, Walter Brown *physician, educator*
†Shultz, Edward Joseph *holdings company executive*
Smith, Robert Freeman *history educator*
Smith, Robert Nelson *former government official, anesthesiologist*
Spitzer, John Brumback *lawyer*
Standaert, Frank George *medical research administrator, physician*
Stankey, Suzanne M. *editor*
†Stark, Charles H., III *architectural firm executive*
Steadman, David Wilton *museum official*
Stewart, Mark Carroll *lawyer*
Strobel, Martin Jack *motor vehicle and industrial component manufacturing and distribution company executive*
Thompson, Gerald E. *historian, educator*
Toadvin-Bester, Josephine Vesella *academic administrator, educator*
Tuschman, James Marshall *lawyer*
Weber, Max O. *retired glass fiber products manufacturing company executive*
Willey, John Douglas *retired newspaper executive*
Wittmann, Otto *art museum executive*
Wolfe, Warren Dwight *lawyer*
Young, Don J. *federal judge*
Zrull, Joel Peter *psychiatry educator*

Troy
Davies, Alfred Robert *physician, educator*

Twinsburg
†Hoven, Dwayne *retail executive*
†Raven, Gregory Kurt *retail executive*
Solganik, Marvin *real estate executive*

University Heights
Bloch, Andrea Lynn *physical therapist*
Cook, Alexander Burns *museum curator, artist, educator*
Kelly, Joseph Francis *theology educator*

Upper Arlington
†Mincy, Homer F. *school system administrator*

Van Wert
Duprey, Wilson Gilliland *retired librarian*
Liljegren, Frank Sigfrid *artist, art association official*

Vandalia
Farley, Paul Emerson *manufacturing company executive*
†Smith, Marjorie Aileen Matthews *museum director*
†Subotnick, Stuart *food service executive*
Welter, William Michael *marketing and advertising executive*

Vermilion
Vance, Elbridge Putnam *mathematics educator*

Wapakoneta
†Brading, Charles Richard *state representative*

Warren
Alli, Richard James, Sr. *electronics executive, service executive*
Johns, Charles Alexander *hospital administrator*
Nader, Robert Alexander *judge, lawyer*
†Rennert, Ira Leon *heavy manufacturing executive*
Rossi, Anthony Gerald *lawyer*

Washington Court House
Fultz, Clair Ervin *former banker*

Waterford
Riley, Nancy Mae *vocational home economics educator*

Wellston
Lillich, Alice Louise *secondary education educator*

West Chester
Ofte, Donald *environmental executive, former management consultant*
Rishel, James Burton *manufacturing executive*

Westerville
Conley, Sarah Ann *health facility administrator*
Davis, Joseph Lloyd *state council educational administrator, consultant*
DeVore, Carl Brent *college president, educator*
Günther, Marian W(aclaw) J(an) *theoretical physicist*
Kollat, David Truman *management consultant*
Milligan, Frederick James *lawyer*
Smith, C. Kenneth *corporate executive*
Willke, Thomas Aloys *university official, statistics educator*
Yoder, Amos *university research official*

Westlake
Bisson, Edmond Emile *mechanical engineer*
Huff, Ronald Garland *mechanical engineer*
Myers, Ira Thomas *physicist*

Wickliffe
Bardasz, Ewa Alice *chemical engineer*
Bares, William G. *chemical company executive*
Coleman, Lester Earl *chemical company executive*
Dunn, Horton, Jr. *organic chemist*
Hsu, Roger Y. K. *lawyer*
Kidder, Fred Dockstater *lawyer*
Pevec, Anthony Edward *bishop*
Rosica, Gabriel Adam *corporate executive, engineer*

Wilberforce
Gupta, Vijay Kumar *chemistry educator*
Svager, Thyrsa Anne Frazier *university administrator, retired educator*
Walker-Taylor, Yvonne *retired college president*

Willoughby
Abelt, Ralph William *bank executive*
Campbell, Talmage Alexander *newspaper editor*
Figgie, Harry E., Jr. *corporate executive*
Harthun, Luther Arthur *lawyer*
Hassell, Peter Albert *electrical and metallurgical engineer*
Paine, Charles William Eliot *arboretum executive, horticulturist*

Wintersville
Becker, William A(lbert) *real estate developer*

Wooster
August, Robert Olin *journalist*
Colclaser, H. Alberta *lawyer, retired government official*
Copeland, Henry Jefferson, Jr. *college president*
Gates, Richard Daniel *manufacturing company executive*
Hickey, Damon D. *library director*
Lafever, Howard Nelson *plant breeder, geneticist, educator*
Loess, Henry Bernard *psychology educator*
Meehan, Joseph Gerard *retired manufacturing executive*
†Payne, Thomas L. *university official*
Schmitt, Wolfgang Rudolph *consumer products executive*
Stuart, James Fortier *musician, artistic director*
Weidensaul, Thomas Craig *university administrator, researcher*
Williams, Walter W. *consumer products manufacturing executive*

Worthington
Bernhagen, Lillian Flickinger *school health consultant*
Compton, Ralph Theodore, Jr. *electrical engineering educator*
Guthrie, Henry Lee *retail executive*
Idol, James Daniel, Jr. *chemist, educator, inventor, consultant*
Winter, Chester Caldwell *physician, surgery educator*

Xenia
Bigelow, Daniel James *aerospace executive*
Nutter, Zoe Dell Lantis *public relations executive, retired*

Yellow Springs
Fogarty, Robert Stephen *historian, educator, editor*
Graham, P(recious) Jewel *lawyer, educator, social worker*
Guskin, Alan E. *university president*
Hamilton, Virginia (Mrs. Arnold Adoff) *author*
Lacey, Beatrice Cates *psychophysiologist*
Lacey, John Irving *psychologist, physiologist, educator*
Trolander, Hardy Wilcox *engineering executive, consultant*

Youngstown
Bell, Carol Willsey *certified genealogist*
†Bowers, Bege K. *English educator*
†Brothers, Barbara *English language educator*
†Buchanan, C. Robert *architectural firm executive*
Butterworth, Jane Rogers Fitch *physician*
Catoline, Pauline Dessie *small business owner*
Cochran, Leslie Herschel *university administrator*
Coleman, Esther Mae Glover *educator*
Courtney, William Francis *food and vending service company executive*
Cushwa, William Wallace *machinery parts company executive*
DeBartolo, Edward John, Jr. *professional football team owner, real estate developer*
Fok, Thomas Dso Yun *civil engineer*
Gaylord, Sanford Fred *physician*
Gillis, Bernard Thomas *chemistry educator*
†Logan, Richard Parker *newspaper editor*
†Mastriana, Robert Alan *architect*
Mumaw, James Webster *lawyer*
Nadler, Myron Jay *lawyer*
Powers, Paul J. *manufacturing company executive*
Pridham, Herbert H. *retired trust company executive, lawyer, foundation administrator*
Przelomski, Anastasia Nemenyi *retired newspaper editor*
Roth, Daniel Benjamin *lawyer, business executive*
†Schwartz, David *retail executive*
Sokolov, Richard Saul *lawyer*
Stevens, Paul Edward *lawyer*
†Trucksis, Theresa A. *library director*
Tucker, Don Eugene *retired lawyer*
†Zona, Louis Albert *art museum director, educator*

Zanesville
Duhs, William Andrew *banker*
Durant, Charles Edward, Jr *medical facility administrator*
Irvin, Helen Arlene *vocational education educator*
Micheli, Frank James *lawyer*
Ray, John Walker *otolaryngologist, educator, broadcast commentator*
Truby, John Louis *corporate executive*

OKLAHOMA

Ada
†Anoatubby, Bill *governor*
†Stafford, Donald Gene *chemistry educator*
Walker, Billy Kenneth *computer science educator, academic administrator*

Altus
†Cotner, Howard Paul *state legislator, land title abstractor*

Anadarko
Pain, Charles Leslie *lawyer*

Antlers
Stamper, Joe Allen *lawyer*

Ardmore
†Thompson, John E. *principal*

Bartlesville
Allen, W. Wayne *oil industry executive*
Armstrong, Oliver Wendell *oil company executive*
Arnold, Philip Mills *retired oil company executive*
Clay, Harris Aubrey *chemical engineer*
Cox, Glenn Andrew, Jr. *petroleum company executive*
Doty, Donald D. *retired banker*
†Dunlap, James Robert *contractor, state legislator*
Hankinson, Risdon William *chemical engineer*
Hogan, J(ohn) Paul *chemistry researcher, consultant*
†Johnson, Marvin Merrill *chemist*
Kaiser, Jean Morgan *real estate broker*
†Owen, Raymond Harold *minister*
Paul, William George *lawyer*
Silas, Cecil Jesse *retired petroleum company executive*
Wallace, Robert Glenn *petroleum company executive*

Bethany
Arnold, Donald Smith *chemical engineer, consultant*
Davis, Harrison Ransom Samuel, Jr. *English language educator*
†Leggett, James Daniel *church administrator*
Leupp, Edythe Peterson *retired educator, administrator*
Mercer, Ronald L. *retired manufacturing executive*

Broken Arrow
Chambers, Richard Lee *geoscientist, researcher*
Elad, Emanuel *industrial instrumentation executive*
Janning, Sister Mary Bernadette *nun, retired association executive*

Chickasha
Beets, Freeman Haley *retired government official*
Feaver, John Clayton *philosopher, educator*
Good, Leonard Phelps *artist*

Durant
Baskin, Vlasta Jana Marie *language educator*
†Garrett, Scott *vocational school administrator*
†Mickle, Billy Arthur *lawyer, state legislator*
Williams, Larry Bill *university president*

Edmond
Ashford, George Allen *financial planner*
Brown, William Ernest *dentist*
Caire, William *biologist, educator, assistant dean*
Griggy, Kenneth Joseph *food company executive*
Nelson, John Woolard *neurology educator, physician*
Nigh, George *university administrator, former governor*
†Raburn, Randall K. *school system administrator*
Simpson, Zelma Alene *librarian*
Standard, James Noel *newspaper editor*

Elk City
Francis, Talton Loe *hospital administrator*

Enid
Jones, Stephen *lawyer*
Musser, William Wesley, Jr. *lawyer*
Peck, Robert David *academic administrator, educator*
Ward, Llewellyn O(rcutt), III *oil producer*

Goodwell
Smith, Kim Lee *educator*

Guthrie
†Davis, Frank Wayne *lawyer*

Guymon
Wood, Donald Euriah *lawyer*

Kingfisher
Baker, Thomas Edward *lawyer, accountant*

Lawton
Brooks, (Leslie) Gene *cultural association administrator*
†Coffey, Wallace E. *chairman Comanche Indian tribe*
Cooke, Wanda (Cookie Cooke) *hearing aid specialist*
†Hooper, Roy B. *state senator, insurance broker*
Moore, Roy Dean *judge*
†Reno, Jennifer *principal*
†Young, J. A. *bishop*

Mangum
Ford, Linda Lou *dietitian*

Mcalester
Cornish, Richard Pool *lawyer*
†Stipe, Gene *state senator*

Miami
Lovell, James Frederick *academic administrator*

Midwest City
Smith, Wayne Calvin *chemical engineer*

Moore
Moore, Dalton, Jr. *petroleum engineer*

Muskogee
Kent, Bartis Milton *physician*
Ruby, Russell (Glenn) *lawyer*
Seay, Frank Howell *federal judge*

Norman
Affleck, Marilyn *sociology educator*
Albert, Lois Eldora Wilson *archaeologist*
Atkinson, Gordon *chemistry educator*
Bauer, George W. *publishing company executive*
Bell, Robert Eugene *anthropologist educator*
Bert, Charles Wesley *mechanical and aerospace engineer, educator*
Boke, Norman Hill *botanist*
†Branch, David Reed *astrophysicist, educator*
Brown, Elvin J. *lawyer*
Brown, Sidney DeVere *history educator*
Bryant, Celia Mae Small *music educator*
Burton, Ron D. *educational foundation executive*
Campbell, John Morgan *retired chemical engineer*
Carey, Thomas Devore *baritone, educator*
Carpenter, Charles Congden *zoologist, educator*
Cella, Francis Raymond *economist, research consultant*
Ciereszko, Leon Stanley *chemistry educator*
Corr, Edwin Gharst *ambassador*
Cosier, Richard A. *business educator, consultant*
Crane, Robert Kendall *engineering educator, researcher, consultant*
Cross, George Lynn *foundation administrator, former university president*
Dary, David Archie *journalism educator, author*
de Stwolinski, Gail Rounce Boyd *music theory and composition educator*
Dille, John Robert *physician*
Donahue, Hayden Hackney *mental health institute administrator, medical educator, psychiatric consultant*
Doviak, Richard James *atmospheric scientist, engineer*
Dryhurst, Glenn *chemistry educator*
Eek, Nathaniel Sisson *retired fine arts educator*
Egle, Davis Max *mechanical engineering educator*
Elkouri, Frank *legal educator*
Estes, James Russell *botanist*
†Fairbanks, Robert Alvin *lawyer*
†Fears, Jesse Rufus *academic dean*
Fuerbringer, Alfred Ottomar *clergyman*
Gal-Chen, Tzvi *geophysicist, meteorologist, educator*
Glad, Paul Wilbur *history educator*
Hagan, William Thomas *history educator*
Hemingway, Richard William *lawyer, educator*
Henderson, Arnold Glenn *architect, educator*
Henderson, George *educational sociologist, educator*
Herstand, Theodore *theatre artist, educator*
Hinshaw, Lerner Brady *physiology educator*
Hodgell, Murlin Ray *university dean*
Hodges, Thompson Gene *librarian*
Hollon, William Eugene *historian, educator, author*
Hutchison, Victor Hobbs *biologist, educator*
Kadir, Djelal *university educator, editor periodical, consultant*
Kemp, Betty Ruth *librarian*
Kessler, Edwin *meteorology educator, consultant*
Kondonassis, Alexander John *economist, educator*
Lamb, Peter James *meteorology educator, researcher, consultant*
Lee, Sul Hi *library administrator*
Leonhardt, Thomas Wilburn *director library technical services, librarian*
Lis, Anthony Stanley *business administration educator*
Lowitt, Richard *history educator*
Maddox, Robert Alan *atmospheric scientist*
Mankin, Charles John *geology educator*
Mares, Michael Allen *ecologist, educator*
Nebergall, Roger Ellis *speech educator*
Owens, Rochelle *poet, playwright*
Ross, Allan Anderson *music educator, university official*
Schindler, Barbara Francois *school administrator*
†Schnell, Gary D. *zoology educator, administrator*
Sharp, Paul Frederick *former university president, educational consultant*
†Sherman, Mary Angus *public library administrator*
Toperzer, Thomas Raymond *art museum director*
Trimble, Preston Albert *retired judge*
Van Auken, Robert Danforth *business administration educator, management consultant*
Van Horn, Richard Linley *university administrator*
Weber, Jerome Charles *education and human relations educator, former academic dean and provost*
Zelby, Leon Wolf *electrical engineering educator, consulting engineer*

Nowata
Osborn, Ann George *retired chemist*

Oklahoma City
Abernathy, Jack Harvey *petroleum, utility company and banking executive*
Abram, Darlene Ruth Sheppard *educator, consultant*
Ackerman, Raymond Basil *advertising agency executive*
†Adcock, James Michael *oil company executive, lawyer*
Alaupovic, Alexandra Vrbanic *artist, educator*
Alexander, Patrick Byron *zoological society executive*
Allen, Robert Dee *lawyer*

Alley, Wayne Edward *federal judge, retired army officer*
Almond, David R. *lawyer*
Anderson, Kenneth Edwin *writer, educator*
Andrews, Robert Frederick *religious organization administrator, retired bishop*
Angel, Arthur Ronald *lawyer, consultant*
Anthony, Robert Holland *state official*
Austin, Gerald Grant *wholesale food distribution company executive*
†Ball, Leonard F. *lawyer, architectural firm executive*
Ball, Rex Martin *architect*
†Bastin, Gary Charles *state legislator*
Beltran, Eusebius Joseph *archbishop*
†Beutler, Randy Leon *rancher, state legislator*
†Bishop, William T. *food company executive*
Bogardus, Carl Robert, Jr. *radiologist, educator*
Bohanon, Luther L. *federal judge*
Bohanon, Richard Lee *federal judge*
Booth, Glenna Greene *genealogical researcher*
Boston, William Clayton *lawyer*
†Boyd, Betty *government official*
†Boyd, Laura Wooldridge *state legislator*
Branch, John Curtis *biology educator, lawyer*
Brandt, Edward Newman, Jr. *physician, educator*
Brawner, Lee Basil *librarian*
Bresler, Mark Irwin *rehabilitation engineer*
Brown, Kenneth Ray *banker*
Browne, John Robinson *banker*
Brumley, David Lee *corporate human resources executive*
Buchanan, Robert Taylor *plastic surgeon*
Burch, Melvin Earl *lawyer, bank executive*
†Caldwell, Warren A. (Tony Caldwell) *state legislator, real estate management company executive*
Cameron, Charles Metz, Jr. *physician, medical educator*
Campbell, David Gwynne *petroleum executive, geologist*
Cantrell, Charles Leonard *lawyer, educator*
Carter, L. Philip *neurosurgeon, consultant*
Cauthron, Robin J. *federal judge*
Champlin, Richard H. *lawyer, insurance company executive*
Clark, Robert Lloyd, Jr. *librarian*
Coats, Andrew Montgomery *lawyer, former mayor*
†Cole, Helen *state leglislator*
Collins, William Edward *aeromedical administrator, researcher*
†Comchoc, Rudolph A. *food distribution company executive*
Comp, Philip Cinnamon *medical researcher*
Coover-Clark, Carol *architect*
Couch, James Russell, Jr. *neurology educator*
Court, Leonard *lawyer*
Crabtree, Jack Turner *lawyer*
Cunningham, Stanley Lloyd *lawyer*
Danforth, Louis Fremont *banker, educator*
Daugherty, Frederick Alvin *federal judge*
Davis, Emery Stephen *wholesale food company executive*
Deckert, Gordon Harmon *psychiatrist, educator*
Dell'Orco, Robert T. *cell biologist, researcher*
Dew, Jess Edward *chemical engineer*
Dunlap, E.T. *retired educational administrator, consultant*
Dunn, Parker Southerland *retired chemical company consultant*
Durland, Jack Raymond *lawyer*
Everett, Mark Allen *dermatologist, educator*
†Fair, Michael Edward *state senator*
†Fallin, Mary Copeland *state representative*
Fellers, James Davison *lawyer*
Felton, Warren Locker, II *surgeon*
Fishburne, John Ingram, Jr. *obstetrician-gynecologist, educator*
†Ford, Charles Reed *state senator*
Ford, Michael Raye *lawyer*
Forni, Patricia Rose *nursing educator, university dean*
†Garrett, Sandy Langley *school system administrator*
Gaylord, Edward Lewis *publishing company executive*
Gourley, James Leland *editor, publishing executive*
Gumerson, Jean Gilderhus *health foundation executive*
Halverstadt, Donald Bruce *urologist, educator*
Hambrick, Marvin K. *energy company executive*
Hargrave, Rudolph *state supreme court justice*
Harlan, Ross Edgar *retired utility company executive, writer, lecturer, consultant*
Harlow, James Gindling, Jr. *utility executive*
Harrington, Gary Burnes *controller*
Hartsuck, Jean Ann *chemist*
Haywood, B(etty) J(ean) *anesthesiologist*
†Hefner, Jerry W. *state legislator, concrete block plant executive*
Heimann, William Emil *retired lawyer*
Hemry, Jerome Eldon *lawyer*
Hendrick, Howard H. *lawyer, state senator*
Henley, Everett Scott *health care marketing firm executive*
†Henry, Brad *state legislator, lawyer*
Henry, Claudette *state official*
Hodges, Ralph B. *state supreme court justice*
Holder, Lee *educator and university dean emeritus*
Holloway, William J., Jr. *federal judge*
Hough, Jack Van Doren *otologist*
Hupfeld, Stanley Francis *health care executive*
Ille, Bernard Glenn *insurance company executive*
Irwin, Pat *federal magistrate judge*
Johnson, James Terence *college president, lawyer, clergyman*
Johnson, Lonnie *special education educator*
Jones, Robert Lee *religion educator*
†Keller, Bryan J. *lawyer*
†Kelley, Carl Ed(win) *editor*
Kennedy, John H., Jr. *former state official*
†Kertok, Michael Bowers *architect, interior designer*
Kilbourne, Lewis Buckner *food service company executive*
Kimerer, Neil Banard, Sr. *psychiatrist, educator*
Kirkpatrick, John Elson *oil company executive, retired naval reserve officer*
Lambird, Mona Salyer *lawyer*
Lane, James Franklin *judge*
Lavender, Robert Eugene *state supreme court justice*
†Leftwich, Keith C. *state senator, economic development consultant*
Legg, William Jefferson *lawyer*
Leonard, Timothy Dwight *federal judge*
Lester, Andrew William *lawyer*
†Lewis, C. A. *church administrator*
Lewis, Wilbur Curtis *surgeon*
Lhevine, Dave Bernard *radiologist, educator*
†Locke, William Sweet *manufacturing executive*
Loving, Susan B. *state attorney general*
Lynn, C(harles) Stephen *franchising company executive*
Lynn, Thomas Neil, Jr. *medical center administrator, physician*
Macer, Dan Johnstone *retired hospital administrator*
Magarian, Robert Armen *medicinal chemist, researcher, educator*
Marshall, Gerald Robert *consultant*
Mason, Betty G(wendolyn) Hopkins *school system administrator*
†Massion, Walter Herbert *anesthesiologist, educator*
McCoy, Wesley Lawrence *musician, conductor, educator*
McKenny, Jere Wesley *energy firm executive*
Mc Pherson, Frank Alfred *manufacturing corporate executive*
Mee, Herb, Jr. *natural resource/environmental services executive*
Meeks, Patricia Lowe *secondary education educator*
†Meyers, Theodore A. *food products executive*
Mildren, Jack *lieutenant governor*
†Miles-LaGrange, Vicki *prosecutor*
Milsten, Robert B. *lawyer*
Miskovsky, George, Sr. *lawyer*
Moler, Edward Harold *lawyer*
Moll, John Edgar *wholesale grocery company executive*
†Moody, Robert M. *bishop*
Moore, Joanne Iweita *pharmacologist, educator*
†Morgan, Judith A. *law librarian*
Necco, Alexander David *lawyer, educator*
†Nelson, Charles E. *bank holding executive*
Nesbitt, Charles Rudolph *state agency administrator*
†Nichols, J. Larry *energy company executive, lawyer*
Noakes, Betty L. *elementary education educator*
Norick, Ronald J. *mayor of Oklahoma City*
Oehlert, William Herbert, Jr. *cardiologist, administrator, educator*
O'Keeffe, Hugh Williams *oil industry executive*
Opala, Marian P(eter) *state supreme court justice*
Painton, Ira Wayne *retired securities executive*
Payne, Gareld Gene *vocal music educator, medical transcriptionist*
Peace, H. W., II *oil company executive*
Pishkin, Vladimir *psychologist, educator*
Pitts, Bill *museum director*
†Ponder, Alonza *church administrator*
†Pope, Tim L. *state legislator, consultant*
Price, B. Byron *museum director*
†Raydon, Max E. *consumer products company executive*
Reynolds, Norman Eben *lawyer*
Robison, Clarence, Jr. *surgeon*
†Ross, William Jarboe *lawyer*
Rossavik, Ivar Kristian *obstetrician/gynecologist*
Russell, David L. *federal judge*
Ryan, Patrick J. *electric utility company executive*
†Schmidt, Fred C. *architect*
Scott, Lawrence Vernon *microbiology educator*
Scribner, Ronald Kent *microbiologist*
Seideman, Ruth Evelyn Young *nurse educator*
Simmons, Jesse Doyle *minister, educator*
Smith, Clodus Ray *academic administrator*
Smith, Robert Walter *food company executive*
Snider, John Joseph *lawyer*
Solomon, Dan Eugene *bishop*
Spencer, Melvin Joe *hospital administrator, lawyer*
Steinhorn, Irwin Harry *lawyer, educator, corporate executive*
Stephens, Denny *librarian*
†Stewart, C.C., Jr. *mechanical engineer*
Summers, Hardy *state supreme court justice*
Taft, Richard George *lawyer*
†Taylor, Stratton *state senator, lawyer*
Thompson, Lee Bennett *lawyer*
Thompson, Ralph Gordon *federal judge*
Thurman, William Gentry *medical research foundation executive, pediatric hematology and oncology physician, educator*
Tolbert, James R., III *financial executive*
†Triplett, E. Eugene *editor*
Troelstra, Arne *physics educator*
Turpen, Michael Craig *lawyer*
Underwood, Bernard Edward *religious organization administrator*
Valentine, Alan Darrell *symphony orchestra executive*
Verity, George Luther *lawyer*
Walker, C. Eugene *psychology educator*
Walker, Jerald Carter *university administrator, minister*
Walsh, Lawrence Edward *lawyer*
Walters, David *governor*
†Weedn, Trish *state legislator*
Werries, E. Dean *food distribution company executive*
West, Lee Roy *federal judge*
Wheat, Willis James *university dean, management educator*
†Wickens, Donald Lee *engineer executive, consultant, rancher*
Williams, George Rainey *surgeon, educator*
Williams, Richard Donald *retired wholesale food company executive*
Williams, William Ralston *retired bank and trust company executive*
Wilson, Alma *state supreme court justice*
Woodruff, Judson Sage *lawyer*
Woods, Pendleton *college offical, author*
Zuhdi, Nazih *surgeon*

Oktaha
Taylor, Clayton Charles *oil company executive, rancher*

Pauls Valley
Hope, Garland Howard *lawyer, retired judge*

Pawhuska
Strahm, Samuel Edward *veterinarian*

Ponca City
Bolene, Margaret Rosalie Steele *bacteriologist, civic worker*
Northcutt, Clarence Dewey *lawyer*

Poteau
Harper, S. Birnie *bakery executive*

Pryor
†Burdick, Larry G. *school system administrator*

Purcell
Lucas, Roy Edward, Jr. *minister*

Sand Springs
Ackerman, Robert Wallace *steel company executive*

Shawnee
Agee, Bob R. *university president, educator, minister*
McCaffree, Brother Benedict *museum director*

Stillwater
Agnew, Theodore Lee, Jr. *historian, educator*
Bantle, John Albert, II *zoology educator*
Bell, Kenneth John *chemical engineer*
Berlin, Kenneth Darrell *chemistry educator, consultant, researcher*
Boger, Lawrence Leroy *university president emeritus*
Browning, Charles Benton *university dean, agricultural educator*
Brusewitz, Gerald Henry *agricultural engineering educator, researcher*
Bynum, Jack Edward, Jr. *sociology educator*
Campbell, John Roy *animal scientist educator, academic administrator*
Case, Kenneth Eugene *industrial engineering educator*
Confer, Anthony Wayne *veterinary pathologist, educator*
Cooper, Donald Lee *physician*
Durham, Norman Nevill *microbiologist, scientist, educator*
Ewing, Sidney Alton *veterinary medical educator, parasitologist*
Fischer, LeRoy Henry *historian, educator*
Folks, J. Leroy *statistician, educator*
Gorin, George *retired chemistry educator*
Grischkowsky, Daniel Richard *research scientist, educator*
Haan, Charles Thomas *agricultural engineering educator*
Hooper, Billy Ernest *medical association administrator*
Jadlow, Joseph Martin *economics educator*
Johnson, Edward Roy *library director*
Kamm, Robert B. *former academic administrator, educator, author, diplomat*
Langwig, John Edward *retired wood science educator*
†Lawson, F. D. *bishop*
Leach, Franklin Rollin *biochemistry educator*
Lu, Huizhu *computer scientist, educator*
Luebke, Neil Robert *philosophy educator*
Maddox, Robert Nott *chemical engineer, educator*
Matoy, Elizabeth Ann *publishing executive*
Mc Collom, Kenneth Allen *retired university dean*
Mc Farland, Frank Eugene *university official*
Mize, Joe Henry *industrial engineer, educator*
Moomaw, Ronald Lee *economics educator*
†Nofziger, David Lynn *soil physicist, educator*
†Noyes, Ronald T. *agricultural engineering educator*
Owens, Fredric Newell *animal nutritionist, educator*
Parcher, James Vernon *civil engineering educator, consultant*
Poole, Richard William *economics educator*
†Quinn, Art Jay *veterinarian*
Sandmeyer, Robert Lee *university dean, economist*
Shearer, John Clyde *economics consultant, labor arbitrator, international manpower consultant*
Shirley, Glenn Dean *writer*
†Thompson, David Russell *agricultural engineering educator, academic dean*
Turner, Wayne Connelly *industrial engineer, educator*

Tahlequah
†Mankiller, Wilma Pearl *tribal leader*
†Rozell, Herbert *construction executive, senator*
Webster, Edgar Lewis *sociology educator, program director*

Tinker AFB
Pray, Donald George *aerospace engineer*

Tulsa
Abbott, William Thomas *claim specialist*
Ahmadieh, Aziz *metallurgy materials science educator*
Alexander, John Robert *hospital administrator, internist*
Anderson, Peer LaFollette *petroleum corporation executive*
Arrington, John Leslie, Jr. *lawyer*
†Baker, Thomas L. *protective services official*
Barnes, James E. *energy company executive*
†Barnett, Howard Gentry, Jr. *publishing executive, lawyer*
Beasley, William Rex *judge*
Bell, Roseanne *business owner, consultant*
Berlin, Steven Ritt *oil company financial official*
Biolchini, Robert Fredrick *lawyer*
Blackstock, LeRoy *lawyer*
Bonsall, Joseph Sloan, Jr. *singer*
Bowen, William Augustus *financial consultant*
Braumiller, Allen Spooner *oil and gas exploration company executive, geologist*
Breck, Howard Rolland *geophysicist*
Brett, Thomas Rutherford *federal judge*
Brightmire, Paul William *judge*
Bryant, Hubert Hale *lawyer*
Buckley, Thomas Hugh *historian, educator*
Bump, Larry J. *engineering and construction company executive*
Bynum, George T., III (Ted Bynum) *biomedical company executive*
Callaham, Thomas Hunter *former business executive*
Calvert, Delbert William *chemical company executive*
Calvert, Jon Channing *family practice physician*
Clark, Roy *singer, musician, business executive*
Cole, Clyde Curtis, Jr. *association executive*
Collins, John Roger *aerospace company executive*
Cook, Harold Dale *federal judge*
Cooper, Richard Casey *lawyer*
Cox, William Jackson *bishop*
†Craft, Joseph W., III *corporate lawyer*
Crawford, B(urnett) Hayden *lawyer*
†Cullison, Robert Virl *state senator*
Culp, Even Asher *communications educator*
Daniel, Samuel Phillips *lawyer*
Donaldson, Robert Herschel *university president*
Dotson, George Stephen *drilling company executive*
Dunn, Clark Allan *civil engineer, educator*
Earlougher, Robert Charles, Sr. *petroleum engineer*
Eaton, Leonard James, Jr. *banker*
Elkins, Lloyd Edwin, Sr. *petroleum engineer, energy consultant*
†Eriksen, Vernon Lee *manufacturing engineering executive*
Farrell, John L., Jr. *lawyer, business executive*
Fate, Martin Eugene, Jr. *utility company executive*
Fender, Freddy (Baldemar Huerta) *singer*
Frey, Martin Alan *lawyer, educator*
Gable, G. Ellis *lawyer*
Gaddis, Richard William *educational administrator, education consultant*
Gentry, Bern Leon, Sr. *minority consulting company executive*
Gottschalk, Sister Mary Therese *nun, hospital administrator*
Graham, Tony M. *attorney*
Hale, Richard Lee *magazine editor*
Hall, Ronald E. *oil company executive*
Haring, Robert Westing *newspaper editor*
Hawkins, Francis Glenn *banker, lawyer*
Helmerich, Hans Christian *oil company executive*
Helmerich, Walter Hugo, III *oil company executive*
Henderson, Robert Waugh *retired religion educator, minister*
Hood, Charles Hurlburt *advertising agency executive*
Horkey, William Richard *retired diversified oil company executive*
Horn, Myron Kay *consulting petroleum geologist, author, educator*
†Horner, Maxine Edwyna Cissel *state legislator*
Howard, Gene Claude *lawyer, former state senator*
Howe, Robert Melvin *oil company executive*
†Howerton, Alvin *retail executive*
Huber, Fritz Godfrey *physical education educator, excercise physiologist*
Hulings, Norman McDermott, Jr. *energy consultant, former company executive*
†Huls, Harrison *wholesale and retail grocery company executive*
Ingram, Charles Clark, Jr. *energy company executive*
Janssen, Erwin T. *health science foundation administrator, psychiatrist*
Jasinski, Roman Larkin *artistic director*
Jedel, Peter Harold *investment executive*
Jones, Jenk, Jr. *newspaper editor*
Jones, Jenkin Lloyd *retired newspaper publisher*
Jones, Robert Lawton *architect, planner, educator*
Kalbfleisch, John McDowell *cardiologist, educator*
Keating, Francis Anthony, II *lawyer*
Kihle, Donald Arthur *lawyer*
Killin, Charles Clark *lawyer*
King, Peter Cotterill *former utilities executive*
†Kitchen, Brent A. *airport executive*
Knaust, Clara Doss *retired elementary educator*
†Knowles, Billy C. *architect*
Kothe, Charles Aloysius *lawyer*
Kruse, David Louis, II *transportation company executive*
Langholz, Robert Wayne *lawyer, investor*
Larkin, Moscelyne *retired artistic director, dancer*
Lewis, Ceylon Smith, Jr. *physician*
Lewis, John Furman *lawyer, oil company executive*
Lowd, Judson Dean *oil and gas processing equipment manufacturing executive*
Luthey, Graydon Dean, Jr. *lawyer*
Major, John Keene *radio broadcasting executive*
McConnell, Charles Goodloe *service company executive*
McCormick, Donald *architect, composer*
Milsten, David Randolph *lawyer*
Mojtabai, Ann Grace *author, educator*
Narwold, Lewis Lammers *paper products manufacturer*
Neas, John Theodore *petroleum company executive*
Nettles, John Barnwell *obstetrics and gynecology educator*
Newman, Richard Oakley *utilities executive, consultant*
O'Brien, Darcy *English educator, writer*
O'Toole, Allan Thomas *electric utility executive*
Oxley, John Thurman *ranching and investments executive, former petroleum company executive*
Parker, Robert Lee, Sr. *petroleum engineer, drilling company executive*
Parker, Robert Lee, Jr. *drilling company executive*
†Philion, James Robert *business executive*
Plunket, Daniel Clark *pediatrician*
†Powell, Sara Jordan *musician, religious worker*
Roberts, (Granville) Oral *clergyman*
Robertson, Peter James *oil company executive*
Rubenstein, Bernard *orchestra conductor*
†Rubottom, Donald Julian *management consultant*
Sanditen, Edgar Richard *investment company executive*
Savage, M. Susan *mayor*
Schmidt, Sister Mary Sylvia (Patricia Ella Nora Schmidt) *nun*
Schwartz, Bernard *lawyer, educator*
†Scott, J. D. *oil company executive*
Seymour, Stephanie Kulp *federal judge*
Shafer, J. M. *utility administrator*
†Smith, Jerry Lee *state senator*
Smothers, William Edgar, Jr. *geophysical exploration company treasurer*
Sterban, Richard Anthony *singer*
Stover, Phil Sheridan, Jr. *investment consultant*
Taylor, Joe Clinton *judge*
Thomas, Robert Eggleston *former corporate executive*
Tompkins, Robert George *physician*
†Troccoli, Joan Carpenter *museum director*
Upton, Howard B., Jr. *management columnist, lawyer*
Wagner, John Leo *federal judge, lawyer*
Walker, Floyd Lee *lawyer*
Wesenberg, John Herman *association executive*
White, Ralph Dallas *retired health insurance executive*
Williams, David Rogerson, Jr. *engineer, business executive*
Williams, John Horter *civil engineer, oil, gas, telecommunications and allied products distribution company executive*
Williams, Joseph Hill *diversified industry executive*
†Williams, Penny *state legislator*
Williford, Richard Allen *oil executive, flight simulator company executive*
Woodrum, Patricia Ann *librarian*

Vinita
Curnutte, Mark William *lawyer*
Neer, Charles Sumner, II *orthopaedic surgeon, educator*

Wanette
Thompson, Joyce Elizabeth *retired home economics educator*

Warr Acres
†Phillips, Richard C. *real estate executive*

Washington
Sliepcevich, Cedomir M. engineering educator

Watonga
Hoberecht, Earnest abstract company executive, former newspaper executive

Weatherford
Hamm, Donald Ivan retired chemistry educator, university dean
†Hoke, Sheila Wilder librarian

OREGON

Albany
Ball, Douglas Schelling oil, gas and mining consultant
†Dooley, George Joseph, III metallurgist
Norman, E. Gladys business computer educator, consultant
Wood, Kenneth Arthur newspaper editor emeritus, writer

Applegate
Boyle, (Charles) Keith artist, educator

Ashland
Addicott, Warren Oliver geologist, educator
Bornet, Vaughn Davis former history and social science educator, research historian
Coffey, Marvin Dale biology educator
Cox, Joseph William academic administrator
Farrimond, George Francis, Jr. management educator
Grover, James Robb retired chemist, editor
Hay, Richard Laurence theater scenic designer
Hemp, Ralph Clyde retired reinsurance company executive, consultant, arbitrator, umpire
Hirschfeld, Gerald Joseph cinematographer
Houston, John Albert political science educator
Kreisman, Arthur higher education consultant, humanities educator emeritus
Levy, Leonard Williams history educator, author
Mularz, Theodore Leonard architect
Smith, G(odfrey) T(aylor) academic administrator
Walt, Harold Richard rancher

Astoria
Bainer, Philip La Vern retired college president
Haskell, Donald McMillan lawyer

Baker City
Graham, Beardsley management consultant

Beaverton
Bosch, Samuel Henry electronics company executive
Chang, David Ping-Chung business consultant, architect
Cymbala, Robert Joseph communications company executive
Henderson, George Miller foundation executive, former banker
Knight, Philip H(ampson) shoe manufacturing company executive
Masi, Edward A. computer company executive
Montagna, William scientist
Pond, Patricia Brown library science educator, university administrator
Rattner, Justin supercomputer research manager

Bend
†Babcock, Walter Christian, Jr. membrane company executive
†Clarno, Beverly Ann state legislator, farmer
Connolly, Thomas Joseph bishop
†Hanes, Clifford Ronald religious denomination administrator
Hurley, James Vincent lawyer
†Luke, Dennis Robert state legislator, home building company executive
Mayer, Richard Dean mathematics educator
Wonser, Michael Dean retired public affairs director, art educator

Brookings
Maxwell, William Stirling retired lawyer
Olsen, Edward Gustave education educator emeritus

Burns
†Timms, Eugene Dale wholesale business owner, state senator

Cannon Beach
Greaver, Harry artist
Landon, Sealand Whitney lawyer

Clackamas
Merrill, William Dean architect, medical facility planning consultant

Coos Bay
Shepard, Robert Carlton English language educator

Coquille
Taylor, George Frederick newspaper publisher, editor

Corvallis
Becker, Boris William business educator
Becker, Robert Richard biochemist, educator
Byrne, John Vincent academic administrator
†Caldwell, Douglas Ray oceanographer, educator
Castle, Emery Neal agricultural and resource economist, educator
Chambers, Kenton Lee botany educator
Davis, John Rowland university administrator
Drake, Charles Whitney physicist
Engelbrecht, Rudolf electrical engineering educator
Evans, Harold J. plant physiologist, biochemist, educator
Forbes, Leonard engineering educator
Frakes, Rod Vance plant geneticist, educator
Frazier, William A. retired horticulturist
†George, Melvin Ray library director, consultant
Gillis, John Simon psychologist, educator
Godfrey, Samuel Addison retired telephone company executive
Hall, Don Alan editor, writer
†Hall, Philip G. engineering executive
Hansen, Hugh Justin agricultural engineer
Harter, Lafayette George, Jr. economics educator emeritus
†Hassebroek, Lyle G. engineering company executive
Horne, Frederick Herbert academic administrator, chemistry educator
Hunt, Donald R. retired librarian
Keller, George Henrik marine geologist
Knudsen, James George chemical engineer, educator
Koller, Loren D. veterinary medicine educator
Kronstad, Warren Ervind genetics educator, researcher
Mac Vicar, Robert William retired university administrator
Miner, John Ronald agricultural engineer
Mohler, Ronald Rutt electrical engineering educator
Moore, Thomas Carrol botanist, educator
Morita, Richard Yukio microbiology and oceanography educator
†Murphy, Thomas Allen government research administrator, scientist
Oldfield, James Edmund nutrition educator
Olleman, Roger Dean industry consultant, former metallurgical engineering educator
Parker, Donald Fred college dean, human resources management educator
Pearson, Albert Marchant food science and nutrition educator
Petersen, Bent Edvard mathematician, educator
†Reed, Donald James biochemistry educator
Shoemaker, David Powell chemist, educator
†Skelton, John Edward computer science educator, consultant
Sleight, Arthur William chemist, educator
Sollitt, Charles Kevin ocean engineering educator, laboratory director
Somero, George Nicholls biology educator
Tarrant, Robert Frank soil science educator, researcher
Temes, Gabor Charles electrical engineering educator
Thomas, Thomas Darrah chemistry educator
Towey, Richard Edward economics educator
Trappe, James Martin mycologist
Van Holde, Kensal Edward biochemistry educator
Verts, Lita Jeanne university administrator
†Welty, James R. mechanical engineer, educator
Westwood, Melvin Neil horticulturist, pomologist
Wilkins, Caroline Hanke consumer agency administrator, political worker
Willis, David Lee radiation biology educator
Yeats, Robert Sheppard geologist, educator
Young, J. Lowell soil chemist, biologist
Young, Roy Alton university administrator, educator
Zauner, Christian Walter exercise physiologist, exercise science educator, exercise rehabilitation consultant
Zobel, Donald Bruce botany educator
Zwahlen, Fred Casper, Jr. journalism educator

Dillard
†Ford, Kenneth lumber, wood products company executive

Eugene
Acker, Martin Herbert psychotherapist, educator
Aikens, C(lyde) Melvin anthropology educator, archaeologist
Andrews, Fred Charles mathematics educator
Bailey, Exine Margaret Anderson soprano, educator
Baker, Alton Fletcher, Jr. newspaper editor
Baker, Edwin Moody retired newspaper publisher
Becker, Wesley Clemence psychology educator emeritus
Bennett, Robert Royce engineering and management consultant
Birn, Raymond Francis historian, educator
Boekelheide, Virgil Carl chemistry educator
Boggs, Sam, Jr. geology educator
Chezem, Curtis Gordon physicist, former retail executive
Clark, Chapin DeWitt law educator
Coffin, Thomas M. federal magistrate judge
Crasemann, Bernd physicist, educator
Dasso, Jerome Joseph real estate educator, consultant
Davis, Richard Malone economics educator
Dawes, Carol J. clinical psychologist
Decker Slaney, Mary Teresa Olympic athlete
Deshpande, Nilendra Ganesh physics educator
Donnelly, Marian Card art historian, educator
Donnelly, Russell James physicist, educator
Eisert, Debra Claire pediatric psychologist
Flanagan, Latham, Jr. surgeon
Franklin, Jon Daniel journalist, science writer, educator
Frohnmayer, David Braden university president
Gall, Meredith Damien (Meredith Mark Damien Gall) education educator, author
Girardeau, Marvin Denham physics educator
Griffith, Osbie Hayes chemistry educator
†Hildebrand, Carol Ilene librarian
Hildreth, Clifford retired economist, educator
Hogan, Michael R(obert) federal judge
†Holser, William Thomas geochemistry educator, geologist
Holzapfel, Christina Marie biologist
†Hosticka, Carl Joseph academic administrator, educator, legislator
Ismach, Arnold Harvey journalism educator
Khang, Chulsoon economics educator
Lemert, James Bolton journalist, educator
Littman, Richard Anton psychologist, educator
Matthews, Brian W. molecular biology educator
Mazo, Robert Marc chemistry educator
McGuire, Timothy William economics and management educator, dean
McTigue, Bernard Francis curator, consultant
Mikesell, Raymond Frech economics educator
Morrison, Perry David librarian, educator
Mowday, Richard Thomas management educator
Mumford, William Porter, II lawyer
Nissel, Martin radiologist, consultant
Noyes, Richard Macy physical chemist, educator
Osborn, Ronald Edwin minister, church history educator
Pascal, C(ecil) Bennett classics educator
Peticolas, Warner Leland physical chemistry educator
Piele, Philip Kern education infosystems educator
Reinmuth, James E. college dean
†Rendall, Steven Finlay language educator, editor, translator, critic
Sahlstrom, E(lmer) B(ernard) lawyer
Sanders, Jack Thomas religious studies educator
Schellman, John A. chemistry educator
Scoles, Eugene Francis legal educator, lawyer
Sherriffs, Ronald Everett communications and film educator
Slocum, Barclay veterinary orthopedic surgeon
Sprague, George Frederick geneticist
Starr, Grier Forsythe retired pathologist
†Stirling, Isabel Ann science librarian
Stone, Joe Allan economics educator
Tull, Donald Stanley marketing educator
Tykeson, Donald Erwin broadcasting executive
von Hippel, Peter Hans chemistry educator
†Walker, Hill M. educator
Walton, Ralph Ervin community mental health services administrator
Wickes, George English educator, writer
Wiley, Carl Ross timber company executive
†Wilhelm, Kate (Katy Gertrude) author

Florence
Ericksen, Jerald Laverne educator, engineering scientist
Gray, Augustine Heard, Jr. computer consultant

Gleneden Beach
Marks, Arnold journalist

Grants Pass
Naylor, John Thomas telephone company executive
Smith, Barnard Elliot management educator

Gresham
†Caldwell, Robert John newspaper editor
Light, Betty Jensen Pritchett former college dean
Nicholson, R. Stephen organization administrator
Poulton, Charles Edgar natural resources consultant

Hillsboro
Gerlach, Robert Louis research and development executive, physicist

Klamath Falls
Ehlers, Eleanor May Collier (Mrs. Frederick Burton Ehlers) civic worker
Wells, Lu artist

La Grande
Carey, Willard Keith lawyer
Gilbert, David Erwin university president, physicist

Lake Oswego
Gawf, John Lee foreign service officer
Kupel, Frederick John counselor
Ladehoff, Robert Louis bishop
Le Shana, David Charles seminary president
Thong, Tran scientist, engineer, researcher
Worsley, John Clayton architect

Lincoln City
Gehrig, Edward Harry electrical engineer, consultant

Marylhurst
Kelley, George Gregory business educator, management consultant

McMinnville
Goodrich, Kenneth Paul college dean
McGillivray, Karen elementary school educator
Walker, Charles Urmston college administrator

Medford
Barnum, William Laird pedodontist
Bunten, John William school system administrator
Cutler, Kenneth Ross investment company and mutual fund executive
Hennion, Reeve Lawrence communications executive
Keener, John Wesley management consultant
O'Connor, Karl William lawyer
†Skelton, Douglas H. architect
Sours, James Kingsley association executive, former college president
†Straus, David A. architectural firm executive

Monmouth
Forcier, Richard Charles information technology educator, computer applications consultant
Meyers, Richard Stuart college president
Shay, Roshani Cari political science educator
White, Donald Harvey physicist, educator

Myrtle Point
Walsh, Don marine consultant, executive

Newport
Gordon, Walter architect
Kennedy, Richard Jerome writer
Langrock, Karl Frederick former academic administrator
Weber, Lavern John marine life administrator, educator

Oakland
Smelt, Ronald retired aircraft company executive

Otter Rock
Eaton, Leonard Kimball retired architecture educator
Kassner, Michael Ernest materials science educator, researcher

Pendleton
Bloom, Stephen Michael lawyer, judge
Klepper, Elizabeth Lee physiologist
Kottkamp, John Harlan lawyer
Lund, Steve agronomist, research administrator
†Smiley, Richard Wayne research center administrator, researcher

Pleasant Hill
Kesey, Ken writer

Port Orford
Drinnon, Richard history educator

Portland
Abbott, Carl John urban studies and planning educator
Abravanel, Allan Ray lawyer
Adelman, Rick professional basketball coach
Ahuja, Jagdish Chand mathematics educator
Anderson, Herbert H. lawyer
Artaud-Wild, Sabine Marie research dietitian
Arthur, Michael Elbert lawyer
Babcock, Robert Evans lawyer
Bach, Richard D. lawyer
Bailey, Robert C. opera company executive
Bakkensen, John Reser lawyer
†Barmack, Neal Herbert neuroscientist
Bartlett, Thomas Alva educational administrator
Bates, Richard Mather dentist
Bauer, Louis Edward retail bookstore executive, educator
Beatty, John Cabeen, Jr. judge
Bennett, Douglas Carleton academic administrator
Bennett, William Michael physician
†Benson, George L. school system administrator
Benson, John Alexander, Jr. physician, educator
Berthelsdorf, Siegfried psychiatrist
Bhatia, Peter K. editor, journalist
Biggs, Hugh Lawry lawyer
†Bishop, B. H. textile manufacturing executive
Blanford, J(ohn) William department store company executive
Blumel, Joseph Carlton university president
Booth, Brian Geddes lawyer
Boyman, John Edward George individual/organizational transition consultant
Bragdon, Paul Errol foundation administrator
Brenneman, Delbert Jay lawyer
Brim, Armand Eugene health care executive
Browne, Joseph Peter librarian
Brummett, Robert Eddie pharmacology educator
Bull, Bergen Ira equipment manufacturing company executive
Burns, James M. federal judge
Butler, Leslie Ann advertising executive, portrait artist
Cable, John Franklin lawyer
Campbell, Charles Joy fishery biologist
Campbell, John Richard pediatric surgeon
Cantlin, Richard Anthony lawyer
†Carlesimo, P. J. (Peter J. Carlesimo) basketball coach
Carlsen, Clifford Norman, Jr. lawyer
Carmack, Mildred Jean lawyer
Carver, Loyce Cleo clergyman
Cateora, Philip Rene business educator, author
Chernoff, Daniel Paregol patent lawyer
†Clarke, J(oseph) Henry dental educator, dentist
Claycomb, Cecil Keith biochemist, educator
Collins, Maribeth Wilson foundation executive
Commerford, Kathleen Anne psychologist
Congdon, Marsha B. telecommunications executive
Conkling, Roger Linton consultant, business administration educator, retired utility executive
Connor, William Elliott physician, educator
Cooley, Edward H. castings manufacturing company executive
Cooper, Ginnie library director
Crabbs, Roger Alan publisher, consultant, small business owner, educator
Crawshaw, Ralph psychiatrist
Cronyn, Marshall William chemistry educator
Crow, William Beryl lawyer
Crowell, John B., Jr. lawyer, former government official
†Cusma, Rena zoological park administrator
Dahl, Joyle Cochran lawyer
Davidson, Crow Girard lawyer
Davis, James Allan gerontologist, educator
Dean, E. Joseph lawyer
DeChaine, Dean Dennis lawyer
Deering, Thomas Phillips lawyer
DePreist, James Anderson conductor
Dew, William Waldo, Jr. bishop
Dotten, Michael Chester lawyer
Drexler, Clyde professional basketball player
Drummond, Gerard Kasper lawyer, retired minerals company executive
Dunne, Thomas Gregory chemistry educator, researcher
Eakin, Margaretta Morgan lawyer
Edwards, Richard Alan lawyer
Eichinger, Marilynne H. museum administrator
Ellis, Barnes Humphreys lawyer
Epstein, Edward Louis lawyer
Eshelman, William Robert librarian, editor
Faust, John Roosevelt, Jr. lawyer
Fell, James F. lawyer
Feuerstein, Howard M. lawyer
Flowerree, Robert Edmund retired forest products company executive
Foehl, Edward Albert chemical company executive
Fogg, George Kephart lawyer
Foley, Ridgway Knight, Jr. lawyer, writer
Franz, Robert Warren banker
Franzke, Richard Albert lawyer
†Frasca, Robert John architect
Fraunfelder, Frederick Theodore ophthalmologist, educator
Frazier, J(ohn) Phillip manufacturing company executive
†Freiser, Leonard Harold engineering library director
Frisbee, Don Calvin retired utilities executive
Frolick, Patricia May educator
Fronk, William Joseph retired machinery company executive
Frye, Helen Jackson federal judge
Geddes, Robert Dale lawyer
Georges, Maurice Ostrow lawyer
Gerow, Edwin Mahaffey Indic culture educator
Gilkey, Gordon Waverly curator, artist
Girard, Leonard Arthur lawyer
Girard, Leonard Arthur lawyer, corporate executive
Glasgow, William Jacob lawyer
Glick, Richard Myron lawyer
Glickman, Harry professional basketball team executive
Goldfarb, Timothy Moore hospital administrator
†Graves, Earl William, Jr. journalist
Gray, John Delton retired manufacturing company executive
†Green, Cyril Kenneth retail company executive
Green, David William lawyer
Greenlick, Merwyn Ronald health services researcher
Greenstein, Merle Edward import/export company executive
Greer, Monte Arnold physician, educator
Griffith, Stephen Loyal lawyer
Gunsul, Brooks R. W. architect
†Hacker, Thomas Owen architect
Hagenstein, William David consulting forester
Hager, Orval O. lawyer
Halle, John Joseph lawyer
†Halverson, Gerald B. insurance company executive
Hanna, Harry Mitchell lawyer
Hardy, Randall Webster utility executive
Harrison, Ken L. holding company and electric utility executive
Hart, C. Allan lawyer
Hathaway, Paul L., Jr. natural gas company executive

†Hatt, Peter McLeod *advertising executive*
Heatherington, J. Scott *retired osteopathic physician and surgeon*
†Hebe, James L. *trucking executive*
†Heiner, Lawrence Elden *mineral company executive*
Helmer, M. Christie *lawyer*
Hergenhan, Kenneth William *lawyer*
Herndon, Robert McCulloch *experimental neurologist*
Hilbert, Bernard Charles *retired union official*
Hill, Andrew William *jazz musician, composer*
Hill, Francis Frederick *gas company executive*
Hill, Wilmer Bailey *administrative law judge*
Hinkle, Charles Frederick *lawyer, clergyman, educator*
Hofer, Judith K. *retail company executive*
Hoffman, Jack Leroy *lawyer*
Holman, Donald Reid *lawyer*
Holmes, Michael Gene *lawyer*
Houghton, Donald Cary *pathology educator*
Howorth, David Bishop *lawyer*
Huenemann, Ruben Henry *clergyman*
Hutchens, Tyra Thornton *physician, educator*
Jacob, Nancy Louise *financial consultant*
Jacob, Stanley Wallace *surgeon, educator*
Jenkins, Donald John *art museum administrator*
Jensen, Edmund Paul *bank holding company executive*
†Johnston, Virginia Evelyn *editor*
†Jones, Alan C. *grocery company executive*
Jones, Richard Theodore *biochemistry educator*
Jones, Robert Edward *federal judge*
Josephson, Richard Carl *lawyer*
Jungers, Francis *oil consultant*
Katz, Vera *mayor, former college administrator, state legislator*
Kendall, John Walker, Jr. *medical educator, researcher, university dean*
Kennedy, Jack Leland *lawyer*
Kester, Randall Blair *lawyer*
†Kilbourn, Lee Ferris *architect, specifications writer*
Kilkenny, John F. *federal judge, lawyer*
Kinzer, Donald Louis *retired historian, educator*
Kitchel, Jan Kelly *lawyer*
Kohler, Peter Ogden *physician, educator, university president*
Kolde, Bert *professional basketball team executive*
Kristof, Ladis Kris Donabed *political scientist, author*
Kuntz, Joel Dubois *lawyer*
Lang, Philip David *former state legislator, insurance company executive*
†Lanz, Robert Francis *corporate financial officer*
Larpenteur, James Albert, Jr. *lawyer*
Lawrence, Sally Clark *educational administrator*
Leavy, Edward *federal judge*
Leedy, R. Allan, Jr. *lawyer*
Leedy, Robert Allan *retired lawyer*
Lees, Martin Henry *physician*
Lendaris, George Gregory *electrical educator*
Levada, William Joseph *archbishop*
†Lim, John K. *state senator, business executive*
Lindley, Thomas Ernest *environmental lawyer, law educator*
Livingston, Louis Bayer *lawyer*
Lobitz, Walter Charles, Jr. *physician, educator*
Long, Sarah Ann *librarian*
Love, William Edward *lawyer*
Maclean, Charles (Bernard) *transition, performance recognition and workplace violence prevention consultant*
Mainwaring, William Lewis *publishing company executive, author*
Maloney, Robert E., Jr. *lawyer*
†Mapes, Jeffrey Robert *journalist*
Marsh, Malcolm F. *federal judge*
Martin, Lucy Z. *public relations executive*
Marvin, Roy Mack *metal products executive*
Matarazzo, Joseph Dominic *psychologist*
Matarazzo, Ruth Gadbois *psychology educator*
McCall, William Calder *oil and chemical company executive*
McClanahan, Mark C. *lawyer*
McClave, Donald Silsbee *association executive*
McKinley, Loren Dhue *museum director*
Meighan, Stuart Spence *hospital consultant, internist, writer*
Merlo, Harry Angelo *forest products executive*
Michael, Gary Linn *architect*
Miller, Robert G. *retail company executive*
Miller, William Richey, Jr. *lawyer*
Mooney, Michael Joseph *academic administrator, philosopher*
Moore, Conrad Lee *lawyer*
†Moose, Charles A. *state official*
†Morgan, James Earl *librarian, administrator*
Morse, Lowell Wesley *real estate executive,banking*
Mowe, Gregory Robert *lawyer*
Murphy, Francis Seward *journalist*
Myers, Clay *retired investment management company executive*
Nagel, Stanley Blair *construction and investment executive*
Nash, Frank Erwin *lawyer*
Nofziger, Sally Alene *diversified utility company executive*
Nunn, Robert Warne *lawyer*
O'Hanlon, James Barry *lawyer*
Olsen, Kurt *investment company executive, adviser*
Olson, Donald Ernest *retired physician*
Olson, Roger Norman *health service administrator*
†Orloff, Chet *cultural organization administrator*
O'Scannlain, Diarmuid Fionntain *federal judge*
Pamplin, Robert Boisseau, Sr. *consumer products executive*
Panner, Owen M. *federal judge*
†Parsons, J. A. *paper and wood products company executive*
Pearson, David Petri *chemist*
†Peressini, William Edward *financial services executive*
Peterman, Mark H. *lawyer*
Pope, Peter T. *forest products company executive*
Porter, Terry *professional basketball player*
Press, Edward *consulting physician, treasurer*
Pruitt, Charles Joseph *lawyer*
Pyle, Donald Hanson *lawyer*
Qutub, Carol Hotelling *elementary education educator*
Raaf, John Elbert *neurosurgeon, educator*
Ramaley, Judith Aitken *university president, endocrinologist*
†Ramsby, Mark Delivan *lighting designer and consultant*
Redden, James Anthony *federal judge*
Reiten, Richard G. *electric power industry executive*
Replogle, William H., II *lawyer*
Richards, Herbert East *minister emeritus, commentator*
Richardson, Campbell *lawyer*
Richter, Peter Christian *lawyer*
Riker, William Kay *pharmacologist, educator*
Ritz, Richard Ellison *architect, architectural historian, writer*
†Roberts, Gary *lawyer*
†Rooks, Judith Pence *family planning, maternal health care, midwifery consultant*
Rosenbaum, Lois Omenn *lawyer*
†Rowe, Sandra Mims *newspaper editor*
Roy, Richard E. *lawyer*
Rubin, Bruce Alan *lawyer*
Rutherford, William Drake *investment executive, lawyer*
Rutsala, Vern A. *poet, English language educator, writer*
Rutzick, Mark Charles *lawyer*
Sand, Thomas Charles *lawyer*
Scott, Lewis Kelly *lawyer*
Seil, Fredrick John *neuroscientist, neurologist*
†Sevetson, Donald James *minister, church administrator*
Sherrer, Charles David *college dean, clergyman*
Short, Robert Henry *retired utility executive*
Simpson, Robert Glenn *lawyer*
Skopil, Otto Richard, Jr. *federal judge*
Smith, Milton Ray *computer company executive, lawyer*
†Spencer, Peter Simner *neurotoxicologist*
Spiekerman, James Frederick *lawyer*
Squier, Leslie Hamilton *psychology educator*
Stalnaker, John Hulbert *physician*
†Stastny, Donald Joseph *architect*
Staver, Leroy Baldwin *banker*
Steiner, Kenneth Donald *bishop*
†Steinfeld, Ray, Jr. *museum administrator, food products executive*
Sterling, Donald Justus, Jr. *retired newspaper editor*
Stevason, John C. *lawyer*
Stevens, Wendell Claire *anesthesiology educator*
Stewart, Milton Roy *lawyer*
Stickel, Frederick A. *publisher*
†Stickel, Patrick Francis *publishing executive, newspaper*
†Stoyanov, Milan *lumber products company executive*
Sugg, John Logan (Jack Sugg) *advertising executive*
Sullivan, Edward Joseph *lawyer, educator*
Sutter, Harvey Mack *engineer,consultant*
Swan, Kenneth Carl *physician, surgeon*
Swank, Roy Laver *physician, educator, inventor*
Swindells, William, Jr. *lumber and paper company executive*
Taylor, Carson William *electrical engineer*
Taylor, Robert Brown *medical educator*
Terkla, Louis Gabriel *retired university dean*
†Thurston, George R. *lumber company executive*
Tilbury, Roger Graydon *lawyer, rancher*
Van Hassel, Henry John *dentist, educator, university dean*
Van Valkenburg, Edgar Walter *lawyer*
Vaughan, Thomas James Gregory *historian*
Waddingham, John Alfred *artist, journalist*
Waggoner, James Clyde *lawyer*
Waldschmidt, Paul Edward *clergyman*
Walters, Stephen Scott *lawyer*
†Warner, David Gill *wholesale food distributing company executive*
Warren, Robert Carlton *manufacturing company executive*
Weaver, Delbert Allen *lawyer*
Webb, Jere Michael *lawyer*
Weber, George Richard *financial consultant, writer*
Westwood, James Nicholson *lawyer*
Whinston, Arthur Lewis *lawyer*
White, Douglas James, Jr. *lawyer*
†White, John *food marketing executive*
Whiteley, Benjamin Robert *insurance company executive*
Whitsell, Helen Jo *lumber executive*
Wiener, Norman Joseph *lawyer*
Wiens, Arthur Nicholai *psychology educator*
Williams, Buck *professional basketball player*
Wilson, Owen Meredith, Jr. *lawyer*
Winnowski, Thaddeus Richard (Ted Winnowski) *bank executive*
Wintermute, Marjorie McLean *architect, educator*
†Wohler, Jeffery Wilson *newspaper editor*
Wood, Erskine Biddle *lawyer*
†Wood, Marcus Andrew *lawyer*
†Woodward, Stephen Richard *newspaper editor*
Wren, Harold Gwyn *arbitrator, lawyer, legal educator*
Wright, Charles Edward *lawyer*
Wyse, William Walker *lawyer*
Yates, Keith Lamar *retired insurance company executive*
Zalutsky, Morton Herman *lawyer*
Zimmer, Norman Cunningham *architect*
Zimmerman, Gail Marie *medical foundation executive*
†Zook, Ronald Z. *school system administrator*

Riddle
†Markham, Bill *timber and logging company owner*

Roseburg
Plummer, Charles McDonald *retired community college administrator*
Whelan, William Anthony *forest products company executive*

Saint Helens
†Federici, Tony *small business owner, state legislator*

Salem
†Andersen-Wyckoff, R. G. *retail executive, small business owner, mayor*
Archer, Stephen Hunt *economist, educator*
†Bebe, Kathy *principal*
†Billman, Jennifer *elementsry school principal*
†Bradbury, William Chapman, III *state senator*
Carson, Wallace Preston, Jr. *state supreme court chief justice*
†Derfler, Eugene L. *real estate broker*
†Dukes, Joan *state legislator*
Fadeley, Edward Norman *state supreme court justice*
†Gold, Shirley Jeanne *state legislator, labor relations specialist*
Graber, Susan P. *judge*
†Hamby, Jeannette *state legislator*
†Hill, Jim *state official*
Hudson, Jerry E. *university president*
Johnson, Robert Raymond *management consultant, educator*
†Jolin, Peggy *state legislator*
Keisling, Phillip Andrew *state official*
Kulongoski, Theodore R. *state attorney general*
†Mack, Patricia *secondary school principal*
†Mannix, Kevin Leese *lawyer*
†Naito, Lisa Heather *state legislator*
†Oakley, Carolyn Le *state legislator, small business owner*
O'Connell, Kenneth John *state justice*
†Payne, Michael *state legislator*
Peterson, Edwin J. *state supreme court justice, retired*
Pierre, Joseph Horace, Jr. *commercial artist*
Rasmussen, Neil Woodland *insurance agent*
Roberts, Barbara *governor*
†Roberts, Frank *state senator*
Trueblood, Paul Graham *emeritus educator, author, editor*
Turnbaugh, Roy Carroll *archivist*
Unis, Richard L. *state supreme court justice*
Van Hoomissen, George Albert *state supreme court justice*
†VanLeeuwen, Liz Susan (Elizabeth VanLeeuwen) *state legislator, farmer,*
Weight, George Dale *banker, educator*
†Yih, Mae Dunn *state legislator*

Scio
†Hayden, Cedric L. *state legislator, dentist*

Siletz
Jennings, Jesse David *anthropology educator*

Sisters
Baxter, John Lincoln, Jr. *manufacturing company executive*
Keppler, Donald John *secondary education educator*

South Beach
Gilbert, David Heggie *consultant, retired educational publisher*

Springfield
†Beyer, Lee Louis *public administrator*
†Detlefsen, William David, Jr. *chemist, administrator*
Kimball, Reid Roberts *psychiatrist*
Lutes, Donald Henry *architect*

Sunriver
Clough, Ray William, Jr. *civil engineering educator*
Davenport, Wilbur Bayley, Jr. *electrical engineering educator*
Fosmire, Fred Randall *retired forest products company executive*
Jamison, Harrison Clyde *former oil company executive, petroleum exploration consultant*

Talent
McGill, Esby Clifton *former college official*

Terrebonne
Siebert, Diane Dolores *author, poet*

Tigard
Berglund, Carl Neil *electronics company executive*
Nokes, John Richard *retired newspaper editor, author*

Troutdale
†Minnis, John Martin *state legislator, protective services official*

Tualatin
Broome, John William *retired architect*
Brown, Robert Wallace *mathematics educator*
†Longaker, Nancy *elementary school principal*

West Linn
Bradley, Lester Eugene *retired steel and rubber products manufacturing executive*
†Treffinger, Karl Edward *architectural firm executive*

Wilsonville
Gross, Hal Raymond *bishop*
Isberg, Reuben Albert *radio communications engineer*
Karalis, John Peter *computer company executive, lawyer*
Meyer, Jerome J. *diversified technology company executive*
Yocam, Delbert Wayne *communication company executive*

Yachats
Gerdemann, James Wessel *plant pathologist, educator*

PENNSYLVANIA

Abington
Ayoub, Ayoub Barsoum *mathematician, educator*
Drudy, Patrick *psychologist, human relations consultant, import and export company executive*
Dunn, Linda Kay *physician*
Lapayowker, Marc Spencer *radiologist*
Pilla, Felix Mario *hospital administrator*
Stolp, Lauren Elbert *speech pathologist*

Akron
†Lapp, John Allen *religious organization administrator*

Albrightsville
Wilson, George Wharton *newspaper editor*

Alcoa Center
†Bridenbaugh, Peter Reese *industrial research executive*
Pien, Shyh-Jye John *mechanical engineer*

Alexandria
Horn, John Chisolm *management consultant*

Allentown
Afflerbach, Roy C., II *senator, consultant*
Agger, James H. *lawyer*
Allen, Anna Foster *librarian*
Anderson, Paul Edward *cement company executive*
Armstrong, W(illiam) Warren *advertising agency executive*
Baker, Dexter Farrington *manufacturing company executive*
Bannon, George *economics educator, department chairman*
Bednar, Charles Sokol *political scientist, educator*
Berman, Muriel Mallin *civic worker*
Berman, Philip I. *foundation administrator*
Blume, Peter Frederick *museum director*
Brown, Robert Wayne *lawyer*
†Dent, Charles Wieder *state legislator*
Donaldson, John Anthony *manufacturing executive*
Donley, Edward *manufacturing company executive*
Doughty, George Franklin *airport administrator*
Frank, Bernard *lawyer*
Gabel, Ronald Glen *telecommunications executive*
Gadomski, Robert Eugene *chemical and industrial gas company executive*
Gaylor, Donald Hughes *surgeon, educator*
Gewartowski, James Walter *electrical engineer*
Goldey, James Mearns *physicist*
Hansel, James Gordon *chemical engineer, educator*
Hecht, William F. *electric power industry executive*
Heitmann, George Joseph *business educator, consultant*
Holt, Leon Conrad, Jr. *lawyer, business executive*
Jackson, William MacLeod *management consultant*
Jodock, Darrell Harland *minister, religion educator*
Kelly, David Hoover *chemical company executive*
Krambeck, Robert Harold *communications executive, researcher*
Lovett, John Robert *chemical company executive*
Moller, Hans *artist*
Nagel, Edward McCaul *lawyer, former utilities executive*
Platt, William Henry *lawyer*
†Ritter, Karen A(nne) *state legislator*
Rushton, Brian Mandel *chemical company executive*
†Sacks, Patricia Ann *librarian, consultant*
Samuels, Abram *stage equipment manufacturing company executive*
Shire, Donald Thomas *retired air products and chemicals executive, lawyer*
Shorts, Gary K. *newspaper publisher*
Singhal, Kishore *engineering administrator*
Smith, Warren L. *electrical engineer, physicist*
†Stephanoff, Kathryn *library director*
Taylor, Arthur Robert *college president, business executive*
Wagner, Harold A. *industrial gas and chemical company executive*
Welsh, Thomas J. *bishop*
†Willistein, Paul August *newspaper editor*
Winters, Arthur Ralph, Jr. *chemical and cryogenic engineer, consultant*

Allison Park
Backus, John King *former chemical company research administrator*
Hadidian, Dikran Yenovk *librarian, clergyman*
Herrington, John David, III *lawyer*
Jacobs, Daniel Kenneth *school system administrator*
LaDow, C. Stuart *consultant financial services*
Miller, William Evans, Jr. *retired lawyer*
Osby, Larissa Geiss *artist*

Altoona
†Jubelirer, Robert C. *lawyer, state senator*
Meadors, Allen Coats *health administrator, educator*
†Miller, Gerald E. *bishop*
†Rossman, William J. *banker*
†Suckling, Robert McCleary *architect*

Ambler
Learnard, William Ewing *marketing executive*
Lengyel, Alfonz *art history, archeology and museology educator*

Ambridge
Frey, William Carl *bishop, academic administrator*

Annville
Ehrhart, Carl Yarkers *retired minister, retired college administrator*
McGill, William James, Jr. *academic administrator*
Synodinos, John Anthony *academic administrator*

Ardmore
†Gutwirth, Marcel Marc *French literature educator*
Kline, George Louis *author, translator, retired philosophy and literature educator*
Scott, Bill *advertising agency executive*
Stanley, Edward Alexander *geologist, forensic scientist, technical and academic administrator*

Aston
†Aldrich, Ronald Robert *health system administrator*
Barnett, Samuel Treutlen *international company executive*
Carroll, Claire Barry *special education educator*

Avondale
Friel, Daniel Denwood, Sr. *manufacturing executive*

Bala Cynwyd
Ackoff, Russell Lincoln *systems sciences educator*
Bausher, Verne C(harles) *banker*
Benenson, James, Jr. *industrialist*
†Bentivegna, Peter Ignatius *architectural company executive*
Cades, Stewart Russell *lawyer, communications company executive*
†Driscoll, Edward Carroll *construction management firm executive*
†Elkman, Stanley *advertising executive*
Field, Joseph Myron *broadcast executive*
Furlong, Edward V., Jr. *paper company executive*
Garrity, Vincent Francis, Jr. *lawyer*
Katz, Julian *gastroenterologist, educator*
†Kleppe, Martin I. *bank executive*
Manko, Joseph Martin, Sr. *lawyer*
Marden, Philip Ayer *physician, educator*
Marinakos, Plato Anthony *medical center administrator*
McGill, Dan Mays *insurance business educator*
Miller, L. Martin *accountant, financial planning specialist*
Pendergrass, Teddy (Theodore D. Pendergrass) *musician*
Quay, Thomas Emery *lawyer*
†Schwartz, Charles D. *broadcast executive*
†Tuckerman, Donald M. *advertising executive*

Bangor
Wolf, Stewart George, Jr. *physician, medical educator*

Barnesboro
Moore, David Austin *pharmaceutical company executive, consultant*

Beaver
Dible, Dennis D. *executive editor*
Gordon, Frank Wallace *newspaper publisher*
Helmick, Gayle Johnston *elementary education educator*

Beaver Falls
Ledebur, Linas Vockroth, Jr. *lawyer*

Belle Vernon
Wapiennik, Carl Francis *manufacturing firm executive, planetarium and science institute executive*

Bellefonte
Howland, Bette *writer*

Bensalem
Bishop, Howard Stuart *management consultant*
†Faijean, Francois *metal products executive*
†Iacovetti, Benedict John *company executive*
Kang, Benjamin Toyeong *writer, clergyman*
Moser, Milton John *collection agency executive, consultant*
†Wachs, David V. *apparel executive*

Berwyn
Brundage, Russell Archibald *retired data processing executive*
Brunner, Lillian Sholtis *nurse, author*
Bryant, James Wesley *investment executive*
Fry, Clarence Herbert *retail executive*
Kane, Jonathan *lawyer*
Lund, George Edward *retired electrical engineer*
Markle, John, Jr. *lawyer*
Odell, Herbert *lawyer*
Watters, Edward McLain, III *lawyer*
Wood, Thomas E. *lawyer*

Bethel Park
Korchynsky, Michael *metallurgical engineer*
O'Donnell, William James *engineering executive*

Bethlehem
†Alhadeff, Jack Abraham *biochemist, educator*
Allen, Eugene Murray *chemist*
Barnette, Curtis Handley *steel company executive, lawyer*
Barsness, Richard Webster *management educator, administrator*
Beedle, Lynn Simpson *civil engineering educator*
Beidler, Peter Grant *English educator*
Benz, Edward John *retired clinical pathologist*
Bergethon, Kaare Roald *educational consultant, former college president*
Billingsley, Charles Edward *transportation company executive*
Boylston, Benjamin Calvin *steel company executive*
Brozek, Josef *psychology educator, scientist*
Campbell, Donald Thomas *psychologist, educator*
Church, Thomas Trowbridge *former steel company executive*
Connors, Leo Gerard *consultant, former finance company executive*
Dahlke, Walter Emil *electrical engineering educator*
Dowling, Joseph Albert *historian, educator*
Durkee, Jackson Leland *civil engineer*
†Fairbairn, Ursula Farrell *human resources executive*
Fisher, John William *civil engineering educator*
Fowler, W(yman) Beall *physics educator*
Frankel, Barbara Brown *cultural anthropologist*
Gardiner, Keith Mattinson *engineering educator*
Gates, Elmer D. *business executive*
Georgakis, Christos *chemical engineer educator, consultant, researcher*
†Ghosh, Bhaskar Kumar *statistics educator, researcher*
Greene, David Mason *retired English language educator*
Hartmann, Robert Elliott *manufacturing company executive*
Haynes, Thomas Morris *philosophy educator*
Heindel, Ned Duane *chemistry educator*
Hertzberg, Richard Warren *materials science and engineering educator, researcher*
Hobbs, James Beverly *business administration educator, writer*
†Howell, John R. *banker*
Jordan, John Allen, Jr. *steel company executive*
Kanofsky, Alvin Sheldon *physicist*
Karakash, John J. *engineering educator*
Kerchner, Charles Frederick, Jr. *electronics executive, engineer*
Lewis, Andrew Lindsay, Jr. (Drew Lewis) *transportation and natural resources executive*
†Lewis, Drew *rail transportation and holding company executive*
Likins, Peter William *university president*
Lindgren, John Ralph *philosophy educator*
Martin, Roger Harry *college president*
Murphy, Warren Burton *writer, screenwriter*
Penny, Roger Pratt *management executive*
Pense, Alan Wiggins *metallurgical engineer, academic administrator*
Rivlin, Ronald Samuel *mathematics educator emeritus*
†Roberts, Malcolm John *steel company executive*
Roberts, Richard *mechanical engineering educator*
Schwartz, Eli *economics educator, writer*
Sclar, Charles Bertram *geology educator, researcher*
Smolansky, Oles M. *humanities educator*
Smyth, Donald Morgan *chemical educator, researcher*
Snyder, John Mendenhall *medical administrator, retired thoracic surgeon*
†Spillman, Robert Arnold *architect*
Stuart, Gary Miller *railroad executive*
Tuzla, Kemal *mechanical engineer, scientist*
Varnerin, Lawrence John *physicist*
Viest, Ivan M(iroslav) *consulting structural engineer*
von Bernuth, Carl W. *diversified corporation executive, lawyer*
Watkins, George Daniels *physics educator*
†Wei, Robert Peh-Ying *mechanics educator*
Weidner, Richard Tilghman *physicist, educator*
Wenzel, Leonard Andrew *engineering educator*
Williams, Walter Fred *steel company executive*

Birdsboro
Hill, Lenora Mae *astrologer*

Blandon
†Nulty, George P. *food products company executive*

Bloomsburg
Miller, David Jergen *insurance executive*
Vann, John Daniel, III *university administrator, historian*

Blue Bell
Abramson, Leonard *healthcare organization executive*
Barron, Harold Sheldon *lawyer*
Blechschmidt, Edward Allan *computer systems executive*
Braun, Reto *computer systems company executive*
Brendlinger, LeRoy R. *college president*
†Carey, Joseph A., Jr. *electronics executive*
Ehrlich, Everett Michael *federal official, computer company executive*
Elliott, John Michael *lawyer*
Fawley, John Jones *retired banker*
Ganoe, Charles Stratford *banker*
Hirsch, Robert W. *environmental consulting, engineering and construction company executive*
Keppler, William Edmund *multinational company executive*
Millar, Victor E. *information services executive*
Neff, P. Sherrill *health care executive*
Swansen, Samuel Theodore *lawyer*
Tomlinson, J. Richard *engineering services company executive*
Unruh, James Arlen *business machines company executive*
Vollmar, John Raymond *electrical engineer*
†Wise, Allen Floyd *insurance executive*
Young, Jere Arnold *lawyer, management consultant*
Yuhas, Alan Thomas *investment management executive*

Boiling Springs
Hoefling, John Alan *former army officer, corporation executive*

Boyertown
†Jilk, Lawrence T., Jr. *banker*

Brackenridge
Bozzone, Robert P. *steel company executive*

Bradford
Rice, Lester *electronics company executive*

Bradfordwoods
Davis, Nathan Tate *musician, educator*

Bridgeville
Keddie, Roland Thomas *physician, hospital administrator, lawyer*
†Nicholson, Peter Joseph *construction company executive*

Bristol
Arkles, Barry Charles *chemist*
Hutton, Ann Hawkes *state official*
†McEwen, Joseph, Jr. *distributing company executive*

Broomall
†Cohen, Philip D. *book publishing executive*
Russo, John Peter *musician, composer*
Stewart, Allen Warren *lawyer*

Brownsville
Dryburg, Ann *secondary education educator*

Bryn Athyn
Kintner, William Roscoe *political science educator emeritus*

Bryn Mawr
Ballam, Samuel Humes, Jr. *retired corporate director*
Barth, Charles Fredrik *aerospace engineer*
Berliner, Ernst *chemistry educator*
Braha, Thomas I. *business executive*
Brand, Charles Macy *history educator*
Broido, Arnold Peace *music publishing company executive*
Brunt, Manly Yates, Jr. *psychiatrist*
Carroll, Mary Colvert *corporate executive*
Chadwick, H. Beatty *lawyer*
Crawford, Maria Luisa Buse *geology educator*
Dayton, Samuel Grey, Jr. *investment banker*
de Laguna, Frederica *anthropology educator emeritus, consultant*
Dorian, Nancy Currier *linguistics educator*
Driskill, John Ray *association executive*
Dudden, Arthur Power *historian, educator*
Dunlop, Robert Galbraith *retired petroleum company executive*
Fanus, Pauline Rife *librarian*
Gaisser, Julia Haig *classics educator*
Goutman, Lois Clair *retired drama educator*
Havens, Timothy Markle *investment advisory firm executive*
Hoffman, Howard Stanley *experimental psychologist, educator*
Hoopes, Janet Louise *educator, psychologist*
Huth, Edward Janavel *physician, editor*
King, Willard Fahrenkamp (Mrs. Edmund Ludwig King) *Spanish language educator*
Krausz, Michael *philosopher, educator*
Lafarge, Catherine *dean*
Lane, Barbara Miller (Barbara Miller-Lane) *humanities educator*
†Lotman, Herbert *food processing executive*
Mallory, Frank Bryant *chemistry educator*
Mc Lean, William L., III *publisher*
McPherson, Mary Patterson *academic administrator*
†Noone, Robert Barrett *plastic surgeon*
Pettit, Horace *allergist, consultant*
Porter, Judith Deborah Revitch *sociologist, educator*
Ridgway, Brunilde Sismondo *archaeology educator*
Rubinstein, Alvin Zachary *political science educator, author*
Salmon, John Hearsey McMillan *historian, educator*
Stapleton, Katharine Laurence *English educator, writer*
Stucky, Steven (Edward) *composer*
Tanis, James Robert *library director, history educator, clergyman*

Turbidy, John Berry *investor, management consultant*
Walton, Clarence *political science and history educator*
Weese, Samuel H. *academic administrator*

Buck Hill Falls
Meditz, Walter Joseph *engineering consultant*

Burlington
Herrold, Kenneth Frederick *psychologist, educator*

Bushkill
Muesing Ellwood, Edith Elizabeth *writer, researcher, publisher, editor*

Butler
Kane, Marilyn Elizabeth *small business owner*
†Kosar, John E. *architectural firm executive*
Zehfuss, Lawrence Thomas *hardware supply company executive*

Cambridge Springs
Hughes, William Frank *mechanical and electrical engineering educator*

Camp Hill
†Grass, Martin Lehrman *business executive*
†Johnston, Thomas McElree, Jr. *church administrator*
Keller, John Richard *insurance company executive*
Nowak, Jacquelyn Louise *retirement home administrator, realtor, consultant*
Richey, Robert Lee *architect*
Robertson, James Colvert *insurance company executive*
Robinson, Ronald Michael *health care financial executive, financial consultant*
†Ross, Samuel D., Jr. *insurance company executive*
Slane, Charles Joseph *chain drug store executive*
†Spiers, Tomas Hoskins, Jr. *architect*
Sullivan, Barry Michael *finance executive*
Wellington, John Stanley *lawyer, former state official*

Canonsburg
†Mascetta, Joseph Anthony *principal*

Carlisle
Clarke, Walter Sheldon *federal government official, instructor*
Fish, Chet *publishing consultant, writer*
Fox, Arturo Angel *Spanish language educator*
†Fox, James Robert *law librarian, educator*
Fritschler, A. Lee *college president, public policy educator*
Graham, William Patton, III *plastic surgeon, educator*
Jacobs, Norman G(abriel) *sociologist, educator*
Lewis, Claude, Jr. *retired shoe company executive*
Long, Howard Charles *physics educator emeritus*
†Noddle, Allan S. *food products executive*
Schiffman, Joseph Harris *literary historian, educator*
Stachacz, John Charles *librarian*
Talley, Carol Lee *newspaper editor*

Carlisle Barracks
Simpson, Daniel H. *ambassador*
Stofft, William A. *career officer*

Center Valley
Cramer, Morgan Joseph, Jr. *international management executive*
Gambet, Daniel G(eorge) *college president, clergyman*

Central City
Brown, Robert Alan *retired construction materials company executive*

Chadds Ford
Brown, Charles Daniel *retired chemical company executive*
Duff, James Henry *museum director, environmental administrator*
Isakoff, Sheldon Erwin *chemical engineer*

Chalfont
Clifford, Maurice Cecil *physician, former college president, foundation executive*

Chambersburg
Furr, Quint Eugene *marketing executive*
Gelbach, Martha Harvey *genealogist*
Rumler, Robert Hoke *agricultural consultant, retired association executive*

Cheltenham
Weinstock, Walter Wolfe *systems engineer*

Chester
Bruce, Robert James *university president*
Buck, Lawrence Paul *academic administrator*
Clark, James Edward *physician, medical educator*
Frank, Amalie Julianna *computer science, electrical engineering and mathematics educator, consultant*
Lederer-Antonucci, Yvonne *management information educator, consultant*
Moll, Clarence Russel *university president emeritus, consultant*
Rosko, Michael Daniel *health science facility administrator, educator*

Clarion
†Caldwell-Wood, Naomi Rachel *library media specialist*
Foreman, Thomas Alexander *dentist*
Mc Cabe, Gerard Benedict *library administrator*

Clarks Summit
Alperin, Irwin Ephraim *clothing company executive*
Ross, Adrian E. *retired drilling manufacturing company executive*

Clearfield
Pride, Douglas Spencer *minister*
Ulerich, William Keener *publishing company executive*

Coatesville
Bucher, John Henry *metallurgical consultant, technology manager*

Gehring, David Austin *physician, adminstrator, cardiologist*
Meyers, Frederick M. *diversified industrial products and service company executive*
Nocks, James Jay *psychiatrist*
†Strauser, Simeon John *academic administrator*

Cochranville
Sazegar, Morteza *artist*

Collegeville
Cawthorn, Robert Elston *health care executive*
Cordes, Eugene Harold *biochemist*
Dupuis, Claude Paul *pharmaceutical company executive*
Kun, Kenneth A. *business executive*
Popp, James Alan *toxicologist, toxicology executive*
Richter, Richard Paul *academic administrator*
Smalley, Christopher Joseph *pharmaceutical company professional*
†Stoughton, W. Vickery *hospital administrator*
Tretter, James Ray *pharmaceutical company executive*

Connellsville
Sember, June Elizabeth *elementary education educator*

Conshohocken
Boenning, Henry Dorr, Jr. *investment banker*
Cohen, Alan *civil engineer*
†Cohen, Lita Indzel *state legislator*
Cunningham, James Gerald, Jr. *transportation company executive*
Froman, Ann Dolores *computer education educator*
Rippel, Harry Conrad *mechanical engineer, consultant*
Rounick, Jack A. *lawyer*
Spaeth, Karl Henry *chemical company executive, lawyer*
Tily, Stephen Bromley, III *bank executive*

Coopersburg
Eckardt, Arthur Roy *religion studies educator emeritus*
†Spira, Joel Solon *electronics company executive*

Cooperstown
Hogg, James Henry, Jr. *education educator*

Coraopolis
Koepfinger, Joseph Leo *utilities executive*
Kohun, Frederick Gregg *information scientist, economist, educator*
†Nelson, Donald J. *engineering executive*
Shaw, Richard Leslie *engineering company executive*

Cranberry Township
Bashore, George Willis *bishop*
Birch, Jack Willard *psychologist, educator*
Pond, Martin Allen *academic dean emeritus*

Cresson
Pierce, Edward Franklin *college president*

Danville
Ackerman, F. Kenneth, Jr. *health facility administrator*
Kazem, Ismail *radiation oncologist, educator, health science facility administrator*
Morgan, Howard Edwin *physiologist*
Pierce, James Clarence *surgeon*

Delaware Water Gap
Woods, Philip Wells (Phil Woods) *jazz musician composer*

Devon
Brody, Aaron Leo *food and packaging consultant*
Lindros, Eric Bryan *professional hockey player*
Niehaus, Robert James *investment banking executive*
O'Malley, John Edward *medical association administrator, physician*

Dillsburg
Bowers, Glenn Lee *association executive*
Jackson, George Lyman *nuclear medicine physician*

Douglassville
Burke, Peter Arthur *microbiologist, chemist*

Dover
Hayek, William Edward *investment counsel, financial consultant*

Doylestown
Brink, Frank, Jr. *biophysicist, former educator*
Cathcart, Harold Robert *hospital administrator*
Davis, Carole Joan *psychologist*
Holstrom, Carleton Arthur *brokerage house executive*
Long, Ronald Alex *real estate and financial consultant, educator*
Maser, Frederick Ernest *clergyman*
Mishler, John Milton (Yochanan Menashsheh ben Shaul) *natural sciences educator, academic administrator*
Purpura, Peter Joseph *museum curator, exhibition designer*
Rusch, Hugh Leonard *corporate executive*
Smith, Charles Paul *newspaper publisher*

Dresher
Taddei, Edward P. *school system administrator*

Drexel Hill
Alexander, Lloyd Chudley *author*
†Loeper, F. Joseph *state senator*
Martino, Michael Charles *entertainer, musician*
†McAllister, Wayne R. *principal*
Perkins, Ralph Linwood *business executive, public health administration specialist*
Schiazza, Guido Domenic (Guy Schiazza) *educational association administrator*
Thompson, William David *minister, homiletics educator*

Drums
Palance, Jack *actor*

Du Bois
Brunk, Samuel Frederick oncologist
†Morris, Trisha Ann librarian

Durham
†Dean, Frederick Bernard holding company executive

Eagles Mere
Moore, Mechlin Dongan business consultant
Sample, Frederick Palmer former college president

East Butler
Mielcuszny, Albert John wholesale distribution executive
Pentz, Paul hardware company executive

East Stroudsburg
Briggs, Philip James political science educator, author, lecturer
Crackel, Theodore Joseph historian
Frazetta, Frank artist
Gilbert, James Eastham academic administrator

Easton
Ashby, Richard James, Jr. bank executive, lawyer
Cooke, Jacob Ernest history educator, author
†Gaertner, Johannes Alexander retired art history educator, author
Grunberg, Robert Leon Willy nephrologist
Gurin, Richard Stephen manufacturing company executive
Holmes, Larry professional boxer
†Humphrey, J. Steven museum director
Reibman, Jeanette Fichman state senator
Van Antwerpen, Franklin Stuart federal judge

Edinboro
Cox, Clifford Laird university administrator, musician
Diebold, Foster Frank university president
Fleischauer, John Frederick English language educator, academic administrator
Kemenyffy, Steven artist, art educator

Eighty Four
Capone, Alphonse William retired industrial executive

Elizabethtown
Hoy, Harold Joseph marketing educator, retail executive, management consultant
Madeira, Robert Lehman association executive
†Mann, Lowell D. religious organization executive
Ritsch, Frederick Field academic administrator, historian

Elkins Park
Bayliss, George Vincent art educator, artist
Davidson, Abraham A. art historian, photographer
Fussell, Catharine Pugh biological researcher
†Moore, Peter John architect

Emmaus
Beldon, Sanford T. publisher
Bowers, Klaus D(ieter) retired electronics research development company executive
Bricklin, Mark Harris magazine editor, publisher

Erie
Bentz, Warren Worthington federal bankruptcy judge
†Boyes, Karl W. state legislator
Bracken, Charles Herbert banker
De Witt, William Gerald retired paper company executive
Gottschalk, Frank Klaus real estate executive
Gray, Robert Beckwith engineer
†Hazuda, Ronald A. church administrator
Hedrick, Charles Lynnwood holding company executive
Hendl, Walter conductor, pianist, composer
Hey, John Charles electronics company executive
Hsu, Bertrand Dahung mechanical engineer
Lilley, John Mark university provost and dean
Lund, David Harrison lawyer
Mead, Edward Mathews newspaper executive
Mencer, Glenn Everell federal judge
Merwin, Robert Freeman manufacturing company executive
Nygaard, Richard Lowell federal judge
Poydock, Mary Eymard nun, educational administrator, biologist, educator
†Ridge, Michele Moore librarian
†Rowley, Robert Deane, Jr. bishop
†Savocchio, Joyce A. mayor
Trautman, Donald W. bishop
Vanco, John L. art museum director
†Weber, Herman C., Jr. architect
Zuern, David Ernest bank executive

Erwinna
Geldmacher, Robert Carl software corporation executive
Richman, Joan F. television consultant

Exeter
Stocker, Joyce Arlene retired secondary education educator

Export
Wagner, Charles Leonard electrical engineer, consultant

Exton
Lewis, Thomas B. specialty chemical company executive
†Mayville, Gail M. environmental consultant
Penrose, Charles, Jr. association executive
Sanford, Richard D. computer company executive

Fairview
Duval, Albert Frank paper company executive

Fairview Village
Kisielowski, Eugene engineering executive

Farmington
Witt, Charles E. coal company executive

Farrell
Sander, Malvin Gustav lawyer

Fayetteville
†Kocek, Stephanie Susan theater executive

Feasterville Trevose
McCaughan, John F. chemical company executive

Felton
Shoemaker, Eleanor Boggs television production company executive

Ferndale
Folk, James sales executive

Flourtown
Lambert, Joan Dorety elementary education educator
Lee, Adrian Iselin, Jr. journalist

Fogelsville
Ault, James Mase bishop

Fort Washington
Blumberg, Donald Freed management consultant
Buescher, Adolph Ernst (Dolph Buescher) aerospace company executive
Deric, Arthur Joseph management consultant, lawyer
Urbach, Frederick physician, educator

Frazer
Godwin, Pamela June insurance company executive
†Kennedy, Donald Davidson, Jr. insurance company executive

Furlong
Parker, Jennifer Ware chemical engineer, researcher

Gaines
Beller, Martin Leonard retired orthopaedic surgeon

Gettysburg
Bohner, Dean Arlington insurance executive
Boritt, Gábor Szappanos history educator
†Cisneros, Jose A. historical site administrator
Hale, James Russell religious studies educator, minister
Mainwaring, Thomas Lloyd motor freight company executive
Plischke, Elmer political science educator

Gibsonia
Cauna, Nikolajs physician, medical educator
Shoub, Earle Phelps chemical engineer, educator

Gladwyne
Acton, David lawyer
Booth, Harold Waverly finance and investment company executive, lawyer
Geisel, Cameron Meade, Jr. investment professional
Hasselman, Richard B. consultant, retired railroad executive
Mc Donald, Robert Emmett conglomerate executive
Nelson, Waldo Emerson physician, educator
Patten, Lanny Ray industrial gas industry executive

Glen Mills
Churchill, Stuart Winston chemical engineering educator

Glenshaw
†Ghaznavi, John Jahangir investment company executive

Glenside
Apperson, Jack Alfonso retired army officer, business executive
Forman, Edgar Ross mechanical engineer
Frudakis, Zenos Antonios sculptor, artist
Johnson, Waine Cecil dermatologist
Landman, Bette Emeline academic administrator

Grantham
†Byers, John A. bishop
†Chubb, Harold D. church official
Sider, E(arl) Morris minister
†Sider, Harvey Ray minister, church administrator

Great Valley
Frazer, Jack Winfield chemistry researcher

Greensburg
Birchem, Regina cell biologist, environment consultant, educator
Boyle, JoAnne Woodyard college president
Dykema, Henry L. manufacturing company financial executive
Guyker, William Charles, Jr. electrical engineer, researcher
Harrell, Edward Harding newspaper executive
McDowell, Michael David lawyer, utility executive

Greentown
Forcheskie, Carl S. former apparel company executive

Greenville
†Farina, Andrew church administrator
†King, David O. orthodontist, state legislator
Stuver, Francis Edward former railway car company executive
Zimmer, Albert Arthur education educator

Grove City
Brenner, Frederic James biology educator, ecological consultant
†Fargo, Howard Lynn legislator
MacKenzie, Charles Sherrard college president

Gwynedd
Bryant, Robert Parker retired food service and lodging executive
Zumeta, Bertram William retired economist

Gwynedd Valley
†Feenane, Sister Mary Alice principal

Hanover
Bechtel, Jean Patricia elementary education educator

Harleysville
Craugh, Joseph Patrick, Jr. insurance company executive, lawyer
Daller, Walter E., Jr. banking executive
†McCarter, Michael G. insurance company executive
Mitchell, Bradford William insurance executive, lawyer
Ruth, Alpheus Landis dairy farmer

Harrisburg
Alexander, William Herbert business educator, former construction company executive, former army officer
Allen, Heath Ledward lawyer
†Andrezeski, Anthony (Buzz Andrezeski) state senator
Angino, Richard Carmen lawyer
Antoun, Annette Agnes newspaper editor, publisher
†Armstrong, Gibson E. state senator
†Armstrong, Thomas Errol state legislator
Ball, William Bentley lawyer
Banks, Albert Victor, Jr. state official
Cadieux, Roger Joseph physician, mental health care executive
Caldwell, William Wilson federal judge
Campbell, Carl Lester banker
Carnahan, Frances Morris magazine editor
Casey, Robert P. governor
Cate, Donald James mechanical enginee, consultant
Cawley, James Hughes lawyer
Cline, Andrew Haley lawyer
Cramer, John McNaight lawyer
Dattilo, Nicholas C. bishop
†Dawida, Michael M. state senator
Diehm, James Warren lawyer, educator
Dietz, John Raphael consulting engineer executive
†Edmiston, Guy S., Jr. bishop
†Farmer, Elaine F. state legislator
Fortier, John Bertram museum director, historian
Fossel, Peter VanBrunt magazine editor and publisher
†Fumo, Vincent Joseph state senator, bank executive, real estate developer, lawyer
†Geist, Richard A. engineering executive, state legislator
Giusti, Joseph Paul engineering education and development director, retired university chancellor
†Glass, Brent D. state commission administrator
Goell, James Emanuel electronics company executive
Gover, Raymond Lewis newspaper publisher
Grass, Alexander retail company executive
Groves, George H. holding company executive
†Gruitza, Michael congressman
Handler, Mimi editor, writer
†Harley, Ellen A. state legislator
Holl, Edwin G. state senator
Hudson, William Jeffrey, Jr. manufacturing company executive
†Itkin, Ivan state legislator
†Jones, Roxanne Harper state legislator
Kelly, Robert Edward, Jr. lawyer
Kimmel, Robert Irving corporate communication design consultant, former state government official
King, William J. bank executive
Klein, Michael D. lawyer
Kury, Franklin Leo lawyer
Lear, John writer, editor
Lourie, Norman Victor government official, social worker
Marley, James Earl manufacturing company executive
May, Felton Edwin bishop
McCormick, James Harold academic administrator
McInnes, Harold A. manufacturing company executive
†McNutt, Charlie Fuller, Jr. bishop
†Mead, James Matthew insurance company executive
Mitchell, Brenda K. state secretary
Moritz, Milton Edward security consultant
Narigan, Harold W. manufacturing company executive
Neilson, Winthrop Cunningham, III communications executive, financial communications consultant
Newland, Larry J. orchestra conductor
Newsome, William Roy, Jr. state official
†Nyce, Robert Eugene state legislator, tax accountant
Parker, Sara Ann librarian
Peechatka, Walter Norman government official
Preate, Ernest D., Jr. state attorney general
Raab, Walter Ferdinand manufacturing company executive
†Rabena, Kathleen A. indurance company executive
Rambo, Sylvia H. federal judge
Redmond, James Melvin medical association administrator
Richards, James Ward geologist
†Rudy, Ruth Corman state legislator
†Schwartz, Allyson Y state senator
Singel, Mark Stephen state official
Stabler, Donald Billman business executive
Stanchak, John Edward magazine editor
Termini, Roseann Bridget lawyer
Warshaw, Allen Charles lawyer
West, James Joseph lawyer
Weston, R. Timothy lawyer, government adminstrator
Zimmerman, LeRoy S. lawyer, former state attorney general
Zook, Merlin Wayne meteorologist

Hatboro
Hull, Lewis Woodruff manufacturing company executive

Hatfield
†Garis, Mark church administrator

Haverford
Allen, Theresa Ohotnicky neurobiologist, consultant
Baney, John Edward insurance company executive
Bemis, Hal Lawall engineering and business executive
Bogash, Richard retired pharmaceutical company executive
Davison, John Herbert music educator, academic administrator
Freeman, Michael Stuart library director
Frick, Sidney Wanning lawyer
Heath, Douglas Hamilton psychology educator
Jorden, Eleanor Harz linguist, educator
Jurney, Dorothy Misener journalist, editor
Kessinger, Tom G. college president
Lazar, Anna chemist
McGlinn, Frank Cresson Potts lawyer
Merrill, Arthur Alexander financial analyst
Northrup, Herbert Roof economist, business executive
Partridge, Robert Bruce astronomy educator
Stroud, James Stanley retired lawyer
Talucci, Samuel James retired chemical company executive
Thimann, Kenneth Vivian biology educator
Zalinski, Edmund Louis Gray insurance executive, mutual funds and real estate executive, investor

Havertown
Brinker, Thomas Michael finance executive
Payne, William Taylor, Jr. former hospital administrator, travel agency owner

Hawley
Conley, Clare Dean retired magazine editor

Hazleton
Denise, Robert Phillips craft company executive
†Gatty, Eugene B. school system administrator
Miller, David Emanuel physics educator, researcher

Hellertown
McCullagh, James Charles publishing company executive

Hershey
Anderson, Allan Crosby hospital executive
Biebuyck, Julien Francois anesthesiologist, educator
Bomgardner, William Earl retired association executive, photographer
Cary, Gene Leonard psychiatrist
†Christ, William Frank food manufacturing company executive
Davis, Dwight cardiologist, educator
Evarts, Charles McCollister orthopaedic surgeon
Eyster, Mary Elaine hematologist, educator
Farrell, Eugene George editor
Kauffman, Gordon Lee, Jr. surgeon, educator
Krieg, Arthur Frederick pathologist
Lang, Carol Max veterinarian, educator
Leaman, David Martin cardiologist
Lehman, Lois Joan medical librarian
Lehr, William, Jr. food products executive
Lipton, Allan medical educator
McInerney, Joseph John biomedical engineer, educator
Naeye, Richard L. pathologist, educator
Pierce, William Schuler cardiac surgeon, educator
Rapp, Fred virologist
Rohner, Thomas John, Jr. urologist
Severs, Walter Bruce pharmacology educator, researcher
Stump, Troy Elwood zoo director
†Vesell, Elliot Saul pharmacologist, educator
Waldhausen, John Anton surgeon, educator
Wassner, Steven Joel pediatric nephrologist, educator
Wolfe, Kenneth L. food products manufacturing company executive
Zelis, Robert Felix cardiologist, educator
Zimmerman, Richard Anson food company executive
Zoumas, Barry Lee food products company executive, nutritionist

Holland
†Reinard, Roy congressman

Hollidaysburg
Bloom, Lawrence Stephen retired clothing company executive

Honesdale
Barbe, Walter Burke education educator
Brown, Kent Louis, Jr. magazine editor

Horsham
Alter, Dennis holding company executive
Boswell, Gary Taggart electronics company executive
Brenner, Ronald John pharmaceutical industry executive
†Duff, Donald James religious organization administrator
Goff, Kenneth Wade electrical engineer
†Hakimoglu, Ayhan electronics company executive
Hart, Alex Way banker
Hook, Jerry B. pharmaceutical company executive
Logue, John Joseph psychologist
McNulty, Carrell Stewart, Jr. manufacturing company executive, architect
†Strock, Gerald E. school system administrator
Wesselink, David Duwayne finance company executive
†Woodruff, Harrison D., Jr. principal

Hummelstown
Custer, John Charles investment broker
Moffitt, Charles William insurance sales executive

Huntingdon
Durnbaugh, Donald Floyd church history educator, researcher
Neff, Robert Wilbur church official, educator

Huntingdon Valley
Forman, Howard Irving lawyer, former government official
Jaffe, Marvin Eugene pharmaceutical company executive, neurologist
Liberti, Paul A. biotechnology executive, inventor, entrepreneur, consultant
Toll, Robert Irwin lawyer, real estate developer
West, A(rnold) Sumner chemical engineer

Indiana
Engler, W. Joseph, Jr. lawyer
Jones, Shelley Pryce chemical company executive
Kegel, William George mining company executive
Mc Cauley, R. Paul criminologist, educator
Perlongo, Daniel James composer
Pettit, Lawrence Kay university president
†Steelman, Sara Gerling state legislator
Thibadeau, Eugene Francis educator, consultant

Irvine
Koedel, John Gilbert, Jr. forge company executive

Jenkintown
Baldwin, David Rawson *retired university administrator*
Beavers, Ellington McHenry *chemical company executive*
†Clemmer, Leon *architect, planner*
Colman, Wendy *psychoanalyst*
Driehuys, Leonardus Bastiaan *conductor*
Greenspan-Margolis, June E. *psychiatrist*
Hankin, Elaine Krieger *psychologist, researcher*
Haythornthwaite, Robert Morphet *civil engineer, educator*
Mifsud, Lewis *electrical engineer, fire origin investigator, physicist*
Nerenberg, Aaron *lawyer*
Reese, Francis Edward *retired chemical company executive, consultant*
Sadoff, Robert Leslie *psychiatrist*
Seid, Ruth (Jo Sinclair) *author*
Silver, Leonard J. *insurance and risk management company executive*

Johnstown
Alcamo, Frank Paul *retired educator*
†Antonazzo, Nicholas Orlando *lawyer, corporate real estate executive*
Glosser, William Louis *lawyer*
Gunter, John Brown, Jr. *real estate executive*
Kuhn, Howard Arthur *engineering executive, educator*
†Miloro, Frank P. *church official, religious studies educator*
†Nicholas, (Richard G. Smisko) *bishop*
Pasquerilla, Frank James *real estate developer and manager*
Saltz, Howard Joel *newspaper editor*
Simmons, Elroy, Jr. *retired utility executive*
Wise, Robert Lester *utilities executive*
†Wozniak, John N. *state legislator, realtor*
†Yurcisin, John *church official*

Jones Mills
Fish, Paul Waring *lawyer*

Kennett Square
Allam, Mark Whittier *veterinarian, former university administrator*
Barr, David Charles *healthcare executive*
Beck, Dorothy Fahs *social researcher*
Bronner, Edwin Blaine *history educator*
Leymaster, Glen R. *former medical association executive*
Martin, George (Whitney) *writer*
May, Harold Edward *chemical company executive*
Naeve, Milo Merle *museum curator*
Nason, John William *retired college president, educational consultant*
Perera, George A. *physician*
Vainstein, Rose *educator, librarian*
Vining, Elizabeth Gray *author*

Kimberton
Douglas, Bryce *former pharmaceutical company executive*
Williams, Lawrence Soper *photographer*

King Of Prussia
Bramson, Robert Sherman *lawyer*
Carroll, Margaret Ann *chemist*
Cash, Francis Winford *health care executive*
†Dungan, Ronald Samuel *utility executive*
†Foster, John Hallett *health facility executive*
Gardella, Libero Anthony *pharmaceutical development executive*
Kopple, Kenneth D. *chemistry researcher, educator*
†Langton, Raymond Benedict, III *manufacturing company executive*
Miller, Alan B. *hospital management executive*
Minter, Philip Clayton *communications company executive*
Olexy, Jean Shofranko *English educator*
P'an, Albert Yuan *corporate executive*
Poste, George Henry *pharmaceutical company executive*
†Wulff, Harald P. *chemicals executive*

Kingston
†Lemmond, Charles D., Jr. *lawyer, state senator*
Marko, Andrew Paul *school system administrator*
Weisberger, Barbara *choreographer, artistic director, educator*

Knox
Rupert, Elizabeth Anastasia *retired university dean*

Kutztown
Dougherty, Percy H. *geographer, educator*
Ghiglia, Oscar Alberto *classical guitarist*
McFarland, David E. *university president*
Ring, Rodney Everett *religion educator*
Sunderland, Ray Thoburn *education educator, administrator*

Lafayette Hill
Dixon, Fitz Eugene, Jr. *professional baseball team executive*
Green, Rose Basile (Mrs. Raymond S. Green) *poet, author, educator*
King, Leon *financial services executive*

Lake Ariel
Tague, Charles Francis *retired engineering, construction and real estate development company executive*

Lake Harmony
Polansky, Larry Paul *court administrator, consultant*

Lancaster
Adams, William White *manufacturing company executive*
Brown, Joseph A. *lawyer, business executive*
†Cody, William Henry *journal editor*
Deaver, Everette Allen *diversified manufacturing company executive*
†Decker, Thomas E. *construction company executive*
Dubble, Curtis William *pastor*
Duroni, Charles Eugene *lawyer, food products executive*
Ebersole, Mark Chester *emeritus college president*
Ellis, Calvert N. *former college president*
Eshleman, Silas Kendrick, III *psychiatrist*
Freeman, Clarence Calvin *financial executive*

Fried, Jeffrey Michael *health care administrator*
Glick, Garland Wayne *retired theological seminary president*
†Hennessey, Joseph E. *chemicals executive*
Hess, Earl Hollinger *laboratory executive, chemist*
High, S. Dale *diversified company executive*
Joseph, John *history educator*
Kelly, Robert Lynn *advertising agency executive*
Kneedler, Alvin Richard *university administrator*
Louden, James Keith *management consultant, executive*
†Shaw, Charles Raymond *journalist*
†Shenk, Willis Weidman *newspaper executive*
Stephenson, Donald Grier, Jr. *government studies educator*
Taylor, Norman William *economics educator*
Troupe, Terry Lee *holding company banker*
Wedel, Paul George *retired hospital administrator*
Woods, Susanne *university dean*

Landenberg
Aldrich, Nancy Armstrong *psychotherapist, clinical social worker*
Lee, Robert John *pharmacologist*

Langhorne
Babb, Wylie Sherrill *college president*
Brafford, William Charles *lawyer*
Willis, Wesley Robert *college administrator*

Lansdale
†Baughn, Juan R. *high school principal*
Callender, John Hancock *architect*
Esterhai, John Louis *lawyer*
Lovelace, Robert Frank *health science facility administrator, researcher*
†Riebman, Leon *electronics company executive*
Schnable, George Luther *chemist*

Lansdowne
†Popovics, Sandor *civil engineer, educator, researcher*
Zingraff, Michael, Jr. *magazine editor*

Latrobe
Dumm, Demetrius Robert *priest, educator*
Murtha, John Francis *priest, academic administrator, history educator*
Underwood, James Martin *business executive*

Lebanon
Arnold, Edward Henry *transportation executive*
†Brightbill, David John *state legislator*
McMindes, Roy James *aggregate company executive*

Lehigh Valley
Kocsis, James Paul *artist, publisher*

Lemoyne
Zimmerman, Charles Hinckley *former financial executive*

Leola
McElhinny, Wilson Dunbar *banker*

Lewisburg
Anderson, John Whiting *economics educator*
Candland, Douglas Keith *psychology educator*
Edgerton, Mills Fox, Jr. *foreign language educator*
Harclerode, Jack Edgar *biologist*
Jump, Chester Jackson, Jr. *clergyman, church official*
Lu, David John *history educator, writer*
†Main, A. Donald *bishop*
Neuman, Nancy Adams Mosshammer *civic leader*
Payne, Michael David *English language educator*
Ray, David Scott *mathematics educator*
Sojka, Gary Allan *biologist, educator, university official*
†Stern, Gerald *poet*

Ligonier
Mellon, Seward Prosser *investment executive*
Pilz, Alfred Norman *manufacturing company executive*
Schmidt, Adolph William *retired ambassador*

Lincoln University
Gaymon, William Edward *psychology educator*
Williams, Willie, Jr. *physicist, educator*

Lititz
Bolinger, Robert Stevens *banker*

Lock Haven
Almes, June *secondary education educator, librarian*
Snowiss, Alvin L. *lawyer*
Willis, Craig Dean *university president*

Lumberville
Frank, F. Alexander *retired savings and loan executive, lawyer*
Katsiff, Bruce *artist*

Lyon Station
Bowers, Richard Philip *manufacturing executive*
Breidegam, DeLight Edgar, Jr. *battery company executive*

Macungie
Gavin, Austin *retired lawyer*

Malvern
Churchill, Winston John *lawyer, investment firm executive*
Ewing, Joseph Neff, Jr. *lawyer*
Gillespie, Mary Krempa *psychologist, consultant*
Kyle, Terrence Wayne *health care data processing executive*
McIntosh, L(orne) William *marketing executive*
McNamara, John F. *health services company executive*
Michaelis, Arthur Frederick *health care company executive*
Patterson, Scott David *lawyer*
†Swymer, Stephen *principal*
Zurawski, Vincent Richard, Jr. *biotechnology company executive, research scientist*

Manchester
Owens, Marilyn Mae *art educator*

Manheim
Spangler, Daisy Kirchoff *educational consultant*

Manns Choice
Jones, Oliver Hastings *consulting economist*

McConnellsburg
†Diller, Charles Herbert, Jr. *corporate professional*

Meadville
Adams, Earl William, Jr. *economics educator*
Cable, Charles Allen *mathematician*
Foster, Catherine Rierson *manufacturing company executive*
Hogan, James Charles *classicist, educator*
Katope, Christopher George *English language educator*

Mechanicsburg
Filipiak, Francis Leonard *naval officer*
†Greer, Robert B., III *orthopaedist*
†Ortenzio, Rocco Anthony *health care executive*

Mechanicsville
Bye, Ranulph DeBayeux *artist, author*

Media
Clauss, Alfred *architect*
†Dunlap, Richard Frank *school system administrator*
Elman, Gerry Jay *lawyer*
Fehnel, Edward Adam *chemist, educator*
Hand, Brian Edward *science association administrator*
Peabody, William Tyler, Jr. *retired paper manufacturing company executive*
†Price, Donald *retail executive*
Resnick, Stewart Allen *diversified company executive*
†Rothchild, Loren *toy manufacturing executive*
Schrom, Gerard Killard *lawyer*
Smith, David Gilbert *political science educator*
Sutton, Jonathan Stone *landscape architect*

Melrose Park
Prince, Morton Bronenberg *physicist*

Mendenhall
Reinert, Norbert Frederick *patent lawyer, retired chemical company executive*

Mercer
Brady, Wray Grayson *mathematician, educator*

Mercersburg
†Burgin, Walter Hotchkiss, Jr. *educational administrator*

Merion Station
First, Joseph Michael *retired legal and management consultant*
Littell, Franklin Hamlin *theologian, educator*

Middleburg
Kline, David Lamar *concrete block manufacturing company executive*

Middlesex
Finlay, Robert Derek *food company executive*

Middletown
Kaynak, Erdener *marketing educator, consultant editor*

Milford
Le Guin, Ursula Kroeber *author*
Snyder, Richard Lee *consumer products company executive*

Millersburg
Woodside, Robert Elmer *lawyer, former judge*

Millersville
Caputo, Joseph Anthony *university president*
Mallery, Anne Louise *elementary educator, consultant*
Taggie, Benjamin Fredrick *university official, educator*

Monroeville
Carney, Ann Vincent *secondary education educator*
Creagan, Robert Joseph *consulting nuclear engineer*
†Hoffman, Donald Howard *transportation executive*
Jacobi, William Mallett *nuclear engineer, consultant*
Lin, Ming Shek *allergist, immunologist*
Maclay, William Nevin *retired manufacturing and construction company executive*
Mandel, Herbert Maurice *civil engineer*
Murphy, William James *materials characterization company executive, metallurgical engineer*
Nemeth, Edward Joseph *process research specialist*
Parker, James Roger *chemist*
Penman, Paul Duane *nuclear power laboratory executive*
Ryan, Christopher Richard *construction company executive*

Montoursville
Woolever, Naomi Louise *retired editor*

Morgan
McQuillen, Albert Lawrence, Jr. *steel company executive*

Morgantown
McGraw, James Michael *manufacturing company executive*

Morrisville
Heefner, William Frederick *lawyer*
Muth, Robert James *metal company executive, lawyer*

Mount Gretna
Cooper, Jane Todd (J. C. Todd) *poet, writer, educator*

Mount Joy
Eichler, Franklin Roosevelt *petroleum products distributor and services company executive*

---

†Zook, Donald Roy *missions administrator*

Mountainhome
Buttz, Charles William *outdoor advertising executive*

Murrysville
Colborn, Harry Walter *electrical engineering consultant*
McWhirter, James Herman *consulting engineering business executive, financial planner*

Myerstown
Robson, Barbara S. *elementary education educator*
†Schock, Franklin H. *clergy member, church administrator*
†Seilhamer, Ray A. *academic administrator*

Narberth
Barnes, Norman Frank *food company executive*
Grenald, Raymond *architectural lighting designer*
Hires, William Leland *psychologist, consultant*
Nathanson, Neal *epidemiologist, virologist, educator*
Newhall, John Harrison *management consultant*
Wagner, Frederick Balthas, Jr. *historian, retired surgery educator*

Nazareth
Herrick, Robert Ford *personnel consultant*

New Brighton
†O'Leary, John P., Jr. *plastic company executive*

New Castle
White, Thomas *hospital administrator*

New Florence
Olson, Clinton Louis *foreign service officer, former ambassador*

New Holland
†Kennedy, William T. *retail executive*
†Marquart, Clifford Lynn *food company executive*
†Ruggeri, Riccardo *automotive sales executive*

New Hope
Braymer, Marguerite Annetta *optical company executive*
Knight, Douglas Maitland *educational administrator, optical executive*
Koljian, Hollis Ann *educational association administrator*
Williamson, Frederick Beasley, III *rubber company executive*

New Kensington
Jarrett, Noel *chemical engineer*
Miller, Albert Jay *retired librarian emeritus, educator*

New Oxford
Frock, J. Daniel *transportation executive, retired manufacturing company executive*

New Wilmington
Deegan, John, Jr. *academic administrator, educator*
Remick, Oscar Eugene *college president*

Newry
Bradley, Audrey Laverne *educator*

Newtown
Bohning, Elizabeth Edrop *foreign language educator*
Carlson, David Emil *physicist*
Cohen, Myer *former international organization official*
Denoon, Clarence England, Jr. *business executive*
Henshaw, Jonathan Cook *manufacturing company executive*
Keenan, Terrance *foundation executive*
Keyes, Fenton *consultant, writer*
Leibholz, Stephen Wolfgang *physicist, engineering company executive, entrepreneur*
Long, Harry (On-Yuen Eng) *chemist, rubber science and technology consultant*
Peroni, Peter A., II *psychologist, educator*
Pfeiffer, John Edward *author*
Selden, William Kirkpatrick *educational consultant*
Somers, Anne Ramsay *medical educator*
Thompson, Carol Lewis *editor*

Newtown Square
Bower, Ward Alan *management consultant, lawyer*
Critz, Richard Laurens *magazine editor, architectural consultant*
Graf, Arnold Harold *employee benefits executive, financial planner*
Staats, Dean Roy *retired reinsurance executive*
Steinman, Robert Cleeton *accountant*
Strausz-Hupé, Robert *ambassador, author*
Turner, George Pearce *consulting company executive*

Norristown
Aman, George Matthias, III *lawyer*
†Case, Andrew J. *educational administrator*
Clemens, Alvin Honey *insurance company executive*
†Fertell, Paul Adolph *manufacturing company executive*
Flint, Daniel Waldo Boone *lawyer*
Folmar, Larry John *lawyer*
†Hellauer, James Carroll *insurance company executive*
†Kaltenbacher, Philip D(avid) *industrialist, former public official*
Wetherill, Eikins *lawyer, stock exchange executive*

North East
Ayrault, Evelyn West *psychologist, writer*

Oil City
Baum, Herbert Merrill *motor oil company executive*
†Berry, James D., III *oil company executive*
Callahan, Gerald William *lawyer, oil company executive*
†Hutchinson, Scott Edward *state legislator*
Olson, Robert Edward *coal mining executive*
Wood, Quentin Eugene *oil company executive*

Oreland
Smith, Gordon Ross *retired English language educator*

Orrtanna
Newman, Doris Jean district sales manager

Paoli
Blankley, Walter Elwood manufacturing company executive
Ferrell, David Lee public relations consultant
Gotshall, Jan Doyle financial planner
Hancox, Robert Ernest financial services company executive
†Hedberg, Robert Daniel venture capitalist
†Kornfeld, Allan A. manufacturing company executive

Peach Glen
Carey, Dean Lavere fruit canning company executive

Peckville
†Mellow, Robert James state senator

Penllyn
Beyer, Karl Henry, Jr. pharmacologist

Perkasie
Ferry, Joan Evans school counselor

Philadelphia
Aaron, Kenneth Ellyot lawyer
Abbott, Frank Harry lawyer
Abel, Andrew Bruce finance and economics educator
Abrahams, Robert David lawyer, author
Abramowitz, Robert Leslie lawyer
Abrams, Jules Clinton psychologist
Ackerman, Alvin S. lawyer
Adams, Barbara lawyer
Adams, F. Gerard economist, educator
Agersborg, Helmer Pareli K. pharmaceutical company executive, researcher
Agus, Zalman S. physician, educator
Aiken, Linda Harman nurse, sociologist, educator
Ajzenberg-Selove, Fay physicist, educator
Ake, John Notley lawyer, former investment services executive
Albert, Jeffrey B. lawyer
†Albertini, William Oliver telecommunications industry executive
Albright, Hugh Norton mathematics educator
Allen, Eric Andre professional football player
Alter, Jean Victor French language educator
Alter, Milton neurologist, educator
Amenta, Peter Sebastian anatomist, researcher, educator
Anders, Jerrold Paul lawyer
Anderson, E. Clive lawyer
Anderson, Rolph Ely marketing educator
†Ando, Albert K. economist, educator
†Andrews, Edwin Joseph pathology educator, academic administrator
†Andrisani, Paul J(oseph) academic dean, academic administrator, business educator, management consultant
Angell, M(ary) Faith federal magistrate judge
Apfel, Jerome B. lawyer
Arce, A. Anthony psychiatrist
Aregood, Richard Lloyd editor
Armstrong, Stephen Wales lawyer
†Arnold, Lee library director
Aronson, Carl Edward pharmacology and toxicology educator
Aronstein, Martin Joseph lawyer, educator
Asbury, Arthur Knight neurologist, educator
Auerbach, Alan Jeffrey economist
Austrian, Robert physician, educator
Auten, David Charles lawyer
Auth, Tony artist
Avery, William Joseph packaging manufacturing company executive
Axam, John Arthur library consultant
†Azoulay, Bernard chemicals company executive
Babbel, David Frederick finance educator
Baccini, Laurance Ellis lawyer
Bachman, Arthur lawyer
Bacon, Edmund Norwood city planner
Bailey, Elizabeth Ellery economics educator
Bailey, Harry Augustine, Jr. political science educator
†Bailin, Michael A. social research firm executive
†Baker, Houston Alfred, Jr. English language educator
Bales, John Foster, III lawyer
Ballengee, James McMorrow lawyer
Baltzell, E(dward) Digby sociologist
Banerji, Ranan Bihari mathematics and computer science educator
Bantel, Linda Mae art museum director
Barchi, Robert Lawrence neuroscience educator, clinical neurologist, neuroscientist
Bardeen, William Leonard electric utility executive
Barker, Clyde Frederick surgeon, educator
Barlett, Donald L. journalist
Barrett, James Edward, Jr. management consultant
Barrett, John J(ames), Jr. lawyer
Bartle, Harvey, III federal judge
Bartlett, Allen Lyman, Jr. bishop
Bartlett, Desmond William engineering company executive
Bartolini, Anthony Louis lawyer
Baserga, Renato Luigi pathology educator
Bates, James Earl college president
Batterman, Steven Charles engineering mechanics and bioengineering educator
Baughman, Jon A. lawyer
†Bauman, Robert Patten diversified company executive
Bayer, Margret Helene Janssen biologist, research scientist
†Beauchamp, Gary Keith physiologist
Bechtle, Louis Charles federal judge
Becker, Edward Roy federal judge
Beckman, Donald lawyer
Beckman, Hester Finke interior designer
Behrman, Jere Richard economics educator
Belinger, Harry Robert business executive
Bell, Whitfield Jenks, Jr. historian
Bellack, Alan Scott clinical psychologist
Benfey, Otto Theodor chemist, editor, historian of science
Benson, Morton educator, lexicographer
Berger, David lawyer
Berger, Harold lawyer, engineer
Berger, Lawrence Howard lawyer
Bergholtz, Norbert F. lawyer
Berkley, Emily Carolan lawyer
Berkman, Richard Lyle lawyer
Bernard, John Marley lawyer, educator
Bernstein, George L. lawyer, accountant
Bershad, Jack R. lawyer
Bevilacqua, Anthony Joseph Cardinal cardinal
Bianchi, Carmine Paul pharmacologist
Biava, Luis musician
Bibbo, Marluce physician, educator
Biezup, John Thomas lawyer
Bilaniuk, Larissa Tetiana neuroradiologist, educator
Bildersee, Robert Alan lawyer
Binder, David Franklin lawyer, author
Binder, Lucy Simpson utility company executive
Binswanger, Frank G., Jr. realty company executive
Binzen, Peter Husted columnist
Bishop, Harry Craden surgeon
Bissinger, H(arry) G(erard) journalist
Black, Albert Pershing, Jr. health care executive
Black, Allen Decatur lawyer
Blades, Herbert William diversified consumer products company executive
Blicher, Bert finance company executive
Block, Isaac Edward association executive
Bloom, Michael Anthony lawyer
Bludman, Sidney Arnold theoretical physicist, astrophysicist
Bluemle, Lewis William, Jr. medical educator
Blumberg, Baruch Samuel academic administrator, research scientist
Blume, Marshall Edward finance educator
Boasberg, Leonard W. reporter
Bodine, James Forney retired civic leader
Boehne, Edward George banker
Bogutz, Jerome Edwin lawyer
Boldt, David Rhys journalist
Bookspan, Michael Lloyd musician
Borer, Edward Turner investment banker
Bowditch, Nathaniel Rantoul brokerage house executive
†Bower, John Arnold, Jr. architect, educator
Bowman, Edward Harry business science educator
Bradley, Raymond Joseph lawyer
Brady, John Paul psychiatrist
Brady, Luther W., Jr. physician, radiation oncology educator
Braverman, Elliott Kenneth lawyer
Brawner, Gerald Theodore lawyer
Breitenfeld, Frederick, Jr. public broadcasting executive, educator
Brenan, Denis V. lawyer
Brest, Albert N. cardiology educator
Breuninger, Tyrone musician
Bridger, Wagner H. psychiatrist, educator
Bright, Joseph Coleman lawyer
Brighton, Carl Theodore orthopedic surgery educator
Brind'Amour, Rod Jean professional hockey player
†Brinster, Barry public relations company executive
Brinster, Ralph Lawrence biologist
Briscoe, Jack Clayton lawyer
Britt, Earl Thomas lawyer
Brobeck, John Raymond physiology educator
†Brockman, Stanley K. medical educator, physician, cardiothoracic surgeon
Brodsky, Julian A. broadcasting services, telecommunications company executive
Brody, Anita Blumstein federal judge
Broom, William Wescott retired newspaper executive
Brown, Denise Scott architect, urban planner
Brown, Richard P., Jr. lawyer
Brown, Stephen D. lawyer
Brown, William Hill, III lawyer
Browne, Michael Leon lawyer
Browne, Stanhope Stryker lawyer
Brownstein, Barbara Lavin geneticist, educator, university official
Buckwalter, Ronald Lawrence federal judge
Buerk, Donald Gene medical educator, biomedical engineer
Buerkle, Jack Vincent sociologist, educator
Burke, Daniel William college president emeritus, English educator
Burstein, Elias physicist, educator
Cahn, Edward N. federal judge
Callé, Craig R.L. packaging executive
Calman, Robert Frederick mining executive
Calvert, Jay H., Jr. lawyer
Cameron, John Clifford lawyer, health science facility administrator
Campbell, Robert H. oil company executive
Cander, Leon physician, educator
Carey, Arthur Bernard, Jr. editor, writer, columnist
Carmi, Shlomo mechanical engineering educator, scientist
Carnecchia, Baldo M., Jr. lawyer
Carson, Timothy Joseph lawyer
†Carter, Edward Carlos, II librarian, historian
Carter, Frederick James professional basketball coach
Casper, Charles B. lawyer
Cass, David economist, educator
Chait, Arnold radiologist
Chance, Britton biophysics and physical chemistry educator emeritus
Chance, Henry Martyn, II engineering executive
Cherken, Harry Sarkis, Jr. lawyer
†Cherry, John Paul health science association director, researcher
Cheston, George Morris lawyer
†Cheston, Morris, Jr. zoological park administrator
Cheston, Warren Bruce research institute administrator
Childress, Scott Julius medicinal chemist
Chimples, George lawyer
†Chinsamy, Anusuya paleobiologist, researcher
Christman, Robert Alan podiatric radiologist
Chung, Edward Kooyoung cardiologist, educator, author
Clark, Frederic William lawyer
Clark, George Roberts retired trust company executive
Clark, John Arthur lawyer
†Clark, John J. economics and finance educator
Clauser, Donald Roberdeau musician
Clayton, Constance school system administrator
Clearfield, Harris Reynold physician
†Clothier, Isaac H., IV lawyer
Cloues, Edward Blanchard, II lawyer
Cohen, David Walter university chancellor, periodontist, educator
Cohen, Deborah Fuchs lawyer
Cohen, Felix Asher lawyer
Cohen, Frederick lawyer
Cohen, Hennig English educator
Cohen, Ira Myron aeronautical and mechanical engineering educator
Cohen, Jeffrey M. physicist
Cohen, Stanley pathologist, educator
Cohen, Sylvan M. lawyer
Cohn, Mildred biochemist, educator
Collier-Evans, Demetra Frances veterans' benefits counselor
Collings, Robert L. lawyer
Collons, Rodger Duane decision sciences educator
Colman, Robert Wolf physician, medical educator
Comer, Nathan Lawrence psychiatrist, educator
Comfort, Robert Dennis lawyer
Comisky, Hope A. lawyer
Comisky, Marvin retired lawyer
Conn, Rex Boland, Jr. physician, educator
Cook, Don author, retired foreign correspondent
Cooke, M(erritt) Todd banker
Cooke, Sara Mullin Graff daycare provider, kindergarten teacher
Cooney, J(ohn) Gordon lawyer
Cooper, Richard Lee newspaper editor, journalist
Cooperman, Barry S. educational administrator, educator, scientist
Copeland, Adrian Dennis psychiatrist
Corrigan, John Edward government official
Cortner, Jean Alexander physician, educator
Cox, Douglas Lynn financial service executive
†Cox, Robert Harold physiology educator
Cox, Roger Frazier lawyer
Coyne, Frank J. insurance company executive
Cramer, Harold lawyer
Cramer, Richard Charles artist, educator
Crawford, James Douglas lawyer
Creech, Hugh John chemist
Crough, Daniel Francis lawyer, insurance company executive
Crowell, Richard Lane microbiologist
†Cruger, Lorenzo civil engineer
Crumb, George Henry composer, educator
Cullen, James G. telecommunications industry executive
Cummins, John David economics educator, consultant
Cunningham, Randall professional football player
Cutler, Neal Evan gerontologist, educator
Dabby, Sabah Salman chemical engineer
Dagit, Charles Edward, Jr. architect, educator
Dalinka, Murray Kenneth radiologist, educator
Daly, Charles Arthur health services administrator
†Daly, John M. surgeon
Dalzell, Stewart federal judge
Damsgaard, Kell Marsh lawyer
D'Angelo, Christopher Scott lawyer
D'Angio, Giulio John radiologist, educator
Daulton, Darren Arthur professional baseball player
Dauth, Frances Kutcher journalist, newspaper editor
†Davidson, Steven J. emergency physician
Davis, Alan Jay lawyer
Davis, Allen Freeman history educator, author
Davis, Raymond, Jr. chemist, researcher, educator
Davis, Robert Harry physiology educator
Dean, Michael M. lawyer
Dean, Morris Jonathan lawyer
Dean-Zubritsky, Cynthia Marian psychologist, reseacher
†DeBenedictis, Nicholas, Jr. chamber of commerce executive
DeBunda, Salvatore Michael lawyer
de Cani, John Stapley statistician, educator
Delacato, Carl Henry education educator
DeLaura, David Joseph English language educator
†De Leon, Clark newspaper columnist
De Lone, H. Francis lawyer
†DeLong, James Clifford aviation administrator
Deming, Frank Stout lawyer
Denenberg, Herbert Sidney journalist, lawyer, former state official
Denious, Robert Wilbur lawyer
Dennis, Edward S(pencer) G(ale), Jr. lawyer
Denworth, Raymond K. lawyer
Depp, (O.) Richard, III obstetrician-gynecologist, educator
Detweiler, David Kenneth veterinary physiologist, educator
Devlin, Thomas McKeown biochemist
d'Harnoncourt, Anne museum director
Diamond, Paul Steven lawyer
DiBerardino, Marie Antoinette developmental biologist, educator
†DiBona, G. Fred, Jr. insurance company executive
Dichter, Mark S. lawyer
Dilks, Park Bankert, Jr. lawyer
Dinoso, Vicente Pescador, Jr. physician, educator
DiPalma, Joseph Rupert pharmacology educator
Di Stefano, Anthony Ferdinand optometry educator, educational administrator
Ditter, John William, Jr. federal judge
Djerassi, Isaac physician, medical researcher
Dolson, Franklin Robert columnist
†Doman, Janet Joy association executive
Donoghue, Norman E., II lawyer
Donohue, James J. lawyer
Doran, Thomas E. lawyer
Doran, William Michael lawyer
Dorfman, John Charles lawyer
Dorsky, Alvin H. lawyer
†Doty, Richard Leroy medical researcher
Drake, Donald Charles journalist
Drake, William Frank, Jr. lawyer
Driscoll, Lee Francis, Jr. corporate director, lawyer
Dubin, Leonard lawyer
DuBois, Jan Ely federal judge
Duffy, Francis Ramon sociology educator
†Duncan, Mariano baseball player
†Dunlap, Albert John venture capitalist
Dunn, Wendell Earl, III management consultant, educator
Durham, James W. lawyer
Dworetzky, Joseph Anthony lawyer
†Dykstra, Lenny (Leonard Kyle Dkystra) baseball player
Dyson, Robert Harris museum director, archaeologist
Eagleson, William Boal, Jr. banker
Earley, Laurence Elliott medical educator
†Edelson, Alan Martin medical publisher, neurophysiologist
Edwards, Stephen Allen lawyer
Ehrlich, George Edward rheumatologist, international pharmaceutical consultant
Eichelman, Burr Simmons, Jr. psychiatrist, researcher, educator
Eisenstein, Bruce Allan electrical engineering educator
Eisenstein, Toby K. microbiology educator
Eisworth, Barry Neil architect, educator
Eldredge, Clifford Murray hospital administrator
Elliott, William Homer, Jr. lawyer
Emerson, S. Jonathan lawyer
Emory, Hugh Mercer lawyer
Engelman, Karl physician
Epstein, William Eric health science facility administrator
Erickson, Ralph O. botany educator
Erslev, Allan Jacob physician, educator
Erving, Julius Winfield former professional basketball player, business executive
Esser, Carl Eric lawyer
Evan, William Martin sociologist, educator
Evans, Audrey Elizabeth physician, educator
Everett, Carl Bell lawyer
Fader, Henry Conrad lawyer
Fagin, Claire Mintzer nursing educator, administrator
Fala, Herman C. lawyer
Falk, I. Lee lawyer
Falkie, Thomas Victor mining engineer, natural resources company executive
Fallon, Christopher Chaffee, Jr. lawyer
†Fancher, Charles B. newspaper publishing executive
Farage, Donald J. lawyer, educator
Farber, Emmanuel pathology and biochemistry educator
Farnam, Walter Edward insurance company executive
Farwell, Russ professional hockey team executive
Featherman, Bernard steel company executive
Fegley, Kenneth Allen systems engineering educator
Feirson, Steven B. lawyer
Feldman, Albert Joseph lawyer
Felts, George William, Sr. special education educator
Feninger, Claude industry management services company executive
Ferber, Arthur Henry engineering executive
Fiebach, H. Robert lawyer
Fielding, Allen Fred oral and maxillofacial surgeon, educator
Fine, Lawrence B. lawyer
†Finet, Scott law librarian
Finney, Graham Stanley management consultant
Fisher, Aron Baer physiology and medicine educator
Fisher, Linda A. lawyer
Fisher, Marshall Lee decision sciences director, educator
Fishman, Alfred Paul physician
Fitts, Donald Dennis chemist, educator
Flaherty, John Edward, Jr. lawyer
Flanagan, Joseph Patrick, Jr. lawyer
Flaxman, Howard Richard lawyer
Flexner, Louis Barkhouse anatomist, educator
Foglietta, Thomas Michael congressman
Foner, Philip S. history educator, author
Ford, Kenneth William physicist
†Foreman, Gene Clemons newspaper editor
Forster, Robert Elder, II retired physiology educator
Foti, Margaret Ann association executive, editor
Foulke, William Green banker
Fox, Lawrence J. lawyer
Fox, Reeder Rodman lawyer
Fox, Renée Claire sociology educator
Frank, Harvey lawyer, writer
Frankel, Francine Ruth political science educator
Frankel, Sherman physicist
Frankl, William Stewart cardiologist, educator
Frantz, Charles anthropology educator
Freed, Edmond Lee podiatrist
Freedman, Robert Louis lawyer
Freeland, Michael Willis lawyer
Fregosi, James Louis professional baseball team manager
Freiman, David Burl radiologist
Freyd, Peter John mathematician, computer scientist, educator
Friedman, Frank Bennett lawyer
Friedman, Murray civil rights official, historian
Friedman, Sidney A. financial services executive
Friedman, Steven Lewis lawyer
Friend, Theodore Wood, III foundation executive, historian
Frohlich, Kenneth R. insurance executive
Fromm, Eli engineering educator
Fryman, Louis William lawyer
Fullam, John P. federal judge
Fuller, John Garsed Campbell food and drug company executive
Fuller, William Henry, Jr. professional football player
Furth, John Jacob molecular biologist, pathologist, educator
Fussell, Paul author, English literature educator
Futcher, Palmer Howard physician, educator
Gable, Fred Burnard pharmacist, author
Gabrielson, Ira Wilson physician, educator
Gadsden, Thomas P. lawyer
Gaither, William Samuel consultant
Gamble, Harry T. professional football team executive
García, Celso-Ramón obstetrician and gynecologist
Garcia, Rudolph lawyer
Garfield, Eugene information scientist, author, publisher
Garrison, Walter R. corporate executive
Gartland, John Joseph physician, writer
†Gaul, Gilbert M. reporter
Gawthrop, Robert Smith, III federal judge
†Gendron, Michèle Marguerite Madeleine librarian
Genkin, Barry Howard lawyer
Gerbner, George communications educator, university dean emeritus
Gerhart, Frederick John lawyer
German, Edward Cecil lawyer
Gerrity, Thomas P. dean
Giese, William Herbert tax accountant
Gilbert, Harry Ephraim, Jr. hotel executive
Giles, James T. federal judge
Giles, William Yale professional baseball team executive
Giordano, Nicholas Anthony stock exchange executive
Glanton, Richard H. lawyer
Glassman, Howard Theodore lawyer
Glassmoyer, Thomas Parvin lawyer
Glazer, Ronald Barry lawyer
Glick, John H. oncologist, medical educator
Glicksman, Russell Allen insurance and human resources executive; executive recruiter
Golaski, Walter Michael manufacturing executive
Goldberg, Martin physician, educator
Goldberg, Morton Edward pharmacologist
Goldberg, Richard Robert lawyer
Golden, Gerald Samuel national medical board executive
Goldin, Judah Hebrew literature educator
†Goldman, Yale E. physiologist, educator
Goldsmith, Martin H. health care executive
†Goldsmith, Philip Robert banker
Goldsmith, Sidney physician, scientist, inventor
Goldstein, William Marks lawyer
Goldstine, Herman Heine mathematician, association executive
Gonick, Paul urologist
Goodchild, John Charles, Jr. advertising and public relations executive

Goodenough, Ward Hunt *anthropologist, educator*
Goodman, Charles Schaffner *marketing educator*
Goodman, David Barry Poliakoff *physician, educator*
Goodrich, Herbert Funk, Jr. *lawyer*
Gordon, George Minot *manufacturing executive*
†Goren, Denise Lynne *deputy mayor*
Gorenberg, Charles Lloyd *financial services executive*
Gornish, Gerald *lawyer*
†Gossett, Joyce *religious organization administrator*
Gough, John Francis *lawyer*
Graffman, Gary *pianist*
Graham, Alexander John *classics educator*
Gralish, Tom *photographer*
Granoff, Gail Patricia *lawyer*
Grant, M. Duncan *lawyer*
Grant, Richard W. *lawyer*
Gray, Gordon L. *communications educator*
Green, Clifford Scott *federal judge*
Greenberg, Marshall Gary *marketing research consultant*
Greenberg, Peter Steven *lawyer*
Greenfield, Bruce Harold *lawyer, banker*
Griffen, Ward O., Jr. *surgeon, educator, medical board executive*
Grodnitzky, Alan Scot *lawyer*
Gross, Irwin Lee *lawyer, corporate executive*
Gross, Larry Paul *communications educator*
Grossman, Sanford Jay *economics educator*
Grove, David Lavan *lawyer*
Guckes, William Ruhland, Jr. *insurance executive*
Guenther, George Carpenter *travel company executive*
Guyer, Paul David *philosophy educator, writer*
Hackney, Francis Sheldon *university president*
Hagen, James Alfred *marketing executive*
Haley, Vincent Peter *lawyer*
Hall, Charles P(otter), Jr. *educator consultant*
Hall, Robert J. *newspaper executive*
†Halsey, Ashley, III *newspaper editor*
Hameka, Hendrik Frederik *chemist, educator*
Hamilton, Ralph West *plastic surgeon, educator*
Hamilton, Stephen David Derwent *lawyer*
Hamlin, Arthur Tenney *librarian*
Hammond, Charles Ainley *clergyman*
Hand, Peter James *neurobiologist, educator*
Hansell, John Royer *physician*
Hargens, Charles William, III *electrical engineer, consultant*
Harker, Robert Ian *geologist, educator*
Harkins, John Graham, Jr. *lawyer*
Harvey, Colin Edwin *veterinary medicine educator*
Harvey, John Adriance *psychology and pharmacology educator, researcher, consultant*
†Harvey, William J. *religious service organization, religious publication editor*
Haskin, Donald Lee *bank executive*
Hatoff, Howard Ira *labor lawyer*
Haugaard, Niels *pharmacologist*
Hauptfuhrer, George Jost, Jr. *lawyer*
Havas, Peter *physicist, educator*
Haviland, Bancroft Dawley *lawyer*
Haydanek, Ronald Edward *lawyer*
Hayes, John Freeman *architect*
Haynes, Gary Allen *newspaper editor, journalist*
Hazard, Geoffrey Cornell, Jr. *law educator*
Heilig, William Wright *coal and manufacturing company executive*
†Heilman, Wesley Marvin, III *architect*
Heim, Robert Charles *lawyer*
Helfand, Arthur E. *podiatrist*
Henderson, J(oseph) Welles *lawyer*
Hennessy, Joseph H. *lawyer*
†Henrich, William Joseph, Jr. *lawyer*
Henry, Ragan A. *lawyer, broadcaster*
Hess, Hans Ober *lawyer*
Hess, Sidney Wayne *management educator*
†Heuser, Frederick J. *historian*
Hextall, Ron *professional hockey player*
Higgins, Frederick Benjamin, Jr. *environmental engineering educator, college dean*
Hildebrand, David Kent *statistics educator*
Hirschmann, Ralph Franz *chemist*
Hodavance, Robert S. *lawyer*
Hoelscher, Robert James *lawyer*
Hoenigswald, Henry Max *linguist, educator*
Hoffman, Alan Jay *lawyer*
Hoffman, Daniel (Gerard) *literature educator, poet*
Hoffman, Jerome A. *lawyer*
Hollins, David Michael *professional baseball player*
†Holloman, Margaret *elementary school principal*
Holloway, Hiliary Hamilton *lawyer, banker*
Holmes, Norman Leonard *lawyer*
†Holtzer, Howard *anatomy educator*
†Homme, David C. *architect*
Honnold, John Otis, Jr. *law educator*
Horvath, Joseph John *lawyer, insurance company executive*
Howard-Carter, Theresa *archaeologist*
Hudak, Thomas F(rancis) *finance company executive*
†Hughes, Daniel I. *oil company executive, real estate investor*
Hughes, Thomas Parke *history educator*
Humenuk, William Anzelm *lawyer, partner*
Humes, James Calhoun *lawyer, communications consultant, author*
Hunter, James Austen, Jr. *lawyer*
Hurvich, Leo Maurice *experimental psychologist, educator, vision researcher*
Hussar, Daniel Alexander *pharmacy educator*
Hutchinson, Pemberton *coal company executive*
Hutchinson, William David *federal judge*
Hutton, Herbert J. *federal judge*
†Iams, David Aveling *journalist, columnist*
Iglewicz, Boris *statistician, educator*
Intemann, Robert Louis *physics educator, researcher*
Iskrant, John Dermot *lawyer*
Izenour, Steven *architect*
Jackendoff, Nathaniel *finance educator*
Jackson, Doris Kelly *principal*
Jackson, Laird Gray *physician, educator*
Jacovini, Joseph Henry *lawyer*
Jaffe, Paul Lawrence *lawyer*
Jameson, Dorothea *sensory psychologist*
Jamieson, David Donald *lawyer*
Janzen, Daniel Hunt *biology educator*
Jaron, Dov *biomedical engineer, educator*
Jellinek, Miles Andrew *lawyer*
Jennings, James Walsh *lawyer*
Jensh, Ronald Paul *anatomist, educator*
Johnson, Craig Norman *investment banker*
†Johnson, E. Marshall *biology educator, toxicologist*
Johnson, Elmer Marshall *toxicologist, teratologist*
Johnson, Joseph Eggleston, III *physician, educator*
Jones, Loren Farquhar *electronics executive*
†Jones, O. T. *bishop*
Jones, Robert Jeffries *lawyer*
Jones, Robert Mead, Jr. *lawyer*
Jones, Thomas Chester *reinsurance company executive*
Jordan, Clifford Henry *management consultant*
Jordan, Joe J. *architect*
†Josephs, Babette *legislator*
Joyce, Michael J. *accountant*
Joyce, Philip Halton *journalist*
Joyce, Robert Joseph *insurance executive*
Joyner, J(ames) Curtis *federal judge*
Justice, Jack Burton *lawyer*
Kadison, Richard Vincent *mathematician, educator*
Kahn, James Robert *lawyer*
Kahn, Sigmund Benham *internist, dean*
Kaji, Akira *microbiology scientist, educator*
Kalman, Arnold I. *lawyer*
Kardon, Robert *mortgage company executive*
Katherine, Robert Andrew *chemical company executive*
Katz, Harold *professional basketball team executive*
Katz, Marvin *federal judge*
Kauffman, Bruce William *lawyer, former state supreme court justice*
Kaufman, David Joseph *lawyer*
Kay, Jack Garvin *chemist, educator*
Kaye, Donald *physician, educator*
Kaye, Robert *pediatrics educator*
†Kazanjian, Haig Hagop, Jr. *medical scientist, physician, educator*
Kee, Howard Clark *religion educator*
Keenan, Mary Ann *orthopaedic surgeon, researcher*
Keene, John Clark *lawyer, educator*
Keller, George Charles *academic administrator*
Kellett, Morris C. *lawyer*
Kelley, William Thomas *marketing educator*
Kelly, James McGirr *federal judge*
Kelly, Robert F. *federal judge*
Kempin, Frederick Gustav, Jr. *lawyer, educator*
Kendall, Robert Louis, Jr. *lawyer*
Kenworthy, Thomas Bausman *lawyer*
Kephart, William Milton *sociologist, educator, author*
Kessler, Alan Craig *lawyer*
Kessler, Mark Keil *lawyer*
Kim, Synja P. *corporate business planner*
Kimball, Harry Raymond *medical association executive, educator*
Kimberly, John Robert *management educator, consultant*
Kimelman, Donald Bruce *newspaper editor*
King, Maxwell E. P. *newspaper editor*
Kircher, Philip G. *lawyer*
Kise, James Nelson *architect, urban planner*
Kissick, William Lee *physician, educator*
Kittredge, Thomas M. *lawyer*
Klasko, Herbert Ronald *lawyer, law educator, writer*
Klauder, N. Jeffrey *lawyer*
Klaus, William Robert *lawyer*
Klausner, Samuel Zundel *sociologist, educator*
Klayman, Barry Martin *lawyer*
Klein, Abraham *physics educator, researcher*
Klein, Howard Bruce *lawyer, law educator*
Klein, Julia Meredith *newspaper reporter*
Klein, Lawrence Robert *economist, educator*
Klein, Michael Lawrence *research chemist, educator*
Klein, Robert *manufacturing company executive*
Klein, Samuel Edwin *lawyer*
Kleinzeller, Arnost *physiologist, physician, emeritus educator*
Kligerman, Morton M. *radiologist*
Kline, Thomas Richard *lawyer*
Knauer, Georg Nicolaus *classical philologist*
Knobler, Nathan *art educator*
†Knoll, David E. *petroleum refining company executive*
Knopp, Marvin Isadore *mathematics educator*
Knudson, Alfred George, Jr. *medical geneticist*
Koelle, George Brampton *university pharmacologist, educator*
Kohn, Harold Elias *lawyer*
Kolansky, Harold *physician, psychiatrist, psychoanalyst*
Kolb, Nancy Dwyer *museum director*
Kopecky, Kenneth John *economics educator*
Kopp, Charles Gilbert *lawyer*
Koprowski, Hilary *microbiology educator, medical scientist*
Korsyn, Irene Hahne *marketing executive*
Kotite, Rich *professional football coach*
Kraemer, Michael Frederick *lawyer*
Kraft, Robert Alan *history of religion educator*
Kramer, Meyer *lawyer, editor, clergyman*
Krampf, John Edward *lawyer*
Kresh, J. Yasha *cardiovascular researcher, educator*
Kritchevsky, David *biochemist, educator*
Krol, John Cardinal *retired archbishop*
†Kruhly, James Oleg *architect*
Kruk, John Martin *professional baseball player*
†Krutsick, Robert Stanley *science center executive*
Krzyzanowski, Richard Lucien *lawyer, corporate executive*
Ksansnak, James E. *service management company executive*
Ku, Y. H. *engineering educator*
Kundel, Harold Louis *radiologist, educator*
Kupperman, Louis Brandeis *lawyer*
Kurland, Seymour *lawyer*
Laddon, Warren Milton *lawyer*
Ladman, A(aron) J(ulius) *anatomist, educator*
Laibson, Peter Robert *ophthalmologist*
Lambert, George Robert *lawyer*
Lambertsen, Christian James *environmental physiologist, physician, educator*
Landis, Edgar David *services business company executive*
Lang, Richard Warren *economist, banker*
†Langacker, Paul George *physics educator*
Larsen, Terrance A. *bank holding company executive*
Larson, Donald Clayton *physics educator, consultant*
Laufer, Igor *radiologist*
LaValley, Frederick J. M. *lawyer*
Lawley, Alan *materials engineering educator*
Lawson, John Quinn *architect*
Leary, Michael Warren *journalist*
†Leatherbee, William Bell *architect*
Le Clair, Charles George *artist, retired dean*
Leddy, John Henry *lawyer*
†Lederer, Marie A. *politcal campaign organizer*
Ledwith, James Robb *lawyer*
Ledwith, John Francis *lawyer*
Lee, Charles *emeritus English language and literature educator, arts critic*
Lee, Chong-Sik *political scientist, educator*
Leech, Noyes Elwood *lawyer, educator*
Lefer, Allan Mark *physiologist*
Lehr, Michael *lawyer*
Leibovitz, Mitchell G. *retail executive*
Leimkuhler, Gerard Joseph, Jr. *financial holding company executive*
Leiter, Robert Allen *journalist, magazine editor*
Lent, John Anthony *journalist, educator*
Leonard, Thomas Aloysius *lawyer*
Levin, A. Leo *law educator, retired government official*
Levin, Murray Simon *lawyer*
Levine, Herbert Samuel *economics educator, research consultant*
Levine, Rhea Joy Cottler *anatomy educator*
Levit, Edithe Judith *physician, medical association administrator*
Levitt, Israel Monroe *astronomer*
Levy, Dale Penneys *lawyer*
Levy, Robert Isaac *physician, educator, research director*
Lewin, Moshe *historian, educator*
Lewis, Christopher Alan *lawyer*
Lewis, Claude Aubrey *columnist*
Lewis, George Withrow *business executive*
Lewis, John Hardy, Jr. *lawyer*
Lewis, Paul Le Roy *pathology educator*
†Lewis, Thomas John, III *hospital administrator*
†Li, Weiye *ophthalmologist, biochemist, educator*
Libonati, Michael Ernest *lawyer, educator, writer*
Lichtenstein, Lawrence Jay *lawyer*
Lichtenstein, Robert Jay *lawyer*
†Liebman, Paul Arno *biophysicist, educator*
Lief, Harold Isaiah *psychiatrist*
Lillie, Charisse Ranielle *lawyer, educator*
Lipkin, Edward B. *real estate developer*
Lipman, Frederick D. *lawyer*
Lippincott, Philip Edward *paper products company executive*
Listgarten, Max Albert *periodontics educator*
Litt, Mitchell *chemical engineer, educator, bioengineer*
Litwack, Gerald *biochemistry educator, academic administrator*
Live, Israel *microbiologist, educator*
Llewellyn, J. Bruce *food products executive*
Lloyd, Albert Lawrence, Jr. *German language educator*
Lodish, Leonard Melvin *marketing educator, entrepreneur*
Loeb, Vernon Frederick *journalist*
Loewenstein, Benjamin Steinberg *lawyer*
Lombard, John James, Jr. *lawyer*
Longnecker, David E. *anesthesiologist, educator*
†LoSciuto, Leonard Anthony *psychologist, educator*
Louchheim, Frank Pfeifer *management consultant*
Lovelady, Steven M. *newspaper editor*
Loveless, George Group *lawyer*
Lowery, William Herbert *lawyer*
Lu, Ponzy *molecular biology educator*
Lucas, John Harding, Jr. *professional basketball coach*
Lucey, John David, Jr. *lawyer*
Lucid, Robert Francis *English educator*
†Ludden, David *Asian studies educator*
Ludwig, Edmund Vincent *federal judge*
Lundy, Joseph E. *lawyer*
Luscombe, Herbert Alfred *physician, educator*
Lustbader, Philip Lawrence *lawyer*
Lyon, William Carl *sports columnist*
Lytle, Richard Harold *university administrator*
MacGregor, David Bruce *lawyer*
Maclay, Donald Merle *lawyer*
Madeira, Edward W(alter), Jr. *lawyer*
Madigan, Martha *photographer, artist, photography educator*
Madow, Leo *psychiatrist, educator*
Madva, Stephen Alan *lawyer*
Magargee, W(illiam) Scott, III *lawyer*
Magarity, Gregory T. *lawyer*
Magaziner, Fred Thomas *lawyer*
Magaziner, Henry Jonas *architect*
Magee, Wayne Edward *biochemistry educator, researcher*
Maguire, Henry Clinton, Jr. *dermatologist*
Mai, Elizabeth Hardy *lawyer*
Maitin, Sam(uel Calman) (Sam Maitin) *artist*
Malamud, Daniel *biochemistry educator*
Mancall, Elliott Lee *neurologist, educator*
Mangione, Jerre Gerlando *author, educator*
Mann, Theodore R. *lawyer*
Mannino, Edward Francis *lawyer*
Mansfield, Carl Major *radiation oncology educator*
Mansfield, Edwin *economist, educator*
Mansmann, Herbert C., Jr. *physician, educator*
Mardar, Dianna *reporter*
Marion, David H. *lawyer*
Marple, Dorothy Jane *retired church executive*
Marshall, Bryan Edward *anesthesiologist, educator*
Marshall, Donald Tompkins *industrial distribution executive*
Mason, Theodore W. *lawyer*
Masterson, Thomas A. *lawyer*
Mastroianni, Luigi, Jr. *physician, educator*
Mather, Barbara W. *lawyer*
Mathes, Stephen Jon *lawyer*
Matschinsky, Franz Maximilian *biochemistry and biophysics educator, researcher*
Matsumoto, Teruo *surgeon, educator*
Mattoon, Peter Mills *lawyer*
Maurer, Paul Herbert *biochemist, educator*
Maxey, David Walker *lawyer*
Maxman, Susan Abel *architect*
Mayock, Robert Lee *internist*
Mazzatenta, Rosemary Dorothy *school administrator*
McCabe, James J. *lawyer*
McDougall, Walter Allan *history educator*
McElroy, Richard P. *lawyer*
McGinley, Joseph Patrick *brokerage house executive*
McGlynn, Joseph Leo, Jr. *federal judge*
McHarg, Ian Lennox *landscape architect, regional planner, educator*
McKeever, John Eugene *lawyer*
McKenna, Thomas Morrison, Jr. *social services organization executive*
†Mc Mahon, Charles Joseph, Jr. *materials science educator*
McMenamin, Richard F. *lawyer*
McNeill, Corbin Asahel, Jr. *utility executive*
McQuiston, Robert Earl *lawyer*
Means, John Barkley *foreign language educator, association executive*
Meigs, John Forsyth *lawyer*
Mella, Arthur John *insurance company executive*
†Melnick, William *advertising executive*
Melvin, John Lewis *physical and rehabilitation physician, educator*
Mendels, Joseph *psychiatrist, educator*
†Menken, Jane Ava *demographer, educator*
Mensing, Stephen Gustav *bishop*
Merrifield, Dudley Bruce *business educator, former government official*
Merritt, John C. *investment banker*
Mesirov, Leon Isaac *lawyer*
Metzker, Ray K. *photographer*
Meyer, Leonard B. *musician, educator*
Meyer, Paul William *arboretum director, horticulturist*
Meyers, Howard L. *lawyer*
Meyerson, Martin *university executive, educator*
†Mezzacappa, Dale Veronica *journalist*
Michael, Henry N. *geographer, anthropologist*
Micko, Alexander S. *financial executive*
Milbourne, Walter Robertson *lawyer*
Miller, Barry *academic administrator, psychologist*
†Miller, Charles Q. *engineering company executive*
Miller, Henry Franklin *lawyer*
Miller, Leonard David *surgeon*
Miller, Margery K. *lawyer*
Miller, Ronald Eugene *regional science educator*
Milone, Francis Michael *lawyer*
Ming, Si-Chun *pathologist, educator*
Minisi, Anthony S. *lawyer*
Mirabello, Francis Joseph *lawyer*
Mirick, Henry Dustin *architect*
Misher, Allen *college president*
Mitchell, Ehrman Burkman, Jr. *architect*
Mitchell, Howard Estill *human resources educator, consultant*
Mode, Charles J. *mathematician, educator*
Montgomery, David Paul *professional baseball team executive*
Montgomery, Edward Alembert, Jr. *developer*
Moore, Acel *journalist*
Moore, Michael Scott *law and philosophy educator*
Morgan, Arlene Notoro *newspaper editor, reporter, recruiter*
Morikawa, Dennis J. *lawyer*
†Morlok, Edward Karl *engineering educator, consultant*
Morris, George Norton *insurance company executive*
Morris, Thomas Bateman, Jr. *lawyer*
Morrison, Donald Franklin *statistician, educator*
Mosher, Paul H. *research library administrator, author, consultant*
Moss, Arthur Henshey *lawyer*
Moss, Roger William, Jr. *historian, writer, administrator*
Mostovoy, Marc Sanders *conductor*
Moyer, F. Stanton *financial executive, advisor*
Mudd, Emily Hartshorne *counselor, educator, researcher*
Mulholland, S. Grant *urologist*
Mulholland, Terence John (Terry Mulholland) *professional baseball player*
Mullen, Eileen Anne *training and development executive*
Mulroney, John Patrick *chemical company executive*
†Munch, David Edward *management executive*
Murdoch, Lawrence Corlies, Jr. *retired banker, economist*
Murphey, Murray Griffin *history educator*
Murray, Terry (Terence Rodney Murray) *professional hockey team coach*
Murrell, Thomas W., III *lawyer*
Myers, Kenneth Raymond *lawyer*
Nadel, Marvin *retired engineering and management consulting firm executive*
Nadley, Harris Jerome *accountant, educator, writer*
Nalle, Peter Devereux *publishing company executive*
Narin, Stephen B. *lawyer*
Nast, Dianne Martha *lawyer*
Naughton, James Martin *newspaper editor*
Naylor, Robert Ernest, Jr. *chemical company executive*
Neilson, Benjamin Reath *lawyer*
Nelson, Nels Robert *drama critic*
Neubauer, Joseph *business executive*
Newbold, Arthur *lawyer*
Newburger, Frank L., Jr. *retired investment broker*
Newcomer, Clarence Charles *federal judge*
†Newman, Sanders David *lawyer*
News, Kathryn Anne *editor, educator, writer*
Nichols, Charles Warren *ophthalmologist*
Niewiarowski, Stefan *physiology educator, biomedical research scientist*
Nix, Robert N(elson) C(ornelius), Jr. *state supreme court chief justice*
Nixon, Eugene Ray *chemist, educator*
Nofer, George Hancock *lawyer*
Noordergraaf, Abraham *biophysics educator*
Nowell, Peter Carey *pathologist, educator*
Nussbaum, Paul Eugene *journalist*
O'Brien, Robert Thomas *investment company executive*
O'Brien, William Jerome, II *lawyer*
O'Connor, Joseph A., Jr. *lawyer*
O'Donnell, G. Daniel *lawyer*
O'Leary, Dennis Joseph *lawyer*
Olsen, George Allen *engineering executive*
†Olshin, Samuel E. *architect*
Ominsky, Harris *lawyer*
O'Neill, Thomas Newman, Jr. *federal judge*
Oppenheimer, Jane Marion *biologist, historian, educator*
O'Reilly, Timothy Patrick *lawyer*
Orlando, Danielle *opera company administrator*
Osborne, Frederick Spring, Jr. *academic administrator*
Oswald, Stanton S. *lawyer*
Padova, John R. *federal judge*
Padulo, Louis *university administrator*
Paglia, Camille *writer, educator*
Pagliaro, James Domenic *lawyer*
Pak, Hyung Woong *foundation executive, educator*
Palmer, Richard Ware *lawyer*
Palmer, Russell Eugene *investment executive*
Panitch, Lois Ponnock Krebs *health care foundation executive*
Panzer, Mitchell Emanuel *lawyer*
Paone, Peter *artist*
Paquette, Joseph F., Jr. *utility company executive*
Parish, Lawrence Charles *physician, editor*
Parke, Jo Anne Mark *publishing company executive*
Parmiter, James Darlin *safety engineer*
Parry, Lance Aaron *newspaper executive*
Patel, Ronald Anthony *editor newspaper*
Patrick, George W. *lawyer*
Peachey, Lee DeBorde *biology educator*
†Pearson, Davis *architect*
Peirce, Donald Oluf *elementary education educator*
Pelham, Fran O'Byrne *writer, teacher*
Pelkaus, Edward Egils *civil engineer*
Pellicciotti, Patricia M. *management consultant, financial analyst*
Pepe, Frank A. *cell and developmental biology educator*
†Pepper, Jane G. *bank executive*
Percy, Ann Buchanan *museum curator*

Perkins, George Holmes architectural educator, architect
Perlmutter, Felice Davidson social work administration educator
Perry, Robert Palese molecular biologist, educator
Peters, Edward Murray history educator
Peterson, Charles Emil architect
Pipes, Daniel writer, editor
Pipes, Wesley O'Feral civil engineering educator
Pittinger, Wilbur Barke medical center executive
†Pizzi, Charles Peter association president
Pollack, Michael lawyer
Pollack, Solomon Robert bioengineering educator
Porter, Gerald Joseph mathematician, educator
†Porter, Jill journalist
Porter, Roger John medical research administrator, neurologist, pharmacologist
Posner, Edward Martin lawyer
†Postlewaite, Andrew William economics and public policy educator
Potamkin, Meyer P. mortgage banker
Potsic, William Paul physician, educator
Poul, Franklin lawyer
Powell, Walter Hecht labor arbitrator
Powers, Richard Augustine, III federal judge
Pratter, Gene E. K. lawyer
Premack, David psychologist
Preston, Samuel Hulse demographer
Preston, Seymour Stotler, III manufacturing company executive
Prevoznik, Stephen Joseph anesthesiologist
Price, Robert Stanley lawyer
Pritchard, James Bennett archaeologist, educator, author
Prockop, Darwin Johnson biochemist, physician
Promislo, Daniel lawyer
†Prowler, Donald Marc architect
Quinn, John Albert chemical engineering educator
Rabinowitz, Howard K. physician, educator
Rabinowitz, Samuel Nathan lawyer
Rachofsky, David J. lawyer
Rackow, Julian Paul lawyer
Rahenkamp, John Edward landscape architecture and planning company executive
Rainey, Arthur H. lawyer
Ralph, Thomas A. lawyer
†Rand, Samuel advertising executive
Rauch, John Keiser, Jr. architect
Reagan, Harry Edwin, III lawyer
Reath, George, Jr. lawyer
†Reber, Stanley Roy insurance company executive
Redeker, James Russell lawyer
Reed, Alan L. lawyer
Reed, Clarence Raymond association executive
Reed, Lowell A., Jr. federal judge
Reed, Michael Haywood lawyer
Regan, Robert Charles English language educator
Reich, Abraham Charles lawyer
Reich, Morton Melvyn marketing communications company executive
Reid, John Mitchell biomedical engineer
Reinecke, Robert Dale ophthalmologist
Reiss, John Barlow lawyer
Reitz, Curtis Randall lawyer, educator
Remenick, Seymour artist, educator
Rendell, Edward Gene mayor
Rescorla, Robert Arthur psychology educator
Rhoads, Jonathan Evans surgeon
Richette, Lisa Aversa judge
Rickels, Karl psychiatrist, physician, educator
Rima, Ingrid Hahne economics educator
Rimel, Rebecca Webster foundation executive
Rimerman, Morton Walter utility executive
Riordan, John Thomas management consultant
Ripley, Edward Franklin investment company executive
†Rivas, Joyce Margaret advertising executive
Rizzo, Richard C. lawyer
Roberts, Carl Geoffrey lawyer
Roberts, Jay pharmacologist, educator
Roberts, Ralph Joel cable television, telephone communications and background music company executive
†Roberts, William Henry architect
Robinson, Robert L. financial service company executive, lawyer
Robreno, Eduardo C. federal judge
Rocher, Ludo humanities educator
Rodin, Judith Seitz academic administrator, educator
Rogers, Fred Baker medical educator
Rohrlich, George Friedrich social economist
Roomberg, Lila Goldstein lawyer
Root, Franklin Russell business educator
Root, Stanley William, Jr. lawyer
Rorke, Lucy Balian neuropathologist
Rosato, Francis Ernest surgeon
Rose, Robert Lawrence lawyer, financial services company executive
Rosen, Gerald Harris physicist, consultant, educator
Rosenberg, Charles Ernest historian, educator
Rosenberg, David Alan military historian, educator
Rosenberg, Robert Allen psychologist, educator, optometrist
Rosenbleeth, Richard Marvin lawyer
Rosenbloom, Bert marketing educator
†Rosenbloom, Joel molecular biologist, educator
Rosenbloom, Sanford M. lawyer
Rosenfield, Bruce Alan lawyer
Rosenstein, James Alfred lawyer
†Rosenthal, Robert Jon newspaper editor, journalist
Rosoff, William A. lawyer
Ross, Daniel R. lawyer
Ross, George Martin investment banker
Ross, James Francis philosophy educator
Ross, Leonard Lester anatomist
Ross, Murray Louis lawyer, business executive
Ross, Roderic Henry insurance company executive
†Rossi, Steven B. newspaper publishing executive
†Rotell, Thomas M. publishing executive
Rouse, Andrew Miles business consultant
†Rovera, Giovanni Aurelio medical educator, scientist
Rowan, Richard Lamar business management educator
†Rowell, Lester John, Jr. insurance company executive
Rubin, Emanuel pathologist, educator
Rudolf, Max symphony and opera director
Rulon, Richard R. lawyer
Rumpf, John Louis university official, civil engineer, educator
Rutman, Robert Jesse biochemist, educator
†Ryan, Desmond film critic
Ryan, Leonard Eames administrative law judge
Rybczynski, Witold Marian architect, educator, writer
Rykwert, Joseph architecture and art history educator
Sabat, Richard J. lawyer
Sabloff, Jeremy Arac archaeologist
†Sage, Louis E. environmental science executive
Saks, Stephen Howard accountant
Salganicoff, Leon pharmacology educator
Salmoiraghi, Gian Carlo physiologist, educator
†Salvatore, Frank A. state legislator
Samson, Peter lawyer
†Samsot, Robert Louis newspaper editor, consultant
†Sandler, Abraham minister
Santomero, Anthony M. business educator
Santos, Adele Naude architect, educator
Sanyour, Michael Louis, Jr. financial services company executive
Sartorius, Peter S. lawyer
Satinsky, Barnett lawyer
Saul, Ralph Southey financial service executive
Savitz, Samuel J. actuarial consulting firm executive
Sawallisch, Wolfgang conductor
Sax, Helen Spigel lawyer
Saylor, Peter M. architect
Scandura, Joseph Michael education researcher, software engineer
†Schad, Mike professional football player
Schaedler, Russell William microbiologist, physicians, educator
†Schaffer, Jan newspaper editor
Schaub, Harry Carl lawyer
Scher, Howard Dennis lawyer
†Schidlow, Daniel pediatrician, medical association administrator
Schimmel, Allan rail company executive
Schmidt, Michael Jack former professional baseball player
Schneider, Carl W. lawyer
Schneider, Jan obstetrics and gynecology educator
Schneider, Pam Horvitz lawyer
Schneider, Richard Graham lawyer
Scholl, David Allen federal judge
Schotland, Donald Lewis neurologist, educator
Schumacher, H(arry) Ralph internist, researcher, medical educator
Schumann, William Henry, III financial executive
Schwan, Herman Paul electrical engineering and physical science educator, research scientist
Schwartz, Gordon Francis surgeon, educator
Schwartz, Robert M. lawyer
Schwarz, Robert Devlin art dealer
Scirica, Anthony Joseph federal judge
Scott, Donald Allison lawyer
Scott, Michael Timothy lawyer
Scott, Robert Montgomery museum executive, lawyer
Scott, William Proctor, III lawyer
Searcy, Jarrell D. (Jay) sportswriter
†Searcy, Jay Sportswriter
Sebold, Russell Perry, III Romance languages educator, author
Segal, Bernard Gerard lawyer
Segal, Bernard Louis physician, educator
Segal, Irving Randall lawyer
Segal, Robert Martin lawyer
Segrè, Nina lawyer
Sevy, Roger Warren retired pharmacology educator
Sewell, Darrel Leslie art museum curator
Shah, Bipin Chandra banker
†Shapiro, Howie newspaper editor
Shapiro, Norma Sondra Levy federal judge
Shapiro, Raymond L. lawyer
†Shapiro, Sandor Solomon hematologist
Sharbaugh, Thomas J. lawyer
Shatz, Stephen Sidney mathematician, educator
Shaw, Mari Gursky lawyer
Shecter, Howard L. lawyer
Sheehan, Donald Thomas university administrator
Shelkrot, Elliot Louis librarian
Shen, Benjamin Shih-Ping scientist, engineer, educator
Shepard, Geoffrey Carroll corporate lawyer
Shestack, Jerome Joseph lawyer
Shiekman, Laurence Zeid lawyer
Shields, Jerry Allen ophthalmologist, educator
Shields, Robert Emmet lawyer
Shils, Edward B. management educator, lawyer
Shockman, Gerald David microbiologist, educator
Shoemaker, Innis Howe art museum curator
Shoup, Michael C. newspaper reporter, editor
Showers, Ralph Morris electrical engineer educator
Shusterman, Murray H. lawyer
Shuter, Bruce Donald lawyer
Siembieda, Matthew John lawyer
Sigmond, Robert M. medical economist
Silberberg, Donald H. neurologist
Silvers, Willys Kent geneticist
†Sims, Armita B. principal
Siskind, Ralph Walter lawyer
Sivin, Nathan historian, educator
†Skalka, Anna Marie molecular biologist, virologist
Sloviter, Dolores Korman federal judge
Sloviter, Henry Allan medical educator
Small, Henry Gilbert information scientist, researcher
Smith, John Francis, III lawyer
Smith, Lloyd musician
Smith, Raymond W. telecommunications company executive
Smith, Robert Rutherford university dean, communication educator
Smolin, Ronald Philip publisher
Snider, Edward Malcolm professional hockey club executive
Snider, Harold Wayne risk and insurance educator
Snider, Jay T. professional hockey team executive
Snyder, Lee H. lawyer
Snyder, Ralph Sheldon lawyer
Solano, Carl Anthony lawyer
Solmssen, Peter university president
Soloff, Louis Alexander physician, educator
Solomon, Phyllis Linda mental health sciences educator, researcher
Solomon, Vita Petrosky artist
Somers, Hans Peter lawyer
Sorgenti, Harold Andrew petroleum and chemical company executive
Sovie, Margaret Doe nursing administrator, college dean
Spaeth, Edmund Benjamin, Jr. lawyer, law educator, former judge
Spaeth, George Link physician, ophthalmology educator
Spandorfer, Merle Sue artist, educator, author
Spector, Harvey M. osteopathic physician
Spector, Martin Wolf lawyer, business executive
Spencer, Steven D. lawyer
Spikol, Art editor, writer, illustrator
Spiro, Walter Anselm advertising and public relations agency executive
Spolan, Harmon Samuel banker
Sprague, James Mather medical scientist, educator
Stack, Stephen A., Jr. lawyer
Stakias, G. Michael lawyer
†Stalberg, Zachary newspaper editor
Staloff, Arnold Fred financial executive
Starr, Allan H. lawyer
Stecklow, Steve journalist
Steel, Howard Haldeman pediatric orthopaedic surgeon
Steele, James B. journalist
Steinberg, Bernard D. electrical engineer, educator, researcher
Steinberg, Robert Philip lawyer
Steinhardt, Paul Joseph physics educator, consultant
Stern, Joan Naomi lawyer
Sternberg, Donna Udin lawyer
Stevens, Rosemary A. academic dean, public health and social history educator
Stewart, James Gathings insurance company executive
Stewart, Robert Forrest, Jr. lawyer
Stiller, Jennifer Anne lawyer
†Storm, Jonathan Morris television critic
Strawbridge, Peter S. department store executive
Strickler, Matthew M. lawyer
Stunkard, Albert James physician, educator
Stuntebeck, Clinton A. lawyer
Subak, John Thomas lawyer
Sudak, Howard Stanley physician, psychiatry educator
Sugarman, Robert Jay lawyer
Sulyk, Stephen archbishop
Summers, Anita Arrow public policy and management educator
Summers, Clyde Wilson law educator
Summers, Robert economics educator
Sunderman, Frederick William physician, educator, author, musician
Suplee, Dennis Raymond lawyer
Sutman, Francis Xavier university dean
Sutnick, Alton Ivan dean, educator, researcher, physician
Swichar, Edward lawyer
Swinburne, Herbert Hillhouse architect
Sykes, David Terrence lawyer
Tague, Barry Elwert securities trader
†Taichman, Norton Stanley pathology educator
†Tait, Elaine restaurant critic
Tait, John Edwin insurance company executive
†Takiff, Jonathan Henry B. journalist
Tarbox, Frank Kolbe insurance company executive
Tasman, William Samuel ophthalmologist, medical association executive
Taubman, Paul James economics educator
Taylor, Wilson H. diversified financial company executive
Temin, Michael Lehman lawyer
Terry, John Joseph transportation investor
Thackray, Arnold Wilfrid historian, educator
Thomas, Frank M., Jr. lawyer
Thomas, Regina O'Brien lawyer
Thompson, Sheldon Lee refining company executive
Thomson, Keith Stewart science museum administrator, writer
†Thrower, John E. architectural firm executive
Thurston, David E. lawyer, general counsel
Tierney, Brian Patrick advertising and public relations executive
Tiger, Ira Paul lawyer
Tise, Larry Edward historian, historic site director
Tomazinis, Anthony Rodoflos city planning educator
Tomiyasu, Kiyo consulting engineer
Toolan, Brian Paul newspaper editor
Torg, Joseph Steven orthopedic surgeon, educator
Torregrossa, Joseph Anthony lawyer
Tourtellotte, Charles Dee physician, educator
Tucker, David newspaper editor
†Tunnessen, Walter William, Jr. pediatrician
Turner, Franklin Delton bishop
†Turow, Joseph Gregory communication educator
Tyng, Anne Griswold architect
†Ugen, Kenneth Eugene medical researcher
Undercofler, J(onas) Clayton lawyer
Vaira, Peter Francis lawyer
Valentini, Robert M. telecommunications industry executive
Veith, Richard Lee oil company executive
Venturi, Robert architect
Vernon, Shirley Jane architect, educator
†Vinh, Binh architect
Vitek, Vaclav materials scientist
Volpicelli, Stephen L. lawyer
von Seldeneck, Judith Metcalfe executive search firm executive
Wachman, Marvin university chancellor
Wadden, Thomas Antony psychology educator
Wagner, Thomas Joseph lawyer, insurance company executive
Wald, Martin lawyer
Waldman, Jay Carl federal judge
Wales, Walter D. physicist, educator
Walker, Herschel football player
Walker, Kent lawyer
Wallace, Anthony Francis Clarke anthropologist, educator
Wallace, David Alexander architect, educator
Wallace, Herbert William physician, surgery educator, researcher
†Wallace, Linda Suzan journalist
†Walls, William Walton, Jr. helicopter company executive
Walters, Christopher Kent lawyer
Wambold, Judson J. lawyer
†Ward, Butch newspaper editor
Ward, Hiley Henry journalist, educator
†Warner, Frank Wilson, III mathematics educator
Warner, Theodore Kugler, Jr. lawyer
Washington, Grover, Jr. musician, producer, composer, arranger
Waskow, Arthur Ocean theologian, educator
Watson, Bernard Charles foundation administrator
Webber, John Bentley orthopedic surgeon
Weber, Janet M. nurse
Weidner, Roswell Theodore artist
Weil, Jeffrey George lawyer
Wein, Alan Jerome urologist, educator, researcher
Weiner, Warren retail executive
Weisberg, Morris L. retired lawyer
Weisz, Paul B(urg) physicist, chemical engineer
Wellington, Ralph Glenn lawyer
Wendt, Henry, III pharmaceutical company executive
Wernick, Richard Frank composer, conductor
Wetzel, Carroll Robbins lawyer
Whatmough, J. Jeremy T. railway executive
White, Albert J. health products executive
White, Warren Wurtele retailing executive
Whiteside, William Anthony, Jr. lawyer
Whitman, Bradford F. lawyer
Whitman, Jules Isidoré lawyer
Whybrow, Peter Charles psychiatrist, educator
Wiener, Ronald Martin lawyer
Wiener, Thomas Eli lawyer
Wiksten, Barry Frank communications executive
Wild, Richard P. lawyer
Wilde, Norman Taylor, Jr. investment banking company executive
Wilder, Robert George advertising and public relations executive
†Wilkinson, Signe cartoonist
Williams, Juanita Lundy elementary education educator
†Wilmot, Louise C. career military officer
Wilson, Bruce Brighton transportation executive
Wilson, James Lawrence chemical company executive
Wilson, Marjorie Price physician, medical commission executive
Wilson, Samuel Mack university dean, educator
Wind, Yoram Jerry marketing and management educator
Winfrey, Marion Lee television critic
Winkler, Sheldon dentist, educator
Witt, Thomas Powell lawyer
Wixon, Rufus retired accounting educator
Woestendiek, (William) John, Jr. reporter
Wolf, Robert B. lawyer
Wolfbein, Seymour Louis economist, educator
Wolfgang, Marvin Eugene sociologist, criminologist, educator
Wolitarsky, James William securities industry executive
Wolkin, Paul Alexander lawyer, former institute executive
Wollman, Harry medical educator
Wood, William Philler lawyer
Woodruff, Margaret Smith lawyer
Woods, Richard Seavey accountant, educator
Wright, Minturn Tatum, III lawyer
Wrobleski, Jeanne Pauline lawyer
Wruble, Brian Frederick investment management company executive
Wysocki, F(elix) Michael lawyer
Yanoff, Myron ophthalmologist
Yohn, William Hendricks, Jr. federal judge
Young, Andrew Brodbeck lawyer
†Young, Donald Stirling clinical pathology educator
Young, Robert Crabill medical researcher, science facility administrator, internist
Yunis, Jorge Jose geneticist, pathologist, educator
Zemel, Jay Norman electrical engineer, educator
Ziegler, Donald Robert accountant
Ziff, Lloyd Richard lawyer
Ziga, Kathleen lawyer
Ziomek, Thomas John lawyer
Zivitz, Stephen Charles lawyer
†Zucchino, David Alan newspaper journalist
Zucker, William retired business educator
Zurmuhle, Robert Walter physicist
Zweiman, Burton physician, scientist, educator

Philipsburg

Reiter, Daisy K. elementary education educator

Phoenixville

Lukacs, John Adalbert historian, retired educator
Wright, Jean Norman elementary education educator

Pittsburgh

Aaron, Marcus, II lawyer
Aaronson, Joel P. lawyer
Abdelhak, Sherif Samy health science executive
Agnew, Franklin Ernest, III former food company executive
Alberts, Robert Carman author
Alexander, James Eckert editor
Allen, Thomas E. obstetrician/gynecologist
Alstadt, Lynn Jeffery lawyer
Alvarez, Paul Hubert communications and public relations consultant
†Ambrose, Donetta federal judge
Amon Parisi, Cristina Hortensia mechanical engineering educator, researcher
†Anderson, Gary Allan professional football player
Anderson, John Leonard chemical engineering educator
Anderson, John Robert psychology and computer science educator
Andersson, Craig Remington chemical company executive
Anthony, Edward Mason linguistics educator
Apone, Carl Anthony journalist
Aranson, Michael J. lawyer
Arkus, Leon Anthony art consultant, former museum director
Armstrong, David J. lawyer
Armstrong, Jack Gilliland lawyer
Aronson, Mark Berne real estate broker, consultant
Arthur, John Morrison retired utility executive
†Astorino, Louis Don architect
Baier, George Patrick lawyer, electrical engineer
Balada, Leonardo composer, educator
†Balas, Egon applied mathematician, educator
Baldisseri, Marie Rosanne physician
Bardyguine, Patricia Wilde ballerina, ballet theatre executive
Barmen, Stewart B. lawyer
†Barone, Eugene J. medical products executive
Barry, Herbert, III psychologist
Bartley, Burnett Graham, Jr. oil company and manufacturing executive
Basinski, Anthony Joseph lawyer
Beachley, Michael Charles radiologist
Bearman, Toni Carbo information scientist
Beck, Paul Augustine lawyer
Behrend, William Louis electrical engineer
Bell, Jay Stuart professional baseball player
Belnap, Nuel Dinsmore, Jr. philosophy educator
Bender, Charles Christian retail home center executive
Benson, Stuart Wells, III lawyer
Berkman, Marshall L. manufacturing company executive
Berliner, Hans Jack computer scientist
Berman, Malcolm Frank health facility administrator
Bernier, George Matthew, Jr. physician, medical educator, medical school dean
Bernt, Benno Anthony financial and business executive
Berry, Guy Curtis polymer science educator, researcher
Bevan, William, III lawyer
Biondi, Manfred Anthony physicist, educator
Birks, Neil metallurgical engineering educator, consultant

Bjorhovde, Reidar civil engineer, educator, researcher, consultant
Black, Alexander lawyer
Bleil, Walter G. lawyer
Blenko, Walter John, Jr. lawyer
Bloch, Alan Neil federal judge
Bloom, William Millard furnace design engineer
Blumstein, Alfred urban and public affairs educator
Bobrow, Davis Bernard public policy educator
Bogdanovich, Joseph James food company executive
Bohlin, Peter Quarfordt architect
Bonessa, Dennis R. lawyer
Borkovic, David Allen lawyer
Borle, André Bernard physiologist
Bothner-By, Aksel Arnold chemist
Boyd, William, Jr. business advisor, banker
†Brenenborg, David C. architectural firm executive
Brennan, Carey M. lawyer
Brewer, William Dixon manufacturing executive
†Briskman, Louis J. lawyer
Brosky, John G. judge
Broussard, Elsie Rita physician, educator, researcher
Brown, Bobby R. coal company executive
Brown, David Ronald lawyer
Bryant, Randal Everitt computer science educator, consultant
Buchanan, James Junkin classics educator
Buerger, David Bernard lawyer
†Buford, Earl, Jr. protective services official
Burbea, Jacob N. mathematics educator
Burger, Herbert Francis advertising agency executive
Burnham, Donald Clemens manufacturing company executive
Cahouet, Frank Vondell banker
Caldwell, John Gilmore oil and gas exploration and production executive
Candris, Laura A. lawyer
Capobianco, Tito opera director
Caretto, Albert Alexander chemist, educator
Carr, Walter James, Jr. research physicist, consultant
Carroll, Holbert Nicholson political science educator
†Carter, Donald K. architectural firm executive
Casasent, David Paul electrical engineering educator, data processing executive
Casey, Robert J. international trade association executive
Cassidy, William Arthur geology and planetary science educator
Catell, Grace Louise nursing educator
Chamberlain, Denise Kay lawyer, banking counsel
Chao, Chong-Yun mathematics educator
Charap, Stanley Harvey electrical engineering educator
Cheever, George Martin lawyer
Chenery, Robin metals manufacturing executive
Chiang, Shiao-Hung chemical engineering educator
†Choyke, Wolfgang Justus physicist
Christiano, Paul P. academic administrator, civil engineering educator
†Christof, Joseph S. D., II lawyer
†Chun, Sun W. energy technology administrator
Clack, Jerry classics educator
Clark, Gary M. electronics executive
Clark, Richard A. lawyer
Clyde, Larry Forbes banker
Cohen, Bernard Leonard physicist, educator
Cohill, Maurice Blanchard, Jr. federal judge
Colen, Frederick Haas lawyer
Coltman, John Wesley physicist
Coney, Aims C., Jr. lawyer, labor-management negotiator
Connell, Janice T. lawyer, author, arbitrator, business executive
Connors, Eugene Kenneth lawyer
Conti, Joy Flowers lawyer
Cooper, Adrian football player
Cooper, Thomas Louis lawyer
Cooper, William Marion physician
Corry, Charles Albert steel and energy company executive
Costello, Thomas Patrick manufacturing executive
Courtsal, Donald Preston manufacturing company executive, financial consultant
Cowan, Barton Zalman lawyer
Cowden, Jere Lee management consultant
Cowher, Bill professional football coach
Craig, David W. judge
Craig, Edward Armstrong, III lawyer
†Craig, John Gilbert, Jr. newspaper editor
†Croan, Robert James music critic, singer
Croneberger, Robert Bruce, Jr. library director
Cummins, James Dale coal executive
Curtis, Gregory Dyer investment company executive, foundation administrator, lawyer, author, poet
Cutler, John Charles physician, educator
Cyert, Richard Michael former university president, economist
Dameshek, H(arold) Lee physician
Damianos, Sylvester architect, sculptor
†Danforth, Douglas Dewitt manufacturing company executive
Daniel, Robert Michael lawyer
Dauler, L. Van V., Jr. chemicals executive
Davidson, George A., Jr. utility company executive
Davis, John Phillips, Jr. lawyer
†Davis, Lewis U., Jr. lawyer
Davis, Otto Anderson economics educator
Dawes, Robyn Mason psychology educator
Dawson, Mary Ruth curator
Day, Maurice Jerome automobile parts distributing company executive
DeForest, Walter Pattison, III lawyer
deGroat, William Chesney pharmacology educator
Delaney, John Francis neurologist, psychiatrist
Delano, Jonathan William lawyer
Dell, Ernest Robert lawyer
Demmler, John Henry lawyer
Demmler, Ralph Henry lawyer
Dempsey, Jerry Edward service company executive
†DeSena, Alphonse Thomas science museum director
Deskins, Wilbur Eugene mathematician, educator
Detre, Katherine Maria physician
Detre, Thomas psychiatrist, educator
Diamond, Gustave federal judge
Dibianca, Joseph Philip finance executive
Dinman, Bertram David consultant, retired aluminum company executive
DiPietro, Melanie lawyer
Director, Stephen William electrical engineering educator, researcher
Dixit, Balwant Narayan pharmacology and toxicology educator
Dodds, Robert James, Jr. retired lawyer
Doerfler, Leo G. audiology educator
†Doerr, Ronald H. steel company executive
Donahoe, David Lawrence state and city official
Donnelly, Thomas Joseph lawyer
Doty, Robert Walter lawyer
Drescher, Seymour history educator, writer
Ducanis, Alex Julius education educator
Duffin, Richard James mathematician, educator
Dugan, John F. lawyer
Dybeck, Alfred Charles labor arbitrator
Eaton, Joseph W. sociology educator
Echement, John R. banker
Eckert, Jean Patricia elementary education educator
Edelman, Harry Rollings, III engineering and construction company executive
Ehrenwerth, David Harry lawyer
Emmerich, Werner Sigmund physicist
Epperson, David Ernest dean, educator
Erb, James J. lawyer
Evans, Bruce Dwight lawyer
Fairbanks, Frank Bates manufacturing company executive
†Fajt, Gregory Charles state legislator
Fararo, Thomas John sociologist, educator
Farley, Andrew Newell lawyer
Fawcett, David Blakley, Jr. lawyer
Feczko, William Albert radiologist
Feingold, David Sidney microbiology educator
Feller, Robert Livingston chemist, art conservator
Fenves, Steven Joseph civil engineer
Ferguson, Mary Anne Heyward language professional, educator
Ferguson, Sanford Barnett lawyer
Fernsler, John Paul lawyer
†Ficco, James Vincent, III advertising executive
Fienberg, Stephen Elliott statistician
Figgins, David Forrester construction company executive
Fine, Milton hotel company executive, lawyer
Fireman, Philip pediatrician, allergist, immunologist, medical association executive
Fischer, Richard Lawrence metal products executive
Fischhoff, Baruch psychologist, educator
Fisher, Bernard surgeon, researcher, educator
†Fisher, D. Michael state senator, lawyer
Fisher, James Aiken industrial marketing executive
Fishman, Libby G. lawyer
Flaherty, John P., Jr. state supreme court justice
Flatley, Lawrence Edward lawyer
Fletcher, Ronald Darling microbiologist
Flinn, Michael J. lawyer
Foreman, John Daniel financial executive
Fort, James Tomlinson lawyer
Fox, Cyril A., Jr. law educator
Foxen, Richard William manufacturing company executive
Frank, Philip Lawrence mechanical engineer, consultant
Frank, Ronald W. lawyer, financier
Franklin, Kenneth Ronald franchise company executive, consultant
†Freeman, Edmund J. heavy manufacturing executive
†Friday, Gilbert Anthony, Jr. pediatrician
Friede, Samuel A(rnold) health care executive
Froehlich, Fritz Edgar telecommunications educator and scientist
Gaffney, Paul Cotter physician
Gale, Robert Lee retired American literature educator and critic
Gallagher, Daniel P., Jr. lawyer
Garrett, Sylvester arbitrator
Geiger, Gene Edward engineer, educator
Genge, William Harrison advertising executive, writer
Gerjuoy, Edward physicist, lawyer
Gerlach, G. Donald lawyer
Gill, Thomas James, III physician, educator
†Gindroz, Raymond L. architect
Gold, Harold Arthur lawyer
Goldberg, Mark Joel lawyer
Goldstein, Gerald research psychologist
Gollin, Susanne Merle cytogeneticist, cell biologist
Gottfried, Byron Stuart engineering educator
Graf, Edward Louis, Jr. lawyer, finance executive
Grant, Daniel Gordon computer consulting company executive
Gray, Charles Buffum theatrical director, producer
†Green, Isaac church administrator
†Grefenstette, Carl G. medical products and real estate executive
†Griffin, Donald Spray mechanical engineer, consultant
Griffiths, Robert Budington physics educator
Grinberg, Meyer Stewart educational institute executive
Grossmann, Ignacio Emilio chemical engineering educator
Groves, Michael banker
Grunbaum, Adolf philosophy educator, author
Gurtin, Morton Edward mathematics educator
Hackney, William Pendleton lawyer
Hall, Charles Allan numerical analyst, educator
Hallen, Philip Burgh foundation administrator
Hamilton, Howard Britton electrical engineer, educator
Hammer, Harold Harlan oil company financial executive
Hammond, Paul Young political scientist, educator
Hannan, Robert William retail pharmaceutical company executive
Hardesty, Robert Lynch surgeon, educator
Hardie, James Hiller lawyer
Harff, Charles Henry lawyer, diversified industrial company executive
Harper, Matrid Thaisa health care administrator
Harris, Ann Birgitta Sutherland art historian
Harrold, Ronald Thomas research scientist
Hartman, Ronald G. lawyer
Harty, James Quinn lawyer
Harvey, Calvin Rea lawyer
Harvey, Thomas J. priest, social service organization executive
†Hathaway, Alden Moinet bishop
Hayes, Ann Louise English educator, consultant, poet
Hedquist, Jan P. advertising company executive
Heilman, Carl Edwin lawyer
Heinz, Drue foundation administrator
Hellman, Arthur David law educator, consultant
Henry, Susan Armstrong biology educator, university dean
Hercules, David Michael chemistry educator, consultant
Herndon, James Henry orthopedic surgeon, educator
Herrington, Donald Francis financial services executive
Hershey, Colin Harry management consultant
Hershey, Dale lawyer
Hershey, Nathan lawyer, educator
Hickman, Leon Edward lawyer, business executive
Higgins, James Henry retired banker
Hill, John Howard lawyer
†Hillman, Henry L. investment company executive
†Hingson, Luke Lockhart charitable foundation executive
Hingson, Robert Andrew physician, educator, inventor, farmer, poet
Hitt, Leo N. lawyer, educator
Ho, Chien biological sciences educator
Hoburg, James Frederick electrical engineering educator
Hodges, Margaret Moore author, educator
Hoffstot, Henry Phipps, Jr. lawyer
Hofmann, Klaus biochemistry educator, researcher
Hollingsworth, Samuel Hawkins, Jr. bassist
Hollinshead, Earl Darnell, Jr. lawyer
†Holz, Richard Lee lawyer
Holzner, Burkart sociologist, educator
Horan, Justin Thomas retired association executive
Horowitz, Don Roy instrument company executive
Hough, Thomas Henry Michael lawyer
Hovis, John Herbert association executive
Howard, Lawrence Cabot international affairs educator
†Howard, Thomas Bailey, Jr. construction materials company executive
†Howland, Robert Herbert psychiatrist
Hsu, Cho-yun history educator
†Hu, William Hsun physical metallurgy educator, materials scientist
Humphrey, Watts Sherman technical executive, author
Hung, Tin-Kan engineering educator, researcher
Hunter, David Wittmer security brokerage executive
Huntington, James Cantine, Jr. equipment manufacturing company executive
Ijiri, Yuji accounting and economics educator
Irwin, Joe Robert banker
Ismail, Yahia Hassan dentist, educator
Janis, Allen Ira retired physicist, educator
Jasnow, David Michael physics educator
Jegasothy, Brian Vasanthakumar dermatology educator
Jehle, Michael Edward financial executive
Johnson, Robert Alan lawyer
†Johnston, Edward Joseph professional hockey team executive
Johnston, Phillip Michael museum director, curator
Jones, Craig Ward lawyer
Jones, Fred Richard financial executive
Jordan, Angel Goni electrical and computer engineering educator
Jordan, Michael Hugh electrical and electronics company executive
Josey, E(lonnie) J(unius) librarian, educator, former state administrator
Joyner, Claude Reuben, Jr. physician, medical educator
Junker, Edward P., III diversified financial services company executive
Kaczmarski, Michael John controller, company executive
Kadane, Joseph B. statistics educator
Kaplan, John photojournalist, consultant, educator
Katarincic, Joseph Anthony lawyer
Katz, Arnold economics educator
Katz, Saul Milton economist, social scientist, educator
Kaufman, William Morris research institute administrator, engineer
Kearney, Hugh Francis historian, educator
Kearney, Kerry A. lawyer
Kearns, John J., III lawyer
Keefe, William Joseph political science educator
Kenrick, Charles William lawyer
Kent, Allen library and information sciences educator
Kerr, William Gregg lawyer
Ketchum, David Storey retired fundraising executive
Ketter, David Lee lawyer
†Khonsari, Michael M. engineering educator
Kiger, Robert William botanist, science historian, educator
Kilmann, Ralph Herman business educator
King, James Edward museum director
King, Peter J. lawyer
King, William Richard business educator, consultant
Kisslinger, Leonard Sol Physicist, educator
Klett, Edwin Lee lawyer
Knapp, George Robert lawyer
Knox, Charles Graham lawyer
Kocisko, Stephen John clergyman
Koedel, Robert Craig minister, historian, educator
Kolodner, Ignace Izaak mathematician, educator
Krasik, Carl lawyer
Kriebel, Charles Hosey management sciences educator
†Kronk, Claude F. heavy manufacturing executive
†Krutz, Ronald L. computer engineer
Kryder, Mark Howard computer and electrical engineering educator, consultant
Krysinski, Linda Ann editorial office supervisor
†Kuhn, James Craighead, Jr. lawyer
Kupfer, David J. psychiatry educator
La Rue, Henry Aldred consultant, former oil company executive
Laughlin, David Eugene materials science educator, metallurgical consultant
†Lauterbach, Hans pharmaceutical company executive
Lauterbach, Robert Emil steel company executive
Lave, Judith Rice economics educator
Lave, Lester Bernard economist, educator, researcher
†Lazzara, Robert Ralph cardiothoracic surgeon
Leak, Allison G. health science facility administrator, nurse
Lee, Donald John federal judge
Lehoczky, John Paul statistics educator
Leiter, Donald Eugene religious organization executive
LeMelle, Tilden John political science educator, editor, college official
Lemieux, Mario professional hockey player
†Leo, Peter Andrew newspaper columnist
Lewis, Jessica Helen (Mrs. Jack D. Myers) physician, educator
Lewis, Richard Allan financial planner
Lewis, Timothy K. federal judge
Leyland, James Richard professional baseball team manager
Li, Ching-Chung electrical engineering, computer science educator
Lidz, Charles Wilmanns sociologist
Limbach, Walter F. construction company executive
London, Alan E. lawyer
Longest, Beaufort Brown health services administration educator, research director
Losacco, Lesley Herdt supervisor, educator
Lovett, Robert G. lawyer
Lowery, Clinton Hershey former naval officer
Luthy, Richard Godfrey environmental engineering educator
Maazel, Lorin conductor, musician
Machatzke, Heinz Wilhelm chemical company executive
†MacLeod, Gordon Kenneth physician, educator
Majors, Johnny (John Terrill Majors) university athletic coach
Mansmann, Carol Los federal judge, law educator
Mansmann, J. Jerome lawyer
†Marshall, Thomas chemical company executive
Martin, Bruce Douglas university official, chemist
Masoner, Paul Henry counseling educator
Massalski, Thaddeus Bronislaw material scientist, educator
†Massey, Gerald J. philosophy educator
Mathieson, Andrew Wray investment management executive
Matthews, Jack psychologist, speech pathologist, educator
Matzke, Gary Roger pharmacologist, educator, researcher
Maximos, (Maximos Demetrios Aghiorgoussis) bishop
May, Charles Kent lawyer
†Mayernik, David John state legislator, lawyer
Mazeski, Edward James, Jr. lawyer, corporate secretary
†Mazur, Mark James economics educator
Mc Anulty, Henry Joseph university administrator
McAvoy, Bruce Ronald scientist, consultant
McCall, Dorothy Kay social worker, psychotherapist
McCallum, Bennett Tarlton economics educator
Mc Cartney, Robert Charles lawyer
McClelland, James L. psychology educator, cognitive scientist
†McCoid, Donald James bishop
McConomy, James Herbert lawyer
McConomy, Thomas Arthur chemical company executive
McCullough, M. Bruce lawyer
Mc Cune, Barron Patterson federal judge
†McDonald, C. W. mining executive
Mc Dowell, John B. bishop
Mc Featters, Dale Stitt retired electric company executive
McGonigle, John William lawyer, investment company executive
McGough, Walter Thomas lawyer
McGough, Walter Thomas, Jr. lawyer
McGovern, John Joseph former air pollution control association executive, consultant
McGuinn, Martin Gregory banker, lawyer
†McIntosh, DeCourcy Eyre museum director
Mc Kenzie, Ray anesthesiologist, educator
McLaughlin, John Sherman lawyer
†McMaster, James Henry orthopaedic surgeon
McMichael, Francis Clay civil engineering educator, environmental engineering consultant
McWilliams, Betty Jane science administrator, communication disorders educator, researcher
Medonis, Robert Xavier lawyer
Mehrabian, Robert academic administrator
Meiksin, Zvi H. electrical engineering educator
Meisel, Alan law educator
Mellon, Richard Prosser charitable foundation executive
Meltzer, Allan H. economist, educator
Mesa-Lago, Carmelo economist, educator
Messner, Robert Thomas lawyer, banking executive
Miller, David William historian, educator
†Miller, Donald art critic
Miller, Harbaugh lawyer
Miller, James Robert lawyer
Miller, Patricia G. lawyer
Milnes, Arthur George electrical engineer, educator
Milsom, Robert Cortlandt banker
Modell, John historian, educator
Moeller, Audrey Carolyn energy company executive, corporate secretary
Moore, Pearl B. nurse
Moore, Richard Allan mathematics educator
Moore, Robert Yates neuroscience educator
Morby, Jeffrey Lewis banker, investment banker
Moriarty, Richard William pediatrician
Morice, Joseph Richard history educator
Moritz, Donald I. energy company executive
Morton, James Davis lawyer
Moura, José Manuel Fonseca electrical engineer
Mueller, Gerd Dieter financial and administrative executive
Mullen, Joseph Patrick professional hockey player
†Mullins, William Wilson physical metallurgist
Mulloney, Peter Black steel, oil and gas executive
Munsch, Martha Hartle lawyer
Murdoch, David Armor lawyer
†Murphy, John N. mining executive, researcher, electrical engineer
Murphy, Lawrence Thomas professional hockey player
†Murphy, Tom mayor
Murray, John Edward, Jr. lawyer, educator, university president
Murrin, Regis Doubet lawyer
Muto, Susan Annette religion educator, academic administrator
Myers, Eugene Nicholas otolaryngologist, otolaryngology educator
Myers, Marlee S. lawyer
Nathanson, Harvey Charles electrical engineer
Needleman, Herbert Leroy psychiatrist, pediatrician
Neuman, Charles P. electrical and computer engineering educator, consultant
Newlin, William Rankin lawyer
Noll, Charles Henry former professional football coach
Nordenberg, Mark Alan legal educator, university administrator
Norris, James Harold lawyer, partner
Norton, Eunice pianist
†Nowak, Joseph J. metal products executive
Nuernberg, William Richard lawyer
Ober, Russell John, Jr. lawyer
O'Brien, Charles Maryon, Jr. hospital administrator
O'Brien, Thomas Henry bank holding company executive
O'Connor, Donald Thomas lawyer
O'Connor, Edward Gearing lawyer
O'Connor, John Dennis chancellor, biology educator
Oehmler, George Courtland corporate executive
Ogul, Morris Samuel political science educator, consultant
†Oles, Paul Joseph planetarium administrator
Olson, Stephen M(ichael) lawyer
O'Neill, Paul Henry aluminum company executive
O'Reilly, Anthony John Francis food company executive

Ostern, Wilhelm Curt *retired holding company executive*
Page, Lorne Albert *physicist, educator*
Papadakos, Nicholas Peter *state supreme court justice*
Parkes, Kenneth Carroll *ornithologist*
Partanen, Carl Richard *biology educator*
Pasnick, Raymond Wallace *labor union official, editor*
Patrick, Craig *professional hockey team executive*
Patten, Charles Anthony *management consultant, arbitrator, retired manufacturing company executive, author*
Patton, Robert Frederick *lawyer, banker*
†Paul, John *health care executive*
Paul, Robert Arthur *steel company executive*
Paulston, Christina Bratt *linguistics educator*
Pearson, Nathan Williams *investment management executive*
Pekruhn, John Edward *retired architect, educator*
Perfido, Ruth S. *lawyer*
Perlman, Mark *economist, educator*
Perloff, Robert *psychologist, educator*
Petrov, Nicolas *dance educator, choreographer*
Pettit, Frederick Sidney *metallurgical engineering educator, researcher*
†Pham, Si Mai *cadiothoracic surgeon, medical educator*
Phillips, James Macilduff *material handling company executive, engineering and manufacturing executive*
Phillips, Larry Edward *lawyer*
Pitts, Samuel Richard *technology company executive*
Plowman, Jack Wesley *lawyer*
Pohl, Paul Michael *lawyer*
Pois, Joseph *lawyer, educator*
Pomeroy, Thomas Wilson, Jr. *lawyer, former state supreme court justice*
†Porter, Irwin W. *food store chain executive*
Porter, Milton *investment executive*
Post, Peter David *lawyer*
Powderly, William H., III *lawyer*
Prado, Gerald M. *investment banker*
Pratt, Richard Houghton *physics educator*
Price, Trevor Robert Pryce *psychiatrist, educator*
Propst, John Leake *lawyer*
Prorok, Robert Francis *lawyer*
Prosperi, Louis Anthony *lawyer*
Pugliese, Robert Francis *lawyer, business executive*
Quinn, John E. *lawyer*
Rabin, Bruce Stuart *immunologist, physician, educator*
Rago, Ann D'Amico *public relations professional*
Raimondi, Albert Anthony *mechanical engineer*
Randolph, Robert DeWitt *lawyer*
Rawski, Evelyn Sakakida *history educator*
Reed, W. Franklin *lawyer*
Reif, Eric Peter *lawyer*
Renner, Simon Edward *steel company executive*
†Rescher, Nicholas *philosophy educator*
†Resnick, Lauren B. *special education research administrator*
Restivo, James John, Jr. *lawyer*
Rheinboldt, Werner Carl *mathematics educator, researcher*
Rich, Thomas Hurlbut *corporate identity consulting company executive*
Ries, William Campbell *lawyer*
Rimer, John Thomas *foreign language educator, academic administrator, writer, translator*
Ritchey, Patrick William *lawyer*
Robinson, William M. *lawyer*
Rogers, Bryan Leigh *artist, art educator*
Rogers, Fred McFeely *television producer and host*
Rogers, Robert Mark *physician*
Rohr, James Edward *banker*
Rohrer, Ronald Alan *electrical and computer engineering educator, consultant*
†Romoff, Jeffrey Alan *university officer, health care executive*
Romualdi, James Philip *engineering educator*
†Roof, Robert L. *broadcast executive, sales executive*
Rooney, Daniel M. *professional football team executive*
Rose, Evans, Jr. *lawyer*
Rosenberg, Jerome Laib *chemist, educator*
Rosenberger, Bryan David *lawyer*
Rosenkranz, Herbert S. *environmental toxicology educator*
Ross, Madelyn Ann *newspaper editor*
Roth, Alvin Eliot *economics educator*
Roth, Loren *psychiatrist*
Roth, William George *manufacturing company executive*
Russell, Stanley G., Jr. *accountant*
Rust, William James *retired steel company executive*
Ruttenberg, Harold Joseph *manufacturing executive*
Ryan, John Thomas, Jr. *business executive*
Ryan, John Thomas, III *safety equipment company executive*
Saalman, Howard *architectural historian, educator*
†Sandman, Dan D. *lawyer*
Sante, William Arthur, II *aerospace and manufacturing company executive*
Sanzo, Anthony Michael *health care executive*
†Sax, Martin *crystallographer*
Scanlon, Eugene Francis *lawyer*
Schaub, Marilyn McNamara *religion educator*
Scheinholtz, Leonard Louis *lawyer*
Schieffelin, Laurie Graham *editor*
Schliebs, Charles Allan *lawyer*
Schmidt, Edward Craig *lawyer*
Schultz, Jerome Samson *biochemical engineer, educator*
Schwab, Arthur James *lawyer*
Schwass, Gary L. *utilities executive*
Schwendeman, Paul William *lawyer*
Sculley, David W. *food company executive*
Sekerka, Robert Floyd *physics educator, scientist*
†Seligson, Mitchell A. *Latin American studies educator*
Sell, William Edward *legal educator*
Sensenich, Ila Jeanne *lawyer, magistrate judge*
Shapiro, Alvin Philip *physician, educator*
Shaw, Mary M. *computer science educator*
Sheon, Aaron *art historian, educator*
Siewiorek, Daniel Paul *computer science educator, researcher*
Siker, Ephraim S. *anesthesiologist*
Silverman, Arnold Barry *lawyer*
Simaan, Marwan A. *electrical engineering educator*
Simmermon, James Everett *credit bureau executive*
Simmons, Richard P. *steel company executive*
Simon, Herbert A(lexander) *social scientist*
Simonds, John Ormsbee *landscape architect*
Singer, Paul Meyer *lawyer*
Slack, Edward Dorsey, III *financial systems professional, consultant*
Smith, Charles Raymond, Jr. *lawyer*
Smith, David Brookman *federal judge*
Smith, Phillip Hartley *steel company executive*
Smith, William J. *lawyer*
Spanovich, Milan *civil engineer*
Stahl, Laddie L. *electrical engineer, manufacturing company executive*
Standish, William Lloyd *federal judge*
Stargell, Willie (Wilver Dornel Stargell) *professional sports team coach, former baseball player*
Starzl, Thomas Earl *physician, educator*
Stearns, Peter Nathaniel *history educator*
Stein, Arland Thomas *lawyer*
Stern, Theodore *electric company executive*
Stevens, Kevin Michael *professional hockey player*
Strader, James David *lawyer*
Strauss, Robert Philip *economics educator*
Stroyd, Arthur Heister *lawyer*
Stuckeman, Herman Campbell *architectural engineer*
Sukiennik, Leopold Jonah *civil, structural engineer, consultant*
Sussna, Edward *economist, educator*
†Suzuki, Jon Byron *dean, periodontist, educator*
Swaim, Joseph Carter, Jr. *lawyer*
Swain, William Grant *landscape architect*
Swann, Lynn Curtis *sportscaster*
Sweeney, Clayton Anthony *lawyer, business executive*
Symons, Edward Leonard, Jr. *lawyer, educator, investment advisor*
Tarr, Joel Arthur *history and public policy educator*
†Taylor, D. Lansing *cell biology educator*
Thomas, John Edward *manufacturing company executive*
Thomas, W(illiam) Bruce *retired steel, oil, gas company executive*
Thompson, Gerald Luther *operations research and applied mathematics educator*
Thompson, Thomas Martin *lawyer*
Thorne, John Reinecke *business educator, venture capitalist*
Thorpe, Leon Ferber *real estate investment company executive*
Tierney, John William *chemical engineering educator*
†Tilton, Robert Daymond *chemical engineer*
Tobin, William Thomas *retail executive*
Toker, Franklin K. *art history educator, archaeologist, foundation executive*
Trapp, Frank Anderson *art educator*
Troen, Philip *physician, educator*
Trottier, Bryan John *profession sports team coach, former professional hockey player*
Tungate, David E. *lawyer, educator*
Turnbull, Gordon Keith *metal company executive, metallurgical engineer*
Turner, Harry Woodruff *lawyer*
Ubinger, John W., Jr. *lawyer*
Ulmer, Daniel C., Jr. *diversified financial services company executive*
Van Dusen, Albert Clarence *university official*
Van Kirk, Thomas L. *lawyer*
Van Slyke, Andrew James *professional baseball player*
†Vaughn, Gordon E. *bishop*
Vogeley, Clyde Eicher, Jr. *engineering educator, artist, consultant*
von Schack, Wesley W. *energy holding company executive*
Voss, James Frederick *psychologist, educator*
†Wagner, Lawrence M. *diversified financial services company executive*
Wald, Niel *medical educator*
Wallace, Richard Christopher, Jr. *school system administrator, educator*
Wallace, William Edward *engineering educator, scientist*
Wallman, George *hospital and food services administrator*
Walsh, Michael Francis *advertising executive*
Walton, James M. *investment company executive*
Walton, Jon David *lawyer*
Ward, Thomas Jerome *lawyer*
Watts, William Edward *retail company executive*
Weaver, Charles Henry *business consulting executive*
Webb, William Hess *lawyer*
Wehmeier, Helge H. *chemical, health care and imaging technologies company executive*
Weingartner, Rudolph Herbert *philosophy educator*
Weis, Joseph Francis, Jr. *federal judge*
Weis, Konrad Max *retired chemical company executive*
Weisgerber, Edward Victor *lawyer*
Welfer, Thomas, Jr. *utility company executive*
Wentley, Richard Taylor *lawyer*
Werner, Gerhard *pharmacologist, psychoanalyst, educator*
Westerberg, Arthur William *chemical engineering educator*
White, Robert Marshall *physicist, educator*
Wilcock, James William *corporation executive, retired capital equipment manufacturing company executive*
Wilde, Patricia *artistic director*
Wilkins, David George *fine arts educator*
Will, James Fredrick *steel company executive*
Willard, Mark Alan *lawyer*
Williams, Charles David *oil and steel company executive*
Williams, John Wesley *fine arts educator*
Williams, Louis Stanton *glass and chemical manufacturing executive*
Williams, Lynn Russell *labor union official*
Williams, Max Lea, Jr. *engineer, educator*
Williams, William Orville *mathematics educator*
Wilson, Charles Reginald *real estate executive*
Winter, Peter Michael *physician, anesthesiologist, educator*
Wolken, Jerome Jay *biophysicist, educator*
Woo, Savio Lau-Yuen *bioengineering educator*
Woodson, Roderick Kevin *professional football player*
Woodward, Thomas Aiken *lawyer*
Woolls, Esther Blanche *library science educator*
Wright, Thomas David *lawyer, entrepreneur*
Wuerl, Donald W. *bishop*
Wynblatt, Paul Pinhas *materials science educator, researcher*
Yankovic, Judith E. *banker, human resources consultant*
Yates, John Thomas, Jr. *chemistry educator, researcher*
Yorsz, Stanley *lawyer*
Young, Hugh David *physics educator, writer, organist*
Youngner, Julius Stuart *microbiologist, educator*
Zanardelli, John Joseph *health facility administrator*
Zandin, Kjell Bertil *management consulting executive*
Zappala, Stephen A. *state supreme court justice*
Ziegler, Donald Emil *federal judge*
Zimmerman, Scott Franklin *lawyer*
Zoffer, H. Jerome *educator, university dean*

Plymouth Meeting
Gilstein, Jacob Burrill *physicist*
Gleklen, Donald Morse *investment company executive*
Green, Raymond S(ilvernail) *retired radio station executive*
Katz, Gerald *management consultant*
Kostinsky, Harvey *clinical and electrical engineer*
Litman, Raymond Stephen *retired banker*
Nobel, Joel J. *physician*
Siegal, Jacob J. *management and financial consultant*
Yarnall, D. Robert, Jr. *entrepreneur, investor*

Polk
Hall, Richard Clayton *psychologist, consultant, researcher*

Port Allegany
Failey, George Leo, Jr. *retired public utility executive*

Port Royal
Wert, Jonathan Maxwell, II *management consultant*

Pottstown
Hylton, Thomas James *editorial writer*
Lenfest, Harold Fitz Gerald *cable television executive, lawyer*
Ruth, Thomas Griswold *history educator*

Pottsville
Kholoussy, A. Mohsen *surgeon, educator*

Punxsutawney
†Cook, Gayland Braun *banker, utility company executive*

Radnor
Arader, Walter Graham *financial consultant*
Barletta, Joseph Francis *newspaper executive, lawyer*
Brown, W(illiam) Thacher *investment firm executive*
†Burns, Denver P. *forestry researcher*
Burtis, Theodore Alfred *oil company executive*
†Follman, John P. *engineering comprnay executive*
Harrison, Robert Drew *management consultant*
Marland, Alkis Joseph *leasing company executive, computer science educator, financial planner*
Paier, Adolf Arthur *computer software and services company executive*
Pool, Patricia Stewart *editor in chief*
†Russell, Daniel Francis *hospital administrator*
Stearns, Milton Sprague, Jr. *financial executive*
†Yoh, Harold Lionel, Jr. *engineering, construction and management company executive*
Youman, Roger Jacob *editor, writer*
Zimmermann, R. Peter *financial executive*

Reading
Beaver, Howard Oscar, Jr. *wrought specialty alloys manufacturing company executive*
Bell, Frances Louise *medical technologist*
†Byers, Edward W. *library director*
Cardy, Robert Willard *speciality steel company executive*
†Cate, Patrick O'Hair *mission executive*
Cottrell, G. Walton *manufacturing executive*
Dersh, Rhoda E. *management consultant, business executive*
Dietrich, Bruce Leinbach *planetarium and museum administrator, astronomer, educator*
Ehlerman, Paul Michael *industrial battery manufacturing company executive*
Erdman, Carl L. N. *retired banker*
Fiore, Nicholas Francis *special alloys and materials company executive*
Fording, Edmund Howard, Jr. *chemical executive*
Hafer, Frederick Douglass *utility executive*
Harner, Paul B. *gray iron foundry executive*
Hawkins, Arthur *battery manufacturing executive*
†Hawkins, Arthur Michael *automotive executive*
Hildreth, Eugene A. *physician, educator*
Hollander, Herbert I. *consulting engineer*
Huyett, Daniel Henry, III *federal judge*
Itin, James Richard *financial executive*
Johnson, Gerard G. *apparel company executive*
Johnson, Robert Joseph *corporate lawyer*
Knerr, Reinhard H. *communications executive*
†Lakin, Edwin A. *retail executive*
Mattern, Donald Eugene *association executive*
McCullough, Samuel Alexander *banker*
Mengel, Philip R(ichard) *investment banker*
Moll, Lloyd Henry *banker*
†Pearson, Douglas N. *battery manufacturing company executive*
Pugh, Lawrence R. *apparel executive*
Roedel, Paul Robert *steel company executive*
Roesch, Clarence Henry *banker*
†Rohrer, Samuel Edward *state legislator*
Rothermel, Daniel Krott *lawyer, holding company executive*
Rutter, Elizabeth Jane *assistant corporate secretary*
Sauer, Elissa Swisher *nursing educator*
Smith, Alexander Forbes, III *engineering consulting firm executive*
Snyder, Clair Allison *banker*
Sparks, David Emerson *bank holding company executive*
Sullivan, Charles Bernard *hospital administrator*
Troutman, E. Mac *federal judge*

Ridley Park
Clark, John H., Jr. *lawyer*

Riegelsville
†Panshin, Alexei *author*

Rochester
†LaValle, Gerald J. *state senator*

Rohrerstown
Stauffer, Sarah Ann *political worker*

Rosemont
Nixon, Agnes Eckhardt *television writer, producer*
Reuschlein, Harold Gill *university dean*

Royersford
†Carriker, Roy C. *physicist*

Ruffs Dale
Slebodnik, Tressa Ann *elementary education educator*

Rydal
Black, Thomas Donald *retired religious organization administrator*
Kirkland, Bryant Mays *clergyman*

Sagamore
†Cornell, William Harvey *clergyman*

Saint Davids
Baird, John Absalom, Jr. *college official*
Bertsch, Frederick Charles, III *business executive*
Bovaird, Brendan Peter *lawyer*
Heebner, Albert Gilbert *economist, banker, educator*
Maahs, Kenneth Henry, Sr. *religion educator*

Saint Marys
Johnson, J. M. Hamlin *manufacturing company executive*
Shobert, Erle Irwin, II *management consultant*

Saltsburg
Pidgeon, John Anderson *headmaster*

Sayre
Moody, Robert Adams *neurosurgeon*
Thomas, John Melvin *surgeon*

Schuylkill Haven
Loder, Michael Wescott *librarian*

Scottdale
Cutrell, Benjamin Elwood *publisher*
†Miller, Levi *publishing administrator*

Scranton
Campion, Carol-Mae Sack *librarian*
Cimini, Joseph Fedele *law educator, lawyer, former magistrate*
Conaboy, Richard Paul *federal judge*
De Celles, Charles Edouard *theologian, educator*
Guerrise, Patrick P. *manufacturing company executive*
Haggerty, James Joseph *lawyer*
Hoffman, Barbara Ann *English educator*
†Horton, Joseph Julian, Jr. *academic dean, educator*
Howley, James McAndrew *lawyer*
Janoski, Henry Valentine *banker, former investment counselor, realtor*
Kosik, Edwin Michael *federal judge*
Lynett, George Vincent *newspaper publisher*
Maislin, Isidore *hospital administrator*
Myers, Morey Mayer *lawyer*
Nealon, William Joseph, Jr. *federal judge*
Nee, Sister Mary Coleman *college president emeritus*
O'Brien, Kevin James *museum director*
O'Malley, Carlon Martin *judge*
Panuska, Joseph Allan *university president*
Parente, William Joseph *political science educator*
Passon, Richard Henry *university administrator*
Preate, Ernest D., Sr. *lawyer*
Reap, Sister Mary Margaret *college administrator*
Staff, Mary Clare *special education educator*
†Stetler, Larry D. *banker*
Timlin, James Clifford *bishop*
Turock, Jane Parsick *nutritionist*

Selinsgrove
Diers, Hank H. *drama educator, playwright, director*
Putterman, Florence Grace *artist, printmaker*

Sellersville
Loux, Norman Landis *psychiatrist*

Seneca
†Spring, Paull E. *bishop*

Sewickley
Barry, John Kevin *lawyer*
Chaplin, James Crossan, IV *securities firm executive*
Newell, Byron Bruce, Jr. *clergyman, former naval officer*
Roemer, William Frederick *banker*
Snyder, William Penn, III *manufacturing company executive*

Sharon
Epstein, Louis Ralph *retired wholesale grocery executive*
Rosenblum, Harold Arthur *grocery distribution executive*
Sheen, Martin (Ramon Estevez) *actor*

Shippensburg
Ceddia, Anthony Francis *university administrator*
†Crowe, Virginia Mary *librarian*
Luhrs, H. Ric *toy manufacturing company executive*
Stone, Susan Ridgaway *marketing educator*

Shiremanstown
Bouvier, Janet Laubach *educator*

Sinking Spring
Wilson, Terrence Raymond *manufacturing executive*

Skytop
Popham, Lewis Charles, III *hotel corporation director, former university dean*

Slippery Rock
Aebersold, Robert Neil *university president*

Solebury
Anthonisen, George Rioch *sculptor, artist*
Valentine, H. Jeffrey *legal association executive*

Somerset
Funari, John H. *editor, consultant*

Souderton
Hoeflich, Charles Hitschler *banker*

South Canaan
†Herman *bishop*

South Gibson
Acker, Raymond Abijah *minister*

Southampton
DaCosta, Edward Hoban *plastics and electronics manufacturing company executive*
Omlor, John Joseph *business consultant*
Zocholl, Stanley Ernest *electronics executive*

Spring City
Blanchard, Norman Harris *retired pharmaceutical company executive*
Mayerson, Hy *lawyer*

Spring Grove
Helberg, Shirley Adelaide Holden *artist, educator*
Norris, Thomas Clayton *paper company executive*
Wand, Richard Walton *paper company executive*

Spring House
Coltoff, Beth Jamie *psychologist, small business owner*
†Emmons, William David *chemist*
Payn, Clyde Francis *technology company executive, consultant*
†Rorke, Edwin Grant, Jr. *manufacturing company executive*
Thorne, John Watson, III *advertising and marketing executive*
Wilson, Hugh Shannon *retired manufacturing company executive, consultant*

Springfield
†Ruiz, Jose R. *podiatric surgeon*

Springtown
Hunt, John Wesley *English language educator*

Star Junction
Baldwin, Clarence Jones, Jr. *electrical engineer, manufacturing company executive*

State College
Asbell, Bernard *English educator, author*
Bergman, Ernest L. *biologist*
Bittner, Carl S. *retired university educator*
DeVoss, James Thomas *community foundation administrator, retired*
Doms, Keith *library director*
Farr, Jo-Ann Hunter *psychologist*
Ferguson, John Henry *retired political science educator*
Fischer, Floyd Brand *educational and management consultant*
Foderaro, Anthony Harolde *nuclear engineering educator*
Forth, Stuart *librarian*
Gordon, Richard Lewis *mineral economics educator*
Gould, Peter Robin *geographer, educator*
Grimes, Dale Mills *electrical engineering educator*
Haas, John C. *architect*
Harris, Dale Benner *psychology educator*
Henderson, Robert Earl *mechanical engineer*
Hettche, L. Raymond *research director*
Hoffa, Harlan Edward *retired university dean, art educator*
Johnstone, Henry Webb, Jr. *philosophy educator*
Kockelmans, Joseph J. *philosopher, educator*
Landy, Richard Allen *consultant*
Miller, E. Willard *geographer*
Morrow, David Austin, III *veterinary medical educator*
Myers, Joel Norman *meteorologist, business executive*
Olson, Donald Richard *mechanical engineering educator*
Phillips, Janet Colleen *educational association executive, editor*
Robinett, Betty Wallace *linguist*
†Rusinko, Frank, Jr. *fuels and materials scientist*
Scott, Charles Edward *philosophy educator*
Thompson, Fred Clayton *engineering executive, consultant*

Strafford
Horwitz, Orville *cardiologist, educator*

Strasburg
Lindsay, George Carroll *former museum director*

Stroudsburg
Gasink, Warren Alfred *speech communication educator*

Sumneytown
Gordon, David Jamieson *tenor*

Swarthmore
Bannister, Robert Corwin, Jr. *history educator*
Barr, Robert Alfred, Jr. *college dean*
Beeman, Richard Roy *historian*
Bilaniuk, Oleksa Myron *physicist, educator*
Blackburn, Thomas Harold *English language professional, educator*
Bloom, Alfred Howard *college president*
Carey, William Bacon *pediatrician, educator*
Cornelsen, Rufus *clergyman*
Devin, (Philip) Lee *dramaturg, theater educator*
Durkan, Michael Joseph *librarian*
Flemister, Launcelot Johnson *physiologist, educator*
Frost, Jerry William *religion and history educator, library administrator*
Gaustad, John Eldon *astronomy educator*
Hammons, James Hutchinson *chemistry educator, researcher*
Heaps, Marvin Dale *food services company executive*
Hopkins, Raymond Frederick *political science educator*
Kaufman, Antoinette D. *business services company executive*
Keith, Jennie *anthropology educator, author*
Kelemen, Charles F. *computer science educator*
Krendel, Ezra Simon *systems engineering consultant, educator*
Lacey, Hugh Matthew *philosophy educator*
LeGros, Susan Packard *lawyer*
Lippincott, Sarah Lee *astronomer, graphologist*
North, Helen Florence *classicist, educator*
Ostwald, Martin *classics educator emeritus*
Pagliaro, Harold Emil *English language educator*
Pasternack, Robert Francis *chemistry educator*
Saffran, Bernard *economist, educator*
†Sawyers, Claire Elyce *arboretum director*
Shaull, Richard *theologian, educator*
Snyder, Susan Brooke *English literature educator*
Swing, Peter Gram *music educator*
Wright, Harrison Morris *historian, educator*

Tannersville
Moore, James Alfred *ski company executive, lawyer*

Telford
Luscinski, Steven Michael *corporate executive*

Titusville
Peaslee, Margaret Mae Hermanek *zoology educator*

Torrance
Bullard, Ray Elva, Jr. *retired psychiatrist, hospital administrator*

Tunkhannock
Jones, Edward White, II *lawyer*

Turtle Creek
†Michlovic, Thomas A. *member House of Representatives*

Tyrone
Simpson, Cary Hatcher *broadcasting station executive*

Uniontown
Eberly, Robert Edward *oil and gas production company executive*
Foster, James Caldwell *academic dean, historian*

Unionville
De Marino, Donald Nicholson *international business executive, former federal agency administrator*
Forney, Robert Clyde *retired chemical industry executive*

University Park
Allcock, Harry R. *chemistry educator*
†Amateau, Maurice Francis *materials scientist, educator*
Ameringer, Charles D. *history educator*
Anderson, John Mueller *retired philosophy educator*
Andrews, George Eyre *mathematics educator*
Antle, Charles Edward *statistics educator*
Aplan, Frank Fulton *metallurgical engineering educator*
Arnold, Douglas Norman *mathematics educator*
†Askov, Eunice May *education educator*
Aspaturian, Vernon Varaztat *political science educator, consultant, author*
Baisley, Robert William *music educator*
Barnes, Hubert Lloyd *geochemistry educator*
Bennett, Peter Dunne *marketing educator*
†Bernheim, Robert Allan *chemistry educator*
Bernlohr, Robert William *biochemist, educator, researcher*
Bieniawski, Zdzislaw Tadeusz *mineral engineer, educator, consultant*
Blackadar, Alfred Kimball *meteorologist, educator*
Bollag, Jean-Marc *soil biochemistry educator, consultant*
Bose, Nirmal Kumar *electrical engineering, mathematics educator*
Brault, Gerard Joseph *French language educator*
Brenchley, Jean Elnora *microbiologist, researcher*
Brown, John Lawrence, Jr. *electrical engineering educator*
Brownawell, Woodrow Dale *mathematics educator*
Buskirk, Elsworth Robert *physiologist, educator*
Cahir, John Joseph *meteorologist, educational administrator*
Castleman, Albert Welford, Jr. *physical chemist, educator*
Chang, Parris Hsu-cheng *government official, political science educator, writer*
Coleman, Michael Murray *polymer science educator*
Cosgrove, Daniel Joseph *biology educator*
Davids, Norman *engineering science and mechanics educator, researcher*
De Armas, Frederick Alfred *foreign language educator*
†Dong, Cheng *bioengineering educator*
Dunson, William Albert *biology educator*
Dupuis, Victor Lionel *curriculum and instruction educator emeritus*
Dutton, John Altnow *meteorologist, educator*
Eckhardt, Caroline Davis *comparative literature educator*
Edwards, Robert Roy *English literature and comparative literature educator*
Engel, Alfred Julius *chemical engineering educator*
†Feller, Irwin *think-tank executive, economics educator*
Feng, Tse-yun *computer engineer, educator*
Filippelli, Ronald Lee *college dean, labor studies and industrial relations educator*
Fonash, Stephen Joseph *engineering educator*
Ford, Donald Herbert *psychologist, educator*
Fowler, H(oratio) Seymour *retired science educator*
Fox, Richard Henry *soil science educator*
Frank, Robert Worth, Jr. *English language educator*
Frankl, Daniel Richard *educator, physicist*
Friedman, Robert Sidney *political science educator*
German, Randall Michael *materials science educator, consultant*
Golany, Gideon Salomon *urban designer*
Goldschmidt, Arthur Eduard, Jr. *historian, educator*
Gouran, Dennis Stephen *communications educator*
Guthrie, Helen A. *nutrition educator, consultant*
Ham, Inyong *industrial engineering educator*
Hammond, J. D. *insurance educator*
Harkness, William Leonard *statistician, educator*
Helfferich, Friedrich G. *chemical engineer, educator*
†Herman, Roger M. *physicist, educator*
†Hogan, Dennis Patrick *university educator*
Holl, John William *engineering educator*
Hood, Lamartine Frain *college dean*
Hosler, Charles Luther, Jr. *meteorologist, educator*
Howell, Benjamin Franklin, Jr. *geophysicist, educator*
Humphrey, Arthur Earl *university administrator*
Jackman, Lloyd Miles *chemistry educator*
Jacobs, Harold Robert *mechanical engineering educator*
Jaffe, Austin Jay *business administration educator*
Jordan, Bryce *corporate director, retired university president*
†Jurs, Peter Christian *chemistry educator*
Kabel, Robert Lynn *chemical engineering educator*
Kim, Ke Chung *entomology and biodiversity educator, researcher*
Klaus, Elmer Erwin *chemical engineering educator, consultant*
Klein, Philip Alexander *economist*
†Koopman, Gary *acoustic administrator*
Kurtz, Stewart Kendall *physics educator, researcher*
Lakshminarayana, Budugur *aerospace engineering educator*
Lampe, Frederick Walter *chemistry educator, consultant*
Larson, Russell Edward *university provost emeritus, consultant agriculture research and development*
Leslie, Donald Wilmot *landscape architecture educator*
Lewis, Peirce Fee *geographer, educator*
Lima, Robert *Hispanic studies and comparative literature educator*
†Lindsay, Bruce George *statistics educator*
Lindstrom, Eugene Shipman *biologist, academic administrator*
Lombra, Raymond Eugene *economist, educator*
†Macdonald, Digby Donald *scientist, science administrator*
Maier-Katkin, Daniel *criminology educator, administrator*
†Manbeck, Harvey B. *agriculturist, educator*
Martorana, Sebastian Vincent *educational consultant*
Mathews, John David *electrical engineering educator, consultant*
Maxson, Linda Ellen *biologist, educator*
Mayers, Stanley Penrose, Jr. *public health educator*
McCormick, Barnes Warnock *aerospace engineering educator*
†McDonnell, Archie Joseph *environmental engineer*
McKeown, James Charles *accounting educator, consultant*
†McWhirter, John Ruben *chemical engineering educator*
Mentzer, John Raymond *electrical engineer, educator*
Morris, Philip John *aerospace engineering educator*
Nelsen, Hart Michael *sociologist, educator*
Nisbet, John Stirling *electrical engineering educator*
Osborn, Elburt Franklin *former geochemistry educator, research scientist*
Pashek, Robert Donald *economics educator emeritus*
Paterno, Joseph Vincent *college football coach*
Pazur, John Howard *biochemist, educator*
Porterfield, Neil Harry *landscape architect, planner*
†Ramani, Raja Venkat *mining engineering educator*
†Rashid, Kamal A. *international programs director, educator*
Ray, William Jackson *psychologist*
Rose, Adam Zachary *economist, educator*
Rosen, Stanley Howard *humanities educator*
Roy, Rustum *interdisciplinary materials researcher, educator*
Ruud, Clayton Olaf *engineering educator*
Schaie, K(laus) Warner *human development and psychology educator*
Schmalstieg, William Riegel *Slavic languages educator*
Schrader, William Joseph *accountant, educator*
Seaburg, Paul Allen *structural engineer, educator*
Starling, James Lyne *university administrator*
Stern, Robert Morris *psychology educator, psychophysiology researcher*
Thatcher, Sanford Gray *publishing executive*
Thomas, Joab Langston *academic administrator, biology educator*
Thompson, William, Jr. *engineering educator*
Thuering, George Lewis *industrial engineering educator*
Tittmann, Bernhard Rainer *engineering science and mechanics educator*
Traverse, Alfred *palynology educator, clergyman*
Tukey, Loren Davenport *pomology educator, researcher*
Turgeon, Alfred Joseph *agronomy educator, head department*
Van Dommelen, David B. *artist, educator*
†Vannice, M. Albert *chemical engineering educator, researcher*
Villafranca, Joseph J. *biochemistry educator*
Walden, Daniel *social sciences educator*
Walker, Eric Arthur *consulting engineer, institute executive*
†Walker, Paul Norvell *agricultural and biological engineering educator*
Wartik, Thomas *chemistry educator, former college dean*
Webb, Ralph Lee *mechanical engineering educator*
†Webster, Peter John *meteorology educator*
Weintraub, Stanley *arts and humanities educator, author*
Werner, John Ellis *steel executive, technological economic development executive, metallurgist*
West, Paul Noden *author, English educator*
Wheeler, C. Herbert *architect, consultant, educator*
White, William Blaine *geochemist, educator*
Williams, Edward Vinson *music history educator*
Winograd, Nicholas *chemist*
Witzig, Warren Frank *nuclear engineer, educator*
Wyand, Martin Judd *economics educator, retired military officer*
Yu, Francis T. S. *electrical engineering educator, researcher, consultant*

Upper Darby
†Apfel, Gail *principal*
Gasparro, Frank *sculptor*
Hurley, Harry James, Jr. *dermatologist*

Upper Saint Clair
†Dunkis, Patricia B. *principal*
Stephenson, Robert Clay *commercial real estate developer*

Valley Forge
Basile, Neal Fahr *environmental consulting firm executive*
Besson, Michel Louis *manufacturing company executive*
Brewer, Oliver Gordon, Jr. *corporate executive*
†Buckles, Michael A. *religious organization executive*
†Carlson, Beverly Clark *historical society administrator*
†Collemer, Craig A. *religious organization administrator*
Croney, J. Kenneth *lawyer*
Dachowski, Peter Richard *manufacturing executive*
Erb, Doretta Louise Barker *polymer applications scientist*
Erb, Robert Allan *physical scientist*
†Gonzales, Hector M. *church administrator*
†González, Héctor *church official*
Green, Norman Marston, Jr. *minister*
Hilyard, James Emerson *manufacturing company executive*
†Housam, Ruth *religious organization administrator*
Huml, Donald Scott *manufacturing company executive*
†Kim, Jean B. *religious organization executive*
†McDermott, Dona M. *curator*
†McPhee, Richard S. *church administrator*
Miller, Robert Wiley *educational foundation executive*
Moulton, Hugh Geoffrey *lawyer, business executive*
Mundt, Ray B. *diversified industry executive*
Olson, James Robert *consulting engineer*
†Penfield, Carole H. (Kate Penfield) *minister, church official*
Rassbach, Herbert David *manufacturing executive*
†Renquest, Richard A. *religious organization executive*
Schaefer, Adolph Oscar, Jr. *advertising agency executive*
†Smith, G. Elaine *religious organization executive*
†Smith, Gordon E. *religious arganization executive*
†Sundquist, John A. *religious organization executive*
Sutton, James Andrew *diversified utility company executive*
†Wade, Cheryl H. *church official*
†Weiss, Daniel Edwin *clergyman, educator*
†Wright-Riggins, Aidsand F. *religious organization executive*

Verona
Potts, Gerald Neal *manufacturing company executive*

Villanova
Bersoff, Donald Neil *lawyer, psychologist*
Dobbin, Edmund J. *university administrator*
Dorian, Harry Aram *financial consultant, former bank executive*
Edwards, John Ralph *chemist, educator*
Helmetag, Charles Hugh *foreign language educator*
†Keating, Daniel Joseph, III *construction company executive*
Lambert, William G. *journalist, consultant*
Melby, Edward Carlos, Jr. *veterinarian*
Nolan, Patrick Joseph *screenwriter, playwright, educator*
Phares, Alain Joseph *physicist, educator*
Steg, Leo *research and development executive*
Sullivan, Richard Cyril *retired transportation executive*
White, Robert Edward *chemical engineering educator, consultant*

Wallingford
Herpel, George Lloyd *marketing educator*
†Rice, Robert H. *principal*

Warminster
Finnegan, Laurence Patrick, Jr. *manufacturing company executive*
Tatnall, George Jacob *aeronautical engineer*
Tolson, Jay Henry *lawyer, industrial instrument company executive*
Whinnery, James Elliott *aerospace medical scientist, flight surgeon*

Warren
Waterston, William King *minister, educator, academic administrator*

Warrendale
Hartwig, Thomas Leo *civil engineer*
Rumbaugh, Max Elden, Jr. *professional society administrator*
Schmidt, Jack *mechanical engineer, electrical engineer*

Warrington
Shaw, Milton Herbert *conglomerate executive*

Washington
Burnett, Howard Jerome *college president*
Erdner, Jon W. *small business owner, securities trader*
Hays, Lewis W. *writer, amateur baseball executive*
Kastelic, Robert Frank *aerospace company executive*
Piatt, Jack Boyd *manufacturing executive*
Richman, Stephen I. *lawyer*

Washington Crossing
Stone, Ezra Chaim *theatrical producer and director, educator, actor, writer, farmer*

Wayne
Andes, Charles Lovett *museum executive, technology association executive*
Atkins, Joseph P. *otorhinolaryngologist*
Baldwin, Frank Bruce, III *lawyer*
Berg, Jean Horton Lutz *writer*
†Blumenthal, Richard Allen *lawyer*
Bricklin, Patricia Ellen *psychologist, educator*
Carroll, Robert W. *retired business executive*
Chimerine, Lawrence *economist*
Christy, John Gilray *financial company executive*
Clelland, Richard Cook *statistics educator, university administrator*
†Coane, James Edwin, III *information technology executive*
†DeCarlo, A. J. *lumber company executive*
de Rivas, Carmela Foderaro *psychiatrist, hospital administrator*
Etris, Samuel Franklin *association executive*
Frye, Roland Mushat *literary historian, theologian*
Gallagher, Terrence Vincent *editor*
Garrison, Guy Grady *librarian, educator*
Griffith, Edward, II *lawyer*
†Gross, Lawrence Alan *lawyer*
Guernsey, Louis Harold *retired oral and maxillofacial surgeon, educator*
Hedges, Donald Walton *lawyer*
Hess, Eugene Lyle *biologist, retired association executive*
Hill, Virgil Lusk, Jr. *naval officer, academic administrator*
Kraftson, Raymond H. *corporate executive*
Kunkel, Russell J. *bank holding company executive*
Lefevre, Thomas Vernon *retired utility company executive, lawyer*
Lewis, James Earl *investment banker*
†Martino, Rocco Leonard *computer systems executive*
Norris, Charles Head, Jr. *lawyer, financial executive*
Pearson, Willard *former army officer*
Peterson, Raymond A. *paper company executive*

Robinowitz, Joe Reece publishing executive
†Russell, Kent hospital administrator
Sims, Robert John financial planner
Suer, Marvin David architect
†West, Alfred Paul, Jr. financial services executive
Wolcott, Robert Wilson, Jr. consulting company executive
Woodbury, Alan Tenney lawyer
Yoskin, Jon William insurance company executive

Waynesboro
Benchoff, James Martin manufacturing company executive
Holzman, Howard Eugene health services executive
Kirk, Daniel Lee physician, consultant

Wellsboro
†Baker, Matthew Edward state legislator

Wernersville
Himmelberger, Richard Charles vocational school educator
Mackey, Sheldon Elias minister

West Chester
Bogle, Hugh Andrew chemical company executive
Diller, Barry entertainment company executive
Dwyer, Francis Gerard chemical engineer, researcher
Green, Andrew Wilson economist, lawyer, educator
Hipple, Walter John English language educator
Jamison, Philip artist
Judson, Franklyn Sylvanus lawyer, consultant
Kim, James Joo-Jin electronics company executive
McKeldin, William Evans management consultant
Mecca, Joseph Nicholas manufacturing company executive
Mulligan, James Francis retired business executive, lawyer
Pollock, Roy Van Horn pharmaceutical company animal health researcher
Schindler, Peter David child and adolescent psychiatrist
†Smith, Lee A. architect
Swope, Charles Evans bank executive, lawyer
Thompson, A(nsel) Frederick, Jr. environmental engineering and consulting company executive
Tomlinson, Charles Wesley, Jr. advertising executive
Weston, Roy Francis environmental consultant
Yarosewick, Stanley J. academic administrator, physicist

West Conshohocken
†Ball, John H. construction executive
Capizzi, Robert Lawrence physician
Miller, Paul Fetterolf, Jr. investment company executive
Richard, Scott F. portfolio manager
Schein, Philip Samuel physician, educator, pharmaceutical executive

West Mifflin
Clayton, John Charles scientist, researcher

West Point
Abrams, William Bernard pharmaceutical company executive, physician
Callahan Graham, Pia Laaster medical researcher, virology researcher
Grossman, William medical researcher, educator
Hilleman, Maurice Ralph virus research scientist
Sherwood, Louis Maier physician, scientist, pharmaceutical company executive

Westtown
Backe, John David communications corporation executive

Wexford
Boyd, Robert Wright, III lamp company executive
Clokey, Frank R. lawyer

Wilkes Barre
†Bevevino, Frank finance company executive
†Bevevino, Frank H. food products executive
†Bogdan, James E. chief financial officer
Breiseth, Christopher Neri academic administrator
Elias, Robert Gerald educational administrator, educator
Falkowitz, Daniel clothing manufacturing company executive
Hobbs, William Barton Rogers company executive
Lackenmier, James Richard college president, priest
Ogren, Robert Edward biologist, educator
Olszewski, Laurence Michael academic administrator
†Parente, Charles Eugene telecommunications executive
†Pollock, Kenneth Leslie manufacturing executive
Rosenn, Max federal judge
Ru Dusky, Basil Michael cardiologist, consultant
†Sordoni, Andrew J., III communications company executive, construction company executive
†Thomas, Reginald Harry, Sr. minister

Williamsport
Bryant, Martha J. accountant
†Davis, William (Doyle) banker
Douthat, James Evans college administrator
Ertel, Allen Edward lawyer, former congressman
Facey, Karlyle Frank financial executive, consultant
Largen, Joseph retailer, furniture manufacturer, book wholesaler
Lattimer, Gary Lee physician
†Lessman, Janice Trojan financial services executive
McClure, James Focht, Jr. federal judge
Muir, Malcolm federal judge
Rafferty, Michael Robert editor, columnist

Willow Grove
†Asplundh, Christopher B. tree service company executive
†Asplundh, Robert H. tree service company executive
Berkoff, Charles Edward pharmaceutical executive
Kulicke, C(harles) Scott business executive
Spikes, John Jefferson, Sr. forensic toxicologist, pharmacologist

Willow Street
†Piscopo, Rich evangelist
Stright, I. Leonard educational consultant

Windber
Furigay, Rodolfo Lazo surgeon

Worcester
McAdam, Will electronics consultant

Wycombe
Denoon, David Baugh Holden economist, educator, consultant

Wyncote
Baldridge, Robert Crary retired biochemistry educator
Bersh, Philip Joseph psychologist, educator
†Burton, DeWitt A. bishop
†Sasso, Sandy rabbi

Wynnewood
Bordogna, Joseph engineer, educator
Boyer, Vincent Saull energy consultant
Bozzelli, Andrew Joseph, Jr. valve company executive
Campbell, Alan Keith business educator
Connor, James Edward, Jr. retired chemical company executive
Doherty, Henry Joseph anesthesiologist, medical hypnotist
Flanagan, Joseph Charles ophthalmologist
Freeman, Morton S. former bar association executive, retired lawyer
Hodges, John Hendricks physician, educator
†Kelly, Paul E., Jr. metal products executive
†Kelly, Paul Edward, Sr. metals company executive
Khouri, Fred John political science educator
Kruger, Arthur Newman speech communication educator, author
La Blanc, Charles Wesley, Jr. financial consultant
Maxwell, John Raymond artist
Meyers, Mary Ann writer, consultant
Peskin, Matt Alan professional society administrator
Phillips, Almarin economics educator, consultant
Singer, Samuel L(oewenberg) journalist
Weinhouse, Sidney biochemist, educator

Wyomissing
Boyer, Robert Allen physics educator
†Cellucci, Peter T. principal
Garr, Carl Robert manufacturing company executive
Sidhu, Jay S. banking executive

Yardley
Crane, Barbara Joyce publishing consulting executive, author
Desai, Cawas Jal distribution company executive
Elliott, Frank Nelson retired college president
Kressler, James Phillip investment and operations company executive
Newsom, Carolyn Cardall management consultant
Somma, Beverly Kathleen English education educator
Zulker, Charles Bates broadcasting company executive

York
Bartels, Bruce Michael health care executive
Conway, Nancy Ann publisher, editor
Dresher, James T. manufacturing executive
Fink, David Ream, Jr. retired hospital education director
Forchheimer, Otto Louis retired chemical company executive
Garner, Edward Markley, II manufacturing executive
Hetzel, Dennis Richard communications executive
Horn, Russell Eugene, Jr. printing executive
Jacobs, Donald Warren dentist
Keiser, Paul Harold hospital administrator
Klingaman, Robert LeRoy golf professional
†Pokelwaldt, Robert N. manufacturing company executive
†Pullo, Robert Wayne banker
Rosen, Raymond health facility executive
†Schmidt, John C. bank executive
Thornton, George Whiteley manufacturing executive
Welber, David Alan accountant

Youngstown
Palmer, Arnold Daniel professional golfer

Zionsville
Fleming, Richard chemical company executive

RHODE ISLAND

Barrington
Carpenter, Charles Colcock Jones physician, educator
Horton, John Alden advertising agency executive
O'Toole, John Dudley retired utility executive, consultant

Block Island
Kingsbury, Read Austin retired journalist

Bristol
Wilcox, Harry Wilbur, Jr. retired corporate executive

Central Falls
†Issa, Daniel J. state senator

Charlestown
Ungaro, Joseph Michael newspaper publishing executive, consultant

Coventry
†Day, Jennie D. state legislator
†Inman, Edward Salisbury, III educator, state legislator
†Spear, Raymond E. school system administrator

Cranston
Crooks, W. Spencer artist, educator
Fang, Pen Jeng engineering executive and consultant
†Fitzpatrick, William P. computer programmer/analyst, state legislator
Gill, Carole O'Brien family therapist
†Sasso, Eleanor Catherine state legislator
†Simonian, John S. lawyer
Thielsch, Helmut John engineering company executive

East Greenwich
Dence, Edward William, Jr. lawyer, banker
Flynn, Richard James lawyer
Weiss, Alan management consultant, author

East Providence
†DeGoes, John V. school system administrator
†Hay, Robert J. plastics manufacturing executive

Greenville
Calo, Joseph Manuel chemical engineering educator

Greenwich
Valenti, Leo Frank electronics company executive

Jamestown
Potter, Clarkson Nott publishing consultant
Todd, Thomas Abbott architect, urban designer
Winnert, Franklin Roy consultant, former building materials manufacturing executive

Johnston
Patin, Robert White insurance company executive
Subramaniam, Shivan Sivaswamy insurance company executive

Kingston
Alexander, Lewis McElwain geographer, educator
Biller, Henry Burt psychologist, educator
Carothers, Robert Lee academic administrator
Cruickshank, Alexander Middleton chemistry educator
Driver, Rodney David mathematics educator, state legislator
Futas, Elizabeth Dorothy library and information studies educator, program director
Gelles, Richard James sociology and psychology educator
Gitlitz, David Martin Hispanic studies educator
Goos, Roger Delmon mycologist
Horn, Francis Henry former educational administrator
Kim, Yong Choon philosopher, theologian, educator
Leete, William White artist
MacLaine, Allan Hugh English language educator
Nixon, Scott West oceanography science educator
Polk, Charles electrical engineer, educator, biophysicist
Rohm, Robert Hermann sculptor
Ross, James Barrett finance and insurance educator
Roxin, Emilio Oscar mathematics educator
†Schmidt, Charles T. labor research organization administrator
Tufts, Donald Winston electrical engineering educator
Verma, Ghasi Ram mathematics educator
†White, Frank M. mechanical engineer, educator
Youngken, Heber Wilkinson, Jr. former university administrator, pharmacy educator
Zucker, Norman Livingston political scientist, educator, author
Zuehlke, Richard William scientific conference manager

Lincoln
†Barr, John Douglas, II entrepreneur, state legislator
Burgdoerfer, Jerry J. marketing and distribution executive
Carter, Wilfred Wilson financial executive, controller
Gulvin, David Horner electric company executive

Little Compton
Bullerjahn, Eduard Henri architect
MacKowski, John Joseph retired insurance company executive

Manville
Eno, Paul Frederick editor

Middletown
Buell, William Ackerman radio broadcasting executive
Whitman, Ruth poet, educator, translator

Narragansett
†Leinen, Margaret Sandra oceanographic researcher
Pouliot, Assunta Gallucci business school owner and director
Sigurdsson, Haraldur oceanography educator, researcher

Newport
Baker, Winthrop Patterson, Jr. broadcasting executive
Brennan, Joseph Gerard philosophy educator
†Burgin, William Lyle architect
Coelho, Joseph Richard religious organization administrator
Cohen, Arthur Abram lawyer
Gleiman, Lubomir philosophy educator
†Graziano, Catherine Elizabeth nursing educator
Hayward, John Tucker management consultant
Holloway, Jerome Knight publisher, former military strategy educator, retired foreign service officer
Levie, Howard S(idney) lawyer, educator, author
Spurr, Daniel editor
Strasser, Joseph C. career military officer, academic administrator
West, Richard Vincent art museum official
†Wurman, Richard Saul architect

North Kingstown
†Feroce, John state senator, optical company executive
†Kondon, E. Jane principal
Paolino, Richard Francis manufacturing company executive
†Sharpe, Henry Dexter, Jr. manufacturing company executive

Pawtucket
Carleton, Richard Allyn cardiologist
Davison, Charles Hamilton financial executive
†Gaschen, Francis Allen lawyer
Hassenfeld, Alan Geoffrey toy company executive
Heyman, Lawrence Murray printmaker, painter
Neff, Edward August manufacturing company executive
O'Neill, John T. toy company executive
Robbins, Donald Michael lawyer
Verrecchia, Alfred J. toy company executive

Portsmouth
Baker, Walter Louis engineering company executive
Becken, Bradford Albert engineering executive

Providence
Adams, Thomas Randolph bibliographer, librarian, historian
†Algiere, Dennis Lee state senator
Amaral, Joseph Ferreira surgeon
Ames, Robert San retired manufacturing company executive
Anderson, James Alfred psychology educator
Anton, Thomas Julius political science, public policy educator, consultant
Arant, Patricia Slavic languages and literature educator
Arcaro, Harold Conrad, Jr. lawyer, educator
Aronson, Stanley Maynard physician, educator
Avery, Donald Hills metallurgist, educator, ethnographer
Banchoff, Thomas Francis mathematics educator
†Benoit, Nancy Louise state legislator, educator
Beyer, Robert Thomas physicist, educator
Blough, Donald S. psychology educator
Borod, Richard Melvin lawyer
Boyle, Francis Joseph federal judge
Bray, Philip James physicist
Bready, Richard Lawrence manufacturing company executive
Brock, Dan Willets philosophy educator
Calia, Vincent Frank psychologist, educator
Callahan, Harry Morey photographer
Campbell, Edwin Denton educational administrator
†Caprio, Frank T. lawyer, state legislator
Carlotti, Stephen Jon lawyer
Carpenter, Gene Blakely crystallography and chemistry educator
Cassill, Ronald Verlin author
Charniak, Eugene computer scientist, educator
Church, Russell Miller psychology educator
Cianci, Vincent Albert, Jr. lawyer, mayor
Clifton, Rodney James engineering educator, civil engineer, consultant
†Coderre, Elaine Ann state representative
Coffey, Sean Owen former state senator, lawyer
Cook, Albert Spaulding comparative literature and classics educator, writer
Cooper, Gordon Mayo retired manufacturing company executive
Cooper, Leon N. physicist, educator
Costellese, Linda E. Grace banker
Courage, Thomas Roberts lawyer
Crooks, Bruce Philip banker
Cunningham, John Fabian college president, philosophy educator
Curran, Joseph Patrick lawyer
Dafermos, Constantine Michael applied mathematics educator
Dahlberg, Albert Edward biochemistry educator
Damon, William Van Buren developmental psychologist, educator
Davis, Philip J. mathematician
Davis, Robert Paul physician, educator
†Dickinson, Brian Ward columnist
†Dimeo, Thomas P. construction company executive, real estate developer
†Dodge, James H. energy industry executive
Donnelly, Kevin William lawyer
Donovan, Bruce Elliot classics educator, university dean
Dowben, Robert Morris physician, scientist
†Dowling, Sarah T. lawyer, state official
Downing, Brian Thomas business executive
†Dujardin, Richard Charles journalist
†Earle, Nathaniel Cabot board of trade executive
Elbaum, Charles physicist, educator, researcher
Enteman, Willard Finley philosophy educator
Erikson, George Emil (Erik Erikson) anatomist, archivist, historian, educator, information specialist
Estrup, Peder Jan physics and chemistry educator
Farmer, Malcolm, III lawyer
Farmer, Susan Lawson broadcasting executive, former secretary of state
Farrell, Margaret Dawson lawyer
Feinstein, Alan Shawn author, financial adviser
Feldman, Walter Sidney artist
Field, Noel Macdonald, Jr. lawyer
Fiering, Norman (Sanford) historian, library administrator
Findley, William Nichols mechanical engineering educator
Fleming, Wendell Helms educator, mathematician
†Fogarty, Charles Joseph senator
Fornara, Charles William historian, classicist, educator
Freiberger, Walter Frederick mathematics educator, actuarial science consultant, educator
Frerichs, Ernest Sunley religious studies educator
Freund, Lambert Ben engineering educator, researcher, consultant
Galletti, Pierre Marie medical science educator, artificial organ scientist
Gardner, Thomas Earle investment banker, financial consultant
Garrison, Mark Joseph political science educator, former diplomat
Gasbarro, Pasco, Jr. lawyer
Gelineau, Louis Edward bishop
Gerbi, Susan Alexandra biology educator
Gerritsen, Hendrik Jurjen physics educator, researcher
Gibbs, June Nesbitt state senator
Gilbane, Jean Ann (Mrs. Thomas F. Gilbane) construction company executive
†Gilbane, William James building company executive
Gleason, Abbott history educator
Glicksman, Arvin S(igmund) radiologist, physician
Glicksman, Maurice engineering educator, former dean and provost
Goddard, Robert Hale Ives investment executive
Goldstein, Sidney sociology educator, demographer
Goodman, Elliot Raymond political scientist, educator
†Goodwin, Maryellen state legislator
†Gorham, Bradford lawyer
Gorton, Arlene Elizabeth physical education educator
Gould, Richard Allan anthropologist, archaeologist, educator
Graboys, George retired bank executive
Greene, Edward Forbes chemistry educator
Greer, David S. university dean, physician, educator
Gregorian, Vartan academic administrator
Grimm, William Richard lawyer
Grossman, Herschel I. economics educator
Gurland, Joseph engineering educator
Hagopian, Jacob federal judge
Hamblett, Stephen newspaper publishing executive
Hamolsky, Milton William physician
Hardymon, James Franklin diversified products company executive

†Harper, Michael S. *English language educator*
Harris, Richard John *diversified holding company executive*
Hartmann, George Herman *retired manufacturing company executive*
†Hawkins, Brian Lee *academic administrator, educator*
Hazeltine, Barrett *electrical engineer, educator*
Heath, Dwight Braley *anthropologist, educator*
†Henseler, Suzanne Marie *legislator, social studies educator, majority whip*
Hindle, Edward Francis *lawyer*
†Hirsch, David H. *English, American literature and Judaic studies educator, academic administrator*
Holden, Raymond Henry *clinical psychologist*
Honig, Edwin *comparative literature educator, poet*
Hopkins, Jacques Vaughn *lawyer*
Hopmann, Philip Terrence *political science educator*
†Houghton, Anthony *physics educator, research scientist*
Howes, Lorraine de Wet *fashion designer, educator*
†Hunt, George Nelson *bishop*
†Jenkins, Richard Dale *actor, theatre director*
Johnson, Vahe Duncan *lawyer*
Jordy, William Henry *art history educator*
Joukowsky, Artemis A. W. *private investor*
†Kane, Agnes Brezak *pathologist, educator*
Kean, John Vaughan *lawyer*
Kersh, DeWitte Talmadge, Jr. *lawyer*
Kim, Jaegwon *philosophy educator*
Klyberg, Albert Thomas *historical society administrator*
Knopf, Paul Mark *immunoparasitologist*
Koelb, Clayton Talmadge *insurance company executive*
†Kreykes, William *health care management executive*
Kucera, Henry *linguistics educator*
Kushner, Harold Joseph *mathematics educator*
Lagueux, Ronald Rene *federal judge*
Landow, George Paul *English literature and art educator, writer*
†Lederman, Michael G. *consumer products company executive*
Leonard, Barbara M *secretary of state, federal agency administrator, state agency administrattor*
Lesko, Leonard Henry *Egyptologist, educator*
†Levin, Frank S. *physicist, educator*
Lewis, David Carleton *medical educator, university center director*
Licht, Richard A. *lawyer*
Little, Dennis Gage *diversified business executive*
Liu, Joseph T. C. *engineering educator*
Loferski, Joseph John *electrical engineering educator*
Lombardi, Alfred Samuel *lawyer*
Long, Beverly Glenn *lawyer*
†Lyle, John William, Jr. *state senator, lawyer, social studies educator*
Manchester, Robert D. *venture capitalist*
Mandle, Earl Roger *university president, former museum administrator*
†Maris, Humphrey John *physicist, educator*
Marsh, Robert Mortimer *sociologist, educator*
Marshall, Jean McElroy *physiologist*
†Martin, John *critic*
Mason, Edward Allen *chemistry educator, scientist*
†Mathieu, Helen M. *state legislator*
McCann, Gail Elizabeth *lawyer*
Mc Donald, Charles J. *physician, educator*
McIlvane, Edward James *artist, instructor, designer*
†Mc Intosh, Douglas J. *insurance company executive*
McMahon, Eleanor Marie *education educator*
McWalters, Peter *state agency administrator*
Mehlman, Edwin Stephen *endodontist*
†Méras, Phyllis Leslie *journalist*
Metrey, George David *social work educator, academic administrator*
Milhaven, John Giles *religious studies educator*
Monteiro, Lois Ann *medical science educator*
†Mueller, Frederick *principal*
Munir, Yusuf *vocational education administrator*
Murray, Florence Kerins *state supreme court justice*
Murray, Terrence *banker*
Nazarian, John *academic administrator, mathematics educator*
Needleman, Alan *mechanical engineering educator*
Nelson, Ron *composer, conductor, educator*
Neu, Charles Eric *historian, educator*
Nussbaum, Martha Craven *philosophy and classics educator*
Ockerse, Thomas *graphic design educator*
O'Donnell, Charles Patrick *retired newspaper executive, consultant*
Oh, William *physician*
Olsen, Hans Peter *lawyer*
†Owens, Robert Warren *energy company executive*
Papitto, Ralph Raymond *manufacturing company executive*
Parks, Robert Emmett, Jr. *medical science educator*
Pearce, George Hamilton *archbishop*
Pendergast, John Joseph, III *lawyer*
Perkins, Whitney Trow *political science educator emeritus*
Petrocelli, Americo William *higher education commissioner*
Pierce, Richard Hilton *lawyer*
Pine, Jeffrey Barry *state attorney general*
Pipkin, Allen Compere, II *mathematician, educator*
Poole, William *economics educator, consultant*
Preparata, Franco Paolo *computer science and engineering educator*
Putnam, Michael Courtney Jenkins *classics educator*
Putterman, Louis G. *economics educator*
Reed, Walter Gurnee Dyer *lawyer*
Reeder, John P., Jr. *religious studies educator*
Resmini, Ronald Joseph *lawyer*
Ribbans, Geoffrey Wilfrid *Spanish educator*
Richman, Marc Herbert *forensic engineer, educator*
Rieger, Philip Henri *chemistry educator, researcher*
Robinson, William Philip, III *lawyer*
Rohr, Donald Gerard *history educator*
Rosenberg, Bruce Alan *English language educator, author*
Rothman, Frank George *biology educator, biochemical genetics researcher, academic administrator*
†Rueschemeyer, Dietrich *sociology educator*
Ryder, Harl Edgar *economist, educator*
St. Florian, Friedrich Gartler *architect, educator, university dean*
Salesses, John Joseph *university administrator*
Salter, Lester Herbert *lawyer*
†Sanderson, Edward French *state official*
Savage, John Edmund *computer science educator, researcher*
Schevill, James Erwin *poet, playwright*
†Schobel, George *insurance company executive*
Scholes, Robert Edward *English language educator*
Schottland, Edward Morrow *hospital adminstrator*
Schupack, Mark Barry *economist, educator*
Selya, Bruce Marshall *federal judge*
Shaw, Ronald Ahrend *physician, educator*
Shepp, Bryan Eugene *psychologist, educator*
Sherman, Deming Eliot *lawyer*
Silver, Paul Allen *lawyer*
Sinclair, Joseph Samuels *broadcasting company executive, retail merchant*
Sizer, Theodore R. *education educator*
Smoke, Richard *political scientist, political psychologist*
Soutter, Thomas D. *lawyer*
Spilka, Mark *English educator*
Staples, Richard Farnsworth *lawyer*
Stultz, Newell Maynard *political science educator*
Sundlun, Bruce *governor*
†Svengalis, Kendall Frayne *law librarian*
Symonds, Paul Southworth *mechanical engineering educator, researcher*
Tauc, Jan *physics educator*
Tella, Luigi *accountant*
Terras, Victor *Slavic languages and comparative literature educator*
Thomson, Paul van Kuykendall *priest, educator*
Tillinghast, Charles Carpenter, Jr. *aviation and financial consultant*
Tobin, Bentley *lawyer*
Torres, Ernest C. *federal judge*
Trueblood, Alan Stubbs *former modern language educator*
Vavala, Domenic Anthony *medical scientist, educator, retired air force officer*
†Vecchio, Anthony Joseph *zoological park administrator*
Votolato, Arthur Nicholas, Jr. *federal judge*
Walker, Howard Ernest *lawyer*
Watkins, John Chester Anderson *newspaper publisher*
Watkins, William, Jr. *electric power industry executive*
Weaver, Barbara Frances *librarian*
Weinstein, Arnold Louis *literature educator*
Weisberger, Joseph Robert *state supreme court justice*
Weissfeld, Joachim Alexander *lawyer*
Weygand, Robert A. *lieutenant governor, landscape architect*
†Whitcomb, Robert Bassett *journalist, editor*
White, Erskine Norman, Jr. *management company executive*
Widgoff, Mildred *physicist, educator*
Williams, Lea Everard *history educator*
Wood, Gordon Stewart *historian, educator*
Wooding, Peter Holden *interior and industrial designer*
Woolf, William Blauvelt *association executive*
Wrenn, James Joseph *East Asian studies educator*
Wunderlich, Alfred Leon *artist, art educator*
Wyatt, William Frank, Jr. *philology educator*
Wyman, James Vernon *newspaper executive*

Riverside
†McElroy, Sister Maureen *secondary school principal*

Rumford
Cote, Louise Roseann *creative director, designer*

Saunderstown
Donovan, Gerald Alton *retired academic administrator, former university dean*
Knauss, John Atkinson *federal agency administrator, oceanographer, educator, former university dean*
Leavitt, Thomas Whittlesey *museum director, educator*

Smithfield
Haas, William Paul *humanities educator, former college president*
Trueheart, William E. *academic administrator*

South Kingstown
Berman, Allan *psychologist, educator*

Tiverton
Davis, Stephen Edward *lawyer*

Wakefield
Eddy, Edward Danforth *academic administrator, educator*
Fair, Charles Maitland *neuroscientist, author*
Gifford, Harry Cortland Frey *health educator*
Mason, Scott MacGregor *entrepreneur, inventor, consultant*
Moore, George Emerson, Jr. *geologist, educator*

Warwick
Blount, William Allan *broadcasting executive*
†Knowles, Charles Timothy *lawyer, state legislator*
Kruse, James Joseph *merchant banker*
†Revens, John Cosgrove, Jr. *state senator, lawyer*

Watch Hill
Rees, Charles H. G. *retired financial officer, investor, consultant*

West Greenwich
Breakstone, Robert Albert *computer and government services company executive*
†Markowicz, Victor *video company executive*

West Kingston
Abell, Paul Irving *retired chemistry educator*
Haring, Howard Jack *magazine editor*

West Warwick
Clary, Alexia Barbara *management company executive*
Galkin, Robert Theodore *company executive*

Westerly
Day, Chon *cartoonist*
Hennessy, Dean McDonald *lawyer, multinational corporation executive*
Reiland, Lowell Keith *sculptor*
Verdier, Philippe M(aurice) *art historian*

SOUTH CAROLINA

Aiken
Alexander, Robert Earl *university chancellor, educator*
†Begley, R. T. *nuclear science administrator*
Cowan, Carolyn Cannon *early childhood educator*
Cutting, Robert Thomas *army officer, physician*
Dickson, Paul Wesley, Jr. *physicist*
Gleichauf, John George *ophthalmologist*
Hanna, Carey McConnell *securities and investments executive*
Hofstetter, Kenneth John *research chemist*
†Rains, Darrell Ross *bank controller*
†Rudnick, Irene Krugman *lawyer, state legislator, educator*
Simons, Charles Earl, Jr. *federal judge*
Smith, Gregory White *writer*
Williamson, Thomas Garnett *nuclear engineering and engineering physics educator*

Anderson
Anderson, George Ross, Jr. *federal judge*
Carroll, Edward Perry *instrumental music educator, conductor*
Elks, William Chester, Jr. *manufacturing executive*
Gleason, Ralph Newton *economic development consultant*
Glenn, Michael Douglas *lawyer*
Goodner, Homer Wade *process control reliability engineer, process safety risk analysis specialist, industrial process system failure risk consultant*
†Harris, Patrick Bradley *state legislator, real estate broker*
Hearne, Stephen Zachary *minister, educator*
Hendrix, James Easton *textiles executive*
Mitchell, Thomas Wayne *newspaper editor*
†Oglesby, Daniel Kirkland, Jr. *hospital administrator*
Watkins, William Law *lawyer, retired*
†Woodward, Karen Callison *school system administrator*
Young, Marjorie Willis *writer, editor*

Arcadia
Dent, Frederick Baily *mill executive, former ambassador, former secretary of commerce*

Beaufort
Day, John Sidney *management sciences educator*
Harvey, William Brantley, Jr. *lawyer, former lieutenant governor*
Ogburn, Charlton *writer*

Bennettsville
Kinney, William Light, Jr. *newspaper editor, publisher*

Camden
Daniels, John Hancock *agricultural products company executive*
Furman, Hezekiah Wyndol Carroll *lawyer*

Chapin
Branham, Mack Carison, Jr. *retired theological seminary executive, minister*

Charleston
Addlestone, Nathan Sidney *metals company executive*
Adelman, Saul Joseph *astronomy educator, researcher*
Anderson, Charles Roberts *English language educator*
Anderson, Ivan Verner, Jr. *newspaper publisher*
Anderson, Marion Cornelius *surgeon, medical educator*
Apple, David Joseph *ophthalmology educator*
Ashley, Franklin Bascom *theater educator, writer*
†Bailey, James Julian *real estate executive*
Barclay, James Ralph *psychologist, educator*
Basler, Thomas G. *librarian, administrator, educator*
Bell, Norman Howard *physician, endocrinologist, educator*
Berglund, Robin G. *biochemist, former corporate executive*
Bowman, Daniel Oliver *psychologist*
Brumgardt, John Raymond *museum administrator*
Brusca, Richard Charles *zoologist, researcher, educator*
Burrell, Victor Gregory, Jr. *marine scientist*
†Buvinger, Jan *library director*
Cannon, Hugh *lawyer*
Carek, Donald J(ohn) *child psychiatry educator*
Carr, Robert Stuart *federal magistrate judge*
Cheng, Thomas Clement *parasitologist, immunologist, educator, author*
Colwell, John Amory *physician*
Conyers, Abda Johnson, III *theology educator, writer*
†Crawford, Fred Allen, Jr. *cardiothoracic surgeon, educator*
Creasman, William Thomas *obstetrician-gynecologist, educator*
Curtis, Marcia *university dean*
Daniell, Herman Burch *pharmacologist*
Delli Colli, Humbert Thomas *chemist, product development specialist*
Dobson, Richard Lawrence *dermatologist, educator*
Donehue, John Douglas *newspaper public relations executive*
Edwards, James Burrows *university president, oral surgeon*
Farr, Charles Sims *lawyer*
Fenn, Jimmy O'Neil *physicist*
Gadsden, Richard Hamilton *clinical biochemistry educator*
Gaillard, John Palmer, Jr. *former government official, former mayor*
Garrett, Gordon Henderson *lawyer*
Gilbreth, Frank Bunker, Jr. *retired communications executive, writer*
Gillette, Paul Crawford *pediatric cardiologist*
Gleason, John Martin *community development consultant*
†Goff, R. Garey *architect*
Grimball, William Heyward *lawyer*
Grimsley, James Alexander, Jr. *university administrator, retired army officer*
Hawkins, Falcon Black, Jr. *federal judge*
Hoel, David Gerhard *state administrator, statistician, scientist*
†Hoerter, Sam Spalding *transportation executive*
Hogan, Arthur James *portfolio manager*
Hogan, Edward Leo *neurologist*
Hughes, Blake *retired architectural institute administrator, publisher*
Ivey, Robert Carl *artistic director, educator, choreographer*
Johnson, Allen Huggins *physician, educator*
†Langley, Lynne Spencer *newspaper editor, columnist*
La Via, Mariano Francis *physician, pathology and laboratory medicine educator*
Legerton, Clarence William, Jr. *gastroenterologist, educator*
LeRoy, Edward Carwile *rheumatologist*
Lucas, Frank Edward *architect*
†Maize, John Christopher *dermatology educator*
Manigault, Peter *media executive*
Margolius, Harry Stephen *pharmacologist, physician*
Martin, Roblee Boettcher *retired cement manufacturing executive*
Mc Devitt, Joseph Bryan *retired university administrator, retired naval officer*
McGee, Hall Thomas, Jr. *newspaper, radio and television executive*
McGinty, John B. *orthopaedic surgeon, educator*
Moore, William Vincent *political science educator*
Mulholland, Angela Broadway *lawyer*
Newberry, William Marcus *physician, educator, university administrator*
Norton, David C. *federal judge*
O'Brien, Paul Herbert *surgeon*
Ogawa, Makio *physician*
Othersen, Henry Biemann, Jr. *pediatric surgeon, physician, educator*
Overton, Marcus Lee *performing arts administrator*
Pearson, Margit Linnea *real estate company executive*
Pincus, Michael Stern *department chairman, language educator*
†Porter, Thomas Joseph, Jr. *writer, songwriter*
Raghupathi, Ragu S. *manufacturing executive*
Reilly, David Henry *university dean*
Rivers, John Minott, Jr. *corporate professional*
Rosebrough, Walter M., Jr. *manufacturing executive*
†Salmon, Edward Lloyd, Jr. *bishop*
†Schmitt, Robert Christian *architect, interior designer*
Schreadley, Richard Lee *writer, retired newspaper editor*
Scott, Henry Lawrence *concert pianist-humorist*
Simons, Albert, Jr. *lawyer*
Simson, Jo Anne *anatomy and cell biology educator*
Smith, J. Roy *education educator*
†Smith, W. Stuart *hospital administrator*
Stahl, David *orchestra and opera conductor*
Swanson, Arnold Arthur *biochemistry educator*
Tarleton, Larry Wilson *newspaper editor*
Thompson, David B. *bishop*
Watts, Claudius Elmer, III *retired air force officer*
†Wilcox, Arthur Manigault *newspaper editor*
Wilson, Frederick Allen *medical educator, medical center administrator, gastroenterologist*
Winthrop, John *investment company executive*
Wyrick, Charles Lloyd, Jr. *publisher, writer, editor*

Chester
†Short, Linda Huffstetler *state senator*

Clemson
Adams, John Quincy, III *nuclear engineer*
Boykin, Joseph Floyd, Jr. *librarian*
†Bunn, Joe Millard *agricultural engineering educator*
Burch, Elmer Earl *management educator*
Byars, Betsy (Cromer) *author*
Calhoun, Richard James *English language educator*
Chisman, James Allan *industrial engineering educator, consultant*
Clayton, Donald Delbert *astrophysicist, nuclear physicist, educator*
Couch, James Houston *industrial engineer, educator*
Cox, Headley Morris, Jr. *lawyer, educator*
DesMarteau, Darryl Dwayne *chemistry and geology educator*
Griffin, Villard Stuart, Jr. *geology educator*
†Han, Young Jo *agricultural engineer, educator*
Hays, Sidney Brooks *retired entomology educator*
Hicks, Edwin Hugh *accountant*
Kenelly, John Willis, Jr. *mathematician, educator*
Lennon, A. Max *university administrator*
Leonard, Michael Steven *industrial engineering educator*
†Morr, Charles Vernon *food science educator*
Paul, Frank Waters *mechanical engineer, educator, consultant*
Pursley, Michael Bader *electrical engineering educator, communications systems research and consulting*
Riley, Helene Maria Kastinger *germanist*
Spain, James Dorris, Jr. *biochemist, educator*
Trevillian, Wallace Dabney *economics educator, retired dean*
Underwood, Richard Allan *English language educator*
Vogel, Henry Elliott *retired university dean and physics educator*
†von Recum, Andreas F. *bioengineer*
Williamson, Robert Elmore *agricultural engineering educator*
Young, Joseph Laurie *architecture educator*

Clinton
Cornelson, George Henry, IV *retired textile company executive*
Orr, Kenneth Bradley *college president*
Vance, Robert Mercer *textile manufacturing company executive, banker*

Clover
Peacock, A(lvin) Ward *textile company executive*

Columbia
Abel, Francis Lee *physiology educator*
Adams, Gregory Burke *lawyer, educator*
Adams, John Hurst *bishop*
Adams, Weston *diplomat, lawyer*
Adcock, David Filmore *radiologist, educator*
†Aelion, C. Marjorie *educator*
Almond, Carl Herman *surgeon, physician, educator*
Altekruse, Joan Morrissey *preventive medicine educator*
Amidon, Roger Lyman *health administration educator*
Anderson, Joseph Fletcher, Jr. *federal judge*
†Aull, James Stroud *bishop*
Averyt, Gayle Owen *insurance executive*
Bailey, George Screven *lawyer*
Beckham, William Arthur *bishop*

Belasco, Simon French language and linguistics educator
Bethea, Joseph Benjamin bishop
Bjontegard, Arthur Martin, Jr. foundation executive
Blanton, Hoover Clarence lawyer
Blount, Evelyn religious organization administrator
Boggs, Jack Aaron banker, municipal government official
Brown, Arnold health science facility administrator
Brubaker, Lauren Edgar minister, religion educator
Bruccoli, Matthew Joseph English educator, publisher
Callaham, Betty Elgin librarian
Campbell, Carroll Ashmore, Jr. governor, former congressman
Carlisle, William Aiken architect
Case, George Tilden, Jr. marketing professional
Chapman, Robert Foster federal judge
Chastain, Randall Meads lawyer, educator
Cilella, Salvatore George, Jr. museum director
Clark, David Randolph wholesale grocer
Clower, Robert Wayne economics educator, consultant
Cohn, Elchanan economics educator
Cole, Benjamin Theodore biologist
Conrad, Paul Ernest transportation consultant
Cooper, William Allen, Jr. audiologist
Cope, Larry Morgan employee assistance provider, coordinator
†Cork, Holly A. state legislator
†Courson, John Edward state senator, insurance company executive
Crim, Reuben Sidney newspaper publishing executive
Culik, Karel computer scientist, educator
Davis, Keith Eugene psychologist, educator, consultant
Dawson, Wallace Douglas, Jr. geneticist
Dickey, James poet, novelist, filmmaker, critic
Donald, Alexander Grant psychiatrist
Duffie, Virgil Whatley, Jr. state official
Duffy, John Joseph academic administrator, history educator
Eastman, Caroline Merriam computer science educator
Edgar, Walter Bellingrath historian
Edge, Ronald Dovaston physics educator
Ernst, Edward Willis electrical engineering educator
Finkel, Gerald Michael lawyer
Folsom, John Roy savings and loan executive
Foster, Robert Watson legal educator
Friedman, Myles Ivan education educator
Fryer, John Stanley management science educator
Geckle, George Leo, III English language educator
†Giese, Warren Kenneth health and physical education educator, state senator
Ginsberg, Leon Herman social work educator
†Golightly, Donald Edward architect
†Gray, Katherine Wilson newspaper editor
†Gressette, Lawrence M., Jr. utilities executive
Haimbaugh, George Dow, Jr. lawyer, educator
†Hallman, Harry M., Jr. retired oil company executive
Hamilton, Clyde Henry federal judge
Hancock, Harriet Daniels lawyer
Hardin, James Neal German and comparative literature educator
†Harvin, Charles Alexander, III state legislator
Hatch, David Lincoln sociology educator
Hatch, Mary Gies German language educator
Heider, Karl Gustav anthropology educator
Horger, Edgar Olin, III obstetrics and gynecology educator
Howard-Hill, Trevor Howard English language educator
†Hultstrand, Charles John architect
Humphries, John O'Neal physician, educator, university dean
Hupp, Jack Scott civic administrator
Inkley, Scott Russell, Jr. state agency administrator
Jervey, Harold Edward, Jr. medical education consultant, retired
Johnson, Herbert Alan history and law educator, lawyer, chaplain
Johnson, James Bek, Jr. library director
Kahn, Herman Bernard construction company executive
Kay, Carol McGinnis literature educator
Kiker, Billy Frazier economics educator
King, John Ethelbert, Jr. education educator, former academic administrator
†Land, John Calhoun, III lawyer, state legislator
†Lander, James Albert retired military officer, state senator
†Leatherman, Hugh Kenneth, Sr. state senator, business executive
Lee, Alexandra Saimovici civil engineer
LeFever, Michael Grant state agency administrator
Lindley, James Gunn bank executive
Long, Eugene Thomas, III philosophy educator, administrator
Lumpkin, John Henderson retired banker
†Macaulay, Alexander Stephens state senator
Marchant, Trelawney Eston national guard officer, lawyer
Marion, Andrew Burnet lawyer
Martin, Charles Wallace travel executive, retired university administrator
Matthews, Steve Allen lawyer
Mc Cullough, Ralph Clayton, II lawyer, educator
McGill, Jennifer Houser non-profit association administrator
Medlock, Thomas Travis state attorney general
Melton, Gary Bentley psychology and law educator
Miles, Jim state official
Mishler, William, II political science educator
Morris, Earle Elias, Jr. state official, business executive
Morris, James Aloysius economist, educator
Myerson, Joel Arthur English language educator, researcher
Nelson-Mayson, Linda Ruth art museum curator
Newton, Rhonwen Leonard microcomputer consultant
Nexsen, Julian Jacobs lawyer
Nielsen, Barbara Stock state education official
Nolte, William Henry English language educator
Norman, George Buford, Jr. foreign language educator
Norton, Hugh Stanton economist, educator
Ott, Jack M. mathematics educator
Palms, John Michael university president
Patterson, Grady Leslie, Jr. state treasurer
Perry, Matthew J., Jr. federal judge
Pritchett, Samuel Travis finance and insurance educator, researcher
Rawlinson, Helen Ann librarian
Reeves, George McMillan, Jr. comparative literature educator, educational administrator
Reichard, William Thomas, III insurance company executive
†Rhoad, Thomas N., Jr. farmer, state legislator, retired mail carrier
Roberts, Edward Calhoun retired lawyer
Robinson, Christopher Thomas artist
†Rogers, Timothy Folk lawyer
Rone, William Eugene, Jr. newspaper editor
†Royall, Robert Venning, Jr. banker
Secor, Donald Terry, Jr. geologist, educator
Shedd, Dennis W. federal judge
Sheheen, Fred Roukos education association administrator
Sloan, Frank Keenan lawyer, writer
Smith, Franklin Sumner, Jr. retired insurance executive
†Smith, James Roland state legislator
†Smith, J(efferson) Verne state senator, business executive
Splittgerber, Fredric Lee education educator
Sproat, John Gerald historian
Starr, Harvey political scientist
Tate, Harold Simmons, Jr. lawyer
Teague, Peyton Clark chemist, educator
†Thelen, Gil newspaper editor
Toal, Jean Hoefer lawyer, state supreme court justice
Toombs, Kenneth Eldridge librarian
Vernberg, Frank John marine and biological sciences educator
†Waites, Candy Yaghjian state official
Walker, Richard Louis former ambassador, educator, author
Warren, Charles David library administrator
†Watabe, Norimitsu biology and marine science educator
Waugh, John David university administrator, engineering educator, consultant
Weatherbee, Donald Emery political scientist, educator
Weir, Robert McColloch history educator
Wells, Robert Steven law association executive
West, Rexford Leon banker
Whitlock, Edward Madison, Jr. civil engineer
Wilder, Ronald Parker economics educator
†Wilson, George Larry computer software company executive
†Wofford, Sandra Smith (Sandi Smith Wofford) legislator
Wolfe, George B. lawyer

Conway
Moore, Richard Harlan biologist, college administrator
Sharples, D. Kent college administrator

Darlington
Chandler, A. Lee state supreme court justice
Samuel, Josie Harris secondary educator

Dataw Island
Dietz, Earl Daniel retired foundation company executive

Dillon
Webb, Ronald Wayne hospital administrator

Due West
Koonts, Jones Calvin retired education educator
Ruble, Randall Tucker theologian, educator, academic administrator

Easley
Dark, Alvin Ralph public relations executive
Failing, George Edgar editor, clergyman, educator
Goldman, Joseph Elias advertising executive
Grantham, George Leighton lawyer, banker, utility company executive
†Robinson, Alfred Burgess, Jr. lawyer

Florence
Burns, William A. museum administrator, author
Dixon, Gale Harllee drug company executive
†Glover, Maggie Wallace state legislator
Guest, Karl Macon retired paper and container manufacturing company executive
†Harwell, B(axter) Hicks lawyer, state legislator
Houck, Charles Weston federal judge
†Kittrell, Benjamin Upchurch agronomist
Smith, Walter Douglas retired college president
Strong, Roger Lee mathematics educator
Wagner, John Garnet pharmacy educator
†Ward, Dennis S. architect

Fort Mill
†Bonds, C. Joseph school system administrator
Elisha, Walter Y. textile manufacturing company executive
†Hodge, Bobby Lynn mechanical engineer
Horten, Carl Frank textile manufacturing company executive
Kelbley, Stephen Paul consumer products executive
Mantle, John Edward newspaper publisher

Gaffney
Perry, Gaylord Jackson former professional baseball player

Gastonia
Carson, John Little historical theology educator, clergyman

Georgetown
Allison, Christopher FitzSimons bishop
McGrath, James Charles, III financial services company executive, lawyer, consultant
Moore, Albert Cunningham lawyer, insurance company executive

Goose Creek
†Evans, V. Bond aluminum components manufacturing company executive
†Johnson, Johnnie bishop

Greenville
Alberga, Alta Wheat artist
Bates, George William obstetrician, gynecologist, educator
Bauknight, Clarence Brock wholesale and retail company executive
Bellantoni, Maureen Blanchfield manufacturing and distribution executive
Boliek, Luther C. bank executive
Bonner, Jack Wilbur, III psychiatrist, educator, administrator
†Brown, George Edward chemical engineer, consultant
Brown, Wilbur C. college director
Burkhardt, J. Bland, Jr. hospital administrator
†Callahan, Ralph Wilson, Jr. advertising agency executive
Carpenter, William Levy mechanical engineer
†Christopher, Socrates S. engineering executive
Cloer, Carl Thomas, Jr. education educator
†Collins, Marshall J., Jr. consumer products company executive
Cook, Paul M(artin), II mathematics educator
Crabtree, John Henry, Jr. retired English educator
Eskew, Rhea Taliaferro newspaper publisher
†Eskola, David Anund television columnist
Fayonsky, James Leon financial planner
Fitzgerald, Eugene Francis management consultant
Freeman, William Ernest, Jr. architect
Friedman, Steven M. textile company executive
†Frist, Thomas Ferran philanthropic organization executive
Gilkerson, Yancey Sherard writer, former editor
†Grimes, J. William cable television executive
Hagood, William Milliken, III lawyer
†Haskins, Terry Edward lawyer, politician
Henderson, James Marvin advertising agency executive
Herlong, Henry Michael, Jr. federal judge
Hill, Grace Lucile Garrison education educator, consultant
Hipp, Francis Moffett insurance executive
Hipp, William Hayne insurance and broadcasting executive
†Hodges, Harland E. apparel executive
Horton, James Wright retired lawyer
Hunt, Walter Kenneth, III insurance company executive
Hunter, Jerry E. textile company executive
James, William Richard lawyer
Jones, Bob, Jr. academic administrator, educator, lecturer, minister
Kilgore, Donald Gibson, Jr. pathologist
†LeBlanc, L(ouis) Christian architect
†Leonhardt, Thomas C. engineering company executive
Maddrey, E. E., II textile company executive
†Magill, Dodie Burns early childhood education educator
Mann, James Robert congressman
Mebane, William deBerniere newspaper publisher
Mims, Thomas Jerome insurance executive
†Mitchell, Theo Walker lawyer
Moore, Alfred Michael insurance broker executive
†Neal, James Austin architect
Pamplin, Robert Boisseau, Jr. agricultural company executive, minister, writer
Parente, Emil J. chemical engineering executive
Parsell, David Beatty modern language educator
Payne, G(eorge) Frederick educational director
Plumstead, William Charles quality engineer, consultant
Rainsford, Bettis C. textile company executive
Roe, Thomas Anderson building supply company executive
Scruggs, Jack Gilbert retired chemical executive
Smith, Morton Howison religious organization administrator, educator
Smith, Philip Daniel academic administrator, education educator
†Stone, Charles Rivers apparel manufacturing company executive
Stultz, Thomas Joseph newspaper executive
†Suitt, Thomas Howard construction company executive
Theodore, Nick Andrew lietenant governor
Thompson, Robert Thomas lawyer
Todd, John Dickerson, Jr. lawyer
†Torrence, Roderick Clark advertising executive
Traxler, William Byrd lawyer
Traxler, William Byrd, Jr. federal judge
Varin, Roger Robert textile executive
Walker, Wesley M. lawyer
Walters, Johnnie McKeiver lawyer
Wearn, Wilson Cannon retired media executive
Wilkins, William Walter, Jr. federal judge

Greenwood
Fox, Richard Shirley zoology educator
Jackson, Larry Artope retired college president
Sigety, Charles Edward lawyer, medical products executive

Greer
Gallman, Clarence Hunter textile executive
Lane, James Garland, Jr. diversified industry executive

Harleyville
†Sugarman, Burt construction company executive

Hartsville
Browning, Peter Crane packaging company executive
Coker, Charles Westfield diversified manufacturing company executive
Daniels, James Douglas academic administrator
DeLoach, Harris E(ugene), Jr. lawyer, manufacturing company executive
Ingram, Gladys Almenas secondary school educator
King, Russell C., Jr. manufacturing company executive
Menius, Espie Flynn, Jr. electrical engineer

Hilton Head
Adams, William Hensley ecologist, educator
Gruchacz, Robert S. real estate executive
Rulis, Raymond Joseph manufacturing company executive, consultant

Hilton Head Island
Batten, William Milfred retired stock exchange executive
Becker, Karl Martin lawyer, investment company executive
Birk, Robert Eugene retired physician, educator
Brock, Karena Diane ballerina, educator, choreographer
Brown, Arthur Edmon, Jr. retired army officer
Carr, David Turner physician
Cunningham, William Henry retired food products executive
Davis, Milton Wickers, Jr. chemical engineer, educator
Eden, Lee Smythe broadcasting executive
Harty, James D. former manufacturing company executive
Hornor, Frank Berkshire banker
Huckins, Harold Aaron chemical engineer
Kaley, Arthur Warren financial consulting company executive
Lewis, Gene Evans retired medical equipment company executive
Little, Thomas Mayer public relations executive
Male, Roy Raymond English language educator
McKinney, Donald Lee magazine editor
Mersereau, Hiram Stipe wood products company consultant
Mirse, Ralph Thomas former college president
Mulhollan, Paige Elliott retired university president
Patton, Joseph Donald, Jr. management consultant
Pritchard, Dalton Harold retired electronics research engineer
Radest, Howard Bernard clergyman, educator
Rose, William Shepard, Jr. lawyer, former federal official
Russell, Allen Stevenson retired aluminum company executive
Santos, George Wesley physician, educator
Scarminach, Charles Anthony lawyer
Simpson, John Wistar energy consultant, former manufacturing company executive
Stein, Bernard Alvin business consultant
Stoll, Richard Edmund retired manufacturing executive
Vadnais, Alfred William lawyer
Windman, Arnold Lewis retired mechanical engineer

Hollywood
Hull, Edward Whaley Seabrook freelance writer, consultant

Hopkins
Clarkson, Jocelyn Adrene medical technologist

Inman
†Reese, Glenn G. state senator, food products executive

Johns Island
Behnke, Wallace Blanchard, Jr. consultant, engineer, retired utility executive
Cameron, Thomas William Lane investment company executive
Failla, Patricia McClement biomedical and environmental research adminstrator
Gamble, William Belser, Jr. physician
Mackaness, George Bellamy retired pharmaceutical company executive
Ross, Paul physician, radiologist

Kershaw
Lucas, Dean Hadden educator

Kiawah Island
Dyal, William M., Jr. retired college president

Lake City
TruLuck, James Paul, Jr. dentist, vintner

Lancaster
Bundy, Charles Alan foundation executive

Landrum
Hilton, Ordway document examiner
Pauley, Robert Reinhold broadcasting executive, financial executive

Laurens
Moncrief, James Loring school principal

Leesville
Crumley, James Robert, Jr. retired clergyman

Lexington
†Gatch, Charles Edward, Jr. middle school principal
Miller, Ben Neely physician
Timmerman, George Bell, Jr. judge
Wilkins, Robert Pearce lawyer

Little River
Uzenda, Jara Carlow technical writer

Mauldin
†Phillips, James Oscar minister

Moncks Corner
†Law, James Norris state legislator, wholesale distribution executive
Morris, Henry Allen, Jr. publisher
†Rainear, Robert E. utilities executive

Mount Pleasant
Cooley, Kathleen Shannon speech-language pathologist

Mullins
Stonesifer, Richard James retired humanities and social science educator

Murrells Inlet
Noble, Joseph Veach fine arts administrator
Tarbox, Gurdon Lucius, Jr. museum executive

Myrtle Beach
Dail, Hilda Lee psychotherapist
Harwell, David Walker retired state supreme court chief justice
Madory, James Richard hospital administrator, former air force officer
Patton, Wendell Melton, Jr. retired management educator, consulting psychologist, college president

Newberry
Bost, Raymond Morris college administrator
Layton, William Isaac mathematics educator
Pope, Thomas Harrington, Jr. lawyer

North
Moran, John Bernard government official

North Augusta
Pritchard, Constance Jenkins career development trainer, consultant

North Charleston
Mc Aleece, Donald John mechanical engineering educator
Zucker, Jerry energy systems manufacturing executive

North Myrtle Beach
Atkinson, Harold Witherspoon utilities consultant, real estate broker
Hampton, Robert K., Sr. environmental and industrial specialist, real estate associate, consultant

Orangeburg
Babb, Julius Wistar, III cardiovascular surgeon
Graule, Raymond S(iegfried) metallurgical engineer
Sims, Edward Howell editor, publisher

Pawleys Island
Alexander, William D., III civil engineer, consultant, former army air force officer
†Cepluch, Robert J. retired mechanical engineer

Piedmont
†McMahand, Willie Bee clergyman, construction company executive

Ridgeland
Smart, Jacob Edward consultant

Rock Hill
Bristow, Robert O'Neil writer, educator
Click, John William communication educator
Du Bois, Paul Zinkhan library director
Viault, Birdsall Scrymser history educator

Saint Helena Island
Herzbrun, David Joseph retired advertising executive, consultant
Pinkerton, Robert Bruce mechanical engineer

Salem
Gentry, Robert Cecil meteorological consultant, research scientist
Jones, Charles Edward mechanical engineer
Van Buren, William Benjamin, III retired pharmaceutical company executive

Seneca
Clausen, Hugh Joseph retired army officer
Hudgin, Donald Edward retired research company executive, editor, consultant
Wise, Milton B. animal science educator

Simpsonville
Kucij, Timothy Michael engineer, composer, organist, pianist, conductor, minister, theologian

Spartanburg
Cavin, William Pinckney chemist, educator
†Courtney, Charles Tyrone lawyer, state legislator
Fudenberg, Herman Hugh immunologist, educator
†Glenn, Robert E. elementary school principal
Leonard, Walter Raymond retired biology educator
Lesesne, Joab Mauldin, Jr. college president
Lindsay, Bryan Eugene educator, musician, writer
Mc Gehee, Larry Thomas university administrator
Milliken, Roger textile company executive
Owens, Hilda Faye academic administrator, management/leadership development consultant, human resource trainer
Patterson, Elizabeth Johnston former congresswoman
Russell, Donald Stuart federal judge
†Smith, William Douglas lawyer
Stephens, Bobby Gene college administrator, consultant
Wilde, Edwin Frederick mathematics educator
Williams, John Cornelius lawyer

Sullivans Island
Romaine, Henry Simmons investment consultant

Sumter
Finney, Ernest Adolphus, Jr. state supreme court chief justice
Olsen, Thomas Richard, Sr. air force officer

Surfside Beach
McCrensky, Edward international consultant, former organization executive

Townville
Wright, George Cullen electronics company executive

Walterboro
Johnson, Daniel McDonald (Dan Johnson) newspaper editor
Marvin, Robert Earle landscape architect
McLeod, Walton James, Jr. lawyer

West Columbia
Carter, Saralee Lessman immunologist, microbiologist
Faust, John William, Jr. electrical engineer, educator
Hand, Herbert Hensley management educator, executive, consultant, inventor
Ochs, Robert David history educator
Parker, Harold Talbot history educator
†Wilson, Addison Graves (Joe Wilson) lawyer, state senator

Williamston
Davis, Michael Todd textile company administrator

Winnsboro
King, Robert Thomas editor, free-lance writer

SOUTH DAKOTA

Aberdeen
Ehli, Gerald James education educator
†Lawler, James F. state senator
Richards, Carlyle Edward magistrate judge

Baltic
†Wagner, Michael Dickman state representative, small business owner

Belle Fourche
Wuest, George W. state supreme court justice

Beresford
Jensen, Shirley Wulff sales executive

Brandon
†Jones, Chet R. state senator, communications executive

Britton
Farrar, Frank Leroy lawyer, former governor of South Dakota

Brookings
Bailey, Harold Stevens, Jr. educational administrator, retired education admin
Gilbert, Howard Alden economics educator
Hugghins, Ernest Jay biology educator
McClure-Bibby, Mary Anne former state legislator
†Moore, Raymond A. agricultural educator
Morgan, Walter retired poultry science educator
Storry, Junis Oliver retired engineering educator
Swiden, Ladell Ray research center administrator
Sword, Christopher Patrick microbiologist, university dean
Wagner, Robert Todd university president, sociology educator

Burbank
Simmons, Joseph Thomas accountant, educator

Chamberlain
Gregg, Robert Lee pharmacist
†Saukerson, Eleanor state legislator

Charleston
Evans, Allen Donald real estate company executive

Edgemont
Bennett, Charles Leo management consultant, rancher

Elk Point
†Chicoine, Roland Alvin farmer, state official

Freeman
Waltner, John Randolph bank executive

Gregory
Bolliger, Eugene Frederick surgeon

Hurley
†Rasmussen, Roberta A. state legislator

Huron
Reynolds, R. John university administrator
Schmidt, Albert Daniel utility executive
Wilkens, Robert Allen utilities executive, electrical engineer

Keystone
†Wenk, Daniel N. landmark site administrator

Madison
Tunheim, Jerald Arden academic administrator, physics educator

Mitchell
†Widman, Paul Joseph insurance agent

North Sioux City
Waitt, Ted computer company executive

Parker
Zimmer, John Herman lawyer

Pierre
Amundson, Robert A. state supreme court justice
Barnett, Mark William state attorney general
Bonaiuto, John A. state education official
†Dunn, James Bernard mining company executive, state legislator
Hazeltine, Joyce state official
Henderson, Frank Ellis state supreme court justice
Johnson, Julie Marie lawyer, lobbyist
Kolbe, Jane Boegler state librarian
Kundert, Alice E. state legislator
Miller, Robert Arthur state supreme court chief justice
Miller, Walter Dale governor
†Pederson, Gordon Roy state legislator, retired military officer
Porter, Donald James federal judge
Russell, James Donald Murray hospital administrator
Sabers, Richard Wayne state supreme court justice
†Stensland, Linda L. state senator
Thompson, Charles Murray lawyer

Platte
Pennington, Beverly Melcher financial services company executive

Prairie City
†Wishard, Della Mae state legislator

Rapid City
Battey, Richard Howard federal judge
†Bickett, Robert Winston insurance executive
Chaput, Charles J. bishop
Corwin, Bert Clark optometrist
Erickson, John Duff mining engineering educator
Foye, Thomas Harold lawyer
Gowen, Richard Joseph electrical engineering educator, college president
†Green, Sharon Vincentine counselor, consultant
Gries, John Paul geologist
Hughes, William Lewis former university official, electrical engineer
†Jones, David L. architect
†Landguth, Daniel P. utility executive
Lisenbee, Alvis Lee structural geologist, educator
Quinn, Robert Henry surgeon, medical school administrator
Ramakrishnan, Venkataswamy civil engineer, educator
Riemenschneider, Albert Louis engineering educator
Schleusener, Richard August college president
Scofield, Gordon Lloyd mechanical engineer, educator
Sykora, Harold James military officer
Undlin, Charles Thomas banker
Wingert, Robert Irvin obstetrician, gynecologist

Selby
†Akre, Donald J. school system administrator

Sherman
†Rogen, Mark Endre state senator, farmer

Sioux Falls
Balcer, Charles Louis college president emeritus, educator
†Billion, John Joseph orthopedic surgeon, state representative
Brendtro, Larry Kay psychologist, educator
Carlson, Marilyn A. English language educator
Carlson, Robert James bishop
†Caselli, Robert Eugene state legislator, retired education administrator
Christensen, David Allen manufacturing company executive
†Cowles, Ronald Eugene church administrator
Dertien, James LeRoy librarian
Dudley, Paul V. bishop
Ecker, Peder Kaloides federal judge
†Eitrheim, Norman Duane bishop
Fenton, Lawrence Jules pediatric educator
Flora, George Claude retired neurology educator, neurologist
Gibbs, Frank P. federal judge
Grupp, Carl Alf art educator, artist
Hoskins, John H. urologist, educator
Huseboe, Doris Louise college administrator, educator, arts consultant
Jaqua, Richard Allen pathologist
Johnson, Thomas Floyd college president, educator
Jones, John Bailey federal judge
†Kirby, Dan Laird lawyer
†Kirby, Joe P. insurance company executive
Koch, Ralph Richard architect
†Koetzle, Gil state legislator, fire fighter, professional association administrator
Morse, Peter Hodges ophthalmologist, educator
†Nelson, Pamela state legislator
†Paisley, Keith W. state senator, small business owner
†Piersol, Lawrence L. federal judge
Richards, LaClaire Lissetta Jones (Mrs. George A. Richards) social worker
Rigsbee, William Alton insurance company executive
†Sandness, William John health care executive
Smith, Murray Thomas transportation company executive
Taplett, Lloyd Melvin human resources management consultant
Tucker, William Vincent vocational evaluator, former college president
Van Demark, Robert Eugene, Sr. orthopedic surgeon
Wegner, Karl Heinrich physician, educator
Wiebe, Richard Herbert reproductive endocrinologist, educator
Wollman, Roger Leland federal judge
†Zawada, Edward Thaddeus, Jr. physician, educator

Spearfish
Erickson, Richard Ames physicist, emeritus educator

Vermillion
Asher, Betty Turner academic administrator
Carlson, Loren Merle political science educator
Clem, Alan Leland political scientist
Clifford, Sylvester retired communication educator
Dahlin, Donald C(lifford) political science educator
†Green, Vincent Scott writer
Hagen, Arthur Ainsworth pharmacologist
Hazlett, James Stephen university administrator
†Langworthy, Thomas Allan microbiologist, educator
Milton, John Ronald English language educator, author
Milton, Lynn Leonharda elementary and secondary school educator
Neuhaus, Otto Wilhelm biochemistry educator
Richardson, James Alexander exercise science educator, wellness center director
†Struck, Judy Kay special education specialist

Volga
Moldenhauer, William Calvin soil scientist

Wall
†Poppe, Kenneth C. school system administrator

Watertown
Hillestad, Gertrude Delene former public utilities specialist

Wessington
†Lockner, Vera Joanne farmer, rancher, legislator

Wessington Springs
†Morford-Burg, JoAnn state senator, investment company executive

Yankton
Hirsch, Robert William lawyer
Sokol, Dennis Allen hospital administrator

TENNESSEE

Antioch
†Malone, Tom bible college president
†Reeds, Roger church administrator
†Thomas, Roy L. minister
†Vallance, James church administrator, religious publication editor
†Waddell, R. Eugene minister
†Wisehart, Mary Ruth academic administrator
Worthington, Melvin Leroy minister, writer

Ashland City
†Lindahl, Herbert Winfred appliance manufacturing executive

Athens
Guinn, Charles Clifford, Jr. lawyer
Thompson, Verdine Mae financial planner, tax preparer
†Wilson, Ben elementary school principal

Bellevue
Ford, Jesse Hill author

Brentwood
Bennett, Harold Clark clergyman, religious organization administrator
†Dalton, James Edgar, Jr. health facility administrator
†Hauk, Donald Benjamin automotive parts company executive
Ragsdale, Richard Elliot hospital management executive
Sullivan, James Thomas printing company executive
†Thompson, Keith M. automotive supply executive
Tucker, Tanya Denise singer
Zimmerman, Raymond retail chain executive

Bristol
Anderson, Jack Oland retired college official
Cauthen, Charles Edward, Jr. college president, former retail executive
Harkrader, Charles Johnston, Jr. surgeon
Riggs, Benjamin Clapp, Jr. building products manufacturing company executive

Brownsville
Kalin, Robert retired mathematics educator

Chapel Hill
Christman, Luther Parmalee university dean emeritus, consultant

Chattanooga
†Albright, Ray C. banker, state senator
Anderson, Lee Stratton newspaper publisher, editor
†Ashley, Jim R. newspaper editor
Bahner, Thomas Maxfield lawyer
Baker, Merl engineering educator
Callahan, North author, educator
Charlton, Shirley Marie instructional supervisor
Colbert, Robert B., Jr. apparel company executive
Cox, Ronald Baker engineering and management consultant, university dean
Cress, George Ayers artist, educator
†Derthick, Alan Wendell architect
Edgar, R(obert) Allan federal judge
†Falcon, Charles consumer products company executive
Feinberg, Edward Burton ophthalmologist, educator
Gore, Barry Maurice electrical engineer
†Guerry, Alexander drug and chemical company executive
Hall, Thor religion educator
Hanlin, Hugh Carey retired life insurance company executive
Hardy, Thomas Cresson insurance company executive
Harris, Marquita Bolden school librarian
Holmberg, Albert William, Jr. publishing company executive
Holmberg, Ruth Sulzberger publishing company executive
Johnston, Hampton L. photography corporation executive
†Knight, Ralph H. consumer products company executive
†Long, Tom insurance company executive
MacManus, Yvonne Cristina editor, videoscripter, writer, consultant
Martin, Chester Y. sculptor, painter
†McFarland, Jane Elizabeth librarian
Milburn, Herbert Theodore federal judge
Mills, Charles G. photography company executive
Mills, Olan, II photography company executive
Mohney, Ralph Wilson minister
Neely, Paul newspaper editor
Obear, Frederick Woods university chancellor
†Palmer, Stanton Dean newspaper editor
Porter, Dudley, Jr. environmentalist, foundation executive, lawyer
Powers, John Y. federal judge
Probasco, Scott Livingston bank executive
Proctor, John Franklin lawyer
†Ragon, Robert Ronald clergyman
Saeks, Richard Ephraim electrical engineer
St. Goar, Edward wholesale food cooperative executive
St. Goar, Herbert food corporation executive
Scarbrough, Cleve Knox, Jr. museum director
Sheehy, Thomas Daniel apparel and textile manufacturing company executive
Smith, Gordon Laidlaw, Jr. manufacturing company executive
†Sudderth, Robert J., Jr. bank executive
Summitt, Robert Murray circuit judge
Thow, George Bruce surgeon
†Travis, W. Vance, Jr. architect
†Tucker, Stanley R. headmaster
†Turner, Brenda Kaye state legislator
Walker, Winston Wakefield, Jr. insurance company executive
Witherspoon, John Knox, Jr. investment banking executive
Witt, Raymond Buckner, Jr. lawyer
Zodhiates, Spiros George association executive

Clarksville
Birdsong, William Herbert, Jr. retired brigadier general
Carlin, James Boyce elementary education educator, consultant
Lester, James Dudley classicist, educator
Smith, Gregory Dale lawyer

Cleveland
†Albert, Leonard religious organization executive
†Alford, Delton religious organization executive
†Betancourt, Esdras religious organization executive
†Chambers, O. Wayne religious organization executive
†Crisp, Sam church administrator
†Fisher, Richard A. lawyer, state legislator
†Fisher, Robert Elwood minister, church official
†Gillum, Perry Eugene college president, minister
Hughes, Ray Harrison minister, church official
†Jackson, Joseph Essard religious organization administrator
†Jones, E. L. church admininistrator
†Moffett, B. J. church administrator
†Murray, Billy Dwayne, Sr. church administrator
†Nichols, John D. church administrator
†O'Neal, Timothy D. church administrator
†Pemberton, Donald T. church administrator

†Rayburn, Billy J. church administrator
†Reyes, Jose Antonio, Sr. minister
†Riley, Jerlena church administrator
†Robinson, Julian B. church administrator
†Sheeks, Bill F. minister
†Stockburger, Harold E., Jr. state legislator, insurance agency executive
†Sustar, T. David religious organization executive
†Taylor, William Al church administrator
Tomlinson, Milton Ambrose clergyman
†Varlack, Adrian church administrator
†Vaughan, Roland church administrator
†Vest, R. Lamar church administrator
†White, Robert church administrator

Clinton
Birdwell, James Edwin, Jr. retired banker

Collegedale
†Bennett, Peggy Elizabeth librarian, library director, educator

Columbia
Chafin, William Vernon, Jr. business consultant
Curry, Beatrice Chesrown English educator
Pryor, Harold S. retired college president

Cookeville
Chowdhuri, Pritindra electrical engineer, educator
Coorts, Gerald Duane horticulturist, educator, college dean
Hearn, Edell Midgett university dean, teacher educator
Peters, Ralph Martin education educator
Sissom, Leighton Esten mechanical engineering educator, dean, consultant
Volpe, Angelo Anthony university administrator, chemistry educator

Cordova
Baer, Ben Kayser cotton merchant
Cooke, Edward William corporate executive, former naval officer
Dean, Jimmy meat processing company executive, entertainer
Hunt, Gregory Lynn writer, author
Springfield, James Francis lawyer, banker

Dandridge
Comer, Evan Philip manufacturing company executive

Dickson
†Thomas, Janey Sue elementary school principal

Dyersburg
Bell, Helen Cherry chemistry educator
†Nerren, George N. school system administrator
†Taylor, Billy D. principal
Wiggins, Jerome Meyer apparel textile industry financial executive

Franklin
†Brown, Joseph D. school system administrator

Gallatin
Ramer, Hal Reed college president

Gatlinburg
†Pope, Randall Ray retired national park superintendent

Germantown
Ewing, William Hickman, Jr. lawyer
Shockley, Thomas Dewey electrical engineering educator

Goodlettsville
Wilkins, Rita Denise multimedia design consultant

Greenbrier
Newell, Paul Haynes, Jr. engineering educator, former college president

Greeneville
Austin, Tom Noell retired tobacco company executive
Hull, Thomas Gray federal judge
Smith, Myron John, Jr. librarian, author

Hendersonville
Allen, Duane David singer
Axton, Hoyt Wayne singer, composer
Bare, Robert Joseph (Bobby Bare) country music singer, songwriter
Cash, June Carter singer
Davis, Robert Norman hospital administrator
Hill, William Thomas geological consultant
McCaleb, Joe Wallace lawyer
Sanders, Steve singer

Hermitage
Anderson, James William, III performing artist, composer
Chambers, Curtis Allen clergyman, church communications executive
Lockmiller, David Alexander lawyer, educator

Jackson
Ewing, Frank Crockett marketing entrepreneur, photographer
Hazlewood, Judith Evans librarian
Lipshie, Joseph apparel manufacturing company executive
†Maynard, Terrell Dennis minister
Moss, James Taylor hospital administrator
Todd, James Dale federal judge

Jefferson City
Bahner, Carl Tabb retired chemistry educator, researcher
Ball, Louis Oliver, Jr. music educator
Baumgardner, James Lewis history educator
†Benson, Stanley Hugh librarian

Jellico
Hausman, Keith Lynn hospital administrator, physical therapist
†Walden, Jasper church adminsitrator

Johnson City
Adebonojo, Festus O. medical educator
Alfonso, Robert John university administrator
Berk, Steven Lee internist, educator
Coogan, Philip Shields pathologist
Dyer, Allen Ralph psychiatrist
Huang, Thomas Tao-shing chemistry educator
Mc Cormick, William Frederick forensic pathologist, neuropathologist
Skalko, Richard Gallant anatomist, educator
Votaw, Charles Lesley academic dean
Yavas, Ugur marketing educator
Zayas-Bazan, Eduardo foreign language educator

Jonesborough
Weaver, Kenneth gynecologist, researcher

Kingsport
Coover, Harry Wesley manufacturing company executive
Findley, Don Aaron manufacturing company executive
Giggey, James Walker chemical company executive
Head, William Iverson, Sr. retired chemical company executive
Holmes, Jerry Dell organic chemist
†Matthews, Vincent, III oil company executive
Scott, H(erbert) Andrew retired chemical engineer
†Siirola, Jeffrey John chemical engineer
†Venable, Richard Sherman motor carrier business executive, state legislator
Watkins, William H(enry) electrical engineer
Young, Howard Seth chemist, researcher

Kingston
Manly, William Donald metallurgist
Oran, Geraldine Ann educator

Knoxville
Acker, Joseph Edington retired cardiology educator
Alexeff, Igor physicist, electrical engineer, educator
Ambrester, Marcus LaRoy communication educator, program administrator
Anderson, Edward Riley state supreme court justice
Armistead, Willis William university administrator, veterinarian
Arnett, Foster Deaver lawyer
Ashe, Victor Henderson mayor
†Atchley, Ben state senator
Bailey, Joel Furness mechanical engineering educator
Bailey, John Milton electrical engineering educator
Bateman, Veda Mae industrial psychologist, management consultant
†Bell, H. Jenkins clergyman, bishop
Bell, Thomas Rowe retired natural gas transmission company executive
Blake, Gerald Rutherford banker
Blass, William Errol physics and astronomy educator
Boling, Edward Joseph university president emeritus, educator
Bose, Bimal Kumar electrical engineering educator
Brady, Patrick French literature educator
†Bressler, Marcus N. consulting engineer
Brockett, Ralph Grover adult education educator
Brott, Walter Howard cardiac surgeon, educator, retired army officer
Burkhart, John Henry physician
Chapman, Jefferson museum director
Christenbury, Edward Samuel lawyer
Cole, William Edward economics educator, consultant
Conger, Bob Vernon plant and soil science educator
Coulson, Patricia Bunker endocrinologist
†Crowell, Craven H., Jr. federal agency administrator
Cutler, Everette Wayne history educator
Danko, Joseph Christopher metals engineer, university official
Dean, Charles Henry, Jr. retired government official
Dean, John Aurie chemist, author, chemistry educator emeritus
Dillard, W. Thomas lawyer
Eisenberg, Lee B. communications executive
Fain, Paul Kemp, Jr. financial planner
Finn, Peter Michael television production executive
Fisher, John Hurt English language educator
Freeman, Richard Merrell business consultant
Froula, James DeWayne national honor society director, engineer
German, Ronald Stephen health care facility administrator
†Goforth, E. Jack security firm executive
Gonzalez, Rafael Ceferino electrical engineering educator
†Goodfriend, Robert M. apparel executive
Green, Eleanor Myers veterinarian, educator
†Griffiths, José-Marie information science educator
Hagood, Lewis Russell lawyer
Hall, O. Glen university dean
Hammond, Edwin Hughes geography educator
Harris, Charles Edgar retired wholesale distribution company executive
†Haslam, James A., II petroleum sales executive
†Haslam, James A., III petroleum sales executive
Herndon, Anne Harkness sales executive
Hohenberg, John journalist, educator
Holton, Raymond William botanist, educator
Howard, Lewis Spilman lawyer
Hung, James Chen engineer, educator, consultant
Jacobs, Kenneth A. composer, educator
Jarvis, James Howard, II federal judge
†Jenkins, Roger Lane retail executive
Jordan, (William) Hamilton (McWhorter) corporate and international communications consultant
Jordan, Robert Leon federal judge
Kliefoth, A(rthur) Bernhard, III neurosurgeon
Lange, Robert Dale internist, educator, medical researcher
LeVert, Francis Edward nuclear engineer
Lietzke, Milton Henry chemistry educator
Lucas, John Allen lawyer
Mahan, Gerald Dennis physics educator, researcher
Malec, William Frank utilities company executive
Mamantov, Gleb chemistry educator, consultant
Martin, James Robert plastics company executive
Mayfield, T. Brient, IV media and computer executive
Mc Carty, Bruce architect
†McCarty, Douglas Hayes architect
Mc Dow, John Jett agricultural engineering educator
†Mc Hargue, Carl Jack research laboratory administator
Mercer, Charles Wayne health care executive
Moser, Harold Dean historian
Murrian, Robert Phillip federal judge, educator
Natelson, Stephen Ellis neurosurgeon
Nielsen, Alvin Herborg university dean, physicist
O'Connell, Anthony J. bishop
Phillips, Jerry Juan law educator
Phillips, Thomas Wade lawyer
Prados, John William educational administrator
Rayson, Edwin Hope lawyer
Rentenbach, Thomas Joseph civil engineer
†Richards, Stephen Harold engineering educator
†Richardson, Don Orland agricultural educator
Roth, J(ohn) Reece electrical engineer, educator, researcher, consultant
Rukeyser, William Simon journalist
†Sanders, William Evan bishop
Sanger, Herbert Shelton, Jr. lawyer, former government official
Schmidt, Benno Charles, Jr. lawyer, educator
Schweitzer, George Keene chemistry educator
Sharp, Aaron John botanist, educator
Sherman, Gordon Rae computer science educator
Singletary, Michael Willis journalism, educator
†Solomon, Alan physician, medical oncologist and clinical investigator
Springer, John K. securities dealer
Stegmayer, Joseph Henry housing industry executive
Stringfield, Hezz, Jr. contractor, financial consultant
Sublett, Carl Cecil artist
Teeter, Dwight Leland, Jr. journalism educator
Trahern, Joseph Baxter, Jr. humanities educator
Trevor, Kirk David Niell orchestra conductor, cellist
Tschantz, Bruce Allen civil engineer, educator
Uhrig, Robert Eugene nuclear engineer, educator
Vance, Stanley Charles management educator
†Vinson, William C. architectural firm executive
Vogel, Howard H. lawyer
Walsh, Joanne Elizabeth educator, librarian
Waters, John B. lawyer
†Watson, Patricia L. library director
Wheeler, John Watson lawyer
Whittle, Christopher media executive, entrepreneur
Wicks, Wesley D. biochemistry educator
Williams, Thomas Ffrancon chemist, educator
Williamson, Handy, Jr. agricultural economist, educator
Wunderlich, Bernhard physical chemistry educator
Wust, Carl John microbiology and medical biology educator

La Follette
Eads, Ora Wilbert clergyman, church official
McDonald, Miller Baird management consultant, columnist, historian

La Vergne
†Forrest, Henry J. manufacturing company executive
Hubbard, Julia Faye accountant
Pfeffer, Philip Maurice distribution company executive

Lafayette
Wolford, Dennis Arthur hospital administrator

Lebanon
Daniels, Charlie musician, songwriter
†Rochelle, Robert Thomas lawyer, state senator

Lenoir City
Breazeale, Mack Alfred physics educator
Gerwels, Laurenn Barker public relations executive
Wilson, Frank Elmore physician, medical administrator

Lookout Mountain
Leitner, Paul R. lawyer
Rymer, S. Bradford, Jr. retired appliance manufacturing company executive
Wyeth, Andrew artist
Wyeth, James Browning artist

Loudon
Jones, Robert Gean religion educator

Louisville
Wheeler, George William university provost, physicist, educator
†Williams, Timothy Wayne finance company executive

Luttrell
Milligan, Mancil Wood mechanical and aerospace engineering educator

Madison
Kennedy, Matthew Washington pianist, educator
Wells, Kitty (Muriel Deason Wright) country western singer

Martin
Peckham, Robert Dabney French language and literature educator
Smith, Robert Mason university dean

Maryville
Ackerman, Ora Ray health facility administrator
Brigance, Albert Henry educational writer
Inscho, Barbara Pickel mathematics educator
†Koella, Carl Ohm, Jr. lawyer, state senator
Oakes, Lester Cornelius retired electrical engineer, consultant

Memphis
Abston, Dunbar, Jr. management executive
†Adamson, John church administrator
†Adsit, Russell Allan landscape designer
Allen, James Henry magistrate judge
Allen, Newton Perkins lawyer
Allison, Beverly Gray seminary president, evangelism educator
Andrews, William Eugene construction and services company executive
Apple, John Boyd elevator company executive
Armstrong, Walter Preston, Jr. lawyer
Babin, Richard Weyro surgeon, educator
Bardos, Denes Istvan research scientist, medical company executive
Battle, Allen Overton, Jr. psychologist, educator
Berry, Robert Vaughan electrical, electronic manufacturing company executive
Broadhurst, Jerome Anthony lawyer
Brode, Marvin Jay lawyer, former state legislator
†Brooks, P. A., II bishop
Brown, Aaron Clifton, Jr. magistrate judge
Brown, Bailey federal judge
Bruce, Marvin Ernest corporate executive
Buchignani, Leo Joseph lawyer
Buckman, Robert Henry chemical company executive
Burch, Lucius Edward, Jr. lawyer
Burgess, Melvin protective services official
Butts, Herbert Clell dentist, educator
†Campbell, Bruce Emerson, Jr. banker
Canale, Dee James neurosurgeon, educator
Canon, Robert Morris performing arts executive, opera producer
Carroll, Billy Price artist
Carter, Michael Allen college dean, nursing educator
Chesney, Russell Wallace pediatrician
†Christopher, Robert Paul physician
Clark, Ross Bert, II lawyer
Clarkson, Andrew MacBeth retail executive
Cody, Walter James Michael lawyer, former state official
Copper, John Franklin Asian studies educator, consultant
Cox, Clair Edward, II urologist, medical educator
†Cox, Larry D. airport terminal executive
Cox, Terry Allen telecommunications executive
Crane, Laura Jane research chemist
Crist, William Miles physician
†Crump, Metcalf architect
†Cunningham, Ronald M. religious education director
Depperschmidt, Thomas Orlando economist, educator
Desiderio, Dominic Morse, Jr. chemistry and neurochemistry educator
Dickson, Alex Dockery bishop
Diggs, Walter Whitley health science facility administrator
Drescher, Judith Altman library director
Dunathan, Harmon Craig college dean
Dunavant, William Buchanan, Jr. small business owner
Dunnigan, T. Kevin electrical and electronics manufacturing company executive
†Echols, James agricultural products supplier
†Elliott, Maurice Wallner health care system administrator
Emery, Sue bulletin editor, owner bridge studio
†Evans, James Mignon architect
†Evans, John S. bank executive
Fain, John Nicholas biochemistry educator
Foote, Shelby author
†Ford, John N. state senator, funeral director
Forell, David Charles financial executive
†Formanek, Peter Raemin automobile parts company executive
Franklin, Stanley Phillip computer scientist, mathematician, cognitive scientist, educator
Freeman, Bob A. microbiology educator
Friedman, Robert Michael lawyer
†Garrott, Thomas M. bank executive
Gerald, Barry radiology educator, neuroradiologist
Gibbons, Julia Smith federal judge
Gilman, Ronald Lee lawyer
Goodman, Benjamin lawyer
Gourley, Dick R. college dean
Granger, David Mason marketing, public relations executive
Greiner, Morris Esty, Jr. broadcast executive
Griffin, Tom former editor, writer
Haizlip, Henry Hardin, Jr. real estate consultant, former banker
†Hamilton, W. W. church administrator
†Harrover, Roy Perkins architect
†Harvey, Albert C. lawyer
Heimberg, Murray pharmacologist, biochemist, physician, educator
Hendren, Gary E. retail executive
Herenton, Willie W. mayor
Hooks, Benjamin Lawson civil rights advocate, brokerage house executive
Horn, Ralph bank executive
Horton, Odell federal judge
Howe, Martha Morgan microbiologist, educator
Hughes, Walter Thompson physician, pediatrics educator
Hunt, James Calvin academic administrator, physician
Hyatt, David Hudson manufacturing executive
†Hyde, Joseph R., III wholesale food distribution executive
Ingram, Alvin John surgeon
Jenkins, Ruben Lee chemical company executive
Johnson, James Gibb physician
Johnson, Johnny research psychologist, consultant
Johnson, Robert Lewis, Jr. retail company executive
Johnston, Archibald Currie geophysics educator, research director
†Jones, Walk Claridge, III architect
†Kelley, Robert C. construction industry executive
Kellogg, Frederic Hartwell civil engineer, educator
Kennedy, David Stewart federal judge
Knight, H. Stuart law enforcement official, consultant
Langford, Walter Martin retired greeting card and gift wrap manufacturing executive
Langton, Bryan D. hotel executive
Lasslo, Andrew medicinal chemist, educator
Ledsinger, Charles Albert, Jr. hotel, gaming executive
†Lieberman, Phillip Louis allergist, educator
†Looney, J. Carson architectural firm executive
†Macklin, F. Douglas bishop
Manire, James McDonnell lawyer
†Martin, William A. business executive
Mauer, Alvin Marx physician, medical educator
Mays, Penny Sandra radiologic technologist, academic administrator
McCalla, Jon P. federal judge
McCommon, Hubert risk management consultant
McEachran, Angus newspaper editor
McMinn, William A. chemicals company executive
McPherson, Larry E(ugene) photographer, educator
McRae, Robert Malcolm, Jr. federal judge
Mealor, William Theodore, Jr. geography educator, university administrator, consultant
†Mendel, Maurice audiologist, educator
Miller, Neil Austin biology educator
Mulholland, Kenneth Leo, Jr. health care facility administrator
†Nager, Larry Mark music critic, journalist
Neely, Charles Lea, Jr. retired physician
Nesin, Jeffrey D. academic administrator
Noble, Douglas Ross museum administrator
Noel, Randall Deane lawyer
Nolly, Robert J. hospital administrator, pharmaceutical science educator
Nuber, Richard Howard civic association executive, insurance company executive, state legislator
O'Donnell, William Hugh English educator
Pate, James Wynford surgeon

†Perry, Floyde E., Jr. *bishop*
Piazza, Marguerite *opera singer, actress, entertainer*
†Porter, W. L. *bishop*
Pourciau, Lester John *librarian*
Powell, Joseph Herbert *hospital administrator*
Presley, Priscilla *actress*
Purcell, William Paul *medicinal chemistry educator*
†Ramirez, Michael P. *editorial cartoonist*
Ramsey, Marjorie Elizabeth *early childhood education educator*
Ranta, Richard Robert *university dean*
Rawlins, Benjamin W., Jr. *bank holding company executive*
†Reeves, Sam T. *argicultural products company executive*
†Reynolds, Stephen Curtis *hospital administrator*
Rich, Charles Allan *singer*
Riss, Murray *photographer, educator*
†Roberts, C. Frank *broadcast executive*
Runyan, John William, Jr. *medical educator*
Satre, Philip Glen *corporate executive, lawyer*
Schelp, Richard Herbert *mathematics educator*
Shanklin, Douglas Radford *physician*
†Shorb, Gary Seymour *hospital administrator*
Shugart, Cecil Glenn *physics educator*
Smith, Frederick Wallace *transportation company executive*
†Smith, Whitney Bousman *music and drama critic*
Solomon, Solomon Sidney *endocrinologist, pharmacologist, scientist*
Stagg, Louis Charles *English language and literature educator*
†Stokes, Henry Arthur *journalist*
Streibich, Harold Cecil *lawyer*
Sullivan, Eugene Joseph *food service company executive*
Sullivan, Jay Michael *medical educator*
Summer, Harry Harmon *marketing educator and consultant*
Summitt, Robert Layman *pediatrician, educator*
Tate, Stonewall Shepherd *lawyer*
Terry, Ronald Anderson *bank holding company executive*
†Thomas, Nathaniel Charles *clergyman*
Tibbs, Martha Jane Pullen *civic worker*
Todd, Virgil Holcomb *clergyman, religion educator*
†Tucker, Jack R., Jr. *architectural firm executive*
Turner, Jerome *federal judge*
Waddell, Alfred Moore, Jr. *investment company executive*
Wallis, Carlton Lamar *librarian*
Wellford, Harry Walker *federal judge*
Wheeler, Orville Eugene *university dean, civil and mechanical engineering educator*
Whitesell, Dale Edward *retired association executive, natural resources consultant*
Wilcox, Harry Hammond *retired medical educator*
Wildman, Gary Cecil *chemist*
Williams, David Russell *music educator*
Wise, George Urban *botanic garden administrator, horticulturist, entomologist*
Yeates, Zeno Lanier *retired architect*
Young, Irma Jean *elementary education educator*

Monteagle
Lytle, Andrew Nelson *author, editor*

Morristown
Cordover, Ronald Harvey *business executive, venture capitalist*
Olmstead, Francis Henry, Jr. *plastics industry executive*

Mount Juliet
Kerr, Charles Randall *florist*
LeDoux, Chris Lee *country musician*
Sweetman, Brian Jack *organic, analytical chemist, educator*

Murfreesboro
Adams, W. Andrew *health care executive*
Aden, Robert Clark *retired computer information systems educator*
Berry, Mary Tom *education educator*
†Bookner, Becci Jane *school system administrator*
Ford, William F. *banker*
Hayes, Janice Cecile Osgard *education educator*
Huhta, James Kenneth *university official, historian, educator, consultant*
Rob, Peter *computer information systems educator*
Wyatt, Robert Odell *journalism educator*
Youree, Beverly B. *library science educator*

Nashville
Abumrad, Naji *surgeon, educator*
†Adkins, Cecelia N. *church administrator*
Alexander, Andrew Lamar (Lamar Alexander) *lawyer, former secretary of education*
Allbritton, Cliff *publisher*
Anderson, Lynn (Rene Anderson) *singer*
Atkins, Chester Burton *record company executive, guitarist, publisher*
Aubrey, Roger Frederick *psychology and education educator*
Banks, John Houston *mathematics educator*
Bass, James Orin *lawyer*
Battle, William Robert (Bob Battle) *newspaper executive*
Bender, Harvey W., Jr. *cardiac and thoracic surgeon*
Benson, Edwin Welburn, Jr. *trade association executive*
Bernard, Louis Joseph *surgeon, educator*
Berry, William Wells *lawyer*
†Binkley, Yildiz Barlas *library director*
Black, Clint *country singer, musician*
Blumstein, James Franklin *legal educator, lawyer, consultant*
Bogguss, Suzy *country music singer, songwriter*
Bolian, George Clement *health care executive, physician*
Bolinger, John C., Jr. *management consultant*
Boorman, Howard Lyon *history educator*
Bostick, Charles Dent *lawyer, educator*
Bottorff, Dennis C. *banker*
Bowen, Barbara Cherry *French and comparative literature educator*
†Bowen, James *record company executive*
†Boyd, Theophilus Bartholomew, III *publishing company executive*
†Boyer, James Floyd *land surveyor, state legislator*
Bradford, James C., Jr. *brokerage house executive*
†Bradshaw, William *museum director*
†Bragg, John Thomas *state legislator, retired businessman*
Brau, Charles Allen *physics educator*
Bredesen, Philip Norman *mayor*
Brodersen, Arthur James *electrical engineer*
Brooks, Garth (Troyal Garth Brooks) *country music singer*
Brooks, Kix *musician*
Brophy, Jeremiah Joseph *former army officer*
Brown, Joe Blackburn *lawyer*
†Brown, Tommie Florence *social work educator*
Brush, Clinton E., III *retired architect*
Buckles, Stephen Gary *economist, educator*
Burgess, Roger *church official*
Burnett, Lonnie Sheldon *obstetrics and gynecology educator*
Burson, Charles W. *state attorney general*
Burt, Alvin Miller, III *anatomist, cell biologist, educator, writer*
Buttrick, David Gardner *religion educator*
Byrd, Benjamin Franklin, Jr. *surgeon, educator*
Cadzow, James Archie *engineering educator, researcher*
Calhoun, Calvin Lee, Sr. *physician*
Carter, James McCord *television producer, personality*
Cawthon, William Connell *operations management consultant*
Chapman, John Edmon *university dean, pharmacologist, physician*
Chaudhuri, Dilip Kumar *engineering educator*
Cheek, James Howe, III *lawyer*
Chytil, Frank *biochemist*
Clark, Frank Rinker, Jr. *retired pipeline company executive*
Clouse, Robert Wilburn *communication executive, educator*
Coen, Daniel Kennedy, Jr. *aeronautical engineer*
Cohen, Stanley *biochemistry educator*
†Coleman, Martin M. *protective services official*
Conkin, Paul Keith *history educator*
†Connery, W. Hudson *health facility administrator*
Cook, Ann Jennalie *English language educator*
Cook, Charles Wilkerson, Jr. *former banker, county official*
Cook, George Edward *electrical engineering educator, consultant*
†Cooper, Jerry W. *state senator*
Cordaro, Matthew Charles *utility executive, energy developer, engineer*
Covington, Robert Newman *lawyer, educator*
Crabtree, Bruce Isbester, Jr. *architect*
†Crants, Doctor R., Jr. *entrepreneur*
Crofford, Oscar Bledsoe, Jr. *internist, medical educator*
Crowell, Rodney J. *country music recording artist, songwriter*
Culbertson, Katheryn Campbell *lawyer*
Cunningham, Leon William *biochemist, educator*
Cunningham, Neil Lewis *retired banker*
Daane, James Dewey *banker*
D'Agostino, James Samuel, Jr. *financial executive*
Damon, William Winchell *economics educator*
Darnell, Riley Carlisle *secretary of state, lawyer*
Daughtrey, Martha Craig *federal judge*
Davis, Danny (George Joseph Nowlan) *musician*
Davis, James Verlin *insurance brokerage executive*
Dean, Billy (William Howard Dean) *country singer, songwriter*
Dedman, Bertram Cottingham *retired insurance company executive*
Deer, James Willis *lawyer*
Dettbarn, Wolf-Dietrich *neurochemist, pharmacologist, educator*
†Diamond, Michael P. *obstetrician-gynecologist, educator*
Diffie, Joe *country singer, songwriter*
†DiLorenzo, Joseph L. *health care company executive*
Doody, Margaret Anne *English educator*
†Duer, Shirley Powell *state legislator*
Dunn, Ronnie *musician*
†Dye, Hank *public relations executive*
Dykes, Archie Reece *financial services executive*
Earle, Steve *country rockabilly musician*
Echols, Robert L. *federal judge*
Eckenfelder, William Wesley, Jr. *environmental engineer*
Emans, Robert LeRoy *academic administrator, education educator*
†Fagan, A. Rudolph *minister*
Faust, A. Donovan *communications executive*
Feaster, Robert K. *publishing company executive*
Fels, Rendigs *economist, educator*
Finegan, Thomas Aldrich *economist*
Fischer, Patrick Carl *computer scientist, educator*
†Fish, Donald Winston *lawyer, health care company executive*
Fitzgerald, Edmund Bacon *electronics industry executive*
Flanagan, Van Kent *journalist*
Fleming, Samuel M. *banker*
†Forlines, Franklin Leroy *minister, educator*
Forstman, Henry Jackson *theology educator, university dean*
Fort, Tomlinson *chemist, chemical engineering educator*
Fowinkle, Eugene W. *physician, medical center administrator*
Frey, Herman S. *publishing company executive*
Frist, Thomas Fearn, Jr. *hospital management company executive*
Fry, Malcolm Craig *clergyman*
†Garcia, Ephrahim *mechanical engineering educator*
Gaultney, John Orton *life insurance agent, consultant*
Gavish, Bezalel *computer science operations research, information systems educator*
Gayle, Crystal *singer*
Geisel, Martin Simon *college dean, educator*
Gentry, Teddy *country musician*
Gillmor, John Edward *lawyer*
Gleaves, Edwin Sheffield *librarian*
†Gobbell, Ronald Vance *architect*
†Golson, Sister Afton Almeda *health facility administrator, nun*
†Gove, Walter R. *sociology educator*
Graham, Hugh Davis *history educator*
Granner, Daryl Kitley *physiology and medicine educator*
Grantham, Dewey Wesley *historian, educator*
Gray, Allen Gibbs *metallurgist, materials engineer, editor*
Greenwood, Lee Melvin *singer*
Gulmi, James Singleton *apparel manufacturing company executive*
Guthrie, James Williams *education educator*
Guy, Sharon Kaye *state agency executive*
Hahn, George Thomas *materials engineering educator, researcher*
Hall, Douglas Scott *astronomy educator*
Hall, Hugh David *dentist, physician, educator*
Halperin, John William *English literature educator*
Hamilton, Joseph Hants, Jr. *physicist, educater*
Hamilton, Russell George, Jr. *academic dean, Spanish and Portuguese language educator*
†Hamm, Richard L. *church administrator*
Hampton, Ralph Clayton, Jr. *pastoral studies educator, clergyman*
Hancock, M(arion) Donald *political science educator*
Hanselman, Richard Wilson *entrepreneur*
Harden, Lydia Dixon *editor*
Hardman, Joel Griffeth *pharmacologist*
†Harper, Thelma *state legislator*
Harrawood, Paul *civil engineering educator*
Harris, Emmylou *singer*
Harris, J(acob) George *health care company executive*
Harris, Stacy *print and broadcast journalist*
Harris, Thomas Raymond *biomedical engineer, educator*
Harrison, Clifford Joy, Jr. *banker*
Hart, Richard Banner *lawyer*
Hartford, John Cowan *singer, songwriter*
Harwell, Aubrey Biggs *lawyer*
Heard, (George) Alexander *retired educator and chancellor*
Hefner, James A. *academic administrator*
Heiser, Arnold Melvin *astronomer*
Henderson, Milton Arnold *association executive*
Hess, Bernard Andes, Jr. *chemistry educator*
Hieronymus, Clara Booth Wiggins *journalist*
Higgins, Thomas A. *federal judge*
Hinshaw, Carroll Elton *economics educator*
†Hohlfeld, Pauline *pharmaceutical executive*
Holladay, Wendell Gene *physics educator*
Holsen, Robert Charles *accountant*
House, Robert William *electrical engineering educator emeritus*
Hummell, Burton Howard *food distribution company executive*
Inagami, Tadashi *biochemist, educator*
†Ingram, E. Bronson *oil industry executive*
†Ireson, Roger William *religious organization administrator, minister, educator*
Ivey, William James *foundation executive, writer, producer*
Jackson, Alan *country songwriter, singer*
Jemison, Theodore Judson *religious organization administrator*
Johnson, Hollis Eugene, III *foundation executive*
Johnson, James Harold *lawyer*
Jones, George *country music singer, songwriter*
Kaas, Jon H. *psychology educator*
†Kaizaki, Yoichiro *automotive executive*
Kaludis, George *management consultant, book company executive, educator*
†Kavass, Igor Ivar *law educator, law librarian, consultant*
†Kidd, Florence *principal*
†Kisber, Matthew Harris *state legislator*
Kono, Tetsuro *biochemist, physiologist, educator*
Krantz, Sanford Burton *physician*
Kuhn, Paul Hubert, Jr. *investment counsel*
Lachs, John *philosopher, educator*
Land, Richard Dale *minister, religious organization administrator*
Langstaff, George Quigley, Jr. *retired footwear company executive*
Lawrence, Thomas Patterson *public relations executive*
Lazenby, Fred Wiehl *insurance company executive*
Ledyard, Robins Heard *lawyer*
Lee, Brenda (Brenda Mae Tarpley) *singer, entertainer*
Levinson, L(eslie) Harold *lawyer, educator*
Lynch, John Brown *plastic surgeon, educator*
Lyon, Philip K(irkland) *lawyer*
MacNaughton, Donald Sinclair *health care company executive*
Madden, Paul Herman *education educator*
Mahanes, David James, Jr. *retired distillery executive*
Maier, Harold Geistweit *legal educator, lawyer*
Maihafer, Harry James *retired banker, former army officer*
Mandrell, Barbara Ann *singer, entertainer*
†Martin, Charles Neil, Jr. *health care management company executive*
Masters, John Christopher *psychologist, educator, writer*
Mattea, Kathy *vocalist, songwriter*
May, Joseph Leserman (Jack) (Jack May) *lawyer*
McClanahan, Larry Duncan *civil engineer, consultant*
McCoy, Thomas Raymond *lawyer, educator*
Mc Creary, James Franklin *banker, lawyer*
†McKnight, Joe Nip *farmer, state senator, small business owner*
Mc Murry, Idanelle Sam *educational consultant*
McWherter, Ned Ray *governor*
McWhorter, Ralph Clayton *health care company executive*
Meacham, William Feland *neurological surgeon, educator*
†Merrills, Roy *telecommunications industry executive*
Merritt, Gilbert Stroud *federal judge*
†Miller, Richard L. *architectural executive*
Mills, Liston Oury *theology educator*
Monroe, William Smith *mandolin player, singer*
Moore, William Grover, Jr. *management consultant, former air freight executive, former air force officer*
Morgan, Lorrie (Loretta Lynn Morgan) *country singer*
†Mosig, Gisela *molecular biology educator*
Nelson, Edward Gage *merchant banking investment company executive*
Nixon, John Trice *federal judge*
†O'Brien, Anna Belle Clement *state senator*
O'Brien, Charles H. *state supreme court justice*
†Ono, Masatoshi *tire manufacturing executive*
Orgebin-Crist, Marie-Claire *biologist*
Orth, David Nelson *physician, educator*
†Osborne, C. William *transportation executive*
Osias, Richard Allen *international financier, investor, real estate investment executive, corporate investor*
Oslin, K. T. (Kay Toinette Oslin) *country singer*
Ossoff, Robert Henry *otolaryngological surgeon*
Parker, Frank Leon *environmental engineering educator, consultant*
Partain, Clarence Leon *radiologist, nuclear medicine physician, educator, administrator*
Pearl, Minnie (Sarah Ophelia Colley Cannon) *entertainer*
Peebles, James W. *publishing executive*
Pendergrass, Henry Pancoast *physician, radiology educator*
Perry, Lewis Curtis *historian, educator*
†Person, Curtis S., Jr. *lawyer, state senator*
Petracek, Michael Ray *surgeon*
Picirilli, Robert Eugene *clergyman, college dean, writer*
Pickens, David Richard, Jr. *retired surgeon, educator*
Polley, Dale Whitcomb *finance company executive*
†Ponder, Henry *university president, economist*
Potter, John Leith *mechanical and aerospace engineer, educator, consultant*
Prine, John *singer, songwriter*
Pruett, Jeanne *singer, songwriter*
†Purcell, William Paxson, III *congressman*
Rabbitt, Edward Thomas *singer, songwriter*
†Rayburn, Ted Rye *newspaper editor*
Reid, Lyle *judge*
†Richards, James E. *pharmaceutical executive*
Richmond, Samuel Bernard *management educator*
Riley, Harris DeWitt, Jr. *pediatrician*
Roaden, Arliss Lloyd *higher education executive director, former university president*
Roberts, Kenneth Lewis *investor, lawyer, foundation administrator*
Roberts, Sandra *editor*
Robertson, David *clinical pharmacologist, physician, educator*
Robinson, Roscoe Ross *nephrologist, educator*
Rogers, Roy (Leonard Franklin Slye) *country musician, actor*
Ross, Joseph Comer *physician, educator, academic administrator*
†Russell, Clifford Springer *economics and public policy educator*
Russell, Fred McFerrin *journalist, author, lawyer*
Sanders, Jay William *audiology educator*
Sanders, Paul Hampton *lawyer, emeritus educator, arbitrator/mediator*
Sanford, Valerius *lawyer*
Sawyers, John Lazelle *surgeon*
Scheffman, David Theodore *economist, management educator, consultant*
Schnelle, Karl Benjamin, Jr. *chemical engineering educator, consultant, researcher*
Schoggen, Phil H(oward) *psychologist, educator*
Schumaker, Larry Lee *mathematics educator*
Scott, Henry William, Jr. *surgeon, educator*
†Seale, James Millard *religious organization administrator, clergyman*
Shell, Owen G., Jr. *banker*
Sherburne, Donald Wynne *philosopher, educator*
Sims, Wilson *lawyer*
Skaggs, Ricky *country musician*
Smith, James Forest, Jr. *retired banker*
Smith, Samuel Boyd *history educator*
Speece, Richard Eugene *civil engineer, educator*
Spencer, Harry Chadwick *minister*
Spengler, Dan Michael *orthopedic surgery educator, researcher, surgeon*
Spores, Ronald Marvin *anthropology educator, ethnohistorian*
Stahlman, Mildred Thornton *pediatrics and pathology educator, researcher*
Standel, Richard Reynold, Jr. *lawyer, communications executive*
Stewart, David Marshall *librarian*
Story, James Clinton *medical educator*
Stringfield, Charles David *hospital administrator*
Strupp, Hans Hermann *psychologist, educator*
Stuart, Marty *country music singer, musician, songwriter*
Stumpf, Samuel Enoch *philosophy educator*
Sullivan, Allen Trousdale *securities company executive*
Sullivan, Walter Laurence *writer, educator*
Sutherland, Frank *editor*
Sutton, Barrett Boulware *former insurance company executive*
Swensson, Earl Simcox *architect*
Tarbell, Dean Stanley *chemistry educator*
Taylor, Robert Bonds *instructional designer*
Thompson, Almose Alphonse *lawyer, educator*
†Thompson, Travis *psychology educator, administrator, researcher*
Thornton, Spencer P. *ophthalmologist, educator*
Tillis, Mel(vin) *musician, songwriter*
Tippin, Aaron *country music singer, songwriter*
†Tolk, Norman Henry *physics educator*
Tomlinson, Gus *biology educator*
Trautman, Herman Louis *lawyer, educator*
Urmy, Norman B. *hospital administrator*
Van, George Paul *international money management executive*
van Eys, Jan *pediatrician, educator, administrator*
Van Mol, Louis John, Jr. *public relations executive*
Van Shelton, Ricky *country music singer, songwriter*
Voegeli, Victor Jacque *history educator, dean*
von Raffler-Engel, Walburga *linguist, lecturer, writer*
Wagoner, Porter *country music singer, composer*
Walden, Philip Michael *recording company executive, publishing company executive*
†Walker, Arthur Lonzo *religious organization administrator*
Wang, Taylor Gunjin *science administrator, astronaut, educator*
Waters, Roger *rock musician*
Weeks, Robert Andrew *materials science researcher, educator*
Weingartner, H(ans) Martin *finance educator*
Wert, James Junior *materials scientist, educator*
†Westmoreland, Barry Keith *state legislator*
†Whaley, Vernon *church administrator*
†Whitefield, Anne C. *secondary school principal*
Wilder, John Shelton *lieutenant governor, president senate*
†Willcott, Mark Robert, III *chemist, educator, researcher*
Wire, William Shidaker, II *retired apparel and footwear manufacturing company executive*
Wiseman, Thomas Anderton, Jr. *federal judge*
Wyatt, Joe Billy *university chancellor*
Youree, Gene Tassey *tool design engineer*
Zibart, Michael Alan *wholesale book company executive*

Oak Ridge
Auerbach, Stanley Irving *ecologist, environmental scientist, educator*
Beasley, Cloyd Orris, Jr. *physicist, researcher*
Boyle, William R. *science administrator*
†Burtis, Carl A., Jr. *chemist*
Cain, Victor Ralph *nuclear engineer*
Cawley, Charles Nash *enviromental scientist*
Gardiner, Donald Andrew *statistician, consultant*
Garrett, Jerry Dale *nuclear physicist*
†Genung, R. K. *physical sciences research administrator*
†Gifford, Franklin Andrew, Jr. *meteorologist*
Gooch, Patricia Carolyn *cytogeneticist*
†Hawsey, Robert Alan *engineering laboratory executive*

Hosker, Rayford Peter, Jr. *air pollution research scientist*
Jasny, George Roman *retired energy company executive*
Kasten, Paul Rudolph *nuclear engineer, educator*
†Kelly, James Michael *soil scientist*
Kliewer, Kenneth Lee *computational scientist, research administrator*
Krause, Manfred Otto *physicist*
Larson, Bennett Charles *solid state physicist, researcher*
Luxmoore, Robert John *soil and plant scientist*
Macfarlane, Alastair Iain Robert *business executive*
Maienschein, Fred C. *physicist*
†Plasil, Franz *physicist*
Postma, Herman *physicist, consultant*
†Poutsma, Marvin L. *chemical research administration*
Raridon, Richard Jay *computer specialist*
Renshaw, Amanda Frances *physicist, nuclear engineer*
Rosenthal, Murray Wilford *chemical engineer, science administrator*
Satchler, George Raymond *physicist*
Scott, Charles David *chemical engineer*
†Sellin, Ivan Armand *physicist, educator, researcher*
Skinner, Dorothy M. *biologist, educator*
†Slusher, Kimberly Goode *researcher*
Spray, Paul *surgeon*
Thomas, John Edwin *retired university administrator*
Totter, John Randolph *biochemist*
Trauger, Donald Byron *nuclear engineering laboratory administrator*
Trivelpiece, Alvin William *physicist, corporate executive*
Turov, Daniel *financial writer, investment executive*
†Veigel, Jon Michael *corporate professional*
†Waters, Dean A. *engineering executive*
Weinberg, Alvin Martin *physicist*
Whittle, Charles Edward, Jr. *consultant, lecturer*
Wilkinson, Michael Kennerly *physicist*
Wooten, Hollis Darwin *engineer*
Zucker, Alexander *physicist, administrator*

Oliver Springs
Davis, Sara Lea *pharmacist*

Paris
Williams, Hank, Jr. *country music singer, songwriter*

Pleasant View
Davis, Alfred Lewis *manufacturing company executive*

Pulaski
Dowdy, Ronald Raymond *academic administrator*

Sewanee
Croom, Frederick Hailey *college administrator, mathematics educator*
Croom, Henrietta Brown *biology educator*
Dunkly, James Warren *theological librarian*
Kepple, Thomas Ray, Jr. *college administrator*
Puckette, Stephen Elliott *mathematics educator, mathematician*
†Spears, Monroe Kirk *educator, author*
Stirling, Edwin Murdoch *English educator, critic*
Williamson, Samuel Ruthven, Jr. *historian, university administrator*
Yeatman, Harry Clay *biologist, educator*

Seymour
Steele, Ernest Clyde *retired insurance company executive*

Signal Mountain
Cooper, Robert Elbert *state supreme court justice*

Tullahoma
Antar, Basil Niman *engineering educator*
Collins, S. Ruth *education educator*
Franke, John Charles *human resources executive*
Gossick, Lee Van *corporate executive, retired air force officer*
†Pate, Samuel Ralph *engineering corporation executive*
Whitfield, Jack Duane *advanced technology services and engineering company executive*
†Wu, Ying Chu Lin Susan *engineering company executive, engineer*

Williamsport
Dysinger, Paul William *physician, educator, health consultant*

TEXAS

Abilene
Boone, Billy Warren *lawyer, judge*
Boyll, David Lloyd *broadcasting company executive*
Clayton, Lawrence Ray *university dean, literary critic, biographer*
Davis, Burl Edward *social sciences research consulting company executive, communications educator*
†Fleshman, Jim J. *zoological park administrator*
†Hunter, Robert Dean (Bob Hunter) *state legislator, retired academic administrator*
Kim, Thomas Kunhyuk *college administrator*
Retzer, Kenneth Albert *mathematics educator*
Shimp, Robert Everett, Jr. *university administrator, historian*
Specht, Alice Wilson *library director*
Stephens, Brad *oil industry executive*
Wilson, Stanley P. *retired lawyer*

Addison
Springer, Stanley G. *lawyer*

Allen
†Leach, Sheryl *television show creator*

Alpine
Morgan, Raymond Victor, Jr. *university administrator, mathematics educator*

Alvin
Lukens, Betty Faye *health facility manager*

Amarillo
Ayad, Joseph Magdy *psychologist*
Ball, Charles Elihue *association consultant*
Brainard, Jayne Dawson (Mrs. Ernest Scott Brainard) *civic worker*
Hilbert, Stephen C. *insurance company executive*
Keaton, Lawrence Cluer *engineer, consultant*
Madden, Wales Hendrix, Jr. *lawyer*
†Marmaduke, John H. *retail executive*
Matthiesen, Leroy Theodore *bishop*
Neal, A. Curtis *retired lawyer*
Petty, John Ernest *education specialist, consultant*
Robinson, Mary Lou *federal judge*
†Smithee, John True *lawyer, state legislator*
†Snell, Mary Kay Holmes *librarian, researcher*
Spies, Dennis J. *editor*
Sprowls, Robert Wayne *veterinarian, laboratory administrator*
Stiff, John Sterling *development company executive*
Streu, Raymond Oliver *financial planner, securities executive*
Strickland, Anita Maurine *retired business educator, librarian*
Von Eschen, Robert Leroy *electrical engineer, consultant*

Arlington
Anderson, Dale Arden *aerospace engineer, educator*
Ayres, Ray Morris *business management educator*
Brown, (James) Kevin *professional baseball player*
Burkart, Burke *geology educator, researcher*
Burson, Betsy Lee *librarian*
Canseco, Jose *professional baseball player*
Carey, Milburn Ernest *musician, educator*
Carney, Kim *economics educator*
Clark, Will (William Nuschler Clark, Jr.) *professional baseball player*
Cole, Richard Louis *political scientist, educator*
Dickinson, Roger Allyn *business administration educator*
Duncan, Thomas Alton *editor*
Elias, Harold John *artist, educator*
Franco, Julio Cesar *professional baseball player*
Fung, Adrian Kin-Chiu *electrical engineering educator, researcher*
Furubotn, Eirik Grundtvig *economics educator*
Gonzalez, Juan *professional baseball player*
Greenspan, Donald *mathematician, educator*
Grieve, Thomas Alan *professional baseball manager*
Han, Chien-Pai *statistics educator*
Kennedy, Kevin Curtis *professional baseball team manager*
Malone, Edwin Scott, III *radio and television producer, public relations consultant*
McCuistion, Robert Wiley *lawyer, hospital administrator, management consultant*
Mc Elroy, John Harley *electrical engineering educator*
Meadows, Jennifer Elizabeth *retired editor,tattoo artist*
Mullendore, Walter Edward *economist*
Murnane, Thomas George *public health veterinarian, military*
Nelson, Wallace Boyd *economics and business administration educator*
†O'Neill, James J. *food service company executive*
Payne, Fred R(ay) *aerospace engineering educator, researcher*
Perkins, Bob(by) F(rank) *geologist, dean*
Pickard, Myrna Rae *college dean*
Pomerantz, Martin *chemistry educator, researcher*
Qasim, Syed Reazul *civil engineering educator, researcher*
Ramsey, Charles Eugene *sociologist, educator*
Rodriguez, Ivan *professional baseball player*
Rose, Edward W. (Rusty) *professional sports team executive*
Russell, Andrew Milo *music educator*
Ryan, Nolan *former professional baseball player*
Sampras, Pete *tennis player*
Schieffer, J. Thomas *professional baseball team executive*
Schimelpfenig, C(larence) W(illiam), Jr. *chemistry educator*
Smith, Charles Isaac *geology educator*
Sobol, Harold *research dean, retired communication equipment manufacturing executive*
Stevens, Gladstone Taylor, Jr. *industrial engineer*
Thompson, Carson R. *retail, manufacturing company executive*
Wiig, Elisabeth Hemmersam *audiologist, educator*
Wiseman, Carl Donald *metallurgy educator, consultant*
Wright, James Edward *judge*

Austin
Abell, Creed W. *pharmacy educator*
Abraham, Jacob A. *computer engineering educator, consultant*
Adams, Warren Sanford, II *retired food company executive, lawyer*
Adcock, Willis Alfred *electrical engineer, educator*
Aggarwal, Jagdishkumar Keshoram *electrical and computer engineering educator, research administrator*
Ahearn, Patricia Jean *lawyer*
Alexander, Drury Blakeley *architectural educator*
†Alich, John Arthur *manufacturing company executive*
Allday, Martin Lewis *lawyer*
Allison, John Robert *lawyer, educator, author*
Alpert, Mark Ira *marketing educator*
Amsel, Abram *experimental psychologist, educator*
Antokoletz, Elliott Maxim *music educator*
†Ardis, Susan Barber *librarian, educator*
Armstrong, Neal Earl *civil engineering educator*
Ashworth, Kenneth Hayden *state educational commissioner*
Austin, David Mayo *social work educator*
Ayres, Robert Moss, Jr. *retired university president*
Bailey, Philip Sigmon *chemistry educator*
Baker, Lee Edward *biomedical engineering educator*
Bard, Allen Joseph *chemist, educator*
Barker, Daniel Stephen *geology educator*
Barlow, Joel William *chemical engineering educator*
Barnes, Jay William, Jr. *architect, rancher*
Barr, Howard Raymond *architect*
Barrera, Elvira Puig *counselor, therapist, educator*
†Bartlett, Joe Michael *school system administrator*
Bash, Frank Ness *astronomer, educator*
Bean, Frank D(awson) *sociology and demography educator*
Beard, Leo Roy *civil engineer*
Beckey, Sylvia Louise *lawyer*
Bengtson, Roger Dean *physicist*
Berdahl, Robert Max *historian, educator*
Bernstein, Robert *retired physician, state official, former army officer*
Biesele, John Julius *biologist, educator*
Billings, Harold Wayne *librarian, editor*
Bissex, Walter Earl *lawyer*
†Black, Charles Layton *rancher, state legislator*
Black, James Sinclair *architect, educator*
Blair, Calvin Patton *retired business administration educator*
Blake, Robert Rogers *psychologist, behavioral science company executive*
Bledsoe, Woodrow Wilson *mathematics and computer sciences educator*
Blodgett, Warren Terrell *public affairs educator*
Bobbitt, Philip Chase *lawyer, educator, writer*
Boggs, James Ernest *chemistry educator*
Bonjean, Charles Michael *foundation executive, sociologist, educator*
Bordie, John George *linguistics educator*
Box, Barry Glenn *aerospace engineer, military officer*
Box, John Harold *architect, educator, academic dean*
Boyer, Mildred Vinson *foreign language educator emeritus*
Boyer, Robert Ernst *geologist, educator*
†Braasch, Steven Mark *advertising executive*
Brager, Walter S. *retired food products corporation executive*
†Branch, Brenda *library director*
Braybrooke, David *philosopher, educator*
Breen, John Edward *civil engineer, educator*
Brewer, Thomas Bowman *retired university president*
Brinkley, Fred Sinclair, Jr. *state agency administrator, pharmacist*
Brock, James Rush *chemical engineering educator*
Brockett, Oscar Gross *theatre educator*
Bronaugh, Edwin Lee *research scientist, consultant*
Bronson, Franklin H. *zoology educator*
†Brown, J. E. (Buster Brown) *state senator, lawyer*
Brown, Norman Donald *history educator*
†Brown, Richard Malcolm, Jr. *botany educator*
Buchanan, Bruce, II *political science educator*
Bullock, Robert D. (Bob) *lieutenant governor, lawyer*
Burnham, Walter Dean *political science educator*
Burns, Ned Hamilton *civil engineering educator*
Byrd, Linward Tonnett *lawyer, rancher*
Campion, Alan *chemistry educator*
Cannon, William Bernard *retired university educator*
Cantilo, Patrick Herrera *lawyer*
Cardozier, Virgus Ray *higher education educator*
Carleton, Don Edward *history center administrator, educator, writer*
Carlton, Donald Morrill *research, development and engineering executive*
Carpenter, Elizabeth Sutherland *library consultant, author, equal rights leader*
Carrasquillo, Ramon Luis *civil engineering educator, consultant*
Carter, Shelby Henry, Jr. *communications executive, educator*
Causey, Robert Louis *philosopher, educator, consultant*
Chavarria, Ernest Montes, Jr. *international trade, business and finance consultant, lecturer*
Christian, George Eastland *political consultant*
Clark, Charles T(aliferro) *retired business statistics educator*
†Cleaves, Peter Shurtleff *academic administrator*
Cleland, Charles Carr *psychologist, educator*
Cline, Clarence Lee *language professional*
Conine, Ernest *newspaper commentator, writer*
Cook, Chauncey William Wallace *retired food products company executive*
Cook, J. Rowland *lawyer*
Cooke, Carlton Lee, Jr. *mayor*
Crain, William Henry *retired curator*
Crenshaw, Ben *professional golfer*
Crosby, Alfred Worcester *history educator*
†Croslin, Charles Wilburn, Jr. *architect*
Crum, Lawrence Lee *banking educator*
Culp, George Hart *computer executive, consultant*
Culp, Joe C(arl) *electronics executive*
Cundiff, Edward William *marketing educator*
Cunningham, William Hughes *university chancellor, marketing educator*
†Dalton, Don *principal*
†Danburg, Debra *state legislator*
Danielson, Wayne Allen *journalism and computer science educator*
Davis, Donald Gordon, Jr. *librarian, educator*
Davis, Edward Mott *anthropology educator and researcher*
Davis, Robert Larry *lawyer*
Dawson, Robert Oscar *lawyer, educator*
Deal, Ernest Linwood, Jr. *banker*
Deisler, Paul Frederick, Jr. *retired oil company executive*
Delevoryas, Theodore *botanist, educator*
Dell, Michael S. *manufacturing executive*
Deming, David Lawson *art educator*
†Denny, Mary Craver *state legislator, rancher*
Derounian, Steven Boghos *lawyer, retired judge*
de Vaucouleurs, Gerard Henri *astronomer, educator*
†de Wette, Frederik Willem *physics educator*
De Witt, Bryce Seligman *physics educator*
De Witt-Morette, Cécile *physicist*
Dijkstra, Edsger Wybe *computer science educator, mathematician*
Divine, Robert Alexander *history educator*
Doenges, Rudolph Conrad *finance educator*
Doggett, Lloyd *state supreme court justice*
Doluisio, James Thomas *pharmacy educator*
Dougal, Arwin Adelbert *electrical engineer, educator*
Dougherty, John Chrysostom, III *lawyer*
Duncombe, Raynor Lockwood *astronomer*
Dupuis, Russell Dean *electrical engineer, research scientist*
Durbin, Richard Louis, Sr. *healthcare admnistration consultant*
Durden, Christopher John *entomologist, paleontologist, museum curator*
Dusansky, Richard *economist, educator*
†Eckels, Robert Allen *state legislator*
Edwards, Wayne Forrest *paper company executive*
Ellison, Samuel Porter, Jr. *geologist, educator*
Epstein, Jeremiah Fain *anthropologist, educator*
Ersek, Robert Allen *plastic surgeon, inventor*
Erskine, James Lorenzo *physics educator*
Evans, David Stanley *astronomy educator*
Evans, Walter Reed *engineering executive, consultant*
Fair, James Rutherford, Jr. *chemical engineering educator, consultant*
Farrell, Edmund James *English language educator, author*
Fernea, Robert Alan *cultural anthropology and Middle Eastern studies educator, consultant*
Fisher, William Lawrence *geologist, educator*
Folk, Robert Louis *geologist, educator*
Folkers, Karl August *chemistry educator*
Fonken, Gerhard Joseph *chemistry educator, university administrator*
Foss, Donald John *research psychologist, educator*
Fowler, David Wayne *architectural engineering educator*
Fowler, Nola Faye *political consultant, rancher*
Fox, Marye Anne *chemistry educator*
France, Newell Edwin *corporation executive*
Francis, Bill Dean *university dean, artist*
†Frank, Karl Heinz *civil engineer, educator*
Franklin, Billy Joe *international education consultant*
Franklin, G(eorge) Charles *academic administrator*
Friedman, Alan Warren *humanities educator*
Frost, Joe Lindell *education educator*
Galbraith, James Kenneth *public affairs and government educator*
Galinsky, Gotthard Karl *classicist, educator*
Gambrell, James Bruton, III *lawyer, educator*
Gammage, Robert Alton (Bob Gammage) *state supreme court justice*
Gangstad, John Erik *lawyer*
Gardiner, William Cecil, Jr. *chemist, educator*
Garner, Harvey Louis *computer scientist, consultant, electrical engineering educator*
Garwood, William Lockhart *federal judge*
†Gates, Charles W., Sr. *city official*
Gavenda, J(ohn) David *physicist*
Gentle, Kenneth William *physicist*
George, Walter Eugene, Jr. *architect*
Gerry, Martin Hughes, IV *federal agency administrator, lawyer*
Gibson, William Willard, Jr. *law educator*
Gill, Clark Cyrus *retired education educator*
Gillman, Leonard *mathematician, educator*
Girling, Bettie Joyce Moore *home health executive*
Girling, Robert George William, III *business owner*
Glade, William Patton, Jr. *economics educator*
Gleeson, Austin Michael *physicist, educator*
Glenn, Norval Dwight *sociologist, educator*
Gloyna, Earnest Frederick *environmental engineer, educator*
Goldstein, E. Ernest *lawyer*
Goldstein, Peggy R. *sculptor*
Golemon, Ronald Kinnan *lawyer*
Gonzalez, Raul A. *state supreme court justice*
†Gooch, William DeWitt *librarian*
Goodenough, John Bannister *engineering educator, research physicist*
Gould, Lewis Ludlow *historian*
Gracy, David Bergen, II *archivist, information science educator, writer*
†Grady, Charles E. *advertising executive*
Granof, Michael H. *accounting educator*
Grant, Verne Edwin *biology educator*
Gray, Kenneth Eugene *petroleum engineering educator*
Green, Peter Morris *classics educator, writer, translator*
Greene, John Joseph *lawyer*
Greenhill, Joe R. *former chief justice state supreme, lawyer*
Greig, Brian Strother *lawyer*
Griffy, Thomas Alan *physics educator*
Guerin, John William *artist*
Gustafsson, Lars Erik Einar *writer, educator*
Haas, Joseph Marshall *petroleum consultant*
Hall, Beverly Adele *nursing educator*
Hall, Michael Garibaldi *education educator*
Hamermesh, Daniel Selim *economics educator*
Hamilton, Dagmar Strandberg *lawyer, educator*
Hamilton, Robert Woodruff *law educator*
Hancock, Ian Francis (O Yanko le Redžosko) *linguistics educator*
Hannah, John H., Jr. *state official*
Harms, Robert Thomas *linguist, educator*
Harris, Ben Maxwell *education educator*
Harris, Richard Lee *engineering executive, retired army officer*
Harrison, Richard Wayne *lawyer*
Hart, Roderick P. *communications educator, researcher, author*
Hartshorne, Charles *philosopher, retired educator*
Hayes, Patricia Ann *university president*
Hearst, Gladys Whitley Henderson *writer*
Hecht, Nathan Lincoln *state supreme court justice*
Helburn, Isadore B. *arbitrator, mediator, educator*
Heller, Adam *chemist, researcher*
Helmreich, Robert Louis *psychologist, educator*
Henderson, George Ervin *lawyer*
Herman, Kenneth Neil *journalist*
Herman, Robert *physics educator*
Hester, Thomas Roy *anthropologist*
High, Timothy Griffin *artist, educator, writer*
Hightower, Jack English *state supreme court justice, former congressman*
Himmelblau, David Mautner *chemical engineer*
Hinojosa-Smith, Roland *English language educator, writer*
Ho, Paul Siu-Chung *physics educator*
Holtzman, Wayne Harold *psychologist, educator*
Holz, Robert Kenneth *geography educator*
Hopper, Robert William *speech communication educator*
Houston, Samuel Lee *computer programmer systems analysis company executive*
Howell, John Reid *mechanical engineer, educator*
Hubbs, Clark *zoologist, researcher*
Hudspeth, Emmett LeRoy *physicist, educator*
Huff, David L. *geography educator*
Huie, William Orr *legal educator*
Hull, David George *aerospace engineering educator, researcher*
Hunter, J(ohn) Robert *insurance commissioner*
Hurd, Richard Nelson *pharmaceutical company executive*
Hurley, Laurence Harold *medicinal chemistry educator*
Huston, Ted Laird *psychology educator*
Ikard, Frank Neville, Jr. *lawyer*
Ingram, Denny Ouzts, Jr. *lawyer, educator*
Inman, Bobby Ray *investor, former electronics executive*
†Iscoe, Ira *psychology educator, director human development institute*
Ivins, Molly *writer*
Jackson, Eugene Bernard *librarian*
Jackson, William Vernon *library science and Latin American studies educator*
Jacobson, Antone Gardner *zoology educator*
Jannuzi, F. Tomasson *economics educator*
Jazayery, Mohammad Ali *foreign languages and literature educator emeritus*
Jefferys, William Hamilton, III *astronomer*
Jeffrey, Robert Campbell *university dean*
Jenkins, Lawrence Eugene *retired aeronautics company executive*
Jennings, Coleman Alonzo *dramatics educator*
Jentz, Gaylord Adair *law educator*
Jirsa, James Otis *civil engineering educator*
Johanson, Stanley Morris *legal educator*

Johnson, Corwin Waggoner *lawyer, educator*
Johnson, Lady Bird (Mrs. Lyndon Baines Johnson) *widow of former President of U.S.*
Johnson, Mildred Snowden *nursing educator*
Johnson, Sam D. *federal judge*
Jordan, Barbara C. *lawyer, educator, former congresswoman*
Jordan, Terry Gilbert *geography educator*
Kalthoff, Klaus Otto *zoology educator*
Katz, Michael Ray *Slavic languages educator*
Kendrick, David Andrew *economist, educator*
Kennamer, Lorrin Garfield, Jr. *retired university dean*
Kennan, Kent Wheeler *composer, educator*
King, Carole *composer, singer*
King, Robert D. *linguistics educator, university dean*
Kinney, William Rudolph, Jr. *accounting educator, researcher*
Kirk, Lynda Pounds *biofeedback therapist, neurotherapist*
†Klein, Dale Edward *nuclear engineering educator*
Knight, Gary *lawyer, educator, publisher*
Koen, Billy Vaughn *mechanical engineering educator*
Koile, Earl *psychologist, educator*
Koros, William John *chemical engineering educator*
†Kozmetsky, George *computer science educator*
†Kreisle, Matthew F., III *architectural firm executive*
†Kronkosky, Preston C. *educational think-tank executive*
Lagowski, J(oseph) J(ohn) *chemist*
LaGrone, Alfred Hall *electrical engineering educator*
Laine, Katie Myers *communications consultant*
Lam, Simon Shin-Sing *computer science educator*
Lamb, Jamie Parker, Jr. *mechanical engineer, educator*
†Landes, Robert Paul *architect*
Lanham, Elizabeth *retired management educator*
†Lariviere, Richard Wilfred *Asian studies educator, consultant*
Larson, Kermit Dean *accounting educator*
Laycock, Harold Douglas *law educator, writer*
Lehmann, Ruth Preston Miller *literature educator*
Lehmann, Winfred Philipp *linguistics educator*
Leiden, Carl *political scientist, educator*
†Leon, Tomas Carlos *foreign exchange broker*
Levinson, Sanford Victor *legal educator*
Levy, Michael Richard *publishing executive*
†Little, Emily Browning *architect*
†Livingston, William Samuel *university administrator, polital scientist*
Loehlin, John Clinton *psychologist, educator*
López-Morillas, Juan *Spanish and comparative literature educator*
Lopreato, Joseph *sociology educator, author*
Lord, William Jackson, Jr. *communication educator*
Louis, William Roger *historian, educator, editor*
Lundelius, Ernest Luther, Jr. *vertebrate paleontologist, educator*
Mackey, Louis Henry *philosophy educator*
Mackovic, John *college football coach, athletic director*
Magee, Stephen Pat *economics and finance educator*
Manosevitz, Martin *psychologist*
Marcus, Harris Leon *mechanical engineering and materials science educator*
Mark, Hans Michael *aerospace engineering educator, physicist*
Marshall, F. Ray *public affairs educator*
Martin, Frederick Noel *audiologist*
Matheson, Daniel Nicholas, III *lawyer*
Mathias, Reuben Victor (Vic Mathias) *real estate executive, investor*
Mauzy, Oscar Holcombe *lawyer, retired state supreme court justice*
Maxwell, Arthur Eugene *oceanographer, marine geophysicist, educator*
May, Robert George *accounting educator*
Mayers, Roy *publishing executive*
Mayes, Wendell Wise, Jr. *broadcasting company executive*
Mc Carthy, John Edward *bishop*
McCuistion, Peg Orem *hospice administrator*
†McCullough, Benjamin Franklin *transportation researcher, educator*
McDaniel, Myra Atwell *lawyer, former state official*
Mc Donald, Stephen Lee *economics educator*
McFadden, Dennis *psychology educator*
†McFarland, Lawrence D. *photographer, educator*
McGarry, William Andrew, Jr. *career counselor*
McGinnis, Charles Irving *civil engineer*
McGinnis, Robert Campbell *lawyer*
Mc Ketta, John J., Jr. *chemical engineering educator*
Meacham, Standish *historian, educator*
Megaw, Robert Neill Ellison *English educator*
Meno, Lionel R. *state education official*
Mercer, Melvin Ray *electrical engineer, educator*
Mersky, Roy Martin *law educator, librarian*
Metcalfe, Tom Brooks *chemical engineering educator*
Michener, James Albert *author*
Middleton, Christopher *Germanic languages and literature educator*
Middleton, Harry Joseph *library administrator*
Misra, Jayadev *computer science educator*
Monti, Stephen Arion *university administrator, chemistry educator*
Moore, James Robert *geological oceanographer*
Morales, Dan *state attorney general*
Moulthrop, James Sylvester *research engineer, consultant*
Mourelatos, Alexander Phoebus Dionysiou *humanities educator*
Mullen, Ron *insurance company executive*
Mullins, Charles Brown *physician, academic administrator*
Nasworthy, Carol Cantwell *education and public policy professional*
Newton, Charles Chartier *architect*
†Nichols, Steven Parks *mechanical engineer, academic administrator*
Northington, David K. *research center director, botanist, educator*
Nowlin, James Robertson *federal judge*
Oakes, Melvin Ervin Louis *physics educator*
Oates, Carl Everette *lawyer*
†Oden, John Tinsley *engineering mechanics educator, consultant*
Oram, Robert W. *library administrator*
Otis, Jack *social work educator*
Painton, Russell Elliott *lawyer, mechanical engineer*
Palaima, Thomas Gerard *Classics educator, researcher*
Paredes, Americo *English language educator*
Park, Thomas Joseph *biology researcher, educator*
Paul, Donald Ross *chemical engineer, educator*
Payne, Eugene Edgar *insurance company executive*
Payne, John Ross *rare books and archives appraisal-consulting company executive, library science educator*
Payne, Tyson Elliott, Jr. *retired insurance executive*
†Perry, David Brian *architect*
Peterson, Robert Allen *marketing educator*
Phillips, Frances Marie *history educator*
Phillips, Thomas Royal *judge*
Pickens, Franklin Ace *lawyer*
†Pinkston, Russell Fountain *music composition educator*
†Polkinghorn, James B. *architectural firm executive*
Polomé, Edgar Charles *foreign language educator*
Pope, Andrew Jackson, Jr. (Jack Pope) *retired state supreme court chief justice*
Powers, Pike, Jr. *lawyer*
Pradzynski, Andrzej Henryk *chemist*
Preeg, William Edward *oil company executive*
Prentice, Norman Macdonald *clinical psychologist*
Prigogine, Vicomte Ilya *physics educator*
Ray, Cread L., Jr. *retired state supreme court justice*
Reavley, Thomas Morrow *federal judge*
Reed, Lester James *biochemist, educator*
†Reeder, William Glase *zoologist, museum administrator*
Reid, Jackson Brock *psychologist, educator*
Rhyne, Vernon Thomas, III *electrical engineer, consultant*
Rich, John Martin *humanities educator, researcher*
Richards, Ann Willis *governor*
†Richards-Kortum, Rebecca Rae *biomedical engineering educator*
Rippey, Donald Taylor *education educator*
Roach, James Robert *political science educator*
Roberts, Bill Glen *retired fire chief, investor, consultant*
Robertson, Jack Clark *accounting educator*
Roessner, Roland Gommel *architect, educator*
Rogers, Lorene Lane *university president emeritus*
Rollins, Henry Moak *former oil drilling equipment company executive, consultant*
Rostow, Elspeth Davies *political science educator*
Rostow, Walt Whitman *economist, educator*
Roueche, John Edward, II *education educator, leadership program director*
Ruud, Millard Harrington *former legal association administrator, retired educator*
Rylander, Henry Grady, Jr. *mechanical engineering educator*
Sandberg, Irwin Walter *electrical and computer engineering educator*
Sargent, Ben *political cartoonist*
Schapery, Richard Allan *engineering educator*
Schechter, Robert Samuel *chemical engineer, educator*
Schmandt-Besserat, Denise *archaeologist, educator*
Schmitt, Karl Michael *retired political scientist*
Schulz-Widmar, Russell Eugene *musician, educator, composer*
Seung, Thomas Kaehao *philosophy educator*
Shapiro, Sander Wolf *lawyer*
Sharir, Yacov *artistic director, choreographer*
Sharp, John Malcolm, Jr. *geology educator*
Sherman, Edward Francis *lawyer, educator*
Sherman, Max Ray *lawyer, academic executive, former state senator*
Short, Byron Elliott *engineering educator*
Shurley, Jay Talmadge *psychiatrist, medical educator, polar explorer, author*
Simpson, Beryl Brintnall *botany educator*
†Sims, Bill *state senator, business executive*
Smith, Alfred Goud *anthropologist, educator*
Smith, Bert Kruger *mental health services professional, consultant*
Smoluchowski, Roman *physicist, emeritus educator*
Snell, Esmond Emerson *biochemist*
Sommerfeld, Raynard Matthias *accounting educator*
Southerland, Louis Feno, Jr. *architect*
Sparks, Sam *federal judge*
Spears, Franklin Scott *retired supreme court justice*
†Speck, Lawrence W. *architect*
†Spertus, Philip *investment company executive*
Spiro, Herbert John *political scientist, politician, educator, ambassador*
Spruce, Everett Franklin *artist*
†Staley, Thomas Fabian *language professional, academic administrator*
Starr, Richard Cawthon *botany educator*
Steinfink, Hugo *chemical engineering educator*
Stephen, John Erle *lawyer, consultant*
Stetson, Daniel Everett *museum director*
Stice, James Edward *chemical engineer, educator*
†Stoffa, Paul L. *geophysicist, educator*
Stone, Leon *banker*
Stoner, James Lloyd *retired foundation executive, clergyman*
Straiton, Archie Waugh *electrical engineering educator*
Strauser, Robert Wayne *lawyer*
Sturley, Michael F. *law educator*
Sullivan, Teresa Ann *law and sociology educator, academic administrator*
Summers, Edward Lee *accounting educator*
Sutherland, William Owen Sheppard *English language educator*
Sutton, Harry Eldon *geneticist, educator*
Sutton, John F., Jr. *law educator, university dean, lawyer*
Swartzlander, Earl Eugene, Jr. *engineering educator, former electronics company executive*
Swinney, Harry Leonard *physics educator*
Szebehely, Victor G. *aeronautical engineer*
Taber, Robert Clinton *retired army officer*
Tapley, Byron Dean *aerospace engineer, educator*
Teague, Hyman Faris *former publishing company executive*
Temple, Larry Eugene *lawyer*
Tesar, Delbert *machine systems and robotics educator, researcher, manufacturing consultant*
Thiessen, Delbert Duane *psychologist*
Thomajan, Robert *lawyer, management and financial consultant*
†Thompson, Garfield *congressman*
Thornberry, William Homer *federal judge*
Thornton, Joseph Scott *research institute executive, materials scientist*
Thurston, George Butte *mechanical and biomedical engineering educator*
Tigar, Michael Edward *lawyer, educator*
Tinic, Seha Mehmet *finance educator*
Todd, Bruce M. *mayor*
Todd, William Burton *English language and literature educator*
Topfer, Morton Louis *communications company executive*
Tottenham, Terry Oliver *lawyer*
Tucker, Richard Lee *civil engineer, educator*
Turner, Billie Lee *botanist, educator*
Tyler, Ronnie Curtis *historian*
Uhlenbeck, Karen Keskulla *mathematician, educator*
Vande Hey, James Michael *corporate executive, former air force officer*
Velz, John William *literature educator*
Vliet, Gary Clark *mechanical engineering educator*
Vykukal, Eugene Lawrence *wholesale drug company executive*
Wadlington, Warwick Paul *English language educator*
Wagner, William Bradley *lawyer*
Wahlberg, Philip Lawrence *former bishop, legislative liaison*
Walker, James Roy *microbiologist*
Walton, Charles Michael *civil engineering educator*
Watson, Elizabeth Marion *protective services official*
Webb, Wayne E., Jr. *lawyer, engineer*
Weddington, Sarah Ragle *lawyer, educator*
Wehring, Bernard William *nuclear engineering educator*
Weinberg, Louise *lawyer, educator, author*
Weintraub, Russell Jay *lawyer, educator*
Weintraub, Sidney *economist, educator*
Weismann, Donald Leroy *art educator, artist, filmmaker, writer*
Welch, Ashley James *engineering educator*
Weldon, William Forrest *electrical and mechanical engineer, educator*
Welsch, Glenn Albert *accounting educator*
Werbow, Stanley Newman *language educator*
†West, George Edgar (Buddy) *congressman*
West, Glenn Edward *business organization executive*
Wheeler, John Craig *astrophysicist, writer*
Wheeler, Marshall Ralph *zoologist, educator*
Whitbread, Thomas Bacon *English educator, author*
White, John Michael *chemistry educator*
†Whitmire, John *state senator*
Whitmore, Jon Scott *theater educator*
Willerman, Lee *psychologist, educator*
Williams, Mary Pearl *judge, lawyer*
†Willson, C. Grant *chemistry educator, engineering educator*
Wilson, Robert Henry *English educator*
Winegar, Albert Lee *computer systems company executive*
Wissler, Eugene Harley *chemical engineer, educator*
Witt, Robert Charles *finance educator*
Wolf, Harold Arthur *finance educator*
Woodson, Herbert Horace *electrical engineering educator*
Wright, Charles Alan *lawyer, educator, author*
Wright, Stephen Gailord *civil engineering educator, consultant*
Young, Phyllis Casselman *music educator*
Yudof, Mark G. *lawyer, educator, academic administrator*
Ziegler, Daniel Martin *chemist, educator*
Zimmerman, Louis Seymour *lawyer*

Baird
Rodenberger, Charles Alvard *aerospace engineer, consultant*

Baytown
Mendelson, Robert Allen *polymer scientist, rheologist*
Williams, Drew Davis *surgeon*

Beaumont
Brentlinger, William Brock *college dean*
Cobb, Howell *federal judge*
Cobb, Leslie Davis *utility executive*
Coe, (Matchett) Herring *sculptor*
Donnelly, Joseph Lennon *utility company executive*
Fisher, Joseph Jefferson *federal judge*
†Gagne, Mary *secondary school principal*
Ganter, Bernard J. *bishop*
Gray, Enid Maurine *city official, director of libraries*
Long, Alfred B. *retired oil company executive, consultant*
Lord, Evelyn Marlin *mayor*
Norton, James Adolphus *higher education administrator and consultant, retired academic administrator, political science educator*
Schell, Richard A. *federal judge*
Sethna, Beheruz Nariman *academic dean, marketing and management educator*
Smith, David Ryan *museum director*
Smith, Floyd Rodenback *utilities executive*

Bedford
Lieber, David Leslie *journalist*

Bellaire
†Carter, Don W. *architect*
Lancaster, Carroll Townes, Jr. *corporate executive*
Mayo, Clyde Calvin *organizational psychologist*
†Schechter, Sue Ann *state legislator*

Bellville
Bishop, James A. *architect, writer*
Dittert, J. Lee, Jr. *lawyer*

Belton
Harrison, Benjamin Leslie *retired army officer*
Parker, Bobby Eugene, Sr. *college president*
Shoemaker, Robert Morin *retired army officer, county government official*

Bertram
Albert, Susan Wittig *writer, English educator*

Blanco
Finley, James Edward *independent oil operator*

Blue Ridge
Comola, James Paul *legislative and environmental consultant*

Boerne
Dixon, Robert James *aerospace consultant, former air force officer, former aerospace company executive*

Brooks AFB
Carroll, Robert Eugene *flight surgeon*
Convertino, Victor Anthony *physiologist, educator, research scientist*
Cox, Ann Bruger *biological scientist, editor, researcher*
Irving, George Washington, III *military officer, research director, veterinarian*

Brownsville
Farst, Don David *zoo director, veterinarian*
Fitzpatrick, John J. *bishop*
Garza, Reynaldo G. *federal judge*
Garza, Roberto Jesus *education educator*
†Lucio, Eduardo Andres, Jr. *state senator*
San Pedro, Enrique *bishop*
Santa-Coloma, Bernardo *secondary school educator, counselor*
Vela, Filemon B. *federal judge*

Brownwood
DeHay, Jerry Marvin *business consultant*
Jarvis, Oscar T., Jr. *dean, education educator*

Bryan
Dirks, Kenneth Ray *pathologist, medical educator, army officer*
Hubert, Frank William Rene *retired university system chancellor*
Kellett, William Hiram, Jr. *retired architect, engineer, educator*
Röller, Herbert Alfred *biology scientist, educator*
Samson, Charles Harold, Jr. (car) *retired engineering educator, consultant*
Sulik, Edwin (Pete Sulik) *health care administrator*
Van Arsdel, Eugene Parr *tree pathologist, consultant meteorologist*

Bullard
Buckner, John Hugh *retired real estate broker, retired construction company executive, retired air force officer*

Burleson
Prior, Boyd Thelman *management consultant*

Bushland
†Howell, Terry Allen *agricultural engineer*
Unger, Paul Walter *soil scientist*

Caldwell
Sebesta, Charles Joseph, Jr. *lawyer*

Carrollton
Bentley, Clarence Edward *savings and loan executive*
Butler, Abbey J. *pharmaceutical distribution company executive*
Estrin, Melvyn J. *computer products company executive*
Grimes, Mary Woodworth *educational consultant*
†Heath, Richard W. *cosmetic company executive*
†Maher, Sheila *secondary school principal*
Miller, Marvin Edward *building materials company executive*
Miller, Ronald Alan *marketing consultant*
Powell, Bill Jake *newspaper executive*
Schulz, Richard Burkart *electrical engineer, consultant*
Smart, David Louis *retired finance executive*
Wilson, Douglas Larone *education consultant*

Cedar Hill
Hickman, Traphene Parramore *library director, storyteller, library and library building consultant*

Channelview
Johnson, Gus LaRoy *marine chemist, safety consultant*

Clarendon
Roper, Beryl Cain *library director*

Cleburne
MacLean, John Ronald *lawyer*
Urban, Carlyle Woodrow *retired lawyer*

College Station
Adkisson, Perry Lee *university system chancellor*
Anderson, Aubrey Lee *oceanographer, educator*
Anderson, Duwayne Marlo *earth and polar scientist, university administrator*
†Arnowitt, Richard Lewis *physics educator, researcher*
Barton, Derek Harold Richard *chemist*
Bass, George Fletcher *archaeology educator*
†Batchelor, Bill *civil engineering educator*
Beaver, Bonnie Veryle *veterinarian, educator*
Berg, Robert Raymond *geologist, educator*
Berner, Leo De Witte, Jr. *retired oceanographer*
Berthold, Dennis Alfred *English language educator*
Bhattacharyya, Shankar Prashad *electrical engineer, educator*
Black, Samuel Harold *microbiology and immunology educator*
Blakley, George Robert, Jr. *mathematician, computer scientist*
Borlaug, Norman Ernest *agricultural scientist*
Boyer, Lester Leroy, Jr. *architecture educator, consultant*
Bryant, Vaughn Motley, Jr. *botany and anthropology educator*
Calhoun, John C., Jr. *academic administrator*
Cannon, Garland *English language educator*
Carpenter, Delbert Stanley *educational administration educator*
Carter, Neville Louis *geophysicist, educator*
†Chiou, George Chung-Yih *pharmacologist, educator*
Christian, James Wayne *economist*
Christiansen, James Edward *agricultural educator*
†Chui, Charles Kam-Tai *mathematics educator*
Clearfield, Abraham *chemistry educator*
Cocanougher, Arthur Benton *university dean, former business administration educator*
Cochran, Robert Glenn *nuclear engineering educator*
Conole, Richard Clement *management consultant*
Conway, Dwight Colbur *chemistry educator*
Copp, James Harris *sociologist, educator*
Cotton, Frank Albert *chemist, educator*
Crumbley, Donald Larry *accounting educator, writer, consultant*
Davenport, Manuel Manson *philosophy educator*
Dethloff, Henry Clay *history educator*
De Vaul, Richard Allan *medical school administrator*
Dixon, Joe Boris *soil science educator*
†Ehsani, Mehrdad (Mark) *electrical engineering educator, consultant*
Erlandson, David Alan *education administration educator*
†Ewing, Richard Edward *mathematics, chemical and petroleum engineering educator*
Fackler, John Paul, Jr. *chemistry educator*
Fedorchik, Bette Joy Winter *foreign language professional*

Fisher, Richard Forrest *soils educator, academic administrator*
Fletcher, Leroy Stevenson *mechanical engineer, educator*
Friedman, Melvin *geology educator, college dean*
Gage, E. Dean *university administrator*
Gordone, Charles *playwright*
Greenhut, Melvin Leonard *economist, educator*
†Gunn, Clare Alward *consultant, writer, retired educator*
Haden, Clovis Roland *university administrator, engineering educator*
Haensly, Patricia A. *psychology educator*
Hall, Kenneth Richard *chemical engineering educator, consultant*
Hall, Timothy C. *biology educator, consultant*
Ham, Joe Strother, Jr. *physics educator*
Hann, Roy William, Jr. *civil engineer, educator*
Harris, William James, Jr. *research administrator, educator*
Hassan, Yassin Abdel *engineer, educator*
Henry, Rene Arthur, Jr. *university official*
Herbich, John Bronislaw *engineering educator*
Hoadley, Irene Braden (Mrs. Edward Hoadley) *librarian*
Holland, Charles Donald *chemical engineer, educator*
Jordan, Wayne Robert *water resources executive, crop physiology educator*
Knight, James Allen *psychiatrist, educator*
Knobel, Dale Thomas *university administrator*
Knutson, Ronald Dale *economist, educator, academic admnistrator*
Kohel, Russell James *geneticist*
†Laane, Jaan *chemistry educator*
†Latimer, George Webster, Jr. *chemist*
Lee, William John *petroleum engineering educator, consultant*
Lowery, Lee Leon, Jr. *civil engineer*
†Lusas, Edmund William *food processing research executive*
Lytton, Robert Leonard *civil engineer, educator*
Manning, Walter Scott *accountant, former educator, consultant*
Martell, Arthur Earl *chemistry educator*
Mathewson, Christopher Colville *engineering geologist, educator*
McCrady, James David *veterinarian, educator*
Mc Dermott, John Joseph *philosophy educator*
McIntyre, John Armin *physics educator*
Milford, Murray Hudson *soil science educator*
Mobley, William Hodges *academic administrator*
†Nachman, Ronald James *research chemist*
Nance, Joseph Milton *history educator*
†Natowitz, Joseph B. *chemistry educator, administrator, researcher*
Neff, Ray Quinn *electric power consultant*
†Neill, William Harold, Jr. *biological science educator*
O'Connor, Rod *chemist, inventor*
Orville, Richard Edmonds *atmospheric science educator*
Padberg, Daniel Ivan *agricultural economics educator, researcher*
Page, Robert Henry *engineer, educator, researcher*
Painter, John Hoyt *electrical engineer*
Parzen, Emanuel *statistical scientist*
Patton, Alton DeWitt *electrical engineering educator, consultant, research administrator*
Peddicord, Kenneth Lee *academic administrator*
Pierce, Kenneth Ray *veterinary medicine educator*
Plum, Charles Walden *retired business executive and educator*
Prescott, John Mack *biochemist, retired university administrator*
Price, Alvin Audis *university administrator, educator emeritus*
Rabins, Michael Jerome *mechanical engineer, educator*
†Reddell, Donald Lee *agricultural engineer*
†Reddy, J. Narasimha *mechanical engineering educator*
Reed, Raymond Deryl *architect*
Rhode, David Leland *mechanical engineering educator, consultant*
Richardson, Herbert Heath *mechanical engineer, educator, institute director*
Rosberg, David William *plant sciences educator*
†Rowe, Gilbert Thomas *oceanography educator*
Sanchez, David Alan *science administrator*
Scott, Alastair Ian *chemistry educator*
†Shadduck, John Allen *veterinary pathologist*
Sis, Raymond Francis *veterinarian, educator*
Slocum, R.C. *university athletic coach*
Solecki, R. Stefan *anthropologist, educator*
Stanton, Robert James, Jr. *geologist, educator*
Steffy, John Richard *nautical archaeologist, educator*
Summers, Max (Duanne) *entomologist, scientist, educator*
†Tassinary, Louis George *psychology educator, director laboratory*
Trennepohl, Gary Lee *finance educator*
Unterberger, Betty Miller *history educator, writer*
Vandiver, Frank Everson *institute administrator, former university president, author, educator*
Van Riper, Paul Pritchard *political science educator*
†Varner, Dickson D. *veterinarian*
Way, James Leong *pharmacology and toxicology educator*
Wichern, Dean William *business educator*
Wilding, Lawrence Paul *pedology educator, soil science consultant*
Wilson, Don Whitman *archivist, historian*
†Woodcock, David Geoffrey *architect, educator*
†Wysk, Richard A. *engineering educator, researcher*
†Yao, James Tsu-Ping *civil engineer*

Colleyville
Love, Ben Howard *organization executive*

Columbus
Hamilton, T. Earle *retired educator, honor society executive*

Comanche
Droke, Edna Faye *elementary education educator*

Commerce
Bell, William Jack *journalism educator*
Grimshaw, James Albert, Jr. *English language educator*
Morris, Jerry Dean *academic administrator*
Tuerk, Richard Carl *English language educator*

Corpus Christi
Bateman, John Roger *investment holding company executive*
Berryhill, Henry Lee, Jr. *geologist*
Branscomb, Harvie, Jr. *lawyer*
Canales, Herbert Glenn *librarian*
Cartwright, Charles Nelson *lawyer*
Cole, June Robertson *psychotherapist*
Cutlip, Randall Brower *retired psychologist, former college president*
Doty, James Edward *pastor, psychologist*
Early, William James *education educator*
Furgason, Robert Roy *university official, chemical engineering educator*
Gracida, Rene Henry *bishop*
Gutierrez, Arturo Luis *school system administrator*
Haas, Paul Raymond *petroleum company executive*
Head, Hayden Wilson, Jr. *federal judge*
Heinz, Walter Ernst Edward *retired chemical executive*
†Hext, George D. *airport terminal executive*
†House, David Augusta *newspaper editor*
†Hunter, Todd Ames *lawyer*
McMillen, James Thomas *lawyer*
Paulson, Bernard Arthur *oil company executive, consultant*
Pivonka, Leonard Daniel *priest*
Roels, Oswald Albert *oceanographer, educator, business executive*
Rose, Larry Lee *newspaper executive*
Schmidt, Richard S. *federal judge*
†Sullivan, Stephen Wentworth *publisher*
Turner, Elizabeth Adams Noble (Betty Turner) *former mayor, Chamber of Commerce executive*
Ullberg, Kent Jean *sculptor*
Wood, James Allen *lawyer*
Wooster, Robert *history educator*

Crockett
Gibbs, James Howard *broadcast executive*

Crosby
†Ohsol, Ernest Osborne *consulting chemical engineer*

Crowell
Binnion, John Edward *educator*

Dallas
Ablon, Arnold Norman *accountant*
Abney, Frederick Sherwood *lawyer*
Acker, Rodney *lawyer*
Adamo, Kenneth R. *lawyer*
Adelizzi, Robert Frederick *bank executive*
Adkins, M. Douglas *lawyer*
Agnich, Richard John *lawyer, electronics company executive*
Akin, Henry David *lawyer*
Albers, John Richard *beverage company executive*
Alford, Margaret Suzanne *lawyer*
†Allen, John Carlton *minister*
Allen, Terry Devereux *urologist, educator*
†Anders, John *newspaper columnist*
Anderson, Barbara McComas *lawyer*
Anderson, E. Karl *lawyer*
Anderson, Jack Roy *health care company executive*
Anderson, Robert Theodore *music educator, organist*
Anderson, Ron Joe *hospital administrator, physician, educator*
Anglin, Michael Williams *lawyer*
†Arbuckle, Scott G. *manufacturing company executive*
Ardoin, John Louis *music editor*
Armour, James Lott *lawyer*
†Arnold, George Lawrence *advertising company executive*
Ash, Mary Kay Wagner *cosmetics company executive*
Aston, James William *banker*
Atkins, Samuel James, III *banker*
Ausere, Joe Morris *food manufacturing company executive*
Babcock, Charles Lynde, IV *lawyer*
†Bach, James A. *food company executive*
Baer, Henry *lawyer*
Baggett, W. Mike *lawyer*
Bahr, Conrad Charles, III *financial management executive, consultant*
†Bailon, Gilbert *newspaper editor*
Baker, Robert Woodward *airline executive*
Barbee, Linton E. *lawyer*
†Barnes, John R. *petroleum company executive*
Barnes, Robert Vertreese, Jr. *masonry contractor executive*
Barrett, Colleen Crotty *airline executive*
Bartlett, Richard C. *cosmetics executive, writer*
Baskin, Leland Burleson *pathologist, educator, researcher*
Beck, Abe Jack *retired business executive, retired air force officer*
Beck, Mary Constance *bank executive*
Beck, Robert Louis *marketing executive, lawyer, foundation executive*
†Bell, Benjamin Clayton, Jr. *public relations executive*
Bell, John Lewis McCulloch *manufacturing executive*
†Benjet, Mervyn *computer company executive*
Berbary, Maurice Shehadeh *physician, military officer, hospital administrator, educator*
Berkeley, Marvin H. *former university dean*
Berry, Buford Preston *lawyer*
†Bersano, Bob *newspaper editor*
Besing, Ray Gilbert *lawyer*
Biegler, David W. *gas company executive*
Birkeland, Bryan Collier *lawyer*
Bishop, Bryan Edwards *lawyer*
Bishop, Gene Herbert *corporate executive*
Blachly, Jack Lee *lawyer*
Blackburn, Charles Lee *oil company executive*
†Blackstone, Kevin *sports columnist*
Blau, Charles William *lawyer, former government official*
Blessen, Karen Alyce *free-lance illustrator, designer*
Blessing, Edward Warfield *petroleum company executive*
Blevins, Gary Lynn *architect, real estate broker, real estate appraiser*
Bliss, Robert Harms *lawyer*
Blomquist, Carl Gunnar *cardiologist*
†Blow, Steve *newspaper columnist*
†Blumenthal, Karen *newspaper editor*
Bolling, Alexander Russell, Jr. *retired military officer, business executive*
Bollon, Arthur Peter *genetic engineer, educator, biotechnology company executive*
Bonesio, Woodrow Michael *lawyer*
Bonney, Samuel Robert *lawyer*
Bonte, Frederick James *radiology educator, physician*
Boone, Michael Mauldin *lawyer*
Boone, Oliver Kiel *lawyer*
Boren, Benjamin N. *lawyer*
†Boyce, Charles A. *oil company executive, lawyer, arbitrator*
Braden, David Rice *architect*
Bradley, John Andrew *hospital management company executive*
Bradshaw, Lillian Moore *retired library director*
Branson, Mary Lou *family therapist, military agency administrator*
Brin, Royal Henry, Jr. *lawyer*
Brister, Bill H. *lawyer, former judge*
Bromberg, Alan Robert *law educator*
Bromberg, Henri Louie, Jr. *lawyer*
Bromberg, John E. *lawyer*
Brooks, E. R. (Dick Brooks) *utility company executive*
Brooks, James Elwood *geologist, educator*
Brown, Benjamin A. *gas, oil industry executive*
Brown, Michael Stuart *geneticist*
†Brown, Stephen Bryan *real estate editor*
†Browne, Richard Harold *statistician, consultant*
Bruene, Warren Benz *electronic engineer*
†Bryant, L. Gerald *health care administrator*
Buchholz, Donald Alden *stock brokerage company executive*
Buchmeyer, Jerry *federal judge*
Bucy, J. Fred *retired electronics company executive*
Budzinsky, Armin Alexander *investment banker*
Bumpas, Stuart Maryman *lawyer*
Burke, William Temple, Jr. *lawyer*
Burns, Scott *columnist*
Burnside, John Wayne *medical educator, university official*
Busbee, Kline Daniel, Jr. *lawyer, public international law educator*
Bux, William John *lawyer*
Byers, Brent Eugene *architect*
Byrd, David Lamar *oral surgeon educator*
Cahill, William Joseph, Jr. *utility company executive*
†Cain, David *state legislator, lawyer*
†Caldwell, Louise Phinney *historical researcher, community volunteer*
Campbell, Donald K. *theological seminary administrator, educator*
†Campbell, Roy E. *diversified company executive*
Campfield, Regis William *law educator*
Carlton, Dean *lawyer*
Carter, Donald *professional basketball team executive*
Carver, John W(illiam), Jr. *hospital administrator*
Casey, Albert Vincent *business policy educator, retired business executive*
†Casey, John T. *medical products executive*
†Castle, John Raymond, Jr. *lawyer*
Cavanagh, Harrison Dwight *ophthalmic surgeon*
Chapman, George C. *lawyer*
Cherryholmes, James Gilbert *construction consultant, real estate agent*
†Clark, C. A. W. *church administrator*
Clements, William Perry, Jr. *former governor, corporate executive*
Cline, Bobby James *insurance company executive*
Cochran, George Calloway, III *retired banker*
Cochran, Kendall Pinney *economics educator*
Coldwell, Philip Edward *financial consultant*
Coleman, Robert Winston *lawyer*
Collins, Michael Homer *lawyer*
Collins, Michael James *investment company executive*
Comini, Alessandra *art historian, educator*
†Compton, Bob *newspaper editor*
Conant, Allah B., Jr. *lawyer*
Cook, Gary Raymond *university president, clergyman*
Copley, Edward Alvin *lawyer*
Copp, Emmanuel Anthony *oil company executive*
†Correu, James M. *newspaper publishing executive*
Costa, Victor Charles *fashion designer*
Costello, John Francis, Jr. (Jack Costello) *lawyer*
†Cott, Burl Gene *transportation company executive*
Countryman, Edward Francis *historian, educator*
Cowart, T(homas) David *lawyer*
Cowling, David Edward *lawyer*
Cox, James William *newspaper executive*
Cox, Rody P(owell) *medical educator, internist*
Crain, Gayla Campbell *lawyer*
Crain, John Walter *historian*
Crandall, Robert Lloyd *airline executive*
†Craycroft, Jack *owner architectural company*
Creany, Cathleen Annette *television station executive*
Creel, Luther Edward, III *lawyer*
Crow, F. Trammell *real estate company executive*
Crowley, James Worthington *lawyer*
Crowson, James Lawrence *lawyer, financial company executive*
Cruikshank, Thomas Henry *energy services and engineering executive*
Cummings, Brian Thomas *public relations company executive*
†Cunyus, George Marvin *oil company executive*
Curran, Geoffrey Michael *lawyer*
Dale, Erwin Randolph *lawyer, author*
Davis, Clarice McDonald *lawyer*
Dean, David Allen *lawyer*
DeBusk, Manuel Conrad *lawyer*
Decherd, Robert William *newspaper and broadcasting executive*
†Dedman, Robert Henry *sales executive*
Demarest, Sylvia M. *lawyer*
Denahan, Joseph Anthony *mining company financial executive*
†DeOre, Bill *editorial cartoonist*
DePaola, Dominick Philip *college president, dean*
Dillard, Robert Lionel, Jr. *lawyer, former life insurance executive*
Dillon, David Anthony *journalist, lecturer*
Dillon, Donald Ward *management consultant*
Doke, Marshall J., Jr. *lawyer*
Domagala, Richard Edward *sales executive*
Dozier, David Charles, Jr. *marketing public relations and advertising executi*
†Dufner, Edward Joseph *newspaper editor*
Durham, Michael Jonathan *transportation company executive*
Dutton, Diana Cheryl *lawyer*
Dyess, Bobby Dale *lawyer*
Dykes, Virginia Chandler *occupational therapist*
Eberhart, Robert Clyde *biomedical engineering educator, researcher*
Eddleman, William Roseman *lawyer*
†Edwards, Carl Elmo, Jr. *lawyer*
Edwards, George Alva *physician, educator*
Edwards, Marvin Earle *superintendent of schools*
Eichenwald, Heinz Felix *physician*
Einspruch, Burton Cyril *psychiatrist*
Emerson, Walter Caruth *artist, educator*
Emery, Herschell Gene *lawyer*
Engleman, Donald James *lawyer*
Enix, Agnes Lucille *editorial consultant*
Ericson, Ruth Ann *psychiatrist*
†Erwin, O. Scott *golf recreational facility executive, consultant*
Esquivel, Agerico Liwag *research physicist*
Estabrook, Ronald Winfield *chemistry educator*
†Estell, Richard J. *insurance company executive*
Estep, Robert Lloyd *lawyer*
Evans, Roger *lawyer*
Everbach, Otto George *lawyer*
Everett, C. Curtis *lawyer*
Fanning, Barry Hedges *lawyer*
Fanning, Robert Allen *lawyer*
Farrington, Jerry *utility holding company executive*
Farris, Louis Anthony, Jr. *banker*
Feiner, Joel S. *psychiatrist*
Feld, Alan David *lawyer*
Feldman, H. Larry *lawyer*
Fennell, Thomas E. *lawyer*
Fenner, Suzan Ellen *lawyer*
Fiddick, Paul William *broadcasting company executive*
Fielder, Charles Robert *oil industry executive*
Finkelstein, William Berndt *lawyer*
Fish, A. Joe *federal judge*
Fisher, Gene Jordan *retired chemical company executive*
Fishman, Edward Marc *lawyer*
Fitzwater, Sidney Allen *federal judge*
Flanagan, Christie Stephen *lawyer*
Flatt, Adrian Ede *surgeon*
Flegle, Jim L. *lawyer*
†Fleming, Jon Hugh *business executive*
Flores, Marion Thomas *advertising executive*
Fogelman, Morris Joseph *physician*
Fontana, Robert Edward *electrical engineering educator, retired air force officer*
Fordtran, John Satterfield *physician*
Fordyce, Edward Winfield, Jr. *lawyer*
Forsythe, Earl Andrew *lawyer, steel company executive*
Fortado, Michael George *lawyer*
Foster, William Edwin (Bill Foster) *nonprofessional basketball coach*
Fowler, Robert Glen *exploration company executive*
Free, Mary Moore *anthropologist*
Freling, Richard Alan *lawyer*
French, Joseph Jordan, Jr. *lawyer*
Frenkel, Eugene Phillip *physician*
Friedheim, Jan V. *education administrator*
Frisbie, Curtis Lynn, Jr. *lawyer*
†Fulton, Duncan Thomas, III *architect*
Gage, John *opera company executive*
Gage, Tommy Wilton *pharmacologist, dentist, pharmacist, educator*
Galecke, Robert Michael *financial company executive*
†Galloway, Randy *newspaper sports columnist*
Galt, John William *actor*
Gandy, Dean Murray *lawyer*
Gant, Norman Ferrell, Jr. *obstetrician-gynecologist*
†Gardiner, John William *insurance company executive*
Garson, Greer *actress*
Geiger, Ken *photojournalist*
†George, Kenneth S. *health facility administration*
Gibbs, James Alanson *geologist*
Gibson, William Edward *banker*
Gifford, Porter William *retired construction materials manufacturing company executive*
Gilbert, Paul H. *engineering executive, consultant*
Gilchrist, Henry *lawyer*
Gill, David Brian *electrical engineer, educator*
Gilleland, Richard A. *health care company executive*
Gillilan, William J, III *construction company executive*
Gilman, Alfred Goodman *pharmacologist, educator*
Gilmore, Jerry Carl *lawyer*
Giordano, Saverio Paul *professional association executive*
Glancy, Walter John *lawyer*
Godfrey, Cullen Michael *lawyer*
Goldberg, Irving Loeb *federal judge*
Goldstein, Joseph Leonard *physician, medical educator, molecular genetics scientist*
Goodell, Sol *retired lawyer*
Goodstein, Barnett Maurice *lawyer*
†Goolsby, Tony *state legislator*
Gores, Christopher Merrel *lawyer*
Goss, James Walter *oil company executive*
Gossen, Emmett Joseph, Jr. *motel chain executive, lawyer*
Goyne, Roderick A. *lawyer*
Grahmann, Charles V. *bishop*
Green, Cecil Howard *consulting geophysicist, educator*
Greenstone, James Lynn *psychotherapist, mediator, consultant, author, educator*
Griffith, Dotty (Dorothy Griffith Stephenson) *journalist, speaker*
Griffith, James William *engineer, consultant*
Grimes, David Lynn *communications company executive*
Grissom, Gerald Homer *lawyer*
Grogan, Timothy James *corporate support executive, retired army officer*
Gump, Richard Anthony *lawyer*
Haas, Samuel Douglas *lawyer*
Haayen, Richard Jan *university official, insurance company executive*
Haddock, Ronald Wayne *oil company executive*
Hafner, Dudley H. *health agency executive*
†Haggar, Edmond Ralph *apparel manufacturing company executive*
Haire, William J. *healthcare executive*
†Halbreich, Jeremy L. *newspaper publishing executive*
†Hall, Cheryl *newspaper editor*
Hamilton, David Lee *retired environmental company executive*
Hamilton, Earle Grady, Jr. *architect*
Hamon, Richard Grady *lawyer*
†Harasta, Cathy Ann *journalist*
Harbin, John Pickens *oil well company executive*
Hardy, Tom Charles, Jr. *medical equipment and insurance claims management executive*
Harper, Harlan, Jr. *lawyer*
Harrington, Marion Ray *ophthalmologist*
†Harris, David, Jr. *minister*
Harris, Leon A., Jr. *writer*
Harris, Lucy Brown *accountant, consultant*
Harrison, Frank *former university president*
Hart, John Clifton *lawyer*
†Hartnett, Will Ford *lawyer*

Hauer, John Longan lawyer
Hauptfuhrer, Robert Paul oil company executive
Hawkins, Jack Wade lawyer
Haworth, Charles Ray lawyer
†Haynes, J. Neauell clergyman, bishop
†Hearne, Carl N. mortgage company executive
†Hegi, Frederick B., Jr. mobile home manufacturing executive
Henkel, Kathryn G. lawyer
Hennessy, Daniel Kraft lawyer
†Herbener, Mark Basil bishop
Hester, Linda Hunt university dean, counselor
Hewett, Arthur Edward real estate developer, lawyer
Hicks, Marion Lawrence, Jr. (Larry Hicks) lawyer, shareholder
Higginbotham, Patrick Errol federal judge
Hill, John Rutledge, Jr. retired construction materials company executive
Hille, Robert Arthur healthcare executive
Hinshaw, Chester John lawyer
Hirl, J. Roger petrochemical company executive
Hirsch, Laurence Eliot business executive, lawyer
Hitt, David Hamilton hospital executive
Hodge, George Lowrance cosmetics company executive
Hoffman, Harold Wayne advertising agency executive
Holmes, Bert Otis E., Jr. retired newspaperman
Horchow, S(amuel) Roger theater producer
Horton, Paul Bradfield lawyer
Howie, John Robert lawyer
Howland, Grafton Dulany financial counselor
Hudnall, David Harrison financial executive
†Hudson, C. B., Jr. insurance company executive
†Hudspeth, Albert James biomedical researcher, educator
Huey, Ward L(igon), Jr. media executive
Huffman, Gregory Scott Combest lawyer
Hughes, Joe Kenneth retired beverage company executive
†Hughes, L. Keith lawyer
Hughes, Vester Thomas, Jr. lawyer
Humann, Walter Johann corporation executive
Hunt, David Ford lawyer
†Hunt, Ray Lee petroleum company executive
Hunter, Kermit Houston writer, former university dean
Hunter, Robert Grams English language educator
Hurst, John L., III (Jack Hurst) chemical company executive
†Ibach, Robert Daniel, Jr. library director
Irwin, Ivan, Jr. lawyer
Jackson, Phillip Ellis lobbyist, consultant
†Jacobson, Gary newspaper business editor
Jeffett, Frank Asbury former oil company and insurance company executive, business consultant
†Jenkins, Chester P. religious organization, church administration
†Jenkins, James Michael restaurant company executive
Jenkins, M. T. Pepper anesthesiologist, educator
Jobe, Larry Alton business executive
†Johnson, Jerry D. lawyer
Johnson, Judith Kay lawyer
Johnson, Richard Clayton engineer, physicist
Johnson, Richard Craig lawyer
Jones, Dale P. service company executive
Jones, James Fleming, Jr. Romance language educator, university administrator
Jones, Philip Davis computer service publishing consultant
Joplin, Julian Mike lawyer
Jordan, Karen Leigh travel editor
Jordan, Robert W. lawyer
Jordan, William Davis lawyer
Junkins, Jerry R. electronics company executive
Kaplan, Norman Mayer medical educator
Keiffer, Edwin Gene electronics industry company executive
†Keiser, R. L. gas and oil industry executive
†Keith, Carter O. advertising company executive
Keithley, Bradford Gene lawyer
Kelleher, Herbert David airline executive, lawyer
Kemp, Harris Atteridge architect
Kemper, Robert Van anthropologist, educator
Kendall, Joe federal judge
Kennedy, Marc J. lawyer
Kent, David Charles lawyer
†Kessler, Tom newspaper editor
Khan, Amanullah physician
Kilby, Jack St. Clair electrical engineer
Kinnebrew, Jackson Metcalfe lawyer
Kluge, John Werner broadcasting and advertising executive
Kneipper, Richard Keith lawyer
†Knowles, True H. food products executive
Kolb, Nathaniel Key, Jr. architect
Konrad, Dusan chemist
†Korba, Robert W. communications executive
Korman, Ira Bruce health care consultant, advisor
Kramer, Robert Ivan pediatrician
Kutner, Janet art critic, book reviewer
Lacy, John Ford lawyer
Lafving, Brian Douglas lawyer
La Jone, Jay Allen lawyer
Lan, Donald Paul, Jr. lawyer
Lancaster, John Lynch, III lawyer
Lancaster, Sally Rhodus philathropy consultant
Landers, James Michael (Jim) international editor
Landry, Jane Lorenz architect
Landry, Tom (Thomas Wade Landry) former professional football coach
Lane, Alvin Huey, Jr. management consultant
Lane, Marvin Maskall, Jr. electronics company executive
Lang, Douglas Steward lawyer
Langer, Ralph Ernest journalist
Lang-Miers, Elizabeth Ann lawyer
Langston, Roy A. insurance company consultant
Lawson, Andrew Lowell, Jr. defense industry company executive
Lee, George Terry, Jr. lawyer
†Lee, J. E. bishop
Lee, Sidney Phillip chemical engineer, state senator
†Leedom, John Nesbett distribution company executive, state senator
Lerner, Alan Burton financial service executive, lawyer
Levenson, Stanley Richard public relations and advertising executive
Levin, Richard C. lawyer
Levine, Harold lawyer
Lewis, Jerry M. psychiatrist, educator
†Lewis, John P. bank executive
†Leyden, Edward E. secondary school principal
Lifson, Kalman Alan management consultant, retail executive
Lites, James professional hockey team executive
Little, Jack Merville lawyer
†Livingston, Grover D. newspaper publishing executive
Lomax, John H. financial service company executive
Lombard, Richard Spencer lawyer
Longyear, Russell Hammond retail executive
Low, Paul M. mortgage banking executive, food service executive
Lowell, Cym Hawksworth lawyer
Lowenberg, Michael lawyer
Luce, Thomas Warren, III former chief justice, lawyer
Lundy, Victor Alfred architect, educator
†Lysaught, Thomas Francis publishing company executive
MacMahon, Paul advertising executive
Maddrey, Willis Crocker medical educator, internist, academic administrator, consultant, researcher
Maguire, Cary McIlwaine oil company executive
Mahr, George Joseph, Jr. financial service executive, real estate developer
Maloney, Robert B. federal judge
Mankoff, Ronald Morton lawyer
Mantle, Mickey Charles former baseball player, marketing consultant
Margerison, Richard Wayne diversified industrial company executive
Maris, Stephen S. lawyer, educator
Marshall, Harold D. leasing and financial services company executive
Marshall, Schuyler Bailey, IV lawyer
Martin, Mark lawyer
Martin, Richard Kelley lawyer
Mason, Barry Jean retired banker
Massman, Richard Allan lawyer
Matthews, Clark J(io), II retail executive, lawyer
Maycock, Ian David oil executive
Mays, Gerald Avery (Jerry Mays) engineering executive, consultant
McAlester, Arcie Lee, Jr. geologist, educator
Mc Cann, Samuel McDonald physiologist, educator
Mc Clelland, Robert Nelson surgeon, educator
McClure, Frederick Donald investment banker, lawyer
McCord, William Charles retired diversified energy company executive
McCormack, William Arthur lawyer
McCormick, James Clarence business consultant
McCormick, James Edward oil company executive
McCullough, George Bierce oil company executive
†McCune, M. Davis architect
Mc Elhaney, John Hess lawyer
McElvain, David Plowman manufacturing company financial executive
McGaw, Kenneth Roy wholesale distribution executive
McGowan, Patrick Francis lawyer
McGregor, Martin Luther, Jr. lawyer
McKnight, Joseph Webb law educator, historian
McLain, Maurice Clayton lawyer, real estate executive
McLane, David Glenn lawyer
Mc Lemore, Robert Henry petroleum engineer, consultant
McNamara, Lawrence John lawyer
McNamara, Martin Burr lawyer, oil and gas company executive
Mc Quillan, Joseph Michael finance company executive
†McTeer, Robert D. bank executive
McWilliams, Mike C. lawyer
Mears, Rona Robbins lawyer
Mebus, Robert Gwynne lawyer
Meek, Paul Derald oil and chemical company executive
Menges, John Kenneth, Jr. lawyer
Meyer, Richard Jonah broadcast executive, consultant
Middleton, Linda Jean Greathouse lawyer
Mighell, Kenneth John lawyer
Miller, Kirk attorney
Miller, William science administrator
Mills, Jerry Woodrow lawyer
Modano, Michael professional hockey player
Moneypenny, Edward William oil and gas mining executive
Mong, Robert William, Jr. managing editor
Monsees, James Eugene engineering executive, consultant
Montgomery, Edward Benjamin physicist, retired educator
Montoya, Regina T. lawyer, government official
Moore, Stanley Ray lawyer
Moore, Thomas Joseph financial company executive
Morgan, Larry Ronald minister
Morgan, Steven Michael lawyer
Morris, Rebecca Robinson lawyer
†Morrison, Lionel B. architect
Mow, Robert Henry, Jr. lawyer
Mullin, Francis Isaac beverage company executive
Mullinax, Otto B. lawyer
Murad, John Louis occupational safety and health consultant
Murphy, John Carter economics educator
Murphy, John Joseph manufacturing company executive
Musa, Samuel Albert electronics company executive
Nash, Michaux, Jr. banker
Neaves, William Barlow cell biologist, educator
†Nelson, Steven Douglas lawyer
New, William Neil physician, retired naval officer
Nichols, Henry Louis lawyer
Nordlund, William Chalmers lawyer
Norgard, Michael Vincent microbiology educator, researcher
Notestine, Wilbur Edmund energy company executive, lawyer
Nurenberg, David oil company executive
Nye, Erle Allen utilities executive, lawyer
O'Leary, Robert W. hospital operations company executive
Osborne, Burl newspaper publisher, editor
Palmer, Ronald Leigh lawyer
Parker, Angelo Pan lawyer
†Parker, Barry James Charles retail executive
Parker, Emily Ann lawyer
Pastine, Maureen Diane librarian
Patterson, Joseph Redwine lawyer
Patterson, Ronald Paul publishing company executive, clergyman
Paul, M(alcolm) Lee psychology educator
Pearce, Ronald retired cosmetic company executive
†Peckham, Barry newspaper publishing executive
†Pederson, Rena newspaper editor
Pell, Jonathan Laurence artistic administrator
Penegar, Kenneth Lawing law educator
Perot, H. Ross investments and real estate group executive, data processing services company executive
Perry, Kenneth Walter integrated oil company executive
Peterson, Edward Adrian lawyer
Pettey, Walter Graves, III lawyer
Petty, Charles Sutherland pathologist
Pew, John Glenn, Jr. lawyer
Phelan, Robin Eric lawyer
Philipson, Herman Louis, Jr. investment banker
†Phillips, Billy Byron distribution executive, electronics executive
Pickens, Thomas Boone, Jr. oil company executive
Pike, Kenneth Lee linguist, educator
Pingree, Bruce Douglas lawyer
Pistor, Charles Herman, Jr. former banker, academic administrator
Pleasant, James Scott lawyer
†Pogue, Mack real estate company executive
Portman, Glenn Arthur lawyer
Powell, Boone, Jr. hospital administrator
Powell, Larry Randall columnist
Powell, Michael Vance lawyer
Pratt, Edward Taylor, Jr. real estate company executive
†Price, Don Herbert architect
Price, John Aley lawyer
Price, J(ohn) William paper industry executive
Price, Robert Eben judge
Pride, Charley singer
Pritzker, Leon statistician, consultant
Profusek, Robert Alan lawyer
†Prude, Elaine S. principal
Pryor, Richard Walter telecommunications executive, retired air force officer
Purnell, Maurice Eugene, Jr. lawyer
Rabin, Stanley Arthur metal products manufacturer
Race, George Justice pathology educator
Radford, Norman DePue, Jr. lawyer
Raggio, Kenneth Gaylord lawyer
Raggio, Louise Ballerstedt lawyer
Ram, Chitta Venkata physician
Ray, Bradley Stephen petroleum geologist
Ray, George Einar lawyer
Reagan, Barbara Benton economics educator
Reid, Langhorne, III merchant banker
Revell, Oliver Burgan government official
Rice, Darrel Alan lawyer
Richardi, Ralph Leonard airline executive
Richards, Jeanne Herron artist
Ries, Edward Richard petroleum geologist, consultant
Riggs, Arthur Jordy retired lawyer
Riggs, Leonard, II emergency medicine physician, emergency care services executive
Ringle, Brett Adelbert lawyer
Ritchie, Robert Field lawyer
Rivera, Richard E. food products executive
†Robbins, Frank Ernest linguistics educator, administrator
Robbins, Ray Charles manufacturing company executive
Roberts, Harry Morris, Jr. lawyer
Robertson, Beverly Carruth steel company executive
Robertson, Ted Zanderson judge
Robinson, Hugh Granville real estate development company executive
Robinson, Lawrence Dewitt lawyer
Rochon, John Philip cosmetics company executive
Rodgers, John Hunter lawyer
†Roeser, Ross Joseph audiologist, educator
†Roger, Richard R. personal care industry executive
Rogers, Ralph B. industrial business executive
Rogers, Richard Raymond cosmetics company executive
†Rone, B. J. financial executive
Rosenberg, David Howard lawyer, mediator, marketing executive
Rosenberg, Roger Newman neurologist, educator
†Rosenstein, Ira M. beverage products executive
Rosson, Glenn Richard building products and furniture company executive
Rouse, Eloise Meadows foundation executive
†Roy, Clarence Leslie landscape architect
Rubottom, Roy Richard, Jr. retired diplomat and educator, consultant
Russell, S. G., III (Jacky Russell) principal
†Rutherford, Howard Don marketing executive
St. Claire, Frank Arthur lawyer
St. James, Lyn business owner, professional race car driver
St. John, Bill Dean diversified equipment and services company executive
St. John, Bob journalist, columnist, author
Salazar, Ramiro S. library administrator
†Salvaggio, Tony Joe banker
Sanders, Harold Barefoot, Jr. federal judge
Sanford, Jay Philip physician, government official
Savage, Scott David broadcast executive
Savage, Wallace Hamilton lawyer
Schmieder, Frank Joseph banker, business executive
Schoenbrun, Larry Lynn lawyer
Schreiber, Sally Ann lawyer
Schwartz, Irving Donn architect
†Schwartz, Marilyn columnist
†Scott, Manuel church administrator
See, Robert Fleming, Jr. lawyer
Seldin, Donald Wayne physician, educator
Sewell, James Leslie engineering company executive
Shapiro, Robert Alan retail executive
Sheeder, Robert Elwood lawyer
Sheehan, James Patrick media company executive
Sheinberg, Israel computer company executive
†Sherrod, Blackie newspaper sports columnist
Shimer, Daniel Lewis corporate executive
Short, David Gaines food company executive
Shoup, Andrew James, Jr. oil company executive
Shower, Robert Wesley financial executive
Siegel, Thomas Louis lawyer
†Siegfried, Tom newspaper editor
Simmons, Harold C. sugar company executive
†Simmons, James F. textiles executive
Sizer, Phillip Spelman consultant, retired oil field services executive
Slater, Oliver Eugene bishop
Smith, Cece venture capitalist
Smith, David Lee newspaper editor
Smith, Edwin Ide pediatric surgeon
Smith, Russell L. film critic
Smith, Sue Frances newspaper editor
Smith, William Randolph (Randy Smith) health care management association executive
†Snetzer, Michael Alan multi-industry executive
†Snyder, Leslie newspaper editor
Snyder, William D. photojournalist
Solender, Robert Lawrence financial and real estate corporation officer
Solis, Jorge Antonio federal judge
†Solomon, William Tarver general construction company executive
Sonju, Norm Arnold professional sports team manager, executive
Sparkman, Robert Satterfield retired surgeon, educator
Spiegel, Lawrence Howard advertising executive
Sprague, Charles Cameron medical foundation president
†Srere, Paul A. biochemist, educator
†Stacy, Dennis William architect
Stalcup, Joe Alan lawyer, clergyman
†Starks, Richard newspaper publishing executive
Staubach, Roger Thomas real estate executive, former professional football player
Steinberg, Lawrence Edward lawyer
Steinhart, Ronald G. banker
Stembridge, Vernie A(lbert) pathologist, educator
Steorts, Nancy Harvey international management consultant
Stewart, Robert H., III banker
Stilwell, John Quincy lawyer
Stockard, James Alfred lawyer
Stone, Marvin Jules immunologist, physician, educator
Storey, Charles Porter lawyer
Strange, Donald Ernest health care company executive
Strauss, Robert Schwarz lawyer, former ambassador
Stuart, Lawrence David, Jr. lawyer
†Stuart, Norton Arlington, Jr. data processing manufacturing executive
†Sturns, Vernell airport terminal executive
Sudbury, David Marshall corporate lawyer
†Sudduth, William McLean museum director
Swanson, Wallace Martin lawyer
Swinton, Gwendolyn Delores secondary education educator
Taylor, Ramona Garrett financial services company executive
Tedford, William Howard, Jr. psychologist
Terry, Marshall Northway, Jr. English language educator, author
Thau, William Albert, Jr. lawyer
Thomas, Robert Lee financial services company executive, consultant
Thompson, Jesse Eldon vascular surgeon
Thorson, Marcelyn Marie applied art educator
Thrash, Purvis James, Sr. retired oil field equipment and service company executive
†Thurston, Stephen John pastor
Trevino, Lee Buck professional golfer
True, Roy Joe lawyer
Tubb, James Clarence lawyer
Tucker, Laurey Dan lawyer
Turley, Windle lawyer
†Turpin, Jack A. electronics executive
Tygrett, Howard Volney, Jr. lawyer
Valentine, Foy Dan clergyman
Vanatta, John Crothers, III physiologist, physician, educator
Vanderveld, John, Jr. waste disposal company executive
Veach, Robert Raymond, Jr. lawyer
Vergne-Marini, Pedro Juan physician
Vetter, James George, Jr. lawyer
†Vitetta, Ellen S. microbiologist educator, immunologist
Vogel, Donald Stanley gallery executive, artist
Walkowiak, Vincent Steven lawyer
Wall, Sidney Smith Roderick, Jr. architectural firm executive, architect, consultant
Wallace, William C. airline executive
Wallace, William Ray fabricated steel manufacturing company executive
Wallenstein, James Harry lawyer
Walvoord, John Flipse seminary president, chancellor, theologian
Warren, Kelcy L. engineering executive
Watson, Jim Albert lawyer
Webb, Lance bishop
Weber, William P. electronics company executive
Weekley, Frederick Clay, Jr. lawyer
†Weeks, Jerome C. writer, drama critic
Weiland, Stephen Cass lawyer
Welch, Carol Ann oil company executive
Wenrich, John William college president
Werner, Seth Mitchell advertising executive
West, William Beverley, III lawyer
White, James Richard lawyer
Whitman, Reginald Norman railroad official
Whitson, James Norfleet, Jr. diversified company executive
Wilber, Robert Edwin corporate executive
Wildenthal, C(laud) Kern physician, educator
Wiles, Charles Preston minister
Wilhelm, Walter Tinkham software systems company executive
Willey, Paul Wayne financial executive
†Williams, David Kendall architect
†Williams, Gordon L. aircraft manufacturing executive
Williams, James Alexander lawyer
Williams, Martha Spring psychologist
Williams, Thomas (Jack Williams) finance company executive
Willingham, Clark Suttles lawyer
†Willrich, Mason utility company executive
Wilson, Claude Raymond, Jr. lawyer
Wilson, Jean Donald endocrinologist, educator
†Wilson, Lawrence Alexander construction company executive
†Wilson, Trisha interior architectural designer
Winkel, Judy Kay lawyer
Winn, Edward Burton lawyer
Winters, J. Otis industry consultant
Wise, Marvin Jay lawyer
Witmer, John Albert librarian
†Wuntch, Philip Samuels journalist, film critic
Wyly, Charles Joseph, Jr. corporate executive
Yanagisawa, Samuel Tsuguo electronics executive
Young, Barney Thornton lawyer
†Young, Norma artistic director
Ziebarth, Karl Rex international transportation consultant
Ziff, Morris internist, rheumatologist, educator
Zimmerman, S(amuel) Mort(on) electrical and electronics engineering executive
Zisman, Barry Stuart lawyer
Zumwalt, Richard Dowling flour mill executive

Del Valle
Browne, Jackson singer, songwriter

Denison
Farr, Reeta Rae special education administrator

Denton
Berry, Joe Wilkes *academic administrator, English educator*
Brock, Horace Rhea *accounting educator*
Brown, John Fred *steel company executive*
Brownell, Blaine Allison *university administrator, history educator*
Clogan, Paul Maurice *English language and literature educator*
†Elder, Mark Lee *university research administrator, writer*
Golden, David Edward *physicist*
Grose, B. Donald *library administrator*
Hurley, Alfred Francis *university administrator, historian*
Kamman, William *historian, educator*
Kesterson, David Bert *English language educator*
Latham, William Peters *composer, former educator*
Lawhon, John E., III *lawyer, former county official*
†Leslie, Marvin Earl *minister*
Miller, Tom Polk *architect*
Nichols, Irby Coghill, Jr. *historian, educator, entrepreneur*
Palermo, Judy Hancock *art educator*
Preston, Thomas Ronald *English language educator, researcher*
Redding, Rogers Walker *physics educator*
Renka, Robert Joseph *computer science educator, consultant*
Rhoades, Warren A., Jr. *retired mechanical engineer*
Schwalm, Fritz Ekkehardt *biology educator*
Snapp, Elizabeth *librarian, educator*
Swigger, B. Keith *dean*
Thompson, Leslie Melvin *college dean, educator*
Toulouse, Robert Bartell *retired college administrator*
Vaughn, William Preston *historian, educator*
Westmoreland, Reginald Conway *journalism educator*

DFW Airport
Lowden, Scott Richard *lawyer*

Diboll
Grum, Clifford J. *manufacturing company executive*

Dripping Springs
Ballard, Mary Melinda *financial communications and investment banking firm executive*
Rios, Evelyn Deerwester *columnist, musician, artist, writer*

Eden
Boyd, John Hamilton *osteopath*

Edinburg
Esparza, Thomas, Sr. *academic athletics administrator*
Mulhern, John David *former academic dean, educator*
Nance, Betty Love *librarian*
Vassberg, David Erland *history educator*

El Paso
Bailey, Kenneth Kyle *history educator*
Bernau, Simon John *mathematics educator*
Bruhn, John Glyndon *university official, educator*
Carroll, Edwin Winford *architect*
Cassidy, Richard Thomas *hotel executive, defense industry consultant, retired army officer*
Coleman, Edmund Benedict *university dean*
Coleman, Howard S. *engineer, physicist*
Cook, Clarence Sharp *physics educator*
Crossen, John Jacob *radiologist, educator*
Day, James Milton *foundation executive, English educator*
Feuille, Richard Harlan *lawyer*
Francis, Larry *mayor*
Friedkin, Joseph Frank *consulting engineering executive*
†Fry, L(eo) Marcus, Jr. *hospital administrator*
Grieves, Robert Belanger *engineering educator*
Hardaway, Robert Morris, III *physician, educator, retired army officer*
Heger, Herbert Krueger *education educator*
†Henry, Samuel Lawrence *financial executive*
Himelstein, Peggy Donn *psychologist*
Hoskins, Curtis Lynn *utility executive*
Hudspeth, Harry Lee *federal judge*
Ingle, Henry Thomas *university official*
Jesurún, Harold Méndez *obstetrician-gynecologist, educator*
Jurey, Wes *chamber of commmerce executive*
Kidd, Gerald Steele, II *endocrinologist, educator*
†Kimmel, Herbert David *psychology educator*
Leach, Joseph Lee *English language educator, author*
Marshall, Richard Treeger *lawyer*
Mitchell, Paula Rae *nursing educator*
Natalicio, Diana Siedhoff *university president*
Ornstein-Galicia, Jacob Leonard (Jack Ornstein-Galicia) *foreign language educator, linguist, author*
Pena, Raymundo Joseph *bishop*
Riter, Stephen *university dean, electrical engineer*
Roberts, Ernst Edward *marketing consultant*
Ruesch, Janet Carol *federal judge*
Schmidt, L. Lee, Jr. *university official*
Schnadig, Edgar Louis *entrepreneur, management consultant*
Shapiro, Stephen Richard *retired air force officer, physician*
Smith, Tad Randolph *lawyer*
Stoddard, Ellwyn R. *sociology and anthropology educator*
Tackett, Stephen Douglas *education services specialist*
Treadwell, Hugh Wilson *publishing executive*
von Tungeln, George Robert *retired university administrator, economics consultant*
Wise, William Allan *oil company executive, lawyer*

Euless
†Draper, James Thomas (Jimmy Draper) *clergyman*
Paran, Mark Lloyd *lawyer*

Floresville
Alexander, William Carter *physiologist, educator*
Alvarez, Olga M. *elementary education educator*

Flower Mound
Gooch, Brian Eugene *health care executive, policy analyst, consultant*
Kolodny, Stanley Charles *oral surgeon, air force officer*
†Morrish, Thomas Jay *golf course architect*

Forney
Cates, Don Tate *mayor, lawyer*

Fort Hood
†Hughes, William Foster *career officer, surgeon, obstetrician, gynecologist*

Fort Sam Houston
Pruitt, Basil Arthur, Jr. *surgeon, army officer*

Fort Worth
Allmand, Linda F(aith) *library director*
Anderson, John Quentin *rail transportation executive*
Appel, Bernard Sidney *electrical company executive*
Ard, Harold Jacob *library administrator*
Arena, M. Scott *pharmaceutical company executive*
Auping, Michael G. *curator*
Bass, Perry Richardson *oil company executive*
Battista, Orlando Aloysius *scientist, author, executive, inventor*
Belew, David Owen, Jr. *judge*
Berg, Ericson *insurance company executive*
Bolen, Bob *retail merchant, university administrator*
Bousquette, William Charles *financial executive*
Brosseau, Charles Martin, Jr. *hospital administrator*
Brown, C. Harold *lawyer*
Brown, Richard Lee *lawyer*
Buckley, Betty Bob *journalist, consultant*
Burroughs, Jack Eugene *ceramic engineering executive*
†Calkins, Loren Gene *church executive, clergyman*
Carrico, Fred Allen *aircraft manufacturing company executive*
Chalk, John Allen *lawyer*
Clark, Emory Eugene *financial planning executive*
Cliburn, Van (Harvey Lavan Cliburn, Jr.) *concert pianist*
Connor, Richard L. *publisher, editor*
Crane, Neal Dahlberg *manufacturing company executive*
Cunningham, Atlee Marion, Jr. *aeronautical engineer*
†Cunningham, Raymond Clement *glass company executive*
Dagnon, James Bernard *human resources executive*
Davis, Jimmie Dan *newspaper editor*
Dean, Beale *lawyer*
Dean, Margo *artistic director*
Dees, Sandra Kay Martin *psychologist, research consultant*
Delaney, Joseph P. *bishop*
de Tonnancour, Paul Roger Godefroy *library administrator*
Diwoky, Roy John *petroleum executive*
Dominiak, Geraldine Florence *accounting educator*
Doran, Robert Stuart *mathematician, educator*
Doris Ann, (Doris Ann Scharfenberg) *producer, former broadcasting company executive*
Erisman, Fred Raymond *English literature educator*
Franks, Jon Michael *lawyer*
Gearhart, Marvin *oil company executive*
Geren, Preston Murdoch, Jr. *architect, engineer*
†Gideon, Randall Clifton *architectural firm executive*
Gilbert, James Cayce *minister*
Ginsburg, Marcus *lawyer*
Giordano, John Read *conductor*
Granger, Kay *mayor*
Greenhill, William Duke *lawyer*
Greenwood, William E. *rail transportation executive*
Grinstein, Gerald *transportation executive*
Gross, John Birney *retired minister*
Gutsche, Carl David *chemistry educator*
Herlihy, James Edward *retail executive*
Hill, Mark C. *lawyer*
Hogan, Ben *golfer, business executive*
Hurley, Linda Kay *psychologist*
Hyde, Clarence Brodie, II *oil company executive*
Jensen, Harlan Ellsworth *veterinarian, educator*
Jurgensen, Warren Peter *psychiatrist, educator*
Kelly, Dee J. *lawyer*
Kenderdine, John Marshall *petroleum engineer, retired army officer*
†Kent, D. Randall, Jr. *engineering company executive*
Landolt, Robert George *chemistry educator*
Law, Thomas Hart *lawyer*
Lawrence, Teleté Zorayda *speech and voice pathologist, educator*
Leone, George Frank *pharmaceutical executive*
†Lesok, Eddie Monroe *lawyer*
Lorenzetti, Ole John *pharmaceutical research executive, ophthalmic research and development executive*
Mack, Theodore *lawyer*
Malone, Dan F. *journalist*
Martin, Harold Eugene *publishing executive, consultant*
McBryde, John Henry *federal judge*
McConnell, Michael Arthur *lawyer*
Mc Kinney, James Carroll *baritone, educator*
†McMillen, Howard Lawrence *municipal government official*
McWhiney, Grady *history educator*
Means, Terry Robert *federal judge*
Michero, William Henderson *retired retail trade executive*
†Miller, Brian Keith *airline executive*
Minton, Jerry Davis *lawyer, former banker*
†Mowery, Anna Renshaw *state legislator*
Muhlert, Jan Keene *art museum director*
Munn, Cecil Edwin *lawyer*
Newport, John Paul *philosophy of religion educator, former academic administrator*
Newsom, Douglas Ann Johnson *writer, journalism educator*
Nichols, James Richard *civil engineer, consultant*
Nichols, Robert Leighton *civil engineer*
†Nourse, Robert E. M. *consumer products company executive*
†Otto, Donald R. *museum director*
Painter, Henry *museum director*
†Peipert, James Raymond *journalist*
Peters, Lawrence H. *management educator, consultant*
†Philpot, Marion Timothy *healthcare executive*
†Pillsbury, Edmund Pennington *museum director*
†Pope, Clarence Cullam, Jr. *bishop*
†Price, Debbie M. *journalist, newspaper editor*
Price, Larry C. *photojournalist*
†Price, Michael Howard *journalist, critic, cartoonist*
Quarles, Carroll Adair, Jr. *physicist, educator*
Ratliff, William Durrah, Jr. *lawyer*
†Ravel, Dilip N. *pharmaceutical executive*
Ray, Paul Richard, Jr. *executive search consultant*
Record, Phillip Julius *newspaper executive*
Reinecke, Manfred G. *chemistry educator*
Reuter, Frank Theodore *history educator*
†Rivera, Angel (Andy) Manuel *retired career officer, city official*
Roach, John Vinson, II *retail company executive*
Roberts, Leonard H. *retail executive*
†Saenz, Michael *college president*
Salih, Halil Ibrahim *political science educator*
Scearse, Patricia Dotson *nurse educator, college dean*
†Schollmaier, Edgar H. *pharmaceutical products company executive*
Shosid, Joseph Lewis *government official*
Smith, William Burton *chemist, educator*
†Stout, Edward L., Jr. *diversified corporation executive*
Suggs, Marion Jack *minister, college dean*
Tade, George Thomas *university dean*
Teegarden, Kenneth Leroy *clergyman*
Thornton, Charles Victor *metals executive*
Tinsley, Jackson Bennett *newspaper editor*
Trimble, Wanda Nell *special education educator*
Tucker, William Edward *university chancellor, clergyman*
Turner, Loyd Leonard *advertising executive, public relations executive*
Walsh, F. Howard *oil producer, rancher*
Webb, Theodore Stratton, Jr. *aerospace executive, consultant*
Wertz, Spencer K. *philosophy educator*
Wheaton, David Joe *aerospace manufacturing company executive*
†Willis, Doyle *lawyer, state legislator*
Winn, Herschel Clyde *retail electronics company executive*
Worcester, Donald Emmet *history educator, author*
Yarbro, James Wesley *financial executive*
Zimmerman, Bill J. *oil company executive, lawyer*

Galveston
†Arens, James F. *anesthesiologist, educator*
Bailey, Byron James *otolaryngologist, medical association executive*
Baker, Robert Ernest, Jr. *foundation executive*
Baron, Samuel *microbiologist, physician*
Barratt, Ernest Stoelting *psychologist, educator*
Bircher, Edgar Allen *lawyer*
Bonchev, Danail Georgiev *chemist, educator*
Budelmann, Bernd Ulrich *zoologist, educator*
Burns, Chester Ray *medical history educator*
Caldwell, Garnett Ernest *lawyer*
Calverley, John Robert *physician, educator*
Carrier, Warren Pendleton *retired university chancellor, writer*
Clay, Orson C. *insurance company executive*
Clayton, William Howard *retired university president*
Cooper, Cary W(ayne) *pharmacology educator*
Daeschner, Charles William, Jr. *physician, educator*
Dawson, Earl Bliss *obstetrics and gynecology educator*
Ewing, George H. *pipeline company executive*
Fisher, Seymour *psychologist, educator*
Giam, Choo-Seng *marine science educator*
Gibson, Hugh *federal judge*
Goodwin, Jean McClung *psychiatrist*
†Grant, J(ohn) Andrew, Jr. *medical educator, allergist*
†Herndon, David N. *surgeon*
Hilton, James Gorton *pharmacologist*
James, Thomas Naum *cardiologist, educator*
Kent, Samuel B. *federal judge*
Kurosky, Alexander *biochemist, educator*
Lefeber, Edward James, Sr. *physician*
Levin, William Cohn *hematologist, former university president*
McLeod, E. Douglas *real estate developer, lawyer*
Merrell, William John, Jr. *oceanography educator*
Norman, Dudley Kent *hospital administrator, nurse*
Ogra, Pearay L. *physician, educator*
Otis, John James *civil engineer*
†Phillips, Linda Goluch *plastic surgeon, educator, researcher*
Powell, Don Watson *medical educator, physiology researcher*
Powell, Leslie Charles, Jr. *obstetrics and gynecology educator*
Prakash, Satya *biology educator*
Sandstead, Harold Hilton *medical educator*
Santschi, Peter Hans *marine sciences educator*
Schreiber, Melvyn Hirsh *radiologist*
Schwartz, Aaron Robert *lawyer, former state legislator*
Seinsheimer, Joseph Fellman, Jr. *insurance executive*
Sheppard, Louis Clarke *biomedical engineer, educator*
Smith, David English *physician, educator*
Smith, Edgar Benton *physician*
Smith, Jerome Hazen *pathologist*
Thompson, Edward Ivins Brad *biological chemistry and genetics educator, molecular endocrinologist, department chairman*
Thompson, James Charles *surgeon*
Tyson, Kenneth Robert Thomas *surgeon, educator*
Weigel, Paul Henry *biochemistry educator, researcher, consultant*
Welch, Ronald J. *actuary*
Willis, William Darrell, Jr. *neurophysiologist, educator*
Würsig, Bernd Gerhard *marine biology educator*
Yielding, K. Lemone *physician*

Garland
Adams, Christopher Steve, Jr. *defense electronics corporation executive, former air force officer*
†Driver, Joe L. *insurance consultant*
McGill, Maurice Leon *financial executive*
McGrath, James Thomas *real estate investment company executive*
Wagers, Robert Shelby *engineering director*

Gary
†Speer, James *religious organization administrator*

Georgetown
Browning, Grayson Douglas *philosophy educator*
Davis, O. L., Jr. *education educator, researcher*
Du Bar, Jules Ramon *geologist, retired educator*
†Gerding, Thomas Graham *medical products company executive*
Girvin, Eb Carl *biology educator*
Lord, William Grogan *financial holding company executive*
Neville, Gwen Kennedy *anthropology educator*
Rosenthal, Michael Ross *academic administrator, dean*
Shilling, Roy Bryant, Jr. *college president*
Weyrauch, Paul Turney *retired army officer*

Granbury
Killebrew, James Robert *architectural engineering firm executive*
McWilliams, Chris Pater Elissa *social studies educator*
Scogin, Martha Aduddell *counselor*
Wisler, Charles Clifton, Jr. *retired cotton oil company executive*

Grand Prairie
Busse, Lu Ann *audiologist*
†Childs, Hymen *broadcasting corporation executive*
†Ritterhouse, Kathy Lee *librarian*
Scott, Dorothy Elaine *elementary education educator*
Wietholter, William James *automotive parts manufacturing company executive*

Granger
Horton, Claude Wendell *physicist, educator*

Grapevine
Holley, Cyrus Helmer *management consulting service executive*
Smith, Lee Herman *business executive*

Greenville
Johnston, John Thomas *engineering executive*

Hale Center
Courtney, Carolyn Ann *school librarian*
†Laney, James Earl *state representative, speaker of the house, farmer*

Hallettsville
Baber, Wilbur H., Jr. *lawyer*

Harlingen
Ephraim, Charles *lawyer*
Farris, Robert Gene *transportation company executive*
Johnson, Orrin Wendell *lawyer*
†Solis, Jim *lawyer, state legislator*

Heath
Kolodey, Fred James *lawyer*

Hemphill
Boren, Hollis Grady *retired physician*

Henderson
†Sadler, Paul Lindsey *lawyer, state legislator*

Hillsboro
Auvenshine, William R. *academic administrator*

Hollywood Park
Rosencrans, Evan William *retired air force officer*

Horseshoe Bay
Lesikar, Raymond Vincent *business administration educator*
Ramey, James Melton *chemist*

Houston
†Ablott, Vance Randall *science foundation administrator*
Adair, Red (Paul Neal Adair) *oil well problem control specialist*
Addison, Linda Leuchter *lawyer*
Adelman, Graham Lewis *lawyer*
†Aguilar, Melissa Ward *newspaper editor*
Ahart, Jan Fredrick *electrical manufacturing company executive*
Akers, William Walter *chemical engineering educator*
Albrecht, Kay Montgomery *primary school educator, consultant, child advocate*
Alderman, Richard Mark *legal educator, lawyer, television and radio commentator*
Alexander, Michael Lee *music educator, cellist*
Alexander, Neil Kenton *lawyer*
Alexanian, Raymond *hematologist*
Alford, Bobby Ray *physician, educator, university official*
Allen, Don Lee *dentistry educator*
Allen, Kenneth Dale *insurance executive, corporate counsel*
Allender, John Roland *lawyer*
Allison, Robert James, Jr. *oil and gas company executive*
†Allison, William V. *oil industry executive*
Amundson, Neal Russell *chemical engineer, mathematician, educator*
Anderson, Claire W. *computer gifted and talented educator*
Anderson, Eric Severin *lawyer*
Anderson, Richard Carl *geophysical exploration company executive*
Anderson, Robert Dennis *lawyer*
Anderson, Thomas Dunaway *lawyer, retired*
Anderson, William (Albion), Jr. *oil and gas producer, investment banker*
†Andrews, Glenn T. *oil company executive*
Andrews, Lavone D. *architect*
†Andrews, Mark Edwin, III *oil and gas exploration company executive*
Anthony, Donald Barrett *engineering executive*
†Appel, Stanley Hersh *neurologist*
Armour, Laurance Hearne, Jr. *banker*
Arntzen, Charles Joel *bioscience educator*
†Arrowsmith, Peter D. *engineering executive*
†Ashby, Lynn Cox *newspaper editor*
†Atlas, Nancy Friedman *lawyer, mediator, arbitrator*
Atlas, Scott Jerome *lawyer*
Austin, Harry Guiden *engineering and construction company executive*
Auston, David Henry *university administrator, educator*
†Avery, Nathan Mark *oilfield equipment and services company executive*
Bagwell, Louis Lee *lawyer*
Bailar, Benjamin Franklin *academic administrator, administration educator*
Bailey, Charles Lyle *insurance company executive*
Bair, Royden Stanley *architect*
Balch, Charles M. *surgeon, educator*
Baldwin, John Charles *surgeon, researcher*
Ball, Lewis Edwin, II *manufacturing company executive*
Bambace, Robert Shelly *lawyer*
Bankston, Gene Clifton *oil and gas consultant*
Barlow, Jim B. *newspaper columnist*
Barnett, Edward William *lawyer*
Barney, Charles Lester *petroleum company executive*

Barrett, John Adams *lawyer*
Barrow, Thomas Davies *oil and mining company executive*
Barthelme, Donald *architect*
Baskin, David Stuart *neurosurgeon*
Bast, Robert Clinton, Jr. *research scientist, medical educator*
Batsakis, John George *pathology educator*
Baugh, John Frank *wholesale company executive*
Bayko, Emil Thomas *lawyer*
Bean, Alan LaVern *space artist, retired astronaut*
Beasley, Robert Palmer *epidemiologist, dean, educator*
Bech, Douglas York *lawyer*
Beck, John Robert *pathologist, information scientist*
Becker, Frederick Fenimore *cancer center administrator, pathologist*
Beghini, Victor Gene *oil company executive*
Bellatti, Lawrence Lee *lawyer*
†Benitez, Maurice Manuel *bishop*
†Bennett, Richard Gerald *gas company executive*
Benninger, Edward C., Jr. *petroleum and natural gas company executive*
Bentsen, Kenneth Edward *architect*
Berg, David Howard *lawyer*
†Bernal, Ivan *chemistry educator*
Berra, Yogi (Lawrence Peter Berra) *professional baseball coach*
Berry, James Declois *special education and history educator*
Berry, Julianne Elward *polymer and colloid chemist, researcher, inventor*
†Berry, Michael A. *physician, consultant*
Bhandari, Arvind *oncologist*
Bickel, Stephen Douglas *insurance company executive*
Billingsley, David Stuart *researcher*
Bischoff, Susan Ann *newspaper editor*
Bistline, F. Walter, Jr. *lawyer*
Bizzell, Bobby Gene *academic administrator*
Black, Norman William *federal judge*
Blackshear, A. T., Jr. *lawyer*
Bliss, Ronald Glenn *lawyer*
Bluestein, Edwin A., Jr. *lawyer*
Bodey, Gerald Paul *oncologist, educator*
†Bonham, Donald L. *food service executive*
Bonica, John R. *lawyer*
Bonnet, Beatriz Alicia *interpreter, translator, flutist*
Bonneville, Richard Briggs *petroleum exploration and production executive*
Bookout, John Frank, Jr. *oil company executive*
Boosey, John Arthur *management consultant, engineer*
Boren, William Meredith *manufacturing executive*
Borget, Lloyd George *architect*
Boston, Charles D. *lawyer*
Botley, Calvin *lawyer*
Bousquet, Thomas Gourrier *lawyer*
Bovay, Harry Elmo, Jr. *retired engineering company executive*
Bowen, W. J. *gas company executive*
†Bower, Arthur Michel *advertising agency executive*
†Bowersox, Thomas H. *executive*
Boyd, John E. *lawyer*
Brackley, William Lowell *aviation management consultant*
Brandenstein, Daniel Charles *astronaut, retired naval officer*
Brandt, I. Marvin *chemist, engineer*
Brann, Richard Roland *lawyer*
Brannon, H(ezzie) Raymond, Jr. *petroleum engineer, oil company scientist*
Brantley, John Randolph *lawyer*
†Brents, Daniel R. *architectural firm executive*
Bridger, Baldwin, Jr. *electrical engineer*
Bridges, David Manning *lawyer*
Brinsmade, Lyon Louis *lawyer*
Brinson, Gay Creswell, Jr. *lawyer*
Brito, Dagobert Llanos *economics educator*
Brotzen, Franz Richard *materials science educator*
Brown, Dennison Robert *mathematician, educator*
Brown, Jack Harold Upton *physiology educator, university official, biomedical engineer*
Brown, Jean William *advertising and public relations executive*
Brown, Lewis Arnold *management consultant*
Brown, Sara Lou *accounting firm executive*
Brundrett, George L(ee), Jr. *lawyer*
Bryan, James Lee *oil field service company executive*
†Bryan, J(ames) P(erry), Jr. *energy company executive*
Bryant, John Bradbury *economics educator, consultant*
Buchanan, Dennis Michael *manufacturing and holding company executive*
Buckingham, Edwin John, III *lawyer*
Bue, Carl Olaf, Jr. *retired federal judge*
Bui, Khoi Tien *college counselor*
†Bunch, Fred C. *newspaper picture editor*
Bungo, Michael William *physician, educator, science administrator*
Burch, Voris Reagan *lawyer*
Burdette, Walter James *surgeon, educator*
Burdine, John A. *hospital administrator, nuclear medicine educator*
Burguieres, Philip *energy service and manufacturing company executive*
Burke, Kevin Charles Antony *geologist*
Busch, Harris *medical educator*
Bush, Barbara Pierce *volunteer, wife of former President of the United States*
Bush, George Herbert Walker *former President of the United States*
Butler, William Thomas *college president, physician, educator*
†Byars, Carlos *newspaper reporter*
Caddy, Michael Douglas *lawyer*
Cain, Gordon A. *chemicals company executive*
Caldwell, James Wiley *lawyer*
Calhoun, Frank Wayne *lawyer, former state legislator*
Calhoun, Harold *architect*
†Caltrider, Thomas Lewis *environmental company executive*
Cameron, Bruce Francis *data processing executive*
Cameron, Richard Douglas *military officer, psychiatrist*
Camfield, William Arnett *art educator*
†Cannady, William Tillman *architect, educator*
Cantrell, William Allen *psychiatrist, educator*
Capps, Ethan LeRoy *oil company executive*
Carameros, George Demitrius, Jr. *natural gas company executive*
Cardus, David *physician*
Carlin, Edward Robert *retail store executive*
†Carlquist, Robert E. *newspaper publishing executive*
Carmody, James Albert *lawyer*
Carrington, Samuel Macon, Jr. *French language educator*
Carroll, James Vincent, III *lawyer*
Carroll, Michael M. *academic dean, mechanical engineering educator*
Carroll, Philip Joseph *oil company executive*
Carter, John Boyd, Jr. *oil operator, bank executive*
†Caskey, Charles Thomas *biology and genetics educator*
Castillo, Leonel Jabier *communications and promotions executive, consultant*
†Catell, Robert Barry *gas utility executive*
Cater, James Thomas *financial and investment planner*
Catlin, Francis Irving *physician*
Caudill, William Howard *lawyer*
Cernan, Eugene A. *management company executive, former astronaut*
Chalmers, David B. *petroleum executive*
Chamberlain, Joseph Wyan *astronomer, educator*
†Chaney, John Douglas *financial executive*
Chang, Robert Huei *library director*
Chapman, Alan Jesse *mechanical engineering educator*
†Chase, John Saunders *architect*
Cheavens, Joseph D. *lawyer*
Childress, Raymond Clay, Jr. *professional football player*
Chiste, Robert Matthew *energy company executive*
Chu, Paul Ching-Wu *physicist*
†Chu, Wei-Kan *physicist, educator*
Cizik, Robert *manufacturing company executive*
Claiborn, Stephen Allan *investment banker*
Clark, Carolyn Archer *technologist, scientist*
†Clark, Malcolm Dowdles *manufacturing company executive*
Clark, Pat English *lawyer*
Clark, Ron D(ean) *cosmetologist*
†Clark, Scott *newspaper editor*
Clarke, Robert Logan *lawyer, partner*
Clayton, William Lewis *retired utility executive*
†Cline, C. Bob *natural gas company executive*
Clore, Lawrence H. *lawyer*
Cobb, Daniel W., Jr. *editor, media consultant*
†Code, James Manley Wayne *manufacturing executive*
Cofran, George Lee *management consultant*
Coghlan, Kelly Jack *lawyer*
Cole, Aubrey Louis *management consultant, forest products company executive*
†Collins, Terry *professional baseball manager*
Collins, Vincent Patrick *radiologist, physician, educator*
Condit, Linda Faulkner *economist*
Conger, Franklin Barker *oil company executive*
Cook, B. Thomas *lawyer*
Cook, Eugene Augustus *lawyer*
Cooley, Andrew Lyman *corporation executive, former army officer*
Cooley, Denton Arthur *surgeon, educator*
Coon, Julian Barham *energy company executive*
Cooper, Paul *composer, educator*
Corral, Edward Anthony *fire marshal*
Corriere, Joseph N., Jr. *urologist, educator*
†Cotros, Charles H. *food products company executive*
Couch, J. O. Terrell *lawyer, former oil company executive*
Couch, Jesse Wadsworth *retired insurance company executive, consultant*
Couch, Robert Barnard *physician, educator*
Cowan, Finis Ewing *federal judge*
Cox, James Talley *lawyer*
Crawford, David Coleman *retired diversified manufacturing company executive*
Crispin, Andre Arthur *international trading company executive*
†Criswell, Ann *newspaper editor*
Crites, Omar Don, Jr. *lawyer*
Crooker, John H., Jr. *lawyer*
†Crowley, Joseph Paul *insurance company executive*
Crystal, Jonathan Andrew *executive recruiter*
Cullom, Hale Ellicott *investment company executive*
†Cunningham, Dan *newspaper editor*
Cunningham, R. Walter *venture capitalist*
Cunningham, Tom Alan *lawyer*
Curfiss, Robert Clinton *lawyer*
Curl, Robert Floyd, Jr. *chemistry educator*
Currie, John Thornton (Jack Currie) *retired investment banker*
Curry, Alton Frank *lawyer*
†Cuthbertson, James *healthcare executive*
†Cutler, John Earl *landscape architect*
Dack, Christopher Edward Hughes *lawyer*
Daily, James L., Jr. *retired financial executive*
Dartez, Franklin *banker*
Davenport, Joseph Dale *insurance executive*
Davis, Martha Algenita Scott *lawyer*
Davis, Rex Lloyd *insurance company executive*
Dawn, Frederic Samuel *chemical and textile engineer*
Dawood, Mohamed Yusoff *obstetrician, gynecologist*
DeBakey, Lois *science communications educator, writer, lecturer, editor, scholar*
DeBakey, Michael Ellis *cardiovascular surgeon, educator*
DeBakey, Selma *science communication educator, writer, editor, lecturer*
De Bremaecker, Jean-Claude *geophysics educator*
Decker, Hannah Shulman *history educator*
de Kanter, Ellen Ann *language professional, educator*
†Del Franco, Ray *consumer products company executive*
De Main, John *conductor, music director*
DeMenil, Dominique *art collector, philanthropist*
DeMent, James Alderson, Jr. *lawyer*
DeMoss, Harold R., Jr. *federal judge*
Dennis, John Emory, Jr. *mathematics educator*
Denny, Otway B., Jr. *lawyer*
†Derrick, James V., Jr. *lawyer*
DesBarres, John P. *energy company executive*
Devlin, Robert Manning *financial services company executive*
Dickey, Duval Frederick *business consultant, former energy company executive*
†Dillard, Max Murray *international drilling contractor*
Dillon, Clifford Brien *retired lawyer*
Dilworth, James Weldon *lawyer*
Dimitry, Theodore George *lawyer*
Dinkins, Carol Eggert *lawyer*
Dishman, Cris Edward *professional football player*
Djerejian, Edward Peter *academic institute director, former diplomat*
Dodd, Gerald Dewey, Jr. *radiologist, educator*
Dodson, D. Keith *engineering and construction company executive*
Dole, Linda Ann Ingols *lawyer*
Donie, Scott *Olympic athlete, platform diver*
Dosher, John Rodney *consulting management consultant*
Douglas, Frank Fair *architect, graphic designer*
Douglass, John Jay *lawyer, educator*
Downes, Robin *library director*
Drabek, Doug (Douglas Dean Drabek) *baseball player*
Drew, Katherine Fischer *history educator*
Drury, Leonard Leroy *retired oil company executive*
Dudrick, Stanley John *surgeon, educator*
†Duke, Michael B. *aerospace scientist*
†Dunbar, Bonnie J. *engineer, astronaut*
Duncan, Charles William, Jr. *investor, former government official*
Dunlap, James Lapham *petroleum company executive*
Dunlop, Fred Hurston *lawyer*
DuPont, Herbert Lancashire *medical educator, researcher*
Dutton, Uriel Elvis *lawyer*
Dykes, Osborne Jefferson, III *lawyer*
Eastep, Larry Gene *construction company executive*
Eastland, S. Stacy *lawyer*
Ebaugh, Helen Rose *sociology educator, researcher*
Edens, Donald Keith *oil company executive*
Edwards, Victor Henry *chemical engineer*
†Efron, Jeanette Oshman *retail executive*
Eichberger, LeRoy Carl *stress analyst, mechanical engineering consultant*
Elers, Karl Emerson *mining company executive*
Elkins, James Anderson, Jr. *banker*
†Ellerbeck, Ronald L. *oil industry executive*
†Ellis, Rodney Glenn *investment banking firm director*
†Elmer, Augustus *shipping company executive*
Engelhardt, Hugo Tristram, Jr. *physician, educator*
Englesmith, Tejas *actor, producer, curator*
†Erikson, Sheldon R. *oil field services company executive*
Estes, Carl Lewis, II *lawyer*
Eubank, J. Thomas *lawyer*
Ewell, Vincent Fletcher *lawyer*
Ewing, John Kirby *real estate, oil and investment executive*
Fabricant, Jill Diane *technology company executive*
Falick, James *architect*
†Fant, Patrick Joseph *radio station general manager*
Farenthold, Frances Tarlton *lawyer*
Farmer, Joe Sam *petroleum company executive*
Feigin, Ralph David *pediatrician, educator*
Feldcamp, Larry Bernard *lawyer*
Feldt, J(ohn) Harrell *lawyer*
Ferguson, Jennifer Lee Berry *education educator*
†Ferguson, John C. *airport terminal executive*
Ferguson, Robert R., III *airline company executive*
Ferrand, Jean C. *oil company executive*
Finch, Michael Paul *lawyer*
Fiorenza, Joseph A. *bishop*
Fishman, Marvin Allen *pediatrician, neurologist, educator*
Flack, Joe Fenley *county and municipal official, former insurance executive*
Focht, John Arnold, Jr. *geotechnical engineer*
Foreman, George *boxer*
Fort, John Franklin, III *manufacturing company executive*
Fortenbach, Ray Thomas *retired lawyer*
Foster, Charles Crawford *lawyer, educator*
Foster, Dale Warren *government educator, management consultant, real estate broker, accountant*
Foster, Joe B. *oil company executive*
Fowler, Robert Asa *consultant, business director, diplomat*
Foyt, A(nthony) J(oseph), Jr. *auto racing crew chief, former professional auto racer*
Frank, George Willard (Will Frank) *oil company executive, consultant*
Frank, Hilda Rhea Kaplan *dancer*
Frankhouser, Homer Sheldon, Jr. *engineering and construction company executive*
Freeman, Marjorie Schaefer *mathematics educator*
Freireich, Emil J *hematologist, educator*
French, Layne Bryan *lawyer, investor, volunteer*
Friedberg, Thomas Harold *insurance company executive*
†Frieden, Kit *newspaper editor*
†Friedkin, Thomas H. *automotive executive*
†Fuchs, Bernard *apparel executive*
†Fukuyama, Tohru *organic chemistry educator*
Fulwiler, Robert Neal *oil company executive*
Gagnon, Stewart Walter *lawyer*
Gallerano, Andrew John *retail company executive*
†Gamel, Wendell Wesley *business executive*
Gano, John *lawyer*
Garber, Alan J(oel) *medical educator*
Gardner, Everette Shaw, Jr. *information sciences educator*
†Garner, Thomas Ward *petroleum company executive*
Garrett, Jasper Patrick *lawyer*
†Garrison, Martha *oil industry executive*
Garrison, Truitt B. *architect*
Garten, David B. *lawyer*
Gayle, Gibson, Jr. *lawyer*
Gee, Thomas Gibbs *lawyer, retired federal judge*
Geer, Ronald Lamar *mechanical engineering consultant, retired oil company executive*
Geis, Duane Virgil *investment banker*
Gentry, Hubert, Jr. *lawyer*
George, Deveral D. *editor, journalist, advertising consultant*
Georgiades, William Den Hartog *university dean*
Gerard, Roy Dupuy *oil company executive*
Germany, Daniel Monroe *aerospace engineer*
†Geraughty, David R. *newspaper editor*
Gibson, Everett Kay, Jr. *space scientist, geochemist*
Gibson, Jerry Leigh *oil company executive*
Gibson, Michael Addison *chemical engineering company executive*
Gibson, Peggy Kathryn *marketing professional*
Gibson, Robert Lee *astronaut*
Gidley, John Lynn *engineering executive*
Gilbert, Harold Stanley *warehousing company executive*
Gildenberg, Philip Leon *neurosurgeon*
†Gillis, Stephen Malcolm *academic administrator, economics educator*
Gissel, L. Henry, Jr. *lawyer*
Glassman, Armand Barry *physician, pathologist, scientist, educator, administrator*
†Godchaux, Frank Area, III *food company executive*
Goff, Robert Burnside *retired food company executive*
Goldsmith, Billy Joe *trade association executive*
†Goldstein, Jack Charles *lawyer*
Goodman, Herbert Irwin *petroleum company executive*
Gordon, Wendell Chaffee *economics educator*
Gordon, William Edwin *physicist, engineer, educator, university official*
Gore, Thomas Jackson *construction executive*
Gorski, Daniel Alexander *art educator*
Gotto, Antonio Marion, Jr. *internist, educator*
Gottschalk, Arthur William *music company executive and educator*
Gould, Kenneth Lance *physician, educator*
Gover, Alan Shore *lawyer*
Gower, Bob G. *gas and oil industry executive*
†Graham, David Yates *gastroenterologist*
Graham, Michael Paul *lawyer*
Gray, Archibald Duncan, Jr. *lawyer*
Gray, Robert Steele *publishing executive, editor*
Grayson, Charles Jackson, Jr. *research association executive*
Green, Gene *congressman*
†Griffin, Linda Gillan *fashion editor*
Grossman, Robert George *physician, educator*
†Gruben, Karl Taylor *law librarian*
Gruber, Ira Dempsey *historian, educator*
Guinn, David Crittenden *petroleum engineer, drilling and exploration company executive*
Gunn, Albert Edward, Jr. *internist, lawyer, hospital and university administrator*
Guynn, Robert William *psychiatrist, educator*
Haas, Merrill Wilber *geologist, oil company executive*
†Hackerman, Norman *chemist, university president*
Hafner, Joseph A., Jr. *food company executive*
Halbouty, Michel Thomas *geologist, petroleum engineer, petroleum operator*
†Hale, Leon *newspaper columnist*
Hall, Robert Joseph *physician, medical educator*
Halloran, Bernard Thorpe *lawyer*
†Hamilton, Phyllis *principal*
Hammack, Gladys Lorene Mann *reading specialist, educator*
†Hammond, Ken *newspaper magazine editor*
Hammond, Michael Peter *music educator, dean*
Hansen, Paula Renee *health care administrator*
Hanson, Jerry Clinton *lawyer*
†Harasim, Paul Houck *columnist, educator*
†Hardcastle, Kenneth Lloyd *oil company executive*
Hardin, George Cecil, Jr. *petroleum consultant*
Hargrove, James Ward *financial consultant*
Harmon, Melinda Furche *federal judge*
Harper, Alfred John, II *lawyer*
Harper, Michael John Kennedy *obstetrics and gynecology educator*
Harrington, Bruce Michael *lawyer, investor*
Harris, Nell H. *retired public relations executive, real estate broker, writer*
Harris, Richard Foster, Jr. *insurance company executive*
Harrison, Otto R. *oil industry executive*
Hart, James Whitfield, Jr. *corporate public affairs executive, lawyer*
Hartsfield, Henry Warren, Jr. *astronaut*
Harvey, F. Reese *mathematics educator*
Harvin, David Tarleton *lawyer*
Harvin, William Charles *lawyer*
Haskell, Thomas Langdon *history educator*
Hasling, Jill Freeman *meteorologist*
Haymes, Robert C. *physicist, educator*
Haymond, Paula J. *psychologist, diagnostician*
Haynes, Karen Sue *university dean, social work educator*
Haynie, Thomas Powell, III *physician*
Haywood, Theodore Joseph *physician, educator*
Heckler, Walter Tim *association executive*
†Hedrick, Kirby L. *petroleum company executive*
Heimbinder, Isaac *construction company executive, lawyer*
†Heinsen, Lindsay *newspaper editor*
†Helburn, Stephen *oceaneering company executive*
Helland, George Archibald, Jr. *equipment manufacturing company executive, former government official, management consultant*
Hellums, Jesse David *chemical engineering educator and researcher*
†Henderson, Nathan H. *bishop*
Hendrix, Dennis R. *energy company executive*
Henington, David Mead *library director*
Henning, George Thomas, Jr. *chemical company executive*
Henning, Susan June *biomedical researcher*
†Henry, John Cooper *journalist*
Hermann, Robert John *lawyer, corporate executive*
Hesse, Martha O. *natural gas company executive*
Hiatt, John David *broadcast company executive*
Hipple, James Blackman *financial executive*
Hirsch, Edward Mark *poet, English language educator*
Hittner, David *federal judge*
Ho, Yhi-Min *university dean, economics educator*
Hobby, William Pettus *broadcast executive*
Hodges, Ann *television editor, newspaper columnist*
Hodo, Edward Douglas *university president*
Hoffman, Philip Guthrie *former university president*
†Hoglund, Forrest Eugene *petroleum company executive*
Holcomb, William A. *real estate broker, consultant, retired oil and gas exploration, pipeline executive*
Holland, Merle Susan *psychologist*
Hollister, Leo Edward *physician, educator*
Hollyfield, John Scoggins *lawyer*
Holmes, Ann Hitchcock *journalist*
Holmes, Darrell *tourism consultant*
Holmquest, Donald Lee *physician, astronaut, lawyer*
Holovak, Mike *sports association exec*
Holstead, John Burnham *lawyer*
Homeyer, Howard C. *energy consultant*
Honeycutt, George Leonard *photographer*
Hook, Harold Swanson *insurance company executive*
Hornak, Anna Frances *library administrator*
†Horning, Marjorie G. *biochemistry educator*
Horvitz, Paul Michael *finance educator*
†Howard, R. L. *oil industry executive*
Hoyt, Kenneth M. *federal judge*
Hoyt, Mont Powell *lawyer*
Hsu, Thomas Tseng-Chuang *civil engineer, educator*
†Huang, Elsie Lee *principal*
Hudspeth, Chalmers Mac *lawyer, educator*
†Huff, John Rossman *oil service company executive*
Huffington, Roy Michael *ambassador*
Hughes, Lynn Nettleton *federal judge*
Hungerford, Ed Vernon, III *physics educator*
†Huntoon, Carolyn Leach *physiologist*
Hurd, Charles W. *lawyer*
Hurwitz, Charles Edwin *oil company executive*
Hutcheson, Joseph Chappell, III *lawyer*
Hutcheson, Thad T., Jr. *business and international lawyer*
Illig, Carl *lawyer*

Smith, Lloyd Hilton *independent oil and gas producer*
Smith, Michael Alexis *petroleum geologist*
Smith, Robert, III *banker*
Smith, William Randolph *lawyer*
Snedeker, Robert D. *air transportation executive*
Snider, Robert Larry *management consultant*
†Snyder, Mike *newspaper editor*
Soliz, Joseph Guy *lawyer*
Sonfield, Robert Leon, Jr. *lawyer*
†SoRelle, Ruth Doyle *medical writer, journalist*
Spalding, Andrew Freeman *lawyer*
†Spanos, Pol Dimitrios *engineering educator*
Spira, Melvin *plastic surgeon*
Staine, Ross *lawyer*
†Stanley, Jack H. *newspaper publishing executive*
†Stanworth, R. Howard *eye care company executive*
†Steele, James Harlan *former public health veterinarian, educator*
Steen, Wesley Wilson *former bankruptcy judge, lawyer*
Stehlin, John Sebastian, Jr. *surgeon*
Stephens, Delia Marie Lucky *lawyer*
Stevenson, Ben *choreographer, ballet company executive*
Stewart, Cornelius James, II *utilities company executive*
Still, Charles Henry *lawyer*
Stormer, John Charles, Jr. *geology educator, mineralogist*
Stradley, William Jackson *lawyer*
Streng, William Paul *lawyer, educator*
Stryker, Steven Charles *lawyer*
Stuart, Walter Bynum, IV *lawyer*
Sudbury, John Dean *religious foundation executive, petroleum chemist*
Susman, Morton Lee *lawyer*
Susman, Stephen Daily *lawyer*
†Suter, Jon Michael *academic library director, educator*
Swanson, Roy Joel *lawyer*
†Sweeney, John W., III *newspaper executive*
Sykora, Donald D. *utility company excutive*
Symons, James Martin *environmental engineer, educator*
Szalkowski, Charles Conrad *lawyer*
Talwani, Manik *geophysicist, educator*
Tapia, Richard Alfred *mathematics educator*
Tarrance, Vernon Lance, Jr. *behavior research executive*
†Tauber, Orner J., Jr. *petrochemical company executive*
Templeton, Robert Earl *engineering and construction company executive*
Terrell, G. Irvin *lawyer*
Tetzlaff, Theodore R. *lawyer*
Thagard, Norman E. *astronaut*
†Thayer, Keith B. *engineering company executive*
Thomas, Orville C. *physician*
Thompson, Guy Bryan *investment company executive*
Thomsen, Charles Burton *engineering design company executive*
Thorne, Joye Holley *special education administrator*
Thorpe, Otis Henry *professional basketball player*
Thrall, Robert McDowell *mathematician, educator*
Tomjanovich, Rudolph *professional athletic coach*
Travis, Andrew David *lawyer*
†Tronchon, Claude *chemical executive*
Trusty, Roy Lee *former oil company executive*
Tucker, Anne Wilkes *curator, photographic historian and critic, lecturer*
Tucker, Randolph Wadsworth *engineering executive*
Tuerff, James Rodrick *insurance company executive*
Turner, William Wilson *hospital administrator*
Tyndall, Marshall Clay, Jr. *banker*
†Urban, Stanley T. *hospital administrator*
†Vaeth, Nancy Ann *sales executive*
Valencia, Jaime Alfonso *chemical engineer*
Vallbona, Carlos *physician*
Van Caspel, Venita Walker *financial planner*
Vance, Carol Stoner *lawyer*
Van Fleet, George Allan *lawyer*
†Van Lanen, James L. *natural resource company executive*
Varner, David Eugene *lawyer, energy company executive*
Vaughan, Eugene H. *investment company executive*
Waggoner, James Virgil *chemicals company executive*
Wagner, Donald Bert *health care administrator*
Wagner, Paul Anthony, Jr. *education educator*
Wainerdi, Richard Elliott *medical center executive*
Wakefield, Stephen Alan *lawyer*
Wakil, Salih Jawad *biochemistry educator*
Walbridge, Willard Eugene *broadcasting executive*
Walker, Esper Lafayette, Jr. *civil engineer*
Walker, William Easton *surgeon, educator, lawyer*
Wallingford, John Rufus *lawyer*
Walls, Carmage *newspaper publisher*
Walls, Martha Ann Williams (Mrs. B. Carmage Walls) *newspaper executive*
Wang, Chao-Cheng *mathematician, engineer*
Ward, Bethea *artist, small business owner*
†Watson, C. L. (Chuck Watson) *gas industry executive*
Watson, John Allen *lawyer*
Weaver, Hilda *counselor, psychotherapist*
Webb, Jack M. *lawyer*
†Webb, Marty Fox *principal*
Weber, Fredric Alan *lawyer*
Weber, Wilford Alexander *education educator*
Weinstein, Roy *physics educator, researcher*
Welch, Byron Eugene *communications educator*
Welch, Harry Scoville *lawyer, retired gas pipeline company executive*
Welch, Robert Morrow, Jr. *lawyer*
Wellin, Keith Sears *investment banker*
Wells, Benjamin Gladney *lawyer*
Wells, Damon, Jr. *investment company executive*
†Wells, Raymond O., Jr. *mathematics educator, researcher*
Werlein, Ewing, Jr. *federal judge, lawyer*
†Wesselski, Clarence J. *aerospace engineer*
Wharton, Thomas H(eard), Jr. *lawyer*
†White, Cecile Holmes *religion editor*
Wickliffe, Jerry L. *lawyer*
Wilde, Carlton D. *lawyer*
Wilde, William Key *lawyer*
†Wilford, Dan Sewell *hospital administrator*
†Wilhelm, Marilyn *private school administrator*
Wilkinson, Bruce W. *corporate executive, lawyer*
Williams, Edward Earl, Jr. *entrepreneur, educator*
Williams, James Lee *financial industries executive*
Williams, Percy Don *lawyer*
Williams, Robert Leon *psychiatrist, neurologist, educator*
Williams, Temple Weatherly, Jr. *internist, educator*
Williamson, Peter David *lawyer*
Williamson, Sam *lawyer*
Wilson, Carl Weldon, Jr. *construction company executive, civil engineer*
Wilson, Clarence Ivan *banker*
Wilson, Edward Converse, Jr. *oil and natural gas production company executive*
Wilson, James William *lawyer*
Wilson, Patricia Potter *library science educator, educational and library consultant*
Winslow, Robert Albert *retired petroleum industry executive, consultant*
Winton, James C. *lawyer*
Wold, Finn *biochemist, educator*
Wolf, Erving *oil company executive*
†Wood, D. Dale *oil and gas industry executive*
Wood, Ivan, Jr. *lawyer*
Wood, Jack Calvin *health care consultant, lawyer*
†Woodard, Robert E. *bishop*
Woodhouse, John Frederick *food distribution company executive*
Woods, James Dudley *manufacturing company executive*
Woodson, Benjamin Nelson, III *insurance executive*
Wray, Marc Frederick *minerals company executive*
Wray, Thomas Jefferson *lawyer*
Wren, Robert James *aerospace engineering manager*
Wright, Robert Payton *lawyer*
Wyatt, Oscar Sherman, Jr. *energy company executive*
Yokubaitis, Roger T. *lawyer*
York, James Martin *lawyer*
Young, John Watts *astronaut*
Young, William John *French educator, university president emeritus*
Youngblood, J. Craig *lawyer*
Youngblood, Ray Wilson *publishing company executive*
Yu, Aiting Tobey *engineering executive*
Zech, William Albert *manufacturing company executive*
Zeff, Stephen Addam *accounting educator*
†Zerr, Emil Martin *construction company executive*
Zivley, Walter Perry *lawyer*
Zlatkis, Albert *chemistry educator*
Zodrow, George Roy *economist, educator*

Humble
Brown, Samuel Joseph, Jr. *mechanical engineer*

Hunt
Price, Donald Albert *veterinarian, consultant*

Huntsville
Anisman, Martin Jay *academic administrator*
Biles, Robert Erle *political science educator*
Bruce, Amos Jerry, Jr. *psychology educator*
†Flanagan, Timothy James *criminal justice educator, university official*
Lea, Stanley E. *artist, educator*
Vick, Marie *retired health science educator*
Warner, Laverne *education educator*

Hurst
Dodd, Sylvia Bliss *special education educator*
†Jackson, Donald *waste management executive*
Kidwell, Georgia Brenner *elementary education educator*
Mc Keen, Chester M., Jr. *business executive*

Industry
Huitt, Jimmie L. *rancher, oil, gas, real estate investor*

Ingram
Hughes, David Michael *oil service company executive*

Irving
Aikman, Troy *football player*
Baird, David Leach, Jr. *lawyer, petroleum and chemical company executive*
†Barclay, George M. *banker*
Bayne, James Elwood *oil company executive*
Belknap, John Corbould *financial executive*
Bolinger, Corbin Eugene *finance company executive*
†Callahan, Frank T. *engineering executive*
Cannon, Francis V., Jr. *academic administrator, electrical engineer, economist*
Clark, Priscilla Alden *elementary education educator*
Clarke, Jack Graeme *consultant, retired petroleum company executive*
Collins, Stephen Barksdale *health care executive*
Cooper, Kathleen Bell *economist*
Donnelly, Barbara Schettler *medical technologist*
Elliott, Frank Wallace *lawyer, educator*
†Faulkner, David J. *computer company executive*
Gidel, Robert Hugh *real estate investor*
Gomersall, Earl Raymond *business executive*
†Groussman, Dean G. *retail executive*
Haley, Charles Lewis *professional football player*
Halter, Jon Charles *magazine editor, writer*
Hansen, Nick Dane *lawyer*
Hendrickson, Constance Marie McRight *chemist, consultant*
Hess, Edwin John *oil company executive*
†Hickey, John Michael *insurance company executive*
Hughes, John Farrell *finance company executive*
Hughes, Keith William *banking and finance company executive*
Irvin, Michael Jerome *professional football player*
Jack, James E. *financial service company executive*
Jones, Jerry (Jerral Wayne Jones) *professional football team executive*
Le Vine, Duane Gilbert *petroleum company executive*
Levy, Lester A. *sanitation company executive*
†Lindner, James D. *computer company executive*
†Lively, H(oward) Randolph, Jr. *retail company executive*
Lundy, Roland *publishing executive*
Lutz, Matthew Charles *geologist, oil company executive*
Martin, Thomas Lyle, Jr. *university president*
†McBrayer, H. Eugene *retired petroleum industry executive*
Metevier, James F. *finance company executive*
Mueller, James Bernhard *anesthesiologist, pain management consultant*
Mundy, William Greg *telecommunications company executive, lawyer*
†Munger, Sharon *market research firm executive*
Novacek, Jay McKinley *professional football player*
†Olson, Herbert Theodore *trade association executive*
Perry, Charles Edward *university administrator*
Pickett, Edwin Gerald *financial executive*
Potter, Robert Joseph *technical research and business executive*
†Raper, Bobby Joe *airlines company executive, mayor*
†Rees, Frank William, Jr. *architect*
Roberts, C. Kenneth *lawyer*
Sasseen, Robert Francis *university president*
†Simon, Dolph B(ertram) H(irst) *lawyer, jewelry company executive*
Smith, Emmitt J., III *professional football player*
Sommerfeldt, John Robert *historian*
Stahl, David Edward *association executive*
†Stepnoski, Mark Matthew *professional football player*
Stuckey, Scott Sherwood *editor*
†Swartz, Robert Mark *high technology manufacturing financial executive*
†Switzer, Barry *football coach*
Temerlin, Liener *advertising agency executive*
Walwer, Frank Kurt *university dean*
†Ward, Patrick J. *oil industry executive*
Wells, Leonard Nathaniel David, Jr. *lawyer*
Wicks, William Withington *retired public relations executive*
†Williams, Erik George *professional football player*
Zahn, Donald Jack *lawyer*

Jacksonville
†Blaylock, James Carl *clergyman, librarian*
†Pruitt, William Charles, Jr. *minister, educator*

Kerrville
Cook, John Alfred *sculptor, medallist, educator*
Dozier, William Everett, Jr. *newspaper editor and publisher*
Harkey, Ira Brown, Jr. *newspaperman, educator, author*
Holloway, Leonard Leveine *former university president*
†Kunz, Sidney *entomologist*
Lich, Glen Ernst *writer, ethnographer, government official, educator*
Matlock, (Lee) Hudson *civil engineer, consultant*
Wilson, William Howard *exploration geologist, oil and gas operator*

Kilgore
Rorschach, Richard Gordon *lawyer*

Killeen
†Brincat, John Nicholas *finance company executive*
Perry, John Wesley, Sr. *psychotherapist*

Kingsville
Cecil, David Rolf *mathematician, educator*
Ibanez, Manuel Luis *university official, biological sciences educator*
Robins, Gerald Burns *education educator*

Kingwood
Brinkley, Charles Alexander *geologist*
Davies, David Keith *geologist*

Lackland AFB
Anderson, Edgar R., Jr. *career officer, hospital administrator, physician*

Lake Jackson
Tasa, Kendall Sherwood *chemistry educator*

Lancaster
Wendorf, Denver Fred, Jr. *anthropology educator*

Laredo
Condon, Maria del Carmen *elementary education educator*
Kazen, George Philip *federal judge*
Kim, Earnest Jae-Hyun *import/export company executive*
†Zaffirini, Judith *state senator*

League City
Meinke, Roy Walter *electrical engineer, consultant*

Levelland
Walker, James Kenneth *judge*

Lewisville
Bickel, Herbert Jacob, Jr. *corporation executive*
†Downing, Clayton W. *school system administrator*
Vacca, John Joseph, Jr. *television executive*

Liberty Hill
Vance, Zinna Barth *artist, writer*
West, Felton *newspaper writer*

Lindale
Bockhop, Clarence William *retired agricultural engineer*
Wilson, Leland Earl *petroleum engineering consultant*

Llano
Walter, Virginia Lee *psychologist, educator*

Longview
Brannon, Clifton Woodrow, Sr. *evangelist, lawyer*
Crain, Bluford Walter, Jr. *architect*
Folzenlogen, P. D. *petrochemical executive*
LeTourneau, Richard Howard *retired college president*
†McMichael, Ronald L. *superintendent*

Lubbock
Allison, Cecil Wayne *insurance company executive*
†Anderson, Noble *dairy products executive*
Archer, James Elson *engineering educator*
Askins, Billy Earl *education educator, consultant*
Bricker, Donald Lee *surgeon*
Buesseler, John Aure *ophthalmologist, management consultant*
Cartwright, Walter Joseph *sociology educator*
†Cochran, Joseph Wesley *law librarian, educator*
Collins, Harker *manufacturing executive, economist, publisher, marketing, financial, business and legal consultant*
Connor, Seymour Vaughan *historian, writer*
Conover, William Jay *statistics educator*
Cummings, Sam R. *federal judge*
Curl, Samuel Everett *university dean, agricultural scientist*
Dregne, Harold Ernest *agronomy educator*
Dudek, Richard Albert *engineering educator*
†Duncan, Robert Lloyd *lawyer*
Eddleman, Floyd Eugene *retired English language educator*
Frazier, Eugene Richard *designer*
Gilliam, John Charles *economist, educator*
Glass, Carson McElyea *lawyer*
Graves, Lawrence Lester *university dean emeritus*
Green, Joseph Barnet *neurologist*
Haragan, Donald Robert *university administrator, geosciences educator*
Hartman, James Theodore *physician, educator*
Havens, Murray Clark *political scientist, educator*
Hentges, David John *microbiology educator*
Higdon, David Leon *English language educator*
†Hulsey, Sam Byron *bishop*
Jackson, Francis Charles *physician, surgeon*
Johnson, James Robert *accountant*
Jonish, James Edward *economist, educator*
Kelsey, Clyde Eastman, Jr. *philosophy and psychology educator*
Kenny, Alexander Donovan *pharmacology educator*
Ketner, Kenneth Laine *philosopher, educator*
Kiesling, Ernst Willie *civil engineering educator*
Koh, Pun Kien *retired educator, metallurgist, consultant*
Kristiansen, Magne *electrical engineer, educator*
Kurtzman, Neil A. *medical educator*
Lawless, Robert William *academic administrator*
Lemley, Steven Smith *academic administrator*
Maunder, Addison Bruce *agronomic research company executive*
May, Donald Robert Lee *ophthalmologist, retina and vitreous surgeon, educator, academic administrator*
McManigal, Shirley Ann *university dean*
†Messer, Robert H. *obstetrician/gynecologist, educator*
Mittemeyer, Bernhard Theodore *physician, academic administrator*
Mittler, Gene Allen *art educator*
Murray, Grover Elmer *geologist, educator*
Pasewark, William Robert *management consultant, author*
Pearce, William Martin *history educator*
Perry, Malcolm Oliver *vascular surgeon*
Portnoy, William Manos *electrical engineering educator*
Purdom, Thomas James *lawyer*
†Rippel, Jeffrey Alan *library director*
Robinson, G. Wilse *molecular spectroscopist, educator*
Rushing, Jane Gilmore *writer*
Schake, Lowell Martin *animal science educator*
Sears, Robert Stephen *finance educator*
†Shine, Henry Joseph *chemistry educator*
Shires, George Thomas *surgeon, physician, educator*
Skoog, Gerald Duane *science educator*
Stem, Carl Herbert *business educator*
Walker, Warren Stanley *English educator*
†Watson, W. H. *bishop*
Wendt, Charles William *soil physicist, educator*
Williams, Darryl Marlowe *medical educator*
Wolfe, Verda Nell *pension consultant, financial planner*
†Wood, Richard Courtney *library director, educator*
Woolam, Gerald Lynn *surgeon*

Lufkin
†Brookshire, Wiley Eugene *cinsumer products company executive*
Cardwell, Horace Milton *communications company executive*
Denman, Joe Carter, Jr. *retired forest products company executive*
Ericson, Roger Delwin *lawyer, forest resource company executive*
Migl, Donald Raymond *optometrist, pharmacist*

Mabank
Beets, Hughla Fae *retired educator*

Marble Falls
Cross, Christopher *recording artist, songwriter, singer*

Marshall
†Magrill, Rose Mary *library director*

Mcallen
†Ashley, J. Thomas, III *architect*
Hinojosa, Ricardo H. *federal judge*
Ramirez, Mario Efrain *physician*

Mesquite
Bullock, Norma Kathryn Rice *chemical research professional*
Vaughan, Joseph Lee, Jr. *education educator, consultant*
†Williams, John Elbert, Jr. *library services director*

Mexia
Guerin, Dean Patrick *food products executive*

Midland
Bullock, Maurice Randolph *lawyer*
Chappell, Clovis Gillham, Jr. *lawyer*
†Craddick, Thomas Russell *investor, state representative*
Luckett, Paul Herbert, III *manufacturing executive*
Morrow, William Clarence *lawyer*
Ott, Wendell Lorenz *art museum director, artist*
Reed, Joel Leston *diversified manufacturing company executive*
†Wagner, Cyril, Jr. *metals manufacturing company executive*

Mineral Wells
Harmon Brown, Valarie Jean *hospital laboratory director, information systems executive*

Missouri City
Griffin, Oscar O'Neal, Jr. *writer, former oil company executive*

Montgomery
Holman, Charles Richardson *chemical company executive*
Tharp, Benjamin Carroll, Jr. *architect*

Moody
McNiel, Norbert Arthur *retired educator*

Mount Pleasant
Ogburn, Wayne Lee *health science facility administrator*

Nacogdoches
Clagett, Arthur F(rank) *psychologist, sociologist, qualitative research writer, retired sociology educator*
Fish, Stewart Allison *obstetrician-gynecologist*
Kallsen, Theodore John *retired English language educator*
Worrell, Albert Cadwallader *forest economics educator*

Natalia
Wright, Douglas Ray *academic and vocational counselor*

Navasota
Norris, Chuck (Carlos Ray) *actor*

New Braunfels
Dunn, Charlotte Valborg Lund *elementary education educator*
Fomon, Samuel Joseph *physician, educator*
Johnson, Marion Phillip *hospital administrator*
Wilson, James Lee *retired geology educator, consultant*

North Austin
Ahlschwede, Arthur Martin *church educational official*

North Richland Hills
Cunningham, Larry J. *city official*

Odessa
Boyd, Claude Collins *education advisor*
Gilliland, William Elton *retired lawyer*
Lee, Nelda S. *artist, art appraiser and dealer, film producer*
Reeves, Robert Grier LeFevre *geology educator, scientist*
Shaw, Scott *photojournalist*
Sorber, Charles Arthur *academic administrator*

Orange
Adkins, John E(arl), Jr. *chemist*
Eldredge, Bruce Beard *museum director*

Overton
Randel, Ronald Dean *physiologist, educator*

Pampa
Cain, Donald Ezell *judge*
Warner, John William *lawyer*

Pasadena
Gilley, Mickey Leroy *musician*
Zimmerer, Ann(a) Morgan *lawyer, consulting psychologist, genealogist*

Pittsburg
Pilgrim, Lonnie (Bo) *poultry production company executive*

Plainview
Duvall, Wallace Lee *management educator, consultant*
Galle, Richard Lynn *association executive, former municipal official*

Plano
Alberthal, Lester M., Jr. *information processing services executive*
Bain, Travis Whitsett, II *manufacturing and retail executive*
Bode, Richard Albert *retired financial executive*
Bonet, Frank Joseph *lawyer*
Brock, Dee Sala *television executive, educator, writer, consultant*
Donald, James L. *communications company executive*
Fernandes, Gary Joe *electronic data processing company executive*
Finley, Glenna *author*
†Friedlander, D. Gilbert *lawyer*
Kranzow, Ronald Roy *lawyer*
Lee, Allan Wren *clergyman*
Neppl, Walter Joseph *retired retail store executive*
Odeh, Aziz Salim *retired oil company scientist*
Schuh, Frank Joseph *drilling engineering company executive, consultant*
†Sedei, Donald James *art director*
Senderling, Jon Townsend *journalist, public affairs specialist*
†Thompson, J. Ken *gas, oil industry executive*

Port Aransas
Lehmann, William Leonardo *electrical engineer, educator*
Wohlschlag, Donald Eugene *zoologist, marine ecologist, educator emeritus*

Port Arthur
Cash, Carol Vivian *sociologist*
Gipson, Robert Malone *research administrator*
†Parker, Carl *state senator*

Portland
Grubbs, Donald Ray *welder, educator*

Post
Earl, Lewis Harold *economics and management consultant*

Pottsboro
Thomas, Ann Van Wynen *lawyer, educator*

Prairie View
Becton, Julius Wesley, Jr. *army officer*
Boyd-Brown, Lena Ernestine *history educator, education consultant*
Coe, Elizabeth Beaubien *English language educator*
Jones, Barbara Ann Posey *dean*
Prestage, Jewel Limar *political science educator*
Robinson, Carrie C. *English educator*

Presidio
Hill, Celia Ann *educator*

Red Oak
Henderson, Edwin Harold *minister*

Rhome
Brammer, Barbara Rhudene *retired secondary education educator*

Richardson
Adamson, Dan Klinglesmith *science association executive*
Berry, Brian Joe Lobley *geographer, political economist, urban planner*
Biard, James Robert *electrical engineer*
†Breard, Benjamin Allen *art dealer*
Brown, Ollie Dawkins *psychotherapist, scientific researcher*
†Coleman, Rogers King *insurance company executive*
Cordell, Robert James *geologist*
†Denton, Jere Michael *oil company executive*
Dunn, David E. *university dean*
Edge, Harold Lee *manufacturing executive*
Gary, John *singer*
Goldberg, Leonard *television and movie producer*
†Gray, Donald Melvin *molecular and cell biology educator*
†Hanson, William Bert *physics educator, science administrator*
Johnson, Francis Severin *physicist*
Kinsman, Frank Ellwood *engineering executive*
Landisman, Mark *geophysicist, educator*
†Langmead, Jeffrey P. *insurance company executive*
Lutz, Raymond Price *industrial engineer, educator*
McDaniel, Dolan Kenneth *oil exploration service company executive*
Nevill, William Albert *chemistry educator*
†Orr, David E. *electronics executive*
Pervin, William Joseph *computer science educator*
Redman, Timothy Paul *English language educator, author, chess federation administrator*
Rutford, Robert Hoxie *university president*
Schrimsher, Jerry James *diversified financial services company executive*
†Wildenthal, Bryan Hobson *university administrator*

Richmond
Barratt, Cynthia Louise *pharmaceutical company executive*
Willis, David Edwin *retired geophysicist*

Roanoke
Bradshaw, Terry *sports announcer, former professional football player*

Rockdale
†Kubiak, Dan *state legislator*

Rockwall
House, Robert William *music educator*
Wallace, Mary Elaine *opera director, author*

Round Rock
LaShelle, Charles Stanton *lawyer, insurance company executive*

Rowlett
Toler, James Larkin *real estate executive*

Rusk
Hassell, Morris William *judge*

Salado
Cutler, Morene Parten *civic worker*
Parks, Lloyd Lee *oil company executive*

San Angelo
Chatfield, Mary Van Abshoven *librarian*
Coe, Robert Stanford *retired management educator*
Davison, Elizabeth Jane Linton *education educator*
†Junell, Robert Alan *lawyer*
Messbarger, Edward Joseph *physical education educator, university coach*
Pfeifer, Michael David *bishop*
Torres, David *Spanish language educator*
Vincent, Lloyd Drexell *university president*

San Antonio
Abramson, Hyman Norman *engineering and science research executive*
Adams, James R. *telecommunications executive*
Ahmad, Shair *mathematics educator*
Aldave, Barbara Bader *law educator, lawyer*
Allison, Stephen Philip *lawyer*
†Alvarado, Leo G. *lawyer, law educator*
Anderson, George Kenneth *air force officer, physician*
Aust, Joe Bradley *surgeon, educator*
Baker, Floyd Wilmer *surgeon, retired army officer*
Ball, M(ary) Isabel *chemistry educator, dean*
†Barnes, Gail *historic site administrator*
Barrow, Charles Wallace *university dean*
Barton, James Cary *lawyer*
Bass, Bob *professional basketball team executive*
Bates, David Quentin, Jr. *lawyer, pharmaceutical executive*
Bellows, Thomas John *political scientist, educator*
Benson, Charles Edward *aircraft company executive*
Benz, George Albert *retired economist, educator*
Berg, Thomas *manufacturing executive*
Betts, Austin Wortham *retired research company executive*
Biery, Evelyn Hudson *lawyer*
Bishop, Charles Landon *air force officer*
Blystone, Robert Vernon *developmental cell biologist, educator, textbook consultant*
Bowman, Barbara Hyde *biologist, geneticist, educator*
†Boyers, John Martin *principal*
Brown, Robert *manufacturing executive*
Bryan, Richard Ray *real estate development executive, construction executive*
Budalur, Thyagarajan Subbanarayan *chemistry educator*
Burch, James Leo *science research institute executive*
Burke, Michael Donald *oil and gas company executive*
Burton, Russell Rohan *aerospace scientist, researcher*
†Butt, Charles C. *food service executive*
Butt, Howard Edward, Jr. *grocery chain executive, foundation executive*
Byrnes, Victor Allen *ophthalmologist*
Cahill, William Randall *health facility executive*
Calgaard, Ronald Keith *university president*
Carmack, George *newspaper editor*
Carpenter, John Wilson, III *management consultant, retired air force officer, educational administrator*
Carroll, William Marion *financial services executive*
Carson, Robin D. *zoological park administrator*
Catto, Henry Edward *former government official, former ambassador*
Caudill, Howard Edwin *Anglican bishop, educator*
Clark, Leif Michael *federal judge*
Cloud, Bruce Benjamin, Sr. *construction company executive*
†Compton, Clinton E. *principal*
†Conly, Michael J. *communications company executive, television executive*
Coronado, Jose Ricardo *hospital administrator*
Corum, B. H. *health care company executive*
Cory, William Eugene *retired consulting company executive*
Cousins, Margaret *author, editor*
†Crews, Donald Roy *lawyer, communications company executive*
Croft, Harry Allen *psychiatrist*
Cruz-Romo, Gilda *soprano*
Dazey, William Boyd *retired lawyer*
†Delmer, Merle W. *pathologist*
Deviney, Marvin Lee, Jr. *research institute scientist, program manager*
Donaldson, Willis Lyle *research institute administrator*
Doyle, Frank Lawrence *geologist, hydrologist, executive*
Duncan, A. Baker *investment banker*
Durbin, Richard Louis, Jr. *lawyer*
Elliot, Sean Michael *professional basketball player*
Fagan, Wayne Irwin *lawyer*
Fawcett, Robert Earl, Jr. *retired banker*
Felicella, Frank George *retail executive*
Fink, Lyman Roger *retired manufacturing executive*
†Finley, Donald J. *medical writer*
Flores, Patrick F. *archbishop*
Fox, Michael W. *lawyer*
Franklin, Larry Daniel *communications company executive*
†Frazer, Robert Lee *landscape architect*
Free, William John *lawyer, communications executive*
Freeman, Howard Lee, Jr. *financial executive*
†Freeman, Philip Dayne *lawyer*
†Freter, Mark Allen *marketing and public relations executive, consultant*
Fretthold, Timothy Jon *lawyer*
Frost, Thomas Clayborne *banker*
Fuhrmann, Charles J., II *investment and finance consultant*
Furino, Antonio *economist, educator*
Garcia, Hipolito Frank (Hippo Garcia) *federal judge*
†Garcia, June Marie *library director*
†Garcia, Linda *secondary school principal*
Garza, Emilio M(iller) *federal judge*
Gates, Mahlon Eugene *applied research executive, former government official, former army officer*
Gibbons, Robert Ebbert *university official*
Goelz, Paul Cornelius *university dean*
Goland, Martin *research institute executive*
Gonzalez, Hector Hugo *nurse, educator, consultant*
Greehey, William Eugene *energy company executive*
Green, Phillip Dale *banker*
Greenberg, Nat *orchestra administrator*
Gresham, Gary Stuart *wholesale grocery executive, accountant*
Grubb, Robert Lynn *computer system designer*
Gudinas, Donald Jerome *banker, retired army officer*
Guenther, Jack Egon *lawyer*
Hamm, William Joseph *retired physics educator*
Hanahan, Donald James *biochemist, educator*
Hardberger, Phillip Duane *judge, lawyer, journalist*
Harte, Houston Harriman *newspaper, broadcasting executive*
†Haywood, Norcell Dan *architect*
Hemminghaus, Roger Roy *energy company executive, chemical engineer*
Henderson, Arvis Burl *data processing executive, biochemist*
Henderson, Dwight Franklin *dean, educator*
†Hernandez, Christine *educator*
Herres, Robert Tralles *insurance company executive*
†Hochhauser, Richard Michael *marketing professional*
Holcomb, M. Staser *insurance executive*
Holguin, Alfonso Hudson *physician, educator*
Hornbeak, John Earl *hospital administrator*
Horner, Richard Elmer *retired telecommunications company executive*
Howard, George Salladé *conductor, music consultant, educator*
Howard, M. Francine *chemist*
Hyland, Douglas K. S. *museum administrator, educator*
†Iglehart, T. D. *bishop*
Issleib, Lutz E. *beverage company executive*
Jacobson, David *rabbi*
Johnson, Hansford Tillman *retired air force officer*
Jones, Daniel Hare *librarian*
Jones, James Richard *business administration educator*
†Juhasz, Stephen *editor, consultant*
Kalter, Seymour Sanford *virologist, educator*
Keck, James Moulton *retired advertising and marketing executive, retired air force officer*
Kellman, Steven G. *literature educator, author*
Kelly, Mae Baker *secondary education educator*
Kelly, Robert Lee *lawyer, evangelist*
Kersnowski, Frank Louis *modern language educator*
†Kibler, Craig Morton *editor, columnist, poet*
Kilpatrick, Charles Otis *newspaper editor, publisher*
Kilpatrick, Mark Kevin *newspaper editor*
King, Ronald Baker *federal judge*
Kirkpatrick, Samuel Alexander *university president, social and policy sciences educator*
Klaerner, Curtis Maurice *former oil company executive*
Kotas, Robert Vincent *research physician, educator*
Krier, Joseph Roland *chamber of commerce executive, lawyer*
Kutchins, Michael Joseph *airport executive*
Lackan, Siewchan *principal, school system administrator*
Lahourcade, John Brosius *service company executive*
Langlinais, Joseph Willis *academic administrator*
Larson, Doyle Eugene *electronics company executive, retired air force officer*
Laurence, Dan H. *author, literary and dramatic specialist*
Leavitt, Audrey Faye Cox *television programming executive*
†Ledford, Frank Finley, Jr. *surgeon, army officer*
Lee, William Franklin, III *association administrator*
Leeper, Michael Edward *retired army officer, retired corporation executive*
Leies, John Alex *academic administrator, educator, clergyman*
Lenke, Joanne Marie *publishing executive*
Leon, Robert Leonard *psychiatrist, educator*
Lindholm, Ulric Svante *engineering research institute executive*
Lowry, A. Robert *federal government railroad arbitrator*
Lyle, Robert Edward *chemist*
Lynch, Robert Martin *lawyer, educator*
Maas, James Weldon *psychiatrist*
Macon, Jane Haun *lawyer*
Macon, Richard Laurence *lawyer*
Manning, Noel Thomas *publishing company executive*
Marbut, Robert Gordon *communications, cable and broadcast executive*
Marek, Vladimir *ballet director, educator*
Masoro, Edward Joseph, Jr. *physiology educator*
Matthews, Dan Gus *lawyer*
Matthews, Wilbur Lee *lawyer*
Mays, L. Lowry *broadcast executive*
Mc Allister, Gerald Nicholas *retired bishop, clergyman*
McClane, Robert Sanford *bank holding company executive*
Mc Dermott, Robert Francis *insurance company executive*
Mc Fee, Arthur Storer *physician*
Mc Giffert, John Rutherford *retired cultural institute director, retired army officer*
McGuire, William Dennis *health care system executive*
†McLelland, Stan L. *energy company executive, lawyer*
Meyer, George Gotthold *psychiatrist, educator*
Miles, Janice Ann *news reporter*
Miller, Larry Joseph *oil and gas company executive*
Mitchell, George Washington, Jr. *physician, educator*
Moder, John Joseph *academic administrator, priest*
†Montecel, Maria Robledo (Cuca Robledo Montecel) *educational association administrator*
Neel, Spurgeon Hart, Jr. *physician, retired army officer*
Oujesky, Helen M. *microbiology educator*
Padgett, Shelton Edward *lawyer*
Parks, Madelyn N. *nurse, retired army officer, university official*
†Perez, Andrew, III *architect*
Persellin, Robert Harold *physician*
Pestana, Carlos *physician, educator*
Post, Gerald Joseph *retired banker, retired air force officer*
Prado, Edward Charles *federal judge*
Quirarte, Jacinto *art historian*
†Randall, Charles Harry *architect*
Ranson, Guy Harvey *clergyman, religion educator*
Regan, William Joseph, Jr. *insurance company executive*
Reiser, Leroy Franklin, Jr. *marketing consultant*
Reuter, Stewart Ralston *radiologist, lawyer, educator*
Rhame, William Thomas *land development company executive*
Ritchie, Richard Lee *communications company executive, former railroad and forest products company executive*
Robinson, David *basketball player*
Roper, Paul Holmes *hospital administrator*
Rosoff, Leonard, Sr. *retired surgeon, medical educator*
Schenker, Steven *physician, educator*
Schlueter, David Arnold *law educator*
Schlueter, Linda Lee *law educator*
Schneider, Bobby Dean *financial consultant*
Schneider, William Henry *retired army officer*
Schulte, Josephine Helen *historian, educator*
†Shih, Chia Shun *educator, consulting engineer*
Siler-Khodr, Theresa Marie *biochemistry educator*
Smith, Reginald Brian Furness *anesthesiologist, educator*
Smith, Richard Thomas *electrical engineer*
Spears, Sally *lawyer*
Spector, Joseph Robert *retired diversified manufacturing executive*
Stebbins, Richard Henderson *electronics engineer, peace officer, security consultant*
Steen, John Thomas, Jr. *lawyer*
Stone, William Harold *geneticist, educator*
Story, Jim Lewis *neurosurgeon, educator*
Sueltenfuss, Sister Elizabeth Anne *university president*
Suttle, Dorwin Wallace *federal judge*
Terracina, Roy David *food executive*
Thornton, William James, Jr. *composer, music educator*
Townsend, Frank Marion *pathology educator*
Trench, William Frederick *mathematics educator*
Truett, Lila Flory *economics educator*
†Van de Putte, Leticia *pharmacist, state official*
†Van Vorst, Charles Brian *health facility administrator*
Vazquez, Gilbert Falcon *lawyer*
Wagener, James Wilbur *social science educator*
West, Robert Van Osdell, Jr. *retired petroleum executive*
Westbrook, Joel Whitsitt, III *lawyer*
Whitacre, Edward E., Jr. *telecommunications executive*
Whitt, Robert Ampudia, III *advertising executive, marketing professional*
Whittington, Floyd Leon *economist, business consultant, retired oil company executive, foreign service officer*
Wiedeman, Geoffrey Paul *physician, air force officer*
Wilson, Janie Menchaca *nursing educator, researcher*
Wimpress, Gordon Duncan, Jr. *corporate consultant, foundation executive*
Witherspoon, John Marshall *advertising executive*
Wolff, Nelson W. *mayor*
Wood, Frank Preuit *educator, former air force officer*
Young, James Julius *university administrator, former army officer*
Young, Olivia Knowles *retired librarian*
†Zachry, Henry Bartell, Jr. *construction company executive*

San Marcos
Bechtol, William Milton *education educator*
Byrom, Jack Edwards *educational administrator*
Cassidy, Patrick Edward *chemist, educator*
Moore, Betty Jean *retired education educator*
Schultz, Clarence Carven, Jr. *sociology educator*
Supple, Jerome H. *university president*
Weinberger, George Martin *political scientist, government infosystems specialist*

Schulenburg
Clark, I. E. *publisher*

Seabrook
Earle, Kenneth Martin *retired neuropathologist*
Sterling, Shirley Frampton *artist, educator*

Sealy
Young, Milton Earl *retired petroleum production company executive*

Seguin
Mims, Forrest Marion, III *science writer*
Moline, Jon Nelson *philosopher, educator, college president*
†Moline, Sandra Lois *librarian*
Oestreich, Charles Henry *college president*
†Selig, Marvin *metal products company executive*

Sherman
Brown, Paul Neeley *federal judge*
Fuller, Anne Elizabeth Havens *English educator, consultant*
Page, Oscar C. *academic administrator*

Silsbee
Ashcraft, David Lee *forest products company executive*

Southlake
George, David Webster *architect*
Norris, Richard Anthony *accountant*

Spearman
Archer, Carl Marion *oil and gas company executive*

Spring
Battle, Thomas Peyton *lawyer*
Frison, Paul Maurice *health care executive*
Goldenberg, George *pharmaceutical company executive*
Hurley, Robert Joseph *lawyer*

Stafford
Brinkley, Elise Hoffman *biofeedback counselor, marriage and family therapist, nurse*
Franks, Charles Leslie *banker*

Stephenville
Christopher, Joe Randell *English language educator*
Collier, Boyd Dean *finance educator, management consultant*
Dees, Lynne *artist*
King, Clyde Richard *journalism educator, writer*
Koestler, Fred *historian, educator*

Stratford
Woods, John William *lawyer*

Sugar Land
Bartolo, Adolph Marion *food company executive*
Kempner, Isaac Herbert, III *sugar company executive*
Kempner, James Carroll *sugar company executive*
McMahon, Edward Francis *oil industry executive, consultant*
Oller, William Maxwell *retired energy company executive, retired naval officer*
Preng, David Edward *management consultant*
Welch, William Henry *oil service company executive, consultant*

Sulphur Springs
†McKenzie, Kenneth *retail grocery executive*

Temple
†Delisi, Dianne White *state legislator*
Dyck, Walter Peter *gastroenterologist, educator*
Montgomery, Johnny Lester *physician, radiologist*
Morrison, Gary Brent *hospital administrator*
Skelton, Byron George *federal judge*
Swartz, Jon David *psychologist, educator*

Texarkana
Cross, Irvie Keil *religious organization executive*
Hill, Imogene Penton *school administrator*
Reinheimer, Robert, Jr. *architect*
Selby, Roy Clifton, Jr. *neurosurgeon*
†Silvey, James L. *religious publisher*
†Tucker, Bobby Glenn *minister*
†Young, Dennis Ray *insurance agent*

The Woodlands
Anderson, Dale *film production executive*
Ashley, Lawrence Atwell, Jr. *former construction executive, management consultant*
Clark, Bernard F. *natural gas company executive*
Connell, Joseph Edward *retired insurance executive*
Levy, Robert Edward *biotechnology company executive*
Logan, Mathew Kuykendall *journalist*
†Neumann, W. Michael *chemicals executive*
†Porter, W. Arthur *research center executive*
Sullivan, James Hall *hospital administrator*
Topazio, Virgil William *university official*
White, Robert Winslow *oilfield service company executive*

Tyler
†Albertson, Christopher Adam *librarian*
Bell, Henry Marsh, Jr. *banking executive*
Blair, James Walter, Jr. *machinery company executive*
Davidson, Jack Leroy *academic administrator*
Frankel, Donald Leon *oil service company executive*
†Gann, Benard Wayne *air force officer*
Guin, Don Lester *insurance company executive*
Guthrie, Judith K. *federal judge*
Justice, William Wayne *federal judge*
Kronenberg, Richard Samuel *physician, educator*
Nelson, Kenwyn Gordon *surgeon*
Odom, Oris Leon, II *finance educator, financial consultant*
Parker, Robert M. *federal judge*
Rudd, Leo Slaton *psychology educator, minister*
Smith, James Edward *petroleum engineer, consultant*
Steger, William Merritt *federal judge*
†Taylor, Jimmie F. *accountant, controller*
Warner, John Andrew *foundry executive*
Yaden, Senka Long *biology educator*

Univ Of Texas At Arlington
†Ferrier, Richard Brooks *architecture educator, architect*
Sundel, Martin *social work educator, psychologist*

Uvalde
Ramsey, Frank Allen *veterinarian, retired army officer*

Valley Mills
Evans, Clifford Jessie *manufacturing executive, land developer*

Van
†Cottrell, Ralph *religious organization executive*

Vanderpool
St. John, Billy Eugene *oil company executive*

Vega
Cook, Clayton Henry *rancher*

Victoria
Fellhauer, David E. *bishop*
†Hunter, Don Michael *banker*
Stubblefield, Page Kindred *banker*

Waco
Achor, L(ouis) Joseph Merlin *neuroscience and psychology educator*
†Averitt, Barry Kip *state legislator*
Baird, Robert Malcolm *philosophy educator, researcher*
Barcus, James Edgar *English literature educator*
Belew, John Seymour *academic administrator, chemist*
†Bonnell, Pamela Gay *library administrator*
Brooks, Roger Leon *university president*
Campbell, Stanley Wallace *history educator*
Chewning, Richard Carter *religious business ethics educator*
Coley, Betty *librarian*
Collmer, Robert George *English language educator*
Colvin, (Otis) Herbert, Jr. *musician, educator*
Cutter, Charles Richard, III *classics educator*
†Denton, Betty *lawyer, state representative*
Flanders, Henry Jackson, Jr. *religion educator*
Goode, Clement Tyson *English language educator*
Henke, Emerson Overbeck *accountant, educator*
Herring, Jack William *English language educator*
Hillis, William Daniel *university administrator*
Kagle, Joseph Louis, Jr. *artist, arts administrator*
Lamkin, Bill Dan *psychologist, educator, consultant*
Lindsey, Jonathan Asmel *library administrator, educator*
†Mann, Robert Allen *banker*
Mc Call, Abner Vernon *law educator, retired university administrator*
Meyer, Paul James *communications company executive*
Miller, Robert T. *political science educator*
Odell, Patrick Lowry *mathematics educator*
Osborne, Harold Wayne *sociology educator, consultant*
Pedrotti, Leno Stephano *physics educator*
Preddy, Raymond Randall *newspaper publisher*
Progar, Dorothy *retired library director*
Rapoport, Bernard *life insurance company executive*
Rose, John Thomas *finance educator*
†Smith, Calvin Bruce *museum director*
Smith, Cullen *lawyer*
Smith, Walter S., Jr. *federal judge*
Sternberg, Daniel Arie *musician, conductor, educator*
Tolbert, Charles Madden *sociology educator*
Wendorf, Hulen Dee *law educator, author, lecturer*
Wilson, John Ross *retired law educator*
Wood, James E., Jr. *religion educator, author*

Warda
Kunze, George William *retired soil scientist*

Waxahachie
Tschoepe, Thomas *bishop*

Webster
Lindner, Kenneth Edward *academic administrator and chemistry educator emeritus*
Rappaport, Martin Paul *internist, nephrologist, educator*

Weslaco
†Amador, Jose Manuel *plant pathologist, research center administrator*
Collins, Anita Marguerite *research geneticist*
†King, Edgar G. *agricultural researcher*
Lingle, Sarah Elizabeth *research scientist*

Wharton
Abell, Thomas Henry *judge*

Whitehouse
Baker, Rebecca Louise *musician, music educator, consultant*

Wichita Falls
Cummins, Shirley Jean *psychologist*
Jones, William Houston *stock brokerage executive, financial consultant*
Reyes, Nicholas Carlos *photographer*
Rodriguez, Louis Joseph *university administrator*
Sarni, Vincent Anthony *manufacturing company executive*
Sund, Eldon Harold *chemistry educator*

Wilford Hall USAF Hosp
Cissik, John Henry *air force career officer, medical researcher*
Klepac, Robert Karl *psychologist, consultant*

Wimberley
Busch, Arthur Winston *environmental engineer, educator, consultant*
Ellis, John *small business owner*
Skaggs, Wayne Gerard *financial services company executive*

Winnsboro
Fairchild, Raymond Eugene *oil company executive*

Woodlands
Mitchell, George P. *gas and petroleum company executive*
Sharman, Richard Lee *communications executive*

Woodsboro
Rooke, Allen Driscoll, Jr. *civil engineer*

Yoakum
Williams, Walter Waylon *lawyer, pecan grower*

UTAH

Altamont
†Evans, Beverly Ann *school administrator, state legislator*

Bountiful
†Burningham, Kim Richard *former state legislator*
Oveson, W(ilford) Val *state official, accountant*

Brigham City
†Call, Osborne Jay *retail executive*

Cedar City
Sherratt, Gerald Robert *college president*

Corinne
Ferry, Miles Yeoman *state official*

Eskdale
Beeston, Joseph Mack *metallurgist*

Gusher
†King, Felton *bishop*

Kaysville
†Simons, Marlene J. *state legislator, rancher*

Layton
†Barlow, Haven J. *state legislator, realtor*

Logan
Aust, Steven Douglas *biochemistry, biotechnology and toxicology educator*
Bennett, James Austin *retired animal science educator*
Clark, Clayton *electrical engineering educator*
Dorst, Howard Earl *entomologist*
Ellsworth, Samuel George *historian, educator*
Hargreaves, George Henry *civil and agricultural engineer, researcher*
†Hillyard, Lyle William *lawyer*
Jackson, LeRoy Eugene (Lee Jackson) *microbiologist, researcher*
Keller, Jack *agricultural engineering educator, consultant*
Rasmussen, Harry Paul *horticulture and landscape educator*
†Roberts, Richard N. *psychologist*
Salisbury, Frank Boyer *plant physiologist, educator*
Scouten, William Henry *chemistry educator, academic administrator*
Shaver, James Porter *education educator, university dean*
Sigler, William Franklin *environmental consultant*
†Steed, Allan J. *physical science research administrator*
Vest, Hyrum Grant, Jr. *horticultural sciences educator*

Murray
Volberg, Herman William *electronic engineer, consultant*

Ogden
Balsiger, David Wayne *television director, author, researcher, producer*
Browning, Roderick Hanson *banker*
Buckner, Elmer La Mar *insurance executive*
Buss, Walter Richard *geology educator*
†Davidson, Thomas Ferguson *chemical engineer*
Garrison, U. Edwin *military, space and defense products manufacturing company executive*
Hardy, Duane Horace *federal agency administrator, educator*
Harris, R. Robert *lawyer*
†Hatch, Randall Clinton *journalist*
Larson, Brent T. *broadcasting executive*
†Lassen, Laurence E. *forester*
McKell, Cyrus M. *college dean, plant physiologist*
†Montgomery, Robert F. *state legislator, retired surgeon, cattle rancher*
†Protzman, Grant Dale *university administrator, state legislator*
Smith, Robert Bruce *college administrator*
Stewart, Isaac Daniel, Jr. *state supreme court justice*
Thompson, Paul Harold *university president*
Trundle, W(infield) Scott *publishing executive newspaper*
Welch, Garth Larry *chemistry educator*
Wilson, James Rigg *aircraft manufacturing company executive*

Orderville
Zornes, Milford *artist*

Orem
Ashton, Alan C. *computer software company executive*
Bastian, Bruce Wayne *software company executive*
Green, John Alden *university director study abroad program*
Jacobson, Alfred Thurl *petroleum executive*
Leifson, June *nursing science educator, university administrator*
Plothow, Roger Henry *college official, consultant*

Park City
Ebbs, George Heberling, Jr. *management consulting company executive*
Fey, John Theodore *insurance company executive*
Mahre, Phil *alpine ski racer, race car driver*
†Moe, Thomas Sven (Tommy Moe) *olympic athlete*
Peterson, Howard George Finnemore *sports executive*
†Trahant, Mark N. *newspaper editor*
Wardell, Joe Russell, Jr. *pharmacologist*

Provo
Abbott, Charles Favour, Jr. *lawyer*
Albrecht, Sterling Jean *university library director*
Alexander, Thomas Glen *history educator*
Allred, Ruel A. *education educator*
Arrington, Leonard James *history educator*
Bahr, Howard Miner *sociologist, educator*
Bartlett, Leonard Lee *communications educator, retired advertising agency executive, advertising historian*
Bergin, Allen Eric *clinical psychologist, educator*
Blake, George Rowland *soil science educator, water resources research administrator*
Brown, Bruce Leonard *psychology educator*
Buck, William Fraser, II *marketing executive*
†Chadwick, Bruce Albert *sociology educator*
Christiansen, John Rees *sociologist, educator*
Clark, Bruce Budge *humanities educator*
†Downey, Howard R. *librarian*
Forster, Merlin Henry *foreign languages educator, author, researcher*
Fry, Earl H. *political scientist, educator*
Gibbons, LeRoy *developer, fundraiser*
Hafen, Bruce Clark *academic administrator*
Hall, Howard Tracy *chemist*
Harlow, LeRoy Francis *organization and management educator emeritus, author*
Hart, Edward LeRoy *poet, educator*
Hunt, H(arold) Keith *business management educator, marketing consultant*
Jensen, Clayne R. *university administrator*
Jonsson, Jens Johannes *electrical engineering educator*
Kimball, Edward Lawrence *legal educator, lawyer*
Kunz, Phillip Ray *sociologist, educator*
Lee, Rex E. *university president, lawyer*
†Lundberg, Constance K. *law educator*
Lyon, James Karl *German educator*
Merritt, LaVere Barrus *engineering educator, civil engineer*
Moore, Hal G. *mathematician, educator*
†Noorda, Raymond J. *computer software company executive*
Peer, Larry Howard *literature educator*
Pope, Bill Jordan *chemical engineering educator, business executive*
Porter, Blaine Robert Milton *psychology/sociology educator*
Porter, Bruce Douglas *federal agency administrator, educator, writer*
Robinson, Donald Wilford *mathematics educator*
Smith, Maurice Edward *lawyer, business consultant*
Smith, Nathan McKay *library and information sciences educator*
Smoot, Leon Douglas *university dean, chemical engineering educator*
Snow, Karl Nelson, Jr. *public management educator, university administrator, former state senator*
Stahmann, Robert F. *education educator*
Strasser, William Carl, Jr. *retired college president, educator*
Thomas, Darwin LaMar *sociology educator*
†Valentine, John Lester *state legislator, lawyer*
Whitman, Dale Alan *lawyer, educator*
Wilson, Ramon B. *agricultural economics educator, administrator*
Woodbury, Lael Jay *theatre educator*

Roy
†Peterson, Douglas Shurtleff *state legislator, packaging company official*

Saint George
Beesley, H(orace) Brent *savings and loan executive*
Belnap, Norma Lee Madsen *musician*
†Peterson, Steven H. *school system administrator*

Salt Lake City
Abildskov, J. A. *cardiologist, educator*
Alter, Edward T. *state treasurer*
Anderson, Arthur Salzner *publishing company executive, marketing executive*
Anderson, Charles Ross *civil engineer*
†Anderson, Grant Allen *librarian*
Anderson, Joseph Andrew, Jr. *retired apparel company executive, retail consultant*
Anderson, Kent Taylor *lawyer*
Anderson, Stephen Hale *federal judge*
†Baird, Delpha *state legislator*
Baker, Charles DeWitt *research and development company executive*
†Ballard, Melvin Russell, Jr. *church official*
†Bates, George Edmonds *bishop*
Baucom, Sidney George *lawyer*
Bauer, A(ugust) Robert, Jr. *surgeon, educator*
Beall, Burtch W., Jr. *architect*
Bean, Scott W. *state education official*
Benjamin, Lorna Smith *psychologist*
Bennett, Janet Huff *legislative staff member*
Berkes, Howard *radio news reporter*
Berman, Daniel Lewis *lawyer*
†Black, Wilford Rex, Jr. *state senator*
†Blackner, Boyd Atkins *architect*
Bozich, Anthony Thomas *transportation industry consultant, retired motor freight company executive*
Brady, Rodney Howard *broadcast company executive, former college president, former government official*
Bragg, David Gordon *physician, radiology educator*
†Brems, David Paul *architect*
Brewer, Stanley R. *wholesale grocery executive*
Brierley, James Alan *research administrator*
Brown, Carolyn Smith *communications educator, consultant*
Buchi, Mark Keith *lawyer*
†Buffmire, Judy Ann *state legislator, psychologist, consultant*
†Buttars, Gerald Anderson *librarian*
Carnahan, Orville Darrell *state legislator, retired college president*
Cash, R(oy) Don *gas and petroleum company executive*
†Chong, Richard David *architect*
Christensen, Ray Richards *lawyer*
Christopher, James Walker *architect, educator*
Clark, Glen Edward *federal judge*
Cook, M(elvin) Garfield *chemical company executive*
†Crane, Steve *architectural firm executive*
Dahlstrom, Donald Albert *chemical and metallurgical engineering educator, former equipment manufacturing company executive*
†Daniels, George Nelson *architect*
†Davis, Gene *state legislator*
†Day, Gerald W. *wholesale grocery company executive*
Day, Joseph Dennis *librarian*

De Vries, Kenneth Lawrence *mechanical engineer, educator*
Dick, Bertram Gale, Jr. *physics educator*
Drew, Clifford James *academic dean, special education and educational psychology educator*
Durham, Christine Meaders *state supreme court justice*
Eakle, Arlene H. *genealogist*
Eccles, Spencer Fox *banker*
†Edwards, William Foster *oil and gas company executive*
Eernisse, Errol Peter *electronics company executive, scientist*
Elkins, Glen Ray *service company executive*
Evans, Max Jay *historical society administrator*
†Evans, Wayne Cannon *communications and public relations executive*
Faust, James E. *church official*
Fehr, J. Will *newspaper editor*
Feucht, Donald Lee *research institute executive*
Flanagan, John Theodore *language professional, educator*
Foltz, Rodger Lowell *chemistry educator, mass spectroscopist*
Frary, Richard Spencer *international consulting company executive*
Furr, James William, Jr. *financial planner, consultant*
†Gallivan, John William *publisher*
Gandhi, Om Parkash *electrical engineer*
Garn, Edwin Jacob (Jake Garn) *former senator*
Ghiselin, Brewster *author, English language educator emeritus*
†Giddings, J. Calvin *chemistry educator*
Giles, Gerald Lynn *psychology,learning enhancement,computer educator*
Goodey, Ila Marie *psychologist*
Graham, Jan *state attorney general*
Grant, David Morris *chemistry educator*
Greene, John Thomas, Jr. *federal judge*
Gregory, Herold La Mar *chemical company administrator*
Grosser, Bernard Irving *psychiatry educator*
Gunnell, Dale Ray *hospital administrator*
Haight, David B. *church official*
†Hales, Robert D. *church official*
Hall, Gordon R. *retired state supreme court chief justice*
Hamill, Mark Richard *actor*
Hammond, M(ary) Elizabeth Hale *pathologist*
Hanson, Roger Kvamme *librarian*
Hart, John *artistic director*
Hatch, George Clinton *television executive*
Hatch, Wilda Gene *broadcast company executive*
Heiner, Clyde Mont *energy company executive*
Hembree, James D. *retired chemical company executive*
Hemingway, W(illiam) David *banker*
Herzberg, Frederick *psychologist, educator*
Hilbert, Robert Backus *county water utility administrator*
Hill, George Richard *chemistry educator*
†Hill, Stephen D. *chemical engineer, federal agency administrator*
Hinckley, Gordon B. *church official*
Hogan, Mervin Booth *mechanical engineer, educator*
Holbrook, Donald Benson *lawyer*
†Holding, R. Earl *oil company executive*
Holtkamp, James Arnold *lawyer, legal educator*
Hornacek, Jeffrey John *professional basketball player*
Howe, Richard Cuddy *state supreme court justice*
†Howell, Scott Newell *computer company executive, state legislator*
Hunter, Howard William *lawyer, church official*
Huntsman, Jon M. *chemical company executive*
†Jacobsen, Stephen Charles *biomedical engineer, educator*
†Janerich, Dwight Thomas *epidemiologist, researcher*
Jarvis, Joseph Boyer *retired university administrator*
Jenkins, Bruce Sterling *federal judge*
Joklik, Günther Franz *mining company executive*
†Jones, Clark David *restaurant executive, accountant*
Kendell, Ross Ezra *banker*
Knight, Joseph Adams *pathologist*
Layden, Francis Patrick (Frank Layden) *professional basketball team executive, former coach*
Lease, Ronald Charles *financial economics educator*
Leavitt, Michael Okerlund *governor, insurance executive*
Lee, Glenn Richard *medical administrator, educator*
Leonard, Glen M. *museum administrator*
Lewis, Leonard J. *lawyer*
Losse, John William, Jr. *mining company executive*
Lueders, Edward George *author, poet, educator, editor*
Lund, Victor L. *retail food company executive*
Lunt, Jack *lawyer*
Mabey, Ralph R. *lawyer*
Madsen, Arch Leonard *broadcasting company executive*
Madsen, Brigham Dwaine *history educator*
†Madsen, Floyd A. *laboratory director*
Malone, Karl *professional basketball player*
Manning, Brent V. *lawyer*
Mason, James Ostermann *public health administrator*
Maxwell, Neal A. *church official*
Mayfield, David Merkley *genealogy director*
McCleary, Lloyd E(verald) *education educator*
McKay, Monroe Gunn *federal judge*
Mc Murrin, Sterling Moss *philosophy educator*
Meldrum, Peter Durkee *venture capital company executive*
Melich, Doris S. *public service worker*
Melich, Mitchell *lawyer*
Middleton, Anthony Wayne, Jr. *urologist, educator*
Miller, Jan Dean *metallurgy educator*
Mock, Henry Byron *lawyer, writer, consultant*
Monson, David Smith *accountant, former congressman*
†Monson, Gregory Brammer *lawyer*
Monson, Thomas Spencer *church official, publishing company executive*
Mortimer, William James *newspaper publisher*
Moser, Royce, Jr. *physician, medical educator*
†Myrin, N. Alarik *senator, rancher, investor*
Nebeker, Stephen Bennion *lawyer*
Nelson, Roger Hugh *management educator, business executive*
Nelson, Russell Marion *surgeon, educator*
Nielsen, Greg Ross *lawyer*
†Nordgren, Bradley J. *advertising executive*
Norton, Delmar Lynn *candy company executive, video executive*
Oaks, Dallin Harris *lawyer, church official*
Oblad, Alexander Golden *chemistry educator, research chemist*
O'Brien, Paul Jerry *newspaper publishing executive*
Odell, William Douglas *physician, scientist, educator*
O'Halloran, Thomas Alphonsus, Jr. *physicist, educator*
Olson, Randall J. *ophthalmologist, educator*
†Osherow, Jacqueline Sue *poet, English language educator*
†Ostler, O. Don *jewelry, emblem manufacturing company executive*
Ottley, Jerold Don *choral conductor, educator*
Overall, James Carney, Jr. *pediatrics educator*
Owen, Amy *library director*
Pace, Nathan Leon *anesthesiologist, educator*
†Packer, Boyd K. *church official*
†Parker, Scott Smith *hospital administrator*
†Parkinson, Richard A. *consumer products company executive*
Parry, Robert Walter *chemistry educator*
Partridge, William Schaubel *physicist, research company executive*
Paulsen, Vivian *magazine editor*
†Perry, L. Tom *church official, merchant*
Pershing, David Walter *chemical engineering educator, researcher*
Peterson, Chase N. *university president*
Phillips, Ted Ray *advertising agency executive*
Plumley, S. Patric *retail executive*
Renzetti, Attilio David *physician*
Richmond, Thomas G. *chemistry educator*
Roberts, Jack Earle *lawyer, ski resort operator, wood products company executive, real estate developer*
†Robison, Barbara Ann *retired newspaper editor*
Roth, John Roger *geneticist, biology educator*
Sam, David *federal judge*
†Samuelson, Cecil O. *health care facility executive*
Sandquist, Gary Marlin *engineering educator*
Sanguinetti, Eugene Frank *art museum administrator, educator*
Scott, Howard Winfield, Jr. *temporary help company executive*
Scott, James Raymond *obstetrics and gynecology educator*
†Scott, Richard G. *church official*
Scowcroft, John Major *petroleum refinery process development executive*
Seader, Junior DeVere *chemical engineering educator*
Shelledy, James Edwin, III *editor*
Sillars, Malcolm Osgood *communications educator*
Silverstein, Joseph Harry *conductor, musician*
Simmons, Harris H. *banker*
Simmons, Roy William *banker*
Skidmore, Rex Austin *social work educator*
Sloan, Jerry (Gerald Eugene Sloan) *professional basketball coach*
Smart, Charles Rich *retired surgeon*
Smith, Arthur Kittredge, Jr. *university official, political science educator*
Smith, Eldred Gee *church leader*
Sohn, Hong Yong *metallurgical and chemical engineering educator*
Stanford, Melvin Joseph *management consultant, retired educator, academic administrator*
Steensma, Robert Charles *English language educator*
Steiner, Richard Russell *conglomerate executive*
Stockham, Thomas Greenway, Jr. *electrical engineering educator*
Stockton, John Houston *professional basketball player*
†Stowe, Neal P. *architect*
†Straight, Richard Coleman *photobiologist*
Stringfellow, Gerald B. *engineering educator*
Swenson, James Reed *physician, educator*
Thurman, Samuel David *legal educator*
Tyler, Frank Hill *medical educator*
†Van Treese, James Bryan *book publishing and investment company executive*
Velick, Sidney Frederick *research biochemist, educator*
Wadsworth, Harold Wayne *lawyer*
Walker, Olene S. *lieutenant governor*
Ward, John Robert *physician, educator*
Warnick, Charles Terry *research biochemist*
Weigand, William Keith *bishop*
†Wharton, Blaze Douglas *county official*
Winder, David Kent *federal judge*
†Wirthlin, Joseph B. *church official*
Wolf, Harold Herbert *pharmacy educator*
Wong, Kuang Chung *anesthesiologist*
Zaharia, Eric Stafford *developmental disabilities program administrator*
Zeamer, Richard Jere *engineer, executive*
Zimmerman, Michael David *state supreme court chief justice*

Sandy
Bennett, Carl McGhie *engineering company executive, consultant, army reserve and national guard officer*
Jorgensen, Leland Howard *aerospace research engineer*
Schneiter, George Malan *golf professional, development company executive*
York, Theodore Robert *consulting company executive*

South Jordan
Bangerter, Norman Howard *building contractor, developer, former governor*

Springville
Hall, Derek Harry *natural health products company sales executive*
†Haymond, J. Brent *chemical company executive, state legislator*

Tremonton
Kerr, Kleon Harding *former state senator, educator*
Thompson, (Gerry) Maxine Leak *supply technician, inventory consultant*

Vernal
Siddoway, Henry Ralph *company executive*

West Jordan
†Shepherd, Paul H. *elementary school educator*

West Valley City
†Peterson, Millie M. *state legislator*

VERMONT

Arlington
Nowicki, George Lucian *chemical company executive*

Barnard
Larson, John Hyde *retired utilities executive*

Bennington
Adams, Pat *artist, educator*
Brownell, David Wheaton *editor*
Coleman, Elizabeth *college president*
Dixon, William Robert *musician, composer, educator*
Gagliardi, Lee Parsons *federal judge*
Garret, Paula Lyn *publishing company executive*
Kaplan, Harold *humanities educator, author*
Killen, Carroll Gorden *electronics company executive*
†Luckey, Laura Colby *museum director*
Perin, Donald Wise, Jr. *former association executive*
Sandy, Stephen *writer, educator*

Bradford
Kaplow, Leonard Samuel *pathologist, educator*

Brattleboro
Akins, Zane Vernon *association executive*
Cohen, Richard *grocery company executive*
Cummings, Charles Rogers *lawyer*
Gregg, Michael B. *health science association administrator, epidemiologist*
Howland, William Stapleton *anesthesiologist, educator*
Lappe, Frances Moore *author, lecturer*
Oakes, James L. *federal judge*
Sarle, Charles Richard *health facility executive*
Weigand, James Gary *utility company executive, former military officer*

Bristol
Kompass, Edward John *consulting editor*

Brookfield
Gerard, James Wilson *book distributor*
Newton, Earle Williams *editor, museum director, library and museum consultant*

Burlington
Albee, George Wilson *psychology educator*
†Albertini, Richard Joseph *molecular geneticist, educator*
Anderson, Richard Louis *electrical engineer*
Bartlett, Richmond Jay *soil chemistry educator, researcher*
Carlisle, Lilian Matarose Baker (Mrs. E. Grafton Carlisle, Jr.) *author, lecturer*
Cram, Reginald Maurice *retired air force officer*
Cutler, Stephen Joel *sociologist*
Daniels, Robert Vincent *history educator, former state senator*
Davis, John Herschel *surgeon, educator*
†Della Santa, Laura *principal*
Dinse, John Merrell *lawyer*
†Grimes, Barbara Lauritzen *housing and community affairs administrator*
Hall, Robert William *philosophy and religion educator*
Hartwell, Samuel Adams *manufacturing company executive*
†Heinrich, Bernd *biologist, zoology educator*
Lawson, Robert Bernard *psychology educator*
†Low, Robert B. *physiology educator*
Lucey, Jerold Francis *pediatrician*
Martin, Allen *lawyer*
Martin, Rebecca Reist *librarian*
Mead, Philip Bartlett *physician, administrator*
Pacy, James Steven *political science professor*
Parker, Fred I. *federal judge*
Pinder, George Francis *engineering educator, scientist*
Riddick, Daniel Howison *obstetrics and gynecology educator, priest*
Salmon, Thomas Paul *lawyer, academic administrator*
Sampson, Samuel Franklin *sociology educator*
Sanders, Bernard (Bernie Sanders) *congressman*
Scrase, David Anthony *German language educator*
Smallwood, Franklin *political science educator*
Sobel, Burton Elias *physician, educator*
†Swenson, Daniel Lee *bishop*
Taylor, James Howard *hospital administrator*
Weiger, John George *foreign language educator*
White, William North *chemistry educator*
Wick, Hilton Addison *lawyer*

Calais
Elmslie, Kenward Gray *retired publishing company executive, author*

Cavendish
Shapiro, David *artist, art historian*

Charlotte
Hong, Richard *pediatrician, educator*
Kiley, Daniel Urban *landscape architect, planner*
McCoubrey, R. James *advertising executive*
Moore, Stephen Gates *banking executive*

Chester
Coleman, John Royston *innkeeper, author*
†Farrar, Aili R. *cartographic draftsperson*

Chittenden
Haley, John Charles *financial executive*

Colchester
Reiss, Paul Jacob *college president*

Danby
†Mitchell, John McKearney *manufacturing company executive*

Dorset
Ketchum, Richard Malcolm *editor, writer*

East Calais
Gahagan, James Edward, Jr. *artist*
Meiklejohn, Donald *philosophy educator*

East Dorset
Armstrong, Jane Botsford *sculptor*

East Wallingford
Bluhm, Norman *artist*

Essex Junction
Pricer, Wilbur David *electrical engineer*
†Sweetser, Gene Gilman *quality assurance professional, state legislator*
†Sweetser, Susan W. *state legislator, lawyer, advocate*

Fair Haven
†Larkin, John Paul, II *state legislator*
†Pentkowski, Raymond J. *superintendent*

Gaysville
Dawson, Wilfred Thomas *marketing executive, consultant*

Greensboro
Hill, Lewis Reuben *horticulturist, nursery owner*

Hartland
Tooker, George *artist*

Hinesburg
Ross, Charles Robert *lawyer, consultant*

Londonderry
Bigelow, David Skinner, III *management consultant*

Lyndon Center
Myers, Rex Charles *academic dean*

Lyndonville
Williams, Peggy Ryan *academic administrator*

Manchester
Fellows, Diana Potenzano *educational administrator*
†Freed, Walter Everett *petroleum company executive, state representative*
Hooper, Arthur William *consultant, former association executive*
†Kouwenhoven, Gerrit Wolphertsen *museum director*
Mills, Gordon Lawrence *financial executive*
Wilbur, James Benjamin, III *philosopher, educator*
Yager, Hunter *advertising executive*

Manchester Center
Gould, James Spencer *financial consultant*

Marlboro
Olitski, Jules *artist*

Middlebury
Andrews, David Henry *anthropology educator*
Clifford, Nicholas Rowland *history educator, college administrator*
Colander, David Charles *economist, educator*
Ferm, Robert Livingston *religion educator*
Gibson, Eleanor Jack (Mrs. James J. Gibson) *psychology educator*
Gleason, Robert Willard *chemistry educator, college dean*
Hitchcock, Harold Bradford *retired biology educator, zoologist*
Jacobs, Travis Beal *historian, educator*
Lamberti, Marjorie *history educator*
Landgren, Craig Randall *biology educator*
†Langrock, Peter Forbes *lawyer*
McCardell, John Malcolm, Jr. *college administrator*
O'Brien, George Dennis *university president, retired*
Patterson, William Bradford *surgical oncologist*
Saul, George Brandon, II *biology educator*
Vail, Van Horn *German educator*
Wilson, George Wilton *economics educator*

Montpelier
Allen, Frederic W. *state supreme court justice*
Amestoy, Jeffrey Lee *state attorney general*
†Backus, Jan *state legislator*
Barbieri, Christopher George *association executive*
Bertrand, Frederic Howard *insurance company executive*
Brandenburg, Richard George *university dean, management educator*
Brock, James Sidney *lawyer*
†Carlson, Mary Ann *state legislator, hotel executive*
†Carroll, John Marcus Conlon *state senator, consultant*
†Crosby, George Miner *state legislator*
Dean, Howard *governor*
Diamond, M. Jerome *lawyer, former state official*
†Gear, Sara Moreau *state legislator*
†Granai, Edwin *state senator*
Guild, Alden *lawyer*
Harding, John Hibbard *insurance company executive*
Hooper, Don *secretary of state*
†Illuzzi, Vincent *state senator, lawyer*
Klinck, Patricia Ewasco *state official*
†Kroger, Althea *state legislator*
Leland, Lawrence *insurance executive*
†McGarey Madkour, Mary Elaine Bliss *state legislator*
†Metcalf, Michael Warren *state senator, educator*
Morse, James L. *state supreme court justice*
†Paquin, Edward H., Jr. *state legislator*
†Ready, Elizabeth M. *state legislator*
†Rivers, Cheryl P. *state legislator*
†Smith, Ruth R. *state legislator*
Snelling, Barbara *state official*
†Steele, Karen Kiarsis *state legislator*

Morrisville
†Roberts, Carolyn C. *hospital administrator*
Simonds, Marshall *lawyer*

Newport
Guerrette, Richard Hector *priest, management consultant*

North Bennington
Belitt, Ben *poet, educator*
Holden, James Stuart *federal judge*
Kimpel, Benjamin Franklin *philosophy educator emeritus, writer*

North Pomfret
Guernsey, Otis Love, Jr. *critic, editor*

Northfield
Schneider, Richard William *university president*
†Wick, William S. *clergyman, chaplain*

Norwich
Byrne, John Joseph, Jr. insurance executive
Fitzhugh, William Wyvill, Jr. printing company executive
†Japikse, David mechanical engineer, manufacturing executive
Naumann, Robert Bruno Alexander chemist, physicist, educator
Payson, Henry Edwards forensic psychiatrist, educator
Post, Avery Denison church official
Smith, Markwick Kern, Jr. management consultant
Snapper, Ernst mathematics educator
Stetson, Eugene William, III film and television writer and producer

Norwick
Lundquist, Weyman Ivan lawyer

Pawlet
Buechner, Carl Frederick minister, author

Peacham
Barnes, Harry G., Jr. retired ambassador
Engle, James Bruce ambassador
Lederer, William Julius author

Perkinsville
Harris, Christopher publisher, designer, editor

Randolph
†Angell, Philip Alvin, Jr. lawyer

Rutland
Billings, Franklin Swift, Jr. federal judge
Cook, George Wallace Foster retired lawyer, tree farmer
†Ferraro, Betty Ann corporate administrator, state senator
Griffin, James Edwin utilities executive
Keyser, Frank Ray, Jr. lawyer, former governor of Vermont
Stafford, Robert Theodore lawyer, former senator
†Webb, Thomas Crawford utilities company executive
Wright, William Bigelow financial executive

Saint Johnsbury
†Mayo, Bernier L. secondary school principal
Trelfa, Richard Thomas paper company executive

Shaftsbury
Bubriski, Kevin Ernest photographer, educator

Sharon
Phillips, Ellis Laurimore, Jr. legal educator, foundation executive

Shelburne
Sawabini, Wadi Issa retired dentist
Sheldon, David Frederick museum director, headmaster

South Burlington
Hackett, Luther Frederick insurance company executive
Johnson, Robert Eugene physiologist
Kebabian, Paul Blakeslee librarian
Kenyon, Judith primary school educator
†Pizzagalli, James construction executive
Terris, Milton physician, educator

South Londonderry
†Coleman, Wendell Lawrence state legislator, farmer
Spiers, Ronald Ian diplomat

South Royalton
Kempner, Maximilian Walter law school dean, lawyer
Williams, Norman law educator, city planner

South Strafford
Novick, Sheldon M. author, lawyer

South Woodstock
Crowl, John Allen retired publishing company executive

Springfield
Garinger, Louis Daniel religion educator

Stowe
Anderson, Rudolph J., Jr. lawyer

Taftsville
Johnson, Philip Martin lawyer

Thetford
Hoagland, Mahlon Bush biochemist, educator

Thetford Center
Brown, Robert Goodell management consultant

Thetford Hill
Paley, Grace author, educator

Waitsfield
Raphael, Albert Ash, Jr. lawyer

Waterbury
Adams, Charles Jairus lawyer
Bunting, Charles I. academic administrator
†Cohen, Bennett R. ("Ben" Cohen) food products executive
†Greenfield, Jerry food products executive

West Brattleboro
Barber, Orion Metcalf, II publishing consultant, book packager

West Burke
Van Vliet, Claire artist

Weston
Kasnowski, Chester Nelson artist, educator

White River Junction
Barton, Gail Melinda psychiatrist, educator
Fayerweather, John management and international business specialist, educator
Halperin, George Bennett education educator, retired naval officer
Linnell, Robert Hartley environment, safety consultant

Williston
Mc Kay, Robert James, Jr. pediatrician, educator

Windsor
Furnas, Howard Earl business executive, educator, retired government official
Seldes, George author

Winooski
Wilson, Mary Louise learning systems company executive

Woodstock
Blackwell, David Jefferson insurance company executive
Browning, Robert Masters management consultant
Debevoise, Thomas McElrath lawyer, educator

VIRGINIA

Abingdon
Widener, Hiram Emory, Jr. federal judge
Williams, Glen Morgan federal judge
Wilson, Samuel Grayson federal judge

Airlie
Clayton, James Edwin foundation executive, journalist

Alexandria
Abbott, Preston Sargent psychologist
Abell, Richard Bender lawyer, federal official
†Ackerman, Roy Alan research and development executive
Adams, Ranald Trevor, Jr. retired air force officer
Alderson, Margaret Northrop arts administrator, educator, artist
Alexander, Fred Calvin, Jr. lawyer
Allen, Fred Cary retired army officer
†Anderson, Robert Barber architect
Armstrong, C. Torrence lawyer
Babcock, Jack Emerson retired army officer, educator, corporate executive
Bachus, Walter Otis retired army general, former association executive
Bailar, Barbara Ann professional society executive, statistician, researcher
†Baird, Charles F. think-tank executive
†Baker, Brent Harold foundation executive
Baroody, Michael Elias public policy institution executive
†Bartholomew, Byron Simpson, Jr. engineering services company executive
Berger, Patricia Wilson retired librarian
Berman, Alan physicist
Bernsen, Harold John political affairs consultant, retired naval officer
Biberman, Lucien Morton physicist
Birely, William Cramer investment banker
Blake, John Francis former government agency official, consultant
Blumenthal, David A. lawyer
†Bolger, Robert Joseph retired trade association executive
Bostetter, Martin V. B., Jr. bankruptcy court judge
Bowman, Richard Carl defense consultant, retired air force officer
Brenner, Alfred Ephraim physicist
Brickell, Charles Hennessey, Jr. marine engineer, retired military officer
Brinkema, Leonie Milhomme federal judge
Broide, Mace Irwin public affairs consultant
Brown, Frederic Joseph army officer
Brown, Quincalee association executive
†Brownfeld, Allan Charles columnist
†Budde, Mitzi Marie Jarrett librarian
Burke, Kelly Howard former air force officer, business executive
Byrd-Lawler, Barbara Ann association executive
Byrne, John Edward writer, retired government official
Byrnside, Oscar Jehu, Jr. association executive
Cacheris, James C. federal judge
Campbell, Francis James retired chemist
Casey, Michael Kirkland business executive, lawyer
Chamberlain, Adrian Ramond executive
Chao, Elaine L. philanthropic organization executive
Choromokos, James, Jr. consultant, former government official
Christensen, Bruce LeRoy public broadcasting executive
Christie, Thomas Philip government administrator
Clarey, Donald Alexander government affairs consultant
Clower, William Dewey association executive
†Cohen, Bernard S. lawyer
Collins, Frank Charles, Jr. industrial and service quality specialist
Condrill, Jo Ellaresa logistics executive, speaker
Conger, Clement Ellis foreign service officer, curator
Connally, Ernest Allen retired federal agency administrator
Connell, John Gibbs, Jr. former government official
Cook, Charles William aerospace consultant, educator
Cooper, B. Jay public relations executive
Cooper, Charles Donald association executive, editor, retired career officer
Cooper, Kenneth Banks business executive, former army officer
Corson, Walter Harris sociologist
Covone, James Michael automotive parts import and distribution company executive
Cowles, Roger William government audit executive
†Cross, Eason, Jr. architect
Darling, Thomas, Jr. retired rural electrification specialist
Dawalt, Kenneth Francis former army officer, former aerospace company executive
Dawson, Samuel Cooper, Jr. motel company executive
Day, Melvin Sherman information company executive
Devine, Donald J. management and political consultant
Dies, Douglas Hilton international trade consultant
Dietrich, Laura Jordan international policy advisor
Dobson, Donald Alfred electrical engineer
Doeppner, Thomas Walter electrical engineer, educator, consultant
†Donnelly, John Francis federal official
Donohue, Thomas Joseph transportation association executive
Dorsey, James Francis, Jr. naval officer
Downs, Michael Patrick retired marine corps officer
Duncan, John Bonner housing development consultant
Duncan, Stephen Mack lawyer
Eckhart, Myron, Jr. marine engineer
Ellis, Thomas Selby, III federal judge
Ensslin, Robert Frank, Jr. retired military officer
Evans, Grose former curator, retired educator
Evans, H. Bradley, Jr. lawyer
†Fahey, John M., Jr. book publishing executive
Fichenberg, Robert Gordon newspaper editor, consultant
Finnell, Dallas Grant fundraising executive
Fisher, Donald Wayne medical association executive
Fleming, Douglas Riley journalist, publisher, public affairs consultant
Foisie, Philip Manning retired journalist, media consultant
Foster, Luther Hilton former university president, educational consultant
Foster, Robert Francis communications executive
Fozard, John William engineer, designer, consultant, educator
Garrison, Preston Jones association consultant
Goldstein, Jerome Charles professional association executive, surgeon, otolaryngologist
Gray, John Edmund chemical engineer
†Greener, William I., III communications executive
Greenstein, Ruth Louise research institute executive, lawyer
Hagan, Robert Leslie consulting company executive
†Hagemann, Kenneth L., Sr. federal official, career officer
Hampton, E. Lynn municipal finance administrator
Hansan, Mary Anne marketing professional
Harding, Trewitt DeLano stockbroker
Harris, Thomas Everett government official, lawyer, retired
Hartsock, Linda Sue educational and management development executive
Havens, Harry Stewart former federal assistant comptroller general, government consultant
Heacock, Phillip Kaga aerospace executive
Helman, Gerald Bernard government official
Hilton, Claude Meredith federal judge
Hilton, Robert Parker, Sr. national security affairs consultant, retired naval officer
Hobbs, Michael Edwin broadcasting company executive
†Hodder, Kenneth Lasett social services administrator
Holland, Dianna Gwin real estate broker
Hoyt, F(rank) Russell association executive
Huffman, Delton Cleon, Jr. pharmaceuticals executive
Hughes, Grace-Flores former federal agency administrator, management consulting executive
Hussey, Ward MacLean lawyer, government official
Irions, Charles Carter trade association executive
†Johnson, Edgar M. psychologist
Johnson, Robert Gerald federal agency consultant
Johnson, William David retired university administrator
Keith, Donald Raymond retired army officer, business executive
Kennedy, Mary Virginia diplomat
Kilcline, Thomas John naval officer
Kitt, Loren Wayne musician
Klotz, John Wesley electronics consultant
Kolar, Mary Jane association executive
Kopp, Eugene Paul lawyer
Lancaster, Bruce Morgan investment adviser, lecturer, retired diplomat
Lasser, Howard Gilbert chemical engineer, consultant
Laurent, Lawrence Bell communications executive, former journalist
Lawson, Jennifer broadcast executive
Lenz, Edward Arnold trade association executive, lawyer
Lion, Paul Michel, III transportation engineer, executive
Litke, Donald Paul business executive, retired military officer
†Locigno, Paul Robert public affairs executive
Loevi, Francis Joseph, Jr. consulting company executive
†Losey, Michael Robert association executive
Lundeberg, Philip Karl curator
Mandil, I. Harry nuclear engineer
Mann, Seymour Zalmon political science and public administration educator emeritus, union official
Marsh, Robert Thomas corporate executive, retired air force general
Masterson, Kleber Sanlin, Jr. physicist
Mathis, William Lowrey lawyer
†Matthews, Stuart aircraft manufacturing company executive
†McClure, Roger John lawyer
McCulloch, William Leonard association executive
†McFarland, Richard B. engineering company executive
McFarlin, Robert Paul army officer
Mc Lucas, John Luther aerospace company executive
McMillan, Charles William consulting company executive
Mc Mullen, Thomas Henry retired air force officer
McNair, Carl Herbert, Jr. army officer, aeronautical engineer
Merrick, Roswell Davenport association executive
Messing, Frederick Andrew, Jr. action lobbyist
Miller, Jerome Gilbert criminologist
Miller, Martin John lawyer
†Milling, Marcus Eugene, Sr. geologist
Mitchell, Joseph Brady military historian, author
Molholm, Kurt Nelson federal agency administrator
†Moody, W. Jarvis think-tank executive
Mosely, Linda Hays surgeon
Muir, Warren R. chemist, toxic substances specialist
Mulvihill, John Gary information services administrator
†Murray, Robert J. think-tank executive
Murray, Russell, II aeronautical engineer, defense analyst, consultant
Myers, Denys Peter, Jr. architectural historian
Newburger, Beth Weinstein medical telecommunications company executive
O'Brien, Patrick Michael library administrator
Olson, Warren Kinley operations research analyst, engineer, physicist
†Osborn, William C. personnel organization executive
†Ottenhoff, Robert George television executive
Palma, Dolores Patricia urban planner
Parsons, Henry McIlvaine psychologist
Pastin, Mark Joseph executive consultant, professional society administrator
Perkins, A. William printing executive
Peterson, David Andreas lawyer, government official, educator
Pitt, Robert Healy, II international marketing executive
Plitt, Jeanne Given librarian
Porter, Elsa Allgood writer, lecturer
Pringle, Robert Maxwell diplomat
Pulling, Ronald Wilson, Sr. aviation systems planner, civil engineer, consultant
Puscheck, Herbert Charles federal administrator
Rall, Lloyd Louis civil engineer
Rector, John Michael lawyer, association executive
Regan, Donald Thomas financier, writer, lecturer
Rice, Sue Ann education administrator, industrial and organizational psychologist
Richardson, Robert Charlwood, III management consultant, retired air force officer
†Ritter, James William architect, educator
†Roley, Jerry bank executive
Rose, Susan Porter federal commission administrator
Rosenkranz, Robert Bernard military officer
Rowden, William Henry naval officer
Saint, Crosbie Edgerton retired army officer
Salomon, Leon Edward career officer
Sanfelici, Arthur H(ugo) editor, writer
†Sava, Samuel G. educational association administrator
†Sayre, Edward Vale chemist
†Scheupelein, Robert John government official
Schultz, Franklin M. lawyer
Scurlock, Arch Chilton chemical engineer
Senese, Donald Joseph former government official
Shannon, Thomas Alfred association executive
Shapiro, Maurice Mandel astrophysicist
Shuster, Robert G. electronics company executive, consultant
Smith, Carl Richard association executive, former air force officer
Smith, J. Brian advertising executive, public affairs consultant, campaign management firm executive
Smith, Jeffrey Greenwood industry executive, retired army officer
Smith, William Young consultant, former air force officer
Spiro, Robert Harry, Jr. foundation and business executive, educator
Stafford, Thomas Patten retired military officer, former astronaut
Stanley, Robert Warren association executive
Stempler, Jack Leon aerospace company executive
Straub, Peter Thornton lawyer
†Straw, Edward M. career officer, federal agency administrator
Strickland, Nellie B. library program director
Sturtevant, Brereton retired lawyer, former government official
Swinburn, Charles lawyer
Thomas, Billy Marshall retired army officer
Thomas, William Griffith lawyer
Thompson, LeRoy, Jr. radio engineer, army reserve officer
†Ticer, Patricia mayor
Tidman, Derek Albert physics researcher
Toulmin, Priestley, III geologist
Tyl, Noel Jan baritone, astrologer
Vander Myde, Paul Arthur engineering services executive
Voorhees, John Henry military officer
Vuono, Carl E. army officer
Watson, George William lawyer, legal consultant
Weinert, Donald G(regory) association executive, engineer
White, Gordon Eliot historian
Whitney, Marvin Edward adult education educator
†Wilding, James Anthony airport administrator
Williams, Justin W. government official
Willis, Clayton broadcaster, corporation executive, former government official, educator, arts consultant, photojournalist, lecturer
Wilner, Morton Harrison retired lawyer
Wolicki, Eligius Anthony nuclear physicist, consultant
Woods, John LaRue international education consultant
Woolley, Mary Elizabeth research administrator
Yates, Jeffrey McKee trade association executive
Yoder, Edwin Milton, Jr. columnist, educator, editor, writer
Yonkman, Fredrick Albers lawyer, management consultant
Zarro, Janice Anne lawyer
Ziegler, Ronald Louis association executive, former government official
Zook, Donovan Quay foreign service officer

Annandale
Abdellah, Faye Glenn retired public health service executive
Ballard, Edward Brooks landscape architect
Binder, Richard Allen hematologist, oncologist
Critchfield, Richard Patrick journalist
Faraday, Bruce John scientific research company executive, physicist
Guthrie, Edward Everett government executive, lawyer
Guthrie, John Reiley retired army officer, business executive
Khim, Jay Wook high-tech research and development, professional service company executive
Lewis, Charles Leonard psychologist
Matuszko, Anthony Joseph research chemist, administrator
McCaffree, Burnham Clough, Jr. retired naval officer
Mc Kee, Fran retired naval officer
Nowak, Jan Zdzislaw writer, consultant
Pollard, David Edward editor
Richstein, Abraham Richard lawyer
Rogers, Stephen Hitchcock former ambassador
Shamburek, Roland Howard physician
Simonian, Simon John surgeon, scientist, educator
Speakes, Larry Melvin public relations executive
Stage, Thomas Benton psychiatrist
†Strohsahl, George Henry, Jr. retired rear admiral, consultant
Tontz, Robert L. government official
Williams, James Arthur retired army officer, information systems company executive

Appomattox
†Montgomery, Jon B. *museum administrator*

Arlington
Ackerson, Jeffrey Townsend *computer systems executive*
Adreon, Harry Barnes *architect*
Aggrey, Orison Rudolph *former ambassador, university administrator*
Allen, Ernest Eugene *non-profit organization executive, lawyer*
Angell, Wayne D. *economist, banker*
Anns, Philip Harold *international trading executive, former pharmaceutical company executive*
Anthony, Robert Armstrong *lawyer, law educator*
Ary, T. S. *federal official, geologist*
Aukland, Elva Dayton *biologist, educator*
Bader, Michael Haley *lawyer, broadcasting executive*
Bailey, Amos Purnell *clergyman, syndicated columnist*
Bailly, Henri-Claude Albert *consulting services executive*
†Banister, G. Huntington *federal official*
Bardon, Marcel *government official*
Barnes, Wesley Edward *energy and environmental consulting company executive*
Barnhart, Beverly Jean *meteorologist*
Barrera, Manuel *foreign service officer*
Barrett, Lida Kittrell *mathematics educator*
Bartlett, Bruce Reeves *economist*
Bartlett, Elizabeth Susan *audio-visual specialist*
Bast, James Louis *trade association executive*
Bautz, Laura Patricia *astronomer*
Beggs, James Montgomery *former government official*
Belen, Frederick Christopher *lawyer*
Bennett, John Joseph *professional services company executive*
Benzinger, Raymond Burdette *lawyer, educator*
Berg, John Richard *chemist, former federal government executive*
Berg, Sister Marie Majella *university chancellor*
Bode, Barbara *foundation executive*
Bodley, Harley Ryan, Jr. *editor, writer, broadcaster*
Boek, Walter Erwin *university president, educator, anthropologist, scientist*
†Bohannon, James Everett *talk show host, newscaster, reporter*
Bolster, Archie Milburn *retired foreign service officer*
Borchers, Robert Reece *physicist and administrator*
Boyle, Robert Patrick *retired government agency consultant, lawyer*
Brenner, Edgar H. *lawyer*
Bridgewater, Albert Louis *science foundation administrator*
†Britt, Harold C. *physicist*
Brown, James Harvey *neuroscientist, government research administrator*
Brown, Robert Lyle *foreign affairs consultant*
Brunson, Burlie Allen *defense contractor executive*
†Buechner, Jack William *lawyer, former congressman*
Bullard, Marcia Lynn *weekly magazine editor*
Burdetsky, Ben *business administration educator, dean*
Burgess, David *lawyer*
Bye, Raymond Erwin, Jr. *federal agency administrator*
Campanella, Anton J. *telephone company executive*
Cargo, William Ira *retired foreign service officer*
Carr, Kenneth Monroe *naval officer*
Carretta, Albert Aloysius *lawyer, educator*
Carter, William Walton *physicist*
Casazza, John Andrew *electrical engineer, business executive*
Case, Charles Carroll *retired army officer*
Cetron, Marvin Jerome *management executive*
Chapman, Donald D. *retired naval officer, lawyer*
†Chapple, Thomas Leslie *lawyer*
†Chavez, Linda *government official*
Chipman, Susan Elizabeth *psychologist*
Clayton, William E. *naval officer*
†Clements, John Brian *broadcasting executive*
Cocklin, Robert Frank *association executive*
Coe, Paul Francis *demographer, economist*
Cohen, Ronald Eli *journalist*
Cole, Benjamin Richason *newspaper executive*
Collins, Eileen Louise *economist*
Collins, Philip Reilly *lawyer, educator*
Cook, Richard Kelsey *aerospace industry executive*
Correll, John Thomas *magazine editor*
Cox, Henry *research company executive, research engineer*
Curley, John J. *diversified media company executive*
Curley, Thomas *newspaper executive*
Curry, George Edward *journalist*
†Curtis, Richard A. *newspaper editor*
†Davis, Walter J., Jr. *rear admiral*
Dillaway, Robert Beacham *engineering and management consultant*
Dillon, Francis Richard *air force officer, retired*
Dolan, William David, Jr. *physician*
Drayton, William *lawyer, management consultant*
Easton, John Jay, Jr. *lawyer*
Edmondson, William Brockway *retired foreign service officer*
Elliott, R Lance *lawyer*
Ensminger, Luther Glenn *chemist*
Entzminger, John Nelson, Jr. *government research agency executive, electronic engineer*
Everett, Warren Sylvester *consultant, former government official*
Ewers, John Canfield *museum administrator*
Fabian, John M. *former astronaut, air force officer*
†Fabian, John McCreary *non-profit company executive, astronaut*
Faris, Frank Edgar *marketing executive*
Fernandez, Henry A. *healthcare administration executive, lawyer*
Fish, Howard Math *aerospace industry executive*
†Fleming, Michael John *trade association executive*
†Fling, Jacqueline Ann *library administrator*
Flowers, Harold Lee *consulting aerospace engineer*
Fraser, James Cavender *research center executive*
Freeman, Neal Blackwell *communications corporation executive*
Friedheim, Jerry Warden *foundation executive*
Funseth, Robert Lloyd Eric Martin *international consultant, lecturer, retired senior foreign service officer*
Gaines, Alan McCulloch *government official, educator*
Garcia, Oscar Nicolas *computer science educator*
Garvey, Robert Robey, Jr. *former government official*
Gianturco, Delio E. *corporate executive*
Gilbert, Arthur Charles *aerospace engineer, consulting engineer*
Giordano, Andrew Anthony *retired naval officer*
Gniewek, Raymond Louis *newspaper editor*
Gottschalk, John Simison *biologist*
Greinke, Everett Donald *corporate executive, international programs consultant*
Haddock, Raymond Earl *career officer*
Hagn, George Hubert *electrical engineer, researcher*
Hall, Carl William *agricultural and mechanical engineer*
Haq, Bilal Ul *national science foundation program director, researcher*
Hatch, Monroe W., Jr. *military officer, association executive*
Hays, James Fred *geologist, educator*
Hazard, Neil Livingstone *corporation financial executive*
Held, Joe Roger *veterinarian, epidemiologist*
Henderson, John Brown *economist*
Hendrickson, Jerome Orland *trade association executive, lawyer*
Hess, Milton Siegmund *computer company executive*
Hittle, James D. *writer, business consultant*
Houston, Paul David *school association administrator*
Hu, Sue King *middle school educator*
Hugler, Edward C. *lawyer, federal and state government*
Huston, Harris Hyde *legal consultant*
Jackson, William Paul, Jr. *lawyer*
Jennings, Madelyn Pulver *communications company human resources executive*
John, Martha Tyler *dean, education educator*
Johns, Michael Douglas *public policy analyst, writer, former government official*
†Jurgensen, Karen *newspaper editor*
Kaiser, Philip Mayer *diplomat*
Keating, John Richard *bishop*
Kelley, Paul Xavier *retired marine corps officer*
Kem, Richard Samuel *retired army officer*
Kiko, Philip George *lawyer*
Kingsley, Daniel Thain *public affairs executive*
Kiraly, Karch (Charles Frederick Kiraly) *professional volleyball player*
†Knipling, Edward Fred *retired research entomologist, agricultural administrator*
Knowlton, William Allen *business executive, consultant*
Korman, James William *lawyer*
Krauss, Michael Ian *law educator*
Kriegsman, William Edwin *consulting firm executive*
Lane, Neal Francis *university provost, physics researcher, federal administrator*
Langworthy, Everett Walter *association executive, natural gas exploration company executive*
Law, David Holbrook *insurance executive*
Lederman, Leonard Lawrence *government research executive*
Leland, Marc Ernest *trust advisor, lawyer*
Lester, Barnett Benjamin *editor, foreign affairs officer*
Lewis, Hunter *financial advisor, publisher*
Lino, Marisa Rose *diplomat*
Lisanby, James Walker *retired naval officer*
Lloyd, Kent *education policy research and public interest executive, educator*
Lockard, John Allen *naval officer*
London, J. Phillip *information technology company executive*
Long, Madeleine J. *mathematics and science educator*
†Lorell, Monte *newspaper editor*
MacDougall, William Lowell *magazine editor*
Malley, Robert Joseph *manufacturing company executive*
Malone, William Grady *lawyer*
Marcuccio, Phyllis Rose *association executive, editor*
Marshall, Charles Burton *political science consultant*
Martin, Edgar Thomas *telecommunications consultant, lawyer*
Mathis, Mark Jay *lawyer*
McCorkindale, Douglas Hamilton *publishing company executive, corporate lawyer*
McDermott, Francis Owen *lawyer*
McGinley, Edward Stillman, II *naval officer*
†McMasters, Paul Kenneth *foundation executive*
†McNamara, Tom *newspaper editor*
†McWethy, John Fleetwood *journalist*
Melickian, Gary Edward *trade association executive*
Mense, Allan Tate *research scientist, engineer*
Merritt, Jack Neil *retired army officer*
Meyer, Richard Townsend *service company executive*
Michael, Larry Perry *broadcasting company executive*
Miller, Loye Wheat, Jr. *journalist, corporate communications specialist*
Miller, Thomas Hulbert, Jr. *former marine corps officer*
Mirrielees, James Fay, III *publishing executive*
Moore, John Hampton *academic administrator*
Morgan, Bruce Ray *international consultant*
Morris, John Woodland *businessman, former army officer*
†Müller, Ronald Ernst *economist*
Munsell, Elsie Louise *lawyer*
Muris, Timothy Joseph *law educator*
Murray, Jeanne Morris *computer scientist, educator, consultant*
Nalen, Craig Anthony *government official*
Neikirk, William Robert *journalist*
Nejelski, Paul Arthur *judge*
Neuharth, Allen Harold *newspaper publisher*
Nida, Jane Bolster (Mrs. Dow Hughes Nida) *retired librarian*
Nielsen, Aldon Dale *retired government agency official, economist*
Noland, Royce Paul *association executive, physical therapist*
Norwood, Bernard *economist*
Olmsted, George Hamden *retired banking and insurance company executive*
O'Neill, Brian *research organization administrator*
Oren, John Birdsell *retired coast guard officer*
Paynter, Harry Alvin *retired trade association executive*
†Pelaez, Marc Y.E. *federal official, career officer*
Peterson, Paul Quayle *retired university dean, physician*
†Pitts, Nathaniel Gilbert *science and technology director*
†Policinski, Eugene Francis *newspaper editor*
Price, Randall Craig *not for profit association executive*
†Prichard, Peter S. *newspaper editor*
Prince, Julius S. *retired foreign service officer, physician*
Pyatt, Everett Arno *government official*
Quigg, Donald James *lawyer*
Quinn, John Collins *publishing executive, newspaper editor*
Rabun, John Brewton, Jr. *social services agency administrator*
Rackmales, Robert *diplomat*
Rahman, Muhammad Abdur *mechanical engineer*
Raymond, David Alan *business executive, former government official*
Reed, Paul Allen *artist*
Rees, Clifford Harcourt, Jr. (Ted Rees) *retired air force officer, association executive*
Riegel, Kurt Wetherhold *environmental protection, occupational safety and health*
†Ritter, Hal *newspaper editor*
Roberts, James Milnor, Jr. *association executive*
Robinson, Kenneth Leonard, Jr. *trade association executive*
†Rockefeller, Sharon Percy *broadcast executive*
Romney, Carl F. *seismologist*
†Rosenthal, Robert M. *automotive sales executive*
Ross, Jimmy Douglas *army officer*
Rossotti, Charles Ossola *computer consulting company executive*
Saafeld, Fred Erich *naval researcher officer*
Sander, Raymond John *government executive*
Sands, Frank Melville *investment manager*
Sawhill, John Crittenden *businessman, economist, university president, government official*
Scarborough, Robert Henry, Jr. *coast guard officer*
Schaefer, Thomas J. *bank executive*
Schofield, Seth Eugene *air transport company executive*
Seely, James Michael *consultant, retired naval officer, small business owner*
Shaud, John Albert *association executive, former air force officer*
Shepard, James J. *government official*
Simonson, David C. *retired newspaper association executive*
Simpson, John Mathes *newspaper editor*
Sinclair, Rolf Malcolm *physicist*
Singer, S(iegfried) Fred *geophysicist, educator*
Smalley, Robert Manning *government official*
Smeal, Eleanor Cutri *organization executive*
Smith, Elise Fiber *international non-profit development agency administrator*
†Smith, Janet Erlene *advertising executive*
Smith, Numa Lamar, Jr. *lawyer*
Smith, Stanley Roger *professional tennis player*
†Snow, Robert Anthony *journalist*
Stahl, O(scar) Glenn *writer, lecturer, former government official*
Stokes, B. R. *transportation consultant*
Stolgitis, William Charles *professional society executive*
Stover, David Frank *lawyer*
Strean, Bernard M. *retired naval officer*
Sullivan, Cornelius Wayne *marine biology researcher, educator*
Sutton, George Walter *research laboratory executive, mechanical engineer*
†Swanson, Dane Craig *naval officer, pilot*
Tanzer, Lester *editor*
Taylor, Lawrence Palmer *diplomat*
Teem, John McCorkle *retired association executive, consultant*
Thomas, Jimmy Lynn *financial executive*
Thurman, Maxwell R. *retired army officer*
Tice, Raphael Dean *army officer*
Umminger, Bruce Lynn *government official, scientist, educator*
†Van Doren, Emerson Barclay *administrative judge*
Van Landingham, Leander Shelton, Jr. *lawyer*
Verburg, Edwin Arnold *federal agency administrator*
†Vesper, Carolyn T. *newspaper publishing executive*
Volgenau, Douglas *career officer*
Wagner, Louis Carson, Jr. *retired army officer*
Wakefield, Richard Alan *energy consulting firm executive*
Waring, John Alfred *retired research writer, lecturer, consultant*
Wayland, Russell Gibson, Jr. *geology consultant, retired government official*
Weidemann, Celia Jean *social scientist, international business development consultant*
†Weiss, Susan *newspaper editor*
Wells, Christine *foundation executive*
†Wendelin, Rudolph Andrew *artist*
Wilcox, Harvey John *lawyer*
Wilkniss, Peter E. *foundation administrator, researcher*
Willenson, Kim Jeremy *publisher, journalist, author*
Williams, Luther Steward *biologist, federal agency administrator*
Wilson, Minter Lowther, Jr. *retired officers association executive*
Wilson, Roy Kenneth *retired education association executive, consultant*
Yankwich, Peter Ewald *chemistry educator*
Young, Paul Ruel *computer scientist, administrator*
Zakheim, Dov Solomon *economist, government official*
Zirkind, Ralph *physicist*
Zorthian, Barry *communications executive*
Zumwalt, Elmo Russell, Jr. *retired naval officer*

Ashburn
Bolton, John Robert *lawyer, federal official*
Boyne, Walter James *writer, former museum director*
Cooke, John Kent *professtional sports management executive*
†Johnson, Tim *professional football player*

Ashland
†Baker, Stephen M. *school system administrator*
d'Evegnee, Charles Paul *lawyer*
Henshaw, William Raleigh *middle school educator*
Inge, Milton Thomas *American literature and culture educator, author*
Payne, Ladell *college president*

Bassett
Spilman, Robert Henkel *furniture company executive*

Basye
Putnam, George W., Jr. *army officer*

Bedford
Haymes, Harmon Hayden *economist, educator*

Belle Haven
Sarsten, Gunnar Edward *mechanical engineer, construction executive*

Berryville
White, Eugene Vaden *pharmacist*

Blacksburg
Ash, Philip *psychologist*
Barden, John Allan *horticulturist*
Bauer, Henry Hermann *chemistry and science educator*
Baumgartner, Frederic Joseph *history educator*
Blackwell, William Allen *electrical engineering educator*
Bliznakov, Milka Tcherneva *architect*
Brown, Gary Sandy *electrical engineering educator*
Brown, Gregory Neil *university administrator, forest physiology educator*
Bryant, Clifton Dow *sociologist, educator*
Cairns, John, Jr. *environmental science educator, researcher*
Carlisle, Ervin Frederick *university provost*
Carter, Dean *artist*
Colmano, Germille *physiology educator, biophysics researcher*
Comparin, Robert Anton *mechanical engineering educator*
Cowles, Joe Richard *biology educator*
Currie, Leonard James *architect, planner, educator*
de Wolf, David Alter *electrical engineer, educator*
Doswald, Herman Kenneth *German language educator, academic administrator*
Dukore, Bernard Frank *theatre arts and humanities educator, writer*
Fabrycky, Wolter Joseph *engineering educator, author, industrial and systems engineer*
Giovanni, Nikki *poet*
Good, Irving John *statistics educator, philosopher of science*
Grover, Norman LaMotte *theologian, philosopher*
Haugh, Clarence Gene *agricultural engineering educator*
Herndon, James Francis *retired political science educator*
Hibbard, Walter Rollo, Jr. *retired engineering educator*
Jacobs, Ira *electrical engineering educator, former telecommunications company executive*
Jensen, Walter Edward *lawyer, educator*
†Jones, James Beverly *mechanical engineering educator*
Killough, Larry Neil *accounting educator*
Krutchkoff, Richard Gerald *statistics educator, researcher*
Landen, Robert Geran *historian, university administrator*
Lucas, J. Richard *retired mining engineering educator*
Meirovitch, Leonard *engineering educator*
Mo, Luke Wei *physicist, educator*
†Modransky, Paula D. *veterinarian, educator*
Moore, James Mendon *industrial engineering educator, consultant*
Moore, Laurence John *business educator*
†Morton, John *engineering educator, researcher*
†Munford, Joan Hardie *member House of Delegates, corporate executive*
Murray, Thomas Michael *civil engineering educator, consultant*
Musser, Stanton Richard *retired air force officer*
†Nayfeh, Ali Hasan *engineering educator*
Ogliaruso, Michael Anthony *chemist, educator*
Olin, Robert Floyd *mathematics educator and researcher*
Peacock, Markham Lovick, Jr. *English educator*
Phadke, Arun G. *electrical engineering educator*
Pitt, Joseph Charles *philosophy educator*
Price, Dennis Lee *industrial engineer, educator*
Randall, Clifford Wendell *civil engineer*
†Rappaport, Theodore Scott *electrical engineering educator*
Robertson, James Irvin, Jr. *historian, educator*
Rodriguez-Camilloni, Humberto Leonardo *architect, historian, educator*
Sgro, Joseph Anthony *psychologist, educator*
Shepard, Jon Max *sociologist*
Siau, John Finn *wood scientist, educator*
Smeal, Paul Lester *retired horticulture educator*
Smith, Robert McNeil *university dean*
Squires, Arthur Morton *chemical engineer, educator*
Steger, Charles William *university administrator*
Stewart, Kent Kallam *analytical biochemistry educator*
Stutzman, Warren Lee *electrical engineer, educator*
Talbot, Richard Burritt *veterinarian, educator*
Ulloa, Justo Celso *Spanish educator*
Weaver, Pamela Ann *hospitality research professional*
Wilkins, Tracy Dale *microbiologist, educator*
Yousten, Allan Arthur *microbiologist, educator*

Boston
†Fisher, John Morris *association official, educator*

Bridgewater
Geisert, Wayne Frederick *retired college president*

Bristol
†Deppen, Douglas *bank executive*
Jones, James Parker *lawyer*

Broad Run
Hinkle, Barton Leslie *retired electronics company executive*
Kotz, Nathan Kallison (Nick Kotz) *news correspondent*

Burke
Boatright, James Francis *air force official*
Dean, John Wilson, Jr. *business consultant, retired army officer*
Fisher, James Burke *publishing company executive*
†Kaminski, Paul Garrett *investment banker, consultant*
O'Connor, Edward Cornelius *army officer*
Pollard, Joseph Augustine *advertising and public relations consultant*
Wood, C(harles) Norman *air force officer*

Castleton
Hahn, James Maglorie *former librarian, farmer*

Catlett
Scheer, Julian Weisel *business executive, author*

Chantilly
Miller, Donald Eugene *aerospace electronics executive*

O'Brien, Robert John, Jr. *public relations executive, former government official, air force officer*
Slayton, Gus *association executive*
Sroka, John Walter *trade association executive*
Stone, Thomas Edward *defense consultant, retired naval officer*

Charlotte Court House
Hoffman, William *author*

Charlottesville
Abraham, Henry Julian *political science educator*
Abraham, Kenneth Samuel *law educator*
Ainsworth, Mary Dinsmore Salter *psychologist, educator*
Alden, Douglas William *French language educator*
Alford, Neill Herbert, Jr. *law educator*
Allinson, Gary Dean *Japanese studies educator*
Barnett, Benjamin Lewis, Jr. *physician, educator*
Barolsky, Paul *art history educator*
Barrett, Eugene J. *researcher, medical educator, physician*
Battestin, Martin Carey *English educator*
Beard, Richard Leonard *education educator emeritus*
Bednar, Michael John *architecture educator*
Beller, George Allan *medical educator*
Benjamin, Albert, III *retired naval officer, oil company executive*
Bergin, Thomas Francis *lawyer*
†Berkeley, Edmund, Jr. *activist, educator*
Berne, Robert Matthew *physiologist, educator*
Bierstedt, Robert *sociologist, author*
Biltonen, Rodney Lincoln *biochemistry and pharmacology educator*
Block, Gene David *biologist, educator, science administrator*
Bonnie, Richard Jeffrey *legal educator, lawyer*
Boring, John Wayne *physicist, educator*
Bosserman, Joseph Norwood *architecture educator*
Bradbeer, Clive *biochemistry and microbiology educator, research scientist*
Brandt, Richard Martin *education educator*
Brill, Arthur Sylvan *biophysics educator*
Broome, Oscar Whitfield, Jr. *accounting educator, administrator*
Brown, Rita Mae *author*
†Browne, Henry James *architect*
Bull, George Albert *retired banker*
Bunch, John Blake *photographer, writer, educator*
Cahill, Cornelius *manufacturing executive*
Cano-Ballesta, Juan *Spanish language educator*
Cantrell, Robert Wendell *otolaryngologist, head and neck surgeon, educator*
Carey, Robert Munson *university dean, physician*
Cargile, James Thomas *philosophy educator*
Carpenter, Richard Amon *chemist*
Casey, John Dudley *writer, English language educator*
Casteen, John T., III *university administrator*
Catlin, Avery *engineering and computer science educator, writer*
Cawley, Edward Philip *physician, educator*
†Celli, Vittorio *physics educator*
Cherno, Melvin *humanities educator*
Chevalier, Roger Alan *astronomy educator, consultant*
Childress, James Franklin *theology and medical educator*
Clark, Reuben Grove, Jr. *lawyer*
Claude, Inis Lothair, Jr. *political scientist, educator*
Cohen, Edwin Samuel *lawyer, educator*
Coleman, Almand Rouse *accounting educator*
Colker, Marvin Leonard *classics educator*
Colley, John Leonard, Jr. *educator, author, management consultant*
Cooper, James Michael *academic dean, education educator*
Corse, John Doggett *university official, lawyer*
Courtney, Edward *classics educator*
Craig, James William *physician, educator, university dean*
Crigler, B. Waugh *federal judge*
Davis, Edward Wilson *business administration educator*
Davis, John Staige, IV *physician*
Deese, James Earle *psychologist, educator*
Denommé, Robert Thomas *foreign language educator*
Derthick, Martha Ann *political science educator*
Desjardins, Claude *physiology educator*
Detmer, Don Eugene *medical educator, administrator, surgeon*
Diamond, Cora Ann *philosopher, educator*
Dorning, John Joseph *nuclear engineering, engineering physics and applied mathematics educator*
Dove, Rita Frances *English language educator, writer*
Dreifuss, Fritz Emanuel *neurologist, educator*
Dunn, Mary Jarratt *public relations executive*
Edgerton, Milton Thomas, Jr. *reconstructive and hand surgeon, educator*
Edlich, Richard French *biomedical engineering educator*
Epstein, Robert Marvin *anesthesiologist, educator*
Essig, Nancy Claire *publishing executive*
Eustis, Albert Anthony *lawyer, diversified industry corporate executive*
Farr, Barry Miller *physician, epidemiologist*
Fechner, Robert Eugene *pathology educator*
Fletcher, John Caldwell *bioethicist, religious studies educator*
Flickinger, Charles John *anatomist, educator*
Foard, Susan Lee *editor*
Fogarty, Gerald Philip *church history educator, priest*
Forbes, John Douglas *architectural and economic historian*
Frantz, Ray William, Jr. *retired librarian*
Fredrick, Laurence William *astronomer, educator*
Frieden, Charles Leroy *university library administrator*
Friesen, Wolfgang Otto *biology educator*
Gaden, Elmer Lewis, Jr. *chemical engineering educator*
Garrett, George Palmer, Jr. *creative writing and English language educator, writer*
Garrett, Reginald Hooker *biology educator, researcher*
Gaskin, Felicia *biochemist, educator*
Gianniny, Omer Allan, Jr. *humanities educator*
Gillenwater, Jay Young *urologist, educator*
Goodell, Horace Grant *environmental sciences educator*
Gottesman, Irving Isadore *psychiatric genetics educator, consultant*
Graebner, Norman Arthur *history educator*
Greene, Virginia Carvel *chemist*
Grimes, Russell Newell *chemistry educator, inorganic chemist*
Grisham, Charles Milton *biochemist, educator*
Gross, Charles Wayne *physician, educator*
†Gugelot, Piet Cornelis *physics educator*
Guiton Hill, Bonnie F. *federal official, adviser*
Gwaltney, Jack Merrit, Jr. *physician, educator, scientist*
Haigh, Robert William *business administration educator*
Haimes, Yacov Yosseph *systems and civil engineering educator, consultant*
Halseth, Michael James *medical center administrator*
Hamilton, Howard Laverne *zoology educator*
Handy, Alice Warner *state agency administrator*
Harbert, Guy Morley, Jr. *obstetrician-gynecologist*
Hartt, Julian Norris *religion educator*
Havran, Martin Joseph *historian, educator, author*
Henderson, Stanley Dale *lawyer, educator*
Henry, Laurin Luther *government and foreign affairs educator*
Herakovich, Carl Thomas *civil engineering, applied mechanics educator*
Hereford, Frank Loucks, Jr. *physicist, educator*
Hirsch, Eric Donald, Jr. *English language educator, educational reformer*
Hodous, Robert Power *lawyer*
Hoel, Lester A. *civil engineering educator*
Holt, Charles Asbury *economics educator*
Hook, Edward Watson, Jr. *physician, educator*
Hopkins, Paul Jeffrey *Asian studies educator, author, translator*
Horgan, Cornelius Oliver *applied mathematics and applied mechanics educator*
Hornberger, George Milton *environmental science educator*
Horton, Madeline Mary *financial planner, consultant*
Howard, Arthur Ellsworth Dick *legal educator*
Howards, Stuart S. *physician, educator*
Hudson, John Lester *chemical engineering educator*
Huet, Marie-Hélène Jaqueline *foreign language educator*
Hutchinson, Thomas Eugene *biomedical engineering educator*
Hymes, Dell Hathaway *anthropologist*
Inigo, Rafael Madrigal *electrical engineering educator*
Jane, John Anthony *neurosurgeon, educator*
Johnson, W(alker) Reed *nuclear engineering educator*
Johnson, William Richard *economist*
Jones, Rayford Scott *surgeon, medical educator*
†Jordan, Daniel Porter, Jr. *foundation administrator, history educator*
Kadner, Robert Joseph *microbiology educator*
Kassell, Neal Frederic *neurosurgeon*
Kattwinkel, John *physician, pediatrics educator*
Keats, Theodore Eliot *physician, radiology educator*
Kellermann, Kenneth Irwin *astronomer*
Kellogg, Robert Leland *English language educator*
†Kelly, Thaddeus E. *medical geneticist*
Kerr, Anthony Robert *space scientist*
Kett, Joseph Francis *historian, educator*
Kitch, Edmund Wells *lawyer, educator, private investor*
Kitchin, James D., III *obstetrician-gynecologist, educator*
Kohler, Charlotte *language professional, educator*
Kolb, Harold Hutchison, Jr. *English language educator*
†Kowalsky, Adrian Dion *publishing executive*
Kraehe, Enno Edward *history educator*
Krzysztofowicz, Roman *systems engineering educator, consultant*
Kuhlmann-Wilsdorf, Doris *physics and materials science educator*
Landess, Fred S. *lawyer*
Lang, Cecil Yelverton *English language educator*
Langbaum, Robert Woodrow *English language educator, author*
Lanham, Betty Bailey *anthropologist, educator*
Lankford, Francis Greenfield, Jr. *education educator emeritus*
Lee, Jen-shih *biomedical engineering educator*
Leffler, Melvyn P. *history educator*
Leng, Shao Chuan *political science educator*
Levenson, Jacob Clavner *English language educator*
Loo, Beverly Jane *publishing company executive*
Lyons, John David *French, Italian and comparative literature educator*
MacAvoy, Thomas Coleman *glass manufacturing executive, educator*
Mandell, Gerald Lee *physician, medicine educator*
Mansfield, Lois Edna *mathematics educator, researcher*
Martin, Nathaniel Frizell Grafton *mathematician, educator*
Martin, Robert Bruce *chemistry educator*
Matson, Robert Edward *management educator, management consultant*
Mattauch, Robert Joseph *electrical engineering educator*
McCallum, Richard Warwick *medical researcher, clinician, educator*
†McCartney, O. Kenton, III *commercial banker*
McCarty, Richard Charles *psychology educator*
Mc Culloch, Frank W. *lawyer, government official, educator, arbitrator*
McGann, Jerome John *English language educator*
McGee, Gary Calvin *lawyer*
Mc Kinney, George Wesley, Jr. *banking educator*
Mc Quillen, Michael Paul *physician*
McVey, Eugene Steven *electrical engineering educator, consultant*
Meador, Daniel John *lawyer, educator*
Meem, James Lawrence, Jr. *nuclear scientist*
Meiburg, Charles Owen *business administration educator*
Menaker, Shirley Ann Lasch *psychology educator, academic administrator*
Michael, James Harry, Jr. *federal judge*
Middleditch, Leigh Benjamin, Jr. *lawyer, educator*
Mikalson, Jon Dennis *classics educator*
Miller, Joseph Calder *academic dean, historical consultant, editor*
Monroe, Brooks *investment banker*
Moore, John Norton *lawyer, diplomat, educator*
Morgan, Raymond F. *plastic surgeon*
Morton, Jeffrey Bruce *aerospace engineering educator*
Muller, William Henry, Jr. *surgeon, educator*
Murray, Joseph James, Jr. *zoologist*
Nelson, Raymond John *English literature educator, university dean, author*
Newman, James Wilson *business executive*
Newsom, David Dunlop *foreign service officer, educator*
Nolan, Stanton Peelle *surgeon, educator*
Norgren, C. Neil *manufacturing executive*
O'Connell, Jeffrey *lawyer, educator*
O'Neal, William B. *retired architectural educator*
O'Neil, Robert Marchant *university administrator, law educator*
Ortega, James McDonough *mathematician, educator*
Owen, John Atkinson, Jr. *physician, educator*
Parrish, David Walker, Jr. *legal publishing company executive*
Pate, Robert Hewitt, Jr. *counselor educator*
Perkins, Marvin Earl *psychiatrist, educator*
Perkins, William Allan, Jr. *retired lawyer*
Perry, Marvin Banks, Jr. *retired college president*
Peterson, Kent Wright *physician*
Peterson, Merrill Daniel *history educator*
†Phillips, Lawrence H., II *neurologist*
Platts-Mills, Thomas Alexander E. *immunologist, educator, researcher*
Poggi, Gianfranco *sociology educator*
Priest, Hartwell Wyse *artist*
Pullen, Edwin Wesley *anatomist, university dean*
Rader, Louis T. *corporation executive, educator*
Redden, Kenneth Robert *lawyer, writer, educator*
Reynolds, Albert Barnett *nuclear engineer, educator*
Reynolds, Robert Edgar *academic administrator, physician*
Rhoads, Steven Eric *political science educator*
Roberts, Morton Spitz *astronomer*
Robinson, Mildred Wigfall *law educator*
†Root, James Benjamin *landscape architect*
Rorty, Richard McKay *philosophy educator*
Rosenblum, John William *business educator*
Rosenblum, Marvin *mathematics educator*
Rotch, William *business administration educator*
Rowlingson, John Clyde *anesthesiologist, educator, physician*
Ruben, Leonard *retired art educator*
†Rubin, David Lee *French literature educator, critic, editor, publisher*
Sacksteder, Frederick Henry *former foreign service officer*
†Sarazin, Craig Leigh *astronomer*
Scarr, Sandra Wood *psychology educator, researcher*
Scharlemann, Robert Paul *religious studies educator, clergyman*
Schuker, Stephen Alan *historian*
Scott, Nathan Alexander, Jr. *minister, educator, literary critic*
Sedgwick, Alexander *historian, educator*
Self, James Reed *librarian*
Shackelford, George Green *historian*
Shannon, Edgar Finley, Jr. *English language educator*
Shaw, Donald Leslie *Spanish language educator*
Shenkir, William Gary *business educator*
Sherman, Roger *economics educator*
Shugart, Herman Henry *environmental sciences educator, researcher*
Sihler, William Wooding *finance educator*
Simmonds, James Gordon *mathematician, educator*
Simmons, Alan John *philosophy educator*
Simpson, R(obert) Smith *author, retired diplomat*
Slaughter, Edward Ratliff, Jr. *lawyer*
Snavely, William Pennington *economics educator*
†Sokel, Walter H. *German language and literature educator*
Somlyo, Andrew Paul *physiology, physics and cardiology educator*
Song, Xiaotong *physicist, educator*
Sorensen, Thomas Chaikin *financial executive*
Spacks, Patricia Meyer *English educator*
Spearing, Anthony Colin *English educator*
Starke, Edgar Arlin, Jr. *metallurgist, educator*
Stenberg, Carl W(aldamer), III *academic program director, educator*
Stevenson, Ian *psychiatrist, educator*
Stocker, Arthur Frederick *classics educator*
Stone, David Deaderick *physician, educator*
Stroud, Robert Edward *lawyer*
Stubbs, Kendon Lee *librarian*
Sundberg, Richard Jay *chemistry educator*
Suratt, Paul Michael *physician, researcher*
Sykes, Gresham M'Cready *sociologist, educator*
Taylor, Peyton Troy, Jr. *gynecologic oncologist, educator*
Taylor, Samuel James *mathematics educator*
Teates, Charles David *radiologist, educator*
†Tewksbury, Charles G. *textiles technology executive*
Thompson, Anthony Richard *electrical engineer, astronomer*
Thompson, David William *business educator*
Thompson, Kenneth W(infred) *educational director, author, editor, administrator, social science educator*
Thorner, Michael Oliver *medical educator, research center administrator*
Townsend, Miles Averill *aerospace and mechanical engineering educator*
Trent, Robert Harold *business educator*
Triggiani, Roberto *mathematics educator*
Turner, Robert Foster *lawyer, educator, former government official, writer*
Underwood, Paul Benjamin *obstetrician, educator*
Vanden Bout, Paul Adrian *astronomer, physicist, educator*
Vaughan, Joseph Lee *language educator*
Velimirovic, Milos M. *music educator*
Villar-Palasi, Carlos *pharmacology educator*
Wadlington, Walter James *legal educator*
Wagner, Robert Roderick *microbiologist, oncology educator*
Wagner, Roy *anthropology educator, researcher*
Walker, William Laurens *lawyer, educator*
Waxman, Ronald *computer engineer*
Weary, Peyton Edwin *medical educator*
Weber, Hans Jürgen *physics educator*
Westfall, Carroll William *architectural historian*
Whitaker, John King *economics educator*
White, George Edward *legal educator, lawyer*
†Whitehead, John Wayne *law educator, organization administrator, author*
Wilhelm, Morton *surgery educator*
Wilkinson, James Harvie, III *federal judge*
Wills, Michael Ralph *medical educator*
Worrell, Anne Everette Rowell *newspaper publisher*
Wright, Charles Penzel, Jr. *poet*
Wright, Theodore Robert Fairbank *biologist, educator*
Wulf, William Allan *computer information scientist, educator*
Zunz, Olivier Jean *history educator*

Chatham
Leonard, Edward Paul *naval officer, dentist, educator*

Chesapeake
Dickson, Suzanne Elizabeth (Sue Dickson) *primary school educator*
Forehand, Margaret P. *library director*
Gibbs, William Eugene *scientific consultant*
Jones, John Lou *arbitrator, retired railroad executive*
Orr, Joel Nathaniel *computer graphics consultant*

Chester
Gray, Frederick Thomas, Jr. *actor, educator*

Chesterfield
Congdon, John Rhodes *corporate executive*
Copeland, Jean Parrish *school system administrator, school board executive*
Morris, James Carl *architect*
Wilson, Dorothy Ann *retired special education educator*

Christiansburg
Roberts, Ruby Altizer *poet, author, fiction*

Clifton
Hennesy, Gerald Craft *artist*

Culpeper
Covey, Charles William *marine consultant*
†Davies, John Jenkyn, III *lawyer*
Landa, William Robert *foundation executive*

Danville
Barker, Willie G., Jr. *agriculture executive*
Conway, French Hoge *lawyer*
Dibrell, Louis Nelson, III *tobacco company executive*
Goodson, Louie Aubrey, Jr. *retired bank executive*
Kiser, Jackson L. *federal judge*
Owen, Claude Bernard, Jr. *tobacco company executive*
Talbott, Frank, III *lawyer*

Draper
Gilmer, B. von Haller *retired educator, industrial psychologist*

Dumfries
Gill, William Albert, Jr. *government official*
Heiser, Joseph Miller, Jr. *retired army officer, business executive, author*
Mc Dowell, Charles Eager *lawyer, retired military officer*

Earlysville
Caplow, Theodore *sociologist*

East Stone Gap
Combs, Jo Karen Kobeck *artist, writer*

Emory
†Dawsey, James Marshall *religious studies educator, minister*

Evington
Fortune, Laura Catherine Dawson *elementary educator*

Faber
Friede, Eleanor Kask *editor, publisher*

Fairfax
Aksyonov, Vassily Pavlovich *author*
Arntson, Peter Andrew *lawyer*
Baer, Robert Jacob *retired army officer*
Bailey, Helen McShane *historian*
Barth, Michael Carl *economist*
†Bausch, Richard C. *writer, educator*
Bennett, James Thomas *economics educator*
†Benton, Robert *automotive executive*
Bloomquist, Dennis Howard *lawyer*
Boneau, C. Alan *psychology educator, researcher*
Boone, James Virgil *engineering executive*
Buchanan, James McGill *economist, educator*
Buzzell, Robert Dow *management educator*
Cantus, H. Hollister *engineering corporation executive*
Church, Randolph Warner, Jr. *lawyer*
Codding, Frederick Hayden *lawyer*
Cook, Gerald *electrical engineering educator*
Cotter, William Joseph *retired grain company executive*
Cullison, Alexander C. (Doc Cullison) *society administrator*
Denning, Peter James *computer scientist, engineer*
Dennis, Rutledge Melvin *sociology educator, researcher*
Dettinger, Garth Bryant *surgeon, physician, retired air force officer, county health officer*
Dobson, Allen *economist*
Drenz, Charles Francis *retired army officer*
Edwards, James Owen *engineering and construction company executive*
†Elias, Antonio L. *aeronautical engineer, aerospace executive*
†Field, Joanne T. *school board executive*
Fink, Lester Harold *engineering company executive, educator*
Folk, Thomas Robert *lawyer*
Gardner, Richard Hartwell *oil company executive*
Gollobin, Leonard Paul *chemical engineer*
Gross, Patrick Walter *business executive, management consultant*
Groves, Hurst Kohler *lawyer, oil company executive*
Hancock, Alton Guy *lawyer*
Hanuschak, George Alan *statistician*
Harlan, Stephen Donald *accountant*
Hoenmans, Paul John *oil company executive*
Hopson, Everett George *lawyer*
Johnson, George William *university president*
Jones, Carleton Shaw *information systems company executive, lawyer*
Jones, George Fleming *diplomat*
Kash, Don Eldon *political science educator*
Kauderer, Bernard Marvin *retired naval officer*
Kieffer, Jarold Alan *policy and management consultant, writer*
Klauberg, William Joseph *technical services company executive*
†Leidinger, William John *clinic administrator*
Lipset, Seymour Martin *sociologist, political scientist, educator*
Mandeville, Robert Clark, Jr. *former naval officer, business executive*
Martin, George Wilbur *association executive*

Mc Pherson, John Barkley aerospace consultant, retired military officer
Moore, Robert Edward research company executive
Morowitz, Harold Joseph biophysicist, educator
Mund, Richard Gordon foundation executive
Murray, Allen Edward oil company executive
†Noto, Lucio A. gas and oil industry executive
Otis, Glenn Kay retired army officer, research and engineering company executive
Ozernoy, Leonid Moissey astrophysicist
Palmer, James Daniel information technology educator
Pan, Elizabeth Lim information systems company executive
Perdue, Christine H. lawyer
Pitchell, Robert J. business executive
Puckorius, Theodore D. consulting company executive
Pugh, Arthur James retired department store executive, consultant
†Renna, Eugene A. petroleum company executive
Rubin, Robert Joseph physician, health care consultant
Sage, Andrew Patrick, Jr. systems information and software engineering educator
Sanderson, Douglas Jay lawyer
†Schrock, Simon retail executive
Schulman, Joseph Daniel physician, medical geneticist, reproductive biologist, educator
Sganga, John B. furniture holding company executive
Sheehan, Edward James technical consultant, former government official
Spitzberg, Irving Joseph, Jr. lawyer, corporate executive
Steger, Meritt Homer lawyer
†Stitt, William C. engineering executive
Stokely, Hugh Lawson economist, publisher
†Tipermas, Marc engineering executive
Trefil, James S. physicist, educator
Uffelman, Malcolm Rucj electronics company executive, electrical engineer
Vaughn, Karen Iversen economics educator
Walker, Betsy Ellen computer products and services company executive
†Ward, George Truman architect
Warfield, John Nelson engineering educator, consultant
West, Bob pharmaceutical company executive
Willauer, Whiting Russell systems integration company executive
†Woods, Jane Haycock state legislator

Fairfax City
Hollans, Irby Noah, Jr. association executive

Fairfax Station
Johansen, Eivind Herbert corporate executive, former army officer
Scanlon, Charles Francis army officer, retired, defense consultant
Starry, Donn Albert former aerospace company executive, former army officer
Taylor, Eldon Donivan government official

Falls Church
Barkley, Paul Haley, Jr. architect
Beach, Robert Oliver, II computer company executive
Benson, William Edward (Barnes) geologist
Block, John Rusling former secretary of agriculture
Boucouvalas, Marcie adult education educator
†Braendel, Douglas Arthur healthcare executive
Bucur, John Charles neurological surgeon
Burg, Ruth Cooper (Thelma Breslauer) administrative judge
Calkins, Gary Nathan lawyer
Calkins, Susannah Eby retired economist
Cardwell, Nancy Lee editor
Cleland, Sherrill college president
Cohn, Samuel Maurice economic and management consultant
Connery, Robert Howe educator, author
Cooper, Arthur Irving former association executive
Deardourff, John D. political consultant
de la Colina, Rafael diplomat
†Devaney, Everett M. health care executive
Diamond, Robert Michael lawyer
Donovan, Robert John retired journalist
Duesenberg, Robert H. lawyer
Ehrlich, Bernard Herbert lawyer, association executive
Ehrlich, S(aul) Paul, Jr. physician, consultant, former government official
Feldmann, Edward George pharmaceutical chemist
Fink, Charles Augustin behavioral systems scientist
Geithner, Paul Herman, Jr. banker
Gouse, S. William, Jr. engineering executive, scientist
Gray, D'Wayne retired marine corps officer
Green, James Wyche sociologist, anthropologist, psychotherapist
Harley, William Gardner retired communications consultant
Hart, C(harles) W(illard), Jr. zoologist, curator
Hart, Herbert Michael military officer
Hazel, John Tilghman, Jr. lawyer, real estate developer
Heldstab, John Christian army officer
Jennings, Thomas Parks lawyer
†Johnson, Clifford Ivery army officer, federal agency administrator
Kaplow, Herbert Elias journalist
†Keegan, John Eugene architect
Keesling, Karen Ruth lawyer
Kroesen, Frederick James army officer
LaNoue, Alcide Moodie medical corps officer, health care administrator
Lantz, Phillip Edward corporate executive, consultant
Larson, Richard Gustaf army officer
Layman, Lawrence naval officer
LeBlanc, Hugh Linus political science educator, consultant
Ledwig, Donald Eugene association executive
Lorenzo, Michael engineer, government official, real estate broker
Marsh, John O(tho), Jr. lawyer, former government official
Masterson, Kleber Sandlin former organization executive, retired naval officer
Mellor, James Robb defense company executive
Morse, Marvin Henry judge
Mortensen, Robert Henry landscape architect
Nashman, Alvin Eli computer company executive
Nelson, Thomas William management consultant, former government official
Nickle, Dennis Edwin electronics engineer, church deacon
Oesterling, Wendy Lee sales and marketing executive
Orben, Robert editor, writer
Palmer, Stephen Eugene, Jr. government official
Pendleton, Elmer Dean, Jr. retired military officer, international consultant
Post, Howard Allen forest industry specialist
Reiter, Joseph Henry judge
Robie, William Randolph lawyer, government official
Rose, Wil foundation executive
Rosenberg, Theodore Roy financial executive
Safer, John artist, lecturer
Schumaker, Clarence Joseph university educator, sociologist, civilian military emplyee
Simokaitis, Frank Joseph air force officer, lawyer
Skoler, Daniel Lawrence lawyer, writer
Spector, Louis retired federal judge, lawyer, arbitrator, consultant
Spindel, William chemistry educator, scientist, educational administrator
Theismann, Joseph Robert former professional football player, announcer
Villarreal, Carlos Castaneda engineering executive
Waldo, (Clifford) Dwight political science educator
Webb, William John public relations counsel
Weiss, Armand Berl economist, association management executive
Whitehead, Kenneth Dean author, translator, retired federal government official
Wilson, Ewen Maclellan economist
Wright, Wiley Reed, Jr. lawyer
Young, John Hardin lawyer
Zalokar, Robert H. bank executive

Farmville
Dorrill, William Franklin academic administrator, political scientist, educator

Flint Hill
Dietel, William Moore former foundation executive

Fort Belvoir
Diercks, Frederick Otto government official
Lajoie, Roland army officer
Menoher, Paul Edwin, Jr. army officer
†Norris, Michael R. engineering administrator
Scott, David Bytovetzski dental research and forensic odontology consultant

Fort Defiance
Livick, Malcolm Harris school administrator

Fort Lee
Sterling, Keir Brooks historian, educator

Fort Myer
Blackwell, Paul Eugene army officer
Shalikashvili, John Malchase military career officer

Franconia
†Keating, Gladys Brown state legislator

Franklin
Cobb, G. Elliott, Jr. lawyer

Fredericksburg
Corcoran, John Joseph federal judge
Dennis, Donald Daly retired librarian
Dorman, John Frederick genealogist
Farmer, James civil rights leader, former trade union official
Jamison, John Ambler retired circuit judge
Keplinger, Duane architectural executive
†Krick, Robert Kenneth historian, writer
Leitch, Alma May city official
Margileth, Andrew Menges physician, former naval officer
Rowe, Charles Spurgeon newspaper publishing and broadcasting executive
Schmutzhart, Berthold Josef sculptor, educator, art and education consultant
Snapp, Roy Baker lawyer

Front Royal
Douglas, J(ocelyn) Fielding toxicologist, consultant
Overton, Joseph Allen, Jr. association official

Gate City
†Quillen, Ford Carter lawyer, state legislator

Glen Allen
†Devany Serio, Catherine clinical psychologist
Fife, William Franklin retired drug company executive
Murphey, Robert Stafford pharmaceutical company executive
†Seymour, Harlan Francis computer services company executive
Williams, William Clyde physician

Gloucester
Donaldson, Coleman duPont aerodynamics and aerospace consulting engineer
Fang, Joong mathematician, philosopher, educator
Powell, Bolling Raines, Jr. lawyer, educator

Gloucester Point
Perkins, Frank Overton marine scientist, educator
Roberts, Morris Henry, Jr. marine biology educator

Gordonsville
Marshall, Victor Fray physician, educator

Great Falls
Anderson, William Robert corporate executive
Anfinson, Thomas Elmer foundation executive
Douma, Jacob Hendrick hydraulic engineer, consultant
Foryst, Carole mortgage broker
Garrett, Wilbur Eugene magazine editor
Hughes, Alan Richard aerospace company executive
Jacobson, Richard Lee lawyer, educator
MacGowan, Charles Frederic retired chemical company executive
Railton, William Scott lawyer
Schwartz, Robert Terry professional association executive
Sims, John Rogers, Jr. lawyer
Zimmermann, Warren former foreign service officer

Grundy
†Smith, Jack food service executive

Halifax
Greenbacker, John Everett lawyer

Hampden Sydney
Joyner, Weyland Thomas physicist, educator, business consultant
†Kniffen, Donald Avery astrophysicist, educator, researcher
Porterfield, William Wendell chemist, educator

Hampton
†Allario, Frank aerospace science research administrator
Brauer, Harrol Andrew, Jr. broadcasting executive
Brown, Loretta Ann Port physician, geneticist
†Bushnell, Dennis Meyer mechanical engineer, researcher
Clark, Leonard Vernon aerospace engineer
†Corlett, William Albert aerospace engineer
Drummond, James Everman technology transfer company executive, former army officer
Duberg, John Edward aeronautical engineer, educator
Goers, Melvin Armand retired army officer
Hightower, John Brantley arts administrator
Holloway, Paul Fayette aerospace executive
Houbolt, John Cornelius physicist
Joshi, Suresh Meghashyam research engineering executive
Noor, Ahmed Khairy engineering educator, researcher
Pandey, Dhirendra Kumar mechanical engineer, scientist
Patty, Anna Christine middle school educator
Sobieski, Jaroslaw aerospace engineer
†Stern, Joseph Aaron services contracting executive
†Tenney, Darrel R. materials science administrator
Whitcomb, Richard Travis aeronautical consultant

Harrisonburg
Arthur, Thomas Hahn theater educator, director
Carrier, Ronald Edwin university administrator
Cline, Paul Charles political science educator, state legislator
Darazsdi, James Joseph food processing executive
Ivory, Ming Marie political scientist
Lemish, Donald Lee university athletics director
Muth, George Edward former art and drafting supply company executive
Palmer, Forrest Charles librarian, educator
Pettus, Alvin Morris program administrator
Rollman, Steven Allan communication educator

Haymarket
Moseley, Mark DeWayne retired professional football player

Haysi
Deel, George Moses elementary education educator

Heathsville
McKerns, Charles Joseph lawyer
Winkel, Raymond Norman avionics manufacturing executive, retired naval officer

Herndon
Arnberg, Robert Lewis mathematician
Crossfield, Albert Scott aeronautical science consultant, pilot
Doebler, James Carl naval officer, engineering executive
Holton, A. Linwood, Jr. lawyer
Kopf, Eugene Herbert management consultant, electrical engineer
Peck, Dallas Lynn geologist
Pollard, Charles William lawyer
Schaer, Werner computer services executive
Scripps, Edward Wyllis newspaper publisher
Spragens, William Clark public policy educator, consultant
Vogel, Frederick John diplomat
Wilson, Douglas Lawson research center director

Hillsboro
Farwell, Byron Edgar writer

Hinton
Keeler, James Leonard food products company executive

Hopewell
Leake, Preston Hildebrand tobacco research executive

Hot Springs
Richey, Herbert Southall, II coal company executive

Huddleston
Kopp, Richard Edgar electrical engineer
Singleton, Samuel Winston physician, pharmaceutical company executive

Hume
Barr, Joseph Walker retired corporate director

Ivy
†Loving, Raymond Franklin, Jr. real estate broker, golf course architect
Selden, Richard Thomas economist, educator

Kilmarnock
Gilruth, Robert Rowe aerospace consultant
Maxwell, W(ilbur) Richard management consultant

King George
Hoglund, Richard Frank research and technical executive
Newhall, David, III former federal government official

Kinsale
Gould, Gordon physicist, retired optical communications executive

Ladysmith
Provencher, Roger Arthur international consultant

Lakeridge
Bales, Richard Henry Horner conductor, composer
†Garon, Richard Joseph, Jr. deputy minority staff director, political worker
Moran, Robert Daniel lawyer

Lanexa
Kirk, Maurice Blake lawyer, educator

Langley AFB
Hobbs, Roy Jerry military career officer, health services administrator
Loh, John M. career military officer

Leesburg
Ecker, G. T. Dunlop hospital administration executive
LeHane, Louis James consulting company executive
†Mims, William Cleveland lawyer, state legislator
Mitchell, Russell Harry dermatologist

Lexington
Badgett, Lee Douglas academic administrator
Burnette, Ollen Lawrence, Jr. historian
Cash, Frank Errette, Jr. foreign service officer
DeVogt, John Frederick management science and business ethics educator, consultant
Elmes, David Gordon psychologist, educator
Evans, John Maurice English language educator
Gaines, James Edwin, Jr. librarian
Herrick, Bruce Hale economics educator
Hickman, Cleveland Pendleton, Jr. biology educator
Hughes, Delos Dyson political science educator
James, D(orris) Clayton history educator
Jarrard, Leonard Everett psychologist, educator
Kirgis, Frederic Lee, Jr. legal educator
Knapp, John Williams college president
Leach, Maurice Derby, Jr. librarian
Martin, Joseph Ramsey philosophy educator
McAhren, Robert Willard history educator
Pemberton, Harrison Joseph educator, philosopher
Phillips, Charles Franklin, Jr. economist, educator
Read, Beverly Money military officer
Seeger, Michael musician, singer, folklorist
Stuart, Walker Dabney, III poet, author, English language educator
Sullivan, Barry lawyer, educator
Trandel, Richard Samuel mechanical engineer, educator
Tyree, Lewis, Jr. retired compressed gas company executive, inventor, technical consultant
Warner, Harry Hathaway financial consultant
Watt, William Joseph academic administrator, chemistry educator
†Wiant, Sarah Kirsten law library director, educator
Winfrey, John Crawford economist, educator

Lightfoot
Morris, Robert Louis management consultant

Lively
Gallimore, Robert Stephenson news service executive

Locust Grove
Baratz, Morton Sachs economic consultant, writer

Lorton
Francis, Richard Haudiomont government administrator
Hazard, John Wharton author, editorial consultant

Louisa
Lanyon, Wesley Edwin retired museum curator, ornithologist

Lynchburg
Barkley, Henry Brock, Jr. research and development executive
Britton, Donald W. insurance company executive
Butler, John Alden insurance company executive
Crow, Harold Eugene physician, family medicine educator
Dolan, Ronald Vincent insurance company executive
Duff, Ernest Arthur political scientist, educator
Falwell, Jerry L. clergyman
Fath, George R. electrical engineer, communications executive
Hinnant, Hilari Anne educational association administrator
McRorie, William Edward life insurance company executive
Morland, John Kenneth sociology and anthropology educator
Quillian, William Fletcher, Jr. retired banker, former college president
Snead, George Murrell, Jr. army officer, scientist, consultant
Stephens, Bart Nelson former foreign service officer
Stewart, George Taylor insurance executive
Wingfield, John Ernest insurance broker,financial executive

Madison
Ince, Eugene St. Clair, Jr. cryptologist, retired naval officer

Manakin Sabot
Robertson, Linwood Righter electric utility executive

Manassas
Geerdes, James (Divine Geerdes) chemical company executive
Holmes, Marjorie Rose author
†Marshall, Robert G. state legislator
Neal, Richard Glenn educational management company executive
Parrish, Frank Jennings food company executive
Smith, Vme (Verna Mae Edom Smith) sociology educator, freelance writer, photographer

Manassas Park
Bussard, Robert William physicist

Markham
Katzen, Jay Kenneth consultant, former foreign service officer

Marshall
Hayward, Charles Winthrop retired railroad company executive
Seder, Arthur Raymond, Jr. lawyer

Maurertown
Macleod, John Amend lawyer

Mc Kenney
Doyle, John Robert, Jr. *writer*

Mc Lean
Adler, Larry *marketing executive*
Albrecht, Mark Jennings *diversified high technology company executive*
Anderson, David Lloyd *defense industry executive*
Appler, Thomas L. *lawyer*
Bartow, Randy David *publishing executive*
†Bass, Roger William *architect*
Berteau, David John *federal official*
†Betsold, Robert John *federal agency administrator*
Bisbee, Gerald Elftman, Jr. *investment company executive*
Bolan, Robert S. *association executive*
†Bollerer, Fred L. *banker*
Brendsel, Leland C. *federal mortgage company executive*
†Brown, Billy Ross *agriculture association executive*
Brown, Thomas C., Jr. *lawyer*
Buck, Alfred Andreas *physician, epidemiologist*
Byrne, Gary Cecil *banker*
Byrnes, Arthur Francis *retired federal official*
Cahill, Harry Amory *diplomat, educator*
†Callahan, Vincent Francis, Jr. *publisher, state legislator*
Cannon, Mark Wilcox *government official, business executive*
Capone, Lucien, Jr. *management consultant, former naval officer*
Carnicero, Jorge Emilio *aeronautical engineer, business executive*
Chadsey, William Lloyd, III *business executive*
†Chatelain, Leon, III *architectural firm executive*
Chiogioji, Melvin Hiroaki *government official*
Collins, James Foster *government official*
Cook, Harry Clayton, Jr. *lawyer*
Cooper, John Allen Dicks *medical educator*
Corson, J. Jay, IV *lawyer*
Cotterill, Carl Hayden *government official*
Cowhill, William Joseph *retired naval officer, consultant*
Davis, Bennie Luke *air force officer*
Davis, William Columbus *educator, writer, lecturer*
Deal, George Edgar *corporate executive*
Dean, Lydia Margaret Carter (Mrs. Halsey Albert Dean) *nutrition coordinator, author, consultant*
De Carbonnel, François Eric *management consultant*
Dempsey, James Raymon *industrial executive*
Donald, James Robert *federal agency official, economist, outdoors writer*
Doyle, Frederick Joseph *government research scientist*
Duncan, Robert Clifton *retired government official*
Dupuy, Trevor Nevitt *historian, research executive*
Enger, Walter Melvin *consulting engineer, former navy officer*
Estren, Mark James *management and media consultant, TV producer*
Ewing, Charles Boal, Jr. *real estate company executive*
Finberg, Donald Richard *foundation administrator*
Fitzpatrick, John Malcolm *manufacturing executive*
Franklin, Jude Eric *electronics executive*
Friel, Thomas Patrick *association executive*
Fromm, Joseph *retired magazine editor, foreign affairs consultant*
Gammon, James Alan *lawyer*
Gardenier, John Stark, II *statistician, management scientist*
Gary, Charles Lester *professional association consultant, educator*
Gavazzi, Aladino A. *retired medical center administrator*
Glenn, David Wright *mortgage executive*
Glines, Carroll Vane, Jr. *magazine editor*
Graybeal, Sidney Norman *national security executive, former government official*
Groennings, Sven Ole *academic administrator, higher education educator, corporate executive*
Halaby, Najeeb E. *financier, lawyer*
Hambrick, Jackson Reid *lawyer, retired educator, writer*
Hashim, Elinor Marie *librarian*
Healy, Theresa Ann *former ambassador*
Hendon, Robert Caraway *retired transportation and manufacturing company executive, consultant*
Herge, J. Curtis *lawyer*
Hicks, C. Thomas, III *lawyer*
Hoffman, Ronald Bruce *biophysicist, life scientist, human factors consultant*
Hopkins, Thomas Matthews *former naval officer*
Howe, Jonathan Trumbull *naval officer*
Hyde, John Paul *retired air force officer*
James, Daniel J. *management consultant*
Jennings, Jerry D. *communications company executive*
Kahne, Stephen James *systems engineer, educator, academic administrator, engineering executive*
Kane, John Dandridge Henley, Jr. *naval officer*
Kennedy, Cornelius Bryant *lawyer*
Kimmel, H. Steven *engineering executive*
Kiviat, Philip Jay *computer services company executive*
Klinedinst, Duncan Stewart *lawyer*
Kolombatovic, Vadja Vadim *management consulting company executive*
Laning, Robert Comegys *retired physician, former naval officer*
Layson, William McIntyre *research consulting company executive*
†Leto, James J. *artificial intelligence executive*
Lotz, Denton *minister, church official*
Luttig, J. Michael *federal judge*
Mand, Martin G. *financial executive*
Marino, Michael Frank *lawyer*
Markels, Michael, Jr. *environmental consulting firm executive*
Mars, Forrest E., Jr. *candy company executive*
Mars, John F. *candy company executive*
Mason, Scott Aiken *management consultant*
McCambridge, John James *civil engineer*
McCullough, R. Michael *management consultant*
Mc Fate, Patricia Ann *educator, foundation executive, scientist*
McInerney, James Eugene, Jr. *association executive*
Mehuron, William Otto *electronics company executive*
Morrison, David Lee *chemist, research institute executive*
Murphy, Thomas Patrick *lawyer*
Nassikas, John Nicholas *lawyer*
Neel, Samuel Ellison *lawyer*
Ney, Robert Terrence *lawyer*
Parker, Scott Lane *management consultant*
Paschall, Lee McQuerter *retired communications consultant*
Phillips, Rufus Colfax, III *planning consultant*
Prichard, Edgar Allen *lawyer*
Prince, Andrew Steven *lawyer, former government official*
Ramsey, Lloyd Brinkley *retired savings and loan executive, retired army officer*
Rau, Lee Arthur *lawyer*
Rhyne, Charles Sylvanus *lawyer*
Ring, James Edward Patrick *mortgage insurance company executive*
Rogers, Thomas Francis *foundation administrator*
Ryan, John Franklin *multinational company executive*
Searles, Dewitt Richard *retired investment firm executive, retired air force officer*
Shanklin, Richard Vair, III *mechanical engineer*
Shevel, Wilbert Lee *information systems executive*
Shirley, Graham Edward *management executive*
Silveira, Milton Anthony *aerospace engineering executive*
†Sitkoff, Theodore *public management executive*
Smith, Russell Jack *former embassy official, research consultant, author*
Smith, Thomas Eugene *investment company executive, financial consultant*
Snyder, Franklin Farison *hydrologic engineering consultant*
Sollenberger, Howard Edwin *retired government official*
Sonnemann, Harry *electrical engineer, consultant*
Sowle, Donald Edgar *management consultant*
Stephens, William Theodore *lawyer, business executive*
Stitt, David Tillman *lawyer*
Struelens, Michel Maurice Joseph Georges *political science educator, foreign affairs consultant*
Stump, John Sutton *lawyer*
Svahn, John Alfred *government official*
Talbot, Lee Merriam *ecologist, environmental specialist, consultant*
Tansill, Frederick Joseph *lawyer*
Thomas, Lydia Waters *research and development executive*
Topping, Peter *historian, educator*
Traver, Courtland Lee *lawyer*
Trotter, Haynie Seay *lawyer*
Trout, Maurice Elmore *foreign service officer*
Turner, Stansfield *former government official, lecturer, writer, teacher*
†Urquhart, Glen Taylor *real estate development company executive, government planning administrator*
Vandemark, Robert Goodyear *retired retail company executive*
†Waylan, Cecil Jerome *telecommunications executive*
Wirthlin, Richard Bitner *research strategist*
Wümpelmann, Knud Aage Abildgaard *clergyman, religious organization administrator*
Yager, Joseph Arthur, Jr. *economist*

Mechanicsville
†Balser, Glennon *church administrator*

Merrifield
Moffett, Margaret J. *public affairs executive*
†Scott, James Martin *state legislator, healthcare system executive*

Middleburg
Beddall, Thomas Henry *lawyer*
Collins, James Lawton, Jr. *retired army officer*
Cooke, Jack Kent *diversified company executive*
Spilhaus, Athelstan *meteorologist, oceanographer*
Spillane, Mickey (Frank Morrison Spillane) *author*

Midlothian
Davis, Emma-Jo Levey *retired government executive, publishing executive*
Jones, John Evan *medical educator*
Rodgers, Eugene *writer*
Sanders, Helen Caravas *art educator*
Stringham, Luther Winters *economist, administrator*

Millwood
Grupe, Warren Edward *pediatrician, educator*

Mineral
Speer, Jack Atkeson *publisher*

Moneta
Armistead, Moss William, III *retired newspaper executive*
Pfeuffer, Robert John *musician*

Montpelier Station
†Scott, Christopher *executive director cultural trust, author*

Montross
Fountain, Robert Roy, Jr. *farmer, retired industrial executive, naval officer*

Morattico
Dawson, Carol Gene *writer, consultant*

Mount Jackson
Sylvester, George Howard *retired air force officer*

Mount Vernon
†Horstman, Neil Williard *museum administrator*

Nellysford
French, Charles Ezra *economist, educational and agricultural consultant*

Newington
Foster, Eugene Lewis *engineering executive*

Newport News
†Banks, Charles A. *manufacturing executive*
†Barnes, Myrtle Sue Snyder *editor*
Bateman, Fred Willom *retired judge*
Bernhardt, John Bowman *banker*
Brink, Gerald R. *hospital executive*
Camp, Hazel Lee Burt *artist*
†Cantrell, Joseph Doyle *newspaper company executive*
Cardman, Lawrence S. *physics educator*
Cox, Alvin Earl *shipbuilding executive*
Cuthrell, Carl Edward *lawyer, educator, clergyman*
Dart, Charles Edward *retired consultant*
Davis, Jack Wayne, Jr. *newspaper editor*
†Duval, Barry Eugene *mayor, real estate executive*
Fricks, William Peavy *shipbuilding company executive*
†Hamilton, Phillip A. *principal, state legislator*
Hubbard, Harvey Hart *aeroacoustician, noise control engineer, consultant*
Isgur, Nathan Gerald *physicist, educator*
Morris, James Matthew *history educator*
†Peebles, David L. *light manufacturing executive*
Perry, Donald A. *cable television consultant*
Phillips, William Ray, Jr. *shipbuilding executive*
Santoro, Anthony Richard *academic administrator*
Smith, Walter Tilford *shipbuilding company executive*
†Wilkinson, William Durfee *museum director*
Young, Maurice Isaac *mechanical and aerospace engineering educator*

Norfolk
Adams, David Huntington *judge*
Ahrari, M. E. *political science educator, researcher, consultant*
Andrews, Mason Cooke *obstetrician-gynecologist, educator, mayor*
Andrews, William Cooke *physician*
Baird, Edward Rouzie, Jr. *lawyer*
Barry, Richard Francis, III *publishing executive*
Batten, Frank *newspaper publisher, cable broadcaster*
Bazin, Nancy Topping *English language educator*
Blount, Robert Haddock *corporate executive, retired naval officer*
Bonney, Hal James, Jr. *federal judge*
Bullington, James R. *ambassador*
†Campbell, Cole C. *journalist, educator*
Clarke, J. Calvitt, Jr. *federal judge*
†Clemins, Archie Ray *naval officer*
†Copeland, Howard E. *lawyer*
Cranford, Page Deronde *lawyer, executive*
Crenshaw, Francis Nelson *lawyer*
Csanady, Gabriel Tibor *oceanographer, meteorologist, environmental engineer*
Cutchins, Clifford Armstrong, III *banker*
Dandridge, Rita Bernice *English language educator*
Davey, John Michael *military career officer*
Devine, Charles Joseph, Jr. *urologist, educator*
Doumar, Robert George *federal judge*
Dyar, Kathryn Wilkin *pediatrician*
El-Mahdi, Anas Morsi *radiation oncologist*
Etheridge, James Edward, Jr. *academic administrator, pediatrics educator*
Faulconer, Robert Jamieson *pathologist, educator*
Fitzpatrick, William Henry *retired journalist*
Garlette, William Henry Lee *army officer*
Geib, Philip Oldham *physician, retired naval officer*
Glickman, Albert Seymour *psychologist, educator*
Goode, David Ronald *transportation company executive*
†Granuzzo, Andrew Aloysius *career officer*
Greene, Douglas George *humanities educator, author, publisher*
†Guy, Louis Lee, Jr. *environmental engineer*
Hoffman, Walter Edward *federal judge*
Ives, Ronn Brian *artist, educator*
†Jackson, Raymond A. *federal judge*
Jones, Franklin Ross *education educator*
Jones, Howard Wilbur, Jr. *gynecologist*
Jones, Leon Herbert, Jr. (Herb Jones) *artist*
Julian, Michael *grocery company executive*
Kern, Howard Paul *hospital administrator*
Koch, James Verch *academic administrator, economist*
Lester, Richard Garrison *radiologist, educator*
Lind, James Forest *surgeon, educator*
Lucking, Robert A. *English literature educator*
Maly, Kurt John *computer science educator*
Marchello, Joseph Maurice *mathematics and physical science educator*
Mark, Peter *director, conductor*
Martin, Roy Butler, Jr. *museum director, retired broker*
Mauz, Henry Herrward, Jr. *naval officer*
Mc Gaughy, John Bell *civil engineer*
McKinnon, Arnold Borden *transportation company executive*
†Miller, Yvonne Bond *state senator, educator*
†Mitchell, Glenn R. *hospital administrator*
Morgan, Henry Coke, Jr. *lawyer*
Moses, Paul Davis *career officer*
Musgrave, Thea *composer, conductor*
Myers, Donald Allen *university dean*
†Olson, Phillip Roger *naval officer*
Perry, Ruth Anna *English language educator*
Prince, William Taliaferro *federal judge*
Rephan, Jack *lawyer*
Ritter, Alfred Francis, Jr. *cable television executive*
Robb, Nathaniel Heyward, Jr. *national guard officer, real estate executive*
Rose, Paul Edward *publishing company executive*
Ruchelman, Leonard Isadore *urban studies and public administration educator*
Ryan, Louis Farthing *lawyer*
Schellenberg, Karl Abraham *biochemist*
†Scott, Kenneth R. *transportation executive*
Shannon, John Sanford *railway executive, lawyer*
Sheetz, Richard LaTrelle *retired association executive*
†Sizemore, William Howard, Jr. *newspaper editor*
Smith, Rebecca Beach *federal judge*
Timms, A. Jackson *lawyer*
Tolmie, Donald McEachern *lawyer*
Train, Harry Depue, II *retired naval officer*
Vest, Frank Harris, Jr. *bishop*
†Wagner, James Dennis *communications executive*
Wallace, William Hall *academic dean, educator, economist*
Watts, Dave Henry *corporate executive*
Wei, Benjamin Min *computer engineering educator*
†Williams, Sue Darden *library director*
Wilson, Lloyd Lee *organization administrator*
Wiltse, James Clark *civil engineer*
Winslow, Janet Lucas *elementary education educator*
Wynne, John Oliver *newspaper, broadcast and cable executive*

North Springfield
Hugin, Adolph Charles (Eugene) *lawyer, engineer, inventor, educator*

Norton
Earls, Donald Edward *lawyer*

Oakton
Curry, Thomas Fortson *electronics engineer, defense industry executive*
Shrier, Stefan *mathematician, educator*
Wolff, Edward A. *electronics engineer*

Occoquan
Johnson, Frank Stanley, Jr. *communications executive, retired government official*
Wolle, William Down *foreign service officer*

Onancock
Kidd, Rebecca Montgomery (Louise Kidd) *artist*

Orange
Cortada, James N. *mayor, former diplomat*
Dunnington, Walter Grey, Jr. *lawyer, retired food and tobacco executive*
Poulson, Richard J. M. *lawyer*

Orlean
Kulski, Julian Eugeniusz *architect, planner, educator*

Palmyra
Leslie, William Cairns *metallurgical engineering educator*
Mulckhuyse, Jacob John *energy conservation and environmental consultant*
Ramsey, Forrest Gladstone, Jr. *engineering company executive*
White, Luther Wesley *lawyer*

Penn Laird
Wise, Charles Conrad, Jr. *former government official, author*

Petersburg
Berry, Lemuel, Jr. *academic dean, music educator*
Dance, Gloria Fenderson *dance studio executive, ballet administrator*
Williams, Gertie Boothe *retired home school coordinator*

Poquoson
Yard, Rix Nelson *former athletic director*

Portsmouth
Brown, James Andrew *naval architect*
†Burgess, Dean *library director*
Mapp, Alf Johnson, Jr. *writer, historian*
McDaniel, William J. *career military officer*
Spong, William Belser, Jr. *lawyer, educator*
†Thomas, Ted, Sr. *minister*
Trumble, Richard Dwain *superintendent of schools, consultant*
†Webb, Gloria O. *mayor*

Purcellville
Conte, Joseph John, II *meteorologist, management consultant*
Sharples, Winston Singleton *automobile importer and distributor*

Quantico
Davis, James Richard *military officer*
†Joy, James R. *retail executive*
Wallenborn, Janice Rae *elementary education educator*

Radford
James, Carolyne Faye (Clarity James) *mezzo-soprano*
Lamb, Lester Lewis *hospital administrator*
Thomas, Robert Wilburn *broadcasting and advertising executive*
Wille, Lois Jean *retired newspaper editor*

Rapidan
Grimm, Ben Emmet *former library director and consultant*
Williams, Langbourne Meade *retired minerals company executive*

Reston
Ayers, George Edward Lewis *higher education association executive*
†Bannister, Dan R. *professional and technical services company executive*
Barton, Paul Booth, Jr. *geologist*
Black, Cathleen Prunty *newspaper executive*
Blanchard, Townsend Eugene *service companies executive*
Blum, John Curtis *agricultural economist*
Brett, Robin *geologist*
Brosseau, Irma Finn *business executive, management consultant*
Brown, James Robert *air force officer*
Calio, Anthony John *scientist, business executive*
Cannistraro, Nicholas, Jr. *newspaper executive*
Cerf, Vinton Gray *telecommunications company executive*
Christ, Thomas Warren *electronics research and development company executive, sociologist*
Clark, Sandra Helen Becker *geologist*
Cohen, Philip *hydrogeologist*
Curry, John Joseph *professional organization executive*
Davis, George Lynn *aerospace company executive*
Doe, Bruce Roger *geologist*
Drew, Russell Cooper *physicist*
Duscha, Lloyd Arthur *engineering executive*
Dyer, Timothy J. *educational association administrator*
Eaton, Gordon Pryor *geologist, research director*
Fredette, Richard Chester *computer specialist*
Gates, James David *association executive*
Goldman, Ralph Morris *political science educator*
Goodwin, Robert Delmege *retired association executive*
Hamilton, Robert Morrison *geophysicist*
Heginbotham, Jan Sturza *sculptor*
Hope, Samuel Howard *accreditation organization executive*
Huebner, John Stephen *geologist*
Humphreys, David John *lawyer, trade association executive*
Kramish, Arnold *technical consultant, author*
Lewis, Arthur Dee *corporation executive*
Mallette, Malcolm Francis *newspaper editor, educator*
Masters, Charles Day *geologist*
Metcalf, William Henry, Jr. *architect*
†Moore, Daniel L. *architect*
Mumzhiu, Alexander *machine vision, image processing engineer*
Murdoch, Robert Waugh *cement and construction materials company executive*
Nysmith, Charles Robert *management consultant*
Payne, Roger Lee *geographer*
Pojeta, John, Jr. *geologist*

Pyle, Thomas Alton intructional television and motion picture executive
Rose, Michel construction materials company executive
Ross, Malcolm mineralogist, crystallographer
Sato, Motoaki geologist, researcher
Scheeler, James Arthur architect
Schelling, John Paul lawyer, consultant
Schleede, Glenn Roy energy market and policy consultant
Sherman, William Courtney foreign service officer
Troester, Carl Augustus, Jr. association consultant
Walzer, William Charles church official, interdenominational religious publishing agency executive
Waxman, Pearl Latterman early childhood educator
Wilkinson, Edward Anderson, Jr. retired naval officer, business executive
†Zigel, James M. aircraft manufacturing executive

Richmond

Ackell, Edmund Ferris university president
Ackerly, Benjamin Clarkson lawyer
Adams, John Buchanan, Jr. advertising agency executive
Addiss, Stephen art history educator, artist, composer
†Allen, George Felix governor
Alpert, Janet A(nne) title insurance company executive
Anderson, James Frederick clergyman
Anderson, Leonard Gustave retired lawyer, retired business executive
Aron, Mark G. corporate executive, lawyer
Ayres, Stephen McClintock physician, educator
Bagby, Daniel Gordon minister
Bagley, Philip Joseph, III lawyer
Baker, Donald Parks journalist, educator
Baliles, Gerald L. lawyer, former governor
Baretski, Charles Allan political scientist, librarian, educator, historian, municipal official
Barker, Thomas Carl health administration educator
Batzli, Terrence Raymond lawyer
Belcher, Dennis Irl lawyer
†Benedetti, Joseph B. lawyer
Berry, William Willis retired utility executive
Beyer, Donald Sternoff, Jr. lieutenant governor
Black, Robert Perry retired banker, executive
Blanchard, Lawrence Eley, Jr. lawyer, corporation executive
Blatt, Elizabeth Kempske museum administrator
Booker, Lewis Thomas lawyer
Bourke, William Oliver retired metal company executive
Bowles, Aubrey Russell, III lawyer
Bradley, Sterling Gaylen microbiology and pharmacology educator
Brame, Joseph Robert, III lawyer
Brasfield, Evans Booker lawyer
†Briggs, Edward Burton, Jr. religion writer
†Broaddus, John Alfred, Jr. bank executive, economist
Brockenbrough, Henry Watkins lawyer
Brooks, Robert Franklin, Sr. lawyer
Brown, Aubrey Neblett, Jr. minister, editor
Brush, Carey Wentworth retired college administrator, history educator
†Bryan, Charles Faulkner, Jr. historical society director
Bryan, David Tennant media company executive
Bryan, John Stewart, III newspaper publisher
Bunzl, Rudolph Hans retired diversified manufacturing company executive
Burke, John K(irkland), Jr. lawyer
Burrus, Robert Lewis, Jr. lawyer
Bush, Thomas Norman lawyer
†Bustard, Clarke music critic, newswriter, radio producer
Butzner, John Decker, Jr. federal judge
Campbell, Thomas Corwith, Jr. economics educator
Capps, Thomas Edward holding company executive
Carrell, Daniel Allan lawyer
Carrico, Harry Lee state supreme court chief justice
Carter, Joseph Carter, Jr. lawyer
Catlett, Richard H., Jr. retired lawyer
†Chichester, John H. state senator
Christie, Laurence Glenn, Jr. surgeon
Clement, Alvis Macon former utilities executive
Clinard, Robert Noel lawyer
Cohn, David Stephen lawyer
Compton, Asbury Christian state supreme court justice
Compton, Olin Randall consulting electrical engineer, researcher
†Costa, Robert Nicholas library director
Coudriet, Charles Edward banker
†Crowl, R(ichard) Bern aluminum company executive
†Cunningham, Jean Wooden lawyer, educator, state legislator
Cutchins, Clifford Armstrong, IV lawyer
Dabney, H. Slayton, Jr. lawyer
Dabney, Virginius author
Dahlenburg, Lyle Marion investment company executive
Dandoy, Suzanne Eggleston physician, state agency executive
Daniel, Beth professional golfer
Davenport, Bradfute Warwick, Jr. lawyer
Davis, Douglas Whitfield lawyer
†Davis, Norwood H., Jr. health insurance corporation executive
Denny, Collins, III lawyer
Dickinson, Alfred James realtor
Dicks, John G., III lawyer
Dillon, James Lee media company executive, newspaper publisher
Dilworth, Robert Lexow military officer
Donnahoe, Alan Stanley newspaper executive
Dray, Mark S. lawyer
†Dresser, Paul Alton, Jr. paper and forest products executive
Dunn, Leo James obstetrician, gynecologist, educator
†Easterling, William K. plastics and chemicals executive
Ellis, Andrew Jackson, Jr. lawyer
Elmore, Edward Whitehead lawyer
Epps, Augustus Charles lawyer
Ermer, James transportation company executive
Estes, Gerald Walter newspaper executive
Evans, James Stanley communications company executive
Farnham, James Edward lawyer
Fay, Frederic Albert former government official
Ferry, Andrew Peter ophthalmic surgeon, medical educator
Fields, William Jay investment banker
Fischer, Carl Robert health care facility administrator
Fox, Joseph Carter pulp and paper manufacturing company executive
Franko, Bernard Vincent pharmacologist
Freed, David Clark artist
Freeman, George Clemon, Jr. lawyer
Freeman, Robert Mallory banker
Freund, Emma Frances medical technologist
Fuller, Reginald Horace clergyman, biblical studies educator
†Gartlan, Joseph V., Jr. state senator
Gary, Richard David lawyer
Gasch, Manning lawyer
Geisler, Ernest Keith, Jr. lawyer
†George, Lester golf course architectural firm executive
Gewanter, Harry Lewis pediatric rheumatologist
Giblin, Patrick David banker
†Gillispie, Charles Stephenson, Jr. publishing and printing executive
Goldman, Israel David hematologist, oncologist
Goodykoontz, Charles Alfred newspaper editor, retired
Gordon, Thomas Christian, Jr. former justice
Gorr, Louis Frederick investment consultant
Gottwald, Bruce Cobb chemical company executive
Gottwald, Floyd Dewey, Jr. chemical company executive
Graves, H. Brice lawyer
Gray, Clarence Jones foreign languages educator, dean emeritus
Gross, Paul Allan health service executive
Hackney, Virginia Howitz lawyer
Hagan, Randall Lee manufacturing executive
†Hall, Franklin Perkins lawyer, banker, state official
Hall, James Curtis business and economics educator
Hall, Stephen Charles lawyer
Hamel, Dana Bertrand academic administrator
Hamill, A(llen) William finance executive
Hancock, William Glenn lawyer
Hanneman, Rodney Elton metallurgical engineer
Hardage, Page Taylor health care administrator
Hardy, Richard Earl rehabilitation counseling educator, clinical psychologist
Harris, Henry Hiter, Jr. banker
Hatch, Robert Norris banker
Haynes, Boyd Withers, Jr. surgeon
Heilman, E. Bruce academic administrator
Hellmuth, William Frederick, Jr. economics educator
Helwig, Arthur Woods chemical company executive
Henderson, Bernard Levie, Jr. former state official, funeral service executive
Henley, Vernard William banker
Hettrick, George H. lawyer
Hicks, Thomas Howard retail executive
Higgins, Kenneth Raymond landscape architect
Hintz, Robert Louis transportation company executive
Holder, Richard Gibson metal products executive
Hong, James Ming industrialist, venture capitalist
Horsley, Waller Holladay lawyer
†Howell, Janet D. state legislator
Huntley, Robert Edward Royall lawyer, business executive, former university president
Jacobs, Harry Milburn, Jr. advertising executive
Jacobs, James Paul insurance executive
James, Allix Bledsoe retired university president
James, Gene Albert farmers cooperative executive
Jandl, Henry Anthony architect, educator
Jezuit, Leslie James manufacturing company executive
Joel, William Lee, II interior and lighting designer
Jones, Catesby Brooke retired banker
Jones, David Eugene pharmaceutical company executive
Kasen, Stewart Michael retail executive
Kay, John Franklin, Jr. lawyer
Kay, Saul pathologist
Kearfott, Joseph Conrad lawyer
Kendig, Edwin Lawrence, Jr. physician, educator
†Kenney, Walter T. mayor
Kessler, Neil Stanton lawyer
Kevorkian, Richard artist
Kilpatrick, Robert Donald retired insurance company executive
King, Robert Leroy business administration educator
Koontz, Warren Woodson, Jr. urologist, educator
†Lambert, Benjamin Joseph, III optometrist, state legislator
Laskin, Daniel M. oral and maxillofacial surgeon, educator
Laverge, Jan tobacco company executive
Lawrence, Walter, Jr. surgeon
Lawton, Nancy artist
Ledbetter, David Oscar lawyer
†Lee, Peter James bishop
Leith, John Haddon clergyman, theology educator
Levit, Jay J(oseph) lawyer
Lewis, Frances Aaronson retail company executive
Lewis, Judith A. nursing educator, women's health nurse
Lewis, Sydney retail company executive
Leyden, Donald Elliott chemist, researcher
Lindholm, John Victor business executive
Manning, William Raymond retired state official
Martenstein, Thomas Ewing lawyer
Mathews, Roderick Bell lawyer
Mauck, Henry Page, Jr. medical and pediatrics educator
Mauro, John Baptist retired marketing researcher
McClard, Jack Edward lawyer
Mc Cue, Carolyn Moore retired pediatric cardiologist
†McDonald, Frank Albert, Jr. personnel director
McDonough, Reginald Milton religious organization executive
McElligott, James Patrick, Jr. lawyer
McGee, Henry Alexander, Jr. chemical engineering educator
Mc Grath, Lee Parr author, public relations executive
Mc Namara, Rieman, Jr. retired banker
McVey, Henry Hanna, III lawyer
Mellette, M. Susan Jackson physician, educator, researcher
Merhige, Robert Reynold, Jr. federal judge
Miller, Lewis Nelson, Jr. banker
Miller, Nan Louise museum director
†Milmoe, Patrick J. lawyer
Modlin, George Matthews university chancellor emeritus
Moore, Andrew Taylor, Jr. banker
Moore, Thurston Roach lawyer
Morrill, Richard Leslie university administrator
Morris, Dewey Blanton lawyer
Morton, Marshall Nay treasurer
Munsey, Virdell Everard, Jr. utility executive
Neathawk, Roger Delmore marketing company executive
†Neman, Daniel Louis movie critic
Newbrand, Charles Michael advertising firm executive
†Nielsen, Steven B. medical products executive
†Nolen, Frank William state senator, engineer, farmer
Norfleet, Robert F., Jr. banking executive
Oakey, John Martin, Jr. lawyer
Oken, Donald Edward physician, educator
Osdene, Thomas Stefan tobacco company executive, chemist
Owen, Duncan Shaw, Jr. physician, medical educator
†Owen, Howard Wayne journalist, writer
Palik, Robert Richard mechanical engineer
Palmore, Fred Wharton, III lawyer
Pasco, Hansell Merrill retired lawyer
Patterson, James Willis pathology and dermatology educator
Patterson, Robert Hobson, Jr. lawyer
Pauley, Stanley Frank manufacturing company executive
Payne, Robert E. federal judge
Pendleton, Eugene Barbour, Jr. business executive
Peters, David Frankman lawyer
Pinckney, C. Cotesworth lawyer
Plaisted, Harris Merrill, III real estate executive
Poff, Richard Harding state supreme court justice
Pollard, Overton Price state agency executive, lawyer
Pope, Robert Dean lawyer
Powell, Kenneth Edward lawyer
Powell, Lewis Franklin, III lawyer
Powell, Virginia W. lawyer
†Puller, Linda Todd state legislator
†Radecki, Catherine psychologist
Rainey, Gordon Fryer, Jr. lawyer
†Raper, Mark Irvin public relations, advertising executive
Rawlings, James Scott architect
Reveley, Walter Taylor, III lawyer
Reynolds, David Parham metals company executive
†Reynolds, Randolph Nicklas aluminum company executive
Rhodes, James T. electric power industry executive
Richardson, David Walthall cardiologist, educator, consultant
Roach, Edgar Mayo, Jr. lawyer
Robertson, William Franklin publishing executive
Robins, Edwin Claiborne, Sr. retired pharmaceutical company executive
Rogers, Isabel Wood religious studies educator
Rogers, James Edward paper company executive
Rogula, James Leroy consumer products company executive
Rolfe, Robert Martin lawyer
Roop, Ralph Goodwin retired oil marketing company executive
Rosbe, William Louis lawyer
Rowley, Frank Selby, Jr. artist
Rudlin, David Alan lawyer, educator
Rutledge, Paul E., III insurance company executive
Sadler, Graham Hydrick library administrator
Saine, Carroll Lee banker
Satterthwaite, Cameron B. physics educator
Savage, William Woodrow education educator
†Schewel, Elliot Sidney state senator
Schwarzschild, Patricia Michaelson lawyer
Schwarzschild, William Harry, Jr. banker
†Self, Phyllis C. health sciences librarian
Shands, William Ridley, Jr. lawyer
Shapiro, Gary Michael philosophy educator
Sharer, John Daniel lawyer
Sharp, Richard L. retail company executive
Simmons, S. Dallas university president
Simpson, John Noel hospital administrator
Slater, Thomas Glascock, Jr. lawyer
Slaughter, Alexander Hoke lawyer
Smith, R. Gordon lawyer
Sniffin, John Harrison retail executive
Spahn, Gary Joseph lawyer
Spain, Jack Holland, Jr. lawyer
Spencer, James R. federal judge
Spivey, Joseph M., III lawyer
Stephenson, Roscoe Bolar, Jr. state supreme court justice
Stettinius, Wallace communications executive
Stockton, Thomas B. bishop
Strickland, William Jesse lawyer
Sullivan, Walter Francis bishop
Sweeney, Arthur Hamilton, Jr. metal manufacturing executive, retired army officer
Swezey, Charles Mason Christian ethics educator, administrator
Talley, Charles Richmond commercial banking executive
Thomas, John Charles lawyer, former state supreme court justice
Thompson, Francis Neal financial services consultant
Thompson, Paul Michael lawyer
Thompson, William Taliaferro, Jr. internist, educator
Thorp, Benjamin A., III paper manufacturing company executive
Tice, Douglas Oscar, Jr. federal judge
Tilghman, Richard Granville banker
Totten, Randolph Fowler lawyer
Trani, Eugene Paul university president, educator
Treadway, John David history educator
Trott, Sabert Scott, II marketing professional
†Trotti, John Boone librarian, educator
Troy, Anthony Francis lawyer
Trumble, Robert Roy business educator
Tuck, Grayson Edwin real estate agent, former natural gas transmission executive
Twomey, Wililam Eldred, Jr. lawyer
Tyson, John C. state official
Urofsky, Melvin Irving historian, educator
†Vallarino, Lidia M. chemistry educator
†Waddell, Charles Lindy state senator
Waddell, William Robert lawyer
Wakeham, Helmut Richard Rae chemist, consulting company executive
Walker, Charles B. chemicals company executive
Walsh, James Hamilton lawyer
Walsh, William Arthur, Jr. lawyer
Ward, John Wesley retired pharmacologist
Warrick, James Craig banker
Warthen, Harry Justice, III lawyer
Watkins, Hays Thomas retired railroad executive
Watts, Daniel Thomas university dean, pharmacologist
Watts, Stephen Hurt, II lawyer
†Wechsler, Andrew Stephen surgery educator
Weinberg, Robert Stephen ophthalmologist
Wellford, Hill B., Jr. lawyer
†Wells, James M., III bank executive
Wheeler, R(ichard) Kenneth lawyer
White, Hugh Vernon, Jr. lawyer
Wilder, Lawrence Douglas former governor
Williams, Loretta Dodson financial advisor, investment broker
Williams, Richard Leroy federal judge
Williams, Robert C. paper company executive
Wilson, James Milton, III bank executive
Witt, Walter Francis, Jr. lawyer
Wolf, Barry genetics, pediatric educator
Wood, Jeanne Clarke charitable organization executive
Word, Thomas S., Jr. lawyer
†Yu, Robert Kuan-jen biochemistry educator

Roanoke

Adams, James E. bank executive
Al-Zubaidi, Amer Aziz physicist, educator
†Beagle, Benjamin Stuart, Jr. columnist
Bell, Houston Lesher, Jr. hospital administrator
Berry, John Coltrin insurance executive
Bond, Victoria Ellen conductor, composer
Butler, Manley Caldwell lawyer
Caudill, David L. bank executive
Dalhouse, Warner Norris banker
Dillard, Richard Henry Wilde English language professional, educator, author
†Edwards, J. Randolph medical products executive
Fishwick, John Palmer lawyer, retired railroad executive
Hamrick, Joseph Thomas mechanical engineer, aerospace company executive
Husted, John Edwin geologist, educator
Johns, Dolores Yuille educational administrator
Landon, Forrest M. newspaper editor
†Layman, Mark Leslie newspaper editor
Light, Arthur Heath bishop
Marmion, William Henry retired bishop
Merker, Frank Ferdinand retired hospital administrator
Pearson, Henry Clyde federal judge
Reggia, Frank electrical engineer
†Robertson, Thomas L. health facility administrator
Rugaber, Walter Feucht, Jr. newspaper executive
†Shaffner, Patrick Noel architectural engineering executive
†Shaftman, Fredrick Krisch telephone communications executive
†Shamy, Edward Thomas newspaper columnist
Sowers, William Armand civil engineer
Stanley, Ralph bluegrass musician
Steinhardt, Ralph Gustav, Jr. chemist
†Thompson, Ron Everett religious organization, church administrator
†Tota, Frank Peter school system administrator
Turk, James Clinton federal judge
Warren, William Kermit newspaper managing editor
†Woodrum, Clifton A., III lawyer, state legislator

Roseland

Fetter, Robert Barclay retired administrative sciences educator

Rosslyn

Adair, John Joseph federal agency administrator

Round Hill

Coll, Helen F. banker
Pugh, Marion Stirling archaeologist, author
Sadd, William Wheeler trade association executive

Ruckersville

Soderbergh, Steven Andrew filmmaker

Salem

†Bansemer, Richard Frederick bishop
Brand, Edward Cabell retail executive
Chakravorty, Ranes Chandra surgeon, educator
Fisher, Charles Harold chemistry educator, researcher
Gring, David M. academic administrator
Lane, Lawrence Jubin electrical engineer, consultant
Walker, Loren Haines electrical engineer
Willet, Richard A. engineering company executive

Seaford

Hammer, Jacob Myer physicist, consultant
Jenkins, Margaret Bunting human resource executive

Smithfield

Luter, Joseph Williamson, III meat packing and processing company executive

South Hill

Brooks, Arlene Sheffield secondary education educator

Sperryville

Armor, David J. sociologist
Mc Carthy, Eugene Joseph writer, former senator

Spotsylvania

Arnhoff, Franklyn Nathaniel psychologist, sociologist, educator
Hardy, Dorcas Ruth government relations and public policy consultant
†Houck, R(obert) Edward state senator, educational administrator
†Orrock, Robert Dickson agricultural education educator, state legislator

Spottswood

Fredricksen, Cleve Laurance thoroughbred horse farm owner, real estate investor

Spring Grove

Daniel, Robert Williams, Jr. business executive, former congressman

Springfield

Broome, Paul Wallace engineering research and development executive
Bruen, John Dermot computer systems company executive
Bush, Norman research and development executive
Duff, William Grierson electrical engineer
Fedewa, Lawrence John information systems company executive
Gawalt, Gerard W(ilfred) historian, writer
Larson, Reed Eugene association executive
McLaurin, Ronald De political analyst, consultant, author, journalist
Nong artist, sculptor
Peters, Charles William research and development company manager

Sebastian, Richard Lee physicist, executive
†Singleton, John Knox hospital administrator
Steele, Lendell Eugene research scientist
Stottlemyer, David Lee government official

Stanleytown
Stanley, Thomas Bahnson, Jr. investor

Staunton
Balsley, Philip Elwood entertainer
Cochran, George Moffett retired judge
Hammaker, Paul M. retail executive, business educator, author

Stephens City
Leeper, Charles Kendal engineering consultant

Sterling
†Acker, C. Edward airline executive
Buchanan, William Walter publisher
†Colgan, Charles Joseph corporate professional, state senator
Harris, Paul Lynwood aerospace transportation executive
Witek, James Eugene public relations executive

Suffolk
Birdsong, George Yancy manufacturing company executive
Carroll, George Joseph pathologist, educator
Hines, Angus Irving, Jr. petroleum marketing executive
Hope, James Franklin mayor, civil engineer, consultant

Susan
Ambach, Dwight Russell retired foreign service officer

Sweet Briar
Armstrong, Gregory Timon religion educator, minister
Hill, Barbara Ann academic administrator, consultant
McClenon, John Raymond chemistry educator
Miller, Reuben George economics educator

Tazewell
†Weeks, Ross Leonard, Jr. museum foundation executive

Upperville
di Zerega, Thomas William former energy company executive, lawyer
Smart, Stephen Bruce, Jr. business and government executive

Urbanna
Hudson, Jesse Tucker, Jr. financial executive
Salley, John Jones university administrator, oral pathologist

Verona
de Vaux, Peter Fordney advertising consultant

Vienna
Argow, Keith Angevin association executive,forester
Bartlett, John Wesley consulting firm executive
Beaty, Orren, Jr. writer, former governmental affairs consultant, former association executive
Binder, Leonard James magazine editor, retired
Blevins, Charles Russell publishing executive
Cartier, Brian Evans association executive
Chamberlain, Diane psychotherapist, author, clinical social worker
Chandler, Hubert Thomas former army officer
Chen, William Shao-Chang retired army officer
Davis, Cabell Seal, Jr. naval officer
Eash, Joseph J. technology executive
Fasser, Paul James, Jr. labor arbitrator
Ghormley, Ralph McDougall retired naval officer
Giovacchini, Robert Peter toxicologist, manufacturing executive, retired
Hatch, Harold Arthur retired military officer
Henry, Charles Robert army officer
Holmes, Bradley Paul information technology consultant
Hood, William Clarence international banking official
Howard, Daggett Horton lawyer
Hughes, Thomas Joseph retired naval officer
Jackson, Dempster McKee retired naval officer
Jackson, Juanita Wallace educational consultant
Jahn, Laurence Roy retired biologist, institute executive
Keiser, Bernhard Edward engineering company executive, consulting telecommunications engineer
†Kohler, Karl Eugene architect
Krejci, Stanley Leon computer software company financial executive
Kumar, Verinder accountant, financial executive
Lewis, Boyd De Wolf publisher,editor, writer
Lillard, Mark Hill, III computer consulting executive, former air force officer
Lyons, Paul Michael producer, film
Mc Arthur, George journalist
McKay, Carol Ruth photographic editor
Razzano, Frank Charles lawyer
†Roth, James engineering company executive
Savoca, Antonio Litterio technology company executive
Schneider, Peter Raymond research scientist, juvenile justice consultant
Van Stavoren, William David management consultant, retired government official
Walker, Edward Keith, Jr. business executive, retired naval officer
Webb, William Loyd, Jr. army officer
West, Richard Luther military association executive, defense consultant, retired army officer
Woodward, Kenneth Emerson retired mechanical engineer

Vinton
†Cranwell, C. Richard lawyer

Virginia Beach
Alexander, William Powell business consultant
Asher, Garland Parker investment holding company executive
Barriskill, Maudanne Kidd primary school educator
Becker, Boris professional tennis player
Brickell, Edward Ernest, Jr. management executive
El-Fayoumy, Joanne Patricia Quinn writer, poet
Farrell, Paul Edward dentist, retired naval officer, educator
Freyss, David producer, director
Green, Barbara-Marie publisher, journalist
Harrison, William Wright retired banker
Kreyling, Edward George, Jr. railroad executive
Lichtenberg, Byron K. futurist, manufacturing executive, space flight consultant
†Lisota, Gary Martin business executive
†May, David L., Jr. architectural firm executive
Mayer, William Dixon pathologist, educator
Merchant, Donald Joseph microbiologist
Oberndorf, Meyera E. mayor
Oldfield, Edward Charles, Jr. retired naval officer, communications company executive
Robertson, Pat (Marion Gordon Robertson) religious broadcasting executive
Sanderson, James Richard naval officer, planning and investment company consultant
†Sekulow, Jay Alan lawyer
Seward, William W(ard), Jr. author, educator
†Sims, Martha J. library director
Smith, A. Robert editor, author
†Stolle, Kenneth William laywer
Tarbutton, Lloyd Tilghman motel executive, franchise consultant, hair care consultant
†Wardrup, Leo C. state legislator
Weller, Robert N(orman) hotel executive
Wick, Robert Thomas retired supermarket executive
Wiggins, Samuel Paul education educator
Williams, John Rodman theologian, educator

Warm Springs
†Deeds, Robert Creigh lawyer, state legislator

Warrenton
Larese, Edward John management company executive
Peisner, Arthur Mann consumer products industry executive
vom Baur, Francis Trowbridge retired lawyer

Warsaw
Hirsch, Charles Bronislaw retired religion educator and administrator

Waterford
Pollack, Reginald Murray painter

Waynesboro
Rippe, Peter Marquart museum administrator

White Stone
Wroth, James Melvin former army officer, computer company executive

Williamsburg
Axtell, James Lewis history educator
Baker, Donald Scott communications executive
Ball, Donald Lewis retired English language educator
Baranowski, Frank Paul energy consultant, former government official
Birney, Robert Charles retired academic administrator, psychologist
Bolender, Carroll Herdus retired air force officer, consultant
Braun, Richard Lane lawyer, university administrator
Brinkley, Joseph Willard association executive
Cantlay, George Gordon retired army officer
Chappell, Miles Linwood, Jr. art history educator
Dittman, Duane Arthur management consultant
Edwards, Jack Donald education educator
Esler, Anthony James historian, novelist
Finn, A. Michael public relations executive
Finn, Thomas Macy religion educator
†Friedman, Herbert psychology educator
Geddy, Vernon Meredith, Jr. lawyer
Geoffroy, Kevin Edward education educator
Godwin, R. Wayne chemicals company executive
Goodwin, Bruce Kesseli geology educator, researcher
†Grayson, George W. congressman
Gross, Robert Alan history educator
Harris, James Franklin philosophy educator
Heller, James Stephen law librarian
Herbert, Albert Edward, Jr. interior, industrial designer
Herrmann, Benjamin Edward former insurance executive
†Hornsby, Bruce Randall composer, musician
Jacoby, William Jerome, Jr. internist, retired military officer
Kottas, John Frederick business administration educator
Lange, Carl James psychology educator
Longsworth, Charles R. foundation administrator
Marcus, Paul lawyer, educator
Marshall, Nancy Haig library administrator
McGiffert, Michael history educator, editor
Mc Kean, John Rosseel Overton university dean
Mc Knight, John Lacy physics educator
McLane, Henry Earl, Jr. philosophy educator
Messmer, Donald Joseph business management educator, marketing consultant
Nettels, Elsa English language educator
Noël Hume, Ivor retired antiquary, consultant
O'Connell, William Edward, Jr. finance educator
Orwoll, Robert Arvid chemistry educator
Parkany, John business educator, international financial consultant
Parker, Donald Howard landscape architect
Pearson, Roy Laing business administration educator
Quittmeyer, Charles Loreaux business educator
Roseberg, Carl Andersson sculptor, educator
Siegel, Robert Ted physicist
†Sipes, Larry L. lawyer
Smith, Roger Winston political theorist, educator
Smolla, Rodney Alan lawyer, educator
Spitzer, Cary Redford avionics consultant, electrical engineer
Starnes, William Herbert, Jr. chemist, educator
Sullivan, Timothy Jackson legal educator, academic administrator
Tate, Thaddeus W(ilbur), Jr. (Thad Tate) history educator, historical institute executive, historian
Walters, Harry N. manufacturing company executive
Warren, William Herbert business administration educator
Whyte, James Primrose, Jr. former legal educator
†Wilburn, Robert Charles institute executive

Winchester
†Bechamps, Gerald J. surgeon
Byrd, Harry Flood, Jr. newspaper executive, former senator
Holland, James Tulley plastic products company executive
Jamison, Richard Bryan airport consultant
Ludwig, George Harry physicist
Murtagh, John Edward chemist, alcohol production consultant
Pavsek, Daniel Allan banker, educator
Tisinger, Catherine Anne college dean
Turner, William Richard retired aeronautical engineer, consultant
Whiting, Henry H. state supreme court justice

Wise
Ellsworth, Lucius Fuller academic administrator
Peake, Richard Henry, Jr. English language educator
Smiddy, Joseph Charles retired college chancellor
Yun, Peter Subueng economics educator

Woodbridge
Breene, Norma Wylie special education educator
Dillaber, Philip Arthur budget/resource analyst, economist, consultant
Peck, Dianne Kawecki architect

Woodstock
Walker, Charles Norman retired insurance company executive

Wytheville
Hansen, B(obby) J. management consultant, real estate investor and developer

Yorktown
†Gould, Alec historic park administrator

WASHINGTON

Anacortes
Businger, Joost Alois atmospheric scientist, educator
Ives, Burl (Icle Ivanhoe) singer, actor
Mc Cracken, Philip Trafton sculptor
Randolph, Carl Lowell chemical company executive
Spaulding, John Pierson public relations executive, marine consultant
Stitt, William D. small business owner, marketing professional, consultant

Ashford
Briggle, William James federal agency administrator

Auburn
Creighton, John W., Jr. forest products company executive
†Cross, Virginia E. tribal council leader, educational consultant
†Lapinski, Donald elementary school principal
Sata, Lindbergh Saburo psychiatrist, physician, educator
Whitmore, Donald Clark retired engineer

Bainbridge Is
Bowden, William Darsie interior designer
Huntley, James Robert government official, international affairs scholar and consultant
Randlett, Mary Willis photographer
†Schmidt, Karen Anne travel company executive, state legislator
Warns, Raymond H. judge

Battle Ground
Hansen, James Lee sculptor

Belfair
Walker, E. Jerry retired clergyman

Bellevue
Akutagawa, Donald psychologist, educator
Armstrong, Dickwin Dill chamber of commerce executive
†Baker, Jackson Arnold container shipping company executive
Chen, Ching-Hong medical biochemist, researcher
Clark, Richard Walter educator, consultant
Dow, Daniel Gould electrical engineering educator
Edde, Howard Jasper engineering executive
Eigsti, Roger Harry insurance company executive
Elliott, Richard Wayne lawyer
†Engebrecht, Richard E. diversified distribution company executive
Faris, Charles Oren civil engineer
Fremouw, Edward Joseph physicist
Gottlieb, Alan M. advertising and broadcasting executive, writer
Graham, John Robert, Jr. financial executive
Groten, Barnet energy company executive
Habbestad, Kathryn Louise writer
Hackett, Carol Ann Hedden physician
Hannah, Lawrence Burlison lawyer
Knoepfler, Peter Tamas psychiatrist, organizational consultant
Koontz, Alfred Joseph, Jr. financial and operating management executive, consultant
McReynolds, Neil Lawrence electric utility company executive
Melby, Orville Erling retired banker
Mutschler, Herbert Frederick retired librarian
Olson, Hilding Harold surgeon, educator
Otterholt, Barry L. technology management consultant
Pigott, Charles McGee transportation equipment manufacturing executive
Puckett, Allen Weare health care information systems executive
Reudink, Douglas Otto John communications company executive, researcher
Roddis, Richard Stiles Law insurance company executive, consultant, legal educator
Roselle, Richard Donaldson industrial, marine and interior designer
Ryles, Gerald Fay private investor, consultant
Schairer, George Swift aeronautical engineer
Shih, Benedict Chesang investment company executive
Smith, George Lester lawyer
†Stephenson, Robert Baird energy company executive
Sullivan, James Jerome lawyer, consultant
Szablya, John Francis electrical engineer, consultant
Walsh, John Breffni aerospace consultant
Warren, James Ronald retired museum director, author, columnist
Wright, Theodore Otis forensic engineer

Bellingham
Albrecht, Albert Pearson electronics engineer, consultant
Bestwick, Warren William retired construction company executive
Critchlow, B. Vaughn research facility administrator, researcher
†DeLorme, Roland L. director, headmaster
Diers, Carol Jean psychology educator
Doerper, John Erwin food writer
Fullmer, Donald Kitchen insurance executive
Helsell, Robert M. construction executive
Jansen, Robert Bruce consulting civil engineer
†Landis, Wayne G. environmental toxicologist
Morse, Karen Williams academic administrator
Naylor, Harry Brooks microbiologist
Packer, Mark Barry lawyer, financial consultant, foundation official
Pierce, George Adams university administrator, educator
Rhoads, James Berton archivist, former government official, consultant, educator
Self, Charles Edwin financial consultant, retail company executive
Skinner, Knute Rumsey poet, English educator
Whisenhunt, Donald Wayne history educator

Bothell
Blackburn, John Lewis consulting engineering executive
Icenhower, Rosalie B. retired elementary school principal
McDonald, Michael Lee career officer, healthcare administrator

Burlington
Zeretzke, Frederick Frank H. artist, educator

Carlsborg
Bouquet, Francis Lester physicist

Centralia
Kirk, Henry Port academic administrator

Cheney
Drummond, Marshall Edward business educator, university administrator
Gerber, Sanford Edwin audiologist

Clark County
Holley, Lawrence Alvin retired labor union official

Colfax
Webster, Ronald B. lawyer

College Place
Andreasen, Niels-Erik Albinus religious educator
Gaskell, Carolyn Suzanne librarian
Jonish, Arley Duane retired bibliographer
Thompson, Alden Lloyd biblical studies educator, author

Dayton
McFarland, Jon Weldon county commissioner

Deer Harbor
Hoag, Paul Sterling architect

East Wenatchee
Bennett, Grover Bryce engineering consultant

Eastwood
Anders, William Alison aerospace and defense manufacturing executive

Edmonds
†Galster, Richard W. engineering geologist
Paul, Ronald Stanley research institute executive
Terrel, Ronald Lee civil engineer, business executive, educator

Edwalla
†Barr, Scott state legislator

Ellensburg
Comstock, Dale Robert mathematics educator
Jacobs, Robert Cooper political scientist, consultant
Jones, Jerry Lynn chemistry educator
Moore, Thomas David academic administrator

Enumclaw
Vernier, Richard foreign language educator, author

Everett
King, Indle Gifford industrial designer, educator
Toyer, Richard Henry accountant

Fairchild AFB
Munn, Eufemia Tobias elementary school principal

Federal Way
Boling, Joseph Edward numismatist, retired military officer
Curtis, Arnold Bennett lumber company executive
Hayek, Carolyn Jean judge
Lane, Robert Casey lawyer
McNeese, Jack Marvin communications executive
†von Reichbauer, Peter Graves senator

Freeland
Freehill, Maurice F. retired educational psychology educator

Friday Harbor
Blinks, John Rogers physiology and biophysics educator
Daum, David Ernest machinery manufacturing company executive
Geyman, John Payne physician, educator
MacGinitie, Walter Harold psychologist
McCreary, Dustin Campbell lawyer, arbitrator
Palmer, Norman Dunbar political scientist, educator, author

Gig Harbor
Canter, Ralph Raymond *psychology educator, research director*
Huyler, Jean Wiley *media and interpersonal communications consultant, hypnotherapist*
Robinson, James William *retired management consultant*

Grandview
Ferguson, Bettie Jean *secondary education educator*

Grayland
Ransom, Bill *author*

Greenbank
Grant, Robert Yearington *former government official*
Tuell, Jack Marvin *retired bishop*

Hansville
Griffin, DeWitt James *architect, real estate developer*

Issaquah
Barchet, Stephen *physician, former naval officer*
Benveniste, Jacob *retired physicist*
Dehlinger, Peter *geophysics educator*
Pearson, Belinda Kemp *economist, consultant*
Tenenbaum, Michael *steel company executive*

Kalama
Liang, Jason Chia *research chemist*

Kenmore
MacKenzie, Peter Sean *computer service company*

Kennewick
Stevens, Henry August *insurance agent, educator*
Wistisen, Martin J. *agricultural business executive*

Kent
Filley, Laurence Duane *computer programmer, consultant*
Goo, Abraham Meu Sen *retired aircraft company executive*
Hebeler, Henry Koester *retired aerospace and electronics executive*
†Johnson, Dennis D. *elementary school principal*
†Kelly, Patrick *school system administrator*
Pierce, Danny Parcel *artist, educator*
Sourapas, Steve James *manufacturing executive*

Kingston
Pichal, Henri Thomas *electronics engineer, physicist, consultant*

Kirkland
Alberg, Tom Austin *communications executive, lawyer*
Allen, Chuck *football team executive*
Ayars, Albert Lee *former school superintendent*
Bernard, James William *corporate executive*
Butler, William A. *lawyer*
Flores, Thomas R. *professional football team executive*
†Gregory, Matthew J. *architectural firm executive*
Kennedy, Cortez *professional football player*
McCaw, Craig O. *communications executive*
McDonald, Joseph Lee *insurance broker*
Parrish, John Brett *manufacturing executive*
Rosett, Ann Doyle *librarian*
Sinegal, James D. *variety store wholesale business executive*
Wenk, Edward, Jr. *civil engineer, policy analyst, educator*

La Conner
Knopf, Kenyon Alfred *economist, educator*
Robbins, Tom *author*

Lacey
Cosand, Joseph Parker, Jr. *education educator emeritus*
Spangler, David Robert *college administrator, engineer*

Lake Spokane
Payne, Arlie Jean *parent education administrator*

Lake Stevens
†Quigley, Kevin Walsh *lawyer, state legislator*

Langley
Bitts, Todd Michael *sales and marketing consultant*
Legters, Lyman Howard *historian*
Medlock, Ann *non-profit organization executive, writer, lecturer*

Liberty Lake
†DeMerritt, Ted C. *microprocessor company executive*

Longview
Kenagy, John Warner *surgeon*
Wollenberg, Richard Peter *paper manufacturing company executive*

Lummi Island
Ewing, Benjamin Baugh *environmental engineering educator, consultant*

Lynnwood
Bear, Gregory Dale *writer, illustrator*
†Benzel, Brian L. *superintendent*
Jenes, Theodore George, Jr. *retired military officer*
Knutzen, Raymond Edward *retired law educator, consultant*

Manchester
Fearon, Lee Charles *chemist*

Marysville
Philpott, Larry La Fayette *horn player*

Mazama
Hogness, John Rusten *physician, academic administrator*

Medina
Schlotterbeck, Walter Albert *manufacturing company executive, lawyer*

Mercer Island
Bowne, Martha Hoke *magazine editor, consultant*
Bridgforth, Robert Moore, Jr. *aerospace engineer*
Coe, Robert Campbell *surgeon*
Culp, Gordon Louis *consulting engineering executive*
Elgee, Neil Johnson *physician*
Gould, Alvin R. *international business executive*
Haviland, James West *physician*
Kelm, Linda *opera singer*
Spitzer, Jack J. *banker*
Steinhardt, Henry *photographer*
†Vining, Glen W., Jr. *insurance company executive*

Mill Creek
Corbally, John Edward *foundation director*
Holmstrom, David Edwin Arthur *mortgage banking executive, consultant*

Moses Lake
Footer, Samuel Joseph *manufacturing company executive*

Mount Vernon
Black, Donald Bruce *controller, arbitrator*
Cammock, Earl E. *surgeon*
†Hall, David Ramsay *architect*
Klein, Henry *architect*

Mountlake Terrace
†Lockwood, Donald A. *insurance company executive*
†Woods, Betty *insurance company executive*

Mukilteo
Jenkins, James Stanley *architect*

Olympia
Alfers, Gerald Junior *bank executive, retired*
Andersen, James A. *state supreme court chief justice*
†Anderson, Ann *state legislator*
Billings, Judith A. *state education official*
Blake, Ann Beth *psychologist*
Brachtenbach, Robert F. *state supreme court justice*
†Chappell, David Jay *language educator, state legislator*
†Cooke, Suzette Allen *state representative*
†Cothern, Barbara Shick *real estate investor, state legislator*
Dolliver, James Morgan *state supreme court justice*
Durham, Barbara *state supreme court justice*
†Flemming, Stanley Lalit Kumar *family practice physician, state legislator*
Gregoire, Christine O. *state attorney general*
Guy, Richard P. *state supreme court justice*
Haseltine, James Lewis *artist, consultant*
†Haugen, Mary Margaret *state legislator*
Johnson, Charles William *state supreme court justice*
†Kessler, Lynn Elizabeth *state legislator*
†Kohl, Jeanne E. *state legislator, sociologist, educator*
Lind, Carl Bradley *retired museum director*
†Long, Jeanine Hundley *state legislator*
Manning, Farley *investment company executive*
Mastrodonato, George Carl *lawyer*
†McDonald, Daniel Robert *senator*
Munro, Ralph Davies *state government official*
Mylroie, Willa Wilcox *transportation engineer, regional planner*
Nesbit, Robert Carrington *historian*
†Norwood, Deborah Anne *law librarian*
O'Brien, Robert S. *state official*
†Ogden, Valeria Juan *management consultant, state representative*
Pritchard, Joel *state lieutenant governor*
†Rayburn, Margaret *state legislator*
Reilly, Robert Joseph *counselor*
†Rinehart, Nita *state senator*
†Shin, Paull Hobom *investment company executive*
†Silver, Jean *state legislator, accountant*
Smith, Charles Z. *state supreme court justice*
†Spanel, Harriet Rosa Albertsen *state senator*
†Thomas, Brian Chester *state legislator, engineer*
Utter, Robert French *state supreme court justice*
†Valle, Georgette Wald *state legislator*
†Wang, Arthur C. *state legislator, lawyer, educator*
†Wojahn, R. Lorraine *state legislator*
Zussy, Nancy Louise *librarian*

Pasco
Yoshino, George *food products executive*

Pierce County
Bourgaize, Robert G. *economist*

Point Townsend
Harrington, LaMar *curator, museum director*

Port Angeles
Chase, John David *university dean, physician*
Hart, Edwin James *chemist*
Muller, Willard C(hester) *writer*
Osborne, Richard Hazelet *anthropology and medical genetics educator*
Ross, Robert King *retired educator*
Warren, Henry Clay, Jr. *naturalist*

Port Ludlow
Gullander, Werner Paul *retired consultant, retired corporate executive*
Ward, Louis Emmerson *retired physician*

Port Townsend
Buhler, Jill Lorie *editor, writer*
†Lamoreaux, Joyce *educational institute executive*

Prosser
Miller, David Eugene *soil scientist, researcher*
†Proebsting, Edward Louis, Jr. *retired research horticulturist*

Pullman
Barnes, Charles D. *neuroscientist, educator*
Bennett, Edward Moore *historian, educator*
Bertramson, B. Rodney *agronomist*
Blakeslee, Leroy Lawrence *agricultural economist*
Bustad, Leo Kenneth *veterinary educator, college administrator*
Catton, William Robert, Jr. *sociology educator*
Crosby, Glenn Arthur *chemistry educator*
†Dillman, Donald Andrew *sociologist, educator*
Dodgen, Harold Warren *chemistry and physics educator*
Fowles, George Richard *physicist, educator*
Funk, William Henry *environmental engineering educator*
George, Thomas Frederick *chemistry educator*
Gustafsson, Borje Karl *veterinarian, educator*
Henson, James Bond *veterinary pathologist*
†Hildebrandt, Darlene Myers *information scientist*
Hirth, John Price *metallurgical engineering educator*
Hosick, Howard Lawrence *cell biology educator, academic administrator*
Kallaher, Michael Joseph *mathematics educator*
†Kapteyn, Henry Cornelius *physics educator*
Markin, Rom J. *college dean, marketing educator, academic administrator*
McSweeney, Frances Kaye *psychology educator*
†Murnane, Margaret Mary *physics educator*
Nakata, Herbert Minoru *retired microbiology educator, academic administrator*
Pomeranz, Yeshajahu *cereal chemist, technologist*
Ryan, Clarence Augustine, Jr. *biochemistry educator*
Schrader, Lawrence Edwin *plant physiologist, educator*
Sheldon, Charles Harvey *political science educator*
Short, James Franklin, Jr. *sociology educator, researcher*
Smith, Robert Victor *university administrator*
Smith, Samuel Howard *university president, plant pathologist*
†Stock, David Earl *mechanical engineering educator*
Warner, Dennis Allan *psychology educator*
Wilson, Robert Burton *veterinary and medical educator*
Young, Francis Allan *psychologist*

Redmond
Beeson, Paul Bruce *physician*
Erxleben, William Charles *lawyer, data processing executive*
Gates, William Henry, III *software company executive*
Herres, Phillip Benjamin *computer software executive*
Mollman, John Peter *book publisher, consultant electronic publishing*
Narodick, Sally G. *corporate executive*
Rossano, August Thomas *environmental engineering educator*
†Smith, William Ward *aerospace executive*

Renton
Tajon, Encarnacion Fontecha (Connie Tajon) *retired educator, association executive*

Richland
Albaugh, Fred William *nuclear engineer, retired research and development executive*
Bair, William J. *radiation biologist*
Barr, Carlos Harvey *lawyer*
Beck, Joe Eugene *environmental health scientist, educator*
Bush, Spencer Harrison *metallurgist*
Campbell, Milton Hugh *chemist*
Cochran, James Alan *mathematics educator*
Colson, Steven Douglas *research director, chemistry educator*
Counsil, William Glenn *electric utility executive*
Elderkin, Charles Edwin *meteorologist*
Evans, Ersel Arthur *engineering consulting executive*
Forsen, Harold Kay *engineering executive*
†Janata, Jiri *biomedical engineer, educator*
McDowell, Robin Scott *physical chemist*
Moore, Emmett Burris, Jr. *physical chemist*
Nolan, John Edward *retired electrical corporation executive*
†Piippo, Steve *educational program director*
Pond, Daniel James *technology planning and analysis program manager, technology transferand deployment*
Rebagay, Teofila Velasco *chemist, chemical engineer*
†Ryans, Yvonne *principal*
Wehner, Alfred Peter *inhalation toxicologist, biomedical scientist*
Wiley, William Rodney *microbiologist, administrator*
Zirkle, Lewis Greer *physician, executive*

Ritzville
†Schoesler, Mark Gerald *state legislator, farmer*

Seattle
Aagaard, George Nelson *medical educator*
Abelson, Herbert Traub *pediatrician, educator*
Ackerley, Barry *professional basketball team executive, communications company executive*
Adams, Hazard Simeon *English educator, author*
Albrecht, Richard Raymond *airplane manufacturing company executive, lawyer*
Aldrich, Robert Anderson *physician*
Alexander, Edward Russell *disease research administrator*
Alkire, John D. *lawyer*
Alps, Glen Earl *printmaker, educator*
Andersen, Niels Hjorth *chemistry educator, biophysics researcher, consultant*
Anderson, Arthur G., Jr. *chemistry educator*
Anderson, Peter MacArthur *lawyer*
Anderson, Richard Powell *thoracic surgeon, educator*
Anderson, Rick Gary *newspaper columnist*
†Anderson, Ross *columnist*
Andrew, Lucius Archibald David, III *bank executive*
Andrews, J. David *lawyer*
Andrews, Richard Otis *museum director*
Ansell, Julian S. *physician, urology educator*
Aoki, John H. *hotel chain executive*
Armstrong, Charles G. *professional baseball executive, lawyer*
Arnold, Robert Morris *banker*
†Aron, William *marine biology administrator*
Arons, Arnold Boris *physicist, educator*
Averill, Lloyd James, Jr. *religion educator*
Babb, Albert Leslie *biomedical engineer, educator*
Bain, William James, Jr. *architect*
Bangsund, Edward Lee *aerospace company executive*
Banks, James Albert *educational research director, educator*
Barash, David Philip *psychology and zoology educator*
Bargreen, Melinda Lueth *music critic*
Barry, Christopher John *lawyer*
Bassett, Edward Powers *university official*
Bassetti, Fred Forde *architect*
Bassingthwaighte, James Bucklin *physiologist, educator, medical researcher*
Baum, William Alvin *astronomer, educator*
Bayley, Christopher T. *international investment banking executive*
Beetham, Stanley Williams *international management consultant*
Beezer, Robert Renaut *federal judge*
Behler, Diana Ipsen *Germanic language and literature educator*
Behnke, Carl Gilbert *beverage franchise executive*
Beighle, Douglas Paul *lawyer*
Bekemeyer, Dennis Lee *lawyer*
Bell, Jeffrey Donald *bank executive*
Benedetti, Thomas Joseph *obstetrician-gynecologist, educator*
Bensussen, Estelle Esther *writer, illustrator, artist*
Berger, Paul Eric *artist, photographer*
Bernard, Eddie Nolan *oceanographer*
Bevan, Donald Edward *retired marine science educator, university dean*
Beyers, William Bjorn *geography educator*
Bierman, Charles Warren *physician, educator*
Bierman, Edwin Lawrence *physician, educator*
Birmingham, Richard Joseph *lawyer*
Black, W. L. Rivers, III *lawyer*
Blagg, Christopher Robin *nephrologist*
Blake, Robert Wallace *aeronautical engineer, consultant*
Blandau, Richard Julius *physician, educator*
Blethen, William Kingsley, Jr. *newspaper publishing executive*
Block, Robert Jackson *investment banker*
Blom, Daniel Charles *lawyer, investor*
Blumenfeld, Charles Raban *lawyer*
Boardman, David *newspaper editor*
Boaz, Doniella *psychotherapist, consultant*
Boba, Imre *history educator*
Bodansky, David *physicist, educator*
Boeder, Thomas L. *lawyer*
Boman, Marc Allen *lawyer*
Bond, Dorothy M. *medical/surgical and geriatrics nurse*
Bonica, John Joseph *anesthesiologist, educator*
Borden, Weston Thatcher *chemistry educator*
Borgatta, Edgar F. *social psychologist, educator*
Bornstein, Paul *physician, biochemist*
Bosmajian, Haig Aram *speech communication educator*
†Bosworth, Thomas Lawrence *architect, educator*
Botimer, Allen Ray *retired surgeon, retirement center administrator*
†Bounds, Christopher E. *food service executive*
Bourque, Philip John *business economist, educator*
†Bowden, Douglas McHose *neuropsychiatric scientist, educator, research center administrator*
Bowen, Jewell Ray *academic dean, chemical engineering educator*
Boylan, Merle Nelson *librarian*
Brammer, Lawrence Martin *psychology educator*
Brandauer, Frederick Paul *Asian language educator*
†Brazier, Robert G. *transportation executive*
Breslow, Norman Edward *biostatistics educator, researcher*
Brier, Evelyn Caroline *retired investment company executive, business consultant*
Bronsdon, Melinda Ann *microbiologist*
Brooke, Francis John, III *foundation administrator*
Brooks, Julie Anne *lawyer*
Brothers, Lynda Lee *lawyer*
Brown, Frederick Calvin *physicist, educator*
†Brown, Kristi *principal*
Brown, Lowell Severt *physicist, educator*
Brownlee, Donald Eugene, II *astronomer, educator*
Bryant, Hilda Marie *journalism educator*
Buck, Robert Follette *banker, lawyer*
Buckner, Philip Franklin *newspaper publisher*
Burgess, Charles Orville *history educator*
Burkhart, William Henry *lawyer*
Burman, David John *lawyer*
Burrows, Elizabeth MacDonald *religious organization executive, educator*
Butler, Timothy Harold *lawyer*
Butow, Robert Joseph Charles *history educator*
†Buursma, William F. *architect*
†Bystrom, Arne *architect*
Cable, Donald Aubrey *lawyer*
Cameron, Mindy *newspaper editor*
Campbell, Robert Hedgcock *investment banker*
Carlsen, James Caldwell *musicologist, educator*
Carlsen, Mary Baird *clinical psychologist*
Carlson, Dale Arvid *university dean*
Caro, Ivor *dermatologist*
Cavanaugh, Michael Everett *lawyer*
Celentano, Francis Michael *artist, art educator*
†Chapman, Bruce Kerry *institute executive*
Char, Patricia Helen *lawyer*
Chihuly, Dale Patrick *artist*
Chisholm, Margaret Elizabeth *retired library director*
Christian, Gary Dale *chemistry educator*
Christiansen, Walter Henry *aeronautics educator*
†Cichanski, Gerald *golf course architect*
Claflin, Arthur Cary *lawyer*
†Clapp, Melvin Carl *gas distributing company executive*
Clark, Kenneth Courtright *retired physics and geophysics educator*
Clark, Robert Newhall *electrical and aeronautical engineering educator*
Clarkson, Lawrence William *airplane company executive*
Cline, Robert Stanley *air freight company executive*
Clinton, Gordon Stanley *lawyer*
Clinton, Richard M. *lawyer*
Coburn, Robert Craig *philosopher*
Cochran, Wendell *science editor*
Cockburn, John F. *retired banker*
Coffman, Sandra Jeanne *psychologist*
Coldewey, John Christopher *English literature educator*
Collett, Robert Lee *financial company executive*
†Collins, Theodore John *lawyer*
Condit, Philip Murray *aerospace executive, engineer*
Corker, Charles Edward *retired lawyer, educator*
Corr, Kelly *lawyer*
†Cosgrove, Benjamin A. *retired aerospace company executive*
Cosway, Richard *legal educator*
Coughenour, John Clare *federal judge*
Couser, William Griffith *medical educator, academic administrator, nephrologist*
†Coviello, Vincent F., Jr. *insurance company executive*
Cox, Frederick Moreland *retired university dean, social worker*
Coxe, Weld *management consultant*
Coyle, Marie Bridget *microbiology educator, laboratory director*
Creager, Joe Scott *geology and oceanography educator*
Criminale, William Oliver, Jr. *applied mathematics educator*

Cross, Harry Maybury retired law educator, consultant
Cullen, James Douglas banker, finance company executive
Culp, Mildred Louise corporate executive
Cunningham, Janis Ann lawyer
Curtis, James Austin actuary consultant
Dahl, Lance Christopher lawyer
Dale, David C. physician, medical educator
D'Ambrosio, Charles Anthony, Sr. economist, educator
Danelo, Peter Anthony lawyer
Davidson, Robert William science foundation director
Davis, Earl James chemical engineering educator
Davis, John MacDougall lawyer
Day, Alexandra (Sandra L. Woodward Darling) illustrator, designer
Day, Robert Winsor research administrator
Debro, Julius university dean, sociology educator
†Dederer, Michael E. public relations executive
Dehmelt, Hans Georg physicist
Denniston, Martha Kent business owner, author
Denny, Brewster Castberg retired university dean
Derham, Richard Andrew lawyer
†Dermanis, Paul Raymond architect
de Tornyay, Rheba nurse, university dean emeritus, educator
DeVore, Paul Cameron lawyer
Dickinson, Calhoun lawyer
Dietrich, William Alan reporter
DiJulio, Peter Stephen lawyer
Dillard, Marilyn Dianne property manager
Dimmick, Carolyn Reaber federal judge
Donaldson, James Adrian otolaryngology educator
Donaldson, Lauren R. fisheries biology and radiobiology educator emeritus
Donohue, James Patrick lawyer
Dorkin, Frederic Eugene lawyer
Dorpat, Theodore Lorenz psychoanalyst
Duncan, Elizabeth Charlotte marriage and family therapist, educator
Dunn, Richard John English language educator
Dunne, Thomas geology educator
Dunnell, Robert Chester archaeologist, educator
Du Pen, Everett George sculptor, educator
Durham, Robert Lewis architect
Duryee, David Anthony management consultant
Dworkin, Samuel Franklin dentist, psychologist
Dwyer, William L. federal judge
†Dyer, Philip E. insurance company executive
Edmondson, W(allace) Thomas limnologist, educator
Edwards, John Stuart zoology educator, researcher
Eggers, David Frank, Jr. chemistry educator
Elgin, Ron Alan advertising executive
Ellegood, Donald Russell publishing executive
Elliott, Jeanne Marie Koreltz transportation executive
Ellis, Eva Lillian artist
Ellis, James Reed lawyer
Ellis, John W. professional baseball team executive, utility company executive
Ellison, Herbert Jay history educator
Engel, Thomas chemistry educator
Etcheson, Warren Wade business administration educator
Evans, Bernard William geologist, educator
Evans, Charles Albert microbiology educator
Evans, Daniel Jackson consultant, former senator
Evans, Ellis Dale psychologist, educator
Evans, Trevor Heiser advertising executive
Even, Jan newspaper editor
Fancher, Michael Reilly newspaper editor, newspaper publishing executive
Farris, Jerome federal judge
Faulstich, James R. bank executive
Favorite, Felix oceanographer
Fetters, Norman Craig, II banker
Fialkow, Philip Jack academic administrator, medical educator
Fiedler, Fred Edward psychology educator, management consultant
Figley, Melvin Morgan radiologist, physician, educator
Finlayson, Bruce Alan chemical engineering educator
Fischer, Edmond Henri biochemistry educator
Fitzpatrick, Thomas Mark lawyer
Fitzsimons, Patrick S. police chief
Fix, Wilbur James department store executive
Fletcher, Betty B. federal judge
Floss, Heinz G. chemistry educator, scientist
Forbes, David Craig musician
Fortson, Edward Norval physics educator
Fox, Kenneth shipbuilder, naval engineer, water transit consultant
Freed, Aaron David architect
Freeny, Patrick Clinton radiology educator, consultant
Funk, Robert Norris college president, lawyer
Gardner, Jill Christopher neuroscientist
Garlid, Kermit Leroy engineering educator
Gates, William H. lawyer
Geballe, Ronald physicist, university dean
†Gelb, Michael H. chemistry educator
Gerberding, William Passavant university president
Gerhart, James Basil physics educator
Gerrodette, Charles Everett real estate company executive, consultant
Gerstenberger, Donna Lorine humanities educator
Gessel, Stanley Paul emeritus soil science educator
Gibaldi, Milo university dean
Giblett, Eloise Rosalie hematology educator
Giles, Robert Edward, Jr. lawyer
Gillis, Steven biotechnology company executive
Gissing, Bruce aerospace company executive
Gittinger, D. Wayne lawyer
Givan, Boyd Eugene aircraft company executive
Glover, Karen E. lawyer
Godden, Jean W. columnist
Goeltz, Thomas A. lawyer
Goodell, Brian Wayne oncologist, medical educator
Goodlad, John Inkster education educator, author
Gorans, Gerald Elmer accountant
Gordon, Milton Paul biochemist, educator
†Gordon, Patrick A. architectural firm executive
Gore, William Jay political science educator
Gouldthorpe, Kenneth Alfred Percival publisher, state official
Gouterman, Martin Paul chemistry educator
Graham, C(lyde) Benjamin, Jr. physician
Graham, Stephen Michael lawyer
Gray, Marvin Lee, Jr. lawyer
Grayston, J. Thomas medical and public health educator
Green, Gertrude Dorsey psychologist, author
Green, Joshua, III banker
Greenan, Thomas J. lawyer
Greene, John Burkland lawyer
Gregory, Norman Wayne chemistry educator, researcher
Griffey, Ken, Jr. (George Kenneth Griffey, Jr.) baseball player
Groman, Neal Benjamin microbiology educator
Gross, Edward retired sociologist, educator
†Grossman, Robert James architect
Guntheroth, Warren Gaden physician
†Guralnick, Michael J. medical research administrator
Guy, Arthur William electrical engineering educator, researcher
†Gwinn, Mary Ann newspaper reporter
Hackett, John Peter dermatologist
Halver, John Emil nutritional biochemist
Haman, Raymond William lawyer
Hamilton, Gary Glen sociology educator
Hansen, Wayne W. lawyer
Hanson, Kermit Osmond business administration educator, university dean emeritus
Haralick, Robert Martin electrical engineering educator
Harder, Virgil Eugene business administration educator
Hargiss, James Leonard ophthalmologist
Harmon, Daniel Patrick classics educator
†Harris, Claude fire department chief
Hartl, John George film critic
Hastings, L(ois) Jane architect, educator
†Hazelton, Penny Ann law librarian, educator
Heath, George Ross oceanographer, university dean
Heer, Nicholas Lawson Arabist-Islamist educator
Hellmann, Donald Charles political science educator
†Hellström, Ingegerd business executive
Henderson, Dan Fenno lawyer, educator
Henderson, Maureen McGrath medical educator
Henkel, Cathy newspaper sports editor
Henley, Ernest Mark physics educator, university dean emeritus
Herring, Susan Weller anatomist
Hertzberg, Abraham aeronautical engineering educator, university research scientist
Hewitt, Edwin mathematician, educator
Hiatt, Peter library educator
Hille, Bertil physiology educator
Hills, Regina J. journalist
Hilpert, Edward Theodore, Jr. lawyer
†Hinshaw, Mark Larson architect, urban planner
Hodge, Paul William astronomer, educator
Hodson, William Alan pediatrician
Hoerni, Jean Amédée electronics consultant
Hoffman, Allan Sachs chemical engineer, educator
Hofmann, Douglas Allan lawyer
Holtby, Kenneth Fraser aircraft manufacturing company consultant
Hood, Leroy Edward biologist
Hornbein, Thomas Frederic anesthesiologist
Horton, Elliott Argue, Jr. lawyer, business consultant
Houck, John Candee research facility administrator, biochemist
†Houk, Benjamin Noah ballet dancer
†Hudson, Leonard Dean physician
Hunkins, Francis Peter education educator
Hunt, Earl Busby psychologist
Hunter, Theodore Paul lawyer, energy consultant
Huston, John Charles law educator
Hutcheson, Mark Andrew lawyer
Hutchinson, William Burke surgeon, research center director
Ingalls, Robert Lynn physicist, educator
Inlow, Edgar Burke political science educator
Isaki, Lucy Power Slyngstad lawyer
Ishimaru, Akira electrical engineering educator
Israel, Allen D. lawyer
Jacobson, Phillip Lee architect, educator
Jaeger, David Arnold aerospace company executive
Jameson, Henry C. lawyer
Jans, James Patrick mathematics educator
Jenkins, Speight opera company executive, writer
Jenkins, William Maxwell banker
Jennerich, Edward John university official and dean
Johnson, Bruce Edward Humble lawyer
Johnson, Randall David (Randy Johnson) professional baseball player
Johnson, Wayne Eaton former drama critic, writer, editor
Johnston, Norman John architecture educator
†Johnston, R. Bruce lawyer
Jonassen, James O. architect
Jones, Edward Louis historian, educator
Jones, Frank Ray biotechnology company executive, researcher
†Jones, Grant Richard landscape architect, planner
†Jones, Johnpaul architect
Jonsen, Albert R. medical ethics educator
Joppa, Robert Glenn aeronautics educator
Judson, C(harles) James (Jim Judson) lawyer
Kalina, Robert Edward physician, educator
Kane, Alan Henry lawyer
Kane, Christopher lawyer
Kaplan, Barry Martin lawyer
Kapur, Kailash Chander industrial engineering educator
Kareken, Francis A. lawyer
Karl, George professional basketball coach
†Karr, James Richard ecologist, researcher, educator
†Keith, Donald Malcolm physician
Kellogg, Kenyon P. lawyer
Kelly, Carolyn Sue newspaper executive
Kemp, Shawn T. professional basketball player
†Kennedy, David Michael environmental scientist
Kenney, Richard Laurence poet, English language educator
Keyt, David philosophy and classics educator
Killeen, Michael John lawyer
Killinger, Kerry Kent bank executive
Kippenhan, Charles Jacob mechanical engineer, retired educator
Kirby, William Murray Maurice medical educator
Kirkendall, Richard Stewart historian, educator
Klebanoff, Seymour Joseph medical educator
Klee, Victor La Rue mathematician, educator
Knechtges, David Richard Chinese and East Asian studies educator
Kobayashi, Albert Satoshi mechanical engineering educator
Koehler, Reginald Stafford, III lawyer
Kolb, Keith Robert architect, educator
Korg, Jacob English literature educator
Kraft, Donald Bowman advertising agency executive
Kraft, George Howard physician, educator
Krebs, Edwin Gerhard biochemistry educator
Kruckeberg, Arthur Rice botanist, educator
Kruse, Paul Robert retired librarian, educator
Kuhrau, Edward W. lawyer
Kummert, Richard Osborne lawyer, educator
†Kunze, Eric physical oceanographer, educator
Kwiram, Alvin L. physical chemistry educator, university official
Lacitis, Erik journalist
Ladd, James Roger international business consultant
Laird, Charles David zoology and genetics educator, researcher
LaPoe, Wayne Gilpin retired business executive
Lauritzen, Peter Owen electrical engineering educator
LaVeck, Gerald DeLoss physician, educator
Lawrence, Jacob artist, educator
†Lee, John Marshall mathematics educator
Leitzell, Terry Lee lawyer
Leland, David D. timber company executive
Lemly, Thomas Adger lawyer
Lingafelter, Edward Clay, Jr. chemistry educator
Loeser, John David neurosurgeon, educator
Lombard, David Norman lawyer
Loper, Robert Bruce theater director, educator
Lord, Jere Johns retired physics educator
Lovett, Wendell Harper architect
Lowry, Mike governor, former congressman
Lubatti, Henry Joseph physicist, educator
Lyden, Fremont James political science educator
MacDonald, Andrew Stephen management consulting firm executive
Mackey, Sally Schear retired religious organization administrator
MacLachlan, Douglas Lee marketing educator
Mah, Feng-hwa economics educator
†Malcolm, Garold Dean architect
Mallory, V(irgil) Standish geologist, educator
Mandeville, Gilbert Harrison consulting engineering executive
Margon, Bruce Henry astrophysicist, educator
†Marriott, David M. public relations executive
Marshall, Scott advertising agency executive
†Martens, David Baker publishing executive
Martin, George Coleman aeronautical engineer
Martin, George M. pathologist, gerontologist
Martin, Joan Callaham psychologist, educator
Martinez, Edgar professional baseball player
Mason, James Tate surgeon
Matchett, William H(enry) English literature educator
†Matheson, Kent D. school system administrator
Matthews, Donald Rowe political scientist, educator
Mauer, Michael Leonard banker
†McAleer, William H. software company financial executive
McCann, Richard Eugene lawyer
McConnell, Calvin Dale clergyman
Mc Donald, James Michael, Jr. research institute consultant
Mc Feron, Dean Earl mechanical engineer
Mc Govern, Walter T. federal judge
†McKay, John lawyer
McKay, Michael Dennis lawyer
McKeown, Mary Margaret lawyer
McKey, Thomas J. lawyer
McKinnon, James Buckner real estate sales executive, writer, researcher
McMillan, John A. retail executive
McNeely, Mark Hall advertising executive
Meagher, Cynthia Nash journalist
Meditch, James Stephen electrical engineering educator
Merendino, K. Alvin surgical educator
Merrill, Ronald Thomas geophysicist, educator
†Meyer, C. Richard architect
Michael, Ernest Arthur mathematics educator
Michalik, John James law school administrator
Mickelwait, Lowell Pitzer lawyer
†Miles, Don Clifford architect
†Miles, Edward Lancelot marine studies educator, consultant, director
Moch, Robert Gaston lawyer
Monsen, Elaine Ranker nutritionist, educator, editor
†Moore, Benjamin theatrical producer
Moore, Daniel Charles physician
Moore, James R. lawyer
Moore, Malcolm Arthur lawyer
†Morgan, Jeff research engineer
Morrill, Richard Leland geographer, educator
Morse, John Moore architect, planner
Mottet, Norman Karle pathologist, educator
Motulsky, Arno Gunther geneticist, physician, educator
Mueller, Gerhard G(ottlob) accounting educator
Muilenburg, Robert Henry hospital administrator
Mullin, J. Shan lawyer
Mullins, Donald Hugh lawyer
Murphy, Thomas Joseph archbishop
Mussehl, Robert Clarence lawyer
Nakatani, Roy Eiji biologist, educator
†Nalder, Eric Christopher investigative reporter
Narver, John Colin business administration educator
Nellermoe, Leslie C. lawyer, partner
†Nelson, James Alonzo radiologist, educator
Nelson, Marshall J. lawyer
Nelson, Wendel Lane medicinal chemist, educator
†Nester, Eugene William microbiology educator, immunology educator
Neurath, Hans biochemist, educator
Newmeyer, Frederick Jaret linguist, educator
†Niemi, Janice state legislator, lawyer
Nijenhuis, Albert mathematician, educator
Nishitani, Martha dancer
†Noe, James Alva judge
Noe, Jerre Donald computer science educator
Noll, Jonathan Boyd lawyer
Nordstrom, Bruce A. department store executive
Nordstrom, John N. department store executive
†Nudelman, Phillip M. insurance company executive
Odegaard, Charles Edwin history educator
†O'Donnell, Wilson Edward historical society director
Oehler, Richard William lawyer
Ojemann, George A. neurosurgeon, medical association executive
O'Leary, Thomas Howard resources executive
Olsen, Harold Fremont lawyer
Olson, David John political science educator
Olson, James William Park architect
Olstad, Roger Gale science educator
O'Malley, Robert Edmund, Jr. mathematics educator
Omenn, Gilbert Stanley university dean, physician
Orians, Gordon Howell biology educator
Owen, John journalist
Pacholski, Richard Francis retired securities company executive, financial consultant
Page, Roy Christopher periodontist, educator
Palm, Gerald Albert lawyer
Parker, Omar Sigmund, Jr. lawyer
Parks, Patricia Jean lawyer
Parsons, A. Peter lawyer
Paul, Thomas Frank lawyer
Pawula, Kenneth John artist, educator
Payne, Ancil Horace retired broadcasting executive
Pease, Carol Helene oceanographer
†Perkin, Gordon Wesley international health agency executive
Perrin, Edward Burton health services researcher, biostatistician, public health educator
Petersdorf, Robert George medical educator, association executive
Petrie, Gregory Steven lawyer
Phillips, Josef Clayton insurance and investment company executive
Piniella, Louis Victor professional baseball team manager
Pinkerton, Guy Calvin savings and loan executive
Piven, Peter Anthony architect, management consultant
Pocker, Yeshayau chemistry, biochemistry educator
Polk, William Merrill architect
Pollack, Gerald Harvey bioengineering educator
Pollak, Robert Andrew economist
Polonis, Douglas Hugh engineering educator
Porter, Stephen Cummings geologist, educator
Potter, Karl Harrington philosophy educator
Powell, George Van Tuyl lawyer
Pratt, David Terry mechanical engineering educator, combustion researcher
Prentke, Richard Ottesen lawyer
Pressly, Thomas James history educator
Prins, David speech pathologist, educator
Privat, Jeannette Mary bank librarian
Prosterman, Roy L. law educator, development specialist
Ptacek, William H. library director
Pusch, William Gerard lawyer
Pyke, Ronald mathematics educator
Pyle, Kenneth Birger historian, educator
Pym, Bruce Michael lawyer
Quimby, George Irving anthropologist, former museum director
Rabinovitch, Benton Seymour chemist, educator emeritus
Raible, Peter Spilman minister
Raisbeck, James David aircraft design executive
Ravenholt, Reimert Thorolf epidemiologist
Read, Charles Raymond, Sr. business executive
Redman, Eric lawyer
Reed, Richard John retired meteorology educator
†Reed, William G., Jr. paper company executive
Reinhardt, William Parker chemical physicist, educator
Rhines, Peter Broomell oceanographer, atmospheric scientist
Rice, Norman B. mayor
Riddell, Richard Harry lawyer
Rieke, Paul Victor lawyer
Rinearson, Peter Mark journalist, author, software developer
Ritter, Daniel Benjamin lawyer
Rives, William D. lawyer
Robb, Bruce former insurance company executive
Robb, John Wesley religion educator
Robertson, William Osborne physician
Robinson, Gary Dale aerospace company executive
Robkin, Maurice Abraham nuclear engineer, educator
†Rockey, Jay public relations company executive
Ross, Austin health care executive
Ross, Russell pathologist, educator
Rothstein, Barbara Jacobs federal judge
†Ruddy, James W. lawyer
Runstad, Judith Manville lawyer
Rupp, John Norris lawyer
Russell, David Allison aeronautical engineering educator
Russell, Francia ballet director, educator
†Sanders, James J. architect
Sandler, Michael David lawyer
Saracino, Samuel Francis lawyer
Sarason, Irwin G. psychology educator
Saunders, William Lockwood financial consultant
Saxberg, Borje Osvald management educator
†Schafer, James Henry newspaper company executive
Scheidel, Thomas Maynard speech communication educator
Scher, Allen Myron physiologist, educator
Schiffman, Harold Fosdick Asian language educator
Schilling, John Albert surgeon
Schoenfeld, Walter Edwin manufacturing company executive
Schomaker, Verner chemist, educator
Schwab, Evan Lynn lawyer
Scott, John Carlyle gynecologist, oncologist
Scribner, Belding Hibbard medical educator, nephrologist
Segal, Jack mathematics educator
Shapiro, J. Peter lawyer
Shepard, Thomas Hill physician, educator
Sherman, John Clinton geography educator
Shrontz, Frank Anderson airplane manufacturing executive
Shulkin, Jerome lawyer
Siefert, Richard Carl lawyer
Simcox, Craig Dennis aeronautical engineer
Simkin, Peter Anthony physician, educator
Singer, Sarah Beth poet
Sizemore, Herman Mason, Jr. newspaper executive
Skilling, John Bower structural and civil engineer
Sleicher, Charles Albert chemical engineer
Smith, Andrew Vaughn telephone company executive
†Smith, Donald William airport manager
Smith, Jeffrey L. (The Frugal Gourmet) cook, writer
Smith, Moncrieff Hynson psychology educator
Smith, Orville Auverne physiology educator
Smith, Payton lawyer
Smulyan, Jeffrey radio station executive, owner pro baseball team
Soltys, John Joseph, Jr. lawyer
Spafford, Michael Charles artist
Spindel, Robert Charles electrical engineering educator
Spinrad, Bernard Israel physicist, educator
Spitzer, Hugh D. lawyer
Squires, William Randolph, III lawyer
†Stanton, Michael John newspaper editor
Staryk, Steven S. violinist, concertmaster, educator
Stear, Edwin Byron corporate executive
Steinberg, Jack lawyer
Stenchever, Morton Albert physician, educator
Stern, Edward Abraham physics educator
Stevens, Clyde Benjamin, Jr. property manager, retired naval officer
Stewart, Robert Andrew lawyer
Stowell, Kent ballet director
Strandjord, Paul Edphil physician, educator
Strandness, Donald Eugene, Jr. surgeon
Stuiver, Minze geological sciences educator
Sugar, Peter Frigyes historian
†Sullivan, Daniel J. artistic director
Sullivan, William James university president

†Sundberg, Richard architectural firm executive
Sutter, Joseph F. aeronautical engineer, consultant, retired airline company executive
Swanson, August George physician, retired association executive
Swanson, Donald Alan geologist
Swanson, Phillip Dean neurologist
Sweeney, David Brian lawyer
Tallman, Richard C. lawyer
Tausend, Fredric Cutner lawyer, university dean
Tenney, William Frank pediatrician
Terrell, W(illiam) Glenn university president emeritus
Thomas, David Phillip forestry educator, college administrator
Thomas, Edward Donnall physician, researcher
Thompson, Arlene Rita nursing educator
Thorbeck, Thomas George lawyer
Thornton, Dean Dickson retired airplane company executive
Thorpe, James Alfred utilities executive
Thorson, Lee A. lawyer
Thouless, David James physicist, educator
†Tracy, Mary E. principal
Treadgold, Donald Warren historian, educator
Treiger, Irwin Louis lawyer
†Trump, Eddie holding company executive
†Trump, Julius holding company executive
Tucker, Gary Jay physician, educator
Tukey, Harold Bradford, Jr. horticulture educator
Turner, Wallace L. reporter
Turnovsky, Stephen John economics educator
Utevsky, David lawyer
van den Berghe, Pierre Louis sociologist, anthropologist
Van Orden, Phyllis Jeanne librarian, educator
Vecci, Raymond Joseph airline executive
Venkata, Subrahmanyam Saraswati electrical engineering educator, electri energy and power researcher
Vesper, Karl Hampton business and mechanical engineering educator
†Voorhees, John Lloyd columnist
Voorhees, Lee R., Jr. lawyer
Wagner, Patricia H. lawyer
Wagoner, David Everett lawyer
Wagoner, David Russell author, educator
Wallace, John Michael meteorology educator
Wan, Frederic Yui-Ming mathematician, educator
†Warner, Vincent W. bishop
Washington, James Winston, Jr. artist, sculptor
Weaver, Lois Jean physician, educator
Webb, Eugene English language educator
Weinberg, John Lee federal judge
Weissman, Eugene Yehuda chemical engineer
Weitkamp, William George nuclear physicist
Welliver, Albertus Delmar aerospace manufacturing company executive
Wellner, Jon August statistician, educator
Wells, Christopher Brian lawyer
Wells, Judee Ann lawyer
Whalen, Jerome Demaris lawyer
†Whalen, Michael P. architect
Whitford, Joseph P. lawyer
Whitsitt, Robert James professional basketball team executive
†Wiborg, James Hooker chemicals distribution company executive
Wilets, Lawrence physics educator
Williams, J. Vernon lawyer
Williams, Jerald Arthur mechanical engineer
Williams, John A. (Jack Williams) newspaper publishing executive
Williams, Robert Walter physics educator
Williams, Walter Baker mortgage banker
Williamson, Don newspaper columnist
Wilske, Kenneth Ray internist, rheumatologist, researcher
Winterbauer, Richard Hill physician, medical researcher
Witham, Barry Bates drama educator
Wolfle, Dael Lee public affairs educator
Wood, Stuart Kee engineering manager
Woodruff, Gene Lowry nuclear engineer, university dean
Wooster, Warren S(criver) marine science educator
Wott, John Arthur arboretum and botanical garden executive, horticulture educator
Wright, Eugene Allen federal judge
Wright, Willard Jurey lawyer
Yantis, Phillip Alexander audiologist, educator
Yarington, Charles Thomas, Jr. surgeon, administrator
†Young, Jeffry John psychologist, gerontologist, educator, consultant
Ziadeh, Farhat J. Middle Eastern studies educator
Zilly, Thomas Samuel federal judge
Zunker, Richard E. insurance company executive

Sequim
Barton, Jay university administrator, biologist
Beaton, Roy Howard retired nuclear industry executive
Meacham, Charles Harding government official
Ramsey, William Ray association executive

Shelton
Barnard, Michael Dana orthopedic surgeon
Wolbrink, Donald Henry landscape architect, city planner

Silverdale
Walske, M(ax) Carl, Jr. physicist

Spanaway
†Campbell, Thomas J. legislator, chiropractor
†Westbrook, T. L. bishop

Spokane
Bakker, Cornelis B. psychiatrist, educator
Bender, Betty Wion librarian
Benson, Allen B. chemist, educator, consultant
†Bolstad, D. D. federal agency administrator
Burr, Robert Lyndon library director
†Cowles, William Stacey publisher
Davis, Scott Livingston banker, lawyer
†Dellwo, Dennis A. state legislator
Eliassen, Jon Eric utility company executive
Evoy, John Joseph psychology educator
Foster, Ruth Mary dental association administrator
Fowler, Betty Janmae dance company director, editor
Gibson, Melvin Roy pharmacognosy educator
Giller, Edward Bonfoy retired government official, retired air force officer
Gray, Alfred Orren journalism educator, research and communications consultant
Green, Dale Monte retired judge
Hendershot, Carol Miller physical therapist
Herdrich, Norman Wesley magazine editor
†Hester, Gerald LeRoy retired school system administrator
†Keller, Robert M. bishop
Kirschbaum, James Louis property manager
Klobucher, John Marcellus federal judge
Koegen, Roy Jerome lawyer
Kossel, Clifford George retired philosophy educator, clergyman
Lamp, John Ernest lawyer
Leahy, Gerald Philip hospital administrator
Lindsay, Donald Parker former savings bank executive
Matters, Clyde Burns former college president
McClellan, David Lawrence physician
McWilliams, Edwin Joseph banker
Mielke, Clarence Harold, Jr. hematologist
Moe, Orville Leroy racetrack executive
†Moyer, John Arthur obstetrician/gynecologist, state senator
Nicolai, Eugene Ralph public relations consultant, editor, writer
Nielsen, William Fremming federal judge
Novak, Terry Lee public adminstration educator
Nyman, Carl John, Jr. university dean and official
Odegard, Richard Erwin banker
Polley, Harvey Lee retired missionary and educator
Quackenbush, Justin Lowe chief federal judge
†Reitemeier, (Timothy) George chamber of commerce executive, public relations executive
Roberts, Larry Paul broadcasting executive
Robinson, Herbert Henry, III educator, therapist
Robinson, William P. academic administrator, consultant, speaker
Rowe, Marjorie Douglas retired social services administrator
†Sandifur, Cantwell Paul, Sr. mortgage company executive
Skylstad, William S. bishop
Stacy, Gardner W. chemical scientist, educator, lecturer
Storey, Francis Harold business consultant, retired bank executive
†Terry, Frank Jeffrey bishop
Van Sickle, Frederick L. federal judge
Wirt, Michael James library director
Woodard, Alva Abe business consultant

Tacoma
Anderson, Arthur Roland engineering company executive, civil engineer
Brevik, J. Albert communications consultant
Bryan, Robert J. federal judge
Carlson, Frederick Paul electronics executive
Champ, Stanley Gordon scientific company executive
Chen, Stephen Shau-tsi psychiatrist, physiologist
Crisman, Mary Frances Borden librarian
Edington, Robert Van university official
Erickson, Richard L. wood products company executive
Felker, Robert Stratton lawyer, consultant
Ferris, James Leonard paper company executive
Foley, Thomas Michael financial executive
Gordon, Joseph Harold lawyer
Graves, Ray lawyer
Graybill, David Wesley chamber of commerce executive
Greene, Mott Tuthill historian
Gregory, Arthur Stanley retired chemist
Grenley, Philip urologist
Hansen, Edward Allen music educator, organist
Harris, James Martin architect
Hendley, Ashley Preston, Jr. clinical social worker
Holman, Kermit Layton chemical engineer
Hutchings, George Henry food company executive
Jungkuntz, Richard Paul university provost emeritus
King, Gundar Julian retired university dean
Le Roy, Bruce Murdock historian
Liddle, Alan Curtis architect
†Maynard, Steven Harry writer
Meyer, Richard Schlomer food company executive
Miller, Judson Frederick lawyer, former military officer
Minnerly, Robert Ward headmaster
Odlin, Richard Bingham retired banker
Otten, Thomas zoological park director
Owen, Thomas Walker banker, broker
Philip, William Warren banker
Pierce, Susan Resneck academic administrator, English educator
Rieke, William Oliver foundation director, medical educator, former university president
†Robison, William Thomas trade association executive
Rudolph, Wallace Morton legal educator
Russell, James Sargent retired naval officer
Schuyler, Robert Len investment company executive
Shanaman, Fred Charles, Jr. business consultant
Smith, Leo Gilbert hospital administrator
†Steele, Anita Martin (Margaret Anne Martin) law librarian, legal educator
Thompson, Ronald Edward lawyer
Weyerhaeuser, George Hunt forest products company executive
Wiegman, Eugene William minister, former college administrator
Wills, J. Robert academic administrator, drama educator, writer
†Wold, David C. bishop

Vancouver
†Bingham, H. Raymond finance executive
Campbell, Scott newspaper publishing company executive
Chartier, Vernon Lee electrical engineer
Ferguson, Larry Emmett educational administrator
Firstenburg, Edward William banker
†Herrera, David Patrick historic site administrator
Kleweno, Gilbert H. lawyer
Larson, Charles Lester television writer, producer, author
Mangino, Kristin Mikalson secondary education educator
†Robinson, Charles E. telecommunications industry executive
†Smith, Linda A. state legislator
Vingo, James Ray transportation executive

Vashon
Biggs, Barry Hugh lawyer
†Munson, Dee Allison food marketing executive, consultant

Walla Walla
Edwards, Glenn Thomas history educator
Hayner, Herman Henry lawyer
Hayner, Jeannette Clare state legislator
Perry, Louis Barnes retired insurance company executive
Stevens, David economics educator
Yaple, Henry Mack library director

Washougal
†Schorzman, Clarice B. principal

Wenatchee
†Foreman, Dale Melvin lawyer, state official

Yakima
George, Francis bishop
Hornstein, Pamela Kathleen educational administrator, educator
Hovis, James Brunton federal judge
McDonald, Alan Angus federal judge
Meshke, George Lewis drama and humanities educator
Suko, Lonny Ray lawyer

WEST VIRGINIA

Athens
Marsh, Joseph Franklin, Jr. emeritus college president, educational consultant

Barboursville
Bradley, Robert Lee surgeon

Beckley
†Baligar, Virupax C. research soil scientist
Hallanan, Elizabeth V. federal judge
Rhoades, Marye Frances paralegal
Voigt, Paul Warren research geneticist

Bethany
Cooey, William Randolph economics educator
Cummins, Delmer Duane academic administrator, historian
Sandercox, Robert Allen college official, clergyman

Bluefield
Blaydes, James Elliott ophthalmologist
Faber, David Alan federal judge

Bridgeport
Timms, Leonard Joseph, Jr. gas company executive

Buckhannon
†Riggs, Dale Flint state legislator, retired coal operator

Charles Town
Layva, David lawyer
McDonald, Angus Wheeler farmer

Charleston
†Adams, Richard M. bank executive
†Atkinson, Robert Poland bishop
Bailey, Larrie (John) state treasurer
†Baronner, Robert Francis banker
Basham, Debra Ann archivist
Bennett, Robert Menzies retired gas pipeline company executive
†Blatnik, Thais Frances state legislator
†Border, Larry Willis pharmacist
Brotherton, William T., Jr. state supreme court justice
†Brown, Bonnie Louise state legislator
Brown, James Knight lawyer
†Burdette, Keith state senator
Burns, Thomas C. communication company executive
Caperton, W. Gaston governor
†Chafin, Harry Truman state senator
†Chernenko, John G. state senator
†Coe, Pam educational researcher
Cograve, John Edwin judge
Conlin, Thomas (Byrd) conductor
Conway, Richard Ashley environmental engineer
Copenhaver, John Thomas, Jr. federal judge
†Craigo, Oshel B. state senator
Drennen, William Miller, Jr. cultural administrator, film executive, producer, director, mineral resource executive
Gage, Charles Quincey lawyer
Glazer, Frederic Jay librarian
Goodwin, Claude Elbert lawyer, former gas utility executive
Goodwin, Phillip Hugh hospital administrator
†Grant, Richard Lee utility company executive
Greenfield, David Joel editor
†Grimes, Richard Stuart editor, writer
Gunnoe, Nancy Lavenia food executive, artist
Haden, Charles H., II federal judge
Hall, Kenneth Keller federal judge
Haught, James Albert, Jr. journalist, newspaper editor
Hechler, Ken state official, former congressman, political science educator, author
†Heck, Albert Frank neurologist
Kizer, John Oscar lawyer
Knapp, Dennis Raymond federal judge
Lawson, Robert William, Jr. retired lawyer
Marockie, Henry R. state school system administrator
Marstiller, Phyllis C. personal care industry executive
McClaugherty, John Lewis lawyer
Mc Gee, John Frampton communications company executive
Mc Graw, Darrell Vivian, Jr. attorney general
McHugh, Thomas Edward state supreme court justice
†McMillian, John G. oil and natural gas executive
†Michael, M. Blane federal judge
Murchison, David Roderick lawyer
Neely, Richard state supreme court justice
Scott, Olof Henderson, Jr. priest
Snyder, Giles D. H. lawyer, utility company executive
Southworth, Louis Sweetland, II lawyer
Stacy, Charles Brecknock lawyer
†Wehrle, Henry Bernard, Jr. diversified manufacturing company executive
Welch, Edwin Hugh academic administrator
Whittington, Bernard Wiley electrical engineer, consultant
Workman, Margaret Lee state supreme court justice
†Yoder, John Christian state senator, lawyer

Clarksburg
Highland, Cecil Blaine, Jr. newspaper publisher, lawyer, banker
Keeley, Irene Patricia Murphy federal judge
Kidd, William Matthew federal judge
†Kittle, Robert Earl school system administrator
Vrable, John Bernard natural gas company executive

Clay
†Dawson, James G. superintendent
†Gillespie, Larry secondary school principal

Dellslow
Allamong, Betty D. academic administrator

Dunbar
Russell, James Alvin, Jr. college administrator

Elkins
MacConkey, Dorothy I. academic administrator
Maxwell, Robert Earl federal judge
Payne, Gloria Marquette business educator
Van Gundy, James Justin biology educator

Fairmont
†Black, L. Alexander bishop
Hardway, Wendell Gary former college president
Shan, Robert Kuocheng biology educator
Stalder, Florence Lucille educator
Wedge, Dorothy Ann education educator

Glenville
Tubesing, Richard Lee library director

Grafton
Poling, Kermit William minister

Greenville
Warner, Kenneth Wilson, Jr. editor, association publications executive

Harpers Ferry
Carter, Powell Frederick retired naval officer
Nash, Bradley DeLamater transportation executive
White, Thomas Edward government park official
Wright, David George landscape architect

Herndon
Garretson, Richard A. principal

Huntington
Barenklau, Keith Edward safety services company executive
Bowdler, Anthony John physician, educator
Cocke, William Marvin, Jr. plastic surgeon, educator
deBarbadillo, John Joseph metallurgist, management executive
Esposito, Albert Charles ophthalmologist, state legislator
Gould, Alan Brant academic administrator
Hayes, Robert Bruce former college president, educator
Hooper, James William educator
Hubbard, John Lewis chemist, educator, researcher
†Jenkins, John E., Jr. lawyer, educator
Kent, Calvin Albert university administrator
McKernan, John Joseph English language educator
Mufson, Maurice Albert physician, educator
Polan, Nancy Moore artist
Reynolds, Marshall Truman printing company executive
Ritchie, Garry Harlan television broadcast executive
Underwood, Cecil H. company executive, past governor of West Virginia

Institute
Brown, Dallas Coverdale, Jr. history educator, retired army officer
DasSarma, Basudeb chemistry educator
Scott, John Edward librarian
Thorn, Arline Roush English language educator
Wohl, David humanities educator, theatre director

Lahmansville
Snyder, Robert Martin consultant, retired government official

Lewisburg
Ford, Richard Edmond lawyer
Seifer, Judith Huffman sex therapist, educator
Sprouse, James Marshall federal judge
Willard, Ralph Lawrence surgery educator, physician, former college president

Martinsburg
†Lucht, Sondra Moore state senator
Malin, Howard Gerald podiatrist
Rice, Lacy I., Jr. lawyer
Weaver, Thomas Harold health facility administrator
Yoe, Harry Warner retired agricultural economist

Mineral Wells
Prather, Denzil Lewis petroleum engineer

Morgantown
Adler, Lawrence mining engineering consultant
Beattie, Diana Scott biochemistry educator
Biddington, William Robert university administrator, dental educator
Blaydes, Sophia Boyatzies English language educator
Brooks, Dana D. dean
Bucklew, Neil S. university president
Butcher, Donald Franklin statistician, computer scientist
Chen, Ping-fan geologist
Colasanti, Brenda Karen pharmacoloy and toxicology educator
Collier, Clifford Warthen, Jr. landscape architect
Colyer, Dale Keith agricultural economics educator
†Cook, Stephen L. state senator
Dadyburjor, Dady B. chemical engineering educator, researcher
Davis, Leonard McCutchan speech educator
De Vore, Paul Warren technology educator
Fisher, John Welton, II law educator, magistrate judge, university official
Fleming, William Wright, Jr. pharmacology educator

Fodor, Gabor Bela *chemistry educator, researcher*
Fusco, Andrew G. *lawyer*
Gagliano, Frank Joseph *playwright*
Guthrie, Hugh Delmar *chemical engineer*
Hedge, George Albert *physiologist*
Holtan, Boyd DeVere *mathematics educator*
†Isserman, Andrew Mark *economist, university administrator*
Jackson, Ruth Moore *academic administrator*
Keller, Edward Clarence, Jr. *foundation executive, ecologist, statistician, geneticist, educator*
Klein, Ronald Lloyd *electrical engineer, educator*
LaBelle, Thomas Jeffrey *academic administrator*
†Maxwell, Robert Haworth *college dean*
Meitzen, Manfred Otto *religious studies educator*
Morris, William Otis, Jr. *lawyer, educator, author*
Nath, Joginder *genetics and biology educator, researcher*
Ong, Tong-man *microbiologist, educator*
Pyles, Rodney Allen *archivist, county official*
Reese, Hayne Waring *psychologist*
†Schroder, John L., Jr. *retired mining engineer*
Singer, Armand Edwards *foreign language educator*
Smith, Robert Leo *ecologist, wildlife biologist*
Snyder, Irvin Stanley *microbiologist, educator*
Stewart, Guy Harry *university dean emeritus, journalism educator*
Trythall, Harry Gilbert *music educator, composer*
Vest, Marvin Lewis *mathematical educator*
Warden, Herbert Edgar *surgeon, educator*
Weinstein, George William *ophthalmology educator*
Westfall, Bernard G. *university hospital executive*

Mullens
†Staton, W. Richard *lawyer*

Nitro
Lucas, Panola *elementary educator*
Magaw, Roger Wayne *construction company executive*

Parkersburg
†Brum, Brenda *state legislator, librarian*
Cochran, Douglas Eugene *building products company executive*
Crooks, Thomas Jackson *advertising executive*
Fahlgren, H(erbert) Smoot *advertising agency executive*
†Mason, Richard Gordon *lawn and garden tool manufacturing company executive*
Wakley, James Turner *manufacturing company executive*

Philippi
Shearer, Richard Eugene *industrial consultant*
Sizemore, William Christian *college president*

Princeton
White, Benjamin Ballard, Jr. *lawyer*

Ravenswood
†Meyers, Gerald A. *metal products executive*

Salem
Frasure, Carl Maynard *political science educator*
Ohl, Ronald Edward *academic administrator*
Raad, Virginia *pianist, lecturer*

Shenandoah Junction
Prince, Garnett B., Jr. *government official*

Shepherdstown
Elliott, Jean Ann *library administrator*
Hresan, Sally L. *journalism educator*
Riccards, Michael Patrick *academic administrator*

Sistersville
Wright, John Charles Young *oil and gas company executive*

Squire
Dishman, Roberta Crockett *retired educator*

Weirton
Elish, Herbert *manufacturing company executive*

Wellsburg
Price, Verla Blanche *elementary education educator*

West Liberty
Campbell, Clyde Del *academic administrator*
Hunter, John Alfred *English educator*

Wheeling
Chbosky, Fred G. *steel company executive*
†Exley, Ben, III *pharmaceutical company executive*
Good, Laurance Frederic *company executive*
Heceta, Estherbelle Aguilar *anesthesiologist*
Hughes, Mary Elizabeth *interior designer*
Kirkpatrick, Forrest Hunter *management consultant*
Nutting, George Ogden *newspaper publisher*
Phillips, John Davisson *retired lawyer*
Schmitt, Bernard W. *bishop*
Wareham, James Lyman *steel company executive*

White Sulphur Springs
Lanahan, John Stevenson *consultant*

WISCONSIN

Altoona
James, Henry Thomas *former foundation executive, educator*

Amery
Mickelson, Arnold Rust *church commission executive, consultant*

Appleton
Barlow, F(rank) John *mechanical contracting company executive*
Boldt, Oscar Charles *construction company executive*
Buchanan, Robert Campbell *corporate professional*
†Chaney, William Albert *historian, educator*
Froehlich, Harold Vernon *judge, former congressman*
Goldgar, Bertrand Alvin *literary historian, educator*
†Gunderson, Richard L. *insurance company executive*
†Herder, Robert H. *bishop*
†McManus, John Francis *executive*
Platten, Peter Michael, III *bank holding company executive*
Rankin, Arthur David *paper company executive*
Sauter, Charles Herman *banker*
†Schumaker, Dale H. *paper manufacturing company executive*
Warch, Richard *university president*

Ashland
Parsonage, Robert Rue *college president*

Baraboo
Brooks, Edward *dairy products company executive*
Cross, Clyde Cleveland *lawyer*
Parkinson, Greg Thomas *museum director*
Storhoff, Donald C. *agricultural products company executive*

Beaver Dam
Butterbrodt, John Ervin *real estate executive*

Beloit
Cole, J. Weldon *manufacturing executive*
Davis, Harry Rex *political science educator*
Ferrall, Victor Eugene, Jr. *college administrator, lawyer*
Gates, Crawford Marion *conductor, composer*
Simon, Michael Alexander *photographer, educator*
Sovey, William Pierre *manufacturing company executive*
†Weeden, Timothy L. *state legislator*

Brookfield
Corby, Francis Michael, Jr. *manufacturing company executive*
Curfman, Floyd Edwin *engineering educator*
DeLuca, Donald Paul *manufacturing company executive*
Diesem, John Lawrence *information systems executive*
†Grade, Jeffery T. *manufacturing company executive*
Hardman, Harold Francis *pharmacology educator*
Jenkins, William Atwell *university chancellor*
Lessiter, Frank Donald *magazine editor*
Payne, Howard James *insurance company executive*
Schwanz, H(erman) Lee *publishing company executive*
†Snyder, C(laude) Robert *insurance company executive*
Welnetz, David Charles *human resources executive*
Zander, Gaillienne Glashow *psychologist*

Cedarburg
Eley, Lynn W. *political science educator, former mayor*
Schaefer, Gordon Emory *food company executive*
White, Doris Anne *artist*

Cleveland
Butler, Robin Erwin *vocational technical educator*

Columbus
Callahan, Carroll Bernard *lawyer*

Cross Plains
Rodenschmit, Helen Juliana *elementary education educator*

Cudahy
Naimoli, Raymond Anthony *infosystems specialist, financial consultant*

De Pere
Manion, Thomas A. *college president*

Delavan
Donnelly, James Charles *manufacturing company executive*

Dodgeville
End, William Thomas *business executive*

Eau Claire
Berney, Joseph Henry *appliance manufacturing company executive*
Davidson, John Kenneth, Sr. *sociologist, educator, researcher, author, consultant*
Dick, Raymond Dale *psychology educator*
Dunlap, William Phillip *dean*
†Larson, Brian Foix *architect*
Patterson, Donald Lee *music educator*
Richards, Jerry Lee *academic administrator, religious educator*
Schnack, Larry Gene *university chancellor*
Thompson, Glenn Judean *library science educator*
Wantland, William Charles *bishop, lawyer*
Weil, D(onald) Wallace *business administration educator*
†Zien, David Allen *state legislator*

Elkhorn
Dunn, Walter Scott, Jr. *former museum director, consultant*
Reinke, Doris Marie *retired elementary education educator*

Ellison Bay
MacKinney, Arthur Clinton, Jr. *retired university official, psychologist*

Elm Grove
Gorske, Robert Herman *lawyer*
†Grunau, Gary Peter *mechanical contracting executive*
Halvorsen, Morrie Edward *association executive*
Headlee, Raymond *psychoanalyst, educator*
Kolda, Thomas Joseph *non-profit organization executive*

Fish Creek
Abegg, Martin Gerald *retired university president*
Becker, Bettie Geraldine *artist*

Fond Du Lac
Chamberlain, Robert Glenn *retired executive*
Henken, Willard John *retired university dean*
†Stevens, William Louis *bishop*
Treffert, Darold Allen *psychiatrist, author, hospital director*

Fort Atkinson
Albaugh, John Charles *hospital executive*
Knox, William David *publishing company executive*
Meyer, Eugene Carlton *retired editor*
Nesbitt, Arthur Wallace *mail order and manufacturing executive*
Sager, Donald Jack *publisher, former librarian*

Frederic
Rudell, Milton Wesley *aerospace engineer*

Glendale
†Moeser, Elliott *principal*

Grafton
Eber, Lorenz *civil engineer, inventor*

Green Bay
†Bacha, Diane Marie *newspaper editor*
†Backer, David F. *packing company executive*
Banks, Robert J. *bishop*
†Bush, Robert G. *food service executive*
Daley, Arthur James *retired magazine publisher*
De Meuse, Donald Howard *paper products manufacturing executive*
†Favre, Brett Lorenzo *professional football player*
†Gariepy, Corinne *elementary school principal*
Gillett, George Nield, Jr. *business executive*
†Green, Mark Andrew *state legislator, lawyer*
Harlan, Robert Ernest *professional football team executive*
Hempel, Kathleen Jane *paper company executive*
Holmgren, Mike *professional football coach*
Hudson, Halbert Austin, Jr. *retired manufacturing engineer, consultant*
Kennedy, Mark Raymond *retail executive*
Kress, George F. *packaging company executive*
†LaViolette, Catherine Patricia *librarian*
Lenz, Randolph W. *manufacturing company executive*
†Lewis, Gary *trucking executive*
†Meng, John C. *food service executive*
Olson, James Richard *transportation company executive*
Outcalt, David Lewis *academic administrator, mathematician, educator*
Parins, Robert James *professional football team executive, judge*
Parkinson, Ethelyn Minerva *author*
†Poppenhagen, Ronald William *newspaper editor, publishing executive*
Sauvey, Raymond Andrew *museum director*
†Sharpe, Sterling *professional football player*
Wakeman, Fred Joseph *retired paper company executive*

Green Lake
†LaDue, Paul W. *religious organization executive*

Greendale
DeLorenzo, David Joseph *public relations executive*
Gillespie, Rory Andrew *professional association administrator*
Olander, Ray Gunnar *lawyer*
Tucker, William Thomas, III *computer software company executive*

Hales Corners
Michalski, (Żurowski) Wacław *adult education educator*

Hartford
Lopina, Lawrence Thomas *manufacturing executive*

Hartland
Burlingame, Leroy James *manufacturing executive*
†Mc Neil, Donald Lewis *retired multiple association management company executive*
Stamsta, Jean F. *artist*

Hillpoint
†Schultz, Dale W. *state legislator*

Hollandale
Myers, Frances *artist*

Iola
Foerster, Urban Michael, III (Trey Foerster) *newspaper owner, publisher*
Krause, Chester Lee *publishing company executive*
Mishler, Clifford Leslie *publisher*
Rulau, Russell *numismatist, consultant*

Janesville
Diotte, Alfred Peter *investment executive, consultant*
Fitzgerald, James Francis *cable television executive*
Steil, George Kenneth, Sr. *lawyer*
†Stich, Peggy R. *direct marketing executive*
†Wood, Wayne W. *state legislator*

Juneau
Carpenter, David Erwin *county planner*

Kaukauna
Janssen, Gail Edwin *banking executive*

Kenosha
Adler, Seymour Jack *social services administrator*
†Baker, Douglas Finley *library director*
Campbell, F(enton) Gregory *college administrator, historian*
†Cornog, Robert A. *manufacturing executive*
Grover, Robert Lawrence *tool company executive*
†Jacobson, Dennis Leonard *business executive*
Steigerwaldt, Donna Wolf *clothing manufacturing company executive*
Tielke, James Clemens *manufacturing executive*

Kohler
†Kohler, Herbert Vollrath, Jr. *diversified manufacturing company executive*

La Crosse
Anderson, Mary Ann *hospital nursing administrator*
Cleary, Russell George *retired brewery executive*
Corser, David Hewson *pediatrician*
†Felten, Edward Joseph *business executive accountant*
Gelatt, Charles Daniel *manufacturing company executive*
Klos, Jerome John *lawyer*
Medland, William James *college president*
†Metcalf, Jerry D. *wholesale food distribution company executive*
Nix, Edmund Alfred *lawyer*
Paul, John Joseph *bishop*
†Poehling, Robert Edward *plumbing supply company executive*
Rausch, Joan Mary *art historian*
†Webster, Stephen Burtis *physician, educator*

Lake Geneva
Braden, Berwyn Bartow *lawyer*

Lake Nebagamon
Meyer, Karl William *retired university president*

Lancaster
Johnson, Hal Harold Gustav *marketing educator emeritus*

Little Chute
Rice, Ferill Jeane *writer, civic worker*

Madison
Abrahamson, Shirley Schlanger *state supreme court justice*
Adler, Julius *biochemist, biologist, educator*
Ahlquist, Paul Gerald *molecular biology researcher, educator*
Albert, Daniel Myron *ophthalmologist, educator*
Aldag, Ramon John *management and organization educator*
Ammerman, Robert Ray *philosopher, educator*
Anderson, Louis Wilmer, Jr. *physicist, educator*
Anderson, Odin Waldemar *sociologist, educator*
Andreano, Ralph Louis *economist, educator*
†Armstrong, Gregory Davenport *arboretum administrator*
Arny, Deane Cedric *former plant pathology educator, researcher*
Askey, Richard Allen *mathematician*
Auen, Michael H. *lawyer*
Bablitch, William A. *state supreme court justice*
Bach-y-Rita, Paul *neurophysiologist, rehabilitation medicine specialist*
Badura-Skoda, Paul (Ludwig Badura) *pianist*
Baeumer, Max Lorenz *literature historian*
†Bailey, Sturges Williams *geologist, educator*
Baldwin, Gordon Brewster *lawyer, educator*
Baldwin, Robert Edward *economics educator*
Barca, Peter William *congressman*
Barger, Vernon Duane *physicist, educator*
Barnes, Robert F *agronomist*
Barnhill, Charles Joseph, Jr. *lawyer*
Baron, Alma Fay S. *management educator*
Barrows, Richard Lee *economics educator, academic administrator*
Barschall, Henry Herman *physics educator*
Bartell, Jeffrey Bruce *lawyer*
Bass, Paul *pharmacology educator*
Beachley, Norman Henry *mechanical engineer, educator*
Beck, Anatole *mathematician, educator*
Beck, Stanley Dwight *retired entomology educator, researcher*
†Becker, David *artist, educator*
Belzer, Folkert Oene *surgeon*
Bennett, Kenneth Alan *biological anthropologist*
Bentley, Charles Raymond *geophysics educator*
Berg, William James *French language educator, writer, translator*
Berkowitz, Leonard *psychology educator*
Bernstine, Daniel O'Neal *law educator, university dean*
Berthouex, Paul Mac *civil and environmental engineer, educator*
Bincer, Adam Marian *physicist, educator*
Bird, Robert Byron *chemical engineering educator, author*
Bisgard, Gerald Edwin *biosciences educator, researcher*
Bjoraker, Walter Thomas *agricultural and vocational educator emeritus*
Blaedel, Walter John *chemist, retired educator*
Blankenburg, William Burl *journalism educator*
Bless, Robert Charles *astronomy educator*
Bloodworth, J. M. Bartow, Jr. *physician, educator*
Bogue, Allan G. *history educator*
†Bollinger, John Gustave *engineering educator, college dean*
Botez, Dan *physicist*
Boutwell, Roswell Knight *oncology educator*
Boyle, William Charles *civil engineering educator*
Brembeck, Winston Lamont *educator*
†Brennan, Robert Walter *association executive*
†Bretherton, Francis P. *aerospace engineering executive*
Brock, Thomas Dale *microbiology educator*
Brock, William Allen, III *economics educator, consultant*
Bromley, Daniel Wood *economics educator, consultant*
Brown, Arnold Lanehart, Jr. *pathologist, educator, university dean*
†Bruhn, Hjalmar Diehl *retired agricultural engineer, educator*
Bryson, Reid Allen *meteorology educator*
Bubenzer, Gary Dean *agricultural engineering educator, researcher*
†Buettner, Carol Ann *state legislator*
Bugge, Lawrence John *lawyer*
Bula, Raymond J. *agronomist*
Bullock, William Henry *bishop*
Bunge, Charles Albert *library science educator*
Burgess, James Edward *newspaper publisher, executive*
Burgess, Richard Ray *oncology educator, molecular biology researcher, biotechnology consultant*
†Burke, Brian B. *state senator, lawyer*
Burkholder, Wendell Eugene *entomologist*
Burris, Robert Harza *biochemist, educator*
Busby, Edward Oliver *former dean*
Callen, James Donald *nuclear engineer, plasma physicist, educator*
Carbone, Paul Peter *oncologist, educator, administrator*
Casey, Charles Philip *organic chemist, educator*
Cassens, Robert Gene *food scientist*
†Cassidy, Frederic Gomes *humanities educator*
Cassinelli, Joseph Patrick *astronomy educator*
Chang, Y. Austin *materials engineer, educator*
Chapman, Loren J. *psychology educator*
Chow, Tse-Tsung *foreign language and literature educator, author, poet*
Churchwell, Edward Bruce *astronomer, educator*
Ciplijauskaite, Birute *humanities educator*

Clark, David Leigh marine geologist, educator
Cleland, W(illiam) Wallace biochemistry educator
Cliver, Dean Otis virologist, educator
Coberly, Camden Arthur chemical engineering educator
†Code, Arthur Dodd astrophysics educator
Coffman, Edward McKenzie history educator
Cohen, Bernard Cecil political scientist, educator
Colás, Antonio Espada medical educator
Colescott, Warrington Wickham artist, printmaker, educator
Connors, Kenneth Antonio chemist
Converse, James Clarence agricultural engineering educator
Cooper, John Milton, Jr. history educator, author
Cornwell, Charles Daniel physical chemist, educator
Courtenay, William James historian, educator
Craddock, (John) Campbell geologist, educator
Crandall, Lee Walter civil and structural engineer
Cronon, E(dmund) David, Jr. history educator, historian
Cronon, William history educator
Crow, James Franklin retired genetics educator
Culbertson, John Mathew economist, educator
Curry, Robert Lee lawyer
Curtiss, Charles Francis chemist, educator
Dahl, Lawrence Frederick chemistry educator, researcher
Daie, Jaleh science educator, administrator, researcher
†Darling, Alberta Statkus state legislator, marketing executive, former art museum executive
Davis, Erroll Brown, Jr. utility executive
Davis, Richard musician, music educator
Day, Roland Bernard state supreme court justice
de Boor, Carl mathematician
Dembo, Lawrence Sanford English educator
Dembski, Stephen Michael composer, university music composition professor
Denevan, William Maxfield geographer, educator
DeNovo, John August history educator
Denton, Frank M. newspaper editor
Derzon, Gordon M. hospital administrator
DeVries, Marvin Frank mechanical engineering educator
Dewey, Gene Lawrence librarian
Dietmeyer, Donald Leo electrical engineer
Dodson, Vernon Nathan physician, educator
Dolan, Terrence Raymond neurophysiology educator
Dott, Robert Henry, Jr. geologist, educator
Doyle, James E(dward) state attorney general
Draper, Norman Richard statistician, educator
Duffie, John Atwater chemical engineer, educator
†Duffie, Neil Arthur mechanical engineering educator, researcher
DuRose, Stanley Charles, Jr. insurance executive
Earl, Anthony Scully former governor
Easterday, Bernard Carlyle veterinary medicine educator
Ebben, James Adrian college president
Ebel, Marvin Emerson physicist,educator
Eisinger, Peter K(endall) political science educator
Ellis, Arthur Baron chemist, educator
Emmert, Gilbert Arthur engineer, educator
†Enslin, Jon S. bishop
Epstein, William experimental psychologist
Erhard, Michael Paul lawyer
Ershler, William Baldwin biogerontologist, educator
Evanson, Elizabeth Moss editor
Evenson, Merle Armin chemist, educator
Fahien, Leonard August physician, educator
†Fanlund, Paul G. newspaper editor
Farley, Eugene Shedden, Jr. physician, educator
†Farrow, Margaret Ann state legislator
Felstehausen, Herman Henry natural resources-land planning educator
Fennema, Owen Richard food chemistry educator
Ferry, John Douglass chemist
Fiedler, Patrick James circuit court judge
Field, Henry Augustus, Jr. lawyer
Finman, Ted lawyer, educator
Fitchen, Allen Nelson publisher
Fleischman, Stephen art center director
Foell, Wesley Kay engineer, energy and environmental scientist, educator, consultant
Forster, Francis Michael physician, educator
Foster, George William, Jr. lawyer, educator
Fowler, Barbara Hughes classicist
Fox, Michael Vass Hebrew educator, rabbi
Frautschi, Walter Albert contract and publications printing company executive
Fritz, Bruce Morrell photographer
Fry, William Frederick physics educator
Frykenberg, Robert Eric historian
Gallagher, John Sill, III astronomer
Garver, Thomas Haskell curator, art consultant, writer
Gavin, Mary Jane medical, surgical nurse
Gehl, Eugene Othmar power company executive, lawyer
Gilboe, David Dougherty physiology educator
Goldberger, Arthur Stanley economics educator
Goodman, Robert Merwin agriculturalist, plant biologist, university educator
Gorski, Jack biochemistry educator
Graf, Truman Frederick agricultural economist, educator
Greaser, Marion Lewis science educator
Green, Theodore, III engineering and science educator
Greenfield, Norman Samuel psychologist, educator
Greenwald, Caroline Meyer artist
Grossman, Joel B(arry) political science educator
Hagedorn, Donald James phytopathologist, educator, agricultural consultant
Hall, David Charles zoo director, veterinarian
Haller, Archibald Orben sociologist, educator
Hamalainen, Pekka Kalevi historian, educator
Hamerow, Theodore Stephen history educator
Hansen, W. Lee economics educator, author
Harr, Lucy Loraine public relations executive
Harrington, Fred Harvey history educator
Harvey, John Grover mathematics educator
†Haslanger, Philip Charles journalist
Hauck, Roger Paul corporate executive
Hauser, Robert Mason sociologist, demographer, educator
†Hayner, Stephen A. academic organization administrator
Heberlein, Thomas Addison sociology educator
Hedden, Gregory Dexter environmental science educator, consultant
Heffernan, Nathan Stewart state supreme court chief justice
†Heins, Richard M. insurance company executive
†Helbach, David Walter state senator
Helstad, Orrin L. lawyer, legal educator
Herndon, Terry Eugene insurance executive
Hershkowitz, Noah physicist, educator
Heymann, S. Richard lawyer
Hickman, James Charles business and statistics educator, business school dean
Higby, Gregory James historical association administrator, historian
Hildebrand, Daniel Walter lawyer
Hill, Charles Graham, Jr. chemical engineering educator
†Hinkfuss, Rosemary state legislator
Hinsdill, Ronald Dwight bacteriology educator, immunotoxicologist
Hokin, Lowell Edward biochemist, educator
Holbrook, John Scott, Jr. lawyer
Hollingsworth, Joseph Rogers history and sociology educator, writer
Hopen, Herbert John horticulture educator
Houghton, David Drew meteorologist, educator
Howe, Herbert Marshall classics educator
Hoyt, James Lawrence journalism educator, athletic administrator
†Huelsman, Joanne B. state legislator
†Hunter, John Patrick newspaper editor
Hurst, James Willard legal educator
Huston, Norman Earl nuclear engineering educator
Ihde, Aaron John history of science educator emeritus
Inman, Ross Banks biochemistry and biophysics educator
Jackson, Carl Robert obstetrician/gynecologist
Jackson, Marion Leroy agronomist, soil scientist
Javid, Manucher J. neurosurgeon
Jeanne, Robert Lawrence entomologist, educator, researcher
Jefferson, James Walter psychiatry educator
Johnson, Alton Cornelius management educator
Johnson, Millard Wallace, Jr. mathematics and engineering educator
Johnson, Richard Arnold statistics educator, consultant
Johnson, Roland A. conductor, music director
Jones, James Edward, Jr. law educator emeritus
Kaesberg, Paul Joseph virology researcher
Karavolas, Harry J(ohn) biochemist, educator
†Kauffman, Stephen Blair law librarian, law educator
Keesey, Ulker Tulunay ophthalmology and psychology educator, researcher
†Kelling, Keith A. soil scientist
Kelly, Douglas medieval and foreign literature educator
Kepecs, Joseph Goodman physician, educator
Kingdon, Robert McCune historian, educator
Kirk, Thomas Kent research scientist
Klein, Sheldon computational linguist, educator
Kleinhenz, Christopher foreign language educator, researcher
Klug, Scott Leo congressman
Knoll, Erwin author, editor
Knowles, Richard Alan John English language educator
Koval, Charles Francis entomologist, agricultural administrator, educator
Kraushaar, William Lester physicist, educator
†Krusick, Margaret Ann state legislator
†Kulcinski, Gerald LaVerne nuclear engineer, educator
†Kumar, Anand medical educator, researcher
Kunicki, Walter J. state legislator
Kurtz, Thomas Gordon mathematics educator
Kutler, Stanley Ira history and law educator, author
Laessig, Ronald Harold pathology educator, state official
La Follette, Douglas J. secretary of state
Lagally, Max Gunter physics educator
Lambert, Philip psychologist, educator, consultant
Langer, Richard J. lawyer
Lardy, Henry Arnold biochemist, biological sciences educator
Larsen, Edwin Merritt retired chemist, educator
Larson, John David life insurance company executive, lawyer
†Lawler, James Edward physics educator
Lawson, David E. architect
Lefert, Gerald W. hospital administrator
Lemberger, August Paul university dean, pharmacy educator
Levin, Jacob Joseph mathematician, educator
Levine, Solomon Bernard business and economics educator
Lewis, Herbert Samuel anthropologist, educator
†Linton, Barbara J. state legislator
Littlefield, Vivian Moore nursing educator, administrator
Lobeck, Charles Champlin, Jr. pediatrics educator
Long, Willis Franklin electrical engineering educator, researcher
Loper, Carl Richard, Jr. metallurgical engineer, educator
†Lorge, William D. state legislator, farmer
†Lorman, Barbara K. state senator
Lotterman, Hal artist, educator
Lovell, Edward George engineering mechanics educator
Lower, Richard Lawrence horticulture educator, researcher
Luening, Robert Adami agricultural economics educator emeritus
Lyall, Katharine C(ulbert) academic administrator, economics educator
MacKendrick, Paul Lachlan classics educator
Mackie, Frederick David retired utility executive
Mac Kinney, Archie Allen, Jr. physician
Maher, Louis James, Jr. geologist, educator
Maki, Dennis G. medical educator, researcher, clinician
Maloney, Michael James research scientist
†Mare, Robert Denis sociology educator, demography researcher
Marks, Elaine French language educator
Marth, Elmer Herman bacteriologist, educator
Martin, Robert David federal judge, law educator
Marton, Laurence Jay clinical pathologist, educator, researcher
Marwell, Gerald sociology educator, research consultant
†Mathis, John Samuel astronomy educator
†Mathwich, Dale F. insurance company executive
McBeath, Andrew Alan orthopedic surgery educator
McCabe, Robert Albert wildlife ecology educator
McCallum, James Scott lieutenant governor, former state senator
Mc Camy, James Lucian former political science educator
McCarty, Donald James education educator
Mc Clellan, Catharine anthropologist, educator
McCubbin, Hamilton I. social scientist, educator, researcher
McDonald, Barbara Ann marketing educator
McNelly, John Taylor journalist, educator
Mebane, David Cummins lawyer
Meloon, Robert A. retired newspaper publisher
Miller, Frederick William publisher, lawyer
Miller, James Alexander oncologist, educator
†Miller, Richard Ulric business and industrial relations educator
Mitby, Norman Peter college president
†Moen, Rodney Charles state senator, retired naval officer
Mohs, Frederic Edward surgeon, educator
Moore, Edward Forrest computer scientist, mathematician, former educator
Morton, Stephen Dana chemist
Mosse, George L. history educator, author
Mueller, Willard Fritz economics educator
Mukerjee, Pasupati chemistry educator
Muller, H(enry) Nicholas, III historical society director
Mullins, Jerome Joseph real estate developer, consulting engineer
Mulvihill, Edward Robert language educator
Murphy, Robert Brady Lawrence lawyer
Nelson, Oliver Evans, Jr. geneticist, educator
Netzer, Lanore A(gnes) retired educational administration educator
Nevin, John Robert business educator, consultant
Newcomb, Eldon Henry retired botany educator
Nichols, Donald Arthur economist, educator
Niemann, Bernard John, Jr. land and geographical system educator, researcher, consultant
Niemi, Peter G. library administrator
Nordby, Eugene Jorgen orthopedic surgeon
Novotny, Donald Wayne electrical engineering educator
O'Brien, James Aloysius foreign language educator
†Odden, Allan Robert education educator
Olson, Norman Fredrick food science educator
†Otte, Clifford state legislator
†Pampel, Roland D. computer company executive
†Panzer, Mary E(llen) state legislator
†Pariza, Michael Willard research institute executive, microbiology and toxicology educator
Pasch, Maurice Bernard lawyer
Pella, Milton Orville retired science educator
†Pempel, T. J. political science educator
Penniman, Clara political scientist, educator
Perkins, Merle Lester French language educator
Perlman, D(avid) biochemist, educator
Peters, Henry Augustus neuropsychiatrist
†Pierce, Harvey R. insurance company executive
Pillaert, E(dna) Elizabeth museum curator
Pitot, Henry Clement, III physician, educator
†Plewa, John Robert state senator
Policano, Andrew J. university dean
Pondrom, Lee Girard physicist, educator
†Poniewaz, Kenneth Anthony banker
†Porter, Andrew Calvin educational administrator, psychology educator
†Porter, Cloyd Allen state representative
Powell, Barry Bruce classicist
Powers, Richard Dale agricultural journalism educator
Prange, Roy Leonard, Jr. lawyer
Pray, Lloyd Charles geologist, educator
†Prosser, David Thomas, Jr. state representative, lawyer
Ragatz, Thomas George lawyer
Raushenbush, Walter Brandeis law educator
Ray, W. Harmon chemical engineering educator, consultant, author
Reynolds, Ernest West physician, educator
Rice, Joy Katharine psychologist, educational policy studies and women's studies educator
†Rich, Daniel Hulbert chemist
Richards, Hugh Taylor physics educator
Rideout, Walter Bates English educator
Ring, Gerald J. real estate developer, insurance executive
Ris, Hans zoologist, educator
Risser, Fred A. state senator
Roberts, Leigh Milton psychiatrist
Robinson, Arthur Howard geography educator
Robinson, Stephen Michael applied mathematician, educator
Rosser, Annetta Hamilton composer
Rothstein, Eric English educator
Rowe, George Giles cardiologist, educator
Rowe, John Westel retired organic chemist
Rowlands, Robert Edward engineering educator
Rudd, Dale Frederick retired chemical engineer
†Rude, Brian David state legislator
Rueckert, Roland Rudyard virologist, educator
†Rutkowski, James Anthony state legislator
†Sackett, Joseph Frederic radiologist, educator, administrator
Sample, Nathaniel Welshire architect
Savage, Blair deWillis astronomer, educator
Schleck, Roth Stephen banker
Schulz, Rockwell Irwin health administration educator
Schutta, Henry Szczesny neurologist, educator
Seevers, Charles Junior foundation executive, psychologist
Seireg, Ali A(bdel Hay) mechanical engineer
Sequeira, Luis plant pathology educator
Sewell, Richard Herbert historian, educator
Sewell, William Hamilton sociologist
Shabaz, John C. federal judge
Shain, Irving retired chemical company executive
Shaw, Joseph Thomas Slavic languages educator
Shea, Jeremy Charles lawyer
†Sheffield, Lewis Glosson physiologist
Shohet, Juda Leon electrical and computer engineering educator, researcher, high technology company executive
†Silbaugh, Rudy Lamont state legislator
Simone, Beverly S. academic administrator
Singer, Marcus George philosopher, educator
Skiles, James Jean electrical and computer engineering educator
Skilton, John Singleton lawyer
†Skinner, James Lauriston chemist, educator
Skoog, Folke Karl botany educator
Smalley, Eugene Byron plant pathology educator, forest pathologist, mycologist
Smith, Michael James industrial engineering educator
Sobkowicz, Hanna Maria neurology researcher
Soglin, Paul R. mayor, lawyer
Sonnedecker, Glenn Allen historian of pharmacy
Sprecher, Peter Leonard, Jr. financial services company executive
†Stern, Steve J. cultural organization administrator, history educator
Stewart, Warren Earl chemical engineer, educator
Strasma, John Drinan economist, educator
Stremler, Ferrel G. engineering educator, administrator
Strier, Karen Barbara anthropology educator
Susman, Millard geneticist, educator
†Swoboda, Lary Joseph state legislator
Swoboda, Ralph Sande credit union official, lawyer
Szybalski, Waclaw molecular geneticist, educator
†Taylor, Carolyn L. principal
Tedeschi, John Alfred historian, librarian
Temkin, Harvey Leon lawyer
†Theobald, H. Rupert political scientist
Thesen, Arne industrial engineering educator
Thiesenhusen, William Charles agricultural economist
Thompson, Cliff F. lawyer, educator
Thompson, Howard Elliott business educator
Thompson, Tommy George governor
Tibbitts, Theodore William horticulturist, researcher
†Tishler, William Henry landscape architect, educator
Tomar, Russell Herman pathologist, educator, researcher
†Turner, Robert Lloyd state legislator
†Urban, Frank Henry dermatologist, state legislator
Vandell, Kerry Dean real estate and urban economics educator
†Vansina, Jan Maria Jozef historian, educator
Vaughan, Worth Edward chemistry educator
†Vergeront, Susan Bowers state legislator, public relations consultant
Vondrasek, Frank Charles, Jr. utilities executive
Vowles, Richard Beckman educator
Wagner, Burton Allan lawyer
Wahba, Grace statistician, educator
Waldo, Robert Leland retired insurance company executive
Waldron, Ellis Leigh retired political science educator
Walker, Duard Lee medical educator
Walker, William Ray broadcasting executive
Walsh, David Graves lawyer
Wang, Herbert Fan geophysics educator
†Ward, David academic administrator, educator
Webster, John Goodwin biomedical engineering educator, researcher
Wedemeyer, Charles A. educator
Weinbrot, Howard David English educator
Weiss, Mareda Ruth university administrator
†Welch, Robert Thomas state representative
Welker, Wallace Irving neurophysiologist, educator
Wermers, Donald Joseph registrar
West, Robert Culbertson chemistry educator
Westman, Jack Conrad child psychiatrist, educator
Whiffen, James Douglass surgeon, educator
Whitburn, Gerald state agency administrator
White, William Fredrick lawyer
Whitney, Robert Michael lawyer
Wilcox, Michael Wing lawyer
Wilde, John artist, educator
Wirz, George O. bishop
Witiak, Donald Theodore academic dean, medicinal chemistry educator
Wolman, J. Martin retired newspaper publisher
Wright, Erik Olin sociology educator
Young, Merwin Crawford political science educator
†Young, Rebecca Mary Conrad state legislator
†Yu, Hyuk chemist, educator
Yuill, Thomas MacKay university administrator, microbiology educator
Zaleski, Michael Louis state official, lawyer
Zimmerman, Howard Elliot chemist, educator
Zobel, Robert Leonard state government official
Zweifel, David Alan newspaper editor

Manitowish Waters

Laidig, William Rupert retired paper company executive

Manitowoc

Logan, Lox Albert, Jr. museum director
Muchin, Arden Archie lawyer, director
Scheving, Lawrence Einar scientist, anatomy educator
Trader, Joseph Edgar orthopedic surgeon

Marion

Simpson, Vinson Raleigh manufacturing company executive

Marshfield

David, Barbara Marie medical, surgical nurse
Fye, W. Bruce, III cardiologist
Jaye, David Robert, Jr. retired hospital administrator
Sautter, Richard Daniel physician, administrator
Stueland, Dean Theodore emergency physician

Mauston

Gross, Carol Jeanne court clerk

Medford

Sebold, Duane David food manufacturing executive

Menasha

Aurand, Calvin W., Jr. specialized printing company executive
Baird, Roger Allen retired corporation executive
†Decker, William Joseph superintendent
Gorsalitz, Jeannine Liane elementary school educator
Henseler, Gerald Anthony printing company executive

Menomonee Falls

†Herma, John retail executive
†Kellogg, William S. retail executive

Mequon

Burroughs, Charles Edward lawyer
Buuck, R(oland) John university president
Dohmen, Frederick Hoeger retired wholesale drug company executive
Felde, Martin Lee advertising agency executive, accountant
†Stevens, Brooks industrial designer, educator
†Watson-Boone, Rebecca A. educator

Middleton

Eriksson, Larry John electrical engineer
Ferry, James Allen physicist, electrostatics company executive
Herb, Raymond G. physicist, manufacturing company executive
Ostrom, Meredith Eggers retired geologist

Milton
Hosler, Russell John *retired education educator*

Milwaukee
Abraham, William John, Jr. *lawyer*
Abramoff, Peter *biology educator*
Aita, Carolyn Rubin *physicist*
Alverson, William H. *lawyer*
Aman, Mohammed Mohammed *university dean, library and information science educator*
Ambrosius, Mark Ralph *hospital administrator*
†Ament, F. Thomas *county government official*
Arbit, Bruce *direct marketing executive, consultant*
†Armstrong, Douglas Dean *movie critic*
Arreola, Philip *police officer*
Auer, James Matthew *art critic, journalist*
Babler, Wayne E., Jr. *lawyer*
†Bader, Alfred Robert *chemist*
Balbach, George Charles *technology company executive*
Bannen, John T. *lawyer*
Barbee, Lloyd Augustus *lawyer*
Barnes, Paul McClung *lawyer*
Barron, Russell J. *lawyer*
Bartel, Fred Frank *consulting engineer executive*
†Bateman, C. Barry *airport terminal Executive*
Battocletti, Joseph Henry *electrical engineer, biomedical engineer, educator*
Bauer, Bruce Richard *lawyer*
Bauer, Chris Michael *banker*
Beals, Vaughn Le Roy, Jr. *motorcycle and RV manufacturing executive*
Beckwith, David E. *lawyer*
Behrendt, David Frogner *journalist*
Bell, Darryl Stephen *lawyer*
Berkoff, Marshall Richard *lawyer*
Berman, Fred Jean *art educator, painter, photographer*
Bero, Ronald Arthur *banker*
Bhore, Jay Narayan *psychiatrist*
Bicha, Karel Denis *historian, educator*
Biehl, Michael Melvin *lawyer*
Biller, Joel Wilson *lawyer, former foreign service officer*
Binder, Robert Lawrence *lawyer*
Bishop, Charles Joseph *manufacturing company executive*
Bloom, James Edward *commodity trading and financial executive*
†Bluestone, Stanton J. *department store chain executive*
Blum, Lawrence Philip *educational psychology educator*
Boese, Gilbert Karyle *cultural organization executive*
Boettcher, Harold Paul *engineer, educator*
Bortin, Mortimer M. *physician*
Bowen, Michael Anthony *lawyer, writer*
Brody, James Patrick *lawyer*
Brown, Edith *social worker*
Bruce, Jackson Martin, Jr. *lawyer*
Bruett, Till Arthur *banker*
Burgess, Richard Ball *food products executive*
Burkert, Robert Randall *artist*
Burstein, Sol *consultant, retired utility company executive, engineer*
Busch, John Arthur *lawyer*
Cannon, David Joseph *lawyer*
Carozza, Davy Angelo *Italian language educator*
Case, Karen Ann *lawyer*
Casey, John Alexander *lawyer*
Casper, Richard Henry *lawyer*
Chait, Jon Frederick *corporate executive, lawyer*
Chan, Shih Hung *mechanical engineering educator, consultant*
Chapman, William Paul *retired automatic control manufacturing company executive*
Checota, Joseph Woodrow *real estate business executive*
Christiansen, Jon Peter *lawyer*
Christiansen, Keith Allan *lawyer*
Clark, James Richard *lawyer*
Cleary, John Washington *lawyer*
Clevert, Charles Nelson, Jr. *federal judge*
Condon, Robert Edward *surgeon, educator*
Connolly, Gerald Edward *lawyer*
Connolly, L. William *lawyer*
Conrad, Kelley Allen *industrial and organizational psychologist*
Cooper, Richard Alan *hematologist, college dean*
Croak, Francis R. *lawyer*
Curran, Thomas J. *federal judge*
Cutler, Richard Woolsey *lawyer*
Daily, Frank J(erome) *lawyer*
Dalton, Harry *professional baseball team executive*
Davis, Thomas William *college administrator, electrical engineering educator*
Davis, Walter Stewart *lawyer*
DiUlio, Albert Joseph *university president, priest*
Downey, John Wilham *composer, pianist, conductor, educator*
Drummond, Robert Kendig *lawyer*
Duback, Steven Rahr *lawyer*
Dunleavy, Janet Frank Egleson *English language educator*
Dunleavy, Michael Joseph *professional basketball coach*
Dupies, Donald Albert *civil engineer, consultant*
Dziewanowski, Marian Kamil *history educator*
Ehrmann, Thomas William *lawyer*
Elias, Paul S. *marketing executive*
†Erdmann, August *protective services official*
Ericson, James Donald *lawyer, insurance executive*
Esterly, Nancy Burton *physician*
Farris, Trueman Earl, Jr. *retired newspaper editor*
†Faude, William Davison *advertising executive*
Feitler, Robert *shoe company executive*
Fibich, Howard Raymond *retired newspaper editor*
Fink, Jordan Norman *physician, educator*
Fischer, Michael Davin *lawyer*
Fitzsimonds, Roger Leon *bank holding company executive*
Florsheim, Richard Steven *lawyer*
†Florsheim, Thomas W. *shoe manufacturing company executive*
Foster, Richard *journalist*
Fraedrich, Royal Louis *magazine editor, publisher*
Frankiewicz, Marcia Jean *telemarketing executive*
Frautschi, Timothy Clark *lawyer*
Friedman, James Dennis *lawyer*
Friedman, Melvin Jack *language professional, literature educator*
Fromstein, Mitchell S. *temporary office services company executive*
Gaggioli, Richard Arnold *mechanical engineering educator*
Gallagher, Richard S. *lawyer*
Gallop, Jane (Anne) *women's studies educator, writer*
Garner, Phil *professional baseball manager*
Garnier, Robert Charles *management consultant*
Gefke, Henry Jerome *lawyer*
Gemignani, Joseph Adolph *lawyer*
Gengler, Sister M. Jeanne *hospital administrator*
†George, Gary Raymond *state senator*
Ghiardi, James Domenic *lawyer, educator*
Gissler, Sigvard Gunnar, Jr. *journalism educator, former newspaper editor*
Goetsch, John Hubert *utility company executive*
Goggins, John Francis *dentist, university administrator*
†Goldsmith, Christopher C. *museum director*
Goodkind, Conrad George *lawyer*
Graef, Luther William *civil engineer*
Green, Edward Anthony *museum director*
†Greenler, Robert George *physics educator, researcher*
Groethe, Reed *lawyer*
Groiss, Fred George *lawyer*
Grossberg, Sidney Edward *microbiology educator*
Gunnlaugsson, Gordon Harvey *bank executive*
Haas, George Edward *lawyer*
Habush, Robert Lee *lawyer*
Hachey, Thomas Eugene *British and Irish history educator, consultant*
Halloran, William Frank *university dean*
Hankin, Bernard Jacob *lawyer*
†Hannah, Stephen *newspaper editor*
Hanthorn, Dennis Wayne *performing arts association administrator*
Harding, Victor Mathews *lawyer*
Harrington, John Timothy *lawyer*
Harvieux, Anne Marie *psychotherapist*
Hase, David John *lawyer*
Hassan, Ihab Habib *English and comparative literature educator, author*
Hatch, Michael Ward *lawyer*
†Hatton, Janie R. Hill *principal*
Hawkins, Brett William *political science educator*
Haworth, Daniel Thomas *chemistry educator*
Hayes, Paul Gordon *journalist*
Hazelwood, John A. *lawyer*
†Hefty, Thomas R. *insurance company executive*
Heinen, James Albin *electrical engineering educator*
Helbert, Clifford L. *graphic designer, journalism educator*
Hendee, William Richard *medical physics educator, university official*
Hinshaw, Edward Banks *broadcasting company executive*
Hoffer, Robert Morrison *retired holding company executive*
Hoffman, Nathaniel A. *lawyer*
Hollenbach, Sister Ruth *college president*
Holz, Harry George *lawyer*
Hopkins, Edward Donald *manufacturing executive*
Horsman, Reginald *history educator*
Humber, Wilbur James *psychologist*
Huntington, David Mack Goode *foundation administrator*
Huston, Kathleen Marie *library administrator*
Huston, Margo *journalist*
Ihlenfeldt, Dale Elwood *judge*
Jache, Albert William *retired chemistry educator, scientist*
Jacobs, Burleigh Edmund *foundry executive*
†Jaksic, Ivan A. *history educator*
James, Charles Franklin, Jr. *engineering educator*
†Jansen, Daniel Ervin *professional speedskater, marketing professional, former Olympic athlete*
†Jaques, Damien Paul *theater critic*
Jenkins, William Ivy *hospital administrator*
Johannes, John Roland *political science educator, college dean*
Johnson, Geneva Bolton *human service organization executive*
Joseph, Jules K. *retired public relations executive*
Joslyn, Jay Thomas *arts critic*
Jost, Lawrence John *lawyer*
Joyce, Michael Stewart *foundation executive, political science educator*
Kahlor, Robert Arnold *communications company executive*
Kamps, Charles Q. *lawyer*
Karl, Max Henry *insurance company executive*
Kelly, Francis Daniel *lawyer*
Kendall, Leon Thomas *finance and real estate educator, retired insurance company executive*
Kerr, Dorothy Marie Burmeister *consultant, marketing executive*
Kessler, Joan F. *lawyer*
Keuler, Roland Leo *retired shoe company executive*
Keulks, George William *university dean, chemistry educator*
Keyes, James Henry *manufacturing company executive*
Killian, William Paul *industrial corporate executive*
Kinnamon, David Lucas *lawyer*
Kneiser, Richard John *accountant*
Kochar, Mahendr Singh *physician, educator, administrator, researcher, writer, consultant*
Kringel, Jerome Howard *lawyer*
Kritzer, Paul Eric *media executive, communications lawyer*
Kubale, Bernard Stephen *lawyer*
†Kuester, Dennis J. *banker*
Kurtz, Harvey A. *lawyer*
LaBudde, Roy Christian *lawyer*
Laikin, George Joseph *lawyer*
Landis, Fred *mechanical engineering educator*
Laun, Arthur Henry, Jr. *lawyer*
Lavers, Richard Marshall *lawyer*
Lawrence, Willard Earl *mathematics, statistics and computer science educator emeritus*
Le Duc, Don Raymond *lawyer, educator*
Leonard, Richard Hart *journalist*
Levit, William Harold, Jr. *lawyer*
Listach, Pat Alan *professional baseball player*
Long, Robert Eugene *banker*
Lubar, Sheldon Bernard *venture capitalist*
†Lueders, Wayne Richard *lawyer*
Lydolph, Paul Edward *geography educator*
†Lynett, William Ruddy *publishing, broadcasting company executive*
†MacDonald, Michael R. *retail executive*
†MacDonough, John N. *beverage company executive*
MacGregor, David Lee *lawyer*
Machulak, Edward Leon *real estate, mining and advertising company executive*
MacIver, John Kenneth *lawyer*
Maio, F. Anthony *lawyer*
Manning, Kenneth Paul *food company executive*
Marcus, Ben *business executive*
Marcus, Stephen Howard *hospitality and entertainment company executive*
Marringa, Jacques Louis *manufacturing company executive*
Martin, Quinn William *lawyer*
Martin, Vincent Lionel *manufacturing company executive*
Mayer, Henry Michael *mass transit consultant*
Maynard, John Ralph *lawyer*
McCanles, Michael Frederick *English language educator*
†McCann, Dennis J. *columnist*
McCauley, Michael Stephen *lawyer*
McCollow, Thomas James *communications company executive*
Mc Gaffey, Jere D. *lawyer*
McGarity, Margaret Dee *federal judge*
McKinney, Venora Ware *librarian*
McSweeney, Maurice J. (Marc) *lawyer*
Meisner, Mary Jo *editor*
Meldman, Clifford Kay *lawyer*
Meldman, Robert Edward *lawyer*
Miller, David Hewitt *environmental scientist, writer*
Miller, Keith *insurance company executive*
Moberg, David Oscar *sociology educator*
Morris, G. Ronald *automotive executive*
Mosher, George Allan *manufacturing company executive*
Mulcahy, Charles Chambers *lawyer, educator*
Mulcahy, Robert William *lawyer*
Namdari, Bahram *surgeon*
Niederjohn, Russell James *electrical and computer engineering educator*
Ninneman, Richard Canney *lawyer*
Noelke, Paul *lawyer*
Norquist, John Olof *mayor*
Novak, Victor Anthony *semi-retired manufacturing company executive*
Olson, Frederick Irving *retired history educator*
Olson, John Marshall *lawyer*
Osborn, Guy A. *food products company executive*
O'Shaughnessy, James Patrick *lawyer*
O'Toole, Robert Joseph *manufacturing company executive*
†Palay, Gilbert *temporary help services company executive*
Panenka, James Brian Joseph *financial company executive*
Parker, Charles Walter, Jr. *consultant, retired equipment company executive*
Paull, Richard Allen *geologist, educator*
Paulson, Belden Henry *political scientist*
Pelisek, Frank John *lawyer*
Pelton, Ralph A. *insurance company executive*
Perlman, Richard Wilfred *economist, educator*
†Petering, David Harold *chemistry educator*
Phillips, Thomas John *lawyer*
Pindyck, Bruce Eben *lawyer, corporate executive*
Pisciotta, Anthony Vito *physician, educator*
Poehlmann, JoAnna *artist, illustrator, designer*
Powell, Edmund William *lawyer*
Precourt, Lyman Arthur *lawyer*
Quade, Quentin Lon *political science educator*
Ramsey, Paul Willard *metallurgical engineer, welding engineering consultant*
Randa, Rudolph Thomas *federal judge*
Randall, William Seymour *leasing company executive*
Raynor, John Patrick *university administrator*
Read, Sister Joel *college administrator*
Reedy, George Edward *educator, author, lecturer*
Reid, Robert Lelon *college dean, mechanical engineer*
†Remsen, Charles Cornell, III *microbiologist, research administrator, educator*
Rice, Robert Marshall *social worker*
Richman, Stephen Erik *lawyer*
†Risch, Richard William *horticultural manager*
Ritz, Esther Leah *civic worker, volunteer, investor*
Roeming, Robert Frederick *foreign language educator*
Ryan, Patrick Michael *lawyer*
Samson, Allen Lawrence *bank executive*
Samson, Richard Max *investments and real estate executive*
Sanderson, Gary Warner *food company executive*
Sankovitz, James Leo *director of development, lobbyist*
Sapp, John Raymond *lawyer*
Schaleben, Arville *newspaper editor, writer, educator*
Scheinfeld, James David *travel agency executive*
Schenk, Quentin Frederick *retired social work educator, mayor*
Schenker, Eric *university dean, economist*
Schmitz, Dolores Jean *educator*
Schnoll, Howard Manuel *investment banking and managed asset consultant*
Schnur, Robert Arnold *lawyer*
Schrader, Thomas F. *utilities executive*
Schroeder, John H. *university administrator, history educator*
Schuenke, Donald John *insurance company executive*
Schultz, Richard Otto *ophthalmologist, educator*
Schur, Leon Milton *educator, economist*
Schwartz, Harold Albert *retired newspaper company executive*
Schwartz, Joseph *English language educator*
Scrabeck, Jon Gilmen *dental eductor*
Scrivner, Thomas William *lawyer*
Selig, Allan H. (Bud Selig) *professional baseball team executive*
Shapiro, James Edward *federal judge*
Shea, Donald Richard *political science educator*
Shiely, John Stephen *company executive, lawyer*
Shindell, Sidney *medical educator, physician*
Shriner, Thomas L., Jr. *lawyer*
†Sim, Richard Guild *business executive*
†Slocum, Elizabeth *newspaper editor*
†Smith, Guy W. *health care executive*
Smith, James John *physiologist*
Smith, Lois Ann *real estate executive*
Soergel, Konrad Hermann *physician*
Spann, Wilma Nadene *principal*
Spitzer, Robert Ralph *academic administrator emeritus*
Spore, Keith Kent *newspaper editor*
Stadtmueller, Joseph Peter *federal judge*
Stafl, Adolf *obstetrician, gynecologist, educator*
Steinmiller, John F. *professional basketball team executive*
Sterner, Frank Maurice *industrial executive*
Stone, Thomas S. *lawyer*
Stratton, Frederick Prescott, Jr. *manufacturing executive*
Stromberg, Roland Nelson *historian*
Surridge, Stephen Zehring *lawyer, writer*
Swanson, Roy Arthur *classicist, educator*
Swick, Herbert Morris *medical educator, neurologist*
Szmanda, Lucille Marie *vocational school educator*
Teerlink, Richard Francis *motor company executive*
Terry, Leon Cass *neurologist, educator*
Teschner, Richard Rewa *retired lawyer*
Thrall, Arthur Alvin *artist*
Uecker, Bob *actor, radio announcer, former baseball player, TV personality*
Van Antwerpen, Regina Lane *underwriter, insurance company executive*
Van Vugt, Eric J. *lawyer*
Vaughn, Gregory Lamont *professional baseball player*
Vespa, Ned Angelo *photographer*
†Vice, Jon Earl *hospital executive*
Viets, Hermann *college president, consultant*
Wallace, Harry Leland *lawyer*
Walmer, Edwin Fitch *lawyer*
Walters, Ronald Ogden *finance company executive*
Walters, William LeRoy *physics educator*
Warren, Richard M. *experimental psychologist, educator*
Wawrzyn, Ronald M. *lawyer*
Weakland, Rembert G. *archbishop*
Weber, Charles Edward *management educator*
Weber, Robert George *lawyer*
Weil, Herman *psychology educator*
Weise, Charles Martin *zoology educator*
Wenzler, William Paul *architect*
White, Walter Hiawatha, Jr. *lawyer*
Whyte, George Kenneth, Jr. *lawyer*
Widera, G. E. O. *materials engineering educator, consultant*
Wiedenman, Jere Wayne *lawyer*
Wigdale, James B. *bank executive*
Wikenhauser, Charles Joseph *zoological park director*
Wiley, Edwin Packard *lawyer*
Will, Trevor Jonathan *lawyer*
Wills, Robert Hamilton *newspaper executive*
Yontz, Kenneth Fredric *medical and chemical company executive*
†Youker, James Edward *radiologist*
Zeidler, Frank P. *former association administrator, mayor, arbitrator, mediator, fact-finder*
Zelazo, Nathaniel K. *engineering executive*
Zigman, Robert S. *public relations executive, hospital executive*
Ziperski, James Richard *lawyer, trucking company executive*
†Zober, Norman Alan *health facility administrator*
Zore, Edward John *insurance company investment executive*

Minocqua
Utt, Glenn S., Jr. *motel investments and biotech industry company executive*

Monroe
†Deininger, David George *federal judge*
Kittelsen, Rodney Olin *lawyer*

Montello
Burns, Robert Edward *editor, publisher*

Mosinee
Janis, Donald Emil *corporate controller*
†Radt, Richard Louis *paper company executive*

Muskego
Stefaniak, Norbert John *business administration educator*

Nashotah
Hansen, Robert Wayne *judge, editor*

Neenah
Bergstrom, Dedric Waldemar *retired paper company executive*
†Brophy, George Thomas *building products company executive*
Fetzer, Edward Frank *transportation company executive*
Heaster, Arlene L. *chemical engineer*
†Parker, Richard E. *building products manufacturing company executive*
Proctor, Nick Hobert *toxicologist, pharmacologist*
Stanton, Thomas Mitchell *lawyer, educator*

Neillsville
Stockwell, Richard E. *journalist, business executive*

Nekoosa
Sigler, LeRoy Walter *banker, lawyer, entrepreneur*

New Franken
Weidner, Edward William *university chancellor, political scientist*

New Glarus
Marsh, Robert Charles *writer, music critic*

New London
Fitzgerald, Laurine Elisabeth *university dean, educator*

Oak Creek
†Clark, Harry Wilber *administrator*
Robertson, Michael Swing *religious association administrator*

Oconomowoc
Reich, Rose Marie *retired art educator*

Onalaska
Wilson, Anthony Vincent *business executive, mechanical engineer*

Oregon
Dorner, Peter Paul *retired economist, educator*
Sloan, Richard *artist*

Oshkosh
Barwig, Regis Norbert James *priest*
Burke, Redmond A. *priest, librarian, educator*
Burr, John Roy *philosophy educator*
Dempsey, Timothy Michael *lawyer*
Goodson, Raymond Eugene *automotive executive*
Gruberg, Martin *political science educator*
Hulsebosch, Charles Joseph *truck manufacturing company executive*
Jones, Norma Louise *librarian, educator*
†Poberezny, Thomas *museum adminstrator*
Reinke, Leonard Herman *architect*

Osseo
Wright, Rodney H. *architect*

Pewaukee
Dickson, John R. *food products company executive, dairy products company executive*
Lee, Jack (Jim Sanders Beasley) *broadcast executive*
†Quadracci, Harry R. *printing company executive*
†Quadracci, Harry V. *printing company executive, lawyer*
†Ranus, Robert D. *food marketing executive*

Platteville
Al Yasiri, Kahtan Abbass *college dean*
†Brodbeck, William Jan *retail executive*

Plover
Peanasky, Robert Joseph *biochemist, medical educator*

Plymouth
Gentine, Lee Michael *marketing professional*

Port Edwards
Veneman, Gerard Earl *paper company executive*

Racine
Batten, Michael Ellsworth *manufacturing company executive*
Bernberg, Bruce Arthur *consumer products and printing executive*
Boyd, William Beaty *retired foundation executive*
Bray, Charles William, III *foundation executive*
Campbell, Edward Joseph *retired machinery company executive*
Carlson, Robert John *manufacturing company executive*
Coates, Glenn Richard *lawyer*
Crawford, Gerald Marcus *lawyer*
Fitch, Robert McLellan *business and technology consultant*
George, William Douglas, Jr. *consumer products company executive*
Gunnerson, Robert Mark *manufacturing company executive, accountant, lawyer*
Harlan, Jean Durgin *psychologist, writer, consultant*
Hart, Robert Camillus *lawyer, company executive*
Jacobson-Wolf, Joan Elizabeth *minister*
Johnson, Samuel Curtis *wax company executive*
Klein, Gabriella Sonja *communications executive*
Konz, Gerald Keith *manufacturing company executive*
†Malone, Terence S. *chemical company executive*
Savage, Richard T. *manufacturing company executive*
Swanson, Robert Lee *lawyer*

Rhinelander
Saari, John William, Jr. *lawyer*

Rice Lake
†Knutson, Gerhard I. *bishop*

Richland Center
Meyer, Edwin Dale, Sr. *school system administrator*

Ripon
Ashley, Robert Paul, Jr. *English literature educator*
Miller, George H. *historian, educator*
Northrop, Douglas Anthony *English educator, college official and dean*
Stott, William Ross, Jr. *college president*

River Falls
†Harsdorf, Sheila Eloise *state legislator, farmer*
Johnson, James Robert *ceramic engineer, educator*
Smith, Clyde Curry *historian, educator*
Thibodeau, Gary A. *university administrator*

River Hills
Silverman, Albert A. *retired lawyer, manufacturing company executive*
Smith, Jane Farwell *civic worker*

Sayner
Southwick, Harry Webb *surgeon*

Sheboygan
†Brewer, Warren Wesley *principal*
Buchen, John Gustave *retired judge*
Gore, Donald Ray *orthopedic surgeon*
†Longo, George P. *superintendent*

Silver Lake
Hellum, Perry K. *school system administrator*

South Milwaukee
Kitzke, Eugene David *research management executive*

Spring Green
Sisson, Everett Arnold *industrial developer, business executive*

Stevens Point
†Arneson, Arne Jon *librarian*
Ballard, Larry Coleman *insurance company executive*
Makholm, Mark Henry *lawyer, former insurance company executive*
Paul, Justus Fredrick *historian, educator*
Salinger, Robert Meredith *lawyer*
Sanders, Keith R. *university chancellor*
Seramur, John C. *bank executive*
Stevens, Dwight Marlyn *educational administrator*

Stone Lake
Kissinger, Harold Arthur *retired army officer*

Stoughton
Ellery, John Blaise *communications educator emeritus*
Kuhn, Peter Mouat *atmospheric physicist*

Sun Prairie
Allen, Ronald Royce *communication educator*
Eustice, Francis Joseph *lawyer*
Mischke, Carl Herbert *religious association executive, retired*

Superior
Feldman, Egal *historian, educator*
Fliss, Raphael M. *bishop*

Thiensville
Berry, William Martin *financial consultant*
Kostecke, B. William *utilities executive*
Lee, Tong Hun *economics educator*
Roselle, William Charles *librarian*

Tomah
Kenyon, Kyle *lawyer*
Shim, Jae Yong *physician*

Twin Lakes
Fleischer, John Richard *secondary education educator*

Verona
Schroeder, Henry William *publisher*

Walworth
Sissons, John Roger *educational administrator*

Waterloo
Kay, Dennis Matthew *operations manager*

Watertown
Henry, Carl Ferdinand Howard *theologian*

Waukesha
Falcone, Frank S. *college president*
Gehrke, Allen Charles *corporation executive*

Waunakee
Berthelsen, John Robert *printing company executive*

Wausau
Derwinski, Dennis Anthony *dentist*
Nemirow, Arnold Myles *manufacturing executive*
†Niederhofer, Laurence John *metals company executive*
Orr, San Watterson, Jr. *lawyer*
†Paprocki, John Thomas *controller*
Slayton, John Arthur *electric motor manufacturing executive*
†Weinberger, Leon Joseph *insurance company executive*

Wauwatosa
†Hollister, Winston Ned *pathologist*

West Allis
Feinsilver, Donald Lee *psychiatry educator*

West Bend
Gardner, Robert Joseph *general and thoracic surgeon*
Karpowitz, Anthony Victor *college dean emeritus*
Rodney, Joel Morris *dean*
Styve, Orloff Wendell, Jr. *electrical engineer*

Whitewater
Bhargava, Ashok *economics educator*
Carrara, Arthur Alfonso *architect, designer, painter, graphic designer*
Culbertson, Frances Mitchell *psychology educator*
Gibbens, John Monnett *economics educator*
Refior, Everett Lee *labor economist, educator*
Rosner, Jorge *therapist, institute director*
Schallenkamp, Kay *college administrator*
Verma, Krishnanand *mathematics educator, consultant*

Williams Bay
Harper, Doyal Alexander, Jr. *astronomer, educator*
Hobbs, Lewis Mankin *astronomer*
Kron, Richard G. *astrophysicist, educator*

Wisconsin Rapids
Brennan, Patrick Francis *printing paper manufacturing executive*
Engelhardt, LeRoy A. *retired paper company executive*
Kenney, Richard John *paper company finance executive*
Mead, George Wilson, II *paper company executive*

WYOMING

Afton
Hunsaker, Floyd B. *accountant*
†Lowe, James Allen *school superintendent*

Bondurant
Shepard, Paul Howe *ecology educator, author, lecturer*

Burns
Suyematsu, Toshiro *lawyer*

Casper
Bostwick, Richard Raymond *retired lawyer*
Donley, Russell Lee, III *engineering executive, former state representative*
†Hinchey, Bruce Alan *environmental engineering company executive*
Kennerknecht, Richard Eugene *sales executive*
Lowe, Robert Stanley *lawyer*
Meenan, Patrick Henry *state legislator*
†Nagel, Patricia Jo *non-profit public policy administrator, lawyer*
Perkins, Dorothy A. *marketing professional*
Rosenthal, Jack *broadcasting executive*
†Sadler, Dick Sherman *state official*
Stroock, Thomas Frank *business executive*
True, Henry Alfonso, Jr. *entrepreneur*
Wilde, David George *electrical engineer, consultant*
Wold, John Schiller *geologist, former congressman*

Centennial
Russin, Robert Isaiah *sculptor, educator*

Cheyenne
Barrett, James E. *federal judge*
Brimmer, Clarence Addison *federal judge*
Brorby, Wade *federal judge*
Brown, Charles Stuart *retired state supreme court justice*
Cardine, Godfrey Joseph *state supreme court justice*
†Cubin, Barbara Lynn *state legislator, public relations consultant*
Drummer, Donald Raymond *financial services executive*
Freudenthal, Steven Franklin *lawyer*
Golden, Michael *state supreme court justice*
†Hanes, John G. *lawyer, state legislator*
†Hansen, Matilda *state legislator*
Hart, Joseph H. *bishop*
Hirst, Wilma Elizabeth *psychologist*
Horton, Bernard Francis *newspaper editor*
Hunton, Donald Bothen *retired internist*
Johnson, Alan Bond *federal judge*
Johnson, Wayne Harold *librarian, county official*
Karpan, Kathleen Marie *state official, lawyer, journalist*
Kathka, David Arlin *state parks and cultural resources administrator, state archivist*
†Lummis, Cynthia Marie *lawyer, rancher*
Macy, Richard J. *state judge*
Mc Clintock, Archie Glenn *lawyer*
Meyer, Joseph B. *state attorney general*
†Mockler, Esther Jayne *state legislator*
Noe, Guy *social services administrator*
Ohman, Diana J. *school system administrator*
†Ray, Michael Franklyn *chemical company executive*
Rooney, John Joseph *lawyer, former state supreme court justice*
Rose, Robert R., Jr. *lawyer*
Schuman, Gerald Eugene *soil scientist*
Smith, Stanford Sidney *state treasurer*
Sullivan, Michael John *governor, lawyer*
Thomas, Richard Van *state supreme court justice*
Thomson, Thyra Godfrey *former state official*
Wittler, Shirley Joyce *former state official, state commissioner*

Cody
Hassrick, Peter Heyl *museum director*
Housel, Jerry Winters *lawyer*
Hynek, Frederick James *architect*
Jackson, Harry Andrew *artist*
†Shreve, Peg *educator*

Daniel
Parker, H. Lawrence *rancher, investor, retired investment banker*

Douglas
Sanford, Leroy Leonard *rancher*

Dubois
†Betts, Robert Budd, Jr. *dude ranch owner*

Fort Laramie
†Hageman, James C. *rancher*

Gillette
†Enzi, Michael Bradley *accountant, state legislator*

Green River
†Boswell, Christopher Orr *broadcast journalist*
Marty, Lawrence A. *lawyer, magistrate judge*

Greybull
†Miller, Carroll S. *dentist, legislator*

Jackson
Bommer, Timothy J *judge*
Downer, Eugene Debs, Jr. *editor, publisher*
Gordon, Stephen Maurice *manufacturing company executive, rancher*
Hansen, Clifford Peter *rancher*
†LaLonde, Robert Frederick *state senator*
†Law, Clarene Alta *innkeeper, state legislator*
Moeller, Robert Charles, III *fine arts consultant*
Schuster, Robert Parks *lawyer*
Tessler, Allan Roger *lawyer*
Thulin, Walter Willis *real estate company executive*
Watt, James Gaius *lawyer, former government official, legal consultant*

Jackson Hole
Adler, Warren *novelist, producer, playwright*

Kemmerer
Clark, Michael *artist, educator*

Lander
†Tipton, Harry Basil, Jr. *state legislator, physician*

Laramie
Boresi, Arthur Peter *author, educator*
Caldwell, Daniel Ralston *microbiology educator*
Chai, Winberg *political science educator, foundation chair*
Christensen, Martha *mycologist, educator*
Cottam, Keith M. *librarian, educator, administrator*
Dickman, Francois Moussiegt *former foreign service officer*
Ferris, Clifford Duras *electrical engineer, bioengineer, educator*
Flach, Victor H. *designer, educator*
Grandy, Walter Thomas, Jr. *physicist*
Gressley, Gene Maurice *history educator*
Hardy, Deborah Welles *history educator*
†Hartman, Ronald Lee *plant systematist*
†Jones, Bob Gordon *bishop*
†Kearley, Timothy G. *law librarian, consultant*
†Kinney, Lisa Frances *state senator*
Langlois, Walter Gordon *foreign language educator*
Long, Francis Mark *electrical engineer, educator*
†Maxfield, Peter C. *law educator, university dean, lawyer*
Meyer, Edmond Gerald *energy and natural resources educator, resources scientist, entrepreneur, former chemistry educator*
Mingle, John Orville *engineer, educator, lawyer, consultant*
Nye, Eric William *language educator*
Rechard, Paul Albert *civil engineering consulting company executive*
Reif, (Frank) David *artist, educator*
Roark, Terry Paul *university president*
Smith, Thomas Shore *lawyer*
Speight, James Glassford *research company executive*
Sutherland, Robert L. *engineering company executive, educator*
Williams, Roger Lawrence *historian, educator*

Moose
Craighead, Frank Cooper, Jr. *ecologist*
†Neckels, Jack *park superintendent*

Rawlins
†Vasey, William Joseph *director college outreach program, state legislator*

Riverton
†Bebout, Eli Daniel *oil executive*
Clark, Stanford E. *accountant*
Girard, Nettabell *lawyer*
†Peck, Robert A. *newspaper publisher*
Tippets, Dennis Wilcock *mineral exploration executive, state legislator*

Rock Springs
†Baumberger, Don R. *school system administrator*
†Blackwell, Samuel Eugene *state legislator*

Sheridan
Mc Ewan, Leonard *former judge*

Teton Village
Ellwood, Paul Murdock, Jr. *health policy analyst, consultant*

Wheatland
Bunker, John Birkbeck *cattle rancher, retired sugar company executive*
Mickelsen, Einer Bjegaard *judge*

Wilson
Breitenbach, Mary Louise McGraw *psychologist, drug rehabilitation counselor*
Eliot, Robert Salim *physician*
Fritz, Jack Wayne *communications and marketing company executive*
Lawroski, Harry *nuclear engineer*
Sage, Andrew Gregg Curtin, II *corporate investor, manager*

Worland
Woods, Lawrence Milton *airline company executive*

TERRITORIES OF THE UNITED STATES

AMERICAN SAMOA

Pago Pago
Coleman, Peter Tali *former governor*
Faleali'i, Logoleo T. V. *educational services administrator*
Fung-Chen-Pen, Emma Talauna Solaita *librarian, program director*
Kruse, F. Michael *judge*
†Lutu, Afoa Moega *legislator, lawyer*
†Tulafono, Togiola T.A. *senator*
Varghese, Mary *secondary education educator*

GUAM

Agana
Ada, Joseph Franklin *territorial governor*
†Blaz, Anthony Crisostomo *U.S. territorial legislator*
†Bordallo, Madeleine Mary (Mrs. Ricardo Jerome Bordallo) *wife of former governor of Guam*
Burr, Hiram Hale, Jr. *air force officer*
Crisostomo, Manny *photographer*
Cruz, Benjamin Joseph Franquez *territory judge*
Diaz, Ramon Valero *judge*
Duenas, Laurent Flores *nursing administrator*
Ladd-Powell, Roberta Kay *horsebreeder, marketing executive*
Lamorena, Alberto C., III *judge*
†Lee, Chin-Tian *academic administrator, agricultural studies educator*
†Lujan, Pilar C. *senator*
Mallo-Garrido, Josephine Ann *marketing manager*
Perez, Gerald S. A. *retail executive educator*
†Reyes, Edward Diego *lieutenant governor*
San Agustin, Joe Taitano *Guam senator, financial institution executive, management researcher*
Tock, Joseph *lawyer*
†Unpingco, Antonio Reyes *senator*
Unpingco, John Walter Sablan *federal judge*
Uyehara, Harry Yoshimi *library educator*

Tamuning
Camacho, Eduardo Garcia *finance company executive, insurance agent*

NORTHERN MARIANA ISLANDS

Saipan
Dela Cruz, Jose Santos *state supreme court chief justice*
†Maratita, Mametto Ulloa *congressman*
†San Nicolas, Henry Deleon Guerrero *territory senator*

PUERTO RICO

Adjuntas
†Altieri Rosado, José Aníbal *principal*

Bayamon
Santacana, Guido E. *physiology educator*

Caparra
†Pont, Marisara *public relations executive*

Carolina
†Figueroa, Iván *lawyer*

Catano
†Behar, Abraham *construction engineer*

Coto Laurel
†Basols, Jose Andres *high school director and principal, priest*

Guaynabo
Cruz Aponte, Ramón Aristides *foundation administrator, educator*

Hato Rey
Ferrer, Miguel Antonio *brokerage firm and investment bank executive*

Humacao
Castrodad, Felix A. *university administrator*

Mayaguez
Hernandez-Avila, Manuel Luis *physical oceanography educator, researcher, administrator, consultant*
Miskimen, George William *neurobiologist, educator*

Ponce
Sala, Luis Francisco *surgeon, educator*
Torres Oliver, Juan Fremiot *bishop*

Rincon
Morris, Victor Franklin, Jr. *meteorology educator*

Rio Piedras
Bangdiwala, Ishver Surchand *statistician, educator*
Perez, Victor *medical technologist, laboratory director*
Santiago, Juan Jose *secondary school president*

San Juan
Acevedo, Hector Luis *mayor*
†Acevedo-Vilá, Aníbal *state legislator, lawyer*
Acosta, Raymond Luis *federal judge*
Amadeo, Jose H. *physician, educator*
†Behar-Ybarra, Elias *civil, structural engineer*
Bonnet, Juan Amedee *nuclear engineer, educator*
†Caro Tirado, Rafael *congressman*
Carreras, Francisco José *former university president, foundation executive*
Carrion, Richard *bank executive*
Cerezo, Carmen Consuelo *federal judge*
†De Castro Font, Jorge A. *state legislator*
De Jesús, Nydia Rosa *physician, anesthesiologist*
†Fernández-Coll, Fred *microbiologist, food technology laboratory director*
Fuste, Jose Antonio *federal judge*
Gierbolini-Ortiz, Gilberto *federal judge*
Gonzalez, Jose Ramón *academic administrator*
†Hernández-Agosto, Miguel Angel *Puerto Rican official*
Hernandez-Denton, Federico *territory supreme court justice*
†Hernández Torres, Zaida *state legislator*
Laffitte, Hector Manuel *federal judge*
†Lugo, Ariel E. *ecologist, botanist, federal agency administrator*
†Marrero Hueca, Angel *state legislator*
Marvel, Thomas Stahl *architect*
Matheu, Federico Manuel *university chancellor*
†McClintock, Kenneth Davison *state legislator*
†Navas de Leon, Luis Felipe *senator, lawyer*
†Orkand, Richard Kenneth *neurobiologist, researcher, educator*
†Ortiz Velazquez, Rolando *territory legislator, lawyer*
Pérez, Angel Alvarez *bank executive*
Perez-Gimenez, Juan Manuel *federal judge*
Pieras, Jaime, Jr. *federal judge*
Ramirez-Rivera, Jose *physician*
Rodriguez-del Valle, Nuri *microbiology educator*
Sahai, Hardeo *medical educator*
†San Antonio Mendoza, Oscar A. *state legislator*
Thompson, Annie Figueroa *academic director, educator*
Toppel, Milton *retired retail food store executive*
Torruella, Juan R. *federal judge*
Trías-Monge, Jose *lawyer, former territory supreme court chief justice*
†Valentin Acevedo, Freddy *senator*
†Zayas, Francisco Seijo *legislator, veterinarian*

Santurce
Aponte Martinez, Luis Cardinal *archbishop*
Loubriel, Tere *bank executive*

REPUBLIC OF MARSHALL ISLAND

Majuro
Fields, David Clark *diplomat*

VIRGIN ISLANDS

Charlotte Amalie
Feuerzeig, Henry Louis *lawyer*
Moore, Thomas Kail *chief judge*
†Richardson, Bingley Geraldo *territory legislator*

Christiansted
Finch, Raymond Lawrence *judge*
Gardine, Juanita Constantia Forbes *educator*

Frederiksted
†O'Neal, Lilliana Belardo de *territory senator*
†Pickard, Mary Ann *senator*
Pierce, Lambert Reid *architect*

Saint Thomas
Farrelly, Alexander *governor*
Hodge, Verne Antonio *judge*
†Liburd, Almando Leando *senator*
Miner, Robert Gordon *creative promotional consultant, auctioneer, writer, publisher, actor*

MILITARY ADDRESSES OF THE UNITED STATES

ATLANTIC

APO
Adams, Alvin Philip, Jr. *diplomat, lawyer*
Bowers, Charles R. *ambassador*
Bracete, Juan Manuel *diplomat, lawyer*
Busby, Morris D. *ambassador*
Carner, George *foreign service executive, economic strategist*
Cheek, James Richard *ambassador*
Davidow, Jeffrey *ambassador*
Guinot, Luis, Jr. *lawyer, ambassador*
Hinton, Deane Roesch *ambassador*
Pastorino, Robert Stephen *diplomat, ambassador*
Pryce, William Thornton *foreign service officer*
†Rifenburg, Raymond F. *government official, economist*
Romero, Peter Frank *diplomat*
Sanbrailo, John A. *mission director*
Taylor, Paul Daniel *ambassador*
Whitman, Gerald John *diplomat*

EUROPE

APO
†Aaron, David L. *diplomat*
Baltimore, Richard Lewis, III *foreign service officer*
Barkley, Richard Clark *ambassador*
†Basora, Adrian A. *ambassador*
Bergold, Harry Earl, Jr. *diplomat*
Berry, Ann Roper *diplomat*
Blinken, Donald *ambassador, investment banker*
Borling, John Lorin *military officer*
Boyd, Charles Graham *military officer*
Brew, William Robert *foreign service officer*
†Brown, William Andreas *ambassador*
Carioti, Bruno M. *civil engineer*
Chelberg, Robert Douglas *army officer*
Chong, Vernon *surgeon, physician, Air Force officer*
Davis, John Roger, Jr. *foreign service officer*
Doyle, Justin Emmett *lawyer, government official*
Eizenstat, Stuart E. *ambassador, lawyer*
Elson, Edward Elliott *retail and distribution executive, diplomat*
Flynn, Raymond Leo *ambassador to the Holy See, former mayor*
Gnehm, Edward W., Jr. *ambassador*
Harriman, Pamela Digby Churchill *diplomat, political activist*
Hill, Hugh Kenneth *diplomat, former ambassador*
Holbrooke, Richard Charles Albert *ambassador*
Hornblow, Michael M. *diplomat*
†Hurwitz, Edward *ambassador to Kyrgyzstan*
Hutton, Winfield Travis *management educator, management consultant*
Johnson, Darryl Norman *ambassador*
Keene, Douglas Ralph *diplomat*
Klosson, Michael *foreign service officer*
†Loftus, Thomas Adolph *ambassador*
Miles, Richard *diplomat*
Niles, Thomas Michael Tolliver *ambassador*
Norris, James Arnold *government executive*
Oaks, Robert C. *air force officer*
Petterson, Donald K. *foreign service officer, ambassador*
Pickering, Thomas Reeve *diplomat*
Quinn, Eugene Frederick *government official, clergyman*
Ray, Norman Wilson *career officer*
†Rey, Nicholas A. *ambassador*
Rickert, Jonathan Bradley *foreign service officer*
Ryerson, William Edwin *diplomat*
Santarelli, Eugene David *air force officer*
Scotti, Michael John, Jr. *military medical officer*
†Sundquist, Maria Alexandra *diplomat*
Welch, Charles David *diplomat*
Westley, John Richard *foreign service officer*
Wolters, Curt Cornelis Frederik *foreign service officer*
Yates, John Melvin *ambassador*
†Yates, Walter Harvey, Jr. *career officer*

FPO
†Allen, Lloyd Edward, Jr. *naval officer*
†Boucher, Richard A. *ambassador*
Dertadian, Richard Norman *diplomat*
Gewecke, Thomas H. *foreign service officer*
†Haskins, Michael Donald *naval officer*
†Katz, Douglas Jeffrey *naval officer*
Picotte, Leonard Francis *naval officer*
†Ryan, Thomas D. *naval officer*

PACIFIC

APO
Barry, Robert Louis *diplomat*
Blackburn, Paul Pritchard *federal agency officer*
Burghardt, Raymond Francis, Jr. *foreign service officer*
Hacker, Paul *foreign service officer*
Lambertson, David Floyd *foreign service officer*
Laney, James Thomas *ambassador, educator*
Mondale, Joan Adams *wife of former vice president of U.S.*
†Monjo, John Cameron *ambassador*
†Running, Nels *career officer*
†Teare, Richard W. *ambassador*
†Tomseth, Victor L *ambassador*
Tull, Theresa Anne *ambassador*
†Wolf, John S. *ambassador*

FPO
†Briggs, Steven Russell *naval officer*
†Chorba, Timothy A. *ambassador to Singapore*
Dantone, Joseph John, Jr. *naval officer*
Gilley, Edward Ray *school system administrator*
†Hickey, Robert Philip, Jr. *naval officer*
Hooley, James Robert *oral and maxillofacial surgeon, educator, university dean*
†Johnson, Donald C. *ambassador to Mongolia*
Ogden, Jerome Christopher *foreign service officer*

CANADA

Toronto
Fraser, Donald Alexander Stuart *mathematics educator*

ALBERTA

Banff
Fruchtman, Milton Allen *film and television producer, director*

Beaverlodge
†McElgunn, James Douglas *agriculturist, researcher*

Bentley
Manes, John Dalton *retired hospital administrator, anaesthesiologist*

Calgary
Allard, James Edward *oil company executive*
Armstrong, David Anthony *physical chemist, educator*
Ballem, John Bishop *lawyer, novelist*
Boorman, Philip Michael *chemistry educator, researcher*
†Borbridge, G. *protective services official*
Calkin, Joy Durfée *healthcare consultant, educator*
Campbell, Finley Alexander *geologist*
†Caron, Ernie M. *airport executive*
Child, Arthur James Edward *food company executive*
Cumming, Thomas Alexander *stock exchange executive*
†Curtis, John Barry *bishop*
Dixon, Gordon Henry *biochemist*
Esler, John Kenneth *artist*
Fisher, John Philip *retired printing and publishing company executive*
Forbis, Richard George *archaeologist*
Furnival, George Mitchell *petroleum and mining consultant*
Glockner, Peter G. *civil and mechanical engineering educator*
Gordon, Lorne Bertram *corporate executive*
Hagerman, Allen Reid *oil and gas company executive*
Haskayne, Richard Francis *petroleum company executive*
Hay, William Charles *professional hockey team executive*
Heidemann, Robert Albert *chemical engineering educator, researcher*
†Hollenberg, Morley Donald *research physician, educator*
Hopper, Wilbert Hill *oil industry executive*
Hriskevich, Michael Edward *oil and gas consultant*
Hugh, George M. *pipeline company executive*
Hughes, Margaret Eileen *law educator, former dean*
Hyne, James Bissett *chemistry educator, director research, consultant*
Janes, Robert Roy *museum director, archaeologist,*
Jenkins, Kevin J. *airline company executive*
Jones, Geoffrey Melvill *physiology research educator*
Kentfield, John Alan *mechanical engineering educator*
†King, Dave *professional hockey coach*
King, W. David *professional hockey coach*
Lederis, Karolis Paul (Karl Lederis) *pharmacologist, educator, researcher*
Little, Brian F. *oil company executive*
Lougheed, Peter *lawyer, former Canadian official*
MacDonald, Alan Hugh *librarian, university administrator*
Maclagan, John Lyall *petroleum company executive*
Maher, Peter Michael *university dean*
Maier, Gerald James *natural gas transmission and marketing company executive*
Malik, Om Parkash *electrical engineering educator, researcher*
Markwood, Lewis Ardra *minister*
Matthews, Francis Richard *lawyer*
McCaig, Jeffrey James *transportation company executive*
McCaig, John Robert *transportation executive*
McCready, Kenneth Frank *electric utility executive*
Mc Daniel, Roderick Rogers *petroleum engineer*
McEwen, Alexander Campbell *cadastral studies educator, former Canadian government official, surveying consultant*
McIntyre, Norman F. *petroleum industry executive*
Mc Kinnon, F(rancis) A(rthur) Richard *utility executive*
†Meek, Gerry *library director*
Melvill-Jones, Geoffrey *physician, educator*
†Meyers, Marlene O. *hospital administrator*
Monk, Allan James *baritone*
†Nassichuk, W. W. *geology research administrator*
Neale, E(rnest) R(ichard) Ward *retired university official, consultant*
†Nigg, Benno Maurus *biomechanics educator*
O'Brien, David Peter *oil company executive*
†O'Byrne, Paul J. *bishop*
Okulitch, Vladimir Joseph *geologist, university administrator*
†Paquette, Richard *airport executive*
Parkinson, Dennis *biology educator, soil biology researcher*
Perrin, Robert Maitland *solicitor, oil company executive*
Peterson, Kevin Bruce *newspaper editor, publishing executive*
Pick, Michael Claude *international exploration consultant*
Pierce, Robert Lorne *petrochemical, oil and gas company executive*
Price, Arthur Richard *petroleum company executive*
Priddle, Roland *Canadian government official*
Raeburn, Andrew Harvey *performing arts association executive, record producer*
Rasporich, Anthony Walter *university dean*
Reid, David Evans *pipeline company executive*
Rewcastle, Neill Barry *neuropathology educator*
†Richardson, J. Scott *public service administrator*
Risebrough, Doug *professional hockey team executive*
Roberts, John Peter Lee *cultural advisor, administrator, lecturer, writer*
Seaman, Daryl Kenneth *oil company executive*
Seaman, Donald Roy *investment company executive*
Sello, Allen Ralph *oil company executive*
Southern, Ronald Donald *diversified corporation executive*
Stanford, James M. *oil company executive*
Stebbins, Robert Alan *sociology educator*
†Stell, William Kenyon *neuroscientist, educator*
ter Keurs, Henk E. D. J. *cardiologist, educator*
Thomlison, Ray J. *university dean, educator*
Thorsteinsson, Raymond *geology research scientist*
Travis, Vance Kenneth *business executive*
Varadarajan, Kalathoor *educator, researcher*
Wagner, Norman Ernest *energy company executive, formerly university president*
Watanabe, Mamoru *former university dean, physician, researcher*
Yoon, Ji-Won *virology, immunology and diabetes educator, research administrator*
Zaruby, Walter Stephen *holding company executive*

Camrose
Campbell, John Douglas *minister*

Canmore
Wood, Sharon *mountaineer*

De Winton
Shutiak, James *management consultant*

Drumheller
Naylor, Bruce Gordon *museum director*

Edmonton
Adams, Peter Frederick *university president, civil engineer*
Albritton, William Leonard *physician, microbiologist*
Archer, Violet Balestreri *music educator, composer, pianist, organist, percusionist, adjudicator*
Bach, Lars *wood products engineer, researcher*
Basken, Reginald C. *communications company executive*
Bateman, William Maxwell *retired construction company executive*
Bellow, Donald Grant *mechanical engineering educator*
Bentley, Charles Fred *consulting agrologist*
Berg, Roy Torgny *retired university dean*
Bogusky, Alf *museum director*
†Burnett, George *professional hockey coach*
Clarkson, Geoffrey Peniston Elliott *company executive*
Cook, David Alastair *pharmacology educator*
Cormack, Robert George Hall *botany educator*
Cormie, Donald Mercer *investment company executive*
Cossins, Edwin Albert *biology educator, academic administrator*
Cowie, Bruce Edgar *communications executive*
†Daciuk, Myron Michael *bishop*
Davenport, Paul *university administrator, economics educator*
Davis, Wayne Alton *computer science educator*
Dewhurst, William George *physician, psychiatrist, educator, researcher*
Doyle, Wilfred Emmett *retired bishop*
†Eng, Howard *airport administrator*
Fields, Anthony Lindsay Austin *health facility administrator, oncologist, educator*
Folinsbee, Robert Edward *geologist*
Forsyth, Joseph *Canadian government official*
†Fraser, Catherine Anne *Canadian chief justice*
Freeman, Milton Malcolm Roland *anthropology educator*
†Genge, Kenneth Lyle *bishop*
Gough, Denis Ian *geophysics educator*
Green, Leslie Claude *political science and international law educator*
Green, Ted *professional hockey team coach*
Harris, Walter Edgar *chemistry educator*
Hiruki, Chuji *plant virologist, science educator*
Hislop, Mervyn Warren *health advocate administrator, psychologist*
Horton, William Russell *retired utility company executive*
Hoyt, David Lemire *musician*
Hughes, Linda J. *newspaper publisher*
Israel, Werner *physics educator*
James, Michael N. G. *crystallographer, educator*
Jones, Richard Norman *physical chemist, researcher*
Jungkind, Walter *design educator, consultant*
†Kanasewich, Ernest Roman *physics educator*
Kay, Cyril Max *biochemist*
†Kebarle, Paul *chemistry educator*
†Khanna, Faqir Chand *physics educator*
†Kitching, Peter *physics educator*
Koval, Don O. *electrical engineering educator*
Kratochvil, Byron George *chemistry educator, researcher*
Krotki, Karol Jozef *sociology educator, demographer*
Lechelt, Eugene Carl *psychology educator*
Lemieux, Raymond Urgel *chemistry educator*
Lock, Gerald Seymour Hunter *mechanical engineering educator*
Mac Neil, Joseph Neil *archbishop*
†McDougall, Donald Blake *retired provincial government library official*
McDougall, John Roland *civil engineer*
McKee, Penelope Melna *library director*
Miller, Jack David R. *radiologist, physician, educator*
Miller, Tevie *supernumary justice, academic administrator*
Morgenstern, Norbert Rubin *civil engineering educator*
Offenberger, Allan Anthony *electrical engineering educator*
Patrick, Lynn Allen *lawyer, construction company executive*
Pocklington, Peter H. *business executive*
†Poignant, Gary Donald *newspaper editor*
Prideaux, Gary Dean *linguistics educator*
†Rajotte, Ray V. *biomedical engineer, researcher*
†Reimer, Jan *mayor*
Roskin, Lewis Ross *broadcasting company executive*
†Rostad, Kenneth Leif *provincial government official*
Rostoker, Gordon *physicist, educator*
Rutter, Nathaniel Westlund *geologist, educator*
Sather, Glen Cameron *professional hockey team executive, coach*
Schmid, Horst A. *Canadian provincial administrator*
Scholefield, Peter Gordon *health agency executive*
Schurman, Donald Peter *hospital administrator*
Shoctor, Joseph Harvey *barrister, producer, civic worker*
Smith, Peter John *geographer, educator*
Smith, Richard Carlisle *history educator*
Spencer, Mary Eileen *biochemist, educator*
†Stanway, Paul William *newspaper editor*
Stelck, Charles Richard *geology educator*
Stepney, Philip Harold Robert *museum director*
Stevenson, William Alexander *retired justice of Supreme Court of Canada*
Stollery, Robert *construction company executive*
Sykes, Brian Douglas *biochemistry educator, researcher*
Thompson, Gordon William *dentist, educator*
Towers, T. Gordon *Canadian lieutenant governor*
Twa, Craighton Oliver *power company executive*
Umezawa, Hiroomi *physics educator, researcher*
Vance, Dennis Edward *biochemistry educator*
Wayman, Morris *chemical engineering educator, consultant*
Wood, John Denison *utility company executive*
Woodbridge, Linda *English language educator*

Lethbridge
Cho, Hyun Ju *veterinary research scientist*
Rand, Duncan D. *librarian*
†Sonntag, Bernard H. *agrologist, research executive*

McLennan
†Legare, Henri Francis *archbishop*

Red Deer
Donald, Jack C. *oil company executive*

Saint Paul
†Roy, Raymond *bishop*

Sherwood Park
Finlay, James Campbell *retired museum director*

Smith
Rodnunsky, Sidney *lawyer, educator, Prince of Kiev, Prince of Trabzon, Duke of Chernigov, Count of Riga, Count of Saint John of Alexandria, Baron of Vai*

BRITISH COLUMBIA

Abbotsford
Sifton, Patricia Anne *library educator*

Bamfield
Druehl, Louis Dix *biology educator*

Brentwood Bay
Carrothers, Alfred William Rooke *retired law educator*

Burnaby
Arrott, Anthony Schuyler *physics educator*
†Borden, John Harvey *entomologist, educator*
†Brandhorst, Bruce Peter *biology educator*
†Brantingham, Patricia Louise *criminology educator*
†Brantingham, Paul Jeffrey *criminology educator*
Buitenhuis, Peter Martinus *language professional, educator*
†Copes, Parzival *economist, researcher*
Kitchen, John Martin *historian, educator*

Cobble Hill
Cox, Albert Reginald *academic administrator, physician, retired*
Ling, Daniel *audiology consultant, educator emeritus, former university dean*

Duncan
Hughes, Edward John *artist*

Gibsons
Millard, Peter Tudor *English language educator*

Kaleden
Siddon, Thomas Edward *Canadian government official, environmental consultant*

Kamloops
†Cruickshank, James David *bishop*
†Sabatini, Lawrence *bishop*

Kelowna
†Muggeridge, Derek Brian *dean, engineering consultant*

Nanaimo
Margolis, Leo *marine biologist*
Meadows, Donald Frederick *librarian*
Ricker, William Edwin *biologist*

Nelson
†Mallon, Peter *bishop*

New Westminster
†Fair, James Stanley *hospital administrator*
Gunn, Roderick James *broadcast executive*
Waygood, Ernest Roy *plant physiology educator*

North Vancouver
Gibbs, David George *retired food processing company executive*
Jarrett, Anthony *business executive*
Joyner, John Brooks *museum director*
†Smith, Robert John *health facility administrator*

Penticton
Higgs, Lloyd Albert *astronomer, observatory administrator*

Powell River
Carsten, Arlene Desmet *financial executive*

Prince Rupert
Hannen, John Edward *bishop*

Richmond
Johnston, Rita Margaret *Canadian provincial government official*
Plomp, Teunis (Tony Plomp) *minister*

Saanichton
†Crozier, Lorna *poet, educator*
Little, Carl Maurice *performing arts administrator*

Salt Spring Island
Raginsky, Nina *artist*

Sidney
†Best, Melvyn Edward *geophysicist*
Bigelow, Margaret Elizabeth Barr *mycologist educator*
Davis, John Christopher *zoologist, aquatic toxicologist*
Irving, Edward *geophysicist, educator*
Kendrick, William Bryce *biology educator, author, publisher*
Mann, Cedric Robert *retired institute administrator, oceanographer*
Petrie, William *physicist*
van den Bergh, Sidney *astronomer*
Weichert, Dieter Horst *seismologist, researcher*

Sooke
Booth, Andrew Donald *former university administrator, scientist*

Summerland
Dueck, John *agricultural researcher, plant pathologist*
Looney, Norman Earl *pomologist, plant physiologist*

Vancouver
†Aalto, Madeleine *library administrator*
Aberle, David Friend *anthropologist, educator*
Aguzzi-Barbagli, Danilo Lorenzo *literature educator*
Alleyne, John *dancer, choreographer*
Ames, Michael McClean *university museum director, anthropology educator*
Andrews, John Hobart McLean *education educator*
Anglesio, Franco J. *hotel executive*
Aubke, Friedhelm *chemistry educator*
Baird, Patricia Ann *physician, educator*
Bates, David Vincent *physician, medical educator*
Batts, Michael Stanley *German language educator*
Beagrie, George Simpson *dentist, educator, dean emeritus*
Belzberg, Samuel *real estate investment professional*
Bender, Graham I. *forest products executive*
Bennett, Winslow Wood *mechanical engineer*
Bentley, Peter John Gerald *forest industry company executive*
Bentley, Thomas Roy *literary educator, writer, consultant*
Birch, Murray Patrick *oil industry executive*
Blair, Robert *animal science administrator, educator, researcher*
Bloom, Myer *physicist, educator*
Bonner, Robert William *lawyer*
Bowering, George Harry *writer*
Boyd, David William *mathematician, educator*
Buell, Thomas Allan *lumber company executive*
Bure, Pavel *professional hockey player*
Burhenne, Hans Joachim *physician, radiology educator*
Cairns, H. Alan C. *political scientist, educator*
Campbell, Bruce Alan *market research consultant*
Campbell, Jack James Ramsay *microbiology educator*
Chitty, Dennis Hubert *zoology educator*
Chow, Anthony Wei-Chik *physician*
Clark, Colin Whitcomb *mathematics educator*
Clarke, Garry Kenneth Connal *geophysics educator*
Conway, John S. *history educator*
Copp, Douglas Harold *physiologist, educator*
Craig, Kenneth Denton *psychologist, educator, researcher*
Crawford, Carl Benson *retired civil engineer, government research administrator*
Cynader, Max Sigmund *psychology, physiology, brain research educator, researcher*
Donald, Ian *wood products company executive*
Doyle, Patrick John *otolaryngologist*
Durrant, Geoffrey Hugh *retired English language educator*
†Dykk, LLoyd Henry *journalist*
Eaves, Allen Charles Edward *hematologist, medical agency administrator*
Elkins, David J. *political science educator*
Erickson, Arthur Charles *architect*
†Ericson, Richard Victor *social science and law educator, university administrator*
†Exner, Adam *archbishop*
Feaver, George A. *political science educator*
Feldman, Joel Shalom *mathematician*
Finnegan, Cyril Vincent *retired university dean, zoology educator*
Freeman, Hugh James *gastroenterology educator*
Friedman, Sydney M. *anatomy educator, medical researcher*
Froese, Victor *language educator*
Fryzuk, Michael Daniel *chemistry educator*
Gardiner, William Douglas Haig *bank executive*
Gardom, Garde Basil *former Canadian government official*
Gilbert, John Humphrey Victor *audiologist, speech scientist, educator*
Goldberg, Michael Arthur *land policy and planning educator*
Grace, John Ross *chemical engineering educator*
Granirer, Edmond Ernest *mathematician, educator*
Griffiths, Arthur R. *professional hockey team executive*
Grunder, Arthur Neil *forest products industry executive*
Hallam, Robert J. *performing company executive, consultant*
Hallbauer, Robert Edward *mining company executive*
Hardwick, David Francis *pathologist*
Hardy, Walter Newbold *physics educator, researcher*
Harwood, Brian Dennis *securities industry executive*
Haycock, Kenneth Roy *education administrator*
Head, Ivan Leigh *law educator*
Ho, Samuel Pao-San *economics educator*
Hoar, William Stewart *zoologist, educator*
Holmes, Willard *art gallery director*
Holsti, Kalevi Jacque *political scientist, educator*
Holtby, Douglas Martin *television executive*
Howard, John Lindsay *lawyer, forest industry company executive*
†Howard, T.E. *scientific and research think-tank executive*
Hudson, Donald J. *stock exchange executive*
Hume, Stephen *writer, editor*
Jackson, Stu *professional sports team executive, former university basketball coach*
James, Brian Robert *chemistry educator*
†Jewesson, Peter John *pharmacologist, educator*
Jones, David Robert *zoology educator*
Jordan, Robert Maynard *language and literature professional, educator*
Jull, Edward V. *electrical engineer, radio scientist, educator*
Jurock, Oswald Erich *real estate executive*
Keevil, Norman Bell, Jr. *mining executive*
Kesselman, Jonathan Rhys *economics educator, public policy researcher*
Key, Chapin *hospital administrator*
Kieffer, Susan Werner *geology educator*
†Kiefl, Robert Frances *physicist, educator*
Klohn, Earle Jardine *engineering company executive, consultant*
Klonoff, Harry *psychologist*
Knobloch, Ferdinand J. *psychiatrist, educator*
Knudsen, Conrad Calvert *corporate director*
Kubicek, Robert Vincent *history educator*
Ladner, Thomas E. *lawyer*
Lambert, Michael Malet *hotel company executive*
Langdon, Frank Corriston *political science educator, researcher*
Laponce, Jean Antoine *political scientist*
Larkin, Peter Anthony *zoology educator, university dean and official*
LeBlond, Paul Henri *oceanographer, educator*
Ledsome, John Russell *physician, educator*
Lindsey, Casimir Charles *zoologist*
Lipsey, Richard George *economist, educator*
Lusztig, Peter Alfred *university dean, educator*
Lysyk, Kenneth Martin *judge*
MacCrimmon, Kenneth Robert *management educator*
Mahler, Richard T. *finance executive*
March, Beryl Elizabeth *animal scientist, educator*
†Marshall, Bill *protective services official*
Mathews, William Henry *geologist, educator*
Mattessich, Richard Victor (Alvarus) *business administration educator*
McBride, Barry Clarke *microbiology and oral biology educator, research microbiologist*
McGeer, Edith Graef *neurological science educator emerita*
†McLauchlin, D. L. *building materials manufacturing executive*
Mc Lean, Donald Millis *microbiology, pathology educator, physician*
McLean, Kirk *professional hockey player*
McNeill, John Hugh *university dean*
Meisen, Axel *chemical engineer, university administrator*
Miller, Robert Carmi, Jr. *microbiology educator, university administrator*
Miura, Robert Mitsuru *mathematician, researcher, educator*
Mizgala, Henry F. *physician*
†Mulchey, Ronald Douglas *hospital administrator*
Nafe, John Elliott *geophysicist*
Nemetz, Nathaniel Theodore *lawyer, former chief justice of British Columbia*
Newman, Murray Arthur *aquarium administrator*
†Oberlander, Cornelia Hahn *landscape architect*
Overmyer, Daniel Lee *Asian studies educator*
Ozier, Irving *physicist, educator*
Pacheco-Ransanz, Arsenio *Hispanic and Italian studies educator*
†Patkau, John *architect*
†Patkau, Patricia *architect, architecture educator*
Paty, Donald Winston *neurologist*
Pearson, Richard Joseph *archaeologist, educator*
Peters, Ernest *metallurgy educator, consultant*
Peterson, Leslie Raymond *lawyer*
Phillips, Anthony George *neurobiology educator*
Phillips, Edwin Charles *gas transmission company executive*
†Phillips, John Edward *zoologist, educator*
Pickard, George Lawson *physics educator*
Pincock, Richard Earl *chemistry educator*
Piternick, Anne Brearley *librarian, educator*
Pulleyblank, Edwin George *history educator emeritus, linguist*
Quinn, Pat (John Brian Patrick Quinn) *professional sports team manager*
Raffi, (Raffi Cavoukian) *folksinger, children's entertainer*
Randall, David John *physiologist, zoologist, educator*
Riedel, Bernard Edward *retired pharmaceutical sciences educator*
Robinson, John Lewis *geography educator*
†Rootman, Jack *ophthalmologist, surgeon, pathologist, oncologist, artist*
Rothstein, Samuel *librarian, educator*
Roy, Chunilal *psychiatrist*
Russell, Richard Doncaster *geophysicist, educator, geoscientist*
Saint-Jacques, Bernard *linguistics educator*
Salcudean, Martha Eva *mechanical engineer, educator*
Saunders, Peter Paul *finance company executive*
Saywell, William George Gabriel *foundation administrator*
Seymour, Brian Richard *mathematician*
Shaw, Michael *biologist*
Shearer, Ronald Alexander *economics educator*
Sikora, Richard Innes *philosophy educator*
Sinclair, Alastair James *geology educator*
Sion, Maurice *mathematics educator*
Slaymaker, H. Olav *geography educator*
Slonecker, Charles Edward *anatomist, medical educator, author*
Smethurst, Robert Guy *lawyer*
Smith, Brian Ray Douglas *rail transportation executive, lawyer*
†Smith, Michael *biochemistry educator*
Smith, Raymond Victor *paper products manufacturing executive*
Snider, Robert F. *chemistry educator, researcher*
Solloway, C. Robert *forest products company executive*
Splane, Richard Beverley *social work educator*
Stankiewicz, Wladyslaw Jozef *political scientist, educator*
Stewart, Ross *chemistry educator*
Stone, Robert Ryrie *financial executive*
Suedfeld, Peter *psychologist, educator*
Sutter, Morley Carman *medical scientist*
Swanson, Charles Andrew *mathematics educator*
Tees, Richard Chisholm *psychology educator, researcher*
Thurlbeck, William Michael *pathologist*
Tingle, Aubrey James *pediatric immunologist, research administrator*
Trifonidis, Beverly Ann *lecturer, opera company manager, accountant*
Tyers, Geddes Frank Owen *surgeon*
Underhill, Anne Barbara *astrophysicist*
Unger, Richard Watson *history educator*
Unruh, William G. *physics educator, researcher*
Vogt, Erich Wolfgang *physicist, academic administrator*
Volkoff, George Michael *former physics educator, educational administrator*
Wakefield, Wesley Halpenny *church official*
Warner, Colin Bertram *retired forest products executive*
Warren, Harry Verney *geological sciences educator, consulting geological engineer*
Webber, William Alexander *university administrator, physician*
Wedepohl, Leonhard M. *electrical engineering educator*
Wellington, William George *plant science and ecology educator*
Wheeler, John Oliver *geologist*
White, Ruth Lillian *French language educator, researcher*
Willson, John Michael *mining company executive*
Wilson, Graham McGregor *energy company executive*
Woodcock, George *author*
Young, Lawrence *electrical engineering educator*
Zidek, James Victor *statistician, educator*

Victoria
Antoniou, Andreas *electrical engineering educator*
Barber, Clarence Lyle *economics educator*
Barkley, William Donald *museum director*
Barnes, Christopher Richard *geologist*
Batten, Alan Henry *astronomer*
Bousfield, Edward Lloyd *biologist*
Chard, Chester Stevens *archaeologist, educator*
De Roo, Remi Joseph *bishop*
†Drew, T. John *life science research administrator*
Frame, John Timothy *bishop*
Fyke, Kenneth John *hospital administrator*
Hamilton, Donald Emery *librarian*
†Harcourt, Michael Franklin *premier of Province of British Columbia*
Harris, Christie Lucy *author*
Harvey, Donald *artist, educator*
Horn, Paul Joseph *musician*
Hutchings, John Barrie *astronomer, researcher*
Lam, David *lieutenant governor*
Lind, Niels Christian *civil engineering educator*
Mac Diarmid, William Donald *physician*
Manning, Eric *computer science and engineering educator, university dean, researcher*
Mc Carter, John Alexander *biochemistry educator*
McCoppin, Peter *symphony orchestra conductor*
McTaggart-Cowan, Ian *retired university chancellor*
Morton, Donald Charles *astronomer*
Oke, John Beverley *astronomy educator*
Partridge, Bruce James *lawyer, educator*
Payne, Robert Walter *psychologist, educator*
Segger, Martin Joseph *museum director, art history educator*
Strong, David F. *university administrator*
Welch, S(tephen) Anthony *university dean, Islamic studies and arts educator*
Wiles, David McKeen *chemist*
Wright, Kenneth Osborne *former astronomer*

West Vancouver
Bentall, Shirley Franklyn *lay church leader, author*
Collins, Mary *former Canadian legislator*
Donaldson, Edward Mossop *research scientist, government official*
†Petrina, Anthony J. *mining executive, retired*
Wynne-Edwards, Hugh Robert *geologist, educator, scientist*

White Rock
Cooke, Herbert Basil Sutton *geologist, educator*
Freeze, Roy Allan *engineering consultant*
Huntington, A. Ronald *coal terminal executive*

MANITOBA

Brandon
†Robertson, John Alden *agrologist, researcher*

Churchill
†Rouleau, Reynald *bishop*

Pinawa
†Allan, Colin James *nuclear research and development company executive*

Saint Boniface
Hacault, Antoine Joseph Leon *archbishop*

The Pas
Sutton, Peter Alfred *archbishop*

Winnipeg
Alexander, Norman James *investment consultant*
Altman, Sheldon *retail company executive*
Anderson, David Trevor *law educator*
Angel, Aubie *physician, academic administrator*
Asper, Israel Harold *broadcasting executive*
Barber, Robert Charles *physics educator*
Bigelow, Charles Cross *biochemist, university administrator*
Blanchard, Robert Johnstone Weir *surgeon*
Bowman, John Maxwell *physician, educator*
Burt, Christopher Murray *former newspaper editor, communications consultant*
Cherniack, Saul Mark *non-practicing barrister, solicitor*
Cohen, Albert Diamond *merchandising executive*
Cohen, Harley *civil engineer, science educator*
Converse, William Rawson Mackenzie *librarian*
Curtis, Charles Edward *Canadian government official*
Di Cosimo, Joanne Violet *museum director*
†Dumont, W. Yvon *provincial official*
Eales, John Geoffrey *zoology educator*
Eyre, Ivan *artist*
Ferguson, Robert Bury *mineralogy educator*
Filmon, Gary Albert *Canadian provincial premier, civil engineer*
Fraser, John Foster *management company executive*
Gratzer, George Andrew *mathematics educator*
†Greenberg, Arnold Harvey *pediatrics educator, cell biologist*
Hamerton, John Laurence *geneticist, educator*
†Harder, Helmut *religious organization administrator*
Haworth, James Chilton *pediatrics educator*
†Hawthorne, Frank Christopher *geologist, educator*
Hermaniuk, Maxim *retired archbishop*
Hodne, Thomas Harold, Jr. *architect, educator*
Hogan, Terrence Patrick *psychologist, university administrator*
Housley, Phil F *professional hockey player*
†Hurst, William Donald *civil engineer, consultant*
Israels, Lyonel Garry *hematologist, medical educator*
Jarmus, Stephan Onysym *priest*
Johnson, George *lieutenant governor, physician*
Kaminski, John *dancer*
Kanfer, Julian Norman *biochemist, educator*
Kroetsch, Robert Paul *English language educator, author*
Kuffel, Edmund *electrical engineering educator*
Lang, Otto E. *industry executive, former Canadian cabinet minister*

Lehman, Edwin *minister, head of religious organization*
Liba, Peter Michael *communications executive*
Loxley, John *economics educator*
†Luetkehoelter, Gottlieb Werner (Lee) *bishop, clergyman*
Lyon, Sterling Rufus *justice*
MacKenzie, George Allan *diversified company executive*
Mantsch, Henry Horst *chemistry educator*
Matthews, Patrick John *consumer products company executive*
McGonigal, Pearl *former lieutenant governor*
†McKie, Francis Paul *journalist*
Morrish, Allan Henry *electrical engineering educator*
Naimark, Arnold *university president, physiologist, internist*
Paddock, John *professional hockey team head coach*
Persaud, Trivedi Vidhya Nandan *anatomy educator, researcher, consultant*
Poettcker, Henry *retired seminary president*
Riske, William Kenneth *arts administrator*
Roblin, Duff *Canadian senator*
Ronald, Allan Ross *internal medicine and medical microbiology educator, researcher*
Ross, Robert Thomas *neurologist, educator*
Schaefer, Theodore Peter *chemistry educator*
†Schultz, Harry *health science organization administrator*
Scott, Richard Jamieson *chief justice*
Searle, Stewart A. *transportation equipment holding company executive*
Shenkarow, Barry L. *professional hockey team executive*
Shnier, Alan *real estate executive*
Sjoberg, Donald *bishop*
Smith, Ian Cormack Palmer *biophysicist*
Smith, Michael Anthony *professional hockey team manager*
Spohr, Arnold Theodore *artistic director, choreographer*
Stalker, Jacqueline D'Aoust *academic administrator, educator*
Sutherland, John Beattie *radiologist, health center administrator*
Suzuki, Isamu *microbiology educator, researcher*
Thorfinnson, A. Rodney *hospital administrator*
Watchorn, William Ernest *diversified manufacturing executive*
†Wiebe, Bernie *conflict resolution studies educator*
Wolfart, H. C. *linguistics scholar, author, editor*
Wreford, David Mathews *magazine editor*

NEW BRUNSWICK

Dieppe
Finn, Gilbert *lieutenant governor*

Douglas
Cogswell, Frederick William *English language educator, poet, editor, publisher*

Edmundston
O'Briain, Niall P. *wood products company executive*

Fredericton
Armstrong, Robin Louis *university official, physicist*
Easterbrook, James Arthur *psychology educator*
†Edwards, Viviane M. *educator, editor*
Elkhadem, Saad Eldin Amin *foreign language and literature educator, author, editor, publisher*
Grotterod, Knut *retired paper company executive*
Kennedy, Richard Frederick *English language educator*
Kenyon, Gary Michael *gerontology educator, researcher*
†Lemmon, George Colborne *bishop*
†Lewell, Peter A. *international technology executive, researcher*
Lumsden, Ian Gordon *art gallery director*
McGeorge, Ronald Kenneth *hospital executive*
McKenna, Frank Joseph *Canadian politician, lawyer*
Ruthven, Douglas Morris *chemical engineering educator*
Valenta, Zdenek *chemistry educator*
Vaníček, Petr *geodesist*

Moncton
†Albert, Elide *architect*
Walker, Tennyson A. *corporation executive*

Rothesay
Fairweather, Robert Gordon Lee *lawyer*

Saint Andrews
Anderson, John Murray *operations executive, former university president*
Clark, David R. *executive not-for-profit organization, lawyer*
Scott, William Beverley *ichthyologist*

Saint John
Condon, Thomas J. *university historian*
Logan, Rodman Emmason *judge*
†Thomas, Martin Lewis H. *marine ecologist, educator*
†Troy, J. Edward *bishop*

NEWFOUNDLAND

Corner Brook
Payne, Sidney Stewart *archbishop*
Watts, Harold Ross *hospital administrator*

Saint John's
†Clark, Jack I. *civil engineer, researcher*
†Coady, Larry *marine biology research administrator*
†Crim, Lawrence *marine life research administrator*
Davis, Charles Carroll *aquatic biologist, educator*
Goodridge, Noel Herbert Alan *state supreme court chief justice*
Grattan, Patricia Elizabeth *art gallery director*
†Harvey, Donald F. *bishop*
Idler, David Richard *biochemist, marine scientist, educator*
†Jeffrey, N. E. *marine biology administrator*
Major, Kevin Gerald *writer*
†Mate, Martin *bishop*
May, Arthur W. *former Canadian government official, educator*
Mills, David B. *museum director*
†Murphy, John Joseph *city official, retail executive*
†Penney, Pearce John *retired librarian*

Rochester, Michael Grant *geophysics educator*
†Russell, Frederick William *Canadian provincial official*
Wells, Clyde Kirby *Canadian provincial government official*
Williams, Harold *geology educator*

NORTHWEST TERRITORIES

Iqaluit
†Williams, J. Christopher R. *bishop*

Yellowknife
Ballantyne, Michael Alan *legislator*
Cournoyea, Nellie *Canadian government official*
†Kakfwi, Steve *Canadian government official*
Patterson, Dennis Glen *Canadian government official, lawyer*

NOVA SCOTIA

Antigonish
†Campbell, Colin *bishop*

Bedford
Hennigar, David J. *investment broker*
†Randell, Joseph David *airline executive*

Dartmouth
Bhartia, Prakash *defense research management executive, researcher, educator*
Callaghan, J. Clair *corporate executive*
Elliott, James A. *oceanographer, researcher*
Keen, Charlotte Elizabeth *marine geophysicist, researcher*
Mann, Kenneth Henry *marine ecologist*
Needler, George Treglohan *oceanographer, researcher*
†Nickerson, T. B. *think-tank organization executive*
Platt, Trevor Charles *oceanographer, scientist*
†Ross, David I. *geological administrator*

Halifax
Amey, Lorne James *library science educator*
Badley, Bernard William David *health care executive, physician, educator*
Birdsall, William Forest *librarian*
Borgese, Elisabeth Mann *political science educator, author*
Calda, Pavel *waste management/environmental services executive*
Carrigan, David Owen *history educator*
Carruthers, S. George *medical educator, physician*
Dickey, John Horace *lawyer*
Duvar, Ivan Ernest Hunter *telephone company executive*
Dykstra, Mary Elizabeth *library and information science educator*
Easterbrook, Kenneth Brian *retired microbiologist*
Eayrs, James George *political scientist, educator*
Fillmore, Peter Arthur *mathematician, educator*
Flint, John E. *historian, educator*
Fowler, Charles Allison Eugene *architect, engineer*
Geldart, Donald James Wallace *physics educator*
†Gillis, John William *Canadian legislator, geologist*
Glube, Constance Rachelle *Canadian chief justice*
Gold, Edgar *marine affairs educator, mariner, lawyer*
Gold, Judith Hammerling *psychiatrist*
Goldbloom, Richard Ballon *pediatrics educator*
Gratwick, John *management consulting executive, writer, consultant*
Gray, James *English literature educator*
Hall, Brian Keith *biology educator, author*
Langley, George Ross *medical educator*
Leffek, Kenneth Thomas *chemist, educator*
Macdonald, Joseph Albert Friel *lawyer*
†MacKay-Lyons, Brian Gerald *architect, urban designer, architecture educator*
MacLean, Guy Robertson *retired university president*
Mingo, James William Edgar *lawyer*
Murray, Thomas John (Jock Murray) *former dean of medicine, medical humanities educator*
†O'Dor, Ron *physiologist, marine biology educator*
Ozmon, Kenneth Lawrence *university president, educator*
†Pringle, John D. *ecological research administrator*
Puccetti, Roland Peter *philosopher, educator*
Renouf, Harold Augustus *business consultant*
Riordon, John Bernard *museum director*
†Savage, John P. *provincial official*
Smith, Ronald Emory *telecommunications executive*
Sparling, Mary Christine *art gallery director*
Stairs, Denis Winfield *political science educator*
Thompson, William Grant *management executive*
Tonks, Robert Stanley *pharmacology and therapeutics educator, former university dean*
†Wilson, George Peter *industrial engineer*

Kentville
Baker, George Chisholm *engineering executive, consultant*

Liscomb
Hemlow, Joyce *language and literature educator, author*

Lunenburg
Morrow, James Benjamin *retired sea products company executive*

Mahone Bay
Tolmie, Kenneth Donald *artist, author*

North Sydney
Nickerson, Jerry Edgar Alan *manufacturing executive*

Parrsboro
Hatfield, Leonard Fraser *retired bishop*

Stellarton
Rowe, Allan Duncan *food products executive*
Sobey, David Frank *food company executive*
Sobey, Donald Creighton Rae *real estate developer*

Timberlea
†Verma, Surjit K. *school system administrator*

Truro
Mac Rae, Herbert Farquhar *retired college president*

Wallace
Bidwell, Roger Grafton Shelford *biologist, educator*
Boyle, Willard Sterling *physicist*

Wolfville
Bishop, Roy Lovitt *physics and astronomy educator*
Colville, David Alexander *artist*
Elliott, Robbins Leonard *consultant*
Ogilvie, Kelvin Kenneth *chemistry educator*
Zeman, Jarold Knox *history educator*

ONTARIO

Almonte
Morrison, Angus Curran *aviation executive*

Arnprior
Christie, Andrew George *military officer*

Barrie
Clune, Robert Bell *bishop*

Blenheim
Thompson, Wesley Duncan *grain merchant*

Brampton
Bastian, Donald Noel *bishop, retired*
Beaumont, Donald A. *department store chain executive*
Buckland, Charles Smillie *can company executive*
Burgis, Grover Cornelius *librarian*
Greenhough, John Hardman *business forms company executive*
Prevost, Edward James *paint manufacturing executive*
†VanDeventer, Vernon Earl *dean*

Brantford
†Woodcock, Richard Beverley *health facility administrator*

Brockville
Lafave, Hugh Gordon John *medical association executive, psychiatrist, educator, consultant*

Burlington
Cragg, Laurence Harold *chemist, former university president*
†Daley, R. J. *environmental research director*
†DeGroote, Michael G. *waste management company executive*
†Donelan, Mark Anthony *physicist*
†Elgersma, Ray *religious organization adminstrator*
†Hamilton, Donald Gordon *religious association administrator*
Harris, Philip John *engineering educator*
†Karsten, Albert *religious organization administrator*
†Krishnappan, Bommanna Gounder *fluid mechanics engineer*
Mc Carthy, Thomas James *newspaper executive*

Caledon East
Fallis, Albert Murray *microbiology educator*

Cambridge
Turnbull, Robert Scott *manufacturing company executive*
White, Joseph Charles *manufacturing and retailing company executive*

Chalk River
Buyers, William James Leslie *physicist*
Hardy, John Christopher *physicist*
Milton, John Charles Douglas *nuclear physicist*

Chatham
McGregor, Michael H. *gas company executive*
McKeough, William Darcy *investment company executive*

Clarksburg
Krueger, Ralph Ray *retired geography educator*

Cornwall
Hornby, Thomas Richard *wholesale distribution executive*
La Rocque, Eugene Philippe *bishop*

Deep River
Carmichael, Hugh *physicist*
Hanna, Geoffrey Chalmers *nuclear scientist*
Newcombe, Howard Borden *biologist, consultant*

Don Mills
Applebaum, Louis *composer, conductor*
Atwood, Margaret Eleanor *author*
Budrevics, Alexander *landscape architect*
Cormack, G. J. *real estate executive*
Craig, John Grant *finance management executive*
Di Tomaso, Nick *oil industry executive*
French, William Harold *retired newspaper editor*
Glover, Donald Robert *professional association administrator, former insurance executive*
Hanna, William Brooks *book publisher*
Heisey, William Lawrence *publisher*
Hickey, Brian Edward *publishing executive*
Koster, Emlyn Howard *geologist, educator, Canadian agency executive*
†Mascitelli, Joel *oil industry executive*
Rollason, W. Peter *corporate financial executive*
†Stoddart, Jack Elliott *publishing company executive*

Downsview
Bakht, Baidar *civil engineer, researcher, educator*
Burton, Ian *federal agency administrator, educator, environmental scientist, geographer, author, consultant*
†Dawson, D. Kirk *atmosphiric science research administrator*
Endler, Norman Solomon *psychology educator*
Forer, Arthur H. *biology educator, researcher, editor*
Moens, Peter B. *biology researcher and educator*
Page, Austin P. *property development company executive*
Pritchard, Huw Owen *chemist, educator*
Ribner, Herbert Spencer *physicist, educator*

†Tennyson, Roderick C. *aerospace scientist*
Thomas, Clara McCandless *retired English language educator, biographer*

Dundas
Jones, Frank Edward *sociology educator*
Walker, Gay Hunner Parsons (Mrs. Roger Geoffrey Walker) *science illustrator*

Dunrobin
Dickson, Brian *retired chief justice of Canada*

Etobicoke
Bahadur, Birendra *display specialist, liquid crystal researcher*
Beckley, Michael John *hotel executive*
Ecroyd, Lawrence Gerald *association executive*
Gulden, Simon *lawyer, foods and beverages company executive*
Macdonald, John Barfoot *research foundation executive*
MacKenzie, Lewis Wharton *military officer*
McGuigan, Thomas J. *engineering company executive*
Pelton, John S. *finance company executive*
Snedden, James Douglas *health service management consultant*
Stojanowski, Wiktor J. *mechanical engineer*

Fort Erie
Watson, Stewart Charles *construction company executive*

Fort Smith
†Croteau, Denis *bishop*

Galt
Dobbie, George Herbert *textile manufacturing executive*

Gloucester
Browning, Kurt *Figure Skating Champion*
†Mykytiuk, Alex P. *chemist*

Guelph
Beveridge, Terrance James *microbiology educator, researcher*
Bewley, John Derek *botany researcher, educator*
†Burnside, Edward Blair *geneticist, educator, administrator*
Danby, Kenneth Edison *artist, painter, printmaker*
Dickinson, William Trevor *hydrologist, educator*
Jorgensen, Erik *forest pathologist, educator, consultant*
Karl, Gabriel *physics educator*
Kasha, Kenneth John *crop science educator*
†McLeod, Norman Carl *librarian*
Oaks, B. Ann *plant physiologist, educator*
Sells, Bruce Howard *biomedical sciences educator*
Simpson, John Joseph *physics educator, researcher*
†Steffer, Robert Wesley *clergyman*

Hamilton
Banaschewski, Bernhard *mathematics educator*
Bandler, John William *electrical engineering educator, consultant*
Basinski, Zbigniew Stanislaw *metal physicist, educator*
Basmajian, John Varoujan *medical scientist, educator, physician*
Bienenstock, John *physician, educator*
†Blewett, David Lambert *English literature educator*
Campbell, Colin Kydd *electrical and computer engineering educator, researcher*
†Chadwick, Bruce Allen *advertising agency executive*
Childs, Ronald Frank *chemistry educator, science administrator*
Collins, John Alfred *obstetrician-gynecologist, educator*
Cowan, James Spencer *financial executive*
Crowe, Cameron Macmillan *chemical engineering educator*
Datars, William Ross *physicist, educator*
Davies, John Arthur *physics and engineering educator, scientist*
Garland, William James *engineering physics educator*
Gillespie, Ronald James *retired chemistry educator, writer*
Hill, Graham Roderick *librarian*
†Kenny-Wallace, G. A. *chemical engineer*
King, Leslie John *geography educator*
Lee, Alvin A. *literary educator, author*
Lipton, Daniel Bernard *conductor*
MacLean, David Bailey *chemistry educator, researcher*
†McAnanama, Judith *library executive*
Mc Kay, Alexander Gordon *classics educator*
McMulkin, Francis John *steel company executive*
Miles, John Frederick *manufacturing company executive*
Morrow, Robert Maxwell *mayor*
Mueller, Charles Barber *surgeon, educator*
Parnas, David Lorge *computer scientist, engineer, educator*
Phoenix, Paul Joseph *steel manufacturing company executive*
Preston, Melvin Alexander *physicist, educator*
Priestner, Edward Bernard *manufacturing company executive*
Roland, Charles Gordon *physician, medical historian, educator*
Root, L. Allen *treasurer, financial executive*
Ryan, Ellen Bouchard *psychology educator, gerontologist*
St-Aubin, Arthur *Canadian federal agency executive*
Schwarcz, Henry Philip *geologist, educator*
Shaw, Denis Martin *university dean, former geology educator*
Shaw, John Firth *orchestra administrator*
Spenser, Ian Daniel *chemist educator*
Sprung, Donald W. L. *physics educator*
Stanbury, Robert Douglas George *lawyer, executive*
Taylor, James Hutchings *chancellor, retired diplomat*
Telmer, Frederick Harold *steel products manufacturing executive*
†Thode, Henry George *chemistry educator*
†Tonnos, Anthony *bishop*
Uchida, Irene Ayako *cytogenetics educator, researcher*
Walker, Roger Geoffrey *geology educator, consultant*

Hearst
†Despatie, Roger *bishop*

Islington
Foster, John Stanton *nuclear engineer*
White, Adrian Michael Stephen *financial executive*
Wykes, Edmund Harold *retired insurance company executive*

Kanata
Colbourne, Edwin Denis *telecommunications company executive*
†Hunter, Edward Stewart *clergy member*
Morrison, John A. *health products company executive*

Kincardine
†Glynn, Peter Alexander Richard *health facility manager*

King City
Stevens, Sinclair McKnight *Canadian government official*

Kingston
Akenson, Donald Harman *historian, educator*
Bacon, David Walter *chemical engineering educator*
Batchelor, Barrington de Vere *civil engineer, educator*
Berry, John Widdup *psychologist*
Bisby, Mark Ainley *physiology educator*
Boag, Thomas Johnson *physician*
Campbell, L(ouis) Lorne *mathematics educator*
Canvin, David Thomas *biologist, educator*
Coleman, Albert John *mathematics educator*
Ewan, George Thomson *physicist, educator*
Flynn, T(homas) Geoffrey *biochemistry educator*
Furter, William Frederick *chemical engineer, university dean*
Hamilton, Albert Charles *English language educator*
Hancock, Geoffrey White *magazine editor, writer*
Kaliski, Stephan Felix *economics educator*
Kaufman, Nathan *pathology educator, physician*
Leggett, William C. *biology educator, educational administrator*
Low, James A. *physician*
Mac Kenzie, Norman Hugh *educator, writer*
McDonald, Arthur Bruce *physics educator*
McGeer, James Peter *research executive, consultant*
Meisel, John *political scientist*
Price, Raymond Alexander *Canadian government official, geologist, educator*
Read, Allan Alexander *minister*
Ribenboim, Paulo *mathematics educator*
Riley, Anthony William *German language and literature educator*
Sayer, Michael *physics educator*
Sen, Paresh Chandra *electrical engineering educator*
†Spence, Francis John *archbishop*
Spencer, John Hedley *biochemistry educator*
Stanley, James Paul *printing company executive*
Stewart, Alec Thompson *physicist*
Szarek, Walter Anthony *chemist, educator*
†Turpin, David Howard *dean*
Uffen, Robert James *geophysics educator, engineer*
Wyatt, Gerard Robert *biology educator, researcher*

Kitchener
Huras, William David *bishop*
MacDonald, Wayne Douglas *publisher*
Pollock, John Albon *broadcasting and manufacturing company executive*
†Winger, Roger Elson *church administrator*

Lions Bay
Bartholomew, Gilbert Alfred *retired physicist*

London
Alford, William Parker *physics educator*
Allan, Ralph Thomas Mackinnon *insurance company executive*
Anderson, Oliver Duncan *consulting statistician, educator*
Bancroft, George Michael *chemical physicist, educator*
Barr, Murray Llewellyn *former anatomy educator*
†Bauer, Michael Anthony *computer scientist, educator*
Bembridge, John Anthony *newspaper editor*
Borwein, David *mathematics educator*
Brooks, Vernon Bernard *neuroscientist, educator, author*
Buck, Carol Kathleen *medical educator*
Carroll, Kenneth Kitchener *biochemist, nutritionist, educator*
†Code, William Robert *geography educator, consultant*
Collins, Thomas Joseph *English language educator*
†Cornies, Larry Alan *journalist, educator*
Creighton, Dale Edward *insurance company executive*
Crncich, Tony Joseph *retired pharmacy chain executive*
Cunningham, Gordon Ross *financial executive*
Dales, Samuel *microbiologist, virologist, educator*
Davenport, Alan Garnett *civil engineer, educator*
Desbarats, Peter Hullett *journalist, academic administrator*
Dreimanis, Aleksis *emeritus geology educator*
Dunn, Wesley John *dental educator*
Edgar, Shirley Anne *librarian, educator*
Ehrman, Joachim Benedict *mathematics educator*
Frelick, Linden Frederick *hospital executive*
Fyfe, William Sefton *geochemist, educator*
Gerber, Douglas Earl *classics educator*
†Hassen, Philip C. *health facility executive*
Henderson, Robert Jules *food service executive*
Hennessey, Frank Martin *strategic planning executive*
Inculet, Ion I. *electrical engineering educator, consultant*
Johnston, Charles Bernie, Jr. *business educator*
Kimura, Doreen *psychology educator, researcher*
Laidler, David Ernest William *economics educator*
Lala, Peeyush Kanti *medical scientist, educator*
Livick, Stephen *fine art photographer*
Locke, Michael *zoology educator*
MacBain, William Halley *minister, theology educator, seminary chancellor*
Marotta, Joseph Thomas *medical educator*
McLeod, Philip R. *publishing executive*
McWhinney, Ian Renwick *physician, medical educator*
Orser, Earl Herbert *insurance company executive*
Osbaldeston, Gordon Francis *business educator, former government official*
Paivio, Allan Urho *psychology educator*
Pearson, Norman *urban planner, administrator, academic and planning consultant, writer*
†Peterson, Leslie Ernest *bishop*
Poole, Nancy Geddes *art gallery director, writer*
Quigley, Robert Murvin *engineering educator, research consultant*
Reaney, James Crerar *dramatist, poet, educator*
Roach, Margot Ruth *biophysicist, educator*
†Scott, W. Peter *bishop*
†Sherlock, John Michael *bishop*
Stewart, Harold Brown *biochemist*
Stothers, John B. *chemistry educator*
Valberg, Leslie Stephen *medical educator, physician, researcher*
†Warntz, William *theoretical geography educator*
Weedon, Alan Charles *chemist, educator*
Widdrington, Peter Nigel Tinling *professional baseball team executive*
†William, David *director, actor*
Wilson, Gerald Einar *mechanical and industrial engineer, business executive*
Wonnacott, Ronald Johnston *economics educator*
Zeigler, Earle Frederick *physical education-kinesiology educator*

Maberly
Kennett, William Alexander *retired Canadian government official, consultant*

Manotick
Hobson, George Donald *retired geophysicist*
Prince, Alan Theodore *former government official, engineering consultant*

Markham
Burns, H. Michael *financial services company executive*
Fitzhenry, Robert Irvine *publisher*
Stronach, Frank *automobile parts manufacturing executive*

Milton
Georgije, Djokic *bishop*

Mississauga
Allen, Clive Victor *lawyer, communications company executive*
Astington, John Harold *English educator*
Barkin, Martin *pharmaceutical company executive, physician*
Davies, Michael Norman Arden *lawyer, electric company executive*
DeGrandis, Donald James *communications executive*
Evans, John Robert *former university president, physician*
Hooper, Wayne Nelson *clergy member*
Lewis, William Leonard *food products executive*
†MacKinnon, David C. *research and development company executive*
Mac Knight, James *minister*
MacNaughton, John David Francis *aerospace company executive*
†Mills, Donald McKenzie *librarian*
Perkin, Reginald Lewis *physician, educator*
Peterson, Oscar Emmanuel *pianist*
Ross, Thomas McCallum *association executive*
Ryan, Noel *librarian, consultant*
Sonnenberg, Hardy *data processing company research and development executive, engineer*
†Strachen, Graham *pharmaceutical company executive*
Turnbull, Adam Michael Gordon *financial executive, accountant*
Vice, David G. *retired telecommunications company executive*
Williams, James B. *retail electronics company executive*

Mowat Block, Toronto
Rose, Jeffrey Raymond *public servant, trade union executive*

Nepean
Beare-Rogers, Joyce Louise *former research executive*
Bishop, Claude Titus *retired biological sciences research administrator, editor*
Bowness, Rick (Richard Gary Bowness) *professional hockey coach*
Cornell, Peter McCaul *economic consultant, former government official*
Firestone, Bruce M. *professional hockey team executive*
Kallmann, Helmut Max *music historian, retired music librarian*

Niagara Falls
†Mullan, Donald William *bishop*

Niagara-on-the-Lake
Newton, Christopher *artistic director*
Olley, Robert Edward *economist, educator*
Scott, Campbell *artist*

Nobleton
Embleton, Tony Frederick Wallace *retired Canadian government official*

North York
†Adelman, Howard *philosophy educator*
Arthurs, Harry William *legal educator, former university president*
Bohme, Diethard Kurt *chemistry educator*
Brown, Donald Robert *lawyer, oil company executive*
Bryant, Josephine Harriet *library executive*
Buzacott, John Alan *engineering educator*
Carrothers, Gerald Arthur Patrick *environmental and city planning educator*
Carswell, Allan Ian *physics educator*
Castel, Jean Gabriel *lawyer*
Cumming, Glen Edward *art gallery director*
Davey, Kenneth George *biologist, university official*
Davidson-Arnott, Frances E. *library science educator*
Godson, Warren Lehman *meteorologist*
Granatstein, Jack Lawrence *history educator*
Land, Reginald Brian *library administrator*
Lastman, Melvin D. *mayor*
Lee, Eugene *theatrical set designer*
Macdonald, Hugh Ian *university president emeritus, economist, educator*
MacDonald, Ian Duncan *commercial credit information executive*
MacKenzie, Donald Murray *hospital administrator*
Regan, David *brain researcher, educator*
Richmond, Anthony Henry *sociologist, emeritus educator*
Tulving, Endel *psychologist, educator*
Wleugel, John Peter *manufacturing company executive*
Woodruff, Laurie *oil industry executive*
Yarlow, Loretta *art museum director*

Nova Scotia
Pottie, Roswell Francis *science and technology consultant*

Oakville
Barlow, Kenneth James *management consultant*
Holmes, James *consumer products company executive*
Mattson, Bradford Craig *manufacturing company executive*
Wilburn, Marion Turner *library and information scientist educator, consultant*

Oshawa
Peapples, George Alan *automotive executive*

Ottawa
Allen, George W. *deputy commissioner*
Alper, Anne Elizabeth *professional association executive*
Alper, Howard *chemistry educator*
†Anderson, David *Canadian government official*
Ansary, Hassan Jaber *transportation executive*
Armstrong, Henry Conner *former Canadian government official, consultant*
Augustyn, Frank Joseph *dancer, artistic director*
Austin, Jacob (Jack Austin) *Canadian senator*
†Babcock, Elkanah Andrew *geologist*
†Barnhart, Gordon *Canadian government official*
Beauchamp, Pierre *real estate association executive*
Beaudoin, Gérald-A(rmand) *lawyer, educator, senator*
Beehan, Cathy *government official, lawyer*
Bell, Phillip Michael *curator*
Bezanson, Keith Arthur *administrative educational executive*
Blachut, Teodor Josef *research scientist*
Blais, Pierre *Canadian government minister*
Blanchard, James J. *ambassador, former governor of Michigan*
†Blondin-Andrew, Ethel *Canadian government official*
Bonin, Bernard *bank executive*
Borcoman, James Willmott *museum curator*
†Bouchard, Lucien *Canadian legislator*
†Bradford, Karleen *writer*
Brooks, David Barry *resource economist*
Brown, Jack Ernest *information scientist*
Carey, Paul Richard *biophysicist, scientific administrator*
Champagne, Andrée *Canadian government official*
†Chan, Raymond *Canadian government official*
Charest, Jean J. *Canadian government official, legislator*
†Chiasson, Donat *archbishop*
†Chrétien, (Joseph Jacques) Jean *Canadian government official, lawyer*
Clark, Charles Joseph (Joe Clark) *Canadian government official, former prime minister*
Clark, Ian Douglas *Canadian government official*
Clemenhagen, Carol Jane *health facility executive*
†Clermont, Georges C. *Canadian government official, lawyer*
Clever, W(arren) Glenn *editor, publishing executive, poet, writer, educator*
Cockshutt, Eric Philip *engineering executive, research scientist*
†Coleman, John Morley *transportation research director*
†Collenette, David *Canadian government official*
Collin, Arthur Edwin *Canadian government official*
Copeland, Miles Alexander *electrical engineer educator, consultant*
†Copps, Sheila Maureen *Canadian deputy prime minister*
Corkery, James Caldwell *Canadian government executive, mechanical engineer*
Cory, Peter deCarteret *Canadian Supreme Court justice*
Csörgö, Miklós *statistician*
Cullen, Jack Sydney George Bud *federal judge*
d'Aquino, Thomas *lawyer, business council chief executive*
Davey, Clark William *newspaper publisher*
†Davis, B. *physical science administrator*
Dawson, Donald Andrew *mathematics educator, researcher*
Deacon, Paul Septimus *retired publishing, communications company executive*
de Bold, Adolfo J. *pathology and physiology educator, research scientist*
de Chastelain, A(lfred) John G(ardyne) D(rummond) *Canadian army officer, diplomat*
Dence, Michael Robert *research director*
Dlab, Vlastimil *mathematics educator, researcher*
Doyle, Richard James *Canadian senator, former editor*
Dray, William Herbert *philosophy educator*
†Dupuy, Michel *Canadian government official*
Eastman, Harry Claude MacColl *economics educator*
Edwards, Henry Percival *psychology educator, dean*
†Eggleton, Arthur C. *member of Parliament, cabinet minister*
Emery, Alan Roy *museum executive*
Epp, Arthur Jacob *Canadian government official*
†Erickson, W. H. *Metallury administrator*
†Fairbairn, Joyce *Canadian senator*
Falconer, David Duncan *electrical engineering educator*
Fallis, Alexander Graham *chemistry educator*
†Ferron, J. *mineralogy administrator*
†Finestone, Sheila *Canadian legislator*
Flichel, Eugene Anthony *banker*
Fowler, Robert Ramsay *Canadian deputy defence minister*
Franca, Celia *ballet director, choreographer, dancer, narrator*
Frappier, Gilles *librarian*
Fraser, John Allen *Canadian government official*
Freedman, Charles *bank executive*
Friesen, Henry George *endocrinologist, educator*
Frith, Royce Herbert *Canadian senator, retired lawyer*
Georganas, Nicolas D. *electrical engineering educator*
†Gerrard, Jon *Canadian government official*
†Gervais, Marcel Andre *bishop*
Gillingham, Bryan Reginald *music educator*
Giroux, Robert-Jean-Yvon *Canadian government official*
Gold, Lorne W. *Canadian government official*
Goldbloom, Victor Charles *commissioner, pediatrician*
Gonthier, Charles Doherty *Canadian Supreme Court justice*
†Goodale, Ralph *Canadian government official*
Goulard, Guy Yvon *lawyer*
Grace, John William *Canadian government official*
†Gratton, Jean *clergyman*
Gravelle, Pierre *Canadian government official*
†Gray, Herbert Eser *canadian government official*
Griller, David *economics and technology consultant*
†Gruchy, Charles George *museum administrator*
Gussow, William Carruthers *petroleum engineer*
Hagen, Paul Beo *physician, medical scientist*
Halliday, Ian *astronomer*
Halstead, John G. H. *educator, diplomat, consultant*
Hamelin, Marcel *historian, educator*
Harington, Charles Richard *vertebrate paleontologist*
Haworth, Richard Thomas *geophysicist, science director*
Heald, Darrel Verner *Canadian federal judge*
Herzberg, Gerhard *physicist*
Hewitt, John Stringer *nuclear engineer*
Himms-Hagen, Jean Margaret *biochemist*
Hnatyshyn, Ramon John *governor general, commander in chief, lawyer*
Holmes, John Leonard *chemistry educator*
Holzman, Jacquelin *mayor*
Homulos, Peter Stephen *government executive*
Howe, Bruce Iver *government official*
Hubbard, Ruth *federal official*
Hughes, Stanley John *mycologist*
Hurteau, Gilles David *obstetrician, gynecologist, educator, university dean*
Iacobucci, Frank *lawyer, educator, jurist*
Ingold, Keith Usherwood *chemist, educator*
Inkster, Norman David *police commissioner*
†Itzkovitch, Irwin J. *metallurgy administrator*
Jackson, Charles Ian *writer, consultant*
Jackson, W. Bruce *ophthalmology educator, researcher*
Jerome, James Alexander *Canadian federal justice*
Johnson, Albert Wesley *political science educator*
Jubinville, Alain Maurice Joseph *retired economist, banker*
Karsh, Yousuf *photographer*
Kates, Morris *biochemist, educator*
†Keon, Wilbert Joseph *cardiologist, surgeon, educator*
Kind, Richard John *engineering educator*
Kingsley, Jean-Pierre *government official*
Kirkwood, David Herbert Waddington *Canadian government official*
Kitchen, Paul Howard *government and association management consultant*
Kroeger, Arthur *former Canadian government administrator, educator*
Labbé, Paul *export corporation executive*
La Forest, Gerard Vincent *justice*
LaHay, David George Michael *ballet company director*
Lamer, Antonio *Canadian supreme court chief justice*
Lander, Donald H. *postal agency executive*
Landriault, Jacques Emile *retired bishop*
Landry, Robert Edward *public policy consultant*
LaRocque, Judith Anne *federal official*
Lavoie, Lionel A. *physician, medical executive*
Legget, Robert Ferguson *civil engineer*
Lewis, Douglas Grinslade *Canadian minister, parliament member*
L'Heureux-Dube, Claire *judge*
†Lister, Earle Edward *animal science consultant*
Lithwick, Norman Harvey *economics educator*
Lossing, Frederick Pettit *chemist*
†MacDonald, Joseph Faber *bishop*
MacEachen, Allan Joseph *senator*
MacFarlane, John Alexander *former federal housing agency administrator*
MacGuigan, Mark R. *Canadian federal judge*
MacKay, William Andrew *judge*
Macklem, Michael Kirkpatrick *publisher*
MacLaren, Roy *publisher, Canadian federal legislator*
MacLeod, John Munroe *radio astronomer, academic administrator*
Mac Neill, James William *Canadian government official, international consultant*
Macphail, Moray St. John *mathematics educator emeritus*
Macquarrie, Heath Nelson *Canadian government official*
Mahoney, Patrick Morgan *judge*
Major, Jean-Louis *author, French literature educator*
†Major, John C. *judge*
Malouin, Jean-Louis *university dean, educator*
Manera, Anthony S. *broadcasting executive*
†Manley, John *Canadian government official*
†Manning, Preston *political organization worker*
†Marchi, Sergio *Canadian government official*
†Marleau, Diane *Canadian legislator*
Marleau, Robert *federal clerk*
Marmet, Paul *physicist*
†Marsters, Gerald Frederick *aerospace science and technology executive*
†Martin, Paul *Canadian federal official*
†Mayman, Shlomo Alex *engineering executive*
McAvity, John Gillis *museum director, association executive, museologist*
McCabe, Michael *broadcast executive*
McGrath, James Aloysius *Canadian provincial official*
†McGregor, G. *engineering research administrator*
McKellar, Andrew Robert *physicist, researcher*
McLachlin, Beverley *supreme court judge*
McLaren, Digby Johns *geologist, educator*
†McLaughlin, Audrey *Canadian politician*
†McLellan, A. Anne *member of Canadian parliament*
Mc Rae, Kenneth Douglas *political scientist, educator*
Mc Whinney, Edward Watson *Canadian government legislator*
Mirza, Shaukat *engineering educator, researcher, consultant*
Moore, William John Myles *electrical engineer, researcher*
Morand, Peter *research agency executive*
Morden, John Reid *Canadian federal agency administrator*
Muldoon, Francis Creighton *Canadian federal judge*
Murphy, Edmund Michael *Canadian government agency administrator, demographer*
Murray, Lowell *Canadian senator*
Nordin, Vidar John *forestry educator, consultant*

†Ouellet, André Canadian government official
Paquet, Gilles economist, university administrator
Penney, Alphonsus Liguori archbishop
Pepin, Jean-Luc retired Canadian government official, political science lecturer
Peppler, William Norman aviation association executive
Perrault, Raymond Canadian legislator, senator
Perry, Malcolm Blythe biologist
†Peters, Douglas Dennison member of parliament
Philogene, Bernard J. R. academic administrator, science educator
Poulin, Marie-Paule Canadian government official
Puddington, Ira Edwin chemist
Ramsay, Donald Allan physical chemist
Rawson, Bruce Strathearn government official, lawyer
Redhead, Paul Aveling physicist
Redway, Alan Arthur Sydney Canadian legislator, lawyer
Reid, Timothy business organization executive
Robertson, Robert Gordon retired Canadian government official
†Robichaud, Fernand Canadian government official
Robichaud, Louis Joseph Canadian senator
†Rock, Allan Michael federal official
Roland, Anne registrar Supreme Court of Canada
Roots, Ernest Frederick scientific advisor emeritus
Rummery, Terrance Edward nuclear engineering executive, researcher
Ryan, William Francis priest
†St. Germain, Gerry member of parliament
St-Onge, Denis Alderic geologist, research scientist
Schneider, William George chemist, research consultant
Scott, Marianne Florence librarian, educator
Seaden, George civil engineer
Sharp, Mitchell William adviser to prime minister
Shaw, Edgar Albert George research association executive
Sheflin, Michael John Edward transportation commissioner
†Shoemaker, John Michael law enforcement official
†Siebrand, Willem theoretical chemist, science editor
Sinha, Ramesh Chandra plant pathologist
Smith, Wilfred Irvin former Canadian government official
Soper, James Herbert botanist, curator
Sopinka, John Supreme Court of Canada justice
Spicer, Erik John retired Canadian parliamentary librarian
Squire, Anne Marguerite religious leader
Staines, David McKenzie English educator
Stanford, Joseph Stephen federal official, diplomat, lawyer
†Stewart, Christine Susan Canadian legislator
†Stone, Jeffrey Jay film critic, journalist, writer
Storey, Kenneth Bruce biology educator
Suthren, Victor J. H. museum director
Sylvestre, Jean Guy former national librarian of Canada
Szlazak, Anita Christina Canadian government official
Tait, John Charles Canadian deputy minister of justice
Tassé, Roger lawyer, former Canadian government official
Templeton, Ian Malcolm physicist
Thibault, J(oseph) Laurent service company executive
Thomson, Shirley Lavinia museum director
†Tobin, Brian Canadian government official
Topp, George Clarke soil physicist
†Torgerson, David Franklyn chemist, research facility administrator
Urie, John James lawyer, retired Canadian federal judge
Vallance-Jones, Alister physicist
Varshni, Yatendra Pal physicist
Veizer, Ján geology educator
Wallot, Jean-Pierre archivist, historian
Watt, Robert Douglas Canadian government official
Waugh, Douglas Oliver William pathology educator
Weatherill, John Frederick William arbitrator
Weiner, Gerry government official
Whitehead, J. Rennie science consultant
Whitham, Kenneth science and technology consultant
Whyte, Anne Veronica social science researcher, educator
Wilson, Bertha Canadian justice
Withers, Ramsey Muir government consultant, former government official
Yalden, Maxwell Freeman Canadian diplomat
Yeomans, Donald Ralph Canadian government official, consultant
†Young, Doug Canadian government official

Owen Sound
Adams, John David Vessot manufacturing company executive
Jones, Phyllis Edith nursing educator
Morley, Lawrence Whitaker geophysicist, remote sensing consultant

Pembroke
†Windle, Joseph Raymond bishop

Petawawa
†Elchuk, Steve chemist

Peterborough
†Doyle, James Leonard bishop
Hutchinson, Thomas Cuthbert ecology and environmental educator
Symons, Thomas H. B. historian, educator
Theall, Donald Francis retired university president
Young, Scott Alexander television journalist, author

Pontypool
Kniewasser, Andrew Graham company director

Rexdale
Gregory, James Michael professional hockey league executive
Hyland, Geoffrey Fyfe energy company executive
†Joseph, Emanuel church administrator
Lutgens, Harry Gerardus food company executive
Stermac, Anthony George professional association executive

Richmond Hill
Bolton, Charles Thomas astronomer
Fernie, John Donald astronomer, educator
Garrison, Robert Frederick astronomer, educator
Howe, James Tarsicius insurance company executive
MacRae, Donald Alexander astronomy educator
Marshall, Donald Stewart company executive

Ridgeway
Jacobs, Eleanor Alice retired clinical psychologist, educator

Rockwood
Eichner, Hans German language and literature educator

Saint Catharines
O'Mara, John Aloysius bishop
Terasmae, Jaan geology educator
White, Terrence Harold academic administrator, sociologist

Saint Catherines
Florio, Ermanno conductor, music administrator

Sault Sainte Marie
Banerjee, Samarendranath orthopedic surgeon
Savoie, Leonard Norman transportation company executive

Scarborough
Bassnett, Peter James librarian
Besse, Ronald Duncan publishing company executive
†Inkpen, Ross McKay publishing company executive
†Isley, John Charles publishing company executive
†Krajicek, Mark Andrew lawyer
Mitchell, Arthur Harris newspaper columnist
Sparshott, Francis Edward poet, educator

Schumacher
†Lawrence, Caleb James bishop

Spencerville
†Farley, Lawrence clergyman

St Catharines
Fulton, Thomas Benjamin retired bishop

Stittsville
Tellier, Henri retired Canadian military officer

Stratford
Neville, John actor, director

Sudbury
Havel, Jean Eugène Martial author, educator

Thornbury
Keyes, Gordon Lincoln history educator

Thornhill
Nimmons, Phillip Rista composer, conductor, clarinetist, educator

Thunder Bay
†Harrison, Karen A. library director
Locker, J. Gary university official, civil engineering educator
Rosehart, Robert George university president, chemical engineer

Timmins
†Cazabon, Gilles bishop

Toronto
Aird, John Black lawyer, university official, former lieutenant governor
Alberti, Peter William otolaryngologist
Allen, Peter Ackerman mining executive
Alomar, Roberto Velazquez professional baseball player
Anderson, Reid Bryce ballet company artistic director
Apple, B. Nixon lawyer
†Arnold, Neil David farm and industrial equipment company executive
Arthur, James Greig mathematics educator
Astman, Barbara Ann artist, educator
Athanassoulas, Sotirios (Sotirios of Toronto) bishop
Atkinson, Lloyd Charles bank executive
Atwood, Harold Leslie physiology and zoology educator
Baillie, Alexander Charles, Jr. banker
Balderrama, Fernando Hiriart electrical utility company executive
Balmain, Keith George electrical engineering educator, researcher
Bandeen, Robert Angus management corporation executive
Barford, Ralph MacKenzie investment executive
Barrett, Matthew W. bank executive
Beckwith, John musician, composer, educator
Beigie, Carl Emerson economist, research administrator, educator
Bell, J. A. Gordon retired banker
Belzberg, Brent Stanley financial executive
Berton, Pierre journalist, author
Bickford, James Gordon banker
Birnbaum, Eleazar language proffessional
Black, Conrad Moffat publishing corporate executive
Blissett, William Frank English literature educator
Blundell, William Richard Charles electric company executive
Bodsworth, Fred author, naturalist
Boland, Janet Lang judge
Bone, Bruce Charles mining and manufacturing executive
Bonnycastle, Lawrence Christopher retired corporate director
†Boot, Sonja Sunni media specialist
Boswell, Philip John opera administrator
Bouissac, Paul Antoine language professional
Boultbee, John Arthur publishing executive
Bradshaw, Richard James conductor
Braithwaite, J(oseph) Lorne real estate executive
Brendon, Rupert Timothy Rundle advertising agency executive
Bristow, David Ian lawyer
Brook, Adrian Gibbs chemistry educator
Brooks, Robert Leslie bank executive
Brown, Gregory Michael psychiatrist, educator, research director
Brown, W. Michael publishing compnay executive
Bruce, William Robert physician, educator
†Brumer, Paul William chemical physicist, educator
†Bunting, Christopher Henry public relations executive
Burns, Pat professional hockey coach
Bush, John Arthur Henry mining company executive, lawyer
Buttrick, John Arthur economist, educator
Cable, Howard Reid composer, conductor
Cameron, Peter Alfred Gordon corporate executive
Campbell, Donald Graham communications company executive
Carder, Paul Charles advertising executive
Carnegie, James Gordon association executive
Carter, Gerald Emmett retired archbishop
Carter, Joseph Chris (Joe Carter) professional baseball player
†Casson, Alan Graham thoracic surgeon, researcher
Caty, J. Charles investment association executive
Chalupka, Edward Stephen professional sports association executive
Chodos, Robert Irwin editor, writer
Cinader, Bernhard immunologist, gerontologist, scientist, educator
Clancy, Louis John newspaper editor, journalist
Clark, Samuel Delbert sociology educator
Clarkson, Max Boydell Elliott printing company executive, business educator
Cobbold, Richard Southwell Chevallier biomedical engineer, educator
Cockwell, Jack Lynn financial executive
Cohen, Marshall diversified international corporation executive
Coleman, John Hewson financial consultant
Colgrass, Michael Charles composer
Collins, Jerry Allan association executive
Colombo, John Robert poet, editor, writer
Conacher, Desmond John classics educator
Connell, Philip Francis food industry executive
Cook, Stephen Arthur mathematics and computer science educator
Cooper, Marsh Alexander mining company executive
Corrigan, Harold Cauldwell accountant
Cowan, Charles Gibbs lawyer, corporate executive
Coxeter, Harold Scott Macdonald mathematician
Crawley, Alexander Radford performing artist, composer
Crean, John Gale hat manufacturer
Creighton, John Douglas newspaper publisher
†Cruickshank, John Douglas newspaper editor
†Cryer, Thomas Wilfred chartered accountant
Cullen, Barry John professional hockey player
Dale, Robert Gordon business executive
Davies, Robertson author
Davis, (Horace) Chandler mathematics educator
Davis, William Grenville lawyer, former premier of Ontario
Davison, Edward Joseph electrical engineering educator
Deacon, David Emmerson advertising executive
Dean, William George geography educator
De Groot, John real estate development executive
Dembroski, George Steven investment banker
DeMone, Robert Stephen hotel company executive
Denham, Frederick Ronald management consultant
Diamond, Abel Joseph architect
Dickens, Bernard Morris law educator
Dimma, William Andrew real estate executive
Dodd, Lionel G. holding company executive
Doherty, Tom (Thomas Storen, Jr.) art director, set designer
Donais, Gary Warren lawyer
Downing, John Henry newspaper editor, journalist, columnist
Dryer, Douglas Poole retired philosophy educator
Dubin, Charles Leonard federal judge
Dunford, Robert A. diversified business executive
Dunlop, David John geophysics educator, researcher
Dyment, John Joseph financial executive
Eagles, Stuart Ernest business executive
Ediger, Nicholas Martin energy resources company executive, consultant
Egan, Vincent Joseph journalist, newspaper columnist
†Egoyan, Atom film director
Eisen, Leonard food and retail company executive
Eklof, Svea Christine ballet dancer
Eldred, Gerald Marcus performing arts association executive
Elliott, R(oy) Fraser lawyer, holding and management company executive
Ellis, Peter Hudson health science facility administrator
Elting, Everett E. advertising agency executive
Endrenyi, Janos research engineer
Evans, Gregory Thomas commissioner, retired justice
Eyton, John Trevor lawyer, business executive
Falle, Daisy Carolyne professional society administrator
Farquharson, Gordon MacKay lawyer
Fasick, Adele Mongan library science educator
Feldbrill, Victor conductor
Ferguson, Kingsley George psychologist
Fernandez, Tony (Octavio Antonio Castro Fernandez) baseball player
Fierheller, George Alfred communications company executive
Fife, Edward H. landscape architecture educator
Finlay, Terence Edward bishop
Fletcher, Cliff professional hockey team executive
Flood, A. L. (Al Flood) bank executive
Fowke, Edith Margaret Fulton author, English language educator emeritus
Fraser, William Neil government official
Freedman, Harry composer
†Freedman, Theodore Jarrell healthcare executive
Freeman, Graham P. M. food company executive
Friedlander, John Benjamin mathematics educator
Friendly, Lynda Estelle theatre marketing and communications executive
†Friesen, James pediatrics research administrator
Fullerton, R. Donald banker
Furse, James Robert communications industry executive
Gairdner, John Smith securities investment dealer
Galloway, David Alexander publishing company executive
Ganczarczyk, Jerzy Jozef civil engineering educator, wastewater treatment consultant
Ganoza-Becker, Maria Clelia biochemistry educator
Gardner, John Robert insurance company executive
Gartner, Michael Alfred professional hockey player
Gaston, Cito professional baseball manager
Gee, Gregory Williams lawyer
George, Peter James economist, educator
Gillespie, Alastair William former Canadian government official
Gillick, Patrick professional baseball team executive
†Gilmour, Doug professional hockey player
Glasco, Kimberly ballet dancer
Godfrey, John Morrow lawyer, retired Canadian senator
Godfrey, Paul Victor newspaper publisher
Godsoe, Peter Cowperthwaite banker
Goffart, Walter André history educator
Goldberg, David Meyer biochemistry educator
Goldenberg, Andrew Avi mechanical engineering educator
Goldenberg, Gerald Joseph physician, educator
Goldfarb, Martin sociologist
Goodrich, Maurice Keith business forms, systems and services company executive
Goring, David Arthur Ingham chemical engineering educator, scientist
Goring, Peter Allan Elliott real estate executive
Gotlib, Lorraine justice, former lawyer
Gotlieb, Allan E. former ambassador
Gotlieb, Calvin Carl computer scientist, educator
Gotlieb, Phyllis Fay Bloom author
Graham, Allister P. diversified company executive
Graham, James Edmund service management executive
Graham, John Webb lawyer
Graham, Kathleen Margaret (K. M. Graham) artist
Graham, Victor Ernest French language educator
Grayson, Albert Kirk Near Eastern studies educator
Greben, Stanley Edward psychiatrist, educator, author, editor
Greenwood, Lawrence George banker
Gregor, Tibor Philip management consultant
Greig, Thomas Currie retired financial executive
Greiner, Peter Charles mathematics educator, researcher
Grendler, Paul Frederick history educator
Griffin, Scott manufacturing executive
Grosland, Emery Layton banker
Grossman, Irving architect
Halperin, John Stephen mathematics educator
Ham, James Milton engineering educator
Hankinson, James Floyd business executive
Harris, Nicholas George publisher
Hartley, Stuart Leslie diversified company executive, accountant
Harvey, George Edwin communications company executive
Harwood, Vanessa Clare ballet dancer
Hawton, Robert P. advertising executive
Hayes, Derek Cumberland banking executive, lawyer
Hayhurst, James Frederick Palmer career and business consultant
Hayne, David Mackness retired French language educator
Haynes, Robert Hall biophysicist, educator
Helleiner, Gerald Karl economics educator
Hentgen, Patrick George professional baseball player
Herbert, Stephen W. hospital executive
Hirst, Peter Christopher consulting actuary
Hofmann, Theo biochemist, educator
Hollander, Samuel economist, educator
Honderich, Beland Hugh publisher
Honderich, John Allen newspaper editor
Hore, John Edward commodity futures educator
Horsey, William Grant corporation executive
Houston, Stanley Dunsmore public relations executive
Hudson, Alan Roy neurosurgeon, medical educator, hospital administrator
Hungerford, John Girdlestone foundation executive
Hurlbut, Robert St. Clair finance company executive
Iannuzzi, Daniel Andrew publishing and broadcasting executive
Innanen, Larry John lawyer, food products executive
Irwin, Samuel Macdonald toy company executive
Israelievitch, Jacques H. violinist, conductor
Ivey, Donald Glenn physics educator
Jackman, Henry Newton Rowell Canadian provincial official
Jackson, Bruce Leslie publishing company financial executive
Jacob, Ellis entertainment company executive
James, Robert Scott historic organization executive
†James, William mining company executive
Janischewskyj, Wasyl electrical engineering educator
Jay, Charles Douglas religion educator, college administrator, clergyman
Jervis, Robert E. chemistry educator
Jewison, Norman Frederick film producer, director
†Johnson, Robert Eugene historian, academic administrator
Johnston, Malcolm Carlyle bank executive
Johnston, Robert Donaghy cultural organization administrator
Jolley, David newspaper executive
Kain, Karen Alexandria ballet dancer
†Kaiser, Nicholas physicist, educator
Kalant, Harold pharmacology educator, physician
Kalow, Werner pharmacologist, toxicologist
Karakas, Rita S. television broadcast executive
Kay, James Fredrick retailer
Keenan, Anthony Harold Brian catalog company executive
Kerr, David Wylie natural resource company executive
Kidd, Robert Hugh financial executive, accountant
King, John Charles Peter newspaper editor
Kirby, Charles William, Jr. dancer, choreographer
Kluge, Holger banking executive
Koken, Bernd Krafft forest products company executive
Korey-Krzeczowski, George J. M. Kniaz university administrator, management consultant
Korthals, Robert W. bank executive
Kosich, George John retail executive
Kossuth, Selwyn Barnett trade association consultant
Kostuch, Mitchell John venture capital company executive, publisher
Kovrig, Bennett political scientist, educator
Kramer, Burton graphic designer, educator
Kresge, Alexander Jerry chemistry educator
Kruger, Arthur Martin economics educator, university official
†Kudelka, James ballet dancer, choreographer
Kuerti, Anton Emil pianist, composer
Kunov, Hans biomedical and electrical engineering educator
Kushner, Eva academic administrator, educator, author
†Kutz-Harder, Helga religious organization executive
†Kuwabara, Bruce Bunji architect
Landsberg, Michele journalist
Lane, Patrick poet
Lanthier, John Spencer accounting company executive
Lanthier, Ronald Ross retired manufacturing company executive
Laurie, John Veldon business financial executive, accountant
Lavoie, Serge principal dancer

Leech, James William *manufacturing and technology company executive*
†Lewis, Robert *periodical editor, journalist*
L'Heureux, Willard John *real estate lawyer*
Light, Walter Frederick *telecommunications executive*
Lindsay, Roger Alexander *investment executive*
Lindsay, William Kerr *surgeon*
Lipowski, Zbigniew Jerzy *psychiatrist, educator*
List, Roland *physicist, educator, former UN official*
Litherland, Albert Edward *physics educator*
Livergant, Harold Leonard *health services executive*
Liversage, Richard Albert *zoologist, educator*
Logan, Frank Henderson *banker*
Lombardi, John Barba-Linardo *broadcasting executive*
Lowe, Donald Cameron *corporate director*
Lowry, Glenn David *art gallery director*
Lowy, Frederick Hans *psychiatrist, university center director, former university dean*
Lyons, Joseph Chisholm *lawyer*
Macaulay, Colin Alexander *mining engineer*
Macaulay, Hugh L. *retail company executive*
Macdonald, Donald Stovel *lawyer*
MacDougall, Hartland Molson *trust company executive*
MacIntosh, Robert Mallory *association executive*
Mack, Edward Gibson *retired business executive*
Mackiw, Vladimir Nicholaus *metallurgical consultant*
MacLennan, David Herman *research scientist, educator*
MacLeod, William Brian *hospital executive*
Mak, Tak Wah *biochemist*
Malloy, Michael Terrence *journalist, newspaper editor*
Mann, George Stanley *real estate and financial services corporation executive*
Manning, Charles Terrill *lawyer*
Marshall, Marvin Giffin *real estate company executive*
Marshall, Paul Macklin *oil company executive*
Martin, Robert William *utilities executive, retired*
†Matathia, Ira Leslie *advertising agency executive*
Matthews, Paul Deacon *steel company executive*
†McAuliffe, Jane Dammen *Middle Eastern and Islamic studies educator*
McClymont, Kenneth Ross *power systems engineer, consultant*
†McCoomb, Lloyd A. *transportation executive*
Mc Culloch, Ernest Armstrong *physician, educator*
Mc Gibbon, Pauline Mills *former Canadian government official, former university chancellor*
McGiverin, Donald Scott *retail company executive*
†McKenna, Marianne *architect*
McMurtry, R. Roy *chief justice*
McNeil, John D. *insurance company executive*
McNeill, John *museum administrator*
McNeill, K(enneth) G(ordon) *medical physicist*
†Meadows, George Lee *communications company executive*
Meagher, George Vincent *mechanical engineer*
†Mercier, Eileen Ann *forest products executive*
Mercurio, Renard Michael *real estate corporation executive*
Michals, George Francis *investment and business development executive*
Miller, Anthony Bernard *physician, medical researcher*
Miller, Anthony G. *advertising executive*
Millgate, Michael (Henry) *retired English educator*
Minto, Clive *retail company executive*
Moffat, John William *physics educator*
Molitor, Paul Leo *professional baseball player*
Montgomery, Donald Russell *labor consulting firm executive*
Moore, Carole Irene *chief librarian*
Morey, Carl Reginald *musicologist, academic administrator*
†Morgan, Peter F. *English educator, philosophy educator*
Morgan, Wayne Philip *art and popular culture exhibition producer*
Moriyama, Raymond *architect*
Morra, Bernadette *fashion journalist, columnist*
Mowat, Farley McGill *writer*
Munk, Peter *mining executive*
Munro, John Henry Alexander *economics educator, writer*
Murasugi, Kunio *mathematician, educator*
Murray, Anne *singer*
Mustard, James Fraser *research institute executive*
Naldrett, Anthony James *geology educator*
Nesbitt, Lloyd Ivan *podiatrist*
Nesbitt, Mark *management consultant*
Neufeld, Edward Peter *economist*
Newman, Peter Charles *journalist*
Nisbet, Joanne *ballet mistress*
Norris, Geoffrey *geology educator, consultant*
Nuttall, Grant *oil company executive*
Oberlander, Ronald Y. *paper manufacturing company executive*
O'Brien, Michael John *classics educator*
Ogilvie, Richard Ian *clinical pharmacologist*
Oland, Sidney M. *brewing and entertainment company executive*
Olerud, John Garrett *professional baseball player*
Oliphant, Betty *ballet school director*
†Olive, David Michael *magazine writer, magazine editor*
Osborne, Ronald Walter *communications executive*
Osler, Gordon Peter *retired utility company executive*
Ostry, Bernard *broadcasting executive*
Ostry, Sylvia *economist*
Owens, Joseph *clergyman*
Packer, Katherine Helen *retired library educator*
Pankratz, Henry J. *management consultant*
Parr, James Gordon *writer*
†Payne, Thomas Charles *architect*
Payton, Thomas William *corporate executive*
Pedersen, Paul Richard *composer, educator*
Peterson, David Robert *former premier of Ontario*
Peterson, Robert Byron *petroleum company executive*
Petrillo, Leonard Philip *corporate securities executive, lawyer*
Plaut, Wolf Gunther *minister, author*
Polanyi, John Charles *chemist, educator*
Porter, Ivan *company executive*
Posluns, Wilfred M. *manufacturing and retailing company executive*
Potts, Douglas Gordon *neuroradiologist*
†Potvin, Felix *professional hockey player*
Powis, Alfred *natural resources company executive*
Pratt, Robert Cranford *political scientist, educator*
Prichard, John Robert Stobo *academic administrator, law educator*
Prugovecki, Eduard *mathematical physicist, educator, author*
Rae, Robert Keith *Canadian premier of Ontario*
Rakoff, Vivian Morris *psychiatrist, writer*
Rapoport, Anatol *peace studies educator, mathematical biologist*
Rapson, William Howard *chemical engineering educator*
Rasky, Harry *producer, director, writer*
Rathke, Sheila Wells *advertising and public relations executive*
†Rauhala, Ann Elaine *newspaper editor, columnist*
Redford, Donald Bruce *historian, archaeologist*
Reid, Terence C. W. *corporation executive*
Rhodes, Andrew James *medical microbiologist*
Rickerd, Donald Sheridan *foundation executive*
Rimrott, Friedrich Paul Johannes *engineer, educator*
Ritchie, Cedric Elmer *banker*
Rogers, Edward Samuel *communications company executive*
Rogers, Harry G. *Canadian government official*
Roman-Barber, Helen *corporate executive*
Rombout, Luke *museum designer, administrator*
Ronald, Thomas Iain *financial services executive*
Ronald, William *artist*
Rooney, Paul George *mathematics educator*
Ross, Henry Raymond *advertising executive and legal counsel*
Ross, Murray George *social science educator, university president emeritus*
Rothstein, Aser *radiation biology educator*
Rowe, David John *physics educator*
Runnalls, (Oliver) John (Clyve) *nuclear engineering educator*
Rusnell, Joanne D. *brewery, entertainment business executive*
Ryan, James Franklin *oil company executive*
Saddlemyer, Ann (Eleanor Saddlemyer) *English educator, critic, theater historian*
Salama, C. Andre Tewfik *electrical engineering educator*
Salter, Robert Bruce *orthopaedic surgeon, researcher, educator*
Schaefer, Carl Fellman *artist*
Scheininger, Lester *lawyer, administrator religious organization*
Schogt, Henry Gilius *foreign language educator*
Schramek, Tomas *ballet dancer*
†Schwenger, Frances *library director*
Scott, Steven Donald *geology educator, researcher*
Seagram, Norman Meredith *corporate executive*
Seaquist, Ernest Raymond *astronomy educator*
Sedra, Adel Shafeek *electrical engineering educator, university administrator*
Seeman, Philip *pharmacology educator, neurochemistry researcher*
Seltzer, Ronald *retail company executive*
Semak, Michael William *photographer, educator*
Semlyen, Adam *electrical engineering educator*
Sessle, Barry John *university administrator, researcher*
†Shaffer, Donald S. *retail executive*
Sharpe, Charles Richard *retail company executive*
Shaw, Ian Alexander *accountant, mining company executive*
Shearing, George Albert *pianist, composer*
Sheinin, Rose *biochemist, educator*
†Shields, Carol Ann *writer, educator*
Silk, Frederick C.Z. *consumer products company executive*
Silver, Malcolm David *pathologist, educator*
Singleton-Wood, Allan James *publishing executive*
Skinner, Alastair *accountant*
Skvorecky, Josef Vaclav *English educator, novelist*
Slemon, Gordon Richard *electrical engineering educator*
Sloan, David Edward *corporate director*
Smith, David Todd *publishing company executive*
Smith, Kenneth Carless *electrical engineering educator*
Smith, Peter William Ebblewhite *electrical engineering educator, scientist*
Smith, Raymond *dancer*
Smith, Stephen Alexander *retail and wholesale food distribution company executive*
†Sole, Michael Joseph *cardiologist*
Sopko, Michael D. *mining company executive*
Stackhouse, Richard Gilbert *retired financial company executive*
Stadelman, William Ralph *foundation executive*
Stavro, Steve A. *professional hockey team executive*
Stefanschi, Sergiu *dancer*
Stoicheff, Boris Peter *physicist, educator*
Strong, Maurice Frederick *hydro-electric power company executive, former United Nations official*
Styles, Richard Geoffrey Pentland *retired banker*
Synan, Edward Aloysius, Jr. *clergyman, former institute president*
Tall, Franklin David *mathematician, neurolinguistic programming master practitioner*
Taylor, Allan Richard *banker*
Taylor, Harry William *physics educator*
Taylor, Paul Albert *banker*
Ten Cate, Arnold Richard *dentistry educator*
Thall, Burnett Murray *newspaper executive*
Thomas, Alan Richard *natural resources products executive*
Thomas, Kenneth Glyndwr *mining executive*
†Thomson, Kenneth R. (Lord Thomson of Fleet) *publishing executive*
Thomson, Richard Murray *banker*
†Thornley, Shirley Blumberg *architect*
Tidwell, Thomas Tinsley *chemistry educator*
Tighe, James C. *publisher*
Till, James Edgar *scientist*
Tobe, Stephen Solomon *zoology educator*
Tremaine, Scott Duncan *astrophysicist*
Tsui, Lap-Chee *molecular genetics educator*
†Turner, Craig *journalist*
Turner, Gerald Phillip *hospital administrator*
Turner, John Napier *former prime minister of Canada, legislator*
Turner, Peter Merrick *retired manufacturing company executive*
Turner, Robert Edward *psychiatrist, educator*
Tushingham, (Arlotte) Douglas *museum administrator*
Vance, James *retired manufacturing company executive, lawyer*
van Ginkel, Blanche Lemco *architect, educator*
Van Houten, Stephen H. *manufacturing company executive*
Venetsanopoulos, Anastasios Nicolaos *electrical engineer, educator*
†Venter, Ronald Daniel *mechanical engineering educator, researcher, administrator*
Volpé, Robert *endocrinologist*
Walker, Ronald C. *oil company executive*
Ward, Duane *professional baseball player*
†Watson, Paul *photojournalist*
Webb, Anthony Allan *banker*
†Webster, Jill Rosemary *historian, educator*
Weldon, David Black *financial executive*
Weston, Willard Galen *diversified holdings executive*
Wetzel, Heinz *foreign language educator*
Wevers, John William *retired Semitic languages educator*
Whaley, John Alexander *finance company executive, lawyer*
White, Calvin John *zoo executive, financial manager, zoological association executive*
White, Devon Markes *professional baseball player*
Whittington, Stuart Gordon *chemistry educator*
Wilder, Valerie *ballet company director*
Wiley, Judith *association executive*
Wilkins, Ormsby *music director, conductor, pianist*
Wilson, Ian Edwin *cultural organization administrator, archivist*
Wilson, Lois M. *minister*
Wilson, Thomas Arthur *economics educator*
Winter, Frederick Elliot *fine arts educator*
Witkowsky, Gizella *dancer*
Wolfe, Harold Joel *lawyer, business executive*
Wolfe, Jonathan A. *food wholesaler, retailer*
Wonham, Walter Murray *electrical engineer, educator*
Wood, Neil Roderick *real estate development company executive*
Worton, Ronald Gilbert *geneticist, educator*
†Yates, Keith *chemistry educator*
Yip, Cecil Cheung-Ching *biochemist, educator*
Zemans, Joyce Pearl *art historian, Canadian arts administrator*
Zimmerman, Adam Hartley *mining and forest industries company executive*

Toronto-Etobicoke
Kurys, Jurij-Georgius *environmental engineer, scientist, consultant*

Unionville
Nichols, Harold Neil *corporate executive, former pipeline company executive*
†Rusnak, Michael *bishop*
Suddick, Patrick Joseph *defense systems company executive*

Vanier
Davidson, Alexander T. *geographer, professional society administrator*

Waterdown
Hawkrigg, Melvin Michael *finance company executive*

Waterloo
Aczel, Janos Dezso *mathematics educator*
Berczi, Andrew Stephen *academic administrator*
Carty, Arthur John *university dean*
Cornell, Paul Grant *history educator*
Downey, James *university president*
Falding, Harold Joseph *sociology educator*
Fisher, Edward Joseph *optometrist, educator*
Gladwell, Graham Maurice Leslie *mathematician, civil engineering educator*
Green, Arthur Nelson *artist, educator*
Haworth, Lawrence Lindley *philosophy educator*
Hynes, Hugh Bernard Noel *biology educator*
†Kay, Jeanne *dean, educator*
†Kraus, Michael *minister*
MacGregor, Kenneth Robert *former insurance company executive*
Masterman, Jack Verner *insurance company executive*
McCauley, Robert William *biologist, educator*
Morgan, Alan Vivian *geologist, educator*
Nash, Peter Hugh John *geographer, educator, planner*
Paldus, Josef *mathematics educator*
Pindera, Jerzy Tadeusz *mechanical and aeronautical engineer*
Qualter, Terence Hall *retired political science educator*
†Rudin, Alfred *chemistry educator emeritus*
Sherbourne, Archibald Norbert *civil engineering educator*
Smith, Rowland James *English language educator*
Sprott, David Arthur *statistics and psychology educator*
Stewart, Cameron Leigh *mathematics educator*
Suits, Bernard Herbert *philosophy educator*
†Thomas, Richard Lynn *geologist, researcher, educator, director university geecology center*
†Thomson, Neil R. *civil engineering educator*
Urquhart, Tony *artist, educator*
Vlach, Jiri *electrical engineering educator, researcher*
Warner, Barry Gregory *geographer*
Wright, Douglas Tyndall *former university president, company director, engineering educator*

Welland
Wintermans, Joseph Jack Gerard Francis *financial services executive*

Weston
McIntyre, John George Wallace *real estate development and management consultant*

Willowdale
Binder, Herbert R. *drug store chain executive*
Bloom, David Ronald *retail drug company executive*
Bulloch, John Frederick Devon *association executive*
Dean, Geoffrey *book publisher*
Glass, Irvine Israel *aerospace educator, researcher*
Hallman, H(enry) Theodore, Jr. *artist, textile designer*
Harris, Sydney Malcolm *retired judge*
Irwin, John Wesley *publisher*
Kerner, Fred *book publisher, writer*
Krakauer, Albert Alexander *pharmacist, retail executive*
MacDonald, Brian Scott *educational administrator*
McDonald, William Henry *manufacturing executive*
Swartz, Malcolm Gilbert *retail executive, restaurateur*
Turnbull, John Cameron *pharmacist, consultant*

Windsor
Auld, Frank *psychologist, educator*
Dirksen-Morrison, Jean *library administrator*
Drake, Gordon William Frederic *physics educator*
Ferguson, James Peter *distilling company executive*
Giffen, John A. *distillery executive*
Hackam, Reuben *electrical engineering educator*
Ianni, Ronald William *university president and vice chancellor, lawyer*
Jones, William Ernest *chemistry educator*
Landry, G. Yves *automotive company executive*
Thibert, Roger Joseph *clinical chemist, educator*
Whitney, Barry Lyn *religious studies educator*

Winnipeg
†Wall, Leonard J. *bishop*

Yarker
Smallman, Beverley N. *biology educator*

York
†Brown, Fergy J. *mayor*

PRINCE EDWARD ISLAND

Charlottetown
Baker, Ronald James *English language educator, university administrator*
Callbeck, Catherine S. *Canadian government official*
Carruthers, Norman Harry *Canadian province supreme court justice*
Eliot, Charles William John *university president, educator*
†MacAulay, Lawrence A. *Canadian government official*
Reid, Marion L. *lieutenant governor, educator*
Severance, Christopher Churchill *museum director*

Monticello
Gingras, Gustave *physician*

QUEBEC

Athelstan
Ness, Owen McGregor *retired aluminum company executive*

Ayers Cliff
Beament, Thomas Harold (Tib Beament) *artist, printmaker, educator*

Beaconsfield
Harder, Rolf Peter *graphic designer, painter*

Boucherville
†Martel, Jacques G. *materials engineer administrator*

Chelsea
Warren, Jack Hamilton *trade policy advisor*

Chicoutimi
Couture, Jean Guy *bishop*
St-Onge, Guy Claude *hospital administrator*

Dorval
Bachynski, Morrel Paul *physicist*
Brown, Robert Ellis *transportation company executive, former Canadian government official*

Fleurimont
Simoneau, Normand J. *hospital administrator*

Hull
†Axworthy, Lloyd *Canadian government official*
Ebacher, Roger *archbishop*
†Irwin, Ron *Canadian government official*
MacDonald, George Frederick *anthropologist, Canadian museum director*
Massé, Marcel *Canadian official*

Ile des Soeurs
Dagenais, Marcel Gilles *economist, educator*

Ile Perrot
Tomlinson, George Herbert *retired industrial company research executive*

Joliette
Audet, Rene *bishop*

Laval
David, Michel Louis *geostatistician, consultant*
†Frisque, Gilles *forestry engineer*
Guindon, Yvan *pharmaceutical company research executive*
Juillet, Chantal *violinist*
Kluepfel, Dieter *microbiologist*
Pichette, Claude *former banking executive, university rector, research executive*

Leclercville
Morin, Pierre Jean *retired management consultant*

Longueuil
Caplan, L(azarus) David *manufacturing company executive*
†Hubert, Bernard *bishop*
Lussier, Gaetan *Canadian government official*
Smith, Elvie Lawrence *aircraft company executive*

Mirabel
Ginzburg, Rubin *airport executive, electrical engineer*

Montpellier
Poirier, Louis Joseph *neurology educator*

Montreal
Adamkiewicz, Vincent Witold *microbiology and immunology educator, researcher*
Alou, Felipe Rojas *professional baseball manager*
Andrew, Frederick James *telecommunications company executive*
Audet, Henri *communications executive*
Bagnall, Graham Edward *financial executive*
Baxter, Donald William *physician, educator*
Beardmore, Harvey Ernest *retired physician, educator*

Beaubien, Philippe de Gaspe, II communications executive
Beauchamp, Jacques wood products executive
Beaudoin, François financial company executive
Beaudoin, Laurent industrial, recreational and transportation company executive
†Beauregard, Luc public relations executive
Becklake, Margaret Rigsby physician, educator
Belanger, Pierre Rolland university dean, electrical engineering educator
†Béliveau, Jules journalist
Benson, Kenneth Samuel corporate executive
Bentley, Kenneth Chessar oral surgeon, educator
Bérard, André bank executive
Bertos, Rigas Nicholas art history educator
Berube, Jacques B. communications company executive
Beugnot, Bernard Andre Henri French literature educator
Bisson, Claude chief justice of Quebec
Black, William Gordon transportation executive
†Bouchard, Jacques advertising executive
†Boucher, Raymond Gabriel advertising executive
Bougie, Jacques metal processing executive
Bourassa, Robert former Premier of Québec
†Bourgeault, Jean-Jacques air transportation executive
†Bouthillier, André public relations executive, consultant
Braide, Robert David broadcast executive
Brecher, Irving economics educator
Brecher, Michael political science educator
Brierley, John E. C. legal educator, former university dean
Brisebois, Marcel museum director
Brochu, Claude Renaud professional baseball team executive
Bronfman, Charles Rosner distillery executive
Bruemmer, Fred writer, photographer
Burgess, John Herbert physician, educator
Burns, James William business executive
Bussieres, Yvan supermarket chain executive
Caillé, André gas distribution company executive
Cameron, Alastair Duncan engineering consultant
Carbonneau, Guy professional hockey player
Cardinal, Marcelin artist
Carroll, Robert Lynn biology educator, vertebrate paleontologist, museum curator
Castonguay, Claude corporate director, lawyer, former senator
Cedraschi, Tullio investment management company executive
Chagnon, Andre broadcast executive
Chan, Tak Hang chemist, educator
Chang, Thomas Ming Swi medical scientist, biotechnologist
Charney, Melvin artist, architect, educator
Charron, André Joseph Charles Pierre theologian, educator, former dean
Chateau, John-Peter D(avid) economics and finance educator, mining company executive
Chevrier, Jean Marc psychologist, publisher, author
Chiriaeff, Ludmilla Gorny ballet company executive, ballet dancer, choreographer
†Chretien, Michel physician, educator, administrator
Cleghorn, John Edward banker
Clermont, Yves Wilfrid anatomy educator, researcher
Cloutier, Gilles Georges academic administrator, research executive
Colas, Emile Jules lawyer
Colosimo, Robert labor relations executive
Corey, Ronald professional hockey team executive
Corinthios, Michael Jean George electrical engineering educator
Courtois, B. A. communications executive
Courtois, Edmond Jacques lawyer
Couture, Armand civil engineer
Crawford, Purdy consumer products and services company executive
Crowston, Wallace Bruce Stewart management educator
Cruess, Richard Leigh surgeon, university dean
Cuello, Augusto Claudio Guillermo medical research scientist, author
Cyr, J. V. Raymond telecommunications and management holding company executive
Daly, Gerald accountant
Damphousse, Vincent professional hockey player
Dansereau, Pierre ecologist
Davidson, Colin Henry university educator
Dealy, John Michael chemical engineer, educator
Deegan, Derek James transportation executive
Demers, Jacques professional hockey team coach
De Mori, Renato computer science educator, researcher
Derome, Jacques Florian meteorology educator
Desjardins, Pierre consumer goods company executive
Desmarais, Paul finance company executive
Des Marais, Pierre, II communications holding company executive
Des Roches, Antoine newspaper executive
†DesRoches, Pierre director
de Takacsy, Nicholas Benedict physicist, educator
†Dingwall, David Canadian government official
†Dubé, Ghyslain earth scientist
Dubuc, André investment consulting company executive
Dubuc, Serge mathematics educator
Ducros, Pierre Y. information technology consulting and systems management executive
Dudek, Stephanie Zuperko psychology educator
†Dufour, Jean-Marie economics researcher, educator
Dufresne, Guy Georges mining company executive
Duquette, Dan professional baseball team executive
Duquette, Jean-Pierre French language and literature educator
Dutoit, Charles conductor
Edward, John Thomas chemist, educator
Eisenberg, Adi chemist
Elie, Jean André investment banker
Fanning, William James professional baseball team executive, radio and television broadcaster
Farnell, Gerald William engineering educator
Feindel, William Howard neurosurgeon, consultant
†Fontaine, Gilles physics educator
Fortin, Joseph André forestry educator, researcher
Freedman, Samuel Orkin university official
Freeman, Carolyn Ruth radiation oncologist
French, Stanley George university dean, philosophy educator
Fridman, Josef Josel telecommunications company executive
†Fyffe, Les earth scientist
Gabbour, Iskandar city and regional planning educator
Gagné, Paul E. paper company executive
†Gallagher, Tanya Marie speech pathologist, educator
Gardner, Richard Kent retired librarian, educator, consultant
Gaudry, Roger chemist, university official
†Gaulin, Jean gas distribution company executive
Genest, Jacques physician, researcher, administrator
Gibbs, Sarah Preble biologist, educator
Gillespie, Thomas Stuart lawyer
Girard, Jacques communications executive
†Gjedde, Albert Hellmut neuroscientist, neurology educator
Gold, Alan B. former Canadian chief justice
Gold, Phil physician, educator
Goltzman, David endocrinologist, educator, researcher
Granger, Luc Andre university dean, psychologist
Grissom, Marquis Dean professional baseball player
Guenette, Francoise legal affairs executive
Gulkin, Harry arts administrator, film producer
Haccoun, David electrical engineering educator
Hall, Douglas John minister, educator
Hamel, Reginald history educator
Hancox, Ralph publisher
Hantho, Charles Harold textile executive
Hart, William D., Jr. food retailing company executive
Hay, Allan Stuart chemist, educator
Henderson, William Boyd engineering executive
Herling, Michael steel company executive
Herz, Carl Samuel mathematician
Hobday, John Charles foundation administrator
Hoffmann, Peter Conrad Werner history educator
†Hurtubise, Jacques editor
Ikawa-Smith, Fumiko anthropologist, educator
†Imorde, Henry K. earth scientist
Ivanier, Isin manufacturing company executive
Ivanier, Paul steel products manufacturing company executive
Jacobs, Peter Daniel Alexander architecture and landscape architecture educator
Jasmin, Gaetan pathologist, educator
Johnston, David Lloyd academic administrator, lawyer
Johnstone, Rose Mamelak (Mrs. Douglas Johnstone) biochemistry educator
Jolicoeur, Paul molecular biologist
Jonas, John Joseph metallurgical engineering educator
Jonassohn, Kurt sociologist, educator
Kannengiesser, Charles A. theology educator
Kearney, Robert communications company executive
Kinsley, William Benton literature educator
Kirkpatrick, John Gildersleeve lawyer
Labelle, Eugene Jean-Marc airport director general
Lacoste, Paul lawyer, educator, university official
Ladanyi, Branko civil engineer
Lajeunesse, Marcel university administrator, educator
Lalonde, Marc lawyer, former Canadian government official
Lamarre, Bernard engineering, contracting and manufacturing advisor
†Lamarre, Daniel public relations company executive
Landry, Roger D. publishing company executive
Langleben, Manuel Phillip physics educator
Lanyi, Alexander Sandor rail transportation executive
Large, John Andrew library and information service educator
Laurin, Pierre finance company executive
Lawson, Jane Elizabeth bank executive
Leblanc, Hugues philosophy educator
Leblond, Charles Philippe anatomy educator, researcher
Lehmann, Heinz Edgar psychiatrist, consultant, researcher
Leroy, Claude physics educator, researcher
Lessard, Michel M. finance company executive
Levine, Martin David computer science and electrical engineering educator
Levitt, Brian Michael consumer products and services company executive, lawyer
Little, Alan Brian obstetrician, gynecologist, educator
†Lord, Guy J.H. lawyer, Canandian government official
Lussier, Jean-Paul dentistry educator
Maag, Urs Richard statistics educator
MacDonald, R(onald Angus) Neil physician, educator
MacKinnon, Rodrick Keith corporate administration executive, lawyer
Maclachlan, Gordon Alistair biology educator, researcher
Mac Lean, Lloyd Douglas surgeon
Major, André radio producer, writer, educator
Manson, Paul David retired military officer, electronics executive
Marcoux, Yvon financial executive, lawyer
Mark, Shew-Kuey Tommy physics educator
Marsan, Jean-Claude architect, urban planner, educator
Martin, Jean Claude health management educator
Masse, Yvon H. transportation company executive
McEwen, Jean painter
Mc Gregor, Maurice cardiologist, medical educator
McLelland, Joseph Cumming philosophy educator, former university dean
Melzack, Ronald psychology educator
Mercier, Francois lawyer
Messier, Pierre lawyer, manufacturing company executive
Milic-Emili, Joseph physician, educator
Miller, Michael Chilcott d'Elboux metal products executive
Milner, Brenda Atkinson Langford neuropsychologist
Milner, Peter Marshall psychology educator
Mintzberg, Henry management educator, researcher, writer
Molson, Eric H. corporate company executive
Montcalm, Norman Joseph lawyer
Monty, Jean Claude telecommunications company executive
Moore, Sean pathologist, educator
Morgera, Salvatore Domenic electrical engineering educator, researcher
Morin, Yves-Charles linguistics educator, researcher
Morton, David aluminum company executive
Moser, William Oscar Jules mathematics educator
Mulder, David S. cardiovascular surgeon
Mulroney, (Martin) Brian former prime minister of Canada
Murphy, Beverley Elaine Pearson scientist, administrator, physician, educator
Mysak, Lawrence Alexander oceanographer, climatologist, mathematician, educator
Nadeau, Bertin F. diversified company executive
†Nattel, Stanley cardiologist, research scientist
Nault, Fernand choreographer
Nayar, Baldev Raj political science educator
†Neveau, Jean printing company executive
Normandeau, Andre Gabriel criminologist, educator
†Noumoff, Samuel J. political scientist, researcher
O'Brien, John Wilfrid economist, university president emeritus, educator
Olivella, Barry James financial executive
O'Neill, Brian Francis professional hockey executive
Orban, Edmond Henry political science educator
Ormsby, Eric Linn library administrator, researcher
Osmond, Dennis Gordon medical educator, researcher
Paidoussis, Michael Pandeli mechanical engineering educator
Paikowsky, Sandra Roslyn art historian
Pal, Prabir Kumar aluminium company executive
Panneton, Jacques librarian
Papineau-Couture, Jean composer, educator
Peladeau, Pierre publishing company executive
Pelletier, Louis Conrad surgeon, educator
Pépin, Marcel broadcast executive
Perlin, Arthur Saul chemistry educator
Pfeiffer, J(ohn) David mechanical engineering educator, consultant
Picard, Laurent management educator, administrator, consultant
Pinard, Gilbert Daniel psychiatrist, educator
Pinard, Raymond R. pulp and paper consultant
†Pinsky, Leonard geneticist
Plaa, Gabriel Leon toxicologist, educator
Plourde, Gerard company director
†Podgorsak, Ervin B. medical physicist, educator, administrator
Poissant, Charles-Albert paper manufacturing company executive
Poitras, Pierre aerospace and transportation products company executive
Popovici, Adrian law educator
Pound, Richard William Duncan lawyer, accountant
Pratte, Lise lawyer, corporate secretary
Prus, Victor Marius architect, urbanist
Purdy, William Crossley chemist, educator
Ramachandran, Venkatanarayana Deekshit electrical engineering educator
Raynauld, Andre economist, educator
Redfern, John D. manufacturing company executive
Redwood, Richard George civil engineering educator, researcher
Régnier, Marc Charles lawyer, corporate executive
†Rhodes, Lawrence artistic director
Richardson, Gisele management company executive
Richler, Mordecai writer
Ritchie, Robert Jamieson transportation executive
Robb, James Alexander lawyer
Rolland, Lucien G. paper company executive
†Romanelli, G. Jack journalist
Roskies, Ethel psychology educator
Rothman, Melvin L. judge
Roy, Armand Joseph military officer
Roy, Patrick professional hockey player
Royer, Raymond transportation equipment manufacturing company executive
Rugeroni, Ian aluminum company executive
Saint-Jacques, Madeleine advertising agency executive
†Saint-Pierre, Guy engineering executive
St.-Pierre, Jacques statistics educator, consultant
Sandor, Thomas biochemist
Sandorfy, Camille chemistry educator
Sattler, Rolf plant morphologist, educator
Saumier, Andre finance executive
†Sauvageau, Philippe library director
†Savard, Claude A. food service executive
Savard, Serge professional hockey team executive
Schwartz, Roy Richard holding company executive
Scott, I. B. railroad executive
Scriver, Charles Robert medical scientist, human geneticist
Selvadurai, Antony Patrick Sinnappa civil engineering educator, applied mathematician, consultant
Shaw, Robert Fletcher retired civil engineer
Shea, William Rene historian, philosopher of science, educator
†Shepherd, Harvey Lawrence religion reporter
Sheppard, Claude-Armand lawyer
Silverthorne, Michael James classics educator
Silvester, Peter Peet electrical engineer, educator, consultant
Simons, John H. electronics manufacturing company executive
Sirois, Gerard pharmacy educator
Skup, Daniel molecular biologist, educator, researcher
Smith, James Hamilton paper, packaging, construction material and chemicals company executive
Smith, Philip Edward Lake anthropology educator
Solomon, Samuel biochemistry educator, administrator
†Somerville, Margaret Anne Ganley law educator
Sonea, Sorin I. microbiologist
Sourkes, Theodore Lionel biochemistry educator
Speirs, Derek James diversified corporation financial executive
†Stanners, Clifford Paul molecular biologist, cell biologist, biochemistry educator
†Stewart, Jane psychology educator
Stinson, William W. business executive
Stoneman, William Hambly, III professional baseball team executive
Suen, Ching Yee computer scientist and educator, researcher
†Sykes, Stephanie Lynn library director, archivist, museum director
Szabo, Denis criminologist, educator
Szanto, George novelist, playwright
Taras, Paul physicist, educator
Tavenas, François civil engineer, educator
Taylor, Claude I. airlines executive
Tellier, Paul M. Canadian railway transportation executive
Terreault, R. Charles management educator, researcher
Thompson, John Douglas financier
Toole, David George pulp and paper products executive
Torrey, David Leonard investment banker
†Tousignant, Jacques human resources executive, lawyer
Tremblay, Andre Gabriel lawyer, educator
Tremblay, Rodrigue economics educator
Trigger, Bruce Graham anthropology educator
Trudeau, Pierre Elliott lawyer, former Canadian prime minister
Turcotte, Jean-Claude archbishop
Turmel, Jean Bernard banker
Uzan, Bernard Franck general and artistic director
Vaillancourt, Jean-Guy sociology educator
Van Vliet, Carolyne Marina physicist, educator
Vennat, Michel lawyer
Vikis-Freibergs, Vaira psychologist, educator
Wallace, Philip Russell retired physics educator
Waller, Harold Myron political science educator
Webster, Norman Eric journalist, charitable foundation administrator
†Weir, D. Robert metallurgical engineer, engineering executive
Weir, Stephen James financial executive
†Wesemael, François physics educator
Whitehead, Michael Anthony chemistry educator
Wilson, Lynton Ronald telecommunications company executive
Wohl, Robert Allen lawyer, aerospace executive
Woszczyk, Wieslaw Richard audio engineering educator, researcher
Yong, Raymond Nen-Yiu civil engineering educator
Zames, George David electrical engineer, educator

Mount Royal
Chauvette, Claude R. building materials company administrator
Glezos, Matthews consumer products and services company executive
†Trudel, Pierre law educator, researcher

North Hatley
Gustafson, Ralph Barker poet, educator
†Jones, Douglas Gordon retired literature educator

Outremont
Domaradzki, Theodore Felix Slavic studies educator, editor
Gouin, Serge corporate executive
Larose, Roger former pharmaceutical company executive, former university administrator
Letourneau, Jean-Paul business association executive and consultant
Levesque, Rene Jules Albert former physicist

Pointe Claire
Bolker, Henry Irving retired chemist, research institute director, educator
Cohen, Charles F. retail executive
Lederman, Frank L. scientist, research center administrator
Wrist, Peter Ellis pulp and paper company executive

Pontiac
Hlavina, Rasto R(astislav) sculptor

Quebec
Asselin, Martial Canadian lieutenant governor
Aubut, Marcel lawyer, sports association official
Belanger, Gerard economics educator
Couture, Jean G. surgeon, educator
†Crawford, Marc professional hockey coach
Engel, Charles Robert chemist, educator
†Filion, Louis Jacques business and economics educator
Gervais, Michel academic administrator
Joly, Jean Robert microbiologist, medical educator
Jovanovic, Miodrag surgeon, educator
Labrie, Fernand physician
Lafleur, Guy professional hockey player
Laliberté-Bourque, Andrée museum director
La Rochelle, Pierre-Louis civil engineering educator
Lecours, Michel electrical engineering educator
LeMay, Jacques lawyer
Lussier, Jacques business management educator, university dean
Migue, Jean Luc economics educator
Normand, Robert lawyer
Page, Michel biochemist
Pagé, Pierre professional hockey executive
Paradis, Andre librarian
†Porter, John Robert art history educator, curator, writer
Potvin, Pierre physiologist, educator
Poussart, Denis Jean-Marie electrical engineering educator, consultant
Rochette, Louis shipowner
Stavert, Alexander Bruce bishop
Stein, Charles retired lawyer
Theodorescu, Radu Amza Serban mathematician, educator
Tremblay, Marc Adélard anthropologist, educator
Trudel, Marc J. botanist
Verge, Pierre legal educator

Rimouski
Blanchet, Bertrand archbishop
Levesque, Louis bishop
Sirois, Raymond telecommunications administrator
†Walton, Alan oceanographer

Rock Forest
Lamirande, Emilien historian, educator

Rosemere
Adrian, Donna Jean librarian

Rouyn-Noranda
Hamelin, Jean-Guy bishop

Saint Adele
†Rousseau-Vermette, Mariette artist

Saint-Hubert
†Doré, Roland dean, science association director
Lindberg, Garry Martin aeronautical engineer, Canadian government official

Saint Hyacinthe
Langevin, Louis-de-Gonzague bishop

Saint Jerome
Joly, Jean-Gil medical biochemist, internist, administrator, researcher, educator
†Valois, Charles bishop

Saint Lambert
Archambault, Louis sculptor
Brossard, Maurice biotechnology company executive

Saint Laurent
Boulet, Lionel research administrator

Harris, Hollis Loyd *airline executive*

Saint Luc
Marcoux, Jules Edouard *physicist, educator, writer*

Saint Romuald
†Lafond, Pierre *forest engineer*

Saint-Sauveur
Hanigan, Lawrence *retired railway executive*

Saint Sauveur des Monts
Dunsky, Menahem *retired advertising agency executive, communications consultant, painter*

Sainte Anne de Bellevue
Broughton, Robert Stephen *irrigation and drainage engineering educator, consultant*
Buckland, Roger Basil *university dean, educator, vice principal*
Grant, William Frederick *geneticist, educator*
MacLeod, Robert Angus *microbiology educator, researcher*
Steppler, Howard Alvey *agronomist*

Sainte-Croix
Grenier, Fernand *geographer, consultant*

Sainte-Foy
Beaulieu, Jacques Alexandre *physicist*
†Boudoux, Michel *environmental research executive*
†Cardinal, André *phycologist, educator*
Denis, Paul-Yves *geography educator*
†Lagassé, Pierre Philippe *exercise science educator*
Legendre, Louis *biological oceanography educator, researcher*
Maranda, Guy *oral maxillofacial surgeon, Canadian health facility executive, educator*
Montgrain, Noël *academic administrator*
Murray, Warren James *educator, philosopher*
Pasquier, Joël *music educator*

Sherbrooke
Bureau, Michel André *pediatrician, pulmonologist, faculty dean*
de Margerie, Jean-M. *ophthalmology educator*
Deslongchamps, Pierre *chemistry educator*
Fortier, Jean-Marie *archbishop*
†Tremblay, André-Marie *physicist*

Sillery
Couture, Maurice *archbishop*

Trois Rivières
†Lavallee, H.-Claude *chemical engineer, researcher*
Noel, Laurent *bishop, educator*

Valleyfield
†Lebel, Robert *bishop*

Varennes
Bartnikas, Raymond *electrical engineer, educator*
Krishnayya, Chandra Pasupulati *research engineer, consultant*
Maruvada, Pereswara Sarma *engineering executive, researcher*
St. Jean, Guy *electric power industry executive*
Vijh, Ashok Kumar *chemistry educator, researcher*

Verdun
†Delisle, Gilles Y. *telecommunications executive*
Ferguson, Michael John *electronics and communications educator*
Paré, Jean-Jacques *civil engineer, geotechnical and dam safety consultant*

Ville de Laval
Pavilanis, Vytautas *microbiology educator, physician*
Siemiatycki, Jack *epidemiologist, biostatistician, educator*

Ville Saint Laurent
Kivenko, Kenneth *aerospace industry executive*

Westmount
†Charbonneau, Guy *Canadian senator, insurance company executive*
Dunbar, Maxwell John *oceanographer, educator*
Fortier, L. Yves *former Canadian ambassador to the UN, lawyer*
Gordonsmith, John Arthur Harold *collection agency executive*
Jasper, Herbert Henri *neuroscience researcher, consultant, writer*
Kessler, Jacques Isaac *gastroenterologist, educator*
McIlhone, John Thomas *educational administrator*
Spalding, James Stuart *retired telecommunications company executive*

SASKATCHEWAN

Gravelbourg
†Delaquis, Noel *bishop*

Prince Albert
†Morand, Blaise E. *bishop*

Regina
†Archer, Douglas Robert *mayor, insurance services executive*
Balfour, Reginald James *lawyer*
Bayda, Edward Dmytro *judge*
Bays, Eric *bishop*
Dalla-Vicenza, Mario Joseph *steel company financial executive*
Davis, Gordon Richard Fuerst *biologist, translator*
Driedger, Florence Gay *social agency executive, social work educator, consultant*
†Fedoruk, Sylvia O. *Canadian provincial official, educator*
Genereux, Robert James *consulting engineer*
Hewitt, James J. *credit corporation executive*
†Holm, Roy K. *church administrator*
Hughes, Robert Lachlan *newspaper executive*
Laschuk, Roy Bogdan *lawyer*
MacKay, Harold Hugh *lawyer*
Mollard, John Douglas *engineering and geology executive*
Nuttall, Richard Norris *state agency administrator*
Oko, Andrew Jan *art gallery director, curator*
Phillips, Roger *steel company executive*
Powell, Trevor John David *archivist*
Romanow, Roy John *provincial government official, barrister, solicitor*
†Sifton, Michael Clifford *broadcaster, publisher*
Stark-Adamec, Cannie *psychology educator, researcher*

Regina Beach
Barber, Lloyd Ingram *retired university president*

Saltcoats
Farquharson, Walter Henry *minister, church official*

Saskatoon
†Babiuk, Lorne Alan *virologist, immunologist, research administrator*
Baker, Robert John *agronomy educator*
Bell, John Milton *agricultural science educator*
Belovanoff, Olga *retired health care facility administrator*
Billinton, Roy *engineering educator*
Blakeney, Allan Emrys *Canadian government official, lawyer*
Bornstein, Eli *artist, sculptor*
Brewster, Elizabeth Winifred *English language educator, poet, novelist*
Carr, Roy Arthur *agricultural products processing research organization executive*
Childers, Charles Eugene *potash mining company executive*
†Dayday, Henry *mayor*
Emson, Harry Edmund *pathology educator, bioethicist*
†Filevich, Basil *bishop*
Gupta, Madan Mohan *engineering educator, researcher*
Habbick, Brian Ferguson *pediatrician, community health and epidemiology educator*
Harvey, Bryan Laurence *crop science educator*
†Henry, Keith Douglas *architect*
Hirose, Akira *physics educator, researcher*
Huang, Pan Ming *soil science educator*
Ish, Daniel Russell *law educator, academic adminstrator*
Jacobson, Sverre Theodore *retired minister*
Jaques, Louis Barker *pharmacologist*
Johnson, Dennis Duane *pharmacologist, educator*
Keegan, David Lloyd *psychiatrist, educator*
Kennedy, Marjorie Ellen *librarian*
Knight, Arthur Robert *technical institute administrator*
Knott, Douglas Ronald *college dean, agricultural sciences educator, researcher*
Kumar, Surinder *electrical engineering educator, consultant*
Kupsch, Walter Oscar *geologist*
†Mahoney, James P. *bishop*
McCallum, Kenneth James *retired university dean, chemistry and chemical engineering educator*
†Morgan, Thomas Oliver *bishop*
Nikiforuk, Peter N. *university dean*
Peterson, Bill *publishing executive*
Randhawa, Bikkar Singh *educational psychologist, educator*
Sachdev, Mohindar Singh *engineering educator*
Shokeir, Mohamed Hassan Kamel *medical geneticist, educator*
Stewart, John Wray Black *college dean*

YUKON TERRITORY

Whitehorse
Ferris, Ronald Curry *bishop*
†Lobsinger, Thomas *bishop*
McKinnon, John Kenneth (Ken) *Candian commissioner*
†Ostashek, John *government leader*
Penikett, Antony David John *Canadian government official*
†Phelps, Willard *Canadian government official*

MEXICO

Aristoteles
Akel, Ollie James *oil company executive*

Chihuahua
Almeida Merino, Adalberto *archbishop*

Cuernavaca
Mora, Francisco *artist, printmaker*

Garza Garcia
†Paez, Rafael Roberto *holding company executive*

Guadalajara
Garibay-Gutierrez, Luis *physician, educator*
†Rivera-Aceves, Carlos *Mexican governor, lawyer*

Juarez
Torres Medina, Emilio *oncologist, consultant*

Matamoros
Chavolla Ramos, Francisco Javier *bishop*

Mexico City
†Arau, Alfonso *film director*
Arellano, Ignacio *advertising executive*
Aspe, Pedro *Mexican government official*
†Azcarraga Milmo, Emilio *communication company executive*
Baer, George Martin *veterinarian, researcher*
Brown, Kenneth Charles *manufacturing company executive*
Bruton, John Macaulay *trade association executive*
del Conde, Teresa *museum director, art historian, researcher*
Diaz-Coller, Carlos *physician*
†Dudley, Craig James *executive recruiter*
†Ellison, Katherine Esther *journalist*
Favela-Lozoya, Fernando *civil engineer, educator*
Friedeberg, Pedro *painter, sculptor, designer*
Godinez Flores, Ramon *auxiliary bishop*
Guizar, Ricardo Diaz *clergyman*
Jones, James R. *ambassador, former congressman, lawyer*
Koenigsberger, Gloria S. *astrophysicist*
Lacouture, Felipe Ernesto *museum consultant*
Lozoya-Thalmann, Emilio *Mexican government official*
Martinez-Tejeda, Juan J. *manufacturing company executive*
Mendelejis, Leonardo Nierman *artist*
Paz, Octavio *poet, Mexican diplomat*
Peimbert, Manuel *astronomer*
Rajaram, Sanjaya *agricultural scientist, plant breeder*
Riviello Bazán, Antonio *government official*
Rodriguez Gallardo, Adolfo *library director, historian*
Rogers, John Ellsworth *lawyer*
Salinas de Gortari, Carlos *president of Mexico*
Serra Puche, Jaime Jose *Mexican government official*
Solana Morales, Fernando *diplomat, financier, educator*
Velasco, Eugenio *advertising executive*
Whitaker, Pernell *professional boxer*

Monterrey
†Garcia, Socrates Rizzo *Mexican governor*
†Ruiz, Othon *financial executive*

Morelia
Alcaraz Figueroa, Estanislao *clergyman*
Warren, J. Benedict *retired history educator*

Morelos
Illich, Ivan *researcher, educator*

Puebla
Zehe, Alfred Fritz Karl *physics educator*

Saltillo
Villalobos Padilla, Francisco *bishop*

Tijuana
Ochoa, Quintin *lawyer*

Veracruz
Ranzahuer, Guillermo Gonzalez *bishop*

ARGENTINA

Bahía Blanca
Cardozo, Miguel Angel *telecommunications engineering educator*

Buenos Aires
Balve, Beba Carmen *research center administrator*
Gennadios, (Gennadios Chrysoulakis) *bishop*
Sacerdote, Manuel Ricardo *banker*

ARMENIA

Yerevan
Gilmore, Harry J. *ambassador*

AUSTRALIA

Adelaide
Twidale, C(harles) R(owland) *geomorphologist, educator*
Wiskich, Joseph Tony *botany educator, researcher*

Avalon
West, Morris Langlo *novelist*

Belair
Briggs, Geoffrey Hugh *retired librarian*

Brighton
Bennett, Frank Cantelo, Jr. *retired diplomat*

Brisbane
English, Francis Peter *ophthalmologist, educator*

Bundoora
Isaac, Rhys Llywelyn *historian, educator*
James, Bruce David *chemistry educator*

Canberra
Gani, Joseph Mark *statistics educator, administrator, researcher*

City Beach
Pelczar, Otto *electrical engineer*

Greenwich
Westerberg, Verne Edward *magazine publisher*

Hobart
Munger, Bryce L. *physician, educator*

Kensington
Rayward, Warden Boyd *librarian, educator*

Melbourne
Lawson, Francis Colin *chemical company executive*
Mc Gimpsey, Ronald Alan *oil company executive*

Menai
Nowotny, Janusz *materials scientist*

Nedlands
Oxnard, Charles Ernest *anatomist, anthropologist, human biologist, educator*

Norfolk Island
McCullough Robinson, Colleen *author*

Perth
Skodon, Emil Mark *diplomat*

Potts Point
Beresford, Bruce *film director*

Randwick
Hall, Peter Francis *physiologist*

Ringwood
Base, Graeme Rowland *illustrator, author*

Rockhampton
Lynch, Thomas Brendan *pathologist*
Zelmer, Amy Elliott *health science educator*

Sydney
Guerin, Didier *magazine executive*
Hinde, John Gordon *lawyer, solicitor*
†Miller, George *film director*
Murdoch, (Keith) Rupert *publisher*
Salsbury, Stephen Matthew *historian, educator*

West Perth
Woods, Thomas Brian *physician*

AUSTRIA

Gaz
Weisstein, Ulrich Werner *English literature educator*

Leoben
Fettweis, Günter Bernhard Leo *mining engineering educator*

Maria Enzersdorf
Vetter, Herbert *physician, educator*

Vienna
Eagleton, William Lester, Jr. *foreign service officer*
Faulkner, Julia Ellen *opera singer*
Frankl, Viktor E. *psychiatrist, author*
†Hunt, Swanee G. *ambassador to Austria*
Jackovich, Victor *ambassador*
Kagel, Mauricio *multi-media composer, director*
Lo Bello, Nino *author, journalist*
Ludwig, Christa *mezzo-soprano*
Niederreiter, Harald Guenther *mathematician, researcher*
Oberhuber, Konrad Johannes *art museum curator, educator*
Steinbruckner, Bruno Friedrich *foreign language educator*
†Swihart, James W., Jr. *diplomat*

BAHAMAS

Aboco
Goodloe, John Duncan, IV *real estate company executive*

Grand Cayman
McIntire, Jerald Gene *investment executive, former municipal official*

Nassau
Templeton, John Marks *investment counsel, financial analyst*

BANGLADESH

Dhaka
Abeyesundere, Nihal Anton Aelian *health organization representative*

BARBADOS

Bridgetown
Barrow, Dame Ruth Nita *governor-general*
Hughes, G. Philip *diplomat*

BELARUS

Minsk
†Swartz, David H. *ambassador*

BELGIUM

Antwerp
De Craene, Jacques Maria *plastics company executive, retired judge, arbitrator*
Uyttenbroeck, Frans Joseph *gynecologic oncologist*

Beerse
Janssen, Paul Adriaan Jan *pharmaceutical company executive*

Blanden
Holleweg dit Wegman, Willy *management expert, educator, entrepreneurship development specialist*

Brussels
Branegan, James Augustus, III *journalist*
Bustin, George Leo *lawyer*
Calingaert, Michael *international consultant*
Glazer, Barry David *lawyer*
†Hunter, Robert Edwards *ambassador, diplomat*
Jadot, Jean Lambert Octave *clergyman*
†Janssen, Paul-Emmanuel *bank executive*
Kempe, Frederick Schumann *newspaper editor, author*
Liebman, Howard Mark *lawyer*

Loutrel, Claude Yves *corporate official*
†Mestrallet, Gérard *association executive*
Oberreit, Walter William *lawyer*
Paul, Robert Carey *lawyer*
Portal, Gilbert Marcel Adrien *oil company executive*
Smith, Turner Taliaferro, Jr. *lawyer*
Walker, Darcy Lynn *banker*

Ghent
de Leenheer, Andreas Prudent *medical biochemistry and toxicology educator*

Heverlee
De Schryver, Frans Carl *chemistry educator*
L'abbe, Gerrit Karel *chemist*

Lens
Peat, Randall Dean *defense analysis company executive, retired air force officer*

Liège
Calvaer, Andre J. *electrical science educator, consultant*

Louvain-la-Neuve
Sintzoff, Michel *computer scientist, educator*

Strombeek Bever
Mancel, Claude Paul *household product company executive*

BERMUDA

Hamilton
Kramer, Donald *insurance executive*
Stempel, Ernest Edward *insurance executive*

Pembroke
Wiedemann, Joseph Robert *insurance company executive*

Tuckers Town
Heizer, Edgar Francis, Jr. *venture capitalist*

BOLIVIA

La Paz
Gelbard, Robert Sidney *ambassador*

BRAZIL

Curitiba
Berman, Marcelo Samuel *mathematics and physics educator, cosmology researcher, retial businessman*

Minas Gerais
Cimbleris, Borisas *engineering educator, writer*

Rio de Janeiro
Costa Neto, Adelina *chemistry educator, consultant*
DaMatta, Roberto Augusto *anthropologist*
de Biasi, Ronaldo Sergio *materials science educator*
Leite, Carlos Alberto *physician, medical educator*
Mercier, Jacques Louis *consulting and investment company executive*
Sales, Eugenio de Araujo Cardinal *archbishop*

São Paulo
Fernicola, Nilda Alicia Gallego Gándara de *pharmacist, biochemist*
Korolkovas, Andrejus *pharmaceutical chemistry educator*

Salvador
Davidson, Ralph Kirby *economist, retired foundation executive, consultant*
Silva, Benedicto Alves de Castro *surgeon, educator*

BRITISH VIRGIN ISLANDS

Tortola
Green, Leon, Jr. *mechanical engineer*

CAPE VERDE

Praia
McNamara, Francis T. *ambassador*
†Segars, Joseph M. *ambassador*

CENTRAL AFRICAN REPUBLIC

Bangui
†Gribbin, Robert E., III *ambassador*

CHAD

N'Djamena
Pope, Laurence E., II *ambassador*

CHANNEL ISLANDS

Jersey
Durrell, Gerald Malcolm *zoologist, author*

CHILE

Concepción
Trzebiatowski, Gregory L. *education educator*

La Serena
Eggen, Olin Jeuck *astrophysicist, administrator*

Puente Alto
Beshears, Charles Daniel *consultant, former insurance executive*

Santiago
Cotter, Michael William *foreign service officer*
Kamman, Curtis Warren *ambassador*
†Strommen, Clifford H. *headmaster*
†Whelan, James Robert *communications executive, internation trade, investment consultant, author, educator*
Wilkey, Malcolm Richard *retired ambassador, former federal judge*

Valparaiso
Hernandez-Sanchez, Juan Longino *electrical engineering educator*

CHINA

Beijing
Chen, Naixing *thermal science educator, researcher*
Gish, Norman Richard *oil industry executive*
Hua, Tong-Wen *chemistry educator, researcher*
Leng, Xin-Fu *chemist, educator*
Liang, Junxiang *aeronautics and astronautics engineer, educator*
Roy, J(ames) Stapleton *ambassador*
Zhang, Li-Xing *physician, medical facility executive*
Zhang, Ping *aerospace engineering educator*

Shanghai
Wang, Ji-Qing (Chi-Ching Wong) *acoustician, educator*

Wuhu
Mo, Jiaqi *mathematics educator*

Xi'an
Fan, Changxin *electrical engineering educator*

COLOMBIA

Cali
Voysest, Oswaldo *agronomist, researcher*

COSTA RICA

San José
Hoffman, Irwin *orchestra conductor*

CROATIA

Zagreb
Galbraith, Peter W. *ambassador*

CUBA

Havana
Kouri, Gustavo Pedro *virologist*

CZECH REPUBLIC

Ceske Budejovice
Sláma, Karel *biologist, zoologist*

Prague
Kalkus, Stanley *librarian, administrator, consultant*
Macek, Karel *analytical chemistry educator*

DENMARK

Bagsvaerd
Sørensen, Erik *health care company executive*

Bronshoj
Skylv, Grethe Krogh *rheumatologist, anthropologist*

Copenhagen
Bohr, Aage Niels *physicist*
†Hansen, Ole *physicist*

Grasted
Wiin-Nielsen, Aksel Christopher *meteorologist educator*

Hoersholm
Jensen, Ole *energy researcher*

Holte
Elliott, George Arthur *mathematician, educator*

Roskilde
Heydorn, Kaj *science laboratory administrator*

Vedbaek
Nordqvist, Erik Askbo *shipping company executive*

ECUADOR

Quito
Casals, Juan Federico *economist, consultant*
Torres, Guido Adolfo *water treatment company executive*

EGYPT

Cairo
El-Hamalaway, Mohamed-Younis Abd-El-Samie *computer engineering educator*
El-Sayed, Karimat Mahmoud *physics and crystallography educator*
Khan, Amir U. *agricultural engineering consultant*
Miller, Harry George *education educator*

Giza
Salem, Ibrahim Ahmed *electrical engineer, consultant, educator*

ENGLAND

Balcombe
Scofield, Paul *actor*

Berkshire
Hall, Arnold Alexander *aeronautical, mechanical and electrical executive*

Birmingham
Banowetz, Joseph Murray *musician, music educator*
Fry, Maxwell John *economist, educator*

Brighton
Cornforth, Sir John Warcup *chemist*

Brighton East Sussex
Watkin, David *film director, cinematographer*

Buckinghamshire
Elegant, Robert Sampson *journalist, author*
Forbes, Bryan *actor, writer, director*

Cambridge
Acheson, Roy Malcolm *epidemiologist, educator*
Buiter, Willem Hendrik *economics educator*
Carpenter, Adelaide Trowbridge Clark *geneticist*
Hawking, Stephen W. *astrophysicist, mathematician*
†Hawthorne, Sir William (Rede) *aerospace and mechanical engineer, educator*
Hodgkin, Sir Alan Lloyd *biophysicist*
Hutton, Warwick Blair *writer, illustrator*
Kermode, (John) Frank *literary critic, educator*
Meade, James Edward *economist*
Milstein, César *molecular biologist*
Needham, Joseph *biochemist, historian of science, Orientalist*
Paton Walsh, Jill *author*
Perutz, Max Ferdinand *molecular biologist*
Sanger, Frederick *retired molecular biologist*
Steiner, George (Francis Steiner) *author, educator*
Todd, Alexander Robertus (Baron Todd of Trumpington) *chemistry educator*

Chiswick
Nelson, John Wilton *symphonic conductor*

Claverton Down
Buchanan, Robert Angus *archaeology educator*

Cornwall
Dark, Philip John Crosskey *anthropologist, educator*

Coventry
Trigg, Roger Hugh *philosophy educator*

Cranbrook
Hattersley-Smith, Geoffrey Francis *retired government research scientist*

East Sussex
Wilson, Leroy *retired glass manufacturing company executive*

Eastbourne,
Baylen, Joseph O. *retired history educator*

Hampshire
Suhrbier, Klaus Rudolf *hydrodynamicist, naval architect*

Hartlepool
Smyth, Reginald (Reggie Smythe) *cartoonist*

Hingham
Pollini, Francis *author*

Hove
Kitchin, Laurence Tyson *liberal arts and drama educator, author*

Hull
Shorter, John *chemistry lecturer*

Iver Heath
Kubrick, Stanley *producer, director, writer*

Kent
Stewart, Mary Florence Elinor *author*

Leicester
Harijan, Ram *technology transfer researcher*

Linton
Kendrew, John Cowdery *molecular biologist, former college president*

London
Adams, George Bell *lawyer*
Albert, Robert Alan *lawyer*
Aliki, (Aliki Liacouras Brandenberg) *author, illustrator children's books*
Ambler, Eric *writer*
Amis, Sir Kingsley *novelist*
Andrews, Anthony *actor*
Arnott, Eric John *ophthalmologist*
Asfoury, Zakaria Mohammed *physician*
Ashkenazy, Vladimir Davidovich *concert pianist, conductor*
Aspbury, Herbert Francis *bank executive*
Ballard, James Graham *writer*
Band, David *investment banker*
Barnett, Bill Marvin *publishing company executive*

Barocci, Robert Louis *former advertising executive, entrepreneur*
Barshai, Rudolf Borisovich *conductor*
Bart, Lionel *composer, lyricist*
Bates, Alan (Arthur Bates) *actor*
Bates, Malcolm Rowland *corporate director*
Batla, Raymond John, Jr. *lawyer*
Bawden, Nina (Mary) *author*
Baxendell, Sir Peter (Brian) *petroleum engineer*
†Beck, Jeff *musician, composer, vocalist*
Bee, Robert Norman *banker*
Beharrell, Steven Roderic *lawyer*
Bell, Theodore Augustus *advertising executive*
Berger, Thomas Jan *financial company executive*
Biddle, Adrian *cinematographer*
Bigbie, John Taylor *lawyer, banker*
Binney, Robert Harry *bank executive*
Bischoff, Winfried Franz Wilhelm *merchant banker*
Boccardi, Louis Donald *news agency executive*
Bokaemper, Stefan *hotel executive*
Bonynge, Richard *opera conductor*
Bowie, David (David Robert Jones) *musician, actor*
Branagh, Kenneth *actor, director*
Bream, Julian *classical guitarist and lutanist*
Brown, Peter Stewart *lawyer*
Catto of Cairncatto, Baron Stephen Gordon *banker*
Cellan-Jones, James Gwynne *television director*
Chappell, Anthony Gordon *banker*
Christie, Julie *actress*
Chubb, Joseph *lawyer*
Clarke, Arthur Charles *author*
Cleese, John Marwood *writer, businessman, comedian*
Cleve, George *conductor*
Codron, Michael Victor *theatrical producer*
Cole, Richard A. *lawyer*
Collins, Paul John *banker*
Comfort, Alexander *physician, author*
Condon, Richard Thomas *author*
Conti, Tom *actor, writer, director*
Cook, Jan *recording industry executive*
Cowles, Fleur (Mrs. Tom M. Meyer) *author, artist*
Craig, Stuart N. *film production designer*
Crowe, William James, Jr. *diplomat*
Curry, Tim *actor*
Day-Lewis, Daniel *actor*
Deal, Timothy *diplomat, government executive*
de Bellaigue, Eric *media consultant, securities analysis specialist*
Dehennin, Herman Baron *diplomat*
Deighton, Len *author*
Dibble, Gordon Lynch *engineering company executive*
Dickinson, Peter *composer*
Douglas, Mary Tew *anthropology and humanities educator*
Drabble, Margaret *writer*
Eddo, James Ekundayo *industrial chemist, chemicals executive*
Elizabeth II, Her Majesty (Elizabeth Alexandra Mary) *Queen of United Kingdom of Great Britain and Northern Ireland, and her other Realms and Territories, head of the Commonwealth, defender of the faith*
Ewart, Gavin Buchanan *poet, writer*
Ewing, Maria Louise *soprano*
Fabricant, Arthur E. *lawyer, corporate executive*
Fenton, Thomas Trail *journalist*
Fine, Anne *author*
Follett, Ken (Symon Myles) *author*
Forsyth, Frederick *author*
Foster, Sir Norman Robert *architect*
Fowles, John *author*
Francke, Albert, III *lawyer*
Fraser, Lady Antonia *writer, editor*
Gaines, Peter Mathew *lawyer*
Ghiaurov, Nicolai *opera singer*
Gielgud, Sir (Arthur) John *actor, director*
Gilbert, Patrick Nigel Geoffrey *organization executive*
Gillam, Patrick John *oil company executive*
Gordon, Jeffrey I. *lawyer*
Grabske, William John *engineering and construction company executive*
Grade, Lew *entertainment corporation executive*
Green, Richard Lancelyn (Gordon) *editor, writer*
Greenbury, Sir Richard *food service executive*
Greener, Anthony *beverage company executive*
Gummer, Peter Selwyn *public relations executive*
Habgood, Anthony John *corporate executive*
Hale, Charles Martin *stockbroker*
†Hall, Peter Geoffrey *urban and regional planning educator*
Hall, Sir Peter Reginald Frederick *theater opera and film director*
Hallissey, Michael *accounting company executive*
Hampshire, Susan *actress*
Hare, David *playwright*
Harper, Heather Mary *soprano*
Harris, Howard Elliott *consulting company executive*
Harris, William Cecil *insurance company consultant*
Harrison, George *musician*
Hawthorne, Nigel Barnard *actor*
Hayden, Richard Michael *investment banker*
Hendricks, Barbara *opera singer, recitalist*
Higgins, Jack (Harry Patterson) *author*
Hite, Shere D. *author, cultural historian*
Hoban, Russell Conwell *author*
Hogwood, Christopher Jarvis Haley *music director, educator*
Holm, Ian *actor*
Hopkins, Sir Anthony (Philip) *actor*
Hornyak, Eugene Augustine *bishop*
Hoskins, Bob (Robert William Hoskins) *actor*
Hudson, Manley O., Jr. *lawyer*
Hughes, Ted *poet, author*
Hughes, Winifred Shirley *writer, illustrator*
Hunter Blair, Pauline Clarke *author*
Hurt, John Vincent *actor*
Idle, Eric *actor, screenwriter*
Irons, Jeremy John *actor*
James, P(hyllis) D(orothy) (Baroness James of Holland Park of Southwold in County of Suffolk) *author*
John, Elton Hercules (Reginald Kenneth Dwight) *musician*
Johnson, Thomas Edward *lawyer*
Jones, Terry *film director, author*
Jordan, Neil Patrick *film director*
Jourdren, Marc Henri *investment banker*
Kane, George Joseph *humanities educator*
Kies, David M. *lawyer*
Kingham, Richard Frank *lawyer*
Kingsley, Ben *actor*
Kirkby, Maurice Anthony *oil company executive*
Kitaj, R. B. *artist*
Kopech, Robert Irving *banker*
Kuper, Adam Jonathan *anthropologist, educator*

Kureishi, Hanif *author*
Lanigan, Denis George *retired advertising agency executive*
Laurie, James Andrew *journalist, broadcaster*
Leaf, Robert Stephen *public relations executive*
le Carré, John (David John Moore Cornwell) *author*
Lessing, Doris (May) (May Lessing) *writer*
Le Vien, John Douglas (Jack Le Vien) *motion picture and television producer, director*
Lloyd Webber, Sir Andrew *composer*
Lynne, Gillian Barbara *choreographer, dancer, actress*
Mackintosh, Cameron *musical theater producer*
Mallinckrodt, George W. *bank executive*
Marriner, Sir Neville *orchestra conductor*
Matthei, Warren Douglas *investment company executive*
Mayer, Peter *publisher*
McGinnis, Marcy Ann *television news executive producer*
McIntyre, Donald Conroy *opera singer, baritone*
McKellen, Ian *actor*
McLeod, Wilson Churchill *lawyer*
†McNulty, Dermot *public relations executive*
Mellon, John *publishing executive*
Metzger, Barry *lawyer*
Miller, Jonathan Wolfe *theater and film director, physician*
Minton, Yvonne Fay *mezzo-soprano*
†Mirren, Helen *actress*
Montero, Fernan Gonzalo *advertising executive*
Moreno, Glen Richard *banker*
Morris, Desmond *author*
Morrison, William David *lawyer*
†Mulford, David Campbell *banking executive*
Naipaul, Vidiadhar Surajprasad *author*
Nelson, Bernard Edward *lawyer*
Newburg, Andre W. G. *lawyer*
†Newmarch, Michael George *insurance company executive*
Norman, David Mark *human resource executive*
Nunn, Trevor Robert *director*
Ogden, Peter James *investment banker*
Oldman, Gary *actor*
O'Mahony, Jeremiah Francis *financial executive*
O'Toole, Peter *actor*
Owers, Brian Charles *holding company executive*
†Oxenbury, Helen *children's writer, illustrator*
†Palin, Michael Edward *writer, actor*
†Pennant-Rea, Rupert Lascelles
Philipsborn, John David *former banker, consultant*
Pinter, Harold *playwright*
Pleasants, Henry *music critic*
Pleasence, Donald *actor*
Plowright, Joan Anne *actress*
Porter, Lord George *chemist, educator*
Previn, Andre *composer, conductor*
Pritchett, Sir Victor Sawdon *author*
Puttnam, David Terence *film producer*
Randour, Paul A(lfred) *lawyer*
Rattle, Simon *conductor*
Read, Piers Paul *author*
Ricci, Ruggiero *violinist, educator*
Rice, Timothy Miles Bindon *stage and screenwriter, broadcaster*
†Rigg, Diana *actress*
Ross, Euan Macdonald *pediatrician, educator*
Saatchi, Maurice *communications and marketing company executive*
†Sainsbury of Preston Candover, Lord John Davan (Baron Sainsbury of Preston Candover) *corporate executive*
Salonen, Esa-Pekka *conductor*
Scardino, Albert James *journalist*
Schaufuss, Peter *dancer, producer, choreographer, ballet director*
Schlesinger, John Richard *film, opera and theater director*
†Self, Larry D. *architectural firm executive*
Serebrier, José *musician, conductor, composer*
Serota, Nicholas Andrew *art gallery director*
Shaw, Sir Neil McGowan *sugar, cereal-starch refining company executive*
Shaw, Richard John Gildroy *insurance executive*
Sheehy, Sir Patrick *manufacturing and service company executive*
Smith, Dame Maggie *actress*
Sorrell, Martin Stuart *marketing executive*
Spark, Muriel Sarah *writer*
Starr, Ringo (Richard Starkey) *musician, actor*
Steen, Norman Frank *marketing executive*
Stevens, Robert Bocking *lawyer, educator*
Sting, (Gordon Matthew Sumner) *musician, songwriter, actor*
Stoppard, Tom (Tomas Straussler) *playwright*
Streator, Edward James *diplomat*
Sutherland, Dame Joan *retired soprano*
Symon, Lindsay *neurological surgery educator*
Taylor, Jonathan Francis *agribusiness executive*
Tebaldi, Renata *opera singer*
Tennstedt, Klaus *conductor*
Thomas, Allen Lloyd *lawyer, private investor*
Thomas, Barbara Singer *lawyer*
Thompson, Emma *actress*
Treasure, John Albert Penberthy *advertising executive*
Tuohy, William *correspondent*
Tureck, Rosalyn *concert artist, author, editor, educator*
Ustinov, Sir Peter Alexander *actor, director, writer*
Van Culin, Samuel *religious organization administrator*
Vane, John Robert *pharmacologist*
Vaness, Carol *soprano*
Van Meter, John David *lawyer*
Vansittart, Peter *novelist, lecturer, critic*
Wallis, Diana Lynn *artistic director*
Warren, Edus Houston, Jr. *investment management executive*
Wilkinson, Geoffrey *chemist, educator*
Winner, Michael Robert *film director, writer, producer*
Zinnemann, Fred *film director*
Zschau, Marilyn *singer*

Malmesbury
Shober, Wharton *bioscience company executive*

Manchester
Knowlton, Thomas A. *food products executive*

Middlesex
Francis, Freddie *film producer and director*
Hancock, Ellen Marie *communications executive*
Lester, Richard *film director*

Milford on Sea
Styan, John Louis *English literature and theater educator*

Milton Keynes
Daniel, John Sagar *academic administrator, metallurgist*

Newcastle upon Tyne
Cookson, Dame Catherine Ann *author*

Oxford
Aldiss, Brian Wilson *author*
Cairncross, Sir Alexander Kirkland *university chancellor, economist*
Carey, John *English language educator, literary critic*
Dawes, Geoffrey Sharman *medical researcher*
Gottmann, Jean *geographer, educator*
Guillery, Rainer Walter *anatomy educator*
†Gulbrandsen, Natalie Webber *religious association administrator*
Hirsch, Peter Bernhard *metallurgist*
Howe, Daniel Walker *historian, educator*
May, Robert McCredie *biology educator*
Segal, Erich *author, educator*
†Williams, William Stanley Cossom *physics educator and researcher*

Oxfordshire
Wilson, James Ray *international business educator*

Poole
Gray, Kenneth John *engineering executive*
Stokes, Donald Gresham *vehicle company executive*

Richmond Green
Attenborough, Sir Richard Samuel *actor, producer, director, goodwill ambassador*

Rottingdean
Matthews, John Floyd *writer, educator*

Sandys
Stigwood, Robert Colin *theater, movie, television and record producer*

Stroud
Robinson, John Beckwith *development management consultant*

Suffolk
Clement, John *food products company executive*
Stauderman, Bruce Ford *advertising agency executive*

Surrey
Petrek, William Joseph *college president emeritus*

Trumpington Cambs
Santoni, Ronald Ernest *philosophy educator*

Uxbridge
Healey, Derek Edward *composer*

Walmer Deal
Symons, Julian Gustave *author*

Walton on Thames
Olney, Robert C. *diversified products manufacturing executive*

Warwick
Hands, Terence David (Terry Hands) *theater director*

West Dayton
Caskey, William Joslin *food products executive*

West Sussex
†Aiken, Joan (Delano) *author*

Whitchurch
Adams, Richard George *writer*

Wiltshire
Gabriel, Peter *vocalist, composer*

Windlesham
Tarallo, Angelo Nicholas *industrial gas and health care company executive, lawyer*

ESTONIA

Tallinn
Callow, Keith McLean *judge*

ETHIOPIA

Addis Ababa
†Baas, Marc A. *ambassador*
Haile Giorgis, Workneh *civil engineer*

FIJI

Suva
Usher, Sir Leonard Gray *retired news association executive*

FINLAND

Helsinki
†Siimestö, Orvo Kalervo *financial executive*
Varmavuori, Anneli *chemical society administrator, chemist*

Kuopio
Hakola, Hannu Panu Aukusti *psychiatry educator*

Tampere
Nikkari, Tapio Urho *medical biochemistry educator*

FRANCE

Aix les Bains
Tabau, Robert Louis *rheumatologist, researcher*

Amiens
Chacron, Joseph *mathematics educator*

Annet-sur-Marne
†Vasarely, Victor *artist*

Arles Cedex
Clergue, Lucien Georges *photographer*

Aulnay-sous-Bois
Shahin, Majdi Musa *biologist*

Ballan Mire
Delbarre, Bernard *pharmacologist, consultant*

Beduer
Ezelle, Robert Eugene *diplomat*

Belves
Raphael, Frederic Michael *author*

Bonnes
Ogilvy, David Mackenzie *advertising executive*

Bordeaux
Gouyon, Paul Cardinal *archbishop*

Boulogne-Billancourt
Dellis, Frédy Michel *car rental company executive*

Cedex
Bourdais de Charbonniere, Eric *financial executive*

Chartres
Benoit, Jean-Pierre Robert *pneumologist, consultant*

Chatenay-Malabry
Fabre, Raoul François *electronics company executive*
Perrault, Georges Gabriel *chemical engineer*

Courbevoie
Desmarescaux, Philippe *chemical company executive, engineer*

Creteil
Robert, Leslie Ladislas *research center administrator, consultant*

Fontainebleu
Ayres, Robert Underwood *environmental economics and technology educator*
Churchill, Neil Center *entrepreneur, educator*

Genlis
van Raalte, John A *research and engineering management executive*

Gouvieux
Fraser, David William *epidemiologist*

Joinville
Greer, Joseph Epps *architect*

Lauris
Spivak, Jonathan M. *journalist*

Laval
Sauvé, Georges *surgeon*

Le Plessis Robinson
Régnier, François Jean *pharmaceutical company executive*

Levauois
†de Pouzilhac, Alain Duplessis *advertising executive*

Longjumeau
Kapandji, Adalbert Ibrahim *orthopedic surgeon*

Lyons
Meunier, Pierre Jean *medical educator*

Marseilles
Dumitrescu, Lucien Z. *aerospace researcher*
Vague, Jean Marie *endocrinologist*

Montpellier
Michel, Henri Marie *medical educator*

Nanterre
Nguyen-Trong, Hoang *physician, consultant*

Neuilly
Hamilton, Robert William *lawyer*

Neuilly-sur-Seine
O'Neill, Lawrence Daniel *lawyer, consultant*
Ophuls, Marcel *film director and producer*
Presby, J. Thomas *financial advisor*

Orsay
Deutsch, Claude David *physicist, educator*
Fiszer-Szafarz, Berta (Berta Safars) *research scientist*
Reich, Robert Claude *metallurgist, physicist*

Paris
Abboud, Ann Creelman *lawyer*
†Annaud, Jean-Jacques *film director, screenwriter*
Arnault, Bernard Jean *trade company executive*
Bathias, Claude *materials science educator, consultant*
Baum, Axel Helmuth *lawyer*
Behrstock, Julian Robert *publishing consultant, writer*
Ben Amor, Ismäil *obstetrician/gynecologist*
Biala, Janice *artist*
Bommelaer, Alain *finance company executive*
Boulez, Pierre *composer, conductor*
Cochran, John M., III *lawyer*
Collomb, Bertrand Pierre *cement company executive*
Cone, Sydney M., III *lawyer*
Cornell, Robert Arthur *international government official*
Cousteau, Jacques-Yves *marine explorer, film producer, writer*
Craig, William Laurence *lawyer*
Dausset, Jean *immunologist*
Davidson, Alfred Edward *lawyer*
Dean, John Gunther *diplomat*
De Givenchy, Hubert James Marcel Taffin (Givenchy) *fashion designer*
de Havilland, Olivia Mary *actress*
De Lyrot, Alain Herve *editor*
DuBois, Jean Gabriel *pharmaceutical executive, pharmacist*
Dubs, Patrick Christian *publisher*
Ferriter, John Pierce *diplomat*
Gallant, Mavis *author*
Gontier, Jean Roger *internist, physiology educator, consultant*
Gottschalk, Charles M. *international relations consultant*
Goupy, Jacques Louis *chemiometrics engineer*
Hintz, Bernd Jurgen *consumer goods manufacturing company executive*
Houël, Patrick *financial executive*
Huffstodt, Karen *soprano*
Iseman, Joseph Seeman *lawyer*
Jaclot, Francois Charles *manufacturing executive*
Jacob, François *biologist*
Jolas, Betsy *composer*
†Konvitz, Josef Wolf *history educator, international civil servant*
Kurtz, Eugene Allen *composer, educator, consultant*
Lacroix, Christian Marie Marc *fashion designer*
Lagerfeld, Karl Otto *fashion designer*
Landers, Steven E. *lawyer*
Larounis, George Philip *manufacturing company executive*
Larson, Alan Philip *federal official*
Lecerf, Olivier Maurice Marie *construction company executive*
LeGoffic, Francois *biotechnology educator*
Lehn, Jean-Marie Pierre *chemistry educator*
Levee, John Harrison *artist, designer*
Levy, Etienne Paul Louis *surgical department administrator*
Lubell, Harold *economic consultant*
MacCrindle, Robert Alexander *lawyer*
Marcus, Claude *advertising executive*
Marton, Eva *opera singer*
Masurel, Jean-Louis Antoine Nicolas *industrialist*
McGurn, William Barrett, III *lawyer*
Myerson, Jacob Myer *former foreign service officer*
Nême, Jacques *economist*
Polanski, Roman *film director, writer, actor*
Rampal, Jean-Pierre Louis *flutist*
Rawlings, Boynton Mott *lawyer*
Renouf, Edda *artist*
Riggs, John Hutton, Jr. *lawyer*
Rohmer, Eric (Henri Joseph Scherer) *film director*
Rosenberg, Pierre Max *museum curator*
Roudybush, Franklin *diplomat, educator*
Roussel, Lee Dennison *diplomat*
Roux, Ambroise Marie Casimir *business executive*
Salans, Carl Fredric *lawyer*
†Suard, Pierre Henri Andre *power company executive*
Teboul, Albert *nuclear engineer, nuclear energy industry executive*
†Vinciguerra, Jean-Louis *finance company executive*
Vuitton, Henry-Louis *designer*
Williams, C(harles) K(enneth) *poet, literature and writing educator*
Wolrich, Peter M. *lawyer*
Yuechiming, Roger Yue Yuen Shing *mathematics educator*

Ramatuelle
Collins, Larry *author, journalist*

Rognac
Castel, Gérard Joseph *physician*

Strasbourg
Barnes, Shirley Elizabeth *foreign service officer*
Schlegel, Justin J. *psychological consultant*

Thonon-les-Bains
Savin, Ronald Richard *chemical company executive, inventor*

Vaucluse
Pfriem, Bernard Aldine *artist*

Velizy-Villacoublay
Musikas, Claude *chemical researcher*

GERMANY

Ascheberg
Voss, Werner Konrad Karl *architect, engineer*

Berlin
Abbado, Claudio *conductor*
Anderson, David *former ambassador*
Fischer-Dieskau, Dietrich *baritone*
Palmer, R(obie Marcus Hooker) Mark *banker*
Selle, Burkhardt Herbert Richard *physicist*
Stachel, John Jay *physicist, educator*
Tiedemann, Heinz *biochemist*

Bielefeld
Lauven, Peter Michael *anesthesiologist*
Muller, Achim *chemistry educator*

Böblingen
Mühe, Erich *surgical educator*

Bonn
Fleming, Joseph Benedict *newspaperman*

Cologne
Stuhl, Oskar Paul *organic chemist*
Ungers, Oswald M. *architect, educator*

Darmstadt
†Hofmann, Karl Heinrich *mathematics educator*
Lichtenthaler, Frieder Wilhelm *chemist, educator*

Dortmund
Freund, Eckhard *electrical engineering educator*

Dresden
Schreier, Peter *tenor*

Düsseldorf
Nickel, Horst Wilhelm *psychology educator*
Olson, Sigmund Lars *corporate finance executive*
Richter, Gerhard *artist*

Finning
English, Charles Brand *retired lawyer*

Frankfurt
Ammann, Jean-Christophe *art curator*
Duus, Peter *neurology educator*
Tholey, Paul Nikolaus *psychology educator, physical education educator*

Freiburg
Schaefer, Hans-Eckart *pathologist*

Garching
Grieger, Günter *physicist*

Gladbeck
Geisler, Linus Sebastian *physician, educator*

Göttingen
Eigen, Manfred *physicist*
Lorenz-Meyer, Wolfgang *aeronautical engineer*
†Sheldrick, George Michael *chemistry educator, crystallographer*
Tietze, Lutz Friedjan *chemist, educator*
Wedemeyer, Erich Hans *physicist*

Greifswald
Teuscher, Eberhard *pharmacist*

Groebenzell
Chandrasekhar, Bellur Sivaramiah *physics educator*

Gütersloh
Wössner, Mark Matthias *media company executive*

Hamburg
Jensen, Elwood Vernon *biochemist*
Müller-Eberhard, Hans Joachim *medical research scientist, administrator*
Neumeier, John *choreographer, ballet company director*
Ramsey, Bill (William McCreery) *singer, actor, composer-lyricist, television executive*

Hannover
Döhler, Klaus Dieter *pharmaceutical and development executive*

Heidelberg
Staab, Heinz A. *chemist*

Hemsbach
Froessl, Horst Waldemar *business executive, data processing developer*

Jülich
Krasser, Hans Wolfgang *physicist*
Stengel, Eberhard Friedrich Otto *botanist*

Kaiserslautern
Immesberger, Helmut *lawyer*

Katlenburg-Lindau
Hagfors, Tor *institute director*

Kelkheim
Haeske, Horst *physicist*

Kiel
Brockhoff, Klaus K. L. *marketing and management educator*

Kruft
Lekim, Dac *chemist*

Küssaberg
Lyndon, Maynard *architect*

Ladenburg
Traub, Peter *biochemist*

Leipzig
Hielscher, Udo Artur *business administration and finance educator*

Lüneberg
Linde, Robert Hermann *economics educator*

Mainz
Gütlich, Philipp *chemistry educator*
Meisel, Werner Paul Ernst *physicist*

Mannheim
Steffens, Franz Eugen Aloys *computer science educator*

Münster
Maltese, George John *mathematics educator*
Spevack, Marvin *English educator*

Munich
Araiza, Francisco (José Francisco Araiza Andrade) *opera singer*
Berg, Jan Mikael *science educator*
Binnig, Gerd Karl *physicist*
Bodlaj, Viktor *electrical engineer*
Born, Gunthard Karl *aerospace executive*
Chapman, Wes *dancer*
Fassbaender, Brigitte *opera singer*
Fischer, Ernst Otto *chemist, educator*
Giacconi, Riccardo *astrophysicist, educator*
Goodman, Alfred *composer, musicologist*
†Kniehl, Hans Joachim *construction company executive*
Paumgartner, Gustav *hepatologist, educator*
Saur, Klaus G. *publisher*
Scharbert, Josef *retired theology educator*
Stiegler, Karl Drago *mathematician*
von Minckwitz, Bernhard *publishing company executive*
Whetten, Lawrence Lester *international relations educator*

Neckargemuend
Kirchmayer-Hilprecht, Martin *geologist*

Nuremberg
Doerries, Reinhard René *modern history educator*

Paderborn
Belli, Fevzi *computing science educator, consultant*

Pforzheim
Voit, Franz Johann, Jr. *financial consultant*

Stuttgart
Kramer, Horst Emil Adolf *physical chemist*
Szirmai, Endre Anreas Franz *physician, writer*

Wachtberg-Villiprott
Gutman, Roy William *reporter*

Weinheim
†Köhler, Hans Dirk *publisher*

Wuppertal
Schubert, Guenther Erich *pathologist*

GHANA

Accra
Brown, Kenneth L. *ambassador*
Korangteng, Daniel Agyei *minister*

Kumasi
Sarpong, Peter Kwasi *bishop*

GRAND CAYMAN ISLAND

Crockett, James Grover, III *musician, former music publisher*

GREECE

Athens
Androutsellis-Theotokis, Paul *civil engineer*
Hatzakis, Michael *electrical engineer, research executive*
Iakovidis, Spyros Eustace *archaeology educator*
Katsikadelis, John *civil engineering educator*
Screttas, Constantinos George *chemistry educator*
Sekeris, Constantine Evangelos *biochemistry educator*

Halandri
†Dorbis, John *school system administrator*

Kalamaki
Cacouris, Elias Michael *economist, consultant*

Thessaloniki
Tsagas, Grigorios Fotios *mathematics educator*

GRENADA

Saint George's
Brunson, Joel Garrett *pathologist, educator*

GUINEA

Conakry
Saloom, Joseph A., III *diplomat*

HONG KONG

Hong Kong
Choo, Yeow Ming *lawyer*
Chu, Franklin Dean *lawyer*
Collins, Charles Roland *lawyer*
Enlow, Fred Clark *banker*
Goodman, Stephen H. *investment bank executive*
Halperin, David Richard *lawyer*
Harris, Randy A. (Alan Harris) *investment executive, lawyer*
Kwong, Peter Kong Kit *bishop*
Lehner, Urban Charles *journalist*
Lui, Ming Wah *electronics executive*
Magarity, Russell Lynn *banker*
Rowe, Kevin S. *banker*
†Sherrill, Joseph Harlan, Jr. *tobacco company executive*
Tanner, Douglas Alan *lawyer*
Tse, Edmund Sze-Wing *insurance company executive*
Wong, Wing Keung *trading, electronics company executive, physician*

Kowloon
Burns, Robert Henry *hotel executive*
Chang, Leroy L. *physicist*

Chiang, Samuel Edward *theological educator, humanities educator*
Liou, Ming-Lei *electrical engineer*
Lui, Ng Ying Bik *engineering educator, consultant*

Peninsula
Pisanko, Henry Jonathan *command and control communications company executive*

Sha Tin
Kao, Charles Kuen *electrical engineer, educator*

Wanchai
van Hoften, James Dougal Adrianus *business executive, former astronaut*

ICELAND

Reykjavik
Jolson, Alfred James *bishop*
Jónatansson, Halldór *utility company executive*
Thorarensen, Oddur C.S. *pharmacist*

INDIA

Calcutta
Kothari, Bijay Singh *accountant*

Chandigarh
†Saboo, Rajendra K. *manufacturing executive*

Madras
Chandra Sekharan, Pakkirisamy *forensic scientist*

New Delhi
Gregorios, Paulos Mar *archbishop, metropolitan of Delhi*

Yavatmal
Ward, Daniel Thomas *bishop*

IRAN

Tehran
†Dinkha, Mar, IV *church administrator*
Sharifi, Iraj Alagha *organic chemistry educator*

IRELAND

Ballyvaughan
Wicks, Eugene Claude *art educator*

Dalkey
Leonard, Hugh (John Keyes Byrne) *playwright*

Donegal
Friel, Brian (Bernard Patrick Friel) *author*

Galway
Lavelle, Seán Marius *clinical informatics educator*

Mullingar
Donleavy, James Patrick *writer, artist*

Wicklow
McCaffrey, Anne Inez *author*

ISLE OF MAN

Peel
Wakeman, Rick *entertainer, composer*

ISRAEL

Haifa
Galil, Uzia *electronics company executive*
Peled, Abraham *computer company executive*

Herzliya
Bitan, Giora Yoav *computer systems executive*

Jerusalem
†Abington, Edward Gordon, Jr. *diplomat*
†Arnon, Michael *finance company executive*
Bronner, Ethan Samuel *news correspondent*
Davis, Moshe *historian*
Rosenne, Meir *lawyer, government agency administrator*
Schindler, Pesach *rabbi, educator, author*

Ra'ananna
Hayon, Elie M. *chemist, educator*

Savyon
Bushinsky, Jay (Joseph Mason) *journalist, radio commentator, television correspondent*

Tel Aviv
Mehta, Zubin *conductor, musician*
Rubin, Barry Mitchel *foreign policy analyst, writer*

ITALY

Camerino
Miyake, Akio *biologist, educator*

Florence
Cecil, Charles Harkless *artist, educator*
Pope-Hennessy, John Wyndham *art historian*

Frattocchie Marino
Storaro, Vittorio *cinematographer*

Messina
Gimbo, Angelo *veterinary pathology educator, researcher*

Nigro, Aldo *physiology and psychology educator*

Milan
Bellobono, Ignazio Renato *chemist, educator*
Bondi, Enrico *educator*
†Calasso, Roberto *writer, publisher*
Ferré, Gianfranco *fashion designer, artistic director*
Poluzzi, Amleto *chemical company consultant*
Sindoni, Elio *physics educator*
Valcavi, Umberto *chemistry educator*

Naples
Tarro, Giulio *virologist*

Novara
Pernicone, Nicola *catalyst consultant*

Padua
Rosati, Mario *mathematician, educator*

Pavia
di Jeso, Fernando *biochemistry educator*

Pontedera
Grotowski, Jerzy *theater director, acting educator*

Ravenna
Muti, Riccardo *orchestra and opera conductor*

Rome
Ahrens, William Henry *architect*
Alegi, Peter Claude *lawyer*
†Antonioni, Michelangelo *film director*
Audet, Leonard *theologian*
Bafile, Corrado Cardinal *clergyman*
†Baum, William Wakefield Cardinal *former church official*
Bertolucci, Bernardo *film director*
†Casolino, Vincenzo *library director*
Cassiers, Juan *diplomat*
Dashow, James *composer*
Hjort, Howard Warren *international organization official, economist*
Levi-Montalcini, Rita *neurobiologist, researcher*
Loren, Sophia *actress*
Lynch, Edward Stephen *corporate executive*
Marchand, J. C. de Montigny *Canadian public servant*
Rossmiller, George Eddie *agricultural economist*
Wynn, Coy Wilton *journalist*
Zeffirelli, Franco *theater and film director*
Zimolo, Armando *insurance company executive*

San Donato
Roggero, Arnaldo *polymer chemistry executive*

Siena
Berio, Luciano *composer, conductor, educator*

Trieste
Salam, Abdus *physicist, educator*

Turin
Agnelli, Giovanni *industrial executive*

Venice
Pasinetti, Pier Maria *author*

JAMAICA

Mona Kingston
Ferguson, Marjorie Delores *nursing educator*

JAPAN

Aichi-ken
Yukei, Hasebe Yoshikazu *religious studies educator*

Ashiya
Yukio, Takeda *engineering educator*

Chiba
Yamada, Shinichi *mathematician, computer scientist, educator*

Ehime
Sakai, Yoshiro *chemistry educator*

Fukuoka
Aizawa, Keio *biology educator*
Omura, Tsuneo *medical educator*
Shirai, Takeshi *physician*

Gotsu
Hirayama, Chisato *healthcare facility administrator, physician, educator*

Hachioji
Shimoji, Sadao *applied mathematics educator, engineer*

Hirakata
Nakanishi, Tsutomu *pharmaceutical science educator*

Hiroshima
Harkness, Donald Richard *hematologist, educator*
Kobayashi, Naomasa *biology educator*
Tahara, Eiichi *pathologist, educator*

Hokkaido
Saito, Shuzo *electrical engineering educator*

Ibaraki
Ishii, Yoshinori *geophysics educator*
Yamada, Keiichi *engineering educator, university official*

Ise
Hayashi, Takemi *physics educator*

Isehara
Morita, Kazutoshi *psychology educator, consultant*

JAPAN

Ishikawa
Konishi, Kenji *geology educator*
Nasu, Shoichi *electrical engineering educator*

Iwate
Kawauchi, Hiroshi *hormone science educator*

Kanagawa
Maeda, Toshihide Munenobu *spacecraft system engineer*
Matsubara, Tomoo *software scientist*
Saitoh, Tamotsu *pharmacology educator*
Swarz, Sahl *sculptor*

Kanazawa
Kawamura, Mitsunori *material scientist, civil engineering educator*

Kawasaki
Taniuchi, Kiyoshi *mechanical engineering educator*
Terada, Yoshinaga *economist*

Kita-ku
Ohnami, Masateru *mechanical engineering educator*

Kitakyushu
Okubo, Toshiteru *health science facility administrator, educator*
Takeda, Yoshiyuki *chemical company executive*

Kobe
Masai, Mitsuo *chemical engineer, educator*
Tani, Shohei *pharmacy educator*
Yamabe, Shigeru *medical educator*

Koganei
Akiyama, Masayasu *chemistry educator*

Koriyama,
Ohama, Yoshihiko *architectural engineer, educator*

Kurashiki
Masamoto, Junzo *chemist, researcher*

Kyoto
Araki, Takeo *chemistry educator*
Fukui, Kenichi *chemist*
Kawabata, Nariyoshi *chemistry educator*
Nagao, Makoto *electrical engineering educator*
Shoichi, Ida *artist, printmaker, painter, sculptor*
Tachiwaki, Tokumatsu *chemistry educator*
Yamana, Shukichi *chemistry educator*

Meguro-ku
Sakamoto, Munenori *engineer educator, researcher, chemist*

Minato-ku
Doi, Masayuki *credit card company executive*
Ito, Masatoshi *retail executive*

Miyakonojo
Eto, Morifusa *chemistry educator*

Miyazaki
Meyer, Ruth Krueger *museum administrator, art historian*

Muroran
Fu, Yuan Chin *chemical engineering educator*

Nagano
Ito, Kentaro *electrical engineering educator*

Nagoya
Abe, Yoshihiro *ceramic engineering educator*
Kato, Masanobu *lawyer, educator*
Murakami, Edahiko *chemistry educator*
Shioiri, Takayuki *pharmaceutical science educator*
Yoshida, Tohru *science and engineering educator*

Nara
Hayashi, Tadao *engineering educator*

Narashino
Inazumi, Hikoji *chemical engineering educator*

Neyagawa
Motoba, Toshio *physics educator*

Niigata
Asakura, Hitoshi *internal medicine educator*

Nishinomiya
Ogida, Mikio *history of religion educator*

Okayama
Furuya, Tsutomu *plant chemist and biochemist, educator*
Oda, Takuzo *biochemistry educator*
Torii, Sigeru *chemistry educator*
Ubuka, Toshihiko *biochemistry educator*

Okinawa
Noda, Yutaka *physician, otolaryngologist*

Okubo
Nishimura, Susumu *biologist*

Osaka
Aoki, Ichiro *theoretical biophysics systems science educator*
Horiuchi, Atsushi *physician, educator*
Ikeda, Kazuyosi *physicist, poet*
Kobayashi, Mitsue *chemistry educator*
†Mima, Kunioki *physicist, educator*
Osumi, Masato *utility company executive*
Sakaguchi, Genji *food microbiologist, educator*
Sakamoto, Ichitaro *oceanologist, consultant*
Solberg, Norman Robert *lawyer*
Watanabe, Toshiharu *ecologist, educator*
Yoneyama, Hiroshi *chemistry educator*

Otsu
Matsuura, Teruo *chemistry educator*
Takemoto, Kiichi *chemistry educator*

Sagamihara
Okui, Kazumitsu *biology educator*

Sakai-Gun
Ise, Norio *chemistry educator*

Sambu-Gun
Morishige, Fukumi *surgeon*

Sapporo
Fukuda, Morimichi *medical educator*

Sendai
Oikawa, Atsushi *pharmacology educator*
Oikawa, Hiroshi *materials science educator*
Okuyama, Shinichi *physician*
Shoji, Sadao *soil scientist*
Sone, Toshio *acoustical engineering educator*

Setagaya-Ku
Kurosawa, Akira *film director*

Seto
Rin, Zengi *economic history educator*

Shibuya-ku
Torii, Shuko *psychology educator*

Shiga
Makigami, Yasuji *transportation engineering educator*

Shimizu
Uyeda, Seiya *geophysics educator*

Shimonoseki
Sekitani, Toru *otolaryngologist, educator*

Shimotsuga
Ichimura, Tohju *pediatrician, educator*

Shinjyuku-ku
Honami, Shinji *mechanical engineer educator*

Tenri
Miyata, Gen *history of religion educator*

Tochigi
Iida, Shuichi *physicist,educator*
Takasaki, Etsuji *urology educator*

Togane
Uchiyama, Shoichi *mechanical engineer*

Tokorozawa
Nakamura, Hiroshi *urology educator*

Tokyo
Akasaki, Toshiro *machinery manufacturing executive*
Akera, Tai *pharmacologist*
Aoyama, Hiroyuki *structural engineering educator*
Armacost, Michael Hayden *ambassador, government official*
Atobe, Yasuzo *financial company executive*
Azuma, Takamitsu *architect, educator*
Churchill, James Allen *lawyer*
Drabkin, David *lawyer*
Franklin, William Emery *corporate executive*
Fujii, Hironori Aliga *aerospace engineer, educator*
Fujii, Keishi *bank executive*
Hashimoto, Kunio *architect, educator*
Hayashi, Taizo *hydraulics researcher, educator*
Hideaki, Okada *information systems specialist*
Hori, Yukio *scientific association administrator, engineering educator*
†Inagaki, Masao *advertising agency executive*
Ishii, Akira *medical parasitologist, malarialogist, allergologist*
†Ishikawa, Rokuro *construction company executive*
Isozaki, Arata *architect*
Iwakura, Yoshio *chemistry educator*
Johnson, Keith Gilbert *heavy equipment company executive*
†Kajima, Shoichi *warehouse executive*
†Kaku, Ryuzaburo *precision instruments manufacturing company executive*
Kamiya, Yoshio *research chemist, educator*
Kaneko, Hisashi *engineering executive, electrical engineer*
Kawachi, Michael Tateo *lawyer*
Kigoshi, Kunihiko *geochemistry educator*
Kitazawa, Koichi *materials science educator*
Koehler, John Edget *electronics company executive*
†Kogure, Gohei *advertising executive*
Koshi, Masaki *engineering educator*
Krisher, Bernard *foreign correspondent*
Kurita, Chushiro *writer, engineering educator, researcher*
Kusama, Yayoi *sculptor, painter*
Kuwahara, Mitsunori *judicial scrivener, consultant*
Makihara, Minoru *diversified corporation executive*
Makino, Shojiro (Mike Makino) *chemicals executive*
Masuda, Gohta *physician, educator*
†Miyazawa, Akira *advertising executive*
Morita, Akio *electronics company executive*
Musha, Toshimitsu *physicist, educator*
Nagai, Tsuneji *pharmaceutics educator*
Naito, Takeshi *investment company executive*
Nakagaki, Masayuki *chemist*
†Narita, Yutaka *advertising executive*
Nomura, Shigeaki *aerospace engineer*
Nozoe, Tetsuo *organic chemist, research consultant*
Ohe, Shuzo *chemical engineer, educator*
†Ohga, Norio *electronics executive*
Oliver, Steven Wiles *banker*
Ori, Kan *political science educator*
Oshita, Koji *advertising executive*
Ranney, Maurice William *chemical company executive*
Reid, Edward Snover *lawyer*
Sakurai, Kiyoshi *economics educator*
†Simons, Lewis Martin *journalist*
Smith, Robert Lee *photographic company executive*
Suami, Tetsuo *chemistry educator*
Taguchi, Yoshitaka *architect*
Takahashi, Keiichi *zoology educator*
Terao, Toshio *physician, educator*
Torii, Tetsuya *retired science educator*
Tsuchida, Eishun *chemistry educator*

Tsuda, Kyosuke *organic chemist, science association administrator*
Watanabe, Kouichi *pharmacologist, educator*

Tondabayashi
Nozato, Ryoichi *metallurgy educator, researcher*

Toshima-Ku
Furuichi, Susumu *physics researcher*

Toyama
Hayashi, Mitsuhiko *physics educator*

Toyonaka
Kishimoto, Uichiro *biophysicist*

Toyota
Miyachi, Iwao *electrical engineering educator*

Toyota Aichi
Toyoda, Eiji *automobile manufacturing company executive*

Tsukuba
Esaki, Leo *physicist*
Koga, Tatsuzo *aerospace engineer, educator*
Nannichi, Yasuo *engineering educator*

Tsukuba-shi, Ibaraki-ken
Kobayashi, Susumu *data processing executive, super computer consultant*

Uji
Yasumoto, Kyoden *food science educator*

Urawa
Hiyama, Tetsuo *biochemistry educator*
Narasaki, Hisatake *analytical chemist*

Yamaguchi
Suzuki, Nobutaka *chemistry educator*

Yamanashi-ken
Onaya, Toshimasa *internal medicine educator*

Yokohama
Asawa, Tatsurō *chemistry researcher*
Kaneko, Yoshihiro *cardiologist, researcher*
Niki, Katsumi *chemist, educator*
Ogawa, Seiichiro *chemistry educator*
Tanaka, Nobuyoshi *engineering consultant*

KENYA

Mbita South Nyanza
Khan, Zeyaur Rahman *entomologist*

Mombasa
†Schmiel, Eugene *foreign service officer*

LATVIA

Riga
Silins, Ints M. *ambassador*

LUXEMBOURG

Luxembourg Ville
Elliott, Lawrence *writer*

MALAYSIA

Penang
Das, Kumudeswar *food and biochemical engineering educator*

MARTINIQUE

Anses d'Arlet
Price, Richard *anthropologist, author*

MAURITANIA

Nouackchott
Brown, Gordon Stewart *diplomat*

MICRONESIA

Chuuk, Caroline Islands
Neylon, Martin Joseph *bishop*

MONACO

Lacets Saint-Léon
Kimmle, Manfred *investment company executive*

WHO'S WHO IN AMERICA

Stade Louie
Davies, Gareth John *trade association executive*

MOROCCO

Casablanca
Cary, Anne O. *diplomat*

MOZAMBIQUE

Maputo
Jett, Dennis Coleman *ambassador*
†Jon de Vos, Peter *former U.S. ambassador to Mozambique*

NAMIBIA

Windhoek
†Holmes, Genta Hawkins *diplomat*

THE NETHERLANDS

Amsterdam
Averill, Bruce Alan *chemistry educator*
Baer, Jo *painter*
Kels, James *publishing executive*
†Vinken, Pierre Jacques *publishing executive, neurosurgeon*
Walker, William Ross *accountant*
Wiegman, Lenore Ho *chemist*

Bunnik
van Dyke, Jacob *civil engineer*

Delft
Moulijn, Jacob A. *chemical technology educator*

Goor
Bonting, Sjoerd Lieuwe *biochemist, priest*

Hilversum
De Waart, Edo *conductor*

Leiden
Banta, Henry David *physician, researcher*

Maastricht
Van Praag, Herman Meir *psychiatrist, educator, administrator*

The Hague
Allison, Richard Clark *judge*
†Herkstroter, Cornelius *oil industry executive*
Kylián, Jirí *choreographer*
†Nones Sucre, Carlos Enrique *political organization executive*
Van Wachem, Lodewijk Christiaan *petroleum company executive*

NEW CALEDONIA

Noumea
Curlook, Walter *mining company executive*

NEW ZEALAND

Bay of Islands
Veysey, Arthur Ernest *reporter, administrator, biographer*

NIGER

Niamey
†Davison, John S. *ambassador*

NIGERIA

Lagos
†Carrington, Walter C. *ambassador*

NORWAY

Lilleström
Borgen, Ole Edvard *bishop, educator*

Oslo
Fagerhol, Magne Kristoffer *immunologist*
Haug, Roar Brandt *architect*

Staranger
Fitzpatrick, Whitfield Westfeldt *lawyer*

Trondheim
Forssell, Börje Andreas *electronics engineer, educator, consultant*
Rokstad, Odd Arne *chemical engineer*
Svaasand, Lars Othar *electronics researcher*

PAKISTAN

Faisalabad
Irfan, Muhammad *pathology educator*

Hyderabad
Ali, Syed Wajahat *physical chemist, researcher*

Karachi
Shroff, Firoz Sardar *merger and acquisition professional*

Lahore
†Geoffrey, Iqbal (Mohammed Jawaid Iqbal Jafree) *artist, lawyer*

PANAMA

Balboa
Rubinoff, Ira *biologist, research administrator, conservationist*

Panama
Tarte, Rodrigo *agriculture and natural resources educator, resea*

PARAGUAY

Asunción
Ferreira Falcon, Magno *economist*

PERU

Lima
French, Edward Ronald *plant pathologist*
Gutiérrez, Gustavo *priest, educator, theologian*

THE PHILIPPINES

Legaspi Village
Quasha, William Howard *lawyer*

Malabon Manila
Pizarro, Antonio Crisostomo *agricultural educator, researcher*

Musuan
†Lao, Mardonio Magadan *history educator, researcher, farmer*

Pasay City
Lim, Sonia Yii *minister*

POLAND

Łódź
Zieliński, Jerzy Stanisław *scientist, electrical engineering educator*

Gdańsk
Jagoda, Jerzy Antoni *marine engineer*

Kraków
Noga, Marian *electrical engineer*
Pytko, Stanisław Jerzy *mechanical engineering educator*

Lodz
Guzek, Jan Wojciech *physiology educator*

Poznan
Golab, Wlodzimierz Andrzej *biologist, geographer, librarian*

Warsaw
Engelberg, Stephen Paul *reporter*
Koscielak, Jerzy *scientist, science administrator*
Semadeni, Zbigniew Wladyslaw *mathematician, educator*
Tarnecki, Remigiusz Leszek *neurophysiology educator, laboratory director*

PORTUGAL

Braga
Rocha, Armandino Cordeiro Dos Santos *accountant, educator, auditor*

Coimbra
Cunha-Vaz, Jose Guilherme Fernandes *ophthalmologist*

Funchal
Mayda, Jaro *lawyer, educator, author, consultant*

Lisbon
Berger, Jason *artist, printmaker*
De Almeida, Antonio Castro Mendes *surgery educator*
Villax, Ivan Emeric *chemical engineer, researcher*

QATAR

Doha
†Hambley, Mark Gregory *ambassador*

REPUBLIC OF KOREA

Chonju
Kang, Sung Kyew *medical educator*
Park, Byeong-Jeon *engineering educator*

Pohang
Choi, Sang-il *physics educator, researcher*

Seoul
Kang, Bin Goo *biologist*
Kim, Moon-Il *metallurgical engineering educator*
Ko, Myoung-Sam *control engineering educator*
Park, Won-Hoon *chemical engineer*

Taejon
Kim, Sung Chul *polymer engineering educator*
Lee, Choochon *physics educator, researcher*

REPUBLIC OF PANAMA

Panama
Thoman, Henry Nixon *food industry executive*

RUSSIA

Moscow
Atkin, William F. *lawyer*
†Keniaykin, Valery Fedorovich *Russian diplomat*

Novosibirsk
Aleksandrov, Leonid Naumovitsh *physicist, educator, researcher*

Saint Petersburg
Gosnell, Jack Leslie *diplomat*

Voronezh
Kostin, Vladimir Alexeevich *mathematics educator*

SAINT LUCIA

Castries
Felix, Kelvin Edward *archbishop*

SAUDI ARABIA

Al Khobar
Ashadawi, Ahmed Ali *computer consultancy company executive*

Dhahran
Warne, Ronson Joseph *mathematics educator*

Riyadh
Chaudhary, Shaukat Ali *ecologist, plant taxonomist*
†Olayan, Suliman Saleh *finance company executive*

SCOTLAND

Aberdeen
†Rousseau, George Sebastian *Eighteenth-century studies educator, chamber musician*

Cellardyke
Roff, William Robert *history educator, writer*

Clydebank
Krakoff, Irwin Harold *pharmacology and oncology educator*

Dumfriesshire
Godden, Rumer *author*

Edinburgh
Buchan, Hamish Noble *securities analyst*
McMaster, Brian John *artistic director*
Miller, James *construction company executive*

Glasgow
Courtney, James McNiven *chemist*

Gullane
Collins, Jeffrey Hamilton *research facility administrator, electrical engineering educator*

Peebles
Hooper, John Edward *retired physicist, researcher*

Saint Andrews
Lenman, Bruce Philip *historian, educator*

Stirling
Kleinpoppen, Hans Johann Willi *physics educator, researcher*

SINGAPORE

Singapore
Ho, Thomas Inn Min *computer scientist, educator*
Liu, Chang Yu *engineering educator*
McMahon, Paul Francis *international management executive*
Reed, John G. *lawyer*

SLOVENIA

Ljubljana
Sicherl, Pavle *economics educator, consultant*
Stusek, Anton *mechanical engineer, researc*

SOUTH AFRICA

Brooklyn
Smith, Edwin David *electrical engineer*

Johannesburg
Mendelsohn, Dennis *chemical pathology educator, consultant*

Klippoortjie
†Els, Theodore Ernest *professional golfer*

Port Elizabeth
Fugard, Athol Harold *playwright, actor, director*

SPAIN

Barcelona
de Larrocha, Alicia *concert pianist*
García Márquez, Gabriel José *author*
Jackson, Gabriel *historian*
Subirana, Juan Antonio *polymer chemist, educator*

Galilea, Mallorca
Ulbricht, John *artist*

Madrid
Álvarez Rendueles, José Ramón *bank executive*
†Babcock, Michael Joseph *retail company executive*
Berganza Vargas, Teresa *mezzo-soprano*
Feltenstein, Harry David, Jr. *chemical executive*
Frühbeck de Burgos, Rafael *conductor*
†Trueba, Fernando *film director and producer, screenwriter*

Mallorco
Raff, Joseph Allen *publishing company executive, author*

Oviedo
Garcia-Moran, Manuel *surgeon*

Santander
Ballesteros, Severiano *professional golfer*

Santiago De Compostela
Balseiro Gonzalez, Manuel *management executive, consultant*

Valencia
Sentandreu, Rafael *microbiologist*

SRI LANKA

Colombo
Schaffer, Teresita Currie *federal official*
Spain, James William *political scientist, writer, investor*

SWEDEN

Falun
Helgesson, Lars-Ake *manufacturing executive*

Gothenburg
Andersson, Leif Per Roland *construction company executive*
Bona, Christian Maximilian *dentist, psychotherapist*
Gyllenhammar, Pehr Gustaf *retired automobile company executive, writer*

Linköping
Schröder, Harald Bertel *aerospace industry executive*

Lund
Abdulla, Mohamed *physician, educator*
Grimmeiss, Hermann Georg *physics educator, researcher*
Welin, Walter *financial advisor*

Malmö
Cronberg, Stig *infectious diseases educator*

Nykoping
Kivikas, Toivelemb *physicist, executive*

Stockholm
Fernandez-Moran, Humberto *biophysicist*
Hagson, Carl Allan *utilities executive*
†Johnson, Antonia Axson *company executive*
Lindberg, Helge *aviation consultant*
McNown, John Stephenson *hydraulic engineer, educator*
Möller, Göran *immunology educator*
†Redman, Charles Edgar *diplomat*
Robinson, Hobart Krum *management consulting company executive*
Samuelsson, Bengt Ingemar *medical chemist*
†Siebert, Thomas L. *ambassador to Sweden*
Soederstrom, Elisabeth Anna *opera singer*

SWITZERLAND

Basel
Arber, Werner *microbiologist*
Reichstein, Tadeus *botanist, scientist, educator*

Bern
†Lawrence, M. Larry *ambassador*

Berne
Polke, Sigmar *artist*

Biel
Scheftner, Gerold *marketing executive*

Büsingen
Friede, Reinhard L. *neuropathologist, educator*

Burgdorf
Haeberlin, Heinrich Rudolf *electrical engineering educator*

Fribourg
Gurley, Franklin Louis *lawyer, military historian*
Hatschek, Rudolf Alexander *electronics company executive*

Gais
Langenegger, Otto *hydrogeologist*

Geneva
Abram, Morris Berthold *lawyer, diplomat*
Baladi, André *economist, financier*
Ballin, William Christopher *international shipping, investments and energy, advisor to corporations and government*
Barenboim, Daniel *conductor, pianist*
Barnes, Thomas Joseph *migration program administrator*
Bogsch, Arpad *diplomat*
De Pfyffer, Andre *lawyer*
Halle, Louis Joseph *author, educator*
Harigel, Gert Günter *physicist*
Henderson, Ralph Hale *physician*
Hofmann, Albert Josef *physicist*
Junz, Helen B. *economist*
Ledogar, Stephen J. *diplomat*
Morgenstern, Sheldon Jon *symphony orchestra conductor*
O'Regan, Richard Arthur *editor, retired foreign correspondent*
Overseth, Oliver Enoch *physicist, educator*
Polunin, Nicholas *environmentalist, author, editor*
Purcell, James Nelson, Jr. *international organization administrator*
Rabinowicz, Théodore *neuropathology educator*
Rubbia, Carlo *physicist*
Steinberger, Jack *physicist, educator*

Lausanne
Bloemsma, Marco Paul *investor*
Borel, Georges Antoine *gastroenterologist, consultant*
Caste, Jean F. *financial advisor*
Delaloye, Bernard *retired nuclear medicine physician*
Stingelin, Valentin *research center director, mechanical engineer*

Lucerne
Sherwin, James Terry *lawyer, window covering company executive*

Lugano
Ricci, Giovanni Mario *financial company executive*

Montreux
Cronin, Robert Francis Patrick *cardiologist, educator*

Rouille
Godard, Jean-Luc *film director*

Rueschlikon
Rohrer, Heinrich *physicist*

Staad
Moore, Roger George *actor*

Valais
Chase, Morris *international management consultant*

Vaud
Joseph, Michael Anthony *marketing executive*

Wallisellen
Kolbe, Hellmuth Walter *acoustical engineer, sound recording engineer*

Zürich
†Gut, Rainer Emil *banker*

Zurich
Barnevik, Percy Nils *electrical company executive*
†Dunitz, Jack David *retired chemistry educator, researcher*
Hauser, Helmut Otmar *biochemistry educator*
Hepgular, Yasar Metin *architectural engineering educator, consultant*
Kalman, Rudolf Emil *mathematician, researcher, systems scientist*
Lanford, Oscar Erasmus, III *mathematics educator*
Mueller, Stephan *geophysicist, educator*
Nievergelt, Jurg *computer science educator*
Panitz, Lawrence Herbert *lawyer*
Peterson, M. Roger *manufacturing executive, retired air force officer*

TAIWAN

Chung-Li
Hong, Zuu-Chang *engineering educator*
Tseng, Tien-Jiunn *physics educator*

Hsinchu
Liu, Ti Lang *physics educator*

Kaohsiung
Yeh, Kung Chie *electrical engineer*

Tainan
†Huang, Ting-Chia *chemical engineering educator, researcher*

Taipei
Chang, Chun-hsing *psychologist, educator*
Ch'in, Michael Kuo-hsing *international conference management executive*
Dai, Peter Kuang-Hsun *government official, aerospace executive*
Ma, Cheung-Shyang (Robert Ma) *reproductive physiology educator, geneticist*
Pao, Yih-Hsing *engineer, educator*
Yang, Chin-Ping *chemist, engineering educator*

TANZANIA

Dar Es Salaam
†DeJarnette, Edmund *ambassador*

THAILAND

Bangkok
Carlson, Mitchell Lans international technical advisor
Ludwig, Harvey Fred environmental engineer
Lyman, David lawyer
†Singh, Gajendra agricultural engineering educator
Stueart, Robert D. college dean, librarian, educator

TRINIDAD

Port of Spain
Cowal, Sally Grooms diplomat

TURKEY

Ankara
Inalcik, Halil historian, educator
Nuber, Philip William air force officer

TURKMENISTAN

Ashgabat
McCall, John Patrick college president, educator

TURKS AND CAICOS ISLANDS

Provinciales
Johnston, Samuel Thomas entertainment company executive

UKRAINE

Kiev
†Miller, William G. ambassador to Ukraine

UNITED ARAB EMIRATES

Al-Ain
Kiwan, Abdul Mageed Metwally chemistry educator

URUGUAY

Montevideo
Ventura, Oscar Nestor chemistry educator, researcher

VATICAN CITY

Vatican City
John Paul II, His Holiness Pope (Karol Jozef Wojtyla) bishop of Rome
†Szoka, Edmund Casimir Cardinal cardinal

VENEZUELA

Caracas
Farrell, Rodger Edward consumer products executive
Nakano, Tatsuhiko chemist, researcher, educator
Rangel-Aldao, Rafael biochemist
Sáez, Alberto M. physics educator

Caripe
Pereira, Jose Francisco plant physiologist

WALES

Cardiff
Morris, William Allan engineer

WEST INDIES

Granada
Barrett, James Thomas immunologist, educator

Grenada
Taylor, Keith Breden physician, educator

Montserrat
Diggs, J(esse) Frank retired magazine editor

ADDRESS UNPUBLISHED

Aaron, Betsy journalist
Aaron, Roy Henry entertainment company executive, lawyer
Abadi, Fritzie artist, educator
Abbe, Elfriede Martha sculptor, graphic artist
Abel, Harold psychologist, educator, university president
†Abele, Fred Raymond metal processing executive
Abell, Murray Richardson retired medical association administrator
Abere, Andrew Evan economist
Ablin, Richard Joel immunologist, educator
Aboody, Albert Victor accountant
Abraham, George G. retired packing company executive
Abramowicz, Janet painter, print-maker
Abzug, Bella Savitzky lawyer, former congresswoman
Achorn, Robert Comey retired newspaper publisher
Ackerman, Jack Rossin investment banker
Ackerman, Melvin investment company executive
Adam, John, Jr. insurance company executive emeritus
Adam, Orval Michael retired financial executive, lawyer
Adamovich, Shirley Gray retired librarian, state official
Adams, Arlin Marvin retired judge, counsel to law firm
Adams, Edwin Melville former foreign service officer, actor, author, lecturer
Adams, James Blackburn former state government official, former federal government official, lawyer
Adams, James Thomas surgeon
Adams, Oscar William, Jr. retired state supreme court justice
Adams, Paul Winfrey lawyer, business executive
Adaskin, Murray composer
Adato, Perry Miller documentary producer, director, writer
Addy, George Arthur retired judge
Adelman, Richard Charles gerontology educator, researcher
†Adelman, Robert Paul retired construction company executive, lawyer
Adelson, Mervyn Lee entertainment and communication industry executive
Aden, Arthur Laverne office systems company executive
Adisman, I. Kenneth prosthodontist
Adkins, Claudia K. nursing educator
Adler, Gerald film and television executive, lawyer
†Adler, Richard Melvin architect, planner
Agnew, Spiro Theodore former Vice President of U.S.
Ahearne, John Francis scientific research society administrator, researcher
Aikens, Martha Brunette national park service administrator
Ajemian, Robert Myron journalist
Akasofu, Syun-Ichi geophysicist
Albino, George Robert business executive
Alda, Alan actor, writer, director
Aldrich, Franklin Dalton research physician
Aldrich, Patricia Anne Richardson retired magazine editor
Aldrin, Buzz former astronaut, science consultant
Alfvén, Hannes Olof Gosta physicist
Alibrandi, Joseph Francis diversified industrial company executive
Alig, Frank Douglas Stalnaker construction company executive
Aljian, James Donovan investment company executive
Allan, Hugh James Pearson bishop
†Allen, Andrew Marshall advertising executive
Allen, Charles Eugene college administrator, agriculturist
Allen, George former congressman
Allen, Marilyn Myers Pool theater director, video producer
Allen, Theodore Earl computer company executive
Allen, Woody (Allen Stewart Konigsberg) actor, filmmaker, author
Allerton, John Stephen association executive
Alligood, Elizabeth H. special education educator
†Allison, John McComb aeronautical engineer, retired
Allshouse, Merle Frederick foundation executive
Almen, Louis Theodore retired college president
Almgren, Herbert Philip bank executive
Almond, Paul film director, producer, writer
Aloff, Mindy writer
Alpert, Hollis writer
Altan, Taylan engineering educator, mechanical engineer, consultant
Altman, Irwin psychology educator
Altshuler, Alan Anthony dean, political scientist
†Altshuler, Kenneth Z. psychiatrist
Alvi, Zahoor Mohem radiological physicist
Alvord, Joel Barnes bank executive
Amann, Charles Albert mechanical engineer
Ambrose, James Richard consultant, retired government official
Ambrozic, Aloysius Matthew archbishop
Ames, Donald Paul retired aerospace company executive, researcher
Ames, Oakes physicist, educator
Amon, Arthur Howard, Jr. real estate consultant, retired retailing executive
Amstutz, Daniel Gordon intergovernmental organization executive, former grain dealer, government official
Anaple, Elsie Mae medical, surgical and geriatrics nurse
Anastasi, Anne (Mrs. John Porter Foley, Jr.) psychology educator
Anastasi, William Joseph artist
†Ancker-Johnson, Betsy physicist, retired automotive company executive
Anderer, Joseph Henry textile company executive
†Anderson, Bob state legislator, business executive
Anderson, Fletcher Neal chemical executive
Anderson, Geoffrey Allen lawyer
Anderson, James Arthur mining company executive
Anderson, John Firth church administrator, librarian
Anderson, John Rogers Canadian diplomat
Anderson, Joseph Norman executive consultant, former food company executive, former college president
Anderson, Keith retired lawyer, retired banker
Anderson, Michael L. financial planning manager
Anderson, Ned, Sr. Apache tribal chairman
Anderson, Nils, Jr. former government official, retired business executive, industrial historian
Anderson, Stanton Dean lawyer
Anderson, Thomas Patrick mechanical engineer, educator
Anderson, Wayne Carl public information officer
Anderson-Spivy, Alexandra writer, editor
Andolsek, Ludwig J. association executive
Andrade, Edna artist, art educator
†Andras, Oscar Sidney oil company executive
Andreas, Dwayne Orville business executive
Andreoli, Thomas Eugene physician
Andretti, Mario (Gabriele) former professional race car driver
Andretti, Michael Mario race car driver
Andreuzzi, Denis chemical company executive
†Andrews, Curtis Dickerman, Jr. state legislator, insurance company official
Andrews, Julie actress, singer
Andrews, Michael Allen (Mike Andrews) congressman, lawyer
Andrews, William Frederick manufacturing executive
Andriole, Stephen John information systems executive
Andrisani, John Anthony editor, author, golf consultant
Angell, Richard Bradshaw philosophy educator
Angle, John Charles retired life insurance company executive
Anglemire, Kenneth Norton retired publishing company executive, writer, environmentalist, lawyer
†Angotti, Anthony J. advertising executive
Anguiano, Lupe business executive
Angulo, Gerard Antonio financial executive, investor, consultant
Anker, Peter Louis equity research director
Annenberg, Walter H. philanthropist, diplomat, editor, publisher, broadcaster
Annus, John Augustus artist
Ansbacher, Charles Alexander conductor, musician
Anselmini, Jean-Pierre communication corporation executive
Anspach, Herbert Kephart retired appliance company executive, patent attorney
Anthony, Earl Roderick professional bowler
Anthony, Piers science fiction writer
Appenzeller, Otto neurologist, researcher
Applebaum, Eugene retail drug store chain executive
Apruzzi, Gene retired stockbroker
Apted, Michael D. film director
Aptheker, Herbert historian, lecturer
†Aragon, Manny M. state legislator
Aranda, Miguel Angel surgeon, educator
Archer, Anne actress
Archer, Jeffrey Howard author, politician
†Archetto, Paul Henry secondary education educator, state legislator
Archibald, Nolan D. household and industrial products company executive
Archibold, Mildred Haynes bilingual education educator
Arcos, Cresencio S. ambassador
Arden, Sherry W. publishing company executive
Arenal, Julie (Mrs. Barry Primus) choreographer
Arenberg, Julius Theodore, Jr. retired accounting company executive
Argun, Fatima Hatice international consultant, specialist
Ariyoshi, George Ryoichi lawyer, business consultant, former governor Hawaii
Arlen, Michael J. writer
Arlidge, John Walter utility company executive
†Armacost, John Cooper packaging company executive
Armacost, Mary-Linda Sorber Merriam college president
Armey, Richard Keith congressman
Armistead, Thomas Boyd, III television and film producer
Armour, David Edward Ponton association executive
Armstrong, Anne Legendre (Mrs. Tobin Armstrong) former ambassador, corporate director
Armstrong, F(redric) Michael retired insurance company executive
Armstrong, John Allan business machine company research executive
Armstrong, Neil A. former astronaut
Armstrong, Thomas Newton, III museum director
Armstrong, Warren Bruce university president, historian, educator
Armstrong, William Henry lawyer
Arnaud, Claude Donald, Jr. physician, educator
†Arnett, Edward McCollin chemistry educator, researcher
Arnold, David Burton tooling systems company executive
Arnold, Duane Wade-Hampton minister, educator
Arnold, Henri cartoonist
Arnold, Jerome Gilbert lawyer
Arnold, William Howard nuclear fuel executive
Arnott, Howard Joseph biology educator, university dean
Arova, Sonia ballet educator, administrator
†Arrarás, José E. state legislator
Arthur, Beatrice actress
†Arthur, Rochelle Linda art director
Aschauer, Charles Joseph, Jr. corporate director, former company executive
Ashby, Clifford Charles theatre arts educator, historian
Ashcraft, Charles Olin business educator
Askey, William Hartman lawyer, federal magistrate judge
Askin, Leon artistic director, actor, producer, writer
†Aspen, Alfred William international trading company executive
Assante, Armand actor
Atherton, William actor
Atkinson, Bill designer
Atkinson, Dewey Franklin retired educational administrator
Attoe, Wayne Osborne architecture educator, author, designer
Atwood, Genevieve geologist
Au, Tung civil engineer, educator, consultant
Auberjonois, René Murat actor
Audet, Paul Andre retired newspaper executive
Aumont, Jean-Pierre actor, author
Auriemma, Louis Francis printing company executive
Aurin, Robert James entrepreneur
Austin, Ralph Leroy chemicals executive
Austin, Robert Clarke naval officer
Autin, Ernest Anthony, II chemist, educator
Avalon, Frankie singer, actor
Avian, Bob choreographer, producer
Axelrad, Irving Irmas lawyer, motion picture producer
Axilrod, Stephen Harvey investment banker, economist
Azarnoff, Daniel Lester pharmaceutical company consultant
Baack, John Edward publishing consultant
Babb, Frank Edward lawyer, executive
Babbitt, Samuel Fisher university administrator
Bacharach, Melvin Lewis venture capitalist
Bachert, Robert Frederic mathematician, systems analyst
Backlund, Ralph Theodore magazine editor
Bacon, George Edgar pediatrician, educator
†Baddour, Phillip A. lawyer, state legislator
Badham, John MacDonald motion picture director
Bageris, John artist, educator
Baggett, Donnis Gene journalist, editor
†Bagley, Amy L. state legislator
Bagley, William Thompson lawyer
Baier, Edward John former public health official, industrial hygiene engineer, consultant
Bailey, Francis Lee lawyer
Bailey, Henry John, III retired lawyer, educator
Bain, William Donald, Jr. lawyer, chemical company executive
Baker, Edward Kevin retail executive
Baker, Henry S., Jr. retired banker
Baker, Joe Don actor
Baker, Laurence Howard oncology educator
Baker, Margery Louise elementary education educator
Baker, Richard Hugh congressman
Baker, Robert M. L., Jr. academic administrator
Bakula, Scott actor
†Baldauf, Jill Christine advertising executive
Baldwin, Alec (Alexander Rae Baldwin, III) actor
Baldwin, C. Andrew, Jr. retired science educator
Baldwin, DeWitt Clair, Jr. physician, educator
Baldwin, George Curriden physicist, educator
Baldwin, William Russell foundation executive, optometrist
Ball, John Robert medical association executive
Ball, Lawrence retired physical scientist
†Ballou, James Howland architect
Balsam, Martin Henry actor
Balter, Alan conductor, music director
Bamberger, Gerald Francis plastics marketing consultant
Bambrick, James Joseph labor economist, labor relations executive
Bandeen, William Reid retired meteorologist
Bangs, John Kendrick lawyer, foundation executive, former chemical company executive
Banks, Robert Sherwood lawyer
Bannard, Walter Darby artist, art critic
Banner, Larry Shyres educator, athlete, consultant
Bantry, Bryan entrepreneur
Barbee, George E. L. financial services executive
Barca, George Gino winery executive, finanial investor
Barger, William James management consultant
†Barkeley, Norman A. vehicle manufacturing company executive
Barker, Mary Katherine retired nurse
†Barker, Robert biochemistry educator
†Barlow, William K. lawyer, state legislator
Barnebey, Kenneth Alan food company executive
Barnes, Joanna author, actress
Barnett, Vincent MacDowell, Jr. political science educator
†Barnett, William Allen finance executive
Barnhart, Jo Anne B. government official
Barnhill, Henry Grady, Jr. lawyer
Barnhouse, Lillian May Palmer retired medical, surgical nurse, researcher, civic worker
Barone, John Anthony university provost emeritus
Barrack, William Sample, Jr. petroleum company executive
Barrett, Barbara McConnell lawyer
Barrett, Izadore retired fisheries research administrator
Barrett, Jane Hayes lawyer
Barrett, Joseph Michael advertising and marketing consultant, educator
Barrett, William Joel investment banker
Barringer, J(ohn) Paul transportation executive, retired diplomat and career service executive
Barron, Charles Elliott retired electronics executive
Barron, Dennis H. retail executive
Barrow, Frank Pearson, Jr. retired energy company executive
Barrows, Robert Guy scriptwriter
Barselou, Paul Edgar actor, writer
Bartels, Gerald Lee association executive
Barth, Frances Dorothy artist
Bartholomew, Donald Dekle engineering executive, inventor
Bartlett, James Williams psychiatrist, educator
Bartlett, Steve mayor
Bartling, Theodore Charles oil company executive
Barton, Joe Linus congressman
Barton, Peter Richard, III communications executive
Bartunek, Joseph Wenceslaus magistrate judge
Bascom, Willard Newell research engineer, scientist
Basford, Robert Eugene retired biochemistry educator, researcher
Basham-Tooker, Janet Brooks geropsychologist, educator
Bass, Norman Herbert physician, scientist, university and hospital administrator, health care executive
Bass, Robert Olin manufacturing executive
Bassett, Barbara Wies editor, publisher
Bassett, Elizabeth Ewing (Libby Bassett) writer, editor
Bassist, Donald Herbert academic administrator
Batalden, Paul Bennett pediatrician, health care educator
Bates, Charles Turner lawyer, educator
Bates, Donald Lloyd civil engineer, retired
Bateson, Mary Catherine anthropology educator
Batignani, Laurie A. communications professional
Battle, Frank Vincent, Jr. lawyer
Bauer, Caroline Feller author
Bauer, Richard Carlton nuclear engineer
Bauer, Victor John pharmaceutical company executive
Baughman, J. Ross photographer, writer, educator
Bauman, Richard Arnold coast guard officer
Baumgartner, John H. refining and petroleum products company executive
Baxter, Cecil William, Jr. retired college president
Baxter, Stephen Bartow retired history educator
†Bayliff, Bradford W. state legislator, law firm official
Baym, Gordon Alan physicist, educator
Beach, Edward Latimer writer
Beadle, John Grant manufacturing company executive
Beal, Merrill David conservationist, museum director
†Beals, Nancy Farwell state legislator
†Beard, Alfred (Butch) professional sports coach
†Beard, Charles Walter veterinarian, researcher
Beasley, Barbara Starin sales executive, marketing professional
Beattie, Nora Maureen insurance company executive, actuary
†Beatts, Anne Patricia writer, producer
Beatty, Ned actor
Beatty, (Henry) Warren actor, producer, director
Becich, Raymond Brice healthcare-dispute resolution consultant
†Beck, Jeffrey Dengler banking executive
Becker, JoAnn Elizabeth insurance company executive
Becker, Walter Heinrich vocational school educator
†Bednarz, Nadine mathematics educator, director research center
Beebe, John Eldridge financial service executive
Beglarian, Grant foundation executive, composer, consultant

Begley, Ed, Jr. *actor*
†Behannon, Kenneth Wayne *retired astrophysicist*
Behl, Wolfgang *sculptor, retired educator*
Beighey, Lawrence Jerome *packaging company executive*
Beisel, Daniel Cunningham *former newspaper publisher*
Beiser, Helen Ruth *psychiatrist*
Belafonte, Harry *singer, concert artist, actor*
Beldock, Myron *lawyer*
†Bell, Clarence Deshong *lawyer, state senator*
Bell, Haney Hardy, III *lawyer*
Bell, Terrel Howard *education educator*
Bellamy, James Carl *insurance company executive*
Belles, Anita Louise *health care researcher*
Beltz, Herbert Allison *financial consultant*
Bender, Gary Nedrow *television sportscaster*
Bender, James Frederick *psychologist, educator, university dean*
Benjamin, Edward A. *lawyer*
Benjamin, James Cover *controller, manufacturing company executive*
Bennett, John Roscoe *computer company executive*
Bennett, Richard Thomas *retired manufacturing executive*
Benney, Douglas Mabley *marketing executive, consultant*
Benton, Fletcher *sculptor*
Benton, Robert Dean *retired university dean*
Ben Tré, Howard *artist*
Bentsen, Lloyd *U.S. secretary of treasury, former senator*
Benzle, Curtis Munhall *artist, educator*
Bercovitch, Sacvan *English language professional, educator*
Berdanier, Carolyn Dawson *nutrition educator, researcher*
†Berg, Rick Alan *state representative, real estate investor*
Bergan, William Luke *lawyer*
Bergen, Candice *actress, writer, photojournalist*
Berger, Frank Stanley *consultant*
Berger, Lawrence Douglas *lawyer*
Berger, William Ernest *newspaper publisher*
Bergman, Hermas John (Jack Bergman) *retired college administrator*
Bergman, Klaus *utility executive, lawyer*
Berk, Ann E. *author*
Berkovich, Gary A. *architect*
Berlin, Beatrice Winn *visual artist, printmaker*
Berlinger, Warren *actor*
Berlowitz Tarrant, Laurence *biotechnologist, university administrator*
Berman, Laura *freelance writer*
Bernard, Jami *film critic, author*
Bernard, Richard Lawson *geneticist, retired*
Bernhardt, Arthur Dieter *building industry executive and consultant*
Bernhardt, Melvin *theater director*
Bernstein, Elmer *composer, conductor*
Bernstein, Laurel *publishing executive*
Bernstein, Lester *editorial consultant*
Berra, Robert Louis *chemicals consultant*
Berry, Janis Marie *lawyer*
Berry, Richard Lewis *author, magazine editor, lecturer, programmer*
Berry, Robert Worth *lawyer, educator, retired army officer*
Bertelsman, William Odis *federal judge*
Bertin, John Joseph *aeronautical engineer, educator, researcher*
Bertinelli, Valerie *actress*
Bertolett, Craig Randolph *mechanical engineer consultant*
Berzon, Betty *psychotherapist*
Betti, John Anso *federal official, former automobile manufacturing company executive*
Beveridge, James MacDonald Richardson *former college president*
Beyer, Gordon Robert *foreign service officer*
Beyer, La Vonne Ann *special education educator*
Bhagat, Surinder Kumar *environmental engineering educator*
Biagi, Richard Charles *retail executive, real estate consultant*
Biedenharn, Lawrence C., Jr. *physicist, educator*
†Biegel, David Eli *social worker, educator*
Bierley, Paul Edmund *musician, author, publisher*
Bierwirth, John Cocks *retired aerospace manufacturing executive*
Biesdorf, Heinz Bernard *retired economist, educator*
Bigelow-Lourie, Anne Edwige *graphic designer*
Biggs, Arthur Edward *retired chemical manufacturing company executive*
Binder, Amy Finn *public relations company executive*
†Bingham, Louise H. *artist, art educator*
Bini, Dante Natale *architect, industrial designer*
Birchfield, John Kermit, Jr. *lawyer*
Birkenstock, James Warren *business machine manufacturing company executive*
Birkhoff, Garrett *mathematician, educator*
†Bischoff, Robert Henry *bank executive*
Bishop, Charles Edwin *university president emeritus, economist*
Bishop, Raymond Holmes, Jr. *physician, retired army officer*
Bishop, (Ina) Sue Marquis *psychiatric and mental health nurse educator, researcher, administrator*
Bishop, William Squire *commercial finance company executive*
Bissell, Allen Morris *engineer, consultant*
Bissell, James Dougal, III *motion picture production designer*
Bjerknes, Michael Leif *dancer*
Bjornson, Maria *theatrical designer*
Black, Richard Bruce *business executive, consultant*
Blacker, Harriet *public relations executive*
Blackstock, Joseph Robinson *newspaper editor*
Blackstone, Harry Bouton, Jr. *magician, actor*
Blackwell, Earl *publishing executive, writer*
Blackwell, Ronald Eugene *livestock consultant*
Blaine, Davis Robert *valuation consultant executive*
Blair, Charles Melvin *scientist, manufacturing company executive*
Blair, Fred Edward *association executive*
Blake, John Edward *car rental company executive*
Blake, Jules *biotechnology consultant*
Blaney, Connie Gayle *importer and broker*
†Blank, Richard Glenn *religious organization administrator, counselor*
Blasco, Alfred Joseph *business and financial consultant*
Blatt, Harold Geller *lawyer*
Bliley, Thomas Jerome, Jr. *congressman*
Bliss, William Stanley, Jr. *manufacturing company executive*
Bloch, Erich *electrical engineer, former science foundation administrator*
Block, Emil Nathaniel, Jr. *military officer*
Block, William *newspaper publisher*
Blodgett, William Arthur *public relations executive*
Blomberg, Susan Ruth *training executive*
Blomgren, Bruce Holmes *motivational speaker*
Blood, Archer Kent *retired foreign service officer*
Bloom, Edward Alan *Englsih language educator, author*
Bloom, Frank *corporation executive, consultant*
Bloom, Hyman *artist*
Bloomquist, Kenneth Gene *music educator, university bands director*
†Blossom, Beverly *choreographer, dance educator*
Blow, George *lawyer*
†Bluechel, Alan *state senator, wood structural components manufacturing company executive*
Bluemle, Robert Louis *lawyer*
Blum, Barbara Davis *banker*
Boal, Dean *arts center administrator, educator*
Boatright, Ann Long *dancer, pianist, music educator, choreographer*
Bochner, Hart *actor*
Bock, Jerry (Jerrold Lewis) *composer*
Bodanszky, Miklos *chemist, educator*
Boeker, Paul Harold *academic official, diplomat*
Boell, Edgar John *biology educator*
Bogdanich, Walt *journalist*
Bogosian, Eric *performance artist, actor*
Bogue, Philip Roberts *consultant*
Bohannan, Paul James *anthropologist, writer, former university administrator*
Boho, Dan L. *lawyer*
Boileau, Oliver Clark, Jr. *aerospace company executive*
Bok, Sissela *philosopher, writer*
Bolen, David B. *ambassador, former corporation executive*
†Boley, Donna Jean *state legislator*
Boling, Robert Bruce *physical education educator*
Bolingbroke, Robert A. *consumer products company executive*
†Bollback, Anthony George *minister*
Bolsterli, Margaret Jones *English educator*
Boner, Eleanor Katz *lawyer*
Bonerz, Peter *actor, director*
Bonito Oliva, Achille *curator*
Bonn, Ethel May *psychiatrist, educator*
Bonneau, Frederic Daniel *business consultant*
Bonner, Jack *public relations company executive*
Bonner, John Tyler *biology educator*
Boomer, Walter Eugene *marine officer*
Bootle, William Augustus *retired federal judge*
Boozer, Howard Rai *state education official*
Borchers, Mary Amelia *middle school educator*
Borda, Richard Joseph *management consultant*
†Borecky, Isidore *bishop*
Borg, Ruth I. *mental health nurse, long-term medical nurse*
Borgnine, Ernest *actor*
Borgstahl, Kaylene Denise *health facility administrator*
Bork, Robert Heron *lawyer, author, former federal judge*
Borow, Richard Henry *lawyer*
Borten, William H. *research company executive*
Bortz, Paul Isaac *media, sport and entertainment consultant*
Borum, Rodney Lee *business executive*
Bosakov, Joseph Blagoev (Metropolitan Bishop Joseph) *bishop*
Bosco, Anthony Gerard *bishop*
Bose, Anjan *electrical engineering educator, researcher, consultant*
†Bosse, Malcolm Joseph, Jr. *professional language educator, author*
Bossier, Albert Louis, Jr. *shipbuilding company executive*
Boswell, Thomas Murray *sports columnist, writer*
Bothwell, John Charles *archbishop*
Boucher, Laurence James *university dean, chemist*
Boulet, Roger Henri *art gallery director, curator*
Bouton, James Alan *author, entrepreneur, sportscaster, former professional baseball player*
Bova, Benjamin William *author, editor, educator*
Bowen, David Reece *foundation director, former congressman*
Bower, Jean Ramsay *court administrator, lawyer*
Bowie, E(dward) J(ohn) Walter *hematologist, researcher*
Bowles, Barbara Landers *investment company executive*
Bowles, Paul Frederick *composer, author*
Bowman, Scotty *professional hockey coach*
Bowne, Shirlee Pearson *credit union executive, real estate executive*
Box, Dwain D. *former judge*
Box, George Edward Pelham *statistics educator*
Boxall, Richard George *construction materials company executive*
Boxer, Stanley Robert *artist, sculptor*
Boyatt, Thomas David *former ambassador*
Boyd, Francis Virgil *retired accounting educator*
Boyd, Liona Maria *musician*
Boyd, Stuart Robert *military officer*
Boykin, Robert Heath *banker*
Boyle, Peter *actor*
Boyle, Richard John *art historian, author*
Boyles, James Kenneth *retired banker*
Bracken, Peg *author*
Braden, Charles Hosea *physicist, university administrator*
Braden, George Walter, II (Lord of Bover) *company executive*
†Bradford, Jackie Edward *army officer, health care administrator*
Bradford, Robert Edward *supermarket executive*
Bradley, Patricia Ellen *professional golfer*
Brady, George Moore *real estate executive, mortgage banker*
Brady, Nicholas Frederick *former secretary of treasury*
Braen, Bernard Benjamin *psychology educator*
Brain, George Bernard *university dean*
Braker, William Paul *aquarium executive, ichthyologist*
Brammer, Elizabeth Hedwig *administrator*
Brancato, Leo John *manufacturing company executive*
Brand, John Charles *chemistry educator*
Brand, Myles *academic administrator*
Brandl, John Edward *public affairs educator*
Brando, Marlon, Jr. *actor*
Branscomb, Anne Wells *communications consultant*
Brantz, George Murray *retired lawyer*
Branyan, Robert Lester *retired university administrator*
Bratt, Nicholas *investment management and research company executive*
Braun, Jerome Irwin *lawyer*
Brazier, Don Roland *retired railroad executive*
Brazil, Jeff *reporter*
Brengel, Fred Lenhardt *manufacturing company executive*
Brennan, Donna Lesley *public relations company executive*
Brennan, Eileen Regina *actress*
Brennan, T. Casey *writer*
Brennan, Terrence Michael *publisher*
Brennen, Stephen Alfred *international business consultant*
Brenner, Albert *production designer, sculptor*
Brenner, David *comedian*
Brent, Robert Leonard *physician, educator*
Brett, Barbara Jeanne *publisher*
Brettell, Richard Robson *art consultant*
Brewer, Carey *fund raising executive*
Brewer, David Meredith *retired computer company executive*
Brewer, Leslie G. *psychiatrist*
Briccetti, Joan Therese *symphony orchestra manager, management consultant*
Bricker, William Rudolph *retired organization executive*
Brickman, Ravelle *public relations writer and consultant*
†Brigham, David Lewis *investment management company executive*
Bright, Harold Frederick *university provost emeritus, consultant*
Brill, Winston Jonas *microbiologist, educator, research director, publisher and management consultant*
Brimacombe, James Keith *metallurgical engineering educator, researcher, consultant*
Brinberg, Herbert Raphael *information management, publishing company executive*
Brinckerhoff, Richard Charles *retired manufacturing company executive*
Brink, Richard Edward *lawyer*
Britt, John Roy *banker*
Broadwater, James E. *publisher*
Brode, David B. *investment counselor*
Brodhead, David Crawmer *lawyer*
Brodian, Laura *broadcasting and illustration studio executive, professional illustrator*
Brodie, Howard *artist*
Brodnax, Margaret O'Bryan *retired English language educator*
Brodsky, David M. *lawyer*
†Brodsky, Richard Louis *state legislator*
Bronfman, Peter Frederick *independent investor*
Brooke, Ralph Ian *dental educator, vice provost, university dean*
†Brooker, Robert Elton, Jr. *manufacturing company executive*
Brookner, Anita *writer, educator*
Brooks, Albert (Albert Einstein) *actor, writer, director*
Brooks, James Sprague *retired national guard officer*
Brooks, Maurice Edward *engineering executive, consultant*
Brooks, Michael Paul *urban planning educator*
Brosnan, Pierce *actor*
Broude, Ronald *music publisher*
Browder, Felix Earl *mathematician, educator*
Brower, Charles Nelson *lawyer, judge*
Brown, Barton *retired automotive company executive*
Brown, Bennett Alexander *former banker*
Brown, Britt *retired publishing company executive*
Brown, Bruce Maitland *philanthropy consultant*
Brown, David Grant *university president*
Brown, Donald Douglas *transportation company executive, retired air force officer, consultant*
Brown, Earle *composer, conductor*
Brown, Gary Ross *lawyer, magistrate*
Brown, Henry Bedinger Rust *financial management company executive*
Brown, Jim (James Nathaniel Brown) *film actor, former professional football player*
Brown, Marcia Joan *author, artist, photographer*
Brown, Robert Laidlaw *state supreme court justice*
Brown, Ruth *rhythm and blues singer*
Brown, Sandra Jean *banker*
Brown, William Ferdinand *artist, writer*
Browne, Diana Gayle *artist, social services*
Browne, Edmund John Phillip *oil company executive*
Browning, Colin Arrott *retired banker*
†Browning, James E. *architectural firm executive*
Broyles, William Dodson, Jr. *author, editor*
Brubaker, Crawford Francis, Jr. *government official, aerospace consultant*
Bruce, James Edmund *retired utility company executive*
Brumberg, G. David *historical center administrator, history bibliographer*
Brune, David Hamilton *financial corporation executive, lawyer*
Bruzda, Francis Joseph *investment executive, former banker*
Bryant, Cecil Farris *lawyer, retired insurance company executive*
Bryant, Gail Annette Grippen *nurse, educator*
†Bubrick, Melvin Phillip *surgeon*
Buchanan, John MacLennan *Canadian provincial official*
Buchanan, Patrick Joseph *journalist*
Buckels, Marvin Wayne *savings and loan executive*
Buckley, William Elmhirst *publishing consultant*
Buffkins, Archie Lee *public television executive*
Bujold, Tyrone Patrick *lawyer*
Bulla, Clyde Robert *writer*
Bullard, Helen (Mrs. Joseph Marshall Krechniak) *sculptor*
Bullins, Ed *author*
Bullock, Theodore Holmes *biologist, educator*
Bullough, Bonnie *nurse, educator*
Bumbery, Joseph Lawrence *diversified telecommunications company executive*
Bunch, Franklin Swope *architect*
Bunch, Jennings Bryan, Jr. *electrical engineer*
Bunim, Mary-Ellis *television producer*
Bunn, George *legal educator, writer*
Bunning, Jim *congressman, former professional baseball player*
Bunton, Lucius Desha, III *federal judge*
Burchman, Leonard *government official*
Burge, James Darrell *personnel, government relations executive*
Burge, John Wesley, Jr. *electric manufacturing company executive, consultant*
Burger, Leslie Morton *physician, army officer*
Burger, Warren Earl *former chief justice of U.S. supreme court, academic administrator*
Burk, Sylvia Joan *petroleum landman, freelance writer*
Burke, Edmond Wayne *judge*
Burki, Fred Albert *labor union official*
Burlew, John Swalm *research scientist*
Burlingame, James Montgomery, III *lawyer*
Burns, J(ohn) Scott *lawyer*
Burns, Nancy Kay *drug abuse services professional*
Burns, Richard Francis *mechanical engineer*
Burrell, Craig Donald *physician, educator*
Burrington, David Edson *journalist*
Burroughs, Franklin Troy *academic administrator*
Burstyn, Ellen (Edna Rae Gillooly) *actress*
†Burton, Joseph Alfred *state legislator*
Bury, John *theatre designer, consultant*
Busby, John Arthur, Jr. *architect*
Busey, Gary *actor, musician*
Busfield, Timothy *actor*
Bush, Charles Vernon *telecommunications executive*
Bush, Guy Louis *biology educator*
†Bushnell, Bill *theatrical director, producer*
Busse, Leonard Wayne *banker, financial consultant*
Bussgang, Julian Jakob *electronics engineer*
Butkus, Dick *actor, former professional football player*
Butler, Eugene L. *oil field equipment company executive*
Butler, Jack Fairchild *semiconductors company executive*
Butler, Robert Leonard *sales executive*
Butler, Robert Thomas *retired advertising executive*
†Butterfield, Alexander Porter *business executive, former government official, retired air force officer*
Butts, Virginia *corporate public relations executive*
Buxton, Winslow Hurlbert *diversified manufacturing company executive*
Buzard, James Albert *management consultant*
Byrd, Lloyd Garland *civil engineer*
Byrne, David *musician, composer, artist, director*
Cachia, Pierre Jacques *Middle East languages and culture educator, researcher*
†Cahn, Robert Nathan *physicist*
Caine, Raymond William, Jr. *retired public relations executive*
Cairns, Theodore LeSueur *chemist*
Caldwell, Warren Frederick *investment company executive*
Califano, Joseph Anthony, Jr. *lawyer, public health policy educator, writer*
Callahan, Joseph Murray *magazine editor*
Callander, Bruce Douglas *journalist, free-lance writer*
Callard, David Jacobus *investment banker*
Callow, William Grant *retired state supreme court justice*
Calvert, James Francis *manufacturing company executive, retired admiral*
Calvert, William Preston *radiologist*
Camdessus, Michel (Jean) *international association executive*
Cameron, J. Elliot *retired parochial educational system administrator*
Cameron, Lucille Wilson *retired dean of libraries*
Camp, Clifton Durrett, Jr. *newspaper consultant, rancher*
Camp, Joseph Shelton, Jr. *film producer, director, writer*
Campanelli, Pauline Eble *artist*
Campbell, Alice Shaw *retired accountant, poet*
†Campbell, Arlington Fichtner *military officer*
Campbell, Avril Kim *Canadian legislator, justice official*
Campbell, Byron Chesser *publishing company executive*
†Campbell, Craig Stewart *landscape architect, town planner*
Campbell, Henry Cummings *librarian*
Campbell, Jackson Justice *medievalist, educator*
Campbell, James Arthur *professional baseball team executive*
Campbell, Patton *stage designer, educator*
Campbell, Raymond McKinly *psychologist, educator, consultant, researcher*
Campbell, Richard Alden *business consultant*
Canin, Stuart Victor *violinist*
Cannon, Dyan *actress*
Cannon, Isabella Walton *mayor*
Cantarella, Francesco Paquin *retail executive*
Cantliffe, Jeri Miller *artist, art educator*
Cantone, Vic *political cartoonist*
Cantril, Albert H(adley) *public opinion analyst*
Capek, Vlastimil *retired radiologist, educator*
Capice, Philip Charles *television production executive*
Caplan, Ralph *design writer, consultant*
Caplovitz, Coleman David *physician*
Cardy, Andrew Gordon *hotel executive*
Carey, Dennis Clarke *executive search consultant*
Carey, Francis James *investment banker*
Carey, Gerard V. *banker*
Carey, Martin Conrad *gastroenterologist, molecular biophysicist, educator*
Caricari, Carl *computer company executive*
Carlquist, Sherwin *biology and botany educator*
Carlson, Elvin Palmer *military officer*
Carlson, Natalie Traylor *publisher*
Carlyss, Earl Winston *musician*
Carman, George Henry *retired physician*
Carney, Arthur William Matthew *actor*
Carothers, Steven Michael *artist, designer, writer*
Carpenter, Derr Alvin *landscape architect*
†Carpenter, Dorothy Fulton *state legislator*
Carpenter, Kenneth John *nutrition educator*
Carpenter, Malcolm Scott *astronaut, oceanographer*
Carpenter, Myron Arthur *manufacturing company executive*
Carr, Harold Noflet *investment corporation executive*
†Carr, Michael Leon *professional sports team executive, former professional basketball player*
Carradine, Keith Ian *actor, singer, composer*
Carrol, Robert Kelton *lawyer*
Carroll, Bernard James *psychiatrist*
Carroll, Marshall Elliott *architect*
Carson, Johnny *television personality*
Carter, Elliott Cook, Jr. *composer*
Carter, Herbert Edmund *former university official*
Carter, (William) Hodding, III *television and newspaper journalist*
Carter, Hugh Clendenin *mechanical consulting engineer*
Carter, John Swain *museum administrator, consultant*
Carter, Joseph Edwin *former nickel company executive, writer*
Carter, Nanette Carolyn *artist*
Carter, Richard Duane *business educator*
Carter, Ronald *musician*
Carter, Rosalynn Smith *wife of former President of U.S.*

Carter, William George, III army officer
Cartier, Celine Paule librarian, administrator, consultant
Carver, Calvin Reeve public utility holding company director
Carville, (Chester) James, Jr. political consultant
Cascio, Anna Theresa playwright, screenwriter
Casdin, Jeffrey Whitman investment company executive
Casey, John Thomas health services agency executive
Casey, Robert Reisch lawyer
Cash, Johnny entertainer
Casper, Gerhard academic administrator, law educator
Casselman, William E., II lawyer
Cassidy, John Harold lawyer
Cassini, Oleg Lolewski fashion designer, manufacturer
Castle, James Cameron information systems executive
Castle, Robert Woods advertising agency executive
Caswell, Dorothy Ann Cottrell arts administrator
Catacosinos, William James utility company executive
Cates, Phoebe actress
Catlin, B. Wesley microbiologist
Cattani, Maryellen B. lawyer
Ceci, Louis J. former state supreme court justice
Cesnik, James Michael union official, newspaperman
†Chaikof, Elliot Lorne vascular surgeon
†Chain, Beverly Jean communications executive
Chamberlain, George Arthur, III manufacturing company executive, venture capitalist
Chamberlain, (George) Richard actor
Chamberlain, William Edwin, Jr. management consultant
Chamberlin, Michael Meade lawyer
Chambers, Richard H. federal judge
Chandler, Alfred Dupont, Jr. historian, educator
Chandler, Harry Edgar author
Chandler, John Herrick college president
†Chandler, John Parker Hale, Jr. state senator
Chandler, William Everett brokerage house executive
Chandra, Pramod art history educator
Channing, Stockard (Susan Stockard) actress
Chapman, Tracy singer, songwriter
Chapman, William baritone
Chappell, Robert E. banker
†Charlton, Betty Jo state legislator
Charlton, Gordon Taliaferro, Jr. retired bishop
Charlton, Jesse Melvin, Jr. management educator, lawyer
Charry, Michael R(onald) musician, conductor
Chase, Clinton Irvin psychologist, educator, business executive
Chase, James Richard college official
Chase-Riboud, Barbara Dewayne sculptor, writer
Chawla, Krishan Kumar materials engineer, educator, consultant
Chelberg, Bruce Stanley holding company executive
Chellas, Brian Farrell philosophy educator
Chen, Di electro-optic company executive, consultant
Chenhall, Robert Gene former museum director, consultant, author
Chercover, Murray television executive
Chernichaw, Mark television, film and interactive multimedia executive, producer, director, international media consultant
Chernoff, Amoz Immanuel hematologist, consultant
Chernoff, Robert rabbi
Cherryh, C. J. writer
Chester, John Ervin medical supplies company executive
Cheston, Theodore C. electrical engineer
Chevalier, Paul Edward retired retail executive, lawyer
Childers, Perry Robert government agency administrator
Chin, Hong Woo oncologist, educator, researcher
Chinn, Thomas Wayne typographic company executive
Chinni, Peter Anthony artist
Chinoy, Helen Krich theater historian
Chisholm, Shirley Anita St. Hill former congresswoman, educator, lecturer
Chmielinski, Edward Alexander electronics company executive
Choi, Man-Duen mathematics educator
Christensen, Albert Sherman federal judge
Christensen, Robert A. lawyer
Christiansen, Christian Carl, Jr. management consultant
Christine, Virginia Feld actress
Christoffersen, Ralph Earl chemist
Christopher, Russell Lewis baritone
Christopher, Sharon A. Brown bishop
Chryssis, George Christopher business executive
Chu, Benjamin Thomas Peng-Nien chemistry educator
Church, Eugene Lent physicist, consultant
Churchill, Mary Carey public relations executive
†Churchill, Robert Wilson state legislator, lawyer
Chyu, Chi-Oy Wei educator
Ciccone, Anne Panepinto artist
Cirese, Robert Charles economist, real estate investment counselor
Claiborne, Craig author, editor cookbooks
Clampitt, Amy Kathleen writer, editor
Clark, Alicia Garcia political party official
Clark, Candy actress
Clark, Claudia J. educational administration, speech, language and learning disabilities professional
Clark, Donald Otis lawyer
Clark, Larry photographer
Clark, Mary Higgins author, business executive
Clark, Maxine retail executive
Clark, Peter Bruce newspaper executive
Clark, Robert Phillips newspaper editor, consultant
Clark, Thomas Lloyd English linguistics educator
Clark, William, Jr. ambassador
†Clarke, Harold lawyer
Clarke, Henry Lee ambassador, U.S. foreign service officer
Clarke, Lambuth McGeehee college president emeritus
Clarke, Malcolm filmmaker
Clary, Everett Burton lawyer, retired
Claver, Robert Earl television director, producer
Claytor, Richard Anderson retired federal agency executive
Clement, Hope Elizabeth Anna librarian
Clemetson, Charles Alan Blake physician
Cliff, Judith Anita author, biblical studies lecturer
Cliff, Ronald Laird energy company executive
Clifton, Russell B. banking and mortgage lending consultant, retired mortgage company executive
Close, Glenn actress
Closset, Gerard Paul forest products company executive
Cloud, Stanley Wills journalist, editor, writer
Clouston, Ross Neal retired food and related products company executive
Cluff, E. Dale librarian, educator, administrator
Clymer, Wayne Kenton bishop
Cobb, John Boswell, Jr. clergyman, educator
Cobb, John Cecil, Jr. (Jack Cobb) communications specialist and executive
Cobb, Miles Alan lawyer
Cobb, Ruth artist
Cobb, Virginia Horton artist, educator
Cobham, William Emanuel, Jr. musician
Coble, Howard congressman, lawyer
Coburn, D(onald) L(ee) playwright
Coburn, Harry L. foreign service officer
Coburn, James actor
Cochran, Thad senator
Cockrum, William Monroe, III investment banker, consultant, educator
Cody, Iron Eyes actor
Coffee, Joseph Denis, Jr. college chancellor emeritus
Coffey, John Louis federal judge
Coffman, Stanley Knight, Jr. English educator, former college president
†Cohen, Aaron M. media executive
Cohen, Alexander H. theatrical and television producer
Cohen, Allan Richard broadcasting executive
Cohen, B. Stanley physician
Cohen, Mark Herbert broadcasting company executive
Cohn, Avern Levin federal judge
Cohn, Leonard Allan retired chemical company executive
Coke, Frank Van Deren museum director, photographer
Colaianni, Joseph Vincent judge
Colbert, Claudette (Lily Chauchoin) actress
Cole, Brady Marshall retired naval officer
Cole, Clifford Adair clergyman
Cole, Jerome Foster research company executive
Coleman, Dabney W. actor
Coleman, Lewis Waldo bank executive
Coleman, Nancy Pees environmental toxicologist
Coleman, Robert Lee lawyer
Collier, Gaylan Jane drama educator
Collier, Herman Edward, Jr. retired college president
Collier, Oscar literary agency consultant, writer
Collins, Jackie writer
Collins, Joan Henrietta actress
†Collins, John Francis landscape architect, educator
Collins, Michael aerospace consultant, former astronaut
Collins, Robert Frederick federal judge
Colman, Edward Brof film director, cinematographer
Colodny, Edwin Irving lawyer, retired airline executive
Colonnier, Marc Leopold neuroanatomist, educator
Colton, Nelson Burton industrial company executive
Comaneci, Nadia gymnast
Compton, Norma Haynes retired university dean
Compton, W. Dale physicist
Condayan, John foreign service officer
Condit, Doris Elizabeth historian
Condry, Robert Stewart retired hospital administrator
Cone, Edward Toner composer, emeritus music educator
Congdon, Thomas B., Jr. author
†Conklin, Michael L. newspaper columnist
Conlon, Harry B., Jr. banking company executive
Connell, George Edward university president, scientist
Connelly, Sharon Rudolph lawyer, federal official
Connors, Mike (Krekor Ohanian) actor
Conole, Clement Vincent corporate executive
†Conover, Charles Todd banker
Console, Frank Milton savings and loan association executive
Consoli, Marc-Antonio composer
Constant, Clinton chemical engineer, consultant
†Constantine, Kevin professional hockey coach
Conway, James Valentine Patrick forensic document examiner, former postal service executive
Conway, Robert P. art dealer
Cook, Beth Marie writer, poet, municipal housing technician
Cook, Charles Beckwith, Jr. securities company executive
Cook, Charles Emerson electrical engineer
Cook, Fielder producer, director
Cook, Fred James journalist, author
Cook, Julian Abele, Jr. federal judge
Cook, Stanton R. media company executive
Cooke, Eileen Delores retired librarian
Cooley, James William retired executive researcher
Cooney, Barbara illustrator, author
Cooney, John Thomas retired banker
†Coonts, Stephen Paul novelist
Coop, Frederick Robert retired city manager
Cooper, Alice (Vincent Furnier) vocalist, composer
Cooper, Charles Gordon insurance consultant, former executive
Cooper, Charles Justin lawyer, former government official
Cooper, E. Camron retired oil company executive
Cooper, Francis Loren advertising executive
Cooper, Hal television director
Cooper, Jackie actor, director, producer
Cooper, Jon Hugh public television executive
Cooper, Norton J. liquor and wine company executive
Cope, Alfred Haines political scientist, educator
Cope, Jeannette Naylor human resources consultant
Cope, Robert Gary management educator, consultant
Coplans, John Rivers artist
Coplin, Mark David lawyer
Copperfield, David (David Kotkin) illusionist, director, producer, writer
Coppie, Comer Swift state official
Corber, Robert Jack lawyer
Corcoran, Barbara Asenath author
Corddry, Paul Imlay retired food products company executive
Corey, Jeff actor, director, educator
Corey, Kenneth Edward geography and urban planning educator, researcher
Coriell, Lewis Lemon physician, research institute administrator
Cork, Edwin Kendall business and financial consultant
Cormier, Jean G. communications company executive
Corrales, Patrick coach, former professional baseball manager
Cortese, Richard Anthony computer company executive
†Corwin, Laura J. lawyer
Cosby, Bill actor, entertainer
†Coscarelli, Don film writer, film director
Cossa, Dominic Frank baritone
Costas, Robert Quinlan (Bob Costas) sportscaster
Costello, James Joseph retired electrical manufacturing company executive
Costner, Kevin actor
Cotrubas, Ileana opera singer, lyric soprano, retired
Couchman, Robert George James human services consultant
Coughlan, William David association executive
Cougill, Roscoe McDaniel mayor, retired air force officer
Courtney, Charles Edward government official
Couturier, Ronald Lee services company executive, consultant
Coval-Apel, Naomi Miller dentist
Coven, Berdeen psychotherapist
Cover, Franklin Edward actor
†Cowenhoven, Garret Peter state legislator, educator
Cowles, John, Jr. publisher, fitness instructor
Cowley, William Eugene former manufacturing company executive
Cox, David Brummal accounting firm executive
Cox, J. William physician, health services administrator
Cox, James Clarence hospital administrator
Cox, John Francis retired cosmetic company executive
Cox, Wilford Donald retired food company executive
Cozan, Lee clinical research psychologist
†Crabtree, Davida Foy minister
Craft, Edmund Coleman automotive parts manufacturing company executive
Cramer, John Sanderson health care executive
Cramer, Robert Vern retired college president, director scholarship program, consultant
Cramer, William F. capitol goods executive
Crampton, Esther Larson educator
Crandles, George Marshal retired insurance company executive
Cranin, Marilyn Sunners landscape designer
Craw, Freeman (Jerry Craw) graphic artist
†Crawford, Carol Tallman government executive
Crawford, Kenneth Charles educational institute executive, retired government official
Crawford, Muriel Laura lawyer, author, educator
Crawford, William Walsh retired consumer products company executive
Creech, John Lewis retired scientist, consultant
Creigh, Thomas, Jr. utility executive
Critoph, Eugene retired physicist, nuclear research company executive
Cromwell, Florence Stevens occupational therapist
Cronkhite, Leonard Wolsey, Jr. physician, consultant, research foundation executive
Cronson, Robert Granville state auditor
Crook, Jacquelyn Elaine Terry elementary education educator, librarian
Crosby, Norman Lawrence comedian
Cross, Alexander Dennis business consultant, former chemical and pharmaceutical executive
†Cross, Elmo Garnett, Jr. lawyer, state senator
†Crossley, Francis Rendel Erskine engineering educator
†Crossley, Francis Rendel Erskine engineering educator
Crouse, Lindsay actress
Crowley, Joseph Michael electrical engineer, educator
Crowther, James Earl radio and television executive
Crowther, Richard Layton architect, consultant, researcher, author, lecturer
Croxton, Fred(erick) E(mory), Jr. retired information specialist, consultant
Cruise, Tom (Tom Cruise Mapother, IV) actor
Csia, Susan Rebecca lawyer, oil company executive
Cuatrecasas, Pedro Martin research pharmacologist
Cuevas, Milton Joseph publishing company executive
Culbertson, Philip Edgar corporate executive
Cull, Robert Robinette electric products manufacturing company executive
Cullen, James Thaddeus, Jr. broadcast executive
Cullum, John actor, singer
Culp, William Newton retired insurance executive
Culvahouse, Arthur Boggess, Jr. lawyer
Culverwell, Albert Henry historian
Culwell, Charles Louis retired manufacturing company executive
Cummer, William Jackson former oil company executive, investor
Cummin, Alfred S(amuel) retired chemist
Cumming, Robert Hugh artist, photographer
Cummings, Constance actress
Cummings, David William artist, educator
Cummings, Josephine Anna writer
Cunningham, Isabella Clara Mantovani advertising educator
Currier, Ruth dancer, choreographer and educator
Curry, James Trueman, Jr. retired mining company executive
Curry, Nancy Ellen education educator, psychoanalyst, psychologist
Curry, Richard Orr history educator and freelance writer
Curson, Theodore musician
Curti, Merle Eugene historian, educator
Curtin, David Stephen newswriter
Curtis, James L. psychiatrist
Curtis, Mary Ellen (Mary Curtis Horowitz) publishing company executive
Cushing, Frederic Sanford publishing company executive
Cushman, Paul physician, educator
Cussler, Clive Eric author
Cyr, Conrad Keefe federal judge
Czarnecki, Gerald Milton banker
Dabbs, Henry Erven television and film producer, educator
Daeschner, Richard Wilbur former food company executive
Dafoe, Willem actor
D'Agostino, Stephen I. bottling company executive
Dahl, Bren Bennington screenwriter
Dahlgren, Carl Herman Per educator, arts administrator
Dailey, Irene actress, educator
Dailey, Janet novelist
Dake, Marcia Allene nursing educator, university dean
Dale, Wesley John chemistry educator
Daltrey, Roger musician
Daly, James Joseph bishop
Daly, James William physician, educator
Daly, William James retired health industry distributing company executive
Dalziel, Robert David retired telecommunications executive
D'Amato, Alfonse M. senator
D'Amato, Anthony Roger recording company executive
Dana, Jerilyn ballet company administrator
Danesh, Hossain Banadaki psychiatrist, writer, international consultant
Daniel, Elbert Clifton journalist
Daniels, James Maurice physicist
Danilowicz, Delores Ann pediatric cardiologist, pediatrics educator
Danis, Peter G., Jr. office products company executive
Dannenberg, Martin Ernest retired insurance company executive
Danner, Blythe Katharine (Mrs. Bruce W. Paltrow) actress
Danoff, I. Michael art center director, writer, educator
Danza, Tony actor
D'Arcangelo, Allan Matthew artist
Dasburg, John Harold airline executive
Daub, Hal former congressman
Daugherty, Alfred Clark manufacturing company executive
Davenport, Chester lawyer
Davenport, Ernest Harold university official, accountant
Davenport, Lawrence Franklin school system administrator
David, Paul Theodore political science educator emeritus
Davidovsky, Mario composer
Davidson, John financial advisory executive
Davidson, Mayer B. medical educator, researcher
Davis, Anna Jane Ripley elementary education educator
Davis, Carl George software engineer
Davis, Darrell L. automotive executive
Davis, George Alfred financial executive
Davis, Henry Jefferson, Jr. former naval officer
Davis, Laurence Laird coal company executive
Davis, Luther writer, producer
Davis, Mac singer, songwriter
Davis, Monte Vincent nuclear engineer, educator
Davis, Roger Edwin lawyer, retired discount chain executive
†Davis, Theodore Roosevelt bishop, contractor
Davison, Beaumont retired university administrator
Dawkins, Marva Phyllis psychologist
Dawson, Horace Greeley, Jr. former diplomat, government official
DeAlessandro, Joseph Paul insurance company executive
Dean, Dearest (Lorene Glosup) songwriter
Dean, Francis Hill landscape architect, educator
†Deane, Marjorie Schlesinger fashion merchandising executive
Deane, Thomas Andersen retired banker
De Antoni, Edward Paul cancer control research scientist
DeBartolo, Edward J., Sr. real estate developer
De Blasi, Tony (Anthony Armando De Blasi) artist
de Blij, Harm Jan geography educator, editor
Debs, Barbara Knowles academic administrator
DeCamp, Graydon journalist
Dechar, Peter Henry artist
Decker, Gilbert Felton manufacturing company executive
Decker, Hans Wilhelm retired finance company executive
Deems, Andrew William health facility administrator
De Felitta, Frank Paul producer, writer, director
DeFleur, Melvin Lawrence sociologist, journalism educator
De Frank, Vincent conductor
DeGray, Thomas Alan private school educator
Deisenhofer, Johann biochemistry educator, researcher
Dekker, Maurits publisher, editor
de la Garza, Eligio (Kika de la Garza) congressman
Delano, Hugh Stafford newspaper sports journalist, author
Delany, Logan Drummond, Jr. financial consultant, investor
Dell'Olio, Louis fashion designer
De Loach, Bernard Collins, Jr. retired physicist
De Looper, Willem Johan artist, museum curator
Del Rio-Diaz, Estyne psychologist
Del Tredici, David composer
de Luce, Virginia entertainer
De Luise, Dom actor
Delza-Munson, Elizabeth dancer, choreographer, educator
DeMark, Richard Reid retired insurance company executive
de Marneffe, Francis psychiatrist, hospital administrator
Dembeck, Mary Grace artist, writer
De Mornay, Rebecca actress
†Demuzio, Vince T. state senator
Deneuve, Catherine (Catherine Dorleac) actress
†Denisco, Ralph Andrew ice cream industry executive
Denneny, James Clinton, Jr. business consultant
Denny, James McCahill retail executive
Denton, David Edward retired education educator
†Denton, M. Bonner research chemistry educator
DePalma, Ralph George surgeon, educator
Depkovich, Francis John retired retail chain executive
Derbes, Daniel William corporate executive
De Salva, Salvatore Joseph pharmacologist, toxicologist
De Santis, Anthony restaurant, theatre executive
De Simone, Daniel V. engineering association executive, engineer
Detra, Ralph William research laboratory administrator
Devane, William actor
Devlin, Michael Coles bass-baritone
Dewhurst, William Harvey psychiatrist
Diamond, Stuart lawyer, journalist
Diaz, Justino bass-baritone
Dibner, David Robert architect
Di Cicco, Joseph Nicholas, Jr. chemical engineer
Dicke, Robert Henry educator, physicist
†Dickerson, Lon Richard library administrator
Dickerson, Nancy (Whitehead) free lance television producer, news correspondent
Dickes, Robert psychiatrist
Dickinson, Angie (Angeline Brown) actress
Dickinson, William Richard retired geologist and educator
Dickman, James Bruce photojournalist

Dickson, James Francis, III *surgeon*
Diehl, Deborah Hilda *lawyer*
Diemer, Emma Lou *composer, music educator*
Diener, Erwin *immunologist*
Diener, Royce *corporate director, retired health care services company executive*
†DiFebo, Valerie *advertising executive*
Diffrient, Niels *industrial designer*
Di Giovanni, Anthony *retired coal mining company executive*
Dill, Laddie John *artist*
Dille, Earl Kaye *utility company executive*
Dills, James Arlof *retired publishing company executive*
Dinkel, John George *magazine editor*
Dirks, Leslie Chant *communications and electronics company executive*
Dirksen, Richard Wayne *canon precentor, organist, choirmaster*
Dirvin, Gerald Vincent *retired consumer products company executive*
Disch, Thomas M(ichael) *author*
Dishy, Bob *actor*
†Disney, Jeffrey F. *banker*
Di Spigna, Tony *graphic designer*
Dixon, Ernest Thomas, Jr. *retired bishop*
Dixon, Louis Frederick *information sciences and telecommunications consulting executive*
Dobbel, Rodger Francis *interior designer*
Dobler, Donald William *retired college dean, consultant, corporate executive*
Dobriansky, Lev Eugene *economist, educator, diplomat*
†Docker, John Thornley *religious organization administrator, minister*
†Doderer, Minnette Frerichs *state legislator*
Dodson, Donald Mills *restaurant executive*
Dodson, Samuel Robinette, III *investment banker*
Dogançay, Burhan C. *artist, photographer, sculptor*
Doherty, Charles Vincent *investment counsel executive*
Doherty, Thomas Joseph *financial services industry consultant*
Dohrmann, Russell William *manufacturing company executive*
Doig, Ivan *writer*
Dolan, Edward Francis *writer*
Dolan, Peter Robert *marketing executive*
Dole, Arthur Alexander *psychology educator*
Dole, Robert Paul *retired appliance manufacturing company executive*
Dolenz, Mickey (George Michael Dolenz) *singer, actor*
Dolin, Samuel Joseph *composer, educator*
Dominick, David DeWitt *lawyer, rancher, environmentalist*
Donahue, Elinor *actress*
Donath, Fred Arthur *geologist, geophysicist*
Donath, Therese *author, artist*
Donohue, George L. *mechanical engineer*
Donovan, James Robert *business equipment company executive*
Donovan, Walter Edgar *retired mayor*
Dore, Fred Hudson *retired state supreme court chief justice*
Dorland, Dodge Oatwell *investment advisor*
Dorman, Richard Frederick, Jr. *association executive, consultant*
Dorn, Dolores *actress*
Dorros, Irwin *retired telecommunications executive*
Dorsey, Frank James *grocery company executive*
Dorsey, Rhoda Mary *academic administrator, retired*
Dotson, Donald L. *lawyer*
Doty, James Robert *lawyer*
Doty, Philip Edward *accountant*
Doud, Wallace C. *retired information systems executive*
Douglas, James Holley *former state official*
Douglass, Harry Robert *architect, health care consultant, educator*
Douglass, John Michael *internist*
†Dowd, Clark Wayne *lawyer, state legislator*
Dowden, Albert Ricker *corporate executive, lawyer*
Dowie, Ian James *management consultant*
Downes, Rackstraw *artist*
Doyle, John Laurence *manufacturing company executive*
†Doyle, Peter W. *painter, illustrator*
Dozier, Glenn Joseph *medical, surgical products distribution executive*
Dozier, James Lee *former army officer*
Drabble, Bernard James *Canadian government official*
Dragon, William, Jr. *footwear and apparel company executive*
†Drake, Ervin Maurice *composer, author*
Drake, Rodman Leland *investment manager consultant*
Drebus, Richard William *pharmaceutical company executive*
Drennen, William Miller *federal judge*
Dressel, Barry *museum administrator*
Drew, Elizabeth Heineman *publishing executive*
Drew, Walter Harlow *retired paper manufacturing company executive*
Drexler, Michael David *advertising agency executive*
Driscoll, William Michael *corporation executive*
Driver, Lottie Elizabeth *librarian*
Drucker, Peter Ferdinand *writer, consultant, educator*
Drummond, Dorothy Weitz *geography education consultant, educator, author*
Drummond, Sally Hazelet *artist*
Dubuc, Carroll Edward *lawyer*
Dudick, Michael Joseph *bishop*
Duerr, Herman George *retired publishing executive*
Duff, John Bernard *college president, former city official*
Duffy, James Henry *author, former lawyer*
Duffy, Martin Edward *management consultant, economist*
†Dugan, Michael Kevin *furniture manufacturing company executive*
Dugan, Patrick Raymond *microbiologist, university dean*
Dull, William Martin *engineering executive*
Dumont, Allan Eliot *physician, educator*
DuMont, Bruce *political correspondent*
Duncan, David Douglas *photojournalist, author*
Duncan, Donald William *retired lawyer*
Duncan, Sandy *actress*
†Dunford, David Joseph *foreign service officer, ambassador*
Dungworth, Donald L. *veterinary educator, consultant*
Dunham, Benjamin Starr *editor, arts administrator*
Dunn, Mignon *mezzo-soprano*
Dunn, Warren Howard *retired lawyer, brewery executive*
Dunworth, John *retired college president*
Duppstadt, Marlyn Henry *financial executive*
Durham, G. Robert *diversified manufacturing company executive*
Durning, Charles *actor*
Durr, Robert Joseph *construction firm executive, mechanical engineer*
Dutile, Fernand Neville *law educator*
†Dutson, Thayne R. *university dean*
Dutton, John Coatsworth *retired consulting engineering executive*
Duvall, Robert *actor*
Dyer, Geraldine Ann (Geri Dyer) *artist, poet*
Dyer, Wayne Walter *psychologist, author, radio and television personality*
Dymond, Lewis Wandell *lawyer, mediator, educator*
Dysart, Richard A. *actor*
†Dyson, Arthur Thomas *architect, educator*
Dziubla, Robert W. *lawyer*
Eagan, Sherman G. *producer, communications executive*
Eagle, Jack *commercial actor, comedian*
Eaglet, Robert Danton *electrical engineer, aerospace consultant, retired military officer*
Eaker, Ira *publishing executive*
Earle, Arthur Percival *textile executive*
East, Don Gaylord *computer engineer, archaeologist, writer*
Eastham, Alan Walter, Jr. *foreign service officer, lawyer*
Easton, Glenn Hanson, Jr. *management and insurance consultant, federal official, naval officer*
Easton, Michelle *foundation executive*
Eaton, Merrill Thomas *psychiatrist, educator*
Eaton, William Charles *retired mechanical engineer*
Ebb, Fred *lyricist, librettist*
Eberle, Charles Edward *paper and consumer products executive*
†Eberly, Joseph Henry *physics educator, consultant*
†Ebitz, David MacKinnon *art historian, museum director*
†Eck, Dorothy Fritz *state senator*
Eckenhoff, James Edward *physician, educator*
Eddy, Don *artist*
Eddy, Esther Dewitz *retired pharmacist*
Edel, Abraham *philosophy educator*
Edelstein, Jerome Melvin *bibliographer*
Edgar, Thomas Flynn *chemical engineering educator*
Edmunds, (Arthur) Lowell *philology educator*
Edmundson, Charles Wayne *mechanical engineer, communications executive*
Edwards, Charles *neuroscientist, educator*
Edwards, Ernest Preston *biologist*
Edwards, Geoffrey Hartley *newspaper publisher*
Edwards, Jerome *lawyer*
Edwards, Larry David *physician, academic dean*
Edwards, Patrick Ross *former retail company executive, lawyer, management consultant*
Edwards, Ryan Hayes *baritone*
Egan, Wesley William, Jr. *ambassador*
Egelston, Roberta Riethmiller *writer*
†Eglee, Charles Hamilton *television writer, producer*
Ehrlich, Amy *editor, writer*
Ehrling, Sixten *orchestra conductor*
Eicher, George John *aquatic biologist*
Eihusen, Virgil R. *retired manufacturing company executive*
Ein, Daniel *allergist*
Eischen, Michael Hugh *retired railroad controller*
Eisen, Henry *retired pharmacy educator*
Eisenhower, John Sheldon Doud *former ambassador, author*
Ekstract, Richard Evan *publishing executive*
Elder, Mark Philip *conductor*
Elgart, Larry Joseph *orchestra leader*
Elikann, Lawrence S. (Larry Elikann) *television and film director*
Eliot, Theodore Lyman, Jr. *international consultant*
Elizondo, Hector *actor*
Elkind, Mort William *creative and business consultant*
Elliot, Jared *financial management consultant*
Elliott, David LeRoy *mathematician, educator, engineering educator*
Elliott, Lois Lawrence *audiology and otolaryngology educator*
Ellis, Emory Nelson, Jr. *retired lawyer*
Ellis, Harold Bernard *civil engineer*
Ellis, Howard Woodrow *evangelist, creative agent, clergyman, artist, author*
Ellison, Eugene Curtis *radio station executive*
†Ellison, Robert M. *new correspondent*
Ellner, Paul Daniel *clinical microbiologist*
Ellwanger, Mike (Cyril Albert Ellwanger) *retired utility executive*
Elsner, Sidney Edgar *journalist*
Elstner, Richard Chesney *structural engineer*
Elverum, Gerard William, Jr. *retired electronic and diversified company executive*
Ely, Joe *singer and songwriter*
Ely, Paul C., Jr. *electronics company executive*
Embry, Carmen Dianne Wheeler *psychologist*
Emerson, Ann Parker *dietician, educator*
Emerson, Daniel Everett *retired communications company executive, executive advisor*
†Emert, Timothy R. *lawyer*
Emery, Sherman Raymond *editorial consultant*
Emmons, Robert Duncan *diplomat*
End, Henry *interior and industrial designer*
†Engelke, George L., Jr. *banker*
English, Bruce Vaughan *museum director and executive, environmental consultant*
English, Richard D. *lawyer, diplomat, government official*
Engman, Lewis August *lawyer, trade association executive*
Enloe, Cortez Ferdinand, Jr. *magazine publisher, physician*
Erb, Richard Louis Lundin *resort and hotel executive*
Erdeljac, Daniel Joseph *retired concrete pipe company executive*
Erden, Sybil Isolde *artist*
Erickson, Alan Eric *librarian*
Erlenmeyer-Kimling, L. *psychiatric and behavior genetics researcher, educator*
Erlicht, Lewis Howard *broadcasting company executive*
Erwin, Elmer Louis *vintager, cement consultant*
Erwin, Judith Ann (Judith Ann Peacock) *writer, photographer, lawyer*
Eschenbrenner, Gunther Paul *engineering consultant*
Esposito, Giancarlo *actor*
Esposito, Philip Anthony (Phil) *professional sports team executive*
Eštes, Clarissa Pinkola *psychologist, analyst, writer*
Estes, Jack Charles *oil service company executive, scientist*
Estrin, Herbert Alvin *financial consultant, entertainment company executive*
Esty, John Cushing, Jr. *writer, lecturer, consultant*
Ettre, Leslie Stephen *chemist*
†Eugster, Albrecht Konrad *veterinarian, laboratory director*
Evanoff, George C. *corporate executive*
†Evans, Marsha Johnson *naval officer*
Evans, Victor Miles *retired funeral home/cemetery company executive*
Evdokimova, Eva *prima ballerina assoluta, choreographer, director, producer*
Everdell, William *lawyer*
Everhart, Rex *actor, director, photographer*
Evstatieva, Stefka *opera singer*
Ewell, Miranda Juan *journalist*
Ewen, H.I. *physicist*
Ewing, Raymond Charles *retired ambassador*
Ewing, Wayne Turner *coal company executive*
Fabares, Shelley *actress*
Faherty, Patricia Bernadette *secondary education educator*
Fahey, Joseph Francis, Jr. *banker, financial consultant*
Fahringer, Catherine Hewson *retired savings and loan executive*
Falcone, Nola Maddox *financial company executive*
Falsey, John Henry, Jr. *television producer*
Fang, Joseph Pe Yong *chemistry educator*
Fanwick, Ernest *corporate lawyer*
Farah, Joseph Francis *newspaper editor, writer*
Farinella, Paul James *retired cultural institution executive*
Fariss, Bruce Lindsay *endocrinologist, educator*
Farley, John Michael *steel industry consultant*
Farley, Lloyd Edward *education educator*
Farmakides, John Basil *lawyer*
Farquhar, Robin Hugh *university president*
Farris, Robert Earl *transportation consultant*
Farrow, Mia Villiers *actress*
Faruqui, G. Ahmad *engineering consultant*
Farwell, Harold Frederick, Jr. *English language educator*
Fassio, Virgil *newspaper publishing company executive*
Faulkner, Lloyd C. *veterinary medicine educator*
†Fawcett, Farrah Leni *actress, model*
Fay, Conner Martindale *management consultant*
Fazio, Evelyn M. *publisher*
Feehan, Thomas Joseph *financial executive*
Fehr, Lola Mae *nursing association director*
Feiffer, Jules *cartoonist, writer, playwright*
Fein, Adrienne Myra *nursing educator*
Feinberg, Herbert *apparel and beverage executive*
Feirstein, Frederick *poet, playwright, psychoanalyst*
Feldman, Thomas Myron *director, lighting director, director of photography, film company executive*
Feldstein, Joshua *academic administrator*
Felix, David *economics educator*
Feller, Robert William Andrew *baseball team public relations executive, retired baseball player*
Fenello, Michael John *aviation consultant, retired government agency executive*
Fenger, Manfred *retired manufacturing executive*
Fenichel, Norman Stewart *public relations and advertising agency executive*
Fenoglio-Preiser, Cecilia Mettler *pathologist, educator*
Ferguson, Glenn Walker *university president*
Ferguson, Maynard *trumpeter, band leader*
Ferguson, Robert *financial services executive, writer*
Ferlinz, Jack *cardiologist, medical educator*
Fernandez-Arrondo, Maria del Carmen *secondary education educator*
Ferre, Antonio Luis *newspaper publisher*
Feshbach, Norma Deitch *psychologist, educator*
Fetler, Andrew *author, educator*
†Fetterly, Lynn Lawrence *real estate broker/ developer*
†Feurig, Thomas Leo *health care executive*
Fibiger, John Andrew *life insurance company executive*
Field, Arthur Norman *lawyer*
Field, Charles William *metallurgical engineer, small business owner, consultant*
Field, George Sydney *retired research director*
Field, Sally *actress*
Fielding, Harold Preston *bank executive*
Fields, Freddie *producer, agent*
Fields, Leo *former jewelry company executive, investor*
Fields, William Hudson, III *magazine publisher*
Fife, Jonathan Donald *higher education educator*
Filchock, Ethel *education educator, poet*
Filerman, Michael Herman *television producer*
†Filizetti, Gary John *construction executive*
Filston, Howard Church *pediatric surgeon, educator*
Finder, Theodore Roosevelt *retired lawyer*
Finger, Harold B. *energy, space, nuclear energy and urban affairs consultant*
Fink, John Francis *newspaper editor*
Finucane, Richard Daniel *corporate medical director, retired food products executive*
Fiorito, Edward Gerald *lawyer*
Fippinger, Grace J. *retired telecommunications company executive*
Firestone, Evan Richard *arts educator and administrator*
Fischer, Eugene H. *air force officer*
Fischer, William Donald *retired food executive*
Fischmar, Richard Mayer *company financial executive, consultant*
Fish, Janet Isobel *artist*
Fishman, Bernard *mechanical engineer*
Fitch, Steven Joseph *retired chemicals executive*
Fitzgeorge, Harold James *former oil and gas company executive*
Fitzgerald, Edward Earl *publishing executive, author*
Fitzgerald, Geraldine *actress*
Fitzmaurice, Laurence Dorset *banking executive*
Fitzpatrick, Sean Kevin *advertising agency executive*
Flaschen, Steward Samuel *high technology company executive*
†Flavin, Dan *artist*
Fleischer, Gerald Albert *industrial engineer, educator*
†Fleisher, David L. *business communications and market research services executive*
Fleming, Charles Clifford, Jr. *retired airline and jet aircraft sales company executive*
Fletcher, Louise *actress*
Flick, John Edmond *lawyer*
Flinner, Beatrice Eileen *library and media sciences educator*
Flipse, John Edward *naval architect, mechanical engineer*
Flitcraft, Richard Kirby, II *former chemical company executive*
Florence, Paul Smith *agronomist, business owner*
Foley, Daniel Edmund *real estate development executive*
Folkens, Alan Theodore *clinical and pharmaceutical microbiologist*
Folkman, David H. *apparel wholesale executive*
Foote, Evelyn Patricia *military officer, consultant*
Ford, Ashley Lloyd *lawyer, retired consumer products company executive*
Ford, Ford Barney *retired government official*
Ford, Harrison *actor*
Ford, Jerry Lee *products company executive*
Ford, Judith Ann *retired natural gas distribution company executive*
Ford, Nancy Louise *composer, scriptwriter*
Ford, Wendell Hampton *senator*
Ford, William Francis *retired bank holding company executive*
Forester, Russell *artist*
Forman, Miloš *film director*
Forsythe, Henderson *actor*
Fort, Randall Martin *former federal official*
Fortier, D'Iberville *communications consultant*
Fortinberry, Glen W. *advertising executive*
Foss, Lukas *composer, conductor, pianist*
Fossier, Mike Walter *consultant, retired electronics company executive*
Foster, Charles Henry Wheelwright *former foundation officer, consultant,author*
Foster, Edson L. *retired mining and manufacturing company executive, consultant*
Foster, Robert Lawson *retired judge, deacon*
Foster, Stephen Kent *banker*
Fouch, Stephanie Saunders *advertising executive*
Fowler, Donald Raymond *retired lawyer, educator*
Fowler, John Moore *financial service company executive*
Fowler, Raymond David *financial executive*
Fowlie, Eldon Leslie *retired library administrator*
Fox, Gerald Lynn *retired oral and maxillofacial surgeon*
Fox, Lawrence *company executive*
Fox, Michael Wilson *veterinarian, animal behaviorist*
Frame, Russell William *retired electronics executive*
Francis, Sam *artist*
Frank, Edgar Gerald *retired financial executive*
Frank, Sanders Thalheimer *physician, educator*
Frankel, Arnold J. *chemical company executive*
†Frankel, Glenn *journalist*
†Franken, Robert E. *news correspondent*
Frankenberger, Bertram, Jr. *investor, consultant*
†Frankfurt, Stephen O. *advertising agency executive*
Franklin, Barbara Kipp *financial planner, investment adviser*
Franklin, John Hope *historian, educator, author*
Franklin, Kenneth L(inn) *astronomer*
Franklin, Margaret Lavona Barnum (Mrs. C. Benjamin Franklin) *civic leader*
Franklin, Michael Harold *arbitrator, lawyer, consultant*
Fraser, Campbell *business consultant*
Fraser, Donald C. *engineering executive, educator*
Fraser, Donald MacKay *former mayor, former congressman*
Fraser, Kathleen Joy *poet, creative writing educator*
Frauenfelder, Hans *physicist, educator*
Frawley, Patrick Joseph, Jr. *corporate executive*
Fredricks, Richard *baritone*
Fredrickson, Donald Sharp *physician, scientist*
Freedman, Russell Bruce *author*
Freeman, Arthur *veterinarian, retired association administrator*
Freeman, Graydon LaVerne *retired publishing company executive*
Freeman, Meredith Norwin *former college president, education educator*
Freeman, Russell Adams *lawyer*
Freilicher, Jane *artist*
Freitag, Harlow *computer scientist, corporate executive*
French, Clarence Levi, Jr. *retired shipbuilding company executive*
French, Glendon Everett, Jr. *health care executive*
Frere, Maurice Herbert *retired soil scientist*
†Freston, Thomas E. *cable television programming executive*
Frick, Ivan Eugene *college president emeritus*
Fried, Walter Rudolf *engineer, aerospace scientist*
Frieder, Gideon *computer science and engineering educator*
Friedlander, Robert Lynn *health education and health management consultant*
Friedman, Donald Joseph *stock brokerage executive*
Friedman, Eugene Warren *surgeon*
Friedman, Martin *arts adviser, retired museum director*
†Friedman, Mildred *designer, educator, curator*
Frieling, Gerald Harvey, Jr. *specialty steel company executive*
Frierson, Jimmie Lou *vocational education educator*
Fritz, Rene Eugene, Jr. *manufacturing executive*
Frost, David (Paradine) *author, producer, columnist*
Frost, J. Ormond *otolaryngologist, educator*
Fry, Doris Hendricks *museum curator*
Fryer, Thomas Waitt, Jr. *writer*
Fuentes, Carlos *writer, former ambassador*
Fugh, John Liu *military officer, lawyer*
Fuhrman, Robert Alexander *aerospace company executive*
Fuld, Richard Severin, Jr. *investment banker*
Fuller, James Chester Eedy *retired chemical company executive*
Fuller, Robert Ferrey *lawyer, investor*
Fuller, Stephen Herbert *business administration educator*
Fulton, James Franklin *industrial designer*
Gable, Carol Brignoli *pharmacoeconomics researcher*
Gaffney, Thomas *banker*
†Gage, Delwyn Orin *state senator, accountant, oil producer*
Gagnon, Edith Morrison *ballerina, singer, actress*
Gainey, Robert Michael *professional hockey coach, former player*
Gajdusek, Daniel Carleton *pediatrician, research virologist*
Galbraith, John Semple *history educator*
Galfo, Armand James *statistics educator*
Gallegly, Elton William *congressman*
Galloway, William Joyce *physicist, consultant*
Gamble, E. James *lawyer, accountant*
Gammon, Samuel Rhea, III *association executive, former ambassador*
Gandy, Charles David *interior designer*
Gantz, Carroll Melvin *industrial design consultant, consumer product designer*
Ganz, Lowell *screenwriter, television producer*

Garcia, Alexander orthopaedic surgeon
Garcia, Jerry (Jerome John Garcia) guitarist, composer
Garcia-Granados, Sergio Eduardo brokerage house executive
Gardner, James Albert investment and real estate executive
Gardner, Warner Winslow lawyer
Gardner, William Michael library administrator
Garfield, Brian Wynne author
Garfield, Robert Edward newspaper columnist
Garfunkel, Art singer, actor
Garner, James (James Scott Bumgarner) actor
Garrard, Don Edward Burdett operatic and concert singer
Garrison, Richard Christopher advertising agency executive
Gartenberg, Seymour Lee retired recording company executive
Garvey, Evelyn Jewel mental health nurse
Gaspar, Anna Louise retired elementary school teacher, consultant
Gasper, Jo Ann association executive
Gass, William H. author, educator
Gates, Larry actor
Gatlin, Larry Wayne singer, songwriter
Gavin, Herbert James consultant, retired air force officer
Gay, William Ingalls veterinarian, health science administrator
Geddes, Jane professional golfer
Geddes, Robert architect, educator
Geer, Stephen DuBois retired journalist
Gehm, Denise Charlene ballerina, arts administrator
Geiselhart, Lorene Annetta elementary education educator
Geissinger, Frederick Wallace investment banker
Geitgey, Doris Arlene retired nursing educator, dean
Geller, Seymour retired educator, researcher
Gelles, Harry P. investment banker, land investor
Gelman, Larry actor
Gemignani, Michael Caesar clergyman, retired educator
Gendell, Gerald Stanleigh retired public affairs executive
Gens, Ralph Samuel electrical engineering consultant
†Gensler, M. Arthur, Jr. architect
Geoffroy, Charles Henry retired travel company executive
Geoghegan, John Joseph retired publisher
Geoppinger, William Anthony meat processing company executive
Georgas, John William beverage manufacturing company executive
George, Joyce Jackson lawyer, former judge
Gerald, Michael Charles pharmacy educator, college dean
Gerard, Jean Broward Shevlin former ambassador, lawyer
Gerhardt, Jon Stuart mechanical engineer, engineering educator
†Gerner, Randolph Henry architect
Gers, Seymour psychiatrist
Gerstein, Esther sculptor
Gertenbach, Robert Frederick medical research organization executive, accountant, lawyer
Getting, Ivan Alexander physicist, former aerospace company executive
Gevantman, Judith financial analyst, consultant
Giacomini, Giuseppe tenor
†Giacomino, Robert Richard advertising executive
Giardina, Paul Anthony environmental nuclear engineer, thoroughbred horse investment specialist
Gibson, Mel actor
†Gibson, Robert N. hospital executive
†Giddings, Helen personnel management executive
†Gilb, Dagoberto writer, carpenter
Gilbert, Kenneth Albert harpsichordist
†Gilbert, Nancy Louise librarian
†Gilbertz, Larry E. state legislator, entrepreneur
Gilchrist, Ellen Louise writer
Gilchrist, James Beardslee banker
Gilder, George Franklin writer
Gilford, Leon business executive and consultant
Gilinsky, Victor physicist
Gill, Henry Herr photojournalist
Gill, William Robert soil scientist
Gillam, Max Lee lawyer
Gillespie, Gerald Ernest Paul comparative literature educator, writer
Gillespie, Gwain Homer financial executive
Gillespie, Nellie Redd state official, academic administrator
Gillespie, Robert James manufacturing company executive
Gillette, Stanley C. apparel manufacturing company executive
Gilliam, Terry Vance film director, actor, illustrator, writer
Gilreath, Warren Dean retired packaging company executive
Gilroy, Frank Daniel playwright
†Gilson, Barbara Frances editor
Ginsburg, Iona Horowitz psychiatrist
Giordano, Richard Vincent chemical executive
Giordano, Tony director
Girzone, Joseph F. retired priest, writer
Giulianti, Mara Selena mayor, civic worker
Giusti, Robert George artist, educator
Giusti, William Roger lawyer
Givens, Robin actress
Glancz, Ronald Robert lawyer
Glasberg, Laurence Brian finance executive, private investor
Glashow, Sheldon Lee physicist, educator
Glass, Dorothea Daniels physiatrist, educator
Glass, Kenneth Edward management consultant
Glassock, Richard James nephrologist
Gleijeses, Mario holding company executive
Glennon, Harrison Randolph, Jr. retired shipping company executive
Glick, J. Leslie biotechnology company executive
Glick, Ruth Burtnick author, lecturer
Glover, Crispin Hellion actor
Glover, William Harper theater critic
Glower, Donald Duane university executive, mechanical engineer
Glück, Louise Elisabeth poet
Gluys, Charles Byron retired marketing management consultant
Glynn, Carlin (Carlin Masterson) actress
Gobel, John Henry lawyer
Goble, Paul author, illustrator, artist
Godino, Rino Lodovico retired petroleum and chemical company executive
Goebert, Robert J. banking executive
Goewey, Gordon Ira university administrator
Goforth, William Clements lawyer
Gogarty, William Barney oil company executive, consultant
Goin, Olive Bown biologist
Goldberg, Samuel retired mathematician, foundation officer
Goldberg, Victor Joel retired data processing company executive
Goldberg, Whoopi (Caryn Johnson) actress
Goldberger, Arthur Earl, Jr. industrial engineer, consultant
Goldberger, Blanche Rubin sculptor, jeweler
Goldblum, Jeff actor
Goldfine, Howard microbiology and biochemistry educator, researcher
Goldhirsh, Bernard A. publisher
Goldman, Alan Ira investment banking executive
Goldman, Alfred Emmanuel marketing research consultant
Goldman, Gerald Hillis beverage distribution company executive
Goldovsky, Boris musician
Goldstein, Walter Elliott biotechnology executive
Goldston, Stephen Eugene community psychologist, educator, consultant
Goldwater, John Leonard publisher, writer
†Golum, Robert Bruce journalist
Good, Daniel James manufacturing executive
Good, Linda Lou elementary education educator
Good, Walter Raymond business executive
Goode, Janet Weiss primary and secondary educator
Goodkin, Michael Jon publishing company executive
Goodman, Erika dancer, actress
Goodwill, Margaret Jane artist
Goodwin, Barbara A. retired nurse, military officer
Gordan, Gilbert Saul physician, educator
Gordis, David Moses academic administrator, rabbi
†Gordly, Avel Louise state legislator, community activist
Gordon, Bonnie Heather writer, editor
Gordon, Cyrus Herzl Orientalist, educator
Gordon, Janine M. advertising agency executive
†Gordon, Richard Joseph gas distribution company executive
Gordon, Stewart George manufacturing company executive
Gore, Sadie Lou elementary education educator
Gorham, William organization executive
Gorme, Eydie singer
Goss, Porter J. congressman
Gossett, Louis, Jr. actor
Gould, Morton composer, conductor
Goulet, Lorrie sculptor
Gounaris, Anne Demetra biochemistry educator, researcher
Govan, Gladys Vernita Mosley retired critical care and medical/surgical nurse
Goyan, Michael Donovan stockbroker, investment executive
Grabemann, Karl W. lawyer
Grace, Marcia Bell advertising executive
Graebner, James Herbert transportation executive
Graf, Steffi professional tennis player
Graff, Luisita Mariano women's health nurse, nursing administrator
Graff, William architect
Grafton, Sue novelist
Graham, James Herbert dermatologist
Grandi, Attilio engineering consultant
Grandy, James Frederick retired electronics business executive, consultant
Grant, Alexander Marshall ballet director
Grant, Frederick Anthony investment banker
Grant, James Colin banker
Grant, James Francis international business and defense consultant, retired air force officer
Gray, David Lawrence retired air force officer
Gray, Donna Mae former agricultural products executive, bookkeeper
Gray, Francine du Plessix author
Gray, Harry Joshua electrical engineer, educator
Gray, James Peyton computer scientist
Gray, John Lathrop, III advertising agency executive
Gray, Richard Alexander, Jr. retired chemical company executive
Greaves, James Louis art conservator
Greaves, William Garfield film director, producer
Greber, Robert Martin financial investments executive
Greeley, Andrew Moran sociologist, author
Green, Barbara Strawn psychotherapist
Green, David Thomas retired surgical company research and development executive, inventor
Green, Flora Hungerford lactation consultant, nurse
†Green, George radio executive
Green, Joseph Martin psychiatrist, educator
Green, Mark Joseph lawyer, author
Green, Nancy Loughridge newspaper executive
Green, Richard Calvin, Jr. utility company executive
Green, Thomas George architect
Greenberg, Albert art director
†Greenberg, Arnold Elihu water quality specialist
Greenberg, Milton corporation executive
Greenburg, Dan author
Greene, Elinore Aschah speech and drama professional, writer
Greene, Laurence Whitridge, Jr. surgical educator
Greene, Lynne Jeannette fashion designer
Greenfield, Helen Meyers real estate executive, publishing company executive, inspection and test service executive
Greenwald, Gerald industrial company executive
Greenway, John Selmes hotel owner
Greenwood, Frank information scientist
Greer, Carl Crawford petroleum company executive
Greer, Germaine author
Gregg, (Alvis) Forrest professional football coach, former college football coach
Gregg, Michael W. manufacturing executive
Gregory, Myra May educator, religious organization administrator
Grewe, John Mitchell orthodontist, educator
Griffin, Campbell Arthur, Jr. lawyer
Griffin, James Anthony bishop
Griffith, Clark Calvin, II lawyer
Griffith, Daniel Boyd automotive products executive
Griffith, Melanie actress
Grinstead, William Carter, Jr. retired coal and minerals company executive
†Grobman, Arnold Brams retired biology educator and academic administrator
Groening, Matthew writer, cartoonist
Grogan, Kevin museum director
Gromen, Richard John historian, educator
Groome, Reginald Kehnroth hotel executive
Grosbard, Ulu director
Gross, Paul Randolph biologist, academic administrator
Gross, Ruth Taubenhaus physician
†Gross, Terry R. radio producer, host
Grossman, John Joseph retired editor
Grove, Brandon Hambright, Jr. diplomat
Grove, Kalvin M(yron) lawyer
Gruber, Fredric Francis financial planning and investment research executive
Gruber, Thomas A. marketing executive
†Grubiak, James Frank chewing gum executive
†Grueskin, William Steven editor
Grund, Walter James, Jr. retired gynecologist
Gryder, Rosa Meyersburg toxicologist, consultant
Gschwind, Donald management and engineering consultant
Gudnitz, Ora M. Cofey secondary school educator
Guild, Nelson Prescott retired state education official
Guillemette, Gloria Vivian dressmaker, designer
Guinness, Sir Alec actor
Gulcher, Robert Harry aircraft company executive
†Gulick, David Miller advertising executive
Gulledge, Sandra Smith publicist
Gummel, Hermann Karl retired physicist, laboratory administrator
Gund, Gordon management executive
Gundelfinger, Ralph Mellow insurance company executive
Gundersen, Wayne Campbell management consultant, oil and gas consultant
Gunderson, Ted Lee security consultant
Gurney, Daniel Sexton race car manufacturing company executive, racing team executive
†Gurney, James Marshall artist, writer
Gutfreund, John H. investment banker
Guthrie, Edgar King artist
Guthrie, Janet professional race car driver
Guthrie, Robert Val psychologist
Guthrie, Wallace Nessler, Jr. naval officer
Gutierrez, Lino diplomat
Gutmann, Reinhart Bruno clergyman, social worker
Gutsch, William Anthony, Jr. astronomer
Guttentag, Joseph Harris lawyer, educator
Guttman, Irving Allen opera stage director
Guyton, Samuel Percy retired lawyer
Haas, Carolyn Buhai publisher, writer, consultant
†Haas, Charlie screenwriter
Hackel-Sims, Stella Bloomberg lawyer, former government official
Hackett, Buddy actor
Hackett, Robert John lawyer
Haddock, Harold, Jr. retired accounting firm executive
Haegele, John Ernest business executive
Haeger, Phyllis Marianna retired association management company executive
Haering, Rudolph Roland retired physics educator, researcher
Hafner, Thomas Mark lawyer
Hagel, Raymond Charles publishing company executive, educator
Hager, Robert Worth retired aerospace company executive
Haggerty, Robert Johns physician, educator
Hahn, Mary Downing author
Hairston, William Russell, Jr. author, playwright
Halaby, Samia Asaad artist, educator, computer artist
Halberstam, Heini mathematician
Haley, George Brock, Jr. lawyer
Half, Robert personnel recruiting executive, author
Halfen, David publishing executive
Hall, Adrienne Ann advertising agency executive
Hall, Conrad L. cinematographer
Hall, Donald poet
Hall, Jack Gilbert lawyer, business executive
Hall, James Parker financial consultant
Hall, James Stanley jazz guitarist, composer
Hall, Janice soprano
Hall, Jay retired social psychologist
Hall, John Hopkins lawyer, retired
Hall, John Marshall food industry consultant
Hall, Milton Reese retired oil company executive
Hall, Monty television producer, actor
Hall, Thomas Forrest naval officer
Halleck, Charles White lawyer, former judge
Hallett, William Jared nuclear engineer
Halliday, William Ross retired physician, speleologist, writer
Halmi, Robert film producer
Halmos, Imre Hubertus insurance company executive
Halpin, Daniel William civil engineering educator, consultant
Halsey, James Albert international entertainment impressario, theatrical producer, talent manager
†Hambidge, Douglas Walter archbishop
Hamblen, John Wesley computer scientist, genealogist
Hameister, Lavon Louetta farm manager, social worker
Hamill, Dorothy Stuart professional ice skater
Hamill, (William) Pete newspaper columnist, author
Hamilton, Allan Corning retired oil company executive
†Hamilton, Calvin Sargent planning consultant, retired city official
Hamilton, James Marvie electronics company executive
Hamilton, Lyman Critchfield, Jr. multi-industry executive
Hamilton, William Frank management educator
Hamilton, William Howard laboratory executive
Hamilton, Willie L. utility executive
Hamlin, Dan William accountant, management consultant
Hamlin, Sonya B. communications specialist
Hamlisch, Marvin composer
Hammer, Joyce Mae gifted and talented education educator
Hammerschmidt, John Paul retired congressman, lumber company executive
Hammond, Robert Lee retired feed company executive
Hamner, Earl Henry, Jr. author, producer, television and film writer
Hampton, Lionel Leo composer, conductor, entertainer
†Hampton, Mark interior designer
Hancock, John Coulter telecommunications company executive
Handler, Harold Robert lawyer
Handy, Edward Otis, Jr. financial services executive
Handy, William Talbot, Jr. bishop
Hanford, George Hyde retired educational administrator
Hankins, Mary Denman elementary school educator
Hanks, Robert Jack writer, consultant, former naval officer
Hanley, Charles psychology educator
Hanmer, Stephen Read, Jr. government executive
Hanna, John A. finance and administration executive
Hannay, N(orman) Bruce chemist, industrial research and business consultant
Hanners, David journalist
Hansbury, Vivien Holmes educator
Hansen, James V. congressman
Hansen, Shirley Jean energy consulting executive, professional association administrator
Hanson, Carl Malmrose financial company executive
Hanson, Jo artist
Hanzlik, Rayburn DeMara lawyer
Harari, Hananiah artist
Harbutt, Charles photographer
Harden, Patrick Alan journalist, news executive
Harder, Robert Clarence state official
†Hardesty, Christopher Scott oil and mining company executive
Hardin, Clifford Morris retired university chancellor, retired executive
Hardin, Hal D. lawyer, former U.S. attorney, former judge
Hardin, Paul, III chancellor
Hardy, Gyme Dufault social worker
Hare, Frederick Kenneth geography and environmental educator, university official
Harlan, Robert Warren retired charitable association executive
Harmon, Robert Gerald health consultant
Harnack, Don Steger lawyer
Harper, W(alter) Joseph financial consultant
Harrell, Henry Howze tobacco company executive
Harrigan, Anthony Hart author
Harriman, John Howland lawyer
Harrington, Jean Patrice former college president
Harris, Barbara actress
Harris, D. George entrepreneur
Harris, David Philip crisis management for underperforming corporations
Harris, Elliott Stanley toxicologist
Harris, Gregory Scott management services executive
Harris, Howard Hunter oil company executive
†Harris, Joseph theatrical producer
Harris, Marcelite Jordan air force officer
Harris, Margaret pianist, conductor, composer
Harris, Richard (Richard St. John) actor
Harris, Robert Norman advertising and communications educator
Harris, Roy Hartley electrical engineer
Harris, William John retired management holding company executive, consultant
Harrison, Charles Maurice lawyer, former communications company executive
Harrison, William Burwell, Jr. banker
Harryhausen, Ray Frederick special effects expert
Harshbarger, Dwight psychologist, management consultant
Hart, Arthur Alvin historian, author
Hart, Dorothy actress
Hart, Evelyn ballet dancer
Hartell, John artist, retired art educator
Hartley, Grace Van Tine foundation administrator
Hartman, John Wheeler publisher
Hartman, Margaret J. biologist, educator, university official
Hartman, Phil Edward actor
Hartnett, Thomas Patrick health care management executive
Harton, John James utility executive
Hartsell, Samuel David insurance agent
†Haskew, George M., Jr. utility executive
Haskins, James English language educator, writer
Hasselmeyer, Eileen Grace medical research administrator
Hasselmo, Nils university official, linguistics educator
Hast, Adele editor, historian
Hatano, Sadashi molecular biology educator
Hatch, Orrin Grant senator
Hatchett, Edward Earl retired aerospace manufacturing company executive
Hatfield, W. C. banking consultant
Hauenstein, George Carey life insurance executive
Hausman, Arthur Herbert electronics company executive
Hauver, Constance Longshore lawyer
Havlicek, John former professional basketball player
Havoc, June actress
Hawes, Alexander Boyd, Jr. newspaper editor, journalist
Hawk, Phillip Michael service corporation executive
†Hawk, Robert Dooley wholesale grocery company executive
Hawkes, John humanities educator, author
Hawkins, Lawrence Charles management consultant, educator
Hawkins, Osie Penman, Jr. baritone
Hayes, David Vincent sculptor
Hayes, Gladys Lucille Allen community care organization official, poet, writer
Hayes, Janet Gray business manager, former mayor
Hayes, John Patrick retired manufacturing company executive
Hayes, Marilyn Jo communications educator, writer
Hayes, Mary Phyllis savings and loan association executive
Hayes, Peter Lind actor, writer
†Hayne, Harriet Ann state legislator, rancher
Hays, Thomas Chandler holding company executive
Headley, Anne Renouf technology commercialization financier
Healton, Donald Carney federal agency administrator
Heard, John actor
Hearn, J(ames) Woodrow bishop
†Hearn, John Patrick biologist, educator
Heath, Percy jazz bassist
Heath, Richard Eddy lawyer
Heath, Richard Murray retired hospital administrator
Hebner, Paul Chester retired oil company executive, consultant
Hecht, Chic ambassador, former senator
Hecht, Emil retired housing and financial company executive
†Heck, Larry Jack vocational school administrator, state legislator
†Heckart, Eileen actress
Heckler, John Maguire stockbroker, investment company executive
Hediger, Gary Roddy property management company executive
Hedrick, Basil Calvin state agency administrator, ethnohistorian, educator, museum and cultural institutions consultant
Heeschen, David Sutphin astronomer, educator
Heffernan, Wilbert Joseph social worker, educator
Hegarty, George John university administrator, English educator

Heggie, Robert James steel company executive
Heilbrun, Carolyn Gold English literature educator
Heilman, Marlin Grant photographer
Heilmann, Christian Flemming corporate executive
Heiman, David Gilbert lawyer
Heiman, Grover George, Jr. magazine editor, author
Heine, Ursula Ingrid biologist, researcher, artist
Heiney, John Weitzel former utility executive
Helander, Bruce Paul art dealer, artist
Helfgott, Roy B. economist, educator
Heller, Dorothy artist
Heller, Ronald Gary manufacturing company executive, lawyer
†Hellmers, Norman Donald historic site director
Helm, DeWitt Frederick, Jr. association executive
Helman, Alfred Blair retired college president, education consultant
Helms, J. Lynn former government agency administrator
Helms, W. Richard lawyer
Helprin, Mark author
Helton, Thelma Ann elementary education educator
†Helzberg, Barnett C. company executive
Hemann, Raymond Glenn aerospace research company executive
Hemmer, James Paul lawyer
Hemond, Roland A. professional baseball team executive
Henderson, Charles Brooke research company executive
Hendry, Jean Sharon psychopharmacologist
Henes, Donna Urban Shaman celebration artist, ritualist, writer
Henkel, Arthur John, Jr. investment banker
Henle, Peter economic consultant, arbitrator
Henner, Marilu actress
Henning, Doug illusionist
†Henry, John Raymond sculptor
†Henry, Suzanne Jane government executive
Hepburn, Katharine Houghton actress
Hepper, Carol artist, educator
Herbert, Ira C. food processing company executive
Herbert, John Warren forest products executive
Herbig, Günther conductor
Herbst, Jurgen history and education educator
Hering, Doris Minnie dance critic
Herington, Cecil John classics educator
Heris, Toni psychologist, psychotherapist
Herman, Chester Joseph physician
Herman, Hank writer
Herman, Joan Elizabeth insurance company executive
Hernández, William Héctor, Jr. government official
Herriot, James (James Alfred Wight) veterinary surgeon, author
Herrmann, Walter retired laboratory administrator
Hersey, David Kenneth theatrical lighting designer
Hertz, Kenneth Theodore health care executive
Herz, George Peter chemical engineer,industrial consultant
Herz, Michael Joseph marine environmental scientist
†Herzberg, Thomas artist, illustrator
Herzfeld, Charles Maria physicist
Heskett, Luvina Hylton elementary education educator
Hess, David Willard journalist
Hesse, Christian August mining industry consultant
Heston, Charlton (John Charlton Carter) actor
Hetzron, Robert linguist, educator
Hewes, Laurence Ilsley, III lawyer, management and legal consultant
Heymann, C(lemens) David author
Heymann, Philip B. law educator, academic director
Hiatt, Arnold shoe manufacturer, importer, retailer
Hiatt, Robert Nelson consumer products executive
†Hibbs, William Ernest, III priest
Hickey, Joseph Michael, Jr. investment banker
Hickson, Joan Bogle actress
Higginbotham, John Taylor lawyer
Hildebrandt, Theodore Ware computer scientist
Hilding, Jerel Lee music and dance educator, former dancer
Hill, Arthur actor
Hill, Harold Nelson, Jr. lawyer
Hiller, Arthur motion picture director
Hiller, Wendy actress
†Hiller, William Arlington agriculture executive
Hillerman, Tony writer, former journalism educator
Hilliard, Sam Bowers geography educator
Hilton, Clifford Thomas clergyman
Himmelfarb, Milton editor, educator
Hinckle, Warren James, III journalist
Hine, Daryl poet
Hingle, Pat actor
Hinkley, Everett David, Jr. scientist,business executive
Hinson, Howard Houston petroleum company executive
Hirose, Teruo Terry surgeon
Hirsch, Horst Eberhard business consultant
Hirschberg, Vera Hilda writer
Hirsh, Norman Barry management consultant
Hirst, Heston Stillings former insurance company executive
Hitchborn, James Brian telecommunications executive
Hitchcock, Walter Anson educational consultant, retired educational administrator
Hite, Elinor Kirkland oil company human resources consultant
†Hixon, Allen Wentworth landscape architect, land planner
Hobbs, J. Edwin retired utility executive
Hoch, Frederic Louis medical educator
Hoch, Roland Franklin lawyer, retired utilities corporation executive
Hock, Morton entertainment advertising executive
Hodges, Paul Joseph securities analyst
Hodson, Nancy Perry real estate agent
Hoeg, Donald Francis chemist, consultant, former research and development executive
Hoffman, S. David lawyer, engineering educator
Hofmann, Paul Bernard health care consultant
Hogan, Mark investment company executive
Hogan, Robert Henry trust company executive, investment strategist
Hogan, Thomas Francis federal judge
Hoge, James Fulton, Jr. magazine editor
Hoggard, Lara Guldmar conductor, educator
Hoi, Samuel Chuen-Tsung dean
Holgate, George Jackson university president
Holiday, Edith Elizabeth former presidential adviser, cabinet secretary
Holland, David Thurston former editor
Holland, James Paul utility company executive
Holland, James Richard, Jr. business executive
Holland, Randy James state supreme court justice
Holland, Robert Campbell anatomist, educator
Holldobler, Berthold Karl zoologist, educator
†Holliday, Robert Kelvin state senator, former newspaper executive
Hollis, William S. management consultant
Holloran, Thomas Edward business educator
Holloway, Robert Ross archaeologist, educator
Holm, Celeste actress
Holmer, Edwin Carl retired petrochemical company executive
Holmes, Kathryn Louise medical technologist
Holster, Robert Marc health care information company executive
Holt, Douglas Eugene consulting engineer, retired business executive
Holt, Marjorie Sewell lawyer, retired congresswoman
Holt, Patricia Lester book review editor
Homestead, Susan psychotherapist
Honeystein, Karl lawyer, entertainment company executive
Hooper, Gerry Don information systems professional, consultant
Hoopes, Townsend Walter former association executive, former government official
Hoover, Francis Louis educator, gemologist, jewelry designer, appraiser fine arts and gems, writer
Hoover, John Elwood former military officer, consultant, writer
Hope, Bob actor, comedian
Horan, Hume Alexander diplomat, association executive
Horner, Matina Souretis retired college president, corporate executive
Hornick, Katherine Joyce Kay artist, small business owner
Horowitz, Beverly Phyllis occupational therapist
Horsch, Kathleen Joanne social services administrator, educator, consultant
Horton, Robert Baynes railroad company executive
Horton, Wilfred Henry mathematics educator
Horwitz, Donald Paul lawyer
Hostettler, Stephen John naval officer
Hough, George Anthony, III journalism educator
Houghton, Katharine actress
House, Charles Staver judge
Houser, William Douglas telecommunications company executive, former naval officer
Houstoun, Lawrence Orson, Jr. development consultant
Howard, Charles L. chemist, educator
Howard, Dean Denton electrical engineer, researcher, consultant
Howard, Donald Searcy banker
Howard, Jack Rohe retired newspaperman
†Howard, James Joseph, III utility company executive
Howard, James Webb investment banker, lawyer, engineer
Howard, Richard (Joseph Howard) poet, literary translator
Howe, John Perry materials science educator, research consultant
Howe, John Prentice, III health science center executive, physician
Howell, Donald Lee lawyer
Howell, William Robert retail company executive
Hoyt, Mary Finch author, editor, media consultant, former government official
†Hoyt, Stanley Charles retired research administrator, entomologist
Hubbard, Elizabeth actress
Hubbe, Henry Ernest financial forecaster, funds manager
Hubley, Reginald Allen publisher
†Hudlin, Reginald Alan director, writer, producer
Hudnut, David Beecher retired leasing company executive, lawyer
Hudson, Franklin Donald diversified company executive
Huffman, James Thomas William oil exploration company executive
Hughes, Eugene Morgan university president
Hughes, George David business educator
Hughes, Michaela Kelly actress, dancer
Hughes, Richard Gene computer executive, consultant
†Hugley, Carolyn Fleming state legislator
Hulbert, Bruce Walker corporate executive, banker
Hull, Bobby (Robert Marvin Hull) former professional hockey player
Humke, Ramon L. utility executive
Hummel, Gene Maywood retired bishop
Huning, Deborah Gray actress, dancer, audiologist
Hunt, Bryan artist
Hunt, Joe Harold retired utility company executive
Hunt, Ronald Duncan veterinarian, educator, pathologist
Hunt, Ronald Forrest lawyer
Hunter, Duncan Lee congressman
Hunter, Holly actress
Hunter, Kim (Janet Cole) actress
Hunter, Richard Grant, Jr. neurologist, executive
Hunter, Ross film producer
Huntley, Robert Ross physician, educator
†Hurn, Raymond Walter religious order administrator
Hurst, John Emory, Jr. retired airline executive
Hurt, William actor
Husain, Taqdir mathematics educator
†Huston, Nancy Louise writer, educator
Hutchinson, John Woodside applied mechanics educator, consultant
Hutner, Herbert L. financial consultant, lawyer
Huttenback, Robert Arthur academic administrator, educator
†Hybl, William Joseph foundation executive,lawyer
Hyde, Robert Burke, Jr. retired business executive
Hyman, Seymour Charles arbitrator
†Hyman, Trina Schart illustrator
Iacocca, Lido Anthony (Lee Iacocca) former automotive manufacturing executive
†Iannone, Dorothy visual artist, writer
Ichino, Yoko ballet dancer
Idaszak, Jerome Joseph economic journalist
Ikle, Richard Adolph lawyer
Ilutovich, Leon organization executive
Ingersoll, Paul Mills banker
Ingle, James Chesney, Jr. geology educator
Inglis, James telecommunications company executive
Inman, Cullen Langdon telecommunications scientist
Inouye, David William zoology educator
Intilli, Sharon Marie television director, small business owner
Inui, Thomas Spencer physician, educator
†Ipsen, Grant Ruel insurance and investments professional
Iqbal, Zafar biochemist, neurochemist
Irani, Raymond Reza electro-mechanical company executive
Ireland, Norma Olin writer, scholarly, researcher
Irey, Charlotte York dance educator
Irsay, Robert professional football team executive, construction company executive
Irvine, John Alexander lawyer
Irving, Amy actress
Irving, George Steven actor
Irving, John Winslow writer
Irving, Terry (Edward B. Irving, III) television producer
Irwin, Robert Walter artist
Isaac, Steven Richard advertising executive
Isaacs, Kenneth S(idney) psychoanalyst, educator
Isaacs, Susan novelist, screenwriter
Isaacson, Edith Lipsig civic leader
Isakow, Selwyn financier
†Isom, Dotcy Ivertus, Jr. bishop
Istomin, Marta Casals performing arts administrator
†Iverson, David M. church executive
†Ives, S. Clifton minister
Ivry, Alfred Lyon foreign language and literature educator
Jackson, Carmault Benjamin, Jr. physician
Jackson, Elmer Joseph lawyer, oil and gas company executive
†Jackson, Nagle stage director, playwright
Jackson, Rudolph Ellsworth pediatrician, educator
Jackson, Victor Louis retired naturalist
Jacobi, Derek George actor
Jacobs, Abigail Conway biochemist
Jacobs, Ilene B. electrical equipment company executive, treasurer
Jacobs, Wilbur Ripley writer, history educator
Jacobsen, Arthur business and financial consultant
Jacobson, Herbert Laurence diplomat
Jacobson, James Bassett insurance executive
Jacoby, Stanley Arthur retired manufacturing executive
Jacques, Andre Charles financial consultant
Jaffe, Stanley Richard film producer, director
Jaicks, Frederick Gillies retired steel company executive
Jaicomo, Ronald James lawyer
Jakubauskas, Edward Benedict college president
†James, Arlo Dee state legislator, retired mining maintenance executive
James, Earl Eugene, Jr. aerospace engineering executive
Jameson, Victor Loyd retired magazine editor
Jamieson, Michael Lawrence lawyer
Jamison, John Callison business educator, investment banker
Janko, May graphic artist
Jankovich, Sam professional football team executive
Janowiak, Robert Michael engineering organization executive
Jansen, Angela Bing artist, educator
Janulaitis, M. Victor consulting company executive
Jarrett, Keith pianist, composer
Jarvis, William Esmond Canadian government official
Jedenoff, George Alexander steel consultant
Jefferson, John Daniel political activist
Jeffries, Robert Alan physicist
†Jenkins, Darrell Lee librarian
Jenney, Neil Franklin, Jr. artist, philosopher
Jennings, Joseph Ashby banker
†Jennings, Max newspaper editor
Jennings, Waylon country musician
†Jensen, Jack Michael publishing executive
Jensen, Marvin Eli retired agricultural engineer
Jensen, Robert Trygve lawyer
Jepson, Robert Scott, Jr. international investment banking specialist
Jernstedt, Richard Don public relations executive
Jiler, William Laurence publisher
Jimenez, Luis Alfonso, Jr. sculptor
Jinks, Robert Larry retired newspaper publisher
Joanou, Phillip advertising executive
John, K. K. (John Kuruvilla Kaiyalethe) minister
John, Ralph Candler retired college president, educator
Johnson, Arnold Ivan civil engineer
Johnson, (Francis) Benjamin actor
Johnson, Clifford Andrew, III financial executive
Johnson, Clifton Herman historian archivist, former research center director
Johnson, Cyrus Edwin grain farmer, former food products executive
Johnson, Dewey E(dward) dentist
Johnson, Diane Lain novelist, critic
Johnson, Don Wayne actor
Johnson, Everett Ramon retired college dean
Johnson, Ferd retired cartoonist, color artist
Johnson, Frank Edward newspaper editor
Johnson, Irving Stanley pharmaceutical company executive, scientist
Johnson, J. J. trombonist
Johnson, Joe William engineering educator, consultant
Johnson, Malcolm Clinton, Jr. publishing consultant
Johnson, Marlene M. social services professional
Johnson, Mary Elizabeth Susan health care planner
Johnson, Reggie professional boxer
Johnson, Robert Maurice newspaper executive
Johnson, Rogers Bruce retired chemical company executive
Johnson, Warren Donald retired pharmaceutical executive, former air force officer
Johnson, William E. manufacturing company executive
Johnson-Masters, Virginia E. (Mrs. William H. Masters) psychologist
Johnston, James Monroe, III air force officer
Johnston, Thomas John management consultant
Jokl, Alois Louis electrical engineer
†Jones, Anita Katherine computer scientist, educator
Jones, David Charles retired air force officer, former chairman Joint Chiefs of Staff
Jones, Jack Dellis oil company executive
†Jones, Jerrauld C. lawyer
Jones, Lawrence Neale university dean, minister
Jones, Regina Nickerson public relations executive
Jones, Robert Alonzo economist
Jones, Robert Henry corporate executive
Jones, Shirley actress, singer
Jones, Tommy Lee actor
Jones, Walton Linton internist, former government official
Jordan, Fred publishing company executive
Jordan, Lois Heywood real estate developer
Jordan, Thomas Fredrick physics educator
Jordan, William Bryan, Jr. art historian
Jorden, William John writer, retired diplomat
Joseph, Judith R. publishing executive
†Joslin, David Bruce bishop
Jourdain, Alice Marie philosopher, retired educator
Jovanovich, Peter William publishing executive
†Joyce, Burton Montgomery natural resources company executive
Judd, Naomi country musician, singer, songwriter, author
Judd, Wynonna country western musician
Judelson, David N. company executive
Judge, Rosemary Ann oil company executive
Juenemann, Sister Jean hospital administrator
Just, Ward Swift author
Kadota, Takashi Theodore mathematician, electrical engineer
Kahanovsky, Luis physical therapist
Kahn, Albert Michael artist, designer
Kahn, Charles Howard architect, educator
Kahn, David dermatologist, educator
Kahn, Madeline Gail actress
Kahn, Susan Beth artist
Kalina, Richard artist
Kalish, Donald philosophy educator
Kalkwarf, Leonard V. minister
Kamen, Martin David physical biochemist
Kane, Michael Joseph director
Kanin, Fay screenwriter
Kapcsandy, Louis Endre building construction and manufacturing executive, chemical engineering consultant
Kaplan, Leonard Eugene accountant
Kapor, Mitchell David foundation executive
Kaprielian, Walter advertising executive
†Karahalios, Sue M. Compton secondary education educator
Karawina, Erica artist, stained glass designer
†Kardos, Paul James insurance company executive
Karls, John B. retired educational administrator
Karnaugh, Maurice computer scientist, educator
Karp, David communications executive, writer
Karp, Sherman aerospace consultant
Kasem, Casey (Kemal Amin Kasem) radio and television personality
Kaser, David librarian, educator, consultant
Kasimer, Solomon charitable organization executive
Kaskowitz, Edwin association executive
Kasperczyk, Jürgen business executive, member Parliament, educator
Kaster, Laura A. lawyer
Kastor, Frank Sullivan English language educator
Katz, Henry insurance executive, retired
Katz, Leon packaging company executive
Kaufman, Jane artist
Kaufman, Paula T. librarian
Kauger, Yvonne state supreme court justice
Kavalek, Lubomir chess expert
Kavanagh, Kevin Patrick insurance company executive
Kavner, Julie actress
Kazan, Elia theatrical, motion picture director and producer, author
Keach, Stacy, Sr. producer, director
Keala, Francis Ahloy security executive
Kearns, James Joseph artist
Kebblish, John Basil retired coal company executive, consultant
Kee, Sharon Phillips lawyer
Keegan, Kenneth Donald financial consultant, retired oil company executive
Keeler, William Henry archbishop
Keenan, Mike professional hockey team coach
†Keigler, John E. aerospace engineer
Keiper, Marilyn Morrison educator
Keisler, H(oward) Jerome mathematics educator
Keith, Brian Michael actor
Kellam, Norma Dawn medical, surgical nurse
Keller, Paul advertising agency executive
Kelley, Jackson DeForest actor
Kellock, Alan C(onverse) book publishing executive
Kellogg, Carol Kay neuroscientist, researcher
Kelly, Alonzo Hyatt, Jr. retired automotive company engineering executive
Kelly, Anthony Odrian flooring manufacturing company executive
Kelly, Aurel Maxey judge
Kelly, Dennis John lawyer
Kelly, Ellsworth artist, sculptor
Kelly, Kevin drama critic
Kelly, Nancy Folden arts administrator
Kempf, Cecil Joseph naval officer
Kempfer, Homer association executive
Kendall, Christopher (Christopher Wolff) conductor, lutenist
Kendrick, Budd Leroy psychologist
Kendrick, Joseph Trotwood former foreign service officer, writer, consultant
Kennedy, Adrienne Lita playwright
Kennedy, Beverly (Kleban) Burris financial consultant, agent, registered representative
Kennedy, Harvey Edward science information publishing executive
†Kennedy, Karen Syence advertising executive
Kennedy, William Francis lawyer
Kenny, Douglas Timothy psychology educator, former university president
Kenny, Patrick Edward publishing executive
Kent, Donald Charles physician
Kent, Howard Lees obstetrician/gynecologist
Kerber, Ronald Lee industrial corporation executive
Kerins, Francis Joseph college president
Kern, Irving John retired food company executive
Kernan, Barbara Desind senior government executive
Kerr, James Winslow pipe line company executive
†Kerr, Leslie A. landscape architect
Kerstetter, Michael James retired manufacturing company executive
Kersting, Edwin Joseph retired university dean
Kertz, Hubert Leonard telephone company executive
Kerwin, Larkin physics educator
†Kevorkian, Jack pathologist
Key, Ted cartoonist
Keyes, Margaret Naumann home economics educator
Keyes, Saundra Elise newspaper editor
†Keyser, Charles Lovett, Jr. bishop
Khouri, Callie Ann screenwriter
Kieffer, Joyce Loretta health science facility administrator, educator
Kiley, Richard Paul actor
Kilpatrick, Georgia Lee nursing educator
Kilpatrick, James Jackson, Jr. columnist, author
Kimmel, George Stuart engineering company executive
Kinder, James Allen lobbyist, professional services firm executive, consultant
King, Algin Braddy marketing educator
King, David Roy lawyer
King, Edward William retired transportation executive
King, Imogene M. nurse, educator
King, James B. federal official
King, John Francis lawyer

King, John Quill Taylor *science center administrator, college administrator emeritus*
King, Larry L. *playwright, actor*
King, Morgana *jazz vocalist*
†King, Patricia Ann *law educator*
King, S(anford) MacCallum *business owner, consultant*
King, Stephen Edwin *novelist, screenwriter, director*
King, Susan Bennett *retired glass company executive*
King, William Collins *oil company executive*
King, William Douglas *retired executive*
Kingsbery, Walton Waits, Jr. *retired accountant*
Kinnell, Galway *writer*
Kinsella, William Patrick *author, educator*
Kinzer, James Raymond *retired pipeline company executive*
Kipniss, Robert *artist*
Kirk, Paul *architect*
Kirkendall, Donald Eugene *federal agency official*
Kirschenmann, Henry George, Jr. *management consultant, former government official, accountant*
Kirsteuer, Ernst Karl Eberhart *biologist, curator*
Kirts, Wayne Charles *interior designer*
Kirven, Gerald *lawyer*
Klapper, Carol Lorraine *magazine publisher*
Kleiman, Alan Boyd *artist*
Kleiman, Ansel *retired electronics company executive*
Kleiman, Bernard *lawyer*
Klein, Edward Joel *editor, author, lecturer*
Klemme, Howard Charles *lawyer*
Klett, Gordon A. *retired savings and loan association executive*
Kliebhan, Sister M(ary) Camille *academic administrator*
Kline, Kevin Delaney *actor*
Klippstatter, Kurt L. *conductor, music director*
Klombers, Norman *association executive, retired*
Kloss, Gene (Alice Geneva Glasier) *artist*
Kloster, Einar *corporate executive*
Knab, Donald Ralph *corporate executive*
Knauer, Virginia Harrington (Mrs. Wilhelm F. Knauer) *consumer consultant, former government official*
Knight, Janet Ann *elementary education educator*
Knipp, Helmut *service executive*
Knobil, Ernst *physiologist*
Knoll, Florence Schust *architect, designer*
Knox, Ernest Rudder *retired college president*
Kocaoglu, Dundar F. *engineering executive, industrial and civil engineering educator*
Kochta, Ruth Martha *art gallery owner*
Koehler, Rudolph August *manufacturing company executive*
Koenig, Allen Edward *higher education consultant*
Kohlmeyer, Ida Rittenberg *artist*
Kolko, Gabriel *historian, educator*
Kolm, Henry Herbert *physicist, electric research company executive*
Koltai, Stephen Miklos *mechanical engineer, consultant, economist*
Kolton, Paul *business executive*
Komidar, Joseph Stanley *librarian*
Komisar, David Daniel *retired university provost*
Komkov, Vadim *mathematician, educator*
Kondo, Masatoshi S. *pharmaceutical executive, educator*
Koner, Pauline *dancer, choreographer*
Kongabel, H. Fred *industrial construction company executive*
Konigsburg, Elaine Lobl *author*
Koning, Hans (Hans Koningsberger) *author*
Konnyu, Ernest Leslie *former congressman*
Kooken, John Frederick *retired bank holding company executive*
Koonts, Robert Henry *lawyer, retired corporation executive*
Koppett, Leonard *columnist, journalist, author*
Korab, Arnold Alva *corporate executive*
Korda, Reva *advertising executive, writer*
Kordisch, Mary Schroller *retired zoology educator, genetic consultant*
Kormondy, Edward John *university official, biology educator*
Korn, Peter A. *city manager, public administration educator*
Korpal, Eugene Stanley *banker, former army officer*
Korsgaard, Christine Marion *philosophy educator*
Korwek, Alexander Donald *management consultant*
Kosarin, Jonathan Henry *lawyer*
Kosuth, Joseph *artist*
Kotler, Steven *investment banker*
Kozlowski, Theodore Thomas *botany educator, research director, author, editor*
†Kraichnan, Robert Harry *theoretical physicist, consultant*
Kramberg, Heinz-Gerhard *ecomomist, educator*
Kramer, Dale Vernon *English language educator*
Kramer, Larry *writer*
Kramer, Reuben Robert *sculptor*
Krantz, Judith Tarcher *novelist*
Krantz, Stephen Falk *motion picture producer*
†Krantz, Steven George *mathematics educator*
Kraslow, David *retired newspaper publishing executive, reporter, author, consultant*
Kratt, Peter George *lawyer*
Krause, Bernard Leo *bioacoustician, sonic artist, composer*
Krause, Werner William *plastics company executive*
Krauthammer, Charles *columnist, editor*
Kravitz, Rubin *chemist*
Kreitzer, Lois Helen *personal investor*
Krepinevich, Kevin W. *social welfare organization administrator, educator*
Kretschmer, Frank F., Jr. *electrical engineer, researcher, consultant*
Krey, Robert Dean *education educator emeritus*
Kristensen, Marlene *early childhood educator*
Kristofferson, Karl Eric *writer*
Kristofferson, Kris *singer, songwriter, actor*
Krogh, Lester Christensen *retired research and development executive*
Kropp, David Arthur *retired landscape architect*
Kruck, Donna Jean *special education educator, consultant*
Kruger, Weldon Dale *oil company executive, consultant*
Krulak, Charles Chandler *marine officer*
Krull, Charles Fred *food research executive, geneticist*
Kryza, E(lmer) Gregory *financial planner, international affairs advisor, former ambassador*
Kucera, Daniel William *bishop*
†Kucey, Reginald Matthew *research scientist, microbiology researcher*
Kudrnac, Kristian Ivoj *chemical executive*
Kuehn, James Marshall *newspaper editor*
Kuhn, James Paul *management consultant*
Kuhn, Margaret (Maggie Kuhn) *organization executive*
Kulik, Rosalyn Franta *food company executive, consultant*
Kumler, Kipton Cornelius *photographer, consultant*
Kump, Ernest Joseph *architect, consultant*
Kundera, Milan *writer, educator*
Kuper, George Henry *research and development institute executive*
Kupferman, Meyer *composer*
†Kurfess, Thomas Roland *mechanical engineering educator*
Kurth, Carl Ferdinand *electrical engineer, researcher*
Kurtz, Gary Douglas *film producer*
Kurtz, Lloyd Sherer, Jr. *lawyer*
Kushinka, Joyce Williams *secondary education educator*
Kushner, Harvey David *management consultant*
Kushner, Robert Ellis *artist*
Kuske, Edward Alan *chemical company executive*
Kusserow, Richard Phillip *government official*
Kutrzeba, Joseph S. *theatrical and film producer, director*
Kutyna, Donald Joseph *air force officer*
†Kuzma, David Richard *natural gas company executive*
Kwak, Sung *conductor, music director*
Kwiat, Joseph J. *English educator, playwright*
Kyle, John Hamilton *publishing executive*
LaBarre, Carl Anthony *retired government official*
La Blanc, Robert Edmund *consulting company executive*
La Bonté, C(larence) Joseph *weight reducing company executive*
Labrecque, Richard Joseph *manufacturing company executive*
Lacey, Cloyd Eugene *retired insurance company executive*
Lacey, John William Charles *computer systems consultant*
Lackey, Larry Alton, Sr. *lawyer, real estate developer*
Lackland, John *lawyer*
Lacy, Alan Jasper *consumer products executive*
Lacy, Joseph Newton *architect*
Ladd, Cheryl (Cheryl Stopplemoor) *actress*
Ladd, Joseph Carroll *retired insurance company executive*
Ladly, Frederick Bernard *health services and financial services company executive*
Lafley, Alan Frederick *retired banker*
Lagos, George Peter *lawyer*
Lahti, Christine *actress*
Laidlaw, Robert Richard *publishing company executive*
Laitin, Joseph *journalist, former government spokesman and public relations consultant*
Lally, Michael David *writer, actor*
Lamalie, Robert Eugene *retired executive search company executive*
†Lamattina, Lawrence E. *advertising agency executive*
Lambert, Samuel Waldron, III *lawyer*
Lambro, Donald Joseph *columnist*
†Lancaster, Carol Roanne *federal official*
Lancaster, Edwin Beattie *insurance company executive*
Lancaster, Robert Samuel *lawyer, educator*
Landauer, Jeramy Lanigan *publishing company executive*
Lande, James Avra *lawyer, engineering and construction company executive*
Landel, Robert Franklin *physical chemist, rheologist*
Landers, Ann (Mrs. Esther P. Lederer) *columnist*
Landesman, Fredric Rocco *theatre executive*
Landgren, George Lawrence *electrical engineer, consultant*
†Landis, Geoffrey Alan *physicist, writer*
Landis, James David *publishing company executive, retired, author*
Landon, Robert Gray *retired manufacturing company executive*
Lane, Burton (Burton Levy) *composer*
†Lane, Joseph C. *financial services executive*
Langdon, George Dorland, Jr. *association executive*
Langenberg, Frederick Charles *business executive*
Langenfeld, Douglas Eugene *accountant*
†Langer, Ray Fritz *retired insurance executive*
Langerak, Esley Oren *retired research chemist*
Langworthy, William Clayton *college official*
Laning, J. Halcombe *retired computer scientist*
Lankford, Duane Gail *investment banker, mountaineer*
Lantz, Joanne Baldwin *university chancellor emerita*
Lantz, Kenneth Eugene *consulting firm executive*
Lanzillotti, Robert Franklin *economist, educator*
Lardner, Ring Wilmer, Jr. *author*
Largman, Kenneth *strategic analyst, strategic defense analysis company executive*
Larizadeh, M(ohammed) R(eza) *business educator*
Larkin, Joan *poet, English educator*
†La Rocca, Isabella *artist*
Larson, David Bruce *research epidemiologist*
Larson, George Charles *magazine editor, writer*
Larson, Mel *retired marketing professional, corporate executive, helicopter pilot*
Larson, Robert Frederick *public broadcasting company executive*
Larson, Russell George *magazine and book publisher*
Lasry, Jean-Michel *mathematics educator*
Lassiter, Kenneth T. *photography educator, consultant*
Lassner, Keith Michael *publishing executive*
Lateef, Yusef (Bill Evans) *composer, educator*
Lathlaen, Robert Frank *retired construction company executive*
Lauper, Cyndi *musician*
Laurent, Robert Louis, Jr. *manufacturing executive*
Laux, James Michael *historian, educator*
Lavidge, Robert James *marketing research executive*
Lavington, Michael Richard *venture capital company executive*
Lawrence, Jerome *playwright, director, educator*
Lawrence, Linda Hiett *writer, administrator*
Lawson, David Jerald *bishop*
†Lawton, Jonathan Frederick *screenwriter*
Laycraft, James Herbert *judge*
Lazarovic, Karen *money manager, investment consultant*
†Lazarus, Margaret Louise *film producer and director*
†Lazay, Paul Duane *telecommunications manufacturing company executive*
Lea, Lorenzo Bates *lawyer*
Leal, Herbert Allan Borden *former university chancellor, former government official*
Leaman, Jack Ervin *landscape architect, community/regional planner*
Leavy, Herbert Theodore *publisher*
Leb, Arthur S. *lawyer*
Lebor, John F(rancis) *retired department store executive*
Lechevalier, Hubert Arthur *microbiology educator*
Le Dain, Gerald Eric *retired Canadian Supreme Court justice*
Leder, Philip *geneticist, educator*
Lederman, Marie Jean *English language educator*
Ledford, Jack Clarence *retired aircraft company executive, former air force officer*
Lee, Dan M. *state supreme court justice*
Lee, James Matthew *Canadian politician*
Lee, John Franklin *retired lawyer, retired association executive*
Lee, Michele *actress*
Lee, William Chien-Yeh *communications executive, educator*
Lee, William Saul (Bill Lee) *artist, writer*
†Leean, Joseph *state legislator*
†Leff, Ilene J(oan) *management consultant, corporate and goverment executive*
Leff, Joseph Norman *yarn manufacturing company executive*
Leff, Sandra H. *gallery director, consultant*
Lefferts, George *writer, producer, director*
Leggett, Roberta Jean (Bobbi Leggett) *association executive*
Lego, Paul Edward *retired corporation executive*
Lehman, Christopher M. *international business consultant*
Lehman, John F., Jr. *industrialist*
†Lehmann, Michael Stephen *film director*
Lehrer, Thomas Andrew *songwriter, entertainer, lecturer*
Leighton, David Struan Robertson *retired education educator*
Leighton, Frances Spatz *writer, journalist*
Leis, Henry Patrick, Jr. *surgeon, educator*
Leith, James Clark *economics educator*
Leizear, Charles William *retired information services executive*
Lejins, Peter Pierre *criminologist, sociologist, educator*
Lennon, Joseph Luke *college official, priest*
Lennox, Donald D(uane) *automotive and housing components company executive*
León, Tania Justina *composer, music director, pianist*
Leonard, John Peter *diplomat*
Leonard, Stanley Sprenger *symphony musician*
Lerman, Jeanette Paula *communications executive*
Lerner, Harry *lawyer, consultant*
Lerner, Herbert J. *accountant*
Lesher, John Lee, Jr. *consulting services company executive*
Lesko, Harry Joseph *transportation company executive*
Leslie, Gerrie Allen *immunologist*
Lester, Virginia Laudano *educational director*
Levack, Arthur Paul *history educator emeritus*
Le Van, Daniel Hayden *business executive*
Levenson, Harvey Stuart *manufacturing company executive*
Levenson, Marc David *optics and lasers specialist, scientist*
Leventhal, Nathan *performing arts executive, lawyer*
Leventhal, Robert Stanley *academic administrator*
Levi, Josef Alan *artist*
Levi, Maurice David *economics educator*
Levin, Jack *physician, educator, biomedical investigator*
Levin, Morton D(avid) *artist, printmaker, educator*
†Levinson, Herbert Sherman *civil and transportation engineer*
Levitsky, Melvyn *foreign service officer*
Levy, Arthur James *public relations executive, writer*
Levy, David *lawyer, insurance company executive*
Levy, David Alfred *immunology educator, physician, scientist*
Levy, Louis Edward *retired accounting firm executive*
Levy, Sam Malcolm *advertising executive*
Lewis, Alexander, Jr. *oil company executive*
Lewis, Gregg Allan *editor, writer*
Lewis, James Lee, Jr. *actuary*
Lewis, Martin R. *paper company executive*
Lewis, Norman *English language educator, writer*
Lewis, Rita Hoffman *plastic products manufacturing company executive*
Lewis, Rolland Wilton *real estate manager*
Lewis, Samuel Winfield *retired government official, former ambassador*
Lichstein, Herman Carlton *microbiology educator emeritus*
Liebeler, Susan Wittenberg *lawyer*
Lieberman, Louis (Karl Lieberman) *artist*
Lienhart, James Lee *graphic designer*
Lightstone, Ronald *lawyer*
Lillibridge, John Lee *retired airline executive*
Lilly, Edward Guerrant, Jr. *retired utility company executive*
Linane, William Edward *corporate real estate executive*
Linda, Gerald *advertising and marketing executive*
Lindars, Laurence Edward *retired health care products executive*
Lindbergh, Anne Spencer Morrow (Mrs. Charles Augustus Lindbergh) *author*
Linde, Hans Arthur *state supreme court justice*
Linde, Maxine Helen *lawyer, business executive, private investor*
Lindegren, Jack Kenneth *educator*
Lindfors, Viveca *actress*
Lindsay, Dale Richard *research administrator*
Lindsay, Franklin Anthony *business executive, author*
Lindsay, John Vliet *former mayor, former congressman, author, lawyer*
†Lindsay, Reginald Carl *federal judge*
Lindsey, D. Ruth *physical education educator*
Link, Arthur Stanley *history educator, editor*
Link, Mae Mills (Mrs. S. Gordden Link) *space medicine historian and consultant*
Link, William Theodore *television writer, producer*
Linxwiler, Louis Major, Jr. *retired finance company executive*
Lipinsky, Carol *business owner*
Lipman, Ira Ackerman *security service company executive*
Lippman, Barry *publishing executive*
Lipscomb-Brown, Edra Evadean *retired childhood educator*
Lipsitt, Lewis Paeff *psychology educator*
Lipsky, Stephen Edward *engineering executive, electronic warfare engineer*
Lipson, Paul S. *lawyer*
Liskamm, William Hugo *architect, urban planner, educator*
Littler, Gene Alec *professional golfer*
Littleton, Harvey Kline *artist*
Littman, Earl *advertising and public relations executive*
Littner, Ner *psychoanalyst, psychiatrist*
Liu, Ernest K. H. *international banking executive, international financial consultant*
Lively, Edwin Lester *retired oil company executive*
Lively, John Pound *magazine editor, publisher*
Livingston, Robert Burr *neuroscientist, educator*
Livingstone, Susan Morrisey *healthcare administrator*
Lloyd, Joseph Wesley *physicist, researcher*
Lloyd, Kate Rand *magazine editor*
Lloyd, Michael Jeffrey *recording producer*
Lobanov-Rostovsky, Oleg *arts association executive*
Locke, Norton *hotel management and construction company executive*
Lockhart, Aileene Simpson *retired dance, kinesiology and physical education educator*
Lockwood, Robert W. *management consultant*
Lockwood, Theodore Davidge *former academic administrator*
Lodge, Arthur Scott *mechanical engineering educator*
Lodge, David Williams *retired corporation executive*
Logan, James Kenneth *federal judge*
Logan, John Francis *electronics company executive*
Lohmuller, Martin Nicholas *bishop*
Lohrer, Richard Baker *investment consultant*
Lomas, Bernard Tagg *college president emeritus*
Long, Alvin William *title insurance company executive*
Longnaker, John Leonard *retired insurance company executive, lawyer*
Longstreet, Harry Stephen *television producer, director, scriptwriter*
Longstreet, Stephen (Chauncey Longstreet) *author, painter*
Lonneke, Michael Dean *radio and television marketing executive*
Lopez, Barry Holstun *writer*
Lopez, Benito Moleiro, Jr. *lawyer, college administrator*
Loppnow, Milo Alvin *clergyman, former church official*
Loquasto, Santo *theatrical set designer*
Lorant, Stefan *author*
Lord, Roy Alvin *retired publisher*
Lord, Walter *author*
Loring, Gloria Jean *singer, actress*
Loser, Joseph Carlton, Jr. *law school dean, retired judge*
Loss, John C. *architect, retired educator*
Lotz, Arthur William *retired engineering and construction company executve*
Loube, Samuel Dennis *physician*
Loughery, Kevin Michael *professional basketball coach*
Loughlin, Mary Anne Elizabeth *television news anchor*
Loughran, James Newman *philosophy educator, former university president*
Lousberg, Sister Mary Clarice *hospital executive*
Louttit, James Russell *publishing company executive*
Lovell, Robert Gibson *retired physician, educator*
Lovell, Walter Carl *engineer, inventor*
Lovinger, Warren Conrad *emeritus university president*
Low, Emmet Francis, Jr. *mathematics educator*
Low, Harry William *judge*
Low, James Patterson *professional association executive*
Lowden, John L. *retired corporate executive*
Lowe, John, III *consulting civil engineer*
Lowe, Rob *actor*
Lowrie, Walter Olin *management consultant*
Lubin, Steven *concert pianist, musicologist*
†Lubinsky, Menachem Y. *communications executive*
Lucas, Rhett Roy *artist, lawyer*
Lucas, William Ray *aerospace consultant*
Luche, Thomas Clifford *foreign service officer*
Ludden, John Franklin *financial economist*
Ludlam, James Edward, III *insurance company executive*
Ludwig, Allan Ira *photographer, artist, author*
Ludwikowski, Rett Ryszard *law educator, researcher*
Luger, Donald R. *engineering company executive*
Lukas, J. Anthony *journalist*
Lund, David Nathan *artist*
Lundgren, Leonard, III *retired secondary education educator*
Lupberger, Edwin Adolph *utility executive*
Lupu, Radu *pianist*
Lutz, Carl Freiheit *academic administrator*
Lyman, Richard R. *journalist*
†Lynch, John Daniel *educator, state legislator*
Lynch, Patricia Gates *broadcasting organization executive consultant, former ambassador*
Lynch, Thomas Francis *archeologist, educator*
Lynch, Thomas Peter *securities executive*
Lynds, Beverly Turner *retired astronomer*
Lyng, Richard Edmund *former secretary of agriculture*
Lynne, Jeff *rock musician, composer*
Lyons, John Ormsby *English language educator*
Macal, Zdenek *conductor*
†Macaulay, David (Alexander) *author*
MacCarthy, Talbot Leland *civic volunteer*
†Macchia, Joseph Dominick *insurance company executive*
Macdonald, Donald Ian *health care administrator*
†MacDonald, Stewart Dixon *ornithologist, ecologist, biologist*
Mac Dowell, Andie *actress*
MacFarlane, Andrew Walker *media specialist, educator*
MacLachlan, Alexander *chemical company executive, retired*
MacLean, John Angus *former premier of Prince Edward Island*
MacLennan, Beryce Winifred *psychologist*
MacMillan, Kip Van Metre *foundation executive*
Macmillan, William Hooper *university dean, educator*
MacMinn, Aleene Merle B(arnes) *newspaper editor, columnist, educator*
Macnee, (Daniel) Patrick *actor*
MacQueen, Robert Moffat *solar physicist*
Madden, Richard Blaine *forest products executive*
†Maddin, Robert *metallurgist educator*
Madeira, Francis King Carey *conductor, educator*
Madera, Joseph J. *bishop*
Maehl, William Harvey *historian, educator*
Maehl, William Henry *historian, university administrator*

Maehr, Martin Louis *psychology educator*
Maestrone, Frank Eusebio *diplomat*
Maglich, Bogdan Cveta *physicist*
Magnuson, Robert Martin *retired hospital administrator*
Magor, Louis Roland *conductor*
Maguire, Robert Francis, III *real estate investor*
Magurno, Richard Peter *lawyer*
†Mai, Chao Chen *engineer*
Maier, Alfred *neuroscientist*
†Maillet, Antonine *author, educator*
Maiman, Theodore Harold *physicist*
Makepeace, Darryl Lee *consulting company executive*
Malkin, Myron Samuel *physicist, management consultant*
Malkinson, Frederick David *dermatologist*
Mallory, Arthur Lee *university dean, retired state official*
Mallory, William Barton, III *corporate lawyer*
Malone, Edward H. *financial executive*
Malone, James William *bishop*
Malott, Adele Renee *editor*
Malpas, Robert *company executive*
†Maltzan, Michael Thomas *architect*
Mamet, David Alan *playwright, director*
Manchester, Kenneth Edward *electronics executive, consultant*
Mandino, Og *author*
†Maness, Anthony Ray *retired naval officer*
Mangan, Frank Thomas *advertising executive*
Manganaro, Francis Ferdinand *naval officer*
Mangione, Chuck (Charles Frank Mangione) *jazz musician, composer*
Mangold, Sylvia Plimack *artist*
Manley, Joan A(dele) Daniels *retired publisher*
Manley, John Hugo *computing technology executive, educator*
Mann, Clarence Charles *real estate company official*
Mann, Emily Betsy *writer, artistic director, theater and film director*
Mann, Jim (James William Manousos) *editor, publisher*
Mann, Jonathan Max *international agency administrator*
Manne, Henry Girard *lawyer, educator*
Mannes, Elena Sabin *film and television producer, director*
Mansouri, Lotfollah *opera stage director*
†Maragos, Andrew George *state representative, stockbroker, consultant*
Maranda, Pierre Jean *anthropologist, writer*
†Marbert, Larry David *newspaper publishing executive*
Marchant, Maurice Peterson *librarian, educator*
†Marchessault, Robert H. *chemical engineer*
Marcus, Greil Gerstley *critic*
Marinaro, Edward Francis *actor*
Marinis, Thomas Paul, Jr. *lawyer*
Marino, Joseph Anthony *retired publishing executive*
Mark, Mary Ellen *photographer*
Markle, Roger A(llan) *retired oil company executive*
Markovitz, Alvin *molecular biologist, geneticist*
Marks, Leonard, Jr. *retired corporate executive*
Marks, Raymond H. *chemical company executive*
Marks, Russell Edward, Jr. *consultant*
Marlatt, Jerry Ronald *lawyer*
Maroni, Paul L. *finance executive*
Marple, Gary Andre *management consultant*
Marr, Carmel Carrington *lawyer, retired state official*
Marrington, Bernard Harvey *retired automotive company executive*
Marshak, Robert Reuben *former university dean, medical educator, veterinarian*
Marshall, Charles *communications company executive*
Marshall, Charles Noble *railroad executive*
Marshall, E. G. *actor*
Marshall, Garry *film producer, director, writer*
Marshall, Gerald Francis *optical engineer, consultant, physicist*
Marshall, Richard *art historian, curator*
†Marsico, Ronald S. *state legislator*
Martin, Albert Charles *manufacturing executive, lawyer*
†Martin, Edwin William, Jr. *pharmaceutical marketing consultant, copywriter*
Martin, Lee *mechanical engineer*
Martin, Louis Edward *retired library director*
Martin, Murray Simpson *librarian, writer, consultant*
Martin, Noel *graphic design consultant, educator*
Martin, Preston *financial services executive*
Martin, Robert Roy *retired securities brokerage company exxecutive*
Martyl, (Mrs. Alexander Langsdorf, Jr.) *artist*
Marvin, William Glenn, Jr. *former foreign service officer*
Marx, Anne (Mrs. Frederick E. Marx) *poet*
Mascotte, John Pierre *insurance executive*
Masiello, Rocco Joseph *airlines and aerospace manufacturing executive*
Masnari, Nino Antonio *electrical engineer, educator*
Mason, Frank Henry, III *automobile company executive, leasing company executive*
Massa, Salvatore Peter *psychologist*
Mast, Stewart Dale *retired airport manager*
Masterson, Peter *actor, director*
Mastroianni, Marcello *actor*
Mathews, Harry Burchell *poet, novelist, educator*
Mathews, Robert Earl, II *insurance company executive*
Mathews, William Edward *neurological surgeon, educator*
Mathis, Sharon Bell *author, elementary educator, librarian*
Matthews, Cari Pineiro *lawyer, author*
Matthews, John Louis *military officer, educator*
Matthews, L. White, III *railroad executive*
Matthiessen, Peter *author*
Mattingly, Mack F. *US ambassador, former US senator, entrepreneur*
Mattingly, William Earl *lawyer*
May, Kenneth Nathaniel *food industry consultant*
May, Rollo *psychoanalyst*
Mayfield, Robert Charles *university official, geography educator*
Mayhew, Lawrence Lee *electronics company executive*
Mayne, Wiley Edward, Jr. *lawyer*
Mayo, Robert Porter *banker*
Mayoras, Donald Eugene *corporate executive, speaker, consultant, educator*
Mayron, Melanie *actress, writer*
Mazankowski, Donald Frank *Canadian government official*
Mazursky, Paul *screenwriter, theatrical director and producer*
McAbeer, Sara Carita *school administrator*
McArdle, John Edward *management consultant*
McBain, Diane Jean *actress, writer*
McBurney, Margot B. *librarian*
McCabe, Charles Law *retired manufacturing company executive, management consultant*
McCall, John Anthony *banker*
McCandless, J(ane) Bardarah *emeritus religion educator*
McCann, Elizabeth Ireland *theater, television and motion picture producer, lawyer*
McCarragher, Bernard John *retired manufacturing company executive*
McCarthy, J. Thomas *lawyer, educator*
McCarthy, Kevin Joseph *academic dean, music educator*
McCarthy, Vincent Paul *lawyer*
Mc Carthy, Walter John, Jr. *retired utility executive*
McCarthy, William J. *retired labor union executive*
McCartney, (James) Paul *musician*
McCarty, Dennis L. *insurance executive*
McCauley, John Francis *geologist*
McClendon, Sarah Newcomb *news service executive, writer*
McClung, John Robinson, Jr. *retired advertising company executive*
Mc Clymont, Hamilton *entertainment industry executive*
Mc Connell, Edward Bosworth *legal organization administrator, lawyer*
McConnell, Elliott Bonnell, Jr. *oil company executive*
McConnell, James Guy *lawyer*
McConner, Stanley Jay, Sr. *academic administrator*
McCormick, John Owen *retired comparative literature educator*
McCormick, Michael D. *lawyer*
Mc Cormick, William Martin *broadcast executive*
†McCorquodale, Dan A. *state senator*
McCown, Hale *retired judge*
†McCoy, Matthew William *state official, human resource manager*
Mc Coy, Tidal Windham *former government official*
McCracken, John Harvey *painter, sculptor*
Mc Curley, Robert Lee, Jr. *lawyer, educator*
McDade, William Joseph *manufacturing consulting company executive*
McDarrah, Gloria Schoffel *editor, author*
McDermott, Agnes Charlene Senape *philosophy educator*
McDermott, Kevin J. *engineering educator, consultant*
McDowell, Malcolm *actor*
McEachern, William Donald *lawyer*
McEntire, Reba N. *country singer*
Mc Fadden, George Linus *retired army officer*
McFall, Catherine Gardner *poet, critic, educator*
McGee, Craig Heslin *insurance company executive*
Mc Gill, Archie Joseph *venture capital and business speaker*
McGillis, Kelly *actress*
McGillivray, Donald Dean *agricultural products executive*
McGough, John Paul *conveyor and power transmission company executive*
Mc Govern, George Stanley *former senator*
Mc Gowan, James Atkinson *business executive, financial consultant*
†McGraw, Warren Randolph, II *lawyer, state legislator*
Mc Guigan, James Edward *physician, scientist, educator*
McGuire, Blanche *marketing professional*
McGuirk, Terrence *former broadcasting company executive*
McHale, Paul *congressman, lawyer*
McHenry, Robert (Dale) *editor*
McHugh, Earl Stephen *dentist*
McHugh, John James *consultant*
McIlvaine, Joseph Peter *professional baseball team executive*
McIntosh, Carolyn *principal*
McIntosh, Rhodina Covington *lawyer*
Mc Intyre, Robert Allen, Jr. *business turnaround executive*
Mc Kayle, Donald Cohen *choreographer, director, writer*
McKean, Robert Jackson, Jr. *retired lawyer*
McKenna, Quentin Carnegie *tool company executive*
McKenna, Terence Patrick *insurance company executive*
McKinney, Donald *art gallery director, art dealer*
McKinnon, Daniel Wayne, Jr. *naval officer*
McLaughlin, Ann *educational administrator, former federal official, lecturer, advisor*
McLean, Walter Franklin *former Canadian government official*
Mc Mahon, George Joseph *academic administrator*
McNeal, Shay *advertising executive*
McNeeley, Donald Robert *steel company executive*
McNeil, George Joseph *painter*
McNeil, Steven Arthur *food company executive*
McNitt, Joseph Edward *lawyer*
McNulty, Henry Bryant *journalist*
McNutt, William James *consulting engineer*
McPhedran, Norman Tait *surgeon, educator*
Mc Phee, John Angus *writer*
Mc Pheeters, Edwin Keith *architect, educator*
McPherson, James Alan *writer, educator*
Mc Pherson, Robert Donald *retired lawyer*
McQuilkin, John Robertson *religion educator, academic administrator, writer*
McRae, Thomas Kenneth *retired investment company executive*
†McSorley, Cisco *lawyer*
McVicker, Jesse Jay *artist, educator*
McWethy, Patricia Joan *association executive*
McWilliams, Bruce Wayne *marketing professional*
Mead, Beverley Tupper *physician, educator*
Meade, Everard Kidder, Jr. *retired broadcasting and publishing executive*
Meads, Donald Edward *management services company executive*
Meaker, Marijane Agnes *author*
Meara, Anne *actress, writer*
Medina, Kathryn Bach *book editor*
Medley, Donald Matthias *retired education educator, consultant*
Medlock, Donald Larson *lawyer*
Mednick, Murray *playwright*
Mednick, Robert *accountant*
Medzihradsky, Fedor *biochemist, educator*
Meehan, John Joseph, Jr. *hospital administrator*
Meeker, Guy Bentley *banker*
Meier, Henry George *architect*
Meindl, James Donald *electrical engineering educator, administrator*
Meister, Steven Gerard *cardiologist, educator*
Melady, Thomas Patrick *university president, ambassador, author, public policy expert, educator*
Melczek, Dale J. *bishop*
Melillo, Joseph Vincent *producer, performing arts*
Melnick, Joseph L. *virologist, educator*
Melody, Michael Edward *publishing company executive*
†Melsheimer, William C. *principal*
Melvin, Ben Watson, Jr. *petroleum and chemical manufacturing executive*
Melvin, T. Stephen *manufacturing company executive*
Menchel, Donald *television executive*
Menchú, Rigoberta *human rights activist*
Mende, Robert Graham *retired engineering association executive*
Mendicino, V. Frank *lawyer*
Mendonsa, Arthur Adonel *city official*
Mendoza, George *poet, author*
Meneeley, Edward Sterling *artist*
Menendez, Carlos *financial executive, banker*
Menhall, Dalton Winn *lawyer, insurance executive, professional association administrator*
Menn, Julius Joel *research scientist*
Menotti, Gian Carlo *composer*
Mercer, Edwin Wayne *lawyer*
Meredith, Burgess *actor*
Meredith, James Howard *association executive, farmer, consultant*
Merlis, George *television producer*
Merriam, J. Alec *leasing executive*
Merrick, David (David Margulois) *theatrical producer*
Merrill, James *poet, playwright*
Merrill, Jean Fairbanks *writer*
Merrill, Lindsey *music educator*
Meserve, Walter Joseph *drama studies educator, publisher*
Messenkopf, Eugene John *real estate and business consultant*
Metz, Frank Andrew, Jr. *data processing executive*
Meyer, Greg Charles *psychiatrist*
Meyer, Harold Louis *mechanical engineer*
Meyer, Harry Martin, Jr. *retired health science facility administrator*
Meyer, Lasker Marcel *retail executive*
Meyer, Max Earl *lawyer*
Meyer, Paul William *biblical literature educator emeritus*
Meyer, Pauline Marie *retired special education educator*
Meyers, Richard James *landscape architect*
Mezzatesta, Michael Philip *art museum director*
Mich, Connie Rita *mental health nurse, educator*
Michael, Donald Nelson *social scientist, educator*
†Michaelis, Elias K. *neurochemist*
Michalik, Edward Francis *construction company executive*
Michaud, Michael Alan George *diplomat, writer*
Mickelson, Elliot Spencer *quality assurance professional*
Micks, Don Wilfred *biologist, educator*
Middaugh, Robert Burton *artist*
Middleton, Donald Earl *transportation company executive*
Middleton, Gerard Viner *geology educator*
†Midkiff, J(ohn) Michael *film and video producer and director*
Migden, Chester L. *association executive*
Mikitka, Gerald Peter *investment banker, financial consultant*
Mikulski, Barbara Ann *senator*
Miles, Jeanne Patterson *artist*
Miles, Robert Henry *management educator, consultant, educational administrator*
Milewski, Barbara Anne *pediatrics nurse, neonatal intensive care nurse*
Milhouse, Paul William *bishop*
Millard, Charles Warren, III *museum director, writer*
Miller, Alan Jay *consultant, author*
Miller, Arjay *retired university dean*
Miller, Charles Edmond *library administrator*
Miller, Edward Albert *lawyer*
Miller, Harold Edward *retired manufacturing conglomerate executive, consultant*
Miller, James Vince *university president*
Miller, Jeffrey Grant *law educator*
Miller, Jeffrey Robert *mayor, insurance planner*
†Miller, Jeffrey Veach *biochemist, researcher*
Miller, Leland Bishop, Jr. *food processing company executive*
Miller, Lillie M. *nursing educator*
Miller, Lowell Donald *pharmaceutical company research executive*
†Miller, Marilyn Suzanne *writer, producer, playwright*
Miller, Penelope Ann *actress*
Miller, Reed *lawyer*
Miller, Richard Alan *lawyer, former merger and acquisition and forest products company executive*
Miller, Robert Branson, Jr. *retired newspaper publisher*
Miller, Robert Stevens, Jr. *finance professional*
Miller, Ross Hays *retired neurosurgeon*
Miller, Thormund Aubrey *lawyer*
Millett, Ralph Linwood, Jr. *retired newspaper editor*
Millikan, Clark Harold *physician*
Millimet, Erwin *lawyer*
Mills, Celeste Louise *hypnotherapist, professional magician*
Mills, Eugene Sumner *college president*
Mills, Howard McIlroy *clergyman, denominational executive*
Mills, Robert Lee *president emeritus*
†Mills, Russell Andrew *newspaper publisher*
Millsaps, Fred Ray *investor*
†Milstein, Monroe Gary *retail executive*
Minami, Robert Yoshio *artist, graphic designer*
Miner, A. Bradford *journalist*
Minnix, Bruce Milton *television and theatre director*
Mintz, M. J. *lawyer*
Mintz, Morton Abner *author, former newspaper reporter*
Mirisch, Walter Mortimer *motion picture producer*
Miskowski, Lee R. *automobile executive*
Mislow, Kurt Martin *chemist, educator*
Misrach, Richard Laurence *photographer*
Mitchel, F(rederick) Kent *retired food company executive*
Mitchell, Claybourne, Jr. *retired utilities executive*
Mitchell, Robert Edward *urban planner, international development specialist, educator*
Mitford, Jessica *author*
Mixon, Alan *actor*
Modigliani, Franco *economics and finance educator*
†Moe, Tommy *professional skier, former Olympic athlete*
Moeckel, Bill Reid *retired university dean*
Moeller, Robert John *marketing consultant*
Moessinger, David *television producer, writer, director*
Moffatt, Hugh McCulloch, Jr. *hospital administrator, physical therapist*
Moffatt, Katy (Katherine Louella Moffatt) *musician, vocalist, songwriter*
Moffet, Hugh Lamson *pediatrician*
Moffett, Jonathan Phillip *drummer, musical director, songwriter*
†Mogel, Leonard Henry *author*
Mogelever, Bernard *public relations executive*
Molden, Herbert George *publisher*
Molnar, Anthony William *publishing and training company executive*
Monacelli, Gianfranco *publishing executive*
†Monahan, Edward Charles *academic administrator, marine science educator*
Mondale, Walter Frederick *former vice president of United States, diplomat, lawyer*
Mondor, Kenneth James *financial executive*
Monninger, Robert Harold George *ophthalmologist, educator*
Monsen, Raymond Joseph, Jr. *economist, educator*
†Monson, David Carl *farmer, state legislator*
Montgomery, Parker Gilbert *investment banker*
Montgomery, Roy Delbert *retired gas utility company executive*
Montgomery, Seth David *state supreme court chief justice*
Monty, Charles Embert *utility company executive*
Monty, Gloria *television producer*
Moody, Roland Herbert *retired librarian*
Mooney, John Allen *retired food company executive*
Mooneyhan, Esther Louise *nurse, educator*
Moore, Donald Eugene *retired botanical garden administrator, communications executive*
Moore, John Runyan *agricultural and resource economics educator*
Moore, Melba *actress, singer*
Moore, Powell Allen *former government official, consultant*
Moore, Richard Alan *landscape architect*
Moore, Richard Earl *communications creative director*
Moore, Robert William *professional organization executive*
Moore, Tom *film and theater director*
Moore, Vernon Lee *agricultural consultant, retired food products company executive*
Moore, William Jason *museum director*
Moore, William Leroy, Jr. *career officer, physician*
Moossy, John *neuropathologist, neurologist, consultant*
Moran, Gordon William *papers and fabrics company executive*
Morath, Max Edward *entertainer, composer*
Mordecai, Benjamin *theatrical producer, drama educator*
Morelan, Paula Kay *choreographer*
Moreland, Alvin Franklin *veterinarian*
Morello, Joseph Albert *musician, educator*
Morgan, Edmund Sears *historian*
Morgan, Elizabeth *plastic and reconstructive surgeon*
Morgan, James John *environmental engineering educator*
Morgan, Jane Hale *retired library director*
Morgan, Linda Rogers *editor*
Morgan, Robert Arthur *accountant*
Morgan, Robert Edward *state supreme court justice*
Morgan, Ruth Prouse *academic administrator, educator*
Morgan, Thomas Rowland *retired marine corps officer*
Morgan, William Douglass *diplomat*
Moriarty, Donald William, Jr. *banker*
†Morita, (Noriyuki) Pat *actor, comedian*
Moritz, Charles Worthington *business information and services company executive*
Morley, Malcolm A. *artist*
Morning, John *graphic designer*
Morosky, Robert Harry *private investor, operator*
Morrell, Gene Paul *liquid terminal company executive*
Morrill, Thomas Clyde *insurance company executive*
Morris, Albert Jerome *biological pest control company executive*
Morris, Frank Eugene *banker*
Morris, Marjorie Hale *retail executive, appraiser, artist, writer*
Morris, Robert G(emmill) *retired foreign service officer*
Morris, Willie *author, editor*
Morrison, James R. *retired banker*
Morrison, John Washburn *banker*
Morrison, Shelley *actress*
Morrison, Van *musician, songwriter*
Morrissey, Charles Thomas *historian, educator*
Morrow, Barry Nelson *screenwriter, producer*
Morrow, George Lester *retired oil and gas executive*
Morrow, Rob *actor*
Morse, Leon William *traffic, physical distribution and transportation management executive, consultant*
Mortensen, Peter *banker*
†Mortimer, Doyle Moss *business consultant, state legislator, business owner*
Mortola, Edward Joseph *emeritus university chancellor*
†Morton, Bruce A. *news correspondent*
Morton, Charles Brinkley *retired bishop, former state legislator, lawyer*
Moscona, Aron Arthur *biology educator, scientist*
Moses, Edward Crosby *artist*
Moses, Robert Davis *retired diversified industry executive*
Mosher, Gregory Dean *director*
Mosler, John *retired business executive*
Mosley, Zack Terrell *cartoonist*
Moss, John Emerson *banker, former congressman*
Mott, Nevill (Francis Mott) *physicist, educator, author*
Mott, Stewart Rawlings *business executive, political activist*
Motto, Jerome Arthur *psychiatry educator*
†Moulton-Patterson, Linda *television executive*
Mount, Thomas H(enderson) *independent film producer*
Mountz, Louise Carson Smith *retired librarian*
Mow, Douglas Farris *former naval officer, consultant*
Muckerman, Norman James *priest, writer*
Mudd, Roger Harrison *news broadcaster*
Mudd, Sidney Peter *former beverage company executive*
Mueller, Barbara Ruth *journalist*

Mulcahy, Robert Edward corporation executive, consultant
Mulholland, Robert Edge broadcasting company executive
Mullen, William Joseph, III military analyst, retired army officer
Mulligan, William Hughes lawyer, former federal judge
Mumma, Albert Girard, Jr. architect
Munisteri, Joseph George construction executive
Murdoch, (Jean) Iris author
Muren, Dennis E. visual effects director
Murphy, Benjamin Edward actor
Murphy, Bernard Thomas electronics executive, researcher, consultant
Murphy, David Ridgeway transportation and financial consultant
Murphy, Francis English language educator
Murphy, Lewis Curtis lawyer, former mayor
Murphy, Sandra Robison lawyer
Murphy, S(usan) (Jane Murphy) small business owner
†Murr, James Coleman federal government official
Murray, Albert L. writer, educator
†Murray, David George architect
Murray, Kathryn Hazel former dance director, author
Murray, Leonard Hugh railroad executive
Murray, Robert Gray sculptor
Murrill, Paul Whitfield former utility executive, former university administrator
Musante, Tony (Anthony Peter Musante, Jr.) actor
Musburger, Brent Woody sportscaster
Muskie, Edmund Sixtus lawyer, former secretary of state, former senator
Muson, Howard Henry writer, editor
Mydland, Gordon James judge
Myers, Albert G., Jr. textile manufacturer
Myers, Harold Mathews academic administrator
Myers, Jack Edgar biologist, educator
Myers, John Herman investment management executive
Myers, Mike actor, writer
†Myers, Phillip Samuel mechanical engineering educator
Myerson, Alan director, film and television writer
Myhren, Trygve Edward communications company executive
Myrer, Anton Olmstead author
Nadel, Norman Allen civil engineer
Nagle, David R. lawyer, former congressman
Nahman, Norris Stanley electrical engineer
Nair, Raghavan D. accountant, educator
Nakagawa, Allen Donald radiologic technologist
Nakamura, Kazuo artist
Nangle, John Francis federal judge
†Nankin, Harold advertising agency executive
Napodano, Rudolph Joseph internist, medical educator
Nardi Riddle, Clarine judge
Narita, Hiro cinematographer
Nasgaard, Roald museum curator
Natcher, Stephen Darlington lawyer, business executive
Naughton, James actor
Naylor, Thomas Everett account administrator
Naylor, Thomas Herbert economist, educator, consultant
Neame, Ronald director, producer
Neary, Patricia Elinor ballet director
Nebel, Henry Martin, Jr. literature historian, educator
†Nederlander, James Laurence theater owner, producer
Needham, Lucien Arthur musician, educator
Neel, James Van Gundia geneticist, educator
Neelankavil, James Paul marketing educator, researcher and consultant
Neese, Elbert Haven retired paper machinery manufacturing executive
Neff, Donald Lloyd news correspondent, writer
Neff, Francine Irving (Mrs. Edward John Neff) former federal government official
Neff, Jack Kenneth apparel manufacturing company executive
Negroponte, John Dimitri diplomat
Nehrt, Lee Charles management educator
Nelson, Ben, Jr. air force officer
Nelson, Carl Roger retired lawyer
Nelson, Clifford Arnold retired bank executive
Nelson, Edwin Clarence academic administrator, emeritus
Nelson, Harvey Frans, Jr. retired foreign service officer
Nelson, Martha Jane magazine editor
Nelson, Robert Charles newspaper executive
†Nelson, Robert Gary textile executive
Nelson-Humphries, Tessa (Tessa Unthank) English language educator
Nesheim, Robert Olaf food products executive
Netter, Cornelia Ann real estate broker
Neunzig, Carolyn Miller secondary education educator
Neville, Phoebe choreographer, dancer, educator
Newfarmer, Gerald Earl city manager
Newman, Carol L. lawyer
Newman, Denis merchant banker
Newman, Dennis Collins, Sr. accountant
Newman, Kenneth E. lawyer
Newman, Muriel Kallis Steinberg art collector
Newman, Paul actor, professional race-car driver, food company executive
Newman, Peter Kenneth economist, educator
Newman, Phillip Barbour, III distilling company executive
Newman, Sheldon Oscar computer company executive
Newman, Theodore Roosevelt, Jr. judge
Newton, Wayne entertainer, actor, recording artist
Nicholson, Leland Ross retired utilities company executive, energy consultant
Nicholson, Richard Joseph trust banking executive
Nicholson, Theodore H. educational administrator
Nicklaus, Charles Edward sales training executive
Nicks, Stevie (Stephanie Nicks) singer, songwriter
Nicoll, Charles Samuel physiologist, educator
Niedzielski, Henri Zygmunt French and English language educator
Nielsen, Emiel Theodore, Jr. retired manufacturing company executive
Nielson, Howard Curtis former congressman, retired educator
Niemann, Lewis Keith lamp manufacturing company executive
Nihart, Franklin Brooke museum consultant, writer and editor
Nilsson, Birgit soprano
Ninos, Nicholas Peter retired military officer, medical consultant
Nishimura, Joseph Yo retired retail executive, accountant
Nissinen, Mikko Pekka dancer
Nixon, Marni singer
†Noble, James Ronald trade association executive
Nobles, Laurence Hewit retired geology educator
Nolan, Irene Clare newspaper editor
Nold, Carl Richard state historic parks and museums administrator
Nord, Eric Thomas manufacturing executive
Nordlund, Donald Elmer manufacturing company executive
Norlander, John Allen hotel executive
Norman, Albert George, Jr. lawyer
Norman, Joe G., Jr. chemistry educator, college dean
†Norris, Alfred Lloyd theological seminary president, clergyman
Norris, Martin Joseph lawyer
†Norris, Stephen Leslie merchant banking, tax and finance executive
North, Phil Record retired banker
Norton, Andre Alice author
Norton, Clifford Charles actor, director
Norton, Judy actress
†Nottingham, William Jesse church mission executive, minister
Nour, Samir banker, economic consultant
Nova, Craig writer
Novack, Alvin John physician
Novas, Joseph, Jr. advertising agency executive
Novenstern, Samuel sports marketing and media sales company executive
Novick, Julius Lerner theater critic, educator
Oaks, Maurice David retired pharmaceutical company executive
Ober, Richard Francis, Jr. lawyer, banker
Obolensky, Marilyn Wall (Mrs. Serge Obolensky) metals company executive
O'Brien, J. Willard lawyer, educator
†O'Brien, Jack George artistic director
O'Connell, Philip Raymond retired lawyer, consultant
O'Connor, Doris Julia non-profit fundraiser, consultant
O'Connor, Mary Scranton public relations executive
O'Connor, Richard Donald advertising company executive
Odell, Frank Harold banker
Oelman, Robert Schantz retired manufacturing executive
Ogg, George Wesley retired foreign service officer
O'Hare, James Raymond energy company executive
Oksas, Joan K. former economist, educator
Okuda, Kunio emeritus medical educator
O'Leary, Denis Joseph retired physician, insurance company executive
Oliansky, Joel author, director
Olkinetzky, Sam artist, retired museum director and educator
Olsen, Jack writer
Olsen, Merlin Jay sports analyst, former professional football player
†Olson, Eric G. insurance company executive
Olson, James Clifton historian, university president
Olson, Kenneth Harvey computer company executive
Olson, Paul Richard Spanish literature educator, editor
Olson, William Clinton international affairs educator, author, lecturer
Olstowski, Franciszek chemical engineer, consultant
O'Mahoney, Robert M. lawyer
O'Malley, Thomas Patrick university president
Ondaatje, (Philip) Michael author, educator
Ondrejka, Ronald conductor
O'Neal, Ryan (Patrick Ryan O'Neal) actor
O'Neill, Donald Edmund health science executive
Ononye, Daniel Chuka social scientist
Onslow Ford, Gordon Max painter
Oppenheim, David Jerome musician, educational administrator
Oppenheimer, Joseph corporate director, infosystems consultant
†Oppenheimer, Suzi state senator
Opperman, Danny Gene packaging professional, consultant
Orbach, Jerry actor, singer
Ordal, Caspar Reuben business executive
Orloff, Neil lawyer
Orr, Carol Wallace book publishing executive
Ortiz, Francis Vincent, Jr. retired ambassador
Ortner, Everett Howard magazine editor, writer
†Ortolano, Ralph J. engineering consultant
Orttung, William Herbert chemistry educator
Osborn, Robert Chesley artist, writer
Osborn, William George savings and loan executive
Osborne, James Alfred religious organization administrator
†Osbourne, Ozzy (John Osbourne) vocalist
Osburn, Charles Benjamin librarian, university dean
Osimitz, Dennis Victor lawyer
Osmer-McQuade, Margaret association executive, broadcast journalist
Osrin, Raymond Harold retired political cartoonist
†Osteen, Harry Montague, Jr. banker
Oster, Patrick Ralph journalist
Ostfeld, Leonard S. computer company executive
Ototott, Charles Paddock army officer
Ott, Margaret E. retired nurse and cosmetology educator
Overcash, Reece A., Jr. financial service company executive
Owen, John Laverty human resources executive, consultant
Owens, Charles Vincent, Jr. diagnostic company executive and consultant
Owens, William Arthur military officer
Pace, Charles Robert psychologist, educator
Pace, R(alph) Wayne organizational behavior educator
Pack, Allen S. retired coal company executive
Pack, Richard Morris broadcasting executive
Packard, John Mallory physician
Padgett, George Arthur retired lawyer
Page, Willis conductor
Paglio, Lydia Elizabeth editor
Palade, George Emil biologist, educator
Palladino, Nunzio Joseph retired nuclear engineer
Palliser, Charles writer, educator
Palmer, Dave Richard military officer
Palmer, Gary Andrew portfolio manager
Palmer, Irene Sabelberg university dean and educator emeritus, nurse, researcher, historian
Palmer, Langdon banker
Palmer, Raymond A. medical association administrator, librarian
Palter, Robert Monroe philosophy and history educator
†Pancake, Edwina Howard medical librarian
Pankey, Edgar Edward rancher
Papadopoulos, Stelios B. scientific, medical products company executive
Parent, Rodolphe Jean Canadian air force official, pilot
Parente, Michael electrical engineer
Paretsky, Sara N. writer
Paris, Lucille Marie artist, educator
Parker, Brent Mershon retired medical educator, internist, cardiologist
Parker, David Shannon publishing company executive
Parker, Franklin writer, educator
Parker, George retired pen manufacturing company executive
Parker, Harry John retired psychologist, educator
Parker, Robert Brown novelist
†Parker, Sybil Pam science editor
Parker, Thomas Lee business executive
Parmelee, David Freeland biologist, educator
Parmer, Dan Gerald veterinarian
†Parode, Ann banker, lawyer
Parrish, Alma Ellis elementary education educator
†Parry, Atwell J., Jr. state senator, retailer
Parslow, Philip Leo film producer, film company executive
Parsons, Elmer Earl retired clergyman
Parsons, Irene management consultant
Partington, James Wood naval officer
Pasant, David A. insurance company executive
Pasic, Mary Rose principal
†Passailaigue, Ernest L., Jr. accountant, state senator
Patent, Dorothy Hinshaw author, photographer
Paterson, Robert E. trading stamp company executive
Patinkin, Mandy actor
Patino, Douglas Xavier foundation administrator
Patmos, Adrian Edward university dean emeritus
Patrick, Dennis actor, director
†Patrick, Deval Laurdine lawyer
Patterson, Donis Dean bishop
Patterson, Mary-Margaret Sharp writer, editor, media strategist
Patterson, Robert Hudson library director
Patton, James Richard, Jr. lawyer
Paul, Frank retired consulting company executive
Paul, Gabriel (Gabe Paul) former professional baseball club executive
Paul, Gordon Wilbur marketing educator
Paul, Herbert Morton lawyer, accountant, taxation educator
Paul, Les entertainer, inventor
Paulino, Sister Mary McAuley principal
Paulsen, Frank Robert college dean emeritus
Paulus, Norma Jean Petersen lawyer, school system administrator
Pavlick, Harvey Naylor financial executive
Paycheck, Johnny country western musician
Peacock, Mary Willa magazine editor
Pearce, Paul Francis retired aerospace electronics company executive
Pearlstein, Philip artist
Pearson, Donald Emanual chemist, educator
†Pearson, John Davis naval officer
Pearson, Ralph Gottfrid chemistry educator
Peck, Daniel Farnum chemical company executive
Peck, Gregory actor
Peckham, Donald Eugene retired utilities company executive
Pedersen, Knud George university president
Peers, Michael Geoffrey archbishop
Peiss, Clarence Norman physiology educator, college dean
Péladeau, Marius Beaudoin art consultant, retired museum director
Pelotte, Donald Edmond bishop
Peltier, Eugene Joseph civil engineer, former naval officer, business executive
Penn, Irving photographer
Penn, Sean actor
Pennington, Mary Anne art museum director, museum management consultant, art educator
Pennington, Richard Maier management consultant, retired insurance company executive, lawyer
Pennock, James Roland political scientist, educator
Pentland, Barbara Lally composer
Penzer, Mark lawyer, editor, corporate trainer, former publisher
Penzias, Arno Allan astrophysicist, research scientist, information systems specialist
Peoples, John Arthur, Jr. former university president, consultant
†Pepper, Jeffrey Mackenzie editor-in-chief
Perelman, Leon Joseph paper manufacturing executive, university president
†Perkins, Frederick Myers oil company executive
Perkins, Thomas Keeble oil company researcher
Perle, George composer
Perlman, Itzhak violinist
Perlman, Leonard G. psychologist, rehabilitation specialist, author, educator
Perlov, Dadie management consultant, association executive
Perman, Norman Wilford graphic designer
Perreault, Sister Jeanne college president
Perrin, Gail editor
Perrin, Robert federal government consultant
Perry, George Wilson oil and gas company executive
Perry, J. Warren health sciences educator, administrator
Persky, Lester film producer
Peter, Richard Ector zoology educator
Peters, Ralph Frew investment banker
†Peters, Robert Woolsey architect
Peters, Virginia actress
Peters, William Henry former university dean, marketing educator
Petersen, Susan Jane publishing company executive
Peterson, Ann Sullivan physician, health care consultant
Peterson, Monica (Dorothy Peterson) actress, singer, model, writer
Peterson, Roderick William writer, producer
Petika, David M. municipal government official, educator
Petok, Samuel retired manufacturing company executive
Petrequin, Harry Joseph, Jr. foreign service officer
Petrie, Donald Archibald lawyer, investment banker, publisher
Pettis-Roberson, Shirley McCumber former congresswoman
Pettit, Ghery DeWitt retired veterinary medicine educator
Pettitt, Jay S. architect, consultant
Petykiewicz, Sandra Dickey editor
Pew, Thomas W., Jr. advertising executive
Peyser, Joseph Leonard historical researcher, translator, author
Pflanze, Otto Paul history educator
Phelan, Ellen artist
Phelps, Paulding rheumatologist, internist
Philippi, Ervin William mortician
Phillips, Charles Alan accounting firm executive
Phillips, Gabriel marketing executive
Phillips, George Michael communications executive
Phillips, James Dickson, Jr. federal judge
†Phillips, John David communications executive
Phillips, Kenneth Higbie association executive
Phillips, William George retired food products executive
†Pick, Robert Yehuda orthopedic surgeon, consultant
Pickering, Howard William metallurgy engineer, educator
Pickus, Albert Pierre lawyer
Pielou, Evelyn C. biologist
Pierce, James Robert magazine executive
Pierce, Ponchitta Anne television host, producer, journalist
Pierce, Samuel Riley, Jr. government official, lawyer
Pierce, Scott retired investment company executive
Piergallini, Alfred A. food products executive
Pierskalla, William Peter academic dean, management and engineering educator
Piga, Stephen Mulry lawyer
Pilisuk, Marc community psychology educator
Pillorgé, George John architect, architectural-engineering company executive
†Pinchot, Bronson actor
Pine, Charles Joseph clinical psychologist
Ping, David Thomas senior project engineer
Pinkney, D. Timothy investment company executive
Pinkney, Jerry artist, educator
†Pinter, Gabriel George physiologist
Pinto, Rosalind retired educator, civic volunteer
Piore, Nora Kahn economist, health policy analyst
Pipal, Faustin Anthony savings bank executive
Pirkle, Earl Charnell geologist, educator
Pisney, Raymond Frank international consulting services executive
Pitcher, Griffith Fontaine lawyer
Pitstick, Leslie James food products company executive
†Pitts, Terence Randolph curator and museum director
Plangere, Jules Leon, Jr. media company executive
†Plasier, Lee J. sales executive
Pleshette, Suzanne actress, writer
Pletcher, Eldon editorial cartoonist
Plimpton, Calvin Hastings physician, university president
Plimpton, Peggy Lucas trustee
Plumb, Pamela Pelton consulting company executive, former mayor and councilwoman
Plummer, Amanda actress
Plummer, (Arthur) Christopher (Orme) actor
Plummer, Daniel Clarence, III insurance consultant
Poch, Stephen metallurgical engineer, consultant
Pockell, Leslie M. publishing company executive
Pocock, Frederick James scientist, consultant
Polasek, Edward John electrical engineer, consultant
Policano, Joseph Daniel import company executive
Polikoff, Benet, Jr. lawyer
Polk, James Ray journalist
Polk, Robert Forrest banker
Poll, Martin Harvey film producer
Pollack, Gerald A. economist, government official
Pollack, Joseph retired labor union official
Pollack, Ronald F(rank) foundation executive, lawyer
Pollard, Henry lawyer
Pomraning, Gerald Carlton engineering educator
Ponce de Leon, Michael artist, lecturer, educator
†Pond, Phyllis Joan state legislator
Pool, Douglas Vernon trust company executive
Pool, Philip Bemis, Jr. investment banker
Pooley, Beverley John law educator, librarian
Poor, Janet Meakin landscape designer
Pope, Robert Glynn telecommunications executive
†Poploff, Michelle Jo editor
Porges, Walter Rudolf television news executive
Porosky, Michael real estate and investment company executive
Porteous, Timothy academic administrator
Porter, Daniel Reed, III museum director
Porter, Philip Thomas retired electrical engineer
Portis, Alan Mark physicist, educator
Poser, Ernest George psychologist, educator
Poss, John Claybron corporate executive
†Post, Richard Bennett retired human resources executive
Poston, Tom actor
Pote, Harold William banker
Potok, Chaim author, artist, editor
Potter, James Earl retired international hotel management company executive
Potts, Sandra D. elementary education educator
Potvin, Alfred Raoul engineering executive
Pound, Robert Vivian physics educator
Powell, Clinton Cobb radiologist, physician, former university administrator
Powell, Earl Alexander, III art museum director
Powell, Harvard Wendell former air force officer, business executive
Powers, John R. author
Powers, Stefanie (Stefanie Federkiewicz) actress
Prager, David retired state supreme court chief justice
Prather, Gerald L. management consultant, retired air force officer, judge
Pratt, Edmund Taylor, Jr. pharmaceutical company executive
Precopio, Frank Mario chemical company executive
†Pressman, Thane Andrew consumer products executive
Priaulx, A(llan) publishing executive
Price, Paul Buford physicist, educator
Price, Robert Ira coast guard officer
†Primosch, James Thomas music educator, composer, musician
Prince, (Prince Rogers Nelson) musician, actor
Prince, Milton S. investment company executive
Prins, Robert Jack college administrator
Pritchard, Claudius Hornby, Jr. retired university president
Procter, John Ernest former publishing company executive
Procunier, Richard Werner environmental scientist, administrator
Prokasy, William Frederick academic administrator
Prokopis, Emmanuel Charles communications company executive

Propst, Harold Dean *retired university chancellor*
Provensen, Alice Rose Twitchell *artist, author*
Proxmire, William *former senator*
Prugh, George Shipley *lawyer*
Pruis, John J. *business executive*
Prusiner, Stanley Ben *neurology and biochemistry educator, researcher*
Pryce, Deborah D. *congresswoman*
Pudney, Gary Laurence *television executive*
Pursey, Derek Lindsay *physics educator*
†Purvis, Richard George *former superintendent of schools*
Puryear, Alvin Nelson *management educator*
Pusateri, Lawrence Xavier *lawyer*
Pusey, William Webb, III *retired dean, foreign language educator*
Putnam, Linda Lee *communication educator, researcher*
Quaid, Dennis William *actor*
Quaid, Randy *actor*
Queenan, Joseph Martin, Jr. *writer, magazine editor*
Quehl, Gary Howard *association executive, consultant*
Questrom, Allen I. *retail executive*
Quigley, Leonard Vincent *lawyer*
Quillen, Cecil Dyer, Jr. *lawyer, consultant*
Quinlan, J(oseph) Michael *lawyer*
Quinn, Charles Nicholas *journalist*
Quirico, Francis Joseph *retired state supreme court justice*
Qutub, Musa Yacub *hydrogeologist, educator, consultant*
Raab, Herbert Norman *retail executive*
Rabb, Ellis *actor, director, writer*
Rabinowitz, Mark Allan *lawyer*
Rabó, Jule Anthony *chemical research administrator, consultant*
Rabon, William James, Jr. *architect*
Rader, Dotson Carlyle *author, journalist*
Radice, Anne-Imelda *museum director*
Radin, Norman Samuel *retired biochemistry educator*
Rafelson, Bob *film director*
Ragsdale, Carl Vandyke *motion picture producer*
Raichle, Marcus Edward *radiology, neurology educator*
Rainey, Claude Gladwin *retired health care executive*
Rajki, Walter Albert *manufacturing company executive*
Ralston, Joanne Smoot *public relations counseling firm executive*
Ramanarayanan, Madhava Prabhu *science administrator, researcher, educator*
Ramo, Virginia M. Smith *civic worker*
Ramsey, Claude Swanson, Jr. *former industrial executive*
Ramsey, Stephen Douglas *lawyer*
Randall, Richard Harding, Jr. *art gallery director*
Randall, Richard Rainier *geographer*
Randolph, Judson Graves *pediatric surgeon*
Ransome, Ernest Leslie, III *transportation and retail company executive*
Rapaccioli, Michel Antoine *financial executive*
Rapin, Charles René Jules *computer science educator*
Rask, Michael Raymond *orthopaedist*
Raskin, Michael A. *retail company executive*
Rasor, Dina Lynn *journalist*
†Rassman, Joel H. *real estate company executive, accountant*
Rast, Walter, Jr. *hydrologist, water quality management*
†Ratcliff, James Lewis *administrator*
Rau, Robert Nicholas *pipe distribution executive*
Raucher, Herman *novelist, screenwriter*
Rawls, S(ol) Waite, III *business executive*
Raymer, Donald George *utility company executive*
Raymond, Joan M. *educational administrator*
Raymond, Lee R. *oil company executive*
Rayner, William Alexander *retired newspaper editor*
Raynolds, Harold, Jr. *retired state education commissioner*
Read, Paul E. *horticulture educator*
Reaves, Ray Donald *civil engineer*
Rector, Richard Robert *television executive, producer*
Redbone, Leon *singer, musician*
Redda, Kinfe Ken *chemist, educator*
Reddy, Helen Maxine *singer*
Redeker, Jerrald H(ale) *banker*
Redford, Robert *actor, director*
Redgrave, Vanessa *actress*
Redmont, Bernard Sidney *university dean, journalism educator*
Reed, Adam Victor *psychologist, engineer*
Reed, David *artist*
Reeder, Cecelia Painter *secondary education educator*
Reeder, James Arthur *lawyer*
Rees, Mina (Spiegel) *university administrator*
Reetz, Harold Frank, Jr. *industrial agronomist*
Reeves, Frank Blair *architect, educator*
Reeves, Keanu *actor*
Regnery, Henry *publisher*
Rehm, Leo Frank *civil engineer*
Rehmus, Charles Martin *law educator, arbitrator*
Reich, Herb *editor*
Reich, Robert Bernard *U.S. secretary of labor, political economics educator*
Reiche, Frank Perley *lawyer, former federal commissioner*
Reichman, Fredrick Thomas *artist*
Reichstetter, Arthur Charles *banker*
Reid, Harry *senator*
Reid, Michael J. *international management consultant and educator*
Reidenbaugh, Lowell Henry *retired sports editor*
Reifsnider, Kenneth Leonard *metallurgist, educator*
Reilly, Edward Francis, Jr. *former state senator, federal agency administrator*
Reinhardt, John Edward *former international affairs specialist*
Reinhardt, Stephen Roy *federal judge*
Reinke, Ralph Louis *retired academic administrator*
Reisman, Fredricka Kauffman *education educator*
Reiss, Jerome *lawyer*
Reister, Ruth Alkema *lawyer, business executive*
Reitan, Daniel Kinseth *electrical and computer engineering educator*
Reiter, Glenn Mitchell *lawyer*
Remer, Donald Sherwood *chemical engineer, engineering economist, educator, administrator*
Reminger, Richard Thomas *lawyer*
Renaud, Bernadette Marie Elise *author*
Renda, Dominic Phillip *airline executive*
Renfro, Charles Gilliland *economist*
Reppen, Norbjorn Dag *electrical engineer, consultant*
Resnik, Linda Ilene *marketing and information executive, consultant*
Reston, James Barrett *retired newspaper publishing executive, author,*
Reuber, Grant Louis *banking insurance company executive*
Reuman, Robert Everett *philosophy educator*
Reycraft, George Dewey *lawyer*
Reynolds, Billie I. *financial representative and counselor, former association executive*
Reynolds, Carl Christiansen *government official*
Reynolds, Jack W. *retired utility company executive*
Reynolds, John Charles *communications company executive, management consultant*
Reynolds, John Francis *insurance company executive*
Reynolds, William Bradford *lawyer*
Rhame, Thomas Gene *army officer*
Rhein, Murray Harold *management consultant*
Rhett, John Taylor, Jr. *government official, civil engineer*
Rhodes, Peter Edward *label company executive*
Riasanovsky, Nicholas Valentine *historian, educator*
Rice, Joseph Albert *banker*
Rice, Richard Campbell *retired state official, retired army officer*
Rice, Richard Lee *retired architect*
Rice, Roger Douglas *television executive, artist*
Rice, Stanley Travis, Jr. *poet, English language educator*
Rice, Stuart Alan *chemist, educator*
Rice, Walter Herbert *federal judge*
Rich, John *film and television producer, director*
Richard, Susan Mathis *trade association executive*
Richards, Paul Linford *physics educator, researcher*
Richards, Thomas Carl *air force officer, governmental official*
Richards, Vincent Philip Haslewood *librarian*
Richardson, Charles Clifton *biochemist, educator*
Richardson, Natasha Jane *actress*
Richardson, Robert Dale, Jr. *English language educator*
Richie, Lionel B., Jr. *singer, songwriter, producer*
Richman, Alan *magazine editor*
Richman, Marvin Jordan *real estate developer, investor, educator*
Richman, Paul *semiconductor industry executive, educator*
Richman, Peter *electronics executive*
Richmond, Julius Benjamin *retired physician, health policy educator emeritus*
Rickard, Ruth David *retired history and political science educator*
Rickards, Leonard Myron *oil company executive*
Rickey, George Warren *artist, sculptor, educator*
†Rickman, Tom *screenwriter, director*
Ridder, Paul Anthony *newspaper executive*
Riddle, Donald Husted *former university chancellor*
Rideout, Patricia Irene *operatic, oratorio and concert singer*
Ridloff, Richard *real estate executive, lawyer, consultant*
Riehecky, Janet Ellen *writer*
Rifkin, Ned *museum director*
Righter, Walter Cameron *bishop*
Riley, Terry *composer, musician*
Ringgold, Faith *artist, writer*
Riss, Robert Bailey *insurance company executive*
Robbins, Frances Elaine *educational administrator*
Roberts, Alfred Wheeler, III *lawyer, law firm executive*
Roberts, Doris *actress*
†Roberts, Jacqueline *state legislator, political consultant*
Roberts, James G. *foundation executive*
Roberts, Joan I. *social psychologist, educator*
Roberts, John Glover, Jr. *lawyer*
Roberts, Marie Dyer *computer systems specialist*
Roberts, Samuel Smith *television news executive*
Robertson, A. Haeworth *actuary, benefit consultant, foundation executive*
Robertson, Cliff *actor, writer, director*
Robertson, John Archibald Law *nuclear scientist*
Robertson, Mary Virginia *retired elementary educator*
Robins, Norman Alan *strategic planning consultant, former steel company executive*
†Robinson, Aminah Brenda Lynn *artist*
Robinson, Bob Leo *international investment services executive*
†Robinson, Bruce Butler *physicist*
Robinson, David Adair *neurophysiologist*
Robinson, Edward Joseph *cosmetics company executive*
Robinson, James Arthur *university president emeritus, political scientist*
Robinson, Linda Gosden *communications executive*
Robinson, Marshall Alan *economics educator, foundation executive*
Robison, James Everett *management consulting company executive*
Robles, Rosalie Miranda *elementary education educator*
Rochberg, George *composer, educator*
Rock, Arthur *venture capitalist*
†Rock, Richard Rand *lawyer, state senator*
Rockburne, Dorothea G. *artist*
Rockefeller, Margaretta Fitler Murphy (Happy Rockefeller) *widow of former vice president of U.S. and former governor of N.Y., Nelson Aldrich Rockefeller*
Rodbell, Clyde Armand *distribution executive*
Rodgers, Lawrence Rodney *physician, educator*
Rodino, Peter Wallace, Jr. *former congressman, lawyer*
Rodriguez-Roig, Aida Ivelisse *educational administrator*
Roe, Thomas Coombe *former utility company executive*
Roegner, George Peter *industrial designer*
Roethel, David Albert Hill *consultant*
Roetman, Orvil M. *aerospace company executive*
Rogers, Bernard William *military officer*
†Rogers, Charles Ford, II *architect*
Rogers, David *playwright, novelist, actor*
Rogers, Ginger (Virginia Katherine McMath) *dancer, actress*
Rogers, Kate Ellen *interior design educator*
Rogers, Nathaniel Sims *banker*
Rogers, Rosemary *author*
Rogo, Kathleen *safety engineer*
Rohatsch, Ralph R., Jr. (Bob Rohatsch, Jr.) *career military officer*
Rohr, Davis Charles *aerospace consultant, business executive, retired air force officer*
Rolandi, Gianna *coloratura soprano*
Roller, Duane Henry DuBose *historian of science, educator*
Roller, Thomas Benjamin *manufacturing company executive*
Rollins, Alfred Brooks, Jr. *historian, educator*
Rollo, Mary-Jo Vivian *special education educator*
†Roloff, Michael *writer*
Romans, Donald Bishop *corporate executive*
Romeo, Luigi *linguist, educator*
†Roodman, Richard David *hospital administrator*
Rooke, David Lee *retired chemical company executive*
Rooks, Charles Shelby *minister*
†Rooney, J. Patrick *insurance company executive*
Root, Doris Smiley *art director*
Roper, John Lonsdale, III *shipyard executive*
†Rose, James Turner *aerospace consultant*
Rose, James W. *lawyer*
Rose, Mason H., IV *psychoanalyst*
Rose, Robert John *bishop*
Rose, Rubye Blevins (Patsy Montana) *singer*
Rosemberg, Eugenia *physician, scientist, educator, medical research administrator*
Rosemont, Norman *television producer*
Rosen, Arthur Marvin *advertising executive*
Rosen, Charles Welles *pianist, music educator*
Rosen, Lawrence *anthropology educator*
Rosen, Myor *harpist, educator*
Rosenbaum, Irving M. *retail store executive*
Rosenberg, Alison P. *public policy official*
Rosenberg, Sheli Zysman *lawyer, financial management executive*
Rosenberg, Stuart *film director*
Rosenblatt, Joseph *poet, editor*
Rosenblatt, Roger *writer*
Rosenfield, James Harold *communications executive*
Rosenkoetter, Gerald Edwin *engineering and construction company executive*
Rosenn, Harold *lawyer*
Rosenow, John Henry *surgeon, educator*
Rosenquist, James Albert *artist*
Rosenthal, Arnold H. *film director, producer, graphic designer*
Rosenthal, Arthur Jesse *publisher*
Rosenthal, Ely Manuel (Manny Rosenthal) *retired meat company executive, consultant*
Rosenthal, Sol Roy *preventive medicine educator, researcher*
Ross, Charlotte Pack *suicidologist*
Ross, Donald Roe *federal judge*
Ross, Elinor *soprano*
Ross, Joseph E. *government official, lawyer*
Ross, Robert Joseph *head professional football coach*
Rosselló, Pedro *governor of Puerto Rico*
Rosset, Lisa Krug *editor*
Rossi, Peter Henry *sociology educator*
Rossman, Ruth Scharff *artist, educator*
Rostow, Charles Nicholas *lawyer, educator*
Roth, Michael *lawyer*
Roth, Richard J. *marketing and advertising consulant*
†Roth, Tim *actor*
Roth, Toby *congressman*
Rothing, Frank John *government official*
Rothman, Julius Lawrence *retired English language educator*
Rothwell, Albert Falcon *retired lawyer, retired natural resource company executive*
†Rotman, Arthur *former social welfare administrator*
†Rountree, Neva Dixon *public relations executive*
Rourke, Mickey (Philip Andre Rourke, Jr.) *actor*
Rouse, Roscoe, Jr. *librarian, educator*
Rowe, William Davis *financial services company executive*
Rowlands, Gena *actress*
Royal, Darrell K. *university administrator*
Roybal, Edward R. *congressman*
Rub, Louis John *savings and loan executive*
Rubello, David Jerome *artist*
Rubin, Larry Bruce *writer, reporter*
Rubin, Rick *record producer*
Rubin, Sandra Mendelsohn *artist*
Rubin, Vera Cooper *research astronomer*
Rubin, Zick *psychology educator, lawyer, writer*
Rubinstein, Eva (Anna) *photographer*
Rubis, George *purchasing executive*
Rudd, Paul Ryan *actor, director*
Ruderman, Armand Peter *health economics educator, consultant, volunteer*
Rudin, Anne Noto *former mayor, nurse*
Rudner, Sara *dancer, choreographer*
Rudy, Raymond Bruce, Jr. *retired food company executive*
Rudzki, Eugeniusz Maciej *chemical engineer, consultant*
Ruegg, Donald George *retired railway company executive*
Rüetschi, Paul *electrochemist*
Ruffelle, Frances *actress*
Rugge, Hugo Robert *physicist*
Ruggiero, Matthew John *bassoonist*
Rundquist, Howard Irving *investment banker*
Runge, Donald Edward *food wholesale company executive*
Rush, Norman *author*
Rush, Richard Henry *financier, writer, lecturer*
Russell, Ray *author*
Russell, Theresa Lynn *actress*
Russell, Tomas Morgan *lawyer*
Russo, Jose *pathologist*
Russo, Roy Lawrence *electronic design automation engineer, researcher*
Rutherford, John Sherman, III (Johnny Rutherford) *professional race car driver*
Ruttner, Albert A. *manufacturing company executive*
Ryan, Carl Ray *electrical engineer*
Ryan, George H., Sr. *secretary of state, pharmacist*
†Ryan, James *insurance company executive*
Ryan, John William *association executive*
Ryan, John William, Jr. *construction-related consulting company executive*
Ryan, Meg *actress*
Ryan, Tom Kreusch *cartoonist*
Ryder, Georgia Atkins *university dean, educator*
Ryder, Jack McBride *educational consultant*
Rydz, John S. *manufacturing executive*
Ryland, G(reaner) Neal *financial executive*
Saar, Betye (Irene Saar) *artist*
Sabatini, Nelson John *government official*
Sacha, Robert Frank *osteopathic physician*
†Sacks, Gloria *interior designer*
Sahl, Morton Lyon *comedian*
Said, Kamal E. *accounting educator*
Saint, Eva Marie *actress*
Sajak, Pat *television game show host*
Saks, Gene *theater director, actor*
Salathe, John, Jr. *manufacturing company executive*
Salatka, Charles Alexander *archbishop*
Salbaing, Pierre Alcee *retired chemical company executive*
Saliterman, Richard Arlen *lawyer, educator*
Saltarelli, Eugene A. *retired engineering and construction company executive, consultant*
Saltzman, Philip *television writer, producer*
Samek, Michael Johann *corporation executive*
Sameroff, Arnold Joshua *developmental psychologist, educator, research scientist*
Samper, Joseph Phillip *retired photographic products company executive*
Sams, John Roland *retired mission executive, missionary*
Samson, Alvin *former distributing company executive, consultant*
Samuels, Sherwin L. *lawyer*
Samuelson, Robert Jacob *journalist*
Sanborn, David *alto saxophonist*
Sanchez, Leonedes Monarrize Worthington *fashion designer*
Sanders, Aaron Perry *radiation biophysics educator*
Sanders, John Theodore *federal agency executive, former state education superintendent*
Sanders, Marlene *academic administrator, educator*
Sanders, Wayne R. *manufacturing executive*
Sanders, William George *public relations executive*
Sandor, Gyorgy *pianist*
Sandrich, Jay H. *television director*
Sands, I. Jay *corporate executive, business, marketing and real estate consultant, lecturer, realtor, analyst*
Saneto, Russell Patrick *pediatrician, neurobiologist*
Sanfelippo, Peter Michael *cardiac, thoracic and vascular surgeon*
Santman, Leon Duane *lawyer, former federal government executive*
Sapsowitz, Sidney H. *entertainment and media company executive*
Sargent, John Turner *publisher*
Sarris, Andrew George *film critic*
Sarry, Christine *ballerina*
Sasdi, George P. *utilities company executive*
Saunby, John Brian *petrochemical company executive*
Saunders, Alexander Hall *real estate executive*
Sausser, Robert Gary *retired army officer*
Sauter, Van Gordon *communications executive*
†Sauvage, Lester Rosaire *health facility administrator, cardiovascular surgeon*
Sauvey, Donald (Robert) *retired musical instrument company executive*
Savage, Charles Francis *lawyer*
Savage, Neve Richard *advertising executive*
†Savini, Tom *make-up artist, actor, director*
Saxon, John David *lawyer, educator*
Sayles, Leonard Robert *management educator, consultant*
Sayre, David *physicist*
Sayre, Francis Bowes, Jr. *clergyman*
Scala, James *health care industry consultant, author*
Scandary, E. Jane *special education educator, consultant*
Schachter, Harry *biochemist, educator*
Schachter, Max *retired engineering services company executive*
Schaefer, C. Barry *railroad executive, lawyer, investment banker*
Schaefer, George Louis *theatrical producer and director, educator*
Schafer, Raymond Murray *composer, author*
Schallert, William Joseph *actor*
Scharf, William *artist*
Schatzberg, Jerry Ned (Jerrold Schatzberg) *film director*
Scheel, Nels Earl *financial executive, accountant*
Scheele, Paul Drake *former hospital supply corporate executive*
Schein, Harvey L. *communications executive*
Schenck, Jack Lee *retired electric utility executive*
Schenker, Leo *retired utility company executive*
Schenkkan, Robert Frederic *writer, actor*
Schexnayder, Brian Edward *opera singer*
Schey, John Anthony *metallurgical engineering educator*
Schiaffino, S(ilvio) Stephen *retired medical society executive, consultant*
Schickel, Richard *writer, film critic*
Schiller, Alfred George *veterinarian, educator*
Schiller, Lawrence Julian *motion picture producer, director*
†Schleck, Thomas Todd *financial executive*
Schlensker, Gary Chris *landscaping company executive*
Schley, Reeve, III *artist*
†Schmergel, Gabriel *pharmaceutical company executive*
Schmidt, Benno Charles *corporate executive*
Schmidt, Kenneth Martin *investment banker*
Schmidt, Ruth Ann *retired college president*
Schmitt, George Joseph *chemist*
Schmutz, Charles Reid *university foundation executive*
Schnackenberg, Roy Lee *artist*
Schneider, Janet M. *arts administrator, curator, painter*
Schneider, Phyllis Leah *writer, editor*
Schnucker, Robert Victor *history and religion educator*
Schoen, William Jack *financier*
Schoettler, Gail Sinton *state treasurer*
Schonhorn, Harold *chemist, researcher*
Schoor, Michael Mercier *lawyer, lobbyist*
Schorr, Daniel Louis *broadcast journalist, author, lecturer*
Schrader, Harry Christian, Jr. *retired naval officer*
Schrader, Henry Carl *civil engineer, consultant*
†Schrader, Martin Harry *retired publisher*
Schrager, James E. *financial company executive, educator*
Schreckinger, Sy Edward *advertising executive, consultant*
Schrempf, Detlef *professional basketball player*
Schroeter, Louis C. *retired pharmaceutical company executive*
Schuck, Joyce Haber *author*
Schuck, Peter Horner *lawyer, educator*
†Schuelke, John Paul *religious organization administrator*
Schulter-Ellis, Frances Pierce *anatomist, educator*
Schultz, Eileen Hedy *graphic designer*
Schultz, Philip *poet, novelist, educator*
Schulz, Ralph Richard *publishing consultant*
Schumacher, William Jacob *retired army officer*
†Schur, Susan Dorfman *state legislator*
Schuster, Gary Francis *corporate executive, former news correspondent*
Schuur, Diane Joan *vocalist*
Schwab, Eileen Caulfield *lawyer, educator*

Schwab, John Harris *microbiology and immunology educator*
Schwartz, Carol Levitt *former government official*
Schwartz, Doris Ruhbel *nursing educator, consultant*
Schwartz, John James *association executive, consultant*
Schwartz, Lillian Feldman *artist, filmaker, art analyst, author*
Schwartz, Lloyd Marvin *newspaper and magazine correspondent, broadcaster*
Schwartz, Robert *automotive manufacturing company executive, marketing executive*
Schwartz, Samuel *business consultant, retired chemical company executive*
Schwartz, Stephen Blair *retired information industry executive*
Schwartzberg, Martin M. *chemical company executive*
Schwartzman, Alan *architect*
Schwary, Ronald Louis *motion picture producer*
Schwarzrock, Shirley Pratt *author, lecturer, educator*
Schwarzschild, Martin *astronomer, educator*
Schwebel, Stephen Myron *judge, arbitrator*
Schweickart, Jim *advertising executive, broadcast consultant*
Schweinhart, Richard Alexander *health care company executive*
Schwier, Frederick Warren *manufacturing company executive*
Schwinn, Donald Edwin *environmental engineer*
Scoles, Clyde Sheldon *library director*
Scott, Amy Annette Holloway *nursing educator*
†Scott, Charles Kennard *state senator, cattle rancher*
Scott, Isadore Meyer *former energy company executive*
Scott, John Burt *life insurance executive*
Scott, Thomas Wright *composer, instrumentalist, arranger*
Scott, Waldron *mission executive*
Scruggs, Charles G. *editor*
Scruggs, Earl Eugene *entertainer*
Seamans, William *writer, commentator, former television-radio journalist*
Searle, Rodney Newell *state legislator, farmer, insurance agent*
Sease, Gene Elwood *public relations company executive*
Sebastian, Peter *international affairs consultant, former ambassador*
Seedlock, Robert Francis *engineering and construction company executive*
Seelig, Gerard Leo *management consultant*
Segal, JoAn Smyth *library consultant, organization administrator*
Seibert, Wilson A., Jr. *advertising executive*
Seidel, Frederick Lewis *writer*
Seidel, Glenda Lee *newspaper publisher*
Seidensticker, Edward George *Japanese language and literature educator*
†Seidlits, Curtis Lee, Jr. *lawyer*
Seitz, Raymond George Hardenbergh *diplomat*
Selby, Hubert, Jr. *writer*
Seldes, Marian *actress*
Sells, Boake Anthony *private investor*
Semerad, Roger Dale *consultant*
Sentenne, Justine *corporate ombudsman*
Servan-Schreiber, Jean-Jacques *engineer, author*
Servison, Roger Theodore *investment executive*
Sessions, Robert Paul *former college president and administrator, retired educator, writer*
Sestini, Virgil Andrew *secondary education educator*
†Setzler, Nikki Giles *state senator*
Sewell, Phyllis Shapiro *retail chain executive*
†Seymour, Dale Gilbert *publisher, author, speaker, consultant*
Shadbolt, Douglas *architecture educator, administrator*
Shafran, Hank *public relations agency executive*
Shames, Ervin Richard *food and chemical company executive*
Shank, Maurice Edwin *aerospace engineering executive, consultant*
Shank, Wesley Ivan *retired architect, educator*
Shannon, Iris Reed *nursing educator*
Shapira, David S. *food chain executive*
Shapiro, Debbie Lynn (Lynn Shapiro) *singer, actress, dancer*
Shapiro, Karl Jay *poet, former educator*
Shapiro, Michael Edward *museum director, art historian*
Shapiro, Richard Charles *sales and marketing executive*
Shapiro, Sumner *retired naval officer, business executive*
Sharif-Emami, Jafar *former prime minister of Iran*
†Sharp, Kenneth Travis *cultural organization administrator, editor*
Sharpe, William Forsyth *economics educator*
Sharwell, William Gay *retired university president and company executive*
Shasteen, Donald Eugene *government official*
Shattuck, Cathie Ann *lawyer, former government official*
Shaw, Artie *musician, writer, lecturer*
Shaw, John Frederick *retired naval officer*
Shaw, Melvin Phillip *physicist, engineering educator, psychologist*
Shaw, Richard *artist*
Shaw, Valeen Jones *special education educator, elementary school educator*
Shea, Donald Francis *state supreme court justice*
Shearer, Charles Livingston *academic administrator*
Sheedy, Ally (Alexandra Elizabeth Sheedy) *actress*
Sheehy, Gail Henion *author*
Sheeline, Paul Cushing *hotel executive*
Sheen, Charlie (Carlos Irwin Estevez) *actor*
Shelby, Khadejah E. *retired zoological park administrator*
Sheldon, Brooke Earle *librarian, educator*
Sheldon, Terry Edwin *lawyer, business consultant, advisor*
Sheldon, Thomas Donald *academic administrator*
Sheleski, Stanley John *accountant, comptroller, consultant*
Shellman-Lucas, Elizabeth C. *special education educator, researcher*
Shelton, Karl Mason *management consultant*
Shelton, Sloane *actress*
Shelton, Stephani *broadcast journalist, consultant*
Shepard, Alan Bartlett, Jr. *astronaut, real estate developer*
Shepherd, Mark, Jr. *retired electronics company executive*
Sheppard, Harold Lloyd *gerontologist, educator*
Sher, Paul Phillip *physician, pathologist*
Sheridan, Patrick Michael *finance company executive*
Sheridan, Sonia Landy *artist, retired art educator*
Sherin, Edwin *theatrical and film director, actor*
Sherman, John Foord *biomedical consultant*
Sherman, Richard H. *education educator*
†Sherrill, Thomas Beck *financial planner, state legislator*
Sherwood, (Peter) Louis *retail executive*
Shields, H. Richard *tax consultant,business executive*
Shipley, Lucia Helene *retired chemical company executive*
†Shirley, David Arthur *chemistry educator, science administrator*
Shirley-Quirk, John *concert and opera singer*
Shockley, Edward Julian *aerospace company executive*
Shockley, James Thomas *physics educator*
Shook, Ann Jones *lawyer*
Short, Martin *actor, comedian*
Shoulberg, Harry *artist*
Shoup, Harold Arthur *advertising executive*
Shreve, Susan Richards *author, English literature educator*
Shriber, Maurice Norden *research and manufacturing company executive*
Shughart, Donald Louis *lawyer*
Shultis, Robert Lynn *finance educator, consultant in cost systems, retired professional association executive*
Shumacker, Harris B., Jr. *surgeon, educator, author*
Shur, Michael *electrical engineer, educator, consultant*
†Shure, Myrna Beth *psychologist, educator*
Shute, Richard Emil *government official, engineer*
Shutt, Edwin Holmes, Jr. *consumer products executive*
Shyer, Charles Richard *screenwriter, film director*
Sidjakov, Nicolas *designer, illustrator*
†Siefer, Stuart B. *architect*
Siegel, Jack Morton *retired biotechnology company executive*
Silberman, Laurence Hirsch *federal judge*
Silverman, Jonathan *actor*
†Silverman, Michael *manufacturing company executive*
Silverstein, Barbara Ann *conductor*
Silvius, Donald Joe *educator, administrator*
Simeral, William Goodrich *retired chemical company executive*
Simmons, Bradley Williams *pharmaceutical company executive*
Simmons, Joseph Jacob, III *federal commissioner*
Simmons, Ted Conrad *writer*
Simms, Maria Ester *health services administrator*
Simon, Carly *singer, composer, author*
Simon, Melvin *real estate developer, professional basketball executive*
Simon, Michael Paul *general contractor, realtor*
Simon, Paul *musician, composer*
†Simon, Roger L. *writer*
Simones, Marie Dolorosa *nun, educator*
Simonet, John Thomas *banker*
†Simons, Robert R. *book publishing executive*
Simpson, Frederick James *research administrator*
Simpson, Murray *engineer, consultant*
Simpson, O. J. (Orenthal James Simpson) *former professional football player, actor, sports commentator*
Sims, Kent Otway *economist*
Sincoff, Michael Z. *human resources and marketing professional*
Singer, Markus Morton *retired trade association executive*
Sinicropi, Anthony Vincent *industrial relations and human resources educator*
Sisto, Elena *artist, educator*
Sjostrand, Fritiof Stig *biologist, educator*
Skaff, Joseph John *state agency administrator, retired army officer*
†Skinner, James Stanford *physiologist, educator*
Skolovsky, Zadel *concert pianist, educator*
Skov, Arlie Mason *petroleum engineer, consultant*
Skowronski, Vincent Paul *concert violinist, recording artist, executive producer, producer classical recordings*
†Skratek, Sylvia Paulette *mediator, arbitrator, state legislator*
Skromme, Lawrence H. *consulting agricultural engineer*
Slavitt, David Walton *retired lawyer*
Slayton, William Larew *planning consultant, former government official*
Slewitzke, Connie Lee *retired army officer*
Sloyan, Gerard Stephen *religious studies educator, priest*
Smally, Donald Jay *consulting engineering executive*
Smith, Barbara Anne *healthcare management company consultant*
Smith, Charles Haddon *geoscientist, consultant*
Smith, David Callaway *retired accounting firm executive*
Smith, Donald Nickerson *food service executive*
Smith, Doris Victoria *educational agency administrator*
Smith, Dwight Raymond *ecology and wildlife educator, writer*
Smith, Edward K. *economist, consultant*
Smith, Edward Reaugh *retired lawyer, cemetery and funeral home consultant*
Smith, Fern M. *federal judge*
Smith, Floyd Leslie *insurance company executive*
Smith, Frederick Coe *manufacturing executive*
Smith, Goff *industrial equipment manufacturing executive*
Smith, Hedrick Laurence *journalist, television comentator, author, lecturer*
Smith, Howard McQueen *librarian*
Smith, Jean Chandler *former museum official*
Smith, Joe Mauk *chemical engineer, educator*
Smith, Kenneth Blose *former financial executive*
Smith, Lauren Ashley *lawyer, journalist, clergyman, physicist*
Smith, Laverne Byrd *educational association administrator*
Smith, Lois Arlene *actress, writer*
Smith, Martin Bernhard *journalist*
Smith, Martin Cruz *author*
Smith, Martin Henry *pediatrician*
Smith, Paul Vergon, Jr. *corporate executive, retired oil company executive*
Smith, Richard Grant *retired telecommunications executive, electrical engineer*
Smith, Robert Michael *lawyer*
Smith, Robert Powell *foundation executive, former ambassador*
Smith, Ronald Lynn *health system executive*
Smith, Seymour Maslin *financial advisor, investment banker*
Smith, Stuart Lyon *psychiatrist, corporate executive*
Smith, Thomas Winston *cotton marketing executive*
Smith, V. Kerry *economics educator*
†Smith, Wayne Alan *state legislator, financial executive*
Smith, Wilburn Jackson, Jr. *retired bank executive*
Smither, Howard Elbert *musicologist*
Smock, Raymond William *historian, government official*
Smoot, George Fitzgerald, III *astrophysicist*
Smoot, Wendell McMeans, Jr. *investment counselor*
Smothers, Dick *actor, singer*
Snead, Richard Thomas *restaurant company executive*
Snead, Samuel Jackson *professional golfer*
Sneed, Alberta Neal *retired elementary education educator*
†Snelling, Robert Orren, Sr. *franchising executive*
Snelson, Kenneth Duane *sculptor*
Snetsinger, David Clarence *retired animal feed company executive*
Snider, L. Britt *government executive*
Snortland, Howard Jerome *educational financial consultant*
Snow, John William *railroad executive*
Snowden, Lawrence Fontaine *retired aircraft company executive, retired marine corps general officer*
Snyder, Alan Carhart *insurance company executive*
Snyder, Gary Sherman *poet*
Snyder, William Burton *insurance executive*
Sokal, Robert Reuven *biology educator, author*
Sollender, Joel David *management consultant, financial executive*
Solomon, Robert Charles *philosopher, educator*
Solomon, Susan *chemist, scientist*
Somes, Daniel E. *retired building materials company executive*
Sommer, Howard Ellsworth *textile executive*
Sondheim, Stephen Joshua *composer, lyricist*
Sonnenschein, Hugo Freund *university president, economics educator*
Sorel, Edward *artist*
Sorensen, Robert Holm *diversified technology company executive, retired*
†Sorensen, Sheila *state senator*
Sotirhos, Michael *ambassador*
Souter, David Hackett *U.S. supreme court justice*
Southerland, S. Duane *manufacturing company executive*
Southwick, Charles Henry *zoologist, educator*
Southworth, Jamie MacIntyre *education educator*
Souveroff, Vernon William, Jr. *corporate executive, investor, author*
Spaulding, Frank Henry *librarian*
Spejewski, Eugene Henry *physicist, educator*
Spence, Andrew *artist, painter*
Spence, Glen Oscar *clergyman*
†Spicer, S(amuel) Gary *lawyer, writer*
†Spiegel, Susan *art director*
Spiegelman, Robert Gerald *retired research institute executive*
Spinelli, Jerry *writer*
Spitzer, Lyman, Jr. *astronomer*
Spivack, Frieda Kugler *psychologist, educator, academician, researcher*
Spliethoff, William Ludwig *chemical company executive*
Splitstone, George Dale *retired hospital administrator*
Spollen, John William *lawyer*
Springer, Paul David *lawyer, motion picture company executive*
Springer, Robert Dale *retired air force officer, consultant, lecturer*
†Sprouse, Robert Allen, II *retail chain executive*
Srinivasan, Venkataraman *marketing and management educator*
Sroge, Maxwell Harold *marketing consultant, publishing executive*
Stabile, Benedict Louis *retired academic administrator, retired coast guard officer*
Stacy, Bill Wayne *college president*
Staiger, Ralph Conrad *educational consultant, former educational association executive*
Staker, Robert Jackson *federal judge*
Stamos, John James *judge*
Stamp, Frederick Pfarr, Jr. *federal judge*
Stamper, Malcolm Theodore *aerospace company executive*
Stanfill, Dennis Carothers *business executive*
Stanley, Scott, Jr. *editor*
Stans, Maurice Hubert *retired business consultant, former government official*
Stanton, John Jeffrey *editor, broadcast journalist, government programs director, analyst*
Stanton, Louis Lee *federal judge*
Stanton, Robert John *corporate bank executive, lawyer*
Stapell, Raymond James *lawyer, partner*
Stapleton, Maureen *actress*
Starer, Robert *composer*
Stark, Donald Gerald *pharmaceutical executive*
Starr, David *newspaper editor, publisher*
Starr, Kenneth Winston *lawyer*
Starr, Leon *retired chemical research company executive*
†Stassi, Peter John *advertising agency executive*
†Stearns, Carl David *architect*
Steen, Carlton Duane *private investor, former food company executive*
Stefan, Steve A. *manufacturing company executive*
Stefano, Ross William *leasing company executive*
Steffens, Dorothy Ruth *economist*
Stegall, Daniel Richard *lawyer*
Stein, Dale Franklin *retired university president*
Stein, Paul Arthur *financial services executive*
Steinhauser, Sheldon Eli *sociology educator, diversity consultant, organiza*
Stendahl, Krister *retired bishop*
Stengel, Ronald Francis *management consultant*
†Stennett, William Clinton (Clint Stennett) *radio and television station executive, state legislator*
Stephens, Donald R(ichards) *banker*
Stepp, James Michael *bank executive*
Stern, Arthur Paul *electronics company executive, electrical engineer*
Stern, Charles *foreign trade company executive*
Stern, Daniel *author, executive, educator*
Stern, Milton *chemical company executive*
Sternhagen, Frances *actress*
Stevens, Elliot Leslie *clergyman*
Stevens, May *artist*
Stevens, Warren *actor*
Stevenson, Elizabeth *author, educator*
Steward, H. Leighton *oil company executive*
Stewart, Carleton M. *banker, corporate director*
Stewart, James Maitland *actor*
Stewart, Marsha Beach *sales executive, entertainment executive*
Stewart, Norman Lawrence *university president*
Stewart, Peter Beaufort *retired beverage company executive*
Stewart, Richard Alfred *business executive*
Stewart, Robert William *retired physicist, government research council executive*
Stewart, Thomas James, Jr. *baritone*
Stewart, Thomas Ted *real estate developer, investment banker*
Stickler, Fred Charles *manufacturing company executive*
Stickler, Gunnar Brynolf *pediatrician*
Stiglitz, Joseph Eugene *economics educator*
Stiller, Jerry *actor*
Stines, Fred, Jr. *publisher*
Stinnett, Lee Houston *newspaper association executive*
Stivers, William Charles *forest products company executive*
Stockwell, Sherwood Beach *architect*
Stolarik, M. Mark *history educator*
Stoll, Charles Buckner *publishing executive, consultant*
Stolley, Richard Brockway *journalist*
Stone, James Robert *surgeon*
Storch, Arthur *theater director*
Stotter, Harry Shelton *banker, lawyer*
Strain, James Ellsworth *pediatrician, retired association administrator*
Strait, George *country music vocalist*
†Strandberg, John David *comparative pathologist*
Strangway, David William *university president*
Strasser, Gabor *priest, management consultant*
Stratman, Joseph Lee *petroleum refining company executive, consultant, chemical engineer*
Stratton, Robert *electronics company executive*
Straub, Peter Francis *novelist*
Strauss, Simon David *manufacturing executive*
Stream, Arnold Crager *lawyer, writer*
Street, John Charles *linguistics educator*
Streeter, Richard Henry *lawyer*
Streeter, Tal *sculptor*
Strider, Marjorie Virginia *artist, educator*
Striker, Cecil Leopold *archaeologist, educator*
Striker, Gary E. *scientist, research institution administrator*
Stromberg, Arthur Harold *retired professional services company executive*
Strothman, James Edward *editor*
Stroud, Robert Michael *biophysicist, educator, biotechnologist*
Struebing, Robert Virgil *retired oil company executive*
Stuart, Mary *actress*
Stuckwisch, Clarence George *university administrator*
Studebaker, John Milton *utilities engineer, consultant, educator*
Stults, Walter Black *management consultant, former trade organization executive*
Stumpe, Warren Robert *scientific, engineering and technical services company executive*
Sturtevant, Julian Munson *biophysical chemist, educator*
Styron, William *writer*
Suenholz, Herman Harry *banker*
Sugarman, Samuel Louis *retired oil transportation and trading company executive, horse breeder*
Suhler, John Stuart *investment banker*
†Sullivan, Barry F. *banker*
Sullivan, Daniel Joseph *writer*
Sullivan, George Edward *author*
Sullivan, James Lenox *clergyman*
Sullivan, Leon Howard *clergyman*
Sullivan, Michael Patrick *marine officer*
Sullivan, Nicholas G. *science educator, speleologist*
Sullivan, Roger Winthrop *retired foreign service officer, consultant*
Sumichrast, Jozef *illustrator, designer*
Summerfield, John Robert *textile curator*
Sundaresan, Mosur Kalyanaraman *physics educator*
Sunderman, Duane Neuman *chemist, research institute executive*
Sundstrom, Aileen Lois *speech educator*
Sunell, Robert John *retired army officer*
Suppes, Patrick *statistics, education, philosophy and psychology educator*
Suput, Ray Radoslav *librarian*
Surrey, Philip Henry *artist, educator*
Sussman, Barry *author, public opinion analyst and pollster, journalist*
Sutcliffe, James H. *insurance company executive*
Sutherland, Kiefer *actor*
Sutton, Dolores *actress, writer*
Sutton, Julia Sumberg *musicologist, dance historian*
Sutton, Willis Anderson, Jr. *sociology educator*
Swan, George Steven *lawyer, educator*
Swanberg, Edmund Raymond *investment counselor*
Swanger, Sterling Orville *appliance manufacturing company executive*
†Swanson, Paul Rubert *minister*
†Swanson, Peter Carl *editor*
Swanson, Rune E. *financial executive*
Swanstrom, Thomas Evan *economist*
Swayze, John Cameron, Sr. *news commentator*
Swift, Harold Augustus *health association executive*
Swig, Roselyne Chroman *art advisor*
Swihart, John Marion *retired aircraft manufacturing company executive*
†Swindler, Daris Ray *physical anthropologist, forensic anthropologist*
Swit, Loretta *actress*
Switzer, Maurice Harold *publisher*
Swope, Donald Downey *retired banker*
Sze, Andy Hok-Fan *transportation executive*
†Szynaka, Edward M. *library director, consultant*
Taber, Edward Albert, III *investment executive*
Tachmindji, Alexander John *systems engineering consultant*
Takal, Peter *artist*
Talbot, Howard Chase, Jr. *retired museum administrator*
Talingdan, Arsenio Preza *health science administrator*
Tallchief, Maria *ballerina*
Tallett, Elizabeth Edith *biopharmaceutical company executive*
Talley, Robert Morrell *aerospace company executive*
†Talmadge, Philip Albert *state senator, lawyer*
Tan, Amy Ruth *writer*
Tancredi, Laurence Richard *law and psychiatry educator, administrator*
Tandler, Bernard *cell biology educator*
Tanner, Laurel Nan *education educator*
Tansor, Robert Henry *investor*
Tapley, James Leroy *retired lawyer, railway corporation executive*
Taplin, Frank E., Jr. *trustee education and arts institutions and associations*

Tarr, David William *political scientist, educator*
†Tasco, Frank John *insurance brokering company executive*
†Tate, F. Wayne *federal agency administrator*
Tate, Manford Ben *guided missile scientist, investor*
Tatlock, Anne M. *trust company executive*
Taubman, A. Alfred *real estate developer*
Taylor, David George *retired banker*
Taylor, Guy Watson *symphonic conductor*
Taylor, Hugh Pettingill, Jr. *geologist, educator*
Taylor, John Jackson (Jay) *writer retired foreign service officer*
Taylor, Kristin Clark *media specialist*
†Taylor, Lynn *public relations executive*
Taylor, Millard Benjamin *concertmaster, educator*
Taylor, Peter Matthew Hillsman *author*
Taylor, Richard Wirth *political science educator*
Teeple, Fiona Diane *librarian, lawyer*
Teitelbaum, Irving *retail executive*
Temam, Roger M. *mathematician*
Templeton, Carson Howard *engineering executive, policy analyst*
†Templeton, John Alexander, II *coal company executive*
Tenney, Stephen Marsh *physiologist, educator*
terHorst, Jerald Franklin *public affairs counsel*
Terkel, Susan Neiburg *author*
Textor, Robert Bayard *cultural anthropology writer, consultant, educator*
Thackray, Richard Irving *psychologist*
Thal, Herbert Ludwig, Jr. *electrical engineer, engineering consultant*
Thaxter, Phyllis St. Felix *actress*
Theroux, Paul Edward *author*
Thiel, Philip *design educator*
Thiele, Howard Nellis, Jr. *lawyer*
Thiessen, Gordon George *banker*
Thom, Douglas Andrew *paper company executive*
Thomas, Franklin Augustine *foundation executive*
Thomas, Karen P. *composer, conductor*
Thomas, Ross Elmore *author*
†Thompson, Charles Kevin *architect, lighting designer*
Thompson, J. Andy *bank executive*
Thompson, Jack Edward *mining company executive*
Thompson, Ralph Newell *former chemical corporation executive*
Thompson, Richard Stephen *management consultant*
Thompson, Robert Elliott *columnist, writer*
Thomson, Grace Marie *nurse, minister*
Thornburg, Frederick Fletcher *diversified business executive, lawyer*
Thornburg, Lacy Herman *judge*
Thorne, Barbara Lockwood *guidance counselor, secondary education educator*
Thorstenberg, (John) Laurence *oboe and English horn player*
Threefoot, Sam Abraham *physician, educator*
Threet, Jack Curtis *oil company executive*
Threlkeld, Richard Davis *broadcast journalist*
Throckmorton, William Robert, Sr. *sociologist*
†Thuillier, Richard Howard *meteorologist*
Tichenor, Donald Keith *association executive*
Tiedge-Lafranier, Jeanne Marie *editor*
Tienken, Arthur T. *retired foreign service officer*
Tillman, Montague Epps *school superintendent*
Timmons, William Milton *retired cinema arts educator, publisher, free-lance writer, film maker*
Tippett, Willis Paul, Jr. *automotive and textile company executive, retired*
Tisdale, Stuart Williams *holding company executive*
Tobias, Andrew Previn *columnist, lecturer*
Tobin, Michael Edward *banker*
Toensing, Victoria *lawyer*
Toevs, Alden Louis *management consultant*
Tokofsky, Jerry Herbert *film producer*
Toledo-Pereyra, Luis Horacio *transplant surgeon, researcher, educator*
Tolentino, Casimiro Urbano *lawyer*
Toll, Maynard Joy, Jr. *investment banker*
Tomas, Jerold F. V. *business executive, management consultant*
†Tomasi, Donald Charles *architect*
Tombros, Peter George *pharmaceutical company executive*
Tompsett, Michael Francis *defense research director*
Tomsovic, Edward Joseph *college dean*
Tonello-Stuart, Enrica Maria *political economist*
Tongue, Paul Graham *financial executive*
Tonjes, Marian Jeannette Benton *education educator*
Tonkyn, Richard George *retired oil and gas company executive, researcher, consultant*
Toor, Herbert Lawrence *chemical engineering educator, researcher*
†Topinka, Judy Baar *state legislator*
Torn, Rip (Elmore Rual Torn, Jr.) *actor, director*
Tourino, Ralph Gene *career officer*
Tovish, Harold *sculptor*
Tower, Joan Peabody *composer, educator*
Towers, (Augustus) Robert, Jr. *English educator, writer*
†Towery, Matthew Allen, Sr. *lawyer*
Travanti, Daniel John *actor*
Travis, Randy Bruce *musician*
Travolta, John *actor*
Trelease, Allen William *historian, educator*
Treynor, Jack Lawrence *financial advisor, educator*
Trigg, Paul Reginald, Jr. *lawyer*
Trilling, Diana *writer*
Trilling, Helen Regina *lawyer*
Trimble, Paul Joseph *lawyer*
Triolo, Peter *advertising agency executive, marketing educator, consultant*
Tripplehorn, Jeanne *actress*
Trombino, Roger A. *investment banker*
Troy, B. Theodore *direct mail advertising executive*
Trudeau, Garretson Beekman (Garry Trudeau) *cartoonist*
Trueman, William Peter Main *broadcaster, newspaper columnist*
Truman, Margaret *author*
Trump, Donald John *real estate developer*
Tsai, Wen-Ying *sculptor, painter, engineer*
Tucci, Daniel Patrick *chemicals executive*
Tucker, H. Richard *oil company executive*
Tucker, Paul William *retired petroleum company executive*
Tucker, Ruth M. *elementary education educator*
Tuft, Mary Ann *former association executive*
Tumbleson, Arthur Louis *civil engineer, contractor*
Turco, Richard Peter *atmospheric scientist*
Turkin, Marshall William *symphony orchestra, festival and opera administrator, arranger, composer*
Turnbull, Fred Gerdes *electronics engineer*
Turnbull, John Neil *retired chemical company executive*
Turner, Henry Brown *finance executive*
Turner, Lana (Julia Jean Mildred Frances Turner) *actress*
Turner, Lee S., Jr. *consultant*
Turner, Robert Comrie *composer*
Turner, Robert Hal *telecommunications and computer executive*
Turnoff, William Charles *judge*
Turok, Paul Harris *composer, music reviewer*
Tutwiler, Margaret DeBardeleben *communications executive*
Tyson, H. Michael *bank executive*
†Tytler, Linda Jean *communications and public affairs executive, state legislator*
Ubell, Earl *television science editor*
Udall, Morris King *former congressman*
Uehlinger, John Clark *marketing executive*
Ugrin, Béla *video producer*
Uhrich, Richard Beckley *hospital executive, physician*
Ulrich, Richard William *finance executive*
Uman, Martin Allan *electrical engineering educator, researcher, consultant*
†Unithan, Dolly *visual artist*
Untermeyer, Charles G. (Chase) *government official*
Upbin, Shari *theatrical producer, director, agent, educator*
Updike, John Hoyer *writer*
Urbantke, Hugh Edmund *business educator, economist*
Urdang, Laurence *lexicographer, publisher*
Ussery, Luanne *communications consultant*
Vachon, Serge Jean *bank executive*
Vajeeprasee Thongsak, Thomas *business planning executive*
Vaky, Viron Peter *diplomacy educator, former foreign service officer*
Valens, Evans Gladstone *sculptor, printmaker, author, former television producer, director*
Valentine, William Newton *physician, educator*
†Valenza, Janet *advertising executive*
Van Allsburg, Chris *author, artist*
van Bruchem, Jan *retired broadcasting executive*
Vance, Lee *publishing company executive, consultant*
Vandenberg, Peter Ray *magazine publisher*
Vanderhoof, Irwin Thomas *life insurance company executive*
Vandevender, Barbara Jewell *elementary education educator, farmer*
Van Dreser, Merton Lawrence *ceramic engineer*
Van Duyn, Mona Jane *poet*
van Dyck, Nicholas Booraem *minister, foundation official*
Van Heijst, Jakob *library administrator*
Vanier, Jacques *physicist*
van Itallie, Jean-Claude *playwright*
†Van Meter, Jan Rodden *public relations executive*
Van Ness, John Ralph *museum administrator*
Van Patten, Joyce Benignia *actress*
Van Tassel, James Henry *retired electronics executive*
van't Hoff, Winfried C. J. *retired diversified manufacturing executive*
Van Valin, Clyde Emory *bishop*
Van Vinkenroye du Waysaeck, Fedia Maurice Gilles *financial services executive*
Vassil, Pamela *graphic designer*
Vaughan, John Charles, III *horticultural products executive*
Vega, J. William *aerospace engineering executive, consultant*
Velzy, Charles O. *mechanical engineer*
Ventre, Francis Thomas *environmental design and policy educator*
†Verdecchia, Guillermo Luis *playwright*
Vernon, Carl Atlee, Jr. *retired wholesale food distributor executive*
†Veronis, George *geophysicist, educator*
Verplanck, William Samuel *psychologist, educator*
Ver Vynck-Potter, Virginia Mary *construction executive*
Verwoerdt, Adriaan *psychiatrist*
Vickrey, Robert Edward, Jr. *petroleum engineer*
Vidal, Gore *writer*
Villella, Edward Joseph *ballet dancer, choreographer, artistic director*
Vincent, Hal Wellman *marine corps officer, investor*
Viorst, Milton *writer*
Virgo, Julie Anne Carroll *management consultant*
Vishnevskaya, Galina Pavlovna *soprano, opera company director*
†Vognild, Larry L. *state senator*
Voight, Jon *actor*
Voigt, Cynthia *author*
Voketaitis, Arnold Mathew *bass-baritone, educator*
Volcker, Paul A. *economist*
Volkhardt, John Malcolm *food company executive*
Vollmer, Richard Wade *federal judge*
Volpe, Edmond L(oris) *college president*
von Brock, A. Raymond *architect*
Von Drehle, Ramon Arnold *lawyer*
von Hoffman, Nicholas *writer, former journalist*
Voorhees, James Dayton, Jr. *lawyer*
Voss, Omer Gerald *truck company executive*
†Vowell, Jack C. *state legislator, investor*
Waddle, John Frederick *former retail chain executive*
Wadley, M. Richard *consumer products executive*
Wagman, Robert John *journalist, author*
Wagner, Julia A(nne) *retired editor*
Wagner, Richard *business executive, former baseball team executive*
Wagner, Sigurd *electrical engineering educator, researcher*
Walch, W. Stanley *lawyer*
Waldhauser, Cathy Howard *financial services executive*
Waldrop, Gideon William *composer, conductor, former president music school*
Walker, Craig Michael *lawyer*
Walker, Gordon Davies *former government official, writer, lecturer, consultant*
Walker, James William, Jr. *lawyer*
Walker, John Sumpter, Jr. *lawyer*
Walker, Mary L. *lawyer*
Walkup, John Frank *electrical engineer, educator*
Wall, M. Danny *financial services consultant*
Wall, Robert Emmet *educational administrator, novelist*
Wallace, William Augustine *philosophy and history educator*
Wallach, Eli *actor*
Waller, Gary Fredric *English language educator, poet*
Walner, Robert Joel *lawyer*
Walsh, Jeremiah Edward, Jr. *government official*
Walsh, Joseph Fidler *recording artist, record producer*
Walsh, William Albert *business executive, former naval officer*
Walston, Ray *actor*
Walter, J. Jackson *consultant*
†Walter, James W. *diversified manufacturing executive*
Walter, John Robert *printing company executive*
Walter, Martin Edward *mathematician, educator*
Walters, Vernon Anthony *ambassador*
Walthall, Lee Wade *artistic director, dancer*
Walton, Harold Vincent *former agricultural engineering educator, academic administrator*
Waltrip, Darrell Lee *professional stock car driver*
Wambaugh, Joseph *author*
†Wampler, Jon R. *health financial administrator*
Wapenhans, Willi Adolf *banking executive*
Warner, Jack, Jr. *motion picture and television producer, writer*
Warnken, Douglas Richard *publishing consultant*
Washington, Valora *foundation administrator*
Washington, Walter *retired college president*
Wasserstein, Wendy *playwright*
Waters, Betty Lou *newspaper reporter, writer*
Waters, David Rogers *retail executive*
Waters, John *film director, writer, actor*
†Watson, James D., Jr. *principal*
†Watson, Robert Barden *physicist*
Watson, W. Robert *financial advisor, consultant*
Watt, John H. *financial executive*
Watts, Glenn Ellis *union official*
Watts, Ronald Lester *retired military officer*
Waymouth, John Francis *physicist, consultant*
Weaver, Edward T. *foundation executive, educator*
†Weaver, Howard Cecil *newspaper editor*
Webb, Charles Richard *retired university president*
Weber, Eugen *historian, educator, author*
Weber, Julian L. *lawyer, former publishing and entertainment company executive*
Webster, Robert David *lawyer*
Wechter, Vivienne Thaul *artist, poet, educator*
Weckesser, Ernest Prosper, Jr. *publisher, educator*
Weclew, Robert George *lawyer, educator*
Weddig, Lee J(ohn) *trade association executive*
Wehrle, Martha Gaines *state legislator*
Weikart, David Powell *educational research foundation administrator*
Weikert, Jerard Lee *real estate broker*
Weil, Rolf Alfred *economist, university president emeritus*
Weiland, Charles Hankes *lawyer*
Weinberg, Robert Leonard *retired lawyer*
Weinberg, Steven *physics educator*
Weinberger, Arnold *retired electrical engineer*
Weiner, Louis Max *retired mathematics educator*
Weinschel, Bruno Oscar *engineering executive, physicist*
Weinstein, Arnold Abraham *playwright, theater educator*
Weir, Kenneth Wynn *marine corps officer, experimental test pilot*
Weir, Paul Joseph *retired corporation executive*
Weir, Thomas Charles *banker*
Weisburger, Elizabeth Kreiser *chemist, editor*
Weisman, Lorenzo David *investment banker*
Weismantel, Gregory Nelson *management consultant and software executive*
Weiss, Michael Allen *retail executive*
Weiss, Michael James *chemistry educator*
Weiss, William Lee *retired communications executive*
Weissman, Jack (George Anderson) *editor*
Weitzman, Bruce H. *lawyer*
Welch, Oliver Wendell *retired pharmaceutical executive*
Weld, Tuesday Ker (Susan Ker Weld) *actress*
†Weldon, Jeffrey Alan *state senator, historical research company executive*
Wells-Carr, Elizabeth Antoinette *educational leadership trainer*
†Welton, Theodore Allen *theoretical physics educator, consultant*
Wendt, George Robert *actor*
Werman, Thomas Ehrlich *record producer*
†Werneburg, Kenneth Roger *mining company executive*
Werth, Andrew M. *telecommunications executive*
Wessler, Richard Lee *psychology educator, psychotherapist*
Wesson, William Simpson *retired paper company executive*
Wettig, Patricia *actress*
Wetzel, Donald Truman *engineering company executive*
Wexler, Jacqueline Grennan (Mrs. Paul J. Wexler) *former association executive and college president*
Weymar, F. Helmut *commodities trading company executive, economist*
Whalen, Charles William, Jr. *author, business executive, educator*
Whistler, Roy Lester *chemist, educator, industrialist*
White, Augustus Aaron, III *orthopaedic surgeon*
White, Gerald Andrew *chemical company executive*
White, James Arthur *college president*
†White, Randy *retired professional football player*
White, Richard Clarence *lawyer*
White, Robb *author*
White, Robert Frederick *landscape architect*
White, Willis Sheridan, Jr. *retired utilities company executive*
Whitehead, Richard Lee *insurance company executive*
Whitehouse, Alton Winslow, Jr. *retired oil company executive*
Whitesell, John Edwin *motion picture company executive*
Whitley, Nancy O'Neil *retired radiology educator*
Whitlock, Bennett Clarke, Jr. *retired association executive*
Whitney, Phyllis Ayame *author*
Whitten, Dolphus, Jr. *former university administrator, educational consortium executive*
Whyte, William Hollingsworth *writer*
Wicker, Thomas Grey *retired journalist*
Widmark, Richard *actor*
Wiebe, Leonard Irving *radiopharmacist, educator*
Wiebenson, Dora Louise *architectural historian, educator, author*
Wien, Stuart Lewis *retired supermarket chain executive*
Wiesen, Donald Guy *retired diversified manufacturing company executive*
Wiesner, John Joseph *retail executive*
Wiessler, David Albert *correspondent*
†Wigdor, Lawrence A. *chemical company executive*
†Wilder, Donny *state legislator, retired newspaper publisher*
Wildhack, William August, Jr. *lawyer*
Wiley, Richard Arthur *lawyer*
Wilhelm, Joseph Lawrence *archbishop*
Wilhelmsen, Harold John *accountant, operations controller*
Wilkens, Leonard Randolph, Jr. (Lenny Wilkens) *professional basketball coach*
Wilkerson, Charles Edward *architect*
Wilkins, Roger Carson *retired insurance company executive*
Wilkinson, Doris Yvonne *medical sociology educator*
Wilkinson, Milton James *ambassador*
Wilkinson, Stanley Ralph *agronomist*
Will, Joanne Marie *food and consumer services executive, communications consultant, writer*
Will, Mari Maseng *communications consultant*
Wille, Wayne Martin *retired editor*
Willenbecher, John *artist*
Willey, Gordon Randolph *retired anthropologist, archaeologist, educator*
Williams, Arthur *engineering consultant*
Williams, Barbara Jean May *state official*
Williams, Betty Lourene *manager, consultant, volunteer*
Williams, Brown F *television media services company executive*
Williams, Charles Wesley *technical executive, researcher*
Williams, Earle Carter *retired professional services company executive*
Williams, Gordon Roland *librarian*
Williams, Joseph Theodore *oil and gas company executive*
Williams, Louis Clair, Jr. *public relations executive*
Williams, Patrick Moody *composer*
Williams, Raymond Crawford *veterinarian anatomy educator*
Williams, Richard Clarence *retired librarian*
Williams, Robert Lyle *corporate executive, consultant*
Williams, Roger Stewart *physician*
Williams, Ronald Oscar *systems engineer*
Williams, Ted (Theodore Samuel Williams) *former baseball player, former manager, consultant*
Williams, William John, Jr. *lawyer*
Williamson, Fletcher Phillips *real estate executive*
Williamson, Laird *stage director, actor*
†Williamson, Michael *writer*
Williamson, Myrna Hennrich *retired army officer, lecturer, consultant*
Willig, Karl Victor *computer firm executive*
Willis, Bruce Walter *actor, singer*
Wills, Charles Francis *former church executive, retired career officer*
Wills, William Ridley, II *former insurance company executive, historian*
†Wilner, Judith *journalist*
Wilson, Almon Chapman *surgeon, physician, retired naval officer*
Wilson, Basil Wrigley *oceanographic engineering consultant, artist, author*
Wilson, Colin Henry *writer*
Wilson, Hugh Steven *lawyer*
Wilson, Jane *artist*
Wilson, Kenneth Geddes *physics research administrator, educator*
Wilson, Lanford *playwright*
†Wilson, Richard Alexander *career officer*
Wilson, Roy Gardiner *real estate developer*
Wilson, Sloan *author, lecturer*
Winder, Robert Owen *mathematician, computer engineering executive*
Winslow, Alfred Akers *retired government official*
Winter, Alan *publishing company executive*
Winter, John Dawson, III *performer, songwriter*
Winters, Jonathan *actor*
Winters, Nola Frances *food company executive*
Winters, Shelley (Shirley Schrift) *actress*
Winwood, Stephen Lawrence *musician, composer*
Wise, Patricia *lyric coloratura*
Wiseman, Jay Donald *photographer, mechanical contractor, designer*
Witcher, Daniel Dougherty *retired pharmaceutical company executive*
Witt, Hugh Ernest *technology consultant*
Witte, Merlin Michael *oil company executive*
Wittich, John Jacob *retired college president, educational administrator, corporation consultant*
Wittner, Loren Antonow *lawyer, former public relations executive*
Woerner, Robert Lester *landscape architect*
Wolf, Dale Edward *state official*
Wolf, Hans Abraham *retired pharmaceutical company executive*
Wolf, Rosalie Joyce *financial executive*
Wolfberg, Melvin Donald *corporate vice president, college president, consultant, optometrist*
Wolfe, Gregory Baker *international relations educator*
Wolfe, Theodore Joseph *food company executive*
Wolff, Peter Adalbert *physicist, educator*
Wolfman, Ira Joel *editor, writer*
Wolfman Jack, (Robert Weston Smith) *radio personality*
Wollert, Gerald Dale *retired food company executive, investor*
Wolner, Rena Meryl *publisher*
Wolters, Oliver William *history educator*
Womach, Emily Hitch *retired banker and marketing and public relations executive*
Wommack, W(illiam) W(alton) *retired manufacturing company executive*
Wonders, William Clare *geography educator*
Wong, David Yue *academic administrator, physics educator*
Wood, Allen John *electrical engineer, consultant*
Wood, David Charles *lawyer, finance company executive*
Wood, Diane Pamela *lawyer*
Wood, Marian Starr *publishing company executive*
Wood, Presnall Hansel *editor, minister*
Wood, Robert Coldwell *political scientist*
Woodall, Jack David *manufacturing company executive*
Wooden, John Robert *former basketball coach*
Woodhouse, Derrick Fergus *ophthalmologist*
Wooding, Gayle McAfee *nursing educator, consultant*
Woodruff, Virginia *television and radio host, producer*
Woods, Geraldine Pittman *health education consultant, educational consultant*
Woods, Phyllis Michalik *elementary education educator*
Woodward, Clinton Benjamin, Jr. *civil engineering educator*
Woodward, Joanne Gignilliat *actress*
Woodward, Thomas Morgan *actor*
Woosnam, Ian Harold *professional golfer*
Work, William *retired association executive*
Worrell, Richard Vernon *orthopedic surgeon, educator*
Worth, Gary James *communications executive*

Worthen, John Edward *university president*
Wright, Ann Elizabeth *physicist, educator*
†Wright, Earl Jerome *pastor, bishop*
Wright, James David *sociology educator, writer*
Wright, Sir (John) Oliver *retired diplomat*
Wright, Randolph Earle *retired petroleum company executive*
Wroblewski, Celeste Judine *non-profit civic association executive*
Wulff, John Kenneth *controller*
Wurdinger, Victoria *writer*
Wussler, Robert Joseph *broadcasting executive, media consultant*
Wyatt, Lenore *civic worker*
Wyckoff, Margo Gail *pyschologist*
Wylie, Clarence Raymond, Jr. *mathematics educator*
Wyman, Jane (Sarah Jane Fulks) *actress*
Wyman, Louis Crosby *state justice, former senator, former congressman*
Wyngaarden, James Barnes *physician*
Yack, Patrick Ashley *editor*

Yamane, George Mitsuyoshi *oral diagnosis and radiology educator*
Yanagitani, Elizabeth *optometrist*
†Yannello, Karen Marie *lawyer*
Yarborough, N. Patricia *human resources educator, human resources executive*
Yarbro, Alan David *lawyer*
Yarbrough, Marilyn Virginia *lawyer, educator*
Yarrow, Peter *folksinger*
Yates, Charles Richardson *former arts center executive*
Yates, David John C. *chemist, researcher*
Yates, Elton G. *retired petroleum industry executive*
Yeager, Mark L. *lawyer*
Yearwood, Donald Robert *oil and shipping executive*
Yellen, Linda Beverly *film director, writer, producer*
Yeo, Ronald Frederick *librarian*
Yetto, John Henry *corporation president*
†Yeutter, Clayton Keith *political organization executive, counselor to President of United States*
Yoakam, Dwight *country western musician*

Yochelson, Bonnie Ellen *museum curator, art historian*
Yoder, Carl W. *banker*
Yolton, John William *philosopher, educator*
Yost, William Albert *psychology educator, hearing researcher*
Young, John Alan *electronics company executive*
Young, Leo *electrical engineer*
Young, Margaret Buckner *civic worker, author*
Young, Margaret Chong *elementary education educator*
Young, Virgil M. *education educator*
Yovicich, George Steven Jones *civil engineer*
Zacks, Sumner Irwin *pathologist*
Zaffaroni, Alejandro C. *biochemist, medical research company executive*
Zajac, Jack *sculptor, painter*
Zaliouk, Yuval Nathan *conductor*
Zandman, Felix *electronics executive*
Zanetti, Joseph Maurice, Jr. *corporate executive*
Zeigler, L(uther) Harmon *political science educator*
Zekman, Terri Margaret *graphic designer*

Zelazny, Roger Joseph *author*
Zelinsky, Paul O. *illustrator, painter, author*
Zevon, Warren *singer, songwriter*
Zhou, Ming De *aeronautical scientist, educator*
Zick, John Walter *retired accounting company executive*
Ziegler, Jack (Denmore) *cartoonist*
Zilkha, Ezra Khedouri *banker*
Zimm, Bruno Hasbrouck *physical chemistry educator*
Zimmer, Donald William *former professional baseball manager*
Zinnen, Robert Oliver *general management executive*
Ziock, Klaus Otto Heinrich *physics educator*
Zischke, Douglas Arthur *foreign service officer*
Zoellick, Robert Bruce *corporate executive, lawyer*
Zuckerman, Martin Harvey *personnel director*
Zuckerman, Richard Engle *lawyer, educator*
Zufryden, Fred S. *academic administrator, marketing educator, researcher*
Zwislocki, Jozef John *neuroscience educator, researcher*

Professional Index

†New name in *Who's Who in America*, 49th Edition

AGRICULTURE

UNITED STATES

ALABAMA

Anniston
Andrews, Glenn *farmer, former congressman*

Tuskegee Institute
Hill, Walter A. *agricultural sciences educator, researcher*

CALIFORNIA

Los Angeles
Dickason, James Frank *land and farming company executive*

Madera
Silk, Bertram Edward *winery executive*

Modesto
Crawford, Charles McNeil *winery science executive*
†Gallo, Ernest *vintner*

Palo Alto
Sandmeier, Ruedi Beat *agricultural research executive*

Rutherford
Eisele, Milton Douglas *viticulturist*

Sacramento
Wightman, Thomas Valentine *rancher, researcher*

San Francisco
Hills, Austin Edward *vineyard executive*

San Luis Obispo
McCorkle, Robert Ellsworth *agribusiness educator*

Sierra Madre
Whittingham, Charles Edward *thoroughbred race horse owner and trainer*

COLORADO

Cedaredge
†Acquafresca, Steven Joseph *fruitgrower, consultant, state legislator*

Glenwood Springs
Gallagher, David Kent *agricultural vegetation manager, consultant*

DELAWARE

Dover
†Carey, V. George *farmer, state legislator*

DISTRICT OF COLUMBIA

Washington
Brady, Nyle C. *international consultant, science educator*
Branstool, Charles Eugene *farmer, federal agency administrator*
Kay, Thomas Oliver *agricultural consultant*
Schmidt, Berlie Louis *agricultural research administrator*

FLORIDA

Clermont
Chandler, Robert Flint, Jr. *international agriculture consultant*

GEORGIA

Atlanta
Brooks, David William *farmer cooperative executive*
Stimpert, Michael Alan *agricultural products company executive*

HAWAII

Honolulu
Ching, Chauncey Tai Kin *agricultural economics educator*

Waialua
Singlehurst, Dona Geisenheyner *horse farm owner*

IDAHO

Boise
Simplot, John R. *agribusiness executive*

Twin Falls
†Jones, Douglas Raymond *farming executive, state legislator*

ILLINOIS

Bloomington
Baer, Kenneth Peter *farmer cooperative executive*
Stevenson, Ernest Vail *retired farmer cooperative executive*
Webb, O. Glenn *farm supplies company executive*

Chicago
Mundlak, Yair *agriculture and economics educator*

Kenilworth
Clary, Rosalie Brandon Stanton *timber farm executive*

Northfield
Bruns, Nicolaus, Jr. *retired agricultural chemicals company executive, lawyer*

Urbana
Bentley, Orville George *retired agricultural educator, dean emeritus*
Courson, Roger Lee *agricultural educator*
Hill, Lowell Dean *agricultural marketing educator*

INDIANA

Indianapolis
French, Philip Franks *agricultural cooperative corporate executive*
Hegel, Carolyn Marie *farmer, farm bureau executive*

Lakeville
†Mangus, Richard W. *farmer*

IOWA

Ames
Jacobson, Norman L. *retired agricultural educator, researcher*
†Mullen, Russell E. *agricultural studies educator*

Muscatine
Kautz, Richard Carl *chemical and feed company executive*

KANSAS

Atchison
Cray, Cloud Lanor, Jr. *grain products company executive*

Haven
Schlickau, George Hans *cattle breeder, professional association executive*

Manhattan
†McKee, Richard Miles *animal studies educator*

KENTUCKY

Midway
Clay, Robert N. *thoroughbred breeder*

MICHIGAN

East Lansing
Paul, Eldor Alvin *agriculture, ecology educator*

MINNESOTA

Minneapolis
Joseph, Burton M. *grain merchant*

Paynesville
†Bertram, Jeff Nickolas *farmer, state legislator*

Saint Paul
†Dille, Stephen Everett *farmer, state legislator, veterinarian*
†Hansen, L(eslie) B. *agricultural studies educator*
†Sviggum, Steven A. *farmer, state representative*
Zylstra, Stanley James *farmer, food company executive*

MISSOURI

Chillicothe
Hamilton, Max Chester *farmer, writer*

Kansas City
Berg, W. Robert *agricultural products company executive*
†Frost, James E. *agricultural organization executive*

Springfield
Strickler, Ivan K. *dairy farmer*

NEBRASKA

Dakota City
Haines, Perry Vansant *cattle company executive*

Grand Island
Dobesh, Ernest Leonard *farmer, mayor*

NEVADA

Las Vegas
Koho, Clarence Herbert *agriculture laboratory executive, biologist, researcher*

NEW HAMPSHIRE

Concord
†Schotanus, Merle William *fruit grower, state legislator*

Lyme
Swan, Henry *forester, consultant*

NEW MEXICO

Cebolla
Berryman, Donald Carroll *cattle rancher*

NEW YORK

Elmont
Stephens, Woodford Cefis (Woody Stephens) *horse trainer, breeder*

Ithaca
Bail, Joe Paul *agricultural educator emeritus*

Rochester
Pease, Donald E. *dairy farmer, food products company executive*

NORTH DAKOTA

Cando
†Nicholas, Eugene Joseph *farmer, state representative*

Lefor
†Martin, Clarence *farmer, state legislator*

Regent
†Krauter, Aaron Joseph *farmer, state senator*

Sanborn
†Gerntholz, Gereld Felix *farmer, state representative*

Williston
†Rennerfeldt, Earl Ronald *farmer, rancher*

OHIO

Columbus
Casey, Raymond Richard *agricultural business executive*
†Holmes, Robert G. *agricultural studies educator*

Germantown
Lansaw, Charles Ray *rendering industry consultant*

OKLAHOMA

Oklahoma City
†Beutler, Randy Leon *rancher, state legislator*

Tulsa
Oxley, John Thurman *ranching and investments executive, former petroleum company executive*

OREGON

Ashland
Walt, Harold Richard *rancher*

PENNSYLVANIA

Harleysville
Ruth, Alpheus Landis *dairy farmer*

SOUTH CAROLINA

Columbia
†Rhoad, Thomas N., Jr. *farmer, state legislator, retired mail carrier*

SOUTH DAKOTA

Brookings
†Moore, Raymond A. *agricultural educator*

Elk Point
†Chicoine, Roland Alvin *farmer, state official*

Wessington
†Lockner, Vera Joanne *farmer, rancher, legislator*

TENNESSEE

Cordova
Baer, Ben Kayser *cotton merchant*

Memphis
†Echols, James *agricultural products supplier*

Nashville
†McKnight, Joe Nip *farmer, state senator, small business owner*

TEXAS

College Station
Christiansen, James Edward *agricultural educator*

Industry
Huitt, Jimmie L. *rancher, oil, gas, real estate investor*

Vega
Cook, Clayton Henry *rancher*

VIRGINIA

Mc Lean
†Brown, Billy Ross *agriculture association executive*

Montross
Fountain, Robert Roy, Jr. *farmer, retired industrial executive, naval officer*

Richmond
James, Gene Albert *farmers cooperative executive*

Spotsylvania
†Orrock, Robert Dickson *agricultural education educator, state legislator*

Spottswood
Fredricksen, Cleve Laurance *thoroughbred horse farm owner, real estate investor*

WEST VIRGINIA

Charles Town
McDonald, Angus Wheeler *farmer*

WYOMING

Douglas
Sanford, Leroy Leonard *rancher*

Dubois
†Betts, Robert Budd, Jr. *dude ranch owner*

Fort Laramie
†Hageman, James C. *rancher*

Jackson
Hansen, Clifford Peter *rancher*

Wheatland
Bunker, John Birkbeck *cattle rancher, retired sugar company executive*

TERRITORIES OF THE UNITED STATES

GUAM

Agana
Ladd-Powell, Roberta Kay *horsebreeder, marketing executive*

CANADA

ONTARIO

Ottawa
†Lister, Earle Edward *animal science consultant*

ENGLAND

Oxfordshire
Wilson, James Ray *international business educator*

ADDRESS UNPUBLISHED

†Aspen, Alfred William *international trading company executive*
Blackwell, Ronald Eugene *livestock consultant*
Erwin, Elmer Louis *vintager, cement consultant*
Hameister, Lavon Louetta *farm manager, social worker*
Johnson, Cyrus Edwin *grain farmer, former food products executive*
†Monson, David Carl *farmer, state legislator*
Pankey, Edgar Edward *rancher*

ARCHITECTURE AND DESIGN

UNITED STATES

ALABAMA

Auburn
Millman, Richard George *architect, educator*

Birmingham
†Barrow, Richard Edward *architect*
Collier, Felton Moreland *architect, planner, developer, detention, and recreation consultant, lecturer*

Huntsville
Jones, Harvie Paul *architect*

Mobile
Winter, Arch Reese *architect*

Montgomery
†Brock, Eugene C. *landscape architect*

Tuskegee
Pryce, Edward Lyons *landscape architect*

ALASKA

Anchorage
†Kumin, Jonathan P. *architectural firm executive*
Maynard, Kenneth Douglas *architect*

ARIZONA

Carefree
Beadle, Alfred Newman *architect*
Robbins, Conrad W. *naval architect*

Green Valley
Schirmer, Henry William *architect*

Mesa
†Shill, Victor Lamar *architect*

New River
Bruder, William Paul *architect*

Paradise Valley
†Blumer, Harry Maynard *architect*

Phoenix
Adams, Gail Hayes *interior designer*
DeBartolo, Jack, Jr. *architect*
Elmore, James Walter *architect, retired university dean*
†Gwozdz, Kim Elizabeth *interior designer*
Hawkins, Jasper Stillwell, Jr. *architect*
Laartz, Esther Elizabeth *interior designer*
Lendrum, James Thoburn *architect*
Schiffner, Charles Robert *architect*
†Winslow, Paul David *architect*

Scottsdale
Clapp, James Ford, Jr. *architect*
†Douglas, John Clifton *architect*
Hill, John deKoven *architect*
†Panks, Gary Allen *golf course architect*
Rutes, Walter Alan *architect*
Soleri, Paolo *architect, urban planner*

Sedona
Iverson, Wayne Dahl *landscape architect, consultant*

Sonoita
Cook, William Howard *architect*

Sun City West
Mc Cune, John Francis, III *retired architect*

Tempe
†Abell, James Logan *architect*
Goodwin, Kemper *architect, retired*
Mc Sheffrey, Gerald Rainey *architect, educator, city planner*
Thums, Charles William *designer, consultant*
Walker, Theodore Delbert *landscape architect*

Tucson
†Breckenridge, Klindt Duncan *architect*
Chafee, Judith Davidson *architect*
Dinsmore, Philip Wade *architect*
Gourley, Ronald Robert *architect, educator*

Jones, Warren David *landscape architect, landscape architecture educator*
Mc Connell, Robert Eastwood *architect, educator*
Nelson, Edward Humphrey *architect*
†Riggs, John B. *architect*
†Wallach, Leslie Rothaus *architect*
Zube, Ervin Herbert *landscape architect, geographer, educator*

ARKANSAS

Fayetteville
Burggraf, Frank Bernard, Jr. *landscape architect, educator*
Jones, Euine Fay *architect, educator*
Jones, Fay *architect*
Smart, Clifton Murray, Jr. *architect, educator*

Little Rock
Blass, Noland, Jr. *retired architect*
Cromwell, Edwin Boykin *architect*
Levy, Eugene Pfeifer *architect*
Truemper, John James, Jr. *architect*
†Wilcox, Jerry C. *architect*

CALIFORNIA

Altadena
Ziegler, Raymond Stewart *architect*

Bakersfield
†McAlister, Michael Hillis *architect*

Berkeley
†Arbegast, David Elwood *landscape architect*
Burger, Edmund Ganes *architect*
Cardwell, Kenneth Harvey *architect, educator*
Eckbo, Garrett *landscape architect, urban designer*
Hester, Randolph Thompson, Jr. *landscape architect, educator*
Hunt, Frank Bouldin *architect, water color artist*
Lyndon, Donlyn *architect, educator*
Olsen, Donald Emmanuel *architect, educator*
Paulling, John Randolph, Jr. *naval architecture educator, consultant*
Stoller, Claude *architect*

Beverly Hills
Eisenshtat, Sidney Herbert *architect*
†Myers, Barton *architect*

Bodega Bay
King, Leland W. *architect*

Burbank
Watson, Raymond Leslie *architect*

Campbell
Richards, Lisle Frederick *architect*

Carmel
Merrill, William Dickey *architect*

Carmichael
Hummel, Fred Ernest *architect*

Corona
Ohmert, Richard Allan *architect*

Corona Del Mar
Dorius, Kermit Parrish *architect*
Jacobs, Donald Paul *architect*
Yeo, Ron *architect*

Coronado
Wagener, Hobart D. *retired architect*

Costa Mesa
†Olson, Cal Oliver *golf architect*

Culver City
†Moss, Eric Owen *architect*
†Ray, Mary-Ann *architect, educator*

Dana Point
†Robinson, Theodore G. *golf course architect*

El Cerrito
Komatsu, S. Richard *architect*

Fallbrook
Burge, Henry Charles *architect*

Fresno
Darden, Edwin Speight, Sr. *architect*
Patnaude, William E. *architect*
†Pings, Anthony Claude *architect*
†Putman, Robert Dean *golf course architect*
†Saito, Paul Makoto *landscape architect*

Glendale
Colby, Barbara Diane *interior designer, consultant*

Irvine
†Danielian, Arthur Calvin *architect*
Kraemer, Kenneth Leo *architect, urban planner, educator*
Paul, Courtland Price *landscape architect, planner*

La Jolla
Baesel, Stuart Oliver *architect*

Lafayette
†Harlock, Michael J. *architect*

Laguna Hills
Burrows, Gates Wilson *retired architect*

Long Beach
†Tyrnauer, Herbert H. *design educator, industrial design consultant*

Los Angeles
†Adams, William Wesley, III *architect*

Aroni, Samuel *architecture and urban planning educator*
†Axon, Donald Carlton *architect*
Berry, Richard Douglas *architectural educator, urban planner and designer*
Blankenship, Edward G. *architect*
†Bobrow, Michael Lawrence *architect*
†Brotman, David J. *architectural firm executive*
Dworsky, Daniel Leonard *architect*
Fickett, Edward Hale *architect, planner, arbitrator*
†Israel, Franklin David *architect*
†Jacob, Paul F., III *architectural firm executive*
†Johnson, Scott *architect*
†Kaliski, John *architectural firm executive*
Kline, Lee B. *architect*
Li, Gerald *architect, film producer*
Martin, Albert Carey *architect*
Mc Carty, Paul James, Jr. *architect*
Moe, Stanley Allen *architect, consultant*
Nelson, Mark Bruce *interior designer*
†Neutra, Dion *architect*
†Phelps, Barton Chase *architect, educator*
†Refuerzo, Ben J. *architectural educator, architectural firm executive*
†Tanzmann, Virginia Ward *architect*
†Terrell, Joseph Alcasar *interior designer*
Thoman, John Everett *architect, mediator*
†Thomas, Julia Dessery *space designer*
Verger, Morris David *architect, planner*
†Wheel, Lesley *design firm executive*

Manhattan Beach
†Blanton, John Arthur *architect*

Marina Del Rey
†Tanaka, Ted Tokio *architect, educator*

Marshall
Evans, Robert James *architect*

Menlo Park
Sidells, Arthur F. *architect*

Mill Valley
D'Amico, Michael *architect, urban planner*
†Pflueger, John Milton *architect*

Mojave
Rutan, Elbert L. (Burt Rutan) *aircraft designer*

Monterey
Shaw, William Vaughan *architect*

Mount Shasta
Anderson, Lee Roger *landscape architect, solar, environmental, recreation and site planner*

Mountain View
Kobza, Dennis Jerome *architect*

Newport Beach
†Bauer, Jay S. *architect*
Bissell, George Arthur *architect*
Dougherty, Betsey Olenick *architect*
†Morgridge, Howard Henry *architect*
Richardson, Walter John *architect*
†Strock, Arthur Van Zandt *architect*
Wimberly, George James *architect*

Oakland
Brocchini, Ronald Gene *architect*
†Dommer, Donald Duane *architect*
Matsumoto, George *architect*
†Nicol, Robert Duncan *architect*

Orinda
Odermatt, Robert Allen *architect*

Oxnard
O'Connell, Hugh Mellen, Jr. *architect, retired*

Palm Springs
Frey, Albert *architect*

Palo Alto
Jones, Robert Trent, Jr. *golf course architect*
†Knott, Donald Joseph *golf course architect*
†Linn, Gary Dean *golf course architect*

Pasadena
†Heaton, Culver *architect*
Thomas, Joseph Fleshman *architect*

Pleasant Hill
Hassid, Sami *architect, educator*

Pleasanton
†Dunbar, Frank Rollin *landscape architect*
Fehlberg, Robert Erick *architect*

Pomona
Lyle, John Tillman *landscape architecture educator*

Rancho Cucamonga
†Christopher, Gaylaird Wiley *architect*

Rancho Mirage
Chambers, Milton Warren *architect*

Rancho Palos Verdes
Lunden, Samuel Eugene *architect*

Redding
Buffum, Nancy Kay *interior designer*

Redondo Beach
Shellhorn, Ruth Patricia *landscape architect*

Sacramento
Cox, Whitson William *architect*
Lionakis, George *architect*
Nacht, Daniel Joseph *architect*
Wasserman, Barry L(ee) *architect*

San Diego
Blumenfeld, Alfred Morton *industrial design consultant, educator*
Delawie, Homer Torrence *architect*
†Donaldson, Milford Wayne *architect, educator*

Harmon, Harry William *architect, former university administrator*
Henderson, John Drews *architect*
†Holl, Walter John *architect, interior designer*
Hope, Frank Lewis, Jr. *retired architect*
†Livingston, Stanley C. *architect*
Paderewski, Clarence Joseph *architect*
†Rosen, Manuel Morrison *architect, educator*
†Stepner, Michael Jay *architect*
Wilson, Richard Allan *landscape architect*

San Francisco
†Armsby, Robert *architect*
Bull, Henrik Helkand *architect*
†Del Campo, Martin Bernardelli *architect*
Dodge, Peter Hampton *architect*
Emmons, Donn *architect*
Esherick, Joseph *architect, educator*
Field, John Louis *architect*
Hardison, Donald Leigh *architect*
†Helmich, Pamela Pence *architect*
†Homsey, George W. *architectural firm executive*
†Hooper, Roger Fellowes *architect*
†House, Steven Lindsay *architect, graphic designer*
†Judd, Bruce Diven *architect*
Kriken, John Lund *architect*
MacDonald, Donald William *architect*
†MacLeamy, Patrick *architectural firm executive*
Marquis, Robert B. *architect*
†Mc Laughlin, Herbert E. *architect*
†Moris, Lamberto Giuliano *architect*
Painter, Michael Robert *landscape architect, urban designer*
†Raeber, John Arthur *architect, construction specifier consultant*
†Ream, James Terrill *architect, sculptor*
Rockrise, George Thomas *architect*
Rockwell, Burton Lowe *architect*
Simon, Cathy Jensen *architect*
Sowder, Robert Robertson *architect*
†Taggart, Paulett Long *architect, educator*
†Thistlethwaite, David Richard *architect*
Turnbull, William, Jr. *architect*
Valentine, William Edson *architect*
Volkmann, Daniel George, Jr. *architect*

San Jose
†Tanaka, Richard Koichi, Jr. *architect, planner*

San Luis Obispo
Deasy, Cornelius Michael *architect*
†Fraser, Bruce Douglas, Jr. *architect, artist*
Rodman, Harry Eugene *architect, educator, acoustical and illumination consultant*

San Rafael
Elliott, Edward Procter *architect*
Engstrom, Eric Gustaf *interior and graphic designer, artist*
†Thompson, Peter L. H. *landscape architect, architectural firm executive*

Santa Barbara
Frizzell, William Kenneth *architect*
Kruger, Kenneth Charles *retired architect*
Powell, Herbert J. *architect*

Santa Clara
†Kwock, Royal *architect*

Santa Cruz
†Oberdorfer, Jeff *architect, firm executive*

Santa Monica
†Eizenberg, Julie *architect*
Gehry, Frank Owen *architect*
†Koning, Hendrik *architect*
Mayne, Thom *architect*
Miller, Leroy Benjamin *architect*
Naidorf, Louis Murray *architect*
†Van Tilburg, Johannes *architectural firm executive*
Wou, Leo S. *architect, planner*

Santa Rosa
†Fream, Ronald Warren *golf course architect*
†Knight, William Hutton *architectural firm executive*
Roland, Craig Williamson *architect*

Sausalito
Leefe, James Morrison *architect*
†Werner, William Arno *architect*

Seal Beach
Rossi, Mario Alexander *architect*

Sonoma
Allen, Rex Whitaker *architect*
Lackey, Lawrence Bailis, Jr. *retired architect, urban designer*
Woodbridge, John Marshall *architect, urban planner*

South Pasadena
Girvigian, Raymond *architect*

Sunset Beach
Faulkner, Adele Lloyd *interior designer, color consultant*

Tarzana
Smith, Mark Lee *architect*

Venice
†Ehrlich, Steven David *architect*

Walnut Creek
Caddy, Edmund Harrington Homer, Jr. *architect*

West Hollywood
Luckman, Charles *architect*

COLORADO

Aspen
Caudill, Samuel Jefferson *architect*
†Ensign, Donald H. *landscape architect*
†Gustafson, James Arthur *architect*

Boulder
Carlson, Devon McElvin *architect, educator*

†Vander Vorste, James LeRoy *architect*

Colorado Springs
Kelsey, Floyd Lamar, Jr. *architect*
Phibbs, Harry Albert *interior designer, professional speaker, lecturer*

Denver
†Abo, Ronald Kent *architect*
Anderson, John David *architect*
†Berg, Karl *architectural firm executive*
Brownson, Jacques Calmon *architect*
Cowley, Gerald Dean *architect*
†Decker, David B. *architect, educator*
†Dominick, Peter Hoyt, Jr. *architect*
Fuller, Kenneth Roller *architect*
Havekost, Daniel John *architect*
Hoover, George Schweke *architect*
Hornbein, Victor *architect*
†Larson, Dayl Andrew *architect*
†Mason, Ronald Leonard *architect*
Prosser, John Martin *architect, educator, urban design consultant*
Steenhagen, Robert Lewis *landscape architect, consultant*
Wirkler, Norman Edward *architectural, engineering, construction management firm executive*
†Zeigel, Henry Alan *architect*

Evergreen
†Gerou, Phillip Howard *architect*

Fort Collins
Ellis, Spencer Percy *landscape architect*

Greenwood Village
†Eccles, Matthew Alan *golf course designer, landscape architect*

Lakewood
†Franta, Gregory Esser *architect, energy consultant*

Vail
†Hopkins, Pamela Withers *architect*

CONNECTICUT

Avon
†Johnson, Dean Adams *landscape architect*

Branford
Blake, Peter Jost *architect*

Cheshire
Rowland, Ralph Thomas *architect*

Darien
Spilman, Raymond *industrial designer*

Essex
Grover, William Herbert *architect*
Harper, Robert Leslie *architect, educator*
Simon, Mark *architect*

Greenwich
Barnum, William Milo *architect*
de Mar, Leoda Miller *fabric and wallcovering designer*
Mock, Robert Claude *architect*

Hamden
Cherry, Edward Earl *architect*
Roche, (Eamonn) Kevin *architect*

Kent
Kilham, Walter H., Jr. *architect*

Morris
Sherwood, Thorne *architect*

New Canaan
Bergmann, Richard Ronald *architect, photographer*
Risom, Jens *furniture designer, manufacturing executive*

New Haven
†Clarke, Fred W. *architectural firm executive*
†Cosham, Don *architect*
†Newick, Craig David *architect*
†Newman, Herbert S. *architect, educator*
Pelli, Cesar *architect*
Platner, Warren *architect*
Rolland, Peter George *landscape architect*
Roth, Harold *architect*
†Woerner, Peter Kurt *architect, builder*

North Branford
Gregan, Edmund Robert *landscape architect*

North Haven
†Hoffmann, John J. *architect*

Norwalk
Irving, Michael Henry *architect*

Norwich
Sharpe, Richard Samuel *architectural company executive*

Old Greenwich
Rossman, Janet Kay *architectural interior designer*

Orange
Miller, Henry Forster *architect*

Ridgefield
Bye, Arthur Edwin, Jr. *landscape architect*

Southport
†Parker, David Scott *architect*

Stamford
Cavallon, Betty Gabler *interior designer*

Waterbury
Cohen, Andrew Stuart *architect, landscape architect*

Westport
†Brown, Mona *architect*
†Ferris, Roger Patrick *architect*

DELAWARE

Wilmington
Dayton, Richard Lee *architect*

DISTRICT OF COLUMBIA

Washington
†Baranes, Shalom *architectural firm executive*
†Barr-Kumar, Raj *architect*
†Bowie, Calvert S. *architect*
†Britt, Stanford R. *architect*
Brodie, M. J. (Jay Brodie) *architect, city planner*
†Bryant, Robert Edward *architect*
Coffin, Laurence Edmondston, Jr. *landscape architect, urban planner*
Cox, Warren Jacob *architect*
†Cragg, Nelson Randolph, Jr. *architect*
Cude, Reginald Hodgin *architect*
†Czinkota, Ilona Vigh *architect*
Daileda, David Allen *architect*
†Deupi, Carlos *architect*
Ensign, William Lloyd *architect*
Florance, Colden l'Hommedieu Ruggles *architect*
Fry, Louis Edwin, Jr. *architect*
†Giegengack, Richard A. *architect*
†Glass, Elliott Michael *architect*
†Gordon, Harry T. *architectural firm executive*
Hartman, George Eitel *architect*
†Hellmuth, George William *architect*
Jacobsen, Hugh Newell *architect*
†Keune, Russell Victor *architect, architectural association executive*
Keyes, Arthur Hawkins, Jr. *architect*
MacDonald, William Lloyd *architectural historian*
†McDuffie, Harvey Thomas, Jr. *architect*
Mc Gaughan, Alexander Stanley *architect*
Miller, Iris Ann *landscape architectural consultant, educator*
Moore, Arthur Cotton *architect*
†Murray, Christopher Charles, III *architect*
†Oehme, Wolfgang Walter *landscape architect*
Oehrlein, Mary Lou *architect*
†Ramberg, Walter Dodd *architect*
†Reid, Joseph Browning *architect*
Schlesinger, B. Frank *architect, educator*
Siegel, Lloyd H. *architect, real estate developer, consultant*
Spreiregen, Paul David *architect, planner, author*
Vosbeck, Robert Randall *architect*
White, George Malcolm *architect*
Wright, Thomas William Dunstan *architect*
Yerkes, David Norton *architect*

FLORIDA

Anna Maria
Aubry, Eugene Edwards *architect*

Boca Raton
McLeod, John Wishart *architect*
Turano, Emanuel Nicolas *architect*

Bonita Springs
†Trudnak, Stephen Joseph *landscape architect*

Boynton Beach
Stubbins, Hugh A(sher), Jr. *architect*

Bradenton
Keane, Gustave Robert *architect, consultant*

Clearwater
Bertram, Frederic Amos *architect*

Coral Gables
†Spear, Laurinda Hope *architect*
Warburton, Ralph Joseph *architect, engineer, planner, educator*

Daytona Beach
†Amick, William Walker *golf course architect*

Deland
MacMahon, Charles Hutchins, Jr. *architect*

Delray Beach
Rippeteau, Darrel Downing *architect*

Fernandina Beach
†Burns, Stephen Redding *golf course architect*

Fort Lauderdale
†Dickinson, Richard *landscape architect*
Singer, Donald Ivan *architect*
Stone, Edward Durell, Jr. *landscape architect*

Gainesville
Schueller, Wolfgang Augustus *architectural educator, writer*

Hobe Sound
Graham, Bruce John *architect*

Hollywood
Harringer, Olaf Carl *architect, museum consultant*

Jacksonville
†Barley, John McKim, II *architect*
†Broward, Robert C. *architect*
†Jenkins, Leerie Thurman, Jr. *architecture engineering planning firm executive*
†Morgan, William N. *architect, educator*
Pappas, Ted Phillip *architect*
Rumpel, Peter Loyd *architect, educator, artist*
Smith, Ivan Huron *architect*
†Walker, Robert Charles *golf course architect*

Jupiter
†Fazio, Tom *golf course designer and architect, architectural firm executive*

Lakeland
Peterson, N. Curtis, Jr. *landscape architect, former state senator*

Maitland
Braun, Charles Stuart *architect*

Marco
Thorson, Oswald Hagen *architect*

Melbourne
†Ehrig, John Paul *architect*

Miami
Arango, Jorge Sanin *architect*
†Atlas, Randall I. *architect, criminologist*
Feito, Jose *architect*
†Fort-Brescia, Bernardo *architect*
Graboski, Thomas Walter *designer, artist*
Hampton, Mark Garrison *architect*
Knight, Charles Frasuer *architect*
Lapidus, Morris *retired architect, interior designer*
Nicholson, William Mac *naval architect, marine engineer, consultant*
Parker, Alfred Browning *architect*
†Plater-Zyberk, Elizabeth Maria *architectural educator*
Reed, George Francis *architect*
Telesca, Francis Eugene *architect*
†Weller, John Albert, Jr. *landscape architect*

Mount Dora
Hoag, Arthur Howard, Jr. *retired architect*

Naples
†Lewis, Gordon Gilmer *golf course architect*

Orlando
Arnett, Warren Grant *interior designer*

Palm Beach
Wheelock, Morgan Dix, Jr. *landscape architect*
Wirtz, Willem Kindler *garden and lighting designer, public relations consultant*

Palm Beach Gardens
Christian, Robert Henry *architect*

Pensacola
Bullock, Ellis Way, Jr. *architect*
†Woolf, Kenneth Howard *architect*

Ponce Inlet
†Connor, Edward Hollis, III *golf course architect*

Port Saint Lucie
Clark, Harold Steve *architect*

Saint Petersburg
Ginn, Ronn *architect, urban planner, general contractor*
Wedding, Charles Randolph *architect*

Sarasota
Abbott, J. Carl *architect, planner, inventor, educator*
†Smith, Mark Hallard *architect*

Stuart
†Ankrom, Charles Franklin *golf course architect, consultant*
Jefferson, Peter Augustus *architect*

Tampa
†Abell, Jan Mary *architect*
Holmes, Dwight Ellis *architect*
Howey, John Richard *architect*
Jennewein, James Joseph *architect*
Walker, H(erbert) Leslie, Jr. *architect*

Venice
Appel, Wallace Henry *retired industrial designer*

Winter Haven
Burns, Arthur Lee *architect*

GEORGIA

Athens
Morrison, Darrel Gene *landscape architecture educator*
Stovall, Allen D. *landscape architect, educator*

Atlanta
Alexander, Cecil Abraham *retired architect, consultant, educational director*
†Amisano, Joseph *architect*
Bainbridge, Frederick Freeman, III *architect*
†Balke, Robert Roy *architect*
†Bradfield, Richard H. *architectural firm executive*
Cooper, Jerome Maurice *architect*
†Daniels, Stanley L. *architect*
†Diedrich, Richard Joseph *architect*
†Elam, Merrill L. *architectural firm executive*
†Farrington, Frank *architect*
Fash, William Leonard *retired architecture educator, college dean*
†Guest, Rita Carson *interior designer*
†Hoover, Ray C., III *architect*
†Hughes, Rufus R., II *architectural firm executive, architectural educator*
Jova, Henri Vatable *architect*
Lewcock, Ronald Bentley *architect, educator*
Mc Intosh, James Eugene, Jr. *interior designer*
†Miller, Robert James *architect, educator*
Moulthrop, Edward Allen *architect, artist*
Portman, John C., Jr. *architect, developer*
Pulgram, William Leopold *architect, space designer*
†Rauh, Richard Paul *architect*
Smith, Joseph Newton, III *retired architect, educator*
†Surber, Eugene Lynn *architect*
†Ventulett, Thomas Walker, III *architect*
†Williams, Thomas Franklin *architect*

Augusta
†Woodhurst, Robert Stanford, Jr. *architect*

Cohutta
†Little, Thomas Michael *architect*

Fayetteville
Harris, Dorothy Clark *interior architect, designer, design instructor*

Macon
Dunwody, Eugene Cox *architect*

Norcross
Crymes, Ronald Jack *draftsman,structural steel detailer*

Rome
Janowski, Thaddeus Marian *architect*

Roswell
†DeVictor, D. J. *landscape architect*

HAWAII

Honolulu
†Ayer, David Clay *architect*
Botsai, Elmer Eugene *architect, educator, former university dean*
Cain, Raymond Frederick *landscape architect, planning company executive*
†Cruthers, Evan Douglas *architect*
†Hale, Nathan Robert *architect*
†Hamada, Duane Takumi *architect*
Hara, Ernest Hideo *architect*
Hong, Norman G. Y. *architect*
†Lau, Charles Kwok-Chiu *architect, architectural firm executive*
†Onishi, Patrick Tomeo *architect*
Sutton, Charles Richard *architect, designer*
Toyomura, Dennis Takeshi *architect*
Yeh, Raymond Wei-Hwa *architect, educator*

Kahului
Riecke, Hans Heinrich *architect*

Kaneohe
†Fisette, Scott Michael *golf course designer*

IDAHO

Boise
Cline, Glen Edwin *architect, planner*
†Hunsucker, (Carl) Wayne *architectural firm executive, educator*

Sun Valley
†Bryant, Woodrow Wesley *architect*
†McMillen, Darryl Charles *architect*

ILLINOIS

Champaign
Baker, Jack Sherman *architect, designer, educator*
Replinger, John Gordon *architect*

Chicago
Allan, Stanley Nance *architect*
Amstadter, Laurence *retired architect*
†Balasi, Mark Geoffrey *architect*
†Barney, Carol Ross *architect*
Beeby, Thomas H. *architect*
†Bellas, Jean *architect*
†Belluschi, Anthony C. *architect*
Blutter, Joan Wernick *interior designer*
†Bowman, John *architectural firm executive*
Brubaker, Charles William *architect*
Buenz, John Buechler *architect*
Butler, Richard Dean *interior designer*
Campbell, Wendell Jerome *architect*
Conte, Richard Nicholas *architect*
Cook, Richard Borreson *architect*
†Cooke, Robert Phillip *architect*
Curatolo, Alphonse Frank *architect*
Dubin, Arthur Detmers *architect*
Dubin, Martin David *architect*
Eyerman, Thomas Jude *architect*
Gordon, Ezra *architect, educator*
Grunsfeld, Ernest Alton, III *architect*
Hackl, Donald John *architect*
†Haymes, David Allen *architect*
Holabird, John Augur, Jr. *retired architect*
Jahn, Helmut *architect*
Keck, William *architect*
Kerbis, Gertrude Lempp *architect*
Kiel, William Frederick *architectural specifications consultant*
Kurtich, John William *architect, film-maker, educator*
Legge Kemp, Diane *architect, landscape architect*
Lohan, Dirk *architect*
Macsai, John *architect*
Manny, Carter Hugh, Jr. *architect, foundation administrator*
Matthei, Edward Hodge *architect*
†McCullagh, Grant Gibson *architect*
McCurry, Margaret Irene *architect, educator*
Moses, Irving Byron *architect*
Moutoussamy, John Warren *architect*
†Pappageorge, George C. *architect*
†Phillips, Frederick Falley *architect*
Quebe, Jerry Lee *architect*
Schirn, Janet Sugerman *interior designer*
Schlossman, John Isaac *architect*
Schroeder, Douglas Fredrick *architect*
Smith, Adrian Devaun *architect*
Sobel, Walter Howard *architect*
Terp, Dana George *architect*
Tigerman, Stanley *architect, educator*
Tobin, Calvin Jay *architect*
Torgersen, Torwald Harold *architect, designer*
†Valerio, Joseph M. *architectural firm executive, educator*
†VanderBeke, Patricia K. *architect*
Vinci, John Nicholas *architect, educator*
†Vrechek, George G. *architectural firm executive*
†Weber, Hanno *architect*
Weese, Benjamin Horace *architect*
Weese, Cynthia Rogers *architect, educator*
Wildermuth, Gordon Lee *architect*
Wilkes, Delano Angus *architect*

Deerfield
†O'Donnell, Lawrence James *architect*

Pigozzi, Raymond Anthony *architect*

Downers Grove
Kirkegaard, R. Lawrence *architectural acoustician*
†Ryan, John Michael *landscape architect*

Evanston
Bowman, Monroe Bengt *architect*
Friedman, Hans Adolf *architect*
Salzman, Arthur George *architect*
†Zolomij, Robert William *landscape architect, consultant*

Geneva
Conterato, Bruno Paul *architect*

Glenview
†Bradtke, Philip Joseph *architect*
Taylor, D(arl) Coder *architect*

Hinsdale
Anderson, Harry Frederick, Jr. *architect*
†Mikos, David Edward *architect*

Lake Forest
Bennett, Edward Herbert, Jr. *architect*

Libertyville
Krolopp, Rudolph William *industrial designer, consultant*
Thominet, Maurice J. *architect*

Northfield
Glass, Henry Peter *industrial designer, interior architect, educator*
Otis, James, Jr. *architect*

Oak Park
†Bell, Robert Alan *architect*
Worley, Marvin George, Jr. *architect*

Peoria
†Crawford, John Wickham *architect*
Hackler, John Byron, III *architect*
†Kenyon, Leslie Harrison *architect*

Riverside
†Potokar, Richard Albert *architect*

Rockford
†Bradley, Charles MacArthur *architect*

Schaumburg
†Walker, Robert Giles, Jr. *architect*

Skokie
Siegal, Burton Lee *product designer, consultant, inventor*

Springfield
Gucker, Jane Gleason *architect*

Urbana
†Poss, Jeffrey Scott *architect, educator*
Riley, Robert Bartlett *landscape architect*

Western Springs
Darrell, George Albert *architect*

Winnetka
Piper, Robert Johnston *architect, urban planner*
Weber, John Bertram *architect*

INDIANA

Carmel
Eden, Barbara Janiece *commercial and residential interior designer*
Mc Laughlin, Harry Roll *architect*

Evansville
Dailey, Donald Earl *industrial design consultant*

Fort Wayne
Cole, Kenneth Duane *architect*

Indianapolis
†Alexander, Gary Lee *architect*
†Altemeyer, Donald Blaine *architect*
Bennett, Claire Richardson *landscape architect*
†Browne, William Albert, Jr. *architectural firm executive*
†Sobieray, Richard Joseph *architect*
Woollen, Evans *architectural firm executive*

Michigan City
†Brockway, Lee J. *architect*

Mishawaka
†Ponko, William Reuben *architect*
†Troyer, LeRoy Seth *architect*

Muncie
Sappenfield, Charles Madison *architect, educator*

Rockville
Davis, William Eugene *architect*

South Bend
Horsbrugh, Patrick *architect, educator*

West Lafayette
†Molnar, Donald Joseph *landscape architecture educator*

IOWA

Ames
Kainlauri, Eino Olavi *architect*
Palermo, Gregory Sebastian *architect*

Cedar Rapids
Healey, Edward Hopkins *architect*
†Stone, Herbert Marshall *architect*

Davenport
Burgess, Janet Helen *interior designer*

Des Moines
†Herbert, Charles Emmet *architect*
†Lewis, Calvin Fred *architect, educator*
†Vande Krol, Jerry Lee *architect*

Iowa City
Neumann, Roy Covert *architect*

Waterloo
Broshar, Robert Clare *architect*

KANSAS

Lawrence
Dean, Thomas Scott *architect, educator*
Grabow, Stephen Harris *architecture educator*

Manhattan
Foerster, Bernd *architecture educator*
Kremer, Eugene R. *architecture educator*

Topeka
†Karst, Gary Gene *architect*
Schneider, Raymond Clinton *architect, educator*

Wichita
Ellington, Howard Wesley *architect*

KENTUCKY

Lexington
Girone, Vito Anthony *architect, city planner, educator emeritus, artist*
Romanowitz, Byron Foster *architect, engineer*
Scruggs, John Dudley *landscape architect*
Wallace, Donald Querk *architect, civil engineer*

Louisville
†Smith, Jeffrey Coursen *architect*
Ward, Jasper Dudley, III *architect*

LOUISIANA

Alexandria
Brocato, Joseph Myron *architect*

Baton Rouge
Brockway, William Robert *architect*
Desmond, John Jacob *architect*
Lee, Betty Redding *architect*
Reich, Robert Sigmund *retired landscape architect*
Schwing, Charles E. *architect*
Shih, Jason Cheng *architecture and engineering educator and consultant, university director*
Williamson, William Floyd, Jr. *architect*

Metairie
Colbert, Charles Ralph *architect*

New Orleans
Blitch, James Buchanan *architect*
†Blitch, Ronald Buchanan *architect*
Filson, Ronald Coulter *architect, educator, college dean*
†Frantz, Phares Albert *architect*
Latorre, Robert George *naval architecture and engineering educator*
†McNaughton, Eugene Eean *architect, educator*
Mirzai, Pirooz (Victor Mirzai) *architect, educator, consultant*
†Steinmetz, Deborah Susan *interior designer*
†Steinmetz, Robert Charles *architect*
†Waggonner, Joseph David, III *architect*
Wilson, Samuel, Jr. *architect*

Shreveport
†Elberson, Edwin Wallace *architect*
Haas, Lester Carl *architect*

MAINE

Canaan
†Zikorus, Albert M. *landscape architect*

Castine
Hartmann, William Edward *architect*

New Harbor
Fradley, Frederick Macdonell *architect*

South Harpswell
Barnes, George William *architecture and engineering company executive*

MARYLAND

Annapolis
†Lee, T. Girard *architect*
Wilkes, Joseph Allen *architect*

Baltimore
Adams, Harold Lynn *architect*
Anderson, Gary Dean *architect, educator*
Ayers, Richard Winston *architect*
Bridges, Leon *architect*
†Clark, John Baker, II *architect*
Donkervoet, Richard Cornelius *architect*
Ford, John Gilmore *interior designer*
†Hord, Edward Marshall *architect*
Rogers, Archibald Coleman *architect*
†Snead, James Arrington *architect*
Trostel, Michael Frederick *architect*
†Ziger, Steven G. *architectural firm executive*

Beltsville
†Parker, Stephen L. *architectural firm executive*

Bethesda
Auerbach, Seymour *architect*
Callmer, James Peter *architect*
Dawson, John Frederick *architect*
Hoenack, August Frederick *architect*
Morgan, William Bruce *naval architect*
†Oudens, Gerald Francis *architect, architectural firm executive*
Schwinn, Robert James *architect*
Spurling, Everett Gordon, Jr. *architect, construction specifications consultant*

Bowie
Stone, Edward Harris, II *landscape architect*

Chestertown
†Newlin, Peter Caverly *architect*

Chevy Chase
Faulkner, Winthrop Waldron *architect*
Freeman, Raymond Lee *landscape architect, planning consultant*

College Park
Lewis, Roger Kutnow *architect, educator, author*

Columbia
†Askew, Laurin Barker, Jr. *architect*
Slater, John Blackwell *landscape architect*

North Potomac
†Bavier, Robert Newton, III *architect*
†Passantino, Richard J. *architect*

Olney
Delmar, Eugene Anthony *architect*

Port Republic
Miller, Ewing Harry *architect*

Rockville
Elliott, Benjamin Paul *architect*
Horowitz, Harold *architect*

Salisbury
†Becker, Thomas McKean *architect*

Silver Spring
Senseman, Ronald Sylvester *architect*

Temple Hills
Miller, John Richard *interior designer*

MASSACHUSETTS

Amherst
Cornish, Geoffrey St. John *golf course architect*
Rupp, William John *architect*

Arlington
†Fletcher, Norman Collings *architect*

Belmont
†Frey, John Ward *landscape architect*
Gui, James Edmund *architect*

Boston
†Acton, Lloyd Phelps, Jr. *architect*
†Alexander, James Garth *architect*
†Bargmann, Joel David *architect*
†Bertman, Richard Jay *architect*
†Bourque, Michael H. *interior designer*
†Clancy, John M. *architectural firm executive*
†Davis, Michael Richard *architect*
Dean, Robert Charles *architect*
Elkus, Howard Felix *architect*
Finegold, Maurice Nathan *architect*
Flansburgh, Earl Robert *architect*
Forbes, Peter *architect*
Glassman, Herbert Haskel *architect*
Goody, Joan *architect*
†Graham, Gary L. *architect*
†Heineman, Robert M. *architectural firm executive*
Hsiung, Robert Yuan Chun *architect*
†Koetter, Fred *architectural firm executive, educator, dean*
†Manfredi, David Peter *architect*
†McKinnell, Noel Michael *architect, educator*
†Notter, George Madison, Jr. *architect*
†Payette, Thomas Martin *architect*
†Rawn, William Leete, III *architect*
Shepley, Hugh *architect*
Stull, Donald LeRoy *architect*
Tappé, Albert Anthony *architect*
†Wallace, David Dunsmore *architect*
†Wood, Henry Austin *architect*

Boxboro
Gary, Benjamin Walter, Jr. *landscape architect*

Brookline
Spring, Bernard Polmer *architect*

Cambridge
Anderson, Stanford Owen *architect, architectural historian, educator*
Bluestone, Hugh Lawrence *architect*
Bruck, Ferdinand Frederick *architect*
Bruck, Phoebe Ann Mason *landscape architect*
Burns, Carol J. *architect, educator*
Campbell, Robert *architect, writer*
Daley, Royston Tuttle *architect*
Green, Richard John *architect*
†Hamner, W. Easley *architect*
Harkness, John Cheesman *architect*
Harris, Charles Ward *landscape architect and educator, land development consultant, editor*
†Hass, Michael Shepherdson *architect*
†Johnson, Carol Roxane *landscape architect*
†Kobus, Richard Lawrence *architectural company executive*
†Krieger, Alex *architecture and design educator*
†Kruger, Kenneth *architect*
†Luchetti, Robert James *architect, industrial designer*
Madsen, Peter Eric *architecture and real estate development firms executive*
†Man, Lawrence Kong *architect, entrepreneur*

Maybank, Joseph *architect, architectural resources company executive*
McCue, Gerald Mallon *architect*
†Moneo, José Rafael *architecture educator*
Newman, John Nicholas *naval architect educator*
Notkin, Leonard Sheldon *architect*
Oommen, George *architect*
Payne, Harry Morse, Jr. *architect*
†Pollock, Wilson F. *architectural firm executive*
Porter, William Lyman *architect, educator*
Rosenfeld, Walter David, Jr. *architect, writer*
Rowe, Peter Grimmond *architecture educator, researcher*
Schwartz, Martha *landscape architect, educator, artist*
Sekler, Eduard Franz *architect, educator*
Szabo, Albert *architect, educator*
†Torroella, Mario Jaime *architect, artist*
†Tsoi, Edward Tze Ming *architect, interior designer, urban planner*
Ward, Robertson, Jr. *architect*

Concord
Cutting, Heyward *designer, planner*

East Orleans
MacMillan, Douglas Clark *naval architect*

Essex
McMillen, Louis Albert *architect*

Lexington
Harkness, Sarah Pillsbury *architect*
Pierce, Walter S. *architect*

Lincoln
Merrill, Vincent Nichols *landscape architect*

Marlborough
†Lawrence, Peter Gordon *design management executive*

Medford
Goldstein, Charles Henry *architect, consultant*

Nantucket
Lethbridge, Francis Donald *architect*

Newton
Oles, Paul Stevenson (Steve Oles) *architect, perspectivist, educator*

Newton Center
†Walker, Bradford C. *architect*

Randolph
†Lee, M. David *architect*
Ross, Edward Joseph *architect*

Shirley
Field, Hermann Haviland *architect, educator*

Somerville
†Korobkin, Barry Jay *architect*
Safdie, Moshe *architect*

Topsfield
Peirce, John Wentworth *architect*

Uxbridge
†Silva, Brian Maurice *landscape architect*

Waltham
Feldman, Mark Russel *architect, policy consultant*

Watertown
Crissman, James Hudson *architect*
Dawson, Stuart Owen *landscape architect, urban designer*
†Lampkin, M. Martha *architect, city planner*
†Ward, Alan L. *architectural landscape designer*

Wayland
Huygens, Remmert William *architect*

West Springfield
Engebretson, Douglas Kenneth *architect*

Weston
Sturgis, Robert Shaw *architect*
†Wacker, John Lee *landscape architect*

Winthrop
†Costantino, Frank Mathew *architectural illustrator*

Worcester
Carlson, Suzanne Olive *architect*

MICHIGAN

Ann Arbor
Benford, Harry Bell *naval architect*
Christman, James Edward *landscape architect*
†Cox, John William *architect, educator*
†Fry, Richard E. *architectural firm executive*
†Mc Gibbon, William *landscape architect*
Metcalf, Robert Clarence *architect, educator*
Paulsen, Serenus Glen *architect, educator*
Snyder, Jeanne Anne *interior designer, educator*

Birmingham
Birkerts, Gunnar *architect*
Bublys, Algimantas Vladas *architect*
†Powell, Robert Barrows *architectural firm executive*
Ziegelman, Robert Lee *architect*

Bloomfield Hills
Allen, Maurice Bartelle, Jr. *architect*
Brown, Jack Wyman *architect*

Detroit
Diehl, Gerald George *architect*
†Francis, Edward D. *architect*
Kessler, William Henry *architect*
†Margerum, Roger Williams, Jr. *architect*
†Mikon, Arnold *architect*
†Roehling, Carl *architect*

Youngren, Ralph Park *architect*

Flint
Tomblinson, James Edmond *architect*

Grand Rapids
†Stevenson, William Alexander *architect*
Vrancken, Robert Danloy *facilities management educator*
Wold, Robert Lee *architect, engineer*

Kalamazoo
Carver, Norman Francis, Jr. *architect, photographer*
O'Boyle, Robert L. *landscape architect*

Saline
Frank, Richard Calhoun *architect*

Southfield
†Redstone, Daniel Aaron *architect*
Redstone, Louis Gordon *architect*
Van Dine, Harold Forster, Jr. *architect*

Traverse City
Brown, Paul Bradley *architect*

MINNESOTA

Duluth
†Salmela, David Daniel *architect*
Whiteman, Richard Frank *architect*

Eden Prairie
†Dunwiddie, Foster Wilfred *architect, educator*

Minneapolis
Bentz, Frederick Jacob *architect*
†Carmody, John *architectural educator*
Cavin, William Brooks *architect*
†Clemence, Roger Davidson *landscape architect, educator*
Degenhardt, Robert Allan *architectural and engineering firm executive*
Eyberg, Donald Theodore, Jr. *architect*
Hargens, William Garman *architect*
Jacob, Bernard Michel *architect*
†Mahaffey, Gary John *architect*
Martin, Roger Bond *landscape architect, educator*
Mulfinger, Dale *architect*
†Parker, Leonard Sam *architect, educator*
†Rand, Peter Anders *architect*
†Rapson, Ralph *architect, educator*
†Susanka, Sarah Hills *architect*
†Van Housen, Thomas Corwin, III *architect, designer, builder*

Northfield
Sovik, Edward Anders *architect*

Saint Paul
Close, Elizabeth Scheu *architect*
Close, Winston Arthur *retired architect*
Faricy, Richard Thomas *architect*
Lein, Malcolm Emil *architect*
†Rafferty, Craig Elliot *architect, educator*

Virginia
†Damberg, John Paul *architect*

MISSISSIPPI

Columbus
†Ivy, Robert Adams, Jr. *architect, writer*
†Kaye, Samuel Harvey *architect, educator*

Hattiesburg
Traylor, Joan Sadler *interior design educator*

Jackson
Biggs, Thomas Jones *architect*
Burns, Robert, Jr. *architect, freelance writer, artist*
Harrison, Robert Vernon McElroy *architect*
†Timmer, Wayne F. *architectural firm executive*

Mississippi State
Bishop, Calvin Thomas *landscape architect, educator*
†Man, Cameron Robert James *landscape architect*
Martin, Edward Curtis, Jr. *landscape architect, educator*

Starkville
†Ford, Robert MacDonald, III *architect, educator*

MISSOURI

Ballwin
†Kern, Gary L. *golf course architect*

Clayton
†Christner, Theodore Carroll *architect*
Turner, Terry Madison *architect*

Kansas City
†Abend, Stephen Neil *architect*
Baker, Robert Thomas *interior designer*
Conrad, William Merrill *architect*
Seligson, Theodore H. *architect, interior designer, art consultant*

Saint Louis
Becker, Rex Louis *architect*
†Burkett, Randy James *lighting designer*
Burks, Verner Irwin *architect*
Cameron, Paul Scott *architect*
†Chivetta, Anthony Joseph *architect*
†Cotton, W(illiam) Philip, Jr. *architect*
†Hastings, Bryce *architect*
Hellmuth, George Francis *architect*
Ittner, H. Curtis *architect*
Kultermann, Udo *architectural and art historian*
†Lickhalter, Merlin Eugene *architect*
Lovelace, Eldridge Hirst *retired landscape architect, city planner*
Mertz, Stuart Moulton *landscape architect*

Michaelides, Constantine Evangelos *architect, educator*
†Obata, Gyo *architect*
Pickens, Buford Lindsay *architectural educator, historian*
Teasdale, Thomas Hennings *architect*
Thalden, Barry R. *architect*

Springfield
Liu, Yuan Hsiung *drafting and design educator*
Ownby, Jerry Steve *landscape architect, educator*

Webster Groves
Kramer, Gerhardt Theodore *architect*

MONTANA

Bozeman
DeHaas, John Neff, Jr. *retired architecture educator*
†Mattson, George Arthur *architect*

Great Falls
Davidson, David Scott *architect*
Hoiland, Andrew Calvin *architect*

NEBRASKA

Bellevue
†Hinz, Calvin L. *architectural firm executive*
†Raynor, Dennis L. *architect, firm executive*

Lincoln
Morrow, Andrew Nesbit *interior designer, business owner*
†Stange, James Henry *architect*
Steward, Weldon Cecil *architecture educator, architect, consultant*

Omaha
†Bowen, Gary Roger *architect*
†Polsky, Donald Perry *architect*

NEVADA

Las Vegas
†Marnell, Anthony Austin, II *architect*

Reno
†Casazza, Ralph Anthony *architect*

NEW HAMPSHIRE

Fremont
Richardson, Artemas P(artridge) *landscape architect*

Hanover
Brooks, H. Allen *architectural educator, author, lecturer*
†White, Cleveland Stuart, Jr. *architect*

Holderness
Cutler, Laurence Stephan *architect, urban designer, advertising executive, educator*

Jaffrey
Alderman, Bissell *architect*

Manchester
†Brensinger, Barry L. *architectural firm executive*
†Mires, Dennis Burnard *architect*

Meredith
†Williams, Christopher P. *architect*

Nashua
Carter, John Avery *architect*
†Rudolph, John W. *architectural firm executive*

New London
Phillips, Roscoe Wendell, Jr. *architect*
†Sheerr, Deirdre McCrystal *architectural firm executive*

Portsmouth
Lyman, William W., Jr. *retired architect*
†Somes, James Hamilton, Jr. *architect*
†Warner, James M. *architect*

NEW JERSEY

Camden
Eshbach, William Wallace *architect*

Cherry Hill
†Ignarri, Robert Joseph *architect*
†Radey, Frank Herbert, Jr. *architect*

Clifton
†Rigolo, Arthur Emil *architect*

Florham Park
Bottelli, Richard *architect*

Hackensack
†Schmidt, Ronald Hans *architect*

Hightstown
†O'Connor, Eugene Francis *architect*

Livingston
Oishi, Satoshi *architectural and engineering executive*

Long Valley
†Goldstein, Eliot Warren *architect, planner*

Mahwah
Hollerith, Richard, Jr. *industrial designer, consultant*

Medford
Dunn, Roy J. *landscape architect*

Montclair
†Boyd, Hugh Alan *architect*
†Jones, Rees Lee *golf course architect*

Moorestown
†Hassinger, Herman A. *architect*

Morristown
†Nadaskay, Raymond *architect*

Newark
Greenfield, Sanford Raymond *architect*
†Horii, Howard Nobuo *architect, educator*
Mahler, Harry Bez *architect, planner*

Oradell
†Wells, Peter Raymond *architect*

Paramus
†DiGeronimo, Suzanne Kay *architect*

Piscataway
†Liotta, Raymond C. *landscape architect, golf course design consultant*

Princeton
†Colquhoun, Alan H. *architectural educator*
†Ford, Jeremiah, III *architect*
Graves, Michael *architect, educator*
Hillier, J(ames) Robert *architect*
Holt, Philetus Havens, III *architect*
†Kehrt, Allan W. *architectural firm executive*
Lerner, Ralph *architect, university dean*
†Sussna, Robert Earl *architect*

Somerville
†Shive, Richard Byron *architect*

South Orange
De Varis, Panayotis Eric *architect*

Wayne
Jones, Deborah *architect*

NEW MEXICO

Alameda
Hooker, Van Dorn *architect, artist*

Albuquerque
†Campbell, C. Robert *architect*
Pearl, George Clayton *architect*
†Sabatini, William Q. *architect*

Placitas
Pirkl, James Joseph *industrial designer, educator*

Santa Fe
Conron, John Phelan *architect*
Leon, Bruno *architect, educator*

NEW YORK

Albany
Morgan, George Jefferson *interior designer*

Armonk
Behr, Richard Henry *architect, educator*

Bedford
†Benedek, Armand *landscape architect*
Damora, Robert Matthew *architect*

Berlin
Stephens, Donald Joseph *retired architect*

Binghamton
†Bearsch, Lee Palmer *architect, city planner*

Brooklyn
Delson, Sidney Leon *architect*
†Ireys, Alice Recknagel *landscape architect*
†Weston, I. Donald *architect*

Buffalo
Coles, Robert Traynham *architect*
†Markwart, Paul Martin *architect*

Carmel
Carruth, David Barrow *landscape architect*

Cold Spring
Brill, Ralph David *architect, real estate developer, venture capitalist*
Sherman, Suzette *interior design consultant*

Cranberry Lake
Glavin, James Edward *landscape architect*

East Hampton
Damaz, Paul F. *architect*

Fayetteville
Sears, Bradford George *landscape architect*

Garden City
Accordino, Frank Joseph *architect, car rental company executive*

Greenlawn
Stevens, John Richard *architectural historian*

Greenvale
†Webel, Richard Karl *landscape architect*

Hastings On Hudson
†Weinstein, Edward Michael *architect, consultant*

Ithaca
†Hoffman, Lawrence *architect*

Sims, William Riley, Jr. *design and facility management educator, consultant*

Katonah
Baker, John Milnes *architect*

Locust Valley
Bentel, Frederick Richard *architect, educator*
Bentel, Maria-Luise Ramona Azzarone (Mrs. Frederick R. Bentel) *architect, educator*

Long Island City
†Sadao, Shoji *architect*

Malverne
Engoren, Sampson Seymour *interior designer*

Manhasset
Grossi, Olindo *architect, educator*
Schiller, Arthur A. *architect, educator*

Marcellus
Lafferty, Richard Thomas *architect*

New York
Abramovitz, Max *architect*
†Agha, Mahmoud F. *architectural firm executive*
Aldea, Patricia *architect*
Alpern, Andrew *architect, lawyer*
†Ambasz, Emilio *architect, industrial designer, graphic designer*
Anderson, Ross Sherwood *architect*
Annese, Domenico *landscape architect*
†Arsene, Vladimir *architect*
Baker, James Barnes *architect*
†Baquero, José Maria *architect, artist*
Barnes, Edward Larrabee *architect*
Barnett, Jonathan *architect, city planner*
†Barratt, Michael Scott *architect*
Beckhard, Herbert *architect*
Belle, John Leighton *architect, planner*
†Berg, Wayne *architect, educator*
†Bland, Frederick Aves *architect*
Blinder, Richard Lewis *architect*
Bond, J. Max, Jr. *architect, educational administrator*
Bookhardt, Fred Barringer, Jr. *architect*
Breines, Simon *architect*
Brennan, Henry Higginson *architect*
†Broches, Paul Elias *architect*
†Buatta, Mario *interior designer*
Burgee, John Henry *architect*
Butler, Jonathan Putnam *architect*
†Buttrick, Harold *architect*
Cavaglieri, Giorgio *architect*
Chan, Lo-Yi Cheung Yuen *architect*
Cobb, Henry Nichols *architect*
Colin, Georgia Talmey *interior designer*
†Dattner, Richard *architect, educator*
†David, Theoharis Lambros *architect, educator*
†Davis, Jerry Albert *architect*
†De Santo, Samuel J. *architectural firm executive, educator*
De Vido, Alfredo Eduardo *architect*
Diamond, Freda *designer, home furnishings consultant, lecturer*
Edelman, Harold *architect*
Edelman, Judith Hochberg *architect*
Eisenman, Peter David *architect, educator*
Fitch, James Marston *architectural preservationist, architectural historian, critic*
Fitzsimmons, Sophie Sonia *interior designer*
†Fleischer, Joseph Linden *architect*
†Fox, Robert Frederick, Jr. *architect*
Franzen, Ulrich J. *architect*
Freed, James Ingo *architect*
Friedberg, Marvin Paul *landscape architect*
Gatje, Robert Frederick *architect*
Georgopoulos, Maria *architect*
Ginsberg, David Lawrence *architect*
Glaser, Milton *interior designer*
†Goldberg, Steven M. *architect*
Guise, David Earl *architect, educator*
Gwathmey, Charles *architect*
Halpin, Anna Marie *architect*
Halsband, Frances *architect*
Hardy, Hugh *architect*
†Hariri, Gisue *architect, educator*
Heisel, Ralph Arthur *architect*
†Hinz, Theodore Vincent *architect*
Holl, Steven Myron *architect*
Holub, Martin *architect*
Holzman, Malcolm *architect*
Houston, James Archibald *designer, author, artist*
†Hoyt, Charles King *architect, editor*
Jacobs, Stephen Benjamin *architect, planner, developer*
Johnson, Philip Cortelyou *architect*
†Kingsland, James Arthur *architect*
Kissiloff, William *industrial designer*
Kliment, Robert Michael *architect*
Kliment, Stephen Alexander *architect, editor*
Knowles, Edward F(rank) *architect*
Kohn, A. Eugene *architect*
†Kondylis, Costas Andrew *architect*
†Kuhn, Denis Glen *architectural firm executive*
Ladau, Robert Francis *architect, planner*
Lee, Sarah Tomerlin *design executive*
Lefferts, Gillet, Jr. *architect*
Leigh, Stephen *industrial designer*
Liebman, Theodore *architect*
†Lupo, Frank Michael *architect*
†Macaluso, Michael Joseph, Sr. *architect*
Mack, Daniel Richard *furniture designer*
Masey, Jack *exhibition designer*
†McCarthy, Michael Anthony *architecture executive*
Meier, Richard Alan *architect*
†Melamede, Ada Karmi *architectural firm executive*
†Owen, Sylvia *interior design executive*
†Pasanella, Giovanni *architect, architectural educator*
Pasanella, Marco *furniture designer*
Pei, Ieoh Ming *architect*
†Perkins, Lawrence Bradford, Jr. *architect*
Platt, Charles Adams *architect, planner*
Pokorny, Jan Hird *architect*
†Polshek, James Stewart *architect*
Pomerance, Ralph *retired architect*
Pomeroy, Lee Harris *architect*
Quennell, Nicholas *landscape architect, educator*
Rhodes, James Whitfield *architect*
†Ricci, Kenneth *architect*
Robertson, Jaquelin Taylor *architect, educator*
Robinson, James LeRoy *architect, educator, developer*
Rosenblatt, Arthur Isaac *architect, former museum director*

Rosenblatt, Lester *naval architect*
Rossant, James Stephane *architect*
Roth, Richard, Jr. *architect*
Rutkin, Seymour *architect*
†Saladino, John F. *architect, interior decorator, furniture designer*
†Scutt, Der *architect*
Silver, Paul *architect*
†Slomanson, Lloyd H. *architect, musician*
Smith, G. E. Kidder *architect, author*
†Smith-Miller, Henry Houck *architect*
Smotrich, David Isadore *architect*
Snibbe, Richard W. *architect*
Stein, Carl *architect*
†Stein, Martin Donald *architect*
Stephens, Olin James, II *naval architect, yacht designer*
†Stern, Robert Arthur Morton *architect, educator*
Swanke, Albert Homer *architect*
Tabler, William Benjamin *architect*
Tafel, Edgar *architect*
Todd, David Fenton Michie *architect*
Varney, Carleton Bates, Jr. *interior designer, columnist, educator, author*
Vignelli, Massimo *architecture and design executive*
Voorsanger, Bartholomew *architect*
Walker, Kenneth Henry *architect*
White, Norval Crawford *architect*
†White, Samuel Giltinan *architect*
†Williams, Tod Culpan *architect*

Oakdale
Tompkins, Daniel D. *landscape architect, horticulturist*

Pittsford
†Gates, Martha Meyer *architect*

Rensselaerville
Dudley, George Austin *architect, planning consultant, educator*

Rochester
†Chapin, Louis William, III *architect*
Hai, Carol Sue *interior designer*

Rye
†Anderson, Allan *architectural firm executive*

Schenectady
†Feibes, Werner Louis *architect*

South Nyack
†Degenshein, Jan *architect, planner*

Staten Island
Greene, Bradford Marson *landscape architect*

Syracuse
Lee, Kermit James, Jr. *architect, educator*
Skoler, Louis *architect, educator*

Troy
Haviland, David Sands *architectural educator, researcher, administrator*

Uniondale
†Corva, Angelo Francis *architect*

Wappingers Falls
Johnson, Jeh Vincent *architect*

Watermill
D'Urso, Joseph Paul *designer*

Weedsport
†Cichello, Samuel Joseph *architect*

White Plains
Papp, Laszlo George *architect*
Rose, William Allen, Jr. *architect*

Woodstock
Hoyt, Earl Edward, Jr. *industrial designer*

NORTH CAROLINA

Asheville
King, Joseph Bertram *architect*

Barnardsville
Acito, Daniel Joseph *interior designer*

Chapel Hill
†Dixon, Frederick Dail *architect*
Godschalk, David Robinson *architect, urban development planner, educator*
†Guthridge, Richard Clay *designer*

Charlotte
†Bost, Walter Lee *architect, printing company executive*
†Ferebee, Stephen Scott, Jr. *architect*
†Gunn, Robert T. *architectural firm executive*
†Huberman, Jeffrey Allen *architect*
Shive, Philip Augustus *architect*
†Turner, Thomas Patrick *architect*

High Point
Kleeman, Walter Benton, Jr. *interior and furniture designer, consultant, author*

Lumberton
Lee, Elizabeth Bobbitt *architect*

Pinehurst
†Maples, Dan *golf course designer*

Pisgah Forest
Albyn, Richard Keith *retired architect*

Raleigh
Bell, Richard Chevalier *landscape architect*
†Burns, Norma DeCamp *architect*
Burns, Robert Paschal *architect, educator*
Clarke, Lewis James *landscape architect*
†Flournoy, William Louis, Jr. *landscape architect*

Godwin, James Beckham *retired landscape architect*
Hunter, Edgar Hayes *architect*
Hunter, Margaret King *architect*
Johnson, Marvin Richard Alois *architect*
†Malecha, Marvin John *architect, academic administrator*
Smith, Macon Strother *architect*

Winston Salem
Butner, Fred Washington, Jr. *architect*
†Oppermann, Joseph Kay *architect*
†Walter, Lloyd Guy, Jr. *architect*

OHIO

Akron
Castronovo, Thomas Paul *architect, consultant*

Berea
Pattison, Robert Maynicke *architect*

Chagrin Falls
Cordes, Loverne Christian *interior designer*
Dunning, Ann Marie *architect*

Cincinnati
Alexander, James Marshall, Jr. *architect, retired educator*
†Brown, William J. *architect, consultant*
Glendening, Everett Austin *architect*
†Goetzman, Bruce Edgar *architecture educator*
†Gossman, Craig Eugene *architect*
Luckner, Herman Richard, III *interior designer*
Meisner, Gary Wayne *landscape architect*
Nielsen, George Lee *architect*
Preiser, Wolfgang Friedrich Ernst *architect, educator, consultant, researcher*
Roomann, Hugo *architect*
†Senhauser, John Crater *architect*
†Thrun, Robert Read *architect*

Cleveland
Behnke, William Alfred *landscape architect, planner*
Bowen, Richard Lee *architect*
†Bucchieri, Stephen Joseph *architect*
†Dewald, Ernest Leroy *landscape architect*
†Eberhard, William Thomas *architect*
†Fleischman, Richard *architect*
Gibans, James David *architect*
†Kelly, John Terence *architect*
Little, Robert Andrews *architect, designer, painter*
Madison, Robert Prince *architect*
†Melsop, James William *architect*
Sande, Theodore Anton *architect, educator, foundation executive*
†Zung, Thomas Tse-Kwai *architect*

Columbus
†Böhm, Friedrich (Friedl) K.M. *architectural firm executive*
Carpenter, Jot David *landscape architect, educator*
†Kirk, Ballard Harry Thurston *architect*
Koncelik, Joseph Arthur *industrial design educator*
†Moody, Curtis Jerome *architect*
Tully, Richard Lowden *architect*
Weinhold, Virginia Beamer *interior designer*

Cuyahoga Falls
Haag, Everett Keith *architect*

Dayton
Betz, Eugene William *architect*
Klink, Robert Michael *consulting engineer, management consultant*

Lima
†Bassett, James H. *landscape architect*

North Canton
George, Donald James *architecture educator, administrator*

Oxford
Zwirn, Robert *architect, architecture educator*

Toledo
†Hills, Arthur W. *architectural firm executive*
†Martin, Robert Edward *architect*
†Stark, Charles H., III *architectural firm executive*

Youngstown
†Buchanan, C. Robert *architectural firm executive*
†Mastriana, Robert Alan *architect*

OKLAHOMA

Norman
Henderson, Arnold Glenn *architect, educator*

Oklahoma City
Ball, Rex Martin *architect*
Coover-Clark, Carol *architect*
†Kertok, Michael Bowers *architect, interior designer*
†Schmidt, Fred C. *architect*

Tulsa
Jones, Robert Lawton *architect, planner, educator*
†Knowles, Billy C. *architect*
McCormick, Donald *architect, composer*

OREGON

Ashland
Mularz, Theodore Leonard *architect*

Clackamas
Merrill, William Dean *architect, medical facility planning consultant*

Lake Oswego
Worsley, John Clayton *architect*

Medford
†Skelton, Douglas H. *architect*
†Straus, David A. *architectural firm executive*

Newport
Gordon, Walter *architect*

Otter Rock
Eaton, Leonard Kimball *retired architecture educator*

Portland
†Frasca, Robert John *architect*
Gunsul, Brooks R. W. *architect*
†Hacker, Thomas Owen *architect*
†Kilbourn, Lee Ferris *architect, specifications writer*
Michael, Gary Linn *architect*
Ritz, Richard Ellison *architect, architectural historian, writer*
†Stastny, Donald Joseph *architect*
Wintermute, Marjorie McLean *architect, educator*
Zimmer, Norman Cunningham *architect*

Springfield
Lutes, Donald Henry *architect*

Tualatin
Broome, John William *retired architect*

West Linn
†Treffinger, Karl Edward *architectural firm executive*

PENNSYLVANIA

Altoona
†Suckling, Robert McCleary *architect*

Bala Cynwyd
†Bentivegna, Peter Ignatius *architectural company executive*

Bethlehem
†Spillman, Robert Arnold *architect*

Butler
†Kosar, John E. *architectural firm executive*

Camp Hill
Richey, Robert Lee *architect*
†Spiers, Tomas Hoskins, Jr. *architect*

Elkins Park
†Moore, Peter John *architect*

Erie
†Weber, Herman C., Jr. *architect*

Jenkintown
†Clemmer, Leon *architect, planner*

Lansdale
Callender, John Hancock *architect*

Media
Clauss, Alfred *architect*
Sutton, Jonathan Stone *landscape architect*

Philadelphia
Beckman, Hester Finke *interior designer*
†Bower, John Arnold, Jr. *architect, educator*
Brown, Denise Scott *architect, urban planner*
Dagit, Charles Edward, Jr. *architect, educator*
Eiswerth, Barry Neil *architect, educator*
Hayes, John Freeman *architect*
†Heilman, Wesley Marvin, III *architect*
†Homme, David C. *architect*
Izenour, Steven *architect*
Jordan, Joe J. *architect*
Kise, James Nelson *architect, urban planner*
†Kruhly, James Oleg *architect*
Lawson, John Quinn *architect*
†Leatherbee, William Bell *architect*
Magaziner, Henry Jonas *architect*
Maxman, Susan Abel *architect*
McHarg, Ian Lennox *landscape architect, regional planner, educator*
Mirick, Henry Dustin *architect*
Mitchell, Ehrman Burkman, Jr. *architect*
†Olshin, Samuel E. *architect*
†Pearson, Davis *architect*
Perkins, George Holmes *architectural educator, architect*
Peterson, Charles Emil *architect*
†Prowler, Donald Marc *architect*
Rahenkamp, John Edward *landscape architecture and planning company executive*
Rauch, John Keiser, Jr. *architect*
†Roberts, William Henry *architect*
Rybczynski, Witold Marian *architect, educator, writer*
Rykwert, Joseph *architecture and art history educator*
Santos, Adele Naude *architect, educator*
Saylor, Peter M. *architect*
Swinburne, Herbert Hillhouse *architect*
†Thrower, John E. *architectural firm executive*
Tyng, Anne Griswold *architect*
Venturi, Robert *architect*
Vernon, Shirley Jane *architect, educator*
†Vinh, Binh *architect*
Wallace, David Alexander *architect, educator*

Pittsburgh
†Astorino, Louis Don *architect*
Bohlin, Peter Quarfordt *architect*
†Brenenborg, David C. *architectural firm executive*
†Carter, Donald K. *architectural firm executive*
Damianos, Sylvester *architect, sculptor*
†Gindroz, Raymond L. *architect*
Pekruhn, John Edward *retired architect, educator*
Saalman, Howard *architectural historian, educator*
Simonds, John Ormsbee *landscape architect*
Swain, William Grant *landscape architect*

State College
Haas, John C. *architect*

University Park
Leslie, Donald Wilmot *landscape architecture educator*
Porterfield, Neil Harry *landscape architect, planner*
Wheeler, C. Herbert *architect, consultant, educator*

Wayne
Suer, Marvin David *architect*

West Chester
†Smith, Lee A. *architect*

RHODE ISLAND

Jamestown
Todd, Thomas Abbott *architect, urban designer*

Little Compton
Bullerjahn, Eduard Henri *architect*

Newport
†Burgin, William Lyle *architect*
†Wurman, Richard Saul *architect*

Providence
St. Florian, Friedrich Gartler *architect, educator, university dean*
Wooding, Peter Holden *interior and industrial designer*

SOUTH CAROLINA

Charleston
†Goff, R. Garey *architect*
Lucas, Frank Edward *architect*
†Schmitt, Robert Christian *architect, interior designer*

Clemson
Young, Joseph Laurie *architecture educator*

Columbia
Carlisle, William Aiken *architect*
†Golightly, Donald Edward *architect*
†Hultstrand, Charles John *architect*

Florence
†Ward, Dennis S. *architect*

Greenville
Freeman, William Ernest, Jr. *architect*
†LeBlanc, L(ouis) Christian *architect*
†Neal, James Austin *architect*

Walterboro
Marvin, Robert Earle *landscape architect*

SOUTH DAKOTA

Rapid City
†Jones, David L. *architect*

Sioux Falls
Koch, Ralph Richard *architect*

TENNESSEE

Chattanooga
†Derthick, Alan Wendell *architect*
†Travis, W. Vance, Jr. *architect*

Knoxville
Mc Carty, Bruce *architect*
†McCarty, Douglas Hayes *architect*
†Vinson, William C. *architectural firm executive*

Memphis
†Adsit, Russell Allan *landscape designer*
†Crump, Metcalf *architect*
†Evans, James Mignon *architect*
†Harrover, Roy Perkins *architect*
†Jones, Walk Claridge, III *architect*
†Looney, J. Carson *architectural firm executive*
†Tucker, Jack R., Jr. *architectural firm executive*
Yeates, Zeno Lanier *retired architect*

Nashville
Brush, Clinton E., III *retired architect*
Crabtree, Bruce Isbester, Jr. *architect*
†Gobbell, Ronald Vance *architect*
†Miller, Richard L. *architectural executive*
Swensson, Earl Simcox *architect*

TEXAS

Austin
Alexander, Drury Blakeley *architectural educator*
Barnes, Jay William, Jr. *architect, rancher*
Barr, Howard Raymond *architect*
Black, James Sinclair *architect, educator*
Box, John Harold *architect, educator, academic dean*
†Croslin, Charles Wilburn, Jr. *architect*
George, Walter Eugene, Jr. *architect*
†Kreisle, Matthew F., III *architectural firm executive*
†Landes, Robert Paul *architect*
†Little, Emily Browning *architect*
Newton, Charles Chartier *architect*
†Perry, David Brian *architect*
†Polkinghorn, James B. *architectural firm executive*
Roessner, Roland Gommel *architect, educator*
Southerland, Louis Feno, Jr. *architect*
†Speck, Lawrence W. *architect*

Bellaire
†Carter, Don W. *architect*

Bellville
Bishop, James A. *architect, writer*

Bryan
Kellett, William Hiram, Jr. *retired architect, engineer, educator*

College Station
Boyer, Lester Leroy, Jr. *architecture educator, consultant*
Reed, Raymond Deryl *architect*

†Woodcock, David Geoffrey *architect, educator*

Dallas
Blevins, Gary Lynn *architect, real estate broker, real estate appraiser*
Braden, David Rice *architect*
Byers, Brent Eugene *architect*
†Craycroft, Jack *owner architectural company*
†Fulton, Duncan Thomas, III *architect*
Hamilton, Earle Grady, Jr. *architect*
Kemp, Harris Atteridge *architect*
Kolb, Nathaniel Key, Jr. *architect*
Landry, Jane Lorenz *architect*
Lundy, Victor Alfred *architect, educator*
†McCune, M. Davis *architect*
†Morrison, Lionel B. *architect*
†Price, Don Herbert *architect*
†Roy, Clarence Leslie *landscape architect*
Schwartz, Irving Donn *architect*
†Stacy, Dennis William *architect*
Wall, Sidney Smith Roderick, Jr. *architectural firm executive, architect, consultant*
†Williams, David Kendall *architect*
†Wilson, Trisha *interior architectural designer*

Denton
Miller, Tom Polk *architect*

El Paso
Carroll, Edwin Winford *architect*

Flower Mound
†Morrish, Thomas Jay *golf course architect*

Fort Worth
Geren, Preston Murdoch, Jr. *architect, engineer*
†Gideon, Randall Clifton *architectural firm executive*

Houston
Andrews, Lavone D. *architect*
Bair, Royden Stanley *architect*
Barthelme, Donald *architect*
Bentsen, Kenneth Edward *architect*
Borget, Lloyd George *architect*
†Brents, Daniel R. *architectural firm executive*
Calhoun, Harold *architect*
†Cannady, William Tillman *architect, educator*
†Chase, John Saunders *architect*
†Cutler, John Earl *landscape architect*
Douglas, Frank Fair *architect, graphic designer*
Falick, James *architect*
Garrison, Truitt B. *architect*
Jackson, R. Graham *architect*
King, Jonathan *architectural researcher, educator*
Lawrence, Charles Edmund *architect*
Mc Ginty, John Milton *architect*
McGinty, Milton Bradford *architect, real estate development executive*
Moorhead, Gerald Lee *architect*
Morehead, James Caddall, Jr. *architect, educator*
Morris, Seth Irwin *architect*
†Neuhaus, Julius Victor, III *architect*
†Neuhaus, William Oscar, III *architect*
†Owens, Gary Steven *architect*
†Perkins, Britten Lee *architectural firm executive*
Pierce, George Foster, Jr. *architect*

Irving
†Rees, Frank William, Jr. *architect*

Longview
Crain, Bluford Walter, Jr. *architect*

Lubbock
Frazier, Eugene Richard *designer*

Mcallen
†Ashley, J. Thomas, III *architect*

Montgomery
Tharp, Benjamin Carroll, Jr. *architect*

San Antonio
†Frazer, Robert Lee *landscape architect*
†Haywood, Norcell Dan *architect*
†Perez, Andrew, III *architect*
†Randall, Charles Harry *architect*

Southlake
George, David Webster *architect*

Texarkana
Reinheimer, Robert, Jr. *architect*

Univ Of Texas At Arlington
†Ferrier, Richard Brooks *architecture educator, architect*

UTAH

Salt Lake City
Beall, Burtch W., Jr. *architect*
†Blackner, Boyd Atkins *architect*
†Brems, David Paul *architect*
†Chong, Richard David *architect*
Christopher, James Walker *architect, educator*
†Crane, Steve *architectural firm executive*
†Daniels, George Nelson *architect*
†Stowe, Neal P. *architect*

VERMONT

Charlotte
Kiley, Daniel Urban *landscape architect, planner*

Chester
†Farrar, Aili R. *cartographic draftsperson*

VIRGINIA

Alexandria
†Anderson, Robert Barber *architect*
†Cross, Eason, Jr. *architect*
†Ritter, James William *architect, educator*

Annandale
Ballard, Edward Brooks *landscape architect*

Arlington
Adreon, Harry Barnes *architect*

Blacksburg
Bliznakov, Milka Tcherneva *architect*
Currie, Leonard James *architect, planner, educator*
Rodriguez-Camilloni, Humberto Leonardo *architect, historian, educator*

Charlottesville
Bednar, Michael John *architecture educator*
Bosserman, Joseph Norwood *architecture educator*
†Browne, Henry James *architect*
O'Neal, William B. *retired architectural educator*
†Root, James Benjamin *landscape architect*

Chesterfield
Morris, James Carl *architect*

Fairfax
†Ward, George Truman *architect*

Falls Church
Barkley, Paul Haley, Jr. *architect*
†Keegan, John Eugene *architect*
Mortensen, Robert Henry *landscape architect*

Fredericksburg
Keplinger, Duane *architectural executive*

Mc Lean
†Bass, Roger William *architect*
†Chatelain, Leon, III *architectural firm executive*

Orlean
Kulski, Julian Eugeniusz *architect, planner, educator*

Portsmouth
Brown, James Andrew *naval architect*

Reston
Metcalf, William Henry, Jr. *architect*
†Moore, Daniel L. *architect*
Scheeler, James Arthur *architect*

Richmond
†George, Lester *golf course architectural firm executive*
Higgins, Kenneth Raymond *landscape architect*
Jandl, Henry Anthony *architect, educator*
Joel, William Lee, II *interior and lighting designer*
Rawlings, James Scott *architect*

Vienna
†Kohler, Karl Eugene *architect*

Virginia Beach
†May, David L., Jr. *architectural firm executive*

Williamsburg
Herbert, Albert Edward, Jr. *interior, industrial designer*
Parker, Donald Howard *landscape architect*

Woodbridge
Peck, Dianne Kawecki *architect*

WASHINGTON

Bainbridge Is
Bowden, William Darsie *interior designer*

Bellevue
Roselle, Richard Donaldson *industrial, marine and interior designer*

Deer Harbor
Hoag, Paul Sterling *architect*

Everett
King, Indle Gifford *industrial designer, educator*

Hansville
Griffin, DeWitt James *architect, real estate developer*

Kirkland
†Gregory, Matthew J. *architectural firm executive*

Mount Vernon
†Hall, David Ramsay *architect*
Klein, Henry *architect*

Mukilteo
Jenkins, James Stanley *architect*

Seattle
Bain, William James, Jr. *architect*
Bassetti, Fred Forde *architect*
†Bosworth, Thomas Lawrence *architect, educator*
†Buursma, William F. *architect*
†Bystrom, Arne *architect*
†Cichanski, Gerald *golf course architect*
†Dermanis, Paul Raymond *architect*
Durham, Robert Lewis *architect*
Freed, Aaron David *architect*
†Gordon, Patrick A. *architectural firm executive*
†Grossman, Robert James *architect*
Hastings, L(ois) Jane *architect, educator*
†Hinshaw, Mark Larson *architect, urban planner*
Jacobson, Phillip Lee *architect, educator*
Johnston, Norman John *architecture educator*
Jonassen, James O. *architect*
†Jones, Grant Richard *landscape architect, planner*
†Jones, Johnpaul *architect*
†Kolb, Keith Robert *architect, educator*
Lovett, Wendell Harper *architect*
†Malcolm, Garold Dean *architect*
†Meyer, C. Richard *architect*
†Miles, Don Clifford *architect*
Morse, John Moore *architect, planner*
Olson, James William Park *architect*
Piven, Peter Anthony *architect, management consultant*
Polk, William Merrill *architect*

†Sanders, James J. *architect*
†Sundberg, Richard *architectural firm executive*
†Whalen, Michael P. *architect*

Shelton
Wolbrink, Donald Henry *landscape architect, city planner*

Tacoma
Harris, James Martin *architect*
Liddle, Alan Curtis *architect*

WEST VIRGINIA

Harpers Ferry
Wright, David George *landscape architect*

Morgantown
Collier, Clifford Warthen, Jr. *landscape architect*

Wheeling
Hughes, Mary Elizabeth *interior designer*

WISCONSIN

Eau Claire
†Larson, Brian Foix *architect*

Madison
Felstehausen, Herman Henry *natural resources-land planning educator*
Lawson, David E. *architect*
Niemann, Bernard John, Jr. *land and geographical system educator, researcher, consultant*
Sample, Nathaniel Welshire *architect*
†Tishler, William Henry *landscape architect, educator*

Mequon
†Stevens, Brooks *industrial designer, educator*

Milwaukee
Wenzler, William Paul *architect*

Oshkosh
Reinke, Leonard Herman *architect*

Osseo
Wright, Rodney H. *architect*

Whitewater
Carrara, Arthur Alfonso *architect, designer, painter, graphic designer*

WYOMING

Cody
Hynek, Frederick James *architect*

TERRITORIES OF THE UNITED STATES

PUERTO RICO

San Juan
Marvel, Thomas Stahl *architect*

VIRGIN ISLANDS

Frederiksted
Pierce, Lambert Reid *architect*

CANADA

BRITISH COLUMBIA

Vancouver
Erickson, Arthur Charles *architect*
†Oberlander, Cornelia Hahn *landscape architect*
†Patkau, John *architect*
†Patkau, Patricia *architect, architecture educator*

MANITOBA

Winnipeg
Hodne, Thomas Harold, Jr. *architect, educator*

NEW BRUNSWICK

Moncton
†Albert, Elide *architect*

NOVA SCOTIA

Halifax
Fowler, Charles Allison Eugene *architect, engineer*
†MacKay-Lyons, Brian Gerald *architect, urban designer, architecture educator*

ONTARIO

Don Mills
Budrevics, Alexander *landscape architect*

Toronto
Diamond, Abel Joseph *architect*
Fife, Edward H. *landscape architecture educator*
Grossman, Irving *architect*

†Kuwabara, Bruce Bunji *architect*
†McKenna, Marianne *architect*
Moriyama, Raymond *architect*
†Payne, Thomas Charles *architect*
†Thornley, Shirley Blumberg *architect*
van Ginkel, Blanche Lemco *architect, educator*

QUEBEC

Montreal
Jacobs, Peter Daniel Alexander *architecture and landscape architecture educator*
Marsan, Jean-Claude *architect, urban planner, educator*
Prus, Victor Marius *architect, urbanist*

SASKATCHEWAN

Saskatoon
†Henry, Keith Douglas *architect*

ENGLAND

London
Foster, Sir Norman Robert *architect*
†Self, Larry D. *architectural firm executive*

FRANCE

Joinville
Greer, Joseph Epps *architect*

GERMANY

Ascheberg
Voss, Werner Konrad Karl *architect, engineer*

Cologne
Ungers, Oswald M. *architect, educator*

Küssaberg
Lyndon, Maynard *architect*

ITALY

Rome
Ahrens, William Henry *architect*

JAPAN

Tokyo
Azuma, Takamitsu *architect, educator*
Hashimoto, Kunio *architect, educator*
Isozaki, Arata *architect*
Taguchi, Yoshitaka *architect*

NORWAY

Oslo
Haug, Roar Brandt *architect*

ADDRESS UNPUBLISHED

†Adler, Richard Melvin *architect, planner*
Attoe, Wayne Osborne *architecture educator, author, designer*
†Ballou, James Howland *architect*
Berkovich, Gary A. *architect*
Bini, Dante Natale *architect, industrial designer*
†Browning, James E. *architectural firm executive*
Bunch, Franklin Swope *architect*
Busby, John Arthur, Jr. *architect*
†Campbell, Craig Stewart *landscape architect, town planner*
Carpenter, Derr Alvin *landscape architect*
Carroll, Marshall Elliott *architect*
†Collins, John Francis *landscape architect, educator*
Cranin, Marilyn Sunners *landscape designer*
Crowther, Richard Layton *architect, consultant, researcher, author, lecturer*
Dean, Francis Hill *landscape architect, educator*
Dibner, David Robert *architect*
Diffrient, Niels *industrial designer*
Dobbel, Rodger Francis *interior designer*
Douglass, Harry Robert *architect, health care consultant, educator*
†Dyson, Arthur Thomas *architect, educator*
End, Henry *interior and industrial designer*
Flipse, John Edward *naval architect, mechanical engineer*
†Friedman, Mildred *designer, educator, curator*
Fulton, James Franklin *industrial designer*
Gandy, Charles David *interior designer*
Gantz, Carroll Melvin *industrial design consultant, consumer product designer*
Geddes, Robert *architect, educator*
†Gensler, M. Arthur, Jr. *architect*
†Gerner, Randolph Henry *architect*
Graff, William *architect*
Green, Thomas George *architect*
†Hampton, Mark *interior designer*
†Hixon, Allen Wentworth *landscape architect, land planner*
Kahn, Charles Howard *architect, educator*
†Kerr, Leslie A. *landscape architect*
Kirk, Paul *architect*
Kirts, Wayne Charles *interior designer*
Knoll, Florence Schust *architect, designer*
Kropp, David Arthur *retired landscape architect*
Kump, Ernest Joseph *architect, consultant*
Lacy, Joseph Newton *architect*
Leaman, Jack Ervin *landscape architect, community/ regional planner*
Liskamm, William Hugo *architect, urban planner, educator*
Loss, John C. *architect, retired educator*
†Maltzan, Michael Thomas *architect*
Mc Pheeters, Edwin Keith *architect, educator*

Meier, Henry George *architect*
Meyers, Richard James *landscape architect*
Moore, Richard Alan *landscape architect*
Mumma, Albert Girard, Jr. *architect*
†Murray, David George *architect*
†Peters, Robert Woolsey *architect*
Pettitt, Jay S. *architect, consultant*
Pillorgé, George John *architect, architectural-engineering company executive*
Poor, Janet Meakin *landscape designer*
Rabon, William James, Jr. *architect*
Reeves, Frank Blair *architect, educator*
Rice, Richard Lee *retired architect*
Roegner, George Peter *industrial designer*
†Rogers, Charles Ford, II *architect*
Rogers, Kate Ellen *interior design educator*
†Sacks, Gloria *interior designer*
Schwartzman, Alan *architect*
Shadbolt, Douglas *architecture educator, administrator*
Shank, Wesley Ivan *retired architect, educator*
†Siefer, Stuart B. *architect*
†Stearns, Carl David *architect*
Stockwell, Sherwood Beach *architect*
†Thompson, Charles Kevin *architect, lighting designer*
†Tomasi, Donald Charles *architect*
von Brock, A. Raymond *architect*
White, Robert Frederick *landscape architect*
Wiebenson, Dora Louise *architectural historian, educator, author*
Wilkerson, Charles Edward *architect*
Woerner, Robert Lester *landscape architect*

ARTS: LITERARY. *See also* COMMUNICATIONS MEDIA.

UNITED STATES

ALABAMA

Guntersville
Sparkman, Brandon Buster *educator, writer, consultant*

Monroeville
Kniskern, Maynard *editor, writer*

ALASKA

Fairbanks
Helmericks, Harmon *author, explorer*

ARIZONA

Bisbee
Eastlake, William Derry *author*

Flagstaff
Cline, Platt Herrick *author*

Mesa
Gaylor, Walter *writer, military historian*

Paradise Valley
Carey, Ernestine Gilbreth (Mrs. Charles E. Carey) *writer, lecturer*

Phoenix
Stahl, Richard G. C. *journalist, editor*

Tempe
Raby, William Louis *author*

Tucson
Ingalls, Jeremy *poet, educator*
Kingsolver, Barbara Ellen *writer*
Mockridge, Norton *writer, editor*
Russ, Joanna *writer, English language educator*
Speare, Elizabeth George *writer*
Vicker, Ray *writer*

ARKANSAS

Eureka Springs
Dragonwagon, Crescent *writer*

Fayetteville
Jones, Douglas Clyde *author*
Williams, Miller *poet, translator*

Little Rock
Brown, Dee Alexander *author*

CALIFORNIA

Alamo
Bolles, Richard Nelson *author, clergyman*

Altadena
Burden, Jean (Prussing) *poet, writer, editor*

Arcadia
Sloane, Beverly LeBov *educational writer, consultant*

Berkeley
Bradley, Marion Zimmer *novelist, editor, educator*
Burger, Robert Eugene *author, chess expert*
Callenbach, Ernest *writer, editor*
Clark, Thomas Willard *poet*
Jordan, June M. *poet, English language educator*
Kingston, Maxine Hong *author*
Meltzer, David *author, musician*
Milosz, Czeslaw *poet, author, educator*
Ogg, Wilson Reid *poet, lyricist, curator, publisher, lawyer, educator*
Temko, Allan Bernard *writer*

Beverly Hills
Barker, Clive *author, artist, screenwriter, director*
Bass, Ronald *screenwriter*
†Benedek, Barbara *screenwriter*
†Boam, Jeffrey David *screenwriter*
†Brickman, Paul *film writer, director*
Crichton, (John) Michael *author, film director*
†Crowe, Cameron *screenwriter*
†Curtin, Valerie *screenwriter, actress*
†David, Larry *television scriptwriter*
Essex, Harry J. *screenwriter, novelist*
Eszterhas, Joseph A. *film scriptwriter*
†Frank, Harriet *screenwriter*
Gelbart, Larry *writer, producer*
†Getchell, Robert *screenwriter*
†Goldman, Bo *screenwriter, director*
Goldman, William *writer*
†Koepp, David *screenwriter*
Livingston, Myra Cohn *poet, writer, educator*
Marx, Arthur (Julius) *author, playwright, director*
†Meyer, Nicholas *screenwriter, director*
Meyers, Nancy Jane *screenwriter, producer*
Niven, Laurence Van Cott *author*
†Peters, Charles Victor *screenwriter*
†Pierson, Frank Romer *screenwriter, director*
†Proft, Pat *screenwriter, film producer*
†Ravetch, Irving *screenwriter*
†Rosenthal, Mark David *screenwriter*
Ross, Stanley Ralph *writer, publisher, producer, software manufacturing executive*
†Rudnick, Paul *playwright, screenwriter*
Schulian, John (Nielsen Schulian) *screenwriter, author*
Schulman, Tom *film writer*
†Schumacher, Joel *film writer, director*
†Shanley, John Patrick *screenwriter*
Shepard, Sam (Samuel Shepard Rogers) *playwright, actor*
†Star, Darren *television writer*
†Torokvei, Peter John *writer, director, actor, producer*
Towne, Robert *screenwriter*
Ward, David Schad *screenwriter, film director*
Weller, Michael *playwright, screenwriter*
†Willingham, Calder Baynard, Jr. *novelist, playwright, screenwriter*

Burbank
White, Loray Betty *writer, actress, producer*

Carmel
Aurner, Robert Ray *author, corporate executive*

Chico
Keithley, George *writer*

Claremont
Mezey, Robert *poet, educator*

Concord
Anderberg, Roy Anthony *journalist*
Headding, Lillian Susan (Sally Headding) *writer, forensic clairvoyant*

Cromberg
Kolb, Ken Lloyd *writer*

Cupertino
Zobel, Louise Purwin *author, educator, writing consultant*

Cypress
Edmonds, Ivy Gordon *writer*

Danville
Mc Millan, Terry *writer, educator*

Davis
Beagle, Peter Soyer *writer*
Major, Clarence Lee *novelist, poet, educator*
McPherson, Sandra Jean *poet, educator*

Fair Oaks
Inglis, Andrew Franklin *author, consultant*

Fairfax
Gores, Joseph Nicholas *novelist, scriptwriter*

Fresno
Levine, Philip *poet, educator*

Gardena
Baker, Lillian L. *author, historian, artist, lecturer*

Georgetown
Lengyel, Cornel Adam (Cornel Adam) *author*

Glendora
Phillips, Jill Meta *author, critic, astrologer*

Healdsburg
Erdman, Paul Emil *author*

Kensington
Mc Cann, Cecile Nelken *writer*
Nathan, Leonard Edward *writer, educator*

La Jolla
Antin, David *poet, critic*

Laguna Beach
Taylor, Theodore Langhans *author*

Laguna Hills
Rabe, David William *playwright*

Landers
Landers, Vernette Trosper *writer, educator, association executive*

Los Angeles
†Anderson, Jane A. *scriptwriter*
†Barry, Julian *playwright, screenwriter*
Basil, Douglas Constantine *author, educator*
Blake, Michael *writer*
Bloch, Robert Albert *author*
Bochco, Steven *screenwriter, television producer*
†Brach, Gérard *screenwriter*
Branch, Taylor *writer*
†Briley, John Richard *writer*
Carabillo, Virginia A. (Toni Carabillo) *writer, editor, graphic designer*
Carpenter, John Howard *screenwriter, director*
Cecchetti, Giovanni *poet, Italian language educator, literary critic*
†Chetwynd, Lionel *screenwriter, producer, director*
Cohen, Leonard (Norman Cohen) *poet, novelist, musician, songwriter*
Corwin, Norman *writer, director, producer*
Crow, John Armstrong *writer, educator*
Epstein, Julius J. *screenwriter, playwright, producer*
Flicker, Ted *scriptwriter, director, actor*
Fuller, Samuel *scriptwriter, film director*
Highwater, Jamake *author, lecturer*
†Hudlin, Warrington *writer, producer, director*
Kinosian, Janet Marie *journalist*
Lachman, Morton *writer, theatrical director and producer*
†Launer, Dale Mark *screenwriter*
Lee, Walter William, Jr. *film writer, consultant, publishing executive*
Leonard, Elmore John *novelist, screenwriter*
†Maddock, Brent Ritter *screenwriter*
Mandel, Babaloo *scriptwriter*
†Matheson, Richard Burton *author, scriptwriter*
Mc Kuen, Rod *poet, composer, author*
†McWilliams, Peter *poet*
Miller, Jason *playwright*
Noguchi, Thomas Tsunetomi *author, forensic pathologist*
†Peoples, David Webb *screenwriter*
Puzo, Mario *author*
†Rayfiel, David *screenwriter*
†Richter, W. D. *screenwriter, director, producer*
Robert, Patrick *playwright*
Rubin, Bruce Joel *screenwriter*
Schrader, Paul Joseph *film writer, director*
Shagan, Steve *screenwriter, novelist, film producer*
Shapiro, Mel *playwright, director, drama educator*
Shore, Herbert *playwright, poet, theatre director, educator*
Shusterman, Neal Douglas *author, screenwriter*
Steel, Ronald Lewis *author, historian, educator*
†Tally, Ted *screenwriter*
Thomas, Shirley *author, educator, business executive*
Westheimer, David Kaplan *novelist*
†Wilson, Steven Seth *writer, producer*

Los Gatos
Dowdell, Dorothy Florence *novelist*

Marina Del Rey
†Zaillian, Steven *screenwriter, director*

Mariposa
Shields, Allan Edwin *writer, photographer, retired educator*

Murphys
Scott, Otto *writer*

Newport Beach
Dovring, Karin Elsa Ingeborg *author, playwright, communication analyst*

North Hollywood
Ribman, Ronald Burt *playwright*

Oakland
Foley, Jack (John Wayne Harold Foley) *poet, writer, editor*
Schacht, Henry Mevis *writer, consultant*
Silverberg, Robert *author*

Pacific Grove
Davis, Robert Edward *writer, former communication educator*
Fleischman, Paul *author*

Palo Alto
Berger, Joseph *author, educator, counselor*

Palos Verdes Estates
Bach, Marcus *author, educator*

Petaluma
Pronzini, Bill John (William Pronzini) *author*

Piedmont
Phillips, Betty Lou (Elizabeth Louise Phillips) *author*

Ramona
Cesinger, Joan *author*

Redondo Beach
Battles, Roxy Edith *novelist, consultant, educator*

San Diego
Hart, Anne *author*
Jaffe, Harold *writer, educator*

San Francisco
Adams, Leon David *author*
†Bantock, Nick *writer, illustrator*
Bowers, Edgar *poet, educator*
Ferlinghetti, Lawrence *poet*
Ferris, Russell James, II *freelance ghostwriter*
Gaines, Ernest J. *author*
Ginsberg, Allen *poet, photographer, musician*
Gunn, Thom(son) (William) *poet*
Jundis, Orvy Lagasca *writer, consultant*
Lai, Him Mark *writer*
Leonard, George Jay *author*
Maupin, Armistead Jones, Jr. *writer*
Olsen, Tillie *author*
Patterson, Richard North *writer, lawyer*
Sachs, Marilyn Stickle *author, lecturer, editor*
Saunders, Sally Love *poet, educator*
Whalen, Philip Glenn *poet, novelist*
Wilcox, Collin M. *author*

San Jose
Steele, Shelby *writer, educator*

San Mateo
Korn, Walter *writer*

San Rafael
Turner, William Weyand *author*

Santa Barbara
Bock, Russell Samuel *author*
Corman, Cid (Sidney Corman) *poet, editor*
Cunningham, Julia Woolfolk *author*
Davidson, Eugene Arthur *author*
Easton, Robert (Olney) *author, environmentalist*
Jackson, Beverley Joy Jacobson *columnist, lecturer*
Smith, Michael Townsend *author, stage director*

Santa Monica
Cowan, Andrew Glenn *television writer*
Fleischman, Albert Sidney (Sid Fleischman) *writer*
†Graff, Todd *screenwriter*
Stone, Oliver William *screenwriter, director*

Sherman Oaks
Ellison, Harlan Jay *author, screenwriter*

Sonoma
Kizer, Carolyn Ashley *poet, educator*

Stanford
Conquest, (George) Robert (Acworth) *writer, historian, poet, critic, journalist*
Gardner, John William *writer, educator*
Girard, René Noel *author, educator*
Lindenberger, Herbert Samuel *writer, literature educator*
Stockdale, James Bond *writer, research scholar, retired naval officer*

Studio City
Parish, James Robert *author, cinema historian*
Pournelle, Jerry Eugene *author*
Shavelson, Melville *writer, theatrical producer and director*

Sunnyvale
Yep, Laurence Michael *author*

Venice
Eliot, Alexander *author, critic, historian*

West Hollywood
Black, David *writer, educator, producer*
†Black, Shane *screenwriter*
Dorsey, Helen Danner (Johna Blinn) *writer, author, educator*
Fisher, Terry Louise *television writer*
Grasshoff, Alex *writer, producer, director*
Ludwig, William *screenwriter*

COLORADO

Boulder
Dorn, Edward Merton *poet, educator*
Folsom, Franklin Brewster *author*
Kaye, Evelyn Patricia (Evelyn Patricia Sarson) *author, publisher, travel expert*
Metzger, H(owell) Peter *writer*
Waldman, Anne Lesley *poet, performer, editor, publisher, educational administrator*

Canon City
Bendell, Donald Ray *writer, director, poet*

Colorado Springs
Yaffe, James *author*

Denver
Ducker, Bruce *novelist, lawyer*
MacGregor, George Lescher, Jr. *freelance writer, brokerage house executive*
Mead, Beverly Mirium Anderson *writer, educator*

Estes Park
Hillway, Tyrus *author, educator*

Greeley
†Willis, Connie (Constance E. Willis) *author*

Vail
Knight, Constance Bracken *writer*
Wilson, Brandon Laine *writer, advertising and public relations consultant, explorer*

CONNECTICUT

East Haven
Scarf, Margaret (Maggie Scarf) *author*

Essex
Keppel, John *writer, former diplomat*

Fairfield
Barone, Rose Marie Pace *writer, former educator*
Clark, Eleanor *author*

Greenwich
Ewald, William Bragg, Jr. *author, consultant*

Guilford
Bryan, Courtlandt Dixon Barnes *author*
Peters, William *author, producer, director*

Madison
Carlson, Dale Bick *writer*

Middletown
Horgan, Paul *writer, educator*
Manchester, William *writer*

New Canaan
Packard, Vance Oakley *writer*
Powers, Thomas Moore *author*
Prescott, Peter Sherwin *writer*

New Haven
Gallup, Donald Clifford *bibliographer, educator*
†Howard, Maureen *writer*

New Preston
Randall, Bob *writer*

Old Lyme
St. George, Judith Alexander *author*

Old Saybrook
Hamilton, Donald Bengtsson *author*

Roxbury
Anderson, Robert Woodruff *playwright, novelist, screenwriter*
Gurney, Albert Ramsdell *playwright, novelist, educator*
Miller, Arthur *playwright, author*

Sandy Hook
Kellogg, Steven *author*

Southport
Weller, Tom *author*

Waterford
Commire, Anne *playwright*

West Cornwall
Klaw, Spencer *writer, editor, educator*

Westbrook
Hall, Jane Anna *writer, model*

Weston
Kilty, Jerome Timothy *playwright, stage director, actor*

Westport
Hotchner, Aaron Edward *author*
Martin, Ralph Guy *writer*
Safran, Claire *writer, editor*
Walden, Amelia Elizabeth (Mrs. John William Harmon) *author*

Willimantic
Clements, Bruce *author*

Wilton
Kopit, Arthur *playwright*

DELAWARE

Newark
Merrill, James Mercer *history educator, writer*

DISTRICT OF COLUMBIA

Washington
Abrams, Elliott *writer, foreign affairs consultant and analyst*
Alperovitz, Gar *author*
Arndt, Richard T. *writer, consultant*
Bacon, Donald Conrad *author, editor*
Baldrige, Letitia *writer, management training consultant*
Barnet, Richard Jackson *author, educator*
Burnham, David Bright *writer*
Burnham, Sophy *writer*
Burns, David Mitchell *writer, musician, former diplomat*
Cavnar, Samuel Melmon *author, publisher, activist*
Coffin, Tristram *writer, editor*
Dixon, Jeane *author, lecturer, realtor, columnist*
George, Gerald William *author, administrator*
Haggerty, James Joseph *writer*
Hecht, Anthony Evan *poet*
Kornberg, Warren Stanley *science journalist*
Lilienthal, Alfred M(orton) *author, editor*
MacKaye, William Ross *writer*
May, Stephen *writer, former government official*
McCarthy, Abigail Quigley *writer, columnist, educator*
Miller, Hope Ridings *author*
Naifeh, Steven Woodward *writer*
O'Doherty, Brian *playwright, filmmaker*
Ramsay, William Charles *writer*
Raskin, Marcus Goodman *writer, educator*
Smith, Stuart Seaborne *writer, government official, union official*
Tannen, Deborah Frances *writer, linguist*
Taquey, Charles Henri *writer, consultant*
Viorst, Judith Stahl *author*
Weaver, Warren, Jr. *writer*
Whalen, Richard James *author, consultant*
Wouk, Herman *writer*

FLORIDA

Belleair Beach
Fuentes, Martha Ayers *playwright*

Boca Raton
Herst, Herman, Jr. *writer*
Keyes, Daniel *author*

Boynton Beach
Heckelmann, Charles Newman (Charles Lawton) *author, publishing consultant*

Bradenton
Wendt, Lloyd *writer*

Captiva
Fadiman, Clifton *writer, editor, radio and television entertainer*

Clearwater
Carlson, Natalie Savage *author*
Horton, Donna Alberg *technical writer*

Coral Gables
Latham, Jean Lee *writer*
Minahan, John English *author*

Daytona Beach
Mc Collister, John Charles *writer, clergyman, educator*

Delray Beach
Coyle, William *educator*

Fort Myers
Powell, Richard Pitts *writer*

Gainesville
†Haldeman, Joe William *novelist*
Pierce, Robert Nash *writer*
Smith, Jo Anne *writer, retired educator*

Indialantic
Lewis, Richard Stanley *author, former editor*

Jacksonville
Slaughter, Frank Gill *author, physician*

Miami
Morgan, Marabel *author*
Rockstein, Morris *science writer, editor, consultant*

Naples
Card, Orson Scott (Byron Walley) *writer*
Montgomery, Ruth Shick *author*

Palm Beach
Hall, Kathryn Evangeline *writer, lecturer*

Saint Augustine
Edwards, Page Lawrence, Jr. *author, archivist, historical society administrat*
Oliver, Elizabeth Kimball *writer, historian*

Saint Petersburg
Carlson, Jeannie Ann *writer*
Meinke, Peter *writer, retired educator*

Sarasota
†Hayes, Joseph *author*
Irwin, Theodore *writer*
Weeks, Albert Loren *author, educator, journalist*

Tampa
Battle, Jean Allen *writer, educator*
†Loft, Kurt *science writer, music critic*

Tavernier
Zim, Herbert Spencer *author, educator*

Venice
Shaw, Bryce Robert *author*

Winter Park
Balliett, Gene (Howard Eugene Balliett) *writer, lecturer*

GEORGIA

Atlanta
Horsman, David A. Elliott *author, financial services executive, educator*
Marsh, Carole *author, photographer, publisher*
Slappey, Sterling Greene *writer, journalist, researcher*

Augusta
Taylor, Janelle Diane Williams *writer*

Decatur
†Cassity, (Allen) Turner *poet*

Fayetteville
Burch, Robert Joseph *writer*

Savannah
Hale, Charlotte *author, publishing executive*
Windsor, Patricia Frances (Katonah Summertree) *author, educator, lecturer*

HAWAII

Honolulu
Day, Arthur Grove *author, educator*
Edel, (Joseph) Leon *biographer, educator*
Statler, Oliver Hadley *writer*

ILLINOIS

Alton
Schlafly, Phyllis Stewart *author*

Chicago
Anshaw, Carol *writer*
Bellow, Saul C. *writer*
Brashler, William *author*
Brooks, Gwendolyn *writer, poet*
†Buck, Genevieve Carol *fashion journalist*
Carpenter, Allan *author, editor, publisher*
Colter, Cyrus *novelist, lawyer*
Kotlowitz, Alex *writer, journalist*
Lach, Alma Elizabeth *food and cooking writer, consultant*
Litweiler, John Berkey *writer, editor*
Manelli, Donald Dean *screenwriter, film producer*
Nims, John Frederick *educator*
Stern, Richard Gustave *author, educator*
Terkel, Studs (Louis) (Louis Terkel) *author, interviewer*
Turow, Scott F. *lawyer, author*

Des Plaines
Kudenholdt, Sharon Sue *freelance author*

Elburn
Etter, David Pearson *poet, editor*

Evanston
Gibbons, William Reginald, Jr. *poet, editor*
Mitchell, Kendall *writer, literary critic*
Samuels, Ernest *author, educator*

Lake Forest
Hughes, John W. *film producer, screenwriter, film director*

Oak Park
Bowman, James Henry *writer*

Palatine
Pohl, Frederik *writer*

Park Forest
Putnam, Robert E. *writer, editor*

Urbana
Lieberman, Laurence *poet, educator*

Wilmette
Nash, Jay Robert, III *author, playwright, publisher*

INDIANA

Beverly Shores
Ruzic, Neil Pierce *author, publisher, scientist*

Bloomington
†Komunyakaa, Yusef (James Willie Brown, Jr.) *poet*
Mitchell, Bert Breon *literary translator*

Chesterton
Petrakis, Harry Mark *author*

Frankfort
Borland, Kathryn Kilby *author*

Muncie
Eddy, Darlene Mathis *poet, educator*

Notre Dame
Kerrigan, (Thomas) Anthony *writer, translator*

South Bend
Black, Virginia Morrow *writer*

IOWA

Ames
Smiley, Jane Graves *author, educator*

Iowa City
Justice, Donald Rodney *poet, educator*

KANSAS

Hutchinson
Baumer, Beverly Belle *journalist*

Lawrence
Burroughs, William Seward *writer*

Manhattan
Davis, Kenneth Sidney *writer*

Shawnee Mission
Keach, Margaret Sally *writer, lecturer*

KENTUCKY

Lexington
Davenport, Guy Mattison, Jr. *author, retired educator*

Louisville
Davenport, Gwen (Mrs. John Davenport) *author*

Port Royal
Berry, Wendell *author, English educator*

LOUISIANA

Baton Rouge
Madden, David *author*

Hammond
Kemp, John Randolph *journalist, author*

Lake Charles
Butler, Robert Olen *writer, educator*

New Orleans
Grau, Shirley Ann (Mrs. James Kern Feibleman) *writer*
Pizer, Donald *author, educator*

MAINE

Blue Hill
Kherdian, David *author*
Lowry, James David *author, consultant*

Brooksville
Kleiner, Richard Arthur *writer, editor*

Castine
Booth, Philip *poet, educator*

East Blue Hill
Taylor, Samuel Albert *playwright*

Milbridge
Enslin, Theodore Vernon *poet*

North Brooklin
Yglesias, Helen Bassine *author, educator*

Orono
Wilson, Dorothy Clarke *author*

Phippsburg
Mc Lanathan, Richard (Barton Kennedy) *author, consultant*

Portland
MacKinnon, Bernard Leo *writer*

Rockland
Taylor, Roger Conant *writer*

South Berwick
Carroll, Gladys Hasty *author*

MARYLAND

Baltimore
Barth, John Simmons *writer, educator*
Davis, Curtis Carroll *writer, reviewer, critic*
Epstein, Daniel Mark *poet, dramatist*
Truesdell, Clifford Ambrose, III *author, editor*
Tyler, Anne (Mrs. Taghi M. Modarressi) *author*

Bethesda
Clark, Blake *author, business executive*
Dyer, Frederick Charles *writer, consultant*
Free, Ann Cottrell *writer*
Hartmann, Robert Trowbridge *author, consultant*
Henze, Paul Bernard *author, former government official*
McNamara, Francis John *writer*
Meredith, William (Morris Meredith) *poet, English language educator*
Naylor, Phyllis Reynolds *author*
Vosburgh, Frederick George *writer, editor*

Brookeville
Wilson, Vincent Joseph, Jr. *writer, historian, publisher*

Chevy Chase
Weisman, John *author*

Cockeysville Hunt Valley
Jacobsen, Josephine Winder Boylan *author*

College Park
Whittemore, Edward Reed, II *poet, retired educator*

Edgewater
Holm, Jeanne Marjorie *author, consultant, government official, former air force officer*

Fort Washington
Cameron, Rita Giovannetti *writer, publisher*

Silver Spring
Ball, Anne H. *writer, editor, public relations consultant*
Brooks, Bruce Delos *writer*

Upper Marlboro
Smith, Ralph Lee *author, musician*

MASSACHUSETTS

Amherst
Jenkins, Paul Randall *poet, editor*
Langland, Joseph Thomas *author, emeritus educator*
Tate, James Vincent *poet, English educator*

Bedford
Kennedy, X. J. (Joseph Kennedy) *writer*

Boston
Andre, Rae *writer, organizational behavior educator*
Angelou, Maya *author*
†Appelbaum, Diana Karter *author*
Carroll, James *author*
Childress, Alice *playwright*
Conroy, Pat (Donald Patrick Conroy) *writer*
Davis, William Arthur *writer, editor*
Greenwald, Sheila Ellen *writer, illustrator*
Hailey, Arthur *writer*
Jones, Rodney G. *poet, English educator*
Lowry, Lois (Hammersberg) *author*
McCraw, Thomas Kincaid *author, educator*
Murchie, Guy *author*
Pinsky, Robert Neal *poet, educator*
Pynchon, Thomas *author*
†Say, Allen *children's writer, illustrator*
Shattuck, Roger Whitney *author, educator*
Steig, William *author, artist*
Terrill, Ross Gladwin *author, educator*
Wakefield, Dan *author, screenwriter*
Walcott, Derek Alton *poet, playwright*
Wiesel, Elie *writer, educator*

Brewster
Hay, John *writer*

Byfield
Kozol, Jonathan *author*

Cambridge
Alfred, William *author, educator*
Bernays, Anne Fleischman *writer, educator*
Heaney, Seamus Justin *poet, educator*
Kaplan, Justin *author*
Lamport, Felicia (Mrs. Benjamin Kaplan) *writer*
Rey, Margret Elizabeth *retired writer, prose, juvenile*
Yergin, Daniel Howard *writer, consultant*

Chestnut Hill
Lowell, Juliet *author*

Concord
Edmonds, Walter Dumaux *author*
Moore, Robert Lowell, Jr. (Robin Moore) *author*

Cummington
Wilbur, Richard Purdy *writer, educator*

Dover
Smith, William Henry Preston *writer, editor, former corporate executive*

Edgartown
Treat, Lawrence *author*

Gardner
Wagenknecht, Edward *author*

Great Barrington
Aigner, Lucien L. *writer, photographer*

Hatfield
Yolen, Jane Hyatt *author*

Lanham
Horowitz, David Joel *author*

Lenox
Novak, William Arnold *author, lecturer*

Leominster
Cormier, Robert Edmund *writer*

Lincoln
Donald, David Herbert *author, history educator*

Marblehead
Kemelman, Harry *author*

Needham
Walworth, Arthur *author*

Newton
Heins, Ethel L. *children's literature consultant, critic*
Porter, Jack Nusan *writer, sociologist, historian, Jewish activist*

North Amherst
Andersen, Richard Arnold *author, writing consultant*
Lester, Julius B. *author*

North Egremont
Le Comte, Edward Semple *author, educator*

Northampton
MacLachlan, Patricia *author*

Norton
Norris, Curtis Bird *writer, journalist*

Provincetown
Oliver, Mary *poet*

Rockport
Deedy, John Gerard, Jr. *writer*

Somerville
†Wheeler, Katherine Frazier (Kate Wheeler) *writer*

South Hadley
Brodsky, Joseph (Alexandrovich) *poet, educator*
†Desai, Anita *writer*
Viereck, Peter *poet, historian, educator*

Stockbridge
Gibson, William *author*

Truro
Woolley, Catherine (Jane Thayer) *author*

Waltham
Ellenbogen, George *poet, educator*
Hindus, Milton *writer, literature educator*
Zohn, Harry *author, educator*

Wellesley
Jacobs, Ruth Harriet *poet, playwright, sociologist, gerontologist*

Wellfleet
Piercy, Marge *poet, novelist, essayist*

West Newbury
Coit, Margaret Louise *writer*
Dooley, Ann Elizabeth *freelance writers cooperative executive, editor*

Weston
Press, Aida Kabatznick *writer*
Wind, Herbert Warren *writer*

Westport
Howard, James Merriam, Jr. *education writer*

Yarmouth Port
Gorey, Edward St. John *author, artist*

MICHIGAN

Ann Arbor
Fraser, Russell Alfred *author, educator*

Battle Creek
Cline, Charles William *poet, rhetoric and literature educator*

Detroit
†Albom, Mitch David *sports columnist*
†Desmet, Kathleen Marie (Kate Desmet) *journalist*
Ethridge, James Merritt *writer, former publishing company executive*
Madgett, Naomi Long *educator, editor, poet*
Mandel, Leon, III *author*
McWilliams, Michael G. *writer, television critic*

East Lansing
Wakoski, Diane *poet*

Kalamazoo
Light, Christopher Upjohn *writer, computer musician*

MINNESOTA

Chanhassen
Rose, Elizabeth (Patricia H. Burke) *author, environmental poisoning specialist, satirist*

Duluth
Wood, Douglas *author, composer, musician*

Luverne
Manfred, Frederick Feikema (Feike Feikema) *writer*

Minneapolis
Baker, John Stevenson (Michael Dyregrov) *writer*
Bly, Robert *poet*
Browne, Michael Dennis *poet, educator*
Korotkin, Fred *writer, philatelist*
Teachout, Noreen Ruth *writer*

Saint Paul
Kenyon, Jane Jennifer *poet, writer*

Spring Grove
Hellyer, Clement David *writer*

MISSISSIPPI

Jackson
Welty, Eudora *author*

MISSOURI

Fairfax
Cleveland, Edna Charlotte *writer, typist*

Kansas City
Bombeck, Erma Louise (Mrs. William Bombeck) *author, columnist*
Martin-Bowen, (Carole) Lindsey *freelance writer*

Saint Charles
Castro, Jan Garden *author, arts consultant, educator*

Saint Louis
Broeg, Bob (Robert William Broeg) *writer*
Elkin, Stanley Lawrence *author, literature educator*
Finkel, Donald *poet*
Long, Helen Halter *author, publishing executive, educator*
†McKissack, Patricia Carwell *children's book author*

Viburnum
West, Roberta Bertha *writer*

MONTANA

Livingston
Harrison, James Thomas (Jim Harrison) *author*

Mc Leod
Hjortsberg, William Reinhold *author*
Mc Guane, Thomas Francis, III *author, screenwriter*

NEVADA

Reno
Wheeler, Sessions Samuel *former foundation executive, author*

NEW HAMPSHIRE

Concord
Lederer, Richard Henry *writer, educator, columnist*

Hanover
Eberhart, Richard *poet*

Walpole
Gooding, Judson *writer*

NEW JERSEY

Andover
†Gioseffi, Daniela *poet, author, educator*

Cape May Court House
Cohen, Daniel Edward *writer*
Cohen, Susan Lois *author*
†Kurtz, James Eugene *freelance writer, minister*

East Brunswick
Avallone, Michael Angelo *author*

Englewood
Downes, John *writer, editor*
Gambee, Eleanor Brown *writer, lecturer, civic worker*

Hopewell
Halpern, Daniel *poet, editor, educator*

Jersey City
†Myers, Walter Dean *young adult's book author*

Lawrenceville
Norback, Craig Thomas *author*

Madison
Gibson, William Ford *author*

Montclair
Alexander, Fernande Gardner *writer, photographer*

Morristown
Tesch, Lorraine Barbara *medical technology assessment writer*

Newark
Dickson, Jim *playwright, stage director*
†Hadas, Rachel *poet, educator*
Moskowitz, Sam (Sam Martin) *author, editor, publisher*

Paramus
Fader, Shirley Sloan *writer*

Princeton
Draper, Theodore *author*
Funk, Peter V. K. *writer, scholarly, lexical semanticist*
Morrison, Toni (Chloe Anthony Morrison) *novelist*
Oates, Joyce Carol *author*
Putnam, Peter Brock *author, lecturer*
Ragno, Nancy Nickell *educational writer*
†Rampersad, Arnold *writer, literature educator*
Weiss, Theodore Russell *poet, editor*

Rockaway
Ruch, William Vaughn *author, consultant, educator*

Salem
Foster, Paul *playwright*

Short Hills
Gitner, Deanne *writer*

Somerset
Plenty, Royal Homer *writer*

Somerville
Hyde, Mary Morley Crapo (Viscountess Eccles) *author*
Johnson, Nicholas *writer, lawyer, lecturer*

Stockton
Tunley, Roul *author*

Teaneck
Roth, June Doris Spiewak *author*

West Orange
Rayfield, Gordon Elliott *playwright, political risk consultant*

NEW MEXICO

Albuquerque
Evans, Max Allen *writer, artist*
Whiddon, Carol Price *writer, editor, consultant*

Corrales
Page, Jake (James K. Page, Jr.) *writer, editor*

Las Cruces
Medoff, Mark Howard *playwright, screenwriter, novelist*

Placitas
Dunmire, William Werden *author, photographer*

Portales
Williamson, Jack (John Stewart Williamson) *writer*

Santa Fe
Bergé, Carol *author*
Connell, Evan Shelby, Jr. *author*
Martin, George Raymond Richard *author*
Tarn, Nathaniel *poet, translator, educator*

Taos
Dickey, Robert Preston *author, educator, poet*

NEW YORK

Albany
Kennedy, William Joseph *novelist, educator*

Annandale On Hudson
Kelly, Robert *poet, educator*
†Manea, Norman *writer, educator*

Barrytown
Higgins, Dick (Richard Carter Higgins) *writer, publisher, composer, artist*

Bedford Hills
Ludlum, Robert *author*

Bronx
Greenberg, Blu *author*
Pellowski, Anne Rose *author, consultant, educator, former librarian*

Bronxville
†Doty, Mark *poet*

Brooklyn
Chernow, Ron *writer, columnist*
Kuskin, Karla *writer, illustrator*
Purdy, James *writer*
Swenson, Karen *poet, journalist*

Buffalo
Creeley, Robert White *author, English educator*
Federman, Raymond *novelist, English and comparative literature educator*
Feldman, Irving *poet*

Cambridge
Guma, Greg William *producer, writer*

Chappaqua
George, Jean Craighead *author, illustrator*
Lundberg, Ferdinand Edgar *author*

Circleville
Hazan, Marcella Maddalena *author, educator, consultant*

Cold Spring Harbor
Freeman, Ira Henry *author, journalist*

Croton On Hudson
Henderson, Harry Brinton, Jr. *author, editor*

Dobbs Ferry
Fritz, Jean Guttery *writer*

East Hampton
Ignatow, David *poet*
Jacobs, Helen Hull *writer*

Erieville
Snodgrass, W. D. *writer, educator*

Esopus
Tetlow, Edwin *author*

Flushing
Allen, Ralph Gilmore *dramatist, producer, drama educator*
Goldsmith, Howard *writer, consultant*

Fulton
Long, Robert Emmet *author*

Great Neck
Hurwitz, Johanna (Frank) *author, librarian*
Mc Quade, Walter *author*

Guilderland
†Nordley, Gerald David *writer, investor*
Persico, Joseph Edward *author*

Hamilton
Berlind, Bruce Peter *poet, educator*
Busch, Frederick Matthew *writer, literature educator*

Hempstead
Hijuelos, Oscar *novelist*

Hicksville
Kneitel, Thomas Stephen *writer, consultant, editor*

Hudson Falls
Bronk, William *writer, retail businessman*

Huntington
Bendiner, Robert *writer, editor*

Huntington Station
†Schell, Jonathan Edward *writer*

Interlaken
Bleiler, Everett Franklin *writer, publishing company executive*

Irvington
Massie, Robert Kinloch *author*

Ithaca
Ammons, Archie Randolph *poet, English educator*
Lurie, Alison *author*

Jamaica
Paolucci, Anne Attura *playwright, poet, English and comparative literature educator*

Jamesville
Mazer, Norma Fox *writer*

Johnson City
Aswad, Betsy (Betsy Becker) *writer*
Sargent, Pamela *writer*

Kings Point
Bloom, Murray Teigh *author*

Larchmont
Diforio, Robert G. *literary agent*
Kerr, Jean *writer*

Locust Valley
McGee, Dorothy Horton *writer, historian*

Montauk
Lavenas, Suzanne *editor*

Munnsville
Carruth, Hayden *poet*

New Rochelle
Branch, William Blackwell *playwright, producer*
Saperstein, David Allan *novelist, screenwriter, film director*

New York
Abbott, George *playwright, director, producer*
Adams, Alice *writer*
Adams, Douglas Noel *writer*
Adler, Renata *writer*
†Akins, Ellen *writer*
Albee, Edward Franklin *author, playwright*
Allen, Jay Presson *writer, producer*
Allen, Roberta L. *fiction and nonfiction writer, conceptual artist*
Amory, Cleveland *writer*
Anderson, Poul William *author*
Angell, Roger *writer, magazine editor*
Ashton, Dore *author, educator*
Atlas, James Robert *writer*
Auchincloss, Louis Stanton *writer*
Auel, Jean Marie *author*
Auster, Paul *writer*
Avi, (Avi Wortis) *author*
†Baitz, Jon Robin *playwright*
Balliett, Whitney *writer, critic*
Baraka, Amiri (LeRoi Jones) *author*
Barzun, Jacques *author, literary consultant*
Bauer, Marion Dane *writer*
Beattie, Ann *author*
Beim, Norman *playwright, actor, director*
Bel Geddes, Joan *author*
Benchley, Peter Bradford *author*
Benedikt, Michael *poet, educator, author, editor, free-lance consultant*
†Benjamin, Alan *children's book author and editor*
Benn, T(heodore) Alexander (Alec Benn) *writer*
Bentley, Eric *author, playwright, comparative literature educator*

Berenstain, Janice *author, illustrator*
Berenstain, Stanley *author, illustrator*
Berg, David *author, artist*
Berkow, Ira Harvey *author, journalist*
Bernard, Kenneth (Otis Bernard) *poet, author, playwright*
Berton, Lee *writer*
Birmingham, Stephen *writer*
Blatty, William Peter *writer*
Bliven, Bruce, Jr. *writer*
Block, Lawrence *author*
Blos, Joan W. *author, critic, lecturer*
Blume, Judy Sussman *author*
†Bolt, Thomas *writer, artist*
Bourdon, David *art critic, writer, editor*
Bourjaily, Vance *novelist*
Bradbury, Ray Douglas *author*
Bradford, Barbara Taylor *writer, journalist, novelist*
Bradford, Richard Roark *writer*
Braun, Lilian Jackson *writer*
Brenner, Erma *author*
Breuer, Lee *writer, theatrical director, producer, actor*
Brickman, Marshall *screenwriter, director*
Brodkey, Harold Roy *writer*
†Bujold, Lois McMaster *science fiction writer*
Burland, Brian Berkeley *novelist, poet, artist, scenarist, playwright*
Burnshaw, Stanley *writer*
Calisher, Hortense (Mrs. Curtis Harnack) *author*
Cameron, Eleanor *author*
†Canin, Ethan *writer*
Caputo, Philip Joseph *author, journalist, screenwriter*
Caras, Roger Andrew *author, motion picture company executive, television correspondent, radio commentator*
†Carlson, P(atricia) M(cElroy) *writer*
Caro, Robert Allan *author*
Cartland, Barbara *author*
†Chopra, Deepak *writer*
Clancy, Thomas L. *novelist*
Clark, Matt *science writer*
Clavell, James *author, screenwriter, producer, director, playwright*
Cleary, Beverly Atlee (Mrs. Clarence T. Cleary) *author*
Cohen, Miriam *writer, educator*
Cook, Robin *author*
Cooper, Paulette Marcia *writer*
Coppel, Alfred *author*
Corman, Avery *author*
Corso, Gregory Nunzio *poet*
†Coulter, Catherine *writer*
†Coupland, Douglas C. *writer*
Crews, Harry Eugene *author*
Cryer, Gretchen *playwright, lyricist, actress*
Curry, Jane Louise *writer*
Danto, Arthur Coleman *author, philosophy educator*
†Danziger, Paula *author*
Davis, Lorraine Jensen *writer, editor*
Decter, Midge *writer*
de Hartog, Jan *writer*
DeLillo, Don *author*
Demaris, Ovid (Ovid Desmarais) *author*
Denker, Henry *playwright, author, director*
Deveraux, Jude (Jude Gilliam White) *writer*
Diamant, Anita *literary agent*
Diamonstein-Spielvogel, Barbaralee *writer, television interviewer/ producer*
Didion, Joan *author*
Dillard, Annie *author*
Doctorow, Edgar Lawrence *novelist, English educator*
Doerr, Harriet *writer*
Donaldson, Stephen Reeder *author*
Drury, Allen Stuart *writer*
Dunne, Dominick *writer*
Dunne, John Gregory *author*
Eckert, Allan W. *author*
Ellis, Bret Easton *author*
Ephron, Nora *writer*
Espy, Willard Richardson *author*
†Esquivel, Laura *writer*
Fallaci, Oriana *writer, journalist*
Fast, Howard Melvin *author*
Fast, Julius *author, editor*
Fierstein, Harvey Forbes *playwright, actor*
Flanagan, Thomas James Bonner *writer, fiction, non-fiction*
Flatley, Guy *writer, magazine editor*
Fleming, Alice Carew Mulcahey (Mrs. Thomas J. Fleming) *author*
Fleming, Thomas James *writer*
Fletcher, Colin *author*
Flexner, James Thomas *author*
Foote, Horton *playwright, scriptwriter*
Fornes, Maria Irene *playwright, director*
Fox, Paula (Mrs. Martin Greenberg) *author*
Francis, Dick (Richard Stanley Francis) *novelist*
Frank, Gerold *writer*
French, Marilyn *author, critic*
Friedan, Betty *author, feminist leader*
Friedman, B(ernard) H(arper) *writer*
Friedman, Mickey (Michaele T. Friedman) *novelist*
Fulghum, Robert L. *author, lecturer*
Fuller, Charles *playwright*
Furnas, Joseph Chamberlain *writer*
Gaddis, William *writer*
Gelber, Jack *playwright, director*
Giblin, James Cross *author, editor*
Gill, Brendan *writer*
Gleick, James *writer, software designer*
†Goldman, Francisco *writer*
Goldman, James *playwright, screenwriter, novelist*
Goldsmith, Barbara *author, social historian, journalist*
Goodman, George Jerome Waldo (Adam Smith) *author, television journalist, editor*
Gordimer, Nadine *author*
Gordon, David *playwright, director, choreographer*
Gordon, Mary Catherine *author*
Goulden, Joseph Chesley *author*
†Grant, Cynthia D. *writer*
Green, Adolph *playwright, lyricist*
Green, Gerald *author*
Greene, A(lvin) C(arl) *author*
Grimes, Martha *author*
Grisham, John *writer*
Grumbach, Doris *novelist, editor, critic, educator, bookseller*
Guare, John *playwright*
Guest, Barbara *author, poet*
Guest, Judith Ann *author*
Hall, Susan *author, film producer*
Hamburger, Philip (Paul) *writer*
Hardwick, Elizabeth *author*
Harris, Aurand *playwright*
Harris, Thomas *author*
Harrison, William Neal *author, educator*
Hauptman, William *playwright*
Haynes, Todd *film writer, producer, director*
Hazzard, Shirley *author*
Heller, Joseph *writer*
Hemming, Roy G. *writer, magazine editor, broadcaster*
Henley, Arthur *author, editor, television consultant*
Henley, Beth *playwright, actress*
Henry, Marguerite *author*
Hentoff, Nathan Irving *writer*
Herzog, Arthur, III *author*
†Hill, Elizabeth Starr *writer*
†Hillman, Howard Budrow *author, editor, publisher, consultant*
Hines, Anna Grossnickle *author, illustrator*
Hinton, S(usan) E(loise) *author*
Hinz, Dorothy Elizabeth *writer, editor, international corporate communications and public affairs specialist*
Hoagland, Edward *author*
†Hoffman, Alice *writer*
Hoffman, William M. *playwright, editor*
†Holabird, Katherine *children's book author*
Holland, Isabelle Christian *author*
Holroyd, Michael *author*
Holzer, Hans *author*
Horovitz, Israel Arthur *playwright*
†Howe, Tina *playwright*
Hunter, Evan (Ed Mc Bain) *author*
Hwang, David Henry *playwright, screenwriter*
Hyams, Joe *writer*
Inez, Colette *poet*
Innaurato, Albert Francis *playwright*
Jacker, Corinne Litvin *playwright*
Jaffe, Rona *author*
Jakes, John *author*
Janeway, Elizabeth Hall *author*
Jhabvala, Ruth Prawer *author*
†Johnson, Angela *children's book author*
Johnson, Charles *writer, teacher*
†Johnson, Denis *poet, writer*
Jones, Diana Wynne *writer*
Jong, Erica Mann *author, poet*
Kanin, Garson *writer, theatrical director*
Katz, William Loren *author*
Kauffmann, Stanley Jules *author*
Kaufman, Bel *author, educator*
Kazin, Alfred *writer*
Kehret, Peg *writer*
Kidder, (John) Tracy *writer*
Kingsley, Sidney *playwright*
Kisner, Jacob *poet, editor*
Klein, T(heodore) E(ibon) D(onald) *writer*
Kobler, John *writer*
Koch, Kenneth *poet, playwright*
Koerner, James David *author, foundation executive, consultant*
Koke, Richard Joseph *author, exhibit designer, museum curator*
Koontz, Dean Ray *writer*
Kostelanetz, Richard *writer, artist*
Kotlowitz, Robert *writer,editor*
Kotzwinkle, William *author*
Kramer, Jane *author*
Kubly, Herbert *author, educator*
Kumin, Maxine Winokur *author, poet*
Kunitz, Stanley Jasspon *poet, editor, educator*
Kuralt, Charles Bishop *writer, former television news correspondent*
Kushner, Tony *playwright*
Lader, Lawrence *writer*
Lahr, John *author*
Lapierre, Dominique *author, historian*
Lapine, James Elliot *playwright, director*
Leavitt, David Adam *writer*
Lelchuk, Alan *author, educator*
L'Engle, Madeleine (Mrs. Hugh Franklin) *author*
Levertov, Denise *poet*
Levin, Ira *author, playwright*
Levine, Israel E. *writer*
Levoy, Myron *author*
Linney, Romulus *author, educator*
Lionni, Leonard *author, artist*
Lish, Gordon *author, educator, editor*
†Loman, Michael *scriptwriter, television producer*
Lord, M. G. *writer*
Lucas, Craig *playwright, screenwriter*
Maas, Peter *writer*
Mailer, Norman *author*
†Malgieri, Nick *chef, author*
Martin, Ann Matthews *writer, juvenile*
Mason, Bobbie Ann *novelist, short story writer*
Maxwell, William *writer*
†Mayle, Peter *writer*
Mayne, William *writer*
McCarthy, Cormac *writer*
Mc Clure, Michael Thomas *poet, playwright, educator*
McCullough, David *author*
Mcdonald, Gregory Christopher *author*
Mc Ginniss, Joe *writer*
McInerney, Jay *author*
McKinley, (Jennifer Carolyn) Robin *writer*
McMeen, Albert Ralph, III *writer, lecturer*
McMurtry, Larry *author*
McNally, Terrence *playwright*
Mee, Charles L., Jr. *playwright, historian, editor*
Mehta, Ved (Parkash) *writer, literature and history educator*
Meltzer, Milton *author*
Merwin, William Stanley *poet*
Mitchell, Joseph (Quincy) *writer*
Mitgang, Herbert *author, journalist*
Mooney, Ted (Edward Comstock Mooney) *writer*
Moore, Brian *writer*
†Moore, Susanna *writer*
Morgan, (George) Frederick *poet, editor*
Morgan, Robin Evonne *poet, author, journalist, activist, editor*
Morris, Wright *novelist, critic*
Morrow, Lance *writer*
Morton, Frederic *author*
Munro, Alice *author*
Neely, Mark E., Jr. *writer*
Neier, Aryeh *author, human rights organization administrator*
†Nelson, Richard John *playwright*
Nixon, Joan Lowery *writer*
Norman, Marsha *playwright*
Offit, Sidney *writer, educator*
O'Rourke, P. J. (Patrick Jake O'Rourke) *writer, humorist*
Ozick, Cynthia *author*
Paterson, Katherine Womeldorf *writer*
Patterson, Jerry Eugene *author*
Peck, Richard Wayne *novelist*
Phillips, Ethel C. (Mrs. Lloyd J. Phillips) *writer*
Philp, Richard Nilson *writer, editor*
Pirsig, Robert Maynard *author*
†Plain, Belva *writer*
Plimpton, George Ames *writer, editor, television host*
Pogrebin, Letty Cottin *writer, lecturer*
†Pomerantz, Charlotte *writer*
Post, Emily (Elizabeth Lindley Post) *author*
†Prelutsky, Jack *author*
Price, Reynolds *novelist, poet, playwright, essayist, educator*
Proulx, Edna Annie *writer*
Rechy, John Francisco *author*
Reed, Ishmael Scott *writer*
Regan, Sylvia *playwright*
Reig, June Wilson *writer, director, producer*
Reiss, Alvin *writer*
†Remnick, David J. *magazine writer*
Rhodes, Richard Lee *writer*
Rice, Anne *author*
Rich, Adrienne *writer*
Robbins, Harold *author*
Rollin, Betty *author, television journalist*
Rooney, Andrew Aitken *writer, columnist*
Root, William Pitt *poet, educator*
Rosenthal, Macha Louis *author, educator*
Rossner, Judith *novelist*
Rosten, Leo Calvin (Leonard Q. Ross) *author, political scientist*
Roth, Henry *writer*
Roth, Philip *writer*
Rothenberg, Jerome *author*
Sainer, Arthur *writer, theater educator*
Sale, (John) Kirkpatrick *writer*
Salinger, Jerome David *author*
Sanders, Lawrence *author*
Saul, John Woodruff, III *writer*
Saylor, Steven Warren *writer, prose, fiction*
Schapiro, Herb *playwright, educator*
Schisgal, Murray Joseph *playwright*
Schlesinger, Arthur (Meier), Jr. *writer, educator*
†Schnackenberg, Gjertrud Cecelia *poet*
Schulberg, Budd *author*
Schulman, Grace *poet, English language educator*
Schwed, Peter *author, retired editor and publisher*
†Scieszka, Jon *children's author*
Seaman, Barbara (Ann Rosner) *author*
Segal, Lore *writer*
Sendak, Maurice Bernard *writer, illustrator*
Seth, Vikram *writer*
Settle, Mary Lee *author*
Shaffer, Peter Levin *playwright*
Shange, Ntozake *playwright, poet*
Shapiro, Harvey *poet*
Shawn, Wallace *playwright, actor*
Sheehan, Susan *writer*
Sheldon, Sidney *author*
Shepard, Elaine Elizabeth *writer, lecturer*
Shulevitz, Uri *author, illustrator*
Simmons, Charles *author*
†Simmons, Dan *science fiction writer*
Simon, Neil *playwright, television writer*
Slade, Bernard *playwright*
Smith, Robert Kimmel *author*
Smith, William Jay *author*
Solzhenitsyn, Aleksandr Isayevich *author*
Sonnenberg, Ben *playwright, poet, editor*
Soule, Gardner Bosworth *author*
Southall, Ivan Francis *author*
†Spencer, LaVyrle *writer*
Spencer, Scott *novelist*
Spiegelman, Art *author, cartoonist*
Spoto, Donald *writer, educator*
Steegmuller, Francis *author*
Steel, Danielle Fernande *author*
Stein, Joseph *playwright*
Steinem, Gloria *writer, editor, lecturer*
Stevens, Shane *novelist*
Stevenson, William Henri *author*
†Stine, R(obert) L(awrence) *children's book author*
Stone, Peter *playwright, scenarist*
Stone, Robert Anthony *author*
Stowers, Carlton Eugene *writer*
Strand, Mark *poet*
Swann, Brian *writer, humanities educator*
Talese, Gay *writer*
Taylor, Clyde Calvin, Jr. *literary agent*
Terry, Megan *playwright, performer , photographer*
Tesich, Steve *author*
Thompson, Hunter Stockton *author, political analyst, journalist*
Toffler, Alvin *author*
Tomkins, Calvin *writer*
Uhry, Alfred Fox *playwright*
Ulanov, Barry *author, educator*
Uris, Leon *author*
van Vogt, Alfred Elton *author*
Vonnegut, Kurt, Jr. *writer*
Wager, Walter Herman *author, communications director*
Walker, Alice Malsenior *author*
Wallach, Ira *writer*
†Waller, Robert James *writer*
Ward, Geoffrey Champion *author, editor*
Wasserman, Albert *writer, director*
Wasserman, Dale *playwright*
Watt, Douglas (Benjamin Watt) *writer, critic*
Weidman, Jerome *author*
Wender, Phyllis Bellows *literary agent*
Weschler, Lawrence Michael *writer, journalist*
Westlake, Donald Edwin *author*
White, Edmund Valentine *author*
Wilson, August *playwright*
Wilson, F(rancis) Paul *novelist*
Winsor, Kathleen *writer*
Wise, David *author, journalist*
†Wolf, Naomi *writer*
Wolfe, Thomas Kennerly, Jr. *writer, journalist*
†Wolff, Virginia Euwer *writer, secondary education educator*
Wright, Laurali R. (Bunny Wright) *writer*
†Yorinks, Arthur *children's author*
Yuncker, Barbara *science writer*
Zahn, Timothy *writer*
Zara, Louis *author, editor*
Zindel, Paul *author*
Zolotow, Charlotte Shapiro *author, editor*

Newburgh
Severo, Richard *writer*

North White Plains
Hearon, Shelby *writer, lecturer, educator*

Oceanside
Mills, James Spencer *author*

Palisades
Berger, Thomas Louis *author*
Davis, Dorothy Salisbury *author*

Plainview
Linn, Edward Allen *writer*

Port Washington
Blakeslee, Alton Lauren *scientific writer*

Poughkeepsie
Bird, Caroline *author*
Willard, Nancy Margaret *writer, educator*

Quogue
Laurents, Arthur *playwright*

Riverdale
Moss, Stanley *poet*

Rochester
Hoch, Edward Dentinger *author*
Rothberg, Abraham *author, educator, editor*
Seessel, Adam H. *writer, journalist*

Rockville Centre
Conrad, Pam *author*

Roslyn Heights
Faber, Adele *author, educator*

Sag Harbor
Sheed, Wilfrid John Joseph *author*

Sagaponack
Appleman, Marjorie (M. H. Appleman) *playwright, educator, poet*

Scarborough
Hopkins, Lee Bennett *writer, educator*

Schenectady
Robbins, Daniel *author, art history educator*

Southampton
Knowles, John *author*

Staten Island
Porter, Darwin Fred *writer*

Stony Brook
Kott, Jan K. *writer, scholar*

Syracuse
Wolff, Tobias (Jonathan Ansell Wolff) *author*

Valley Stream
Rachlin, Harvey Brant *author, music publishing company executive*

Waccabuc
Hall, Elizabeth *writer*

West Nyack
Pringle, Laurence Patrick *writer*

White Plains
†Fjelde, Rolf Gerhard *translator, writer*

Woodmere
Abramson, Martin *author, journalist*

Woodstock
Godwin, Gail Kathleen *author*

Yonkers
Kresh, Paul *author, editor*

NORTH CAROLINA

Banner Elk
Isbell, Robert *writer*

Beaufort
Hayman, Carol Bessent *poet, author*

Blowing Rock
Haley, Gail E(inhart) *author*

Chapel Hill
Betts, Doris June Waugh *author, English language educator*
Dareff, Hal *author, editor, publisher*
Spencer, Elizabeth *author*

Durham
†Dorfman, Ariel *writer, educator*
Dunbar, Leslie Wallace *writer, consultant*
Tebbel, John *writer, educator*

Greensboro
Sewell, Elizabeth *author, English educator*
Watson, Robert Winthrop *poet, English language educator*

Hendersonville
Moore, John Travers *poet, author*

Newport
Little, Loyd Harry, Jr. *author*

Pinehurst
Blake, Joan Johnston Wallman *playwright, lyricist*

Raleigh
Murray, Elizabeth Davis Reid *writer, lecturer*

Southern Pines
Yarborough, William Pelham *writer, lecturer, retired army officer, consultant*

Winston Salem
Ehle, John Marsden, Jr. *writer*

Hanes, Frank Borden *author, farmer, former business executive*
†Mandelbaum, Allen *poet, English language and literature educator*

OHIO

Cincinnati
Hornbaker, Alice Joy *author*

Cleveland
Gleisser, Marcus David *author, lawyer, journalist*
Kovel, Ralph M. *author, authority on antiques*
Kovel, Terry Horvitz (Mrs. Ralph Kovel) *author, antiques authority*
Sandburg, Helga *author*
Stadtler, Beatrice Horwitz *author*

Kent
Rylant, Cynthia *author*

Yellow Springs
Hamilton, Virginia (Mrs. Arnold Adoff) *author*

OKLAHOMA

Norman
Owens, Rochelle *poet, playwright*

Oklahoma City
Anderson, Kenneth Edwin *writer, educator*

Stillwater
Shirley, Glenn Dean *writer*

Tulsa
Mojtabai, Ann Grace *author, educator*

OREGON

Eugene
†Wilhelm, Kate (Katy Gertrude) *author*

Newport
Kennedy, Richard Jerome *writer*

Pleasant Hill
Kesey, Ken *writer*

Portland
Rutsala, Vern A. *poet, English language educator, writer*

Salem
Trueblood, Paul Graham *emeritus educator, author, editor*

Terrebonne
Siebert, Diane Dolores *author, poet*

PENNSYLVANIA

Ardmore
Kline, George Louis *author, translator, retired philosophy and literature educator*

Bellefonte
Howland, Bette *writer*

Bethlehem
Murphy, Warren Burton *writer, screenwriter*

Bushkill
Muesing Ellwood, Edith Elizabeth *writer, researcher, publisher, editor*

Drexel Hill
Alexander, Lloyd Chudley *author*

Harrisburg
Lear, John *writer, editor*

Jenkintown
Seid, Ruth (Jo Sinclair) *author*

Kennett Square
Martin, George (Whitney) *writer*
Vining, Elizabeth Gray *author*

Lafayette Hill
Green, Rose Basile (Mrs. Raymond S. Green) *poet, author, educator*

Lewisburg
†Stern, Gerald *poet*

Milford
Le Guin, Ursula Kroeber *author*

Mount Gretna
Cooper, Jane Todd (J. C. Todd) *poet, writer, educator*

Newtown
Pfeiffer, John Edward *author*

Philadelphia
Fussell, Paul *author, English literature educator*
Mangione, Jerre Gerlando *author, educator*
Paglia, Camille *writer, educator*
Pelham, Fran O'Byrne *writer, teacher*
Pipes, Daniel *writer, editor*

Pittsburgh
Alberts, Robert Carman *author*
Hodges, Margaret Moore *author, educator*
†Leo, Peter Andrew *newspaper columnist*

Riegelsville
†Panshin, Alexei *author*

Rosemont
Nixon, Agnes Eckhardt *television writer, producer*

University Park
West, Paul Noden *author, English educator*

Villanova
Nolan, Patrick Joseph *screenwriter, playwright, educator*

Wayne
Berg, Jean Horton Lutz *writer*

RHODE ISLAND

Middletown
Whitman, Ruth *poet, educator, translator*

Providence
Cassill, Ronald Verlin *author*
Feinstein, Alan Shawn *author, financial adviser*
Schevill, James Erwin *poet, playwright*

SOUTH CAROLINA

Aiken
Smith, Gregory White *writer*

Anderson
Young, Marjorie Willis *writer, editor*

Beaufort
Ogburn, Charlton *writer*

Clemson
Byars, Betsy (Cromer) *author*

Columbia
Dickey, James *poet, novelist, filmmaker, critic*

Greenville
Gilkerson, Yancey Sherard *writer, former editor*

Hollywood
Hull, Edward Whaley Seabrook *freelance writer, consultant*

Little River
Uzenda, Jara Carlow *technical writer*

Rock Hill
Bristow, Robert O'Neil *writer, educator*

SOUTH DAKOTA

Vermillion
†Green, Vincent Scott *writer*

TENNESSEE

Bellevue
Ford, Jesse Hill *author*

Chattanooga
Callahan, North *author, educator*

Cordova
Hunt, Gregory Lynn *writer, author*

Memphis
Foote, Shelby *author*

Monteagle
Lytle, Andrew Nelson *author, editor*

TEXAS

Austin
Gustafsson, Lars Erik Einar *writer, educator*
Hearst, Gladys Whitley Henderson *writer*
Ivins, Molly *writer*
Michener, James Albert *author*

Bertram
Albert, Susan Wittig *writer, English educator*

College Station
Gordone, Charles *playwright*

Dallas
Harris, Leon A., Jr. *writer*
Hunter, Kermit Houston *writer, former university dean*
†Weeks, Jerome C. *writer, drama critic*

Fort Worth
Newsom, Douglas Ann Johnson *writer, journalism educator*

Houston
Hirsch, Edward Mark *poet, English language educator*
†SoRelle, Ruth Doyle *medical writer, journalist*

Kerrville
Lich, Glen Ernst *writer, ethnographer, government official, educator*

Liberty Hill
West, Felton *newspaper writer*

Lubbock
Rushing, Jane Gilmore *writer*

Plano
Finley, Glenna *author*

San Antonio
Cousins, Margaret *author, editor*
†Finley, Donald J. *medical writer*
Laurence, Dan H. *author, literary and dramatic specialist*

Seguin
Mims, Forrest Marion, III *science writer*

UTAH

Provo
Hart, Edward LeRoy *poet, educator*

Salt Lake City
Ghiselin, Brewster *author, English language educator emeritus*
†Osherow, Jacqueline Sue *poet, English language educator*

VERMONT

Bennington
Sandy, Stephen *writer, educator*

Brattleboro
Lappe, Frances Moore *author, lecturer*

Burlington
Carlisle, Lilian Matarose Baker (Mrs. E. Grafton Carlisle, Jr.) *author, lecturer*

North Bennington
Belitt, Ben *poet, educator*

Norwich
Stetson, Eugene William, III *film and television writer and producer*

Peacham
Lederer, William Julius *author*

South Strafford
Novick, Sheldon M. *author, lawyer*

Thetford Hill
Paley, Grace *author, educator*

Windsor
Seldes, George *author*

VIRGINIA

Alexandria
Porter, Elsa Allgood *writer, lecturer*

Annandale
Nowak, Jan Zdzislaw *writer, consultant*

Arlington
Hittle, James D. *writer, business consultant*
Stahl, O(scar) Glenn *writer, lecturer, former government official*

Ashburn
Boyne, Walter James *writer, former museum director*

Blacksburg
Giovanni, Nikki *poet*

Charlotte Court House
Hoffman, William *author*

Charlottesville
Brown, Rita Mae *author*
Casey, John Dudley *writer, English language educator*
Simpson, R(obert) Smith *author, retired diplomat*
Wright, Charles Penzel, Jr. *poet*

Christiansburg
Roberts, Ruby Altizer *poet, author, fiction*

Fairfax
Aksyonov, Vassily Pavlovich *author*
†Bausch, Richard C. *writer, educator*

Falls Church
Connery, Robert Howe *educator, author*
Orben, Robert *editor, writer*
Whitehead, Kenneth Dean *author, translator, retired federal government official*

Hillsboro
Farwell, Byron Edgar *writer*

Lexington
Stuart, Walker Dabney, III *poet, author, English language educator*

Lorton
Hazard, John Wharton *author, editorial consultant*

Manassas
Holmes, Marjorie Rose *author*

Mc Kenney
Doyle, John Robert, Jr. *writer*

Middleburg
Spillane, Mickey (Frank Morrison Spillane) *author*

Midlothian
Rodgers, Eugene *writer*

Portsmouth
Mapp, Alf Johnson, Jr. *writer, historian*

Richmond
Dabney, Virginius *author*

Sperryville
Mc Carthy, Eugene Joseph *writer, former senator*

Virginia Beach
El-Fayoumy, Joanne Patricia Quinn *writer, poet*
Seward, William W(ard), Jr. *author, educator*

WASHINGTON

Bellevue
Habbestad, Kathryn Louise *writer*

Bellingham
Doerper, John Erwin *food writer*
Skinner, Knute Rumsey *poet, English educator*

Grayland
Ransom, Bill *author*

La Conner
Robbins, Tom *author*

Lynnwood
Bear, Gregory Dale *writer, illustrator*

Port Angeles
Muller, Willard C(hester) *writer*

Seattle
Bensussen, Estelle Esther *writer, illustrator, artist*
Kenney, Richard Laurence *poet, English language educator*
Singer, Sarah Beth *poet*
Wagoner, David Russell *author, educator*

Tacoma
†Maynard, Steven Harry *writer*

WEST VIRGINIA

Morgantown
Gagliano, Frank Joseph *playwright*

WISCONSIN

Green Bay
Parkinson, Ethelyn Minerva *author*

Little Chute
Rice, Ferill Jeane *writer, civic worker*

WYOMING

Laramie
Boresi, Arthur Peter *author, educator*

CANADA

BRITISH COLUMBIA

Saanichton
†Crozier, Lorna *poet, educator*

Vancouver
Bowering, George Harry *writer*
Woodcock, George *author*

Victoria
Harris, Christie Lucy *author*

NEWFOUNDLAND

Saint John's
Major, Kevin Gerald *writer*

ONTARIO

Don Mills
Atwood, Margaret Eleanor *author*

London
Reaney, James Crerar *dramatist, poet, educator*

Ottawa
†Bradford, Karleen *writer*
Jackson, Charles Ian *writer, consultant*
Major, Jean-Louis *author, French literature educator*

Scarborough
Sparshott, Francis Edward *poet, educator*

Sudbury
Havel, Jean Eugène Martial *author, educator*

Toronto
Bodsworth, Fred *author, naturalist*
Colombo, John Robert *poet, editor, writer*
Davies, Robertson *author*
Fowke, Edith Margaret Fulton *author, English language educator emeritus*
Gotlieb, Phyllis Fay Bloom *author*
Lane, Patrick *poet*
Mowat, Farley McGill *writer*
Parr, James Gordon *writer*

QUEBEC

Montreal
Bruemmer, Fred *writer, photographer*
Richler, Mordecai *writer*
Szanto, George *novelist, playwright*

North Hatley
Gustafson, Ralph Barker *poet, educator*

MEXICO

Mexico City
Paz, Octavio *poet, Mexican diplomat*

AUSTRALIA

Avalon
West, Morris Langlo *novelist*

Norfolk Island
McCullough Robinson, Colleen *author*

AUSTRIA

Vienna
Lo Bello, Nino *author, journalist*

ENGLAND

Cambridge
Hutton, Warwick Blair *writer, illustrator*
Paton Walsh, Jill *author*
Steiner, George (Francis Steiner) *author, educator*

Hingham
Pollini, Francis *author*

Kent
Stewart, Mary Florence Elinor *author*

London
Aliki, (Aliki Liacouras Brandenberg) *author, illustrator children's books*
Ambler, Eric *writer*
Amis, Sir Kingsley *novelist*
Ballard, James Graham *writer*
Bawden, Nina (Mary) *author*
Clarke, Arthur Charles *author*
Cleese, John Marwood *writer, businessman, comedian*
Condon, Richard Thomas *author*
Cowles, Fleur (Mrs. Tom M. Meyer) *author, artist*
Deighton, Len *author*
Drabble, Margaret *writer*
Ewart, Gavin Buchanan *poet, writer*
Fine, Anne *author*
Follett, Ken (Symon Myles) *author*
Forsyth, Frederick *author*
Fowles, John *author*
Fraser, Lady Antonia *writer, editor*
Hare, David *playwright*
Higgins, Jack (Harry Patterson) *author*
Hite, Shere D. *author, cultural historian*
Hoban, Russell Conwell *author*
Hughes, Ted *poet, author*
Hughes, Winifred Shirley *writer, illustrator*
Hunter Blair, Pauline Clarke *author*
James, P(hyllis) D(orothy) (Baroness James of Holland Park of Southwold in County of Suffolk) *author*
Kureishi, Hanif *author*
le Carré, John (David John Moore Cornwell) *author*
Lessing, Doris (May) (May Lessing) *writer*
Morris, Desmond *author*
Naipaul, Vidiadhar Surajprasad *author*
†Oxenbury, Helen *children's writer, illustrator*
†Palin, Michael Edward *writer, actor*
Pinter, Harold *playwright*
Pritchett, Sir Victor Sawdon *author*
Read, Piers Paul *author*
Rice, Timothy Miles Bindon *stage and screenwriter, broadcaster*
Spark, Muriel Sarah *writer*
Stoppard, Tom (Tomas Straussler) *playwright*
Vansittart, Peter *novelist, lecturer, critic*

Newcastle upon Tyne
Cookson, Dame Catherine Ann *author*

Oxford
Aldiss, Brian Wilson *author*
Segal, Erich *author, educator*

Rottingdean
Matthews, John Floyd *writer, educator*

Walmer Deal
Symons, Julian Gustave *author*

West Sussex
†Aiken, Joan (Delano) *author*

Whitchurch
Adams, Richard George *writer*

FRANCE

Belves
Raphael, Frederic Michael *author*

Paris
Gallant, Mavis *author*
Williams, C(harles) K(enneth) *poet, literature and writing educator*

Ramatuelle
Collins, Larry *author, journalist*

IRELAND

Dalkey
Leonard, Hugh (John Keyes Byrne) *playwright*

Donegal
Friel, Brian (Bernard Patrick Friel) *author*

Mullingar
Donleavy, James Patrick *writer, artist*

Wicklow
McCaffrey, Anne Inez *author*

ITALY

Milan
†Calasso, Roberto *writer, publisher*

Venice
Pasinetti, Pier Maria *author*

JAPAN

Tokyo
Kurita, Chushiro *writer, engineering educator, researcher*

LUXEMBOURG

Luxembourg Ville
Elliott, Lawrence *writer*

SCOTLAND

Dumfriesshire
Godden, Rumer *author*

SPAIN

Barcelona
García Márquez, Gabriel José *author*

SOUTH AFRICA

Port Elizabeth
Fugard, Athol Harold *playwright, actor, director*

SWITZERLAND

Geneva
Halle, Louis Joseph *author, educator*
Polunin, Nicholas *environmentalist, author, editor*

ADDRESS UNPUBLISHED

Aloff, Mindy *writer*
Alpert, Hollis *writer*
Anderson-Spivy, Alexandra *writer, editor*
Anthony, Piers *science fiction writer*
Archer, Jeffrey Howard *author, politician*
Arlen, Michael J. *writer*
Barnes, Joanna *author, actress*
Barrows, Robert Guy *scriptwriter*
Bassett, Elizabeth Ewing (Libby Bassett) *writer, editor*
Bauer, Caroline Feller *author*
Beach, Edward Latimer *writer*
†Beatts, Anne Patricia *writer, producer*
Berk, Ann E. *author*
Berry, Richard Lewis *author, magazine editor, lecturer, programmer*
Bova, Benjamin William *author, editor, educator*
Bracken, Peg *author*
Brennan, T. Casey *writer*
Brookner, Anita *writer, educator*
Brown, Marcia Joan *author, artist, photographer*
Broyles, William Dodson, Jr. *author, editor*
Bulla, Clyde Robert *writer*
Bullins, Ed *author*
Cascio, Anna Theresa *playwright, screenwriter*
Chandler, Harry Edgar *author*
Cherryh, C. J. *writer*
Claiborne, Craig *author, editor cookbooks*
Clampitt, Amy Kathleen *writer, editor*
Clark, Mary Higgins *author, business executive*
Coburn, D(onald) L(ee) *playwright*
Collier, Oscar *literary agency consultant, writer*
Collins, Jackie *writer*
Congdon, Thomas B., Jr. *author*
Cook, Beth Marie *writer, poet, municipal housing technician*
†Coonts, Stephen Paul *novelist*
Corcoran, Barbara Asenath *author*
†Coscarelli, Don *film writer, film director*
Cummings, Josephine Anna *writer*
Cussler, Clive Eric *author*
Dahl, Bren Bennington *screenwriter*
Dailey, Janet *novelist*
Davis, Luther *writer, producer*
Disch, Thomas M(ichael) *author*
Doig, Ivan *writer*
Dolan, Edward Francis *writer*
Drucker, Peter Ferdinand *writer, consultant, educator*
Duffy, James Henry *author, former lawyer*
Egelston, Roberta Riethmiller *writer*
†Eglee, Charles Hamilton *television writer, producer*
Erwin, Judith Ann (Judith Ann Peacock) *writer, photographer, lawyer*
Esty, John Cushing, Jr. *writer, lecturer, consultant*
Feirstein, Frederick *poet, playwright, psychoanalyst*
Fetler, Andrew *author, educator*
Fraser, Kathleen Joy *poet, creative writing educator*
Freedman, Russell Bruce *author*
Frost, David (Paradine) *author, producer, columnist*
Fryer, Thomas Waitt, Jr. *writer*
Fuentes, Carlos *writer, former ambassador*
Garfield, Brian Wynne *author*

Gass, William H. *author, educator*
†Gilb, Dagoberto *writer, carpenter*
Gilchrist, Ellen Louise *writer*
Gilroy, Frank Daniel *playwright*
Glick, Ruth Burtnick *author, lecturer*
Glück, Louise Elisabeth *poet*
Goble, Paul *author, illustrator, artist*
Gordon, Bonnie Heather *writer, editor*
Grafton, Sue *novelist*
Gray, Francine du Plessix *author*
Greenburg, Dan *author*
Greer, Germaine *author*
Groening, Matthew *writer, cartoonist*
†Haas, Charlie *screenwriter*
Hahn, Mary Downing *author*
Hairston, William Russell, Jr. *author, playwright*
Hall, Donald *poet*
Hamner, Earl Henry, Jr. *author, producer, television and film writer*
Hanks, Robert Jack *writer, consultant, former naval officer*
Harrigan, Anthony Hart *author*
Helprin, Mark *author*
Herman, Hank *writer*
Heymann, C(lemens) David *author*
Hillerman, Tony *writer, former journalism educator*
Hine, Daryl *poet*
Hirschberg, Vera Hilda *writer*
Howard, Richard (Joseph Howard) *poet, literary translator*
Hoyt, Mary Finch *author, editor, media consultant, former government official*
†Huston, Nancy Louise *writer, educator*
Ireland, Norma Olin *writer, scholarly, researcher*
Irving, John Winslow *writer*
Isaacs, Susan *novelist, screenwriter*
Jacobs, Wilbur Ripley *writer, history educator*
Johnson, Diane Lain *novelist, critic*
Jorden, William John *writer, retired diplomat*
Just, Ward Swift *author*
Kanin, Fay *screenwriter*
Kennedy, Adrienne Lita *playwright*
Khouri, Callie Ann *screenwriter*
King, Larry L. *playwright, actor*
King, Stephen Edwin *novelist, screenwriter, director*
Kinnell, Galway *writer*
Kinsella, William Patrick *author, educator*
Konigsburg, Elaine Lobl *author*
Koning, Hans (Hans Koningsberger) *author*
Kramer, Larry *writer*
Krantz, Judith Tarcher *novelist*
Kristofferson, Karl Eric *writer*
Lally, Michael David *writer, actor*
Lardner, Ring Wilmer, Jr. *author*
Larkin, Joan *poet, English educator*
Lawrence, Jerome *playwright, director, educator*
†Lawton, Jonathan Frederick *screenwriter*
Leighton, Frances Spatz *writer, journalist*
Lindbergh, Anne Spencer Morrow (Mrs. Charles Augustus Lindbergh) *author*
Link, William Theodore *television writer, producer*
Longstreet, Stephen (Chauncey Longstreet) *author, painter*
Lopez, Barry Holstun *writer*
Lorant, Stefan *author*
Lord, Walter *author*
†Macaulay, David (Alexander) *author*
†Maillet, Antonine *author, educator*
Mamet, David Alan *playwright, director*
Mandino, Og *author*
Mann, Emily Betsy *writer, artistic director, theater and film director*
Marx, Anne (Mrs. Frederick E. Marx) *poet*
Mathews, Harry Burchell *poet, novelist, educator*
Mathis, Sharon Bell *author, elementary educator, librarian*
Matthiessen, Peter *author*
Mazursky, Paul *screenwriter, theatrical director and producer*
McFall, Catherine Gardner *poet, critic, educator*
Mc Phee, John Angus *writer*
McPherson, James Alan *writer, educator*
Meaker, Marijane Agnes *author*
Mednick, Murray *playwright*
Mendoza, George *poet, author*
Merrill, James *poet, playwright*
Merrill, Jean Fairbanks *writer*
†Miller, Marilyn Suzanne *writer, producer, playwright*
Mintz, Morton Abner *author, former newspaper reporter*
Mitford, Jessica *author*
†Mogel, Leonard Henry *author*
Morris, Willie *author, editor*
Morrow, Barry Nelson *screenwriter, producer*
Murdoch, (Jean) Iris *author*
Murray, Albert L. *writer, educator*
Muson, Howard Henry *writer, editor*
Myrer, Anton Olmstead *author*
Norton, Andre Alice *author*
Nova, Craig *writer*
Oliansky, Joel *author, director*
Olsen, Jack *writer*
Ondaatje, (Philip) Michael *author, educator*
Palliser, Charles *writer, educator*
Paretsky, Sara N. *writer*
Parker, Franklin *writer, educator*
Parker, Robert Brown *novelist*
Patent, Dorothy Hinshaw *author, photographer*
Patterson, Mary-Margaret Sharp *writer, editor, media strategist*
Potok, Chaim *author, artist, editor*
Powers, John R. *author*
Queenan, Joseph Martin, Jr. *writer, magazine editor*
Rader, Dotson Carlyle *author, journalist*
Raucher, Herman *novelist, screenwriter*
Renaud, Bernadette Marie Elise *author*
Rice, Stanley Travis, Jr. *poet, English language educator*
Riehecky, Janet Ellen *writer*
Rogers, David *playwright, novelist, actor*
Rogers, Rosemary *author*
†Roloff, Michael *writer*
Rosenblatt, Joseph *poet, editor*
Rosenblatt, Roger *writer*
Rubin, Larry Bruce *writer, reporter*
Rush, Norman *author*
Russell, Ray *author*
Schenkkan, Robert Frederic *writer, actor*
Schickel, Richard *writer, film critic*
Schneider, Phyllis Leah *writer, editor*
Schuck, Joyce Haber *author*
Schultz, Philip *poet, novelist, educator*
Schwarzrock, Shirley Pratt *author, lecturer, educator*
Seamans, William *writer, commentator, former television-radio journalist*
Seidel, Frederick Lewis *writer*
Selby, Hubert, Jr. *writer*

Shapiro, Karl Jay *poet, former educator*
Sheehy, Gail Henion *author*
Shreve, Susan Richards *author, English literature educator*
Shyer, Charles Richard *screenwriter, film director*
Simmons, Ted Conrad *writer*
†Simon, Roger L. *writer*
Smith, Martin Cruz *author*
Snyder, Gary Sherman *poet*
Spinelli, Jerry *writer*
Stern, Daniel *author, executive, educator*
Stevenson, Elizabeth *author, educator*
Straub, Peter Francis *novelist*
Styron, William *writer*
Sullivan, Daniel Joseph *writer*
Sullivan, George Edward *author*
Sussman, Barry *author, public opinion analyst and pollster, journalist*
Tan, Amy Ruth *writer*
Taylor, John Jackson (Jay) *writer retired foreign service officer*
Taylor, Peter Matthew Hillsman *author*
Terkel, Susan Neiburg *author*
Theroux, Paul Edward *author*
Thomas, Ross Elmore *author*
Timmons, William Milton *retired cinema arts educator, publisher, free-lance writer, film maker*
Trilling, Diana *writer*
Truman, Margaret *author*
Updike, John Hoyer *writer*
Van Allsburg, Chris *author, artist*
Van Duyn, Mona Jane *poet*
van Itallie, Jean-Claude *playwright*
†Verdecchia, Guillermo Luis *playwright*
Vidal, Gore *writer*
Viorst, Milton *writer*
Voigt, Cynthia *author*
von Hoffman, Nicholas *writer, former journalist*
Wambaugh, Joseph *author*
Wasserstein, Wendy *playwright*
Weinstein, Arnold Abraham *playwright, theater educator*
Whalen, Charles William, Jr. *author, business executive, educator*
White, Robb *author*
Whitney, Phyllis Ayame *author*
Whyte, William Hollingsworth *writer*
†Williamson, Michael *writer*
Wilson, Colin Henry *writer*
Wilson, Lanford *playwright*
Wilson, Sloan *author, lecturer*
Wurdinger, Victoria *writer*
Zelazny, Roger Joseph *author*

ARTS: PERFORMING

UNITED STATES

ALABAMA

Birmingham
Pirkle, George Emory *television and film actor, director*
Polivnick, Paul *conductor, music director*
Sutowski, Thor Brian *choreographer*

Huntsville
Beary, Shirley Lorraine *music educator*

Mentone
Herndon, Mark *musician*

Point Clear
Englund, Gage Bush *dancer, educator*

Tuscaloosa
Goossen, Jacob Frederic *composer, educator*
Rafferty, James Patrick *violinist, violin educator*

ALASKA

Indian
Wright, Gordon Brooks *musician, conductor, educator*

ARIZONA

Flagstaff
Aurand, Charles Henry, Jr. *music educator*

Fountain Hills
Hegyi, Julius *conductor, musician*

Glendale
Neff, John *recording engineer, producer*

Paradise Valley
Alcantara, Theo *conductor*

Phoenix
Albright, Lois *operetta company executive director*
Allen, Russell Plowman *symphony orchestra executive*
Aschaffenburg, Walter Eugene *composer, music educator*
Sedares, James L. *conductor*
Shane, Bob *singer*
Shaw, Lillie Marie King *vocalist*

Scottsdale
Moeck, Walter F. *conductor, music director*
Wolfgang, Bonnie Arlene *musician, bassoonist*

Sedona
Gregory, James *actor*

Tempe
Lombardi, Eugene Patsy *orchestra conductor, violinist, educator, recording artist*

Tucson
Bernhardt, Robert *music director, conductor*
Cook, Gary Dennis *music educator*

Roe, Charles Richard *baritone*
Ross, Glynn *opera administrator*
Seaman, Arlene Anna *musician, educator*

ARKANSAS

Little Rock
†Booth, Richard Donald *radio station executive*

CALIFORNIA

Albany
Boris, Ruthanna *dancer, choreographer, dance therapist, educator*

Anza
Skelton, Red (Richard Skelton) *comedian, artist*

Bakersfield
Owens, Buck (Alvis Edgar, Jr.) *singer, musician, songwriter*

Belvedere Tiburon
Power, Jules *television producer*

Berkeley
Dresher, Paul Joseph *composer, music educator, performer*
Dugger, Edwin Ellsworth *composer, educator*
Hutcherson, Bobby *jazz vibraphonist*
Imbrie, Andrew Welsh *composer, educator*
Wood, David Kennedy Cornell *choreographer, educator*
Zaentz, Saul *motion picture producer*

Beverly Hills
†Adams, Jane *actress*
Albert, Edward *actor, photographer*
Alexander, Jason (Jay Scott Greenspan) *actor*
Alice, Mary (Mary Alice Smith) *actress*
Allen, Karen Jane *actress*
Anderson, Loni Kaye *actress*
Anderson, Richard Dean *actor*
Arquette, Rosanna *actress*
August, Bille *film director*
Avildsen, John Guilbert *film director*
Bacon, Kevin *actor*
Bailey, John *cinematographer*
Baker, Anita *singer*
Bancroft, Anne (Mrs. Mel Brooks) *actress*
†Barrymore, Drew *actress*
Basinger, Kim *actress*
Bates, Kathy *actress*
†Bauer, Marty *agent*
Baxter, Meredith *actress*
Beals, Jennifer *actress*
Bellisario, Donald P. *television director*
Belushi, James *actor*
Benatar, Pat (Pat Andrzejewski) *rock singer*
Bening, Annette *actress*
†Benjamin, Richard *actor, director*
Benson, Robby *actor, director, writer, producer*
Berenger, Tom *actor*
Berle, Milton (Milton Berlinger) *actor*
Bernhard, Harvey *producer*
Bill, Tony *actor, producer, director*
Bishop, Joey (Joseph Abraham Gottlieb) *comedian*
Bisset, Jacqueline *actress*
Bolton, Michael *singer, songwriter*
Bridges, Beau (Lloyd Vernet Bridges, III) *actor*
Bridges, Jeff *actor*
Bridges, Lloyd *actor*
Brightman, Sarah *singer, actress*
Brokaw, Norman Robert *management company executive*
Bronson, Charles (Charles Buchinsky) *actor*
Brooks, Mel *producer, director, writer, actor*
Burnett, Carol *actress, comedienne, singer*
Burton, Al *producer, director, writer*
Burton, Tim *film director*
Cage, Nicholas (Nicholas Coppola) *actor*
Caine, Michael *actor*
†Carrey, Jim *actor*
Channing, Carol *actress*
Chaplin, Geraldine *actress*
Cheech, (Richard Anthony Marin) *actor, writer, director*
Cher, (Cherilyn Sarkisian) *singer, actress*
Chong, Thomas *comedian, writer, director, musician*
Chritton, George A. *film producer*
Clayburgh, Jill *actress*
Coen, Ethan *film producer, writer*
Coen, Joel *film director, writer*
†Cohen, Larry *film director, producer, screenwriter*
Collins, Pauline *actress*
Connery, Sean (Thomas Connery) *actor*
†Coolidge, Martha *film director*
Corbin, Barry *actor, writer*
Corman, Eugene Harold *motion picture producer*
Costa-Gavras, (Konstaninos Gavras) *director, writer*
Coyote, Peter (Peter Cohon) *actor*
Crenna, Richard *actor*
Cristofer, Michael *actor, author*
Culkin, Macaulay *actor*
Culp, Robert *actor, writer, director*
Curtin, Jane Therese *actress, writer*
Curtis, Jamie Lee *actress*
Curtis, Tony (Bernard Schwartz) *actor*
Cusack, John *actor*
Cusak, Joan *actress*
Daly, Timothy *actor*
D'Angelo, Beverly *actress*
Danson, Ted *actor*
Davis, Geena (Virginia Davis) *actress*
Davison, Bruce *actor*
Dawber, Pam *actress*
†Dearden, James *director, screenwriter*
Delany, Dana *actress*
De Laurentiis, Dino *motion picture producer*
DeNiro, Robert *actor*
Dennehy, Brian *actor*
Depardieu, Gerard *actor*
Depp, Johnny *actor*
Dern, Bruce MacLeish *actor*
Dern, Laura Elizabeth *actress*
Devito, Danny Michael *actor*
Dobson, Kevin *actor*
Doherty, Shannen *actress*
Douglas, Kirk (Issur Danielovitch Demsky) *actor, motion picture producer*
Douglas, Michael Kirk *actor, film producer, director*
Downey, Robert, Jr. *actor*
Dunaway, (Dorothy) Faye *actress*
Eden, Barbara Jean *actress*
Eikenberry, Jill *actress*
Elkins, Hillard *producer*
Elliott, Robert B. *comedian*
Elwes, Cary *actor*
Evans, Linda *actress*
Evans, Robert J. *motion picture producer, actor*
Evigan, Greg *actor, musician*
†Fahey, Jeff *actor*
Fargo, Louis James *film director*
Feldshuh, Tovah S. *actress*
Finney, Albert *actor, director*
Fitzgerald, Ella *singer*
Flaum, Marshall Allen *television producer, writer, director*
Fleischer, Richard O. *film director*
Foch, Nina *actress, creative consultant, educator*
Fonda, Bridget *actress*
Foster, Jodie (Alicia Christian Foster) *actress*
Fox, Charles Ira *composer, conductor*
Fox, Michael J. *actor*
Foxworth, Robert Heath *actor, director*
Frankenheimer, John Michael *film and stage director*
Franklin, Aretha *singer*
†Frears, Stephen *film director*
Freberg, Stan(ley) (Victor Freberg) *satirist*
Furth, George *actor, playwright*
Garr, Teri (Ann) *actress*
Gere, Richard *actor*
Gilbert, Melissa *actress*
Gillard, Stuart Thomas *film and television director, writer*
Glenn, (Theodore) Scott *actor*
Gless, Sharon *actress*
Gould, Elliott *actor*
†Grant, Hugh *actor*
Graves, Peter *actor*
†Grey, Jennifer *actress*
Grey, Joel *actor*
Griffin, Merv Edward *entertainer, television producer, entrepreneur*
Griffith, Andy (Andrew Samuel Griffith) *actor*
Grodin, Charles *actor, writer, director*
Guardino, Harry *actor*
†Hackford, Taylor *film director, producer*
Hagman, Larry *actor*
Hamel, Veronica *actress*
†Hamilton, Linda *actress*
Hanks, Tom *actor*
Hannah, Daryl *actress*
†Hanson, Curtis *director, writer*
†Harlin, Renny (Renny Lauri Mauritz Harjola) *film director*
Harmon, Mark *actor*
Harper, Valerie *actress*
Harrelson, Woody *actor*
Harris, Mel (Mary Ellen Harris) *actress*
Haskell, Peter Abraham *actor*
†Hawke, Ethan *actor*
Hawn, Goldie *actress*
Headly, Glenne Aimée *actress*
Helgenberger, Marg *actress*
Helmond, Katherine *actress*
Henry, Buck *actor, writer*
Herrmann, Edward Kirk *actor*
Hershey, Barbara (Barbara Herzstein) *actress*
Hesseman, Howard *actor*
Hill, Walter *film director, writer, producer*
Hines, Gregory Oliver *actor, dancer*
Hopper, Dennis *actor, writer, photographer, film director*
†Horn, Alan *motion picture company executive*
Howard, Ron *director, actor*
Hulce, Tom *actor*
Hunt, Helen *actress*
Hunt, Linda *actress*
Hunt, Peter Huls *director, theatrical lighting designer*
†Hurd, Gale Anne *film producer*
Huston, Anjelica *actress*
Hutton, Timothy *actor*
†Jackson, Samuel L. *actor*
Jillian, Ann (Ann Jura Nauseda) *actress, singer*
Jones, David Hugh *theater, film and television director*
Jones, Dean Carroll *actor*
Jordan, Glenn *theater director*
Kasdan, Lawrence Edward *film director, screenwriter*
Kaufman, Philip *film director*
Keaton, Diane *actress*
Kelly, Gene Curran *dancer, actor, director*
Kilmer, Val *actor*
King, Alan *entertainer*
Kirkwood, Gene *motion picture producer*
†Kravitz, Lenny *singer*
Kurtz, Swoosie *actress*
Ladd, Diane *actress*
Landis, John David *film director, writer*
Lange, Jessica *actress*
Laurie, Piper (Rosetta Jacobs) *actress*
Lawrence, Steve *entertainer*
Leachman, Cloris *actress*
Leary, Denis *comedian*
Lee, Peggy (Norma Delores Egstrom) *singer, actress*
Leibman, Ron *actor*
Leigh, Janet (Jeanette Helen Morrison) *actress*
Lemmon, Jack (John Uhler Lemmon, III) *actor*
Leonard, Robert Sean *actor*
Levinson, Barry L. *film director*
†Levy, Eugene *actor, director, screenwriter*
Lewis, Juliette *actress*
Linkletter, Arthur Gordon *radio and television broadcaster*
Liotta, Ray *actor*
Lithgow, John Arthur *actor, director*
Little, Richard Caruthers (Rich Little) *comedian, impressionist, actor*
†Locklear, Heather *actress*
Loggia, Robert *actor*
Loggins, Kenny (Kenneth Clarke Loggins) *singer, songwriter*
Long, Shelley *actress*
Lynch, David K. *film director, writer*
Mann, Michael K. *producer, director, writer*
Manoff, Dinah Beth *actress*
Manulis, Martin *film producer*
Marshall, (C.) Penny *actress, director*
Mason, Marsha *actress, director, writer*
Mason, Pamela Helen *actress, producer, writer*
Masterson, Mary Stuart *actress*
Mastrantonio, Mary Elizabeth *actress*
Matlin, Marlee *actress*
Matz, Peter S. *composer, conductor, arranger*
McDonnell, Mary *actress*
McGavin, Darren *actor, director, producer*
McNaughton, John D. *director*
Mc Tiernan, John *film director*
Menges, Chris *cinematographer, film director*
Mercer, Marian *actress*
Meyer, Ron *agent*
Modine, Matthew Avery *actor*
Moloney, Jay *agent*
Moore, Demi (Demi Guynes) *actress*
Mulligan, Robert Patrick *film director, producer*
Nabors, James Thurston *actor, singer*
†Neeson, Liam *actor*
Neill, Sam *actor*
Nelson, Judd *actor*
Neuwirth, Bebe *dancer, actress*
Newton-John, Olivia *singer, actress*
Nichols, Mike *stage and film director*
Nicholson, Jack *actor, director, producer*
Nicita, Rick *agent*
Nimoy, Leonard *actor, director*
Noble, James Wilkes *actor*
Nykvist, Sven Vilhem *cinematographer*
O'Hara, Catherine *actress, comedienne*
Olin, Ken *actor*
Ovitz, Michael S. *artists agency executive*
†Pantoliano, Joe *actor*
†Paquin, Anna *actress*
Parker, Alan William *film director, writer*
Penderecki, Krzysztof *composer, conductor*
†Perez, Rosie *actress, choreographer*
Perkins, Elizabeth Ann *actress*
Perry, Luke (Coy Luther Perry, III) *actor*
Pesci, Joe *actor*
Peters, Jon *film producer, film company executive*
†Petersen, Wolfgang *film director*
Petrie, Daniel Mannix *film, theatre and television director*
Pfeiffer, Michelle *actress*
Pitt, Brad *actor*
Poitier, Sidney *actor, director*
Ponty, Jean-Luc *violinist, composer, producer*
Pop, Iggy (James Newell Osterberg) *composer, singer, musician*
†Ptak, John A. *talent agent*
Quinn, Aidan *actor*
Ramis, Harold Allen *film director, screenwriter, actor*
Ransohoff, Martin *motion picture producer*
Rapke, Jack *agent*
Rea, Stephen *actor*
†Red, Eric *film director, screenwriter*
Reiner, Carl *actor, writer, director*
Reiner, Rob *actor, writer, director*
Reitman, Ivan *film director, producer*
Reynolds, Gene *television producer, director*
Richards, Michael *actor, comedian*
†Richardson, Patricia *actress*
Riegert, Peter *actor*
Robards, Jason Nelson, Jr. *actor*
Robbins, Tim (Timothy Francis Robbins) *actor*
Roberts, Eric *actor*
†Robinson, Phil Alden *film director*
Roeg, Nicolas Jack *film director*
Rolle, Esther *actress*
Rollins, Howard Ellsworth, Jr. *actor*
Romero, George A. *film director*
†Rudolph, Alan *film director*
Ruehl, Mercedes *actress*
Russell, Kurt Von Vogel *actor*
Ryder, Winona (Winona Laura Horowitz) *actress*
†Sadwith, James Steven *screenwriter, director*
Sager, Carole Bayer *lyricist, singer*
†Schlatter, George H. *producer, director, writer*
Scorsese, Martin *film director, writer*
Scott, Ridley *film director*
Seagal, Steven *actor*
Seinfeld, Jerry *comedian*
Selleck, Tom *actor*
Sharif, Omar (Michael Shalhoub) *actor*
†Sheridan, Jim *director, screenwriter*
Simmons, Jean *actress*
Singleton, John *director, screenwriter*
Sinise, Gary *actor*
Skerritt, Tom *actor*
Slater, Christian *actor*
Slater, Helen Rachel *actress*
Smith, Will (Fresh Prince) *actor, rap singer*
Snipes, Wesley *actor*
Spacek, Sissy (Mary Elizabeth Spacek) *actress*
Spader, James *actor*
Spheeris, Penelope *film director*
Spielberg, Steven *motion picture director, producer*
Stack, Robert Langford *actor*
Stallone, Sylvester Enzio *actor, writer, director*
Stamos, John *actor*
Steel, Dawn *motion picture producer*
Steenburgen, Mary *actress*
Stefano, Joseph William *film and television producer, author*
Stern, Daniel *actor*
Stewart, Patrick *actor*
Stoltz, Eric *actor*
Stone, Sharon *actress*
Strasberg, Susan *actress, writer, educator*
Strauss, Peter *actor*
Streep, Meryl (Mary Louise Streep) *actress*
Sutherland, Donald *actor*
Tambor, Jeffrey *actor, theatre director, educator*
Terry, Clark *musician*
†Thompson, Caroline Warner *film director, screenwriter*
Thompson, Larry Angelo *producer, lawyer, personal manager*
Tomei, Marisa *actress*
Torme, Mel(vin) (Howard Torme) *musician, jazz vocalist*
Trumbull, Douglas *film director, writer, creator special effects*
Tucker, Michael *actor*
Turner, Janine *actress*
Turturro, John *actor*
Tyson, Cicely *actress*
Uggams, Leslie *entertainer*
Ullman, Tracey *actress, singer*
Urich, Robert *actor*
Van Ark, Joan *actress*
Van Dyke, Dick *actor, comedian*
†Van Sant, Gus, Jr. *director, screenwriter*
Wagner, Lindsay J. *actress*
Wagner, Robert *actor*
Walken, Christopher *actor*
Wedgeworth, Ann *actress*
Weir, Peter Lindsay *film director*
Welch, Raquel *actress*
Weston, Paul *composer, arranger, conductor*
White, Betty *actress, comedienne*
White, Jesse Marc *actor*
†Williams, JoBeth *actress*
Williams, Treat (Richard Williams) *actor*
†Wincer, Simon *film director*
Winkler, Henry Franklin *actor*
Winkler, Irwin *motion picture producer*
Wise, Robert *film producer, director*
†Wood, Elijah *actor*
Woodard, Alfre *actress*
Woods, James Howard *actor*
Yates, Peter *director, producer*
York, Michael (Michael York-Johnson) *actor*
Yorkin, Bud (Alan Yorkin) *producer, director*
Zerbe, Anthony *actor*
Zimmerman, Don *film editor*

Big Bear Lake
Miles, Vera *actress*

Bolinas
Murch, Walter Scott *director, writer, film editor, sound designer*

Burbank
Allen, Tim *actor, comedian*
Berman, Bruce *entertainment company executive*
Berry, Bill *popular musician*
Bruckheimer, Jerry *producer*
Buck, Peter *musician, guitarist*
Burke, Michele Christine *make-up artist*
†Cameron, James *film director, screenwriter, producer*
Clark, Dick *performer, producer*
Clark, Susan (Nora Goulding) *actress*
†Clements, Ronald Francis *animation director*
Cooder, Ry *recording artist, guitarist*
Coolidge, Rita *singer*
Costello, Elvis (Declan Patrick McManus) *musician, songwriter*
de Cordova, Frederick Timmins *television producer, director*
Donner, Richard *film director, producer*
Eastwood, Clint *actor, director, former mayor*
Fagen, Donald *musician*
Flanagan, Tommy (Lee) *jazz pianist*
Fleetwood, Mick *musician*
†Gold, Jeffrey Alan *record company executive*
†Griffith, Robert Douglas *broadcasting company executive*
Guy, Buddy *blues guitarist*
Ingram, James *rhythm and blues songwriter, performer*
Isaak, Chris *popular musician, singer, songwriter, actor*
Karras, Alex *actor, former professional football player*
Ketchum, Hal Michael *country music singer, songwriter*
Lanois, Daniel *record producer, musician, popular*
Lavin, Linda *actress*
Leno, Jay (James Douglas Muir Leno) *comedian, writer*
Marsalis, Branford *musician*
Mathis, Johnny *singer*
Mc Vie, Christine Perfect *musician*
Menken, Alan *composer*
Milchan, Arnon *film producer*
Mills, Mike *popular musician*
Nardino, Gary *television and motion picture producer*
Ohlmeyer, Donald Winfred, Jr. *film and television producer*
Pryor, Richard *actor, writer*
Rauch, Paul David *television producer*
Rich, Lee *entertainment industry executive*
Robinson, James G. *businessman, film production executive*
Rundgren, Todd *musician, record producer*
Seals, Dan Wayland *country music singer*
Severinsen, Doc (Carl H. Severinsen) *conductor, musician*
Silver, Joel *producer*
Simpson, Don *film producer*
Steiger, Rod *actor*
Stewart, Roderick David *singer*
Stipe, Michael *musician*
Strasser, Robin *actress*
†Thomas, Betty *actress*
†Thomas, Jay *actor*
Tritt, Travis *country music singer, songwriter*
Weintraub, Jerry *motion picture producer, executive*
Wonder, Stevie (Stevland Morris) *singer, musician, composer*

Burlingame
Ward, William Reed *composer, educator*

Calabasas
Kanaly, Steven Francis *actor*
Young, Terence *motion picture director*

Carmel
Novak, Kim (Marilyn Novak) *actress*

Century City
Bishop, Stephen *singer, songwriter*
Bogdanovich, Peter *film director, writer, producer, actor*

Chatsworth
Woodruff, Tom, Jr. *special effects designer*

Claremont
Herschensohn, Bruce *film director, writer*

Concord
Clooney, Rosemary *singer, popular and jazz*
Jackson, Milton (Bags Jackson) *jazz musician*

Culver City
Abdul, Paula (Julie) *singer, dancer, choreographer*
Boorman, John *film director, producer, screenwriter*
Brooks, James L. *writer, director, producer*
Guber, Peter *producer*
Levine, Alan J. *entertainment company executive*
Melnick, Daniel *film producer*
Nathanson, Michael *film company executive*
Reiser, Paul *actor, comedian*
Stark, Ray *motion picture producer*
†Tarantino, Quentin *film director, screenwriter*
Wayans, Damon *actor*
Zucker, David *director*

Davis
Rosen, Jerome *composer, clarinetist, educator*
Swift, Richard G(ene) *composer, educator*

Encino
Goodman, John actor
Hubbard, Frederick Dewayne trumpeter
Majors, Lee actor
Nielsen, Leslie actor
Stanton, Harry Dean actor
Zsigmond, Vilmos cinematographer, director

Fairfax
Novello, Don writer, comedian, actor

Fish Camp
Schneider, Arthur Paul retired videotape and film editor, author

Fresno
Gerster, Robert Gibson composer
Harvey, Raymond Curtis conductor

Fullerton
Karson, Burton Lewis musician
Timm, Laurance Milo musician, educator

Glendale
Schifrin, Lalo composer

Granada Hills
Carradine, David actor, director

Hemet
Bible, Frances Lillian mezzo-soprano, educator

Hollywood
Carter, Bennett Lester (Benny Carter) musician, composer, conductor
Jordan, Stanley musician
Klingman, Lynzee film editor
Koch, Howard Winchel film and television producer
Lewis, Huey (Hugh Anthony Cregg, III) singer, composer, bandleader
Little Richard, (Richard Wayne Penniman) recording artist, pianist, songwriter, minister
Marshall, Frank W. film producer, director
Salomon, Mikael cinematographer, director
Strock, Herbert Leonard motion picture producer, director, editor, writer
Wayans, Keenen Ivory actor, producer
Wilder, Billy motion picture director, writer, producer

Irvine
Cohen, Robert Stephen drama educator
Penrod, James Wilford choreographer, dancer

Kentfield
Halprin, Anna Schuman (Mrs. Lawrence Halprin) dancer

La Jolla
Harkins, Edwin L. music educator, performer
McAnuff, Des artistic director
Ogdon, Wilbur composer, music educator
Reynolds, Roger Lee composer

Laguna Hills
Herold, Ralph Elliott motion picture arts educator

Long Beach
Falletta, Jo Ann musician
Walker, Mallory Elton tenor

Los Angeles
Aaron, Paul film and television producer and director
Abramson, Rochelle Susan violinist
Ackerman, Bettye Louise (Mrs. Sam Jaffe) actress
Adams, Bryan vocalist, composer
Aiello, Danny actor
Allen, Debbie actress, dancer, director, choreographer
Alley, Kirstie actress
Allman, Gregg musician
Amos, John actor, producer, director
Anderson, Daryl actor
Anderson, Michael Joseph film director
Anderson, Richard Norman actor, film producer
Anka, Paul singer, composer
Arnold, Tom actor, comedian, producer
Ashforth, Alden musician, educator
Asner, Edward actor
Astin, John Allen actor, director, writer
Bacharach, Burt composer, conductor
Bain, Conrad Stafford actor
Baker, Kathy Whitton actress
Bakshi, Ralph film and television producer, director
Baldwin, William actor
Banner, Bob television producer, director
Barbera, Joseph motion picture and television producer, cartoonist
Barker, Robert William television personality
Barkin, Ellen actress
Barrie, Barbara Ann actress
Barry, Gene actor
Barry, Philip Semple television and film producer
Bassett, Angela actress
Bell, Lee Phillip television personality
Bennett, Harve (Harve Fischman) television and film producer, writer
Bergman, Alan lyricist, writer
Bergman, (Ernst) Ingmar film director, writer
Bernhard, Sandra actress, comedienne, singer
†Berry, Halle actress
Boerlage, Frans Theodoor opera director, music educator
Bono, Sonny Salvatore singer, composer, former mayor
Boone, Pat (Charles Eugene Boone) singer, actor
Bosley, Tom actor
Bostwick, Barry actor
Braun, Zev motion picture and television producer
Brest, Martin film director
Brimley, Wilford actor
Broccoli, Albert Romolo motion picture producer
Broderick, Matthew actor
Brolin, James (James Brunderlin) actor
Brown, Iona violinist, orchestra director
Brunner, Robert Francis composer, conductor
Buckley, Betty Lynn actress
Burrows, James television and motion picture director, producer
Caan, James actor, director
Campbell, Glen singer, entertainer
Cannell, Stephen Joseph television writer, producer, director
Canter, Stanley Stanton motion picture producer
Carlin, George Denis comedian
Carroll, Pat actress
†Carter, Nell actress, singer
†Caruso, David actor
Cates, Gilbert film, theater, television producer and director
Champlin, Charles Davenport television host, book critic, writer
Charisse, Cyd (Tula Ellice Finklea) actress, dancer
Charles, Glen television producer
Charles, Les television producer
Charles, Ray (Ray Charles Robinson) musician, singer, composer
Chase, Chevy (Cornelius Crane Chase) comedian, actor, author
Chomsky, Marvin J. director
Christopher, William actor
Cimino, Michael film director, writer
Clay, Andrew Dice (andrew clay silverstein) comedian
Cocker, Joe vocalist, composer
Cole, Natalie Maria singer
Corea, Chick (Armando Corea) pianist, composer
Corman, Roger William motion picture producer, director
†Craig, Sidney Richard theatrical agent
†Craven, Wes film director
†Cronenberg, David film director
Crystal, Billy comedian, actor
†Curtis, Daniel M. film director
Cyrus, Billy Ray country music performer
D'Accone, Frank Anthony music educator
Daly, Tyne actress
Dangerfield, Rodney (Jack Roy Dangerfield) comedian, actor, author
Daniels, Jeff actor
†Dante, Joe film director
Daviau, Allen cinematographer
Davidson, Gordon theatrical producer, director
†Davis, Andrew film director, screenwriter
Davis, Ossie actor, author
Dee, Ruby (Ruby Dee Davis) actress, writer, director
de Passe, Suzanne record company executive
Deschanel, Caleb cinematographer, director
Dewell, Michael theater executive, writer, producer, translator
Dey, Susan actress
Diamond, Matthew Philip artistic director, choreographer, dancer
†Dillingham, Charles, III entertainment executive
Dillman, Bradford actor
Domino, Fats (Antoine Domino) pianist, singer, songwriter
†Dooley, Paul actor, writer
Dorn, Wanda Faye talent agent
†Dr. Dre, (Andre Young) rapper, record producer
Dreyfuss, Richard Stephan actor
Duffy, Patrick actor
†Duritz, Adam musician
Edwards, Blake film director
Elfman, Danny composer
Eno, Brian (Brian Peter George St. John De La Salle Eno) composer, musician, producer
Estevez, Emilio actor, writer, director
Falk, Peter actor
Farnsworth, Richard actor, former stuntman
Farrell, Mike actor
Fenn, Sherilyn actress
Ferrell, Conchata Galen actress
Fishburne, Laurence, III actor
Flanagan, Fionnula Manon actress, writer, producer
Fleischmann, Ernest Martin music administrator
Fogelberg, Daniel Grayling composer, recording artist
Ford, Glenn (Gwylin Samuel Newton Ford) actor
Forrest, Frederic actor
Forsythe, John actor
Franciosa, Anthony (Anthony Papaleo) actor
Franklin, Bonnie Gail actress
Freeman, Morgan actor
Frey, Glenn songwriter, vocalist, guitarist
Friedkin, William film director
Fuller, Larry choreographer, director
Gallagher, Peter actor
Gamble, Tracy Joseph television producer, writer, lawyer
Garcia, Andy actor
Getty, Estelle actress
Gibbons, Leeza television talk show host
Gibbs, Marla (Margaret Gibbs) actress
Giles, Anne Diener flutist
Glover, Danny actor
†Glover, John actor
Goldberg, Gary David producer, writer
Goldsmith, Jerry composer
Goldwyn, Samuel John, Jr. motion picture producer
Goodman, David Bryan musician, educator
Gordon, Lawrence film producer
Gorman, Cliff actor
Gould, Harold actor
Grammer, Kelsey actor
Grant, Amy singer, songwriter
Grant, Lee (Lyova Haskell Rosenthal) actress, director
Gray, Linda actress
Green, Guy Mervin Charles film director
Guest, Christopher actor, director, screenwriter
Guttenberg, Steve actor
Hackman, Gene actor
Haden, Charles jazz bassist, composer
Hall, Arsenio television talk show host, comedian
Hamlin, Harry Robinson actor
Hammer, (Stanley Kirk Burrell) musician
Hancock, Herbert Jeffrey (Herbie Hancock) composer, pianist, publisher
Hanna, William Denby motion picture and television producer, cartoonist
Harris, Susan television producer
Harry, Deborah Ann singer
Hart, Mary television talk show host
†Hartke, Stephen Paul composer, educator
Hartman, Lisa (Lisa Hartman Black) actress, singer
Hemion, Dwight Arlington television producer, director
Hemmings, Peter William orchestra and opera administrator
Henderson, Florence (Florence Henderson Bernstein) actress, singer
Hertzberg, Paul Stuart producer, publisher, writer
Hettler, Paul visual effects producer
Holbrook, Hal (Harold Rowe Holbrook, Jr.) actor
Howard, Sandy motion picture producer
Howe, John Thomas film director, educator
Huddleston, David William actor, producer
Hughes, Barnard actor
†Hutton, Lauren (Mary Laurence Hutton) actress, model
Ice Cube, (O'Shea Jackson) rap singer, actor
Ice-T, (Tracy Marrow) rap singer, actor
Ireland, Kathy actress
Jackson, Isaiah conductor
Jackson, Janet Damita singer, dancer
Jackson, Mary actress
Jackson, Michael (Joseph) singer
Jarrott, Charles film and television director
Jeter, Michael actor
Joffe, Charles motion picture producer, comedy management executive
Jones, Henry actor
Jones, James Earl actor
Jones, Tom singer
Kagan, Jeremy Paul director, filmmaker
Kane, Carol actress
Kaneko, Mitsuru production company executive, animation producer
Kaplan, Jonathan Stewart film writer, director
Keach, Stacy, Jr. actor, director, producer, writer, musician, composer
Kellerman, Sally Claire actress
Kennedy, George actor
Kennedy, Kathleen film producer
Kercheval, Ken actor
Kidman, Nicole actress
Kinski, Nastassja (Nastassja Nakszynski) actress
†Kirkland, Sally actress
Kleiser, John Randal motion picture director
Knotts, Don actor
Koch, Howard W., Jr. film producer
Korman, Harvey Herschel actor
Kotcheff, William Theodore (Ted Kotcheff) director
Kramer, Stanley E. motion picture producer, director
Lambro, Phillip composer, conductor, pianist
Lancaster, Burt(on) actor
Langella, Frank actor
Lansing, Sherry Lee motion picture production executive
Larroquette, John Bernard actor
Lawrence, Vicki Schultz singer, dancer, comedienne
Lear, Norman Milton producer, writer, director
Lee, Christopher Frank Carandini actor, author
Lenz, Kay actress
Leo, Malcolm producer, director, writer
Leonard, Sheldon television producer, director
Leonetti, Matthew Frank cinematographer
Leritz, Lawrence choreographer, dancer, actor
Levy, Norman motion picture company executive
Lewis, Shari puppeteer, entertainer
Lewitzky, Bella choreographer
Limato, Edward Frank talent agent
Lloyd, Christopher actor
Lloyd, Emily (Emily Lloyd Pack) actress
Loughnane, Lee David trumpeter
Louis-Dreyfus, Julia actress
Lovitz, Jon actor, comedian
Lowe, Chad actor
Lyne, Adrian director
†Lynn, Jonathan Adam director, writer, actor
Mackerras, Sir (Alan) Charles (Mac Laurin) conductor
Magner, Martin theatrical producer and director
Malden, Karl (Malden Sekulovich) actor
Malkovich, John actor
Manilow, Barry singer, composer, arranger
Mann, Delbert film, theater, television director and producer
Manson, Eddy Lawrence composer, conductor, arranger, producer, clarinetist, harmonica virtuoso
Martin, Dean (Dino Crocetti) actor, singer
Martin, Ernest H. theatrical and motion picture executive
Martin, Steve comedian, actor
Mason, Marshall W. theater director
Matthau, Walter actor
Mc Callum, David actor
Mc Clanahan, Rue (Eddi-Rue Mc Clanahan) actress
McDonald, Jeanne Gray (Mrs. John B. McDonald) television producer
Mc Dowall, Roddy actor
Mc Guire, Dorothy Hackett actress
McQueen, Justice Ellis (L. Q. Jones) actor, director
†Medak, Peter film director
Merkert, George visual effects producer
Michael, George (Gergios Kyriakou Panayiotou) musician, singer, songwriter
Michelson, Lillian motion picture researcher
Miles, Joanna actress, playwright
Miller, Dennis comedian
Mills, Donna actress
Mischer, Donald Leo television director and producer
Mitchell, Joni (Roberta Joan Anderson) singer, songwriter
Mitchum, Robert Charles Durman (Charles Mitchum) actor
†Moore, Michael film director
†Moranis, Rick actor
Moreno, Rita actress
Morris, Garrett actor, singer
Moses, Gilbert film and theatre director
Mossman, Thomas Mellish, Jr. television manager
Mueller, Carl Richard theater arts educator, author
Muldaur, Diana Charlton actress
Mulligan, Richard M. actor, writer
Munzer, Cynthia Brown mezzo-soprano
Murphy, Eddie comedian, actor
Nelligan, Kate (Patricia Colleen Nelligan) actress
Nesmith, Michael film producer, video specialist
Neville, Aaron musician
Neville, Art musician
Neville, Charles musician
Neville, Cyril musician
Newhart, Bob entertainer
O'Connor, Carroll actor, writer, producer
O'Day, Anita Belle Colton entertainer, singer
O'Donnell, Rosie comedienne, actress
†Olin, Lena Maria Jonna actress
Olmos, Edward James actor
O'Neal, Tatum actress
Parton, Dolly Rebecca singer, composer, actress
†Perry, Joe guitarist
Petty, Tom rock guitarist, band leader, composer
†Pierce, David Hyde actor
Pollack, Daniel concert pianist
Post, Markie actress
Post, Mike composer
Potts, Annie actress
†Pressman, Michael film director
Priestley, Jason actor
Principal, Victoria actress
†Purcell, Lee actress
Rabinovitz, Jason film and television consultant
Rafkin, Alan television and film director
Raimi, Samuel M. film director
Raitt, Bonnie Lynn singer, musician
Randolph, John actor
Ratzenberger, John Deszo actor, writer, director
Reaney, Gilbert musician, educator
†Reinhold, Judge (Edward Ernest Reinhold, Jr.) actor
Richman, Peter Mark actor, painter, writer
Rickles, Donald Jay comedian, actor
Rickman, Alan actor
Riley, Jack actor, writer
Ritchie, Michael Brunswick film director and producer
Rivers, Joan entertainer
Robertson, Robbie musician, popular
Robinson, Smokey singer, composer
Rogers, Kenneth Ray entertainer, recording artist
†Rollins, Henry musician, author, publisher
Roos, Frederick Ried film producer
Ross, Herbert David film director
Rosten, Irwin writer, producer, director
Rubin, Stanley Creamer producer
Ruskin, Joseph Richard actor, director
Rydell, Mark film director, producer, actor
Sanders, Richard Kinard actor
Sarandon, Susan Abigail actress
Sayles, John Thomas film director, writer, actor
Schell, Maximilian actor, director
†Schepisi, Fred director, screenwriter
†Schroeder, Barbet G. director
Scott, Campbell actor
Scott, George Campbell actor, director
Seger, Bob musician
Seidelman, Arthur Allan director
Seymour, Jane actress
Shandling, Garry comedian, scriptwriter, actor
Shatner, William actor
Shepherd, Cybill actress, singer
Shire, David Lee composer
Shorter, Wayne musician
Silverman, Fred television producer
Skotak, Robert F. film production company executive
Slonimsky, Nicolas conductor, composer
Smits, Jimmy actor
Smothers, Tom actor, singer
Snyder, Allegra Fuller dance educator
Sorvino, Paul actor
Spelling, Aaron film and television producer, writer
†Stanfill, Shelton G. performing arts administrator
Stapleton, Jean (Jeanne Murray) actress
Stevenson, Robert Murrell music educator
Stiers, David Ogden actor, conductor
Stockwell, Dean actor
Stowe, Madeleine actress
Streisand, Barbra Joan singer, actress, director
Swayze, Patrick actor, dancer
Taylor, Meshach actor
Tesh, John television talk show host
Tewkesbury, Joan F. film director, writer
Thomas, Marlo (Margaret Julia Thomas) actress
†Thurman, Uma Karuna actress
Tomlin, Lily actress
Townsend, Robert film director
Trebek, Alex television game show host
Trembly, Dennis Michael musician
Turner, Kathleen actress
Turner, Tina (Anna Mae Bullock) singer
†Tyler, Steven singer
Urioste, Frank J. film editor
Van Damme, Jean-Claude (Jean-Claude Van Varenberg) actor
Van Patten, Dick Vincent actor
Vaughn, Robert (Francis Vaughn) actor
Vereen, Ben actor, singer, dancer
Waits, Thomas Alan composer, actor, singer
Ward, Fred actor
†Ward, Sela actress
Warren, Lesley Ann actress
Washington, Denzel actor
Waterston, Samuel Atkinson actor
Whitaker, Forest actor
Whitmore, James Allen actor
†Wiatt, James Anthony theatrical agency executive
Wickes, Mary actress
Wilder, Gene actor, director, writer
Williams, John Towner composer, conductor
Williams, Mark Alvin writer, director, producer
Williams, Paul Hamilton composer, singer
Williams, Robin actor, comedian
Williams, Russell, II production sound mixer
Wilson, Brian Douglas recording artist, composer, record producer
Wilson, Nancy singer
Winfield, Paul Edward actor
Winger, Debra actress
Winters, Barbara Jo musician
Winters, Ralph E. film editor
Wood, Karen Sue theatre manager, stage producer, consultant
Wyman, William George musician
Young, Loretta (gretchen young) actress
Young, Robert (George Young) actor
Zemeckis, Robert L. film director
Zucker, Jerry producer, director

Malibu
Elliott, Sam actor
Felton, Norman Francis motion picture producer
Gail, Maxwell Trowbridge, Jr. actor, director, musician
Hancock, John D. film director
Klugman, Jack actor
Nolte, Nick actor
Perlman, Rhea actress

Marina Del Rey
Waite, Ralph actor

Menlo Park
Baez, Joan Chandos folk singer

Mill Valley
Kleiman, Harlan Philip film company executive
Padula, Fred David filmmaker

Millbrae
Li, David Wen-Chung television company executive

Mission Hills
Krieg, Dorothy Linden soprano, performing artist, educator

Newbury Park
Issari, Mohammad Ali *film producer, educator, consultant*

North Hollywood
Blake, Robert (Michael Gubitosi) *actor*
Buffett, Jimmy *singer, songwriter*
Flowers, A. D. (Adlia Douglas Flowers) *retired special effects expert*
Frost, Mark *director, producer, writer*
Mirisch, Marvin Elliot *motion picture producer*
Reynolds, Debbie (Mary Frances Reynolds) *actress*

Northridge
†Molen, Gerald Robert *film producer*

Oakland
Cray, Robert *guitarist, singer, songwriter*

Oceanside
Erickson, Frank William *composer*

Pacific Palisades
Albert, Eddie (Edward Albert Heimberger) *actor*
†Clark, Bob H. *film director*
Fonda, Jane *actress*
Horner, Harry *art director, performing arts designer*
Keaton, Michael *actor, comedian*
Kovacs, Laszlo *cinematographer*
Zipper, Herbert *symphony conductor*

Palm Springs
Caesar, Sid *actor, comedian*

Palo Alto
Nanney, Herbert Boswell *musician, educator*

Palo Cedro
Haggard, Merle Ronald *songwriter, recording artist*

Palos Verdes Peninsula
Ebsen, Buddy (Christian Ebsen, Jr.) *actor, dancer*

Pebble Beach
Cameron, JoAnna *actress, director*

Rancho Palos Verdes
Lima, Luis Eduardo *tenor*

Sacramento
Nice, Carter *conductor, music director*

San Diego
Burge, David Russell *concert pianist, composer, piano educator*
Campbell, Ian David *opera company director*
Flettner, Marianne *cultural organization administrator*
Noehren, Robert *organist, organ builder*
†Noel, Craig *performing arts company executive, producer*
Sasaki, Tatsuo *musician*
Ward-Steinman, David *composer, music educator*

San Francisco
Allemann, Sabina *ballet dancer*
Balin, Marty (Martyn Jerel Buchwald) *musician*
Bennett, William *oboist*
Berman, Joanna *dancer*
Bischof, Merriem Lanova *artistic director, choreographer, educator*
Blomstedt, Herbert Thorson *conductor, symphony director*
Borne, Bonita H. *ballet dancer, assistant artistic director*
Breeden, David *clarinetist*
Brubeck, David Warren *musician*
Bullin, Christine Neva *arts administrator*
Caniparoli, Val William *choreographer, dancer*
†Castilla, Antonio *ballet dancer*
Cisneros, Evelyn *dancer*
Collins, Jeremy *dancer*
Coppola, Francis Ford *film director, producer, writer*
Drayer, Cynthia *dancer*
Eilenberg, Lawrence Ira *theater educator, artistic director*
†Festinger, Richard *music educator, composer*
Getty, Gordon Peter *composer, philanthropist*
Haire, James *theatrical producer*
†Harrington, Rex *ballet dancer*
Hastings, Edward Walton *theater director*
Hooker, John Lee *singer, guitarist*
Kantner, Paul *musician*
Kobler, Raymond *concertmaster*
LeBlanc, Tina *dancer*
†Legate, Stephen *ballet dancer*
Lilly, Shannon Jeanne *dancer*
Maffre, Muriel *ballet dancer*
Pastreich, Peter *orchestra executive director*
Peterson, Wayne Turner *composer, pianist*
Runnicles, Donald *conductor*
Santana, Carlos *guitarist*
Sheinfeld, David *composer*
Stowell, Christopher R. *dancer*
Susa, Conrad *composer*
Tomasson, Helgi *dancer, choreographer, dance company executive*
Van Dyck, Wendy *dancer*
†Waldo, Katita *ballet dancer*
†Zhukov, Yuri *ballet dancer*

San Jose
Dalis, Irene *mezzo-soprano, opera company administrator, music educator*
Gregory, Cynthia Kathleen *ballerina*

San Rafael
Brevig, Eric *special effects expert, executive*
Burtt, Ben *sound designer, director, editor*
Carson, Dave *special effects expert, executive*
Farrar, Scott *special effects expert, executive*
Goldman, Clint Paul *graphics expert, producer*
Gorman, Ned *film producer*
Healy, Janet *graphics expert, producer*
Jessup, Harley William *graphics expert, art director*
Joblove, George H. *graphics and special effects expert*
Kay, Douglas *graphics expert, executive*
Kennedy, Thomas *executive producer*
Lesh, Philip Chapman *musician, composer*

Lucas, George W., Jr. *film director, producer, screenwriter*
Mann, Jeff *special effects expert, executive*
Nicholson, Bruce *graphics expert, executive*
Owens, Michael *graphics expert, executive*
Ralston, Ken *graphics expert*
Sheldon, Gary *conductor, music director*
Squires, Scott *special effects expert, executive*

Santa Ana
St. Clair, Carl *conductor, music director*

Santa Barbara
Brant, Henry *composer*
Gimbel, Norman *lyricist, music publisher, television producer*
Messick, Don *actor*
Ohyama, Heiichiro *music educator, violist, conductor*
Wayland, Newton Hart *conductor*

Santa Clarita
Powell, Mel *composer*

Santa Cruz
Mumma, Gordon *composer, educator, author*
Winston, George *keyboardist, recording company executive*

Santa Monica
Alenikov, Vladimir *motion picture director and writer*
Bedelia, Bonnie *actress*
Black, Noel Anthony *television and film director*
Chartoff, Robert Irwin *film producer*
De Palma, Brian Russell *film director, writer*
Diamond, Neil Leslie *singer, composer*
Farentino, James *actor*
Feitshans, Fred Rollin (Buzz Feitshans) *film producer*
Gossage, James Dearl *quality department aide*
Jarreau, Alwyn Lopez *singer*
Leaf, Paul *producer, director, writer*
MacLaine, Shirley *actress*
Mahal, Taj (Henry St. Clair Fredericks) *composer, musician*
Owens, Gary *broadcast personality, entrepreneur, author*
Pisano, A. Robert *entertainment company executive, lawyer*
Schultz, Michael *stage and film director, film producer*
Schwarzenegger, Arnold Alois *actor, author*
Scott, Tony *film director*
Watrous, William Russell *trombonist, composer, conductor*
Watson, Doc (Arthel Lane Watson) *vocalist, guitarist, banjoist, recording artist*
†Weber, Samuel Lloyd *tap dancer, choreographer*
Wexler, Haskell *film producer, cameraman*

Sausalito
Slick, Grace Wing *singer*

Sherman Oaks
Almeida, Laurindo *guitarist, composer*
Arnold, Roseanne *actress, comedienne*
Buckingham, Lindsey *musician*
Burton, Levardis Robert Martyn (Levar Burton) *actor*
Champion, Marge (Marjorie Celeste Champion) *actress, dancer, choreographer*
†Cherones, Thomas Harry, Jr. *television producer, director*
Conrad, Robert (Conrad Robert Falk) *actor, singer, producer, director*
Cossette, Pierre *agent, producer*
Easton, Sheena *rock vocalist*
Gilmore, Art *television performer*
Janis, Conrad *actor, jazz musician, art dealer, film producer, director*
Jourdan, Louis (Louis Gendre) *actor*
Kanter, Hal *writer, producer, director*
Kennedy, Burt Raphael *film director*
Lamas, Lorenzo *actor, race car driver*
Landau, Martin *actor*
Mc Kean, Michael *actor*
Montalban, Ricardo *actor*
Ross, Marion *actress*
Silliphant, Stirling Dale *motion picture writer, producer, novelist*
Stevens, Andrew *actor, producer, writer, director*
Williams, Billy Dee *actor*

Simi Valley
Beck, Mat *special effects expert, photographer*
Bigelow, Michael *film director, visual effects expert*
Durst, Eric *television and commercial director*
Hoover, Richard *special effects expert, film director*
Shartle, Keith Robert *producer*
Yeatman, Hoyt *special effects expert, executive*

Stanford
Cohen, Albert *musician, educator*
Lyons, Charles R. *drama educator*

Studio City
Autry, Gene (Orvon Gene Autry) *actor, radio entertainer, broadcasting executive, baseball team executive*
Aykroyd, Daniel Edward *writer, actor*
Bloodworth-Thomason, Linda *television producer, writer*
Carsey, Marcia Lee Peterson *television producer*
Duvall, Shelley *actress*
English, Diane *executive producer, writer television*
Gautier, Dick *actor, writer*
Goldthwait, Bob *comedian, actor*
Harrison, Gregory *actor*
Kenney, H(arry) Wesley, Jr. *producer, director*
Leider, Gerald J. *motion picture and television company executive*
†Malone, Nancy *actor, director, producer*
Metcalf, Laurie *actress*
Moore, Mary Tyler *actress*
Needham, Hal *director, writer*
Peerce, Larry *film director*
Reynolds, Burt *actor, director*
von Zerneck, Frank Ernest *television producer*
Werner, Tom *television producer, professional baseball team executive*
Westmore, Michael George *make-up artist*

Tarzana
Abbott, Philip *actor*

Topanga
Redgrave, Lynn *actress*

Torrance
Harness, William Edward *tenor*

Turlock
Goedecke, David Stewart *music educator, band educator, trumpet player*

Universal City
Davies, Raymond Douglas *musician, songwriter*
Day, Doris (Doris von Kappelhoff) *singer, actress*
†Kemp, Barry Michael *writer, producer*
LaBelle, Patti *singer*
Lansbury, Angela Brigid *actress*
Lovett, Lyle *musician*
Lynn, Loretta Webb (Mrs. Oliver Lynn, Jr.) *singer*
†Meat Loaf, (Marvin Lee Aday) *popular musician, actor*
Nelson, Craig T. *actor*
Pollack, Sydney *film director*
Van Dyke, Jerry *actor, comedian*
Yearwood, Trisha *country music singer, songwriter*

Valley Village
Diller, Phyllis *actress, author*

Van Nuys
Allen, Stephen Valentine Patrick William *television comedian, author, pianist, songwriter*
Conway, Tim *comedian*
†Gordon, Stuart *film and theater producer, director, playwright*
Ivey, Judith *actress*
MacLachlan, Kyle *actor*

Venice
Grimshaw, Paul *producer*
O'Neill, Edward *actor*

West Hills
†Jones, Dennis Edmund *film producer*
Straight, Beatrice Whitney *actress*

West Hollywood
†Bartel, Paul *film director*
Bass, Barbara DeJong *film assistant director, free-lance writer*
Beal, John *actor, director, narrator*
Benson, George *guitarist*
Bloom, Claire *actress*
Blumofe, Robert Fulton *motion picture producer, association executive*
Bogart, Paul *film director*
Brandauer, Klaus Maria *actor*
Burns, George *actor, comedian*
Carr, Allan *film and stage producer, celebrity representative*
Conniff, Ray *conductor, composer, arranger*
Conti, Bill *film composer*
Denver, John (Henry John Deutschendorf, Jr.) *singer, songwriter*
Erman, John *film director*
Fisher, Carrie Frances *actress, writer*
Haley, Jack, Jr. (John J. Haley) *director, producer, writer, executive*
†Hallstrom, Lasse *director*
Henley, Don *singer, drummer, songwriter*
Ingels, Marty *theatrical agent, television and motion picture production executive*
Jackson, Joe *musician, singer, composer, songwriter*
†Kerr, Deborah Jane *actress*
Kidder, Margot *actress*
Leigh, Jennifer Jason (Jennifer Leigh Morrow) *actress*
Lewis, Richard *actor, comedian*
Males, William James *film producer, make-up artist*
Marsalis, Wynton *musician*
May, Elaine *actress, theatre and film director*
†McKagan, Duff (Michael McKagan) *bassist*
Milius, John Frederick *film writer, director*
Moore, Dudley Stuart John *actor, musician*
Mull, Martin *comedian, singer*
Phillips, Julia Miller *film producer*
Reid, Antonio (L. A. Reid) *musician, songwriter*
Roberts, Julia Fiona *actress*
Ronstadt, Linda Marie *singer*
Rose, W. Axl (William Bruce Bailey) *singer*
Russell, Ken (Henry Kenneth Alfred Russell) *film and theatre director*
†Sargent, Joseph Daniel *motion picture and television director*
†Shaiman, Marc *composer, arranger, orchestrator*
Shaye, Robert Kenneth *cinema company executive*
Sherman, Robert B(ernard) *composer, lyricist, screenwriter*
Slash, (Saul Hudson) *guitarist*
Taylor, James Vernon *musician*
Verhoeven, Paul *film director*
von Sydow, Max (Carl Adolf von Sydow) *actor*
Young, Neil *musician, songwriter*

Westlake Village
Rooney, Mickey (Joe Yule, Jr.) *actor*

Woodland Hills
†Crowe, Christopher *director, screenwriter*
Horne, Lena *singer*
Newman, Randy *singer, songwriter, musician*
Scheimer, Louis *film and television producer*
Taylor, Rowan Shaw *music educator, composer, conductor*
Wester, Keith Albert *film and television recording engineer, television executive*

COLORADO

Basalt
Feliciano, José *entertainer*
Kazan, Lainie (Lainie Levine) *singer, actress*
Sinatra, Frank (Francis Albert Sinatra) *singer, actor*
Williams, Joe *jazz and blues singer*

Boulder
Brakhage, James Stanley *filmmaker, educator*
Duckworth, Guy *musician, educator*
Fink, Robert Russell *music theorist, university dean*

Sarson, John Christopher *television producer, director, writer*
Symons, James Martin *theater and dance educator*

Colorado Springs
Wilkins, Christopher Putnam *conductor*

Denver
†Bearden, Thomas Howard *news program producer, correspondent*
Ceci, Jesse Arthur *violinist*
Fredmann, Martin *artistic director ballet, educator, choreographer*
Keats, Donald Howard *composer, educator*
Rule, Daniel Rhodes *opera company executive*
Schwartz, Cherie Anne Karo *storyteller*

Grand Junction
Thomas, Mark Stanton *flutist*

Ridgway
Weaver, Dennis *actor*

CONNECTICUT

Bridgeport
Katz, Susan Audrey *producer, director, writer*

Chester
Hays, David Arthur *theater producer, stage designer*

Cos Cob
Donahue, Barbara Lynn Sean *television producer*

Danbury
Nelson, Willie *musician, songwriter*

East Haddam
Borton, John Carter, Jr. (Terry Borton) *producer, theater*

Fairfield
Mc Lean, Don *singer, instrumentalist, composer*
Wolff, Steven Alexander *arts and entertainment consultant*

Greenwich
Tiegs, Cheryl *model, designer*

Hartford
Hawkanson, David Robert *theater managing director*
Lamos, Mark *artistic director, administrator, actor*
Lyman, Peggy *dancer, choreographer, educator*
Mc Lean, Jackie *jazz saxophonist, educator, composer, community activist*
Osborne, George Delano *arts director*

Litchfield
Winter, Paul Theodore *musician*

New Haven
Baker, Robert Stevens *educator, organist*
Brainard, Paul Henry *musicologist, music educator*
Brown, Arvin Bragin *theater director*
French, Richard Frederic *emeritus music educator*
Friedman, Erick *concert violinist, educator*
Gilman, Richard *author, drama educator*
Laderman, Ezra *composer, educator, college dean*
†Nolan, Victoria Holmes *theater director*
Rosenblum, M. Edgar *theater director*
Tirro, Frank Pascale *music educator, author, composer*

Norwalk
Brown, Beatrice *symphony conductor*
Caro, Warren *theatrical executive, lawyer*

Ridgefield
Pilbrow, Richard *theatre consultant, lighting designer*
Wyton, Alec *composer, organist*

South Norwalk
Albanese, Licia *operatic soprano*

Stamford
Nierenberg, Roger *symphony conductor*

Storrs
Wood, Wendy Deborah *filmmaker*

Storrs Mansfield
Birdman, Jerome Moseley *drama educator, consultant*

Washington
Pendleton, Moses Robert Andrew *dancer, choreographer*

Washington Depot
Chase, Alison *modern dancer, choreographer, teacher*
Mandler, Susan Ruth *dance company administrator*
Tracy, Michael Cameron *choreographer, performer*

Waterford
White, George Cooke *theater director, foundation executive*

West Redding
Kipnis, Igor *harpsichordist, fortepianist, critic*
Mathews, Carmen Sylva *actress*

Weston
Fredrik, Burry *theatrical producer, director*
Schnitzer, Robert C. *theater administrator*

Westport
Rose, Reginald *television writer, producer*

DELAWARE

Wilmington
†Edelman, David Scott *arts administrator, performer*

Gunzenhauser, Stephen Charles *conductor*

DISTRICT OF COLUMBIA

Washington
Alexander, Jane *actress*
Ames, Frank Anthony *percussionist, film producer*
†Andrews, Jessica L. *performing arts company executive*
Armstrong, Richard Burke *retired television director*
Brown, Oscar, Jr. *writer, entertainer*
Crawford-Mason, Clare Wootten *television producer, journalist*
Day, Mary *artistic director, ballet company executive*
Dukert, Betty Cole *television producer*
Feinstein, Martin *opera director*
Forrest, Sidney *clarinetist, music educator*
Guggenheim, Charles E. *film, television producer, political media consultant*
Harpham, Virginia Ruth *violinist*
Hay, George Austin *actor, producer, director, musician, artist*
Hewitt, Frankie Lea *theater producer*
Kahn, Michael *stage director*
Kendall, Peter Landis *television news executive*
†Klenk, Ann Shirley *television production executive*
Landau, Saul *filmmaker, writer*
Lehrman, Margaret McBride *news executive, producer*
Levalier, Dotian *harpist*
Makris, Andreas *composer*
McLaughlin, John Joseph *broadcast executive, television producer, journalist*
Mosettig, Michael David *television producer, writer*
Parris, Robert *composer*
Pasmanick, Kenneth *bassoonist*
†Pincus, Ann Terry *television executive*
Russell, Mark *comedian*
Silverman, Ira Norton *news producer*
Southern, Hugh *performing arts consultant*
Stevens, George, Jr. *film and television producer, writer, director*
Stevens, Milton Lewis, Jr. *trombonist*
Stevens, Roger Lacey *theatrical producer*
Thayer, Edwin Cabot *musician*
Thulean, Donald Myron *symphony conductor*
†Wager, Douglas Charles *artistic director*
Whedon, Margaret Brunssen *television and radio producer*

FLORIDA

Boca Raton
Blanton, Jeremy *dance company director*
Fengler, John Peter *television producer, director, advertising executive*
Gordon, Marjorie *opera director, coloratura soprano, educator*

Deland
Sorensen, Jacki Faye *choreographer, aerobic dance company executive*

Eastpoint
Hoffer, Thomas William *communication educator*

Fort Lauderdale
Alberg, Mildred Freed *film and television producer, writer*
Gill, Richard Thomas *opera singer, economic analyst*
Holland, Beth *actress*
Randi, James (Randall James Hamilton Zwinge) *magician, writer, educator*

Fort Walton Beach
Clements, Bernadette Stone *ballet director*

Gainesville
Bodine, Willis Ramsey, Jr. *music educator, organist*
Kushner, David Zakeri *musicologist, educator*
White, John David *composer, theorist, cellist*

Jacksonville
Swenson, Courtland Sevander *retired musician*

Lake Buena Vista
Mc Mahon, Ed *television personality*

Largo
Fournier, Serge Raymond-Jean *orchestra conductor*

Miami
Brady, Alexander Childs *dancer*
Bufman, Zev *stage producer, theater chain executive*
Catanzaro, Tony *dancer*
Estefan, Gloria Maria *singer, songwriter*
Gibb, Maurice *vocalist, songwriter*
Gibb, Robin *vocalist, songwriter*
Heuer, Robert Maynard, II *opera company executive*
†Milian, Emilio M. *broadcasting executive*
Reed, Alfred *retired composer, conductor*
Sandoval, Arturo *jazz musician*
Stephan, Egon, Sr. *cinematographer, film equipment company executive*
Waters, Willie Anthony *opera and orchestra conductor*

Naples
Dickie, Brian *opera director*
Jones, Edward Magruder *television producer and writer, correspondent*
White, Roy Bernard *theater executive*

North Miami
Cliff, Jimmy (James Chambers) *vocalist, composer*

North Palm Beach
Hayman, Richard Warren Joseph *conductor*

Odessa
Lister, Thomas Mosie *composer, lyricist, publishing company executive, minister*

Orlando
Boehle, William Randall *music educator emeritus*
Grant, Raymond Thomas *arts administrator*
Swedberg, Robert Mitchell *opera company director*

Punta Gorda
†Kavanaugh, Frank James *film producer, educator*

Saint Petersburg
Carroll, Charles Michael *music educator*
Cook, Marian Alice *musician*

Sarasota
†Booker, Margaret Elizabeth *theater director, artistic director, performing arts educator*
McCollum, John Morris *tenor*
Powers, Dudley *musician*
Smith, Richard Emerson (Dick Smith) *make-up artist*

Spring Hill
Youngman, Henny *comedian*

Sun City Center
†Fleischman, Sol Joseph, Sr. *retired television broadcasting executive*

Tallahassee
Harsanyi, Janice *soprano, educator*
Housewright, Wiley Lee *music educator*
Kirk, Colleen Jean *conductor, educator*

Tampa
Bujones, Fernando Calleiro *ballet dancer*
Hankenson, E(dward) Craig, Jr. *performing arts executive*

West Palm Beach
Robinson, Raymond Edwin *musician, music educator, writer*

GEORGIA

Athens
Staub, August William *drama educator, theatrical producer*

Atlanta
†Babyface, (Kenny Edmunds) *songwriter*
Kennedy, Alfred Doby *performing arts administrator*
Lane, Louis *musician, conductor*
Levi, Yoel *orchestra conductor*
†Ottinger, Richard Estes *public broadcasting executive*
Robinson, Florence Claire Crim *composer, conductor, educator*
Shaw, Robert Lawson *symphony orchestra conductor*
†Turner, Ed Sims *broadcast executive, writer*

Buford
Ziegler, Delores *mezzo-soprano*

Columbus
Patrick, Carl Lloyd *theatre executive*

Decatur
Strawn-Hamilton, Frank *jazz musician, folksinger, composer and arranger, educator*

Macon
Marshall, Howard Lowen *music educator, musicologist*
Rich, Arthur Lowndes *music educator*

Roswell
Siepi, Cesare *opera singer*

HAWAII

Honolulu
Ho, Donald Tai Loy *entertainer, singer*
Johanos, Donald *orchestra conductor*
Langhans, Edward Allen *drama and theater educator*
McGinn, Susan Frances *musician*
Smith, Barbara Barnard *music educator*

Kula
Becker, Walter *guitarist, record producer*

IDAHO

Coeur D Alene
Duke, Patty (Anna Marie Duke) *actress*

Moscow
Bray, R(obert) Bruce *music educator*

Pocatello
Stanek, Alan Edward *music educator*

ILLINOIS

Alton
Schnabel, John Henry *music educator*

Bloomington
Brown, Jared *theater director, educator, writer*
Vayo, David Joseph *composer, music educator*

Buffalo Grove
Denov, Sam *musician*
Siegel, Sid *composer, lyricist*

Champaign
Fredrickson, L(awrence) Thomas *composer*
Garvey, John Charles *violist, conductor, retired music educator*

Chicago
Aitay, Victor *violinist, music educator*
Akos, Francis *violinist*
Bartoletti, Bruno *conductor*
†Conte, Lou *artistic director, choreographer*
Duell, Daniel Paul *artistic director, choreographer, lecturer*
Eaton, John C. *composer, educator*
Ekstrom, Robert Carl *musician, music educator, choral director, singer*
Elliot, Willard Somers *musician, composer*
†Falls, Robert Arthur *artistic director*
Favors, Malachi *jazz musician, bassist*
Fogel, Henry *orchestra administrator*
Foldi, Andrew Harry *singer, educator*
Gonzalez, Ruben *professional musician*
Gossett, Philip *musicologist*
Hall, Tom T. *songwriter, performer*
Hillis, Margaret *conductor, musician*
Janson, Patrick *singer, actor, conductor, educator*
Jean, Kenneth *conductor*
Knapp, Donald Roy *musician, educator*
Krainik, Ardis *opera company executive*
Lewis, Ramsey Emanuel, Jr. *pianist, composer*
Maggio, Michael John *artistic director*
Mahoney, John *actor*
Miller, Frederick Staten *music educator, academic administrator*
Mourek, Joseph Edward *musician*
Peck, Donald Vincent *musician*
Peters, Gordon Benes *musician*
Pikler, Charles *musician*
Ran, Shulamit *composer*
†Schulfer, Roche Edward *theater director*
Schweikert, Norman Carl *musician*
Sedelmaier, John Josef *film director, cinematographer*
Shapey, Ralph *composer, conductor, educator*
Solti, Sir Georg *conductor*
Turner, Lynne Alison (Mrs. Paul H. Singer) *harpist*
†Wang, Albert James *violinist, educator*
Webster, Albert Knickerbocker *consultant in performing arts*
Winfrey, Oprah *television talk show host, actress, producer*
Zajicek, Jeronym *music educator*
Zlatoff-Mirsky, Everett Igor *violinist*

De Kalb
Bach, Jan Morris *composer, educator*

East Saint Louis
Dunham, Katherine *choreographer, dancer, anthropologist*

Evanston
Eberley, Helen-Kay *opera singer, classical record company executive, poet*
Galati, Frank Joseph *stage and opera director, educator, screen writer, actor*
Giordano, August Thomas (Gus Giordano) *choreographer, dancer*
Karlins, M(artin) William *composer, educator*
Kujala, Walfrid Eugene *musician, educator*
Paynter, John Philip *conductor*
Reimer, Bennett *music educator, writer*

Highland Park
Grimmer, Margot *dancer, choreographer, director*
Mehta, Zarin *music association administrator*

Mount Prospect
Sweet, Cody *performing artist, non-verbal communication expert*

Northbrook
Gangware, Edgar Brand, Jr. *retired music educator*
Magad, Samuel *orchestra concertmaster, conductor*
Slattery, James Joseph (Joe Slattery) *actor*

Oak Park
Neil, William *composer*

Park Forest
†Billig, Etel Jewel *theater director, actress*

River Forest
†Columbus, Chris Joseph *film director, screenwriter*
Rimbach, Evangeline Lois *music educator*

Rockford
Hendershott Love, Arles June *television news director*
Ward, Sylvan Donald *music conductor, educator*

Skokie
Childers, John Henry *talent company executive, personality representative*

University Park
Strukoff, Rudolf Stephen *music educator*

Urbana
Boardman, Eunice *music educator*
Brün, Herbert *composer*
Elyn, Mark *opera singer, educator*
Melby, John B. *composer, educator*
Warfield, William Caesar *singer, actor, educator*
Wisniewski, Thomas Joseph *music educator*

Villa Park
Willis, John Fristoe *concertmaster*

Wilmette
Merrier, Helen *actress, director*

INDIANA

Bloomington
Brown, Keith *musician, educator*
Klotman, Robert Howard *music educator*
Mac Watters, Virginia Elizabeth *singer, music educator, actress*
Orrego-Salas, Juan Antonio *composer, retired music educator*
Pagels, Jürgen Heinrich *balletmaster, dance educator, dancer, choreographer, author*
Phillips, Harvey *musician, music educator*
Rousseau, Eugene Ellsworth *musician, music educator, consultant*
Samuelsen, Roy *bass-baritone*
Sebok, Gyorgy *pianist, educator*
Svetlova, Marina *ballerina, choreographer, educator*
Williams, Camilla *soprano, voice educator*

Fort Wayne
Sack, James McDonald, Jr. *radio and television producer, marketing executive*

Indianapolis
Johnson, David Allen *singer, songwriter, investor*
Jones, Robert C. *symphony orchestra administrator*
Suzuki, Hidetaro *violinist*

Michigan City
Musgrave, Charles Edward *music director, correctional facility official*

Terre Haute
Ashbrook, William Sinclair, Jr. *music educator, musicologist*
Cowden, Robert Laughlin *music educator*

Upland
Shulze, Frederick Bennett *music educator*

West Lafayette
Wright, Alfred George James *band symphony orchestra conductor, educator*

IOWA

Dubuque
Hemmer, Paul Edward *musician, broadcasting executive*

Indianola
Larsen, Robert LeRoy *artistic director*

Iowa City
Kottick, Edward Leon *music educator, harpsichord maker*
Mather, Betty Bang *musician, educator*
Mather, Roger Frederick *music educator, freelance technical writer*

KANSAS

Kansas City
Stoskopf, William Howard *retired music educator*

Lawrence
Duerksen, George Louis *music educator, music therapist*
Pozdro, John Walter *music educator, composer*
Tsubaki, Andrew Takahisa *theater director, educator*

Wichita
Chen, Zuohuang *conductor*

KENTUCKY

Louisville
Luvisi, Lee *concert pianist*
Smillie, Thomson John *opera producer*
Smith, Lawrence Leighton *conductor*

LOUISIANA

Baton Rouge
Constantinides, Dinos Demetrios (Constantine Constantinides) *music educator, composer, conductor*
Mathews, Sharon Walker *ballet educator, artistic director*
Norem, Richard Frederick, Sr. *musician, music educator*

Metairie
Best, Eugene Crawford, Jr. *musician*

New Orleans
Baron, John Herschel *music educator, musicologist*
Cosenza, Arthur George *opera director*
Fountain, Peter Dewey, Jr. (Pete Fountain) *clarinetist*
Gonzales, Brother Alexis (Joseph M. Gonzales) *theater and communications educator*
Monachino, Francis Leonard *music educator*

MAINE

Blue Hill Falls
Stookey, Noel Paul *folksinger, composer*

Boothbay Harbor
Lenthall, Franklyn *theatre historian*

Brunswick
Schwartz, Elliott Shelling *composer, author, music educator*

Castine
Davis, Peter Frank *filmmaker, author*

Gouldsboro
Wexler, Ginia Davis *singer, association executive*

Portland
Shimada, Toshiyuki *orchestra conductor, music director*

Surry
Sopkin, George *cellist, music educator*

MARYLAND

Baltimore
Epstein, Selma *pianist, musicologist, author, artist, critic*
Harrison, Michael *opera company executive*
Ivey, Jean Eichelberger *composer*
Yannuzzi, William A(nthony) *conductor*
Zinman, David Joel *conductor*

Chestertown
Clarke, Garry Evans *composer, educator, musician, administrator*

College Park
Aylward, Thomas James, Jr. *communication arts and theatre educator*
Moss, Lawrence Kenneth *composer, educator*

Davidsonville
Mahaffey, Redge Allan *movie producer, director, writer*

Gaithersburg
Whallon, Evan Arthur, Jr. *orchestra conductor*

Hagerstown
Tuckwell, Barry Emmanuel *musician, music educator*

Lutherville Timonium
Hambleton, Thomas Edward *theatrical producer*

MASSACHUSETTS

Allston
Bley, Carla Borg *jazz composer*
Metheny, Patrick Bruce *musician*
Sanders, Pharoah *saxophonist, composer*

Amherst
Bestor, Charles Lemon *composer, educator*
Brandon, Liane *filmmaker, educator*

Boston
Armand, Patrick *dancer*
Barker, Edwin Bogue *musician*
Bauer, Elaine Louise *ballet dancer*
Cassilly, Richard *tenor*
Cogan, Robert David *composer, school official*
Curtin, Phyllis *music educator, former dean, operatic singer*
Dederer, William Bowne *music educator, dean*
Di Domenica, Robert Anthony *musician, composer*
Gang, Stephen R. *motion picture executive, consultant*
Haas, Kenneth Gregg *orchestra executive*
Hampton, Henry Eugene, Jr. *film and television producer*
Harvey, Leslie Leo (Les Harvey) *composer, production company executive*
Hoyt, Herbert Austin Aikins *television producer*
Jochum, Veronica *pianist*
MacCombie, Bruce Franklin *composer, college administrator*
Marks, Bruce *artistic director, choreographer*
McKinley, William Thomas *composer, performer, educator*
McPhee, Jonathan *music director, conductor*
Miller, J. Philip *television producer, director, educator*
Moriarty, John *opera administrator, artistic director*
Peyton, Malcolm C. *composer*
Rotenberg, Sheldon *violinist*
Row, Peter L. *musician, educator*
Sasson, Michel *conductor*
†Sellars, Peter *theater director*
Totenberg, Roman *violinist, music educator*
Young, Laura *dance educator, choreographer*

Brookline
Blake, Ran *jazz pianist, composer*
Epstein, Alvin *actor, director, singer, mime*
Krasner, Louis *concert violinist*

Cambridge
de Varon, Lorna Cooke *choral conductor*
Epstein, David Mayer *composer, conductor*
Erdely, Stephen Lajos *music educator*
Harbison, John *composer*
Kim, Earl *composer*
Kirchner, Leon *composer, pianist, conductor*
Langstaff, John Meredith *musician*
Martino, Donald James *composer, educator*
Orchard, Robert John *theater producer, educator*
Pinkham, Daniel *composer*
Rands, Bernard *composer, educator*
Russell, George Allen *composer, musicologist*
Sims, Ezra *composer*
Wiseman, Frederick *filmmaker*
†Wunderlich, Renner *film producer, cinematographer*

Charlestown
Armstrong, Nancy L. *soprano, voice coach*

Dedham
Firth, Everett Joseph *timpanist*
Magner, Jerome Allen *entertainment company executive*

Framingham
Bogard, Carole Christine *lyric soprano*

Lee
†Miller, Samuel Aaron *dance association executive*

Lenox
Curtis, William Edgar *conductor, composer*

Marstons Mills
Vila, Robert Joseph *television host, designer, real estate developer*

Medford
Anderson, Thomas Jefferson, Jr. *composer, educator*
Burnim, Kalman Aaron *theatre educator emeritus*

Nantucket
Rorem, Ned *composer, author*

Natick
Gomberg, Sydelle *dancer educator*

Newton
Caldwell, Sarah *opera producer, conductor, stage director and administrator*
Price, Roland John Stuart *dancer*

Newton Center
Schuller, Gunther Alexander *composer*

Northampton
Naegele, Philipp Otto *violinist, violist, music educator*

Plymouth
Gregory, Dick *comedian, civil rights activist*

Truro
Falk, Lee Harrison *performing arts executive, cartoonist*

Waltham
Berger, Arthur Victor *music educator, composer, critic*
Boykan, Martin *composer, music educator*
Titcomb, Caldwell *music and theatre historian*
Wyner, Yehudi *composer, pianist, conductor, educator*

Williamstown
Shainman, Irwin *music educator, musician*

Woburn
Freund, Mitchell David *cable television executive, producer, director*

MICHIGAN

Ann Arbor
Bassett, Leslie Raymond *composer, educator*
Bolcom, William Elden *musician, composer, educator, pianist*
Boylan, Paul Charles *music educator, academic administrator*
Buyse, Leone Karena *orchestral musician, educator*
Finney, Ross Lee *composer*
Lillya, Clifford Peter *musician, educator*
Nugent, Theodore Anthony *musician*
†Rosseels, Gustave Alois *music educator*
Sparling, Peter David *dancer, dance educator*

Coldwater
†Spittle, James Pratt *theatre administrator*

Detroit
Calarco, N. Joseph *theatre educator*
Di Chiera, David *performing arts impresario*
Jarvi, Neeme *conductor*
Young, Gordon Ellsworth *composer, organist*

East Lansing
Johnson, Theodore Oliver, Jr. *musician, educator*
Kirk, Edgar Lee *musician, educator*

Flint
Diemecke, Enrique Arturo *conductor*

Grand Rapids
Comet, Catherine *conductor*
Hardy, Michael C. *performing arts administrator*
Smith, Peter Wilson *symphony orchestra administrator*

Grosse Pointe
Smith, Leonard Bingley *musician*

Kalamazoo
Zupko, Ramon *composer, music professor*

Lansing
Kluge, Len H. *director, actor, theater educator*

Saginaw
Najar, Leo Michael *conductor, arranger, educator*

MINNESOTA

Bloomington
Smith, Henry Charles, III *symphony orchestra conductor*

Duluth
Coffman, Phillip Hudson *music educator, arts administrator*

Hopkins
Mayeron, Carol Ann *Cantor*

Mankato
Hustoles, Paul John *theater educator*

Minneapolis
Anderson, Clyde Bailey *musician, educator*
Fetler, Paul *composer*
Fleezanis, Jorja Kay *violinist, educator*
†Houlton, Loyce J. *artistic director, choreographer*
Martenson, Edward Allen *theater manager*
Miller, John William, Jr. *bassoonist*
Ovitsky, Steven Alan *musician, symphony orchestra executive*
Skrowaczewski, Stanislaw *conductor, composer*
Ware, D. Clifton *singer, educator*
Wright, (James) Garland *artistic director*

Saint Paul
Assink, Brent E. *performing arts executive*
Corn, Joseph Edward, Jr. *arts management consultant*
Paulus, Stephen Harrison *composer*
Tecco, Romuald Gilbert Louis Joseph *violinist, concertmaster*

White Bear Lake
Gutchë, Gene *composer*

MISSOURI

Branson
Williams, Andy *entertainer*

Columbia
Archer, Stephen Murphy *theater educator*

Joplin
Harris, Robert A. *music educator*

Kansas City
Bolender, Todd *choreographer*
†Costin, James D. *performing company executive*
†Keathley, George *performing arts executive*
Patterson, Russell *conductor, opera executive*
Williams, Wade Hampton, III *motion picture producer, director, distributor*

Maryland Heights
Dokoudovsky, Nina Ludmila *dance educator*

Saint Louis
†Bernstein, Mark D. *theater director*
Gaddes, Richard *performing arts administrator*
Graham, Colin *stage director*
Slatkin, Leonard Edward *conductor, music director, pianist*
Stewart, John Harger *voice educator*
†Woolf, Steven Michael *artistic director*
Wright, Tamela Jean (T.J. Wright) *disc jockey, entertainer*

Springfield
Orms, Howard Raymond *dramatics educator*
Spicer, Holt Vandercook *speech and theater educator*

Warrensburg
Smith, Dolores Maxine Plunk *dancer, educator*

Wentzville
Berry, Chuck (Charles Edward Anderson Berry) *singer, composer*

MONTANA

Missoula
Knowles, William Leroy (Bill) *television news producer, journalism educator*

NEBRASKA

Chadron
Winkle, William Allan *music educator*

Omaha
Hangen, Bruce Boyer *conductor, music director*

NEVADA

Las Vegas
Ann-Margret, (Ann-Margret Olsson) *actress, performer*
Atkins, Cholly (Charles Atkinson) *choreographer, consultant*
Capelle, Madelene Carole *international opera singer, educator, soprano*
Goulet, Robert Gerard *singer, actor*
Healy, Mary (Mrs. Peter Lind Hayes) *singer, actress*
Knight, Gladys (Maria) *singer*
Lewis, Jerry (Joseph Levitch) *comedian*
Wiemer, Robert Ernest *film and television producer, writer, director*

NEW HAMPSHIRE

Hanover
Hill, Errol Gaston *drama educator, director, author*

Lyme
Darion, Joe *librettist, lyricist*

Plymouth
Swift, Robert Frederic *music educator*

Walpole
Burns, Kenneth Lauren *filmmaker, historian*

NEW JERSEY

Andover
Klein, Joseph Michelman *musical director*

Camden
Polin, Claire *musician*

East Brunswick
Mooney, William Piatt *actor*

Englewood
Bullough, John Frank *organist, music educator*
Zwilich, Ellen Taaffe *composer*

Fords
Brown, James *singer, broadcasting executive*

Fort Lee
†Ramsey, Douglas Kenneth *television anchor, journalist*

Glen Ridge
Bracken, Eddie (Edward Vincent) *actor, director, writer, singer, artist*

Haworth
Shields, Brooke Christa Camille *actress, model*

Hope
Laine, Cleo (Clementina Dinah Dankworth) *singer*

Madison
†Monte, Bonnie J. *performing company executive*

Maplewood
Weston, Randy (Randolph Edward Weston) *pianist, composer*

Millburn
†Cohen, Geoffrey Merrill *theater executive*

Montclair
Walker, George Theophilus, Jr. *composer, pianist, music educator*

New Brunswick
Hurst, Gregory Squire *artistic director, director, producer*
Lettvin, Theodore *concert pianist*
Roussakis, Nicolas *composer, music educator*
Yttrehus, Rolv Berger *composer, educator*

Newark
Jones, Etta *singer*
Morgenstern, Dan Michael *jazz historian, educator, editor*
Silipigni, Alfredo *opera conductor*

Newfield
McKee, Mary Elizabeth *producer*

Princeton
Babbitt, Milton Byron *composer*
Estey, Audree Phipps *artistic director*
Levy, Kenneth *music educator*
Spies, Claudio *composer, educator*
Westergaard, Peter Talbot *composer, music educator*

River Vale
Moderacki, Edmund Anthony *music educator, conductor*

Rutherford
Law, Janet Mary *music educator*

Secaucus
Pinsker, Penny Collias (Pangeota Pinsker) *television producer*

South Plainfield
Ferry, Bryan *singer, songwriter*

Teaneck
Kay, Ulysses Simpson *composer, educator*

Tenafly
Rosenberger, Walter Emerson *percussionist, educator*

Warren
Maull, George Marriner *music director, conductor*

West Orange
Berman, Mona S. *actress, playwright, theatrical director and producer*

Wood Ridge
Castagnetta, Grace Sharp *pianist, piano educator*

NEW MEXICO

Albuquerque
Dressel, Diane Lisette *dancer, choreographer, electrical designer*
Evans, Bill (James William Evans) *dancer, choreographer, educator, arts administrator*
Hamilton, Jerald *musician*
Shedd, Ben Alvin *film producer, director, production company executive*

Portales
Paschke, Donald Vernon *music educator*

Santa Fe
Ballard, Louis Wayne *composer*
Baustian, Robert Frederick *conductor*
Buckley, Richard Edward *conductor*
Crosby, John O'Hea *conductor, opera manager*
Erdman, Barbara *visual artist*
Mann, Herbie *flutist*
Robertson, Stewart *conductor*
Subotnick, Morton *composer, clarinetist*

Taos
Murphey, Michael Martin *country western singer, songwriter*

NEW YORK

Albany
†Papiernik, Richard Lawrence *editor, business columnist*

Amherst
Coover, James Burrell *music educator*

Astoria
Koszarski, Richard *film historian, writer*
†McCormick, Douglas Walter *cable, broadcast executive*

Bayside
Zinn, William *violinist, composer, business executive*

Beacon
Flagello, Ezio Domenico *basso*

Brockport
Fagan, Garth *choreographer, artistic director, educator*

Bronx
†Sherman, Judith Dorothy *producer, recording company owner, recording engineer*

Bronxville
Biscardi, Chester *composer, educator*
Farber, Viola Anna *dancer, choreographer*
†Schönberg, Bessie *dance educator*

Brooklyn
Carter, Betty (Lillie Mae Jones) *jazz singer, songwriter*
†Castro, Nikki Marie *dancer*
Dodge, Charles Malcolm *composer, music educator*
Gaston, Oland P. *music educator*
†Hopkins, Karen *art administrator*
Jarman, Joseph *jazz musician*
Lee, Spike (Shelton Jackson Lee) *filmmaker*
Lichtenstein, Harvey *performing arts executive*
Silver, Horace Ward Martin Tavares *composer, pianist*

Buffalo
Manes, Stephen Gabriel *concert pianist, educator*
Valdes, Maximiano *orchestra director*

Cortland
Anderson, Donna Kay *musicologist, educator*

Dobbs Ferry
Kapp, Richard P. *conductor, arts administrator*

East Hampton
Dello Joio, Norman *composer*
Paxton, Tom *songwriter, entertainer, author*

East Setauket
Layton, Billy Jim *composer*

Fairport
Haylett, Margaret Wendy *television director, engineer*

Flushing
Moriarty, Michael *actor*
†Smaldone, Edward Michael *composer*

Forest Hills
Lipkin, Seymour *pianist, conductor, educator*
Polakoff, Abe *baritone*
Prager, Alice Heinecke *music company executive*
Silver, Sheila Jane *composer, music educator*

Fredonia
Jordan, Robert *concert pianist, educator*

Garden City
Schenck, Andrew Craig *conductor, music director*

Geneva
Berta, Joseph Michel *music educator, musician*

Germantown
Rollins, (Theodore) Sonny *composer, musician*

Gilbertsville
Roos, Casper *actor*

Great Neck
Brand, Oscar *folksinger, author, educator*
Kraft, Leo Abraham *composer*
Lees, Benjamin *composer*

Greenfield Center
Conant, Robert Scott *harpsichordist, music educator*

Hastings On Hudson
Wolfe, Stanley *composer, educator*

Hempstead
Chapman, Ronald Thomas *musician, educator*

Hollis
†Vai, Steve *guitarist*

Hopewell Junction
Walden, Stanley Eugene *composer, clarinetist*

Ithaca
Hsu, John Tseng Hsin *music educator, cellist, gambist, barytonist, conductor*
Husa, Karel Jaroslav *composer, conductor, educator*

Jamaica
Desser, Maxwell Milton *art director, filmstrip producer*

Jamesville
George, Earl *composer, conductor, critic*

Lindenhurst
Farrell-Logan, Vivian *actress*

Long Eddy
Hoiby, Lee *composer, concert pianist*

Massapequa Park
Zizzo, Alicia *concert pianist*

New Kingston
†Maffei, Dorothy Jean *theatre manager*

New Rochelle
Klein, Arthur Luce *theatrical company executive*
Markinson, Martin *theatre owner, producer*
Merrill, Robert *baritone*
Primus, Pearl *dancer, choreographer*

New York
†Aaron, Lynn *dancer*
Abraham, F(ahrid) Murray *actor, educator*
Abrams, Muhal Richard *pianist, composer*
Adams, Joey *comedian, author*
Adler, Richard *composer, lyricist*
Ailes, Roger Eugene *television producer, consultant*
Akalaitis, JoAnne *theater director, writer, actress*
Akiyoshi, Toshiko *jazz composer, pianist*
Alexopoulos, Helene *ballet dancer*
Allen, Betty (Mrs. Ritten Edward Lee, III) *mezzo-soprano*
†Allen, Nancy *musician, educator*
Allers, Franz *orchestra conductor*
†Almodóvar, Pedro *filmmaker*
Altman, Robert B. *film director, writer, producer*
Alvary, Lorenzo *bass*
Amara, Lucine *opera and concert singer*
Ameling, Elly *soprano*
†Amos, Tori *singer, musician*
Amram, David Werner *composer, conductor, musician*
Anderson, Laurie *performance artist*
Arkin, Alan Wolf *actor*
Armitage, Karole *dancer, choreographer*
Arnold, Eddy *singer*
Arpino, Gerald Peter *performing company executive*
Arron, Judith Hagerty *concert hall executive*
Asakawa, Takako *choreograper, dance teacher*
†Ashdown, Marie Matranga (Mrs. Cecil Spanton Ashdown, Jr.) *writer, lecturer*
Ashley, Elizabeth *actress*
Ashley, Merrill *ballerina*
†Avni, Ran *artistic director*
Ax, Emanuel *pianist*
Bacall, Lauren *actress*
Baker-Riker, Margery *television executive*
†Balaban, Bob *actor, director*
Barbee, Victor *ballet dancer*
Barber, Russell Brooks Butler *television producer*
Barker, Charles *conductor*
Barsalona, Frank Samuel *theatrical agent*
Bartoli, Cecilia *coloratura soprano, mezzo soprano*
Baryshnikov, Mikhail *ballet dancer*
Basden, Cameron *assistant ballet mistress, dancer*
Battle, Kathleen Deanna *soprano*
Baudendistel, Daniel *dancer*
†Beatty, Talley *choreographer*
Becofsky, Arthur Luke *arts administrator, writer*
Bedford, Brian *actor*
Bednar, Rudy Gerard *television producer, director*
Beeson, Jack Hamilton *composer, educator, writer*
Behrens, Hildegard *soprano*
Belkin, Boris David *violinist*
†Bell, Richard *arts education executive*
†Belle, Regina *popular musician*
Bellson, Louis Paul *drummer*
Benichou, Pascal *dancer*
Bennett, Tony (Anthony Dominick Benedetto) *entertainer*
Benton, Nicholas *theater producer*
Benton, Robert *film director, screenwriter*
Berezin, Tanya *artistic director, actress*
†Bergman, Andrew *motion picture director*
Bergman, Marilyn Keith *writer, lyricist*
Bergonzi, Carlo *tenor*
Berlind, Roger Stuart *stage and film producer*
Berman, Lazar *pianist*
†Berman, Martin M. *television producer*
Bernardi, Mario *conductor*
Bernstein, Elliot Louis *television executive*
Berry, Walter *baritone*
Betts, Dicky (Richard Forrest Betts) *guitarist, songwriter, vocalist*
Bikel, Theodore *actor, singer*
Binkerd, Gordon Ware *composer*
Birkenhead, Thomas Bruce *theatrical producer and manager, educator*
Bishop, André *artistic director, producer*
†Black, Shawn Morgado, . *dancer*
Blades, Ruben *singer, songwriter, composer*
Boal, Peter Cadbury *dancer*
Bocca, Julio *dancer*
Boelzner, Gordon *orchestral conductor*
Boggs, Gil *principal ballet dancer*
Bonazzi, Elaine Claire *mezzo-soprano*
Bon Jovi, Jon *rock singer, composer*
Bono, (Paul Hewson) *singer, songwriter*
Borda, Deborah *symphony orchestra executive*
Borge, Victor *entertainer, comedian, pianist*
Bosco, Philip Michael *actor*
Bowden, Sally Ann *choreographer, teacher, dancer*
Bown, Patti (Ann Bown) *musician, composer*
Bradford, Robert Ernest *motion picture producer*
Braun, Craig Allen *producer*
†Braxton, Toni *popular musician*
†Brechner, Stanley *artistic director*
Bregman, Martin *film producer*
Brendel, Alfred *concert pianist*
Brewster, Robert Gene *concert singer, educator*
†Brinkley, Christie *model*
Brockway, Merrill LaMonte *television producer and director*
Brooks, Tyrone *dancer*
Brothers, Joyce Diane *television personality, psychologist*
Brown, David *motion picture producer, writer*
Brown, Trisha *dancer*
Browne, Leslie *dancer, actress*
Browning, John *pianist*
Bumbry, Grace *soprano*
Burke, Chris *actor*
Burrell, Kenneth Earl *guitarist, composer*
†Bush, Gage *ballet mistress*
Bush, Kate (Catherine Bush) *singer, songwriter*
Button, Richard Totten *television and stage producer, former figure skating champion*
Caldwell, Zoe *actress, director*
Calegari, Maria *ballerina*
†Campbell, Naomi *model*
Cantrell, Lana *actress, singer*
Capalbo, Carmen Charles *director, producer*
Caples, Richard James *dance company executive, lawyer*
Cardenes, Andres Jorge *violinist, music educator*
Carelli, Gabor Paul *opera singer*
Carey, Mariah *vocalist, songwriter*
Cariou, Len Joseph *actor, director*
Carlson, Marvin Albert *theater educator*
Carpenter, Mary-Chapin *country music singer*
Carpenter, Patricia *music educator*
Carreras, José *tenor*
Carver, Brent *actor*
Carvey, Dana *actor, stand up comedian*
Casei, Nedda *mezzo-soprano*
Cash, Rosanne *country singer, songwriter*
Cazeaux, Isabelle Anne Marie *retired musicology educator*
Charnin, Martin *theatrical director, lyricist, producer*
†Checker, Chubby (Ernest Evans) *popular musician*
Chester, Giraud *television executive*
Chou, Wen-chung *composer*
Christensen, Dieter *ethnomusicologist, educator*
Chryst, Gary *ballet dancer*
Clapton, Eric *musician*
Clarke, Hope *choreographer*
Cohen, Isidore Leonard *violinist, educator*
Cohen, Selma Jeanne *dance historian*
Cohn, Sam *motion picture and theatrical agent*
Cole, Vinson *tenor*
Coleman, Cy *pianist, composer, producer*
Coleman, George Edward *tenor, alto and soprano saxophonist*
Coleman, Ornette *composer, instrumentalist*
Collins, Judy Marjorie *singer, composer*
Comden, Betty *writer, dramatist, lyricist, performer*
Comissiona, Sergiu *conductor*
Como, Perry *singer*
Conlon, James Joseph *conductor*
Connick, Harry, Jr. *jazz musician, actor, singer*
Conway, Kevin *actor, director*
Cook, Bart R. *dancer*
Cooper, Marilyn *actress*
Corigliano, John Paul *composer*
Corry, Carl *dancer*
Corsaro, Frank Andrew *theater, musical and opera director*
Cossotto, Fiorenza *mezzo-soprano*
Cowan, Richard *vocalist*
Crawford, Cindy *model*
Crespin, Regine *soprano*
Crivello, Anthony *actor*
Crystal, Lester Martin *television producer*
Culhane, Shamus *producer, author*
Cunningham, Merce *dancer*
Curtis, Paul James *mime*
Dakin, Christine Whitney *dancer, educator*
†Daldry, Stephen *theatrical director*
Dale, Jim *actor*
Dalrymple, Jean Van Kirk *theatrical producer, publicist, author*
d'Amboise, Christopher *ballet dancer, artistic director, choreographer*
d'Amboise, Jacques Joseph *dancer, choreographer*
†Daniels, Aaron Martin *broadcasting executive*
Danilova, Alexandra *ballet dancer, choreographer*
Danitz, Marilynn Patricia *choreographer*
Darling, Robert Edward *designer, stage director*
Darvarova, Elmira *violinist, concertmaster*
David, Hal *lyricist*
Davidovich, Bella *pianist*
Davidson, Joy Elaine *mezzo-soprano*
Davies, Dennis Russell *conductor, music director, pianist*
†Davies, Martha Hill *dance educator*
Davis, Andrew Frank *conductor*
Davis, Leonard *violist*
Dawn, Deborah *dancer*
de Cou, Emil *conductor*
De Johnette, Jack *musician*
†de la Falaise, Lucie *model*
DeLay, Dorothy (Mrs. Edward Newhouse) *violinist, educator*
Demme, Jonathan *director, producer, writer*
Dennis, Robert (Arthur) (Arthur Dennis) *composer, educator*
Dichter, Misha *concert pianist*
Dicterow, Glenn Eugene *violinist*
†Diekmann, Nancy Kassak *stage producer*
Di Franco, Loretta Elizabeth *lyric coloratura soprano*
Diggins, Peter Sheehan *ballet company administrator*
Dillon, Matt *actor*
Dispeker, Thea *artists' representative*
Dodson, Daryl Theodore *ballet administrator, arts consultant*
Domingo, Placido *tenor*
Donahue, Phil *television personality*
Dowell, Anthony James *ballet dancer*
Downes, Edward Olin Davenport *musicologist, critic, radio broadcaster*
Downs, Hugh Malcolm *radio and television broadcaster*
Druck, Mark *director, producer, writer*
Druckman, Jacob Raphael *composer*
Duchin, Peter Oelrichs *musician*
†Duddy, Joan Frances *performing arts administrator, dancer*
Duffy, Nicole *dancer*
Dufour, Val (Albert Valery Dufour) *actor*
Dukakis, Olympia *actress*
Dulaine, Pierre *ballroom dancer*
Dunham, Christine *dancer*
Dunleavy, Rosemary *ballet dancer*
Dunn, Susan *singer*
Dylan, Bob (Robert Allen Zimmerman) *singer, composer*
Eger, Joseph *conductor, music director*
Elias, Rosalind *mezzo-soprano*
Ellington, Mercer Kennedy *trumpeter, conductor, composer*
Elliott, Chris *actor*
†Emick, Jarrod *actor*
Englander, Roger Leslie *television producer, director*
Entremont, Philippe *conductor, pianist*
Eschenbach, Christoph *conductor, pianist*
Esperian, Kallen Rose *soprano*
Estes, Simon Lamont *opera singer, bass-baritone*
Etheridge, Melissa *singer, songwriter*
†Evangelista, Linda *model*
†Evans, Abigail Winifred *theatrical executive*
Evans, Jerry Norman *television director*
Evans, Lee *composer, musician, educator*
†Everhart, Angie *model*
†Everly, Jack *conductor*
†Fabio, (Fabio Lanzoni) *model*
Fairbanks, Douglas Elton, Jr. *actor, producer, writer, corporation director*
Farberman, Harold *conductor, composer*
Farley, Carole *soprano*
Farrell, Eileen *soprano*
Farrell, Suzanne *ballerina*
Fates, Joseph Gilbert *television producer*
Feist, Gene *theater director*
Feld, Eliot *dancer, choreographer*
Ferri, Alessandra Maria *ballet dancer*
Fetter, Theodore Henry *entertainment consultant*
Feuer, Cy *motion picture and theatrical producer, director*
Fiorato, Hugo *conductor*
Firkušny, Rudolf *pianist, music educator*
Fischer, Lindsay Koehler *dancer*
Fisher, Jules Edward *producer, lighting designer, theatre consultant*
Flack, Roberta *singer*
Flatt, Ernest Orville *choreographer, director*
Fodor, Eugene Nicholas *concert violinist*
†Fontana, Thomas Michael *producer, scriptwriter*
Forbes, Barbara *ballet dancer*
Ford, Eileen Otte (Mrs. Gerard W. Ford) *modeling agency executive*
Foreman, Laura *dancer, choreographer, performance artist, writer, educator*
Foreman, Richard *theater director, playwright*
Forst, Judith Doris *mezzo-soprano*
Foster, Frances *actress*
Frampton, Peter *singer, musician*
†Frankel, David Alexander *television commercial producer*
Frankel, Gene *theater director, author, producer, educator*
Freizer, Louis A. *radio news producer*
Freni, Mirella *soprano*
Fricke, Janie (Jane Marie Fricke) *singer*
Friend, Jonathan Joseph *opera administrator*
Frisell-Schröder, Sonja Bettie *opera producer, stage director*
Fryer, Robert Sherwood *theatrical producer*
Fugate, Judith *ballet dancer*
†Gaines, Boyd *actor*
Galway, James *flutist*
Gamson, Annabelle *dancer*
Gates, Jodie *dancer*
Gattie, Erma Charlotte *opera singer*
Gazzara, Ben *actor*
†Geddie, William Fredrick *television producer*
†Gersten, Bernard *theatrical producer*
Giannini, Cynthia *dancer*
Gibb, Barry *vocalist, songwriter*
Gideon, Miriam *composer*
Gifford, Kathie Lee *television personality*
Gilbert, Pia S. *musical educator, composer*
Gill, Vince *country musician, singer*
Glass, Philip *composer, musician*
Glazer, Esther *violinist*
Gleason, Joanna *actress*
Godunov, Alexander Boris *ballet dancer, actor*
†Goodacre, Jill *model*
Goode, Richard Stephen *pianist, educator*
Gottlieb, Morton Edgar *theatrical and film producer*
Graff, Randy *actress*
Graffin, Guillaume *ballet dancer*
Grant, Merrill Theodore *producer*
Grappelli, Stephane *jazz violinist*
Graves, Lorraine Elizabeth *dancer, educator, coach*
Gray, Diane *dancer, choreographer*
Gray, Spalding *actor, writer, performance artist*
Greco, Jose *choreographer*
Green, Al *singer, clergyman*
Greene, Shecky *entertainer*
Greenhouse, Bernard *cellist, educator*
Grillo, Joann Danielle *mezzo-soprano*
Grizzard, George *actor*
†Grose, Molly Pickering *performing company executive*
†Grove, Barry *theater executive*
Grusin, Dave *film composer, record producer, performer*
Guettel, Henry Arthur *retired arts executive*
Gurin, Meg *dancer*
Gurnee, Hal *television director*
Hadley, Jerry *opera singer*
Hagen, Uta Thyra *actress*
Hall, Daryl *musician*
Hancock, Gerre Edward *musician*
Hardy, Gordon Alfred *music educator, music school president*
†Harkarvy, Benjamin *dance director*
Harnick, Sheldon Mayer *lyricist*
Harrell, Lynn Morris *cellist*
Harris, Ed(ward Allen) *actor*
Harris, Julie (Ann) *actress*
Harrow, Nancy (Mrs. Jan Krukowski) *jazz singer, songwriter, editor*
Harth, Sidney *musician, educator*
Harvey, Cynthia *ballet dancer*
Hasso, Signe Eleonora Cecilia *actress*
Hastings, Baird *conductor, music educator, writer*
Hastings, Donald Francis *actor, writer*
†Haubert, Alaine *ballet dancer*
Hawkins, Erick *dancer, choreographer*
Hayes, Isaac *composer, singer*
Hays, Kathryn *actress*
Hebert, Bliss Edmund *opera director*
Hedlund, Ronald *baritone*
Hemingway, Mariel *actress*
Henderson, Joe *jazz tenor saxophonist*
Henderson, Skitch (Lyle Russell Cedric) *pianist, conductor*
Herman, Jerry *composer-lyricist*
†Herrera, Paloma *dancer*
†Hess, Robert B. *producer*
†Hetfield, James *singer*
Hewitt, Don S. *television news producer*
Heyward, Andrew John *television producer*
Hiatt, John *musician, country, popular*
Hill, George Roy *film director*
Hill, Robert Arthur *ballet dancer*
Hirsch, Judd *actor*
Hlinka, Nichol *dancer*
Hoffman, Dustin Lee *actor*
Holder, Geoffrey *dancer, actor, choreographer, director*
Hollander, Lorin *pianist*
Holliday, Jennifer Yvette *singer, actress*
Holliday, Polly Dean *actress*
Holloway, David *baritone*
Horiuchi, Gen *professional dancer*
Horn, Shirley *vocalist, pianist*
Horne, Marilyn *mezzo-soprano*
Houghton, Charles Norris *stage director, author, educator*
Houston, Whitney *vocalist, recording artist*
Hovhaness, Alan *composer*
Howard, David *ballet school administrator*
Hubbe, Nikolaj *dancer*
Humperdinck, Engelbert (Arnold George Dorsey) *singer*
†Hunter, Rachel *model*
Hyman, Earle *actor, educator*
†Hytner, Nicholas *theatrical director*
Iglesias, Julio (Julio Jose Iglesias De La Cueva) *singer, songwriter*
†Iman, (Iman Abdulmajid) *model*
Ivory, James Francis *film director*
Jackson, Anne (Anne Jackson Wallach) *actress*
Jackson, Glenda *actress*
Jacobs, Bernard B. *theater executive*
Jacobs, Jim *actor, playwright, composer, lyricist*
Jaffe, Susan *ballerina*
Jagger, Mick (Michael Philip Jagger) *singer, musician*
Jamison, Judith *dancer*
†Jefferson, Denise *dance school director*
Jenkins, Leroy *violinist, composer*
†Jerome, Albert David *broadcasting company executive*
Joel, Billy (William Martin Joel) *musician*
Johansen, David (Buster Poindexter) *popular musician, actor*
Johnson, James M. *orchestra executive*
†Johnson, Kate *dancer*
Johnson, Virginia Alma Fairfax *ballerina*
Jones, Bill T. *dancer, choreographer*
Jones, Gwyneth *soprano*
†Jones, Rickie Lee *singer, songwriter*
Julia, Raul *actor*
Jung, Doris *dramatic soprano*
Kalmanoff, Martin *composer*
Kamlot, Robert *performing arts executive*
Kamm, Laurence Richard *television producer, director*
Kander, John Harold *composer*

†Kaplan, Richard James producer, director, writer, educator, consultant
Karchin, Louis Samuel composer
Kassel, Virginia Weltmer television producer, writer
Kaye, Judy actress
Keene, Christopher conductor, author, librettist, musician
Keeshan, Bob television producer, actor
Kellman, Barnet Kramer film, stage and television director
Kellogg, Cal Stewart, II conductor, composer
†Kent, Julie Ann ballet dancer, actress, model
Kent, Linda Gail dancer
Khan, Chaka (Yvette Marie Stevens) singer
Khanzadian, Vahan tenor
Kidd, Michael (Milton Greenwald) choreographer, director
Kinberg, Judy television producer, director
King, B. B. (Riley B. King) singer, guitarist
King, Woodie, Jr. producer, actor, director
Kirkland, Gelsey dancer
†Kirschen, Robert Steven music director
Kirstein, Lincoln ballet promoter
Kistler, Darci Anna ballet dancer
Kitt, Eartha Mae actress, singer
Klein, Robert comedian, actor
Kness, Richard Maynard tenor
Kolpakova, Irina dancer, educator, coach
Kozlov, Leonid ballet dancer
Kozlova, Valentina ballerina
Kraus, Alfredo (Alfredo Kraus Trujillo) tenor
Krawitz, Herman Everett television producer
Krone, Gerald Sidney theatrical and television producer
Krosnick, Joel cellist
Krupska, Danya (Mrs. Ted Thurston) theater director, choreographer
Lacy, Steve jazz musician
La Fosse, Robert ballet dancer
Landesman, Heidi set designer
Lane, Nathan (Joseph Lane) actor
lang, k. d. (Katherine Dawn Lang) country music singer, composer
Lang, Pearl dancer, choreographer
Langham, Michael theatrical director
Lansbury, Edgar George theatrical producer
Lansing, Robert Howell actor, director
Lasser, Louise actress
Leach, Robin producer, writer, television host
Lear, Evelyn soprano
Leber, Steven Edward film producer, corporate executive
Lee, Dai-Keong composer
LeFrak, Francine theatre and film producer
Leland, Sara ballet master
Lemesh, Nicholas Thomas designer, filmmaker
Lennox, Annie rock musician
Leppard, Raymond John conductor, harpsichordist
Letterman, David television personality, comedian, writer
Levine, James conductor, pianist, artistic director
Levy, Marvin David composer
Lewis, Allan conductor, ballet company music director
Lewis, Jerry Lee country-rock singer, musician
Libin, Paul theatre executive, producer
Liebermann, Lowell composer, pianist, conductor
Lightfoot, Gordon Meredith singer, songwriter
Limbaugh, Rush Hudson radio and talk show host
Lincoln, Abbey (Anna Marie Woolridge, Gaby Lee, Aminata Moseka) jazz singer
Linden, Hal actor, singer
Lipman, Samuel musician, music critic
Livengood, Victoria Ann opera singer
Livingston, Jay Harold composer, lyricist
LL Cool J, (James Todd Smith) rap singer, actor
Lockett, Pierre dancer
Loney, Glenn Meredith drama educator
Lopez, Lourdes ballerina
Lortel, Lucille theatrical producer
Loudon, Dorothy actress
Louis, Murray dancer, choreographer, dance teacher
Loveless, Patty (Patty Ramey) country music singer
Lubovitch, Lar dancer, choreographer
Lucas, James E(vans) operatic director
Lucci, Susan actress
Luders, Adam ballet dancer
Ludgin, Chester Hall baritone, actor
Luening, Otto composer, conductor, flutist, educator
Lumet, Sidney film director
Lunden, Joan television personality
LuPone, Patti actress
Ma, Yo Yo cellist
†Macpherson, Elle model
Macurdy, John Edward basso
Madonia, Valerie dancer
Madonna, (Madonna Louise Veronica Ciccone) singer, actress
Malina, Judith actress, director, producer, writer
Malle, Louis film director
Maltby, Richard Eldridge, Jr. theater director, lyricist
Mamlok, Ursula composer, educator
Mann, Robert Nathaniel violinist
Mann, Theodore theatrical producer and artistic director
Mantegna, Joe Anthony actor, playwright
Maraynes, Allan Lawrence filmmaker, television producer
Marceau, Marcel pantomimist, actor, director, painter, poet
Marceau, Yvonne ballroom dancer
Marsee, Susanne Irene lyric mezzo-soprano
Marsh, Jean Lyndsey Torren actress, writer
Martin, Andrea Louise actress, comedienne, writer
Martin, Elliot Edwards theatrical producer
Martins, Nilas dancer
Martins, Peter ballet master, choreographer, dancer
Mason, Jackie comedian, actor
Masur, Kurt conductor
Mata, Eduardo conductor
Matalon, Vivian theatrical director
Maxwell, Carla Lena dancer, choreographer, educator
Mayfield, Curtis Lee musician
†Maynard, Parrish ballet dancer
Mazzo, Kay ballet dancer, educator
Mazzola, John William former performing arts center executive, consultant
†McDonald, Audra Ann actress
McDormand, Frances actress
McFerrin, Bobby singer, musician, composer and conductor
McKenzie, Kevin Patrick ballet dancer
McKerrow, Amanda ballet dancer
†Mclaughlin, Mark John media director
†McMenamy, Kristen model
McRae, Carmen singer
Meadow, Lynne (Carolyn Meadow) theatrical producer and director
Mellencamp, John (John Cougar) singer, songwriter
Menuhin, Yehudi violinist
Merchant, Ismail Noormohamed film producer
Meyer, Kerstin mezzo-soprano, music educator
Michaels, Joseph Eugene television director
Michaels, Lorne television writer, producer
Midler, Bette singer, entertainer, actress
Midori, (Midori Goto) classical violinist
Miller, Mildred opera singer, recitalist
Millo, Aprile Elizabeth opera singer
Milnes, Sherrill Eustace baritone
Minnelli, Liza singer, actress
Mintz, Shlomo conductor, violist, violinist
Mitchell, Arthur dancer, choreographer
Mitchell, Leona Pearl soprano
Monk, Debra actress
Monk, Meredith Jane artistic director, composer, choreographer, film maker, director
Moore, Kathleen dancer
Moore, Sonia theatre administrator, researcher
Morris, James Peppler bass-baritone
Morris, Mark choreographer
Morse, Robert Alan actor
Moseley, Carlos DuPre former music executive, musician
†Moss, Kate model
Mossbrucker, Tom dancer
Muller, Jennifer choreographer, dancer
Mulligan, Gerald Joseph (Gerry Mulligan) composer, arranger, musician, songwriter
Muradian, Vazgen composer, viola d'amore player
†Murphy, Donna actress
Murphy, Rosemary actress
Namath, Joseph William entertainer, former professional football player
Nash, Graham William singer, composer
Neal, Philip dancer
Neblett, Carol soprano
Nederlander, James Morton theater executive
Nero, Peter pianist, conductor, composer, arranger
Nichols, Kyra ballerina
Norman, Jessye soprano
Nucci, Leo baritone
Nugent, Nelle theater, film and television producer
O'Brien, Conan writer, performer, talk show host
O'Brien, Orin Ynez musician, educator
O'Connor, Sinead singer, songwriter
†O'Donoghue, Michael producer, director, writer, actor
O'Horgan, Thomas Foster composer, director
Oliveira, Elmar violinist
Orr, Terrence S. dancer
Ostrum, Dean Gardner actor, calligrapher
Owen, Lynn Rasmussen soprano, voice educator
Owen, Michael ballet dancer
Ozawa, Seiji conductor, music director
Oznowicz, Frank Richard (Frank Oz) puppeteer, film director
Pacino, Al (Alfredo James Pacino) actor
Pakula, Alan J. producer, director
Pardo, Dominick George (Don Pardo) broadcasting announcer
Parker, Maceo jazz musician, alto saxophone
Parkinson, Georgina ballet mistress
Parks, Gordon Roger Alexander Buchanan film director, author, photographer, composer
Parsons, David artistic director, choreographer
Parsons, Estelle actress
Pavarotti, Luciano lyric tenor
Pellegrini, Anna Maria soprano
Penn, Arthur Hiller film and theatre producer
Pennario, Leonard concert pianist, composer
Perahia, Murray pianist
Peress, Maurice symphony conductor, musicologist
Perlmutter, Alvin Howard television and film producer
Perry, Douglas opera singer
Perry, Ronald dancer
Peters, Bernadette (Bernadette Lazzara) actress
Peters, Roberta soprano
Peterson, Kirk Charles ballet dancer
Philbin, Regis television personality
†Pirner, David musician, songwriter
Plunkett, Maryann actress
Poor, Peter Varnum producer, director
Porizkova, Paulina model, actress
Porter, Karl Hampton orchestra musical director, conductor
Porter, Stephen Winthrop stage director
Price, Leontyne concert and opera singer
Prince, Harold theatrical producer
Prosky, Robert Joseph actor
Protas, Ron dance company executive
Pryce, Jonathan actor
Puente, Tito Anthony orchestra leader, composer, arranger
Queler, Eve conductor
Questel, Mae actress
Quilico, Louis baritone
Quinn, Anthony Rudolph Oaxaca actor, writer, artist
Quintero, Jose theatrical director
Rachleff, Owen Spencer (Owen Spencer Rackleff) actor, author
Raimondi, Ruggero opera singer
†Raines, Joan Binder literary agent
Ramey, Samuel Edward bass soloist
Ramsay, Gustavus Remak actor
Rand, Calvin Gordon arts and education producer and consultant
Randall, Tony (Leonard Rosenberg) actor
†Randazzo, Anthony dancer
Randolph, David conductor
Ransom, Jeremy ballet dancer
Raphael, Sally Jessy talk-show host
Rawls, Eugenia actress
Reed, Pamela actress
Reeve, Christopher actor
Reich, Steve composer
†Renick, Kyle artistic director
†Rennie, Milbrey Tower television news producer
Renvall, Johan ballet dancer
Resnik, Regina operatic singer
Reyes, Andre ballet dancer
Rhodes, Samuel violist
Ricciarelli, Katia soprano
†Richard, Ellen theater executive
Richards, Keith musician
Richards, Lloyd George theatrical director, university administrator
Richardson, David John ballet dancer, educator
Richardson, Miranda actress
†Richter, Richard William television producer
Rivera, Chita (Conchita del Rivero) actress, singer, dancer
Rivera, Geraldo television personality, journalist
Rizzo, Francis arts administrator, writer, stage director
Roach, Maxwell Lemuel musician
Robbins, Jerome choreographer, director
Roberts, Tony (David Anthony Roberts) actor
Robison, Paula Judith flutist
Rodgers, Nile musician, record producer
Rodriguez, Beatriz ballerina
Roerick, William (George) (William Roehrick) actor, author
Rollins, Jack motion picture producer
Roney, Wallace musician
Rosen, Nathaniel Kent cellist
Rosenberger, Carol concert pianist
Ross, Diana singer, actress, entertainer, fashion designer
Rossellini, Isabella model, actress
Rostropovich, Mstislav Leopoldovich musician
Roy, Melinda dancer
Rudel, Julius conductor
Rysanek, Leonie soprano
Saddler, Donald Edward choreographer, dancer
Sade, (Helen Folasade Adu) singer, songwriter
Sadler, Eric recording industry executive
Sagami, Kim dancer
Salgado, Lissette dancer
Salonga, Lea actress, singer
Salvador, Sal jazz musician, guitarist, music educator, composer
Sandler, Jenny dancer
Saunders, Arlene opera singer
Scardino, Don artistic director
Schechner, Richard theater director, author, educator
Scheeder, Louis theater producer, director, educator
Schickele, Peter composer
†Schiffer, Claudia model
Schnabel, Karl Ulrich pianist
Schnell, Joseph dancer
Schorer, Suki ballet educator
Schroeder, Aaron Harold songwriter
Schwartz, Stephen Lawrence composer, lyricist
Schwarz, Gerard Ralph conductor, musician
Scofield, John jazz guitarist
Scott, Willard Herman radio and television performer
Scotto, Renata soprano
Sedaka, Neil singer, songwriter
Seeger, Pete songwriter
Segal, George actor
Seidelman, Susan film director
Seltzer, Leo filmmaker, educator, lecturer
Seraphine, Danny Peter drummer
Serkin, Peter pianist
Shaffer, Paul musician, bandleader
Shane, Rita opera singer
Shaw, (Francis) Harold performing arts administrator
Shelley, Carole Augusta actress
Shellman, Eddie J. ballet dancer, teacher, choreographer
Short, Robert Waltrip (Bobby Short) entertainer, author
Shostakovich, Maxim Dmitriyevich symphonic conductor
Shull, Richard Bruce actor
Sidney, Sylvia (Sophia Kossow) actress
Siegel, Marc Monroe television and film producer, writer, director
Sills, Beverly (Mrs. Peter B. Greenough) opera company director, coloratura soprano
Silver, Joan Micklin film director, screenwriter
Silver, Ron actor, director
†Silvers, Sally choreographer, performing company executive
Simmons, Gene musician
Simon, Joanna singer
Smith, Anna Deavere actress, playwright
†Smith, Anna Nicole model
Smith, James Oscar (Jimmy Smith) jazz organist
Smith, Lowell dancer
Smith, Malcolm Sommerville bass
Smuin, Michael choreographer, director, dancer
†Sobel, Shepard Michael artistic director
Solomon, Maynard Elliott music historian, former recording company executive
Solomons, Gus, Jr. (Gustave Martinez) choreographer, dancer, writer
Solov, Zachary choreographer, ballet artist
Sontag, Susan film and theatre director
Sorel, Claudette Marguerite pianist
Soto, Jock dancer
Soviero, Diana Barbara soprano
Soyer, David cellist, music educator
Spacey, Kevin actor
Spinella, Stephen actor
Sprecher, Baron William Gunther pianist, composer, conductor, diplomat
Springsteen, Bruce singer, songwriter, guitarist
Stapp, Olivia Brewer opera singer
Stern, Howard Allan radio disc jockey, television show host
Stern, Isaac violinist
Stills, Stephen musician, vocalist, composer
Stilwell, Richard Dale baritone
Stoltzman, Richard Leslie clarinetist
Storke, William Frederick Joseph film producer
Strasfogel, Ian opera company director
Stratas, Teresa (Anastasia Strataki) opera singer
Stretton, Ross ballet dancer
Styne, Jule composer, producer
Summers, Andy (Andrew James Somers) popular musician
Swados, Elizabeth A. composer, director, writer
Taddei, Giuseppe baritone
Talmi, Yoav conductor, composer
Taylor, Cecil Percival pianist, composer, educator
Taylor, Elizabeth Rosemond actress
†Taylor, Nicole Renée model
Taylor, Paul choreographer
Taylor, Regina actress
Tcherkassky, Marianna Alexsavena ballerina
Te Kanawa, Kiri opera and concert singer
Terborgh, Bert dancer
Tetley, Glen choreographer
Tharp, Twyla dancer, choreographer
Thomas, Michael Tilson symphony conductor
Thomas, Richard actor
Thorne, Francis composer
Tillis, Pam country singer, songwriter
Townshend, Peter musician, composer, singer
Tracey, Margaret dancer
Tree, Michael violinist, violist, educator
Trzetrzelewska, Basia musician, vocalist
Tune, Tommy (Thomas James Tune) musical theater director, dancer, choreographer, actor
†Turlington, Christy model
Turrentine, Stanley William musician
Ullmann, Liv actress
†Ulrich, Lars drummer
Uppman, Theodor concert and opera singer, voice educator
Upshaw, Dawn soprano
†Valletta, Amber model
Vandross, Luther singer
Van Halen, Eddie guitarist, rock musician
†Vedder, Eddie singer
†Vendela model
Verdon, Gwen (Gwyneth Evelyn) actress, dancer, choreographer
Volpe, Joseph opera company administrator
von Furstenberg, Betsy actress, writer
Von Stade, Frederica mezzo-soprano
Voultsos-Vourtzis, Pericles Count composer, conductor, educator, author, former honorary consul to Grenada
Wadsworth, Charles William pianist
Wagner, Alan Cyril television and film producer
Walker, Sandra mezzo-soprano
Walker, Wendy Joy ballet mistress
†Wallace, Robert F. dancer
Warden, Jack actor
Warfield, Gerald Alexander composer, writer
Warwick, Dionne singer
Washington, Shelley Lynne dancer
Waters, Sylvia dance company artistic director
Watts, André concert pianist
Watts, Heather ballerina
Weaver, Fritz William actor
Weaver, Sigourney (Susan Alexandra Weaver) actress
†Webb, Veronica fashion model, journalist
Weisgall, Hugo David composer, conductor
Weller, Peter actor
†Wenders, Wim film director
Wexler, Peter John producer, director, set designer
Whelan, Wendy ballet dancer
White, John Simon opera director
Whitehead, Robert theatrical producer
Whitener, William Garnett dancer, choreographer
Wiest, Dianne actress
Williams, Donald Maxey dancer, singer, actor
†Williams, Lucinda country musician
Williams, Stanley ballet dancer and teacher
Williams, Tony jazz drummer
Williams, Vanessa recording artist, actress
Williamson, Liz (Elizabeth Anne Ray Williamson) choreographer, dancer, educator
Willis, Gordon cinematographer
Wilson, Robert M. theatrical artist
†Wincenc, Carol concertizing flutist, educator
Wittstein, Edwin Frank stage and film production designer
Woetzel, Damian Abdo ballet dancer, educator
Woitach, Richard conductor, pianist
Wolfe, George C. theater director, producer, playwright
Wood, Ronald musician
Woodman, William E. theater, opera and television director
Worth, Irene actress
†Wright, Jeffrey actor
Wuorinen, Charles Peter composer
Wynette, Tammy singer
Yeager, Cheryl Lynn ballet dancer
Yellin, Victor Fell composer, music educator
Yeston, Maury composer, lyricist, educator
†Zaks, Jerry theatrical director, actor
Zawinul, Josef bandleader, composer, keyboardist, synthesist
Zhu, Ai-Lan opera singer
Zukerman, Pinchas concert violinist, violist, conductor
Zylis-Gara, Teresa Gerarda soprano

Nyack
Hendin, David Bruce literary agent, author, consultant, numismatist

Oswego
Nesbitt, Rosemary Sinnett theatre educator

Palisades
†Bracco, Lorraine actress
Cavett, Dick entertainer
Keitel, Harvey actor
Krainin, Julian Arthur film director, producer, writer, cinematographer
Murray, Bill actor, writer

Pittsford
Benson, Warren Frank composer, educator

Poughkeepsie
Wilson, Richard Edward composer, pianist, music educator

Pound Ridge
Ostrow, Stuart theatrical producer

Purchase
Lamagra, Anthony James concert pianist, television host, music educator

Quogue
Macero, Teo composer, conductor

Rego Park
Cronyn, Hume actor, writer, director
Tandy, Jessica actress

Riverdale
Hubley, Faith Elliott filmmaker, painter, animator

Rochester
Adler, Samuel Hans conductor, composer
Diamond, David Leo composer
Hodkinson, Sydney Phillip composer, educator
Horak, Jan-Christopher film studies educator, curator
Kowalke, Kim H. music educator, musicologist, conductor, foundation executive
Laires, Fernando concert piano educator
Marcellus, John Robert, III trombonist, educator
Rouse, Christopher Chapman, III composer
Schwantner, Joseph composer, educator
Weiss, Howard A. violinist, concertmaster, conductor, music educator

Saratoga Springs
Porter, David Hugh pianist, classicist, academic administrator, liberal arts educator

Sea Cliff
Popova, Nina *dancer, choreographer, director*

Sparkill
Dahl, Arlene *actress, author, designer, cosmetic executive*

Stony Brook
Baron, Samuel *flutist*

Syracuse
Akiyama, Kazuyoshi *conductor*
Driver, Robert Baylor, Jr. *opera administrator*
†Thompson, Tazewell Alfred *artistic director, writer*

Tarrytown
Kroll, Nathan *film producer, director*

Tuxedo Park
Shore, Howard Leslie *composer*

Washingtonville
Castel, Nico *tenor, educator*

White Plains
Magaziner, Elliot Albert *musician, conductor, educator*

Yonkers
Baumel, Herbert *violinist, conductor*

Yorktown Heights
Rosenfeld, Steven Ira *artistic director, music publisher*

NORTH CAROLINA

Asheville
Baker, Robert Hart *conductor*
Weed, Maurice James *composer, retired music educator*

Chapel Hill
Best, Winfield Judson *writer, television producer, public relations consultant*
Ellis, Michael *theatrical producer*
Hammond, David Alan *stage director, educator*
Newman, William Stein *music educator, author, pianist, composer*
Powell, Carolyn Wilkerson *music educator*

Charlotte
Smith, Arthur *radio and television producer, composer*

Durham
Bryan, Paul Robey, Jr. *musician, educator*
†Caesar, Shirley *gospel singer, evangelist*
Ward, Robert *composer, conductor, educator*

Greensboro
Gutter, Robert Harold *conductor, music educator*
Middleton, Herman David, Sr. *theater educator*

Greenville
Chauncey, Beatrice Arlene *music educator*

Jacksonville
Daugherty, Robert Michael *music educator, composer*

Raleigh
Casey, Ethel Laughlin *concert and opera singer*
Zimmermann, Gerhardt *conductor*

Winston Salem
Johnson, Norman *music director, opera producer, educator*
Perret, Peter James *symphony conductor*
Trautwein, George William *conductor*

OHIO

Akron
Poll, Heinz *choreographer, artistic director*
Schubert, Barbara Schuele *performing company executive*

Athens
Glidden, Robert Burr *musician, educator, academic administrator*

Berea
Strew, Suzanne Claflin *choreographer, dance educator*

Cincinnati
Belew, Adrian *guitarist, singer, songwriter, producer*
de Blasis, James Michael *artistic director, producer, stage director*
DeLeone, Carmon *conductor, musician, educator*
Hoffman, Joel Harvey *composer*
Kunzel, Erich, Jr. *conductor, arranger, educator*
Lopez-Cobos, Jesus *conductor*
Samuel, Gerhard *orchestra conductor, composer*
Tocco, James *pianist*

Cleveland
Alfieri, Lisa Gwyneth *ballet dancer, teacher*
Bamberger, David *opera company executive*
Erb, Donald *composer*
Giannetti, Louis Daniel *film educator, film critic*
Holderfield, Marilyn Ida *jazz vocalist*
Hruby, Frank M. *musician, critic, educator*
Keegan, Jane *opera and music theatre producer*
McConnell, Michael *opera company director*
Mc Farlane, Karen Elizabeth *concert artists manager*
Morris, Thomas William *symphony orchestra administrator*
Nahat, Dennis F. *artistic director, choreographer*
von Dohnányi, Christoph *musician, conductor*

Columbus
Brown, Firman Hewitt, Jr. *drama educator, theatrical director*
Drvota, Mojmir *cinema educator, author*
Haddad, George Richard *musician, educator*
Harris, Donald *composer*
Lowe, Clayton Kent *visual imagery, cinema, and video educator*
Russell, William Fletcher, III *opera company director*

Dayton
Schwarz, Josephine Lindeman *retired ballet company director, choreographer*
Walters, Jefferson Brooks *musician, retired real estate broker*

North Ridgeville
Nagy, Robert David *tenor*

Oberlin
Boe, David Stephen *musician, educator, college dean*

Oxford
Lehmkuhl, Lois D. *music educator*

Steubenville
Johnson, Micah William *television newscaster, director*

Strongsville
Oltman, C. Dwight *conductor, educator*

Toledo
Massey, Andrew John *conductor, composer*

Wooster
Stuart, James Fortier *musician, artistic director*

OKLAHOMA

Norman
Bryant, Celia Mae Small *music educator*
Carey, Thomas Devore *baritone, educator*
de Stwolinski, Gail Rounce Boyd *music theory and composition educator*
Eek, Nathaniel Sisson *retired fine arts educator*
Herstand, Theodore *theatre artist, educator*
Ross, Allan Anderson *music educator, university official*

Oklahoma City
McCoy, Wesley Lawrence *musician, conductor, educator*
Payne, Gareld Gene *vocal music educator, medical transcriptionist*
Valentine, Alan Darrell *symphony orchestra executive*

Tulsa
Bonsall, Joseph Sloan, Jr. *singer*
Clark, Roy *singer, musician, business executive*
Fender, Freddy (Baldemar Huerta) *singer*
Jasinski, Roman Larkin *artistic director*
Larkin, Moscelyne *retired artistic director, dancer*
†Powell, Sara Jordan *musician, religious worker*
Rubenstein, Bernard *orchestra conductor*
Sterban, Richard Anthony *singer*

OREGON

Ashland
Hirschfeld, Gerald Joseph *cinematographer*

Eugene
Bailey, Exine Margaret Anderson *soprano, educator*

Portland
Bailey, Robert C. *opera company executive*
DePreist, James Anderson *conductor*
Hill, Andrew William *jazz musician, composer*

PENNSYLVANIA

Bala Cynwyd
Pendergrass, Teddy (Theodore D. Pendergrass) *musician*

Bradfordwoods
Davis, Nathan Tate *musician, educator*

Broomall
Russo, John Peter *musician, composer*

Bryn Mawr
Goutman, Lois Clair *retired drama educator*
Stucky, Steven (Edward) *composer*

Delaware Water Gap
Woods, Philip Wells (Phil Woods) *jazz musician composer*

Drexel Hill
Martino, Michael Charles *entertainer, musician*

Drums
Palance, Jack *actor*

Erie
Hendl, Walter *conductor, pianist, composer*

Fayetteville
†Kocek, Stephanie Susan *theater executive*

Harrisburg
Newland, Larry J. *orchestra conductor*

Haverford
Davison, John Herbert *music educator, academic administrator*

Indiana
Perlongo, Daniel James *composer*

Jenkintown
Driehuys, Leonardus Bastiaan *conductor*

Kingston
Weisberger, Barbara *choreographer, artistic director, educator*

Kutztown
Ghiglia, Oscar Alberto *classical guitarist*

Philadelphia
Biava, Luis *musician*
Bookspan, Michael Lloyd *musician*
Breuninger, Tyrone *musician*
Clauser, Donald Roberdeau *musician*
Crumb, George Henry *composer, educator*
Graffman, Gary *pianist*
Meyer, Leonard B. *musician, educator*
Mostovoy, Marc Sanders *conductor*
Orlando, Danielle *opera company administrator*
Rudolf, Max *symphony and opera director*
Sawallisch, Wolfgang *conductor*
Smith, Lloyd *musician*
†Storm, Jonathan Morris *television critic*
Washington, Grover, Jr. *musician, producer, composer, arranger*
Wernick, Richard Frank *composer, conductor*

Pittsburgh
Balada, Leonardo *composer, educator*
Bardyguine, Patricia Wilde *ballerina, ballet theatre executive*
Capobianco, Tito *opera director*
†Croan, Robert James *music critic, singer*
Gray, Charles Buffum *theatrical director, producer*
Hollingsworth, Samuel Hawkins, Jr. *bassist*
Maazel, Lorin *conductor, musician*
Norton, Eunice *pianist*
Petrov, Nicolas *dance educator, choreographer*
Rogers, Fred McFeely *television producer and host*
Wilde, Patricia *artistic director*

Selinsgrove
Diers, Hank H. *drama educator, playwright, director*

Sharon
Sheen, Martin (Ramon Estevez) *actor*

Sumneytown
Gordon, David Jamieson *tenor*

Swarthmore
Devin, (Philip) Lee *dramaturg, theater educator*
Swing, Peter Gram *music educator*

University Park
Baisley, Robert William *music educator*
Williams, Edward Vinson *music history educator*

Washington Crossing
Stone, Ezra Chaim *theatrical producer and director, educator, actor, writer, farmer*

RHODE ISLAND

Providence
†Jenkins, Richard Dale *actor, theatre director*
Nelson, Ron *composer, conductor, educator*

SOUTH CAROLINA

Anderson
Carroll, Edward Perry *instrumental music educator, conductor*

Charleston
Ashley, Franklin Bascom *theater educator, writer*
Ivey, Robert Carl *artistic director, educator, choreographer*
Overton, Marcus Lee *performing arts administrator*
†Porter, Thomas Joseph, Jr. *writer, songwriter*
Scott, Henry Lawrence *concert pianist-humorist*
Stahl, David *orchestra and opera conductor*

Greenville
†Grimes, J. William *cable television executive*

Hilton Head Island
Brock, Karena Diane *ballerina, educator, choreographer*

TENNESSEE

Brentwood
Tucker, Tanya Denise *singer*

Hendersonville
Allen, Duane David *singer*
Axton, Hoyt Wayne *singer, composer*
Bare, Robert Joseph (Bobby Bare) *country music singer, songwriter*
Cash, June Carter *singer*
Sanders, Steve *singer*

Hermitage
Anderson, James William, III *performing artist, composer*

Jefferson City
Ball, Louis Oliver, Jr. *music educator*

Knoxville
Jacobs, Kenneth A. *composer, educator*
Trevor, Kirk David Niell *orchestra conductor, cellist*

Lebanon
Daniels, Charlie *musician, songwriter*

Madison
Kennedy, Matthew Washington *pianist, educator*
Wells, Kitty (Muriel Deason Wright) *country western singer*

Memphis
Canon, Robert Morris *performing arts executive, opera producer*
Piazza, Marguerite *opera singer, actress, entertainer*
Presley, Priscilla *actress*
Rich, Charles Allan *singer*
Williams, David Russell *music educator*

Mount Juliet
LeDoux, Chris Lee *country musician*

Nashville
Anderson, Lynn (Rene Anderson) *singer*
Black, Clint *country singer, musician*
Bogguss, Suzy *country music singer, songwriter*
Brooks, Garth (Troyal Garth Brooks) *country music singer*
Brooks, Kix *musician*
Carter, James McCord *television producer, personality*
Crowell, Rodney J. *country music recording artist, songwriter*
Davis, Danny (George Joseph Nowlan) *musician*
Dean, Billy (William Howard Dean) *country singer, songwriter*
Diffie, Joe *country singer, songwriter*
Dunn, Ronnie *musician*
Earle, Steve *country rockabilly musician*
Gayle, Crystal *singer*
Gentry, Teddy *country musician*
Greenwood, Lee Melvin *singer*
Harris, Emmylou *singer*
Hartford, John Cowan *singer, songwriter*
Jackson, Alan *country songwriter, singer*
Jones, George *country music singer, songwriter*
Lee, Brenda (Brenda Mae Tarpley) *singer, entertainer*
Mandrell, Barbara Ann *singer, entertainer*
Mattea, Kathy *vocalist, songwriter*
Monroe, William Smith *mandolin player, singer*
Morgan, Lorrie (Loretta Lynn Morgan) *country singer*
Oslin, K. T. (Kay Toinette Oslin) *country singer*
Pearl, Minnie (Sarah Ophelia Colley Cannon) *entertainer*
Prine, John *singer, songwriter*
Pruett, Jeanne *singer, songwriter*
Rabbitt, Edward Thomas *singer, songwriter*
Rogers, Roy (Leonard Franklin Slye) *country musician, actor*
Skaggs, Ricky *country musician*
Stuart, Marty *country music singer, musician, songwriter*
Tillis, Mel(vin) *musician, songwriter*
Tippin, Aaron *country music singer, songwriter*
Van Shelton, Ricky *country music singer, songwriter*
Wagoner, Porter *country music singer, composer*
Waters, Roger *rock musician*

Paris
Williams, Hank, Jr. *country music singer, songwriter*

TEXAS

Arlington
Carey, Milburn Ernest *musician, educator*
Malone, Edwin Scott, III *radio and television producer, public relations consultant*
Russell, Andrew Milo *music educator*

Austin
Antokoletz, Elliott Maxim *music educator*
Brockett, Oscar Gross *theatre educator*
Jennings, Coleman Alonzo *dramatics educator*
Kennan, Kent Wheeler *composer, educator*
King, Carole *composer, singer*
†Pinkston, Russell Fountain *music composition educator*
Schulz-Widmar, Russell Eugene *musician, educator, composer*
Sharir, Yacov *artistic director, choreographer*
Whitmore, Jon Scott *theater educator*
Young, Phyllis Casselman *music educator*

Dallas
Anderson, Robert Theodore *music educator, organist*
Gage, John *opera company executive*
Galt, John William *actor*
Garson, Greer *actress*
Horchow, S(amuel) Roger *theater producer*
Pell, Jonathan Laurence *artistic administrator*
Pride, Charley *singer*
†Young, Norma *artistic director*

Del Valle
Browne, Jackson *singer, songwriter*

Denton
Latham, William Peters *composer, former educator*

Fort Worth
Cliburn, Van (Harvey Lavan Cliburn, Jr.) *concert pianist*
Dean, Margo *artistic director*
Doris Ann, (Doris Ann Scharfenberg) *producer, former broadcasting company executive*
Giordano, John Read *conductor*
Mc Kinney, James Carroll *baritone, educator*

Houston
Alexander, Michael Lee *music educator, cellist*
Cooper, Paul *composer, educator*
De Main, John *conductor, music director*
Englesmith, Tejas *actor, producer, curator*
Frank, Hilda Rhea Kaplan *dancer*
Gottschalk, Arthur William *music company executive and educator*
Hammond, Michael Peter *music educator, dean*
Jones, Samuel *conductor*
Moffatt, Joyce Anne *performing arts executive*
Rose, Beatrice Schroeder (Mrs. William H. Rose) *harpist, educator*
Stevenson, Ben *choreographer, ballet company executive*

Marble Falls
Cross, Christopher *recording artist, songwriter, singer*

Navasota
Norris, Chuck (Carlos Ray) *actor*

Pasadena
Gilley, Mickey Leroy *musician*

Richardson
Gary, John *singer*
Goldberg, Leonard *television and movie producer*

Rockwall
House, Robert William *music educator*
Wallace, Mary Elaine *opera director, author*

San Antonio
Cruz-Romo, Gilda *soprano*
Greenberg, Nat *orchestra administrator*
Howard, George Sallad é *conductor, music consultant, educator*
Marek, Vladimir *ballet director, educator*
Thornton, William James, Jr. *composer, music educator*

Waco
Colvin, (Otis) Herbert, Jr. *musician, educator*
Sternberg, Daniel Arie *musician, conductor, educator*

Whitehouse
Baker, Rebecca Louise *musician, music educator, consultant*

UTAH

Ogden
Balsiger, David Wayne *television director, author, researcher, producer*

Provo
Woodbury, Lael Jay *theatre educator*

Saint George
Belnap, Norma Lee Madsen *musician*

Salt Lake City
Hamill, Mark Richard *actor*
Hart, John *artistic director*
Ottley, Jerold Don *choral conductor, educator*
Silverstein, Joseph Harry *conductor, musician*

VERMONT

Bennington
Dixon, William Robert *musician, composer, educator*

VIRGINIA

Alexandria
Kitt, Loren Wayne *musician*
Tyl, Noel Jan *baritone, astrologer*

Arlington
†Bohannon, James Everett *talk show host, newscaster, reporter*

Blacksburg
Dukore, Bernard Frank *theatre arts and humanities educator, writer*

Charlottesville
Velimirovic, Milos M. *music educator*

Chester
Gray, Frederick Thomas, Jr. *actor, educator*

Harrisonburg
Arthur, Thomas Hahn *theater educator, director*

Lakeridge
Bales, Richard Henry Horner *conductor, composer*

Lexington
Seeger, Michael *musician, singer, folklorist*

Moneta
Pfeuffer, Robert John *musician*

Norfolk
Mark, Peter *director, conductor*
Musgrave, Thea *composer, conductor*

Petersburg
Dance, Gloria Fenderson *dance studio executive, ballet administrator*

Radford
James, Carolyne Faye (Clarity James) *mezzo-soprano*

Roanoke
Bond, Victoria Ellen *conductor, composer*
Stanley, Ralph *bluegrass musician*

Ruckersville
Soderbergh, Steven Andrew *filmmaker*

Staunton
Balsley, Philip Elwood *entertainer*

Vienna
Lyons, Paul Michael *producer, film*

Virginia Beach
Freyss, David *producer, director*

Williamsburg
†Hornsby, Bruce Randall *composer, musician*

WASHINGTON

Anacortes
Ives, Burl (Icle Ivanhoe) *singer, actor*

Marysville
Philpott, Larry La Fayette *horn player*

Mercer Island
Kelm, Linda *opera singer*

Seattle
Forbes, David Craig *musician*
†Houk, Benjamin Noah *ballet dancer*
Jenkins, Speight *opera company executive, writer*
Loper, Robert Bruce *theater director, educator*
†Moore, Benjamin *theatrical producer*
Nishitani, Martha *dancer*
Russell, Francia *ballet director, educator*
Staryk, Steven S. *violinist, concertmaster, educator*
Stowell, Kent *ballet director*
†Sullivan, Daniel J. *artistic director*
Witham, Barry Bates *drama educator*

Spokane
Fowler, Betty Janmae *dance company director, editor*

Tacoma
Hansen, Edward Allen *music educator, organist*

Vancouver
Larson, Charles Lester *television writer, producer, author*

WEST VIRGINIA

Charleston
Conlin, Thomas (Byrd) *conductor*
Drennen, William Miller, Jr. *cultural administrator, film executive, producer, director, mineral resource executive*

Morgantown
Trythall, Harry Gilbert *music educator, composer*

Salem
Raad, Virginia *pianist, lecturer*

WISCONSIN

Beloit
Gates, Crawford Marion *conductor, composer*

Eau Claire
Patterson, Donald Lee *music educator*

Madison
Badura-Skoda, Paul (Ludwig Badura) *pianist*
Davis, Richard *musician, music educator*
Dembski, Stephen Michael *composer, university music composition professor*
Johnson, Roland A. *conductor, music director*
Rosser, Annetta Hamilton *composer*

Milwaukee
Downey, John Wilham *composer, pianist, conductor, educator*
Hanthorn, Dennis Wayne *performing arts association administrator*
Uecker, Bob *actor, radio announcer, former baseball player, TV personality*

WYOMING

Green River
†Boswell, Christopher Orr *broadcast journalist*

Jackson Hole
Adler, Warren *novelist, producer, playwright*

CANADA

ALBERTA

Banff
Fruchtman, Milton Allen *film and television producer, director*

Calgary
Monk, Allan James *baritone*
Roberts, John Peter Lee *cultural advisor, adminstrator, lecturer, writer*

Edmonton
Archer, Violet Balestreri *music educator, composer, pianist, organist, percussionist, adjudicator*
Hoyt, David Lemire *musician*

BRITISH COLUMBIA

Saanichton
Little, Carl Maurice *performing arts administrator*

Vancouver
Alleyne, John *dancer, choreographer*
Hallam, Robert J. *performing company executive, consultant*
Raffi, (Raffi Cavoukian) *folksinger, children's entertainer*
Trifonidis, Beverly Ann *lecturer, opera company manager, accountant*

Victoria
Horn, Paul Joseph *musician*
McCoppin, Peter *symphony orchestra conductor*

MANITOBA

Winnipeg
Kaminski, John *dancer*
Riske, William Kenneth *arts administrator*
Spohr, Arnold Theodore *artistic director, choreographer*

ONTARIO

Don Mills
Applebaum, Louis *composer, conductor*

Hamilton
Lipton, Daniel Bernard *conductor*
Shaw, John Firth *orchestra administrator*

London
†William, David *director, actor*

Mississauga
Peterson, Oscar Emmanuel *pianist*

Niagara-on-the-Lake
Newton, Christopher *artistic director*

Ottawa
Augustyn, Frank Joseph *dancer, artistic director*
Franca, Celia *ballet director, choreographer, dancer, narrator*
Gillingham, Bryan Reginald *music educator*
LaHay, David George Michael *ballet company director*

Saint Catherines
Florio, Ermanno *conductor, music administrator*

Stratford
Neville, John *actor, director*

Thornhill
Nimmons, Phillip Rista *composer, conductor, clarinetist, educator*

Toronto
Anderson, Reid Bryce *ballet company artistic director*
Beckwith, John *musician, composer, educator*
Boswell, Philip John *opera administrator*
Bradshaw, Richard James *conductor*
Cable, Howard Reid *composer, conductor*
Colgrass, Michael Charles *composer*
Crawley, Alexander Radford *performing artist, composer*
Doherty, Tom (Thomas Storen, Jr.) *art director, set designer*
†Egoyan, Atom *film director*
Eklof, Svea Christine *ballet dancer*
Eldred, Gerald Marcus *performing arts association executive*
Feldbrill, Victor *conductor*
Freedman, Harry *composer*
Glasco, Kimberly *ballet dancer*
Harwood, Vanessa Clare *ballet dancer*
Israelievitch, Jacques H. *violinist, conductor*
Jewison, Norman Frederick *film producer, director*
Kain, Karen Alexandria *ballet dancer*
Kirby, Charles William, Jr. *dancer, choreographer*
†Kudelka, James *ballet dancer, choreographer*
Kuerti, Anton Emil *pianist, composer*
Lavoie, Serge *principal dancer*
Murray, Anne *singer*
Nisbet, Joanne *ballet mistress*
Oliphant, Betty *ballet school director*
Pedersen, Paul Richard *composer, educator*
Rasky, Harry *producer, director, writer*
Schramek, Tomas *ballet dancer*
Shearing, George Albert *pianist, composer*
Smith, Raymond *dancer*
Stefanschi, Sergiu *dancer*
Wilder, Valerie *ballet company director*
Wilkins, Ormsby *music director, conductor, pianist*
Witkowsky, Gizella *dancer*

QUEBEC

Laval
Juillet, Chantal *violinist*

Montreal
Chiriaeff, Ludmilla Gorny *ballet company executive, ballet dancer, choreographer*
†DesRoches, Pierre *director*
Dutoit, Charles *conductor*
Gulkin, Harry *arts administrator, film producer*
Major, André *radio producer, writer, educator*
Nault, Fernand *choreographer*
Papineau-Couture, Jean *composer, educator*
†Rhodes, Lawrence *artistic director*
Uzan, Bernard Franck *general and artistic director*
Woszczyk, Wieslaw Richard *audio engineering educator, researcher*

Sainte-Foy
Pasquier, Joël *music educator*

MEXICO

Mexico City
†Arau, Alfonso *film director*

AUSTRALIA

Potts Point
Beresford, Bruce *film director*

Sydney
†Miller, George *film director*

AUSTRIA

Vienna
Faulkner, Julia Ellen *opera singer*
Kagel, Mauricio *multi-media composer, director*
Ludwig, Christa *mezzo-soprano*

COSTA RICA

San José
Hoffman, Irwin *orchestra conductor*

ENGLAND

Balcombe
Scofield, Paul *actor*

Birmingham
Banowetz, Joseph Murray *musician, music educator*

Brighton East Sussex
Watkin, David *film director, cinematographer*

Buckinghamshire
Forbes, Bryan *actor, writer, director*

Chiswick
Nelson, John Wilton *symphonic conductor*
Vaness, Carol *soprano*

Iver Heath, Bucks
Kubrick, Stanley *producer, director, writer*

London
Andrews, Anthony *actor*
Ashkenazy, Vladimir Davidovich *concert pianist, conductor*
Barshai, Rudolf Borisovich *conductor*
Bart, Lionel *composer, lyricist*
Bates, Alan (Arthur Bates) *actor*
†Beck, Jeff *musician, composer, vocalist*
Biddle, Adrian *cinematographer*
Bonynge, Richard *opera conductor*
Bowie, David (David Robert Jones) *musician, actor*
Branagh, Kenneth *actor, director*
Bream, Julian *classical guitarist and lutanist*
Cellan-Jones, James Gwynne *television director*
Christie, Julie *actress*
Cleve, George *conductor*
Codron, Michael Victor *theatrical producer*
Conti, Tom *actor, writer, director*
Curry, Tim *actor*
Day-Lewis, Daniel *actor*
Dickinson, Peter *composer*
Ewing, Maria Louise *soprano*
Ghiaurov, Nicolai *opera singer*
Gielgud, Sir (Arthur) John *actor, director*
Hall, Sir Peter Reginald Frederick *theater opera and film director*
Hampshire, Susan *actress*
Harper, Heather Mary *soprano*
Harrison, George *musician*
Hawthorne, Nigel Barnard *actor*
Hendricks, Barbara *opera singer, recitalist*
Hogwood, Christopher Jarvis Haley *music director, educator*
Holm, Ian *actor*
Hopkins, Sir Anthony (Philip) *actor*
Hoskins, Bob (Robert William Hoskins) *actor*
Hurt, John Vincent *actor*
Idle, Eric *actor, screenwriter*
Irons, Jeremy John *actor*
John, Elton Hercules (Reginald Kenneth Dwight) *musician*
Jones, Terry *film director, author*
Jordan, Neil Patrick *film director*
Kingsley, Ben *actor*
Le Vien, John Douglas (Jack Le Vien) *motion picture and television producer, director*
Lloyd Webber, Sir Andrew *composer*
Lynne, Gillian Barbara *choreographer, dancer, actress*
Mackintosh, Cameron *musical theater producer*
Marriner, Sir Neville *orchestra conductor*
McIntyre, Donald Conroy *opera singer, baritone*
McKellen, Ian *actor*
Miller, Jonathan Wolfe *theater and film director, physician*
Minton, Yvonne Fay *mezzo-soprano*
†Mirren, Helen *actress*
Nunn, Trevor Robert *director*
Oldman, Gary *actor*
O'Toole, Peter *actor*
Pleasence, Donald *actor*
Plowright, Joan Anne *actress*
Previn, Andre *composer, conductor*
Puttnam, David Terence *film producer*
Rattle, Simon *conductor*
Ricci, Ruggiero *violinist, educator*
†Rigg, Diana *actress*
Salonen, Esa-Pekka *conductor*
Schaufuss, Peter *dancer, producer, choreographer, ballet director*
Schlesinger, John Richard *film, opera and theater director*
Serebrier, José *musician, conductor, composer*
Smith, Dame Maggie *actress*
Starr, Ringo (Richard Starkey) *musician, actor*
Sting, (Gordon Matthew Sumner) *musician, songwriter, actor*
Sutherland, Dame Joan *retired soprano*
Tebaldi, Renata *opera singer*
Tennstedt, Klaus *conductor*
Thompson, Emma *actress*
Tureck, Rosalyn *concert artist, author, editor, educator*
Ustinov, Sir Peter Alexander *actor, director, writer*
Wallis, Diana Lynn *artistic director*
Winner, Michael Robert *film director, writer, producer*
Zinnemann, Fred *film director*
Zschau, Marilyn *singer*

Middlesex
Francis, Freddie *film producer and director*
Lester, Richard *film director*

Richmond Green
Attenborough, Sir Richard Samuel *actor, producer, director, goodwill ambassador*

Sandys
Stigwood, Robert Colin *theater, movie, television and record producer*

Uxbridge
Healey, Derek Edward *composer*

Warwick
Hands, Terence David (Terry Hands) *theater director*

Wiltshire
Gabriel, Peter *vocalist, composer*

FRANCE

Neuilly-sur-Seine
Ophuls, Marcel *film director and producer*

Paris
†Annaud, Jean-Jacques *film director, screenwriter*
Boulez, Pierre *composer, conductor*
de Havilland, Olivia Mary *actress*
Huffstodt, Karen *soprano*
Jolas, Betsy *composer*
Kurtz, Eugene Allen *composer, educator, consultant*
Marton, Eva *opera singer*
Polanski, Roman *film director, writer, actor*
Rampal, Jean-Pierre Louis *flutist*
Rohmer, Eric (Henri Joseph Scherer) *film director*

GERMANY

Berlin
Abbado, Claudio *conductor*
Fischer-Dieskau, Dietrich *baritone*

Dresden
Schreier, Peter *tenor*

Hamburg
Neumeier, John *choreographer, ballet company director*
Ramsey, Bill (William McCreery) *singer, actor, composer-lyricist, television executive*

Munich
Araiza, Francisco (José Francisco Araiza Andrade) *opera singer*
Chapman, Wes *dancer*
Fassbaender, Brigitte *opera singer*
Goodman, Alfred *composer, musicologist*

GRAND CAYMAN ISLAND

Crockett, James Grover, III *musician, former music publisher*

ISLE OF MAN

Peel
Wakeman, Rick *entertainer, composer*

ISRAEL

Tel Aviv
Mehta, Zubin *conductor, musician*

ITALY

Frattocchie Marino
Storaro, Vittorio *cinematographer*

Pontedera
Grotowski, Jerzy *theater director, acting educator*

Ravenna
Muti, Riccardo *orchestra and opera conductor*

Rome
†Antonioni, Michelangelo *film director*
Bertolucci, Bernardo *film director*
Dashow, James *composer*
Loren, Sophia *actress*
Zeffirelli, Franco *theater and film director*

Siena
Berio, Luciano *composer, conductor, educator*

JAPAN

Setagaya-Ku
Kurosawa, Akira *film director*

THE NETHERLANDS

Hilversum
De Waart, Edo *conductor*

The Hague
Kylián, Jirí *choreographer*

SCOTLAND

Edinburgh
McMaster, Brian John *artistic director*

SPAIN

Barcelona
de Larrocha, Alicia *concert pianist*

Madrid
Berganza Vargas, Teresa *mezzo-soprano*
Frühbeck de Burgos, Rafael *conductor*
†Trueba, Fernando *film director and producer, screenwriter*

SWEDEN

Stockholm
Soederstrom, Elisabeth Anna *opera singer*

SWITZERLAND

Geneva
Barenboim, Daniel *conductor, pianist*
Morgenstern, Sheldon Jon *symphony orchestra conductor*

Rouille
Godard, Jean-Luc *film director*

Staad
Moore, Roger George *actor*

ADDRESS UNPUBLISHED

Adaskin, Murray *composer*
Adato, Perry Miller *documentary producer, director, writer*
Adelson, Mervyn Lee *entertainment and communication industry executive*
Alda, Alan *actor, writer, director*
Allen, Marilyn Myers Pool *theater director, video producer*
Allen, Woody (Allen Stewart Konigsberg) *actor, filmmaker, author*
Almond, Paul *film director, producer, writer*
Andrews, Julie *actress, singer*
Ansbacher, Charles Alexander *conductor, musician*
Apted, Michael D. *film director*
Archer, Anne *actress*
Arenal, Julie (Mrs. Barry Primus) *choreographer*
Armistead, Thomas Boyd, III *television and film producer*
Arova, Sonia *ballet educator, administrator*
Arthur, Beatrice *actress*
Ashby, Clifford Charles *theatre arts educator, historian*
Askin, Leon *artistic director, actor, producer, writer*
Assante, Armand *actor*
Atherton, William *actor*
Auberjonois, René Murat *actor*
Aumont, Jean-Pierre *actor, author*
Avalon, Frankie *singer, actor*
Avian, Bob *choreographer, producer*
Badham, John MacDonald *motion picture director*
Baker, Joe Don *actor*
Bakula, Scott *actor*
Baldwin, Alec (Alexander Rae Baldwin, III) *actor*
Balsam, Martin Henry *actor*
Balter, Alan *conductor, music director*
Barselou, Paul Edgar *actor, writer*
Beatty, Ned *actor*
Beatty, (Henry) Warren *actor, producer, director*
Begley, Ed, Jr. *actor*
Belafonte, Harry *singer, concert artist, actor*
Bergen, Candice *actress, writer, photojournalist*
Berlinger, Warren *actor*
Bernhardt, Melvin *theater director*
Bernstein, Elmer *composer, conductor*
Bertinelli, Valerie *actress*
Bierley, Paul Edmund *musician, author, publisher*
Bjerknes, Michael Leif *dancer*
Blackstone, Harry Bouton, Jr. *magician, actor*
Bloomquist, Kenneth Gene *music educator, university bands director*
†Blossom, Beverly *choreographer, dance educator*
Boatright, Ann Long *dancer, pianist, music educator, choreographer*
Bochner, Hart *actor*
Bock, Jerry (Jerrold Lewis) *composer*
Bogosian, Eric *performance artist, actor*
Bonerz, Peter *actor, director*
Borgnine, Ernest *actor*
Bortz, Paul Isaac *media, sport and entertainment consultant*
Bowles, Paul Frederick *composer, author*
Boyd, Liona Maria *musician*
Boyle, Peter *actor*
Brando, Marlon, Jr. *actor*
Brennan, Eileen Regina *actress*
Brenner, David *comedian*
Briccetti, Joan Therese *symphony orchestra manager, management consultant*
Brooks, Albert (Albert Einstein) *actor, writer, director*
Brosnan, Pierce *actor*
Brown, Earle *composer, conductor*
Brown, Jim (James Nathaniel Brown) *film actor, former professional football player*
Brown, Ruth *rhythm and blues singer*
Bunim, Mary-Ellis *television producer*
Burstyn, Ellen (Edna Rae Gillooly) *actress*
Busey, Gary *actor, musician*
Busfield, Timothy *actor*
†Bushnell, Bill *theatrical director, producer*
Butkus, Dick *actor, former professional football player*
Byrne, David *musician, composer, artist, director*
Camp, Joseph Shelton, Jr. *film producer, director, writer*
Canin, Stuart Victor *violinist*
Cannon, Dyan *actress*
Capice, Philip Charles *television production executive*
Carlyss, Earl Winston *musician*
Carney, Arthur William Matthew *actor*
Carradine, Keith Ian *actor, singer, composer*
Carson, Johnny *television personality*
Carter, Elliott Cook, Jr. *composer*
Carter, (William) Hodding, III *television and newspaper journalist*
Carter, Ronald *musician*
Cash, Johnny *entertainer*
Caswell, Dorothy Ann Cottrell *arts administrator*
Cates, Phoebe *actress*
Chamberlain, (George) Richard *actor*
Channing, Stockard (Susan Stockard) *actress*
Chapman, Tracy *singer, songwriter*
Chapman, William *baritone*
Charry, Michael R(onald) *musician, conductor*
Chercover, Murray *television executive*
Christine, Virginia Feld *actress*
Christopher, Russell Lewis *baritone*
Clark, Candy *actress*
Clarke, Malcolm *filmmaker*
Claver, Robert Earl *television director, producer*
Close, Glenn *actress*
Cobham, William Emanuel, Jr. *musician*
Coburn, James *actor*
Cody, Iron Eyes *actor*
Cohen, Alexander H. *theatrical and television producer*
Colbert, Claudette (Lily Chauchoin) *actress*
Coleman, Dabney W. *actor*
Collier, Gaylan Jane *drama educator*
Collins, Joan Henrietta *actress*
Colman, Edward Brof *film director, cinematographer*
Cone, Edward Toner *composer, emeritus music educator*
Connors, Mike (Krekor Ohanian) *actor*
Consoli, Marc-Antonio *composer*
Cook, Fielder *producer, director*
Cooper, Alice (Vincent Furnier) *vocalist, composer*
Cooper, Hal *television director*
Cooper, Jackie *actor, director, producer*
Copperfield, David (David Kotkin) *illusionist, director, producer, writer*
Corey, Jeff *actor, director, educator*
Cosby, Bill *actor, entertainer*
Cossa, Dominic Frank *baritone*
Costner, Kevin *actor*
Cotrubas, Ileana *opera singer, lyric soprano, retired*
Cover, Franklin Edward *actor*
Crosby, Norman Lawrence *comedian*
Crouse, Lindsay *actress*
Cruise, Tom (Tom Cruise Mapother, IV) *actor*
Cullum, John *actor, singer*
Cummings, Constance *actress*
Currier, Ruth *dancer, choreographer and educator*
Curson, Theodore *musician*
Dabbs, Henry Erven *television and film producer, educator*
Dafoe, Willem *actor*
Dailey, Irene *actress, educator*
Daltrey, Roger *musician*
Dana, Jerilyn *ballet company administrator*
Danner, Blythe Katharine (Mrs. Bruce W. Paltrow) *actress*
Danza, Tony *actor*
Davidovsky, Mario *composer*
Davis, Mac *singer, songwriter*
Dean, Dearest (Lorene Glosup) *songwriter*
De Felitta, Frank Paul *producer, writer, director*
De Frank, Vincent *conductor*
Del Tredici, David *composer*
de Luce, Virginia *entertainer*
De Luise, Dom *actor*
Delza-Munson, Elizabeth *dancer, choreographer, educator*
De Mornay, Rebecca *actress*
Deneuve, Catherine (Catherine Dorleac) *actress*
Devane, William *actor*
Devlin, Michael Coles *bass-baritone*
Diaz, Justino *bass-baritone*
Dickerson, Nancy (Whitehead) *free lance television producer, news correspondent*
Dickinson, Angie (Angeline Brown) *actress*
Diemer, Emma Lou *composer, music educator*
Dishy, Bob *actor*
Dolenz, Mickey (George Michael Dolenz) *singer, actor*
Dolin, Samuel Joseph *composer, educator*
Donahue, Elinor *actress*
Dorn, Dolores *actress*
†Drake, Ervin Maurice *composer, author*
Duncan, Sandy *actress*
Dunn, Mignon *mezzo-soprano*
Durning, Charles *actor*
Duvall, Robert *actor*
Dysart, Richard A. *actor*
Eagan, Sherman G. *producer, communications executive*
Eagle, Jack *commercial actor, comedian*
Ebb, Fred *lyricist, librettist*
Edwards, Ryan Hayes *baritone*
Ehrling, Sixten *orchestra conductor*
Elder, Mark Philip *conductor*
Elgart, Larry Joseph *orchestra leader*
Elikann, Lawrence S. (Larry Elikann) *television and film director*
Elizondo, Hector *actor*
Ely, Joe *singer and songwriter*
Esposito, Giancarlo *actor*
Evdokimova, Eva *prima ballerina assoluta, choreographer, director, producer*
Everhart, Rex *actor, director, photographer*
Evstatieva, Stefka *opera singer*
Fabares, Shelley *actress*
Falsey, John Henry, Jr. *television producer*
Farrow, Mia Villiers *actress*
†Fawcett, Farrah Leni *actress, model*
Feldman, Thomas Myron *director, lighting director, director of photography, film company executive*
Ferguson, Maynard *trumpeter, band leader*
Field, Sally *actress*
Fields, Freddie *producer, agent*
Filerman, Michael Herman *television producer*
Fitzgerald, Geraldine *actress*
Fletcher, Louise *actress*
Ford, Harrison *actor*
Ford, Nancy Louise *composer, scriptwriter*
Forman, Miloš *film director*
Forsythe, Henderson *actor*
Foss, Lukas *composer, conductor, pianist*
Fredricks, Richard *baritone*
†Freston, Thomas E. *cable television programming executive*
Gagnon, Edith Morrison *ballerina, singer, actress*
Ganz, Lowell *screenwriter, television producer*
Garcia, Jerry (Jerome John Garcia) *guitarist, composer*
Garfunkel, Art *singer, actor*
Garner, James (James Scott Bumgarner) *actor*
Garrard, Don Edward Burdett *operatic and concert singer*
Gates, Larry *actor*
Gatlin, Larry Wayne *singer, songwriter*
Gehm, Denise Charlene *ballerina, arts administrator*
Gelman, Larry *actor*
Giacomini, Giuseppe *tenor*
Gibson, Mel *actor*
Gilbert, Kenneth Albert *harpsichordist*
Gilliam, Terry Vance *film director, actor, illustrator, writer*
Giordano, Tony *director*
Givens, Robin *actress*
Glover, Crispin Hellion *actor*
Glynn, Carlin (Carlin Masterson) *actress*
Goldberg, Whoopi (Caryn Johnson) *actress*
Goldblum, Jeff *actor*
Goldovsky, Boris *musician*
Goodman, Erika *dancer, actress*
Gorme, Eydie *singer*
Gossett, Louis, Jr. *actor*
Gould, Morton *composer, conductor*
Grant, Alexander Marshall *ballet director*
Greaves, William Garfield *film director, producer*
†Green, George *radio executive*
Griffith, Melanie *actress*
Grosbard, Ulu *director*
†Gross, Terry R. *radio producer, host*
Guinness, Sir Alec *actor*
Guttman, Irving Allen *opera stage director*
Hackett, Buddy *actor*
Hall, Conrad L. *cinematographer*
Hall, James Stanley *jazz guitarist, composer*
Hall, Janice *soprano*
Hall, Monty *television producer, actor*
Halmi, Robert *film producer*
Halsey, James Albert *international entertainment impressario, theatrical producer, talent manager*
Hamlisch, Marvin *composer*
Hampton, Lionel Leo *composer, conductor, entertainer*
Harris, Barbara *actress*
†Harris, Joseph *theatrical producer*
Harris, Margaret *pianist, conductor, composer*
Harris, Richard (Richard St. John) *actor*
Harryhausen, Ray Frederick *special effects expert*
Hart, Dorothy *actress*
Hart, Evelyn *ballet dancer*
Hartman, Phil Edward *actor*
Havoc, June *actress*
Hawkins, Osie Penman, Jr. *baritone*
Hayes, Peter Lind *actor, writer*
Heard, John *actor*
Heath, Percy *jazz bassist*
†Heckart, Eileen *actress*
Henes, Donna Urban Shaman *celebration artist, ritualist, writer*
Henner, Marilu *actress*
Henning, Doug *illusionist*
Hepburn, Katharine Houghton *actress*
Herbig, Günther *conductor*
Heston, Charlton (John Charlton Carter) *actor*
Hickson, Joan Bogle *actress*
Hilding, Jerel Lee *music and dance educator, former dancer*
Hill, Arthur *actor*
Hiller, Arthur *motion picture director*
Hiller, Wendy *actress*
Hingle, Pat *actor*
Hoggard, Lara Guldmar *conductor, educator*
Holm, Celeste *actress*
Hope, Bob *actor, comedian*
Houghton, Katharine *actress*
Hubbard, Elizabeth *actress*
†Hudlin, Reginald Alan *director, writer, producer*
Hughes, Michaela Kelly *actress, dancer*
Huning, Deborah Gray *actress, dancer, audiologist*
Hunter, Holly *actress*
Hunter, Kim (Janet Cole) *actress*
Hunter, Ross *film producer*
Hurt, William *actor*
Ichino, Yoko *ballet dancer*
Intilli, Sharon Marie *television director, small business owner*
Irey, Charlotte York *dance educator*
Irving, Amy *actress*
Irving, George Steven *actor*
Irving, Terry (Edward B. Irving, III) *television producer*
Istomin, Marta Casals *performing arts administrator*
†Jackson, Nagle *stage director, playwright*
Jacobi, Derek George *actor*
Jaffe, Stanley Richard *film producer, director*
Jarrett, Keith *pianist, composer*
Jennings, Waylon *country musician*
Johnson, (Francis) Benjamin *actor*
Johnson, Don Wayne *actor*
Johnson, J. J. *trombonist*
Jones, Shirley *actress, singer*
Jones, Tommy Lee *actor*
Judd, Naomi *country musician, singer, songwriter, author*
Judd, Wynonna *country western musician*
Kahn, Madeline Gail *actress*
Kane, Michael Joseph *director*
Kasem, Casey (Kemal Amin Kasem) *radio and television personality*
Kavner, Julie *actress*
Kazan, Elia *theatrical, motion picture director and producer, author*
Keach, Stacy, Sr. *producer, director*
Keith, Brian Michael *actor*
Kelley, Jackson DeForest *actor*
Kelly, Nancy Folden *arts administrator*
Kendall, Christopher (Christopher Wolff) *conductor, lutenist*
Kiley, Richard Paul *actor*
King, Morgana *jazz vocalist*
Kline, Kevin Delaney *actor*
Klippstatter, Kurt L. *conductor, music director*
Koner, Pauline *dancer, choreographer*
Krantz, Stephen Falk *motion picture producer*
Krause, Bernard Leo *bioacoustician, sonic artist, composer*
Kristofferson, Kris *singer, songwriter, actor*
Kupferman, Meyer *composer*
Kurtz, Gary Douglas *film producer*
Kutrzeba, Joseph S. *theatrical and film producer, director*
Kwak, Sung *conductor, music director*
Ladd, Cheryl (Cheryl Stopplemoor) *actress*
Lahti, Christine *actress*
Landesman, Fredric Rocco *theatre executive*
Lane, Burton (Burton Levy) *composer*

Lateef, Yusef (Bill Evans) *composer, educator*
Lauper, Cyndi *musician*
†Lazarus, Margaret Louise *film producer and director*
Lee, Michele *actress*
Lefferts, George *writer, producer, director*
†Lehmann, Michael Stephen *film director*
Lehrer, Thomas Andrew *songwriter, entertainer, lecturer*
León, Tania Justina *composer, music director, pianist*
Leonard, Stanley Sprenger *symphony musician*
Leventhal, Nathan *performing arts executive, lawyer*
Lindfors, Viveca *actress*
Lobanov-Rostovsky, Oleg *arts association executive*
Lockhart, Aileene Simpson *retired dance, kinesiology and physical education educator*
Longstreet, Harry Stephen *television producer, director, scriptwriter*
Loring, Gloria Jean *singer, actress*
Lowe, Rob *actor*
Lubin, Steven *concert pianist, musicologist*
Lupu, Radu *pianist*
Lynne, Jeff *rock musician, composer*
Macal, Zdenek *conductor*
Mac Dowell, Andie *actress*
Macnee, (Daniel) Patrick *actor*
Madeira, Francis King Carey *conductor, educator*
Magor, Louis Roland *conductor*
Mangione, Chuck (Charles Frank Mangione) *jazz musician, composer*
Mannes, Elena Sabin *film and television producer, director*
Mansouri, Lotfollah *opera stage director*
Marinaro, Edward Francis *actor*
Marshall, E. G. *actor*
Marshall, Garry *film producer, director, writer*
Masterson, Peter *actor, director*
Mastroianni, Marcello *actor*
Mayron, Melanie *actress, writer*
McBain, Diane Jean *actress, writer*
McCann, Elizabeth Ireland *theater, television and motion picture producer, lawyer*
McCartney, (James) Paul *musician*
Mc Clymont, Hamilton *entertainment industry executive*
McDowell, Malcolm *actor*
McEntire, Reba N. *country singer*
McGillis, Kelly *actress*
Mc Kayle, Donald Cohen *choreographer, director, writer*
Meara, Anne *actress, writer*
Melillo, Joseph Vincent *producer, performing arts*
Menotti, Gian Carlo *composer*
Meredith, Burgess *actor*
Merlis, George *television producer*
Merrick, David (David Margulois) *theatrical producer*
Merrill, Lindsey *music educator*
Meserve, Walter Joseph *drama studies educator, publisher*
†Midkiff, J(ohn) Michael *film and video producer and director*
Miller, Penelope Ann *actress*
Minnix, Bruce Milton *television and theatre director*
Mirisch, Walter Mortimer *motion picture producer*
Mixon, Alan *actor*
Moessinger, David *television producer, writer, director*
Moffatt, Katy (Katherine Louella Moffatt) *musician, vocalist, songwriter*
Moffett, Jonathan Phillip *drummer, musical director, songwriter*
Monty, Gloria *television producer*
Moore, Melba *actress, singer*
Moore, Tom *film and theater director*
Morath, Max Edward *entertainer, composer*
Mordecai, Benjamin *theatrical producer, drama educator*
Morelan, Paula Kay *choreographer*
Morello, Joseph Albert *musician, educator*
†Morita, (Noriyuki) Pat *actor, comedian*
Morrison, Shelley *actress*
Morrison, Van *musician, songwriter*
Morrow, Rob *actor*
Mosher, Gregory Dean *director*
†Moulton-Patterson, Linda *television executive*
Mount, Thomas H(enderson) *independent film producer*
Mudd, Roger Harrison *news broadcaster*
Muren, Dennis E. *visual effects director*
Murphy, Benjamin Edward *actor*
Murray, Kathryn Hazel *former dance director, author*
Musante, Tony (Anthony Peter Musante, Jr.) *actor*
Myers, Mike *actor, writer*
Myerson, Alan *director, film and television writer*
Narita, Hiro *cinematographer*
Naughton, James *actor*
Neame, Ronald *director, producer*
Neary, Patricia Elinor *ballet director*
†Nederlander, James Laurence *theater owner, producer*
Needham, Lucien Arthur *musician, educator*
Neville, Phoebe *choreographer, dancer, educator*
Newman, Paul *actor, professional race-car driver, food company executive*
Newton, Wayne *entertainer, actor, recording artist*
Nicks, Stevie (Stephanie Nicks) *singer, songwriter*
Nilsson, Birgit *soprano*
Nissinen, Mikko Pekka *dancer*
Nixon, Marni *singer*
Norton, Clifford Charles *actor, director*
Norton, Judy *actress*
†O'Brien, Jack George *artistic director*
Ondrejka, Ronald *conductor*
O'Neal, Ryan (Patrick Ryan O'Neal) *actor*
Oppenheim, David Jerome *musician, educational administrator*
Orbach, Jerry *actor, singer*
†Osbourne, Ozzy (John Osbourne) *vocalist*
Page, Willis *conductor*
Parslow, Philip Leo *film producer, film company executive*
Patinkin, Mandy *actor*
Patrick, Dennis *actor, director*
Paul, Les *entertainer, inventor*
Paycheck, Johnny *country western musician*
Peck, Gregory *actor*
Penn, Sean *actor*
Pentland, Barbara Lally *composer*
Perle, George *composer*
Perlman, Itzhak *violinist*
Persky, Lester *film producer*
Peters, Virginia *actress*
Peterson, Monica (Dorothy Peterson) *actress, singer, model, writer*
Peterson, Roderick William *writer, producer*
Pierce, Ponchitta Anne *television host, producer, journalist*
†Pinchot, Bronson *actor*
Pleshette, Suzanne *actress, writer*
Plummer, Amanda *actress*
Plummer, (Arthur) Christopher (Orme) *actor*
Poll, Martin Harvey *film producer*
Poston, Tom *actor*
Powers, Stefanie (Stefanie Federkiewicz) *actress*
†Primosch, James Thomas *music educator, composer, musician*
Prince, (Prince Rogers Nelson) *musician, actor*
Quaid, Dennis William *actor*
Quaid, Randy *actor*
Rabb, Ellis *actor, director, writer*
Rafelson, Bob *film director*
Ragsdale, Carl Vandyke *motion picture producer*
Redbone, Leon *singer, musician*
Reddy, Helen Maxine *singer*
Redford, Robert *actor, director*
Redgrave, Vanessa *actress*
Reeves, Keanu *actor*
Rich, John *film and television producer, director*
Richardson, Natasha Jane *actress*
Richie, Lionel B., Jr. *singer, songwriter, producer*
†Rickman, Tom *screenwriter, director*
Rideout, Patricia Irene *operatic, oratorio and concert singer*
Riley, Terry *composer, musician*
Roberts, Doris *actress*
Roberts, Samuel Smith *television news executive*
Robertson, Cliff *actor, writer, director*
Rochberg, George *composer, educator*
Rogers, Ginger (Virginia Katherine McMath) *dancer, actress*
Rolandi, Gianna *coloratura soprano*
Rose, Rubye Blevins (Patsy Montana) *singer*
Rosemont, Norman *television producer*
Rosen, Charles Welles *pianist, music educator*
Rosen, Myor *harpist, educator*
Rosenberg, Stuart *film director*
Rosenthal, Arnold H. *film director, producer, graphic designer*
Ross, Elinor *soprano*
†Roth, Tim *actor*
Rourke, Mickey (Philip Andre Rourke, Jr.) *actor*
Rowlands, Gena *actress*
Rudd, Paul Ryan *actor, director*
Rudner, Sara *dancer, choreographer*
Ruffelle, Frances *actress*
Ruggiero, Matthew John *bassoonist*
Russell, Theresa Lynn *actress*
Ryan, Meg *actress*
Sahl, Morton Lyon *comedian*
Saint, Eva Marie *actress*
Sajak, Pat *television game show host*
Saks, Gene *theater director, actor*
Saltzman, Philip *television writer, producer*
Sanborn, David *alto saxophonist*
Sandor, Gyorgy *pianist*
Sandrich, Jay H. *television director*
Sarry, Christine *ballerina*
†Savini, Tom *make-up artist, actor, director*
Schaefer, George Louis *theatrical producer and director, educator*
Schafer, Raymond Murray *composer, author*
Schallert, William Joseph *actor*
Schatzberg, Jerry Ned (Jerrold Schatzberg) *film director*
Schexnayder, Brian Edward *opera singer*
Schiller, Lawrence Julian *motion picture producer, director*
Schuur, Diane Joan *vocalist*
Schwary, Ronald Louis *motion picture producer*
Scott, Thomas Wright *composer, instrumentalist, arranger*
Scruggs, Earl Eugene *entertainer*
Seldes, Marian *actress*
Shapiro, Debbie Lynn (Lynn Shapiro) *singer, actress, dancer*
Shaw, Artie *musician, writer, lecturer*
Sheedy, Ally (Alexandra Elizabeth Sheedy) *actress*
Sheen, Charlie (Carlos Irwin Estevez) *actor*
Shelton, Sloane *actress*
Sherin, Edwin *theatrical and film director, actor*
Shirley-Quirk, John *concert and opera singer*
Short, Martin *actor, comedian*
Silverman, Jonathan *actor*
Silverstein, Barbara Ann *conductor*
Simon, Carly *singer, composer, author*
Simon, Paul *musician, composer*
Skolovsky, Zadel *concert pianist, educator*
Skowronski, Vincent Paul *concert violinist, recording artist, executive producer, producer classical recordings*
Smith, Lois Arlene *actress, writer*
Smothers, Dick *actor, singer*
Sondheim, Stephen Joshua *composer, lyricist*
Stapleton, Maureen *actress*
Starer, Robert *composer*
Sternhagen, Frances *actress*
Stevens, Warren *actor*
Stewart, James Maitland *actor*
Stewart, Thomas James, Jr. *baritone*
Stiller, Jerry *actor*
Storch, Arthur *theater director*
Strait, George *country music vocalist*
Stuart, Mary *actress*
Sutherland, Kiefer *actor*
Sutton, Dolores *actress, writer*
Swit, Loretta *actress*
Tallchief, Maria *ballerina*
Taylor, Guy Watson *symphonic conductor*
Taylor, Millard Benjamin *concertmaster, educator*
Thaxter, Phyllis St. Felix *actress*
Thomas, Karen P. *composer, conductor*
Thorstenberg, (John) Laurence *oboe and English horn player*
Tokofsky, Jerry Herbert *film producer*
Torn, Rip (Elmore Rual Torn, Jr.) *actor, director*
Tower, Joan Peabody *composer, educator*
Travanti, Daniel John *actor*
Travis, Randy Bruce *musician*
Travolta, John *actor*
Tripplehorn, Jeanne *actress*
Turkin, Marshall William *symphony orchestra, festival and opera administrator, arranger, composer*
Turner, Lana (Julia Jean Mildred Frances Turner) *actress*
Turner, Robert Comrie *composer*
Turok, Paul Harris *composer, music reviewer*
Ugrin, Béla *video producer*
Upbin, Shari *theatrical producer, director, agent, educator*
Van Patten, Joyce Benignia *actress*
Villella, Edward Joseph *ballet dancer, choreographer, artistic director*
Vishnevskaya, Galina Pavlovna *soprano, opera company director*
Voight, Jon *actor*
Voketaitis, Arnold Mathew *bass-baritone, educator*
Waldrop, Gideon William *composer, conductor, former president music school*
Wallach, Eli *actor*
Walsh, Joseph Fidler *recording artist, record producer*
Walston, Ray *actor*
Walthall, Lee Wade *artistic director, dancer*
Warner, Jack, Jr. *motion picture and television producer, writer*
Waters, John *film director, writer, actor*
Weld, Tuesday Ker (Susan Ker Weld) *actress*
Wendt, George Robert *actor*
Wettig, Patricia *actress*
Widmark, Richard *actor*
Williams, Patrick Moody *composer*
Williamson, Laird *stage director, actor*
Willis, Bruce Walter *actor, singer*
Winter, John Dawson, III *performer, songwriter*
Winters, Jonathan *actor*
Winters, Shelley (Shirley Schrift) *actress*
Winwood, Stephen Lawrence *musician, composer*
Wise, Patricia *lyric coloratura*
Wolfman Jack, (Robert Weston Smith) *radio personality*
Woodruff, Virginia *television and radio host, producer*
Woodward, Joanne Gignilliat *actress*
Woodward, Thomas Morgan *actor*
Wyman, Jane (Sarah Jane Fulks) *actress*
Yarrow, Peter *folksinger*
Yellen, Linda Beverly *film director, writer, producer*
Yoakam, Dwight *country western musician*
Zaliouk, Yuval Nathan *conductor*
Zevon, Warren *singer, songwriter*

ARTS: VISUAL

UNITED STATES

ALABAMA

Birmingham
†Cullum, Mark Edward *editorial cartoonist*

Huntsville
Wilson, Allan Byron *graphics company executive*

Montgomery
Schwarz, Joseph Edmund *artist*

ALASKA

Anchorage
Sharp, Anne Catherine *artist, educator*

Cordova
Bugbee-Jackson, Joan *sculptor*

Fayetteville
Wilson, Charles Banks *artist*

ARIZONA

Apache Junction
Bothwell, Dorr *artist*

Green Valley
Page, John Henry, Jr. *artist, educator*

Lake Montezuma
Burkee, Irvin *artist*

Oracle
Rush, Andrew Wilson *artist*

Paradise Valley
Heller, Jules *artist, writer*

Payson
Rich, Frances Luther *sculptor*

Phoenix
deMatties, Nicholas Frank *artist, art educator*
Dignac, Geny (Eugenia M. Bermudez) *sculptor*
McGuire, Maureen A. *artist*

Prescott
Farrar, Elaine Willardson *artist*
Stasack, Edward Armen *artist*

Scottsdale
Chase, James Keller *retired artist, museum director, educator*
Curtis, Philip C. *artist*
Golden, Libby *artist*
Lang, Margo Terzian *artist*
Scholder, Fritz *artist*

Tempe
Grigsby, Jefferson Eugene, Jr. *artist, educator*
Klett, Mark C. *photographer, educator*
Turk, Rudy Henry *artist, retired museum director*

Tucson
Conant, Howard Somers *artist, educator*
Flint, Willis Wolfschmidt (Willi Wolfschmidt) *artist*
Golden, Judith Greene *artist, educator*
Kingery, William David *ceramics and anthropology educator*

ARKANSAS

State University
Lindquist, Evan *artist, educator*

CALIFORNIA

Albion
Martin, Bill *artist, art educator*

Altadena
Ikegawa, Shiro *artist*

Aptos
Woods, Gurdon Grant *sculptor*

Aromas
Nutzle, Futzie (Bruce John Kleinsmith) *artist, author, cartoonist*

Bakersfield
Reep, Edward Arnold *artist*

Berkeley
Abel, Ray *graphic artist*
Genn, Nancy *artist*
Hartman, Robert Leroy *artist, educator*
Kasten, Karl Albert *painter, printmaker*
Klein, Lynn E. *artist*
Kriz, Vilem Francis *photographer, educator*
Miyasaki, George Joji *artist*
Rapoport, Sonya *artist*
Simpson, David William *artist, educator*
Voulkos, Peter *artist*
Wall, Brian Arthur *sculptor*
Washburn, Stan *artist*

Beverly Hills
Acheson, James *costume designer*
Berman, Eleanore (Lazarof) *artist*
Klausen, Raymond *sculptor, television/theatre production designer*

Bodega
Hedrick, Wally Bill *artist*

Bolinas
Harris, Paul *sculptor*

Brisbane
Anargyros, Spero *sculptor*

Burbank
†Heiden, Jeri McManus *art director*

Carmel
Kennedy, John Edward *art dealer, appraiser, curator*
Weston, Theodore Brett *photographer*

Carmichael
Sahs, Majorie Jane *art educator*

Carpinteria
Hansen, Robert William *artist, educator*

Carson
Hirsch, Gilah Yelin *artist, writer*

Claremont
Benjamin, Karl Stanley *artist, educator*
Blizzard, Alan *artist*
Casanova, Aldo John *sculptor*
Reiss, Roland Martin *artist, educator*

Corona Del Mar
Brandt, Rexford Elson *artist*
Delap, Tony *artist*

Costa Mesa
Muller, Jerome Kenneth *painter, editor, psychologist*

Culver City
†Bluth, Don *animator, director, screenwriter*

Davis
DePaoli, Geri M. *artist, art historian*

Dillon Beach
Petersen, Roland *artist, printmaker*

Escondido
Barrio, Raymond *author, artist*
Sternberg, Harry *artist*

Fallbrook
Ragland, Jack Whitney *artist*

Fullerton
Curran, Darryl Joseph *photographer, educator*
Smith, Joachim *artist*

Garden Grove
Ortlieb, Robert Eugene *sculptor*

Hayward
Ramos, Melvin John *artist, educator*

Healdsburg
Conrat, Richard Fraenkel *photographer, educator, mechanical contractor*

Indio
Lloyd, Douglas George *watercolor artist, educator*

Inverness
Welpott, Jack Warren *photographer, educator*

Irvine
Kingman, Dong *artist, educator*

Kensington
Loran, Erle *artist*

La Jolla
Antin, Eleanor *artist*
Cuevas, Jose Luis *painter, illustrator*
Imana, Jorge Garron *artist*
Monaghan, Eileen *artist*
Whitaker, Eileen Monaghan *artist*

Lafayette
Kapp, Eleanor Jeanne *impressionistic artist, writer, researcher*

Laguna Niguel
Pierce, Hilda (Hilda Herta Harmel) *painter*

Lagunitas
Holman, Arthur Stearns *artist*

Long Beach
Dean, Charles Thomas *industrial arts educator, academic administrator*
Ferreira, Armando Thomas *sculptor, educator*

Los Angeles
Adam, Ken *production designer*
Bass, Saul *graphic designer, filmmaker*
Batres, Eduardo *computer model builder, animator*
†Bayless, Raymond *artist*
Burkhardt, Hans Gustav *artist*
Danziger, Louis *graphic designer, educator*
Davis, Ronald *artist, printmaker*
Dillon, Paul Sanford *artist*
Ewing, Edgar Louis *artist, educator*
Galanos, James *fashion designer*
Greiman, April *graphic designer*
Harp, Rufus William *set decorator*
Hebald, Milton Elting *sculptor*
Johnston, Ynez *artist*
Kanemitsu, Matsumi *artist*
Ketchum, Robert Glenn *photographer, print maker*
Kienholz, Lyn Shearer *international arts projects coordinator*
Kirschner, David *animation entertainment company executive*
Lark, Raymond *artist, art scholar*
Lewis, Samella Sanders *artist, educator*
Natzler, Otto *ceramic artist*
Pederson, Con *animator*
Rankaitis, Susan *artist*
Rodgers, Aggie Guerard *costume designer*
Starr, Steven Dawson *photographer*
Von Brandenstein, Patrizia *production designer*
Weil, Jerry *animator*
Welch, Bo (Robert W. Welch, III) *production designer*
Welles, Melinda Fassett *artist, educator*
Woelffer, Emerson Seville *artist*
Young, Joseph Louis *artist*

Marina Del Rey
Valentine, De Wain *artist*

Mariposa
Rogers, Earl Leslie *artist, educator*

Mendocino
Alexander, Joyce Mary *illustrator*

Mill Valley
Ihle, John Livingston *artist, educator*

Modesto
Bucknam, Mary Olivia Caswell *artist*

Monterey
Bowman, Dorothy Louise *artist*
Bradford, Howard *graphic artist, painter*

Morgan Hill
Freimark, Robert (Bob Freimark) *artist*

Napa
Garnett, William *photographer*

Newport Beach
Spitz, Barbara Salomon *artist*

North Hollywood
†Kaminski, Janusz Zygmuni *photographer*

Northridge
Bassler, Robert Covey *sculptor, educator*
Danin, Mary Ann *artist, designer, educator*
Harden, Marvin *artist, educator*

Oakland
Beasley, Bruce Miller *sculptor*
Dickinson, Eleanor Creekmore *artist, educator*
Leon, Dennis *sculptor*
Melchert, James Frederick *artist*
Okamura, Arthur *artist, educator, writer*
Rath, Alan T. *sculptor*

Oxnard
Perrier, Barbara Sue *artist*

Pacific Palisades
Chesney, Lee Roy, Jr. *artist*

Palm Springs
Maree, Wendy *painter, sculptor*

Palo Alto
Dater, Judy Lichtenfeld *photographer*

Pasadena
Howe, Graham Lloyd *photographer, curator*
Newman, Joyce Kligerman *sculptor*
Zammitt, Norman *artist*

Pebble Beach
Mortensen, Gordon Louis *artist, printmaker*

Petaluma
Mc Chesney, Robert Pearson *artist*
Reichek, Jesse *artist*

Pinole
Gerbracht, Robert Thomas (Bob Gerbracht) *painter, educator*

Portola Valley
†De Alessi, Ross Alan *lighting designer*

Poway
Harlan, Roma Christine *portrait painter*

Richmond
Wessel, Henry *photographer*

Sacramento
†Dalkey, Fredric Dynan *artist*

San Clemente
Cederquist, John *artist*

San Diego
Albuquerque, Lita *artist*
Chandler, Floyd Copeland *fine arts educator*
Jackson, Everett Gee *painter, illustrator*
Linton, Roy Nathan *graphic arts company executive*

San Francisco
Adams, Mark *artist*
Beall, Dennis Ray *artist, educator*
Bechtle, Robert Alan *artist, educator*
Chin, Sue Soone Marian (Suchin Chin) *conceptual artist, portraitist, photographer, community affairs activist*
Hershman, Lynn Lester *artist*
Hobbs, Carl Fredric *artist, filmmaker, author*
Holland, Tom *artist, educator*
Howard, David E. *artist*
Jones, Pirkle *photographer, educator*
Lobdell, Frank *artist*
Mach, David *artist*
Martin, Fred *artist, college administrator*
McClintock, Jessica *fashion designer*
McNamara, John Stephen *artist, educator*
Neri, Manuel *artist, educator*
Oliveira, Nathan *artist, educator*
Raciti, Cherie *artist*
Saunders, Raymond Jennings *artist, educator*
Stermer, Dugald Robert *designer, illustrator, writer, consultant*
Van Hoesen, Beth Marie *artist, printmaker*
Wiley, William T. *artist*

San Jose
Estabrook, Reed *artist, educator*

San Luis Obispo
Dickerson, Colleen Bernice Patton *artist, educator*

San Marino
Medearis, Roger Norman *artist*

San Pedro
Crutchfield, William Richard *artist, educator*

San Rafael
Napoles, Veronica Kleeman *graphic designer, consultant*

Santa Barbara
Eguchi, Yasu *artist*
Paradise, Phil(ip Herschel) *artist*

Santa Clarita
Fritzke, Audrey Elmere *artist*

Santa Cruz
Rydell, Amnell Roy *artist, landscape architect*
Summers, Carol *artist*

Santa Monica
Arnoldi, Charles Arthur *painter, sculptor*
Foulkes, Llyn *artist, educator*
Jenkins, George *stage designer, film art director*
Kauffman, Robert Craig *artist, sculptor*
Stern, Jan Peter *sculptor*

Santa Rosa
Barr, Roger Terry *sculptor*
Crossland, Harriet Kent *artist*
Monk, Diana Charla *artist, stable owner*
Rider, Jane Louise *artist, educator*

Sausalito
Kuhlman, Walter Egel *artist, educator*
Tift, Mary Louise *artist*

Soda Bay
Fletcher, Leland Vernon *artist*

Sonora
Price, Joe *artist, educator*

South Pasadena
Askin, Walter Miller *artist, educator*

Stockton
Oak, Claire Morisset *artist, educator*

Summerland
Calamar, Gloria *artist*

Torrance
Everts, Connor *artist*

Venice
Bengston, Billy Al *artist*
Berlant, Anthony *artist*
Eversley, Frederick John *sculptor, engineer*
Rady, Elsa *artist*

Victorville
Bascom, Earl Wesley *artist, sculptor, writer*

West Hills
Freas, Frank Kelly *illustrator*

West Hollywood
Hockney, David *artist*

Whittier
Bayer, William Martin *photographer, educator*

Windsor
Hayes, Vertis Clemon *painter, sculptor, educator*

Yreka
McFadden, Leon Lambert *artist, inventor*

COLORADO

Aspen
Berkó, Ferenc *photographer*
Soldner, Paul Edmund *artist, ceramist, educator*

Aurora
Hickman, Grace Marguerite *artist*

Boulder
Balog, James Dennis *photographer*
Matthews, Eugene Edward *artist*
Matthews, Wanda Miller *artist*

Colorado Springs
Blanchette, Jeanne Ellene Maxant *artist, educator, performer*
Goehring, Kenneth *artist*

Denver
Norman, John Barstow, Jr. *designer, educator*

Larkspur
Bierbaum, Janith Marie *artist*

Louisville
Day, Robert Edgar *retired artist, educator*
Qualley, Charles Albert *fine arts educator*

Telluride
Smith, Samuel David *artist, educator*

University Of Colorado
Chamberlin, Henry Scott *artist, educator*

Wiley
Dooley, Jennie Lee *art educator*

CONNECTICUT

Bethel
Ajay, Abe *artist*

Bloomfield
Hammer, Alfred Emil *artist, educator*

Bridgeport
Kovatch, Jak Gene *artist*

Brookfield
Westermann, Horace Clifford *sculptor*
†Whelan, Michael Raymond *artist, illustrator*

Cornwall Bridge
Pfeiffer, Werner Bernhard *artist, educator*

Cos Cob
Kane, Margaret Brassler *sculptor*

Danbury
Caparn, Rhys (Mrs. Herbert Johannes Steel) *sculptor*

Essex
Curtis, Alva Marsh *artist*

Georgetown
Roberts, Priscilla Warren *artist*

Greenwich
Perless, Robert L. *sculptor*

Kent
Cronin, Robert Lawrence *sculptor, painter*

Meriden
Bertolli, Eugene Emil *sculptor, goldsmith, designer, consultant*

Mystic
Bates, Gladys Edgerly *sculptor*

New Canaan
Caesar, Henry A., II *sculptor*
Holch, Eric Sanford *artist*
Richards, Walter DuBois *artist, illustrator*

New Haven
Bailey, William Harrison *artist, educator*
Chaet, Bernard Robert *artist, educator*
de Bretteville, Sheila Levrant *art educator, art director, artist*
Johnson, Lester Fredrick *artist*
Lindroth, Linda (Linda Hammer) *artist*
Papageorge, Tod *photographer, educator*
Pease, David Gordon *artist, educator*

Norwalk
Perry, Charles Owen *sculptor*

Old Lyme
Chandler, Elisabeth Gordon (Mrs. Laci De Gerenday) *sculptor, harpist*
de Gerenday, Laci Anthony *sculptor*

Ridgefield
Julian, Alexander, II *menswear designer*

Sherman
Goodspeed, Barbara *artist*

Stamford
Austin, Darrel *artist*
Strosahl, William Austin *artist, art director*

Storrs Mansfield
Zelanski, Paul John *art educator, author*

Warren
Abrams, Herbert E. *artist*
Gray, Cleve *artist*

West Cornwall
Prentice, Tim *sculptor, architect*

Simont, Marc *artist*

West Hartford
Glasson, Lloyd *sculptor, educator*
Uccello, Vincenza Agatha *artist, director, educator emerita*

West Haven
Eisenman, Alvin *educator, graphic designer*
Lee, Ming Cho *set designer*

Weston
Bleifeld, Stanley *sculptor*
Cadmus, Paul *artist, etcher*
Rand, Paul *graphic designer, educator*

Westport
Silk, George *photographer*

Wilton
Stuart, Kenneth James *illustrator, art director*

DELAWARE

Hockessin
Sawin, Nancy Churchman *educator, artist, historian*

New Castle
Almquist, Don *illustrator, artist*

Newark
Moss, Joe Francis *sculptor, painter*
Rowe, Charles Alfred *artist, designer, educator*

Wilmington
Reilley, James Clark *artist, cartoonist, small business owner*

DISTRICT OF COLUMBIA

Washington
Blair, James Pease *photographer, retired*
Costigan, Constance Frances *artist, educator*
Danziger, Joan *sculptor*
DiPerna, Frank Paul *photographer, educator*
Donaldson, Jeff Richardson *visual artist, educator*
Gilliam, Sam *artist*
Gossage, John Ralph *photographer*
Grupe, Barbara Ann Pandzik *artist, museum administrator*
Gumpert, Gunther *artist*
Halstead, Dirck S. *photographer, journalist*
Jones, Lois Mailou (Mrs. Vergniaud Pierre-Noel) *artist, educator*
Millon, Henry Armand *fine arts educator, architectural historian*
Perlmutter, Jack *artist, lithographer*
Polan, Annette Lewis *artist*
Power, Mark *journalist, photographer, educator*
Puryear, Martin *artist*
Stevenson, A. Brockie *artist*
Summerford, Ben Long *retired artist, educator*
Suro, Dario *artist, diplomat*
Truitt, Anne Dean *artist*

FLORIDA

Bal Harbour
Bernay, Betti *artist*

Boca Raton
Amen, Irving *artist*
Marca-Relli, Conrad *artist*
Ortlip, Paul Daniel *artist*
Russo, Kathleen Marie *art educator*

Boynton Beach
Plossu, Bernard Pierre *photographer*

Bradenton
Doenecke, Carol Anne *artist*
Hodgell, Robert Overman *artist, art educator*

Delray Beach
Draper, Line Bloom (Line B. Draper-Rubba) *artist*
Ross, Beatrice Brook *artist*

Englewood
Sisson, Robert F. *photographer, writer, lecturer, educator*

Fernandina Beach
D'Agnese, Helen Jean *artist*

Flagler Beach
Nebil, Corinne Elizabeth *artist*

Fort Lauderdale
Hanson, Duane Elwood *sculptor*

Fort Myers
Schwartz, Carl Edward *artist, printmaker*

Gainesville
Craven, Roy Curtis, Jr. *art educator, art gallery director*
Kerslake, Kenneth Alvin *art educator, printmaker*
Murray, Ernest Don *artist, educator*
Uelsmann, Jerry Norman *photographer*
Williams, Hiram Draper *artist, educator*

Hobe Sound
Frank, Mary *sculptor, artist*

Holmes Beach
Neustadt, Barbara Mae *artist, illustrator, etcher*

Jacksonville
Mikulas, Joseph Frank *graphic designer, educator, painter*

Lake Worth
Stevens, William John *management consultant, writer, inventor, former association executive*

Melbourne
Stark, Bruce Gunsten *artist*

Miami
Alexenberg, Mel *art educator*
Morgan, Andrew Wesley *artist, educator*
Strickland, Thomas Joseph *artist*

Naples
Eldridge, David Carlton *art appraiser*
Vickrey, Robert Remsen *artist*

New Port Richey
Robichaud, Phyllis Ivy Isabel *artist, educator*

Palm Beach
Kaplan, Muriel Sheerr *sculptor*

Plant City
Holland, Gene Grigsby (Scottie Holland) *artist*

Quincy
Lindquist, Mark Alvin *artist*

Sarasota
Altabe, Joan Augusta Berg *artist, writer, art and architecture critic*
Chamberlain, John Angus *sculptor*
Eliscu, Frank *sculptor*
Sawyer, Helen Alton *artist*
Solomon, Syd *artist*

Sebastian
Pieper, Patricia Rita *artist, photographer*

Siesta
Held, Philip *artist*

Surfside
Albert, Calvin *sculptor*

Tallahassee
Harper, William C. *artist, educator*

Tampa
Wilson, Wallace *art educator, artist*

Winter Park
Holt, Georgina L. *ceramic artist*

GEORGIA

Alpharetta
Byrd, Bette Jean *artist, author*

Athens
Herbert, James Arthur *artist, filmmaker*
Kent, Robert B. *artist, educator*

Atlanta
Beattie, George *artist*
Grumet, Priscilla Hecht *fashion specialist, consultant, writer*
†Guberman, Sidney Thomas *painter, writer*
McLean, James Albert *artist, educator*

Augusta
Rosen, James Mahlon *artist, art historian, educator*

Decatur
Loehle, Betty Barnes *artist, painter*

Mount Berry
Mew, Thomas Joseph, III (Tommy Mew) *artist, educator*

Savannah
Alley, James Pinckney, Jr. *computer art and graphic design educator*

HAWAII

Haiku
Cost, James Peter *artist*

Honolulu
Amor, Simeon, Jr. *photographer, historian*
Betts, Barbara Stoke *artist, educator*
Kenda, Juanita Echeverria *artist, educator*

Lahaina
Sato, Tadashi *artist*

IDAHO

Saint Maries
Carlson, George Arthur *artist*

ILLINOIS

Champaign
Jackson, Billy Morrow *artist, retired art educator*
Kotoske, Roger Allen *artist, educator*

Chicago
Africano, Nicholas *artist*
Avison, David *photographer*
Bender, Janet Pines *artist*
Boggess, Thomas Phillip, III *graphic arts company executive*
Bowman, Leah *fashion designer, consultant, photographer, educator*
Crane, Barbara Bachmann *photographer, educator*
Feeley, Henry Joseph, Jr. (Hank Feeley) *artist, former advertising agency executive*
Gehr, Mary *illustrator, painter, printmaker*
Goetz, John Bullock *graphic designer*
Goldstein, Fern *fine artist, custom designer, design consultant*
Gray, Richard *art dealer, consultant, holding company executive*

Heinecken, Robert Friedli *art educator, artist*
Himmelfarb, John David *artist*
Horn, Milton *sculptor*
Jachna, Joseph D. *photographer, educator*
Josephson, Kenneth Bradley *artist, educator*
Kearney, John Walter *sculptor, painter*
King, Andre Richardson *architectural graphic designer*
Klement, Vera *artist*
Koga, Mary *artist, photographer, social worker*
Lerner, Nathan Bernard *artist*
Mintz, Harry *artist, educator*
Nutt, Jim *artist*
Paschke, Edward F. *artist, illustrator*
Paul, Arthur *artist, graphic designer, illustrator, art and design consultant*
Pizzi, Pier Luigi *costume and scenic designer, film director*
Ramberg, Christina *artist, educator*
Regensteiner, Else Friedsam (Mrs. Bertold Regensteiner) *textile designer, educator*
Saul, Peter *artist*
Skrebneski, Victor *photographer*
Whitney, Patrick Foster *design educator*

De Kalb
Ashmann, Jon *art professor, designer*
Even, Robert Lawrence *art educator*

Edwardsville
Malone, Robert Roy *artist, art educator*

Evanston
Conger, William Frame *artist, educator*
Vanderstappen, Harrie Albert *Far Eastern art educator*

Lombard
Ahlstrom, Ronald Gustin *artist*

River Forest
Sloan, Jeanette Pasin *artist*
White, Philip Butler *artist*

Riverside
Howlett, Carolyn Svrluga *art educator*

Scales Mound
Lieberman, Archie *photographer, writer*

Waukegan
Bleck, Virginia Eleanore *illustrator*

Winnetka
Pattison, Abbott Lawrence *sculptor*
Plowden, David *photographer*
Sharboneau, Lorna Rosina *artist, educator, writer*

INDIANA

Bloomington
Barnes, Robert Merton *artist, educator*
Lowe, Marvin *artist*
Markman, Ronald *artist, educator*
O'Hearn, Robert Raymond *stage designer*
Pozzatti, Rudy Otto *artist*

Indianapolis
Block, Amanda Roth *artist*

Lowell
Boller, Carole Ann *visual artist*

Madison
Gunter, Frank Elliott *artist*

Morgantown
Boyce, Gerald G. *artist, educator*

Muncie
Connally, Sandra Jane Oppy *art educator*

Notre Dame
Lauck, Anthony Joseph *artist, retired art educator, priest*

Terre Haute
Lamis, Leroy *artist, retired educator*

West Lafayette
Ichiyama, Dennis Yoshihide *design educator, consultant*

IOWA

Davenport
Jecklin, Lois Underwood *art corporation executive, consultant*

Des Moines
†Cambridge, Daniel Arthur *creative director*
Reece, Maynard Fred *artist, author*

Iowa City
Schmidt, Julius *sculptor*

KANSAS

Lawrence
Brawley, Robert Julius *artist, art educator*
Papanek, Victor *designer, educator, writer*

Ottawa
Howe, William Hugh *artist*

Shawnee Mission
†Hershman, Mark Steven *lighting designer*

KENTUCKY

Bowling Green
†Richards, Jody *art educator, artist*

Lexington
Boyer, Lillian Buckley *artist, educator*
Henderson, Hubert Platt *fine arts association executive*

LOUISIANA

New Orleans
Azaceta, Luis Cruz *artist*
Lovejoy, Barbara Campbell *sculptor, architectural designer*
O'Meallie, Kitty *artist*
Steg, J(ames) L(ouis) *artist*
Thornell, Jack Randolph *photographer*

MAINE

Bath
Ipcar, Dahlov *illustrator, painter, author*
Webb, Todd (Charles Clayton Webb) *photographer, writer*

Boothbay Harbor
Cavanaugh, Tom Richard *artist, antiques dealer, retired art educator*
Eames, John Heagan *etcher*
Grossman, Morton S. *artist*

Cushing
Magee, A. Alan *artist*

Damariscotta
Robinson, Walter George *arts management and funding consultant*

Gorham
Bearce, Jeana Dale *artist, educator*

Jefferson
Fiore, Joseph Albert *artist*

Kennebunk
Betts, Edward *artist*
Escalet, Frank Diaz *art gallery owner, artist, educator*

Little Deer Isle
Mc Closkey, Robert *artist*

Monhegan Island
Hudson, Jacqueline *artist*

New Harbor
Lyford, Cabot *sculptor*

North Fryeburg
Bolomey, Roger Henry *sculptor*

Port Clyde
Thon, William *artist*

Vinalhaven
Indiana, Robert *artist*

Wiscasset
†Leslie, Seaver *artist*

York Beach
Davison, Nancy Reynolds *artist*

MARYLAND

Baltimore
Carper, Gertrude Esther *artist, marina owner*
Hartigan, Grace *artist*
Pittman, Carolyn *artist*
Rembski, Stanislav *artist, portrait painter*
Rothschild, Amalie Rosenfeld *artist*

Bethesda
Hart, Betty Miller *artist*

Brentwood
†Kaskey, Raymond John *sculptor*

Centreville
Amos, James Lysle *photographer*

Chevy Chase
Asher, Lila Oliver *artist*
Calfee, William Howard *sculptor, painter*
Ginzburg, Yankel *artist*
Kainen, Jacob *artist, former museum curator*

College Park
DeMonte, Claudia Ann *artist, educator*
Lapinski, Tadeusz Andrew *artist, educator*

Gaithersburg
Bochicchio-Ausura, Jill Arden *photographer*

Greenbelt
Blackwell, Camellia Ann *art educator*

Silver Spring
Barkin, Robert Allan *graphic designer, newspaper executive, consultant*
Peiperl, Adam *kinetic and video sculptor*

Springfield
Delaney, Jean M. *art educator*

MASSACHUSETTS

Allston
Katayama, Toshihiro *artist, educator*

Amherst
Hendricks, James Powell *artist*
Holmes, Helen Bequaert *researcher*

Liebling, Jerome *photographer, educator*
Schmalz, Carl Nelson, Jr. *artist, educator, printmaker*

Andover
Cook, Christopher Capen *artist, educator, museum director*
Lloyd, Robert Andrew *art educator*

Ashland
Gohlke, Frank William *photographer*

Boston
Ablow, Joseph *artist, educator*
†Cevoli, Victor *graphic designer*
Fink, Joanna Elizabeth *art dealer*
Gibran, Kahlil *sculptor*
Handford, Martin John *illustrator, author*
Isaacs, Helen Coolidge Adams (Mrs. Kenneth L. Isaacs) *artist*
Pineda, Marianna *sculptor, educator*
Preston, Malcolm *artist, art critic*
Smith, Keith A. *artist*
Stone, James J. *artist*
†Wiesner, David *illustrator, children's writer*
†Yamamoto, Tamotsu *art educator*

Brookline
Barron, Ros *artist*
Swan, Barbara *artist*
Wilson, John *artist*

Cambridge
Ackerman, James Sloss *fine arts educator*
Alcalay, Albert S. *artist, educator*
Berndt, Jerry W. *photographer, film producer*
Feininger, Theodore Lux *artist*
Mazur, Michael *artist*
Mc Kie, Todd Stoddard *artist*
Piene, Otto *artist, educator*
Reimann, William Page *artist, educator*
Rosenfield, John Max *art educator*

Chilmark
Geyer, Harold Carl *artist, writer*
Low, Joseph *artist*

Concord
Ihara, Michio *sculptor*

Conway
Mallary, Robert *sculptor*

Gloucester
Curtis, Roger William *artist, educator*
Duca, Alfred Milton *artist*
Hancock, Walker Kirtland *sculptor*

Hull
Burgess, David Lowry *artist*

Leeds
Baskin, Leonard *sculptor, graphic artist*

Lenox
LiMarzi, Joseph *artist*

Leyden
Garston, Gerald Drexler *artist*

Manchester
Lothrop, Kristin Curtis *sculptor*

Montague
Coughlin, Jack *printmaker, sculptor, art educator*

Natick
Geller, Esther (Bailey Geller) *artist*

Needham
Hunter, Elizabeth Ives-Valsam *fashion consultant*

Newton
Ranalli, Daniel *artist, writer*

Newtonville
Polonsky, Arthur *artist, educator*

North Brookfield
Neal, Avon *artist, author*
Parker, Ann (Ann Parker Neal) *photographer, graphic artist*

North Eastham
Simmel, Marianne Lenore *graphic designer*

Northampton
Rupp, Sheron Adeline *photographer, educator*

Norwell
Brett, Jan Churchill *illustrator, author*
Wentworth, Murray Jackson *artist, educator*

Orange
Bate, Judith Ellen *artist*

Rockport
Nicholas, Thomas Andrew *artist*
Strisik, Paul *artist*

Sherborn
Pickhardt, Carl Emile, Jr. *artist*

Somerville
†Bakanowsky, Louis Joseph *visual arts educator, architect, artist*

South Hadley
Hall, Lee *artist, educator*

Sudbury
Aronson, David *artist, retired art educator*

Topsfield
Webster, Larry Russell *artist*

Waltham
Bohlen, Nina *artist*

Wellfleet
Hopkins, Budd *artist, writer*

Westford
Bowman, George Leo *artist*

Westwood
Philbrick, Margaret Elder *artist*

Wilbraham
Gale, William Henry *artist*

Winchester
Neuman, Robert Sterling *art educator, artist*

MICHIGAN

Ann Arbor
Cassara, Frank *artist, printmaker*
Kamrowski, Gerome *artist*
Leonard, Joanne *photographer, educator*

Birmingham
Ortman, George Earl *artist*

Bloomfield Hills
McCoy, Katherine Braden *designer, educator*
McCoy, Michael Dale *designer, educator*
Slade, Roy *artist, college president, museum director*

Detroit
Kachadoorian, Zubel *artist, educator*
Moldenhauer, Judith A. *graphic design educator*

East Lansing
Leepa, Allen *artist, educator*

Glenn
Rizzolo, Louis B. M. *artist, educator*

Grand Rapids
Blovits, Larry John *retired art educator*
Bolt, Eunice Mildred DeVries *artist*

Kalamazoo
Kayser, Thomas Arthur *art consultant*

Port Huron
Rowark, Maureen *fine arts photographer*

Riverdale
Kirby, Kent Bruce *artist, educator*

Royal Oak
Fredericks, Marshall Maynard *sculptor*

MINNESOTA

Duluth
Chee, Cheng-Khee *artist*

Edina
Saltzman, William *painter, sculptor, designer*

Minneapolis
Dugmore, Edward *artist*
Hallman, Gary L. *photographer, educator*
Larkin, Eugene David *artist, educator*
Myers, Malcolm Haynie *artist, art educator*
Preuss, Roger E(mil) *artist*
Rose, Thomas Albert *artist, art educator*

Northfield
Dittmann, Reidar *art educator*

Red Wing
Biederman, Charles Joseph *artist*

Rochester
Husband, Richard Lorin, Sr. *consulting company executive*

MISSISSIPPI

Meridian
Marshall, John Steven *artist, educator, museum administrator*

MISSOURI

Columbia
Larson, Sidney *art educator, artist, writer, painting conservator*

Kansas City
Bransby, Eric James *muralist, educator*
Lee, Margaret Norma *artist*

Saint Louis
DesRosiers, Roger I. *artist, educator*
Duhme, H(erman) Richard, Jr. *sculptor, educator*
†Lazorko, Anthony, Jr. *art director*
McGarrell, James *artist, educator*
Pulitzer, Emily S Rauh (Mrs. Joseph Pulitzer, Jr.) *art consultant*
Trova, Ernest Tino *artist, sculptor*

Sibley
Morrow, Elizabeth *sculptress, educator, museum association administrator, business owner*

Springfield
King, (Jack) Weldon *photographer*

Webster Groves
Osver, Arthur *artist*

MONTANA

Browning
Scriver, Robert Macfie *sculptor*

Hot Springs
Erickson, James Gardner *retired artist, cartoonist*

Missoula
Rippon, Thomas Michael *art educator, artist*

NEBRASKA

Omaha
Horning, Jerome Kay *artist, educator*

NEVADA

Henderson
Turner, Florence Frances *ceramist*

Reno
Newberg, Dorothy Beck (Mrs. William C. Newberg) *portrait artist*

NEW HAMPSHIRE

Exeter
Dailey, Daniel Owen *artist, educator, designer*

Francestown
Milton, Peter Winslow *artist*

Hanover
Boghosian, Varujan Yegan *sculptor*

Jaffrey
Hillsmith, Fannie L. *artist*

Manchester
Dobbins, James Joseph *artist*

Rindge
Sandback, Frederick Lane *artist*

NEW JERSEY

Asbury
Konrad, Adolf Ferdinand *artist*

Bayonne
Gorman, William David *artist, graphic artist*

Bernardsville
Coheleach, Guy Joseph *artist*

Blairstown
Bean, Bennett *artist*

Bridgewater
Patton, Diana Lee Wilkoc *artist*

Califon
Rosen, Carol Mendes *artist*

Cranbury
Lee-Smith, Hughie *artist, educator*

Cresskill
Smyth, Craig Hugh *fine arts educator*

East Brunswick
Nemser, Robert Solomon *visual communications consultant, art director, designer, educator*

Edison
Behr, Marion Ray *artist, author*

Englewood
Anuszkiewicz, Richard Joseph *artist*
Casarella, Edmond *sculptor, printmaker*

Fair Lawn
Parker, Adrienne Natalie *art educator, art historian, lecturer*

Hightstown
Howard, Barbara Sue Mesner *artist*

Iselin
Tice, George A(ndrew) *photographer*

Jersey City
†Gurevich, Grigory *visual artist, educator*
Serra-Badue, Daniel Francisco *artist, educator*

Lakehurst
Case, Elizabeth *artist, writer*

Milford
Carter, Clarence Holbrook *artist*

Montclair
Beerman, Miriam *artist, educator*

New Brunswick
Goffen, Rona *art educator*

Park Ridge
De Pol, John *artist*

Piscataway
Goodyear, John Lake *artist, educator*
Ortiz, Raphael Montañez *performance artist, educator*
Young, James Earl *ceramics educator, educational administrator*

Princeton
Bunnell, Peter Curtis *photography and art educator, museum curator*
Canright, Sarah Anne *artist, educator*
Carlson, Charlotte Booth *book illustrator*
George, Thomas *artist*
Grabar, Oleg *art educator*
Savage, Naomi *photographer*
Seawright, James L., Jr. *artist, educator*
Wilmerding, John *art history educator, museum curator*

Rockleigh
†Heslin, Cathleen Jane *artist, designer, entrepreneur*

Roosevelt
Landau, Jacob *artist*

Rumson
Cocker, Barbara Joan *marine artist, interior designer*

Rutherford
Petrie, Ferdinand Ralph *illustrator, artist*

Short Hills
Good, Joan Duffey *artist*

Stillwater
Finkelstein, Louis *retired art educator*

Stockton
Mahon, Robert *photographer*
Schoenherr, John (Carl) *artist, illustrator*

Summit
Nessen, Ward Henry *typographer, lawyer*
Rousseau, Irene Victoria *sculptor*

Tenafly
Koons, Irvin Louis *design executive, graphic artist, consultant*

Toms River
Unger, Howard Albert *artist, photographer, educator*

Trenton
Chavooshian, Marge *artist, educator*

Upper Montclair
Coes, Kent Day *artist*

Ventnor City
Frudakis, Evangelos William *sculptor*
Robbins, Hulda Dornblatt *artist, printmaker*

Verona
Ayaso, Manuel *artist*

Wayne
Haxton, David *computer animator, artist, director, computer graphics educator*
Katz, Leandro *artist*

NEW MEXICO

Albuquerque
Adams, Clinton *artist, historian*
Antreasian, Garo Zareh *artist, lithographer, art educator*
Armstrong, Glenn Garnett *artist, retired postal executive*
Barrow, Thomas Francis *artist, educator*
Hahn, Betty *artist, photographer, educator*
Witkin, Joel-Peter *photographer*

Corrales
Eaton, Pauline *artist*

Ruidoso Downs
Knapp, Thomas Edwin *sculptor, painter*

Santa Fe
Ancona, George Ephraim *photographer, film producer, author*
Chicago, Judy *artist*
Clift, William Brooks, III *photographer*
Grover, Phyllis Bradman *artist, consultant*
Hatch, John Davis *design consultant, art historian*
Longley, Bernique *artist, sculptor*
Loriaux, Maurice Lucien *artist, ecclesiologist*
Scheinbaum, David *photography educator*
Shubart, Dorothy Louise *artist, educator*

Silver City
Sturgen, Winston *photographer, printmaker, artist*

Taos
Bell, Larry Stuart *artist*
Crespin, Leslie Ann *artist*

NEW YORK

Alfred
Billeci, Andre George *art educator, sculptor*
Higby, (Donald) Wayne *artist, educator*

Amagansett
†Opper, John *painter, retired educator*

Annandale On Hudson
Sullivan, Jim *artist*

Armonk
Elson, Charles *stage designer, educator*

Babylon
Haley, Priscilla Jane *artist, printmaker*

Bayside
Goldstein, Milton *art educator, printmaker, painter*

Bearsville
Wickiser, Ralph Lewanda *painter, educator, author*

Bedford
Weinman, Robert Alexander *sculptor*

Binghamton
Ippolito, Angelo *artist, educator*
Schwartz, Aubrey Earl *artist*

Bloomington
Ruffing, Anne Elizabeth *artist*

Bridgehampton
Jackson, Lee *artist*

Bronx
Adams, Alice *sculptor*
†Kassoy, Hortense (Honey Kassoy) *artist*
Schwam, Marvin Albert *graphic design company executive*

Brooklyn
Anderson, Lennart *artist*
Artschwager, Richard Ernst *artist*
Battle, Turner Charles, III *art educator, educational association administrator*
Carlile, Janet Louise *artist, educator*
Carruthers, Walter Edward Royden (Roy Carruthers) *graphic designer, artist*
Clark, Peggy *theatrical lighting designer*
Cornell, Thomas Browne *artist, educator*
DeCarava, Roy R. *photographer, educator*
Delson, Elizabeth *artist*
Dinnerstein, Harvey *artist*
Dinnerstein, Simon Abraham *artist, educator*
Grado, Angelo John *artist*
Jackson, Sarah Jeanette *sculptor, graphic artist, copier artist, bookmaker*
Jones, Susan Emily *fashion educator, administrator, educator*
Lederman, Stephanie Brody *artist*
†Lipski, Donald G. *sculptor*
Pearlstein, Seymour *artist*
Pfaffman, William Scott *sculptor*
Ries, Martin *artist, educator*
Rocco, Ron *artist*
Schaefer, Marilyn Louise *artist, writer, educator*
Shechter, Ben-Zion *artist, illustrator*
Shechter, Laura Judith *artist*
Snyder, Joan *artist*
Sonenberg, Jack *artist*
Swirsky, Judith Perlman *arts administrator, consultant*

Buffalo
Berlin, Lorna Chumley *artist*
Chryssa *sculptor*
Piccillo, Joseph *artist*
Rogovin, Milton *photographer, retired optometrist*

Buskirk
Johanson, Patricia Maureen *artist, architect, park designer*

Campbell Hall
Greenly, Colin *artist*

Clarence
Hubler, Julius *artist*

Climax
Adler, Lee *artist, educator, marketing executive*

Congers
Gussow, Alan *artist, sculptor*

Corning
Buechner, Thomas Scharman *artist, retired glass manufacturing company executive, museum director*

Cross River
Smith, Lawrence Beall *artist*

Croton On Hudson
†Rubinfien, Leo H. *photographer, filmmaker*

Cutchogue
Dank, Leonard Dewey *medical illustrator, audio-visual consultant*

Douglaston
Costa, Ernest Fiorenzo *graphic designer*

East Hampton
Lassaw, Ibram *sculptor, painter*
Praetorius, William Albert, Sr. *artist, former advertising and real estate executive*
Richenburg, Robert Bartlett *artist, retired art educator*
Stein, Ronald Jay *artist, airline transport pilot*

Elmhurst
†Wachsteter, George *illustrator*

Flushing
Bruder, Harold Jacob *artist, educator*
Carlson, Cynthia Joanne *artist, educator*
Laderman, Gabriel *artist*

Fly Creek
Dusenbery, Walter Condit *sculptor*

Forest Hills
Crystal, Boris *artist*
Gayner, Esther K. *artist*
Tewi, Thea *sculptor*

Franklin Square
Indiviglia, Salvatore Joseph *artist, retired naval officer*

Great Neck
Seidler, Doris *artist*

Greenvale
Leipzig, Arthur *photographer, educator emeritus*
Soreff, Stephen Mayer *artist*

Hawthorne
Sandbank, Henry *photographer, film director*

Hillsdale
Richards, Joseph Edward *artist*

Holland
Blair, Robert Noel *artist*

Hoosick Falls
Hatfield, David Underhill *artist*

Hudson
Avedisian, Edward *artist*

Huntington
Twardowicz, Stanley Jan *artist, photographer*

Huntington Station
Barron, Barbara Marilyn *fibre artist*

Irvington
Holden, Donald *author, artist*

Ithaca
Grippi, Salvatore William *artist*
Mikus, Eleanore Ann *artist*
Poleskie, Stephen Francis *artist, educator*
Squier, Jack Leslie *sculptor, educator*

Jackson Heights
Kanidinc, Salahattin *graphic artist, consultant art director*
Schiavina, Laura Margaret *artist*

Jamaica
Cade, Walter, III *artist, musician, singer, actor*

Jeffersonville
Craft, Douglas Durwood *artist*
Harms, Elizabeth Louise *artist*

Katonah
Giobbi, Edward Giacchino *artist*
Toney, Anthony *artist*

Larchmont
Tobey, Alton Stanley *artist*

Locust Valley
Lippold, Richard *sculptor*

Long Island City
Di Suvero, Mark *sculptor*
Donneson, Seena Sand *artist*
Gussow, Roy *sculptor, educator*

Mahopac Falls
†Karimi, Reza *artist*

Merrick
Cariola, Robert Joseph *artist*

Middle Village
Meyers, Edward *photographer, writer, publisher*

Middletown
Blumenthal, Fritz *printmaker*

Mount Kisco
Couture, Ronald David *art administrator, design consultant*

New Rochelle
Nienburg, George Frank *photographer*
Slotnick, Mortimer H. *artist*

New York
Abboud, Joseph M. *fashion designer*
Abeles, Sigmund M. *artist, printmaker*
Abish, Cecile *artist*
Abrams, Vivien *artist*
Abularach, Rodolfo Marco Antonio *artist*
Acconci, Vito (Hannibal) *conceptual artist*
Adams, Dennis Paul *artist*
Adams, Edward Thomas (Eddie Adams) *photographer*
Adolfo, (Adolfo F. Sardiña) *fashion designer*
Adri, (Adrienne Steckling) *fashion designer*
Adrian, Barbara (Mrs. Franklin C. Tramutola) *artist*
Aldredge, Theoni Vachliotis *costume designer*
Allard, Linda Marie *fashion designer*
Allner, Walter Heinz *designer, painter, art director*
Andre, Carl *sculptor*
Anthony, William Graham *artist*
Antonakos, Stephen *sculptor*
Antupit, Samuel Nathaniel *art director*
Appel, Karel *artist, illustrator*
Arcilesi, Vincent Jasper *artist*
Arman, Armand Pierre *sculptor*
Armani, Giorgio *fashion designer*
Avedon, Richard *photographer*
Aycock, Alice *artist*
Azuma, Norio *artist, art dealer*
Banerjee, (Bimal) *artist, educator*
†Banks, Jeffrey *fashion designer*
Baranik, Rudolf *artist*
Barnard, Scott *artist consultant*
Barnes, Jhane Elizabeth *fashion design company executive, designer*
Barnet, Will *artist, educator*
Barrett, Bill *sculptor*
Bartle, Annette Gruber (Mrs. Thomas R. Bartle) *artist, writer, photographer*
Bartlett, Jennifer Losch *artist*
†Bartlett, John *fashion designer*
Bass, Joel Leonard *artist*
Bateman, Robert McLellan *artist*
Beal, Jack *artist*
Beatty, John Lee *scenic designer*
Beck, Rosemarie *artist, educator*
Beene, Geoffrey *fashion designer*
Bellin, Milton Rockwell *artist*
Benglis, Lynda *artist, sculptor*
Ben-Haim, Zigi *artist*
Berger, Oscar *artist*
Bergson, Maria *designer*
Berlind, Robert Elliot *artist*
Berman, Ariane R. *artist*
Bernard, Walter *art director*
Bernstein, Theresa *artist*
Berthot, Jake *artist*
Bhavsar, Natvar Prahladji *artist*
Billian, Cathey R. *sculptor, educator*
Blaine, Nell *artist, printmaker*
Blanc, Peter (William Peters Blanc) *sculptor, painter*
Blass, Bill (William Ralph Blass) *designer apparel, home furnishings*
Blechman, R. O. *artist, filmmaker*
Block, John Douglas *auction house executive*
Boardman, Seymour *artist*
Bochner, Mel *artist*
Boley Bolaffio, Rita *artist*
Bonino, Fernanda *art dealer*
Boothe, Power *visual artist, educator, filmmaker, set designer*
Borofsky, Jonathan *artist*
Botero, Fernando *artist*
Bourgeois, Louise *sculptor*
Bradley, Lisa M. *artist*
Brandt, Grace Borgenicht *art dealer*
Brandt, Warren *artist*
Bricken, Barry Irwin *fashion designer*
Brooks, Diana D. *auction house executive*
Brown, Robert Delford *artist*
Bunts, Frank Emory *artist*
Burlingame, Lloyd Lamson *design instructor*
Cajori, Charles Florian *artist, educator*
Caldwell, Susan Hanes *art dealer*
Campbell, Ronald Neil *magazine designer*
Carnase, Thomas Paul *graphic designer, typographic consultant*
†Carter, Kevin *photographer*
Casebere, James Edward *artist*
Catlett, Elizabeth *sculptor, printmaker, educator*
Cesarani, Sal *fashion designer*
Charlesworth, Sarah E. *photographer, conceptual artist*
Chen, Chi (Chen Chi) *artist*
Chermayeff, Ivan *graphic designer*
Christo, (Christo Vladimirov Javacheff) *artist*
Chwast, Seymour *graphic artist*
Claiborne, Liz (Elisabeth Claiborne Ortenberg) *fashion designer*
Clarke, John Clem *artist*
Close, Charles Thomas (Chuck Close) *artist*
Cohen, Arthur Morris *artist*
Cohen, Cora *artist*
Cole, Max *artist*
Cole, Sylvan, Jr. *art dealer*
Colker, Edward *artist, educator*
Conover, Robert Fremont *artist, educator*
Cooper, Mario *artist, educator*
Cooper, Paula *art dealer*
Cortor, Eldzier *artist, printmaker*
Cowles, Charles *art dealer*
Crile, Susan *artist*
†Cunningham, Bill *photographer*
Currie, Bruce *artist*
Dajani, Virginia *arts administrator*
Dallmann, Daniel F. *artist, educator*
Dana, F(rank) Mitchell *theatrical lighting designer*
Daphnis, Nassos *artist*
Davidovich, Jaime *video artist, researcher*
Davidson, Nancy Brachman *artist, educator*
Davis, Douglas Matthew *artist, educator, author*
Davison, Daniel Pomeroy *fine arts auction executive*
de Champlain, Vera Chopak *artist, painter*
Deem, George *artist*
†De Harak, Rudolph *painter, graphic designer*
de Kooning, Willem *artist*
de la Renta, Oscar *fashion designer*
Demaria, Walter *sculptor*
Denes, Agnes C. *environmental artist*
Denhof, Miki *graphic designer*
Dennis, Donna Frances *sculptor, art educator*
†dePaola, Thomas Anthony *illustrator, children's author*
des Rioux, Deena Victoria Coty *artist, graphics designer*
Di Meo, Dominick *artist, sculptor, painter*
Di Mitri, Piero *fashion designer*
Dine, Jim *artist*
Dintenfass, Terry *art dealer*
Dobbs, John Barnes *artist, educator*
Dodd, Lois *artist, art professor*
Donati, Enrico *artist*
Draper, William Franklin *artist, portrait and landscape painter*
Drucker, Mort *commercial artist*
Duff, John Ewing *sculptor*
Dyyon, Frazier (LeRoy Frazier) *artist*
†Egielski, Richard *illustrator*
Eisen, Mark *fashion designer*
Eisenberg, Sonja Miriam *artist*
Elder, Eldon *stage designer, theatre consultant*
Eliot, Lucy Carter *artist*
Elman, Naomi Geist *artist, producer*
Enders, Elizabeth McGuire *artist*
Erwitt, Elliott Romano *photographer, cinematographer*
Estes, Richard *artist*
Evans, John *artist*
Faulkner, Frank M. *artist*
Faurer, Louis *photographer*
Federico, Gene *graphic designer*
Feigen, Richard L. *art dealer*
Feiler, Jo Alison *artist*
Feininger, Andreas Bernhard Lyonel *photographer*
Findlay, Michael Alistair *auction house executive, poet*
Fischer, Carl *photographer, graphic artist*
†Fisher, Rick *lighting designer*
Fleischman, Lawrence Arthur *art dealer, publisher, consultant*
Frankenthaler, Helen *artist*
Freeman, Elaine Lavalle *sculptor*
Freeman, Mark *artist*
Freeman, Peter Craig *art dealer*
Frumkin, Allan *art dealer*
Fugate-Wilcox, Terry *artist*
Gagosian, Larry *art dealer*
†Gammell, Stephen *illustrator*
Gechtoff, Sonia *artist*
Geismar, Thomas H. *graphic designer*
Geissbuhler, Stephan *graphic designer*
Georges, Paul Gordon *artist*
Gibson, Ralph H(olmes) *photographer*
Glasco, Joseph Milton *artist*
Gleason, John James *theatrical lighting designer*
Goertz, Augustus Frederick, III *artist*
Gold, Albert *artist*
Goldberg, Michael *artist*
Goldin, Leon *artist, educator*
†Goldstein, Gary Alan *creative director*
Golub, Leon Albert *artist*
Gottschall, Edward Maurice *graphic arts company executive*
Graves, Nancy Stevenson *artist*
Gray, George *mural painter*
Griefen, John Adams *artist, educator*
Grooms, Red *artist*
Grossman, Nancy *artist*
Gutman, Robert William *retired fine arts educator*
†Haacke, Hans Christoph Carl *artist, educator*
Haber, Ira Joel *artist, art educator*
Haerer, Carol *artist*
Haessle, Jean-Marie Georges *artist*
Hallam, Beverly (Beverly Linney) *artist*
Hardison, Ruth Inge *sculptor*
Hardy, Thomas Austin *sculptor*
Harmon, Lily *artist, author*
Hasen, Burton Stanley *artist*
†Hazlitt, Donald Robert *artist*
Heiloms, May (Mrs. Samuel Heiloms) *artist*
Held, Al *artist, educator*
Heliker, John *artist*
Helman, Joseph Arthur *art dealer*
Herrera, Carolina *fashion designer*
Hilfiger, Tommy *fashion designer*
Hill, Clinton *artist*
†Hios, Theodore *painter, graphic artist*
Hirschfeld, Albert *artist*
Hoff, Margo *artist, printmaker, muralist*
Holland, Bradford Wayne *artist*
Holt, Nancy Louise *artist*
†Holzer, Jenny *artist*
†Hould-Ward, Ann *theatrical costume designer*
Hull, Cathy *artist, illustrator*
†Hultberg, John *artist*
Hunt, Richard *sculptor*
Incandela, Gerald Jean-Marie *artist*
Ireland, Patrick *artist*
Isley, Alexander Max *graphic designer, lecturer*
Jackson, Ward *artist*
Jacobs, Marc *fashion designer*
Jacquette, Yvonne Helene *artist*
Jaffe, Nora *artist*
Jampolis, Neil Peter *designer*
Jaudon, Valerie *artist*
Jenkins, Paul *artist*
Johns, Jasper *artist*
Johnson, Betsey Lee *fashion designer*
Jonas, Joan *artist*
Jones, Edward Powis *artist*
Judson, Jeannette Alexander *artist*
Kahn, Wolf *artist*
Kaish, Luise Clayborn *sculptor*
Kaish, Morton *artist, educator*
Kamali, Norma *fashion designer*
Kan, Diana Artemis Mann Shu *artist*
Kanovitz, Howard *artist*
Karan, Donna (Donna Faske) *fashion designer*
Karp, Marshall Warren *creative director, writer*
Katz, Alex *artist*
Katz, Hilda *artist*
Katzen, Lila Pell *sculptor*
Katzman, Herbert Henry *artist*
Kaz, Nathaniel *sculptor*
Kelly, James *artist*
Kemper, Randolph E. *fashion designer*
Kennedy, Ian Glen *art appraiser*
Kepets, Hugh Michael *artist*
Kim, Willa *costume designer*
Kinstler, Everett Raymond *artist*
Kirk, Alexis Vemian *designer*
†Kirshenbaum, Richard Warren *creative director*
Kleemann, Ronald Allen *artist*
Klein, Calvin Richard *fashion designer*
Klotz, Florence *costume designer*
Kner, Andrew Peter *art director*
Konzal, Joseph Charles *sculptor*
Koppelman, Chaim *artist*
Koppelman, Dorothy Myers *artist, consultant*
Korman, Barbara *artist, educator*
Kors, Michael (Karl Anderson, Jr.) *fashion designer*
†Kosstrin, Jane Edith *designer*
Krementz, Jill *photographer, author*
Krushenick, Nicholas *artist*
Lane, Kenneth Jay *jewelry designer*
Lane, Lois N. *artist*
Lang, Daniel S. *artist*
La Noue, Terence David *artist, educator*
Lanyon, Ellen (Mrs. Roland Ginzel) *artist, educator*
Lash, Stephen Sycle *auction company executive*
Lasker, Jonathan Lewis *artist*
Lasker, Joseph L. *artist, illustrator*
Lauren, Ralph *fashion designer*
Lechay, James *artist, emeritus art educator*
Lee, Catherine *sculptor, painter*
Lehr, Janet *art dealer*
Lehrer, Leonard *artist, educator*
Leiber, Gerson August *artist*
Leiber, Judith Maria *designer, manufacturer*
Leibovitz, Annie *photographer*
Levine, David *artist*
Levy, Benjamin *artist*
LeWitt, Sol *artist*
Liberman, Alexander *artist, editor*
Loengard, John Borg *photographer; editor*
Loring, John Robbins *artist*
Loving, Alvin Demar, Jr. *artist, educator*
Lucchesi, Bruno *sculptor*
MacIver, Loren *artist*
Mackie, Robert Gordon *costume and fashion designer*
Mackler, Tina *artist*
Madsen, Loren Wakefield *sculptor*
Mangold, Robert Peter *artist*
Manning, Jack *photographer, columnist, author*
Marion, John Louis *fine arts auctioneer and appraiser*
Marisol, (Marisol Escobar) *sculptor*
Martin, Agnes *artist*
Massey, Stephen Charles *auctioneer*
Max, Peter *artist*
McCarthy, Denis *artist, educator*
McCully, Emily Arnold *illustrator,writer*
McDarrah, Fred William *photographer, editor, writer, photography reviewer*
Mc Gowin, William Edward *artist*
McKenzie, Mary Beth *artist*
Meisel, Louis Koenig *art dealer, art historian, writer*
Meisel, Steven *advertising photographer*
Meiselas, Susan Clay *photographer*
Mendelson, Haim *artist, educator, art gallery director*
Menses, Jan *artist, draftsman, etcher, lithographer, muralist*
Meyers, Dale (Mrs. Mario Cooper) *artist*
Michals, Duane *photographer*
Miller, Lee Anne *artist, educator*
Miller, Nicole Jacqueline *fashion designer*
Miller, Richard Kidwell *artist, actor, educator*
Miller, Richard McDermott *sculptor*
Miss, Mary *artist*
Miyake, Issey *fashion designer*
Mizrahi, Isaac *fashion designer*
Morath, Inge *photographer*
Morgan, Jacqui *illustrator, painter, educator*
Mori, Hanae *fashion designer*
Morris, Robert *artist*
Murphy, Catherine *painter*
Murphy, John Cullen *illustrator*
Murray, Elizabeth *artist*
Musser, Tharon *theatrical lighting designer, theatre consultant*
Neiman, LeRoy *artist*
Nelson, Richard *lighting designer, consultant*
Neuhaus, Max *artist, composer*
Newman, Arnold *photographer*
Newman, Elias *artist*
Notarbartolo, Albert *artist*
Ohlson, Douglas Dean *artist*
Oldenburg, Claes Thure *artist*
Oldham, Todd *fashion designer*
Owsley, David Thomas *art consultant, appraiser, lecturer, author*
Pace, Stephen Shell *artist, educator*
Parker, Nancy Winslow *artist, writer*
Parker, Olivia *photographer*
Parker, Robert Andrew *artist*
Pascal, David *artist*
†Pavlika, Holly Ann *art director*
Pearson, Henry Charles *artist*
Peckolick, Alan *graphic designer*
Pepper, Beverly *artist, sculptor*
Peress, Gilles *photographer*
Perlis, Donald M. *artist*
Perls, Klaus Gunther *art dealer*
Phillips, Anthony Mark *auction house executive*
Pimsler, Alvin J. *artist*
Pinsker, Essie Levine *sculptor, former advertising and public relations executive*
Pool, Mary Jane *design consultant, author, lecturer*
Poons, Larry *artist*
Poor, Anne *artist*
Porter, Liliana Alicia *artist, printmaker*
Quackenbush, Robert Mead *artist, author, psychoanalyst*
Quaytman, Harvey *painter*
Quisgard, Liz Whitney *artist, sculptor*
Rabinowitch, David George *sculptor*
Racz, Andre *artist, engraver, educator*
Raffael, Joseph *artist*
Raffo, Steve *artist*
Rauschenberg, Robert *artist*
Reddy, Krishna Narayana *artist, educator*
Reid, Robert Dennis *artist, educator*
Reininghaus, Ruth *artist*
Remington, Deborah Williams *artist*
Resika, Paul *artist*
Resnick, Marcia Aylene *photographic artist, educator*
Resnick, Milton *artist*
Rodriguez, Geno (Eugene Rodriguez) *artist, arts administrator*
Roehm, Carolyne Jane *fashion designer*
Rose, Herman *artist*
Rose, Leatrice *artist, educator*
Rosenhouse, Irwin J. *artist, designer*
Rosenthal, Tony (Bernard) *sculptor*
Ross, Charles *artist*
Roth, Ann *costume designer*
Rothenberg, Susan *artist*
Ruben, Richards *artist, educator*
Rubin, Lawrence Edward *art dealer*
Ruscha, Edward *artist*
Ryman, Robert Tracy *artist*
St. Clair, Michael *art dealer*
Sainty, Guy Stair *art dealer*
Saks, Arnold *graphic designer*
Salle, David *artist*
Savelli, Angelo *artist*
Scavullo, Francesco *photographer*
Schapiro, Miriam *artist*
Scher, Paula Joan *graphic designer*
Schnabel, Julian *artist*
Schneider, JoAnne *artist*
Schrag, Karl *artist*
Schwartz, Daniel Bennett *artist*
Schwartz, Eugene M. *art collector, patron*
Scully, Sean Paul *artist*
Searle, Ronald *artist*
Secunda, Arthur (Holland Secunda) *artist*
Segal, George *sculptor*
Seliger, Charles *artist*
†Seliger, Mark Alan *photographer*
Serra, Richard *sculptor*
Shamask, Ronaldus *fashion designer*
Shapiro, Babe *artist*
Shapiro, Joel Elias *artist*
Shaw, (George) Kendall *artist, educator*
Sherman, Cindy *artist*
Shikler, Aaron *artist*
Shore, Stephen *photographer*
Shuff, Lily *artist, wood engraver*
Silverman, Burton Philip *artist*
Simpson, Adele *costume designer*
†Sis, Peter *illustrator, children's book author, artist, filmmaker*
Skupinski, Bogdan Kazimierz *artist*
†Sky, Alison *artist, designer*
Slavin, Arlene *artist*
Slavin, Neal *photographer*
Sleigh, Sylvia *artist, educator*
Smith, Leon Polk *artist*
Smith, Shirley *artist*
Smith, Vincent DaCosta *artist*
Soffer, Sasson *artist, sculptor*
Solman, Joseph *artist*
Sonneman, Eve *artist*
Sperakis, Nicholas George *artist*
Stamos, Theodoros *artist*
Stanley, Bob *artist*
Starn, Douglas *artist, photographer*
Starn, Mike P. *artist, photographer*
Stefanelli, Joseph James (Joe Stefanelli) *artist*
Steinberg, Saul *artist*
Steir, Pat Iris *artist*
Stella, Frank Philip *artist*
†Sterling, David M. *graphic designer*
Stiebel, Gerald Gustave *art dealer*
Sugarman, George *artist*
Sui, Anna *fashion designer*
Sultan, Donald Keith *artist, printmaker*
Surrey, Milt *artist*
Sutton, Pat Lipsky *artist, educator*
Swain, Robert *artist*
Thrall, Donald Stuart *artist*
Tilton, James Floyd *theatrical designer, art director*
Tipton, Jennifer *lighting designer*
Tobias, Julius *sculptor*
Trigere, Pauline *fashion designer*
Tscherny, George *graphic designer*
†Tyler, David A. *auction house executive*
†Tyler, Richard *fashion designer*

Upright, Diane Warner *auction house executive*
van den Akker, Koos *fashion designer*
Vass, Joan *fashion designer*
Versace, Gianni *fashion designer*
Vittadini, Adrienne *fashion designer*
Viviano, Sam Joseph *illustrator*
Von Furstenberg, Diane Simone Michelle *fashion designer*
Von Ringelheim, Paul Helmut *sculptor*
Wagner, Robin Samuel Anton *stage and set designer*
Wald, Sylvia *artist*
Walton, Anthony John (Tony Walton) *theater and film designer, book illustrator*
†Wang, Vera *fashion designer*
Watson, Albert MacKenzie *photographer*
Wegman, William George *artist*
Weitz, John *fashion designer, writer*
Weschler, Anita *sculptor, painter*
Wesley, John Mercer *artist*
Williams, Garth Montgomery *illustrator*
Williams, William Thomas *artist, educator*
Willis, Thornton Wilson *painter*
Winsor, Jackie *artist*
Wolins, Joseph *artist*
Wong, Kwan Shut *art appraiser, artist*
Woodman, Timothy *artist*
Wunderman, Jan Darcourt *artist*
Wurmfeld, Sanford *artist, educator*
Yelle, Richard Wilfred *artist, product designer*
York, Richard Travis *art dealer*
†Young, Ed (Tse-chun) *illustrator, children's author*
Youngerman, Jack *artist, sculptor*
Zabriskie, Virginia M. *art dealer*
Zakanitch, Robert Rahway *artist*
Zapf, Hermann *book and type designer*
Zipprodt, Patricia *costume designer*
Zlowe, Florence Markowitz *artist*
Zox, Larry *artist*

North White Plains
Erla, Karen *artist, painter, collagist, printmaker*

Ossining
Cober, Alan Edwin *artist, illustrator, printmaker, educator*

Oswego
Fox, Michael David *art educator, visual imagist artist*

Palisades
Knowlton, Grace Farrar *sculptor, photographer*

Peekskill
Rosenberg, Marilyn R. *artist, visual poet*

Piermont
Der Harootian, Khoren *sculptor*

Pittsford
Lyttle, Douglas Alfred *photographer, educator*

Pleasantville
Robinson, Jay (Thurston Robinson) *artist*

Pound Ridge
Ferro, Walter *artist*

Rhinebeck
Clutz, William (Hartman Clutz) *artist, educator*
Rabinovich, Raquel *artist, sculptor*

Rochester
Engelmann, Lothar Klaus *photographic science educator*
Margolis, Richard Martin *photographer, educator*
Merritt, Howard Sutermeister *retired art educator*
Mertin, Roger *photographer*
Paley, Albert Raymond *art educator, sculptor*
Saisselin, Remy Gilbert *fine arts educator*

Rock Hill
Schary, Emanuel *artist*

Rye
Troller, Fred *graphic designer, painter, visual consultant, educator*

Sagaponack
Butchkes, Sydney *artist*
Isham, Sheila Eaton *artist*

Saratoga Springs
Upton, Richard Thomas *artist*

Scarsdale
Breinin, Raymond *painter, sculptor*
Fendelman, Helaine *art appraiser*
Gialleonardo, Victor *graphic designer*

Shady
Ruellan, Andree *artist*

Shelter Island
Culbertson, Janet Lynn *artist*

Shoreham
Spier, Peter Edward *artist, author*

Snyder
Breverman, Harvey *artist*

South Salem
Howard, Joan Alice *artist*

Southampton
Fuller, Sue *artist*
Lichtenstein, Roy *artist*
Silverstein, Louis *art director, designer, editor*

Sterling
Seawell, Thomas Robert *artist, retired educator*

Stony Brook
Pekarsky, Melvin Hirsch *artist*
Pindell, Howardena Doreen *artist*

Syracuse
Thomas, Sidney *fine arts educator, researcher*

Tappan
Dell, Robert Christopher *geothermal sculptor, scenic artist*
Nickford, Juan *sculptor, educator*

Tarrytown
Savage, Whitney Lee *artist, filmmaker*

Tuxedo Park
Domjan, Joseph (Spiri Domjan) *artist*

Utica
Pribble, Easton *artist*

Wainscott
Russo, Alexander Peter *artist, educator*

Wallkill
Koch, Edwin Ernest *artist, interior decorator*

Warwick
Franck, Frederick Sigfred *artist, author, dental surgeon*

Water Mill
Mac Whinnie, John Vincent *artist*
Rosenberg, Alex Jacob *art dealer, curator, fine arts appraiser, educator*

Westbury
Barboza, Anthony *photographer, artist*
Sherbell, Rhoda *artist, sculptor*

White Plains
Marci-Mariani, Anita *designer, illustrator*
Nickerson, Ruth *sculptor*

Woodstock
Banks, Rela *sculptor*
Fortess, Karl Eugene *artist, lithographer*

Yorktown Heights
Jones, Lauretta Marie *artist, graphic designer, computer interface designer*
Laventhol, Henry L(ee) (Hank Laventhol) *artist, etcher*

NORTH CAROLINA

Asheville
Jones, J. Kenneth *art dealer, former museum administrator*
Rufa, Robert Henry *artist, writer, editor*

Burnsville
†Bernstein, William Joseph *glass artist, educator*
Doyle, John Lawrence *artist*

Chapel Hill
Ness, Albert Kenneth *artist, educator*
Stipe, Robert Edwin *design educator*

Davidson
Jackson, Herb *artist, educator*

Fearrington Village
Schwinn-Jordan, Barbara (Barbara Schwinn) *painter*

Greensboro
Barker, Walter William, Jr. *artist, educator*

Laurinburg
Nance, Tony Max-Perry *designer, illustrator*

Pinehurst
Twitty, James Watson *artist*

Sanford
Higgins, George Edward *sculptor*

Winston Salem
Faccinto, Victor Paul *artist, gallery administrator*

NORTH DAKOTA

Bismarck
Solberg, Nellie Florence Coad *artist*

OHIO

Ashville
Beckman, Judith *art educator*

Aurora
Lawton, Florian Kenneth *artist, educator*

Bowling Green
Ocvirk, Otto George *artist*

Cincinnati
Brod, Stanford *graphic designer, educator*
Knipschild, Robert *artist, educator*
Rexroth, Nancy Louise *photographer*
Sullivan, Connie Castleberry *artist, photographer*
Wygant, Foster Laurance *art educator*

Cleveland
Beling, Helen *sculptor*
Cassill, Herbert Carroll *artist*
Fenton, Alan *artist*
McVey, William Mozart *sculptor*
Seltzer, Phyllis Estelle *painter, printmaker*

Columbus
Beverley, Jane Taylor *artist*
Kuehn, Edmund Karl *artist*

Hilliard
Cupp, David Foster *photographer, journalist*

Oberlin
Arnold, Paul Beaver *artist, educator*

Olmsted Township
Laessig, Robert H. *artist*

Perrysburg
Autry, Carolyn *artist, art history educator*

Seven Hills
Stanczak, Julian *artist, educator*

Shaker Heights
Held, Lila M. *art appraiser*

Toledo
McGlauchlin, Tom *artist*

Van Wert
Liljegren, Frank Sigfrid *artist, art association official*

OKLAHOMA

Chickasha
Good, Leonard Phelps *artist*

Oklahoma City
Alaupovic, Alexandra Vrbanic *artist, educator*

OREGON

Applegate
Boyle, (Charles) Keith *artist, educator*

Ashland
Hay, Richard Laurence *theater scenic designer*

Cannon Beach
Greaver, Harry *artist*

Klamath Falls
Wells, Lu *artist*

Portland
Waddingham, John Alfred *artist, journalist*

Salem
Pierre, Joseph Horace, Jr. *commercial artist*

PENNSYLVANIA

Allentown
Moller, Hans *artist*

Allison Park
Osby, Larissa Geiss *artist*

Cochranville
Sazegar, Morteza *artist*

East Stroudsburg
Frazetta, Frank *artist*

Edinboro
Kemenyffy, Steven *artist, art educator*

Elkins Park
Bayliss, George Vincent *art educator, artist*

Glenside
Frudakis, Zenos Antonios *sculptor, artist*

Kimberton
Williams, Lawrence Soper *photographer*

Lehigh Valley
Kocsis, James Paul *artist, publisher*

Lumberville
Katsiff, Bruce *artist*

Mechanicsville
Bye, Ranulph DeBayeux *artist, author*

Narberth
Grenald, Raymond *architectural lighting designer*

Philadelphia
Auth, Tony *artist*
Cramer, Richard Charles *artist, educator*
Gralish, Tom *photographer*
Knobler, Nathan *art educator*
Le Clair, Charles George *artist, retired dean*
Madigan, Martha *photographer, artist, photography educator*
Maitin, Sam(uel Calman) (Sam Maitin) *artist*
Metzker, Ray K. *photographer*
Paone, Peter *artist*
Remenick, Seymour *artist, educator*
Schwarz, Robert Devlin *art dealer*
Solomon, Vita Petrosky *artist*
Spandorfer, Merle Sue *artist, educator, author*
Weidner, Roswell Theodore *artist*

Pittsburgh
Rogers, Bryan Leigh *artist, art educator*
Trapp, Frank Anderson *art educator*
Wilkins, David George *fine arts educator*
Williams, John Wesley *fine arts educator*

Selinsgrove
Putterman, Florence Grace *artist, printmaker*

Solebury
Anthonisen, George Rioch *sculptor, artist*

Spring Grove
Helberg, Shirley Adelaide Holden *artist, educator*

University Park
Van Dommelen, David B. *artist, educator*

Upper Darby
Gasparro, Frank *sculptor*

West Chester
Jamison, Philip *artist*

Wynnewood
Maxwell, John Raymond *artist*

RHODE ISLAND

Cranston
Crooks, W. Spencer *artist, educator*

Kingston
Leete, William White *artist*
Rohm, Robert Hermann *sculptor*

Pawtucket
Heyman, Lawrence Murray *printmaker, painter*

Providence
Callahan, Harry Morey *photographer*
Feldman, Walter Sidney *artist*
Howes, Lorraine de Wet *fashion designer, educator*
McIlvane, Edward James *artist, instructor, designer*
Ockerse, Thomas *graphic design educator*
Wunderlich, Alfred Leon *artist, art educator*

Rumford
Cote, Louise Roseann *creative director, designer*

Westerly
Reiland, Lowell Keith *sculptor*

SOUTH CAROLINA

Columbia
Robinson, Christopher Thomas *artist*

Greenville
Alberga, Alta Wheat *artist*

SOUTH DAKOTA

Sioux Falls
Grupp, Carl Alf *art educator, artist*

TENNESSEE

Chattanooga
Cress, George Ayers *artist, educator*
Martin, Chester Y. *sculptor, painter*
Mills, Charles G. *photography company executive*
Mills, Olan, II *photography company executive*

Knoxville
Sublett, Carl Cecil *artist*

Lookout Mountain
Wyeth, Andrew *artist*
Wyeth, James Browning *artist*

Memphis
Carroll, Billy Price *artist*
McPherson, Larry E(ugene) *photographer, educator*
Riss, Murray *photographer, educator*

TEXAS

Arlington
Elias, Harold John *artist, educator*

Austin
Deming, David Lawson *art educator*
Goldstein, Peggy R. *sculptor*
Guerin, John William *artist*
High, Timothy Griffin *artist, educator, writer*
†McFarland, Lawrence D. *photographer, educator*
Spruce, Everett Franklin *artist*
Weismann, Donald Leroy *art educator, artist, filmmaker, writer*

Beaumont
Coe, (Matchett) Herring *sculptor*

Corpus Christi
Ullberg, Kent Jean *sculptor*

Dallas
Blessen, Karen Alyce *free-lance illustrator, designer*
Costa, Victor Charles *fashion designer*
Emerson, Walter Caruth *artist, educator*
Richards, Jeanne Herron *artist*
Thorson, Marcelyn Marie *applied art educator*

Houston
Camfield, William Arnett *art educator*
DeMenil, Dominique *art collector, philanthropist*
Gorski, Daniel Alexander *art educator*
Honeycutt, George Leonard *photographer*
King, Kay Wander *design educator, fashion designer, consultant*
Long, Meredith J. *art dealer*
O'Neil, John *artist*
Schorre, Louis Charles, Jr. *artist*
Sherwood, Bette Wilson *artist*
Ward, Bethea *artist, small business owner*

Huntsville
Lea, Stanley E. *artist, educator*

Kerrville
Cook, John Alfred *sculptor, medallist, educator*

Liberty Hill
Vance, Zinna Barth *artist, writer*

Lubbock
Mittler, Gene Allen *art educator*

Odessa
Lee, Nelda S. *artist, art appraiser and dealer, film producer*

Plano
†Sedei, Donald James *art director*

Richardson
†Breard, Benjamin Allen *art dealer*

Seabrook
Sterling, Shirley Frampton *artist, educator*

Stephenville
Dees, Lynne *artist*

Waco
Kagle, Joseph Louis, Jr. *artist, arts administrator*

Wichita Falls
Reyes, Nicholas Carlos *photographer*

UTAH

Orderville
Zornes, Milford *artist*

VERMONT

Bennington
Adams, Pat *artist, educator*

Cavendish
Shapiro, David *artist, art historian*

East Calais
Gahagan, James Edward, Jr. *artist*

East Dorset
Armstrong, Jane Botsford *sculptor*

East Wallingford
Bluhm, Norman *artist*

Hartland
Tooker, George *artist*

Marlboro
Olitski, Jules *artist*

Shaftsbury
Bubriski, Kevin Ernest *photographer, educator*

West Burke
Van Vliet, Claire *artist*

Weston
Kasnowski, Chester Nelson *artist, educator*

VIRGINIA

Alexandria
Alderson, Margaret Northrop *arts administrator, educator, artist*

Arlington
Reed, Paul Allen *artist*
†Wendelin, Rudolph Andrew *artist*

Blacksburg
Carter, Dean *artist*

Charlottesville
Bunch, John Blake *photographer, writer, educator*
Priest, Hartwell Wyse *artist*
Ruben, Leonard *retired art educator*

Clifton
Hennesy, Gerald Craft *artist*

East Stone Gap
Combs, Jo Karen Kobeck *artist, writer*

Falls Church
Safer, John *artist, lecturer*

Fredericksburg
Schmutzhart, Berthold Josef *sculptor, educator, art and education consultant*

Newport News
Camp, Hazel Lee Burt *artist*

Norfolk
Ives, Ronn Brian *artist, educator*
Jones, Leon Herbert, Jr. (Herb Jones) *artist*

Onancock
Kidd, Rebecca Montgomery (Louise Kidd) *artist*

Reston
Heginbotham, Jan Sturza *sculptor*

Richmond
Addiss, Stephen *art history educator, artist, composer*
Freed, David Clark *artist*
Kevorkian, Richard *artist*
Lawton, Nancy *artist*
Rowley, Frank Selby, Jr. *artist*

Springfield
Nong *artist, sculptor*

Waterford
Pollack, Reginald Murray *painter*

Williamsburg
Roseberg, Carl Andersson *sculptor, educator*

WASHINGTON

Anacortes
Mc Cracken, Philip Trafton *sculptor*

Bainbridge Is
Randlett, Mary Willis *photographer*

Battle Ground
Hansen, James Lee *sculptor*

Burlington
Zeretzke, Frederick Frank H. *artist, educator*

Kent
Pierce, Danny Parcel *artist, educator*

Mercer Island
Steinhardt, Henry *photographer*

Olympia
Haseltine, James Lewis *artist, consultant*

Seattle
Alps, Glen Earl *printmaker, educator*
Berger, Paul Eric *artist, photographer*
Celentano, Francis Michael *artist, art educator*
Chihuly, Dale Patrick *artist*
Day, Alexandra (Sandra L. Woodward Darling) *illustrator, designer*
Du Pen, Everett George *sculptor, educator*
Ellis, Eva Lillian *artist*
Lawrence, Jacob *artist, educator*
Pawula, Kenneth John *artist, educator*
Spafford, Michael Charles *artist*
Washington, James Winston, Jr. *artist, sculptor*

WEST VIRGINIA

Huntington
Polan, Nancy Moore *artist*

WISCONSIN

Beloit
Simon, Michael Alexander *photographer, educator*

Cedarburg
White, Doris Anne *artist*

Fish Creek
Becker, Bettie Geraldine *artist*

Hartland
Stamsta, Jean F. *artist*

Hollandale
Myers, Frances *artist*

Madison
†Becker, David *artist, educator*
Colescott, Warrington Wickham *artist, printmaker, educator*
Fritz, Bruce Morrell *photographer*
Greenwald, Caroline Meyer *artist*
Lotterman, Hal *artist, educator*
Wilde, John *artist, educator*

Milwaukee
Berman, Fred Jean *art educator, painter, photographer*
Burkert, Robert Randall *artist*
Helbert, Clifford L. *graphic designer, journalism educator*
Poehlmann, JoAnna *artist, illustrator, designer*
Thrall, Arthur Alvin *artist*
Vespa, Ned Angelo *photographer*

Oregon
Sloan, Richard *artist*

WYOMING

Centennial
Russin, Robert Isaiah *sculptor, educator*

Cody
Jackson, Harry Andrew *artist*

Jackson
Moeller, Robert Charles, III *fine arts consultant*

Kemmerer
Clark, Michael *artist, educator*

Laramie
Flach, Victor H. *designer, educator*
Reif, (Frank) David *artist, educator*

CANADA

ALBERTA

Calgary
Esler, John Kenneth *artist*

Edmonton
Jungkind, Walter *design educator, consultant*

BRITISH COLUMBIA

Duncan
Hughes, Edward John *artist*

Salt Spring Island
Raginsky, Nina *artist*

Victoria
Harvey, Donald *artist, educator*

MANITOBA

Winnipeg
Eyre, Ivan *artist*

NOVA SCOTIA

Mahone Bay
Tolmie, Kenneth Donald *artist, author*

Wolfville
Colville, David Alexander *artist*

ONTARIO

Dundas
Walker, Gay Hunner Parsons (Mrs. Roger Geoffrey Walker) *science illustrator*

Guelph
Danby, Kenneth Edison *artist, painter, printmaker*

London
Livick, Stephen *fine art photographer*

Niagara-on-the-Lake
Scott, Campbell *artist*

North York
Lee, Eugene *theatrical set designer*

Ottawa
Karsh, Yousuf *photographer*

Toronto
Astman, Barbara Ann *artist, educator*
Graham, Kathleen Margaret (K. M. Graham) *artist*
Kramer, Burton *graphic designer, educator*
Morgan, Wayne Philip *art and popular culture exhibition producer*
Ronald, William *artist*
Schaefer, Carl Fellman *artist*
Semak, Michael William *photographer, educator*
Winter, Frederick Elliot *fine arts educator*

Waterloo
Green, Arthur Nelson *artist, educator*
Urquhart, Tony *artist, educator*

Willowdale
Hallman, H(enry) Theodore, Jr. *artist, textile designer*

QUEBEC

Ayers Cliff
Beament, Thomas Harold (Tib Beament) *artist, printmaker, educator*

Beaconsfield
Harder, Rolf Peter *graphic designer, painter*

Montreal
Cardinal, Marcelin *artist*
Charney, Melvin *artist, architect, educator*
McEwen, Jean *painter*

Pontiac
Hlavina, Rasto R(astislav) *sculptor*

Saint Adele
†Rousseau-Vermette, Mariette *artist*

Saint Lambert
Archambault, Louis *sculptor*

SASKATCHEWAN

Saskatoon
Bornstein, Eli *artist, sculptor*

MEXICO

Cuernavaca
Mora, Francisco *artist, printmaker*

Mexico City
Friedeberg, Pedro *painter, sculptor, designer*
Mendelejis, Leonardo Nierman *artist*

AUSTRALIA

Ringwood, Victoria
Base, Graeme Rowland *illustrator, author*

ENGLAND

London
Craig, Stuart N. *film production designer*
Kitaj, R. B. *artist*

FRANCE

Annet-sur-Marne
†Vasarely, Victor *artist*

Arles Cedex
Clergue, Lucien Georges *photographer*

Paris
Biala, Janice *artist*
De Givenchy, Hubert James Marcel Taffin (Givenchy) *fashion designer*
Lacroix, Christian Marie Marc *fashion designer*
Lagerfeld, Karl Otto *fashion designer*
Levee, John Harrison *artist, designer*
Renouf, Edda *artist*
Vuitton, Henry-Louis *designer*

Vaucluse
Pfriem, Bernard Aldine *artist*

GERMANY

Dusseldorf 30
Richter, Gerhard *artist*

IRELAND

Ballyvaughan, County Clare
Wicks, Eugene Claude *art educator*

ITALY

Florence
Cecil, Charles Harkless *artist, educator*

Milan
Ferré, Gianfranco *fashion designer, artistic director*

JAPAN

Kanagawa
Swarz, Sahl *sculptor*

Kyoto
Shoichi, Ida *artist, printmaker, painter, sculptor*

Tokyo
Kusama, Yayoi *sculptor, painter*

THE NETHERLANDS

Amsterdam
Baer, Jo *painter*

PAKISTAN

Lahore
†Geoffrey, Iqbal (Mohammed Jawaid Iqbal Jafree) *artist, lawyer*

PORTUGAL

Lisbon
Berger, Jason *artist, printmaker*

SPAIN

Galilea, Mallorca
Ulbricht, John *artist*

SWITZERLAND

Berne
Polke, Sigmar *artist*

ADDRESS UNPUBLISHED

Abadi, Fritzie *artist, educator*
Abbe, Elfriede Martha *sculptor, graphic artist*
Abramowicz, Janet *painter, print-maker*
Anastasi, William Joseph *artist*
Andrade, Edna *artist, art educator*
Annus, John Augustus *artist*
†Arthur, Rochelle Linda *art director*
Atkinson, Bill *designer*
Bageris, John *artist, educator*
Bannard, Walter Darby *artist, art critic*
Barth, Frances Dorothy *artist*
Baughman, J. Ross *photographer, writer, educator*
Behl, Wolfgang *sculptor, retired educator*
Benton, Fletcher *sculptor*
Ben Tré, Howard *artist*
Benzle, Curtis Munhall *artist, educator*
Berlin, Beatrice Winn *visual artist, printmaker*
Bigelow-Lourie, Anne Edwige *graphic designer*
†Bingham, Louise H. *artist, art educator*
Bissell, James Dougal, III *motion picture production designer*
Bjornson, Maria *theatrical designer*
Bloom, Hyman *artist*
Boal, Dean *arts center administrator, educator*
Boxer, Stanley Robert *artist, sculptor*
Brenner, Albert *production designer, sculptor*
Brettell, Richard Robson *art consultant*
Brodie, Howard *artist*
Brown, William Ferdinand *artist, writer*
Browne, Diana Gayle *artist, social services*
Bullard, Helen (Mrs. Joseph Marshall Krechniak) *sculptor*
Bury, John *theatre designer, consultant*
Campanelli, Pauline Eble *artist*
Campbell, Patton *stage designer, educator*
Cantliffe, Jeri Miller *artist, art educator*
Caplan, Ralph *design writer, consultant*
Carothers, Steven Michael *artist, designer, writer*
Carter, Nanette Carolyn *artist*
Cassini, Oleg Lolewski *fashion designer, manufacturer*
Chase-Riboud, Barbara Dewayne *sculptor, writer*
Chinn, Thomas Wayne *typographic company executive*
Chinni, Peter Anthony *artist*

Ciccone, Anne Panepinto *artist*
Clark, Larry *photographer*
Cobb, Ruth *artist*
Cobb, Virginia Horton *artist, educator*
Conway, Robert P. *art dealer*
Cooney, Barbara *illustrator, author*
Coplans, John Rivers *artist*
Craw, Freeman (Jerry Craw) *graphic artist*
Cumming, Robert Hugh *artist, photographer*
Cummings, David William *artist, educator*
D'Arcangelo, Allan Matthew *artist*
†Deane, Marjorie Schlesinger *fashion merchandising executive*
De Blasi, Tony (Anthony Armando De Blasi) *artist*
Dechar, Peter Henry *artist*
Dell'Olio, Louis *fashion designer*
De Looper, Willem Johan *artist, museum curator*
Dembeck, Mary Grace *artist, writer*
Dill, Laddie John *artist*
Di Spigna, Tony *graphic designer*
Dogançay, Burhan C. *artist, photographer, sculptor*
Donath, Therese *author, artist*
Downes, Rackstraw *artist*
†Doyle, Peter W. *painter, illustrator*
Drummond, Sally Hazelet *artist*
Dyer, Geraldine Ann (Geri Dyer) *artist, poet*
Eddy, Don *artist*
Erden, Sybil Isolde *artist*
Firestone, Evan Richard *arts educator and administrator*
Fish, Janet Isobel *artist*
†Flavin, Dan *artist*
Forester, Russell *artist*
Francis, Sam *artist*
Freilicher, Jane *artist*
Gerstein, Esther *sculptor*
Giusti, Robert George *artist, educator*
Goldberger, Blanche Rubin *sculptor, jeweler*
Goodwill, Margaret Jane *artist*
Goulet, Lorrie *sculptor*
Greenberg, Albert *art director*
Greene, Lynne Jeannette *fashion designer*
†Gurney, James Marshall *artist, writer*
Guthrie, Edgar King *artist*
Halaby, Samia Asaad *artist, educator, computer artist*
Hanson, Jo *artist*
Harari, Hananiah *artist*
Harbutt, Charles *photographer*
Hartell, John *artist, retired art educator*
Hayes, David Vincent *sculptor*
Heilman, Marlin Grant *photographer*
Helander, Bruce Paul *art dealer, artist*
Heller, Dorothy *artist*
†Henry, John Raymond *sculptor*
Hepper, Carol *artist, educator*
Hersey, David Kenneth *theatrical lighting designer*
†Herzberg, Thomas *artist, illustrator*
Hoover, Francis Louis *educator, gemologist, jewelry designer, appraiser fine arts and gems, writer*
Hornick, Katherine Joyce Kay *artist, small business owner*
Hunt, Bryan *artist*
†Hyman, Trina Schart *illustrator*
†Iannone, Dorothy *visual artist, writer*
Irwin, Robert Walter *artist*
Janko, May *graphic artist*
Jansen, Angela Bing *artist, educator*
Jenney, Neil Franklin, Jr. *artist, philosopher*
Jimenez, Luis Alfonso, Jr. *sculptor*
Kahn, Albert Michael *artist, designer*
Kahn, Susan Beth *artist*
Kalina, Richard *artist*
Karawina, Erica *artist, stained glass designer*
Kaufman, Jane *artist*
Kearns, James Joseph *artist*
Kelly, Ellsworth *artist, sculptor*
Kipniss, Robert *artist*
Kleiman, Alan Boyd *artist*
Kloss, Gene (Alice Geneva Glasier) *artist*
Kohlmeyer, Ida Rittenberg *artist*
Kosuth, Joseph *artist*
Kramer, Reuben Robert *sculptor*
Kumler, Kipton Cornelius *photographer, consultant*
Kushner, Robert Ellis *artist*
†La Rocca, Isabella *artist*
Lassiter, Kenneth T. *photography educator, consultant*
Lee, William Saul (Bill Lee) *artist, writer*
Levi, Josef Alan *artist*
Levin, Morton D(avid) *artist, printmaker, educator*
Lieberman, Louis (Karl Lieberman) *artist*
Lienhart, James Lee *graphic designer*
Littleton, Harvey Kline *artist*
Loquasto, Santo *theatrical set designer*
Lucas, Rhett Roy *artist, lawyer*
Ludwig, Allan Ira *photographer, artist, author*
Lund, David Nathan *artist*
Mangold, Sylvia Plimack *artist*
Mark, Mary Ellen *photographer*
Martin, Noel *graphic design consultant, educator*
Martyl, (Mrs. Alexander Langsdorf, Jr.) *artist*
McCracken, John Harvey *painter, sculptor*
McNeil, George Joseph *painter*
McVicker, Jesse Jay *artist, educator*
Meneeley, Edward Sterling *artist*
Middaugh, Robert Burton *artist*
Miles, Jeanne Patterson *artist*
Minami, Robert Yoshio *artist, graphic designer*
Misrach, Richard Laurence *photographer*
Morley, Malcolm A. *artist*
Morning, John *graphic designer*
Moses, Edward Crosby *artist*
Murray, Robert Gray *sculptor*
Nakamura, Kazuo *artist*
Newman, Muriel Kallis Steinberg *art collector*
Olkinetzky, Sam *artist, retired museum director and educator*
Onslow Ford, Gordon Max *painter*
Osborn, Robert Chesley *artist, writer*
Paris, Lucille Marie *artist, educator*
Pearlstein, Philip *artist*
Péladeau, Marius Beaudoin *art consultant, retired museum director*
Penn, Irving *photographer*
Perman, Norman Wilford *graphic designer*
Phelan, Ellen *artist*
Pinkney, Jerry *artist, educator*
Ponce de Leon, Michael *artist, lecturer, educator*
Provensen, Alice Rose Twitchell *artist, author*
Reed, David *artist*
Reichman, Fredrick Thomas *artist*
Rickey, George Warren *artist, sculptor, educator*
Ringgold, Faith *artist, writer*
†Robinson, Aminah Brenda Lynn *artist*
Rockburne, Dorothea G. *artist*
Root, Doris Smiley *art director*
Rosenquist, James Albert *artist*
Rossman, Ruth Scharff *artist, educator*
Rubello, David Jerome *artist*
Rubin, Sandra Mendelsohn *artist*
Rubinstein, Eva (Anna) *photographer*
Saar, Betye (Irene Saar) *artist*
Sanchez, Leonedes Monarrize Worthington *fashion designer*
Scharf, William *artist*
Schley, Reeve, III *artist*
Schnackenberg, Roy Lee *artist*
Schultz, Eileen Hedy *graphic designer*
Schwartz, Lillian Feldman *artist, filmaker, art analyst, author*
Shaw, Richard *artist*
Sheridan, Sonia Landy *artist, retired art educator*
Shoulberg, Harry *artist*
Sidjakov, Nicolas *designer, illustrator*
Sisto, Elena *artist, educator*
Snelson, Kenneth Duane *sculptor*
Sorel, Edward *artist*
Spence, Andrew *artist, painter*
†Spiegel, Susan *art director*
Stevens, May *artist*
Streeter, Tal *sculptor*
Strider, Marjorie Virginia *artist, educator*
Sumichrast, Jozef *illustrator, designer*
Surrey, Philip Henry *artist, educator*
Swig, Roselyne Chroman *art advisor*
Takal, Peter *artist*
Thiel, Philip *design educator*
Tovish, Harold *sculptor*
Tsai, Wen-Ying *sculptor, painter, engineer*
†Unithan, Dolly *visual artist*
Valens, Evans Gladstone *sculptor, printmaker, author, former television producer, director*
Vassil, Pamela *graphic designer*
Wechter, Vivienne Thaul *artist, poet, educator*
Willenbecher, John *artist*
Wilson, Jane *artist*
Wiseman, Jay Donald *photographer, mechanical contractor, designer*
Zajac, Jack *sculptor, painter*
Zekman, Terri Margaret *graphic designer*
Zelinsky, Paul O. *illustrator, painter, author*

ASSOCIATIONS AND ORGANIZATIONS. *See also* specific fields.

UNITED STATES

ALABAMA

Auburn
Teague, Sam Fuller *association executive, educator,*

Birmingham
Carter, Frances Tunnell (Fran Carter) *fraternal organization administrator*
Gross, Iris Lee *association executive*
†Newton, Don Allen *association executive*
Parker, Israel Frank *national association consultant*
†Rynearson, W. John *association executive*

Mobile
McCann, Clarence David, Jr. *special events coordinator, museum curator and director, artist*

Montgomery
Oswalt, (Eugene) Talmadge *educational administrator*

ALASKA

Juneau
†Nicholia, Irene Kay *organization administrator*
†Thomas, Edward K. *tribal executive, educator*

Nome
†Timbers, RoseAnn S. *association executive*

Unalakleet
†Katchatag, Stanton Oswald *civic and political worker*

ARIZONA

Phoenix
†DeMenna, Kevin Bolton *lobbyist*

Scottsdale
Carney, Richard Edgar *foundation executive*
Foss, Joe *association executive, speaker*
Jacobson, Frank Joel *cultural organization adminisrator*
†Smith, Jesse Morgan, Jr. *association executive, consultant*

Sedona
Keane, Mark Edward *public executive and educator*

Sun City
Jones, Alexander Elvin *retired foundation executive*

Tempe
Baker, Roland Jerald *association executive*

Tucson
Belk, John Blanton *educational and cultural organization executive*
†Grand, Marcia *civic worker*
Parry, Pamela Jeffcott *association executive, art librarian*
Riggs, Frank Lewis *foundation executive*
†Toppel, Alan Herman *organization executive*

Window Rock
Zah, Peterson *American Indian tribal executive*

ARKANSAS

Camden
†Smith, Judy Seriale *social services administrator*

Glenwood
Klopfenstein, Philip Arthur *financial development officer, historical researcher*

Morrilton
Havener, Robert Dale *agricultural institute administrator*

Stuttgart
†Smith, Kevin Andrew *non-profit corportation executive*

CALIFORNIA

Alamo
Lee, Richard *martial arts educational executive*

Anaheim
Hughes, Allan Bebout *chamber of commerce executive*

Atherton
Heyns, Roger William *retired foundation executive and educator*

Belvedere Tiburon
Cook, Lyle Edwards *retired fund raising executive, consultant*

Big Sur
†Donovan, Steven Robert *institute executive*

Campbell
Throndson, Edward Warner *residential association administrator*

Canoga Park
Lederer, Marion Irvine *cultural administrator*

Carlsbad
†Vincent, John Graham *administrator*

Carmel
Pinkham, Frederick Oliver *foundation executive, consultant*

Claremont
Hale, Doty Doherty *educational administrator*
Rankin, Robert *retired educational foundation executive*
Wrigley, Elizabeth Springer (Mrs. Oliver K. Wrigley) *foundation executive*

Coarsegold
†Wyatt, Jane Ellen *tribal leader*

Covina
†Jackson, John Jay *association administrator, minister*

Gardenia
Crismond, Linda Fry *association executive*

Hayward
Critzer, William Ernest *association executive*

Healdsburg
Canfield, Grant Wellington, Jr. *association administrator, management consultant*

Irvine
Moore, David Lewis *trade association executive*
Young, Robert Anthony *association director*

Long Beach
Lee, Isaiah Chong-Pie *social worker, educator*
Muchmore, Don Moncrief *museum, foundation, educational, financial fund raising and public opinion consulting firm administrator*

Los Alamitos
†Myers, Edwin *think-tank executive*

Los Altos
Wickham, Kenneth Gregory *retired army officer, institute official*
†Wilbur, Colburn Sloan *foundation administrator*

Los Angeles
Caldwell-Portenier, Patty Jean Grosskopf *advocate, educator*
Chassman, Leonard Fredric *labor union administrator*
Ennis, Thomas Michael *health foundation executive*
Gumpel, Glenn J. *association executive*
Headlee, Rolland Dockeray *association executive*
Hubbs, Donald Harvey *foundation president*
Mack, J. Curtis, II *civic organization administrator*
Orsatti, Alfred Kendall *organization executive*
Reagan, Nancy Davis (Anne Francis Robbins) *volunteer, wife of former President of United States*
Shakely, John Bower (Jack Shakely) *foundation executive*
Shmavonian, Gerald S. *association executive*
Williams, Harold Marvin *foundation official*
Wilson, Eugene Rolland *foundation executive*

Menlo Park
Gardner, David Pierpont *foundation executive*
Morrison, James Ian *research institute executive*
Nichols, William Ford, Jr. *foundation executive, business executive*
Pallotti, Marianne Marguerite *foundation administrator*

Monrovia
†Seiple, Robert Allen *Christian relief organization executive*

Mountain View
Michalko, James Paul *library association administrator*

Newbury Park
†McCune, Sara Miller *foundation executive, publisher*

North Hollywood
Grasso, Mary Ann *theatre association administrator*

Oakland
Callos, Phyllis Marie *association executive*
Macmeeken, John Peebles *foundation executive*

Oceanside
Roberts, James McGregor *retired professional association executive*

Ojai
Mankoff, Albert William *cultural organization administrator, consultant*

Orange
†Reed, David Andrew *foundation executive*

Orinda
Cooper, Clare Dunlap *civic worker, writer*

Palo Alto
Bills, Robert Howard *political party executive*
†Duggan, Susan J. *educational administrator*
Karp, Nathan *political activist*
Rosenzweig, Robert Myron *educational consultant*

Pebble Beach
Gianelli, William Reynolds *foundation administrator, civil engineering consultant, former federal agency commissioner*

Ridgecrest
Nason, Patricia Anne Woodward *museum educator, consultant*

Riverside
†Pick, Arthur Joseph, Jr. *chamber of commerce executive*

Rowland Heights
Perfetti, Robert Nickolas *career education coordinator, educator*

Sacramento
Hay, John Thomas *trade association executive*

San Andreas
Breed, Allen Forbes *correctional administrator*

San Bernardino
Bellis, David James *public administration educator*

San Diego
Atchison, Richard Calvin *trade association director*
Carleson, Robert Bazil *public policy consultant, corporation executive*
†Dolan, James Michael, Jr. *zoological society executive*
Grosser, T.J. *administrator, developer, fundraiser*
Lane, Gloria Julian *foundation administrator*
Swoap, David Bruce *children's relief administrator*

San Francisco
†Arian, David *labor union official*
Collins, Dennis Arthur *foundation executive*
Eastham, Thomas *foundation administrator*
Fisher, Robert M. *foundation administrator, university administrator*
Henderson, Horace Edward *public affairs consultant, author*
Jacobs, John Howard *association executive*
Mikuriya, Mary Jane *educational agency administrator*
Shirpser, Clara *former Democratic national committeewoman*
Stauffer, Thomas Michael *educational administrator*
Thelen, Max, Jr. *foundation executive, lawyer*

San Jose
Bennett, Charles Turner *social welfare administrator*

San Juan Capistrano
Horn, Deborah Sue *organization administrator, writer, editor*

San Marino
Hull, Suzanne White *retired cultural institution administrator, writer*

San Rafael
Lee, Robert *association executive, former theological educator, consultant, author*

Santa Ana
†Metzler, Michael *chamber of commerce executive*

Santa Monica
Liddicoat, Richard Thomas, Jr. *association executive*
Rich, Michael David *research corporation executive, lawyer*
Thomson, James Alan *research company executive*

Santa Rosa
Burton, Nanci L. *professional association administrator, management consultant*

Scotts Valley
Bourret, Marjorie Ann *educational advocate, consultant*

Sonoma
Stadtman, Verne August *former foundation executive, editor*

South Pasadena
Staehle, Robert L. *foundation executive*

Stanford
Lyman, Richard Wall foundation and university executive, historian
†Matisoff, Susan cultural research organization administrator
Raisian, John public policy institute executive, economist
Stone, William Edward association executive

Trinidad
Marshall, William Edward historical association executive

Woodland Hills
†O'Meara, Sara foundation administrator
Sigholtz, Sara O'Meara non-profit organization executive

Woodside
Blum, Richard Hosmer Adams foundation executive

COLORADO

Aspen
Harth, Robert James music festival executive

Aurora
Fish, Ruby Mae Bertram (Mrs. Frederick Goodrich Fish) civic worker
†Hutchins, Charles Larry educational association administrator, consultant
Motz, Kenneth Lee former farm organization official

Boulder
Neinas, Charles Merrill athletic association executive

Castle Rock
Graf, Joseph Charles retired foundation executive

Colorado Springs
Killian, George Ernest association executive
MacLeod, Richard Patrick foundation administrator

Denver
†Craig, Lexie Ferrell career development specialist, career guidance counselor, educator
†Daley, Richard Halbert foundation executive
Darkey, Kermit Louis association executive, lawyer
Harris, Ellen Gandy (Mrs. J. Ramsay Harris) civic worker
Hirschfeld, Arlene F. civic worker, homemaker
Hixon, Janet Kay Erickson nursing association administrator, educator
Hogan, Curtis Jule union executive, industrial relations consultant
Konrad, Peter Allen foundation administrator
Neiser, Brent Allen professional association director
Nelson, Bernard William foundation executive, educator, physician
Reynolds, Collins James, III association administrator

Englewood
Chesser, Al H. union official
Massey, Leon R. association executive

Snowmass
†Lovins, L. Hunter public policy institute executive

CONNECTICUT

East Haven
Hegyi, Albert Paul association executive, lawyer

Fairfield
Polin, Jane Louise foundation official

Greenwich
Slavin, Simon social administration educator
Taylor, Sir Cyril (Julian Hebden) education association administrator, consultant

Guilford
Logan, John Arthur, Jr. retired foundation executive

Hamden
Resnick, Idrian Navarre foundation administrator

Hartford
Bickford, Christopher Penny association executive
Connelly, William Howard retired foundation executive
Decko, Kenneth Owen association executive

Lyme
Greene, Joseph Nathaniel, Jr. former foundation executive, former diplomat

Madison
Houghton, Alan Nourse association executive, educator, consultant

Mystic
Smith, Norman Clark fund raising consultant

New Canaan
Mountcastle, Katharine Babcock foundation executive
Thomsen, Donald Laurence, Jr. institute executive, mathematician

New Haven
Brewster, Carroll Worcester fund administrator
Dechant, Virgil C. fraternal organization administrator
Theodore, Eustace D. alumni association executive, management consultant

New London
Wetmore, Thomas Trask, III retired foundation administrator, retired coast guard officer

Newington
†Sumner, David George association executive

Norwalk
†Bullard, Edward Payson, IV non-profit executive
Dresher, William Henry research association executive

Old Greenwich
Bonner, Charles William, III community services executive, newspaper writer
Slack, Lewis organization administrator

Old Lyme
Bond, Niles Woodbridge cultural institute executive, former foreign service officer

Old Saybrook
Spencer, William Courtney foundation executive, international business executive

Riverside
Coulson, Robert retired association executive, lawyer

Southport
Pifer, Alan (Jay Parrish) former foundation executive

Stamford
Brakeley, George Archibald, Jr. fund raising counsel
Kaufman, John E. retired association executive
Mc Namara, Francis Joseph, Jr. foundation executive, lawyer
Sharp, Daniel Asher foundation executive, corporate consultant

West Redding
Schramm, John Clarendon foundation executive

Westport
Levinger, Beryl Beth cultural organization administrator, consultant

Wilton
Forger, Robert Durkin retired professional association administrator

DELAWARE

Dover
Ornauer, Richard Lewis retired educational association administrator

Newark
Mitchell, Peter Kenneth, Jr. educational consultant, association administrator

Wilmington
†Cartwright, Albert Thomas association executive
Peterson, Russell Wilbur former association executive, former state governor

DISTRICT OF COLUMBIA

Washington
Able, Edward H. association executive
Ahmann, Mathew Hall social action organization administrator, consultant
†Alberts, Bruce Michael foundation administrator, biochemist
Allnutt, Robert Frederick organization executive, lawyer
Ambach, Gordon Mac Kay education association official
†Andersen, Per Pinstrup think-tank executive, agricultural research administrator
Anderson, Dean William educational administrator
†Andrews, Laureen E. foundation administrator
Appleberry, James Bruce higher education association president
Arlook, Ira Arthur public interest association executive
Atherton, Alfred Leroy, Jr. foundation executive, former foreign service officer
Atwell, Robert Herron association executive
AuCoin, Les lobbyist, former congressman
Babby, Ellen Reisman education administrator
Bader, William Banks foundation executive, former corporate executive
Bagge, Carl Elmer association executive, lawyer, consultant
Bahr, Morton trade union executive
†Baldi, Patricia Ann association executive
Ball, Robert M. social security, welfare and health policy specialist, writer, lecturer
Banzhaf, John F., III organization executive,lawyer
†Barbour, Haley political organization administrator, law partner, former federal official
†Baroody, William Joseph, Jr. research institute executive
Barrow, Robert Earl agricultural organization administrator
†Bartlett, Charles J. think-tank executive
Bartlett, Charles Leffingwell foundation executive, former newspaperman
Bayne, J. Phillip educational association administrator
Beazley, Hamilton Scott volunteer health organization executive
Bell, Thomas Devereaux, Jr. public affairs company executive
Bender, David Ray library association executive
Benjamin, Ernst professional association executive
Biller, Morris (Moe Biller) union executive
Bishop, Barry Chapman professional society executive, scientist
Bissell, Richard Etter association administrator
†Bleviss, Deborah Lynn association executive
Blitzer, Charles educational administrator
Boaz, David Douglas foundation executive
Bond, Julian civil rights leader
Bond, Richard Norman political activist
Bonosaro, Carol Alessandra professional association executive,former government official
Book, Edward R. association executive
Bookbinder, Hyman H(arry) public affairs counselor
Borut, Donald J. association executive
Bourne, Francis Stanley foundation administrator
Boyle, John Edward Whiteford cultural organization administrator
Boyle, Renée Kent cultural organization executive, translator, editor
Bradley, Mitchell Hugh professional society administrator, retired career officer
Brobeck, Stephen James consumer advocate
†Brown, David R. think-tank executive
†Brown, Lawrence Clifton, Jr. foundation administrator
Brown, William Robert association executive, consultant
Brownlee, Paula Pimlott association executive
Bryant, Anne Lincoln association executive
Buchanan, Peter McEachin educational association executive
Butynski, William national association administrator
Cain, Becky C. association executive
Calhoun, John Alfred social services administrator
Cameron, Don R. association director
Campbell, Wallace Justin social welfare administrator, economist
Canes, Michael Edwin trade association administrator, economist
Carey, Ronald labor union leader
Carney, David Mitchel political party official
Cashmore, Patsy Joy speechwriter, editor, author, consultant, educator
†Cavanaugh, John think-tank executive
Cavaney, Red trade association administrator
Cheney, Lynne V. humanities educator, writer
Chilcote, Samuel Day, Jr. association executive
Clark, Wendell Mark travelers organization executive
Cochran, John Thomas professional association executive
Coia, Arthur A. labor union executive
†Collie, H. Cris trade association executive
Cooper, Josephine Smith trade association and public relations executive
Cope, James Dudley association executive
†Covey-Toperoff, Janice Margaret director of publications
Cox, Geraldine Vang engineering executive
Cramer, James Perry association executive, publisher, educator, architectural historian
Crane, Edward Harrison, III institute executive
Croser, Mary Doreen educational association executive
Crutchfield, Sam Shaw, Jr. association executive, lawyer
Curran, R. T. foundation executive
Damgard, John Michael trade association executive
Deets, Horace association executive
Denney, George Covert, Jr. organization administrator
DiBona, Charles Joseph association executive
†Dillon, Robert Sherwood non-profit educational organization executive
†Ditlow, Clarence M. think-tank executive
Dole, Elizabeth Hanford charitable organization administrator, former secretary of labor, former secretary of transportation
Donahue, Thomas Reilly trade union official
Dorn, Jennifer Lynn charitable organization administrator
Eisenberg, Pablo Samuel non-profit organization executive
Elders, Minnie Joycelyn public health administrator, endocrinologist
Eller, Joseph Burton, Jr. trade association executive
Elsey, George McKee association executive
Engel, Ralph manufacturers association executive
English, Glenn association executive, former congressman
†Feeney, Richard Joseph trade association executive, journalist
Fink, Matthew Pollack trade association executive, lawyer
Finkle, Jeffrey Alan professional association executive
Foard, Douglas W. educational association administrator
Francois, Francis Bernard association executive, lawyer
Friedman, Miles trade association executive, financial services company executive, university lecturer
Fritz, Thomas Vincent association and business executive, accountant
Futrell, Basil Lee association executive
Futrell, Mary Alice Hatwood education association administrator
Georgine, Robert Anthony union executive
†Ginsberg, Mark R. social welfare administrator
Goldman, Aaron foundation executive, writer
Golodner, Jack labor association official
Goslin, David Alexander research administrator, sociologist
Granick, Lois Wayne association administrator
†Green, Monica peace organization director
Green, Shirley Moore political organization director
Greenstein, Robert M. non-profit organization director
Griffenhagen, George Bernard trade association executive
Guenther, Kenneth Allen business association executive, economist
Hall, Samuel M., Jr. career educator, career development consultant
Handelsman, M. Gene association administrator
†Hanley, Edward Thomas union official
Hansell, William Howard, Jr. association executive
Harbrant, Robert Francis labor union executive
Hartman, Arthur A. international business consultant
†Haseltine, John B. think-tank executive
Healey, John G. human services organization executive
Herbst, Robert LeRoy organization executive
Hermanson Ogilvie, Judith foundation executive
Hills, John Merrill public policy research center executive, former educational administrator
Hobart, Lawrence Scott service organization administrator
Holbrook, Douglas Cowen labor union administrator
Holloway, James Lemuel, III foundation executive, retired naval officer
Howard, Jack union executive
Hoyt, John Arthur humane society executive
Huband, Frank Louis educational association executive
Hughes, Thomas Lowe foundation executive
Hymel, Gary Gerard lobbyist
Imig, David Gregg educational association executive
Ireland, Patricia association executive
Isaacs, Amy Fay political organization executive
Jacobson, Michael Faraday consumer advocate, writer
†Joe, Thomas think-tank
†Johnson, Willa Ann think-tank executive
Johnston, Laurance Scott foundation director
†Jones, Elaine R. civil rights advocate
Kamber, Victor Samuel political consultant
Kavanaugh, Everett Edward, Jr. trade association executive
Keeny, Spurgeon Milton, Jr. association executive
Kelly, Eugene Walter, Jr. counseling and human services educator, director
Kempner, Jonathan L. professional society administrator
Kirkland, Joseph Lane (Lane Kirkland) labor union official
Kleinknecht, Christian Frederick Masonic official
Kline, Raymond Adam professional organization executive
Knapp, Richard Maitland association executive
†Knebel, John Albert trade association executive
†Kossak, Shelley think-tank executive
†Kruse, Dennis K. think-tank executive, career officer
Kurth, Walter Richard association executive
†Lachance, Janice Rachel labor union executive, lawyer
Lampl, Peggy Ann association administrator
LaPidus, Jules Benjamin association executive
Larson, Charles Fred association executive
Lawson, Richard Laverne trade association executive, retired military officer
Lesher, Richard Lee association executive
Leven, Ann Ruth arts administrator
Lewis, Ann Frank political analyst, commentator, columnist
Liederman, David Samuel child welfare administrator
Lightner, Candace Lynne advocate, government relations consultant
Lilley, James Roderick foreign relations expert, former federal government official
Lively, Carol A. association executive
Low, Stephen foundation executive, educator, former diplomat
Loy, Frank Ernest foundation executive
†Lucassen, Sigurd labor union administrator
Magazine, Alan Harrison association executive, consultant
Magrath, C. Peter educational association executive
Marlowe, Howard David lobbyist, public affairs company executive
Masters, Edward E. association executive, former foreign service officer
McClintic, Howard Gresson foundation executive
McCloskey, J(ohn) Michael association executive
†McEntee, Gerald W. labor union official
McGlotten, Robert Miller labor union official
Mc Kay, Emily Gantz civil rights professional
McLennan, Barbara Nancy trade association executive, lawyer
McNamee, Sister Catherine educational association executive
McNulty, Robert Holmes civic association executive
McSteen, Martha Abernathy organization executive
Messner, Howard Myron professional association executive
Metz, Douglas Wilber association executive, lawyer
Miller, John Francis association executive, social scientist
†Mitchell, Louis Livingston consortium executive
Mossinghoff, Gerald Joseph lawyer, association executive
Mtewa, Mekki foundation administrator
†Munson, Richard congressional coalition policy analyst
†Murphy, Kenneth Ray non-governmental organization executive
†Murphy, Patrick Vincent foundation executive
Murray, James Joseph, III association executive
Myers, Samuel Lloyd education association executive
Nader, Ralph consumer advocate, lawyer, author
Nash, Bernard Elbert association executive
Nelson, Charles Edward foundation/government executive
Nicholson, Richard Selindh educational association administrator
Norton, James J. union official
O'Day, Paul Thomas trade association executive
Ogilvie, Donald Gordon bankers association executive
†O'Hagan, Malcolm Edward trade association administrator
O'Keefe, William Francis association executive
Oliver, Daniel foundation fellow, lawyer
†Onto, John think-tank executive
Paulson, Stanley Fay association executive
Pearson, Roger organization executive
Perez, Lillian non-profit association administrator
Peterson, Esther consumer advocate
Pines, Burton Yale broadcasting executive
†Pinstrup-Andersen, Per educational administrator
Porter, Elisabeth Scott (Leezee Porter) political worker
Radin, Alex former association executive, consultant
Reger, Lawrence Lee association executive
Reich, Alan Anderson association executive
†Richards, Cory demographic think-tank executive
Richardson, Ann Bishop foundation executive, lawyer
Roberts, James Cleveland foundation executive
Robinson, Leonard Harrison, Jr. international government consultant, business executive
Rodman, Peter Warren foreign policy specialist
Rogers, John S. union official
Romero-Barceló, Carlos Antonio former chairman New Progressive Party, former governor, lawyer, real estate agent
Rosenberg, Sarah Zacher institute arts administration executive, humanities administration consultant
Rosenker, Mark Victor trade association executive
Rother, John Charles association executive, lawyer
Rudder, Catherine E. political science association administrator
Russell, William Joseph association executive
†Salvado, August J. think-tank executive
Sampson, Robert Neil association executive
Samuel, Howard David union official
Scanlon, Patrick Michael lawyer
Scanlon, Terrence Maurice foundation administrator
Schlossberg, Stephen I. international official
Schosberg, Paul Alan trade association executive
Schubert, Richard Francis foundation administrator
†Schuman, Michael think-tank executive
Schweiker, Richard Schultz trade association executive, former senator
†Seldman, Neil Norman cultural organization administrator
†Sever, Tom labor union administrator
Sewell, John Williamson research association executive
Shanker, Albert labor union official
Shaw, Russell Burnham association executive, author

Shriver, Eunice Mary Kennedy (Mrs. Robert Sargent Shriver, Jr.) *civic worker*
Sims, Robert Bell *professional society administrator, public affairs official, newspaper publisher*
Skadden, Donald Harvey *professional society executive, accounting educator*
Smedley, Lawrence Thomas *organization executive*
Spence, Sandra *association executive*
Splete, Allen Peterjohn *association executive, educator*
Sprague, Edward Auchincloss *association executive, economist*
Staats, Elmer Boyd *foundation executive, former government official*
†Stapleton, Jean *think-tank executive*
Stone, Jeremy Judah *association executive*
Strachan, David E. *trade association executive*
Strong, Henry *foundation executive*
Sugarman, Jule M. *professional society administrator, former public administrator*
Tanguy, Charles Reed *foundation administrator, consultant, former foreign service officer*
Tape, Gerald Frederick *former association executive*
†Tarr-Whelan, Linda Jane *political organization administrator*
Taylor, Robert William *association executive*
†Thomas, Ralph C., III *trade association administrator, lawyer*
Tipton, E. Linwood *trade association executive*
Tobias, Robert Max *labor leader, lawyer*
Tonkin, Leo Sampson *educational foundation administrator*
†Trumka, Richard Louis *labor leader, lawyer*
Ture, Norman Bernard *public policy research organization executive*
Unsell, Lloyd Neal *energy organization executive, former journalist*
Van Nelson, Nicholas Lloyd *business council executive*
Vaught, Wilma L. *foundation executive, retired air force officer*
Veliotes, Nicholas Alexander *professional association executive, former ambassador and assistant secretary of state*
Vetter, Betty McGee *commission executive*
Wait, Carol Grace Cox *organization administrator*
Walker, John Denley *foundation director, former government official*
Warden, Richard Dana *government labor union official*
Warren, David Liles *educational association executive*
Weber, Susan *research organization executive*
Wertheimer, Fredric Michael *association executive*
Weyrich, Paul Michael *political organizations executive*
White, Margita Eklund *television association executive*
†Whitehead, John C. *think tank executive*
†Wilhelm, David *political organization administrator*
Willging, Paul Raymond *trade association executive*
Williams, Eddie Nathan *research institution executive*
Williams, Maurice Jacoutot *development organization executive*
Williams, Ronald L. *pharmaceutical association executive*
Wilson, Glen Parten *association administrator*
Wingerter, Eugene Joseph *association executive*
Wiseman, Laurence Donald *trade association executive*
†Wolfe, Leslie R. *think-tank executive*
Woodall, Samuel Roy, Jr. *trade association executive*
Yost, Paul Alexander, Jr. *foundation executive, retired coast guard officer*
†Yzaguirre, Raul Humberto *civil rights administrator*
†Zuck, Alfred Miller *association executive*
†Zwick, Charles J. *think-tank executive*

FLORIDA

Altamonte Springs
Wilson, George Peter *association executive*

Arcadia
†Turnbull, David John (Chief Piercing Eyes-Penn) *cultural association executive*

Boca Raton
Fey, Dorothy (Mrs. George Jay Fey) *former association executive*

Bonita Springs
Miller, Richard Dwight *professional association executive*

Boynton Beach
Falk, Bernard Henry *trade association executive*

Cypress Gardens
Gobie, Henry Macaulay *philatelic researcher, retired postal executive*

Daytona Beach
Collyer, Robert B. *association executive*

Delray Beach
Stewart, Patricia Carry *foundation administrator*

Englewood
Schultz, Arthur Joseph, Jr. *retired trade association executive*

Fort Lauderdale
Wynne, Brian James *former association executive, consultant*

Gainesville
Baughman, George Fechtig *foundation executive*

Hallandale
Contney, John Joseph *association executive*

Hollywood
Graves, Walter Albert *retired association executive, editor*

Jacksonville
Boyles, Carol Ann Patterson *career development educator*

Miami
Brinkman, Paul Del(bert) *foundation executive*
Courshon, Carol Biel *civic worker*
Cullom, William Otis *trade association executive*
Dickason, John Hamilton *foundation executive*
Hills, Lee *foundation administrator, newspaper executive, consultant*
†Rosenberg, Mark B. *think-tank executive*
VanBrode, Derrick Brent, IV *association executive*
Weber, Nancy Walker *charitable trust administrator*

Naples
Rowe, Herbert Joseph *retired trade association executive*

Nokomis
Peters, Farnsley Lewellyn *retired association executive*

North Miami Beach
Beckley, Donald K. *fundraiser*

Orlando
†Ball, Joseph E. *association executive*

Osprey
Crispin, Mildred Swift (Mrs. Frederick Eaton Crispin) *civic worker, writer*

Palm Beach
Chittick, Elizabeth Lancaster *association executive, women's rights activist*
Ferrin, Allan Wheeler *association executive*
Rinker, Ruby Stewart *foundation administrator*

Palm City
Wirsig, Woodrow *magazine editor, trade organization executive, business executive*

Pensacola
Furlong, George Morgan, Jr. *retired naval officer, museum foundation executive*

Ponte Vedra Beach
Beman, Deane Randolph *association executive*

Saint Augustine
Baker, Norman Henderson *association executive*
Davis, Bertram George *association executive, lawyer*

Saint Petersburg
Shank, Clare Brown Williams *political leader*

Sanibel
Ball, Armand Baer *former association executive, consultant*

South Pasadena
Minton, Joseph Paul *retired safety organization executive*

Tallahassee
Ryll, Frank Maynard, Jr. *association executive*

Tampa
Zeno, Phyllis Wolfe *association executive, editor*

Tarpon Springs
Byrne, Richard Hill *counselor, educator*

Tequesta
Luster, George Orchard *professional society administrator*

Vero Beach
Brim, Orville Gilbert, Jr. *former foundation administrator, author*

Wesley Chapel
Holloway, Marvin Lawrence *retired automobile club executive, rancher, vintager*

West Palm Beach
Hoewing, Mark Wesley *real estate association executive*
McBride, Nancy Allyson *child resource center administrator*

Winter Park
Olsson, Nils William *former association executive*

GEORGIA

Americus
Fuller, Millard Dean *charitable organization executive, lawyer*

Atlanta
†Beard, Rick *cultural organization administrator*
Clarke, Clifford Montreville *health foundation executive*
Glassick, Charles Etzweiler *cultural organization administrator*
Kelly, William Watkins *educational association executive*
King, Coretta Scott (Mrs. Martin Luther King, Jr.) *educational association administrator, lecturer, writer, concert singer*
Merritt, Lynn Garnard *trade association executive*
Scott, William Fred *cultural organization administrator*
Sears, Curtis Thornton, Jr. *educational administrator*
Thumann, Albert *association executive, engineer*
Tipping, William Malcolm *social services administrator*
Wylly, Barbara Bentley *performing arts association administrator*
Young, Andrew *clergyman, civil rights leader, former mayor, former ambassador, former congressman*

Augusta
Davison, Frederick Corbet *foundation executive*

Decatur
Robb, Felix Compton *association executive, consultant*

Greenville
Johnson, Hardwick Smith, Jr. *school psychologist*

Norcross
†Cullison, William Lester *association executive*

Savannah
Beals, L(oren) Alan *association executive*

Stone Mountain
Wingate, Henry Taylor, Jr. *foundation administrator, fundraiser*

Winterville
Shockley, W. Ray *travel trade association executive*

HAWAII

Honolulu
Jordan, Amos Azariah, Jr. *foreign affairs educator, retired army officer*
Lee, Beverly Ing *educational administrator*
Olmsted, Ronald David *foundation executive, consultant*
Robinson, Robert Blacque *association executive*

ILLINOIS

Arlington Heights
Fellers, James Davison, Jr. (Dave Fellers) *professional association executive*
Nerlinger, John William *association executive*

Bedford Park
Herbert, Victor James *association executive*

Champaign
Clark, Roger Gordon *educational administrator*
Eilbracht, Lee Paul *retired association executive*

Chicago
†Baker, James Nettleton *railroad association executive*
Barker, Emmett Wilson, Jr. *trade association executive*
Bottom, Dale Coyle *association executive*
Chacko, Samuel *association official*
Creighton, Neal *foundation administrator, retired military officer*
Cyr, Arthur *association executive*
Daniel, David Logan *retired state welfare agency administrator*
Detmer, Lawrence McCormick *professional society administrator*
Dolan, Thomas Christopher *association executive*
Donnell, Harold Eugene, Jr. *association executive*
Dykla, Edward George *social services administrator*
†Engman, John Daniel *non-profit foundation administrator*
Epstein, Laura *social work educator, consultant*
Feldstein, Charles Robert *fund raising consultant*
Fetridge, Bonnie-Jean Clark (Mrs. William Harrison Fetridge) *civic volunteer*
Furman, James Merle *foundation executive*
Gardner, James Harkins *educational organization executive*
Hayes, Richard Johnson *association executive, lawyer*
Heineman, Natalie (Mrs. Ben W. Heineman) *civic worker*
†Huston, John Leo *trade association executive*
Jackson, David Munro *association executive*
Jackson, Jesse Louis *civic and political leader, clergyman*
Jonas, Harry S. *professional society administrator*
Koenig, Bonnie *non-profit organization administrator*
MacDougal, Gary Edward *foundation trustee, director, arts manager*
Mercer, David Robinson *association executive*
Minow, Josephine Baskin *civic worker*
Murphy, Ellis *association management executive*
Olsen, Rex Norman *trade association executive*
Palmer, Robert Erwin *association executive*
Peterson, Mildred Othmer (Mrs. Howard R. Peterson) *lecturer, writer, librarian, civic leader*
Richman, Harold Alan *social welfare policy educator*
Rielly, John Edward *association executive*
Rodgers, James Foster *association executive, economist*
Scalish, Frank Anthony *labor union administrator*
Sigmon, Joyce Elizabeth *association executive*
Simmons, Adele Smith *foundation president, former educator*
Sullivan, Peggy (Anne) *association executive*
Williams, Harold Milton *trade association executive*

Crystal Lake
Chamberlain, Charles James *railroad labor union executive*

De Kalb
†Kleppner, Paul *social studies think-tank administrator*

Des Plaines
Neel, Judy Murphy *association executive*
Newman, Wade Davis *trade association executive*
†Shoults, Harold E. *social services administrator*

Elgin
Kelly, Matthew Edward *association executive*

Elk Grove Village
Best, Willis D. *retired international union official*

Elmhurst
Hildreth, R(oland) James *foundation executive, economist*

Evanston
Abnee, A. Victor *trade association executive*
Bernstein, Susan Powell *development and fundraising consultant*
Gordon, Julie Peyton *foundation administrator*
Kreml, Franklin Martin *educational administrator, association executive*
Thrash, Patricia Ann *association executive*
Yoder, Frederick Floyd *fraternity executive*

Franklin Park
Tompson, Marian Leonard *association executive*

Galena
Hermann, Paul David *retired association executive*

Highland Park
Gordon, Edward *music association executive*

Itasca
Gilchrest, Thornton Charles *association executive*

La Grange Park
Webster, Lois Shand *association executive*

Lake Bluff
Schreiber, George Richard *association executive, writer*

Lake Forest
Fuhs-Smith, Wendy L. *foundation executive*

Long Grove
Connor, James Richard *foundation administrator*

Mooseheart
O'Hollaren, Paul Joseph *former international fraternity administrator*

Northbrook
Crowell, Edward Prince *retired association executive*
Degen, Bernard John, II *association executive*

Northfield
Cartwright, Howard E(ugene) *retired association executive*

Oak Brook
Stauffer, Delmar J. *professional association executive*

Park Ridge
Howlett, Phyllis Lou *athletics conference administrator*
Kukla, Robert John *association executive*
Raffel, Louis B. *association executive*

Peoria
Smith, Clyde R. *counselor educator*

Rosemont
Good, William Allen *professional society executive*

Schaumburg
Boston, Leona *organization executive*
Keil, M. David *international association executive*
Roach, William Russell *training and education executive*

Skokie
Gleason, John Patrick, Jr. *trade association executive*

Springfield
Blackman, Jeanne A. *lobbyist*

Villa Park
O'Leary, Dennis Sophian *medical organization executive*

Wheeling
Smith, Justine Townsend *recreational association executive*

Wilmette
Brink, Marion Francis *association executive*
Hansen, Andrew Marius *retired library association executive*

Winnetka
Andersen, Kenneth Benjamin *retired association executive*
Owens, Luvie Moore *association executive*

INDIANA

Bloomington
Thiagarajan, Sivasailam *educational association administrator, educator*

Greenwood
Means, George Robert *organization executive*

Indianapolis
Barcus, Robert Gene *educational association administrator*
Butler, Wilford Arthur *association executive*
†Clark, Charles M., Jr. *educational institution administrator, researcher*
Conley, James Daniel *retired foundation executive*
Dortch, Carl Raymond *former association executive*
Kreegar, Phillip Keith *educational administrator*
Marsolais, Harold Raymond *association executive*
Stein, Carole Ruth *social services administrator, researcher*
Sweezy, John William *political party official*
Vereen, Robert Charles *retired trade association executive*
Wooden, Reba Faye Boyd *guidance counselor*

Santa Claus
Platthy, Jeno *cultural association executive*

IOWA

Cedar Rapids
Huber, Rita Norma *civic worker*
†Wieck, Paul H. *fraternal organization executive*

Center Point
Neenan, Thomas Francis *association executive, consultant*

Des Moines
Powell, Sharon Lee *social welfare organization administrator*

Smith, Mary Louise *politics and public affairs consultant*

Iowa City
†Ferguson, Richard L. *educational administrator*
Froeschle, Robert Edward *professional association administrator*

Johnston
†Churchill, Steven Wayne *fund-raising consultant*

Larchwood
Zangger, Russell George *organization executive, flying school executive*

KANSAS

Kansas City
Bechtholdt, Henry Wilbert *international union executive*
Campbell, Joseph Leonard *trade association executive*

Lawrence
Bowman, Laird Price *retired foundation administrator*
Schilling, John Michael *golf course executive*

Overland Park
Green, John Lafayette, Jr. *education executive*

Prairie Village
Souders, James P. *professional association executive*
Stock, Gregg Francis *retired association executive*

Topeka
Menninger, Roy Wright *medical foundation executive, psychiatrist*
Powers, Ramon Sidney *historical society administrator, historian*

KENTUCKY

Corbin
Barton-Collings, Nelda Ann *political activist, newspaper, bank and nursing home executive*

Lexington
†Houlihan, Ed *association executive*

Louisville
Peebles, Robert Alvin *horse breed registry executive*
†Strachan, Gladys *executive director*

LOUISIANA

Baton Rouge
Robertson, George Leven *retired association executive*

Franklin
Fairchild, Phyllis Elaine *counselor*

New Orleans
†Butler, Edward Scannell *organization executive*
Cody, Wilmer St. Clair *educational administrator*
Monroe, James Walter *organization executive*

MAINE

Augusta
Billings, Richard Whitten *association executive*
Gervais, Paul Nelson *foundation administrator, psychologist, public relations executive*

Brunswick
Chandler, John, Jr. *retired educational consultant*

Yarmouth
Hertz, Willard Joel *foundations and nonprofit organizations consultant*

MARYLAND

Annapolis
Brady, Frank Benton *retired technical society executive*
†Shea, Walter James *labor union executive*

Baltimore
Backas, James Jacob *foundation administrator*
Battle, Mark Garvey *social services executive*
Chavis, Benjamin Franklin, Jr. *civil rights advocate, minister*
Fuentealba, Victor William *professional society administrator*
Hartman, Charles Henry *association executive, educator*
Jernigan, Kenneth *association executive*
McCarthy, Carol M. *health care association executive, lawyer*

Bethesda
Beall, Robert Joseph *foundation executive*
Briggs, Shirley Ann *organization executive*
Brouha, Paul *association executive, fishery-wildlife biologist*
Cooney, David Martin *organization administrator, retired naval officer*
Day, Robert Dwain, Jr. *foundation executive, lawyer*
Fri, Robert Wheeler *non-profit research executive*
Grau, John Michael *trade association executive*
Higgins, Robert Louis *trade association executive*
Larson, Clarence Edward *association executive*
Lewis, David *association executive*
Meredith, Ellis Edson *association and business executive*
Reichard, John Francis *association executive*
Salisbury, Franklin Cary *foundation executive, lawyer*
Salisbury, Tamara Paula *foundation executive*

Saunders, Charles Baskerville, Jr. *retired association executive*
†Shapiro, Irving S. *medical think-tank executive*
Small, William Edwin, Jr. *association executive*
von Kann, Clifton Ferdinand *aviation and space executive, financial consultant*
†Walter, Robert *think-tank executive, career officer*
Wright, Helen Patton *association executive*
†Zinn, Dale W. *think-tank executive*

Chevy Chase
Cross, Christopher T. *association executive*
Sauer, Richard John *association executive*
Vanderryn, Jack *philanthropic foundation administrator*

College Park
Stephens, John Frank *association executive, researcher*
Stover, Carl Frederick *foundation executive*
Toll, John Sampson *association administrator, former university administrator, physics educator*

Elkton
Scherf, Christopher N. *association executive*

Faulkner
Freeze, James Donald *administrator, clergyman*

Fort Washington
Coffey, Matthew B. *association executive*

Germantown
Price, William James *organization executive*

Hyattsville
McLin, William Merriman *foundation administrator*

Kensington
LaGasse, Alfred Bazil, III *association executive*

Lutherville
Tebay, James Elwood *retired foundation executive*

Mitchellville
Kendall, Katherine Anne *social worker*

Oxford
Stanley, Edmund Allport, Jr. *foundation administrator, philanthropist*

Potomac
Hammond, Harold Francis *former association executive*
Noonan, Patrick Francis *conservation executive*
Rhode, Alfred Shimon *business consultant, educator*

Rockville
Anderson, Walter Dixon *trade association management consultant*
Hawkins, James Alexander, II *mental health fund executive*
Huber, John Michael *director non-profit organization*
Josephs, Melvin Jay *professional society administrator*
†Leshner, Alan Irvin *science foundation administrator*
Spahr, Frederick Thomas *association executive*

Silver Spring
Dale, Charles *trade association executive*
Fanelli, Joseph James *retired public affairs executive, consultant*
Fockler, Herbert Hill *foundation executive*
Hayman, Harry *association executive, electrical engineer*
Odland, Gerald Clark *association executive*
Winston, Michael Russell *foundation executive, historian*
Young, Kenneth *union official*

MASSACHUSETTS

Amherst
Benson, Lucy Peters Wilson *political and diplomatic consultant*
Hewlett, Horace Wilson *former educational administrator, association executive*

Boston
Deissler, Mary A. *foundation executive*
Hammock, John Calvin *international economic developer, consultant*
Mc Carthy, Patrick Edward *institute president*
Mitchell, Peter McQuilkin *educational administrator*
Sullivan, James Leo *organization executive*
Tarlov, Alvin Richard *former philanthropic foundation administrator, physician, educator, researcher*
Tucker, Louis Leonard *historical society administrator*

Cambridge
Bloomfield, Richard J. *international relations executive*
Charren, Peggy *consumer activist*
Kovach, Bill *educational foundation administrator*
Orlen, Joel *association executive*
Tyler, Lewis Adair *not-for-profit organization executive*
Voss, John *retired association executive*
Wenger, Luke Huber *educational association executive, editor*

Chestnut Hill
Fouraker, Lawrence Edward *social and business organizations director, former business administration educator*
Hunt-Clerici, Carol Elizabeth *academic personnel assistant*
Plaut, James Sachs *foundation executive*

Concord
Morgan, Charles Sumner *retired association executive*

Dorchester
Daly, Charles Ulick *foundation executive, investor*

Great Barrington
Gilmour, Robert Arthur *foundation executive, educator*

Hyannis
Kennedy, Rose Fitzgerald (Mrs. Joseph P. Kennedy) *philanthropist*

Milford
Desmarais, Maurice *trade association administrator*

Newton
Tannenwald, Leslie Keiter *educational administrator*

Williamstown
Taylor, Alfred Hendricks, Jr. *former foundation executive*

MICHIGAN

Ann Arbor
†Cole, Juan R.I. *cultural organization administrator*
Diana, Joseph A. *retired foundation executive*
†Dirks, Nicholas B. *cultural research organization administrator/history educator*
Guardo, Carol J. *association executive*
Kennedy, David Boyd *foundation executive, lawyer*
Radock, Michael *foundation executive*
Ware, Richard Anderson *foundation executive*

Battle Creek
Brown, Norman A. *foundation executive*
Davis, Laura Arlene *foundation administrator*
DeVries, Robert Allen *foundation administrator*
Grace, Helen Kennedy *foundation administrator*
Mawby, Russell George *foundation executive*
Pattullo, Andrew *former foundation executive*

Bloomfield Hills
Bianco, Joseph Paul, Jr. *foundation and art museum executive*

Dearborn
Brennan, Leo Joseph, Jr. *foundation executive*

Detroit
Bieber, Owen F. *labor union official*
†Casstevens, Bill J. *labor union administrator*
Scherer, Karla *foundation executive, venture capitalist*
Schuster, Elaine *civil rights professional, state official*
Sheffield, Horace Lindsey, Jr. *union official*
Smith, Frank Earl *association executive*
†Vaitkevicius, Vainutis K. *foundation administrator, medical educator*

East Lansing
Munger, Benson Scott *association executive*

Farmington
Lakritz, Isaac *fundraising organization executive*

Flint
White, William Samuel *foundation executive*

Grosse Pointe
Gilbert, Ronald Rhea *organization executive, lawyer*

Madison Heights
O'Hara, Thomas Edwin *association executive*
Pricer, Wayne Francis *counseling administrator*

Midland
Dow, Herbert Henry, II *foundation executive*

Southfield
Fleming, Mac Arthur *labor union administrator*

Troy
Marshall, John Elbert, III *foundation executive*

University Center
Miller, Roberta Balstad *science administrator*

Ypsilanti
Corriveau, Arlene Josephine *educational specialist*
McNutt, Kristen Wallwork *consumer affairs executive*

MINNESOTA

Hopkins
Burke, Steven Francis *organization executive*

Minneapolis
Johnson, John Warren *association executive*
King, Robert Cotton *association consultant*
Kolehmainen, Jan Waldroy *association executive*
O'Keefe, Thomas Michael *foundation executive*

Rochester
Wojcik, Martin Henry *foundation development official*

Saint Cloud
Henry, Edward LeRoy *former foundation executive, consultant, college president, public official*

Saint Paul
Archabal, Nina M(archetti) *historical society director*
Doermann, Humphrey *foundation administrator*
Fesler, David Richard *foundation director*
Goff, Lila Johnson *historical society administrator*

Saint Peter
Nelsen, William Cameron *foundation president, former college president*

Wayzata
Shannon, James Patrick *foundation consultant, retired food company executive*

Winona
Preska, Margaret Louise Robinson *institute executive*

MISSISSIPPI

Fayette
La Salle, Arthur Edward *historic foundation executive*

Jackson
Penick, George Dial, Jr. *foundation executive*
Thrash, Edsel E. *educational administrator*

MISSOURI

Columbia
Palo, Nicholas Edwin *professional society administrator*

Earth City
Anderhalter, Oliver Frank *educational organization executive*

Independence
Potts, Barbara Joyce *historical society executive*

Joplin
Williams, Rex Enoch *international union representative*

Kansas City
Bugher, Robert Dean *association executive*
Fries, James Lawrence *trade association executive*
†Levi, Peter Steven *chamber of commerce executive, lawyer*
Vander Clute, Howard Edmund, Jr. *association executive*

Marshall
Tweito, Eleanor Marie *social services administrator*

Maysville
Bram, Isabelle Mary Rickey McDonough (Mrs. John Bram) *civic worker*

North Kansas City
Hartley, Richard Glendale *association executive*

Saint Louis
Hunter, Earle Leslie, III *professional association executive*
Suelflow, August Robert *historical institute administrator, educator*

Springfield
Himstedt, Ronald Eugene *union official*

MONTANA

Billings
Sample, Joseph Scanlon *foundation executive*

Harrison
Jackson, Peter Vorious, III *retired association executive*

NEBRASKA

Lincoln
†Crosby, LaVon Kehoe Stuart *civic leader*
Hodges, Clarence Eugene *charitable organization executive, former government official*
Rosenow, John Edward *foundation executive*
Swartz, Jack *association executive*

Omaha
Batchelder, Anne Stuart *former publisher, political party official*
Bell, C(lyde) R(oberts) (Bob Bell) *association executive*
Flickinger, Thomas Leslie *hospital alliance executive*
Monasee, Charles Arthur *healthcare foundation executive*
Roskens, Ronald William *association administrator*

Seward
Vrana, Verlon Kenneth *professional society administrator, conservationist*

NEVADA

Carson City
Ayres, Janice Ruth *social service executive*

Henderson
Freyd, William Pattinson *fund raising executive, consultant*

Las Vegas
Polk-Matthews, Josephine Elsey *school psychologist*

Pahrump
Hersman, Marion Frank *professional administrator, lawyer*

Reno
McHardy, Louis William *professional association executive, educator*

NEW HAMPSHIRE

Concord
Crosier, John David *association administrator*

Francestown
White, Ruth O'Brien (Mrs. Wallace B. White) *civic worker*

Greenfield
Caverly, Gardner A. *foundation executive*

Washington
Halverson, Wendell Quelprud *former educational association executive, clergyman, educator*

NEW JERSEY

Bernardsville
Cooperman, Saul *foundation administrator*

Bogota
Condon, Francis Edward *foundation administrator, retired chemistry educator*

Camden
Wellington, Judith Lynn *cultural organization administrator*

Cedar Grove
Brownstein, Alan P. *health foundation executive, consultant*
Thiel, Thelma King *foundation executive*

Cliffside Park
Pushkarev, Boris S. *research foundation director, writer*

Cranbury
Rector, Milton Gage *social work educator, former association executive*

Edison
Maeroff, Gene I. *educational association administrator, journalist*

Englewood
Orlando, George (Joseph) *union executive*

Jersey City
McGhee, Elaine Simmons *school director, consultant*
Niemiec, Edward Walter *professional association executive*

Kendall Park
Goldberg, Bertram J. *social agency admininistrator*

Kinnelon
Schafer, John Stephen *foundation administrator*

Montclair
Campbell, Stewart Fred *foundation executive*
Schlesinger, Stephen Lyons *foundation executive, nurseryman*

Montvale
Scopes, Gary Martin *professional association executive*

New Vernon
Dugan, John Leslie, Jr. *foundation executive*

Newark
†Schoon, Richard G. *association executive*

Paramus
Plucinsky, Constance Marie *school counselor, supervisor*

Pennington
†Calvo, Roque John *association executive*

Princeton
Boyer, Ernest LeRoy *foundation executive*
Cohen, Alan Barry *foundation executive*
Hearn, Ruby Puryear *foundation executive*
Jellinek, Paul S. *foundation executive, health economist*
Kaufman, Nancy J. *health foundation executive*
Knight, Walter Early *association executive*
Rhett, Haskell Emery Smith *foundation executive, educator*
Stern, Gail Frieda *historical association director*

Ramsey
Eklund, Donald Arthur *trade association executive*

Red Bank
Meredith, George (Marlor) *association executive, writer*

River Edge
†Kempner, Michael W. *public relations executive*

Rumson
†Brenner, Theodore Engelbert *retired trade association executive*
Freeman, David Forgan *foundation executive*

Scotch Plains
Ungar, Manya Shayon *volunteer, consultant*

South Orange
Sontag, Frederick H. *public affairs and research consultant*

Tenafly
Kullberg, John Francis *association executive*

Trenton
Pollock, John Crothers, III *opinion research executive, educator*

Voorhees
†Myslowka, Myron William (Ron Myslowka) *labor union executive*

Westwood
Mastroserio, Joe *association consultant*

NEW MEXICO

Albuquerque
Mitovich, John *association executive*

Angel Fire
Dillon, Robert Morton *retired association executive, architectural consultant*

Santa Fe
Chatfield, Cheryl Ann *non profit organization executive, educator*

NEW YORK

Albany
Ashe, Bernard Flemming *lawyer*
Carovano, John Martin *not-for-profit adminstrator, conservationist*

Amherst
Clark, Donald Malin *association executive*

Armonk
Bergson, Henry Paul *association executive*

Bedford Hills
Waller, Wilhelmine Kirby (Mrs. Thomas Mercer Waller) *civic worker, organization official*

Briarcliff Manor
Luck, Edward Carmichael *association executive*

Buffalo
†Brandt, Barbara Berryman *cultural organization administrator*
Glickman, Marlene *social organization administrator*

Clinton
Couper, Richard Watrous *foundation executive, educator*

Flushing
Fichtel, Rudolph Robert *retired association executive*
Hoffman, Merle Holly *political activist, social psychologist, author*
Madden, Joseph Daniel *trade association executive*
Sutherland, Alan Roy *association executive*

Garrison
Pierpont, Robert *fund raising executive, consultant*

Huntington Bay
Schulz, William Frederick *human rights association executive*

Kingston
Arnold, William Edwin *foundation adminstrator*

Larchmont
Hinerfeld, Ruth J. *civic organization executive*

Long Island
Ulrich, Werner Richard *union education administrator*

Mamaroneck
Allensworth, Dorothy Alice *education foundation administrator*

Merrick
Doyle, James Aloysius *retired association executive*

Mount Kisco
Senkier, Robert Joseph *foundation administrator, educator*

New Paltz
†Hasbrouck, Kenneth Edward *professional society administrator*

New York
Aaron, Chloe Wellingham *association executive*
Allmendinger, Paul Florin *retired engineering association executive*
Aronson, Esther Leah *association administrator, psychotherapist*
Astor, Brooke *foundation executive, civic worker*
Barnes, Jack Whittier *political party official*
Barondess, Linda Hiddemen *professional society executive*
Bausch, James John *foundation executive*
Beardsley, Theodore S(terling), Jr. *association executive*
Beckham, Edgar Frederick *foundation administrator*
Belden, David Leigh *professional association executive, engineering educator*
Benham, Isabel Hamilton *think tank company executive*
Benson, Lenore J. *association executive*
Berkman, Lillian *foundation executive, corporation executive, art collector*
Berresford, Susan Vail *philanthropic foundation executive*
Berry, Nancy Michaels *nonprofit development executive*
Betanzos, Amalia V. *social services administrator*
Bird, Mary Lynne Miller *association executive*
Braverman, Robert Jay *international consultant, public policy educator*
Brief, Henry *association executive*
Brown, Terrence Charles *art association executive, researcher, lecturer*
Buckman, Thomas Richard *foundation executive, educator*
Calabrese, Rosalie Sue *professional arts administrator, writer*
Campbell, Colin Goetze *foundation president*
Cantor, Alexandra S. E. *professional society administrator*
Cashin, Richard Marshall *international aid official*
Cassella, William Nathan, Jr. *organization executive*
Catley-Carlson, Margaret *association executive*
Chapin, Schuyler Garrison *cultural affairs executive, university dean*
Christopher, Maurine Brooks *foundation administrator, writer, editor*
Clarke, Garvey Elliott *educational association administrator, lawyer*
Cole, Elma Phillipson (Mrs. John Strickler Cole) *social welfare executive*
Conarroe, Joel Osborne *foundation administrator, educator, editor*
Cornez, Gerald H. *association executive*
Cross, William Redmond, Jr. *corporate director, foundation executive*
David, Miles *association and marketing executive*
Davis, Karen Padgett *fund executive*
Davis, Kathryn Wasserman *foundation executive, writer, lecturer*
Deffenbaugh, Ralston H., Jr. *immigration agency executive, lawyer*
Dennis, Everette Eugene, Jr. *foundation executive, journalism educator, media critic, author*
Derryck, Vivian Lowery *executive non-profit organization*
Diamond, Irene *foundation administrator*
†DiTolla, Alfred W. *international union executive*
Dressner, Howard Roy *foundation executive, lawyer*
Egle, Jack *educational association executive*
Einiger, Carol Blum *foundation executive*
Eisenberg, Alan *association executive*
Ekman, Richard *foundation executive, educator*
Elam, Leslie Albert *association executive*
Elliott, Eleanor Thomas *foundation executive, civic leader*
Emmert, Richard Eugene *professional association executive*
Engelhardt, Sara Lawrence *organization executive*
Fabian, Larry Louis *non-profit foundation executive*
†Fehr, Donald M. *baseball union executive*
Feist, Leonard *association executive*
Ferguson, Frances Hand *volunteer, civic worker*
Finberg, Barbara Denning *foundation executive*
Fox, Daniel Michael *foundation administrator, author*
Franklin, Phyllis *professional association administrator*
Freid, Jacob *association executive, educator*
Freund, Gerald *foundation administrator*
Furuhata, Taketo (Mike Furuhata) *trading company executive*
Gallagher, Edward Peter *arts association administrator*
Garrison, John Raymond *organization executive*
Gaudieri, Millicent Hall *association executive*
Glasser, Ira Saul *civil liberties organization executive*
Goldmark, Peter Carl, Jr. *foundation executive*
Grant, James Pineo *international organization executive*
Grant, Leonard Tydings *educational association president*
†Gray, Robert Loren *association executive*
Gray, William H., III *association executive, former congressman*
Grimaldi, Nicholas Lawrence *social services administrator*
Hall, Gus (Arvo Kusta Halberg) *political party official*
Halpern, Charles Robert *foundation executive, educator, lawyer*
Hammett, William M. H. *foundation executive*
Handberg, Irene Deak *educational executive*
Harris, David Alan *not-for-profit organization executive*
Harrod, B(illy) J(oe) *professional association executive*
Hart, Kitty Carlisle *arts administrator*
Hartford, Huntington *financier, art patron*
Hartley, Duncan *fund raising executive*
Hendricks, Edward David *association executive*
Heslin, James J. *association executive*
Hesselbein, Frances Richards *foundation executive, consultant*
Hester, James McNaughton *foundation administrator*
Hester, Melvyn Francis *labor union executive*
Holman, Margaret Mezoff *fund raising consultant*
Holtzman, Ellen A. *foundation executive*
Hoxie, Ralph Gordon *educational administrator, author*
Innis, Roy Emile Alfredo *organization official*
Jacob, John Edward *social service agency executive*
Jacobson, Gaynor I. *retired association executive*
Janklow, Linda LeRoy *civic worker, volunteer*
Jedlicka, Judith Ann *organization executive*
Jerome, Fred Louis *science organization executive*
†Jones, Elaine *civil rights advocate*
Kahan, Marlene *professional association executive*
Kahn, Alfred Joseph *social worker and planner, educator*
Kane, Herman William *research company executive, political scientist*
Kaplan, Robert Arthur *association executive*
Karr, Norman *association executive*
Kaskell, Peter Howard *association executive, lawyer*
Kennedy, Moorhead *foundation administrator*
†Krasno, Richard Michael *educational organization executive, educator*
Labunski, Stephen Bronislaw *association executive*
Lamb, George Richard *foundation executive*
Larkin, June Noble *foundation executive*
Lawson-Johnston, Peter Orman *foundation executive*
†Lee, Clement William Khan *association administrator*
Lubic, Ruth Watson *association executive, nurse-midwife*
Luce, Henry, III *foundation executive*
Mahoney, Margaret Ellerbe *foundation executive*
Mangan, Mona *association executive, lawyer*
Maraldo, Pamela Jean *nursing association executive, lecturer, consultant*
Marks, Edward B. *international social service administrator*
†Mazur, Jay J. *trade union official*
McCord, Alice Bird *association executive*
†Michel, Harriet R. *association executive*
Milbank, Jeremiah *foundation executive*
Miller, Harvey S. Shipley *foundation trustee*
Miller, Lenore *labor union official*
Millett, Katherine Murray (Kate Millett) *political activist, sculptor, artist, writer*
Moloney, Thomas Walter *consulting firm executive*
Moran, Martin Joseph *fund raising company executive*
Muse, Martha Twitchell *foundation executive*
Odenweller, Robert Paul *philatelist association executive, airline pilot*
Olyphant, David *cultural, educational association executive*
O'Neill Bidwell, Katharine Thomas *fine arts association executive, performing arts executive*
Phillips, Russell Alexander, Jr. *foundation executive*
Piereson, James Eugene *foundation administrator*
Preston, Frances W. *performing rights organization executive*
Price, Hugh B. *foundation executive, lawyer*
Rattazzi, Serena *art museum and association administrator*
†Rhodes, Milton *arts association administrator*
Riordan, John Thomas *trade association executive*
Robinson, David Zav *foundation administrator*
Rolfe, Robin Ann *trade association executive, lawyer*
†Rosoff, Jeannie I. *association administrator*
Sabinson, Harvey Barnett *cultural organiztion administrator*
†Sackman, Ruth *foundation executive*
†Samers, Bernard Norman *fund raising organization executive*
Sawyer, John Edward *foundation officer*
Schubart, Mark Allen *arts and education executive*
Schwartz, Felice N. *social activist, educator*
Scullion, Tsugiko Yamagami *non-profit organization executive*
Seessel, Thomas Vining *civic organization executive*
Shea, Dion Warren Joseph *educational association executive, physicist*
Singer, Arthur Louis, Jr. *foundation executive*
Slater, Joseph Elliott *educational institute administrator*
Slutsky, Lorie Ann *foundation executive*
Smith, Datus Clifford, Jr. *former foundation executive*
Smith, J. Kellum, Jr. *foundation executive, lawyer*
†Solender, Stephen David *philanthropic organization executive*
Straus, Oscar S., II *foundation executive*
Sussman, Leonard Richard *foundation executive*
Swing, John Temple *lawyer, association executive*
Torrence, (John) Richard *administrator, special events producer*
Townley, Preston *association executive, former dean*
†Troubetzkoy, Alexis S. *foundation administrator, educator*
Tudryn, Joyce Marie *professional society administrator*
Turnbaugh, Douglas Blair *arts administration executive, author*
†Wang, Charles Pei *social service administrator*
Watson, John Lawrence, III *trade association executive*
Wattleton, Alyce Faye *association executive*
Weeks, David Frank *foundation administrator*
†Weintraub, Daniel Ralph *social welfare administrator*
Wellington, Sheila Wacks *foundation administrator, psychiatry educator*
Wohlgelernter, Beth *organization executive*
Wright, Hugh Elliott, Jr. *association executive, writer*

Pittsford
Dorsey, Eugene Carroll *former foundation and communications executive*

Princeton
Karel, Frank, III *foundation executive*

Richfield Springs
Mc Kelvey, John Jay, Jr. *retired foundation executive*

Rochester
DeMarco, Roland R. *foundation executive*
Pacala, Leon *retired assocation executive*

Scarsdale
Bernstein, Irving *international organization executive*
Ferry, Wilbur Hugh *foundation consultant*
Rosow, Jerome Morris *institute executive*
Sullivan, Adèle Woodhouse *organization official*
Wile, Julius *former corporate executive, educator*

Schenectady
Chestnut, Harold *foundation administrator, engineering executive*

Seneca Falls
Butler, Susan Lowell *association executive, writer*

Suffern
Zecca, John Andrew *retired association executive*

Tarrytown
Dobkin, John Howard *art administrator*
†Dorland, Byrl Brown *civic worker*
Goldin, Milton *fund raising counsel, author*
Rath, Bernard Emil *trade association executive*

Tonawanda
Browning, James Franklin *professional society executive*

White Plains
Cooke, Lloyd Miller *former organization executive*
Howse, Jennifer Louise *foundation administrator*
Jensen, Grady Edmonds *association executive*

Yonkers
Karpatkin, Rhoda Hendrick *consumer information organization executive, lawyer*

NORTH CAROLINA

Asheville
Gabriel, Robert *art association administrator*

Carrboro
Greenslade, Forrest Charles *international health care executive*

Charlotte
Love, Franklin Sadler *retired trade association executive*
McCall, Billy Gene *charitable trust executive*
Stair, Frederick Rogers *retired foundation executive, former seminary president*
Wenner, Gene Charles *arts foundation executive*

Durham
Bevan, William *retired foundation executive*
Rosenthal, Julian Bernard *lawyer, association executive*

Greensboro
Kornegay, Horace Robinson *trade association executive, former congressman, lawyer*
Ulmer, Walter F., Jr. *leadership development executive, former army officer*

High Point
Brackett, Douglas Lane *trade association executive*

Research Triangle Park
Martin, William Royall, Jr. *association executive*

Winston Salem
Carter, Henry Moore, Jr. *foundation executive*
Gleason, Norman Dale *association executive*

OHIO

Akron
Frank, John V. *foundation executive*
†Martino, Frank Dominic *union executive*

Avon Lake
†McLaughlin, Ronald Paul *labor union administrator*

Beachwood
Swank, Emory Coblentz *world affairs consultant, lecturer*

Chardon
Reinhard, Sister Mary Marthe *educational organization administrator*

Cincinnati
Blanken, Sarah S. *retired foundation administrator*
†Conley, Robert T. *educational administrator*
Hiatt, Marjorie McCullough *service organization executive*

Circleville
Scherer, Robert Davisson *retired association executive*

Cleveland
Bergholz, David *foundation administrator*
Boyd, Richard Alfred *foundation administrator*
Jenson, Jon Eberdt *association executive*
Luttner, Edward F. *career management consultant*
†Russell, Valerie Eileen *social service executive*
Wadsworth, Homer Clark *foundation consultant*

Columbus
Barker, Judy *foundation executive*
Blair, William Travis (Bud Blair) *retired organization executive*
Cole, Charles Chester, Jr. *educational administrator*
Hamilton, Harold Philip *fund raising executive*
Luck, James I. *foundation executive*
†Ness, Gary Clifford *historical society administrator*
Newman, Diana S. *community foundation executive*
Sharp, Paul David *institute administrator*

Dayton
Crowe, Shelby *educational specialist, consultant*
Daley, Robert Emmett *foundation executive*
Mathews, David *foundation executive*
Schwartzhoff, James Paul *foundation executive*

Girard
Wolanin, Sophie Mae *civic worker, tutor, scholar, lecturer*

Materials Park
Langer, Edward L. *association executive*

Mentor
Andrassy, Timothy Francis *trade association executive*

Middletown
Clinton, Mariann Hancock *association executive*

Oberlin
Distelhorst, Garis Fred *association executive*

Oxford
Miller, Robert James *association executive*

OKLAHOMA

Lawton
Brooks, (Leslie) Gene *cultural association administrator*

Norman
Burton, Ron D. *educational foundation executive*

Oklahoma City
Gumerson, Jean Gilderhus *health foundation executive*

Tulsa
Cole, Clyde Curtis, Jr. *association executive*
Wesenberg, John Herman *association executive*

OREGON

Beaverton
Henderson, George Miller *foundation executive, former banker*

Corvallis
Wilkins, Caroline Hanke *consumer agency administrator, political worker*

Klamath Falls
Ehlers, Eleanor May Collier (Mrs. Frederick Burton Ehlers) *civic worker*

Medford
Sours, James Kingsley *association executive, former college president*

Portland
Bragdon, Paul Errol *foundation administrator*
Collins, Maribeth Wilson *foundation executive*
Hilbert, Bernard Charles *retired union official*
McClave, Donald Silsbee *association executive*
†Orloff, Chet *cultural organization administrator*

PENNSYLVANIA

Allentown
Berman, Muriel Mallin *civic worker*
Berman, Philip I. *foundation administrator*

Bryn Mawr
Carroll, Mary Colvert *corporate executive*
Driskill, John Ray *association executive*

Dillsburg
Bowers, Glenn Lee *association executive*

Drexel Hill
Schiazza, Guido Domenic (Guy Schiazza) *educational association administrator*

Elizabethtown
Madeira, Robert Lehman *association executive*

Exton
Penrose, Charles, Jr. *association executive*

Harrisburg
Lourie, Norman Victor *government official, social worker*

Hershey
Bomgardner, William Earl *retired association executive, photographer*

Lewisburg
Neuman, Nancy Adams Mosshammer *civic leader*

New Hope
Koljian, Hollis Ann *educational association administrator*

Newtown
Keenan, Terrance *foundation executive*

Perkasie
Ferry, Joan Evans *school counselor*

Philadelphia
†Bailin, Michael A. *social research firm executive*
Block, Isaac Edward *association executive*
Bodine, James Forney *retired civic leader*
Collier-Evans, Demetra Frances *veterans' benefits counselor*
†Doman, Janet Joy *association executive*
Foti, Margaret Ann *association executive, editor*
Friedman, Murray *civil rights official, historian*
Friend, Theodore Wood, III *foundation executive, historian*
†Lederer, Marie A. *politcal campaign organizer*
McKenna, Thomas Morrison, Jr. *social services organization executive*
Montgomery, Edward Alembert, Jr. *developer*
Mullen, Eileen Anne *training and development executive*
Pak, Hyung Woong *foundation executive, educator*
Panitch, Lois Ponnock Krebs *health care foundation executive*
Perlmutter, Felice Davidson *social work administration educator*
†Pizzi, Charles Peter *association president*
Reed, Clarence Raymond *association executive*
Rimel, Rebecca Webster *foundation executive*
Watson, Bernard Charles *foundation administrator*

Pittsburgh
Casey, Robert J. *international trade association executive*
Dybeck, Alfred Charles *labor arbitrator*
Grinberg, Meyer Stewart *educational institute executive*
Hallen, Philip Burgh *foundation administrator*
Heinz, Drue *foundation administrator*
†Hingson, Luke Lockhart *charitable foundation executive*
Horan, Justin Thomas *retired association executive*
Hovis, John Herbert *association executive*
Ketchum, David Storey *retired fundraising executive*
Mellon, Richard Prosser *charitable foundation executive*
Pasnick, Raymond Wallace *labor union official, editor*
Williams, Lynn Russell *labor union official*

Reading
Mattern, Donald Eugene *association executive*

Rohrerstown
Stauffer, Sarah Ann *political worker*

State College
DeVoss, James Thomas *community foundation administrator, retired*
Phillips, Janet Colleen *educational association executive, editor*

University Park
†Feller, Irwin *think-tank executive, economics educator*

Valley Forge
†Carlson, Beverly Clark *historical society administrator*
Miller, Robert Wiley *educational foundation executive*

Warrendale
Rumbaugh, Max Elden, Jr. *professional society administrator*

Wayne
Etris, Samuel Franklin *association executive*

Wynnewood
Freeman, Morton S. *former bar association executive, retired lawyer*
Peskin, Matt Alan *professional society administrator*

RHODE ISLAND

Kingston
†Schmidt, Charles T. *labor research organization administrator*

Providence
Campbell, Edwin Denton *educational administrator*
†Earle, Nathaniel Cabot *board of trade executive*
Klyberg, Albert Thomas *historical society administrator*
Woolf, William Blauvelt *association executive*

SOUTH CAROLINA

Charleston
Hughes, Blake *retired architectural institute administrator, publisher*

Columbia
Bjontegard, Arthur Martin, Jr. *foundation executive*
Hupp, Jack Scott *civic administrator*
McGill, Jennifer Houser *non-profit association administrator*
Sheheen, Fred Roukos *education association administrator*

Dataw Island
Dietz, Earl Daniel *retired foundation company executive*

Greenville
†Frist, Thomas Ferran *philanthropic organization executive*

Lancaster
Bundy, Charles Alan *foundation executive*

Surfside Beach
McCrensky, Edward *international consultant, former organization executive*

TENNESSEE

Chattanooga
Zodhiates, Spiros George *association executive*

Knoxville
Froula, James DeWayne *national honor society director, engineer*

Memphis
Hooks, Benjamin Lawson *civil rights advocate, brokerage house executive*
Nuber, Richard Howard *civic association executive, insurance company executive, state legislator*
Tibbs, Martha Jane Pullen *civic worker*
Whitesell, Dale Edward *retired association executive, natural resources consultant*

Nashville
Benson, Edwin Welburn, Jr. *trade association executive*
Henderson, Milton Arnold *association executive*
Ivey, William James *foundation executive, writer, producer*
Johnson, Hollis Eugene, III *foundation executive*

TEXAS

Amarillo
Ball, Charles Elihue *association consultant*
Brainard, Jayne Dawson (Mrs. Ernest Scott Brainard) *civic worker*

Austin
Barrera, Elvira Puig *counselor, therapist, educator*
Bonjean, Charles Michael *foundation executive, sociologist, educator*
†Kronkosky, Preston C. *educational think-tank executive*
McGarry, William Andrew, Jr. *career counselor*
Stoner, James Lloyd *retired foundation executive, clergyman*
West, Glenn Edward *business organization executive*

College Station
Vandiver, Frank Everson *institute administrator, former university president, author, educator*

Colleyville
Love, Ben Howard *organization executive*

Dallas
Branson, Mary Lou *family therapist, military agency administrator*
Giordano, Saverio Paul *professional association executive*
Jackson, Phillip Ellis *lobbyist, consultant*
Lancaster, Sally Rhodus *philathropy consultant*
Rouse, Eloise Meadows *foundation executive*

El Paso
Day, James Milton *foundation executive, English educator*
Tackett, Stephen Douglas *education services specialist*

Galveston
Baker, Robert Ernest, Jr. *foundation executive*

Granbury
Scogin, Martha Aduddell *counselor*

Houston
Bui, Khoi Tien *college counselor*
Crispin, Andre Arthur *international trading company executive*
Goldsmith, Billy Joe *trade association executive*
Grayson, Charles Jackson, Jr. *research association executive*
Heckler, Walter Tim *association executive*
Johns, Sheryl Lightfoot *philanthropic foundation executive*
Knotts, Glenn R(ichard) *foundation administrator*
Nicholson, Patrick James *retired university administrator and foundation president, author*

Irving
†Olson, Herbert Theodore *trade association executive*
Stahl, David Edward *association executive*

Plainview
Galle, Richard Lynn *association executive, former municipal official*

Port Arthur
Cash, Carol Vivian *sociologist*

Richardson
Adamson, Dan Klinglesmith *science association executive*

Salado
Cutler, Morene Parten *civic worker*

San Antonio
†Hernandez, Christine *educator*
Krier, Joseph Roland *chamber of commerce executive, lawyer*
†Montecel, Maria Robledo (Cuca Robledo Montecel) *educational association administrator*

UTAH

Provo
Gibbons, LeRoy *developer, fundraiser*

Salt Lake City
Evans, Max Jay *historical society administrator*
Melich, Doris S. *public service worker*

VERMONT

Bennington
Perin, Donald Wise, Jr. *former association executive*

Brattleboro
Akins, Zane Vernon *association executive*

Manchester
Hooper, Arthur William *consultant, former association executive*

Montpelier
Barbieri, Christopher George *association executive*

White River Junction
Linnell, Robert Hartley *environment, safety consultant*

VIRGINIA

Airlie
Clayton, James Edwin *foundation executive, journalist*

Alexandria
Bachus, Walter Otis *retired army general, former association executive*
Bailar, Barbara Ann *professional society executive, statistician, researcher*
†Baird, Charles F. *think-tank executive*
†Baker, Brent Harold *foundation executive*
†Bolger, Robert Joseph *retired trade association executive*
Brown, Quincalee *association executive*
Byrd-Lawler, Barbara Ann *association executive*
Byrnside, Oscar Jehu, Jr. *association executive*
Chao, Elaine L. *philanthropic organization executive*
Clower, William Dewey *association executive*
Cooper, Charles Donald *association executive, editor, retired career officer*
Dietrich, Laura Jordan *international policy advisor*
Finnell, Dallas Grant *fundraising executive*
Garrison, Preston Jones *association consultant*
Goldstein, Jerome Charles *professional association executive, surgeon, otolaryngologist*
Greenstein, Ruth Louise *research institute executive, lawyer*
†Hodder, Kenneth Lasett *social services administrator*
Hoyt, F(rank) Russell *association executive*
Irions, Charles Carter *trade association executive*
Kolar, Mary Jane *association executive*
Lenz, Edward Arnold *trade association executive, lawyer*
†Losey, Michael Robert *association executive*
McCulloch, William Leonard *association executive*
Merrick, Roswell Davenport *association executive*
Messing, Frederick Andrew, Jr. *action lobbyist*
†Moody, W. Jarvis *think-tank executive*
†Murray, Robert J. *think-tank executive*
Rector, John Michael *lawyer, association executive*
†Sava, Samuel G. *educational association administrator*
Shannon, Thomas Alfred *association executive*
Smith, Carl Richard *association executive, former air force officer*
Spiro, Robert Harry, Jr. *foundation and business executive, educator*
Stanley, Robert Warren *association executive*
Weinert, Donald G(regory) *association executive, engineer*
Yates, Jeffrey McKee *trade association executive*
Ziegler, Ronald Louis *association executive, former government official*

Arlington
Allen, Ernest Eugene *non-profit organization executive, lawyer*
Bailly, Henri-Claude Albert *consulting services executive*
Bast, James Louis *trade association executive*
Bode, Barbara *foundation executive*
Cocklin, Robert Frank *association executive*
†Fleming, Michael John *trade association executive*
Friedheim, Jerry Warden *foundation executive*
Hendrickson, Jerome Orland *trade association executive, lawyer*

Langworthy, Everett Walter *association executive, natural gas exploration company executive*
Lloyd, Kent *education policy research and public interest executive, educator*
Marcuccio, Phyllis Rose *association executive, editor*
†McMasters, Paul Kenneth *foundation executive*
Melickian, Gary Edward *trade association executive*
Noland, Royce Paul *association executive, physical therapist*
Paynter, Harry Alvin *retired trade association executive*
Price, Randall Craig *not for profit association executive*
Roberts, James Milnor, Jr. *association executive*
Robinson, Kenneth Leonard, Jr. *trade association executive*
Shaud, John Albert *association executive, former air force officer*
Smeal, Eleanor Cutri *organization executive*
Smith, Elise Fiber *international non-profit development agency administrator*
Stolgitis, William Charles *professional society executive*
Teem, John McCorkle *retired association executive, consultant*
Wells, Christine *foundation executive*
Wilkniss, Peter E. *foundation administrator, researcher*
Wilson, Minter Lowther, Jr. *retired officers association executive*
Wilson, Roy Kenneth *retired education association executive, consultant*

Boston
†Fisher, John Morris *association official, educator*

Chantilly
Slayton, Gus *association executive*
Sroka, John Walter *trade association executive*

Charlottesville
†Jordan, Daniel Porter, Jr. *foundation administrator, history educator*

Culpeper
Landa, William Robert *foundation executive*

Fairfax
Cullison, Alexander C. (Doc Cullison) *society administrator*
Martin, George Wilbur *association executive*
Mund, Richard Gordon *foundation executive*

Fairfax City
Hollans, Irby Noah, Jr. *association executive*

Falls Church
Cooper, Arthur Irving *former association executive*
Ledwig, Donald Eugene *association executive*
Masterson, Kleber Sandlin *former organization executive, retired naval officer*
Rose, Wil *foundation executive*

Flint Hill
Dietel, William Moore *former foundation executive*

Fredericksburg
Farmer, James *civil rights leader, former trade union official*

Front Royal
Overton, Joseph Allen, Jr. *association official*

Great Falls
Anfinson, Thomas Elmer *foundation executive*
Schwartz, Robert Terry *professional association executive*

Lynchburg
Hinnant, Hilari Anne *educational association administrator*

Manassas
Neal, Richard Glenn *educational management company executive*

Mc Lean
Bolan, Robert S. *association executive*
Finberg, Donald Richard *foundation administrator*
Friel, Thomas Patrick *association executive*
Gary, Charles Lester *professional association consultant, educator*
Mc Fate, Patricia Ann *educator, foundation executive, scientist*
McInerney, James Eugene, Jr. *association executive*
Rogers, Thomas Francis *foundation administrator*

Montpelier Station
†Scott, Christopher *executive director cultural trust, author*

Norfolk
Sheetz, Richard LaTrelle *retired association executive*
Wilson, Lloyd Lee *organization administrator*

Reston
Ayers, George Edward Lewis *higher education association executive*
Curry, John Joseph *professional organization executive*
Dyer, Timothy J. *educational association administrator*
Gates, James David *association executive*
Goodwin, Robert Delmege *retired association executive*
Hope, Samuel Howard *accreditation organization executive*
Troester, Carl Augustus, Jr. *association consultant*

Richmond
Wood, Jeanne Clarke *charitable organization executive*

Round Hill
Sadd, William Wheeler *trade association executive*

Spotsylvania
Hardy, Dorcas Ruth *government relations and public policy consultant*

Springfield
Larson, Reed Eugene *association executive*

Tazewell
†Weeks, Ross Leonard, Jr. *museum foundation executive*

Vienna
Argow, Keith Angevin *association executive, forester*
Cartier, Brian Evans *association executive*
West, Richard Luther *military association executive, defense consultant, retired army officer*

Williamsburg
Brinkley, Joseph Willard *association executive*
Longsworth, Charles R. *foundation administrator*
†Wilburn, Robert Charles *institute executive*

WASHINGTON

Clark County
Holley, Lawrence Alvin *retired labor union official*

Langley
Medlock, Ann *non-profit organization executive, writer, lecturer*

Mill Creek
Corbally, John Edward *foundation director*

Seattle
Brooke, Francis John, III *foundation administrator*
†Chapman, Bruce Kerry *institute executive*

Sequim
Ramsey, William Ray *association executive*

Spokane
†Reitemeier, (Timothy) George *chamber of commerce executive, public relations exective*
Rowe, Marjorie Douglas *retired social services administrator*

Tacoma
Graybill, David Wesley *chamber of commerce executive*
Rieke, William Oliver *foundation director, medical educator, former university president*
†Robison, William Thomas *trade association executive*

WISCONSIN

Altoona
James, Henry Thomas *former foundation executive, educator*

Elm Grove
Halvorsen, Morrie Edward *association executive*
Kolda, Thomas Joseph *non-profit organization executive*

Greendale
Gillespie, Rory Andrew *professional association administrator*

Kenosha
Adler, Seymour Jack *social services administrator*

Madison
†Brennan, Robert Walter *association executive*
Higby, Gregory James *historical association administrator, historian*
Muller, H(enry) Nicholas, III *historical society director*
†Porter, Andrew Calvin *educational administrator, psychology educator*
Seevers, Charles Junior *foundation executive, psychologist*
†Stern, Steve J. *cultural organization administrator, history educator*

Milwaukee
Huntington, David Mack Goode *foundation administrator*
Johnson, Geneva Bolton *human service organization executive*
Joyce, Michael Stewart *foundation executive, political science educator*
Ritz, Esther Leah *civic worker, volunteer, investor*
Zeidler, Frank P. *former association administrator, mayor, arbitrator, mediator, fact-finder*

Racine
Boyd, William Beaty *retired foundation executive*
Bray, Charles William, III *foundation executive*

River Hills
Smith, Jane Farwell *civic worker*

WYOMING

Cheyenne
Noe, Guy *social services administrator*

TERRITORIES OF THE UNITED STATES

PUERTO RICO

Guaynabo
Cruz Aponte, Ramón Aristides *foundation administrator, educator*

CANADA

ALBERTA

Calgary
Raeburn, Andrew Harvey *performing arts association executive, record producer*

BRITISH COLUMBIA

Vancouver
†Howard, T.E. *scientific and research think-tank executive*
Saywell, William George Gabriel *foundation administrator*

NEW BRUNSWICK

Fredericton
†Lewell, Peter A. *international technology executive, researcher*

Saint Andrews
Clark, David R. *executive not-for-profit organization, lawyer*

NOVA SCOTIA

Dartmouth
†Nickerson, T. B. *think-tank organization executive*

Wolfville
Elliott, Robbins Leonard *consultant*

ONTARIO

Don Mills
Glover, Donald Robert *professional association administrator, former insurance executive*

Etobicoke
Ecroyd, Lawrence Gerald *association executive*

Mississauga
Ross, Thomas McCallum *association executive*

Mowat Block
Rose, Jeffrey Raymond *public servant, trade union executive*

Ottawa
Alper, Anne Elizabeth *professional association executive*
Beauchamp, Pierre *real estate association executive*
Bezanson, Keith Arthur *administrative educational executive*
Landry, Robert Edward *public policy consultant*
†Manning, Preston *political organization worker*
Peppler, William Norman *aviation association executive*
Reid, Timothy *business organization executive*
Shaw, Edgar Albert George *research association executive*

Pontypool
Kniewasser, Andrew Graham *company director*

Rexdale
Stermac, Anthony George *professional association executive*

Toronto
Collins, Jerry Allan *association executive*
Falle, Daisy Carolyne *professional society administrator*
Hayhurst, James Frederick Palmer *career and business consultant*
Hungerford, John Girdlestone *foundation executive*
James, Robert Scott *historic organization executive*
Johnston, Robert Donaghy *cultural organization administrator*
Kossuth, Selwyn Barnett *trade association consultant*
MacIntosh, Robert Mallory *association executive*
Montgomery, Donald Russell *labor consulting firm executive*
Rickerd, Donald Sheridan *foundation executive*
Wiley, Judith *association executive*
Wilson, Ian Edwin *cultural organization administrator, archivist*

Willowdale
Bulloch, John Frederick Devon *association executive*

QUEBEC

Laval
Pichette, Claude *former banking executive, university rector, research executive*

Montreal
Hobday, John Charles *foundation administrator*

Outremont
Letourneau, Jean-Paul *business association executive and consultant*

Saint Laurent
Boulet, Lionel *research administrator*

SASKATCHEWAN

Regina
Driedger, Florence Gay *social agency executive, social work educator, consultant*

MEXICO

Mexico City
Bruton, John Macaulay *trade association executive*

BELGIUM

Brussels
Calingaert, Michael *international consultant*
†Mestrallet, Gérard *association executive*

ENGLAND

Oxford
†Gulbrandsen, Natalie Webber *religious association administrator*

FINLAND

Helsinki
Varmavuori, Anneli *chemical society administrator, chemist*

ITALY

Rome
Hjort, Howard Warren *international organization official, economist*

MONACO

Stade Louie
Davies, Gareth John *trade association executive*

THE NETHERLANDS

The Hague
†Nones Sucre, Carlos Enrique *political organization executive*

SWITZERLAND

Geneva
Barnes, Thomas Joseph *migration program administrator*
Purcell, James Nelson, Jr. *international organization administrator*

ADDRESS UNPUBLISHED

Allerton, John Stephen *association executive*
Allshouse, Merle Frederick *foundation executive*
Amstutz, Daniel Gordon *intergovernmental organization executive, former grain dealer, government official*
Anderson, Ned, Sr. *Apache tribal chairman*
Andolsek, Ludwig J. *association executive*
Annenberg, Walter H. *philanthropist, diplomat, editor, publisher, broadcaster*
Armour, David Edward Ponton *association executive*
Baldwin, William Russell *foundation executive, optometrist*
Bartels, Gerald Lee *association executive*
Beglarian, Grant *foundation executive, composer, consultant*
Blair, Fred Edward *association executive*
Bowen, David Reece *foundation director, former congressman*
Brewer, Carey *fund raising executive*
Bricker, William Rudolph *retired organization executive*
Burki, Fred Albert *labor union official*
Camdessus, Michel (Jean) *international association executive*
Cesnik, James Michael *union official, newspaperman*
Clark, Alicia Garcia *political party official*
Coughlan, William David *association executive*
De Simone, Daniel V. *engineering association executive, engineer*
Dorman, Richard Frederick, Jr. *association executive, consultant*
Easton, Michelle *foundation executive*
Eliot, Theodore Lyman, Jr. *international consultant*
Farinella, Paul James *retired cultural institution executive*
Farris, Robert Earl *transportation consultant*
Foster, Charles Henry Wheelwright *former foundation officer, consultant, author*
Franklin, Margaret Lavona Barnum (Mrs. C. Benjamin Franklin) *civic leader*
Gammon, Samuel Rhea, III *association executive, former ambassador*
Gasper, Jo Ann *association executive*
Gertenbach, Robert Frederick *medical research organization executive, accountant, lawyer*
Gorham, William *organization executive*
Hanford, George Hyde *retired educational administrator*
Harlan, Robert Warren *retired charitable association executive*
Hartley, Grace Van Tine *foundation administrator*
Helm, DeWitt Frederick, Jr. *association executive*
Hoopes, Townsend Walter *former association executive, former government official*
Horsch, Kathleen Joanne *social services administrator, educator, consultant*
†Hybl, William Joseph *foundation executive, lawyer*
Ilutovich, Leon *organization executive*
Isaacson, Edith Lipsig *civic leader*
Jefferson, John Daniel *political activist*
Johnson, Marlene M. *social services professional*
Kapor, Mitchell David *foundation executive*
Kasimer, Solomon *charitable organization executive*
Kaskowitz, Edwin *association executive*
Kempfer, Homer *association executive*
Kinder, James Allen *lobbyist, professional services firm executive, consultant*
Knauer, Virginia Harrington (Mrs. Wilhelm F. Knauer) *consumer consultant, former government official*
Krepinevich, Kevin W. *social welfare organization administrator, educator*
Kuhn, Margaret (Maggie Kuhn) *organization executive*
Langdon, George Dorland, Jr. *association executive*
Largman, Kenneth *strategic analyst, strategic defense analysis company executive*

Lee, John Franklin *retired lawyer, retired association executive*
Leggett, Roberta Jean (Bobbi Leggett) *association executive*
Low, James Patterson *professional association executive*
MacCarthy, Talbot Leland *civic volunteer*
MacMillan, Kip Van Metre *foundation executive*
Mann, Jonathan Max *international agency administrator*
McCarthy, William J. *retired labor union executive*
McLaughlin, Ann *educational administrator, former federal official, lecturer, advisor*
McWethy, Patricia Joan *association executive*
Menchú, Rigoberta *human rights activist*
Mende, Robert Graham *retired engineering association executive*
Meredith, James Howard *association executive, farmer, consultant*
Migden, Chester L. *association executive*
Moore, Robert William *professional organization executive*
†Noble, James Ronald *trade association executive*
O'Connor, Doris Julia *non-profit fundraiser, consultant*
Osmer-McQuade, Margaret *association executive, broadcast journalist*
Patino, Douglas Xavier *foundation administrator*
Phillips, Kenneth Higbie *association executive*
Plimpton, Peggy Lucas *trustee*
Pollack, Joseph *retired labor union official*
Pollack, Ronald F(rank) *foundation executive, lawyer*
Quehl, Gary Howard *association executive, consultant*
Ramo, Virginia M. Smith *civic worker*
Richard, Susan Mathis *trade association executive*
Roberts, James G. *foundation executive*
Roethel, David Albert Hill *consultant*
Rosenberg, Alison P. *public policy official*
Ross, Charlotte Pack *suicidologist*
†Rotman, Arthur *former social welfare administrator*
Ryan, John William *association executive*
Schiaffino, S(ilvio) Stephen *retired medical society executive, consultant*
Schwartz, John James *association executive, consultant*
Segal, JoAn Smyth *library consultant, organization administrator*
†Sharp, Kenneth Travis *cultural organization administrator, editor*
Singer, Markus Morton *retired trade association executive*
Smith, Laverne Byrd *educational association administrator*
Smith, Robert Powell *foundation executive, former ambassador*
Stinnett, Lee Houston *newspaper association executive*
Taplin, Frank E., Jr. *trustee education and arts institutions and associations*
Thomas, Franklin Augustine *foundation executive*
Thorne, Barbara Lockwood *guidance counselor, secondary education educator*
Tichenor, Donald Keith *association executive*
Tuft, Mary Ann *former association executive*
Wall, Robert Emmet *educational administrator, novelist*
Walter, J. Jackson *consultant*
Washington, Valora *foundation administrator*
Watts, Glenn Ellis *union official*
Weaver, Edward T. *foundation executive, educator*
Weddig, Lee J(ohn) *trade association executive*
Weikart, David Powell *educational research foundation administrator*
Wexler, Jacqueline Grennan (Mrs. Paul J. Wexler) *former association executive and college president*
Whitlock, Bennett Clarke, Jr. *retired association executive*
Work, William *retired association executive*
Wroblewski, Celeste Judine *non-profit civic association executive*
Wyatt, Lenore *civic worker*
†Yeutter, Clayton Keith *political organization executive, counselor to President of United States*
Young, Margaret Buckner *civic worker, author*

ATHLETICS

UNITED STATES

ALABAMA

Bessemer
Allison, Robert Arthur *retired professional stock car driver*

Birmingham
Starr, Bart (Bryan Bartlett Starr) *former professional football coach, former professional football player*

Talladega
Adams, James Wilson *physical education educator*

Tuscaloosa
Stallings, Gene Clifton *professional, university athletic coach*

ALASKA

Wasilla
Butcher, Susan Howlet *dog kennel owner, sled dog racer*

ARIZONA

Mesa
Unser, Bobby (Robert William Unser) *professional auto racer, television commentator*

Phoenix
Barkley, Charles Wade *professional basketball player*
Camarillo, Richard Jon *professional football player*
Colangelo, Jerry John *professional basketball team executive*

Fitzsimmons, (Lowell) Cotton *professional basketball executive, former coach*
†Johnson, Kevin *professional basketball player*
Majerle, Daniel Lewis *professional basketball player, olympic athlete*
Manning, Danny (Daniel Ricardo Manning) *professional basketball player*
Van Arsdale, Dick *professional basketball team executive*
Westphal, Paul *professional basketball coach*

Tempe
Bidwill, William V. *professional football executive*
Clark, Gary C. *football player*
Joyner, Seth *professional football player*
Ryan, James (Buddy Ryan) *professional football coach*
Simmons, Clyde *professional football player*
Wilson, Lawrence Frank (Larry Wilson) *professional football team executive*

Tucson
Olson, Lute *university athletic coach*

ARKANSAS

Conway
Titlow, Larry Wayne *physical education and kinesiology educator*

Fayetteville
Richardson, Nolan *university athletic coach*

CALIFORNIA

Anaheim
Frontiere, Georgia *professional football team executive*
Herzog, Whitey (Dorrel Norman Elvert Herzog) *professional baseball team executive*
Jackson, Bo (Vincent Edward Jackson) *professional baseball, former football player*
Knox, Chuck (Charles Robert Knox) *professional football coach*
†Lachemann, Marcel *professional baseball manager*
Langston, Mark *professional baseball player*
Stark, Milton Dale *sports association executive*

Beverly Hills
Fleming, Peggy Gale *professional ice skater*
Shoemaker, Bill (William Lee Shoemaker) *retired jockey*

Coronado
Axelson, Joseph Allen *professional athletics executive*

Danville
Behring, Kenneth E. *professional sports team owner*

El Segundo
Ball, Jerry Lee *professional football player*
Brown, Timothy Donell *professional football player*
Davis, Allen *professional football team executive*
Gossett, Jeffrey Alan *professional football player*
Herrera, John *professional football team executive*
Hostetler, Jeff W. *professional football player*
Ismail, Raghib (Rocket Ismail) *professional football player*
Jaeger, Jeff Todd *professional football player*
Mosebar, Donald Howard *professional football player*
Shell, Art *professional football team coach*
Townsend, Greg *professional football player*
Wisniewski, Stephen Adam *professional football player*

Fullerton
Garrido, Augie *university athletic coach*

Garden Grove
Banks, Ernest (Ernie Banks) *business executive, former professional baseball player*

Hayward
Morgan, Joe Leonard *former professional baseball player, investment company executive*

Huntington Beach
†Ho, Derek *professional surfer*

Inglewood
Abdul-Jabbar, Kareem (Lewis Ferdinand Alcindor) *former professional basketball player*
Beverley, Nick *hockey team executive*
Gretzky, Wayne *professional hockey player*
Johnson, Earvin (Magic Johnson) *professional sports team executive, former professional basketball coach*
Kurri, Jari *professional hockey player*
McNall, Bruce *professional sports executive, numismatist*
Melrose, Barry James *professional hockey team coach*
Mlakar, Roy A. *professional hockey team executive*
Robitaille, Luc *professional hockey player*
Sharman, William *professional basketball team executive*
Vachon, Rogatien Rosaire (Rogie Vachon) *professional hockey team executive*
West, Jerry Alan *professional basketball team executive*
Worthy, James *professional basketball player*

Long Beach
Brisco, Valerie *track and field athlete*

Los Angeles
Baylor, Elgin Gay *professional basketball team executive*
Chamberlain, Wilton Norman *former professional basketball player*
De La Hoya, Oscar *Olympic athlete, boxer*
Dismukes, Valena Grace Broussard *physical education educator*
†Fitch, William C. *professional basketball coach*
Frazier, Joe *retired professional boxer, performer*
Harrick, Jim *university athletic coach*

Hershiser, Orel Leonard, IV *professional baseball player*
Karros, Eric Peter *professional baseball player*
Lasorda, Thomas Charles (Tommy Lasorda) *professional baseball team manager*
Levy, Louis *chess master*
O'Malley, Peter *professional baseball club executive*
Piazza, Michael Joseph *professional baseball player*
Raveling, George *university athletic coach*
Rothenberg, Alan I. *professional sports association executive, lawyer*
Sterling, Donald T. *professional basketball team executive*
Watts, Quincy *track and field athlete*
†Weiss, Robert William (Bob) *professional basketball coach*

Malibu
Louganis, Greg E. *former Olympic athlete, actor*

Mentone
Stockton, David Knapp *professional golfer*

Napa
Miller, John Laurence *professional golfer*

Oak Park
Caldwell, Stratton Franklin *kinesiologist*

Oakland
Alderson, Richard Lynn *professional baseball team executive*
Dolich, Andrew Bruce *professional baseball team executive*
Eckersley, Dennis Lee *professional baseball player*
Finnane, Daniel F. *professional basketball team executive*
Haas, Walter J. *professional baseball team executive*
Hardaway, Tim (Timothy Duane Hardaway) *basketball player*
Henderson, Rickey Henley *professional baseball player*
†Lanier, Bob *professional sports team executive, former basketball player*
La Russa, Tony, Jr. (Anthony La Russa, Jr.) *professional baseball manager*
McGwire, Mark *professional baseball player*
Mullin, Chris(topher) Paul *professional basketball player*
Nelson, Donald Arvid (Nellie Nelson) *professional basketball coach*
Pierce, Ricky Charles *professional basketball player*
Sierra, Ruben Angel *professional baseball player*

Palm Springs
Jumonville, Felix Joseph, Jr. *physical education educator, realtor*

Rancho Santa Fe
Stadler, Craig Robert *professional golfer*

Rancho Santa Margarita
Griffith Joyner, Florence DeLorez *track and field athlete*

Sacramento
Reynolds, Jerry Owen *professional basketball executive*
Russell, Bill *professional basketball team executive*
St. Jean, Garry *professional basketball coach*
Thomas, Jim *professional basketball team executive*

San Bernardino
Weiny, George Azem *physical education educator, consultant*

San Diego
Benes, Andrew Charles *professional baseball player*
Freeman, Dick *professional baseball team executive*
Gwynn, Anthony Keith (Tony Gwynn) *professional baseball player*
Riggleman, James David *professional baseball team manager*
†Seau, Junior (Jr. Tiana Seau) *professional football player*
Spanos, Alexander Gus *professional football team executive*
White, Reggie (Reginald Howard White) *professional football player*

San Francisco
Baker, Dusty (Johnnie B. Baker, Jr.) *professional baseball team manager*
Beck, Rodney Roy *professional baseball player*
Bonds, Barry Lamar *professional baseball player*
Burkett, John David *professional baseball player*
Magowan, Peter Alden *professional baseball team executive, grocery chain executive*
Mays, Willie Howard, Jr. *former professional baseball player*
Mc Covey, Willie Lee *former professional baseball player*
McGee, Willie *professional baseball player*
Strawberry, Darryl *professional baseball player*
Swift, William Charles *professional baseball player, olympic athlete*
Thompson, Robert Randall (Robby Thompson) *professional baseball player*
Williams, Matt (Matthew Derrick Williams) *baseball player*

San Jose
Savage, Arthur L. *professional hockey team executive*

Santa Clara
Dent, Richard Lamar *professional football player*
†Hanks, Merton Edward *professional football player*
McDonald, Tim *professional football player*
McIntyre, Guy Maurice *professional football player*
Oates, Bart Steven *professional football player*
Rice, Jerry Lee *professional football player*
Seifert, George *professional football coach*
Young, Steven *professional football player*

Sausalito
Casals, Rosemary *professional tennis player*

Sherman Oaks
†Dodd, Mike (M.D.) *volleyball player*
†Dodd, Patty Drozco *volleyball player*

Hamilton, Scott Scovell *professional figure skater, former Olympic athlete*
†Hovland, Tim (The Hov) *volleyball player*
†Rock, Angela *volleyball player*
†Smith, Sinjin *volleyball player*
†Steffes, Kent *volleyball player*
†Stoklos, Randy (Stokey) *volleyball player*
†Timmons, Steve (Red) *volleyball player*

Spring Valley
†Runge, Paul Edward *baseball umpire, realtor*

Stanford
Van Derveer, Tara *university athletic coach*
Walsh, William *football coach*

Walnut
Ashford, Evelyn *track and field athlete*

Walnut Creek
Hallock, C. Wiles, Jr. *athletic official*

COLORADO

Aspen
Sullivan, Danny *professional race car driver*

Colorado Springs
†Armstrong, Lance *professional cyclist*
Austin, Timothy *Olympic athlete, boxer*
Barrowman, Mike *Olympic athlete, swimmer*
Barton, Greg *Olympic athlete, kayak racer*
Bates, Michael *Olympic athlete, track and field*
Berkoff, David *Olympic athlete, swimmer*
Biondi, Matt *Olympic athlete, swimmer*
Burgess, Greg *Olympic athlete, swimming*
Byrd, Chris *Olympic athlete, boxer*
Carmichael, Nelson *skier*
Conley, Mike *track and field athlete*
Dees, Tony *Olympic athlete, track and field*
Dello Joio, Norman *Olympic athlete, equestrian*
Devers, Gail *track and field athlete*
Diebel, Nelson *Olympic athlete, swimmer*
Dimas, Trent *Olympic athlete, gymnast*
Doehrin, James *Olympic athlete, track and field*
Eldredge, Todd *figure skater*
Essick, Raymond Brooke, III *amateur sports administrator*
Foth, Bob *Olympic athlete, riflery*
Gray, Johnny *Olympic athlete, track and field*
Greene, Joe *Olympic athlete, track and field*
Groebli, Werner Fritz (Mr. Frick) *professional ice skater, realtor*
Hartwell, Erin *Olympic athlete, cycling*
Jacobi, Joe *Olympic athlete, canoeist*
Jager, Tom *Olympic athlete, swimmer*
Johnson, Dave *Olympic athlete, track and field*
†Kerrigan, Nancy *professional figure skater, former Olympic athlete*
†Lace, Jerry E. *executive*
Lenzi, Mark *Olympic athlete, springboard diver*
Lewis, Steve *Olympic athlete, track and field*
Marsh, Michael *track and field athlete*
†McIntyre, Liz *Olympic athlete*
Mitchell, Dennis *Olympic athlete, track and field*
Morales, Pablo *Olympic athlete, swimmer*
Morris, Jason *Olympic athlete*
Moses, Edwin *track and field athlete*
Murray, Ty (The Kid) *professional rodeo cowboy*
†Peterson, Amy *Olympic athlete*
Pierce, Jack *Olympic athlete, track and field*
Rouse, Jeff *Olympic athlete, swimmer*
Simpkins, Charles *Olympic athlete, track and field*
Stewart, Melvin *Olympic athlete, swimmer*
Strausbaugh, Scott David *Olympic athlete, canoeist*
†Street, Picabo *Olympic athlete*
Stulce, Mike *Olympic athlete, track and field*
Turner, Cathy *Olympic athlete*
Yamaguchi, Kristi Tsuya *ice skater*
Young, Kevin *track and field athlete*

Denver
Baylor, Don Edward *professional baseball manager*
Bickerstaff, Bernard Tyrone, Sr. *professional basketball team executive*
Galarraga, Andres Jose *professional baseball player*
Gebhard, Bob *professional baseball team executive*
Issel, Daniel Paul *professional basketball coach*
Mutombo, DiKembe *professional basketball player*

Englewood
Atwater, Stephen Dennis *professional football player*
Beake, John *professional football team executive*
†Craw, Nicholas Wesson *motor sports association executive*
Elway, John Albert *professional football player*
Phillips, Wade *professional football team coach*
†Sharpe, Shannon *professional football player*

Littleton
Kearney, Joseph Laurence *athletic conference administrator*

CONNECTICUT

Greenwich
Gaston, Don F. *professional basketball executive*

Hartford
Burke, Brian *hockey team executive*
Francis, Emile Percy *professional hockey team executive*
Gordon, Richard H. *professional hockey team executive*
Holmgren, Paul *professional hockey coach*

New London
Pinhey, Frances Louise *physical education educator*

DISTRICT OF COLUMBIA

Washington
Blair, Bonnie *professional speedskater, former Olympic athlete*
Casserly, Charley *professional football team executive*
Gibbs, Joe Jackson *former professional football coach, professional sports team executive*

Green, Darrell *professional football player*
Jordan, Michael Jeffery *baseball player, retired professional basketball player*
Lachey, James Michael *professional football player*
Lohmiller, John M. (Chip Lohmiller) *professional football player*
Thompson, John *college basketball coach*
†Turner, Norv *professional football coach*
Upshaw, Gene *sports association executive*

FLORIDA

Boca Raton
Evert, Christine Marie (Chris Evert) *retired professional tennis player*

Coral Gables
Erickson, Dennis *university football coach*

Davie
Shula, Don Francis *professional football coach*

Daytona Beach
Alcott, Amy Strum *professional golfer*
Earnhardt, (Ralph) Dale *professional race car driver*
Inkster, Juli *professional golfer*
King, Betsy *professional golfer*
Mallon, Meg *professional golfer*
†Marlin, Sterling *professional race car driver*
Mochrie, Dottie *professional golfer*
Petty, Kyle *professional stock car driver*
†Reeves, Donna Andrews *golfer*
Sheehan, Patty *professional golfer*
Whitworth, Kathrynne Ann *professional golfer*
Yarborough, William Caleb *former professional stock car race driver*

Fort Lauderdale
Barger, Carl *professional sports team executive*
Fitzpatrick, Mark *professional hockey player*
Holtzman, Gary Yale *recreational facility executive*
Murray, Bryan Clarence *professional sports team executive*
†Torrey, William Arthur *professional hockey team executive*
Vanbiesbrouck, John *professional hockey player*

Fort Myers
Peete, Calvin *professional golfer*

Gainesville
Liquori, Martin William, Jr. *athlete, business executive, television commentator*
Lopez, Andy *university athletic coach*
Singer, Robert Norman *motor behavior educator*
Spurrier, Steve *university athletic coach*

Hobe Sound
Norman, Greg *professional golfer*

Hollywood
Di Maggio, Joseph Paul *former professional baseball player*

Hollywood Hills
King, Alma Jean *former health and physical education educator*

Miami
†Carr, Chuck (Charles Lee Glenn Carr, Jr.) *baseball player*
Harvey, Bryan Stanley *professional baseball player*
Jones, Eddie J. *professional football team executive*
Lachemann, Rene George *professional sports manager*
Robbie, Timothy John *professional football team executive*
Santiago, Benito Rivera *professional baseball player*
Sheffield, Gary Antonian *professional baseball player*
†Sims, Keith *professional football player*
†Smith, Steven Delano *professional basketball player*
Webb, Richmond Jewel *professional football player*

Miami Beach
Cunningham, Billy (William John Cunningham) *professional basketball team executive, television sportscaster*
Schaffel, Lewis *professional basketball team executive*

Naples
Sullivan, Haywood Cooper *professional baseball team executive*

North Palm Beach
Nicklaus, Jack William *professional golfer*

Ocoee
Rose, Peter Edward *former professional baseball player and manager*

Opa Locka
Greene, Joe (Charles Edward Greene) *former professional football player*
Jackson, Keith Jerome *football player*
Kosar, Bernie, Jr. *professional football player*
Marino, Daniel Constantine, Jr. *professional football player*

Orlando
Hill, Brian *professional basketball team coach*
O'Neal, Shaquille Rashaun *professional basketball player*
Stephenson, Jan Lynn *professional golfer*

Ormond Beach
Wendelstedt, Harry Hunter, Jr. *umpire*

Palm Beach Gardens
Awtrey, Jim L. *sports association executive*
Calcevecchia, Mark *professional golfer*
Daly, John *professional golfer*
Mize, Larry *professional golfer*
Player, Gary Jim *professional golfer*
Rodriguez, Chi Chi (Juan Rodriguez) *professional golfer*
Sabatini, Gabriela *tennis player*

Panama City
Green, Hubert *professional golfer*

Pompano Beach
Elder, Robert Lee *professional golfer*

Ponte Vedra Beach
Agassi, Andre Kirk *tennis player*
Azinger, Paul *professional golfer*
Chang, Michael *tennis player*
Cook, John *professional golfer*
Couples, Fred *golfer*
Edberg, Stefan *professional tennis player*
Faxon, Brad *professional golfer*
Floyd, Raymond *professional golfer*
Forsman, Dan *professional golfer*
Janzen, Lee *professional golfer*
Kite, Thomas O., Jr. *professional golfer*
Love, Davis, III *professional golfer*
Pavin, Corey *professional golfer*
Price, Nick *professional golfer*
Stewart, (William) Payne (Payne Stewart) *professional golfer*
Wadkins, Lanny *professional golfer*
Zoeller, Fuzzy *professional golfer*

Sarasota
Graham, Otto Everett, Jr. *retired athletic director*

Tallahassee
Bowden, Bobby *university athletic coach*

Tampa
†Crisp, Terry Arthur *professional hockey coach*
Munoz, Michael Anthony *professional football player*
Nakamura, Yoshio *professional sports team executive*
Savard, Denis *professional hockey player*
Wyche, Samuel David *professional football coach*

GEORGIA

Athens
Dooley, Vincent Joseph *college athletics administrator*

Atlanta
Aaron, Hank (Henry L. Aaron) *professional baseball team executive*
†Arani, Ardy A. *professional sports marketing executive, lawyer*
Avery, Steven Thomas *professional baseball player*
Babcock, Peter Heartz *professional sports executive*
Barry, Rick (Richard Francis Dennis Barry, III) *former professional basketball player, broadcaster*
Blauser, Jeffrey Michael *professional baseball player*
Cox, Bobby (Robert Joe) *professional baseball manager*
Gearon, John Michael *professional basketball team executive*
Glavine, Tom (Thomas Michael Glavine) *baseball player*
Justice, David Christopher *baseball player*
Kasten, Stanley Harvey *sports association executive*
Maddux, Greg (Gregory Alan Maddux) *baseball player*
McGriff, Fred (Frederick Stanley McGriff) *baseball player*
Pendleton, Terry Lee *baseball player*
Smith, Peter John *professional baseball player*
Smoltz, John Andrew *professional baseball player*
Willis, Kevin Alvin *professional basketball player*

Suwanee
†Hebert, Bobby Joseph, Jr. *professional football player*
†Jones, June *professional football coach*
Rison, Andre *football player*
Sanders, Deion Luwynn *baseball and football player*
†Sanders, Ricky Wayne *professional football player*
†Shelley, Elbert Vernell *professional football player*
Smith, Taylor *professional football team executive*

HAWAII

Ewa Beach
Williamson, J(ohn) Craig *professional golfer*

ILLINOIS

Belleville
Connors, Jimmy (James Scott Connors) *professional tennis player*

Centralia
Wargo, Tom *professional golfer*

Chicago
Belfour, Ed *professional hockey player*
Bell, George Antonio *professional baseball player*
Carrier, Mark Anthony *professional football player*
Chelios, Christos K *professional hockey player*
Einhorn, Edward Martin (Eddie Einhorn) *professional baseball team executive*
Fisk, Carlton Ernest *retired professional baseball player*
Grace, Mark Eugene *professional baseball player*
Guillen, Ozzie (Oswaldo Jose Barrios Guillen) *baseball player*
Himes, Laurence Austin *professional baseball executive*
Ivan, Thomas Nathaniel *professional hockey team executive*
Jackson, Philip Douglas *professional basketball coach*
King, Billie Jean Moffitt *professional tennis player*
Krause, Jerry (Jerome Richard Krause) *professional basketball team executive*
Lamont, Gene *professional baseball team manager*
McCaskey, Edward W. *professional football team executive*
McDowell, Jack Burns *professional baseball player*
Meyer, Raymond Joseph *former college basketball coach*
Myers, Randall Kirk *professional baseball player*
Pippen, Scottie *professional basketball player*
Pizer, Howard Charles *professional baseball team executive, lawyer*
Raines, Tim *professional baseball player*
Reinsdorf, Jerry Michael *professional baseball team executive, real estate executive, lawyer*
Roenick, Jeremy *professional hockey player*
Sutter, Darryl *professional hockey coach*
Thomas, Frank Edward *baseball player*
†Trebelhorn, Thomas Lynn *professional baseball team manager*
Ventura, Robin Mark *professional baseball player*
Williams, Billy Leo *professional baseball coach*
Wirtz, Arthur Michael, Jr. *professional hockey team executive*

Lake Forest
†Jones, Dante Delaneo *professional football player*
McCaskey, Michael B. *professional football team executive*
Singletary, Michael *retired professional football player*
Wannstedt, David Raymond *professional football team coach*
†Woolford, Donnell *professional football player*

Rockford
Lynn, Janet (Janet Lynn Nowicki Salomon) *professional figure skater*

Schaumburg
Payton, Walter (Sweetness) *professional race car driver, former professional football player*

Urbana
Thompson, Margaret M. *physical education educator*

INDIANA

Bloomington
Counsilman, James Edward *physical education educator*
Knight, Bobby *college basketball coach*

Indianapolis
Andretti, John *professional race car driver*
Brown, Lawrence Harvey (Larry Brown) *basketball coach*
Emtman, Steven Charles *professional football player*
Irsay, James Steven *professional football team executive*
Irvine, George *professional basketball coach*
Marchibroda, Ted (Theodore Joseph Marchibroda) *professional football coach*
†Miller, Reginald Wayne *professional basketball player*
Simon, Herbert *professional basketball team executive*
Stark, Rohn Taylor *professional football player*
Walsh, Donnie *sports club executive*

Muncie
Park, Sung Jae *physical education educator*

Notre Dame
Holtz, Louis Leo *college football coach*

Ogden Dunes
Mulvaney, Mary Jean *physical education educator*

South Bend
MacLeod, John *college basketball coach*

Speedway
Unser, Alfred, Jr. *professional race car driver*

Terre Haute
Campbell, Judith May *physical education educator*

IOWA

Iowa City
Balukas, Jean *professional pocket billiard player*
Fry, Hayden *university athletic coach*

KANSAS

Lawrence
Williams, Roy *university athletic coach*

Overland Park
Byrne, Catherine *swimmer*

Shawnee Mission
Byers, Walter *athletic association executive*
Watson, Thomas Sturges *professional golfer*

Westwood
Schultz, Richard Dale *national athletic organizations executive*

KENTUCKY

Lexington
Pitino, Richard *college basketball coach*

Louisville
Crum, Denny Edwin (Denzel Crum) *nonprofessional basketball coach*

LOUISIANA

Baton Rouge
Brown, Dale Duward *basketball coach*

Grambling
Robinson, Eddie Gay *college football coach*

Metairie
Andersen, Morten *football player*
Benson, Tom *professional football executive*
Finks, James Edward *professional football club executive, consultant*
†Jackson, Rickey *professional football player*
Johnson, Vaughan *football player*
Mills, Samuel Davis, Jr. *professional football player*
Mora, James Ernest *professional football coach*
†Roaf, William *professional football player*
†Turnbull, Renaldo *professional football player*

MARYLAND

Baltimore
Baines, Harold Douglass *professional baseball player*
Cruz, Bobby *professional boxer*
Mussina, Michael Cole *professional baseball player*
Oates, Johnny *professional baseball team manager*
Ripken, Calvin Edwin, Jr. (Cal Ripken) *professional baseball player*
Robinson, Frank *former professional baseball manager*
Seaman, Tony *university athletic coach*
Taylor, Meldrick *professional boxer, Olympic athlete*

Bethesda
Leonard, Sugar Ray (Ray Charles Leonard) *professional boxer*

Hyattsville
†Schoenfeld, Jim *professional hockey coach*

Landover
Lynam, Jim *professional basketball coach*
Nash, John N. *professional basketball team executive*
O'Malley, Susan *professional basketball team executive*
Pollin, Abe *professional basketball executive, builder*
Sachs, Jerry *professional basketball team executive*
Unseld, Westley Sissel *former professional basketball coach*

Lutherville Timonium
Shriver, Pamela Howard *professional tennis player*

MASSACHUSETTS

Boston
Auerbach, Red (Arnold Jacob Auerbach) *professional basketball team executive*
Bird, Larry Joe *professional basketball player*
Bourque, Ray *professional hockey player*
Clemens, (William) Roger *professional baseball player*
Cooper, Scott Kendrick *professional baseball player*
Dawson, Andre Fernando *professional baseball player*
Ford, Chris *professional basketball coach*
†Gavitt, Dave *professional sports team executive*
Gorman, James Lou *professional baseball team executive*
Harrington, John Leo *baseball company executive, foundation administrator*
Hobson, Butch *major league baseball team manager*
Iafrate, Al Anthony *professional hockey player*
McHale, Kevin Edward *former professional basketball player*
Neely, Cam *professional hockey player*
Oates, Adam R. *professional hockey player*
Orr, Bobby (Robert Gordon Orr) *former hockey player*
Rodgers, William Henry *professional runner*
Sinden, Harry *professional hockey team executive*
Sutter, Brian *professional hockey coach*
†Vaughn, Maurice Samuel *baseball player*
Viola, Frank John, Jr. *professional baseball player*
Volk, Jan *professional basketball team manager*
Wilkins, (Jacques) Dominique *professional basketball player*
Yastrzemski, Carl Michael *former baseball player, public relations executive*

Bridgewater
Anderson, Marcia Kay *physical education educator*

Cambridge
Parker, Harry Lambert *university rowing coach*

Foxboro
Armstrong, Bruce Charles *professional football player*
Orthwein, James B. *professional football team executive*
Parcells, Bill (Duane Charles Parcells) *professional football coach*
Sullivan, William Hallisey, Jr. *professional football team executive*

Needham
Cowens, David William (Dave Cowens) *former professional basketball player, basketball school executive, insurance executive*

Quincy
Lydon, Mary C. *physical education educator*

Springfield
Kerr, Tim *professional hockey player*

West Springfield
Butterfield, Jack Arlington *hockey league executive*

MICHIGAN

Ann Arbor
Moeller, Gary *university athletic coach*

Auburn Hills
Chaney, Don *professional basketball coach*
Dumars, Joe, III *professional basketball player*
Robertson, Alvin Cyrrale *professional basketball player*
Thomas, Isiah Lord, III *former professional basketball player, basketball executive*

Berrien Springs
Ali, Muhammad (Cassius Marcellus Clay) *former professional boxer*

Detroit
Anderson, Sparky (George Lee Anderson) *professional baseball team manager*
Cheveldae, Tim *professional hockey player*
Coffey, Paul *professional hockey player*
Davis, Eric Keith *professional baseball player*
Devellano, James Charles *professional hockey manager*
Fielder, Cecil Grant *professional baseball player*
Fryman, David Travis *professional baseball player*
Hearns, Thomas *professional boxer*
Ilitch, Marian *professional hockey team executive*
Ilitch, Michael *professional hockey team executive*
Yzerman, Steve *professional hockey player*

Pontiac
Blades, Horatio Benedict (Bennie Blades) *professional football player*
Brown, Lomas, Jr. *professional football player*
Fontes, Wayne *professional football team head coach*
Gray, Mel *professional football player*
Sanders, Barry *football player*
Schmidt, Chuck *professional football team executive*
Spielman, Chris *professional football player*
Swilling, Pat *professional football player*

Traverse City
Howe, Gordon *former professional hockey player, sports association executive*

MINNESOTA

Bloomington
Allen, Mary Louise Hook *physical education educator*

Eden Prairie
Carter, Anthony *football player*
Doleman, Christopher John *professional football player*
Green, Dennis *professional football coach*
Headrick, Roger Lewis *professional sports executive*
Hinton, Christopher Jerrod *professional football player*
Jordan, Steven Russell *professional football player*
McDaniel, Randall Cornell *professional football player*
Moon, Warren *professional football player*
Skoglund, John C. *former professional football team executive*
Thomas, Henry Lee, Jr. *professional football player*

Mankato
†Taylor, Glen *professional sports team executive, printing and graphics company executive*

Minneapolis
Aguilera, Richard Warren (Rick Aguilera) *professional baseball player*
Bell, Jerry *professional sports team executive*
Carlton, Steven Norman *former professional baseball player*
Clarke, Robert Earle (Bobby Clarke) *hockey executive*
Fox, Howard Tall, Jr. *professional baseball team executive*
Kelly, Tom (Jay Thomas Kelly) *major league baseball club manager*
Laettner, Christian Donald *professional basketball player*
LeMond, Gregory James *professional bicycle racer*
Lowe, Sidney *professional basketball coach*
Mack, Shane Lee *professional baseball player, olympic athlete*
MacPhail, Andy *professional baseball team executive*
Nanne, Louis Vincent *professional hockey team executive*
Pohlad, Carl R. *professional baseball team executive, bottling company executive*
Puckett, Kirby *professional baseball player*
Ratner, Harvey *professional basketball team owner*
Stein, Bob *professional basketball team executive*
Winfield, David Mark *professional baseball player*
Wolfenson, Marv *professional basketball team executive*

MISSISSIPPI

Itta Bena
Ware, William Levi *physical education educator, researcher*

MISSOURI

Bridgeton
Joyner-Kersee, Jacqueline *track and field athlete*

Kansas City
Allen, Marcus *professional football player*
Alt, John *football player*
Appier, (Robert) Kevin *professional baseball player*
Brett, George Howard *baseball executive, former professional baseball player*
†Collins, Mark *professional football player*
Cone, David Brian *professional baseball player*
Hunt, Lamar *professional football team executive*
McRae, Hal (Harold Abraham McRae) *major league baseball team manager*
Montana, Joseph C., Jr. *professional football player*
Montgomery, Jeffrey Thomas *professional baseball player*
Peterson, Carl *professional football team executive*
Robinson, Spencer T. (Herk Robinson) *professional baseball team executive*
Schottenheimer, Martin Edward *professional football coach*
Smith, Neil *professional football player*
Steadman, Jack W. *professional football team executive*
Thompson, Bennie *professional football player*

Saint Louis
Caron, Ronald Jacques *professional sports team executive*
Gibson, Robert *broadcaster, former baseball player*
Hull, Brett A. *professional hockey player*
Irwin, Hale S. *professional golfer*
Jefferies, Gregory Scott *professional baseball player*
Maxvill, Dal *professional baseball team executive*
Musial, Stan(ley) (Frank Musial) *baseball executive, hotel and restaurant executive*
Plager, Bob *professional hockey coach*
Quinn, Jack J. *professional hockey team executive*
Schoendienst, Albert Fred (Red Schoendienst) *professional baseball coach, former baseball player*
Smith, Ozzie (Osborne Earl Smith) *professional baseball player*
Tewksbury, Robert Alan *professional baseball player*
Torre, Joseph Paul (Joe Torre) *professional baseball team manager*

NEBRASKA

Lincoln
Osborne, Tom *college football coach*

NEVADA

Las Vegas
Massimino, Roland V. *university basketball coach*

NEW JERSEY

East Orange
Bowe, Riddick Lamont *professional boxer*
Gibson, Althea *professional tennis player, golfer, state official*
Holyfield, Evander *boxer*
†Moorer, Michael *professional boxer*

East Rutherford
Aufzien, Alan L. *professional sports team executive*
†Beard, Butch *professional basketball coach*
†Coleman, Derrick D. *professional basketball player*
Daly, Chuck (Charles Jerome) *former professional basketball coach*
Lamoriello, Louis Anthony *professional hockey team executive*
Lemaire, Jacques *professional hockey coach*
Mann, Bernie *professional basketball team executive*
Mara, Wellington T. *professional football team executive*
Reed, Willis *professional basketball team executive, former head coach*
Reeves, Daniel Edward *professional football coach*
Young, George Bernard, Jr. *professional football team executive*

Far Hills
Fay, David B. *sports association executive*

Jersey City
Bavasi, Peter Joseph *professional baseball team executive*

Milltown
Bradley, Edward William *sports foundation executive*

Princeton
Tierney, Bill *university athletic coach*

Union
Pasvolsky, Richard Lloyd *parks, recreation, and environment educator*

NEW MEXICO

Albuquerque
Unser, Al *professional auto racer*

NEW YORK

Bronx
Abbott, Jim (James Anthony Abbott) *baseball player*
Boggs, Wade Anthony *professional baseball player*
Key, Jimmy (James Edward Key) *professional baseball player*
Lawn, John C. *professional baseball team executive, former federal government official*
Mattingly, Donald Arthur *professional baseball player*
Showalter, Buck (William Nathaniel Showalter, III) *major league baseball team manager*
Smith, Lee Arthur *professional baseball player*
Steinbrenner, George Michael, III *professional baseball team executive, shipbuilding company executive*

Buffalo
Fuhr, Grant *professional hockey player*
Hawerchuk, Dale *professional hockey player*
Lafontaine, Pat *professional hockey player*
Meehan, Gerry *professional hockey team executive*
Muckler, John *professional hockey coach*

Cooperstown
Carew, Rodney Cline *batting coach, former professional baseball player*
Jenkins, Ferguson Arthur, Jr. (Fergie Jenkins) *former baseball player*

Flushing
Bonilla, Bobby (Roberto Martin Antonio Bonilla) *baseball player*
Cashen, J. Frank *professional baseball team executive*
Doubleday, Nelson *professional baseball team executive*
Gooden, Dwight Eugene *professional baseball player*
Green, Dallas (George Dallas Green) *professional baseball team manager*
Johnson, Howard Michael *baseball player*
Saberhagen, Bret *professional baseball player*

Hempstead
†Carroll, Pete *professional football coach*
Coslet, Bruce N. *professional football coach*
Esiason, Boomer (Norman Julius Esiason) *professional football player*
Gutman, Steve *professional football team executive*
†Lewis, Mo *professional football player*
Lott, Ronnie (Ronald Mandel Lott) *professional football player*
†Lowery, Dominic Gerald (Nick) *professional football player*
†Meola, Tony *professional football player, former professional soccer player*
Monk, Art *football player*
Steinberg, Dick *professional football team executive*

Lake Success
Stevens, Gary *professional jockey*

New York
Amonte, Anthony Lewis *professional hockey player*
Arcaro, Eddie (George Edward) *sports broadcasting journalist, former jockey*
Arias, Jimmy *professional tennis player*
Austrian, Neil R. *football league executive*
Brooksbank, Randolph Wood *broadcasting executive*
Brown, Robert William *baseball league executive, physician*
†Campbell, Colin (Soupy) *professional hockey coach*
Capriati, Jennifer Maria *professional tennis player*
Cauthen, Steve *jockey*
Checketts, David Wayne *professional basketball team executive*
†Coleman, Leonard S., Jr. *sports association executive*
Cordero, Angel T., Jr. *jockey*
DeBusschere, David Albert *former professional basketball player and team executive, brokerage firm executive*
Ewing, Patrick Aloysius *professional basketball player*
Fires, Earlie Stancel *jockey*
Frazier, Walt (Clyde Frazier) *former professional basketball player, radio announcer, television anaylst*
Garrison-Jackson, Zina *tennis player*
Gilbert, Bradley *professional tennis player, Olympic athlete*
Gourdine, Simon Peter *professional basketball executive*
†Graves, Adam *professional hockey player*
Jackson, Reginald Martinez *former professional baseball player*
King, Don *boxing promoter*
Krickstein, Aaron *professional tennis player*
Krone, Julie *jockey*
Leetch, Brian *hockey player*
Mayotte, Timothy Spencer *professional tennis player*
†McClelland, Timothy Reid *baseball umpire*
Mc Enroe, John Patrick, Jr. *professional tennis player*
McEnroe, Patrick *professional tennis player*
Messier, Mark *professional hockey player*
Monroe, Vernon Earl, Jr. *former professional basketball player*
†Neilson, Roger *professional hockey coach*
Palmer, James Alvin *baseball commentator*
Pelé, (Edson Arantes do Nascimento) *professional soccer player*
Pincay, Laffit, Jr. *jockey*
Powell, Mike *olympic athlete, track and field*
Reneberg, Richard (Richey Reneberg) *professional tennis player*
†Richter, Michael Thomas *professional hockey player*
Riley, Patrick James *professional basketball coach*
Rostagno, Derrick *professional tennis player*
Rozelle, Pete (Alvin Ray Rozelle) *former commissioner National Football League*
Schramm, Texas E. *football league executive*
Seaver, Tom (George Thomas Seaver) *former professional baseball player*
Spinks, Michael *professional boxer*
Stein, Gilbert *professional hockey executive*
Stern, David Joel *basketball association executive*
Stram, Hank Louis *former professional football coach, television and radio commentator*
Tagliabue, Paul John *national football league commissioner*
Thomas, Debi (Debra J. Thomas) *ice skater*
Velasquez, Jorge Luis, Jr. *jockey*
†Ward, Charlie *professional basketball player*
Washington, MaliVai *professional tennis player*
Weiss, Donald L(ogan) *sports association executive*
White, William Dekova (Bill White) *baseball league executive*
Zahnd, Richard Hugo *professional sports team executive, lawyer*

Orchard Park
Bennett, Cornelius *professional football player*
Hull, Kent *football player*
Kelly, Jim (James Edward Kelly) *professional football player*
Levy, Marvin Daniel *professional football coach*
Reed, Andre Darnell *professional football player*
Smith, Bruce *professional football player*
Talley, Darryl Victor *professional football player*
Tasker, Steven Jay *professional football player*
Thomas, Thurman *professional football player*

Rochester
Crane, Irving Donald *pocket billiards player*

Syracuse
Simmons, Roy, Jr. *university athletic coach*

Uniondale
Bossy, Michael *professional hockey player*
†Henning, Lorne Edward *professional hockey coach*

Utica
Trojan, Penelope Ann *physical education educator*

White Plains
Wheaton, David *professional tennis player*

NORTH CAROLINA

Chapel Hill
Klarmann, Dave *university athletic coach*
Smith, Dean Edwards *university basketball coach*

Charlotte
Bristow, Allan Mercer *professional basketball coach*
Johnson, Larry Demetric *professional basketball player*
†Mourning, Alonzo *professional basketball player*
†Parish, Robert L. *professional basketball player*
Shinn, George *professional basketball executive*
Stolpen, Spencer *professional sports team executive*

Durham
Krzyzewski, Mike *university athletic coach*
Little, Larry Chatmon *head football coach*

Randleman
Petty, Richard *professional race car driver*

OHIO

Akron
Monacelli, Amieto *professional bowler*
Ozio, David *professional bowler*

Berea
Belichick, Bill *professional football coach*
Byner, Earnest Alexander *professional football player*
Modell, Arthur B. *professional football team executive*
Perry, Michael Dean *professional football player*
Rypien, Mark Robert *football player*

Canton
†Dorsett, Anthony Drew (Tony Dorsett) *former professional football player*
Elliott, Peter R. *athletic organization executive*
†Grant, Bud (Harold Peter Grant) *retired professional football coach*
†Johnson, Jimmy *former professional football player*
†Kelly, Leroy *former professional football player*
†Smith, Jackie *former professional football player*

Cincinnati
Bench, Johnny Lee *former professional baseball player*
Brown, Mike *professional sports team executive*
Gant, Ron (Ronald Edwin Gant) *baseball player*
Johnson, Davey (David Allen Johnson) *baseball team manager*
Kelly, Roberto Conrado (Bobby Kelly) *professional baseball player*
Knowlton, Austin E. (Dutch Knowlton) *professional football team executive*
Larkin, Barry Louis *professional baseball player*
Mitchell, Kevin Darrell *baseball player*
Sawyer, John *professional football team executive*
Schott, Marge *professional baseball team executive*
Shula, David D. *professional football team coach*

Cleveland
Adubato, Richard Adam (Richie Adubato) *professional basketball coach*
Alomar, Sandy, Jr. (Santos Velazquez Alomar) *baseball player*
Baerga, Carlos Obed Ortiz *professional baseball player*
Belle, Albert Jojuan *professional baseball player*
Courier, Jim (James Spencer Courier, Jr.) *tennis player*
Fratello, Michael Robert *professional basketball coach*
Hargrove, Mike (Dudley Michael Hargrove) *professional baseball team manager*
Lofton, Kenneth *professional baseball player*
Lopez, Nancy *professional golfer*
Murray, Eddie Clarence *professional baseball player*
Nance, Larry Donnell *professional basketball player*
Navratilova, Martina *professional tennis player*
Rothstein, Ronald *professional basketball coach*
Salazar, Alberto *Olympic professional runner*
Seles, Monica *tennis player*
Strange, Curtis Northrop *professional golfer*

Columbus
Ayers, Randy *university athletic coach*

Fairfield
Robertson, Oscar Palmer *former professional basketball player, chemical company executive*

Oxford
Pont, John *football coach, educator*

Richfield
Daugherty, Brad(ley) (Lee) *professional basketball player*
Embry, Wayne Richard *basketball executive*
Price, (William) Mark *professional basketball player*

Shaker Heights
Eakin, Thomas Capper *sports promotion executive*

Youngstown
DeBartolo, Edward John, Jr. *professional football team owner, real estate developer*

OKLAHOMA

Tulsa
Huber, Fritz Godfrey *physical education educator, excercise physiologist*

OREGON

Eugene
Decker Slaney, Mary Teresa *Olympic athlete*

Portland
Adelman, Rick *professional basketball coach*
†Carlesimo, P. J. (Peter J. Carlesimo) *basketball coach*
Drexler, Clyde *professional basketball player*
Glickman, Harry *professional basketball team executive*
Kolde, Bert *professional basketball team executive*
Porter, Terry *professional basketball player*
Williams, Buck *professional basketball player*

PENNSYLVANIA

Devon
Lindros, Eric Bryan *professional hockey player*

Easton
Holmes, Larry *professional boxer*

Lafayette Hill
Dixon, Fitz Eugene, Jr. *professional baseball team executive*

Philadelphia
Allen, Eric Andre *professional football player*
Brind'Amour, Rod Jean *professional hockey player*
Carter, Frederick James *professional basketball coach*
Cunningham, Randall *professional football player*
Daulton, Darren Arthur *professional baseball player*
†Duncan, Mariano *baseball player*
†Dykstra, Lenny (Leonard Kyle Dkystra) *baseball player*
Erving, Julius Winfield *former professional basketball player, business executive*
Farwell, Russ *professional hockey team executive*
Fregosi, James Louis *professional baseball team manager*
Fuller, William Henry, Jr. *professional football player*
Gamble, Harry T. *professional football team executive*
Giles, William Yale *professional baseball team executive*
Hextall, Ron *professional hockey player*
Hollins, David Michael *professional baseball player*
Katz, Harold *professional basketball team executive*
Kotite, Rich *professional football coach*
Kruk, John Martin *professional baseball player*
Lucas, John Harding, Jr. *professional basketball coach*
Montgomery, David Paul *professional baseball team executive*
Mulholland, Terence John (Terry Mulholland) *professional baseball player*
Murray, Terry (Terence Rodney Murray) *professional hockey team coach*
†Schad, Mike *professional football player*
Schmidt, Michael Jack *former professional baseball player*
Snider, Edward Malcolm *professional hockey club executive*
Snider, Jay T. *professional hockey team executive*
Walker, Herschel *football player*

Pittsburgh
†Anderson, Gary Allan *professional football player*
Bell, Jay Stuart *professional baseball player*
Cooper, Adrian *football player*
Cowher, Bill *professional football coach*
†Johnston, Edward Joseph *professional hockey team executive*
Lemieux, Mario *professional hockey player*
Leyland, James Richard *professional baseball team manager*
Majors, Johnny (John Terrill Majors) *university athletic coach*
Mullen, Joseph Patrick *professional hockey player*
Murphy, Lawrence Thomas *professional hockey player*
Noll, Charles Henry *former professional football coach*
Patrick, Craig *professional hockey team executive*
Rooney, Daniel M. *professional football team executive*
Stargell, Willie (Wilver Dornel Stargell) *professional sports team coach, former baseball player*
Stevens, Kevin Michael *professional hockey player*
Trottier, Bryan John *profession sports team coach, former professional hockey player*
Van Slyke, Andrew James *professional baseball player*
Woodson, Roderick Kevin *professional football player*

University Park
Paterno, Joseph Vincent *college football coach*

Washington
Hays, Lewis W. *writer, amateur baseball executive*

York
Klingaman, Robert LeRoy *golf professional*

Youngstown
Palmer, Arnold Daniel *professional golfer*

RHODE ISLAND

Providence
Gorton, Arlene Elizabeth *physical education educator*

SOUTH CAROLINA

Columbia
†Giese, Warren Kenneth *health and physical education educator, state senator*

Gaffney
Perry, Gaylord Jackson *former professional baseball player*

SOUTH DAKOTA

Vermillion
Richardson, James Alexander *exercise science educator, wellness center director*

TEXAS

Arlington
Brown, (James) Kevin *professional baseball player*
Canseco, Jose *professional baseball player*
Clark, Will (William Nuschler Clark, Jr.) *professional baseball player*
Franco, Julio Cesar *professional baseball player*
Gonzalez, Juan *professional baseball player*
Grieve, Thomas Alan *professional baseball manager*
Kennedy, Kevin Curtis *professional baseball team manager*
Rodriguez, Ivan *professional baseball player*
Rose, Edward W. (Rusty) *professional sports team executive*
Ryan, Nolan *former professional baseball player*
Sampras, Pete *tennis player*
Schieffer, J. Thomas *professional baseball team executive*

Austin
Crenshaw, Ben *professional golfer*
Mackovic, John *college football coach, athletic director*

College Station
Slocum, R.C. *university athletic coach*

Dallas
Carter, Donald *professional basketball team executive*
Foster, William Edwin (Bill Foster) *nonprofessional basketball coach*
Landry, Tom (Thomas Wade Landry) *former professional football coach*
Lites, James *professional hockey team executive*
Mantle, Mickey Charles *former baseball player, marketing consultant*
Modano, Michael *professional hockey player*
Sonju, Norm Arnold *professional sports team manager, executive*
Trevino, Lee Buck *professional golfer*

Fort Worth
Hogan, Ben *golfer, business executive*

Houston
Berra, Yogi (Lawrence Peter Berra) *professional baseball coach*
Childress, Raymond Clay, Jr. *professional football player*
†Collins, Terry *professional baseball manager*
Dishman, Cris Edward *professional football player*
Donie, Scott *Olympic athlete, platform diver*
Drabek, Doug (Douglas Dean Drabek) *baseball player*
Foreman, George *boxer*
Foyt, A(nthony) J(oseph), Jr. *auto racing crew chief, former professional auto racer*
Holovak, Mike *sports association exec*
Jeffires, Haywood Franklin *professional football player*
Kile, Darryl Andrew *professional baseball player*
Lewis, Carl *Olympic track and field athlete*
Marr, David Francis *professional golfer, television announcer, golf course architect, journalist*
Matthews, Bruce Rankin *professional football player*
McClane, Drayton, Jr. *professional baseball team executive*
McMullen, John J. *professional hockey team executive*
Munchak, Michael Anthony *professional football player*
Olajuwon, Hakeem Abdul *professional basketball player*
Pardee, Jack (John Perry Pardee) *professional football coach*
Patterson, Steve *professional hockey team executive*
Smith, Al Frederick *professional football player*
Thorpe, Otis Henry *professional basketball player*
Tomjanovich, Rudolph *professional athletic coach*

Irving
Aikman, Troy *football player*
Haley, Charles Lewis *professional football player*
Irvin, Michael Jerome *professional football player*
Jones, Jerry (Jerral Wayne Jones) *professional football team executive*
Novacek, Jay McKinley *professional football player*
Smith, Emmitt J., III *professional football player*
†Stepnoski, Mark Matthew *professional football player*
†Switzer, Barry *football coach*
†Williams, Erik George *professional football player*

San Angelo
Messbarger, Edward Joseph *physical education educator, university coach*

San Antonio
Bass, Bob *professional basketball team executive*
Elliot, Sean Michael *professional basketball player*
Robinson, David *basketball player*

UTAH

Park City
Mahre, Phil *alpine ski racer, race car driver*
†Moe, Thomas Sven (Tommy Moe) *olympic athlete*
Peterson, Howard George Finnemore *sports executive*

Salt Lake City
Hornacek, Jeffrey John *professional basketball player*
Layden, Francis Patrick (Frank Layden) *professional basketball team executive, former coach*
Malone, Karl *professional basketball player*
Sloan, Jerry (Gerald Eugene Sloan) *professional basketball coach*
Stockton, John Houston *professional basketball player*

Sandy
Schneiter, George Malan *golf professional, development company executive*

VIRGINIA

Arlington
Kiraly, Karch (Charles Frederick Kiraly) *professional volleyball player*
Smith, Stanley Roger *professional tennis player*

Ashburn
Cooke, John Kent *professtional sports management executive*
†Johnson, Tim *professional football player*

Falls Church
Theismann, Joseph Robert *former professional football player, announcer*

Haymarket
Moseley, Mark DeWayne *retired professional football player*

Richmond
Daniel, Beth *professional golfer*

Virginia Beach
Becker, Boris *professional tennis player*

WASHINGTON

Kirkland
Allen, Chuck *football team executive*
Flores, Thomas R. *professional football team executive*
Kennedy, Cortez *professional football player*

Seattle
Ackerley, Barry *professional basketball team executive, communications company executive*
Armstrong, Charles G. *professional baseball executive, lawyer*
Ellis, John W. *professional baseball team executive, utility company executive*
Griffey, Ken, Jr. (George Kenneth Griffey, Jr.) *baseball player*
Johnson, Randall David (Randy Johnson) *professional baseball player*
Karl, George *professional basketball coach*
Kemp, Shawn T. *professional basketball player*
Martinez, Edgar *professional baseball player*
Piniella, Louis Victor *professional baseball team manager*
Whitsitt, Robert James *professional basketball team executive*

Spokane
Moe, Orville Leroy *racetrack executive*

WISCONSIN

Green Bay
†Favre, Brett Lorenzo *professional football player*
Harlan, Robert Ernest *professional football team executive*
Holmgren, Mike *professional football coach*
Parins, Robert James *professional football team executive, judge*
†Sharpe, Sterling *professional football player*

Milwaukee
Dalton, Harry *professional baseball team executive*
Dunleavy, Michael Joseph *professional basketball coach*
Garner, Phil *professional baseball manager*
†Jansen, Daniel Ervin *professional speedskater, marketing professional, former Olympic athlete*
Listach, Pat Alan *professional baseball player*
Selig, Allan H. (Bud Selig) *professional baseball team executive*
Steinmiller, John F. *professional basketball team executive*
Vaughn, Gregory Lamont *professional baseball player*

CANADA

ALBERTA

Calgary
Hay, William Charles *professional hockey team executive*
†King, Dave *professional hockey coach*
King, W. David *professional hockey coach*
Risebrough, Doug *professional hockey team executive*

Canmore
Wood, Sharon *mountaineer*

Edmonton
†Burnett, George *professional hockey coach*
Green, Ted *professional hockey team coach*
Sather, Glen Cameron *professional hockey team executive, coach*

BRITISH COLUMBIA

Vancouver
Bure, Pavel *professional hockey player*
Griffiths, Arthur R. *professional hockey team executive*
Jackson, Stu *professional sports team executive, former university basketball coach*
McLean, Kirk *professional hockey player*
Quinn, Pat (John Brian Patrick Quinn) *professional sports team manager*

MANITOBA

Winnipeg
Housley, Phil F *professional hockey player*
Paddock, John *professional hockey team head coach*
Shenkarow, Barry L. *professional hockey team executive*
Smith, Michael Anthony *professional hockey team manager*

ONTARIO

Gloucester
Browning, Kurt *Figure Skating Champion*

London
Widdrington, Peter Nigel Tinling *professional baseball team executive*
Zeigler, Earle Frederick *physical education-kinesiology educator*

Nepean
Bowness, Rick (Richard Gary Bowness) *professional hockey coach*
Firestone, Bruce M. *professional hockey team executive*

Rexdale
Gregory, James Michael *professional hockey league executive*

Toronto
Alomar, Roberto Velazquez *professional baseball player*
Burns, Pat *professional hockey coach*
Carter, Joseph Chris (Joe Carter) *professional baseball player*
Chalupka, Edward Stephen *professional sports association executive*
Cullen, Barry John *professional hockey player*
Fernandez, Tony (Octavio Antonio Castro Fernandez) *baseball player*
Fletcher, Cliff *professional hockey team executive*
Gartner, Michael Alfred *professional hockey player*
Gaston, Cito *professional baseball manager*
Gillick, Patrick *professional baseball team executive*
†Gilmour, Doug *professional hockey player*
Hentgen, Patrick George *professional baseball player*
Molitor, Paul Leo *professional baseball player*
Olerud, John Garrett *professional baseball player*
†Potvin, Felix *professional hockey player*
Stavro, Steve A. *professional hockey team executive*
Ward, Duane *professional baseball player*
White, Devon Markes *professional baseball player*

QUEBEC

Montreal
Alou, Felipe Rojas *professional baseball manager*
Brochu, Claude Renaud *professional baseball team executive*
Carbonneau, Guy *professional hockey player*
Corey, Ronald *professional hockey team executive*
Damphousse, Vincent *professional hockey player*
Demers, Jacques *professional hockey team coach*
Duquette, Dan *professional baseball team executive*
Fanning, William James *professional baseball team executive, radio and television broadcaster*
Grissom, Marquis Dean *professional baseball player*
O'Neill, Brian Francis *professional hockey executive*
Roy, Patrick *professional hockey player*
Savard, Serge *professional hockey team executive*
Stoneman, William Hambly, III *professional baseball team executive*

Quebec
†Crawford, Marc *professional hockey coach*
Lafleur, Guy *professional hockey player*
Pagé, Pierre *professional hockey executive*

Sainte-Foy
†Lagassé, Pierre Philippe *exercise science educator*

MEXICO

Mexico City
Whitaker, Pernell *professional boxer*

SOUTH AFRICA

Klippoortjie
†Els, Theodore Ernest *professional golfer*

SPAIN

Santander
Ballesteros, Severiano *professional golfer*

ADDRESS UNPUBLISHED

Andretti, Mario (Gabriele) *former professional race car driver*
Andretti, Michael Mario *race car driver*
Anthony, Earl Roderick *professional bowler*
†Beard, Alfred (Butch) *professional sports coach*
Boling, Robert Bruce *physical education educator*
Bowman, Scotty *professional hockey coach*
Bradley, Patricia Ellen *professional golfer*
Campbell, James Arthur *professional baseball team executive*
†Carr, Michael Leon *professional sports team executive, former professional baseball player*
Comaneci, Nadia *gymnast*
†Constantine, Kevin *professional hockey coach*
Corrales, Patrick *coach, former professional baseball manager*
Esposito, Philip Anthony (Phil) *professional sports team executive*
Feller, Robert William Andrew *baseball team public relations executive, retired baseball player*
Gainey, Robert Michael *professional hockey coach, former player*
Geddes, Jane *professional golfer*
Graf, Steffi *professional tennis player*
Gregg, (Alvis) Forrest *professional football coach, former college football coach*
Guthrie, Janet *professional race car driver*
Hamill, Dorothy Stuart *professional ice skater*
Havlicek, John *former professional basketball player*
Hemond, Roland A. *professional baseball team executive*
Hull, Bobby (Robert Marvin Hull) *former professional hockey player*
Irsay, Robert *professional football team executive, construction company executive*
Jankovich, Sam *professional football team executive*
Johnson, Reggie *professional boxer*
Kavalek, Lubomir *chess expert*
Keenan, Mike *professional hockey team coach*
Lindsey, D. Ruth *physical education educator*
Littler, Gene Alec *professional golfer*
Loughery, Kevin Michael *professional basketball coach*
McIlvaine, Joseph Peter *professional baseball team executive*
†Moe, Tommy *professional skier, former Olympic athlete*

Paul, Gabriel (Gabe Paul) *former professional baseball club executive*
Ross, Robert Joseph *head professional football coach*
Rutherford, John Sherman, III (Johnny Rutherford) *professional race car driver*
Schrempf, Detlef *professional basketball player*
Snead, Samuel Jackson *professional golfer*
Waltrip, Darrell Lee *professional stock car driver*
†White, Randy *retired professional football player*
Wilkens, Leonard Randolph, Jr. (Lenny Wilkens) *professional basketball coach*
Williams, Ted (Theodore Samuel Williams) *former baseball player, former manager, consultant*
Wooden, John Robert *former basketball coach*
Woosnam, Ian Harold *professional golfer*
Zimmer, Donald William *former professional baseball manager*

BUSINESS. *See* FINANCE; INDUSTRY.

COMMUNICATIONS. *See* COMMUNICATIONS MEDIA; INDUSTRY: SERVICE.

COMMUNICATIONS MEDIA. *See also* ARTS: LITERARY.

UNITED STATES

ALABAMA

Anniston
Ayers, Harry Brandt *editor, publisher, columnist*

Auburn
Barker, Larry Lee *communications educator*

Birmingham
Bailey, Thomas Edward *newspaper editor, book publisher*
Casey, Ronald Bruce *journalist*
Crichton, Douglas Bentley *editor, writer*
†Finebaum, Paul Alan *sports columnist*
Hanson, Victor Henry, II *newspaper publisher*
†Hanson, Victor Henry, III *publishing executive*
†Hester, Wayne *journalist*
Jackson, Harold *journalist*
†Kemp, Kathryn deVan *newswriter, photographer*
Kennedy, Joe David, Jr. (Joey Kennedy) *editor*
Phillips, James Linford *agricultural affairs reporter, editor*
†Reeves, Garland Phillip *newspaper editor*
Scarritt, Thomas Varnon *newspaper editor*
†Seitz, Karl Raymond *editor*
Stephens, James T. *publishing executive*
Walker, Evelyn *retired educational television executive*

Jacksonville
Merrill, Martha *instructional media educator*

Mobile
Hearin, William Jefferson *newspaper publishing company executive*
†Tatum, Gordon, Jr. *fine arts editor, critic*
Taylor, Thomas Alexander, III *newspaper editor*
†Thomson, H. Bailey *editor*

Montgomery
Amberg, Richard Hiller, Jr. *newspaper executive*
†Brown, William Blake *newspaper editor*
Teague, Larry Gene *editor*

Tuscaloosa
Mac Donald, Malcolm Murdoch *editor, publisher*
Reinhart, Kellee Connely *journalist*

ALASKA

Anchorage
Atwood, Robert Bruce *publisher*
Lindauer, John Howard, II *newspaper publisher*
Pearson, Larry Lester *journalism educator, communication consultant*
Strohmeyer, John *former editor, writer*
Thomas, Lowell, Jr. *author, lecturer, former lieutenant governor Alaska, former state senator*
†Unruh, Leon Dale *newspaper editor*

ARIZONA

Casa Grande
Kramer, Donovan Mershon, Sr. *newspaper publisher*

Chandler
†Stellrecht, Fritz *newspaper publishing executive*

Flagstaff
Hammond, Howard David *retired botanist and editor*
Smyth, Joel Douglas *newspaper executive*

Glendale
Joseph, Gregory Nelson *media critic*

Green Valley
Lasch, Robert *former journalist*
Perry, Roger Lawrence *printing executive*

Phoenix
Benson, Stephen R. *editorial cartoonist*
Bergamo, Ron *broadcasting company executive*
†Caputo, Salvatore *critic*
Cheshire, William Polk *newspaper columnist*
Early, Robert Joseph *magazine editor*
Edens, Gary Denton *broadcasting executive*
Ellison, Cyril Lee *publisher*
Genrich, Mark L. *newspaper editor*
Harelson, Hugh *magazine publisher*
Kolbe, John William *newspaper columnist*
†Leach, John Franklin *newspaper editor, journalism educator*
Might, Thomas Owen *newspaper company executive*
Moyer, Alan Dean *retired newspaper editor*
Oppedahl, John Fredrick *newspaper editor*
Schatt, Paul *newspaper editor*
Steckler, Phyllis Betty *publishing company executive*
Weil, Louis Arthur, III *newspaper publishing executive*

Scottsdale
Fox, Kenneth L. *retired newspaper editor, writer*
Gorsuch, John Wilbert *publisher*
Smyth, Bernard John *retired newspaper editor*
Walsh, Mason *retired newspaperman*

Sedona
Chicorel, Marietta Eva *publisher*
Sasmor, James Cecil *publisher representative, educator*

Sun City West
Edwards, F(loyd) Kenneth *journalist, educator, management consultant, marketing executive*

Tempe
Frischknecht, Lee Conrad *retired broadcasting executive*
Richards, Gale Lee *communications educator*
Sabine, Gordon Arthur *educator, writer*

Tucson
Hatfield, Charles Donald *newspaper executive*
Hutchinson, Charles Smith, Jr. *book publisher*
Neal, James Madison, Jr. *editor*
Roos, Nestor Robert *consultant*
Weber, Samuel *editor*

ARKANSAS

Dermott
Kinney, Abbott Ford *radio broadcasting executive*

Eureka Springs
Sackett, Ross DeForest *publisher*

Little Rock
Friedlander, Edward Jay *journalism educator*
Greenberg, Paul *newspaperman*
†Harrison, Eric E. *journalist, entertainer*
†Lutgen, Robert R. *newspaper editor*
Portis, Charles McColl *reporter, writer*
Simmons, Bill *newsman*
Starr, John Robert *retired newspaper editor, political columnist*
†Wassell, Irene Martin *food editor*

Mountain Home
Anderson, Kenneth Norman *retired magazine editor, author*

CALIFORNIA

Agoura Hills
Chagall, David *journalist, author*
Teresi, Joseph *publishing executive*

Alameda
Klein, Marc S. *editor, publishing executive*

Alhambra
Duke, Donald Norman *publisher*

Alpine
Greenberg, Byron Stanley *newspaper and business executive, consultant*

Avila Beach
Kamm, Herbert *journalist*

Belmont
Lake, David S. *publisher, lawyer*

Belvedere Tiburon
Kramer, Lawrence Stephen *journalist*
Moffitt, Phillip William *magazine editor*

Berkeley
Bagdikian, Ben Haig *journalist, emeritus university educator*
Browne, Walter Shawn *journalist, chess player*
Clark, James Henry *publishing company executive*
Craib, Ralph Grant *reporter*
Drechsel, Edwin Jared *retired magazine editor*
Lesser, Wendy *literary magazine editor, writer, consultant*
Littlejohn, David *journalism educator, writer*
†Weidman, Anna Kathryn *publishing company financial executive*

Beverly Hills
Beck, Marilyn Mohr *columnist*
Buyse, Emile Jules *film company executive*
Chernin, Peter *motion picture company executive*
Cort, Robert W. *film company executive*
Corwin, Stanley Joel *book publisher*
Dore, Bonny Ellen *film and television production company executive*
†Grushow, Sandy *broadcast executive*
Harris, Jordan *record company executive*
Heller, Paul Michael *film company executive, producer*
Jenner, Bruce *sportscaster, former Olympic athlete*
Johnson, Jimmy *sports commentator, former professional football coach*
Kellner, Jamie *broadcasting executive*
Kerkorian, Kirk *motion picture company executive, consultant*
Levy, David *broadcasting executive*
Lewine, Robert F. *broadcasting company executive*
Madden, John *television sports commentator, former professional football coach*
†Mark, John *film company executive*
Menon, Vijaya Bhaskar *recording and entertainment company executive*
Obst, Lynda Rosen *film company executive, producer, screenwriter*
Rush, Herman E. *television executive*
Salhany, Lucille S. *broadcast executive*
Spikings, Barry Peter *film company executive*
Thompson, Tina Lewis Chryar *publisher*
Zanuck, Richard Darryl *motion picture company executive*

Burbank
Arkoff, Samuel Z. *motion picture executive, producer*
Brogliatti, Barbara Spencer *television and motion picture executive*
Daly, Robert Anthony *film executive*
Disney, Roy Edward *broadcasting company executive*
Fisher, Lucy J. *motion picture company executive*
Hoberman, David *motion picture company executive*
Katzenberg, Jeffrey *motion picture studio executive*
Mestres, Ricardo A., III *motion picture company executive*
Moonves, Leslie *television company executive*
Roth, Joe *motion picture company executive*
Salzman, David Elliot *entertainment industry executive*
Semel, Terry *motion picture company executive*
Vajna, Andy *film company executive*
Wolper, David Lloyd *motion picture and television executive*

Burlingame
Mendelson, Lee M. *film company executive, writer, producer, director*

Camarillo
DePatie, David Hudson *motion picture company executive*

Cambria
Blundell, William Edward *journalist, consultant*

Capistrano Beach
Lewis, Jack (Cecil Paul Lewis) *publishing executive, editor*

Carlsbad
Brown, Jack *magazine editor*
Lynn, Fredric Michael *sportscaster, former professional baseball player*
Pawlik, Robert Altenloh *publisher, editor*

Carson
Davidson, Mark *writer, educator*

Chatsworth
Rawitch, Robert Joe *newspaper editor*

Chico
Greb, Gordon Barry *educator, writer*

Corona Del Mar
Crump, Spencer *publisher, business executive*

Costa Mesa
Jensen, Gerald Randolph *editor and graphics designer*

Culver City
Canton, Mark *motion picture company executive*
Martin, Gary O. *film company executive*
Medavoy, Mike *motion picture company executive*
Rosenfelt, Frank Edward *motion picture company executive*
Tinker, Grant A. *broadcasting executive*

Cupertino
Reed, Robert Daniel *publisher*

Del Mar
Kaye, Peter Frederic *newspaper editor*

El Cajon
Fike, Edward Lake *newspaper editor*

El Centro
Lokey, Frank Marion, Jr. *broadcast executive, consultant*

Emeryville
Schwartz, David Marcus *magazine editor-in-chief*
†Winton, Charlie Bradley *publishing executive*

Encino
Karlin, Myron D. *motion picture executive*

Forestville
Benyo, Richard Stephen *magazine editor, writer*

Frazier Park
Nelson, Harry *journalist, medical writer*

Fresno
Kees, Beverly *newspaper editor*
Rehart, Burton Schyler *journalism educator, freelance writer*
Tatarian, Hrach Roger *journalist*
†Wilson, Rhea *newspaper editor*

Half Moon Bay
Bonham, George Wolfgang *magazine editor, writer, foundation executive*

Hollywood
Israel, David *journalist, screenwriter, producer*
Rudin, Scott *film company executive*
Schaefer, Carl George Lewis *writer, public relations and advertising executive*

Huntington Beach
Frye, Judith Eleen Minor *editor*

Irvine
Bartkus, Richard Anthony *magazine publisher*
Lesonsky, Rieva *editor in chief*
Power, F. William *newspaper publisher*
Robinson, Rob *publishing company executive*
Segal, D. Robert *publishing and broadcast company executive*

La Canada Flintridge
Fry, Donald Owen *broadcasting company executive*

La Jolla
Copley, David C. *newspaper publishing company executive*
Copley, Helen Kinney *newspaper publisher*
Jones, Charlie *television sports announcer*
Walker, Harold Osmonde *newspaper and cable television executive*

La Mesa
Douglas, Stewart *publishing executive, rancher*

Lafayette
Alexander, Kenneth Lewis *editorial cartoonist*

Laguna Beach
†Adler, Jeffrey D. *political consultant, public affairs consultant, crisis management expert*

Laguna Hills
James, Sidney Lorraine *television executive*

Lakewood
Fenwick, James H(enry) *editor*

Long Beach
†Christensen, Christina Marie *newspaper columnist*
Hennessy, Thomas Anthony *columnist*
Lobdell, Robert Charles *retired newspaper executive*
†Ruszkiewicz, Carolyn Mae *newspaper editor*
†Zappe, John Paul *city editor, educator*

Los Alamitos
†Ayling, Henry Faithful *editorial director, consultant*

Los Altos
†Miller, Ronald Grant *journalist*

Los Angeles
Ansen, David B. *critic, writer*
Archerd, Army (Armand Archerd) *columnist, television commentator*
Askin, Richard Henry, Jr. *entertainment company executive*
Barham, Patte (Mrs. Harris Peter Boyne) *publisher, author, columnist*
Bart, Peter Benton *newspaper editor, film producer, novelist*
Belnap, David Foster *journalist*
Berman, Arthur Malcolm *newspaper editor*
Bernheimer, Martin *music critic*
Billiter, William Overton, Jr. *journalist*
Boyarsky, Benjamin William *journalist*
Busby, Jheryl *record company executive*
Camron, Roxanne *editor*
Cannon, Louis Simeon *journalist, author*
Cardone, Bonnie Jean *photojournalist*
Cate, Benjamin Wilson Upton *journalist*
Chandler, Otis *publisher*
Charen, Mona *syndicated columnist*
Clarke, Peter *communications and health educator*
Coffey, C. Shelby, III *newspaper editor*
Conrad, Paul Francis *editorial cartoonist*
Cotliar, George J. *newspaper editor*
Crippens, David Lee *broadcast executive*
†Dahlburg, John-Thor Theodore *newspaper correspondent*
Day, Anthony *newspaper correspondent*
Del Olmo, Frank *newspaper editor*
Delugach, Albert Lawrence *journalist*
Dobson, Bridget McColl Hursley *television executive and writer*
Draznin, Jules Nathan *journalism and public relations educator, consultant*
Dunnahoo, Terry (Mrs. Thomas William Dunnahoo) *editor, author*
Dwyre, William Patrick *journalist, public speaker*
Erburu, Robert F. *media and information company executive*
Falk, EuGene L. *publishing executive*
Field, Ted (Frederick Field) *film and record industry executive*
†Fifield, James G. *recording industry executive*
Firstenberg, Jean Picker *film institute executive*
Flanigan, James J(oseph) *journalist*
Foster, Mary Christine *motion picture and television executive*
Friedman, Robert Lee *film company executive*
Garry, William James *magazine editor*
†Garza, Oscar *newspaper editor*
Glass, Herbert *music critic, lecturer, editor*
†Grant, David *broadcasting executive*
Grazer, Brian *film company executive*
†Groves, Martha *newspaper writer*
Hall, Jeffrey Stuart *newspaper executive*
†Harbert, Ted *broadcast executive*
Hart, John Lewis (Johnny Hart) *cartoonist*
Hearst, George Randolph, Jr. *publishing executive, diversified ranching and real estate executive*
†Higby, Lawrence *newspaper publishing executive*
Hinton, Leslie Frank *media executive*
Hogarth, Burne *cartoonist, illustrator*
Horowitz, David Charles *consumer commentator, newspaper columnist*
†Isinger, William R. *newspaper publishing executive*
Jarmon, Lawrence *developmental communications educator*
Jimirro, James P. *broadcasting and telecommunications executive*
Jones, Quincy *producer, composer, arranger, conductor, trumpeter*
Katleman, Harris L. *television executive*
Kingsley, Walter Ingalls *television executive*
Knight, Christopher Allen *art critic*
Ladd, Alan Walbridge, Jr. *motion picture company executive*
Laventhol, David Abram *newspaper editor*
Lipstone, Howard Harold *television executive*
†Lozano, Ignacio Eugenio, Jr. *newspaper editor*
MacLeod, Robert Fredric *editor, publisher*
Maltin, Leonard *television commentator, writer*
Mancuso, Frank G. *entertainment company executive*
†Margulies, Lee *newspaper editor*
Marion, Douglas Welch *magazine editor*
Marsh, Dave Rodney *writer, publisher, editor*

Martinez, Al *journalist, screenwriter*
Maxwell, Donald Stanley *publishing executive*
Michel, Donald Charles *editor*
Miles, Jack (John Russiano) *journalist, book columnist*
Miller, Norman Charles, Jr. *newspaper editor*
Murray, James Patrick *newspaper columnist*
Neufeld, Mace *film company executive*
Nogales, Luis Guerrero *communications company executive*
O'Reilly, Richard Brooks *journalist*
Parks, Michael Christopher *journalist*
†Paulson, David L. *newspaper publishing executive*
Perenchio, Andrew Jerrold *film and television executive*
Perlmutter, Donna *music and dance critic*
Plate, Thomas Gordon *newspaper editor*
Polovets, Alexander *editor, publisher*
Purcell, Patrick B. *motion picture company executive*
Ray, Kelley *production company technical director*
†Rehme, Robert G. *film company executive*
Reich, Kenneth Irvin *journalist*
†Rense, Paige *editor, publishing company executive*
Rich, Alan *music critic, editor, author*
Rosenzweig, David *newspaper editor*
†Rourke, Mary *newspaper editor*
Sagansky, Jeff *broadcast executive*
Saltzman, Joseph *journalist, producer, educator*
Sansweet, Stephen Jay *journalist, author*
Sarnoff, Thomas Warren *television executive*
†Saylor, Mark *newspaper editor*
Saylor, Mark Julian *editor*
†Schlosberg, Richard T., III *newspaper publishing executive*
Schneider, Charles I. *newspaper executive*
Schneider, Wolf *magazine editor, writer*
†Scott, Kelly *newspaper editor*
Scully, Vincent Edward *sports broadcaster*
Shaw, David Lyle *journalist, author*
Shuster, Alvin *journalist, newspaper editor*
Sigband, Norman Bruce *management communication educator*
Sinay, Hershel David *publisher*
Smith, Jack Clifford *journalist, author*
Smith, Lane Jeffrey *automotive journalist, technical consultant*
Spero, Stanley Leonard *broadcast executive*
Stern, Leonard Bernard *television and motion picture production company executive*
Stoddard, Brandon *film and television company executive*
Stolberg, Sheryl Gay *journalist*
†Sweeney, Judith L. *newspaper publishing executive*
†Tanen, Ned Stone *motion picture company executive*
Tartikoff, Brandon *broadcast executive*
Thomas, Robert Joseph *columnist, author*
†Tortorici, Peter Frank *television executive*
Townley, Jon *production company creative director*
Ward, Leslie Allyson *journalist, editor*
Weinstein, Harvey *film company executive*
Weinstein, Robert *film company executive*
†Williams, Phillip L. *newspaper publishing executive*
†Wolinsky, Leo C. *newspaper editor*
Wright, Donald Franklin *newspaper executive*
Yablans, Frank *film company executive, motion picture producer*
†Zacchino, Narda *newspaper editor*

Los Gatos
Meyers, Ann Elizabeth *sports broadcaster*

Marina Del Rey
Doebler, Paul Dickerson *publishing management executive*
Smith, George Drury *publisher, editor, collagist, writer*

Marysville
Hardie, Robert C. *newspaper publishing executive*

Menlo Park
Browne, Millard Child *former newspaper editor*
Litfin, Richard Albert *retired news organization executive*
Marken, William Riley *magazine editor*
Wolaner, Robin Peggy *magazine publisher*

Mill Valley
Leslie, Jacques Robert, Jr. *journalist*

Modesto
LaMont, Sanders Hickey *journalist*
†Potts, Erwin Rea *newspaper executive*

Monterey
Benjamin, David Joel, III *radio broadcasting executive*
Dedini, Eldon Lawrence *cartoonist*
Ketcham, Henry King *cartoonist*
Miller, Susan Heilmann *publishing executive*

Mountain View
Broadbent, Thomas Valentine *publisher*

Napa
Muedeking, George Herbert *editor*

Newbury Park
McCune, David Franklin *publisher*

Newport Beach
Bryant, Thos Lee *magazine editor*
Dean, Paul John *magazine editor*
†Homan, Rich *magazine editor*
†Little, Lawrence Michael *publishing company executive*

North Hollywood
Bishop, Kathryn Elizabeth *film company executive, writer*
Boyle, Barbara Dorman *motion picture company executive*
Hulse, Jerry *journalist*
Loper, James Leaders *broadcasting executive*

Northridge
Devol, Kenneth Stowe *journalism educator*

Novato
Pfeiffer, Phyllis Kramer *newspaper company executive*

Oakland
Clancy, Thomas Gerald *newspaper company executive*
McKinney, Judson Thad *broadcast executive*
†Poole, Monte LaRue *sports columnist, consultant*
Wood, Larry (Mary Laird) *journalist, author, university educator, public relations executive, environmental consultant*

Pacific Grove
†Roberts, William M. *publishing executive*

Palm Desert
Hartman, Ashley Powell *publishing executive, journalist, educator*

Palm Springs
Behrmann, Joan Metzner *newspaper editor*
Browning, Norma Lee (Mrs. Russell Joyner Ogg) *journalist*
Jones, Milton Wakefield *publisher*

Palmdale
Grooms, Larry Willis *newspaper editor*

Palo Alto
Latimer, Douglas Hamilton *publishing executive*

Paradise
Fulton, Len *publisher*

Pasadena
Bergholz, Richard Cady *political writer*
Diehl, Digby Robert *journalist*
Drutchas, Gerrick Gilbert *investigator*
Hessler, Curtis Alan *newspaper publishing company executive*
Spector, Phil *record company executive*
Wood, Nathaniel Fay *editor, writer, public relations consultant*

Paso Robles
Brown, Benjamin Andrew *journalist*

Piedmont
Knight, Jeffrey William *publishing and marketing executive*

Pleasanton
†Cochnar, Robert John *newspaper executive*
†Surrence, Matthew Michael *critic, journalist*
†Wevurski, Peter John *newspaper editor*

Portola Valley
Garsh, Thomas Burton *publisher*

Richmond
Doyle, William Thomas *retired newspaper editor*

Riverside
†Foreman, Thomas Elton *drama critic*
†Garrett, John Cecil *newspaper editor*
Hays, Howard H. (Tim Hays) *editor, publisher*
†Maas, Sally Ann *newspaper editor, journalist*
Mc Laughlin, Leighton Bates, II *journalism educator, former newspaperman*
McQuern, Marcia Alice *newspaper publishing executive*
Opotowsky, Maurice Leon *newspaper editor*
†Scott, Loretta Bernadette *newspaper editor*
Sokolsky, Robert Lawrence *journalist, entertainment writer*

Ross
Godwin, Sara *writer*

Sacramento
Baltake, Joe *film critic*
†Blum, Deborah *reporter*
Bottel, Helen Alfea *columnist, writer*
†Dexter, Peter Whittemore *columnist, writer*
Endicott, William F. *journalist*
†Glackin, William Charles *arts critic, editor*
†Haugen, D. Peter *theatre critic*
Knudson, Thomas Jeffery *journalist*
†Lundstrom, Marjie *newswriter*
McClatchy, James B. *editor, newspaper publisher*
†McGrath, Daniel Bernard *newspaper editor*
Schrag, Peter *editor, writer*
†Shaw, Eleanor Jane *newspaper editor*
Slater, Manning *broadcasting consultant*
†Swatt, Stephen Benton *communications executive, consultant*
Walsh, Denny Jay *reporter*
†Walters, Daniel Raymond *political columnist*
Williams, Arthur Cozad *broadcasting executive*

San Anselmo
Keough, James Gordon *publishing executive, editor*

San Bernardino
Burgess, Mary Alice (Mary Alice Wickizer) *publisher*
Garson, Arnold Hugh *newspaper editor*
†Reginald, Robert *publisher, university library cataloger, researcher*

San Carlos
Barnard, William Calvert *retired news service executive*

San Clemente
Singer, Kurt Deutsch *news commentator, author, publisher*
Stallknecht Roberts, Clois Freda *publisher, publicist*
Wray, Karl *newspaper broker, former newspaper owner and publisher*

San Diego
†Bell, Gene *newspaper publishing executive*
Bennett, Ronald Thomas *photojournalist*
Bolman, Pieter Simon Heinrich *publishing company executive, physicist*
Derrough, Neil E. *television executive*
Freedman, Jonathan Borwick *journalist, author, lecturer*
Hope, Douglas Olerich *newspaper editor*
†Jones, Welton H., Jr. *critic*
Kaufman, Julian Mortimer *broadcasting company executive, consultant*
Klein, Herbert George *newspaper editor*
Kopp, Harriet Green *communication specialist*
Krulak, Victor Harold *newspaper executive*
Mc Kinnon, Clinton D. *editor, former congressman*
Mickelson, Sig *broadcasting executive, educator*
Morgan, Neil *author, newspaper editor, lecturer, columnist*
Pfeffer, Rubin Harry *publishing executive*
Pfeiffer, John William *publisher, management consultant*
†Pincus, Robert Lawrence *art critic, cultural historian*
†Ristine, Jeffrey Alan *reporter*
†Rowe, Peter A. *newspaper columnist*
Salamone, Gary P. (Pike Salamone) *newspaper editor-in-chief, cartoonist*
†Scher, Valerie Jean *music critic*
Simms, Maria Kay *publishing and computer services executive*
Steen, Paul Joseph *retired broadcasting executive*
Warren, Gerald Lee *newspaper editor*
†Winner, Karin *newspaper editor*

San Francisco
Baker, Kenneth *art critic, writer*
Batlin, Robert Alfred *editor*
†Bauer, Michael *newspaper editor*
Beckmann, Jon Michael *publisher*
Benet, Thomas Carr *journalist*
Bonetti, David *art critic*
†Briebart, Jack *newspaper editor*
Caen, Herb *newspaper columnist, author*
Carman, John Elwin *journalist*
†Carroll, Jon *newspaper columnist*
Chapin, Dwight Allan *columnist, writer*
†Curley, John Peter *sports editor*
Dewey, Phelps *publishing executive*
Dickey, Glenn Ernest, Jr. *sports columnist*
†Donnally, Patricia Broderick *newspaper fashion editor*
Duscha, Julius Carl *journalist*
Garchik, Leah Lieberman *journalist*
German, William *newspaper editor*
†Graham, Robert Arlington *newspaper entertainment editor*
Graysmith, Robert *political cartoonist, author*
Hearst, William Randolph, III *newspaper publisher*
Hochschild, Adam *writer, commentator, journalist*
Hoppe, Arthur Watterson *columnist*
Horne, Grant Nelson *corporate communications specialist*
Hoyem, Andrew Lewison *publisher*
Hyde, Stuart Wallace *educator, author*
Jenkins, Bruce *sportswriter*
Kahn, Alice Joyce *columnist*
Kobayashi, Tom Toru *motion picture company executive*
†Lara, Adair *columnist, writer*
Luckow, Lynn D. W. *publishing executive*
†Lufkin, Liz *newspaper editor*
Meyer, Thomas James *editorial cartoonist*
Nachman, Gerald Weil *columnist, critic, author*
Nichols, Robert Edmund *editor, writer, journalist*
O'Flaherty, Terrence *journalist*
Osterhaus, William Eric *television executive*
†Ostler, Scott *newspaper sports columnist*
Perlman, David *science editor, journalist*
Rice, Jonathan C. *educational television executive*
Roberts, Gerald Jeffrey *newspaper editor, journalist*
†Roberts, Jerry *newspaper editor*
†Rosenheim, Daniel Edward *journalist, newspaper editor*
Rubenstein, Steven Paul *newspaper columnist*
Rusher, William Allen *writer, commentator*
Ryan, Joan *sportswriter*
†Saunders, Debra J. *columnist*
Schwarz, Glenn Vernon *editor*
Shulgasser, Barbara *writer*
Sias, John B. *multi-media company executive*
†Sinton, Peter *newspaper editor*
Spander, Art *sportswriter*
Steinberg, Michael *music critic, educator*
Susskind, Teresa Gabriel *publisher*
Thieriot, Richard Tobin *publisher*
Tulsky, Fredric Neal *journalist*
Wilner, Paul Andrew *journalist*
Wilson, Matthew Frederick *newspaper editor*
†Winn, Steven Jay *critic*
Wright, Rosalie Muller *newspaper and magazine editor*

San Jose
Bentel, Dwight *emeritus journalism educator*
Carey, Peter Kevin *reporter*
Ceppos, Jerome Merle *newspaper editor*
Elder, Robert Laurie *newspaper editor*
Frymer, Murry *columnist, theater critic, critic-at-large*
Ingle, Robert D. *newspaper editor*
†Lovell, Glenn Michael *film critic*
†Migielicz, Geralyn *photojournalist*
Ritzheimer, Robert Alan *educational publishing executive*
†Sumrall, Harry *journalist*
Trombley, William Holden *journalist*
†Trounstine, Philip J. *editor, journalist*

San Marcos
Barnes, Howard G. *film company executive, film and video producer*

San Mateo
Carter, Michelle Adair *editor*
Goldstein, Morris *publishing company executive*

San Rafael
Roffman, Howard *motion picture company executive*

Santa Ana
Cheverton, Richard E. *newspaper editor*
Humes, Edward *journalist, writer*
Katz, Tonnie *newspaper editor*
†Stern, Sherry Ann *journalist*

Santa Barbara
Ackerman, Marshall *publishing company executive*
Brantingham, Barney *journalist, writer*
Campbell, William Steen *writer, magazine publisher*
Gallagher, James Wes *journalist*
Gibney, Frank Bray *publisher, editor, writer, foundation executive*
Mitchell, Maurice B. *publishing executive, educator*
Smith, Robert Nathaniel *broadcasting executive, lawyer*
Tapper, Joan Judith *magazine editor*
Taylor, Stuart Symington *editor, publisher*
Wiemann, John Moritz *communications educator, consultant*

Santa Clara
McVay, John Edward *professional football club executive*

Santa Monica
Alpert, Herb *record company executive, musician*
†Baer, Walter S. *executive*
Dreyfuss, John Alan *journalist*
Holzman, D. Keith *record company executive, producer, arts consultant*
Jacobson, Sidney *editor*
Price, Frank *motion picture and television company executive*

Santa Rosa
Person, Evert Bertil *newspaper and radio executive*
Pipal, George Henry *journalist*
Swofford, Robert Lee *newspaper editor, journalist*

Sausalito
Brand, Stewart *editor, writer*

Serl Beach
Caesar, Vance Roy *newspaper executive*

Sierra Madre
Dewey, Donald William *magazine editor and publisher, writer*

Somis
Gius, Julius *retired newspaper editor*

South San Francisco
Alvarez, Robert Smyth *editor, publisher*

Stanford
Abel, Elie *reporter, broadcaster, educator*
Barnes, Grant Alan *book publisher*
Breitrose, Henry S. *communications educator*
Chaffee, Steven Henry *communication educator*
Maharidge, Dale Dimitro *journalist, educator*
Nelson, Lyle Morgan *communications educator*
Risser, James Vaulx, Jr. *journalist, educator*

Stockton
Whittington, Robert Bruce *retired publishing company executive*

Studio City
Self, William Edwin *film company executive*

Tarzana
Lowy, Jay Stanton *music industry executive*
Shaw, Carole *editor, publisher*
Shaw-Cohen, Lori Eve *magazine editor*

Thousand Oaks
Hale, William Bryan, Jr. *newspaper editor*
Kehrer, Daniel M. *publishing executive, author, journalist*
Van Mols, Brian *publishing executive*

Torrance
Adelsman, (Harriette) Jean *newspaper editor*
†Young, Scott *recording tape distributor*

Universal City
Haas, Harold Murray *motion picture company executive*
Horowitz, Zachary I. *entertainment company executive*
Lindheim, Richard David *television company executive*
Masket, Edward Seymour *television executive*
Paul, Charles S. *motion picture and television company executive*
Pollock, Thomas P. *motion picture company executive*
Sheinberg, Sidney Jay *recreation and entertainment company executive*
Teller, Alvin Norman *music industry executive*
Wasserman, Lew R. *film, recording and publishing company executive*
Young, J. Anthony *entertainment company executive*

Van Nuys
Blinder, Martin S. *publishing company executive*
†Fraser, Julia Diane *publishing executive*
Sludikoff, Stanley Robert *publisher, writer*

Venice
†Shapazian, Robert Michael *publishing executive*

Ventura
Kirman, Charles Gary *photojournalist*

Walnut Creek
Haswell, T. Clayton *newspaper editor*
†Haswell, T. Clayton *newspaper editor*
†Lesher, Margaret Lisco *newspaper publishing, songwriter*
Satz, Louis K. *publishing executive*

West Hollywood
Byrne, Edward Blake *broadcasting company executive*
Fein, Irving Ashley *television and motion picture executive*
Friedman, Arthur Meeker *magazine editor, professional motorcycle racer*
Geffen, David *recording company executive, producer*
Kassar, Mario F. *film production company executive*
Sloan, L. Lawrence *publishing executive*
Van Buren, Abigail (Pauline Friedman Phillips) *columnist, author, writer, lecturer*

Whittier
Loughrin, Jay Richardson *mass communications educator, consultant*

Woodland Hills
Auger, David J. *newspaper publisher*
†DeWitt, Barbara Jane *journalist*
Fisher, Gerald Saul *publisher, financial consultant, lawyer*
Gray, Thomas Stephen *newspaper editor*
Neill, William Alexander *magazine editor*
Rapoport, Ronald Jon *journalist*
†Rosenthal, Philip David *columnist*

COLORADO

Boulder
Birkenkamp, Dean Frederick *editor, publishing executive*
Bowers, John Waite *communication educator*
Hill, Harold Eugene *communications educator*
Rienner, Lynne Carol *publisher*

Colorado Springs
Anderson, N. Christian, III *newspaper executive*
†Hall, Brian Howard *publishing executive*
Nolan, Barry Hance *publishing company executive*
Witte, Randall Erwyn *publisher*
Zapel, Arthur L. *book publishing executive*

Crawford
Mosher, Lawrence Forsyth *journalist*

Denver
Barnewall, Gordon Gouverneur *news analyst, educator*
†Bates, James Robert *newspaper editor*
†Bradley, Jeff(rey) M. *arts critic*
Brom, Libor *journalist, educator*
Cubbison, Christopher Allen *editor*
Dobbs, Gregory Allan *journalist*
Drake, Sylvie (Jurras Drake) *theater critic*
†Dubroff, Henry Allen *journalist*
Engdahl, Todd Philip *newspaper editor*
†Giffin, Glenn Orlando, II *music critic, writer, newspaper editor*
†Green, Charles Walter *newspaper editor*
†Hamblin, Kenneth Lorenzo *radio talk show host, columnist*
Hesse, Stephen Max *newspaper executive*
†May, Clifford Daniel *newspaper editor, journalist*
McGowan, Joseph Anthony, Jr. *news executive*
McKibben, Ryan Timothy *newspaper executive*
†Movshovitz, Howard Paul *film critic, educator*
Myers, Harry J., Jr. *publisher*
Omura, James Matsumoto *journalist, editor, publisher*
Otto, Jean Hammond *journalist*
Schneider, Gene W. *cable television company executive, movie theater executive*
Spencer, Frederick Gilman *newspaper editor in chief*
Stephenson, Toni Edwards *publisher, investment management executive*
Udevitz, Norman *publishing executive*
Ulevich, Neal Hirsh *photojournalist*

Durango
Ballantine, Morley Cowles (Mrs. Arthur Atwood Ballantine) *newspaper editor*

Englewood
Beddow, David Pierce *broadcasting and cable executive*
†Strutton, Larry D. *newspaper executive*

Fort Collins
Christiansen, Norman Juhl *retired newspaper publisher*
Sons, Raymond William *journalist*

Georgetown
Stern, Mort(imer) P(hillip) *journalism and communications educator, academic administrator, consultant*

Golden
Baron, Robert Charles *publishing executive*

Lakewood
Hosokawa, William K. *newspaper columnist, author*

Longmont
Davis, Donald Alan *author, news correspondent, lecturer*
†Stewart, William Gene *broadcast executive*

Middletown
MacLam, Helen *editor, periodical*

Pueblo
Rawlings, Robert Hoag *newspaper publisher*

Univ Of Denver
Dance, Francis Esburn Xavier *communication educator*

Winter Park
Johnson, William Potter *newspaper publisher*

CONNECTICUT

Bridgeport
Henderson, Albert *publishing company executive, dairy executive, consultant*
Thomas, Dudley Breckinridge *newspaper pubisher*

Bristol
†Bornstein, Steven M. *broadcast executive*
Simms, Phillip *sports commentator, former professional football player*

Brookfield
Reynolds, Jean Edwards *publishing executive*

Cheshire
Chamberlain, John Rensselaer *columnist*

Chester
Cobb, Hubbard Hanford *magazine editor, writer*

Cornwall Bridge
Galazka, Jacek Michal *publishing company executive*

Cos Cob
Hauptman, Michael *broadcasting company executive*
Senter, William Joseph *publishing company executive*

Danbury
Leish, Kenneth William *publishing company executive*
Lisimachio, Jean Louis *book publishing executive*

Darien
Allen, Joseph Henry *retired publishing company executive*
Becker, Ralph Edward *broadcast executive, consultant*
Brooke, Avery Rogers *publisher, writer*
Kobak, Hope McEldowney *publishing executive*
Post, David Alan *broadcast executive, producer*

East Granby
Hostetter, Amos Barr, Jr. *cable television executive*

Essex
Kenyon, Charles Moir *publishing company executive*

Fairfield
Cox, Richard Joseph *former broadcasting executive*
Limpitlaw, John Donald *retired publishing executive, clergyman*

Greens Farms
Deford, Frank *sportswriter, television and radio commentator, author*
Fiske, Edward Bogardus *newspaper editor, journalist, lecturer*

Greenwich
Bogart, Robert B. *publishing company executive*
Chapman, Gilbert Whipple, Jr. *publishing company executive*
Collins, Richard Lawrence *magazine editor, publisher, author*
Gately, George (Gallagher Gately) *cartoonist*
Hanson, Maurice Francis (Maury Hanson) *retired magazine publisher and editor*
Johnson, Herbert Michael *publisher*
Keogh, James *journalist*
Lurie, Ranan Raymond *political analyst, political cartoonist, artist, lecturer*
Pfeiffer, Jane Cahill *former broadcasting company executive, consultant*
Rukeyser, Louis Richard *economic commentator*
Schutz, Herbert Dietrich *publishing executive*
Shaffer, David H. *publishing company executive*
Shepard, Thomas Rockwell, Jr. *publishing consultant*

Hartford
†Endrst, James Bryan *television critic, columnist*
†Englehart, Robert Wayne, Jr. *cartoonist*
†Golden, Louis Joseph *business news editor*
Harden, Jon Bixby *publishing executive*
†Horgan, Denis Edward *journalist*
King, Richard Hood *newspaper executive*
†Koupal, Raymond *newspaper publishing executive*
Lumsden, Lynne Ann *publishing company executive*
†Noel, Don Obert, Jr. *newspaper columnist*
†Pach, Peter Barnard *newspaper columnist and editor*
†Renner, Gerald Anthony *journalist*
†Roessner, Barbara *journalist*
Schweitzer, N. Tina *photojournalist, television producer, director, writer, international consultant public relations, media relations, government relations*
†Zakarian, John J. *journalist*

Ivoryton
Bendig, William Charles *editor, artist, publisher*

Lakeville
Barnes, Robert Goodwin *publishing consultant*
Estabrook, Robert Harley *journalist*

Madison
Azarian, Martin Vartan *publishing company executive*
Egbert, Emerson Charles *publisher*
Platt, Sherman Phelps, Jr. *publishing consultant*
Purcell, Bradford Moore *publishing company executive*

Middletown
Balay, Robert Elmore *magazine editor, reference librarian*
Cumming, Robert Emil *editor*
D'Oench, Russell Grace, Jr. *consultant*
Hoey, Edwin Anderson *editor, writer*
Marteka, Vincent James, Jr. *magazine editor, writer*

New Canaan
Hanson, Joseph J. *publishing executive*
Thomas, Robert Dean *publisher*

New Haven
†Butler, David J. *newspaper editor*
Hoover, Roland Armitage *publisher, printer*
Leeney, Robert Joseph *newspaper editor*
McClatchy, J. D. *editor, writer, educator*
Rush, William John *newspaper executive*
Ryden, John Graham *publishing executive*

New London
MacCluggage, Reid *newspaper editor, publisher*

Newtown
Cayne, Bernard Stanley *editor*

Niantic
Driskill, Clarence *publishing executive*

North Haven
Thorpe, James, III *publisher*
Walker, Fred Elmer *broadcasting executive*

Norwalk
Bowman, Robert Gibson *publishing company executive*
Hayashida, Ralph Francis *educational publishing company executive*
Partch, Kenneth Paul *editor, consultant*
Rawlins, Christopher John *publishing executive, director*

Old Greenwich
Islan, Gregory deFontaine *cable television executive*
Kenyon, Robert Edwin, Jr. *magazine journalist, magazine consultant, lecturer*

Old Lyme
†Bessie, Simon Michael *publisher*

Old Saybrook
Jensen, Oliver Ormerod *editor, writer*

Ridgefield
Forbes, James Wendell *publishing consultant*

Riverside
Isaacson, Gerald Sidney *publishing company executive*

Salem
Diamond, Sigmund *educator, editor*

Sharon
Gordon, Nicholas *broadcasting executive*

Shelton
Forbes, Richard E. *retired publishing company executive*
McCurdy, Charles Gribbel *publishing company executive*
Wham, William Neil *publisher*

Sherman
Valeriani, Richard Gerard *news broadcaster*

Stamford
Aylesworth, Thomas Gibbons *editor, author*
Bigelow, Eugene Thayer, Jr. *media company executive*
Britt, Glenn Alan *media company executive*
Chiddix, James Alan *broadcast engineering executive*
Conover, Harvey *retired publisher*
Dixon, John Morris *magazine editor*
Frese, Walter Wenzel *publisher*
Johnson, Martin Allen *publisher*
Kaff, Albert Ernest *journalist, author*
Lane, Hana Umlauf *editor*
O'Neill, Robert Edward *business journal editor*
Paul, Thomas A. *book publisher*
Rowe, William John *newspaper publishing executive*
†Sayers, Richard James *newspaper editor*
Tow, Leonard *television executive*
Veronis, Peter *publisher*
Wilensky, Julius M. *publishing company executive*

Trumbull
Doherty, Donna Kathryn *editor*
Ferm, David G. *magazine publisher*
FitzGerald, James W. *publishing executive*
†Galvin, Terry *magazine editor*
Seitz, Nicholas Joseph *magazine editor*
†Tarde, Gerard *magazine editor*

Waterbury
Pape, William James, II *newspaper publisher*

West Cornwall
Klaw, Barbara Van Doren *author, editor*

West Granby
Conland, Stephen *publishing company executive*

West Hartford
Glixon, David M(orris) *editor*

West Haven
Ellis, Lynn Webster *management educator, telecommunications consultant*

Westport
Angle, Richard Warner, Jr. *not-for-profit and publishing executive*
Britt, David Van Buren *educational communications executive*
†Bronson, Carole *publishing executive*
Brooks, Andrée Aelion *journalist, educator, author*
Brooks, Babert Vincent *publisher*
Davis, Joel *publisher*
†Dunton, James Raynor *publisher*
Enos, Randall *cartoonist, illustrator*
Hagelstein, Robert Philip *publisher*
Joseph, Michael Thomas *broadcast consultant*
Knopf, Alfred, Jr. *retired publisher*
Kramer, Sidney B. *publisher, lawyer, literary agent*
McCormack, Donald Paul *newspaper consultant*
McCormack, Patricia Seger *independent press service editor, journalist*
Meckler, Alan Marshall *publisher, author*
Murphy, Thomas John *publishing executive*
Ross, John Michael *editor, magazine publisher*
Sabin, James Thomas *publisher*
Weissman, Robert Evan *publisher, financial information company executive*

Wilton
Cutler, Theodore John *cable company executive*
†Morris, Michael J. *book publishing executive*
Pemberton, Jeffery Kenneth *publisher*

DELAWARE

New Castle
Cansler, Leslie Ervin *retired newspaper editor*

Wilmington
†DeVivo, Sal J. *newspaper executive*
Kusheloff, David Leon *journalist*
Lockman, Norman Alton *newspaper editor, columnist*

DISTRICT OF COLUMBIA

Washington
†Adams, Lorraine *reporter*
Adams, Robert Edward *journalist*
Alexander, Charles Thomas *journalism educator*
Anderson, John Weir *editor*
Andrews, John Frank *editor, author, educator*
†Andrews, Wyatt *news correspondent*
†Anthan, George Peter *news reporter and correspondent*
Anton, Frank A. *publishing executive*
Apple, Raymond Walter, Jr. *journalist*
Arnett, Peter *journalist*
Arnold, Gary Howard *film critic*
Arnovitz, Benton Mayer *editor*
Auerbach, Stuart Charles *journalist*

Aug, Stephen M. *business journalist*
Bailey, Charles Waldo, II *journalist, author*
Bancroft, Elizabeth Abercrombie *publisher, analytic chemist*
†Bandow, Douglas Leighton *editor, columnist, policy consultant*
Barbash, Fred *journalist, author*
†Barnes, Frederic Wood, Jr. *journalist*
Barone, Michael D. *journalist*
Barrett, Laurence Irwin *journalist*
Beach, Walter Eggert *publishing organization executive*
Beale, Betty (Mrs. George K. Graeber) *columnist, writer*
Beecher, William Manuel *government official*
†Begleiter, Ralph J. *correspondent*
Beltz, William Albert *publisher*
Bentley, James Luther *journalist*
Bierbauer, Charles *broadcast executive, cable*
Block, Herbert Lawrence (Herblock) *editorial cartoonist*
Bogle, Robert W. *publishing executive, trade association administrator*
Bradlee, Benjamin Crowninshield *executive editor*
Braestrup, Peter *editor*
Branigin, William Joseph *journalist*
Brazaitis, Thomas Joseph *journalist*
Breathed, Berkeley *cartoonist*
Bredemeier, Kenneth Herbert *journalist*
†Brewster-Walker, Sandra JoAnn *public relations executive, publishing executive, genealogist, historian, consultant*
Brinkley, David *news commentator*
Broder, David Salzer *reporter*
Brown, John Patrick *newspaper executive, financial consultant*
Brown, Richard Laurence *broadcast executive*
Bruno, Harold Robinson, Jr. *journalist*
Buchwald, Art *columnist, writer*
†Bury, Christopher Robert *journalist*
Burzynski, Norman Stephen *editor*
Busch, Richard *magazine editor*
Byrd, Joann Kathleen *newswriter*
Byrne, Carol Susan *newspaper reporter*
Carlson, Richard Warner *diplomat, journalist, federal agency administrator, broadcast executive*
†Carmody, John *newspaper columnist*
Carto, Willis Allison *publishing executive*
Chronister, Gregory Michael *newspaper editor*
†Clift, Eleanor *newspaper correspondent*
Clurman, Michael *newspaper publishing executive*
Cocco, Marie Elizabeth *journalist*
Cohen, Richard Martin *journalist*
Cohn, Victor Edward *journalist*
Coll, Stephen Wilson *journalist*
Compton, Ann Woodruff *news correspondent*
Conroy, Sarah Booth *columnist, novelist, speaker, editor*
Cosgrove, John Patrick *editor*
Cowan, Edward *journalist*
Cowen, Eugene Sherman *broadcasting executive*
Crenshaw, Albert Burford *journalist*
Crewdson, John Mark *journalist, author*
Cromley, Allan Wray *journalist*
Cromley, Raymond Avolon *syndicated columnist*
†Crowley, Candy Alt *news correspondent*
Cutler, Bernard Joseph *editor in chief, writer*
Dancy, John Albert *news correspondent*
Daniel, Leon *journalist, newspaper columnist, editor*
Dash, Leon DeCosta, Jr. *journalist*
Davis, Evelyn Y. *editor, writer, publisher, investor*
Davis, S. Gareth *publishing executive*
Davis, Sid *journalist*
Deane, James Garner *magazine editor, conservationist*
Dearth, Jeffrey L. *magazine publisher*
de Borchgrave, Arnaud *editor, writer, lecturer*
Denlinger, John Kenneth *journalist*
Denton, Laurie R. *newspaper editor*
Dickinson, William Boyd, Jr. *editorial consultant*
Dillin, John Woodward, Jr. *newspaper correspondent*
Dillman, Grant *journalist*
Dirda, Michael *book critic*
†Dixon, Phillip *newspaper editor*
Doan, Michael Frederick *editor*
Donaldson, Samuel Andrew *journalist*
Dorn, James Andrew *editor*
Downie, Leonard, Jr. *newspaper editor, author*
Drew, Elizabeth *television commentator, journalist*
†Dunsmore, Barrie *television news correspondent*
Edsall, Thomas Byrne *reporter*
Edwards, Bob (Robert Alan Edwards) *radio news anchor*
Edwards, Julia Spalding *journalist*
Elfin, Mel *magazine editor*
†Engberg, Eric Jon *news correspondent*
Epstein, Joseph *editor, writer, educator*
Epstein, Kalman Noel *newspaper publishing company executive*
Epstein, Sidney *editor*
Evans, Rowland, Jr. *newspaper columnist*
Feld, Karen Irma *columnist, journalist, public speaker*
Felton, Gordon H. *retired publishing executive*
Ferguson, Thomas H. *newspaper executive*
Fields, Suzanne Bregman *syndicated columnist*
Foote, Timothy Gilson *editor*
†Forgey, Benjamin Franklin *architecture and art critic*
Francis, Samuel Todd *columnist*
Frank, Richard Sanford *magazine editor*
†Franzen, Byron T. (John Franzen) *media specialist*
Furgurson, Ernest Baker, Jr. (Pat Furgurson) *journalist*
†Gannon, James Patrick *newspaper editor*
Gart, Murray Joseph *journalist, newspaper editor*
Geyer, Georgie Anne *syndicated columnist, educator, author, biographer*
Gilliam, Dorothy Butler *columnist*
†Gilmour, Craddock Matthew, Jr. (Sandy Gilmour) *television news correspondent*
Glaser, Vera Romans *journalist*
Glass, Andrew James *newspaper editor*
Glassman, James Kenneth *editor, writer, publishing executive*
Graham, Donald Edward *publisher*
Graham, Fred Patterson *journalist, lawyer*
Graham, Katharine *newspaper executive*
Grapin, Jacqueline G. *journalist*
Graves, William P. E. *editor*
Gray, Ralph *editor, writer*
Greenfield, Meg *journalist*
Greenwood, William Warren *journalist*
Grefé, Richard *public broadcasting executive*
Gregory, Bettina Louise *journalist*
†Griffith, Patricia King *journalist*

Grosvenor, Gilbert Melville *journalist, educator, business executive*
Gruenberg, Mark Jonathan *correspondent*
Gunther, Marc *television writer*
Gwaltney, Corbin *editor, publishing executive*
Hackl, Alphons J. *publisher*
Hadar, Mary Ellen *newspaper editor*
Hager, Robert *journalist*
†Hales, Linda *newspaper editor*
Hallinan, Joseph Thomas *journalist, correspondent*
†Halsey, Linda *newspaper editor*
Hamachek, Ross Frank *media company executive*
†Hamrick, Mark Alan *radio news reporter*
Harden, Blaine Charles *journalist*
Hartman, (Howard) Carl *newspaperman*
Harwood, Richard Lee *journalist, newspaper editor*
Hecht, Marjorie Mazel *editor*
Herbers, Tod Arthur *publisher*
Herman, Andrea Maxine *newspaper editor*
Hersh, Seymour M. *journalist*
Hey, Robert Pierpont *editor association bulletin*
Hillgren, Sonja Dorothy *journalist*
Hinden, Stanley Jay *newspaper editor*
†Hinson, Hal *film critic*
Hoagland, Jimmie Lee *newspaper editor*
†Holliman, John *news broadcaster*
†Horyn, Cathy *newspaper editor*
Hume, Brit (Alexander Britton Hume) *journalist*
Hunt, Albert R. *newspaper executive*
†Ignatius, David *newspaper editor*
Innerst, Preston Eugene *newspaper editor, journalist*
Irvine, Reed John *media critic, corporation executive*
Jankowski, Gene F. *broadcasting executive*
Johnson, Haynes Bonner *journalist, author*
Johnson, Robert Louis *cable television company executive*
Jones, Leonade Diane *newspaper publishing company executive*
Jones, Philip Howard *broadcast journalist*
Kaiser, Robert Greeley *newspaper editor*
Karayn, James, Jr. *broadcasting executive*
Karmin, Monroe William *senior editor*
Kaulkin, Donna Brookman *editor, writer*
Kempley, Rita A. *film critic, editor*
Kempster, Norman Roy *journalist*
Kern, Harry Frederick *editor*
†Kilborn, Peter Thurston *journalist*
Kilian, Michael David *journalist, columnist, writer*
King, Larry (Larry Zeiger) *broadcaster, radio personality*
King, Nina Davis *journalist*
Kinsley, Michael E. *magazine editor*
Kiplinger, Austin Huntington *editor, publisher*
Kiplinger, Knight A. *journalist, publisher*
Kirk, Donald *journalist*
Klass, Philip Julian *technical journalist, electrical engineer*
Knight, Athelia Wilhelmenia *journalist*
Koppel, Ted *broadcast journalist*
Kornheiser, Anthony I. *journalist*
Laessig, Walter Bruce *publishing executive*
Lanouette, William John *writer, public policy analyst*
Lardner, George, Jr. *journalist*
†LeBrecht, Thelma Jane Mossman *reporter*
Leeds, Charles Alan *publishing executive*
Lehrer, James Charles *television journalist*
Lepkowski, Wil (Wilbert Charles Lepkowski) *journalist*
Lescaze, Lee Adrien *editor*
Leubsdorf, Carl Philipp *newspaper executive*
Levey, Robert Frank *newspaper columnist*
Levine, Irving Raskin *news commentator, author, lecturer*
Lewis, Charles Joseph *journalist*
Limpert, John Arthur *editor*
Loker, Elizabeth St. John *newspaper executive*
Lorsung, Thomas Nicholas *director, editor-in-chief*
Lowe, Felix Caleb *publishing executive*
Lubar, Jeffrey Stuart *journalist*
†Lutz, Theodore *newspaper publishing executive*
Mack, Raymond Francis *newspaper executive*
Mac Nelly, Jeffrey Kenneth *cartoonist*
Malarkey, Martin Francis, Jr. *cable television executive*
Malone, Julia Louise *news reporter, White House correspondent*
Mankiewicz, Frank F. *journalist*
Maraniss, David *reporter*
†Marquis, Christopher Holliday *newspaper correspondent*
Martin, John Joseph *journalist*
Mater, Gene P. *communications consultant*
Maxa, Rudolph Joseph, Jr. *journalist*
Maynes, Charles William *editor, former government official*
McAllister, William Howard, III *newspaper reporter, columnist*
Mc Curdy, Patrick Pierre *editor, consultant*
†McDowell, Charles R. *columnist, news analyst*
†Mc Grory, Mary *columnist*
McLellan, Joseph Duncan *critic, journalist*
Means, Marianne *political columnist*
Mears, Walter Robert *journalist*
†Melendy, David Russell *broadcast journalist*
Merrill, Philip *publisher*
†Merry, Robert William *publishing executive*
Meszar, Frank *publishing executive, former army officer*
†Meyer, Lawrence Robert *journalist*
Meyerson, Adam *magazine editor, foundation executive*
Michelson, Edward J. *journalist*
†Miklaszewski, James Alan *television news correspondent*
Mitchell, Andrea *journalist*
Morris, Daniel Kearns *journalist*
Moser, Donald Bruce *magazine editor*
Murphy, Caryle Marie *foreign correspondent*
Murphy, Reg *publishing executive*
†Naylor, Brian *news correspondent*
†Neighmond, Patricia *reporter*
Nelson, John Howard (Jack Howard Nelson) *journalist*
Nelson, Lars-Erik *newspaperman*
Novak, Robert David Sanders *newspaper columnist, television commentator*
Nover, Naomi *journalist, editor, author*
O'Brien, Timothy Andrew *writer, journalist, lawyer*
Oppel, Richard Alfred *newspaper executive*
†Orr, J. Scott *newspaper correspondent*
Parshall, Gerald *journalist*
†Paxson, Richard *newspaper editor*
Peirce, Neal R. *journalist*
Peter, Frances Marchbank *author, editor, research agency administrator, writer, strategic planner*
†Peters, Charles Given, Jr. *editor*
Pettit, William Thomas *broadcasting journalist*
Phlegar, Benjamin Focht *retired magazine editor*
Pincus, Walter Haskell *editor*
Plante, William Madden *news correspondent*
Poteete, Robert Arthur *editor*
†Potter, Deborah Ann *news correspondent, educator*
Povich, Shirley Lewis *columnist, former sports editor*
Powell, Anne Elizabeth *editor*
Prah, Pamela Marie *journalist*
Prina, L(ouis) Edgar *journalist*
Pruden, James Wesley *newspaper editor, columnist*
Putzel, Michael *journalist*
Quinn, Sally *journalist*
Quinn-Judge, Paul Malachy *journalist*
†Rabel, Ed *news correspondent*
Radewagen, Fred *publisher, organization executive*
†Randall, Gene *news correspondent, anchor*
Rankin, Robert Arthur *journalist*
Raspberry, William James *journalist*
Richard, Paul *art critic*
Richman, Phyllis Chasanow *newspaper critic*
Ridgeway, James Fowler *journalist*
†Rivas-Vazquez, Ana Victoria *press secretary*
Roberts, Corinne Boggs (Cokie Roberts) *correspondent, news analyst*
Roberts, Steven Victor *journalist*
Rogers, Warren Joseph, Jr. *journalist*
Rollins, Sherrie Sandy *publishing executive*
Rooney, William Richard *magazine editor*
†Rose, Lloyd *theatre critic*
Rosen, Gerald Robert *editor*
Rosenbloom, Morris Victor *author, publisher, public relations executive, government official*
Rosenfeld, Stephen Samuel *newspaper editor*
†Rosenthal, Andrew *newspaper editor*
Ross, Robinette Davis *publisher*
Ross, Wendy Clucas *newspaper editor, journalist*
Rowan, Carl Thomas *columnist*
Rowen, Hobart *journalist*
Rowson, Richard Cavanagh *publisher*
Ruby, Michael *magazine executive*
†Russert, Timothy J. *broadcast executive*
Safire, William *journalist, author*
Salinger, Pierre Emil George *journalist*
Scali, John Alfred *journalist*
Scheibel, Kenneth Maynard *journalist*
†Schiavone, Louise L. *political correspondent, news analyst*
†Schiff, Margaret Scott *newspaper publishing executive*
Schneider, Keith Hilary *news correspondent, journalist*
Schram, Martin Jay *journalist*
†Schwartz, Amy Elizabeth *editorial writer, columnist*
Seidman, L(ewis) William *television chief commentator*
Semas, Philip Wayne *editor*
†Serafin, Barry D. *television news correspondent*
†Sesno, Frank *television correspondent*
Shales, Thomas William *writer, journalist, television and film critic*
Shanks, Hershel *editor, writer*
Shannon, Donald Hawkins *retired newspaperman*
Sharpe, Rochelle Phyllis *journalist*
Shaw, Bernard *television journalist*
Shaw, Gaylord *newspaper executive*
Sheehan, Neil *reporter, scholarly writer*
Sherman, Charles Edwin *broadcasting executive, educator*
†Shiner, Josette Sheeran *editor*
Shogan, Robert *news correspondent*
†Shribman, David M. *editor*
Sidey, Hugh Swanson *correspondent*
Siegel, Robert Charles *broadcast journalist*
Silver, Brian Quayle *broadcast journalist, educator, musician*
Simon, Roger *newspaper columnist, author*
Simpson, Carole *broadcast journalist*
Skene, G(eorge) Neil *publisher, lawyer*
Sloyan, Patrick Joseph *journalist*
Smith, Dean *communications advisor, arbitrator*
Smith, Jack Prescott *journalist*
Smith, Stephen Grant *journalist*
Smith, Terence Fitzgerald *television news correspondent*
Solomon, George M. *newspaper editor*
Spears, Gregory Luttrell *journalist*
Sperling, Godfrey, Jr. *journalist*
Spoon, Alan Gary *communications and publishing executive*
Stamberg, Susan Levitt *radio broadcaster*
Steele, John Lawrence *journalist*
Stepp, Laura Sessions *journalist*
Stern, Carl Leonard *former news correspondent, federal official*
Stewart, John Daugherty *publishing company executive*
Stone, Marvin Lawrence *journalist, government official*
Sullivan, John Fox *publisher*
Szulc, Tad *journalist, commentator*
Taishoff, Lawrence Bruce *publishing company executive*
†Talbott, Strobe *journalist*
†Terzian, Philip Henry *journalist*
Thomas, Helen A. (Mrs. Douglas B. Cornell) *newspaper bureau executive*
Thompson, Edward Kramer *editor, publisher*
Thompson, Richard C. *magazine executive*
Tolchin, Martin *newspaper reporter, author*
Toledano, Ralph de *columnist, author, photographer*
Tolson, John J. *editor*
Totenberg, Nina *journalist*
Toth, Robert Charles *correspondent, journalist*
Trafford, Abigail *editor, writer, columnist*
Tufty, Harold Guilford *editor, publisher*
Valenti, Jack Joseph *motion picture executive*
Van Bennekom, Pieter *news service executive*
Vaslef, Nicholas P. *broadcasting executive*
Vernon, Weston, III (Wes Vernon) *journalist*
VerStandig, John David *broadcasting executive, investor*
Vise, David Allan *journalist*
Wallach, John Paul *newspaper editor*
Warren, Albert *publishing executive*
Watson, George Henry, Jr. *broadcast executive, journalist*
Weiner, Timothy Emlyn *newspaper journalist*
West, Donald Valentine *editor, journalist*
West, Marvin Leon *sports editor*
White, Robert M., II *newspaper executive, editor, columnist*
Will, George Frederick *editor, political columnist, news commentator*
Wilson, Robert Spencer *magazine editor*
Winter, Thomas Swanson *editor, newspaper executive*
Witcover, Jules Joseph *newspaper columnist, author*
Woodruff, Judy Carline *broadcast journalist*
Woodward, Robert Upshur *newspaper reporter, writer*
†Wooten, James Terrell *journalist*
Yardley, Jonathan *journalist, columnist*
Young, Patrick *editor*
Zelnick, Carl Robert *news correspondent*
Zimmerman, Richard Gayford *journalist*

FLORIDA

Babson Park
Morrison, Kenneth Douglas *newspaper columnist*

Bradenton
McFarland, Richard Macklin *retired journalist*
†White, Dale Andrew *journalist*

Clearwater
Darack, Arthur J. *editor*
†Pinch, John G. *radio executive*

Daytona Beach
Davidson, Herbert M. (Tippen), Jr. *newspaper publisher*
†Davidson, Josephine F. *newspaper editor*
Gardner, Joseph Lawrence *editor, writer*
Mechem, Charles Stanley, Jr. *former broadcasting executive, golf association executive*

Deerfield Beach
Hochberger, Simon *communications educator*

Delray Beach
Cary, James Donald *journalist*
Peoples, Thomas Edward *publisher, executive, writer*
Shannon, Stephen Quinby, Jr. *broadcasting human resources executive*

Dover
Pearson, Walter Donald *editor, columnist*

Dunedin
Geer, James Hamilton *retired broadcasting company executive*

Eustis
Trussell, Charles Tait *columnist*

Fort Lauderdale
†Aleff, Andrea Lee (Andy Aleff) *newspaper editor*
Cryer, Eugene Edward *newspaper editor*
de Leon, Lidia Maria *magazine editor*
Eisner, Will *publishing company executive*
Gilbert, Anne Wieland *journalist*
†Greenberger, Sheldon Lee *newspaper advertising executive*
†Keller, Larry Allan *reporter*
Klein, Bernard *publishing company executive*
Maucker, Earl Robert *newspaper editor*
Parkyn, John William *editor, writer*
Pettijohn, Fred Phillips *retired newspaper executive, consultant*
Randolph, Jennings, Jr. (Jay Randolph) *sportscaster*
†Schulte, Frederick James *newpaper editor*
†Smith, James Edward *newspaper company executive*
†Tenaglia, John Franc *broadcasting executive*

Fort Myers
Barbour, Hugh Revell *publisher*
Barbour, William Rinehart, Jr. *retired book publisher*

Fort Walton Beach
Phillips, Loyal *newspaper executive*

Gainesville
Bedell, George Chester *retired publisher*
Davis, Horance Gibbs, Jr. *retired educator, journalist*
Hollien, Harry Francis *speech and communications scientist, educator*
Kenney, Thomas Frederick *broadcasting executive*

Goldenrod
Carmichael, William Jerome *publishing company executive*

Greenwood
Goode, Stephen Hogue *publishing company executive*

Hollywood
Fell, Frederick Victor *publisher*
Korngold, Alvin Leonard *broadcasting company executive*
McQueen, Scott Robert *broadcasting company executive*

Jacksonville
†Brown, Lloyd Harcourt, Jr. *newspaper editor*
Fredrickson, Arthur Allan *retired publishing company executive*
Hartmann, Frederick William *newspaper editor*
†Hulin-Salkin, Belinda *newspaper editor*
†Kress, Mary Elizabeth *newspaper editor*
Loomis, Henry *former broadcasting company executive, former government official*
Manning, Arthur Brewster *newspaper editor*
Morris, William Shivers, III *newspaper executive*
Vincent, Norman Fuller *broadcasting executive*
Walters, John Sherwood *retired newspaperman*

Jupiter
Anderson, Thomas J. *publisher, rancher, public speaker, syndicated columnist*

Lake Mary
Strang, Stephen Edward *magazine editor, publisher*

Lakeland
Perez, Louis Michael *newspaper editor*

Lantana
Calder, Iain Wilson *publishing company executive*

Marco
Lavin, John Halley *editor, author*

Wheeler, Warren G(age), Jr. *retired publishing executive*

Melbourne
Krieger, Robert Edward *publisher*
Spezzano, Vincent Edward *newspaper publisher*

Melrose
Burt, Alvin Victor, Jr. *journalist*

Miami
†Anger, Paul *newspaper Sports Editor*
Balmaseda, Liz *columnist*
Barry, Dave *columnist, author*
Batten, James Knox *newspaper executive*
†Birger, Larry *newspaper editor, columnist*
Black, Creed Carter *newspaper executive*
†Bubnow, Vic *newspaper publishing executive*
Buchanan, Edna *journalist*
Chapman, Alvah Herman, Jr. *newspaper executive*
†Clifton, Douglas C. *newspaper editor*
Cohen, Alex *retired publisher*
†Dickey, Arden *newspaper publishing executive*
†Dolen, Christine Arnold *theater critic*
†Dubocq, Tom *newspaper reporter*
†Fichtner, Margaria *newspaper editor*
†Fontaine, John C. *newspaper company executive*
Gerber, Seymour *publishing company executive*
†Hampton, Jim *newspaper editor*
Hampton, John Lewis *newspaper editor*
Harless, Byron Brittingham *newspaper executive*
Harris, Douglas Clay *newspaper executive*
Hoyt, Clark Freeland *journalist, newspaper editor*
Kleinberg, Howard J. *newspaper columnist*
Kram, Michael Arnold *magazine publisher*
Lawrence, David, Jr. *newspaper editor, publisher*
Lewis, John Milton *cable television company executive*
Miller, Gene Edward *newspaper reporter and editor*
†Natoli, Joe *newspaper publishing executive*
†Pancake, John *newspaper editor*
†Pitts, Leonard Garvey, Jr. *columnist, writer*
Pope, John Edwin, III *newspaper sports editor*
†Quintana, Mack *newspaper publishing executive*
†Reisinger, Sandra Sue *journalist, lawyer*
†Roberts, Brian L. *cable company executive*
Russell, James Webster, Jr. *newspaper editor, columnist*
Sanchez, Robert Francis *journalist*
Savage, James Francis *editor*
†Seline, Rex *reporter*
Shaklan, Allen Yale *broadcast executive*
Shoemaker, Don (Donald Cleavenger Shoemaker) *columnist*
†Shroder, Tom *newspaper editor*
†Sonsky, Steve *newspaper editor*
†Steinback, Robert Lamont *newspaper columnist*
Suarez, Roberto *newspaper publishing executive*
†Terilli, Samuel A., Jr. *newspaper publishing executive*
†Verdeja, Sam *newspaper publishing executive*
†Weitzel, Peter Andre *editor, newspaper*
Wickstrom, Karl Youngert *publishing company executive*
Williamson, William Paul, Jr. *journalist*

Miami Beach
Filosa, Gary Fairmont Randolph V., II *film company executive, financier*
Meyer, Sylvan Hugh *editor, magazine executive, author*
Michaels, Willard A. *retired broadcasting executive*
Wax, William Edward *photojournalist*

Mount Dora
Goodwin, Harry Eugene *journalist, educator*

Naples
Arthur, William Bolling *retired editor*
Clapp, Roger Howland *retired newspaper executive*
Conant, Colleen Christner *newspaper editor*
Gordon, Martin *publisher, print dealer*
Hobbs, Ranald Purcell *publisher*
Kennedy, Robert Emmet *retired newspaperman*
Mc Combs, G. B. *publishing company executive*
Wodlinger, Mark Louis *broadcast executive*
Wyant, Corbin A. *newspaper publisher*

New Smyrna Beach
Makela, Benjamin R. *editor, research director*

North Fort Myers
Rogliano, Aldo Thomas *publishing executive*

North Palm Beach
Edwards, William James *broadcasting executive*

Orlando
Argirion, Michael *editor*
Aronow, Neil Arthur *publishing company executive*
Berry, Stephen Joseph *reporter*
Bollen, Roger *cartoonist*
†Dunn, William Bruna, III *journalist*
†Guest, Larry Samuel *newspaper columnist*
Haile, L. John, Jr. *journalist, newspaper executive*
Healy, Jane Elizabeth *newspaper editor*
Ivey, James Burnett *political cartoonist*
†Maupin, Elizabeth Thatcher *theater critic*
†Morgan, Richard T. *publishing executive*
†Reese, Charles Edgar *columnist*
Williamson, Thomas Arnold *publishing company executive*
Wolski, Patrick Edward *newspaper executive*

Osprey
Allen, George Howard *publishing management consultant*
Strongin, Theodore *journalist*

Palm Beach
Pryor, Hubert *editor, writer*
Roberts, Margaret Harold *editor, publisher*
Stoneman, Samuel Sidney *cinema company executive*

Palm Beach Gardens
Baker, Jean Mary *cable television executive*

Palm Coast
Franco, Annemarie Woletz *editor*

Pensacola
Bowden, Jesse Earle *newspaper editor, author, cartoonist, journalism educator*

Plant City
Tully, Darrow *newspaper publisher*

Pompano Beach
Roen, Sheldon R. *publisher, psychologist*

Port Charlotte
†Flanders, Jefferson *publishing executive*

Port Saint Lucie
Sommers, Robert Thomas *editor, publisher, author*

Saint Augustine
Nolan, Joseph Thomas *journalism educator, communications consultant*

Saint Petersburg
Barnes, Andrew Earl *newspaper editor*
Belich, John Patrick, Sr. *journalist*
Benbow, Charles Clarence *retired writer, critic*
Foley, Michael Francis *newspaper executive*
Haiman, Robert James *newspaper editor, journalism educator*
†Hull, Anne Victoria *journalist*
Martin, Susan Taylor *newspaper editor*
†O'Hearn, John Howard *publishing company executive*
Patterson, Eugene Corbett *retired editor, publisher*
Pittman, Robert Turner *retired newspaper editor*
Schuck, Marjorie Massey *publisher, editor, consultant*
†Snider, Eric Ross *music critic*
†Tash, Paul C. *editor-in-chief*

Sarasota
Burket, Harriet (Mrs. Francis B. Taussig) *editor*
Estrin, Richard William *newspaper editor*
Grubbs, Elven Judson *retired newspaper publisher*
†Handelman, Jay Harold *theater critic*
Loomis, Wesley Horace, III *former publishing company executive*
MacDonald, Robert Taylor *newspaper executive*
Marino, Eugene Louis *publishing company executive*
McFarlin, Diane H. *newspaper editor*
†North, Marjorie Mary *columnist*
Proffitt, Waldo, Jr. *newspaper editor*
Wilson, Kenneth Jay *writer*

Stuart
Murchake, John *publishing executive*
Shurick, Edward Palmes *television executive, rancher*
Slade, Gerald Jack *publishing company executive*

Tallahassee
Dadisman, Joseph Carrol *newspaper executive*
Heldman, Louis Marc *newspaper editor*
Morgan, Lucy W. *journalist*
†Shaw, Robert D., Jr. *newspaper editor*
Stiff, Robert Martin *newspaper editor*

Tampa
Benjamin, Robert Spiers *foreign correspondent, writer, publicist*
Dunn, Henry Hampton *television commentator, former editor*
Harvill, H. Doyle *newspaper publisher*
†Locker, Raymond Duncan *editor*
Nevins, Albert J. *publisher, editor, author*
Roberts, Edwin Albert, Jr. *newspaper editor, journalist*

Venice
Corrigan, William Thomas *retired broadcast news executive*

Vero Beach
Leonsis, Theodore John *publishing company executive*
Petersmeyer, C(harles) Wrede *retired broadcasting executive, venture capitalist*

West Palm Beach
Fairbanks, Richard Monroe *broadcasting company executive*
Giuffrida, Tom A. *publisher*
O'Hara, Thomas Patrick *managing editor*
†Passy, Charles *arts critic*
Rivers, Marie Bie *broadcasting executive*
Sears, Edward Milner, Jr. *newspaper editor*
Turner, David Reuben *publisher, author*
Wright, Donald Conway *editorial cartoonist*

GEORGIA

Athens
Agee, Warren Kendall *journalism educator*
Feldman, Edmund Burke *art critic*
Fink, Conrad Charles *journalism educator, communications consultant*
Hester, Albert Lee *journalism educator*
Holder, Howard Randolph, Sr. *broadcasting company executive*

Atlanta
†Berry, Dennis *newspaper publishing executive*
Bisher, James Furman *journalist, author*
Bridgewater, Herbert Jeremiah, Jr. *radio host*
Chambers, Anne Cox *newspaper executive*
Cross, Joyce Annette Oscar *newscaster*
†Dollar, Steve *music critic*
Dotson, Robert Charles *news correspondent*
Easterly, David Eugene *newspaper executive*
Eckert, Michael Joseph *cable and broadcast television executive*
Ellis, Elmo Israel *broadcast executive, consultant, newspaper columnist*
†Ezell, Reva Gross *radio station manager, writer*
Gilmer, Harry Wesley *publishing executive, educator*
Harris, Henry Wood *cable television executive*
Harrison, John Raymond *retired newspaper executive, foundation executive*
Hayes, Sarah Hall *magazine editor, educator*
Holzel, David Benjamin *newspaper editor*
†Hulbert, Daniel J. *theater critic, entertainment writer*
Johnson, Wyatt Thomas, Jr. (Tom Johnson) *cable news executive*
Jones, J. Kenley *journalist*
Kennedy, James C. *publishing and media executive*
†Kloer, Philip Baldwin *television critic*
†Korn, Steven W. *broadcasting company executive, corporate lawyer*
Lamkin, William Pierce *editor*
Loory, Stuart Hugh *journalist*
†Martin, Ron *newspaper editor in chief*
Merdek, Andrew Austin *publishing executive, lawyer*
Pantel, Stan Roy *newspaper publishing executive*
†Pucket, Susan *newspaper editor*
Reeves, Alexis Scott *journalist*
Rierson, Robert Leak *broadcasting executive, television writer*
†Ringel, Eleanor *film critic*
Rosenfeld, Arnold Solomon *newspaper editor*
†Salter, Sally *reporter*
†Schrutt, Norman *broadcast company executive*
Schwartz, William A(llen) *broadcasting and cable executive*
†Seabrook, Charles *reporter*
Sibley, Celestine (Mrs. John C. Strong) *columnist, reporter*
Tarver, Jackson Williams *newspaper executive*
Teepen, Thomas Henry *newspaper editor, journalist*
Tharpe, Frazier Eugene *journalist*
Tierney, Michael Stewart *newspaper editor*
Toner, Mike *journalist*
Tucker, Cynthia Anne *journalist*
Turner, Ted (Robert Edward Turner) *television executive*
Van Horn, Lecia Joseph *television newswriter*
†Walter, John W., Jr. *newspaper editor*
Weber, Owen *broadcast executive*
Whitt, Richard Ernest *reporter*
†Yother, Michele *publisher*

Augusta
†Folker, James Edward, Jr. *newspaper editor*

Columbus
Watson, Billy *publishing executive, newspaper*

Decatur
Knight, Walker Leigh *editor, publisher, clergyman*

Gainesville
Duffy, Thomas Edward *publisher*

Macon
†Haynes-Hooks, Ella Mae *journalist*
Savage, Randall Ernest *journalist*
Yancy, Cecil Henton, Jr. *editor*

Marietta
Dunwoody, Kenneth Reed *magazine editor*

Oxford
Sitton, Claude Fox *newspaper editor*

Roswell
Peterson, Donald Robert *magazine editor, vintage automobile consultant*

Savannah
Coffey, Thomas Francis, Jr. *editor*
Tobey, Carl Wadsworth *retired publisher*

Sea Island
Carter, Don Earl *newspaper editor, publisher*

Stone Mountain
Le Roy, L. David *journalist*
Speed, Billie Cheney (Mrs. Thomas S. Speed) *retired editor, journalist*

HAWAII

Honolulu
Chaplin, George *newspaper editor*
Chung, Kea Sung *television broadcasting executive*
Flanagan, John Michael *editor, publisher*
Gialanella, Philip Thomas *newspaper publisher*
Jellinek, Roger *editor*
Keir, Gerald Janes *newspaper editor*
†Krauss, Robert *newspaper columnist, author*
Simonds, John Edward *newspaper editor*
Smyser, Adam Albert *newspaper editor*
Sparks, Robert William *publishing executive*
Twigg-Smith, Thurston *newspaper publisher*

IDAHO

Caldwell
Gipson, Gordon *publishing company executive*

Coeur D Alene
Rolphe, Ben Richard, Jr. *publishing company executive*

Idaho Falls
Harris, Darryl Wayne *publishing executive*

ILLINOIS

Arlington Heights
Baumann, Daniel E. *newspaper executive*
†Lampinen, John A. *newspaper editor*
†Paddock, Robert Young *publisher*
†Paddock, Stuart R., Jr. *publishing executive*
†Ray, Douglas *newspaper editor*
†terHorst, Cheryl Ann *journalist*

Barrington
Bash, Philip Edwin *publishing executive*

Belleville
Berkley, Gary L. *newspaper publisher*

Bloomington
Merwin, Davis Underwood *newspaper executive*
†Wills, Edgar W. (Bill) *newspaper editor*

Burr Ridge
Sund, Jeffrey Owen *publishing company executive*

Carbondale
Hart, James Warren *athletic director, restaurant owner, former professional football player*

Carol Stream
Berkley, James Donald *editor*
Coffman, Roy Walter, III *publishing company executive*
Franzen, Janice Marguerite Gosnell *magazine editor*
Myra, Harold Lawrence *publisher*
Shorney, George Herbert *publishing executive*
Taylor, Kenneth Nathaniel *publishing executive, author*
Yancey, Philip David *editor, author*

Carpentersville
Wilson, Delbert Ray *publisher, author*

Champaign
Foreman, John Richard *journalist*
†McCulloh, Judith Marie *editor*
Meyer, August Christopher, Jr. *broadcasting company executive, lawyer*
Vedder, Byron Charles *newspaper executive*

Chicago
Abrams, Susan Elizabeth *book editor, publisher*
Anderson, Jon Stephen *newswriter*
Artner, Alan Gustav *art critic, journalist*
Balz, Douglas Charles *journalist*
Beck, Joan Wagner *journalist*
Bell, Clark Wayne *business editor, educator*
†Bennett, Beverly *newspaper editor*
Bennett, Lerone, Jr. *magazine editor, author*
Blakely, Robert John *retired journalist, educator*
Boers, Terry John *sportswriter, radio and television personality*
Brickhouse, John B. (Jack Brickhouse) *sports broadcaster*
Brissie, Eugene Field, Jr. *publisher*
Britton, Dennis A. *newspaper editor*
Brotman, Barbara Louise *columnist, writer*
Brumback, Charles Tiedtke *newspaper executive*
Brummel, Mark Joseph *magazine editor*
Callaway, Karen A(lice) *journalist*
Camper, John Jacob *writer, university administrator*
Cappo, Joseph C. *publisher*
Caray, Harry Christopher *sports announcer*
†Champion, Charles F. *newspaper publishing executive*
Chapman, Stephen James *columnist*
Christiansen, Richard Dean *newspaper editor*
†Ciccone, Richard *newspaper editor*
Coffey, Raymond Richard *newspaper editor, journalist*
Cohodes, Eli Aaron *publisher*
Connors, Dorsey *television and radio commentator, newspaper columnist*
Constant, Anita Aurelia *publisher*
Cooper, Ilene Linda *magazine editor, author*
Crain, Gertrude Ramsay *publishing company executive*
Crain, Rance *publishing company executive*
Crawford, William Basil, Jr. *journalist*
Cross, Robert Clark *journalist*
Curwen, Randall William *journalist, editor*
D'Alexander, William Joseph *publishing company executive*
Darby, Edwin Wheeler *newspaper financial columnist*
†Davis, Andrew Bashaw *publishing executive*
DeBat, Donald Joseph *newspaper editor*
Dimond, Robert Edward *publisher*
Dodds, Claudette La Vonn *radio executive and consultant*
†Dold, Robert Bruce *journalist*
†Donovan, Dianne Francys *journalist, literary editor*
Downing, Joan Forman *editor*
Ebert, Roger Joseph *film critic*
Elleman, Barbara *editor*
Essex, Joseph Michael *visual communication planner*
Feder, Robert *television and radio columnist*
Ferrara, Stephen Arthur *publishing company executive, editor*
Fetridge, Clark Worthington *publisher*
Field, Marshall *business executive*
Figge, Frederick Henry, Jr. *retired publishing executive*
Fink, John *editor, newspaper*
Foster, Irene Parks *special projects administrator*
Frank, Stanley Donald *publishing company executive*
Fuller, Jack William *writer, newspaper executive*
Gaines, William Chester *journalist*
Geannopulos, Nicholas George *publisher*
Gies, Thomas Anthony *publishing company executive*
Goldberg, Stephanie Benson *editor, writer, lawyer*
Goldsborough, Robert Gerald *publishing executive, author*
Gradowski, Stanley Joseph, Jr. *publishing company executive*
Graham, Jarlath John *publishing executive*
Granger, Bill *columnist*
Grant, Dennis *newspaper publishing executive*
Greene, Robert Bernard, Jr. (Bob Greene) *broadcast television correspondent, columnist, author*
†Grenesko, Donald C. *publishing company executive*
†Griffin, Howard *newspaper publishing executive*
Griffin, Jean Latz *newspaper reporter*
Gruber, William Paul *journalist*
Gwinn, Robert P. *publishing executive*
Haddix, Carol Ann Mighton *journalist*
Hall, Lee Boaz *publishing company consultant, author*
Harvey, Paul *news commentator, author, columnist*
Hay, Howard *newspaper publishing executive*
Hefner, Christie Ann *international media and marketing executive*
Hefner, Hugh Marston *editor in chief*
Hengstler, Gary Ardell *publisher, editor, lawyer*
Herguth, Robert John *columnist*
Hewitt, Brian *journalist*
Higgins, Jack *editorial cartoonist*
Hlavacek, Roy George *publishing executive, magazine editor*
†Holton, Lisa *newspaper editor*
†Hornung, Mark *newspaper editor*
†Huntley, Robert Stephen *newspaper editor*
Hurst, Charles Jackson *newspaper columnist*
Husar, John Paul *newspaper columnist, television panelist*
Hynes, Mary Ann *publishing executive, lawyer*
Johnson, John H. *publisher, consumer products executive, chairman*
Kaiserlian, Penelope Jane *publishing company executive*
Kazik, John Stanley *newspaper executive*
Kelley, Michael John *newspaper editor*
Kennett, Robert L. *publisher*
Kisor, Henry Du Bois *newspaper editor, critic, columnist*
Klaviter, Helen Lothrop *magazine editor*
Knight, Robert Milton *independent journalist, educator*
Koester, Robert Gregg *record company executive*
Kotulak, Ronald *newspaper science writer*
Krueger, Bonnie Lee *editor, writer*
Kupcinet, Irv *columnist*
Kyle, Robert Campbell, II *publishing executive*
Larson, Roy *journalist, publisher*
Lazarus, George Milton *newspaper columnist*
Leckey, Andrew A. *financial columnist*
Lehrman, Nat *magazine editor*
Lewis, Sylvia Gail *journalist*
†Lincicome, Bernard Wesley *journalist*
Lipinski, Ann Marie *newspaper editor*
Litzsinger, Paul Richard *publishing company executive*
Locher, Richard Earl *editorial cartoonist*
Longworth, Richard Cole *journalist*
Lundberg, George David, II *medical editor, pathologist*
Lyon, Jeffrey *journalist, author*
Lyons, Jeffrey *film critic*
†Lythcott, Marsha S. *newspaper editor*
Madigan, John William *publishing executive*
Mariotti, Jay Anthony *journalist*
Markus, Robert Michael *journalist*
McCarron, John Francis *columnist*
McDaniel, Charles-Gene *journalism educator, writer*
Mc Guirt, Wayne Robert *publishing company executive*
McIntyre, Kathryn Joan *publisher, editorial director*
Mc Keel, Sam Stewart *newspaper executive*
Medved, Michael *film critic, author*
Migala, Lucyna Jozefa *broadcast journalist, arts administrator, radio station executive*
Miller, Mark *newspaper editor*
Nadler, Mark B. *executive editor*
Nault, William Henry *publishing executive*
Neal, Steven George *journalist*
†Nelson, William Bruce *newspaper company executive*
Neubauer, Charles Frederick *investigative reporter*
Nicholls, David G. *editor*
Nordstrand, Raymond William *broadcasting company executive*
Norton, Peter Bowes *publishing company executive*
O'Dell, James E. *newspaper publishing executive*
Orr, Richard Tuttle *journalist*
Page, Clarence E. *newspaper columnist*
Parisi, Joseph (Anthony) *magazine editor, writer-consultant, educator*
Peerman, Dean Gordon *magazine editor*
Pemberton, Scott Bender *editor, publishing executive*
Peres, Judith May *journalist*
Perlis, Michael Steven *magazine publisher*
Pesmen, Sandra (Mrs. Harold William Pesmen) *editor*
Petacque, Arthur M. *journalist*
†Philipson, Morris *university press director*
†Pierson, Don *sports columnist*
Plotnick, Harvey Barry *publishing executive*
Plotnik, Arthur *publishing executive*
Pope, Kerig Rodgers *magazine executive*
Puerner, John *newspaper publishing executive*
Quaal, Ward Louis *broadcast executive*
Quade, Victoria Catherine *editor, writer*
Reedy, Jerry Edward *editor, writer*
Renshaw, Charles Clark, Jr. *retired publishing executive*
Rice, Linda Johnson *publishing executive*
Rice, William Edward *newspaper columnist*
Rodgers, Johnathan *broadcast executive*
Roeper, Richard *columnist*
†Rosenbloom, Steve *sportswriter*
Royko, Mike *newspaper columnist*
Rubin, Bonnie Miller *journalist*
†Rynkiewicz, Stephen Michael *journalist*
†Sachs, Lloyd Robert *entertainment critic, writer*
Scanlan, Thomas Cleary *publishing executive, editor*
Sengstacke, John Herman Henry *publishing company executive*
Shere, Dennis *publishing executive*
Shuman, Nicholas Roman *journalist, educator*
Simonson, Margaret *newspaper publishing executive*
Siskel, Gene (Eugene Kal Siskel) *film critic*
†Sneed, Michael (Michele) *columnist*
Soeteber, Ellen *journalist, newspaper editor*
Stone, Steven Michael *sports announcer, former baseball player*
Terry, Clifford Lewis *journalist*
†Tyner, Howard A. *newspaper editor, journalist*
Varro, Barbara Joan *health journal editor*
†Veitch, Michael J. *newspaper publishing executive*
†Verdi, Robert William *sports columnist*
von Rhein, John Richard *music critic, editor*
†Wallace, Julia Diane *newspaper editor*
Wasik, John Francis *editor, writer, publisher*
Wasiolek, Edward *literary critic, language and literature educator*
Weber, Arthur *publisher*
Weinberg, Lila Shaffer *writer, editor*
Weintraub, Joseph Barton *publishing executive*
Wells, Joel Freeman *editor, author*
Wier, Patricia Ann *publishing executive*
Williams, Carl Chanson *publishing company executive*
Wilson, Gahan *cartoonist, author*
Wolfe, Sheila A. *journalist*
Wycliff, Noel Don *journalist, newspaper editor*
Youngman, Owen Ralph *newspaper editor*
Yuenger, James Laury *newspaper editor*
Zaslow, Jeffrey Lloyd *syndicated columnist*
Zekman, Pamela Lois (Mrs. Fredric Soll) *reporter*
Zorn, Eric J. *newspaper columnist*

Chicago Heights
Hurd, Byron Thomas *newspaper executive*

Crystal Lake
Keller, William Francis *publishing consultant*

De Kalb
Vance Siebrasse, Kathy Ann *newspaper publishing executive*

Deerfield
Massie, Edward Lindsey, Jr. *publishing company executive*
Thorne, Oakleigh Blakeman *publishing company executive*

Des Plaines
Babb, Michael Paul *engineering magazine editor*
Clapper, Lyle Nielsen *magazine publisher*
Clapper, Marie Anne *magazine publisher*
Gillette, Halbert Scranton *publisher*
Henrikson, Lois Elizabeth *photojournalist*
Kelly, Timothy Michael *magazine publisher*
Klemens, Thomas Lloyd *editor*
Kuennen, Thomas Gerard *magazine editor*
Shoup, Wesley Dale *publishing company executive*
Tory, John A. *newspaper publishing executive*
Wallace, Jane Young (Mrs. Donald H. Wallace) *editor*
Young, Richard Alan *publishing company executive*

Dixon
Shaw, Thomas Douglas *newspaper executive*

Elgin
†Mehlis, David Lee *publishing executive*

Elk Grove Village
Halloran, James Joseph *editor*

Elmhurst
Ephland, John Russell *magazine editor*

Evanston
†Borcover, Alfred Seymour *journalist*
Haiman, Franklyn Saul *author, communications educator*
Jacobs, Norman Joseph *publishing company executive*
Janeway, Michael Charles *journalism educator, school dean*
Jones, Robert Russell *magazine editor*
Kuenster, John Joseph *magazine editor*
Lavine, John M. *journalism educator, newspaper publisher*
Lyles, Jean Elizabeth Caffey *journalist*
McDougal, Alfred Leroy *publisher*
†McGee, Julia Ann *publishing company executive*
Otwell, Ralph Maurice *retired newspaper editor*
Peck, Abraham *editor, writer, educator, magazine consultant*
Swanton, Virginia Lee *publishing company administrator, editor*
Wagner, Durrett *former publisher, picture service executive*
White, Willmon Lee *magazine editor*
Wills, Garry *journalist, educator*

Glen Ellyn
Crumbaugh, Lee Forrest *publisher, consultant*
Kirkpatrick, Clayton *former newspaper executive*

Glenview
Mabley, Jack *newspaper columnist, communications consultant*
†Nyquist, Kathleen A. *publishing executive*

Highland Park
Johnson, Curtis Lee *publisher, editor, writer*
Rutenberg-Rosenberg, Sharon Leslie *journalist*

Homewood
Grunwald, Arnold Paul *communications executive, engineer*

Jacksonville
Hack, Carole Mae *media generalist*

Lake Bluff
Felknor, Bruce Lester *editorial consultant*

Lake Forest
Krouse, Ann Wolk *publishing executive*
Morgan, Richard Thomas *publishing executive*
Schulze, Franz, Jr. *art critic, educator*

Lincolnwood
Astrin, Marvin H. *broadcasting company executive*
Pattis, S. William *publisher*

Litchfield
Jackson, David A. *retired newspaper editor*

Matteson
Leak, Alberta Hedgley *newspaper editor*

Mount Vernon
Withers, W. Russell, Jr. *broadcast executive*

Naperville
Spiotta, Raymond Herman *consulting editor*

Normal
Mc Knight, William Warren, Jr. *publisher*

Northbrook
Snader, Jack Ross *publishing company executive*

Northfield
Hotze, Charles Wayne *publisher, printer*

Oak Brook
Honeywell, Larry Gene *publishing company executive, travel company executive*

Park Ridge
Peterson, Richard Elton *publisher*
Tosh, Nancy Peckham *magazine editor*

Peoria
Dancey, Charles Lohman *newspaper executive*
McConnell, John Thomas *newspaper executive, publisher*
†Peak, William Roy *newspaper editor*
†Slane, Henry Pindell *broadcasting executive*

Peru
Carus, André Wolfgang *educational publishing firm executive*
Carus, Marianne *magazine editor*

Quincy
†Dorsey, Jeffrey Alan *broadcaster*

River Grove
Follett, Robert John Richard *publisher*

Rolling Meadows
Grogan, Kenneth Augustine *publishing company executive*

Schaumburg
Edmunds, Jane Clara *communications consultant*

Skokie
Breen, Thomas John *form publishing company executive*
McNally, Andrew, III *printer, publisher*
McNally, Andrew, IV *publishing executive*
Wildermuth, Roger Gregory *publishing company executive*

Springfield
Clarke, John Patrick *newspaper publisher*
Heintz, Jack *publishing company executive*
Resnick, Joel H. *motion picture distributing executive*
Thomas, Payne Edward Lloyd *publisher*

Urbana
Littlewood, Thomas Benjamin *journalism educator*
Peterson, Theodore Bernard *retired journalism educator*

Wauconda
†Bolchazy, Ladislaus J. *publishing company executive*

Wheaton
Beers, V(ictor) Gilbert *publishing executive*
Kelly, Robert Thomas *publisher*
Sweeney, Mark Owen *publisher*
Taylor, Mark Douglas *publishing executive*

Wilmette
Biedron, Theodore John *newspaper executive*
Henry, Alan Pemberton *newspaper editor, journalist*

Winnetka
Mancuso, James Vincent *automobile columnist*

INDIANA

Bedford
Schurz, Scott Clark *journalist, publisher*

Bloomington
Gough, Pauline Bjerke *magazine editor*
Jacobi, Peter Paul *journalism educator, author*
Lee, Don Yoon *publisher, academic researcher and writer*
Weaver, David Hugh *journalism educator, communications researcher*

Elkhart
Dille, John Flint, Jr. *newspaper and broadcasting executive*

Evansville
Jackson, Bill D. *newspaper editor*
Riechmann, Fred B. *retired newspaper publisher*
Ryder, Thomas Michael *newspaper editor*

Fort Wayne
Klugman, Stephan Craig *newspaper editor*
Lockwood, Robert Philip *publishing executive*
†Pellegrene, Thomas James, Jr. *editor, researcher*
Sandeson, William Seymour *cartoonist*

Franklin
Jacobs, Harvey Collins *newspaper editor, writer*

Greencastle
Bingham, Jinsie Scott *broadcast company executive*

Greensburg
Small, Ralph Milton *publisher, clergyman*

Huntingburg
Matthews, William Edmund *newspaper and travel magazine publisher*

Indianapolis
†Allan, Marc D. *music critic*
Applegate, Malcolm W. *newspaper executive*
†Birky, Nathan Dale *publishing company executive*
Born, Emily Marie *editor, association executive*
Caperton, Albert Franklin *newspaper editor*
Cohen, Gabriel Murrel *editor, publisher*
†Drawbaugh, Kevin Alan *newspaper editor*
†Fleming, Marcella *journalist*
Fortune, William Lemcke *journalist*
†Fuson, Wayne Edward *sports editor*
†Garmel, Marion Bess Simon *journalist*
Greenwald, John Edward *magazine executive*
†Headden, Susan M. *reporter*
†Higgins, William Robert, III *journalist*
†Lyst, John Henry *journalist*
Phillippi, Wendell Crane *editor*
Pulliam, Eugene Smith *newspaper publisher*
†Pulliam, Russell Bleecker *editor, elder*
Russell, Frank Eli *newspaper publishing executive*
†SerVaas, Beurt Richard *corporate executive*
†Staff, Charles Bancroft, Jr. *music and theater critic*
Thomas, Beth Eileen Wood (Mrs. Raymond O. Thomas) *editor*
†Van Valin, John E. *publisher*
Werner, Charles George *cartoonist*
Wheeler, Daniel Scott *publishing executive, editor*
Wright, David Burton *retired newspaper publishing company executive*

Martinsville
Kendall, Robert Stanton *newspaper editor, journalist*

Muncie
Bell, Stephen Scott (Steve Bell) *journalist, educator*
Kumbula, Tendayi Sengerwe *journalism educator*

New Haven
Chapman, Reid Gillis *former broadcasting company executive*

Notre Dame
Langford, James Rouleau *university press administrator*
Rice, (Ethel) Ann *publishing executive, editor*

Peru
Stackhouse, John Wesley *publishing executive*

Richmond
†Talbot, Ann *editor*

South Bend
Schurz, Franklin Dunn, Jr. *media executive*

Terre Haute
Meany, John Joseph *newspaper publisher*

IOWA

Ames
Gartner, Michael Gay *editor, television executive*

Cedar Falls
Carlson, Jerry Alan *editor*
†Slife, Harry Gene *broadcast executive, former state senator*

Cedar Rapids
†Hladky, Joseph F., Jr. *newspaper publisher, broadcasting executive*
Hladky, Joseph F., III *publishing executive*
Quarton, William Barlow *broadcasting company executive*

Davenport
Gottlieb, Richard Douglas *media executive*
Schermer, Lloyd G. *publishing and broadcasting company executive*

Des Moines
Boyle, Bruce James *publisher*
Burnett, Robert A. *publisher*
Edwards, Charles C., Jr. *newspaper publisher*
Flansburg, James Sherman *editor, columnist*
Jordan, David Loran *editor*
Kerr, William T. *publishing company executive*
Kruidenier, David *newspaper executive*
†Lawless, James L. *editor, columnist*
LemMon, Jean Marie *editor in chief periodical*
Little, Christopher Mark *publishing company executive, lawyer*
MacDonald, Kenneth *journalist, former editor*
Peterson, David Charles *photojournalist*
Rehm, Jack Daniel *publishing executive*
†Simbro, William Charles *journalist*
Van Zante, Shirley Mae *magazine editor*
Witke, David Rodney *newspaper editor*

Dubuque
Brown, William Clifford *publishing company executive*
Husfloen, Kyle Douglas *editor*

Iowa City
Hardt, Hanno Richard Eduard *communications educator*
Keller, Eliot Aaron *broadcasting executive*
Zimmer, Paul Jerome *editor, poet*

Sioux City
Krenz, Dean Albert *newspaper publisher*

Spirit Lake
Hedberg, Paul Clifford *broadcasting executive*

West Des Moines
Alumbaugh, JoAnn McCalla *magazine editor*
Dooley, Donald John *publishing executive*

KANSAS

Coffeyville
Seaton, Richard Melvin *newspaper and broadcasting executive*

Fort Scott
Emery, Frank Eugene *publishing executive*

Hutchinson
Buzbee, Richard Edgar *newspaper editor*

Lawrence
Eblen, George Thomas (Tom Eblen) *journalist*
Ginn, John Charles *journalism educator, former newspaper publisher*
Levine, Stuart George *editor, English literature educator, author*
Orel, Harold *literary critic, educator*
Pickett, Calder Marcus *retired journalism educator*
Simons, Dolph Collins, Jr. *newspaper publisher*
Woodward, Frederick Miller *publisher*

Manhattan
Marsh, Harry Dean *journalism educator*
Seaton, Edward Lee *newspaper editor and publisher*

Marion
Meyer, Bill *newspaper publisher, editor*

Saint Marys
Latham, Dudley Eugene, III (Del Latham) *printing and paper converting executive*

Strawn
†Lawrence, Douglass Ray *radio station executive, state legislator*

Topeka
Peavler, Nancy Jean *editor*
Powers, Harris Pat *broadcasting executive*
Stauffer, John H. *newspaper and broadcast executive*
†Stauffer, Peter Wallace *newspaper executive*
Stauffer, Stanley Howard *newspaper and broadcasting executive*

Wichita
†Claassen, Sherida Dill *newspaper editor*
†Curtright, Robert Eugene *newspaper critic and columnist*
†Getz, Robert Lee *newspaper columnist*
Hatteberg, Larry Merle *photojournalist*

KENTUCKY

Covington
Trimble, Vance Henry *retired newspaper editor*

Goshen
Strode, William Hall, III *photojournalist, publisher*

Lexington
Allison, James Claybrooke, II *broadcasting executive*
Henson, Glenda Maria *newspaper writer*
Keeling, Larry Dale *journalist*
Kelly, Timothy Michael *newspaper editor*
Owens, Lewis E. *newspaper executive*

Louisville
Bingham, George Barry, Jr. *publishing and broadcasting executive*
Bullard, Claude Earl *newspaper, commercial printing and radio and television executive*
Carpenter, Marj Collier *news director*
†Drury, Ralph Leon *newspaper executive*
†Ellison, William Louie, Jr. *newspaper editor, journalist*
Hawpe, David Vaughn *newspaper editor, journalist*
MacKinnon, Cyrus Leland *retired newspaper executive*
McIntyre, Robert Donald *publishing executive, consultant*
Melnykovych, Andrew O. *journalist*
Tallichet, Leon Edgar *retired publishing executive, financial administrator*
†Tinsley, Tuck, III *book publishing executive*
Towles, Donald Blackburn *retired newspaper publishing executive*
Woolsey, Frederick William *retired journalist, music critic*

Pewee Valley
Gill, George Norman *newspaper publishing company executive*

Trappist
Hart, Patrick Joseph *editor*

LOUISIANA

Alexandria
Smith, Joe Dorsey, Jr. *newspaper executive*

Baker
Roberson, Patt Foster *mass communications educator*

Baton Rouge
Dalrymple, Margaret Fisher *university press editor, writer*
Giles, William Elmer *journalism educator, former newspaper editor*
Gilmore, Clarence Percy *writer, magazine editor*
†Hatfield, Jack Daniel *newspaper editor*
†Jenkins, Louis (Woody) *television executive, state legislator*
Manship, Charles Phelps, Jr. *newspaper executive, retired association executive*
Manship, Douglas *broadcast and newspaper executive*
Phillabaum, Leslie Ervin *publisher*

Covington
†Stroup, Sheila Tierney *columnist*

Gretna
Calhoun, Milburn *publishing executive, rare book dealer, physician*

Lafayette
Lenox, Charles N(ewton), Jr. *newspaper editor*

Lake Charles
Beam, James C. (Jim Beam) *editor, newspaper*

Metairie
Costello, Joseph Mark, III *broadcasting and motion picture executive*

New Orleans
†Amoss, Walter James, III *editor*
†Ball, Millie (Mildred Porteons Ball) *editor, journalist*
Corey, Orlin Russell *publisher, editor*
†Dodds, Richard Crofton *theater critic*
Ferguson, Charles Austin *retired newspaper editor*
Phelps, Ashton, Jr. *newspaper publisher*
†Pope, John M. *journalist*
Roesler, Robert Harry *newspaper editor*
Toussaint, Allen Richard *recording studio executive, composer, pianist*

Shreveport
Beaird, Charles T. *publishing executive*
Lazarus, Allan Matthew *retired newspaper editor*
†Tiner, Stanley Ray *business communications executive, former editor*

MAINE

Bangor
Warren, Richard Jordan *newspaper publisher*
Warren, Richard Kearney *newspaper publisher*

Camden
Anderson, George Harding *broadcasting company executive*
Thomas, (Charles) Davis *editor*

Cape Elizabeth
Emerson, Paul Carlton *retired publishing executive*

Castine
Hall, David *sound archivist, writer*
Zehring, Karen *information executive*

Damariscotta
Blake, Bud (Julian Watson) *cartoonist*

Ellsworth
Dudman, Richard Beebe *communications company executive, journalist*
Wiggins, James Russell *newspaper editor*

Lincoln
Kneeland, Douglas Eugene *retired newspaper editor*

Portland
†Chisholm, Colin Alexander Joseph, III *media professional*
Harte, Christopher McCutcheon *newspaper executive*
McGorrill, Bruce Courtney *broadcasting executive*
†Neavoll, George Franklin *newspaper editor*
Silverman, George Alan *broadcasting executive*
Ureneck, Louis Adam *newspaper editor*

Rockport
Fernald, Harold Allen *publishing executive*
Jackson, David Pingree *publishing executive*

Sebago Lake
Murray, Wallace Shordon *publisher, educator*

Sedgwick
Schroth, Thomas Nolan *editor*

Thorndike
Treleaven, Phillips Albert *retired publishing company executive*

MARYLAND

Annapolis
Casey, Edward Dennis *newspaper editor*
Chambers, Ronald D. *book publishing executive*
Jackson, Elmer Martin, Jr. *newspaper executive*

Baltimore
Beckenstein, Myron *journalist*
Bor, Jonathan Steven *journalist*
Brunson, Dorothy Edwards *broadcasting executive*
Carroll, John Sawyer *newspaper editor*
Digges, Dudley Perkins *retired editor*
Dorsey, John Russell *art critic, journalist*
Finnegan, Sara Anne *publisher*
Gardner, R. H. (Rufus Hallette Gardner, III) *retired drama and film critic*
Glasgow, Jesse Edward *newspaper editor*
Goellner, Jack Gordon *publishing executive*
†Hirsh, Allan T., III *book publisher*
Hirsh, Allan Thurman, Jr. *publishing executive*
Houck, James I. *newspaper editor*
†Jenkins, Carrell Ray *newspaper editor*
Magida, Arthur Jay *newspaper editor, writer*
Marimow, William Kalmon *journalist*
†Moeller, Philip Theodore *newspaper business editor*
Montgomery, Paula Kay *school editor, publishing executive*
†Passano, E. Magruder, Jr. *publishing executive*
Passano, Edward Magruder *printing company executive*
Rabb, Bernard Paul *book publisher, consultant*
†Rodricks, Daniel John *columnist, television commentator*
†Rousuck, J. Wynn *theater critic*
Scott, Frederick Isadore, Jr. *editor, business executive*
Sterne, Joseph Robert Livingston *newspaper editor*
Stevens, Elisabeth Goss (Mrs. Robert Schleussner, Jr.) *writer, journalist*
Tepper, Michael Howard *publishing company executive*
Williams, Harold Anthony *retired newspaper editor*

Bethesda
Cornish, Edward Seymour *magazine editor*
Harney, Kenneth Robert *editor, columnist*
Herman, Edith Carol *journalist*
Iglehart, John K. *journalist*
Kamenske, Bernard Harold *journalist, communications specialist*
Kohlmeier, Louis Martin, Jr. *newspaper reporter*
Larrabee, Donald Richard *publishing company executive*
Massa, Paul Peter *publisher*
Mc Kenna, James Aloysius *broadcasting executive, former lawyer*
Morton, Herbert Charles *editor, economist*
Nessen, Ronald Harold *public affairs executive*
Otte, Ruth L. *cable television executive*
Paro, Tom Edward *broadcasting company executive*
Phillips, Kevin Price *columnist, author*
Pickerell, James Howard *photojournalist*
Pratt, Dana Joseph *publishing consultant*
Roberts, Chalmers McGeagh *reporter*
Rubin, William *editor*
Shipler, David Karr *journalist, correspondent, author*
Sulkin, Sidney *editor, writer*

Bowie
Towle, Laird Charles *book publisher*

Chevy Chase
Adler, James Barron *publisher*
Chaseman, Joel *media executive*

College Park
Cleghorn, Reese *journalist, educator*
Grunig, James Elmer *communications educator, researcher, public relations consultant*
Hiebert, Ray Eldon *journalism educator, author, consultant*

Columbia
Barrow, Lionel Ceon, Jr. *communications and marketing consultant*
Trohan, Walter *newspaperman*

Easton
Lockwood, Willard Atkinson *publisher*

Frederick
Beran, Denis Carl *publisher*
Delaplaine, George Birely, Jr. *newspaper editor, cable television executive*

Gaithersburg
Deutsch, Judith Sloan *journalist, newspaper editor*
Marozsan, John Robert *publishing company executive*
Wicklein, John Frederick *journalist, educator*

Germantown
Christian, John Kenton *organization executive, publisher, writer, marketing consultant*

Grantsville
Ruddell, Gary Ronald *publisher*

Hagerstown
Fisher, Charles Worley *editor*
†Warner, Harry Backer, Jr. *retired journalist, freelance writer*

Havre De Grace
Wetter, Edward *broadcasting executive*

Landover
Poile, David Robert *professional hockey team executive*

Lanham
Nagan, Peter Seymour *publisher*

Lanham Seabrook
Fellers, Raymond *publisher*

Lusby
Radcliffe, Redonia Wheeler (Donnie Radcliffe) *journalist, author*

Lutherville Timonium
Cedrone, Louis Robert, Jr. *critic*

Mitchellville
Phelps, Flora L(ouise) Lewis *editor, anthropologist, photographer*

Owings Mills
Holdridge, Barbara *book publisher*

Potomac
Fox, Arthur Joseph, Jr. *editor*
Kessler, Ronald Borek *journalist*
Munroe, Pat *retired newsman*

Rockville
Karnow, Stanley *journalist, writer*
Matthews, Daniel George *editorial consultant*
Regeimbal, Neil Robert, Sr. *journalist*

Salisbury
Kleiman, Gary Howard *broadcast, advertising and cellular communications consultant*

Silver Spring
Barber, Ben Bernard Andrew *journalist*
Eiserer, Leonard Albert Carl *publishing executive*
Flieger, Howard Wentworth *editor*
Hegstad, Roland Rex *magazine editor*
Howze, Karen Aileen *newspaper editor, lawyer, multi-cultural communications consultant*
†Kabela, Frank, Jr. *broadcast executive*
Mooney, James Hugh *newspaper editor*
Myers, Evelyn Stephenson *editor, writer*
Whitten, Leslie Hunter, Jr. *author, newspaper reporter*

Stevenson
Jacobs, Bradford McElderry *newspaper editor*

Thurmont
Lucey, Charles Timothy *journalist, author*

MASSACHUSETTS

Acton
Kittross, John Michael *retired communications educator*

Allston
Becton, Henry Prentiss, Jr. *broadcasting company executive*

Amherst
Wilcox, Bruce Gordon *publisher*

Bedford
Brady, Upton Birnie *editor*
Goodman, William Beehler *editor, literary agent*

Boston
Adams, Phoebe-Lou *journalist*
Ames, Damaris *publishing executive*
†Bailey, Stephen *newspaper reporter*
Beatty, Jack J. *magazine editor*
Berger, Francine Ellis *radio executive, educator*
Berman, William H. *publishing company executive*
Burack, Sylvia Kamerman *editor, publisher*
Caldwell, Gail *book critic*
Carr, Jay Phillip *critic*
†Carroll, Matthew Shaun *reporter*
†Chinlund, Christine *newspaper editor*
Cohen, Rachelle Sharon *journalist*
Cohn, Robert Mark *publishing executive*
Collins, Monica Ann *journalist*
†Cook, David *editor*
Cousy, Bob Joseph *sports commentator*
Curtis, Christopher Michael *magazine editor*
Danziger, Jeff *political cartoonist, writer*
Darehshori, Nader Farhang *publishing sales executive*
Davison, Peter *editor, poet*
†Donovan, Helen W. *newspaper editor*
†Driscoll, John S. *newspaper editor*
Eder, Richard Gray *newspaper critic*
†Eisner, Alan S. *newspaper editor*
Eldridge, Larry (William Lawrence Eldridge) *journalist*

†Everitt, Charles Bell *publishing executive*
Fanning, Katherine Woodruff *editor, journalism educator*
†Feder, Donald Albert *syndicated columnist*
Feeney, Mark *newspaper editor*
Fletcher, Suzanne Wright *physician, educator*
†Flint, Anthony Evans *journalist*
†Gendron, George *magazine editor*
Gibson, Barry Joseph *magazine editor*
Godine, David Richard *publishing company executive*
†Greene, Leonard J. *newspaper columnist*
Grossfeld, Stan *newspaper photography executive, author*
Hayward, Charles E. *publishing company executive*
Higgins, George Vincent *journalist, lawyer, author*
Jenks, Homer Simeon *newspaper editor, free-lance writer*
†Jones, Donald Wayne *publisher*
†Julian, Sheryl *newspaper writer*
†Kassirer, Jerome Paul *editor-in-chief*
†Katz, Larry *writer*
†Kauffman, Godfrey *newspaper publishing executive*
†Kimball, George E., III *sports columnist*
†King, Nick *Newspaper editor*
Klarfeld, Jonathan Michael *journalism educator*
Knight, Norman *broadcast executive*
Knox, Richard Albert *journalist*
Larkin, Michael John *newspaper editor, journalist*
Lawrence, Merloyd Ludington *editor*
†Lee, Donald Young (Don Lee) *publishing executive, editor, writer*
Lewis, Anthony *newspaper columnist*
Lichtenberg, Margaret Klee *publishing company executive*
Lyman, Henry *retired publisher, marine fisheries consultant*
Manning, Robert Joseph *editor*
†Manning, Thomas Allen *publishing company executive*
Manning, William Frederick *wire service photographer*
McArdle, John *publishing company executive*
McKibben, Gordon Charles *journalist, correspondent*
McMullin, Ruth Roney *retired publishing company executive*
Menzies, Ian Stuart *newspaper editor*
†Modugno, Maria *publishing executive*
Moore, Francis Daniels *retired surgeon, educator, consultant, editor*
Morgan, Frank Brown Webb, Jr. *journalist, consultant*
†Morris, Gerald Douglas *newspaper editor*
Mulvoy, Thomas F., Jr. *newspaper editor, journalist*
Newman, Richard Alan *publisher, editor and consultant*
Purcell, Patrick Joseph *newspaper publisher*
†Robinson, Walter *newspaper editor*
†Rodman, Oliver *newspaper publishing executive*
†Sales, Robert Julian *newspaper editor*
†Schwartz, Lloyd *music critic, poet*
Silvey, Anita Lynne *editor*
Skwar, Donald R. *newspaper editor*
Smyth, Peter Hayes *radio executive*
Storin, Matthew Victor *newspaper editor*
Strothman, Wendy Jo *book publisher*
Szep, Paul Michael *editorial cartoonist*
Taylor, Benjamin B. *newspaper publishing executive*
†Taylor, Stephen Emlyn *publishing executive*
†Turek, Sonia Fay *journalist*
Utiger, Robert David *medical editor*
Wallraff, Barbara Jean *magazine editor, writer*
Walton, Bill (William Theodore Walton, III) *sportscaster*
Whitworth, William A. *magazine editor*
†Yemma, John *newspaper editor*
Zellman, Ande *editor*

Cambridge
Aronson, Michael Andrew *editor*
Bowes, Frederick, III *publishing executive*
Donald, Aida DiPace *publishing executive*
Nordell, Hans Roderick *journalist, editor*
Rubin, Jerome Sanford *publishing company executive, lawyer*
Sisler, William Philip *publishing executive*
Squire, James Robert *retired publisher, consultant*
Trainor, Bernard Edmund *journalist, educator, retired marine corps officer*
Urbanowski, Frank *publishing company executive*
Wilcox, Maud *editor*

Chatham
Leighten, Edward Henry *publisher, consultant*

Chestnut Hill
Levy, James Peter *publishing company executive*
Tarr, Robert Joseph, Jr. *publishing executive, retail executive*

Concord
Kasputys, Joseph Edward *corporate executive, economist*

Dorchester
Brelis, Matthew Dean Burns *journalist*
Bruzelius, Nils Johan Axel *journalist*
Goodman, Ellen Holtz *journalist*
Greenway, Hugh Davids Scott *journalist*
Hatfield, Julie Stockwell *journalist, newspaper editor*
Huff, William Braid *publication company executive*
Kaufman, Jonathan Reed *journalist*
Kingsbury, Arthur French, III *newspaper publishing executive*
Larkin, Alfred Sinnott, Jr. *newspaper editor*
Leland, Timothy *newspaper executive*
Ockerbloom, Richard C. *newspaper executive*
Stanger, David N. *newspaper publishing executive*
Taylor, William Osgood *newspaper executive*

East Orleans
Nenneman, Richard Arthur *retired publishing executive*

Gloucester
Baird, Gordon Prentiss *publisher*

Great Barrington
Syer, Warren Bertram *publisher*

Groton
Smith, Alan Harvey *former editor*

Harwich
Thorndike, Joseph Jacobs, Jr. *editor*

Hingham
Replogle, David Robert *publishing company executive*

Holden
Botty, Kenneth John *editor, newspaper executive*

Holyoke
Dwight, William, Jr. *former newspaper executive, restaurateur*

Hyannis
Himstead, Scott *newspaper publisher*
White, Timothy Oliver *newspaper editor*

Ipswich
Berggren, Dick *editor*

Kingston
Stair, Gobin *publishing executive, painter, graphic designer*

Lawrence
Gowdy, Curtis *sportscaster*

Lexington
Bursma, Albert, Jr. *publishing company executive*
Korte, Loren A. *publishing company executive*
Kotelly, George Vincent *editor, writer*

Lincoln
Adams, Thomas Boylston *writer*
Schwann, William Joseph *publisher, musician, discographer*

Lowell
Osenton, Thomas George *publisher*

Marshfield
Mc Carthy, Thomas Patrick *magazine publisher*

Needham
†Kilburn, Donald C. *publishing company executive*
Lebowitz, Marshall *publishing company executive*

New Bedford
Ragsdale, James Marcus *editor*

Newton
Forsberg, Roy Walter *publishing company executive*
Krakoff, Robert Leonard *publishing executive*
Mason, Charles Ellis, III *magazine editor*
Sbordon, William G. *publisher*
Stundza, Thomas John *journalist*
Thompson, Stephen Arthur *publishing executive*

North Adams
Thurston, Donald Allen *broadcasting executive*

North Chatham
Rowlands, Marvin Lloyd, Jr. *publishing and communications consultant*

North Quincy
Porter, John Stephen *television executive*

Northampton
†Blomberg, Marcia Christine *newspaper editor*

Norwell
†Rolnik, Zachary Jacob *senior editor, publisher*
†Smith, Jeffrey K. *publishing executive*

Orange
Preece, Warren Eversleigh *editor*

Quincy
†Lippincott, Joseph P. *photojournalist, educator*

Reading
†Stone, Warren R. *book publishing executive*

Richmond
Sexton, William Cottrell *journalist*

Rockport
Bissell, Phil (Charles P. Bissell) *cartoonist*

South Harwich
Micciche, Salvatore Joseph *journalist, lawyer*

South Wellfleet
Macauley, Robie Mayhew *retired editor*

Southbridge
†Ghiglione, Loren Frank *newspaper editor*

Springfield
Esposito, Joseph John *publishing company executive*
Friedman, Arnold S. *newspaper editor*
†Garvey, Richard Conrad *journalist*
†Gordon, Ronni Anne *journalist*
Haggerty, Thomas Francis *newspaper editor*
†Long, Brian Joseph *newspaper publishing executive*
Mish, Frederick Crittenden *editor*
†Morse, John M. *book publishing executive*
†Norton, Peter J. *publishing executive*
†Stanley, Thomas E. *publishing company executive*

Stockbridge
Rich, Philip Dewey *publishing executive*

Sudbury
Hillery, Mary Jane Larato *editor, producer, television host, columnist, reserve army officer*

Wayland
O'Connell, Paul Edmund *publisher*
Williams, James P., Jr. (Jay Williams) *broadcasting executive*

Wellesley
Gladstone, Richard Bennett *retired publishing company executive*
Myers, Arthur M. *journalist, author*

Wellfleet
Dugger, Ronnie E. *writer, publisher*

Weston
DeVito, Richard A(nthony) *publisher*
Oelgeschlager, Guenther Karl *publisher*

Westwood
Borgman, George Allan *journalist*

Wilmington
Sabosik, Patricia Elizabeth *publisher, editor*

Winchester
Ewing, David Walkley *magazine editor*

Woburn
†Klein, Michael James *broadcast executive, engineer*

Worcester
†Janensch, Paul *newspaper editor*
†Magiera, Frank Edward *journalist, critic*

MICHIGAN

Ann Arbor
Beaver, Frank Eugene *communication educator, film critic and historian*
Bedard, Patrick Joseph *editor, writer, consultant*
†Csere, Csaba *magazine editor*
Day, Colin Leslie *publisher*
Eisendrath, Charles Rice *journalism educator, manufacturer, farmer, consultant*
Fitzsimmons, Joseph John *publishing executive*
Stowe, Leland *journalist, writer*
†Veit, Werner *newspaper executive*
Yates, Brock Wendel *editor, journal*

Auburn Hills
Donald, Larry Watson *sports journalist*

Bay City
†McDermott, Larry Arnold *newspaper publisher*

Birmingham
Dirks, Lee Edward *newspaper executive*

Bloomfield
Brown, Lynette Ralya *journalist, publicist*

Bloomfield Hills
James, William Ramsay *cable television executive*

Colon
Walsh, Loren Melford *retired journal editor*

Detroit
†Anstett, Pat *newspaper editor*
Ashenfelter, David Louis *editor and former newspaper reportor*
†Bainbridge, Leesa *newspaper editor*
Bradford, Christina *newspaper editor*
Bray, Thomas Joseph *journalist, editor*
†Bullard, George *newspaper editor*
Burzynski, Susan Marie *newspaper editor*
Cantor, George Nathan *journalist*
Colby, Joy Hakanson *art critic*
DeRamus, Betty Jean *columnist*
DeVine, (Joseph) Lawrence *drama critic*
Dickerson, Brian *editor, periodical*
Diebolt, Judy *managing editor, newspaper*
Elsila, David August *editor*
Falls, Joseph Francis *sportswriter, editor*
†Freedman, Eric *journalist*
†Gerstel, Judith Ross *film critic*
Giles, Robert Hartmann *newspaper editor*
†Givhan, Robin Deneen *journalist*
Green, Jerome Frederic *sportswriter, journalist*
Guinn, John Rockne *music critic*
Hill, Draper *editorial cartoonist*
†Hutton, Carole Leigh *newspaper editor*
Kelleher, Timothy John *publishing company executive*
Kiska, Timothy Olin *newspaper columnist*
†Kushma, David William *journalist*
†Laitner, Bill *reporter*
†Lannon, Linnea *newspaper editor*
†Laughlin, Nancy *newspaper editor*
†McGruder, Robert *newspaper publishing executive*
Meriwether, Heath J. *newspaper editor*
†Mitzelfeld, Jim *newspaper reporter*
†O'Gorman, Kathy *newspaper editor*
†Olmstead, Laurence Daniel *journalist*
†Parry, Dale D. *newspaper editor*
Pepper, Jonathon Lester *newspaper columnist*
†Richardson, Joan *reporter*
†Ross-Flanigan, Nancy *reporter*
Ruffner, Frederick G., Jr. *book publisher*
Shine, Neal James *newspaper editor*
Smyntek, John Eugene, Jr. *newspaper editor*
Spina, Anthony *photojournalist*
†Stark, Susan R. *Film Critic*
Stroud, Joe Hinton *newspaper editor*
†Sylvain, Rick *newspaper editor*
†Talbert, Bob *newspaper columnist*
Teagan, John Gerard *newspaper executive*
†Thomas, Jacqueline Marie *journalist, editor*
Turnley, David Carl *photojournalist*
†Vega, Frank J. *newspaper publishing executive*
Vincent, Charles Eagar, Jr. *sports columnist*
Waldmeir, Peter Nielsen *journalist*
†Watson, Susan *newspaper columnist*
White, Joseph B. *reporter*

East Grand Rapids
Bolinder, Scott W. *publishing company executive*

East Lansing
Greenberg, Bradley Sander *communications educator*
†Johnson, J. David *communication educator*
Lowe, Kenneth Stephen *magazine editor*
Ralph, David Clinton *communications educator*

Farmington Hills
Harwell, William Earnest (Ernie Harwell) *broadcaster*

Flint
†McKesson, Michael Alan *journal editor*

Grand Rapids
Baker, Richard Lee *book publishing company executive*
Gundry, Stanley N. *publishing company executive*
Lloyd, Michael Stuart *newspaper editor*
Ryskamp, Bruce E. *publishing executive*

Grosse Pointe
Christian, Edward Kieren *radio station executive*
McWhirter, Glenna Suzanne (Nickie McWhirter) *newspaper columnist*
Whittaker, Jeanne Evans *newspaper columnist*

Jackson
Weaver, Franklin Thomas *newspaper executive*

Kalamazoo
Gilmore, James Stanley, Jr. *broadcast executive*

Marquette
Manning, Robert Hendrick *development director*

Mount Pleasant
Orlik, Peter Blythe *media educator, author, musician*

Northville
Opre, Thomas Edward *magazine editor, film company executive, corporate travel company executive*

Plymouth
Scott, George Ernest *publisher, writer*

Pontiac
McIntyre, Bruce Herbert *publishing company executive*

Saginaw
Chaffee, Paul Charles *newspaper editor*
Thatcher, Rex Howard *newspaper publisher*

Southfield
Brown, June *journalist*

Suttons Bay
Skinner, Thomas *broadcasting and film executive*

Whitehall
Youngquist, Alvin Menvid, Jr. *publisher, editor*

Williamston
Landis, Elwood Winton *retired newspaper editor*

Ypsilanti
Evans, Gary Lee *communications educator and consultant*

MINNESOTA

Annandale
Johnson, Jon E. *editor, periodical*

Duluth
Billig, Thomas Clifford *publishing and marketing executive*
Latto, Lewis M., Jr. *broadcasting company executive*

Eagan
Opperman, Dwight Darwin *publishing company executive*

Fergus Falls
†Rinden, David Lee *editor*

Mankato
Larson, Michael Len *newspaper editor*

Minneapolis
†Albright, Susan *Newspaper editor*
Anderson, Albert Esten *publisher*
Bisping, Bruce Henry *photojournalist*
Brings, Lawrence Martin *publisher*
†Buoen, Roger *newspaper editor*
Carter, Roy Ernest, Jr. *journalist, educator*
Cope, Lewis *newspaper reporter*
†Cowles, John, III *newspaper publishing executive*
Crosby, Jacqueline Garton *journalist*
Degnan, Joseph *magazine editor*
†Engebrecht, Julie *newspaper sports editor*
Flanagan, Barbara *journalist*
Franklin, Robert Brewer *journalist*
Hull, William Henry *publishing company executive*
†Ison, Christopher John *investigative reporter*
†Johnson, Cheryl *newspaper columnist*
Jones, William Arnold *writer, former newspaper columnist*
Kilzer, Louis Charles *journalist*
Kinderwater, Joseph C. (Jack Kinderwater) *publishing company executive*
†Klobuchar, James John *columnist*
Kramer, Joel Roy *journalist, newspaper executive*
Laing, Karel Ann *magazine publishing executive*
Lerner, Harry Jonas *publishing company executive*
†Marshall, Sherrie *newspaper editor*
†McEnroe, Paul *reporter*
McGuire, Timothy James *newspaper editor, lawyer*
Meador, Ron *newspaper editor, writer*
Moraczewski, Robert Leo *publisher*
Murphy, Joseph Edward, Jr. *broadcast executive*
Nixon, Raymond Blalock *journalist, educator*
Salyer, Stephen Lee *broadcast executive*
Scallen, Thomas Kaine *broadcasting executive*
Seaman, William Casper *news photographer*
†Slovut, Gordon *reporter*
†Smetanka, Mary Jane *reporter*
†Strickler, Jeff *newspaper movie critic*
Swartz, Donald Everett *television executive*
†Vaughan, Peter H. *theater critic*
Watson, Catherine Elaine *journalist*
White, Robert James *newspaper editor, columnist*
Wright, Frank Gardner *newspaper editor*

Youngblood, Richard Neil *columnist*
Ziebarth, E. William *news analyst, educator*

Minnetonka
Carey, Gregory Brian *magazine publisher*
Ehlert, John Ambrose *publisher*

Northfield
Hvistendahl, Joyce Kilmer *journalism and communications educator*

Red Wing
Seymour, Arthur Hallock *retired newspaper editor*

Rochester
Boldan, Kelton John (Kelly Boldan) *editor, journalist*

Saint Joseph
Rowland, Howard Ray *mass communications educator*

Saint Louis Park
Dahl, Christopher T. *broadcasting executive*

Saint Paul
†Boxmeyer, Donald Harold *columnist*
Doctor, Kenneth Jay *editor*
†Elrod, Bernett Richard (Sam Elrod) *newspaper editor*
Finnegan, John Robert, Sr. *retired newspaper executive*
†Fogg, James W. *printing company executive*
Fryxell, David Allen *publishing executive, newspaper editor*
Green, Philip Bevington *publishing company executive*
Henry, John Thomas *retired newspaper executive*
Hubbard, Stanley Stub *broadcast executive*
Keillor, Garrison Edward *writer, radio host, storyteller*
Kling, William Hugh *broadcasting executive*
Lund, Bert Oscar, Jr. *publisher*
Lundy, Walker *newspaper editor*
†Ostman, Eleanor A. *food writer*
Ridder, Bernard Herman, Jr. *newspaper publisher*

MISSISSIPPI

Biloxi
Hash, John Frank *broadcasting executive*
Weeks, Roland, Jr. *newspaper publisher*

Brandon
Buckley, Frank Wilson *newspaper executive*

Gulfport
Yeager, Andrea Wheaton *editor*

Jackson
Downing, Margaret Mary *newspaper editor*
Henderson, W. Guy *editor, minister*
Mc Gregor, Donald Thornton *newspaper editor, journalist*
Saunders, Doris Evans *editor, educator, business executive*
†Todd, Chris *photojournalist*

University
Hannah, Barry *educator, writer*

Yazoo City
Breese, Frank Chandler, III *newsprint company executive, lawyer*
Brown, Marion Lipscomb, Jr. *publisher, retired chemical company executive*

MISSOURI

Columbia
Atwater, James David *journalist, educator*
Taft, William Howard *journalism educator*

Independence
Vaughan, Luva D. *motion picture theatre executive*

Jefferson City
Ganey, Terry Joseph *journalist, author*

Joplin
Hughes, Fred George *retired newspaper publisher*

Kansas City
†Anderson, David Charles *media specialist*
Anderson, James Keith *retired magazine editor*
†Andrews, Kathleen W. *book publishing executive*
Batiuk, Thomas Martin *cartoonist*
†Brisbane, Arthur Seward *newspaper editor*
Burg, George Roscoe *journalist*
Busby, Marjorie Jean (Marjean Busby) *journalist*
†Cantrell, (Thomas) Scott *newspaper editor, music critic*
Davis, James Robert *cartoonist*
†Dozois, Gardner *editor, writer*
Fox, Thomas Charles *editor, writer*
Frauens, Marie *editor, researcher*
Guisewite, Cathy Lee *cartoonist*
Gusewelle, Charles Wesley *journalist*
Ingram, Robert Palmer *magazine publisher*
Kipp, Robert Almy *greeting card company executive*
Larson, Gary *cartoonist*
Martin, Donna Lee *publishing company executive*
Mc Meel, John Paul *newspaper syndicate and publishing executive*
McSweeney, William Lincoln, Jr. *publishing executive*
Oliphant, Patrick *editorial cartoonist*
Olson, Kay Melchisedech *magazine editor*
Palmer, Cruise *newspaper editor*
Payne, James Leroy *newspaper publishing executive*
Petosa, Jason Joseph *publisher*
Scott, James White *newspaper editor*
Stites, C. Thomas *journalist, publisher*
Tammeus, William David *journalist, columnist*
†Taylor, Jeff *reporter*
Thornton, Thomas Noel *publishing executive*
Townsend, Harold Guyon, Jr. *publishing company executive*

Watterson, Bill *cartoonist*
Wilson, Tom *cartoonist, greeting card company executive*

Liguori
O'Connor, Francine Marie *magazine editor*

Saint Joseph
Lockwood, George J. *newspaper editor*

Saint Louis
†Barnes, Harper Henderson *movie critic*
Bauman, George Duncan *former newspaper publisher*
Bohle, Bruce William *editor*
Buck, Jack *sportscaster*
Christopher, Glenn A. *publishing company executive*
Dames, Joan Foster (Mrs. Urban L. Dames) *magazine editor, columnist*
Dierdorf, Daniel Lee (Dan Dierdorf) *football analyst, sports commentator, former professional football player*
Dill, John Francis *publishing company executive*
Domjan, Laszlo Karoly *newspaper executive*
Elkins, Ken Joe *broadcasting executive*
Engelhardt, Thomas Alexander *editorial cartoonist*
†Freeland, A. Jerome *publishing executive*
Gauen, Patrick Emil *newspaper correspondent*
Goldberg, Norman Albert *music publisher, writer*
Higgins, Edward Aloysius *newspaper editor*
Janecke, Ronald Brian *newspaper editor, journalist, sports columnist*
Kanne, Marvin George *newspaper publishing executive*
Killenberg, George Andrew *newspaper consultant, former newspaper editor*
Korando, Donna Kay *journalist*
Lipman, David *multimedia company executive*
†Mette, Virgil Louis *publishing executive, biology educator*
Mink, Eric P. *newspaper columnist*
Noonan, Ray John *retired newspaper editor*
Olson, Clarence Elmer, Jr. *newspaper editor*
Penniman, Nicholas Griffith, IV *newspaper publisher*
Peters, Frank Lewis, Jr. *retired arts editor*
Pollack, Joe *newspaper critic and columnist, free-lance writer*
Pulitzer, Michael Edgar *publishing executive*
Richmond, Richard Thomas *journalist*
†Sauer, Georgia Booras *newspaper writer*
Waters, Richard *retired publishing company executive*
Wiley, Gregory Robert *publisher*
Woo, William Franklin *newspaper editor*

Springfield
†Champion, Norma Jean *communications educator, state legislator*
Champion, Richard Gordon *editor, journalism educator*
Dearmore, Thomas Lee *retired journalist*
Glazier, Robert Carl *publishing executive*
†Jacobi, Fredrick Thomas *newspaper publisher*
†Sylvester, Ronald Charles *newspaper writer*

Webb City
Blanset, Robert James *newspaper editor*

MONTANA

Big Fork
Blumberg, Nathan(iel) Bernard *journalist, educator, writer and publisher*

Billings
†Rye, David Blake *television news anchor*

Columbia Falls
Ruder, Melvin Harvey *retired newspaper editor*

Helena
Malcolm, Andrew Hogarth *journalist, writer*

Kalispell
James, Marion Ray *magazine founder, publisher and editor*

Livingston
Feldstein, Albert B. *retired editor, artist, writer*

NEBRASKA

Lincoln
Dyer, William Earl, Jr. *retired newspaper editor*
Hillegass, Clifton Keith *publisher*
Raz, Hilda *editor-in-chief periodical, educator*
†Spellman, J. R. *book publishing executive*

Omaha
Andersen, Harold Wayne *director, contributing editor, newspaper executive*
Davis, Chip *record producer, arranger*
Howe, G(ary) Woodson *newspaper editor*

NEVADA

Las Vegas
†Flippin, Perry Welch *newspaper editor*
†Hill, Michael John *newspaper editor*
Rossin, Herbert Yale *television broadcaster*

Reno
Evans, Larry Melvyn *newspaper columnist, chess expert*
Miller, Newton Edd, Jr. *communications educator*

NEW HAMPSHIRE

Dublin
†Avery, Stephen Goodrich *publishing company sales executive*
Hale, Judson Drake, Sr. *editor*

Goffstown
Gillmore, Robert *syndicated columnist, author, editor, publisher*

Hancock
Herman, George Edward *radio and television correspondent*

Hanover
Mc Farland, Thomas L. *book publishing executive*
Rutter, Frances Tompson *publisher*

Henniker
Cowan, Stuart DuBois *publisher, consultant, writer*

Hollis
Lerner, Arnold Stanley *radio station executive*

Jackson
Johnson, Ned (Edward Christopher Johnson) *publishing company executive*

Jaffrey
Von Eckardt, Wolf *design critic, educator*

Lyme
Dwight, Donald Rathbun *newspaper publisher, corporate communications executive*

Manchester
†Adams, James W. *journalist*
Loeb, Nackey Scripps *publisher*
McQuaid, Joseph Woodbury *newspaper executive*
Perkins, Charles, III *newspaper editor*

Nashua
Bickford, Andrew Thomas *newspaper publisher*
Holton, Robert Page *publishing executive*

Portsmouth
Hopkins, Jeannette E. *book publisher, editor*
Thornhill, Arthur Horace, Jr. *retired book publisher*

NEW JERSEY

Asbury Park
Jobson, Thomas Wootten *retired editor*

Bloomfield
Vincent, Tony *cable television/radio executive and personality*

Bridgewater
Freeman, Henry McCall *newspaper publisher*
Harrigan, Laura G. *newspaper editor*
Healey, Lynne Kover *editor, broadcaster, writer, educator*

Brigantine
Birdwhistell, Ray L. *retired folklore and communication educator*

Califon
Hannigan, Frank *sportswriter, television writer and commentator, golf course design consultant*

Cedar Grove
Spagnardi, Ronald Lee *publishing executive*

Cherry Hill
Biddle, Daniel R. *reporter*
Callaway, Ben Anderson *journalist*
Rudman, Solomon Kal *magazine publisher*

Cranbury
Reichek, Morton Arthur *retired magazine editor, writer*
Yoseloff, Julien David *publishing company executive*
Yoseloff, Thomas *publisher*

Cranford
Bodian, Nat G. *publishing, marketing consultant, author, lecturer, lexicographer*

Deal
Becker, Richard Stanley *music publisher*

East Brunswick
Thompson, Robert McBroom *publishing executive*

East Rutherford
Taylor, Lawrence *sports commentator, former professional football player*

Edison
Comstock, Robert Ray *journalism educator, newspaper editor*
Hunter, Michael *publishing executive*

Elmwood Park
Scudder, Richard B. *newspaper executive*

Englewood
†Caulo, Ralph Daniel *publishing executive*
Friedman, Emanuel *publishing company executive*

Englewood Cliffs
Bradler, James Edward *publishing company executive*
Butterfield, Bruce Scott *publishing company executive*
†Glasser, Lynn Schreiber *publisher*
†Glasser, Stephen Andrew *publishing executive, lawyer*
Guiher, James Morford, Jr. *publisher*
Haltiwanger, Robert Sidney, Jr. *book publishing executive*
Hurst, Kenneth Thurston *publisher*

Florham Park
Mott, Vincent Valmon *publisher, author*

Fort Lee
Fischel, Daniel Norman *publishing consultant*
†Gharib, Susie *television newscaster*
†Insana, Ronald Gerard *newscaster*
†Sturtevant, Peter Mann, Jr. *television news executive*
Williams, Edwin William *publisher*

Hackensack
Ahearn, James *newspaper columnist*
†Benfield, Richard Ernest *journalist*
†Blomquist, David Wels *journalist*
†Mack, Patricia Johnson *newspaper editor*
Margulies, James Howard *editorial cartoonist*
†Pennington, William Mark *sportswriter*
†Waixel, Vivian *journalist*

Haddonfield
Cheney, Daniel Lavern *retired magazine publisher*

Harvey Cedars
Elliott, Joseph Gordon, Jr. *retired newspaper executive*

Hawthorne
†Fry, Ronald William *publishing executive*

Hillside
Enslow, Ridley Madison, Jr. *book publisher*

Hoboken
Regazzi, John James, III *publishing executive*

Holmdel
Wyndrum, Ralph W., Jr. *communications company executive*

Jersey City
Ingrassia, Paul Joseph *publishing executive*
Katz, Colleen *editor in chief*
Shildneck, Barbara Jean *accounting magazine editor*
Wagner, Douglas Walker Ellyson *journal editor*
Williams, Alan Davison *publishing company executive*

Long Branch
Lagowski, Barbara Jean *writer, book editor*

Mahwah
Bram, Leon Leonard *publishing company executive*
Eiger, Richard William *publisher*
†Lynch, Kevin A. *book publishing executive*
†Schecter, M. *book publishing executive*

Maplewood
†Hammond, Caleb Dean, III *publishing executive*
†Hammond, Kathleen Doorish *publishing executive*

Margate City
Kennedy, Berenice Connor (Mrs. Jefferson Kennedy, Jr.) *magazine executive, writer, consultant*

Marlton
Forbes, Gordon Maxwell *sports journalist, commentator*

Medford
Hogan, Thomas Harlan *publisher*

Metuchen
Daub, Albert Walter *publishing executive*
Horrocks, Norman *publisher*

Midland Park
Koster, John Peter, Jr. *journalist, author*

Millburn
Liben, Michael Paul *magazine publisher*
Raff, Gilbert *publishing company executive*

Montclair
Brownrigg, Walter Grant *cartoonist, corporate executive*
Gogick, Kathleen Christine *magazine editor, publisher*
Hardin, John Alexander *retired broadcasting consultant*
Jacoby, Tamar *journalist, author*
Sabin, William Albert *editor*

Montvale
Pfister, James Joseph *publishing company executive*
Sifton, David Whittier *magazine editor*

Montville
Galella, Ronald Edward *photojournalist*

Morris Plains
Bruggink, Herman *publishing executive*
Rakay, William R. *publishing company executive*

Morristown
Ahl, David Howard *writer, editor*
Suchodolski, Ronald Eugene *publishing company executive*

Murray Hill
Wagner, Edward Kurt *publishing company executive*

Neptune
†Clurfeld, Andrea *editor, food critic*
†Colantoni, Alfred Daniel *newspaper executive*
Lass, E(rnest) Donald *communications company executive*
Ollwerther, William Raymond *newspaper editor*
†Plangere, Jules L., III *newpaper company executive*
†Strauss, Robert Seth *critic*

New Brunswick
Horowitz, Irving Louis *publisher, educator*

New Providence
Barnes, Sandra Henley *publishing company executive*
Cooper, Carol Diane *publishing company executive*
Siegel, Ira Theodore *publishing executive*
†Walker, Stanley P. *publishing executive*

Newark
†Allen, David *newspaper editor*
†Bartner, Martin *newspaper executive*
Bishop, Gordon Bruce *journalist*
†Braun, Robert *newspaper editor*
Canfield, William Newton *editorial cartoonist*
†Cocchia, Neal *newspaper editor*
†Everett, Richard G. *newspaper editor*
Gillett, Jonathan Newell *publishing executive*
†Greendorfer, Terese Grosman *fashion editor*
†Harrison, Charles *newspaper editor*
†Kanzler, George *journalist, critic*
†Klein, Willie *newspaper editor*
†Lenehan, Art *newspaper editor*
†Martinez, Arturo *newspaper editor*
†Maske, Monica *newspaper editor*
†Newhouse, Mark William *publishing executive*
Pye, Mort *newspaper editor*
†Sleed, Joel *newspaper editor*
Wolper, Allan L. *journalist, educator*

Newton
Carstens, Harold Henry *publisher*

Northvale
Aronson, Jason *publisher*
†Kurzweil, Arthur *publisher, writer, educator*

Oldwick
Snyder, Arthur *publishing company executive*

Paramus
Underwood, Steven Clark *publishing executive*

Park Ridge
Noyes, Robert Edwin *publisher, writer*

Parsippany
Geyer, Thomas Powick *newspaper publisher*

Passaic
Levine, David M. *newspaper editor*

Pennington
Harris, Frederick George *publishing company executive*

Piscataway
†Fogiel, Max *publishing executive*

Plainsboro
†Talkington, William Ale *publishing company executive*

Pleasantville
†Briant, Maryjane *newspaper editor*
Hopson, James Warren *newspaper publisher*
†Linz, Carla Jean *newspaper editor*

Princeton
†Austin, Danforth Whitley *newspaper executive*
Buttenheim, Edgar Marion *publishing executive*
Doherty, Leonard Edward *financial publishing company executive*
Lippincott, Walter Heulings, Jr. *publishing executive*
O'Donnell, Laurence Gerard *newspaper editor*
†Palsho, Dorothea Coccoli *information services executive*
Weiss, Renée Karol *editor, writer, musician*
Wilson, Donald Malcolm *publishing executive*

Ridgewood
Anderson, Thomas Kemp, Jr. *editor*
Economaki, Chris Constantine (Christopher Economaki) *publisher, editor*
Kiernan, Richard Francis *publisher*

Rumson
Robinson, William Wheeler *editor*

Saddle River
Buckler, Beatrice *editor*
Dowden, Carroll Vincent *publishing company executive*

Secaucus
Bender, Bruce F. *book publishing executive*
Thomas, Ian Leslie Maurice *publisher*

Short Hills
Winter, Ruth Grosman (Mrs. Arthur Winter) *journalist*

Sparta
Spence, Robert Leroy *publishing executive*

Stockholm
dePaolo, Ronald Francis *editor, publisher*

Summit
LeDuc, J. Adrien M. *publishing company executive, consultant*
Scudder, Edward Wallace, Jr. *newspaper and broadcasting executive*

Tenafly
Vinocur, M. Richard *publisher*

Trenton
†Bilotti, Richard *newspaper publisher*
Kelly, Thomas Joseph, III *photojournalist*
Stewart, Barbara Elizabeth *free-lance magazine editor, artist*
†Weissman, Daniel *journalist*

Tuckerton
Egan, Roger Edward *publishing executive*

Verona
Meyer, Helen (Mrs. Abraham J. Meyer) *retired editorial consultant*

Woodstown
Koehler, George Applegate *broadcasting company executive*

NEW MEXICO

Albuquerque
†Burton, Johanna King *journalist*
Danziger, Jerry *broadcasting executive*
Goldston, Barbara M. Harral *editor*
Guthrie, Patricia Sue *newspaper reporter, free-lance writer*
Hadas, Elizabeth Chamberlayne *publisher*
Johnson, Robert Hersel *journalist*
Lang, Thompson Hughes *publishing company executive*
Looney, Ralph Edwin *journalist, editor, author, photographer*
Mc Million, John Macon *retired newspaper publisher*
†Stieber, Tamar *newswriter*
†Welsome, Eileen *journalist*

Glorieta
Mc Coy, Robert Baker *publisher*

Las Cruces
Dickinson, James Gordon *editor*

Los Alamos
Mendius, Patricia Dodd Winter *editor, educator, writer*

Reserve
Tackman, Arthur Lester *newspaper publisher, management consultant*

Santa Fe
†Calloway, Larry *columnist*
Drabanski, Emily Ann *editor*
Ettinger, Richard Prentice *publishing company executive*
Forsdale, (Chalmers) Louis *education and communication educator*
Mc Kinney, Robert Moody *newspaper editor and publisher*

NEW YORK

Albany
†Eastman, William Don *publishing executive*
Lynch, Daniel *newspaper editor, writer*
Morga Bellizzi, Celeste *editor*
Murray, David *journalist, author*
†Reynolds, Joseph P. *publishing executive, educational consultant*
Rosenfeld, Harry Morris *editor*

Armonk
Sharpe, Myron Emanuel *publisher, editor, writer*

Astoria
Douglas, Eileen *news broadcaster*

Baldwin Place
Kurian, George Thomas *publisher*

Ballston Spa
Barba, Harry *publisher, editor, author, educator*

Bayport
Poli, Kenneth Joseph *editor*

Bedford
Bowman, James Kinsey *publishing company executive, rare book specialist*

Bellport
Hughes, Elinor Lambert *drama and film critic*

Briarcliff Manor
Zimmar, George Peter *publishing executive, psychology educator*

Briarwood
Danna, Jo J. *publisher, author, anthropologist*

Bridgehampton
Phillips, Warren Henry *publisher*

Bronx
Carrick, Bruce Robert *publishing company executive*
Moritz, Charles Fredric *book editor*
†Rizzuto, Phillip Francis (Scooter) *former sports broadcaster, former professional baseball player*
Weins, Leo Matthew *publishing company executive*
Zalaznick, Sheldon *editor, journalist*

Bronxville
Barnhart, Clarence Lewis *lexicographer, editor*
Lombardo, Philip Joseph *broadcasting company executive*
Noble, James Kendrick, Jr. *media industry consultant*

Brooklyn
Bianco, Anthony Joseph, III *newswriter*
Bode, Walter Albert *editor*
Carlson, Ralph Lawrence *book publisher*
Federici, William Vito *newspaper reporter*
Friis, Erik Johan *editor, publisher*
Harvey, Edmund Huxley, Jr. (Tad Harvey) *editor*
Lobron, Barbara L. *writer, editor*
Moore, Arthur James *editor*
Sanford, David Boyer *writer, editor*
Schmidt, Fred (Orval Frederick Schmidt) *editor*
Walsh, George William *publishing company executive, editor*

Brookville
Huber, Don Lawrence *publisher*

Buffalo
†Brady-Borland, Karen *reporter*
Collins, J. Michael *public broadcasting executive*
†Curran, Robert *columnist*
Goldhaber, Gerald Martin *communication educator, author, consultant*
Halpert, Leonard Walter *retired editor*
†Ireland, Barbara Hennig *newspaper editor*
Light, Murray Benjamin *newspaper editor*
†Okun, Janice *food editor*
†Robinson, David Clinton *reporter*
†Spencer, Foster Lewis *newspaper editor*
Toles, Thomas Gregory *editorial cartoonist*
†Trotter, Herman Eager, Jr. *music critic*
Urban, Henry Zeller *newspaperman*
†Vogel, Michael N. *journalist, writer, historian*

Campbell Hall
Ottaway, James Haller, Jr. *newspaper publisher*

Chappaqua
Gstalder, Herbert William *publisher*

Clifton Park
Kleinschrod, Walter Andrew *publishing company executive, author, journalist*

Croton On Hudson
Coleman, Earl Maxwell *publishing company executive*
Kahn, Roger *author*
Karales, James Harry *photojournalist*
Miranda, Robert Nicholas *publishing company executive*
Nelson, Charles Arthur *publisher, consultant*
Straka, Laszlo Richard *publishing consultant*

Delmar
Mangouni, Norman *publisher*

Dobbs Ferry
Cohen, Philip Francis *publishing company executive*
Holtz, Sidney *publishing company executive*
Levy, Alan Joseph *editor, journalist, writer*
Simon, Lothar *publishing company executive*
Whiting, John Randolph *publisher, writer, editor*

East Hampton
De Bruhl, Arthur Marshall *writer, editor, publishing consultant*

East Northport
Reed, Robert Monroe *publishing executive*

Farmingdale
Steckler, Larry *publisher, editor*

Floral Park
Chatoff, Michael Alan *legal editor*

Flushing
Cathcart, Robert Stephen *mass media consultant*
Kiner, Ralph McPherran *sports commentator, former baseball player*

Forest Hills
Levine, Charles Michael *publishing company executive, consultant*
Stinson, Richard James *editor*

Fort Covington
Dunwich, Gerina *magazine editor, author*

Garden City
Olcott, William Alfred *magazine editor*

Goshen
Goodreds, John Stanton *newspaper publisher*

Grand Island
White, Ralph David *retired editor and writer*

Great Neck
Fiel, Maxine Lucille *journalist, behavioral analyst, lecturer*
Panes, Jack Samuel *publishing company executive*
Roth, Harvey Paul *publisher*
Rubin, Irving *editor*
Velie, Lester *journalist*

Hamilton
Edmonston, William Edward, Jr. *publisher*

Harrison
McCaffrey, Neil *publishing executive*

Hauppauge
Reis, Don *publishing executive*

Hawthorne
†Koffler, Richard Max *publishing company executive, author, translator*
†Scheffler, Eckart Arthur *publisher*

Hempstead
Adams, Robert Hugo *business news publisher, English teacher*
Masheck, Joseph Daniel *art critic, educator*

Hicksville
Salsberg, Arthur Philip *publishing company executive*
Tinghitella, Stephen *publishing company executive*

Huntington
Christiansen, Donald David *editor, publisher, electrical engineer*
Connor, J. Robert *editor*
Holahan, Richard Vincent *former magazine and book publisher*

Huntington Station
†Tollerson, Ernest *newspaper editor*

Irvington
Lugenbeel, Edward Elmer *publisher*

Ithaca
Bourne, Russell *publisher, author*
Conklin, Gordon Leroy *retired editor*
Kendler, Bernhard *editor*
Schwartz, Donald Franklin *communication educator*

Jackson Heights
Sklar, Morty E. *publisher, editor*

Jamestown
Goldman, Simon *broadcasting executive*

Katonah
Fry, John *magazine editor*
Krefting, Robert J(ohn) *publishing company executive*
Raymond, Jack *journalist, public relations executive, foundation executive*
Shanaphy, Edward John *publishing executive*

Kinderhook
Lankhof, Frederik Jan *publishing executive*

Kings Park
Greene, Robert William *media consultant*

Larchmont
Kerr, Walter F. *retired drama critic, author*

Locust Valley
Zulch, Joan Carolyn *retired medical publishing company executive*

Long Beach
Robbins, Jeffrey Howard *media consultant, research writer, educator*

Mamaroneck
Hettich, Arthur Matthias *editor*

Manhasset
Leeds, Lilo J. *publishing executive*
Rostky, George Harold *editor*
Wallace, Richard *editor, writer*
Wallace, Richard K. *editor, journalist*

Maryknoll
Gormley, Robert John *book publisher*

Mattituck
†Paulsen, Joanna *publishing executive*

Melville
Asimov, Stanley *newspaper executive*
†Bass, Elizabeth *editor*
†Bengelsdorf, Peter *newspaper editor*
Brandt, Robert Frederic, III *newspaper editor, journalist*
Colen, B. D. *journalist*
Cooke, Robert William *science journalist*
†Dooley, James C. *newspaper editor*
Fox, Douglas Brian *newspaper publishing company executive*
Hall, Charlotte Hauch *newspaper editor*
Hildebrand, John Frederick *newspaper columnist*
Isenberg, Steven Lawrence *newspaper executive*
Kahn, David *editor, author*
Klurfeld, James Michael *journalist*
Lynn, James Dougal *newspaper editor, journalist*
Marro, Anthony James *newspaper editor*
Moran, Paul James *journalist, columnist*
Payne, Leslie *newspaper editor, columnist, journalist, author*
Redder, Thomas H. *newspaper publishing executive*
†Robins, Marjorie Kaplan *newspaper editor*
†Roel, Ron *newspaper editor*
Schneider, Howard Stewart *newspaper editor, educator*
†Sommer, Jeff *journalist*
Toedtman, James Smith *newspaper editor, journalist*
Woldt, Harold Frederick, Jr. *newspaper publishing executive*

Middle Village
Kolatch, Alfred Jacob *publisher*

Middletown
†Bedell, Barbara Lee *newspaperwoman*
†Gaydos, Robert John *newspaper editor*
†Kennedy, William Townsend *newspaper executive*
†Sprick, Dennis Michael *critic, copy editor*

Mineola
Cirker, Hayward *publisher*

Montauk
First, Wesley *publishing company executive*

Mount Kisco
Pastorelle, Peter John *film company executive, radiological services and waste management company executive*

Mount Vernon
Mc Neill, Charles James *publishing executive*

New City
Elberg, Darryl Gerald *publisher, educator*

New Rochelle
Nolte, Judith Ann *magazine editor*
Saunders, Rubie Agnes *former magazine editor, author*

New York
Abelson, Alan *columnist*
Abercrombie, Stanley *magazine editor*
Abrahams, William Miller *editor, author*
Achtert, Walter Scott *publisher*
†Adams, Seibert Gruber, Jr. *publisher*
Addison, Herbert John *publishing executive*
Albert, Marv *sportscaster, program director*
Alexander, Shana *journalist, author, lecturer*
Allison, Wick *publishing executive*
†Alpern, David Mark *magazine editor, broadcast journalist and producer*
Alter, Jonathan Hammerman *journalist*
Ambrose, Daniel Michael *publishing executive*
†Amdur, Neil *sports editor, writer*
Amster, Linda Evelyn *newspaper executive, consultant*
†Andersen, Kurt Byars *magazine editor, critic, writer*
Anderson, Bradley Jay *cartoonist*
Anderson, David Poole *sportswriter*
Anderson, Jack Northman *newspaper columnist*
Anderson, Walter Herman *magazine editor*
Andrews, Frederick Franck *newspaper editor*
Angier, Natalie Marie *science journalist*
Antilla, Susan *journalist*
Antonell, Walter John *publishing executive*
Appleton, Myra *magazine editor, writer*
Arcara, James Amadeus *broadcasting company executive*
Arenson, Karen Wattel *journalist*
Arledge, Roone *television executive*
Arnold, Kenneth Lloyd *publisher, playwright*
Arnold, Martin *journalist*
Asahina, Robert James *editor, publishing company executive*
Asen, Shel F. *publishing company executive*
Asher, Aaron *editor, publisher*
†Atkinson, Paul C. *newspaper publishing executive*
†Attkisson, Sharyl T. *news correspondent, writer*
Auchincloss, Kenneth *magazine editor*
Austin, Gabriel Christopher *publisher*
Babson, Irving K. *publishing company executive*
Bache, Theodore Stephen *recording company executive*
Bahash, Robert J. *publishing executive*
Bahr, Lauren S. *publishing company executive*
Bahrenburg, D. Claeys *publishing executive*
Bailey, Janet Dee *publishing company executive*
Bakal, Carl *writer, public relations counsel, photojournalist*
Baker, Elizabeth Calhoun *magazine editor*
Baker, Russell Wayne *columnist, author*
Baker, William Franklin *public broadcasting company executive*
Baker, William George *publishing company financial executive*
Baldassano, Corinne Leslie *radio executive*
Ball, John Paul *publishing company executive*
Ballantine, Ian *publisher*
Bandier, Martin *music publisher*
†Baquet, Dean Paul *investigative reporter*
Baranski, Joan Sullivan *publisher*
Barnes, Clive Alexander *drama and dance critic*
Barnes, Duncan *magazine editor, writer*
Baron, Carolyn *editor, author, publishing executive*
Barrett, Loretta Anne *publishing executive*
Barron, James Turman *journalist*
Barry, Edward William *publisher*
Barry, Lynda *cartoonist, playwright, author*
Barry, William Garrett, III *publishing company executive*
Bartley, Robert LeRoy *newspaper editor*
Baruch, Ralph M. *communications executive*
†Bazell, Robert Joseph *science correspondent*
Beardsley, Charles William *engineering publisher, editor, writer*
Becker, Don Crandall *newspaper executive*
Begell, William *publisher*
Bemis, Mary *editor-in-chief, magazine*
Bennack, Frank Anthony, Jr. *publishing company executive*
†Bennett, Edward A. *broadcast company executive*
Bercovitch, Hanna Margareta *editor*
Berger, Eric *magazine editor*
Berkwitt, George Joseph *editor*
Bernstein, Carl *author, journalist*
Bernstein, Richard Allen *publishing company executive*
Bernstein, Robert Louis *book publishing company executive*
Berrien, James Stuart *magazine publisher*
Berry, Joyce Charlotte *university press editor*
Bewkes, Jeff *television broadcasting company executive*
Biewen, Robert L. *publishing executive*
†Bite-Dickson, Guna *newspaper editor*
Black, Hillel Moses *publisher*
Black, Neil Spencer *magazine publishing executive*
†Black, Rosemary *newspaper editor*
Blair, William Granger *retired newspaperman*
Bleiberg, Robert Marvin *retired financial editor*
Bliven, Naomi *book reviewer*
Blyth, Myrna Greenstein *publishing executive, editor, author*
Blythe, William LeGette, II *editor, writer*
Boehm, David Alfred *publisher, producer*
†Boehm, Lincoln A. *publishing company executive*
Bonniwell, Katherine *magazine executive*
†Borden, Elizabeth B. *publishing executive*
Borders, William Alexander *journalist*
Bosley, John Scott *editor*
†Bouloukos, Don P. *broadcast company executive*
Boultinghouse, Marion Craig Bettinger *editor*
Boundas, Louise Gooch *editor*
Boyce, Joseph Nelson *journalist*
Brack, Reginald Kufeld, Jr. *publisher*
Bradford, John Carroll *retired magazine executive*
Bradley, Edward R. *news correspondent*
Brady, James Winston *writer, television commentator*
Brant, Sandra *magazine publisher*
Braziller, George *publisher*
†Brecher, John *newspaper editor*
†Breindel, Eric Marc *editor, columnist, educator*
Brennan, Timothy William *entertainment company executive*
Breslin, Jimmy *columnist, author*
Brewer, John Charles *journalist*
Brice, John R. *publishing sales manager*
Briggs, Jean Audrey *publishing company executive*
†Brill, Steven *magazine editor*
Brimelow, Peter *journalist*
Brody, Jacqueline *editor*
Brody, Jane Ellen *journalist*
Brokaw, Thomas John *television broadcast executive, correspondent*
Brooks, Geraldine *reporter, correspondent*
Broun, Heywood Hale *author, broadcaster, actor*
Brown, Helen Gurley *writer, editor*
Brown, Les (Lester Louis) *journalist*
Brown, Marvin S. *publisher*
Brown, Tina *magazine editor*
†Browne, Arthur *newspaper editor*
Browne, Malcolm Wilde *journalist*
Browne, Morgan Trew *editor*
Bryant, Gay *magazine editor, writer*
Brydon, Donald James *media consultant, former news service executive*
Buckley, Priscilla Langford *magazine editor*
Buckley, Virginia Laura *editor*
Buckley, William Frank, Jr. *magazine editor, writer*
Buhagiar, Marion *editor, author*
Burenga, Kenneth L. *publishing executive*
Burgheim, Richard Allan *magazine editor*
Burns, John F. *reporter*
Bussell, Mark Stephen *newspaper picture editor*
Bylinsky, Gene Michael *magazine editor*
Byrne, Gerard Anthony *publishing company executive, marketing consultant*
†Caldwell, Earl *newspaper columnist*
Callum, Myles *magazine editor, writer*
†Campbell, Robert Chambers *critic, playwright*
†Campi, John G. *newspaper publishing executive*
Canby, Vincent *film critic*
Cantwell, Mary *journalist*
Cappon, Rene Jacques *news editor*
Carr, Gladys Justin *publishing company executive*
†Carroll, Kent *book publishing executive*
†Carter, Graydon *editor*
Carter, John Mack *publishing company executive*
†Carter, Sylvia *journalist*
Chancellor, John William *former news correspondent*
Chandler, Kenneth A. *newspaper editor*
Chase, Sylvia B. *journalist*
†Chernoff, Allan *correspondent*
Cherry, Rona Beatrice *magazine editor, writer*
†Chesnutt, Jane *publishing executive*
†Chiles, Nick *newspaper reporter*
Chimsky, Mark Evan *editorial executive*
Chook, Paul Howard *publishing executive*
Christian, Darrell L. *journalist*
Chung, Constance Yu-hwa (Connie Chung) *broadcast journalist*
Clabby, William Robert *editor*
Clurman, Richard Michael *journalist*
Cohen, Jeff *media critic, columnist*
Colasuonno, Louis Christopher *newspaper editor*
Colbourn, Frank Edwin *communications educator*
Collins, Bud *sports commentator*
Connolly, William Gerard *newspaper editor*
Conway, David Antony *corporate executive*
Cook, James *magazine editor*
Cooke, Alfred Alistair *correspondent, broadcaster*
Cooney, Joan Ganz *broadcasting executive*
Cooper, Arthur Martin *magazine editor*
Cooper, Guy *editor periodical*
Corcoran, David *newspaper editor*
Corliss, Richard Nelson *critic, magazine editor*
Cornell, George W. *journalist*
Corporon, John Robert *broadcasting executive*
†Cose, Ellis *magazine editor*
Cosell, Howard (Howard William Cohen) *sports journalist*
Costello, Gerald Michael *editor*
†Cotler, Joanna *children's book editor, artist*
Couric, Katherine *broadcast journalist*
Court, Kathryn Diana *editor*
†Cox, Winston H. *television executive*
Craig, George *publishing executive*
Crawford, Harold Bernard *publisher*
Crawley, John Boevey *publisher*
†Crier, Catherine *television news correspondent*
Crist, Judith *film and drama critic*
Croce, Arlene Louise *critic*
Cronkite, Walter *radio and television news correspondent*
Cross, Theodore Lamont *publisher, author*
†Crow, Elizabeth *publishing company executive*
Crow, Elizabeth Smith *publishing company executive*
Crowdus, Gary Alan *film company executive*
Culhane, John William *journalist, author, film historian*
†Cunningham, Jeffrey Milton *publishing executive*
Cuozzo, Steven David *newspaper editor*
†Curry, Ann *broadcast journalist*
Curry, Jack *magazine editor*
†Cutie, James A. *newspaper publishing executive*
Daly, Charles Patrick *publishing company executive*
Daly, Joe Ann Godown *publishing company executive*
†Daly, Margaret V. *magazine editor*
†Daly, Michael *newspaper columnist*
D'Angelo, Joseph Francis *publishing company executive*
Daniels, Faith *newscaster*
†Daniels, Joanne D. *publisher*
Danzig, Frederick Paul *newspaper editor*
†Danzig, Robert James *newspaper executive*
Davis, Clive Jay *record company executive*
Davis, Orlin Ray *publisher, consultant*
†Davoe, David *publishing executive*
†Decker, Bob *newspaper editor*
Dedman, Bill *journalist*
Deems, Richard Emmet *magazine publisher*
Deitz, Paula *magazine editor*
Dekker, Marcel *publishing company executive*
Derow, Peter Alfred *publishing company executive*
Deutsch, Martin Bernard Joseph *editor, publisher*
Diamond, Robert Stephen *publishing company executive*
Dillingham, Robert Bulger *publishing executive*
Dionne, Joseph Lewis *publishing company executive*
Disney, Anthea *editor*
Dobell, Byron Maxwell *magazine consultant*
Doherty, Thomas *publisher*
Dojny, Richard Francis *publishing company executive*
Dolgen, Jonathan L. *motion picture company executive*
Dolger, Jonathan *editor, literary agent*
†Donald, Roger Thomas *publishing executive*
Dormann, Henry O. *magazine publisher*
†Dornemann, Michael *book publishing executive*
Drapkin, Arnold Howard *consulting picture editor, journalist, program director*
Drasner, Fred *newspaper publishing executive*
†Drewry, Elizabeth *newspaper publishing executive*
†Duff, John Richard *book publisher*
Duggan, Dennis Michael *newspaper editor*
Duncan, Richard *magazine editor*
Dunn, James Joseph *magazine publisher*
†Dunn, Martin *newspaper editor-in-chief*
Dunne, Thomas Leo *editor, author, publisher*
Dupuy, Frank Russell, Jr. *magazine publisher*
Duva, Philip *publishing executive*
Dystel, Jane Dee *literary agent*
Ebersol, Dick *television broadcasting executive*
Eckman, Fern Marja *journalist*
Edmiston, Mark Morton *publishing company executive*
Eisenstaedt, Alfred *photojournalist*
Ellerbee, Linda *broadcast journalist*
Elliman, Donald *magazine company executive*
Elliott, Osborn *journalist, educator, former university dean*
Ellis, Charles Richard *publishing executive*
Ellsworth, Arthur Whitney *publishing consultant*
†Emerson, Ken *newspaper editor*
Enberg, Dick *sportscaster*
Epstein, Barbara *editor*
Epstein, Jason *publishing company executive*
Erbsen, Claude Ernest *journalist*
Erlanger, Steven Jay *journalist*
Ertegun, Ahmet Munir *record company executive*
†Esposito, Richard Joseph *journalist*
Esterow, Milton *magazine editor, publisher*
Evans, Edward Parker *former publishing company executive*
†Evans, Harold M. *publishing executive, writer*
†Everette, Cheryl *newspaper editor*
Fairchild, John Burr *publisher*
Faludi, Susan C. *journalist, scholarly writer*
Farber, Jackie *editor*
Fargis, Paul McKenna *publishing consultant, book developer, editor*
†Faris, Peter *newspaper publishing executive*
†Farney, Dennis *journalist*
†Feders, Sid *journalist, television producer*

Feinberg, Samuel retired newspaper columnist
†Feiwel, Jean Leslie editorial director
Feniger, Jerome Roland, Jr. broadcasting executive
Ferber, Samuel publishing executive
Feretic, Eileen Susan editor
Ferrara, Peter Biagio, Jr. radio broadcast executive
Fertig, Howard publisher, editor
†Fields, Joyce M. publishing company executive
Finberg, Alan Robert retired newspaper executive, lawyer
Fine, Donald Irving editor, publisher
Fine, Michael Joseph publishing and communications company executive
†Fiore, Mary magazine editor
Fish, Hamilton public interest executive
Fisher, Arthur magazine editor
Fisher, David Woodrow editor, publisher
Fisher, Gary Alan publishing executive
Fishman, James H. magazine executive
†Fitzgerald, James E. newspaper publiching executive
Flagg, Jeanne Bodin editor
†Flanagan, Bernard newspaper publishing executive
Flanagan, Dennis journalist
Florio, Steven T. magazine executive
Foley, Joseph Bernard business publishing executive
†Fondiller, David Stewart journalist
Forbes, Christopher (Kip Forbes) publisher
Forbes, Malcolm Stevenson, Jr. publishing executive
Forbes, Timothy Carter publisher
†Forst, Donald newspaper editor
†Fox, Stephen Cress television correspondent, writer
Fox, Sylvan journalist
Frank, James Aaron magazine editor, author
Frankel, Max journalist, newspaper editor
Franks, Lucinda Laura journalist
Frawley, Sean Paul publishing executive
Freedgood, Anne Goodman editor
Freedman, Albert Z. publishing company executive
Friedheim, Eric Arthur publisher, editor
†Friedman, Fredrica Schwab editor, publisher
†Friedman, J. Roger publisher
Friedman, Joshua M. journalist, educator
Friedman, Robert editor
Friendly, Fred W. journalist, educator
Frith, Margaret publishing company executive
Fuchs, Joseph Louis magazine publisher
Fuchs, Michael J. television executive
Furlong, Charles Richard broadcasting executive
Gaines, James Russell magazine editor, author
Gainsburg, Roy Ellis publishing executive
Galassi, Jonathan White book publishing company executive
Gallo, William Victor cartoonist
Galotti, Donna publishing executive
Galotti, Ronald magazine publisher
Gandolf, Raymond L. media correspondent
Garagiola, Joe sports broadcaster
Garratt, Graham publishing executive
†Gatti, Frank R. publishing executive
Gazouleas, Panagiotis J. journalist
Geis, Bernard book publisher
Geiser, Elizabeth Able publishing company executive
Gelb, Arthur newspaper editor
Gelb, Leslie Howard organization president, lecturer
Gellermann, Henry journalist, cultural organization administrator
Gerhardt, Lillian Noreen magazine editor
Germano, William Paul publisher
Gewirtz, Gerry editor
Gibson, Charles DeWolf broadcast journalist
Giddins, Gary Mitchell music critic, columnist
Gifford, Frank Newton sportscaster, commentator
Gillespie, Sarah Ashman newspaper syndicate executive
†Gilman, Richard H. newspaper publishing executive
Giniger, Kenneth Seeman publisher
Ginzburg, Ralph editor, writer
Giraldi, Robert Nicholas film director
Giroux, Robert editor, book publisher, author
Glaser, Robert Leonard television executive
Glass, Daniel S. record company executive
Gold, Sylviane entertainment editor, writer, critic
†Goldberg, Bernard R. news correspondent
Goldberg, Sidney editor
Goldberger, Paul Jesse architecture critic, writer, educator, editor
†Golden, Soma newspaper editor
†Golden, Stephen publishing executive, forest products company executive
Goldsmith, Arthur Austin magazine editor
Goldsmith, Robert Lewis youth association magazine executive
Goldstein, Norm editor, writer
Gollin, Albert Edwin media research executive, sociologist
Gollob, Herman Cohen publishing company executive, editor
Golson, George Barry editor
†Gooding, Richard newspaper editor
Goodman, Jordan Elliot journalist
†Goodstein, Les newspaper publishing executive
Gopnik, Adam editor, writer
†Gordon, Elizabeth Jane publisher
Gorham, David L. newspaper executive
Gotlieb, Irwin I. broadcast executive
Gottlieb, Paul publishing company executive
Gottlieb, Robert Adams publisher
Goulazian, Peter Robert broadcasting executive
Graham, Howard Barrett publishing company executive
Gralla, Lawrence publishing company executive
Gralla, Milton publisher
†Gralnick, Jeff broadcasting company executive
†Grann, Phyllis publisher, editor
Grant, Virginia Annette newspaper editor, journalist
Graves, Earl Gilbert publisher
Gray, Barry Sherman radio commentator
Grebow, Edward television executive, banker
Green, Ashbel publishing executive, book editor
Green, Dan publishing company executive
Green, George Joseph publishing executive
Greenberg, Freddi Jane editor-in-chief, magazine
Greenfield, (Henry) Jeff news analyst
Greenwald, Martin publishing company executive
Grenquist, Peter Carl publishing executive
Grey, Linda book publisher
Grigsby, Henry Jefferson, Jr. editor
Grimsley, Will Henry author
Gropp, Louis Oliver editor in chief
Grose, William Rush publishing executive
Groseclose, Everett Harrison editor
†Grossman, Barbara Susanne publisher
Grossman, Janice publisher
Guccione, Anthony Joseph, II media entrepreneur, cable television executive
Guccione, Robert Charles Joseph Edward Sabatini publisher
Gumbel, Bryant Charles broadcaster
Gunther, Jane Perry (Mrs. John Gunther) editor, writer
†Gwertzman, Bernard newspaper editor
Habeeb, Virginia Thabet magazine editor
Hager, Larry Stanley book editor, publishing executive
Haiken, Leatrice Brown periodical editor
Halberstam, David journalist, author
Hall, Nancy Christensen publishing company executive, author, editor
Harris, Ann S. editor
Harris, Charles Frederick book publishing executive
Harris, Louis public opinion analyst, columnist
Harrison, Gerald publisher
Hartford, William H. magazine editor, writer, lecturer
Hauck, Marguerite Hall broadcasting executive, antique dealer
Hauser, Gustave M. cable and electronic communications company executive
†Hayon, Jack publishing executive
Hearst, Randolph Apperson publishing executive
Hechinger, Fred Michael newspaper editor, columnist, foundation executive
Heckscher, August journalist, author, foundation executive
Heffner, Richard Douglas educator, historian, communications consultant, television producer
†Helferich, Gerard Marion book editor
Heloise columnist, lecturer, broadcaster, author
†Henley, Deborah newspaper editor
Henninger, Daniel Paul editor
Hensler, Guenter Manfred record company executive
Hentoff, Margot columnist
Herbert, Bob newspaper columnist
†Herman, John Joseph publisher
Hertz, Leon publishing executive
†Hertzberg, Daniel journalist
Hertzberg, Hendrik magazine editor, writer
Heuer, Kenneth John publishing company executive
Hewes, Henry drama critic
Heyworth, James O. communications company executive
Hicks, Tyler Gregory publishing company executive, writer
Hill, Norman Julius publisher, author, editor, playwright
Hill, Pamela television executive
Hills, Frederic Wheeler editor, publishing company executive
Hinds, Thomas Sheldon publisher, organization executive
Hirsch, George Aaron publisher
Hirsch, Roseann Conte publisher
Hiss, Tony writer
†Hockenberry, John television journalist
Hoeflin, Ronald Kent philosopher, test designer, journal publisher
Hoeft, Julius Albert publishing company executive
†Hoelterhoff, Manuela Vali newspaper editor, critic
Hoff, Syd(ney) cartoonist, author
Hoffman, Michael Eugene editor, publisher, museum curator
Hoge, Warren M. newspaper and magazine editor
Hollenbeck, Ralph Anthony retired editor, book reviewer
Hollinshead, Byron Sharpe, Jr. publishing company executive
Holmes, Miriam H. publisher
Holstein, Marilyn Anne publishing company executive
Holt, Donald Dale magazine editor
Honan, William Holmes journalist, writer
House, Karen Elliott company executive, former editor, reporter
Howatson, Marianne publisher
Hoyt, Seth publisher
†Hufham, Barbara Frances publishing executive, lawyer
Hughes, Allen music critic
Hughes, Robert Studley Forrest art critic
†Hunter-Gault, Charlayne journalist
Hurley, Cheryl Joyce publishing company executive
Hutchens, John Kennedy journalist, editor
Huxtable, Ada Louise architecture critic
†Hyatt, Jim newspaper editor
Ibarguen, Alberto newspaper executive
Iger, Robert A. broadcast executive
†Ingraham, David Wood broadcast executive
Isaacson, Walter Seff editor
Isay, Jane Franzblau publisher
Jackel, Lawrence publishing company executive
†Jackson, David Parker radio news anchor
Jackson, Keith MacKenzie television commentator, writer, producer
Jaffe, Leo motion picture executive
Jameson, Richard magazine editor, film critic
Jamieson, Edward Leo magazine editor
†Jamieson, Robert John television journalist
Janson, Joseph Bror, II editor, publishing executive
Janssen, Peter Anton magazine editor and publisher
Jaroff, Leon Morton magazine editor
Jarriel, Thomas Edwin correspondent
Jellinek, George broadcast executive, writer, music educator
Jennings, Frank Gerard editor
Jennings, Peter Charles television anchorman
Jensen, Michael Charles journalist, lecturer, author
Jones, Alex S. reporter
†Jones, Colin Howard publishing company executive
Jones, David Rhodes newspaper editor
Jones, Gwenyth Ellen director information systems
Jones, Landon Y., Jr. magazine editor
Jones, Laurie Lynn magazine editor
Jones, William Randall publisher
†Jordan, Susan newspaper editor
Jordan, Wilma Elizabeth Hacker publishing executive
Kael, Pauline film critic, author
Kagan, Julia Lee magazine editor
Kahn, Jenette Sarah publishing company executive
Kahn, Joseph Gabriel newspaperman
Kahn, Robert Theodore photojournalist
†Kalech, Marc newspaper editor
Kaminsky, Howard publisher
Kann, Peter Robert journalist, business reporting and services company executive
Karpel, Craig S. journalist, editor
†Karten, Terry book editor
†Katalinich, Peggy newspaper editor
Katz, Phyllis Pollak magazine publisher and editor
†Kaufman, Victor A. film company executive
Keane, Bil cartoonist
Keating, Cornelius Francis record company executive
†Kehr, David film critic
†Keller, Bill journalist
Kellogg, David publisher
Kelly, L. Thomas magazine publisher, museum director
†Kenney, Martin Edward, Jr. publishing company executive
Keppler, Herbert publishing company executive
†Kerrison, Ray newspaper columnist
Kesting, Theodore magazine editor
†Kiechel, Walter, III magazine editor
Kifner, John William journalist, newspaper correspondent
†Kirshbaum, Laurence J. book publishing executive
Kismaric, Carole Lee editor, writer, book packaging company executive
Kissel, Howard William drama critic
Kiwitt, Sidney motion picture production consultant
†Klipper, Mitchell S. book publishing executive
Kluberdanz, Wallace publishing executive
Knell, Gary Evan media executive, lawyer
Knobler, Peter Stephen magazine editor, writer
Kolatch, Myron magazine editor
†Koons, Linda Gleitsman editor
Koontz, Richard Harvey financial printing company executive
Koppelman, Charles record company executive
Koren, Edward Benjamin cartoonist, educator
Korman, Lewis J. film company executive, consultant, lawyer
Korner, Anthony David publisher
Kosner, Edward A(lan) magazine editor and publisher
Koster, Elaine Landis publishing executive
Kozodoy, Neal magazine editor
Kreh, Kent Q. magazine publishing executive
Krenek, Debby newspaper editor
Krents, Milton Ellis broadcast executive
†Kriney, Marilyn Walker publishing executive
Kristof, Nicholas Donabet journalist
Kroft, Steve news correspondent, editor
Krzyzanowski, Eve broadcasting executive
Kubek, Anthony Christopher (Tony Kubek) sports announcer
Kuhn, Michael motion picture company executive
†Kull, F. Thomas, Jr. newspaper publishing executive
Kurtis, William Horton (Bill Kurtis) broadcast journalist
†Kurtz, Michael J. newspaper publishing executive
Lachenbruch, David editor, writer
LaForce, William Leonard, Jr. photojournalist
Laird, Robert Winslow journalist
†Lalli, Cele Goldsmith editor
†Lalli, Frank magazine editor
Lamirande, Arthur Gordon editor
Lamm, Donald Stephen publishing company executive
Lamont, Lansing journalist, public affairs executive, author
Landau, Peter Edward editor
Landau, Sidney I. publishing executive, lexicographer
Lane, Nancy editor
Lansner, Kermit Irvin editor, consultant
Lapham, Lewis Henry editor, author, television host
†Larsen, Anne editor
Laughlin, James publishing company executive, writer, lecturer
†Laybourne, Geraldine broadcasting executive
Lazarus, Mell cartoonist
Leach, Michael Glen publisher
Leahy, Michael Joseph newspaper editor
Lederer, Edith Madelon journalist
LeDoux, Harold Anthony cartoonist, painter
Lee, Stan (Stanley Martin Lieber) cartoon publisher, writer
Lehmann-Haupt, Christopher Charles Herbert book reviewer
Lelyveld, Joseph Salem newspaper editor, correspondent
Leo, Jacqueline magazine editor-in-chief
Leser, Bernard H. publishing executive
†Leventhal, Kathy Neisloss magazine publisher
Levin, Alan M. television journalist
Levin, Gerald Manuel publishing company executive
Levin, Martin P. publishing executive, lawyer
†Levine, Ellen R. magazine editor
Levine, Richard James publishing executive
Levine, Suzanne Braun magazine editor
†Levinson, Warren Mitchell broadcast journalist
Levitas, Mitchel Ramsey editor
Levitz, Paul Elliot publishing executive
Levy, Alain M. record company executive
Lewis, Flora journalist
Lewis, Russell T. newspaper publishing executive
Liebman, Milton publisher, journalist
Lilien, Mark Ira publishing, retailing and systems executive
Lingeman, Richard Roberts editor, writer
Linz, Werner Mark publishing executive
Littlefield, Martin (Martin Kleinwald) book publishing executive
Loeb, Marshall Robert journalist, magazine editor
Longley, Marjorie Watters newspaper executive
†Loomis, Carol J. journalist
Loomis, Robert Duane publishing company executive, author
Lorenz, Lee Sharp cartoonist
Losee, Thomas Penny, Jr. publisher
Low, Richard H. broadcasting executive, producer
Lund, Peter Anthony broadcast executive
†Lynch, James C. newspaper editor
Lynch, William Dennis, Jr. broadcast journalist
†Lyne, Susan magazine editor
MacArthur, John Roderick C. G. (Rick MacArthur) magazine publisher, journalist
Macdonald, Clifford Palmer editor, writer
Machlin, Milton Robert magazine editor, writer
MacKenzie, John Pettibone journalist
MacNeil, Robert Breckenridge Ware broadcast journalist
Macri, Theodore William book publisher
Macro, Lucia Ann editor
Madden, John Kevin publishing executive
Malabre, Alfred Leopold, Jr. journalist, author
Malamed, Seymour H. motion picture company executive
Mallardi, Michael Patrick broadcasting company executive
Mandelsberg-Weiss, Rose Gail editor in chief
Mantell, Suzanne editor
Mapes, Glynn Dempsey newspaper editor
Mapes, Lynn Calvin publishing executive
Marchioni, Allen publishing company executive
Mardenborough, Leslie A. newspaper publishing company executive
Marella, Philip Daniel broadcasting company executive
Marlette, Douglas Nigel editorial cartoonist, comic strip creator
Martin, Judith Sylvia journalist, author
†Maslin, Janet film critic
Mastromonaco-Adler, Ellen G. publishing company executive
Mathews, Jack Wayne journalist, film critic
Mathews, Linda McVeigh newspaper editor
†Matloff, Robert Leonard publisher
Mattson, Walter Edward retired publishing company executive
Mauldin, William H. (Bill Mauldin) cartoonist
Maurer, Gilbert Charles media company executive
Mayer, Margery Weil publishing executive
Mazzola, Anthony Thomas editor, art consultant, designer
McCandless, Carolyn Keller entertainment, media company executive
McCarver, James Timothy sportscaster
Mc Cormack, Thomas Joseph publishing company executive
Mc Cormick, Kenneth Dale retired editor
Mc Crie, Robert Delbert editor, publisher, educator
McDonell, Robert Terry magazine editor, novelist
Mc Fadden, James Patrick publisher
†Mc Fadden, Robert Dennis reporter
Mc Ginnis, Arthur Joseph publisher
McGraw, Harold Whittlesey, Jr. publisher
McGraw, Robert Pierce publishing executive
Mc Guire, Alfred James former basketball coach, sports equipment company executive, basketball commentator
†McInnis, Helen Louise publishing company executive
McIntyre, Douglas Alexander magazine publisher
Mc Kay, Jim television sports commentator
Mc Keown, William Taylor magazine editor, author
McLaughlin, Mary Rittling magazine editor
McManus, Jason Donald editor
Mc Pherson, Paul Francis publishing company executive
Mc Queeney, Henry Martin, Sr. publisher
McQuillen, Harry A. publishing company executive
Meagher, Mark Joseph publishing company executive
Mehta, A. Sonny publishing company executive
Melvin, Russell Johnston magazine publishing consultant
Mencher, Melvin journalist, retired educator
†Messineo, Karen newspaper publishing executive
Metz, Robert Roy publisher, editor
Meyer, Karl Ernest journalist
Meyer, Pucci newspaper editor
Meyer, Susan E. publisher
Meyers, John Allen magazine publisher
Michaels, Alan Richard sports commentator
Michaels, James Walker magazine editor
Mikita, Joseph Karl broadcasting executive
†Millard, Wenda Harris magazine publisher
Miller, Donald LeSessne publishing executive
Miller, Gerri magazine editor, writer
Miller, Robert L. publishing company executive
Miller, Roberta Davis editor
Minard, Everett Lawrence, III journalist, magazine editor
Minick, Michael publishing executive
†Mirabella, Grace magazine publishing executive
Modell, Frank cartoonist, writer
Mohler, Mary Gail magazine editor
Molho, Emanuel publisher
†Montorio, John Angelo magazine editor
Mooney, Richard E. editorial writer
Moore, John Dennis publisher
Moore, Oliver Semon, III publishing executive, consultant
Morgado, Robert music company executive
Morgan, Thomas Bruce media and public affairs executive, author
†Morris, Douglas Peter recording company executive
Moskin, John Robert editor, writer
Moyers, Bill D. journalist
Muller, Henry James journalist, magazine editor
Mulligan, Hugh Augustine journalist
Mulvoy, Mark journalist
Munro, J. Richard publishing company executive
†Murphy, Ann Pleshette magazine editor-in-chief
Murphy, Barry John publishing executive
Murphy, Thomas S. media company executive
Muth, John Francis newspaper editor, columnist
Myers, William S. magazine publishing executive
Nagourney, Herbert publishing company executive
Naiburg, Irving B., Jr. publisher
†Nardin, Theodore Celeste publisher
Nathan, Paul S. editor, writer
Navasky, Victor Saul magazine editor
Nederlander, Robert E. entertainment and television executive, lawyer
Needham, Richard Lee magazine editor
Neff, Craig periodical editor
Neilly, Andrew Hutchinson, Jr. publisher
Nelson, Lindsey sportscaster
†Neufeld, Victor television executive
Neuthaler, Paul David publisher
Newbauer, John Arthur editor
†Newcomb, Jonathan publishing executive
†Newfield, Jack columnist
†Newhouse, Nancy R. newspaper editor
Newhouse, Samuel I., Jr. publishing executive
Newman, Rachel magazine editor
Nibley, Andrew Mathews editorial executive
Nied, Thomas H. publishing company executive
†Nielsen, Nancy publishing executive
Niles, Nicholas Hemelright publisher
Norville, Deborah news correspondent
Novitz, Charles Richard television executive
Novogrod, Nancy Ellen editor
Nyren, Neil Sebastian publisher, editor
Oakes, John Bertram writer, editor
Ober, Eric W. broadcasting executive
O'Brian, Jack journalist
†O'Brien, Geoffrey Paul editor
O'Brien, John M. newspaper publishing company executive
Ochs, Michael editor, librarian, music educator
†Ohannessian, Griselda Jackson publishing executive
Olafsson, Olafur J. publishing company executive
Oliver, Stephanie Stokes magazine editor
O'Neil, James Peter financial printing company executive
†Oppenheim, Ellen W. media director, advertising executive
Oresman, Donald entertainment and publishing company executive, corporate lawyer
Osgood, Charles news broadcaster, journalist
Osnos, Peter Lionel Winston publishing executive
Ostling, Richard Neil journalist, author, broadcaster
Pace, Eric Dwight journalist
†Pagnozzi, Amy columnist
Pandolfi, Francis P. publishing executive
Paneth, Donald J. editor, writer
Paradise, Robert Richard publishing executive

Parker, Maynard Michael *journalist, magazine executive*
Parker, Mel *editor*
Patten, John W. *magazine publisher*
Patton, Joëlle Delbourgo *publishing executive*
Paugh, Thomas Francis *magazine editor, writer, photographer*
Pauley, Jane *television journalist*
Pearlstine, Norman *media company executive*
Penglase, Frank Dennis *publishing company executive*
Penn, Stanley William *journalist,columnist*
†Penney, Alexandra *magazine editor-in-chief, writer*
Peper, George Frederick *editor*
†Perlman, Gilbert E. *publishing executive*
Perry, Frank *motion picture executive, director, producer, writer*
Petersen, Raymond Joseph *publishing company executive*
Peterson, Kristina *publishing company executive*
Petzal, David Elias *editor, writer*
Peyronnin, Joseph Felix, III *network news executive*
†Philips, George *publishing company executive*
†Phillips, William Dodd *book publishing executive*
Picower, Warren Michael *magazine editor*
Piel, Gerard *editor, publisher*
Pittman, Robert Warren *entertainment executive*
Podd, Ann *newspaper publishing executive*
Podhoretz, Norman *magazine editor, writer*
Pollak, Richard *writer, editor*
†Pollak, William L. *newspaper publishing executive*
Pomerance, Norman *publishing company executive*
Pope, Leavitt Joseph *broadcast company executive*
†Poussaint, Renee Francine *journalist*
Povich, (Maurice) Maury Richard *broadcast journalist, talk show host, television producer*
Pratt, Michael Theodore *book publishing company executive, marketing, sales and publishing specialist*
Preiss, David Lee *publishing company executive*
Prestbo, John Andrew *newspaper editor, journalist, author*
Primis, Lance Roy *newspaper executive*
Princz, Judith *publishing executive*
Quigley, Martin Schofield *publishing company executive, educator*
Quindlen, Anna *journalist, author*
Quinn, Jane Bryant *journalist, writer*
Quinson, Bruno Andre *publishing executive*
Raab, Selwyn *journalist*
Rabiner, Susan *editor*
Ragan, David *publishing company executive*
Raines, Howell Hiram *newspaper editor, journalist*
Rainier, Robert Paul *publisher*
Ramond, Charles Knight, II *financial forecaster, publisher*
Randinelli, Tracey Anne *magazine editor*
†Raphael, Frank Lewis *broadcast executive*
Rashad, Ahmad (Bobby Moore) *sports broadcaster, former professional football player*
Rasmus, John A. *magazine executive*
Rather, Dan *broadcast journalist*
Rauch, Rudolph Stewart, III *periodical editor, journalist*
Rawson, Eleanor S. *publishing company executive*
Reed, James Donald *journalist, author*
Reed, Rex *author, critic*
†Regan, Judith T. *editor*
Reichl, Ruth Molly *restaurant critic*
Reid-Crisp, Wendy *publishing executive*
Reidy, Carolyn Kroll *publisher*
†Reilly, Edward T., Jr. *publisher*
Reilly, William Francis *publishing company executive*
Reuther, David Louis *children's book publisher, writer*
†Reverand, Diane *publisher, editor*
Reynolds, Warren Jay *retired publisher*
Rhoads, Geraldine Emeline *editor*
Rich, Frank Hart *critic*
Richardson, Midge Turk *magazine editor*
†Richter, Georg *book publishing executive*
Ridder, Eric *newspaper publisher*
Rideout, Philip Munroe *publishing company executive*
Rigby, Paul Crispin *artist, cartoonist*
†Riggio, Leonard *book publishing executive*
†Riggs, Andy J., Jr. *newspaper publishing executive*
Riggs, Michael David *magazine editor, writer*
Robinson, Maurice Richard, Jr. *publishing executive*
Robinson, Richard *publishing company executive*
Rockwell, John Sargent *music critic, journalist*
Rogalin, Roger Richard *publishing executive*
Rogers, Mary Martin *publishing company executive*
Rogin, Gilbert Leslie *editor, author*
Rolontz, Robert *recording company executive*
Ronson, Raoul R. *publishing executive*
Rose, Charles *television journalist*
†Rosenblum, Constance *newspaper editor*
Rosenfield, Jay Gary *publisher*
Rosenthal, Jacob (Jack Rosenthal) *newspaper editor*
Rosenthal, Lucy Gabrielle *writer, editor, educator*
Ross, Brian Elliott *news correspondent*
Ross, Elise Jane *newspaper executive*
Ross, Norman Alan *publisher*
Rosset, Barnet Lee, Jr. *publisher*
Rothberg, Gerald *editor, publisher*
Rubin, Harry Meyer *entertainment industry executive*
Rubin, Norman Julius *columnist*
Rubin, Stephen Edward *editor, journalist*
†Ruinsky, Sam *newspaper publishing executive*
Rukeyser, M. S., Jr. *television consultant, writer*
Rushnell, Squire Derrick *television executive*
†Russell, Charles F. *newspaper publishing executive*
Ryan, Michael E. *newspaper publishing executive*
Ryan, Michael Edmond *communications company executive, lawyer*
Ryan, Regina Claire (Mrs. Paul Deutschman) *editor, book packager, literary agent*
Saal, Hubert Daniel *journalist*
Sachs, Susan F. *publishing executive*
Safer, Morley *journalist*
Sagendorf, Bud (Forrest Cowles Sagendorf) *cartoonist*
Salembier, Valerie Birnbaum *publishing executive*
Saltz, Carole Pogrebin *publisher*
Sanders, Richard Louis *assistant managing editor*
Sapinsky, Joseph Charles *magazine executive, photographer*
Sarazen, Richard Allen *media company executive*
Sarnoff, William *publishing company executive*
Saunders, Dero Ames *writer, editor*
Sawyer, (L.) Diane *television journalist*
Sawyer, Forrest *newscaster*
Scarborough, Charles Bishop, III *broadcast journalist, writer*
Scardino, Marjorie Morris *publishing company executive*
Schaap, Richard Jay *journalist*
Schanberg, Sydney Hillel *newspaper editor, columnist*
Schieffer, Bob *broadcast journalist*
Schiffrin, Andre *publisher*
Schlosser, Herbert S. *broadcasting company executive*
Schmemann, Serge *journalist*
Schmertz, Mildred Floyd *editor, writer*
Schmidt, Stanley Albert *editor, writer*
Schmitz, Robert Allen *publishing executive, investor*
†Schneider, Martin Aaron *photojournalist, ecologist, engineer, writer, artist, television director, public intervenor, educator, university instructor, lecturer*
Schneiderman, David Abbott *publisher, journalist*
Schonberg, Harold Charles *music critic, columnist*
†Schragis, Steven M. *publisher, lawyer*
Schulz, Charles Monroe *cartoonist*
Schwartz, Jack Theodore *retired publisher*
Scribner, Charles, III *publisher, art historian, lecturer*
Seaman, Alfred Barrett *journalist*
Segal, Jonathan Bruce *editor*
Seligman, Daniel *editor*
†Settipani, Frank G. *news correspondent*
†Seymore, James W., Jr. *magazine editor*
Sharbel, Jean M. *editor*
Shatzkin, Leonard *publishing consultant*
†Shaw, Ray *financial publishing company executive*
†Shear, Matthew Joel *publishing executive*
Shepard, Stephen Benjamin *journalist, magazine editor*
Sherak, Thomas Mitchell *motion picture company executive*
†Sherr, Lynn Beth *TV news correspondent*
Shestack, Melvin Bernard *editor, author, filmmaker, television producer*
Shnayerson, Robert Beahan *editor*
Shortz, Will *puzzle editor*
†Shriver, Maria Owings *news correspondent*
Shuker, Gregory Brown *publishing and production company executive*
†Sidrane, Michelle Diana *publishing executive*
Siegal, Allan Marshall *newspaper editor*
Siegel, Alan Michael *communications and design consultant*
Siegel, Joel Steven *television news correspondent*
Siegel, Marvin *newspaper editor*
†Sifton, Elisabeth *book publisher*
Silberman, Charles Eliot *magazine editor, author*
Silberman, James Henry *editor, publisher*
Silverman, Stephen M. *journalist, author, television scriptwriter*
Silvers, Robert Benjamin *editor*
Silverstein, Shelby (Shel Silverstein) *author, cartoonist, composer, folksinger*
Simmons, Russell *recording industry executive*
Simon, John Ivan *film and drama critic*
Simonson, Lee Stuart *broadcast company executive*
†Singerman, Martin *newspaper publishing executive*
Singleton, Donald Edward *journalist*
Sischy, Ingrid Barbara *magazine editor, art critic*
Skillin, Edward Simeon *magazine publisher*
†Skinner, Peter Graeme *publishing executive, lawyer*
Smith, Clarence O'Farrell *publishing company executive*
Smith, Corlies Morgan *publishing executive*
†Smith, Derek Armand *publishing company executive*
Smith, Joseph Phelan *film company executive*
Smith, Liz (Mary Elizabeth Smith) *newspaper columnist, broadcast journalist*
Smith, Richard Mills *editor in chief, magazine executive*
Snyder, Richard Elliott *publishing company executive*
†Solem, Karen Lynn *publishing executive*
Soren, Tabitha L. *television newscaster, writer*
Sparano, Vincent Thomas *editor*
Spence, James Robert, Jr. *television sports executive*
Spring, Michael *editor, writer*
Stahl, Lesley R. *journalist*
Stanger, Ila *writer, editor*
Staniar, Burton B. *entertainment company executive*
Steiger, Paul Ernest *newspaper editor, journalist*
Steinfeld, Thomas Albert *publisher*
Steinfels, Margaret O'Brien *editor*
Stern, Robert D. *publishing executive*
Stern, Roslyne Paige *magazine publisher*
Stewart, James B. *journalist*
†Stossel, John *news analyst*
†Strachan, William Bruce *publisher, editor*
Straus, Roger W., Jr. *publishing company executive*
Straus, Roger W, III *book publishing executive, photographer*
Stringer, Howard *television executive*
Stuart, Carole *publishing executive*
Stuart, Lyle *publishing company executive*
Sugihara, Kenzi *publishing executive*
Sullivan, Anne Elizabeth *publishing executive*
Sullivan, Thomas John *communications company executive*
Sullivan, Walter Seager *editor, author*
Sulzberger, Arthur Ochs *newspaper executive*
Sulzberger, Arthur Ochs, Jr. *newspaper publisher*
Summerall, Pat (George Allan Summerall) *sportscaster*
Sussman, Gerald *publishing company executive*
Sutton, Kelso Furbush *publishing executive*
Sutton-Straus, Joan M. *journalist*
Sweezy, Paul Marlor *editor, publisher*
Swenson, Eric Pierson *publishing company executive*
Swift, Isabel Davidson *editorial director*
Taber, Carol A. *magazine publisher*
Tagliaferro, John Anthony *broadcasting company executive*
Talese, Nan Ahearn *publishing company executive*
Talley, Truman Macdonald *publisher*
Targ, William *editor, writer*
Tash, Martin Elias *publishing company executive*
Taylor, Humphrey John Fausitt *information services executive*
Taylor, Sherril Wightman *broadcasting company executive*
Temple, Wick *journalist*
Ternes, Alan Paul *editor*
Teubner, Ferdinand Cary, Jr. *publishing company executive*
Thomas, Brooks *publishing company executive*
Thomas, John Cox, Jr. *publisher*
Thompson, Martin Christian *news service executive*
Tigay, Alan Merrill *editor*
Tilberis, Elizabeth *editor in chief*
Timothy, Raymond Joseph *television executive*
Tisch, Laurence Alan *broadcast corporation executive*
†Tober, Barbara D. (Mrs. Donald Gibbs Tober) *editor*
†Toff, Nancy Ellen *book editor*
Tomlinson, James Francis *retired news agency executive*
†Townsend, Charles H. *publishing executive*
Traina, Albert Salvatore *publishing executive*
Trillin, Calvin Marshall *columnist*
†Tryhane, Gerald *newspaper publishing executive*
Tucker, Alan David *publisher*
Ubell, Robert Neil *editor, publisher, consultant, literary agent*
Uchitelle, Louis *journalist*
†Ungaro, Susan Kelliher *magazine editor*
Urdang, Alexandra *book publishing executive*
Valenti, Carl M. *newspaper publisher*
Valk, Elizabeth *magazine publisher*
Van Eysinga, Frans W. *publisher*
Van Nostrand, Morris Abbott, Jr. *publisher*
†Van Sant, Peter Richard *news correspondent*
Vaughan, Samuel Snell *editor, author*
Vecsey, George Spencer *sports columnist*
Vega, Marylois Purdy *journalist*
Venza, Jac *broadcast executive*
Verdi, David Joseph *broadcast news executive*
†Vestal, Jeanne Marie Goodspeed *book publishing company executive*
Vick, James Albert *publishing executive, consultant*
Vitale, Alberto Aldo *publishing company executive*
†Vitale, Dick *color commentator, sports writer*
Vitt, Sam B. *communications media services executive*
Vittorini, Carlo *publishing company executive*
Vizard, Frank Joseph *journalist*
von Knorring, Henrik Johan *publisher*
Wachtel, David Edward *magazine publisher*
Waddell, Harry Lee *editor, publisher*
Wade, James O'Shea *publisher*
Wade, Nicholas Michael Landon *journalist*
Wagner, Christina Breuer *publishing company executive*
†Walker, Douglas Craig *publisher*
Walker, Mort *cartoonist*
Wallace, Christopher *broadcast television correspondent*
Wallace, Mike *television interviewer and reporter*
Wallace, Thomas C(hristopher) *editor, literary agent*
†Wallace, Thomas J. *magazine editor-in-chief*
Wallach, Allan Henry *former senior critic*
Walters, Barbara *television journalist*
Walters, Raymond, Jr. *newspaper editor, author*
Wanek, William Charles *public relations executive*
Wang, Arthur Woods *publisher*
Warner, Peter David *publishing executive*
†Wasserman, Marlie P(arker) *publisher*
Waxenberg, Alan M. *publisher*
Weber, Karl William *book publisher*
Weber, Robert Maxwell *cartoonist*
Weberman, Ben *journalist, editor*
Weeks, Brigitte *publishing executive*
†Weill, Gus, Jr. *communications consultant*
Weinberger, Caspar Willard *publishing executive, former secretary of defense*
Weintz, Walter Louis *book publishing company executive*
Wells, Linda Ann *editor-in-chief*
Welsh, Donald Emory *publisher*
Wenner, Jann Simon *editor, publisher*
West, Bernard *investor*
Westerman, Sylvia Hewitt *journalist*
Wham, George Sims *publishing executive*
†Whipple, Judith Roy *book editor*
White, Kate *magazine editor in chief*
†White, Leonard *motion picture company executive*
White, Timothy Thomas Anthony *writer, editor, broadcaster*
Whiteman, Douglas E. *publisher*
†Whitmer, Kevin *newspaper sports editor*
Whitney, Ruth Reinke *magazine editor*
†Widmann, Nancy C. *broadcast executive*
Wiley, Deborah E. *publishing executive*
Wilford, John Noble, Jr. *news correspondent*
†Wilkerson, Isabel *journalist*
Willis, John Alvin *editor*
Wilson, Judy Vantrease *publishing executive*
Windsor, Laurence Charles, Jr. *publishing executive*
Winfrey, Carey Wells *journalist, magazine editor*
Winship, Frederick Moery *journalist*
Wintour, Anna *editor*
Wogan, Robert *broadcasting company executive*
Wright, Robert C. *broadcasting executive*
†WuDunn, Sheryl *journalist, correspondent*
Yablon, Leonard Harold *publishing company executive*
Yellin, Thomas Gilmer *broadcast executive*
Young, Genevieve Leman *publishing executive, editor*
Young, Robert Francis *publisher*
†Yunich, Peter B. *publishing executive*
Zacharius, Walter *publishing company executive*
Zackheim, Adrian Walter *editor*
Zahn, Paula *newscaster*
Zeldin, Richard Packer *publisher*
Ziff, William Bernard, Jr. *publishing executive*
Zimmerman, William Edwin *newspaper editor and publisher*
Zinsser, William Knowlton *editor, writer, educator*
Zuckerman, Mortimer Benjamin *real estate developer, publisher, editor*

North Salem
Larsen, Jonathan Zerbe *journalist*

Nyack
Leiser, Ernest Stern *journalist*

Old Brookville
Fairman, Joel Martin *broadcasting executive*

Ossining
Carter, Richard *publisher, writer*
Ravis, Howard Shepard *conference planner and publishing consultant*
Stein, Sol *publisher, writer, editor in chief*

Piermont
Fox, Matthew Ignatius *publishing company executive*

Pittsford
Woodhull, Nancy Jane *publishing executive*

Plainview
Newman, Edwin Harold *news commentator*

Pleasantville
Grune, George Vincent *publishing company executive*
Oursler, Fulton, Jr. *editor-in-chief, writer*
Ruggiero, Anthony William *direct mail company executive*
†Schadt, James P. *publishing executive*
†Tomlinson, Kenneth Y. *periodical editor in chief*

Port Washington
†Donohue, Peter Joseph *publishing executive*
Jay, Frank Peter *educator, writer*
McGreal, Joseph A., Jr. *publishing company executive*
Simmons, Lee Howard *book publishing company executive*

Poughkeepsie
†Wager, Richard Kenneth *newspaper executive*

Purchase
Sandler, Irving Harry *art critic, art historian*

Purdys
Burlingame, Edward Livermore *publishing company executive*

Queensbury
Winsten, Archer *retired newspaper and movie critic*

Remsenburg
Billman, Irwin Edward *publishing company executive*

Rhinecliff
Dierdorff, John Ainsworth *retired editor*

Rochester
Hyman, Ralph Alan *journalist, consultant*
†Orr, Jim (James D. Orr) *columnist, writer*
Palvino, Jack Anthony *broadcasting executive*
Pearce, William Joseph *public broadcasting executive*

Rome
Waters, George Bausch *newspaper publisher*

Roslyn
Risom, Ole Christian *publishing company executive*

Rye
Erlick, Everett Howard *broadcasting company executive*
Stoller, Ezra *photojournalist*

Sagaponack
Francke, Linda Bird *journalist*

Saratoga Springs
Boyers, Margarita Anne (Peggy Boyers) *editor, periodical, writer, translator*

Scarsdale
Duncan, George Harold *broadcasting company executive*
Frankel, Stanley Arthur *columnist, educator, business executive*
O'Neill, Michael James *editor, author*
Schwartz, Harry *journalist*
Topping, Seymour *publishing executive, newspaper*

Southampton
Louchheim, Donald Harry *journalist*
Sims, Everett Martin *publishing company executive*
Smith, Dennis (Edward) *publisher, author*

Spencertown
Lieber, Charles Donald *publisher*

Staten Island
Diamond, Richard Edward *publisher*
†Newhouse, Donald E. *newspaper publishing executive*

Stony Brook
Booth, George *cartoonist*

Syosset
Rudman, Michael P. *publishing executive*

Syracuse
Balk, Alfred William *journalist*
Bunn, Timothy David *newspaper editor*
Mesrobian, Arpena Sachaklian *publisher, editor, consultant*
Rogers, Stephen *newspaper publisher*
Schulte, Henry Frank *journalism educator*
Stephens, Edward Carl *communications educator, writer*

Tarrytown
Ashburn, Anderson *magazine editor*
Kaplan, Richard *magazine editor*
Neill, Richard Robert *retired publishing company executive*

Troy
Buckley, J. Stephen *newspaper publisher*
Smith, Rex William *journalist*

Unionville
Kemnitz, Thomas Milton *publisher*

Utica
Donovan, Donna Mae *newspaper publisher*

Valley Stream
Lehrer, Stanley *magazine publisher, editorial director, corporate executive*

Waccabuc
Kislik, Richard William *publishing executive*
Thompson, Edward Thorwald *magazine editor*

Wainscott
Henderson, William Charles *editor*

Watertown
Johnson, John Brayton *editor, publisher*

West Hempstead
Pollio, Ralph Thomas *editor, writer, magazine consultant*

White Plains
Benjamin, Theodore Simon *publishing company executive*
Boudreaux, John *public relations specialist*
Cohn, Howard *retired magazine editor*
Ellenbogen, Milton Joseph *publishing executive, editor, writer*
Kisseberth, Paul Barto *publishing executive*
†Sherlock, Gary Fuller *newspaper publisher*

Woodbury
Bell, William Joseph *cable television company executive*
†Dolan, Charles Francis *cable systems company executive*
Randolph, Francis Fitz, Jr. *cable television executive*
Sweeney, Daniel Thomas *cable television company executive*
Tatta, John Louis *cable television executive*

Yonkers
Denver, Eileen Ann *magazine editor*
Eimicke, Victor W(illiam) *publishing company executive*
Landau, Irwin *magazine publishing company executive*

NORTH CAROLINA

Asheville
Banks, James Barber *publishing executive*
Damtoft, Walter Atkinson *editor, publisher*
Pulleyn, S(amuel) Robert *publishing company executive*

Brevard
Phillips, Euan Hywel *publishing executive*

Cary
†Andrews, John Woodhouse *newspaper publisher*
Gehringer, Richard George *publishing executive*
McCarty, Thomas Joseph *publishing company executive*
Reynolds, Edward *book publisher*

Chapel Hill
Boggs, Robert Newell *editor*
Bowers, Thomas Arnold *journalism educator*
Lauder, Valarie Anne *editor, educator*
Meyer, Philip Edward *journalism educator*

Charlotte
†Barrows, Frank Clemence *newspaper editor*
†Brown, Tony *theater and dance critic*
Ethridge, Mark Foster, III *writer, publisher, newspaper consultant*
†Koch, Richard Joseph *lawyer, publishing company executive*
Neill, Rolfe *newspaper executive*
†White, David Lee *journalist*
†Williams, Edwin Neel *newspaper editor*

China Grove
Baker, Ira Lee *journalist, former educator*

Durham
Cooper, Charles Howard *photojournalist, newspaper publishing company executive*
Fulton, Katherine Nelson *journalist*
Hawkins, William E. N. *newspaper editor*
Hayes, Brian Paul *editor, writer*
Rollins, Edward Tyler, Jr. *newspaper executive*
Rossiter, Alexander, Jr. *news service executive, editor*

Edenton
Walklet, John James, Jr. *publishing executive*

Fearrington Village
Bailey, Herbert Smith, Jr. *retired publisher*
Hauser, Charles Newland McCorkle *newspaper consultant*

Garner
Dobyns, Lloyd (Allen) *free-lance journalist*

Gloucester
Price, Marion Woodrow *journalist*

Greensboro
Cline, Ned Aubrey *newspaper editor*
†DuBuisson, Charles David *newspaper editor*
Jellicorse, John Lee *communications and theatre educator*
Smink, Mary Jane *graphic communications technology educator*

Jefferson
Franklin, Robert McFarland *book publisher*

Point Harbor
Heffernan, Phillip Thomas, Jr. *retired publisher*

Raleigh
Daniels, Frank Arthur, Jr. *newspaper publisher*
Daniels, Frank Arthur, III *publishing executive*
Parker, Joseph Mayon *printing and publishing executive*
Powell, Drexel Dwane, Jr. *editorial cartoonist*
Reeves, Ralph B., III *publisher, editor*
†Rogers, Dennis Stanley *columnist, actor, author*
Royster, Vermont (Connecticut) *journalist*
†Skube, Michael *journalist, critic*

Research Triangle Park
May, Michael Lee *magazine editor*

Southern Pines
Ragan, Samuel Talmadge *newspaper editor, publisher, educator, poet laureate*

Tryon
Thayer, Lee *educator, author, consultant*

Waxhaw
Lamparter, William C. *printing and publishing consultant, digital printing and information systems specialist*

Wilmington
Meyer, John *newspaper editor*

Winston Salem
Doster, Joseph C. *newspaper publisher*
Goodman, Joseph Champion *editor*
†Sparber, Gordon Mark *music journalist*

Wrightsville Beach
Mc Ilwain, William Franklin *newspaper editor, writer*

NORTH DAKOTA

Fargo
Dill, William Joseph *newspaper editor*
Lohman, John Frederick *editor*
Marcil, William Christ, Sr. *publisher, broadcast executive*
Paulson, John Doran *newspaper editor, retired*

OHIO

Akron
Allen, William Dale *newspaper editor*
†Cooper, David Booth *newspaper editor*
Dotson, John Louis, Jr. *newspaper executive*
Greenman, John Frederick *newspaper executive*
†Kirksey, Charles Ron *journalist*

Athens
Scott, Charles Lewis *photojournalist*
Stempel, Guido Hermann, III *journalism educator*

Bowling Green
Clark, Robert King *communications educator emeritus, lecturer, consultant, actor, model*

Bucyrus
Moore, Thomas Paul *broadcast executive*

Canton
Fouts, Daniel Francis *sports announcer, former professional football player*

Chagrin Falls
Gillam, James Kennedy *publishing company executive*

Cincinnati
Adams, James Louis *newspaper editor, retired*
Beard, Thomas Lee *magazine editor*
Beckwith, Barbara Jean *journalist*
Blake, George Rowell *newspaper editor, journalist*
†Borgman, James Mark *editorial cartoonist*
†Bronson, Peter William *newspaper editor*
Burleigh, William Robert *newspaper executive*
Dunning, Thomas E. *newspaper editor*
Harmon, Patrick *newspaperman*
Knue, Paul Frederick *newspaper editor*
†Leser, Lawrence A. *broadcasting company executive*
Liss, Herbert Myron *newspaper publisher, communications company executive*
Rogers, Lawrence H., II *retired television executive, investor, writer*
Schottelkotte, Albert Joseph *broadcasting executive*
Scripps, Charles Edward *newspaper publisher*
Servodidio, Pat Anthony *broadcast executive*
†Silvers, Gerald Thomas *publishing executive*
Smith, C. LeMoyne *publishing company executive*
†Whipple, Harry *newspaper publishing executive*
Wigginton, Eugene H. *publishing executive*
Woods, Bruce Walter *editor, poet*

Cleveland
Atherton, James Dale *publishing executive*
†Bennett, Michael *newspaper editor*
Bingham, Richard Donnelly *journal editor, director, educator*
Clark, Gary R. *newspaper editor*
†Connors, Joanna *film critic*
Davis, David Aaron *journalist*
Day, Charles Roger, Jr. *editor in chief*
Drane, Walter Harding *publishing executive, business consultant*
Fabris, James A. *journalist*
Finn, Robert *music critic, educator*
Greer, Thomas H. *newspaper executive*
Hall, David *newspaper editor*
†Harayda, Janice *newspaper book editor, author*
†Holland, Darrell Wendell *newspaper religion editor*
†Kovacs, Rosemary *newspaper editor*
Lebovitz, Harold Paul (Hal Lebovitz) *journalist*
†Long, Robert M. *newspaper publishing executive*
Lucier, P. Jeffrey *publishing executive*
†Lynch, Maxine *newspaper publishing executive*
Machaskee, Alex *newspaper publishing company executive*
†Marino, Sal F. *publisher*
Miyares, Benjamin David *editor, publisher, consultant*
Modic, Stanley John *business editor, publisher*
†Molyneaux, David Glenn *newspaper travel editor*
†Morway, Richard A. *newspaper publishing executive*
Pascarella, Perry James *magazine editor*
Romei, Lura Knachel *magazine editor*
Strang, James Dennis *editor*
Strassmeyer, Mary *newspaper columnist*
†Tipton-Martin, Toni *newspaper editor*
†Urban, Richard *newspaper editor*

Columbus
Barker, Llyle James, Jr. *journalism educator, public relations executive, former military officer*
Barry, James P(otvin) *writer, editor, association executive*
Campbell, Richard Rice *retired newspaper editor*
Charles, Bertram *radio broadcasting executive*
Clark, Christine May *editor, author*
Cox, Mitchel Neal *editor*
†Dawson, Virginia Sue *newspaper editor*
Dervin, Brenda Louise *communications educator*
Fornshell, Dave Lee *educational broadcasting executive*
†Franks, Richard Matthew *newspaper executive*
†Grossberg, Michael Lee *theater critic, writer*
Kefauver, Weldon Addison *publisher*
Massie, Robert Joseph *publishing company executive*
Masterson, Michael Rue *journalist, educator, editor*
Meider, Elmer Charles, Jr. *publishing company executive*
†Murphy, Andrew J., Jr. *newspaper editor*
Sherrill, Thomas Boykin, III *newspaper publishing executive*
Smith, Robert Burns *newspaper magazine executive*
†Strode, George K. *sports editor*
Thomas, Stephen Clair *software publisher, writer, editor, consultant*
Weisgerber, David Wendelin *editor, chemist*
†Wolfe, J. W. *newspaper publishing executive*
Wolfe, John F. *publishing executive*

Dayton
†Cawood, Albert McLaurin (Hap Cawood) *newspaper editor*
Granzow, Paul H. *printing company executive*
Matheny, Ruth Ann *editor*
†Peterson, Skip (Orley R. Peterson, III) *newspaper photographer*
†Stewart, D. L. *newspaper columnist*
Tillson, John Bradford, Jr. *newspaper publisher*

Fairlawn
Herman, Roger Eliot *professional speaker, consultant, futurist, writer*

Kent
Poorman, Paul Arthur *educator, media consultant*

Lakewood
Condon, George Edward *journalist*
†Gordon, Anne Kathleen *editor*

Loudonville
Battison, John Henry *broadcasting executive, consulting engineer*

Oxford
Sanders, Gerald Hollie *communications educator*

Riverside
Willardson, Kimberly Ann Carey *editor, writer, publisher*

Sidney
Laurence, Michael Marshall *magazine publisher, writer*
Lawrence, Wayne Allen *publisher*
Stevens, Robert Jay *magazine editor*

Springfield
Maddex, Myron Brown (Mike Maddex) *broadcasting executive*

Toledo
Block, John Robinson *newspaper publisher*
Block, William Karl, Jr. *newspaper executive*
Gearhart, Thomas Lee *newspaper editor*
†Rosenbaum, Kenneth E. *journalist, editor*
†Royhab, Ronald *journalist, newspaper editor*
Stankey, Suzanne M. *editor*
Willey, John Douglas *retired newspaper executive*

Willoughby
Campbell, Talmage Alexander *newspaper editor*

Wooster
August, Robert Olin *journalist*

Youngstown
†Logan, Richard Parker *newspaper editor*
Przelomski, Anastasia Nemenyi *retired newspaper editor*

OKLAHOMA

Edmond
Standard, James Noel *newspaper editor*

Norman
Bauer, George W. *publishing company executive*
Dary, David Archie *journalism educator, author*

Oklahoma City
Gaylord, Edward Lewis *publishing company executive*
Gourley, James Leland *editor, publishing executive*
†Kelley, Carl Ed(win) *editor*
†Triplett, E. Eugene *editor*

Stillwater
Matoy, Elizabeth Anne *publishing executive*

Tulsa
†Barnett, Howard Gentry, Jr. *publishing executive, lawyer*
Culp, Even Asher *communications educator*
Hale, Richard Lee *magazine editor*
Haring, Robert Westing *newspaper editor*
Jones, Jenk, Jr. *newspaper editor*
Jones, Jenkin Lloyd *retired newspaper publisher*
Major, John Keene *radio broadcasting executive*
Upton, Howard B., Jr. *management columnist, lawyer*

OREGON

Albany
Wood, Kenneth Arthur *newspaper editor emeritus, writer*

Coquille
Taylor, George Frederick *newspaper publisher, editor*

Corvallis
Hall, Don Alan *editor, writer*
Zwahlen, Fred Casper, Jr. *journalism educator*

Eugene
Baker, Alton Fletcher, Jr. *newspaper editor*
Baker, Edwin Moody *retired newspaper publisher*
Franklin, Jon Daniel *journalist, science writer, educator*
Ismach, Arnold Harvey *journalism educator*
Lemert, James Bolton *journalist, educator*
Sherriffs, Ronald Everett *communications and film educator*
Tykeson, Donald Erwin *broadcasting executive*

Gleneden Beach
Marks, Arnold *journalist*

Gresham
†Caldwell, Robert John *newspaper editor*

Portland
Bhatia, Peter K. *editor, journalist*
Crabbs, Roger Alan *publisher, consultant, small business owner, educator*
†Graves, Earl William, Jr. *journalist*
†Johnston, Virginia Evelyn *editor*
Mainwaring, William Lewis *publishing company executive, author*
†Mapes, Jeffrey Robert *journalist*
Murphy, Francis Seward *journalist*
†Rowe, Sandra Mims *newspaper editor*
Sterling, Donald Justus, Jr. *retired newspaper editor*
Stickel, Frederick A. *publisher*
†Stickel, Patrick Francis *publishing executive, newspaper*
†Wohler, Jeffery Wilson *newspaper editor*
†Woodward, Stephen Richard *newspaper editor*

South Beach
Gilbert, David Heggie *consultant, retired educational publisher*

Tigard
Nokes, John Richard *retired newspaper editor, author*

PENNSYLVANIA

Albrightsville
Wilson, George Wharton *newspaper editor*

Allentown
Shorts, Gary K. *newspaper publisher*
†Willistein, Paul August *newspaper editor*

Bala Cynwyd
Field, Joseph Myron *broadcast executive*
†Schwartz, Charles D. *broadcast executive*

Beaver
Dible, Dennis D. *executive editor*
Gordon, Frank Wallace *newspaper publisher*

Bensalem
Kang, Benjamin Toyeong *writer, clergyman*

Broomall
†Cohen, Philip D. *book publishing executive*

Bryn Mawr
Broido, Arnold Peace *music publishing company executive*
Mc Lean, William L., III *publisher*

Carlisle
Fish, Chet *publishing consultant, writer*
Talley, Carol Lee *newspaper editor*

Clearfield
Ulerich, William Keener *publishing company executive*

Doylestown
Smith, Charles Paul *newspaper publisher*

Emmaus
Beldon, Sanford T. *publisher*
Bricklin, Mark Harris *magazine editor, publisher*

Erie
Mead, Edward Mathews *newspaper executive*

Erwinna
Richman, Joan F. *television consultant*

Felton
Shoemaker, Eleanor Boggs *television production company executive*

Flourtown
Lee, Adrian Iselin, Jr. *journalist*

Greensburg
Harrell, Edward Harding *newspaper executive*

Harrisburg
Antoun, Annette Agnes *newspaper editor, publisher*
Carnahan, Frances Morris *magazine editor*
Fossel, Peter VanBrunt *magazine editor and publisher*
Gover, Raymond Lewis *newspaper publisher*
Handler, Mimi *editor, writer*
Stanchak, John Edward *magazine editor*

Haverford
Jurney, Dorothy Misener *journalist, editor*

Hawley
Conley, Clare Dean *retired magazine editor*

Hellertown
McCullagh, James Charles *publishing company executive*

Hershey
Farrell, Eugene George *editor*

Honesdale
Brown, Kent Louis, Jr. *magazine editor*

Johnstown
Saltz, Howard Joel *newspaper editor*

Lancaster
†Cody, William Henry *journal editor*
†Shaw, Charles Raymond *journalist*
†Shenk, Willis Weidman *newspaper executive*

Lansdowne
Zingraff, Michael, Jr. *magazine editor*

Montoursville
Woolever, Naomi Louise *retired editor*

Newtown
Thompson, Carol Lewis *editor*

Newtown Square
Critz, Richard Laurens *magazine editor, architectural consultant*

Philadelphia
Aregood, Richard Lloyd *editor*
Barlett, Donald L. *journalist*
Binzen, Peter Husted *columnist*
Bissinger, H(arry) G(erard) *journalist*
Boasberg, Leonard W. *reporter*
Boldt, David Rhys *journalist*
Breitenfeld, Frederick, Jr. *public broadcasting executive, educator*
Brodsky, Julian A. *broadcasting services, telecommunications company executive*
Broom, William Wescott *retired newspaper executive*
Carey, Arthur Bernard, Jr. *editor, writer, columnist*
Cook, Don *author, retired foreign correspondent*
Cooper, Richard Lee *newspaper editor, journalist*
Dauth, Frances Kutcher *journalist, newspaper editor*
†De Leon, Clark *newspaper columnist*
Denenberg, Herbert Sidney *journalist, lawyer, former state official*
Dolson, Franklin Robert *columnist*
Drake, Donald Charles *journalist*
†Edelson, Alan Martin *medical publisher, neurophysiologist*
†Fancher, Charles B. *newspaper publishing executive*
†Foreman, Gene Clemons *newspaper editor*
†Gaul, Gilbert M. *reporter*
Gerbner, George *communications educator, university dean emeritus*
Gray, Gordon L. *communications educator*
Gross, Larry Paul *communications educator*
Hall, Robert J. *newspaper executive*
†Halsey, Ashley, III *newspaper editor*
Haynes, Gary Allen *newspaper editor, journalist*
†Iams, David Aveling *journalist, columnist*
Joyce, Philip Halton *journalist*
Kimelman, Donald Bruce *newspaper editor*
King, Maxwell E. P. *newspaper editor*
Klein, Julia Meredith *newspaper reporter*
Leary, Michael Warren *journalist*
Leiter, Robert Allen *journalist, magazine editor*
Lent, John Anthony *journalist, educator*
Lewis, Claude Aubrey *columnist*
Loeb, Vernon Frederick *journalist*
Lovelady, Steven M. *newspaper editor*
Lyon, William Carl *sports columnist*
Mardar, Dianna *reporter*
†Mezzacappa, Dale Veronica *journalist*
Moore, Acel *journalist*
Morgan, Arlene Notoro *newspaper editor, reporter, recruiter*
Nalle, Peter Devereux *publishing company executive*
Naughton, James Martin *newspaper editor*
Nelson, Nels Robert *drama critic*
News, Kathryn Anne *editor, educator, writer*
Nussbaum, Paul Eugene *journalist*
Parke, Jo Anne Mark *publishing company executive*
Parry, Lance Aaron *newspaper executive*
Patel, Ronald Anthony *editor newspaper*
†Porter, Jill *journalist*
Roberts, Ralph Joel *cable television, telephone communications and background music company executive*
†Rosenthal, Robert Jon *newspaper editor, journalist*
†Rossi, Steven B. *newspaper publishing executive*
†Rotell, Thomas M. *publishing executive*
†Ryan, Desmond *film critic*
†Samsot, Robert Louis *newspaper editor, consultant*
†Schaffer, Jan *newspaper editor*
Searcy, Jarrell D. (Jay) *sportswriter*
†Searcy, Jay *Sportswriter*
†Shapiro, Howie *newspaper editor*
Shoup, Michael C. *newspaper reporter, editor*
Smolin, Ronald Philip *publisher*
Spikol, Art *editor, writer, illustrator*
†Stalberg, Zachary *newspaper editor*
Stecklow, Steve *journalist*
Steele, James B. *journalist*
†Tait, Elaine *restaurant critic*
†Takiff, Jonathan Henry B. *journalist*
Toolan, Brian Paul *newspaper editor*
Tucker, David *newspaper editor*
†Turow, Joseph Gregory *communication educator*
†Wallace, Linda Suzan *journalist*
†Ward, Butch *newspaper editor*
Ward, Hiley Henry *journalist, educator*
†Wilkinson, Signe *cartoonist*
Winfrey, Marion Lee *television critic*
Woestendiek, (William) John, Jr. *reporter*
†Zucchino, David Alan *newspaper journalist*

Pittsburgh
Alexander, James Eckert *editor*
Apone, Carl Anthony *journalist*
†Craig, John Gilbert, Jr. *newspaper editor*
Kaplan, John *photojournalist, consultant, educator*
Krysinski, Linda Ann *editorial office supervisor*
†Miller, Donald *art critic*
†Roof, Robert L. *broadcast executive, sales executive*
Ross, Madelyn Ann *newspaper editor*
Schieffelin, Laurie Graham *editor*
Swann, Lynn Curtis *sportscaster*

Plymouth Meeting
Green, Raymond S(ilvernail) *retired radio station executive*

Pottstown
Hylton, Thomas James *editorial writer*
Lenfest, Harold Fitz Gerald *cable television executive, lawyer*

Radnor
Barletta, Joseph Francis *newspaper executive, lawyer*
Pool, Patricia Stewart *editor in chief*
Youman, Roger Jacob *editor, writer*

Scottdale
Cutrell, Benjamin Elwood *publisher*
†Miller, Levi *publishing administrator*

Scranton
Lynett, George Vincent *newspaper publisher*

Somerset
Funari, John H. *editor, consultant*

Stroudsburg
Gasink, Warren Alfred *speech communication educator*

Tyrone
Simpson, Cary Hatcher *broadcasting station executive*

University Park
Thatcher, Sanford Gray *publishing executive*

Villanova
Lambert, William G. *journalist, consultant*

Wayne
Gallagher, Terrence Vincent *editor*
Robinowitz, Joe Reece *publishing executive*

West Chester
Diller, Barry *entertainment company executive*

Westtown
Backe, John David *communications corporation executive*

Williamsport
Rafferty, Michael Robert *editor, columnist*

Wynnewood
Meyers, Mary Ann *writer, consultant*
Singer, Samuel L(oewenberg) *journalist*

Yardley
Crane, Barbara Joyce *publishing consulting executive, author*
Zulker, Charles Bates *broadcasting company executive*

York
Conway, Nancy Ann *publisher, editor*

RHODE ISLAND

Block Island
Kingsbury, Read Austin *retired journalist*

Charlestown
Ungaro, Joseph Michael *newspaper publishing executive, consultant*

Jamestown
Potter, Clarkson Nott *publishing consultant*

Manville
Eno, Paul Frederick *editor*

Middletown
Buell, William Ackerman *radio broadcasting executive*

Newport
Baker, Winthrop Patterson, Jr. *broadcasting executive*
Holloway, Jerome Knight *publisher, former military strategy educator, retired foreign service officer*
Spurr, Daniel *editor*

Providence
†Dickinson, Brian Ward *columnist*
†Dujardin, Richard Charles *journalist*
Farmer, Susan Lawson *broadcasting executive, former secretary of state*
Hamblett, Stephen *newspaper publishing executive*
†Martin, John *critic*
†Méras, Phyllis Leslie *journalist*
O'Donnell, Charles Patrick *retired newspaper executive, consultant*
Sinclair, Joseph Samuels *broadcasting company executive, retail merchant*
Watkins, John Chester Anderson *newspaper publisher*
†Whitcomb, Robert Bassett *journalist, editor*
Wyman, James Vernon *newspaper executive*

Warwick
Blount, William Allan *broadcasting executive*

West Greenwich
†Markowicz, Victor *video company executive*

West Kingston
Haring, Howard Jack *magazine editor*

Westerly
Day, Chon *cartoonist*

SOUTH CAROLINA

Anderson
Mitchell, Thomas Wayne *newspaper editor*

Bennettsville
Kinney, William Light, Jr. *newspaper editor, publisher*

Charleston
Anderson, Ivan Verner, Jr. *newspaper publisher*
Gilbreth, Frank Bunker, Jr. *retired communications executive, writer*
†Langley, Lynne Spencer *newspaper editor, columnist*
Manigault, Peter *media executive*
McGee, Hall Thomas, Jr. *newspaper, radio and television executive*
Schreadley, Richard Lee *writer, retired newspaper editor*
Tarleton, Larry Wilson *newspaper editor*
†Wilcox, Arthur Manigault *newspaper editor*
Wyrick, Charles Lloyd, Jr. *publisher, writer, editor*

Columbia
Crim, Reuben Sidney *newspaper publishing executive*
†Gray, Katherine Wilson *newspaper editor*
Rone, William Eugene, Jr. *newspaper editor*
†Thelen, Gil *newspaper editor*

Easley
Failing, George Edgar *editor, clergyman, educator*

Fort Mill
Mantle, John Edward *newspaper publisher*

Greenville
Eskew, Rhea Taliaferro *newspaper publisher*
†Eskola, David Anund *television columnist*
Mebane, William deBerniere *newspaper publisher*
Stultz, Thomas Joseph *newspaper executive*
Wearn, Wilson Cannon *retired media executive*

Hilton Head Island
Eden, Lee Smythe *broadcasting executive*
McKinney, Donald Lee *magazine editor*

Landrum
Pauley, Robert Reinhold *broadcasting executive, financial executive*

Moncks Corner
Morris, Henry Allen, Jr. *publisher*

Orangeburg
Sims, Edward Howell *editor, publisher*

Walterboro
Johnson, Daniel McDonald (Dan Johnson) *newspaper editor*

Winnsboro
King, Robert Thomas *editor, free-lance writer*

TENNESSEE

Chattanooga
Anderson, Lee Stratton *newspaper publisher, editor*
†Ashley, Jim R. *newspaper editor*
Holmberg, Albert William, Jr. *publishing company executive*
Holmberg, Ruth Sulzberger *publishing company executive*
MacManus, Yvonne Cristina *editor, videoscripter, writer, consultant*
Neely, Paul *newspaper editor*
†Palmer, Stanton Dean *newspaper editor*

Goodlettsville
Wilkins, Rita Denise *multimedia design consultant*

Knoxville
Ambrester, Marcus LaRoy *communication educator, program administrator*
Finn, Peter Michael *television production executive*
Hohenberg, John *journalist, educator*
Rukeyser, William Simon *journalist*
Singletary, Michael Willis *journalism, educator*
Teeter, Dwight Leland, Jr. *journalism educator*
Whittle, Christopher *media executive, entrepreneur*

Maryville
Brigance, Albert Henry *educational writer*

Memphis
Emery, Sue *bulletin editor, owner bridge studio*
Greiner, Morris Esty, Jr. *broadcast executive*
Griffin, Tom *former editor, writer*
McEachran, Angus *newspaper editor*
†Nager, Larry Mark *music critic, journalist*
†Ramirez, Michael P. *editorial cartoonist*
†Roberts, C. Frank *broadcast executive*
†Smith, Whitney Bousman *music and drama critic*
†Stokes, Henry Arthur *journalist*

Murfreesboro
Wyatt, Robert Odell *journalism educator*

Nashville
Allbritton, Cliff *publisher*
Atkins, Chester Burton *record company executive, guitarist, publisher*
Battle, William Robert (Bob Battle) *newspaper executive*
†Bowen, James *record company executive*
†Boyd, Theophilus Bartholomew, III *publishing company executive*
Feaster, Robert K. *publishing company executive*
Flanagan, Van Kent *journalist*
Frey, Herman S. *publishing company executive*
Harden, Lydia Dixon *editor*
Harris, Stacy *print and broadcast journalist*
Hieronymus, Clara Booth Wiggins *journalist*
Peebles, James W. *publishing executive*
†Rayburn, Ted Rye *newspaper editor*
Roberts, Sandra *editor*
Russell, Fred McFerrin *journalist, author, lawyer*
Sutherland, Frank *editor*
Walden, Philip Michael *recording company executive, publishing company executive*

TEXAS

Abilene
Boyll, David Lloyd *broadcasting company executive*

Allen
†Leach, Sheryl *television show creator*

Amarillo
Spies, Dennis J. *editor*

Arlington
Duncan, Thomas Alton *editor*
Meadows, Jennifer Elizabeth *retired editor,tattoo artist*

Austin
Conine, Ernest *newspaper commentator, writer*
Danielson, Wayne Allen *journalism and computer science educator*
Herman, Kenneth Neil *journalist*
Laine, Katie Myers *communications consultant*
Levy, Michael Richard *publishing executive*
Mayers, Roy *publishing executive*
Mayes, Wendell Wise, Jr. *broadcasting company executive*
Sargent, Ben *political cartoonist*
Teague, Hyman Faris *former publishing company executive*

Bedford
Lieber, David Leslie *journalist*

Carrollton
Powell, Bill Jake *newspaper executive*

Commerce
Bell, William Jack *journalism educator*

Corpus Christi
†House, David Augusta *newspaper editor*
Rose, Larry Lee *newspaper executive*
†Sullivan, Stephen Wentworth *publisher*

Crockett
Gibbs, James Howard *broadcast executive*

Dallas
†Anders, John *newspaper columnist*
Ardoin, John Louis *music editor*
†Bailon, Gilbert *newspaper editor*
†Bersano, Bob *newspaper editor*
†Blackstone, Kevin *sports columnist*
†Blow, Steve *newspaper columnist*
†Blumenthal, Karen *newspaper editor*
†Brown, Stephen Bryan *real estate editor*
Burns, Scott *columnist*
†Compton, Bob *newspaper editor*
†Correu, James M. *newspaper publishing executive*
Cox, James William *newspaper executive*
Creany, Cathleen Annette *television station executive*
Decherd, Robert William *newspaper and broadcasting executive*
†DeOre, Bill *editorial cartoonist*
Dillon, David Anthony *journalist, lecturer*
†Dufner, Edward Joseph *newspaper editor*
Enix, Agnes Lucille *editorial consultant*
Fiddick, Paul William *broadcasting company executive*
†Galloway, Randy *newspaper sports columnist*
Geiger, Ken *photojournalist*
Griffith, Dotty (Dorothy Griffith Stephenson) *journalist, speaker*
†Halbreich, Jeremy L. *newspaper publishing executive*
†Hall, Cheryl *newspaper editor*
†Harasta, Cathy Ann *journalist*
Holmes, Bert Otis E., Jr. *retired newspaperman*
Huey, Ward L(igon), Jr. *media executive*
†Jacobson, Gary *newspaper business editor*
Jones, Philip Davis *computer service publishing consultant*
Jordan, Karen Leigh *travel editor*
†Kessler, Tom *newspaper editor*
Kutner, Janet *art critic, book reviewer*
Landers, James Michael (Jim) *international editor*
Langer, Ralph Ernest *journalist*
†Livingston, Grover D. *newspaper publishing executive*
†Lysaught, Thomas Francis *publishing company executive*
Meyer, Richard Jonah *broadcast executive, consultant*
Mong, Robert William, Jr. *managing editor*
Osborne, Burl *newspaper publisher, editor*
Patterson, Ronald Paul *publishing company executive, clergyman*
†Peckham, Barry *newspaper publishing executive*
†Pederson, Rena *newspaper editor*
Powell, Larry Randall *columnist*
St. John, Bob *journalist, columnist, author*
Savage, Scott David *broadcast executive*
†Schwartz, Marilyn *columnist*
Sheehan, James Patrick *media company executive*
†Sherrod, Blackie *newspaper sports columnist*
†Siegfried, Tom *newspaper editor*
Smith, David Lee *newspaper editor*
Smith, Russell L. *film critic*
Smith, Sue Frances *newspaper editor*
†Snyder, Leslie *newspaper editor*
Snyder, William D. *photojournalist*
†Starks, Richard *newspaper publishing executive*
†Wuntch, Philip Samuels *journalist, film critic*

Denton
Westmoreland, Reginald Conway *journalism educator*

Dripping Springs
Rios, Evelyn Deerwester *columnist, musician, artist, writer*

El Paso
Treadwell, Hugh Wilson *publishing executive*

Fort Worth
Buckley, Betty Bob *journalist, consultant*
Connor, Richard L. *publisher, editor*
Davis, Jimmie Dan *newspaper editor*
Malone, Dan F. *journalist*
Martin, Harold Eugene *publishing executive, consultant*
†Peipert, James Raymond *journalist*
†Price, Debbie M. *journalist, newspaper editor*
Price, Larry C. *photojournalist*
†Price, Michael Howard *journalist, critic, cartoonist*
Record, Phillip Julius *newspaper executive*
Tinsley, Jackson Bennett *newspaper editor*

Houston
†Aguilar, Melissa Ward *newspaper editor*
†Ashby, Lynn Cox *newspaper editor*
Barlow, Jim B. *newspaper columnist*
Bischoff, Susan Ann *newspaper editor*

†Bunch, Fred C. *newspaper picture editor*
†Byars, Carlos *newspaper reporter*
†Carlquist, Robert E. *newspaper publishing executive*
†Clark, Scott *newspaper editor*
Cobb, Daniel W., Jr. *editor, media consultant*
†Criswell, Ann *newspaper editor*
†Cunningham, Dan *newspaper editor*
DeBakey, Selma *science communication educator, writer, editor, lecturer*
†Fant, Patrick Joseph *radio station general manager*
†Frieden, Kit *newspaper editor*
George, Deveral D. *editor, journalist, advertising consultant*
†Gerraughty, David R. *newspaper editor*
Gray, Robert Steele *publishing executive, editor*
†Griffin, Linda Gillan *fashion editor*
†Hale, Leon *newspaper columnist*
†Hammond, Ken *newspaper magazine editor*
†Harasim, Paul Houck *columnist, educator*
†Heinsen, Lindsay *newspaper editor*
†Henry, John Cooper *journalist*
Hiatt, John David *broadcast company executive*
Hobby, William Pettus *broadcast executive*
Hodges, Ann *television editor, newspaper columnist*
Holmes, Ann Hitchcock *journalist*
†Jetton, Steve *newspaper editor*
Johnson, Richard James Vaughan *newspaper executive*
Johnston, Marguerite *journalist, author*
†Klentz, Renee *newspaper editor*
Klinger, Oliver Cecil *publishing company executive*
†Laird, John B. *newspaper publishing executive*
†Leydon, Joseph Patrick *film critic, journalist*
†Loftis, Jack *newspaper editor*
†Lunn, Judith Saska *newspaper editor, journalist*
†Marshall, Jane P. *newspaper editor*
†Marshall, Thom *columnist*
Massey, Ike *newspaper publishing executive*
Mc David, George Eugene (Gene Mc David) *newspaper executive*
Millar, Jeffery Lynn *columnist*
†Mitchell, Richard Dale *journalist, writer*
Morris, David Hargett *broadcast executive, rancher*
Newberry, Robert Curtis, Sr. *newspaper columnist*
†Oppmann, Andrew James *newspaper editor*
Oren, Bruce Clifford *newspaper editor, artist*
†Palomo, Juan Ramón *columnist*
Pederson, Tony Weldon *newspaper editor*
Ponder, Thomas C. *publishing company executive*
†Powers, Hugh William *newspaper executive*
†Simmon, Jim *newspaper editor*
Singleton, William Dean *newspaper publisher*
†Snyder, Mike *newspaper editor*
†Stanley, Jack H. *newspaper publishing executive*
†Sweeney, John W., III *newspaper executive*
Walbridge, Willard Eugene *broadcasting executive*
Walls, Carmage *newspaper publisher*
Walls, Martha Ann Williams (Mrs. B. Carmage Walls) *newspaper executive*
†White, Cecile Holmes *religion editor*
Youngblood, Ray Wilson *publishing company executive*

Irving
Halter, Jon Charles *magazine editor, writer*
Lundy, Roland *publishing executive*
Stuckey, Scott Sherwood *editor*

Kerrville
Dozier, William Everett, Jr. *newspaper editor and publisher*
Harkey, Ira Brown, Jr. *newspaperman, educator, author*

Lewisville
Vacca, John Joseph, Jr. *television executive*

Lufkin
Cardwell, Horace Milton *communications company executive*

Missouri City
Griffin, Oscar O'Neal, Jr. *writer, former oil company executive*

Odessa
Shaw, Scott *photojournalist*

Plano
Brock, Dee Sala *television executive, educator, writer, consultant*
Senderling, Jon Townsend *journalist, public affairs specialist*

Roanoke
Bradshaw, Terry *sports announcer, former professional football player*

San Antonio
Carmack, George *newspaper editor*
Harte, Houston Harriman *newspaper, broadcasting executive*
†Juhasz, Stephen *editor, consultant*
†Kibler, Craig Morton *editor, columnist, poet*
Kilpatrick, Charles Otis *newspaper editor, publisher*
Kilpatrick, Mark Kevin *newspaper editor*
Lenke, Joanne Marie *publishing executive*
Manning, Noel Thomas *publishing company executive*
Marbut, Robert Gordon *communications, cable and broadcast executive*
Mays, L. Lowry *broadcast executive*
Miles, Janice Ann *news reporter*

Schulenburg
Clark, I. E. *publisher*

Stephenville
King, Clyde Richard *journalism educator, writer*

The Woodlands
Anderson, Dale *film production executive*
Logan, Mathew Kuykendall *journalist*

Waco
Preddy, Raymond Randall *newspaper publisher*

UTAH

Ogden
†Hatch, Randall Clinton *journalist*
Larson, Brent T. *broadcasting executive*
Trundle, W(infield) Scott *publishing executive newspaper*

Park City
†Trahant, Mark N. *newspaper editor*

Salt Lake City
Anderson, Arthur Salzner *publishing company executive, marketing executive*
Berkes, Howard *radio news reporter*
Brady, Rodney Howard *broadcast company executive, former college president, former government official*
Brown, Carolyn Smith *communications educator, consultant*
Fehr, J. Will *newspaper editor*
†Gallivan, John William *publisher*
Hatch, George Clinton *television executive*
Hatch, Wilda Gene *broadcast company executive*
Madsen, Arch Leonard *broadcasting company executive*
Mortimer, William James *newspaper publisher*
O'Brien, Paul Jerry *newspaper publishing executive*
Paulsen, Vivian *magazine editor*
†Robison, Barbara Ann *retired newspaper editor*
Shelledy, James Edwin, III *editor*
†Van Treese, James Bryan *book publishing and investment company executive*

Tremonton
Thompson, (Gerry) Maxine Leak *supply technician, inventory consultant*

VERMONT

Bennington
Brownell, David Wheaton *editor*
Garret, Paula Lyn *publishing company executive*

Bristol
Kompass, Edward John *consulting editor*

Brookfield
Newton, Earle Williams *editor, museum director, library and museum consultant*

Calais
Elmslie, Kenward Gray *retired publishing company executive, author*

Dorset
Ketchum, Richard Malcolm *editor, writer*

North Pomfret
Guernsey, Otis Love, Jr. *critic, editor*

Perkinsville
Harris, Christopher *publisher, designer, editor*

South Woodstock
Crowl, John Allen *retired publishing company executive*

West Brattleboro
Barber, Orion Metcalf, II *publishing consultant, book packager*

Winooski
Wilson, Mary Louise *learning systems company executive*

VIRGINIA

Alexandria
†Brownfeld, Allan Charles *columnist*
Christensen, Bruce LeRoy *public broadcasting executive*
†Fahey, John M., Jr. *book publishing executive*
Fichenberg, Robert Gordon *newspaper editor, consultant*
Fleming, Douglas Riley *journalist, publisher, public affairs consultant*
Foisie, Philip Manning *retired journalist, media consultant*
Foster, Robert Francis *communications executive*
Hobbs, Michael Edwin *broadcasting company executive*
Lawson, Jennifer *broadcast executive*
†Ottenhoff, Robert George *television executive*
Perkins, A. William *printing executive*
Sanfelici, Arthur H(ugo) *editor, writer*
Willis, Clayton *broadcaster, corporation executive, former government official, educator, arts consultant, photojournalist, lecturer*
Yoder, Edwin Milton, Jr. *columnist, educator, editor, writer*

Annandale
Critchfield, Richard Patrick *journalist*
Pollard, David Edward *editor*

Arlington
Bodley, Harley Ryan, Jr. *editor, writer, broadcaster*
Bullard, Marcia Lynn *weekly magazine editor*
†Clements, John Brian *broadcasting executive*
Cohen, Ronald Eli *journalist*
Cole, Benjamin Richason *newspaper executive*
Correll, John Thomas *magazine editor*
Curley, John J. *diversified media company executive*
Curley, Thomas *newspaper executive*
Curry, George Edward *journalist*
†Curtis, Richard A. *newspaper editor*
Gniewek, Raymond Louis *newspaper editor*
†Jurgensen, Karen *newspaper editor*
Lester, Barnett Benjamin *editor, foreign affairs officer*
†Lorell, Monte *newspaper editor*
MacDougall, William Lowell *magazine editor*
McCorkindale, Douglas Hamilton *publishing company executive, corporate lawyer*
†McNamara, Tom *newspaper editor*
†McWethy, John Fleetwood *journalist*
Michael, Larry Perry *broadcasting company executive*
Miller, Loye Wheat, Jr. *journalist, corporate communications specialist*
Mirrielees, James Fay, III *publishing executive*
Neikirk, William Robert *journalist*
Neuharth, Allen Harold *newspaper publisher*
†Policinski, Eugene Francis *newspaper editor*
†Prichard, Peter S. *newspaper editor*
Quinn, John Collins *publishing executive, newspaper editor*
†Ritter, Hal *newspaper editor*
†Rockefeller, Sharon Percy *broadcast executive*
Simonson, David C. *retired newspaper association executive*
Simpson, John Mathes *newspaper editor*
†Snow, Robert Anthony *journalist*
Tanzer, Lester *editor*
†Vesper, Carolyn T. *newspaper publishing executive*
†Weiss, Susan *newspaper editor*
Willenson, Kim Jeremy *publisher, journalist, author*

Broad Run
Kotz, Nathan Kallison (Nick Kotz) *news correspondent*

Burke
Fisher, James Burke *publishing company executive*

Charlottesville
Essig, Nancy Claire *publishing executive*
Foard, Susan Lee *editor*
†Kowalsky, Adrian Dion *publishing executive*
Loo, Beverly Jane *publishing company executive*
Parrish, David Walker, Jr. *legal publishing company executive*
Worrell, Anne Everette Rowell *newspaper publisher*

Faber
Friede, Eleanor Kask *editor, publisher*

Falls Church
Cardwell, Nancy Lee *editor*
Donovan, Robert John *retired journalist*
Kaplow, Herbert Elias *journalist*

Fredericksburg
Rowe, Charles Spurgeon *newspaper publishing and broadcasting executive*

Great Falls
Garrett, Wilbur Eugene *magazine editor*

Hampton
Brauer, Harrol Andrew, Jr. *broadcasting executive*

Harrisonburg
Rollman, Steven Allan *communication educator*

Herndon
Scripps, Edward Wyllis *newspaper publisher*

Lively
Gallimore, Robert Stephenson *news service executive*

Mc Lean
Bartow, Randy David *publishing executive*
Fromm, Joseph *retired magazine editor, foreign affairs consultant*
Glines, Carroll Vane, Jr. *magazine editor*

Mineral
Speer, Jack Atkeson *publisher*

Moneta
Armistead, Moss William, III *retired newspaper executive*

Newport News
†Barnes, Myrtle Sue Snyder *editor*
†Cantrell, Joseph Doyle *newspaper company executive*
Davis, Jack Wayne, Jr. *newspaper editor*
Perry, Donald A. *cable television consultant*

Norfolk
Barry, Richard Francis, III *publishing executive*
Batten, Frank *newspaper publisher, cable broadcaster*
†Campbell, Cole C. *journalist, educator*
Fitzpatrick, William Henry *retired journalist*
Ritter, Alfred Francis, Jr. *cable television executive*
Rose, Paul Edward *publishing company executive*
†Sizemore, William Howard, Jr. *newspaper editor*
Wynne, John Oliver *newspaper, broadcast and cable executive*

Radford
Thomas, Robert Wilburn *broadcasting and advertising executive*
Wille, Lois Jean *retired newspaper editor*

Reston
Black, Cathleen Prunty *newspaper executive*
Cannistraro, Nicholas, Jr. *newspaper executive*
Mallette, Malcolm Francis *newspaper editor, educator*
Pyle, Thomas Alton *intructional television and motion picture executive*

Richmond
Baker, Donald Parks *journalist, educator*
Bryan, David Tennant *media company executive*
Bryan, John Stewart, III *newspaper publisher*
†Bustard, Clarke *music critic, newswriter, radio producer*
Dillon, James Lee *media company executive, newspaper publisher*
Donnahoe, Alan Stanley *newspaper executive*
Estes, Gerald Walter *newspaper executive*
†Gillispie, Charles Stephenson, Jr. *publishing and printing executive*
Goodykoontz, Charles Alfred *newspaper editor, retired*
†Neman, Daniel Louis *movie critic*
†Owen, Howard Wayne *journalist, writer*
Robertson, William Franklin *publishing executive*

Roanoke
†Beagle, Benjamin Stuart, Jr. *columnist*
Landon, Forrest M. *newspaper editor*
†Layman, Mark Leslie *newspaper editor*
Rugaber, Walter Feucht, Jr. *newspaper executive*
†Shamy, Edward Thomas *newspaper columnist*
Warren, William Kermit *newspaper managing editor*

Sterling
Buchanan, William Walter *publisher*

Vienna
Binder, Leonard James *magazine editor, retired*
Blevins, Charles Russell *publishing executive*
Lewis, Boyd De Wolf *publisher,editor, writer*
Mc Arthur, George *journalist*
McKay, Carol Ruth *photographic editor*

Virginia Beach
Green, Barbara-Marie *publisher, journalist*
Robertson, Pat (Marion Gordon Robertson) *religious broadcasting executive*
Smith, A. Robert *editor, author*

Winchester
Byrd, Harry Flood, Jr. *newspaper executive, former senator*

WASHINGTON

Mercer Island
Bowne, Martha Hoke *magazine editor, consultant*

Port Townsend
Buhler, Jill Lorie *editor, writer*

Redmond
Mollman, John Peter *book publisher, consultant electronic publishing*

Seattle
Anderson, Rick Gary *newspaper columnist*
†Anderson, Ross *columnist*
Bargreen, Melinda Lueth *music critic*
Blethen, William Kingsley, Jr. *newspaper publishing executive*
Boardman, David *newspaper editor*
Bryant, Hilda Marie *journalism educator*
Buckner, Philip Franklin *newspaper publisher*
Cameron, Mindy *newspaper editor*
Cochran, Wendell *science editor*
Culp, Mildred Louise *corporate executive*
Dietrich, William Alan *reporter*
Ellegood, Donald Russell *publishing executive*
Even, Jan *newspaper editor*
Fancher, Michael Reilly *newspaper editor, newspaper publishing executive*
Godden, Jean W. *columnist*
Gouldthorpe, Kenneth Alfred Percival *publisher, state official*
†Gwinn, Mary Ann *newspaper reporter*
Hartl, John George *film critic*
Henkel, Cathy *newspaper sports editor*
Hills, Regina J. *journalist*
Johnson, Wayne Eaton *former drama critic, writer, editor*
Kelly, Carolyn Sue *newspaper executive*
Lacitis, Erik *journalist*
†Martens, David Baker *publishing executive*
Meagher, Cynthia Nash *journalist*
†Nalder, Eric Christopher *investigative reporter*
Owen, John *journalist*
Payne, Ancil Horace *retired broadcasting executive*
Rinearson, Peter Mark *journalist, author, software developer*
†Schafer, James Henry *newspaper company executive*
Sizemore, Herman Mason, Jr. *newspaper executive*
Smulyan, Jeffrey *radio station executive, owner pro baseball team*
†Stanton, Michael John *newspaper editor*
Turner, Wallace L. *reporter*
†Voorhees, John Lloyd *columnist*
Williams, John A. (Jack Williams) *newspaper publishing executive*
Williamson, Don *newspaper columnist*

Spokane
†Cowles, William Stacey *publisher*
Gray, Alfred Orren *journalism educator, research and communications consultant*
Herdrich, Norman Wesley *magazine editor*
Roberts, Larry Paul *broadcasting executive*

Vancouver
Campbell, Scott *newspaper publishing company executive*

WEST VIRGINIA

Charleston
Greenfield, David Joel *editor*
†Grimes, Richard Stuart *editor, writer*
Haught, James Albert, Jr. *journalist, newspaper editor*

Clarksburg
Highland, Cecil Blaine, Jr. *newspaper publisher, lawyer, banker*

Greenville
Warner, Kenneth Wilson, Jr. *editor, association publications executive*

Huntington
Reynolds, Marshall Truman *printing company executive*
Ritchie, Garry Harlan *television broadcast executive*

Parkersburg
Crooks, Thomas Jackson *advertising executive*

Shepherdstown
Hresan, Sally L. *journalism educator*

Wheeling
Nutting, George Ogden *newspaper publisher*

WISCONSIN

Brookfield
Lessiter, Frank Donald *magazine editor*
Schwanz, H(erman) Lee *publishing company executive*

Fort Atkinson
Knox, William David *publishing company executive*
Meyer, Eugene Carlton *retired editor*
Sager, Donald Jack *publisher, former librarian*

Green Bay
†Bacha, Diane Marie *newspaper editor*
Daley, Arthur James *retired magazine publisher*
†Poppenhagen, Ronald William *newspaper editor, publishing executive*

Iola
Foerster, Urban Michael, III (Trey Foerster) *newspaper owner, publisher*
Krause, Chester Lee *publishing company executive*
Mishler, Clifford Leslie *publisher*

Janesville
Fitzgerald, James Francis *cable television executive*

Madison
Blankenburg, William Burl *journalism educator*
Burgess, James Edward *newspaper publisher, executive*
Denton, Frank M. *newspaper editor*
Evanson, Elizabeth Moss *editor*
†Fanlund, Paul G. *newspaper editor*
Fitchen, Allen Nelson *publisher*
†Haslanger, Philip Charles *journalist*
Hoyt, James Lawrence *journalism educator, athletic administrator*
†Hunter, John Patrick *newspaper editor*
Knoll, Erwin *author, editor*
McNelly, John Taylor *journalist, educator*
Meloon, Robert A. *retired newspaper publisher*
Miller, Frederick William *publisher, lawyer*
Walker, William Ray *broadcasting executive*
Wolman, J. Martin *retired newspaper publisher*
Zweifel, David Alan *newspaper editor*

Menasha
Henseler, Gerald Anthony *printing company executive*

Milwaukee
†Armstrong, Douglas Dean *movie critic*
Auer, James Matthew *art critic, journalist*
Behrendt, David Frogner *journalist*
Farris, Trueman Earl, Jr. *retired newspaper editor*
Fibich, Howard Raymond *retired newspaper editor*
Foster, Richard *journalist*
Fraedrich, Royal Louis *magazine editor, publisher*
Gissler, Sigvard Gunnar, Jr. *journalism educator, former newspaper editor*
†Hannah, Stephen *newspaper editor*
Hayes, Paul Gordon *journalist*
Hinshaw, Edward Banks *broadcasting company executive*
Huston, Margo *journalist*
†Jaques, Damien Paul *theater critic*
Joslyn, Jay Thomas *arts critic*
Kritzer, Paul Eric *media executive, communications lawyer*
Leonard, Richard Hart *journalist*
†Lynett, William Ruddy *publishing, broadcasting company executive*
†McCann, Dennis J. *columnist*
Meisner, Mary Jo *editor*
Reedy, George Edward *educator, author, lecturer*
Schaleben, Arville *newspaper editor, writer, educator*
Schwartz, Harold Albert *retired newspaper company executive*
†Slocum, Elizabeth *newspaper editor*
Spore, Keith Kent *newspaper editor*
Wills, Robert Hamilton *newspaper executive*

Montello
Burns, Robert Edward *editor, publisher*

Neillsville
Stockwell, Richard E. *journalist, business executive*

New Glarus
Marsh, Robert Charles *writer, music critic*

Pewaukee
Lee, Jack (Jim Sanders Beasley) *broadcast executive*

Stoughton
Ellery, John Blaise *communications educator emeritus*

Verona
Schroeder, Henry William *publisher*

Waterloo
Kay, Dennis Matthew *operations manager*

WYOMING

Casper
Rosenthal, Jack *broadcasting executive*

Cheyenne
Horton, Bernard Francis *newspaper editor*

Jackson
Downer, Eugene Debs, Jr. *editor, publisher*

Riverton
†Peck, Robert A. *newspaper publisher*

TERRITORIES OF THE UNITED STATES

GUAM

Agana
Crisostomo, Manny *photographer*
Mallo-Garrido, Josephine Ann *marketing manager*

CANADA

ALBERTA

Calgary
Fisher, John Philip *retired printing and publishing company executive*
Peterson, Kevin Bruce *newspaper editor, publishing executive*

Edmonton
Hughes, Linda J. *newspaper publisher*
†Poignant, Gary Donald *newspaper editor*
Roskin, Lewis Ross *broadcasting company executive*
†Stanway, Paul William *newspaper editor*

BRITISH COLUMBIA

New Westminster
Gunn, Roderick James *broadcast executive*

Vancouver
†Dykk, LLoyd Henry *journalist*
Holtby, Douglas Martin *television executive*
Hume, Stephen *writer, editor*

MANITOBA

Winnipeg
Asper, Israel Harold *broadcasting executive*
Burt, Christopher Murray *former newspaper editor, communications consultant*
†McKie, Francis Paul *journalist*
Wreford, David Mathews *magazine editor*

ONTARIO

Burlington
Mc Carthy, Thomas James *newspaper executive*

Don Mills
French, William Harold *retired newspaper editor*
Hanna, William Brooks *book publisher*
Heisey, William Lawrence *publisher*
Hickey, Brian Edward *publishing executive*
†Stoddart, Jack Elliott *publishing company executive*

Kingston
Hancock, Geoffrey White *magazine editor, writer*

Kitchener
MacDonald, Wayne Douglas *publisher*

London
Bembridge, John Anthony *newspaper editor*
†Cornies, Larry Alan *journalist, educator*
Desbarats, Peter Hullett *journalist, academic administrator*
McLeod, Philip R. *publishing executive*

Markham
Fitzhenry, Robert Irvine *publisher*

Ottawa
Clever, W(arren) Glenn *editor, publishing executive, poet, writer, educator*
Davey, Clark William *newspaper publisher*
Deacon, Paul Septimus *retired publishing, communications company executive*
Macklem, Michael Kirkpatrick *publisher*
MacLaren, Roy *publisher, Canadian federal legislator*
Manera, Anthony S. *broadcasting executive*
McCabe, Michael *broadcast executive*
†Stone, Jeffrey Jay *film critic, journalist, writer*

Peterborough
Young, Scott Alexander *television journalist, author*

Scarborough
Besse, Ronald Duncan *publishing company executive*
†Inkpen, Ross McKay *publishing company executive*
†Isley, John Charles *publishing company executive*
Mitchell, Arthur Harris *newspaper columnist*

Toronto
Berton, Pierre *journalist, author*
Black, Conrad Moffat *publishing corporate executive*
†Boot, Sonja Sunni *media specialist*
Boultbee, John Arthur *publishing executive*
Clancy, Louis John *newspaper editor, journalist*
Creighton, John Douglas *newspaper publisher*
†Cruickshank, John Douglas *newspaper editor*
Downing, John Henry *newspaper editor, journalist, columnist*
Egan, Vincent Joseph *journalist, newspaper columnist*
Fierheller, George Alfred *communications company executive*
Galloway, David Alexander *publishing company executive*
Godfrey, Paul Victor *newspaper publisher*
Harris, Nicholas George *publisher*
Honderich, Beland Hugh *publisher*
Honderich, John Allen *newspaper editor*
Iannuzzi, Daniel Andrew *publishing and broadcasting executive*
Jolley, David *newspaper executive*
Karakas, Rita S. *television broadcast executive*
King, John Charles Peter *newspaper editor*
Landsberg, Michele *journalist*
†Lewis, Robert *periodical editor, journalist*
Lombardi, John Barba-Linardo *broadcasting executive*
Malloy, Michael Terrence *journalist, newspaper editor*
Morra, Bernadette *fashion journalist, columnist*

Newman, Peter Charles *journalist*
†Olive, David Michael *magazine writer, magazine editor*
Ostry, Bernard *broadcasting executive*
†Rauhala, Ann Elaine *newspaper editor, columnist*
Singleton-Wood, Allan James *publishing executive*
Smith, David Todd *publishing company executive*
Thall, Burnett Murray *newspaper executive*
†Thomson, Kenneth R. (Lord Thomson of Fleet) *publishing executive*
Tighe, James C. *publisher*
†Turner, Craig *journalist*
†Watson, Paul *photojournalist*

Willowdale
Dean, Geoffrey *book publisher*
Irwin, John Wesley *publisher*
Kerner, Fred *book publisher, writer*

QUEBEC

Montreal
Beaubien, Philippe de Gaspe, II *communications executive*
†Béliveau, Jules *journalist*
Braide, Robert David *broadcast executive*
Chagnon, Andre *broadcast executive*
Des Marais, Pierre, II *communications holding company executive*
Des Roches, Antoine *newspaper executive*
Girard, Jacques *communications executive*
Hancox, Ralph *publisher*
†Hurtubise, Jacques *journalist*
Landry, Roger D. *publishing company executive*
Peladeau, Pierre *publishing company executive*
Pépin, Marcel *broadcast executive*
†Romanelli, G. Jack *journalist*
Webster, Norman Eric *journalist, charitable foundation administrator*

SASKATCHEWAN

Regina
Hughes, Robert Lachlan *newspaper executive*

Saskatoon
Peterson, Bill *publishing executive*

MEXICO

Mexico City
†Ellison, Katherine Esther *journalist*

AUSTRALIA

Greenwich
Westerberg, Verne Edward *magazine publisher*

Sydney
Guerin, Didier *magazine executive*
Murdoch, (Keith) Rupert *publisher*

BELGIUM

Brussels
Branegan, James Augustus, III *journalist*
Kempe, Frederick Schumann *newspaper editor, author*

ENGLAND

Buckinghamshire
Elegant, Robert Sampson *journalist, author*

Cambridge
Kermode, (John) Frank *literary critic, educator*

Hartlepool
Smyth, Reginald (Reggie Smythe) *cartoonist*

London
Barnett, Bill Marvin *publishing company executive*
Boccardi, Louis Donald *news agency executive*
Cook, Jan *recording industry executive*
de Bellaigue, Eric *media consultant, securities analysis specialist*
Fenton, Thomas Trail *journalist*
Grade, Lew *entertainment corporation executive*
Green, Richard Lancelyn (Gordon) *editor, writer*
Laurie, James Andrew *journalist, broadcaster*
Mayer, Peter *publisher*
McGinnis, Marcy Ann *television news executive producer*
Mellon, John *publishing executive*
Pleasants, Henry *music critic*
Scardino, Albert James *journalist*
Tuohy, William *correspondent*

FEDERAL REPUBLIC GERMANY

Wachtberg-Villiprott
Gutman, Roy William *reporter*

FIJI

Suva
Usher, Sir Leonard Gray *retired news association executive*

FRANCE

Lauris
Spivak, Jonathan M. *journalist*

Paris
Behrstock, Julian Robert *publishing consultant, writer*
De Lyrot, Alain Herve *editor*
Dubs, Patrick Christian *publisher*

GERMANY

Bonn
Fleming, Joseph Benedict *newspaperman*

Munich
Saur, Klaus G. *publisher*
von Minckwitz, Bernhard *publishing company executive*

Weinheim
†Köhler, Hans Dirk *publisher*

HONG KONG

Hong Kong
Lehner, Urban Charles *journalist*

ISRAEL

Jerusalem
Bronner, Ethan Samuel *news correspondent*

Savyon
Bushinsky, Jay (Joseph Mason) *journalist, radio commentator, television correspondent*

ITALY

Rome
Wynn, Coy Wilton *journalist*

JAPAN

Tokyo
Krisher, Bernard *foreign correspondent*
†Simons, Lewis Martin *journalist*

THE NETHERLANDS

Amsterdam
Kels, James *publishing executive*
†Vinken, Pierre Jacques *publishing executive, neurosurgeon*

NEW ZEALAND

Bay of Islands
Veysey, Arthur Ernest *reporter, administrator, biographer*

POLAND

Warsaw
Engelberg, Stephen Paul *reporter*

SPAIN

Mallorco
Raff, Joseph Allen *publishing company executive, author*

SWITZERLAND

Geneva
O'Regan, Richard Arthur *editor, retired foreign correspondent*

TURKS AND CAICOS ISLANDS

Provinciales
Johnston, Samuel Thomas *entertainment company executive*

WEST INDIES

Montserrat
Diggs, J(esse) Frank *retired magazine editor*

ADDRESS UNPUBLISHED

Aaron, Betsy *journalist*
Aaron, Roy Henry *entertainment company executive, lawyer*
Achorn, Robert Comey *retired newspaper publisher*
Adler, Gerald *film and television executive, lawyer*
Ajemian, Robert Myron *journalist*
Aldrich, Patricia Anne Richardson *retired magazine editor*
Andrisani, John Anthony *editor, author, golf consultant*
Anglemire, Kenneth Norton *retired publishing company executive, writer, environmentalist, lawyer*
Arden, Sherry W. *publishing company executive*
Arnold, Henri *cartoonist*
Audet, Paul Andre *retired newspaper executive*
Baack, John Edward *publishing consultant*
Backlund, Ralph Theodore *magazine editor*
Baggett, Donnis Gene *journalist, editor*
Bassett, Barbara Wies *editor, publisher*
Batignani, Laurie A. *communications professional*

Beisel, Daniel Cunningham former newspaper publisher
Bender, Gary Nedrow television sportscaster
Berger, William Ernest newspaper publisher
Berman, Laura freelance writer
Bernard, Jami film critic, author
Bernstein, Laurel publishing executive
Bernstein, Lester editorial consultant
Blackstock, Joseph Robinson newspaper editor
Blackwell, Earl publishing executive, writer
Block, William newspaper publisher
Bogdanich, Walt journalist
Boswell, Thomas Murray sports columnist, writer
Bouton, James Alan author, entrepreneur, sportscaster, former professional baseball player
Brazil, Jeff reporter
Brennan, Terrence Michael publisher
Brett, Barbara Jeanne publisher
Brinberg, Herbert Raphael information management, publishing company executive
Broadwater, James E. publisher
Brodian, Laura broadcasting and illustration studio executive, professional illustrator
Broude, Ronald music publisher
Brown, Britt retired publishing company executive
Buchanan, Patrick Joseph journalist
Buckley, William Elmhirst publishing consultant
Buffkins, Archie Lee public television executive
Burrington, David Edson journalist
Callahan, Joseph Murray magazine editor
Callander, Bruce Douglas journalist, free-lance writer
Camp, Clifton Durrett, Jr. newspaper consultant, rancher
Campbell, Byron Chesser publishing company executive
Cantone, Vic political cartoonist
Carlson, Natalie Traylor publisher
Chernichaw, Mark television, film and interactive multimedia executive, producer, director, international media consultant
Clark, Peter Bruce newspaper executive
Clark, Robert Phillips newspaper editor, consultant
Cloud, Stanley Wills journalist, editor, writer
Cohen, Allan Richard broadcasting executive
Cohen, Mark Herbert broadcasting company executive
†Conklin, Michael L. newspaper columnist
Cook, Fred James journalist, author
Cook, Stanton R. media company executive
Cooper, Jon Hugh public television executive
Costas, Robert Quinlan (Bob Costas) sportscaster
Cowles, John, Jr. publisher, fitness instructor
Crowther, James Earl radio and television executive
Cuevas, Milton Joseph publishing company executive
Cullen, James Thaddeus, Jr. broadcast executive
Curtin, David Stephen newswriter
Curtis, Mary Ellen (Mary Curtis Horowitz) publishing company executive
Cushing, Frederic Sanford publishing company executive
Dahlgren, Carl Herman Per educator, arts administrator
D'Amato, Anthony Roger recording company executive
Daniel, Elbert Clifton journalist
DeCamp, Graydon journalist
Dekker, Maurits publisher, editor
Delano, Hugh Stafford newspaper sports journalist, author
Dickman, James Bruce photojournalist
Dills, James Arlof retired publishing company executive
Dinkel, John George magazine editor
Drew, Elizabeth Heineman publishing executive
Duerr, Herman George retired publishing executive
DuMont, Bruce political correspondent
Duncan, David Douglas photojournalist, author
Dunham, Benjamin Starr editor, arts administrator
Eaker, Ira publishing executive
Edwards, Geoffrey Hartley newspaper publisher
Ehrlich, Amy editor, writer
Ekstract, Richard Evan publishing executive
Ellison, Eugene Curtis radio station executive
†Ellison, Robert M. new correspondent
Elsner, Sidney Edgar journalist
Emery, Sherman Raymond editorial consultant
Enloe, Cortez Ferdinand, Jr. magazine publisher, physician
Erlicht, Lewis Howard broadcasting company executive
Ewell, Miranda Juan journalist
Farah, Joseph Francis newspaper editor, writer
Fassio, Virgil newspaper publishing company executive
Fazio, Evelyn M. publisher
Feiffer, Jules cartoonist, writer, playwright
Ferre, Antonio Luis newspaper publisher
Fields, William Hudson, III magazine publisher
Fink, John Francis newspaper editor
Fitzgerald, Edward Earl publishing executive, author
†Frankel, Glenn journalist
†Franken, Robert E. news correspondent
Freeman, Graydon LaVerne retired publishing company executive
Garfield, Robert Edward newspaper columnist
Gartenberg, Seymour Lee retired recording company executive
Geer, Stephen DuBois retired journalist
Geoghegan, John Joseph retired publisher
Gilder, George Franklin writer
Gill, Henry Herr photojournalist
†Gilson, Barbara Frances editor
Glover, William Harper theater critic
Goldhirsh, Bernard A. publisher
Goldwater, John Leonard publisher, writer
†Golum, Robert Bruce journalist
Goodkin, Michael Jon publishing company executive
Green, Nancy Loughridge newspaper executive
Grossman, John Joseph retired editor
†Grueskin, William Steven editor
Haas, Carolyn Buhai publisher, writer, consultant
Hagel, Raymond Charles publishing company executive, educator
Halfen, David publishing executive
Hamill, (William) Pete newspaper columnist, author
Hanners, David journalist
Harden, Patrick Alan journalist, news executive
Hartman, John Wheeler publisher
Hast, Adele editor, historian
Hawes, Alexander Boyd, Jr. newspaper editor, journalist
Hayes, Marilyn Jo communications educator, writer
Heiman, Grover George, Jr. magazine editor, author
Hering, Doris Minnie dance critic
Hess, David Willard journalist
Himmelfarb, Milton editor, educator
Hinckle, Warren James, III journalist
Hoge, James Fulton, Jr. magazine editor
Holland, David Thurston former editor
Holt, Patricia Lester book review editor
Hough, George Anthony, III journalism educator
Howard, Jack Rohe retired newspaperman
Hubley, Reginald Allen publisher
Idaszak, Jerome Joseph economic journalist
Jameson, Victor Loyd retired magazine editor
†Jennings, Max newspaper editor
†Jensen, Jack Michael publishing executive
Jiler, William Laurence publisher
Jinks, Robert Larry retired newspaper publisher
Johnson, Ferd retired cartoonist, color artist
Johnson, Frank Edward newspaper editor
Johnson, Malcolm Clinton, Jr. publishing consultant
Johnson, Robert Maurice newspaper executive
Jordan, Fred publishing company executive
Joseph, Judith R. publishing executive
Jovanovich, Peter William publishing executive
Kellock, Alan C(onverse) book publishing executive
Kelly, Kevin drama critic
Kennedy, Harvey Edward science information publishing executive
Kenny, Patrick Edward publishing executive
Key, Ted cartoonist
Keyes, Saundra Elise newspaper editor
Kilpatrick, James Jackson, Jr. columnist, author
Klapper, Carol Lorraine magazine publisher
Klein, Edward Joel editor, author, lecturer
Koppett, Leonard columnist, journalist, author
Kraslow, David retired newspaper publishing executive, reporter, author, consultant
Krauthammer, Charles columnist, editor
Kuehn, James Marshall newspaper editor
Kyle, John Hamilton publishing executive
Laidlaw, Robert Richard publishing company executive
Laitin, Joseph journalist, former government spokesman and public relations consultant
Lambro, Donald Joseph columnist
Landauer, Jeramy Lanigan publishing company executive
Landers, Ann (Mrs. Esther P. Lederer) columnist
Landis, James David publishing company executive, retired, author
Larson, George Charles magazine editor, writer
Larson, Robert Frederick public broadcasting company executive
Larson, Russell George magazine and book publisher
Lassner, Keith Michael publishing executive
Leavy, Herbert Theodore publisher
Lewis, Gregg Allan editor, writer
Lippman, Barry publishing executive
Lively, John Pound magazine editor, publisher
Lloyd, Kate Rand magazine editor
Lloyd, Michael Jeffrey recording producer
Lonneke, Michael Dean radio and television marketing executive
Lord, Roy Alvin retired publisher
Loughlin, Mary Anne Elizabeth television news anchor
Louttit, James Russell publishing company executive
Lukas, J. Anthony journalist
Lyman, Richard R. journalist
Lynch, Patricia Gates broadcasting organization executive consultant, former ambassador
MacFarlane, Andrew Walker media specialist, educator
MacMinn, Aleene Merle B(arnes) newspaper editor, columnist, educator
Malott, Adele Renee editor
Manley, Joan A(dele) Daniels retired publisher
Mann, Jim (James William Manousos) editor, publisher
†Marbert, Larry David newspaper publishing executive
Marcus, Greil Gerstley critic
Marino, Joseph Anthony retired publishing executive
McClendon, Sarah Newcomb news service executive, writer
Mc Cormick, William Martin broadcast executive
McDarrah, Gloria Schoffel editor, author
McGuirk, Terrence former broadcasting company executive
McHenry, Robert (Dale) editor
McNulty, Henry Bryant journalist
Meade, Everard Kidder, Jr. retired broadcasting and publishing executive
Medina, Kathryn Bach book editor
Melody, Michael Edward publishing company executive
Menchel, Donald television executive
Miller, Robert Branson, Jr. retired newspaper publisher
Millett, Ralph Linwood, Jr. retired newspaper editor
†Mills, Russell Andrew newspaper publisher
Miner, A. Bradford journalist
Molden, Herbert George publisher
Molnar, Anthony William publishing and training company executive
Monacelli, Gianfranco publishing executive
Morgan, Linda Rogers editor
†Morton, Bruce A. news correspondent
Mosley, Zack Terrell cartoonist
Mueller, Barbara Ruth journalist
Mulholland, Robert Edge broadcasting company executive
Musburger, Brent Woody sportscaster
Neff, Donald Lloyd news correspondent, writer
Nelson, Martha Jane magazine editor
Nelson, Robert Charles newspaper executive
Nolan, Irene Clare newspaper editor
Novick, Julius Lerner theater critic, educator
Olsen, Merlin Jay sports analyst, former professional football player
Orr, Carol Wallace book publishing executive
Ortner, Everett Howard magazine editor, writer
Osrin, Raymond Harold retired political cartoonist
Oster, Patrick Ralph journalist
Pack, Richard Morris broadcasting executive
Paglio, Lydia Elizabeth editor
Parker, David Shannon publishing company executive
†Parker, Sybil Pam science editor
Peacock, Mary Willa magazine editor
†Pepper, Jeffrey Mackenzie editor-in-chief
Perrin, Gail editor
Petersen, Susan Jane publishing company executive
Petykiewicz, Sandra Dickey editor
Pierce, James Robert magazine executive
Plangere, Jules Leon, Jr. media company executive
Pletcher, Eldon editorial cartoonist
Pockell, Leslie M. publishing company executive
Polk, James Ray journalist
†Poploff, Michelle Jo editor
Porges, Walter Rudolf television news executive
Priaulx, A(llan) publishing executive
Pudney, Gary Laurence television executive
Putnam, Linda Lee communication educator, researcher
Quinn, Charles Nicholas journalist
Rasor, Dina Lynn journalist
Rayner, William Alexander retired newspaper editor
Rector, Richard Robert television executive, producer
Regnery, Henry publisher
Reich, Herb editor
Reidenbaugh, Lowell Henry retired sports editor
Reston, James Barrett retired newspaper publishing executive, author, lecturer
Rice, Roger Douglas television executive, artist
Richman, Alan magazine editor
Ridder, Paul Anthony newspaper executive
Rosenthal, Arthur Jesse publisher
Rosset, Lisa Krug editor
Rubin, Rick record producer
Ryan, Tom Kreusch cartoonist
Samuelson, Robert Jacob journalist
Sapsowitz, Sidney H. entertainment and media company executive
Sargent, John Turner publisher
Sarris, Andrew George film critic
Sauter, Van Gordon communications executive
Schorr, Daniel Louis broadcast journalist, author, lecturer
†Schrader, Martin Harry retired publisher
Schulz, Ralph Richard publishing consultant
Schwartz, Lloyd Marvin newspaper and magazine correspondent, broadcaster
Scruggs, Charles G. editor
Seidel, Glenda Lee newspaper publisher
†Seymour, Dale Gilbert publisher, author, speaker, consultant
Shelton, Stephani broadcast journalist, consultant
†Simons, Robert R. book publishing executive
Simpson, O. J. (Orenthal James Simpson) former professional football player, actor, sports commentator
Smith, Hedrick Laurence journalist, television comentator, author, lecturer
Smith, Martin Bernhard journalist
Stanley, Scott, Jr. editor
Stanton, John Jeffrey editor, broadcast journalist, government programs director, analyst
Starr, David newspaper editor, publisher
†Stennett, William Clinton (Clint Stennett) radio and television station executive, state legislator
Stines, Fred, Jr. publisher
Stoll, Charles Buckner publishing executive, consultant
Stolley, Richard Brockway journalist
Strothman, James Edward editor
†Swanson, Peter Carl editor
Swayze, John Cameron, Sr. news commentator
Switzer, Maurice Harold publisher
Taylor, Kristin Clark media specialist
Thompson, Robert Elliott columnist, writer
Threlkeld, Richard Davis broadcast journalist
Tiedge-Lafranier, Jeanne Marie editor
Tobias, Andrew Previn columnist, lecturer
Trudeau, Garretson Beekman (Garry Trudeau) cartoonist
Trueman, William Peter Main broadcaster, newspaper columnist
Ubell, Earl television science editor
Urdang, Laurence lexicographer, publisher
van Bruchem, Jan retired broadcasting executive
Vance, Lee publishing company executive, consultant
Vandenberg, Peter Ray magazine publisher
Wagman, Robert John journalist, author
Wagner, Julia A(nne) retired editor
Warnken, Douglas Richard publishing consultant
Waters, Betty Lou newspaper reporter, writer
†Weaver, Howard Cecil newspaper editor
Weckesser, Ernest Prosper, Jr. publisher, educator
Weissman, Jack (George Anderson) editor
Werman, Thomas Ehrlich record producer
Whitesell, John Edwin motion picture company executive
Wicker, Thomas Grey retired journalist
Wiessler, David Albert correspondent
Wille, Wayne Martin retired editor
†Wilner, Judith journalist
Winter, Alan publishing company executive
Wolfman, Ira Joel editor, writer
Wolner, Rena Meryl publisher
Wood, Marian Starr publishing company executive
Wood, Presnall Hansel editor, minister
Wussler, Robert Joseph broadcasting executive, media consultant
Yack, Patrick Ashley editor
Ziegler, Jack (Denmore) cartoonist

EDUCATION. For postsecondary education, *See also* specific fields.

UNITED STATES

ALABAMA

Auburn
Alderman, Charles Wayne business educator
Galbraith, Ruth Legg retired university dean, home economist
Muse, William Van university president
†Owens, John Murry dean
Philpott, Harry Melvin former university president
Reeve, Thomas Gilmour academic administrator
Rouse, Roy Dennis retired university dean
Voitle, Robert Allen college dean, physiologist

Bessemer
Clarke, McKinley A. secondary educator

Birmingham
Barker, Samuel Booth former university dean, physiology and biology educator
Bennett, Joe Claude university president
Berte, Neal Richard college president
Carter, John Thomas retired educational administrator, writer
Clarke, Juanita M. Waiters education educator
Corts, Thomas Edward university president
Fincher, John Albert college official, consultant
Glaze, Robert Pinckney retired university administrator
Goldman, Jay university dean, industrial engineer, educator
†Gross, Michael S. secondary school principal
Hendley, Dan Lunsford retired university official
Hull, William Edward provost, theology educator
Lee, James Michael education educator
Mc Callum, Charles Alexander university official
Pewitt, James Dudley academic administrator
Sibley, William Arthur academic administrator, physics educator, consultant

Brewton
Jones, Sherman J. academic administrator, management educator

Dothan
Garner, Alto Luther retired education educator
†Harrison, Thomas E. academic official

Florence
Potts, Robert Leslie academic administrator

Gadsden
†Hill, Anita Griffith principal
†Taylor, Fred M. school system administrator

Guntersville
Patterson, Harold Dean superintendent of schools

Huntsville
Ball, Howard Guy education specialist educator
Franz, Frank Andrew academic administrator
Leslie, Lottie Lyle retired educator
Lundquist, Charles Arthur university official
Reaves, Benjamin F. academic administrator

Jacksonville
Boswell, Rupert Dean, Jr. academic administrator, mathematics educator
Dunaway, William Preston education educator emeritus
McGee, Harold Johnston university president

Jasper
Rowland, David Jack college chancellor

Livingston
Green, Asa Norman university president

Madison
Brannan, Eulie Ross education consultant

Maplesville
Nichols, J. Hugh education and economic development consultant

Maxwell AFB
Kline, John Alvin academic administrator

Mobile
Baker, Amanda Sirmon academic administrator, nursing educator
Byrd, Gwendolyn Pauline school system superintendent
†Copeland, Lewis principal
Rewak, William John university president, clergyman
Vacik, James Paul university administrator
Whiddon, Frederick Palmer university president

Montgomery
†Baker, Clifford Cornell state educational administrator
†Bobo, Thomas school system administrator
Cater, Douglass former college president, former government official, writer, editor
Johnson, Andrew Emerson, III educational administrator
Williams, James Orrin university administrator, educator

Muscle Shoals
†Smith, Harry Delano educational administrator

Normal
†Henson, David B. academic administrator

Orange Beach
Bennett, James Jefferson higher education consultant

Prattville
Moorer, Frances Earline Green vocational educator

Rainbow City
Browning, Leslie O. middle school educator

Russellville
†Clemmons, Robert W. school system administrator

Talladega
Johnson, Joseph Benjamin university president

Troy
Adams, Ralph Wyatt, Sr. university chancellor emeritus
†Hawkins, Jack, Jr. academic administrator
Long, John Maloy university dean
Marsicano, Hazel Elliott education educator

Tuscaloosa
Austin, Philip Edward university chancellor
Mitchell, Herbert Hall former university dean, educational consultant
†Sayers, Roger academic administrator
Taaffe, James Griffith university administrator, educator
Turner, Philip Michael university official and dean, author

Tuskegee
Payton, Benjamin Franklin college president

ALASKA

Anchorage
Behrend, Donald Fraser university administrator
Byrd, Milton Bruce college president, former business executive
†Davis, Bettye Jean academic administrator, state official

†Holthouse, Rita J. secondary school principal
Mitchell, Michael Kiehl elementary and secondary education educator, minister
†Trotter, F(rederick) Thomas university president
Young, Bettye Jeanne secondary education educator

Barrow
Trainor, Jerry Allen vocational education professional

Fairbanks
Alexander, Vera dean, marine science educator
†Doran, Timothy Patrick principal
†Drew, James Vandervort university administrator
Komisar, Jerome Bertram university administrator
Ray, Charles Kendall retired university dean
†Reichardt, Paul Bernard dean, chemistry educator
Wadlow, Joan Krueger university chancellor
Wood, William Ransom former university president, city official, corporate executive

Haines
Haas, June F. special education educator, consultant

Juneau
†Lind, Marshall L. academic administrator

Saint Paul
†Dishman, Leland Lee school system administrator

Tuntutuliak
Daniel, Barbara B. secondary education educator

Valdez
†Rogers, Harry school system administrator

ARIZONA

Flagstaff
Hooper, Henry Olcott university dean, physicist
Lovett, Clara Maria university administrator, historian

Glendale
†Altersitz, Janet Kinahan principal
Voris, William educational administrator

Green Valley
Carpenter, John Everett retired principal, educational consultant
Smith, Raymond Lloyd former university president, consultant

Mesa
Belok, Michael Victor education educator
Garwood, John Delvert former college administrator
Johnson, Mary Elizabeth elementary education educator

Page
Hart, Marian Griffith retired educator

Peoria
Jones, Lillie Agnes retired educator

Phoenix
†Dewalt, Judith K. elementary school principal
Donnelly, Charles Robert retired college president
Duvall, Joann retired special education educator
†Ebert, Richard J. principal
†Fitzgerald, Joan principal
†Forsyth, Ben Ralph academic administrator, medical educator
Gibbs, William Harold university administrator
†Williams, Bill academic administrator

Prescott
Russo, Joseph Frank former college president

Scottsdale
Gordon, Rena Joyce health services researcher, educator
Hill, Louis Allen, Jr. former university dean, consultant

Sierra Vista
†Lokensgard, Jon A. school system administrator

Sun City
Corcoran, Eileen Lynch special education educator emerita

Sun City West
Cohen, Abraham J. (Al Cohen) educational administrator

Sun Lakes
Johnson, Marian Ilene education educator
Thompson, Loring Moore retired college administrator, writer

Tempe
Abraham, Willard B. special education educator
Cheatham, Glenn Wallace leisure studies educator, consultant, researcher
Coor, Lattie Finch university president
†Kelly, Rita Mae professor, researcher
Marsh, Roberta Reynolds educator, consultant
Overman, Glenn Delbert college dean emeritus
Sackton, Frank Joseph university official, lecturer, retired army officer

Tucson
†Abrams, Eric R. principal
Barich, Dewey Frederick emeritus educational administrator
Beverly, Theria M. reading educator
†Bowers, William S. educator
†Cate, Rodney Michael academic administrator
Chidester, Otis Holden retired secondary education educator
†Clement, Nicholas I. principal
Harcleroad, Fred Farley education educator
Heins, Marilyn college dean, pediatrics educator, author
†Hershberger, Robert Glen dean, architect
Humphrey, John Julius university program director, historian, writer
Johnson, John Gray retired university chancellor
†Kaltenbach, C. Colin dean, educator
Leavitt, Jerome Edward childhood educator
Nelson, Lawrence Olaf administrative educator
Pacheco, Manuel Trinidad university president
Reid, Charles Phillip Patrick academic administrator, researcher, professor
Smerdon, Ernest Thomas academic administrator
Stoffle, Carla Joy dean university library
Weaver, Albert Bruce university administrator
Wilson, John Lewis university official

ARKANSAS

Arkadelphia
Dunn, Charles DeWitt academic administrator
Elrod, Ben Moody academic administrator
Grant, Daniel Ross retired university president
†Thomas, Herman L. school system administrator

Batesville
Griffith, John Vincent academic official

Beebe
†Owen, William Harold, Jr. academic administrator

Camden
†Brown, George J. academic administrator

Clarksville
†Stephenson, C. Gene academic administrator

Conway
Thompson, Winfred Lee university president, lawyer

Fayetteville
Farrell, Karolyn Kay McMillan adult education educator
Ferritor, Daniel E. university official
Knowles, Malcolm Shepherd education educator
Madison, Bernard L. academic dean, mathematics educator
Oxford, Charles William university dean, chemical engineer
Schoppmeyer, Martin William education educator
Vorsanger, Fred S. university administrator
Williams, Doyle Z. university dean, educator

Fort Smith
†Gooden, Benny L. school system administrator

Hot Springs Village
Robinson, Donald Walter university dean

Jonesboro
Smith, Eugene Wilson retired university president and educator

Little Rock
†Anderson, Joel E. academic administrator
Fribourgh, James Henry university administrator
Gray, John Wylie university dean, consultant
†Hathaway, Charles E. academic administrator
Keaton, William Thomas academic administrator, pastor
Smith, Charles Wilson, Jr. university dean
Truex, Dorothy Adine retired university administrator

Magnolia
Brinson, Harold Thomas university president emeritus
†Gamble, Steven G. academic administrator

Pine Bluff
†Davis, Lawrence A. academic administrator

Searcy
†Burks, David Basil academic administrator, educator

Springdale
†Hill, Peggy Sue principal
†Rogers, Jerry principal
†Rollins, Jimmy Don school system administrator

State University
Fowler, Gilbert L. dean, educator
Mangieri, John Nicholas university administrator

CALIFORNIA

Alameda
Verrill, Kathleen Wills special education educator

Anaheim
Balch, Glenn McClain, Jr. academic administrator, minister, author
†Jackson, David Robert school system administrator
McGarry, Eugene L. university official

Anaheim Hills
Grose, Elinor Ruth retired elementary education educator

Angwin
Maxwell, D. Malcolm college president

Apple Valley
Mays, George Walter, Jr. educational administrator, educator, consultant

Aptos
Bohn, Ralph Carl educational consultant, retired educator

Arcata
Bowker, Lee Harrington academic administrator
Mc Crone, Alistair William university president

Artesia
†Ferris, Pauline principal
†Moffett, Kenneth Lee superintendent schools

Azusa
Bonner, Patricia J. academic dean
†Felix, Richard E. academic administrator
Gray, Paul Wesley university dean

Bakersfield
Arciniega, Tomas Abel university president
†Hefner, John principal

Bayside
†Bank, Ron principal

Berkeley
Bender, Richard university dean, architect, educator
Clifford, Geraldine Joncich (Mrs. William F. Clifford) education educator
Elberg, Sanford Samuel university administrator
†Freedman, Sarah Warshauer education educator
Glenny, Lyman Albert retired education educator
Kerr, Clark university president emeritus
Maslach, George James former university official
Merrill, Richard James educational director
Miles, Raymond Edward former university dean, organizational behavior and industrial relations educator
Montgomery, Roger dean
Park, Roderic Bruce retired university chancellor
Rice, Robert Arnot school administrator
Tien, Chang-Lin chancellor

Bonita
Barnard, Arlene secondary education educator
Jacobsen, Adolf M.B. university administrator, former naval officer

Brea
Shell, Billy Joe retired university president

Burbank
Godwin, Annabelle Palkes retired early childhood education educator
Sago, Paul Edward college administrator

Burlingame
Clover, Haworth Alfred elementary school educator, historian
†Kennedy, Shannon Ray education educator

California City
Friedl, Rick former academic administrator, lawyer

Cambria
Wallen, Vera S. school superintendent

Campo
Charles, Blanche retired elementary education educator

Carmel
Faul, George Johnson former college president
Lockhart, Brooks Javins retired college dean
Longman, Anne Strickland educational consultant

Carmichael
McHugh, James Joseph retired associate dean

Carson
Brownell, John Arnold former university president
Detweiler, Robert Chester university president, historian

Castro Valley
Dance, Maurice Eugene college administrator

Chico
†Esteban, Manuel Antonio university administrator, educator
Stephens, William Leonard university provost

Chula Vista
Clement, Betty Waidlich literacy educator, consultant

Claremont
Albrecht, Paul Abraham dean
Alexander, John David, Jr. college administrator
Bekavac, Nancy Yavor academic administrator, lawyer
Douglass, Enid Hart educational program director
†Fucaloro, Anthony Frank academic dean
Liggett, Thomas Jackson retired seminary president
Maguire, John David university administrator, educator, writer
Massey, Marilyn Chapin academic administrator
Pedersen, Richard Foote academic administrator
Platt, Joseph Beaven former college president
Riggs, Henry Earle college president, engineering management educator
Stanley, Peter William college president
Stark, Jack Lee college president
Tanenbaum, Basil Samuel college dean, engineering educator
Wettack, F. Sheldon academic administrator

Clovis
Driscoll, Glen Robert former university president

Coronado
Trent-Ota, Jane Suzanne elementary school educator

Cotati
†Arminana, Ruben university president, educator

Daly City
Martin, Bernard Lee former college dean

Davis
Hullar, Theodore Lee university chancellor
Pritchard, William Roy former university system administrator
Smiley, Robert Herschel university dean
Tomlinson-Keasey, Carol Ann university administrator
Vanderhoef, Larry Neil university administrator

Del Mar
Sullivan, Romaine Brust school system administrator

Downey
Ashton, Lillian Hazel Church adult education educator
†Gothold, Stuart E. school system administrator, education educator

Encino
Erickson, Lawrence Wilhelm education educator

Escondido
Moore, Marc Anthony university administrator, writer, retired military officer

Fair Oaks
Branch, Robert Lee retired educational administrator

Fontana
†Lardieri, Anthony J. school system administrator

Fortuna
Fullerton, Gail Jackson university president

Fremont
Brown, David Richard school system administrator, minister
de Roque, Barbara Penberthy special education educator, consultant
Ours, Marian Leah elementary education educator
Sanders, Adrian Lionel gifted and talented education educator

Fresno
†Andresen, Claudia principal
Dandoy, Maxima Antonio education educator emeritus
Haak, Harold Howard university president
Klassen, Peter James academic administrator, history educator
Welty, John Donald university president

Fullerton
Atwell, Margaret Ann education educator
Borst, Philip West academic administrator
Donoghue, Mildred Ransdorf education educator
Gordon, Milton Andrew academic administrator
Hopping, Richard Lee college president
Hugstad, Paul Steven college dean
McGinnis, Joán Adell secondary school educator
Smith, Ephraim Philip university dean, educator

Glendale
Whalen, Lucille academic administrator

Glendora
Schiele, Paul Ellsworth, Jr. educator, writer

Hayward
McCune, Ellis E. retired university system chief administrator, higher education consultant
†Rees, Norma S. university president, educator
Resnikoff, George Joseph university dean, mathematics and statistics educator emeritus
Tontz, Jay Logan university dean, educator

Huntington Park
Johnson, Patricia Hardy early childhood specialist pre-school provider

Inglewood
Guzy, Marguerita Linnes educator
†Jefferson, Bernard S. academic administrator
Kimble, Bettye D. retired educational administrator

Irvine
Garrison, Clayton university dean
†Halm, Dennis Ray academic administrator
Wilkening, Laurel Lynn university official, planetary scientist

La Canada Flintridge
Lamson, Robert Woodrow retired school system administrator

La Jolla
Atkinson, Richard Chatham university chancellor, cognitive psychologist, educator
Dreilinger, Charles Lewis (Chips Dreilinger) dean
Frieman, Edward Allan university administrator, educator
Spooner, Charles Edward university administrator, health educator
Stewart, John Lincoln university administrator

La Mesa
Tarson, Herbert Harvey university administrator emeritus

La Mirada
Lingenfelter, Sherwood Galen university provost, anthropology educator

La Verne
Morgan, Stephen Charles academic administrator

Lafayette
Dietz, Donald Arthur vocational education educator

Lake Elsinore
Wilson, Sonja Mary secondary education educator, consultant

Lakeport
Summerill, John Frederick retired mortuary science college dean and educator

Lakewood
Bogdan, James Thomas secondary education educator, electronics researcher and developer

Livermore
Dyer, Richard Hutchins risk management executive

Loma Linda
Klooster, Judson academic administrator, dentistry educator

Long Beach
Anatol, Karl W. E. provost

Beljan, John Richard *university administrator, medical educator*
Fornia, Dorothy Louise *educator*
Lathrop, Irvin Tunis *retired academic dean, educator*
Lauda, Donald Paul *university dean*
Munitz, Barry *chief university administrator, English literature educator, business consultant*
Thompson, William Ancker *intramural and recreational sports director, educator*

Los Altos
Drachler, Norman *retired education educator*

Los Angeles
Astin, Alexander William *education educator*
Borsting, Jack Raymond *business administration educator*
Bratt, Bengt Erik *academic administrator, consulting engineer*
Calhoun, Ollie Arlene *elementary education educator*
Carden, Joy Cabbage *education executive*
Cleveland, Carl S(ervice), Jr. *academic administrator, educator, physician*
†Cobb, Jewel Plummer *former college president, educator*
Cohen, S(tephen) Marshall *philosophy educator*
Coughlin, Sister Magdalen *college chancellor*
Dewey, Donald Odell *university dean*
Dixon, Andrew Derart *retired academic administrator*
Ellsworth, Frank L. *university administrator*
Hayes, Robert Mayo *university dean, library and information science educator*
Hoffman, Neil James *art school executive*
Hubbard, John Randolph *university president emeritus, history educator, diplomat*
Ireland, Robert Abner, Jr. *education consultant*
Jackson, Kingsbury Temple *educational contract consultant*
Kennelly, Sister Karen Margaret *college administrator*
Lazzaro, Anthony Derek *university administrator*
Lieber, David Leo *university president*
Mandel, Joseph David *university official, lawyer*
Melbo, Irving Robert *retired education educator*
Merrifield, Donald Paul *university chancellor*
Prager, Susan Westerberg *dean, law educator*
†Rosser, James Milton *university president*
Sample, Steven Browning *university president*
Schneider, Edward Lewis *academic administrator, research administrator*
Shea, Robert Stanton *academic administrator*
Shutler, Mary Elizabeth *academic administrator*
Silverman, Leonard M. *university dean, electrical engineering educator*
Slaughter, John Brooks *university president*
Spitzer, William George *university dean, physicist, educator, researcher*
Steinberg, Warren Linnington *school principal*
Taylor, Leigh Herbert *college dean*
Topping, Norman Hawkins *former university chancellor*
†Tuckson, Reed V. *university president*
Wagner, William Gerard *university dean, physicist, consultant, information scientist, investment manager*
Wazzan, Ahmed R(assem) Frank *engineering educator, dean*
†Wexler, Robert *university administrator*
Young, Charles Edward *university chancellor*

Los Gatos
Hartinger, Patricia B. Curran *elementary school educator*
†Simonson, Ted *principal*

Malibu
Davenport, David *university president, lawyer*
Young, Matt Norvel, Jr. *retired university chancellor*

Manhattan Beach
Brooks, Edward Howard *college administrator*

Mission Viejo
Sabaroff, Rose Epstein *retired education educator*

Modesto
†Bairey, Marie *principal*

Montebello
Dible, Rose Harpe McFee *special education educator*

Moraga
Anderson, Brother Mel *academic administrator*

Mountain View
†Bowler, James S. *educational administrator*

North Hollywood
Thurston, Alice Janet *former college president*

Northridge
Bianchi, Donald Ernest *academic administrator, biology educator*
Ellner, Carolyn Lipton *university dean, consultant*
Wilson, Blenda Jacqueline *university chancellor*

Novato
Patterson, W. Morgan *college president*

Oakland
Adwere-Boamah, Joseph *school district administrator*
Dibble, David Van Vlack *educator of visually impaired, lawyer*
†Farley, Thelma *principal*
Goldstine, Stephen Joseph *college administrator*
Isaac Nash, Eva Mae *educator*
†Mitrano, Joseph Charles *school principal*
Peltason, Jack Walter *university administrator*

Ojai
†Wyman, Willard G. *headmaster*

Orange
†Doti, James L. *academic administrator*
Gerhard, Nancy Lucile Dege *educator*
Hamilton, Harry Lemuel, Jr. *academic administrator*

Orinda
†Gilbert, Robert W. *secondary school principal*
†Glasser, Charles Edward *academic administrator*

Oxnard
Frodsham, Olaf Milton *music educator*
Hill, Alice Lorraine *secondary education educator, researcher*
Lawson, William Harold *college dean, labor economist*

Pacoima
Irving, Harry Rayfield *secondary education educator*

Palm Desert
Sicuro, Natale Anthony *academic administrator*

Palm Springs
Aikens, Donald Thomas *educational administrator, consultant*

Palo Alto
Attig, John Clare *history educator, consultant*
Cohen, Elizabeth G. *education and sociology educator, researcher*

Palos Verdes Peninsula
Weaver, John Carrier *university president emeritus*

Paramount
Cook, Karla Joan *elementary education educator*

Pasadena
Everhart, Thomas Eugene *university president, engineering educator*
Gilman, Richard Carleton *retired college president*
Meye, Robert Paul *retired seminary administrator, writer*
†Stolper, Edward Manin *geology educator*

Pebble Beach
Sullivan, James Francis *university administrator*

Pinole
Grogan, Stanley Joseph, Jr. *consultant*

Point Arena
Kohl, Herbert Ralph *education educator*

Pomona
Baker, Frederick John *education educator*
Eaves, Ronald Weldon *university administrator*
Fleck, Raymond Anthony, Jr. *university administrator*
†Suzuki, Bob H. *university president*

Poway
†Brose, Cathy *principal*
Shippey, Lyn *reading center director*

Rancho Cucamonga
Hattar, Michael Mizyed *secondary education educator, mathematics educator*

Rancho Mirage
Scholl, Allan Henry *retired school system administrator, education consultant*

Rancho Palos Verdes
Fischer, Robert Blanchard *university administrator, researcher*
McFadden, Thomas *academic administrator*

Redding
Ballew, Nellie Hester *retired secondary school educator*
Treadway, Douglas Morse *academic administrator*

Redlands
Appleton, James Robert *university president, educator*

Redondo Beach
Marsee, Stuart (Earl) *educational consultant, retired*

Reseda
†Anstad, Neil *director*

Rialto
Jackson, Betty Eileen *music and elementary school educator*

Riverside
Balow, Irving Henry *retired education educator*
Donlan, Dan M. *education educator*
Fleischer, Everly Borah *academic administrator*
†Geraty, Lawrence Thomas *academic administrator, archaeologist*
Hodgen, Maurice Denzil *financial development administrator, educator*
Inacker, Charles John *academic dean, business educator*
Perkins, Van L. *university administrator, educator, conservationist*
Tuck, Russell R., Jr. *college president*
Wilson, Jeanette Kurtz *elementary and middle school educator, behavior specialist*
Yacoub, Ignatius I. *university dean*

Rohnert Park
Babula, William *university dean*

Rosemead
Hansen, Robert Dennis *educational administrator*

Sacramento
Gerth, Donald Rogers *university president*
Merwin, Edwin Preston *educator*
Riles, Wilson Camanza *educational consultant*
Stegenga, Preston Jay *international education consultant*

San Andreas
Millsaps, Rita R. *elementary school educator*

San Bernardino
Evans, Anthony Howard *university president*

San Diego
Charles, Carol Morgan *education educator*
Day, Thomas Brennock *university president*

Feinberg, Lawrence Bernard *university dean, psychologist*
Golding, Brage *former university president*
†Hays, Garry D. *academic administrator*
Hughes, Author E. *university president, association executive*
Lee, Jerry Carlton *university administrator*
Lomeli, Marta *secondary education educator*
Maurer, Lawrence Michael *acting school administrator, educator*
†McBrayer, Sandra L. *educational director, homeless outreach educator*
Morris, Henry Madison, Jr. *education educator*
Netter, Irene M. *secondary education educator*
Owen, Sally Ann *gifted and talented education educator*
Schade, Charlene Joanne *adult education educator*
Schwartz, Alfred *university dean*
Walker, Donald Ezzell *retired academic administrator*

San Dimas
Cameron, Judith Lynne *secondary education educator, hypnotherapist*

San Fernando
Tanis, Norman Earl *retired university dean, library expert*

San Francisco
†Ammiano, Tom *school system administrator*
Bashir, Naheed *university administrator*
Cain, Leo Francis *retired special education educator*
Corrigan, Robert Anthony *university president*
Counelis, James Steve *education educator*
Cunningham, Arthur Francis *university dean, marketing educator*
Dullea, Charles W. *university chancellor emeritus, priest*
Gray, Frances M. *retired college president, lecturer*
Heaton, Jean *early childhood educator*
Kleinberg, David Lewis *education administrator*
Kozloff, Lloyd M. *university dean, educator, scientist*
Krevans, Julius Richard *university administrator, physician*
Lo Schiavo, John Joseph *university executive*
Naegele, Carl Joseph *university academic administrator, educator*
†Rippel, Clarence W. *academic administrator*
Schlegel, John Peter *university president*
Wallace, Arthur, Jr. *college dean*

San Jose
†Collett, Jennie *principal*
†Cruz, B. Robert *academic administrator*
†Evans, James Handel *university president, architect, educator*
Okerlund, Arlene Naylor *university official*

San Lorenzo
†Glenn, Jerome T. *secondary school principal*

San Luis Obispo
Bailey, Philip Sigmon, Jr. *academic dean, chemistry educator*
Baker, Warren J(oseph) *university president*
Ericson, Jon Meyer *academic administrator, rhetoric theory educator*
†Wentz, Janet *principal*

San Marcos
Lilly, Martin Stephen *university dean*

San Marino
Footman, Gordon Elliott *educational administrator*

San Mateo
†Poulos, Gary Peter *school system administrator*

San Quentin
Anderson, Douglas Sanford *vocational supervisor*

San Rafael
Fink, Joseph Richardson *college president*

Santa Ana
†Castruita, Rudy *school system administrator*

Santa Barbara
Allaway, William Harris *university adminstrator*
Boyan, Norman J. *retired education educator*
Dahl, John Anton *education educator emeritus*
Louis, Barbra Schantz *dean*
Mac Intyre, Donald John *college president*
Sinsheimer, Robert Louis *former educational administrator*
Sprecher, David A. *university administrator, mathematician*
Uehling, Barbara Staner *academic administrator*
Winter, David Kenneth *college president*
Yang, Henry T.Y. *university chancellor, educator*

Santa Clara
Facione, Peter Arthur *dean, philosophy and education educator*
Locatelli, Paul Leo *university administrator*

Santa Clarita
Lavine, Steven David *college president*

Santa Cruz
Mc Henry, Dean Eugene *academic administrator emeritus*

Santa Rosa
†Christiansen, Peggy *principal*

Seaside
Wilson, Robin Scott *university president, writer*

Stanford
Bridges, Edwin Maxwell *education educator*
Gibbons, James Franklin *university dean, electrical engineering educator*
Gross, Richard Edmund *education educator*
Henriksen, Thomas Hollinger *university official*
Kays, William Morrow *university administrator, mechanical engineer*
Massy, William Francis *education educator, academic administrator*

†Palm, Charles Gilman *university official*
Rice, Condoleezza *academic administrator, political scientist*
Strena, Robert Victor *research laboratory manager*

Stinson Beach
Metz, Mary Seawell *university dean, retired college president*

Stockton
†Atchley, Bill Lee *university president*
DeRicco, Lawrence Albert *college president emeritus*
Fish, Tom *vocational school educator*
Jantzen, J(ohn) Marc *retired education educator*
Klinger, Wayne Julius *secondary education educator*
Sorby, Donald Lloyd *university dean*
Thompson, Thomas Sanford *former college president*

Susanville
Blake, Larry Jay *academic administrator*

Thousand Oaks
†Luedtke, Luther S. *academic administrator*
Miller, Jerry Huber *university chancellor*
†Pflueger, Kenneth Edgar *university administrator, minister*

Tulare
Sickels, William Loyd *secondary educator*

Turlock
Amrhein, John Kilian *dean*
Kerschner, Lee R(onald) *university president, political science educator*

Twentynine Palms
Clemente, Patrocinio Ablola *psychology educator*

Vacaville
Emery, Rita Dorothy *physical education educator*
Wisneski, Mary Jo Elizabeth *reading specialist, educator*

Ventura
†McElroy, Charlotte Ann *principal*

Villa Park
Writer, Sharon Lisle *science educator*

Vista
†Johnson, Alan *principal*
Tiedeman, David Valentine *research education educator*

Walnut Creek
Grufman, Marjorie Jule *elementary art educator*
Morgan, Elmo Rich *former university official*

Westlake Village
Steadman, Lydia Duff *elementary school educator, symphony violinist*

Westminster
Ryan, James Edwin *industrial arts educator*

Whittier
Ash, James Lee, Jr. *academic administrator*
Drake, E Maylon *academic administrator*
Hurley, Eileen Beverly *school system administrator*
Newsom, Will Roy *former college president*
Tunison, Elizabeth Lamb *education educator*

Woodland Hills
Zeitlin, Herbert Zakary *retired college president*

COLORADO

Alamosa
Fulkerson, William Measey, Jr. *college president*

Aurora
†Jarvis, Mary G. *principal*

Bellvue
Bennett, Jim *retired university official*

Boulder
†Albino, Judith E. N. *university president*
Anderson, Ronald Delaine *education educator*
Corbridge, James Noel, Jr. *chancellor, educator*
Danilov, Victor Joseph *museum management program director, consultant, writer, educator*
Ekstrand, Bruce Rowland *university administrator, psychology educator*
Enarson, Harold L. *emeritus university president*
Gabridge, Michael Gregory *university administrator, science administrator*
Sirotkin, Phillip Leonard *educational administrator*
Williams, James Franklin, II *university dean, librarian*

Colorado Springs
Adams, Bernard Schroder *retired college president*
†Burnley, Kenneth S. *school system administrator*
Grady, Dolores Anne *academic administrator, educator, consultant*
†Mohrman, Kathryn *academic administrator*
Twardowski, Thomas John *college president*
Wilcox, Rhoda Davis *educator*
Worner, Lloyd Edson *retired college president*

Denver
Antonoff, Steven Ross *educational consultant, author*
Ballard, Jack Stokes *educator*
Brainard, Edward Axdal *academic administrator*
†Buechner, John C. *academic administrator*
Byyny, Richard Lee *academic administrator*
Clarke, David Marshall *academic administrator, priest*
Cowee, John Widmer *retired university chancellor*
Craine, Thomas Knowlton *academic administrator*
DePew, Marie Kathryn *retired secondary educator*
Fulginiti, Vincent *university dean*
Mc Clenney, Byron Nelson *community college administrator*
Messer, Donald Edward *theological school president*
†Palmreuter, Kenneth Richard Louis *principal*

Poynter, James Morrison travel educator
Ritchie, Daniel Lee university administrator
Whatley, Lisa vocational school administrator
Witkowski-Garcia, Phyllis Josephine early childhood specialist, headstart consultant
Zaranka, William F. academic administrator, author

Durango
Jones, Joel Mackey college president

Englewood
Shields, Marlene Sue elementary school educator

Fort Collins
Anderson, B(enard) Harold educational administrator
Harper, Judson Morse university administrator, consultant, educator
Jaros, Dean university official
Yates, Albert Carl university administrator, chemistry educator

Fort Morgan
Bond, Richard Randolph college administrator, legislator
Perdue, James Everett university vice chancellor emeritus

Glenwood Springs
Mayer, Dennis Marlyn academic administrator

Golden
Mueller, William Martin former academic administrator, metallurgical engineering educator

Grand Junction
Kribel, Robert Edward academic administrator, physicist
Moberly, Linden Emery educational adminstrator

Greeley
Duff, William Leroy, Jr. university dean, busiiness educator
Hause, Jesse Gilbert former college president
Schulze, Robert Oscar university dean

Keystone
†Craig, Robert Wallace educational administrator

Lakewood
†Beckman, L. David academic administrator
Mc Bride, Guy Thornton, Jr. college president emeritus
Milan, Marjorie Lucille early childhood educator
†West, Marjorie Edith elementary education educator

Leadville
†McCabe, James R. school system administrator

Littleton
†Chavez, Cile school superintendent

Pueblo
Byrnes, Lawrence William dean
†Shirley, Robert Clark university president, strategic planning consultant, educator
Sisson, Ray L. dean

Sterling
Milander, Henry Martin community college president

Univ Of No Colo
†Lujan, Herman D. university president

Westminster
Reed, John Howard school administrator

CONNECTICUT

Bloomfield
†Hilsenrath, Baruch M. principal

Bridgeport
†Garcia, Edna I. secondary education educator

Cheshire
†Wallace, Ralph superintendent

Danbury
Hawkes, Carol Ann university dean
†Roach, James R. academic administrator
Stewart, Albert Clifton college dean, marketing educator

Fairfield
Cernera, Anthony Joseph academic administrator
Eigel, Edwin George, Jr. university president, mathematics educator
Kelley, Aloysius Paul university president, priest
Smith, Clifford Vaughn, Jr. academic administrator

Falls Village
Purcell, Dale college administrator, consultant

Farmington
†Hartley, Harry J. academic administrator

Glastonbury
†Hatch, D. Patricia P. principal

Granby
†Pestka, Stanley secondary school principal

Groton
English, James Fairfield, Jr. former college president

Hamden
Bennett, Harry Louis college educator

Hartford
Loomis, Worth (Alfred Worthington Loomis) college president, manufacturer
Stoker, Warren Cady university president

Madison
Peterkin, Albert Gordon retired education educator

Middlebury
†Coleman, Robert Elliott secondary education educator

Middletown
Kerr, Clarence William university administrator, retired

New Britain
Beal, Dallas Knight university president
Dethy, Ray Charles former university dean, management educator, consultant
Frost, James Arthur former university president
Jestin, Heimwarth B. retired university administrator
Judd, Richard Louis academic administrator
Shumaker, John William university president

New Haven
Aaslestad, Halvor Gunerius university official
†Cappelli, Mary Antoinette principal
Ebbert, Arthur, Jr. retired university dean
Lamar, Howard Roberts educational administrator, historian
Lorimer, Linda Koch college official
Mullen, Frank Albert university official, clergyman
†Wegener, Peter Paul educator, author

New London
Gaudiani, Claire Lynn academic administrator

Newington
Vassar, William Gerald gifted and talented education educator

Northford
James, Virginia Stowell elementary education educator

Norwalk
†Perschino, Arthur J. secondary school principal
Wiggins, Charles educator

Ridgefield
Norman, Richard Arthur educator

Southport
Miles, Leland Weber university president

Storrs
Nieforth, Karl Allen university dean, educator

Stratford
Rozarie, Vera Jean school district administrator

Trumbull
†Norcel, Jacqueline Joyce Casale educational administrator

Wallingford
†Cirasuolo, Joseph J. school system administrator
†Hay, Leroy E. school system administrator

West Hartford
Lawson, Jonathan Nevin academic administrator
Pustilnik, Jean Todd elementary education educator
Tonkin, Humphrey Richard university president

West Haven
†DeNardis, Lawrence J. academic administrator

Wethersfield
†Edwards, Kenneth S. principal

Willimantic
†Carter, David George, Sr. university administrator

Wolcott
†Gerace, Robert F. secondary school principal

DELAWARE

Dover
Delauder, William B. academic administrator
†Sorenson, Liane Beth McDowell university administrator, state legislator

Lewes
†Wilson, James L. superintendent

Milford
†Moses, Charles E. superintendent

New Castle
Morton, Hazel Caudle elementary education educator

Newark
Allen, Rocelia J. retired special education educator
Roselle, David Paul university administrator, mathematician
Schiavelli, Melvyn David university provost, chemistry educator, researcher

Wilmington
†Desien, Mary Donna principal
Graves, Thomas Ashley, Jr. educational administrator
Olson, Leroy Calvin retired educational administration educator
Renshaw, John Hubert secondary education educator

DISTRICT OF COLUMBIA

Washington
†Adams, Linette M. principal
Alatis, James Efstathios university dean
Alton, Bruce Taylor educational consultant
†Arkin, William Morris military and political analyst
Arnez, Nancy Levi educational leadership educator
Barrett, Richard David fundraising consultant
Battle, Lucius Durham former educational institution administrator, former diplomat
Bolling, Landrum Rymer former academic administrator, writer, consultant
Bowker, Albert Hosmer university dean
Brown, Jeanne Pinkett physical education educator
†Bulger, Roger James academic health center executive
Burris, James Frederick academic dean, educator
Chandler, John Wesley educational consultant
Chater, Shirley Sears university administrator
Cheek, James Edward university president
Childress, Fay Alice university administrator
Cornett, Richard Orin research educator, consultant
Cortright, Jane Brigid Moynahan educational administrator
Donley, Rosemary university official
Dougherty, Jude Patrick dean
East, Maurice Alden academic dean, political scientist
Ellis, Brother Patrick (H. J. Ellis) academic administrator
Fisher, Alfred Foster university administrator
Fisher, Miles Mark, IV education educator
†Fosler, R. Scott academic administrator, federal agency administrator
Gaff, Jerry Gene academic administrator
Graves, Ruth Parker educational executive
Halperin, Samuel education and training policy analyst
Harrison, Rosalie Thornton (Mrs. Porter Harmon Harrison) retired educator
†Herbert, James Charles education executive
Herbster, William Gibson university administrator, consultant
†Higgins, William Robert college administrator
Holden, John Bernard former college president, educator
Horan, Harold Eugene university administrator, former diplomat
†Hudson, Philip academic director
†Jenifer, Franklyn Green academic administrator
Jenkins, John Smith academic dean, lawyer
Jones, Alice Samuels elementary education educator, reading specialist
Jones-Wilson, Faustine Clarisse education educator emeritus
Jordan, Irving King academic administrator
Keeley, Robert Vossler academic administrator, retired ambassador
Kent, Jill Elspeth academic administrator, lawyer, former government official
Kreuter, Gretchen V. college president
Kupperman, Robert Harris university official
Leon, Donald Francis university dean, medical educator
Lieberman, Myron educational consulting firm executive
MacDonald, John Thomas educational administrator
†Mattar, Philip institute director, editor
Maxwell, David E. academic administrator, educator
McGrory, Mary Kathleen academic administrator
†Melendez, Sara E. academic administrator
Miller, Carroll Lee Liverpool educational researcher
Nelson, Charles J. university administrator, international consultant, diplomat, consultant
O'Donovan, Leo Jeremiah university president, theologian, priest
Ostar, Allan William higher education consultant
Packard, George Randolph university dean, journalist, educator
Parrish, Alvin Edward former university dean, medical educator
†Preer, Jean Lyon university administrator, educator
†Price, Mary Kathleen lawyer, law librarian, library administrator
Pruitt, Anne Loring university administrator, educator
Remick, Forrest Jerome, Jr. academic administrator
Robinson, Ruth Harris elementary education educator
Rogers, Sharon J. university administrator
Salamon, Linda Bradley university dean, English literature educator
Scott, Joyce Alaine university official
Shoemaker, Cynthia Cavenaugh Jones academic director
Smith, Anne Bowman academic administrator, editor
Smuckler, Ralph Herbert university dean, political science educator
Solomon, Henry university dean
Steigman, Andrew L. academic dean
Stone, Elizabeth Wenger retired dean
Sullivan, Charles university dean, educator, author
Tipton, Paul S. former college president, association executive
Trachtenberg, Stephen Joel university president
Turaj, Frank university dean, literature and film educator
†Tuttle, Jerry community education and development consultant
†Whitfield, Princess D. principal
Wolfman, Brunetta Reid education educator
Woods, Harriett Ruth academic administrator
Young, Kenneth Evans educational consultant

FLORIDA

Alachua
Marston, Robert Quarles university president
Thornton, J. Ronald technologist

Avon Park
Cornelius, Catherine Petrey college president

Babson Park
Cloud, Linda Beal retired secondary school educator

Boca Raton
Arden, Eugene retired university provost
Arnold, Walter Martin vocational education educator
Burns, Gerald Phillip education educator
Catanese, Anthony James academic administrator
Hille, Stanley James university dean
†Lampi, Juanita principal
Murray, John Ralph former college president
Ross, Donald Edward university administrator
†Tennies, Robert Hunter headmaster
Turbeville, Gus emeritus college president

Bonita Springs
Johnson, Franklyn Arthur academic administrator
†Lane, William C., Jr. principal

Magill, Samuel Hays retired college administrator, higher education consultant

Bradenton
Jain, Mohinder (Mona Jain) daycare administrator, educator

Clearwater
Youngberg, Robert Stanley principal, consultant

Coral Gables
Moss, Ambler Holmes, Jr. university dean, lawyer, former ambassador
Murfin, Ross C university dean, English educator
Yarger, Sam Jacob dean, educator

Coral Springs
†Vandiver, Frances principal

Dade City
†Rine, Susan principal

Deland
Brakeman, Louis Freeman former university administrator
Dascher, Paul Edward academic dean, accounting educator
Duncan, Pope Alexander college administrator
Gill, Donald George education educator
Langston, Paul T. music educator, university dean, composer
Lee, Howard Douglas university president
Morland, Richard Boyd retired educator

Fort Lauderdale
Adams, Alfred Hugh college president
Feldman, Stephen university president
Fischler, Abraham Saul university president
McMahon-Dumas, Carmen Elethea education educator
Young, Lois Catherine Williams public administrator, consultant
Young, William Benjamin special education educator

Fort Myers
Cyphert, Frederick Ralph academic administrator
Gerdes, Lillian Anna elementary education educator
†Hughes, Judi E. principal
Tyrer, John Lloyd headmaster emeritus

Fort Pierce
Sampson, Bonita Lippard health occupations educator

Gainesville
Bryan, Robert Armistead university administrator, educator
Challoner, David Reynolds university official, physician
†Cheek, Jimmy Geary university dean, agricultural education and communications educator
Clark, Elmer J. education educator
Finger, Kenneth Franklin academic administrator
Lombardi, John V. university administrator, historian
Lowenstein, Ralph Lynn university dean
Neims, Allen Howard univeristy dean, medical scientist
Penland, Arnold Clifford, Jr. college dean, educator
Sharp, Bert Lavon retired education educator, retired university dean
Sorensen, Andrew Aaron provost
Viessman, Warren, Jr. academic dean, civil engineering educator, researcher
Woeste, John Theodore academic administrator
York, E. Travis, Jr. academic administrator, former university chancellor, consultant

Green Cove Springs
Yelton, Eleanor O'Dell reading specialist

Groveland
Hamilton, Rhoda Lillian Rosen educator, consultant

Hollywood
Goldberg, Icchok Ignacy retired special education educator

Hudson
Sarnecki, Thomas George special education educator

Indian Rocks Beach
Rocheleau, James Romig academic administrator

Jacksonville
Barrett, S. Barre academic administrator, art educator
Brady, James Joseph academic administrator
Brann, William Paul retired university administrator, consultant
Colby, Lestina Larsen secondary education educator
Gunning, John Thaddeus retired superintendent
†Herbert, Adam William, Jr. university president
Kinne, Frances Bartlett chancellor
Metzler, Mary Fink elementary education educator
Osborn, Marvin Griffing, Jr. educational consultant
Reese, Dorothy Harmon special education educator
Seroka, James Henry academic program director, educator

Jensen Beach
Kraynak, Helen special education consultant

Key West
†Henriquez, Armando Joseph superintendent

Lakeland
Davis, Robert Aldine college president
Wade, Ben Frank college administrator

Largo
†Gall, Keith D. director
†Hinesley, J. Howard superintendent

Longboat Key
Johnson, Carroll Frye educational consultant

Maitland
Whitlock, Luder Gradick, Jr. seminary president

Marianna
Flowers, Virginia Anne *academic administrator emerita*

Mayo
Durham, Guinevere McCabe *educational administrator, writer, consultant*

Melbourne
Edwards, David Northrop *university administrator*
†Hollingsworth, Abner Thomas *university dean*
Noonan, Norine Elizabeth *academic administrator, researcher*
Weaver, Lynn Edward *academic administrator, consultant, editor*

Melrose
Meyer, Harvey Kessler, II *retired academic administrator*

Miami
Bitter, John *university dean emeritus, musician, businessman, diplomat*
Cohen, Eugene Erwin *university health institute administrator, accounting educator emeritus*
†Le Duc, Albert Louis, Jr. *college official*
†Maidique, Modesto Alex *academic administrator*
O'Farrill, Francisca Josefina *early childhood educator*
Stiehm, Judith Hicks *university official, political science educator*
Thornton, Sandi Tokoa *secondary education educator*
†Williams, James A. *principal*

Miami Beach
Gitlow, Abraham Leo *retired university dean*

Miami Shores
O'Laughlin, Sister Jeanne *university administrator*

Monticello
Hooks, Mary Linda *adult education educator*

Mount Dora
Santini, John Amedeo *educational consultant*

Naples
Abbott, John Sheldon *law school dean and chancellor emeritus*

North Miami Beach
†Terry, Morton *academic administrator, physician*

Opa Locka
†Hopton, Janice *elementary school principal*

Orange City
Gorman, Burton William *retired education educator*

Orange Park
Ratzlaff, Judith L. *secondary school educator*

Orlando
†Hitt, John Charles *university president*
Medin, Julia Adele *educator, researcher*

Oviedo
Martin, Judson Phillips *retired education educator*

Palm City
Ammarell, John Samuel *retired college president, former security services executive*

Palm Coast
Dickson, David Watson Daly *retired college president*
Godfrey, Eutha Marek *elementary education educator, consultant*

Penney Farms
Kimbrough, Ralph Bradley *educational administration educator emeritus*

Pensacola
Gregory, Flaudie Stewart *special education educator*
†Marx, Morris Leon *academic administrator*

Pinellas Park
†Athanson, Mary Catheryne *elementary school principal*

Placida
Schwarting, Arthur Ernest *university dean*

Ponte Vedra Beach
Hartzell, Karl Drew *retired dean*

Port Charlotte
Norris, Dolores June *elementary educator*

Punta Gorda
Hill, Richard Earl *academic administrator*

Rockledge
Sutton, Betty Sheriff *elementary education educator*

Saint Augustine
Proctor, William Lee *college president*

Saint Leo
Mouch, Frank Messman *college president, priest*

Saint Petersburg
Armacost, Peter Hayden *college president*
Jacob, Bruce Robert *dean, academic administrator, law educator*
Kuttler, Carl Martin, Jr. *college president*
Nussbaum, Leo Lester *retired college president, consultant*
Peterson, Arthur Laverne *former college president*
Southworth, William Dixon *retired education educator*

Sarasota
Adams, Richard Towsley *university president, educational consultant*
Christ-Janer, Arland Frederick *college president*
Downey, John Charles *university dean, zoology educator*
†Highland, Marilyn M. *principal*
Tatum, Joan Glennalyn John *business, vocational educator*

Satellite Beach
†St John, Constance R. *school system administrator*

Sebastian
Mauke, Otto Russell *retired college president*

Spring Hill
Rojas, Victor Hugo *retired vocational education educator*

Starke
Loper, George Wilson, Jr. *physical education educator*

Sun City Center
Fields, Ralph Raymond *education educator*

Tallahassee
Adams, Perry Ronald *former college administrator*
Baum, Werner A. *former academic administrator, meteorologist*
†Burnette, Ada M. Puryear *educational administrator*
Crider, Irene Perritt *educator, consultant*
Early, Johnnie L., II *pharmacy educator*
Gil, Lazier *university dean*
Hafner, Lawrence Erhardt *education educator*
†Humphries, Frederick S. *university president*
McTarnaghan, Roy E. *acadamic administrator*
Morgan, Robert Marion *educational research educator*
Reed, Charles Bass *university system chancellor*
†Voran, James F. *principal*

Tampa
Anderson, Robert Henry *education educator*
Bondi, Joseph Charles, Jr. *education educator, consultant*
Brown, John Lott *retired university president, educator*
Givens, Paul Ronald *former university chancellor*
Heck, James Baker *university official*
Hegarty, Thomas Joseph *academic administrator*
McCook, Kathleen de la Peña *university educator*
Meisels, Gerhard George *academic administrator, chemist, educator*
Ruffer, David Gray *college president*
Sanchez, Mary Anne *secondary school educator*
Smith, Donn L. *university dean*
Troxell, Raymond Robert, Jr. *college administrator*
Wade, Thomas Edward *university research administrator, electrical engineering educator*
Weiner, Irving Bernard *university administrator, psychologist, educator*

Thonotosassa
Grant, Pauline Larry *owner and director daycare center, consultant*

University Of Miami
Foote, Edward Thaddeus, II *university president, lawyer*

Venice
Jamrich, John Xavier *retired university administrator*
Thomas, David Ansell *retired university dean*

West Palm Beach
Corts, Paul Richard *academic administrator*
Turner, Arthur Edward *college administrator*

Winter Haven
Peck, Maryly VanLeer *college president, chemical engineer*

Winter Park
Bornstein, Rita *academic administrator*
Fernandez, Joseph Anthony *educational administrator*
Mc Kean, Hugh Ferguson *college president, painter, writer*
Mc Kean, Keith Ferguson *former education educator*

Zephyrhills
Jernstrom, Joan *secondary education educator*

GEORGIA

Alpharetta
†Kingrea, Ann B. *principal*

Americus
Capitan, William Harry *college president*
†McGrady, Clyde A. *secondary school principal*
Stanford, Henry King *college president*

Athens
Buccino, Alphonse *university dean*
Cutlip, Scott Munson *university dean*
Douglas, Dwight Oliver *university administrator*
Fincher, Cameron Lane *educator*
Hunt, Jacob Tate *special education educator emeritus*
Newsome, George Lane, Jr. *education educator*
Tillman, Murray Howell *instructional technology educator*
Younts, Sanford Eugene *university administrator*

Atlanta
Bright, David Forbes *academic administrator, classics and comparative literature educator*
Caprio, Anthony S. *university official*
Chace, William Murdough *university administrator*
†Clough, Gerald Wayne *academic administrator*
Cole, Johnnetta Betsch *academic administrator*
†Cole, Thomas Winston, Jr. *chancellor, college president, chemist*
Dees, Julian Worth *academic administrator*
†Fowler, Andrea *teachers academy administrator*
†Fox, James Harold, Jr. *superintendent of schools*
Frye, Billy Eugene *university administrator, biologist*
Godard, James McFate *retired educational consultant*
Greenberg, Raymond Seth *dean, educator*
Hogan, John Donald *college dean, finance educator*
Jones, George Henry *university dean, research administrator, biology educator*
Jordan, Elizabeth Clark *elementary education educator*
Keiller, James Bruce *college dean, clergyman*
Keith, Leroy, Jr. *college president*
Kraft, Arthur *academic dean*
†Lewis, Larry Lynn *college official, minister, denominational official*
Matula, Richard A(llan) *academic administrator*
O'Neil, Daniel Joseph *research executive*
Pattillo, Manning Mason, Jr. *academic administrator*
Patton, Carl Vernon *academic administrator, educator*
†Ragan, Harold James *retired educator, senator*
Sink, John Davis *leadership consultant, scientist*
Stanton, Donald Sheldon *university administrator*
Suttles, William Maurrelle *university administrator, clergyman*
Tummala, Rao Ramamohana *engineering educator*

Augusta
Bloodworth, William Andrew, Jr. *academic administrator*
Martin, Willie Pauline *secondary education educator, illustrator*
Puryear, James Burton *college administrator*
Tedesco, Francis Joseph *medical college president, educator*

Brunswick
Harper, Janet Sutherlin Lane *educational administrator, writer*

Buford
Carswell, Virginia Colby *primary school educator, special education educator*

Carrollton
Johnson, Harris Tucker *educational institution administrator*
Morris, Robert Christian *education educator*

Cleveland
Raznoff, Beverly Shultz *education educator*

Cochran
Welch, Joe Ben *academic administrator*

Dalton
†Thomason, Frank W. *superintendent*

Decatur
Carey, John Jesse *academic administrator, religion educator*
Myers, Orie Eugene, Jr. *university official*
Wilkinson, Ben *chancellor, evangelist, ministry organizer, writer*

Douglas
King, Ruby Thompson *secondary education educator, civic worker*
Purvis, Mary Ruth Moore *special education educator*

Duluth
†Neuman, Ted R. *principal*

East Point
†Gloster, Hugh Morris *retired college president, college association consultant*

Fairburn
Montague, Mary Ellen *social studies educator*

Folkston
Crumbley, Esther Helen Kendrick *educator, realtor*

Gainesville
Burd, John Stephen *academic administrator, music educator*

Jasper
Parrish, Carmelita *secondary school educator*

La Grange
Ault, Ethyl Lorita *academic administrator*
Gordon, Robert Edward *university administrator*
Murphy, Walter Young *college president, clergyman*

Mableton
Day, Afton J. *elementary school educator and administrator*

Macon
†Bayliss, Mary Rosina *principal*
†Godsey, R(aleigh) Kirby *university president*
Innes, David Lyn *university official, educator*
Smith, Constance Lewis *educator*
Steeples, Douglas Wayne *university vice president, consultant, researcher*

Marietta
Cheshier, Stephen Robert *university president, electrical engineer*
Hall, George Ralph *school system administrator*
Rocker, Peggy Bland *retired home economics educator*
Siegel, Betty Lentz *college president*

Milledgeville
Engerrand, Doris Dieskow *business educator*

Monroe
Lynch, Lillian *educator*

Mount Berry
Mathis, Luster Doyle *college administrator, political scientist*
Shatto, Gloria McDermith *college administrator, economist*

Newnan
Cowles, Milly *education educator*

Perry
†Hinnant, Tony *superintendent*

Saint Simons Island
†Tomberlin, William G. *principal*

Sautee Nacoochee
Miller, Wilbur Randolph *retired university administrator*

Savannah
Burnett, Robert Adair *university administrator, history educator*

Statesboro
Black, Charlene Rushton *university official, sociology educator*

Thomson
†Smith, Robert L. *principal*

Toccoa Falls
Alford, Paul Legare *college and religious foundation administrator*

Valdosta
Bailey, Hugh Coleman *university president*
Peace, Barbara Lou Jean *education educator*
Scruggs, Betty Joyce Clenney *public school administrator*

Washington
Wills, Olive Boline *elementary education educator*

Winterville
Anderson, David Prewitt *university dean*

Young Harris
Yow, Thomas Sidney, III *college administrator*

HAWAII

Eleele
Takanishi, Lillian K. *elementary school educator*

Hilo
†Perrin, Kenneth Lynn *university chancellor*

Honolulu
Alm, Richard Sanford *education educator*
Bess, Henry David *dean*
Dolly, John Patrick *university dean, educational psychologist*
Enoki, Donald Yukio *curriculum specialist*
Greenfield, David W. *academic dean, ichthyologist*
Harrison, Jeremy Thomas *dean*
Ikeda, Moss Marcus Masanobu *educational administrator, lecturer, consultant*
Inaba, Lawrence Akio *educational director*
Jackson, Miles Merrill *university dean*
Keith, Kent Marsteller *academic administrator, corporate executive, government official, lawyer*
†King, Arthur R., Jr. *education educator, researcher*
Matsuda, Fujio *director academic research*
Moreno, Rose Lani *secondary schools administrator*
Pickens, Alexander Legrand *education educator*
Ramler, Siegfried *school administrator*
Wright, Chatt Grandison *academic administrator*

Kailua
†Tam, William *secondary school principal*
†Tokumaru, Roberta *principal*

Kailua Kona
Clewett, Kenneth Vaughn *college official*
Feaver, Douglas David *university dean, classics educator*

Kaneohe
†Kamiyama, Linda *elementary school principal*

Laie
Bradshaw, James R. *business educator*

Makawao
Mascho, George Leroy *education educator emeritus*

IDAHO

Boise
Barr, Robert Dale *university dean, educator*
Crane, Charles Arthur *college president*
Griffin, Sylvia Gail *reading specialist*
Maloof, Giles Wilson *academic administrator, educator*
†Ruch, Charles P. *university official*
Steinfort, James Richard *university program director*
Woodard, Larry L. *Bible college official*

Caldwell
Hendren, Robert Lee, Jr. *academic administrator*

Craigmont
†McPherson, James L. *school system administrator*

Lewiston
†Morgan, Glen D. *superintendent*

Mc Call
Evans, Darrell J. *art educator*

Moscow
Bartlett, Robert Watkins *academic dean, metallurgist*
†Hendee, John Clare *college dean, natural resources educator*
Zinser, Elisabeth Ann *university president*

Pocatello
Bowen, Richard Lee *academic administrator, political science educator*
Nelson, Arthur Alexander, Jr. *university dean, pharmacist*
Sagness, Richard Lee *education educator, former academic dean*

ILLINOIS

Arlington Heights
Roderick, William Rodney *academic administrator*

Aurora
†Zarle, Thomas H. *university president*

Bloomington
Gregor, Marlene Pierce *primary educator, elementary science consultant*
Myers, Minor, Jr. *college administrator, political science educator*
Watkins, Lloyd Irion *university president*

Carbondale
Casey, John P. *special education educator*
Covington, Patricia Ann *university administrator*
Dixon, Billy Gene *academic administrator*
Elkins, Donald Marcum *associate dean, agronomy educator*
Guyon, John Carl *university administrator*
†Mead, John Stanley *university administrator*
Snyder, Carolyn Ann *university dean, librarian*

Carlinville
Mc Conagha, Glenn Lowery *chancellor emeritus*

Champaign
Cammack, Trank Emerson *retired university dean*
Dulany, Elizabeth Gjelsness *university press administrator*
Estabrook, Leigh Stewart *dean, library science educator*
Peshkin, Alan *education educator*
Schowalter, William Raymond *college dean, educator*
Spodek, Bernard *curriculum educator*

Charleston
Buckellew, William Franklin *education educator*
Jorns, David Lee *university president*
Laible, Jon Morse *college dean, former mathematics educator*
Rives, Stanley Gene *university president emeritus*

Chicago
Abularach, Gloria Nancy *education specialist*
Alexandroff, Mirron (Mike Alexandroff) *academic administrator*
Appelson, Wallace Bertrand *academic administrator*
Bearden, Patricia Ann *education educator*
Begando, Joseph Sheridan *former university chancellor, educator*
Bernadetta, Sister Maria *special education educator*
Bornholdt, Laura Anna *university administrator*
Bowman, Barbara Taylor *academic administrator*
Burton, Erlie P. *academic administrator*
Caldwell, Ethel Louise Lynch *academic administrator*
Champagne, Ronald Oscar *academic administrator, mathematics educator*
Coe, Donald Kirk *university official*
Collens, Lewis Morton *university president, legal educator*
Cross, Dolores Evelyn *university administrator, educator*
†Felton, Cynthia *principal*
Finch, Herman Manuel *academic administrator*
Flynn-Franklin, Gertrude Elizabeth *elementary education educator, social worker*
Graham, Patricia Albjerg *education educator, foundation executive*
Gross, Theodore Lawrence *university administrator, author*
Heckmann, Irvin Lee *former college dean, educator*
Henikoff, Leo M., Jr. *academic administrator, medical educator*
Houston, Simpson Pete *secondary education educator*
Johnson, Beverly June *librarian, educator*
Karlin, Bernard Richard *principal*
Kasbeer, Stephen Frederick *university official*
Kloc, Emily Alvina *elementary principal*
Lamb, Gordon Howard *academic administrator*
Lewis, Philip *educational and technical consultant*
Lynn, Laurence Edwin, Jr. *university administrator, educator*
Matasar, Ann B. *former dean, business and political science educator*
Meyer, Donald Gordon *college dean, educator*
Meyers, Dorothy *educator, writer*
†Minogue, John P. *academic administrator, priest, educator*
†Mosley, Elaine Christian Savage *principal, chief education officer, consultant*
Nero, Ellie Theresa *elementary education educator*
O'Reilly, Charles Terrance *university dean*
†Piderit, John J. *academic administrator*
Pollick, G. David *academic administrator*
†Raven, Corinne *principal*
Richardson, John Thomas *university chancellor, clergyman*
Schieser, Hans Alois *education educator*
†Schommer, Carol Marie *principal*
Schroeder, W(illiam) Widick *educator*
Schubert, William Henry *curriculum studies educator*
Smith, Kenneth Bryant *seminary administrator*
Stelmack, Gloria Joy *elementary education educator*
Stukel, James Joseph *university official, mechanical engineering educator*
Sulkin, Howard Allen *college president*
Swanson, Don Richard *university dean*
Swanson, Patricia K. *university administrator, librarian*
Taylor, John Wilkinson *education educator*
Thomas, Marion May *educational program coordinator*
Turner, Sadie Lee *elementary educator*
Wasan, Darsh Tilakchand *university official, chemical engineer educator*
Watkins, Cheryl Denise *special education educator*
Yamakawa, Allan Hitoshi *university administrator*

Clarendon Hills
Gorski, Nancy Anne *elementary education educator*

Crystal Lake
Linklater, Isabelle Stanislawa Yarosh-Galazka (Lee Linklater) *secondary education educator*

Danville
Braun, Harry Jean *college president*

De Kalb
La Tourette, John Ernest *academic administrator*
Monat, William Robert *university official*

Decatur
†McCray, Curtis Lee *university president*

Deerfield
Fodrea, Carolyn Wrobel *educational researcher, publisher*
Meyer, Kenneth Marven *academic administrator*

Des Plaines
†Coburn, James LeRoy *educational administrator*

East Moline
Puffer, Richard Judson *retired college chancellor*

Edwardsville
Kovarik, M. Leora *elementary principal*
Lazerson, Earl Edwin *university president emeritus*
Potthast, Ray Joseph *secondary education educator*

Elgin
Weber, Harm Allen *former college president*

Eureka
Hearne, George Archer *academic administrator*

Evanston
†Bufe, Noel Carl *program director*
Christian, Richard Carlton *university dean, former advertising agency executive*
†Gellman, Aaron Jacob *transportation center administrator, engineering educator*
Herron, Orley R. *college president*
Ihlanfeldt, William *university administrator, consultant*
Kern, Charles William *university official, chemistry educator*
Kerr, Thomas Jefferson, IV *academic official*
Mack, Raymond Wright *university provost*
Miller, Thomas Williams *former university dean*
Scott, Walter Dill *education educator*
Shanafield, Harold Arthur *educator*
Weber, Arnold R. *university president*
Zarefsky, David Harris *academic administrator, communication studies educator*

Glen Ellyn
McAninch, Harold D. *college president*
Patten, Ronald James *dean*

Glencoe
Grabow, Beverly *learning disability therapist*

Glenview
Corley, Jenny Lynd Wertheim *educator*
†McGrew, Jean B. *superintendent*
Traudt, Mary B. *elementary education educator*

Grayslake
Brown, Sandra Lee *educational consultant*

Greenville
Stephens, William Richard *college president emeritus*

Highland Park
Mordini, Marilyn Heuer *physical education educator*

Hinsdale
Burrows, Donald Albert *college dean*
†Lynch, Charles J. *secondary school principal*

Jacksonville
Pfau, Richard Anthony *college president*

Kankakee
†Bowling, John C. *academic administrator*

Kewanee
Damron, Marvin Arthur *principal*

Lake Forest
†Bransfield, Joan *principal*
Hotchkiss, Eugene, III *college president emeritus*
†Kreischer, Gary C. *secondary school principal*

Lewistown
Novak, Martha Lois *elementary education educator*

Libertyville
†Kremkau, Paul *principal*
†Mraz, Alana L. *elementary school principal*

Lincolnshire
†DuFour, Richard P. *school system administrator*

Lisle
Becker, Richard Charles *college president*

Lynwood
Dyer-Dawson, Diane Faye *educational administrator*

Macomb
Malpass, Leslie Frederick *retired university president*
Wagoner, Ralph Howard *academic administrator, educator*
Witthuhn, Burton Orrin *university official*

Madison
Pope, Sarah Ann *elementary education educator*

Mattoon
Sherline, Harold Albert *adult education professional*

Metamora
Crow, Mary Jo Ann *elementary education educator*

Minooka
Flatness, Mary Linda *educational administrator*

Monmouth
Haywood, Bruce *college president*

Murphysboro
Brewer, Donald Louis *school superintendent*
Jacobs, Robert *education educator emeritus*

Naperville
†Scullen, Thomas G. *superintendent*
Wilde, Harold Richard *college president*

Normal
Bolen, Charles Warren *university dean*
Matsler, Franklin Giles *higher education educator*
Strand, David Axel *university executive*
Wallace, Thomas Patrick *university administrator*

North Chicago
†Hawkins, Richard Albert *life sciences educator, administrator*
Johnson, Lucille Merle Brown *elementary school principal*

Oak Forest
Hull, Charles William *special education educator*

Oak Park
Adelman, William John *university labor and industrial relations educator*
Davis, Christine Eurich *elementary education educator*
Denne, Joan Mallery *educator*

Orland Park
Denys, Edward Paul *education educator*

Palatine
Zandier, Fred F. *special education educator*

Pecatonica
Smith, Janet Faye *special education educator*

Pekin
Herbstreith, Yvonne Mae *primary education educator*
Wherry, Nancy Jeanne *elementary education educator*

Peoria
Brazil, John Russell *academic administrator*
Murphy, Sharon Margaret *university official, educator*

Poplar Grove
Hullah, Ann Marie *elementary education educator*

Quincy
Toal, James Francis *academic administrator*

River Forest
Krentz, Eugene Leo *university president, educator, minister*
Lund, Sister Candida *college chancellor*
Murray, Sister Jean Carolyn *college president*

Riverdale
Saulsbury, Ruth Eva *retired special education educator*

Rock Island
Brauch, Merry Ruth Moore *gifted education consultant*
Horstmann, James Douglas *college official*
Tredway, John Thomas *college president*

Rockford
Howard, John Addison *former college president, institute executive*
†Marelli, Sister M. Anthony *secondary school principal*
Steele, Carl Lavern *academic administrator*
Whitsell, Doris Benner *retired educator*

South Holland
Schaap, Marcia *special education educator*

Springfield
Giesecke, G(ustav) Ernst *education educator emeritus*
†Layzell, Thomas D. *academic administrator*
Lynn, Naomi B. *university president, public administration educator*
†Mervis, Louis *school system administrator*
Moy, Richard Henry *academic dean, educator*
Poorman, Robert Lewis *higher education consultant, academic administrator*
Taylor, Mary Kathleen *school system administrator*

Sterling
Albrecht, Beverly Jean *special education educator*

Summit Argo
Urban, Patricia A. *elementary school educator*

Sycamore
Johnson, Yvonne Amalia *elementary education educator, science consultant*

Urbana
Aiken, Michael Thomas *academic administrator*
Bloomfield, Daniel Kermit *college dean, physician*
Carey, James William *university dean, educator, researcher*
Feinberg, Walter *cultural values and ethics director*
Gomes, Wayne Reginald *college dean*
Holt, Donald A. *university administrator, agronomist, consultant, researcher*
Ikenberry, Stanley Oliver *university president*
Mc Conkie, George Wilson *education educator*
Resek, Robert William *university administrator*
Shuman, R(obert) Baird *academic program director, writer, english educator, educational consultant*
Wedgeworth, Robert *university librarian, dean, former association exe*
Weir, Morton Webster *retired university chancellor and educator*
Wilson, Winnie Ruth *elementary education educator, reading specialist*

Venice
Purdes, Alice Marie *secondary education educator*

Villa Park
†Devlin, Barbara Jo *school district administrator*

Washington
McKinney-Keller, Margaret Frances *retired special education educator*

Wilmette
Smutny, Joan Franklin *academic director, educator*

Winnetka
†Lindsay, Dianna Marie *educational administrator*

INDIANA

Anderson
†Edwards, James L. *university president*
Nicholson, Robert Arthur *college president*

Angola
Elliott, Carl Hartley *former university president*

Berne
†Lehman, Doyle *superintendent*

Bloomington
Arnove, Robert Frederick *education educator*
Bain, Wilfred Conwell *former university dean, music educator, opera theater director*
Barnes, A. James *academic dean*
Ehrlich, Thomas *university administrator, law educator*
Gousha, Richard Paul *education educator*
Gros Louis, Kenneth Richard Russell *university chancellor*
Hopkins, Jack Walker *former university administrator, environmental educator*
†Johnson, Owen Verne *program director*
Mehlinger, Howard Dean *education educator*
Mobley, Tony Allen *university dean, recreation educator*
Otteson, Schuyler Franklin *former university dean, educator*
Ryan, John William *retired university president*
Warren, Donald *university dean, education educator*
Webb, Charles Haizlip, Jr. *university dean*
Wells, Herman B *university chancellor*
Wentworth, Jack Roberts *business educator, consultant*
Williams, Edgar Gene *university administrator*

Carmel
†Hartman, Robert D. *superintendent*

Crawfordsville
Ford, Andrew Thomas *university dean, educational administrator*

Culver
Manuel, Ralph Nixon *private school executive*

East Chicago
Vis, Mary A. Murga *elementary education educator*

Elwood
Vance, Joan Emily Jackson (Mrs. Norval E. Vance) *elementary school educator*

Evansville
Graves, Wallace Billingsley *retired university executive*
Vinson, James Spangler *university president*

Fishers
Gatto, Louis Constantine *retired college president*

Fort Wayne
Andorfer, Donald Joseph *academic administrator, educator*
Lewark, Carol Ann *special education educator*
Pease, Ella Louise *elementary education educator*

Gary
Richards, Hilda *university administrator*
Roberts, Samuel Alden *secondary education educator*
†Smith, Vernon G. *education educator, state representative*

Goshen
Stoltzfus, Victor Ezra *academic administrator*

Greencastle
Bottoms, Robert Garvin *academic administrator*

Greentown
†Healy, Stephen C. *seconadry school principal*

Hammond
Delph, Donna Jean (Maroc) *education educator, consultant, university administrator*

Highland
Gregory, Marian Frances *educator, counselor*

Indianapolis
Bannister, Geoffrey *university president, geographer*
Barcus, Mary Evelyn *primary school educator*
Bepko, Gerald Lewis *academic administrator, law educator, lecturer, consultant, lawyer*
†Davis, F. Benjamin *academic administrator*
Engledow, Jack Lee *college administrator, consultant, researcher*
Evans, Daniel Fraley *college administrator, banker, retail executive*
Felicetti, Daniel A. *academic administrator, educator*
Gilmore, H. William *college dean, dentistry educator*
†Gould, Karen J. *elementary school principal*
†Hardin, Boniface *academic administrator*
Huffman-Hine, Ruth Carson *adult education administrator, educator*
Ilchman, Warren Frederick *university administrator, political science educator*
†Klinker, Sheila Ann J. *middle school educator, state legislator*
Silver, David Mayer *former university official*
Speth, Gerald Lennus *education educator, business programs director*
†Stern, Raymond *principal*
Voos, William John *university administrator, artist, art educator*

Kokomo
†Hill, Emita Brady *academic administrator*

Lafayette
Andrews, Frederick Newcomb *emeritus university administrator*

Lebanon
Ohmart, Sally Jo *elementary education educator*

Marion
†Barnes, James Byron *university president*
Dixon, Ruth Ann Storey *education educator*

Merrillville
Magry, Martha J. *elementary education educator*

Muncie
Marsh, Helen Unger *retired educational administrator*
Shondell, Donald Stuart *physical education educator*
Wheeler, David Laurie *university dean*

Munster
Sherman, Mona Diane *school system administrator*

New Albany
Crooks, Edwin William *former academic administrator*
Rand, Leon *university administrator*

Newport
Weeks, Catherine Claire *elementary education educator*

Notre Dame
Castellino, Francis Joseph *university dean*
Crosson, Frederick James *former university dean, humanities educator*
Hatch, Nathan Orr *university administrator*
O'Meara, Onorato Timothy *academic administrator, mathematician*

Pendleton
†Phenis, Nancy Sue *educational administrator*

Rensselaer
Banet, Charles Henry *college president, clergyman*

Richmond
†Nelms, Charlie *academic administrator*
Wood, Richard J. *college president*

Saint Mary Of The Woods
Doherty, Sister Barbara (Ann Doherty) *academic administrator*

South Bend
Charles, Isabel *university administrator*
Mills, Nancy Anne *elementary education educator*

Terre Haute
Gilman, David Alan *education educator, editor*
Grimley, Liam Kelly *special education educator*
Hulbert, Samuel Foster *college president*
Hunt, Effie Neva *former college dean, former English educator*
Jerry, Robert Howard *education educator*
Kicklighter, Clois Earl *academic administrator*
Landini, Richard George *university president, emeritus English educator*
Leach, Ronald George *university dean, librarian*
†Moore, John W. *academic administrator*
Moore, John William *university administrator*
Van Til, William *education educator, writer*

Upland
Kesler, Jay Lewis *university administrator*

Valparaiso
Harre, Alan Frederick *university president*
Hillila, Bernhard Hugo Paul *education educator*
Miller, John Albert *university administrator, marketing consultant*
Mundinger, Donald Charles *college president retired*
Schnabel, Robert Victor *retired academic administrator*

West Lafayette
Baumgardt, Billy Ray *university official, agriculturist*
Beering, Steven Claus *university president, medical educator*
Frick, Gene Armin *university administrator*
Gentry, Don Kenneth *academic dean*
Haring, Marilyn Joan *academic dean*
†Lechtenberg, Victor L. *university administrator*
Moskowitz, Herbert *management educator*
†Newby, Timothy James *education educator, researcher*
Ringel, Robert Lewis *university administrator*
Shertzer, Bruce Eldon *education educator*
Stone, Marguerite Beverley *former university dean, former dean of students*
Weidenaar, Dennis Jay *college dean*

Westville
Alspaugh, Dale William *university administrator, aeronautics and astronautics educator*

Zionsville
Hansen, Arthur Gene *former academic administrator, consultant*

IOWA

Ames
Christensen, George Curtis *university official*
Crabtree, Beverly June *college dean*
Ebbers, Larry Harold *education educator*
Jischke, Martin C. *academic administrator*
Manatt, Richard *education educator*
†Rice, Ronald Max *superintendent*
Topel, David Glen *college dean, animal science educator*

Cedar Falls
Curris, Constantine William *university president*

Cedar Rapids
Brown, John Edward *college president*
Feld, Thomas Robert *college president*
†Ledford, Sandra *principal*
†Plagman, Ralph *principal*

Davenport
Copes, Marvin Lee *college dean*
Moeller, Donald Joseph *academic administrator, educator*
Rogalski, Edward J. *university administrator*
†Wenz, Richard L. *school system and church administrator*

Des Moines
Canfield, Earle Lloyd *university dean, mathematics educator*
Ferrari, Michael Richard, Jr. *university administrator*
Marker, David George *university president*
Puotinen, Arthur Edwin *college president, clergyman*

Dubuque
Agria, John Joseph *college official*
Dunn, M. Catherine *college administrator, educator*
Peterson, Walter Fritiof *academic administrator*
Toale, Thomas Edward *school system administrator, priest*

Fort Dodge
Pratt, Diane Adele *elementary education educator*

Grinnell
†Fitzgerald, Michael J. *secondary school principal*
Walker, Waldo Sylvester *academic administrator*

Indianola
Jennings, Stephen Grant *academic administrator*

Iowa City
Bruch, Delores Ruth *education educator, musician*
Dickeson, Robert Celmer *retired university president, corporation president, political science educator*
Mc Leran, James Herbert *university dean, oral surgeon*
Rawlings, Hunter Ripley, III *university administrator*
Schulz, Rudolph Walter *university dean*
Skorton, David Jan *university official, physician, educator*
Vaughan, Emmett John *academic dean, insurance educator*

Lamoni
Higdon, Barbara J. *college president*

Mount Pleasant
Haselmayer, Louis August *college president emeritus*

Oakdale
Spriestersbach, Duane Caryl *university administrator, speech pathology educator*

Ottumwa
†Roseberry, Donald G. *chief administrator*

Sioux Center
Hulst, John B. *academic administrator*

Sioux City
Tommeraasen, Miles *college president*
Wick, Sister Margaret *college administrator*

Storm Lake
Briscoe, Keith G. *college president*

Waterloo
Kober, Arletta Refshauge (Mrs. Kay L. Kober) *educational administrator*

Waverly
Vogel, Robert Lee *college administrator, clergyman*

West Des Moines
Kimm, Dorothy Allene *elementary education educator*

KANSAS

Baldwin City
Keeling, Joe Keith *academic administrator, provost*
Lambert, Daniel Michael *academic administrator*

Downs
La Barge, William Joseph *tutor, researcher*

El Dorado
Edwards, James Lynn *educational administrator*
Flaming, Iretha Mae *elementary education educator*

Emporia
Glennen, Robert Eugene, Jr. *university president*

Goodland
Sharp, Glenn (Skip Sharp) *vocational education administrator*

Hays
Budke, Charles Henry *secondary education educator*
Hammond, Edward H. *university president*

Hiawatha
Pennel, Marie Lucille Hunziger *elementary education educator*

Kansas City
Whelan, Richard J. *director special education and pediatrics programs, academic administrator*

Lawrence
Budig, Gene Arthur *university chancellor*
Crowe, William Joseph *dean of libraries, educator*
Frederickson, Horace George *former college president, public administration educator*
Locke, Carl Edwin, Jr. *academic administrator, engineering educator*
Pinet, Frank Samuel *former university dean*
Turnbull, Ann Patterson *special education educator, consultant*

Leavenworth
Clifford, Brother Peter *academic administrator, religious educator*

Manhattan
Chang, Amos Ih-Tiao *retired educator*
Coffman, James Richard *academic administrator, veterinarian*
Kruh, Robert F. *university administrator*

Mc Pherson
Mason, Stephen Olin *academic administrator*

Paola
Cleary, William Richard *superintendent of schools*

Pittsburg
Sullivan, Frank Victor *academic dean, industrial arts educator*
Wilson, Donald Wallin *university president, educator*

Russell
Anschutz, Mary Anna *special education educator*

Salina
†Tompkins, John Andrew *school system administrator*

Shawnee Mission
†Kaplan, Marjorie Ann Pashkow *school district administrator*
Steele, Dorothy Pauline *retired elementary education educator*

Topeka
†Shuler, Howard L. *superintendent*
Thompson, Hugh Lee *university president*

Vassar
Visser, John Evert *university president emeritus, historian*

Winfield
Willoughby, John Wallace *former college dean, provost*

KENTUCKY

Berea
Hager, Paul Calvin *college administrator, educator*

Bowling Green
Haynes, Robert Vaughn *university administrator, historian*
Meredith, Thomas C. *academic administrator*
Murrell, Estelle C. *elementary school educator*

Crestwood
†Upchurch, Paul *principal*

Danville
Adams, Michael F. *academic administrator, political communications specialist*
Breeze, William Hancock *college administrator*
†Rowland, Robert E. *secondary school principal*
Spragens, Thomas Arthur *educational consultant*

Harrodsburg
Cummins, Bonnie Norvell *gifted and talented education educator*
Lunger, Irvin Eugene *university president emeritus, clergyman*

Highland Heights
Boothe, Leon Estel *university president*

Hopkinsville
Riley, Thomas Leslie *retired college president*

Lexington
Blanton, Jack Christopher *academic administrator*
Bosomworth, Peter Palliser *university medical administrator*
Hemenway, Robert E. *university administrator, language educator*
†Kuc, Joseph A. *educator, consultant*
Logan, Joyce Polley *education educator*
Manley, Margaret Edwards *primary education educator*
Robinson, Thomas Christopher *academic administrator, educator*
Shipley, David Elliott *university dean, lawyer*
Singletary, Otis Arnold, Jr. *university president emeritus*
†Turner, Larry William *educator*
Wethington, Charles T., Jr. *academic administrator*

London
Early, Jack Jones *college administrator*

Louisville
Berman, Edward Henry *education educator*
Ekstrom, William Ferdinand *college administrator*
†Ferguson, Duncan Sheldon *education administrator*
Garfinkel, Herbert *university official*
Gummere, Walter Cooper *educator, consultant*
Hazen, Elizabeth Frances *special education educator*
†Hoye, Robert Earl *higher education educator, health care consultant*
Kmetz, Donald R. *academic administrator*
Nystrand, Raphael Owens *university dean, educator*
Swain, Donald Christie *university president, history educator*
Taylor, Robert Lewis *academic administrator*

Mayfield
Harris, Isaac Henson *university dean*

Murray
Hunt, Charles Brownlow, Jr. *university dean, musician*
Kurth, Ronald James *university president, retired naval officer*

Paducah
Broady, Fannie Marie *vocational school educator*

Richmond
Funderburk, H(enry) Hanly, Jr. *college president*
Kirkpatrick, Dorothy Louise *education educator, program coordinator*
Martin, Robert Richard *emeritus college president, former senator*

Saint Catherine
Collins, Martha Layne *college president, former governor*

Wilmore
McKenna, David Loren *seminary president, clergyman*

LOUISIANA

Arnaudville
LaGrange, Claire Mae *special education educator*

Baton Rouge
Boyce, Bert Roy *university dean, library and information science educator*
†Brun, Judith *principal*
Caffey, H(orace) Rouse *academic administrator, consultant*
Copping, Allen Anthony *university president*
Davis, William Eugene *university administrator*
†Hancock, Paul Byron *headmaster*
Mc Cameron, Fritz Allen *university administrator*
†Phills, Bobby Ray *dean, agricultural research director*
Prestage, James Jordan *university chancellor*
Rabideau, Peter Wayne *university dean, chemistry educator*
Soderbergh, Peter Andrew *educator*
Wheeler, Otis Bullard *academic administrator, educator emeritus*
Williams, Hulen Brown *former university dean*
Woodin, Martin Dwight *retired university system president*

Covington
†Bankston, Terry *school system administrator*

Hammond
Cook, Myrtle *special education educator*
Parker, Clea Edward *university president*
Smith, Grant Warren, II *university administrator, physical sciences educator*

Kenner
Cook, Willie Chunn *elementary education educator*

Lafayette
Andrew, Catherine Vige *elementary education educator*

Lake Charles
Hebert, Robert D. *academic administrator*

Luling
Smith, Raymond Kermit *former educational administrator*

Mansfield
Smelley, Joyce Marie *special education supervisor*

Metairie
Flake, Leone Elizabeth *special education educator*
†Johnson, Beth Michael *principal*
Murphy, Alvin Leo *educational administrator*

Minden
†Doerge, Everett Gail *retired school system administrator, congressman*

Monroe
Jones, Emma Jean *principal*

Napoleonville
†Gunnell, William N. *school system administrator*

Natchitoches
Alost, Robert Allen *university executive*

New Iberia
†Cavalier, David J. *school system administrator*

New Orleans
Abad, Rosario Dalida *elementary educator*
†Berlin, Charles I. *audiologist, scientist*
Campbell, Margaret M. *academic dean*
Carter, James Clarence *university administrator*
Cook, Samuel DuBois *university president, political scientist*
Gordon, Joseph Elwell *university official, educator*
Hamlin, James Turner, III *university dean, physician*
†Hassenboehler, Donalyn *principal*
Johnson, Lee Harnie *dean, educator*
Kelly, Eamon Michael *university president*
Mackin, Cooper Richerson *university chancellor*
McFarland, James W. *academic administrator*
†McMahon, Maeve *principal*
Reddix, Rowena Pinkie *retired elementary school principal*
†Riedlinger, Brian A. *principal*
Rigby, Perry Gardner *medical center administrator, educator, former university dean, physician*
Vanselow, Neal Arthur *university administrator, physician*
Walsh, John Joseph *medical school administrator, physician*
Washington, Robert Orlanda *university administrator, former university dean*

Pineville
Matthews, Betty Parker *special education educator*

Ruston
Freasier, Aileen W. *special education educator*
Maxfield, John Edward *retired university dean*
Reneau, Daniel D. *university administrator*
Taylor, Foster Jay *retired university president*

Shreveport
Darling, John Rothburn, Jr. *university administrator, educator*

Slidell
†Faust, Marilyn B. *elementary school principal*

Thibodaux
Worthington, Janet Evans *academic director, English language educator*

MAINE

Auburn
Farwell, Margaret Wheeler *elementary education educator*

Bangor
Warford, Malcolm Lyle *seminary president, theology educator*

Bar Harbor
Swazey, Judith Pound *institute president, sociomedical science educator*

Biddeford
Ford, Charles Willard *university administrator, educator*

Bridgton
†Thompson, Larry A. *principal*

Brunswick
Edwards, Robert Hazard *college president*
Greason, Arthur LeRoy, Jr. *university administrator*

Caribou
†McElwain, Franklin Roy *educational administrator*

Cumberland Foreside
Dill, William Rankin *college president*

Damariscotta
Johnson, Arthur Menzies *retired college president, historian, educator*

Farmington
Kalikow, Theodora J. *academic administrator*

Kennebunk
†McConnell, David M. *secondary school principal*

Lewiston
Harward, Donald *academic official*

North Windham
Hart, Loring Edward *academic administrator*
†Libby, James Delmas *educator, marketing consultant*

Oakland
†Albanese, J. Duke *school system administrator*

Old Orchard Beach
†Bartner, Jay B. *school system administrator*

Orono
Coupe, John Donald *university official, economics educator*
Hutchinson, Frederick Edward *university president*
Rauch, Charles Frederick, Jr. *academic official*
†Wiersma, G. Bruce *dean, forest resources educator*

Portland
Gilmore, Roger *academic administrator*

Southwest Harbor
Rabineau, Louis *academic administrator, former state official*

Spruce Head
Bird, John Adams *educational consultant*

Waterville
Cotter, William Reckling *college president*

West Brownfield
Kloskowski, Vincent John, Jr. *educational consultant, writer*

MARYLAND

Adelphi
Langenberg, Donald Newton *academic administrator, physicist*

Annapolis
Calvin, Teresa Ann B. *secondary education educator*
Ness, Frederic William *former academic administrator, educator, consultant*
Nuesse, Celestine Joseph *educational administrator*

Baltimore
Bowser, Geneva Beatrice *secondary school educator, principal*
Brown, John Walter *vocational education supervisor*
Chylinski-Polubinski, Roger *academic administrator*
†Ferrara, Steven *educational administrator, researcher, consultant*
Fitzgerald, Thomas Rollins *university administrator*
Furst, Norma Fields *academic administrator*
Glynn, Edward *college administrator*
Grasmick, Nancy S. *superintendent*
King, Ora Sterling *education educator*
Klitzke, Theodore Elmer *former college dean, arts consultant*
Lafferty, Joyce G. Zvonar *retired educator*
Laric, Michael Victor *academic administrator*
Lazarus, Fred, IV *college president*
†McPartland, James Michael *university official*
Moszkowski, Lena Iggers *educator*
Nwagbaraocha, Joel Onukwugha *college president, educator*
Reese, Errol Lynn *university administrator, dentist*
Reid, Lauretta Glasper *retired principal*
Richardson, William Chase *university administrator*
Ross, Richard Starr *medical school dean emeritus, physician, cardiologist*
†Simon, David *principal*
Smith, Hoke LaFollette *university president*

Berlin
Crawford, Norman Crane, Jr. *academic administrator, consultant*

Bethesda
Corn, Milton *academic dean, physician*
Dykstra, Vergil Homer *retired academic administrator*
Gleazer, Edmund John, Jr. *retired education educator*
Lystad, Robert Arthur Lunde *retired university dean, educator*
Meltzer, Jack *consultant, retired college dean*
Pemberton, Melissie Collins *retired elementary education educator*

Clinton
Averett-Short, Geneva Evelyn *college administrator*

College Park
Berman, Louise Marguerite *education educator*
Birnbaum, Robert *higher education educator*
Dieter, George Elwood, Jr. *university dean*
Dorsey, John Wesley, Jr. *university administrator, economist*
Fallon, Daniel *university administrator*
Finkelstein, Barbara *education educator*
†Hardy, Robert Charles *human development educator*
Hey, Nancy Henson *educational administrator*
Massey, Thomas Benjamin *academic administrator*
Mayer, William Emilio *dean*
Polakoff, Murray Emanuel *university dean, economics and finance educator*
Prentice, Ann Ethelynd *academic adminstrator*
Scannell, Dale Paul *dean, university educator*
Seefeldt, Carol *education educator*

Columbia
Bruley, Duane Frederick *academic administrator, consultant, engineer*
Whiting, Albert Nathaniel *former university chancellor*

Ellicott City
†Hickey, Michael E. *school system administrator*
†Phelps, Catherine *elementary school principal*

Frederick
Brown, Frederick James *education educator*
Church, Martha Eleanor *college president*
†Farmer, Noel T., Jr. *school system administrator*

Frostburg
Gira, Catherine Russell *university president*
Root, Edward Lakin *university dean, educator*

Gaithersburg
†Karch, Karen Brooke *principal*

Greenbelt
†Boarman, Gerald L. *principal*

Hagerstown
Palmisano, Sister Maria Goretti *principal*

Hampstead
Staub, Martha Lou *elementary school educator*

Hyattsville
†Moylan, John L. *secondary school principal*
Rodgers, Mary Columbro *university chancellor, English educator, author*

Kensington
Jackson, Mary Jane McHale *principal*

La Plata
Merrick, Barbara Barnhart *school administrator*

Landover
Drahmann, Brother Theodore *academic administrator*

Laurel
Gottsman, Earl Eugene *academic administrator*
Wales, Sister Patrice *school system administrator*

Mardela Springs
Harcum, Louise Mary Davis *retired elementary education educator*

Mount Rainier
Steinbach, Donald Ervin *middle school educator*

North Bethesda
†Stansfield, Charles W. *educational administrator*

Oakland
Farrar, Richard Bartlett, Jr. *secondary education educator, wildlife biology consultant*

Oxford
Waetjen, Walter Bernhard *university president emeritus*

Princess Anne
Hytche, William Percy *university president*

Queenstown
Mc Laughlin, David Thomas *academic administrator, business executive*

Rockville
Au, Mary Lee *school system administrator*
Sparks, David Stanley *university administrator*

Sandy Spring
Cope, Harold Cary *former university president, higher education association executive*

Silver Spring
Butler, Broadus Nathaniel *retired university administrator*
Geiger, Anne Ellis *secondary educator*
Holloway, William Jimmerson *retired educator*
Pearman, Reginald James *educational administrator*
Raphael, Coleman *business school dean*
†Sampugnaro, Trudy M. *principal*

Stevensville
Kent, James A. *university dean, author, consultant*

Takoma Park
McLain, Sandra Brignole *art educator*

Towson
Caret, Robert Laurent *university administrator, author*
Chappell, Annette M. *university dean*
Hildebrand, Joan Martin *education educator*
Mark, Michael Laurence *academic administrator*

Upper Marlboro
†Elwood, Patricia *educator, political consultant*

Westminster
Chambers, Robert Hunter, III *college president, American studies educator*

MASSACHUSETTS

Amherst
†Adrion, William Richards *academic administrator, computer and information sciences educator, author*
Anderson, Ronald Trent *art educator*
Bischoff, David Canby *university dean*
Gerety, Tom *college administrator, educator*
Marcum, James Benton *college dean*
O'Brien, Richard Desmond *university administrator, neurobiologist*
Pouncey, Peter Richard *college president, classics educator*
Prince, Gregory Smith, Jr. *academic administrator*
Rosbottom, Ronald Carlisle *academic administrator, French culture and literature educator*

Andover
Wise, Kelly *private school educator, photographer, critic*

Arlington
Fulmer, Vincent Anthony *retired college president*
LaFauci, Horatio Michael *education educator emeritus*

Babson Park
Glavin, William Francis *academic administrator*

Bedford
†Aronstein, Laurence W. *middle school principal*

Boston
Argyris, Chris *organizational behavior educator*
Banks, Henry H. *academic dean, physician*
Chobanian, Aram Van *medical school dean, cardiologist*
Curry, John Anthony, Jr. *university administrator*
†Davies, Don *educator*
Eisner, Sister Janet Margaret *college president*
El-Baz, Farouk *program director, educator*
Estabrooks, Gordon Charles *secondary education educator*
Greene, Robert Allan *former university administrator*
Henry, Joseph Louis *university dean*
Hooker, Michael Kenneth *college president*
Kirkpatrick, Edward Thomson *college administrator, mechanical engineer*
Lesser, Laurence *music conservatory president, cellist, educator*
Milley, Jane Elizabeth *academic administrator*
O'Connell, Kevin George *priest, fundraiser, former college president*
O'Neil, William Francis *academic administrator*
Penney, Sherry Hood *university chancellor, educator*
Rittner, Carl Frederick *educational administrator*
Robinson, Sumner Martin *college administrator*
Ronayne, Michael Richard, Jr. *academic dean*
Sargent, David Jasper *university executive, lawyer*
Sessoms, Allen Lee *academic administrator, former diplomat, physicist*
Shira, Robert Bruce *university administrator, oral surgery educator*
Silber, John Robert *university president*
Van Domelen, John Francis *academic administrator*
Watts, Charles Henry, II *university administrator*
Westling, Jon *university administrator*

Bridgewater
Bardo, John William *university administrator*
Rondileau, Adrian *college president*
Tinsley, Adrian *college president*

Brookline
Mesch, Barry *academic administrator*

Burlington
†Connors, Richard J. *principal*

Cambridge
Breneman, David Worthy *former university president, economics educator*
Cavanagh, Richard Edward *academic administrator, consultant, writer*
Cazden, Courtney B(orden) *education educator*
Clark, William Cummin *academic director, educator*
Conway, Jill Kathryn Ker *former college president*
†Eisenberg, Carola *university academic director, psychiatrist*
Emerson, Anne Devereux *university administrator*
Eurich, Nell P. *educational consultant*
Fischer, Kurt Walter *education educator*
Fox, John Bayley, Jr. *university dean*
Ganley, Oswald Harold *university official*
Gray, Paul Edward *academic official*
Johnson, Howard Wesley *former university president, business executive*
McArthur, John Hector *university dean, business educator*
McKenna, Margaret Anne *college president*
Ragone, David Vincent *former university president*
Rudenstine, Neil Leon *academic administrator, educator*
Sharp, Phillip Allen *academic administrator, biologist, educator*
†Slater, Jonathan E. *director*
Smith, Ronald Lee *academic administrator, public policy educator*
Thiemann, Ronald Frank *dean, religion educator*
Vest, Charles Marstiller *university administrator*
Whitlock, Charles Preston *former university dean*
Wilson, Linda Smith *university administrator*

Centerville
Kiernan, Owen Burns *educational consultant*

Chestnut Hill
Altbach, Philip *comparative education director, educator*
Monan, James Donald *college president*

Danvers
Traicoff, George *college president*

Dorchester
Steller, Arthur Wayne *educational administrator*
Washington, Mary Louise *retired elementary and special education educator*

Duxbury
Mc Carthy, D. Justin *college president*

Easthampton
†Grubbs, Dennis H. *secondary school principal*

Fall River
Ingles, James H. *learning resources academic director*

Fitchburg
Mara, Vincent Joseph *college president*

Framingham
Atsumi, Ikuko *management school administrator, educator*

Haverhill
Dimitry, John Randolph *college president*

Kingston
†Squarcia, Paul Andrew *school superintendent*

Lexington
Mack, Jane Louise *early childhood educator, administrator*

Longmeadow
Wright, Jeanette Tornow *college president*

Mansfield
†Rosa, Edward A. *principal*

Medford
Bernstein, I(rving) Melvin *university official and dean, materials scientist*
DiBiaggio, John A. *university administrator*
Gittleman, Sol *university official, humanities educator*
Mancke, Richard Bell *university dean, economics educator*
Mumford, George Saltonstall, Jr. *former university dean, astronomy educator*
Swap, Walter Charles *academic dean, psychology educator*

Milton
†Giuliano, Frank J., Jr. *school system administrator*
Ingold, Catherine White *academic administrator*

Newton Center
Shannon, David Thomas *theological seminary executive*

North Andover
McGovern, Barbara Elizabeth Ann *elementary educator*

North Dartmouth
Andersen, Laird Bryce *university administrator*
Waxler, Robert Phillip *university educator, consultant*

Northampton
Dunn, Mary Maples *college president*

Rockport
Bakrow, William John *college president emeritus*

Roxbury
Short, Janet Marie *principal*

Salem
Harrington, Nancy D. *college president*
Miaskiewicz, Theresa Elizabeth *secondary educator*

Saugus
Austill, Allen *dean emeritus*

Sheffield
†Haworth, Donald Robert *educator, retired association executive*

South Dartmouth
Ward, Richard Joseph *university official, educator, author*

South Hadley
Kennan, Elizabeth Topham *college president*

Southwick
MacEwan, Barbara Ann *middle school educator*

Springfield
Miller, Beverly White *college president*
Riddle, James Douglass *college administrator*

Swampscott
Truog, Dean-Daniel Wesley *educator, consultant*

Taunton
†Donly, Michael J. *headmaster*

Waltham
Adamian, Gregory Harry *academic administrator*
Reinharz, Jehuda *university president, history educator*

Westborough
Jackson, Frederick Herbert *educational administrator*

Westfield
Applbaum, Ronald Lee *academic administrator*

Weston
Megley, Sheila *university executive, administrator, English educator*

Westwood
Funkhouser, Elmer Newton, Jr. *retired academic official*

Worcester
Berth, Donald Frank *university official, consultant*
Brooks, John Edward *college president*
Clements, Kevin Anthony *dean, electrical engineering educator, consultant*
Grogan, William Robert *university dean*
Hagan, Joseph Henry *college president*
Lutz, Francis Charles *university dean, civil engineering educator*
Onorato, Nicholas Louis *program director, economist*
Strauss, Jon Calvert *university president*
Traina, Richard Paul *university president*

Yarmouth Port
Hall, James Frederick *retired college president*

MICHIGAN

Adrian
Caine, Stanley Paul *college administrator*

Albion
Vulgamore, Melvin L. *college president*

Allendale
Niemeyer, Glenn Alan *academic administrator, history educator*

Alma
Stone, Alan Jay *college administrator*
Swanson, Robert Draper *college president*

Ann Arbor
Anderson, Austin Gothard *university administrator, lawyer*
†Davis, Wayne Kay *university dean, educator*
Duderstadt, James Johnson *university president*
Eggertsen, Claude Andrew *education educator*
Fleming, Suzanne Marie *university official, chemistry educator*
†Jelinek, Fran *school system administrator*
Kirkpatrick, Dorothy Ann *early childhood education educator*
Lewis, Robert Enzer *lexicographer, educator*
Paul, Ara Garo *university dean*
Porter, John Wilson *education executive*
Robbins, Jerry Hal *educational administration educator*
Stark, Joan Scism *education educator*
Van Houweling, Douglas Edward *university administrator, educator*
Whitaker, Gilbert Riley, Jr. *academic administrator, business economist*

Bay City
Zuraw, Kathleen Ann *special education and physical education educator*

Berrien Springs
Lesher, William Richard *university president*

Bloomfield Hills
†Doyle, Jill J. *elementary school principal*
†Hillman, Donald M. *middle school principal*

Brighton
†Jensen, Baiba *principal*

Carsonville
†Kummerow, Arnold A. *superintendent of schools*

Coloma
Tallman, Clifford Wayne *school system administrator, consultant*

Dearborn
Brucker, Eric *academic administrator*
Fair, Jean Everhard *education educator*
Morshead, Richard Williams *philosophy of education educator*

Detroit
Adamany, David Walter *university administrator*
Cortada, Rafael Leon *university president*
Cox, Clifford Ernest *deputy superintendent, chief information officer*
Fay, Sister Maureen A. *university president*
†Hough, Leslie Seldon *educational administrator*
Jackson, Robert Lee, II *university administrator*
Lee, James Edward, Jr. *educational administrator*
McGriff, Deborah *school system administrator*
Rezabek, Christina JoAnn *adult education educator*
Richards, Frederick Edward Maxwell *school system administrator*
Shay, John E., Jr. *college president*
†Snead, David L. *assistant education superintendent*

East Lansing
Andrew, Gwen *university dean, retired*
Bettinghaus, Erwin Paul *university dean*
†Brophy, Jere Edward *education educator, researcher*
Byerrum, Richard Uglow *college dean*
Hickey, Howard Wesley *education educator*
Johnson, Tom Milroy *academic dean, medical educator, physician*
Mackey, Maurice Cecil *university president, economist, lawyer*
Rudman, Herbert Charles *education educator*
Saul, William Edward *academic administrator, civil engineering educator*
Snoddy, James Ernest *education educator*
Wronski, Stanley Paul *education educator*

Farmington
Elder, Jean Katherine *education administrator*

Flint
Duckett, Bernadine Johnal *elementary principal*
Lorenz, John Douglas *college official*
Simmons, Robert Randolph *principal*

Frankfort
Acker, Nathaniel Hull *retired educational administrator*

Grand Rapids
Calkins, Richard W. *college president*
Deihl, Charles L. *college president*
Delnick, Martha Joyce *elementary education educator*
Diekema, Anthony J. *college president*
VanHarn, Gordon Lee *college provost*
†Vinton, Samuel R., Jr. *academic administrator*

Grosse Pointe
†Robie, Joan *elementary school principal*

Gwinn
Lasich, Vivian Esther Layne *secondary education educator*

Haslett
Hotaling, Robert Bachman *community planner, educator*

Hastings
Adrounie, V. Harry *dean, environmental scientist, educator*

Highland
†Doyle, James H. *school system administrator*

Highland Park
Omar, Ameenah E.P. *college dean*

Hillsdale
Roche, George Charles, III *college administrator*

Holland
Hill, JoAnne Francis *elementary education educator*
Jacobson, John Howard, Jr. *college president*
Nyenhuis, Jacob Eugene *college official*
Van Wylen, Gordon John *former college president*

Houghton
Tompkins, Curtis Johnston *university president*

Kalamazoo
Barrett, Nancy Smith *university administrator*
Bryan, Lawrence Dow *college administrator*
Haenicke, Diether Hans *university president*
†Stufflebeam, Daniel LeRoy *education educator*

Kincheloe
Light, Kenneth Freeman *college administrator*

Lansing
Brennan, Thomas Emmett *law school president*

Livonia
Van de Vyver, Sister Mary Francilene *academic administrator*

Maple City
Morris, Donald Arthur Adams *college president*

Marquette
Heldreth, Leonard Guy *university administrator*
Vandament, William Eugene *academic administrator, educator*

Midland
Barker, Nancy Lepard *college official*
Hyde, Geraldine Veola *secondary education educator, retired*

Monroe
Siciliano, Elizabeth Marie *secondary art educator*

Mount Clemens
Darby, Lewis Randal *special education educator*
†Fraser, Blanche E. *school system administrator*

Mount Pleasant
Lippert, Robert J. *administrator and culinary arts educator, consultant*

Muskegon
Austin, William Lamont *educational consultant, former superintendent of schools*
Stevenson, James Lyall *academic administrator*

Newaygo
†Grodus, Edward T. *secondary school principal*

Olivet
Bassis, Michael Steven *academic administrator*

Pontiac
Decker, Peter William *academic administrator*

Portland
†Adams, Bill *principal*

Rochester
Packard, Sandra Podolin *university president*
Polis, Michael Philip *academic administrator, electrical engineering educator*

Rockford
Duzan, Dee *elementary school principal*

Southfield
Chambers, Charles MacKay *university president*
†Olsen, Douglas H. *superintendent*

Spring Arbor
Cherem, Barbara Frances *educational program director, professor*

Three Rivers
Allen, Janet Louise *school system administrator*

Traverse City
†Bourdo, G. F. *principal*
Rosser, Richard Franklin *education consultant*
Warrington, Willard Glade *former university official*
Zimmerman, Paul Albert *retired college president, minister*

University Center
Gilbertson, Eric Raymond *academic administrator, lawyer*

West Bloomfield
†Childress, Carl T. *principal*
†Peterson, Esther *secondary school principal*

Williamsburg
Goodell, Warren Franklin *retired university administrator*

Wixom
Boynton, Irvin Parker *educational administrator*

Ypsilanti
Boone, Morell Douglas *academic administrator, information and instructional technology educator*
Goldenberg, Ronald Edwin *university dean*
Gwaltney, Thomas Marion *education educator, researcher*
Sullivan, Thomas Patrick *college president*

MINNESOTA

Bloomington
Krueger, Eugene Rex *academic program director*
Kuntz, Lila Elaine *secondary education educator*

Circle Pines
†McClellan, John R. *school system administrator*

Cokato
†Thomas, Paul S. *principal*

Collegeville
Reinhart, Dietrich Thomas *university president, history educator*

Dassel
†Kay, Craig *principal*

Duluth
Franks, Ronald Dwyer *university dean, psychiatrist, educator*
Leland, Paula Susan *educational administrator, educator*

Eden Prairie
McCoy, Gerald Leo *superintendent of schools*

Elysian
Nickerson, James Findley *education consultant*

Grand Rapids
King, Sheryl Jayne *secondary education educator, counselor*

Hopkins
†Passi, Beth *school administrator*

Minneapolis
Anderson, Charles S. *college president, clergyman*
Bowie, Norman Ernest *university official, educator*
Cantelon, John Edward *academic administrator*
Davis, Julia McBroom *college dean, speech pathology and audiology educator*
DiGangi, Frank Edward *academic administrator*
Ferrera, Robert James *superintendent of schools*
Gardner, William Earl *university dean*
George, Melvin Douglas *university official*
†Hertogs, Mary Helen *educational administrator*
Hoyer, Harvey Conrad *retired college president, clergyman*
Kidwell, David Stephen *academic administrator*
Lindell, Edward Albert *former college president, religious organization administrator*
Matson, Wesley Jennings *educational administrator*
Merwin, Jack Clifford *retired education educator*
Petersen, Anne Cheryl *university official and dean, educator*
Philipson, Willard Dale *curriculum and instructional educator*
Rand, Sidney Anders *retired college administrator*
Schuh, G(eorge) Edward *university dean, agricultural economist*
Slorp, John S. *academic administrator*

Minnetonka
Vanstrom, Marilyn June *elementary education educator*

Moorhead
Dille, Roland Paul *college president*
Treumann, William Borgen *university dean*

Morris
Johnson, David Chester *university chancellor, sociology educator*

Northfield
Berwald, Helen Dorothy *education educator*

Osseo
Hersch, Russell LeRoy *secondary education educator*
†Ramsey, Mark *school system administrator*

Saginaw
Stauber, Marilyn Jean *educator, consultant*

Saint Cloud
Berling, John George *academic dean*

Saint Louis Park
†Dooley, David J. *elementary school principal*
Svendsbye, Lloyd August *college president, clergyman, educator*

Saint Paul
†Brushaber, George Karl *academic president, minister*
Gavin, Robert Michael, Jr. *college president*
Graham, Charles John *university educator, former university president*
Huber, Sister Alberta *college president*
Keffer, Charles Joseph *academic administrator*
MacTaggart, Terrence Joseph *academic administrator*
Matteson, Robert Eliot *former college administrator*
Osnes, Larry G. *academic administrator*
Pampusch, Anita Marie *academic administrator*
Powers, David Richard *educational administrator*

Stillwater
†Anderson, Burnell *principal*

Waseca
Frederick, Edward Charles *university official*

Wayzata
Fish, James Stuart *college dean, advertising consultant*

Winona
DeThomasis, Brother Louis *college president*
Krueger, Darrell William *academic administrator*
Towers, James Mc *education educator*

MISSISSIPPI

Amory
Brown, James Leaman, Jr. *vocational education educator*

Canton
Hill, Ronald Guy *craft school director*

Cleveland
Wyatt, Forest Kent *university president*

Clinton
Nobles, Lewis *college president*

Columbus
Fant, Joseph Lewis, III *retired junior college president*
Rent, Clyda Stokes *university president*

Gulfport
Daffron, Martha *retired education educator*

Hattiesburg
Lucas, Aubrey Keith *university president*
Noonkester, James Ralph *retired college president*
Saucier Lundy, Karen *college dean, educator*

Holly Springs
Beckley, David Lenard *academic administrator*

Jackson
Burnham, Tom *state school system administrator*
†Dodson, William H. *school system administrator*
Harmon, George Marion *college president*
Williams, William Lane *university administrator, anatomist*

Meridian
†Drawdy, Larry A. *school system administrator*
Phillips, Patricia Jeanne *retired educational administrator, consultant*

Mississippi State
Hawkins, Merrill Morris *college administrator*
Lee, John Edward, Jr. *university administrator*
†Mabry, Donald Joseph *university administrator, history educator*
McRae, John Malcolm *college dean, architect*
Powe, Ralph Elward *university administrator*
†Thompson, Warren S. *dean, academic administrator*
Vasek, Richard Jim *academic dean*
Zacharias, Donald Wayne *university president*

Oxford
Moorhead, Sylvester Andrew *education educator retired*

Perkinston
Parker, Ora Dean Simmons *elementary school educator*

Shelby
Campany, Sarah Wilson *special education educator*

Starkville
Martin, Theodore Krinn *former university administrator*
Mercer, H. Dwight *university dean, veterinarian*

University
†Ferris, William Reynolds *folklore educator*
Leary, William James *educational administrator*
Meador, John Milward, Jr. *university dean*
Sam, Joseph *retired university dean*
Smith, Allie Maitland *university dean*
Turner, Robert Gerald *university chancellor*
Walton, Gerald Wayne *university administrator*

MISSOURI

Boonville
Cline, Dorothy May Stammerjohn (Mrs. Edward Wilburn Cline) *educator*

California
Wood, Mary Marie *business educator*

Clayton
†Kohm, Barbara *principal*
Zimmerman, Harold Seymour *elementary school educator*

Clinton
†Deskins, Gary *school system administrator*

Columbia
Adams, Algalee Pool *college dean, art educator*
Burchett, Betty Martela *science education educator*
Gysbers, Norman Charles *education educator*
Hatley, Richard V(on) *education educator*
Lenox, Mary Frances *academic dean*
McCollum, Clifford Glenn *college dean emeritus*
Miller, Paul Ausborn *adult education educator*
Monroe, Haskell M., Jr. *university professor*
Russell, George Albert *university president*
Sampson, Patsy Hallock *college president*
Wheeler, Otis V., Jr. *public school principal*

Creve Coeur
Dodge, Paul Cecil *academic administrator*

Fenton
Korn, Irene Elizabeth *elementary education educator, consultant*

Florissant
†Bartlett, Robert James *principal*
Ordinachev, Joann Lee *special education counselor and administrator*

Fulton
Barnett, Jahnae Harper *academic administrator*
Davidson, Robert Laurenson Dashiell *college president emeritus, philatelist*

Gallatin
Wilsted, Joy *elementary education educator, reading specialist, consultant*

Hillsboro
Adkins, Gregory D. *academic administrator*

Independence
†Henley, Robert Lee *school system administrator*

Jefferson City
Scott, Gary Kuper *academic administrator*

Joplin
Pulliam, Frederick Cameron *educational administrator*

Kansas City
†Durig, James Robert *college dean*
Eubanks, Eugene Emerson *education educator, consultant*
Farris, Jefferson Davis *university administrator*
Fonne, Hiram A. *dean*
†Isler, Mamie *secondary school principal*
Johnson, Dora Myrtle Knudtson *principal*
Kramer, Lawrence John *college president*
Nease, Stephen Wesley *college president*
Savage, Thomas Joseph *college president, governance and planning consultant, educator, priest*
Thomas, Larry Wayne *secondary school educator*
Van Ackeren, Maurice Edward *college administrator*

Kirksville
Warren, Russell Glen *academic administrator*

Liberty
Tanner, Jimmie Eugene *college dean*

Manchester
†Warner, Vinnie *principal*

Maryland Heights
Hampton, Margaret Josephine *secondary education educator, decorating consultant*

Maryville
Hubbard, Dean Leon *university president*
†Jonagan, Glenn E. *principal*

Moberly
Pelfrey, Lloyd Marvin *college president*

Parkville
Breckon, Donald John *academic administrator*

Rolla
French, Eunice Pelafigue *university international programs administrator*
Warner, Don Lee *dean emeritus*

Saint Louis
†Allen, Renee *principal*
†Barth, Karl Luther *retired seminary president*
Biondi, Lawrence *university administrator, priest*
Bloomberg, Terry *early childhood education administrator*
Bohne, Jeanette Kathryn *mathematics and science educator*
Byrnes, Christopher Ian *academic dean, researcher*
Cain, James Nelson *arts school administrator*
Chandler, James Barton *international education consultant*
Conaway, Mary Ann *professional counselor, educator*
Danforth, William Henry *university chancellor, physician*
Deal, Joseph Maurice *university dean, art educator, photographer*
Douglas, Mary Younge Riley *secondary education educator*
Ellis, Dorsey Daniel, Jr. *dean*
Gerdine, Leigh *retired academic administrator*
†Gilligan, Sandra Kaye *private school director*
Gordon, Larry Dean *elementary education educator*
Hayes, Alice Bourke *university official, biology educator*
Henle, Robert John *former university president*
Hunter, Thom Hugh *seminary administrator*
King, Morris Kenton *medical school dean*
Koff, Robert Hess *academic program director*
Lovin, Keith Harold *university administrator, philosophy educator*
Mahan, David James *school superintendent*
†Marsh, James C., Jr. *secondary school principal*
McFarland, Mary A. *elementary/secondary school educator/administrator*
Mitchell, Carol *daycare administrator*
Mulligan, Robert William *university official, clergyman*
†O'Neill, Sheila *principal*
Pfefferkorn, Michael Gene, Sr. *secondary education educator, writer*
Pflueger, M(elba) Lee *academic administrator*
Preus, Jacob Aall Ottesen *former seminary president and church executive*
Ramming, Michael Alexander *school system administrator*
Reinert, Paul Clare *university chancellor emeritus*
†Spainhower, James Ivan *retired college president*
Touhill, Blanche Marie *university chancellor, history-education educator*
Turner, Harold Edward *education educator*
†Virgil, Robert L. *dean*
Wandling, Marilyn Elizabeth Branson *art educator*
Watkins, Hortense Catherine *middle school educator*
Weiss, Robert Francis *former academic administrator, religious organization administrator, consultant*
Wirth, Arthur George *education educator*

Springfield
Ames, Jimmy Ray *education educator*
Moore, John Edwin, Jr. *college president*
Stovall, Richard L. *academic administrator*

Warrensburg
Elliott, Eddie Mayes *college president*

Webster Groves
†Schenkenberg, Mary Martin *principal*

West Plains
Gunter, DeVona Elizabeth *special education educator*

Willow Springs
Evins, Marylou *special education educator*

MONTANA

Antelope
Olson, Betty-Jean *elementary education educator*

Arlee
Gregory, Russell Arthur *education and training consultant*

Billings
Carpenter, Bruce H. *academic administrator*
DeRosier, Arthur Henry, Jr. *college president*
Evans, Judith Christien Lunbeck *elementary school principal*
Heiny, Robert Wayne *special education educator*
†McCracken, Joe C. *school system administrator*
Surwill, Benedict Joseph, Jr. *college dean, educator*

Bozeman
Goering, Kenneth Justin *college administrator*

Dayton
Catalfomo, Philip *university dean*

Kalispell
†Dowell, Timothy John *educator*
Ormiston, Patricia Jane *educator*

Missoula
Dennison, George Marshel *academic administrator*
Fisher, William Henry *education educator*
Kindrick, Robert LeRoy *academic administrator, English educator*
†Kraft, Dennis *school system administrator*
†Winston, Bente *academic administrator*

NEBRASKA

Auburn
Winegardner, Rose Mary *special education educator*

Bellevue
Muller, John Bartlett *college president*

Boys Town
†Peter, Val Joseph *social service administrator, educator, priest*

Columbus
†Bellum, Fred Lewis *school system administrator*

Daykin
Rife, Ronald Eugene *elementary education educator*

Gretna
†Riley, Kevin M. *principal*

Hastings
†Larsen, Glen L. *school system administrator*

Lincoln
Bradley, Richard Edwin *retired university president*
Childs, Gayle B(ernard) *retired education educator*
Grew, Priscilla Croswell *university official, geology educator*
Hendrickson, Kent Herman *dean, librarian*
Hermance, Lyle Herbert *education educator*
Janzow, Walter Theophilus *retired college administrator*
Laursen, Paul Herbert *retired university educator*
Nelson, Darrell Wayne *university administrator*
Rogers, Vance Donald *former university president*
Spanier, Graham Basil *university administrator, family sociologist*
White, John Wesley, Jr. *university president*

Madison
Say, Marlys Mortensen (Mrs. John Theodore Say) *school system administrator*

Omaha
Bauer, Otto Frank *university official, communication educator*
†Fjell, Mick *principal*
Haselwood, Eldon LaVerne *education educator*
McEniry, Robert Francis *education educator*
Morrison, Michael Gordon *university president, clergyman, history educator*
Newton, John Milton *acadmeic administrator, psychology educator*
O'Brien, Richard L(ee) *academic administrator, physician, cell biologist*
Schlessinger, Bernard S. *retired university dean*
†Tucker, Michael *elementary school principal*

Scottsbluff
†Fritschen, Robert David *educational administrator, animal science educator, researcher*
†Weichenthal, Burton A. *educational administrator, beef specialist*

Wayne
Mash, Donald J. *college president*

NEVADA

Battle Mountain
†Hensley, E. Leon *school system administrator*

Glenbrook
Buscaglia, (Felice) Leo(nardo) *special education educator, author*

Hawthorne
Graham, Lois Charlotte *retired educator*

Henderson
Benson, James DeWayne *university administrator*

Incline Village
Hiatt, Robert Worth *former university president*
White, Richard Hugh *dean student affairs*

Las Vegas
†Brown, Lori Lipman *secondary school educator*
Cwerenz-Maxime, Virginia Margaret *secondary education educator*
Iorio, John Emil *retired education educator*
McDonald, Malcolm Gideon *education educator*
Zehm, Stanley James *education educator*

Lovelock
†Kiley, James P. *retired school system administrator*

North Las Vegas
†Regan, John Bernard (Jack Regan) *community relations executive, assemblyman*

Reno
Cain, Edmund Joseph *education educator, emeritus dean*
Clarke, Janice Cessna *educational administrator*
Crowley, Joseph Neil *academic administrator*
Daugherty, Robert Melvin, Jr. *university dean, medical educator*
Humphrey, Neil Darwin *university president, retired*
Loveless, Edward Eugene *education educator, musician*

NEW HAMPSHIRE

Amherst
†Collins, Paul D. *principal*
†Lalley, Richard A. *school system administrator*

Chester
Preston, Faith *college president*

Durham
Faiman, Robert Neil *academic administrator*
Farrell, William Joseph *university chancellor*
Lawson, John H. *university official*
Nitzschke, Dale Frederick *university president*
Palmer, Stuart Hunter *academic dean, sociology educator*
†Powers, John H. *school system administrator*
Ritvo, Roger Alan *university dean, health management-policy educator*
Sproul, Otis Jennings *dean*

Exeter
Erickson, Raymond Leroy *dean, psychologist*

Hanover
Blaydon, Colin Campbell *university professor*
Fox, Edward A. *college dean*
Freedman, James Oliver *university president, lawyer*
Hennessey, John William, Jr. *academic administrator*
Hutchinson, Charles Edgar *engineering school dean*
Rieser, Leonard Moos *college administrator, physics educator*

Henniker
Cummiskey, J. Kenneth *former college president*
O'Connell, William Raymond, Jr. *college president*

Kingston
Curtis, Staton Russell *university dean*

Manchester
Comeau, Reginald Alfred *academic administrator, consultant*
DeFelice, Jonathan Peter *college president, priest*
Gustafson, Richard Alrick *college president*

Nashua
†Jean, Claudette R. *retired elementary educator*

NEW JERSEY

Atlantic Highlands
Crowley, Cynthia Johnson *secondary education educator*
Fink, Dolores Hesse *special education educator*

Belleville
Pincus, George *university dean, engineering educator*

Camden
Gordon, Walter Kelly *provost, English language educator*

Cedar Grove
Nash, Annamarie *secondary education educator*

Cliffside Park
Jaspen, Nathan *educational statistics educator*

East Brunswick
†Fisher, Lucille *principal*
Haupin, Elizabeth C. *retired secondary school educator*
†King, Charles M. *principal*

Edison
Danzis, Rose Marie *emeritus college president*
Renzulli, Mary Ann *parochial education educator*

Elmer
Slavoff, Harriet Emonds *learning disabilities teacher, consultant*

Fair Lawn
†Panella, Elizabeth M. *secondary school principal*

Flemington
Foti, Margaret Mai *education consultant*

Fort Lee
Sugarman, Alan William *educational administrator*

Glassboro
Gephardt, Donald Louis *college official*
James, Herman Delano *college administrator*

Haddon Heights
Gwiazda, Stanley John *university dean*

Hazlet
Leibow, Lois May *educator*

Highland Lakes
Ansorge, Helen J. *retired elementary school educator*

Hoboken
Raveché, Harold Joseph *university administrator, physical chemist*

Jersey City
Foster, Delores Jackson *elementary school principal*
Fox, Thomas George *academic adminstrator, healthscience educator*
Reynolds, Scott Walton *academic administrator*

Lakewood
Williams, Barbara Anne *college president*

Lawrenceville
†Bunting, Josiah, III *college president*
Tharney, Leonard John *education educator, consultant*

Lincroft
Sullivan, Brother Jeremiah Stephen *former college president*

Little Falls
Nash, James John *superintendent*

Lodi
Pivinski, Sister Mary Lorene *academic administrator*

Madison
Kean, Thomas H. *academic administrator, former governor*

Mahwah
Scott, Robert Allyn *college administrator*

Margate City
†Weiss, Mordechai *principal*

Medford
†Konstantinos, K. Kiki *school system administrator*

Mendham
Posunko, Barbara *elementary education educator*

Montclair
†Strobert, Barbara *principal*

New Brunswick
Carman, John Herbert *elementary education educator*
Dill, Ellis Harold *university dean*
Garner, Charles William *educational administration educator, consultant*
Nelson, Jack Lee *education educator*
Tanner, Daniel *curriculum theory educator*

Newark
†Abrams, Roger I. *academic dean, labor arbitrator*
Bergen, Stanley Silvers, Jr. *university president, physician*
Chagnon, Joseph V. *school system administrator*
Fenster, Saul K. *university president*
Hart, Paul *dean, poet, educator*
Hollander, Toby Edward *education educator*
Lanzoni, Vincent *medical school dean*
Murray, Constance Ann *college dean*
Pfeffer, Edward Israel *educational administrator*
Starks, Florence Elizabeth *special education educator*
Thomas, Gary L. *academic administrator*
Wolfe, Lilyan *special education educator, clinician*

North Branch
†Gartlan, Philip M. *secondary school director*

Old Bridge
Swett, Stephen Frederick, Jr. *principal*

Parsippany
Maness, Mildred *reading specialist*
Sommer, Joseph William *educator*

Paterson
Pulhamus, Marlene Louise *elementary school educator*

Phillipsburg
Stull, Frank Walter *educator*

Piscataway
Colaizzi, John Louis *college dean*

Pomona
Farris, Vera King *college president*

Pompton Lakes
Brolsma, Catherine *secondary education educator, educational administrator*

Princeton
Gillespie, Thomas William *theological seminary administrator, religion educator*
Jahn, Robert George *university dean, engineering educator*
Labalme, Patricia Hochschild *educational administrator*
Malkiel, Nancy Weiss *college dean, history educator*
Massa, Conrad Harry *seminary dean*
Shapiro, Harold Tafler *university president, economist*

Rockaway
Allen, Dorothea *secondary school educator*

Rutherford
Mertz, Francis James *academic administrator*
Sarsfield, Luke Aloysius *school system administrator*

Saddle River
Lehmann, Doris Elizabeth *elementary education educator*

Somerville
McCoy, Eileen Carey *academic dean*

South Orange
†Harahan, Robert E. *rector*

Sparta
Harrison, Alice Kathleen *elementary educator*

Spring Lake
Connor, Frances Partridge *education educator*

Springfield
†Merachnik, Donald *superintendent of schools*

Summit
Rossey, Paul William *superintendent of schools*

Teaneck
Pischl, Adolph John *school administrator*

Tenafly
Gerst, Elizabeth Carlsen (Mrs. Paul H. Gerst) *university dean, researcher, educator*
Hartung, Walter Magnus *retired aeronautical college executive*

Totowa
Barbarow, Thomas Steven *public school system administrator*

Trenton
Brown, Dorothea Williams *technology consulting company executive*
Eickhoff, Harold Walter *college president, humanities educator*
Pruitt, George Albert *college president*

Wayne
Benedict, Theresa Marie *mathematics educator*
Goetz, William Walter *education and history educator*
Speert, Arnold *college president, chemistry educator*

West Long Branch
Rouse, Robert Sumner *former college official*
Stafford, Rebecca *college president, sociologist*

West Milford
Kinney, Dorothy Jean *elementary educator*

West New York
Aquino, Felix John *college administrator*

Westwood
Cullen, Ruth Enck *reading specialist, elementary education educator*

NEW MEXICO

Albuquerque
†Anaya, Rudolfo *educator, writer*
Caplan, Edwin Harvey *university dean, accounting educator*
Drummond, Harold Dean *education educator*
Garcia, F. Chris *academic administrator, political science educator, public opinion researcher*
Lattman, Laurence Harold *retired academic administrator*
May, Gerald William *university administrator, educator, civil engineering consultant*
Norman, Ralph David *consulting psychologist, former university administrator*
Paler, Peggy Louise D'Arcy *elementary education educator, education educator*
Peck, Richard Earl *academic administrator, playwright, novelist*
Travelstead, Chester Coleman *former educational administrator*
Woodbridge, Ruth I. *elementary education educator*
†Zink, Lee B. *academic administrator, economist, educator*

Artesia
Sarwar, Barbara Duce *school system administrator*

Cimarron
†Lopez, Joe A. *school system administrator*

Gallup
Boucher, Raymond Joseph *educator*

Las Cruces
†Easterling, Kathy *elementary school principal*
Gale, Thomas Martin *university dean*
Halligan, James Edmund *university administrator, chemical engineer*

Las Vegas
Sanchez, Gilbert *university president, microbiologist, researcher*

Los Alamos
Engel, Emily Flachmeier *school administrator*

Mesilla
Box, Thadis Wayne *university dean emeritus, educator*
Willey, Darrell S. *education educator*

Mesilla Park
Shutt, Frances Barton *special education educator*

Montezuma
†Geier, Philip O., III *academic adminstrator*

Rancho de Taos
Brown, David Warfield *former academic administrator*

Santa Fe
Agresto, John *college president*
Bond, Thomas Alden *university president*
Denman, William Foster *retired academic administrator, educator*

Silver City
Snedeker, John Haggner *university president*

Univ Of New Mexico
Hull, McAllister Hobart, Jr. *retired university administrator*

NEW YORK

Albany
Burke, Joseph C. *university interim chancellor*
Hughs, Richard Earl *business school dean*
Kiepper, James Julius *education educator*
†Kinney, Thomas J. *adult education educator*
Robbins, Cornelius (Van Vorse) *education administration educator*
Thornton, Maurice *university administrator*
Vaccaro, Louis Charles *college president*

Alfred
Coll, Edward Girard, Jr. *university president*
Ott, Walter Richard *academic administrator*

Alfred Station
Love, Robert Lyman *educational consulting company executive*

Auburn
Eldred, Thomas Gilbert *secondary education educator, historian*

Batavia
Steiner, Stuart *college president*

Binghamton
Defleur, Lois B. *university president, sociology educator*
Feisel, Lyle Dean *university dean, electrical engineering educator*

Briarcliff Manor
Radandt, Friedhelm K. *college president*

Brockport
Harter, Michael Thomas *college dean, health sciences consultant*
Studer, Ginny *college dean*
Van de Wetering, John E(dward) *college president*

Bronx
Fernandez, Ricardo R. *university administrator*
†Fleischer, Norman *director of endocrinology, medical educator*
†Iazetti, Anthony M. *school system administrator*
Keane, John Patrick *secondary education educator*
Nathanson, Melvyn Bernard *university provost, mathematician*
Rothstein, Anne Louise *education educator, college official*
Scanlan, Thomas Joseph *college president, educator*

Bronxville
Ilchman, Alice Stone *college president, former government official*

Brooklyn
Birenbaum, William M. *former university president*
Bugliarello, George *university president*
†Comer, John F. *superintendent*
†Gresser, Carol A. *school system administrator*
Kimmich, Christoph Martin *academic administrator, educator*
O'Connor, Sister George Aquin (Margaret M. O'Connor) *college president, sociology educator*
Roess, Roger Peter *university vice president and dean*
Sullivan, Donald *college president*
Wasserman, Arnold Saul *academic dean, industrial design executive*
Williams, Ethel Coger *elementary education educator*
Wolfe, Ethyle Renee (Mrs. Coleman Hamilton Benedict) *college administrator*

Brookville
Woodsworth, Anne *university dean, librarian*

Buffalo
Birch, David William *business manager*
Durand, Henry J., Jr. *academic administrator*
Gemmett, Robert James *university dean, English language educator*
Greiner, William Robert *university administrator, educator, lawyer*
Johnstone, D. Bruce *university administrator*
Kiser, Kenneth M(aynard) *academic dean, chemical engineering educator*
†Ottenbacher, Kenneth J. *dean, educator*
Richardson, F. C. *academic administrator*
Seidl, Fredrick William *dean, social work educator*
Stull, G. Alan *university dean, health professions educator*
Triggle, David John *university dean, consultant*
Wiesen, Richard A. *academic administrator, educator*

Canton
Peterson, Patti McGill *college president*

Castleton On Hudson
Lanford, Oscar Erasmus, Jr. *retired university vice chancellor*

Centerport
Mallett, Helene Gettler *elementary education educator*

Central Islip
Gillespie, Eileen Rose *elementary education educator*

Clifton Park
Schmitt, Roland Walter *retired academic administrator*

Clinton
†Fuller, Ruthann *principal*

Cold Spring Harbor
Huffman, Carol Koster *middle school educator*
Roberts, Francis Joy *educator, journalist*

Coopers Plains
Wilson, Louise Astell Morse *educator, home economist*

Cortland
Clark, James Milford *college president*

Dix Hills
†Murphy, Edward J. *school system administrator*

East Aurora
Spahn, Mary Attea *retired education educator*
Weidemann, Julia Clark *principal, educator*
Woodard, Carol Jane *educational consultant*

East Meadow
Beyer, Norma Warren *educator*

Elmira
Burke, Rita Hoffmann *educational administrator*
Meier, Thomas Keith *college president, English educator*

Elmont
Pilkington, Frances Jean *secondary school educator*

Farmingdale
Cipriani, Frank Anthony *college president*

Floral Park
†Scricca, Diane Bernadette *principal*

Flushing
Brush, George W. *college president*
Carlton, Doreen Charlotte *special education supervisor and administrator*
Kenny, Shirley Strum *college administrator*

Fredonia
MacPhee, Donald Albert *academic administrator*
Mac Vittie, Robert William *retired college administrator*

Freeport
Antoine, Yvetot Marc *university director*

Friendship
Kingdon, Mary Oneida Grace *elementary education educator*

Garden City
Webb, Igor Michael *university administrator*

Garrison
†Grossman, Allen *educational administrator*

Geneseo
Harter, Carol Clancey *university president, English language educator*

Geneva
Hersh, Richard H. *academic administrator*

Glen Head
†Boyrer, Elaine M. *principal*

Glenmont
Block, Murray Harold *educational consultant*
†Robillard, Donald J. *elementary school principal*

Greece
†Ryan-Johnson, Deborah *principal*

Greenvale
Cook, Edward Joseph *college president*
Gillespie, John Thomas *university administrator*
Steinberg, David Joel *academic administrator, historian, educator*

Greenwood
Rollins, June Elizabeth *elementary education educator*

Hamilton
Jones, Howard Langworthy *educational administrator, consultant*

Hauppauge
Oschmann, Joan Edythe *gifted and elementary education educator*

Hempstead
Berliner, Herman Albert *university provost and dean, economics educator*
Chapman, Lenora Rosamond *social service organization director*
Haynes, Ulric St. Clair, Jr. *academic dean*
Shuart, James Martin *university president*

Holland Patent
Giacobbe, Anna Gretchen Steinhauer *elementary education educator*

Horseheads
Cusimano, Adeline Mary *educational administrator*

Houghton
Chamberlain, Daniel Robert *college president*
Luckey, Robert Reuel Raphael *retired academic administrator*

Huntington
D'Addario, Alice Marie *school administrator*

Huntington Station
Braun, Ludwig *educational technology consultant*

Ithaca
Cooke, William Donald *university administrator, chemistry educator*
Corson, Dale Raymond *retired university president, physicist*
Cotton, Dorothy Foreman *former director student activities, consultant*
Craft, Harold Dumont, Jr. *university official, radio astronomer*
Firebaugh, Francille Maloch *university official*
†Hopcroft, John Edward *dean, computer science educator*
†Kalos, Malvin Howard *university researcher, educator, and administrator*
Longin, Thomas Charles *academic administrator*
Merten, Alan Gilbert *university dean*
†Nesheim, Malden C. *university administrator*
Oblak, John Byron *academic administrator*
Phemister, Robert David *college dean*
Rhodes, Frank Harold Trevor *university president, geologist*
†Rhodin, Thor Nathaniel *educational administrator*
Scott, Norman Roy *academic administrator, agricultural engineering educator*
Seibert, Mary Lee *college official*
Streett, William Bernard *university dean, engineering educator*
Tynes, Theodore Archibald *school administrator*
Whalen, James Joseph *college president*

Jamaica
Bartilucci, Andrew Joseph *university administrator*
Harrington, Donald James *university president*

Jamestown
Benke, Paul Arthur *college president*

Jericho
†Mandery, Mathew M. *secondary school principal*

Kenmore
†Vienne, Dorothy Titus *school principal*

Kings Point
Matteson, Thomas T. *academic administrator*
Mazek, Warren F(elix) *academic administrator, economics educator*

Larchmont
Gallaher, Carolyn Combs *secondary education educator*

Long Beach
Thompson, Dorothy Barnard *elementary school educator*

Long Eddy
Van Swol, Noel Warren *secondary education educator*

Loudonville
McConville, William *academic administrator*

Mahopac
†Gould, Sandra M. *elementary school principal*

Malone
Quesnel, Elizabeth Dimick *secondary school educator*

Middle Island
†Mastrion, Guy *secondary school principal*

Middletown
Byrne, Mary Margaret (Meg Byrne) *elementary education educator*

Mill Neck
Grieve, William Roy *education educator, educational association administrator*

Mineola
Salten, David George *university administrator, educator*

Moriches
†Casciano, Paul *principal*

Nanuet
†Gold, Arline *elementary school principal*

New Paltz
Nyquist, Thomas Eugene *academic administrator*

New Rochelle
Gallagher, John Francis *academic administrator, education educator*
Kelly, Sister Dorothy Ann *college president*
Wolotsky, Hyman *retired college dean*

New York
Brademas, John *former university president, former congressman*
Brenner, Egon *university official, education consultant*
Burton, John Campbell *university dean, educator, consultant*
Campbell, Mary Schmidt *dean art school*
†Claster, Jill Nadell *university administrator, history educator*
Cohen, Saul Bernard *former college president, geographer*
Consagra, Sophie Chandler *academy administrator*
Daly, George Garman *college dean, educator*
†Duggan, Rosemary H. *vocational administrator*
Duke, Angier Biddle *retired university chancellor, retired diplomat*
Ehrenkranz, Shirley Malakoff *university dean, social work educator*
Elster, Samuel Kase *college dean, medical educator, physician*
Essandoh, Hilda Brathwaite *kindergarten educator*
Ewers, Patricia O'Donnell *university administrator*
Fanton, Jonathan Foster *university president*
Feldberg, Meyer *university dean*
Fernández-Velazquez, Juan Ramon *university chancellor*
Gartner, Alan P. *university official, author*
†Geiger, H. Jack *medical educator*
Ginsburg, Sigmund G. *academic administrator*
Goren, Arnold Louis *educator, former university official*
Griffiths, Daniel Edward *dean emeritus*
Haffner, Alden Norman *university official*
Harkrader, Milton Keene, Jr. *academic administrator*
Harleston, Bernard Warren *college president*
Hejduk, John Quentin *dean, architect*
†Hershfield, Allan F. *academic administrator*
Heyer, Paul Otto *college president, architect*
Horowitz, Frances Degen *academic administrator, psychology educator*
Iselin, John Jay *university president*
Jeynes, Mary Kay *college dean*
Katsh, Abraham Isaac *university president emeritus, educator*
Klopf, Gordon John *college dean, educational consultant*
Konner, Joan Weiner *university administrator, educator, broadcasting executive, television producer*
†Kopp, Wendy *volunteer program administrator*
Lamm, Norman *academic administrator, rabbi*
Lange, Phil C. *education educator*
Lazarus-Franklin, Paula Guillermina *vocational services administrator*
Lehmann, Frederick Gliessmann *university administrator*
Levine, Arthur Elliott *academic administrator, educator*
Levine, Naomi Bronheim *university administrator*
Liebman, Lance Malcolm *dean, lawyer*
Long, Melvin Durward *university president*
Lynch, Gerald Weldon *college president, psychologist*
Marcus, Steven *dean, English educator*
Marcuse, Adrian Gregory *college administrator*
Marshall, Geoffrey *university administrator*
Maubert, Jacques Claude *headmaster*
Mitchell, John Dietrich *theatre arts institute executive*
Molholt, Pat *university official*
O'Hare, Joseph Aloysius *university president, priest*
Oliva, Lawrence Jay *university official, history educator*
Passow, Aaron Harry *education educator*
Pflaum, Susanna Whitney *college dean*
Polisi, Joseph W(illiam) *college administrator*
Powell, Lillian Marie *music educator*
Pratt, Richardson, Jr. *retired college president*
Reutter, Eberhard Edmund, Jr. *education and law educator*
Reynolds, W(ynetka) Ann *university system administrator, educator*
Rice, Charles Duncan *academic dean, history educator, writer*
Rinsland, Roland DeLano *university official*
Rosen, David Michael *university administrator, public affairs consultant*
Rosenfeld, Herb *educational consultant*
Rosenthal, Albert Joseph *university dean, law educator, lawyer*
Rowe, John Wallis *academic administrator, hospital administrator*
Rowland, Esther E(delman) *college dean*
Rubinstein, Laurence Henry *university administrator, fund raiser*
Rupp, George Erik *university president*
Schwarz, Ralph Jacques *university dean*
Seitz, Frederick *university president emeritus*
Selby, Cecily Cannan *dean, educator, scientist*
Shenker, Joseph *college administrator*
Shields, James Joseph, Jr. *educator, educational administrator, author*
Strumingher, Laura Sharon *academic administrator*
Tapley, Donald Fraser *university official, physician, educator*
Timpane, Philip Michael *college administrator*
Vázquez, José Antonio *education educator*
Violenus, Agnes A. *school system administrator*
Walzer, Judith Borodovko *university administrator, educator*
Waren, Stanley A. *university administrator, theatre and arts center administrator, director*
†Watkins, Stanley *academic director*
Weiner, Annette B. *university dean, anthropology educator*
Weinstein, Sidney *university program director*
Wharton, Clifton Reginald, Jr. *former university president, former government official, former insurance executive*
Yetman, Leith Eleanor *administrator, educator*

Newburgh
†Joyce, Mary Ann *principal*
Saturnelli, Annette Miele *school system administrator*

Niagara Falls
Powers, Bruce Raymond *academic administrator, writer*
Sheeran, Thomas Joseph *education educator, consultant, judge*

Niagara University
O'Connell, Brian James *academic administrator, priest*
O'Leary, Daniel Francis *university dean*

Oakdale
Meskill, Victor Peter *college president, educator*

Old Westbury
Cheek, King Virgil, Jr. *lawyer, educational administrator*
Pettigrew, L. Eudora *university president*
Schure, Alexander *university chancellor*
Schure, Matthew *college president*

Oneonta
Donovan, Alan Barton *college president*

Orangeburg
Hennessy, James Ernest *college official, educator*

Oswego
Geisinger, Kurt Francis *academic dean, psychometrician, educator*
Gerber, Barbara Ann Witter *university dean, educator*
Moody, Florence Elizabeth *education educator, retired college dean*
Weber, Stephen Lewis *academic administrator*

Peekskill
Manthey, Robert Wendelin *educator*

Pittsford
Hess, Donald K. *university administrator*

Pleasantville
†Antonecchia, Donald A. *principal*
†Glotzer, Marilyn *principal*
Pastore, Joseph Michael, Jr. *university administrator, business educator*

Potsdam
Gallagher, Richard Hugo *university official, engineer*
Washburn, Robert Brooks *university dean, composer*

Poughkeepsie
Conklin, D(onald) David *college president*
Fergusson, Frances Daly *college president, educator*
Kim, David Sang Chul *seminary president, publishing executive*
Marshall, Natalie Junemann *university official*

Purchase
Grebstein, Sheldon Norman *university administrator*
Lacy, Bill *college president*
Myers, Catherine R. *academic administrator*

Ransomville
Mayer, George Merton *elementary education educator*

Rochester
Bernstein, Paul *retired academic dean*
Beston, Rose Marie *college president*
Castle, William Eugene *academic administrator*
Cohen, Jules *academic dean, physician, educator*
Everett, Claudia Kellam *special education educator*
Jackson, Thomas Humphrey *university president*
Joynt, Robert James *academic administrator*
Munson, Harold Lewis *education educator*
Pickett, William Lee *academic administrator*
Plosser, Charles Irving *dean, economics educator*
Scalise, Francis Allen *administrator, consultant*
Simone, Albert Joseph *academic administrator*
Sproull, Robert Lamb *retired university president, physicist*
Thompson, Brian John *university provost, optics educator*
†Wager, Barbara *principal*
Woods, John Joseph *executive director*

Rockville Centre
Fitzgerald, Sister Janet Anne *college president*

Rocky Point
Kretschmer, Ingrid Butler *elementary education educator*

Saint Bonaventure
Doyle, Mathias Francis *university president, political scientist, educator*
O'Connell, Neil James *priest, academic administrator*

Saratoga Springs
Hall, James William *college president*

Schenectady
Hull, Roger Harold *college president*
Rycheck, Jayne Bogus (Mrs. Roy Richard Rycheck) *retired educational administrator*

Setauket
Werner, Joseph *retired secondary education educator, administrator*

Shoreham
Reynolds, Carolyn Mary *elementary educator*

Sidney
Haller, Irma Tognola *secondary social studies educator*

Skaneateles
†Sullivan, Walter J. *school system administrator*

Staten Island
Smith, Norman Raymond *college president*

Stony Brook
Edelstein, Tilden Gerald *academic administrator, history educator*
Marburger, John Harmen, III *university president, physics educator*
†Shamash, Yacov *dean, electrical engineering educator*
Smith, John Brewster *dean library sciences, director*

Syosset
Nydick, David *schools superintendent*

Syracuse
Burstyn, Joan Netta *educator*
Charters, Alexander Nathaniel *education educator emeritus*
Goodman, Donald C. *university administrator*
Hiemstra, Roger *adult education educator, writer*
Krathwohl, David Reading *education educator emeritus*
Lillestol, Jane Marie *academic administrator*
Nelli, D. James *school administrator, accountant*
Shaw, Kenneth Alan *university president*
Tolley, William Pearson *former university chancellor, former airline executive*
Weiss, Volker *university administrator, educator*

Troy
Chapman, Sara Simmons *academic administrator, English educator*
Judd, Gary *university administrator*
Kahl, William Frederick *retired college president*
†Le Maistre, Christopher William *educational director*
Pipes, Robert Byron *academic administrator, mechanical engineer*
Richtol, Herbert Harold *academic dean*
†Romond, James *principal*
Wait, Samuel Charles, Jr. *academic administrator, educator*
Watson, Donald Ralph *academic dean, architect, author*

Utica
Boyle, William Leo, Jr. *educational consultant, retired college president*
Simpson, Michael Kevin *college president, political science educator*

Van Hornesville
Case, Everett Needham *former university president, educator*

Wantagh
†DeNapoli, Anthony *middle school principal*

West Point
Galloway, Gerald Edward, Jr. *dean*

White Plains
Peck, Alexander Norman *physical education educator, day camp administrator*

Williamsville
Harnack, Robert Spencer *retired education educator*

Woodside
Burchell, Jeanne Kathleen *primary school educator*

Yonkers
Atkins, Leola Mae *special education educator*
Liggio, Jean Vincenza *artist, educator*
Robinson, Chester Hersey *retired dean*

Yorktown Heights
Hsieh, Hazel Tseng *elementary education educator*

NORTH CAROLINA

Albemarle
Bramlett, Christopher Lewis *academic administrator*

Asheville
Merrill, Edward Clifton, Jr. *emeritus university president*
†Reed, Patsy Bostick *university administrator*
Wilson, Lauren Ross *academic administrator*

Biscoe
McIlvaine, William L. *educational director, computer science educator*

Black Mountain
Holden, Reuben Andrus *retired college president*
Weatherford, Willis Duke, Jr. *college president emeritus*

Bladenboro
Walters, Cathryne Brunson *primary school educator*

Boiling Springs
White, Martin Christopher *academic administrator*

Boone
Auten, Janet Sue *business education educator*
Borkowski, Francis Thomas *university administrator*

Buies Creek
Wiggins, Norman Adrian *university administrator, legal educator*

Chapel Hill
†Campbell, B. (Obby) Jack *university official*
†Carroll, Roy *academic administrator*
Cole, Richard Ray *university dean*
Edwards, Richard LeRoy *academic dean, social work educator, non-profit management consultant*
Fordham, Christopher Columbus, III *university dean and chancellor, medical educator*
Friday, William Clyde *university president emeritus*
Joyner, Leon Felix *university administrator*
MacGillivray, Lois Ann *academic administrator*
Memory, Jasper Durham *academic administrator, physics educator*
Murphy, James Lee *college dean, economics educator*
Spangler, Clemmie Dixon, Jr. *academic administrator*
Tillman, Rollie, Jr. *university official*

Charlotte
Blaschke, Robert Carvel *education coordinator*
Burke, Mary Thomas *university administrator, educator*
†Clark, Ann Blakeney *educational administrator*
Colvard, Dean Wallace *emeritus university chancellor*
Fretwell, Elbert Kirtley, Jr. *university chancellor emeritus, consultant*
Greene, William Henry L'Vel *academic administrator*
Woodward, James Hoyt *university chancellor, engineer*

Creedmoor
Cross, June Crews *music educator*

Cullowhee
Coulter, Myron Lee *retired academic administrator*
Reed, Alfred Douglas *university official*

Davidson
Kuykendall, John Wells *academic administrator, educator*
Spencer, Samuel Reid, Jr. *educational consultant, former university president*

Durham
Beckum, Leonard Charles *academic administrator*
Dowell, Earl Hugh *university dean, aerospace and mechanical engineering educator*
Fleishman, Joel Lawrence *university administrator, journalist, law educator*
Hopkins, Everett Harold *education educator*
Keller, Thomas Franklin *dean, management science educator*
Keohane, Nannerl Overholser *college president, political scientist*
Schmalbeck, Richard Louis *university dean, lawyer*

Elizabeth City
†Twiford, Travis W. *school system administrator*

Elon College
Young, James Fred *college president*

Fayetteville
Hackley, Lloyd Vincent *university administrator, retired air force officer*

Greensboro
Cardwell, Jessie Womack *elementary education educator*
†Clark, Joanne *school system administrator*
Davis-Seaver, Elizabeth Jane *elementary school educator*
Edinger, Lois Virginia *education educator emeritus*
Miller, Robert Louis *university dean, chemistry educator*
Poteet, Daniel P(owell), II *college provost*
Rogers, William Raymond *college president, psychology educator*
Scott, Gloria Dean Randle *academic administrator*
Speight, Velma Ruth *academic director*

Greenville
Bearden, James Hudson *university official*
Eakin, Richard Ronald *academic administrator, mathematics educator*
Howell, John McDade *retired university chancellor, political science educator*
Hudgins, Herbert Cornelius, Jr. *education educator*
Leggett, Donald Yates *university program director*

Hendersonville
†Byrd, Charles L. *school system administrator*
Jones, J(ohn) Charles *education educator*
Payne, Gerald Oliver *elementary education educator*

High Point
Howard, Lou Dean Graham *elementary education educator*
Martinson, Jacob Christian, Jr. *university president*

Kinston
Matthis, Eva Mildred Boney *college official*
Petteway, Samuel Bruce *college president*

Kure Beach
Funk, Frank E. *retired university dean*

Lincolnton
Saine, Betty Boston *elementary education educator*

Mars Hill
Bentley, Fred Blake *academic administrator*

Monroe
†Griffin, Gwyn *secondary school principal*

Montreat
De Jong, Arthur Jay *education consultant, former university president*

Mount Olive
Raper, William Burkette *college president*

Mount Ulla
†Kluttz, Henry G. *principal*

Murfreesboro
Whitaker, Bruce Ezell *college president*

Oxford
†Pruitt, Dorothy J. Gooch *educational administrator*

Pittsboro
Gustafson, Sarah *elementary school educator*
Lewis, Henry Wilkins *university administrator, lawyer, educator*
Robinson, Ormsbee Wright *educational consultant*

Raleigh
†Buchanan, David Royal *associate dean*
Dolce, Carl John *education administration educator*
Fadum, Ralph Eigil *university dean*
Fletcher, Oscar Jasper, Jr. *college dean*

Jividen, Loretta Ann Harper *secondary education educator*
Maidon, Carolyn Howser *academic program administrator*
Malone, Thomas Francis *university administrator, meteorologist*
McKinney, Charles Cecil *investment company executive*
Menius, Arthur Clayton, Jr. *former university dean*
Monteith, Larry King *university chancellor*
Page, Anne Ruth *gifted education educator, education specialist*
Parker, Charles Brand, Jr. *training company executive*
Poulton, Bruce Robert *former university chancellor*
Robinson, Prezell Russell *college administrator*
Rochelle, Lugenia *academic administrator*
Shaw, Talbert O. *university president*
Winstead, Nash Nicks *university administrator, phytopathologist*
†Wynne, Johnny Calvin *university official, plant breeding researcher*

Rockingham
†Robertson, Ralph S. *secondary school principal*

Shelby
Edgar, Ruth R. *educator*

Sparta
Adams, Marion Ruth Allison *special education educator*

Weaverville
Wallin, Franklin Whittelsey *educational consultant, former college president*

West End
Cartwright, William Holman *education educator emeritus*

Wilmington
Cahill, Charles L. *university administrator, chemistry educator*
Leutze, James Richard *academic administrator, television producer and host*
†McManus, Hugh F. *principal*
Wagoner, William Hampton *university chancellor*

Wilson
Hemby, James B., Jr. *college president*

Winston Salem
Ewing, Alexander Cochran *chancellor*
Janeway, Richard *university executive*
Roth, Marjory Joan Jarboe *special education educator*
Stroupe, Henry Smith *university dean*
Thompson, Cleon F., Jr. *university administrator*
Wilson, Edwin Graves *university official*

NORTH DAKOTA

Bismarck
†Evanson, Barbara Jean *middle school education educator*
Stastney, Agnes Florence *principal*

Dickinson
Conn, Philip Wesley *university president*
†Morud, Rollie D. *school system administrator*

Fargo
Ozbun, Jim L. *academic administrator*

Garrison
†Schlieve, Hy C. J. *superintendent*

Grand Forks
Baker, Kendall L. *academic administrator*
Clifford, Thomas John *university president*
Lindquist, Mary Louise *special education educator*
O'Kelly, Bernard *university dean*
Sand, Phyllis Sue Newnam *retired special education educator*

Jamestown
Walker, James Silas *college official*

Minot
Shaar, H. Erik *academic administrator*

OHIO

Ada
Freed, DeBow *college president*
Quick, Albert Thomas *academic law administrator, educator*

Akron
Auburn, Norman Paul *university president*
Barker, Harold Kenneth *former university dean*
Elliott, Peggy Gordon *university president*
†Kelley, Frank Nicholas *dean*
Kodish, Arline Betty *principal*
Seiberling, John Frederick *former congressman, law educator, lawyer*
Stroll, Beverly Marie *elementary school principal*

Alliance
Weber, Ronald Gilbert *retired college president*

Andover
Mathay, John Preston *elementary education educator*

Athens
Bruning, James Leon *university official, educator*
Gallaway, Gladys McGhee *elementary education educator*
Miller, Richard Irwin *education educator, university administrator*
Ping, Charles Jackson *university administrator, educator*

Berea
Malicky, Neal *college president*

Brecksville
Johnson, L. Neil *school system administrator*

Centerville
†Mattia, Frank J. *secondary school principal*

Chagrin Falls
Grasselli, Jeanette Gecsy *university official*
Phillips, Dorothy Ormes *elementary education educator*

Chesapeake
Harris, Bob L(ee) *principal*

Cincinnati
Ashley, Lynn *educational coordinator*
Baas, Robert Miller *school administrator*
Baker, Norman Robert *education educator*
Gosling, David *university administrator*
Gottschalk, Alfred *college president*
Greengus, Samuel *academic administrator, religion educator*
Harrison, Donald Carey *academic administrator, cardiologist*
Hartleb, David Frederick *academic administrator, legal educator*
Hoff, James Edwin *university president*
†Hyre, James G. *educational administrator*
King, James Calvin *university radio director, educator*
Kohl, David *dean, librarian*
Nester, William Raymond, Jr. *university administrator*
Papadakis, Constantine N. *dean, civil engineering educator*
Sanford, Wilbur Lee *elementary education educator*
Steger, Joseph A. *university president*
Voluse, Charles Rodger, III *education educator*
Werner, Robert Joseph *college dean, music educator*
Winkler, Henry Ralph *retired university president, historian*

Cleveland
Bernard, Lowell Francis *academic administrator, educator, consultant*
Calkins, Hugh *elementary school educator*
†Cerone, David *academic administrator*
Cullis, Christopher Ashley *dean, biology educator*
Gronick, Patricia Ann Jacobsen *school system administrator*
Hartley, Robert Frank *education educator, author*
McArdle, Richard Joseph *academic administrator*
McCullough, Joseph *college president emeritus*
Mc Murrin, Lee Ray *educational administrator*
Moss, Thomas Henry *university dean, physicist*
Parker, Robert Frederic *university dean emeritus*
Pytte, Agnar *academic administrator, theoretical physicist*
Stein, Herman David *academic administrator, social sciences and social work educator*
Van Ummersen, Claire A(nn) *university president, biologist, educator*
Weidenthal, Maurice David (Bud Weidenthal) *educational administrator, journalist*
Wertheim, Sally Harris *academic administrator, dean, education educator*
Zdanis, Richard Albert *academic administrator*

Columbus
Alutto, Joseph Anthony *university dean, management educator*
Armes, Walter Scott *vocational school administrator*
Baughman, George Washington, III *retired university official, financial consultant*
Beytagh, Francis Xavier, Jr. *college dean, lawyer*
Bishop, James Joseph *dean*
Blackmore, Josiah H. *university president, lawyer, educator*
Cole, Clarence Russell *college dean*
†Cottrell, David Alton *school system administrator*
Gee, Elwood Gordon *university administrator*
Gunnels, Lee O. *retired finance and management educator*
†Hermann, Charles F. *academic director, political science educator*
Howe, Robert Wilson *education educator*
Koenigsknecht, Roy A. *university dean*
Magliocca, Larry Anthony *education educator*
Marcus, Lola Eleanor *elementary and secondary education educator*
Meuser, Fredrick William *retired seminary president, church historian*
Otte, Paul John *college administrator, consultant, trainer*
Parks, Darrell Lee *vocational education administrator*
Salgia, Tansukh Jawaharlal *academic administrator*
†Silcott, James *principal*
Stephens, Thomas M(aron) *education educator*

Concord
Watterson, Joyce Grande *academy director*

Curtice
Cashen, Elizabeth Anne *elementary school educator*

Dayton
†Bowman, Ed *principal*
Gies, Frederick John *education educator, university dean*
Heft, James Lewis *academic administrator, theology educator*
Martin, James Gilbert *university provost emeritus*
Ponitz, David H. *academic administrator*
Przemieniecki, Janusz Stanislaw *college dean, engineer*
Rowe, Joseph Everett *electrical engineering educator, administrator*
Stander, Joseph William *former university administrator, mathematics educator*
Uphoff, James Kent *education educator*

Defiance
Hodapp, Shirley Jeaniene *curriculum administrator*

Delaware
Courtice, Thomas Barr *college president*

Dublin
Felger, Ralph William *retired military officer, educator*

Fairfield
Dizney, Robert Edward *secondary education educator*

Findlay
Draper, David Eugene *seminary president*

Gambier
Browning, Reed S. *college official*
Jordan, Philip Harding, Jr. *academic administrator*

Granville
Morris, Charles Joseph, Jr. *university provost*
Myers, Michele Tolela *academic administrator*

Harrison
†Stoll, Robert W. *principal*

Hiram
Jagow, Elmer *retired college administrator*
Oliver, G(eorge) Benjamin *academic administrator, philosophy educator*

Jackson
Clark, M. Juanita *vocational education evaluator*

Jamestown
Liem, Darlene Marie *secondary education educator*

Kent
Buttlar, Rudolph Otto *college dean*
Du Mont, Rosemary Ruhig *university dean*
Schwartz, Michael *university president, sociology educator*
Vars, Gordon Forrest *education educator*

Kingston
Mathew, Martha Sue Cryder *retired education educator*

Marietta
Ling, Dwight L. *college administrator, history educator*
McDonough, Patrick Dennis *university executive*

Mechanicsburg
Maynard, Joan *education educator*

Mentor
†Davis, Barbara Snell *principal*

Millersburg
Childers, Lawrence Jeffrey *superintendent of schools*

New Bremen
Poppe, Beverly Reed *special education educator*

New Concord
Speck, Samuel Wallace, Jr. *academic administrator*

New Philadelphia
Doughten, Mary Katherine (Molly Doughten) *retired secondary education educator*
Goforth, Mary Elaine Davey *secondary education educator*

Newark
Fortaleza, Judith Ann *school system administrator*
Greenstein, Julius Sidney *academic administrator*

Oberlin
Carrier, Samuel Crowe, III *college official*
†Dye, Nancy Schrom *academic administrator, history educator*

Oxford
Henry, Ronald James Whyte *university official*
Pearson, Paul Guy *university president emeritus*
Shriver, Phillip Raymond *university president*
Thompson, Bertha Boya *retired educator*

Richfield
†Berkey, Timothy B. *principal*

South Euclid
Loehr, Marla *college president*

Springfield
Dominick, Charles Alva *college official*
Kinnison, William Andrew *university president*
Reck, W(aldo) Emerson *retired university administrator, public relations consultant, writer*

Sugar Grove
Young, Nancy Henrietta Moe *elementary education educator*

Sylvania
Sampson, Earldine Robison *education educator*

Tiffin
Cassell, William Comyn *college president*

Toledo
Billups, Norman Fredrick *college dean, pharmacist*
Horton, Frank Elba *university official, geography educator*
Proefrock, Carl Kenneth *academic medical administrator*
Toadvin-Bester, Josephine Vesella *academic administrator, educator*

Upper Arlington
†Mincy, Homer F. *school system administrator*

Wellston
Lillich, Alice Louise *secondary education educator*

Westerville
DeVore, Carl Brent *college president, educator*
Willke, Thomas Aloys *university official, statistics educator*
Yoder, Amos *university research official*

Wilberforce
Svager, Thyrsa Anne Frazier *university administrator, retired educator*
Walker-Taylor, Yvonne *retired college president*

Wooster
Copeland, Henry Jefferson, Jr. *college president*
†Payne, Thomas L. *university official*
Weidensaul, Thomas Craig *university administrator, researcher*

Yellow Springs
Guskin, Alan E. *university president*

Youngstown
Cochran, Leslie Herschel *university administrator*
Coleman, Esther Mae Glover *educator*

Zanesville
Irvin, Helen Arlene *vocational education educator*

OKLAHOMA

Ardmore
†Thompson, John E. *principal*

Bethany
Leupp, Edythe Peterson *retired educator, administrator*

Durant
†Garrett, Scott *vocational school administrator*
Williams, Larry Bill *university president*

Edmond
Nigh, George *university administrator, former governor*
†Raburn, Randall K. *school system administrator*

Enid
Peck, Robert David *academic administrator, educator*

Lawton
†Reno, Jennifer *principal*

Miami
Lovell, James Frederick *academic administrator*

Norman
†Fears, Jesse Rufus *academic dean*
Hodgell, Murlin Ray *university dean*
Leonhardt, Thomas Wilburn *director library technical services, librarian*
Schindler, Barbara Francois *school administrator*
Sharp, Paul Frederick *former university president, educational consultant*
Van Horn, Richard Linley *university administrator*

Oklahoma City
Abram, Darlene Ruth Sheppard *educator, consultant*
Dunlap, E.T. *retired educational administrator, consultant*
†Garrett, Sandy Langley *school system administrator*
Holder, Lee *educator and university dean emeritus*
Johnson, James Terence *college president, lawyer, clergyman*
Johnson, Lonnie *special education educator*
Mason, Betty G(wendolyn) Hopkins *school system administrator*
Meeks, Patricia Lowe *secondary education educator*
Noakes, Betty L. *elementary education educator*
Smith, Clodus Ray *academic administrator*
Walker, Jerald Carter *university administrator, minister*
Wheat, Willis James *university dean, management educator*
Woods, Pendleton *college offical, author*

Pryor
†Burdick, Larry G. *school system administrator*

Shawnee
Agee, Bob R. *university president, educator, minister*

Stillwater
Boger, Lawrence Leroy *university president emeritus*
Browning, Charles Benton *university dean, agricultural educator*
Kamm, Robert B. *former academic administrator, educator, author, diplomat*
Mc Collom, Kenneth Allen *retired university dean*
Mc Farland, Frank Eugene *university official*
Sandmeyer, Robert Lee *university dean, economist*

Tulsa
Donaldson, Robert Herschel *university president*
Gaddis, Richard William *educational administrator, education consultant*
Knaust, Clara Doss *retired elementary educator*

Wanette
Thompson, Joyce Elizabeth *retired home economics educator*

OREGON

Ashland
Cox, Joseph William *academic administrator*
Kreisman, Arthur *higher education consultant, humanities educator emeritus*
Smith, G(odfrey) T(aylor) *academic administrator*

Astoria
Bainer, Philip La Vern *retired college president*

Bend
Wonser, Michael Dean *retired public affairs director, art educator*

Brookings
Olsen, Edward Gustave *education educator emeritus*

Corvallis
Byrne, John Vincent *academic administrator*
Davis, John Rowland *university administrator*
Horne, Frederick Herbert *academic administrator, chemistry educator*

Mac Vicar, Robert William *retired university administrator*
Parker, Donald Fred *college dean, human resources management educator*
Verts, Lita Jeanne *university administrator*
Young, Roy Alton *university administrator, educator*

Eugene
Frohnmayer, David Braden *university president*
Gall, Meredith Damien (Meredith Mark Damien Gall) *education educator, author*
†Hosticka, Carl Joseph *academic administrator, educator, legislator*
Reinmuth, James E. *college dean*
†Walker, Hill M. *educator*

Gresham
Light, Betty Jensen Pritchett *former college dean*

La Grande
Gilbert, David Erwin *university president, physicist*

Lake Oswego
Le Shana, David Charles *seminary president*

McMinnville
Goodrich, Kenneth Paul *college dean*
McGillivray, Karen *elementary school educator*
Walker, Charles Urmston *college administrator*

Medford
Bunten, John William *school system administrator*

Monmouth
Meyers, Richard Stuart *college president*

Portland
Bartlett, Thomas Alva *educational administrator*
Bennett, Douglas Carleton *academic administrator*
†Benson, George L. *school system administrator*
Blumel, Joseph Carlton *university president*
Frolick, Patricia Mary *educator*
Lawrence, Sally Clark *educational administrator*
Mooney, Michael Joseph *academic administrator, philosopher*
Qutub, Carol Hotelling *elementary education educator*
Ramaley, Judith Aitken *university president, endocrinologist*
Sherrer, Charles David *college dean, clergyman*
Terkla, Louis Gabriel *retired university dean*
†Zook, Ronald Z. *school system administrator*

Roseburg
Plummer, Charles McDonald *retired community college administrator*

Salem
†Bebe, Kathy *principal*
†Billman, Jennifer *elementsry school principal*
Hudson, Jerry E. *university president*
†Mack, Patricia *secondary school principal*

Sisters
Keppler, Donald John *secondary education educator*

Talent
McGill, Esby Clifton *former college official*

Tualatin
†Longaker, Nancy *elementary school principal*

PENNSYLVANIA

Allentown
Taylor, Arthur Robert *college president, business executive*

Allison Park
Jacobs, Daniel Kenneth *school system administrator*

Annville
McGill, William James, Jr. *academic administrator*
Synodinos, John Anthony *academic administrator*

Aston
Carroll, Claire Barry *special education educator*

Beaver
Helmick, Gayle Johnston *elementary education educator*

Bethlehem
Bergethon, Kaare Roald *educational consultant, former college president*
Likins, Peter William *university president*
Martin, Roger Harry *college president*

Bloomsburg
Vann, John Daniel, III *university administrator, historian*

Blue Bell
Brendlinger, LeRoy R. *college president*

Brownsville
Dryburg, Ann *secondary education educator*

Bryn Mawr
Lafarge, Catherine *dean*
McPherson, Mary Patterson *academic administrator*
Weese, Samuel H. *academic administrator*

Canonsburg
†Mascetta, Joseph Anthony *principal*

Carlisle
Fritschler, A. Lee *college president, public policy educator*

Center Valley
Gambet, Daniel G(eorge) *college president, clergyman*

Chester
Bruce, Robert James *university president*

Buck, Lawrence Paul *academic administrator*
Moll, Clarence Russel *university president emeritus, consultant*

Coatesville
†Strauser, Simeon John *academic administrator*

Collegeville
Richter, Richard Paul *academic administrator*

Connellsville
Sember, June Elizabeth *elementary education educator*

Cooperstown
Hogg, James Henry, Jr. *education educator*

Cranberry Township
Pond, Martin Allen *academic dean emeritus*

Cresson
Pierce, Edward Franklin *college president*

Dresher
Taddei, Edward P. *school system administrator*

Drexel Hill
†McAllister, Wayne R. *principal*

Eagles Mere
Sample, Frederick Palmer *former college president*

East Stroudsburg
Gilbert, James Eastham *academic administrator*

Edinboro
Cox, Clifford Laird *university administrator, musician*
Diebold, Foster Frank *university president*

Elizabethtown
Ritsch, Frederick Field *academic administrator, historian*

Erie
Lilley, John Mark *university provost and dean*

Exeter
Stocker, Joyce Arlene *retired secondary education educator*

Flourtown
Lambert, Joan Dorety *elementary education educator*

Glenside
Landman, Bette Emeline *academic administrator*

Greensburg
Boyle, JoAnne Woodyard *college president*

Greenville
Zimmer, Albert Arthur *education educator*

Grove City
MacKenzie, Charles Sherrard *college president*

Gwynedd Valley
†Feenane, Sister Mary Alice *principal*

Hanover
Bechtel, Jean Patricia *elementary education educator*

Harrisburg
McCormick, James Harold *academic administrator*

Haverford
Kessinger, Tom G. *college president*

Hazleton
†Gatty, Eugene B. *school system administrator*

Honesdale
Barbe, Walter Burke *education educator*

Horsham
†Strock, Gerald E. *school system administrator*
†Woodruff, Harrison D., Jr. *principal*

Huntingdon
Neff, Robert Wilbur *church official, educator*

Indiana
Pettit, Lawrence Kay *university president*
Thibadeau, Eugene Francis *educator, consultant*

Jenkintown
Baldwin, David Rawson *retired university administrator*

Johnstown
Alcamo, Frank Paul *retired educator*

Kennett Square
Nason, John William *retired college president, educational consultant*

King Of Prussia
Olexy, Jean Shofranko *English educator*

Kingston
Marko, Andrew Paul *school system administrator*

Knox
Rupert, Elizabeth Anastasia *retired university dean*

Kutztown
McFarland, David E. *university president*
Sunderland, Ray Thoburn *education educator, administrator*

Lancaster
Ebersole, Mark Chester *emeritus college president*
Ellis, Calvert N. *former college president*
Kneedler, Alvin Richard *university administrator*

Woods, Susanne *university dean*

Langhorne
Babb, Wylie Sherrill *college president*
Willis, Wesley Robert *college administrator*

Lansdale
†Baughn, Juan R. *high school principal*

Lock Haven
Almes, June *secondary education educator, librarian*
Willis, Craig Dean *university president*

Malvern
†Swymer, Stephen *principal*

Manchester
Owens, Marilyn Mae *art educator*

Manheim
Spangler, Daisy Kirchoff *educational consultant*

Media
†Dunlap, Richard Frank *school system administrator*

Mercersburg
†Burgin, Walter Hotchkiss, Jr. *educational administrator*

Millersville
Caputo, Joseph Anthony *university president*
Mallery, Anne Louise *elementary educator, consultant*
Taggie, Benjamin Fredrick *university official, educator*

Monroeville
Carney, Ann Vincent *secondary education educator*

Myerstown
Robson, Barbara S. *elementary education educator*
†Seilhamer, Ray A. *academic administrator*

New Hope
Knight, Douglas Maitland *educational administrator, optical executive*

New Wilmington
Deegan, John, Jr. *academic administrator, educator*
Remick, Oscar Eugene *college president*

Newry
Bradley, Audrey Laverne *educator*

Newtown
Selden, William Kirkpatrick *educational consultant*

Norristown
†Case, Andrew J. *educational administrator*

Philadelphia
†Andrisani, Paul J(oseph) *academic dean, academic administrator, business educator, management consultant*
Bates, James Earl *college president*
Blumberg, Baruch Samuel *academic administrator, research scientist*
Clayton, Constance *school system administrator*
Cohen, David Walter *university chancellor, periodontist, educator*
Cooke, Sara Mullin Graff *daycare provider, kindergarten teacher*
Cooperman, Barry S. *educational administrator, educator, scientist*
Delacato, Carl Henry *education educator*
Felts, George William, Sr. *special education educator*
Fisher, Marshall Lee *decision sciences director, educator*
Gerrity, Thomas P. *dean*
Hackney, Francis Sheldon *university president*
†Holloman, Margaret *elementary school principal*
Jackson, Doris Kelly *principal*
Keller, George Charles *academic administrator*
Lytle, Richard Harold *university administrator*
Mazzatenta, Rosemary Dorothy *school administrator*
Meyerson, Martin *university executive, educator*
Miller, Barry *academic administrator, psychologist*
Misher, Allen *college president*
Osborne, Frederick Spring, Jr. *academic administrator*
Padulo, Louis *university administrator*
Peirce, Donald Oluf *elementary education educator*
Rodin, Judith Seitz *academic administrator, educator*
Rumpf, John Louis *university official, civil engineer, educator*
Sheehan, Donald Thomas *university administrator*
†Sims, Armita B. *principal*
Smith, Robert Rutherford *university dean, communication educator*
Solmssen, Peter *university president*
Stevens, Rosemary A. *academic dean, public health and social history educator*
Sutman, Francis Xavier *university dean*
Sutnick, Alton Ivan *dean, educator, researcher, physician*
Wachman, Marvin *university chancellor*
Williams, Juanita Lundy *elementary education educator*
Wilson, Samuel Mack *university dean, educator*

Philipsburg
Reiter, Daisy K. *elementary education educator*

Phoenixville
Wright, Jean Norman *elementary education educator*

Pittsburgh
Christiano, Paul P. *academic administrator, civil engineering educator*
Cyert, Richard Michael *former university president, economist*
Ducanis, Alex Julius *education educator*
Eckert, Jean Patricia *elementary education educator*
Epperson, David Ernest *dean, educator*
Losacco, Lesley Herdt *supervisor, educator*
Martin, Bruce Douglas *university official, chemist*
Mc Anulty, Henry Joseph *university administrator*
Mehrabian, Robert *academic administrator*
O'Connor, John Dennis *chancellor, biology educator*
†Suzuki, Jon Byron *dean, periodontist, educator*

Van Dusen, Albert Clarence *university official*
Wallace, Richard Christopher, Jr. *school system administrator, educator*
Zoffer, H. Jerome *educator, university dean*

Rosemont
Reuschlein, Harold Gill *university dean*

Ruffs Dale
Slebodnik, Tressa Ann *elementary education educator*

Saint Davids
Baird, John Absalom, Jr. *college official*

Saltsburg
Pidgeon, John Anderson *headmaster*

Scranton
†Horton, Joseph Julian, Jr. *academic dean, educator*
Nee, Sister Mary Coleman *college president emeritus*
Panuska, Joseph Allan *university president*
Passon, Richard Henry *university administrator*
Reap, Sister Mary Margaret *college administrator*
Staff, Mary Clare *special education educator*

Shippensburg
Ceddia, Anthony Francis *university administrator*

Shiremanstown
Bouvier, Janet Laubach *educator*

Slippery Rock
Aebersold, Robert Neil *university president*

State College
Hoffa, Harlan Edward *retired university dean, art educator*

Swarthmore
Barr, Robert Alfred, Jr. *college dean*
Bloom, Alfred Howard *college president*

Uniontown
Foster, James Caldwell *academic dean, historian*

University Park
†Askov, Eunice May *education educator*
Dupuis, Victor Lionel *curriculum and instruction educator emeritus*
Filippelli, Ronald Lee *college dean, labor studies and industrial relations educator*
Hood, Lamartine Frain *college dean*
Humphrey, Arthur Earl *university administrator*
Larson, Russell Edward *university provost emeritus, consultant agriculture research and development*
Martorana, Sebastian Vincent *educational consultant*
†Rashid, Kamal A. *international programs director, educator*
Starling, James Lyne *university administrator*
Thomas, Joab Langston *academic administrator, biology educator*
Wartik, Thomas *chemistry educator, former college dean*

Upper Darby
†Apfel, Gail *principal*

Upper Saint Clair
†Dunkis, Patricia B. *principal*

Villanova
Dobbin, Edmund J. *university administrator*

Wallingford
†Rice, Robert H. *principal*

Washington
Burnett, Howard Jerome *college president*

Wernersville
Himmelberger, Richard Charles *vocational school educator*

West Chester
Yarosewick, Stanley J. *academic administrator, physicist*

Wilkes Barre
Breiseth, Christopher Neri *academic administrator*
Elias, Robert Gerald *educational administrator, educator*
Lackenmier, James Richard *college president, priest*
Olszewski, Laurence Michael *academic administrator*

Williamsport
Douthat, James Evans *college administrator*

Willow Street
Stright, I. Leonard *educational consultant*

Wyomissing
†Cellucci, Peter T. *principal*

Yardley
Elliott, Frank Nelson *retired college president*
Somma, Beverly Kathleen *English education educator*

RHODE ISLAND

Coventry
†Inman, Edward Salisbury, III *educator, state legislator*
†Spear, Raymond E. *school system administrator*

East Providence
†DeGoes, John V. *school system administrator*

Kingston
Carothers, Robert Lee *academic administrator*
Horn, Francis Henry *former educational administrator*
Youngken, Heber Wilkinson, Jr. *former university administrator, pharmacy educator*

Narragansett
Pouliot, Assunta Gallucci *business school owner and director*

North Kingstown
†Kondon, E. Jane *principal*

Providence
Cunningham, John Fabian *college president, philosophy educator*
Greer, David S. *university dean, physician, educator*
Gregorian, Vartan *academic administrator*
†Hawkins, Brian Lee *academic administrator, educator*
Mandle, Earl Roger *university president, former museum administrator*
McMahon, Eleanor Marie *education educator*
†Mueller, Frederick *principal*
Munir, Yusuf *vocational education administrator*
Nazarian, John *academic administrator, mathematics educator*
Salesses, John Joseph *university administrator*
Sizer, Theodore R. *education educator*

Riverside
†McElroy, Sister Maureen *secondary school principal*

Saunderstown
Donovan, Gerald Alton *retired academic administrator, former university dean*

Smithfield
Trueheart, William E. *academic administrator*

SOUTH CAROLINA

Aiken
Alexander, Robert Earl *university chancellor, educator*
Cowan, Carolyn Cannon *early childhood educator*

Anderson
†Woodward, Karen Callison *school system administrator*

Chapin
Branham, Mack Carison, Jr. *retired theological seminary executive, minister*

Charleston
Curtis, Marcia *university dean*
Edwards, James Burrows *university president, oral surgeon*
Grimsley, James Alexander, Jr. *university administrator, retired army officer*
Mc Devitt, Joseph Bryan *retired university administrator, retired naval officer*
Reilly, David Henry *university dean*
Smith, J. Roy *education educator*

Clemson
Lennon, A. Max *university administrator*
Vogel, Henry Elliott *retired university dean and physics educator*

Clinton
Orr, Kenneth Bradley *college president*

Columbia
†Aelion, C. Marjorie *educator*
Duffy, John Joseph *academic administrator, history educator*
Friedman, Myles Ivan *education educator*
Kay, Carol McGinnis *literature educator*
King, John Ethelbert, Jr. *education educator, former academic administrator*
Palms, John Michael *university president*
Splittgerber, Fredric Lee *education educator*
Waugh, John David *university administrator, engineering educator, consultant*

Conway
Sharples, D. Kent *college administrator*

Darlington
Samuel, Josie Harris *secondary educator*

Due West
Koonts, Jones Calvin *retired education educator*

Florence
Smith, Walter Douglas *retired college president*

Fort Mill
†Bonds, C. Joseph *school system administrator*

Greenville
Brown, Wilbur C. *college director*
Cloer, Carl Thomas, Jr. *education educator*
Hill, Grace Lucile Garrison *education educator, consultant*
Jones, Bob, Jr. *academic administrator, educator, lecturer, minister*
†Magill, Dodie Burns *early childhood education educator*
Payne, G(eorge) Frederick *educational director*
Smith, Philip Daniel *academic administrator, education educator*

Greenwood
Jackson, Larry Artope *retired college president*

Hartsville
Daniels, James Douglas *academic administrator*
Ingram, Gladys Almenas *secondary school educator*

Hilton Head Island
Mirse, Ralph Thomas *former college president*
Mulhollan, Paige Elliott *retired university president*

Kershaw
Lucas, Dean Hadden *educator*

Kiawah Island
Dyal, William M., Jr. *retired college president*

Laurens
Moncrief, James Loring *school principal*

Lexington
†Gatch, Charles Edward, Jr. *middle school principal*

Newberry
Bost, Raymond Morris *college administrator*

Spartanburg
†Glenn, Robert E. *elementary school principal*
Lesesne, Joab Mauldin, Jr. *college president*
Mc Gehee, Larry Thomas *university administrator*
Owens, Hilda Faye *academic administrator, management/leadership development consultant, human resource trainer*
Stephens, Bobby Gene *college administrator, consultant*

SOUTH DAKOTA

Aberdeen
Ehli, Gerald James *education educator*

Brookings
Bailey, Harold Stevens, Jr. *educational administrator, retired education admin*
Wagner, Robert Todd *university president, sociology educator*

Huron
Reynolds, R. John *university administrator*

Madison
Tunheim, Jerald Arden *academic administrator, physics educator*

Rapid City
Hughes, William Lewis *former university official, electrical engineer*
Schleusener, Richard August *college president*

Selby
†Akre, Donald J. *school system administrator*

Sioux Falls
Balcer, Charles Louis *college president emeritus, educator*
Huseboe, Doris Louise *college administrator, educator, arts consultant*
Johnson, Thomas Floyd *college president, educator*

Vermillion
Asher, Betty Turner *academic administrator*
Hazlett, James Stephen *university administrator*
Milton, Lynn Leonharda *elementary and secondary school educator*
†Struck, Judy Kay *special education specialist*

Wall
†Poppe, Kenneth C. *school system administrator*

TENNESSEE

Antioch
†Malone, Tom *bible college president*
†Wisehart, Mary Ruth *academic administrator*

Athens
†Wilson, Ben *elementary school principal*

Bristol
Anderson, Jack Oland *retired college official*
Cauthen, Charles Edward, Jr. *college president, former retail executive*

Chapel Hill
Christman, Luther Parmalee *university dean emeritus, consultant*

Chattanooga
Charlton, Shirley Marie *instructional supervisor*
Harris, Marquita Bolden *school librarian*
Obear, Frederick Woods *university chancellor*
†Tucker, Stanley R. *headmaster*

Clarksville
Carlin, James Boyce *elementary education educator, consultant*

Cleveland
†Gillum, Perry Eugene *college president, minister*

Columbia
Pryor, Harold S. *retired college president*

Cookeville
Hearn, Edell Midgett *university dean, teacher educator*
Peters, Ralph Martin *education educator*
Volpe, Angelo Anthony *university administrator, chemistry educator*

Dickson
†Thomas, Janey Sue *elementary school principal*

Dyersburg
†Nerren, George N. *school system administrator*
†Taylor, Billy D. *principal*

Franklin
†Brown, Joseph D. *school system administrator*

Gallatin
Ramer, Hal Reed *college president*

Johnson City
Alfonso, Robert John *university administrator*
Votaw, Charles Lesley *academic dean*

Kingston
Oran, Geraldine Ann *educator*

Knoxville
Armistead, Willis William *university administrator, veterinarian*
Boling, Edward Joseph *university president emeritus, educator*
Brockett, Ralph Grover *adult education educator*
Hall, O. Glen *university dean*
Nielsen, Alvin Herborg *university dean, physicist*
Prados, John William *educational administrator*

Louisville
Wheeler, George William *university provost, physicist, educator*

Martin
Smith, Robert Mason *university dean*

Memphis
Allison, Beverly Gray *seminary president, evangelism educator*
Carter, Michael Allen *college dean, nursing educator*
Dunathan, Harmon Craig *college dean*
Gourley, Dick R. *college dean*
Hunt, James Calvin *academic administrator, physician*
Mays, Penny Sandra *radiologic technologist, academic administrator*
Nesin, Jeffrey D. *academic administrator*
Ramsey, Marjorie Elizabeth *early childhood education educator*
Ranta, Richard Robert *university dean*
Wheeler, Orville Eugene *university dean, civil and mechanical engineering educator*
Young, Irma Jean *elementary education educator*

Murfreesboro
Berry, Mary Tom *education educator*
†Bookner, Becci Jane *school system administrator*
Hayes, Janice Cecile Osgard *education educator*
Huhta, James Kenneth *university official, historian, educator, consultant*

Nashville
Chapman, John Edmon *university dean, pharmacologist, physician*
Emans, Robert LeRoy *academic administrator, education educator*
Geisel, Martin Simon *college dean, educator*
Guthrie, James Williams *education educator*
Hamilton, Russell George, Jr. *academic dean, Spanish and Portuguese language educator*
Hefner, James A. *academic administrator*
†Kidd, Florence *principal*
Madden, Paul Herman *education educator*
Mc Murry, Idanelle Sam *educational consultant*
†Ponder, Henry *university president, economist*
†Whitefield, Anne C. *secondary school principal*
Wyatt, Joe Billy *university chancellor*

Oak Ridge
Thomas, John Edwin *retired university administrator*

Pulaski
Dowdy, Ronald Raymond *academic administrator*

Sewanee
Croom, Frederick Hailey *college administrator, mathematics educator*
Kepple, Thomas Ray, Jr. *college administrator*

Tullahoma
Collins, S. Ruth *education educator*

TEXAS

Abilene
Clayton, Lawrence Ray *university dean, literary critic, biographer*
Kim, Thomas Kunhyuk *college administrator*
Shimp, Robert Everett, Jr. *university administrator, historian*

Alpine
Morgan, Raymond Victor, Jr. *university administrator, mathematics educator*

Amarillo
Petty, John Ernest *education specialist, consultant*

Arlington
Pickard, Myrna Rae *college dean*
Sobol, Harold *research dean, retired communication equipment manufacturing executive*

Austin
Ayres, Robert Moss, Jr. *retired university president*
†Bartlett, Joe Michael *school system administrator*
Brewer, Thomas Bowman *retired university president*
Cannon, William Bernard *retired university educator*
Cardozier, Virgus Ray *higher education educator*
†Cleaves, Peter Shurtleff *academic administrator*
Cunningham, William Hughes *university chancellor, marketing educator*
†Dalton, Don *principal*
Francis, Bill Dean *university dean, artist*
Franklin, Billy Joe *international education consultant*
Franklin, G(eorge) Charles *academic administrator*
Frost, Joe Lindell *education educator*
Gill, Clark Cyrus *retired education educator*
Hall, Michael Garibaldi *education educator*
Harris, Ben Maxwell *education educator*
Hayes, Patricia Ann *university president*
Jeffrey, Robert Campbell *university dean*
Kennamer, Lorrin Garfield, Jr. *retired university dean*
†Livingston, William Samuel *university administrator, polital scientist*
Monti, Stephen Arion *university administrator, chemistry educator*
Rippey, Donald Taylor *education educator*
Rogers, Lorene Lane *university president emeritus*
Roueche, John Edward, II *education educator, leadership program director*

Beaumont
Brentlinger, William Brock *college dean*
†Gagne, Mary *secondary school principal*
Norton, James Adolphus *higher education administrator and consultant, retired academic administrator, political science educator*

Sethna, Beheruz Nariman *academic dean, marketing and management educator*

Belton
Parker, Bobby Eugene, Sr. *college president*

Brownsville
Garza, Roberto Jesus *education educator*
Santa-Coloma, Bernardo *secondary school educator, counselor*

Brownwood
Jarvis, Oscar T., Jr. *dean, education educator*

Bryan
Hubert, Frank William Rene *retired university system chancellor*

Carrollton
Grimes, Mary Woodworth *educational consultant*
†Maher, Sheila *secondary school principal*
Wilson, Douglas Larone *education consultant*

College Station
Adkisson, Perry Lee *university system chancellor*
Calhoun, John C., Jr. *academic administrator*
Carpenter, Delbert Stanley *educational administration educator*
Cocanougher, Arthur Benton *university dean, former business administration educator*
De Vaul, Richard Allan *medical school administrator*
Erlandson, David Alan *education administration educator*
Gage, E. Dean *university administrator*
Haden, Clovis Roland *university administrator, engineering educator*
Henry, Rene Arthur, Jr. *university official*
Knobel, Dale Thomas *university administrator*
Mobley, William Hodges *academic administrator*
Peddicord, Kenneth Lee *academic administrator*
Price, Alvin Audis *university administrator, educator emeritus*

Comanche
Droke, Edna Faye *elementary education educator*

Commerce
Morris, Jerry Dean *academic administrator*

Corpus Christi
Early, William James *education educator*
Furgason, Robert Roy *university official, chemical engineering educator*
Gutierrez, Arturo Luis *school system administrator*

Crowell
Binnion, John Edward *educator*

Dallas
Berkeley, Marvin H. *former university dean*
Campbell, Donald K. *theological seminary administrator, educator*
Cook, Gary Raymond *university president, clergyman*
DePaola, Dominick Philip *college president, dean*
Edwards, Marvin Earle *superintendent of schools*
Friedheim, Jan V. *education administrator*
Haayen, Richard Jan *university official, insurance company executive*
Harrison, Frank *former university president*
Hester, Linda Hunt *university dean, counselor*
†Leyden, Edward E. *secondary school principal*
†Prude, Elaine S. *principal*
Russell, S. G., III (Jacky Russell) *principal*
Swinton, Gwendolyn Delores *secondary education educator*
Walvoord, John Flipse *seminary president, chancellor, theologian*
Wenrich, John William *college president*

Denison
Farr, Reeta Rae *special education administrator*

Denton
Berry, Joe Wilkes *academic administrator, English educator*
Brownell, Blaine Allison *university administrator, history educator*
†Elder, Mark Lee *university research administrator, writer*
Hurley, Alfred Francis *university administrator, historian*
Palermo, Judy Hancock *art educator*
Swigger, B. Keith *dean*
Thompson, Leslie Melvin *college dean, educator*
Toulouse, Robert Bartell *retired college administrator*

Edinburg
Esparza, Thomas, Sr. *academic athletics administrator*
Mulhern, John David *former academic dean, educator*

El Paso
Bruhn, John Glyndon *university official, educator*
Coleman, Edmund Benedict *university dean*
Heger, Herbert Krueger *education educator*
Ingle, Henry Thomas *university official*
Natalicio, Diana Siedhoff *university president*
Riter, Stephen *university dean, electrical engineer*
Schmidt, L. Lee, Jr. *university official*
von Tungeln, George Robert *retired university administrator, economics consultant*

Floresville
Alvarez, Olga M. *elementary education educator*

Fort Worth
†Saenz, Michael *college president*
Tade, George Thomas *university dean*
Trimble, Wanda Nell *special education educator*
Tucker, William Edward *university chancellor, clergyman*

Galveston
Carrier, Warren Pendleton *retired university chancellor, writer*
Clayton, William Howard *retired university president*

Georgetown
Davis, O. L., Jr. *education educator, researcher*
Rosenthal, Michael Ross *academic administrator, dean*
Shilling, Roy Bryant, Jr. *college president*

Granbury
McWilliams, Chris Pater Elissa *social studies educator*

Grand Prairie
Scott, Dorothy Elaine *elementary education educator*

Hillsboro
Auvenshine, William R. *academic administrator*

Houston
Albrecht, Kay Montgomery *primary school educator, consultant, child advocate*
Anderson, Claire W. *computer gifted and talented educator*
Auston, David Henry *university administrator, educator*
Bailar, Benjamin Franklin *academic administrator, administration educator*
Berry, James Declois *special education and history educator*
Bizzell, Bobby Gene *academic administrator*
Butler, William Thomas *college president, physician, educator*
Carroll, Michael M. *academic dean, mechanical engineering educator*
Djerejian, Edward Peter *academic institute director, former diplomat*
Ferguson, Jennifer Lee Berry *education educator*
Georgiades, William Den Hartog *university dean*
†Gillis, Stephen Malcolm *academic administrator, economics educator*
†Hamilton, Phyllis *principal*
Hammack, Gladys Lorene Mann *reading specialist, educator*
Haynes, Karen Sue *university dean, social work educator*
Ho, Yhi-Min *university dean, economics educator*
Hodo, Edward Douglas *university president*
Hoffman, Philip Guthrie *former university president*
†Huang, Elsie Lee *principal*
Le Maistre, Charles Aubrey *university official, physician*
Lewis, Cleotrice O. Ney *elementary education educator*
†Lott, Thaddeus *principal*
Maddox, Iris Carolyn Clark *secondary education educator*
Mc Fadden, Joseph Michael *university president*
Meeks, Herbert Lessig, III *school system administrator*
Pickering, James Henry, III *university president*
Pinson, Artie Frances *elementary school educator*
†Quigg, Jean *principal*
Rice, Emily Joy *retired secondary and adult education educator*
†Sheehan, Linda Suzanne *educational administrator*
Thorne, Joye Holley *special education administrator*
Wagner, Paul Anthony, Jr. *education educator*
†Webb, Marty Fox *principal*
Weber, Wilford Alexander *education educator*
†Wilhelm, Marilyn *private school administrator*

Huntsville
Anisman, Martin Jay *academic administrator*
Warner, Laverne *education educator*

Hurst
Dodd, Sylvia Bliss *special education educator*
Kidwell, Georgia Brenner *elementary education educator*

Irving
Cannon, Francis V., Jr. *academic administrator, electrical engineer, economist*
Clark, Priscilla Alden *elementary education educator*
Martin, Thomas Lyle, Jr. *university president*
Perry, Charles Edward *university administrator*
Sasseen, Robert Francis *university president*
Walwer, Frank Kurt *university dean*

Kerrville
Holloway, Leonard Leveine *former university president*

Kingsville
Ibanez, Manuel Luis *university official, biological sciences educator*
Robins, Gerald Burns *education educator*

Laredo
Condon, Maria del Carmen *elementary education educator*

Lewisville
†Downing, Clayton W. *school system administrator*

Longview
LeTourneau, Richard Howard *retired college president*
†McMichael, Ronald L. *superintendent*

Lubbock
Askins, Billy Earl *education educator, consultant*
Curl, Samuel Everett *university dean, agricultural scientist*
Graves, Lawrence Lester *university dean emeritus*
Haragan, Donald Robert *university administrator, geosciences educator*
Lawless, Robert William *academic administrator*
Lemley, Steven Smith *academic administrator*
McManigal, Shirley Ann *university dean*

Mabank
Beets, Hughla Fae *retired educator*

Mesquite
Vaughan, Joseph Lee, Jr. *education educator, consultant*

Moody
McNiel, Norbert Arthur *retired educator*

Natalia
Wright, Douglas Ray *academic and vocational counselor*

New Braunfels
Dunn, Charlotte Valborg Lund *elementary education educator*

Odessa
Boyd, Claude Collins *education advisor*
Sorber, Charles Arthur *academic administrator*

Prairie View
Jones, Barbara Ann Posey *dean*

Presidio
Hill, Celia Ann *educator*

Rhome
Brammer, Barbara Rhudene *retired secondary education educator*

Richardson
Dunn, David E. *university dean*
Rutford, Robert Hoxie *university president*
†Wildenthal, Bryan Hobson *university administrator*

San Angelo
Davison, Elizabeth Jane Linton *education educator*
Vincent, Lloyd Drexell *university president*

San Antonio
Barrow, Charles Wallace *university dean*
†Boyers, John Martin *principal*
Calgaard, Ronald Keith *university president*
†Compton, Clinton E. *principal*
†Garcia, Linda *secondary school principal*
Gibbons, Robert Ebbert *university official*
Goelz, Paul Cornelius *university dean*
Henderson, Dwight Franklin *dean, educator*
Kelly, Mae Baker *secondary education educator*
Kirkpatrick, Samuel Alexander *university president, social and policy sciences educator*
Lackan, Siewchan *principal, school system administrator*
Langlinais, Joseph Willis *academic administrator*
Lee, William Franklin, III *association administrator*
Leies, John Alex *academic administrator, educator, clergyman*
Moder, John Joseph *academic administrator, priest*
Sueltenfuss, Sister Elizabeth Anne *university president*
Wood, Frank Preuit *educator, former air force officer*
Young, James Julius *university administrator, former army officer*

San Marcos
Bechtol, William Milton *education educator*
Byrom, Jack Edwards *educational administrator*
Moore, Betty Jean *retired education educator*
Supple, Jerome H. *university president*

Seguin
Oestreich, Charles Henry *college president*

Sherman
Page, Oscar C. *academic administrator*

Texarkana
Hill, Imogene Penton *school administrator*

The Woodlands
Topazio, Virgil William *university official*

Tyler
Davidson, Jack Leroy *academic administrator*

Waco
Belew, John Seymour *academic administrator, chemist*
Brooks, Roger Leon *university president*
Hillis, William Daniel *university administrator*

Webster
Lindner, Kenneth Edward *academic administrator and chemistry educator emeritus*

Wichita Falls
Rodriguez, Louis Joseph *university administrator*

UTAH

Altamont
†Evans, Beverly Ann *school administrator, state legislator*

Cedar City
Sherratt, Gerald Robert *college president*

Logan
Shaver, James Porter *education educator, university dean*

Ogden
McKell, Cyrus M. *college dean, plant physiologist*
†Protzman, Grant Dale *university administrator, state legislator*
Smith, Robert Bruce *college administrator*
Thompson, Paul Harold *university president*

Orem
Green, John Alden *university director study abroad program*
Plothow, Roger Henry *college official, consultant*

Provo
Allred, Ruel A. *education educator*
Hafen, Bruce Clark *academic administrator*
Jensen, Clayne R. *university administrator*
Lee, Rex E. *university president, lawyer*
Smoot, Leon Douglas *university dean, chemical engineering educator*
Stahmann, Robert F. *education educator*
Strasser, William Carl, Jr. *retired college president, educator*

Saint George
†Peterson, Steven H. *school system administrator*

Salt Lake City
Drew, Clifford James *academic dean, special education and educational psychology educator*
Jarvis, Joseph Boyer *retired university administrator*
McCleary, Lloyd E(verald) *education educator*
Peterson, Chase N. *university president*
Smith, Arthur Kittredge, Jr. *university official, political science educator*

West Jordan
†Shepherd, Paul H. *elementary school educator*

VERMONT

Bennington
Coleman, Elizabeth *college president*

Burlington
†Della Santa, Laura *principal*

Colchester
Reiss, Paul Jacob *college president*

Fair Haven
†Pentkowski, Raymond J. *superintendent*

Lyndon Center
Myers, Rex Charles *academic dean*

Lyndonville
Williams, Peggy Ryan *academic administrator*

Manchester
Fellows, Diana Potenzano *educational administrator*

Middlebury
McCardell, John Malcolm, Jr. *college administrator*
O'Brien, George Dennis *university president, retired*

Montpelier
Brandenburg, Richard George *university dean, management educator*

Northfield
Schneider, Richard William *university president*

Saint Johnsbury
†Mayo, Bernier L. *secondary school principal*

South Burlington
Kenyon, Judith *primary school educator*

South Royalton
Kempner, Maximilian Walter *law school dean, lawyer*

Waterbury
Bunting, Charles I. *academic administrator*

White River Junction
Halperin, George Bennett *education educator, retired naval officer*

VIRGINIA

Alexandria
Foster, Luther Hilton *former university president, educational consultant*
Johnson, William David *retired university administrator*
Rice, Sue Ann *education administrator, industrial and organizational psychologist*
Whitney, Marvin Edward *adult education educator*
Woods, John LaRue *international education consultant*

Arlington
Bartlett, Elizabeth Susan *audio-visual specialist*
Berg, Sister Marie Majella *university chancellor*
Boek, Walter Erwin *university president, educator, anthropologist, scientist*
Houston, Paul David *school association administrator*
Hu, Sue King *middle school educator*
John, Martha Tyler *dean, education educator*
Lane, Neal Francis *university provost, physics researcher, federal administrator*
Moore, John Hampton *academic administrator*
Peterson, Paul Quayle *retired university dean, physician*

Ashland
†Baker, Stephen M. *school system administrator*
Henshaw, William Raleigh *middle school educator*
Payne, Ladell *college president*

Blacksburg
Brown, Gregory Neil *university administrator, forest physiology educator*
Carlisle, Ervin Frederick *university provost*
Smith, Robert McNeil *university dean*
Steger, Charles William *university administrator*

Bridgewater
Geisert, Wayne Frederick *retired college president*

Charlottesville
Beard, Richard Leonard *education educator emeritus*
Brandt, Richard Martin *education educator*
Carey, Robert Munson *university dean, physician*
Casteen, John T., III *university administrator*
Cooper, James Michael *academic dean, education educator*
Corse, John Doggett *university official, lawyer*
Lankford, Francis Greenfield, Jr. *education educator emeritus*
Miller, Joseph Calder *academic dean, historical consultant, editor*
O'Neil, Robert Marchant *university administrator, law educator*
Perry, Marvin Banks, Jr. *retired college president*
Reynolds, Robert Edgar *academic administrator, physician*
Stenberg, Carl W(aldamer), III *academic program director, educator*

Thompson, Kenneth W(infred) *educational director, author, editor, administrator, social science educator*

Chesapeake
Dickson, Suzanne Elizabeth (Sue Dickson) *primary school educator*

Chesterfield
Copeland, Jean Parrish *school system administrator, school board executive*
Wilson, Dorothy Ann *retired special education educator*

Evington
Fortune, Laura Catherine Dawson *elementary educator*

Fairfax
†Field, Joanne T. *school board executive*
Johnson, George William *university president*

Falls Church
Boucouvalas, Marcie *adult education educator*
Cleland, Sherrill *college president*

Farmville
Dorrill, William Franklin *academic administrator, political scientist, educator*

Fort Defiance
Livick, Malcolm Harris *school administrator*

Hampton
Hightower, John Brantley *arts administrator*
Patty, Anna Christine *middle school educator*

Harrisonburg
Carrier, Ronald Edwin *university administrator*
Lemish, Donald Lee *university athletics director*
Pettus, Alvin Morris *program administrator*

Haysi
Deel, George Moses *elementary education educator*

Lexington
Badgett, Lee Douglas *academic administrator*
Knapp, John Williams *college president*
Watt, William Joseph *academic administrator, chemistry educator*

Mc Lean
Groennings, Sven Ole *academic administrator, higher education educator, corporate executive*

Midlothian
Sanders, Helen Caravas *art educator*

Newport News
Santoro, Anthony Richard *academic administrator*

Norfolk
Etheridge, James Edward, Jr. *academic administrator, pediatrics educator*
Jones, Franklin Ross *education educator*
Koch, James Verch *academic administrator, economist*
Myers, Donald Allen *university dean*
Wallace, William Hall *academic dean, educator, economist*
Winslow, Janet Lucas *elementary education educator*

Petersburg
Berry, Lemuel, Jr. *academic dean, music educator*

Poquoson
Yard, Rix Nelson *former athletic director*

Portsmouth
Trumble, Richard Dwain *superintendent of schools, consultant*

Quantico
Wallenborn, Janice Rae *elementary education educator*

Reston
Waxman, Pearl Latterman *early childhood educator*

Richmond
Ackell, Edmund Ferris *university president*
Brush, Carey Wentworth *retired college administrator, history educator*
Hamel, Dana Bertrand *academic administrator*
Heilman, E. Bruce *academic administrator*
James, Allix Bledsoe *retired university president*
Modlin, George Matthews *university chancellor emeritus*
Morrill, Richard Leslie *university administrator*
Savage, William Woodrow *education educator*
Simmons, S. Dallas *university president*
Trani, Eugene Paul *university president, educator*
Watts, Daniel Thomas *university dean, pharmacologist*

Roanoke
Johns, Dolores Yuille *educational administrator*
†Tota, Frank Peter *school system administrator*

Salem
Gring, David M. *academic administrator*

South Hill
Brooks, Arlene Sheffield *secondary education educator*

Sweet Briar
Hill, Barbara Ann *academic administrator, consultant*

Urbanna
Salley, John Jones *university administrator, oral pathologist*

Vienna
Jackson, Juanita Wallace *educational consultant*

Virginia Beach
Barriskill, Maudanne Kidd *primary school educator*
Wiggins, Samuel Paul *education educator*

Williamsburg
Birney, Robert Charles *retired academic administrator, psychologist*
Edwards, Jack Donald *education educator*
Geoffroy, Kevin Edward *education educator*
Mc Kean, John Rosseel Overton *university dean*

Winchester
Tisinger, Catherine Anne *college dean*

Wise
Ellsworth, Lucius Fuller *academic administrator*
Smiddy, Joseph Charles *retired college chancellor*

Woodbridge
Breene, Norma Wylie *special education educator*

WASHINGTON

Auburn
†Lapinski, Donald *elementary school principal*

Bellevue
Clark, Richard Walter *educator, consultant*

Bellingham
†DeLorme, Roland L. *director, headmaster*
Morse, Karen Williams *academic administrator*
Pierce, George Adams *university administrator, educator*

Bothell
Icenhower, Rosalie B. *retired elementary school principal*

Centralia
Kirk, Henry Port *academic administrator*

Ellensburg
Moore, Thomas David *academic administrator*

Fairchild AFB
Munn, Eufemia Tobias *elementary school principal*

Grandview
Ferguson, Bettie Jean *secondary education educator*

Kent
†Johnson, Dennis D. *elementary school principal*
†Kelly, Patrick *school system administrator*

Kirkland
Ayars, Albert Lee *former school superintendent*

Lacey
Cosand, Joseph Parker, Jr. *education educator emeritus*
Spangler, David Robert *college administrator, engineer*

Lake Spokane
Payne, Arlie Jean *parent education administrator*

Lynnwood
†Benzel, Brian L. *superintendent*

Port Angeles
Chase, John David *university dean, physician*
Ross, Robert King *retired educator*

Port Townsend
†Lamoreaux, Joyce *educational institute executive*

Pullman
Markin, Rom J. *college dean, marketing educator, academic administrator*
Smith, Robert Victor *university administrator*
Smith, Samuel Howard *university president, plant pathologist*

Renton
Tajon, Encarnacion Fontecha (Connie Tajon) *retired educator, association executive*

Richland
†Piippo, Steve *educational program director*
†Ryans, Yvonne *principal*

Seattle
Banks, James Albert *educational research director, educator*
Bassett, Edward Powers *university official*
Bowen, Jewell Ray *academic dean, chemical engineering educator*
†Brown, Kristi *principal*
Carlson, Dale Arvid *university dean*
Cox, Frederick Moreland *retired university dean, social worker*
Debro, Julius *university dean, sociology educator*
Denny, Brewster Castberg *retired university dean*
Fialkow, Philip Jack *academic administrator, medical educator*
Funk, Robert Norris *college president, lawyer*
Gerberding, William Passavant *university president*
Gibaldi, Milo *university dean*
Goodlad, John Inkster *education educator, author*
Hunkins, Francis Peter *education educator*
Jennerich, Edward John *university official and dean*
†Matheson, Kent D. *school system administrator*
Michalik, John James *law school administrator*
Omenn, Gilbert Stanley *university dean, physician*
Sullivan, William James *university president*
Terrell, W(illiam) Glenn *university president emeritus*
†Tracy, Mary E. *principal*

Sequim
Barton, Jay *university administrator, biologist*

Spokane
†Hester, Gerald LeRoy *retired school system administrator*
Matters, Clyde Burns *former college president*

Tacoma
Edington, Robert Van *university official*
Jungkuntz, Richard Paul *university provost emeritus*
King, Gundar Julian *retired university dean*
Minnerly, Robert Ward *headmaster*
Pierce, Susan Resneck *academic administrator, English educator*
Wills, J. Robert *academic administrator, drama educator, writer*

Vancouver
Ferguson, Larry Emmett *educational administrator*
Mangino, Kristin Mikalson *secondary education educator*

Washougal
†Schorzman, Clarice B. *principal*

Yakima
Hornstein, Pamela Kathleen *educational administrator, educator*

WEST VIRGINIA

Athens
Marsh, Joseph Franklin, Jr. *emeritus college president, educational consultant*

Bethany
Cummins, Delmer Duane *academic administrator, historian*
Sandercox, Robert Allen *college official, clergyman*

Charleston
†Coe, Pam *educational researcher*
Welch, Edwin Hugh *academic administrator*

Clarksburg
†Kittle, Robert Earl *school system administrator*

Clay
†Dawson, James G. *superintendent*
†Gillespie, Larry *secondary school principal*

Dellslow
Allamong, Betty D. *academic administrator*

Dunbar
Russell, James Alvin, Jr. *college administrator*

Elkins
MacConkey, Dorothy I. *academic administrator*

Fairmont
Hardway, Wendell Gary *former college president*
Stalder, Florence Lucille *educator*
Wedge, Dorothy Ann *education educator*

Herndon
Garretson, Richard A. *principal*

Huntington
Gould, Alan Brant *academic administrator*
Hayes, Robert Bruce *former college president, educator*
Hooper, James William *educator*
Kent, Calvin Albert *university administrator*

Morgantown
Biddington, William Robert *university administrator, dental educator*
Brooks, Dana D. *dean*
Bucklew, Neil S. *university president*
Jackson, Ruth Moore *academic administrator*
LaBelle, Thomas Jeffrey *academic administrator*
†Maxwell, Robert Haworth *college dean*
Stewart, Guy Harry *university dean emeritus, journalism educator*

Nitro
Lucas, Panola *elementary educator*

Philippi
Sizemore, William Christian *college president*

Salem
Ohl, Ronald Edward *academic administrator*

Shepherdstown
Riccards, Michael Patrick *academic administrator*

Squire
Dishman, Roberta Crockett *retired educator*

Wellsburg
Price, Verla Blanche *elementary education educator*

West Liberty
Campbell, Clyde Del *academic administrator*

WISCONSIN

Appleton
Warch, Richard *university president*

Ashland
Parsonage, Robert Rue *college president*

Beloit
Ferrall, Victor Eugene, Jr. *college administrator, lawyer*

Brookfield
Jenkins, William Atwell *university chancellor*

Cleveland
Butler, Robin Erwin *vocational technical educator*

Cross Plains
Rodenschmit, Helen Juliana *elementary education educator*

De Pere
Manion, Thomas A. *college president*

Eau Claire
Dunlap, William Phillip *dean*
Richards, Jerry Lee *academic administrator, religious educator*
Schnack, Larry Gene *university chancellor*

Elkhorn
Reinke, Doris Marie *retired elementary education educator*

Fish Creek
Abegg, Martin Gerald *retired university president*

Fond Du Lac
Henken, Willard John *retired university dean*

Glendale
†Moeser, Elliott *principal*

Green Bay
†Gariepy, Corinne *elementary school principal*
Outcalt, David Lewis *academic administrator, mathematician, educator*

Hales Corners
Michalski, (Żurowski) Wacław *adult education educator*

Kenosha
Campbell, F(enton) Gregory *college administrator, historian*

La Crosse
Medland, William James *college president*

Lake Nebagamon
Meyer, Karl William *retired university president*

Madison
Bernstine, Daniel O'Neal *law educator, university dean*
Busby, Edward Oliver *former dean*
Ebben, James Adrian *college president*
Lemberger, August Paul *university dean, pharmacy educator*
Lyall, Katharine C(ulbert) *academic administrator, economics educator*
McCarty, Donald James *education educator*
Mitby, Norman Peter *college president*
Netzer, Lanore A(gnes) *retired educational administration educator*
†Odden, Allan Robert *education educator*
Policano, Andrew J. *university dean*
Simone, Beverly S. *academic administrator*
†Taylor, Carolyn L. *principal*
Vowles, Richard Beckman *educator*
†Ward, David *academic administrator, educator*
Wedemeyer, Charles A. *educator*
Weiss, Mareda Ruth *university administrator*
Wermers, Donald Joseph *registrar*
Witiak, Donald Theodore *academic dean, medicinal chemistry educator*
Yuill, Thomas MacKay *university administrator, microbiology educator*

Menasha
†Decker, William Joseph *superintendent*
Gorsalitz, Jeannine Liane *elementary school educator*

Mequon
Buuck, R(oland) John *university president*
†Watson-Boone, Rebecca A. *educator*

Milton
Hosler, Russell John *retired education educator*

Milwaukee
Aman, Mohammed Mohammed *university dean, library and information science educator*
Davis, Thomas William *college administrator, electrical engineering educator*
DiUlio, Albert Joseph *university president, priest*
Halloran, William Frank *university dean*
†Hatton, Janie R. Hill *principal*
Hollenbach, Sister Ruth *college president*
Keulks, George William *university dean, chemistry educator*
Raynor, John Patrick *university administrator*
Read, Sister Joel *college administrator*
Reid, Robert Lelon *college dean, mechanical engineer*
Sankovitz, James Leo *director of development, lobbyist*
Schenker, Eric *university dean, economist*
Schmitz, Dolores Jean *educator*
Schroeder, John H. *university administrator, history educator*
Spann, Wilma Nadene *principal*
Spitzer, Robert Ralph *academic administrator emeritus*
Szmanda, Lucille Marie *vocational school educator*
Viets, Hermann *college president, consultant*

New Franken
Weidner, Edward William *university chancellor, political scientist*

New London
Fitzgerald, Laurine Elisabeth *university dean, educator*

Oconomowoc
Reich, Rose Marie *retired art educator*

Platteville
Al Yasiri, Kahtan Abbass *college dean*

Richland Center
Meyer, Edwin Dale, Sr. *school system administrator*

Ripon
Stott, William Ross, Jr. *college president*

River Falls
Thibodeau, Gary A. *university administrator*

Sheboygan
†Brewer, Warren Wesley *principal*
†Longo, George P. *superintendent*

Silver Lake
Hellum, Perry K. *school system administrator*

Stevens Point
Sanders, Keith R. *university chancellor*
Stevens, Dwight Marlyn *educational administrator*

Twin Lakes
Fleischer, John Richard *secondary education educator*

Walworth
Sissons, John Roger *educational administrator*

Waukesha
Falcone, Frank S. *college president*

West Bend
Karpowitz, Anthony Victor *college dean emeritus*
Rodney, Joel Morris *dean*

Whitewater
Schallenkamp, Kay *college administrator*

WYOMING

Afton
†Lowe, James Allen *school superintendent*

Cheyenne
Ohman, Diana J. *school system administrator*

Cody
†Shreve, Peg *educator*

Laramie
Roark, Terry Paul *university president*

Rawlins
†Vasey, William Joseph *director college outreach program, state legislator*

Rock Springs
†Baumberger, Don R. *school system administrator*

TERRITORIES OF THE UNITED STATES

AMERICAN SAMOA

Pago Pago
Faleali'i, Logoleo T. V. *educational services administrator*
Varghese, Mary *secondary education educator*

GUAM

Agana
†Lee, Chin-Tian *academic administrator, agricultural studies educator*

PUERTO RICO

Adjuntas
†Altieri Rosado, José Aníbal *principal*

Coto Laurel
†Basols, Jose Andres *high school director and principal, priest*

Humacao
Castrodad, Felix A. *university administrator*

Rio Piedras
Santiago, Juan Jose *secondary school president*

San Juan
Carreras, Francisco José *former university president, foundation executive*
Gonzalez, Jose Ramón *academic administrator*
Matheu, Federico Manuel *university chancellor*
Thompson, Annie Figueroa *academic director, educator*

VIRGIN ISLANDS

Christiansted
Gardine, Juanita Constantia Forbes *educator*

MILITARY ADDRESSES OF THE UNITED STATES

PACIFIC

APO
Mondale, Joan Adams *wife of former vice president of U.S.*

FPO
Gilley, Edward Ray *school system administrator*

CANADA

ALBERTA

Calgary
Maher, Peter Michael *university dean*
Neale, E(rnest) R(ichard) Ward *retired university official, consultant*
Rasporich, Anthony Walter *university dean*
Thomlison, Ray J. *university dean, educator*
Watanabe, Mamoru *former university dean, physician, researcher*

Edmonton
Adams, Peter Frederick *university president, civil engineer*
Berg, Roy Torgny *retired university dean*
Davenport, Paul *university administrator, economics educator*

BRITISH COLUMBIA

Cobble Hill
Cox, Albert Reginald *academic administrator, physician, retired*

Kelowna
†Muggeridge, Derek Brian *dean, engineering consultant*

Sooke
Booth, Andrew Donald *former university administrator, scientist*

Vancouver
Andrews, John Hobart McLean *education educator*
Finnegan, Cyril Vincent *retired university dean, zoology educator*
Haycock, Kenneth Roy *education administrator*
Lusztig, Peter Alfred *university dean, educator*
McNeill, John Hugh *university dean*
Webber, William Alexander *university administrator, physician*

Victoria
McTaggart-Cowan, Ian *retired university chancellor*
Strong, David F. *university administrator*
Welch, S(tephen) Anthony *university dean, Islamic studies and arts educator*

MANITOBA

Winnipeg
Naimark, Arnold *university president, physiologist, internist*
Poettcker, Henry *retired seminary president*
Stalker, Jacqueline D'Aoust *academic administrator, educator*

NEW BRUNSWICK

Fredericton
Armstrong, Robin Louis *university official, physicist*
†Edwards, Viviane M. *educator, editor*

NOVA SCOTIA

Halifax
MacLean, Guy Robertson *retired university president*
Murray, Thomas John (Jock Murray) *former dean of medicine, medical humanities educator*
Ozmon, Kenneth Lawrence *university president, educator*

Timberlea
†Verma, Surjit K. *school system administrator*

Truro
Mac Rae, Herbert Farquhar *retired college president*

ONTARIO

Brampton
†VanDeventer, Vernon Earl *dean*

Hamilton
Shaw, Denis Martin *university dean, former geology educator*
Taylor, James Hutchings *chancellor, retired diplomat*

Kingston
†Turpin, David Howard *dean*

Mississauga
Evans, John Robert *former university president, physician*

North York
Macdonald, Hugh Ian *university president emeritus, economist, educator*

Ottawa
Malouin, Jean-Louis *university dean, educator*
Philogene, Bernard J. R. *academic administrator, science educator*

Peterborough
Theall, Donald Francis *retired university president*

Saint Catharines
White, Terrence Harold *academic administrator, sociologist*

Thunder Bay
Locker, J. Gary *university official, civil engineering educator*
Rosehart, Robert George *university president, chemical engineer*

Toronto
Korey-Krzeczowski, George J. M. Kniaz *university administrator, management consultant*
Kushner, Eva *academic administrator, educator, author*
Prichard, John Robert Stobo *academic administrator, law educator*
Sessle, Barry John *university administrator, researcher*

Waterloo
Berczi, Andrew Stephen *academic administrator*
Carty, Arthur John *university dean*
Downey, James *university president*
†Kay, Jeanne *dean, educator*
Wright, Douglas Tyndall *former university president, company director, engineering educator*

Willowdale
MacDonald, Brian Scott *educational administrator*

Windsor
Ianni, Ronald William *university president and vice chancellor, lawyer*

PRINCE EDWARD ISLAND

Charlottetown
Eliot, Charles William John *university president, educator*

QUEBEC

Montreal
Belanger, Pierre Rolland *university dean, electrical engineering educator*
Cloutier, Gilles Georges *academic administrator, research executive*
Davidson, Colin Henry *university educator*
Freedman, Samuel Orkin *university official*
French, Stanley George *university dean, philosophy educator*
Granger, Luc Andre *university dean, psychologist*
Johnston, David Lloyd *academic administrator, lawyer*
Lajeunesse, Marcel *university administrator, educator*

Quebec
Gervais, Michel *academic administrator*

Saint-Hubert
†Doré, Roland *dean, science association director*

Sainte Anne de Bellevue
Buckland, Roger Basil *university dean, educator, vice principal*

Sainte-Foy
Montgrain, Noël *academic administrator*
Murray, Warren James *educator, philosopher*

Westmount
McIlhone, John Thomas *educational administrator*

SASKATCHEWAN

Regina Beach
Barber, Lloyd Ingram *retired university president*

Saskatoon
Knight, Arthur Robert *technical institute administrator*
Knott, Douglas Ronald *college dean, agricultural sciences educator, researcher*
McCallum, Kenneth James *retired university dean, chemistry and chemical engineering educator*
Nikiforuk, Peter N. *university dean*
Stewart, John Wray Black *college dean*

CHILE

Concepción
Trzebiatowski, Gregory L. *education educator*

Santiago
†Strommen, Clifford H. *headmaster*

EGYPT

Cairo
Miller, Harry George *education educator*

ENGLAND

Milton Keynes
Daniel, John Sagar *academic administrator, metallurgist*

Surrey
Petrek, William Joseph *college president emeritus*

GREECE

Halandri
†Dorbis, John *school system administrator*

THAILAND

Bangkok
Stueart, Robert D. *college dean, librarian, educator*

TURKMENISTAN

Ashgabat
McCall, John Patrick *college president, educator*

ADDRESS UNPUBLISHED

Allen, Charles Eugene *college administrator, agriculturist*
Alligood, Elizabeth H. *special education educator*
Almen, Louis Theodore *retired college president*
Altshuler, Alan Anthony *dean, political scientist*
†Archetto, Paul Henry *secondary education educator, state legislator*
Armacost, Mary-Linda Sorber Merriam *college president*
Armstrong, Warren Bruce *university president, historian, educator*
Atkinson, Dewey Franklin *retired educational administrator*
Babbitt, Samuel Fisher *university administrator*
Baker, Margery Louise *elementary education educator*
Baker, Robert M. L., Jr. *academic administrator*
Baldwin, C. Andrew, Jr. *retired science educator*
Banner, Larry Shyres *educator, athlete, consultant*
Barone, John Anthony *university provost emeritus*
Bassist, Donald Herbert *academic administrator*
Baxter, Cecil William, Jr. *retired college president*
Becker, Walter Heinrich *vocational school educator*
Bell, Terrel Howard *education educator*
Benton, Robert Dean *retired university dean*
Bergman, Hermas John (Jack Bergman) *retired college administrator*
Beveridge, James MacDonald Richardson *former college president*
Beyer, La Vonne Ann *special education educator*
Bishop, Charles Edwin *university president emeritus, economist*
Blomberg, Susan Ruth *training executive*
Boeker, Paul Harold *academic official, diplomat*
Borchers, Mary Amelia *middle school educator*
Boucher, Laurence James *university dean, chemist*
Brain, George Bernard *university dean*
Brammer, Elizabeth Hedwig *administrator*
Brand, Myles *academic administrator*
Branyan, Robert Lester *retired university administrator*
Bright, Harold Frederick *university provost emeritus, consultant*
Brown, David Grant *university president*
Burroughs, Franklin Troy *academic administrator*
Cameron, J. Elliot *retired parochial educational system administrator*
Cameron, Lucille Wilson *retired dean of libraries*
Carter, Herbert Edmund *former university official*
Casper, Gerhard *academic administrator, law educator*
Chandler, John Herrick *college president*
Chase, James Richard *college official*
Chyu, Chi-Oy Wei *educator*
Clark, Claudia J. *educational administration, speech, language and learning disabilities professional*
Clarke, Lambuth McGeehee *college president emeritus*
Coffee, Joseph Denis, Jr. *college chancellor emeritus*
Collier, Herman Edward, Jr. *retired college president*
Compton, Norma Haynes *retired university dean*
Connell, George Edward *university president, scientist*
Cramer, Robert Vern *retired college president, director scholarship program, consultant*
Crawford, Kenneth Charles *educational institute executive, retired government official*
Crook, Jacquelyn Elaine Terry *elementary education educator, librarian*
Curry, Nancy Ellen *education educator, psychoanalyst, psychologist*
Davenport, Ernest Harold *university official, accountant*
Davenport, Lawrence Franklin *school system administrator*
Davis, Anna Jane Ripley *elementary education educator*
Davison, Beaumont *retired university administrator*
Debs, Barbara Knowles *academic administrator*
DeGray, Thomas Alan *private school educator*
Denton, David Edward *retired education educator*
Dobler, Donald William *retired college dean, consultant, corporate executive*
Dorsey, Rhoda Mary *academic administrator, retired*
Duff, John Bernard *college president, former city official*
Dunworth, John *retired college president*
†Dutson, Thayne R. *university dean*
Faherty, Patricia Bernadette *secondary education educator*
Farley, Lloyd Edward *education educator*
Farquhar, Robin Hugh *university president*
Feldstein, Joshua *academic administrator*
Ferguson, Glenn Walker *university president*
Fernandez-Arrondo, Maria del Carmen *secondary education educator*
Fife, Jonathan Donald *higher education educator*
Filchock, Ethel *education educator, poet*
Freeman, Meredith Norwin *former college president, education educator*
Frick, Ivan Eugene *college president emeritus*
Frierson, Jimmie Lou *vocational education educator*
Gaspar, Anna Louise *retired elementary school teacher, consultant*
Geiselhart, Lorene Annetta *elementary education educator*
Gillespie, Nellie Redd *state official, academic administrator*
Glower, Donald Duane *university executive, mechanical engineer*
Goewey, Gordon Ira *university administrator*
Good, Linda Lou *elementary education educator*
Goode, Janet Weiss *primary and secondary educator*
Gordis, David Moses *academic administrator, rabbi*
Gore, Sadie Lou *elementary education educator*
Gregory, Myra May *educator, religious organization administrator*
Gudnitz, Ora M. Cofey *secondary school educator*
Hammer, Joyce Mae *gifted and talented education educator*
Hankins, Mary Denman *elementary school educator*
Hansbury, Vivien Holmes *educator*
Hardin, Clifford Morris *retired university chancellor, retired executive*
Hardin, Paul, III *chancellor*
Harrington, Jean Patrice *former college president*
Hasselmo, Nils *university official, linguistics educator*
†Heck, Larry Jack *vocational school administrator, state legislator*
Hegarty, George John *university administrator, English educator*
Helman, Alfred Blair *retired college president, education consultant*
Helton, Thelma Ann *elementary education educator*
Heskett, Luvina Hylton *elementary education educator*
Hitchcock, Walter Anson *educational consultant, retired educational administrator*
Hoi, Samuel Chuen-Tsung *dean*
Holgate, George Jackson *university president*
Horner, Matina Souretis *retired college president, corporate executive*
Hughes, Eugene Morgan *university president*
Huttenback, Robert Arthur *academic administrator, educator*
Jakubauskas, Edward Benedict *college president*
John, Ralph Candler *retired college president, educator*
Johnson, Everett Ramon *retired college dean*
Jones, Lawrence Neale *university dean, minister*
†Karahalios, Sue M. Compton *secondary education educator*
Karls, John B. *retired educational administrator*
Keiper, Marilyn Morrison *educator*
Kerins, Francis Joseph *college president*
Kersting, Edwin Joseph *retired university dean*
Kliebhan, Sister M(ary) Camille *academic administrator*
Knight, Janet Ann *elementary education educator*
Knox, Ernest Rudder *retired college president*
Koenig, Allen Edward *higher education consultant*
Komisar, David Daniel *retired university provost*
Kormondy, Edward John *university official, biology educator*
Krey, Robert Dean *education educator emeritus*
Kristensen, Marlene *early childhood educator*
Kruck, Donna Jean *special education educator, consultant*
Kushinka, Joyce Williams *secondary education educator*
Langworthy, William Clayton *college official*
Lantz, Joanne Baldwin *university chancellor emerita*
Lawrence, Linda Hiett *writer, administrator*
Leal, Herbert Allan Borden *former university chancellor, former government official*
Leighton, David Struan Robertson *retired education educator*
Lennon, Joseph Luke *college official, priest*
Lester, Virginia Laudano *educational director*
Leventhal, Robert Stanley *academic administrator*
Lindegren, Jack Kenneth *educator*
Lipscomb-Brown, Edra Evadean *retired childhood educator*
Lockwood, Theodore Davidge *former academic administrator*
Lomas, Bernard Tagg *college president emeritus*
Loser, Joseph Carlton, Jr. *law school dean, retired judge*
Lovinger, Warren Conrad *emeritus university president*
Lundgren, Leonard, III *retired secondary education educator*
Lutz, Carl Freiheit *academic administrator*
†Lynch, John Daniel *educator, state legislator*
Macmillan, William Hooper *university dean, educator*
Mallory, Arthur Lee *university dean, retired state official*
Marshak, Robert Reuben *former university dean, medical educator, veterinarian*
Mayfield, Robert Charles *university official, geography educator*
McAbeer, Sara Carita *school administrator*
McCarthy, Kevin Joseph *academic dean, music educator*
McConner, Stanley Jay, Sr. *academic administrator*
McIntosh, Carolyn *principal*
Mc Mahon, George Joseph *academic administrator*
Medley, Donald Matthias *retired education educator, consultant*
Melady, Thomas Patrick *university president, ambassador, author, public policy expert, educator*
†Melsheimer, William C. *principal*
Meyer, Pauline Marie *retired special education educator*
Miller, Arjay *retired university dean*
Miller, James Vince *university president*
Mills, Eugene Sumner *college president*
Mills, Robert Lee *president emeritus*
Moeckel, Bill Reid *retired university dean*
†Monahan, Edward Charles *academic administrator, marine science educator*
Morgan, Ruth Prouse *academic administrator, educator*
Mortola, Edward Joseph *emeritus university chancellor*
Myers, Harold Mathews *academic administrator*
Naylor, Thomas Everett *account administrator*
Neelankavil, James Paul *marketing educator, researcher and consultant*
Nelson, Edwin Clarence *academic administrator, emeritus*
Neunzig, Carolyn Miller *secondary education educator*
Nicholson, Theodore H. *educational administrator*
†Norris, Alfred Lloyd *theological seminary president, clergyman*
O'Malley, Thomas Patrick *university president*
Palmer, Irene Sabelberg *university dean and educator emeritus, nurse, researcher, historian*
Parrish, Alma Ellis *elementary education educator*
Pasic, Mary Rose *principal*
Patmos, Adrian Edward *university dean emeritus*
Paulino, Sister Mary McAuley *principal*
Paulsen, Frank Robert *college dean emeritus*
Pedersen, Knud George *university president*
Peoples, John Arthur, Jr. *former university president, consultant*
Perreault, Sister Jeanne *college president*
Peters, William Henry *former university dean, marketing educator*
Pierskalla, William Peter *academic dean, management and engineering educator*
Pinto, Rosalind *retired educator, civic volunteer*
Porteous, Timothy *academic administrator*
Potts, Sandra D. *elementary education educator*
Prins, Robert Jack *college administrator*
Pritchard, Claudius Hornby, Jr. *retired university president*
Prokasy, William Frederick *academic administrator*
Propst, Harold Dean *retired university chancellor*
†Purvis, Richard George *former superintendent of schools*
Pusey, William Webb, III *retired dean, foreign language educator*
†Ratcliff, James Lewis *administrator*
Raymond, Joan M. *educational administrator*
Redmont, Bernard Sidney *university dean, journalism educator*
Reeder, Cecelia Painter *secondary education educator*
Rees, Mina (Spiegel) *university administrator*

Reinke, Ralph Louis *retired academic administrator*
Reisman, Fredricka Kauffman *education educator*
Riddle, Donald Husted *former university chancellor*
Robbins, Frances Elaine *educational administrator*
Robertson, Mary Virginia *retired elementary educator*
Robinson, James Arthur *university president emeritus, political scientist*
Robles, Rosalie Miranda *elementary education educator*
Rodriguez-Roig, Aida Ivelisse *educational administrator*
Rollo, Mary-Jo Vivian *special education educator*
Royal, Darrell K. *university administrator*
Ryder, Georgia Atkins *university dean, educator*
Ryder, Jack McBride *educational consultant*
Sanders, Marlene *academic administrator, educator*
Scandary, E. Jane *special education educator, consultant*
Schmidt, Ruth Ann *retired college president*
Sessions, Robert Paul *former college president and administrator, retired educator, writer*
Sestini, Virgil Andrew *secondary education educator*
Sharwell, William Gay *retired university president and company executive*
Shaw, Valeen Jones *special education educator, elementary school educator*
Shearer, Charles Livingston *academic administrator*
Sheldon, Thomas Donald *academic administrator*
Shellman-Lucas, Elizabeth C. *special education educator, researcher*
Sherman, Richard H. *education educator*
Silvius, Donald Joe *educator, administrator*
Simones, Marie Dolorosa *nun, educator*
Sneed, Alberta Neal *retired elementary education educator*
Snortland, Howard Jerome *educational financial consultant*
Sonnenschein, Hugo Freund *university president, economics educator*
Southworth, Jamie MacIntyre *education educator*
Stabile, Benedict Louis *retired academic administrator, retired coast guard officer*
Stacy, Bill Wayne *college president*
Staiger, Ralph Conrad *educational consultant, former educational association executive*
Stein, Dale Franklin *retired university president*
Stewart, Norman Lawrence *university president*
Strangway, David William *university president*
Stuckwisch, Clarence George *university administrator*
Tanner, Laurel Nan *education educator*
Tillman, Montague Epps *school superintendent*
Tomsovic, Edward Joseph *college dean*
Tonjes, Marian Jeannette Benton *education educator*
Tucker, Ruth M. *elementary education educator*
Vandevender, Barbara Jewell *elementary education educator, farmer*
Volpe, Edmond L(oris) *college president*
Washington, Walter *retired college president*
†Watson, James D., Jr. *principal*
Webb, Charles Richard *retired university president*
Wells-Carr, Elizabeth Antoinette *educational leadership trainer*
White, James Arthur *college president*
Whitten, Dolphus, Jr. *former university administrator, educational consortium executive*
Wittich, John Jacob *retired college president, educational administrator, corporation consultant*
Wong, David Yue *academic administrator, physics educator*
Woods, Phyllis Michalik *elementary education educator*
Worthen, John Edward *university president*
Young, Margaret Chong *elementary education educator*
Young, Virgil M. *education educator*
Zufryden, Fred S. *academic administrator, marketing educator, researcher*

ENGINEERING

UNITED STATES

ALABAMA

Auburn
Aldridge, Melvin Dayne *electrical engineering educator*
Cochran, John Euell, Jr. *aerospace engineer, educator, lawyer*
Crocker, Malcolm John *mechanical engineer, noise control engineer, educator*
Irwin, John David *electrical engineering educator*
Jaeger, Richard Charles *electrical engineer, educator, science center director*
Rainer, Rex Kelly *civil engineer, educator*
Schafer, Robert Louis *agricultural engineer, researcher*
Turnquist, Paul Kenneth *agricultural engineer, educator*

Birmingham
Appleton, Joseph Hayne *civil engineer, educator*
Edmonds, William Fleming *retired engineering and construction company executive*
Gilbert, Rodney C. *engineering executive*
Goodrich, Thomas Michael *engineering and construction executive*
†Kennedy, Ted C. *engineering executive*
Kennedy, Theodore Clifford *engineering and construction company executive, consultant*
Miller, Edmond Trowbridge *civil engineer, educator, consultant*
†Williamson, Edward L. *retired nuclear engineer, consultant*

Daphne
Jeffreys, Elystan Geoffrey *geological engineer, petroleum consultant and appraiser*

Huntsville
Costes, Nicholas Constantine *aerospace technologist, government official*
†Dannenberg, Konrad K. *aeronautical engineer*
Daussman, Grover Frederick *electrical engineer, consultant*
Douillard, Paul Arthur *engineering and financial executive, consultant*

Emerson, William Kary *engineering company executive*
Hung, Ru J. *engineering educator*
Kowel, Stephen Thomas *electrical engineer, educator*
Mc Donough, George Francis, Jr. *aerospace engineer*
Moore, Fletcher Brooks *engineering company executive*
Potate, John Spencer, Sr. *engineering company executive, consultant*
Ritter, Alfred *aerospace consultant*
Russell, Lynn Darnell *engineering educator*
†Schroer, Bernard Jon *industrial engineering educator*
Vinz, Frank Louis *electrical engineer*
Wessling, Francis Christopher *mechanical engineer, educator*

Madison
Hawk, Clark Wiliams *mechanical engineering educator*

Mobile
Hamid, Michael *electrical engineering educator, consultant*

Montgomery
Paddock, Austin Joseph *engineering executive*

Orange Beach
Brennan, Lawrence Edward *electronics engineer*

Point Clear
Ferguson, Joseph Gantt *chemical engineer*

Redstone Arsenal
Pittman, William Claude *electrical engineer*

Tuscaloosa
Barfield, Robert F. *mechanical engineer, educator, university dean*
Brown, Jack Cole *civil engineer*
Bryan, Colgan Hobson *aerospace engineering educator*
Frye, John H., Jr. *metallurgical engineering educator*
Griffin, Marvin Anthony *industrial engineer, educator*
Morley, Lloyd Albert *mining engineering educator*

ALASKA

Anchorage
†Leman, Loren Dwight *civil engineer*
Thomas, Howard Paul *civil engineer, consultant*

Fairbanks
Behlke, Charles Edward *civil engineer, former university dean*
Bennett, Fred Lawrence *engineering educator*
Cook, Donald Jean *mineral engineering educator, trade consultant*
Tilsworth, Timothy *environmental and civil engineering educator*
†Zarling, John Paul *mechanical engineering educator*

ARIZONA

Cave Creek
MacKay, John *mechanical engineer*

Chandler
Ratkowski, Donald J. *mechanical engineer, consultant*

Flagstaff
Somerville, Mason Harold *mechanical engineering educator, university dean*

Green Valley
Peterson, Harold Albert *electrical engineer, educator*

Mesa
Fairbanks, Harold Vincent *metallurgical engineer, educator*
Rummel, Robert Wiland *aeronautical engineer, author*

Paradise Valley
Russell, Paul Edgar *electrical engineering educator*

Phoenix
Bachus, Benson Floyd *mechanical engineer, consultant*
Burchard, John Kenneth *chemical engineer*
Chisholm, Tom Shepherd *environmental engineer*
†Freyermuth, Clifford L. *structural engineering consultant*
Jorgensen, Gordon David *engineering company executive*
†Ralston, Mark David *electrical engineer*
Stine, George Harry *consulting engineer, author*
Watson, Harold George *engineering executive, mechanical engineer*

Prescott
Chesson, Eugene, Jr. *civil engineering educator, consultant*

Prescott Valley
Beck, John Roland *environmental consultant*

Rio Verde
Jordan, Richard Charles *engineering executive*

Scottsdale
Blackburn, Jack Bailey *retired civil engineering educator*
Fisher, John Richard *engineering consultant, former naval officer*
Kline, Arthur Jonathan *electronics engineer*

Sun City West
Woodruff, Neil Parker *agricultural engineer*

Tempe
Balanis, Constantine Apostle *electrical engineering educator*

Beakley, George Carroll, Jr. *mechanical engineering educator*
Berman, Neil Sheldon *chemical engineering educator*
Carpenter, Ray Warren *materials scientist and engineer, educator*
Ferry, David Keane *electrical engineering educator*
Karady, George Gyorgy *electrical engineering educator, consultant*
Kaufman, Irving *engineering educator*
Schroder, Dieter Karl *electrical engineering educator*
Shaw, Milton Clayton *mechanical engineering educator*
Singhal, Avinash Chandra *engineering educator*

Tucson
Arnell, Walter James William *mechanical engineering educator, consultant*
Battistelli, Joseph John *electronics executive*
Chen, Chuan Fang *mechanical engineering educator*
Davidson, Lacinda Susan *materials engineer, chemist*
Freeh, Edward James *chemical engineer*
Galloway, Kenneth Franklin *electrical engineering educator*
Ganapol, Barry Douglas *nuclear engineering educator, consultant*
Gross, Joseph Francis *retired bio-engineering educator*
Hunt, Bobby Ray *electrical engineering educator, consultant*
Jones, Roger Clyde *electrical engineer, educator*
Kececioglu, Dimitri Basil *mechanical engineering educator*
Kerwin, William James *electrical engineering educator, consultant*
†Kim, Yi Hwa *industrial hygienist, safety engineer*
Kinney, Robert Bruce *mechanical engineering educator*
Nordby, Gene Milo *agricultural engineering educator*
Porcello, Leonard Joseph *engineering research and development executive*
Preston, Kendall, Jr. *electro-optical engineer*
Prince, John Luther, III *engineering educator*
Renard, Kenneth George *civil engineer*
Sears, William Rees *engineering educator*
Speas, Robert Dixon *aeronautical engineer, aviation company executive*
Wait, James Richard *electrical engineering educator, scientist*
Wygnanski, Israel Jerzy *aerospace engineering educator*
Zeigler, Bernard Phillip *electrical and computer engineering educator*

Youngtown
Gross, Al *electrical engineer, consultant*

ARKANSAS

Conway
Holt, Frank Ross *retired aerospace engineer*

Fayetteville
Andrews, John Frank *civil and environmental engineering educator*
Gaddy, James Leoma *chemical engineer, educator*
LeFevre, Elbert Walter, Jr. *civil engineering educator*

CALIFORNIA

Agoura Hills
Chang, Chong Eun *chemical engineer*

Alameda
Klehs, Henry John Wilhelm *civil engineer*

Alta Loma
Cooper, George Robert *electrical engineer, educator*

Anaheim
Arnwine, William Carrol *industrial engineer*
†Griffin, Gerald D. *engineering company executive*
Hubbard, Charles Ronald *engineering executive*
Prince, Warren Victor *mechanical engineer*

Arcadia
Broderick, Donald Leland *electronics engineer*

Belvedere Tiburon
Elder, Rex Alfred *civil engineer*

Berkeley
Angelakos, Diogenes James *electrical engineering educator*
Berger, Stanley Allan *mechanical engineering educator*
Birdsall, Charles Kennedy *electrical engineer*
Bogy, David B(eauregard) *mechanical engineering educator*
Cairns, Elton James *chemical engineering educator*
†Chopra, Anil Kumar *civil engineering educator*
Denn, Morton Mace *chemical engineering educator*
Desoer, Charles Auguste *electrical engineer*
†Dornfeld, David A. *engineering educator*
Evans, James William *metallurgical educator*
Fatt, Irving *optometry and bioengineering educator*
Finnie, Iain *mechanical engineer, educator*
Frisch, Joseph *mechanical engineer, educator, consultant*
Fuerstenau, Douglas Winston *mineral engineering educator*
Garrison, William Louis *civil engineering educator*
Goldsmith, Werner *mechanical engineering educator*
Grossman, Lawrence Morton *nuclear engineering educator*
Harris, Guy Hendrickson *chemical research engineer*
Hodges, David Albert *electrical engineering educator*
Hsu, Chieh Su *applied mechanics engineering educator, researcher*
Hu, Chenming *electrical engineering educator*
Jewell, William Sylvester *engineering educator*
Leitmann, George *mechanical engineering educator*
Lewis, Edwin Reynolds *biomedical engineering educator*
May, Adolf Darlington *civil engineering educator*
†Mikesell, Walter R., Jr. *mechanical engineer, engineering executive*
Mitchell, James Kenneth *civil engineer, educator*
Monismith, Carl Leroy *civil engineering educator*
Mote, Clayton Daniel, Jr. *mechanical engineer, educator, administrator*

Muller, Richard Stephen *electrical engineer, educator*
Newman, John Scott *chemical engineer, educator*
Oldham, William George *electrical engineering and computer science educator*
Ott, David Michael *engineering company executive*
Pagni, Patrick John *mechanical and fire safety engineering science educator ,*
Pask, Joseph Adam *ceramic engineering educator*
Penzien, Joseph *structural engineering educator*
Pigford, Thomas Harrington *nuclear engineering educator*
Popov, Egor Paul *engineering educator*
Prausnitz, John Michael *chemical engineer, educator*
Schrock, Virgil Edwin *mechanical and nuclear engineer*
Scordelis, Alexander Costicas *civil engineering educator*
Shen, Hsieh Wen *civil engineer, consultant, educator*
Susskind, Charles *engineering educator, author, publishing executive*
Tobias, Charles William *chemical engineer, educator*
Whinnery, John Roy *electrical engineering educator*
White, Richard Manning *electrical engineering educator*
Wiegel, Robert Louis *consulting engineering executive*
Zadeh, Lotfi A. *engineering educator*
Zwoyer, Eugene Milton *consulting engineering executive*

Burbank
†Mullin, Sherman N. *engineering executive*
†Rich, Ben Robert *aerospace executive, aero-thermodynamicist*

Calabasas
Sargent, Ernest Douglas *retired aerospace engineer, educator*

Campbell
Levy, Salomon *mechanical engineer*
Ross, Hugh Courtney *electrical engineer*

Canoga Park
†Gibbs, D.C. *materials engineer administrator*

Carmel
Alsberg, Dietrich Anselm *electrical engineer*
Brahtz, John Frederick Peel *civil engineering educator*

Chico
Allen, Charles William *mechanical engineering educator*

Chula Vista
Wolk, Martin *electronic engineer, physicist*

Claremont
Dym, Clive Lionel *engineering educator*
Molinder, John Irving *engineering educator, consultant*
Monson, James Edward *electrical engineer, educator*
Phillips, John Richard *engineering educator*

Concord
Lee, Low Kee *electronics engineer, consultant*

Corona
Tillman, Joseph Nathaniel *engineer*

Corona Del Mar
Donovan, Allen Francis *aerospace company executive*

Costa Mesa
Richmond, Ronald LeRoy *aerospace engineer*

Culver City
Sensiper, Samuel *consulting electrical engineer*

Cupertino
†Lindsay, Leslie *packaging engineer*

Danville
Maninger, R(alph) Carroll *engineering executive, consultant*
Trezek, George James *mechanical engineer*

Davis
Akesson, Norman Berndt *agricultural engineer, emeritus educator*
Beadle, Charles Wilson *retired mechanical engineering educator*
Brandt, Harry *mechanical engineering educator*
Chancellor, William Joseph *agricultural engineering educator*
Cheney, James Addison *civil engineering educator*
Dorf, Richard Carl *electrical engineering and management educator*
Fridley, Robert Bruce *agricultural engineering educator, academic administrator*
Gardner, William Allen *electrical engineering educator*
†Gates, Bruce Clark *chemical engineer, educator*
Ghausi, Mohammed Shuaib *electrical engineering educator, university dean*
Giedt, Warren Harding *mechanical engineer, educator*
Hakimi, S. Louis *electrical and computer engineering educator*
Kemper, John Dustin *mechanical engineering educator*
Ryu, Dewey Doo Young *biochemical engineering educator*
Tchobanoglous, George *civil engineering educator*
Wang, Shih-Ho *electrical engineer, educator*

Del Mar
†Cutrona, Louis John *engineering executive*
Wilkinson, Eugene Parks *nuclear engineer*

Dinuba
Leps, Thomas MacMaster *civil engineer, consultant*

Downey
Baumann, Theodore Robert *aerospace engineer, consultant, army officer*
Brofman, Woody *astronautical engineer, educator*
Demarchi, Ernest Nicholas *aerospace company executive*

Duarte
Chou, Chung-Kwang *bio-engineer*

Edwards
Deets, Dwain Aaron *aeronautical research engineer*

El Cerrito
Wilke, Charles Robert *chemical engineer, educator*

El Segundo
Gupta, Madhu Sudan *electrical engineering educator*
Mo, Roger Shih-Yah *electronics engineering manager*
†Plummer, James Walter *engineering company executive*
Ricardi, Leon Joseph *electrical engineer*
Tamrat, Befecadu *aeronautical engineer*

Encinitas
Morrow, Charles Tabor *aerospace consulting engineer*

Encino
Acheson, Louis Kruzan, Jr. *aerospace engineer and systems analyst*
Knuth, Eldon Luverne *engineering educator*

Fair Oaks
Smiley, Robert William *industrial engineer*

Folsom
Ettlich, William F. *electrical engineer*

Foster City
Fisk, Edward Ray *civil engineer, author, educator*
Ham, Lee Edward *civil engineer*

Fremont
Wang, Ying Zhe *mechanical and optical engineer*

Fresno
Brahma, Chandra Sekhar *civil engineering educator*

Fullerton
Begovich, Nicholas Anthony *electrical engineer, consultant*

Glendale
Knoop, Vern Thomas *civil engineer, consultant*

Granite Bay
Crossley, Frank Alphonso *former metallurgical engineer*

Hacienda Heights
Love, Daniel Joseph *consulting engineer*

Half Moon Bay
Hidy, George Martel *chemical engineer, executive*

Hawthorne
Ashkenas, Irving Louis *aerospace executive*

Hayward
Flora, Edward Benjamin *research and development company executive, mechanical engineer*

Hermosa Beach
McDowell, Edward R. H. *chemical engineer*

Hillsborough
Blume, John August *consulting civil engineer*

Huntington Beach
Anderson, Raymond Hartwell, Jr. *metallurgical engineer*
†Falcon, Joseph A. *mechanical engineering consultant*
Forkert, Clifford Arthur *civil engineer*

Indian Wells
Pace, Stanley Carter *retired aeronautical engineer*

Irvine
Ang, Alfredo Hua-Sing *civil engineering educator*
Bershad, Neil Jeremy *electrical engineering educator*
Guymon, Gary LeRoy *civil engineering educator, consultant*
Kontny, Vincent L. *engineering and construction company executive*
Korb, Robert William *former materials and processes engineer*
Lurie, Harold *engineer, lawyer*
McCraw, Leslie G. *engineering and construction company executive*
Saunders, Robert Mallough *engineering educator, college administrator*
Sirignano, William Alfonso *aerospace and mechanical engineer, educator*
Sklansky, Jack *electrical and computer engineering educator, researcher*
Slavich, Denis Michael *engineering and construction company executive*
Stubberud, Allen Roger *electrical engineering educator*
Ting, Albert Chia *bioengineering researcher*

Kensington
Oppenheim, Antoni Kazimierz *mechanical engineer*

La Jolla
Breitwieser, Charles John *engineer, educator*
Chang, William Shen Chie *electrical engineering educator*
†Chien, Shu *physiology and bioengineering educator*
Conn, Robert William *engineering science educator*
Counts, Stanley Thomas *aerospace consultant, retired naval officer, retired electronics company executive*
Fung, Yuan-Cheng Bertram *bioengineering educator, author*
Goldman, Stanford *electrical engineer, scientist*
Helstrom, Carl Wilhelm *electrical engineering educator*
Levy, Ralph *engineering executive, consultant*
Milstein, Laurence Bennett *electrical engineering educator, researcher*
Nelles, Maurice *mechanical engineer, author*
Penner, Stanford Solomon *engineering educator*
Rudee, Mervyn Lea *engineering educator, researcher*

†Schmid-Schoenbein, Geert Wilfried *biomedical engineer, educator*
Skalak, Richard *engineering mechanics educator, researcher*
†Sung, Kuo-Li Paul *bioengineering educator*
Williams, Forman Arthur *engineering science educator, combustion theorist*
Wolf, Jack Keil *electrical engineer, educator*

La Selva
Brown, Alan Charlton *retired aeronautical engineer*

Lafayette
Laird, Alan Douglas Kenneth *mechanical engineering educator*

Laguna Hills
Larson, Harry Thomas *electronics engineer*
Lederer, Jerome *aerospace safety engineer, educator*

Lancaster
Hodges, Vernon Wray *mechanical engineer*

Livermore
Carley, James French *chemical and plastics engineer*
Johnson, Roy Ragnar *electrical engineer*
King, Ray John *electrical engineer*

Lompoc
Peltekof, Stephan *systems engineer*

Long Beach
Brent, Paul Leslie *mechanical engineering educator*
Cynar, Sandra Jean *electrical engineering educator*
de Soto, Simon *mechanical engineer*
†Dillon, Michael Earl *engineering executive, mechanical engineer, educator*
Donald, Eric Paul *aeronautical engineer, inventor*
Hildebrant, Andy McClellan *retired electrical engineer*
Roberts, William Harrison *aerospace engineer, consultant, researcher*

Los Alamitos
Iceland, William Frederick *engineering consultant*

Los Altos
Fenn, Raymond Wolcott, Jr. *retired metallurgical engineer*
Fondahl, John Walker *civil engineering educator*
Jones, Robert Thomas *aerospace scientist*
Kazan, Benjamin *research engineer*
†Peterson, Victor Lowell *aerospace engineer, research center administrator*
Sharpe, Roland Leonard *retired engineering company executive, earthquake and structural engineering consultant*

Los Altos Hills
Ginzton, Edward Leonard *engineering corporation executive*

Los Angeles
Ayres, James Marx *mechanical engineer*
Blackwelder, Ron Forest *engineering educator, consultant, researcher*
Brandow, George Everett *civil engineer*
Breuer, Melvin Allen *electrical engineering educator*
Bucy, Richard Snowden *aerospace engineering and mathematics educator, consultant*
Catton, Ivan *mechanical engineer*
Charwat, Andrew Franciszek *engineering educator*
Cheng, Hsien Kei *aeronautics educator*
Cheng, Tsen-Chung *electrical engineering educator*
Chilingarian, George Varos *petroleum, environmental and civil engineering educator*
Chobotov, Vladimir Alexander *aerospace engineer, educator*
Crombie, Douglass Darnill *aerospace communications engineer, former government official*
Cross, Glenn Laban *engineering executive, development planner*
†Dhir, Vijay K. *mechanical engineering educator*
Dorman, Albert A. *consulting engineer executive, architect*
Dougherty, Elmer Lloyd, Jr. *chemical engineering educator, consultant*
Friedlander, Sheldon Kay *chemical engineering educator*
Friedman, George Jerry *aerospace company executive, engineer*
Friedmann, Peretz Peter *aerospace engineer, educator*
†Garmire, Elsa Meints *electrical engineering educator, consultant*
Gaspari, Russell Arthur *electrical engineer*
Hammond, David Greene *engineering company executive, consultant*
Handy, Lyman Lee *petroleum engineer, chemist, educator*
Hovanessian, Shahen Alexander *electrical engineer, educator*
†Incaudo, Joseph A. *engineering company executive*
Itoh, Tatsuo *engineering educator*
Johnston, Roy G. *consulting structural engineer*
Karplus, Walter J. *engineering educator*
†Kiddoo, Robert James *engineering service company executive*
Kleiman, Joseph *engineer, consultant, retired life sciences company executive*
Kuehl, Hans Henry *electrical engineering educator*
†Leal, George D. *engineering company executive*
Lin, Tung Hua *civil engineering educator*
MacKenzie, John Douglas *engineering educator*
Martin, J(ohn) Edward *architectural engineer*
Masri, Sami F(aiz) *civil and mechanical engineering educator, consultant*
Meecham, William Coryell *engineering educator*
Mendel, Jerry Marc *electrical engineering educator*
Mirels, Harold *aerospace engineer*
Mortensen, Richard Edgar *engineering educator*
Muntz, Eric Phillip *aerospace engineering and radiology educator, consultant*
Nadler, Gerald *engineering educator, management consultant*
†Newman, Richard *engineering executive*
Nobe, Ken *chemical engineering educator*
Okrent, David *engineering educator*
O'Neill, Russell Richard *engineering educator*
Orchard, Henry John *electrical engineer*
Perrine, Richard Leroy *environmental engineering educator*
†Perry, Robert Michael *consulting engineering company executive*

Portenier, Walter James *aerospace engineer*
Purcell, Arthur Henry *environmental engineering educator, consultant*
Ramo, Simon *engineering executive*
Rauch, Lawrence Lee *aerospace and electrical engineer, educator*
Rechtin, Eberhardt *aerospace educator*
Rosenstein, Allen Bertram *electrical engineering educator*
Rubin, Izhak *electrical engineering educator, consultant*
Rubinstein, Moshe Fajwel *engineering educator*
Safonov, Michael George *electrical engineering educator, consultant*
Schmit, Lucien André, Jr. *structural engineer*
Scholtz, Robert Arno *electrical engineering educator*
Schumacher, Joseph Charles *chemical engineer*
Seide, Paul *civil engineering educator*
†Speyer, Jason Lee *engineer, educator*
Udwadia, Firdaus Erach *engineering educator, consultant*
Wagner, Christian Nikolaus Johann *materials engineering educator*
Welch, Lloyd Richard *electrical engineering educator, communications consultant*
Wheeler, William Thornton *structural engineer, consultant*
Wiberg, Donald Martin *electrical engineering educator, consultant*
†Willner, Alan Eli *electrical engineer, educator*
Willson, Alan Neil, Jr. *engineering educator, dean*
Yeh, William Wen-Gong *civil engineering educator*
Yen, Teh Fu *civil engineering and environmental educator*
Yue, Alfred Shui-choh *metallurgical engineer, educator*

Los Gatos
Leverett, Miles Corrington *retired nuclear power consultant*
Naymark, Sherman *consulting nuclear engineer*

Los Osos
Cloonan, Clifford B. *electrical engineer, educator*

Malibu
Widmann, Glenn Roger *electrical engineer*

Manhattan Beach
Bradburn, David Denison *engineer, retired air force officer*

Menlo Park
Duda, Richard Oswald *electrical engineering educator, researcher*
Edson, William Alden *electrical engineer*
Honey, Richard Churchill *retired electrical engineer*
Kohne, Richard Edward *retired engineering executive*
Leadabrand, Ray L. *engineering executive, defense industry consultant*
†McCarthy, Roger Lee *mechanical engineer*
Szentirmai, George *electrical engineer, corporate executive*
Turin, George Lewis *electrical engineering educator, university dean*

Mission Hills
Cramer, Frank Brown *engineering executive, combustion engineer, systems consultant*

Moffett Field
†Kerr, Andrew W. *aerodynamics researcher*
Lomax, Harvard *aeronautical research scientist, educator*
McCroskey, William James *aeronautical engineer*
†Park, Chul *aerospace engineer*
Statler, Irving Carl *aerospace engineer*

Monrovia
Mac Cready, Paul Beattie *aeronautical engineer*

Monterey
Butler, Jon Terry *computer engineering educator, researcher*
†Marto, Paul James *mechanical engineering educator, researcher*
Newberry, Conrad Floyde *aerospace engineering educator*
Newton, Robert Eugene *mechanical engineering educator*
Sarpkaya, Turgut *mechanical engineering educator*

Mountain View
Johnson, Noel Lars *biomedical engineer*
Marple, Stanley Lawrence, Jr. *electrical engineer, signal processing researcher*
Peters, Stanley Thomas *materials engineer, consultant, educator*

Napa
Folsom, Richard Gilman *retired mechanical engineer and academic administrator, consultant*

Newport Beach
Sharbaugh, W(illiam) James *plastics engineer, consultant*

Northridge
Bradshaw, Richard Rotherwood *engineering executive*
Jakobsen, Jakob Knudsen *mechanical engineer*
Stout, Thomas Melville *control system engineer*
Torgow, Eugene N. *electrical engineer*

Novato
†Harding, Richard Swick *engineering executive*

Oakland
Ambrose, Tommy W. *chemical engineer, executive*
Borum, William Donald *engineer*
King, Cary Judson, III *chemical engineer, educator, university official*
List, Raymond Edward *engineering and construction executive, management consultant*

Occidental
Rumsey, Victor Henry *electrical engineering educator emeritus*

Orange
Toeppe, William Joseph, Jr. *retired aerospace engineer*

Palo Alto
Baldwin, Gary Lee *electronics engineer, research laboratory administrator*
Brown, David Randolph *electrical engineer*
Childs, Wylie Jones *metallurgical engineer*
Cohen, Karl Paley *nuclear energy consultant*
Friedlander, Benjamin *electrical and computer engineering educator*
Hodge, Philip Gibson, Jr. *mechanical and aerospace engineering educator*
Johnson, Conor Deane *mechanical engineer*
Kino, Gordon Stanley *electrical engineering educator*
Lender, Adam *electrical engineer*
Moll, John Lewis *electronics engineer*
Oliver, Bernard More *electrical engineer, technical consultant*
Partain, Larry Dean *solar research engineer*
Quate, Calvin Forrest *engineering educator*
Rauch, Herbert Emil *electrical engineer*
Taylor, John Joseph *nuclear engineer*
Yuan, Sidney Wei Kwun *cryogenic engineer, consultant*

Palos Verdes Peninsula
Raue, Jorg Emil *electrical engineer*
Spinks, John Lee *engineering executive*
Weiss, Herbert Klemm *aeronautical engineer*

Pasadena
Boulos, Paul Fares *civil and environmental engineer*
†Brennen, Christopher E. *fluid mechanics educator*
Bridges, William Bruce *electrical engineer, researcher, educator*
Carroll, William Jerome *civil engineer*
Coles, Donald Earl *aeronautics educator*
Gould, Roy Walter *engineering educator*
†Hall, William E. *engineering and construction company executive*
Hatheway, Alson Earle *mechanical engineer*
Hilbert, Robert S(aul) *optical engineer*
Hornung, Hans Georg *aeronautical engineering educator, science facility administrator*
Housner, George William *civil engineering educator, consultant*
Hudson, Donald Ellis *civil engineering educator*
Iwan, Wilfred Dean *mechanical engineering educator*
Jacobs, Joseph John *engineering company executive*
Jennings, Paul Christian *civil engineering educator, academic administrator*
Knowles, James Kenyon *applied mechanics educator*
Loven, Andrew Witherspoon *environmental engineering company executive*
Morari, Manfred *chemical engineer, educator*
Nothmann, Gerhard Adolf *retired engineering executive, research engineer*
†Presecan, Nicholas Lee *civil, environmental engineer, consultant*
Sabersky, Rolf Heinrich *mechanical engineer*
Schlinger, Warren Gleason *retired chemical engineer*
Scott, Ronald Fraser *civil engineering educator, engineering consultant*
Seinfeld, John Hersh *chemical engineering educator*
Simon, Marvin Kenneth *electrical engineer, consultant*
Slater, Richard James *engineering company executive*
Springer, Edwin Kent *mechanical engineer*
Stewart, Homer Joseph *engineering educator*
Vanoni, Vito August *hydraulic engineer*
†Wu, Theodore Yao-Tsu *engineer*
†Yamarone, Charles Anthony, Jr. *aerospace engineer, consultant*
Yariv, Amnon *electrical engineering educator, scientist*
Yeh, Paul Pao *electrical and electronics engineer, educator*

Penn Valley
Throner, Guy Charles, Jr. *engineering executive, scientist, engineer, inventor, consultant*

Pico Rivera
Mitzner, Kenneth Martin *electrical engineer*

Pismo Beach
Saveker, David Richard *naval and marine architectural engineering executive*

Playa Del Rey
Copperman, William H *value engineer, consultant*

Pleasanton
Karn, Richard Wendall *civil engineer*

Port Hueneme
†Chapla, P.A. *civil engineering research administrator*

Rancho Santa Fe
Gunness, Robert Charles *chemical engineer*

Redondo Beach
Buchta, Edmund *engineering executive*
Chazen, Melvin Leonard *chemical engineer*
Cohen, Clarence Budd *aerospace engineer*
Hughes, James Arthur *electrical engineer*
†Sackheim, Robert Lewis *aerospace engineer, educator*

Redwood City
Eliassen, Rolf *environmental engineer, emeritus educator*

Richmond
Bertero, Vitelmo Victorio *civil engineer*
Colvin, Lloyd Dayton *electrical engineer*
†Moehle, Jack P. *civil engineer, engineering executive*

Ridgecrest
Pearson, John *mechanical engineer*

Riverside
Beni, Gerardo *electrical and computer engineering educator, robotics scientist*
Carrillo, Gilberto *engineer*
Hackwood, Susan *electrical and computer engineering educator*

Rohnert Park
Lord, Harold Wilbur *electrical engineer, electronics consultant*

Ross
Scott, John Walter *chemical engineer, research management executive*

Sacramento
Bezzone, Albert Paul *structural engineer*
Cavigli, Henry James *petroleum engineer*
Crimmins, Philip Patrick *metallurgical engineer, lawyer*
Forsyth, Raymond Arthur *civil engineer*
Lagarias, John Samuel *engineering executive*

San Bernardino
Holtz, Tobenette *aerospace engineer*

San Carlos
Symons, Robert Spencer *electronics engineer*

San Clemente
White, Stanley Archibald *research electrical engineer*

San Diego
Abalos, Ted Quinto *electronics engineer*
Anderson, Paul Maurice *electrical engineering educator, researcher, consultant*
Beyster, John Robert *engineering company executive*
Chen, Kao *consulting electrical engineer*
Conly, John Franklin *engineering educator, researcher*
†Fernandez, Fernando Lawrence *research company executive, aeronautical engineer*
Huang, Chien Chang *electrical engineer*
Inoue, Michael Shigeru *industrial engineer, electrical engineer*
†Northup, T. Eugene *nuclear engineer*
Safa, Bahram *civil engineer*
St. Clair, Hal Kay *electrical engineer*
Sell, Robert Emerson *electrical engineer*
Sesonske, Alexander *nuclear and chemical engineer*
Slate, John Butler *biomedical engineer*
Tricoles, Gus Peter *electromagnetics engineer, physicist, consultant*
Viterbi, Andrew James *electrical engineering and computer science educator, business executive*
†Wenaas, Eric Paul *electrical engineering executive*

San Francisco
Bechtel, Riley Peart *engineering company executive*
Bechtel, Stephen Davison, Jr. *engineering company executive*
Brooks, William George *engineer*
Cheng, Wan-Lee *mechanical engineer, industrial technology educator*
Chu, Kuang-Han *structural engineer, educator*
Dolby, Ray Milton *engineering company executive, electrical engineer*
Gerwick, Ben Clifford, Jr. *construction engineer, educator*
Gulbenkian, Paul *inventor, conceptual civil engineer*
Hotchkiss, Ralf David *engineer, educator*
Jacobs, Joseph Donovan *engineering firm executive*
†Johnstone, R. C., Jr. *engineering company executive*
Keller, Edward Lowell *electrical engineer, educator*
Lin, Tung Yen *civil engineer, educator*
Luft, Rene Wilfred *civil engineer*
Medwadowski, Stefan J. *consulting engineering executive, educator*
Morrin, Thomas Harvey *engineering research company executive*
Peirano, Lawrence Edward *civil engineer*
Shor, Samuel Wendell Williston *naval engineer*
Yuan, Shao Wen *aerospace engineer, educator*

San Jose
†Chen, Wen H. *engineering executive, educator*
Huang, Francis Fu-Tse *mechanical engineering educator*
McCarthy, Mary Ann Bartley *electrical engineer*
Montgomery, Leslie David *biomedical engineer, cardiovascular physiologist*
Moody, Frederick Jerome *mechanical engineer, consultant thermal hydraulics*
Morimoto, Carl Noboru *computer system engineer, crystallographer*
Rosenheim, Donald Edwin *electrical engineer*
Valentine, Ralph Schuyler *chemical engineer, research director*
†Wilkins, Daniel R. *nuclear engineer, nuclear energy industry executive*

San Luis Obispo
Blattner, Ernest Willi *mechanical engineering educator*
Hasslein, George Johann *architectural engineering educator*
Mc Donald, Henry Stanton *electrical engineer*
Moazzami, Sara *civil engineering educator*

San Marino
Smith, Apollo Milton Olin *retired aerodynamics engineer*

San Mateo
Pappas, Costas Ernest *aeronautical engineer, consultant*

San Pedro
Ellis, George Edwin, Jr. *chemical engineer*
McCarty, Frederick Briggs *electrical engineer*

San Rafael
Holman, Tomlinson *engineer, film educator*

Santa Ana
Jacobsen, Eric Kasner *consulting engineer*
Kelly, James Patrick, Jr. *retired engineering and construction executive*
Zabsky, John Mitchell *engineering executive*

Santa Barbara
†Fredrickson, Glenn Harold *chemical engineering and materials educator*
Iselin, Donald Grote *civil engineering and management consultant*
Laub, Alan John *engineering educator*
Lawrance, Charles Holway *consulting engineer*
Leal, Leslie Gary *chemical engineering educator*
Leckie, Frederick Alexander *mechanical engineer, educator*
Lick, Wilbert James *mechanical engineering educator*
†Majumdar, Arunava *mechanical engineer, educator*
Merz, James Logan *electrical engineering and materials educator, researcher*
Mitra, Sanjit Kumar *electrical and computer engineering educator*
†Pincus, Philip A. *chemical engineering educator*
Wade, Glen *electrical engineer, educator*
Wooldridge, Dean Everett *engineering executive, scientist*

Santa Clara
Chan, Shu-Park *electrical engineering educator*
Hoagland, Albert Smiley *electrical engineer*
†Koffel, Martin M. *engineering company executive*
Parden, Robert James *engineering educator, management consultant*
Siljak, Dragoslav D. *engineering educator*

Santa Cruz
Langdon, Glen George, Jr. *electrical engineer*
Pister, Karl Stark *engineering educator*

Santa Margarita
Thomas, John Bowman *educator, electrical engineer*

Santa Maria
Spellman, John David *retired electrical engineer*

Santa Monica
Bedrosian, Edward *electrical engineer*
Crain, Cullen Malone *electrical engineer*
Gritton, Eugene Charles *nuclear engineer*
Hammond, R. Philip *chemical engineer*
Kayton, Myron *engineering company executive*
Roney, Robert Kenneth *retired aerospace company executive*
Weingarten, Victor I. *engineering educator*

Santa Rosa
†Dwight, Herbert M., Jr. *optical engineer, manufacturing executive*

Saratoga
Cooper, George Emery *aerospace consultant*
Syvertson, Clarence Alfred *aerospace engineering consultant*
Wenzel, James Gottlieb *ocean engineering executive, consultant*

Simi Valley
Deisenroth, Clinton Wilbur *electrical engineer*

Sonoma
Muchmore, Robert Boyer *engineering consultant executive*

Sonora
Walasek, Otto Frank *chemical engineer, biochemist, photographer*

South Pasadena
Glad, Dain Sturgis *retired aerospace engineer, consultant*
Kopp, Eugene Howard *electrical engineer*

South San Francisco
Swanson, Robert A. *genetic engineering company executive*

Spring Valley
Gardner, Leonard Burton, II *industrial automation engineer*

Stanford
Angell, James Browne *electrical engineering educator*
Barkan, Philip *mechanical engineer*
Boudart, Michel *chemist, chemical engineer, educator*
Bracewell, Ronald Newbold *electrical engineering and computer science educator*
Bradshaw, Peter *engineering educator*
Brigham, William Everett *petroleum engineering educator*
†Bryson, Arthur Earl, Jr. *engineering educator*
Cannon, Robert Hamilton, Jr. *aerospace engineering educator*
Carlson, Robert Codner *industrial engineering educator*
Cornell, Carl Allin *civil engineering educator*
Cox, Donald Clyde *electrical engineering educator*
Dunn, Donald Allen *engineering educator, consultant*
Eustis, Robert Henry *mechanical engineer*
Franklin, Gene Farthing *electrical engineering educator, consultant*
Gere, James Monroe *civil engineering educator*
Goodman, Joseph Wilfred *electrical engineering educator*
Gray, Robert Molten *electrical engineering educator*
Harris, Stephen Ernest *electrical engineering and applied physics educator*
Herrmann, George *mechanical engineering educator*
Hoff, Nicholas John *mechanical and aerospace engineer*
Hughes, Thomas Joseph *mechanical engineering educator, consultant*
Kailath, Thomas *electrical engineer, educator*
Kane, Thomas Reif *engineering educator*
Kline, Stephen Jay *mechanical engineer, educator*
Kruger, Charles Herman, Jr. *mechanical engineering educator*
Linvill, John Grimes *engineering educator*
Luenberger, David Gilbert *electrical engineer, educator*
Macovski, Albert *electrical engineering educator*
Mc Carty, Perry Lee *environmental engineer, educator*
McCluskey, Edward Joseph *engineering educator*
Moffat, Robert John *mechanical engineering educator, researcher*
Ortolano, Leonard *civil engineering educator, water resources planner*
Ott, Wayne Robert *environmental engineer*
Pease, Roger Fabian Wedgwood *electrical engineering educator*
Pierce, John Robinson *electrical engineer, educator*
†Reynolds, William Craig *mechanical engineer, educator*
Roth, Bernard *mechanical engineering educator, researcher*
Rott, Nicholas *fluid mechanics educator*
Shah, Haresh C. *civil engineering educator*
Siegman, Anthony Edward *electrical engineer, educator*
Spreiter, John Robert *engineering educator, space physics scientist*
Springer, George Stephen *mechanical engineering educator*
Street, Robert Lynnwood *civil and mechanical engineer*
Thompson, David Alfred *industrial engineer*
Van Dyke, Milton Denman *aeronautical engineering educator*
Vincenti, Walter Guido *aeronautical engineer, emeritus educator*
White, Robert Lee *electrical engineer, educator*
Widrow, Bernard *electrical engineering educator*

Stockton
Heyborne, Robert Linford *electrical engineering educator*

Sunnyvale
Kim, Wan Hee *electrical engineering educator, business executive*
Ma, Fengchow Clarence *agricultural engineering consultant*
Omura, Jimmy Kazuhiro *electrical engineer*
Schubert, Ronald Hayward *retired aerospace engineer*
Zebroski, Edwin Leopold *nuclear engineer consultant*

Tarzana
Hansen, Robert Clinton *electrical engineering consultant*
Macmillan, Robert Smith *electronics engineer*

Temecula
†Feltz, Charles Henderson *former mechanical engineer, consultant*
Minogue, Robert Brophy *retired nuclear engineer*

Thousand Oaks
Krumm, Charles Ferdinand *electrical engineer*
†Shankar, Vijaya V. *aeronautical engineer*

Tiburon
Heacox, Russel Louis *mechanical engineer*

Torrance
Brodsky, Robert Fox *aerospace engineer*
Mason, John Latimer *engineering executive*
Sheh, Robert Bardhyl *environmental management company executive*

Ventura
Gaynor, Joseph *chemical engineering consultant*
Matley, Benvenuto Gilbert (Ben Matley) *computer engineer, educator, consultant*
Wheeler, Harold Alden *retired radio engineer*

Walnut Creek
Crandall, Ira Carlton *consulting electrical engineer*
†Delorme, Jean *mining engineer*
Woodward, Richard Joseph, Jr. *geotechnical engineer*

Westlake Village
Caligiuri, Joseph Frank *engineering executive*

Westminster
Armstrong, Gene Lee *systems engineering consultant, retired aerospace company executive*

Whittier
Lillevang, Omar Johansen *civil engineer*

Woodland Hills
Amerine, Anne Follette *aerospace engineer*
Higginbotham, Lloyd William *mechanical engineer*
Oltman, Henry George, Jr. *retired engineering executive*

COLORADO

Bellvue
Mattson, Roy Henry *retired engineering educator*

Boulder
Avery, Susan Kathryn *electrical engineering educator, researcher*
Barnes, Frank Stephenson *electrical engineer, educator*
Fuchs, Ewald Franz *engineer, educator, consultant*
Fuller, Jackson Franklin *electrical engineering educator*
Geers, Thomas Lange *mechanical engineering educator*
Goble, George G. *civil engineering educator*
Griffiths, Lloyd Joseph *electrical engineering educator, consultant*
Gupta, Kuldip Chand *electrical and computer engineering educator, researcher*
Hanna, William Johnson *electrical engineering educator*
Hill, David Allan *electrical engineer*
Kanda, Motohisa *electronics engineer*
Ma, Mark Tsu-han *electronic engineer*
Maley, Samuel Wayne *electrical engineering educator*
Rodriguez, Juan Alfonso *technology corporation executive*
Sani, Robert LeRoy *chemical engineering educator*
Smith, Ernest Ketcham *electrical engineer*
Sodal, Ingvar Edmund *electrical engineer, scientist*
Timmerhaus, Klaus Dieter *chemical engineering educator*
Uberoi, Mahinder Singh *aerospace engineering educator*
†Utlaut, William Frederick *electrical engineer*

Canon City
Mc Bride, John Alexander *retired chemical engineer*

Colorado Springs
†Allen, J. Lamar *engineering company executive, educator*
Anderson, Lawrence Keith *electrical engineer*
Kohlman, David Leslie *engineering executive, consultant*
Sherman, Donald H. *civil engineer*
Watts, Oliver Edward *engineering consultancy company executive*
Ziemer, Rodger Edmund *electrical engineering educator, consultant*

Conifer
Powers, Edwin Malvin *consulting engineer*

Denver
†Chmelir, John David *engineer, consultant*
†Evans, Ginger Sunday *civil engineer*
Ferguson, Lloyd Elbert *manufacturing engineer*
†Kafadar, Charles Bell *mechanical engineer, engineering executive*
Krill, Arthur Melvin *engineering, architectural and planning company executive*
Mc Candless, Bruce, II *engineer, former astronaut*
Mehring, Clinton Warren *engineering executive*
†Perez, Jean-Yves *engineering company executive*
Poirot, James Wesley *engineering company executive*
Pollard, William Sherman, Jr. *civil engineer, educator*
†Yamamoto, Kaoru *psychology, education educator*

Estes Park
Webb, Richard C. *engineering company executive*

Evergreen
Jesser, Roger Franklyn *former brewing company engineering executive, consultant*
Newkirk, John Burt *metallurgical engineer, administrator*

Fort Collins
†Abt, Steven R. *civil engineering educator, laboratory director*
Boyd, Landis Lee *agricultural engineer, educator*
Cermak, Jack Edward *engineer, educator*
Collins, Royal Eugene *petroleum engineering educator, physicist, consultant*
Frasier, Gary W. *hydraulic engineer*
†Garvey, Daniel Cyril *mechanical engineer*
†Heermann, Dale Frank *agricultural engineer*
Kaufman, Harold Richard *mechanical engineer and physics educator*
Koelzer, Victor Alvin *civil engineer*
Richardson, Everett Vern *hydraulic engineer, educator, administrator*
Sandborn, Virgil Alvin *civil engineer, educator*
Woolhiser, David Arthur *hydraulic engineer*

Golden
Ansell, George Stephen *metallurgical engineering educator, academic administrator*
Danzberger, Alexander Harris *chemical engineer, consultant*
†Haddon, Timothy John *mining engineer*
Hager, John Patrick *metallurgy engineering educator*
Johnstone, James George *engineering educator*
Poettmann, Frederick Heinz *retired petroleum engineering educator*
Salamon, Miklos Dezso Gyorgy *mining educator*

Grand Junction
†Agapito, J. F. T. *mining engineer, mineralogist*

Lakewood
Elkins, Lincoln Feltch *petroleum engineering consultant*
Gayer, John Harrison *engineering executive, consultant*
Lu, Paul Haihsing *mining engineer, geotechnical consultant*

Littleton
Kazemi, Hossein *petroleum engineer*
Kullas, Albert John *management and systems engineering consultant*
Ulrich, John Ross Gerald *aerospace engineer*

Pueblo West
Giffin, Walter Charles *retired industrial engineer, educator, consultant*

Wheat Ridge
Barrett, Michael Henry *civil engineer*
Scherich, Erwin Thomas *civil engineer, consultant*

CONNECTICUT

Bloomfield
Leonberger, Frederick John *electrical engineer, photonics manager*

Branford
Cohen, Myron Leslie *mechanical engineer, business executive*
Izenour, George Charles *mechanical, electrical engineering educator*

Bridgeport
Brunale, Vito John *aerospace engineer*
Hmurcik, Lawrence Vincent *electrical engineering educator*

Cheshire
Fuller, Jack Glendon, Jr. *retired plastics engineer*

Darien
Bays, John Theophanis *consulting engineering executive*
Forman, J(oseph) Charles *chemical engineer, consultant, writer*
Glenn, Roland Douglas *chemical engineer*
McCurdy, Richard Clark *engineering consultant*

East Granby
†Kimberley, John A. *mechanical engineer, consultant*

East Hartford
†Davis, Roger L. *aeronautical engineer*
De Maria, Anthony John *electrical engineer*
Foyt, Arthur George *electronics research administrator*
†Hobbs, David E. *mechanical engineer*
†Johnson, Bruce Virgil *mechanical engineer, physicist, researcher*

Ellington
Setzer, Herbert John *chemical engineer*

Greenwich
Marchand, Nathan *electrical engineer, corporation president*

Groton
Sheets, Herman Ernest *marine engineer*

Hamden
Walker, Charles Allen *chemical engineer, educator*

Hartford
Bronzino, Joseph Daniel *electrical engineer*
†Hajek, Thomas J. *aerospace engineer*
†Wagner, Joel H. *aerospace engineer*
†Weingold, Harris D. *aerospace engineer*

Manchester
Slaiby, Theodore George *aeronautical engineer, consultant*

Mansfield Center
Aldrich, Robert Adams *agricultural engineer*

Meriden
Hou, Kenneth Chaing *biochemical engineer*

Middlefield
Thermenos, Nicholas *engineering company executive*

Middletown
Day, William Hudson *mechanical engineer, turbomachinery company executive*
Loughran, Robert Hall *design-development engineering executive, physicist*

New Canaan
Halverstadt, Robert Dale *mechanical engineer, metals manufacturing company executive*
O'Neill, Patrick Henry *consulting mining engineer*

New Hartford
Hall, Newman A. *retired mechanical engineer*

New Haven
Apfel, Robert Edmund *mechanical engineering educator, applied physicist, research scientist*
Cunningham, Walter Jack *electrical engineering educator*
Horváth, Csaba *chemical engineering educator, researcher*
Narendra, Kumpati Subrahmanya *electrical engineer, educator*

New London
Owsley, Norman Lee *electrical engineer, educator*

Old Saybrook
Elrod, Harold Glenn *retired engineering science educator, consultant*

Rocky Hill
Chuang, Frank Shiunn-Jea *engineering executive, consultant*

Stamford
Rodriguez, J. Louis *civil engineer, land surveyor*

Storrs
†Di Benedetto, Anthony Thomas *chemical engineering educator*
†Galligan, James M. *material sciences educator, researcher*
Long, Richard Paul *civil engineering educator, geotechnical engineering consultant*
Pitkin, Edward Thaddeus *aerospace engineer, consultant*

Storrs Mansfield
DiBenedetto, Anthony Thomas *engineering educator*
McFadden, Peter William *mechanical engineering educator*

Stratford
Zimmerman, Daniel D. *chemical engineer*

Tariffville
Johnson, Loering M. *design engineer, historian, consultant*

Tolland
Wilde, Daniel Underwood *computer engineering educator*

Trumbull
Gladki, Hanna Zofia *civil engineer, hydraulic mixer specialist*

Weston
Offenhartz, Edward *aerospace executive*

Wilton
†Juran, Joseph Moses *engineer*
Rubin, Jacob Carl *mechanical research engineer*
Willoughby, William, II *retired nuclear engineer*

Windsor
†Rocco, Vincent Anthony *consulting firm executive*

DELAWARE

Hockessin
Bischoff, Kenneth Bruce *chemical engineer, educator*
Sproesser, William David, Sr. *engineering executive*

Newark
Allen, Herbert Ellis *environmental chemistry educator*
Cooper, Stuart Leonard *chemical engineering educator, researcher, consultant*
Jones, Russel Cameron *civil engineering educator*
Kennedy, Christopher Robin *ceramist*
Klein, Michael Tully *chemical engineering educator, consultant*
McCullough, Roy Lynn *chemical engineering educator*
†Nye, John Calvin *agricultural engineer, educator*
†Russell, Thomas William Fraser *chemical engineering educator*
Sandler, Stanley Irving *chemical engineering educator*
Sten, Johannes Walter *controls system engineer, consultant*
Szeri, Andras Z. *engineering educator*
Urquhart, Andrew Willard *engineering and business executive*

Seaford
Kittlitz, Rudolf Gottlieb, Jr. *chemical engineer*

Wilmington
Huang, Hua-Feng *electrical engineer, researcher*
Salzstein, Richard Alan *biomedical engineer, researcher*
Science, Carroll Thomas *chemical engineer*

DISTRICT OF COLUMBIA

Washington
Aein, Joseph Morris *electrical engineer*
Arkilic, Galip Mehmet *mechanical engineer, educator*
Bainum, Peter Montgomery *aerospace engineer, consultant*
Brahms, Thomas Walter *engineering institute executive*
Briskman, Robert David *engineering executive*
Cambel, Ali Bulent *engineering educator*
†Caywood, James Alexander, III *transportation engineering company executive, civil engineer*
Cerny, Louis Thomas *civil engineer, association executive*
Chalmers, Franklin Stevens, Jr. *engineering consultant*
Chen, Ho-Hong H. H. *industrial engineering executive, educator*
Dinneen, Gerald Paul *electrical engineer, former government official*
Edelson, Burton Irving *electrical engineering educator*
Eisner, Howard *engineering educator, engineering executive*
Flax, Alexander Henry *aeronautical engineer, science administrator*
Friedman, Arthur Daniel *electrical engineering and computer science educator, investment management company executive*
Giallorenzi, Thomas Gaetano *optical engineer*
Husemann, Robert William *mechanical engineer*
Jones, Howard St. Claire, Jr. *electronics engineering executive*
Kahn, Walter Kurt *engineering and applied science educator*
Katona, Peter Geza *biomedical engineer, educator*
Kaufman, John Gilbert, Jr. *materials engineer*
Kiper, Ali Muhlis *mechanical engineering educator, consultant*
Kirkbride, Chalmer Gatlin *chemical engineer*
Lemer, Andrew Charles *engineer, economist*
Liebowitz, Harold *aeronautical engineering educator, dean emeritus*
Lynch, Charles Theodore, Sr. *materials science engineering researcher, administrator, educator*
†Lynn, Larry *engineering executive*
Mathias, Joseph Simon *metallurgical engineer*
Montgomery, G(eorge) Franklin *electrical engineer, consultant*
Nichols, Kenneth David *consulting engineer*
†Ochs, Walter J. *civil engineer, drainage adviser*
Page, Robert Wesley *engineering and construction company executive, federal official*
Pickholtz, Raymond Lee *electrical engineering educator, consultant*
†Reis, Victor H. *mechanical engineer, government official*
Rojas, Richard Raimond *electrical engineer*
Salmon, William Cooper *mechanical engineer, engineering academy executive*
Shalowitz, Erwin Emmanuel *civil engineer*
Shon, Frederick John *nuclear engineer*
Skolnik, Merrill I. *electrical engineer*
Sorensen, John Noble *mechanical and nuclear engineer*
†Stanley, Thomas P. *chief engineer*
Stanwick, Tad *systems engineering and business management executive*
Stever, Horton Guyford *aerospace scientist and engineer, educator, consultant*
Townsend, Marjorie Rhodes *aerospace engineer, business executive*
Walker, M. Lucius, Jr. *mechanical engineer*
Walters, John Linton *electronics engineer, consultant*
Wang, John Cheng Hwai *communications engineer*
White, Robert Roy *chemical engineer*
Widnall, Sheila Evans *secretary of Air Force, aeronautical educator, university official*
Willenbrock, Frederick Karl *engineer, educator*
Wisniewski, John William *mining engineer, bank engineering executive*
Yang, Tony Tien Sheng *engineering educator*

FLORIDA

Atlantic Beach
Engelmann, Rudolph Herman *electronics consultant*

Boca Raton
Chryssafopoulos, Nicholas *civil engineer*
Lin, Y. K. *engineer, educator*
Rosenthal, Myron Martin *retired electrical engineer, educator, author*

Boynton Beach
Cross, Ralph Emerson *mechanical engineer*
Friedman, Raymond *chemical engineer, fire protection specialist*
Turner, William Benjamin *electrical engineer*

Bradenton
Friedrich, Robert Edmund *retired electrical engineer, corporate consultant*

Cape Canaveral
Clark, John F. *aerospace research and engineering educator*

Cape Coral
Purdy, Alan Harris *biomedical engineer*

Coral Gables
Baddour, Raymond Frederick *chemical engineer, educator, entrepreneur*
†Fung, Kee-Ying *engineer, educator, researcher*
Jury, Eliahu Ibraham *electrical engineer, research educator*
Kline, Jacob *biomedical engineering educator*
Saffir, Herbert Seymour *structural engineer, consultant*
Sumanth, David Jonnakoty *industrial engineer, educator*
Young, Tzay Y. *electrical and computer engineering educator*

Coral Springs
Elmore, Walter A. *electrical engineer, consultant*

Crystal River
Black, Charles Alvin *consulting engineering executive*

Daytona Beach
Geier, George *optical engineering consultant*
Haviland, Robert Paul *engineering executive, author*
Millar, Gordon Halstead *mechanical engineer, agricultural machinery manufacturing executive*
†Sliwa, Steven Mark *engineering executive, academic administrator*

Dundee
Johnson, Gordon Selby *consulting electrical engineer*

Englewood
Suiter, John William *industrial engineer, consultant*

Fort Lauderdale
Fishe, Gerald Raymond Aylmer *engineering executive*

Fort Myers
Mergler, Harry Winston *engineering educator*
Moeschl, Stanley Francis *electrical engineer, management consultant*
†Ölling, Edward Henry *aerospace engineer, consulting firm executive*
Scott, Kenneth Elsner *mechanical engineering educator*

Fort Myers Beach
Arneson, Harold Elias Grant *manufacturing engineer, consultant*

Gainesville
Anghaie, Samim *nuclear engineer, educator*
Block, Seymour Stanton *chemical engineering educator, consultant, writer*
Capehart, Barney Lee *industrial and systems engineer*
†Childers, Donald Gene *electrical engineering educator, researcher*
Couch, Leon Worthington *electrical engineering educator*
†Delfino, Joseph John *environmental engineering sciences educator*
Drucker, Daniel Charles *engineer, educator*
Elzinga, Donald Jack *industrial engineering researcher, educator*
Fossum, Jerry George *electrical engineering educator*
Isaacs, Gerald William *agricultural engineer, educator*
Kurzweg, Ulrich Hermann *engineering science educator*
Lindholm, Fredrik Arthur *electrical engineering educator, researcher*
Malvern, Lawrence Earl *engineering educator, researcher*
Neugroschel, Arnost *electrical engineering educator*
†Ohanian, Mihran Jacob *engineering educator*
Peebles, Peyton Zimmerman, Jr. *electrical engineer, educator*
Phillips, Winfred Marshall *engineer, educator, university administrator*
Price, Donald Ray *agricultural engineer, university administrator*
Schaub, James Hamilton *engineering educator*
Schmertmann, John Henry *civil engineer, educator, consultant*
Shyy, Wei *aerospace, mechanical engineering researcher and educator*
Singley, John Edward, Jr. *environmental engineer, consultant*
Verink, Ellis Daniel, Jr. *metallurgical engineering educator, consultant*
Wethington, John Abner, Jr. *retired nuclear engineering educator*

Indian Harbour Beach
Denaburg, Charles Robert *metallurgical engineer, retired government official*

Jacksonville
Joyce, Edward Rowen *chemical engineer, educator*
Klabosh, Charles Joseph *aerospace research and development executive*
Mueller, Edward Albert *transportation engineer executive*
Russell, David Emerson *mechanical engineer, consultant*
Shivler, James Fletcher, Jr. *retired civil engineer*

Jensen Beach
Kirjassoff, Gordon Louis *consulting civil engineer*

Juno Beach
Migliaro, Marco William *electrical engineer*

Lady Lake
Dore, Stephen Edward, Jr. *retired civil engineer*

Lakeland
Carrier, W(illiam) David, III *geotechnical engineer*

Melbourne
Swalm, Thomas Sterling *aerospace executive, retired military officer*

Miami
†Ajamil, Luis *civil engineer*
Bellero, Chiaffredo John *civil engineer*
de la Guardia, Mario Francisco *electrical engineer*
†Dye, H. Michael *engineering executive*
Khalil, Tarek Mohamed *industrial engineering educator*
Le Mehaute, Bernard Jean *marine physics educator*
Lindquist, Claude S. *electrical and computer engineering educator*
Nagel, Joachim Hans *biomedical engineer, educator*
Schuetzenduebel, Wolfram Gerhard *engineering executive*
Veziroglu, Turhan Nejat *mechanical engineering educator, energy researcher*

Naples
Benedict, Manson *chemical engineer, educator*
George, Charles William *retired aerospace equipment executive*
Jackson, Daniel Francis *engineering scientist, educator*
Suziedelis, Vytautas A. *engineering corporation executive*
†Tanner, Robert Hugh *engineer, consultant*
Widman, Richard Gustave *engineering and construction company executive*
Williams, George Earnest *engineer, retired business executive*

Nokomis
Cather, Donald Warren *civil engineer*

North Miami Beach
Wolfenson, Azi U. *electrical engineer*

Orlando
Buchanan, Walter Woolwine *engineering educator, electrical engineer*
Rice, Stephen Landon *engineering educator*
Roesner, Larry August *civil engineer*
Soileau, Marion Joseph *engineering and physics educator*

Osprey
Coates, Clarence Leroy, Jr. *research engineer, educator*

Palm Bay
Bachmann, Albert Edward *engineering educator*

Panama City
D'Arcy, Gerald Paul *engineering executive, consultant*

Pensacola
McSwain, Richard Horace *materials engineer, consultant*
Watt, Stuart George *engineering contracting company executive*

Ponte Vedra Beach
Schultz, Andrew Schultz, Jr. *industrial engineering educator*

Port Charlotte
Munger, Elmer Lewis *civil engineer, educator*

Saint Cloud
Everett, Woodrow Wilson *electrical engineer, educator*

Saint Petersburg
Collins, Carl Russell, Jr. *architectural and engineering company executive*
Donaldson, Merle Richard *electrical engineering educator, consultant*

Sarasota
Beck, George William *retired industrial engineer*
Hrones, John Anthony *mechanical engineering educator*
Ross, Gerald Fred *engineering executive, researcher*
Veinott, Cyril George *electrical engineer, consultant*
Weeks, Walter LeRoy *electrical engineering educator*

Satellite Beach
Van Arsdall, Robert Armes *engineer, retired air force officer*

Stuart
Morena, John Joseph *manufacturing engineer, executive*

Sun City Center
Jeffries, Robert Joseph *retired engineering educator, business executive*

Tallahassee
Braswell, Robert Neil *scientist, engineer, educator*
†Chen, Ching Jen *mechanical engineering educator, research scientist*
Coloney, Wayne Herndon *civil engineer*
De Forest, Sherwood Searle *agricultural engineer, agribusiness services executive*
Hall, Houghton Alexander *engineering professional*
Harrison, Thomas James *electrical engineer, educator*

Tampa
Ashley, James Robert *electrical engineer, inventor, educator*
Deutsch, Sid *bioengineer, educator*
Givens, Paul Edward *industrial engineer, educator*
†Gregg, Charles W. *engineering executive*
Henning, Rudolf Ernst *electrical engineer, educator, consultant*
Miller, Charles Leslie *civil engineer, planner, consultant*

Venice
Concordia, Charles *consulting engineer*

Vero Beach
Haywood, Oliver Garfield *engineer*

West Palm Beach
Aaron, M. Robert *electrical engineer*
Coar, Richard John *mechanical engineer, aerospace consultant*
†Gillette, Frank C., Jr. *aeronautical engineer*
Koff, Bernard L. *engineering executive*
Olsak, Ivan Karel *civil engineer*

Winter Park
Flick, Carl *electrical engineer, consultant, free-lance author*

GEORGIA

Athens
Kraszewski, Andrzej Wojciech *electrical engineer, researcher*
Nelson, Stuart Owen *agricultural engineer, researcher, educator*
†Verma, Brahm Prakash *agricultural engineer*

Atlanta
Abdel-Khalik, Said Ibrahim *nuclear and mechanical engineering educator*
†Antolovich, Stephen Dale *engineering educator*
Bacon, Louis Albert *retired consulting civil engineer*
Barksdale, Richard Dillon *civil engineer, educator*
Barnwell, Thomas Pinkney, III *electrical engineering educator, business executive*
Bourne, Henry Clark, Jr. *electrical engineering educator, former academic official*
Carlson, Robert Lee *engineering educator*
Dahlke, Wayne Theodore *civil engineer, corporate executive*
Dalrymple, Gordon Bennett *former engineering company executive*
Durbetaki, Pandeli *mechanical engineer, educator, researcher*
Eckert, Charles Alan *chemical engineering educator*
Fitzgerald, John Edmund *civil engineering educator, dean*
†Grace, Donald J. *engineering researcher*
Griffin, Clayton Houstoun *retired power company engineer, lecturer*
Hatch, Henry J. *engineering executive*
Hodges, Dewey Harper *aerospace engineer, educator*
Joy, Edward Bennett *electrical engineer, educator*
Loewy, Robert Gustav *engineering educator, aeronautical engineering executive*
McClellan, James Harold *electrical engineering educator*
Mersereau, Russell Manning *electrical engineering educator, consultant*
Moore, Henry Rogers *civil engineer, railroad operating officer*
Nemhauser, George L. *industrial, systems engineer, operations research educator*
Nerem, Robert Michael *engineering educator, consultant*
†Reedy, Edward K. *system engineer administrator*
Richards, Robert Wadsworth *civil engineer, consultant*
Rodrigue, George Pierre *electrical engineering educator, consultant*
Rousseau, Ronald William *chemical engineering educator, researcher*
Schafer, Ronald William *electrical engineering educator*
Scovil, Roger Morris *engineering company executive*
Smith, Glenn Stanley *electrical engineering educator*
†Stacey, Weston Monroe, Jr. *nuclear engineer, educator*
Su, Kendall Ling-Chiao *engineering educator*
†Teja, Amyn S. *chemical engineering educator, consultant*
Thuesen, Gerald Jorgen *industrial engineer, educator*
†Toler, James C. *electrical engineer*
Webb, Roger Paul *electrical engineer, educator*
White, John Austin, Jr. *engineering educator, dean, consultant*
Wiedeman, John Herman *civil engineer*
Winer, Ward Otis *mechanical engineer, educator*
Wu, James Chen-Yuan *aerospace engineering educator*
†Yoganathan, Ajit Prithiviraj *biomedical engineer, educator*

Dahlonega
Jones, William Benjamin, Jr. *electrical engineering educator*

Doraville
†Wempner, Gerald Arthur *engineering educator*

Jersey
Batchelor, Joseph Brooklyn, Jr. *electronics engineer, consultant*

Kennesaw
Sowers, George Frederick *civil engineer*

Marietta
†Foster, Finley B. *engineering company executive*
Hayes, Robert Deming *electrical engineer, consultant*

Norcross
Harrison, Gordon Ray *engineering executive, consultant, research scientist*
Rouse, William Bradford *systems engineering executive, researcher, educator*

Roswell
Bristow, Preston Abner, Jr. *civil engineer, environmental engineer*

Savannah
Hsu, Ming-Yu *engineer, educator*

HAWAII

Honolulu
Abramson, Norman *electronics executive*
Antal, Michael Jerry, Jr. *mechanical engineering educator*
Cox, Richard Horton *civil engineering executive*
Kohloss, Frederick Henry *consulting engineer*
Koide, Frank Takayuki *electrical engineer*
Minhas, Faqir Ullah *aerospace engineer*
Wang, Jaw-Kai *agricultural engineering educator*
Yee, Alfred Alphonse *structural engineer, consultant*

Kaneohe
Hanson, Richard Edwin *civil engineer*

Kapaau
McFee, Richard *electrical engineer, physicist*

IDAHO

Boise
McKee, Joseph Fulton *engineering and construction executive*
True, Leland Beyer *civil engineer, consultant*
Wilbur, Lyman Dwight *consulting engineering executive*

Idaho Falls
Riemke, Richard Allan *mechanical engineer*
†Woodall, David Monroe *research engineer*

Island Park
Stratford, Ray Paul *electrical engineer, consultant*

Moscow
†DeShazer, James Arthur *agricultural engineer, educator, administrator*
Jackson, Melbourne Leslie *chemical engineering educator and administrator, consultant*
Jacobsen, Richard T. *mechanical engineering educator*
Peterson, Charles Loren *agricultural engineer, educator*

Pocatello
Wilson, Albert Eugene *nuclear engineering educator*

Rigby
Peterson, Erle Vidaillet *retired metallurgical engineer*

ILLINOIS

Argonne
†Chang, Yoon Il *nuclear engineer*
Kumar, Romesh *chemical engineer*

Arlington Heights
†Jenny, Daniel P. *retired engineer*

Carbondale
†Chugh, Yoginder Paul *mining engineering educator*
Orthwein, William Coe *mechanical engineer*
Smith, James Gilbert *electrical engineer*

Champaign
Kruger, William Arnold *consulting civil engineer*
Sechrist, Chalmers F., Jr. *electrical engineering educator*

Chicago
Acs, Joseph Steven *transportation engineering consultant*
Agarwal, Gyan Chand *engineering educator*
Babcock, Lyndon Ross, Jr. *environmental engineer, educator*
Breyer, Norman Nathan *metallurgical engineering educator, consultant*
Budenholzer, Roland Anthony *mechanical engineering educator*
Camras, Marvin *electrical and computer engineering educator, inventor*
Chen, Wai-Kai *electrical engineering and computer science educator, consultant*
Chung, Paul Myungha *mechanical engineer, educator*
Dix, Rollin C(umming) *mechanical engineering educator, consultant*
D'Souza, Anthony Frank *mechanical engineering educator, consultant, researcher*
Epstein, Raymond *engineering and architectural executive*
Epstein, Sidney *architectural engineer*
Gerstner, Robert William *structural engineering educator, consultant*
Graupe, Daniel *electrical and computer engineering educator, systems and biomedical engineer*
Gupta, Krishna Chandra *mechanical engineering educator*
Guralnick, Sidney Aaron *civil engineering educator*
Hartnett, James Patrick *engineering educator*
Hobbs, Marvin *engineering executive*
Kim, H. J. (Shaun Kim) *engineer*
†Kupperman, Melvin *civil engineer, construction and development company executive*
Lin, James Chih-I *biomedical and electrical engineer, educator*
Linden, Henry Robert *chemical engineering research executive*
Markus, Fred H. *engineering and architectural company executive*
McCullough, Henry G(lenn) L(uther) *nuclear engineer*
Michelson, Irving *aerospace engineer*
Miller, Irving Franklin *chemical engineering educator, academic administrator*
Minkowycz, W. J. *mechanical engineering educator*
Murata, Tadao *engineering and computer science educator*
Nelson, Kenneth Edward *consulting engineer*
Nickel, Melvin Edwin *metallurgical engineer*
Noll, Kenneth Eugene *air resources engineering educator*
Novick, David *civil engineer, educator*
Patterson, James William *environmental engineering educator, consultant*
Riddell, Matthew Donald Rutherford *consulting environmental engineer*
Rikoski, Richard Anthony *engineering executive, electrical engineer*
Smith, Spencer Bailey *engineering and business educator*
†Stone, Daniel Hunter *metallurgical engineer, researcher*
Swanson, Bernet Steven *consulting engineer, former educator*
Todd Copley, Judith Ann *materials and metallurgical engineering educator*

Clarendon Hills
Moritz, Donald Brooks *mechanical engineer, consultant*

Decatur
Graf, Karl Rockwell *nuclear engineer*
Koucky, John Richard *metallurgical engineer, manufacturing executive*

Des Plaines
Dlouhy, Phillip Edward *engineering, construction executive*

Dunlap
Bailey, John Maxwell *mechanical engineer, consultant*

Elmhurst
Burton, Darrell Irvin *engineering executive*

Evanston
Achenbach, Jan Drewes *engineer and scientist*
Bankoff, Seymour George *chemical engineer, educator*
Belytschko, Ted Bohdan *civil, mechanical engineering educator*
Brazelton, William Thomas *chemical engineering educator*
Butt, John Baecher *chemical engineering educator*
Carr, Stephen Howard *materials engineer, educator*
Cheng, Herbert Su-Yuen *mechanical engineering educator*
Epstein, Max *electrical engineering educator*
Fine, Morris Eugene *materials engineer, educator*
Frey, Donald Nelson *industrial engineer, educator, manufacturing company executive*
Goldstick, Thomas Karl *biomedical engineering educator*
Haddad, Abraham Herzl *electrical engineering educator, researcher*
Keer, Leon Morris *engineering educator*
Kistler, Alan Lee *engineering educator*
Kliphardt, Raymond A. *engineering educator*
Krizek, Raymond John *civil engineering educator, consultant*
Mah, Richard Sze Hao *chemical engineering educator*
Marhic, Michel Edmond *engineering educator, entrepreneur, consultant*
Murphy, Gordon John *engineering educator*
Ottino, Julio Mario *chemical engineering educator, scientist*
Shah, Surendra Poonamchand *engineering educator, researcher*
Sobel, Alan *electrical engineer, physicist*
Taflove, Allen *electrical engineer, educator, researcher, consultant*
Tankin, Richard Samuel *fluid dynamics educator*
Van Ness, James Edward *electrical engineering educator*

Evergreen Park
Ephraim, Max, Jr. *mechanical engineer*

Gilman
Ireland, Herbert Orin *engineering educator*

Glenview
Adler, Robert *electronics engineer*
Harris, Ronald David *chemical engineer*
Russell, Henry George *structural engineer*
Van Zelst, Theodore William *civil engineer, natural resource exploration company executive*

Hartford
Christian, Nelson Frederick *chemical engineer*

Lake Forest
Lambert, John Boyd *chemical engineer, consultant*

Lemont
Chen, Shoei-Sheng *mechanical engineer*

Lisle
Melsa, James Louis *electrical engineer*

Lombard
†Ahlberg, James E. *technical services company executive*
Branum, William Howell *engineering company executive*

Moline
†Harrington, Roy Edwards *agricultural engineer, author*

Mount Prospect
†Scott, Norman Laurence *engineering consultant*

Naperville
Crawford, Raymond Maxwell, Jr. *nuclear engineer*
Oxenreiter, Maurice Frank *chemical engineer*
Wharton, Lennard *engineering company executive*

North Barrington
Bergstrom, Richard Norman *civil engineer*

Northfield
Fraenkel, Stephen Joseph *engineering and research executive*

Oak Brook
Degerstrom, James Marvin *engineering manager*

Oak Park
Clark, John Peter, III *engineering consultant*

Orland Park
Dyott, Richard Burnaby *research engineering executive*

Palatine
Francis, Philip Hamilton *technology executive*
Novak, Robert Louis *civil engineer, pavement management consultant*

Park Ridge
Bridges, Jack Edgar *electronics engineer*
Ellis, Robert Griswold *engineering executive*

Peoria
†Doyle, Richard Lee *architect, engineer*
†Rainson, Ronald Lee *engineering executive, consultant*

Plainfield
Chakrabarti, Subrata Kumar *marine research engineer*

Rockford
Block, Stanley Marlin *engineering educator, arbitrator*
Eliason, Jon Tate *electrical engineer*

Skokie
Corley, William Gene *engineering research executive*
Hognestad, Eivind *retired civil engineer*
Panarese, William C. *civil engineer*
Siegal, Rita Goran *engineering company executive*

Springfield
†Hahn, Ralph Crane *structural engineer, consultant*
Hanson, Walter Edmund *consulting civil engineer*
Lyons, J. Rolland *civil engineer*
Reed, John Charles *chemical engineer*

Urbana
Addy, Alva Leroy *mechanical engineer*
†Alkire, Richard Collin *chemical engineering educator*
Assanis, Dennis N. (Dionissios Assanis) *mechanical engineering educator*
Axford, Roy Arthur *nuclear engineering educator*
Basar, Tamer *electrical engineering educator*
Bayne, James Wilmer *mechanical engineering educator*
Beck, Paul Adams *metallurgist, educator*
Bergeron, Clifton George *ceramic engineer, educator*
Chao, Bei Tse *mechanical engineering educator*
Chato, John Clark *mechanical engineering educator*
Clausing, Arthur M. *mechanical engineering educator*
Conry, Thomas Francis *mechanical engineering educator, consultant*
Cusano, Cristino *mechanical engineer, educator*
Dobrovolny, Jerry Stanley *engineering educator*
Economy, James *polymer researcher, consultant*
Eden, James Gary *electrical engineering and physics educator, researcher*
Engelbrecht, Richard Stevens *environmental engineering educator*
Gaddy, Oscar Lee *electrical engineering educator*
Goering, Carroll E. *agricultural engineering educator*
Hajj, Ibrahim Nasri *electrical and computer engineering educator*
Hall, William Joel *civil engineer, educator*
Hannon, Bruce Michael *engineer, educator*
Hanratty, Thomas Joseph *chemical engineer, educator*
Hawkins, Neil Middleton *civil engineer, educator*
Herrin, Moreland *civil engineering educator, consultant*
Hess, Karl *electrical and computer engineering educator*
Holonyak, Nick, Jr. *electrical engineering educator*
Huang, Thomas Shi-Tao *electrical engineering educator, researcher*
Hunt, Donnell Ray *agricultural engineering educator*
Kang, Sung-Mo (Steve Kang) *electrical engineering educator*
Kesler, Clyde Ervin *engineering educator*
Kumar, Panganamala Ramana *electrical and computer engineering educator*
†Lauffenburger, Douglas Alan *chemical engineering educator*
May, Walter Grant *chemical engineer*
Mayes, Paul Eugene *engineering educator, technical consultant*
Mazumder, Jyotirmoy *mechanical and industrial engineering educator*
Miley, George Hunter *nuclear engineering educator*
Miller, Robert Earl *engineer, educator*
Ormsbee, Allen Ives *aeronautical and astronautical engineering educator, researcher, consultant*
Pai, Anantha Mangalore *electrical engineering educator, consultant*
Perkins, William Randolph *electrical engineer, educator*
Rao, Nannapaneni Narayana *electrical engineer*
Siess, Chester Paul *civil engineering educator*
Socie, Darrell Frederick *mechanical engineering educator*
Soo, Shao Lee *mechanical engineer, educator*
Stallmeyer, James Edward *engineer, educator*
Swenson, George Warner, Jr. *electronics engineer, radio astronomer, educator*
Tang, Wilson Hon-chung *engineering educator*
Trick, Timothy Noel *electrical and computer engineering educator, researcher*
†Trigger, Kenneth James *manufacturing engineering educator*
Van Valkenburg, Mac Elwyn *electrical engineering educator*
Wert, Charles Allen *metallurgical and mining engineering educator*
Westwater, James William *chemical engineering educator*
White, Robert Allan *mechanical engineering educator*
Yoerger, Roger Raymond *agricultural engineer, educator*

Wilmette
Barnett, Ralph Lipsey *engineering educator*
Muhlenbruch, Carl W. *civil engineer*

INDIANA

Bloomington
Harder, John E. *electrical engineer*

Chesterfield
Fry, Meredith Warren *civil engineer, consultant*

Columbus
Kamo, Roy *engineering company executive*

Evansville
†Gerhart, Philip Mark *mechanical engineering educator*
Hartsaw, William O. *mechanical engineering educator*

Fort Wayne
Lyons, Jerry Lee *mechanical engineer*
Mahmoud, Aly Ahmed *electrical engineering educator*
Quinn, C. Jack *mechanical engineering educator, consultant*
Weatherford, George Edward *civil engineer*
Williams, Walter Jackson, Jr. *electrical engineer, consultant*

Hammond
Neff, Gregory Pall *manufacturing engineering educator, consultant*
Pierson, Edward Samuel *engineering educator, consultant*

Indianapolis
Brannon-Peppas, Lisa *chemical engineer, researcher*
Cones, Van Buren *electronics engineer, consultant*
Monical, Robert Duane *consulting structural engineer*

Lafayette
Emery, Alden Hayes, Jr. *chemical engineer, educator*
Etzel, James Edward *environmental engineering educator*
Fox, Robert William *mechanical engineering educator*
Geddes, Leslie Alexander *bioengineer, physiologist, educator*
Gustafson, Winthrop Adolph *aeronautical and astronautical engineering educator*
Mc Laughlin, John Francis *civil engineer, educator*
Ott, Karl Otto *nuclear engineering educator, consultant*

Muncie
Bennon, Saul *electrical engineer, transformer consultant*

Notre Dame
Gray, William Guerin *civil engineering educator*
Jerger, Edward William *mechanical engineer, university dean*
Kohn, James Paul *engineering educator*
Michel, Anthony Nikolaus *electrical engineering educator, researcher*
Sain, Michael Kent *electrical engineering educator*
Schmitz, Roger Anthony *chemical engineering educator, academic administrator*
Szewczyk, Albin Anthony *engineering educator*
Varma, Arvind *chemical engineering educator, researcher*

Orleans
Keys, Steven Franklin *chemical engineer*

Princeton
Mullins, Richard Austin *chemical engineer*

Terre Haute
†Smith, Charles Oliver *engineer*
Wheelock, Larry Arthur *engineer, consultant*

West Lafayette
Albright, Lyle Frederick *chemical engineering educator*
Altschaeffl, Adolph George *civil engineer*
Andres, Ronald Paul *chemical engineer, educator*
Barany, James Walter *industrial engineering educator*
Bement, Arden Lee, Jr. *engineering educator*
Bogdanoff, John Lee *aeronautical engineering educator*
Cohen, Raymond *mechanical engineer, educator*
Cooper, James Albert, Jr. *electrical engineering educator*
Dayananda, Mysore Ananthamurthy *materials engineering educator*
Delleur, Jacques William *civil engineering educator*
Dolch, William Lee *retired engineering materials educator*
†Drnevich, Vincent Paul *civil engineering educator*
Eckert, Roger E(arl) *chemical engineering educator*
†Farris, Thomas N. *engineering educator, researcher*
Friedlaender, Fritz Josef *electrical engineering educator*
Fukunaga, Keinosuke *engineering educator*
Grace, Richard Edward *engineering educator*
Hillberry, Ben(ny) M(ax) *mechanical engineering educator*
Hinkle, Charles Nelson *retired agricultural engineering educator*
Incropera, Frank Paul *mechanical engineering educator*
Jacko, Robert Bertram *environmental engineering educator*
Kashyap, Rangasami Lakshmi Narayan *electrical engineering educator*
Landgrebe, David Allen *electrical engineer*
Leimkuhler, Ferdinand Francis *industrial engineering educator*
Liley, Peter Edward *mechanical engineering educator*
Lin, Pen-Min *electrical engineer, educator*
Marshall, Francis Joseph *aerospace engineer*
Mc Gillem, Clare Duane *electrical engineering educator*
Michael, Harold Louis *civil engineering educator*
Neudeck, Gerold Walter *electrical engineering educator*
Ong, Chee-Mun *engineering educator*
Peppas, Nikolaos Athanassiou *chemical engineering educator, consultant*
Pritsker, A. Alan B. *engineering executive, educator*
†Sadeghi, Farshid *engineering educator*
Salvendy, Gavriel *industrial engineer*
Schuhmann, Reinhardt, Jr. *metallurgical engineering educator, consultant*
†Schwartz, Richard John *electrical engineering educator, researcher*
Solberg, James Joseph *industrial engineering educator*
Sozen, Mete Avni *civil engineering educator*
Stevenson, Warren Howard *mechanical engineering educator*
Taber, Margaret Ruth *electrical engineering technology educator, electrical engineer*
Vest, Robert Wilson *ceramic engineering educator*
Viskanta, Raymond *mechanical engineering educator*
Wankat, Phillip Charles *chemical engineering educator*
Williams, Theodore Joseph *engineering educator*

IOWA

Ames
Anderson, Robert Morris, Jr. *electrical engineer*
Basart, John Philip *electrical engineering and radio astronomy researcher, educator*
Baumann, Edward Robert *sanitary engineering educator*
Boylan, David Ray *retired chemical engineer, educator*
Brown, Robert Grover *engineering educator*
Buchele, Wesley Fisher *agricultural engineering educator, consultant*
Burnet, George, Jr. *engineering educator*
Cleasby, John LeRoy *civil engineer, educator*
†Colvin, Thomas Stuart *agricultural engineer, farmer*
Curry, Norval Herbert *retired agricultural engineer*
Ekberg, Carl Edwin, Jr. *civil engineering educator*
Geiger, Randall L. *electrical engineering educator, design engineer*
Iversen, James Delano *aerospace engineering educator, consultant*
Jones, Edwin Channing, Jr. *electrical engineering educator*
Larsen, William Lawrence *materials science and engineering educator*
Larson, Maurice Allen *chemical engineer, educator*
†Mischke, Charles Russell *mechanical engineering educator*
Okiishi, Theodore Hisao *mechanical engineering educator*
Riley, William Franklin *mechanical engineering educator*
Sanders, Wallace Wolfred, Jr. *civil engineer*
Tannehill, John C. *aerospace engineer, educator*
Wilder, David Randolph *materials engineer, consultant*
†Wilhelm, Harley A. *metallurgist, chemist*
Wilson, Lennox Norwood *aeronautical engineering educator*
Young, Donald Fredrick *engineering educator*

Decorah
Erdman, Lowell Paul *civil engineer, land surveyor*

Iowa City
Arora, Jasbir Singh *engineering educator*
Branson, Dan Earle *civil engineer, educator*
Eyman, Earl Duane *electrical science educator, consultant*
Haug, Edward Joseph, Jr. *mechanical engineering educator, simulation research engineer*
Hering, Robert Gustave *mechanical engineer, educator, university administrator*
Lance, George Milward *mechanical engineering educator*
Lonngren, Karl Erik *electrical and computer engineering educator*
Madsen, Donald Howard *engineering educator, consultant*
†Marshall, Jeffrey Scott *mechanical engineer, educator*
Patel, Virendra Chaturbhai *mechanical engineering educator*

Madrid
Handy, Richard Lincoln *civil engineer, educator*

Mason City
Wallace, Ralph Howes *retired engineering company executive*

Muscatine
Fosholt, Sanford Kenneth *consulting engineer*
Stanley, Richard Holt *consulting engineer*
Thomopulos, Gregs G. *consulting engineering company executive*

KANSAS

Lawrence
Benjamin, Bezaleel Solomon *architecture and architectural engineering educator*
Forman, George Whiteman *mechanical design consultant*
Green, Don Wesley *chemical and petroleum engineering educator*
†Holtzman, Julian Charles *electrical engineer*
Leonard, Roy Junior *civil engineering educator*
Lucas, William Max, Jr. *structural engineer, university dean*
Mc Kinney, Ross Erwin *civil engineering educator*
Moore, Richard Kerr *electrical engineering educator*
Muirhead, Vincent Uriel *aerospace engineer*
Rolfe, Stanley Theodore *civil engineer, educator*
Roskam, Jan *aerospace engineer*
Rowland, James Richard *electrical engineering educator*
Smith, Howard Wesley *engineering educator*
Smith, Robert Lee *retired civil engineering educator*
Zerwekh, Robert Paul *engineering administrator, engineering management educator, researcher, consultant, artist*

Lee's Summit
Puglisi, Philip James *electrical engineer*

Manhattan
Appl, Fredric Carl *mechanical engineering educator*
†Fenton, Donald Lee *mechanical engineering educator, consultant*
Johnson, William Howard *agricultural engineer, educator*
Kirmser, Philip George *engineering educator*
Lee, E(ugene) Stanley *industrial engineer, mathematician, educator*
Simons, Gale Gene *nuclear engineering educator, university administrator*

Overland Park
†Baker, Charles H. *engineering company executive*

Pittsburg
Nettels, George Edward, Jr. *mining company executive*

Salina
Crawford, Lewis Cleaver *engineering executive*

Shawnee Mission
Callahan, Harry Leslie *civil engineer*
Heineman, Paul Lowe *consulting civil engineer*
Robinson, Thomas Bullene *retired civil engineer*

Topeka
Comstock, Glen David *civil engineer*
Frazier, John Warren *civil engineer*
Metzler, Dwight Fox *civil engineer, retired state official*

University Of Kansas
Kraft, David Christian *civil engineering educator*

Wichita
Egbert, Robert Iman *electrical engineering educator, academic administrator*
†Ellis, David R. *aeronautical researcher*
Gosman, Albert Louis *mechanical engineering educator*
Mc Kee, George Moffitt, Jr. *civil engineer, consultant*
Sills, Milton D. *engineer, air transportation executive*
†Wentz, William H., Jr. *aerospace engineer, educator*
Wilhelm, William Jean *civil engineering educator*

KENTUCKY

Lexington
†Caroland, William Bourne *structural engineer*
Cremers, Clifford John *mechanical engineering educator*
†Hanson, Mark Todt *engineering mechanics educator*
Heffelbower, Dwight Earl *engineering services company executive*
Jewell, Robert Burnett *engineering company executive*
Nasar, Syed Abu *electrical engineering educator*
Steele, Earl Larsen *electrical engineering educator*
Tauchert, Theodore Richmond *mechanical engineer, educator*
Traynor, Harry Sheehy *engineering consultant*
Walker, John Neal *agricultural engineering educator*

Louisville
Clark, John Hallett, III *consulting engineering executive*
Cornelius, Wayne Anderson *engineering technology educator, consultant*
Garcia, Rafael Jorge *chemical engineer*
Hanley, Thomas Richard *engineering educator*
Ward, Thomas Leon *engineering educator*

LOUISIANA

Baker
Moody, Lamon Lamar, Jr. *civil engineer*

Baton Rouge
Acar, Yalcin Bekir *civil engineer, soil remediation technology executive, educator*
Aghazadeh, Fereydoun *industrial engineer, educator*
Arman, Ara *civil engineering educator*
Chen, Peter Pin-Shan *electrical engineering and computer science educator, data processing executive*
Coates, Jesse *retired chemical engineer*
Cundy, Vic Arnold *mechanical engineer, educator*
Desbrandes, Robert *petroleum engineering educator, consultant*
Gopu, Vijaya K.A. *engineer, consultant*
Marshak, Alan Howard *electrical engineer, educator*
McLaughlin, Edward *chemical engineering educator, dean*
Moody, Gene Byron *engineering executive, small business owner*
†Pike, Ralph Webster *chemical engineer, educator, university official*
†Stopher, Peter Robert *civil and transportation engineering educator, consultant*

Kenner
Siebel, Mathias Paul *mechanical engineer*

Lafayette
Chieri, Pericle Adriano Carlo *educator, consulting mechanical and aeronautical engineer, naval architect*
Domingue, Emery *consulting engineering company executive*
Leon, Benjamin Joseph *electrical engineering educator, consultant*

New Orleans
Lannes, William Joseph, III *electrical engineer*
Lee, Griff Calicutt *civil engineer*
Quirk, Peter Richard *engineering company executive*
Tewell, Joseph Robert, Jr. *electrical engineer*
†Walk, Frank Humphrey *consulting engineer*

Ruston
Barron, Randall Franklin *mechanical engineer, educator, consultant*
Painter, Jack Timberlake *civil engineer*
†Warrington, Robert O'Neil, Jr. *mechanical engineering educator and administrator, researcher*

Shreveport
Demopulos, Chris *engineering company executive*

MAINE

East Boothbay
Smith, Merlin Gale *engineering executive, researcher*

Oakland
†Poulin, Thomas Edward *marine engineer, state legislator, retail business owner*

Orono
Rivard, William Charles *mechanical engineering educator*

Pemaquid Beach
Brown, Donald Vaughn *technical educator, engineering consultant*

Portland
Raisbeck, Gordon *systems engineer*

Prospect Harbor
Shipman, Charles William *chemical engineer*

MARYLAND

Aberdeen Proving Ground
†Paules, Palmer L. *engineering director*

Annapolis
Allen, John Loyd *technical engineering consultant*
DiAiso, Robert Joseph *civil engineer*
†Granger, Robert Alan *aerospace engineer*
Henderson, William Boyd *engineering consulting company executive*
Johnson, Bruce *engineering educator*
Kapland, Mitchell Arthur *engineering firm executive*

Baltimore
Cohn, Marvin *consulting engineering executive*
Corn, Morton *environmental engineer, educator*
Corotis, Ross Barry *civil engineering educator, academic administrator*
Davidson, Frederic McShan *electrical engineering educator*
Degenford, James Edward *electrical engineer, educator*
Donahoo, Melvin Lawrence *aerospace management consultant, industrial engineer*
Donohue, Marc David *chemical engineering educator*
Ellingwood, Bruce Russell *structural engineering researcher*
Fisher, Jack Carrington *environmental engineering educator*
Giddens, Don Peyton *engineering educator, researcher*
Huggins, William Herbert *electrical engineering educator*
Jelinek, Frederick *electrical engineer, educator*
Katz, Joseph Louis *chemical engineer, educator*
Knoedler, Elmer L. *retired chemical engineer*
Long, Robert Radcliffe *fluid mechanics educator*
Mc Cord, Kenneth Armstrong *consulting engineer*
O'Melia, Charles Richard *environmental engineering educator*
Popel, Aleksander S. *engineering educator*
†Prince, Jerry Ladd *engineering educator*
ReVelle, Charles S. *environmental engineer, geophysicist, systems analysis and economics educator*
Sharpe, William Norman, Jr. *mechanical engineer, educator*

Bel Air
Powers, Doris Hurt *engineering company executive*

Bethesda
†Bosnak, Robert J. *mechanical engineer, federal agency administrator*
Cottony, Herman Vladimir *electronic engineer, consultant*
Eden, Murray *electrical engineer, emeritus educator*
Freedman, Joseph *sanitary and public health engineering consultant*
Koltnow, Peter Gregory *engineering consultant*
Saville, Thorndike, Jr. *coastal engineer, consultant*
Sevik, Maurice *engineer*

Burtonsville
†Yang, Jackson *aerospace engineering company executive*

Catonsville
Cadman, Theodore Wesley *chemical engineering educator*

Chevy Chase
Mayers, Jean *aeronautical engineering educator*
Rockwell, Theodore *nuclear engineer*

Clarksburg
Bargellini, Pier Luigi *electrical engineer*
Mahle, Christoph Erhard *electrical engineer*

Clarksville
Brancato, Emanuel Leonard *electrical engineering consultant*

Cockeysville Hunt Valley
Hirsch, Richard Arthur *mechanical engineer*

College Park
Anderson, John David, Jr. *aerospace engineer*
Barbe, David Franklin *electrical engineer, educator*
Blankenship, Gilmer Leroy *electrical engineering educator, engineering company executive*
Cunniff, Patrick Francis *mechanical engineer*
Dally, James William *mechanical engineering educator, consultant*
Ephremides, Anthony *electrical engineering educator*
Gessow, Alfred *aerospace engineer, educator*
Granatstein, Victor Lawrence *electrical engineer, educator*
Gupta, Ashwani Kumar *mechanical engineering educator*
Levine, William Silver *electrical engineering educator*
Ligomenides, Panos Aristides *electrical and computer engineering educator, consultant*
Marcus, Steven Irl *electrical engineering educator*
Newcomb, Robert Wayne *electrical engineer*
†Pai, Shih I. *aeronautical engineer*
Singh, Amarjit *engineering executive, scientist, management consultant*
Smith, Theodore Goodwin *chemical engineering educator*
Taylor, Leonard Stuart *engineering educator, consultant*

Columbia
Hegedus, L. Louis *chemical engineer, research and development executive*

Frederick
Bryan, John Leland *retired engineering educator*

Gaithersburg
Cookson, Alan Howard *electrical engineer, researcher*
Fuhrman, Ralph Edward *civil and environmental engineer*
Hoppes, Harrison Neil *corporate executive, chemical engineer*
Levine, Robert Sidney *chemical engineer*
Pande, Krishna Prasad *electrical engineer, physicist*
Rabinow, Jacob *electrical engineer, consultant*
Ulbrecht, Jaromir Josef *chemical engineer*
Wiederhorn, Sheldon Martin *materials scientist, ceramic engineer*
Wright, Richard Newport, III *civil engineer, government official*

Glen Arm
Mc Cord, Marshal *civil engineer*

Greenbelt
Cooper, Robert Shanklin *engineering executive, former government official*
Fitzmaurice, Michael William *electrical and mechanical engineer*
†O'Mara, Arthur James *civil engineer*

Hunt Valley
Kinstlinger, Jack *engineer executive, consultant*
McKay, Jack Alexander *electronics engineer, physicist*

Kingsville
Pullen, Keats A., Jr. *electronics engineer*

Landover
Freeman, Ernest Robert *engineering executive*

Lanham Seabrook
Blanchard, David Lawrence *aerospace executive, real estate developer*

Laurel
†Billig, Frederick Stucky *mechanical engineer*
Dallman, Paul Jerald *engineer, writer*
Eaton, Alvin Ralph *aeronautical and systems engineer, research and development administrator*
Halushynsky, George Dobroslav *systems engineer*
Perrone, Nicholas *mechanical engineer, business executive*
Sherwood, Aaron Wiley *aerodynamics educator*

Linthicum
Skillman, William Alfred *consulting engineering executive*

North Bethesda
Foa, Joseph Victor *aeronautical engineer, educator*

Potomac
Peters, Frank Albert *retired chemical engineer*

Rockville
Beckjord, Eric Stephen *energy researcher, nuclear engineering educator*
McDonald, Capers Walter *biomedical engineer, corporate executive*
McMahon, Edward Peter *systems engineer, consultant*
Weinberger, Leon Walter *sanitary engineer*

Seabrook
Durrani, Sajjad Haidar *space communications engineer*
Laurenson, Robert Mark *mechanical engineer*

Severna Park
Retterer, Bernard Lee *electronic engineering consultant*

Silver Spring
Blake, Lamont Vincent *electronics consultant*
Eades, James Beverly, Jr. *aeronautical engineer*
Foresti, Roy, Jr. *chemical engineer*
Glenn, Robert Edward *industrial hygienist, trade association executive, former government research administrator*
Hermach, Francis Lewis *consulting engineer*
Mundel, Marvin Everett *industrial engineer*
Scipio, L(ouis) Albert, II *aerospace science engineering educator, architect, military historian*
Shames, Irving Herman *engineering educator*

Sparks
Barr, Irwin Robert *retired aeronautical engineer*

MASSACHUSETTS

Acton
Anderson, Bob *environmental company executive, consultant*
Lee, Shih-Ying *mechanical engineering educator*

Amherst
Abbott, Douglas Eugene *engineering educator*
Akers, Sheldon Buckingham, Jr. *electrical and computer engineering educator*
Berger, Bernard Ben *environmental and civil engineer, former educator and public health officer*
Clayton, Joe Todd *agricultural and food engineering educator*
Franks, Lewis E. *electrical and computer engineering educator, researcher*
Haensel, Vladimir *chemical engineering educator*
Laurence, Robert Lionel *chemical engineering educator*
McIntosh, Robert Edward, Jr. *electrical engineering educator, consultant, electronics executive*
Menon, Premachandran Rama *electrical engineering educator*
Motherway, Joseph Edward *mechanical engineer, educator*
Nash, William Arthur *civil engineer, educator*
Schaubert, Daniel Harold *electrical engineering educator*
Swift, Calvin Thomas *electrical and computer engineering educator*
White, Merit Penniman *engineering educator*

Andover
Jakes, William Chester *electrical engineer*

Arlington
Gumpertz, Werner Herbert *structural engineering company executive*

Ashfield
Nye, Edwin Packard *mechanical engineering educator*

Attleboro
†Buckley, Charles E. *engineering executive*

Bedford
Cronson, Harry Marvin *electronics engineer*
Dill, Melville Reese, Jr. *industrial engineering consultant*
Hicks, Walter Joseph *electrical engineer, consultant*
Jelalian, Albert V. *electrical engineer*
Kovaly, John Joseph *consulting engineering executive, educator*
Ren, Chung-Li *engineer*
Zraket, Charles Anthony *systems research and engineering company executive*

Belmont
Haralampu, George Stelios *electric power engineer, former engineering executive electric utility company*
Keil, Alfred Adolf Heinrich *marine engineering educator*
†Merrill, Edward Wilson *chemical engineering educator*
Seifert, William Walther *electrical engineering educator*

Billerica
Schmidt, James Robert *facilities engineer*

Boston
Anderson, John Edward *mechanical engineering educator*
Davis, Robert Jocelyn *engineering executive*
De Luca, Carlo John *biomedical engineer*
Fine, Samuel *biomedical engineering educator, consultant*
Hines, Marion Ernest *electronic engineering consultant*
McCluskey, Jean Louise *civil and consulting engineer*
Moore, Richard Lawrence *structural engineer, consultant*
Pierce, Allan Dale *engineering educator, researcher*
Raemer, Harold Roy *electrical engineering educator*
Saleh, Bahaa E. A. *electrical engineering educator*
Vershbow, Arthur Emmanuel *mechanical engineer*

Boxboro
Demmer, William Roy *engineering executive*

Braintree
Foster, Arthur Rowe *mechanical engineering educator*

Brookline
Cooney, Charles Leland *chemical and biochemical engineering educator*
Katz, Israel *engineering educator, retired*

Burlington
Kern, Fred Robert, Jr. *engineer*

Cambridge
Abernathy, Frederick H. *mechanical engineering educator*
Argon, Ali Suphi *mechanical engineering educator*
Athans, Michael *electrical engineering educator, consultant*
Baron, Judson Richard *aerospace educator*
Baron, Sheldon *research and development company executive*
Battin, Richard Horace *astronautical engineer*
Beér, János Miklós *engineering educator*
Bras, Rafael Luis *engineering educator*
Brenner, Howard *chemical engineering educator*
Brockett, Roger Ware *engineering and computer science educator*
Brown, Robert Arthur *chemical engineering educator*
Bruce, James Donald *electrical engineering educator*
Budiansky, Bernard *engineering educator*
Chen, Sow-Hsin *nuclear engineering educator, researcher*
Cohen, Morris *engineering educator*
Cohen, Robert Edward *chemical engineering educator, consultant*
Colton, Clark Kenneth *chemical engineering educator*
Crandall, Stephen Harry *engineering educator*
de Neufville, Richard Lawrence *engineering educator*
Drake, Elisabeth Mertz *chemical engineer*
Dubowsky, Steven *mechanical engineering educator*
Duffy, Robert Aloysius *aeronautical engineer*
Dugundji, John *aeronautical engineer*
Elias, Peter *electrical engineering educator*
Emmons, Howard Wilson *engineer, educator, consultant, researcher*
Fano, Robert Mario *electrical engineering educator*
Fay, James Alan *mechanical engineering educator*
Fortmann, Thomas Edward *research and development company executive*
Fujimoto, James G. *electrical engineering educator*
Gallager, Robert Gray *electrical engineering educator*
Gatos, Harry Constantine *engineering educator*
Glaser, Peter Edward *mechanical engineer, consultant*
Greitzer, Edward Marc *aeronautical engineering educator, consultant*
Griffith, Peter *mechanical engineering educator, researcher*
Gyftopoulos, Elias Panayiotis *mechanical and nuclear engineering educator*
Hansen, Kent Forrest *nuclear engineering educator*
†Hansman, Robert John, Jr. *aeronautics and astronautics educator*
Harleman, Donald Robert Fergusson *environmental engineering educator*
†Harrington, Joseph, Jr. *consulting mechanical engineer*
Haus, Hermann Anton *electrical engineering educator*
Heney, Joseph Edward *environmental engineer*
Heywood, John Benjamin *mechanical engineering educator*
Ho, Yu-Chi *electrical engineering educator*
Hoag, David Garratt *aerospace engineer*
Kennedy, Robert Spayde *electrical engineering educator*
Kerrebrock, Jack Leo *aeronautics and astronautics engineering educator*
Kyhl, Robert Louis *electrical engineering educator*
Ladd, Charles Cushing, III *civil engineering educator*
†Langer, Robert Martin *retired chemical engineering company executive, consultant*
Langer, Robert Samuel *chemical, biochemical engineering educator*
Larson, Richard Charles *electrical engineer, educator, operations researcher*
Latanision, Ronald Michael *materials science and engineering educator, consultant*
Lee, Thomas Henry *electrical engineer, educator*
Leehey, Patrick *mechanical and ocean engineering educator*
Longwell, John Ploeger *chemical engineering educator*
Makhoul, John Ibrahim *electrical engineer, researcher*
Mann, Robert Wellesley *biomedical engineer, educator*
Marini, Robert Charles *environmental engineering executive*
Markey, Winston Roscoe *aeronautical engineering educator*
Marks, David Hunter *civil engineering educator*
McGarry, Frederick Jerome *civil engineering educator*
Meyer, John Edward *nuclear engineering educator*
Milgram, Jerome H. *marine and ocean engineer, educator*
Miller, Rene Harcourt *aerospace engineer, educator*
†Mitter, Sanjoy K. *electrical engineering educator*
†Morel, François Marie Michel *civil and environmental engineering educator*
Ogilvie, T(homas) Francis *engineer, educator*
Oppenheim, Alan Victor *electrical engineering educator*
Owen, Walter Shepherd *materials science and engineering educator*
Parthum, Charles Albert *civil engineer*
Penfield, Paul Livingstone, Jr. *electrical engineering educator*
Pian, Theodore Hsueh-Huang *engineering educator, consultant*
Powers, Michael Kevin *architectural and engineering executive*
Probstein, Ronald Filmore *mechanical engineering educator*
Rabinowicz, Ernest *mechanical engineer, tribologist, educator*
Rasmussen, Norman Carl *nuclear engineer*
Reid, Robert Clark *chemical engineering educator*
Rha, ChoKyun *biomaterials scientist and engineer, researcher, educator, inventor*
Rogers, Peter Philips *environmental engineering educator, city planner*
Rohsenow, Warren Max *retired mechanical engineer, educator*
Roos, Daniel *civil engineering educator*
Ruina, Jack Philip *electrical engineer, educator*
Russell, Kenneth Calvin *metallurgical engineer, educator*
Saltzer, Jerome Howard *computer science educator*
Satterfield, Charles Nelson *chemical engineer, educator*
Schreiber, William Francis *electrical engineering educator*
Seamans, Robert Channing, Jr. *astronautical engineering educator*
Siebert, William McConway *electrical engineering educator*
Smith, Joseph LeConte, Jr. *engineering educator, science laboratory administrator*
Smith, Kenneth Alan *chemical engineer, educator*
Staelin, David Hudson *electrical engineering educator, consultant*
Stephanopoulos, Gregory *chemical engineering educator, consultant, researcher*
Stevens, Kenneth Noble *electrical engineering educator*
Suh, Nam Pyo *mechanical engineering educator*
†Szekely, Julian *materials engineering educator*
†Thomas, Edwin L. *materials engineering educator*
Thomas, Harold Allen, Jr. *civil engineer, educator*
Trilling, Leon *aeronautical engineering educator*
Ungar, Eric Edward *mechanical engineer*
Vander Velde, Wallace Earl *aeronautical and astronautical educator*
Vivian, Johnson Edward *retired chemical engineering educator*
†Wang, Daniel I-Chyau *biochemical engineering educator*
Wechsler, Alfred Elliot *consulting company executive, chemical engineer*
Weiss, Thomas Fischer *electrical engineering educator, biophysicist*
White, David Calvin *electrical engineer, energy educator, consultant*
Whitman, Robert Van Duyne *civil engineer, educator*
Wiesner, Jerome Bert *engineering educator, researcher*
Wuensch, Bernhardt John *ceramic engineering educator*
Yannas, Ioannis Vassilios *polymer science and engineering educator*
†Yip, Sidney *nuclear engineering educator*
Young, Laurence Retman *biomedical engineer, educator*

Charlestown
†Argov, Gideon *engineering company executive*

Chatham
Hester, William Francis *engineering executive*

Chelmsford
Fulks, Robert Grady *engineering computer executive*

Concord
Drew, Philip Garfield *consultant engineering company executive*
Villers, Philippe *mechanical engineer*
Woll, Harry J. *electrical engineer*

East Falmouth
George, M(erton) Baron T(isdale) *aerospace researcher, aviation artist*

Foxboro
Bowditch, Hoel Lawrence *design engineer inventor, consultant*
Ghosh, Asish *control engineer, consultant*
Pierce, Francis Casimir *civil engineer*

Framingham
Bose, Amar Gopal *electrical engineering educator*

Harwich
Bush, Richard James *engineering executive, lay church worker*

Jamaica Plain
Shapiro, Ascher Herman *mechanical engineer, educator, consultant*

Lenox
Shammas, Nazih Kheirallah *environmental engineering educator*

Lexington
Bailey, Fred Coolidge *retired engineering consulting company executive*
Barton, David Knox *engineering executive, radar engineer*
Brookner, Eli *electrical engineer*
Cooper, William Eugene *consultant engineer*
Freed, Charles *engineering consultant, researcher*
Kingston, Robert Hildreth *engineering educator*
McWhorter, Alan Louis *electronics research executive, electrical engineering educator*
Morrow, Walter Edwin, Jr. *electrical engineer, university laboratory administrator*
O'Donnell, Robert Michael *electrical engineering executive*
Osepchuk, John Moses *engineering physicist, consultant*
Winter, David Louis *systems engineer,human factors scientist*

Lincoln
Eschenroeder, Alan Quade *environmental scientist*

Littleton
Fuller, Samuel Henry, III *computer engineer*

Ludlow
Koeninger, Edward Calvin *chemical engineer*

Marblehead
Ehrich, Fredric F. *aeronautical engineer*

Marlborough
Bennett, C. Leonard *consulting engineering executive*
Stiffler, Jack Justin *electrical engineer*

Medford
Astill, Kenneth Norman *mechanical engineering educator*
Balabanian, Norman *electrical engineering educator*
Greif, Robert *mechanical engineering educator*
Howell, Alvin Harold *engineer*
Nelson, Frederick Carl *mechanical engineering educator, university dean*
Sussman, Martin Victor *chemical engineering educator, inventor, consultant*
Uhlir, Arthur, Jr. *electrical engineer, university administrator*

Millbury
Pan, Coda H. T. *mechanical engineering educator, consultant, researcher*

Nantucket
Jesser, Benn Wainwright *chemical engineering and construction company executive*

Natick
†Gionfriddo, Maurice Paul *research and development manager, aeronautical engineer*

Needham
Toner, Walter Joseph, Jr. *transportation engineer, financial consultant*

New Bedford
Chang, Robin *engineering executive*

Newton
Saffran, Kalman *engineering consulting company executive, entrepreneur*

Newton Center
Mark, Melvin *consulting mechanical engineer, educator*

North Dartmouth
Law, Frederick Masom *engineering educator, structural engineering firm executive*

Northampton
Vesely, Alexander *civil engineer*

Northborough
Jeas, William C. *electronics and aerospace engineering executive*

Norwood
Imbault, James Joseph *engineering executive*
Sheingold, Daniel H. *electrical engineer*

Pittsfield
Anderson, John Gaston *electrical engineer*
Feigenbaum, Armand Vallin *systems engineer, systems equipment executive*

Quincy
Mancini, Rocco Anthony *civil engineer*

South Yarmouth
McIlveen, Edward E. *electrical engineer, association executive*

Sudbury
Blum, Seymour L. *ceramic engineer*
Fowler, Charles Albert *electronics engineer*

Swampscott
†Neumann, Gerhard *mechanical engineer*

Wakefield
Goldberg, Harold Seymour *electrical engineer, academic administrator*

Waltham
Hatsopoulos, George Nicholas *mechanical engineer, thermodynamicist, educator*

Watertown
Katz, William Emanuel *chemical engineer*
True, Edward Keene *architectural engineer*

Wellesley
Farnham, Sherman Brett *retired electrical engineer*

Reiss, Martin Harold *engineering executive*

Wellfleet
Jentz, John Macdonald *engineer, travel executive*

West Hyannisport
Corry, Andrew Francis *consulting engineering executive*

West Roxbury
Wiegner, Allen Walter *biomedical engineering educator, researcher*

Westford
Dennison, Byron Lee *electrical engineering educator, consultant*

Weston
Kendall, Julius *consulting engineer*

Wianno
Old, Bruce Scott *chemical and metallurgical engineer*

Wilmington
Faccini, Ernest Carlo *mechanical engineer*
Reeves, Barry Lucas *aerophysics research engineer*

Winchester
Hansen, Robert Joseph *civil engineer*
Hirschfeld, Ronald Colman *retired consulting engineering executive*
Hottel, Hoyt Clarke *consulting chemical engineer*

Worcester
Biederman, Ronald R. *mechanical engineer, educator*
Clarke, Edward Nielsen *engineering science educator*
DeFalco, Frank Damian *civil engineering educator*
Sioui, Richard Henry *chemical engineer*
Weiss, Alvin Harvey *chemical engineering educator, catalysis researcher and consultant*
Wilbur, Leslie Clifford *mechanical engineering educator*
Zwiep, Donald Nelson *mechanical engineering educator, administrator*

Yarmouth Port
Stott, Thomas Edward, Jr. *engineering company executive*

MICHIGAN

Ann Arbor
Adamson, Thomas Charles, Jr. *aerospace engineering educator, consultant*
Akcasu, Ahmet Ziyaeddin *nuclear engineer, educator*
Banks, Peter Morgan *electrical engineering educator*
Becher, William Don *electrical engineering educator, engineering consultant*
†Bhattacharya, Pallab Kumar *electrical engineering educator, researcher*
Bilello, John Charles *materials science and engineering educator*
Bitondo, Domenic *engineering executive*
†Brown, William Milton *electrical engineering educator*
Cain, Charles Alan *electrical engineering educator, researcher*
Calahan, Donald Albert *electrical engineering educator*
†Chaffin, Donald B. *industrial engineer, researcher*
Chen, Michael Ming *mechanical engineering educator*
Clark, John Alden *mechanical engineering educator*
Dow, William Gould *electrical engineer, educator*
England, Anthony Wayne *electrical engineering and computer science educator, astronaut, geophysicist*
Enns, Mark Kynaston *electrical engineer*
Faeth, Gerard Michael *aerospace engineering educator, researcher*
Fox, James Carroll *aerospace engineer, program manager*
Gibala, Ronald *metallurgical engineering educator*
†Gilbert, Elmer Grant *aerospace engineering educator, control theorist*
Gomberg, Henry Jacob *nuclear engineer*
Grant, Michael Peter *electrical engineer*
Haddad, George Ilyas *engineering educator, research scientist*
Haddox, Mark *electronic engineer*
Hanson, Robert Duane *civil engineering educator*
Hayes, John Patrick *electrical engineering and computer science educator, consultant*
Kempe, Lloyd Lute *chemical engineering educator*
Kerr, William *nuclear engineering educator*
Knoll, Glenn Frederick *nuclear engineering educator*
Kozma, Adam *electrical engineer*
Leith, Emmett Norman *electrical engineer, educator*
Liu, Vi-Cheng *aerospace engineering educator*
Macnee, Alan Breck *electrical engineer, educator*
McClamroch, N. Harris *aerospace engineering educator, consultant, researcher*
Meyer, John Frederick *engineering and computer science educator, researcher, consultant*
Nagy, Andrew Francis *engineering educator*
Pehlke, Robert Donald *materials and metallurgical engineering educator*
Petrick, Ernest Nicholas *mechanical engineer*
Pollock, Stephen Michael *industrial engineering educator, consultant*
Richart, Frank Edwin, Jr. *civil engineer, educator*
Root, William Lucas *electrical engineering educator*
Rumman, Wadi (Saliba Rumman) *civil engineer*
Schultz, Albert Barry *engineering educator*
Senior, Thomas Bryan A. *electrical engineering educator, researcher, consultant*
Solomon, David Eugene *engineering company executive*
Tai, Chen-To *electrical engineering educator*
Ulaby, Fawwaz Tayssir *electrical engineering and computer science educator, research center administrator*
Upatnieks, Juris *optical engineer, researcher, educator*
Weber, Walter Jacob, Jr. *engineering educator*
Willmarth, William Walter *aerospace engineering educator*
Wilson, Richard Christian *engineering firm executive*
Wineman, Alan Stuart *mechanical engineering and applied mechanics educator*
Wylie, Evan Benjamin *civil engineering educator, consultant, researcher*
Yeh, Chai *electrical engineer, educator*
Yih, Chia-Shun *fluid mechanics educator*
Young, Edwin Harold *chemical and metallurgical engineering educator*

Big Rapids
Thapa, Khagendra *survey engineering educator*

Bloomfield Hills
†Heinen, Charles M. *retired chemical and materials engineer*
Klingler, Eugene Herman *consulting engineer, educator*
Stivender, Donald Lewis *mechanical engineering consultant*

Clarkston
Erkfritz, Donald Spencer *mechanical engineer*

Dearborn
Cairns, James Robert *mechanical engineering educator*
Chou, Clifford Chi Fong *research engineering executive*
Little, Robert Eugene *mechanical engineering educator, materials behavior researcher, consultant*
Meitzler, Allen Henry *electrical engineering educator, automotive scientist*

Detroit
Beaufait, Frederick W(illiam) *civil engineering educator*
Brammer, Forest Evert *electrical engineering educator*
†Holness, Gordon Victor Rix *engineering executive, mechanical engineer*
Kline, Kenneth Alan *mechanical engineering educator*
Kummler, Ralph H. *chemical engineering educator*
Meisel, Jerome *electrical engineer*
Schmidt, Robert *mechanical and civil engineering educator*
Sengupta, Dipak Lal *electrical engineering and physics educator, researcher*
Stynes, Stanley Kenneth *retired chemical engineer, educator*
Uicker, James Leo *mechanical engineer*
†Uicker, Joseph Bernard *engineering company executive*
Wagner, Harvey Arthur *nuclear engineer*

East Lansing
Andersland, Orlando Baldwin *civil engineering educator*
Asmussen, Jes, Jr. *electrical engineer*
Bickart, Theodore Albert *electrical and computer engineering educator, university dean*
Chen, Kun-Mu *electrical engineering educator*
Cutts, Charles Eugene *civil engineering educator*
Foss, John Frank *mechanical engineering educator*
Goodman, Erik David *engineering educator*
Kreer, John Belshaw *retired electrical engineering educator*
Lloyd, John Raymond *mechanical engineering educator*
Merva, George Ellis *agricultural engineer, educator, researcher*
Mukherjee, Kalinath *materials science and engineering educator, researcher*
Snell, John Raymond *civil engineer*
Soutas-Little, Robert William *mechanical engineer, educator*
Von Tersch, Lawrence Wayne *electrical engineering educator, university dean*

Farmington
Weber, Leo L. *electrical engineer*

Flint
Davis, Stephen Robert *power engineering educator, former academic dean, automotive engineer*
Gratch, Serge *mechanical engineering educator*

Grand Blanc
Tomlinson, James Lawrence *mechanical engineer*

Greenbush
Paulson, James Marvin *engineering educator*

Grosse Pointe
Beltz, Charles Robert *engineering executive*

Houghton
Heckel, Richard Wayne *metallurgical engineering educator*
Huang, Eugene Yuching *civil engineer, educator*
Lumsdaine, Edward *mechanical engineering educator, university dean*
Pelc, Karol I. *engineering management educator, researcher*
Smith, Darrell Wayne *metallurgical engineering educator, consultant*

Kalamazoo
Fitch, W. Chester *industrial engineer*

Madison Heights
Jeffe, Sidney David *automotive engineer*

Midland
Carson, Gordon Bloom *engineering executive*
Meister, Bernard John *chemical engineer*

Monroe
Halthon, John Louis *quality engineer*

Okemos
Giacoletto, Lawrence Joseph *electronics engineering educator, researcher, consultant*

Plymouth
Grannan, William Stephen *safety engineer, consultant*

Rochester
Hovanesian, Joseph Der *mechanical engineering educator*

Romulus
Archer, Hugh Morris *consulting engineer, manufacturing professional*

Southfield
Ellis, Robert William *engineering educator*

Sterling Heights
Dea, David Young Fong *electrical engineer, consultant*

Trenton
Crooks, Archibald Muir, Jr. *engineer, licensed builder*

Warren
Gallopoulos, Nicholas Efstratios *chemical engineer*
Jacovides, Linos Jacovou *electrical engineering research manager*
Lau, Ian Van *safety research engineer, biomechanics expert*
Nagy, Louis Leonard *engineering executive, researcher*

Waterford
Hampton, Phillip Michael *consulting engineering company executive*

MINNESOTA

Brooklyn Park
Peterson, Donn Neal *forensic engineer*

Chanhassen
Thorson, John Martin, Jr. *electrical engineer, consultant*

Litchfield
Johnson, Richard Warren *civil engineer*

Lutsen
Napadensky, Hyla Sarane *engineering consultant*

Madison
Husby, Donald Evans *engineering company executive*

Minneapolis
Arndt, Roger Edward Anthony *hydraulic engineer, educator*
Baker, Michael Harry *chemical engineer*
Bakken, Earl Elmer *electrical engineer, bioengineering company executive*
Cohen, Arnold A. *electrical engineer*
†Crouch, Steven L. *mining engineer*
Davis, Howard Ted *chemical engineering educator*
Eckert, Ernst R. G. *mechanical engineering educator*
Fairhurst, Charles *civil and mining engineering educator*
Fletcher, Edward Abraham *engineering educator*
Galambos, Theodore Victor *civil engineer, educator*
Gerberich, William Warren *engineering educator*
Goldstein, Richard Jay *mechanical engineer, educator*
Isbin, Herbert Stanford *chemical engineering educator*
Johnson, Walter Kline *civil engineer*
Joseph, Daniel Donald *aeronautical engineer, educator*
Kain, Richard Yerkes *electrical engineer, researcher, educator*
Kvalseth, Tarald Oddvar *mechanical engineer, educator*
Lambert, Robert Frank *electrical engineer, educator*
Lee, E. Bruce *electrical engineering educator*
Liu, Benjamin Young-hwai *engineering educator*
Mulich, Steve Francis *safety engineer*
Nathan, Marshall Ira *electrical engineering educator*
Ogata, Katsuhiko *engineering educator*
Oriani, Richard Anthony *metallurgical engineering educator*
†Patankar, Suhas V. *engineering educator*
Persson, Erland Karl *electrical engineer*
Pfender, Emil *mechanical engineering educator*
Porter, William L. *electrical engineer*
Sackett, William Tecumseh, Jr. *electrical engineer*
Scriven, L. E(dward), II *chemical engineering educator, scientist*
Sparrow, Ephraim Maurice *mechanical engineering scientist, educator*
Sterling, Raymond Leslie *civil engineering educator, researcher, consultant*
Weisberg, Leonard R. *research and engineering executive*
Wilson, Theodore Alexander *engineering educator, respiratory physiologist*
Wollenberg, Bruce Frederick *electrical engineering educator, consultant*

Osseo
Haun, James William *chemical engineer, retired food company executive, consultant*

Rochester
Huffine, Coy Lee *retired chemical engineer, consultant*

Saint Cloud
Higgins, Robert Arthur *electrical engineer, educator, consultant*

Saint Paul
Benforado, David M. *environmental engineer*
Fingerson, Leroy Malvin *corporate executive, engineer*
Goodman, Lawrence Eugene *structural analyst, educator*

Stillwater
Sowman, Harold Gene *ceramic engineer, researcher*

MISSISSIPPI

Jackson
Pearce, David Harry *biomedical engineer*

Mississippi State
Cliett, Charles Buren *aeronautical engineer, educator, academic administrator*
Jacob, Paul Bernard, Jr. *electrical engineering educator*
†Taylor, Clayborne Dudley *engineering educator*
†Thompson, Joe Floyd *aerospace engineer, researcher*

Oxford
†Mutchler, Calvin Kendal *hydraulic research engineer*

Starkville
Carley, Charles Team, Jr. *mechanical engineer*
Priest, Melville Stanton *consulting hydraulic engineer*

University
Horton, Thomas Edward, Jr. *mechanical engineering educator*

Vicksburg
Albritton, Gayle Edward *structural engineer*
†Herrmann, Frank A., Jr. *hydraulics laboratory director, researcher*

MISSOURI

Ballwin
Bodner, Herbert *engineering and construction executive*
Cornell, William Daniel *mechanical engineer*

Centralia
Harmon, Robert Wayne *electrical engineering executive*

Chesterfield
†Plunkett, Larry Neil *electrical engineer*
Smith, Lawrence Abner *aeronautical engineer*
Yardley, John Finley *aerospace engineer*

Columbia
Day, Cecil LeRoy *agricultural engineering educator*
Frisby, James Curtis *agricultural engineering educator*
Heldman, Dennis Ray *engineering educator*
Pringle, Oran Allan *mechanical and aerospace engineering educator*
Viswanath, Dabir Srikantiah *chemical engineer*
Warder, Richard Currey, Jr. *mechanical aerospace engineering educator*
Yasuda, Hirotsugu Koge *chemical engineering professor*

Florissant
Martin, Edward Brian *electrical engineer*

Fortuna
Ramer, James LeRoy *civil engineer*

Kansas City
Acheson, Allen Morrow *retired engineering executive*
Adam, Paul James *engineering company executive, mechanical engineer*
Ayres, John Samuel *chemical engineer*
Boyd, John Addison, Jr. *civil engineer*
Campbell, Newton Allen *consulting engineering company executive, consulting electrical engineer*
Davis, F(rancis) Keith *civil engineer*
Karmeier, Delbert Fred *consulting engineer*
Robinson, John Hamilton *civil engineer*
†Skinner, Willis Dean *consulting engineering company executive*
Stewart, Albert Elisha *safety engineer, industrial hygienist*

Kirkwood
Holsen, James Noble, Jr. *retired chemical engineer*

Lake Saint Louis
Czarnik, Marvin Ray *retired aerospace engineer*

Maryland Heights
Beumer, Richard Eugene *engineer, architect, construction firm executive*
†Schwartz, Henry Gerard, Jr. *consulting engineering company executive*
Smith, Brice Reynolds, Jr. *engineering company executive*
Uselton, James Clayton *engineering executive*
†Whitfield, J. D. *engineering executive*

Rolla
Babcock, Daniel Lawrence *chemical engineer, educator*
Barr, David John *civil, geological engineering educator*
Cheng, Franklin Yih *civil engineering educator*
Crosbie, Alfred Linden *mechanical engineering educator*
Day, Delbert Edwin *ceramic engineering educator*
Johnson, James Winston *chemical engineering educator*
Minor, Joseph Edward *civil engineer, educator*
Munger, Paul R. *civil engineering educator*
Omurtag, Yildirim (Bill) *engineering educator*
Saperstein, Lee Waldo *mining engineering educator*
Sauer, Harry John, Jr. *mechanical engineering educator, university administrator*
Tsoulfanidis, Nicholas *nuclear engineering educator*

Saint Joseph
Johnson, Marvin Melrose *consulting industrial engineer*

Saint Louis
Brasunas, Anton de Sales *metallurgical engineering educator*
Breihan, Erwin Robert *civil engineer, consultant*
Briggs, William Benajah *aeronautical engineer*
Brunstrom, Gerald Ray *engineering executive, consultant*
Cairns, Donald Fredrick *engineering educator, management consultant*
Cox, Jerome Rockhold, Jr. *electrical engineer*
Dreifke, Gerald Edmond *electrical engineering educator*
Fascia, Remo Mario *aviation consultant, airplane manufacturing company executive*
Gould, Phillip L. *civil engineering educator, consultant*
Hakkinen, Raimo Jaakko *aeronautical engineer, scientist*
Howard, Walter Burke *chemical engineer*
†Kirberg, Leonard Carl *engineering executive*

†Kugelman, Irwin Jay *civil engineering educator*
McKelvey, James Morgan *chemical engineering educator*
Morgan, Robert Peter *engineering educator*
Moulder, James Edwin *civil engineer*
Muller, Marcel W(ettstein) *electrical engineering educator*
Orton, George Frederick *aerospace engineer*
Paris, Paul Croce *mechanics educator, engineering consultant, researcher*
Peters, David Allen *mechanical engineering educator, consultant*
Prickett, Gordon Odin *mining, mineral and energy engineer*
Ross, Donald Kenneth *consulting engineering executive*
Ross, Monte *electrical engineer*
Ryckman, DeVere Wellington *consulting environmental engineer*
Shipton, Harold William *biomedical engineering educator, researcher*
Shrauner, Barbara Wayne Abraham *electrical engineering educator*
Staley, Robert W. *mechanical engineer, electric company executive*
Sutera, Salvatore Philip *mechanical engineering educator*
Szabo, Barna Aladar *mechanical engineering educator, mining engineer*
Tarn, Tzyh-Jong *electrical engineering educator, researcher*
Winter, David Ferdinand *electrical engineering educator, consultant*
Wolfe, Charles Morgan *electrical engineering educator*
Zurheide, Charles Henry *consulting electrical engineer*

Springfield
Hansen, John Paul *metallurgical engineer*
Nuccitelli, Saul Arnold *civil engineer, consultant*

MONTANA

Bozeman
Berg, Lloyd *chemical engineering educator*
Knox, James Lester *electrical engineer*
Sanks, Robert Leland *environmental engineer, emeritus educator*
Stanislao, Joseph *consulting engineer, educator*

Butte
Studebaker, Irving Glen *engineering educator, researcher*

Great Falls
Walker, Leland Jasper *civil engineer*

Helena
Johnson, David Sellie *civil engineer*

NEBRASKA

Clay Center
Hahn, George LeRoy *agricultural engineer, biometeorologist*

Las Vegas
Haas, Robert John *aerospace engineer*

Lincoln
Bahar, Ezekiel *electrical engineering educator*
Edison, Allen Ray *electrical engineer, educator*
Edwards, Donald Mervin *biological systems engineering educator, university dean*
Elias, Samy E. G. *engineering executive*
†Hanna, Milford A. *agricultural engineering educator*
Splinter, William Eldon *agricultural engineering educator*
Ullman, Frank Gordon *electrical engineering educator*
†Woollam, John Arthur *electrical engineering educator*

Omaha
Coy, William Raymond *civil engineer*
Hultquist, Paul Fredrick *electrical engineer, educator*
Jelensperger, Francis J. *engineering and architectural executive*
Lenz, Charles Eldon *electrical engineering consultant, author*
Matthies, Frederick John *architectural engineer*
Tunnicliff, David George *civil engineer*

NEVADA

Incline Village
Merdinger, Charles John *civil engineer, naval officer, academic adminstrator*

Las Vegas
Boehm, Robert Foty *mechanical engineer, educator, researcher*
†Colston, Bill W. *engineering executive*
Herzlich, Harold J. *chemical engineer*
Messenger, George Clement *engineering executive, consultant*
Wyman, Richard Vaughn *engineering educator, exploration company executive*

Mercury
Schwichtenberg, Daryl Robert *drilling engineer*

Reno
Krenkel, Peter Ashton *engineer, educator*
Middlebrooks, Eddie Joe *environmental engineer*

Sparks
Kleppe, John Arthur *electrical engineering educator, business executive*

NEW HAMPSHIRE

Center Sandwich
Simmons, Alan Jay *electrical engineer, consultant*

Hanover
Browning, James Alexander *engineering company executive,inventor*
Dean, Robert Charles, Jr. *mechanical engineer, entrepreneur, innovator*
Ermenc, Joseph John *mechanical engineering educator*
Long, Carl Ferdinand *engineering educator*
†Marvin, Eugene L. *civil engineer*
Queneau, Paul Etienne *metallurgical engineer, educator*
Stearns, Stephen Russell *civil engineer, forensic engineer, educator*
Wallis, Graham Blair *engineer, educator*

Hollis
†Wright, George Walter *aeronautical engineer, state legislator*

Merrimack
Hower, Philip Leland *semiconductor device engineer*

Nashua
Woodruff, Thomas Ellis *electronics consulting executive*

Pelham
†Borsa, Andrew John *electronics engineering consultant*

Warner
Hunt, Everett Clair *engineering educator, researcher, consultant*

West Lebanon
MacAdam, Walter Kavanagh *consulting engineering executive*

NEW JERSEY

Allendale
Birdsall, Blair *consulting engineering executive*

Bedminster
David, Edward Emil, Jr. *electrical engineer, business executive*

Belle Mead
Singley, Mark Eldridge *agricultural engineering educator*

Bellmawr
Hughes, James Sinclair *electronic engineer and executive*

Bergenfield
Pei, Ming L. *civil engineering educator*

Berkeley Heights
Rabiner, Lawrence Richard *electrical engineer*

Bloomfield
Solomon, Stephen Michael *chemical engineer, company executive*

Chatham
Hinderliter, Richard Glenn *electrical engineer*

Cherry Hill
Parker, Jack Royal *engineering executive*

Clifton
Srinivasachari, Samavedam *chemical engineer*

Clinton
†Atwater, N. William *engineering and construction executive*
Daman, Ernest Ludwig *mechanical engineer*
Newman, Stephen Alexander *chemical engineer, thermodynamicist*
Winkin, Justin Philip *engineering executive*

Cranbury
Wang, Chih Chun *material scientist, business executive*

Cranford
Schink, Frank Edward *electrical engineer*
Sommerlad, Robert Edward *environmental research engineer*

Dover
Kajor, Michael Steven *electrical engineer*
Tatyrek, Alfred Frank *materials engineer, research chemist, consultant*

Edison
Schwalje, Joseph Louis *mechanical engineering consultant*

Egg Harbor City
Melick, George Fleury *mechanical engineer, educator*

Englewood
Deresiewicz, Herbert *mechanical engineering educator*

Englewood Cliffs
Bogert, Ivan Lathrop *sanitary engineer*

Fairfield
Finn, James Francis *consulting engineering executive*

Florham Park
Lieberman, Lester Zane *engineering company executive*

Fort Monmouth
†Campi, Anthony V. *engineering research administrator*
Perlman, Barry Stuart *electrical engineer, researcher*

Franklin Lakes
Lovell, Theodore *electrical engineer, consultant*

Green Village
Castenschiold, Rene *engineering company executive, author, consultant*

Hackensack
Mavrovic, Ivo *chemical engineer*
Michel, Robert Charles *retired engineering company executive*

Haddonfield
Siskin, Edward Joseph *engineering and construction company executive*

Hewitt
Selwyn, Donald *engineering administrator, researcher, inventor, educator*

Hoboken
Boesch, Francis Theodore *electrical engineer, educator*
†Bruno, Michael Stephen *ocean engineering educator, researcher*
†Gans, Manfred *chemical engineer*
Griskey, Richard George *chemical engineering educator*
Savitsky, Daniel *engineer, educator*
Sisto, Fernando *mechanical engineering educator*

Holmdel
Abate, John E. *electrical ar d electronic engineer, communications consultant*
Boyd, Gary Delane *electro-optical engineer, researcher*
Johannes, Virgil Ivancich *electrical engineer*
Li, Tingye *electrical engineer*
Meadors, Howard Clarence, Jr. *electrical engineer*
Opie, William Robert *retired metallurgical engineer*
Ross, Ian Munro *electrical engineer*
Tien, Ping King *electronics engineer*

Jamesburg
Maxwell, Bryce *engineer,educator*

Kinnelon
Haller, Charles Edward *engineering consultant*

Lakehurst
†Raffetto, David J. *engineering administrator*

Lawrenceville
Kihn, Harry *electronics engineer, manufacturing company executive*

Little Falls
Dohr, Donald R. *metallurgical engineer, researcher*

Livingston
Heilmeier, George Harry *electrical engineer, researcher*
Lucky, Robert Wendell *electrical engineer*

Long Branch
Nahavandi, Amir Nezameddin *retired engineering firm executive*

Marlboro
Schwartz, Perry Lester *information systems engineer, consultant*

Mendham
Kaprelian, Edward K. *mechanical engineer, physicist*

Middletown
O'Neill, Eugene Francis *communications engineer*

Morristown
Kurtz, Bruce Edward *chemical engineer, research and development executive*
Personick, Stewart David *electrical engineer*

Mountainside
Gordon, Eugene Irving *electrical and computer engineering educator*

Murray Hill
Cho, Alfred Yi *electrical engineer*
Murthy, Srinivasa K. *engineering corporation executive*

New Brunswick
Eager, George Sidney, Jr. *electrical engineer, business executive*
Katz, Carlos *electrical engineer*
Mc Laren, Malcolm Grant, IV *ceramic engineering educator*
Nawy, Edward George *civil engineer, educator*
Vieth, Wolf Randolph *chemical engineering educator*
Wolfe, Robert Richard *bioresource engineer, educator*

New Providence
Kotynek, George Roy *mechanical engineer, educator, marketing executive*

Newark
Bar-Ness, Yeheskel *electrical engineer, educator*
Bigley, William Joseph, Jr. *control engineer*
Friedland, Bernard *engineer, educator*
Guenzel, Frank Bernhard *chemical engineer*
Hanesian, Deran *chemical engineer, chemistry and environmental science educator, consultant*
Henderson, Dorland John *retired electrical engineer*
Hrycak, Peter *mechanical engineer, educator*
Hsieh, Jui Sheng *mechanical engineer, educator*
Hsu, Cheng-Tzu Thomas *civil engineering educator*
Pfeffer, Robert *chemical engineer, academic administrator, educator*
Pignataro, Louis James *engineering educator*
Spillers, William Russell *civil engineering educator*
Yu, Yi-Yuan *mechanical engineering educator*

North Caldwell
Stevens, William Dollard *consulting mechanical engineer*

Oakland
Bacaloglu, Radu *chemical engineer*

Ocean City
Speitel, Gerald Eugene *consulting environmental engineer*

Oradell
Roe, Kenneth Keith *power and industrial engineering/construction company executive*

Parsippany
Ajmera, Pravin V. *engineer, business and technical consultant*

Pennsauken
Alday, Paul Stackhouse, Jr. *mechanical engineer*

Phillipsburg
†Cooper, Paul *mechanical engineer, research director*

Piscataway
Flanagan, James Loton *electrical engineer, educator*
Freeman, Herbert *computer engineering educator*
Sannuti, Peddapullaiah *electrical engineering educator*
Welkowitz, Walter *biomedical engineer, educator*

Plainfield
Granstrom, Marvin Leroy *civil and sanitary engineering educator*

Princeton
Axtmann, Robert Clark *nuclear and chemical engineering educator*
Ayers, William McLean *electrochemical engineering company executive*
Bartolini, Robert Alfred *electrical engineer, researcher*
Bergman, Richard Isaac *consulting company executive*
Billington, David Perkins *civil engineering educator*
Bogdonoff, Seymour Moses *aeronautical engineer*
Cakmak, Ahmet Sefik *civil engineering educator*
Cinlar, Erhan *engineering educator*
Curtiss, Howard Crosby, Jr. *mechanical engineer, educator*
Denlinger, Edgar Jacob *electronics engineering research executive*
Dickinson, Bradley William *electrical engineering educator*
Durbin, Enoch Job *aeronautical engineering educator*
File, Joseph *research physics engineer*
Gibson, James John *electronics engineer, consultant*
Gillham, John Kinsey *chemical engineering educator*
Glassman, Irvin *mechanical and aeronautical engineering educator, consultant*
Graessley, William Walter *chemical engineering educator*
Johnson, Ernest Frederick *chemical engineer, educator*
Johnson, Walter Curtis *electrical engineering educator*
Karol, Reuben Hirsh *civil engineer, sculptor*
Lam, Sau-Hai *aeronautical engineering educator*
†Law, Chung King *aerospace engineering educator, researcher*
Lechner, Bernard Joseph *consulting electrical engineer*
Lopresti, Philip Vincent *electrical engineer, researcher, consultant*
†Mills, Michael James *architect*
Poor, Harold Vincent *electrical engineering educator*
Saville, Dudley Albert *chemical engineering educator*
Schroeder, Alfred Christian *electronics research engineer*
Socolow, Robert Harry *mechanical and aerospace engineering educator, scientist*
Stengel, Robert Frank *mechanical and aerospace engineering educator*
†Tarbox, Dick *communications engineering executive*
Vahaviolos, Sotirios John *electrical engineer, scientist, corporate executive*
Vanmarcke, Erik Hector *civil engineering educator*
Vann, Joseph McAlpin *nuclear engineer*
Wei, James *chemical engineering educator, academic dean*
Weimer, Paul K(essler) *electrical engineer*

Princeton Junction
Haddad, James Henry *chemical engineering consultant*

Red Bank
Fleischer, Paul E. *electrical engineer*
Hollywood, John Matthew *electronics consultant*
Schneider, Sol *electronic engineer, consultant, researcher*

Ridgefield Park
Case, Gerard Ramon *drafting technician*

Ridgewood
Abplanalp, Glen Harold *civil engineer*

Riverside
Gouda, Moustafa Abdel-Hamid *geotechnical engineer consultant*

Robbinsville
Goldstein, Norman Robert *safety engineer*

Rumson
Rosen, Bernard H. *chemical engineer*

Sea Bright
Plummer, Dirk Arnold *electrical engineer*

Short Hills
Kaye, Jerome R. *retired engineering and construction company executive*
Moore, Robert Condit *civil engineer*

Shrewsbury
Reich, Bernard *telecommunications engineer*

Skillman
Brill, Yvonne Claeys *engineer, consultant*

Somerville
†Beck, Eckardt C. *engineering executive*

Cirello, John environmental management and engineering company executive
†Glenn, Arthur L. engineering company executive

Summit
Fukui, Hatsuaki electrical engineer, art historian

Teaneck
Borg, Sidney Fred mechanical engineer, educator
Ehrlich, Ira Robert mechanical engineering consultant

Tenafly
Lang, Hans Joachim engineering company executive

Teterboro
Zomick, David Alan engineering executive

Toms River
Curreri, John Robert mechanical engineer, consultant
Fanuele, Michael Anthony electronics engineer, research engineer

Trenton
Jester, Roberts Charles, Jr. engineering services company executive

Upper Montclair
Aronson, David chemical and mechanical engineer

Upper Saddle River
Wallace, William, III engineering executive

Warren
Sartor, Anthony Joseph environmental engineer

Wayne
Cheng, David Hong mechanical engineering educator

Whippany
Michaelis, Paul Charles engineering physicist executive

White House Station
Nusim, Stanley Herbert chemical engineer, executive director

Willingboro
Schnapf, Abraham aerospace engineer, consultant

NEW MEXICO

Albuquerque
Bolie, Victor Wayne electrical and computer engineering educator
Carrick, David Stanley electrical engineer
Dorato, Peter electrical and computer engineering educator
Haddad, Edward Raouf civil engineer, consultant
Hall, Jerome William research engineering educator
Howard, William Jack mechanical engineer, retired
Johnson, Stewart Willard civil engineer
Karni, Shlomo electrical engineering educator
Kramarsic, Roman Joseph engineering consultant
McKiernan, John William mechanical engineer
Molzen, Dayton Frank consulting engineering executive
Peck, Ralph Brazelton civil engineering educator, consultant
Westwood, Albert Ronald Clifton metallurgical engineer
Wildin, Maurice Wilbert mechanical engineering educator

Belen
Toliver, Lee mechanical engineer

Farmington
Garretson, Owen Loren engineer

Kirtland A F B
Baum, Carl Edward electromagnetic theorist

Las Cruces
Ford, Clarence Quentin mechanical engineer, educator
Matthews, Larryl Kent mechanical engineering educator
Morgan, John Derald electrical engineer
Thode, Edward Frederick chemical engineer, educator

Los Alamos
Jackson, James F. nuclear engineer
Maraman, William Joseph nuclear engineering company executive
Nunz, Gregory Joseph aerospace engineer and educator
Stoddard, Stephen Davidson ceramic engineer, former state senator

Santa Fe
Baerwald, John Edward traffic and transportation engineer, educator
Miller, Edmund Kenneth retired electrical engineer
Moellenbeck, Albert John, Jr. engineering executive
Phister, Montgomery, Jr. computer engineering consultant, writer

Socorro
Lancaster, John Howard civil engineer

Tijeras
Vizcaino, Henry P. mining engineer, consultant

White Sands Missle Range
Arthur, Paul Keith electronic engineer

NEW YORK

Albany
Happ, Harvey Heinz electrical engineer, educator

Alfred
Frechette, Van Derck ceramic engineer
Spriggs, Richard Moore ceramic engineer, research center administrator

Amherst
Lee, George C. civil engineer, university administrator
Reinhorn, Andrei M. civil engineering educator, consultant

Ballston Lake
Fiedler, Harold Joseph electrical engineer, consultant

Bethpage
Brown, James Kenneth computer engineer
Melnik, Robert Edward aeronautical engineer
Rockensies, John William mechanical engineer

Binghamton
Cornacchio, Joseph Vincent engineering educator, computer researcher, consultant
Jennings, Frank Louis engineering company executive, engineer
Lowen, Walter mechanical engineering educator
Schwartz, Richard Frederick electrical engineering educator

Bronx
Berger, Frederick Jerome electrical engineer, educator
Hovnanian, H. Philip biomedical engineer

Brooklyn
Bertoni, Henry Louis electrical engineering educator
Felsen, Leopold B. engineer, educator
Giordano, Anthony Bruno electrical engineering educator, retired college dean
Goodman, Alvin S. engineering educator, consultant
Helly, Walter Sigmund engineering educator
Kempner, Joseph aerospace engineering educator
Margolin, Harold metallurgical educator
Othmer, Donald Frederick chemical engineer, educator
Pan, Huo-Hsi mechanical engineer, educator
Rice, John Thomas mechanical engineering and architecture educator
Shaw, Leonard Glazer electrical engineering educator, consultant
Shooman, Martin Lawrence electrical engineer, computer scientist, educator

Buffalo
Anderson, Wayne Arthur electrical engineering educator
Ashgriz, Nasser mechanical and aerospace engineer, educator
Benenson, David Maurice engineering educator
†Givi, Peyman science and engineering educator
Kinzly, Robert Edward engineering company executive
Landi, Dale Michael industrial engineer, academic administrator
Liew, Fah Pow mechanical engineer
Meredith, Dale Dean civil engineering educator
Metzger, Ernest Hugh aerospace engineer, scientist
Reismann, Herbert engineer, educator
Ruckenstein, Eli chemical engineering educator
Sarjeant, Walter James electrical and computer engineering educator
Shaw, David Tai-Ko electrical and computer engineering educator, university administrator
Weber, Thomas William chemical engineering educator
Weller, Sol William chemical engineering educator

Chappaqua
O'Neill, Robert Charles consultant, inventor
Pomerene, James Herbert retired computer engineer

Clarence
Greatbatch, Wilson biomedical engineer

Deer Park
Caputi, William James, Jr. engineering company consultant
Taub, Jesse J. electrical engineering researcher

Delmar
Birdsey, Anna Campas civil engineer, architect

East Amherst
†Soong, Tsu-Teh engineering science educator

Elmira
Orsillo, James Edward computer systems engineer, company executive

Endwell
Wagner, Peter Ewing physics and electrical engineering educator

Fairport
Oldshue, James Y. chemical engineering consultant

Farmingdale
Bolle, Donald Martin engineering educator
Bongiorno, Joseph John, Jr. electrical engineering educator
Klosner, Jerome Martin applied mechanics educator
LaTourrette, James Thomas retired electrical engineering and computer science educator
Shmoys, Jerry electrical engineering educator

Fayetteville
Dosanjh, Darshan S(ingh) aeronautical engineer, educator

Flushing
Birnstiel, Charles consulting engineer
†Ryan, William R. mechanical engineer

Garden City
Fleisig, Ross aeronautical engineer, engineering manager

Glen Cove
Conti, James Joseph chemical engineer, educator

Glenham
Douglas, Fred Robert cost engineering consultant

Glenville
Anderson, Roy Everett electrical engineering consultant

Great Neck
Longobardo, Anna Kazanjian mechanical engineer
Shaffer, Bernard William mechanical and aerospace engineering educator

Greenlawn
Bachman, Henry Lee electrical engineer, engineering executive

Griffiss A F B
Diamond, Fred I. electronic engineer

Hauppauge
†Miller, Kenneth Allen electrical engineer

Hawthorne
McConnell, John Edward electrical engineer, company executive

Hempstead
Goldstein, Stanley Philip engineering educator
Maier, Henry B. environmental engineer

Huntington
Papoulis, Athanasios electrical engineering educator

Huntington Station
Agosta, Vito mechanical/aerospace engineering educator
Lanzano, Ralph Eugene civil engineer

Ithaca
Berger, Toby electrical engineer
Booker, John Franklin mechanical engineer, educator
Carlin, Herbert J. electrical engineering educator, researcher
Dalman, Gisli Conrad electrical engineering educator
De Boer, Pieter Cornelis Tobias mechanical and aerospace engineering educator
Dick, Richard Irwin environmental engineer, educator
Dworsky, Leonard B. civil and environmental engineer, educator
Eastman, Lester Fuess electrical engineer, educator
Fine, Terrence Leon electrical engineering and statistics educator
George, Albert Richard aerospace and mechanical engineering educator
Gubbins, Keith Edmund chemical engineering educator
Kramer, Edward John materials science and engineering educator
Leibovich, Sidney engineering educator
Loucks, Daniel Peter environmental systems engineer
Lynn, Walter Royal civil engineering educator, university administrator
Maxwell, William Laughlin industrial engineering educator
†Mc Guire, William civil engineer, educator
McIsaac, Paul Rowley electrical engineer, educator
Meyburg, Arnim Hans transportation engineer, educator, consultant
Nation, John Arthur electrical engineering educator, researcher
O'Rourke, Thomas Denis civil engineer, educator
†Parks, Thomas W. electrical engineering educator, consultant
Phelan, Richard Magruder mechanical engineer
Pope, Stephen Bailey engineering educator
Rehkugler, Gerald Edwin agricultural engineering educator, consultant
Rodríguez, Ferdinand chemical engineer, educator
†Shen, Shan-Fu aeronautical engineering educator, consultant
Shuler, Michael Louis biochemical engineering educator, consultant
Smith, Julian Cleveland, Jr. chemical engineering educator
Sudan, Ravindra Nath electrical engineer, physicist, educator
Thorp, James Shelby electrical engineering educator
†Wang, Kuo-King manufacturing engineer, educator
White, Richard Norman civil and environmental engineering educator
Wolf, Edward Dean electrical engineering educator

Jamaica
Vasilopoulos, Athanasios V. engineering educator

Jericho
Shinners, Stanley Marvin electrical engineer

Katonah
Bashkow, Theodore Robert electrical engineering consultant, former educator

Levittown
Rubin, Arnold Jesse aeronautical engineer

Locust Valley
Schaffner, Charles Etzel consulting engineering executive

Massapequa Park
Plotkin, Martin retired electrical engineer

Millbrook
Johnston, Robert Cossin consulting engineer executive

New Hartford
Maurer, Gernant Elmer metallurgical executive, consultant

New York
Acampora, Anthony Salvator electrical engineer, educator
†Acrivos, Andreas chemical engineering educator
†Ahmad, Jameel civil engineer, researcher, educator
Alexander, Harold bioengineer, educator
Allen, William Frederick, Jr. mechanical engineer
†Augeri, Joseph Leonard packaging engineer
Bardin, Clyde Wayne biomedical researcher and developer of contraceptives
Baron, Melvin Leon civil engineer, consultant
Baum, Eleanor electrical engineering educator, academic administrator
Becker, Herbert P. mechanical engineer
Bendelius, Arthur George engineering firm executive
Binger, Wilson Valentine civil engineer
Boley, Bruno Adrian engineering educator
Boshkov, Stefan Hristov mining engineer, educator
Bove, John Louis chemistry and environmental engineering educator, researcher
Brazinsky, Irving chemical engineering educator
Brodsky, Stanley Martin engineering technology educator, researcher
Brown, Seymour William engineering executive, consultant
Cantilli, Edmund Joseph safety engineering educator, writer
Cheh, Huk Yuk engineering educator, electrochemist
Clarke, Kenneth Kingsley electrical equipment company executive
Cohen, Edward civil engineer
Coler, Myron A(braham) chemical engineer, educator
Cowin, Stephen Corteen biomedical engineering educator, consultant
†Danziger, Bruce Edward structural engineer
De Gaster, Zachary engineering company executive
DiMaggio, Frank Louis civil engineering educator
Eberstein, Arthur biomedical engineering educator, researcher
Fink, Donald Glen engineering executive, editor
Fogel, Irving Martin consulting engineering company executive
Freudenstein, Ferdinand mechanical engineering educator
†Grace, E. engineering executive
Greenfield, Seymour Stephen mechanical engineer
Grossman, Jacob S. structural engineer
Grunes, Robert Lewis engineering consulting firm executive
Happel, John chemical engineer, researcher
Hardesty, Egbert Railey retired engineering firm executive
Harris, Colin Cyril mineral engineer, educator
Keller, Kenneth Harrison engineering educator, science policy analyst
Klein, Morton industrial engineer, educator
Knobler, Alfred Everett ceramic engineer, manufacturing company executive, publisher
Koshar, Louis David civil engineer
Kvint, Vladimir Lev economist, mining engineer, educator
Lai, W(ei) Michael mechanical engineer, educator
Landau, Ralph chemical engineer
Lee, Martin Yongho mechanical engineer
Leonard, Edward F. chemical engineer, educator
Lewis, William Scheer electrical engineer
†Low, Dana Evarts consulting engineer
Lowen, Gerard Gunther mechanical engineering educator
†Luo, Gangming M. mechanical engineer
McAward, Patrick Joseph, Jr. architectural and engineering company executive
Michel, Henry Ludwig civil engineer
†Miele, Joel Arthur, Sr. civil engineer
Mow, Van C. engineering educator, researcher
Ozero, Brian John chemical engineer
Paaswell, Robert Emil civil engineer, educator
Pisetzner, Emanuel structural engineer
Robertson, Leslie Earl structural engineer
Ross, Donald Edward engineering company executive
†Sadegh, Ali M. mechanical engineering educator, researcher, consultant
†Salvadori, Mario mathematical engineer
Schwartz, Mischa electrical engineering educator
Shapiro, Murray structural engineer
Shinnar, Reuel chemical engineering educator, industrial consultant
†Smith, Gordon H. civil engineer
Somasundaran, Ponisseril surface and colloid engineering, applied science educator
Stahl, Frank Ludwig civil engineer
†Stasior, William F. engineering company executive
Subak-Sharpe, Gerald Emil electrical engineer, educator
Teich, Malvin Carl electrical engineering educator
Themelis, Nickolas John metallurgical engineering educator
Vogelman, Joseph Herbert scientific engineering company executive
Watkins, Charles Booker, Jr. mechanical engineering educator
Weidlinger, Paul civil engineer
Weinstein, Herbert chemical engineer, educator
Wheeler, Wesley Dreer marine engineer, naval architect, consultant
Yang, Edward S. electrical engineering educator
Zakkay, Victor aeronautical engineering educator, scientist
Zuck, Alfred Christian consulting mechanical engineer

Newton Falls
Hunter, William Schmidt engineering executive, environmental engineer

Niagara Falls
Dojka, Edwin Sigmund civil engineer

Niskayuna
Johnson, Ingolf Birger retired electrical engineer

Northport
Gebhard, David Fairchild aeronautical engineer, consultant

Old Westbury
Ranu, Harcharan Singh biomedical scientist, administrator, orthopaedic biomechanics educator

Owego
Blahut, Richard Edward electrical engineer
Nolis, William M. aerospace engineer, consultant

Penfield
Battaglini, Frank Paul engineering company executive

Pleasantville
Pike, John Nazarian optical engineering consultant

Port Washington
Bogen, Samuel Adams electrical engineer, consultant

Potsdam
Cotellessa, Robert Francis *retired electrical engineering educator, academic administrator*
Demerdash, Nabeel Aly Omar *electrical engineer*
Hammam, M. Shawky *electrical engineer, educator*
†Wilcox, William Ross *chemical engineering educator, researcher*

Poughkeepsie
Chu, Richard Chao-Fan *mechanical engineer*
Logue, Joseph Carl *electronics engineer, consultant*

Remsenburg
Edwards, Arthur Anderson *retired mechanical engineer*

Rexford
Kirchmayer, Leon Kenneth *retired electrical engineer*

Rochester
Bouyoucos, John Vinton *research and development company executive*
Burns, Stephen James *engineering educator, materials science researcher*
Carstensen, Edwin Lorenz *biomedical engineer, biophysicist*
Cokelet, Giles Roy *biomedical engineering educator*
Feinberg, Martin Robert *chemical engineering educator*
Freckleton, Jon Edward *engineering educator, consultant, retired military officer*
Gans, Roger Frederick *mechanical engineering educator*
Jorne, Jacob *chemical engineer, educator*
Kinnen, Edwin *electrical engineer, educator*
Lessen, Martin *engineering educator, consulting engineer*
McWilliams, C. Paul, Jr. *engineering executive*
Palmer, Harvey John *chemical engineering educator, consultant*
†Parker, Kevin James *electrical engineer educator*

Rome
Coppola, Anthony *electrical engineer*
Gabelman, Irving Jacob *consulting engineering executive, retired government official*

Rye
Lehman, Lawrence Herbert *consulting engineering executive*
Tung, David Hsi Hsin *consulting civil engineer, emeritus engineering educator*

Saint James
Irvine, Thomas Francis, Jr. *mechanical engineering educator*

Schenectady
Barthold, Lionel Olav *engineering executive*
Coffin, Louis Fussell, Jr. *mechanical engineer*
Hedman, Dale Eugene *consulting electrical engineer*
Huening, Walter Carl, Jr. *retired consulting application engineer*
LaForest, James John *retired electrical engineer*
Linville, Thomas Merriam *engineer*
Mafi, Mohammad *civil engineer, educator*
Matta, Ram Kumar *aeronautical engineer*
McMurray, William *consultant, retired electrical engineer*
Panek, Jan *electrical power engineer, consultant*
Ringlee, Robert James *consulting engineering executive*
Walsh, George William *engineering executive*

Setauket
Irving, A. Marshall *marine engineer*
Levine, Sumner Norton *industrial engineer, educator, editor, author, financial consultant*

Slingerlands
Wilcock, Donald Frederick *mechanical engineer*

Stafford
Moran, John Henry, Jr. *electrical engineer, consultant*

Stony Brook
Chang, Sheldon Shou Lien *electrical engineer*
Chen, Chi-Tsong *electrical engineering educator*
Cope, Randolph Howard, Jr. *electronic research and development executive, educator*
Visich, Marian, Jr. *engineering educator, university dean*
Zemanian, Armen Humpartsoum *electrical engineer, mathematician*

Syracuse
Brennan, Paul Joseph *civil engineer, educator*
Eveleigh, Virgil William *electrical and computer engineering educator*
Harrington, Roger Fuller *electrical engineering educator, consultant*
Jefferies, Michael John *electrical engineer*
Konski, James Louis *civil engineer*
LePage, Wilbur Reed *electrical engineering educator*
Libove, Charles *mechanical and aerospace engineering educator*
Liu, Hao-wen *mechanical and aerospace engineering educator, consultant*
Lyman, Frederic A. *mechanical and aerospace engineering educator, researcher*
Pennock, Donald William *retired mechanical engineer*
†Roberts, Robert *engineering organization executive, think-tank executive*
Sargent, Robert George *engineering educator*
Strait, Bradley Justus *electrical engineering educator*
Tully, William P. *civil engineer, academic administrator*
Wiley, Richard Gordon *electrical engineer*

Tarrytown
Anderson, John Erling *chemical engineer*
Bartoo, Richard Kieth *chemical engineer, consultant*

Troy
Abetti, Pier Antonio *consulting electrical engineer, technology management and entrepreneurship educator*
Anderson, John Bailey *electrical engineering educator*
Bergles, Arthur Edward *mechanical engineering educator*
Block, Robert Charles *nuclear engineering and engineering physics educator*
Brunelle, Eugene John, Jr. *mechanical engineering educator*
†Desrochers, Alan Alfred *electrical engineer*
Feeser, Larry James *civil engineering educator, researcher*
Gill, William Nelson *chemical engineering educator*
Glicksman, Martin Eden *materials engineering educator*
Greenwood, Allan N. *engineering educator, researcher*
Horton, John Tod *engineering company executive*
Jones, Owen Craven, Jr. *nuclear and mechanical engineer, educator*
Jordan, Mark Henry *consulting civil engineer*
Krempl, Erhard *mechanics educator, consultant*
Littman, Howard *chemical engineer, educator*
McDonald, John Francis Patrick *electrical engineering educator*
Modestino, James William *electrical engineering educator*
Nelson, John Keith *electrical engineer*
Saridis, George Nicholas *electrical engineer*
Woods, John William *electrical, computer and systems engineering educator, consultant*

Upton
Baron, Seymour *engineering and research executive*
Radeka, Veljko *electronics engineer*
Steinberg, Meyer *chemical engineer*
Susskind, Herbert *biomedical engineer, educator*

Wantagh
Litman, Bernard *electrical engineer, consultant*

Watervliet
Kitchens, Clarence Wesley, Jr. *physical science administrator*

Webster
Johnson, Ray Clifford *mechanical engineering educator, consultant, writer*
†Machell, Arthur R. *retired mechanical engineer, association board member*

West Nyack
Hornik, Joseph William *civil engineer*

Westbury
†Sandler, Gerald Howard *aerospace executive*

White Plains
†Busch, Paul Louis *engineering company executive, consultant*
Foster, John Horace *consulting environmental engineer*
Mitchell, Robert Dale *consulting engineer*
Pirnie, Malcolm, Jr. *consulting engineer*
†Westerhoff, Garret Peter *environmental engineer, executive*

Woodstock
Smith, Albert Aloysius, Jr. *electrical engineer, consultant*

Yorktown Heights
Almasi, George Stanley *electrical engineer, computer scientist*
Dennard, Robert Heath *engineering executive, scientist*
Hong, Se June *computer engineer*
Pugh, Emerson William *electrical engineer*
†Romankiw, Lubomyr Taras *materials engineer*
Terman, Lewis Madison *electrical engineer, researcher*
Troutman, Ronald R. *electrical engineer*

NORTH CAROLINA

Boonville
Reece, Joe Wilson *engineering company executive*

Cary
†Conrad, Hans *materials engineering educator*
Miranda, Constancio Fernandes *civil engineering educator*

Chapel Hill
Baker, Charles Ray *engineering and mathematics educator, researcher*
Coulter, Norman Arthur, Jr. *biomedical engineering educator emeritus*
Eisenbud, Merril *environmental engineer*
Kusy, Robert Peter *biomedical engineering and orthodontics educator*
Lucas, Carol Lee *biomedical engineer*
Okun, Daniel Alexander *environmental engineering educator, consulting engineer*
Stidham, Shaler, Jr. *operations research educator*

Charlotte
Kim, Rhyn Hyun *engineering educator*
King, L. Ellis *civil engineer, educator and administrator*
Rodite, Robert R.R. *engineering scientist, technology strategist*

Columbus
Weber, Ernst *engineering consultant*

Durham
†Bejan, Adrian *mechanical engineering educator*
Casey, H(orace) Craig, Jr. *electrical engineering educator*
Chaddock, Jack Bartley *mechanical engineering educator*
Fisher, Charles Page, Jr. *consulting geotechnical engineer*
Garg, Devendra Prakash *mechanical engineer, educator*
Harman, Charles Morgan *mechanical engineer*
Hochmuth, Robert Milo *mechanical and biomedical engineer, educator*
McElhaney, James Harry *biomedical engineer*
Piatt, William McKinney, III *consulting engineering executive*
Plonsey, Robert *electrical and biomedical engineer*
Strohbehn, John Walter *engineering science educator*
Utku, Senol *civil engineer, computer science educator*

Fuquay Varina
Hairston, William Michael *manufacturing engineer*

Granite Falls
Humphreys, Kenneth King *engineer, educator, association executive*

High Point
Huston, Fred John *automotive engineer*

Highland
Sandor, George Nason *mechanical engineer, educator*

New Bern
Baughman, Fred Hubbard *aeronautical engineer, former naval officer*
Moeller, Dade William *environmental engineer, educator*

Raleigh
Agrawal, Dharma Prakash *engineering educator*
Baliga, Bantval Jayant *electrical engineering educator, consultant*
Beatty, Kenneth Orion, Jr. *chemical engineer*
Bitzer, Donald Lester *electrical engineering educator, retired research laboratory administrator*
Church, Kern Everidge *engineer, consultant*
†Dudziak, Donald John *nuclear engineer, educator*
†Ferrell, James K. *chemical engineering educator, dean*
Gardner, Robin Pierce *engineering educator*
†Gilbert, Charles Gorman *civil engineering educator*
Hanson, John M. *civil engineering and construction educator*
Hauser, John Reid *electrical engineering educator*
Jennings, Burgess Hill *mechanical engineering educator*
Kriz, George James *agricultural research administrator, educator*
Murray, Raymond Le Roy *nuclear engineering educator*
Nagle, Hubert Troy, Jr. *electrical engineering educator*
Nickel, Donald Lloyd *engineering executive*
Rhodes, Donald Robert *electrical engineer, educator*
†Rohrbach, Roger Phillip *agricultural engineer, educator*
Skaggs, Richard Wayne *agricultural engineering educator*
Sorrell, Furman Yates *mechanical engineering educator*
Turinsky, Paul Josef *nuclear engineer, educator*
Williams, Hugh Alexander, Jr. *retired mechanical engineer, consultant*
Zorowski, Carl Frank *engineering educator, university administrator*

Research Triangle Park
Holton, William Coffeen *electrical engineering executive*
Kuhn, Matthew *engineering company executive*
Larsen, Ralph Irving *environmental research engineer*

Salisbury
Kelly, Brendan William *engineering executive*

Washington
Hackney, James Acra, III *industrial engineer, manufacturing company executive*

NORTH DAKOTA

Bismarck
Carmichael, Virgil Wesly *mining, civil and geological engineer, former coal company executive*

OHIO

Akron
Brown, David Rupert *engineering executive*

Alexandria
Palmer, Melville Louis *retired agricultural engineering educator*

Athens
Dinos, Nicholas *engineering educator, administrator*
Robe, Thurlow Richard *engineering educator, university dean*

Brook Park
Bluford, Guion Stewart, Jr. *engineering company executive*
Wilson, Jack *aeronautical engineer*

Canton
Hoecker, David *engineering executive*

Centerville
Keating, Tristan Jack *retired aeronautical engineer*

Chagrin Falls
Cadou, Peter Brosius *mechanical engineer*
Pauly, Bruce Henry *engineering consultant*

Chardon
Nara, Harry Raymond *engineering educator*

Cincinnati
Anno, James Nelson *nuclear engineering scientist, educator*
Arnold, Lynn Ellis *metallurgist, consultant*
Bahr, Donald Walter *chemical engineer*
Bostian, Harry Edward *chemical engineer*
Greenberg, David Bernard *chemical engineering educator*
Hall, Ernest L. *electrical engineer, robotics educator*
Johnson, K(enneth) O(dell) *aerospace engineer*
Katzen, Raphael *consulting chemical engineer*
Kehew, William James *environmental, quality assurance engineering manager*
Kroll, Robert James *aerospace engineering educator*
†Leylek, James H. *aerospace engineer*
Martin, John Bruce *chemical engineer*
McDonough, James Francis *civil engineer, educator*
Middendorf, William Henry *electrical engineering educator*
Niemoller, Arthur B. *electrical engineer*
Rubin, Stanley Gerald *aerospace engineering educator*
Smith, Leroy Harrington, Jr. *mechanical engineer, aerodynamics consultant*
Toftner, Richard Orville *engineering executive*
Weisman, Joel *nuclear engineering educator, engineering consultant*
†Wisler, David Charles *aerospace engineer, educator*

Cleveland
†Anderson, James R. *engineering executive*
Angus, John Cotton *chemical engineering educator*
Baer, Eric *engineering and science educator*
Bahniuk, Eugene *mechanical engineering educator*
Brosilow, Coleman Bernard *chemical engineering educator*
Burghart, James Henry *electrical engineer, educator*
Collin, Robert Emanuel *electrical engineering educator*
Coulman, George Albert *chemical engineer, educator*
Dy Liacco, Tomas Enciso *engineering consulting executive*
Goldstein, Marvin Emanuel *aerospace scientist, research center administrator*
Graham, Robert William *areospace research engineer*
Gruber, Sheldon *electrical engineering educator*
†Hardy, Richard Allen *mechanical engineer, diesel fuel engine specialist*
Jordan, Howard Emerson *retired engineering executive*
Ko, Wen-Hsiung *electrical engineering educator*
Liu, Chung-Chiun *chemical engineering educator*
Madden, James Desmond *forensic engineer*
Martin, Paul Joseph *biomedical engineer, cardiology researcher, educator, consultant*
Mortimer, J. Thomas *biomedical engineering educator*
†Noneman, Edward E. *engineering executive*
Ostrach, Simon *engineering educator*
Pao, Yoh-Han *engineering educator*
†Peckham, P. Hunter *biomedical engineer, educator*
Reisman, Arnold *management science educator*
Reshotko, Eli *aerospace engineer, educator*
Saada, Adel Selim *civil engineer, educator*
†Savinell, Robert Francis *engineering educator*
†Siegel, Robert *heat transfer engineer*

Columbus
Alexander, Carl Albert *ceramic engineer*
Antler, Morton *consulting engineering executive, author, educator*
Bailey, Cecil Dewitt *aerospace engineer, educator*
†Bechtel, Stephen E. *mechanical engineer, educator*
Bedford, Keith Wilson *civil engineering and atmospheric science educator*
†Bhushan, Bharat *mechanical engineer*
Boulger, Francis William *metallurgical engineer*
Brodkey, Robert Stanley *chemical engineering educator*
Cearlock, Dennis Bill *research executive*
Cruz, Jose Bejar, Jr. *engineering educator*
Dickinson, David Walter *welding engineer, educator*
Duckworth, Winston Howard *ceramic engineer*
Dwon, Larry *retired electrical engineer, educator, consultant*
Engdahl, Richard Bott *mechanical engineer*
Ensminger, Dale *mechanical engineer, electrical engineer*
Fenton, Robert Earl *electrical engineering educator*
Gozon, Jozsef Stephan *engineering educator*
Hsu, Hsiung *engineering educator*
Jackson, Curtis Maitland *metallurgical engineer*
Keaney, William Regis *engineering and construction services executive, consultant*
Kennedy, Lawrence Allan *mechanical engineering educator*
Ko, Hsien Ching *electrical engineer, educator*
Ksienski, Aharon Arthur *electrical engineer*
Leissa, Arthur William *mechanical engineering educator*
Miller, Don Wilson *nuclear engineering educator*
Moore, Donald Paul *retired electrical engineer*
Moulton, Edward Quentin *civil engineer, educator*
Ojalvo, Morris *civil engineer, educator*
Peters, Leon, Jr. *electrical engineering educator, research administ*
Rapp, Robert Anthony *metallurgical engineering educator, consultant*
Rubin, Alan J. *environmental engineer, chemist*
†Sahai, Yogeshwar *engineering educator*
St. Pierre, George Roland, Jr. *materials science and engineering administrator, educator*
Satyapriya, Combatore Keshavamurthy *geotechnical engineering executive*
Schwab, Glenn Orville *retired agricultural engineering educator, consultant*
Smith, George Leonard, Jr. *industrial engineering educator*
Uotila, Urho Antti Kalevi *geodesist, educator*
Ware, Brendan John *electrical engineer, electric utility company executive*
Zakin, Jacques Louis *chemical engineering educator*

Dayton
Chattoraj, Shib Charan *chemical engineer*
D'Azzo, John Joachim *electrical engineer, educator*
Goesch, William Holbrook *aeronautical engineer*
Haigh, Peter Leslie *software company executive, consultant*
Holiga, Ludomil Andrew *metallurgical engineer*
Houpis, Constantine Harry *electrical engineering educator*
Kazimierczuk, Marian Kazimierz *electrical engineer, educator*
Keto, John Edwin *consulting electrical engineer*
†Krug, Maurice F. *engineering company executive*
Schell, Allan Carter *electrical engineer*
Schmitt, George Frederick, Jr. *materials engineer*

Dublin
Major, Coleman Joseph *chemical engineer*

Gates Mills
Enyedy, Gustav, Jr. *chemical engineer*

Granville
Jacobs, Richard Allen *industrial engineer*

Hudson
Kirchner, James William *electrical engineer*

Logan
Carmean, Jerry Richard *broadcast engineer*

Lyndhurst Mayfield
Sevin, Eugene *engineer, consultant, educator*

Marblehead
Haering, Edwin Raymond *chemical engineering educator, consultant*

Marion
Tozzer, Jack Carl *civil engineer, surveyor*

Mason
Clarke, W. Hall *engineer*

Middletown
†Gilby, Steve *metallurgical engineering researcher*

Mount Vernon
†Schaub, Fred S. *mechanical engineer*

North Olmsted
Lundin, Bruce Theodore *engineering and management consultant*

Northfield
Baltazzi, Evan Serge *engineering research consulting company executive*

Oxford
Ward, Roscoe Fredrick *engineering educator*

Painesville
Jayne, Theodore Douglas *technical research and development company executive*

Powell
Adeli, Hojjat *civil engineering educator, computer scientist*

Shelby
Moore, Florian Howard *electronics engineer*

Silver Lake
Chrobak, Dennis Steven *chemical engineer*

Springboro
Saxer, Richard Karl *metallurgical engineer, retired air force officer*

Toledo
Farison, James Blair *electrical engineer, educator*
Hauenstein, Henry William *civil engineer*
Hood, Douglas Crary *electronics educator*

Westlake
Bisson, Edmond Emile *mechanical engineer*
Huff, Ronald Garland *mechanical engineer*

Wickliffe
Bardasz, Ewa Alice *chemical engineer*

Willoughby
Hassell, Peter Albert *electrical and metallurgical engineer*

Worthington
Compton, Ralph Theodore, Jr. *electrical engineering educator*

Yellow Springs
Trolander, Hardy Wilcox *engineering executive, consultant*

Youngstown
Fok, Thomas Dso Yun *civil engineer*

OKLAHOMA

Bartlesville
Clay, Harris Aubrey *chemical engineer*
Hankinson, Risdon William *chemical engineer*

Bethany
Arnold, Donald Smith *chemical engineer, consultant*

Midwest City
Smith, Wayne Calvin *chemical engineer*

Moore
Moore, Dalton, Jr. *petroleum engineer*

Norman
Bert, Charles Wesley *mechanical and aerospace engineer, educator*
Campbell, John Morgan *retired chemical engineer*
Crane, Robert Kendall *engineering educator, researcher, consultant*
Egle, Davis Max *mechanical engineering educator*
Zelby, Leon Wolf *electrical engineering educator, consulting engineer*

Oklahoma City
Dew, Jess Edward *chemical engineer*
†Stewart, C.C., Jr. *mechanical engineer*
†Wickens, Donald Lee *engineer executive, consultant, rancher*

Stillwater
Bell, Kenneth John *chemical engineer*
Brusewitz, Gerald Henry *agricultural engineering educator, researcher*
Case, Kenneth Eugene *industrial engineering educator*
Haan, Charles Thomas *agricultural engineering educator*
Maddox, Robert Nott *chemical engineer, educator*
Mize, Joe Henry *industrial engineer, educator*
†Noyes, Ronald T. *agricultural engineering educator*
Parcher, James Vernon *civil engineering educator, consultant*
†Thompson, David Russell *agricultural engineering educator, academic dean*
Turner, Wayne Connelly *industrial engineer, educator*

Tinker AFB
Pray, Donald George *aerospace engineer*

Tulsa
Dunn, Clark Allan *civil engineer, educator*
Earlougher, Robert Charles, Sr. *petroleum engineer*
Elkins, Lloyd Edwin, Sr. *petroleum engineer, energy consultant*
†Eriksen, Vernon Lee *manufacturing engineering executive*
Parker, Robert Lee, Sr. *petroleum engineer, drilling company executive*
Williams, David Rogerson, Jr. *engineer, business executive*
Williams, John Horter *civil engineer, oil, gas, telecommunications and allied products distribution company executive*

Washington
Sliepcevich, Cedomir M. *engineering educator*

OREGON

Corvallis
Engelbrecht, Rudolf *electrical engineering educator*
Forbes, Leonard *engineering educator*
†Hall, Philip G. *engineering executive*
Hansen, Hugh Justin *agricultural engineer*
†Hassebroek, Lyle G. *engineering company executive*
Knudsen, James George *chemical engineer, educator*
Miner, John Ronald *agricultural engineer*
Mohler, Ronald Rutt *electrical engineering educator*
Olleman, Roger Dean *industry consultant, former metallurgical engineering educator*
Sollitt, Charles Kevin *ocean engineering educator, laboratory director*
Temes, Gabor Charles *electrical engineering educator*
†Welty, James R. *mechanical engineer, educator*

Florence
Ericksen, Jerald Laverne *educator, engineering scientist*

Lincoln City
Gehrig, Edward Harry *electrical engineer, consultant*

Myrtle Point
Walsh, Don *marine consultant, executive*

Portland
Lendaris, George Gregory *electrical educator*
Sutter, Harvey Mack *engineer,consultant*
Taylor, Carson William *electrical engineer*

Sunriver
Clough, Ray William, Jr. *civil engineering educator*
Davenport, Wilbur Bayley, Jr. *electrical engineering educator*

Wilsonville
Isberg, Reuben Albert *radio communications engineer*

PENNSYLVANIA

Alcoa Center
Pien, Shyh-Jye John *mechanical engineer*

Allentown
Gewartowski, James Walter *electrical engineer*
Hansel, James Gordon *chemical engineer, educator*
Singhal, Kishore *engineering administrator*
Smith, Warren L. *electrical engineer, physicist*
Winters, Arthur Ralph, Jr. *chemical and cryogenic engineer, consultant*

Berwyn
Lund, George Edward *retired electrical engineer*

Bethel Park
Korchynsky, Michael *metallurgical engineer*
O'Donnell, William James *engineering executive*

Bethlehem
Beedle, Lynn Simpson *civil engineering educator*
Dahlke, Walter Emil *electrical engineering educator*
Durkee, Jackson Leland *civil engineer*
Fisher, John William *civil engineering educator*
Gardiner, Keith Mattinson *engineering educator*
Georgakis, Christos *chemical engineer educator, consultant, researcher*
Karakash, John J. *engineering educator*
Pense, Alan Wiggins *metallurgical engineer, academic administrator*
Roberts, Richard *mechanical engineering educator*
Tuzla, Kemal *mechanical engineer, scientist*
Viest, Ivan M(iroslav) *consulting structural engineer*
†Wei, Robert Peh-Ying *mechanics educator*
Wenzel, Leonard Andrew *engineering educator*

Blue Bell
Hirsch, Robert W. *environmental consulting, engineering and construction company executive*
Tomlinson, J. Richard *engineering services company executive*
Vollmar, John Raymond *electrical engineer*

Bryn Mawr
Barth, Charles Fredrik *aerospace engineer*

Buck Hill Falls
Meditz, Walter Joseph *engineering consultant*

Cambridge Springs
Hughes, William Frank *mechanical and electrical engineering educator*

Chadds Ford
Isakoff, Sheldon Erwin *chemical engineer*

Cheltenham
Weinstock, Walter Wolfe *systems engineer*

Conshohocken
Cohen, Alan *civil engineer*
Rippel, Harry Conrad *mechanical engineer, consultant*

Coraopolis
†Nelson, Donald J. *engineering executive*
Shaw, Richard Leslie *engineering company executive*

Erie
Gray, Robert Beckwith *engineer*
Hsu, Bertrand Dahung *mechanical engineer*

Export
Wagner, Charles Leonard *electrical engineer, consultant*

Fairviewvill
Kisielowski, Eugene *engineering executive*

Fort Washington
Buescher, Adolph Ernst (Dolph Buescher) *aerospace company executive*

Furlong
Parker, Jennifer Ware *chemical engineer, researcher*

Gibsonia
Shoub, Earle Phelps *chemical engineer, educator*

Glen Mills
Churchill, Stuart Winston *chemical engineering educator*

Glenside
Forman, Edgar Ross *mechanical engineer*

Greensburg
Guyker, William Charles, Jr. *electrical engineer, researcher*

Harrisburg
Cate, Donald James *mechanical enginee, consultant*
Dietz, John Raphael *consulting engineer executive*
Giusti, Joseph Paul *engineering education and development director, retired university chancellor*

Haverford
Bemis, Hal Lawall *engineering and business executive*

Hershey
McInerney, Joseph John *biomedical engineer, educator*

Horsham
Goff, Kenneth Wade *electrical engineer*

Huntingdon Valley
West, A(rnold) Sumner *chemical engineer*

Jenkintown
Haythornthwaite, Robert Morphet *civil engineer, educator*
Mifsud, Lewis *electrical engineer, fire origin investigator, physicist*

Johnstown
Kuhn, Howard Arthur *engineering executive, educator*

Lake Ariel
Tague, Charles Francis *retired engineering, construction and real estate development company executive*

Lansdowne
†Popovics, Sandor *civil engineer, educator, researcher*

Monroeville
Creagan, Robert Joseph *consulting nuclear engineer*
Jacobi, William Mallett *nuclear engineer, consultant*
Mandel, Herbert Maurice *civil engineer*
Murphy, William James *materials characterization company executive, metallurgical engineer*

Murrysville
Colborn, Harry Walter *electrical engineering consultant*

New Kensington
Jarrett, Noel *chemical engineer*

Philadelphia
Bartlett, Desmond William *engineering company executive*
Batterman, Steven Charles *engineering mechanics and bioengineering educator*
Carmi, Shlomo *mechanical engineering educator, scientist*
Chance, Henry Martyn, II *engineering executive*
Cohen, Ira Myron *aeronautical and mechanical engineering educator*
†Cruger, Lorenzo *civil engineer*
Dabby, Sabah Salman *chemical engineer*
Eisenstein, Bruce Allan *electrical engineering educator*
Falkie, Thomas Victor *mining engineer, natural resources company executive*
Fegley, Kenneth Allen *systems engineering educator*
Fromm, Eli *engineering educator*
Hargens, Charles William, III *electrical engineer, consultant*
Higgins, Frederick Benjamin, Jr. *environmental engineering educator, college dean*
Jaron, Dov *biomedical engineer, educator*
Ku, Y. H. *engineering educator*
Lawley, Alan *materials engineering educator*
Litt, Mitchell *chemical engineer, educator, bioengineer*
†Mc Mahon, Charles Joseph, Jr. *materials science educator*
†Miller, Charles Q. *engineering company executive*
†Morlok, Edward Karl *engineering educator, consultant*
Olsen, George Allen *engineering executive*
Parmiter, James Darlin *safety engineer*
Pelkaus, Edward Egils *civil engineer*
Pipes, Wesley O'Feral *civil engineering educator*
Quinn, John Albert *chemical engineering educator*
Reid, John Mitchell *biomedical engineer*
Schwan, Herman Paul *electrical engineering and physical science educator, research scientist*
Showers, Ralph Morris *electrical engineer educator*
Steinberg, Bernard D. *electrical engineer, educator, researcher*
Tomiyasu, Kiyo *consulting engineer*
Zemel, Jay Norman *electrical engineer, educator*

Pittsburgh
Amon Parisi, Cristina Hortensia *mechanical engineering educator, researcher*
Anderson, John Leonard *chemical engineering educator*
Behrend, William Louis *electrical engineer*
Birks, Neil *metallurgical engineering educator, consultant*
Bjorhovde, Reidar *civil engineer, educator, researcher, consultant*
Bloom, William Millard *furnace design engineer*
Casasent, David Paul *electrical engineering educator, data processing executive*
Charap, Stanley Harvey *electrical engineering educator*
Chiang, Shiao-Hung *chemical engineering educator*
Director, Stephen William *electrical engineering educator, researcher*
Fenves, Steven Joseph *civil engineer*
Frank, Philip Lawrence *mechanical engineer, consultant*
Geiger, Gene Edward *engineer, educator*
Gottfried, Byron Stuart *engineering educator*
†Griffin, Donald Spray *mechanical engineer, consultant*
Grossmann, Ignacio Emilio *chemical engineering educator*
Hamilton, Howard Britton *electrical engineer, educator*
Hoburg, James Frederick *electrical engineering educator*
Hung, Tin-Kan *engineering educator, researcher*
Jordan, Angel Goni *electrical and computer engineering educator*
†Khonsari, Michael M. *engineering educator*
†Krutz, Ronald L. *computer engineer*
Kryder, Mark Howard *computer and electrical engineering educator, consultant*
Li, Ching-Chung *electrical engineering, computer science educator*
Luthy, Richard Godfrey *environmental engineering educator*
McMichael, Francis Clay *civil engineering educator, environmental engineering consultant*
Meiksin, Zvi H. *electrical engineering educator*
Milnes, Arthur George *electrical engineer, educator*
Moura, José Manuel Fonseca *electrical engineer*
Nathanson, Harvey Charles *electrical engineer*
Neuman, Charles P. *electrical and computer engineering educator, consultant*
Pettit, Frederick Sidney *metallurgical engineering educator, researcher*
Raimondi, Albert Anthony *mechanical engineer*
Rohrer, Ronald Alan *electrical and computer engineering educator, consultant*
Romualdi, James Philip *engineering educator*
Schultz, Jerome Samson *biochemical engineer, educator*
Simaan, Marwan A. *electrical engineering educator*
Spanovich, Milan *civil engineer*
Stuckeman, Herman Campbell *architectural engineer*
Sukiennik, Leopold Jonah *civil, structural engineer, consultant*
Tierney, John William *chemical engineering educator*
†Tilton, Robert Daymond *chemical engineer*
Vogeley, Clyde Eicher, Jr. *engineering educator, artist, consultant*
Wallace, William Edward *engineering educator, scientist*
Westerberg, Arthur William *chemical engineering educator*
Williams, Max Lea, Jr. *engineer, educator*
Woo, Savio Lau-Yuen *bioengineering educator*

Plymouth Meeting
Kostinsky, Harvey *clinical and electrical engineer*

Radnor
†Follman, John P. *engineering comprnay executive*

Reading
Hollander, Herbert I. *consulting engineer*
Smith, Alexander Forbes, III *engineering consulting firm executive*

Star Junction
Baldwin, Clarence Jones, Jr. *electrical engineer, manufacturing company executive*

State College
Foderaro, Anthony Harolde *nuclear engineering educator*
Grimes, Dale Mills *electrical engineering educator*
Henderson, Robert Earl *mechanical engineer*
Olson, Donald Richard *mechanical engineering educator*
Thompson, Fred Clayton *engineering executive, consultant*

Swarthmore
Krendel, Ezra Simon *systems engineering consultant, educator*

University Park
Aplan, Frank Fulton *metallurgical engineering educator*
Bieniawski, Zdzislaw Tadeusz *mineral engineer, educator, consultant*
Bose, Nirmal Kumar *electrical engineering, mathematics educator*
Brown, John Lawrence, Jr. *electrical engineering educator*
Davids, Norman *engineering science and mechanics educator, researcher*
†Dong, Cheng *bioengineering educator*
Engel, Alfred Julius *chemical engineering educator*
Feng, Tse-yun *computer engineer, educator*
Fonash, Stephen Joseph *engineering educator*
Ham, Inyong *industrial engineering educator*
Helfferich, Friedrich G. *chemical engineer, educator*
Holl, John William *engineering educator*
Jacobs, Harold Robert *mechanical engineering educator*
Kabel, Robert Lynn *chemical engineering educator*
Klaus, Elmer Erwin *chemical engineering educator, consultant*
Lakshminarayana, Budugur *aerospace engineering educator*
Mathews, John David *electrical engineering educator, consultant*

McCormick, Barnes Warnock *aerospace engineering educator*
†McDonnell, Archie Joseph *environmental engineer*
†McWhirter, John Ruben *chemical engineering educator*
Mentzer, John Raymond *electrical engineer, educator*
Morris, Philip John *aerospace engineering educator*
Nisbet, John Stirling *electrical engineering educator*
†Ramani, Raja Venkat *mining engineering educator*
Ruud, Clayton Olaf *engineering educator*
Seaburg, Paul Allen *structural engineer, educator*
Thompson, William, Jr. *engineering educator*
Thuering, George Lewis *industrial engineering educator*
Tittmann, Bernhard Rainer *engineering science and mechanics educator*
†Vannice, M. Albert *chemical engineering educator, researcher*
Walker, Eric Arthur *consulting engineer, institute executive*
†Walker, Paul Norvell *agricultural and biological engineering educator*
Webb, Ralph Lee *mechanical engineering educator*
Witzig, Warren Frank *nuclear engineer, educator*
Yu, Francis T. S. *electrical engineering educator, researcher, consultant*

Valley Forge
Olson, James Robert *consulting engineer*

Villanova
White, Robert Edward *chemical engineering educator, consultant*

Warminster
Tatnall, George Jacob *aeronautical engineer*

Warrendale
Hartwig, Thomas Leo *civil engineer*
Schmidt, Jack *mechanical engineer, electrical engineer*

West Chester
Dwyer, Francis Gerard *chemical engineer, researcher*
Thompson, A(nsel) Frederick, Jr. *environmental engineering and consulting company executive*

Wynnewood
Bordogna, Joseph *engineer, educator*

RHODE ISLAND

Cranston
Fang, Pen Jeng *engineering executive and consultant*
Thielsch, Helmut John *engineering company executive*

Greenville
Calo, Joseph Manuel *chemical engineering educator*

Kingston
Polk, Charles *electrical engineer, educator, biophysicist*
Tufts, Donald Winston *electrical engineering educator*
†White, Frank M. *mechanical engineer, educator*

Portsmouth
Baker, Walter Louis *engineering company executive*
Becken, Bradford Albert *engineering executive*

Providence
Clifton, Rodney James *engineering educator, civil engineer, consultant*
Findley, William Nichols *mechanical engineering educator*
Freund, Lambert Ben *engineering educator, researcher, consultant*
Glicksman, Maurice *engineering educator, former dean and provost*
Gurland, Joseph *engineering educator*
Hazeltine, Barrett *electrical engineer, educator*
Liu, Joseph T. C. *engineering educator*
Loferski, Joseph John *electrical engineering educator*
Needleman, Alan *mechanical engineering educator*
Richman, Marc Herbert *forensic engineer, educator*
Symonds, Paul Southworth *mechanical engineering educator, researcher*

SOUTH CAROLINA

Aiken
Williamson, Thomas Garnett *nuclear engineering and engineering physics educator*

Anderson
Goodner, Homer Wade *process control reliability engineer, process safety risk analysis specialist, industrial process system failure risk consultant*

Clemson
Adams, John Quincy, III *nuclear engineer*
†Bunn, Joe Millard *agricultural engineering educator*
Chisman, James Allan *industrial engineering educator, consultant*
Couch, James Houston *industrial engineer, educator*
†Han, Young Jo *agricultural engineer, educator*
Leonard, Michael Steven *industrial engineering educator*
Paul, Frank Waters *mechanical engineer, educator, consultant*
Pursley, Michael Bader *electrical engineering educator, communications systems research and consulting*
†von Recum, Andreas F. *bioengineer*
Williamson, Robert Elmore *agricultural engineering educator*

Columbia
Ernst, Edward Willis *electrical engineering educator*
Lee, Alexandra Saimovici *civil engineer*
Whitlock, Edward Madison, Jr. *civil engineer*

Fort Mill
†Hodge, Bobby Lynn *mechanical engineer*

Greenville
†Brown, George Edward *chemical engineer, consultant*
Carpenter, William Levy *mechanical engineer*
†Christopher, Socrates S. *engineering executive*
†Leonhardt, Thomas C. *engineering company executive*
Plumstead, William Charles *quality engineer, consultant*

Hartsville
Menius, Espie Flynn, Jr. *electrical engineer*

Hilton Head Island
Davis, Milton Wickers, Jr. *chemical engineer, educator*
Huckins, Harold Aaron *chemical engineer*
Windman, Arnold Lewis *retired mechanical engineer*

North Charleston
Mc Aleece, Donald John *mechanical engineering educator*

Orangeburg
Graule, Raymond S(iegfried) *metallurgical engineer*

Pawleys Island
Alexander, William D., III *civil engineer, consultant, former army air force officer*
†Cepluch, Robert J. *retired mechanical engineer*

Saint Helena Island
Pinkerton, Robert Bruce *mechanical engineer*

Salem
Jones, Charles Edward *mechanical engineer*

Simpsonville
Kucij, Timothy Michael *engineer, composer, organist, pianist, conductor, minister, theologian*

West Columbia
Faust, John William, Jr. *electrical engineer, educator*

SOUTH DAKOTA

Brookings
Storry, Junis Oliver *retired engineering educator*

Rapid City
Erickson, John Duff *mining engineering educator*
Gowen, Richard Joseph *electrical engineering educator, college president*
Ramakrishnan, Venkataswamy *civil engineer, educator*
Riemenschneider, Albert Louis *engineering educator*
Scofield, Gordon Lloyd *mechanical engineer, educator*

TENNESSEE

Chattanooga
Baker, Merl *engineering educator*
Cox, Ronald Baker *engineering and management consultant, university dean*
Gore, Barry Maurice *electrical engineer*
Saeks, Richard Ephraim *electrical engineer*

Cookeville
Chowdhuri, Pritindra *electrical engineer, educator*
Sissom, Leighton Esten *mechanical engineering educator, dean, consultant*

Germantown
Shockley, Thomas Dewey *electrical engineering educator*

Greenbrier
Newell, Paul Haynes, Jr. *engineering educator, former college president*

Kingsport
Scott, H(erbert) Andrew *retired chemical engineer*
†Siirola, Jeffrey John *chemical engineer*
Watkins, William H(enry) *electrical engineer*

Knoxville
Bailey, Joel Furness *mechanical engineering educator*
Bailey, John Milton *electrical engineering educator*
Bose, Bimal Kumar *electrical engineering educator*
†Bressler, Marcus N. *consulting engineer*
Danko, Joseph Christopher *metals engineer, university official*
Gonzalez, Rafael Ceferino *electrical engineering educator*
Hung, James Chen *engineer, educator, consultant*
LeVert, Francis Edward *nuclear engineer*
Mc Dow, John Jett *agricultural engineering educator*
Rentenbach, Thomas Joseph *civil engineer*
†Richards, Stephen Harold *engineering educator*
†Richardson, Don Orland *agricultural educator*
Roth, J(ohn) Reece *electrical engineer, educator, researcher, consultant*
Tschantz, Bruce Allen *civil engineer, educator*
Uhrig, Robert Eugene *nuclear engineer, educator*

Luttrell
Milligan, Mancil Wood *mechanical and aerospace engineering educator*

Maryville
Oakes, Lester Cornelius *retired electrical engineer, consultant*

Memphis
Kellogg, Frederic Hartwell *civil engineer, educator*

Nashville
Brodersen, Arthur James *electrical engineer*
Cadzow, James Archie *engineering educator, researcher*
Chaudhuri, Dilip Kumar *engineering educator*
Coen, Daniel Kennedy, Jr. *aeronautical engineer*
Cook, George Edward *electrical engineering educator, consultant*
Eckenfelder, William Wesley, Jr. *environmental engineer*
†Garcia, Ephrahim *mechanical engineering educator*
Hahn, George Thomas *materials engineering educator, researcher*
Harrawood, Paul *civil engineering educator*
Harris, Thomas Raymond *biomedical engineer, educator*
House, Robert William *electrical engineering educator emeritus*
McClanahan, Larry Duncan *civil engineer, consultant*
Parker, Frank Leon *environmental engineering educator, consultant*
Potter, John Leith *mechanical and aerospace engineer, educator, consultant*
Schnelle, Karl Benjamin, Jr. *chemical engineering educator, consultant, researcher*
Speece, Richard Eugene *civil engineer, educator*
Youree, Gene Tassey *tool design engineer*

Oak Ridge
Cain, Victor Ralph *nuclear engineer*
†Hawsey, Robert Alan *engineering laboratory executive*
Kasten, Paul Rudolph *nuclear engineer, educator*
Rosenthal, Murray Wilford *chemical engineer, science administrator*
Scott, Charles David *chemical engineer*
Trauger, Donald Byron *nuclear engineering laboratory administrator*
†Waters, Dean A. *engineering executive*
Wooten, Hollis Darwin *engineer*

Tullahoma
Antar, Basil Niman *engineering educator*
†Pate, Samuel Ralph *engineering corporation executive*
†Wu, Ying Chu Lin Susan *engineering company executive, engineer*

TEXAS

Amarillo
Keaton, Lawrence Cluer *engineer, consultant*
Von Eschen, Robert Leroy *electrical engineer, consultant*

Arlington
Anderson, Dale Arden *aerospace engineer, educator*
Fung, Adrian Kin-Chiu *electrical engineering educator, researcher*
Mc Elroy, John Harley *electrical engineering educator*
Payne, Fred R(ay) *aerospace engineering educator, researcher*
Qasim, Syed Reazul *civil engineering educator, researcher*
Stevens, Gladstone Taylor, Jr. *industrial engineer*

Austin
Abraham, Jacob A. *computer engineering educator, consultant*
Adcock, Willis Alfred *electrical engineer, educator*
Aggarwal, Jagdishkumar Keshoram *electrical and computer engineering educator, research administrator*
Armstrong, Neal Earl *civil engineering educator*
Baker, Lee Edward *biomedical engineering educator*
Barlow, Joel William *chemical engineering educator*
Beard, Leo Roy *civil engineer*
Box, Barry Glenn *aerospace engineer, military officer*
Breen, John Edward *civil engineer, educator*
Brock, James Rush *chemical engineering educator*
Burns, Ned Hamilton *civil engineering educator*
Carlton, Donald Morrill *research, development and engineering executive*
Carrasquillo, Ramon Luis *civil engineering educator, consultant*
Dougal, Arwin Adelbert *electrical engineer, educator*
Dupuis, Russell Dean *electrical engineer, research scientist*
Evans, Walter Reed *engineering executive, consultant*
Fair, James Rutherford, Jr. *chemical engineering educator, consultant*
Fowler, David Wayne *architectural engineering educator*
†Frank, Karl Heinz *civil engineer, educator*
Gloyna, Earnest Frederick *environmental engineer, educator*
Goodenough, John Bannister *engineering educator, research physicist*
Gray, Kenneth Eugene *petroleum engineering educator*
Harris, Richard Lee *engineering executive, retired army officer*
Himmelblau, David Mautner *chemical engineer*
Howell, John Reid *mechanical engineer, educator*
Hull, David George *aerospace engineering educator, researcher*
Jirsa, James Otis *civil engineering educator*
†Klein, Dale Edward *nuclear engineering educator*
Koen, Billy Vaughn *mechanical engineering educator*
Koros, William John *chemical engineering educator*
LaGrone, Alfred Hall *electrical engineering educator*
Lamb, Jamie Parker, Jr. *mechanical engineer, educator*
Marcus, Harris Leon *mechanical engineering and materials science educator*
Mark, Hans Michael *aerospace engineering educator, physicist*
McGinnis, Charles Irving *civil engineer*
Mc Ketta, John J., Jr. *chemical engineering educator*
Mercer, Melvin Ray *electrical engineer, educator*
Metcalfe, Tom Brooks *chemical engineering educator*
Moulthrop, James Sylvester *research engineer, consultant*
†Nichols, Steven Parks *mechanical engineer, academic administrator*
†Oden, John Tinsley *engineering mechanics educator, consultant*
Paul, Donald Ross *chemical engineer, educator*
Rhyne, Vernon Thomas, III *electrical engineer, consultant*
†Richards-Kortum, Rebecca Rae *biomedical engineering educator*
Rylander, Henry Grady, Jr. *mechanical engineering educator*
Sandberg, Irwin Walter *electrical and computer engineering educator*
Schapery, Richard Allan *engineering educator*
Schechter, Robert Samuel *chemical engineer, educator*
Short, Byron Elliott *engineering educator*
Steinfink, Hugo *chemical engineering educator*
Stice, James Edward *chemical engineer, educator*
Straiton, Archie Waugh *electrical engineering educator*
Swartzlander, Earl Eugene, Jr. *engineering educator, former electronics company executive*
Szebehely, Victor G. *aeronautical engineer*
Tapley, Byron Dean *aerospace engineer, educator*
Tesar, Delbert *machine systems and robotics educator, researcher, manufacturing consultant*
Thurston, George Butte *mechanical and biomedical engineering educator*
Tucker, Richard Lee *civil engineer, educator*
Vliet, Gary Clark *mechanical engineering educator*
Walton, Charles Michael *civil engineering educator*
Wehring, Bernard William *nuclear engineering educator*
Welch, Ashley James *engineering educator*
Weldon, William Forrest *electrical and mechanical engineer, educator*
Wissler, Eugene Harley *chemical engineer, educator*
Woodson, Herbert Horace *electrical engineering educator*
Wright, Stephen Gailord *civil engineering educator, consultant*

Baird
Rodenberger, Charles Alvard *aerospace engineer, consultant*

Boerne
Dixon, Robert James *aerospace consultant, former air force officer, former aerospace company executive*

Bryan
Samson, Charles Harold, Jr. (car) *retired engineering educator, consultant*

Bushland
†Howell, Terry Allen *agricultural engineer*

Carrollton
Schulz, Richard Burkart *electrical engineer, consultant*

Channelview
Johnson, Gus LaRoy *marine chemist, safety consultant*

College Station
†Batchelor, Bill *civil engineering educator*
Bhattacharyya, Shankar Prashad *electrical engineer, educator*
Cochran, Robert Glenn *nuclear engineering educator*
†Ehsani, Mehrdad (Mark) *electrical engineering educator, consultant*
Fletcher, Leroy Stevenson *mechanical engineer, educator*
Hall, Kenneth Richard *chemical engineering educator, consultant*
Hann, Roy William, Jr. *civil engineer, educator*
Hassan, Yassin Abdel *engineer, educator*
Herbich, John Bronislaw *engineering educator*
Holland, Charles Donald *chemical engineer, educator*
Lee, William John *petroleum engineering educator, consultant*
Lowery, Lee Leon, Jr. *civil engineer*
Lytton, Robert Leonard *civil engineer, educator*
Mathewson, Christopher Colville *engineering geologist, educator*
Page, Robert Henry *engineer, educator, researcher*
Painter, John Hoyt *electrical engineer*
Patton, Alton DeWitt *electrical engineering educator, consultant, research administrator*
Rabins, Michael Jerome *mechanical engineer, educator*
†Reddell, Donald Lee *agricultural engineer*
†Reddy, J. Narasimha *mechanical engineering educator*
Rhode, David Leland *mechanical engineering educator, consultant*
Richardson, Herbert Heath *mechanical engineer, educator, institute director*
†Wysk, Richard A. *engineering educator, researcher*
†Yao, James Tsu-Ping *civil engineer*

Crosby
†Ohsol, Ernest Osborne *consulting chemical engineer*

Dallas
Bruene, Warren Benz *electronic engineer*
Eberhart, Robert Clyde *biomedical engineering educator, researcher*
Fontana, Robert Edward *electrical engineering educator, retired air force officer*
Gilbert, Paul H. *engineering executive, consultant*
Gill, David Brian *electrical engineer, educator*
Griffith, James William *engineer, consultant*
Kilby, Jack St. Clair *electrical engineer*
Lee, Sidney Phillip *chemical engineer, state senator*
Mays, Gerald Avery (Jerry Mays) *engineering executive, consultant*
Mc Lemore, Robert Henry *petroleum engineer, consultant*
Monsees, James Eugene *engineering executive, consultant*
Sewell, James Leslie *engineering company executive*
Warren, Kelcy L. *engineering executive*

Denton
Rhoades, Warren A., Jr. *retired mechanical engineer*

El Paso
Coleman, Howard S. *engineer, physicist*
Friedkin, Joseph Frank *consulting engineering executive*
Grieves, Robert Belanger *engineering educator*

Fort Worth
Burroughs, Jack Eugene *ceramic engineering executive*
Cunningham, Atlee Marion, Jr. *aeronautical engineer*
Kenderdine, John Marshall *petroleum engineer, retired army officer*
†Kent, D. Randall, Jr. *engineering company executive*
Nichols, James Richard *civil engineer, consultant*
Nichols, Robert Leighton *civil engineer*
Webb, Theodore Stratton, Jr. *aerospace executive, consultant*

Galveston
Otis, John James *civil engineer*

Sheppard, Louis Clarke *biomedical engineer, educator*

Garland
Wagers, Robert Shelby *engineering director*

Granbury
Killebrew, James Robert *architectural engineering firm executive*

Greenville
Johnston, John Thomas *engineering executive*

Houston
Akers, William Walter *chemical engineering educator*
Amundson, Neal Russell *chemical engineer, mathematician, educator*
Anthony, Donald Barrett *engineering executive*
†Arrowsmith, Peter D. *engineering executive*
Bovay, Harry Elmo, Jr. *retired engineering company executive*
Brannon, H(ezzie) Raymond, Jr. *petroleum engineer, oil company scientist*
Bridger, Baldwin, Jr. *electrical engineer*
Chapman, Alan Jesse *mechanical engineering educator*
Dawn, Frederic Samuel *chemical and textile engineer*
†Duke, Michael B. *aerospace scientist*
†Dunbar, Bonnie J. *engineer, astronaut*
Edwards, Victor Henry *chemical engineer*
Eichberger, LeRoy Carl *stress analyst, mechanical engineering consultant*
Focht, John Arnold, Jr. *geotechnical engineer*
Frankhouser, Homer Sheldon, Jr. *engineering and construction company executive*
Geer, Ronald Lamar *mechanical engineering consultant, retired oil company executive*
Germany, Daniel Monroe *aerospace engineer*
Gidley, John Lynn *engineering executive*
Hellums, Jesse David *chemical engineering educator and researcher*
Hsu, Thomas Tseng-Chuang *civil engineer, educator*
†Jeanes, Joe W. *materials engineering executive*
Kenefick, John Henry, Jr. *retired engineering company executive, consultant*
King, Robert Augustin *engineering executive*
†Knight, Tommy E. *civil engineer*
Kobayashi, Riki *chemical engineer, educator*
Krause, William Austin *engineering executive*
Krishen, Kumar *aerospace research technologist*
Lienhard, John Henry *mechanical engineering educator*
Luss, Dan *chemical engineering educator*
†Martin, Craig Lee *engineering company executive*
Matney, William Brooks, VII *electrical engineer, marine engineer*
Matthews, Charles Sedwick *petroleum engineering consultant, research advisor*
McClelland, Bramlette *engineering executive, consultant*
McIntire, Larry Vern *chemical engineering educator*
Miele, Angelo *engineering educator, researcher, consultant, author*
Montijo, Ralph Elias, Jr. *engineering executive*
Moore, Pat Howard *engineering and construction company executive*
†Moore, Walter Parker, Jr. *civil engineering company executive*
Morris, Owen Glenn *engineering corporation executive*
Nordgren, Ronald Paul *engineering educator, researcher*
Ostrofsky, Benjamin *business and engineering management educator, industrial engineer*
Pearson, James Boyd, Jr. *electrical engineering educator*
Powell, Alan *engineer-scientist, educator*
Prats, Michael *petroleum engineer, educator*
Reistle, Carl Ernest, Jr. *petroleum engineer*
Shen, Liang Chi *electrical engineer, educator, researcher*
†Spanos, Pol Dimitrios *engineering educator*
Symons, James Martin *environmental engineer, educator*
†Thayer, Keith B. *engineering company executive*
Thomsen, Charles Burton *engineering design company executive*
Tucker, Randolph Wadsworth *engineering executive*
Valencia, Jaime Alfonso *chemical engineer*
Walker, Esper Lafayette, Jr. *civil engineer*
†Wesselski, Clarence J. *aerospace engineer*
Wilkinson, Bruce W. *corporate executive, lawyer*
Wren, Robert James *aerospace engineering manager*
Yu, Aiting Tobey *engineering executive*

Humble
Brown, Samuel Joseph, Jr. *mechanical engineer*

Irving
†Callahan, Frank T. *engineering executive*

Kerrville
Matlock, (Lee) Hudson *civil engineer, consultant*

League City
Meinke, Roy Walter *electrical engineer, consultant*

Lindale
Bockhop, Clarence William *retired agricultural engineer*
Wilson, Leland Earl *petroleum engineering consultant*

Lubbock
Archer, James Elson *engineering educator*
Dudek, Richard Albert *engineering educator*
Kiesling, Ernst Willie *civil engineering educator*
Koh, Pun Kien *retired educator, metallurgist, consultant*
Kristiansen, Magne *electrical engineer, educator*
Portnoy, William Manos *electrical engineering educator*

Port Aransas
Lehmann, William Leonardo *electrical engineer, educator*

Richardson
Biard, James Robert *electrical engineer*
Kinsman, Frank Ellwood *engineering executive*
Lutz, Raymond Price *industrial engineer, educator*

San Antonio
Abramson, Hyman Norman *engineering and science research executive*
†Shih, Chia Shun *educator, consulting engineer*
Smith, Richard Thomas *electrical engineer*
Stebbins, Richard Henderson *electronics engineer, peace officer, security consultant*

Tyler
Smith, James Edward *petroleum engineer, consultant*

Wimberley
Busch, Arthur Winston *environmental engineer, educator, consultant*

Woodsboro
Rooke, Allen Driscoll, Jr. *civil engineer*

UTAH

Logan
Clark, Clayton *electrical engineering educator*
Hargreaves, George Henry *civil and agricultural engineer, researcher*
Keller, Jack *agricultural engineering educator, consultant*

Murray
Volberg, Herman William *electronic engineer, consultant*

Ogden
†Davidson, Thomas Ferguson *chemical engineer*

Provo
Jonsson, Jens Johannes *electrical engineering educator*
Merritt, LaVere Barrus *engineering educator, civil engineer*
Pope, Bill Jordan *chemical engineering educator, business executive*

Salt Lake City
Anderson, Charles Ross *civil engineer*
Dahlstrom, Donald Albert *chemical and metallurgical engineering educator, former equipment manufacturing company executive*
De Vries, Kenneth Lawrence *mechanical engineer, educator*
Eernisse, Errol Peter *electronics company executive, scientist*
Gandhi, Om Parkash *electrical engineer*
†Hill, Stephen D. *chemical engineer, federal agency administrator*
Hogan, Mervin Booth *mechanical engineer, educator*
†Jacobsen, Stephen Charles *biomedical engineer, educator*
Pershing, David Walter *chemical engineering educator, researcher*
Sandquist, Gary Marlin *engineering educator*
Seader, Junior DeVere *chemical engineering educator*
Sohn, Hong Yong *metallurgical and chemical engineering educator*
Stockham, Thomas Greenway, Jr. *electrical engineering educator*
Stringfellow, Gerald B. *engineering educator*
Zeamer, Richard Jere *engineer, executive*

Sandy
Bennett, Carl McGhie *engineering company executive, consultant, army reserve and national guard officer*
Jorgensen, Leland Howard *aerospace research engineer*

VERMONT

Burlington
Anderson, Richard Louis *electrical engineer*
Pinder, George Francis *engineering educator, scientist*

Essex Junction
Pricer, Wilbur David *electrical engineer*

Norwich
†Japikse, David *mechanical engineer, manufacturing executive*

VIRGINIA

Alexandria
†Ackerman, Roy Alan *research and development executive*
†Bartholomew, Byron Simpson, Jr. *engineering services company executive*
Brickell, Charles Hennessey, Jr. *marine engineer, retired military officer*
Cook, Charles William *aerospace consultant, educator*
Darling, Thomas, Jr. *retired rural electrification specialist*
Dobson, Donald Alfred *electrical engineer*
Doeppner, Thomas Walter *electrical engineer, educator, consultant*
Eckhart, Myron, Jr. *marine engineer*
Fozard, John William *engineer, designer, consultant, educator*
Gray, John Edmund *chemical engineer*
Heacock, Phillip Kaga *aerospace executive*
Klotz, John Wesley *electronics consultant*
Lasser, Howard Gilbert *chemical engineer, consultant*
Mandil, I. Harry *nuclear engineer*
†McFarland, Richard B. *engineering company executive*
Murray, Russell, II *aeronautical engineer, defense analyst, consultant*
Rall, Lloyd Louis *civil engineer*
Scurlock, Arch Chilton *chemical engineer*
Thompson, LeRoy, Jr. *radio engineer, army reserve officer*

Arlington
Casazza, John Andrew *electrical engineer, business executive*
Dillaway, Robert Beacham *engineering and management consultant*
Flowers, Harold Lee *consulting aerospace engineer*
Gilbert, Arthur Charles *aerospace engineer, consulting engineer*
Hagn, George Hubert *electrical engineer, researcher*
Hall, Carl William *agricultural and mechanical engineer*
Rahman, Muhammad Abdur *mechanical engineer*
Sutton, George Walter *research laboratory executive, mechanical engineer*

Belle Haven
Sarsten, Gunnar Edward *mechanical engineer, construction executive*

Blacksburg
Blackwell, William Allen *electrical engineering educator*
Brown, Gary Sandy *electrical engineering educator*
Comparin, Robert Anton *mechanical engineering educator*
de Wolf, David Alter *electrical engineer, educator*
Fabrycky, Wolter Joseph *engineering educator, author, industrial and systems engineer*
Haugh, Clarence Gene *agricultural engineering educator*
Hibbard, Walter Rollo, Jr. *retired engineering educator*
Jacobs, Ira *electrical engineering educator, former telecommunications company executive*
†Jones, James Beverly *mechanical engineering educator*
Lucas, J. Richard *retired mining engineering educator*
Meirovitch, Leonard *engineering educator*
Moore, James Mendon *industrial engineering educator, consultant*
†Morton, John *engineering educator, researcher*
Murray, Thomas Michael *civil engineering educator, consultant*
†Nayfeh, Ali Hasan *engineering educator*
Phadke, Arun G. *electrical engineering educator*
Price, Dennis Lee *industrial engineer, educator*
Randall, Clifford Wendell *civil engineer*
†Rappaport, Theodore Scott *electrical engineering educator*
Squires, Arthur Morton *chemical engineer, educator*
Stutzman, Warren Lee *electrical engineer, educator*

Charlottesville
Dorning, John Joseph *nuclear engineering, engineering physics and applied mathematics educator*
Edlich, Richard French *biomedical engineering educator*
Gaden, Elmer Lewis, Jr. *chemical engineering educator*
Haimes, Yacov Yosseph *systems and civil engineering educator, consultant*
Herakovich, Carl Thomas *civil engineering, applied mechanics educator*
Hoel, Lester A. *civil engineering educator*
Hudson, John Lester *chemical engineering educator*
Hutchinson, Thomas Eugene *biomedical engineering educator*
Inigo, Rafael Madrigal *electrical engineering educator*
Johnson, W(alker) Reed *nuclear engineering educator*
Krzysztofowicz, Roman *systems engineering educator, consultant*
Lee, Jen-shih *biomedical engineering educator*
Mattauch, Robert Joseph *electrical engineering educator*
McVey, Eugene Steven *electrical engineering educator, consultant*
Morton, Jeffrey Bruce *aerospace engineering educator*
Reynolds, Albert Barnett *nuclear engineer, educator*
Thompson, Anthony Richard *electrical engineer, astronomer*
Townsend, Miles Averill *aerospace and mechanical engineering educator*
Waxman, Ronald *computer engineer*

Fairfax
Boone, James Virgil *engineering executive*
Cantus, H. Hollister *engineering corporation executive*
Cook, Gerald *electrical engineering educator*
†Elias, Antonio L. *aeronautical engineer, aerospace executive*
Fink, Lester Harold *engineering company executive, educator*
Gollobin, Leonard Paul *chemical engineer*
Mc Pherson, John Barkley *aerospace consultant, retired military officer*
†Stitt, William C. *engineering executive*
†Tipermas, Marc *engineering executive*
Warfield, John Nelson *engineering educator, consultant*

Falls Church
Gouse, S. William, Jr. *engineering executive, scientist*
Lorenzo, Michael *engineer, government official, real estate broker*
Nickle, Dennis Edwin *electronics engineer, church deacon*
Villarreal, Carlos Castaneda *engineering executive*

Fort Belvoir
†Norris, Michael R. *engineering administrator*

Gloucester
Donaldson, Coleman duPont *aerodynamics and aerospace consulting engineer*

Great Falls
Douma, Jacob Hendrick *hydraulic engineer, consultant*

Hampton
†Bushnell, Dennis Meyer *mechanical engineer, researcher*
Clark, Leonard Vernon *aerospace engineer*
†Corlett, William Albert *aerospace engineer*
Duberg, John Edward *aeronautical engineer, educator*
Joshi, Suresh Meghashyam *research engineering executive*
Noor, Ahmed Khairy *engineering educator, researcher*
Pandey, Dhirendra Kumar *mechanical engineer, scientist*
Sobieski, Jaroslaw *aerospace engineer*

Huddleston
Kopp, Richard Edgar *electrical engineer*

Kilmarnock
Gilruth, Robert Rowe *aerospace consultant*

King George
Hoglund, Richard Frank *research and technical executive*

Lexington
Trandel, Richard Samuel *mechanical engineer, educator*

Lynchburg
Barkley, Henry Brock, Jr. *research and development executive*
Fath, George R. *electrical engineer, communications executive*

Mc Lean
Carnicero, Jorge Emilio *aeronautical engineer, business executive*
Enger, Walter Melvin *consulting engineer, former navy officer*
Kahne, Stephen James *systems engineer, educator, academic administrator, engineering executive*
Kimmel, H. Steven *engineering executive*
Markels, Michael, Jr. *environmental consulting firm executive*
McCambridge, John James *civil engineer*
Shanklin, Richard Vair, III *mechanical engineer*
Silveira, Milton Anthony *aerospace engineering executive*
Snyder, Franklin Farison *hydrologic engineering consultant*
Sonnemann, Harry *electrical engineer, consultant*

Newington
Foster, Eugene Lewis *engineering executive*

Newport News
Hubbard, Harvey Hart *aeroacoustician, noise control engineer, consultant*
Young, Maurice Isaac *mechanical and aerospace engineering educator*

Norfolk
†Guy, Louis Lee, Jr. *environmental engineer*
Mc Gaughy, John Bell *civil engineer*
Wiltse, James Clark *civil engineer*

Oakton
Curry, Thomas Fortson *electronics engineer, defense industry executive*
Wolff, Edward A. *electronics engineer*

Palmyra
Leslie, William Cairns *metallurgical engineering educator*
Ramsey, Forrest Gladstone, Jr. *engineering company executive*

Reston
Davis, George Lynn *aerospace company executive*
Duscha, Lloyd Arthur *engineering executive*
Kramish, Arnold *technical consultant, author*
Mumzhiu, Alexander *machine vision, image processing engineer*

Richmond
Compton, Olin Randall *consulting electrical engineer, researcher*
Hanneman, Rodney Elton *metallurgical engineer*
McGee, Henry Alexander, Jr. *chemical engineering educator*
Palik, Robert Richard *mechanical engineer*

Roanoke
Hamrick, Joseph Thomas *mechanical engineer, aerospace company executive*
Reggia, Frank *electrical engineer*
†Shaffner, Patrick Noel *architectural engineering executive*
Sowers, William Armand *civil engineer*

Salem
Lane, Lawrence Jubin *electrical engineer, consultant*
Walker, Loren Haines *electrical engineer*
Willet, Richard A. *engineering company executive*

Springfield
Broome, Paul Wallace *engineering research and development executive*
Duff, William Grierson *electrical engineer*

Stephens City
Leeper, Charles Kendal *engineering consultant*

Vienna
Eash, Joseph J. *technology executive*
Keiser, Bernhard Edward *engineering company executive, consulting telecommunications engineer*
†Roth, James *engineering company executive*
Woodward, Kenneth Emerson *retired mechanical engineer*

Winchester
Turner, William Richard *retired aeronautical engineer, consultant*

WASHINGTON

Auburn
Whitmore, Donald Clark *retired engineer*

Bellevue
Dow, Daniel Gould *electrical engineering educator*
Edde, Howard Jasper *engineering executive*
Faris, Charles Oren *civil engineer*
Schairer, George Swift *aeronautical engineer*
Szablya, John Francis *electrical engineer, consultant*
Walsh, John Breffni *aerospace consultant*
Wright, Theodore Otis *forensic engineer*

Bellingham
Albrecht, Albert Pearson *electronics engineer, consultant*

Jansen, Robert Bruce *consulting civil engineer*

Bothell
Blackburn, John Lewis *consulting engineering executive*

East Wenatchee
Bennett, Grover Bryce *engineering consultant*

Edmonds
†Galster, Richard W. *engineering geologist*
Terrel, Ronald Lee *civil engineer, business executive, educator*

Kingston
Pichal, Henri Thomas *electronics engineer, physicist, consultant*

Kirkland
Wenk, Edward, Jr. *civil engineer, policy analyst, educator*

Lummi Island
Ewing, Benjamin Baugh *environmental engineering educator, consultant*

Mercer Island
Bridgforth, Robert Moore, Jr. *aerospace engineer*
Culp, Gordon Louis *consulting engineering executive*

Olympia
Mylroie, Willa Wilcox *transportation engineer, regional planner*

Pullman
Funk, William Henry *environmental engineering educator*
Hirth, John Price *metallurgical engineering educator*
†Stock, David Earl *mechanical engineering educator*

Redmond
Rossano, August Thomas *environmental engineering educator*
†Smith, William Ward *aerospace executive*

Richland
Albaugh, Fred William *nuclear engineer, retired research and development executive*
Evans, Ersel Arthur *engineering consulting executive*
Forsen, Harold Kay *engineering executive*
†Janata, Jiri *biomedical engineer, educator*
Pond, Daniel James *technology planning and analysis program manager, technology transferand deployment*

Seattle
Babb, Albert Leslie *biomedical engineer, educator*
Bangsund, Edward Lee *aerospace company executive*
Blake, Robert Wallace *aeronautical engineer, consultant*
Christiansen, Walter Henry *aeronautics educator*
Clark, Robert Newhall *electrical and aeronautical engineering educator*
Davis, Earl James *chemical engineering educator*
Finlayson, Bruce Alan *chemical engineering educator*
Fox, Kenneth *shipbuilder, naval engineer, water transit consultant*
Garlid, Kermit Leroy *engineering educator*
Guy, Arthur William *electrical engineering educator, researcher*
Haralick, Robert Martin *electrical engineering educator*
Hertzberg, Abraham *aeronautical engineering educator, university research scientist*
Hoffman, Allan Sachs *chemical engineer, educator*
Ishimaru, Akira *electrical engineering educator*
Joppa, Robert Glenn *aeronautics educator*
Kapur, Kailash Chander *industrial engineering educator*
Kippenhan, Charles Jacob *mechanical engineer, retired educator*
Kobayashi, Albert Satoshi *mechanical engineering educator*
Lauritzen, Peter Owen *electrical engineering educator*
Mandeville, Gilbert Harrison *consulting engineering executive*
Martin, George Coleman *aeronautical engineer*
Mc Feron, Dean Earl *mechanical engineer*
Meditch, James Stephen *electrical engineering educator*
†Morgan, Jeff *research engineer*
Pollack, Gerald Harvey *bioengineering educator*
Polonis, Douglas Hugh *engineering educator*
Pratt, David Terry *mechanical engineering educator, combustion researcher*
Robkin, Maurice Abraham *nuclear engineer, educator*
Russell, David Allison *aeronautical engineering educator*
Simcox, Craig Dennis *aeronautical engineer*
Skilling, John Bower *structural and civil engineer*
Sleicher, Charles Albert *chemical engineer*
Spindel, Robert Charles *electrical engineering educator*
Sutter, Joseph F. *aeronautical engineer, consultant, retired airline company executive*
Venkata, Subrahmanyam Saraswati *electrical engineering educator, electri energy and power researcher*
Vesper, Karl Hampton *business and mechanical engineering educator*
Weissman, Eugene Yehuda *chemical engineer*
Williams, Jerald Arthur *mechanical engineer*
Wood, Stuart Kee *engineering manager*
Woodruff, Gene Lowry *nuclear engineer, university dean*

Tacoma
Anderson, Arthur Roland *engineering company executive, civil engineer*
Holman, Kermit Layton *chemical engineer*

Vancouver
Chartier, Vernon Lee *electrical engineer*

WEST VIRGINIA

Charleston
Conway, Richard Ashley *environmental engineer*
Whittington, Bernard Wiley *electrical engineer, consultant*

Huntington
deBarbadillo, John Joseph *metallurgist, management executive*

Mineral Wells
Prather, Denzil Lewis *petroleum engineer*

Morgantown
Adler, Lawrence *mining engineering consultant*
Dadyburjor, Dady B. *chemical engineering educator, researcher*
Guthrie, Hugh Delmar *chemical engineer*
Klein, Ronald Lloyd *electrical engineer, educator*
†Schroder, John L., Jr. *retired mining engineer*

WISCONSIN

Brookfield
Curfman, Floyd Edwin *engineering educator*

Elm Grove
†Grunau, Gary Peter *mechanical contracting executive*

Frederic
Rudell, Milton Wesley *aerospace engineer*

Grafton
Eber, Lorenz *civil engineer, inventor*

Green Bay
Hudson, Halbert Austin, Jr. *retired manufacturing engineer, consultant*

Madison
Beachley, Norman Henry *mechanical engineer, educator*
Berthouex, Paul Mac *civil and environmental engineer, educator*
Bird, Robert Byron *chemical engineering educator, author*
†Bollinger, John Gustave *engineering educator, college dean*
Boyle, William Charles *civil engineering educator*
†Bretherton, Francis P. *aerospace engineering executive*
†Bruhn, Hjalmar Diehl *retired agricultural engineer, educator*
Bubenzer, Gary Dean *agricultural engineering educator, researcher*
Callen, James Donald *nuclear engineer, plasma physicist, educator*
Chang, Y. Austin *materials engineer, educator*
Coberly, Camden Arthur *chemical engineering educator*
Converse, James Clarence *agricultural engineering educator*
Crandall, Lee Walter *civil and structural engineer*
DeVries, Marvin Frank *mechanical engineering educator*
Dietmeyer, Donald Leo *electrical engineer*
Duffie, John Atwater *chemical engineer, educator*
†Duffie, Neil Arthur *mechanical engineering educator, researcher*
Emmert, Gilbert Arthur *engineer, educator*
Foell, Wesley Kay *engineer, energy and environmental scientist, educator, consultant*
Green, Theodore, III *engineering and science educator*
Hill, Charles Graham, Jr. *chemical engineering educator*
Huston, Norman Earl *nuclear engineering educator*
†Kulcinski, Gerald LaVerne *nuclear engineer, educator*
Long, Willis Franklin *electrical engineering educator, researcher*
Loper, Carl Richard, Jr. *metallurgical engineer, educator*
Lovell, Edward George *engineering mechanics educator*
Novotny, Donald Wayne *electrical engineering educator*
Ray, W. Harmon *chemical engineering educator, consultant, author*
Rowlands, Robert Edward *engineering educator*
Rudd, Dale Frederick *retired chemical engineer*
Seireg, Ali A(bdel Hay) *mechanical engineer*
Shohet, Juda Leon *electrical and computer engineering educator, researcher, high technology company executive*
Skiles, James Jean *electrical and computer engineering educator*
Smith, Michael James *industrial engineering educator*
Stewart, Warren Earl *chemical engineer, educator*
Stremler, Ferrel G. *engineering educator, administrator*
Thesen, Arne *industrial engineering educator*
Webster, John Goodwin *biomedical engineering educator, researcher*

Middleton
Eriksson, Larry John *electrical engineer*

Milwaukee
Bartel, Fred Frank *consulting engineer executive*
Battocletti, Joseph Henry *electrical engineer, biomedical engineer, educator*
Boettcher, Harold Paul *engineer, educator*
Chan, Shih Hung *mechanical engineering educator, consultant*
Dupies, Donald Albert *civil engineer, consultant*
Gaggioli, Richard Arnold *mechanical engineering educator*
Graef, Luther William *civil engineer*
Heinen, James Albin *electrical engineering educator*
James, Charles Franklin, Jr. *engineering educator*
Landis, Fred *mechanical engineering educator*
Niederjohn, Russell James *electrical and computer engineering educator*
Ramsey, Paul Willard *metallurgical engineer, welding engineering consultant*
Widera, G. E. O. *materials engineering educator, consultant*
Zelazo, Nathaniel K. *engineering executive*

Neenah
Heaster, Arlene L. *chemical engineer*

River Falls
Johnson, James Robert *ceramic engineer, educator*

West Bend
Styve, Orloff Wendell, Jr. *electrical engineer*

WYOMING

Casper
Donley, Russell Lee, III *engineering executive, former state representative*
†Hinchey, Bruce Alan *environmental engineering company executive*
Wilde, David George *electrical engineer, consultant*

Laramie
Ferris, Clifford Duras *electrical engineer, bioengineer, educator*
Long, Francis Mark *electrical engineer, educator*
Mingle, John Orville *engineer, educator, lawyer, consultant*
Rechard, Paul Albert *civil engineering consulting company executive*
Sutherland, Robert L. *engineering company executive, educator*

Wilson
Lawroski, Harry *nuclear engineer*

TERRITORIES OF THE UNITED STATES

PUERTO RICO

Catano
†Behar, Abraham *construction engineer*

San Juan
†Behar-Ybarra, Elias *civil, structural engineer*
Bonnet, Juan Amedee *nuclear engineer, educator*

MILITARY ADDRESSES OF THE UNITED STATES

EUROPE

APO
Carioti, Bruno M. *civil engineer*

CANADA

ALBERTA

Calgary
Glockner, Peter G. *civil and mechanical engineering educator*
Heidemann, Robert Albert *chemical engineering educator, researcher*
Kentfield, John Alan *mechanical engineering educator*
Malik, Om Parkash *electrical engineering educator, researcher*
Mc Daniel, Roderick Rogers *petroleum engineer*

Edmonton
Bach, Lars *wood products engineer, researcher*
Bellow, Donald Grant *mechanical engineering educator*
Koval, Don O. *electrical engineering educator*
Lock, Gerald Seymour Hunter *mechanical engineering educator*
McDougall, John Roland *civil engineer*
Morgenstern, Norbert Rubin *civil engineering educator*
Offenberger, Allan Anthony *electrical engineering educator*
†Rajotte, Ray V. *biomedical engineer, researcher*
Wayman, Morris *chemical engineering educator, consultant*

BRITISH COLUMBIA

Vancouver
Bennett, Winslow Wood *mechanical engineer*
Crawford, Carl Benson *retired civil engineer, government research administrator*
Grace, John Ross *chemical engineering educator*
Jull, Edward V. *electrical engineer, radio scientist, educator*
Klohn, Earle Jardine *engineering company executive, consultant*
Meisen, Axel *chemical engineer, university administrator*
Peters, Ernest *metallurgy educator, consultant*
Salcudean, Martha Eva *mechanical engineer, educator*
Wedepohl, Leonhard M. *electrical engineering educator*
Young, Lawrence *electrical engineering educator*

Victoria
Antoniou, Andreas *electrical engineering educator*
Lind, Niels Christian *civil engineering educator*

White Rock
Freeze, Roy Allan *engineering consultant*

MANITOBA

Winnipeg
Cohen, Harley *civil engineer, science educator*
†Hurst, William Donald *civil engineer, consultant*
Kuffel, Edmund *electrical engineering educator*
Morrish, Allan Henry *electrical engineering educator*

NEW BRUNSWICK

Fredericton
Ruthven, Douglas Morris *chemical engineering educator*

NEWFOUNDLAND

Saint John's
†Clark, Jack I. *civil engineer, researcher*

NOVA SCOTIA

Halifax
†Wilson, George Peter *industrial engineer*

Kentville
Baker, George Chisholm *engineering executive, consultant*

ONTARIO

Burlington
Harris, Philip John *engineering educator*
†Krishnappan, Bommanna Gounder *fluid mechanics engineer*

Downsview
Bakht, Baidar *civil engineer, researcher, educator*

Etobicoke
McGuigan, Thomas J. *engineering company executive*
Stojanowski, Wiktor J. *mechanical engineer*

Hamilton
Bandler, John William *electrical engineering educator, consultant*
Campbell, Colin Kydd *electrical and computer engineering educator, researcher*
Crowe, Cameron Macmillan *chemical engineering educator*
†Kenny-Wallace, G. A. *chemical engineer*

Islington
Foster, John Stanton *nuclear engineer*

Kingston
Bacon, David Walter *chemical engineering educator*
Batchelor, Barrington de Vere *civil engineer, educator*
Furter, William Frederick *chemical engineer, university dean*
Sen, Paresh Chandra *electrical engineering educator*

London
Davenport, Alan Garnett *civil engineer, educator*
Inculet, Ion I. *electrical engineering educator, consultant*
Quigley, Robert Murvin *engineering educator, research consultant*
Wilson, Gerald Einar *mechanical and industrial engineer, business executive*

North York
Buzacott, John Alan *engineering educator*

Ottawa
Cockshutt, Eric Philip *engineering executive, research scientist*
Copeland, Miles Alexander *electrical engineer educator, consultant*
Falconer, David Duncan *electrical engineering educator*
Georganas, Nicolas D. *electrical engineering educator*
Gussow, William Carruthers *petroleum engineer*
Hewitt, John Stringer *nuclear engineer*
Kind, Richard John *engineering educator*
Legget, Robert Ferguson *civil engineer*
†Mayman, Shlomo Alex *engineering executive*
†McGregor, G. *engineering research administrator*
Mirza, Shaukat *engineering educator, researcher, consultant*
Moore, William John Myles *electrical engineer, researcher*
Rummery, Terrance Edward *nuclear engineering executive, researcher*
Seaden, George *civil engineer*

Owen Sound
Morley, Lawrence Whitaker *geophysicist, remote sensing consultant*

Toronto
Balmain, Keith George *electrical engineering educator, researcher*
Cobbold, Richard Southwell Chevallier *biomedical engineer, educator*
Davison, Edward Joseph *electrical engineering educator*
Endrenyi, Janos *research engineer*
Ganczarczyk, Jerzy Jozef *civil engineering educator, wastewater treatment consultant*
Goldenberg, Andrew Avi *mechanical engineering educator*
Goring, David Arthur Ingham *chemical engineering educator, scientist*
Ham, James Milton *engineering educator*
Janischewskyj, Wasyl *electrical engineering educator*
Kunov, Hans *biomedical and electrical engineering educator*
Macaulay, Colin Alexander *mining engineer*
Mackiw, Vladimir Nicholaus *metallurgical consultant*
McClymont, Kenneth Ross *power systems engineer, consultant*
Meagher, George Vincent *mechanical engineer*
Rapson, William Howard *chemical engineering educator*
Rimrott, Friedrich Paul Johannes *engineer, educator*
Runnalls, (Oliver) John (Clyve) *nuclear engineering educator*
Salama, C. Andre Tewfik *electrical engineering educator*
Sedra, Adel Shafeek *electrical engineering educator, university administrator*

Semlyen, Adam *electrical engineering educator*
Slemon, Gordon Richard *electrical engineering educator*
Smith, Kenneth Carless *electrical engineering educator*
Smith, Peter William Ebblewhite *electrical engineering educator, scientist*
Venetsanopoulos, Anastasios Nicolaos *electrical engineer, educator*
†Venter, Ronald Daniel *mechanical engineering educator, researcher, administrator*
Wonham, Walter Murray *electrical engineer, educator*

Toronto-Etobicoke
Kurys, Jurij-Georgius *environmental engineer, scientist, consultant*

Waterloo
Pindera, Jerzy Tadeusz *mechanical and aeronautical engineer*
Sherbourne, Archibald Norbert *civil engineering educator*
†Thomson, Neil R. *civil engineering educator*
Vlach, Jiri *electrical engineering educator, researcher*

Willowdale
Glass, Irvine Israel *aerospace educator, researcher*

Windsor
Hackam, Reuben *electrical engineering educator*

QUEBEC

Boucherville
†Martel, Jacques G. *materials engineer administrator*

Montreal
Cameron, Alastair Duncan *engineering consultant*
Corinthios, Michael Jean George *electrical engineering educator*
Couture, Armand *civil engineer*
Dealy, John Michael *chemical engineer, educator*
Farnell, Gerald William *engineering educator*
Haccoun, David *electrical engineering educator*
Henderson, William Boyd *engineering executive*
Jonas, John Joseph *metallurgical engineering educator*
Ladanyi, Branko *civil engineer*
Lamarre, Bernard *engineering, contracting and manufacturing advisor*
Morgera, Salvatore Domenic *electrical engineering educator, researcher*
Paidoussis, Michael Pandeli *mechanical engineering educator*
Pfeiffer, J(ohn) David *mechanical engineering educator, consultant*
Ramachandran, Venkatanarayana Deekshit *electrical engineering educator*
Redwood, Richard George *civil engineering educator, researcher*
†Saint-Pierre, Guy *engineering executive*
Selvadurai, Antony Patrick Sinnappa *civil engineering educator, applied mathematician, consultant*
Shaw, Robert Fletcher *retired civil engineer*
Silvester, Peter Peet *electrical engineer, educator, consultant*
Tavenas, François *civil engineer, educator*
†Weir, D. Robert *metallurgical engineer, engineering executive*
Yong, Raymond Nen-Yiu *civil engineering educator*
Zames, George David *electrical engineer, educator*

Quebec
La Rochelle, Pierre-Louis *civil engineering educator*
Lecours, Michel *electrical engineering educator*
Poussart, Denis Jean-Marie *electrical engineering educator, consultant*

Saint-Hubert
Lindberg, Garry Martin *aeronautical engineer, Canadian government official*

Saint Romuald
†Lafond, Pierre *forest engineer*

Sainte Anne de Bellevue
Broughton, Robert Stephen *irrigation and drainage engineering educator, consultant*

Trois Rivières
†Lavallee, H.-Claude *chemical engineer, researcher*

Varennes
Bartnikas, Raymond *electrical engineer, educator*
Krishnayya, Chandra Pasupulati *research engineer, consultant*
Maruvada, Pereswara Sarma *engineering executive, researcher*

Verdun
Paré, Jean-Jacques *civil engineer, geotechnical and dam safety consultant*

SASKATCHEWAN

Regina
Genereux, Robert James *consulting engineer*
Mollard, John Douglas *engineering and geology executive*

Saskatoon
Billinton, Roy *engineering educator*
Gupta, Madan Mohan *engineering educator, researcher*
Kumar, Surinder *electrical engineering educator, consultant*
Sachdev, Mohindar Singh *engineering educator*

MEXICO

Mexico City
Favela-Lozoya, Fernando *civil engineer, educator*

ARGENTINA

Bahía Blanca
Cardozo, Miguel Angel *telecommunications engineering educator*

AUSTRALIA

City Beach
Pelczar, Otto *electrical engineer*

AUSTRIA

Leoben
Fettweis, Günter Bernhard Leo *mining engineering educator*

BELGIUM

Liège
Calvaer, Andre J. *electrical science educator, consultant*

BRAZIL

Minas Gerais
Cimbleris, Borisas *engineering educator, writer*

BRITISH VIRGIN ISLANDS

Tortola,
Green, Leon, Jr. *mechanical engineer*

CHILE

Valparaiso
Hernandez-Sanchez, Juan Longino *electrical engineering educator*

CHINA

Beijing
Liang, Junxiang *aeronautics and astronautics engineer, educator*
Zhang, Ping *aerospace engineering educator*

Xi'an
Fan, Changxin *electrical engineering educator*

ECUADOR

Quito
Torres, Guido Adolfo *water treatment company executive*

EGYPT

Cairo
Khan, Amir U. *agricultural engineering consultant*

Giza
Salem, Ibrahim Ahmed *electrical engineer, consultant, educator*

ENGLAND

Cambridge
†Hawthorne, Sir William (Rede) *aerospace and mechanical engineer, educator*

Hampshire
Suhrbier, Klaus Rudolf *hydrodynamicist, naval architect*

London
Baxendell, Sir Peter (Brian) *petroleum engineer*
Dibble, Gordon Lynch *engineering company executive*
Grabske, William John *engineering and construction company executive*

Poole
Gray, Kenneth John *engineering executive*

ETHIOPIA

Addis Ababa
Haile Giorgis, Workneh *civil engineer*

FRANCE

Chatenay-Malabry
Perrault, Georges Gabriel *chemical engineer*

Marseilles
Dumitrescu, Lucien Z. *aerospace researcher*

Paris
Goupy, Jacques Louis *chemiometrics engineer*

Velizy-Villacoublay
Musikas, Claude *chemical researcher*

GERMANY

Dortmund
Freund, Eckhard *electrical engineering educator*

Göttingen
Lorenz-Meyer, Wolfgang *aeronautical engineer*

Munich
Bodlaj, Viktor *electrical engineer*

GREECE

Athens
Androutsellis-Theotokis, Paul *civil engineer*
Hatzakis, Michael *electrical engineer, research executive*
Katsikadelis, John *civil engineering educator*

HONG KONG

Kowloon
Liou, Ming-Lei *electrical engineer*
Lui, Ng Ying Bik *engineering educator, consultant*

Sha Tin
Kao, Charles Kuen *electrical engineer, educator*

ITALY

Milan
Bondi, Enrico *engineer*

JAPAN

Ashiya
Yukio, Takeda *engineering educator*

Hokkaido
Saito, Shuzo *electrical engineering educator*

Ibaraki
Yamada, Keiichi *engineering educator, university official*

Ishikawa
Nasu, Shoichi *electrical engineering educator*

Kanagawa
Maeda, Toshihide Munenobu *spacecraft system engineer*

Kanazawa
Kawamura, Mitsunori *material scientist, civil engineering educator*

Kawasaki
Taniuchi, Kiyoshi *mechanical engineering educator*

Kita-ku
Ohnami, Masateru *mechanical engineering educator*

Kobe
Masai, Mitsuo *chemical engineer, educator*

Koriyama,
Ohama, Yoshihiko *architectural engineer, educator*

Kyoto
Nagao, Makoto *electrical engineering educator*

Meguro-ku
Sakamoto, Munenori *engineer educator, researcher, chemist*

Muroran
Fu, Yuan Chin *chemical engineering educator*

Nagano
Ito, Kentaro *electrical engineering educator*

Nagoya
Abe, Yoshihiro *ceramic engineering educator*
Yoshida, Tohru *science and engineering educator*

Nara
Hayashi, Tadao *engineering educator*

Narashino
Inazumi, Hikoji *chemical engineering educator*

Sendai
Sone, Toshio *acoustical engineering educator*

Shiga
Makigami, Yasuji *transportation engineering educator*

Shinjyuku-ku Tokyo
Honami, Shinji *mechanical engineer educator*

Togane
Uchiyama, Shoichi *mechanical engineer*

Tokyo
Aoyama, Hiroyuki *structural engineering educator*
Fujii, Hironori Aliga *aerospace engineer, educator*
Hayashi, Taizo *hydraulics researcher, educator*
Kaneko, Hisashi *engineering executive, electrical engineer*
Koshi, Masaki *engineering educator*
Nomura, Shigeaki *aerospace engineer*
Ohe, Shuzo *chemical engineer, educator*

Toyota
Miyachi, Iwao *electrical engineering educator*

Tsukuba
Koga, Tatsuzo *aerospace engineer, educator*

Nannichi, Yasuo *engineering educator*

Yokohama
Tanaka, Nobuyoshi *engineering consultant*

MALAYSIA

Penang
Das, Kumudeswar *food and biochemical engineering educator*

THE NETHERLANDS

Bunnik
van Dyke, Jacob *civil engineer*

NORWAY

Trondheim
Forssell, Börje Andreas *electronics engineer, educator, consultant*
Rokstad, Odd Arne *chemical engineer*
Svaasand, Lars Othar *electronics researcher*

POLAND

Łódź
Zieliński, Jerzy Stanisław *scientist, electrical engineering educator*

Gdańsk
Jagoda, Jerzy Antoni *marine engineer*

Kraków
Noga, Marian *electrical engineer*
Pytko, Stanislaw Jerzy *mechanical engineering educator*

PORTUGAL

Lisbon
Villax, Ivan Emeric *chemical engineer, researcher*

REPUBLIC OF KOREA

Chonju
Park, Byeong-Jeon *engineering educator*

Seoul
Kim, Moon-Il *metallurgical engineering educator*
Ko, Myoung-Sam *control engineering educator*
Park, Won-Hoon *chemical engineer*

Taejon
Kim, Sung Chul *polymer engineering educator*

SINGAPORE

Singapore
Liu, Chang Yu *engineering educator*

SLOVENIA

Ljubljana
Stusek, Anton *mechanical engineer, researcher*

SOUTH AFRICA

Brooklyn
Smith, Edwin David *electrical engineer*

SWEDEN

Stockholm
McNown, John Stephenson *hydraulic engineer, educator*

SWITZERLAND

Burgdorf
Haeberlin, Heinrich Rudolf *electrical engineering educator*

Wallisellen
Kolbe, Hellmuth Walter *acoustical engineer, sound recording engineer*

Zurich
Hepguler, Yasar Metin *architectural engineering educator, consultant*

TAIWAN

Chung-Li
Hong, Zuu-Chang *engineering educator*

Kaohsiung
Yeh, Kung Chie *electrical engineer*

Tainan
†Huang, Ting-Chia *chemical engineering educator, researcher*

Taipei
Pao, Yih-Hsing *engineer, educator*

THAILAND

Bangkok
Ludwig, Harvey Fred *environmental engineer*
†Singh, Gajendra *agricultural engineering educator*

WALES

Cardiff
Morris, William Allan *engineer*

ADDRESS UNPUBLISHED

†Allison, John McComb *aeronautical engineer, retired*
Altan, Taylan *engineering educator, mechanical engineer, consultant*
Amann, Charles Albert *mechanical engineer*
Anderson, Thomas Patrick *mechanical engineer, educator*
Au, Tung *civil engineer, educator, consultant*
Bartholomew, Donald Dekle *engineering executive, inventor*
Bascom, Willard Newell *research engineer, scientist*
Bates, Donald Lloyd *civil engineer, retired*
Bauer, Richard Carlton *nuclear engineer*
Bertin, John Joseph *aeronautical engineer, educator, researcher*
Bertolett, Craig Randolph *mechanical engineer consultant*
Bhagat, Surinder Kumar *environmental engineering educator*
Bissell, Allen Morris *engineer, consultant*
Bloch, Erich *electrical engineer, former science foundation administrator*
Bose, Anjan *electrical engineering educator, researcher, consultant*
Brimacombe, James Keith *metallurgical engineering educator, researcher, consultant*
Brooks, Maurice Edward *engineering executive, consultant*
Brooks, Michael Paul *urban planning educator*
Bunch, Jennings Bryan, Jr. *electrical engineer*
Burns, Richard Francis *mechanical engineer*
Bussgang, Julian Jakob *electronics engineer*
Byrd, Lloyd Garland *civil engineer*
Carter, Hugh Clendenin *mechanical consulting engineer*
Chawla, Krishan Kumar *materials engineer, educator, consultant*
Cheston, Theodore C. *electrical engineer*
Collins, Michael *aerospace consultant, former astronaut*
Constant, Clinton *chemical engineer, consultant*
Cook, Charles Emerson *electrical engineer*
†Crossley, Francis Rendel Erskine *engineering educator*
†Crossley, Francis Rendel Erskine *engineering educator*
Crowley, Joseph Michael *electrical engineer, educator*
Davis, Carl George *software engineer*
Davis, Monte Vincent *nuclear engineer, educator*
Di Cicco, Joseph Nicholas, Jr. *chemical engineer*
Donohue, George L. *mechanical engineer*
Dull, William Martin *engineering executive*
Dutton, John Coatsworth *retired consulting engineering executive*
Eaglet, Robert Danton *electrical engineer, aerospace consultant, retired military officer*
East, Don Gaylord *computer engineer, archaeologist, writer*
Eaton, William Charles *retired mechanical engineer*
Edgar, Thomas Flynn *chemical engineering educator*
Edmundson, Charles Wayne *mechanical engineer, communications executive*
Ellis, Harold Bernard *civil engineer*
Elstner, Richard Chesney *structural engineer*
Eschenbrenner, Gunther Paul *engineering consultant*
Faruqui, G. Ahmad *engineering consultant*
Field, Charles William *metallurgical engineer, small business owner, consultant*
Finger, Harold B. *energy, space, nuclear energy and urban affairs consultant*
Fishman, Bernard *mechanical engineer*
Fleischer, Gerald Albert *industrial engineer, educator*
Fraser, Donald C. *engineering executive, educator*
Fried, Walter Rudolf *engineer, aerospace scientist*
Gens, Ralph Samuel *electrical engineering consultant*
Gerhardt, Jon Stuart *mechanical engineer, engineering educator*
Giardina, Paul Anthony *environmental nuclear engineer, thoroughbred horse investment specialist*
Goldberger, Arthur Earl, Jr. *industrial engineer, consultant*
Grandi, Attilio *engineering consultant*
Gray, Harry Joshua *electrical engineer, educator*
Hallett, William Jared *nuclear engineer*
Halpin, Daniel William *civil engineering educator, consultant*
Harris, Roy Hartley *electrical engineer*
Henderson, Charles Brooke *research company executive*
Herz, George Peter *chemical engineer,industrial consultant*
Holt, Douglas Eugene *consulting engineer, retired business executive*
Howard, Dean Denton *electrical engineer, researcher, consultant*
Hutchinson, John Woodside *applied mechanics educator, consultant*
James, Earl Eugene, Jr. *aerospace engineering executive*
Janowiak, Robert Michael *engineering organization executive*
Jensen, Marvin Eli *retired agricultural engineer*
Johnson, Arnold Ivan *civil engineer*
Johnson, Joe William *engineering educator, consultant*
Jokl, Alois Louis *electrical engineer*
Karp, Sherman *aerospace consultant*
†Keigler, John E. *aerospace engineer*
Kimmel, George Stuart *engineering company executive*
Kocaoglu, Dundar F. *engineering executive, industrial and civil engineering educator*
Koltai, Stephen Miklos *mechanical engineer, consultant, economist*
Korab, Arnold Alva *corporate executive*
Kretschmer, Frank F., Jr. *electrical engineer, researcher, consultant*
†Kurfess, Thomas Roland *mechanical engineering educator*
Kurth, Carl Ferdinand *electrical engineer, researcher*
Landgren, George Lawrence *electrical engineer, consultant*
†Levinson, Herbert Sherman *civil and transportation engineer*
Lipsky, Stephen Edward *engineering executive, electronic warfare engineer*
Lodge, Arthur Scott *mechanical engineering educator*
Lovell, Walter Carl *engineer, inventor*
Lowe, John, III *consulting civil engineer*
Luger, Donald R. *engineering company executive*
†Mai, Chao Chen *engineer*
†Marchessault, Robert H. *chemical engineer*
Marshall, Gerald Francis *optical engineer, consultant, physicist*
Martin, Lee *mechanical engineer*
Masnari, Nino Antonio *electrical engineer, educator*
McDermott, Kevin J. *engineering educator, consultant*
McNutt, William James *consulting engineer*
Meindl, James Donald *electrical engineering educator, administrator*
Meyer, Harold Louis *mechanical engineer*
Morgan, James John *environmental engineering educator*
†Myers, Phillip Samuel *mechanical engineering educator*
Nadel, Norman Allen *civil engineer*
Nahman, Norris Stanley *electrical engineer*
Olstowski, Franciszek *chemical engineer, consultant*
†Ortolano, Ralph J. *engineering consultant*
Palladino, Nunzio Joseph *retired nuclear engineer*
Parente, Michael *electrical engineer*
Peltier, Eugene Joseph *civil engineer, former naval officer, business executive*
Pickering, Howard William *metallurgy engineer, educator*
Ping, David Thomas *senior project engineer*
Poch, Stephen *metallurgical engineer, consultant*
Polasek, Edward John *electrical engineer, consultant*
Pomraning, Gerald Carlton *engineering educator*
Porter, Philip Thomas *retired electrical engineer*
Potvin, Alfred Raoul *engineering executive*
Rabó, Jule Anthony *chemical research administrator, consultant*
Reaves, Ray Donald *civil engineer*
Rehm, Leo Frank *civil engineer*
Reifsnider, Kenneth Leonard *metallurgist, educator*
Reitan, Daniel Kinseth *electrical and computer engineering educator*
Remer, Donald Sherwood *chemical engineer, engineering economist, educator, administrator*
Reppen, Norbjorn Dag *electrical engineer, consultant*
Roetman, Orvil M. *aerospace company executive*
Rogo, Kathleen *safety engineer*
Rohr, Davis Charles *aerospace consultant, business executive, retired air force officer*
Rosenkoetter, Gerald Edwin *engineering and construction company executive*
Rudzki, Eugeniusz Maciej *chemical engineer, consultant*
Russo, Roy Lawrence *electronic design automation engineer, researcher*
Ryan, Carl Ray *electrical engineer*
Schachter, Max *retired engineering services company executive*
Schey, John Anthony *metallurgical engineering educator*
Schrader, Henry Carl *civil engineer, consultant*
Schwinn, Donald Edwin *environmental engineer*
Seedlock, Robert Francis *engineering and construction company executive*
Servan-Schreiber, Jean-Jacques *engineer, author*
Shank, Maurice Edwin *aerospace engineering executive, consultant*
Shur, Michael *electrical engineer, educator, consultant*
Simpson, Murray *engineer, consultant*
Skov, Arlie Mason *petroleum engineer, consultant*
Skromme, Lawrence H. *consulting agricultural engineer*
Smally, Donald Jay *consulting engineering executive*
Smith, Joe Mauk *chemical engineer, educator*
Studebaker, John Milton *utilities engineer, consultant, educator*
Stumpe, Warren Robert *scientific, engineering and technical services company executive*
Templeton, Carson Howard *engineering executive, policy analyst*
Thal, Herbert Ludwig, Jr. *electrical engineer, engineering consultant*
Toor, Herbert Lawrence *chemical engineering educator, researcher*
Tumbleson, Arthur Louis *civil engineer, contractor*
Turnbull, Fred Gerdes *electronics engineer*
Turner, Lee S., Jr. *consultant*
Uman, Martin Allan *electrical engineering educator, researcher, consultant*
Van Dreser, Merton Lawrence *ceramic engineer*
Vega, J. William *aerospace engineering executive, consultant*
Velzy, Charles O. *mechanical engineer*
Vickrey, Robert Edward, Jr. *petroleum engineer*
Wagner, Sigurd *electrical engineering educator, researcher*
Walkup, John Frank *electrical engineer, educator*
Walton, Harold Vincent *former agricultural engineering educator, academic administrator*
Weinberger, Arnold *retired electrical engineer*
Weinschel, Bruno Oscar *engineering executive, physicist*
Wetzel, Donald Truman *engineering company executive*
Williams, Arthur *engineering consultant*
Williams, Charles Wesley *technical executive, researcher*
Williams, Ronald Oscar *systems engineer*
Wilson, Basil Wrigley *oceanographic engineering consultant, artist, author*
Wood, Allen John *electrical engineer, consultant*
Woodward, Clinton Benjamin, Jr. *civil engineering educator*
Young, Leo *electrical engineer*
Yovicich, George Steven Jones *civil engineer*

FINANCE: BANKING SERVICES.
See also FINANCE: INVESTMENT SERVICES.

UNITED STATES

ALABAMA

Birmingham
Bailey, Charles Stanley *banker*
†Banton, Julian Watts *banker*
Brock, Harry Blackwell, Jr. *banker*
Gilbert, Roy W., Jr. *banker*
Horsley, Richard D. *banker*
Jones, D. Paul, Jr. *banker, lawyer*
Mackin, J. Stanley *banker*
Malone, Wallace D., Jr. *bank executive*
Moor, Manly Eugene, Jr. *retired banker*
Morgan, Hugh Jackson, Jr. *bank executive*
Nichol, Victor E., Jr. *banking executive*
Northen, Charles Swift, III *banker*
Powell, William Arnold, Jr. *retired banker*
Sellers, Fred Wilson *banker*
Stephens, Elton Bryson *bank executive, service and manufacturing company executive*
Stone, Edmund Crispen, III *banker*
†Watson, William L., III *banker*
Weatherly, Robert Stone, Jr. *banker*
Woodall, Norman Eugene *banker*
Woods, John Witherspoon *banker*

Mobile
Crow, James Sylvester *retired banker, railway executive*
Lott, Kench Lee, Jr. *banker*

Montgomery
Frazer, Nimrod Thompson *investment banker, financial services executive*
Hoffman, Richard William *banker*

ALASKA

Anchorage
Cuddy, Daniel Hon *bank executive*
Rasmuson, Elmer Edwin *banker, former mayor*
Rose, David Allan *investment manager*

ARIZONA

Carefree
Craft, Robert Homan *banker, corporate executive*

Green Valley
Miner, Earl Howard *retired trust banker*

Phoenix
Bimson, Carl Alfred *bank executive*
Bradley, Gilbert Francis *retired banker*
†Bruner, James D. *trust banker*
Donaldson, Wilburn Lester *property management corporation executive*
†Hoffman, Jay Russell *mortgage investment company executive, accountant*
Houseworth, Richard Court *banker*
Huck, Leonard William *banker, retired*

Tubac
Miller, Frederick Robeson *banker*

ARKANSAS

Conway
Daugherty, Billy Joe *banker*

Fort Smith
Francis, Darryl Robert *former banker*

Little Rock
Bisno, Alison Peck *investment banker*
Bowen, William Harvey *banker, lawyer*
†Bradbury, Curt *bank executive*
Breen, John Francis *retired banker*
Butler, Richard Colburn *banker, lawyer*
†Cobb, James Richard *banker*
Gulley, Wilbur Paul, Jr. *former savings and loan executive*
Hatcher, Joe Branch *banker*
McAdams, Herbert Hall, II *banker*
Stephens, Warren A. *banking executive*

CALIFORNIA

Aptos
Dobey, James Kenneth *banker*

Arcadia
Baillie, Charles Douglas *banker*

Baldwin Park
Swartz, Stephen Arthur *banker, lawyer*

Beverly Hills
Goldsmith, Bram *banker*

Burbank
Miller, Clifford Albert *banker, business consultant*

Burlingame
Souter, Robert Taylor *retired banker*

Chatsworth
Montgomery, James Fischer *savings and loan association executive*

Costa Mesa
Riordan, George Nickerson *investment banker*

Escondido
Newman, Barry Ingalls *retired banker, lawyer*
O'Meara, David Collow *retired banker*

Glendale
Cross, Richard John *banker*
Trafton, Stephen J. *banking executive*

Hidden Hills
Hodgdon, Herbert James *savings and loan executive, consultant*

Irvine
Jamshidipour, Yousef *bank executive, financial consultant, financial planner*
Rady, Ernest S. *thrift and loan association executive*

Irwindale
Deihl, Richard Harry *savings and loan association executive*
Rinehart, Charles R. *savings and loan association executive*

La Jolla
Robbins, John Michael, Jr. *mortgage company executive*

La Mesa
Schmidt, James Craig *retired bank executive*

La Puente
Perret, Joseph Aloysius *banker, consultant*

Lafayette
Dethero, J. Hambright *banker*

Laguna Hills
Luhring, John William *former bank executive*

Long Beach
Hancock, John Walker, III *banker*

Los Angeles
Allman-Ward, Michele Ann *bank executive*
Badie, Ronald Peter *banker*
Callender, William Lacey *savings and loan executive, lawyer*
Carson, Edward Mansfield *banker*
Chuang, Harold Hwa-Ming *banker*
Crawford, Philip Stanley *bank executive*
Dockson, Robert Ray *savings and loan executive*
Little, Richard Le Roy *merchant and investment banker*
Martin, Ray *banker*
McKee, Kathryn Dian Grant *banker*
McLarnan, Donald Edward *banker, corporation executive*
Mullane, Donald A. *banker*
Siart, William Eric Baxter *banker*
Van Asperen, Morris Earl *banker*

Modesto
McNickle, Michael M. *bank executive*

Napa
Hill, Orion Alvah, Jr. *retired banker*

Newport Beach
Kemper, Robert L. *savings and loan association executive*
McAlister, Maurice L. *savings and loan association executive*

Oakland
Sandler, Herbert M. *savings and loan association executive*
Sandler, Marion Osher *savings and loan association executive*

Orange
Starr, Richard William *retired banker*

Pacific Palisades
Kridel, James S. *banker*
Rode, James Dean *banker*

Pasadena
Cecil, John Lamont *bank executive, lawyer*
Smith, Richard Howard *banker*
Ulrich, Peter Henry *banker*
Vaughn, John Vernon *banker, industrialist*

Pebble Beach
Burkett, William Andrew *banker*

Petaluma
Morris, Donald James *banker*

Piedmont
Hoover, Robert Cleary *retired bank executive*

Rancho Cordova
Ling, Robert Malcolm *banker, publishing executive*

Sacramento
†Cox, David W. *bank executive*

San Diego
Binkley, Nicholas Burns *banking executive*
Blakemore, Claude Coulehan *banker*
Kendrick, Ronald H. *banker*
†Madresh, Richard William *bank executive*
Reinhard, Christopher John *merchant banking company executive*
Wiesler, James Ballard *retired banker*

San Francisco
†August, Katherine *banker*
†Barron, Patrick Kenneth *bank executive*
Baumhefner, Clarence Herman *banker*
Bloch, Julia Chang *bank executive, former government official*
Bolin, William Harvey *banker*
Coombe, George William, Jr. *banker, lawyer*
Costello, Daniel Walter *bank executive*
Demarest, David Franklin, Jr. *banker, former government official*
Eckersley, Norman Chadwick *banker*
Gomi, Yasumasa *bank executive*

Gordon, Roger L. *savings and loan association executive*
Hazen, Paul Mandeville *banker*
Ikagawa, Tadaichi *banking executive*
Jurdana, Ernest J. *banker, accountant*
Lindh, Patricia Sullivan *banker, former government official*
McLin, Stephen T. *investment banker*
Meyer, Donald Robert *banker, lawyer*
Otto, George John *investment banker*
Parry, Robert Troutt *bank executive, economist*
Peters, Raymond Robert *bank executive*
Peterson, Rudolph A. *banker*
†Readmond, Ronald Warren *investment banking firm executive*
Reichardt, Carl E. *banker*
Rosenberg, Richard Morris *banker*
Schmidt, Chauncey Everett *banker*
Shimizu, Taisuke *bank executive*
Stewart, Samuel B. *banker, lawyer*
Taylor, Glenhall E. *banker*
Trowbridge, Thomas, Jr. *mortgage banking company executive*
Warner, Harold Clay, Jr. *banker, investment management executive*
Williams, Morgan Lloyd *retired investment banker*

San Mateo
Balles, John Joseph *banker, business consultant*
Brubaker, John E. *bank executive*
Douglass, Donald Robert *banker*
†Russell, Charles T. *bank executive*

Santa Barbara
Anderson, Donald Meredith *bank executive*
Tilton, David Lloyd *savings and loan association executive*

Santa Fe Springs
Popejoy, William J. *savings and loan association executive*

Santa Monica
Barren, Bruce Willard *merchant banker*
Morgan, Monroe *retired savings and loan executive*
Mortensen, William S. *banking executive*
Weil, Leonard *banker*

Sonora
Rand, John Fay *retired banker*

Stockton
†Antoci, Mario *savings and loan company executive*
†Barnum, Robert T. *bank executive*

Ventura
Milligan, Arthur Achille *banker*
†Milligan, Marshall *banker*
†Peck, Douglas Montgomery, Jr. *banking executive*

Walnut Creek
McGrath, Don John *banker*
Rhody, Ronald Edward *banker, communications executive*

COLORADO

Colorado Springs
Olin, Kent Oliver *banker*

Denver
Fugate, Ivan Dee *banker, lawyer*
Grant, William West, III *banker*
Holte, Debra Leah *investment executive, financial analyst*
Krane, Robert Alan *banker*
Malone, Robert Joseph *bank executive*
Nicholson, Will Faust, Jr. *bank holding company executive*
Rockwell, Bruce McKee *retired banker, retired foundation executive*

Englewood
†Harding, W. M. *cooperative financial institution executive*
†Sims, Doug *bank executive*

Lakewood
†Orullian, B. LaRae *bank executive*

Pueblo
Horn, Thomas Carl *retired banker*

CONNECTICUT

Avon
Rutland, George Patrick *banker*

Bridgeport
Carson, David Ellis Adams *banker*
†Goodspeed, Norwick Royall Givens *banker*

Darien
de Selding, Edward Bertrand *retired banker*
Mapel, William Marlen Raines *retired banking executive*

East Haddam
Clarke, Logan, Jr. *banker*

Fairfield
Brett, Arthur Cushman, Jr. *banker*
Jewitt, David Willard Pennock *retired banker*

Greenwich
Dianis, Walter Joseph *retired banker*
Egbert, Richard Cook *retired banker*
Massey, James L. *investment banker*
Moller, William Richard, Jr. *banker*
Woelflein, Kevin Gerard *banker*

Hamden
Williams, Edward Gilman *retired banker*

Middletown
Stevens, Robert Edwin *bank executive, former insurance company executive*

New Canaan
Dillon, James M. *banker*

New Haven
Cottrell, Mary-Patricia Tross *banker*
†Kugler, Frank J. *bank executive*

Newtown
Verano, Anthony Frank *banker*

Norfolk
Vagliano, Alexander Marino *banker*

Washington
Hardee, William Covington *banker, lawyer*

Waterbury
Narkis, Robert Joseph *bank executive, lawyer*

West Hartford
Miller, Elliott Cairns *retired bank executive, lawyer*
Newell, Robert Lincoln *retired banker*

Weston
Lindsay, Charles Joseph *banker*

Whitneyville
Miller, Walter Richard, Jr. *banker*

DELAWARE

Dover
Moran, Joseph Milbert *retired banker*

Newark
Cawley, Charles M. *banker*
†Cochran, John R. *bank executive*
†Lerner, Alfred *bank executive*
Wright, Vernon Hugh Carroll *bank executive*

Wilmington
Cecala, Ted Thomas, Jr. *banker, accountant*
†Classon, Bruce David *bank executive*
Corkran, Donald Allen *bank executive*
Mattey, John Joseph *mortgage and investment company executive, real estate analyst, appraiser*
†Porter, John Francis, III *banker*
St. Clair, Jesse Walton, Jr. *retired savings and loan executive*
†Smoot, Richard L(eonard) *banker*
Taylor, Bernard J., II *banker*
†Wakefield, David Dean *banker*

DISTRICT OF COLUMBIA

Washington
Andringa, Calvin Bruce *investment banker*
Applegarth, Paul Vollmer *investment banking and finance executive*
Bibby, Douglas Martin *mortgage association executive*
Billings, Donald Franklin *international banking consultant*
Coreth, Joseph Herman *bank executive*
Coughlin, Timothy Crathorne *bank executive*
Couper, William *banker*
†D'Aniello, Daniel *merchant banker*
Gilbert, Jackson B. *banker*
Hawley, Frederick William, III *bank executive, former federal official*
Husain, Syed Shahid *bank executive*
†Iglesias, Enrique V. *bank executive, former government minister*
Jaycox, Edward Van Kleeck *bank executive*
†Karaosmanoglu, Attila *bank executive, economist*
Kesterman, Frank Raymond *investment banker*
Kimberly, William Essick *investment banker*
Lasko, Warren Anthony *mortgage banker, economist*
LaWare, John Patrick *banker, federal official*
Marsh, Quinton Neely *banker*
Mathias, Edward Joseph *merchant banker*
Miller, G(eorge) William *merchant banker, business executive*
Paquin, Paul Peter *mortgage finance executive*
Preston, Lewis Thompson *banker*
Raines, Franklin Delano *investment banker*
Riley, Joseph Harry *retired banker*
Robinson, Daniel Baruch *banker*
Rodriguez, Rita Maria *bank executive*
Rogers, James Frederick *banker, management consultant*
Rotberg, Eugene Harvey *investment banker, lawyer*
†Seelig, Steven Alfred *government financial executive*
Shihata, Ibrahim Fahmy Ibrahim *development banker, lawyer*
Smilow, Michael A. *mortgage company excecutive*
Stern, Paula *international trade advisor*
Stevenson, Eric Van Cortlandt *lawyer, mortgage banker, real estate executive*
West, Millard Farrar, Jr. *banker*
Yeo, Edwin Harley, III *bank executive*
Young, Harrison Hurst, III *banker*

FLORIDA

Bal Harbour
Behrman, Myron M. *banker, real estate investor*

Bonita Springs
Birky, John Edward *banker, consultant, financial planner*

Boynton Beach
Jacobs, C. Bernard *banker*

Deland
†Renfroe, L. Edwin *bank executive*

Dunedin
Rosa, Raymond Ulric *retired banker*

Fort Lauderdale
Cannon, Herbert Seth *investment banker*
Levi, Kurt *retired banker*
†Robinson, James *bank executive*

Fort Myers
†McLeod, Allan L., Jr. *bank executive*

Holmes Beach
Browning, Henry Prentice *banker*

Jacksonville
Ernest, Albert Devery, Jr. *banker*
Graham, Cynthia Armstrong *banker*
Lane, Edward Wood, Jr. *retired banker*
Lastinger, Allen Lane, Jr. *banker*
Rice, Charles Edward *banker*
Rishel, Richard Clinton *banker*

Lake Worth
Finch, Ronald M., Jr. *savings bank executive*

Maitland
Fichthorn, Luke Eberly, III *investment banker*

Miami
Barnes, Donald Winfree *banker*
Brownell, Edwin Rowland *banker, civil engineer*
Cooper, Thomas Astley *banking executive*
†Coords, Robert H. *bank executive*
Courshon, Arthur Howard *banker, lawyer*
Giller, Norman Myer *banker, architect, author*
Kanter, Joseph Hyman *banker, community developer*
†Mentzer, Carl Forrest *banker*
Rebozo, Charles Gregory *banker*
Scheinberg, Steven Eliot *investment banker*
Smathers, Frank, Jr. *banker, horticulturist*
Stuzin, Charles Bryan *savings and loan association executive*
Taylor, Stephen Dewitt *savings and loan association executive*
Weiner, Morton David *banker, insurance agent*
Wilson, Milner Bradley, III *banker*

Miami Lakes
Ringo, James Joseph *mortgage company executive*

Naples
Craighead, Rodkey *banker*
Hooper, John Allen *retired banker*
Kley, John Arthur *banker*
Martinuzzi, Leo Sergio, Jr. *banker*
Searle, Philip Ford *banker*

North Palm Beach
Connor, John Thomas *retired bank and corporate executive, lawyer*

Ocala
†Harris, Charles Edison *banker, lawyer*

Orange Park
Kirkwood, Maurice Richard *banker*

Orlando
McNulty, Chester Howard *bank holding company executive*

Palm Beach
Curry, Bernard Francis *former banker, consultant*
Korn, David *investor*
Levine, Laurence Brandt *investment banker*

Pompano Beach
Kester, Stewart Randolph *banker*

Ponte Vedra Beach
McMullan, William Patrick, Jr. *banker*
O'Brien, Raymond Vincent, Jr. *banker*

Santa Rosa Beach
Wright, John Peale *retired banker*

Sarasota
Page, George Keith *banker*

South Miami
Benbow, John Robert *banker*

Sun City Center
Sevold, Gordon James *savings and loan executive*

Tampa
Koehn, George Waldemar *bank executive*
†Mirro, Richard Allen *bank executive*

Temple Terrace
Rink, Wesley Winfred *banker*

Tequesta
Turrell, Richard Horton, Sr. *retired banker*

Venice
O'Keefe, Robert James *retired banker*

Vero Beach
Berkovitch, Boris S. *bank executive, lawyer*
Riley, Randy James *banker*
Sheehan, Charles Vincent *investment banker*
Slater, George Richard *retired banker*

West Palm Beach
Lynch, William Walker *savings and loan association executive*
O'Brien, Robert Brownell, Jr. *investment banker, savings bank executive, yacht broker*

GEORGIA

Atlanta
Boland, Thomas Edwin *banker*
Chapman, Hugh McMaster *banker*
Flinn, Patrick L. *bank executive*
Forrestal, Robert Patrick *banker, lawyer*
Hollis, Charles Eugene, Jr. *savings and loan association executive*
†Hutchins, Ralph Edwin, Jr. *banker*
Jackson, Richard Delyn *bank executive*
Monroe, Melrose *retired banker*
†Riddle, Dennis Raymond *banker*
Snelling, George Arthur *banker*

Spiegel, John William *bank executive*
Tschinkel, Sheila Lerner *banker, economist*
†VanLandingham, William Jennings *banker*
Williams, James Bryan *banker*

Douglas
†Palmer, Timothy *bank executive*

Gainesville
†McNeece, Richard A. *bank executive*

Millwood
McCarthy, William Daniel *retired banking educator*

Savannah
Barnes, Benjamin Shields, Jr. *retired banker*
Bell, William Henry, Jr. *banker*

HAWAII

Honolulu
Behnke, Richard Frederick *investment banking executive*
Buchman, Mark Edward *banker*
Chiozzi, Richard Emilio *bank executive*
Dods, Walter Arthur, Jr. *bank executive*
Hoag, John Arthur *bank executive*
Johnson, Lawrence M. *banker*
Midkiff, Robert Richards *consultant*
†Morita, James Masami *banker, lawyer*
Satoh, Yoshiharu *banker*
Stephenson, Herman Howard *banker*
Wolff, Herbert Eric *banker, former army officer*

IDAHO

Boise
†Curran, James J. *banker*
†Ellis, Ted Ellsworth *banker*
Jones, D. Michael *banker*
Speer, William Thomas, Jr. *banker, rancher*

ILLINOIS

Blue Island
Kollmann, Hilda Hanna *banker*

Champaign
Froom, William Watkins *banker*

Chicago
Bakwin, Edward Morris *banker*
Barrow, Charles Herbert *investment banker*
Bartter, Brit Jeffrey *investment banker*
Bouchard, Craig Thomas *international banker*
Brennan, Richard Snyder *lawyer, bank executive*
†Burrus, Clark *banker*
Dancewicz, John Edward *investment banker*
Darr, Milton Freeman, Jr. *banker*
†Doyle, Daniel M. *bank executive*
Eddy, David Latimer *banker*
Finley, Harold Marshall *investment banker*
Fix, John Neilson *banker*
Fox, David Wayne *banker*
Franke, Richard James *investment banker*
Frazier, A. D., Jr. *banker*
Ginley, Thomas J. *banker*
†Goldberg, Sherman I. *banking company executive*
Heagy, Thomas Charles *banker*
Hollis, Donald Roger *banker*
Huber, Richard Leslie *banker*
Hunt, Donald Samuel *banker*
Jahns, Adam A. *banking executive*
†Johnson, Chauncey Paul *banker*
Jones, Richard Melvin *bank executive, former retail executive*
Keehn, Silas *banker*
Kinzie, Raymond Wyant *banker, lawyer*
Klapperich, Frank Lawrence, Jr. *investment banker*
Kramer, Ferdinand *mortgage banker*
Lecker, Abraham *former banker*
Massolo, Arthur James *banker*
Mc Kay, Neil *banker*
Mitchell, Douglas Farrell *trust company executive, lawyer*
Montgomery, Charles Howard *retired bank executive*
Morgan, Howard Campbell *banker*
Mullin, Leo Francis *banker*
O'Connell, Harold Patrick, Jr. *banker*
Pollock, Alexander John *banker*
Rahe, Maribeth Sembach *bank executive*
Roberts, Theodore Harris *banker*
Rowen, Robert G. *savings and loan executive*
Schroeder, Charles Edgar *banker, investment management executive*
Scully, Joseph C. *bank executive*
†Shanahan, Edmond Michael *savings and loan executive*
†Sherman, Robert Frank *banker*
Socolofsky, Jon Edward *banker*
Stirling, James Paulman *investment banker*
Theobald, Thomas Charles *banker*
Thomas, Richard Lee *banker*
Trukenbrod, William Sellery *banker*
†Ulbricht, Robert E. *lawyer, savings and loan executive*
Vander Wilt, Carl Eugene *banker*
West, Byron Kenneth *banker*
Williams, Edward Joseph *banker*

Deerfield
Foght, James Loren *banker*

Des Plaines
†Kubalanza, Ronald J. *bank executive*

Fox River Grove
Abboud, Alfred Robert *banker, consultant, investor*

Highwood
Brown, Lawrence Haas *banker*

Hinsdale
Kinney, Kenneth Parrish *banker, retired*

Hoffman Estates
Weston, Roger Lance *banker*

Joliet
Barber, Andrew Bollons *bank executive*
†Brown, Keith Jeffery *banker*

Kenilworth
Corrigan, John Edward, Jr. *banker, lawyer*

Lake Bluff
Anderson, Roger E. *bank executive*

Lake Forest
Christopherson, Weston Robert *retired bank executive*

Matteson
Yager, Vincent Cook *banker*

Naperville
†Oberwortmann, C. D. *banker*
†O'Meara, Robert P. *banker*
Schilling, Arlo Leonard *bank executive*

Northbrook
Heitmann, Frederick William *bank executive, lecturer*

Northfield
Edelson, Ira J. *venture banker*

Palatine
Fitzgerald, Gerald Francis *banker*

Rolling Meadows
Johnson, Robert Lawrence, Jr. *bank executive*

Springfield
†Ferguson, Mark Harmon *banker, lawyer*
Hudson, Claude Earl *banker*
Lohman, Walter Rearick *banker*

INDIANA

Columbus
Abts, Henry William *banker*
Nash, John Arthur *bank executive*

Crown Point
Bartolome, Joseph S. *bank executive*

Evansville
Hargrave, Robert Webb *banker*

Fort Wayne
Shaffer, Paul E. *banker*

Indianapolis
Dietz, William Ronald *financial services executive, consultant*
Frenzel, Otto N., III *banker*
Givens, David W. *banker*
†Heger, Martin L. *bank executive*
Massey, James D. *bank holding company executive*
Melton, Owen B., Jr. *banking company executive*
†Paine, Andrew J., Jr. *banker*
Risk, John Fred *banker, investment banker*

Lafayette
Howarth, David H. *retired bank executive*

Muncie
Anderson, Stefan Stolen *bank executive*

Portage
Gasser, Wilbert (Warner), Jr. *retired banker*

South Bend
†Jones, Wellington Downing, III *banker*
†Murphy, Christopher Joseph, III *financial executive*
Raclin, Ernestine Morris *banker*

Terre Haute
Smith, Donald Eugene *banker*

Vincennes
Rose, Robert Carlisle *banker*

IOWA

Adel
†Garst, Elizabeth *bank executive*

Bettendorf
Shenk, John Christian, Jr. *retired savings bank executive*

Clinton
Weil, Myron *retired banker*

Des Moines
†Dunlap, Paul D. *bank holding company executive*
†Runger, Donald R. *bank executive*

Fonda
Kuhl, Margaret Helen Clayton (Mrs. Alexius M. Kuhl) *banker*

Johnston
Steele, Betty Louise *retired banker*

Schaller
Currie, James Morton *bank executive*

Sioux City
Hagen, R. E. *bank executive*

KANSAS

Kansas City
†Bond, Richard Lee *banker, state senator*

Leawood
Ballard, John William, Jr. *banker*

Manhattan
Howe, H(ugh) Philip *banker*
Stolzer, Leo William *bank executive*

Overland Park
Dore, James Francis *financial services executive*
Linn, James Herbert *retired banker*

Pratt
Loomis, Howard Krey *banker*

Shawnee Mission
McEachen, Richard Edward *banker, lawyer*
Widder, Willard Graves *retired banker*

Topeka
Dicus, John Carmack *savings and loan association executive*
Johnson, Arnold William *mortgage company executive*

Wichita
Bunten, William Daniel *banker*
Jabara, Francis Dwight *merchant banker, educator, entrepreneur*

KENTUCKY

Frankfort
Adams, Robert Waugh, Jr. *bank executive*

Lexington
Nyere, Robert Alan *banker*

Louisville
Chancey, Malcolm B., Jr. *bank executive*
Davis, Harry Scott, Jr. *banker*
†Hale, Hershel David *bank executive*
Hower, Frank Beard, Jr. *retired banker*

LOUISIANA

Alexandria
Bolton, Robert Harvey *banker*

Baton Rouge
Griffin, G. Lee *banker*
Moyse, Hermann, Jr. *banker*
Urban, Gilbert William *banker*

Covington
Blossman, Alfred Rhody, Jr. *banker*

Lafayette
Stuart, Walter Bynum, III *banker*

New Orleans
Arnof, Ian *banker*
Beason, Amos Theodore *banker*
Milling, R(oswell) King *bank executive, lawyer*
Wakefield, Benton McMillin, Jr. *banker*

MAINE

Andover
Ellis, George Hathaway *retired banker and utility company executive*

Bristol
Schmidt, Thomas Carson *international development banker*

Cumberland Foreside
Harper, Ralph Champlin *retired banker*

Portland
Bonney, Weston Leonard *bank executive*
Grosset, Alexander Donald, Jr. *banker*
Ryan, William J. *bank executive*
Saufley, William Edward *banker, lawyer*

MARYLAND

Baltimore
Baldwin, Henry Furlong *banker*
Barber, John Merrell *banker*
Bramble, Frank P. *bank executive*
Cole, Charles W., Jr. *bank holding company executive*
†Dunn, Edward K., Jr. *banker*
Harvey, F. Barton, Jr. *investment banker*
Harvey, Robert Dixon Hopkins *banker*
Liberto, Joseph Salvatore *banker*
McGuire, James Carroll, Jr. *banking executive*
McGuirk, Ronald Charles *banker*
Murray, Joseph William *banker*
Peck, James Stevenson *banker*
Rank, Larry Gene *executive director*
Ray, Robert Franklin *banker*
Scaggs, Howard Irwin *savings and loan association executive, lawyer*
Schaefer, Robert Wayne *banker*
Shattuck, Mayo Adams, III *investment banking executive*
†Topping, Brian Barclay *trust banker*
Wood, Howard Graham *banker*

Bethesda
Comings, William Daniel, Jr. *mortgage banker, housing development executive*
Lo, Ronald Ping Wong *banker*

Chestertown
Williams, Henry Thomas *retired banker, real estate agent*

Cheverly
Lockyer, Charles Warren, Jr. *corporate executive*

Chevy Chase
Saul, B. Francis, II *bank executive*

Crownsville
Wright, Harry Forrest, Jr. *retired banker*

Easton
Belmont, August *investment banker*

Elkton
Harrington, Benjamin Franklin, III *business consultant*

Ellicott City
Faulstich, Albert Joseph *banking consultant*

Frederick
Hoff, Charles Worthington, III *banker*

Potomac
Schonholtz, Joan Sondra Hirsch *banker, civic worker*

Rockville
Meyer, F. Weller *bank executive*

Silver Spring
Dame, William Page, III *banker, school administrator*

Stevenson
Schnering, Philip Blessed *investment banker*

Timonium
Morrel, William Griffin, Jr. *banker*

MASSACHUSETTS

Boston
Alden, Vernon Roger *corporate director, trustee*
Beal, Ilene *bank executive*
Beinhocker, Gilbert David *investment banker*
Bennett, Rhona *bank administrator, consultant*
Berg, Warren Stanley *retired banker*
Blampied, Peter J. *banker*
Brown, William L. *banker*
Carty, John Lydon *financial services executive*
Cotter, Joseph Francis *bank officer*
Crozier, William Marshall, Jr. *bank holding company executive*
Curry, John Michael *investment banker*
Driver, William Raymond, Jr. *banker*
Elsbree, John Francis *banker*
Finnegan, Neal Francis *banker*
†Gallary, Peter Hayden *financial services company executive*
†Gallaudet, Denison *bank executive*
Gifford, Charles Kilvert *banker*
Gulley, Joan Long *banker*
Hamill, John P. *bank executive*
Hill, Richard Devereux *retired banker*
Laine, Richard R. *banking executive*
Little, Arthur Dehon *investment banker*
Monrad, Ernest Ejner *trust company executive*
Nutt, William James *investment, management and mutual funds company executive*
Phillips, Daniel Anthony *trust company executive*
Ray, William F. *banker*
Stepanian, Ira *banker*
Tangney, Eugene Michael *banker*
Tempel, Jean C. *bank executive*
Vermilye, Peter Hoagland *banker*
Vineburgh, James Hollander *banking executive*
Williams, Charles Marvin *commercial banking educator*

Cambridge
Curtiss, Trumbull Cary *banker*
Edgerly, William Skelton *banker*

Cohasset
Sewall, Tingey Haig *banker*

Dover
Aldrich, Frank Nathan *bank executive*
Crittenden, Gazaway Lamar *retired banker*
Stockwell, Ernest Farnham, Jr. *banker*

Lexington
Fallon, John Golden *banker*
Lawton, Eugene Alfred *banking executive*

Longmeadow
Lo Bello, Joseph David *banking executive*

Lynn
Stark, Dennis Edwin *banker*

Manchester
Bundy, Harvey Hollister *retired bank executive*

Marstons Mills
Wheeler, Richard Warren *banker*

Medford
Sloane, Marshall M. *banker*

New Bedford
McCarter, Robert *banking executive*

North Quincy
Allinson, A. Edward *banking executive*

South Orleans
Fleck, Gustav Peter *former banker, former securities firm executive, clergyman*

Waltham
Riley, Henry Charles *banker*

Weston
Aquilino, Daniel *banker*

Winchester
Brennan, Francis Patrick *banker*

Worcester
Cabot, Harold *banker*
Hunt, John David *retired banker*
Spencer, Harry Irving, Jr. *retired banker*
Titcomb, Woodbury Cole *bank executive, consultant*

MICHIGAN

Ada
Whitney, William Chowning *retired banker, financial consultant*

Ann Arbor
Delonis, Robert J. *bank executive*
Freeth, Douglas Duncan *banker*

Bay City
Van Dyke, Clifford Craig *banker*

Bloomfield Hills
Colladay, Robert S. *trust company executive, consultant*
Houston, E. James, Jr. *bank officer*
Rusin, Edward A. *bank executive*

Detroit
Fisher, Charles Thomas, III *banker*
Harling, Carlos Gene *savings and loan executive*
Hughes, Robert Edwin *banking executive*
Istock, Verne George *banker*
Jeffs, Thomas Hamilton, II *banker*
Miller, Eugene Albert *banker*
Surdam, Robert McClellan *retired banker*

Elk Rapids
Briggs, Robert Peter *banker*

Farmington
Mylod, Robert Joseph *banker*

Farmington Hills
Gladchun, Lawrence L. *banker, lawyer*
Heiss, Richard Walter *banker, consultant*

Flint
†Johnson, Donald E., Jr. *bank executive*
Piper, Mark Harry *retired banker*
†Weeks, Charles R. *bank executive*

Frankfort
Foster, Robert Carmichael *banker*

Grand Rapids
Canepa, John Charles *banking executive*
Sadler, Robert Livingston *banker*

Grosse Pointe
French, John Henry, Jr. *banker*
Richardson, Dean Eugene *retired banker*
Thurber, Cleveland, Jr. *trust banker*

Hamtramck
Weinert, Carl Robert *retired banker*

Kalamazoo
Holland, Harold Herbert *banker*
Klein, Richard Dean *banker*
McCarty, Theodore Frederick *banker*
Smith, Daniel R. *bank holding company executive*

Monroe
Keck, Merel Fogg *bank executive*

Saginaw
Evans, Harold Edward *banker*

Southgate
†Peacock, Lowell *bank executive*

Taylor
Wilkinson, E. G., Jr. *bank executive*

Troy
Fellingham, David Andrew *mortgage banker*
Leach, Ralph F. *banker*
Ricketts, Thomas Roland *savings bank executive*

Warren
†Kassab, Sir Charles Shaw *banker*

MINNESOTA

Bemidji
Bridston, Paul Joseph *strategy consultant*

Eden Prairie
Hanson, Dale S. *banker*

Excelsior
Rich, Willis Frank, Jr. *banker*

Minneapolis
Benson, Donald Erick *holding company executive*
Biller, Leslie Stuart *banker*
Campbell, James Robert *banker*
Cooper, William Allen *banking executive*
Deming, Frederick Lewis *banker*
Gainor, Thomas Edward *banker*
Grundhofer, John F. *banker*
Hetland, James Lyman, Jr. *banker, lawyer, educator*
Huston, Beatrice Louise *banker*
Johnson, Lloyd Peter *banker*
Kovacevich, Richard M. *banker*
Morrison, Clinton Homer *banker*
Murray, Kenneth Richard *banking executive*
Rahn, Alvin Albert *former banker*
Rohr, Daniel C. *banker*
†Schoenke, Richard Warren *banker*
Swanson, Lloyd Oscar *former savings and loan association executive*
Walters, Glen Robert *banker*

Saint Paul
Bjorklund, Frederick *savings and loan association executive*

Williams, Phillip Stephen *banker*

MISSISSIPPI

Gulfport
Pickering, Shelbie Jean *mortgage loan executive*
Schloegel, George Anthony *banker*
Thatcher, George Robert *banker*

Hattiesburg
Barr, Jacob Dexter *banker*

Jackson
†Carter, David Ray *banker*
McMillan, Howard Lamar, Jr. *banker*
Robinson, E. B., Jr. *bank executive*
Sewell, Charles Haslett *banker*
Tullos, John Baxter *banker*

Monticello
Allen, Frank Carroll *retired banker*

Tupelo
†Neelly, Edwin Clyde, III *banker*
†Patterson, Aubrey Burns, Jr. *banker*
Smith, John Willis *banker*

MISSOURI

Jefferson City
Cook, Sam B. *banker*

Kansas City
Aslin, M. M. *banker*
Brown, John O. *banker*
Crider, Stephen Wayne *banker, lawyer*
Davis, John Edward *banking executive*
Hendrickson, Marshall David *banker*
†Hoenig, Thomas M. *bank executive*
Kemper, David Woods, II *banker*
Kemper, James Madison, Jr. *banker*
†Kemper, Jonathan McBride *banker*
Kemper, Rufus Crosby, Jr. *banker*
Murdock, Stuart Laird *retired banker, investment adviser*
Pendleton, Barbara Jean *retired banker*
Reiter, Robert Edward *banker*
Skahan, Paul L(aurence) *bank executive, lawyer*
Vaughan, Kirk William *banker*

Nevada
Morton, John, III *banker*

Saint Louis
Andes, G. Thomas *banker*
Babb, Ralph Wheeler, Jr. *banker*
Badgley, William S. *multi-bank holding company executive*
Barksdale, Clarence Caulfield *banker*
Bealke, Linn Hemingway *bank executive*
Bowen, James Ronald *banker*
Brennan, John Merritt *banker*
Bryant, Ruth Alyne *banker*
Craig, Andrew Billings, III *bank holding company executive*
Dezort, Jacquelyn Louise Link *bank executive*
Gray, Walter Franklin *banker*
Hayes, Samuel Banks, III *banking company executive*
Heisler, John Columbus *investment banker*
Jacobsen, Thomas H(erbert) *banker*
James, William W. *banker*
Jennings, Michael Eugene *banker*
Kling, S(tephen) Lee *banker*
Leonard, Eugene Albert *banker*
MacCarthy, John Peters *banker*
McCarty, Philip Norman *bank holding company executive*
†Quenon, Robert H. *bank executive*
Siteman, Alvin Jerome *banker*
Stoecker, David Thomas *banker*
Walker, Dale Rush *banker*

Springfield
†McCartney, N. L. *investment banker*

Warrensburg
Harmon, Lynn Adrian *banker*

NEBRASKA

Alliance
Knight, Robert Edward *banker*

Lincoln
Stuart, James *banker, broadcaster*
Young, Dale Lee *banker*

Omaha
†Cochran, John R. *bank executive*
Fitzgerald, William Allingham *savings and loan association executive*
†Krohn, Robert Finley *bank executive*
Lauritzen, John Ronnow *banker*
Miller, Morris Folsom *banker*
†Rismiller, David A. *banking company executive*

NEVADA

Las Vegas
†Cheever, Dan J. *bank executive*
Rogers, David Hughes *banker*
Thomas, Peter M. *bank executive*
Troidl, Richard John *banker*

Reno
Binns, James Edward *banker*
Tuxon, Linda Louise *banking officer*

NEW HAMPSHIRE

Hanover
Paganucci, Paul Donnelly *banker, lawyer, former college official*
Weiss, Ira Francis *retired banker*

Lancaster
Drapeau, Phillip David *banking executive*

Manchester
Craig, William Francis *banker*
Thurber, Davis Peabody *banker*

NEW JERSEY

Bordentown
†Walther, John Henry *banker*

Bridgeton
Vogel, Charles A., Jr. *banker*

Bridgewater
Lewis, Donald Emerson *banker*

Chatham
Feeney, John Robert *banker*
Sayles, Thomas Dyke, Jr. *banker*

Cherry Hill
Norton, George Dawson *retired banker*

Cinnaminson
Johnson, Victor Lawrence *banker*

Clifton
Magnus, Frederick Samuel *investment banker*

Colts Neck
French, Charles Ferris, Jr. *banker*

East Brunswick
Georgantas, Aristides William *banking executive*

Edison
Scheuring, Garry Joseph *banker*
Silberstein, Alan Mark *banker*
†Sullivan, Cornelius Francis, Jr. *banking executive*

Egg Harbor City
Dittenhafer, Brian Douglas *banker, economist*
Hamilton, Thomas Herman *savings and loan association executive*

Elizabeth
Chard, Roland Turner *retired banker*
Leonett, Anthony Arthur *banker*

Glen Rock
Feeks, J. Michael *bank executive*

Hightstown
Phelan, Richard Paul *trust company executive*

Jersey City
Howard, Stanley Louis *investment banker*
Nash, Lee J. *banker*
Tugwell, John *bank executive*
Tymon, Leo F., Jr. *banker*
†Wilzig, Siggi Bert *banker*

Lawrenceville
Terracciano, Anthony Patrick *banker*

Montclair
Pierson, Robert David *banker*

Montvale
Sbarbaro, Robert Arthur *banker*

Morristown
Moore, Milo Anderson *banking executive*
†Simon, William Edward *investment banker, former secretary of treasury*

Mountain Lakes
Turnheim, Palmer *financial consultant, banker*

Newark
Newman, Samuel *trust company executive*

Paramus
Birchby, Kenneth Lee *banker*

Parsippany
Gorman, Thomas Francis *tax manager, computer systems developer*
Olsen, Robert John *savings and loan association executive*
Singleterry, Gary Lee *investment banker*

Pennington
Wallace, John Duncan *banker*

Perth Amboy
Gemmell, Joseph Paul *banker*

Princeton
Dornburgh, William Walter *banker*
Haggerty, John Richard *banker*
Mills, Bradford *merchant banker*
Paneyko, Stephen Hobbs *banker*
Roberts, Peter A. *banker*
Semrod, T. Joseph *banker*

Rancocas
Burke, James Joseph *banker*

Red Bank
Dale, Madeline Houston McWhinney *banker*

Roseland
Costanzo, Hilda Alba *retired banker*

Short Hills
Klemme, Carl William *banker*

Shrewsbury
Jones, Charles Hill, Jr. *banker*

Summit
Mueller, Paul Henry *retired banker*

Sussex
Holbert, Theodore Frank *banker*

Tenafly
Levy, Norman Jay *investment banker, financial consultant*

Totowa
Jelliffe, Charles Gordon *banker*

Trenton
Roebling, Mary Gindhart *banker*

Union City
Neilson, Kenneth Thomas *bank executive*

Wayne
Haswell, Carleton Radley *banker*
†Pinyuh, Sam P. *banker*

NEW MEXICO

Albuquerque
†Grady, William G. (Bing Grady) *banker*

Carlsbad
†Kidd, Melvin Don *banker*

Santa Fe
Koessel, Donald Ray *retired banker*

NEW YORK

Albany
Brown, Albert Joseph, Jr. *banker*
Chorbajian, Herbert G. *bank executive*
Robinson, John Bowers, Jr. *bank holding company executive*
Tuttle, Frank James *bank executive*
†Ward, Frank Jay *banker*

Babylon
Keane, Daniel J. *banker*

Bedford
Philip, Peter Van Ness *former trust company executive*

Briarcliff Manor
Carey, James Henry *banker*

Bronx
Howell, Alfred Hunt *former banker*

Bronxville
Arndt, Kenneth Eugene *banker*
Pratt, John Adams, Jr. *bank executive*
Wilson, John Donald *banker, economist*

Brooklyn
Dellomo, Frank A. *banker*
Hamm, Charles John *banker*
Hohenrath, William Edward *retired banker*
†Kraemer, Richard A. *bank executive*
Pollack, Bruce *banker, real estate consultant*
†Reissman, Maurice L. *bank executive*

Buffalo
Cleave, James H. *bank executive*
†Kailbourne, Erland E. *banker*
Kenzie, Ross Bruce *retired banker*
Knox, Northrup Rand *banker*
†Pett, John Lyman *banker*
†Rappolt, William Carl *banker*
Shanahan, Robert B. *banker*
Stainrook, Harry Richard *banker*
Vardon, James Lewes *bank executive*
Wilmers, Robert George *banker*

Clearwater
Torell, John Raymond, III *banker*

Cold Spring Harbor
Hargraves, Gordon Sellers *banker*

Elmont
Cusack, Thomas Joseph *banker*

Fayetteville
Carlson, Russell Charles *banker*

Flushing
Diehl, Stephen Anthony *banker*
Johnson, Thomas Stephen *banker*

Garden City
Desch, Carl William *banker, consultant*
Lovely, Thomas Dixon *banker*

Geneseo
Hickman, John Hampton, III *entrepreneurial investment banker, industrialist, educator*

Glens Falls
Bitner, William Lawrence, III *banker, educator*

Great Neck
Katz, Edward Morris *banker*

Hawthorne
Kane, James Golden *banker*
†Olson, William Furman *bank executive, lawyer*

Hewlett
Dalrymple, Richard William *banker*
Large, James Mifflin, Jr. *banker*
Sickle, Cody T. *banker*

Hicksville
Walsh, Charles Richard *banker*

Ithaca
Smith, Robert Samuel *banker, former agricultural finance educator*

Larchmont
Aburdene, Odeh Felix *banker*
Kaufmann, Henry Mark *mortgage banker*

Locust Valley
Van Rensselaer, Stephen *banker*

Manhasset
Lindow, John Wesley *banker, corporate executive*

Mattituck
†Kanas, John Adam *banker*

Melville
Viklund, William Edwin *banker*

Nanuet
Burden, Ordway Partridge *investment banker*

New York
Abbe, Colman *investment banker*
Aisenbrey, Stuart Keith *trust company official*
Albright, Harry Wesley, Jr. *banking executive, former government official, lawyer*
Altschul, Arthur Goodhart *investment banker*
Bacon, James Edmund *corporate director*
Bacot, John Carter *banker*
Bains, Leslie Elizabeth *banker*
Barkhorn, Henry Charles, III *investment banker*
Barry, Thomas M. *banker*
Beim, David Odell *investment banker, educator*
Bellanger, Serge René *banker*
Benedetto, M. William *investment banker*
Berens, Rodney Bristol *investment banker*
Biggs, Jeremy Hunt *trust company executive*
Blackford, Leo Price *investment banker*
Bohn, John Augustus, Jr. *banker, lawyer*
Boothby, Willard Sands, III *bank executive*
Brenner, Howard Martin *banker*
Brown, G(lenn) William, Jr. *investment banker*
Bruckmann, Donald John *investment banker*
Butcher, Willard Carlisle *banker*
Byrne, James Thomas, Jr. *banker, lawyer*
Cajigal, Joseph A. *financial services executive*
Calise, Ronald Jan *investment banking executive*
Campbell, Douglass *banker*
Cardew, William Joseph *bank executive*
Carter, Marshall Nichols *banker*
Caruso, Victor Guy *investment banker*
Castle, John Krob *merchant banker*
Cayne, James E. *investment banker*
Chevalier, Samuel Fletcher *banker*
Childs, John Farnsworth *investment banker*
Ciechanover, Joseph *banker, lawyer*
Clark, Thomas Carlyle *banker*
Clifford, Stewart Burnett *banker*
Cohen, Irving I. *financial executive*
Coleman, Denis Patrick, Jr. *investment banker*
Comfort, William Twyman, Jr. *banker*
Corcoran, Robert Lee, Jr. *banker*
Corley, Leslie M. *investment banker*
Corrigan, E. Gerald *investment banker*
Dacey, Michael F. *bank executive*
Darst, David Martin *investment banking company executive, writer, educator*
Davis, George Linn *banker*
Dawson, Thomas Cleland, II *financial executive*
DeGroff, Ralph Lynn, Jr. *investment banker*
Dempsey, Louis F(rancis), III *banker*
deVeer, Robert Kipp, Jr. *investment banker*
Douglass, Robert Royal *banker, lawyer*
Doyle, L. F. Boker *trust company executive*
Drakos, Charles Peter *investment banker*
Druker, Henry Leo *investment banker*
Dugan, Edward Francis *investment banker*
Dwek, Cyril S. *banker*
Edelstein, Haskell *banker, tax lawyer*
Elliott, A. Wright *banker*
Farley, Terrence Michael *banker*
Feldberg, Chester Ben *banker, lawyer*
Finocchiaro, Alfonso G. *bank executive*
Fisher, Bennett Lawson *investment executive*
Foulke, William Green, Jr. *banker*
Franz, Donald Eugene, Jr. *merchant banker, security analyst*
Friedberg, Barry Sewell *investment banker*
Fusina, Alessandro Eugenio *banker*
Gallagher, Thomas Joseph *banker*
Galleno, Anthony Massimo *bank executive*
Garver, Robert S. *banker*
George, David Alan *investment banker*
Gerry, Elbridge Thomas, Jr. *banker*
Gibson, William Francis *investment banking executive*
Gillham, Robert *bank executive*
Goldberg, Arthur Abba *merchant banker, financial advisor*
Goodchild, Robert Marshall *trust company executive*
Goodwin, Todd *banker*
Gossett, Robert Francis, Jr. *merchant banker*
Greenstein, Abraham Jacob *mortgage company executive, accountant*
Grimes, Charles B., Jr. *bank executive*
Gruver, William Rolfe *investment banker*
Guenther, Jack Donald *banker*
Guldimann, Till M. *banker*
Hampton, Philip McCune *banker*
Harlan, Leonard Morton *merchant banker*
Hartman, Stephen Jennings, Jr. *banker*
Hassell, Gerald L. *banker*
Heard, Edwin Anthony *banker*
Hedstrom, Mitchell Warren *banker*
Hellmold, Ralph O. *investment banker*
Hendrickson, Charles John *bank executive*
Herregat, Guy-Georges Jacques *banker*
Hertz, Rudolf Heinrich *banker*
Hilliard, Landon *banker*
Hover, John Calvin, II *banker*
†Hunnewell, Francis O. *bank executive*
†Huntington, Lawrence Smith *investment banker*
Ingraham, John Wright *banker*
Joseph, Frederick Harold *investment banker*
Kahana, Aron *bank executive*

Kane, Jay Brassler *banker*
Kaufmann, Mark Steiner *banker*
Keating, Karen Rupert *commercial banker*
Keegan, Gerard C. *bank executive*
Keilin, Eugene Jacob *investment banker, lawyer*
Kilburn, H(enry) T(homas), Jr. *investment banker*
Killefer, Tom *banker*
Kirsch, Arthur William *investment banker*
Klein, Robert Majer *bank executive*
Kretschmer, Paul Robert *investment banker*
†Kruech, Paul C. *bank executive*
Labrecque, Thomas G. *banker*
Lang, Theresa *investment banker*
Larr, Peter *banker*
Lattin, Albert Floyd *banker*
Layton, Donald Harvey *banker*
Lear, Robert William *holding company executive*
LeBlond, Richard Knight, II *banker*
Lesser, Edward Arnold *banker*
†Levin, Neil D. *bank executive*
Lincoln, Edmond Lynch *investment banker*
Lindsay, Robert Van Cleef *trust company executive*
Lipp, Robert I. *bank holding company executive*
Lissack, Michael Robert *investment banker*
Lockhart, James Bicknell, III *investment banker*
Loeb, John Langeloth *banker, broker*
Lohse, Austin Webb *banker*
Londoner, David Jay *investment banker, analyst*
MacEwan, Nigel Savage *merchant banker*
Magdol, Michael Orin *bank executive*
McCann, Edward *investment banker*
McFarland, Alan Roberts *investment banker*
Mc Gillicuddy, John Francis *banker*
Meachin, David James Percy *investment banker, import-export executive*
Meadows, Sharon Marie *investment banker*
Mendell, Oliver M. *banking executive*
Menschel, Robert Benjamin *investment banker*
Merriss, Philip Ramsay, Jr. *banker*
Mesznik, Joel R. *investment banker*
Meyer, Sandra W(asserstein) *management consultant*
Miller, Edward Daniel *banker*
Miller, Richard Jerome *bank executive*
Mintz, Norman Nelson *investment banker, educator*
Muñoz, Carlos Ramón *bank executive*
Murphy, Charles Joseph *investment banker*
Nichols, C. Walter, III *trust company executive*
Nolan, William Joseph, III *banker*
Nuzum, John M., Jr. *banker*
Olds, John Theodore *banker*
Ostergard, Paul Michael *bank executive*
Pados, Frank John, Jr. *trust company executive*
Palmer, Edward Lewis *banker*
Parsons, Richard Dean *banker, lawyer*
Patterson, Ellmore Clark *banker*
Peterkin, DeWitt, Jr. *banker*
Peterson, Peter G. *banker*
Petrie, Donald Joseph *banker*
Pettus, Barbara Wyper *bank executive*
Petty, John Robert *banker*
Pincus, Lionel Irwin *venture banker*
Pirie, Robert S. *investment banker, lawyer*
Poll, Robert Eugene, Jr. *bank executive*
Porretta, Emanuele Peter *bank executive*
Potter, Cary Nicholas *banker*
Prizzi, Jack Anthony *investment banking executive*
Prouty, Norman R. *investment banker*
Pyne, Eben Wright *banker*
Ramsey, Peter Christie *bank executive*
Reed, John Shepard *banker*
Repko, William Clarke *banker*
Rimerman, Ira Stephen *banker*
Rines, S. Melvin *investment banker*
Roach, John Hendee, Jr. *bank executive, investment banker*
Roberts, Donald Munier *banker, trust company executive*
†Roche, John J. *banking company executive, corporate lawyer*
Rockefeller, David *banker*
Rogers, Arthur Merriam, Jr. *banker*
Rossoff, Mack Fredric *investment banker*
Ruding, Herman Onno *banker, former Dutch minister of finance*
Ruffle, John Frederick *banker*
Ryan, Thomas Timothy, Jr. *banker, lawyer, government official*
Salmans, Charles Gardiner *banker*
Sanford, Charles Steadman, Jr. *banker*
Sawabini, Nabil George *banker*
Schneider, Donald Frederic *banker*
Schumacher, Robert Denison *banker*
Schwarz, H. Marshall *trust company executive*
Scopaz, John Matthew *banker*
†Scowcroft, John Arthur *portfolio manager*
Segalas, Hercules Anthony *investment banker*
Seligson, Carl H. *investment banker*
Sendrovic, Israel *bank executive*
Shanks, Eugene B., Jr. *banker*
Shipley, Walter Vincent *banker*
Shuman, Stanley S. *investment banker*
Sim, Craig Stephen *investment banker*
Simmons, John Derek *investment banker*
Slusser, William Peter *investment banker*
Smith, Kathleen Tener *bank executive*
Smith, Peter Bennett *banker*
Smith, Phillips Guy *banker*
Smith, Richard Anthony *investment banker*
Solar, Richard Leon *banker*
Spaeh, Winfried Heinrich *banker*
Spangler, Arnold Eugene *investment banker*
Speciale, Richard *bank executive*
Spelker, Arnold William *banker*
Steffen, Christopher J. *bank executive*
Stein, Howard S. *banker*
Stewart, James M. *merchant banker*
Stewart, James Montgomery *banker*
Strong, Robert S. *banker*
Tarnopol, Michael L. *bank executive*
Tauber, Ronald Steven *investment banker*
†Teitelbaum, William Allen *investment banker*
Tetzeli, Frederick Edward *banker*
Trachtenberg, Matthew J. *bank holding company executive*
Urkowitz, Michael *banker*
van Hengel, Maarten *banker*
Viermetz, Kurt F. *banker*
Von Fraunhofer-Kosinski, Katherina *bank executive*
†Wallace, Robert Fergus *banker*
Warner, Douglas Alexander, III *banker*
Weatherstone, Dennis *trust company executive*
Weil, Frank A. *investment banker, lawyer*
Weill, Sanford I. *banker*
Weiner, Walter Herman *banker, lawyer*
Weiss, Myrna Grace *investment banker, consultant*
Whitcraft, Edward C. R. *investment banker*
Whiteman, H(orace) Clifton *banker*
Whitmore, John Rogers *banker*
Whittemore, Laurence Frederick *private banker*
Wilmerding, Harold Pratt *banker, investment counselor*
Wirz, Pascal Francois *trust company executive*
Wolfensohn, James David *bank executive*
Wolff, William F., III *investment banker*
Wonham, Frederick Stapley *trust bank executive*
Woods, Rodney Ian *banker*
Wriston, Walter Bigelow *retired banker*
Zukerman, Morris E. *investment banker*
Zwerling, Gary Leslie *investment bank executive*

Niskayuna
Whittingham, Harry Edward, Jr. *retired banker*

Oyster Bay
Schwab, Hermann Caspar *banker*

Pittsford
Schubert, John Edward *former banker*

Port Kent
Mc Kee, James, Jr. *retired banker*

Queensbury
Mead, John Milton *banker*

Ridgewood
Jones, Harold Antony *banker*

Rochester
Hargrave, Alexander Davidson *banker, lawyer*
Simon, Leonard Samuel *banker*
Wayland-Smith, Robert Dean *banker*

Scarsdale
Hines, William Eugene *banker*

Shelter Island
Dowd, David Joseph *banker, builder*

Stamford
Bergleitner, George Charles, Jr. *investment banker*

Staten Island
Chapin, Elliott Lowell *retired bank executive*

Syracuse
Bennett, Robert John *banker*
Meyers, Peter L. *banker*
Morton, William Gilbert *banker*
O'Day, Royal Lewis *former banker*

Tonawanda
Haller, Calvin John *banker*
Hettrick, John Lord *banker, manufacturer*

Uniondale
†Guenzel, Rudolf Paul *banker*
Tempest, Harrison F. *bank executive*

Utica
Raymonda, James Earl *banker*
Schrauth, William Lawrence *banker, lawyer*

Valley Cottage
Atha, Stuart Kimball, Jr. *retired banker*

Westbury
Tulchin, Stanley *banker, lecturer, author, business reorganization consultant*

White Plains
Bober, Lawrence Harold *retired banker*
Wilson, Malcolm *banker, lawyer, former governor*

Yonkers
Philipps, Edward William *banker, real estate appraiser*

NORTH CAROLINA

Asheville
Everett, Durward R., Jr. *retired banker*

Charlotte
†Abbott, James A. *mortgage company executive*
Birle, James Robb *investment banker*
Covington, William Clyde, Jr. *banker*
Crutchfield, Edward Elliott, Jr. *banker*
Figge, Fredric J., II *bank executive*
Georgius, John R. *bank executive*
McColl, Hugh Leon, Jr. *banker*
†Powell, Charles Roland *financial services company executive*
Thompson, James William *banker*
Williford, Donald Bratton *bank executive*
†Wilson, Constance Kramer *bank officer*

Durham
Wright, Paul, Jr. *banker*

Gastonia
Teem, Paul Lloyd, Jr. *savings and loan executive*

High Point
Coggins, George Miller, Jr. *strategic planning and finance educator*

Lumberton
Byrne, James Frederick *banker*
Orr, L. Glenn, Jr. *banker*

New Bern
†Nichols, John M. *bank executive*

Pilot Mountain
Ross, Norman Alexander *retired banker*

Pinehurst
Henderson, Paul Audine *banker, consultant*

Raleigh
Barmore, Gregory Terhune *capital mortgage company executive*
Hardin, Eugene Brooks, Jr. *banker*
†Holding, Frank B. *bank executive*
Holding, Lewis R. *banker*

Rocky Mount
Mauldin, Robert Ray *banker*
Powers, James Bascom *banker*
Wilkerson, William Holton *banker*

Tryon
Claud, Joseph Gillette *banker*

Whiteville
†Sasser, Edward Rhone *bank executive*

Wilson
Allison, John Andrew, IV *bank executive*
Stewart, Burton Gloyden, Jr. *banker*
Williamson, Henry Gaston, Jr. *banker*

Winston Salem
Austell, Edward Callaway *banker*
Cotterill, David Lee *banker*
Cramer, John Scott *retired banker*
McNair, John Franklin, III *banker*
Medlin, John Grimes, Jr. *banker*
Runnion, Howard J., Jr. *banker*
Sperry, Michael Winton *banker*
Wanders, Hans Walter *banker*
Watlington, John Francis, Jr. *banker*
Worley, Bland Wallace *banker*

NORTH DAKOTA

Bismarck
Malmberg, John Andrew *bank executive*

Fargo
Mengedoth, Donald Roy *commercial banker*

Grand Forks
Wold, Richard Otto *banker*

Watford City
Stenehjem, Leland Manford *banker*

OHIO

Canton
Carpenter, Noble Olds *banker*

Cincinnati
Brumm, Paul Michael *banker*
†Buenger, Clement Lawrence *banker*
Bullock, John McDonell *banker*
Schaeter, George A., Jr. *banking executive*
Thiemann, Charles Lee *banker*
Waddell, Oliver W. *banker*

Cleveland
Brandon, Edward Bermetz *banker*
Daberko, David A. *banker*
Gillespie, Robert Wayne *banker*
Glickman, Carl David *banker*
Harding, Frank I., III *trust banker*
Heffern, Gordon Emory *banker*
†Horn, Karen Nicholson *banker*
Hottois, Lawrence Daniel *banking executive*
Jones, Theodore William *banker, lawyer*
Koch, Charles Joseph *banker*
Noall, Roger *bank executive*
Obert, Charles Frank *banker*
†Pianalto, Sandra *bank executive*
Robertson, William Richard *banker, holding company executive*
Rupert, John Edward *retired savings and loan executive, business and civic affairs consultant*
Schaut, Joseph William *banker*
Siefers, Robert George *banker*
Simonson, John Alexander *banking executive*
Tung, Theodore Hschum *banker, economist*
Wert, James William *banker*

Columbus
Havens, John Franklin *retired banker*
Hoskins, W. Lee *banker*
Leiter, William C. *banking executive, controller*
Mathews, Robert Edward *banker*
Mc Coy, John Bonnet *banker*
McCoy, John Gardner *banker*
McWhorter, Donald L. *bank executive*
Meiling, George Robert Lucas *bank holding company executive*
Page, Linda Kay *banking executive*
Wobst, Frank Georg *banker*

Dayton
Hawthorne, Douglas Lawson *banker*

Dublin
Gores, Gary Gene *credit union executive*

Elyria
Kreighbaum, John Scott *banker*

Hudson
Wooldredge, William Dunbar *investment banker*

Mansfield
Baker, James Allan *banker*

Newark
McConnell, William Thompson *commercial banker*

Pepper Pike
Mc Call, Julien Lachicotte *banker*

Perrysburg
Yager, John Warren *retired banker, lawyer*

Toledo
Bergsmark, Edwin Martin *trust company executive*
Carson, Samuel Goodman *retired banker, company director*
†Hoffman, James Al *banker*
Kunze, Ralph Carl *savings and loan executive*

Washington Court House
Fultz, Clair Ervin *former banker*

Willoughby
Abelt, Ralph William *bank executive*

Youngstown
Pridham, Herbert H. *retired trust company executive, lawyer, foundation administrator*

Zanesville
Duhs, William Andrew *banker*

OKLAHOMA

Bartlesville
Doty, Donald D. *retired banker*

Oklahoma City
Brown, Kenneth Ray *banker*
Browne, John Robinson *banker*
Danforth, Louis Fremont *banker, educator*
†Nelson, Charles E. *bank holding executive*
Williams, William Ralston *retired bank and trust company executive*

Tulsa
Eaton, Leonard James, Jr. *banker*
Hawkins, Francis Glenn *banker, lawyer*

OREGON

Portland
Franz, Robert Warren *banker*
Jensen, Edmund Paul *bank holding company executive*
Staver, Leroy Baldwin *banker*
Winnowski, Thaddeus Richard (Ted Winnowski) *bank executive*

Salem
Weight, George Dale *banker, educator*

PENNSYLVANIA

Altoona
†Rossman, William J. *banker*

Bala Cynwyd
Bausher, Verne C(harles) *banker*
†Kleppe, Martin I. *bank executive*

Bethlehem
†Howell, John R. *banker*

Blue Bell
Fawley, John Jones *retired banker*
Ganoe, Charles Stratford *banker*

Boyertown
†Jilk, Lawrence T., Jr. *banker*

Conshohocken
Boenning, Henry Dorr, Jr. *investment banker*
Tily, Stephen Bromley, III *bank executive*

Easton
Ashby, Richard James, Jr. *bank executive, lawyer*

Erie
Bracken, Charles Herbert *banker*
Zuern, David Ernest *bank executive*

Gladwyne
Geisel, Cameron Meade, Jr. *investment professional*

Harleysville
Daller, Walter E., Jr. *banking executive*

Harrisburg
Campbell, Carl Lester *banker*
Groves, George H. *holding company executive*
King, William J. *bank executive*

Horsham
Hart, Alex Way *banker*

King Of Prussia
P'an, Albert Yuan *corporate executive*

Lancaster
Troupe, Terry Lee *holding company banker*

Leola
McElhinny, Wilson Dunbar *banker*

Lititz
Bolinger, Robert Stevens *banker*

Lumberville
Frank, F. Alexander *retired savings and loan executive, lawyer*

Philadelphia
Boehne, Edward George *banker*
Clark, George Roberts *retired trust company executive*
Cooke, M(erritt) Todd *banker*
Eagleson, William Boal, Jr. *banker*
Foulke, William Green *banker*
†Goldsmith, Philip Robert *banker*
Haskin, Donald Lee *bank executive*
Kardon, Robert *mortgage company executive*
Larsen, Terrance A. *bank holding company executive*
Murdoch, Lawrence Corlies, Jr. *retired banker, economist*
†Pepper, Jane G. *bank executive*
Potamkin, Meyer P. *mortgage banker*
Ross, George Martin *investment banker*
Shah, Bipin Chandra *banker*
Spolan, Harmon Samuel *banker*

Pittsburgh
Cahouet, Frank Vondell *banker*
Clyde, Larry Forbes *banker*
Echement, John R. *banker*
Groves, Michael *banker*
Higgins, James Henry *retired banker*
Irwin, Joe Robert *banker*
McGuinn, Martin Gregory *banker, lawyer*
Milsom, Robert Cortlandt *banker*
Morby, Jeffrey Lewis *banker, investment banker*
O'Brien, Thomas Henry *bank holding company executive*
Ostern, Wilhelm Curt *retired holding company executive*
Pearson, Nathan Williams *investment management executive*
Rohr, James Edward *banker*
Yankovic, Judith E. *banker, human resources consultant*

Plymouth Meeting
Litman, Raymond Stephen *retired banker*

Punxsutawney
†Cook, Gayland Braun *banker, utility company executive*

Reading
Erdman, Carl L. N. *retired banker*
McCullough, Samuel Alexander *banker*
Mengel, Philip R(ichard) *investment banker*
Moll, Lloyd Henry *banker*
Roesch, Clarence Henry *banker*
Snyder, Clair Allison *banker*
Sparks, David Emerson *bank holding company executive*

Scranton
Janoski, Henry Valentine *banker, former investment counselor, realtor*
†Stetler, Larry D. *banker*

Sewickley
Roemer, William Frederick *banker*

Souderton
Hoeflich, Charles Hitschler *banker*

Wayne
Kunkel, Russell J. *bank holding company executive*

West Chester
Swope, Charles Evans *bank executive, lawyer*

Williamsport
†Davis, William (Doyle) *banker*

Wyomissing
Sidhu, Jay S. *banking executive*

York
†Pullo, Robert Wayne *banker*
†Schmidt, John C. *bank executive*

RHODE ISLAND

Providence
Costellese, Linda E. Grace *banker*
Crooks, Bruce Philip *banker*
Gardner, Thomas Earle *investment banker, financial consultant*
Graboys, George *retired bank executive*
Murray, Terrence *banker*

Warwick
Kruse, James Joseph *merchant banker*

SOUTH CAROLINA

Aiken
†Rains, Darrell Ross *bank controller*

Columbia
Boggs, Jack Aaron *banker, municipal government official*
Folsom, John Roy *savings and loan executive*
Lindley, James Gunn *bank executive*
Lumpkin, John Henderson *retired banker*
†Royall, Robert Venning, Jr. *banker*
West, Rexford Leon *banker*

Greenville
Boliek, Luther C. *bank executive*

Hilton Head Island
Hornor, Frank Berkshire *banker*

SOUTH DAKOTA

Freeman
Waltner, John Randolph *bank executive*

Rapid City
Undlin, Charles Thomas *banker*

TENNESSEE

Athens
Thompson, Verdine Mae *financial planner, tax preparer*

Chattanooga
†Albright, Ray C. *banker, state senator*
Probasco, Scott Livingston *bank executive*
†Sudderth, Robert J., Jr. *bank executive*

Clinton
Birdwell, James Edwin, Jr. *retired banker*

Knoxville
Blake, Gerald Rutherford *banker*

Memphis
†Campbell, Bruce Emerson, Jr. *banker*
†Evans, John S. *bank executive*
†Garrott, Thomas M. *bank executive*
Horn, Ralph *bank executive*
Rawlins, Benjamin W., Jr. *bank holding company executive*
Terry, Ronald Anderson *bank holding company executive*

Murfreesboro
Ford, William F. *banker*

Nashville
Bottorff, Dennis C. *banker*
Cook, Charles Wilkerson, Jr. *former banker, county official*
Cunningham, Neil Lewis *retired banker*
Daane, James Dewey *banker*
Fleming, Samuel M. *banker*
Harrison, Clifford Joy, Jr. *banker*
Maihafer, Harry James *retired banker, former army officer*
Mc Creary, James Franklin *banker, lawyer*
Shell, Owen G., Jr. *banker*
Smith, James Forest, Jr. *retired banker*

TEXAS

Austin
Deal, Ernest Linwood, Jr. *banker*
Stone, Leon *banker*

Carrollton
Bentley, Clarence Edward *savings and loan executive*

Dallas
Adelizzi, Robert Frederick *bank executive*
Aston, James William *banker*
Atkins, Samuel James, III *banker*
Beck, Mary Constance *bank executive*
Cochran, George Calloway, III *retired banker*
Farris, Louis Anthony, Jr. *banker*
Gibson, William Edward *banker*
†Hearne, Carl N. *mortgage company executive*
Hudnall, David Harrison *financial executive*
†Lewis, John P. *bank executive*
Low, Paul M. *mortgage banking executive, food service executive*
Mason, Barry Jean *retired banker*
†McTeer, Robert D. *banker*
Nash, Michaux, Jr. *banker*
Pistor, Charles Herman, Jr. *former banker, academic administrator*
Reid, Langhorne, III *merchant banker*
†Salvaggio, Tony Joe *banker*
Schmieder, Frank Joseph *banker, business executive*
Steinhart, Ronald G. *banker*
Stewart, Robert H., III *banker*

Houston
Armour, Laurance Hearne, Jr. *banker*
Brown, Lewis Arnold *management consultant*
Dartez, Franklin *banker*
Elkins, James Anderson, Jr. *banker*
†Ellis, Rodney Glenn *investment banking firm director*
Geis, Duane Virgil *investment banker*
Knapp, David Hebard *banker*
Osborne, Dee S. *banker*
†Powell, Don Graber *investment company executive*
Smith, Robert, III *banker*
Tyndall, Marshall Clay, Jr. *banker*
Wilson, Clarence Ivan *banker*

Irving
†Barclay, George M. *banker*
Hughes, Keith William *banking and finance company executive*

San Antonio
Fawcett, Robert Earl, Jr. *retired banker*
Frost, Thomas Clayborne *banker*
Green, Phillip Dale *banker*
Gudinas, Donald Jerome *banker, retired army officer*
McClane, Robert Sanford *bank holding company executive*
Post, Gerald Joseph *retired banker, retired air force officer*

Tyler
Bell, Henry Marsh, Jr. *banking executive*

Victoria
†Hunter, Don Michael *banker*
Stubblefield, Page Kindred *banker*

Waco
†Mann, Robert Allen *banker*

UTAH

Ogden
Browning, Roderick Hanson *banker*

Saint George
Beesley, H(orace) Brent *savings and loan executive*

Salt Lake City
Eccles, Spencer Fox *banker*
Hemingway, W(illiam) David *banker*
Kendell, Ross Ezra *banker*
Simmons, Harris H. *banker*
Simmons, Roy William *banker*

VERMONT

Charlotte
Moore, Stephen Gates *banking executive*

VIRGINIA

Alexandria
Birely, William Cramer *investment banker*

Lancaster, Bruce Morgan *investment adviser, lecturer, retired diplomat*
†Roley, Jerry *bank executive*

Arlington
Leland, Marc Ernest *trust advisor, lawyer*
Olmsted, George Hamden *retired banking and insurance company executive*
Schaefer, Thomas J. *bank executive*

Bristol
†Deppen, Douglas *bank executive*

Charlottesville
Bull, George Albert *retired banker*
†McCartney, O. Kenton, III *commercial banker*

Danville
Goodson, Louie Aubrey, Jr. *retired bank executive*

Falls Church
Geithner, Paul Herman, Jr. *banker*
Zalokar, Robert H. *bank executive*

Great Falls
Foryst, Carole *mortgage broker*

Lynchburg
Quillian, William Fletcher, Jr. *retired banker, former college president*

Mc Lean
†Bollerer, Fred L. *banker*
Byrne, Gary Cecil *banker*
Glenn, David Wright *mortgage executive*
Ramsey, Lloyd Brinkley *retired savings and loan executive, retired army officer*
Ring, James Edward Patrick *mortgage insurance company executive*

Newport News
Bernhardt, John Bowman *banker*

Norfolk
Cutchins, Clifford Armstrong, III *banker*

Richmond
Black, Robert Perry *retired banker, executive*
†Broaddus, John Alfred, Jr. *bank executive, economist*
Coudriet, Charles Edward *banker*
Fields, William Jay *investment banker*
Freeman, Robert Mallory *banker*
Giblin, Patrick David *banker*
Harris, Henry Hiter, Jr. *banker*
Hatch, Robert Norris *banker*
Henley, Vernard William *banker*
Jones, Catesby Brooke *retired banker*
Mc Namara, Rieman, Jr. *retired banker*
Miller, Lewis Nelson, Jr. *banker*
Moore, Andrew Taylor, Jr. *banker*
Norfleet, Robert F., Jr. *banking executive*
Saine, Carroll Lee *banker*
Schwarzschild, William Harry, Jr. *banker*
Talley, Charles Richmond *commercial banking executive*
Tilghman, Richard Granville *banker*
Warrick, James Craig *banker*
†Wells, James M., III *bank executive*
Wilson, James Milton, III *bank executive*

Roanoke
Adams, James E. *bank executive*
Caudill, David L. *bank executive*
Dalhouse, Warner Norris *banker*

Round Hill
Coll, Helen F. *banker*

Vienna
Hood, William Clarence *international banking official*

Virginia Beach
Harrison, William Wright *retired banker*

Winchester
Pavsek, Daniel Allan *banker, educator*

WASHINGTON

Bellevue
Melby, Orville Erling *retired banker*

Mercer Island
Spitzer, Jack J. *banker*

Mill Creek
Holmstrom, David Edwin Arthur *mortgage banking executive, consultant*

Olympia
Alfers, Gerald Junior *bank executive, retired*

Seattle
Andrew, Lucius Archibald David, III *bank executive*
Arnold, Robert Morris *banker*
Bell, Jeffrey Donald *bank executive*
Buck, Robert Follette *banker, lawyer*
Campbell, Robert Hedgcock *investment banker*
Cockburn, John F. *retired banker*
Cullen, James Douglas *banker, finance company executive*
Faulstich, James R. *bank executive*
Fetters, Norman Craig, II *banker*
Green, Joshua, III *banker*
Jenkins, William Maxwell *banker*
Killinger, Kerry Kent *bank executive*
Mauer, Michael Leonard *banker*
Pinkerton, Guy Calvin *savings and loan executive*
Williams, Walter Baker *mortgage banker*

Spokane
Davis, Scott Livingston *banker, lawyer*
Lindsay, Donald Parker *former savings bank executive*
McWilliams, Edwin Joseph *banker*
Odegard, Richard Erwin *banker*

†Sandifur, Cantwell Paul, Sr. *mortgage company executive*

Tacoma
Odlin, Richard Bingham *retired banker*
Owen, Thomas Walker *banker, broker*
Philip, William Warren *banker*

Vancouver
Firstenburg, Edward William *banker*

WEST VIRGINIA

Charleston
†Adams, Richard M. *bank executive*
†Baronner, Robert Francis *banker*

WISCONSIN

Appleton
Platten, Peter Michael, III *bank holding company executive*
Sauter, Charles Herman *banker*

Kaukauna
Janssen, Gail Edwin *banking executive*

Madison
†Poniewaz, Kenneth Anthony *banker*
Schleck, Roth Stephen *banker*

Milwaukee
Bauer, Chris Michael *banker*
Bero, Ronald Arthur *banker*
Bruett, Till Arthur *banker*
Fitzsimonds, Roger Leon *bank holding company executive*
Gunnlaugsson, Gordon Harvey *bank executive*
†Kuester, Dennis J. *banker*
Long, Robert Eugene *banker*
Samson, Allen Lawrence *bank executive*
Wigdale, James B. *bank executive*

Nekoosa
Sigler, LeRoy Walter *banker, lawyer, entrepreneur*

Stevens Point
Seramur, John C. *bank executive*

TERRITORIES OF THE UNITED STATES

PUERTO RICO

San Juan
Carrion, Richard *bank executive*
Pérez, Angel Alvarez *bank executive*

Santurce
Loubriel, Tere *bank executive*

CANADA

BRITISH COLUMBIA

Vancouver
Gardiner, William Douglas Haig *bank executive*

ONTARIO

Ottawa
Bonin, Bernard *bank executive*
Flichel, Eugene Anthony *banker*
Freedman, Charles *bank executive*

Toronto
Atkinson, Lloyd Charles *bank executive*
Baillie, Alexander Charles, Jr. *banker*
Barrett, Matthew W. *bank executive*
Bell, J. A. Gordon *retired banker*
Bickford, James Gordon *banker*
Brooks, Robert Leslie *bank executive*
Flood, A. L. (Al Flood) *bank executive*
Fullerton, R. Donald *banker*
Godsoe, Peter Cowperthwaite *banker*
Greenwood, Lawrence George *banker*
Grosland, Emery Layton *banker*
Hayes, Derek Cumberland *banking executive, lawyer*
Johnston, Malcolm Carlyle *bank executive*
Kluge, Holger *banking executive*
Korthals, Robert W. *bank executive*
Logan, Frank Henderson *banker*
MacDougall, Hartland Molson *trust company executive*
Ritchie, Cedric Elmer *banker*
Styles, Richard Geoffrey Pentland *retired banker*
Taylor, Allan Richard *banker*
Taylor, Paul Albert *banker*
Thomson, Richard Murray *banker*
Webb, Anthony Allan *banker*

QUEBEC

Chelsea
Warren, Jack Hamilton *trade policy advisor*

Montreal
Bérard, André *bank executive*
Cleghorn, John Edward *banker*
Lawson, Jane Elizabeth *bank executive*
Marcoux, Yvon *financial executive, lawyer*
Turmel, Jean Bernard *banker*

ARGENTINA

Buenos Aires
Sacerdote, Manuel Ricardo banker

BELGIUM

Brussels
†Janssen, Paul-Emmanuel bank executive
Walker, Darcy Lynn banker

ENGLAND

London
Aspbury, Herbert Francis bank executive
Band, David investment banker
Bee, Robert Norman banker
Binney, Robert Harry bank executive
Bischoff, Winfried Franz Wilhelm merchant banker
Catto of Cairncatto, Baron Stephen Gordon banker
Chappell, Anthony Gordon banker
Collins, Paul John banker
Kopech, Robert Irving banker
Mallinckrodt, George W. bank executive
Moreno, Glen Richard banker
Ogden, Peter James investment banker
Philipsborn, John David former banker, consultant

GERMANY

Berlin
Palmer, R(obie Marcus Hooker) Mark banker

HONG KONG

Hong Kong
Enlow, Fred Clark banker
Magarity, Russell Lynn banker
Rowe, Kevin S. banker

JAPAN

Minato-ku
Doi, Masayuki credit card company executive

Tokyo
Fujii, Keishi bank executive
Oliver, Steven Wiles banker

SPAIN

Madrid
Álvarez Rendueles, José Ramón bank executive

SWITZERLAND

Zürich
†Gut, Rainer Emil banker

ADDRESS UNPUBLISHED

Ackerman, Jack Rossin investment banker
Almgren, Herbert Philip bank executive
Alvord, Joel Barnes bank executive
Axilrod, Stephen Harvey investment banker, economist
Baker, Henry S., Jr. retired banker
Barrett, William Joel investment banker
†Beck, Jeffrey Dengler banking executive
†Bischoff, Robert Henry bank executive
Blum, Barbara Davis banker
Boykin, Robert Heath banker
Boyles, James Kenneth retired banker
Britt, John Roy banker
Brown, Bennett Alexander former banker
Brown, Sandra Jean banker
Browning, Colin Arrott retired banker
Buckels, Marvin Wayne savings and loan executive
Busse, Leonard Wayne banker, financial consultant
Carey, Francis James investment banker
Carey, Gerard V. banker
Chappell, Robert E. banker
Clifton, Russell B. banking and mortgage lending consultant, retired mortgage company executive
Coleman, Lewis Waldo bank executive
Conlon, Harry B., Jr. banking company executive
†Conover, Charles Todd banker
Console, Frank Milton savings and loan association executive
Cooney, John Thomas retired banker
Czarnecki, Gerald Milton banker
Deane, Thomas Andersen retired banker
†Disney, Jeffrey F. banker
Dodson, Samuel Robinette, III investment banker
Dorland, Dodge Oatwell investment advisor
†Engelke, George L., Jr. banker
Fahey, Joseph Francis, Jr. banker, financial consultant
Fahringer, Catherine Hewson retired savings and loan executive
Fielding, Harold Preston bank executive
Fitzmaurice, Laurence Dorset banking executive
Ford, William Francis retired bank holding company executive
Foster, Stephen Kent banker
Gaffney, Thomas banker
Gilchrist, James Beardslee banker
Goebert, Robert J. banking executive
Grant, James Colin banker
Greenwald, Gerald industrial company executive
Harrison, William Burwell, Jr. banker
Hatfield, W. C. banking consultant
Hayes, Mary Phyllis savings and loan association executive
Hogan, Robert Henry trust company executive, investment strategist
Howard, Donald Searcy banker
Hulbert, Bruce Walker corporate executive, banker
Ingersoll, Paul Mills banker
Jennings, Joseph Ashby banker
Klett, Gordon A. retired savings and loan association executive
Kooken, John Frederick retired bank holding company executive
Korpal, Eugene Stanley banker, former army officer
Lafley, Alan Frederick retired banker
Lankford, Duane Gail investment banker, mountaineer
Linane, William Edward corporate real estate executive
Liu, Ernest K. H. international banking executive, international financial consultant
Martin, Preston financial services executive
Mayo, Robert Porter banker
McCall, John Anthony banker
Meeker, Guy Bentley banker
Montgomery, Parker Gilbert investment banker
Moriarty, Donald William, Jr. banker
Morris, Frank Eugene banker
Morrison, James R. retired banker
Morrison, John Washburn banker
Mortensen, Peter banker
Moss, John Emerson banker, former congressman
Nelson, Clifford Arnold retired bank executive
Newman, Denis merchant banker
Nicholson, Richard Joseph trust banking executive
North, Phil Record retired banker
Nour, Samir banker, economic consultant
Odell, Frank Harold banker
Osborn, William George savings and loan executive
†Osteen, Harry Montague, Jr. banker
Palmer, Langdon banker
†Parode, Ann banker, lawyer
Pipal, Faustin Anthony savings bank executive
Polk, Robert Forrest banker
Pool, Douglas Vernon trust company executive
Pote, Harold William banker
Redeker, Jerrald H(ale) banker
Reichstetter, Arthur Charles banker
Reuber, Grant Louis banking insurance company executive
Rice, Joseph Albert banker
Rogers, Nathaniel Sims banker
Rub, Louis John savings and loan executive
Rundquist, Howard Irving investment banker
Simonet, John Thomas banker
Smith, Wilburn Jackson, Jr. retired bank executive
Stanton, Robert John corporate bank executive, lawyer
Stephens, Donald R(ichards) banker
Stepp, James Michael bank executive
Stewart, Carleton M. banker, corporate director
Stotter, Harry Shelton banker, lawyer
Suenholz, Herman Harry banker
Suhler, John Stuart investment banker
†Sullivan, Barry F. banker
Swope, Donald Downey retired banker
Tatlock, Anne M. trust company executive
Taylor, David George retired banker
Thiessen, Gordon George banker
Thompson, J. Andy bank executive
Tobin, Michael Edward banker
Toll, Maynard Joy, Jr. investment banker
Trombino, Roger A. investment banker
Tyson, H. Michael bank executive
Vachon, Serge Jean bank executive
Wapenhans, Willi Adolf banking executive
Weir, Thomas Charles banker
Womach, Emily Hitch retired banker and marketing and public relations executive
Yoder, Carl W. banker
Zilkha, Ezra Khedouri banker

FINANCE: FINANCIAL SERVICES

UNITED STATES

ALABAMA

Auburn
Barth, James Richard finance educator

Birmingham
Baxter, Arthur Pearce financial services marketing company executive
Powers, Edward Latell accountant
†Vogelsang, John Martin financial executive

Huntsville
Graves, Benjamin Barnes business administration educator

Montgomery
Gorland, Ronald Kent corporate executive

Tuscaloosa
Garner, Samuel Paul accounting educator, author
Gup, Benton Eugene banking educator
Lee, Thomas Alexander accountant, educator
Mayer, Morris Lehman marketing educator
Penz, Anton Jacob retired accounting educator

ALASKA

Fairbanks
Rice, Michael Lewis business educator

Juneau
†Bushre, Peter Alvin financial executive

ARIZONA

Phoenix
Burg, Jerome Stuart financial planning consultant
Daniel, James Richard accountant, computer company financial executive
Dougherty, Ronald Jary business owner, accountant
Feldman, Ira S. accountant
Holloway, Edgar Austin retired diversified business executive
Khan, Ahmed Mohiuddin financial/insurance executive
Leonard, George Edmund finance company executive, consultant
Mullen, Daniel Robert treasurer
Robertson, Richard Curtis credit union executive
Stern, Richard David investment company executive
Upson, Donald V. financial executive

Scottsdale
Hansen, Donald W. insurance and financial services executive
Huizingh, William former accounting educator
Randolph, John Maurice financial consultant

Sun City West
Person, Robert John financial management consultant
Schrag, Adele Frisbie business education educator

Tempe
Files, L(awrence) Burke financial consultant
Pany, Kurt Joseph accounting educator, consultant
Poe, Jerry B. financial educator
Treichler, Harvey Albert financial planner

Tucson
Carleton, Willard Tracy finance educator
Guimond, John Patrick financial consultant
Nixon, Robert Obey, Sr. business educator

ARKANSAS

Fayetteville
Cook, Doris Marie accountant, educator
Hay, Robert Dean retired management educator
Rosenberg, Leon Joseph marketing educator

Little Rock
Bethea, William C. financial administrator, lawyer

State University
Ruby, Ralph, Jr. vocational business educator

CALIFORNIA

Alhambra
Siler, Walter Orlando, Jr. retired business executive

Alta Loma
Wu, Seng-Chai financial planner, life insurance agency official

Anaheim
Lano, Charles Jack management auditor

Atherton
Chetkovich, Michael N. accountant

Belvedere Tiburon
Cook, Robert Donald financial service executive

Berkeley
Staubus, George Joseph accounting educator

Beverly Hills
Bailey, William Ralph financial services company executive
†Geuther, Carl Frederick financial services company executive
†Harshfield, Edward Gordon financial services company executive
McGagh, William Gilbert financial consultant
Smith, Robert Harold accountant

Brea
Engleman, David S. diversified financial services executive

Burbank
Peterson, Ralph financial executive
†Shao, Shiu financial executive

Carmel
Steele, Charles Glen retired accountant

Carmichael
Areen, Gordon E. finance company executive

Chatsworth
Palko, Michael James finance company executive

Chula Vista
Chapman, Laurence Arthur finance executive

Compton
Bogdan, Carolyn Louetta financial specialist
†Briskin, Bernard finance executive

Corona Del Mar
Helphand, Ben J. actuary

Coronado
Allen, Charles Richard retired financial executive

Costa Mesa
Hamilton, Michael Scott accounting firm executive

Culver City
Brown, Abbott Louis accountant
Eckel, James Robert, Jr. financial planner

Dana Point
Kesselhaut, Arthur Melvyn financial consultant

Danville
Amon, William Frederick, Jr. finance company executive

Fallbrook
Freeman, Harry Lynwood accountant

Foster City
MacNaughton, Angus Athole finance company executive
Paterson, Richard Denis financial executive

Fresno
Tellier, Richard Davis management educator

Fullerton
Axelson, Charles Frederic retired accounting educator

Glendale
Greenwood, Richard M. finance company executive, bank executive

Glendora
Christofi, Andreas Charalambos finance educator

Irvine
Feldstein, Paul Joseph management educator
Pearson, William James finance company executive

La Jolla
Dorsey, Dolores Florence business executive, corporate treasurer
Dunn, David Joseph financial executive
Simon, Ronald I. finance consultant

La Mesa
Bailey, Brenda Marie accountant

Laguna Beach
Garfin, Louis actuary
Warner, Robert S. company director, former accountant

Los Altos
Hinckley, Gregory Keith financial executive

Los Angeles
†Anderson, George Edward financial services company executive
Broad, Eli financial services and home construction company executive
Brockett, Peter Charles financial executive
Cohen, William Alan marketing educator, author, consultant
Coombs, John Wendell financial service executive
Cummings, Thomas Gerald management educator, consultant
DeBard, Roger investment executive
Engler, George Nichols educator, financial consultant
Feiman, Thomas E. accounting company executive
Frisch, Robert A. financial planning company executive
Gooch, Lawrence Boyd accounting executive
Hein, Leonard William accounting educator
King, Joseph Paul finance executive
Kleingartner, Archie business educator
Knapp, Cleon Talboys business executive
Lane, Marilyn Edith corporate executive
†Lewin, David management educator
Magner, Fredric Michael financial services executive
Meloan, Taylor Wells marketing educator
Miech, Allen C. financial services company executive
Mock, Theodore Jaye accounting educator
Morrison, Donald Graham business educator, consultant
Morrow, Winston Vaughan financial executive
Mosich, Anelis Nick accountant, author, educator, consultant
Nanus, Burton Benjamin management educator, researcher
Ross, William H. accountant
Roussey, Robert Stanley accountant, educator
Stancill, James McNeill finance educator, consultant
Stern, Marc Irwin financial services executive
Tanaka, Togo W(illiam) retired real estate and financial executive
Weston, John Frederick business educator, consultant
Williams, Julie Ford investment specialist

Malibu
Yates, Jere Eugene business educator, management consultant

Menlo Park
Elkus, Richard J. finance and industrial company executive
Fassett, Hugh Gardner investment counselor
McDonald, Warren George accountant, former savings and loan executive

Monrovia
Breen, Thomas Albert financial services executive

Mountain View
Benham, James Mason mutual fund executive

Newport Beach
Frederick, Dolliver H. merchant banker
Masotti, Louis Henry management educator, consultant
Schroeder, Charles Henry corporate treasurer

Northridge
Lehtihalme, Larry (Lauri) K. financial planner

Novato
Varney, Bernard Keith financial executive, consultant

Oakland
Barlow, William Pusey, Jr. accountant
Helvey, Julius Louis, II finance company executive
Lee, Jong Hyuk accountant
Rowlings, Donald George international investment banker
Schwyn, Charles Edward accountant

Orinda
Meadowcroft, Robert Stanley financial investment executive

Oxnard
Lewis, Michael John diversified financial services company executive

Palo Alto
Horngren, Charles Thomas accounting educator
Ivy, Benjamin Franklin, III financial and real estate investment advisor

Palos Verdes Peninsula
Ryker, Charles Edwin *consultant, former aerospace company executive*

Pleasant Hill
Hamilton, Allen Philip *financial advisor*

Pleasanton
Vandenberghe, Ronald Gustave *accountant, real estate developer*

Pollock Pines
Johnson, Stanford Leland *marketing educator*

Pomona
†Johnson, Richard M. *finance company executive*
Patten, Thomas Henry, Jr. *management, human resources educator*

Portola Valley
Berghold, Joseph Philip *finance company executive*

Rancho Mirage
Buskirk, Richard Hobart *marketing educator*
Kocen, Joel Evan *financial planner*

Rancho Santa Fe
Kessler, A. D. *business, financial, investment and real estate advisor, consultant, lecturer, author, broadcaster, producer*

Riverside
Harrison, Ethel Mae *financial executive*

Sacramento
Hanson, Dale *pension fund administrator*
Herman, Irving Leonard *business administration educator*

Salinas
Stevens, Wilbur Hunt *accountant*

San Diego
Bateman, Giles Hirst Litton *finance executive*
Jeub, Michael Leonard *financial executive*
Pierson, Albert Chadwick *business management educator*
Riedy, Mark Joseph *finance educator*
Spanos, Dean A. *business executive*
Tennent, Valentine Leslie *accountant*
West, James Harold *accounting company executive*

San Francisco
Carniglia, Stephen Davis *accountant, real estate consultant, lawyer*
Dinkelspiel, Paul Gaines *investment banking and public financial consultant*
Duff, James George *financial services executive*
Greeley, Robert Emmett *financial analyst*
Gund, George, III *financier*
Harvey, James Ross *finance company executive*
Heller, H(einz) Robert *financial executive*
Herringer, Frank Casper *diversified financial services company executive*
Kahn, Paul Markham *actuary*
Kelly, Thomas Brooke *accounting and consulting firm executive*
Kingsley, Leonard Edward *financial services executive*
Krause, Lawrence Allen *financial adviser, financial planner*
Mayer, Patricia Jayne *financial officer, management accountant*
Mumford, Christopher Greene *corporate financial executive*
Nord, Paul Elliott *accountant*
Palmer, William Joseph *accountant*
Peterson, Harries-Clichy *financial consultant*
Quiban, Estelita Cabrera *controller*
†Schultz, Dean M. *finance company executive*
Thornton, James Ivan, Jr. *financial executive*
Uri, George Wolfsohn *accountant*
Weihrich, Heinz *management educator*
Whitney, David Clay *business educator, consultant, writer*
Wood, George H. *investment executive*

San Jose
Belluomini, Frank Stephen *accountant*
Halverson, George Clarence *business administration educator*

San Luis Obispo
Stream, Jay Wilson *financial consultant*

San Marcos
Melcher, Trini Urtuzuastegui *accounting educator*
Waters, George Gary *financial service executive*

San Mateo
Johnson, Charles Bartlett *mutual fund executive*
†Silver, William Robert *corporate finance executive*

Santa Ana
Hickson, Ernest Charles *financial executive*

Santa Barbara
Mehra, Rajnish *finance educator*

Santa Clara
Delucchi, George Paul *accountant*
Menkin, Christopher (Kit Menkin) *leasing company executive*

Santa Monica
†Bronstein, Gerald Morton *holding company executive*
Mc Intyre, James A. *diversified financial services executive*

Saratoga
†Araquistain, Paul A. *financial professional*

Springs
†Olofson, Roy Leonard *financial executive, accountant*

Stanford
Beaver, William Henry *accounting educator*
Germane, Gayton Elwood *business educator*
Holloway, Charles Arthur *public and private management educator*
Leavitt, Harold Jack *management educator*
McDonald, John Gregory *financial investment educator*
Montgomery, David Bruce *marketing educator*
Pfeffer, Jeffrey *business educator*
Porterfield, James Temple Starke *business administration educator*
Serbein, Oscar Nicholas *business educator, consultant*
Wolfson, Mark Alan *accounting and finance educator*

Torrance
†Sakai, Shinji *finance company executive*

Universal City
Baker, Richard Eugene *controller, corporate executive*
Boulanger, Donald Richard *financial services executive*

Upland
Jones, Nancy Langdon *financial planner, investment advisor*

Whittier
Maxwell, Raymond Roger *accountant*

Woodland Hills
Anaya, Richard Alfred, Jr. *accountant, investment banker*
Robison, Frederick Mason *financial executive*
Taubitz, Fredricka *financial executive*

COLORADO

Aurora
Bauman, Earl William *accountant, government official*

Boulder
Bangs, F(rank) Kendrick *former business educator*
Baughn, William Hubert *former business educator and academic administrator*
Buchanan, Dodds Ireton *business educator, consultant*
Hyland, Laurie Zoe *financial planner*
Mason, Leon Verne *financial planner*
Melicher, Ronald William *finance educator*
Stanton, William John, Jr. *marketing educator, author*

Castle Rock
Eppler, Jerome Cannon *private financial advisor*

Columbine Valley
Wittbrodt, Edwin Stanley *consultant, former bank executive, former air force officer*

Denver
Edwards, Phyllis Mae *accountant, graphologist*
Fernandez, Tomas Isidro *accountant*
Gillis, Paul Leonard *accountant*
Kuper, Dennis Lee *financial officer*
Sandler, Thomas R. *accountant*

Golden
Eaton, Mark Rayner *financial executive*

Greenwood Village
Barnard, Rollin Dwight *retired financial executive*

Littleton
Hadley, Marlin LeRoy *direct sales financial consultant*
Snyder, William Harry *financial advisor*

Wheat Ridge
Gerlick, Helen J. *tax practitioner, accountant*

CONNECTICUT

Bloomfield
Desautelle, William Peter *financial executive*

Bridgeport
DeWerth, Gordon Henry *corporate finance executive*

Danbury
Goldstein, Joel *management science educator, researcher*
Holzman, Robert Stuart *tax consultant*

Darien
Hart, Eric Mullins *finance company executive*
Hubner, Robert Wilmore *consultant, former business machines company executive*
Owen, Robert Vaughan *financial company executive*
Schell, James Munson *financial executive*
Schmalzried, Marvin Eugene *financial consultant*

East Hartford
Mordo, Jean Henri *financial executive*

Enfield
Crocker, Frederick Greeley, Jr. *financial executive*

Fairfield
Cion, Richard M. *financial executive, lawyer*
Golub, Stephen Bruce *accountant, consultant, educator*

Greenwich
†Flagg, George V. *business executive*
Gabelli, Mario J. *diversified financial services company executive*
Horton, Jared C. *retired corporation executive*
Howard, John Arnold *marketing educator*
Lanzit, Stephen Ray *finance company executive, consultant*
McLaughlin, Michael John *financial executive*
Miles, Jesse Mc Lane *retired accounting company executive*
Moonie, Clyde Wickliffe *financial consultant*
†Ordway, John Danton *pension administrator, lawyer, accountant*
Richards, Fred Tracy *finance company executive*
Smith, Rodger Field *financial executive*
Springsteen, David Folger *financial consultant*

Hartford
Gerson, Elliot Francis *financial services executive*
Wyatt, Wilson Watkins, Jr. *finance company and public relations executive*

Middlebury
Todt, Malcolm S. *financial, management consultant*

Milford
†Madigan, Michael Scott *financial executive, treasurer*

New Haven
Buck, Donald Tirrell *finance educator*
Deese, James LaMotte *financial executive*
Fried, Charles A. *accountant,financial executive*
†Galvin, James Norman *financial executive, investment banker*
Vroom, Victor Harold *management consultant, educator*

North Stonington
Nolf, David Manstan *financial executive*

Norwalk
Foster, John McNeely *accounting standards executive*
Mosso, David *accountant*
Northcutt, Robert Hull, Jr. *financial executive*
†Payne, Paul D. *finance company executive*

Ridgefield
†Finneran, Thomas A. *finance company executive*
Ruggles, Rudy Lamont, Jr. *investment banker, consultant*

Shelton
Canosa, Albert Anthony *corporate finance officer*

Stamford
Dewing, Merlin Eugene *diversified financial services company executive*
Fillet, Mitchell Harris *financial services executive*
Frank, Charles Raphael, Jr. *financial executive*
Higgins, Jay Francis *financial service executive*
Hoekwater, James Warren *controller*
Howard, Melvin *financial executive*
†James, John Whitaker, Sr. *financial services executive*
Marsden, Charles Joseph *financial executive*
McCain, Arthur Williamson, Jr. *pension investment consultant*
McLeod, Christopher Kevin *service company executive*
McNear, Barbara Baxter *financial communications executive, consultant*
Morgan, William J. *accounting company executive*
Norman, Geoffrey Robert *financial executive*
O'Connor, Frank M. *business educator, sales professional*
Pacter, Paul Allan *accounting educator*
Quinnell, Bruce Andrew *finance executive*
Reynolds, Robert Louis *financial services executive*
Riggs, James Arthur *financial executive*
Ross, Stuart B. *corporate financial executive*
Sharp, Edgar E. *diversified corporation executive*
†Stauff, Michael Frederick *financial manager*
Wendt, Gary Carl *finance company executive*

Thompson
Fisher, William Thomas *business administration educator*

Waterbury
Hamilton, John Ross *financial consultant, educator*

West Hartford
Farr, Richard Claborn *private investor, corporate executive*

Westport
Ready, Robert James *financial company executive*

Wilton
Billings, Edward Robert *accountant*
Cook, Jay Michael *accounting company executive*
Kangas, Edward A. *accounting firm executive*

DELAWARE

Wilmington
Caspersen, Finn Michael Westby *diversified financial services company executive*
Lukens, Paul Bourne *financial executive*
Pew, Robert Anderson *financial corporation officer*
Rogoski, Patricia Diana *financial executive*
Sidell, Robert Leonard *financial planner, management consultant*
Slook, George Francis *finance company executive*

DISTRICT OF COLUMBIA

Washington
Allbritton, Joe Lewis *diversified holding company executive*
Armstrong, Alexandra *financial advisor*
Arnold, G. Dewey, Jr. *accountant*
Brown, George Leslie *legislative affairs and business development consultant, former manufacturing company executive, former lieutenant governor*
Byron, William James *management educator, former university president*
Calhoun, John Cozart *financial services marketing executive*
de Saint Phalle, Thibaut *investment banker, educator, lawyer, financial consultant*
Droms, William George *finance educator*
Durnil, James B. *accountant*
Edwards, Bert Tvedt *accountant*
Ernstthal, Henry L. *management educator*
Ewing, Samuel Daniel, Jr. *financial executive*
Fischetti, Michael Joseph *accounting educator*
Fitts, C. Austin *investment banker, former federal agency administrator*
Frank, Victor H., Jr. *international financial consultant*
Frankel, Michael Henry *accountant, lawyer*
Grub, Phillip Donald *business educator*
Harrison, Monika Edwards *business development executive*
Johnson, James A. *financial organization executive*
Kanter, Arnold Lee *policy analyst*
Koskinen, John Andrew *asset management executive*
Larsen, Richard Gary *accounting firm executive*
†Lerner, Charles *pension fund administrator, lawyer*
Linowes, Harry Michael *accountant*
Litke, Arthur Ludwig *business executive*
MacLaury, Bruce King *research institution executive*
Malek, Frederic Vincent *finance executive*
McGlone, Denise Marie *financial company executive*
McKinless, Kathy Jean *accountant*
Murphy, James Jackson *actuary, association executive*
Nason, Charles Tuckey *financial services executive*
†Naughton, Paul Francis *financial executive*
Page, Harry Robert *business administration educator*
Parks, James Thomas *financial company executive*
Parrish, Edgar Lee *financial services executive*
Pivik, Robert William *accounting executive*
Ranelli, Raymond A. *accounting firm executive*
†Robinson, Virginia Brown *financial services company executive*
Seale, William Edward *finance educator*
Silver, David *financial executive, lawyer*
Small, Lawrence M. *financial organization executive*
Sockwell, Oliver R., Jr. *financial services company executive*
Stout, Carl Frederick *finance and management executive*
Tuggle, Francis Douglas *management educator*
Walker, David A(lan) *finance educator*
West, Emery Joseph *financial analyst, investment portfolio manager*
West, J. Robinson *petroleum finance company executive, former government official*
Zoeller, Jack Carl *financial executive*

FLORIDA

Apopka
Rufenacht, Roger Allen *accounting educator*

Arcadia
Davis, Bruce Livingston, Jr. *retired accountant*

Aventura
Kliger, Milton Richard *financial services executive*

Boca Raton
Jaffe, Leonard Sigmund *financial executive*
Jessup, Joe Lee *business educator, management consultant*
Kelley, Eugene John *business educator*
Miller, Eugene *financial executive*
Shane, Ronald *financial company executive*
Sigel, Marshall Elliot *financial consultant*

Boynton Beach
Bartholomew, Arthur Peck, Jr. *accountant*

Clearwater
Pendleton, Sumner Alden *financial consultant*

Coral Springs
Luing, Gary Alan *financial management educator*

Deerfield Beach
†Bernstein, Stanley Robert *financial consultant, mortgage broker and banker*

Deland
Horton, Thomas R. *business advisor*

Delray Beach
Bryan, Robert Fessler *former investment analyst*

Englewood
Defliese, Philip Leroy *accountant, educator*

Fort Lauderdale
Becker, Edward A. *accounting educator, consultant*
Miller, Tanfield Charles *accountant*

Gainesville
Abdel-Khalik, Ahmed Rashad *business educator*
Simmons, John Kaul *accounting educator*
Stone, Williard Everard *accountant, educator*

Hernando
Bell, Philip Wilkes *accounting and economics educator*

Hialeah
Kennedy, Thomas Patrick *financial executive*
Shaw, Steven John *retired marketing educator, academic administrator*

Hobe Sound
DeHority, Edward Havens, Jr. *retired accountant, lawyer*
Vanderbilt, Oliver Degray *financier*

Jacksonville
El-Ansary, Adel Ibrahim *business educator*
†Hill, John Steven *accountant*
Lindner, Carl Henry, Jr. *financial holding company executive*
†Sparrow, William Holliday *corporate financial executive*
Tomlinson, William Holmes *management educator, retired army officer*

Jupiter
Ashby, Donald Wayne, Jr. *retired accountant*
Danforth, Arthur Edwards *finance executive*

Largo
Criqui, William Edmund *lighting company financial executive*

Melbourne
Roub, Bryan R(oger) *financial executive*
Sottile, James *financier*

Miami
Coton, Carlos David *finance manager*
Ehrlich, Morton *international finance executive*
Pomeranz, Felix *accounting educator*
von Clemm, Michael *financial executive*
Wolper, Marshall *insurance and financial consultant*

Naples
Fess, Philip Eugene *accountant, educator*

Nokomis
Meyerhoff, Jack Fulton *financial executive*

North Miami Beach
Fishel, Peter Livingston *accounting business executive*

Orlando
Abbott, Edward Leroy *finance executive*
Gray, Anthony Rollin *capital management company executive*
Miller, Charles Edward, Jr. *financial executive*

Palm Beach
Barness, Amnon Shemaya *financial service executive*
Bishop, Warner Bader *finance company executive*
Riefler, Donald Brown *financial consultant*

Palm Beach Gardens
Herrick, John Dennis *consultant, former law firm executive, retired food products executive*

Panama City Beach
Miller, Robert William *personal property appraiser, writer*

Pensacola
Usry, Milton Franklin *accounting educator*

Plantation
Shoemaker, William Edward *financial executive*

Pompano Beach
Mulvey, John Thomas, Jr. *financial consultant*

Punta Gorda
Bulzacchelli, John G. *financial executive*

Ridge Manor
Widmer, Raymond Arthur *financial holding company executive*

Saint Petersburg
Blumenthal, Herman Bertram *accountant*
Freeman, Corinne *financial services, former mayor*
McMurray, Joseph Patrick Brendan *financial consultant*

Sarasota
Arreola, John Bradley *diversified financial service company executive, financial planner*
Bailey, Robert Elliott *financial executive*
Bewley, David Charles *financial planner*
Lambert, John Phillip *financial executive, consultant*
Miles, Arthur J. *financial planner, consultant*
Vestal, Lucian LaRoe *financier*

Tallahassee
Anthony, William Philip *management educator*

Tampa
Alexander, William Olin *finance company executive*
Hernandez, Gilberto Juan *accountant, auditor*
Homan, Paul M. *financial consultant*
Nord, Walter Robert *business administration educator, researcher, consultant*
Velez, Francisco S. *financial planner*

Tequesta
Stanger, John William *finance company executive*

Vero Beach
Hill, Henry Parker *accountant*
Kinard, Hargett Yingling *financial consultant*

West Palm Beach
Eppley, Roland Raymond, Jr. *retired financial services executive*
Hamilton, Neil Alfred *financial executive*
Livingstone, John Leslie *accountant, management consultant, business economist, educator*

Windermere
Graese, Clifford Ernest *retired accountant*

Winter Park
Plane, Donald Ray *management science educator*
Richards, Max De Voe *management educator, consultant, researcher, author*

GEORGIA

Athens
Miller, Herbert Elmer *accountant*

Atlanta
Benston, George James *accountant, economist*
Bleser, Joseph G. *financial executive*
Bragg, John Mackie *actuarial consultant*
†Chalmers, Alan Knight *financial corporation executive*
Cotton, James Perry, Jr. *holding company executive*
Dykes, John Henry, Jr. *finance executive*
Frank, Ronald Edward *marketing educator*
Hawkins, Robert Garvin *management educator, consultant*
Henry, William Ray *business administration educator*
Lobb, William Atkinson *financial services executive*
Manners, George Emanuel *business educator, emeritus dean*
Nelson, Robert Earl, Jr. *financial services company executive*

Parsons, Leonard Jon *marketing educator, consultant*
Phillips, Herbert Alvin, Jr. *retired financial executive*
Rasnake, James Hamilton, Jr. *portfolio manager*
Reichardt, Delbert Dale *financial executive*
Seto, William Roderick *public accounting company executive*
†Stubbs, Thomas Hubert *company executive*
Walker, David Michael *compensation and benefits consultant, accountant*
†Winter, Wilburn Jackson, Jr. *financial executive*
Zimmermann, John *financial consultant*

Columbus
Blanchard, James Hubert *finance company executive*

Decatur
Myers, Clark Everett *retired business administration educator*

Macon
Owens, Garland Chester *accounting educator*

Roswell
Topliss, Harry, Jr. *financial consultant, former corporation executive*

Savannah
Gay, Lee Anderson *financial consultant*
Sortor, Harold Edward *financial executive*

Thomasville
Stepanek, David Leslie *financial services company executive*

Woodstock
Austin, John David *financial executive*

HAWAII

Honolulu
Cotlar, Morton *organizational scientist, educator*
Hook, Ralph Clifford, Jr. *business educator*
Nakagawa, Jean Harue *diversified corporation executive*

IDAHO

Boise
†Ingram, Cecil D. *accountant, state legislator*
Kayser, Donald Robert *financial executive*
†Pomeroy, Horace Burton, III *accountant, corporate executive*

ILLINOIS

AMF Ohare
Fisher, Patricia Sweeney *business executive, lawyer*

Aurora
Halloran, Kathleen L. *financial executive, accountant*

Bannockburn
Zorio, John William *financial services executive*

Belleville
Fietsam, Robert Charles *accountant*

Calumet City
Edwards, James Clifford *finance company executive*

Champaign
Bailey, Andrew Dewey, Jr. *accounting educator*
Brighton, Gerald David *accounting educator*
Bryan, William Royal *finance educator*
Neumann, Frederick Loomis *accounting educator, academic administrator, consultant*
Perry, Kenneth Wilbur *accounting educator*
Schoenfeld, Hanns-Martin Walter *accounting educator*

Chicago
Allgyer, Robert Earl *accounting company executive*
†Almeida, Richard J. *finance company executive*
Blum, Michael Stephen *financial services executive*
Bohne, Carl John, Jr. *accountant*
Bott, Harold Sheldon *accountant, management consultant*
Brice, James John *retired accounting firm executive*
Caccamo, Nicholas James *financial executive*
†Canning, John Anthony, Jr. *venture capital company executive*
Center, Robert A. *accounting firm executive*
Chapman, Alger Baldwin *finance executive, lawyer*
Chlebowski, John Francis, Jr. *financial executive*
Chookaszian, Dennis Haig *financial executive*
Ciccarone, Richard Anthony *financial executive*
†Ciotola, Nicholas Anthony *financial executive*
Cloonan, James Brian *investment executive*
Cotner, C(arol) Beth *financial services company executive*
Eidell, Ronald George *financial executive*
Eppen, Gary Dean *business educator*
Fiorentino, Leon Francis *holding company executive*
Fitzgerald, Robert Maurice *financial executive*
Flanagan, Thomas Patrick *accountant*
French, Kenneth Ronald *finance educator*
Garrigan, Richard Thomas *finance educator, consultant, editor*
Goggin, Joseph Robert *financial consultant*
Hansen, Claire V. *financial executive*
Harding, James Warren *finance company executive*
Hoffman, Philip Andrew *property tax consultant*
†Hunt, Steven J. *media and advertising executive*
Kelly, Robert Donald *consultant*
Koltin, Allan David *accountant*
Krupnik, Vee M. *financial company executive*
Kudish, David J. *financial executive*
Kullberg, Duane Reuben *accounting firm executive*
Lauder, Norma J. *corporate finance executive*
Lennes, Gregory *manufacturing and financing company executive*
Lewis, John D. *financial services company executive*
Litwin, Michael Joseph *finance company executive*
Longman, Gary Lee *accountant*
Lorie, James Hirsch *business administration educator*
Lyman, Arthur Joseph *financial executive*

Mallory, Robert Mark *controller, finance executive*
Mayer, Raymond Richard *business administration educator*
McCormack, Robert Cornelius *investment banker*
Measelle, Richard L. *accountant*
Medvin, Harvey Norman *financial executive, treasurer*
Miller, Merton Howard *finance educator*
Moor, Roy Edward *finance educator*
Moravy, L. Joe *accountant, financial consultant*
Nason, Robert E. *accountant*
Neuhausen, Benjamin Simon *auditor, accountant*
Ott, James Forgan *finance company executive*
†Oulvey, David E. *accountant, brokerage house executive*
Pitts, Robert Eugene, Jr. *marketing educator, consultant*
Rachwalski, Frank Joseph, Jr. *financial executive*
Reilly, Robert Frederick *valuation consultant*
Reiss, Dale Anne *accounting executive*
†Rohlin, Diane Elizabeth *financial public relations executive*
Rosenbaum, Michael A. *investor relations consultant*
Ryan, Leo Vincent *business educator*
Schornack, John James *accountant*
Smith, Freddye L(ee) *financial planner*
Stearns, Neele Edward, Jr. *diversified holding company executive*
†Stelzel, Walter Tell, Jr. *accountant, financial company executive*
Sullivan, Bernard James *accountant*
Thornton, Theodore Kean *investment advisor*
Verschoor, Curtis Carl *business educator, consultant*
Watson, Ben Charles *financial services company executive*
Weil, Roman Lee *accounting educator*
Wishner, Maynard Ira *finance company executive, lawyer*
Yacktman, Donald Arthur *financial executive, investment counselor*
†Zimmerman, Martin E. *financial executive*

De Kalb
Hanna, Nessim *marketing educator*

Decatur
Decker, Charles Richard *business educator*

Deerfield
Boyd, Joseph Don *financial services*
†Donovan, Nancy S. *financial services executive*

Elgin
†Murphy, William Holland *financial executive*

Evanston
Balachandran, Bala Venkataraman *accounting systems educator*
Cassell, Frank Hyde *business educator*
Catlett, George Roudebush *accountant*
Corey, Gordon Richard *financial advisor, former utilities executive*
Duncan, Robert Bannerman *strategy and organizations educator*
Prince, Thomas Richard *accountant, educator*
Revsine, Lawrence *accounting educator, consultant*
Stern, Louis William *marketing educator, consultant*

Freeport
Kleindl, James Nicholas *business educator, consultant*

Geneva
Young, Jack Allison *financial executive*

Itasca
Kendrick, William Monroe *pension manager*

La Grange
Norby, William Charles *financial consultant*

Lake Forest
Reichert, Norman Vernon *financial services consultant*
Van Gorkom, Jerome William *financial executive*
†Vastardis, Anthony George *finance executive*

Lake Zurich
Timbers, Stephen Bryan *financial services company executive*

Lincolnshire
†Ellen, Martin M. *financial services executive*
Macmillan, Douglas Hathaway *financial executive*
O'Connell, Edward Joseph, III *financial executive, accountant*

Long Grove
Mathis, David B. *financial services and insurance company executive*

Naperville
Dranias, Dean Anthony *financial corporation consultant*

Normal
Williams, Michael Roy *marketing research, management educator*

Northbrook
Russell, William Steven *finance executive*

Oak Brook
Schueppert, George Louis *financial executive*
Stonich, Timothy Whitman *financial executive*

Okawville
Schmale, Allen Lee *financial services company executive*

Palatine
Butler, John Musgrave *business financial consultant*
Kasten, Richard John *accountant*

Paris
Russell, Turner Alan *financial executive*

Peoria
Poupard, James J. *controller*

Prospect Heights
Clark, Donald Cameron *financial services company executive*
Larson, Gaylen Nevoy *financial executive*

Rantoul
†Kosick, Howard Allen *accountant, finance executive*

Riverside
Fleck, Gordon Pierce *accounting firm executive*
Perkins, William H., Jr. *finance company executive*

Rockford
†DeLuca, August Frank, Jr. *financial executive*

Rolling Meadows
Bongiorno, John Jacques *financial corporation executive*

Schaumburg
Geiger, Joseph Francis *financial planner*

Skokie
Cunningham, R. John *financial consultant*
Dishman, Leonard I. *accountant*
Pappano, Robert Daniel *corporate treasurer*

Springfield
Travis, Lawrence Allan *accountant*

Urbana
Bedford, Norton Moore *accounting educator*

Villa Park
Grant, Charles Truman *business recapitalization and health care management executive*

Wilmette
Stipp, John Edgar *financial consultant, lawyer*

Winnetka
Fulk, Roscoe Neal *retired accountant*

Wood Dale
Ward, Katheryn Hope *marketing educator and administrator, consultant*

INDIANA

Beech Grove
Clapper, George Raymond *accountant, computer consultant*

Bloomington
Belth, Joseph Morton *retired business educator*
DeHayes, Daniel Wesley *management executive, educator*
Dieterle, Donald Lyle *accountant, educator*
Swanson, Robert Mclean *retired business educator*

Carmel
Pickens, Robert Bruce *accountant*

Columbus
Berman, Lewis Paul *financial executive*
Sales, A. R. *financial executive*

Crown Point
Snearly, Sandra Jo *accountant*

Elkhart
Robinson, Joseph Albert *corporate executive*

Evansville
Brill, Alan Richard *financial executive*
Gaither, John Francis *accountant, consultant*

Goshen
Lehman, Karl Franklyn *accountant*
†Newberry, Richard Alan *corporate executive*

Indianapolis
Brinkerhoff, Tom J. *financial services executive*
Carey, Edward Marshel, Jr. *accounting company executive*
Fisher, Gene Lawrence *financial executive*
Furlow, Mack Vernon, Jr. *financial executive, treasurer*
Goodwin, William Maxwell *financial executive*
Helmkamp, John G. *accounting educator, consultant*
Kaufman, Barton Lowell *financial services company executive*
Khalil, Michael O. *actuary*
Long, Clarence William *accountant*
O'Brien, Frank B. *accounting firm executive*

Notre Dame
Reilly, Frank Kelly *business educator*
Vecchio, Robert Peter *business management educator*

South Bend
†Cohen, Ronald S. *accountant*
Harriman, Gerald Eugene *retired business educator, former university dean*
Wiegand, George Frederick, Sr. *financial services executive*

Terre Haute
Steinbaugh, Robert P. *management and finance educator*

Wabash
Curless, Larry Dean *tax consultant, farm manager*

West Lafayette
Lewellen, Wilbur Garrett *management educator, consultant*

IOWA

Ames
Handy, Charles Brooks *accountant, educator*

Des Moines
†Brinkman, Richard J. financial services company executive
Finley, Gary Roger financial company executive
Hartsook, Larry D. financial executive
Young, Dennis Eugene financial services executive

Iowa City
Collins, Daniel W. accountant, educator
Riesz, Peter Charles marketing educator, consultant

Muscatine
Dvorchak, Thomas Edward financial executive
McMains, Melvin L(ee) controller

Sioux City
Silverberg, David S. financial consultant

Storm Lake
Shafer, Everett Earl business administration educator

Waterloo
Taylor, Lyle Dewey economic development company executive

West Des Moines
Sather, Everett Norman accountant

KANSAS

Emporia
Hashmi, Sajjad Ahmad business educator, university dean

Lawrence
Beedles, William LeRoy finance educator, financial consultant

Lecompton
Conard, John Joseph financial official

Mc Pherson
Hull, Robert Glenn retired financial administrator

Shawnee Mission
Hechler, Robert Lee financial services company executive
Howard, Theodore Walter mutual fund corporation executive

Topeka
McCandless, Barbara J. auditor

Wichita
Knudsen, Darrell G. diversified financial services company executive
Pohlman, Randolph Allen business administration educator, dean
Redman, Peter finance company executive

KENTUCKY

Goshen
Mc Clinton, Donald G. diversified holding company executive

Louisville
Bryant, Oscar Sims, Jr. investment advisor
Daulton, David Coleman actuary

LOUISIANA

Baton Rouge
Bedeian, Arthur George business educator
Booth, George Geoffrey finance educator
Simmons, Dolores Brown finance officer, accountant

Kenner
Scherich, Edward Baptiste retired diversified company executive

Lafayette
Burnam, Paul Wayne accountant, educator

Metairie
†McShan, Clyde Griffin, II financial executive

New Orleans
Hansel, Stephen Arthur holding company executive
Wohleber, Robert Michael treasurer

Thibodaux
Fairchild, Joseph Virgil, Jr. accounting educator

MAINE

Friendship
MacIlvaine, Chalmers Acheson retired financial executive, former association executive

South Portland
†Martin, Joseph Robert financial executive

MARYLAND

Annapolis
McAfee, Lawrance Wiley finance executive

Baltimore
†Ambler, Bruce Melville finance company executive
Barrett, John Anthony printing company financial executive
Blake, Norman Perkins, Jr. finance company executive
Colhoun, Howard Post financial executive
Eanes, Joseph Cabel, Jr. surety company executive
Jacobs, Richard James banker, educator
Kues, Irvin William health care system financial executive
Quinn, Michael Desmond diversified financial services executive
Thomas, Gary Lynn financial executive

Beltsville
Carroll, Stephen John, Jr. business educator

Berlin
Howarth, Thomas tax consultant

Bethesda
Castelli, Alexander Gerard accountant
†Kamerow, Martin Laurence accountant
Lee, John Chonghoon, Sr. financial executive, lawyer, consultant

Chevy Chase
Freeman, Harry Louis financial services company executive

College Park
Kolodny, Richard finance educator

Columbia
Hotchkies, Barry financial executive

Ellicott City
Lakhani, Dilawar accountant, financial planner

Gaithersburg
Boddiger, George Cyrus corporate consultant

Glenwood
Simms, Charles Averill environmental management company executive

Hyattsville
Lovick, Norman accountant

Owings Mills
Kershaw, Robert Alan corporate treasurer

Queenstown
O'Toole, James Joseph business educator

Rockville
Graff, Stuart Leslie accounting executive
Milan, Thomas Lawrence accountant
Ruth, James Perry financial planning executive

Salisbury
Khazeh, Khashayar (Kashi Khazeh) finance educator

Silver Spring
Grubbs, Donald Shaw, Jr. actuary

Woodstock
Price, John Roy, Jr. financial executive

Wye Mills
Schnaitman, William Kenneth finance company executive

MASSACHUSETTS

Allston
Mills, Daniel Quinn business educator, consultant, author
Silk, Alvin John business educator

Bedford
Kouyoumjian, Charles H. diversified financial services company executive
†Wagner, Harvey Alan finance executive

Boston
Akin, Steven Paul financial company executive
Baker, Charles Duane business administration educator, former management executive
Berg, Norman Asplund management educator
Bower, Joseph Lyon business administration educator
Bruns, William John, Jr. business administration educator
Christensen, Carl Roland business administration educator
Christenson, Charles John business educator
Clapp, Eugene Howard, II financial executive
Crook, Robert Wayne mutual funds executive
D'Alessandro, David Francis financial services company executive
DiStasio, James Shannon accountant
Dooley, Arch Richard business administration educator
Eastman, Thomas George investment management executive
Elfner, Albert Henry, III mutual fund management company executive
Gardner, Dorsey Robertson finance company executive
Gifford, Nelson Sage financial company executive
Haber, Robert J. mutual fund manager
Hayes, Robert Herrick technology management educator
Hayes, Samuel Linton, III business educator
Hjerpe, Edward Alfred, III finance and banking executive
Johnson, Edward Crosby, III financial company executive
Kanter, Rosabeth Moss management educator, consultant, writer
Kingman, William Lockwood financial consultant
Kotter, John Paul organizational behavior educator, management consultant
Lane, Harold Edwin retired management educator, consultant
Langermann, John W.R. institutional equity salesperson
Lawrence, Paul Roger retired organizational behavior educator
Lee, Jonathan Owen financial services company executive, lawyer
Leibler, Kenneth Robert financial service executive
Lodge, George C(abot) business administration educator
Lynch, Peter S. retired portfolio manager
Marshall, Martin Vivan business administration educator, business consultant
McFarlan, Franklin Warren business administration educator
†Park, William H(erron) financial executive
Pratt, Albert financial consultant, trustee
†Provost, David Emile financial services executive
Reiling, Henry Bernard business educator
Riley, Robert Edward financial services company executive
Schwartz, Jules Jacob management educator
†Siskind, Paul M. holding company executive
Skinner, Wickham business administration educator
Stevenson, Howard Higginbotham business educator
Stobaugh, Robert Blair business educator, business executive
Temkin, Robert Harvey accountant
Tucker, Richard Lee financial executive
Uyterhoeven, Hugo Emil Robert business educator and consultant
Vatter, Paul August business administration educator, dean
Walton, Richard Eugene business educator
†Webb, Alexander, III portfolio manager
Wheatland, Richard, II fiduciary services executive, museum executive
Wortzel, Lawrence Herbert marketing educator
Young, David William accounting educator

Brighton
Bernstein, Emil Steven financial executive

Brockton
Clark, Carleton Earl tax consultant

Cambridge
Hax, Arnoldo Cubillos management educator, industrial engineer
Leonard, Herman Beukema (Dutch Leonard) public finance and management educator
Little, John Dutton Conant management scientist, educator
†Parker, Sam finance company executive
Pounds, William Frank management educator
Rosenbloom, Richard Selig business administration educator
Safran, Edward Myron financial service company executive

Chestnut Hill
Glynn, Arthur Lawrence business administration and accounting educator

Concord
Smith, Peter Walker finance executive

Dedham
†Lynch, David B. financial executive
Russo, Peter Francis financial executive, accountant

Everett
Jenkins, Alexander, III business executive

Falmouth
Mitchell, Charles Archie financial planning consultant, engineer

Foxboro
†Bush, Raymond T. accountant, corporate professional

Hanover
Hart, Richard Nevel, Jr. finance company executive, financial consultant

Hyannis Port
Ludtke, James Buren business and finance educator

Lexington
Deitcher, Herbert financial executive
Wyss, David Alen financial service executive

Longmeadow
Skelton, Don Richard consulting actuary, retired insurance company executive

Lowell
†Story, Robert P., Jr. financial executive

Needham
Tarsky, Eugene Stanley accountant, management and systems consultant

North Adams
Markou, Peter John business educator, business and tax consultant

Pittsfield
Gregware, James Murray financial planner

Quincy
Pitts, James Atwater financial executive

Salem
Ettinger, Mort marketing educator

South Orleans
Hickok, Richard Sanford accountant

South Yarmouth
Arthur, George Roland accountant,engineer, mathematician

Springfield
†Woods, David Fitzwilliam business, estate and financial planner

Sudbury
Meltzer, Donald Richard treasurer

Taunton
Dykstra, William Henry corporate treasurer

Waltham
Pantazelos, Peter George financial executive

West Springfield
Krach, Mitchell Peter retired financial services executive

Weston
Clayton, Richard Reese holding company executive
Ives, J. Atwood financial executive
Rockwell, George Barcus financial consultant

Wilmington
Bartlett, John Bruen financial executive

Worcester
Graf, Robert Arlan financial services executive
Greenberg, Nathan accountant

MICHIGAN

Ann Arbor
Cornelius, Kenneth Cremer, Jr. finance executive
Crawford, Charles Merle business administration educator
Foster, Alan Herbert financial consultant
Griffin, Carleton Hadlock accountant, educator
Huntington, Curtis Edward actuary
Kim, E. Han finance and business administration educator
Pierpont, Wilbur K. retired acounting educator
Smith, Gary Allen portfolio manager

Battle Creek
Fritz, William Warren accountant, foundation executive

Bingham Farms
Garpow, James Edward financial executive

Birmingham
Catallo, Clarence Guerrino, Jr. financial services company executive

Bloomfield Hills
Cooper, John Arnold financial analyst
Forrester, Alan McKay capital company executive
Marks, Craig management educator, consultant, engineer
Poth, Stefan Michael retired sales financing company executive
Sillman, Herbert Phillip accounting firm executive

Dearborn
Czarnecki, Richard Edward business educator
Odom, William E. automobile finance company executive

Detroit
Adams, William Johnston financial and tax consultant
Baumann, Gary Joseph accountant
Bergeron, Jeffrey David accountant
Dunham, Frank L. accounting company executive
Halperin, Jerome Yale accountant
Krauss, Charles A(nthony), Jr. finance company executive
Massura, Edward Anthony accountant
Nicholson, George Albert, Jr. financial analyst

East Lansing
Sollenberger, Harold Myers accounting educator

Farmington Hills
Fox, Dean Frederick coporate executive

Flint
Rappleye, Richard Kent financial executive, consultant, educator

Holland
†Miglore, Joseph James financial executive

Lansing
Anderton, James Franklin, IV holdings company executive

Lapeer
†Galas, Thomas A. financial executive

Marquette
Camerius, James Walter marketing educator, corporate researcher

Monroe
†Mlocek, Sister Frances Angeline finance director

Okemos
Oberg, Roger Winston management educator

Orchard Lake
Haven, Thomas Kenneth financial consultant
Ingram, Robert John business education educator

Rochester
Horwitz, Ronald M. business administration educator

Saginaw
Doud, Kenneth Eugene, Jr. accountant
Kern, Franklin Lorenz auditor

Southfield
Cantwell, Dennis Michael finance company executive
Peiser, Robert Alan financial executive
Tierney, John Patrick financial services executive

Stanwood
Cawthorne, Kenneth Clifford financial planner

Traverse City
Taylor, Donald Arthur marketing educator

Troy
Wetstein, Gary M. accountant, company executive

Warren
Valerio, Michael Anthony financial executive

West Bloomfield
†Dobb, Barbara Jeane accountant

Ypsilanti
Robek, Mary Frances *business education educator*

MINNESOTA

Hopkins
Haugen, Gerald Alan *financial consultant*

Maple Plain
Larson, Mark Allan *financial executive*

Minneapolis
†Bartkowski, William Patrick *finance company executive*
Berry, David J. *financial services company executive*
†Berryman, Robert Glen *accounting educator, consultant*
†Carpenter, Marshall Le Roy *corporation financial executive*
Diracles, John Michael, Jr. *financial executive*
Falker, John Richard *investor relations counsel*
Hoffmann, Thomas Russell *business management educator*
Jones, Norman M. *finance executive*
King, Richard Harding *financial consultant, retired food processing company executive*
Kinney, Earl Robert *mutual funds company executive*
Miller, Donald Muxlow *accountant, administrator*
Montgomery, Henry Irving *financial planner*
Pillsbury, George Sturgis *investment adviser*
Rudelius, William *marketing educator*
†Saunders, R. Reed *financial services company executive*
†Shipp, Roger Lee *finance company executive*
Sorbo, Allen Jon *actuary, consultant*
Thornton, John T. *corporate financial executive*
Viera, James Joseph *financial executive*
Weiss, James Michael *financial analyst, portfolio manager*

Minnetonka
†Sorensen, Stuart L. *actuary*

Nisswa
Marmas, James Gust *retired businees educator, retired college dean*

Saint Paul
†Bothun, Donald Dean *controller*
Dalton, Howard Edward *accounting executive*
Halverson, Richard Paul *investment management company executive*
Palmer, Roger Raymond *accounting educator*
Reardon, Robert Joseph *financial corporation executive*
Vaughn, John Rolland *auditor*
Zammit, John P. *financial planner*

MISSISSIPPI

Bay Saint Louis
Sidders, Patrick Michael *financial executive*

Jackson
Watts, John McCleave *financial services executive*

Mississippi State
Nash, Henry Warren *marketing educator*

Ocean Springs
Bates, Mable Johnson *business technology educator*

MISSOURI

Blue Springs
†Foudree, Charles M. *financial executive*

Chesterfield
Bradshaw, Stanley J. *financial holding company executive*
Henry, Roy Monroe *financial planner*
Liggett, Hiram Shaw, Jr. *retired diversified industry financial executive*
Neiner, A(ndrew) Joseph *corporate executive*
†Turley, Clarence M. *finance company executive*
Unterreiner, C. Martin *financial advisor*

Clinton
†Schemenauer, Robert George *accountant, state representative*

Columbia
Nikolai, Loren Alfred *accounting educator, author*
Silvoso, Joseph Anton *accounting educator*
Wagner, William Burdette *business educator*

Crestwood
Reitter, Charles Andrew *personal financial planner*

Kansas City
Bloch, Henry Wollman *tax preparation company executive*
Bloch, Thomas Morton *tax company executive*
†Hall, Beth Shand *holding company executive*
Hoffman, Alfred John *mutual fund executive*
†Ramsey, Craig Ray *financial officer*
Sexton, Donald Lee *business administration educator*

Saint Louis
Baloff, Nicholas *business educator, consultant*
Bloemer, Rosemary Celeste *bookkeeper*
Butler, James Lawrence *financial planner*
Dill, Virginia S. *accountant*
Frederick, William Sherrad *manufacturing and retailing company executive*
†Gunn, Russell C. *financial services company executive*
Hewitt, Thomas Edward *financial executive*
Jones, Wilbur Boardman, Jr. *trust company executive*
Kniffen, Jan Rogers *finance executive*
Lamoreux, Frederick Holmes *financial executive*
†Liese, Christopher A. *benefits and financial consulting company owner, state legislator*
Maguire, John Patrick *investment company executive*

---

†Mueller, David Brian *accountant, chief financial officer*
Nemanick, Richard Charles *business executive*
Normile, Michael T. *treasurer*
Roberts, Hugh Evan *business investment services company executive*
Schmidt, Robert Charles, Jr. *finance company executive*
Shapiro, Harold Benjamin *accountant*
Shepperd, Thomas Eugene *accountant*
Thompson, James David *financial services company executive, lawyer*
Walsh, John E., Jr. *business educator, consultant*
Wilson, Betty May *finance company executive*

Springfield
Abraham, Yohannan *management educator*

MONTANA

Great Falls
Christiaens, Chris (Bernard F. Christiaens) *financial analyst, senator*

NEBRASKA

Chadron
Scott, Jerry Don *management and marketing educator*

Fremont
Dunklau, Rupert Louis *personal investments consultant*

Gibbon
Wiley, Ronald LeRoy *financial executive*

Lincoln
Broman, Keith Leroy *finance educator, financial planner*
Cederberg, John Edwin *accountant*
Digman, Lester Aloysius *management educator*
Johnson, Margaret Kathleen *business educator*
Schwendiman, Gary *business administration educator*

Norfolk
Wehrer, Charles Siecke *business educator*

Omaha
Erickson, James Paul *financial service company executive*
Krogstad, Jack Lynn *accounting educator*

NEVADA

Carson City
Larson, Gerald Lee *auditor*

Incline Village
Diederich, J(ohn) William *financial consultant*
Henderson, Paul Bargas, Jr. *economic development consultant*

Las Vegas
Bradshaw, Ira Webb *accountant*

Reno
Neidert, Kalo Edward *accountant, educator*

NEW HAMPSHIRE

Concord
Currie, Glenn Kenneth *financial consultant*

Gilmanton
Osler, Howard Lloyd *controller*

Hampton
Rizzo, Richard David *financial service company executive*

Hanover
Deshpandé, Rohit *marketing educator*
Montgomery, William J. *finance company executive*

Manchester
Epstein, William Stuart *financial executive, trust company executive*

Nashua
Perkins, George William, II *financial services executive, film producer*

NEW JERSEY

Avon By The Sea
Bruno, Grace Angelia *accountant, educator*

Bay Head
Benning, Joseph Francis, Jr. *portfolio manager, financial analyst*

Bridgewater
Cohen, Walter Stanley *accountant, financial consultant*

Camden
Rapaport, Robert M. *financial executive*

Cherry Hill
Newell, Eric James *financial planner, tax consultant, former insurance executive*

Clifton
†Bubba, Joseph L. *financial advisor, state senator*

Clinton
Boyland, Joseph Francis *corporate controller*

Convent Station
Wright, Robert Burroughs *financial consultant*

Denville
†Kimmel, Betty *chief executive officer*

Eatontown
Van Winkle, William *financial planner*

Fairfield
MacKinnon, Walter Allan *employee benefits administration company executive*

Flemington
Russo, Wenona Berrie *business educator*

Glen Rock
Fine, Seymour Howard *marketing educator, lecturer, author, consultant*

Hackensack
Mehta, Jay *financial executive*

Haddonfield
LaBarge, Richard Allen *financial analyst, educator*

Hoboken
Jurkat, Martin Peter *management educator*

Iselin
Hecht, William David *accountant*
Shaw, Alan John *manufacturing and financial corporation executive*

Jackson
Hagberg, Carl Thomas *financial executive*

Jersey City
Dubin, Michael *financial services executive*
Fortune, Robert Russell *financial consultant*
Tognino, John Nicholas *financial services executive*

Liberty Corner
Rajani, Prem Rajaram *transportation company financial executive*

Lincroft
Keenan, Robert Anthony *financial services company executive, educator, consultant*

Mahwah
Carey, William Joseph *retired controller*

Matawan
Kesselman, Bruce Alan *marketing executive, consultant*

Metuchen
Cangemi, Michael Paul *accountant, financial executive*

Monmouth Beach
Herbert, LeRoy James *retired accounting firm executive*

Montvale
Brecht, Warren Frederick *business executive*
†Pitkowsky, Murray *financial executive*

Montville
Klapper, Byron D. *financial company executive*

Morristown
Hesselink, Ann Patrice *financial executive, lawyer*

Mount Laurel
Laubach, Roger Alvin *accountant*

Mountain Lakes
†Hubert, Bernhard *computer company financial executive*

Murray Hill
†Rayner, Robert Martin *financial executive*

New Brunswick
Lee, Cheng-few *finance educator*

New Providence
Symanski, Robert Anthony *treasurer*

Newark
Arabie, Phipps *marketing educator, researcher*
†Gilboy, Thomas V. *financial executive*
Rosenberg, Jerry Martin *business administration educator*

Paramus
Ross, William *financial planner*

Parsippany
Laskowski, Robert Anthony *financial executive*

Phillipsburg
Paige, Richard Bruce *financial information executive*

Pleasantville
Fabietti, Victor Armando *accountant*

Princeton
Appelbaum, Michael Arthur *finance company executive*
Goldman, Clifford Alan *financial advisor*
Harvey, Norman Ronald *finance company executive*
Henkel, William *financial services executive*
Kemmerer, Peter Ream *financial executive*
Tabell, Anthony *financial analyst*

Red Bank
McCann, John Francis *financial services company executive*
Silverman, Herbert R. *corporate financial executive*

Ridgewood
McBride, William Bernard *treasurer*

River Edge
Gass, Manus M. *accountant, business executive*

Roseland
†McElwee, Andrew Allison *finance executive, lawyer*

Rumson
Alexander, Nicholas Anthony *accounting executive*

Rutherford
Liptak, Irene Frances *retired business executive*

Secaucus
Ryan, Daniel Nolan *financial corporation executive*

Short Hills
Mebane, William Black *controller, financial consultant*
Soderlind, Sterling Eugene *newspaper industry consultant*

Southampton
Knortz, Walter Robert *accountant, former insurance company executive*

Summit
Batzer, R. Kirk *accountant*
Vogel, Julius *consulting actuary, former insurance company executive*

Sussex
Sekula, Edward Joseph, Jr. *financial executive*

Teaneck
Forson, Norman Ray *controller*

Tenafly
Lilley, Theodore Robert *financial executive*

Waldwick
Surdoval, Donald James *accounting and management consulting company executive*

Warren
Hartman, David Gardiner *actuary*

West Paterson
Kaufman, Allan M. *actuary, consultant*

Westfield
Boutillier, Robert John *accountant*
Connolly, Ronald Cavanagh *financial services executive*

White House Station
Atieh, Michael Gerard *accountant*

Wyckoff
Abdelrahman, Talaat Ahmad Mohammad *financial executive*

NEW MEXICO

Las Cruces
Peterson, Robin Tucker *marketing educator*

Santa Fe
Watkins, Stephen Edward *accountant*

NEW YORK

Albany
Blount, Stanley Freeman *marketing educator*
Holstein, William Kurt *business administration educator*
†Langlitz, Harold N. *pension fund administrator*
Riley, Victor J., Jr. *financial services company executive*

Amherst
Jen, Frank Chifeng *finance and management educator*

Armonk
Godfrey, Robert R. *financial services executive*

Bedford
Ruppel, George Robert *accountant*

Binghamton
Piaker, Philip Martin *accountant, educator*
Shillestad, John Gardner *financial services company executive*

Bronx
Stuhr, David Paul *business educator, consultant*

Bronxville
Jordan, Louis Hampton *retired accounting educator*
Martin, R. Keith *business and information systems educator, consultant*

Brooklyn
DeBock, Florent Alphonse *controller*
Fischman, Myrna Leah *accountant, educator*
Gordon, Conrad J. *financial executive*
Kunjukunju, Pappy *insurance company financial executive*
Sands, Edith Sylvia Abeloff (Mrs. Abraham M. Sands) *finance educator, author*

Buffalo
Draper, Verden Rolland *accountant*
Flint, Mark Addison *financial executive*
Gruen, David Henry *financial executive, consultant*
Jacobs, Jeremy M. *diversified holding company executive, hockey team owner*
Koontz, Eldon Ray *financial consultant*
†Layton, Rodney Eugene *controller, newspaper executive*

Canton
Pollard, Fred Don *finance company executive*

Chappaqua
Cronin, Raymond Valentine *financial executive*

Chittenango
Cassell, William Walter *retired accounting operations consultant*

Commack
Nelson, Marvin Bernard *financial executive*

East Garden City
Baker, J. A., II *pension architect and plan engineer*

East Hampton
Dalzell, Fred Briggs *consultant*

East Rochester
Murray, James Doyle *accountant*

Floral Park
†Moskowitz, Stanley Alan *financial executive*

Forest Hills
Phelan, Arthur Joseph *financial executive*

Great Neck
Reich, Pauline Carole *international business consultant, author*
†Rubin, Michael *accountant, finance company executive*

Hampton Bays
Yavitz, Boris *business educator and dean emeritus*

Harrison
Serenbetz, Warren Lewis *financial management company executive*

Hastings On Hudson
Shillinglaw, Gordon *accounting educator, consultant, writer*

Hauppauge
†Stoehr, Charles Michael *financial executive*

Hempstead
Montana, Patrick Joseph *management educator*

Huntington
Hayden, Ralph Frederick *accountant, financial consultant*

Huntington Station
Herz, Leonard *financial consultant*

Ithaca
Brunk, Max Edwin *marketing educator emeritus*
Dyckman, Thomas Richard *accounting educator*
Geller, A. Neal *business educator, financial consultant*
Van Houtte, Raymond A. *financial executive*

Jamaica
Aiken, William *accountant*

Kew Gardens
Schnakenberg, Donald G. *financial administrator*

Lake Success
Chafitz, Alan Herbert *financial services company executive*

Larchmont
Fletcher, Denise Koen *strategic and financial consultant*

Long Island City
Brustein, Lawrence *financial executive*

Massapequa
Hughes, Spencer Edward, Jr. *financial executive, consultant*

Merrick
Beckman, Judith Kalb *financial counselor and planner, educator, writer*

Mount Kisco
Keesee, Thomas Woodfin, Jr. *financial consultant*

New Hyde Park
Richards, Bernard *investment company executive*

New Rochelle
Brodie, Norman *retired financial actuary*

New York
Alexander, Barbara Toll *investment banker*
Alper, Merlin Lionel *financial executive*
†Altfest, Lewis Jay *financial and investment advisor*
Altman, Edward Ira *finance educator, consultant, editor*
Anderson, Theodore Wellington *portfolio strategist*
Assael, Henry *marketing educator*
Atwater, Verne Stafford *finance educator*
Auriemmo, Frank Joseph, Jr. *financial holding company executive*
Bains, Harrison MacKellar, Jr. *financial executive*
Baldasaro, P. Michael *tax consultant*
Barnett, Bernard *accountant*
Barry, Mary Alice *retired financial executive*
Belknap, Robert Ernest, III *investment counselor*
Beller, Gary A. *financial services company executive, lawyer*
Berger, Bruce *finance and information services consultant*
Berger, Stephen *financial services company executive*
Berliner, William Michael *business educator*
†Betley, John R. *accountant*
Birch, William Dunham, Jr. *asset manager*
Borelli, Francis J(oseph) (Frank Borelli) *insurance brokerage and consulting firm financial executive*
Borenstein, Abe Isaac *securities industry executive*
Bovin, Denis Alan *finance company executive*
†Boyarski, Joel I. *financial executive*
Brennan, Daniel L. *accounting, consulting firm executive*
Briloff, Abraham Jacob *accountant, educator*
Brocksmith, James G., Jr. *accounting, management consulting firm executive*
Brofman, Lance Mark *portfolio manager, mutual fund executive*
Brooke, Paul Alan *finance company executive*
Bruggeman, Terrance John *corporate executive*
Butterfield, R. Keith *financial company executive*
Byington, Homer Morrison, III *financial consultant*
Caldwell, Philip *financial services company executive, retired automobile manufacturing company executive*
Cantor, Bernard Gerald *financial executive*
Carroll, Thomas Joseph *investment services company executive*
Carthaus, James Arthur *financial service company executive*
Chang, Robert Timothy *fixed-income researcher, consultant*
Chapman, Peter Herbert *investment company executive*
Chenault, Kenneth Irvine *financial services company executive*
Chiarelli, Joseph *accountant, banker*
Claire, Thomas Andrew *treasurer*
Clark, Howard Longstreth, Jr. *finance company executive*
Clauson, James Wilson *accountant*
†Clayton, Jon Kerry *holding company executive*
Cohen, Burton Jerome *financial service executive*
Colby, Marvelle Seitman *business management educator, administrator*
Connor, Joseph E. *accountant*
†Cornstein, David B. *finance executive*
Corr, Gary Alan *finance company executive*
Cotter, Ernest Robert, III *finance company executive*
Cumming, Ian M. *holding company executive*
Curtis, Robert Joseph *financial advisor*
Daley, James E. *accounting firm executive*
Daly, John Neal *investment company executive*
DeMartini, Richard Michael *financial services company executive*
Deupree, Marvin Mattox *business consultant, accountant*
Dimon, James *financial services executive*
†Dirks, Dennis John *financial services executive*
Donaldson, William Henry *financial executive*
†Edelman, Asher Barry *financier*
Edwards, James D. *accounting company executive*
Eforo, John Francis *financial officer*
Eig, Norman *investment company executive*
†Eisner, Richard Alan *accountant*
Emmerman, Michael N *financial analyst*
Erosh, William Daniel *financial services company executive*
Eveillard, Jean-Marie *financial company executive*
Farley, James Bernard *financial services company executive*
Farley, Peggy Ann *finance company executive*
Fishman, Jay Steven *financial services executive*
Fitilis, Theodore Nicholas *portfolio manager*
†Foresman, Bruce Chalfin *treasurer*
Freeburg, Richard Gorman *financial derivatives company executive*
Freedman, Eugene M. *accounting firm executive*
Freiberg, Lowell Carl *financial executive*
Frimerman, Leslie *financial services company executive*
Froewiss, Kenneth Clark *corporate finance executive*
Frommer, Henry *financial executive*
Frost, Robert *financial consulting firm executive*
Garba, Edward Aloysius *financial executive*
Gargana, John Joseph, Jr. *mutual funds executive*
Garrett, Robert *financial advisory executive*
Gaughan, Eugene Francis *accountant*
Geraghty, Kenneth George *financial services company executive*
Gill, Ardian C. *actuary*
Gladstone, William Louis *accountant*
Glynn, Gary Allen *pension fund executive*
Goldberg, Edward L. *financial services executive*
Golden, William Theodore *corporate executive*
Goldman, Robert Irving *financial services company executive*
Goldschmidt, Robert Alphonse *financial executive*
Goldstein, Fred *accountant*
Gollin, Stuart Allen *accountant*
Golub, Harvey *financial services company executive*
Graf, Peter Gustav *accountant, lawyer*
Green, David O. *accounting educator, educational administrator*
Grisi, Jeanmarie Conte *finance executive*
Groves, Ray John *accountant*
†Hajim, Edmund A. *financial services executive*
Halloran, Leo Augustine *retired financial executive*
†Harfst, Jeffrey Loren *accountant*
Harrison, Gilbert Warner *investment banker*
Harrison, John Alexander *financial executive*
Hazen, William Harris *finance executive*
†Hemsley, Maarten D. *business financial executive*
†Hennesey, John M. *diversified financial servies company executive*
Herrera, Paul Fredrick *accountant*
Hewitt, Dennis Edwin *financial executive*
Hibel, Bernard *financial consultant, former apparel company executive*
Hickman, J. Kenneth *accounting company executive*
Horner, Larry Dean *retired accounting firm executive, brokerage firm executive*
Jacey, Charles Frederick, Jr. *accounting company executive, consultant*
Jacobs, Mark Neil *financial services corporation executive, lawyer*
Johnson, Clarke Courtney *finance educator*
Johnson, Freda S. *public finance consultant*
Johnson, J. Chester *financial executive, poet*
Joseph, Michael Sarkies *accountant*
Karpen, Marian Joan *financial executive*
Kaye, Walter *financial executive*
Kelly, Robert J. *accounting firm executive*
Kenney, Jerome P. *finance company executive*
†Kobayashi, Hisao *financial company executive*
Koeppel, Noel Immanuel *financial planner, securities and real estate broker*
Kolb, Jerry Wilbert *accountant*
Kolesar, Peter John *business and engineering educator*
Kopelman, Richard Eric *management educator*
Kotecha, Mahesh Kanjibhai *financial guarantee insurance company executive*
Kovalcik, Kenneth John *accountant*
†Krat, Gary Walden *financial services company executive*
Kravis, Henry R. *venture financier*
Ladjevardi, Hamid *fund manager*
Langer, Horst *financial corporate executive*
Larkins, Gary Thomas *accountant*
Layer, Meredith Mitchum *financial services company executive, public responsibility professional*
Leaf, Roger Warren *business consultant*
Lebouitz, Martin Frederick *financial services industry executive, consultant*
Libby, John Kelway *financial services company executive*
Lieberman, Gail Forman *finance executive*
†Lipton, William James *accountant, lawyer*
†Livnat, Joshua *accounting educator, consultant*
Loeb, Peter Kenneth *money manager*
Loss, Stuart Harold *financial executive*
Lowenthal, Jacob *finance executive*
Lucido, Louis Charles *finance company executive*
MacHale, Joseph P. *financial executive*
Madden, Michael Daniel *finance company executive*
Madonna, Jon C. *accounting firm executive*
Mankin, Robert Stephen *financial executive*
Mantell, Lester J. *business executive*
Martinez, Roman, IV *financial executive*
Mathes, Sorrell Mark *investment banker*
Matthews, Westina L. *finance and banking executive*
Maurer, Jeffrey Stuart *finance executive*
McBride, Rodney Lester *investment counselor*
McCaffrey, William Thomas *financial services company executive*
McCandless, Stephen Porter *financial executive*
McCarthy, Bryant *accounting firm executive*
McDonald, James L. *accounting firm executive*
†McGraw, Harold Whittlesey, III (Terry McGraw) *financial services company executive*
Mc Gruder, Stephen Jones *portfolio manager*
McKessy, Stephen W. *accounting firm executive*
Miller, Donald Keith *asset management executive*
Miller, Neil S. *financial officer, advertising executive*
†Miller, Robert A. *finance company executive*
Monaco, Michael P. *finance company executive*
Morrow, E. Frederic *consultant, retired banker*
Mortimer, Henry Tilford, Jr. *financial assurance executive*
Mosse, Peter John Charles *financial services executive*
†Murchie, Edward Michael *accountant*
Nadel, Elliott *investment firm executive*
Nayden, Denis J. *diversified financial services company executive*
Neff, Robert Arthur *business and financial executive*
Norman, Stephen Peckham *financial services company executive*
O'Brien, William K. *accounting firm executive*
O'Malley, Shaun F. *accounting firm executive*
Peritz, Abraham Daniel *business executive*
Pitti, Donald Robert *financial service company executive*
Posner, Roy Edward *finance executive*
Powers, Richard F., III *finance company executive*
Purcell, Philip James *financial services company executive*
Pyle, Robert Milner, Jr. *financial services company executive*
Rein, Catherine Amelia *financial services executive, lawyer*
Rinaldini, Luis Emilio *investment banker*
Ritch, Herald LaVern *finance company executive*
Roberts, John J. *accounting firm executive*
Robinson, James Dixon, III *corporate executive*
Robinson, Robert Armstrong *pension fund executive*
†Roche, Kevin Joseph *finance executive*
Roethenmund, Otto Emil *financial and banking executive*
Rosenberg, Michael Joseph *financial executive*
†Rosenthal, Imre *financial company executive*
Ross, Coleman DeVane *accountant, insurance company consultant*
Salomon, Robert S., Jr. *portfolio manager*
Salzman, Robert Jay *accountant*
Sandalls, William Thomas, Jr. *financial services company executive*
Sarver, Eugene *finance educator*
Scanlon, Peter Redmond *accountant*
Segal, Martin Eli *retired actuarial and consulting company executive*
Shapoff, Stephen H. *financial executive*
Shaw, Alan Roger *financial executive, educator*
Shern, Stephanie Marie *accountant*
Siguler, George William *financial services executive*
Skwiersky, Paul *accountant*
Smith, Paul Thomas *financial services company executive*
Smith, Winthrop Hiram, Jr. *financial services executive*
†Soldatos, Paul W. *holding company executive*
Soros, George *fund management executive*
Sorter, George Hans *accounting and law educator, consultant*
Starr, Martin Kenneth *management educator*
Stein, Howard *mutual fund executive*
Stephens, Lester John, Jr. *corporate controller*
Stiefler, Jeffrey E. *financial services executive*
Stockman, David Allen *former federal official, congressman, financier*
Stone, David Kendall *financial executive*
Stovall, Robert H(enry) *money management company executive*
Syron, Richard Francis *financial services executive, economist*
Tarantino, Dominic A. *accounting firm executive*
Tavel, Mark Kivey *money management company executive, economist*
Udcoff, George Joseph *financial executive*
Volk, Norman Hans *financial executive*
Walsh, Thomas Gerard *actuary*
Weinbach, Lawrence Allen *accounting executive*
Wiener, Robert Alvin *accountant*
Wieser, Charles Edward *financial consultant*
†Wood, Robert Elkington, II *financial services company executive*
Woodward, M. Cabell, Jr. *financial executive*
Wright, Richard John *business executive*
Zand, Dale Ezra *business management educator*

Newburgh
Apuzzo, Gloria Isabel *accountant*

Pittsford
†Herge, Henry Curtis, Jr. *consulting firm executive*

Plainview
Brill, Steven Charles *financial advisor, lawyer*

Pleasantville
Reps, David Nathan *finance educator*

Port Washington
Sonnenfeldt, Richard Wolfgang *business educator*

Poughkeepsie
Henley, Richard James *healthcare institution administrative and financial officer*

Pound Ridge
Webb, Richard Gilbert *financial executive*

Purchase
Lessin, Andrew Richard *accounting executive*
Noonan, Frank R. *business executive*

Queens
Curzio, Francis Xavier *finance company executive*

Queensbury
Lake, William Thomas *financial consultant*

Rochester
Balderston, William, III *retired banker*
Olson, Russell L. *pension fund administrator*

Roslyn
Verdi, Philip Paul *credit card company executive*

Rye
Beldock, Donald Travis *financial executive*

Syracuse
Marcoccia, Louis Gary *accountant, university administrator*

Tarrytown
Ferrari, Robert Joseph *business educator, former banker*

Thornwood
Chin, Carolyn Sue *business executive*

Wappingers Falls
Hogan, Edward Robert *financial services executive*

Webster
Garg, Devendra *financial executive*
Nicholson, Douglas Robert *accountant*

Yonkers
Augustine, John *accountant*

York
Coleman, David Cecil *financial executive*

NORTH CAROLINA

Boone
Bowden, Elbert Victor *banking, finance and economics author and educator*

Chapel Hill
Brummet, Richard Lee *accounting educator*
Langenderfer, Harold Quentin *accountant, educator*
Perreault, William Daniel, Jr. *business administration educator*
Rosen, Benson *business administration educator*

Charlotte
Anderson, Gerald Leslie *financial executive*
Boyd, Edward Lee *financial executive*
Brigden, Richard Nevius *financial executive*
Smith, James Copeland *controller*
Vane, Terence G., Jr. *finance and insurance company executive, lawyer*
Wentz, Billy Melvin, Jr. *finance executive*

Durham
Bettman, James Ross *management educator*
Staelin, Richard *business administration educator*

Greensboro
Compton, John Carroll *accountant*
Mecimore, Charles Douglas *accounting educator*

Greenville
Hines, Danny Ray *accountant, educator*

Hickory
†Knedlik, Ronald W. *food wholesale and retail executive*

High Point
Johnson, Richard Arthur *factoring credit executive*

Jacksonville
Hutto, James Calhoun *retired financial executive*

New Bern
Degnan, Herbert Raymond *financial executive, lawyer, accountant*

North Wilkesboro
Underwood, Harry Burnham, II *financial executive, accountant*

Raleigh
Glass, Margaret Smyllie *corporate treasurer, lawyer*
Jessen, David Wayne *accountant*

Research Triangle Park
Hagan, John Aubrey *financial executive*

Saxapahaw
Bulla, Ben F. *treasurer*

Weaverville
Boyce, Emily Stewart *retired library and information science educator*

Wilmington
Wade, James Michael *treasurer*

Winston Salem
Mackey, Dallas L. *financial consultant, development officer*

OHIO

Ada
Cooper, Ken Errol *management educator*

Akron
Crawford, Robert John *credit company executive*
Krause, David James *accountant, transportation company executive*
†Ray, Roy Lee *public finance consultant, state legislator*

Alliance
Rockhill, Jack Kerrigan *collections company executive*

Ashland
Cox, Harry Seymour *financial executive*

Athens
Miller, Peggy McLaren *management educator*
Patterson, Harlan Ray *finance educator*
Rakes, Ganas Kaye *finance and banking educator*

Canton
Warner, E. John *manufacturing financial executive*

Chagrin Falls
Strachan, Donald M. *accountant*

Cincinnati
Black, David deLaine *investment consultant*
Carroll, Robert Henry *accountant*
Conaton, Michael Joseph *financial service executive*
DeBrunner, Gerald Joseph *accounting firm executive*
Hayden, Joseph Page, Jr. *finance company executive*
Lawson, Randall Clayton, II *financial executive*
Lindner, Robert David *finance company executive*
Lintz, Robert Carroll *financial holding company executive*
Mantel, Samuel Joseph, Jr. *management educator, consultant*
Sedgwick-Hirsch, Carol Elizabeth *financial executive*
Siekmann, Donald Charles *accountant*
Ullman, Louis Jay *financial executive*
Walker, Michael Claude *finance educator*
Watts, Barbara Gayle *law academic administrator*

Cleveland
Cannon, Norman Lawrence *treasurer*
Dossey, Richard L. *accountant*
Easton, John Edward *accountant, financial executive*
Gelfand, Ivan *investment advisor*
†Goehler, James Lawrence *finance company executive*
Koch, Charles John *credit agency executive*
Lampl, Jack Willard, Jr. *retired finance company executive*
Mayne, Lucille Stringer *finance educator*
Roberts, James Owen *financial planning executive*
Stratton-Crooke, Thomas Edward *financial consultant*

Columbus
Bentz, William Frederick *accounting educator*
Berry, William Lee *business administration educator*
Gerber, William Kenton *financial executive*
Ginter, James Lee *business educator, researcher, consultant*
Grapski, Ladd Raymond *accountant*
†Kyees, John Edward *apparel company executive*
McMaster, Robert Raymond *accountant*
Shook, Robert Louis *business writer*
†Sofranko, Joel E. *pension fund administrator*
String, John F. *financial executive*
Tomassini, Lawrence Anthony *accounting educator, consultant*
Trimble, Marian Alice Eddy *mutual fund executive*

Cuyahoga Falls
Moses, Abe Joseph *international financial consultant*

Dayton
Hoge, Franz Joseph *accounting firm executive*
Walden, James William *accountant, educator*

Dublin
Madigan, Joseph Edward *financial executive, consultant, director*

Harrison
Kocher, Juanita Fay *auditor*

Holland
Kennedy, James L. *accountant*

Lakewood
Seaton, Robert Finlayson *planned giving consultant*

Lancaster
Voss, Jack Donald *international business consultant, lawyer*

Maumee
Tigges, Kenneth Edwin *retired financial executive*

North Canton
Lynham, C(harles) Richard *foundry company executive*

Oxford
Goodell, George Sidney *finance educator*

Painesville
Clement, Daniel Roy, III *accountant, assistant nurse, small business owner*

Pepper Pike
Stroesenreuther, George Dale *financial executive*

Perrysburg
Barbe, Betty Catherine *financial analyst*

Spring Valley
Singhvi, Surendra Singh *finance and strategy consultant*

Toledo
Hartmann, Ann Wilson *financial planner*

---

†Shultz, Edward Joseph *holdings company executive*

OKLAHOMA

Edmond
Ashford, George Allen *financial planner*

Norman
Cosier, Richard A. *business educator, consultant*
Lis, Anthony Stanley *business administration educator*

Oklahoma City
Harrington, Gary Burnes *controller*
Tolbert, James R., III *financial executive*

Tulsa
Bowen, William Augustus *financial consultant*

OREGON

Eugene
Mowday, Richard Thomas *management educator*

Grants Pass
Smith, Barnard Elliot *management educator*

Marylhurst
Kelley, George Gregory *business educator, management consultant*

Portland
Cateora, Philip Rene *business educator, author*
Jacob, Nancy Louise *financial consultant*
†Lanz, Robert Francis *corporate financial officer*
†Peressini, William Edward *financial services executive*
Weber, George Richard *financial consultant, writer*

PENNSYLVANIA

Allentown
Heitmann, George Joseph *business educator, consultant*

Allison Park
LaDow, C. Stuart *consultant financial services*

Bala Cynwyd
Miller, L. Martin *accountant, financial planning specialist*

Bethlehem
Barsness, Richard Webster *management educator, administrator*
Connors, Leo Gerard *consultant, former finance company executive*
Hobbs, James Beverly *business administration educator, writer*

Blue Bell
Yuhas, Alan Thomas *investment management executive*

Camp Hill
Robinson, Ronald Michael *health care financial executive, financial consultant*
Sullivan, Barry Michael *finance executive*

Chester
Lederer-Antonucci, Yvonne *management information educator, consultant*

Dover
Hayek, William Edward *investment counsel, financial consultant*

Durham
†Dean, Frederick Bernard *holding company executive*

Elizabethtown
Hoy, Harold Joseph *marketing educator, retail executive, management consultant*

Gladwyne
Booth, Harold Waverly *finance and investment company executive, lawyer*

Glenshaw
†Ghaznavi, John Jahangir *investment company executive*

Harrisburg
Alexander, William Herbert *business educator, former construction company executive, former army officer*

Haverford
Merrill, Arthur Alexander *financial analyst*

Havertown
Brinker, Thomas Michael *finance executive*

Horsham
Alter, Dennis *holding company executive*
Wesselink, David Duwayne *finance company executive*

Lafayette Hill
King, Leon *financial services executive*

Lancaster
Freeman, Clarence Calvin *financial executive*

Murrysville
McWhirter, James Herman *consulting engineering business executive, financial planner*

Newtown Square
Graf, Arnold Harold *employee benefits executive, financial planner*

Steinman, Robert Cleeton *accountant*

Paoli
Gotshall, Jan Doyle *financial planner*
Hancox, Robert Ernest *financial services company executive*

Philadelphia
Abel, Andrew Bruce *finance and economics educator*
Anderson, Rolph Ely *marketing educator*
Babbel, David Frederick *finance educator*
Blicher, Bert *finance company executive*
Blume, Marshall Edward *finance educator*
Bowman, Edward Harry *business science educator*
Cox, Douglas Lynn *financial service executive*
Friedman, Sidney A. *financial services executive*
Giese, William Herbert *tax accountant*
Goodman, Charles Schaffner *marketing educator*
Gorenberg, Charles Lloyd *financial services executive*
Hess, Sidney Wayne *management educator*
Hudak, Thomas F(rancis) *finance company executive*
Jackendoff, Nathaniel *finance educator*
Joyce, Michael J. *accountant*
Kelley, William Thomas *marketing educator*
Kim, Synja P. *corporate business planner*
Kimberly, John Robert *management educator, consultant*
Ksansnak, James E. *service management company executive*
Leimkuhler, Gerard Joseph, Jr. *financial holding company executive*
Lodish, Leonard Melvin *marketing educator, entrepreneur*
Merrifield, Dudley Bruce *business educator, former government official*
Micko, Alexander S. *financial executive*
Moyer, F. Stanton *financial executive, advisor*
Nadley, Harris Jerome *accountant, educator, writer*
Pellicciotti, Patricia M. *management consultant, financial analyst*
Robinson, Robert L. *financial service company executive, lawyer*
Rosenbloom, Bert *marketing educator*
Rowan, Richard Lamar *business management educator*
Saks, Stephen Howard *accountant*
Santomero, Anthony M. *business educator*
Sanyour, Michael Louis, Jr. *financial services company executive*
Saul, Ralph Southey *financial service executive*
Savitz, Samuel J. *actuarial consulting firm executive*
Schumann, William Henry, III *financial executive*
Shils, Edward B. *management educator, lawyer*
Staloff, Arnold Fred *financial executive*
Taylor, Wilson H. *diversified financial company executive*
Wixon, Rufus *retired accounting educator*
Woods, Richard Seavey *accountant, educator*
Ziegler, Donald Robert *accountant*
Zucker, William *retired business educator*

Pittsburgh
Bernt, Benno Anthony *financial and business executive*
Dibianca, Joseph Philip *finance executive*
Foreman, John Daniel *financial executive*
Franklin, Kenneth Ronald *franchise company executive, consultant*
Herrington, Donald Francis *financial services executive*
Ijiri, Yuji *accounting and economics educator*
Jehle, Michael Edward *financial executive*
Jones, Fred Richard *financial executive*
Junker, Edward P., III *diversified financial services company executive*
Kaczmarski, Michael John *controller, company executive*
Kilmann, Ralph Herman *business educator*
King, William Richard *business educator, consultant*
Lewis, Richard Allan *financial planner*
Russell, Stanley G., Jr. *accountant*
Slack, Edward Dorsey, III *financial systems professional, consultant*
Thorne, John Reinecke *business educator, venture capitalist*
Ulmer, Daniel C., Jr. *diversified financial services company executive*
†Wagner, Lawrence M. *diversified financial services company executive*

Radnor
Arader, Walter Graham *financial consultant*
Stearns, Milton Sprague, Jr. *financial executive*
Zimmermann, R. Peter *financial executive*

Reading
Itin, James Richard *financial executive*

Saint Davids
Bertsch, Frederick Charles, III *business executive*

University Park
Bennett, Peter Dunne *marketing educator*
McKeown, James Charles *accounting educator, consultant*
Schrader, William Joseph *accountant, educator*

Valley Forge
Brewer, Oliver Gordon, Jr. *corporate executive*

Villanova
Dorian, Harry Aram *financial consultant, former bank executive*

Wallingford
Herpel, George Lloyd *marketing educator*

Wayne
Sims, Robert John *financial planner*
†West, Alfred Paul, Jr. *financial services executive*

West Conshohocken
Richard, Scott F. *portfolio manager*

Wilkes Barre
†Bevevino, Frank *finance company executive*
†Bogdan, James E. *chief financial officer*

Williamsport
Bryant, Martha J. *accountant*
Facey, Karlyle Frank *financial executive, consultant*
†Lessman, Janice Trojan *financial services executive*

Wynnewood
Campbell, Alan Keith *business educator*
La Blanc, Charles Wesley, Jr. *financial consultant*

York
Welber, David Alan *accountant*

RHODE ISLAND

Kingston
Ross, James Barrett *finance and insurance educator*

Lincoln
Carter, Wilfred Wilson *financial executive, controller*

Pawtucket
Davison, Charles Hamilton *financial executive*

Providence
Downing, Brian Thomas *business executive*
Harris, Richard John *diversified holding company executive*
Tella, Luigi *accountant*
Tillinghast, Charles Carpenter, Jr. *aviation and financial consultant*

Watch Hill
Rees, Charles H. G. *retired financial officer, investor, consultant*

West Warwick
Galkin, Robert Theodore *company executive*

SOUTH CAROLINA

Charleston
Hogan, Arthur James *portfolio manager*

Clemson
Hicks, Edwin Hugh *accountant*

Columbia
Fryer, John Stanley *management science educator*
Pritchett, Samuel Travis *finance and insurance educator, researcher*

Georgetown
McGrath, James Charles, III *financial services company executive, lawyer, consultant*

Greenville
Fayonsky, James Leon *financial planner*

Hilton Head Island
Kaley, Arthur Warren *financial consulting company executive*

Myrtle Beach
Patton, Wendell Melton, Jr. *retired management educator, consulting psychologist, college president*

SOUTH DAKOTA

Burbank
Simmons, Joseph Thomas *accountant, educator*

Platte
Pennington, Beverly Melcher *financial services company executive*

TENNESSEE

Knoxville
Fain, Paul Kemp, Jr. *financial planner*

La Vergne
Hubbard, Julia Faye *accountant*

Louisville
†Williams, Timothy Wayne *finance company executive*

Memphis
Forell, David Charles *financial executive*

Nashville
D'Agostino, James Samuel, Jr. *financial executive*
Dykes, Archie Reece *financial services executive*
Holsen, Robert Charles *accountant*
Polley, Dale Whitcomb *finance company executive*
Richmond, Samuel Bernard *management educator*
Van, George Paul *international money management executive*
Weingartner, H(ans) Martin *finance educator*

TEXAS

Amarillo
Streu, Raymond Oliver *financial planner, securities executive*
Strickland, Anita Maurine *retired business educator, librarian*

Arlington
Ayres, Ray Morris *business management educator*
Dickinson, Roger Allyn *business administration educator*

Austin
Alpert, Mark Ira *marketing educator*
Blair, Calvin Patton *retired business administration educator*
Crum, Lawrence Lee *banking educator*
Cundiff, Edward William *marketing educator*
Doenges, Rudolph Conrad *finance educator*
Granof, Michael H. *accounting educator*
Kinney, William Rudolph, Jr. *accounting educator, researcher*
Larson, Kermit Dean *accounting educator*

May, Robert George *accounting educator*
Peterson, Robert Allen *marketing educator*
Robertson, Jack Clark *accounting educator*
Sommerfeld, Raynard Matthias *accounting educator*
Summers, Edward Lee *accounting educator*
Tinic, Seha Mehmet *finance educator*
Welsch, Glenn Albert *accounting educator*
Witt, Robert Charles *finance educator*
Wolf, Harold Arthur *finance educator*

Carrollton
Smart, David Louis *retired finance executive*

College Station
Crumbley, Donald Larry *accounting educator, writer, consultant*
Manning, Walter Scott *accountant, former educator, consultant*
Plum, Charles Walden *retired business executive and educator*
Trennepohl, Gary Lee *finance educator*
Wichern, Dean William *business educator*

Dallas
Ablon, Arnold Norman *accountant*
Casey, Albert Vincent *business policy educator, retired business executive*
Coldwell, Philip Edward *financial consultant*
Denahan, Joseph Anthony *mining company financial executive*
Galecke, Robert Michael *financial company executive*
Harris, Lucy Brown *accountant, consultant*
Howland, Grafton Dulany *financial counselor*
Jobe, Larry Alton *business executive*
Lerner, Alan Burton *financial service executive, lawyer*
Lomax, John H. *financial service company executive*
Mahr, George Joseph, Jr. *financial service executive, real estate developer*
Marshall, Harold D. *leasing and financial services company executive*
McCormick, James Clarence *business consultant*
McElvain, David Plowman *manufacturing company financial executive*
Mc Quillan, Joseph Michael *finance company executive*
Moore, Thomas Joseph *financial company executive*
†Rone, B. J. *financial executive*
Shimer, Daniel Lewis *corporate executive*
Shower, Robert Wesley *financial executive*
Solender, Robert Lawrence *financial and real estate corporation officer*
Taylor, Ramona Garrett *financial services company executive*
Thomas, Robert Lee *financial services company executive, consultant*
Willey, Paul Wayne *financial executive*
Williams, Thomas (Jack Williams) *finance company executive*

Denton
Brock, Horace Rhea *accounting educator*

El Paso
†Henry, Samuel Lawrence *financial executive*

Fort Worth
Bousquette, William Charles *financial executive*
Dominiak, Geraldine Florence *accounting educator*
Yarbro, James Wesley *financial executive*

Galveston
Welch, Ronald J. *actuary*

Garland
McGill, Maurice Leon *financial executive*

Georgetown
Lord, William Grogan *financial holding company executive*

Houston
Brown, Sara Lou *accounting firm executive*
Cater, James Thomas *financial and investment planner*
†Chaney, John Douglas *financial executive*
Daily, James L., Jr. *retired financial executive*
Hargrove, James Ward *financial consultant*
Hipple, James Blackman *financial executive*
Horvitz, Paul Michael *finance educator*
Jenkins, Judith Alexander *bank consultant*
Klingel, Martin Allen *investment company executive*
Knauss, Robert Lynn *international business educator, corporate executive*
Ranieri, Lewis S. *financial services company executive*
Rockwell, Elizabeth Dennis *retirement specialist, financial planner*
†Shaper, Stephen Jay *finance company executive*
Van Caspel, Venita Walker *financial planner*
Wells, Damon, Jr. *investment company executive*
Williams, James Lee *financial industries executive*
Zeff, Stephen Addam *accounting educator*

Irving
Belknap, John Corbould *financial executive*
Bolinger, Corbin Eugene *finance company executive*
Hughes, John Farrell *finance company executive*
Jack, James E. *financial service company executive*
Metevier, James F. *finance company executive*
Pickett, Edwin Gerald *financial executive*
†Swartz, Robert Mark *high technology manufacturing financial executive*

Killeen
†Brincat, John Nicholas *finance company executive*

Lubbock
Johnson, James Robert *accountant*
Sears, Robert Stephen *finance educator*
Stem, Carl Herbert *business educator*
Wolfe, Verda Nell *pension consultant, financial planner*

Plainview
Duvall, Wallace Lee *management educator, consultant*

Plano
Bode, Richard Albert *retired financial executive*

Richardson
Schrimsher, Jerry James *diversified financial services company executive*

San Antonio
Carroll, William Marion *financial services executive*
Freeman, Howard Lee, Jr. *financial executive*
Fuhrmann, Charles J., II *investment and finance consultant*
Jones, James Richard *business administration educator*
Schneider, Bobby Dean *financial consultant*

Southlake
Norris, Richard Anthony *accountant*

Stephenville
Collier, Boyd Dean *finance educator, management consultant*

Tyler
Odom, Oris Leon, II *finance educator, financial consultant*
†Taylor, Jimmie F. *accountant, controller*

Waco
Henke, Emerson Overbeck *accountant, educator*
Rose, John Thomas *finance educator*

Wimberley
Skaggs, Wayne Gerard *financial services company executive*

UTAH

Provo
Hunt, H(arold) Keith *business management educator, marketing consultant*

Salt Lake City
Furr, James William, Jr. *financial planner, consultant*
Monson, David Smith *accountant, former congressman*
Nelson, Roger Hugh *management educator, business executive*

VERMONT

Chittenden
Haley, John Charles *financial executive*

Manchester
Mills, Gordon Lawrence *financial executive*

Manchester Center
Gould, James Spencer *financial consultant*

Rutland
Wright, William Bigelow *financial executive*

VIRGINIA

Alexandria
Pastin, Mark Joseph *executive consultant, professional society administrator*
Regan, Donald Thomas *financier, writer, lecturer*

Arlington
Hazard, Neil Livingstone *corporation financial executive*
Lewis, Hunter *financial advisor, publisher*
Sands, Frank Melville *investment manager*
Thomas, Jimmy Lynn *financial executive*

Blacksburg
Killough, Larry Neil *accounting educator*
Moore, Laurence John *business educator*

Charlottesville
Broome, Oscar Whitfield, Jr. *accounting educator, administrator*
Coleman, Almand Rouse *accounting educator*
Davis, Edward Wilson *business administration educator*
Horton, Madeline Mary *financial planner, consultant*
Matson, Robert Edward *management educator, management consultant*
Mc Kinney, George Wesley, Jr. *banking educator*
Rosenblum, John William *business educator*
Shenkir, William Gary *business educator*
Sihler, William Wooding *finance educator*
Sorensen, Thomas Chaikin *financial executive*
Thompson, David William *business educator*
Trent, Robert Harold *business educator*

Fairfax
Buzzell, Robert Dow *management educator*
Harlan, Stephen Donald *accountant*

Falls Church
Rosenberg, Theodore Roy *financial executive*

Lexington
DeVogt, John Frederick *management science and business ethics educator, consultant*
Warner, Harry Hathaway *financial consultant*

Mc Lean
Halaby, Najeeb E. *financier, lawyer*
Mand, Martin G. *financial executive*
Phillips, Rufus Colfax, III *planning consultant*

Richmond
Hamill, A(llen) William *finance executive*
King, Robert Leroy *business administration educator*
Morton, Marshall Nay *treasurer*
Thompson, Francis Neal *financial services consultant*
Trumble, Robert Roy *business educator*

Roseland
Fetter, Robert Barclay *retired administrative sciences educator*

Upperville
Smart, Stephen Bruce, Jr. *business and government executive*

Urbanna
Hudson, Jesse Tucker, Jr. *financial executive*

Vienna
Kumar, Verinder *accountant, financial executive*

Williamsburg
Kottas, John Frederick *business administration educator*
Messmer, Donald Joseph *business management educator, marketing consultant*
O'Connell, William Edward, Jr. *finance educator*
Parkany, John *business educator, international financial consultant*
Pearson, Roy Laing *business administration educator*
Quittmeyer, Charles Loreaux *business educator*
Warren, William Herbert *business administration educator*

WASHINGTON

Bellevue
Graham, John Robert, Jr. *financial executive*
Koontz, Alfred Joseph, Jr. *financial and operating management executive, consultant*

Bellingham
Self, Charles Edwin *financial consultant, retail company executive*

Cheney
Drummond, Marshall Edward *business educator, university administrator*

Everett
Toyer, Richard Henry *accountant*

Redmond
Narodick, Sally G. *corporate executive*

Seattle
Collett, Robert Lee *financial company executive*
Curtis, James Austin *actuary consultant*
Etcheson, Warren Wade *business administration educator*
Gorans, Gerald Elmer *accountant*
Hanson, Kermit Osmond *business administration educator, university dean emeritus*
Harder, Virgil Eugene *business administration educator*
MacLachlan, Douglas Lee *marketing educator*
Mueller, Gerhard G(ottlob) *accounting educator*
Saunders, William Lockwood *financial consultant*
Saxberg, Borje Osvald *management educator*
†Trump, Eddie *holding company executive*
†Trump, Julius *holding company executive*

Tacoma
Foley, Thomas Michael *financial executive*

Vancouver
†Bingham, H. Raymond *finance executive*

WISCONSIN

Eau Claire
Weil, D(onald) Wallace *business administration educator*

Madison
Aldag, Ramon John *management and organization educator*
Baron, Alma Fay S. *management educator*
McDonald, Barbara Ann *marketing educator*
Nevin, John Robert *business educator, consultant*
Sprecher, Peter Leonard, Jr. *financial services company executive*
Swoboda, Ralph Sande *credit union official, lawyer*

Milwaukee
Kendall, Leon Thomas *finance and real estate educator, retired insurance company executive*
Kneiser, Richard John *accountant*
Panenka, James Brian Joseph *financial company executive*
Walters, Ronald Ogden *finance company executive*

Mosinee
Janis, Donald Emil *corporate controller*

Muskego
Stefaniak, Norbert John *business administration educator*

Thiensville
Berry, William Martin *financial consultant*

Wausau
†Paprocki, John Thomas *controller*

Wisconsin Rapids
Kenney, Richard John *paper company finance executive*

WYOMING

Afton
Hunsaker, Floyd B. *accountant*

Cheyenne
Drummer, Donald Raymond *financial services executive*

Gillette
†Enzi, Michael Bradley *accountant, state legislator*

Riverton
Clark, Stanford E. *accountant*

TERRITORIES OF THE UNITED STATES

GUAM

Tamuning
Camacho, Eduardo Garcia *finance company executive, insurance agent*

CANADA

BRITISH COLUMBIA

Powell River
Carsten, Arlene Desmet *financial executive*

Vancouver
MacCrimmon, Kenneth Robert *management educator*
Mahler, Richard T. *finance executive*
Mattessich, Richard Victor (Alvarus) *business administration educator*
Saunders, Peter Paul *finance company executive*
Stone, Robert Ryrie *financial executive*

MANITOBA

Winnipeg
Watchorn, William Ernest *diversified manufacturing executive*

NEW BRUNSWICK

Saint Andrews
Anderson, John Murray *operations executive, former university president*

ONTARIO

Don Mills
Craig, John Grant *finance management executive*
Rollason, W. Peter *corporate financial executive*

Etobicoke
Pelton, John S. *finance company executive*

Hamilton
Cowan, James Spencer *financial executive*
Root, L. Allen *treasurer, financial executive*

Islington
White, Adrian Michael Stephen *financial executive*

London
Cunningham, Gordon Ross *financial executive*
Johnston, Charles Bernie, Jr. *business educator*
Osbaldeston, Gordon Francis *business educator, former government official*

Markham
Burns, H. Michael *financial services company executive*

Mississauga
Turnbull, Adam Michael Gordon *financial executive, accountant*

North York
MacDonald, Ian Duncan *commercial credit information executive*

Toronto
Belzberg, Brent Stanley *financial executive*
Cockwell, Jack Lynn *financial executive*
Coleman, John Hewson *financial consultant*
Corrigan, Harold Cauldwell *accountant*
†Cryer, Thomas Wilfred *chartered accountant*
Dodd, Lionel G. *holding company executive*
Dyment, John Joseph *financial executive*
Greig, Thomas Currie *retired financial executive*
Hankinson, James Floyd *business executive*
Hartley, Stuart Leslie *diversified company executive, accountant*
Hirst, Peter Christopher *consulting actuary*
Hurlbut, Robert St. Clair *finance company executive*
Jackson, Bruce Leslie *publishing company financial executive*
Kidd, Robert Hugh *financial executive, accountant*
Lanthier, John Spencer *accounting company executive*
Laurie, John Veldon *business financial executive, accountant*
Mann, George Stanley *real estate and financial services corporation executive*
Ronald, Thomas Iain *financial services executive*
Skinner, Alastair *accountant*
Sloan, David Edward *corporate director*
Stackhouse, Richard Gilbert *retired financial company executive*
Weldon, David Black *financial executive*
Whaley, John Alexander *finance company executive, lawyer*

Waterdown
Hawkrigg, Melvin Michael *finance company executive*

Welland
Wintermans, Joseph Jack Gerard Francis *financial services executive*

QUEBEC

Montreal
Andrew, Frederick James *telecommunications company executive*
Bagnall, Graham Edward *financial executive*
Beaudoin, François *financial company executive*

Castonguay, Claude *corporate director, lawyer, former senator*
Cedraschi, Tullio *investment management company executive*
Crowston, Wallace Bruce Stewart *management educator*
Daly, Gerald *accountant*
Desmarais, Paul *finance company executive*
Laurin, Pierre *finance company executive*
Lessard, Michel M. *finance company executive*
Mintzberg, Henry *management educator, researcher, writer*
Olivella, Barry James *financial executive*
Picard, Laurent *management educator, administrator, consultant*
Saumier, Andre *finance executive*
Speirs, Derek James *diversified corporation financial executive*
Terreault, R. Charles *management educator, researcher*
Thompson, John Douglas *financier*
Weir, Stephen James *financial executive*

MEXICO

Monterrey
†Ruiz, Othon *financial executive*

ENGLAND

London
Berger, Thomas Jan *financial company executive*
Hallissey, Michael *accounting company executive*
O'Mahony, Jeremiah Francis *financial executive*

FINLAND

Helsinki
†Siimestö, Orvo Kalervo *financial executive*

FRANCE

Cedex
Bourdais de Charbonniere, Eric *financial executive*

Neuilly-sur-Seine
Presby, J. Thomas *financial advisor*

Paris
Bommelaer, Alain *finance company executive*
Houël, Patrick *financial executive*
†Vinciguerra, Jean-Louis *finance company executive*

GERMANY

Düsseldorf
Olson, Sigmund Lars *corporate finance executive*

Kiel
Brockhoff, Klaus K. L. *marketing and management educator*

Pforzheim
Voit, Franz Johann, Jr. *financial consultant*

INDIA

Calcutta
Kothari, Bijay Singh *accountant*

JAPAN

Tokyo
Atobe, Yasuzo *financial company executive*
Makihara, Minoru *diversified corporation executive*

THE NETHERLANDS

Amsterdam
Walker, William Ross *accountant*

PORTUGAL

Braga
Rocha, Armandino Cordeiro Dos Santos *accountant, educator, auditor*

SAUDI ARABIA

Riyadh
†Olayan, Suliman Saleh *finance company executive*

SWEDEN

Lund
Welin, Walter *financial advisor*

SWITZERLAND

Lausanne
Caste, Jean F. *financial advisor*

Lugano
Ricci, Giovanni Mario *financial company executive*

ADDRESS UNPUBLISHED

Aboody, Albert Victor *accountant*
Adam, Orval Michael *retired financial executive, lawyer*
Anderson, Michael L. *financial planning manager*
Angulo, Gerard Antonio *financial executive, investor, consultant*
Arenberg, Julius Theodore, Jr. *retired accounting company executive*
Barbee, George E. L. *financial services executive*
Beebe, John Eldridge *financial service executive*
Beltz, Herbert Allison *financial consultant*
Benjamin, James Cover *controller, manufacturing company executive*
Bishop, William Squire *commercial finance company executive*
Borum, Rodney Lee *business executive*
Bowne, Shirlee Pearson *credit union executive, real estate executive*
Boyd, Francis Virgil *retired accounting educator*
Brown, Bruce Maitland *philanthropy consultant*
Brown, Henry Bedinger Rust *financial management company executive*
Brune, David Hamilton *financial corporation executive, lawyer*
Campbell, Alice Shaw *retired accountant, poet*
Charlton, Jesse Melvin, Jr. *management educator, lawyer*
Chelberg, Bruce Stanley *holding company executive*
Conole, Clement Vincent *corporate executive*
Cox, David Brummal *accounting firm executive*
Davidson, John *financial advisory executive*
Davis, George Alfred *financial executive*
Decker, Hans Wilhelm *retired finance company executive*
Delany, Logan Drummond, Jr. *financial consultant, investor*
Doherty, Thomas Joseph *financial services industry consultant*
Doty, Philip Edward *accountant*
Duppstadt, Marlyn Henry *financial executive*
Eischen, Michael Hugh *retired railroad controller*
Estrin, Herbert Alvin *financial consultant, entertainment company executive*
Falcone, Nola Maddox *financial company executive*
Feehan, Thomas Joseph *financial executive*
Ferguson, Robert *financial services executive, writer*
Fischmar, Richard Mayer *company financial executive, consultant*
Fowler, John Moore *financial service company executive*
Fowler, Raymond David *financial executive*
Fox, Lawrence *company executive*
Frank, Edgar Gerald *retired financial executive*
Franklin, Barbara Kipp *financial planner, investment adviser*
Fuller, Stephen Herbert *business administration educator*
Gevantman, Judith *financial analyst, consultant*
Gillespie, Gwain Homer *financial executive*
Gleijeses, Mario *holding company executive*
Grant, James Francis *international business and defense consultant, retired air force officer*
Gruber, Fredric Francis *financial planning and investment research executive*
Haddock, Harold, Jr. *retired accounting firm executive*
Hall, James Parker *financial consultant*
Hamilton, William Frank *management educator*
Hamlin, Dan William *accountant, management consultant*
Handy, Edward Otis, Jr. *financial services executive*
Hanna, John A. *finance and administration executive*
Hanson, Carl Malmrose *financial company executive*
Harper, W(alter) Joseph *financial consultant*
Hecht, Emil *retired housing and financial company executive*
Hodges, Paul Joseph *securities analyst*
Holloran, Thomas Edward *business educator*
Hubbe, Henry Ernest *financial forecaster, funds manager*
Hughes, George David *business educator*
Hutner, Herbert L. *financial consultant, lawyer*
Isakow, Selwyn *financier*
Jacques, Andre Charles *financial consultant*
Jamison, John Callison *business educator, investment banker*
Johnson, Clifford Andrew, III *financial executive*
Kaplan, Leonard Eugene *accountant*
Keegan, Kenneth Donald *financial consultant, retired oil company executive*
Kennedy, Beverly (Kleban) Burris *financial consultant, agent, registered representative*
King, Algin Braddy *marketing educator*
Kingsbery, Walton Waits, Jr. *retired accountant*
Kolton, Paul *business executive*
Kreitzer, Lois Helen *personal investor*
Kryza, E(lmer) Gregory *financial planner, international affairs advisor, former ambassador*
La Blanc, Robert Edmund *consulting company executive*
†Lane, Joseph C. *financial services executive*
Langenfeld, Douglas Eugene *accountant*
Larizadeh, M(ohammed) R(eza) *business educator*
Lazarovic, Karen *money manager, investment consultant*
Lerner, Herbert J. *accountant*
Lesher, John Lee, Jr. *consulting services company executive*
Levy, Louis Edward *retired accounting firm executive*
Lewis, James Lee, Jr. *actuary*
Linxwiler, Louis Major, Jr. *retired finance company executive*
Malone, Edward H. *financial executive*
Maroni, Paul L. *finance executive*
Mayoras, Donald Eugene *corporate executive, speaker, consultant, educator*
Mc Gowan, James Atkinson *business executive, financial consultant*
Mednick, Robert *accountant*
Menendez, Carlos *financial executive, banker*
Miller, Robert Stevens, Jr. *finance professional*
Mondor, Kenneth James *financial executive*
Morgan, Robert Arthur *accountant*
Nair, Raghavan D. *accountant, educator*
Nehrt, Lee Charles *management educator*
Newman, Dennis Collins, Sr. *accountant*
†Norris, Stephen Leslie *merchant banking, tax and finance executive*
Overcash, Reece A., Jr. *financial service company executive*
Palmer, Gary Andrew *portfolio manager*
†Passailaigue, Ernest L., Jr. *accountant, state senator*
Pennington, Richard Maier *management consultant, retired insurance company executive, lawyer*
Phillips, Charles Alan *accounting firm executive*
Rapaccioli, Michel Antoine *financial executive*
Rawls, S(ol) Waite, III *business executive*
Reynolds, Billie I. *financial representative and counselor, former association executive*
Robertson, A. Haeworth *actuary, benefit consultant, foundation executive*
Rosenberg, Sheli Zysman *lawyer, financial management executive*
Rowe, William Davis *financial services company executive*
Rush, Richard Henry *financier, writer, lecturer*
Ryland, G(reaner) Neal *financial executive*
Said, Kamal E. *accounting educator*
Sayles, Leonard Robert *management educator, consultant*
Scheel, Nels Earl *financial executive, accountant*
†Schleck, Thomas Todd *financial executive*
Schoen, William Jack *financier*
Sheleski, Stanley John *accountant, comptroller, consultant*
Sheridan, Patrick Michael *finance company executive*
Shields, H. Richard *tax consultant,business executive*
Shultis, Robert Lynn *finance educator, consultant in cost systems, retired professional association executive*
Smith, David Callaway *retired accounting firm executive*
Smith, Kenneth Blose *former financial executive*
Smith, Seymour Maslin *financial advisor, investment banker*
†Snelling, Robert Orren, Sr. *franchising executive*
Srinivasan, Venkataraman *marketing and management educator*
Stein, Paul Arthur *financial services executive*
Swanson, Rune E. *financial executive*
Tongue, Paul Graham *financial executive*
Treynor, Jack Lawrence *financial advisor, educator*
Turner, Henry Brown *finance executive*
Ulrich, Richard William *finance executive*
Van Vinkenroye du Waysaeck, Fedia Maurice Gilles *financial services executive*
Waldhauser, Cathy Howard *financial services executive*
Wall, M. Danny *financial services consultant*
Watson, W. Robert *financial advisor, consultant*
Watt, John H. *financial executive*
Wilhelmsen, Harold John *accountant, operations controller*
Wolf, Rosalie Joyce *financial executive*
Wulff, John Kenneth *controller*
Zick, John Walter *retired accounting company executive*

FINANCE: INSURANCE

UNITED STATES

ALABAMA

Birmingham
Dekich, Sherlie Eugene *insurance company executive*
Dover, James Burrell *insurance executive*
McKewen, Jack Leard *insurance sales executive*
Nabers, Drayton, Jr. *insurance company executive*
†Pope, G. Phillip *insurance company executive*
Renneker, Frederick Weyman, III *insurance executive*
†Richey, Ronald Kay *insurance company executive, lawyer*
Rushton, William James, III *insurance company executive*

Mobile
†Rakich, Robert T. *insurance holding company executive*

ARIZONA

Carefree
Wise, Paul Schuyler *insurance company executive*

Green Valley
Brissman, Bernard Gustave *insurance company executive*

Phoenix
Barbanell, Alexander Stanley *insurance marketing company executive*
Melner, Sinclair Lewis *insurance company executive*

Scottsdale
Burr, Edward Benjamin *life insurance company executive, financial executive*
Prisbrey, Rex Prince *insurance agent, underwriter, financial consultant*

Tempe
Christie, Clarence J. *insurance brokerage executive*

Tucson
Martin, Paul Edward *retired insurance company executive*
Ziehler, Tony Joseph *insurance agent*

ARKANSAS

Fayetteville
Dulan, Harold Andrew *former insurance company executive, educator*

Pine Bluff
†Bradford, Jay Turner *insurance executive, state legislator*

CALIFORNIA

Agoura Hills
†Cordon, Frank Joseph *insurance company executive*

Auburn
Jeske, Howard Leigh *life insurance company executive, lawyer*

Burlingame
Bell, Herbert Aubrey Frederick *life insurance company executive*

Costa Mesa
Gore, Thomas Gavin *insurance and securities broker*

Danville
Frederickson, John Marcus *insurance executive*

Diamond Bar
Fisher, Louis Raymond *insurance executive*

Encino
Webster, David Arthur *life insurance company executive*

Garden Grove
Williams, J(ohn) Tilman *insurance executive, real estate broker, city official*

Hemet
Treece, Joseph Charles *insurance broker*

Laguna Hills
Westover, Samuel Lee *insurance company executive*

Los Angeles
Baker, Lawrence Colby, Jr. *insurance company executive*
Carpenter, David Roland *life insurance executive*
Denlea, Leo Edward, Jr. *insurance company executive*
Faulwell, Gerald Edward *insurance company executive*
†Gelfand, Leonard H. *insurance comprnay executive*
Gurash, John Thomas *insurance company executive*
Houston, Ivan James *insurance company executive*
Krumm, William Frederick *insurance company executive*
Neal, Louise Kathleen *life insurance company executive, accountant*
Rinsch, Charles Emil *insurance company executive*
Whitaker, Fred Maynard *insurance agent*

Newport Beach
Gerken, Walter Bland *insurance company executive*
Marcoux, Carl Henry *former insurance executive, writer*
Sutton, Thomas C. *insurance company executive*

Northridge
Norris, Darell Forest *insurance company executive*

Novato
†Hansmeyer, Herbert *insurance company executive*
†Meyer, John F. *insurance company executive*

Oakland
†Skinner, Clifford *insurance company executive*

Palo Alto
Schonbrun, Michael Keith *health care executive*

Pasadena
Bare, Bruce *life insurance company executive*
Bourdeau, Paul Turgeon *insurance company executive*
Simpson, William Arthur *insurance company executive*

Rancho Cordova
†Alenius, John Todd *insurance executive*

Reseda
Roth, Leonard Jerome *financial consultant, insurance agent*

Sacramento
Gray, Myles McClure *insurance company executive*
†Zax, Stanley R. *insurance company executive*

San Diego
Albritton, Robert Sanford *life insurance executive*
Hayes, Robert Emmet *retired insurance company executive, consultant*
Hill, Frank Whitney, Jr. *insurance company executive*
Rotter, Paul Talbott *retired insurance executive*

San Francisco
Broome, Burton Edward *insurance company executive*
Clark, Edgar Sanderford *insurance broker, consultant*
Djordjevich, Michael *insurance company executive*
Drexler, Fred *insurance executive*
Hatfield, Dale Charles *insurance company executive, banker*
†Hill, Arthur Brian *auto insurance company executive*
†Jaeger, Joseph C. *insurance company executive*
Lamberson, John Roger *insurance company executive*
Levine, Norman Gene *insurance company executive*
Murrin, Thomas Edward *insurance company executive*
†Ward, William T. *insurance company executive*
†Webb, J. A. *insurance company executive*

San Marcos
Reed, H(orace) Curtis *insurance company executive, management consultant*

Santa Ana
†Kennedy, Donald Parker *title insurance company executive*

Santa Barbara
Terry, John Timothy *insurance company executive*

Spring Valley
Peterson, Donald Curtis *life care executive, consultant*

Thousand Oaks
Gregory, Calvin *insurance service executive*
†Weinberg, D. Mark *health insurance company executive*

Whittier
Davidson, Alan Charles *insurance executive*

Woodland Hills
†Rotenstreich, Jon W. *insurance company executive*

COLORADO

Aurora
Huff, Paul Emlyn *insurance executive*

Denver
Conroy, Thomas Francis *insurance company executive*
Deering, Fred Arthur *insurance company executive*
Hardy, Wayne Russell *insurance broker*
†Robinson, Carole Ann *insurance executive*

Englewood
Dackow, Orest Taras *insurance company executive*
Manley, Richard Walter *insurance executive*
O'Bryan, William Hall *insurance executive*

Parker
Nelson, Marvin Ray *retired life insurance company executive*

CONNECTICUT

Avon
Armstrong, John Kenaston *insurance and financial services company executive*
†Jarvis, Ronald Dean *life insurance company executive*

Bloomfield
†Dooley, Thomas Howard *insurance company executive*
English, Lawrence P. *insurance company executive*

Collinsville
Ford, Dexter *retired insurance company executive*

Cos Cob
Woodman, Harry Andrews *retired life insurance company executive, consultant*

Fairfield
O'Connell, Robert John *insurance company executive*

Farmington
Kelly, Francis J., Jr. *insurance executive*
Paul, Christian Thomas *retired insurance company executive*

Glenbrook
Schofield, Herbert Spencer, III *insurance agent*

Greenwich
Berkley, William Robert *insurance holding company executive*
Clements, Robert *insurance brokerage executive*
Fuller, Theodore *retired insurance executive*
Heer, Edwin LeRoy *insurance executive*

Hartford
Baird, Zoë *insurance company executive, lawyer*
Benanav, Gary G. *insurance company counsel*
Booth, Richard H. *insurance company executive*
Boyko, Gregory Andrew *insurance company executive*
Brophy, Joseph Thomas *insurance company executive*
Budd, Edward Hey *insurance company executive*
Compton, Ronald E. *insurance and financial services executive*
Conrad, Donald Glover *insurance executive*
†Doyle, Lawrence Sawyer *insurance company executive*
Fiondella, Robert William *insurance company executive*
Frahm, Donald Robert *insurance company executive*
Gingold, George Norman *insurance company executive, lawyer*
Gummere, John *insurance company executive*
Holt, Timothy Arthur *insurance company executive*
†Keating, Thomas Edward *insurance company executive*
†Kenney, John R. *insurance corporation executive, lawyer*
Lautzenheiser, Barbara Jean *insurance executive*
Martin, John J. *insurance company executive*
McLane, James Woods *insurance executive*
Messmore, Thomas Ellison *insurance company executive*
Mueller, Marnie Wagstaff *insurance company executive, economist*
Mullane, Denis Francis *insurance executive*
†Petry, Paul E. *insurance company executive*
Randall, Gerald J. *insurance company executive*
Sargent, Joseph Denny *insurance executive*
Scully, John Carroll *life insurance marketing research company executive*
Stephen, Michael Anthony *insurance company executive*
Westervelt, James Joseph *insurance company executive*
Wilde, Wilson *insurance company executive*
Wilder, Michael Stephen *insurance company executive*

Madison
Anderson, Roy Ryden *former insurance executive, consultant*

Simsbury
Krisher, William K. *former insurance company executive*

Stamford
Bailey, Robert William *reinsurance brokerage executive*
Block, Ruth *retired insurance company executive*
Burton, Arthur Henry, Jr. *insurance company executive*
Chickering, Howard Allen *insurance company executive, lawyer*
Ferguson, Ronald Eugene *reinsurance company executive*
Hudson, Harold Jordon, Jr. *retired insurance executive*
Kellogg, Tommy Nason *reinsurance corporation executive*
Rondepierre, Edmond Francois *insurance company executive*

West Hartford
Abbot, Quincy Sewall *retired insurance executive*

Weston
Thompson, N(orman) David *insurance company executive*

DELAWARE

Wilmington
Nottingham, Robinson Kendall *life insurance company executive*

DISTRICT OF COLUMBIA

Washington
Browne, Ray *insurance broker*
Canapary, Herbert Carton *insurance company executive*
DeHarde, William M. *insurance company executive*
Ellis, Rudolph Lawrence *insurance company executive*
Fowler, Caleb L. *insurance company executive, lawyer*
Freeman, Robert Turner, Jr. *insurance executive*
Lewin, George Forest *former insurance company executive*
Lynn, James Thomas *investment banker, insurance company executive, government executive, lawyer*
Moore, Robert Henry *insurance company executive*
†Pace, Simone J. *insurance executive*
Simpson, Louis A. *insurance company executive*
Smith, Donald Kaye *insurance company executive*
Sormani, Charles Robert *insurance company executive, actuary*
Stark, Nathan Julius *insurance company executive*
Vagley, Robert Everett *insurance association executive*

FLORIDA

Boca Raton
Deppe, Henry A. *insurance company executive*
Leahy, William F. *insurance company executive, lawyer*
Lipsey, John C. (Jack Lipsey) *insurance company executive*
Richardson, R(oss) Fred(erick) *insurance executive*

Boynton Beach
Bryant, Donald Loyd *insurance company executive*
Caras, Joseph Sheldon *life insurance company executive*

Bradenton
Phelan, John Densmore *insurance executive, consultant*

Clearwater
Caronis, George John *insurance executive*

Delray Beach
Sibigtroth, Joseph Clarence *insurance company executive*

Jacksonville
†Gibbons, G. Hunter *insurance executive*
†Gilson, Warren Edwin, Jr. *insurance company executive*
Howell, John Floyd *insurance company executive*
Lyon, Wilford Charles, Jr. *insurance executive*
McCullough, Ray Daniel, Jr. *insurance company executive*
†Parks, Herbert Louis *insurance company executive*
Purcifull, Robert Otis *insurance company executive*
†Verlander, William Ashley *insurance company executive*

Key Largo
Daenzer, Bernard John *insurance company executive, legal consultant*

Marathon
Kolker, Roger Russell *insurance executive*

Miami
Denison, Floyd Gene *insurance executive*
†Johnson, Glendon E. *insurance company executive*
Landon, Robert Kirkwood *insurance company executive*
Mandine, Salvador G. *insurance executive*
Van Wyck, George Richard *insurance company executive*

Murdock
Cross, George R. *insurance consultant*

Naples
Duff, Daniel Vincent *former insurance company executive, former mayor*
Mc Queen, Robert Charles *retired insurance executive*
Parish, John Cook *insurance executive*

Osprey
Woodall, William Leon *retired insurance executive*

Palm Beach Gardens
Lebed, Hartzel Zangwill *insurance company executive*

Pensacola
DeBardeleben, John Thomas, Jr. *retired insurance company executive*

Pompano Beach
Zinman, Jacques *former insurance agency executive*

Port Saint Lucie
Rhodes, Alfred William *former insurance company executive*

Saint Petersburg
Wittner, Ted Philip *insurance company executive*

Tallahassee
Gunter, William Dawson, Jr. (Bill Gunter) *insurance company executive*
Hunt, John Edwin *insurance company executive, consultant*

Tampa
Poe, William Frederick *insurance agency executive, former mayor*

Tequesta
Holmes, Melvin Almont *insurance company executive*

Vero Beach
Feagles, Robert West *insurance company executive*

Village Of Golf
Bates, Edward Brill *retired insurance company executive*

Winter Park
Hoche, Philip Anthony *life insurance company executive*

GEORGIA

Atlanta
Baxter, Robert Hampton, III *insurance executive*
Black, Kenneth, Jr. *insurance executive, educator, author*
Buck, Lee Albert *retired insurance company executive, evangelist*
Burns, Carroll Dean *insurance company executive*
Dodge, William Douglas *risk management, insurance, benefits consultant*
Foxen, Gene Louis *insurance executive*
Gregory, Mel Hyatt, Jr. *retired insurance company executive*
Hilliard, Robert Glenn *insurance company executive, lawyer*
†Johnston, Lynn Henry *insurance company executive*
Peacock, George Rowatt *retired life insurance company executive*
†Shirk, Richard D. *insurance company executive*
Skipper, Harold Dallas, Jr. *insurance educator*

Columbus
Amos, Daniel Paul *insurance executive*
Amos, Paul Shelby *insurance company executive*
Bugg, William Joseph, Jr. *insurance executive*
Cloninger, Kriss, III *insurance company executive*
Diaz-Verson, Salvador, Jr. *investment advisor*

Marietta
Cooper, Keith Harvey *insurance consultant*

HAWAII

Honolulu
Kanehiro, Kenneth Kenji *insurance educator, risk analyst, consultant*
†Kiessling, Ralph J. *health insurance company executive*

IDAHO

Boise
†Black, Max C. *insurance agent*
Lowder, Robert Jackson *insurance agent*

ILLINOIS

Bloomington
Bower, Marvin D. *insurance company executive*
Callis, Bruce *insurance company executive*
Curry, Alan Chester *insurance company executive*
Edmondson, James William (Jay Edmondson) *insurance company executive*
Engelkes, Donald John *insurance company executive*
Johnson, Earle Bertrand *insurance executive*
Joslin, Roger Scott *insurance company executive*
Miller, Duane Leon *insurance company executive*
Nelson, Walter Gerald *insurance company executive*
Rust, Edward Barry, Jr. *insurance company executive, lawyer*
Shelley, Edward Herman, Jr. *retired insurance company executive*
Trosino, Vincent Joseph *insurance company executive*
Vincent, Norman L. *insurance company executive*
Wamboldt, Donald George *insurance executive*
†White, John, Jr. *insurance company executive, farm organization executive*
Wright, Charles Richard *insurance executive*

Champaign
Peterson, Roger Lyman *insurance company executive*

Chicago
Bartholomay, William C. *insurance brokerage company executive, professional baseball team executive*
Bolnick, Howard Jeffrey *insurance company executive*
Conway, Michael Anthony *insurance executive*
Desch, Theodore Edward *health insurance company executive, lawyer*
†Dunphy, Thomas *insurance company executive*
Gill, William Haywood *insurance broker*
Hickey, Kevin Francis *insurance company executive*
Jerome, Jerrold V. *insurance company executive*
Kickler, James Arnold *insurance company executive*
Link, Carl Dean *insurance company executive*
Lorenz, Hugo Albert *insurance executive*
†Marziano, Fredric G. *insurance company executive*
†Mc Caskey, Raymond F. *insurance company executive*
†Murphy, Barth T. *insurance company executive*
Noha, Edward J. *insurance company executive*
O'Connor, Joseph William *reinsurance company executive*
Reichelt, Fred (Ferdinand Herbert Reichelt) *insurance and finance company executive*
Ryan, Patrick G. *insurance company executive*
Rycroft, Donald Cahill *insurance executive*
Shanks, Gerald Robert *insurance company executive*
Stitt, Frederick Hesse *insurance broker*
Tresnowski, Bernard Richard *health insurance company executive*
Vie, Richard Carl *insurance company executive*
Zucaro, Aldo Charles *insurance company executive*

Decatur
Braun, William Joseph *underwriter*
Strong, John David *insurance company executive*

Deerfield
Cruikshank, John W., III *life insurance underwriter*
Halaska, Robert H. *insurance company executive*

Des Moines
†Kelley, Bruce Gunn *insurance company executive, lawyer*

Evanston
Pabst, Edmund G. *retired insurance company executive, lawyer*

Geneva
Goulet, Charles Ryan *retired insurance company executive*

Goreville
Fosse, E(rwin) Ray *insurance company executive*

Highland Park
Boruszak, James Martin *insurance company executive*

Itasca
Grue, Howard Wood *former insurance company executive*

Lake Forest
Brown, Cameron *insurance company consultant*
†Eckert, Ralph John *insurance company executive*
Ford, Donald James *retired insurance company executive, consultant, lawyer*
O'Loughlin, John Kirby *retired insurance executive*
†Peterson, Donald Matthew *insurance company executive*
†Stone, W. Clement *insurance company executive, civic leader*

Lake Zurich
Luecke, Joseph E. *insurance company executive*

Lawrenceville
†Whelan, John M. *insurance company executive*

Libertyville
Kummer, Daniel William *insurance executive*

Long Grove
Fitzpatrick, John Henry *insurance company executive*
Maatman, Gerald Leonard *insurance company executive*
Standbridge, Peter Thomas *insurance company executive*

Morrison
French, Raymond Douglas *insurance agent, realtor,*

Northbrook
Flieder, John Joseph *insurance executive, marketing professional*
Hedien, Wayne Evans *insurance company executive*
Kuby, Edward Raymond *insurance company executive*
Lower, Louis Gordon, II *insurance company executive*
McFadden, Joseph Patrick *insurance company executive*
Resnick, Myron J. *insurance company executive, lawyer*
Saunders, Kenneth D. *insurance company executive, consultant, arbitrator*

Orland Park
Schultz, Barbara Marie *insurance company executive*

Peoria
†Michael, Jonathan Edward *insurance company executive*
†Stephens, Gerald D. *insurance company executive*

Prospect Heights
Clark, Donald Robert *retired insurance company executive*

Rock Island
Cheney, Thomas Ward *insurance company executive*
Lardner, Henry Petersen (Peter Lardner) *insurance company executive*

Schaumburg
†Bolinder, William Howard *insurance company executive*
Nauert, Peter William *insurance company executive*

Springfield
Budinger, Charles Jude *state agency insurance analyst*
Humphrey, Howard C. *insurance company executive*
Stooksbury, Walter Elbert *insurance company executive*
†Tarr, Paul Cresson, III *insurance company executive*

Villa Park
Webb, James Okrum, Jr. *insurance company executive*

Wheaton
Flynn, James Rourke *retired insurance company executive*

INDIANA

Bloomington
Long, John D. *retired insurance educator*

Carmel
†Dick, Rollin Merle *insurance company executive*
†Gongaware, Donald Francis *insurance company executive*
†Hilbert, Stephen C. *insurance company executive*

Fort Wayne
Anker, Robert Alvin *insurance company executive*
Clarke, Kenneth Stevens *insurance company executive*
Dunsire, P(eter) Kenneth *insurance company executive*
Edris, Charles Lawrence *insurance company executive*
Hirschy, Gordon Harold *insurance agent, auctioneer*
Lupke, Duane Eugene *insurance company executive*
Robertson, Richard Stuart *insurance holding company executive*
Rolland, Ian McKenzie *insurance executive*
Vachon, Marilyn Ann *retired insurance company executive*
West, Thomas Meade *insurance company executive*

Indianapolis
†Banks, Lloyd J. *insurance company executive*
Bash, James Francis *insurance company executive*
Christenson, Le Roy Howard *insurance company officer*
Cramer, Betty F. *life insurance company executive*
Heard, William Robert *insurance company executive*
†Huber, Richard C. *insurance company executive*
Husman, Catherine Bigot *insurance company executive, actuary*
†Lytle, L(arry) Ben *insurance company executive, lawyer*
Maginn, M. Joseph *insurance agent*
Mc Carthy, Harold Charles *retired insurance company executive*
McKinney, E. Kirk, Jr. *retired insurance company executive*
Norman, LaLander Stadig *insurance company executive*
Reich, Jack Egan *insurance company executive*
Robinson, Larry Robert *insurance company executive*
Semler, Jerry D. *insurance company executive*
†Whelan, John Martin *insurance executive*
Wolsiffer, Patricia Rae *insurance company executive*

Jasper
Fleck, Albert Henry, Jr. *insurance agency executive*

Leo
†Worman, Richard W. *insurance company executive, state senator*

Monticello
Haskins, Perry Glen *insurance company executive*

Pendleton
Kischuk, Richard Karl *insurance company executive*

South Bend
Wurzburg, Richard Joseph *health insurance executive*

IOWA

Cedar Rapids
†Falconio, Patrick E. *insurance company executive*

Council Bluffs
†Gibson, Richard Charles *insurance company executive*
†Nelson, H. H. Red *insurance company executive*

Des Moines
Ehrle, Roy W. *insurance company executive*
Ellis, Mary Louise Helgeson *insurance company executive*
†Hennesy, Craig *insurance company executive*
Hubbell, James Windsor, Jr. *retired insurance company executive*
Hurd, G. David *insurance company executive*
Hutchison, Theodore Murtagh *insurance company executive*
Kalainov, Sam Charles *insurance company executive*
Kelley, Robb Beardsley *insurance company executive*
Larson, Paul Edward *insurance company executive*
†Newsome, Jon P. *insurance company executive*
†Ray, Robert D. *health insurance company executive*
Richards, Riley Harry *insurance company executive*
Rohm, Charles Edward *insurance company executive*
Schneider, William George *former life insurance company executive*
Speas, Raymond Aaron *retired insurance company executive*
Stauffer, William Albert *insurance company executive*

Fayette
Wenger, Eugene Edward *insurance agent*

West Des Moines
Brooks, Roger Kay *insurance company executive*
Davis, Ronald Arthur *life insurance brokerage executive*
Westerbeck, Kenneth Edward *retired insurance company executive*

KANSAS

Fort Scott
†McCurley, F. C. *insurance company executive*

Overland Park
Oldham, Dale Ralph *life insurance company executive, actuary*

Shawnee Mission
Barton, C. Robert *insurance company executive*
Holliday, John Moffitt *insurance company executive*
†Lakin, Scott Bradley *insurance agent*
Miller, Stanford *insurance consultant*
Shipman, David Norval *healthcare consultant*

Topeka
Abrahams, John Hambleton *life insurance company executive*
†Eisenbarth, Gary *insurance company executive*
†Fricke, Howard R. *insurance company executive*
Heitz, Mark V. *insurance company executive*
Laster, Ralph William, Jr. *insurance company executive, accountant*
†Miller, Thomas L. *insurance company executive*

KENTUCKY

Beulah Heights
†Barthel, F. Ernest *insurance company executive*

Louisville
Bailey, Irving Widmer, II *insurance holding company executive*
Baxter, James William, III *insurance and investment executive*
†Bow, Stephen Tyler, Jr. *insurance company executive*
†Gillis, Frank Lauren *insurance executive*
Hull, John Thomas, Jr. *life insurance company executive*
McCormick, Steven Thomas *insurance company executive*
†Rice, Jerry W. *insurance company executive*
Rosky, Theodore Samuel *insurance company executive*
Speed, John Sackett *insurance company executive*

LOUISIANA

Baton Rouge
†Greer, Robert Stephenson *insurance company executive*
Jay, James Albert *insurance company executive*

New Orleans
Purvis, George Frank, Jr. *life insurance company executive*
Roberts, John Kenneth, Jr. *life insurance company executive*
Trapolin, Frank Winter *retired insurance executive*

MAINE

Portland
Freilinger, James Edward *insurance and investments company executive*
Orr, James F., III *insurance company executive*

South Portland
Dalbeck, Richard Bruce *insurance executive*

MARYLAND

Baltimore
Benedict, Linda Sherk *insurance company executive*
Bradley, Thomas Andrew *insurance company executive*
†Dailey, George R., Jr. *insurance company executive*
Hayes, Charles Lawton *insurance company executive, holding company executive*
Hecht, Alan Dannenberg *insurance executive*
Jenkins, Benjamin Larry *insurance company executive*

Chester
Dabich, Eli, Jr. *insurance company executive*

Easton
Hayes, James Edward *retired insurance executive*

Lutherville
Morgan, James Gilmor *insurance executive*

Mount Airy
Collins, Henry James, III *insurance company executive*

Owings Mills
Disharoon, Leslie Benjamin *retired insurance executive*
†Gloth, Fred M., Jr. *insurance company executive*
Walsh, Semmes Guest *retired insurance company executive*
Wieczynski, Frank Robert *insurance brokerage executive*

Oxford
Radcliffe, George Grove *retired life insurance company executive*

Silver Spring
Jaskot, John Joseph *insurance company executive*

MASSACHUSETTS

Andover
Fitzgerald, Michael Anthony *insurance company executive*

Boston
Aborn, Foster Litchfield *insurance company executive*
†Atherton, William *insurance company executive*
†Boyan, William L., Jr. *insurance company executive*
Brown, Michael *information technology executive*
Brown, Stephen Lee *insurance company executive*
Buckley, Joseph W. *insurance company executive*
Chilvers, Derek *insurance company executive*
Conners, John Brendan *insurance company executive*
Countryman, Gary Lee *insurance company executive*
†Duffy, Kenneth J. *insurance company executive*
Fish, David Earl *insurance company executive*
Gianino, John Joseph *insurance executive*
Gruhl, Robert Herbert *insurance company executive*
†Hirtle, Richard C. *insurance company executive*
Kamer, Joel Victor *insurance company executive, actuary*
†Kelly, Edmund F. *insurance company executive*
King, Kernan Francis *insurance company executive, lawyer*
King, Robert David *insurance company executive*
†La Fontaine, Raymond M. *insurance company executive*
Lykins, Marshall Herbert *insurance company executive*
Maloney, Therese Adele *insurance company executive*
Morton, Edward James *insurance company executive*
Nashe, Carol *insurance executive, consultant*
†Roffey, Robert C., Jr. *insurance company executive*
Rohda, Rodney Raymond *insurance company executive*
Rosensteel, John William *insurance company executive*
Scipione, Richard Stephen *insurance company executive, lawyer*
Shafto, Robert Austin *insurance company executive*
Shemin, Barry L. *insurance company executive*
Toran, Daniel James *insurance executive*
Wangler, William Clarence *insurance company executive*

Brookline
Shaw, Samuel Ervine, II *retired insurance company executive, consultant*

Eastham
McLaughlin, Richard Warren *retired insurance company executive*

Framingham
†Holmes, Jack E. *insurance company executive*
Oleskiewicz, Francis Stanley *retired insurance executive*

Great Barrington
Schenck, Benjamin Robinson *insurance consultant*

Needham
Carey, Robert Williams *retired insurance company executive*

Newton
Rodman, Sumner *insurance executive*

Pittsfield
Cornelio, Albert Carmen *insurance executive*

Salem
O'Brien, Robert Kenneth *insurance company executive*

Springfield
Bixby, Allan Barton *insurance company executive*
Clark, William J. *life insurance company executive*
Clark, William James *insurance company executive*
Finnegan, Thomas Joseph, Jr. *insurance executive, lawyer*
Johnson, Robert Allison *life insurance company executive*
Naughton, John M. *insurance company executive*
Wheeler, Thomas Beardsley *insurance company executive*

Waltham
Bumpus, Frederick Joseph *insurance executive*
Yancey, Wallace Glenn *insurance company executive*

Wellesley
Horn, David Dinsmore *insurance company executive*

West Boylston
Moorefield, James Lee *retired insurance executive, lawyer*

Weston
Mc Elwee, John Gerard *retired life insurance company executive*

Winchester
Cowgill, F(rank) Brooks *retired insurance company executive*

Worcester
Alie, Arthur Henry *financial services company executive*
O'Brien, John F., Jr. *insurance company executive*
Olson, Robert Leonard *retired insurance company executive*
†Soule, Charles Everett *insurance executive*

Yarmouth Port
†Teague, Edward B., III *insurance and investment broker*

MICHIGAN

Battle Creek
†Hutson, Don D. *insurance company executive*

Chelsea
†Holmes, Howard Sumner *association executive*

Detroit
Buselmeier, Bernard Joseph *insurance company executive*
Lindow, Donald August *insurance company executive*
Pero, Joseph John *insurance company executive*

Farmington
Headlee, Richard Harold *insurance company executive*

Lansing
†Arends, Herman J. *insurance company executive*
Saltzman, Robert Paul *insurance company executive*

Port Huron
Haynes, Marcia Margaret *insurance agent*

Southgate
Torok, Margaret Louise *insurance company executive*

Tecumseh
Taylor, Robert Lee *financial services and sales executive, information systems account executive, educator*

MINNESOTA

Chisholm
†Tomassoni, David Joseph *insurance agent, state representative*

Ivanhoe
Hoversten, Ellsworth Gary *insurance executive, producer*

Lake Elmo
Shervheim, Lloyd Oliver *insurance company executive, lawyer*

Minneapolis
†Anderson, Lowell Carlton *insurance company executive*
Barnhill, Howard Eugene *insurance company executive*
Blomquist, Robert Oscar *insurance company executive*
Dubes, Michael J. *insurance company executive*
†Gandrud, Robert P. *insurance company executive*
Guillaume, Marnix Leo Karl *insurance company executive*
Kling, Richard William *insurance executive*
McErlane, Joseph James *insurance company executive*
Mitchell, James Austin *insurance company executive*
†Nicholson, Bruce J. *insurance company executive*
Turner, John Gosney *insurance company executive*

Minnetonka
Anderson, H(arry) Robert *insurance agent*
†Maxwell, Robert Oliver *insurance company executive*
†Robbins, Orem Olford *insurance company executive*

Owatonna
†Buxton, Charles Ingraham, II *insurance company executive*
†Nelson, Kirk N. *insurance company executive*

Red Wing
Vonch, David Lee *insurance agent, writer, financial consultant*

Saint Paul
Bloomfield, Coleman *insurance company executive*
Boudreau, James Lawton *insurance company executive*
Hunstad, Robert Edward *insurance company executive*
Kane, Stanley Phillip *insurance company executive*
Leatherdale, Douglas West *insurance company executive*
Pendergast, Edward Gaylord *insurance company executive*
Troske, L. A. *insurance executive*
Williams, Chester Arthur, Jr. *insurance educator*

Woodbury
†Clancy, Robert J. *insurances company executive*

MISSISSIPPI

Clinton
†Montgomery, Keith Norris, Sr. *insurance executive, state legislator*

Gulfport
†Hewes, William Gardner, III *insurance executive, real estate agent, legislator*

Jackson
Dean, Jack Pearce *retired insurance company executive*
Stovall, Jerry (Coleman Stovall) *insurance company executive*

MISSOURI

Camdenton
Mullens, William Reese *retired insurance company executive*

Eagle Rock
Rowan, Gerald Burdette *insurance company executive, lawyer*

Kahoka
Huffman, Robert Merle *insurance company executive*

Kansas City
Bixby, Walter E. *insurance company executive*
Bradshaw, William David *insurance company executive*
Chastain, Larry Kent *insurance company executive*
Hazlett, James Arthur *insurance administrator*
Hogan, Thomas John *insurance company executive*
Malacarne, C. John *insurance company executive, lawyer*
Mc Gee, Joseph John, Jr. *former insurance company executive*
Merriman, Joe Jack *insurance company executive*
Reaves, Charles William *insurance company executive, writer, educator, investment advisor*
†Sayler, J. W., Jr. *insurance company executive*
†Walker, John Ernst *insurance company executive*

Lees Summit
Timmons, Joseph Dean *insurance company executive*

Saint Louis
†Chomeau, David Douglass *insurance company executive*

Dressel, Roy Robert *insurance company executive*
Haberstroh, Richard David *insurance agent*
Liddy, Richard A. *insurance company executive*
†Redmond, Donald Paul *insurance company executive*
Schumacher, Frederick Carl *former insurance company executive*
Stalnaker, Armand Carl *former insurance company executive, retired educator*
Stith, Richard Taylor, Jr. *insurance company executive*
†Trusheim, H. Edwin *insurance executive*
Williams, Thom Albert *insurance company executive*
†Winer, Warren James *insurance executive*

Springfield
†Ostergren, Gregory Victor *insurance company executive*

NEBRASKA

Holdrege
Hendrickson, Bruce Carl *life insurance company executive*

Lincoln
Arth, Lawrence Joseph *insurance executive*
Day, Richard Putnam *insurance executive*
Haire, James Robert *insurance company individual administration and strategic development executive*
Holdt, Leland LaMar Stark *insurance company executive*
Louis, Kenneth Clair *insurance company executive*
Tyner, Neal Edward *insurance company executive*

Omaha
Ames, George Ronald *insurance marketing executive*
Barrett, Frank Joseph *insurance company executive*
†Bookout, John G. *insurance company executive*
Conley, Eugene Allen *retired insurance company executive*
†Graham, Wayne *insurance company executive*
Haney, J. Terrence *insurance consultant*
Jay, Burton Dean *insurance actuary*
Maginn, John Leo *insurance company executive*
†Myers, Herman E., Jr. *life insurance company executive*
†Schellpeper, Gene Harold *insurance executive*
Skutt, Thomas James *insurance company executive*
Weekly, John William *insurance company executive*

NEW HAMPSHIRE

Concord
Swope, John Franklin *insurance company executive*

Grantham
Boothroyd, Herbert J. *insurance company executive*

Keene
Colby, Kenneth Poole *insurance company executive*

Nashua
Barton, Carl P. *retired insurance company executive*

Sunapee
MacKinnon, Malcolm D(avid) *retired insurance company executive*

NEW JERSEY

Allenhurst
Delaney, William Francis, Jr. *reinsurance broker*

Berkeley Heights
Gottheimer, George Malcolm, Jr. *insurance executive, educator*

Bernardsville
Vairo, Robert John *insurance company executive*

Branchville
Hallowell, Walter Henry *insurance company executive*

Cherry Hill
Beebe, Leo Clair *industrial equipment executive, former educator*

East Orange
Green, David *insurance company executive*

Florham Park
Bossen, Wendell John *insurance company executive*
Erickson, Charles Edward *insurance company executive*
Smith, Robert William *former insurance company executive, lawyer*

Jersey City
Marshall, Philips Williamson *insurance agency executive*
Sanders, Franklin D. *insurance company executive*

Liberty Corner
Miller, Walter Neal *insurance company executive*
†Stoll, Roger G. *health insurance company executive*

Madison
Calligan, William Dennis *retired life insurance company executive*
Leak, Margaret Elizabeth *insurance company executive*

Morristown
Munson, William Leslie *insurance company executive*
Newhouse, Robert J., Jr. *insurance executive*

Mount Tabor
Lender, Herman Joseph *reinsurance company executive*

Mountain Lakes
Cook, Charles Francis *insurance executive*

Neptune
Suozzo, Frank Vincent *insurance company executive*

Newark
Beck, Robert Arthur *insurance company executive*
†Clark, Dewey P. *insurance company executive*
†Dwane, James E. *insurance company executive*
Gerathy, E. Carroll *former insurance executive, real estate developer*
Gillen, James Robert *insurance company executive, lawyer*
Keith, Garnett Lee, Jr. *insurance company investment executive*
Latini, Anthony A. *insurance company financial executive*
Light, Dorothy Kaplan *insurance executive, lawyer*
†Link, William P. *insurance company executive*
†Murray, John Peter *insurance company executive*
Winters, Robert Cushing *insurance company executive*
Zinbarg, Edward Donald *insurance company executive*

Ocean City
Brown, Frederick Harold *insurance company executive*

Parsippany
Waggoner, Leland Tate *insurance company executive*

Plainsboro
Jones, Allen N. *insurance company executive*

Princeton
†Inderbitzin, Paul Herold *reinsurance company executive*
†Jobe, Edward B. *insurance company executive*
Wentz, Sidney Frederick *insurance company executive, foundation executive*

Ridgewood
Knies, Paul Henry *former life insurance company executive*

Rumson
Creamer, William Henry, III *insurance company executive*

Secaucus
Feaster, S. Edward *insurance agent*

Trenton
†Bandish, Dennis Michael *insurance company executive*

Warren
Chubb, Percy, III *insurance company executive*
Georgieff, Gregory *insurance executive*
†Norton, Donn H. *insurance company executive*
O'Hare, Dean Raymond *insurance company executive*
Parker, Henry Griffith, III *insurance executive*
Smith, Dudley Renwick *insurance company executive*
Smith, Richard D. *insurance holding company executive*
Werner, Richard Vincent *insurance company executive*

NEW MEXICO

Las Cruces
Cochrun, John Wesley *insurance agent*

NEW YORK

Armonk
Bailey, William O. *retired insurance company executive*
Elliot, David H. *insurance company executive*

Binghamton
Best, Robert Mulvane *insurance company executive*
Dunn, Melvin Bernard *insurance company executive*
Pearson, Paul Holding *insurance company executive*

Bronxville
Knapp, George Griff Prather *insurance consultant, arbitrator*

Brooklyn
Faison, Seth Shepard *retired insurance broker*

Chappaqua
Harris, David Henry *retired life insurance company executive*

Fayetteville
Sager, Roderick Cooper *retired life insurance company executive*

Irvington
Stimpson, John Hallowell *insurance company executive*

Jericho
Spivack, Henry Archer *life insurance company executive*

Locust Valley
Sunderland, Ray, Jr. *retired insurance company executive*

Malverne
Knight, John Francis *insurance company executive*

Melville
Dixon, Lawrence Paul *insurance company executive*

Merrick
Cherry, Harold *insurance company executive*
O'Brien, Kenneth Robert *life insurance company executive*

New York
Athanassiades, Ted *insurance company executive*
Benjamin, George David *insurance company executive*
†Berstein, Richard A. *insurance company executive*
Biggs, John Herron *insurance company executive*
Blumstein, William A. *insurance company executive*
Briggs, Philip *insurance company executive*
Bundschuh, George August William *insurance company executive*
Bushey, Alan Scott *insurance holding company executive*
Caouette, John Bernard *insurance company executive*
Clapman, Peter Carlyle *insurance company executive, lawyer*
Comey, Dale Raymond *insurance company executive*
Conklin, Thomas J. *insurance company executive*
Crane, Stephen Andrew *insurance company executive*
Creedon, John J. *insurance company executive*
Crystal, James William *insurance company executive*
Decaminada, Joseph Pio *insurance company executive, educator*
Dolan, Raymond Bernard *insurance executive*
Ferrara, Arthur Vincent *insurance company executive*
Forte, Wesley Elbert *insurance company executive, lawyer*
Futia, Leo Richard *former insurance company executive*
Gammill, Lee Morgan, Jr. *insurance company executive*
†Gamper, Albert R., Jr. *insurance executive*
†Gantz, John G., Jr. *insurance company executive*
Garber, Harry Douglas *life insurance executive*
Gavrity, John Decker *insurance company executive*
Gibson, William Shepard *insurance executive*
Gilmore, Robert Gordon *insurance company executive*
Glidden, Allan Hartwell *insurance company executive*
Goodstone, Edward Harold *insurance company executive*
Greenberg, Maurice Raymond *insurance company executive*
Gruber, Alan Richard *insurance company executive*
Hansen, Richard Arthur *insurance company executive, psychologist*
Hauser, Fred P. *insurance company executive*
Hohn, Harry George *insurance company executive, lawyer*
Hutchings, Peter Lounsbery *insurance company executive*
Irvin, Tinsley Hoyt *insurance broker*
Jibaja, Gilbert *insurance company executive*
†Jones, Thomas W. *insurance company executive*
Kamen, Harry Paul *life insurance company executive, lawyer*
†Karter, Jerome *insurance company executive*
Kavee, Robert Charles *insurance company executive*
King, Douglas Lohr *insurance executive, lawyer*
Klein, Paul E. *insurance company executive, lawyer*
Knudsen, Rudolph Edgar, Jr. *insurance company executive*
†Kornreich, Morton Alan *insurance brokerage company executive*
Lamel, Linda Helen *insurance company executive, college president, lawyer*
Lassiter, Phillip B. *insurance company executive*
Lee, J. Daniel, Jr. *insurance company executive*
Lowry, William Ketchin, Jr. *insurance company executive*
†Loynes, John Hamilton *insurance company executive*
†Lynch, Frank Joseph *insurance company executive*
†Mangino, Robert *insurance company executive*
Manton, Edwin Alfred Grenville *insurance company executive*
Martin, James Smith *insurance executive*
Matthews, Edward E. *insurance company executive*
McCormack, John Joseph, Jr. *insurance executive*
Mc Elrath, Richard Elsworth *insurance company executive*
McKillop, Daniel James *insurance company real estate executive*
McLaughlin, Michael John *insurance company executive*
Melone, Joseph James *insurance company executive*
†Meyer, Richard E. *insurance agent*
Morrissey, Dolores Josephine *insurance executive*
Moynahan, John Daniel, Jr. *insurance executive*
Murray, Richard Maximilian *insurance executive*
Nagler, Stewart Gordon *insurance company executive*
†Neeck, Bernard J. *insurance company executive*
Norton, Paul Allen *insurance executive*
†O'Healy, Quill *insurance company executive*
Olsen, David Alexander *insurance executive*
Osterhout, Dan Roderick *insurance executive*
Oxley, Geraldine Motta *insurance company executive*
Papa, Vincent T. *insurance company executive*
Parker, Charles A. *insurance company executive*
†Patrell, Oliver Lincoln *insurance company executive*
Paul, Douglas Allan *insurance executive*
†Procope, Ernesta Gertrude *insurance broker*
Putney, John Alden, Jr. *insurance company executive*
Reuter, Carol Joan *insurance company executive*
Roberts, John Joseph *insurance company executive*
Ross, Donald Keith *retired insurance company executive*
†Sanborn, Robert B. *insurance company executive*
Sandler, Robert Michael *insurance company executive, actuary*
Sargent, Joseph Dudley *insurance executive*
Schwartz, Robert George *retired insurance company executive*
Shinn, Richard Randolph *former insurance executive, former stock exchange executive*
Shur, Walter *retired insurance company executive*
Smith, Alexander John Court *insurance executive*
Smith, John Matthew *insurance company executive*
†Smith, Steven James *insurance company executive*
Somers, John Arthur *insurance company executive*
Spencer, Henry Benning *insurance industry investment advisor*
Stewart, Gordon Curran *insurance information association executive*
Sullivan, Joseph Peter *insurance broker*
Tirakis, Judith Angelina *financial company executive*
Tocklin, Adrian Martha *insurance company executive, lawyer*
Tse, Stephen Yung Nien *insurance executive*
Underhill, Jacob Berry, III *retired insurance company executive*
Vascellaro, Frank John *insurance company executive*
Wolf, James Anthony *insurance company executive*
Woodbury, Marion A. *insurance company executive*
Yalen, Gary N. *insurance company executive*

Point Lookout
Stack, Maurice Daniel *retired insurance company executive*

Poughkeepsie
O'Shea, John P. *insurance executive*

Rockville
Burton, Daniel G. *insurance executive*

Rockville Centre
Friedman, Neil Stuart *insurance company executive*

Schenectady
Lawrence, Albert Weaver *insurance company executive*

Searingtown
Entmacher, Paul Sidney *insurance company executive, physician, educator*

Syosset
Barry, Richard Francis *retired life insurance company executive*

Syracuse
Mannion, John Francis Xavier *insurance company executive*
Marge, Michael *disability prevention specialist*
Whittle, John Joseph *insurance company executive*

Utica
Ehre, Victor Tyndall *insurance company executive*

White Plains
Cohen, Richard Norman *insurance executive*
†Tobin, Steven Michael *insurance company executive*

NORTH CAROLINA

Camden
Hammond, Roy Joseph *reinsurance company executive*

Chapel Hill
Kittredge, John Kendall *retired insurance company executive*
Stewart, Richard Edwin *insurance consulting company executive*

Charlotte
Mendelsohn, Robert Victor *insurance company executive*
Stephens, Louis Cornelius, Jr. *insurance executive*

Durham
Clark, Arthur Watts *insurance company executive*
Clement, William Alexander *insurance compnay executive*
Collins, Bert *insurance executive*
†Philyaw, A. Roger *insurance company executive*

Greensboro
Blackwell, William Ernest *insurance company executive, financial analyst*
Bryan, Joseph McKinley *insurance company executive*
Carr, Howard Ernest *retired insurance agency executive*
Carter, Wilbur Lee, Jr. *retired insurance executive*
Macon, Seth Craven *retired insurance company executive*
Soles, William Roger *insurance company executive*

Pinehurst
†Morgan, Richard Timothy *insurance executive*

Raleigh
†King, George Edward *insurance executive*
Pendleton, Gary H(erman) *life insurance agent*

Rocky Mount
Pitt, Theophilus Harper, Jr. *insurance and real estate company executive*

NORTH DAKOTA

Bismarck
Smith, Richard Ernest *retired insurance company executive*

Fargo
†Payne, Douglas G. *retired insurance company executive*
Swedback, James M. *insurance company executive*

OHIO

Akron
Arnett, James Edward *retired insurance company executive, retired secondary school educator*

Bedford Heights
Moore, Dianne J. Hall *insurance claims administrator*

Cincinnati
Addison, Harry Metcalf *insurance executive*
Aniskovich, Paul Peter, Jr. *insurance company executive*
Byers, Kenneth Vernon *insurance company executive*
†Cantu, John Maurice *insurance company executive*
Clark, James Norman *insurance executive*
†Houser, Dwane Russell *insurance company executive*
Klinedinst, Thomas John, Jr. *insurance agency executive*
Krohn, Claus Dankertsen *insurance company executive*
†Milnes, William Robert, Jr. *insurance company executive*
Morgan, Robert B. *insurance company executive*
†Pike, Larry Ross *insurance executive*
Schiff, John Jefferson *insurance company executive*

Warnemunde, Bradley Lee *insurance company executive*
Weed, Ithamar Dryden *life insurance company executive*
†Williams, William Joseph *insurance company executive*

Columbus
Carlson, Larry Vernon *insurance company executive*
Doyle, Patrick Lee *insurance company executive*
Duryee, Harold Taylor *insurance executive*
Emanuelson, James Robert *retired insurance company executive*
Fisher, John Edwin *insurance company executive*
Frenzer, Peter Frederick *insurance company executive*
Fullerton, Charles William *retired insurance company executive*
Galloway, Harvey Scott, Jr. *insurance company executive*
McFerson, D. Richard *insurance company executive*
Neckermann, Peter Josef *insurance company executive*
Sokol, Saul *insurance agency executive*
Wilhelmy, Odin, Jr. *insurance agent*

Hamilton
Marcum, Joseph LaRue *insurance company executive*
Patch, Lauren Nelson *insurance company executive*

Mayfield Heights
Lewis, Peter Benjamin *insurance company executive*

OKLAHOMA

Oklahoma City
Ille, Bernard Glenn *insurance company executive*

Tulsa
Abbott, William Thomas *claim specialist*
White, Ralph Dallas *retired health insurance executive*

OREGON

Ashland
Hemp, Ralph Clyde *retired reinsurance company executive, consultant, arbitrator, umpire*

Portland
†Halverson, Gerald B. *insurance company executive*
Lang, Philip David *former state legislator, insurance company executive*
Whiteley, Benjamin Robert *insurance company executive*
Yates, Keith Lamar *retired insurance company executive*

Salem
Rasmussen, Neil Woodland *insurance agent*

PENNSYLVANIA

Bala Cynwyd
McGill, Dan Mays *insurance business educator*

Bloomsburg
Miller, David Jergen *insurance executive*

Blue Bell
†Wise, Allen Floyd *insurance executive*

Camp Hill
Keller, John Richard *insurance company executive*
Robertson, James Colvert *insurance company executive*
†Ross, Samuel D., Jr. *insurance company executive*

Frazer
Godwin, Pamela June *insurance company executive*
†Kennedy, Donald Davidson, Jr. *insurance company executive*

Gettysburg
Bohner, Dean Arlington *insurance executive*

Harleysville
Craugh, Joseph Patrick, Jr. *insurance company executive, lawyer*
†McCarter, Michael G. *insurance company executive*
Mitchell, Bradford William *insurance executive, lawyer*

Harrisburg
†Mead, James Matthew *insurance company executive*
†Rabena, Kathleen A. *indurance company executive*

Haverford
Baney, John Edward *insurance company executive*
Zalinski, Edmund Louis Gray *insurance executive, mutual funds and real estate executive, investor*

Jenkintown
Silver, Leonard J. *insurance and risk management company executive*

Newtown Square
Staats, Dean Roy *retired reinsurance executive*

Norristown
Clemens, Alvin Honey *insurance company executive*
†Hellauer, James Carroll *insurance company executive*

Philadelphia
Coyne, Frank J. *insurance company executive*
†DiBona, G. Fred, Jr. *insurance company executive*
Farnam, Walter Edward *insurance company executive*
Frohlich, Kenneth R. *insurance executive*
Glicksman, Russell Allen *insurance and human resources executive; executive recruiter*
Guckes, William Ruhland, Jr. *insurance executive*
Jones, Thomas Chester *reinsurance company executive*
Joyce, Robert Joseph *insurance executive*
Mella, Arthur John *insurance company executive*
Morris, George Norton *insurance company executive*
†Reber, Stanley Roy *insurance company executive*
Ross, Roderic Henry *insurance company executive*
†Rowell, Lester John, Jr. *insurance company executive*
Snider, Harold Wayne *risk and insurance educator*
Stewart, James Gathings *insurance company executive*
Tait, John Edwin *insurance company executive*
Tarbox, Frank Kolbe *insurance company executive*

University Park
Hammond, J. D. *insurance educator*

Wayne
Yoskin, Jon William *insurance company executive*

RHODE ISLAND

Johnston
Patin, Robert White *insurance company executive*
Subramaniam, Shivan Sivaswamy *insurance company executive*

Little Compton
MacKowski, John Joseph *retired insurance company executive*

Providence
Koelb, Clayton Talmadge *insurance company executive*
†Mc Intosh, Douglas J. *insurance company executive*
†Schobel, George *insurance company executive*

SOUTH CAROLINA

Columbia
Averyt, Gayle Owen *insurance executive*
Reichard, William Thomas, III *insurance company executive*
Smith, Franklin Sumner, Jr. *retired insurance executive*

Greenville
Hipp, Francis Moffett *insurance executive*
Hipp, William Hayne *insurance and broadcasting executive*
Hunt, Walter Kenneth, III *insurance company executive*
Mims, Thomas Jerome *insurance company executive*
Moore, Alfred Michael *insurance broker executive*

SOUTH DAKOTA

Mitchell
†Widman, Paul Joseph *insurance agent*

Rapid City
†Bickett, Robert Winston *insurance executive*

Sioux Falls
†Kirby, Joe P. *insurance company executive*
Rigsbee, William Alton *insurance company executive*

TENNESSEE

Chattanooga
Hanlin, Hugh Carey *retired life insurance company executive*
Hardy, Thomas Cresson *insurance company executive*
†Long, Tom *insurance company executive*
Walker, Winston Wakefield, Jr. *insurance company executive*

Nashville
Davis, James Verlin *insurance brokerage executive*
Dedman, Bertram Cottingham *retired insurance company executive*
Lazenby, Fred Wiehl *insurance company executive*
Sutton, Barrett Boulware *former insurance company executive*

Seymour
Steele, Ernest Clyde *retired insurance company executive*

TEXAS

Amarillo
Hilbert, Stephen C. *insurance company executive*

Austin
Mullen, Ron *insurance company executive*
Payne, Eugene Edgar *insurance company executive*
Payne, Tyson Elliott, Jr. *retired insurance executive*

Dallas
Cline, Bobby James *insurance company executive*
†Estell, Richard J. *insurance company executive*
†Gardiner, John William *insurance company executive*
Hardy, Tom Charles, Jr. *medical equipment and insurance claims management executive*
†Hudson, C. B., Jr. *insurance company executive*
Langston, Roy A. *insurance company consultant*

Fort Worth
Berg, Ericson *insurance company executive*

Galveston
Clay, Orson C. *insurance company executive*
Seinsheimer, Joseph Fellman, Jr. *insurance executive*

Garland
†Driver, Joe L. *insurance consultant*

Houston
Allen, Kenneth Dale *insurance executive, corporate counsel*
Bailey, Charles Lyle *insurance company executive*
Bickel, Stephen Douglas *insurance company executive*
Couch, Jesse Wadsworth *retired insurance company executive, consultant*
†Crowley, Joseph Paul *insurance company executive*
Davenport, Joseph Dale *insurance executive*
Davis, Rex Lloyd *insurance company executive*
Devlin, Robert Manning *financial services company executive*
Friedberg, Thomas Harold *insurance company executive*
Harris, Richard Foster, Jr. *insurance company executive*
Hook, Harold Swanson *insurance company executive*
Kellison, Stephen George *insurance executive*
Lindsey, John Horace *insurance executive, museum official*
†Morris, Stewart, Jr. *title insurance company executive*
Poulos, Michael James *insurance company executive*
Skalla, John Lionell *insurance agent*
Tuerff, James Rodrick *insurance company executive*
Woodson, Benjamin Nelson, III *insurance executive*

Irving
†Hickey, John Michael *insurance company executive*

Lubbock
Allison, Cecil Wayne *insurance company executive*

Richardson
†Coleman, Rogers King *insurance company executive*
†Langmead, Jeffrey P. *insurance company executive*

San Antonio
Herres, Robert Tralles *insurance company executive*
Holcomb, M. Staser *insurance executive*
Mc Dermott, Robert Francis *insurance company executive*
Regan, William Joseph, Jr. *insurance company executive*

Texarkana
†Young, Dennis Ray *insurance agent*

The Woodlands
Connell, Joseph Edward *retired insurance executive*

Tyler
Guin, Don Lester *insurance company executive*

Waco
Rapoport, Bernard *life insurance company executive*

UTAH

Ogden
Buckner, Elmer La Mar *insurance executive*

Park City
Fey, John Theodore *insurance company executive*

VERMONT

Montpelier
Bertrand, Frederic Howard *insurance company executive*
Harding, John Hibbard *insurance company executive*
Leland, Lawrence *insurance executive*

Norwich
Byrne, John Joseph, Jr. *insurance executive*

South Burlington
Hackett, Luther Frederick *insurance company executive*

Woodstock
Blackwell, David Jefferson *insurance company executive*

VIRGINIA

Alexandria
Casey, Michael Kirkland *business executive, lawyer*

Arlington
Law, David Holbrook *insurance executive*

Lynchburg
Britton, Donald W. *insurance company executive*
Butler, John Alden *insurance company executive*
Dolan, Ronald Vincent *insurance company executive*
McRorie, William Edward *life insurance company executive*
Stewart, George Taylor *insurance executive*

Richmond
†Davis, Norwood H., Jr. *health insurance corporation executive*
Jacobs, James Paul *insurance executive*
Kilpatrick, Robert Donald *retired insurance company executive*
Rutledge, Paul E., III *insurance company executive*

Roanoke
Berry, John Coltrin *insurance executive*

Williamsburg
Herrmann, Benjamin Edward *former insurance executive*

Woodstock
Walker, Charles Norman *retired insurance company executive*

WASHINGTON

Bellevue
Eigsti, Roger Harry *insurance company executive*
Roddis, Richard Stiles Law *insurance company executive, consultant, legal educator*

Bellingham
Fullmer, Donald Kitchen *insurance executive*

Kennewick
Stevens, Henry August *insurance agent, educator*

Kirkland
McDonald, Joseph Lee *insurance broker*

Mercer Island
†Vining, Glen W., Jr. *insurance company executive*

Mountlake Terrace
†Lockwood, Donald A. *insurance company executive*
†Woods, Betty *insurance company executive*

Seattle
†Coviello, Vincent F., Jr. *insurance company executive*
†Dyer, Philip E. *insurance company executive*
LaPoe, Wayne Gilpin *retired business executive*
†Nudelman, Phillip M. *insurance company executive*
Phillips, Josef Clayton *insurance and investment company executive*
Robb, Bruce *former insurance company executive*
Zunker, Richard E. *insurance company executive*

Walla Walla
Perry, Louis Barnes *retired insurance company executive*

WISCONSIN

Appleton
†Gunderson, Richard L. *insurance company executive*

Brookfield
Payne, Howard James *insurance company executive*
†Snyder, C(laude) Robert *insurance company executive*

Madison
DuRose, Stanley Charles, Jr. *insurance executive*
†Heins, Richard M. *insurance company executive*
Herndon, Terry Eugene *insurance executive*
Larson, John David *life insurance company executive, lawyer*
†Mathwich, Dale F. *insurance company executive*
†Pierce, Harvey R. *Insurance company executive*
Waldo, Robert Leland *retired insurance company executive*

Milwaukee
†Hefty, Thomas R. *insurance company executive*
Karl, Max Henry *insurance company executive*
Miller, Keith *insurance company executive*
Pelton, Ralph A. *insurance company executive*
Schuenke, Donald John *insurance company executive*
Van Antwerpen, Regina Lane *underwriter, insurance company executive*
Zore, Edward John *insurance company investment executive*

Stevens Point
Ballard, Larry Coleman *insurance company executive*

Wausau
†Weinberger, Leon Joseph *insurance company executive*

CANADA

ONTARIO

Islington
Wykes, Edmund Harold *retired insurance company executive*

London
Allan, Ralph Thomas Mackinnon *insurance company executive*
Creighton, Dale Edward *insurance company executive*
Orser, Earl Herbert *insurance company executive*

Richmond Hill
Howe, James Tarsicius *insurance company executive*

Toronto
Gardner, John Robert *insurance company executive*
McNeil, John D. *insurance company executive*
Nesbitt, Mark *management consultant*

Waterloo
MacGregor, Kenneth Robert *former insurance company executive*
Masterman, Jack Verner *insurance company executive*

BERMUDA

Hamilton
Kramer, Donald *insurance executive*
Stempel, Ernest Edward *insurance executive*

Pembroke
Wiedemann, Joseph Robert *insurance company executive*

ENGLAND

London
Harris, William Cecil *insurance company consultant*

†Newmarch, Michael George insurance company executive
Shaw, Richard John Gildroy insurance executive

HONG KONG

Hong Kong
Tse, Edmund Sze-Wing insurance company executive

ITALY

Rome
Zimolo, Armando insurance company executive

ADDRESS UNPUBLISHED

Adam, John, Jr. insurance company executive emeritus
Angle, John Charles retired life insurance company executive
Armstrong, F(redric) Michael retired insurance company executive
Beattie, Nora Maureen insurance company executive, actuary
Becker, JoAnn Elizabeth insurance company executive
Bellamy, James Carl insurance company executive
Cooper, Charles Gordon insurance consultant, former executive
Crandles, George Marshal retired insurance company executive
Culp, William Newton retired insurance executive
Dannenberg, Martin Ernest retired insurance company executive
DeAlessandro, Joseph Paul insurance company executive
DeMark, Richard Reid retired insurance company executive
Fibiger, John Andrew life insurance company executive
Gundelfinger, Ralph Mellow insurance company executive
Halmos, Imre Hubertus insurance company executive
Hartsell, Samuel David insurance agent
Hauenstein, George Carey life insurance executive
Herman, Joan Elizabeth insurance company executive
Hirst, Heston Stillings former insurance company executive
†Ipsen, Grant Ruel insurance and investments professional
Jacobson, James Bassett insurance executive
†Kardos, Paul James insurance company executive
Katz, Henry insurance executive, retired
Kavanagh, Kevin Patrick insurance company executive
Lacey, Cloyd Eugene retired insurance company executive
Ladd, Joseph Carroll retired insurance company executive
Lancaster, Edwin Beattie insurance company executive
†Langer, Ray Fritz retired insurance executive
Long, Alvin William title insurance company executive
Longnaker, John Leonard retired insurance company executive, lawyer
Ludlam, James Edward, III insurance company executive
†Macchia, Joseph Dominick insurance company executive
Mascotte, John Pierre insurance executive
Mathews, Robert Earl, II insurance company executive
McCarty, Dennis L. insurance executive
McGee, Craig Heslin insurance company executive
McHugh, John James consultant
McKenna, Terence Patrick insurance company executive
Morrill, Thomas Clyde insurance company executive
†Olson, Eric G. insurance company executive
Pasant, David A. insurance company executive
Plummer, Daniel Clarence, III insurance consultant
Reynolds, John Francis insurance company executive
Riss, Robert Bailey insurance company executive
†Rooney, J. Patrick insurance company executive
†Ryan, James insurance company executive
Scott, John Burt life insurance executive
Smith, Floyd Leslie insurance company executive
Snyder, Alan Carhart insurance company executive
Snyder, William Burton insurance executive
Sutcliffe, James H. insurance company executive
†Tasco, Frank John insurance brokering company executive
Vanderhoof, Irwin Thomas life insurance company executive
Whitehead, Richard Lee insurance company executive
Wilkins, Roger Carson retired insurance company executive
Wills, William Ridley, II former insurance company executive, historian

FINANCE: INVESTMENT SERVICES

UNITED STATES

ALABAMA

Birmingham
Comer, Donald, III investment company executive
Culp, Charles Allen financial executive
Marks, Charles Caldwell retired investment banker, retired industrial distribution company executive
Massey, Richard Walter, Jr. investment counselor
Tucker, Thomas James investment manager

Montgomery
Blount, Winton Malcolm, III investment executive

Mountain Brook
Haworth, Michael Elliott, Jr. investor, former aerospace company executive

ALASKA

Anchorage
Harris, Roger J. entrepreneur

ARIZONA

Mesa
Tennison, William Ray, Jr. financial planner, stock broker, recreational facility executive

Phoenix
Bansak, Stephen A., Jr. investment banker, financial consultant
Quinsler, William Thomson retired investment advisor

Scottsdale
Doede, John Henry investment company executive

Tucson
Schannep, John Dwight brokerage firm executive

Vail
Maierhauser, Joseph George entrepreneur

ARKANSAS

Fort Smith
Hembree, Hugh Lawson, III diversified holding company executive

Little Rock
McGowan, Michael Benedict investment banker
Morris, Walter Scott investment company executive
Reeves, Rosser Scott, III investment company executive
Stephens, Jackson Thomas investment executive

CALIFORNIA

Agoura Hills
Myers, Phillip Fenton brokerage house executive

Aptos
Zischke, James Braden entrepreneur

Beverly Hills
Mc Kenna, William Edward entrepreneur
Walker, William Tidd, Jr. investment banker

Burlingame
Holmes, Richard Hugh Morris investment management executive

Carmel
Jordan, Edward George business investor, former college president, former railroad executive
Stratton, Thomas Oliver investment banker

Corona Del Mar
Solberg, Ronald Louis investment management company executive

Coronado
Grant, Alan J. business executive

Cupertino
Horn, Christian Friedrich venture capital company executive
†Markkula, A. C., Jr. entrepreneur
Perkins, Thomas James venture capital company executive

Del Mar
Beare, Bruce Riley trading company and sales executive

Escondido
Allen, Donald Vail investment executive, author, concert pianist and organist

Foster City
Turner, Ross James investment corporation executive

Fresno
Buzick, William Alonson, Jr. investor, lawyer, educator
Dauer, Donald Dean investment executive

Goleta
Bartlett, James Lowell, III investment banker

Irvine
†Cowart, Jim Cash secutities trader
Giannini, Valerio Louis investment banker

Laguna Hills
Burns, Donald Snow registered investment advisor, financial and business consultant

Larkspur
Kirk, Gary Vincent investment advisor

Los Angeles
Angeloff, Dann V. investment banking executive
Baker, William Garrett, Jr. investment banker
Bernstein, Arthur Harold venture capital executive
Campbell, Douglas Argyle securities broker
Drew, Paul entrepreneur
Emmeluth, Bruce Palmer investment banker, venture capitalist
Galef, Andrew Geoffrey investment and manufacturing company executive
Gebhart, Carl Grant security broker
Gordy, Berry entrepreneur, record company executive, motion picture executive
Greenstadt, Melvin investor, retired educator
Hurt, William Holman investment management company executive
Hurwitz, Lawrence Neal investment banking company executive
†Johnston, Michael J. brokerage house executive
Kelly, Raymond Francis commodity company executive
Koffler, Stephen Alexander investment banker
Lovelace, Jon B. investment management company executive
Morgan, Todd Michael investment advisor
Nilles, John Mathias (Jack Nilles) entrepreneur
Ogle, Edward Proctor, Jr. investment counseling executive
Tennenbaum, Michael Ernest investment banker
Terry, Thomas Edward investment company executive, lawyer
Winkler, Howard Leslie investment banker, stockbroker, business consultant

Menlo Park
Bissell, Betty Dickson stockbroker
Hoagland, Laurance Redington, Jr. investment executive
Lucas, Donald Leo entrepreneur
Lynch, Charles Allen investment executive, corporate director
McCown, George E. venture banking company executive
Roberts, George R. venture capital company executive
Walsh, William Desmond investor

Newport Beach
Albright, Archie Earl, Jr. investment banker
Fletcher, Douglas Baden investment company executive

Orinda
Campbell-White, Annette Jane venture capitalist
Rosenberg, Barr Marvin investment advisor, economist

Palm Desert
Budge, Hamer Harold mutual fund company executive
Krallinger, Joseph Charles entrepreneur, business advisor, author

Palm Springs
Yantis, Richard William investments executive

Palos Verdes Estates
Mennis, Edmund Addi investment management consultant

Pasadena
Arnott, Robert Douglas investment company executive
Baum, Dwight Crouse investment banking executive
Howes, Benjamin Durward, III mergers and acquisitions executive
Lauter, James Donald stockbroker

San Francisco
Apatoff, Michael John finance executive
Bertelsen, Thomas Elwood, Jr. investment banker
Bond, Cornelius Combs, Jr. investment advisor
Buckner, John Knowles corporate executive
Delaney, Richard James investment banker
Dellas, Robert Dennis investment banker
De Lutis, Donald Conse investment manager, consultant
deWilde, David Michael executive search consultant, financial services executive, lawyer
†Dunn, Richard Joseph investment counselor
George, Michael P. investment banker, lawyer
Halliday, John Meech investment company executive
Hellman, F(rederick) Warren investment advisor
†Hitchcock, Patrick J. investment company executive
Korins, Leopold stock exchange executive
Latzer, Richard Neal investment company executive
McGettigan, Charles Carroll, Jr. investment banker
Pfau, George Harold, Jr. stockbroker
Pottruck, David S. brokerage house executive
Ratzlaff, James W. investment company executive
Redo, David Lucien investment company executive
Rosenberg, Claude Newman, Jr. investment adviser
†Seip, Tom Decker securities executive
Shansby, John Gary investment banker
Shelton, Richard Fottrell investment executive
Stupski, Lawrence J. investment company executive
Tobkin, Christine Anderson investment banker
Turner, Marshall Chittenden, Jr. venture capitalist
Veitch, Stephen William investment counselor
Wiley, Thomas Glen retired investment company executive

San Jose
Hall, Robert Emmett, Jr. investment banker, realtor

San Juan Capistrano
Robinson, Daniel Thomas brokerage company executive

San Leandro
Pansky, Emil John entrepreneur

San Marino
Zimmerman, William Robert entrepreneur, engineering based manufacturing company executive

San Mateo
Fenton, Noel John venture capitalist
†Hawkins, William (Trip), III software executive

Santa Barbara
Vos, Hubert Daniel private investor

Santa Clara
Greene, Frank Sullivan, Jr. business executive

Santa Monica
Richards, David Kimball investor
Sher, Allan L. retired brokerage company executive

Westlake Village
Fredericks, Ward Arthur venture capitalist, food industry consultant

COLORADO

Colorado Springs
Ramsay, Robert Henry investment manager
Tutt, Russell Thayer investment company executive

Denver
Brierly, Keppel retired investment executive
Butler, Owen Bradford securities advisor
Cook, Albert Thomas Thornton, Jr. financial advisor
Imhoff, Walter Francis investment banker
Stephenson, Arthur Emmet, Jr. investment company executive, banker
Wagner, Judith Buck investment firm executive

Englewood
Perry, Mervyn Francis investment company executive

Grand Junction
Sewell, Beverly Jean financial executive

CONNECTICUT

Darien
Lewis, A. Duff, Jr. investment executive
Moltz, James Edward brokerage company executive
Morse, Edmond Northrop investment management executive

Farmington
Bigler, Harold Edwin, Jr. investment company executive
Halligan, Howard Ansel investment management company executive

Greenwich
Baker, Charles Ernest stockbroker
Foley, Thomas C. investor
Kopp, W. Brewster corporate director, advisor
Larned, William Edmund, Jr. international development and venture capital company executive
Lewis, Perry Joshua investment banker
Nevin, Crocker investment banker
Pringle, Lewis Gordon international trade and investment company executive

Guilford
†Boyle, Helen D. entrepreneur

Hartford
Crispin, Robert William investment company executive
O'Keefe, James William, Jr. investment manager and banker

Litchfield
Booth, John Thomas investment banker

Lyme
Friday, John Ernest, Jr. retired securities company executive

New Canaan
Mendez, Albert Orlando industrialist, financier
Pike, William Edward investment company executive
Snyder, Nathan entrepreneur

Norwalk
Hathaway, Carl Emil investment management company executive
Maisano, Phillip Nicholas investment company executive

Old Greenwich
Alley, William Jack holding company executive

Old Saybrook
Schneider, John Arnold business investor

Southbury
Fabiani, Dante Carl industrialist

Southport
Wilbur, E. Packer investment company executive

Stamford
Carpenter, Michael Alan securities firm executive
De Micoli, Salvatore metals commodity executive
Ekernas, Sven Anders investment company executive
Frey, Dale Franklin financial investment company executive, manufacturing company executive
Hawley, Frank Jordan, Jr. venture capital executive
Walton, Alan George venture capitalist

Weston
Daniel, James business executive, writer, former editor

Westport
Kalan, George Richard venture capitalist
Kelly, Paul Knox investment banker
O'Keefe, John David investment specialist
Radigan, Joseph Richard human resources executive
Scheinman, Stanley Bruce venture capital executive, lawyer

Wilton
†Finlayson, John L. commodities company executive
†Ritter, Bruce Commodities Company executive

DELAWARE

Newark
Miller, Michael Barbree investment company executive

Wilmington
Boyer, David Creighton stockbroker
Dewees, Donald Charles securities company executive

DISTRICT OF COLUMBIA

Washington
Ansary, Cyrus A. lawyer, investor

Carley, L. David investment consultant, former college administrator
Countryman, John Russell business executive, former ambassador
Cusick, Ralph A., Jr. investment banking company executive
Douglas, Leslie investment banker
Ellsworth, Robert Fred investment executive, former government official
Farrar, Donald Eugene capital markets advisor
Ferris, George Mallette, Jr. investment banker
Fisher, Robert Dale stockbroker, retired naval officer
Fleming, Robert Wright investment banker
Hardiman, Joseph Raymond investment banking executive
Hartwell, Stephen investment company executive
Isaac, William Michael investment firm executive, former government official
Kelly, Charles J., Jr. investment company executive
Levitt, Arthur, Jr. securities and publishing executive, federal agency administrator
Lister, Harry Joseph financial company executive, consultant
Lurton, Horace VanDeventer brokerage house executive
Macomber, John D. industrialist
Peterson, Charles Hayes trading company executive
Sethness, Charles Olin international financial official
Shrier, Adam Louis investment firm executive
Silby, Donald Wayne investment executive, entrepreneur
Spangler, Scott Michael private investor
Stearns, James Gerry securities company executive
Thompson, Bruce Edward, Jr. brokerage house executive, former government official
Tomlinson, Alexander Cooper investment banker, consultant
Ulmer, Alfred Conrad investment banker
Wortley, George Cornelius business consultant, investor

FLORIDA

Boca Raton
†Mischler, Harland Louis investment company executive

Boynton Beach
Allison, Dwight Leonard, Jr. investor
Davant, James Waring investment banker

Coral Gables
Nunez-Portuondo, Ricardo investment company executive

Daytona Beach
Locke, Edwin Allen, Jr. investment banker

Delray Beach
Holmes, Walter Stephen, Jr. retired financial executive
Jenkins, Stanley Michael stockbroker

Englewood
Simis, Theodore Luckey investment banker, information technology executive

Fort Lauderdale
Huizenga, Harry Wayne entertainment corporation executive, professional sports team executive
Sanders, Howard investment company executive
†Thayer, Charles J. investment banker

Hobe Sound
Fiske, Guy Wilbur investment company executive
Hotchkiss, Winchester Fitch retired investment banker

Jacksonville
Monsky, John Bertrand investment banking executive
Schultz, Frederick Henry investor, former government official
Travis, Forrest investment firm executive

Marco Island
Pettersen, Kjell Will stockbroker, consultant

Miami
Bishopric, Karl investment banker, real estate executive, advertising executive
Bradley, Ronald Calvin investment company executive
Dorion, Robert Charles entrepreneur, investor
Garner, John Michael investment company executive
Gittlin, Arthur Sam industrialist, banker
Wilson, Robert Gordon investment banker, waste management manager
Wolf, Clarence, Jr. stockbroker

Naples
Colbert, Lester Lum investor, lawyer, former automobile executive
†Dover, Clarence Joseph entrepreneur, public and employee relations executive, educator, consultant, communication director
Elliott, Edward investment executive, financial planner
Guarino, Roger Charles consulting company executive
Harvey, Curran Whitthorne, Jr. investment management executive
Oliver, Robert Bruce retired investment company executive

North Palm Beach
Gray, Harry Jack investment executive

Palm Beach
Adduci, Vincent James business executive
Bagby, Joseph Rigsby financial investor
Gundlach, Heinz Ludwig investment banker, lawyer
Halmos, Peter investment company executive
Rudolph, Malcolm Rome investment banker

Palm Beach Gardens
Mergler, H. Kent investment counselor

Pompano Beach
Rifenburgh, Richard Philip investment company executive

Ponte Vedra Beach
Hanigan, Marvin Frank investment company executive, consultant
Krusen, Henry Stanley investment banker
Thorndike, Richard King former brokerage company executive

Saint Petersburg
Emerson, William Allen retired investment company executive
Galbraith, John William securities company executive
Godbold, Francis Stanley investment banker, real estate, oil and gas executive
Mosby, John Davenport, III investment banking executive
Scott, Lee Hansen holding company executive

Sarasota
Levitt, Irving Francis investment company executive

Tampa
Crowe, Eugene Bertrand retired investment counselor
Holder, Harold Douglas, Sr. investor, industrialist

Tierra Verde
Gaffney, Thomas Francis investment company executive

Vero Beach
Glassmeyer, Edward investment banker
Thompson, William David investment banking executive

West Palm Beach
Price, William James, IV investment banker

GEORGIA

Albany
Greene, William Joshua, III investment executive and consultant

Atlanta
Dowling, Roderick Anthony investment banker
†Green, Holcombe Tucker, Jr. investment executive
†Greene, Milton Anthony investment securities executive
Tracy, Thomas Kit investment company executive
Williams, Ralph Watson, Jr. retired securities company executive
Winship, Wadleigh Chichester holding company executive

Sea Island
Brown, Ann Catherine investment company executive
Brown, George Hay investment counselor

HAWAII

Honolulu
Ho, Stuart Tse Kong investment company executive
Mau, William Koon-Hee financier

IDAHO

Challis
†Barrett, Lenore Hardy mining and investment consultant, state legislator

Sun Valley
†Nickelson, Donald Eugene brokerage house executive

ILLINOIS

Barrington
Baxter, Reginald Robert investment company executive
†Farina, Nick Charles investor relations consultant

Chicago
Bergonia, Raymond David venture capitalist
Blair, Bowen investment banker
Blair, Edward McCormick investment banker
Block, Philip Dee, III investment counselor
Brodsky, William J. futures options exchange executive
Buckle, Frederick Tarifero international holding company executive, political and business intelligence analyst
Chaleff, Carl Thomas brokerage house executive
Clarke, Philip Ream, Jr. investment banker
Cole, Franklin Alan investment company executive
Cone, Joseph Jay investment banking officer
Donovan, Thomas Roy futures exchange executive
Ender, John T. investment management executive, banker
Fenton, Clifton Lucien investment banker
Freehling, Stanley Maxwell investment banker
Freehling, Willard Maxwell stockbroker
Gorter, James Polk investment banker
†Hawkinson, John former investment management company executive
Kahn, Herta Hess (Mrs. Howard Kahn) retired stockbroker
Kaufman, Ira Jeffrey investment banker
Kelly, Arthur Lloyd management and investment company executive
Knox, Lance Lethbridge venture capital executive
Lewis, Charles A. investment company executive
†Lincoln, Sandy investment management executive
Livingston, Homer J., Jr. stock exchange executive
Loucks, Ralph Bruce, Jr. investment company executive
McCausland, Thomas James, Jr. brokerage house executive
†McConahey, Stephen George securities company executive
McNeill, Robert Patrick investment counselor
Meers, Henry W. investment banker
Melamed, Leo investment company executive
Miner, Thomas Hawley international entrepreneur
Mukoyama, James Hidefumi, Jr. securities executive
Mulvihill, Terence Joseph investment banking executive
Nash, Donald Gene commodities specialist
Oliver, Harry Maynard, Jr. retired brokerage house executive
†Phillips, Donald W. investment company executive
Podesta, Robert Angelo investment banker
Pritzker, Nicholas J. diversified services corporation executive
Rasin, Rudolph Stephen investment banker
Rhea, Edward Buford, Jr. brokerage house executive
Robertson, Sara Stewart investment company executive
Rogers, John W., Jr. brokerage house executive
Rumsfeld, Donald Henry former government official, corporate executive
Sandner, John Francis commodity futures broker, lawyer
Schulte, David Michael investment banker
Slansky, Jerry William investment company executive
Stead, James Joseph, Jr. securities company executive
Swift, Edward Foster, III investment banker
Waite, Dennis Vernon investor relations consultant
Weitzman, Robert Harold investment company executive
Wilmouth, Robert K. commodities executive
Wirsching, Charles Philipp, Jr. brokerage house executive, investor
Woods, Robert Archer investment counsel
Young, Ronald Faris commodity trader

Deerfield
Howell, George Bedell equity investing and managing executive

Highland Park
Uhlmann, Frederick Godfrey commodity and securities broker
Weinberg, Michael, Jr. commodities broker

Hinsdale
Kelly, Donald Philip entrepreneur

Jacksonville
Olinger, Glenn Slocum entrepreneur, consultant, investor

Lake Forest
Leatham, John Tonkin business executive

Morton Grove
†Shaw, Jeffrey A. commodities trader

Oak Brook
Cooper, Richard Harris investment company executive

Palatine
†Flavin, Patrick Brian investment company executive, securities analyst

Saint Charles
Schultz, Robert Vernon entrepreneur

Skokie
Searle, William Louis investment company executive

Villa Park
McDonnell, Dennis J. securities industry executive

Wilmette
Albright, Townsend Shaul investment banker, government benefits consultant

Winnetka
Mathers, Thomas Nesbit financial consultant
Sick, William Norman, Jr. investment company executive

INDIANA

Fort Wayne
Burns, Thagrus Asher manufacturing company executive, former life insurance company executive

Indianapolis
Fritz, Cecil Morgan investment company executive

Richmond
Passmore, Jan William investment company executive

IOWA

Cedar Falls
Oster, Merrill James entrepreneur, publisher, author, lecturer

KANSAS

Kansas City
Olofson, Tom William private investor, business executive

KENTUCKY

Harrods Creek
Chandler, James Williams retired securities company executive

Louisville
Lomicka, William Henry investor
Porter, Henry Homes, Jr. investor

LOUISIANA

Covington
Files, Mark Willard business and financial consultant

New Orleans
†Copelin, Sherman Nathaniel, Jr. entrepreneur, business executive
Doley, Harold Emanuel, Jr. securities company executive
Levert, John Bertels, Jr. investment executive

MAINE

Manset
Delehanty, Edward John investment company executive

Portland
Powell, Larson Merrill investment advisory service executive

Waterville
Ezhaya, Joseph Bernard brokerage house executive

MARYLAND

Baltimore
Bacigalupo, Charles Anthony brokerage company executive
Brinkley, James Wellons investment company executive
Burgess, R. William, Jr. investment banking executive
Cashman, Edmund Joseph, Jr. investment banker
Collins, George Joseph investment counselor
Curley, John Francis, Jr. securities company executive
Griswold, Benjamin Howell, IV investment banker
Himelfarb, Richard Jay securities firm executive
Hopkins, Samuel retired investment banker
†Hyman, Harris, IV investment banker
Janney, Stuart Symington, III investment company executive
Kent, Edgar Robert, Jr. investment banker
Mason, Raymond Adams brokerage company executive
McManus, Walter Leonard investment executive
Newhall, Charles Watson, III venture capitalist
Ober, Douglas Gary investment company executive
Riepe, James Sellers investment company executive
Semans, Truman Thomas investment company executive
Shaeffer, Charles Wayne investment counselor
Westheimer, Julius Milton investment executive, media financial commentator
Wilson, Robert James Montgomery investment company executive

Bethesda
Corbett, Jack Elliott mutual fund officer, clergyman, author

Chestertown
Sener, Joseph Ward, Jr. securities company executive

Lutherville Timonium
Cappiello, Frank Anthony, Jr. investment advisor

Potomac
Proffitt, John Richard investment banking executive

Queenstown
Bancroft, Paul, III investment company executive, venture capitalist

Riverdale
Guetzkow, Daniel Steere technology company entrepreneur

Rockville
Tripp, Frederick Gerald investment advisor

MASSACHUSETTS

Boston
Bailey, Richard Briggs investment company executive
Bennett, George Frederick investment manager
Calderwood, Stanford Matson investment management executive
Cantella, Vincent Michele stockbroker
†Clay, Landon Thomas investment company executive
Colburn, Kenneth Hersey investment banker
Cox, Howard Ellis, Jr. venture capitalist
de Burlo, Comegys Russell, Jr. investment advisor, educator
Drohan, Thomas H. investment management executive
Elfers, William retired investment company director
Estin, Hans Howard investment executive
Gardner, George Peabody investment banker
Glazer, Donald Wayne business executive, lawyer, educator
Greeley, Walter Franklin management and acquisition corporation executive, lawyer
Hagler, Jon Lewis investment executive
Hobbs, Matthew Hallock investment banker
Kretschmer, Keith Hughes stockbroker
Lee, David Stoddart investment counselor
Loring, Caleb, Jr. investment company executive
†Mc Carthy, Denis Michael investment executive
McDaniels, John Francis investment banker
Mc Neice, John Ambrose, Jr. investment company executive
Morby, Jacqueline venture capitalist
Morrison, Gordon Mackay, Jr. investment company executive
Morton, William Gilbert, Jr. stock exchange executive
Moseley, Frederick Strong, III investment banker
Oates, William Armstrong, Jr. investment company executive
Peckham, John Munroe, III investment executive, author

Pierce, Daniel *investment company executive*
Piret, Marguerite Alice *investment banker*
Roman, William Edward *investment banker*
Romney, W Mitt *investment company executive*
Sobin, Julian Melvin *international consultant*
Stone, David Barnes *investment advisor*
Thorndike, John Lowell *investment executive*
Towles, Stokley Porter *commercial and investment banking executive*
Vinik, Jeffrey *investment portfolio manager*

Cambridge
Babson, David Leveau *retired investment counsel*
Bedrosian, Edward Robert *investment management company executive*
Lloyd, Boardman *investment executive*

Carlisle
Fohl, Timothy *consulting and investment company executive*

Concord
Lombardo, Gaetano (Guy Lombardo) *venture capitalist*
Schiller, Pieter Jon *venture capital executive*

Milton
Kennedy, Thomas Leo *investment management company executive*

Reading
Burbank, Nelson Stone *investment banker*

Stoneham
†Mc Donald, Andrew Jewett *securities firm executive*

Wellesley
Anthony, Edward Lovell, II *retired investments executive*
Beckedorff, David Lawrence *investment manager, computer scientist*
Valente, Louis Patrick (Dan Valente) *technical corporation executive*

Westwood
Gillette, Hyde *investment banker*

Woburn
Eddison, Elizabeth Bole *entrepreneur, information specialist*

MICHIGAN

Beulah
Auch, Walter Edward *securities company executive*

Bloomfield Hills
Benton, Robert Austin, Jr. *investment banker, broker*
Rom, (Melvin) Martin *securities executive*
Suter, Kenneth Harris *personal investments consultant*
†Winograd, Bernard *financial adviser*

Detroit
Brown, William Paul *investment executive*
Callaway, David Henry, Jr. *investment banker*
Lane, James McConkey *investment executive*
Martin, John Gustin *investment banker*
Mengden, Joseph Michael *investment banker*

Lansing
Stevens, J. Paul *entrepreneur*

Oak Park
Novick, Marvin *investment company executive, former automotive supplier executive, accountant*

Traverse City
LeJeune, Dennis Edward *investment counsel*

MINNESOTA

Minneapolis
Foley, Thomas *brokerage house executive*
Froehlke, Robert Frederick *financial services executive*
Gallagher, Gerald Raphael *venture capitalist*
Goldberg, Luella Gross *investment company executive*
Horsch, Lawrence Leonard *corporate revitalization executive, venture capitalist*
Martens, Keith Otto *investment company executive*
Piper, Addison Lewis *securities executive*
Ross, Percy Nathan *business executive, newspaper columnist*

Saint Paul
Rothmeier, Steven George *merchant banker*

Waubun
Christensen, Marvin Nelson *venture capitalist*

MISSISSIPPI

Jackson
Burwell, Dudley Sale *retired investment executive and food executive*

Ripley
Clawson, John Addison *financier, investor*

MISSOURI

Kansas City
Barnes, Peter Crain *stockbroker*
Braude, Michael *commodity exchange executive*
Latshaw, John *entrepreneur*
Rowland, Landon Hill *diversified holding company executive*
Stowers, James Evans, Jr. *investment company executive*

Lees Summit
Korschot, Benjamin Calvin *investment executive*

Saint Louis
Avis, Robert Grier *investment company executive, civil engineer*
Bachmann, John William *securities firm executive*
Bernstein, Donald Chester *brokerage company executive, lawyer*
Buesinger, Ronald Ernest *security and commodity brokerage executive*
Clement, Richard Francis *retired investment company executive*
Costigan, Edward John *investment banker*
Frager, Norman *stockbroker*
Lindner, Kurt Julius *fund management company executive*
Marsh, Miles L. *holding company executive*
Newton, George Addison *investment banker, lawyer*
Stein, Elliot H. *investment broker*
Walker, George Herbert, III *investment banking company executive, lawyer*

MONTANA

Bozeman
Davis, Nicholas Homans Clark *finance company executive*

Helena
Lindgren, Robert Kemper *securities investor, county tax collector*

NEBRASKA

Dakota City
Tinstman, Dale Clinton *investment company executive*

Omaha
Buffett, Warren Edward *corporate executive*
Greer, Randall Dewey *investment company executive*
Sawtell, Stephen M. *private investor, lawyer*
Sokolof, Phil *industrialist, consumer advocate*
Soshnik, Joseph *investment banking consultant*
Velde, John Ernest, Jr. *business executive*

NEVADA

Glenbrook
Jabara, Michael Dean *investment banker*

Incline Village
Dale, Martin Albert *investment banking executive*
Johnson, James Arnold *business consultant, venture capitalist*

Las Vegas
Di Palma, Joseph Alphonse *company executive, lawyer*

Logandale
Smiley, Robert William, Jr. *investment banker*

Smith
Weaver, William Merritt, Jr. *investment banker*

NEW HAMPSHIRE

Concord
Levins, John Raymond *investment advisor, management consultant, educator*

Portsmouth
Morin, Carlton Paul *private investments executive*

NEW JERSEY

Bloomfield
Stella, John Anthony *investment company executive*

Cranford
Bardwil, Joseph Anthony *investments consultant*

East Orange
Howe, James Everett *investment company executive*

Fairfield
Oolie, Sam *investment company executive*

Florham Park
†Lovell, Robert Marlow, Jr. *investment company executive*

Fort Lee
Lippman, William Jennings *investment company executive*

Gladstone
Detwiler, Peter Mead *investment banker*

Hackensack
Delaney, Patrick James *investment company executive*

Jersey City
Dreman, David Nasaniel *investment counselor, security analyst*

Madison
Johnson, William Joseph *stockbroker*

Mendham
Kirby, Allan Price, Jr. *investment company executive*

Montclair
Kidde, John Lyon *investment manager*
Richart, John Douglas *investment banker*

Morristown
Kearns, William Michael, Jr. *investment banker*
Warlick, Robert Patterson *investment management company executive*

Mountain Lakes
Wolff, Ivan Lawrence *venture capitalist*

Newark
Hannon, John Robert *investment company executive*
O'Leary, Paul Gerard *investment executive*

Paramus
Smith, Donald Gene *investment management company executive*

Parsippany
Bean, Bruce Winfield *investment banker, lawyer*

Plainsboro
†Hewitt, N. J. *investment company executive*
Schreyer, William Allen *retired investment firm executive*
Urciuoli, J. Arthur *investment executive*

Princeton
Chamberlin, John Stephen *investor, former cosmetics company executive*
Dilworth, Joseph Richardson *investment banker*
Ehrenberg, Edward *executive, investor*
Johnston, Robert Fowler *venture capitalist*
Schafer, Carl Walter *investment executive*

Red Bank
Weiant, William Morrow *investment banking executive*

Rockleigh
Heslin, John Thomas *entrepreneur, historic preservationist*

Scotch Plains
Bishop, Robert Milton *former stock exchange official*

Short Hills
Bartels, Stanley Leonard *investment banker*
Perez, Bertin John *investment banker*

Summit
Geiger, Richard Lawrence *entrepreneur*

Teaneck
Palitz, Clarence Yale, Jr. *commercial finance executive*

Westfield
Simon, Martin Stanley *commodity marketing company executive, economist*

NEW MEXICO

Albuquerque
†Malina, Robert S. *investment company executive*

Santa Fe
Davis, Shelby M. C. *investment executive, consultant*
Dreisbach, John Gustave *investment banker*
Duval, Michael Raoul *investment banker*
Nurock, Robert Jay *investment analysis company executive*

NEW YORK

Ardsley
Sanders, Robert Martin *commodity trader*

Armonk
Karvelis, Leon J., Jr. *investment company executive*

Bedford Hills
Fissell, William Henry *investment advisor*

Bronxville
Penisten, Gary Dean *entrepreneur*

Brooklyn
Leyh, Richard Edmund, Sr. *retired investment executive*

Buffalo
Irwin, Robert James Armstrong *investment company executive*
Littlewood, Douglas Burden *business brokerage executive*

Chappaqua
Stralem, Pierre *retired stockbroker*

Dobbs Ferry
Grunebaum, Ernest Michael *investment banker*

Garden City
Gordon, Barry Joel *investment advisor*

Glen Head
Sutherland, Donald James *investment company executive*

Glendale
Hess, Karsten *trading company executive*

Great Neck
Fialkov, Herman *investment banker*
Hampton, Benjamin Bertram *brokerage house executive*

Hartsdale
Katz, John *investment banker, business consultant, lawyer*

Ithaca
Ben Daniel, David Jacob *entrepreneurship educator, consultant*

Jamestown
Bargar, Robert Sellstrom *investor*

Larchmont
Sandell, Richard Arnold *international trade executive, economist*

Lloyd Harbor
Deavers, Karl Alan *investment banker*

Locust Valley
Benson, Robert Elliott *investment banker, consultant*

Mill Neck
Phelan, John J., Jr. *former stock exchange executive, corporate director*

Mount Kisco
Singer, Craig *investor, consultant*
Wood, James *broker*

New York
Acampora, Ralph Joseph *brokerage firm executive*
Agostinelli, Robert Francesco *investment banker*
Albers, Charles Edgar *investment manager, insurance executive*
Allen, Herbert *investment banker*
Allison, Herbert Monroe, Jr. *investment firm executive*
Alworth, Sandra Ann *municipal bond salesperson, brokerage house executive*
Ames, George Joseph *investment banker*
Andersen, K(ent) Tucker *investment executive*
Aronson, Edgar David *venture capitalist*
Bach, Arthur James *investment banker*
Ballard, Charles Alan *investment banker*
Barr, Michael Charles *securities analyst, lawyer, investment banker*
Barrett, Robert James, III *investment banker*
Barry, Thomas Corcoran *investment counsellor*
Baylis, Robert Montague *investment banker*
Beale, Christopher William *investment banker*
Bell, Martin Allen *corporate executive*
Bellas, Albert Constantine *investment banker, advisor*
Berger, Andrew L. *investment banker, lawyer*
Beringer, Stuart Marshall *investment banker*
Berlin, Howard Richard *investment advisory company executive*
Berlin, Jordan Stuart *investment company executive*
Bernard, Lewis W. *foundation executive*
Bewkes, Eugene Garrett, Jr. *investment company executive, consultant*
Beyman, Jonathan Eric *investment banker*
Bickford, Jewelle Wooten *investment banker*
Biggs, Barton Michael *investment company executive*
Birkelund, John Peter *investment banking executive*
Blackwell, John Wesley *securities industry executive, consultant*
Blalock, Sherrill *investment advisor*
Boyd, Michael Alan *investment banking company executive, lawyer*
†Brinker, Robert J. *investment company executive, radio talk show host*
Brittenham, Raymond Lee *investment company executive*
Brody, Alan Jeffrey *business executive*
Brody, Eugene David *investment company executive*
Brody, Kenneth David *investment banker*
Brokaw, Clifford Vail, III *investment banker, business executive*
Brown, Fred Elmore *investment executive*
Brown, Ronald *stockbroker*
Brunie, Charles Henry *investment manager*
Buckles, Robert Howard *investment company executive*
Bucko, John Joseph *investment corporation executive*
Bullock, Hugh *investment banker*
Burke, James Joseph, Jr. *investment banker*
Cannaliato, Vincent, Jr. *investment banker, mathematician*
Carey, William Polk *investment banker*
Chalsty, John Steele *investment banker*
Charrier, Michael Edward *investment banker*
Chefitz, Harold Neal *investment banker*
Clarens, John Gaston *investment executive*
Clayton, William L. *investment banking executive*
Cogan, Marshall S. *entrepreneur*
Cohen, Jonathan Little *investment banker*
Cohn, Bertram Josiah *investment banker*
Cole, Carolyn Jo *brokerage house executive*
†Coles, Michael H. *investment banker*
Colombo, Frank V. *securities company executive*
Connor, Robert Patrick *investment company executive*
Cory, Charles Robinson *media investment banker*
Corzine, Jon Stevens *investment banker*
Cox, Archibald, Jr. *investment banker*
Cromwell, Oliver Dean *investment banker*
Crosby, John Griffith *investment banker*
Culp, Michael *securities company executive, research director*
Cushing, Harry Cooke, IV *investment banker*
Danson, Stephen Michael *brokerage firm executive*
†DaPuzzo, Peter James *investment banker, trader, financial consultant*
Darlington, Henry, Jr. *investment broker*
David-Weill, Michel Alexandre *investment banker*
†Davis, J. Morton *investment company executive, economist*
Davis, Martin S. *investment company executive*
Davis, Richard Bruce *investment banker*
Debs, Richard A. *investment banker, government official*
de la Gueronniere, Raphael *securities firm executive*
DeMarco, Robert Thomas *investment company executive*
DeNunzio, Ralph Dwight *investment banker*
Derchin, Michael Wayne *research director, investment banker, financial analyst*
DeRoma, Leonard James *securities firm executive*
Dillon, Clarence Douglas *retired investment company executive*
†DiMartino, Joseph Salvatore *investment company executive*
Doyle, William Stowell *venture capitalist*
Dudack, Gail Marie *brokerage house executive*
DuGan, Gordon F. *investment banker*
†Dyson, Robert R. *investment company executive*
Ebbitt, Kenneth Cooper, Jr. *investment company executive*
Edlow, Kenneth Lewis *securities brokerage executive*
Edwards, James Cook *investment counselor*
Ehinger, Albert Louis, Jr. *securities trader*
Einbender, Alvin H. *securities dealer*
Einiger, Roger W. *brokerage house executive*

Ercklentz, Alexander Tonio *banker*
Evnin, Anthony Basil *venture capital investor*
Fein, Bernard *investments executive*
†Fensterstock, Lee *securities firm executive*
Ferris, Barton Purdy, Jr. *investment banker*
Feskoe, Gaffney Jon *investment banker, management consultant*
Field, William Stephenson *private equity investment company executive*
Fisher, Richard B. *investment banker*
Fiumefreddo, Charles A. *investment management company executive*
Flanigan, Peter Magnus *investment banker*
Fogarty, John Thomas *business executive, former association executive*
Forlano, Anthony *investment company executive*
Fowler, Henry Hamill *investment banker*
Frackman, Richard Benoit *investment banker*
France, Joseph David *securities analyst*
Frank, Frederick *investment banker*
Franklin, Edward Ward *international investment consultant, lawyer, actor*
Frantzen, Henry Arthur *investment company executive*
Fried, Albert, Jr. *investment banker*
Friedenberg, Daniel Meyer *financial investor*
Friedman, Alvin Edward *investment executive*
Friedman, Howard Martin *financial executive*
Furman, Roy Lance *investment banker*
Galbraith, Evan Griffith *investment banker*
Gambee, Robert Rankin *investment banker*
Gant, Donald Ross *investment banker*
Garner, Albert Headden *investment banker*
Garzarelli, Elaine Marie *brokerage house executive, economist*
Gelb, Harold Seymour *investor*
Gellert, Michael Erwin *investment banker*
Gerard, Emanuel *investment banking executive*
Gold, Jeffrey Mark *investment banker, financial adviser*
Goldberg, David Alan *investment banker, lawyer*
Golden, Robert Charles *brokerage house executive*
Gonzalez, Eugene Robert *investment banker*
Gordon, Albert Hamilton *investment banker*
Goren, Alexander Mircea *investment company executive*
Gottesman, David Sanford *investment executive*
Granger, David *investment banker*
Grano, Joseph J., Jr. *securities industry executive*
Grant, William Robert *investment banker*
Grasso, Richard A. *stock exchange executive*
Gray, Arthur, Jr. *investment counselor*
Greenberg, Alan Courtney (Ace Greenberg) *stockbroker*
Greenhill, Robert Foster *investment banker*
Guenther, Paul Bernard *securities company executive*
Guttman, Zoltan Lou *exchange executive*
Haire, John Russell *corporate executive, lawyer*
Hallingby, Paul, Jr. *investment banker*
Hansmann, Ralph Emil *investment executive*
Hart, Gurnee Fellows *investment counselor*
Haskell, John Henry Farrell, Jr. *investment banking company executive*
Hedley, David Van Houten *investment banker*
Heimann, John Gaines *investment banker*
Hennessy, John M. *brokerage house executive*
Herkness, Lindsay Coates, III *securities broker*
Herrmann, Lacy Bunnell *investment company executive, financial entrepreneur, venture capitalist*
Herzog, John E. *securities executive*
Hess, Dennis John *investment banker*
Heyman, George Harrison, Jr. *securities company executive*
Heyman, William Herbert *securities firm executive*
†Higgins, Harrison Scott *investment company executive*
Hill, J(ames) Tomilson *investment banker*
Hobbs, Franklin Warren, IV *investment banker*
Holland, Michael Francis *investment company executive*
Horowitz, Gedale Bob *investment banker*
Howard, Nathan Southard *investment banker, lawyer*
Hu, Joseph Chi-Ping *mortgage securities analyst*
Hultquist, Timothy Allen *investment banker*
Hurford, John Boyce *investment counselor*
Hurst, Robert Jay *securities company executive*
Hussein, Ahmed Dia *investment banker*
Hyman, Seymour *capital and product development company executive*
Jacoby, A. James *securities brokerage firm executive*
Jaffee, Sandra Schuyler *financial executive*
James, Hamilton Evans *investment banking firm executive*
Janiak, Anthony Richard, Jr. *investment banker*
Jenrette, Richard Hampton *investment and insurance company executive*
Jepson, Hans Godfrey *investment company executive*
Jones, Barclay Gibbs, III *investment banker*
†Jordan, John W., II *holding company executive*
Keevil, Philip Clement *investment banker*
Kellogg, Peter R. *securities dealer*
Khayatt, Shaker Albert *investment banker*
Kingsberg, Harold Joseph *investment management company executive*
Klemm, Richard Henry *investment company executive*
Klingenstein, Frederick Adler *investment banking executive*
Koch, Sidney *investment banker*
Kornstein, Don Robert *investment banker*
Krimendahl, Herbert Frederick, II *investment banker*
Krueger, Harvey Mark *investment banker, lawyer*
Lackritz, Marc E. *securities trade association executive*
Lamport, Anthony Matthew *investments and venture capitalist*
Lane, Frederick Carpenter *investment banker*
Lane, Jeffrey Bruce *financial services company executive*
Laren, Kuno *investment banker*
Lasser, Joseph Robert *investment company executive*
Lavine, Lawrence Neal *investment banker*
Lavitt, Mel S. *investment company executive*
Lebec, Alain *investment banker*
Le Buhn, Robert *investment company executive*
Le Fevre, William Mathias, Jr. *brokerage company executive*
Leighton, Lawrence Ward *investment banker*
Levine, Gerald Richard *investment banker, finanical advisor, estate planning and philanthropy specialist, commercial real estate broker*
Levitan, Dan *investment banker*
Levy, Leon *investment company executive*
Lewis, Sherman Richard, Jr. *investment banker*
Lipper, Kenneth *investment banker*
Loeb, John Langeloth, Jr. *investment counselor*
Logan, J. Murray *investment manager*
Loomis, Philip Clark *investment executive*
Ludovici, Anthony *security investment executive*
Lyons, Laurence *securities executive*
Mager, Ezra Pascal *automobile dealership group executive*
Maher, Stephen Albert *investment banker*
Maleska, Martin Edmund *investment banker*
Malin, Robert Abernethy *investment management executive*
Maloney, William Gerard *retired investment company executive*
Manges, James Horace *investment banker*
†Mangold, Glenn E. *securities industry executive*
Marcus, James Stewart *investment banker*
Marks, Edwin S. *merchant banker*
Marron, Donald Baird *investment banker*
Matthews, Gilbert Elliott *investment banker*
Mattone, Vincent J. *investment banker*
Maughan, Deryck C. *investment banker*
Maxwell, Anders John *brokerage house executive*
†Maxwell, Charles Thoburn *petroleum securities analyst*
Mazzilli, Paul John *investment banker*
Mc Carter, Thomas N., III *investment counseling company executive*
McCleary, Benjamin Ward *investment banker*
†McElroy, Edmund G., Jr. *investment company executive*
McGirr, David William John *investment banker*
Mc Lendon, Heath Brian *securities investment company executive*
McMullan, William Patrick, III *investment banker*
Meehan, John Joseph *brokerage house executive*
Menges, Carl Braun *investment banker*
Metz, Emmanuel Michael *investment company executive, lawyer*
Michas, Athanassios N. *investment company executive*
Miller, B. Jack *investment company executive*
Miller, Paul Lukens *investment banker*
Minard, Frank Pell Lawrence *investment manager*
Mintz, Walter *investment company executive*
Moak-Mazur, Connie J. *investment consultant, marketing professional*
Moran, Charles A. *securities executive*
Moran, John A. *investment company executive*
Morris, William Charles *investor*
Morrissey, Thomas Jerome *investment banker*
Most, Nathan *securities exchange executive*
Mountcastle, Kenneth Franklin, Jr. *stockbroker*
†Muenzen, Lee John *commodity trading company executive*
Muller, Robert Henry *securities research company executive*
Muratore, Peter Frederick *securities executive*
Myerberg, Marcia *investment banker*
Nabi, Stanley Andrew *investment executive*
Nazem, Fereydoun F. *venture capitalist, financier*
†Nebb, Edward Alan *investor relations executive*
Necarsulmer, Henry *investment banker*
Needham, George Austin *investment banker*
Neuberger, Roy R. *investment counselor*
Niehoff, Karl Richard Besuden *financial executive*
Niemiec, David Wallace *investment company executive*
Nodelman, Jared Robert *investment advisor*
Obolensky, Ivan *investment banker, foundation consultant, writer, publisher*
O'Connor, Francis X. *securities corporation executive*
†O'Donnell, Richard Walter *lawyer, accountant, brokerage company executive*
Offensend, David Glenn *investment executive*
Offit, Morris Wolf *investment management executive*
Orben, Jack Richard *investment company executive*
Osborne, Stanley de Jongh *investment banker*
Ostrander, Thomas William *investment banker*
Owen, Thomas Llewellyn, Sr. *investment executive*
Panitch, Michael B. *brokerage house executive*
Pardee, Scott Edward *securities dealer*
Paton, Leland B. *investment banker*
†Patrick, Thomas H. *brokerage house executive*
Patterson, Edward *investment banker*
Perlmutter, Louis *investment banker, lawyer*
Phillips, Howard William *investment banker*
Piper, Thomas Laurence, III *investment banker*
Pittaway, David Bruce *investment banker, lawyer*
Pollack, Stephen J. *stockbroker*
Pollicino, Joseph Anthony *investment company executive*
Potter, William James *investment banker*
Pulling, Thomas Leffingwell *investment advisor*
Quain, Mitchell I. *investment executive*
Quick, Thomas Clarkson *brokerage house executive*
Quirk, John James *investment company executive*
Rafferty, Brian Joseph *investor relations consultant*
Rand, Lawrence Anthony *investor and financial relations executive*
Rattner, Steven Lawrence *investment banker*
Reis, Judson Patterson *investment banker*
Rice, James A. *investment company executive*
Richter, Barry *brokerage firm executive*
Ricker, John Boykin, Jr. *insurance counselor*
Riley, Ivers Whitman *stock exchange executive*
Roehm, MacDonell, Jr. *investment firm executive*
Rogers, Eugene Charles *investment firm executive*
Rogers, Theodore Courtney *investment company executive*
Rohatyn, Felix George *investment company executive*
†Rohrbasser, Markus *securities broker executive*
Roosevelt, Theodore, IV *investment banker*
Rose, Robert Neal *brokerage house executive*
Rosen, Benjamin Maurice *venture capitalist*
Rosenbloom, Daniel *investment banker, lawyer*
Rosenwald, E. John, Jr. *brokerage house executive, investment banker*
Rosenwald, William *investment executive, philanthropist*
Rothstein, Gerald Alan *investment company executive*
Rubin, Robert Samuel *investment banker*
Sacerdote, Peter M. *investment banker*
Salomon, Richard *investor*
Samuels, Nathaniel *business executive, government administrator*
†Sardanis, Andrew S. *investment company executive*
†Saunders, Thomas A., III *investment company executive*
Scaturro, Philip David *investment banker*
Schapiro, Morris A. *investment banker*
Schechter, Stephen Lloyd *investment banker*
Schick, Harry Leon *investment company executive*
Schiff, David Tevele *investment banker*
Schless, Phyllis Ross *investment banker*
Schwarzman, Stephen Allen *investment banker*
Seevers, Gary Leonard *investment banker*
Seff, Leslie S. *securities trader*
†Seidler, Lee J. *investment banker*
Seidman, Samuel Nathan *investment banker, economist*
Senior, Enrique Francisco *investment banker*
Shapiro, Mark Lawrence *investment banker*
Shapiro, Robert Frank *investment banking company executive*
†Shaykin, Leonard P. *investor*
Shen, Theodore Ping *investment banker*
Sheppard, William Stevens *investment banker*
Sherva, Dennis G. *investment company executive*
Shinn, George Latimer *investment banker, consultant, educator*
Siebert, Muriel *brokerage house executive,former state banking official*
Siegler, Thomas Edmund *investment banking executive*
Siemer, Fred Harold *securities analyst*
Silverman, Henry Richard *diversified business executive, lawyer*
Silverstein, Howard Alan *investment banker*
Simmons, Hardwick *investment banker*
Sirna, Anthony Alfred, III *investment company executive*
Smethurst, E(dward) William, Jr. *brokerage house executive*
†Smith, H. C. Bowen *investment banker*
Smith, Malcolm Bernard *investment company executive*
Smith, Peter Lawrence *investment banker, lawyer*
Smith, Pierce Reiland *stock brokerage, investment banking executive*
Sorensen, Burton Erhard *investment banker*
Spielvogel, Sidney Meyer *investment banker*
Stamas, Stephen *investment executive*
Steffens, John Laundon *brokerage house executive*
Stein, Bernard *stockbroker*
Stein, David Fred *investment executive*
Steinberg, Joseph Saul *investment company executive*
Steinberg, Robert M. *holding company executive*
Steinberg, Saul Phillip *holding company executive*
Sterling, Robert Lee, Jr. *investment company executive*
Stern, Geoffrey Adlai *investment banker*
Stern, James Andrew *investment banker*
Stiles, Thomas Beveridge, II *investment banking executive*
Stoddard, George Earl *investment company financial executive*
Straton, John Charles, Jr. *investment banker*
Strong, William L., III *investment executive*
Sulimirski, Witold Stanislaw *banker*
Suskind, Dennis A. *investment banker*
†Suzuki, Ryosuke *securities firm executive*
Svenson, Charles Oscar *investment banker*
Tagliaferri, Lee Gene *investment banker*
Tanner, Harold *investment banker*
Taylor, Richard William *investment banker, securities broker*
Terry, F. Davis, Jr. *investment company executive*
Tizzio, Thomas Ralph *brokerage executive*
Topol, Robert Martin *financial services executive, securities trader*
Towbin, A(braham) Robert *investment banker*
Tozer, W. James, Jr. *investment company executive*
Train, John *investment counselor, writer, government official*
Treadway, James Curran *investment company executive, lawyer, former government official*
Tufts, David Albert, Jr. *securities company executive*
Tully, Daniel Patrick *investment company executive*
Tyson, Harry James *investment banker*
Van Dine, Vance *investment banker*
Wachtel, Eli *investment banking executive*
Walters, Milton James *investment banker*
Wareham, Raymond Noble *investment banker*
Wasserstein, Bruce *investment banker*
Watts, Henry Miller, Jr. *stockbroker*
Weathersby, George Byron *investment management executive*
Webster, John Kimball *investment executive*
Weinberg, John Livingston *investment banker*
Weingrow, Howard L. *financial executive, investor*
Weiss, Charles Stanard *investment banker*
Weissman, Paul Marshall *investment company executive*
Wendel, Thomas Michael *financial services company executive*
Whitehead, John Cunningham *investment executive*
Whiting, Richard Brooke *investment banker*
Whitney, Edward Bonner *investment banker*
Wiegers, George Anthony *investment banker*
Wiener, Malcolm Hewitt *investment management company executive*
Wigmore, Barrie Atherton *investment banker*
Williams, Dave Harrell *investment executive*
Wit, Harold Maurice *investment banker, lawyer, investor*
Wolcott, Samuel H., III *investment banker*
Wolitzer, Steven Barry *investment banker*
Yancey, Richard Charles *investment banker*
Zarb, Frank Gustave *investment company executive*
Zeikel, Arthur *investment company executive*
Zeisler, Richard Spiro *investor*
Zeuschner, Erwin Arnold *investment advisory company executive*
Zofnass, Paul Jesse *investment banker*
Zuckerberg, Roy J. *investment banking executive*

Roslyn Heights
Jaffe, Melvin *securities company executive*

Rye
Wagner, Edward Frederick, Jr. *investment management company executive*

Southampton
Atkins, Victor Kennicott, Jr. *investment banker*

Staten Island
Aiken, William Eric *securities research executive*

Syosset
Kantor, Edwin *investment company executive*

Tarrytown
Shaw, Bryan P. H. *retired investment company executive*

Wainscott
Dubow, Arthur Myron *investor, lawyer*

Wantagh
Zinder, Newton Donald *stock market analyst, consultant*

West Hempstead
Brodsky, Irwin Abel *retired stockbroker*

Westbury
Fogg, Joseph Graham, III *investment banking executive*

White Plains
Bagwill, John Williams, Jr. *retired pension fund company executive*

Woodstock
Ober, Stuart Alan *investment consultant, book publisher*

NORTH CAROLINA

Efland
Efland, Simpson Lindsay *entrepreneur*

High Point
Phillips, Earl Norfleet, Jr. *financial services executive*

Monroe
†Griffin, Bobby F. *entrepreneur*

North Wilkesboro
Pardue, Dwight Edward *venture capitalist*

Pinehurst
Lebeck, Warren Wells *commodities consultant*

Raleigh
Anderson, Glenn Elwood *investment banker*
Woodson, Richard Peyton, III *entrepreneur*

Winston Salem
Davis, John Wesley, III *investment banker*
Strickland, Robert Louis *business executive*

NORTH DAKOTA

Fargo
Tallman, Robert Hall *investment company executive*

OHIO

Alpha
James, Francis Edward, Jr. *investment counselor*

Cincinnati
Joseph, David J., Jr. *trading company executive*
Pettengill, Kroger *investment counselor*

Cleveland
Brentlinger, Paul Smith *venture capital executive*
Hook, John Burney *investment company executive*
Mc Fadden, John Volney *retired manufacturing company executive*
Murfin, Donald Leon *investment company executive*
O'Brien, John Feighan *investment banker*
O'Donnell, Thomas Michael *brokerage firm executive*
Roulston, Thomas Henry *investment adviser*
Sherrill, H. Virgil *securities company executive, manufacturing company executive*

Columbus
Barthelmas, Ned Kelton *investment and commercial real estate banker*
Jennings, Edward Harrington *business educator*
Pointer, Peter Leon *investment executive*
Wolfe, John Walton *investment banker*

Dayton
†Berry, John William *investment company executive, retired telephone directory advertising company executive*

Galion
Cobey, Ralph *industrialist*

Lancaster
Hurley, Samuel Clay, III *investment company executive*

Martins Ferry
Gracey, Robert William *account executive, minister*

Toledo
Glowacki, Richard Chester *real estate, brokerage house executive*

OKLAHOMA

Oklahoma City
Marshall, Gerald Robert *consultant*
Painton, Ira Wayne *retired securities executive*

Tulsa
Jedel, Peter Harold *investment executive*
Sanditen, Edgar Richard *investment company executive*
Stover, Phil Sheridan, Jr. *investment consultant*

OREGON

Medford
Cutler, Kenneth Ross *investment company and mutual fund executive*

Portland
Myers, Clay *retired investment management company executive*
Olsen, Kurt *investment company executive, adviser*

Rutherford, William Drake *investment executive, lawyer*

PENNSYLVANIA

Bala Cynwyd
Benenson, James, Jr. *industrialist*

Berwyn
Bryant, James Wesley *investment executive*

Bryn Mawr
Dayton, Samuel Grey, Jr. *investment banker*
Havens, Timothy Markle *investment advisory firm executive*
Turbidy, John Berry *investor, management consultant*

Devon
Niehaus, Robert James *investment banking executive*

Doylestown
Holstrom, Carleton Arthur *brokerage house executive*

Hummelstown
Custer, John Charles *investment broker*
Moffitt, Charles William *insurance sales executive*

Ligonier
Mellon, Seward Prosser *investment executive*

Newtown Square
Turner, George Pearce *consulting company executive*

Paoli
†Hedberg, Robert Daniel *venture capitalist*

Philadelphia
Borer, Edward Turner *investment banker*
Bowditch, Nathaniel Rantoul *brokerage house executive*
†Dunlap, Albert John *venture capitalist*
Giordano, Nicholas Anthony *stock exchange executive*
Johnson, Craig Norman *investment banker*
McGinley, Joseph Patrick *brokerage house executive*
Merritt, John C. *investment banker*
Newburger, Frank L., Jr. *retired investment broker*
O'Brien, Robert Thomas *investment company executive*
Palmer, Russell Eugene *investment executive*
Ripley, Edward Franklin *investment company executive*
Tague, Barry Elwert *securities trader*
Wilde, Norman Taylor, Jr. *investment banking company executive*
Wolitarsky, James William *securities industry executive*
Wruble, Brian Frederick *investment management company executive*

Pittsburgh
Curtis, Gregory Dyer *investment company executive, foundation administrator, lawyer, author, poet*
†Hillman, Henry L. *investment company executive*
Hunter, David Wittmer *security brokerage executive*
Mathieson, Andrew Wray *investment management executive*
Porter, Milton *investment executive*
Prado, Gerald M. *investment banker*
Walton, James M. *investment company executive*

Plymouth Meeting
Gleklen, Donald Morse *investment company executive*
Yarnall, D. Robert, Jr. *entrepreneur, investor*

Radnor
Brown, W(illiam) Thacher *investment firm executive*

Sewickley
Chaplin, James Crossan, IV *securities firm executive*

Wayne
Lewis, James Earl *investment banker*

West Conshohocken
Miller, Paul Fetterolf, Jr. *investment company executive*

Yardley
Kressler, James Phillip *investment and operations company executive*

RHODE ISLAND

Lincoln
†Barr, John Douglas, II *entrepreneur, state legislator*

Providence
Goddard, Robert Hale Ives *investment executive*
Joukowsky, Artemis A. W. *private investor*
Manchester, Robert D. *venture capitalist*

Wakefield
Mason, Scott MacGregor *entrepreneur, inventor, consultant*

SOUTH CAROLINA

Aiken
Hanna, Carey McConnell *securities and investments executive*

Charleston
Winthrop, John *investment company executive*

Hilton Head Island
Batten, William Milfred *retired stock exchange executive*

Johns Island
Cameron, Thomas William Lane *investment company executive*

TENNESSEE

Chattanooga
Witherspoon, John Knox, Jr. *investment banking executive*

Knoxville
Springer, John K. *securities dealer*

Memphis
Waddell, Alfred Moore, Jr. *investment company executive*

Nashville
Bradford, James C., Jr. *brokerage house executive*
†Crants, Doctor R., Jr. *entrepreneur*
Gaultney, John Orton *life insurance agent, consultant*
Hanselman, Richard Wilson *entrepreneur*
Kuhn, Paul Hubert, Jr. *investment counsel*
Nelson, Edward Gage *merchant banking investment company executive*
Osias, Richard Allen *international financier, investor, real estate investment executive, corporate investor*
Roberts, Kenneth Lewis *investor, lawyer, foundation administrator*
Sullivan, Allen Trousdale *securities company executive*

Oak Ridge
Turov, Daniel *financial writer, investment executive*

TEXAS

Austin
Inman, Bobby Ray *investor, former electronics executive*
†Leon, Tomas Carlos *foreign exchange broker*
†Spertus, Philip *investment company executive*

Corpus Christi
Bateman, John Roger *investment holding company executive*

Dallas
Buchholz, Donald Alden *stock brokerage company executive*
Budzinsky, Armin Alexander *investment banker*
Collins, Michael James *investment company executive*
McClure, Frederick Donald *investment banker, lawyer*
Perot, H. Ross *investments and real estate group executive, data processing services company executive*
Philipson, Herman Louis, Jr. *investment banker*
Smith, Cece *venture capitalist*
Whitson, James Norfleet, Jr. *diversified company executive*

El Paso
Schnadig, Edgar Louis *entrepreneur, management consultant*

Fort Worth
Clark, Emory Eugene *financial planning executive*

Garland
McGrath, James Thomas *real estate investment company executive*

Houston
Claiborn, Stephen Allan *investment banker*
Cullom, Hale Ellicott *investment company executive*
Cunningham, R. Walter *venture capitalist*
Currie, John Thornton (Jack Currie) *retired investment banker*
Duncan, Charles William, Jr. *investor, former government official*
Lee, Thomas Joseph, Jr. *entrepreneur, business consultant*
Mackey, William Sturges, Jr. *investor, consultant*
Mischer, Walter M. *diversified company executive, bank holding company executive*
Montle, Paul Joseph *entrepreneur*
Neuhaus, Philip Ross *investment banker*
O'Connor, Ralph Sturges *investment company executive*
Poindexter, John Bruce *entrepreneur*
Thompson, Guy Bryan *investment company executive*
Vaughan, Eugene H. *investment company executive*
Wellin, Keith Sears *investment banker*
Williams, Edward Earl, Jr. *entrepreneur, educator*

San Antonio
Duncan, A. Baker *investment banker*

Stafford
Franks, Charles Leslie *banker*

Wichita Falls
Jones, William Houston *stock brokerage executive, financial consultant*

UTAH

Salt Lake City
Meldrum, Peter Durkee *venture capital company executive*

VIRGINIA

Alexandria
Harding, Trewitt DeLano *stockbroker*

Annandale
Khim, Jay Wook *high-tech research and development, professional service company executive*

Arlington
Anns, Philip Harold *international trading executive, former pharmaceutical company executive*

Burke
†Kaminski, Paul Garrett *investment banker, consultant*

Charlottesville
Monroe, Brooks *investment banker*
Newman, James Wilson *business executive*

Mc Lean
Bisbee, Gerald Elftman, Jr. *investment company executive*
Searles, Dewitt Richard *retired investment firm executive, retired air force officer*
Smith, Thomas Eugene *investment company executive, financial consultant*

Richmond
Dahlenburg, Lyle Marion *investment company executive*
Gorr, Louis Frederick *investment consultant*
Hong, James Ming *industrialist, venture capitalist*
Williams, Loretta Dodson *financial advisor, investment broker*

Stanleytown
Stanley, Thomas Bahnson, Jr. *investor*

Virginia Beach
Asher, Garland Parker *investment holding company executive*

WASHINGTON

Bellevue
Ryles, Gerald Fay *private investor, consultant*
Shih, Benedict Chesang *investment company executive*

Olympia
Manning, Farley *investment company executive*
†Shin, Paull Hobom *investment company executive*

Seattle
Bayley, Christopher T. *international investment banking executive*
Block, Robert Jackson *investment banker*
Brier, Evelyn Caroline *retired investment company executive, business consultant*
Pacholski, Richard Francis *retired securities company executive, financial consultant*

Tacoma
Schuyler, Robert Len *investment company executive*

WISCONSIN

Janesville
Diotte, Alfred Peter *investment executive, consultant*

Milwaukee
Bloom, James Edward *commodity trading and financial executive*
Lubar, Sheldon Bernard *venture capitalist*
Samson, Richard Max *investments and real estate executive*
Schnoll, Howard Manuel *investment banking and managed asset consultant*

WYOMING

Casper
True, Henry Alfonso, Jr. *entrepreneur*

Daniel
Parker, H. Lawrence *rancher, investor, retired investment banker*

Wilson
Sage, Andrew Gregg Curtin, II *corporate investor, manager*

TERRITORIES OF THE UNITED STATES

PUERTO RICO

Hato Rey
Ferrer, Miguel Antonio *brokerage firm and investment bank executive*

CANADA

ALBERTA

Calgary
Cumming, Thomas Alexander *stock exchange executive*
Seaman, Donald Roy *investment company executive*

Edmonton
Cormie, Donald Mercer *investment company executive*
Pocklington, Peter H. *business executive*

BRITISH COLUMBIA

Vancouver
Harwood, Brian Dennis *securities industry executive*
Hudson, Donald J. *stock exchange executive*

MANITOBA

Winnipeg
Alexander, Norman James *investment consultant*

NOVA SCOTIA

Bedford
Hennigar, David J. *investment broker*

ONTARIO

Chatham
McKeough, William Darcy *investment company executive*

Toronto
Barford, Ralph MacKenzie *investment executive*
Caty, J. Charles *investment association executive*
Dembroski, George Steven *investment banker*
Dunford, Robert A. *diversified business executive*
Gairdner, John Smith *securities investment dealer*
Hore, John Edward *commodity futures educator*
Kostuch, Mitchell John *venture capital company executive, publisher*
Lindsay, Roger Alexander *investment executive*
Michals, George Francis *investment and business development executive*
Petrillo, Leonard Philip *corporate securities executive, lawyer*
Weston, Willard Galen *diversified holdings executive*

QUEBEC

Montreal
Dubuc, André *investment consulting company executive*
Elie, Jean André *investment banker*
Schwartz, Roy Richard *holding company executive*
Torrey, David Leonard *investment banker*

BAHAMAS

Grand Cayman
McIntire, Jerald Gene *investment executive, former municipal official*

Nassau
Templeton, John Marks *investment counsel, financial analyst*

BERMUDA

Tuckers Town
Heizer, Edgar Francis, Jr. *venture capitalist*

ENGLAND

London
Hale, Charles Martin *stockbroker*
Hayden, Richard Michael *investment banker*
Jourdren, Marc Henri *investment banker*
Matthei, Warren Douglas *investment company executive*
†Mulford, David Campbell *banking executive*
Warren, Edus Houston, Jr. *investment management executive*

FRANCE

Fontainebleu
Churchill, Neil Center *entrepreneur, educator*

Paris
Masurel, Jean-Louis Antoine Nicolas *industrialist*

HONG KONG

Hong Kong
Goodman, Stephen H. *investment bank executive*
Harris, Randy A. (Alan Harris) *investment executive, lawyer*

ISRAEL

Jerusalem
†Arnon, Michael *finance company executive*

JAPAN

Tokyo
Naito, Takeshi *investment company executive*

MONACO

Lacets Saint-Léon
Kimmle, Manfred *investment company executive*

PAKISTAN

Karachi
Shroff, Firoz Sardar *merger and acquisition professional*

SCOTLAND

Edinburgh
Buchan, Hamish Noble *securities analyst*

SWITZERLAND

Lausanne
Bloemsma, Marco Paul *investor*

ADDRESS UNPUBLISHED

Ackerman, Melvin *investment company executive*
Aljian, James Donovan *investment company executive*
Anker, Peter Louis *equity research director*
Apruzzi, Gene *retired stockbroker*
Aurin, Robert James *entrepreneur*
Bacharach, Melvin Lewis *venture capitalist*
Bantry, Bryan *entrepreneur*
Black, Richard Bruce *business executive, consultant*
Bowles, Barbara Landers *investment company executive*
Bratt, Nicholas *investment management and research company executive*
†Brigham, David Lewis *investment management company executive*
Brode, David B. *investment counselor*
Bronfman, Peter Frederick *independent investor*
Bruzda, Francis Joseph *investment executive, former banker*
Caldwell, Warren Frederick *investment company executive*
Callard, David Jacobus *investment banker*
Carr, Harold Noflet *investment corporation executive*
Casdin, Jeffrey Whitman *investment company executive*
Chandler, William Everett *brokerage house executive*
Cockrum, William Monroe, III *investment banker, consultant, educator*
Cook, Charles Beckwith, Jr. *securities company executive*
Doherty, Charles Vincent *investment counsel executive*
Drake, Rodman Leland *investment manager consultant*
Frankenberger, Bertram, Jr. *investor, consultant*
Friedman, Donald Joseph *stock brokerage executive*
Fuld, Richard Severin, Jr. *investment banker*
Garcia-Granados, Sergio Eduardo *brokerage house executive*
Gardner, James Albert *investment and real estate executive*
Geissinger, Frederick Wallace *investment banker*
Gelles, Harry P. *investment banker, land investor*
Glasberg, Laurence Brian *finance executive, private investor*
Goldman, Alan Ira *investment banking executive*
Goyan, Michael Donovan *stockbroker, investment executive*
Grant, Frederick Anthony *investment banker*
Greber, Robert Martin *financial investments executive*
Gutfreund, John H. *investment banker*
Harris, D. George *entrepreneur*
Hays, Thomas Chandler *holding company executive*
Headley, Anne Renouf *technology commercialization financier*
Heckler, John Maguire *stockbroker, investment company executive*
Henkel, Arthur John, Jr. *investment banker*
Hickey, Joseph Michael, Jr. *investment banker*
Hogan, Mark *investment company executive*
Holland, James Richard, Jr. *business executive*
Howard, James Webb *investment banker, lawyer, engineer*
Jepson, Robert Scott, Jr. *international investment banking specialist*
Kotler, Steven *investment banker*
Lohrer, Richard Baker *investment consultant*
Lynch, Thomas Peter *securities executive*
Marks, Leonard, Jr. *retired corporate executive*
Martin, Robert Roy *retired securities brokerage company executive*
Mc Gill, Archie Joseph *venture capital and business speaker*
McRae, Thomas Kenneth *retired investment company executive*
Mikitka, Gerald Peter *investment banker, financial consultant*
Miller, Alan Jay *consultant, author*
Millsaps, Fred Ray *investor*
Morosky, Robert Harry *private investor, operator*
Myers, John Herman *investment management executive*
Pavlick, Harvey Naylor *financial executive*
Peters, Ralph Frew *investment banker*
Petrie, Donald Archibald *lawyer, investment banker, publisher*
Pierce, Scott *retired investment company executive*
Pinkney, D. Timothy *investment company executive*
Pool, Philip Bemis, Jr. *investment banker*
Prince, Milton S. *investment company executive*
Robinson, Bob Leo *international investment services executive*
Rock, Arthur *venture capitalist*
Schmidt, Kenneth Martin *investment banker*
Sells, Boake Anthony *private investor*
Servison, Roger Theodore *investment executive*
Smoot, Wendell McMeans, Jr. *investment counselor*
Stanfill, Dennis Carothers *business executive*
Steen, Carlton Duane *private investor, former food company executive*
Swanberg, Edmund Raymond *investment counselor*
Taber, Edward Albert, III *investment executive*
Tansor, Robert Henry *investor*
Weisman, Lorenzo David *investment banker*
Weymar, F. Helmut *commodities trading company executive, economist*

FINANCE: REAL ESTATE

UNITED STATES

ALABAMA

Birmingham
Copeland, Hunter Armstrong *real estate executive*

ALASKA

Anchorage
Faulkner, Sewell Ford *real estate executive*

ARIZONA

Bullhead City
Jones, Vernon Quentin *surveyor*

Peoria
Morrison, Manley Glenn *real estate investor, former army officer*

Phoenix
Lewis, Orme, Jr. *real estate company executive, land use adviser*
Rau, David Edward *real estate company executive*
†Spencer, John Andrew *real estate development corporation executive*

ARKANSAS

Bentonville
†Yates, Joe Elton *real estate developer, state senator*

Little Rock
McConnell, John Wesley *real estate-resort developer, corporate executive*

CALIFORNIA

Alamo
Plummer, Marcie Stern *real estate broker*

Belvedere Tiburon
Caselli, Virgil P. *real estate executive*

Berkeley
Catlin, James C. *environmentalist, land use planner, electrical engineer*

Beverly Hills
Bergman, Nancy Palm *real estate investment company executive*
Shapell, Nathan *financial and real estate executive*
Victor, Robert Eugene *real estate corporation executive, lawyer*
Winthrop, John *real estate executive, lawyer*

Big Sur
Cross, Robert Louis *realtor, land use planner, writer*
Owings, Margaret Wentworth *conservationist, artist*

Bonita
Dresser, Jesse Dale *real estate investor*

Campbell
Nicholson, Joseph Bruce *real estate developer*

El Macero
Wheeler, Douglas Paul *conservationist, government official, lawyer*

Foster City
Meredith, Allen Kent *real estate developer*

Hawthorne
Testa, Gabriel *real estate broker*

Inglewood
Buss, Jerry Hatten *real estate executive, sports team owner*

Irvine
Chronley, James Andrew *real estate executive*
Stack, Geoffrey Lawrence *real estate developer*

La Jolla
Anthony, Harry Antoniades *city planner, architect, educator*

Laguna Beach
Hanauer, Joe Franklin *real estate executive*

Laguna Niguel
York, James Orison *real estate executive*

Larkspur
Roulac, Stephen E. *real estate consultant*

Los Angeles
Abernethy, Robert John *real estate developer*
Beban, Gary Joseph *real estate corporation officer*
†Didion, James J. *real estate company executive*
Glazer, Guilford *real estate developer*
Gordon, Milton G. *real estate counselor, consultant*
Grantham, Richard Robert *real estate company executive*
Linsk, Michael Stephen *real estate executive*
†Martin, Vincent Francis, Jr. *real estate investment executive*
Mitchell, Joseph Nathan *real estate company executive*
Tornek, Terry E. *real estate executive*
Wachs, Martin *urban planning educator*

Manhattan Beach
Krienke, Carol Belle Manikowske (Mrs. Oliver Kenneth Krienke) *realtor*

Newport Beach
Kenney, William John, Jr. *real estate development executive*

North Hollywood
Milner, Howard M. *real estate developer, international real estate financier*

Oakland
Fischer, Michael Ludwig *environmental company executive*

Palmdale
Anderson, R(obert) Gregg *real estate company executive*

Palo Alto
Warne, William Elmo *irrigationist*

Rancho Mirage
Gardner, Donald LaVere *development company executive*

Sacramento
Lukenbill, Gregg *real estate developer, professional basketball team executive*

San Diego
Mc Comic, Robert Barry *real estate development company executive, lawyer*

San Francisco
Anthony, Elaine Margaret *real estate executive, interior designer*
Brower, David Ross *conservationist*
Colwell, Kent Leigh *real estate executive*
Davies, Paul Lewis, Jr. *real estate executive*
Freund, Fredric S. *real estate broker, property manager*
Mc Mahan, John William *real estate investment advisor*
Shorenstein, Walter Herbert *commercial real estate development company executive*
†Walther, Roger O. *international education estate executive*
†Woodberry, Paul Francis *real estate executive*

San Jose
Rothblatt, Donald Noah *urban and regional planner, educator*

San Mateo
Bohannon, David D. *community planner and developer*
Leeder, Stuart L. *real estate financial executive*

Santa Ana Heights
Warren, William Robinson *real estate broker*

Torrance
Alter, Gerald L. *real estate executive*

Twain Harte
Kinsinger, Robert Earl *property company executive, educational consultant*

Upland
Lewis, Goldy Sarah *real estate developer, corporation executive*
Lewis, Ralph Milton *real estate developer*

Venice
Rosenthal, Richard Jay *real estate consultant, broker, educator*

COLORADO

Aspen
Dietsch, Alfred John *real estate executive, lawyer*

Breckenridge
†Williams, Samuel *real estate executive*

Denver
Antonoff, Gary L. *real estate executive*

Englewood
Fisher, Bob *real estate broker, franchisor*

CONNECTICUT

Greenwich
Morrison, Fred Beverly *real estate consultant*

New Britain
Adams, John Francis, Jr. *real estate executive*

New Haven
Harrison, Henry Starin *real estate educator, appraiser, entrepreneur*

DELAWARE

Newark
Byrne, John Michael *energy and environmental policy educator, researcher*
Harkins, Roseann Hildebrandt *real estate broker*

Wilmington
Bredin, J(ohn) Bruce *real estate executive*
Gilman, Marvin Stanley *real estate developer, educator*

DISTRICT OF COLUMBIA

Washington
Akridge, John Edward, III *real estate management and development company executive*
Berg, Norman Alf *conservation consultant*
Blackwelder, Brent Francis *environmentalist*
†Cook, Albert George, III *retired parking company executive, consultant*
Golden, Terence C. *realty corporation executive, former government official*
Hanke, Byron Reidt *residential land planning and community associations consultant*
Hollander, Richard Edward *real estate executive*
Meyer, Alden Merrill *environmental association executive*
†Mittermeier, Russell Alan *conservation executive, educator*
Rumford, Lewis, III *real estate company executive*
Sexton, Ken *environmental health scientist*
Stollman, Israel *city planner*

FLORIDA

Boca Raton
Mandor, Leonard Stewart *real estate company executive*

Cedar Key
Starnes, Earl Maxwell *urban and regional planner, architect*

Clearwater
Glindeman, Henry Peter, Jr. *real estate developer*

Coral Gables
Blumberg, David *builder, developer*

Deland
Tedros, Theodore Zaki *appraiser, real estate broker, educator*

Fort Lauderdale
Hirshson, William Roscoe *real estate consultant*
Paulauskas, Edmund Walter *real estate broker*
Sutte, Donald T., Jr. *real estate executive*

Gainesville
Feiss, Carl Lehman *retired urban planning educator*
Stein, Jay M. *planning and design educator, consultant*

Indialantic
McIntyre, Joseph Charles *real estate investor*

Jacksonville
†Bankhead, William Greer, Jr. *real estate administrator*
Clarkson, Charles Andrew *real estate investment executive*
†Koger, Ira M. *real estate executive*
Parker, David Forster *real estate development consultant*

Lake Suzy
Schmidt, Harold Eugene *real estate company executive*

Lakeland
Smith, Levie David, Jr. *real estate appraiser, consultant*

Maitland
Vallee, Judith Delaney *environmentalist, fundraiser*

Melbourne
Michalski, Thomas Joseph *city planner, developer*

Miami
Mozian, Gerard Paul *real estate company executive, business consultant*
Raffel, Leroy B. *real estate development company executive*
Roemer, Elaine Sloane *real estate broker*
Salvaneschi, Luigi *real estate and development executive, business educator*
Stover, James Howard *real estate executive*
†Valdes, Carlos Leonardo *realtor, mortgage broker, state legislator*

Micco
Muller, Henry John *real estate developer*

Mount Dora
Adams, Carl Morgan, Jr. *real estate appraiser, mortgage banker*

New Port Richey
Rhodes, Eric Foster *real estate and insurance executive, consultant*

Palm Beach
Bonan, Seon Pierre *real estate developer*

Ponte Vedra Beach
Moore, Philip Walsh *appraisal company executive*

Rockledge
†Posey, William J. *realtor*

Saint Petersburg Beach
Hurley, Frank Thomas, Jr. *realtor*

Sanibel
Courtney, James Edmond *real estate development*

Sebring
Sherrick, Daniel Noah *real estate broker*

Tallahassee
Avant, David Alonzo, Jr. *realty company executive, photographer*
Johnson, Benjamin F., VI *real estate developer, consulting economist*

Vero Beach
Dillard, Rodney Jefferson *real estate company executive*

West Palm Beach
Wilensky, Alvin *real estate investment trust executive*

GEORGIA

Atlanta
Aulbach, George Louis *property investment company executive*
Charania, Barkat *real estate consultant*
†Cupp, Robert Erhard *golf course designer, land use planner*
†Easton, Loretta J. *real estate executive*
Regenstein, Lewis Graham *conservationist, author, lecturer, speech writer*
Wolbrink, James Francis *real estate investor*

Macon
Jones, John Ellis *real estate broker*

Toccoa
Maypole, John Floyd *real estate holding company executive*

HAWAII

Honolulu
Hufschmidt, Maynard Michael *resources planning educator*
Levine, Aaron *city planner*

Lihue
Cobb, Rowena Noelani Blake *real estate broker*

IDAHO

Idaho Falls
Williams, Phyllis Cutforth *retired realtor*

Payette
Jones, Donna Marilyn *real estate broker, legislator*

Sun Valley
Janss, William Cluff *resort development executive*

ILLINOIS

Chicago
Amato, Isabella Antonia *real estate executive*
Beitler, J. Paul *real estate developer*
†Bluhm, Neil Gary *real estate company executive*
Bynoe, Peter Charles Bernard *real estate developer, legal consultant*
†Claeys, Jerome Joseph, III *real estate company executive*
Eubanks-Pope, Sharon G. *real estate entrepreneur*
Foley, L(ewis) Michael *real estate executive*
†Gerst, C(ornelius) Gary *real estate executive*
Glass, Ronald Lee *real estate executive*
Grabowski, Roger J. *business, intangible assets, real estate appraiser*
Greenberg, Arthur A. *diversified real estate and financial services executive, manufacturing company executive*
†Hill, Arthur J. *real estate company executive*
Levy, Arnold S(tuart) *real estate company executive*
Pezzella, Jerry James, Jr. *investment and real estate corporation executive*
Reschke, Michael W. *real estate executive*
Sen, Ashish Kumar *urban planner, educator*
Stein, Paula Jean Anne Barton *real estate company executive*
Travis, Dempsey Jerome *real estate executive, mortgage banker*

Edwardsville
Ottwein, Merrill William George *real estate company executive, veterinarian*

Flossmoor
Wagner, Alvin Louis, Jr. *real estate appraiser, consultant*

Hinsdale
Merrion, James M. *real estate company officer*
†Wheeler, Paul James *real estate executive*

Itasca
Sheridan, James Leslie *real estate developer*

Lake Zurich
Schultz, Carl Herbert *real estate management and development company executive*

Oak Brook
†Cosenza, G. Joseph *real estate executive*
†Goodwin, Daniel L. *real estate company executive*

Round Lake Park
Corcoran, Gregory Michael *corporate real estate executive*

Saint Charles
Urhausen, James Nicholas *real estate developer, construction executive*

Urbana
Blair, Lachlan Ferguson *urban planner, educator*
Goodman, William I. *urban planner, educator*
Guttenberg, Albert Ziskind *planning educator*

INDIANA

Elkhart
Vite, Frank Anthony *realtor*

Indianapolis
Jewett, John Rhodes *real estate executive*
†Merritt, James W. *real estate developer*
Mullen, Thomas Edgar *real estate consultant*

Jeffersonville
Reisert, Charles Edward, Jr. *real estate executive*

Montpelier
Neff, Kenneth D. *realtor, mayor*

Newburgh
Tierney, Gordon Paul *real estate broker, genealogist*

Terre Haute
Perry, Eston Lee *real estate and equipment leasing company executive*

West Lafayette
Curtis, Kenneth Stewart *land surveyor*

IOWA

Des Moines
Bucksbaum, Martin *real estate developer*
Bucksbaum, Matthew *real estate development company president*
Neis, Arthur Veral *healthcare and development company executive*

Windsor Heights
Ansorge, Iona Marie *retired real estate agent, musician*

KANSAS

Concordia
Casado, Antonio Francisco *retired real estate executive*

Liberal
†Holmes, Carl Dean *landowner, state legislator*

Overland Park
Longan, George Baker, III *real estate executive*

Westwood
Buckner, William Claiborne *real estate broker*

KENTUCKY

Lexington
Gable, Robert Elledy *real estate investment company executive*

LOUISIANA

Baton Rouge
McLindon, Gerald Joseph *planning and environmental design consultant, university dean emeritus*

New Orleans
Villavaso, Stephen Donald *urban planner, lawyer*

MAINE

Bangor
Hunt, Walter L. *real estate and petroleum company executive*

Lincolnville
Williams, Robert Luther *city planning consultant*

Rockport
Duarte, Patricia M. *real estate and insurance broker*

MARYLAND

Baltimore
Apgar, Mahlon, IV *real estate management counselor*
Bart, Polly Turner *commercial real estate developer*
Frank, Robert Allen *real estate investment analyst*

Bethesda
Blair, William Draper, Jr. *conservationist*
Greenwald, Alan Frank *real estate company finance executive, lawyer*
Lee, Edward Brooke, Jr. *real estate executive, fund raiser*
Walker, Mallory *real estate executive*

Columbia
Alexander, Bruce Donald *real estate executive*
Cook, Stephen Bernard *homebuilding company executive*
DeVito, Mathias Joseph *real estate executive*
Hilderbrandt, Donald Franklin, II *urban designer, landscape architect, artist*
McCauley, Richard Gray *real estate developer, lawyer*
McCuan, William Patrick *real estate company executive*
Millspaugh, Martin Laurence *real estate developer, urban development consultant*

Gaithersburg
†Watkins, Michael Dean *town planner*

Laurel
Lavin, Charles Blaise, Jr. *realtor, association executive*
†O'Connor, Harold J. *wildlife research administrator*

Lutherville Timonium
Kerr, Patrick Corbitt *real estate appraiser, consultant*

Rockville
Dockser, William Barnet *real estate, finance and development company executive*

Silver Spring
Bailey, John Martin *transportation planner*
Humphries, Weldon R. *real estate executive*
Kronstadt, Arnold Mayo *community and architectural planner*

MASSACHUSETTS

Amherst
Bentley, Richard Norcross *regional planner, consultant*
Larson, Joseph Stanley *environmentalist, educator, researcher*

Boston
Beal, Robert Lawrence *real estate executive*

Cervieri, John Anthony, Jr. *real estate company officer*
†Colloredo-Mansfeld, Ferdinand *real estate company executive*
Logue, Edward Joseph *development company executive*
Morse, Garlan, Jr. *real estate investment counseling officer*
Radloff, Robert Albert *real estate executive*
Wolbach, William Wellington, Sr. *retired business executive*

Cambridge
†Bernard, Michael Mark *city planning consultant, lawyer*
Fagans, Karl Preston *real estate facilities executive*
Fleming, Ronald Lee *urban designer, administrator, preservation planner, environmental educator*
Spunt, Shepard Armin *real estate executive, management and financial consultant*
Susskind, Lawrence Elliott *urban and environmental planner, educator, mediator*
Vigier, François Claude Denis *city planning educator*

Franklin
Bonin, Paul Joseph *real estate and banking executive*

Hanover
Fantozzi, Peggy Ryone *environmental planner*

Newburyport
Howard, John Tasker *city planner*

Newton
Frieden, Bernard Joel *urban studies educator*

North Reading
Dolan, Edward Corcoran *real estate developer and investor*

Worcester
Brazelton, Roy Dale *real estate executive*

MICHIGAN

Ann Arbor
Clark, Thomas Bertram, Sr. *real estate broker*
Rycus, Mitchell Julian *urban planning educator, urban security and energy planning consultant*
Surovell, Edward David *real estate company executive*

East Lansing
Hamlin, Roger Eugene *urban planning educator, economic and financial analyst*

Farmington
†Shapiro, Mickey *real estate developer, financier*

Grosse Ile
Smith, Veronica Latta *real estate corporation officer*

Kalamazoo
Taborn, Jeannette Ann *real estate investor*

Lansing
Hales, David Foster *natural resources educator*

Saginaw
Cline, Thomas William *real estate leasing company executive, management consultant*

West Bloomfield
Colton, Victor Robert *real estate developer, manufacturing executive*

MINNESOTA

Duluth
Bowman, Roger Manwaring *real estate executive*

Faribault
Turnbull, Charles Vincent *real estate broker*

Minneapolis
Bolan, Richard Stuart *urban planner, educator, researcher*
Dahlberg, Burton Francis *real estate corporation executive*
Stuebner, James Cloyd *real estate developer, contractor*

Minnetonka
Johnson, Kay Durbahn *real estate manager, consultant*

MISSISSIPPI

Meridian
Church, George Millord *real estate executive*

Mississippi State
†Parsons, George William *city planner, educator*

MISSOURI

Kansas City
Dumovich, Loretta *real estate and transportation company executive*
Shutz, Byron Christopher *real estate executive*

Lake Saint Louis
Royal, William Henry *real estate developer, architect*

Saint Joseph
Miller, Lloyd Daniel *real estate agent*

Saint Louis
Meissner, Edwin Benjamin, Jr. *real estate broker*
Morley, Harry Thomas, Jr. *real estate executive*
Schierholz, William Francis, Jr. *real estate developer*

MONTANA

Darby
Brandborg, Stewart Monroe *conservationist, government official*

Great Falls
Stevens, George Alexander *realtor*

NEBRASKA

Norfolk
Wozniak, Richard Michael, Sr. *city and regional planner*

NEW HAMPSHIRE

Hinsdale
†Smith, Edwin O. *real estate executive, state legislator*

NEW JERSEY

Bound Brook
Chandler, Marguerite Nella *real estate corporation executive*

Colts Neck
Rode, Leif *real estate agent*

Haworth
Stokvis, Jack Raphael *urban planner and developer, government agency administrator*

Hightstown
Arnold, Matthew Charles *real estate corporation officer*

Imlaystown
†Richardson, Donald Campbell *land planner, landscape architect*

Mount Laurel
Buchan, Alan Bradley *land planner, consultant, civil engineer*

Mountainside
Good, Allen Hovey *acquisitions broker, real estate broker*

Newark
Simmons, Peter *urban planning educator*
Strum, Brian J. *real estate executive*

Paramus
†Gingras, Paul Joseph *real estate management company executive*

Princeton
Baker, Richard Wheeler, Jr. *real estate executive*
Wood, Eric Franklin *earth and environmental sciences educator*

Red Bank
†Hovnanian, Kevork S. *real estate developer*
Schimpf, John Joseph *real estate developer*

Rochelle Park
Mack, Earle Irving *real estate company executive*

Short Hills
Lax, Philip *land developer, space planner*

Summit
Natkin, Alvin Martin *environmental company executive*

Warren
Lennon, Marilyn Ellen *environmentalist*

Westfield
Bartok, William *environmental technologies consultant*

NEW MEXICO

Albuquerque
Liberman, Ira L. *real estate broker*
Stahl, Jack Leland *real estate company executive*

NEW YORK

Albany
Picotte, Michael Bernard *real estate developer*

Brooklyn
Blackman, Robert Irwin *real estate developer and investor, lawyer, accountant*

Central Islip
McGowan, Harold *real estate developer, investor, scientist, author, philanthropist*

Forest Hills
LeFrak, Richard Stone *real estate developer*

Ithaca
Parsons, Kermit Carlyle *urban planning educator, former university dean*
Saltzman, Sidney *city and regional planning educator*

Jericho
Axinn, Donald Everett *real estate investor, developer*

Larchmont
Levi, James Harry *real estate executive, investment banker*

Mount Kisco
King, Robert John *real estate executive*

Mount Vernon
Rossini, Joseph *contracting and development corporate executive*

New Hyde Park
Jacob, Gary Steven *real estate developer*

New York
Benenson, Edward Hartley *realty company executive*
Berliner, Ruth Shirley *real estate company executive*
Bingham, Bruce Bryan *real estate developer*
Booth, Albert Edward, II *real estate executive*
Cohen, Irving Elias *real estate executive*
Cohen, Lawrence Alan *real estate executive*
Fetscher, Paul George William *commercial real estate corporation executive*
French, Raymond *real estate executive*
Friedman, Howard W. *retired real estate company executive*
Gochberg, Thomas Joel *real estate investor, financial executive*
Goddess, Lynn Barbara *commercial real estate broker*
Goldenberg, Charles Lawrence *real estate company executive*
Gordon, Jacques Nicholas *real estate economist*
Hemmerdinger, H. Dale *real estate executive*
Hernstadt, Judith Filenbaum *city planner, real estate executive, broadcasting executive*
Jenkins, Robert Nesbit *real estate executive*
Kalikow, Peter Stephen *real estate developer, former newspaper owner, publisher*
Lachman, Marguerite Leanne *real estate investment advisor*
†Licari, Joseph *real estate company executive*
Malino, John Gray *real estate executive*
Marder, John G. *real estate investor, marketing consultant, corporate director*
Marshall, Alton Garwood *real estate counselor*
†McClellan, Anne Starr *environmentalist*
Mintz, Stephen Allan *real estate company executive, lawyer*
Morris, Kenneth Baker *mergers, acquisition and real estate executive*
Murray, Thomas Francis *real estate executive*
Newman, William *real estate executive*
Nichols, Carol D. *real estate professional, association executive*
Pasquarelli, Joseph J. *real estate, engineering and construction executive*
Petz, Edwin V. *real estate executive, lawyer*
Purse, Charles Roe *real estate company executive*
Rose, Elihu *real estate executive*
Roskind, E. Robert *real estate company executive*
Ruben, Lawrence *real estate developer, building company executive, lawyer*
Schwerin, Warren Lyons *real estate developer*
Tishman, Robert V. *real estate and construction company executive*
Toote, Gloria E. A. *developer, lawyer, columnist*
Urstadt, Charles Jordan *real estate executive*
Voell, Richard Allen *real estate services company executive*
Warsawer, Harold Newton *real estate appraiser and consultant*
Weiss, Ronald Whitman *real estate executive, lawyer*
Weston, M. Moran, II *educator, real estate developer, banker, clergyman*
Wolf, Peter Michael *investment and land planning consultant, educator, author*
Wood, Christopher L. J. *real estate consulting firm executive*
Zeckendorf, William, Jr. *real estate developer*

Roslyn
Cooper, Milton *real estate development executive*

Stony Brook
Koppelman, Lee Edward *regional planner, educator*

Suffern
Marchetti, Peter Louis *real estate executive*
Ward, William Francis, Jr. *real estate investment banker*

Tarrytown
Raymond, George Marc *city planner, educator*

Westport
Davis, George Donald *land use policy consultant*

Wyandanch
Barnett, Peter John *property development executive, educator*

NORTH CAROLINA

Chapel Hill
Weiss, Shirley F. *urban and regional planner, economist, educator*

Charlotte
Crosland, John, Jr. *real estate developer*
Phillips, Howard Mitchell *real estate developer*

Kinston
Sutton, Frederick Isler, Jr. *realtor*

Winston Salem
Doggett, Aubrey Clayton, Jr. *real estate executive, consultant*

NORTH DAKOTA

Grafton
†Tallackson, Harvey D. *real estate and insurance salesman*

OHIO

Beachwood
Ellett, Alan Sidney *real estate development company executive*
Lerner, Alfred *real estate and financial executive*

Beechwood
Donnem, Roland William *real estate manager, lawyer*

Bellefontaine
Johnson, Renie *real estate executive, publisher*

Canton
Duncan, Joyce Louise *real estate broker*

Cincinnati
†Chatterjee, Jayanta *educator, urban designer*
Hoermann, Edward Richard *urban planning educator*
Le Blond, Patricia Morrison *real estate company executive*
Magnusson, M(arylin) Sue Shirey *real estate executive*
†Schuler, Robert Leo *appraiser, consultant*
Totlis, Gust John *title insurance company executive*
Weiskittel, Ralph Joseph *real estate executive*

Cleveland
Cleary, Martin Joseph *real estate company executive*
Jacobs, Richard E. *real estate executive, sports team owner*
Markos, Chris *real estate company executive*

Columbus
Daub, Berger Ellis *real estate agent*
Pyatt, Leo Anthony *real estate broker*
Voss, Jerrold Richard *city planner, educator, university official*

Dayton
Frydman, Paul *real estate broker and developer*
Stout, Donald Everett *real estate developer, environmental preservationist*
Wertz, Kenneth Dean *real estate executive*

Gates Mills
Schanfarber, Richard Carl *real estate broker*

Hudson
Stec, John Zygmunt *real estate company executive*

Lancaster
Wagonseller, James Myrl *real estate executive*

Mentor
Richter, Hans *real estate broker and developer*

New Albany
Kessler, John Whitaker *real estate developer*

Shaker Heights
Adler, Naomi Samuel *real estate counselor*

Toledo
Batt, Nick *property and investment executive*

Twinsburg
Solganik, Marvin *real estate executive*

Wintersville
Becker, William A(lbert) *real estate developer*

OKLAHOMA

Bartlesville
Kaiser, Jean Morgan *real estate broker*

Warr Acres
†Phillips, Richard C. *real estate executive*

Watonga
Hoberecht, Earnest *abstract company executive, former newspaper executive*

OREGON

Eugene
Dasso, Jerome Joseph *real estate educator, consultant*

Portland
Abbott, Carl John *urban studies and planning educator*
Morse, Lowell Wesley *real estate executive, banking*

Salem
†Derfler, Eugene L. *real estate broker*

PENNSYLVANIA

Doylestown
Long, Ronald Alex *real estate and financial consultant, educator*

Erie
Gottschalk, Frank Klaus *real estate executive*

Exton
†Mayville, Gail M. *environmental consultant*

Johnstown
Gunter, John Brown, Jr. *real estate executive*

Philadelphia
Bacon, Edmund Norwood *city planner*
Binswanger, Frank G., Jr. *realty company executive*
Lipkin, Edward B. *real estate developer*
Tomazinis, Anthony Rodoflos *city planning educator*

Pittsburgh
Aronson, Mark Berne *real estate broker, consultant*
Thorpe, Leon Ferber *real estate investment company executive*
Wilson, Charles Reginald *real estate executive*

University Park
Golany, Gideon Salomon *urban designer*

Upper Saint Clair
Stephenson, Robert Clay *commercial real estate developer*

Valley Forge
Basile, Neal Fahr *environmental consulting firm executive*

SOUTH CAROLINA

Charleston
†Bailey, James Julian *real estate executive*
Gleason, John Martin *community development consultant*
Pearson, Margit Linnea *real estate company executive*

Hilton Head
Gruchacz, Robert S. *real estate executive*

SOUTH DAKOTA

Charleston
Evans, Allen Donald *real estate company executive*

TENNESSEE

Chattanooga
Porter, Dudley, Jr. *environmentalist, foundation executive, lawyer*

Memphis
Haizlip, Henry Hardin, Jr. *real estate consultant, former banker*

Nashville
†Boyer, James Floyd *land surveyor, state legislator*

TEXAS

Amarillo
Stiff, John Sterling *development company executive*

Austin
Mathias, Reuben Victor (Vic Mathias) *real estate executive, investor*

Blue Ridge
Comola, James Paul *legislative and environmental consultant*

Bullard
Buckner, John Hugh *retired real estate broker, retired construction company executive, retired air force officer*

Dallas
Crow, F. Trammell *real estate company executive*
Hamilton, David Lee *retired environmental company executive*
Hewett, Arthur Edward *real estate developer, lawyer*
†Pogue, Mack *real estate company executive*
Pratt, Edward Taylor, Jr. *real estate company executive*
Robinson, Hugh Granville *real estate development company executive*
Staubach, Roger Thomas *real estate executive, former professional football player*

Galveston
McLeod, E. Douglas *real estate developer, lawyer*

Houston
Ewing, John Kirby *real estate, oil and investment executive*
Holcomb, William A. *real estate broker, consultant, retired oil and gas exploration, pipeline executive*
Kollaer, Jim C. *real estate executive, architect*
Lehrer, Kenneth Eugene *real estate advisor, economist, developer, consultant*
Peck, Edwin Russell *real estate management executive*
Rhoades, Floyd *real estate and property manager*

Irving
Gidel, Robert Hugh *real estate investor*

Rowlett
Toler, James Larkin *real estate executive*

San Antonio
Bryan, Richard Ray *real estate development executive, construction executive*
Rhame, William Thomas *land development company executive*

UTAH

Logan
Sigler, William Franklin *environmental consultant*

VIRGINIA

Alexandria
Holland, Dianna Gwin *real estate broker*
Palma, Dolores Patricia *urban planner*

Ivy
†Loving, Raymond Franklin, Jr. *real estate broker, golf course architect*

Lynchburg
Wingfield, John Ernest *insurance broker, financial executive*

Mc Lean
Ewing, Charles Boal, Jr. *real estate company executive*

Upper Saint Clair *(see right column)*

†Urquhart, Glen Taylor *real estate development company executive, government planning administrator*

Palmyra
Mulckhuyse, Jacob John *energy conservation and environmental consultant*

Richmond
Alpert, Janet A(nne) *title insurance company executive*
Dickinson, Alfred James *realtor*
Plaisted, Harris Merrill, III *real estate executive*
Tuck, Grayson Edwin *real estate agent, former natural gas transmission executive*

WASHINGTON

Olympia
†Cothern, Barbara Shick *real estate investor, state legislator*

Seattle
Dillard, Marilyn Dianne *property manager*
Gerrodette, Charles Everett *real estate company executive, consultant*
McKinnon, James Buckner *real estate sales executive, writer, researcher*
Stevens, Clyde Benjamin, Jr. *property manager, retired naval offier*

Spokane
Kirschbaum, James Louis *property manager*

WISCONSIN

Beaver Dam
Butterbrodt, John Ervin *real estate executive*

Madison
Mullins, Jerome Joseph *real estate developer, consulting engineer*
Ring, Gerald J. *real estate developer, insurance executive*
Vandell, Kerry Dean *real estate and urban economics educator*

Milwaukee
Checota, Joseph Woodrow *real estate business executive*
Machulak, Edward Leon *real estate, mining and advertising company executive*
Smith, Lois Ann *real estate executive*

Minocqua
Utt, Glenn S., Jr. *motel investments and biotech industry company executive*

WYOMING

Jackson
Thulin, Walter Willis *real estate company executive*

CANADA

ALBERTA

Calgary
McEwen, Alexander Campbell *cadastral studies educator, former Canadian government official, surveying consultant*

BRITISH COLUMBIA

Vancouver
Belzberg, Samuel *real estate investment professional*
Goldberg, Michael Arthur *land policy and planning educator*
Jurock, Oswald Erich *real estate executive*

MANITOBA

Winnipeg
Shnier, Alan *real estate executive*

NOVA SCOTIA

Stellarton
Sobey, Donald Creighton Rae *real estate developer*

ONTARIO

Burlington
†Daley, R. J. *environmental research director*

Don Mills
Cormack, G. J. *real estate executive*

Downsview
Page, Austin P. *property development company executive*

London
Pearson, Norman *urban planner, administrator, academic and planning consultant, writer*

North York
Carrothers, Gerald Arthur Patrick *environmental and city planning educator*

Toronto
Braithwaite, J(oseph) Lorne *real estate executive*
De Groot, John *real estate development executive*
Dimma, William Andrew *real estate executive*

Goring, Peter Allan Elliott *real estate executive*
L'Heureux, Willard John *real estate lawyer*
Marshall, Marvin Giffin *real estate company executive*
Mercurio, Renard Michael *real estate corporation executive*
Wood, Neil Roderick *real estate development company executive*

Weston
McIntyre, John George Wallace *real estate development and management consultant*

QUEBEC

Montreal
Gabbour, Iskandar *city and regional planning educator*

BAHAMAS

Aboco
Goodloe, John Duncan, IV *real estate company executive*

ENGLAND

London
†Hall, Peter Geoffrey *urban and regional planning educator*

ADDRESS UNPUBLISHED

Amon, Arthur Howard, Jr. *real estate consultant, retired retailing executive*
Beal, Merrill David *conservationist, museum director*
Bernhardt, Arthur Dieter *building industry executive and consultant*
Brady, George Moore *real estate executive, mortgage banker*
Burk, Sylvia Joan *petroleum landman, freelance writer*
Corey, Kenneth Edward *geography and urban planning educator, researcher*
DeBartolo, Edward J., Sr. *real estate developer*
†Fetterly, Lynn Lawrence *real estate broker/developer*
Foley, Daniel Edmund *real estate development executive*
Greenfield, Helen Meyers *real estate executive, publishing company executive, inspection and test service executive*
†Hamilton, Calvin Sargent *planning consultant, retired city official*
Harris, David Philip *crisis management for underperforming corporations*
Hediger, Gary Roddy *property management company executive*
Hodson, Nancy Perry *real estate agent*
Houstoun, Lawrence Orson, Jr. *development consultant*
Jordan, Lois Heywood *real estate developer*
Lewis, Rolland Wilton *real estate manager*
Maguire, Robert Francis, III *real estate investor*
Mann, Clarence Charles *real estate company official*
Messenkopf, Eugene John *real estate and business consultant*
Mitchell, Robert Edward *urban planner, international development specialist, educator*
Netter, Cornelia Ann *real estate broker*
Porosky, Michael *real estate and investment company executive*
†Rassman, Joel H. *real estate company executive, accountant*
Richman, Marvin Jordan *real estate developer, investor, educator*
Ridloff, Richard *real estate executive, lawyer, consultant*
Saunders, Alexander Hall *real estate executive*
Simon, Melvin *real estate developer, professional basketball executive*
Slayton, William Larew *planning consultant, former government official*
Stewart, Thomas Ted *real estate developer, investment banker*
Taubman, A. Alfred *real estate developer*
Trump, Donald John *real estate developer*
Ventre, Francis Thomas *environmental design and policy educator*
Weikert, Jerard Lee *real estate broker*
Williamson, Fletcher Phillips *real estate executive*
Wilson, Roy Gardiner *real estate developer*

GOVERNMENT: AGENCY ADMINISTRATION

UNITED STATES

ALABAMA

Birmingham
Gallups, Vivian Lylay Bess *federal contracting officer*

Mobile
Lager, Robert John *state agency administrator*

Montgomery
Gainous, Fred Jerome *state agency administrator*
Teague, Wayne *state education official*

Tuscaloosa
Flinn, David R. *federal agency research director*

ALASKA

Anchorage
†Porter, Brian Stanley *police chief*

Juneau
Deihl, Michael Allen *federal agency administrator*
Sandor, John Abraham *state agency administrator*
†Scott, William Herbert *state agency administrator*

ARIZONA

Glendale
North, Warren James *government official*

Oro Valley
Rivkind, Perry Abbot *federal railroad agency administrator*

Phoenix
Bishop, C. Diane *state agency administrator, educator*
†Brunacini, Alan Vincent *fire chief*
Garrett, Dennis Andrew *police official*

Sun City West
De Layo, Leonard Joseph *former state education official*

Tucson
Isenhower, Eleanor Anne Hexamer *state government administrator*

ARKANSAS

Mountain Home
Saltzman, Benjamin Nathan *retired state health administrator, physician*

CALIFORNIA

Bakersfield
†Price, Robert O. *police official*

Castro Valley
Palmer, James Daniel *inspector*

Cupertino
Compton, Dale Leonard *retired space agency executive*

Fresno
Rank, Everett George *government official*

Los Angeles
Manning, Donald O. *protective services official*
Williams, Willie *protective services official*

Oakland
†Ewell, P. Lamont *fire department chief*
†Samuels, Joseph, Jr. *police chief*

Rocklin
Ha, Chong Wan *state government executive*

Sacramento
Eu, March Kong Fong *state official*
Muehleisen, Gene Sylvester *retired law enforcement officer, state official*
Strock, James Martin *state agency administrator, lawyer, conservationist*

San Diego
Osby, Robert Edward *protective services official*

San Francisco
Honig, Bill *state educational administrator*

COLORADO

Boulder
Birmingham, Bascom Wayne *retired government official*
Chinnery, Michael Alistair *federal government official, geophysicist*
Gilman, Peter A. *national laboratory administrator, scientist*

Colorado Springs
Leuver, Robert Joseph *former government official, association executive*

Denver
Baumgart, Norbert K. *government official*
†Gonzales, Richard L. *fire department chief*
McGraw, Jack Wilson *government official*
†Michaud, David L. *protective services official*
†Nessi, Dominic *federal agency administrator, instructor*
Randall, William Theodore *state official*
Simons, Lynn Osborn *state education official*

Golden
Clagett, William H., IV *government agency administrator*
Olson, Marian Katherine *emergency management executive, publisher*
Toll, Jack Benjamin *government official*

Grand Junction
Olson, Sylvester Irwin *government official*

Monument
Miele, Alfonse Ralph *former government official*

Vail
Searls, Melvin William, Jr. *government official*

CONNECTICUT

Hartford
Piotrowski, Richard Francis *state agency administrator, council chairman*

New Canaan
†Bosworth, Stephen Warren *foundation executive*

Riverside
†Powers, Claudia McKenna *state government official*

Stamford
Schilling, Albert Henry *former government agency administrator, corporate environmental consultant*

DELAWARE

Dover
delTufo, Theresa Lallana Izon *state official*
Forgione, Pascal D., Jr. *state superintendent*
Lowell, Howard Parsons *government records administrator*

Newark
Keene, William Blair *state education official*

Wilmington
Benson, Barbara Ellen *state agency administrator*
Eichler, Thomas P. *state agency administrator*

DISTRICT OF COLUMBIA

Washington
†Adams, Gordon Merritt *federal agency administrator*
Aikens, Joan Deacon *government official*
Allen, Frederick Warner *federal agency executive*
Anderson, David Turpeau *government official, judge*
Apfel, Kenneth S. *federal government official*
Armstrong, David Andrew *federal agency official, retired army officer*
†Bailey, John E. *federal agency administrator*
†Baker, D. James *federal agency administrator*
†Bane, Mary Jo *federal agency administrator*
†Baquet, Charles R., III *federal agency administrator*
Barrett, Andrew *federal agency administrator*
Barton, William Russell *government official*
Bateman, Paul William *government official, business executive*
Beaumont, Enid Franklin *public administration executive*
Beebe, Cora Prifold *government official*
†Bellamy, Carol *federal agency administrator*
Bennet, Douglas Joseph, Jr. *federal agency administrator*
Bernthal, Frederick Michael *association executive*
Berube, Raymond P. *federal agency administrator*
Biddle, Livingston Ludlow, Jr. *former government official, author*
Bigelow, Donald Nevius *educational administrator, historian, consultant*
Boerrigter, Glenn Charles *educational administrator*
†Brandt, Werner William *federal agency official*
Breger, Marshall J. *government official, legal educator*
Bresee, James Collins *federal agency administrator*
Britten, Gerald Hallbeck *government official*
Broderick, Anthony James *federal government administrator*
Brown, Harold *corporate director, former secretary of defense*
Brown, June Gibbs *government agency official*
Bullard, John Kilburn *federal agency administrator*
Burt, John Alan *federal agency administrator*
Bussard, David Andrew *federal agency administrator*
†Campbell, Donald Alfred *government official*
Carlson, William Dwight *government agency administrator*
†Cashell, Lois D. *federal agency administrator*
Clarke, Richard A. *federal agency administrator*
Clinkscales, William Abner, Jr. *government administrator*
Congel, Frank Joseph *federal agency administrator, physicist*
Conway, John Thomas *government official, lawyer, engineer*
Cooper, Benita Ann *federal agency administrator*
Cooper, Roger Merlin *government administrator, educator*
Cotruvo, Joseph Alfred *federal agency administrator*
Cremona, Vincent Anthony *federal agency administrator*
Cunningham, George Woody *federal official, metallurgical engineer*
Curran, Donald Charles *federal agency administrator, government librarian*
Danaher, James William *federal government executive*
Daniels, Stephen M. *government official*
Dausman, George Erwin *federal official, aeronautical engineer*
†Davies, Tudor Thomas *federal agency administrator*
Dawson, Robert Kent *government relations expert*
Day, Daniel Edgar *government information officer*
Dean, Alan Loren *government official*
†Deer, Ada E. *federal agency official, social worker, educator*
DeMars, Bruce *naval administrator*
Detchon, Bryan Reid *federal agency administrator*
†DiMario, Michael F. *federal agency official, lawyer*
†Donahue, John David *federal official*
Donley, Michael Bruce *federal government executive, financial manager*
Draper, William Henry, III *former United Nations official*
Duggan, Ervin S. *federal agency administrator*
Elliott, Emerson John *federal agency administrator, policy analyst*
†Erdreich, Ben Leader *federal government agency executive*
Finarelli, Margaret G. *government executive*
†Fischer, Dennis James *federal agency administrator*
Fishbaugh, Franklin James *government intelligence officer, researcher, weapons specialist*
Fletcher, Arthur A. *federal official*
Flint, Myles Edward *federal agency administrator, lawyer*
Fouchard, Joseph James *government agency administrator*
Frazier, Henry Bowen, III *government official, lawyer*
Freeh, Louis J. *federal agency administrator*
Fried, Edward R. *government official*
Frohnmayer, John Edward *federal agency administrator*
Frost, Ellen Louise *federal agency administrator*
Funk, Sherman Maxwell *government official*
†Gall, Mary Sheila *federal agency administrator*
Gallegos, Tony Eismail *federal agency administrator*
Gauldin, Michael Glen *federal agency administrator*
Gebbie, Kristine Moore *health official*
Gest, Kathryn Waters *press secretary*
Gibson, Thomas Fenner, III *public affairs consultant, political cartoonist*
Gillingham, Robert Fenton *federal agency administrator, economist*
Gilliom, Judith Carr *government official*
†Ginsburg, Alan *federal agency adminstrator*
Glynn, Thomas P. *federal agency administrator*
Gober, Hershel W. *federal agency official*
Goldin, Daniel S. *government agency administrator*
†Golding, Carolyn May *government administrator*
Good, Mary Lowe (Mrs. Billy Jewel Good) *government official*
Goodman, Roland Alfred *federal agency administrator, former military officer*
Gorn, Janet Marie *government official*
†Gould, William Benjamin, IV *federal official, lawyer, educator*
Grayson, Lawrence Peter *federal educational administrator*
Green, Richard James *federal agency administrator, aerospace engineer*
Greenwood, Mark A. *federal agency administrator, lawyer*
Griffith, Jerry Dice *government official, nuclear engineer*
Guimond, Richard Joseph *federal agency executive, environmental scientist*
Haas, Ellen *federal agency administrator*
†Hackney, Sheldon *federal agency administrator, academic administrator*
†Hagenstad, M. Thomas *federal government administrator*
Haller, Ralph A. *federal agency administrator*
Hallett, Carol Boyd *government official*
Hammond, Jerome Jerald *government program administrator, agricultural economist*
Hannigan, Vera Simmons *federal agency administrator*
†Harris, David Ford *federal agency administrator*
Harris, Wesley L. *federal agency administrator*
Hathaway, William Dodd *federal agency administrator*
†Hayes, Paula Freda *governmental official*
Hedrick, Floyd Dudley *government official, author*
Hervey, Homer Vaughan *federal agency administrator*
†Heumann, Judith *federal agency administrator*
Hill, Jimmie Dale *government official*
Hinch, Gerald K. *federal agency official*
Hitz, Frederick Porter *federal agency administrator, lawyer*
Hogan, John P. *federal agency official*
Hough, Lawrence A. *financial organization executive*
Hove, Andrew Christian *federal agency administrator*
Howerton, Helen Veronica *federal agency administrator*
Hoyt, David Richard *federal agency official*
Hsu, Ming Chen *federal agency administrator*
Hughes, Ann Hightower *economist, government official*
Hundt, Reed Eric *federal official, lawyer*
Hunkele, Lester Martin, III *federal agency administrator*
Hunter, Kenneth James *federal agency adminstrator*
Iklé, Fred Charles *former federal agency administrator, policy advisor, defense expert*
†Itteilag, Anthony L. *government official*
Johnson, Arlene Lytle *government agency official*
Johnson, Ralph Raymond *ambassador, federal agency administrator*
Johnson, Roger *federal agency administrator*
Johnson, Roger W. *federal official, computer manufacturing company executive*
Johnson, Stephen L. *federal agency administrator*
Jordan, John Patrick *government agency executive, research scientist, educator*
Kearney, Stephen Michael *federal agency administrator, treasurer*
†Kearns, David Todd *federal agency administrator*
Kelley, Edward Watson, Jr. *federal agency administrator*
Kilgore, Edwin Carroll *retired government official, consultant*
†Kinghorn, Charles Morgan, Jr. *federal agency administrator*
Kinlow, Eugene *federal agency executive*
Kitzmiller, William Michael *government official*
Klepner, Jerry D. *federal agency administrator*
†Kline, Jerry Robert *government official, ecologist*
Knoll, Jerry *former government official*
Komarek, Thomas Charles *government official*
Kondratas, Skirma Anna *policy analyst*
Kropp, Arthur John *public interest organization executive*
†Kruesi, Frank E. *federal agency administrator*
Kunin, Madeleine May *federal agency administrator, former governor*
†Kutscher, Ronald Earl *federal government executive*
Ladwig, Alan Michael *space policy analyst, author*
Layton, John C. *federal agency administrator*
†Lindsey, Alfred Walter *federal agency official, environmental engineer*
Lord, Jerome Edmund *federal education administrator, writer*
Maas, Joe (Melvin Joseph Maas) *federal agency administrator*
Mahan, Clarence *government official, writer*
Mancher, Rhoda Ross *strategic planner*
Martin, Jerry L. *federal agency administrator*
Marzetti, Loretta A. *government agency executive, policy analyst*
Masten, Charles C. *federal agency administrator*
Maxwell, David Ogden *government official, financial executive*
†Mays, Janice Ann *federal agency administrator, lawyer*
Mc Afee, William *government official*
McCahill, Barry Winslow *federal public affairs official*
McCormick, Robert Junior *government official*
McDonald, Gail Clements *government official*
Mc Fee, Thomas Stuart *government agency administrator*
†McGarry, John Warren *government official*
McKee, Margaret Jean *federal agency executive*
†McLaughlin, Maureen A. *federal agency administrator*
McLucas, William Robert *federal agency director*
McNeill, John Henderson *government official, lawyer*

Meikle, Philip G. *government agency executive*
Meyers, Sheldon *government official*
Mlay, Marian *government official*
Moler, Elizabeth Anne *federal agency administrator, lawyer*
†Moore, Richard Thomas *federal government administrator*
Moos, Eugene *federal agency administrator*
Moose, George E. *government official*
Mosemann, Lloyd Kenneth, II *government official*
Nash, Robert R. (Bob Nash) *under-secretary agriculture rural and small development*
Neal, Darwina Lee *government official*
Nethery, John Jay *government official*
Newhouse, Alan Russell *federal government executive*
Newman, Don Melvin *federal agency administrator*
Newquist, Don *federal agency administrator*
†Norry, Patricia Goodwin *government executive*
Palast, Geri D. *federal agency administrator*
†Patron, June Eileen *federal agency administrator*
†Petersen, Richard Herman *government executive, aeronautical engineer*
Pettengill, Harry Junior *federal agency administrator*
Plowman, R. Dean *federal agriculture agency administrator*
Powers, Charles Henri *federal official*
Quello, James Henry *government official*
Reed, Vincent Emory *federal education official*
Reidy, Gerald Patrick *federal organization executive, arbitrator, mediator, fact-finder*
Reswick, James Bigelow *government official, rehabilitation engineer, educator*
Richardson, Margaret Milner *federal agency administrator, lawyer*
Rieke, Elizabeth Ann *federal agency administrator*
Rogers, Jerry L. *federal agency administrator*
Rogers, Raymond Jesse *federal railroad associate administrator*
Rominger, Richard *federal agency administrator*
Rosamond, John Bell *government official*
Rosendhal, Jeffrey David *federal science agency administrator, astronomer*
†Rothkopf, David Jochanan *federal official*
Rottman, Ellis *public information officer*
Salamone, Philip Joseph *federal agency administrator*
Savage, Phillip Hezekiah *federal agency administrator*
Savage, Xyla Ruth *government official*
Schapiro, Mary *federal agency administrator, lawyer*
Schneider, Mark Lewis *government official*
Schoenberg, Mark George *government agency administrator*
Schoenberger, James Edwin *federal agency administrator*
Searing, Marjory Ellen *government official, economist*
†Seidel, Milton Joseph *government administrator*
†Seignious, George Marion, II *former government official, former college president, retired army officer*
Sessions, William Steele *former government official*
Shank, Fred Ross *federal agency administrator*
Shapiro, Michael Henry *government executive*
†Shearer, P. Scott *government relations professional*
Sherman, Wendy Ruth *federal agency administrator*
Sherwin, Michael Dennis *government official*
Siegel, Richard David *lawyer, former government official*
Sieverts, Frank Arne *government official*
†Slater, Rodney E. *federal administrator*
†Slatkin, Nora *federal agency administrator*
Slocombe, Walter Becker *government official, lawyer*
Smith, Curtis Johnston *government executive*
Smith, Richard Melvyn *government official*
Soderberg, Nancy *federal agency administrator*
Spector, Eleanor Ruth *government executive*
Sphar, Raymond Leslie, Jr. *medical administrator, researcher*
Steele, Ana Mercedes *government official*
Stephens, James M. *federal agency administrator*
Stewart, Frank Maurice, Jr. *federal agency administrator*
Stonehill, Robert Michael *federal agency administrator*
Stoner, John Richard *federal government executive*
Summers, Lawrence *under secretary treasury department*
Swanson, Russell Bruce *federal agency administrator*
Sweedler, Barry Martin *federal agency administrator*
Tarnoff, Peter *governmental official*
Tarrants, William Eugene *government official*
Taylor, Christopher Andrew *securities industry regulation executive*
Taylor, Harold Allen, Jr. *federal agency administrator*
†Thomas, Fred *police chief*
Thomas, James Bert, Jr. *government official*
†Thompson, James Robert, Jr. *federal space center executive*
†Tippeconnic, John W., III *federal agency administrator*
Townsend, Wardell C., Jr. *federal agency administrator*
Trilling, Donald R. *federal agency administrator*
Trodden, Stephen Anthony *federal agency administrator*
Truesdale, John Cushman *government executive*
†Truly, Richard H. *federal agency administrator*
Tuck, John Chatfield *former federal agency administrator, public policy advisor*
†Ulsamer, Andrew George *federal agency manager*
†Vanderveen, John E. *federal agency administrator*
Verhalen, Robert Donald *federal agency executive*
Vogt, Carl William *federal official, lawyer*
Walsh, Edward Patrick *federal agency administrator*
Watson, Harlan L(eroy) *federal official, physicist, economist*
Weber, Thomas Andrew *federal agency executive*
Weiner, Robert Stephen *federal agency administrator*
†Weisberg, Stuart Elliot *federal official, lawyer*
Weiss, Paul Thomas *federal agency executive*
†Wells, Linton, II *federal official*
West, Togo Dennis, Jr. *secretary of Army, former aerospace executive*
Wexler, Anne *government relations and public affairs consultant*
†White, George *government official, physical scientist*
Wilkinson, John Burke *former government official, novelist, biographer*
†Williams, Arthur E. *federal agency administrator*
†Williams, Paul *federal agency administrator*
Wince-Smith, Deborah L. *federal agency administrator*
Winter, Roger Paul *government official*
†Winters, J. Sam *federal official*
Witt, James Lee *federal agency administrator*
Wolfe, Janice E. *business development executive*
Yancik, Joseph John *government official*
Zenowitz, Allan Ralph *government official*

FLORIDA

Bay Pines
†Vogel, Raymond John *federal government executive*

Bradenton
Thompson, Barbara Storck *state official*

Fort Lauderdale
†Cicora, Kenneth Allan *public information officer*

Jacksonville
Harriman, Constance Bastine *federal official*

Melbourne
Cockriel, Russell George, Sr. *crime investigation official*

Miami
Vila, Adis Maria *former government official, lawyer*

North Palm Beach
Oleksiw, Daniel Philip *former foreign service officer, consultant*

Palm Beach
Asencio, Diego C. *state agency administrator, former federal commission administrator, consultant, business executive*

Palm City
Pepitone, Byron Vincent *former government official*

Pensacola
Dixon, James Andrew, Jr. *protective services official*

Saint Augustine
Shortlidge, Richard Lynn, Jr. *foreign affairs consultant, retired foreign service officer, human resource economist*

Tallahassee
Durrence, James Larry *state executive, history educator*
Gould, Bruce Allan *state agency administrator, educator, consultant*
Lewis, Gerald A. *state comptroller*

Tampa
Allen, Timothy Andrew *law enforcement officer*

GEORGIA

Athens
Carter, Mary Eddie *government administrator*

Atlanta
†Bell, Eldrin *protective services official*
Benson, Ronald Edward *state humanities program executive, clergyman, educator*
Collins, Marcus E., Sr. *state agency administrator*
Ebneter, Stewart Dwight *federal agency administrator*
†Hinman, Alan Richard *public health administrator, epidemiologist*
Millar, John Donald *occupational and environmental health consultant, educator*
Tolsma, Dennis Dwayne *federal agency administrator*

Glynco
Rinkevich, Charles Francis *federal official*

Midway
Cobb, John Anthony *retired state veterinarian*

HAWAII

Honolulu
†Chang, Donald S. M. *fire department chief*
†Miyamoto, Owen *state agency administrator*
†Nakamura, Michael S. *protective services official*
Saiki, Patricia (Mrs. Stanley Mitsuo Saiki) *former federal agency administrator, former congresswoman*

IDAHO

Boise
Evans, Jerry Lee *school system administrator*

Moscow
Butterfield, Samuel Hale *former government official and educator*

ILLINOIS

Chicago
Anderson, Douglas Charles *juvenile probation administrator*
Jibben, Laura Ann *state agency administrator*
Orozco, Raymond E. *protective services official*
Prochnow, Herbert Victor *former government official, banker, author*
Rodriguez, Matt L. *protective services professional*
Wilson, Richard Harold *government official*

Evanston
Moskow, Michael H. *federal official*

Hoffman Estates
Laubenstein, Vernon Alfred *state agency administrator*

Springfield
†Mogerman, Susan *state agency administrator*
Shim, Sang Koo *state mental health official*

INDIANA

Indianapolis
Harden, Mary Louise *human resources management specialist*
Kaufman, Karl Lincoln *consultant, former state agency administrator*
Ryan, Earl M. *public affairs analyst*
†Smith, Keith *protective services official*

La Porte
Hiler, John Patrick *former government official, former congressman, business executive*

Notre Dame
Kmiec, Douglas William *government official, law educator*

IOWA

Des Moines
Lepley, William *state education official*

McCallsburg
Lounsberry, Robert Horace *former state government administrator*

KANSAS

Topeka
Droegmueller, Lee *state education official*

KENTUCKY

Frankfort
McDonald, Alice Coig *state education official*

LOUISIANA

Baton Rouge
†Arveson, Raymond G. *state superintendent*
†Brickman, Kenneth Alan *state lottery executive*

New Orleans
Edwards, James Kennedy *quality assurance director, safety-fire protection engineer*
Rodriguez, Myrtle Mary *protective service official*

Shreveport
Greene, Dallas Whorton, Jr. *fire chief*

MAINE

Augusta
Sewell, Dwight A. *state government official*

MARYLAND

Adelphi
Lyons, John W(inship) *government agency administrator, chemist*

Annapolis
Aery, Shaila Rosalie *state educational administrator*
Taussig, Joseph Knefler, Jr. *retired government official, lawyer*

Baltimore
†Couchoud, B. Carlton *federal agency administrator*
DiPentima, Renato Anthony *government agency official*
Guest, James Alfred *public service official*
Hilgenberg, Eve Brantly Handy *government official*
†Martin, George Reilly *federal agency administrator*
Schuster, Charles Roberts *federal government scientist*
Thompson, Lawrence Hyde *federal agency official*

Beltsville
Tso, Tien Chioh *federal agency official, plant physiologist*
van Schilfgaarde, Jan *agricultural engineer, government agricultural service administrator*

Bethesda
Amende, Lynn Meridith *government health scientist*
†Brown, Ann *federal agency administrator*
Burton, Benjamin Theodore *government official*
Campbell, Arthur Andrews *government official*
Chen, Philip S., Jr. *government official*
Dunning, Herbert Neal *government official, physical chemist*
Gutheim, Robert Julius *government official*
Lee, Young Jack *federal agency administrator*
O'Callaghan, Jerry Alexander *government official*
Peterson, Eric Christian *federal agency administrator*
Richardson, John *retired international relations executive*
Schambra, Philip Ellis *federal agency administrator, radiobiologist*
Sprott, Richard Lawrence *government official, researcher*
Walleigh, Robert Shuler *consultant*
Whaley, Storm Hammond *retired government official, consultant*

Bowie
Sullivan, Francis Edward *research administrator*

Chevy Chase
Hudson, Anthony Webster *retired federal agency administrator*
Mulligan, James Kenneth *government official*

Columbia
Hart, Robert Gordon *federal agency administrator*

Fort George G Meade
†McConnell, John Michael *federal agency administrator*

Gaithersburg
Ambler, Ernest *government official*
Hertz, Harry Steven *government official*
Kammer, Raymond Gerard, Jr. *government official*
Prabhakar, Arati *federal administration research director, electrical engineer*
Snell, Jack Eastlake *federal agency administrator*
Warshaw, Stanley Irving *federal agency official*

Greenbelt
†Rothenberg, Joseph Howard *federal agency administrator*

Huntingtown
†Haller, Harlan Thomas *federal agency administrator*

Kensington
Schmerling, Erwin Robert *retired government official*

New Windsor
Culver, Charles George *federal agency administrator, civil engineer*

Potomac
Frey, James McKnight *government official*

Rockville
Aamodt, Roger Louis *federal agency administrator*
†Hoffman, C. Michael *federal agency administrator*
Johnson, Elaine McDowell *federal government administrator*
Kelso, John Hodgson *government official*
Kessler, David A. *health services commissioner*
Rheinstein, Peter Howard *government official, physician, lawyer*
Springer, Michael Louis *federal agency administrator*
Towle, Leland Hill *government official*

Silver Spring
Carnell, Paul Herbert *federal education official*
Friday, Elbert Walter, Jr. *federal agency administrator, meteorologist*
Haynes, Leonard L., III *government official, consultant*
Podgorny, Richard Joseph *government official*

Sykesville
Enoff, Louis D. *international consultant*

Woodbine
Brush, Peter Norman *federal agency administrator, lawyer*

MASSACHUSETTS

Boston
Pierce, Martin E., Jr. *fire commissioner*

MICHIGAN

Belding
Mason, Donald Roger *protective services official, city official*

Detroit
†McKinnon, Isaiah *police chief*
Moss, Leslie Otha *court administrator*

Lansing
Beardmore, Dorothy *state education administrator*

Romulus
Girardin, Burton Lee *retired protective services official*

MINNESOTA

Arden Hills
†Lindmark, Ronald Dorance *retired federal agency administrator*

Minneapolis
Carlson, Norman A. *government official*

MISSISSIPPI

Stoneville
†Putnam, Paul Adin *government agency official*

MISSOURI

Independence
†Mack, Ronald J. *park superintendent*

Jefferson City
Bartman, Robert E. *state education official*
Deck, Robert Alan *state government official*
†Karll, Jo Ann *state agency administrator, lawyer*
McClain, Charles James *state educational administrator*
Parr, Lloyd Byron *state official*

Kansas City
†Bishop, Steven C. *protective services official*
†Fisher, Charles *protective services official*
Getty, Carol Pavilack *government official*

Lambert Airport
Griggs, Leonard LeRoy, Jr. *fedearl agency administrator*

Springfield
Gruhn, Robert Stephen *parole officer*

NEVADA

Carson City
Paslov, Eugene T. *state education official*

Las Vegas
†Broadbent, Robert N. *government official, pharmacist*

NEW HAMPSHIRE

Concord
Brunelle, Robert L. *retired state education director*
Day, Russell Clover *federal agency administrator*
Marston, Charles *state education official*
Mevers, Frank Clement *state archivist, historian*

Exeter
Boggess, Jerry Reid *protective services official*

NEW JERSEY

Atlantic City
Tucci, Mark A. *state agency administrator*

Barrington
Florio, Maryanne J. *state health research scientist*

Fort Monmouth
Kalwinsky, Charles Knowlton *government official*

Morristown
DeLury, Bernard E. *vice president labor relations*

Pennsauken
Connor, Wilda *government health agency administrator*

Trenton
Clymer, Brian William *federal agency administrator*
Wolfe, Deborah Cannon Partridge *government education consultant*

NEW MEXICO

Albuquerque
Gordon, Larry Jean *public health administrator and educator*

Roswell
Lewis, George Raymond *clinical social worker*

Santa Fe
Knapp, Edward Alan *scientist, government administrator*
Morgan, Alan D. *state education official*

NEW YORK

Albany
Knoll, Bruce Evans *state agency administrator*

Greenport
†Breeze, Roger Gerrard *federal agency administrator*

Hadley
Gray-Aldrich, Gretchen Elise *state agency administrator, nursing educator*

Jamaica
Crivelli, Joseph Louis *security specialist*

Lewiston
Kennedy, G. Alfred *federal agency administrator*

New York
Brezenoff, Stanley *bi-state agency administrator*
Ink, Dwight A. *government agency administrator*
Murphy, Eugene Francis *consultant, retired government official*
Novello, Antonia Coello *U.S. surgeon general*
Parker, Susan Brooks *rehabilitation administrator*
†Samuels, Leslie B. *federal agency administrator, lawyer*
Sorensen, Gillian Martin *United Nations official*
Talbot, Phillips *Asian affairs specialist*

Schroon Lake
Swanson, Norma Frances *federal agency administrator*

Woodbury
†Zirkel, Don *public information official*

NORTH CAROLINA

Burlington
Kee, Walter Andrew *former government official*

Corolla
Schrote, John Ellis *retired government executive*

Greensboro
Reed, William Edward *government official, educator*

Pinehurst
Garman, Willard Hershel *former government official, scientist*

Winston Salem
Griscom, Thomas Cecil *presidential assistant, public relations executive*

NORTH DAKOTA

Bismarck
Sanstead, Wayne Godfrey *state superintendent, former lieutenant governor*

OHIO

Alliance
Woods, Rose Mary *consultant, former presidential assistant*

Cincinnati
Fingerhut, Marilyn Ann *federal agency administrator*

Cleveland
†Kovacic, Edward P. *protective services official*
Ross, Lawrence John *federal agency administrator*

Columbus
Barner, Bruce Monroe *state agency administrator*
Deckrosh, Hazen Douglas *state agency administrator, educator*
Ray, Frank David *government agency official*

Dayton
Schorgl, Thomas Barry *arts administrator*

Toledo
Smith, Robert Nelson *former government official, anesthesiologist*

Westerville
Davis, Joseph Lloyd *state council educational administrator, consultant*

OKLAHOMA

Chickasha
Beets, Freeman Haley *retired government official*

Oklahoma City
Collins, William Edward *aeromedical administrator, researcher*
Nesbitt, Charles Rudolph *state agency administrator*

Tulsa
†Baker, Thomas L. *protective services official*

PENNSYLVANIA

Harrisburg
†Glass, Brent D. *state commission administrator*
Peechatka, Walter Norman *government official*

Pittsburgh
†Buford, Earl, Jr. *protective services official*

RHODE ISLAND

Providence
McWalters, Peter *state agency administrator*

Saunderstown
Knauss, John Atkinson *federal agency administrator, oceanographer, educator, former university dean*

SOUTH CAROLINA

Charleston
Gaillard, John Palmer, Jr. *former government official, former mayor*

Columbia
Inkley, Scott Russell, Jr. *state agency administrator*
LeFever, Michael Grant *state agency administrator*
Nielsen, Barbara Stock *state education official*

Greenville
Theodore, Nick Andrew *lietenant governor*

North
Moran, John Bernard *government official*

SOUTH DAKOTA

Pierre
Bonaiuto, John A. *state education official*

TENNESSEE

Knoxville
†Crowell, Craven H., Jr. *federal agency administrator*
Dean, Charles Henry, Jr. *retired government official*

Memphis
Burgess, Melvin *protective services official*
Knight, H. Stuart *law enforcement official, consultant*

Nashville
†Coleman, Martin M. *protective services official*
Guy, Sharon Kaye *state agency executive*

TEXAS

Austin
Ashworth, Kenneth Hayden *state educational commissioner*
Brinkley, Fred Sinclair, Jr. *state agency administrator, pharmacist*
Gerry, Martin Hughes, IV *federal agency administrator, lawyer*
Meno, Lionel R. *state education official*

Roberts, Bill Glen *retired fire chief, investor, consultant*
Watson, Elizabeth Marion *protective services official*

Houston
Corral, Edward Anthony *fire marshal*

UTAH

Ogden
Hardy, Duane Horace *federal agency administrator, educator*

Provo
Porter, Bruce Douglas *federal agency administrator, educator, writer*

VERMONT

Burlington
†Grimes, Barbara Lauritzen *housing and community affairs administrator*

VIRGINIA

Alexandria
Blake, John Francis *former government agency official, consultant*
Choromokos, James, Jr. *consultant, former government official*
Christie, Thomas Philip *government administrator*
Connally, Ernest Allen *retired federal agency administrator*
Connell, John Gibbs, Jr. *former government official*
Cowles, Roger William *government audit executive*
Harris, Thomas Everett *government official, lawyer, retired*
Hughes, Grace-Flores *former federal agency administrator, management consulting executive*
Johnson, Robert Gerald *federal agency consultant*
Molholm, Kurt Nelson *federal agency administrator*
Senese, Donald Joseph *former government official*
Williams, Justin W. *government official*

Annandale
Guthrie, Edward Everett *government executive, lawyer*

Arlington
Ary, T. S. *federal official, geologist*
Bardon, Marcel *government official*
Beggs, James Montgomery *former government official*
Boyle, Robert Patrick *retired government agency consultant, lawyer*
Bye, Raymond Erwin, Jr. *federal agency administrator*
Entzminger, John Nelson, Jr. *government research agency executive, electronic engineer*
Garvey, Robert Robey, Jr. *former government official*
Johns, Michael Douglas *public policy analyst, writer, former government official*
Lederman, Leonard Lawrence *government research executive*
Nalen, Craig Anthony *government official*
Nielsen, Aldon Dale *retired government agency official, economist*
Sander, Raymond John *government executive*
Shepard, James J. *government official*
Verburg, Edwin Arnold *federal agency administrator*

Charlottesville
Guiton Hill, Bonnie F. *federal official, adviser*
Handy, Alice Warner *state agency administrator*

Fairfax Station
Taylor, Eldon Donivan *government official*

Lorton
Francis, Richard Haudiomont *government administrator*

Mc Lean
†Betsold, Robert John *federal agency administrator*
Brendsel, Leland C. *federal mortgage company executive*
Collins, James Foster *government official*
Cotterill, Carl Hayden *government official*
Donald, James Robert *federal agency official, economist, outdoors writer*
Duncan, Robert Clifton *retired government official*
Svahn, John Alfred *government official*
Turner, Stansfield *former government official, lecturer, writer, teacher*

Midlothian
Davis, Emma-Jo Levey *retired government executive, publishing executive*

Morattico
Dawson, Carol Gene *writer, consultant*

Penn Laird
Wise, Charles Conrad, Jr. *former government official, author*

Richmond
Fay, Frederic Albert *former government official*
Pollard, Overton Price *state agency executive, lawyer*
Tyson, John C. *state official*

Rosslyn
Adair, John Joseph *federal agency administrator*

Vienna
Beaty, Orren, Jr. *writer, former governmental affairs consultant, former association executive*

WASHINGTON

Ashford
Briggle, William James *federal agency administrator*

Greenbank
Grant, Robert Yearington *former government official*

Olympia
Billings, Judith A. *state education official*

Seattle
Fitzsimons, Patrick S. *police chief*
†Harris, Claude *fire department chief*

Sequim
Meacham, Charles Harding *government official*

Spokane
†Bolstad, D. D. *federal agency administrator*

WEST VIRGINIA

Charleston
Marockie, Henry R. *state school system administrator*

Harpers Ferry
White, Thomas Edward *government park official*

WISCONSIN

Madison
Fiedler, Patrick James *circuit court judge*
Whitburn, Gerald *state agency administrator*

Milwaukee
Arreola, Philip *police officer*
†Erdmann, August *protective services official*

WYOMING

Casper
†Nagel, Patricia Jo *non-profit public policy administrator, lawyer*

Cheyenne
Karpan, Kathleen Marie *state official, lawyer, journalist*
Kathka, David Arlin *state parks and cultural resources administrator, state archivist*

MILITARY ADDRESSES OF THE UNITED STATES

ATLANTIC

APO
†Rifenburg, Raymond F. *government official, economist*

EUROPE

APO
Quinn, Eugene Frederick *government official, clergyman*

PACIFIC

APO
Blackburn, Paul Pritchard *federal agency officer*

CANADA

ALBERTA

Calgary
†Borbridge, G. *protective services official*
Priddle, Roland *Canadian government official*
†Richardson, J. Scott *public service administrator*

Edmonton
Schmid, Horst A. *Canadian provincial administrator*

BRITISH COLUMBIA

Vancouver
†Marshall, Bill *protective services official*

NEW BRUNSWICK

Fredericton
McKenna, Frank Joseph *Canadian politician, lawyer*

NORTHWEST TERRITORIES

Yellowknife
Patterson, Dennis Glen *Canadian government official, lawyer*

ONTARIO

Downsview
Burton, Ian *federal agency administrator, educator, environmental scientist, geographer, author, consultant*

Kingston
Price, Raymond Alexander *Canadian government official, geologist, educator*

Nova Scotia
Pottie, Roswell Francis *science and technology consultant*

Ottawa
Allen, George W. *deputy commissioner*
Blais, Pierre *Canadian government minister*
†Chrétien, (Joseph Jacques) Jean *Canadian government official, lawyer*
Clark, Ian Douglas *Canadian government official*
Collin, Arthur Edwin *Canadian government official*
Epp, Arthur Jacob *Canadian government official*
Gravelle, Pierre *Canadian government official*
Hubbard, Ruth *federal official*
Inkster, Norman David *police commissioner*
MacFarlane, John Alexander *former federal housing agency administrator*
Mac Neill, James William *Canadian government official, international consultant*
Macquarrie, Heath Nelson *Canadian government official*
†Martin, Paul *Canadian federal official*
Morden, John Reid *Canadian federal agency administrator*
Murphy, Edmund Michael *Canadian government agency administrator, demographer*
†Shoemaker, John Michael *law enforcement official*
†Tobin, Brian *Canadian government official*

Toronto
Fraser, William Neil *government official*
Gillespie, Alastair William *former Canadian government official*
Rogers, Harry G. *Canadian government official*

QUEBEC

Hull
Massé, Marcel *Canadian official*

Montreal
†Lord, Guy J.H. *lawyer, Canandian government official*

SASKATCHEWAN

Regina
†Fedoruk, Sylvia O. *Canadian provincial official, educator*
Nuttall, Richard Norris *state agency administrator*

MEXICO

Mexico City
Lozoya-Thalmann, Emilio *Mexican government official*
Serra Puche, Jaime Jose *Mexican government official*

TAIWAN

Taipei
Dai, Peter Kuang-Hsun *government official, aerospace executive*

ADDRESS UNPUBLISHED

Anderson, Wayne Carl *public information officer*
Boozer, Howard Rai *state education official*
Brubaker, Crawford Francis, Jr. *government official, aerospace consultant*
Childers, Perry Robert *government agency administrator*
Claytor, Richard Anderson *retired federal agency executive*
Conway, James Valentine Patrick *forensic document examiner, former postal service executive*
Courtney, Charles Edward *government official*
†Crawford, Carol Tallman *government executive*
Guild, Nelson Prescott *retired state education official*
Harder, Robert Clarence *state official*
Healton, Donald Carney *federal agency administrator*
Hedrick, Basil Calvin *state agency administrator, ethnohistorian, educator, museum and cultural institutions consultant*
Helms, J. Lynn *former government agency administrator*
Hernández, William Héctor, Jr. *government official*
Keala, Francis Ahloy *security executive*
Kirkendall, Donald Eugene *federal agency official*
Kusserow, Richard Phillip *government official*
LaBarre, Carl Anthony *retired government official*
Lewis, Samuel Winfield *retired government official, former ambassador*
Mc Coy, Tidal Windham *former government official*
†Murr, James Coleman *federal government official*
Perrin, Robert *federal government consultant*
Rhett, John Taylor, Jr. *government official, civil engineer*
Ross, Joseph E. *government official, lawyer*
Shasteen, Donald Eugene *government official*
Shute, Richard Emil *government official, engineer*
Skaff, Joseph John *state agency administrator, retired army officer*
Smith, Doris Victoria *educational agency administrator*
†Tate, F. Wayne *federal agency administrator*
Untermeyer, Charles G. (Chase) *government official*
Walker, Gordon Davies *former government official, writer, lecturer, consultant*
Walsh, Jeremiah Edward, Jr. *government official*
Williams, Barbara Jean May *state official*
Winslow, Alfred Akers *retired government official*

GOVERNMENT: EXECUTIVE ADMINISTRATION

UNITED STATES

ALABAMA

Bessemer
Bains, Lee Edmundson *lawyer, state official*

Birmingham
†Arrington, Richard, Jr. *mayor*
†Bennett, Jim *secretary of state*
Boomershine, Donald Eugene *bureau executive, development official*
Dentiste, Paul George *city and regional planning executive*

Huntsville
Hettinger, Steve *mayor*

Mobile
Delaney, Thomas Caldwell, Jr. *city official*
†Dow, Michael Craig *mayor*

Montgomery
Camp, Billy Joe *state official*
†Dixon, Larry Dean *state official*
Evans, James Harold *state attorney general*
Folsom, James, Jr. *governor*
Latham, Larry Lee *state administrator, psychologist*
Wallace, George Corley *former governor*

ALASKA

Anchorage
†Brown, Kay (Mary Kathryn Brown) *state official*
Fink, Tom *mayor*

Chugiak
†Ondola, George *village official*

Fairbanks
Smith, Robert London *commissioner, retired air force officer, political scientist, educator*
Wolting, Robert Roy *city official*

Juneau
†Botelho, Bruce Manuel *state official, mayor*
Coghill, John Bruce *state official*
Hickel, Walter Joseph *state governor, investment firm executive*

Kodiak
Selby, Jerome M. *mayor*

Kokhanok
†Nelson, John D., Jr. *village administrator*

ARIZONA

Mesa
Rich, David Barry *city official, auditor, accountant*

Phoenix
Frank, Anthony Melchior *federal official, former financial executive*
Johnson, Paul E. *mayor*
Mahoney, Richard *state official*
Symington, Fife *governor*
Woods, Grant *state attorney general*
Woods, Joel Grant *state attorney general*

Scottsdale
†Drinkwater, Herbert R. *mayor*

Sun City
Farwell, Albert Edmond *retired government official, consultant*

Tempe
†Mitchell, Harry E. *mayor, educator*
Tambs, Lewis Arthur *diplomat, historian, educator*

Tucson
Miller, George *mayor*
Volgy, Thomas John *mayor, political science educator*
Williams, Ben Franklin, Jr. *mayor, lawyer*

ARKANSAS

Bella Vista
Medin, Myron James, Jr. *city manager*

Little Rock
Ahlen, John William, III *state official, scientist, educator*
Bryant, Winston *state attorney general*
Lumpkin, JimmieLou Fisher *state official*
McCuen, William James (Bill) *state official*
Tucker, Jim Guy, Jr. *governor*

CALIFORNIA

Berkeley
Rice, Edward Earl *former government official, author*

Beverly Hills
Black, Shirley Temple (Mrs. Charles A. Black) *ambassador, former actress*
Toman, Mary Ann *federal official*

Concord
Davis, Robert Leach *retired government official, consultant*

Coronado
Hostler, Charles Warren *international affairs consultant*

Felicity
Istel, Jacques Andre *mayor*

Fremont
Ball, William *mayor*

Fresno
†Patterson, James *mayor*

Fullerton
†Catlin, Allen Burdett (Buck Catlin) *mayor, former naval officer*

Glendale
Day, John Francis *city official, former savings and loan executive, former mayor*
†Zarian, Larry *mayor*

Hayward
†Sweeney, Michael *mayor*

Inglewood
†Vincent, Edward *mayor*

La Jolla
Klein, David *foreign service officer*
Shakespeare, Frank *ambassador*

Laguna Hills
Hussey, William Bertrand *retired foreign service officer*

Long Beach
Kell, Ernest Eugene, Jr. *mayor, contractor*
Sato, Eunice Noda *former mayor, consultant*

Los Altos
Gray, Robert Donald *mayor*

Los Angeles
Amarat, Issariyaporn Chulajata *diplomat*
Peters, Aulana Louise *government agency commissioner, lawyer*
Reagan, Ronald Wilson *former President of United States*
Remy, Ray *local government official*
Rice, Donald Blessing *former secretary of air force, corporate executive*
Riordan, Richard J. *mayor*
Rudd, Hynda L. *city official*
Schnabel, Rockwell Anthony *ambassador*
Shelton, Turner Blair *diplomat*

Los Gatos
Farley, Philip Judson *former government official*

Menlo Park
Lane, Laurence William, Jr. *retired U.S. ambassador, publisher*

Modesto
Mensinger, Peggy Boothe *retired mayor*

Monterey
†Wright, Mary R. *state park superintendent*

Napa
Battisti, Paul Oreste *county supervisor*

Oakland
Harris, Elihu Mason *mayor*

Oceanside
Lyon, Richard *mayor, retired naval officer*

Ontario
Fatland, James R. *mayor*

Orange
Schoettger, Theodore Leo *city official*

Orinda
Conran, James Michael *state government official*

Pasadena
Bean, Maurice Darrow *retired diplomat*
Hawkey, Philip A. *city manager*

Pomona
Smith, Donna *mayor, small business owner*

Rancho Mirage
Ford, Gerald Rudolph, Jr. *former President of United States*

Rancho Santa Fe
Capen, Richard Goodwin, Jr. *ambassador*

Riverside
†Frizzel, Teresa R. *mayor*
Steckel, Barbara Jean *city financial officer*

Sacramento
Betts, Bert A. *former state treasurer, accountant*
Brown, Kathleen *state treasurer, lawyer*
Covitz, Carl D. *state official, real estate and investment executive*
†Eastin, Delaine Andree *state legislator*
Kemmerly, Jack Dale *state official*
Lungren, Daniel Edward *state attorney general*
McCarthy, Leo Tarcisius *state lieutenant governor*
Nelson, Alan Curtis *government official, lawyer*
†Serna, Joe, Jr. *mayor*
Takasugi, Nao *state official, business developer*
Walston, Roderick Eugene *attorney general*
Whiteside, Carol Gordon *state official, former mayor*
Wilson, Pete *governor of California*

San Diego
Golding, Susan *mayor*
Kenneally, Dennis Michael *government official*
†Partida, Gilbert A. *chamber of commerce executive*

San Francisco
Brown, Edmund Gerald, Jr. (Jerry Brown) *former governor*
†Jordan, Frank M. *mayor*
Rosenthal, James D. *former ambassador, government and foundation executive*
Stone, Michael P. W. *former federal official*
Taylor, John Lockhart *city official*

San Jose
†Gonzales, Ron *city mayor*
Hammer, Susan W. *mayor*

Santa Rosa
Frowick, Robert Holmes *retired diplomat*

Solana Beach
Ernst, Roger Charles *former government official, natural resources consultant, association executive*
Gildred, Theodore Edmonds *ambassador*

Stanford
Reilly, William Kane *former government official, lawyer, conservationist*
Shultz, George Pratt *former secretary of state, economics educator*

Torrance
†Geissert, Katy *mayor*

West Covina
Markham, Clarence Matthew, III *city administrator*

COLORADO

Aurora
†Tauer, Paul E. *mayor, educator*

Colorado Springs
Isaac, Robert Michael *mayor, lawyer*
Milton, Richard Henry *retired diplomat*

Denver
Brown, Keith Lapham *retired ambassador*
Callihan, C. Michael *lieutenant governor, former state senator*
†Kerns, Peggy Shoup *state representative*
Meyer, Natalie *state official*
Norton, Gale *state attorney general*
Romer, Roy R. *governor*
Webb, Wellington E. *mayor*
Zakhem, Sam Hanna *diplomat*

Pueblo
Casey, William Robert, Jr. *ambassador, mining engineer*
Occhiato, Michael Anthony *city official*

CONNECTICUT

Bloomfield
Houston, Howard Edwin *retired government official*

Bridgeport
†Ganim, Joseph P. *mayor*

Bristol
Moffitt, George, Jr. *foreign service officer*

Hartford
Addiss, Susan Silliman *state government administrator*
Blumenthal, Richard *state attorney general*
De Rocco, Andrew Gabriel *state commissioner, educator*
Farren, J. Michael *former government official, lawyer*
Groark, Eunice *state official*
Kezer, Pauline Ryder *state official*
Killian, Robert Kenneth *former lieutenant governor*
†Milner, Thirman L. *mayor*
Weicker, Lowell Palmer, Jr. *governor*

Waterbury
†Bergin, Edward Daniel *mayor*

Wethersfield
Precourt, George Augustine *government official*

DELAWARE

Christiana
†Neal, James Preston *state senator, project engineer*

Dover
Bookhammer, Eugene Donald *state government official*
Carper, Thomas Richard *governor*
Minner, Ruth Ann *state official*

Newark
Woo, S. B. (Shien-Biau Woo) *former lieutenant governor, physics educator*

Wilmington
Ianni, Francis Alphonse *state official, former army officer*
Oberly, Charles Monroe, III *state attorney general*

DISTRICT OF COLUMBIA

Washington
†Abramowitz, Morton I. *former ambassador*
Abshire, David Manker *diplomat, research executive*
†Achtenberg, Roberta *federal official*
Albright, Raymond Jacob *government official*
Allison, Graham Tillett, Jr. *federal government official*
Altman, Roger C. *U.S. Treasury deputy secretary*
Andersen, Robert Allen *government official*
Anschuetz, Norbert Lee *retired diplomat, banker*
†Anthony, Sheila F. *federal official*
Archard, Douglas Bruce *foreign service officer*

Aspin, Les *former U.S. secretary of defense, former congressman*
Atherton, Charles Henry *federal commission administrator*
Atwood, John Brian *federal official, foundation administrator*
Auten, John Harold *government official*
Ayres, Mary Ellen *government official*
Azcuenaga, Mary Laurie *government official*
Babbitt, Bruce Edward *U.S. secretary of the interior*
†Bachula, Gary R. *federal official*
Baena Soares, João Clemente *ambassador*
Bair, Sheila Colleen *commissioner*
Baker, D(onald) James *federal official, oceanographer, administrator*
Baker, John Alexander *retired foreign service officer, federal official*
Baldyga, Leonard J. *diplomat, foreign service officer*
Ballantyne, Robert Jadwin *former foreign service officer, consultant*
Barnett, Robert Warren *diplomat, author*
†Barram, David J. *federal official*
†Barrett, Dennis P. *ambassador to Madagascar*
Barringer, Philip E. *government official*
†Barshefsky, Charlene *diplomat*
Bartholomew, Reginald *diplomat*
Bassin, Jules *foreign service officer*
Bauer, Gary Lee *government official*
†Baumgartner, Eileen Mary *government official*
Beckler, David Zander *government official, science administrator*
Bell, Robert G. *federal agency official*
Bellinger, John B., Jr. *federal official*
Bellows, Michael Donald *foreign service officer*
Benedick, Richard Elliot *diplomat*
Bennett, John E. *diplomat*
†Berg, Olena *federal official*
†Berger, Samuel R. *federal official*
†Berlincourt, Marjorie Alkins *government official*
Bodde, William, Jr. *foreign service officer*
Bolino, John Vincent *federal agency administrator*
Borg, Parker Webb *ambassador*
Bowles, Erskine *federal agency administrator*
Bowsher, Charles Arthur *government official*
Boyd, Thomas Marshall *federal official, lawyer*
Brazeal, Aurelia E. *ambassador*
Brewster, Robert Charles *diplomat, consultant*
†Broadnax, Walter D. *federal official*
Broedling, Laurie Adele *federal official, psychologist, educator*
†Bromwich, Michael Ray *federal official*
Brotzman, Donald Glenn *government official, lawyer*
Brown, Elizabeth Ann *foreign service officer*
†Brown, Jesse *federal official*
Brown, Kent Newville *ambassador*
Brown, Lee Patrick *federal official, law enforcement educator*
Brown, Ronald Harmon *U.S. secretary of commerce, political organization administrator, lawyer*
Brown, William Holmes *government official*
Browner, Carol *federal official*
Brynn, Edward Paul *ambassador*
Calderhead, William Dickson *former foreign service officer*
Camp, Donald A. *diplomat*
†Cantu, Norma V. *federal official*
Carlucci, Frank Charles, III *former secretary of defense*
†Carnes, Bruce M. *federal official*
Carson, Johnnie *ambassador*
Casey, Mary Ann *diplomat*
†Casstevens, Kay L. *federal official*
†Catlett, D. Mark *federal official*
Charles, Kathleen J. *federal agency official*
Cheney, Dick (Richard Bruce Cheney) *former secretary of defense, former congressman*
†Cheshes, Martin L. *ambassador*
†Chrétien, Raymond A.J. *ambassador*
†Christensen, Sally Hayden *government executive*
Christopher, Warren *U.S. secretary of state*
Cisneros, Henry G. *U.S. secretary of housing and urban development*
Clinton, Bill (William Jefferson Clinton) *President of the United States*
Cohen, Bonnie R. *government official*
†Colon, Gilbert *federal official*
†Colvin, Bill D. *government official*
Constable, Elinor Greer *federal official, diplomat*
Cook, Frances D. *diplomat*
Cook, Michael Blanchard *government executive*
Cooke, David Ohlmer *government official*
Courtney, William Harrison *diplomat*
Crawford, William Rex, Jr. *former ambassador*
Crocker, Chester Arthur *diplomat, scholar*
Crowley, John Joseph, Jr. *ambassador*
Crutcher, John William *federal agency commissioner*
Cutler, Walter Leon *diplomat, foundation executive*
Dalton, John Howard *Secretary of the Navy, financial consultant*
†Dameron, William H., III *ambassador*
Danzig, Richard Jeffrey *government official, lawyer*
Dapice, Ronald R. *government official*
Darman, Richard Gordon *investor, former government official, former investment banker, former educator*
Davis, David George *federal agency executive*
†Davis, Marilynn A. *housing agency administrator*
†Dean, Edwin Robinson *government official, economist*
Dean, Leslie Alan *foreign service officer*
DeGeorge, Francis Donald *federal official*
†deLaski, Kathleen M. *federal official*
†DeSeve, G. Edward *federal official*
Deutch, John Mark *federal official, chemist, academic administrator*
de Vos, Peter Jon *ambassador*
Dewhurst, Stephen B. *government official, lawyer*
DeWitt, Charles Barbour *federal government official*
†Dickey, George Edward *federal government executive*
Dobbins, James Francis, Jr. *foreign service officer*
Dodd, Thomas *ambassador, educator*
†Donilon, Thomas E. *federal official*
Downey, Mortimer Leo, III *transportation executive*
Dreyer, David E. *federal official*
Duemling, Robert Werner *diplomat, museum director*
Duffey, Joseph Daniel *federal official*
Dulles, Eleanor Lansing *diplomatic consultant, retired diplomat, educator*
†Durham, Archer L. *federal official, retired career officer*
Dyvig, Peter P. *ambassador*
Eddy, John Joseph *diplomat*
Ein, Melvin Bennett *government official*
†Einaudi, Luigi R. *federal official*
†Eller, Jeff *media affairs director, assistant to President*
Elliott, Lee Ann *federal official*
Ellwood, David T. *federal agency administrator*
Ely-Raphel, Nancy *diplomat*
†Escudero, Stanley *ambassador*
Espy, Mike (Alphonso Michael Espy) *U.S. secretary of agriculture*
Faleomavaega, Eni F. H. *territorial diplomat*
Feinberg, Richard E. *federal official*
Ferrara, Peter Joseph *federal official, lawyer, author, educator*
FitzGerald, William Henry G. *diplomat, corporation executive*
Fitzwater, (Max) Marlin *former government official, press secretary, advertising executive*
Flanigan, Alan H. *ambassador*
†Ford, Charles A. *federal official*
Franklin, Barbara Hackman *former goverment official*
Frasure, Robert Conway *diplomat*
†Freeman, Chas. W., Jr. *ambassador*
Freitag, Robert Frederick *government official*
†Fry, Tom *federal official*
†Gaffney, Susan *federal official*
Galloway, William Jefferson *former foreign service officer*
†Gallucci, Robert Louis *diplomat, federal government official*
†Gati, Toby T. *federal official*
Gearan, Mark D. *federal official*
Geisel, Harold Walter *diplomat*
Gergen, David Richmond *federal official, magazine editor*
Gibbons, John Howard (Jack Gibbons) *government official, physicist*
Gildenhorn, Joseph Bernard *diplomat, lawyer*
Glassman, Jon David *diplomat*
Gore, Albert, Jr. *Vice President of the United States*
Green, Marshall *former ambassador, consultant*
Gribbin, David James, III *federal official*
Haig, Alexander Meigs, Jr. *former secretary of state, former army officer, business executive*
Hale, Marcia L. *federal official*
†Hall, Douglas K. *federal official*
Hall, James Henry *foreign service officer*
Hall, Keith R. *federal official*
†Hamilton, Donald R. *foreign service official*
Hamilton, Donald Reed *foreign service officer*
Hamilton, Milton Holmes, Sr. *government executive, politico-military analyst*
Harrop, William Caldwell *retired ambassador, foreign service officer*
Hart, John P. *federal official*
Harter, Dennis Glenn *diplomat*
†Hawk, Kathleen M. *federal official*
Hawkins, Wilbur *federal official*
Hays, Donald Osborne *retired government official*
Henderson, Donald Ainslie *government science administrator*
Hennemeyer, Robert Thomas *diplomat*
Herman, Alexis M. *federal official*
†Heyman, Ira Michael *government official, university chancellor, law educator*
High, George Borman *executive director, research organization*
Holmes, Henry Allen *government official*
†Holum, John D. *federal official*
Houdek, Robert G. *diplomat*
†Houley, William Purcell *federal official, career officer*
Howard, Robert Elliott *federal official*
†Hughes, Arthur H. *ambassador to Yemen*
Hulings, Joseph Simpson *diplomat*
Huntress, Wesley Theodore, Jr. *government official*
†Irving, Clarence L., Jr. (Larry Irving) *federal official*
Isom, Harriet Winsar *ambassador*
Israel, Lesley Lowe *political consultant*
Jackson, Karl Dion *government official business executive, scholar*
Janis, Michael B. *federal official*
Jesseramsing, Chitmansing *ambassador*
Jeter, Howard F. *ambassador*
Johnson, U. Alexis *diplomat*
†Johnston, Kelly Don *political administrator*
†Kalnay, Eugenia *government official, meteorologist*
Kampelman, Max M. *former ambassador, lawyer*
Kantor, Michael (Mickey Kantor) *federal trade representative*
Kappner, Augusta Souza *government official*
Karelis, Charles Howard *government official*
Kauzlarich, Richard Dale *U.S. ambassador, foreign service officer*
Keating, Robert B. *ambassador*
Keel, Alton Gold, Jr. *ambassador*
†Keith, Kenton W. *ambassador to Qatar*
Kelley, Wayne Plumbley, Jr. *federal official*
Kelly, John Hubert *diplomat*
Kelly, Sharon Pratt *mayor*
†Kelman, Steven Jay *government official*
Kemp, Jack French *association director, former U.S. secretary of housing and urban development, former congressman*
†Kendig, William L. *government official, accountant*
†Kennedy, Patrick F. *federal official*
Kennedy, Richard Thomas *government official*
Kerber, Frank John *diplomat*
Kidd, Charles Vincent *former civil servant, educator*
Killgore, Andrew Ivy *former ambassador*
†Kirby, Harmon E. *ambassador*
Knisely, Robert August *government official, lawyer*
Koch, Bruce R. *diplomat*
Komer, Robert William *government official, consultant*
Kornblum, John Christian *foreign service officer*
Korth, Penne Percy *ambassador*
Kovach, Eugene George *government official, consultant*
Kristol, William *public policy activist*
Krys, Sheldon Jack *foreign service officer*
Kuchel, Roland Karl *ambassador*
Laird, Melvin Robert *former secretary of defense*
Lake, Anthony *federal official*
Lake, Joseph Edward *ambassador*
Lalley, Frank Edward *federal government official*
Lamb, Robert Edward *diplomat*
†Lanpher, E. Gibson *ambassador to Zimbabwe*
La Rocque, Gene Robert *retired naval officer, government official, author*
Lastowka, James Anthony *former federal agency executive, lawyer*
LaVelle, Avis *federal administration official*
Le Baron, Joseph Evan *diplomat*
Lee, Chester Maurice *government official*
Lenahan, Walter Clair *retired foreign service officer*
Leonard, Michael *federal official*
†Levy, Michael B. *federal official*
Lilly, William Eldridge *government official*
†Longanecker, David A. *federal official*
Longstreet, Victor Mendell *government official*
Lord, Winston *diplomat*
Lovell, Malcolm Read, Jr. *public policy institute executive, educator, former government official, former trade association executive*
Lowe, Mary Frances *federal government official*
Lowenstein, James Gordon *former diplomat, international consultant*
Lucas, James Walter *federal government official*
Ludwig, Eugene Allan *U.S. comptroller of the currency, lawyer*
Lyman, Princeton Nathan *foreign service officer*
Lyons, James Robert *federal official*
Madigan, Edward R. *former secretary of agriculture*
Magaw, John W. *federal law enforcement official*
†Magaziner, Ira *federal official*
Maisto, John F. *ambassador*
†Maldon, Alfonso *federal official, retired military officer*
†Malott, Frank Stephen *foreign service officer*
Malott, John Raymond *foreign service officer*
Mansfield, Michael Joseph *former ambassador, former senator*
Mathews, Jessica Tuchman *policy researcher, former government official*
Mc Afee, Marilyn *ambassador*
McCallie, Marshall F. *ambassador*
McCarthy, John Thomas *diplomat*
McConnell, James Michael *federal official*
†McCormack, Richard Thomas Fox *government official*
McCurry, Michael Demaree *government spokesman, press secretary*
Mc Donald, John Warlick *diplomat, global strategist*
†McGue, Christie *federal official*
McGuire, Roger Alan *foreign service officer*
McHenry, Donald F. *former diplomat, international affairs consultant, educator*
McKinley, Brunson *diplomat*
McLarty, Thomas F., III (Mack McLarty) *chief of staff*
†McMichael, Guy H., III *federal official*
McMillen, (Charles) Thomas *federal official*
†McNamara, Thomas Edmund *diplomat*
McNicol, David Leon *federal official*
†Meissner, Doris M. *federal commissioner*
Meyer, Armin Henry *retired diplomat, author, educator*
Michel, James H. *ambassador, lawyer*
Milam, William Bryant *diplomat, economist*
Miller, William Lawrence *government official*
†Mintz, Richard I. *federal official*
Mitchell, Graham Richard *government engineering executive*
Mohler, Brian Jeffery *diplomat*
Moore, Jonathan *diplomat, policy analyst, university administrator*
Moore, Richard Anthony *diplomat, lawyer*
†Moose, Richard M. *federal official*
Morgan, John Davis *government official*
Moscato, Anthony Charles *federal official*
†Mueller, Richard Walter *foreign service officer*
Murphy, Gerald *government official*
Myers, Dee Dee (Margaret Jane Myers) *press secretary*
†Natter, Robert, J. *federal official, military career officer*
Neill, Denis Michael *government relations consulting executive*
Newman, Frank Neil *federal official*
†Noble, Ronald K. *federal official*
Nolan, Jean *federal agency official*
Norland, Donald Richard *retired foreign service officer*
Obee, Kent *foreign service officer*
†O'Bryon, James Fredrick *defense executive*
O'Leary, Hazel R. *U.S. secretary of energy, former power company executive, lawyer*
Ordway, Frederick Ira, III *government official, educator, consultant, researcher, author*
†O'Toole, Tara J. *federal official*
Owen, Henry *former ambassador, consultant*
Oxman, Stephen A. *federal official*
Page, Marcus William *federal official*
Palmer, Ronald DeWayne Faisal *retired diplomat, educator, consultant*
†Palmer, Steven O. *federal official*
Panetta, Leon Edward *federal official, former congressman*
†Pang, Frederick F. Y. *federal official*
Pelletreau, Robert Halsey *diplomat*
Peña, Federico Fabian *U.S. secretary of transportation, lawyer*
Pendleton, Mary Catherine *foreign service officer*
†Perkins, Edward J. *diplomat*
Perle, Richard Norman *government official*
Peters, Lauralee Milberg *diplomat*
Philbin, Edward James *federal agency commissioner, military officer, legal educator, engineer*
Phillips, Karen Borlaug *economist*
Pierce, Margaret Hunter *government official*
Piez, William *government official*
Pistor, Michael T. F. *foreign service officer*
Placke, James A(nthony) *foreign service officer, international affairs consultant*
Plaisted, Joan M. *diplomat*
†Poneman, Daniel Bruce *federal official*
Pridmore, Roy Davis *government official*
Quainton, Anthony Cecil Eden *diplomat*
Ramsey, William C. *ambassador*
Rankin, Haywood Forney *diplomat*
†Raphel, Robin *federal official*
Rasco, Carol Hampton *federal official*
†Rawson, David P. *ambassador*
Rawson, David P. *ambassador*
†Raymond, Victor P. *federal official*
Reade, Lewis Pollock *diplomat, engineer*
Rechcigl, Miloslav, Jr. *government official*
Reed, John Hathaway *former ambassador*
Reeder, Joe Robert *federal official*
Render, Arlene *ambassador*
Reno, Janet *U.S. attorney general*
Retsinas, Nicolas P. *federal official*
Ridgway, Rozanne LeJeanne *foreign policy executive*
Riley, Richard Wilson *U.S. secretary of education*
†Robinson, Sharon Porter *federal official*
Rohr, David Baker *federal agency commissioner*
Rope, William Frederick *foreign service officer*
Rosenthal, Alan Sayre *government official*
Ross, Christopher Wade Stelyan *diplomat*
Ross, Thomas Bernard *federal government official*
†Rugh, William Arthur *diplomat*
Runyon, Marvin Travis *postmaster general*
Ryan, Mary A. *diplomat*
San Martin, Robert L. *federal official*
Sayre, Robert Marion *ambassador*
Scanlan, John Douglas *foreign service officer, former ambassador*
†Scarbrough, Frank Edward *government official*
†Scassa, Eugene L. *ambassador*
Schley, Wayne A. *postal rate commissioner*
†Schroeter, Richard B. *federal official*
Seidman, Ricki *federal official*
Selin, Ivan *federal official*
Sellin, Theodore *foreign service officer, consultant*
Seymour, Jon *federal government official*
†Shafer, Jeffrey R. *federal official*
Shalala, Donna Edna *federal official, political scientist, educator, university chancellor*
†Shattuck, John H. F. *federal official*
Shinn, David Hamilton *diplomat*
Shlaudeman, Harry Walter *retired ambassador*
Shurtleff, Leonard Grant *ambassador*
Siegel, Jack S. *federal official*
Silberman, Rosalie Gaull *federal official*
†Simon, Jeanne Hurley *federal commissioner*
Skol, Michael *diplomat*
†Slagle, Larry B. *federal government executive*
†Smith, Dallas R. *federal official*
Smith, Elaine Diana *foreign service officer*
Smith, Jean Kennedy *ambassador*
Smith, Marshall Savidge *government official, academic dean, education educator*
†Somerville, Walter Raleigh, Jr. *government official*
Sommerfelt, Soren Christian *foreign affairs, international trade consultant, former Norwegian diplomat, lawyer*
Sonnenfeldt, Helmut *former government official, educator, consultant, author*
Sprott, John T. *ambassador*
Steiger, Janet Dempsey *government official*
Stephanopoulos, George Robert *federal official*
†Stoll, Louise Frankel *federal official*
Storing, Paul Edward *foreign service officer*
Streb, Alan Joseph *government official, engineer*
†Stuart, Sandra Kaplan *federal official*
Swing, William Lacy *ambassador*
Szabo, Daniel *government official*
Tarrant, James Richard *foreign service officer*
†Tarullo, Daniel K. *federal official*
†Taylor, William James, III *federal official*
†Tetelman, Alice Fran *city government official*
Thomas, Charles Howard, II *federal official*
Thomas, Scott E. *federal government executive, lawyer*
Thomasson, Patsy *federal official*
Tierney, Susan Fallows *federal official*
†Torres-Gil, Fernando M. *federal official*
Trezise, Philip Harold *government official*
†Tucker, Alvin Leroy *federal government executive*
†Turner, Leslie M. *federal official*
Tuthill, John Wills *former diplomat, educator*
Twaddell, William Hartsthorne *diplomat*
†Underwood, Robert A. *congressional delegate, academic administrator*
†Varney, Christine A. *federal official*
Verville, Elizabeth Giavani *federal official*
Wachtmeister, Count Wilhelm H. F. *diplomat*
Ward, George Frank, Jr. *foreign service officer*
Ward, Jennifer C. *diplomat*
Ware, Thaddeus Van *government official*
Watkins, Birge Swift *real estate investment executive*
Watkins, David *federal official*
†Watkins, James David *government official, naval officer*
Watson, Alexander Fletcher *ambassador*
Watson, Arthur Dennis *government official*
†Watson, Jeffrey Howard *federal official*
†Weise, George J. *commissioner*
Wendt, E. Allan *ambassador*
†Wiedemann, Kent M. *federal official*
Wilcox, Philip C., Jr. *foreign service officer*
Williams, Margaret *federal official*
Williams, Richard Llewellyn *diplomat*
Williamson, Richard Hall *federal official*
Wilson, Joseph Charles, IV *ambassador*
Winter, Andrew J. *ambassador*
Winter, Harvey John *government official*
Wirth, Timothy Endicott *federal official, former senator*
Wisner, Frank George *federal official, foreign service officer*
Withrow, Mary Ellen *federal government treasurer*
Woodward, Robert Forbes *retired government official, consultant*
Woolsey, R. James, Jr. *federal agency administrator*
Worthy, Patricia Morris *municipal official, lawyer*
Ziglar, James W. *former federal official, lawyer, investment banker*

FLORIDA

Dunedin
Carmichael, Mary Mulloy *foreign service officer, educator*

Fort Lauderdale
Anderson, Richard Edmund *city manager, management consultant*
Hanbury, George Lafayette, II *city manager*
Wallace, Joan S. *international development consultant*

Fort Myers
Ball, Robert Michael *government aviation official*

Gainesville
Heflin, Martin Ganier *foreign service officer, international political economist*
Jones, Elizabeth Nordwall *county government official*

Jacksonville
†Austin, Ed *mayor*
Austin, T. Edward (Ed Austin) *mayor*

Lakeland
Hollis, Mark D. *federal official*

Leesburg
Houston, John Coates, Jr. *consultant*

Miami
Clark, Stephen P. *mayor*

North Palm Beach
Fauver, John William *mayor, retired business executive*

Palm City
Henry, David Howe, II *former diplomat and international organization official*

Saint Petersburg
†Fischer, David J. *mayor*
Mc Connell, Robert Chalmers *former city official*

Sarasota
Connor, Robert T. *former government official*
Yordan, Carlos Manuel *foreign service officer*

Tallahassee
Butterworth, Robert A. *state attorney general*
Chiles, Lawton Mainor *governor, former senator*
MacKay, Kenneth "Buddy" Hood *state official, former congressman*
Smith, James C. *secretary of state, former state attorney general*

Tampa
Freedman, Sandra Warshaw *mayor*
Richardson, Edward James *federal government agency official*
Studer, William Allen *county official*

Winter Park
Hawkins, Paula *federal official, former senator*

GEORGIA

Athens
Hillenbrand, Martin Joseph *diplomat, educator*
Mc Whorter, Hezzie Boyd *former collegiate athletic commissioner, English language educator*
Rusk, Dean *educator, former secretary of state*

Atlanta
Bell, Griffin B. *lawyer, former attorney general*
Bowers, Michael Joseph *state attorney general*
†Campbell, Bill *mayor, broadcasting executive*
Carter, Jimmy (James Earl Carter, Jr.) *former President of United States*
Cleland, Joseph Maxwell (Max) *state official*
Miller, Zell Bryan *governor*
Nethercut, Philip Edwin *honorary consul*
Phillips, James D. *diplomat*
Rogers, Werner *state education official*
Schwartz, William B., Jr. *ambassador*
Streeb, Gordon Lee *diplomat, economist*
Sullivan, Louis Wade *former secretary health and human services, physician*

Carrollton
Harrison, Earle *former county official*

Cartersville
Harris, Joe Frank *former governor*

Columbus
Martin, Frank Kieffer *mayor, lawyer*

Decatur
Gay, Robert Derril *county official*
Howard, Pierre *lieutenant governor, president senate*

Saint Simons Island
Douglas, William Ernest *retired government official*

Savannah
Rousakis, John Paul *former mayor*
†Weiner, Susan S. *mayor*

Smyrna
Wallace, Clifford Noble, III *public assembly facility management executive*

HAWAII

Honolulu
Cayetano, Benjamin Jerome *lieutenant governor, former state senator and representative*
Fasi, Frank Francis *mayor*
Salmon, Charles B., Jr. *diplomat*
Waihee, John David, III *governor, lawyer*

IDAHO

Boise
Andrus, Cecil Dale *governor*
Cenarrusa, Pete T. *secretary of state*
EchoHawk, Larry *state attorney general*
Otter, Clement Leroy *lieutenant governor*
Wilson, Jack Fredrick *retired federal government official*

ILLINOIS

Champaign
Semonin, Richard Gerard *state official*

Chicago
Bishop, Oliver Richard *state official*
†Cullerton, John James *state senator, lawyer*
Daley, Richard Michael *mayor*
Lafontant-Mankarious, Jewel (Mrs. Naguib S. Mankarious) *diplomat, lawyer*
Levi, Edward Hirsch *former attorney general, university president emeritus*
†Mosena, David R. *aviation commissioner*
Phelan, Richard John *county administrator, lawyer*
Roque, Roberto Dizon *city official*

Hudson
Mills, Lois Jean *legislative aide, former education educator*

Northfield
Louis, John (Jeffry), Jr. *former ambassador*

Peoria
†Maloof, James A(loysius) *mayor, real estate company executive*

Quincy
Points, Roy Wilson *municipal official*

Springfield
Burris, Roland Wallace *state attorney general*
Edgar, Jim *governor*

Urbana
†Prussing, Laurel Lunt *state official, economist*

Wilmette
Ingersoll, Robert Stephen *former diplomat, federal agency administrator*

INDIANA

Evansville
†McDonald, Frank F., II *mayor*

Fort Wayne
†Helmke, (Walter) Paul, Jr. *mayor, lawyer*

Gary
†Barnes, Thomas Vernon *mayor, lawyer*

Indianapolis
Bayh, Evan *governor*
Carter, Pamela Lynn *state attorney general*
Goldsmith, Stephen *mayor*
Hogsett, Joseph H. *state official*
Knight, Margarett Lee *lawyer, editor*
†Mannweiler, Paul S. *state legislator*
O'Bannon, Frank Lewis *state official, lawyer*
Quayle, J(ames) Danforth *former vice president of United States, investment company executive*

Notre Dame
†Wadsworth, Michael A. *ambassador, director of athletics, former professional football player*

IOWA

Cedar Rapids
Novetzke, Sally Johnson *former ambassador*

Des Moines
Baxter, Elaine *state government official*
Branstad, Terry Edward *governor, lawyer*
Campbell, Bonnie Jean *state attorney general*
Corning, Joy Cole *state official*
Fitzgerald, Michael Lee *state official*

Sioux City
Juon, Lester Allen *utility executive*

Steamboat Rock
†Taylor, Ray *state senator*

KANSAS

Kansas City
Hollenbeck, Marynell *municipal government official*

Mc Pherson
†Steffes, Don C. *state senator*

Topeka
Carlin, John William *former governor*
Finney, Joan McInroy *governor*
Francisco, James L. *lieutenant governor*
Graves, William Preston *state official*
Stephan, Robert Taft *state attorney general*
Thompson, Sally Engstrom *state official*

KENTUCKY

Burkesville
Smith, Paul Traylor *mayor, former business executive, former army officer*

Frankfort
Babbage, Robert A. *state official*
Gorman, Chris *state attorney general*
Jones, Brereton C. *governor*
Mills, Frances Jones *state official*
Patton, Paul E. *state official*

Hebron
†Holscher, Robert F. *county official*

Lexington
†Miller, Pamela Gundersen *mayor*

Louisville
†Abramson, Jerry *mayor*

LOUISIANA

Baton Rouge
Brown, James H., Jr. *state official, lawyer*
Clausen, Sally Ilene *state official*
Edwards, Edwin Washington *governor*
†Fussell, Bonnie Gene *lottery corporation executive*
Ieyoub, Richard Phillip *state attorney general*
McKeithen, Walter Fox *secretary of state*
Schwegmann, Melinda *state official*

New Orleans
Barthelemy, Sidney John *mayor*
Dixon, Irma Muse *state commissioner, former state legislator, social worker*
†Levell, Edward, Jr. *city official*
†Morial, Marc H. *mayor*

MAINE

Augusta
†Amero, Jane Adams *state official*
Carpenter, Michael E. *state attorney general*
Diamond, G. William *secretary of state*
McKernan, John Rettie, Jr. *governor*

Springvale
Eastman, Harland Horace *former foreign service officer*

Topsham
Tierney, James Edward *attorney general*

MARYLAND

Annapolis
Brock, William Emerson *former secretary of labor*
Coulter, James Bennett *state official*
Goldstein, Louis Lazarus *state official*
Maurer, Lucille Darvin *state treasurer*
Meima, Ralph Chester, Jr. *corporate execuitve, former foreign service officer*
Schaefer, William Donald *governor, former mayor*
Steinberg, Melvin Allen *lieutenant governor, lawyer*
†Stup, Janet Anita *delegate state general assembly*

Baltimore
Curran, J. Joseph, Jr. *state attorney general*
†Hutchinson, Leslie E *fiscal programs manager, consultant*
Jones, Raymond Moylan *strategy and public policy educator*
†O'Hare, Thomas J(ames), Jr. *federal commissioner*
Schmoke, Kurt L. *mayor*

Bethesda
†Clark, William Doran *government official*
Clay, Jasper R. *federal government official*
Gallagher, Hubert R. *governmental consultant*
Goldberg, Herman Raphael *government agency official, educator*
†Green, Jerome George *federal government official*
Hannah, Norman Britton *former foreign service officer*
Hempstone, Smith, Jr. *diplomat, journalist*
Ingraham, Edward Clarke, Jr. *foreign service officer*
Jones-Smith, Jacqueline *federal commission administrator, lawyer*
Laingen, Lowell Bruce *diplomat*
Lewis, James Histed *retired foreign service officer*
Lukens, Alan Wood *retired ambassador and foreign service officer*
McManus, Edward Hubbard *government official*
Navarro, Bruce Charles *federal government official, lawyer*
Neumann, Robert Gerhard *ambassador, consultant*
North, William Haven *foreign service officer*
Peck, Edward Lionel *retired foreign service officer, corporate executive*
Rowell, Edward Morgan *foreign service officer, lecturer*
Ruppe, Loret Miller *former ambassador*
Schiavo, A. Mary Fackler *federal official, lawyer*
Vest, George Southall *diplomat*
Walker, Lannon *foreign service officer*

Bowie
Mc Manus, Charles Anthony, Jr. *retired federal official, political and public relations executive*

Braddock Heights
Wirths, Theodore William *public policy consultant*

Chevy Chase
Bush, Frederick Morris *federal official*
Mc Closkey, Robert James *former diplomat*
Pancoast, Edwin C. *retired foreign service officer, writer, researcher*

College Park
Peterson, David Frederick *government agency executive*

Dunkirk
Ewing, Richard Tucker *diplomat, educator, publisher*

Gaithersburg
French, Judson Cull *government official*
†Mills, Kevin Lee *government executive*
†Rollow, Thomas A. *federal official*

Grasonville
Andrews, Archie Moulton *government official*

Kensington
Rogers, Kenneth Norman *retired foreign service officer, lawyer, international political and commercial consultant*
Root, William Alden *export control consultant*

Port Republic
Hughes, Phillip Samuel *government official, social scientist*

Potomac
Nichol, Henry Ferris *former government official, environment consultant*
Shepard, William Seth *government official, diplomat*

Rockville
†Hoobler, James Ferguson *federal executive*
Sacchet, Edward M. *foreign service officer*

Silver Spring
Goott, Daniel *government official, consultant*
Popkin, Roy Sandor *emergency management consultant, writer, researcher*
†Schmitten, Rolland Arthur *government official*

MASSACHUSETTS

Boston
Cellucci, Argeo Paul *state official*
Connolly, Michael Joseph *state official*
Crane, Andrew B. *state official*
Harshbarger, Scott *state attorney general*
Malone, Joseph P. *state treasurer*
Menino, Thomas M. *mayor*
Weld, William Floyd *governor, lawyer*

Brewster
Hemsing, Albert E. *public affairs adviser*

Brookline
Dukakis, Michael Stanley *former governor*

Cambridge
Porter, Roger Blaine *government official, educator*

Concord
Cavazos, Lauro Fred *former U.S. secretary of education, former university president*

Falmouth
Brewer, William Dodd *former ambassador, political science educator emeritus*

Sherborn
Kennedy, Chester Ralph, Jr. *former state official, art director*

Springfield
†Markel, Robert Thomas *mayor*

Waltham
Fuchs, Lawrence Howard *government official, educator*

Wellesley
Levin, Burton *diplomat*
Parker, William H., III *federal official*

MICHIGAN

Ann Arbor
†Sheldon, Ingrid Kristina *mayor*

Detroit
Archer, Dennis Wayne *mayor*
Martin, Fred *municipal official*
†McNamara, Edward Howard *mayor*
Worden, William Michael *city agency administrator, preservation consultant*

Escanaba
Reid, Duane Lee *government official*

Flint
Stanley, Woodrow *mayor*

Grand Rapids
Logie, John Hoult *mayor, lawyer*

Lansing
Austin, Richard H. *state official*
Binsfeld, Connie Berube *lieutenant governor*
Dykhouse, David Jay *commissioner, lawyer*
Engler, John *governor*
Kelley, Frank Joseph *state attorney general*
†McManus, Michelle Ann *state representative, cherry farmer*

Negaunee
Friggens, Thomas George *state official, historian*

Rochester Hills
Farrar, Stephen Prescott *federal official*

Sterling Heights
Koski, Deanna Eleanor *city official, real estate broker, closing officer*

Warren
Bonkowski, Ronald Lawrence *mayor*

MINNESOTA

Cass Lake
†Wadena, Darrell Eugene *indian tribe executive*

Minneapolis
†Belton, Sharon Sayles *mayor*
Joseph, Geri Mack (Geraldine Joseph) *former ambassador, educator*

Moorhead
Sinner, George Albert *former state governor, farmer, corporate executive*

Northfield
Flaten, Robert Arnold *ambassador, retired*

Saint Paul
Carlson, Arne Helge *governor*
Dyrstad, Joanell M. *lieutenant governor*
Growe, Joan Anderson *state official*
Humphrey, Hubert Horatio, III *state attorney general*
McGrath, Michael Alan *state government officer*
Powell, Linda *state education official*

MISSISSIPPI

Carrollton
McConnell, David Stuart *retired federal executive*

Hattiesburg
Rawlings, Paul C. *retired government official*

Jackson
Briggs, Eddie J. *state official*
Ditto, (John) Kane *mayor*
Fordice, Daniel Kirkwood, Jr. (Kirk Fordice) *governor, construction company executive, engineer*
†Fordice, Kirk *governor*
Mabus, Raymond Edwin, Jr. *ambassador, former governor*
Molpus, Dick *state official*
Moore, Mike *state attorney general*
Ray, H. M. *lawyer*
Winter, William Forrest *former governor, lawyer*

Natchez
Parker, Mary Evelyn *former state treasurer*

Ridgeland
Dye, Bradford Johnson, Jr. *former lieutenant governor of Mississippi, lawyer, partner*

Stennis Space Center
Mc Call, Jerry Chalmers *government official*

MISSOURI

Clayton
Osterloh, Everett William *county official*

Harrisonville
White, Ray William, Jr. *county official*

Jefferson City
Carnahan, Mel *governor, lawyer*
Holden, Bob *state official*
Moriarty, Judith Kay Spry *state official*
Nixon, Jeremiah W. (Jay Nixon) *state attorney general*
Wilson, Roger B. *lieutenant governor, school administrator*

Kansas City
Davis, Richard Francis *city government official*
Edwards, Horace Burton *former state official, former oil pipeline company executive, management consultant*
Price, Charles H., II *former ambassador*
†Steele, Kathleen Frances *federal official*

Raytown
†Barnes, James Richard *county official*

Saint Louis
†Bosley, Freeman Robertson, Jr. *mayor*
Farris, Charles Lowell *city official*
†Svetanics, Neil *fire chief*

MONTANA

Billings
Larsen, Richard Lee *former city manager, business, municipal and labor relations consultant, arbitrator*
Rehberg, Dennis R. *state official*

Helena
Marks, Robert L. (Bob Marks) *treasurer ex-officio, rancher*
Mazurek, Joseph P. *state attorney general*
Racicot, Marc F. *governor*

Missoula
Kemmis, Daniel Orra *mayor, author*

NEBRASKA

Grand Island
Mason, Doris Ann *county official*

Lincoln
Beermann, Allen J. *state official*
†Johanns, Michael O. *mayor*
Lutjeharms, Joseph Earl *commissioner*
Moul, Maxine Burnett *state official*
Nelson, E. Benjamin *governor*
Stenberg, Donald B. *state attorney general*

Omaha
Bechtel, James M. *retired civil servant*
Cunningham, Glenn Clarence *government official*
Morgan, P. J. *mayor*

Wood River
Bish, Milan David *former ambassador, consultant*

NEVADA

Carson City
Del Papa, Frankie Sue *state attorney general*
Lau, Cheryl *state official*
Miller, Robert Joseph *governor, lawyer*
Seale, Robert L. *state treasurer*
Wagner, Sue Ellen *state official*

Las Vegas
†Jones, Jan Laverty *mayor*

Reno
†Sferrazza, Peter Joseph *mayor, lawyer*

Yerington
†Stahl, Stacy L. *tribal chairman*

NEW HAMPSHIRE

Bow
†Johnson, C. William *retired federal agent, state representative*

Concord
†Flanagan, Natalie Smith *state representative*
Gardner, William Michael *state official*
Merrill, Stephen *governor*

Grantham
Feldman, Roger Bruce *government official*

Lancaster
†Pratt, Leighton C. *state legislator*

Salem
Sununu, John H. *former chief of staff President of U.S., former governor*

NEW JERSEY

Belle Mead
Stampfl, Rudolf Alois *government official*

East Orange
†Talmadge, Quilla Esther *county management specialist*

Morristown
†Dayson, Diane Harris *superintendent, park ranger*

Newark
James, Sharpe *mayor*

Paterson
†Pascrell, William J., Jr. *mayor, assemblyman*

Trenton
Crane, Samuel *treasurer*
Dalton, Daniel J. *secretary of state*
Haberle, Joan Baker *state official*
†Whitman, Christine Todd *governor*

Woodbridge
Mills, George Marshall *state official, insurance executive*

NEW MEXICO

Albuquerque
†Chavez, Martin Joseph *mayor, attorney*
Clark, Alan Barthwell *city administrator*
Lujan, Manuel, Jr. *former U.S. secretary of the interior, former congressman*
Romo, Gene David *municipal official*

Santa Fe
Gonzales, Stephanie *state official*
King, Bruce *governor*
King, David W. *state treasurer*
Lewis, James Beliven *state government official*
Udall, Thomas *state attorney general*

NEW YORK

Albany
Bradford, Peter Amory *state official*
Chassin, Mark Russell *state official*
Cotter, William Donald *state commissioner, former newspaper editor*
Cuomo, Mario Matthew *governor*
Herman, Robert S. *former state official, economist, educator*
Lundine, Stanley Nelson *state government official, former congressman, lawyer*
Shaffer, Gail S. *state government official*
Sobol, Thomas *state education commissioner*

Bridgehampton
Needham, James Joseph *consultant*

Brooklyn
Garcia, Marc Anthony *diplomat*
†Safir, Howard *fire commissioner*

Buffalo
Millane, Lynn *town official*
Rochwarger, Leonard *former ambassador*

Chappaqua
Laun, Louis Frederick *government official*

Delhi
MacDonald, Robert Bruce *county official*

New York
Abrams, Robert *former state attorney general*
Albright, Madeleine *federal official, political scientist*
Baker, James Estes *foreign service officer*
Boutros-Ghali, Boutros *United Nations official*
Brown, Carroll *diplomat, association executive*
Bundy, McGeorge *former government official, history educator*
Bushnell, John Alden *diplomat, economist*
Chaves, Jose Maria *diplomat, foundation administrator, lawyer, educator*
Cohn, David Herc *retired foreign service officer*
Curley, Walter Joseph Patrick, Jr. *diplomat, investment banker*
Dunham, Donald Carl *diplomat*
Eisenstadt, G. Michael *diplomat, author, lecturer, research scholar*
Gardner, Richard Newton *diplomat, lawyer, educator*
Giuliani, Rudolph W. *mayor, former lawyer*
Katz, Abraham *retired foreign service officer*
Kissinger, Henry Alfred *former secretary of state, international consulting company executive*
Koch, Edward I. *former mayor, lawyer*
Lehman, Orin *retired state official*
Matlock, Jack Foust, Jr. *diplomat*
Murphy, Richard William *retired foreign service officer, Middle East specialist, consultant*
Ney, Edward N. *ambassador, advertising and public relations company executive*
Okun, Herbert Stuart *ambassador, international executive*
†Perales, Cesar Augusto *government official*
Platt, Nicholas *Asian affairs specialist, ambassador*
Rogers, Elizabeth Barlow *municipal park administrator*
†Rosado, David *city official*
†Waldon, Alton Ronald, Jr. *state commissioner*
Walker, Edward S., Jr. *diplomat*
Weil, Leon Jerome *diplomat*
Wells, Melissa Foelsch *foreign service officer*

Plainview
Fulton, Richard *lecture bureau executive*

Port Washington
Navajas-Mogro, Hugo *diplomat*

Watertown
Coe, Benjamin Plaisted *state official*

White Plains
O'Rourke, Andrew Patrick *lawyer, county official*

Williamsville
Danni, F. Robert *municipal official*

NORTH CAROLINA

Advance
Legere, Laurence Joseph *government official*

Charlotte
Edwards, Harold Mills *government official, lawyer*
Martin, James Grubbs *governor*

Durham
Kreps, Juanita Morris *former secretary of commerce*

Foxfire Village
Krebs, Max Vance *retired foreign service officer, educator*

Greensboro
†Nussbaum, V. M., Jr. *former mayor*

Raleigh
Boyles, Harlan Edward *state official*
Cameron, John Lansing *retired government official*
†Cummings, Frances McArthur *state official, retired educational administrator*
Easley, Michael F. *state attorney general*
Edmisten, Rufus Ligh *state official*
†Ellington, John David *state official*
Hunt, James Baxter, Jr. *governor, lawyer*
Wicker, Dennis A. *lieutenant governor*

Southern Pines
Toon, Malcolm *former ambassador*

Warrenton
†Ballance, Frank W., Jr. *state senator, lawyer*

Waynesville
Matlock, Clifford Charles *retired foreign service officer*

Winston Salem
†Wood, Martha Swain *mayor*

NORTH DAKOTA

Bismarck
Gilmore, Kathi *state treasurer*
Heitkamp, Heidi *state attorney general*
Jaeger, Alvin A. (Al Jaeger) *secretary of state*
Myrdal, Rosemarie Caryle *state official, former state legislator*
Schafer, Edward T. *governor of North Dakota*

Fargo
Spaeth, Nicholas John *lawyer, former state attorney general*

OHIO

Akron
Plusquellic, Donald L. *mayor*
Schrader, Helen Maye *retired municipal worker*

Cincinnati
†Qualls, Roxanne *mayor of Cincinnati*
Taft, Robert, Jr. *state official, lawyer, former senator*
Tihany, Leslie Charles *retired foreign service officer, educator*

Cleveland
Chema, Thomas V. *government official, lawyer*
Smercina, Charles Joseph *mayor, accountant*
White, Michael Reed *mayor*

Columbus
DeWine, R. Michael *lieutenant governor, lawyer*
Fisher, Lee I. *state attorney general*
Lashutka, Gregory S. *mayor, lawyer*
Taft, Bob *state official*
Voinovich, George V. *governor*

Medina
†Batchelder, William George, III *attorney general, lawyer, professional society administrator*

Portsmouth
Davis, Donald W. *government official*

Sandusky
Link, Frank Albert *retired city manager*

Toledo
†Finkbeiner, Carleton S. (Carty) *mayor*

OKLAHOMA

Ada
†Anoatubby, Bill *governor*

Lawton
†Coffey, Wallace E. *chairman Comanche Indian tribe*
†Hooper, Roy B. *state senator, insurance broker*

Norman
Corr, Edwin Gharst *ambassador*

Oklahoma City
Anthony, Robert Holland *state official*
†Boyd, Betty *government official*
Henry, Claudette *state official*
Kennedy, John H., Jr. *former state official*
Loving, Susan B. *state attorney general*
Mildren, Jack *lieutenant governor*
Norick, Ronald J. *mayor of Oklahoma City*

Walters, David *governor*

Tahlequah
†Mankiller, Wilma Pearl *tribal leader*

Tulsa
Savage, M. Susan *mayor*

OREGON

Corvallis
†Murphy, Thomas Allen *government research administrator, scientist*

Lake Oswego
Gawf, John Lee *foreign service officer*

Portland
Katz, Vera *mayor, former college administrator, state legislator*
†Moose, Charles A. *state official*

Salem
†Hill, Jim *state official*
Keisling, Phillip Andrew *state official*
Kulongoski, Theodore R. *state attorney general*
Roberts, Barbara *governor*

Springfield
†Beyer, Lee Louis *public administrator*

PENNSYLVANIA

Blue Bell
Ehrlich, Everett Michael *federal official, computer company executive*

Bristol
Hutton, Ann Hawkes *state official*

Carlisle
Clarke, Walter Sheldon *federal government official, instructor*

Carlisle Barracks
Simpson, Daniel H. *ambassador*

Erie
†Savocchio, Joyce A. *mayor*

Harrisburg
Banks, Albert Victor, Jr. *state official*
Casey, Robert P. *governor*
Mitchell, Brenda K. *state secretary*
Newsome, William Roy, Jr. *state official*
Preate, Ernest D., Jr. *state attorney general*
Singel, Mark Stephen *state official*

Ligonier
Schmidt, Adolph William *retired ambassador*

New Florence
Olson, Clinton Louis *foreign service officer, former ambassador*

Newtown
Cohen, Myer *former international organization official*

Newtown Square
Strausz-Hupé, Robert *ambassador, author*

Philadelphia
Corrigan, John Edward *government official*
†DeBenedictis, Nicholas, Jr. *chamber of commerce executive*
†Goren, Denise Lynne *deputy mayor*
Rendell, Edward Gene *mayor*

Pittsburgh
Donahoe, David Lawrence *state and city official*
†Murphy, Tom *mayor*

Turtle Creek
†Michlovic, Thomas A. *member House of Representatives*

University Park
Chang, Parris Hsu-cheng *government official, political science educator, writer*

RHODE ISLAND

Providence
Leonard, Barbara M *secretary of state, federal agency administrator, state agency administrattor*
Petrocelli, Americo William *higher education commissioner*
Pine, Jeffrey Barry *state attorney general*
†Sanderson, Edward French *state official*
Sundlun, Bruce *governor*
Weygand, Robert A. *lieutenant governor, landscape architect*

SOUTH CAROLINA

Columbia
Adams, Weston *diplomat, lawyer*
Campbell, Carroll Ashmore, Jr. *governor, former congressman*
Duffie, Virgil Whatley, Jr. *state official*
Medlock, Thomas Travis *state attorney general*
Miles, Jim *state official*
Morris, Earle Elias, Jr. *state official, business executive*
Patterson, Grady Leslie, Jr. *state treasurer*
†Waites, Candy Yaghjian *state official*
Walker, Richard Louis *former ambassador, educator, author*

SOUTH DAKOTA

Pierre
Barnett, Mark William *state attorney general*
Hazeltine, Joyce *state official*
Miller, Walter Dale *governor*

Watertown
Hillestad, Gertrude Delene *former public utilities specialist*

TENNESSEE

Knoxville
Ashe, Victor Henderson *mayor*

Memphis
Herenton, Willie W. *mayor*

Nashville
Bredesen, Philip Norman *mayor*
Burson, Charles W. *state attorney general*
Darnell, Riley Carlisle *secretary of state, lawyer*
McWherter, Ned Ray *governor*
Roaden, Arliss Lloyd *higher education executive director, former university president*
Wilder, John Shelton *lieutenant governor, president senate*

TEXAS

Austin
Bullock, Robert D. (Bob) *lieutenant governor, lawyer*
Cooke, Carlton Lee, Jr. *mayor*
†Gates, Charles W., Sr. *city official*
Hannah, John H., Jr. *state official*
Hunter, J(ohn) Robert *insurance commissioner*
Morales, Dan *state attorney general*
Richards, Ann Willis *governor*
Todd, Bruce M. *mayor*

Beaumont
Gray, Enid Maurine *city official, director of libraries*
Lord, Evelyn Marlin *mayor*

Brownsville
†Lucio, Eduardo Andres, Jr. *state senator*

Corpus Christi
Turner, Elizabeth Adams Noble (Betty Turner) *former mayor, Chamber of Commerce executive*

Dallas
Clements, William Perry, Jr. *former governor, corporate executive*
Revell, Oliver Burgan *government official*
Rubottom, Roy Richard, Jr. *retired diplomat and educator, consultant*

El Paso
Francis, Larry *mayor*
Jurey, Wes *chamber of commmerce executive*

Forney
Cates, Don Tate *mayor, lawyer*

Fort Worth
Granger, Kay *mayor*
†McMillen, Howard Lawrence *municipal government official*
Shosid, Joseph Lewis *government official*

Houston
Bush, George Herbert Walker *former President of the United States*
Flack, Joe Fenley *county and municipal official, former insurance executive*
Foster, Dale Warren *government educator, management consultant, real estate broker, accountant*
Fowler, Robert Asa *consultant, business director, diplomat*
Huffington, Roy Michael *ambassador*
Lanier, Robert C. (Bob Lanier) *mayor*
Perry, Cynthia Norton Shepard *diplomat*

North Richland Hills
Cunningham, Larry J. *city official*

San Antonio
Catto, Henry Edward *former government official, former ambassador*
Wolff, Nelson W. *mayor*

UTAH

Bountiful
Oveson, W(ilford) Val *state official, accountant*

Salt Lake City
Alter, Edward T. *state treasurer*
Bean, Scott W. *state education official*
Graham, Jan *state attorney general*
Hilbert, Robert Backus *county water utility administrator*
Leavitt, Michael Okerlund *governor, insurance executive*
Walker, Olene S. *lieutenant governor*
†Wharton, Blaze Douglas *county official*

VERMONT

Montpelier
Amestoy, Jeffrey Lee *state attorney general*
Dean, Howard *governor*
Hooper, Don *secretary of state*
Klinck, Patricia Ewasco *state official*
Snelling, Barbara *state official*

Peacham
Barnes, Harry G., Jr. *retired ambassador*
Engle, James Bruce *ambassador*

South Londonderry
Spiers, Ronald Ian *diplomat*

VIRGINIA

Alexandria
Baroody, Michael Elias *public policy institution executive*
Clarey, Donald Alexander *government affairs consultant*
Conger, Clement Ellis *foreign service officer, curator*
†Donnelly, John Francis *federal official*
†Hagemann, Kenneth L., Sr. *federal official, career officer*
Hampton, E. Lynn *municipal finance administrator*
Havens, Harry Stewart *former federal assistant comptroller general, government consultant*
Helman, Gerald Bernard *government official*
Hilton, Robert Parker, Sr. *national security affairs consultant, retired naval officer*
Kennedy, Mary Virginia *diplomat*
Pringle, Robert Maxwell *diplomat*
Puscheck, Herbert Charles *federal administrator*
Rose, Susan Porter *federal commission administrator*
†Scheupelein, Robert John *government official*
†Ticer, Patricia *mayor*
Zook, Donovan Quay *foreign service officer*

Annandale
Rogers, Stephen Hitchcock *former ambassador*
Tontz, Robert L. *government official*

Arlington
Aggrey, Orison Rudolph *former ambassador, university administrator*
†Banister, G. Huntington *federal official*
Barrera, Manuel *foreign service officer*
Bolster, Archie Milburn *retired foreign service officer*
Cargo, William Ira *retired foreign service officer*
†Chavez, Linda *government official*
Edmondson, William Brockway *retired foreign service officer*
Everett, Warren Sylvester *consultant, former government official*
Fernandez, Henry A. *healthcare administration executive, lawyer*
Kaiser, Philip Mayer *diplomat*
Lino, Marisa Rose *diplomat*
†Pelaez, Marc Y.E. *federal official, career officer*
Prince, Julius S. *retired foreign service officer, physician*
Pyatt, Everett Arno *government official*
Rackmales, Robert *diplomat*
Smalley, Robert Manning *government official*
Taylor, Lawrence Palmer *diplomat*
Umminger, Bruce Lynn *government official, scientist, educator*

Charlottesville
Newsom, David Dunlop *foreign service officer, educator*
Sacksteder, Frederick Henry *former foreign service officer*

Dumfries
Gill, William Albert, Jr. *government official*

Fairfax
Jones, George Fleming *diplomat*

Falls Church
Block, John Rusling *former secretary of agriculture*
de la Colina, Rafael *diplomat*
Palmer, Stephen Eugene, Jr. *government official*

Fort Belvoir
Diercks, Frederick Otto *government official*

Fredericksburg
Leitch, Alma May *city official*

Great Falls
Zimmermann, Warren *former foreign service officer*

Herndon
Vogel, Frederick John *diplomat*

King George
Newhall, David, III *former federal government official*

Ladysmith
Provencher, Roger Arthur *international consultant*

Lakeridge
†Garon, Richard Joseph, Jr. *deputy minority staff director, political worker*

Lexington
Cash, Frank Errette, Jr. *foreign service officer*

Lynchburg
Stephens, Bart Nelson *former foreign service officer*

Markham
Katzen, Jay Kenneth *consultant, former foreign service officer*

Mc Lean
Berteau, David John *federal official*
Byrnes, Arthur Francis *retired federal official*
Cahill, Harry Amory *diplomat, educator*
Cannon, Mark Wilcox *government official, business executive*
Chiogioji, Melvin Hiroaki *government official*
Healy, Theresa Ann *former ambassador*
Smith, Russell Jack *former embassy official, research consultant, author*
Sollenberger, Howard Edwin *retired government official*
Trout, Maurice Elmore *foreign service officer*

Newport News
†Duval, Barry Eugene *mayor, real estate executive*

Norfolk
Bullington, James R. *ambassador*

Occoquan
Wolle, William Down *foreign service officer*

Orange
Cortada, James N. *mayor, former diplomat*

Portsmouth
†Webb, Gloria O. *mayor*

Reston
Sherman, William Courtney *foreign service officer*

Richmond
†Allen, George Felix *governor*
Beyer, Donald Sternoff, Jr. *lieutenant governor*
Henderson, Bernard Levie, Jr. *former state official, funeral service executive*
†Kenney, Walter T. *mayor*
Manning, William Raymond *retired state official*
Wilder, Lawrence Douglas *former governor*

Springfield
Stottlemyer, David Lee *government official*

Suffolk
Hope, James Franklin *mayor, civil engineer, consultant*

Susan
Ambach, Dwight Russell *retired foreign service officer*

Virginia Beach
Oberndorf, Meyera E. *mayor*

WASHINGTON

Auburn
†Cross, Virginia E. *tribal council leader, educational consultant*

Bainbridge Is
Huntley, James Robert *government official, international affairs scholar and consultant*

Bellevue
Armstrong, Dickwin Dill *chamber of commerce executive*

Dayton
McFarland, Jon Weldon *county commissioner*

Olympia
Gregoire, Christine O. *state attorney general*
Munro, Ralph Davies *state government official*
O'Brien, Robert S. *state official*
Pritchard, Joel *state lieutenant governor*
†Spanel, Harriet Rosa Albertsen *state senator*

Seattle
Lowry, Mike *governor, former congressman*
Rice, Norman B. *mayor*

Spokane
Giller, Edward Bonfoy *retired government official, retired air force officer*

WEST VIRGINIA

Charleston
Bailey, Larrie (John) *state treasurer*
Caperton, W. Gaston *governor*
Hechler, Ken *state official, former congressman, political science educator, author*
Mc Graw, Darrell Vivian, Jr. *attorney general*

Shenandoah Junction
Prince, Garnett B., Jr. *government official*

WISCONSIN

Juneau
Carpenter, David Erwin *county planner*

Madison
Doyle, James E(dward) *state attorney general*
Earl, Anthony Scully *former governor*
La Follette, Douglas J. *secretary of state*
McCallum, James Scott *lieutenant governor, former state senator*
Soglin, Paul R. *mayor, lawyer*
Thompson, Tommy George *governor*
Zaleski, Michael Louis *state official, lawyer*
Zobel, Robert Leonard *state government official*

Milwaukee
†Ament, F. Thomas *county government official*
Norquist, John Olof *mayor*

WYOMING

Casper
†Sadler, Dick Sherman *state official*

Cheyenne
Meyer, Joseph B. *state attorney general*
Smith, Stanford Sidney *state treasurer*
Sullivan, Michael John *governor, lawyer*
Thomson, Thyra Godfrey *former state official*
Wittler, Shirley Joyce *former state official, state commissioner*

Laramie
Dickman, Francois Moussiegt *former foreign service officer*

TERRITORIES OF THE UNITED STATES

AMERICAN SAMOA

Pago Pago
Coleman, Peter Tali *former governor*

GUAM

Agana
Ada, Joseph Franklin *territorial governor*
†Bordallo, Madeleine Mary (Mrs. Ricardo Jerome Bordallo) *wife of former governor of Guam*
†Reyes, Edward Diego *lieutenant governor*

PUERTO RICO

San Juan
Acevedo, Hector Luis *mayor*

MARSHALL ISLANDS

Majuro
Fields, David Clark *diplomat*

VIRGIN ISLANDS

Saint Thomas
Farrelly, Alexander *governor*

MILITARY ADDRESSES OF THE UNITED STATES

ATLANTIC

APO
Adams, Alvin Philip, Jr. *diplomat, lawyer*
Bowers, Charles R. *ambassador*
Bracete, Juan Manuel *diplomat, lawyer*
Busby, Morris D. *ambassador*
Carner, George *foreign service executive, economic strategist*
Cheek, James Richard *ambassador*
Davidow, Jeffrey *ambassador*
Hinton, Deane Roesch *ambassador*
Pastorino, Robert Stephen *diplomat, ambassador*
Pryce, William Thornton *foreign service officer*
Romero, Peter Frank *diplomat*
Sanbrailo, John A. *mission director*
Taylor, Paul Daniel *ambassador*
Whitman, Gerald John *diplomat*

EUROPE

APO
†Aaron, David L. *diplomat*
Baltimore, Richard Lewis, III *foreign service officer*
Barkley, Richard Clark *ambassador*
†Basora, Adrian A. *ambassador*
Bergold, Harry Earl, Jr. *diplomat*
Berry, Ann Roper *diplomat*
Blinken, Donald *ambassador, investment banker*
Brew, William Robert *foreign service officer*
†Brown, William Andreas *ambassador*
Davis, John Roger, Jr. *foreign service officer*
Eizenstat, Stuart E. *ambassador, lawyer*
Elson, Edward Elliott *retail and distribution executive, diplomat*
Flynn, Raymond Leo *ambassador to the Holy See, former mayor*
Gnehm, Edward W., Jr. *ambassador*
Harriman, Pamela Digby Churchill *diplomat, political activist*
Hill, Hugh Kenneth *diplomat, former ambassador*
Holbrooke, Richard Charles Albert *ambassador*
Hornblow, Michael M. *diplomat*
†Hurwitz, Edward *ambassador to Kyrgyzstan*
Johnson, Darryl Norman *ambassador*
Keene, Douglas Ralph *diplomat*
Klosson, Michael *foreign service officer*
†Loftus, Thomas Adolph *ambassador*
Miles, Richard *diplomat*
Niles, Thomas Michael Tolliver *ambassador*
Norris, James Arnold *government executive*
Petterson, Donald K. *foreign service officer, ambassador*
Pickering, Thomas Reeve *diplomat*
†Rey, Nicholas A. *ambassador*
Rickert, Jonathan Bradley *foreign service officer*
Ryerson, William Edwin *diplomat*
†Sundquist, Maria Alexandra *diplomat*
Welch, Charles David *diplomat*
Westley, John Richard *foreign service officer*
Wolters, Curt Cornelis Frederik *foreign service officer*
Yates, John Melvin *ambassador*

FPO
†Boucher, Richard A. *ambassador*
Dertadian, Richard Norman *diplomat*
Gewecke, Thomas H. *foreign service officer*

APO
Barry, Robert Louis *diplomat*
Burghardt, Raymond Francis, Jr. *foreign service officer*
Hacker, Paul *foreign service officer*
Lambertson, David Floyd *foreign service officer*
Laney, James Thomas *ambassador, educator*
†Monjo, John Cameron *ambassador*
†Teare, Richard W. *ambassador*
†Tomseth, Victor L *ambassador*
Tull, Theresa Anne *ambassador*
†Wolf, John S. *ambassador*

FPO
†Chorba, Timothy A. *ambassador to Singapore*
†Johnson, Donald C. *ambassador to Mongolia*
Ogden, Jerome Christopher *foreign service officer*

CANADA

ALBERTA

Edmonton
Forsyth, Joseph *Canadian government official*
†Reimer, Jan *mayor*
†Rostad, Kenneth Leif *provincial government official*
Towers, T. Gordon *Canadian lieutenant governor*

BRITISH COLUMBIA

Kaleden
Siddon, Thomas Edward *Canadian government official, environmental consultant*

Richmond
Johnston, Rita Margaret *Canadian provincial government official*

Vancouver
Gardom, Garde Basil *former Canadian government official*

Victoria
†Harcourt, Michael Franklin *premier of Province of British Columbia*
Lam, David *lieutenant governor*

MANITOBA

Winnipeg
Curtis, Charles Edward *Canadian government official*
†Dumont, W. Yvon *provincial official*
Filmon, Gary Albert *provincial premier, civil engineer*
Johnson, George *lieutenant governor, physician*
McGonigal, Pearl *former lieutenant governor*

NEW BRUNSWICK

Dieppe
Finn, Gilbert *lieutenant governor*

NEWFOUNDLAND

Saint John's
May, Arthur W. *former Canadian government official, educator*
†Murphy, John Joseph *city official, retail executive*
†Russell, Frederick William *Canadian provincial official*
Wells, Clyde Kirby *Canadian provincial government official*

NORTHWEST TERRITORIES

Yellowknife
Cournoyea, Nellie *Canadian government official*
†Kakfwi, Steve *Canadian government official*

NOVA SCOTIA

Halifax
†Savage, John P. *provincial official*

ONTARIO

Hamilton
Morrow, Robert Maxwell *mayor*
St-Aubin, Arthur *Canadian federal agency executive*

King City
Stevens, Sinclair McKnight *Canadian government official*

Maberly
Kennett, William Alexander *retired Canadian government official, consultant*

Manotick
Prince, Alan Theodore *former government official, engineering consultant*

Nobleton
Embleton, Tony Frederick Wallace *retired Canadian government official*

North York
Lastman, Melvin D. *mayor*

Ottawa
†Anderson, David *Canadian government official*
Armstrong, Henry Conner *former Canadian government official, consultant*
†Barnhart, Gordon *Canadian government official*
Beehan, Cathy *government official, lawyer*
Blanchard, James J. *ambassador, former governor of Michigan*
†Blondin-Andrew, Ethel *Canadian government official*
†Bouchard, Lucien *Canadian legislator*
†Chan, Raymond *Canadian government official*
Charest, Jean J. *Canadian government official, legislator*
Clark, Charles Joseph (Joe Clark) *Canadian government official, former prime minister*
†Clermont, Georges C. *Canadian government official, lawyer*
†Collenette, David *Canadian government official*
†Copps, Sheila Maureen *Canadian deputy prime minister*
Corkery, James Caldwell *Canadian government executive, mechanical engineer*
†Dupuy, Michel *Canadian government official*

Fowler, Robert Ramsay *Canadian deputy defence minister*
†Gerrard, Jon *Canadian government official*
Giroux, Robert-Jean-Yvon *Canadian government official*
Gold, Lorne W. *Canadian government official*
Goldbloom, Victor Charles *commissioner, pediatrician*
†Goodale, Ralph *Canadian government official*
Grace, John William *Canadian government official*
†Gray, Herbert Eser *canadian government official*
Halstead, John G. H. *educator, diplomat, consultant*
Hnatyshyn, Ramon John *governor general, commander in chief, lawyer*
Holzman, Jacquelin *mayor*
Homulos, Peter Stephen *government executive*
Howe, Bruce Iver *government official*
Kingsley, Jean-Pierre *government official*
Kirkwood, David Herbert Waddington *Canadian government official*
Kroeger, Arthur *former Canadian government administrator, educator*
LaRocque, Judith Anne *federal official*
Lewis, Douglas Grinslade *Canadian minister, parliament member*
†Manley, John *Canadian government official*
†Marchi, Sergio *Canadian government official*
McGrath, James Aloysius *Canadian provincial official*
†Ouellet, André *Canadian government official*
Pepin, Jean-Luc *retired Canadian government official, political science lecturer*
Poulin, Marie-Paule *Canadian government official*
Rawson, Bruce Strathearn *government official, lawyer*
Redway, Alan Arthur Sydney *Canadian legislator, lawyer*
Robertson, Robert Gordon *retired Canadian government official*
†Robichaud, Fernand *Canadian government official*
†Rock, Allan Michael *federal official*
Roland, Anne *registrar Supreme Court of Canada*
†St. Germain, Gerry *member of parliament*
Smith, Wilfred Irvin *former Canadian government official*
Stanford, Joseph Stephen *federal official, diplomat, lawyer*
Szlazak, Anita Christina *Canadian government official*
Watt, Robert Douglas *Canadian government official*
Weiner, Gerry *government official*
Withers, Ramsey Muir *government consultant, former government official*
Yalden, Maxwell Freeman *Canadian diplomat*
Yeomans, Donald Ralph *Canadian government official, consultant*
†Young, Doug *Canadian government official*

Toronto
Carnegie, James Gordon *association executive*
Evans, Gregory Thomas *commissioner, retired justice*
Gotlieb, Allan E. *former ambassador*
Jackman, Henry Newton Rowell *Canadian provincial official*
Mc Gibbon, Pauline Mills *former Canadian government official, former university chancellor*
Ostry, Sylvia *economist*
Peterson, David Robert *former premier of Ontario*
Rae, Robert Keith *Canadian premier of Ontario*
Turner, John Napier *former prime minister of Canada, legislator*

York
†Brown, Fergy J. *mayor*

PRINCE EDWARD ISLAND

Charlottetown
Callbeck, Catherine S. *Canadian government official*
†MacAulay, Lawrence A. *Canadian government official*
Reid, Marion L. *lieutenant governor, educator*

QUEBEC

Hull
†Axworthy, Lloyd *Canadian government official*
†Irwin, Ron *Canadian government official*

Longueuil
Lussier, Gaetan *Canadian government official*

Montreal
Bourassa, Robert *former Premier of Québec*
†Dingwall, David *Canadian government official*
Mulroney, (Martin) Brian *former prime minister of Canada*

Quebec
Asselin, Martial *Canadian lieutenant governor*

Westmount
Fortier, L. Yves *former Canadian ambassador to the UN, lawyer*

SASKATCHEWAN

Regina
†Archer, Douglas Robert *mayor, insurance services executive*
Romanow, Roy John *provincial government official, barrister, solicitor*

Saskatoon
Blakeney, Allan Emrys *Canadian government official, lawyer*
†Dayday, Henry *mayor*

YUKON TERRITORY

Whitehorse
McKinnon, John Kenneth (Ken) *Candian commissioner*
†Ostashek, John *government leader*
Penikett, Antony David John *Canadian government official*

†Phelps, Willard *Canadian government official*

MEXICO

Guadalajara
†Rivera-Aceves, Carlos *Mexican governor, lawyer*

Mexico City
Aspe, Pedro *Mexican government official*
Jones, James R. *ambassador, former congressman, lawyer*
Riviello Bazán, Antonio *government official*
Salinas de Gortari, Carlos *president of Mexico*
Solana Morales, Fernando *diplomat, financier, educator*

Monterrey
†Garcia, Socrates Rizzo *Mexican governor*

ARMENIA

Yerevan
Gilmore, Harry J. *ambassador*

AUSTRALIA

Brighton
Bennett, Frank Cantelo, Jr. *retired diplomat*

Perth
Skodon, Emil Mark *diplomat*

AUSTRIA

Vienna
Eagleton, William Lester, Jr. *foreign service officer*
†Hunt, Swanee G. *ambassador to Austria*
Jackovich, Victor *ambassador*
†Swihart, James W., Jr. *diplomat*

BARBADOS

Bridgetown
Barrow, Dame Ruth Nita *governor-general*
Hughes, G. Philip *diplomat*

BELARUS

Minsk
†Swartz, David H. *ambassador*

BELGIUM

Brussels
†Hunter, Robert Edwards *ambassador, diplomat*

BOLIVIA

La Paz
Gelbard, Robert Sidney *ambassador*

CAPE VERDE

Praia
McNamara, Francis T. *ambassador*
†Segars, Joseph M. *ambassador*

CENTRAL AFRICAN REPUBLIC

Bangui
†Gribbin, Robert E., III *ambassador*

CHAD

N'Djamena
Pope, Laurence E., II *ambassador*

CHILE

Santiago
Cotter, Michael William *foreign service officer*
Kamman, Curtis Warren *ambassador*
Wilkey, Malcolm Richard *retired ambassador, former federal judge*

CHINA

Beijing
Roy, J(ames) Stapleton *ambassador*

CROATIA

Zagreb
Galbraith, Peter W. *ambassador*

ENGLAND

London
Crowe, William James, Jr. *diplomat*
Deal, Timothy *diplomat, government executive*
Dehennin, Herman Baron *diplomat*

Elizabeth II, Her Majesty (Elizabeth Alexandra Mary) *Queen of United Kingdom of Great Britain and Northern Ireland, and her other Realms and Territories, head of the Commonwealth, defender of the faith*
Streator, Edward James *diplomat*

ETHIOPIA

Addis Ababa
†Baas, Marc A. *ambassador*

FRANCE

Beduer
Ezelle, Robert Eugene *diplomat*

Paris
Cornell, Robert Arthur *international government official*
Dean, John Gunther *diplomat*
Ferriter, John Pierce *diplomat*
Larson, Alan Philip *federal official*
Myerson, Jacob Myer *former foreign service officer*
Roudybush, Franklin *diplomat, educator*
Roussel, Lee Dennison *diplomat*

Strasbourg
Barnes, Shirley Elizabeth *foreign service officer*

GERMANY

Berlin
Anderson, David *former ambassador*

GHANA

Accra
Brown, Kenneth L. *ambassador*

GUINEA

Conakry
Saloom, Joseph A., III *diplomat*

ISRAEL

Jerusalem
†Abington, Edward Gordon, Jr. *diplomat*

ITALY

Rome
Cassiers, Juan *diplomat*
Marchand, J. C. de Montigny *Canadian public servant*

JAPAN

Tokyo
Armacost, Michael Hayden *ambassador, government official*

KENYA

Mombasa
†Schmiel, Eugene *foreign service officer*

LATVIA

Riga
Silins, Ints M. *ambassador*

MAURITANIA

Nouackchott
Brown, Gordon Stewart *diplomat*

MOROCCO

Casablanca
Cary, Anne O. *diplomat*

MOZAMBIQUE

Maputo
Jett, Dennis Coleman *ambassador*
†Jon de Vos, Peter *former U.S. ambassador to Mozambique*

NAMIBIA

Windhoek
†Holmes, Genta Hawkins *diplomat*

NIGER

Niamey
†Davison, John S. *ambassador*

NIGERIA

Lagos
†Carrington, Walter C. *ambassador*

QATAR

Doha
†Hambley, Mark Gregory *ambassador*

RUSSIA

Moscow
†Keniaykin, Valery Fedorovich *Russian diplomat*

Saint Petersburg
Gosnell, Jack Leslie *diplomat*

SRI LANKA

Colombo
Schaffer, Teresita Currie *federal official*

SWEDEN

Stockholm
†Redman, Charles Edgar *diplomat*
†Siebert, Thomas L. *ambassador to Sweden*

SWITZERLAND

Bern
†Lawrence, M. Larry *ambassador*

Geneva
Bogsch, Arpad *diplomat*
Ledogar, Stephen J. *diplomat*

TANZANIA

Dar Es Salaam
†DeJarnette, Edmund *ambassador*

THAILAND

Bangkok
Carlson, Mitchell Lans *international technical advisor*

TRINIDAD

Port of Spain
Cowal, Sally Grooms *diplomat*

UKRAINE

Kiev
†Miller, William G. *ambassador to Ukraine*

ADDRESS UNPUBLISHED

Adams, Edwin Melville *former foreign service officer, actor, author, lecturer*
Adams, James Blackburn *former state government official, former federal government official, lawyer*
Agnew, Spiro Theodore *former Vice President of U.S.*
Anderson, John Rogers *Canadian diplomat*
Arcos, Cresencio S. *ambassador*
Argun, Fatima Hatice *international consultant, specialist*
Armstrong, Anne Legendre (Mrs. Tobin Armstrong) *former ambassador, corporate director*
Barnhart, Jo Anne B. *government official*
Bartlett, Steve *mayor*
Bentsen, Lloyd *U.S. secretary of treasury, former senator*
Betti, John Anso *federal official, former automobile manufacturing company executive*
Beyer, Gordon Robert *foreign service officer*
Blood, Archer Kent *retired foreign service officer*
Bolen, David B. *ambassador, former corporation executive*
Boyatt, Thomas David *former ambassador*
Brady, Nicholas Frederick *former secretary of treasury*
Buchanan, John MacLennan *Canadian provincial official*
Burchman, Leonard *government official*
Campbell, Avril Kim *Canadian legislator, justice official*
Cannon, Isabella Walton *mayor*
Clark, William, Jr. *ambassador*
Clarke, Henry Lee *ambassador, U.S. foreign service officer*
Coburn, Harry L. *foreign service officer*
Condayan, John *foreign service officer*
Coop, Frederick Robert *retired city manager*
Cope, Jeannette Naylor *human resources consultant*
Coppie, Comer Swift *state official*
Cougill, Roscoe McDaniel *mayor, retired air force officer*
Cronson, Robert Granville *state auditor*
Dawson, Horace Greeley, Jr. *former diplomat, government official*
Donovan, Walter Edgar *retired mayor*
Douglas, James Holley *former state official*
Drabble, Bernard James *Canadian government official*
†Dunford, David Joseph *foreign service officer, ambassador*
Eastham, Alan Walter, Jr. *foreign service officer, lawyer*
Egan, Wesley William, Jr. *ambassador*
Eisenhower, John Sheldon Doud *former ambassador, author*
Emmons, Robert Duncan *diplomat*
Ewing, Raymond Charles *retired ambassador*
Ford, Ford Barney *retired government official*
Fort, Randall Martin *former federal official*
Fraser, Donald MacKay *former mayor, former congressman*
Fugh, John Liu *military officer, lawyer*
Gerard, Jean Broward Shevlin *former ambassador, lawyer*
Giulianti, Mara Selena *mayor, civic worker*
Grove, Brandon Hambright, Jr. *diplomat*
Gutierrez, Lino *diplomat*
Hanmer, Stephen Read, Jr. *government executive*
Hecht, Chic *ambassador, former senator*
†Henry, Suzanne Jane *government executive*
Heymann, Philip B. *law educator, academic director*
Holiday, Edith Elizabeth *former presidential adviser, cabinet secretary*
Horan, Hume Alexander *diplomat, association executive*
Jacobson, Herbert Laurence *diplomat*
Jarvis, William Esmond *Canadian government official*
Kendrick, Joseph Trotwood *former foreign service officer, writer, consultant*
Kernan, Barbara Desind *senior government executive*
King, James B. *federal official*
Korn, Peter A. *city manager, public administration educator*
†Lancaster, Carol Roanne *federal official*
Lee, James Matthew *Canadian politician*
Leonard, John Peter *diplomat*
Levitsky, Melvyn *foreign service officer*
Lindsay, John Vliet *former mayor, former congressman, author, lawyer*
Luche, Thomas Clifford *foreign service officer*
Lyng, Richard Edmund *former secretary of agriculture*
MacLean, John Angus *former premier of Prince Edward Island*
Maestrone, Frank Eusebio *diplomat*
Marvin, William Glenn, Jr. *former foreign service officer*
Mattingly, Mack F. *US ambassador, former US senator, entrepreneur*
Mazankowski, Donald Frank *Canadian government official*
McLean, Walter Franklin *former Canadian government official*
Mendonsa, Arthur Adonel *city official*
Michaud, Michael Alan George *diplomat, writer*
Miller, Jeffrey Robert *mayor, insurance planner*
Mondale, Walter Frederick *former vice president of United States, diplomat, lawyer*
Moore, Powell Allen *former government official, consultant*
Morgan, William Douglass *diplomat*
Morris, Robert G(emmill) *retired foreign service officer*
Neff, Francine Irving (Mrs. Edward John Neff) *former federal government official*
Negroponte, John Dimitri *diplomat*
Nelson, Harvey Frans, Jr. *retired foreign service officer*
Newfarmer, Gerald Earl *city manager*
Ogg, George Wesley *retired foreign service officer*
Ortiz, Francis Vincent, Jr. *retired ambassador*
Petika, David M. *municipal government official, editor*
Petrequin, Harry Joseph, Jr. *foreign service officer*
Pierce, Samuel Riley, Jr. *government official, lawyer*
Raynolds, Harold, Jr. *retired state education commissioner*
Reich, Robert Bernard *U.S. secretary of labor, political economics educator*
Reinhardt, John Edward *former international affairs specialist*
Reynolds, Carl Christiansen *government official*
Rice, Richard Campbell *retired state official, retired army officer*
Rohatsch, Ralph R., Jr. (Bob Rohatsch, Jr.) *career military officer*
Rosselló, Pedro *governor of Puerto Rico*
Rothing, Frank John *government official*
Rudin, Anne Noto *former mayor, nurse*
Ryan, George H., Sr. *secretary of state, pharmacist*
Sabatini, Nelson John *government official*
Sanders, John Theodore *federal agency executive, former state education superintendent*
Schoettler, Gail Sinton *state treasurer*
Schwartz, Carol Levitt *former government official*
Seitz, Raymond George Hardenbergh *diplomat*
Sentenne, Justine *corporate ombudsman*
Sharif-Emami, Jafar *former prime minister of Iran*
Simmons, Joseph Jacob, III *federal commissioner*
Snider, L. Britt *government executive*
Sotirhos, Michael *ambassador*
Sullivan, Roger Winthrop *retired foreign service officer, consultant*
Tienken, Arthur T. *retired foreign service officer*
Vaky, Viron Peter *diplomacy educator, former foreign service officer*
Walters, Vernon Anthony *ambassador*
Wilkinson, Milton James *ambassador*
Wolf, Dale Edward *state official*
Wright, Sir (John) Oliver *retired diplomat*
Zischke, Douglas Arthur *foreign service officer*

GOVERNMENT: LEGISLATIVE ADMINISTRATION

UNITED STATES

ALABAMA

Birmingham
Allen, Maryon Pittman *former senator, journalist, lecturer, interior and clothing designer*

Mobile
†Bedsole, Ann Smith *state senator*
Callahan, H. L. (Sonny Callahan) *congressman*
Edwards, Jack *former congressman, lawyer*

Montgomery
Clark, James S. *congressman*
†Gullatt, Jane *state legislator*
†Walker, Claud Ladale, Sr. *state representative*

Phenix City
†Corbett, James Daniel (Danny) *state senator*

Selma
†Sanders, Hank *state senator, lawyer*

Troy
†Flowers, Steve *state legislator*

Tuscumbia
†Denton, Bobby E. *state senator*

ALASKA

Anchorage
†Nordlund, James Robert *state legislator*
†Pearce, Drue *state legislator*

Eagle River
Cotten, Samuel Richard *former state legislator, fisherman*
†Willis, Edward Charles *legislator*

Fairbanks
†Brice, Tom Luther *state legislator*

Homer
†Phillips, Gail *state legislator*

Juneau
†Grussendorf, Benjamin Franklin, Jr. *state house speaker*
Kelly, Timothy Donahue *state senator*
†Kerttula, Jalmar M. *state senator*
†Mackie, Jerry *state legislator, business owner*
†MacLean, Eileen Panigeo *state legislator*
†Mulder, Eldon Paul *state legislator, real estate agent*
†Rieger, Steven Arthur *state legislator, business consultant*

North Pole
†James, Jeannette Adeline *state legislator, accountant*

ARIZONA

Glendale
†Brewer, Janice Kay *state legislator*
†Wright, Patricia *state legislator*

Huachuca City
†Ortega, Ruben Francisco *state representative*

Phoenix
†Alston, Lela *state senator*
†Beezley, Linda D. *state legislator*
†Blanchard, Charles Alan *state senator*
†Hull, Jane Dee *former state legislator*
†Keegan, John Charles *state legislator, engineer, consultant*
†Kennedy, Sandra Denise *state representative*
†Kyle, Richard Daniel *state legislator, fundraising consultant*
†Lynch, Susan H. *state legislator*
†Pena, Manuel, Jr. *state senator*
†Salmon, Matthew James *state legislator, public relations specialist*
†Solomon, Ruth *state legislator, teacher*
†Springer, Carol *state legislator*
†Steffey, Lela *state legislator, banker*
†Turner, Warren Austin *state legislator*

Queen Creek
Sossaman, James J. *state legislator*

Scottsdale
Goldwater, Barry Morris *former senator*
Pritzlaff, John Charles, Jr. *former state senator*

Sun City West
Smith, Virginia Dodd (Mrs. Haven Smith) *congresswoman*

Tucson
†Day, Ann *state legislator*
†Noland, Patricia Ann *state legislator*
†Resnick, Cindy *state legislator*

ARKANSAS

Dumas
†Schexnayder, Charlotte Tillar *state legislator*

Fayetteville
†Fairchild, Robert Samuel *state legislator, insurance company executive*
†Malone, David Roy *university administrator, state senator*

Foreman
†Horn, Hoye D. *state legislator, farmer*

Fort Smith
†Pollan, Carolyn Joan *state legislator, job research administrator*

Hamburg
†Murphy, N. B. (Nap Murphy) *state congressman, automobile dealer*

Helena
†Cunningham, Ernest *state legislator*

Little Rock
†Bryan, Lloyd Leon (Doc Bryan) *state legislator*
†Chaffin, Charlie Cole *state senator*
†Hinshaw, Jerrold Eldon *state legislator*
†Miles, Travis Anthony *state senator*

Malvern
†Hopkins, George *senator*

North Little Rock
†Hoofman, Cliff *state senator*

Pine Bluff
†Wilkins, Josetta Edwards *state representative*

Russellville
†Hardin, Luther *state senator*

Searcy
†Beebe, Mike *state senator, lawyer*
†Capps, John Paul *state legislator, radio station owner*

CALIFORNIA

Compton
Dymally, Mervyn Malcolm *retired congressman, international business executive*

Fresno
Krebs, John H. *former congressman*
†Maddy, Kenneth Leon *state senator, lawyer*

Glendale
†Russell, Newton Requa *state senator*

Huntington Beach
†Allen, Doris *state legislator*

Los Angeles
†Hayden, Tom *state legislator, author*
†Torres, Art *state senator*
†Watson, Diane Edith *state legislator*

Newport Beach
Badham, Robert E. *former congressman*
Cox, Christopher *congressman*

Rancho Cucamonga
†Ayala, Ruben Samuel *state senator*

Redondo Beach
†Beverly, Robert Graham *state senator, lawyer*

Roseville
†Leslie, Tim *state legislator*

Sacramento
†Bergeson, Marian *state legislator*
†Boatwright, Daniel E. *state legislator*
†Bowler, Larry Dean *state legislator*
Brown, Willie Lewis, Jr. *state legislator, lawyer*
†Caldera, Louis Edward *state legislator, lawyer*
†Connolly, Tom M. *state legislator, lawyer*
†Cortese, Dominic L. *state legislator, farmer*
Holmes, Robert Eugene *state legislative consultant, journalist*
†Isenberg, Phillip L. *state legislator*
†Killea, Lucy Lytle *state legislator*
Knight, William J. (Pete Knight) *state legislator, retired military officer*
†Moore, Gwen *state legislator*
†Presley, Robert Buel *state senator*
†Umberg, Thomas John *state legislator, lawyer*

San Francisco
Cranston, Alan *former senator*
†Marks, Milton *state senator*
Shumway, Norman D. *former congressman*

San Jose
†Alquist, Alfred E. *state senator*
†Vasconcellos, John *state legislator*

COLORADO

Aurora
†Hagedorn, Robert, Jr. *state legislator, educator*
†Ruddick, Stephen Richard *state legislator, lawyer, political consultant*

Boulder
†Mendez, Jana Wells *state senator*

Colorado Springs
†Powers, Ray Lloyd *state senator, dairy farmer, rancher*
†Wells, Jeffrey M. *state senator, lawyer, judge*

Denver
†Agler, Vickie Lyn *state legislator*
†Benavidez, Celina Garcia *state legislator*
†Bishop, Tilman Malcolm *state senator, retired college administrator*
†Faatz, Jeanne Ryan *state legislator*
†Gallagher, Dennis Joseph *state senator, educator*
Hart, Gary W. *former senator, lawyer*
†Johnson, Joan *state senator*
†Meiklejohn, Alvin J., Jr. *state senator, lawyer, accountant*
†Schaffer, Robert Warren *state senator*
†Sullivan, Patrick James *physician, state representative*
†Tebedo, MaryAnne *state legislator*
†Traylor, Claire Guthrie *state senator*
†Weissmann, Paul Martin *state legislator*
†Wham, Dorothy Stonecipher *state legislator*

Golden
†Hopper, Sally *state legislator*

CONNECTICUT

Bristol
†Krawiecki, Edward C., Jr. *state legislator, lawyer*

Hartford
†Balducci, Richard Joseph *state legislator*
†DePino, Chris Anthoney *state legislator*
†Dillon, Patricia Anne *state legislator*
†Eads, M. Adela *state senator*
†Flaherty, Brian John *state legislator, editor*
†Flaherty, Patrick John *state legislator, economist*

†Gunther, George Lackman state senator, natureopathic physician
†Hess, Marilyn Ann state representative
†Joyce, Raymond M. H. state legislator
†Maloney, James Henry state senator, lawyer
†Mattiello, Brian Edward state legislator
†Meotti, Michael Patrick state legislator, lawyer
†Nickerson, William Hoffman state senator, real estate investor
†O'Leary, Cornelius Peter state senator
†Simmons, Robert Ruhl state legislator, educator
†Upson, Thomas Fisher state legislator, lawyer
†Wyman, Nancy S. state legislator
†Young, Leslie Towner state legislator, stockbroker

Meriden
†Mustone, Amelia P. state legislator

New Haven
Stolberg, Irving J. state legislator, consultant

Stafford Springs
†Guglielmo, Tony state legislator, insurance agency executive

Stratford
†Chase, J. Vincent state legislator, shopping center executive

Wallingford
†Fritz, Mary G. state legislator

Westport
†Freedman, Judith Greenberg state senator, importer

DELAWARE

Dover
†Bair, Myrna Lynn state senator
†Cook, Nancy W. state legislator
†George, Orlando John, Jr. state representative, college administrator
†Holloway, Herman M., Sr. state legislator
†Maroney, Jane P. state legislator
†Still, John C., III insurance agent, state senator
†Vaughn, James T. former state police officer, state senator

Millsboro
Cordrey, Richard Stephen senator

Wilmington
†Amick, Steven Hammond lawyer, legislator
†Blevins, Patricia M. state legislator
†Marshall, Robert I. state legislator

DISTRICT OF COLUMBIA

Washington
Abercrombie, Neil congressman
Ackerman, Gary L. congressman
Akaka, Daniel Kahikina senator
Allard, Wayne A. congressman, veterinarian
Andrews, Robert E. congressman
Anthony, Beryl Franklin, Jr. congressman
Applegate, Douglas congressman
Archer, William Reynolds, Jr. (Bill Reynolds) congressman
Bachus, Spencer congressman, lawyer
Baesler, Scotty congressman
Baker, William P. (Bill Baker) congressman
Ballenger, Thomas Cass congressman
Barcia, James A. congressman
Barlow, Tom congressman, sales executive
Barrett, Thomas M. congressman
Barrett, William E. congressman
Bartlett, Roscoe congressman
Bateman, Herbert Harvell congressman
Baucus, Max S. senator
Becerra, Xavier congressman, lawyer
Beilenson, Anthony Charles congressman
Bennett, Robert F. senator
Bereuter, Douglas Kent congressman
Berman, Howard Lawrence congressman
Bevill, Tom congressman, lawyer
Biden, Joseph Robinette, Jr. senator
Bilbray, James Hubert congressman, lawyer
Bilirakis, Michael congressman, lawyer, business executive
Bingaman, Jeff senator
Bishop, Sanford, Jr. congressman
Blackwell, Lucien E. congressman
Blute, Peter I. congressman
Boehlert, Sherwood Louis congressman
Boehner, John A. congressman
Bond, Christopher Samuel (Kit Bond) senator, lawyer
Bonilla, Henry congressman, broadcast executive
Bonior, David Edward congressman
Boren, David Lyle senator
Borski, Robert Anthony congressman
Boucher, Frederick C. congressman, lawyer
Boxer, Barbara senator
Bradley, Bill senator
Breaux, John B. senator, former congressman
Brewster, Bill K. congressman
Brooks, Jack Bascom congressman
Browder, John Glen congressman, educator
Brown, Corrine congresswoman
Brown, George Edward, Jr. congressman
Brown, Hank senator
Brown, Sherrod congressman, former state official
Bryan, Richard H. senator
Bryant, John Wiley congressman
Bumpers, Dale L. senator, former governor
Burns, Conrad Ray senator
Burton, Danny Lee congressman
Buyer, Steve E. congressman, lawyer
Byrd, Robert Carlyle senator
Byrne, Leslie Larkin congresswoman
Calvert, Ken congressman
Camp, Dave congressman
Campbell, Ben Nighthorse senator
Canady, Charles T. congressman, lawyer
Cannon, Howard Walter former senator
Cantwell, Maria E. congresswoman
Cardin, Benjamin Louis congressman
Carlisle, Margo Duer Black chief senatorial staff
Castle, Michael N. congressman, former governor of Delaware, lawyer
Chafee, John Hubbard senator
Chapman, James L. (Jim Chapman) congressman
Clark, Dick former senator, ambassador, foreign affairs specialist
Clay, William Lacy congressman
Clayton, Eva congresswoman
Clement, Bob congressman
Clinger, William Floyd, Jr. congressman
Clyburn, James E. congressman
Coats, Daniel Ray senator
Cohen, William Sebastian senator
Coleman, Ronald D. (Ron Coleman) congressman
Collins, Barbara-Rose congresswoman
Collins, Cardiss congresswoman
Collins, Mac congressman
Combest, Larry Ed congressman
Condit, Gary A. congressman
Conrad, Kent senator
Conyers, John, Jr. congressman
Cooper, James Hayes Shofner (Jim Cooper) congressman, lawyer
Coppersmith, Sam congressman, lawyer
Costello, Jerry F., Jr. congressman, former county official
Coverdell, Paul D. senator
Coyne, William Joseph congressman
Craig, Larry Edwin senator
Cramer, Robert E., Jr. (Bud Cramer) congressman
Crane, Philip Miller congressman
Crapo, Michael Dean congressman, lawyer
Cunningham, Randy congressman
Danforth, John Claggett senator, lawyer, clergyman
Danner, Patsy Ann (Mrs. C. M. Meyer) congresswoman
Darden, George Washington, III (Buddy Darden) congressman, lawyer
Daschle, Thomas Andrew senator
Deal, Nathan congressman, lawyer
De Concini, Dennis senator, lawyer
DeFazio, Peter A. congressman
DeLauro, Rosa congresswoman
DeLay, Thomas D. (Tom DeLay) congressman
Dellums, Ronald V. congressman
de Lugo, Ron congressman
Derrick, Butler Carson, Jr. congressman
Deutsch, Peter congressman, lawyer
Diaz-Balart, Lincoln congressman
Dickey, Jay W., Jr. congressman, lawyer
Dicks, Norman De Valois congressman
Dingell, John David, Jr. congressman
Dixon, Julian Carey congressman
Dodd, Christopher J. senator
Dole, Robert J. senator
Domenici, Pete (Vichi Domenici) senator
Dooley, Calvin Millard congressman
Doolittle, John Taylor congressman
Dorgan, Byron Leslie senator
Dornan, Robert Kenneth congressman
Dreier, David Timothy congressman
Duncan, John J., Jr. congressman
Dunn, Jennifer Blackburn congresswoman
Durbin, Richard Joseph congressman
Durenberger, David Ferdinand senator
Edwards, Chet congressman
Edwards, Don congressman
†Ehlers, Vernon James congressman
Emerson, William congressman
Engel, Elliot L. congressman
English, Karan state representative
Eshoo, Anna Georges congresswoman
Evans, Lane congressman
Everett, Terry congressman, farmer, newspaper executive, bank executive
Ewing, Thomas W. congressman, lawyer
Exon, J(ohn) James senator
Faircloth, Duncan McLauchlin (Lauch Faircloth) senator, businessman, farmer
Farr, Sam congressman
Fawell, Harris W. congressman
Fazio, Vic congressman
Feingold, Russell Dana senator
Fields, Cleo congressman
Fields, Jack Milton, Jr. congressman
Filner, Bob congressman
Fingerhut, Eric D. congressman, lawyer
Fish, Hamilton, Jr. congressman
Flake, Floyd Harold congressman
Foley, Thomas Stephen speaker of the U.S. House of Representatives
Ford, Harold Eugene congressman
Ford, William David congressman, lawyer
Fowler, Tillie Kidd congresswoman
Fowler, Wyche, Jr. senator, former congressman
Frank, Barney congressman
Franks, Gary Alvin congressman, real estate professional
Frost, Jonas Martin, III congressman
Fulbright, James William former senator
Furse, Elizabeth congresswoman, small business owner
Gallo, Dean Anderson congressman
Gejdenson, Sam congressman
Gekas, George William congressman
Gephardt, Richard Andrew congressman
Geren, Preston (Pete Geren) congressman
Gibbons, Samuel Melville (Sam Gibbons) congressman
Gilchrest, Wayne Thomas congressman, former high school educator
Gillmor, Paul E. congressman, lawyer
Gilman, Benjamin Arthur congressman
Gingrich, Newton Leroy (Newt Gingrich) congressman
Glenn, John Herschel, Jr. senator
Glickman, Daniel Robert congressman
Gonzalez, Henry Barbosa congressman
Goodlatte, Robert William congressman, lawyer
Goodling, William F. congressman
Gordon, Barton Jennings (Bart Gordon) congressman, lawyer
Gorton, Slade senator
Graham, D. Robert (Bob Graham) senator, former governor
Gramm, William Philip (Phil Gramm) senator, economist
Grams, Rodney D. congressman, construction executive, television producer and anchor
Grandy, Fred congressman, actor
Grassley, Charles Ernest senator
Greenwood, James Charles congressman
Gregg, Judd senator, former governor
Guarini, Frank J. congressman
Gunderson, Steve Craig congressman
Gutierrez, Luis V. congressman, elementary education educator
Hall, Ralph Moody congressman
Hall, Tony P. congressman
Hamburg, Daniel (Dan Hamburg) congressman
Hamilton, Lee Herbert congressman
Hancock, Mel congressman
Harkin, Thomas Richard senator
Harman, Jane congresswoman, lawyer
Hastert, (J) Dennis congressman
Hastings, Alcee Lamar congressman, former federal judge
Hatfield, Mark O. senator
Hayes, James Alison congressman
Hefley, Joel M. congressman
Heflin, Howell Thomas senator, lawyer, former state supreme court chief justice
Hefner, W. G. (Bill Hefner) congressman
Helms, Jesse senator
Herger, Wally W., Jr. congressman
Hilliard, Earl Frederick congressman, former state senator
Hinchey, Maurice D., Jr. congressman
Hoagland, Peter Jackson congressman, lawyer
Hobson, David Lee congressman, lawyer
Hochbrueckner, George J. congressman
Hoehn, William Edwin federal goverment official
Hoekstra, Peter congressman, manufacturing executive
Hoke, Martin Rossiter congressman
Holden, Tim congressman, protective official
Hollings, Ernest Frederick senator
Horn, (John) Stephen congressman, political science educator
Horton, Frank former congressman, lawyer
Houghton, Amory, Jr. congressman
Hoyer, Steny Hamilton congressman
Huffington, Michael congressman
Hughes, William John congressman
Hutchinson, Tim congressman
Hutto, Earl congressman
Hyde, Henry John congressman
Inglis, Robert D (Bob Inglis) congressman, lawyer
Inhofe, James M. congressman
Inouye, Daniel Ken senator
Inslee, Jay R. congressman, lawyer
Istook, Ernest James, Jr. (Jim Istook) congressman, lawyer
Jacobs, Andrew, Jr. congressman
†Jarvis, Charlene Drew councilmember
Jefferson, William J. (Jeff Jefferson) congressman
Jeffords, James Merrill senator
Johnson, C. Donald, Jr. (Don Johnson) congressman
Johnson, Eddie Bernice congresswoman
Johnson, Nancy Lee congresswoman
Johnson, Samuel (Sam Johnson) congressman
Johnson, Timothy Peter congressman
Johnston, Harry A., II congressman
Johnston, John Bennett, Jr. senator
Kanjorski, Paul Edmund congressman, lawyer
Kaptur, Marcia Carolyn congresswoman
Kasich, John R. congressman
Kassebaum, Nancy Landon senator
Kasten, Robert W., Jr. former senator
Kempthorne, Dirk Arthur senator
Kennedy, Edward Moore senator
Kennedy, Joseph Patrick, II congressman
Kennelly, Barbara B. congresswoman
Kerrey, Bob (J. Robert Kerrey) senator
Kerry, John Forbes senator
Kildee, Dale Edward congressman
Kim, Jay congressman
Kindness, Thomas Norman former congressman, lawyer, consultant
King, Peter T. congressman, lawyer
Kingston, Jack congressman
Kleczka, Gerald D. congressman
Klein, Herbert C. congressman
Klink, Ron congressman, reporter, newscaster
Knollenberg, Joseph (Joe Knollenberg) congressman
Kohl, Herbert senator, professional sports team owner
Kolbe, James Thomas congressman
Kopetski, Mike congressman
Kostmayer, Peter Houston congressman
Kreidler, Mike congressman, optometrist
Kyl, Jon congressman
La Falce, John Joseph congressman, lawyer
Lambert, Blanche M. congresswoman
Lancaster, H(arold) Martin congressman
Lantos, Thomas Peter congressman
LaRocco, Larry congressman
Laughlin, Gregory H. (Greg Laughlin) congressman
Lautenberg, Frank R. senator
Lazio, Rick A. congressman, lawyer
Leach, James Albert Smith congressman
Leahy, Patrick Joseph senator
Lehman, Richard Henry congressman
Lent, Norman Frederick, Jr. former congressman
Levin, Carl senator
Levin, Sander M. congressman
Levitan, Laurence state senator, lawyer
Levy, David A. congressman
Lewis, Jerry congressman
Lewis, John congressman
Lewis, Thomas F., Jr. (Tom Lewis) congressman
Lieberman, Joseph I. senator
Lightfoot, James Ross congressman
Linder, John E congressman, dentist
Lipinski, William Oliver congressman
Livingston, Robert Linlithgow, Jr. (Bob Livingston, Jr.) congressman
Lloyd, Marilyn congresswoman
Long, Jill Lynette congresswoman
Lott, Trent senator
Lowey, Nita M. congresswoman
†Lucas, Frank D. congressman
Lugar, Richard Green senator
Machtley, Ronald Keith congressman, lawyer
Mack, Connie, III (Cornelius Mack) senator
Maloney, Carolyn Bosher congresswoman
Mann, David Scott congressman, lawyer
Manton, Thomas Joseph congressman
Manzullo, Donald A congressman, lawyer
Margolies-Mezvinsky, Marjorie congresswoman
Markey, Edward John congressman
Martinez, Matthew Gilbert congressman
Mathews, Harlan senator
Matsui, Robert Takeo congressman
May, Edgar former state legislator, nonprofit administrator
Mazzoli, Romano Louis congressman
McCain, John Sidney, III senator
Mc Candless, Alfred A. (Al Mc Candless) congressman
McCloskey, Frank congressman
Mc Collum, Ira William, Jr. (Bill Mc Collum) congressman
McConnell, Addison Mitchell, Jr. (Mitch McConnell, Jr.) senator, lawyer
McCrery, James (Jim McCrery) congressman
McCurdy, David Keith (Dave) congressman, lawyer
McDade, Joseph Michael congressman
McDermott, James A. congressman, psychiatrist
McHugh, John Michael congressman, former state senator
McInnis, Scott Steve congressman, lawyer
McKeon, Howard P. (Buck McKeon) congressman, mayor
McKinney, Cynthia Ann congresswoman
McMillan, J(ohn) Alex(ander), III congressman
McNulty, Michael Robert congressman
Meehan, Martin Thomas congressman, lawyer
Meek, Carrie P. congresswoman
Menendez, Robert congressman, lawyer
Metz, Craig Huseman legislative staff
Metzenbaum, Howard Morton senator
Meyers, Jan congresswoman
Mfume, Kweisi congressman
†Mica, Daniel A. congressman
Michel, Robert Henry congressman
Miller, Dan congressman
Miller, George congressman
Mineta, Norman Yoshio congressman
Minge, David congressman, lawyer, law educator
Mink, Patsy Takemoto congresswoman
Mitchell, George John senator, lawyer
Moakley, John Joseph congressman
Molinari, Susan K. congresswoman
Mollohan, Alan B. congressman, lawyer
Montgomery, Gillespie V. (Sonny Montgomery) congressman
Moorhead, Carlos J. congressman
Moran, James Patrick congressman, stockbroker
Morella, Constance Albanese congresswoman
Moseley-Braun, Carol senator
Moynihan, Daniel Patrick senator, educator
Murkowski, Frank Hughes senator
Murphy, Austin John congressman
Murray, Patty senator
Murtha, John Patrick congressman
Myers, John Thomas congressman
Nadler, Jerrold Lewis congressman, lawyer
Neal, Richard Edmund congressman, former mayor
Neal, Stephen Lybrook congressman
Nelson, Gaylord Anton former senator, association executive
Nickles, Donald (Don Nickles) senator
Nunn, Samuel (Sam Nunn) senator
Nussle, James Allen congressman
Oberstar, James L. congressman
Obey, David Ross congressman
Olver, John Walter congressman
Ortiz, Solomon P. congressman
Orton, William H (Bill Orton) congressman, lawyer
Owens, Major Robert Odell congressman
Oxley, Michael Garver congressman
Packard, Ronald congressman
Packwood, Bob senator
Pallone, Frank, Jr. congressman
Parker, Michael (Mike Parker) congressman
Pastor, Ed congressman
Paxon, L. William congressman
Payne, Donald M. congressman
Payne, Lewis Franklin, Jr. (L.F. Payne) congressman
Pell, Claiborne senator
Pelosi, Nancy congresswoman
Penny, Timothy Joseph congressman
Peterson, Collin C. congressman
Peterson, Douglas (Pete Peterson) congressman
Petri, Thomas Evert congressman
Pickett, Owen B. congressman
Pickle, James Jarrell (Jake Pickle) congressman
Pombo, Richard congressman, farmer, rancher
Pomeroy, Earl R. congressman, former state insurance commissioner
Porter, John Edward congressman
Portman, Rob congressman
Poshard, Glenn W. congressman
Pressler, Larry senator
Price, David Eugene congressman, educator
Pryor, David Hampton senator
Quillen, James Henry (Jimmy Quillen) congressman
Quinn, Jack congressman, English language educator, sports coach
Rahall, Nick J., II (Nick Rahall) congressman
Ramstad, Jim congressman, lawyer
Rangel, Charles Bernard congressman
Ravenel, Arthur, Jr. congressman
Reed, John Francis congressman, lawyer
Regula, Ralph congressman, lawyer
Reynolds, Melvin J. (Mel Reynolds) congressman
Richardson, William Blaine congressman
Ridge, Thomas Joseph congressman
Riegle, Donald Wayne, Jr. senator
Robb, Charles Spittal senator, lawyer
Roberts, Charles Patrick congressman
Rockefeller, John Davison, IV (Jay Rockefeller) senator, former governor
Roemer, Timothy J. congressman
Rogers, Harold Dallas (Hal Rogers) congressman
Rohrabacher, Dana congressman
Rose, Charles Grandison, III (Charlie Rose) congressman
Ros-Lehtinen, Ileana congresswoman
Rostenkowski, Dan congressman
Roth, William V., Jr. senator
Roukema, Margaret Scafati congresswoman
Rowland, (James) Roy congressman
Roybal-Allard, Lucille congresswoman
Royce, Edward R. (Ed Royce) congressman
Rudman, Warren Bruce former senator, lawyer
Rush, Bobby L. congressman
Sabo, Martin Olav congressman
St. Germain, Fernand Joseph congressman
Santorum, Rick congressman
Sarbanes, Paul Spyros senator
Sarpalius, William C. (Bill Sarpalius) congressman
Sasser, James Ralph (Jim Sasser) senator
Sawyer, Thomas C. congressman
Saxton, H. James congressman
Schaefer, Dan L. congressman
Schenk, Lynn congresswoman
Schiff, Steven Harvey congressman, lawyer
Schroeder, Patricia Scott (Mrs. James White Schroeder) congresswoman
Schulze, Richard Taylor congressman
Schumer, Charles Ellis congressman
Scott, Robert Cortez congressman, lawyer
Sensenbrenner, Frank James, Jr. congressman, lawyer
Serrano, Jose E. congressman
Sharp, Philip R. congressman
Shaw, E. Clay, Jr. (Clay) congressman
Shays, Christopher congressman
Shelby, Richard Craig senator, former congressman
Shepherd, Karen congresswoman
Shuster, E. G. (Bud) congressman
Simon, Paul senator, educator, author
Simpson, Alan Kooi senator
Sisisky, Norman congressman, soft drink bottler
Skaggs, David E. congressman

Skeen, Joseph Richard *congressman*
Skelton, Isaac Newton, IV (Ike Skelton) *congressman*
Slattery, James Charles *congressman, real estate executive*
Slaughter, Louise McIntosh *congresswoman*
†Smeeton, Thomas Rooney *congressional staff director*
Smith, Christopher Henry *congressman*
Smith, Lamar Seeligson *congressman*
Smith, Neal Edward *congressman*
Smith, Nick *congressman, farmer*
Smith, Robert Clinton *senator*
Smith, Robert Freeman *congressman*
Snowe, Olympia J. *congresswoman*
Solarz, Stephen Joshua *congressman*
Solomon, Gerald Brooks Hunt *congressman*
Specter, Arlen *senator*
Spence, Floyd Davidson *congressman*
Spratt, John McKee, Jr. *congressman, lawyer*
Stark, Fortney Hillman (Pete Stark) *congressman*
Stearns, Clifford Bundy *congressman, business executive*
Stenholm, Charles W. *congressman*
Stevens, Theodore Fulton *senator*
Stokes, Louis *congressman*
Strickland, Ted *congressman, clergyman, psychology educator, psychologist*
Studds, Gerry Eastman *congressman*
Stump, Bob *congressman*
Stupak, Bart T. *congressman, lawyer*
Sundquist, Donald Kenneth (Don Sundquist) *congressman, sales corporation executive*
Swett, Richard Nelson (Dick Swett) *congressman*
Swift, Al *congressman*
Synar, Michael Lynn (Mike Lynn) *congressman*
Talent, James M. *congressman, lawyer*
Tanner, John S. *congressman, lawyer*
Tauzin, Wilbert J., II (Billy Tauzin) *congressman*
Taylor, Charles H. *congressman*
Taylor, Gene *congressman*
Tejeda, Frank *congressman*
Thomas, Craig *congressman*
Thomas, William Marshall *congressman*
Thompson, Bennie G. *congressman*
Thornton, Ray *congressman*
Thurman, Karen *congresswoman*
Thurmond, Strom *senator*
Torkildsen, Peter *congressman*
Torres, Esteban Edward *congressman, business executive*
Torricelli, Robert G. *congressman*
Towns, Edolphus *congressman*
Traficant, James A., Jr. *congressman*
Tucker, Walter Rayford, III *congressman, lawyer, mayor*
Unsoeld, Jolene *congresswoman*
Upton, Frederick Stephen *congressman*
Valentine, I. Tim, Jr. (Tim Valentine) *congressman*
†Van Hollen, Christopher, Jr. *state legislator, lawyer*
Velazquez, Nydia *congresswoman*
Vento, Bruce Frank *congressman*
Visclosky, Peter John *congressman, lawyer*
Volkmer, Harold L. *congressman*
Vucanovich, Barbara Farrell *congresswoman*
Walker, Robert Smith *congressman*
Wallop, Malcolm *senator, rancher*
Walsh, James Thomas *congressman*
Warner, John William *senator*
Washington, Craig A. *congressman*
Waters, Maxine *congresswoman*
Watt, Melvin L. *congressman, lawyer*
Waxman, Henry Arnold *congressman*
Weiss, Gail Ellen *legislative staff director*
Weldon, W(ayne) Curtis *congressman*
Wellstone, Paul *senator*
Wheat, Alan Dupree *congressman, economist*
Whitten, Jamie Lloyd *congressman*
Williams, Pat *congressman*
Wilson, Charles (Charlie Wilson) *congressman*
Wise, Robert Ellsworth, Jr. (Bob Ellsworth) *congressman*
Wofford, Harris Llewellyn *senator, lawyer*
Wolf, Frank R. *congressman, lawyer*
Woolsey, Lynn *congresswoman*
Wyden, Ronald Lee *congressman*
Wynn, Albert R. *congressman*
Yates, Sidney Richard *congressman, lawyer*
Young, C. W. (Bill Young) *congressman*
Young, Donald E. *congressman*
Zeliff, William *congressman*
Zimmer, Richard Alan *congressman, lawyer*

FLORIDA

Cocoa
Bacchus, James L. (Jim Bacchus) *congressman*

Crestview
Sikes, Robert L. F. *former congressman*

Fort Lauderdale
†Dawson, Muriel Amanda *legislator*

Gainesville
†Kirkpatrick, George Grier, Jr. *state legislative*

Jacksonville
Bennett, Charles Edward *former congressman, educator*
†Holzendorf, Betty Smith *state representative*

Largo
†Mortham, Sandra Barringer *state legislator*

Miami
Fascell, Dante B. *lawyer, congressman*
Gordon, Jack David *senator, foundation executive*

Orlando
†Jennings, Toni *state senator, construction company executive*

Pinellas Park
†Brennan, Mary M. *state legislator*

Saint Petersburg
†Wallace, Peter Rudy *state senator*

Tallahassee
†Hawkins, Mary Ellen Higgins (Mary Ellen Higgins) *state legislator, public relations consultant*
†Sindler, Robert Brian *state legislator, veterinarian*
†Wetherell, Virginia Bacon *state legislator, engineering company executive*

Tampa
†Glickman, Ronnie Carl *state official, lawyer*
†Grant, John Audley, Jr. *state senator, lawyer*
†Miller, Lesley James, Jr. *congressman*
†Rush, Brian Paul *state legislator, lawyer*

Winter Park
Mica, John L. *congressman*

GEORGIA

Americus
†Hooks, George Bardin *state senator, insurance and real estate company executive*

Atlanta
†Martin, James Francis *state legislator, lawyer*
†McBee, Mary Louise *state legislator, former academic administrator*
Murphy, Thomas Bailey *state legislator*
†Newbill, Sallie Puller *state senator*
†Purcell, Ann Rushing *state legislator, office manager medical business*
†Scott, David Albert *state senator, advertising agency executive*
†Slotin, Ronald David *state legislator*
†Stanley, LaNett Lorraine *state legislator*

Augusta
Barnard, Druie Douglas, Jr. *former congressman*

Blairsville
†Colwell, Carlton H. *state legislator, construction executive*

Columbus
†Harbison, Ed *state senator, broadcast journalist*

Gainesville
†Hemmer, Jane Reynolds *state senator, real estate executive*

Lawrenceville
†Wall, Clarence Vinson *congressman*

Marietta
†Klein, Edward W., III (Kip Klein) *state legislator, lawyer*
†Vaughan, Jack Dixon, Jr. *state legislator, insurance agent*

Rockmart
†Dean, Nathan D. *state senator*

Smyrna
†Atkins, William A. (Bill) *state legislator*

HAWAII

Hilo
Ushijima, John Takeji *state senator, lawyer*

Honolulu
†Cachola, Romy Munoz *state representative*
†Chang, Anthony Kai Ung *state legislator*
Fong, Hiram L. *former senator*
†George, Mary Shannon *state senator*
†Hagino, Gerald Takao *state senator*
†Hirono, Mazie Keiko *state legislator*
†Ikeda, Donna Rika *state legislator*
†Isbell, Virginia *state legislator*
†Iwase, Randall Yoshio *state senator*
†Kobayashi, Ann H. *state legislator*
†Marumoto, Barbara Chizuko *state legislator*
†Peters, Henry H. *state legislator*
†Takumi, Roy Mitsuo *state representative*
†Tam, Rod *state legislator*
†Tungpalan, Eloise Yamashita *state legislator*
†Young, Jacqueline Eurn Hai *state legislator*

IDAHO

Boise
†Black, Pete *state legislator, educator*
†Darrington, Denton *state senator*
†Gurnsey, Kathleen Wallace *state legislator*
†McLaughlin, Marguerite P. *state senator, logging company executive*
†Reents, Sue *state legislator*
†Ricks, Mark G. *state senator, farmer*
†Stone, Ruby R. *state legislator*
†Taylor, W.O. (Bill) *state legislator, business consultant*

Caldwell
†Kerrick, David Ellsworth *senator lawyer*

Coeur D Alene
†Jenkins, Janet E. *state legislator, lawyer*
†Reed, Mary Lou *state legislator*

Eagle
†Carlson, Herb *state legislator*

Mountain Home
†Wetherell, Claire *state legislator*

Payette
†Hartung, Mary *state legislator*

Pocatello
†Hofman, Elaine D. *state legislator*
†Lloyd, Mary Ellen *state legislator*

Post Falls
†Chamberlain, Barbara Kaye *state legislator*

Rupert
†Antone, Steve *state legislator, farmer*

ILLINOIS

Aurora
†Deuchler, Suzanne Louise *state legislator*
Etheredge, Forest DeRoyce *former state senator, university administrator*
†Lindner, Patricia Reid *state representative, lawyer*

Bolingbrook
†Meyer, James Henry *state representative, insurance broker*

Buffalo Grove
†Clayton, Verna Lewis *state legislator*

Chicago
†Berman, Arthur Leonard *state senator*
†Bugielski, Robert Joseph *state legislator*
†Carroll, Howard William *state senator, lawyer*
†Collins, Earlean *state legislator*
†Davis, Monique D. (Deon Davis) *state legislator*
†Jones, Emil, Jr. *state legislator*
†Morrow, Charles Gay, III *state legislator, utility company representative*
†Palmer, Alice J. *state legislator*
Stevenson, Adlai Ewing, III *lawyer, former senator*

Christopher
†Severns, Penny L. *state legislator*

Des Plaines
†Butler, Marty *state legislator*

Evanston
†Schakowsky, Janice *state legislator*

Hinsdale
Dyer, Goudyloch Erwin *state legislator*

Jacksonville
Findley, Paul *former congressman, author, educator*

Lake Forest
†Frederick, Virginia Fiester *state legislator*

Mokena
Sangmeister, George Edward *congressman, lawyer*

Naperville
†Cowlishaw, Mary Lou *state legislator*

Nashville
†Deering, Terry William *state legislator*

Northfield
†Stern, Grace Mary *state legislator*

Peru
†Weaver, Stanley B. *state senator*

Quincy
†Donahue, Laura Kent *state senator*

Rockford
†Giolitto, Barbara *state representative*

Schaumburg
†Wojcik, Kathleen Louise *state representative*

Springfield
†Currie, Barbara Flynn *state legislator*
†DeAngelis, Aldo A. *state senator*
†Homer, Thomas J. *state legislator*
†Karpiel, Doris Catherine *state legislator*
Madigan, Michael Joseph *state legislator*
†Philip, James (Pate Philip) *state senator*
†Smith, Margaret *state legislator*
†Welch, Patrick Daniel *state senator*

Sterling
†von Bergen Wessels, Pennie Lea *state legislator*

Westchester
†Walsh, Thomas J. *state representative*

Wheaton
†Fawell, Beverly Jean *state legislator*

Zion
†Geo-Karis, Adeline Jay *state senator*

INDIANA

Attica
†Harrison, Joseph William *state senator*

Bedford
†Skillman, Becky Sue *state legislator*

Bloomington
†Simpson, Vi *state senator*

Columbus
†Garton, Robert Dean *state senator*

Dubois
†Heeke, Dennis Henry *state legislator*

Evansville
†Server, Gregory Dale *state legislator, guidance counselor*

Fort Wayne
†Goeglein, Gloria J. *state legislator*
†Moses, Winfield C., Jr. *state legislator*
†Wyss, Thomas John *state senator*

Indianapolis
†Antich, Rose Ann *state legislator*
†Brinkman, Joyce Elaine *state legislator*
†Crosby, Susan *state legislator, mental health services executive*
†Gard, Beverly J. *state legislator*
†Lubbers, Teresa S. *state senator, public relations executive*
†McCarty, William Dennis *state senator, lawyer*
†Miller, Patricia Louise *state legislator, nurse*
†Mills, Morris Hadley *state senator, farmer*
†Paul, Allen E. *state senator*
†Rogers, Earline S. *state legislator*
†Scholer, Sue Wyant *state legislator*
†Wheeler, Harold H. *state senator, utility contractor*

Lawrenceburg
†Bischoff, Robert John *state representative*

Michigan City
†Alevizos, Thomas James *state representative, lawyer*
†Bowser, Anita Olga *state legislator, education educator*

Monticello
†Wolf, Katie Louise *state legislator*

Oldenburg
†Leising, Jean *state legislator*

IOWA

Ames
†Rosenberg, Ralph *state senator, lawyer, consultant, educator*

Cedar Rapids
†Running, Richard V. *state legislator, college official*

Davenport
†Tinsman, Margaret Neir *state senator*

Davis City
†Boswell, Leonard L. *state senator*

Des Moines
†Buhr, Florence D. *state senator*
†Daggett, Horace Clinton *state legislator*
†Deluhery, Patrick John *state senator*
†Dieleman, William Wilbur *state senator*
†Drake, Richard Francis *state senator*
†Garman, Teresa Agnes *state legislator*
†Grubbs, Steven Eric *state representative*
†Grundberg, Betty *state legislator, property manager*
†Murphy, Patrick Joseph *state representative*
†Pate, Paul Danny *state senator, business executive, entrepreneur*
†Rittmer, Sheldon *farmer, senator*
†Schrader, David F. *congressman*
†Szymoniak, Elaine Eisfelder *state senator*
†Varn, Richard James *state legislator, lawyer, consultant*

Fort Dodge
†Kersten, James Burke *state senator, financial investment officer*

Osage
†Koenigs, Deo A. *state representative*

Ottumwa
†Moreland, Michael Joseph *state representative, associate*

KANSAS

Clay Center
Braden, James Dale *former state legislator*

Colby
†Frahm, Sheila *state legislator*

Hesston
†Samuelson, Ellen Banman *state legislator*

Hutchinson
†Kerr, David Mills *state legislator*

Iola
Talkington, Robert Van *state senator*

Kansas City
†Bruns, G(erald) Thomas *state representative, pharmacist*
†Jones, Sherman J. *state senator*

Lawrence
†Winter, Winton Allen, Jr. *lawyer, state senator*

Lenexa
†Parkinson, Mark Vincent *lawyer, state senator*

Manhattan
†Oleen, Lana *state legislator*

Mc Pherson
Nichols, Richard Dale *former congressman, banker*

Olathe
Burke, Paul E., Jr. *state senator, investment banker*

Overland Park
†Vancrum, Robert James *state senator, partner*

Shawnee Mission
†Bogina, August, Jr. *state senator*
†Langworthy, Audrey Hansen *state legislator*

Stanley
†Brown, Nancy J. *state representative*

Topeka
†Lee, Janis K. *state legislator*
†Mays, M. Douglas *state legislator, financial consultant*
†Petty, Marge *state senator*
Sader, Carol Hope *state representative, legal editor*
†Salisbury, Alicia Laing *state legislator*
†Wagnon, Joan *state legislator, association executive*
†Wells, Elaine Louise *state legislator, health care administrator*

Wichita
†Grotewiel, Ken *state representative*
†Harris, Michael Terry *state senator, partner*
†Pottorff, Jo Ann *state legislator*
†Rutledge, Joel R. *state legislator, small business owner*
†Tiahrt, W. Todd *state senator*
†Welshimer, Gwen R. *state legislator, real estate broker, appraiser, tax consultant*

KENTUCKY

Covington
†Harper, Kenneth Franklin *state legislator, real estate broker*

Frankfort
†Blandford, Donald Joseph *state legislator, speaker of the house*
†Johns, Susan D. *state senator*
†Northup, Anne Meagher *state legislator*
†Palumbo, Ruth Ann *state legislator*
†Rogers, John D. *state senator*
†Stumbo, Gregory D. *state legislator*
†Ward, Michael Delavan *former state legislator*

Leitchfield
†Moore, Virgil C. *state senator, retired army officer*

Louisville
†Ackerson, Jon W. *lawyer, state senator*

LOUISIANA

Baton Rouge
†Dimos, Jimmy *state representative*
†Flournoy, Melissa *state legislator*
†Rayburn, B. B. *state senator, farmer*

Grambling
†Wilkerson, Pinkie Carolyn *state legislator, lawyer*

Harahan
†Bowler, Shirley *state legislator*

La Place
†Landry, Ronald Jude *lawyer, state senator*

Marksville
†Riddle, Charles Addison, III *state legislator, lawyer*

New Iberia
†Romero, Craig F. *state senator, cattle farmer*

New Orleans
†Bajoie, Diana E. *state legislator*

Saint Martinville
†Durand, Sydnie Mae *state legislator*

Sunset
†Brinkhaus, Armand J. *lawyer, state senator*

MAINE

Augusta
†Barth, Alvin Ludwig *state legislator*
†Berube, Georgette B. *state legislator*
†Bustin, Beverly Miner *state legislator*
†Cahill, Pamela Lee *state legislator*
†Daggett, Beverly Clark *state legislator*
†Foster, Ruth Sullivan *state senator*
†Kilkelly, Marjorie Lee *state legislator*
†Ludwig, Margaret G. *state legislator*
Martin, John L. *state legislator*
†Simonds, Stephen Paige *state legislator, former university official*
†Titcomb, Bonnie L. *state legislator*
†Tracy, Richard H.C. *state legislator*

Bangor
†Saxl, Jane Wilhelm *state legislator*
†Winn, Julie *state representative*

Brunswick
†Pfeiffer, Sophia Douglass *state legislator, lawyer*

Caribou
†Donnelly, James Owen *state legislator, bank executive*

Dover-Foxcroft
†Cross, Ruel P. *state representative*

Fairfield
†Gwadosky, Dan A. *state legislator*

Hallowell
†Treat, Sharon Anglin *state legislator*

Monmouth
†McCormick, Dale *state legislator*

Portland
Andrews, Thomas H. *congressman*
†Conley, Gerard P. *state senator, railroad clerk*

Town
†Attean, Priscilla Ann *state legislator*

MARYLAND

Aberdeen
†Bonsack, Rose Mary Hatem *state legislator, physician*

Annapolis
†Amoss, William Hamilton *state senator*
†Boergers, Mary H. *senator*
†Cade, John A. *state senator*
†Forehand, Jennie Meador *state legislator*
†Garrott, Idamae T. *state senator*
†Hixson, Sheila Ellis *state legislator*
†Hollinger, Paula Colodny *state senator*
†Kelley, Delores Goodwin *state legislator*
†Klima, Martha Scanlan *state legislator*
†Kopp, Nancy Kornblith *state legislator*
†Lapides, Julian Lee *state senator, lawyer*
†Madden, Martin G. *state legislator, insurance agent*
†Masters, Kenneth Halls *state legislator*
†Menes, Pauline H. *state legislator*
†Mitchell, R. Clayton, Jr. *state legislator*
†Morgan, John Stephen *state representative, materials science researcher*
†Perry, Marsha Gratz *legislator, professional skating coach*
†Piccinini, Janice *state legislator*
†Roesser, Jean Wolberg *state legislator*
†Ruben, Ida Gass *state senator*
†Sauerbrey, Ellen Elaine Richmond *state legislator*
†Winegrad, Gerald William *lawyer, state senator, educator*

Baltimore
Bentley, Helen Delich (Mrs. William Roy Bentley) *congresswoman*
†Della, George Washington, IV *state senator*
†Hoffman, Barbara A. *state legislator*
†Murphy, Nancy L. *state legislator*
†Stone, Norman R., Jr. *state legislator*

Bethesda
Gude, Gilbert *former state and federal legislator, nurseryman, writer*
Steers, Newton Ivan, Jr. *former congressman*

Bowie
†Green, Leo Edward *state legislator*

Frederick
Byron, Beverly Butcher *congresswoman*

Owings Mills
†Montague, Kenneth C. *congressman*

Oxon Hill
†Lawlah, Gloria Gary *state legislator, educator*

Riverdale
†O'Reilly, Thomas Patrick *state senator, lawyer*

Rockville
†Petzold, Carol Stoker *state legislator*

Silver Spring
†Dorman, Arthur *state legislator*
†Sher, Patricia Ruth *state legislator*

Waldorf
†Simpson, James Carroll *state senator*

MASSACHUSETTS

Boston
†Amorello, Matthew John *state senator*
†Berry, Frederick E. *state legislator*
†Bertonazzi, Louis Peter *state senator*
†Brenton, Marianne Webber *state legislator, technical librarian*
†Bulger, William Michael *state senator*
†Casey, Paul C. *state legislator*
†Cleven, Carol Chapman *state legislator*
Cronin, Bonnie Kathryn Lamb *legislative staff executive*
†Donovan, Carol Ann *state legislator*
†Doran, Stephen William *state legislator, mortgage banker*
†Durand, Robert Alan *state senator*
Flaherty, Charles Francis *state speaker of the house*
†Forman, Peter *state legislator*
†Harkins, Lida E. *state legislator, educator*
†Hawke, Robert Douglas *state legislator*
†Hayward, Jeffrey J. *state legislator*
†Hicks, Lucile P. *state legislator*
†Hornblower, Augusta *state legislator*
†Jehlen, Patricia D. *state legislator*
†Melconian, Linda Jean *state senator, lawyer*
†Murphy, Dennis Michael *state legislator*
†Pines, Lois G. *state legislator*
†Rogeness, Mary Speer *state legislator*
†Rogers, John Healy *congressman*
†Rushing, Byron *state legislator*
†Tarr, Bruce Edward *lawyer, state legislator*
†Turkington, Eric Thornton *state legislator, lawyer*
†Walrath, Patricia A. *state legislator*
†Wetmore, Robert Delvey *state senator*

Chelsea
†Birmingham, Thomas *state legislator*

Fall River
†Correia, Robert *state legislator*

Springfield
†Lees, Brian Paul *state senator*

Worcester
†McManus, William Joseph, II *state legislature, lawyer*

MICHIGAN

Ann Arbor
†Pollack, Lana *state senator*

Clinton Township
†Gire, Sharon Lee *state legislator*

Detroit
†Kelly, John Francis *state senator*

East Lansing
Carr, M. Robert (Bob Carr) *congressman*

Lansing
†Bankes, Lyn R. *state legislator*
†Brown, Mary C. *state representative*
Bullard, Willis Clare, Jr. *state legislator*
†Cisky, Jon Ayres *state senator*
†Dobronski, Agnes Marie *state legislator*
†Dolan, Jan Clark *state legislator*
†Emmons, Joanne *state senator*
†Geake, Raymond Robert *state senator*
†Hammerstrom, Beverly Swoish *state representative*
†Harder, Clark Andrew *state representative*
†Harrison, Charlie J., Jr. *state representative*
†Hoffman, Philip Edward *state legislator*
†Kaza, Greg John *state representative, economist*
†Kilpatrick, Carolyn Cheeks *state representative, educator*
†Munsell, Susan Grimes *state legislator, accountant*
†Pitoniak, Gregory Edward *state representative*
†Posthumus, Richard Earl *state senator, farmer*
†Rhead, Kim Alan *state representative*
†Schroer, Mary Bernadette *state representative*
†Schwarz, John J.H. *state senator, surgeon*
†Smith, Virgil Clark *state legislator*
†Stabenow, Deborah Ann *state legislator*
†Stallworth, Alma Grace *state legislator*
†Vaughn, Jackie, III *state legislator*
†Welborn, John Alva *state senator*

MINNESOTA

Austin
†Piper, Pat Kathryn *state senator*

Burnsville
†Morrison, Constance Faith *state legislator, realtor*

Minneapolis
†Oliver, Edward Carl *state senator, retired investment executive*

Mound
†Olson, Gen *state legislator*

North Oaks
†Asch, Marc *state legislator, consultant*

Saint Paul
†Adkins, Betty A. *state legislator*
†Anderson, Ellen Ruth *state senator*
†Benson, Joanne *state legislator*
†Berglin, Linda *state senator*
†Betzold, Donald Richard *state senator*
†Blatz, Kathleen Ann *state legislator*
†Carlson, Lyndon Richard *state legislator, educator*
†Flynn, Carol *state legislator*
†Frederickson, Dennis Russel *state legislator, farmer*
†Greiling, Marion Gail (Mindy Greiling) *state legislator*
†Gutknecht, Gilbert William, Jr. *state legislator, auctioneer*
†Haukoos, Melvin Robert *state representative*
Hughes, Jerome Michael *state senator, educator*
†Johnson, Janet B. *state legislator*
†Krueger, Richard Arnold *state legislator*
†Leppik, Margaret W. *legislator*
†Long, Dee *state legislator*
†Lynch, Teresa Ann *state legislator*
†Marty, John *state senator, writer*
†Mondale, Theodore Adams *state senator*
†Murphy, Mary C. *state legislator*
†Murphy, Steven Leslie *state senator, utilities company official*
†Orfield, Myron Willard, Jr. *state legislator, educator*
†Pappas, Sandra L. *state legislator*
†Pariseau, Patricia *state senator*
†Robertson, Martha Rappaport *state senator, consultant*
†Segal, Gloria May *retired state legislator*
†Solberg, Loren Albin *state legislator, secondary education educator*
Spear, Allan Henry *state senator, historian, educator*
†Vellenga, Kathleen Osborne *state legislator*
†Wagenius, Jean *state representative*

Saint Peter
†Ostrom, Don *state legislator, political science educator*

MISSISSIPPI

Amory
†Bryan, Hob *lawyer, state senator*

Columbia
†Simmons, Miriam Quinn *state legislator*

Greenwood Springs
†Huskey, William Jerome *state legislaator, farmer, retired army officer*

Gulfport
†Guice, Daniel Dicks, Jr. *state legislator*

Jackson
†Bourdeaux, Norma Sanders *state legislator*
†Ford, Timothy Alan *state representative*
†Hall, Dick *state legislator*
†Harden, Alice V. *state legislator*
†Powell, Amy Tuck *state senator, lawyer*
†Rayborn, William Lee *state senator*
†Woodfield, Clyde V. *senator*

Mississippi State
Stennis, John Cornelius *former senator*

Mize
†Thames, Billy Howard *state senator*

New Albany
†Graham, Walter A. *state legislator, agricultural products executive*

MISSOURI

Cameron
Griffin, Bob Franklin *state legislator, lawyer*

Cassville
†Melton, Emory Leon *state legislator, lawyer, publisher*

Eminence
†Staples, Danny Lew *state senator*

Hale
†Danner, Steve *senator*

Hattiesburg
†Saucier, Gene Duane *state legislator, import/export company executive*

Jefferson City
†Caskey, Harold Leroy *state senator*
†Clay, William Lacy, Jr. *state legislator*
†Griesheimer, John Elmer *state representative*
†Hale, David Clovis *state representative*
†Kauffman, Sandra Daley *state legislator*
†Linton, William Carl *state legislator*
†Maxwell, Joe *state representative, lawyer*
†McCarthy, Karen P. *state representative*
†McCarthy, Thomas William, III *state senator*
†McGee, Jacqueline T. *state legislator*
†Olson, Lawrence E. (Gene) *state representative*
†Smith, Todd Patrick *state legislator, marketing professional*
†Treppler, Irene Esther *state senator*
†Waters, Stephen Russell *state legislator*
†Wible, Connie *state legislator*
†Wiggins, Harry *state senator, lawyer*
†Witt, Gary Dean *state legislator*

Normandy
†Goode, Wayne *state senator*

Saint Louis
Eagleton, Thomas Francis *former senator*
Hoblitzelle, George Knapp *former state legislator*
†Shelton, O. L. *state legislator*

MONTANA

Anaconda
†McCarthy, Bea *state legislator*

Billings
†Keating, Thomas Francis *state senator*
†Russell, Angela Veta *state legislator, social worker*
†Vogel, Randy Charles *state legislator, police officer*

Cascade
†Mesaros, Kenneth Lee *rancher, state senator*

Galata
†Aklestad, Gary C. *state legislater*

Great Falls
†Christiaens, Bernard F. *state legislator, innkeeper*

Helena
†Ewer, David *state legislator, bond program officer*
†Jacobson, Judith Helen *state senator*
†Vaughn, Eleanor *state legislator*

Hungry Horse
†Wagner, Douglas T. *state legislator, millwright*

Laurel
†Blaylock, Chet *state legislator*

Miles City
†Bergman, Ellen Marie *state legislator*

Polson
†Harding, Ethel M. *state legislator*

Seeley Lake
†Larson, Donald Edward *state legislator*

NEBRASKA

Lincoln
Curtis, Carl Thomas *former senator*
†Fisher, Dan *state legislator, bank executive*
†Haberman, Rex Stanley *state senator*
†Hillman, Joyce *state legislator*
†Landis, David Morrison *state legislator*
Marsh, Frank (Irving) *former state official*
†Pirsch, Carol McBride *state senator, community relations manager*
†Rasmussen, Jessie K. *state legislator*
†Schimek, DiAnna R. *state legislator*
†Wesely, Donald Raymond *state senator*
†Will, Eric John *state senator*

Omaha
†Abboud, Christopher William *state senator*

Plattsmouth
†Wehrbein, Roger Ralph *state senator*

NEVADA

Carson City
†Glomb, Diana *state legislator*
†Nevin, Leonard Verne *state legislator, retired police officer*

Las Vegas
†Augustine, Kathy Marie *state legislator, primary school educator*
†Gregory, William David (Bill Gregory) *former state legislator, marketing executive*
Hilbrecht, Norman Ty *state legislator, lawyer*
†O'Donnell, William Russell *state senator*

Reno
†Freeman, Vivian Lois *state legislator, retired nurse*
†Raggio, William John *state senator*

Tuscarora
†Rhoads, Dean Allan *state senator, cattle rancher*

Yerington
Dini, Joseph Edward, Jr. *state legislator*

NEW HAMPSHIRE

Alton
†Ziegra, Alice Stevenson *state legislator*

Bridgewater
†Larson, Nils H. *state legislator, resort owner*

Concord
†Arnold, Thomas Ivan, Jr. *retired legislator*
Burns, Harold W. *state representative, insurance company executive*
†Conroy, Janet M. *former state legislator*
†Cote, David Edward *state legislator*
†Delahunty, Joseph Lawrence *state senator, business investor*
†Dunn, Miriam D. *research firm executive, state legislator*
†Durham, Susan B. *state legislator*
†Hazelton, Robert G., III *state legislator*
†Hollingworth, Beverly A. *state senator*
†Hurst, Sharleene Page *state legislator*
†Kane, Cecelia Drapeau *state legislator, registered nurse*
†McLane, Susan Neidlinger *state legislator*
†Newland, Matthew John *state legislator*
†Packard, Bonnie Bennett *state legislator*
†Pignatelli, Debora Becker *state legislator*
†Podles, Eleanor Pauline *state senator*
†Shaw, Randall Francis *state legislator*
†Skinner, Patricia Morag *state legislator*
†Teschner, Douglass Paul *state legislator*
†Wallner, Mary Jane *state legislator, director child care organization*

Derry
†Aranda, Mary Kathryn *state legislator*
†Katsakiores, George N. *state legislator, retired restauranteur*

Dover
†Pelletier, Arthur Joseph *state legislator, industrial arts and computer programming educator*
†Pelletier, Marsha Lynn *state legislator, secondary school educator*

Durham
†Merritt, Deborah Foote *state legislator, small business owner*
Wheeler, Katherine Wells *state legislator*

Etna
†Copenhaver, Marion Lamson *state legislator*

Hanover
†Crory, Elizabeth L. *state legislator*
Guest, Robert Henry *state legislator, management educator*

Manchester
†Arnold, Barbara Eileen *state legislator*

Nashua
†Clemons, Jane Andrea *state legislator*

Newport
†Stamatakis, Carol Marie *state legislator, lawyer*

Pembroke
†Mears, Edgar Harry *state legislator*

Plaistow
†Senter, Merilyn P(atricia) *state legislator, retired freelance reporter*

Plymouth
†Driscoll, William J. *state legislator, retired postmaster*

Raymond
†Warburton, (Nathaniel) Calvin, Jr. *state legislator, retired clergyman*

Rochester
†Hambrick, Patricia *state legislator*

Rumney
†King, Wayne Douglas *state senator*

NEW JERSEY

Bernardsville
†Ewing, John H. *senator*

Emerson
†Rooney, John Edward *state legislator, electrical company executive*

Flemington
†Lance, Leonard *assemblyman*

Florham Park
†Brown, Leanna *state senator*

Linwood
†Gaffney, John Francis *state congressman*

Millburn
†Ogden, Maureen Black *state legislator*

New Brunswick
†Lynch, John A. *lawyer, state senator*

Paramus
†Kosco, Louis F. *senator*

Trenton
†DiFrancesco, Donald T. *state senator*
†Lipman, Wynona M. *state legislator*

Union
†Bassano, C. Louis *state senator, fuel oil company executive*

West Trenton
†LaRossa, Richard Joseph *state legislator, computer consultant*

Woodbury
†Zane, Raymond J. *lawyer, state senator*

NEW MEXICO

Albuquerque
†Benavides, Tom R. *state senator, realtor*
†Carraro, Joseph John *senator, small business owner, consultant*
†Paster, Janice D. *state legislator*
†Rutherford, Thomas Truxtun, II *state senator, lawyer*
Schmitt, Harrison Hagan *former senator, geologist, astronaut, consultant*
†Wray, Tom Charles *state senator, electrical engineering consultant*

Bloomfield
†Donisthorpe, Christine Ann *state legislator*

Carlsbad
†Stell, Joe M., Jr. *state legislator*

Las Cruces
†Porter, William Emme *state legislator, small business owner*

Los Alamos
†Wallace, Jeannette Owens *state legislator*

Questa
†Cisneros, Carlos R. *state senator*

Roswell
†Casey, Barbara A. Perea *state representative, educator*
†Jennings, Timothy Zeph *rancher, state senator*
†Knowles, Richard Thomas *state legislator, retired army officer*

Santa Fe
†Garcia, Mary Jane Madrid *state legislator*
†Howes, Gloria *state legislator*
†Robinson, Shannon *state legislator*
†Sanchez, Raymond G. *state legislator*

Silver City
†Altamirano, Ben D. *merchant, state senator*

NEW YORK

Albany
†Bruno, Joseph L. *state legislator*
†Connelly, Elizabeth Ann *state legislator*
†Farley, Hugh T. *state senator, law educator*
†Galiber, Joseph Lionel *state senator*
†Gottfried, Richard Norman *state legislator*
†Harenberg, Paul E. *state legislator*
†Hoffmann, Nancy Larraine *state legislator*
†Holland, Joseph R. *state senator*
†Johnson, Owen H. *state senator*
†Lack, James J. *state senator, lawyer*
†Leichter, Franz S. *state senator*
†Luster, Martin A. *state legislator*
†Marino, Ralph J. *state legislator*
†Mendez, Olga A. *state legislator*
†Nolan, Howard Charles, Jr. *state senator, lawyer*
†Padavan, Frank *state legislator*
†Paterson, David Alexander *state senator*
†Santiago, Nellie *state legislator*
Singer, Cecile D. *state legislator*
†Skelos, Dean G. *senator*
†Solomon, Martin M. *state senator*
†Stachowski, William T. *state senator*
†Stafford, Ronald B. *state legislator*
†Vitaliano, Eric N. *state legislator, lawyer*
†Volker, Dale Martin *state senator, lawyer*

Binghamton
†Libous, Thomas W. *state senator*

Bronx
†Espada, Pedro, Jr. *state senator*
†Greene, Aurelia *state legislator*
†Velella, Guy J. *state legislator*

Brooklyn
†Halperin, Donald Marc *state senator, lawyer*
†Montgomery, Velmanette *state legislator*
†Smith, Ada L. *state legislator*

East Setauket
†Englebright, Steven Cale *assemblyman*

Herkimer
Mitchell, Donald J. *former congressman*

Mount Kisco
Goodhue, Mary Brier *former state senator, lawyer*

New City
†Gromack, Alexander Joseph *state legislator*

New Windsor
†Calhoun, Nancy P. *state legislator*

New York
Coelho, Tony *former congressman*
Connor, Martin Edward *state senator, lawyer*
†Maltese, Serphin Ralph *state senator, lawyer*
†Ohrenstein, Manfred *state senator, lawyer*
†Silver, Sheldon *lawyer, state legislator*
Speth, James Gustave *United Nations executive, lawyer*

Niagara Falls
†Pillittere, Joseph T. *congressman*

Ossining
†Galef, Sandra Risk *state legislator*

Pearl River
†Colman, Samuel *assemblyman*

Roslyn Heights
†Tully, Michael J., Jr. *state senator*

Syracuse
†DeFrancisco, John A. *state senator, lawyer*
†Nicoletti, Joseph *New York state assemblyman*

Union
Franks, Robert D. (Bob Franks) *congressman*

NORTH CAROLINA

Advance
†Cochrane, Betsy Lane *state senator*

Greensboro
†Seymour, Mary Powell *state senator*

Locust
†Barbee, Bobby Harold *state legislator, insurance agency executive*

Manteo
†Basnight, Marc *state senator*

New Bern
†Perdue, Beverly M. *state legislator, geriatric consultant*

Raleigh
†Blackmon, John (Jerry) *state senator*
†Gottovi, Karen Elizabeth *state legislator, political consultant, researcher*
†Johnson, Joseph Edward *state senator*
†Lemmond, Joseph Shawn *state legislator, insurance agent*
†Miner, David Morris *state representative*
†Ramsey, Liston Bryan *state legislator*
†Sutton, Ronnie Neal *lawyer, state legislator*
†Tally, Lura Self *state legislator*
†Ward, Marvin *state senator, former superintendent of schools*

Wadesboro
†Hightower, Foyle Robert, Jr. *state legislator, ice and fuel company executive*

Washington
†Edwards, Zeno L., Jr. *state legislator, retired dentist*

NORTH DAKOTA

Bismarck
†Cleary, Audrey *state legislator, nurse volunteer*
†Heinrich, Bonnie *state legislator*
†Lips, Evan E. *state senator, insurance company executive*
†Olsen, Dagne B. *state legislator*

Crosby
†Andrist, John M. *state senator*

Fargo
†Mathern, Tim *state senator, social worker*
†Nalewaja, Donna *state legislator*
†Scherber, Catherine A. (Kit Scherber) *state legislator, trainer persons with disabilities*

Grand Forks
†DeMers, Judy Lee *state legislator, dean*
†Poolman, Jim *state legislator*

Hannaford
†Wogsland, Dan *state senator*

Mandan
†Mushik, Corliss *state legislator*

Minot
Haugland, Brynhild *retired state legislator, farmer*
†Krebsbach, Karen K. *state legislator*

Saint Anthony
†Tomac, Steven W. *state senator, farmer*

OHIO

Cleveland
Oakar, Mary Rose *former congresswoman*
†Pringle, Barbara Carroll *state legislator*

Columbus
†Cain, Madeline Ann *state representative*
†Campbell, Jane Louise *state representative*
†Gaeth, Matthew Ben *state senator*
†Gillmor, Karen Lako *state legislator, strategic planner*
†Guthrie, Marc D. *congressman*
†Kearns, Merle Grace *state senator*
†Krebs, Eugene Kehm, II *state legislator*
†Long, Jan Michael *state legislator*
†Maier, Johnnie A., Jr. *state legislator*
†McLin, Rhine Lana *state representative, funeral service executive, educator*
†Meshel, Harry *state senator*
†Montgomery, Betty D. *state legislator*
†Mottley, J. Donald *state legislator, lawyer*
†Nettle, Robert Dale *state legislator, former insurance and real estate broker*
†O'Brien, Jacquelyn Kirtley *state legislator*
†Opfer, Darrell Williams *state representative, educator*
†Prentiss, C.J. *state legislator*
†Riffe, Vernal G., Jr. *state representative*
†Stinziano, Michael Peter *state representative, real estate broker*
†Suhadolnik, Gary C. *state senator*
†Zaleski, Alan Joseph *state legislator*

Hillsboro
†Snyder, Harry Cooper *state senator*

Lima
†Cupp, Robert Richard *state senator, attorney*

Oberlin
Pease, Donald James *former congressman, political educator*

Toledo
†Furney, Linda Jeanne *state legislator*

Wapakoneta
†Brading, Charles Richard *state representative*

OKLAHOMA

Altus
†Cotner, Howard Paul *state legislator, land title abstractor*

Mcalester
†Stipe, Gene *state senator*

Oklahoma City
†Bastin, Gary Charles *state legislator*
†Boyd, Laura Wooldridge *state legislator*
†Caldwell, Warren A. (Tony Caldwell) *state legislator, real estate management company executive*
†Cole, Helen *state legislator*
†Fair, Michael Edward *state senator*
†Fallin, Mary Copeland *state representative*
†Ford, Charles Reed *state senator*
†Hefner, Jerry W. *state legislator, concrete block plant executive*
†Henry, Brad *state legislator, lawyer*
†Leftwich, Keith C. *state senator, economic development consultant*
†Pope, Tim L. *state legislator, consultant*
†Weedn, Trish *state legislator*

Tulsa
†Cullison, Robert Virl *state senator*
†Horner, Maxine Edwyna Cissel *state legislator*
†Smith, Jerry Lee *state senator*
†Williams, Penny *state legislator*

OREGON

Bend
†Clarno, Beverly Ann *state legislator, farmer*
†Luke, Dennis Robert *state legislator, home building company executive*

Portland
†Lim, John K. *state senator, business executive*

Salem
†Bradbury, William Chapman, III *state senator*
†Dukes, Joan *state legislator*
†Gold, Shirley Jeanne *state legislator, labor relations specialist*
†Hamby, Jeannette *state legislator*
†Jolin, Peggy *state legislator*
†Naito, Lisa Heather *state legislator*
†Oakley, Carolyn Le *state legislator, small business owner*
†Payne, Michael *state legislator*
†Roberts, Frank *state senator*
†VanLeeuwen, Liz Susan (Elizabeth VanLeeuwen) *state legislator, farmer,*
†Yih, Mae Dunn *state legislator*

Scio
†Hayden, Cedric L. *state legislator, dentist*

Troutdale
†Minnis, John Martin *state legislator, protective services official*

PENNSYLVANIA

Allentown
Afflerbach, Roy C., II *senator, consultant*
†Dent, Charles Wieder *state legislator*
†Ritter, Karen A(nne) *state legislator*

Altoona
†Jubelirer, Robert C. *lawyer, state senator*

Conshohocken
†Cohen, Lita Indzel *state legislator*

Drexel Hill
†Loeper, F. Joseph *state senator*

Easton
Reibman, Jeanette Fichman *state senator*

Erie
†Boyes, Karl W. *state legislator*

Grove City
†Fargo, Howard Lynn *legislator*

Harrisburg
†Andrezeski, Anthony (Buzz Andrezeski) *state senator*
†Armstrong, Gibson E. *state senator*
†Armstrong, Thomas Errol *state legislator*
†Dawida, Michael M. *state senator*
†Farmer, Elaine F. *state legislator*
†Fumo, Vincent Joseph *state senator, bank executive, real estate developer, lawyer*
†Geist, Richard A. *engineering executive, state legislator*
†Gruitza, Michael *congressman*
†Harley, Ellen A. *state legislator*
Holl, Edwin G. *state senator*
†Itkin, Ivan *state legislator*
†Jones, Roxanne Harper *state legislator*

†Nyce, Robert Eugene *state legislator, tax accountant*
†Rudy, Ruth Corman *state legislator*
†Schwartz, Allyson Y *state senator*

Holland
†Reinard, Roy *congressman*

Indiana
†Steelman, Sara Gerling *state legislator*

Johnstown
†Wozniak, John N. *state legislator, realtor*

Kingston
†Lemmond, Charles D., Jr. *lawyer, state senator*

Lebanon
†Brightbill, David John *state legislator*

Oil City
†Hutchinson, Scott Edward *state legislator*

Peckville
†Mellow, Robert James *state senator*

Philadelphia
Foglietta, Thomas Michael *congressman*
†Josephs, Babette *legislator*
†Salvatore, Frank A. *state legislator*

Pittsburgh
†Fajt, Gregory Charles *state legislator*
†Fisher, D. Michael *state senator, lawyer*
†Mayernik, David John *state legislator, lawyer*

Reading
†Rohrer, Samuel Edward *state legislator*

Rochester
†LaValle, Gerald J. *state senator*

Wellsboro
†Baker, Matthew Edward *state legislator*

RHODE ISLAND

Central Falls
†Issa, Daniel J. *state senator*

Coventry
†Day, Jennie D. *state legislator*

Cranston
†Sasso, Eleanor Catherine *state legislator*

North Kingstown
†Feroce, John *state senator, optical company executive*

Providence
†Algiere, Dennis Lee *state senator*
†Benoit, Nancy Louise *state legislator, educator*
†Coderre, Elaine Ann *state representative*
Coffey, Sean Owen *former state senator, lawyer*
†Fogarty, Charles Joseph *senator*
Gibbs, June Nesbitt *state senator*
†Goodwin, Maryellen *state legislator*
†Henseler, Suzanne Marie *legislator, social studies educator, majority whip*
†Lyle, John William, Jr. *state senator, lawyer, social studies educator*
†Mathieu, Helen M. *state legislator*

Warwick
†Revens, John Cosgrove, Jr. *state senator, lawyer*

SOUTH CAROLINA

Aiken
†Rudnick, Irene Krugman *lawyer, state legislator, educator*

Anderson
†Harris, Patrick Bradley *state legislator, real estate broker*

Chester
†Short, Linda Huffstetler *state senator*

Columbia
†Cork, Holly A. *state legislator*
†Courson, John Edward *state senator, insurance company executive*
†Harvin, Charles Alexander, III *state legislator*
†Leatherman, Hugh Kenneth, Sr. *state senator, business executive*
†Macaulay, Alexander Stephens *state senator*
†Smith, James Roland *state legislator*
†Smith, J(efferson) Verne *state senator, business executive*
†Wofford, Sandra Smith (Sandi Smith Wofford) *legislator*

Florence
†Glover, Maggie Wallace *state legislator*

Greenville
Mann, James Robert *congressman*

Inman
†Reese, Glenn G. *state senator, food products executive*

Moncks Corner
†Law, James Norris *state legislator, wholesale distribution executive*

Spartanburg
Patterson, Elizabeth Johnston *former congresswoman*

West Columbia
†Wilson, Addison Graves (Joe Wilson) *lawyer, state senator*

SOUTH DAKOTA

Aberdeen
†Lawler, James F. *state senator*

Baltic
†Wagner, Michael Dickman *state representative, small business owner*

Brandon
†Jones, Chet R. *state senator, communications executive*

Brookings
McClure-Bibby, Mary Anne *former state legislator*

Chamberlain
†Saukerson, Eleanor *state legislator*

Hurley
†Rasmussen, Roberta A. *state legislator*

Pierre
Kundert, Alice E. *state legislator*
†Pederson, Gordon Roy *state legislator, retired military officer*
†Stensland, Linda L. *state senator*

Prairie City
†Wishard, Della Mae *state legislator*

Sherman
†Rogen, Mark Endre *state senator, farmer*

Sioux Falls
†Caselli, Robert Eugene *state legislator, retired education administrator*
†Koetzle, Gil *state legislator, fire fighter, professional association administrator*
†Nelson, Pamela *state legislator*
†Paisley, Keith W. *state senator, small business owner*

Wessington Springs
†Morford-Burg, JoAnn *state senator, investment company executive*

TENNESSEE

Chattanooga
†Turner, Brenda Kaye *state legislator*

Cleveland
†Stockburger, Harold E., Jr. *state legislator, insurance agency executive*

Kingsport
†Venable, Richard Sherman *motor carrier business executive, state legislator*

Knoxville
†Atchley, Ben *state senator*

Maryville
†Koella, Carl Ohm, Jr. *lawyer, state senator*

Memphis
†Ford, John N. *state senator, funeral director*

Nashville
†Bragg, John Thomas *state legislator, retired businessman*
†Cooper, Jerry W. *state senator*
†Duer, Shirley Powell *state legislator*
†Harper, Thelma *state legislator*
†Kisber, Matthew Harris *state legislator*
†O'Brien, Anna Belle Clement *state senator*
†Person, Curtis S., Jr. *lawyer, state senator*
†Purcell, William Paxson, III *congressman*
†Westmoreland, Barry Keith *state legislator*

TEXAS

Abilene
†Hunter, Robert Dean (Bob Hunter) *state legislator, retired academic administrator*

Austin
†Black, Charles Layton *rancher, state legislator*
†Brown, J. E. (Buster Brown) *state senator, lawyer*
†Danburg, Debra *state legislator*
†Denny, Mary Craver *state legislator, rancher*
†Eckels, Robert Allen *state legislator*
†Sims, Bill *state senator, business executive*
†Thompson, Garfield *congressman*
†West, George Edgar (Buddy) *congressman*
†Whitmire, John *state senator*

Bellaire
†Schechter, Sue Ann *state legislator*

Dallas
†Cain, David *state legislator, lawyer*
†Goolsby, Tony *state legislator*
†Leedom, John Nesbett *distribution company executive, state senator*

Fort Worth
†Mowery, Anna Renshaw *state legislator*

Hale Center
†Laney, James Earl *state representative, speaker of the house, farmer*

Houston
Green, Gene *congressman*

Laredo
†Zaffirini, Judith *state senator*

Midland
†Craddick, Thomas Russell *investor, state representative*

Port Arthur
†Parker, Carl *state senator*

Rockdale
†Kubiak, Dan *state legislator*

Temple
†Delisi, Dianne White *state legislator*

Waco
†Averitt, Barry Kip *state legislator*

UTAH

Bountiful
†Burningham, Kim Richard *former state legislator*

Corinne
Ferry, Miles Yeoman *state official*

Kaysville
†Simons, Marlene J. *state legislator, rancher*

Layton
†Barlow, Haven J. *state legislator, realtor*

Ogden
†Montgomery, Robert F. *state legislator, retired surgeon, cattle rancher*

Provo
†Valentine, John Lester *state legislator, lawyer*

Roy
Peterson, Douglas Shurtleff *state legislator, packaging company official*

Salt Lake City
†Baird, Delpha *state legislator*
Bennett, Janet Huff *legislative staff member*
†Black, Wilford Rex, Jr. *state senator*
†Buffmire, Judy Ann *state legislator, psychologist, consultant*
Carnahan, Orville Darrell *state legislator, retired college president*
†Davis, Gene *state legislator*
Garn, Edwin Jacob (Jake Garn) *former senator*
†Myrin, N. Alarik *senator, rancher, investor*

Tremonton
Kerr, Kleon Harding *former state senator, educator*

West Valley City
†Peterson, Millie M. *state legislator*

VERMONT

Burlington
Sanders, Bernard (Bernie Sanders) *congressman*

Essex Junction
†Sweetser, Susan W. *state legislator, lawyer, advocate*

Fair Haven
†Larkin, John Paul, II *state legislator*

Montpelier
†Backus, Jan *state legislator*
†Carlson, Mary Ann *state legislator, hotel executive*
†Carroll, John Marcus Conlon *state senator, consultant*
†Crosby, George Miner *state legislator*
†Gear, Mary Moreau *state legislator*
†Granai, Edwin *state senator*
†Illuzzi, Vincent *state senator, lawyer*
†Kroger, Althea *state legislator*
†McGarey Madkour, Mary Elaine Bliss *state legislator*
†Metcalf, Michael Warren *state senator, educator*
†Paquin, Edward H., Jr. *state legislator*
†Ready, Elizabeth M. *state legislator*
†Rivers, Cheryl P. *state legislator*
†Smith, Ruth R. *state legislator*
†Steele, Karen Kiarsis *state legislator*

South Londonderry
†Coleman, Wendell Lawrence *state legislator, farmer*

VIRGINIA

Blacksburg
†Munford, Joan Hardie *member House of Delegates, corporate executive*

Fairfax
†Woods, Jane Haycock *state legislator*

Franconia
†Keating, Gladys Brown *state legislator*

Manassas
†Marshall, Robert G. *state legislator*

Mc Lean
†Callahan, Vincent Francis, Jr. *publisher, state legislator*

Merrifield
†Scott, James Martin *state legislator, healthcare system executive*

Newport News
†Hamilton, Phillip A. *principal, state legislator*

Norfolk
†Miller, Yvonne Bond *state senator, educator*

Richmond
†Chichester, John H. *state senator*
†Gartlan, Joseph V., Jr. *state senator*
†Howell, Janet D. *state legislator*
†Nolen, Frank William *state senator, engineer, farmer*
†Puller, Linda Todd *state legislator*
†Schewel, Elliot Sidney *state senator*
†Waddell, Charles Lindy *state senator*

Spotsylvania
†Houck, R(obert) Edward *state senator, educational administrator*

Virginia Beach
†Wardrup, Leo C. *state legislator*

Williamsburg
†Grayson, George W. *congressman*

WASHINGTON

Edwalla
†Barr, Scott *state legislator*

Federal Way
†von Reichbauer, Peter Graves *senator*

Olympia
†Anderson, Ann *state legislator*
†Cooke, Suzette Allen *state representative*
†Haugen, Mary Margaret *state legislator*
†Kessler, Lynn Elizabeth *state legislator*
†Kohl, Jeanne E. *state legislator, sociologist, educator*
†Long, Jeanine Hundley *state legislator*
†McDonald, Daniel Robert *senator*
†Rayburn, Margaret *state legislator*
†Rinehart, Nita *state senator*
†Silver, Jean *state legislator, accountant*
†Thomas, Brian Chester *state legislator, engineer*
†Valle, Georgette Wald *state legislator*
†Wang, Arthur C. *state legislator, lawyer, educator*
†Wojahn, R. Lorraine *state legislator*

Ritzville
†Schoesler, Mark Gerald *state legislator, farmer*

Seattle
†Niemi, Janice *state legislator, lawyer*

Spanaway
†Campbell, Thomas J. *legislator, chiropractor*

Spokane
†Dellwo, Dennis A. *state legislator*

Vancouver
†Smith, Linda A. *state legislator*

Walla Walla
Hayner, Jeannette Clare *state legislator*

WEST VIRGINIA

Buckhannon
†Riggs, Dale Flint *state legislator, retired coal operator*

Charleston
†Blatnik, Thais Frances *state legislator*
†Brown, Bonnie Louise *state legislator*
†Burdette, Keith *state senator*
†Chafin, Harry Truman *state senator*
†Chernenko, John G. *state senator*
†Craigo, Oshel B. *state senator*
†Yoder, John Christian *state senator, lawyer*

Martinsburg
†Lucht, Sondra Moore *state senator*

Morgantown
†Cook, Stephen L. *state senator*

Parkersburg
†Brum, Brenda *state legislator, librarian*

WISCONSIN

Beloit
†Weeden, Timothy L. *state legislator*

Eau Claire
†Zien, David Allen *state legislator*

Green Bay
†Green, Mark Andrew *state legislator, lawyer*

Hillpoint
†Schultz, Dale W. *state legislator*

Janesville
†Wood, Wayne W. *state legislator*

Madison
Barca, Peter William *congressman*
†Buettner, Carol Ann *state legislator*
†Burke, Brian B. *state senator, lawyer*
†Darling, Alberta Statkus *state legislator, marketing executive, former art museum executive*
†Farrow, Margaret Ann *state legislator*
†Helbach, David Walter *state senator*
†Hinkfuss, Rosemary *state legislator*
†Huelsman, Joanne B. *state legislator*
Klug, Scott Leo *congressman*
†Krusick, Margaret Ann *state legislator*
Kunicki, Walter J. *state legislator*
†Linton, Barbara J. *state legislator*
†Lorge, William D. *state legislator, farmer*
†Lorman, Barbara K. *state senator*
†Moen, Rodney Charles *state senator, retired naval officer*
†Otte, Clifford *state legislator*
†Panzer, Mary E(llen) *state legislator*

†Plewa, John Robert *state senator*
†Porter, Cloyd Allen *state representative*
†Prosser, David Thomas, Jr. *state representative, lawyer*
Risser, Fred A. *state senator*
†Rude, Brian David *state legislator*
†Rutkowski, James Anthony *state legislator*
†Silbaugh, Rudy Lamont *state legislator*
†Swoboda, Lary Joseph *state legislator*
†Turner, Robert Lloyd *state legislator*
†Vergeront, Susan Bowers *state legislator, public relations consultant*
†Welch, Robert Thomas *state representative*
†Young, Rebecca Mary Conrad *state legislator*

Milwaukee
†George, Gary Raymond *state senator*

River Falls
†Harsdorf, Sheila Eloise *state legislator, farmer*

WYOMING

Casper
Meenan, Patrick Henry *state legislator*

Cheyenne
†Cubin, Barbara Lynn *state legislator, public relations consultant*
†Hansen, Matilda *state legislator*
†Mockler, Esther Jayne *state legislator*

Jackson
†LaLonde, Robert Frederick *state senator*

Lander
†Tipton, Harry Basil, Jr. *state legislator, physician*

Laramie
†Kinney, Lisa Frances *state senator*

Rock Springs
†Blackwell, Samuel Eugene *state legislator*

TERRITORIES OF THE UNITED STATES

AMERICAN SAMOA

Pago Pago
†Lutu, Afoa Moega *legislator, lawyer*
†Tulafono, Togiola T.A. *senator*

GUAM

Agana
†Blaz, Anthony Crisostomo *U.S. territorial legislator*
†Lujan, Pilar C. *senator*
San Agustin, Joe Taitano *Guam senator, financial institution executive, management researcher*
†Unpingco, Antonio Reyes *senator*

Saipan
†Maratita, Mametto Ulloa *congressman*

NORTHERN MARIANA ISLANDS

Saipan
†San Nicolas, Henry Deleon Guerrero *territory senator*

PUERTO RICO

San Juan
†Acevedo-Vilá, Aníbal *state legislator, lawyer*
†Caro Tirado, Rafael *congressman*
†De Castro Font, Jorge A. *state legislator*
†Hernández-Agosto, Miguel Angel *Puerto Rican official*
†Hernández Torres, Zaida *state legislator*
†Marrero Hueca, Angel *state legislator*
†McClintock, Kenneth Davison *state legislator*
†Navas de Leon, Luis Felipe *senator, lawyer*
†Ortiz Velazquez, Rolando *territory legislator, lawyer*
†San Antonio Mendoza, Oscar A. *state legislator*
†Valentin Acevedo, Freddy *senator*
†Zayas, Francisco Seijo *legislator, veterinarian*

VIRGIN ISLANDS

Charlotte Amalie
†Richardson, Bingley Geraldo *territory legislator*

Frederiksted
†O'Neal, Lilliana Belardo de *territory senator*
†Pickard, Mary Ann *senator*

Saint Thomas
†Liburd, Almando Leando *senator*

CANADA

BRITISH COLUMBIA

West Vancouver
Collins, Mary *former Canadian legislator*

MANITOBA

Winnipeg
Roblin, Duff *Canadian senator*

NORTHWEST TERRITORIES

Yellowknife
Ballantyne, Michael Alan *legislator*

NOVA SCOTIA

Halifax
†Gillis, John William *Canadian legislator, geologist*

ONTARIO

Ottawa
Austin, Jacob (Jack Austin) *Canadian senator*
Champagne, Andrée *Canadian government official*
Doyle, Richard James *Canadian senator, former editor*
†Eggleton, Arthur C. *member of Parliament, cabinet minister*
†Fairbairn, Joyce *Canadian senator*
†Finestone, Sheila *Canadian legislator*
Fraser, John Allen *Canadian government official*
Frith, Royce Herbert *Canadian senator, retired lawyer*
MacEachen, Allan Joseph *senator*
†Marleau, Diane *Canadian legislator*
Marleau, Robert *federal clerk*
†McLaughlin, Audrey *Canadian politician*
†McLellan, A. Anne *member of Canadian parliament*
Mc Whinney, Edward Watson *Canadian government legislator*
Murray, Lowell *Canadian senator*
Perrault, Raymond *Canadian legislator, senator*
†Peters, Douglas Dennison *member of parliament*
Robichaud, Louis Joseph *Canadian senator*
†Stewart, Christine Susan *Canadian legislator*

QUEBEC

Westmount
†Charbonneau, Guy *Canadian senator, insurance company executive*

ADDRESS UNPUBLISHED

Allen, George *former congressman*
†Anderson, Bob *state legislator, business executive*
†Andrews, Curtis Dickerman, Jr. *state legislator, insurance company official*
Andrews, Michael Allen (Mike Andrews) *congressman, lawyer*
†Aragon, Manny M. *state legislator*
Armey, Richard Keith *congressman*
†Arrarás, José E. *state legislator*
†Bagley, Amy L. *state legislator*
Baker, Richard Hugh *congressman*
Barton, Joe Linus *congressman*
†Bayliff, Bradford W. *state legislator, law firm official*
†Beals, Nancy Farwell *state legislator*
†Bell, Clarence Deshong *lawyer, state senator*
†Berg, Rick Alan *state representative, real estate investor*
Bliley, Thomas Jerome, Jr. *congressman*
†Bluechel, Alan *state senator, wood structural components manufacturing company executive*
†Boley, Donna Jean *state legislator*
†Brodsky, Richard Louis *state legislator*
Bunning, Jim *congressman, former professional baseball player*
†Burton, Joseph Alfred *state legislator*
†Carpenter, Dorothy Fulton *state legislator*
†Chandler, John Parker Hale, Jr. *state senator*
†Charlton, Betty Jo *state legislator*
Chisholm, Shirley Anita St. Hill *former congresswoman, educator, lecturer*
†Churchill, Robert Wilson *state legislator, lawyer*
Coble, Howard *congressman, lawyer*
Cochran, Thad *senator*
†Cowenhoven, Garret Peter *state legislator, educator*
D'Amato, Alfonse M. *senator*
Daub, Hal *former congressman*
de la Garza, Eligio (Kika de la Garza) *congressman*
†Demuzio, Vince T. *state senator*
†Doderer, Minnette Frerichs *state legislator*
†Eck, Dorothy Fritz *state senator*
Ford, Wendell Hampton *senator*
†Gage, Delwyn Orin *state senator, accountant, oil producer*
Gallegly, Elton William *congressman*
†Gilbertz, Larry E. *state legislator, entrepreneur*
†Gordly, Avel Louise *state legislator, community activist*
Goss, Porter J. *congressman*
Hammerschmidt, John Paul *retired congressman, lumber company executive*
Hansen, James V. *congressman*
Hatch, Orrin Grant *senator*
†Hayne, Harriet Ann *state legislator, rancher*
†Holliday, Robert Kelvin *state senator, former newspaper executive*
†Hugley, Carolyn Fleming *state legislator*
Hunter, Duncan Lee *congressman*
†James, Arlo Dee *state legislator, retired mining maintenance executive*
Konnyu, Ernest Leslie *former congressman*
†Lean, Joseph *state legislator*
†Maragos, Andrew George *state representative, stockbroker, consultant*
†Marsico, Ronald S. *state legislator*
†McCorquodale, Dan A. *state senator*
†McCoy, Matthew William *state official, human resource manager*
Mc Govern, George Stanley *former senator*
McHale, Paul *congressman, lawyer*
Mikulski, Barbara Ann *senator*
Nielson, Howard Curtis *former congressman, retired educator*
†Oppenheimer, Suzi *state senator*
†Parry, Atwell J., Jr. *state senator, retailer*
Pettis-Roberson, Shirley McCumber *former congresswoman*
†Pond, Phyllis Joan *state legislator*
Proxmire, William *former senator*
Pryce, Deborah D. *congresswoman*
Reid, Harry *senator*
Reilly, Edward Francis, Jr. *former state senator, federal agency administrator*
†Roberts, Jacqueline *state legislator, political consultant*
Rodino, Peter Wallace, Jr. *former congressman, lawyer*
Roth, Toby *congressman*
Roybal, Edward R. *congressman*
†Schur, Susan Dorfman *state legislator*
†Scott, Charles Kennard *state senator, cattle rancher*
Searle, Rodney Newell *state legislator, farmer, insurance agent*
†Setzler, Nikki Giles *state senator*
†Sherrill, Thomas Beck *financial planner, state legislator*
†Smith, Wayne Alan *state legislator, financial executive*
†Sorensen, Sheila *state senator*
†Talmadge, Philip Albert *state senator, lawyer*
†Topinka, Judy Baar *state legislator*
Udall, Morris King *former congressman*
†Vognild, Larry L. *state senator*
†Vowell, Jack C. *state legislator, investor*
Wehrle, Martha Gaines *state legislator*
†Weldon, Jeffrey Alan *state senator, historical research company executive*
†Wilder, Donny *state legislator, retired newspaper publisher*

HUMANITIES: LIBERAL STUDIES

UNITED STATES

ALABAMA

Auburn
Amacher, Richard Earl *literature educator*
Andelson, Robert Vernon *social philosopher, educator*
Lewis, Walter David *historian*
Littleton, Taylor Dowe *humanities educator*
Skelton, Robert Beattie *language educator*

Birmingham
Allen, Lee Norcross *historian, educator*
Benditt, Theodore Matthew *humanities educator*
Hamilton, Virginia Van der Veer *historian, educator*
Irons, George Vernon *history educator*
Morton, Marilyn Miller *genealogy and history educator, lecturer, researcher, tour planner*
Roberts, David Harrill *English language educator*

Huntsville
†Mercieca, Charles *philosophy and political science educator*
Roberts, Frances Cabaniss *history educator*
White, John Charles *historian*

Montgomery
Cornett, Lloyd Harvey, Jr. *retired historian*
Gribben, Alan *English language educator, research consultant*

Tuscaloosa
†Bell, Robert Fred *German language educator*
Hocutt, Max Oliver *philosophy educator*
McDonald, Forrest *historian, educator*
Rembert, Virginia Pitts *art educator, historian, critic*

ALASKA

Anchorage
†Bunde, Con *communication educator, state legislator*

Fairbanks
Krauss, Michael Edward *linguist*

ARIZONA

Bisbee
Hagstrum, Jean Howard *language professional, educator*

Flagstaff
Hallowell, Robert Edward *French language educator*
Poen, Monte M. *history educator, researcher*

Green Valley
Dmytryshyn, Basil *historian, educator*

Peoria
Bergmann, Fredrick Louis *English language educator, theater historian*

Phoenix
†Land, George A. *philosopher, writer, educator, consultant*
Orman, Arthur Allen *English educator educator*

Scottsdale
Donaldson, Scott *English language educator, writer*

Sun City
Oppenheimer, Max, Jr. *foreign language educator, consultant, hypnotherapist*

Surprise
Clark, Lloyd *historian, educator*

Tempe
Brack, O. M., Jr. *English language educator*
Harris, Mark *English educator, author*
Iverson, Peter James *historian, educator*
†MacKinnon, Stephen R. *Asian studies administrator, educator*
Ney, James Walter Edward Colby *English language educator*

Tucson
Austin, John Norman *classics educator*
Birkinbine, John, II *philatelist*
Briggs, Peter Stromme *art historian, curator*
Dinnerstein, Leonard *historian, educator*
Dufner, Max *retired German language educator*
Hucker, Charles Oscar *author, former history educator*
Lamb, Ursula Schaefer *history educator*
Langendoen, Donald Terence *linguistics educator*
Momaday, Navarre Scott *English educator, author*

ARKANSAS

Conway
Kearns, Terrance Brophy *English language educator*
Stiritz, Marette McCauley *English language educator, consultant*

Fayetteville
Faulkner, Claude Winston *language professional*
Gatewood, Willard Badgett, Jr. *historian*
Kinnamon, Keneth *English language educator*

Jonesboro
Elkins, Francis Clark *history educator, university official*

Little Rock
Ferguson, John Lewis *state historian*
Williams, C(harles) Fred *history professor*

Monticello
Babin, Claude Hunter *history educator*

Searcy
Organ, Dennis Michael *English educator*

CALIFORNIA

Antioch
Graham, Lanier *art historian, curator, cultural planner*

Atherton
Bales, Royal Eugene *philosophy educator*

Bakersfield
Boyd, William Harland *historian*

Berkeley
Alter, Robert B. *comparative literature educator and critic*
Anderson, William Scovil *classics educator*
Baas, Jacquelynn *art historian, museum administrator*
Barish, Jonas Alexander *English language educator*
Bouwsma, William James *history educator*
Bronstein, Arthur J. *former linguistics educator*
Cahill, James Francis *art history educator*
Calame, Alexandre Emile *emeritus French literature educator*
Chapman, G. Arnold *Romance Languages educator*
Costa, Gustavo *Italian language educator*
Crews, Frederick Campbell *humanities educator, writer*
Davidson, Donald Herbert *philosophy educator*
Greenblatt, Stephen J. *English language educator*
Grossman, Joan Delaney *language and literature educator*
Gruen, Erich Stephen *classics educator*
Heilbron, John L. *historian*
Herr, Richard *history educator*
Jordan, John Emory *language professional, educator*
Karlinsky, Simon *language educator, author*
Kay, Paul de Young *linguist*
Kerman, Joseph Wilfred *musicologist, critic*
Lichterman, Martin *history educator*
Litwack, Leon Frank *historian, educator*
Long, Anthony Arthur *classics educator*
Maron, Melvin Earl *philosopher, educator*
Mc Cullough, Helen Craig *Oriental languages educator*
Middlekauff, Robert Lawrence *history educator, administrator*
Muscatine, Charles *English educator, author*
Ohala, John Jerome *linguistics educator*
Oliver, Raymond Davies *English educator*
Penzl, Herbert *German language and linguistics educator*
Rauch, Irmengard *linguist, educator*
Scheffler, Samuel *philosophy educator*
Sealey, B. Raphael *classicist, educator*
Seeba, Hinrich Claassen *foreign language educator*
Selz, Peter Howard *art historian, educator*
Sloane, Thomas O. *speech educator*
Tracy, Robert (Edward) *English educator, poetry translator*
Wakeman, Frederic Evans, Jr. *historian*
Wang, William Shi-Yuan *linguistics educator*
Zwerdling, Alex *English educator*

Beverly Hills
Kravitz, Ellen King *musicologist, educator*
Orenstein, (Ian) Michael *philatelic dealer, columnist*

Carmichael
Bloom, John Porter *historian, editor, administrator, archivist*

Chico
Moore, Brooke Noel *philosophy educator*

Chula Vista
Adams, John R. *English educator*

Claremont
Ackerman, Gerald Martin *art historian, consultant*
Barnes, Richard Gordon *English educator, poet*
Burns, Richard Dean *history educator, publisher, author*
Dunbar, John Raine *emeritus English educator*
Goodrich, Norma Lorre (Mrs. John H. Howard) *French and comparative literature educator*
Lofgren, Charles Augustin *legal and constitutional historian*
Louch, Alfred Richard *philosophy educator*
Macaulay, Ronald Kerr Steven *linguistics educator, former college dean*
McKirahan, Richard Duncan, Jr. *classics and philosophy educator*
Neumann, Harry *philosophy educator*
Olson, Richard George *historian, educator*
Pinney, Thomas Clive *English language educator*

Roth, John King *philosopher, educator*
Sontag, Frederick Earl *philosophy educator*
Young, Howard Thomas *foreign language educator*

Culver City
Clodius, Albert Howard *history educator*

Davis
Crummey, Robert Owen *history educator, university dean*
Forbes, Jack D. *ethnohistorian, educator, writer*
Hayden, John Olin *English literature educator, author*
Hays, Peter L. *English language and literature educator*
Hoffman, Michael Jerome *humanities educator*
Jackson, William Turrentine *history educator*
Rothstein, Morton *historian, retired educator*
Waddington, Raymond Bruce, Jr. *English language educator*
Williamson, Alan Bacher *English literature educator, poet, writer*
Willis, Frank Roy *history educator*
Woodress, James Leslie, Jr. *English language educator*

Duarte
Smith, Hallett Darius *retired English literature educator*

El Cerrito
Kuo, Ping-chia *historian, educator*

Fresno
Flores, William Vincent *educator*
Kouymjian, Dickran *art historian, Orientalist, educator*

Gualala
Gaustad, Edwin Scott *historian*

Hayward
Glasrud, Bruce Alden *history educator*
Mayers, Eugene David *philosopher, educator*

Irvine
Hine, Robert Van Norden, Jr. *historian, educator*
Key, Mary Ritchie (Mrs. Audley E. Patton) *linguist, author, educator*
Kluger, Ruth *German language educator, editor*
Krieger, Murray *English educator, author*
Lehnert, Herbert Hermann *foreign language educator*
Lillyman, William John *German language educator*
Mc Culloch, Samuel Clyde *history educator*
Miller, Joseph Hillis *comparative literature educator*
Sutton, Dana Ferrin *classics educator*
Wiener, Jon *history educator*

Kensington
Malkiel, Yakov *linguistics educator*

La Canada Flintridge
Dales, Richard Clark *history educator*

La Jolla
Kitcher, Philip Stuart *philosophy educator*
Langacker, Ronald Wayne *linguistics educator*
Newmark, Leonard Daniel *linguistics educator*
Olafson, Frederick Arlan *philosophy educator*
Ruiz, Ramon Eduardo *history educator*
Wesling, Donald Truman *English literature educator*
Wright, Andrew *English literature educator*

Laguna Beach
Calderwood, James Lee *English literature educator, writer*

Long Beach
Beebe, Sandra E. *English language educator, artist, writer*
Polakoff, Keith Ian *historian, university administrator*
Stetler, Charles Edward *English language educator*
Weinberg, Meyer *humanities educator*

Los Angeles
Alkon, Paul Kent *English language educator*
Allen, Michael John Bridgman *English educator*
Alpers, Edward Alter *history educator*
Amneus, D. A. *English language educator*
Anastos, Rosemary Park *retired foreign language educator*
Andersen, Henning *linguistics educator*
Appleby, Joyce Oldham *historian*
Arora, Shirley Lease *Spanish language educator*
Bahr, Ehrhard *Germanic languages and literature educator*
Bauml, Franz Heinrich *German language educator*
Beckwith, Charles Emilio *English educator*
Birnbaum, Henrik *Slavic languages and literature educator*
Boime, Albert Isaac *art history educator*
Bradshaw, Murray Charles *musicologist*
Braudy, Leo Beal *English language educator, author*
Burns, E(dward) Bradford *history educator*
Burns, Robert Ignatius *historian, educator, clergyman*
Calder, Daniel Gillmore *English language educator*
Dallek, Robert *history educator*
Davidson, Herbert Alan *Near Eastern languages and cultures educator*
Dearing, Vinton Adams *retired English language educator*
Dyck, Andrew Roy *philologist*
Fisch, Max Harold *educator*
Fromkin, Victoria Alexandra *linguist, phonetician, educator*
Fry, Michael Graham *historian, educator*
Göllner, Marie Louise *musicologist, educator*
Greene, Donald Johnson *retired English language educator, author*
Hospers, John *philosophy educator*
Hovannisian, Richard G. *Armenian and Near East history educator*
Hundley, Norris Cecil, Jr. *history educator*
Jorgensen, Paul Alfred *English language educator emeritus*
Kaplan, Robert B. *linguistics educator, consultant, researcher*
Kelly, Henry Ansgar *English language educator*
Kolve, V. A. *English literature educator*
Ladefoged, Peter Nielsen *phonetician*
Laird, David *humanities educator emeritus*
Lehan, Richard D'Aubin *English language educator, writer*
Levine, Philip *classics educator*
Löfstedt, Bengt Torkel Magnus *classics educator*
MacGregor, Geddes *author, philosophy educator*
Manning, Sylvia *English studies educator*
Martines, Lauro *historian, educator*
Moote, A. Lloyd *history educator*
†Nakanishi, Don Toshiaki *Asian studies educator, writer*
Nevius, Blake Reynolds *English literature educator*
Nunis, Doyce Blackman, Jr. *historian, educator*
Puhvel, Jaan *philologist, educator*
Rathbun, John Wilbert *American studies educator*
Rogger, Hans Jack *history educator*
Rouse, Richard Hunter *historian, educator*
Sanjian, Avedis Krikor *Armenian studies educator*
Schaefer, William David *English educator*
Schutz, John Adolph *historian, educator, university dean*
Schwartz, Leon *foreign language educator*
Shideler, Ross Patrick *foreign language and comparative literature educator, author, translator, poet*
Stockwell, Robert Paul *linguist, educator*
Tennyson, Georg Bernhard *English educator*
Toulmin, Stephen Edelston *humanities educator*
†Wills, John Elliot, Jr. *history educator, writer*
Winterowd, Walter Ross *English educator*
Wortham, Thomas Richard *English language educator*
Zwerver, Peter John *linguistics educator*

Menlo Park
Craig, Gordon Alexander *historian, educator*

Mission Viejo
Teitelbaum, Harry *English educator*

Montclair
Haage, Robert Mitchell *retired history educator, organization leader*

Montecito
Rose, Mark Allen *humanities educator*

Monterey
Chung, Kyung Cho *Korean language educator, author*
Kennedy-Minott, Rodney *international relations educator, former ambassador*

Moorpark
Hall, Elton A. *philosophy educator*

Newport Beach
Brown, Giles Tyler *history educator, lecturer*

Northridge
Chen, Joseph Tao *historian, educator*

Pacific Palisades
Garwood, Victor Paul *retired speech communication educator*
Nash, Gary Baring *historian, educator*

Palo Alto
Buss, Claude Albert *history educator*
Dallin, Alexander *history and political science educator*
Elsen, Albert Edward *art history educator*
Guerard, Albert Joseph *retired modern literature educator, author*
Knoles, George Harmon *history educator*

Palos Verdes Peninsula
Thomas, Pearl Elizabeth *English educator*

Pasadena
Bush, Ronald L. *literature educator*
Elliot, David Clephan *historian, educator*
Kevles, Daniel Jerome *history educator, writer*
Kousser, J(oseph) Morgan *history educator*
Searle, Eleanor Millard *history educator*

Piedmont
Putter, Irving *French educator*

Redondo Beach
Ilie, Paul *foreign language educator*

Riverside
Elliott, Emory Bernard *English language educator, educational adminstrator*
Fagundo, Ana Maria *creative writing and Spanish literature educator*
Hanna, Ralph, III *English educator, author*
Ravitch, Norman *history educator*
Reynolds, William Harold *educator, choral conductor, music critic*
Rosenberg, Alexander *philosophy educator, author*
Ross, Delmer Gerrard *historian, educator*
Snyder, Henry Leonard *history educator, bibliographer*
Steadman, John Marcellus, III *English educator*

Rohnert Park
Grivas, Theodore *retired historian, educator*

Sacramento
Adams, Richard Maxwell *English educator*
Meindl, Robert James *English language educator*
Schmitz, Dennis Mathew *English language educator*

San Diego
Brandes, Raymond Stewart *history educator*
Coox, Alvin David *history educator*
Daley, Arthur Stuart *retired humanities educator*
Feinberg, Leonard *English language educator*
Vanderbilt, Kermit *English language educator*

San Francisco
Cherny, Robert Wallace *history educator*
Edwards, John Hamilton *language professional*
Gregory, Michael Strietmann *English language educator*
Needleman, Jacob *philosophy educator, writer*
Satin, Joseph *language professional, university administrator*
Wilczek, John Franklin *history educator*

San Jose
Melendy, Howard Brett *historian, educator*

San Marino
Karlstrom, Paul Johnson *art historian*
†Ridge, Martin *historian, educator*
Rolle, Andrew F. *historian, educator, author*
Thorpe, James *humanities scholar*
Zall, Paul Maxwell *retired English language educator, consultant*

San Rafael
Eekman, Thomas Adam *Slavic languages educator*

Santa Barbara
Atkins, Stuart (Pratt) *German language and literature educator*
Avalle-Arce, Juan Bautista *language educator*
Brownlee, Wilson Elliot, Jr. *history educator*
Chafe, Wallace LeSeur *linguist, educator*
Collins, Robert Oakley *history educator*
Crawford, Donald Wesley *philosophy educator, university official*
Dauer, Francis Watanabe *philosophy educator*
Del Chiaro, Mario Aldo *art historian, archeologist, etruscologist, educator*
Djordjevic, Dimitrije *historian, educator*
Fingarette, Herbert *philosopher, educator*
Fleming, Brice Noel *retired philosophy educator*
Graham, Otis Livingston, Jr. *history educator*
Gunn, Giles Buckingham *English educator, religion educator*
Hay, Eloise Knapp *English language educator*
Hollister, Charles Warren *history educator, author*
Hsu, Immanuel Chung Yueh *history educator*
McGee, James Sears *history educator*
Moir, Alfred Kummer *art history educator*
Renehan, Robert Francis Xavier *Greek and Latin educator*
Russell, Jeffrey Burton *historian, educator*
Sears, Joanne Lewis *retired educator, author*
Wilkins, Burleigh Taylor *philosophy educator*
Zimmerman, Everett Lee *English educator, academic administrator*

Santa Clara
Meier, Matthias S(ebastian) *historian*

Santa Cruz
†Dizikes, John *American studies educator*
Ellis, John Martin *German literature educator*
Lieberman, Fredric *ethnomusicologist, educator*
Lynch, John Patrick *classics educator, university official*
Suckiel, Ellen Kappy *philosophy educator*

Santa Monica
Abrams, Irwin *historian, educator, consultant*
Cathcart, Linda *art historian*

Santa Rosa
Aman, Reinhold Albert *philologist, publisher*

Stanford
Baker, Keith Michael *history educator*
Carnochan, Walter Bliss *retired English educator*
Cole, Wendell Gordon *speech and drama educator*
Degler, Carl Neumann *history educator*
Dekker, George Gilbert *literature educator, literary scholar, writer*
Dunlop, John Barrett *foreign language educator, research institution scholar*
Duus, Peter *history educator*
Eitner, Lorenz Edwin Alfred *art historian, educator*
Fehrenbacher, Don Edward *retired history educator*
Ferguson, Charles Albert *linguist, language consultant*
Follesdal, Dagfinn *philosophy educator*
Frank, Joseph Nathaniel *comparative literature educator*
Fredrickson, George Marsh *history educator*
Gelpi, Albert Joseph *English educator, literary critic*
Gelpi, Barbara Charlesworth *English literature and women's studies educator*
Giraud, Raymond Dorner *retired language professional*
Johnson, John J. *historian, educator*
Kennedy, David Michael *historian, educator*
L'Heureux, John Clarke *English language educator*
Loftis, John (Clyde), Jr. *English language educator*
Lohnes, Walter F. W. *German language and literature educator*
†Middlebrook, Diane Wood *English language educator*
Mommsen, Katharina *German language and literature educator*
Newman-Gordon, Pauline *French language and literature educator*
Nivison, David Shepherd *Chinese and philosophy educator*
Perloff, Marjorie Gabrielle *English and comparative literature educator*
Perry, John Richard *philosophy educator*
Robinson, Paul Arnold *historian, educator, author*
Sheehan, James John *historian, educator*
Sorrentino, Gilbert *English language educator, novelist, poet*
Spitz, Lewis William *historian, educator*
Stansky, Peter David Lyman *historian*
Traugott, Elizabeth Closs *linguistics educator and researcher*
Watt, Ian Pierre *retired English literature educator*

Stockton
Limbaugh, Ronald Hadley *history educator, history center director*

Sylmar
Hoggatt, Clela Allphin *English language educator*

Van Nuys
Zucker, Alfred John *English educator, academic administrator*

Walnut Creek
Judah, Jay Stillson *historian, educator*

Wilmington
Smith, June Burlingame *English educator*

Woodland Hills
Abramson, Albert *television historian, consultant*

COLORADO

Boulder
Bright, William Oliver *linguistics educator*
Brutus, Dennis Vincent *African literature, poetry, creative writing educator*
Fest, Thorrel Brooks *former speech educator, consultant*
Hawkins, David Cartwright *philosophy and history of science, educator*
Hill, Boyd H., Jr. *medieval history educator*
Main, Jackson Turner *history educator*
Mandel, Siegfried *English language educator, deceased*
Pois, Robert August *historian*
Rood, David S. *linguistics educator*
Taylor, Allan Ross *linguist, educator*

Colorado Springs
Cramer, Owen Carver *classics educator*
Hallenbeck, Kenneth Luster *numismatist*
Stavig, Mark Luther *English language educator*

Denver
Breck, Allen du Pont *historian, educator*
Hamilton, William T. *English educator, former academic administrator*
Pfnister, Allan Orel *humanities educator*
Storey, Brit Allan *historian*
Sullivan, Mary Rose *English educator*

Dolores
Kreyche, Gerald Francis *retired philosophy educator*

Fort Collins
Gilderhus, Mark Theodore *historian, educator*
Kennedy, George Alexander *classicist, educator*
Rock, Kenneth Willett *history educator*
Rollin, Bernard Elliot *philosophy educator, consultant on animal ethics*

Golden
Eckley, Wilton Earl, Jr. *humanities educator*
Pegis, Anton George *English educator*
Sneed, Joseph Donald *philosophy educator, author*

Greeley
†Worley, Lloyd Douglas *English educator*

Pueblo
Farwell, Hermon Waldo, Jr. *parliamentarian, educator, speech communicator*

CONNECTICUT

Bridgeport
Allen, Richard Stanley (Dick Allen) *English language educator, author*

Colebrook
Mc Neill, William Hardy *retired history educator, writer*

Danbury
Edelstein, David Simeon *historian, educator*
Toland, John Willard *historian, writer*

Deep River
Hieatt, Allen Kent *language professional, educator*
Hieatt, Constance Bartlett *English language educator*

Fairfield
Lachowicz, Franciszek *foreign language educator*
Newton, Lisa Haenlein *philosophy educator*

Goshen
Berleant, Arnold *philosopher*

Greenwich
Pope, Marvin Hoyle *foreign language educator*

Hamden
Gay, Peter *history educator, author*
Rosenthal, Franz *lanague educator*
Woodward, C. Vann *historian*

Hartford
Cooper, George Brinton *historian, educator*
Mahoney, Michael Robert Taylor *art historian, educator*

Litchfield
Shapiro, Norman Richard *Romance languages and literatures educator*

Mansfield Center
Butler, Francelia McWilliams *retired English language educator, writer*

Middletown
Arnold, Herbert Anton *German language educator*
Briggs, Morton Winfield *Romance language educator*
Buel, Richard Van Wyck, Jr. *history educator, writer, editor*
Gillmor, Charles Stewart *history and science educator, researcher*
Gourevitch, Victor *philosophy educator*
Greene, Nathanael *historian, university official*
Pomper, Philip *history educator*
Reed, Joseph Wayne *American studies educator*
Rose, Phyllis *English language professional, author*
†Slotkin, Richard Sidney *educator, writer*
Wensinger, Arthur Stevens *German language and literature educator, author*

New Britain
Gallo, Donald Robert *English educator*

New Haven
Bloom, Harold *humanities educator*
Blum, John Morton *historian*
Brooks, Peter (Preston) *French and comparative literature educator, writer*
Cooper, Franklin Seaney *speech scientist*
Culler, Arthur Dwight *English language educator*
Davis, David Brion *historian, educator*

Demos, John Putnam *history educator, writer, consultant*
Dupré, Louis *philosopher, educator*
Erlich, Victor *Slavic languages educator*
Geanakoplos, Deno John *history educator*
Glier, Ingeborg Johanna *German language and literature educator*
Greene, Liliane *French educator, editor*
Greene, Thomas McLernon *language professional, educator*
Hallo, William Wolfgang *Assyriologist*
Hanson, Anne Coffin *art historian*
Harries, Karsten *philosophy educator, researcher*
Hartman, Geoffrey H. *language professional, educator*
Hersey, George Leonard *art history educator*
Hollander, John *humanities educator, poet*
Holmes, Frederic Lawrence *science historian*
Holquist, James Michael *Russian and comparative literature educator*
Hyman, Paula E(llen) *history educator*
Insler, Stanley *philologist, educator*
Kagan, Donald *historian, educator*
Kazemzadeh, Firuz *history educator*
Kennedy, Paul Michael *history educator*
Lord, George deForest *English educator*
MacMullen, Ramsay *retired history educator*
Marcus, Ruth Barcan *philosopher, educator, writer, lecturer*
Martz, Louis Lohr *English literature educator*
Miskimin, Harry Alvin *history educator*
Natanson, Maurice Alexander *philosopher, educator*
Nelson, Lowry, Jr. *comparative literature educator*
Outka, Gene Harold *philosophy and Christian ethics educator*
Palisca, Claude Victor *musicologist, educator*
Pelikan, Jaroslav Jan *history educator*
Poirion, Daniel *foreign language educator*
Pollitt, Jerome Jordan *art history educator*
Robinson, Fred Colson *English language educator*
Schenker, Alexander Marian *linguistics educator*
†Scully, Vincent *art historian, retired educator, writer*
†Smith, Gaddis *history professor*
Smith, John Edwin *philosophy educator*
Spence, Jonathan Dermot *historian, educator*
Underdown, David Edward *historian, educator*
Valesio, Paolo *Italian language and literature educator, writer*
Wandycz, Piotr Stefan *history educator*
Whitaker, Thomas Russell *English literature educator*
Winks, Robin William *history educator*

Old Greenwich
Baritz, Loren *history educator*

Storrs
Charters, Ann *biographer, editor, educator*
Coons, Ronald Edward *historian, educator*
Greene, John Colton *retired history educator*
Rosen, William *English language educator*
Shaffer, Jerome Arthur *philosophy educator*

Storrs Mansfield
Abramson, Arthur Seymour *linguistics educator, researcher*
Reed, Howard Alexander *educator, historian*

West Hartford
Chiarenza, Frank John *English language educator*

West Haven
Turner, Frank Miller *historian, educator*

Willimantic
Philips, David Evan *English language educator*

Windsor
Auten, Arthur Herbert *history educator*

Woodbridge
Ecklund, Constance Cryer *French language educator*

DELAWARE

Newark
Bohner, Charles Henry *English language educator*
Capek, Milic *retired philosophy educator*
Day, Robert Androus *English language educator, former library director, editor, publisher*
Halio, Jay Leon *language professional, educator*
Homer, William Innes *art history educator, art expert, author*
Kirch, Max Samuel *modern language educator*
McLaren, James Clark *French educator*
Tolles, Bryant Franklin, Jr. *historian*
Valbuena-Briones, Angel Julian *language educator, author*
Venezky, Richard Lawrence *English educator*
Weslager, Clinton Alfred *historian, writer*
Wolters, Raymond *historian, educator*

DISTRICT OF COLUMBIA

Washington
Allard, Dean Conrad *historian, naval history center director*
Atil, Esin *Islamic art historian, researcher*
Bearss, Edwin C(ole) *historian*
Bedini, Silvio A. *historian, author*
Bennett, Betty T. *English educator, university dean, writer*
†Berry, Mary Frances *history and law educator*
Billington, James Hadley *historian, librarian*
Bloomfield, Maxwell Herron, III *historian, educator*
Broun, Elizabeth *art historian, museum administrator*
Caws, Peter James *philosopher, educator*
Cua, Antonio S. *philosophy educator*
Davidson, Dan Eugene *language educator, educational exchange administrator*
Davison, Roderic Hollett *historian, educator*
De Pauw, Linda Grant *history educator*
Durfee, Harold Allen *philosophy educator*
Fern, Alan Maxwell *art historian, museum director*
Fink, Lois Marie *art historian*
Goode, James Moore *historian*
Hamarneh, Sami Khalaf *historian of medicine and science, author*
Hammond, Deanna Lindberg *linguist*
Heelan, Patrick Aidan *philosophy educator*
Hill, Bennett David *history educator, Benedictine monk, priest*
Hume, Paul Chandler *music editor, music educator*
Kennedy, Robert Emmet, Jr. *history educator*
King, James Cecil *German educator*
Laiou, Angeliki E. *history educator*
Langan, John Patrick *philosophy educator*
Laqueur, Walter *history educator*
Lewis, Douglas *art historian*
Lewis, Emanuel Raymond *historian, librarian, psychologist*
Lloyd, Timothy Charles *folklorist*
Lucas, George Ramsdell, Jr. *philosophy educator*
Miles, Ellen Gross *art historian, museum curator*
Miller, Jeanne-Marie Anderson (Mrs. Nathan J. Miller) *English educator, academic administrator*
Morse, Richard McGee *historian*
Mowat, Barbara Adams *Shakespearian scholar*
Myers, Robert Manson *English educator, author*
Nisbet, Robert A. *historian, sociologist*
Raaflaub, Kurt A. *classics educator*
Rand, Harry Zvi *art historian*
Reed, Berenice Anne *art historian, artist, government official*
Reingold, Nathan *historian*
Robb, James Willis *Romance languages educator*
Roberts, Jeanne Addison *English educator*
†Rothenberg, Marc *historian*
Sachar, Howard Morley *history educator*
Schlagel, Richard H. *philosophy educator*
Schoenbaum, Samuel *English educator*
Schwartz, Richard Brenton *English language educator, university dean, writer*
Shih, J. Chung-wen *Chinese language educator*
Snowden, Frank Martin, Jr. *classics educator*
Taylor, Estelle Wormley *English educator, college dean*
Taylor, Henry Splawn *literature educator, poet, writer*
Van Cleve, John Vickrey *history educator*
Vaslef, Irene *historian, librarian*
Veatch, Robert Marlin *philosophy educator,medical ethics researcher*
Verheyen, Egon *art historian, educator*
Walker, Robert Harris *historian, author, editor*
Washburn, Wilcomb Edward *historian, educator*
Webb, Robert Kiefer *history educator*
Weismiller, Edward Ronald *English language educator, writer*
Weiss, Paul *philosopher, educator*

FLORIDA

Atlantic Beach
Herge, Henry Curtis, Sr. *education educator, dean emeritus*

Beverly Hills
Larsen, Erik *art history educator*

Boca Raton
Sharf, Donald Jack *speech communication educator, researcher*

Bradenton
Allen, James Lovic, Jr. *humanist, writer, retired educator*

Coral Gables
Lemos, Ramon Marcelino *philosophy educator*
McCarthy, Patrick A. *English educator*

Daytona Beach
Osterholm, J(ohn) Roger *humanities educator*

Dunedin
Espy, Charles Clifford *English educator, author, consultant, lecturer, administrator*

Englewood
Marchand, Leslie Alexis *language educator, writer*

Fort Lauderdale
Van Alstyne, Judith Sturges *English language educator*

Fort Myers
Brown, Earl Kent *historian, clergyman*
Solomon, Irvin D. *history educator, author*

Gainesville
Abbott, Thomas Benjamin *speech educator*
Der-Houssikian, Haig *linguistics educator*
Emch-Dériaz, Antoinette Suzanne *historian*
Goldhurst, William *retired humanities and English educator, writer*
Haring, Ellen Stone (Mrs. E. S. Haring) *philosophy educator*
Harrison, John Armstrong *historian, university dean*
†Hartigan, Karelisa Dorothy *classics educator*
Proctor, Samuel *history educator*
Schmeling, Gareth *classics educator*
Stephan, Alexander F. *German language and literature educator*
Storer, Morris Brewster *emeritus philosophy educator*
Wyatt-Brown, Bertram *historian, educator*

Highland Beach
Stimson, Frederick Sparks *Hispanist, educator*

Jacksonville
Harmon, Gary Lee *language professional, educator*
Scholl, Sharon Lynn *humanities educator*

Key Biscayne
Markell, Alan William *linguistic company executive*

Lakeland
Peeler, Scott Loomis, Jr. *foreign language educator*

Lecanto
Brogan, Howard Oakley *English language educator*

Maitland
Nash, Ronald Herman *philosophy educator*

Marathon
Wiecha, Joseph Augustine *linguist, educator*

Miami
Jones y Diez Arguelles, Gastón Roberto *language educator*
Kirsner, Robert *language educator*
Schwartz, Kessel *modern language educator*

Naples
Waller, George Macgregor *historian, educator*

Orlando
Pauley, Bruce Frederick *history educator*

Palm Beach
Artinian, Artine *French literature scholar, collector*

Saint Augustine
Adams, William Roger *historian*
Russell, Josiah Cox *historian, educator*

Sarasota
Hansen, Elisa Marie *art historian*
Hoover, Dwight Wesley *history educator*
Noether, Emiliana Pasca *historian, educator*
Palermo, Joseph *language educator*
Taplin, Winn Lowell *historian, retired senior intelligence operations officer*

Seminole
McGinn, Donald Joseph *English educator*

Tallahassee
Beck, Earl Ray *historian, educator*
Burroway, Janet G. *English language educator, novelist*
Davis, Bertram Hylton *retired English educator*
Dillingham, Marjorie Carter *foreign language educator*
Dorn, Charles Meeker *art education educator*
Frechette, Ernest Albert *foreign language educator emeritus*
Golden, Leon *classicist, educator*
Harper, George Mills *English language educator*
Kaelin, Eugene Francis *philosophy educator*
McCrimmon, James McNab *language educator*
Moore, John Hebron *history educator*
Oldson, William Orville *history educator*

Tampa
†Anton, John Peter *philosophy educator*
Cundiff, Paul Arthur *English language educator*
Perry, James Frederic *philosophy educator, author*
Preto-Rodas, Richard Anthony *foreign language educator*

Tarpon Springs
Thompson, Mack Eugene *history educator*

West Palm Beach
†Greene, Addie Lue *English educator, mayor, state legislator*
Hall, E. Eugene *communication arts educator*

Winter Haven
Kerner, Howard Alex *English and communications educator, writer, literary manager*
Love, John Wesley, Jr. *English language and reading educator*

Winter Park
Sedwick, (Benjamin) Frank *language educator*
Seymour, Thaddeus *English educator*

GEORGIA

Andersonville
†Boyles, Frederick Holdren *historian*

Athens
Dickie, Margaret McKenzie *English language educator*
Freer, Coburn *English language educator*
Kretzschmar, William Addison, Jr. *English language educator*
Lindberg, Stanley William *English language educator, editor*
Mamatey, Victor Samuel *history educator*
Mc Feely, William Shield *historian, writer*
Moore, Rayburn Sabatzky *American literature educator*
†Nute, Donald E., Jr. *philosophy educator*
Steer, Alfred Gilbert, Jr. *foreign language educator*
Wall, Bennett Harrison *history educator*

Atlanta
Bakewell, Peter John *history educator*
Benario, Herbert William *classics educator*
Burns, Thomas Samuel *history educator*
Carter, Dan T. *history educator*
Dillingham, William Byron *literature educator, author*
Fox-Genovese, Elizabeth Ann *humanities educator*
Genovese, Eugene Dominick *historian, educator*
Hartle, Robert Wyman *retired foreign language and literature educator*
Kranzberg, Melvin *history educator*
Kuntz, Marion Lucile Leathers *classicist, historian, educator*
Mafico, Temba Levi Jackson *Old Testament and Semitic languages educator, clergy*
Manley, Frank *English language educator*
Rojas, Carlos *Spanish literature educator*
Sitter, John Edward *English literature educator*
Spivey, Ted Ray *English educator*

Augusta
Cashin, Edward Joseph *history educator*

Decatur
Pepperdene, Margaret Williams *English educator*
Young, James Harvey *historian, educator*

Gainesville
†Wagner, Clarence *historian*

Macon
Cockfield, Jamie Hartwell *history educator*

Marietta
Rainey, Kenneth Tyler *English language educator*

Savannah
Warlick, Roger Kinney *history educator, assistant dean*

HAWAII

Honolulu
Bender, Byron Wilbur *linguistics educator*
Copi, Irving Marmer *philosophy educator*
Dyen, Isidore *linguistic scientist, educator*
Knowlton, Edgar Colby, Jr. *linguist, educator*
Peterson, Barbara Ann Bennett *history educator*
Rapson, Richard L. *history educator*
Seymour, Richard Kellogg *linguist, educator*
Stephan, John Jason *historian, educator*
Varley, Herbert Paul *Japanese language and cultural history educator*

IDAHO

Boise
Nguyen, King Xuan *historian*
Wells, Merle William *historian, state archivist*

Caldwell
Attebery, Louie Wayne *English language educator, folklorist*

Emmett
Farnham, Wallace Dean *historian*

ILLINOIS

Bloomington
Bray, Robert C. *literature educator*

Carbondale
Ammon, Harry *history educator*
†Brown, James Montgomery *English language and literature educator emeritus, academic administrator*
Fladeland, Betty *historian, educator*
Gilbert, Glenn Gordon *linguistics educator*
Hahn, Lewis Edwin *philosopher, retired educator*
Schilpp, Paul Arthur *philosopher, editor, clergyman*
Spees, Emil Ray *philosophy educator*
†Webb, Howard William, Jr. *humanities educator, university official*
Woodbridge, Hensley Charles *retired librarian, foreign languages educator*

Champaign
†Crummey, Donald Edward *history educator*
Friedberg, Maurice *Russian literature educator*
†Koenker, Diana P. *history educator*
†Love, Joseph L. *history educator, cultural studies center administrator*
O'Neill, John Joseph *speech educator*
Smith, Ralph Alexander *cultural and educational policy educator*
Spence, Clark Christian *history educator*

Chicago
Adkins, Arthur William Hope *humanities educator*
Adler, Mortimer Jerome *philosopher, author*
Aronson, Howard Isaac *linguist, educator*
Austen, Ralph A. *historian, educator*
†Berk, Harlan Joseph *numismatist, writer, antiquarian*
Bevington, David Martin *English literature educator*
Biggs, Robert Dale *Near Eastern studies educator*
Booth, Wayne Clayson *English literature and rhetoric educator, author*
Brinkman, John Anthony *historian, educator*
Cohen, Ted *philosophy educator*
Cullen, Charles Thomas *historian, librarian*
Debus, Allen George *history educator*
Dembowski, Peter Florian *foreign language educator*
Erlebacher, Albert *history educator*
Fleischer, Cornell Hugh *history educator*
Frings, Manfred Servatius *philosophy educator*
Gannon, Sister Ann Ida *retired philosophy educator, former college administrator*
Garber, Daniel Elliot *philosophy educator*
Goldsmith, John Anton *linguist, educator*
Grant, Robert McQueen *humanities educator*
Gray, Hanna Holborn *history educator*
Griffin, Mary *English language educator*
Grove, Helen Harriet *historian, artist*
Gutek, Gerald Lee *education and history educator*
Haley, George *Romance languages educator*
Hamp, Eric Pratt *linguist*
Hardy, John Edward *English language educator, author*
Harris, Neil *history educator*
Harvanek, Robert Francis *philosophy educator, clergyman*
Heller, Reinhold August *art educator, consultant*
Hellie, Richard *Russian history educator, researcher*
Helmbold, Nancy Pearce *classical languages educator*
Hunter, J(ames) Paul *English language educator, literary critic, historian*
Hurley, William James, Jr. *English language educator*
Jones, Peter d'Alroy *history educator, author*
Karanikas, Alexander *English language educator, author, actor*
Karl, Barry Dean *historian, educator*
Kazazis, Kostas *linguist, educator*
Keenan, James George *classics educator*
Kolb, Gwin Jackson *language professional, educator*
Lawler, James Ronald *French language educator*
Lieb, Michael *English educator, humanities educator*
Marshall, Donald Glenn *English language and literature educator*
Martinez, Miguel Angel *Spanish language educator*
Miller, James Edwin, Jr. *English language educator*
Mitchell, W. J. T. *English language, literature and visual arts educator, editor*
Najita, Tetsuo *history educator*
Newman, Ralph Geoffrey *literary scholar historian*
Novick, Peter *historian, educator*
Pestureau, Pierre Gilbert *literature educator, literary critic, editor*
Pollock, Sheldon Ivan *language professional, educator*
Redfield, James Michael *humanities and classics educator*

Remini, Robert Vincent *historian, educator*
Rosenheim, Edward Weil *English educator*
Rosenthal, Earl Edgar *art history educator*
Roy, David Tod *Chinese literature educator*
Saller, Richard Paul *classics educator*
Sochen, June *historian*
Tanner, Helen Hornbeck *historian*
Thaden, Edward Carl *history educator*
Vaillancourt, Daniel Gilbert *philosophy educator*

De Kalb
†Aung-Thwin, Michael *history educator*
Hagelman, Charles William, Jr. *language professional, educator*

Edwardsville
Going, William Thornbury *language professional, educator*

Elsah
Hodgson, Peter John *music educator*

Evanston
Cole, Douglas *English literature educator*
Condit, Carl Wilbur *history educator*
De Coster, Cyrus Cole *Spanish language and literature educator*
Fine, Arthur I. *philosopher*
Fox, Edward Inman *education administrator and Spanish educator*
Sheridan, James Edward *history educator*
Ver Steeg, Clarence Lester *historian, educator*
Weil, Irwin *Slavic languages and literature educator*
Werckmeister, Otto Karl *philosopher educator*
Wilks, Ivor Gordon Hughes *historian, educator*
Wright, John *classics educator*

Galesburg
Hane, Mikiso *history educator*

Glenview
Levine, Edwin Burton *retired classics educator*

Joliet
Marion, Marjorie Anne *English educator*

Macomb
Brown, Spencer Hunter *historian*
Spencer, Donald Spurgeon *historian, academic administrator*
Vos, Morris *foreign languages educator, language services consultant*

Monmouth
Johnson, John Prescott *philosophy educator*

Mount Prospect
Stamper, James M. *retired English language educator*

Palatine
Hull, Elizabeth Anne *English language educator*

Peoria
Ballowe, James *English educator, author*

Springfield
Fischoff, Ephraim *humanities educator, sociologist, social worker*
Temple, Wayne Calhoun *historian*

Urbana
Aldridge, Alfred Owen *English language educator*
Andersen, Kenneth Eldon *speech communication educator*
Antonsen, Elmer Harold *Germanic languages and literature educator*
Arnstein, Walter Leonard *historian, educator*
Bateman, John Jay *classics educator*
Bates, James Leonard *historian*
Baym, Nina *English educator*
Broudy, Harry Samuel *retired philosophy educator*
Browne, Gerald Michael *classics educator*
Dawn, Clarence Ernest *history educator*
Gaeng, Paul Ami *foreign language educator*
Haile, H. G. *German language and literature educator*
Hendrick, George *English language educator*
Hurt, James Riggins *English language educator*
Jacobson, Howard *classics educator*
Kachru, Braj Behari *linguist*
Kachru, Yamuna *linguist*
Kim, Chin-Woo *linguist, educator*
Mainous, Bruce Hale *foreign language educator*
†Marcovich, Miroslav *educator*
McColley, Robert McNair *history educator*
Newman, John Kevin *classics educator*
Queller, Donald Edward *historian, educator*
Scanlan, Richard Thomas *classics educator*
Schacht, Richard Lawrence *philosopher, educator*
Solberg, Winton Udell *history educator*
Stein, Arnold *English educator*
Stillinger, Jack Clifford *English educator*
Talbot, Emile Joseph *French educator*
Watts, Emily Stipes *English educator*

Westchester
Masterson, John Patrick *retired English language educator*

Wilmette
Fries, Robert Francis *historian, educator*

INDIANA

Bloomington
Anderson, Judith Helena *English language educator*
Barnstone, Willis (Robert Barnstone) *language literature educator, poet, scholar*
Battenhouse, Roy Wesley *English educator*
Baxter, Maurice Glen *historian, educator*
Boerner, Peter *language and literature educator*
Buelow, George John *musicologist, educator*
Burgan, Mary Alice *English language educator*
Byrnes, Robert Francis *history educator*
Cohen, William Benjamin *historian, educator*
Cole, Bruce Milan *art historian*
Dunn, Jon Michael *philosophy educator*
Edgerton, William B. *foreign language educator*
Ferrell, Robert Hugh *historian, educator*
Foster, Kathleen Adair *art historian, museum curator*
Hanson, Karen *philosopher, educator*
Hess-Lüttich, Ernest Walter Bernhard *Germanic studies educator*
Hodge, Carleton Taylor *linguist, educator*
Juergens, George Ivar *history educator*
Martins, Heitor Miranda *foreign language educator*
†McDowell, John Holmes *folklore educator, institute director*
Oinas, Felix Johannes *foreign language educator*
Pletcher, David Mitchell *history educator*
Rosenberg, Samuel Nathan *French and Italian language educator*
Sebeok, Thomas Albert *linguistics educator*
Simmons, Merle Edwin *foreign language educator*
Sinor, Denis *Orientalist, educator*
†Sperling, Elliot Harris *history educator*
Strohm, Paul Holzworth, Jr. *English language educator, educational administrator*
Westfall, Richard Samuel *historian*
†Wilson, George Macklin *history educator, cultural studies center administrator*
Wittlich, Gary Eugene *music theory educator*

Charlestown
Schmidt, Jakob Edward *medical and medicolegal lexicographer, physician, author, inventor*

Crawfordsville
Barnes, James John *history educator*

Culver
Holaday, Allan Gibson *English educator*

Fort Wayne
Fairchild, David Lawrence *philosophy educator*
Ratliff, Gerald Lee *speech and theatre educator*
Scheetz, Sister Mary JoEllen *English language educator*

Greencastle
DiLillo, Leonard Michael *Spanish educator, researcher, academic administrator*
Phillips, Clifton J. *history educator*
Weiss, Robert Orr *speech educator*

Greenfield
Bettler, Janet Louise Bell *foreign language educator*

Indianapolis
Baetzhold, Howard George *English language educator*
Casebeer, Edwin Frank, Jr. *English language educator*
Geib, George Winthrop *history educator*
Krasean, Thomas Karl *historian*
Plater, William Marmaduke *English language educator, academic administrator*

Notre Dame
Bruns, Gerald L. *English literature educator*
Delaney, Cornelius Francis *philosophy educator*
De Santis, Vincent Paul *educator, historian*
Gabriel, Astrik Ladislas *educator, scholar*
Gutting, Gary Michael *philosophy educator*
MacIntyre, Alasdair *philosophy educator*
McInerny, Ralph Matthew *philosophy educator, author*
Mc Mullin, Ernan Vincent *philosophy educator*
Nugent, Walter Terry King *historian*
O'Rourke, William Andrew *English language educator, author*
Quinn, Philip Lawrence *philosophy educator*
Rosenberg, Charles Michael *art historian, educator*
Sayre, Kenneth Malcolm *philosophy educator*
Walicki, Andrzej Stanislaw *history educator*

Terre Haute
Baker, Ronald Lee *English educator*
Carmony, Marvin Dale *linguist, educator*
De Marr, Mary Jean *English language educator*

Valparaiso
Peters, Howard Nevin *foreign language educator*

West Lafayette
Contreni, John Joseph, Jr. *humanities educator*
Gottfried, Leon Albert *English language educator*
Leitch, Vincent Barry *literary studies educator*
Mc Bride, William Leon *philosopher, educator*
Reichard, Hugo Manley *English literature educator*
Rothenberg, Gunther Erich *history educator*
Woodman, Harold David *historian*

IOWA

Ames
Bruner, Charlotte Hughes *French language educator*
Dobson, John McCullough *historian*
Herrnstadt, Richard Lawrence *American literature educator*
Wilt, Alan Freese *history educator*

Cedar Falls
Maier, Donna Jane-Ellen *history educator*
Thompson, Thomas Henry *philosophy educator*
Wilson, Robley Conant, Jr. *English educator, editor, author*

Cedar Rapids
Lisio, Donald John *historian, educator*

Clinton
†Ollie, C(lifford) Arthur *history educator, state representative*

Davenport
Luzkow, Jack Lawrence *history educator, writer, consultant*

Grinnell
Kissane, James Donald *English literature educator*
Leggett, Glenn *former English language educator, academic administrator*
Wall, Joseph Frazier *historian, educator*

Iowa City
Addis, Laird Clark, Jr. *philosopher, educator, musician*
Andrews, Clarence Adelbert *historian, educator, writer, publisher*
Butchvarov, Panayot Krustev *philosophy educator*
Deligiorgis, Stavros G. *literature educator*
Gerber, John Christian *English language educator*
Goldstein, Jonathan Amos *ancient history and classics educator*
Hawley, Ellis Wayne *historian, educator*
Hornsby, Roger Allen *classics educator*
Kelley, Robert E. *English language educator*
Kerber, Linda Kaufman *historian, educator*
Klaus, Carl Hanna *English language educator*
Percas de Ponseti, Helena *foreign language and literature educator*
Persons, Stow Spaulding *historian, educator*
Raeburn, John Hay *English language educator*
Ringen, Catherine Oleson *linguistics educator*
Sayre, Robert Freeman *English educator*
Schoenbaum, David Leon *historian*
Solbrig, Ingeborg Hildegard *German literature educator*
Steele, Oliver *English educator*
Tomasini, Wallace J(ohn) *art historian, educator, university official*
Trank, Douglas Monty *rhetoric and speech communications educator*
Wachal, Robert Stanley *linguistics educator, consultant*

KANSAS

Dighton
Stanley, Ellen May *historian, consultant*

Lawrence
Alexander, John Thorndike *historian, educator*
Andrews, William Leake *English educator*
Cherniss, Michael David *English educator*
De George, Richard Thomas *philosophy educator*
Eldredge, Charles Child, III *art history educator*
Genova, Anthony Charles *philosophy educator*
†Hurst, George Cameron, III *history educator*
Li, Chu-Tsing *art history educator*
Mc Coy, Donald Richard *historian*
Phillips, Oliver Clyde, Jr. *classics educator*
Quinn, Dennis B. *English language and literature educator*
Robinson, Walter Stitt, Jr. *historian*
Saul, Norman Eugene *history educator*
Schoeck, Richard Joseph *English and humanities scholar*
Seaver, James Everett *historian, educator*
Spires, Robert Cecil *foreign language educator*
Stokstad, Marilyn Jane *art history educator, curator*
Tuttle, William McCullough, Jr. *history educator*
Woelfel, James Warren *philosophy educator*
Worth, George John *English literature educator*
Young, J(ohn) Michael *philosophy educator*

Manhattan
Higham, Robin *historian, editor, publisher*
McCulloh, John Marshall *historian*

Topeka
Wagnon, William Odell, Jr. *university professor*

University Of Kansas
†Kuznesof, Elizabeth Anne *history educator*

KENTUCKY

Bowling Green
Constans, Henry Philip, Jr. *philosopher, educator*
Minton, John Dean *historian, educator*

Danville
Newhall, David Sowle *history educator*

Frankfort
Gale, Steven Hershel *humanities educator*
Geddes, LaDonna McMurray *speech educator*

Highland Heights
Wallace, Harold Lew *historian, educator*

Lexington
Bryant, Joseph Allen, Jr. *English language educator*
Cone, Carl Bruce *history educator*
†Eller, Ronald D *historian, educator*
Madden, Edward Harry *philosopher, educator*
Perdue, Theda *history educator, author*
Perreiah, Alan Richard *philosophy educator*
Warth, Robert Douglas *history educator*

Louisville
Brockwell, Charles Wilbur, Jr. *history educator*
Ford, Gordon Buell, Jr. *English language and linguistics educator, author, hospital industry financial management executive*
Miller, Robert Henry *English educator*
St. Clair, Robert Neal *English language and linguistics educator*

Murray
Pogue, Forrest Carlisle *retired historian*

Richmond
Burkhart, Robert Edward *English language educator*
Shearon, Forrest Bedford *humanities educator*
Witt, Robert Wayne *English educator*

Versailles
Freehling, William Wilhartz *historian, educator*

LOUISIANA

Baton Rouge
Arceneaux, William *historian, educator, association official*
Campbell, Lyle Richard *linguistics educator*
Cooper, William James, Jr. *history educator*
Duffy, John *history educator*
Edgeworth, Robert Joseph *classical languages educator*
Glissant, Edouard Mathieu *French language educator, writer*
Haynes, Leonard L., Jr. *philosophy educator, clergyman*
Olney, James *English language educator*
Roider, Karl Andrew, Jr. *history educator, university dean*
Smith, David Jeddie *American literature educator*
Stanford, Donald Elwin *English educator, editor, poet, critic*

Eunice
Rogers, Donald Onis *language educator*

Hammond
Thorburn, James Alexander *humanities educator*

Lafayette
Nolan, Paul Thomas *retired English and humanities educator*
Poe, (Lydia) Virginia *reading educator*

New Orleans
Ambrose, Stephen Edward *history educator, author*
Cohen, Joseph *English literature educator, writer, business owner*
Greenleaf, Richard Edward *Latin American history educator*
Luza, Radomir Vaclav *historian, educator*
Paolini, Gilbert *literature and science educator*
Poesch, Jessie Jean *art historian*
Reck, Andrew Joseph *philosophy educator*
Roberts, Louise Nisbet *philosopher*
Sellin, Eric *linguist, poet, educator*
Thompson, Annie Laura *foreign language educator*
Woodward, Ralph Lee, Jr. *historian, educator*

Pineville
Howell, Thomas *history educator*

Ruston
Halliburton, Lloyd *Romance philology educator*

Thibodaux
Swetman, Glenn Robert *English language educator, poet*

MAINE

Brunswick
Hodge, James Lee *German language educator*

Orono
Hatlen, Burton Norval *English educator*
Ives, Edward Dawson *folklore educator*

Portland
†Miller, Elizabeth Jane *historian*

Waterville
Bassett, Charles Walker *English language educator*
Hudson, Yeager *philosophy educator, minister*

MARYLAND

Baltimore
Achinstein, Peter Jacob *philosopher, educator*
Baldwin, John Wesley *history educator*
Cacossa, Anthony Alexander *Romance languages educator*
Cohen, Warren I. *history educator*
Cooper, Jerrold Stephen *historian, educator*
Fleishman, Avrom Hirsch *English educator*
Greene, Jack Phillip *historian, educator*
Higham, John *history educator*
Hillers, Delbert Roy *Near East language educator*
Irwin, John Thomas *humanities educator*
Johnson, Michael Paul *history educator*
Judson, Horace Freeland *history of science, writer, educator*
Kessler, Herbert Leon *art historian, educator*
Kurth, Lieselotte *foreign language educator*
Lidtke, Vernon LeRoy *history educator*
Luck, Georg Hans Bhawani *classics educator*
McCarter, P(ete) Kyle, Jr. *Near Eastern studies educator*
Nägele, Rainer *German and comparative literary educator*
Natividad, Evangelia de Hitta *Spanish educator, court interpreter, translator*
Nichols, Stephen George *romance languages educator*
Paulson, Ronald Howard *English and humanities educator*
Peirce, Carol Marshall *English educator*
†Pocock, John Greville Agard *historian, educator*
Ranum, Orest Allen *historian, educator*
Russell-Wood, Anthony John R. *history educator*
Schneewind, Jerome Borges *philosophy educator*
†Walker, Mack *historian, educator*
Ziff, Larzer *English language educator*

Bethesda
†Benson, Elizabeth Polk *Pre-Columbian art specialist*
Curtis, Mark Hubert *historian, former educational association executive*
Duncan, Francis *historian, government official*
Highfill, Philip Henry, Jr. *retired language educator*

Catonsville
Loerke, William Carl *art history educator*

Chestertown
Trout, Charles Hathaway *historian, educator*

Chevy Chase
Goodwin, Ralph Roger *historian, editor*
Key, Kerim Kami *historian, educator*

Chevy Chase Village
Durant, Frederick Clark, III *aerospace history and space art consultant*

Cockeysville Hunt Valley
Peirce, Brooke *English language educator*

College Park
Brown, Peter Gilbert *philosopher, educator*
Dietrich, Martha Jane (Martha Jane Shultz) *genealogist*

Fuegi, John *comparative literature educator, author, filmmaker*
Harlan, Louis Rudolph *history educator, writer*
Holton, William Milne *English language and literature educator*
Lightfoot, David William *linguistics educator*
Olson, Keith Waldemar *history educator*
Oster, Rose Marie Gunhild *foreign language professional, educator*
†Panichas, George Andrew *English language educator, critic, editor*
Pasch, Alan *philosophy educator*
Russell, John David *English literature educator*
†Sagoff, Mark *philosopher, educator, academic administrator*
Yaney, George *history educator*

Columbia
Butcher, (Charles) Philip *English language educator, author*

Darnestown
Knox, Bernard MacGregor Walker *retired classics educator*

Lusby
†Eshelman, Ralph Ellsworth *historian, consultant*

Myersville
Blake, John Ballard *retired historian*

Rockville
Hewlett, Richard Greening *historian*

Saint Michaels
Marshall, Robert Gerald *language educator*

Severna Park
Schick, Edgar Brehob *German literature educator*

Silver Spring
Calinger, Ronald Steve *historian*
Cole, Wayne Stanley *historian, educator*
Doherty, William Thomas, Jr. *historian, retired educator*
Edwards, Kamala Doris *humanities educator*
Papas, Irene Kalandros *English educator, author, poet*

Solomons
Samuels, Sheldon Wilfred *philosophy educator*

Sparks
Suarez-Murias, Marguerite C. *retired language and literature educator*

Towson
Baker, Jean Harvey *history educator*

MASSACHUSETTS

Amherst
Bagg, Robert Ely *English educator, poet*
Baker, Lynne Rudder *philosophy educator*
Bezucha, Robert Joseph *history educator*
Chappell, Vere Claiborne *philosophy educator*
Creed, Robert Payson, Sr. *literature educator*
Hernon, Joseph Martin, Jr. *history educator*
Kinney, Arthur Frederick *literary history educator, author, editor*
Oates, Stephen Baery *history educator*
Partee, Barbara Hall *linguist, educator*
Porter, Dennis Dudley *foreign language educator*
Tager, Jack *historian, educator*
Wideman, John Edgar *English literature educator, novelist*
Wolff, Robert Paul *philosophy educator*
Wyman, David Sword *historian, educator*

Belmont
Buckley, Jerome Hamilton *English language educator*

Boston
†Brandt, Allan M. *medical history educator*
Bromsen, Maury Austin *historian, bibliographer, antiquarian bookseller*
Cardona, Rodolfo *Spanish language and literature educator*
Foss, Clive Frank Wilson *history educator*
Hartmann, Edward George *historian, educator*
Henry, DeWitt Pawling, II *creative writing educator, writer, arts administrator*
Hintikka, Jaakko *philosopher, educator*
Kleiner, Fred Scott *art history and archaeology educator, editor*
Langer, Lawrence Lee *English educator, writer*
Lowry, Bates *art historian, museum director*
Mc Carthy, Joseph Michael *historian*
Menyuk, Paula *developmental psycholinguistics educator*
Miller, Naomi *art historian*
Neville, Robert Cummings *philosophy and religion educator*
Phillips, William *English language educator, editor, author*
Riley, Stephen Thomas *historian, librarian*
Weitzman, Arthur Joshua *English educator*
Wermuth, Paul Charles *retired educator*
†Wiseman, James Richard *classicist, archaeologist, educator*

Brookline
Mc Cormick, Thomas Julian *art history educator*
Wax, Bernard *historian, research consultant, lecturer*

Cambridge
Alexiou, Margaret Beatrice *Greek studies educator*
Anderson-Imbert, Enrique *retired Hispanic literature educator, author*
†Appiah, Kwame Anthony *philosophy educator*
Badian, Ernst *history educator*
Bailyn, Bernard *historian, educator*
Barnet, Sylvan *educator*
Bate, Walter Jackson *English literature educator*
Block, Ned *philosophy educator*
Bolster, Arthur Stanley, Jr. *history educator*
Boolos, George Stephen *philosophy educator*
Bottiglia, William Filbert *humanities educator*
Brustein, Robert Sanford *English language educator, theatre director, author*
Buell, Lawrence Ingalls *English language educator*
Cavell, Stanley *philosophy educator, writer*
Chomsky, Avram Noam *linguistics and philosophy educator*
Clausen, Wendell Vernon *classics educator*
Craig, Albert Morton *Asian studies educator*
Cross, Frank Moore, Jr. *foreign language educator*
Dreben, Burton Spencer *philosopher,educator*
Dunn, Charles William *educator, author*
Dupree, Anderson Hunter *historian, educator*
Dyck, Arthur James *ethicist, educator*
Fanger, Donald Lee *Slavic language and literature educator*
Fleming, Donald Harnish *educator, historian*
Flier, Michael Stephen *Slavic languages educator*
Ford, Franklin Lewis *history educator, historian*
Ford, Patrick Kildea *Celtic studies educator*
Frye, Richard Nelson *historian, educator*
Gates, Henry Louis, Jr. *English language educator*
Goldfarb, Warren (David) *philosophy educator*
†Grabowicz, George Gregory *Slavic studies educator*
Graham, Loren Raymond *historian, educator*
Graubard, Stephen Richards *history educator, editor*
Guthke, Karl Siegfried *foreign language educator*
Halle, Morris *linguist, educator*
Hanan, Patrick Dewes *foreign language professional, educator*
Handlin, Oscar *historian, educator*
Heimert, Alan Edward *humanities educator*
Henrichs, Albert Maximinus *classicist, educator*
Hibbett, Howard Scott *foreign language professional, educator*
Iriye, Akira *historian, educator*
Jones, Robert Emmet *French language educator*
Kalb, Marvin *public policy and government educator*
Keenan, Edward Louis *history educator*
Keyser, Samuel Jay *linguistics educator, university official*
Lee, Leo Ou-fan *Far Eastern languages educator*
Lockwood, Lewis Henry *musicologist, educator*
Lunt, Horace Gray *linguist, educator*
MacMaster, Robert Ellsworth *historian, educator*
Mahoney, Thomas Henry Donald *historian, educator, government official*
Maier, Charles Steven *history educator*
†Malmstad, John Earl *Slavic languages and literature educator*
Marx, Leo *retired American cultural history educator*
Mazlish, Bruce *educator, historian*
Nozick, Robert *philosophy educator, author*
Nykrog, Per *French literature educator*
O'Neil, Wayne *linguist, educator*
Ozment, Steven *historian, educator*
Pian, Rulan Chao *musicologist, scholar*
Pipes, Richard (Edgar) *historian, educator*
Preyer, Robert Otto *English literature educator*
Quine, Willard Van Orman *philosophy educator*
Schama, Simon *historian, educator, author*
Scheffler, Israel *philosopher, educator*
Segal, Charles Paul *classics educator, author*
Sevcenko, Ihor *history and literature educator*
Shinagel, Michael *English literature educator*
Simon, Eckehard (Peter) *foreign language educator*
Smith, Merritt Roe *history educator*
Southern, Eileen (Mrs. Joseph Southern) *music educator*
Sulloway, Frank Jones *historian*
Tarrant, R(ichard) J(ohn) *classicist, educator*
Teeter, Karl van Duyn *retired linguistic scientist, educator*
Thernstrom, Stephan Albert *historian, educator*
Thorburn, David *literature educator*
Tu, Wei-Ming *historian, philosopher, writer*
Vanger, Milton Isadore *history educator*
Vendler, Helen Hennessy *literature educator, poetry critic*
Vermeule, Emily Townsend (Mrs. Cornelius C. Vermeule, III) *classicist, educator*
Ward, John Milton *music educator*
†West, Cornel *philosopher, writer*
Winner, Thomas G. *foreign literature educator*
Wolff, Cynthia Griffin *humanities educator, author*

Chestnut Hill
Barth, John Robert *English educator, priest*
Blanchette, Oliva *philosophy educator*
Casper, Leonard Ralph *American literature educator*
Duhamel, Pierre Albert *English language professional*
Mahoney, John L. *English literature educator*
Valette, Rebecca Marianne *Romance languages educator*

Dedham
Schork, Rudolph Joseph, Jr. *philologist*

Lowell
Shirvani, Hamid *philosophy educator, university dean, critic*

Medford
Bedau, Hugo Adam *philosophy educator*
Caviness, Madeline Harrison *art history educator, researcher*
Ch'en, Li-li *Chinese language and literature educator, writer*
Dennett, Daniel Clement *philosopher, author, educator*
Laurent, Pierre-Henri *history educator*
Simches, Seymour Oliver *language educator*
Wechsler, Judith Glatzer *art historian, filmmaker, educator*

Natick
Current, Richard Nelson *historian, educator*

Needham
Burrell, Sidney Alexander *history educator*

North Dartmouth
Dace, Tish *drama educator*
†Yoken, Mel B. *foreign language educator, author*

Northampton
Elkins, Stanley Maurice *historian, educator*
Ellis, Frank Hale *English literature professional*
Hoyt, Nelly Schargo (Mrs. N. Deming Hoyt) *history educator*
Little, Lester Knox *historian, educator*
Murdock, Mary-Elizabeth *history educator*
Pickrel, Paul *English educator*
Smith, Malcolm Barry Estes *philosophy educator, lawyer*
Vaget, Hans Rudolf *language professional, educator*
von Klemperer, Klemens *historian, educator*

Norton
Dahl, Curtis *English literature educator*
Olson, Roberta Jeanne Marie *art historian, author, educator*
Taylor, Robert Sundling *English educator, art critic*

Randolph
Morrissey, Edmond Joseph *classical philologist*

Rockport
Delakas, Daniel Liudviko *retired foreign language educator*
Walen, Harry Leonard *historian, lecturer, author*

Rutland
Cormick, Albina *foreign language educator*

South Hadley
Berek, Peter *English educator*
Brownlow, Frank Walsh *English language educator*
Ciruti, Joan Estelle *Spanish language and literature educator*
Farnham, Anthony Edward *English language educator*
Herbert, Robert Louis *art history educator*
Johnson, Richard August *English language educator*
Mazzocco, Angelo *language educator*
Quinn, Betty Nye *former classics educator*
Robin, Richard Shale *philosophy educator*

South Yarmouth
Benoit, Leroy James *language educator*

Springfield
Porter, Burton Frederick *philosophy educator, author*

Waltham
Black, Eugene Charlton *historian, educator*
Harth, Erica *French language and comparative literature educator*
Jackendoff, Ray Saul *linguistics educator*
Marshall, Robert Lewis *musicologist, educator*
Staves, Susan *English educator*
Wasserstein, Bernard Mano Julius *historian*

Watertown
Goodheart, Eugene *English language educator*
Rivers, Wilga Marie *foreign language educator*

Wellesley
Ruiz-de-Conde, Justina *retired foreign language educator*

West Barnstable
Corsa, Helen Storm *language professional*

Weston
Higgins, Sister Therese *English educator, former college president*

Williamstown
Bahlman, Dudley Ward Rhodes *history educator*
Dalzell, Robert Fenton, Jr. *historian*
Dew, Charles Burgess *historian, educator*
Graver, Lawrence Stanley *English language professional*
Hyde, John Michael *history educator*
Oakley, Francis Christopher *history educator, former college president*
Payne, Harry Charles *historian, educator*
Pistorius, George *language educator*
†Raab, Lawrence Edward *English educator*
Rudolph, Frederick *history educator*
Stamelman, Richard Howard *French and humanities educator*
Waite, Robert George Leeson *history educator*

Winchester
Smith, Whitney *vexillologist*

Worcester
Billias, George Athan *history educator*
Von Laue, Theodore Herman *historian, educator*
Zeugner, John Finn *history educator, writer*

MICHIGAN

Ann Arbor
Aldridge, John Watson *English language educator, author*
Amann, Peter Henry *historian, educator*
Arthos, John *English language educator*
Bailey, David Roy Shackleton *classics educator*
Bailey, Richard Weld *English educator*
Baker, Sheridan *English educator, author*
Becker, Marvin Burton *historian*
Blotner, Joseph Leo *English language educator*
Bornstein, George Jay *literary educator*
Brandt, Richard Booker *former philosophy educator*
Brown, Deming Bronson *Slavic languages and literature educator*
†Burbank, Jane Richardson *Russian and European studies educator*
Chambers, Leigh Ross *French language educator*
Cowen, Roy Chadwell, Jr. *German language educator*
Crawford, Richard *musicology educator*
Curley, Edwin Munson *philosophy educator*
†Danly, Robert Lyons *Japanese studies educator, author, translator*
D'Arms, John Haughton *classics educator, university dean*
Eby, Cecil DeGrotte *English language educator, writer*
Eisenberg, Marvin *art history educator*
Eisenstein, Elizabeth Lewisohn *historian, educator*
Fader, Daniel Nelson *English language educator*
Feuerwerker, Albert *history educator*
Forsyth, Ilene Haering *art historian*
Gomez, Luis Oscar *Asian and religious studies educator*
Hackett, Roger Fleming *history educator*
Knott, John Ray, Jr. *language professional, educator*
Koenen, Ludwig *classical studies educator*
Konigsberg, Ira *film and literature educator, writer*
McCarus, Ernest Nasseph *language educator*
McDougal, Stuart Yeatman *comparative literature educator, author*
Mersereau, John, Jr. *Slavic languages and literatures educator*
Morgan, Raleigh, Jr. *linguistics educator*
Morris, Phyllis Sutton *philosophy educator*
Munro, Donald Jacques *philosopher, educator*
Murphey, Rhoads *history educator*
Pulgram, Ernst *linguist, philologist, Romance and classical linguistics educator, writer*
Starr, Chester G. *history educator*
Steinhoff, William Richard *English literature educator*
Stolz, Benjamin Armond *foreign language educator*
Super, Robert Henry *English educator*
Trautmann, Thomas Roger *history and anthropology educator*
Weisbuch, Robert Alan *English educator*
Woodcock, Leonard *humanities educator, former ambassador*

Berrien Springs
Schwarz, Richard William *historian, educator*
Waller, John Oscar *English language educator*

Bloomfield Hills
Bonner, Thomas Neville *history and higher education educator*

Detroit
Abt, Jeffrey *art and art history educator*
Kowalczyk, Richard Leon *English language educator, technical writing consultant*
Schindler, Marvin Samuel *foreign language educator*
Small, Melvin *history educator*
van der Marck, Jan *art historian*
Williamson, Marilyn Lammert *English educator, university adminstrator*

East Lansing
Anderson, David Daniel *retired humanities educator, writer, editor*
Appel, John J. *history educator*
Dulai, Surjit Singh *English literature educator, literary critic, editor*
Eadie, John William *history educator*
Falk, Julia S. *linguistics educator*
Fisher, Alan Washburn *historian, educator*
Greer, Thomas Hoag *historian, educator*
Grimes, Margaret Whitehurst *medievalist, educator*
Huzar, Eleanor Goltz *history educator*
Kronegger, Maria Elisabeth *French and comparative literature educator*
Mansour, George P. *Spanish language and literature educator*
Paananen, Victor Niles *English educator*
Platt, Franklin Dewitt *history educator*
Pollack, Norman *history educator*
Silverman, Henry Jacob *history educator*
Whallon, William *literature educator*

Eastpointe
Humita, Tiberius Ted *languages educator*

Flint
Heywood, Robert Wales *history educator*

Grand Rapids
Hoekema, David Andrew *philosophy educator, academic administrator*

Grosse Pointe
Peters, Thomas Robert *writer, educator*

Harbert
Morrissette, Bruce Archer *Romance languages educator*

Hillsdale
Castel, Albert Edward *history educator*

Holland
Quimby, Robert Sherman *retired humanities educator*

Huntington Woods
Gutmann, Joseph *art history educator*

Jackson
Feldmann, Judith G. *language professional, educator*

Kalamazoo
Breisach, Ernst A. *historian, educator*
Gordon, Jaimy *English educator*
Gregory, Ross *history educator, author*
Light, Timothy *linguistics, religious and Asian studies educator, academic administrator*
Maier, Paul Luther *history educator, author, chaplain*
Moritz, Edward *educator, historian*
Waring, Walter Weyler *English language educator*

Lansing
Harvey, Joanne H. *genealogist*

Livonia
Holtzman, Roberta Lee *foreign language educator*

Okemos
Huddleston, Eugene Lee *retired American studies educator*

Rochester
Thomas, S. Bernard *history educator*

Rochester Hills
Matthews, George Tennyson *history educator*

Southfield
Papazian, Dennis Richard *history educator, political commentator*
Stern, Guy *educator, writer*

Sterling Heights
Ice, Orva Lee, Jr. *history educator*

Ypsilanti
Perkins, Bradford *history educator*

MINNESOTA

Bemidji
Paul, Sherman *retired English language educator*

Duluth
Fischer, Roger Adrian *history educator*
Jankofsky, Klaus Peter *medieval studies educator*
Schroeder, Fred Erich Harald *humanities educator*

Minneapolis
Anderson, Chester Grant *English educator*
Bales, Kent Roslyn *English language educator*
Browne, Donald Roger *speech communication educator*
Campbell, Karlyn Kohrs *speech and communication educator*
Conley, Tom Clark *literature educator*
†Eidelman, Terry *philosophy educator, publisher*
Erickson, Gerald Meyer *classical studies educator*
Farah, Caesar Elie *Middle Eastern and Islamic studies educator*
Firchow, Evelyn Scherabon *German educator, author*
Firchow, Peter Edgerly *language professional, educator, author*
Griffin, Edward Michael *language professional, educator*
Kohlstedt, Sally Gregory *history educator*
Layton, Edwin Thomas, Jr. *science and technology history educator, writer*
Lehmberg, Stanford Eugene *historian, educator*
Leppert, Richard David *humanities educator*
McDonald, William Andrew *classics educator*
Noonan, Thomas Schaub *history educator, Russian studies educator*
†Norberg, Arthur Lawrence, Jr. *historian, physicist educator*
Rath, R. John *historian, educator*
Ross, Donald, Jr. *English language educator, university administrator*
Scott, Robert Lee *speech educator*
Sonkowsky, Robert Paul *classicist, educator, actor*
Tracy, James Donald *historian*
Vecoli, Rudolph John *history educator*
Weiss, Gerhard Hans *German language educator*

Minnetonka
Nagel, Paul Chester *historian, writer, lecturer*

Moorhead
Anderson, Jerry Maynard *speech educator*
Coomber, James Elwood *English language educator*

Northfield
Clark, Clifford Edward, Jr. *history educator*
Haworth, Dale Keith *art history educator, gallery director*
Mason, Perry Carter *philosophy educator*
Soule, George Alan *literature educator*

Saint Paul
Kane, Patricia Lanegran *language professional, educator*
Mather, Richard Burroughs *retired Chinese language and literature educator*
Murray, Peter Bryant *English language educator*
Stewart, James Brewer *historian, author, college administrator*
Stewart, Melville Yorke *philosophy educator*
Weiner, Carl Dorian *historian*

Wayzata
Judkins, Donald Ward *retired banker, art historian*

MISSISSIPPI

Biloxi
Hagood, Annabel Dunham *speech communication educator, communication consultant*

Cleveland
Cash, William McKinley *history educator*

Clinton
Bigelow, Martha Mitchell *retired historian*

Columbus
Stringer, Mary Evelyn *art historian, educator*

Hattiesburg
Gonzales, John Edmond *history educator*
Sims, James Hylbert *English educator, former university administrator*

Mississippi State
Donaghy, Henry James *English literature educator, academic administrator*
Lowery, Charles Douglas *history educator, academic administrator*
Parrish, William Earl *history educator*
Shillingsburg, Peter LeRoy *English language educator*
Wiltrout, Ann Elizabeth *foreign language educator*

Rose Hill
Young, Thomas Daniel *retired humanities educator, author*

Starkville
Wolverton, Robert Earl *classics educator*

University
Jordan, Winthrop Donaldson *historian, educator*
Kiger, Joseph Charles *history educator*

MISSOURI

Chesterfield
Bowling, William Glasgow *language professional, educator*

Columbia
Alexander, Thomas Benjamin *history educator*
Anderson, Donald Kennedy, Jr. *English educator*
Bien, Joseph Julius *philosophy educator*
Fulweiler, Howard Wells *language professional*
Geiger, Louis George *historian*
Goodrich, James William *historian, association executive*
Jones, William McKendrey *language professional, educator*
Lago, Mary McClelland *English language educator, author*
Mullen, Edward John, Jr. *Spanish language educator*
Overby, Osmund Rudolf *art historian, educator*
Reid, Loren Dudley *speech educator*
Strickland, Arvarh Eunice *history educator*
Timberlake, Charles Edward *history educator*

Kansas City
Cappon, Alexander Patterson *English language educator*
Hoffmann, Donald *architectural historian*
†McKinley, James C. *English educator, editor*
Miller, Patricia Elizabeth Cleary *American and British literature educator*

Liberty
Harriman, Richard Lee *English language educator*

Marshall
Gruber, Loren Charles *English language educator, writer*

Saint Charles
Barnett, Howard Albert *English language educator*

Saint Louis
Bagley, Mary Carol *educator, writer, broadcaster*
Barmann, Lawrence Francis *history educator*
Benberry, Cuesta Ray *historian*
Berthoff, Rowland Tappan *historian, educator*
Bourke, Vernon Joseph *philosophy educator*
Boyd, Robert Cotton *English educator*
Brown, Virginia Suggs *language arts educator, consultant*
Collins, Margaret Elizabeth *librarian*
Davis, Richard Whitlock *history educator, writer*
Herbert, Kevin Barry John *classics educator*
Hexter, Jack H. *historian, educator*
Krukowski, Lucian *philosophy educator, artist*
Lacy, Norris Joiner *French language and literature educator*
Morrow, Ralph Ernest *historian, educator*
Ruland, Richard Eugene *English and American literature educator, critic, literary historian*
Sale, William Merritt *classicist, educator*
Schwarz, Egon *humanities and German language educator, author, literary critic*
Shea, Daniel Bartholomew, Jr. *English language educator, actor*
Spector, Stanley *foreign language educator*
Ullian, Joseph Silbert *philosophy educator*
Watson, Richard Allan *philosophy educator, writer*
Wellman, Carl Pierce *philosophy educator*
Wheeler, Burton M. *literature educator, higher education consultant, college dean*
Wu, Nelson Ikon *art history educator, author, artist*

MONTANA

Billings
Small, Lawrence Farnsworth *history educator*

Missoula
Weber, Brom *literature educator*

NEBRASKA

Hastings
McEwen, Larry Burdette *retired English language arts and theatre arts educator*

Lincoln
Bailey, Dudley *English educator*
Crompton, Louis William *English literature educator*
Leinieks, Valdis *classicist, educator*
Rawley, James Albert *history educator*
Sawyer, Robert McLaran *history educator*
Stover, John Ford *railroad historian, educator*

Omaha
Bergquist, Gordon Neil *English educator*
Cunningham, William Francis, Jr. *English language educator, university administrator*
Dougherty, Charles John *philosophy and medical ethics educator*
Horning, Ross Charles, Jr. *historian, educator*

NEVADA

Las Vegas
Adams, Charles Lynford *English language educator*
Malek, James Stanley *language professional*
Stevens, Arthur Wilber, Jr. *English language educator, writer, editor*

NEW HAMPSHIRE

Alstead
Lyon, Bryce Dale *historian, educator*

Durham
Hapgood, Robert Derry *English educator*
†Rouman, John Christ *Classics educator*
Ulrich, Laurel Thatcher *historian, educator*
Voll, John Obert *history educator*

Hanover
Arndt, Walter Werner *Slavic scholar, linguist, writer, translator*
Bien, Peter Adolph *English language educator, author*
Daniell, Jere Rogers, II *history educator, consultant*
Doenges, Norman Arthur *classics educator*
Doney, Willis Frederick *philosophy educator*
Gert, Bernard *philosopher, educator*
Mansell, Darrel Lee, Jr. *English educator*
Oxenhandler, Neal *language educator, writer*
Parton, James *historian*
Penner, Hans Henry *historian*
Russell, Robert Hilton *romance languages and literature educator*
Scher, Steven Paul *literature educator*
Sheldon, Richard Robert *Russian language and literature educator*
Wood, Charles Tuttle *history educator*

Laconia
Heald, Bruce Day *English and music educator, historian*

Madbury
Bruce, Robert Vance *historian, educator*

Nashua
Light, James Forest *English educator*

New Castle
Silva, Joseph Donald *English language educator*

Rindge
†Riley, William Allen *history educator, state legislator*

Strafford
Simic, Charles *English language educator, poet*

NEW JERSEY

Bradley Beach
Unger, Irwin *historian, educator*

Camden
Showalter, English, Jr. *French educator*

Cape May
Lassner, Franz George *educator*

Englewood
Beer, Jeanette Mary Scott *foreign language educator*

Frenchtown
Scaglione, Aldo Domenico *language educator*

Highland Park
Pane, Remigio Ugo *Romance languages educator*

Madison
Knox, John, Jr. *philosopher, educator*
Mc Mullen, Edwin Wallace, Jr. *English language educator*

New Brunswick
Gardner, Lloyd Calvin, Jr. *history educator*
Gillette, William *historian, educator*
Grob, Gerald N. *historian, educator*
Hartman, Mary S. *historian*
Kelley, Donald Reed *historian*
Levine, George Lewis *English language educator, literature critic*
†Lewis, David Levering *history educator*
Mc Cormick, Richard Patrick *history educator*
Morrison, Karl Frederick *history educator*
Moynahan, Julian Lane *English language educator, author*
O'Neill, William Lawrence *history educator*
Poirier, Richard *English educator, literary critic*
Reed, James Wesley *social historian, educator*
Stimpson, Catharine Roslyn *English language educator, writer*

Newark
Crew, Louie (Li Min Hua) *language professional, educator*
Estrin, Herman Albert *English language educator*
†Schweizer, Karl Wolfgang *author, historian*
Vevier, Charles *historian, educator, consultant, university administrator*

Princeton
Aarsleff, Hans *linguistics educator*
Beeners, Wilbert John *speech professional, minister*
Benacerraf, Paul Joseph Salomon *philosophy educator*
Bowersock, Glen Warren *historian*
Brombert, Victor Henri *literature educator, author*
Brown, Leon Carl *history educator*
†Cassidy, Brendan Francis *art educator and director*
Champlin, Edward James *classics educator*
Clagett, Marshall *historian, educator*
Coffin, David Robbins *art historian, educator*
Corngold, Stanley Alan *German and comparative literature educator, writer*
Curschmann, Michael Johann Hendrik *German language and literature educator*
de Grazia, Sebastian *political philosopher, author*
Finch, Jeremiah Stanton *English language educator*
Fleming, John Vincent *humanities educator*
George, Emery Edward *foreign language and studies educator*
Goheen, Robert Francis *classicist, educator, former ambassador*
Habicht, Christian Herbert *history educator*
Harman, Gilbert Helms *philosophy educator*
Hollander, Robert B., Jr. *Romance languages educator*
Hunter, Sam *art historian, educator*
Hynes, Samuel *English language educator, author*
Itzkowitz, Norman *history educator*
Jeffery, Peter Grant *musicologist, fine arts educator*
Jordan, William Chester *history educator*
Keeley, Edmund LeRoy *English, creative writing and modern Greek studies educator, author*
Kennan, George Frost *historian, educator, former ambassador,*
Knoepflmacher, Ulrich Camillus *literature educator*
Lange, Victor *language educator, author*
Lewis, Bernard *Near Eastern studies educator*
Lewis, David Kellogg *philosopher, educator*
Litz, Arthur Walton, Jr. *English language educator*
Ludwig, Richard Milton *English literature educator, librarian*
Mahoney, Michael Sean *history educator*
Marks, John Henry *Near Eastern studies educator*
Mc Pherson, James Munro *history educator*
Miner, Earl Roy *English educator*
Nehamas, Alexander *philosophy educator*
Palmer, Robert Roswell *historian, educator*
Paret, Peter *historian*
Peterson, Willard James *Chinese history educator*
Rabb, Theodore K. *historian, educator*
Rigolot, François *French literature educator, literary critic*
Rodgers, Daniel Tracy *history educator*
Schofield, Robert E(dwin) *history educator, academic administrator*
Schorske, Carl Emil *historian, educator*
Setton, Kenneth M. *historian, educator*
Shimizu, Yoshiaki *art historian, educator*
Showalter, Elaine *humanities educator*
Steiner, Robert Lisle *language consultant*
Stone, Lawrence *historian*
Townsend, Charles Edward *Slavic languages educator*
Twitchett, Denis Crispin *historian*
Uitti, Karl David *language educator*
White, Morton Gabriel *philosopher, author*
Wilson, Margaret Dauler *philosophy educator*
Woolf, Harry *historian, educator*
Ziolkowski, Theodore Joseph *comparative literature educator*

Ridgewood
Molnar, Thomas *educator, author*

Scotch Plains
Edwards, Thomas Robert, Jr. *language professional, investment company executive*

Short Hills
Broder, Patricia Janis *art historian, writer*

South Orange
Reilly, George Love Anthony *history educator*

Teaneck
Gordon, Lois Goldfein *English language educator*
Rudy, Willis *historian*
Williams, John A. *English educator, author*

Wayne
O'Connor, John Morris, III *philosophy educator*

West Orange
Osborne, John Walter *historian, educator, author*

NEW MEXICO

Albuquerque
Bahm, Archie John *philosophy educator*
Kutvirt, Duda Chytilova (Ruzena) *scientific translator*
MacCurdy, Raymond Ralph, Jr. *modern language educator*
Nash, Gerald David *historian*
Sturm, Fred Gillette *philosopher, educator*

Corrales
Martin, Harold Clark *humanities educator*

Placitas
Forrest, Suzanne Sims *research historian*

Portales
Matheny, Robert Lavesco *history educator, former university president*

Santa Fe
McLaughlin, Ted John *speech educator*

Taos
Bacon, Wallace Alger *speech communications educator, author*

Univ Of New Mexico
Thorson, James Llewellyn *English language educator*

NEW YORK

Albany
Beharriell, Frederick John *German and comparative literature educator*
Creegan, Robert Francis *philosophy educator*
Donovan, Robert Alan *English educator*
Eckstein, Jerome *philosopher, educator*
Kekes, John *philosopher, educator*
Lenardon, Robert Joseph *classics educator*
Moelleken, Wolfgang Wilfried *Germanic languages and literature educator*
Pohlsander, Hans Achim *classics educator*
Purves, Alan Carroll *English language educator, education educator*
Reese, William Lewis *philosophy educator*
Roberts, Warren Errol *history educator*
Zacek, Joseph Frederick *history educator, international studies consultant, East European affairs specialist*

Alfred
Potter, Barrett George *historian, educator*

Amherst
Gracia, Jorge Jesus Emiliano *philosopher, educator*

Annandale
†Achebe, Chinua *humanist, educator*

Annandale On Hudson
Ashbery, John Lawrence *language educator, poet, playwright*
Frank, Elizabeth *English literature educator, author*

Binghamton
Block, Haskell Mayer *humanities educator*
Gaddis Rose, Marilyn *comparative literature educator, translator*
Kessler, Milton *English language educator, poet*
Sklar, Kathryn Kish *historian, educator*
Stein, George Henry *historian, educator, administrator*

Briarcliff Manor
Leiser, Burton Myron *philosophy and law educator*

Brockport
Marcus, Robert D. *historian, educator*

Stack, George Joseph *philosophy educator*

Bronx
Ansbro, John Joseph *philosophy educator*
Bowers, Francis Robert *literature educator*
Brush, Craig Balcombe *French language and computer educator*
Hallett, Charles Arthur, Jr. *English and humanities educator*
Himmelberg, Robert Franklin *historian, educator*
Karp, Abraham Joseph *historian, rabbi, educator*
Macklin, Ruth *bioethics educator*
†Tusiani, Joseph *foreign language educator, author*
Ultan, Lloyd *historian*
Zeichner, Oscar *historian, educator*

Bronxville
Forester, Erica Simms *decorative arts historian, consultant, educator*
Krupat, Arnold *English educator, writer*
Peters, Sarah Whitaker *art historian, writer, lecturer*
Randall, Francis Ballard *historian, educator, writer*
Swerdlow, Amy *historian, educator, writer*

Brooklyn
Ashley, Leonard Raymond Nelligan *English language educator*
Blasi, Alberto *Romance languages educator, writer*
Brownstone, Paul Lotan *emeritus speech communications and drama educator*
Contino, Rosalie Helene *English educator, costume designer*
Everdell, William Romeyn *humanities educator*
Flam, Jack Donald *art historian, educator*
Hoogenboom, Ari Arthur *historian, educator*
Jofen, Jean *foreign language educator*
King, Margaret Leah *history educator*
Olson, Robert Goodwin *philosophy educator*
†Spector, Robert Donald *language professional, educator*

Buffalo
Allen, William Sheridan *history educator*
Drew, Fraser Bragg Robert *English language educator*
Fiedler, Leslie Aaron *English educator, actor, author*
Hare, Peter Hewitt *philosophy educator*
Iggers, Georg Gerson *history educator*
Kurtz, Paul *philosopher, educator, publisher*
Levine, George Richard *English language educator*
Milligan, John Drane *historian, educator*
Payne, Frances Anne *literature educator, researcher*
Peradotto, John Joseph *classics educator, editor*
Richards, David Gleyre *German educator*
Riepe, Dale Maurice *philosopher, writer, educator, Asian art dealer*
Saveth, Edward Norman *history educator*
Wolck, Wolfgang Hans-Joachim *linguist, educator*

Canton
Goldberg, Rita Maria *foreign language educator*

Clinton
Blackwood, Russell Thorn, III *philosophy educator*
Wagner, Frederick Reese *language professional*

Cortland
Kaminsky, Alice Richkin *English language educator*

Delmar
Odenkirchen, Carl Josef *educator Romance languages and literatures*

East Berne
Grenander, M. E. *English language educator, critic*

Flushing
Hirshson, Stanley Philip *history educator*
Lamont, Rosette Clementine *Romance languages educator, theatre journalist, translator*
Parmet, Herbert Samuel *historian, educator*
Rabassa, Gregory *Romance languages educator, translator*
Tytell, John *English educator, writer*
Wolz, Henry George *philosophy educator*

Fredonia
Fries, Maureen Holmberg *English literature educator*
Sonnenfeld, Marion *linguist, educator*

Garden City
Diamandopoulos, Peter *philosopher, educator*
Jenkins, Kenneth Vincent *literature educator, writer*
Shneidman, J. Lee *historian, educator*

Gardiner
Mabee, Carleton *historian, educator*

Geneseo
Edgar, William John *philosophy educator*
Fausold, Martin Luther *history educator*

Geneva
Caponegro, Mary *English language educator*

Hamilton
Blackton, Charles S(tuart) *history educator*
Busch, Briton Cooper *historian*
Hathaway, Robert Lawton *Romance languages educator*
Jones, Frank William *language educator*
Van Schaack, Eric *art historian, educator*

Harrison
Wadsworth, Frank Whittemore *educator*

Ithaca
Abrams, Meyer Howard *English language educator*
Brazell, Karen Woodard *Japanese literature educator*
Brown, Theodore Morey *art history educator*
Caputi, Anthony *comparative literature educator*
Colby-Hall, Alice Mary *Romance studies educator*
Culler, Jonathan Dwight *English language educator*
Eddy, Donald Davis *English language educator*
Elledge, Scott Bowen *language professional, educator*
Gibian, George *Russian and comparative literature educator*
Gilman, Sander Lawrence *German educator*
Groos, Arthur Bernhard, Jr. *German literature educator*
Hohendahl, Peter Uwe *German language and literature educator*
Kammen, Michael *historian, educator*
Kronik, John William *Romance studies educator*
LaCapra, Dominick Charles *historian*
LaFeber, Walter Frederick *history educator, author*
Lyons, David Barry *philosophy and law educator*
McConkey, James Rodney *English educator, writer*
Norton, Mary Beth *history educator, author*
Polenberg, Richard *history educator*
Porte, Joel Miles *English educator*
Radzinowicz, Mary Ann *language educator*
Rosenberg, Edgar *English and comparative literature educator*
Rossiter, Margaret Walsh *history of science educator*
Shoemaker, Sydney S. *philosophy educator*
Silbey, Joel Henry *history educator*
Strout, Sewall Cushing, Jr. *humanities educator*
Williams, Leslie Pearce *history educator*
Wyatt, David Kent *history educator*

Jamaica
Fay, Thomas A. *philosopher, educator*
Harmond, Richard Peter *educator*

Jericho
Astuto, Philip Louis *retired Spanish educator*

New Paltz
Hathaway, Richard Dean *language professional, educator*
Ryan, Marleigh Grayer *Japanese language educator*

New York
Abel, Reuben *educator*
Alazraki, Jaime *Romance languages educator*
Anderson, Quentin *English language educator, critic*
Apple, Max Isaac *English educator*
Bagnall, Roger Shaler *history educator*
Baker, Paul Raymond *history educator*
Balakian, Anna *foreign language educator, scholar, critic, writer*
Barzilay, Isaac Eisenstein *historian*
Belknap, Robert Lamont *Slavic language educator*
Bender, Thomas *history and humanities educator, writer*
Bielenstein, Hans Henrik August *Oriental studies educator*
Bonfante, Larissa *classics educator*
Brilliant, Richard *art history educator*
Brody, Saul Nathaniel *English literature educator*
Brooks, Jerome Bernard *English and Afro-American literature educator*
Brown, Jonathan *art historian, fine arts educator*
Brown, Milton Wolf *art historian, educator*
Bulliet, Richard Williams *history educator, novelist*
Burrill, Kathleen R. F. (Kathleen R. F. Griffin-Burrill) *Turkologist, educator*
Cahn, Steven M. *philosopher, educator*
Cantor, Norman Frank *history educator, writer*
Castronovo, David *English language educator*
Caws, Mary Ann *French language and comparative literature educator, critic*
Chitty, Arthur Ben *historiographer, consultant*
Cook, Blanche Wiesen *history educator, journalist*
Costello, John Robert *linguistics educator*
Cullen, Patrick Colborn *English educator*
Czerwinski, Edward Joseph *foreign language educator*
Dauben, Joseph Warren *history educator*
Davies, Jane B(adger) (Mrs. Lyn Davies) *architectural historian*
Deak, Istvan *historian, educator*
de Bary, William Theodore *Asian studies educator*
Diver, William *linguistics educator*
Eisler, Colin Tobias *art historian, curator*
Elderfield, John *art historian, museum curator*
Embree, Ainslie Thomas *history educator*
Foner, Eric *historian, educator*
Garrow, David Jeffries *historian, author*
Gerdts, William Henry *art history educator*
Harris, William Vernon *history educator*
Harter, Hugh Anthony *foreign language educator*
Harvey, Donald Joseph *history educator*
Held, Virginia *philosophy educator*
Hovde, Carl Frederick *language professional, educator*
Howe, Florence *English educator, writer, publisher*
Hunter-Stiebel, Penelope *art historian, art dealer*
Huyssen, Andreas *German literature educator*
Jackson, Kenneth Terry *historian, educator*
Karsen, Sonja Petra *Spanish educator emeritus*
Kivette, Ruth Montgomery *English language educator*
Kneller, John William *French language educator*
Kortepeter, Carl Max *history educator, columnist*
Krinsky, Carol Herselle *art history educator*
Kristeller, Paul Oskar *former philosophy educator*
Kroeber, Karl *English language educator*
La Rue, (Adrian) Jan (Pieters) *musicologist, educator, author*
Leavitt, Charles Loyal *English language educator, administrator*
Leibowitz, Herbert Akiba *English language educator, author*
Lencek, Rado L. *Slavic languages educator*
London, Herbert Ira *humanities educator*
Lorch, Maristella De Panizza (Mrs. Inama von Brunnenwald) *Romance languages educator, writer, lecturer*
Low, Anthony *English language educator*
Lowenthal, Constance *art historian*
Maguire, Robert Alan *Slavic languages and literatures educator*
Malefakis, Edward E. *history educator*
Malin, Irving *English educator, literary critic*
Malone, Joseph Lawrence *linguistics educator*
Matthews, William Procter *English educator*
Mayerson, Philip *classics educator*
Maynard, John Rogers *English educator*
Mc Cormick, Edward Allen *foreign language educator*
†Mc Kitrick, Eric Louis *historian, educator*
Meier, August *historian, educator*
Meisel, Martin *English and comparative literature educator*
Meisel, Perry *English educator*
Mendelson, Edward James *English literature educator*
Middendorf, John Harlan *English literature educator*
Morris, Robert C. *historian, archivist, educator*
Mundy, John Hine *history educator*
Myers, Gerald E. *humanities educator*
Nida, Eugene Albert *linguist, minister and author*
Novak, Barbara *art history educator*
Paxton, Robert Owen *historian, educator*
Posner, Donald *art historian*
Potoker, Edward Martin *English language educator, author*
Prince, Carl E. *historian, educator*
Quigley, Austin Edmund *literature and language educator*
Ragusa, Olga Maria *Italian language educator*
Ravitch, Diane Silvers *historian, educator, author, government official*
Rebay, Luciano *Italian literature educator, literary critic*
Reff, Theodore *art historian*
Reiman, Donald Henry *English educator*
Reiss, Timothy James *comparative literature educator, writer*
Riffaterre, Michael *educator, writer*
Rosenberg, John David *English educator, literary critic*
Rosenblum, Robert *art historian, educator*
Rowen, Ruth Halle *musicologist, educator*
Said, Edward W. *English language and literature educator*
Sander, Volkmar *foreign language educator*
Sandler, Lucy Freeman *art historian*
Schapiro, Meyer *retired art history educator*
Scheindlin, Raymond Paul *Hebrew literature educator, translator*
Seigel, Jerrold Edward *historian, writer*
Selig, Karl-Ludwig *language and literature educator*
Semmel, Bernard *historian, educator*
Silverman, Kenneth Eugene *English educator, writer*
Smit, Jacobus Wilhelmus *history educator*
Spector, Johanna Lichtenberg *ethnomusicologist, former educator*
Stade, George Gustav *humanities educator*
Steinberg, Leo *art historian, educator*
Stephens, Gary Ralph *American literature and journalism educator*
Stern, Fritz Richard *historian, educator*
Stevens, Martin *English educator*
Tanselle, George Thomas *English language educator, foundation executive*
Taran, Leonardo *classicist, educator*
Thompson, William Irwin *humanities educator, author*
Tison-Braun, Micheline Lucie *French language educator*
†Treitler, Leo *musicologist, educator*
Turner, Almon Richard *art historian, educator*
Tuttleton, James Wesley *English educator*
Unger, Peter Kenneth *philosophy educator*
Vai, Marjorie Theresa *language educator, university administrator, author*
Valenstein, Suzanne Gebhart *art historian*
Walkowitz, Daniel J. *historian, filmmaker, educator*
Wardwell, Allen *art historian*
Wasser, Henry *English educator, university administrator*
†Weil-Garris Brandt, Kathleen *art historian*
Weinberg, H. Barbara *art historian, educator, curator paintings and sculpture*
Wittreich, Joseph Anthony, Jr. *English language educator, author*
Wixom, William David *art historian, museum administrator, educator*
Woolfenden, William Edward *art administrator and historian*
Wortman, Richard S. *historian, educator*
Yerushalmi, Yosef Hayim *historian, educator*
Yurchenco, Henrietta Weiss *ethnomusicologist, writer*

Oakdale
Kramer, Aaron *English educator emeritus, poet, author*

Old Westbury
Rabil, Albert, Jr. *humanities educator*

Oswego
Smiley, Marilynn Jean *musicologist*
Turco, Lewis Putnam *language professional, educator*

Plattsburgh
Myers, John Lytle *historian*

Poestenkill
Radley, Virginia Louise *humanities educator*

Port Washington
†Williams, George Leo *retired educator*

Potsdam
Harder, Kelsie Brown *retired language professional, educator*

Poughkeepsie
Ahern, John Joseph *Italian studies educator*
Bartlett, Lynn Conant *English literature educator*
Daniels, Elizabeth Adams *English language educator*
Griffen, Clyde Chesterman *retired history educator*
Hytier, Adrienne Doris *French language educator*
Lipschutz, Ilse Hempel *French and Franco-Spanish relations, painting and literature educator*
Winn, Otis Howard *English educator*

Purchase
Clark, Mary Twibill *philosopher, educator*

Putnam Valley
Bracken, Harry McFarland *philosophy educator*

Quogue
Cooke, Robert John *history and law educator*

Rochester
Annunziata, Frank *history educator*
Berman, Milton *history educator*
Carlton, Charles Merritt *linguistics educator*
Chiarenza, Carl *art historian, critic, artist, educator*
Dohanian, Diran Kavork *art historian, educator*
Eaves, Morris Emery *English language educator*
Freeman, Robert Schofield *musicologist, educator, pianist*
Gordon, Dane Rex *philosophy educator, minister*
Hauser, William Barry *history educator, historian*
Herminghouse, Patricia Anne *foreign language educator*
Holmes, Robert Lawrence *philosophy educator*
Horsford, Howard Clarke *English language educator*
Howard, Hubert Wendell *English language educator, academic administrator, choral conductor*
Hoy, Cyrus Henry *language professional, educator*
Johnson, Bruce Marvin *English language educator*
Johnson, James William *English educator, author*
Joyce, John Joseph *English educator*
Klimas, Antanas *linguist, educator*
Kyburg, Henry Guy Ely, Jr. *philosophy and computer science educator*
Mann, Alfred *musicology educator, choral conductor*
Ramsey, Jarold William *English language educator, author*
Watanabe, Ruth Taiko *music historian, library science educator*
Young, Mary Elizabeth *history educator*
Zagorin, Perez *historian, educator*

Sagaponack
Appleman, Philip *educator, writer, poet*

Saint Bonaventure
Dooley, Patrick Kiaran *philosopher, educator*
Wallace, Malcolm Vincent Timothy *classics educator*

Saratoga Springs
Boyers, Robert *English language educator*

Scarsdale
Graff, Henry Franklin *historian, educator*

Schenectady
Morris, John Selwyn *philosophy educator, college president emeritus*
Murphy, William Michael *literature educator, biographer*

Setauket
Simpson, Louis Aston Marantz *English educator, author*

Slingerlands
Ellis, David Maldwyn *history educator*

Southampton
Brophy, James David, Jr. *humanities educator*

Stony Brook
Aronoff, Mark H. *linguistics educator, author, consultant*
Goldberg, Homer Beryl *English language educator*
Ihde, Don *philosophy educator, university administrator*
Kuspit, Donald Burton *art historian, art critic, educator*
Levin, Richard Louis *English language educator*
Mignone, Mario B. *Italian studies educator*
Silverman, Hugh J. *philosophy educator*
Spector, Marshall *philosophy educator*

Suffern
Walsh, James Jerome *philosophy educator*

Syracuse
Alston, William Payne *philosophy educator*
Crowley, John W(illiam) *English language educator*
Denise, Theodore Cullom *philosophy educator*
Hoffman, Arthur Wolf *English language educator*
Ketcham, Ralph *history and political science educator*
Lichtblau, Myron Ivor *language educator*
Peterfreund, Sheldon Paul *educator*
Powell, James Matthew *history educator*
Sternlicht, Sanford *English and theater arts educator, writer*
Sutton, Walter *English educator*
Tatham, David Frederic *art historian, educator*
van Inwagen, Peter Jan *philosophy educator*

Troy
Ahlers, Rolf Willi *philosopher, theologian*
Whitburn, Merrill Duane *English literature educator*

Trumansburg
Taylor, Richard *philosopher, educator*

NORTH CAROLINA

Buies Creek
Funderburk, David B. *history educator, former ambassador*

Chapel Hill
Bain, Robert Addison *English literature educator*
Baron, Samuel Haskell *historian*
Debreczeny, Paul *Slavic language educator, author*
Eaton, Charles Edward *English language educator, author*
Falk, Eugene Hannes *foreign language educator emeritus*
Flora, Joseph M(artin) *English language educator*
Furst, Lilian Renee *language professional, educator*
Heninger, Simeon Kahn, Jr. *English language educator*
Jackson, Blyden *English language educator*
Jones, Houston Gwynne *history educator*
Kohn, Richard H. *historian, educator*
Lee, Sherman Emery *art historian, curator*
Levine, Madeline Geltman *Slavic literatures educator, translator*
Long, Douglas Clark *philosophy educator*
Ludington, Charles Townsend, Jr. *English and American studies educator*
Munsat, Stanley Morris *philosopher, educator*
Nelson, Philip Francis *musicology educator, consultant, choral conductor*
Rubin, Louis Decimus, Jr. *English language and literature educator, writer, publisher*
Schier, Donald Stephen *language educator*
Smith, Sidney Rufus, Jr. *linguist, educator*
Stadter, Philip Austin *classicist, educator*
Strauss, Albrecht Benno *English educator, editor*
Tindall, George Brown *historian, educator*
Tsiapera, Maria *linguistics educator*
Vogler, Frederick Wright *French educator*
Weinberg, Gerhard Ludwig *history educator*
Ziff, Paul *philosophy educator*

Charlotte
Hill, Ruth Foell *language consultant*
Preyer, Norris Watson *history educator*

Cullowhee
Blethen, Harold Tyler, III *history educator*

Davidson
Abernethy, George Lawrence *philosophy educator*

Cole, Richard Cargill *English educator*
Lester, Malcolm *historian, educator*
Williams, Robert Chadwell *history educator*
Zimmermann, T. C. Price *historian, educator*

Durham
Budd, Louis John *English language educator*
†Butters, Ronald Richard *English language educator*
Cady, Edwin Harrison *English language educator, author*
Chafe, William Henry *history educator*
Colton, Joel *historian, educator*
Davidson, Cathy Notari *English language educator, writer*
Davis, Calvin De Armond *historian, educator*
Durden, Robert Franklin *history educator*
Fish, Stanley Eugene *English language and literature educator*
Gleckner, Robert Francis *English language professional, educator*
Golding, Martin Philip *law and philosophy educator*
Hillerbrand, Hans Joachim *historian, university administrator*
Holley, Irving Brinton, Jr. *historian, educator*
Lerner, Warren *historian*
Mauskopf, Seymour Harold *history educator*
Nygard, Holger Olof *English and folklore educator*
Oates, John Francis *classics educator*
Preston, Richard Arthur *historian*
Richardson, Lawrence, Jr. *Latin educator, archeologist*
Ryals, Clyde de Loache *humanities educator*
Sanford, David Hawley *philosophy educator*
Scott, Anne Byrd Firor *history educator*
Smith, Grover Cleveland *English language educator*
Spencer, John Richard *art historian*
Thomas, Jean-Jacques Robert *romance languages educator*
Wardropper, Bruce Wear *language educator*
Williams, George Walton *English educator*

Fayetteville
Bowman, Charles Harwood, Jr. *historian, educator*

Fearrington Village
Abrahamson, James Leonard *history educator*

Greensboro
Bardolph, Richard *historian, educator*
Chappell, Fred Davis *English language educator, poet*
Thompson, James Howard *historian, library administrator*

Greenville
Holt, Robert LeRoi *philosophy educator*

Mars Hill
Jolley, Betty Cornette *history educator*

Raleigh
†Kessel, John Joseph *English language educator, writer*

Research Triangle Park
Connor, Walter Robert *classics educator, humanities center administrator*

West End
Moncure, James Ashby *historian*

Winston Salem
Alderson, William Thomas *historian, consultant*
Barnett, Richard Chambers *historian, educator*
Covey, Cyclone *history educator*
Helm, Robert Meredith *philosophy educator*
Hendricks, J(ames) Edwin *historian, educator, consultant, author*
Scales, James Ralph *history educator, former university president*
Shapere, Dudley *philosophy educator*

NORTH DAKOTA

Bismarck
Newborg, Gerald Gordon *historical agency administrator*

OHIO

Akron
Bryant, Keith Lynn, Jr. *history educator*
Jones, Robert Huhn *history educator*
Knepper, George W. *history educator*
Phillipson, John Samuel *retired English educator*

Athens
Borchert, Donald Marvin *philosopher, educator*
Crowl, Samuel Renninger *English language educator*
Eckes, Alfred Edward, Jr. *historian, international trade analyst*
Gaddis, John Lewis *history educator*
Gustavson, Carl Gustav *historian, educator*
Hamby, Alonzo Lee *historian, educator*
Matthews, Jack (John Harold Matthews) *English educator, writer*
Schneider, Duane Bernard *English literature educator, publisher*
Whealey, Lois Deimel *humanities scholar*

Berea
Blumer, Frederick Elwin *philosophy educator*

Bowling Green
Browne, Ray Broadus *popular culture educator*
Lavezzi, John Charles *art history educator, archaeologist*
Weaver, Richard L., II *speech communication educator*

Chagrin Falls
Rawski, Conrad H(enry) *humanities educator, medievalist*

Cincinnati
Bleznick, Donald William *Romance languages educator*
†Ciani, Alfred Joseph *language professional, dean*
Glenn, Jerry Hosmer, Jr. *foreign language educator*
Huvos, Kornel *linguistics educator*
Lewis, Gene Dale *historian, educator*
Marcus, Jacob Rader *history educator*
Mitchell, Otis Clinton, Jr. *history educator*
Muntz, Ernest Gordon *historian, educator*
†Peck, Abraham Joseph *historian*
Peterson, Gale Eugene *historian*
Schrier, Arnold *historian, educator*

Cleveland
†Benseler, David Price *foreign language educator*
Buchanan, D(aniel) Harvey *art history educator*
Ferguson, Suzanne Carol *English educator*
Friedman, Barton Robert *English educator*
Gibson, Walter Samuel *humanities educator*
Greppin, John Aird Coutts *philologist, editor, educator*
Heald, Morrell *humanities educator*
Milic, Louis Tonko *English educator*
Miller, Genevieve *medical historian*
Olszewski, Edward John *art history educator*
Ornstein, Robert *humanities educator*
Pursell, Carroll Wirth *history educator*
Reeves, Charles Howell *classics educator*
Roth, Jack Joseph *historian, educator*
Salomon, Roger Blaine *English language educator*
Strauss, Walter Adolf *foreign languages educator*
Trawick, Leonard Moses *English educator*
Weinberg, Helen Arnstein *American art and literature educator*

Columbus
Babcock, Charles Luther *classics educator*
Battersby, James Lyons, Jr. *English language educator*
Beja, Morris *English literature educator*
Boh, Ivan *philosophy educator*
Brooks, Keith *educator*
Burnham, John Chynoweth *historian, educator*
Dillon, Merton Lynn *historian, educator*
Hahm, David Edgar *classics educator*
Hare, Robert Yates *music history educator*
Hinshaw, Virgil Goodman, Jr. *philosopher, emeritus educator*
Hoffmann, Charles Wesley *retired foreign language educator*
Jarvis, Gilbert Andrew *humanities educator*
Kuhn, Albert Joseph *English educator*
Lehiste, Ilse *language educator*
Rule, John Corwin *history educator*
Scanlan, James Patrick *philosophy and Slavic studies educator*
Silbajoris, Frank Rimvydas *Slavic languages educator*

Dayton
Harden, Oleta Elizabeth *English educator, university administrator*
Romaguera, Enrique *foreign language educator, corporate interpreter*
Schwartz, Irving Lloyd *history educator emeritus*

Gambier
Sharp, Ronald Alan *English literature educator, author*

Kent
Beer, Barrett Lynn *historian, educator*
Byrne, Frank Loyola *history educator*
Dante, Harris Loy *history educator*
Georgopoulos, Nenos Aristides *philosophy educator*
Harkness, Bruce *English language educator*
Hassler, Donald Mackey, II *English language educator, writer*
James, Patricia Ann *philosophy educator*
Zornow, William Frank *historian, educator*

Marietta
Wilbanks, Jan Joseph *philosopher*

Mentor
Skerry, Philip John *English educator*

Niles
Darlington, Oscar Gilpin *historian, educator*

Oberlin
Colish, Marcia Lillian *history educator*
Greenberg, Nathan Abraham *classics educator*
Long, Herbert Strainge *classics educator*
Spear, Richard Edmund *art history educator*
Young, David Pollock *humanities educator, author*

Oxford
Pratt, William Crouch, Jr. *English language educator*
Winkler, Allan Michael *history educator*

Tiffin
Davison, Kenneth Edwin *American studies educator*
Kramer, Frank Raymond *classicist, educator*

Toledo
Smith, Robert Freeman *history educator*
Thompson, Gerald E. *historian, educator*

Yellow Springs
Fogarty, Robert Stephen *historian, educator, editor*

Youngstown
Bell, Carol Willsey *certified genealogist*
†Bowers, Bege K. *English educator*
†Brothers, Barbara *English language educator*

OKLAHOMA

Bethany
Davis, Harrison Ransom Samuel, Jr. *English language educator*

Chickasha
Feaver, John Clayton *philosopher, educator*

Durant
Baskin, Vlasta Jana Marie *language educator*

Goodwell
Smith, Kim Lee *educator*

Norman
Brown, Sidney DeVere *history educator*
Glad, Paul Wilbur *history educator*
Hagan, William Thomas *history educator*
Hollon, William Eugene *historian, educator, author*
Kadir, Djelal *university educator, editor periodical, consultant*
Lowitt, Richard *history educator*
Nebergall, Roger Ellis *speech educator*

Oklahoma City
Booth, Glenna Greene *genealogical researcher*

Stillwater
Agnew, Theodore Lee, Jr. *historian, educator*
Fischer, LeRoy Henry *historian, educator*
Luebke, Neil Robert *philosophy educator*

Tulsa
Buckley, Thomas Hugh *historian, educator*
O'Brien, Darcy *English educator, writer*

OREGON

Ashland
Bornet, Vaughn Davis *former history and social science educator, research historian*
Levy, Leonard Williams *history educator, author*

Coos Bay
Shepard, Robert Carlton *English language educator*

Eugene
Birn, Raymond Francis *historian, educator*
Donnelly, Marian Card *art historian, educator*
Pascal, C(ecil) Bennett *classics educator*
†Rendall, Steven Finlay *language educator, editor, translator, critic*
Wickes, George *English educator, writer*

Port Orford
Drinnon, Richard *history educator*

Portland
Gerow, Edwin Mahaffey *Indic culture educator*
Kinzer, Donald Louis *retired historian, educator*
Vaughan, Thomas James Gregory *historian*

PENNSYLVANIA

Ambler
Lengyel, Alfonz *art history, archeology and museology educator*

Ardmore
†Gutwirth, Marcel Marc *French literature educator*

Bethlehem
Beidler, Peter Grant *English educator*
Dowling, Joseph Albert *historian, educator*
Greene, David Mason *retired English language educator*
Haynes, Thomas Morris *philosophy educator*
Lindgren, John Ralph *philosophy educator*
Smolansky, Oles M. *humanities educator*

Bryn Mawr
Brand, Charles Macy *history educator*
Dorian, Nancy Currier *linguistics educator*
Dudden, Arthur Power *historian, educator*
Gaisser, Julia Haig *classics educator*
King, Willard Fahrenkamp (Mrs. Edmund Ludwig King) *Spanish language educator*
Krausz, Michael *philosopher, educator*
Lane, Barbara Miller (Barbara Miller-Lane) *humanities educator*
Salmon, John Hearsey McMillan *historian, educator*
Stapleton, Katharine Laurence *English educator, writer*

Carlisle
Fox, Arturo Angel *Spanish language educator*
Schiffman, Joseph Harris *literary historian, educator*

Chambersburg
Gelbach, Martha Harvey *genealogist*

East Stroudsburg
Crackel, Theodore Joseph *historian*

Easton
Cooke, Jacob Ernest *history educator, author*
†Gaertner, Johannes Alexander *retired art history educator, author*

Edinboro
Fleischauer, John Frederick *English language educator, academic administrator*

Elkins Park
Davidson, Abraham A. *art historian, photographer*

Gettysburg
Boritt, Gábor Szappanos *history educator*

Haverford
Jorden, Eleanor Harz *linguist, educator*

Kennett Square
Bronner, Edwin Blaine *history educator*

Lancaster
Joseph, John *history educator*

Lewisburg
Edgerton, Mills Fox, Jr. *foreign language educator*
Lu, David John *history educator, writer*
Payne, Michael David *English language educator*

Meadville
Hogan, James Charles *classicist, educator*
Katope, Christopher George *English language educator*

Narberth
Wagner, Frederick Balthas, Jr. *historian, retired surgery educator*

Newtown
Bohning, Elizabeth Edrop *foreign language educator*

Oreland
Smith, Gordon Ross *retired English language educator*

Philadelphia
Alter, Jean Victor *French language educator*
†Baker, Houston Alfred, Jr. *English language educator*
Bell, Whitfield Jenks, Jr. *historian*
Benson, Morton *educator, lexicographer*
Burke, Daniel William *college president emeritus, English educator*
Cohen, Hennig *English educator*
Davis, Allen Freeman *history educator, author*
DeLaura, David Joseph *English language educator*
Foner, Philip S. *history educator, author*
Graham, Alexander John *classics educator*
Guyer, Paul David *philosophy educator, writer*
†Heuser, Frederick J. *historian*
Hoenigswald, Henry Max *linguist, educator*
Hoffman, Daniel (Gerard) *literature educator, poet*
Hughes, Thomas Parke *history educator*
Knauer, Georg Nicolaus *classical philologist*
Lee, Charles *emeritus English language and literature educator, arts critic*
Lewin, Moshe *historian, educator*
Lloyd, Albert Lawrence, Jr. *German language educator*
Lucid, Robert Francis *English educator*
†Ludden, David *Asian studies educator*
McDougall, Walter Allan *history educator*
Means, John Barkley *foreign language educator, association executive*
Moss, Roger William, Jr. *historian, writer, administrator*
Murphey, Murray Griffin *history educator*
Peters, Edward Murray *history educator*
Regan, Robert Charles *English language educator*
Rocher, Ludo *humanities educator*
Rosenberg, Charles Ernest *historian, educator*
Rosenberg, David Alan *military historian, educator*
Ross, James Francis *philosophy educator*
Sebold, Russell Perry, III *Romance languages educator, author*
Sivin, Nathan *historian, educator*
Thackray, Arnold Wilfrid *historian, educator*
Tise, Larry Edward *historian, historic site director*

Phoenixville
Lukacs, John Adalbert *historian, retired educator*

Pittsburgh
Anthony, Edward Mason *linguistics educator*
Belnap, Nuel Dinsmore, Jr. *philosophy educator*
Buchanan, James Junkin *classics educator*
Clack, Jerry *classics educator*
Drescher, Seymour *history educator, writer*
Ferguson, Mary Anne Heyward *language professional, educator*
Gale, Robert Lee *retired American literature educator and critic*
Grunbaum, Adolf *philosophy educator, author*
Harris, Ann Birgitta Sutherland *art historian*
Hayes, Ann Louise *English educator, consultant, poet*
Hsu, Cho-yun *history educator*
Kearney, Hugh Francis *historian, educator*
†Massey, Gerald J. *philosophy educator*
Miller, David William *historian, educator*
Modell, John *historian, educator*
Morice, Joseph Richard *history educator*
Paulston, Christina Bratt *linguistics educator*
Rawski, Evelyn Sakakida *history educator*
†Rescher, Nicholas *philosophy educator*
Rimer, John Thomas *foreign language educator, academic administrator, writer, translator*
†Seligson, Mitchell A. *Latin American studies educator*
Sheon, Aaron *art historian, educator*
Stearns, Peter Nathaniel *history educator*
Tarr, Joel Arthur *history and public policy educator*
Toker, Franklin K. *art history educator, archaeologist, foundation executive*
Weingartner, Rudolph Herbert *philosophy educator*

Pottstown
Ruth, Thomas Griswold *history educator*

Scranton
Hoffman, Barbara Ann *English educator*

Springtown
Hunt, John Wesley *English language educator*

State College
Asbell, Bernard *English educator, author*
Johnstone, Henry Webb, Jr. *philosophy educator*
Kockelmans, Joseph J. *philosopher, educator*
Robinett, Betty Wallace *linguist*
Scott, Charles Edward *philosophy educator*

Swarthmore
Bannister, Robert Corwin, Jr. *history educator*
Beeman, Richard Roy *historian*
Blackburn, Thomas Harold *English language professional, educator*
Lacey, Hugh Matthew *philosophy educator*
North, Helen Florence *classicist, educator*
Ostwald, Martin *classics educator emeritus*
Pagliaro, Harold Emil *English language educator*
Snyder, Susan Brooke *English literature educator*
Wright, Harrison Morris *historian, educator*

University Park
Ameringer, Charles D. *history educator*
Anderson, John Mueller *retired philosophy educator*
Brault, Gerard Joseph *French language educator*
De Armas, Frederick Alfred *foreign language educator*
Eckhardt, Caroline Davis *comparative literature educator*
Edwards, Robert Roy *English literature and comparative literature educator*
Frank, Robert Worth, Jr. *English language educator*
Goldschmidt, Arthur Eduard, Jr. *historian, educator*
Lima, Robert *Hispanic studies and comparative literature educator*

Rosen, Stanley Howard *humanities educator*
Schmalstieg, William Riegel *Slavic languages educator*
Weintraub, Stanley *arts and humanities educator, author*

Villanova
Helmetag, Charles Hugh *foreign language educator*

Wayne
Frye, Roland Mushat *literary historian, theologian*

West Chester
Hipple, Walter John *English language educator*

Wynnewood
Kruger, Arthur Newman *speech communication educator, author*

RHODE ISLAND

Kingston
Gitlitz, David Martin *Hispanic studies educator*
Kim, Yong Choon *philosopher, theologian, educator*
MacLaine, Allan Hugh *English language educator*

Newport
Brennan, Joseph Gerard *philosophy educator*
Gleiman, Lubomir *philosophy educator*

Providence
Arant, Patricia *Slavic languages and literature educator*
Brock, Dan Willets *philosophy educator*
Cook, Albert Spaulding *comparative literature and classics educator, writer*
Donovan, Bruce Elliot *classics educator, university dean*
Enteman, Willard Finley *philosophy educator*
Fiering, Norman (Sanford) *historian, library administrator*
Fornara, Charles William *historian, classicist, educator*
Gleason, Abbott *history educator*
†Harper, Michael S. *English language educator*
†Hirsch, David H. *English, American literature and Judaic studies educator, academic administrator*
Honig, Edwin *comparative literature educator, poet*
Jordy, William Henry *art history educator*
Kim, Jaegwon *philosophy educator*
Kucera, Henry *linguistics educator*
Landow, George Paul *English literature and art educator, writer*
Lesko, Leonard Henry *Egyptologist, educator*
Neu, Charles Eric *historian, educator*
Nussbaum, Martha Craven *philosophy and classics educator*
Putnam, Michael Courtney Jenkins *classics educator*
Ribbans, Geoffrey Wilfrid *Spanish educator*
Rohr, Donald Gerard *history educator*
Rosenberg, Bruce Alan *English language educator, author*
Scholes, Robert Edward *English language educator*
Spilka, Mark *English educator*
Terras, Victor *Slavic languages and comparative literature educator*
Trueblood, Alan Stubbs *former modern language educator*
Weinstein, Arnold Louis *literature educator*
Williams, Lea Everard *history educator*
Wood, Gordon Stewart *historian, educator*
Wrenn, James Joseph *East Asian studies educator*
Wyatt, William Frank, Jr. *philology educator*

Smithfield
Haas, William Paul *humanities educator, former college president*

Westerly
Verdier, Philippe M(aurice) *art historian*

SOUTH CAROLINA

Charleston
Anderson, Charles Roberts *English language educator*
Pincus, Michael Stern *department chairman, language educator*

Clemson
Calhoun, Richard James *English language educator*
Riley, Helene Maria Kastinger *germanist*
Underwood, Richard Allan *English language educator*

Columbia
Belasco, Simon *French language and linguistics educator*
Bruccoli, Matthew Joseph *English educator, publisher*
Edgar, Walter Bellingrath *historian*
Geckle, George Leo, III *English language educator*
Hardin, James Neal *German and comparative literature educator*
Hatch, Mary Gies *German language educator*
Howard-Hill, Trevor Howard *English language educator*
Johnson, Herbert Alan *history and law educator, lawyer, chaplain*
Long, Eugene Thomas, III *philosophy educator, administrator*
Myerson, Joel Arthur *English language educator, researcher*
Nolte, William Henry *English language educator*
Norman, George Buford, Jr. *foreign language educator*
Reeves, George McMillan, Jr. *comparative literature educator, educational administrator*
Sproat, John Gerald *historian*
Weir, Robert McColloch *history educator*

Greenville
Crabtree, John Henry, Jr. *retired English educator*
Parsell, David Beatty *modern language educator*

Hilton Head Island
Male, Roy Raymond *English language educator*

Mullins
Stonesifer, Richard James *retired humanities and social science educator*

Rock Hill
Viault, Birdsall Scrymser *history educator*

Spartanburg
Lindsay, Bryan Eugene *educator, musician, writer*

West Columbia
Ochs, Robert David *history educator*
Parker, Harold Talbot *history educator*

SOUTH DAKOTA

Sioux Falls
Carlson, Marilyn A. *English language educator*

Vermillion
Milton, John Ronald *English language educator, author*

TENNESSEE

Clarksville
Lester, James Dudley *classicist, educator*

Columbia
Curry, Beatrice Chesrown *English educator*

Jefferson City
Baumgardner, James Lewis *history educator*

Johnson City
Zayas-Bazan, Eduardo *foreign language educator*

Knoxville
Brady, Patrick *French literature educator*
Cutler, Everette Wayne *history educator*
Fisher, John Hurt *English language educator*
Moser, Harold Dean *historian*
Trahern, Joseph Baxter, Jr. *humanities educator*

Martin
Peckham, Robert Dabney *French language and literature educator*

Memphis
Copper, John Franklin *Asian studies educator, consultant*
O'Donnell, William Hugh *English educator*
Stagg, Louis Charles *English language and literature educator*

Nashville
Boorman, Howard Lyon *history educator*
Bowen, Barbara Cherry *French and comparative literature educator*
Conkin, Paul Keith *history educator*
Cook, Ann Jennalie *English language educator*
Doody, Margaret Anne *English educator*
Graham, Hugh Davis *history educator*
Grantham, Dewey Wesley *historian, educator*
Halperin, John William *English literature educator*
Lachs, John *philosopher, educator*
Perry, Lewis Curtis *historian, educator*
Sherburne, Donald Wynne *philosopher, educator*
Smith, Samuel Boyd *history educator*
Stumpf, Samuel Enoch *philosophy educator*
Sullivan, Walter Laurence *writer, educator*
Voegeli, Victor Jacque *history educator, dean*
von Raffler-Engel, Walburga *linguist, lecturer, writer*

Sewanee
†Spears, Monroe Kirk *educator, author*
Stirling, Edwin Murdoch *English educator, critic*
Williamson, Samuel Ruthven, Jr. *historian, university administrator*

TEXAS

Austin
Berdahl, Robert Max *historian, educator*
Bordie, John George *linguistics educator*
Boyer, Mildred Vinson *foreign language educator emeritus*
Braybrooke, David *philosopher, educator*
Brown, Norman Donald *history educator*
Carleton, Don Edward *history center administrator, educator, writer*
Causey, Robert Louis *philosopher, educator, consultant*
Cline, Clarence Lee *language professional*
Crosby, Alfred Worcester *history educator*
Divine, Robert Alexander *history educator*
Farrell, Edmund James *English language educator, author*
Friedman, Alan Warren *humanities educator*
Galinsky, Gotthard Karl *classicist, educator*
Gould, Lewis Ludlow *historian*
Green, Peter Morris *classics educator, writer, translator*
Hancock, Ian Francis (O Yanko le Redžosko) *linguistics educator*
Harms, Robert Thomas *linguist, educator*
Hartshorne, Charles *philosopher, retired educator*
Hinojosa-Smith, Roland *English language educator, writer*
Hopper, Robert William *speech communication educator*
Jazayery, Mohammad Ali *foreign languages and literature educator emeritus*
Katz, Michael Ray *Slavic languages educator*
King, Robert D. *linguistics educator, university dean*
Lehmann, Ruth Preston Miller *literature educator*
Lehmann, Winfred Philipp *linguistics educator*
López-Morillas, Juan *Spanish and comparative literature educator*
Louis, William Roger *historian, educator, editor*
Mackey, Louis Henry *philosophy educator*
Meacham, Standish *historian, educator*
Megaw, Robert Neill Ellison *English educator*
Middleton, Christopher *Germanic languages and literature educator*
Mourelatos, Alexander Phoebus Dionysiou *humanities educator*

Palaima, Thomas Gerard *Classics educator, researcher*
Paredes, Americo *English language educator*
Phillips, Frances Marie *history educator*
Polomé, Edgar Charles *foreign language educator*
Rich, John Martin *humanities educator, researcher*
Seung, Thomas Kaehao *philosophy educator*
†Staley, Thomas Fabian *language professional, academic administrator*
Sutherland, William Owen Sheppard *English language educator*
Todd, William Burton *English language and literature educator*
Tyler, Ronnie Curtis *historian*
Velz, John William *literature educator*
Wadlington, Warwick Paul *English language educator*
Werbow, Stanley Newman *language educator*
Whitbread, Thomas Bacon *English educator, author*
Wilson, Robert Henry *English educator*

College Station
Berthold, Dennis Alfred *English language educator*
Cannon, Garland *English language educator*
Davenport, Manuel Manson *philosophy educator*
Dethloff, Henry Clay *history educator*
Fedorchik, Bette Joy Winter *foreign language professional*
Mc Dermott, John Joseph *philosophy educator*
Nance, Joseph Milton *history educator*
Unterberger, Betty Miller *history educator, writer*

Columbus
Hamilton, T. Earle *retired educator, honor society executive*

Commerce
Grimshaw, James Albert, Jr. *English language educator*
Tuerk, Richard Carl *English language educator*

Corpus Christi
Wooster, Robert *history educator*

Dallas
†Caldwell, Louise Phinney *historical researcher, community volunteer*
Comini, Alessandra *art historian, educator*
Countryman, Edward Francis *historian, educator*
Crain, John Walter *historian*
Hunter, Robert Grams *English language educator*
Jones, James Fleming, Jr. *Romance language educator, university administrator*
Pike, Kenneth Lee *linguist, educator*
†Robbins, Frank Ernest *linguistics educator, administrator*
Terry, Marshall Northway, Jr. *English language educator, author*

Denton
Clogan, Paul Maurice *English language and literature educator*
Kamman, William *historian, educator*
Kesterson, David Bert *English language educator*
Nichols, Irby Coghill, Jr. *historian, educator, entrepreneur*
Preston, Thomas Ronald *English language educator, researcher*
Vaughn, William Preston *historian, educator*

Edinburg
Vassberg, David Erland *history educator*

El Paso
Bailey, Kenneth Kyle *history educator*
Leach, Joseph Lee *English language educator, author*
Ornstein-Galicia, Jacob Leonard (Jack Ornstein-Galicia) *foreign language educator, linguist, author*

Fort Worth
Erisman, Fred Raymond *English literature educator*
McWhiney, Grady *history educator*
Reuter, Frank Theodore *history educator*
Wertz, Spencer K. *philosophy educator*
Worcester, Donald Emmet *history educator, author*

Georgetown
Browning, Grayson Douglas *philosophy educator*

Houston
Bonnet, Beatriz Alicia *interpreter, translator, flutist*
Carrington, Samuel Macon, Jr. *French language educator*
Decker, Hannah Shulman *history educator*
de Kanter, Ellen Ann *language professional, educator*
Drew, Katherine Fischer *history educator*
Gruber, Ira Dempsey *historian, educator*
Haskell, Thomas Langdon *history educator*
Lamb, Sydney MacDonald *linguistics and cognitive science educator*
Martin, James Kirby *historian, educator*
Matusow, Allen Joseph *history educator, academic administrator*
Minter, David Lee *English literature educator*
Patten, Robert Lowry *English language educator*
Russman, Thomas Anthony *philosophy educator*
Young, William John *French educator, university president emeritus*

Irving
Sommerfeldt, John Robert *historian*

Lubbock
Connor, Seymour Vaughan *historian, writer*
Eddleman, Floyd Eugene *retired English language educator*
Higdon, David Leon *English language educator*
Kelsey, Clyde Eastman, Jr. *philosophy and psychology educator*
Ketner, Kenneth Laine *philosopher, educator*
Pearce, William Martin *history educator*
Walker, Warren Stanley *English educator*

Nacogdoches
Kallsen, Theodore John *retired English language educator*

Prairie View
Boyd-Brown, Lena Ernestine *history educator, education consultant*
Coe, Elizabeth Beaubien *English language educator*
Robinson, Carrie C. *English educator*

Richardson
Redman, Timothy Paul *English language educator, author, chess federation administrator*

San Angelo
Torres, David *Spanish language educator*

San Antonio
Kellman, Steven G. *literature educator, author*
Kersnowski, Frank Louis *modern language educator*
Quirarte, Jacinto *art historian*
Schulte, Josephine Helen *historian, educator*

Seguin
Moline, Jon Nelson *philosopher, educator, college president*

Sherman
Fuller, Anne Elizabeth Havens *English educator, consultant*

Stephenville
Christopher, Joe Randell *English language educator*
Koestler, Fred *historian, educator*

Waco
Baird, Robert Malcolm *philosophy educator, researcher*
Barcus, James Edgar *English literature educator*
Campbell, Stanley Wallace *history educator*
Collmer, Robert George *English language educator*
Cutter, Charles Richard, III *classics educator*
Goode, Clement Tyson *English language educator*
Herring, Jack William *English language educator*

UTAH

Logan
Ellsworth, Samuel George *historian, educator*

Provo
Alexander, Thomas Glen *history educator*
Arrington, Leonard James *history educator*
Clark, Bruce Budge *humanities educator*
Forster, Merlin Henry *foreign languages educator, author, researcher*
Lyon, James Karl *German educator*
Peer, Larry Howard *literature educator*

Salt Lake City
Eakle, Arlene H. *genealogist*
Flanagan, John Theodore *language professional, educator*
Lueders, Edward George *author, poet, educator, editor*
Madsen, Brigham Dwaine *history educator*
Mayfield, David Merkley *genealogy director*
Mc Murrin, Sterling Moss *philosophy educator*
Sillars, Malcolm Osgood *communications educator*
Steensma, Robert Charles *English language educator*

VERMONT

Bennington
Kaplan, Harold *humanities educator, author*

Burlington
Daniels, Robert Vincent *history educator, former state senator*
Hall, Robert William *philosophy and religion educator*
Scrase, David Anthony *German language educator*
Weiger, John George *foreign language educator*

East Calais
Meiklejohn, Donald *philosophy educator*

Manchester
Wilbur, James Benjamin, III *philosopher, educator*

Middlebury
Clifford, Nicholas Rowland *history educator, colleg administrator*
Jacobs, Travis Beal *historian, educator*
Lamberti, Marjorie *history educator*
Vail, Van Horn *German educator*

North Bennington
Kimpel, Benjamin Franklin *philosophy educator emeritus, writer*

VIRGINIA

Alexandria
Byrne, John Edward *writer, retired government official*
Mitchell, Joseph Brady *military historian, author*
Myers, Denys Peter, Jr. *architectural historian*
White, Gordon Eliot *historian*

Ashland
Inge, Milton Thomas *American literature and culture educator, author*

Blacksburg
Baumgartner, Frederic Joseph *history educator*
Doswald, Herman Kenneth *German language educator, academic administrator*
Landen, Robert Geran *historian, university administrator*
Peacock, Markham Lovick, Jr. *English educator*
Pitt, Joseph Charles *philosophy educator*
Robertson, James Irvin, Jr. *historian, educator*
Ulloa, Justo Celso *Spanish educator*

Charlottesville
Alden, Douglas William *French language educator*
Allinson, Gary Dean *Japanese studies educator*
Barolsky, Paul *art history educator*
Battestin, Martin Carey *English educator*
Cano-Ballesta, Juan *Spanish language educator*
Cargile, James Thomas *philosophy educator*
Cherno, Melvin *humanities educator*
Colker, Marvin Leonard *classics educator*
Courtney, Edward *classics educator*

Denommé, Robert Thomas *foreign language educator*
Diamond, Cora Ann *philosopher, educator*
Dove, Rita Frances *English language educator, writer*
Forbes, John Douglas *architectural and economic historian*
Garrett, George Palmer, Jr. *creative writing and English language educator, writer*
Gianniny, Omer Allan, Jr. *humanities educator*
Graebner, Norman Arthur *history educator*
Havran, Martin Joseph *historian, educator, author*
Hirsch, Eric Donald, Jr. *English language educator, educational reformer*
Hopkins, Paul Jeffrey *Asian studies educator, author, translator*
Huet, Marie-Hélène Jaqueline *foreign language educator*
Kellogg, Robert Leland *English language educator*
Kett, Joseph Francis *historian, educator*
Kohler, Charlotte *language professional, educator*
Kolb, Harold Hutchison, Jr. *English language educator*
Kraehe, Enno Edward *history educator*
Lang, Cecil Yelverton *English language educator*
Langbaum, Robert Woodrow *English language educator, author*
Leffler, Melvyn P. *history educator*
Levenson, Jacob Clavner *English language educator*
Lyons, John David *French, Italian and comparative literature educator*
McGann, Jerome John *English language educator*
Mikalson, Jon Dennis *classics educator*
Nelson, Raymond John *English literature educator, university dean, author*
Peterson, Merrill Daniel *history educator*
Rorty, Richard McKay *philosophy educator*
†Rubin, David Lee *French literature educator, critic, editor, publisher*
Schuker, Stephen Alan *historian*
Sedgwick, Alexander *historian, educator*
Shackelford, George Green *historian*
Shannon, Edgar Finley, Jr. *English language educator*
Shaw, Donald Leslie *Spanish language educator*
Simmons, Alan John *philosophy educator*
†Sokel, Walter H. *German language and literature educator*
Spacks, Patricia Meyer *English educator*
Spearing, Anthony Colin *English educator*
Stocker, Arthur Frederick *classics educator*
Vaughan, Joseph Lee *language educator*
Westfall, Carroll William *architectural historian*
Zunz, Olivier Jean *history educator*

Fairfax
Bailey, Helen McShane *historian*

Fort Lee
Sterling, Keir Brooks *historian, educator*

Fredericksburg
Dorman, John Frederick *genealogist*
†Krick, Robert Kenneth *historian, writer*

Gloucester
Fang, Joong *mathematician, philosopher, educator*

Herndon
Wilson, Douglas Lawson *research center director*

Lexington
Burnette, Ollen Lawrence, Jr. *historian*
Evans, John Maurice *English language educator*
James, D(orris) Clayton *history educator*
Martin, Joseph Ramsey *philosophy educator*
McAhren, Robert Willard *history educator*
Pemberton, Harrison Joseph *educator, philosopher*

Manassas
Smith, Vme (Verna Mae Edom Smith) *sociology educator, freelance writer, photographer*

Mc Lean
Davis, William Columbus *educator, writer, lecturer*
Dupuy, Trevor Nevitt *historian, research executive*
Topping, Peter *historian, educator*

Newport News
Morris, James Matthew *history educator*

Norfolk
Bazin, Nancy Topping *English language educator*
Dandridge, Rita Bernice *English language educator*
Greene, Douglas George *humanities educator, author, publisher*
Lucking, Robert A. *English literature educator*
Perry, Ruth Anna *English language educator*

Richmond
Gray, Clarence Jones *foreign languages educator, dean emeritus*
Shapiro, Gary Michael *philosophy educator*
Treadway, John David *history educator*
Urofsky, Melvin Irving *historian, educator*

Roanoke
Dillard, Richard Henry Wilde *English language professional, educator, author*

Williamsburg
Axtell, James Lewis *history educator*
Ball, Donald Lewis *retired English language educator*
Chappell, Miles Linwood, Jr. *art history educator*
Esler, Anthony James *historian, novelist*
Gross, Robert Alan *history educator*
Harris, James Franklin *philosophy educator*
McGiffert, Michael *history educator, editor*
McLane, Henry Earl, Jr. *philosophy educator*
Nettels, Elsa *English language educator*
Tate, Thaddeus W(ilbur), Jr. (Thad Tate) *history educator, historical institute executive, historian*

Wise
Peake, Richard Henry, Jr. *English language educator*

WASHINGTON

Bellingham
Whisenhunt, Donald Wayne *history educator*

Enumclaw
Vernier, Richard *foreign language educator, author*

Federal Way
Boling, Joseph Edward *numismatist, retired military officer*

Langley
Legters, Lyman Howard *historian*

Olympia
†Chappell, David Jay *language educator, state legislator*
Nesbit, Robert Carrington *historian*

Pullman
Bennett, Edward Moore *historian, educator*

Seattle
Adams, Hazard Simeon *English educator, author*
Behler, Diana Ipsen *Germanic language and literature educator*
Boba, Imre *history educator*
Bosmajian, Haig Aram *speech communication educator*
Brandauer, Frederick Paul *Asian language educator*
Burgess, Charles Orville *history educator*
Butow, Robert Joseph Charles *history educator*
Carlsen, James Caldwell *musicologist, educator*
Coburn, Robert Craig *philosopher*
Coldewey, John Christopher *English literature educator*
Dunn, Richard John *English language educator*
Ellison, Herbert Jay *history educator*
Gerstenberger, Donna Lorine *humanities educator*
Harmon, Daniel Patrick *classics educator*
Heer, Nicholas Lawson *Arabist-Islamist educator*
Jones, Edward Louis *historian, educator*
Keyt, David *philosophy and classics educator*
Kirkendall, Richard Stewart *historian, educator*
Knechtges, David Richard *Chinese and East Asian studies educator*
Korg, Jacob *English literature educator*
Matchett, William H(enry) *English literature educator*
Newmeyer, Frederick Jaret *linguist, educator*
Odegaard, Charles Edwin *history educator*
Potter, Karl Harrington *philosophy educator*
Pressly, Thomas James *history educator*
Pyle, Kenneth Birger *historian, educator*
Scheidel, Thomas Maynard *speech communication educator*
Schiffman, Harold Fosdick *Asian language educator*
Sugar, Peter Frigyes *historian*
Treadgold, Donald Warren *historian, educator*
Webb, Eugene *English language educator*
Ziadeh, Farhat J. *Middle Eastern studies educator*

Spokane
Kossel, Clifford George *retired philosophy educator, clergyman*

Tacoma
Greene, Mott Tuthill *historian*
Le Roy, Bruce Murdock *historian*

Walla Walla
Edwards, Glenn Thomas *history educator*

Yakima
Meshke, George Lewis *drama and humanities educator*

WEST VIRGINIA

Huntington
McKernan, John Joseph *English language educator*

Institute
Brown, Dallas Coverdale, Jr. *history educator, retired army officer*
Thorn, Arline Roush *English language educator*
Wohl, David *humanities educator, theatre director*

Morgantown
Blaydes, Sophia Boyatzies *English language educator*
Davis, Leonard McCutchan *speech educator*
Singer, Armand Edwards *foreign language educator*

West Liberty
Hunter, John Alfred *English educator*

WISCONSIN

Appleton
†Chaney, William Albert *historian, educator*
Goldgar, Bertrand Alvin *literary historian, educator*

Iola
Rulau, Russell *numismatist, consultant*

La Crosse
Rausch, Joan Mary *art historian*

Madison
Ammerman, Robert Ray *philosopher, educator*
Baeumer, Max Lorenz *literature historian*
Berg, William James *French language educator, writer, translator*
Bogue, Allan G. *history educator*
Brembeck, Winston Lamont *educator*
†Cassidy, Frederic Gomes *humanities educator*
Chow, Tse-Tsung *foreign language and literature educator, author, poet*
Ciplijauskaite, Birute *humanities educator*
Coffman, Edward McKenzie *history educator*
Cooper, John Milton, Jr. *history educator, author*
Courtenay, William James *historian, educator*
Cronon, E(dmund) David, Jr. *history educator, historian*
Cronon, William *history educator*
Dembo, Lawrence Sanford *English educator*
DeNovo, John August *history educator*
Fowler, Barbara Hughes *classicist*
Frykenberg, Robert Eric *historian*
Hamalainen, Pekka Kalevi *historian, educator*
Hamerow, Theodore Stephen *history educator*
Harrington, Fred Harvey *history educator*
Hollingsworth, Joseph Rogers *history and sociology educator, writer*
Howe, Herbert Marshall *classics educator*
Ihde, Aaron John *history of science educator emeritus*
Kelly, Douglas *medieval and foreign literature educator*
Kingdon, Robert McCune *historian, educator*
Klein, Sheldon *computational linguist, educator*
Kleinhenz, Christopher *foreign language educator, researcher*
Knowles, Richard Alan John *English language educator*
Kutler, Stanley Ira *history and law educator, author*
MacKendrick, Paul Lachlan *classics educator*
Marks, Elaine *French language educator*
Mosse, George L. *history educator, author*
Mulvihill, Edward Robert *language educator*
O'Brien, James Aloysius *foreign language educator*
Perkins, Merle Lester *French language educator*
Powell, Barry Bruce *classicist*
Rideout, Walter Bates *English educator*
Rothstein, Eric *English educator*
Sewell, Richard Herbert *historian, educator*
Shaw, Joseph Thomas *Slavic languages educator*
Singer, Marcus George *philosopher, educator*
Tedeschi, John Alfred *historian, librarian*
†Vansina, Jan Maria Jozef *historian, educator*
Weinbrot, Howard David *English educator*

Milwaukee
Bicha, Karel Denis *historian, educator*
Carozza, Davy Angelo *Italian language educator*
Dunleavy, Janet Frank Egleson *English language educator*
Dziewanowski, Marian Kamil *history educator*
Friedman, Melvin Jack *language professional, literature educator*
Gallop, Jane (Anne) *women's studies educator, writer*
Hachey, Thomas Eugene *British and Irish history educator, consultant*
Hassan, Ihab Habib *English and comparative literature educator, author*
Horsman, Reginald *history educator*
†Jaksic, Ivan A. *history educator*
McCanles, Michael Frederick *English language educator*
Olson, Frederick Irving *retired history educator*
Roeming, Robert Frederick *foreign language educator*
Schwartz, Joseph *English language educator*
Stromberg, Roland Nelson *historian*
Swanson, Roy Arthur *classicist, educator*

Oshkosh
Burr, John Roy *philosophy educator*

Ripon
Ashley, Robert Paul, Jr. *English literature educator*
Miller, George H. *historian, educator*
Northrop, Douglas Anthony *English educator, college official and dean*

River Falls
Smith, Clyde Curry *historian, educator*

Stevens Point
Paul, Justus Fredrick *historian, educator*

Sun Prairie
Allen, Ronald Royce *communication educator*

Superior
Feldman, Egal *historian, educator*

WYOMING

Laramie
Gressley, Gene Maurice *history educator*
Hardy, Deborah Welles *history educator*
Langlois, Walter Gordon *foreign language educator*
Nye, Eric William *language educator*
Williams, Roger Lawrence *historian, educator*

CANADA

ALBERTA

Edmonton
Prideaux, Gary Dean *linguistics educator*
Smith, Richard Carlisle *history educator*
Woodbridge, Linda *English language educator*

BRITISH COLUMBIA

Burnaby
Buitenhuis, Peter Martinus *language professional, educator*
Kitchen, John Martin *historian, educator*

Gibsons
Millard, Peter Tudor *English language educator*

Vancouver
Aguzzi-Barbagli, Danilo Lorenzo *literature educator*
Batts, Michael Stanley *German language educator*
Bentley, Thomas Roy *literary educator, writer, consultant*
Conway, John S. *history educator*
Durrant, Geoffrey Hugh *retired English language educator*
Froese, Victor *language educator*
Jordan, Robert Maynard *language and literature professional, educator*
Kubicek, Robert Vincent *history educator*
Overmyer, Daniel Lee *Asian studies educator*
Pacheco-Ransanz, Arsenio *Hispanic and Italian studies educator*
Pulleyblank, Edwin George *history educator emeritus, linguist*
Saint-Jacques, Bernard *linguistics educator*
Sikora, Richard Innes *philosophy educator*
Unger, Richard Watson *history educator*
White, Ruth Lillian *French language educator, researcher*

MANITOBA

Winnipeg
Kroetsch, Robert Paul *English language educator, author*
Wolfart, H. C. *linguistics scholar, author, editor*

NEW BRUNSWICK

Douglas
Cogswell, Frederick William *English language educator, poet, editor, publisher*

Fredericton
Elkhadem, Saad Eldin Amin *foreign language and literature educator, author, editor, publisher*
Kennedy, Richard Frederick *English language educator*

Saint John
Condon, Thomas J. *university historian*

NOVA SCOTIA

Halifax
Carrigan, David Owen *history educator*
Flint, John E. *historian, educator*
Gray, James *English literature educator*
Puccetti, Roland Peter *philosopher, educator*

Liscomb
Hemlow, Joyce *language and literature educator, author*

Wolfville
Zeman, Jarold Knox *history educator*

ONTARIO

Downsview
Thomas, Clara McCandless *retired English language educator, biographer*

Hamilton
†Blewett, David Lambert *English literature educator*
Lee, Alvin A. *literary educator, author*
Mc Kay, Alexander Gordon *classics educator*

Kingston
Akenson, Donald Harman *historian, educator*
Hamilton, Albert Charles *English language educator*
Mac Kenzie, Norman Hugh *educator, writer*
Riley, Anthony William *German language and literature educator*

London
Collins, Thomas Joseph *English language educator*
Gerber, Douglas Earl *classics educator*

Mississauga
Astington, John Harold *English educator*

Nepean
Kallmann, Helmut Max *music historian, retired music librarian*

North York
†Adelman, Howard *philosophy educator*
Granatstein, Jack Lawrence *history educator*

Ottawa
Dray, William Herbert *philosophy educator*
Hamelin, Marcel *historian, educator*
Staines, David McKenzie *English educator*

Peterborough
Symons, Thomas H. B. *historian, educator*

Rockwood
Eichner, Hans *German language and literature educator*

Thornbury
Keyes, Gordon Lincoln *history educator*

Toronto
Birnbaum, Eleazar *language proffessional*
Blissett, William Frank *English literature educator*
Bouissac, Paul Antoine *language professional*
Conacher, Desmond John *classics educator*
Dryer, Douglas Poole *retired philosophy educator*
Goffart, Walter André *history educator*
Graham, Victor Ernest *French language educator*
Grendler, Paul Frederick *history educator*
Hayne, David Mackness *retired French language educator*
†Johnson, Robert Eugene *historian, academic administrator*
†McAuliffe, Jane Dammen *Middle Eastern and Islamic studies educator*
Millgate, Michael (Henry) *retired English educator*
Morey, Carl Reginald *musicologist, academic administrator*
†Morgan, Peter F. *English educator, philosophy educator*
O'Brien, Michael John *classics educator*
Redford, Donald Bruce *historian, archaeologist*
Saddlemyer, Ann (Eleanor Saddlemyer) *English educator, critic, theater historian*
Schogt, Henry Gilius *foreign language educator*
†Shields, Carol Ann *writer, educator*
Skvorecky, Josef Vaclav *English educator, novelist*
†Webster, Jill Rosemary *historian, educator*
Wetzel, Heinz *foreign language educator*
Wevers, John William *retired Semitic languages educator*
Zemans, Joyce Pearl *art historian, Canadian arts administrator*

Waterloo
Cornell, Paul Grant *history educator*
Haworth, Lawrence Lindley *philosophy educator*
Smith, Rowland James *English language educator*
Suits, Bernard Herbert *philosophy educator*

PRINCE EDWARD ISLAND

Charlottetown
Baker, Ronald James *English language educator, university administrator*

QUEBEC

Montreal
Bertos, Rigas Nicholas *art history educator*
Beugnot, Bernard Andre Henri *French literature educator*
Duquette, Jean-Pierre *French language and literature educator*
Hamel, Reginald *history educator*
Hoffmann, Peter Conrad Werner *history educator*
Kinsley, William Benton *literature educator*
Leblanc, Hugues *philosophy educator*
McLelland, Joseph Cumming *philosophy educator, former university dean*
Morin, Yves-Charles *linguistics educator, researcher*
Paikowsky, Sandra Roslyn *art historian*
Shea, William Rene *historian, philosopher of science, educator*
Silverthorne, Michael James *classics educator*

North Hatley
†Jones, Douglas Gordon *retired literature educator*

Outremont
Domaradzki, Theodore Felix *Slavic studies educator, editor*

Quebec
†Porter, John Robert *art history educator, curator, writer*

Rock Forest
Lamirande, Emilien *historian, educator*

SASKATCHEWAN

Saskatoon
Brewster, Elizabeth Winifred *English language educator, poet, novelist*

MEXICO

Morelia
Warren, J. Benedict *retired history educator*

AUSTRALIA

Bundoora
Isaac, Rhys Llywelyn *historian, educator*

Sydney
Salsbury, Stephen Matthew *historian, educator*

AUSTRIA

Gaz
Weisstein, Ulrich Werner *English literature educator*

Vienna
Steinbruckner, Bruno Friedrich *foreign language educator*

ENGLAND

Coventry
Trigg, Roger Hugh *philosophy educator*

Eastbourne,
Baylen, Joseph O. *retired history educator*

Hove
Kitchin, Laurence Tyson *liberal arts and drama educator, author*

London
Kane, George Joseph *humanities educator*

Milford on Sea
Styan, John Louis *English literature and theater educator*

Oxford
Carey, John *English language educator, literary critic*
Howe, Daniel Walker *historian, educator*

Trumpington Cambs
Santoni, Ronald Ernest *philosophy educator*

FRANCE

Paris
†Konvitz, Josef Wolf *history educator, international civil servant*

GERMANY

Münster
Spevack, Marvin *English educator*

Nuremberg
Doerries, Reinhard René *modern history educator*

ISRAEL

Jerusalem
Davis, Moshe *historian*

ITALY

Florence
Pope-Hennessy, John Wyndham *art historian*

THE PHILIPPINES

Musuan
†Lao, Mardonio Magadan *history educator, researcher, farmer*

SCOTLAND

Aberdeen
†Rousseau, George Sebastian *Eighteenth-century studies educator, chamber musician*

Cellardyke
Roff, William Robert *history educator, writer*

Saint Andrews
Lenman, Bruce Philip *historian, educator*

SPAIN

Barcelona
Jackson, Gabriel *historian*

TURKEY

Ankara
Inalcik, Halil *historian, educator*

ADDRESS UNPUBLISHED

Angell, Richard Bradshaw *philosophy educator*
Aptheker, Herbert *historian, lecturer*
Archibold, Mildred Haynes *bilingual education educator*
Baxter, Stephen Bartow *retired history educator*
Bercovitch, Sacvan *English language professional, educator*
Bloom, Edward Alan *Englsih language educator, author*
Bok, Sissela *philosopher, writer*
Bolsterli, Margaret Jones *English educator*
†Bosse, Malcolm Joseph, Jr. *professional language educator, author*
Boyle, Richard John *art historian, author*
Brodnax, Margaret O'Bryan *retired English language educator*
Cachia, Pierre Jacques *Middle East languages and culture educator, researcher*
Campbell, Jackson Justice *medievalist, educator*
Chandler, Alfred Dupont, Jr. *historian, educator*
Chandra, Pramod *art history educator*
Chellas, Brian Farrell *philosophy educator*
Chinoy, Helen Krich *theater historian*
Clark, Thomas Lloyd *English linguistics educator*
Coffman, Stanley Knight, Jr. *English educator, former college president*
Condit, Doris Elizabeth *historian*
Crampton, Esther Larson *educator*
Culverwell, Albert Henry *historian*
Curry, Richard Orr *history educator and freelance writer*
Curti, Merle Eugene *historian, educator*
†Ebitz, David MacKinnon *art historian, museum director*
Edel, Abraham *philosophy educator*
Edmunds, (Arthur) Lowell *philology educator*
Farwell, Harold Frederick, Jr. *English language educator*
Franklin, John Hope *historian, educator, author*
Galbraith, John Semple *history educator*
Gillespie, Gerald Ernest Paul *comparative literature educator, writer*
Gordon, Cyrus Herzl *Orientalist, educator*
Greene, Elinore Aschah *speech and drama professional, writer*
Gromen, Richard John *historian, educator*
Hart, Arthur Alvin *historian, author*
Haskins, James *English language educator, writer*
Hawkes, John *humanities educator, author*
Heilbrun, Carolyn Gold *English literature educator*
Herbst, Jurgen *history and education educator*
Herington, Cecil John *classics educator*
Hetzron, Robert *linguist, educator*
Ivry, Alfred Lyon *foreign language and literature educator*
Johnson, Clifton Herman *historian archivist, former research center director*
Jordan, William Bryan, Jr. *art historian*
Jourdain, Alice Marie *philosopher, retired educator*
Kalish, Donald *philosophy educator*
Kastor, Frank Sullivan *English language educator*
Keyes, Margaret Naumann *home economics educator*
Kolko, Gabriel *historian, educator*
Korsgaard, Christine Marion *philosophy educator*
Kramer, Dale Vernon *English language educator*
Kundera, Milan *writer, educator*
Kwiat, Joseph J. *English educator, playwright*
Laux, James Michael *historian, educator*
Lederman, Marie Jean *English language educator*
Levack, Arthur Paul *history educator emeritus*
Lewis, Norman *English language educator, writer*
Link, Arthur Stanley *history educator, editor*
Link, Mae Mills (Mrs. S. Gordden Link) *space medicine historian and consultant*
Loughran, James Newman *philosophy educator, former university president*
Lyons, John Ormsby *English language educator*
Maehl, William Harvey *historian, educator*
Maehl, William Henry *historian, university administrator*
Marshall, Richard *art historian, curator*
McCormick, John Owen *retired comparative literature educator*
McDermott, Agnes Charlene Senape *philosophy educator*
Morgan, Edmund Sears *historian*
Morrissey, Charles Thomas *historian, educator*
Murphy, Francis *English language educator*
Nebel, Henry Martin, Jr. *literature historian, educator*
Nelson-Humphries, Tessa (Tessa Unthank) *English language educator*
Niedzielski, Henri Zygmunt *French and English language educator*
Olson, James Clifton *historian, university president*
Olson, Paul Richard *Spanish literature educator, editor*
Pace, R(alph) Wayne *organizational behavior educator*
Palter, Robert Monroe *philosophy and history educator*
Peyser, Joseph Leonard *historical researcher, translator, author*
Pflanze, Otto Paul *history educator*
Reuman, Robert Everett *philosophy educator*
Riasanovsky, Nicholas Valentine *historian, educator*
Richardson, Robert Dale, Jr. *English language educator*
Rickard, Ruth David *retired history and political science educator*
Roller, Duane Henry DuBose *historian of science, educator*
Rollins, Alfred Brooks, Jr. *historian, educator*
Romeo, Luigi *linguist, educator*
Rothman, Julius Lawrence *retired English language educator*
Schnucker, Robert Victor *history and religion educator*
Seidensticker, Edward George *Japanese language and literature educator*
Smither, Howard Elbert *musicologist*
Smock, Raymond William *historian, government official*
Solomon, Robert Charles *philosopher, educator*
Stolarik, M. Mark *history educator*
Street, John Charles *linguistics educator*
Sundstrom, Aileen Lois *speech educator*
Sutton, Julia Sumberg *musicologist, dance historian*
Towers, (Augustus) Robert, Jr. *English educator, writer*
Trelease, Allen William *historian, educator*
Wallace, William Augustine *philosophy and history educator*
Waller, Gary Fredric *English language educator, poet*
Weber, Eugen *historian, educator, author*
Wolters, Oliver William *history educator*
Yolton, John William *philosopher, educator*

HUMANITIES: LIBRARIES

UNITED STATES

ALABAMA

Birmingham
Spence, Paul Herbert *librarian*
Stephens, Jerry Wayne *librarian, library director*
Stewart, George Ray *librarian*

Huntsville
†Schremser, Donna Barrett *library executive*

Mobile
Bahr, Alice Harrison *librarian*
Damico, James Anthony *library director*

Montgomery
Harris, Patricia Lea *librarian*

Troy
Thompson, Jean Tanner *retired librarian*

ALASKA

Juneau
Schorr, Alan Edward *librarian, publisher*

ARIZONA

Mesa
Anderson, Herschel Vincent *librarian*

Phoenix
Edwards, Ralph M. *librarian*
Fox, Frances Juanice *retired librarian, educator, retired*
Miele, Anthony William *librarian*

Scottsdale
†Saferite, Linda Lee *library director*

Sun City West
Williams, William Harrison *retired librarian*

Tempe
†Borovansky, Vladimir Theodore *librarian*
†Metros, Mary Teresa *librarian*

Tucson
Altman, Ellen *librarian, educator*
Anderson, Rachael Keller *library administrator*
Dickinson, Donald Charles *library science educator*
†Hurt, Charles *college librarian*
Hurt, Charlie Deuel, III *library school director, educator*
Laird, Wilbur David, Jr. *librarian*
Miller, Liz Rodriguez *public library system director, librarian*
Wolfe, William Jerome *librarian, English language educator*

ARKANSAS

Arkadelphia
†Martin, Marilyn Joan *library director*

Fayetteville
Harrison, John Arthur *library administrator*

Fort Smith
Larson, Larry *librarian*

Little Rock
Compton, Susan LaNell *retired librarian*
†Jones, Phillip Lindsey *librarian*
Mulkey, Jack Clarendon *library director*

State University
Hansard, James William *library director*

CALIFORNIA

Aptos
Heron, David Winston *librarian*

Bakersfield
†Duquette, Diane Rhea *library director*

Belvedere Tiburon
Crockett, Ethel Stacy *librarian*

Berkeley
Buckland, Michael Keeble *librarian, educator*
Danton, Joseph Periam *librarian, educator*
Gregor, Dorothy Deborah *librarian*
†Hanff, Peter Edward *librarian, bibliographer*
Harlan, Robert Dale *library and information studies educator, academic administrator*
Minudri, Regina Ursula *library director, consultant*
Rafael, Ruth Kelson *archivist, librarian, consultant*
Van House, Nancy Anita *library educator*

Carlsbad
Lange, Clifford E. *librarian*

Carmel
Jorgensen, William Ernest *retired librarian*

Commerce
Conover, Robert Warren *librarian*

Corona
†Leo, Karen Ann *library administrator*

Cupertino
Fletcher, Homer Lee *librarian*

Davis
†Grossman, George Stefan *library director, law eductor*
Sharrow, Marilyn Jane *library administrator*

Encino
Wood, Raymund Francis *retired librarian*

Fresno
Gorman, Michael Joseph *library director, educator*
Kallenberg, John Kenneth *librarian*

Fullerton
Ayala, John *librarian, dean*

Glendora
Thompson, John Reed *librarian*

Huntington Beach
†Hayden, Ron L. *library director*

Inglewood
†Alaniz, Miguel José Castañeda *library director*

Irvine
Boyer, Calvin James *librarian*
Euster, Joanne Reed *librarian*

La Jolla
†Goff, William James *librarian*

Long Beach
Lathrop, Ann *librarian, educator*

Los Angeles
Ackerman, Helen Page *librarian, educator*
Borko, Harold *information scientist, psychologist, educator*
Chang, Henry Chung-Lien *library administrator*
Cuadra, Carlos Albert *information scientist, management executive*
Gilman, Nelson Jay *library director*
Lynch, Beverly Pfeifer *library science educator*
†Martinez, Elizabeth *librarian*
Martinez Smith, Elizabeth *librarian*
Polan, Morris *librarian*
†Robinson, Barbara Jõn *librarian*
Shank, Russell *librarian, educator*
Werner, Gloria S. *librarian*

Mill Valley
Dillon, Richard Hugh *librarian, author*
†Hair, William Bates, III *librarian*

Modesto
†Kreissman, Starrett *librarian*

Monterey
Reneker, Maxine Hohman *librarian*

Mountain View
Di Muccio, Mary Jo *retired librarian*

Northridge
†Curzon, Susan Carol *library administrator*

Oakland
†Gomez, Martin *library director*
Howatt, Sister Helen Clare *library director*

Ontario
†Luce, Susan Marie *library director*

Palo Alto
Dassoff, Christine Ellen *library administrator*

Pasadena
Brudvig, Glenn Lowell *library director*
Harmsen, Tyrus George *librarian*

Sacramento
Burns, John Francis *archivist, state official*
†Killian, Richard M. *library director*
Strong, Gary Eugene *librarian*

Salinas
†Shaffer, Dallas Young *library administrator*
Spinks, Paul *retired library director*

San Bernardino
†Anderson, Barbara Louise *library director*
Burgess, Michael *library science educator, publisher*

San Diego
Sannwald, William Walter *librarian*

San Francisco
Dowlin, Kenneth Everett *librarian*
Frantz, John Corydon *librarian*

San Jose
Fish, James Henry *library director*
Healey, James Stewart *library science educator*
Schmidt, Cyril James *librarian*

San Luis Obispo
†Walch, David Bean *librarian, university official*

San Marcos
Ciurczak, Alexis *librarian*

San Marino
Moffett, William Andrew *librarian, educator*
Robertson, Mary Louise *archivist, historian*
Woodward, Daniel Holt *librarian, researcher*

Santa Ana
Richard, Robert John *library director*

Santa Barbara
Boisse, Joseph Adonias *library administrator*
Dougan, Robert Ormes *librarian*
†Keator, Carol Lynne *library director*

Santa Clara
Hopkinson, Shirley Lois *library and information science educator*

Santa Cruz
Dyson, Allan Judge *librarian*

Santa Rosa
†Sabsay, David *library consultant*

Sherman Oaks
Miller, Margaret Haigh *librarian*

Stanford
†Derksen, Charlotte Ruth Meynink *librarian*
†Keller, Michael Alan *librarian, educator, musicologist*
†Ross, Alexander Duncan *art librarian*
Weber, David C(arter) *librarian*

Stockton
†Meyer, Ursula *library director*

Torrance
†Buckley, James W. *librarian*

Ventura
†Adeniran, Dixie Darlene *library administrator*

COLORADO

Boulder
†Gralapp, Marcelee Gayl *librarian*

Colorado Springs
Budington, William Stone *retired librarian*
Margolis, Bernard Allen *library administrator, antique book merchant and appraiser*
Sheridan, John Brian *librarian*

Denver
†Ashton, Rick James *librarian*
†Miller, Sarah Pearl *librarian*

Englewood
Czartolomny, Piotr Antoni *librarian*
Wynar, Bohdan Stephen *librarian, author and editor*

Fort Collins
Chambers, Joan Louise *library director*

Golden
Lerud, Joanne Van Ornum *library administrator*

Greeley
Seager, Daniel Albert *university librarian*

Lakewood
†Knott, William Alan *library director, library management and building consultant*

Pueblo
†Bates, Charles Emerson *library administrator*

CONNECTICUT

Bridgeport
†Johmann, Nancy *librarian*

Fairfield
Bryan, Barbara Day *librarian*
†Kijanka, Dorothy M. *library administrator*

Hartford
†Kaimowitz, Jeffrey Hugh *librarian*

†Martin, Vernon Emil *librarian*
†Wilkie, Everett Cleveland, Jr. *librarian*

Middletown
Adams, John Robert *librarian*

New Britain
Donahugh, Robert Hayden *library administrator*
†Eiselstein, June *library director*

New Haven
Abell, Millicent Demmin *university library administrator*
Franklin, Ralph William *library director, literary scholar*
Oliver-Warren, Mary Elizabeth *library science educator*
Siggins, Jack Arthur *librarian*
Stuehrenberg, Paul Frederick *librarian*

New London
Rogers, Brian Deane *librarian*

Southbury
Usher, Elizabeth Reuter (Mrs. William A. Scar) *retired librarian*

Stamford
†DiMattia, Ernest Anthony, Jr. *library administrator*

Storrs Mansfield
Stevens, Norman Dennison *retired library director*

DELAWARE

Wilmington
Williams, Richmond Dean *library appraiser, consultant*
†Wodjewodzki, Catherine *reference librarian, state legislator*

DISTRICT OF COLUMBIA

Washington
Atiyeh, George Nicholas *library administrator, educator*
Avram, Henriette Davidson *librarian, government official*
†Battin, Patricia Meyer *librarian*
†Baum, Ingeborg Ruth *librarian*
Bledsoe, Ralph Champion *archivist*
Bold, Frances Ann *librarian*
Boorstin, Daniel J. *librarian emeritus, history educator, author, editor*
Broering, Naomi Cordero *librarian*
Bush, Robert Donald *historical preservation director*
Chin, Cecilia Hui-Hsin *librarian*
Clemmer, Dan Orr *librarian*
Cylke, Frank Kurt *librarian*
Daffron, MaryEllen *librarian*
Deel, Frances Quinn *librarian*
Emperado, Mercedes Lopez *librarian*
Fawcett, John Thomas *archivist*
†Franklin, Hardy R. *library director*
Gernand, Bradley Elton *archivist, manuscripts librarian*
Gifford, Prosser *library administrator*
Gifford, Virginia Snodgrass *cataloger, bibliographer*
Gundersheimer, Werner Leonard *library director*
Haas, Warren James *librarian, consultant*
Haley, Roger Kendall *librarian*
Harlem, Susan Lynn *librarian*
Hedges, Kamla King *corporate librarian*
Heiss, Harry Glen *archivist*
Higbee, Joan Florence *librarian*
Jones, Catherine Ann *library administrator*
Karklins, Vija L. *librarian*
Kohlhorst, Gail Lewis *librarian*
†Leonard, Lawrence Edwards *librarian*
Lorenz, John George *librarian, consultant*
Marcum, Deanna Bowling *library administrator*
Martin, Susan Katherine *librarian*
†Mathews, Anne Jones *library director, educator*
†Mikel, Sarah Ann *librarian*
Newton, Virginia *archivist, historian*
Perella, Susanne Brennan *librarian*
†Peterson, Trudy Huskamp *national archivist*
Pruett, James Worrell *librarian, musicologist*
†Ratner, Rhoda Sue *librarian*
Renninger, Mary Karen *librarian*
Reynolds, Gary Kemp *librarian*
Rovelstad, Mathilde Verner *library science educator*
Sahanek, Tatana *librarian, editor*
Sampson, Daphne Rae *library director*
Scott, Catherine Dorothy *librarian, consultant*
Smith, Barbara Jeanne *library administrator*
†Tashjean, Catherine Richardson *librarian*
†Turtell, Neal Timothy *librarian*
Walton, Kathleen Endres *librarian*
Wand, Patricia Ann *librarian*
Wattenmaker, Richard Joel *archive director, art scholar*
Young, Peter Robert *librarian*

FLORIDA

Atlantis
Gough, Carolyn Harley *library director*

Bal Harbour
Gray, Phyllis Anne *librarian*

Boca Raton
Bettmann, Otto Ludwig *picture archivist, graphic historian*

Coral Gables
Rodgers, Frank *librarian*

Gainesville
Canelas, Dale Brunelle *library director*
Goggin, Margaret Knox *librarian, educator*
Harrer, Gustave Adolphus *librarian, educator*
Willocks, Robert Max *retired librarian*

Hialeah
†Clarke, Robert Flanders *librarian, administrator, public health service officer*

Jacksonville
Williams, Judith L. *library administrator*

Lakeland
Reich, David Lee *librarian*

Melbourne
†Henson, Llewellyn Lafayette, III *library director*

Miami
Comras, Rema *library director*
Kozlowski, Ronald Stephan *librarian*
Treyz, Joseph Henry *librarian*

Naples
Chartrand, Robert Lee *information scientist*

Pompano Beach
Trenery, Mary Ellen *librarian*

Saint Petersburg
Hargrave, Victoria Elizabeth *librarian*
Runge, De Lyle Paul *retired library director, consultant*

Sarasota
Kelley, Susan Curtin *writer*

Tallahassee
Robbins, Jane Borsch *library science educator, information science educator*
Rockwood, Ruth H. *former library science educator*
Summers, Frank William *librarian*
Summers, Lorraine Dey Schaeffer *librarian*
Trezza, Alphonse Fiore *librarian, educator*
Wilkins, (George) Barratt *librarian*
Zachert, Martha Jane *retired librarian*

Tampa
Harkness, Mary Lou *librarian*
†Kemp, Thomas Jay *librarian*
Tabor, Curtis Harold, Jr. *library director*

Winter Park
Rogers, Rutherford David *librarian*

GEORGIA

Athens
Potter, William Gray, Jr. *library director*
†Surrency, Erwin Campbell *librarian, educator*

Atlanta
Brown, Lorene B(yron) *library educator, educational administrator*
Cann, Sharon Lee *librarian*
Churchwell, Charles Darrett *librarian*
Drake, Miriam Anna *librarian, educator*
†Dubberly, Ronald Alvah *library director*
Jeschke, Channing Renwick *librarian*
Lawson, A(bram) Venable *librarian, educational administrator*
Miller, Rosalind Elaine *librarian, educator*
Roberts, Edward Graham *librarian*
†Schewe, Donald Bruce *archivist, library director*
Yates, Ella Gaines *library consultant*

Augusta
Rowland, Arthur Ray *librarian*

Bainbridge
Frieling, Thomas Jerome *library director*

Lilburn
Forsee, Joe Brown *library director*

Macon
†Schmidt, Charles J. *library administrator*

Rome
†Overbeck, James A. *library director, educator*

Savannah
Ball, Ardella Patricia *library science educator*

HAWAII

Honolulu
Kane, Bartholomew Aloysius *state librarian*
Stevens, Robert David *librarian, educator*

IDAHO

Boise
†Bolles, Charles Avery *librarian*

Jerome
†Bell, Maxine Toolson *librarian, state legislator*

Moscow
Force, Ronald Wayne *librarian*

ILLINOIS

Carbondale
†Bauner, Ruth Elizabeth *library administrator, reference librarian*

Champaign
Krummel, Donald William *librarian, educator*
Wajenberg, Arnold Sherman *retired librarian, educator*
Wert, Lucille Mathena *librarian, educator*

Chicago
Berry, John Willard *librarian, consultant*

Brown, Richard Holbrook *library administrator, historian*
Elbaz, Sohair Wastawy *library director, consultant*
Gerdes, Neil Wayne *library director*
†Gross, Dorothy-Ellen *library director, dean*
†Hayden, Carla Diane *librarian, educator*
King, David Edgar *librarian, editor*
Knoblauch, Mark George *librarian*
†Lenneberg, Hans *music librarian, educator*
Miletich, Ivo *library and information scientist, bibliographer, educator, linguist, literature research specialist*
†Morrison, Samuel F. *library administrator, chief librarian*
Park, Chung Il *librarian*
Runkle, Martin Davey *library director*
†Samuels, Joel L. *librarian, clergyman*
Scott, Alice H. *librarian*
†Simpson, Donald Bruce *library director*
Stein, Jay Wobith *legal research and education consultant*
Veit, Fritz *librarian*
Waite, Ellen Jane *library director*
Whiteley, Sandra Marie *librarian, editor*
Winger, Howard Woodrow *library educator*

De Kalb
Kies, Cosette Nell *library science educator, consultant*

Decatur
†Moorman, John A. *librarian*

Deerfield
Young, Arthur Price *librarian, educator*

Elgin
†Zack, Daniel Gerard *library director*

Elmhurst
Klatt, Melvin John *library administrator*

Evanston
Bishop, David Fulton *library administrator*
†Cates, Jo Ann *librarian, management consultant*
†Crawford, Susan Y. Young *library director, educator*
Wright, Donald Eugene *retired librarian*

Galesburg
Kirk, Sherwood *librarian*

Jacksonville
Gallas, Martin Hans *librarian*

Joliet
†Johnston, James Robert *library director*

Lake Forest
Miller, Arthur Hawks, Jr. *librarian, consultant*

Maywood
Ellington, Mildred L. *librarian*

Normal
Peterson, Fred McCrae *librarian*

Peoria
†Herring, Susan Kay *library director*
Lindgren, William Dale *librarian*
Watson, Ellen I. *library director*

Quincy
Tyer, Travis Earl *librarian*

River Forest
Brace, William *information science educator*
Marco, Guy Anthony *librarian*
McCusker, Mary Lauretta *library science educator*

Rockford
Chitwood, Julius Richard *librarian*

Schaumburg
Chitwood, Lera Catherine *information professional, manufacturing company manager*

Springfield
†Lamont, Bridget Later *librarian, consultant*
†Petterchak, Janice A. *library director*

Urbana
Brichford, Maynard Jay *archivist*
Mc Clellan, William Monson *library administrator*
Shtohryn, Dmytro Michael *librarian, educator*
Watson, Paula D. *library administrator*

Wheaton
Thompson, Bert Allen *retired librarian*

Wheeling
Hammer, Donald Price *librarian*
Mc Clarren, Robert Royce *librarian*

Wilmington
Anderson, Mary Jane *public library director*

INDIANA

Bloomington
Cagle, William Rea *librarian*
Kudryk, Oleg *librarian*
Rudolph, Lavere Christian *library director*
White, Herbert Spencer *research library educator, university dean*

Evansville
†Howard, Edward Allen *library administrator, consultant*

Fort Wayne
†Jackson, Paul Howard *librarian*
Krull, Jeffrey Robert *library director*

Indianapolis
†Bundy, David Dale *librarian, educator*
Ewick, Charles Ray *librarian*

Fischler, Barbara Brand *librarian*
Gnat, Raymond Earl *librarian*

La Porte
Grott, Geraldine *librarian*

Lafayette
†Posey, Edwin Dalfield *librarian*
VanHandel, Ralph Anthony *librarian*

Notre Dame
†Jacobs, Roger Francis *librarian, educator, lawyer*
Miller, Robert Carl *library director*

Richmond
Farber, Evan Ira *librarian*
Kirk, Thomas Garrett, Jr. *librarian*

Saint Meinrad
Daly, Simeon Philip John *librarian*

South Bend
†Napoli, Donald J. *library director*

Terre Haute
Little, Robert David *library science educator*

West Lafayette
Markee, Katherine Madigan *librarian, educator*
Mobley, Emily Ruth *library dean, educator*

IOWA

Ames
Eaton, Nancy L. *librarian, dean*

Camanche
Rittmer, Elaine Heneke *library media specialist*

Cedar Rapids
†Armitage, Thomas Edward *library director*

Davenport
†Runge, Kay Kretschmar *library director*

Des Moines
Estes, Elaine Rose Graham *librarian*

Grinnell
McKee, Christopher Fulton *librarian, naval historian, educator*

Iowa City
Bentz, Dale Monroe *librarian*

Sioux City
†Olsen, Janus Frederick, III *library director*

West Branch
Mather, Mildred Eunice *retired archivist*
†Smith, Richard Norton *library director*

KANSAS

Enterprise
Wickman, John Edward *librarian, historian*

Lawrence
†Koepp, Donna Pauline Petersen *librarian*

Topeka
Marvin, James Conway *librarian, consultant*

Wichita
Rademacher, Richard Joseph *librarian*

KENTUCKY

Danville
Campbell, Stanley Richard *library services director*

Frankfort
Nelson, James Albert *librarian, state official*

Grayson
Waite, Lemuel Warren *library director*

Lexington
Mason, Ellsworth Goodwin *librarian*
Sineath, Timothy Wayne *librarian, educator, university administrator*
Willis, Paul Allen *librarian*

Louisville
†Deering, Ronald Franklin *librarian, minister*
Edwards, Grace Coleman *librarian*
†Henderson, Harriet *librarian*
VanMeter, Vandelia L. *library director*

Morehead
Besant, Larry Xon *librarian, administrator, consultant*

Owensboro
Eaton, Clara Barbour *librarian*

LOUISIANA

Baton Rouge
Patterson, Charles Darold *librarian, educator*
†Richard, John Benard *library director*

Lacombe
Hendricks, Donald Duane *librarian*

Lafayette
Carstens, Jane Ellen *library science educator*

Metairie
Walsh, Maurice David, Jr. *former librarian, business executive*

New Orleans
Leinbach, Philip Eaton *librarian*
†Taylor, Kenneth Byron, Jr. *librarian, minister, religion educator*
Wilson, C. Daniel, Jr. *library director*

Pineville
Martin, W. Terry *librarian*

Ruston
Wicker, William Walter *librarian*

Shreveport
Pelton, James Rodger *librarian*

MAINE

Orient
Chenevert, Edward Valmore, Jr. *retired librarian, real estate broker*

Portland
Parks, George Richard *librarian*

Presque Isle
McGrath, Anna Fields *library director*

Waterville
Muehlner, Suanne Wilson *library director*

MARYLAND

Annapolis
Howard, Joseph Harvey *retired librarian*
Papenfuse, Edward Carl, Jr. *archivist, state official*
Werking, Richard Hume *librarian, historian, academic administrator*

Baltimore
Bennett, Scott Boyce *librarian*
Magnuson, Nancy *librarian*

Beltsville
Andre, Pamela Q. J. *library director*

Bethesda
Knachel, Philip Atherton *librarian*
Lindberg, Donald Allan Bror *library administrator, pathologist, educator*
†Masys, Daniel Rochard *library director*
Smith, Ruth Lillian Schluchter *librarian*
Tilley, Carolyn Bittner *information manager, technical information specialist*

College Park
Burke, Frank Gerard *archivist*
Wasserman, Paul *library and information science educator*

Columbia
Wolter, John Amadeus *librarian, government official*

Gaithersburg
Klein, Sami Weiner *librarian*

Kensington
Rather, Lucia Porcher Johnson *library administrator*

Potomac
Broderick, John Caruthers *retired librarian, educator*

Rockville
Brandhorst, Wesley Theodore *information manager*
Missar, Charles Donald *librarian*

Savage
Filby, Percy William *library consultant*

Silver Spring
Hackett, John Francis *archivist*
†von Hake, Margaret Joan *librarian*

MASSACHUSETTS

Amherst
Bozone, Billie Rae *librarian, consultant*
Bridegam, Willis Edward, Jr. *librarian*
Talbot, Richard Joseph *library administrator*

Boston
Allen, Nancy Schuster *librarian*
Armstrong, Rodney *librarian*
†Chen, Ching-chih *information science educator, consultant*
Curley, Arthur *library director*
Patterson, Robert Logan *librarian, country and western dance promoter*
Sauer, David Andrew *librarian*

Bridgewater
Neubauer, Richard A. *library science educator, consultant*

Brookline
Tuchman, Maurice Simon *library director*

Cambridge
Bond, William Henry *librarian, educator*
Carpenter, Kenneth E. *librarian, bibliographer*
Cole, Heather E. *librarian*
De Gennaro, Richard *library director*
Hamilton, Malcolm Cowan *librarian, editor, indexer, personnel educator*
†Horrell, Jeffrey Lanier *library administrator*
King, Patricia Miller *library administrator, historian*
Lucker, Jay K. *library administrator, consultant*
Stoddard, Roger Eliot *librarian*
Wendorf, Richard Harold *library director, educator*
Willard, Louis Charles *librarian*

Framingham
†Kuklinski, Joan Lindsey *librarian*
Preve, Roberta Jean *librarian, researcher*

Granby
Edmonds, Anne Carey *librarian*

Lexington
Freitag, Wolfgang Martin *librarian, educator*

Northampton
†Piccinino, Rocco Michael *librarian*

Quincy
†Watson, Warren Edward *retired library administrator*

Salem
†La Moy, William Thomas *library director, editor*

Shrewsbury
Piggford, Roland Rayburn *library and information services consultant*

Springfield
Brennen, Patrick Wayne *library director*
†Costello, Thomas Murray *library and museums executive*
Keough, Francis Paul *librarian*
†Stack, May E. *library director*
Utley, F. Knowlton *library director, educator*

Wakefield
Kelley, John Dennis *librarian*

Waltham
Hahn, Bessie King *library administrator, lecturer*
†Hayes, Sherman L. *library director*

Williamstown
†Gibson, Sarah Ann Scott *art librarian*
Wikander, Lawrence Einar *librarian*

Worcester
Baughman, Susan S. *library director*
Dunlap, Ellen S. *library administrator*
†Johnson, Penelope B. *librarian*
Mc Corison, Marcus Allen *librarian, cultural organization administrator*
Morton, Donald John *librarian*

MICHIGAN

Adrian
Dombrowski, Mark Anthony *librarian*

Allendale
Murray, Diane Elizabeth *librarian*

Ann Arbor
Beaubien, Anne Kathleen *librarian*
Bidlack, Russell Eugene *librarian, educator and dean emeritus*
Carlen, Sister Claudia *librarian*
Dougherty, Richard Martin *library and information science educator*
Dunlap, Connie *librarian*
†Hernandez, Ramon Robert *public library director*
Hessler, David William *information management educator, information systems consultant*
Riggs, Donald Eugene *librarian, university dean*
Slavens, Thomas Paul *information and library studies educator*
Wagman, Frederick Herbert *librarian, educator, deceased*
Wall, Carroll Edward *librarian, publisher*
Warner, Robert Mark *archivist, historian, university dean*
Williams, John Troy *librarian, educator*

Dearborn
†Coady, Reginald Patrick *library director*
Marquis, Rollin Park *retired librarian*

Detroit
Audia, Christina *librarian*
Curtis, Jean Trawick *library director*
†Frenette, Geraldine Gloria *librarian*
†Klont, Barbara Anne *librarian*
Mika, Joseph John *library director, consultant*
Spyers-Duran, Peter *librarian, educator*
†Tong, James *librarian, consultant*

East Lansing
Chapin, Richard Earl *librarian*
De Benko, Eugene *educator, librarian*

Grand Rapids
†Jacobsen, Arnold *archivist*
†Monsma, Marvin Eugene *library director*

Houghton
Krenitsky, Michael V. *librarian*

Kalamazoo
Carlson, Andrew Raymond *archivist*
Grotzinger, Laurel Ann *library science educator*
Lowrie, Jean Elizabeth *librarian, educator*

Lansing
Fry, James Wilson *state librarian*

Midland
†Byers, Rosemarie *library director*

Port Huron
Wu, Harry Pao-Tung *librarian*

Thompsonville
Perry, Margaret *librarian, writer*

Ypsilanti
†Beck, Mary Clare *librarian*

MINNESOTA

Collegeville
Haile, Getatchew *archivist, educator*

Duluth
Pearce, Donald Joslin *librarian*

Minneapolis
Asp, William George *librarian*
Goldberg Kent, Susan *library director*
Huttner, Marian Alice *library administrator*
Shaughnessy, Thomas William *librarian, consultant*
Smith, Eldred Reid *library educator*

Northfield
Hong, Howard Vincent *library administrator, philosophy educator, editor, translator*
Metz, T(heodore) John *librarian, consultant*

Rochester
Key, Jack Dayton *librarian*
Leachman, Roger Mack *librarian*

Saint Paul
Holbert, Sue Elisabeth *archivist, writer, consultant*
Kane, Lucile Marie *archivist, historian*
MacDonald, Roderick *library director*
†Magnuson, Norris Alden *history educator*
Wagner, Mary Margaret *library and information science educator*

Saint Peter
Haeuser, Michael John *library administrator*

MISSISSIPPI

Indianola
Powell, Anice Carpenter *librarian*

Itta Bena
Henderson, Robbye Robinson *library director*

Jackson
†Ballard, Thomas Hickok *library director*
Capers, Charlotte *state archives director emeritus*
Parks, James Franklin, Jr. *librarian*

Ridgeland
Morgan, Madel Jacobs *retired archives and library administrator*

Tupelo
Radojcsics, Anne Parsons *librarian*

MISSOURI

Blue Springs
Nelson, Freda Nell Hein *librarian*

Columbia
Alexander, Martha Sue *librarian*
Almony, Robert Allen, Jr. *librarian, businessman*
Carroll, Carmal Edward *librarian, educator, clergyman*

Hannibal
Dothager, Julie Ann *librarian*

Independence
Ferguson, John Wayne *library director*
†Ferguson, John Wayne, Sr. *librarian*
Strang, Marian Boundy *librarian*
Zobrist, Benedict Karl *library director, historian*

Jefferson City
Winn, Kenneth Hugh *archivist, historian*

Kansas City
Bradbury, Daniel Joseph *library administrator*
La Budde, Kenneth James *librarian*
Pedram, Marilyn Beth *reference librarian*
Zeller, Marilynn Kay *librarian*

Nevada
Hizer, Marlene Brown *library director*

Saint Louis
Guenther, Charles John *librarian, writer*
Holt, Glen Edward *library administrator*
†Smith, Jeffrey E. *library director*

Springfield
†Linnemeyer, Annie *library director*

MONTANA

Billings
†Cochran, William Michael *librarian*

Helena
†Fitzpatrick, Lois Ann *library administrator*

NEBRASKA

Lincoln
Diffendal, Anne P. *archivist, consulting historian*
Robson, John Merritt *library and media administrator*
Wagner, Rod *library director*

Omaha
Tollman, Thomas Andrew *librarian*

NEVADA

Carson City
Rocha, Guy Louis *archivist, historian*

Las Vegas
Curley, Elmer Frank *librarian*
Hunsberger, Charles Wesley *library director*

Reno
Gould, Martha Bernice *librarian*

NEW HAMPSHIRE

Concord
Wiggin, Kendall French *state librarian*

Exeter
Thomas, Jacquelyn May *librarian*

Hanover
Lathem, Edward Connery *librarian, editor, educator*
Otto, Margaret Amelia *librarian*

Manchester
Constance, Joseph William, Jr. *library director*
†Pantano, Richard Thomas *library director*

NEW JERSEY

East Brunswick
Wagman, Gerald Howard *library administrator*

Elizabeth
†Keenan, Joseph James, Jr. *library director*

Hightstown
Brodman, Estelle *librarian, retired educator*

Hoboken
Widdicombe, Richard Palmer *librarian*

Laurel Springs
Cleveland, Susan Elizabeth *library administrator, researcher*

Lawrenceville
Iversen, David Stewart *librarian*

Lodi
Karetzky, Stephen *library director, educator, researcher*

Lyndhurst
Sieger, Charles *librarian*

Madison
Coughlin, Caroline Mary *library director, educator*

New Brunswick
Anderson, James Doig *library and information science educator*
†Becker, Ronald Leonard *archivist*
†Chou, Nelson Lingsun *librarian*
Edelman, Hendrik *library and information science educator*
†Richards, Pamela Spence *library and information studies educator*
Turock, Betty Jane *library and information science educator*

Newark
Boyd, Alex *library director*
†Buck, Anne Marie *library director, consultant*

Princeton
Ferguson, Stephen *librarian*
Fox, Mary Ann Williams *librarian*
Henneman, John Bell, Jr. *library bibliographer*
Joyce, William Leonard *librarian*
Koepp, Donald William *librarian*

Trenton
†Minervino, Louise *librarian*
Russell, Joyce Anne Rogers *librarian*

NEW MEXICO

Albuquerque
†Wright, James Burnell *music librarian*

New Mexico State Capitol
†Watkins, Karen J. *librarian*

Santa Fe
Wolf, Cynthia Tribelhorn *librarian, library educator*

Univ Of New Mexico
Snell, Patricia Poldervaart *librarian, consultant*

NEW YORK

Albany
Aceto, Vincent John *librarian, educator*
Katz, William Armstrong *library science educator*
Paulson, Peter John *librarian, publishing company executive*
Shubert, Joseph Francis *librarian*

Bohemia
Manley, Gertrude Ella *librarian, media specialist*

Bronx
Humphry, James, III *librarian*

Brooklyn
Brandwein, Larry *library administrator*
Clune, John Richard *library administrator*
Corry, Emmett Brother *librarian, educator, researcher, archivist*
†Lawrence, Deirdre Elizabeth *librarian*
Sharify, Nasser *librarian, educator, author*
†Stevenson, Gale *librarian*

Buffalo
Bobinski, George Sylvan *librarian, educator*

Chrisman, Diane J. *librarian*
Cloudsley, Donald Hugh *library administrator*
†Newman, George Charles *library administrator*
Rooney, Paul Monroe *former library administrator*

Chappaqua
Whittingham, Charles Arthur *library administrator, publisher*

Clifton Park
Farley, John Joseph *library science educator emeritus*

Clinton
Anthony, Donald Charles *librarian, educator*

Cornwall On Hudson
Weiss, Egon Arthur *retired library administrator*

Corona
†Jackson, Andrew Preston *library director*

Delmar
Nitecki, Joseph Zbigniew *librarian*

East Setauket
Thom, Joseph M. *librarian*

Great Neck
Pohl, Gunther Erich *retired library administrator*

Hamilton
Bergen, Daniel Patrick *librarian, retired educator*
Noyes, Judith Gibson *library director*

Hempstead
Andrews, Charles Rolland *library administrator*

Hyde Park
Newton, Verne Wester *library director*

Ithaca
Finch, C. Herbert *archivist, library administrator, historian*
Miller, J(ames) Gormly *retired librarian, educator*
Skipper, James Everett *librarian*

Jamaica
Cooke, Constance Blandy *librarian*
†Hammer, Deborah Marie *librarian*

Kings Point
Billy, George John *library director*

Lagrangeville
LaMont, Barbara Gibson *librarian*

New York
†Ashton, Jean Willoughby *library director*
Berger, Pearl *library director*
†Berliner, Barbara *librarian, consultant*
Birnbaum, Henry *librarian*
†Bowen, Jean *music librarian, consultant*
†Brewer, Karen *librarian*
Bristah, Pamela Jean *librarian*
Cassell, Kay Ann *librarian*
Castleberry, May Lewis *librarian,curator,editor*
Colby, Robert Alan *retired library science educator*
Deuss, Jean *librarian*
†El-Erian, Tahani *library administrator*
†Franck, Jane Paul *library administrator*
Gatch, Milton McCormick, Jr. *library administrator, clergyman, educator*
†Giral, Angela *librarian*
Gold, Leonard Singer *librarian, translator*
†Gossage, Wayne *library director, management consultant, executive recruiter*
Gottlieb, Jane Ellen *librarian*
Graves, Fred Hill *librarian*
†Green, David Edward *librarian, priest, translator*
Hewitt, Vivian Ann Davidson (Mrs. John Hamilton Hewitt, Jr.) *librarian*
†Isaacson, Melvin Stuart *library director*
Kasinec, Edward Joseph *library administrator*
LeClerc, Paul *library director*
Logsdon, Richard Henry *retired librarian and educator*
Lohf, Kenneth A. *librarian, writer*
LoSchiavo, Linda Bosco *library director*
†Lubetski, Edith Esther *librarian*
†Lundquist, John Milton *librarian, author, lecturer*
Mattson, Francis Oscar *librarian, rare books curator*
McCormick, Donald E. *librarian, archivist*
Meyerhoff, Erich *librarian, administrator*
†Miller, Philip Efrem *librarian*
Mirsky, Sonya Wohl *librarian, curator*
Moore, Jane Ross *librarian*
Palmer, Robert Baylis *librarian*
Phillpot, Clive James *art librarian*
Pierce, Charles Eliot, Jr. *library director, educator*
Placzek, Adolf Kurt *librarian*
Rabinowitz, Mayer Elya *librarian, educator*
Rachow, Louis A(ugust) *librarian*
Root, Nina J. *librarian*
Sheehy, Eugene Paul *retired librarian, author*
Walker, William Bond *retired librarian*
Wertsman, Vladimir Filip *librarian, information specialist, author*

Ogdensburg
Rusaw, Sally Ellen *librarian*

Oneonta
Johnson, Richard David *librarian*

Pleasantville
†Murdock, William John *librarian*

Poughkeepsie
Emerson, William R. *retired library executive, historian*
Henry, Charles Jay *library director*
Van Zanten, Frank Veldhuyzen *library system director*

Rochester
†Matzek, Richard Allan *library director*
Pitkin, Patricia Albanese *library administrator*
Swanton, Susan Irene *library director*
Wyatt, James Franklin *librarian*

Roslyn
Gelfand, Morris Arthur *librarian, publisher*

Somers
Lane, David Oliver *retired librarian*

Staten Island
Auh, Yang John *librarian, academic administrator*

Syracuse
†Abbott, George Lindell *librarian*
†Eisenberg, Michael Bruce *information studies educator*
Stam, David Harry *librarian*

Troy
Lockett, Barbara Ann *librarian*

Tuckahoe
Silk, Eleana S. *librarian*

Vails Gate
Fife, Betty H. *librarian*

West Point
Watson, Georgianna *librarian*

White Plains
†Ellenbogen, Rudolph Solomon *library curator*

Yonkers
Miller, Jacqueline Winslow *library director*

NORTH CAROLINA

Chapel Hill
Campbell, Jerry Dean *librarian*
Carpenter, Raymond Leonard *information science educator*
†Daniel, Evelyn Hope *library science educator, university dean*
Holley, Edward Gailon *library science educator, former university dean*
Kilgour, Frederick Gridley *librarian, educator*
Moran, Barbara Burns *librarian, educator*

Charlotte
Cannon, Robert Eugene *librarian, public administrator, fund raiser*
Sintz, Edward Francis *librarian*

Davidson
Jones, Arthur Edwin, Jr. *library administrator, English and American literature educator*
Park, Leland Madison *librarian*

Durham
Canada, Mary Whitfield *librarian*
†Gaddis, Dale *library director*
Thorn, Rosemary Kost *librarian*

Fayetteville
†Thrasher, Jerry Arthur *library director*

Greensboro
Miller, Marilyn Lea *library science educator*
Viele, George Brookins *library executive*
Wright, Kieth Carter *librarian, educator*

Greenville
†Lennon, Donald Ray *archivist, historian*

Hendersonville
Peckham, Howard Henry *librarian, educator*

Raleigh
Littleton, Isaac Thomas, III *retired university library administrator, consultant*
Moore, Thomas Lloyd *librarian*

Saluda
Mowery, Bob Lee *librarian*

Washington
Timour, John Arnold *retired librarian, medical bibliography and library science educator*

Wilmington
Haselden, Clyde LeRoy *librarian*

Winston Salem
Roberts, William Hugh, III *library director, consultant*

NORTH DAKOTA

Mayville
Karaim, Betty June *librarian*

OHIO

Akron
Friedman, Richard Everett *librarian*
Rebenack, John Henry *retired librarian*

Athens
Lee, Hwa-Wei *librarian, educator*

Bedford
Parch, Grace Dolores *librarian*

Bluffton
Smucker, Barbara Claassen *former librarian, writer*

Cincinnati
Bestehorn, Ute Wiltrud *retired librarian*
†Proffitt, H. Kevin *archivist*
†Stonestreet, Robert *library director*
Wilson, Lucy Jean *librarian*
Zafren, Herbert Cecil *librarian, educator*

Cleveland
†Abid, Ann B. *art librarian*
Mason, Marilyn Gell *library administrator, writer, consultant*
†Muller, Claudya Barbara *librarian*
Pike, Kermit Jerome *library director*
Rader, Hannelore *library director, consultant*

Columbus
Black, Larry David *library director*
Branscomb, Lewis Capers, Jr. *librarian, educator*
Sawyers, Elizabeth Joan *librarian, administrator*
Studer, William Joseph *library director*
Tiefel, Virginia May *librarian*

Dayton
Chait, William *librarian, consultant*
Helling, James T. *library director*
†Klinck, Cynthia Anne *library director*
O'Brien, Elmer John *librarian, educator*
Wallach, John S(idney) *library administrator*

Lima
Dicke, Candice Edwards *library educator*

Middleburg Heights
Maciuszko, Kathleen Lynn *librarian, educator*

Oberlin
English, Ray *library administrator*

Oxford
Sessions, Judith Ann *librarian, university library dean*

Perrysburg
Danford, Ardath Anne *retired librarian*

Rootstown
Sayre, Jean Williams *librarian, educator*

Springfield
Montag, John Joseph, II *librarian*
Pearson, Norman Ralston *librarian*

Van Wert
Duprey, Wilson Gilliland *retired librarian*

Wooster
Hickey, Damon D. *library director*

Youngstown
†Trucksis, Theresa A. *library director*

OKLAHOMA

Edmond
Simpson, Zelma Alene *librarian*

Norman
Hodges, Thompson Gene *librarian*
Kemp, Betty Ruth *librarian*
Lee, Sul Hi *library administrator*
†Sherman, Mary Angus *public library administrator*

Oklahoma City
Brawner, Lee Basil *librarian*
Clark, Robert Lloyd, Jr. *librarian*
Stephens, Denny *librarian*

Stillwater
Johnson, Edward Roy *library director*

Tulsa
Woodrum, Patricia Ann *librarian*

Weatherford
†Hoke, Sheila Wilder *librarian*

OREGON

Beaverton
Pond, Patricia Brown *library science educator, university administrator*

Corvallis
†George, Melvin Ray *library director, consultant*
Hunt, Donald R. *retired librarian*

Eugene
†Hildebrand, Carol Ilene *librarian*
Morrison, Perry David *librarian, educator*
†Stirling, Isabel Ann *science librarian*

Portland
Browne, Joseph Peter *librarian*
Cooper, Ginnie *library director*
Eshelman, William Robert *librarian, editor*
†Freiser, Leonard Harold *engineering library director*
Long, Sarah Ann *librarian*
†Morgan, James Earl *librarian, administrator*

Salem
Turnbaugh, Roy Carroll *archivist*

PENNSYLVANIA

Allentown
Allen, Anna Foster *librarian*
†Sacks, Patricia Ann *librarian, consultant*
†Stephanoff, Kathryn *library director*

Allison Park
Hadidian, Dikran Yenovk *librarian, clergyman*

Bryn Mawr
Fanus, Pauline Rife *librarian*
Tanis, James Robert *library director, history educator, clergyman*

Carlisle
Stachacz, John Charles *librarian*

Clarion
†Caldwell-Wood, Naomi Rachel *library media specialist*
Mc Cabe, Gerard Benedict *library administrator*

Du Bois
†Morris, Trisha Ann *librarian*

Erie
†Ridge, Michele Moore *librarian*

Harrisburg
Parker, Sara Ann *librarian*

Haverford
Freeman, Michael Stuart *library director*

Kennett Square
Vainstein, Rose *educator, librarian*

New Kensington
Miller, Albert Jay *retired librarian emeritus, educator*

Philadelphia
†Arnold, Lee *library director*
Axam, John Arthur *library consultant*
†Carter, Edward Carlos, II *librarian, historian*
†Gendron, Michèle Marguerite Madeleine *librarian*
Hamlin, Arthur Tenney *librarian*
Mosher, Paul H. *research library administrator, author, consultant*
Shelkrot, Elliot Louis *librarian*

Pittsburgh
Bearman, Toni Carbo *information scientist*
Croneberger, Robert Bruce, Jr. *library director*
Josey, E(lonnie) J(unius) *librarian, educator, former state administrator*
Kent, Allen *library and information sciences educator*
Woolls, Esther Blanche *library science educator*

Reading
†Byers, Edward W. *library director*

Schuylkill Haven
Loder, Michael Wescott *librarian*

Scranton
Campion, Carol-Mae Sack *librarian*

Shippensburg
†Crowe, Virginia Mary *librarian*

State College
Doms, Keith *library director*
Forth, Stuart *librarian*

Swarthmore
Durkan, Michael Joseph *librarian*

Wayne
Garrison, Guy Grady *librarian, educator*

RHODE ISLAND

Kingston
Futas, Elizabeth Dorothy *library and information studies educator, program director*

Providence
Adams, Thomas Randolph *bibliographer, librarian, historian*
Weaver, Barbara Frances *librarian*

SOUTH CAROLINA

Charleston
Basler, Thomas G. *librarian, administrator, educator*
†Buvinger, Jan *library director*

Clemson
Boykin, Joseph Floyd, Jr. *librarian*

Columbia
Callaham, Betty Elgin *librarian*
Johnson, James Bek, Jr. *library director*
Rawlinson, Helen Ann *librarian*
Toombs, Kenneth Eldridge *librarian*
Warren, Charles David *library administrator*

Rock Hill
Du Bois, Paul Zinkhan *library director*

SOUTH DAKOTA

Pierre
Kolbe, Jane Boegler *state librarian*

Sioux Falls
Dertien, James LeRoy *librarian*

TENNESSEE

Chattanooga
†McFarland, Jane Elizabeth *librarian*

Collegedale
†Bennett, Peggy Elizabeth *librarian, library director, educator*

Greeneville
Smith, Myron John, Jr. *librarian, author*

Jackson
Hazlewood, Judith Evans *librarian*

Jefferson City
†Benson, Stanley Hugh *librarian*

Knoxville
†Griffiths, José-Marie *information science educator*
Walsh, Joanne Elizabeth *educator, librarian*
†Watson, Patricia L. *library director*

Memphis
Drescher, Judith Altman *library director*
Pourciau, Lester John *librarian*
Wallis, Carlton Lamar *librarian*

Murfreesboro
Youree, Beverly B. *library science educator*

Nashville
†Binkley, Yildiz Barlas *library director*
Gleaves, Edwin Sheffield *librarian*
Stewart, David Marshall *librarian*

Sewanee
Dunkly, James Warren *theological librarian*

TEXAS

Abilene
Specht, Alice Wilson *library director*

Amarillo
†Snell, Mary Kay Holmes *librarian, researcher*

Arlington
Burson, Betsy Lee *librarian*

Austin
†Ardis, Susan Barber *librarian, educator*
Billings, Harold Wayne *librarian, editor*
†Branch, Brenda *library director*
Carpenter, Elizabeth Sutherland *library consultant, author, equal rights leader*
Davis, Donald Gordon, Jr. *librarian, educator*
†Gooch, William DeWitt *librarian*
Gracy, David Bergen, II *archivist, information science educator, writer*
Jackson, Eugene Bernard *librarian*
Jackson, William Vernon *library science and Latin American studies educator*
Middleton, Harry Joseph *library administrator*
Oram, Robert W. *library administrator*

Cedar Hill
Hickman, Traphene Parramore *library director, storyteller, library and library building consultant*

Clarendon
Roper, Beryl Cain *library director*

College Station
Hoadley, Irene Braden (Mrs. Edward Hoadley) *librarian*
Wilson, Don Whitman *archivist, historian*

Corpus Christi
Canales, Herbert Glenn *librarian*

Dallas
Bradshaw, Lillian Moore *retired library director*
†Ibach, Robert Daniel, Jr. *library director*
Pastine, Maureen Diane *librarian*
Salazar, Ramiro S. *library administrator*
Witmer, John Albert *librarian*

Denton
Grose, B. Donald *library administrator*
Snapp, Elizabeth *librarian, educator*

Edinburg
Nance, Betty Love *librarian*

Fort Worth
Allmand, Linda F(aith) *library director*
Ard, Harold Jacob *library administrator*
de Tonnancour, Paul Roger Godefroy *library administrator*

Grand Prairie
†Ritterhouse, Kathy Lee *librarian*

Hale Center
Courtney, Carolyn Ann *school librarian*

Houston
Chang, Robert Huei *library director*
Downes, Robin *library director*
Henington, David Mead *library director*
Hornak, Anna Frances *library administrator*
Liddell, Leon Morris *educator, librarian*
†Lyders, Richard Arnold *librarian*
Radoff, Leonard Irving *librarian, consultant*
Shapiro, Beth Janet *librarian*
†Suter, Jon Michael *academic library director, educator*
Wilson, Patricia Potter *library science educator, educational and library consultant*

Lubbock
†Rippel, Jeffrey Alan *library director*
†Wood, Richard Courtney *library director, educator*

Marshall
†Magrill, Rose Mary *library director*

Mesquite
†Williams, John Elbert, Jr. *library services director*

San Angelo
Chatfield, Mary Van Abshoven *librarian*

San Antonio
†Garcia, June Marie *library director*
Jones, Daniel Hare *librarian*
Young, Olivia Knowles *retired librarian*

Seguin
†Moline, Sandra Lois *librarian*

Tyler
†Albertson, Christopher Adam *librarian*

Waco
†Bonnell, Pamela Gay *library administrator*
Coley, Betty *librarian*
Lindsey, Jonathan Asmel *library administrator, educator*
Progar, Dorothy *retired library director*

UTAH

Provo
Albrecht, Sterling Jean *university library director*
†Downey, Howard R. *librarian*
Smith, Nathan McKay *library and information sciences educator*

Salt Lake City
†Anderson, Grant Allen *librarian*
†Buttars, Gerald Anderson *librarian*
Day, Joseph Dennis *librarian*
Hanson, Roger Kvamme *librarian*
Owen, Amy *library director*

VERMONT

Burlington
Martin, Rebecca Reist *librarian*

South Burlington
Kebabian, Paul Blakeslee *librarian*

VIRGINIA

Alexandria
Berger, Patricia Wilson *retired librarian*
Mulvihill, John Gary *information services administrator*
O'Brien, Patrick Michael *library administrator*
Plitt, Jeanne Given *librarian*
Strickland, Nellie B. *library program director*

Arlington
†Fling, Jacqueline Ann *library administrator*
Nida, Jane Bolster (Mrs. Dow Hughes Nida) *retired librarian*

Castleton
Hahn, James Maglorie *former librarian, farmer*

Charlottesville
†Berkeley, Edmund, Jr. *activist, educator*
Frantz, Ray William, Jr. *retired librarian*
Frieden, Charles Leroy *university library administrator*
Self, James Reed *librarian*
Stubbs, Kendon Lee *librarian*

Chesapeake
Forehand, Margaret P. *library director*

Fredericksburg
Dennis, Donald Daly *retired librarian*

Harrisonburg
Palmer, Forrest Charles *librarian, educator*

Lexington
Gaines, James Edwin, Jr. *librarian*
Leach, Maurice Derby, Jr. *librarian*

Mc Lean
Hashim, Elinor Marie *librarian*

Norfolk
†Williams, Sue Darden *library director*

Portsmouth
†Burgess, Dean *library director*

Rapidan
Grimm, Ben Emmet *former library director and consultant*

Richmond
†Bryan, Charles Faulkner, Jr. *historical society director*
†Costa, Robert Nicholas *library director*
Sadler, Graham Hydrick *library administrator*
†Self, Phyllis C. *health sciences librarian*
†Trotti, John Boone *librarian, educator*

Springfield
Gawalt, Gerard W(ilfred) *historian, writer*

Virginia Beach
†Sims, Martha J. *library director*

Williamsburg
Marshall, Nancy Haig *library administrator*

WASHINGTON

Bellevue
Mutschler, Herbert Frederick *retired librarian*

Bellingham
Rhoads, James Berton *archivist, former government official, consultant, educator*

College Place
Gaskell, Carolyn Suzanne *librarian*
Jonish, Arley Duane *retired bibliographer*

Kirkland
Rosett, Ann Doyle *librarian*

Olympia
Zussy, Nancy Louise *librarian*

Seattle
Boylan, Merle Nelson *librarian*
Chisholm, Margaret Elizabeth *retired library director*

Hiatt, Peter *library educator*
Kruse, Paul Robert *retired librarian, educator*
Privat, Jeannette Mary *bank librarian*
Ptacek, William H. *library director*
Van Orden, Phyllis Jeanne *librarian, educator*

Spokane
Bender, Betty Wion *librarian*
Burr, Robert Lyndon *library director*
Wirt, Michael James *library director*

Tacoma
Crisman, Mary Frances Borden *librarian*

Walla Walla
Yaple, Henry Mack *library director*

WEST VIRGINIA

Charleston
Basham, Debra Ann *archivist*
Glazer, Frederic Jay *librarian*

Glenville
Tubesing, Richard Lee *library director*

Institute
Scott, John Edward *librarian*

Morgantown
Pyles, Rodney Allen *archivist, county official*

Shepherdstown
Elliott, Jean Ann *library administrator*

WISCONSIN

Eau Claire
Thompson, Glenn Judean *library science educator*

Green Bay
†LaViolette, Catherine Patricia *librarian*

Kenosha
†Baker, Douglas Finley *library director*

Madison
Bunge, Charles Albert *library science educator*
Dewey, Gene Lawrence *librarian*
Niemi, Peter G. *library administrator*

Milwaukee
Huston, Kathleen Marie *library administrator*
McKinney, Venora Ware *librarian*

Oshkosh
Jones, Norma Louise *librarian, educator*

Stevens Point
†Arneson, Arne Jon *librarian*

Thiensville
Roselle, William Charles *librarian*

WYOMING

Cheyenne
Johnson, Wayne Harold *librarian, county official*

Laramie
Cottam, Keith M. *librarian, educator, administrator*

TERRITORIES OF THE UNITED STATES

AMERICAN SAMOA

Pago Pago
Fung-Chen-Pen, Emma Talauna Solaita *librarian, program director*

GUAM

Agana
Uyehara, Harry Yoshimi *library educator*

CANADA

ALBERTA

Calgary
MacDonald, Alan Hugh *librarian, university administrator*
†Meek, Gerry *library director*

Edmonton
†McDougall, Donald Blake *retired provincial government library official*
McKee, Penelope Melna *library director*

Lethbridge
Rand, Duncan D. *librarian*

BRITISH COLUMBIA

Abbotsford
Sifton, Patricia Anne *library educator*

Nanaimo
Meadows, Donald Frederick *librarian*

Vancouver
†Aalto, Madeleine *library administrator*
Piternick, Anne Brearley *librarian, educator*
Rothstein, Samuel *librarian, educator*

Victoria
Hamilton, Donald Emery *librarian*

MANITOBA

Winnipeg
Converse, William Rawson Mackenzie *librarian*

NEWFOUNDLAND

Saint John's
†Penney, Pearce John *retired librarian*

NOVA SCOTIA

Halifax
Amey, Lorne James *library science educator*
Birdsall, William Forest *librarian*
Dykstra, Mary Elizabeth *library and information science educator*

ONTARIO

Brampton
Burgis, Grover Cornelius *librarian*

Guelph
†McLeod, Norman Carl *librarian*

Hamilton
Hill, Graham Roderick *librarian*
†McAnanama, Judith *library executive*

London
Edgar, Shirley Anne *librarian, educator*

Mississauga
†Mills, Donald McKenzie *librarian*
Ryan, Noel *librarian, consultant*

North York
Bryant, Josephine Harriet *library executive*
Davidson-Arnott, Frances E. *library science educator*
Land, Reginald Brian *library administrator*

Oakville
Wilburn, Marion Turner *library and information scientist educator, consultant*

Ottawa
Brown, Jack Ernest *information scientist*
Frappier, Gilles *librarian*
Scott, Marianne Florence *librarian, educator*
Spicer, Erik John *retired Canadian parliamentary librarian*
Sylvestre, Jean Guy *former national librarian of Canada*
Wallot, Jean-Pierre *archivist, historian*

Scarborough
Bassnett, Peter James *librarian*

Thunder Bay
†Harrison, Karen A. *library director*

Toronto
Fasick, Adele Mongan *library science educator*
Moore, Carole Irene *chief librarian*
Packer, Katherine Helen *retired library educator*
†Schwenger, Frances *library director*

Windsor
Dirksen-Morrison, Jean *library administrator*

QUEBEC

Montreal
Gardner, Richard Kent *retired librarian, educator, consultant*
Large, John Andrew *library and information service educator*
Ormsby, Eric Linn *library administrator, researcher*
Panneton, Jacques *librarian*
†Sauvageau, Philippe *library director*
†Sykes, Stephanie Lynn *library director, archivist, museum director*

Quebec
Paradis, Andre *librarian*

Rosemere
Adrian, Donna Jean *librarian*

SASKATCHEWAN

Regina
Powell, Trevor John David *archivist*

Saskatoon
Kennedy, Marjorie Ellen *librarian*

MEXICO

Mexico City
Rodriguez Gallardo, Adolfo *library director, historian*

AUSTRALIA

Belair
Briggs, Geoffrey Hugh *retired librarian*

Kensington
Rayward, Warden Boyd *librarian, educator*

CZECH REPUBLIC

Prague
Kalkus, Stanley *librarian, administrator, consultant*

ITALY

Rome
†Casolino, Vincenzo *library director*

ADDRESS UNPUBLISHED

Adamovich, Shirley Gray *retired librarian, state official*
Campbell, Henry Cummings *librarian*
Cartier, Celine Paule *librarian, administrator, consultant*
Clement, Hope Elizabeth Anna *librarian*
Cluff, E. Dale *librarian, educator, administrator*
Cooke, Eileen Delores *retired librarian*
†Dickerson, Lon Richard *library administrator*
Driver, Lottie Elizabeth *librarian*
Edelstein, Jerome Melvin *bibliographer*
Erickson, Alan Eric *librarian*
Flinner, Beatrice Eileen *library and media sciences educator*
Fowlie, Eldon Leslie *retired library administrator*
Gardner, William Michael *library administrator*
†Gilbert, Nancy Louise *librarian*
†Jenkins, Darrell Lee *librarian*
Kaser, David *librarian, educator, consultant*
Kaufman, Paula T. *librarian*
Komidar, Joseph Stanley *librarian*
Marchant, Maurice Peterson *librarian, educator*
Martin, Louis Edward *retired library director*
Martin, Murray Simpson *librarian, writer, consultant*
McBurney, Margot B. *librarian*
Miller, Charles Edmond *library administrator*
Moody, Roland Herbert *retired librarian*
Morgan, Jane Hale *retired library director*
Mountz, Louise Carson Smith *retired librarian*
Osburn, Charles Benjamin *librarian, university dean*
Patterson, Robert Hudson *library director*
Richards, Vincent Philip Haslewood *librarian*
Rouse, Roscoe, Jr. *librarian, educator*
Scoles, Clyde Sheldon *library director*
Sheldon, Brooke Earle *librarian, educator*
Smith, Howard McQueen *librarian*
Spaulding, Frank Henry *librarian*
Suput, Ray Radoslav *librarian*
†Szynaka, Edward M. *library director, consultant*
Teeple, Fiona Diane *librarian, lawyer*
Van Heijst, Jakob *library administrator*
Williams, Gordon Roland *librarian*
Williams, Richard Clarence *retired librarian*
Yeo, Ronald Frederick *librarian*

HUMANITIES: MUSEUMS

UNITED STATES

ALABAMA

Huntsville
Robb, David Metheny, Jr. *art museum director, art historian*

Mc Calla
Gentry, Vicki Paulette *museum director*

Mobile
Richelson, Paul William *curator*

Tuscaloosa
Jones, Douglas Epps *natural history museum director*

ALASKA

Gustavus
Jensen, Marvin O. *national park superintendent*

ARIZONA

Mesa
†Mead, Tray C. *museum administrator*

Phoenix
†Ballinger, James K. *art museum executive*
Carman, Michael Dennis *museum director*
Grinell, Sheila *museum director*
†Sullivan, Martin Edward *museum director*

San Simon
Zweifel, Richard George *curator*

Tempe
†Zeitlin, Marilyn A. *museum director*

Tucson
†Bermingham, Peter *museum director*
Hancocks, David Morgan *museum director, architect*
Yassin, Robert Alan *museum administrator, curator*

ARKANSAS

Little Rock
DuBois, Alan Beekman *art museum administrator, curator*
Wolfe, Townsend Durant, III *art museum director, curator*

State University
Jones, Charlott Ann *museum director, art educator*

CALIFORNIA

Auburn
Adams, Margaret Bernice *retired museum official*

Bakersfield
Enriquez, Carola Rupert *museum director*

Berkeley
Benedict, Burton *museum director, anthropology educator*
Elliott, James Heyer *retired curator university art museum, fine arts consultant*

Fresno
†Barrett, Robert Daker *arts center executive*
Sobey, Edwin J. C. *museum director, oceanographer, consultant*

La Jolla
†Beebe, Mary Livingstone *curator*
†Davies, Hugh Marlais *museum director*

Laguna Beach
Desmarais, Charles Joseph *museum director, writer, editor*

Los Angeles
Black, Craig Call *museum administrator*
Cohen, Daniel Morris *museum administrator, marine biology researcher*
Koshalek, Richard *museum director, consultant*
Kuwayama, George *curator*
Pal, Pratapaditya *museum curator*
Powell, James Lawrence *museum president*
†Rudolph, Jeffrey N. *museum director*
†Wilson, Thomas Henry *museum director*

Mill Valley
Fuller, Glenn R. *park ranger*

Monterey
Hernandez, Jo Farb *museum and curatorial consultant*
†Powell, David Clark *curator, consultant*

Newport Beach
Botwinick, Michael *museum director*

North Hollywood
Bull, David *fine art conservator*

Oakland
Burns, Catherine Elizabeth *art dealer*
Power, Dennis Michael *museum director*

Redlands
Griesemer, Allan David *museum director*

Riverside
Green, Jonathan William *museum administrator and educator, artist, author*

Sacramento
Gibbs, Barbara Kennedy *art museum director*
†Mette, Joe *museum director*

San Diego
Brezzo, Steven Louis *museum director*
†DiMattio, Terry *historic site administrator*
†Ollman, Arthur Lee *museum director, photographer*
Petersen, Martin Eugene *museum curator*

San Francisco
†Castile, Rand *museum administrator*
†Halsey, Milton B. *military site administrator*
Lane, John Rodger *art museum director*
Leviton, Alan Edward *museum curator*
Lindsay, George Edmund *museum director*
Parker, Harry S., III *art museum administrator*
†Phillips, Sandra Sammataro *curator, educator*
Shangraw, Clarence Frank *museum official*

San Jose
†Callan, Josi Irene *museum director*

San Marino
Skotheim, Robert Allen *museum administrator*
Wark, Robert Rodger *art curator*

Santa Barbara
Gebhard, David *museum director, educator*
Karpeles, David *museum director*
†Perrot, Paul Norman *museum director*

Santa Monica
Walsh, John, Jr. *museum director*

Stanford
Seligman, Thomas Knowles *museum administrator*

West Hollywood
Byrnes, James Bernard *museum director emeritus*

COLORADO

Boulder
Crane, Michael Patrick *art museum administrator, educator*
Hay, William Winn *former museum director, natural history and geology educator*
Lanham, Urless Norton *curator*

Colorado Springs
†Wagner, David J. *art center director*

Denver
Welles, John Galt *museum director*

CONNECTICUT

Hartford
†Faude, Wilson Hinsdale *museum director*
†White, David Oliver *museum executive*

Mystic
Johnston, Waldo Cory Melrose *museum director*

New Haven
Dangremond, David W. *museum administrator, educator*
Hickey, Leo J(oseph) *museum curator, educator*
Robinson, (David) Duncan *museum administrator, art historian*

New London
Knowles, Elizabeth Pringle *art museum director*

Norwalk
Marnane, Joseph Peter *maritime center executive*

Norwich
Gualtieri, Joseph Peter *museum director*

Stamford
Kinsman, Robert Donald *art museum administrator, cartoonist*
Scribner, Barbara Colvin *museum administrator*

Waterbury
Smith, Ann Youngdahl *museum administrator*

DELAWARE

Wilmington
Bruni, Stephen Thomas *art museum director*
Otey, Orlando *music executive, educator, pianist, theorist*
Porter, Glenn *museum and library administrator*

Winterthur
Hummel, Charles Frederick *museum official*
Lanmon, Dwight Pierson *museum director*

DISTRICT OF COLUMBIA

Washington
Abbott, Rebecca Phillips *museum director*
Bader, Franz *retired gallery administrator*
Beach, Milo C. *art museum director*
†Bloomfield, Sara *museum director*
Bowron, Edgar Peters *art museum curator, administrator*
Bretzfelder, Deborah May *museum exhibit designer, photographer*
Brown, John Carter *art museum director emeritus*
Burke, Mary *art gallery administrator*
Cikovsky, Nicolai, Jr. *curator, art history educator*
Cowart, Jack *museum executive*
Crew, Spencer *museum administrator*
Davis, Nancy Ellen *museum director*
Demetrion, James Thomas *art museum director*
Evelyn, Douglas Everett *museum executive*
Fitzgerald, Oscar P., IV *museum administrator*
Freedberg, Sydney Joseph *retired museum curator, retired fine arts educator*
Freudenheim, Tom Lippmann *museum administrator*
Furgol, Edward Mackie *museum curator, historian*
Hand, John Oliver *museum curator*
Hoffmann, Robert Shaw *museum administrator, educator*
Ketchum, James Roe *curator*
Kilbourne, John Dwight *museum and library director*
Levy, David Corcos *museum director*
Lewin, Ann White *museum director*
Lowe, Harry *museum director*
Marsh, Caryl Amsterdam *curator, psychologist*
Mellon, Paul *retired art gallery executive*
Micozzi, Marc Stephen *museum director, physician, educator*
Moffett, Charles Simonton *museum director, curator, writer*
Phillips, Laughlin *museum president, former magazine editor*
†Rahill, Margaret Anne *retired museum curator*
Rodriguez, Belgica *museum director*
Russell, H. Diane *museum curator, educator*
†Sheehan, Michael Terrence *arts administrator, historian, consultant*
Shestack, Alan *museum administrator*
†Sopher, Vicki Elaine *museum director*
†Stanton, Robert *historic site director*
Stewart, Robert Gordon *museum curator*
Sultan, Terrie Frances *curator*
Talbot, Frank Hamilton *museum director, marine researcher*
Viola, Herman Joseph *museum director*
Weil, Stephen Edward *museum official*
†West, W. Richard, Jr. *museum director*
Williams, Sylvia Hill *museum director*
Wolanin, Barbara Ann Boese *art curator, art historian*

FLORIDA

Boca Raton
Selby, Roger Lowell *museum director*

Daytona Beach
Libby, Gary Russell *museum director*

Fort Myers
†Halgrim, Robert P. *museum director*

Gainesville
Bennett, Thomas Peter *museum director, educator, biologist*

Bishop, Budd Harris *museum administrator*
Dickinson, Joshua Clifton, Jr. *museum director, educator*
Wing, Elizabeth Schwarz *museum curator, educator*

Jacksonville
Adams, Henry *museum director*
Dundon, Margo Elaine *museum director*
Schlageter, Robert William *museum administrator*

Miami
Etling, Russell Hull *museum director, production company executive*

Orlando
Davis, William Albert *theme park director*
†Morrisey, Marena Grant *art museum administrator*

Pensacola
†Rasmussen, Robert *museum director*

Sarasota
Harmon, (Loren) Foster *art dealer*

Tallahassee
Palladino-Craig, Allys *museum director*

Tampa
Maass, R. Andrew *museum director*

West Palm Beach
Orr-Cahall, Christina *art gallery director, art historian*

GEORGIA

Atlanta
Davis, Eleanor Kay *museum administrator*
†Hiers, Mary A. *museum director*
†Rathburn, Robert Richard *museum director*
Vigtel, Gudmund *museum director emeritus*

Fort Benning
Grube, Dick DeWayne *museum director*

Macon
†Bundy, John Franklin, Jr. *national monument administrator*

Roswell
Forbes, John Ripley *museum executive, educator*

Savannah
†Cave, Kent R. *national park ranger*
Smith, Gregory Allgire *art museum director*

HAWAII

Honolulu
†Duckworth, Walter Donald *museum executive, entomologist*
Ellis, George Richard *museum administrator*

Kaneohe
Lagoria, Georgianna Marie *curator, writer, editor, visual art consultant*

IDAHO

Pocatello
Jackson, Allen Keith *museum administrator*

ILLINOIS

Brookfield
Pawley, Ray Lynn *zoological park herpetology curator*

Carbondale
Whitlock, John Joseph *museum director*

Chicago
Balzekas, Stanley, Jr. *museum director*
Boyd, Willard Lee *museum administrator, educator, lawyer*
Consey, Kevin Edward *museum administrator*
Druick, Douglas Wesley *museum administrator*
Edelstein, Teri J. *museum administrator, educator*
†Haas, Jonathan *museum research organization executive*
Heltne, Paul Gregory *museum executive*
Jakstas, Alfred John *museum conservator, consultant*
Kahn, James Steven *museum director*
Kamyszew, Christopher D. *museum curator, executive educator, art consultant*
Kubida, Judith Ann *museum administrator*
Lewis, Phillip Harold *museum curator*
Mueller, Gregory M. *museum curator, botanist, researcher*
†Nevling, Lorin Ives, Jr. *museum administrator*
Nordland, Gerald *art museum administrator, historian, consultant*
Wardropper, Ian Bruce *museum curator, educator*
Wilson, Karen Lee *museum curator*
Wood, James Nowell *museum director and executive*
Zukowsky, John Robert *curator*

Homewood
MacMaster, Daniel Miller *museum official emeritus*

Springfield
†Hallmark, Donald Parker *museum director*
Mc Millan, R(obert) Bruce *museum executive, anthropologist*

INDIANA

Bloomington
Calinescu, Adriana Gabriela *museum curator, art historian*
Gealt, Adelheid Maria *museum director*

Elkhart
†Kovach, John Michael *museum director, historian*

Evansville
Streetman, John William, III *museum official*

Indianapolis
Gantz, Richard Alan *museum administrator*
Jontz, Polly *museum director*
Waller, Aaron Bret, III *museum director*

Muncie
Joyaux, Alain Georges *art museum director*

Terre Haute
Quick, Edward Raymond *museum director*

IOWA

Des Moines
†Crosson, David Earl *historical agency administrator*

Iowa City
Prokopoff, Stephen Stephen *art museum director, educator*

KANSAS

Dodge City
Clifton-Smith, Rhonda Darleen *museum curator*

Fort Riley
†Van Meter, Terry *museum director*

Lawrence
Norris, Andrea Spaulding *art museum director*

University Of Kansas
Humphrey, Philip Strong *university museum director*

Wichita
Gurney, Hugh Douglas *historic site administrator*
Wooden, Howard Edmund *museum director, art researcher*

KENTUCKY

Louisville
Becker, Gail Roselyn *museum director*
Morrin, Peter Patrick *museum director*
Ray, Randy Wayne *museum director*

Murray
Hunt, Mark Alan *museum director*

Owensboro
Hood, Mary Bryan *museum director, painter*

LOUISIANA

New Orleans
Bullard, Edgar John, III *museum director*
Fagaly, William Arthur *curator*
†Forman, L. Ronald *park and zoological garden administrator*
Freeman, Montine McDaniel *museum trustee*
Glasgow, Vaughn Leslie *museum curator and administrator*
Platou, Joanne (Dode) *museum director*
Sefcik, James Francis *museum director*

MAINE

Augusta
†Phillips, Joseph Robert *museum director*

Bath
Weber, Jean MacPhail *museum director*

Brunswick
Brown, James Monroe, III *museum administrator*
Watson, Katharine Johnson *art museum director, art historian*

Falmouth
Sadik, Marvin Sherwood *art consultant, former museum director*

Orono
Hartgen, Vincent Andrew *museum director, educator, artist*

Rockland
†Crosman, Christopher Byron *art museum administrator*

MARYLAND

Aberdeen Proving Ground
Atwater, William Felix *museum director*

Baltimore
Bastedo, Ralph W(alter) *museum administrator, educator*
†Fishman, Bernard Philip *museum director*
Hanle, Paul Arthur *museum administrator*
Lehman, Arnold Lester *museum official, art historian*
Ott, John Harlow *museum administrator*
Somerville, Romaine Stec *arts consultant*
†Tyler, John W. *historic site administrator*

MASSACHUSETTS

Acton
†Moir, Ronald Brown, Jr. *museum director*

Amherst
Parkhurst, Charles *museum official*
Sandweiss, Martha A. *museum director, author, American studies educator*

Boston
Brovarski, Edward Joseph *curator, Egyptologist*
†Curran, Emily Katherine *museum director*
Ellis, David Wertz *museum director*
Fairbanks, Jonathan Leo *museum curator*
Freed, Rita Evelyn *curator, Egyptologist*
Hawley, Anne *museum director*
Hills, Patricia Gorton Schulze *curator*
Krakow, Barbara Levy *art gallery executive*
Meister, Mark Jay *museum director, professional society administrator*
Nylander, Jane Louise *museum director*
Stebbins, Theodore Ellis, Jr. *museum curator*
Sutton, Peter Campbell *museum curator*
Vermeule, Cornelius Clarkson, III *museum curator*
Washburn, H. Bradford, Jr. *museum administrator, cartographer, photographer*
Wu, Tung *curator, art historian, art educator*
Zahn, Carl Frederick *museum publications director, designer, photographer*
Zannieri, Nina *museum director*

Brewster
Lindquist, Susan Pratzner *museum executive*

Cambridge
Cohn, Marjorie Benedict *curator, art historian, educator*
†Cuno, James *art museum director*
†Gaskell, Ivan George Alexander De Wend *art museum curator*
Mongan, Agnes *museum curator, art historian, educator*
Mowry, Robert Dean *art museum curator, educator*
Rathbone, Perry Townsend *art museum director*
Seamans, Warren Arthur *museum director*
Slive, Seymour *museum director, fine arts educator*

Duxbury
Vose, Robert Churchill, Jr. *former art gallery executive*

Fitchburg
Timms, Peter Rowland *art museum administrator*

Groton
Silvestro, Clement Mario *museum director, historian*

Lincoln
Master-Karnik, Paul Joseph *art museum director*

Salem
†Goss, Kenneth David *museum director*

Springfield
Muhlberger, Richard Charles *former museum administrator, writer*
Sturges, Hollister, III *museum director*

Waltham
Arena, Albert A. *museum director*

Williamstown
Brooke, David Stopford *art gallery official*
Hamilton, George Heard *curator*

Worcester
Jareckie, Stephen Barlow *museum curator*
King, Anthony Gabriel *museum administrator*
Welu, James A. *art museum director*

MICHIGAN

Alpena
†Bodem, Dennis Richard *museum director*

Ann Arbor
Bailey, Reeve Maclaren *museum curator*
Hennessey, William John *museum director*

Bloomfield Hills
Jacobowitz, Ellen Sue *museum administrator*

Dearborn
Skramstad, Harold Kenneth *museum administrator, consultant*

Detroit
Darr, Alan Phipps *curator*
Lyon, Maud Margaret *museum director*
Peck, William Henry *museum curator, art historian, archaeologist, author, lecturer*
Sachs, Samuel, II *museum director*
Shaw, Nancy Rivard *museum curator, art historian*

East Lansing
Bandes, Susan Jane *museum director, educator*
Dewhurst, Charles Kurt *museum director, curator, folklorist, English educator*

Flint
Germann, Steven James *museum director*
Mahey, John Andrew *museum director*

Grand Rapids
Frankforter, Weldon DeLoss *retired museum administrator*
Sobol, Judith Ellen *museum director, art historian*

Kalamazoo
†Bridenstine, James Aloysius *museum director*
Norris, Richard Patrick *museum director, history educator*

MINNESOTA

Minneapolis
Armstrong, Elizabeth Neilson *curator*
Conforti, Michael Peter *museum curator, art historian*
Halbreich, Kathy *museum director*

King, Lyndel Irene Saunders *art museum director*
Maurer, Evan Maclyn *art museum director*

Saint Paul
Appelhof, Ruth Stevens *museum director, curator, art historian*
Czarniecki, Myron James, III *art museum director, cultural planner*
†Osman, Stephen Eugene *historic site administrator*
Peterson, James Lincoln *museum executive*

MISSOURI

Columbia
Witt, Ruth Elizabeth *retired museum administrator*

Fort Leonard Wood
†Combs, Robert Kimbal *museum director*

Hannibal
Sweets, Henry Hayes, III *museum director*

Kansas City
McKenna, George LaVerne *art museum curator*
Sanchez, Beatrice Rivas *art institute executive, artist*
Scott, Deborah Emont *curator*
Svadlenak, Jean Hayden *museum administrator, consultant*
Ucko, David Alan *museum director*
Wilson, Marc Fraser *art museum administrator and curator*

Saint Joseph
†Chilcote, Gary M. *museum director, reporter*

Saint Louis
Burke, James Donald *museum administrator*
Owyoung, Steven David *curator*
Wint, Dennis Michael *museum director*

Springfield
Berger, Jerry Allen *museum director*

MONTANA

Missoula
†Brown, Robert Munro *museum director*
†Millin, Laura J. *museum director*

West Glacier
Lusk, Harlan Gilbert *national park superintendent*
Mihalic, David Anthony *national park administrator*

NEBRASKA

Kearney
Lund, Virginia Llego *museum director, curator, chemistry educator*

Lincoln
Genoways, Hugh Howard *museum director*

Omaha
Beal, Graham William John *museum director*

NEW HAMPSHIRE

Manchester
Hoffman, Marilyn Friedman *museum director*

Portsmouth
†O'Toole, Dennis Allen *museum director*

NEW JERSEY

Allaire
†Smith, Sibley Judson, Jr. *historic site administrator*

Basking Ridge
Peterson, John Douglas *museum administrator*

Cape May
Cadge, William Fleming *gallery owner, photographer*

Morristown
†Klindt, Steven *art museum director*

New Brunswick
Cate, Phillip Dennis *art museum director*

Princeton
†Rosenbaum, Allen *art museum administrator*

NEW MEXICO

Alamogordo
Way, Jacob Edson, III *museum director*

Albuquerque
Bawden, Garth Lawry *museum director*

Roswell
Ebie, William D. *museum director*

Santa Fe
Becker, Stephen Arnold *museum director*
†Cerny, Charlene Ann *museum director*
Livesay, Thomas Andrew *museum administrator*
Smith, Richard Bowen *national park superintendent*

Taos
Witt, David L. *curator, writer*

NEW YORK

Albany
Levine, Louis David *museum director, archaeologist*
Miles, Christine Marie *museum director*
†Ray, Alan *museum director*

Bronxville
Prakapas, Eugene Joseph *art gallery director*

Brooklyn
Buck, Robert Treat, Jr. *museum director, educator*
Ferber, Linda S. *museum curator*

Buffalo
Schultz, Douglas George *art museum director*
Siener, William Harold *museum director, historian, consultant*

Cooperstown
MacLeish, Archibald Bruce *museum director*

Corning
Ahrens, Kent *museum director, art historian*
Spillman, Jane Shadel *curator, researcher, writer*

Flushing
Friedman, Alan Jacob *museum director*

Huntington
Coraor, John Edward *museum director*
Noll, Anna Cecilia *curator*

Ithaca
Robinson, Franklin Westcott *museum director, art historian*
†Trautmann, Charles Home *museum director, civil engineer*

Katonah
Simpson, William Kelly *curator, Egyptologist, educator*

New York
Baer, Norbert Sebastian *art conservation educator, chemist*
Bandy, Mary Lea *museum official*
Baragwanath, Albert Kingsmill *curator*
Barnett, Vivian Endicott *curator*
Batscha, Robert Michael *museum executive*
Belkov, Meredith Ann *landmark administrator*
Biddle, Flora Miller *art museum administrator*
Bothmer, Dietrich Felix von *museum curator, archaeologist*
Brundage, Susan *art dealer, gallery director*
Castelli, Leo *art dealer*
Castleman, (Esther) Riva *museum curator*
Cohen, Mildred Thaler *art gallery director*
De Ferrari, Gabriella *curator, writer*
de Montebello, Philippe Lannes *museum administrator*
Desai, Vishakha N. *gallery director*
Dinaburg, Mary Ellen *art education and curatorial consultant*
Draper, James David *art museum curator*
Emmerich, Andre *art gallery executive, author*
†Feld, Stuart Paul *art gallery director*
Feldman, Ronald *art gallery director*
Fletcher, Harry George, III *curator*
Freed, Stanley Arthur *museum curator*
Fung, Lance Michael *art gallery director*
Futter, Ellen Victoria *museum administrator*
†Galassi, Peter *museum curator*
Gaudieri, Alexander V. J. *museum administrator*
Gruskin, Mary J. (Mrs. Alan D. Gruskin) *art gallery director emeritus*
Haskell, Barbara *curator*
Hawkins, Ashton *museum executive, lawyer*
Hayward, Jane *museum curator*
Heckscher, Morrison Harris *museum curator, architectural historian*
Hoving, Thomas *museum and cultural affairs consultant, author*
Howat, John Keith *museum executive*
Ives, Colta Feller *museum curator, educator*
Jones, Julie *art museum curator*
Kallir, Jane Katherine *art gallery director, author*
Kardon, Janet *museum director, curator*
Krens, Thomas *museum director*
Krulik, Barbara S. *museum director, curator*
Lerner, Martin *museum curator*
†Levai, Pierre Alexandre *art gallery executive*
Luers, William Henry *art museum administrator*
Lupton, Ellen *curator, graphic designer*
Macdonald, Robert Rigg, Jr. *museum director*
Martin, Mary-Anne *art gallery owner*
Martin, Richard Harrison *curator, art historian*
McFadden, David Revere *museum director and curator*
Mertens, Joan R. *museum curator, art historian*
Messer, Thomas Maria *museum director*
Metcalf, William Edwards *coin museum curator*
Miller, Laurence Glenn *art gallery owner and director*
Morris, Robert Lee *gallery administrator, jewelry designer*
Munhall, Edgar *curator, art history educator*
Murdock, Robert Mead *art consultant, curator*
†Novacek, Michael John *curator, museum administrator*
Oldenburg, Richard Erik *museum director*
Parker, James *retired curator*
Pesner, Carole Manishin *art gallery owner*
Pilgrim, Dianne Hauserman *art museum director*
Pisano, Ronald George *art consultant*
Platnick, Norman I. *curator, arachnologist*
†Rosenbaum, Joan Hannah *museum director*
Rosenthal, Nan *curator, author*
Ross, David A. *art museum director*
Ryskamp, Charles Andrew *museum executive, educator*
Sidamon-Eristoff, Anne Phipps *museum official*
Simon, Ronald Charles *curator*
Storr, Robert *curator painting and sculpture, artist, writer*
†Tucker, Marcia *museum director, curator*
Varnedoe, John Kirk Train *museum curator*
Vuilleumier, Francois *curator*
Wertkin, Gerard Charles *museum director, lawyer*
Wright, Gwendolyn *art center director, writer, educator*

Purchase
†Gedeon, Lucinda Heyel *museum director*

Rochester
Adams, G. Rollie *museum executive*
Enyeart, James L. *museum director*
†Hall, Donald S. *planetarium administrator*
Holcomb, Grant, III *museum director*

Southampton
Lerner, Abram *retired museum director, artist*

Stillwater
†Lindsay, W. Douglas, Jr. *historic site administrator*

Syracuse
Kuchta, Ronald Andrew *art museum director, educator*

Ticonderoga
†Westbrook, Nicholas Kilmer *museum administrator, historian*

Tupper Lake
Welsh, Peter Corbett *museum consultant, historian*

Utica
Schweizer, Paul Douglas *museum director*

Wantagh
Smits, Edward John *museum consultant*

Waterford
Gold, James Paul *museum director*

Woodstock
Cox, James David *art gallery executive*

Youngstown
†Dunnigan, Brian Leigh *historic site administrator*

NORTH CAROLINA

Asheville
Cecil, William A. V., Sr. *landmark director*

Chapel Hill
Bolas, Gerald Douglas *art museum administrator, art history educator*
†Riggs, Timothy Allan *museum curator*

Charlotte
†Evans, Bruce Haselton *art museum director*
†Nicholson, Freda Hyams *museum executive, medical educator*

Durham
Krakauer, Thomas Henry *museum director*

Gastonia
Stout, Richard Alan *museum director*

Greensboro
†von der Lippe, Edward Joseph *museum director*

Manteo
†Hartman, Thomas *historical site adminstrator*

Raleigh
Schneiderman, Richard Steven *museum official*

Salisbury
Shalkop, Robert Leroy *retired museum consultant*

Wilmington
Janson, Anthony Frederick *art educator, former museum curator*
Scheu, David Robert, Sr. *historic site director*

Winston Salem
Cawood, Hobart Guy *historic site administrator*
Gray, James Alexander *historic preservation official*

NORTH DAKOTA

Grand Forks
†Glassheim, Eliot *museum director, state legislator*

OHIO

Akron
Kahan, Mitchell Douglas *art museum director*

Cincinnati
†Burt, DeVere *museum administrator*
King, Elaine A. *curator, art historian, critic*
Long, Phillip Clifford *museum director*
Rogers, Millard Foster, Jr. *art museum director*
†Timpano, Anne *museum director, art historian*

Cleveland
Bergman, Robert Paul *museum administrator, art historian, educator, lecturer*
Mayer, Robert Anthony *art institute executive*
Taylor, J(ocelyn) Mary *museum administrator, zoologist, educator*
Turner, Evan Hopkins *retired art museum director*

Columbus
Rogers, Sarah Jeanne *curator*
Stearns, Robert Leland *curator*

Dayton
Nyerges, Alexander Lee *museum director*

Fremont
†Bridges, Roger Dean *historical agency administrator*

Mentor
†Miller, Frances Suzanne *historic site curator*

Oberlin
Moore, Anne Frances *museum director*

Oxford
Kelm, Bonnie G. *art museum director, educator*

Toledo
Steadman, David Wilton *museum official*
Wittmann, Otto *art museum executive*

University Heights
Cook, Alexander Burns *museum curator, artist, educator*

Vandalia
†Smith, Marjorie Aileen Matthews *museum director*

Youngstown
†Zona, Louis Albert *art museum director, educator*

OKLAHOMA

Norman
Toperzer, Thomas Raymond *art museum director*

Oklahoma City
Pitts, Bill *museum director*
Price, B. Byron *museum director*

Shawnee
McCaffree, Brother Benedict *museum director*

Tulsa
†Troccoli, Joan Carpenter *museum director*

OREGON

Eugene
McTigue, Bernard Francis *curator, consultant*

Portland
Eichinger, Marilynne H. *museum administrator*
Gilkey, Gordon Waverly *curator, artist*
Jenkins, Donald John *art museum administrator*
McKinley, Loren Dhue *museum director*
†Steinfeld, Ray, Jr. *museum administrator, food products executive*

PENNSYLVANIA

Allentown
Blume, Peter Frederick *museum director*

Chadds Ford
Duff, James Henry *museum director, environmental administrator*

Doylestown
Purpura, Peter Joseph *museum curator, exhibition designer*

Easton
†Humphrey, J. Steven *museum director*

Erie
Vanco, John L. *art museum director*

Gettysburg
†Cisneros, Jose A. *historical site administrator*

Harrisburg
Fortier, John Bertram *museum director, historian*

Kennett Square
Naeve, Milo Merle *museum curator*

Philadelphia
Bantel, Linda Mae *art museum director*
d'Harnoncourt, Anne *museum director*
Dyson, Robert Harris *museum director, archaeologist*
Kolb, Nancy Dwyer *museum director*
Percy, Ann Buchanan *museum curator*
Scott, Robert Montgomery *museum executive, lawyer*
Sewell, Darrel Leslie *art museum curator*
Shoemaker, Innis Howe *art museum curator*

Pittsburgh
Arkus, Leon Anthony *art consultant, former museum director*
Dawson, Mary Ruth *curator*
†DeSena, Alphonse Thomas *science museum director*
Johnston, Phillip Michael *museum director, curator*
King, James Edward *museum director*
†McIntosh, DeCourcy Eyre *museum director*

Reading
Dietrich, Bruce Leinbach *planetarium and museum administrator, astronomer, educator*

Scranton
O'Brien, Kevin James *museum director*

Strasburg
Lindsay, George Carroll *former museum director*

Valley Forge
†McDermott, Dona M. *curator*

Wayne
Andes, Charles Lovett *museum executive, technology association executive*

RHODE ISLAND

Newport
West, Richard Vincent *art museum official*

Saunderstown
Leavitt, Thomas Whittlesey *museum director, educator*

SOUTH CAROLINA

Charleston
Brumgardt, John Raymond *museum administrator*

Columbia
Cilella, Salvatore George, Jr. *museum director*
Nelson-Mayson, Linda Ruth *art museum curator*

Florence
Burns, William A. *museum administrator, author*

Murrells Inlet
Noble, Joseph Veach *fine arts administrator*
Tarbox, Gurdon Lucius, Jr. *museum executive*

SOUTH DAKOTA

Keystone
†Wenk, Daniel N. *landmark site administrator*

TENNESSEE

Chattanooga
Scarbrough, Cleve Knox, Jr. *museum director*

Gatlinburg
†Pope, Randall Ray *retired national park superintendent*

Knoxville
Chapman, Jefferson *museum director*

Memphis
Noble, Douglas Ross *museum administrator*

Nashville
†Bradshaw, William *museum director*

TEXAS

Austin
Crain, William Henry *retired curator*
Stetson, Daniel Everett *museum director*

Beaumont
Smith, David Ryan *museum director*

Dallas
†Sudduth, William McLean *museum director*
Vogel, Donald Stanley *gallery executive, artist*

Fort Worth
Auping, Michael G. *curator*
Muhlert, Jan Keene *art museum director*
†Otto, Donald R. *museum director*
Painter, Henry *museum director*
†Pillsbury, Edmund Pennington *museum director*

Houston
Latimer, Roy Truett *museum president*
Lee, Janie C. *art gallery owner*
†Marzio, Peter Cort *museum director*
Tucker, Anne Wilkes *curator, photographic historian and critic, lecturer*

Midland
Ott, Wendell Lorenz *art museum director, artist*

Orange
Eldredge, Bruce Beard *museum director*

San Antonio
†Barnes, Gail *historic site administrator*
Hyland, Douglas K. S. *museum administrator, educator*
Mc Giffert, John Rutherford *retired cultural institute director, retired army officer*

Waco
†Smith, Calvin Bruce *museum director*

UTAH

Salt Lake City
Leonard, Glen M. *museum administrator*
Sanguinetti, Eugene Frank *art museum administrator, educator*

VERMONT

Bennington
†Luckey, Laura Colby *museum director*

Manchester
†Kouwenhoven, Gerrit Wolphertsen *museum director*

Shelburne
Sheldon, David Frederick *museum director, headmaster*

VIRGINIA

Alexandria
Evans, Grose *former curator, retired educator*
Lundberg, Philip Karl *curator*

Appomattox
†Montgomery, Jon B. *museum administrator*

Arlington
Ewers, John Canfield *museum administrator*

Louisa
Lanyon, Wesley Edwin *retired museum curator, ornithologist*

Mount Vernon
†Horstman, Neil Williard *museum administrator*

Newport News
†Wilkinson, William Durfee *museum director*

Norfolk
Martin, Roy Butler, Jr. *museum director, retired broker*

Richmond
Blatt, Elizabeth Kempske *museum administrator*
Miller, Nan Louise *museum director*

Waynesboro
Rippe, Peter Marquart *museum administrator*

Yorktown
†Gould, Alec *historic park administrator*

WASHINGTON

Bellevue
Warren, James Ronald *retired museum director, author, columnist*

Olympia
Lind, Carl Bradley *retired museum director*

Point Townsend
Harrington, LaMar *curator, museum director*

Seattle
Andrews, Richard Otis *museum director*
†O'Donnell, Wilson Edward *historical society director*

Vancouver
†Herrera, David Patrick *historic site administrator*

WISCONSIN

Baraboo
Parkinson, Greg Thomas *museum director*

Elkhorn
Dunn, Walter Scott, Jr. *former museum director, consultant*

Green Bay
Sauvey, Raymond Andrew *museum director*

Madison
Fleischman, Stephen *art center director*
Garver, Thomas Haskell *curator, art consultant, writer*
Pillaert, E(dna) Elizabeth *museum curator*

Manitowoc
Logan, Lox Albert, Jr. *museum director*

Milwaukee
†Goldsmith, Christopher C. *museum director*
Green, Edward Anthony *museum director*

Oshkosh
†Poberezny, Thomas *museum adminstrator*

WYOMING

Cody
Hassrick, Peter Heyl *museum director*

Moose
†Neckels, Jack *park superintendent*

CANADA

ALBERTA

Calgary
Janes, Robert Roy *museum director, archaeologist,*

Drumheller
Naylor, Bruce Gordon *museum director*

Edmonton
Bogusky, Alf *museum director*
Stepney, Philip Harold Robert *museum director*

Sherwood Park
Finlay, James Campbell *retired museum director*

BRITISH COLUMBIA

North Vancouver
Joyner, John Brooks *museum director*

Vancouver
Ames, Michael McClean *university museum director, anthropology educator*
Holmes, Willard *art gallery director*

Victoria
Barkley, William Donald *museum director*
Segger, Martin Joseph *museum director, art history educator*

MANITOBA

Winnipeg
Di Cosimo, Joanne Violet *museum director*

NEW BRUNSWICK

Fredericton
Lumsden, Ian Gordon *art gallery director*

NEWFOUNDLAND

Saint John's
Grattan, Patricia Elizabeth *art gallery director*
Mills, David B. *museum director*

NOVA SCOTIA

Halifax
Riordon, John Bernard *museum director*
Sparling, Mary Christine *art gallery director*

ONTARIO

London
Poole, Nancy Geddes *art gallery director, writer*

North York
Cumming, Glen Edward *art gallery director*
Yarlow, Loretta *art museum director*

Ottawa
Bell, Phillip Michael *curator*
Borcoman, James Willmott *museum curator*
Emery, Alan Roy *museum executive*
†Gruchy, Charles George *museum administrator*
McAvity, John Gillis *museum director, association executive, museologist*
Suthren, Victor J. H. *museum director*
Thomson, Shirley Lavinia *museum director*

Toronto
Lowry, Glenn David *art gallery director*
McNeill, John *museum administrator*
Rombout, Luke *museum designer, administrator*
Tushingham, (Arlotte) Douglas *museum administrator*

PRINCE EDWARD ISLAND

Charlottetown
Severance, Christopher Churchill *museum director*

QUEBEC

Montreal
Brisebois, Marcel *museum director*

Quebec
Laliberté-Bourque, Andrée *museum director*

SASKATCHEWAN

Regina
Oko, Andrew Jan *art gallery director, curator*

MEXICO

Mexico City
del Conde, Teresa *museum director, art historian, researcher*
Lacouture, Felipe Ernesto *museum consultant*

AUSTRIA

Vienna
Oberhuber, Konrad Johannes *art museum curator, educator*

ENGLAND

London
Serota, Nicholas Andrew *art gallery director*

FRANCE

Paris
Rosenberg, Pierre Max *museum curator*

GERMANY

Frankfurt
Ammann, Jean-Christophe *art curator*

JAPAN

Miyazaki
Meyer, Ruth Krueger *museum administrator, art historian*

ADDRESS UNPUBLISHED

Armstrong, Thomas Newton, III *museum director*
Bogue, Philip Roberts *consultant*
Bonito Oliva, Achille *curator*
Boulet, Roger Henri *art gallery director, curator*

Brumberg, G. David *historical center administrator, history bibliographer*
Carter, John Swain *museum administrator, consultant*
Chenhall, Robert Gene *former museum director, consultant, author*
Coke, Frank Van Deren *museum director, photographer*
Danoff, I. Michael *art center director, writer, educator*
Dressel, Barry *museum administrator*
English, Bruce Vaughan *museum director and executive, environmental consultant*
Friedman, Martin *arts adviser, retired museum director*
Fry, Doris Hendricks *museum curator*
Greaves, James Louis *art conservator*
Grogan, Kevin *museum director*
†Hellmers, Norman Donald *historic site director*
Kochta, Ruth Martha *art gallery director*
Leff, Sandra H. *gallery director, consultant*
McKinney, Donald *art gallery director, art dealer*
Mezzatesta, Michael Philip *art museum director*
Millard, Charles Warren, III *museum director, writer*
Moore, William Jason *museum director*
Nasgaard, Roald *museum curator*
Nihart, Franklin Brooke *museum consultant, writer and editor*
Nold, Carl Richard *state historic parks and museums administrator*
Pennington, Mary Anne *art museum director, museum management consultant, art educator*
Pisney, Raymond Frank *international consulting services executive*
†Pitts, Terence Randolph *curator and museum director*
Porter, Daniel Reed, III *museum director*
Powell, Earl Alexander, III *art museum director*
Radice, Anne-Imelda *museum director*
Randall, Richard Harding, Jr. *art gallery director*
Rifkin, Ned *museum director*
Schneider, Janet M. *arts administrator, curator, painter*
Shapiro, Michael Edward *museum director, art historian*
Smith, Jean Chandler *former museum official*
Summerfield, John Robert *textile curator*
Talbot, Howard Chase, Jr. *retired museum administrator*
Van Ness, John Ralph *museum administrator*
Yates, Charles Richardson *former arts center executive*
Yochelson, Bonnie Ellen *museum curator, art historian*

INDUSTRY: MANUFACTURING. See also FINANCE: FINANCIAL SERVICES.

UNITED STATES

ALABAMA

Alexander City
Gade, Marvin Francis *retired paper company executive*

Birmingham
Blount, William Houston *construction materials company executive*
Chrencik, Frank *chemical company executive*
Daniel, Kenneth Rule *former iron and steel manufacturing company executive*
de Windt, Edward Mandell *manufacturing executive*
Fowler, C. Thomas *power equipment manufacturing executive*
Gaffney, Michael Scully *diversified manufacturing company executive*
†Johnsey, Walter F. *manufacturing executive*
Krulitz, Leo Morrion *manufacturing executive*
Neal, Phil Hudson, Jr. *manufacturing company executive*
†Rozendale, David S. *engineering and construction firm executive*
Sklenar, Herbert Anthony *industrial products manufacturing company executive*
Styslinger, Lee Joseph, Jr. *manufacturing company executive*

Huntsville
King, Olin B. *electronics systems company executive*
†Ramsey, V. Bruce *electronics executive*
Sapp, A. Eugene, Jr. *electronics executive*

Lanett
Fowler, Conrad Murphree *retired manufacturing company executive*

Montgomery
Blount, Winton Malcolm, Jr. *manufacturing company executive*
†Findlay, R. B. *paper company executive*
Van Sant, Robert William *manufacturing company executive*

Opelika
Jenkins, Richard Lee *manufacturing company executive*

Sheffield
†Roy, Amit H. *agricultural executive*

Sylacauga
†Felker, G. Stephen *textile company executive*

Tuscaloosa
Williams, Ernest Going *paper company executive*

ALASKA

Anchorage
†Williams, Mark *food products executive*

Juneau
Loescher, Robert Wayne *holding company executive*

ARIZONA

Carefree
Byrom, Fletcher Lauman *chemical manufacturing company executive*
Menk, Louis Wilson *retired manufacturing company executive*
Trimble, George Simpson *industrial executive*

Goodyear
Cabaret, Joseph Ronald *electronics company executive*

Green Valley
Blickwede, Donald Johnson *retired steel company executive*
Ehrenfeld, John Henry *grocery company executive*

Litchfield Park
Reid, Ralph Ralston, Jr. *electronics executive, engineer*

Mesa
DeRosa, Francis Dominic *chemical company executive*

Phoenix
Atutis, Bernard P. *manufacturing company executive*
Carter, Ronald Martin, Sr. *pharmaceutical company executive*
Franke, William Augustus *corporate executive*
Giedt, Bruce Alan *paper company executive*
Goldman, Murray Abraham *semiconductor executive*
Kyl, John Henry *former business executive*
Mardian, Daniel *construction company director*
†McClelland, Norman P. *food products executive*
†Mc Clelland, W. Kent *food products executive*
†Patti, Andrew S. *consumer products company executive*
Paul, Elias *food company consultant*
Rethore, Bernard Gabriel *diversified company executive*
Thomas, Edward Francis, Jr. *synthetic fuel executive*
Weinstein, Allan M. *medical device company executive*

Scottsdale
Grenell, James Henry *retired manufacturing company executive*
Howard, William Gates, Jr. *electronics company executive*
Malsack, James Thomas *retired manufacturing company executive*
Ruhlman, Terrell Louis *business executive*
†Smith, Harlan William *automotive parts manufacturing company executive*
Stuart, Derald Archie *aerospace company consultant*
Walsh, Edward Joseph *toiletries and food company executive*

Sierra Vista
Meyer, William Trenholm *defense company official, real estate executive*

Sun City West
Anderson, Ernest Washington *manufacturing company executive*
Van Horssen, Arden Darrell *retired manufacturing executive*

Tempe
†Akers, Lex A. *electonics director*

Tucson
Eckdahl, Donald Edward *manufacturing company executive*
Green, Robert Scott *biotechnology company executive*
Maxon, Don Carlton *construction company executive, mining company executive*
Meeker, Robert Eldon *retired manufacturing company executive*
Mullikin, Vernon Eugene *aerospace executive*
Speer, Phillip Bradford *commercial business executive*
Sundt, Harry Wilson *construction company executive*
Troup, Thomas James *electronics company executive*

ARKANSAS

Conway
†Morgan, Charles Donald, Jr. *manufacturing executive*

Fort Smith
Flanders, Donald Hargis *manufacturing company executive*
†Goins, Randall *grain company executive*
Hendrickson, Boyde W. *health products executive*
†Marquard, William Albert *diversified manufacturing company executive*
Qualls, Robert L. *manufacturing executive, banker, former state official, educator*

Hiwasse
Sutherland, Gail Russell *retired industrial equipment manufacturing company executive*

Hot Springs Village
Schroeder, Donald Perry *retired food products company executive*

Little Rock
Dyke, James Trester *building materials distributing company executive*
Givens, John Kenneth *manufacturing executive*
†Hickingbotham, Frank D. *food product executive*
†Hickingbotham, Herren C. *food products executive*
McMullin, Carleton Eugene *manufacturing executive*

Rogers
Hudson, James T. *food company executive*
Hudson, Michael T. *food company executive*

Springdale
†Tollett, Leland Edward *food company executive*
Tyson, Donald John *food company executive*

Stuttgart
Bell, Richard Eugene *grain and food company executive*
Jessup, Stewart E. *agricultural products executive*

CALIFORNIA

Alamo
Pritchett, Thomas Ronald *retired metal and chemical company executive*

Anaheim
†Heiner, Dennis Grant *manufacturing company executive*

Aptos
Mechlin, George Francis *electrical manufacturing company executive*

Arcadia
Eck, Dennis K. *supermarket chain executive*
Nelson, Garrett R. *retail food company executive*

Arroyo Grande
Vahsholtz, Robert John *retired manufacturing executive*

Artesia
†Korsmeier, Gary *dairy products executive*

Atherton
Goodman, Sam Richard *electronics company executive*
Hogan, Clarence Lester *retired electronics executive*
Mc Intyre, Henry Langenberg *former business executive, lawyer*

Bakersfield
Akers, Tom, Jr. *cotton broker, consultant*
†Groefsema, Bruce *agricultural products executive*
Hart, Donald Milton *automotive and ranching executive, former mayor*
Lundquist, Gene Alan *cotton company executive*

Berkeley
Berlekamp, Elwyn Ralph *former electronics company executive, mathematics educator*
Cutter, David Lee *pharmaceutical company executive*
Locke, John Whiteman, III *manufacturing company executive*

Beverly Hills
†Ballhaus, William Francis *retired scientific instruments company executive*
Brann, Alton Joseph *aerospace executive*
dePaolis, Potito Umberto *food company executive*
Hoch, Orion Lindel *corporate executive*
†Leonis, John Michael *aerospace executive*
Loeffler, Richard Harlan *retail and technology company executive*
Willson, James Douglas *aerospace executive*

Borrego Springs
Bowers, Bobby Eugene *metal products executive, small business owner*

Brea
†Hulsey, Neven C. *metal products executive*

Buena Park
†Arimoto, Masahiko *electronics company executive*
†Raup, Ronald B. *electronics executive*

Burbank
Gold, Stanley P. *chemical company executive, manufacturing company executive*
Raulinaitis, Pranas Algis *electronics executive*

Calabasas
Egan, John Frederick *electronics executive*
Ghose, Rabindra Nath *technology research company executive*
Kitchen, Lawrence Oscar *aircraft and aerospace corporation executive*
Marafino, Vincent Norman *aerospace company executive*
Pearce, Susan Miriam *aerospace company executive*

Camarillo
Denmark, Bernhardt *manufacturing executive*

Campbell
Sack, Edgar Albert *electronics company executive*

Carlsbad
†Callaway, Ely Reeves, Jr. *golf club manufacturer*
Crooke, Stanley Thomas *pharmaceutical company executive*
Graham, Robert Klark *lens manufacturer*
Randall, William B. *manufacturing company executive*
Schumacher, John Christian *semiconductor materials and air pollution control equipment manufacturing company executive*

Carpinteria
Ehrlich, Grant C(onklin) *business consultant*

Central Valley
†Emmerson, A. A. *sawmill executive*

Chatsworth
Adams, Charles Richard *manufacturing executive*
†Alagem, Beny *electronics executive*
†Van Dine, Robert *cosmetics company executive*

Chula Vista
Goldsmith, Robert Holloway *manufacturing company executive*
†Kerley, James J. *manufacturing executive*

Compton
†Collins, Patrick W. *grocery stores company executive*

Coronado
Brunton, Paul Edward *retired diversified industry executive*

Covina
Fillius, Milton Franklin, Jr. *food products company executive*

Crockett
Somerset, Harold Richard *sugar company executive*

Culver City
Leve, Alan Donald *electronic materials manufacturing company owner, executive*

Cupertino
Bossen, David August *electronics company executive*
Burg, John Parker *signal processing executive*
Gingerich, John Charles *manufacturing company executive*
Mathias, Leslie Michael *electronic manufacturing company executive*
McAdams, Robert, Jr. *electronics executive*

Cypress
†Naganuma, Kazue *automotive executive*

Danville
Arrol, John *corporate executive*
Liggett, Lawrence Melvin *vacuum equipment manufacturing company executive*

Del Mar
Cooper, Martin *electronics company executive*

El Cajon
McClure, Donald Edwin *electrical construction executive, consultant*

Encino
Krueger, Kenneth John *corporate executive*
Roderick, Robert Lee *aerospace executive*

Escalon
Barton, Gerald Lee *food company executive*

Escondido
Darmstandler, Harry Max *business executive, retired air force officer*
Lux, John H. *corporate executive*
†Packer, Russell Howard *automotive company executive*

Fair Oaks
Byrne, John James *retired manufacturing company executive*
Chernev, Melvin *retired beverages executive*

Fallbrook
Dennis, Ward Brainerd *retired aerospace company executive*

Folsom
†Close, Gary E. *pharmaceuticals executive*

Foster City
Wang, Su Sun *chemical company executive, chemist*

Fountain Valley
†Price, Westcott Wilkin, III *health care executive*

Fremont
Domeier, David John *food products executive*

Fresno
†O'Donnell, Thomas Howard *wheelchair manufacturing executive*

Fullerton
Miller, Arnold *electronics executive*
Rosso, Louis T. *scientific instrument manufacturing company executive*

Gilroy
†Blattman, H. Eugene *foods corporation executive*

Glendale
†Crull, Timm F. *food company executive*
†Schult, Robert W. *food products executive*
Seegman, Irvin P. *manufacturing company executive*

Glendora
Cahn, David Stephen *cement company executive*

Goleta
Thom, Richard David *aerospace executive*

Gridley
Tanimoto, George *agricultural executive, farmer*

Hawthorne
Weiss, Max Tibor *aerospace company executive*

Healdsburg
Reed, Thomas Care *business executive*

Hesperia
Butcher, Jack Robert *manufacturing executive*

Hillsborough
Keller, John Francis *retired wine company executive, mayor*

Hollywood
Parks, Robert Myers *appliance manufacturing company executive*
Perkins, William Clinton *company executive*

Indian Wells
Harris, Milton M. *distributing company executive*
Reed, A(lfred) Byron *retired apparel and textile manufacturing company*

Irvine
Alspach, Philip Halliday *manufacturing company executive*
†Beckman, Arnold Orville *analytical instrument manufacturing company executive*
†Haggerty, Charles A. *electronics executive*
Herbert, Gavin Shearer *health care products company executive*
Maestrini, Emilio *industrial projects contracts manager*
Qureshey, Safi U. *electronics manufacturing company executive*
Santoro, Carmelo James *electronics executive*
†Shepherd, William C. *pharmaceutical company executive*
†Sonoguchi, Kazuo *automotive company executive*
Williams, James E. *food products manufacturing company executive*

Irwindale
Groom, John Miller *food company executive*

Jackson
†Halvorson, William *automotive executive*

La Habra
†Golleher, George *food company executive*

La Jolla
Drell, William *chemical company executive*
Monday, John Christian *electronics company executive*
Penhune, John Paul *science company executive, electrical engineer*
Richey, Phil Horace *former manufacturing executive, consultant*
Stevens, Paul Irving *manufacturing company executive*
Todd, Harry Williams *aircraft propulsion system company executive*

La Mesa
Burns, Kenneth Dean *aerospace industry executive, retired air force major general*

La Puente
†Reilly, John E. *automotive executive*
†Sakaino, Kozo *automobile company executive*

Lafayette
Lewis, Sheldon Noah *technology consultant*

Laguna Beach
Bezar, Gilbert Edward *retired aerospace company executive, volunteer*
Wolf, Karl Everett *aerospace and communications corporation executive*
Youngquist, Andrew Lance *construction executive*

Laguna Hills
Miller, Eldon Earl *consultant, retired manufacturing company executive*

Laguna Niguel
Nelson, Alfred John *retired pharmaceutical company executive*

Livermore
Bennett, Alan Jerome *electronics executive, physicist*

Livingston
Fox, Robert August *food company executive*

Long Beach
Anderson, Gerald Verne *aerospace company executive*
McGuire, James Charles *aircraft company executive*
†Seita, Yukifusa *electronics executive*
†Valli, Peter Constantine *manufacturing company executive*

Los Altos
Beer, Clara Louise Johnson *retired electronics executive*
Mullaley, Robert Charles *manufacturing company executive*
Oder, Frederic Carl Emil *retired aerospace company executive, consultant*

Los Angeles
Anderson, Robert *retired manufacturing company executive*
†Aroesty, Sidney A. *medical diagnostic manufacturing company executive*
Ash, Roy Lawrence *business executive*
Bennis, Warren Gameliel *business administration educator, author, consultant*
Broadhurst, Norman Neil *manufacturing executive*
Bromberg, Robert *aerospace company executive*
Burns, Dan W. *manufacturing company executive*
Campion, Robert Thomas *manufacturing company executive*
Corum, William Thomas, III *computer information systems executive*
Currie, Malcolm Roderick *aerospace and automotive executive, scientist*
†Dingwell, Everett W. *food products company executive*
Drake, Hudson Billings *aerospace and electronics company executive*
Forester, Bernard I. *recreational equipment company executive*
Galef, Andrew G. *textiles executive*
Godbold, Wilford Darrington, Jr. *enclosure manufacturing company executive, lawyer*
Golden, Milton M. *paint company executive*
Halamandaris, Harry *aerospace executive*
Handschumacher, Albert Gustave *retired corporate executive*
Holman, Harland Eugene *manufacturing company executive*
Howard, Murray *manufacturing, real estate property management executive, farmer, rancher*
Irani, Ray R. *oil, gas and chemical company executive*
†Jones, Jerve Maldwyn *construction company executive*
†Kelleher, Robert *apparel executive*
Kendall, William Denis *medical electronic equipment company executive*
Korn, Lester Bernard *business executive, diplomat*
Kresa, Kent *aerospace executive*

†Laverty, Roger Montgomery, III *food products executive, lawyer*
Mager, Artur *retired aerospace company executive, consultant*
Mall, William John, Jr. *aerospace executive, retired air force general officer*
†Mettler, Ruben Frederick *former electronics and engineering company executive*
†Norian, Roger W. *glass manufacturing company executive*
Palevsky, Max *industrialist*
Perna, Frank, Jr. *manufacturing company executive*
Ramer, Lawrence Jerome *corporation executive*
†Rutledge, William P. *manufacturing company executive*
Seaver, Richard Carlton *oil field equipment company executive, lawyer*
Segil, Larraine Diane *materials company executive*
Settles, F. Stan, Jr. *manufacturing executive, educator*
Wurmbrand, Harry George *cosmetics company executive*
Wyatt, James Luther *drapery hardware company executive*
†Ziering, Sigi *medical company executive*

Los Gatos
†Millard, Stephens Fillmore *electronics company executive*

Lynwood
†Jorgensen, Earle M. *metal products executive*

Malibu
Smith, George Foster *retired aerospace company executive*

Menlo Park
Bremser, George, Jr. *electronics company executive*
Cook, Paul M. *chemical manufacturing company executive*
†Denend, Leslie George *computer company executive*
Evans, Bob Overton *electronics executive*
Fergason, James L. *optical company executive*
Frisco, Louis Joseph *retired materials science company executive, electrical engineer*
Graham, Howard Holmes *manufacturing executive*
Graham, William James *packaging company executive*
Halperin, Robert Milton *electrical machinery company executive*
Hiller, Stanley, Jr. *manufacturing company executive*
Postlewait, Harry Owen *chemical company executive*
Taft, David Dakin *chemical executive*

Mill Valley
Winskill, Robert Wallace *manufacturing executive*

Milpitas
†Coghlan, Paul *electronics executive*
Huber, Paul E. *electronics industry executive*

Modesto
Ferrucci, Raymond Vincent *retired food company executive*
Shastid, Jon Barton *wine company executive*

Montecito
Meghreblian, Robert Vartan *manufacturing executive, physicist*

Mountain View
Clark, James H. *electronics executive*
Cusumano, James Anthony *chemical company executive, former recording artist*
Elkus, Richard J., Jr. *electronics company executive*
Jarrat, Henri Aaron *semiconductor company executive*
Koo, George Ping Shan *electronics executive*
Mc Nealy, Scott *computer company executive*
Pallakoff, Owen E. *retired electronics executive*
Saifer, Mark Gary Pierce *pharmaceutical executive*

Newport Beach
†Brower, Edgar S. *manufacturing company executive*
Plat, Richard Vertin *corporate finance executive*

Novato
†Carlston, Douglas Gene *computer software executive*

Oakland
Saunders, Ward Bishop, Jr. *retired aluminum company executive*
Serenbetz, Robert *manufacturing executive*
Sullivan, G. Craig *chemical executive*

Oakville
Mondavi, Robert Gerald *winery executive*

Ojai
Weill, Samuel, Jr. *automobile company executive*

Orange
†Martini, Robert Edward *wholesale pharmaceutical and medical supplies company executive*
†Stacho, Zoltan Aladar *construction and engineering company executive*
Steffensen, Dwight A. *medical products and data processing services executive*

Pacific Palisades
Crane, Richard Clement *paper manufacturing company executive*

Palm Desert
Brown, James Briggs *retired business forms company executive*

Palm Springs
Greenbaum, James Richard *liquor distributing company executive, real estate developer*

Palo Alto
Burke, Edmund Charles *retired aerospace company executive*
DeLustro, Frank Anthony *biomedical company executive, research immunologist*
Early, James Michael *electronics research consultant*

Goff, Harry Russell *retired manufacturing company executive*
Hewlett, William (Redington) *manufacturing company executive, electrical engineer*
Hornak, Thomas *electronics company executive*
Johnson, Horace Richard *electronics company executive*
Kennedy, W(ilbert) Keith, Jr. *electronics company executive*
O'Rourke, J. Tracy *manufacturing company executive*
Packard, David *manufacturing company executive, electrical engineer*
†Platt, Lewis Emmett *electronics company executive*
Reagan, Joseph Bernard *aerospace executive*
Rivette, Gerard Bertram *manufacturing company executive*
Staprans, Armand *electronics executive*
Watkins, Dean Allen *electronics executive, educator*

Palos Verdes Peninsula
Dalton, James Edward *aerospace executive, retired air force officer*
Grant, Robert Ulysses *retired manufacturing company executive*
Wilson, Theodore Henry *retired electronics company executive, aerospace engineer*

Pasadena
Adler, Fred Peter *electronics company executive*
Bennett, Joel Herbert *construction company executive*
Caldwell, William Mackay, III *business executive*
Chamberlain, Willard Thomas *retired metals company executive*
Geckler, Richard Delph *metal products company executive*
Jenkins, Royal Gregory *manufacturing executive*
Marlen, James S. *chemical-plastics-building materials manufacturing company executive*
Miller, Charles Daly *business executive*
Neal, Philip Mark *diversified manufacturing executive*
Pieroni, Leonard J. *construction company executive*
Smith, Howard Russell *manufacturing company executive*
Sudarsky, Jerry M. *industrialist*
Tollenaere, Lawrence Robert *industrial products company executive*

Pauma Valley
Dooley, George Elijah *manufacturing executive*

Pebble Beach
Crossley, Randolph Allin *retired corporate executive*

Pittsburg
†Chuderewicz, Leonard H. *heavy industry executive*

Pleasanton
†Perry, James R. *construction company executive*
Stager, Donald K. *construction company executive*
†Tauscher, William Young *pharmaceutical and cosmetic products executive*
Weiss, Robert Stephen *medical manufacturing and services company financial executive*

Portola Valley
Purl, O. Thomas *retired electronics company executive*

Ramona
Vaughn, Robert Lockard *aerospace and astronautics company executive*

Rancho Mirage
Strickman, Arthur Edwin *retired retail executive*

Rancho Santa Fe
Jordan, Charles Morrell *retired automotive designer*

Rancho Santa Margarita
Wong, Wallace *medical supplies company executive, real estate investor*

Redlands
Merritt, Joshua Levering, Jr. *consultant, retired engineering executive*
Skomal, Edward Nelson *aerospace company executive, consultant*

Redondo Beach
Kagiwada, Reynold Shigeru *advanced technology manager*

Redwood City
†Bramson, Edward J. *electronics corporation executive, financial executive*
†Kalinske, Thomas J. *toy company executive*
†Nosler, Peter C. *construction company executive*
Swinerton, William Arthur *retired construction company executive*

Redwood Shores
†Ellison, Lawrence J. *computer software company executive*

Riverside
Crean, John C. *housing and recreational vehicles manufacturing company executive*
Kummer, Glenn F. *automotive executive*
Smith, Elden Leroy *recreational vehicle company executive*
Weide, William Wolfe *housing and recreational vehicles manufacturer*

Sacramento
Aldrich, Thomas Albert *consultant, former brewing executive and air forceofficer*
Baccigaluppi, Roger John *agricultural company executive*

San Carlos
Glenn, Thomas Michael *science and technology executive*
Gutow, Bernard Sidney *packing manufacturing company executive*

San Clemente
Fertik, Ira J. *medical laser company executive*

San Diego
Anjard, Ronald Paul, Sr. *business and industry executive, consultant, educator, technologist, importer*
Arledge, Charles Stone *former aerospace executive, entrepreneur*
Boarman, Patrick Madigan *economics and business administration educator, public official*
Bradley, Francis Xavier *aluminum company executive*
Conner, Dennis *manufacturing executive, yachtsman*
Devine, Brian Kiernan *pet food and supplies company executive*
Duddles, Charles Weller *food company executive*
Goode, John Martin *manufacturing company executive*
Hawran, Paul William *pharmaceutical executive*
Holman, J(ohn) Leonard *retired manufacturing corporation executive*
Howell, Thomas Edwin *manufacturing company executive*
Ivans, William Stanley *electronics company executive*
†Lewis, Alan James *pharmaceutical executive, pharmacologist*
†Lovelace, Alan Mathieson *aerospace company executive*
Maier, Paul Victor *pharmaceutical executive*
Mullane, John Francis *pharmaceutical company executive*
Nassif, Thomas Anthony *business executive, former ambassador*
Price, Robert E. *manufacturing company executive*
†Ray, Gene Wells *industrial executive*
Rice, Clare I. *electronics company executive*

San Francisco
†Brindley, Robert E. *food products executive*
†Chamberlain, David M. *consumer products company executive*
Chiaverini, John Edward *construction company executive*
Colbert, Lester Lum, Jr. *technology products executive*
Dewey, Edward Allen *construction company executive*
†D'Ornellas, Robert W. *food products executive*
Du Bain, Myron *diversified industry executive*
†Fannon, John *paper company executive*
Gates, Milo Sedgwick *construction company executive*
†Grubb, David H. *construction company president*
Haas, Robert Douglas *apparel manufacturing company executive*
Haas, Walter A., Jr. *retired apparel company executive, professional baseball executive*
Hull, Cordell William *business executive*
James, George Barker, II *apparel industry executive*
Jewett, George Frederick, Jr. *forest products company executive*
Kreitzberg, Fred Charles *construction management company executive*
Malson, Rex Richard *drug and health care corporation executive*
Marcus, Robert *aluminum company executive*
†McDowell, David E. *pharmaceutical executive*
Merrill, Harvie Martin *manufacturing executive*
Miller, Paul James *coffee company executive*
Monson, Arch, Jr. *fire alarm manufacturing company executive*
†Mullenix, Travis H. *food products company executive*
†Peppercorn, John Edward *chemical company executive*
Powell, Sandra Theresa *timber company executive*
Saras, James J. *agricultural products, grain company executive*
Scarff, Edward L. *diversified company executive*
Siegel, Louis Pendleton *forest products executive*
†Thacher, Carter Pomeroy *diversified manufacturing company executive*
†Tidball, Robert Nial *financial executive*
Tusher, Thomas William *apparel company executive*
Westerfield, Putney *management consulting executive*
Wilson, Ian Robert *food company executive*
Woodard, Clarence James *manufacturing company executive*
Zellerbach, William Joseph *retired paper company executive*

San Jose
Conner, Finis F. *electronics company executive*
Faggin, Federico *electronics executive*
†Frauenfelder, Lewis *electronics executive*
Hanley, Peter Ronald *corporate executive, engineer, physicist*
Heiman, Frederic Paul *electronics company executive*
†Hootnick, Laurence R. *electronics company executive*
Kasson, James Matthews *electronics executive*
†Lee, Sung W. *electronics executive*
Mitchell, David T. *electronic computing equipment company executive*
Pausa, Clements Edward *electronics company executive*
†Rha, Y. B. *electronics executive*
Rosendin, Raymond Joseph *electrical contracting company executive*
Schroeder, William John *electronics executive*
Scifres, Don R. *semiconductor laser, fiber optics and electronics company executive*
Stockton, Anderson Berrian *electronics company executive, consultant, genealogist*

San Juan Capistrano
†Huta, Henry Nicholaus *manufacturing and service company executive*

San Mateo
Aadahl, Jorg *corporate executive*
Felker, James M. *business executive*

Santa Ana
Buster, Edmond Bate *metal products company executive*
Ware, James Edwin *retired international company executive*

Santa Barbara
Blasingame, Benjamin Paul *electronics company executive*
Bongiorno, James William *electronics company executive*
Heidenheim, Roger Stewart *automotive and electronic consultant*
Potter, David Samuel *former automotive company executive*

Prindle, William Roscoe *consultant, retired glass company executive*

Santa Clara
Amelio, Gilbert Frank *electronics company executive*
Baird, Mellon Campbell, Jr. *electronics industry executive*
Grove, Andrew S. *electronics company executive*
House, David L. *electronics components company executive*
†Krause, L. William *manufacturing company executive*
Moore, Gordon E. *electronics company executive*
Morgan, James C. *electronics executive*

Santa Clarita
DeMieri, Joseph L. *manufacturing company executive*

Santa Cruz
Broadway, Nancy Ruth *landscape design and construction company executive, consultant, model and actress*

Santee
Vanier, Kieran Francis *business forms printing company executive*

Seal Beach
Bacon, Paul Caldwell *training system company executive, aviation consultant, engineering test pilot*
Beall, Donald Ray *multi-industry high-tech company executive*
Black, Kent March *electronics company executive*
Iacobellis, Sam Frank *aerospace company executive*
Merrick, George Boesch *aerospace company executive*

Sherman Oaks
Laney, Michael L. *manufacturing executive*

Simi Valley
†Mow, William *apparel executive*
†Nesi, Vincent *apparel executive*

Solana Beach
Brody, Arthur *industrial executive*
Kempf, Paul Stuart *optics company executive*

South El Monte
Kay, Kenneth Jeffrey *property development company executive*

South Pasadena
White-Thomson, Ian Leonard *chemical company executive*

South San Francisco
Anderson, Margaret Allyn *carpet showroom manager*
Crowley, Jerome Joseph, Jr. *manufacturing company executive*
†Henderson, Thomas James *construction company executive*
Raab, G. Kirk *biotechnology company executive*

Stockton
Hosie, William Carlton *food products company executive*

Sun Valley
Kamins, Philip E. *diversified manufacturing company executive*

Sunnyvale
Evans, Barton, Jr. *analytical instrument company executive*
Fialer, Philip Anthony *research scientist, electronics company executive*
Hind, Harry William *pharmaceutical company executive*
Leeson, David Brent *electronics company executive*
Lewis, John Clark, Jr. *manufacturing company executive*
Rugge, Henry Ferdinand *medical products executive*
Sanders, Walter Jeremiah, III *electronics company executive*
†Tramiel, Jack *computer game company executive*
†Tramiel, Sam *microcomputer and video game company executive*
†Trimble, Charles R. *electronics executive*

Thousand Oaks
†Binder, Gordon M. *health and medical products executive*
†Colburn, Keith W. *electronics executive*
DeLorenzo, David A. *food products executive*
Fitzgerald, Janet Marie *cosmetic company executive, training consultant*

Torrance
†Amemiya, Koichi *motor vehicle company executive*
Bruinsma, Theodore August *retired business executive*
Burnham, Daniel Patrick *manufacturing company executive*
Dankanyin, Robert John *manufacturing executive*
Mann, Michael Martin *electronics company executive*
†Woodhull, John Richard *electronics company executive*

Tustin
Hester, Norman Eric *chemical company technical executive, chemist*
Sognefest, Peter William *manufacturing company executive*

Ukiah
McAllister, (Ronald) Eric *pharmaceutical executive, physician*

Valencia
Davison, Arthur Lee *scientific instrument manufacturing company executive, engineer*

Valley Ford
Clowes, Garth Anthony *electronics executive, consultant*

Van Nuys
Hanlin, Russell L. *citrus products company executive*

Ventura
Huntsinger, Fritz Roy *former offshore equipment manufacturing company executive*

Walnut Creek
Graham, Dee McDonald *food company executive*
Hamlin, Kenneth Eldred, Jr. *retired pharmaceutical company executive*
Roach, John D. C. *manufacturing company executive*
Santos, E(nos) Francis (Frank) *agrochemical company executive*

Watsonville
†Costanzo, Patrick M. *constuction executive*
Roberts, Richard Heilbron *construction company executive*

West Los Angeles
Tamkin, S. Jerome *business executive, consultant*

Westlake Village
Blum, Fred Andrew *electronics company executive*

Whittier
Brown, Thomas Andrew *aircraft and weaponry manufacturing executive*
Conlin, Alfred Thomas *retired food company executive, consultant*

Woodland Hills
Firestone, Morton H. *business management executive*
Goldberg, David Charles *electrical contracting executive*
Weiser, Paul David *manufacturing company executive*

Yorba Linda
Eriksen, Otto Louis *retired manufacturing company executive*
Forth, Kevin Bernard *beverage distributing consultant*

COLORADO

Arvada
Holden, George Fredric *brewing company executive, policy specialist, consultant*

Boulder
Andrews, James Rowland *electronics executive, consultant*
Clark, Melvin Eugene *chemical company executive*
Daughenbaugh, Randall Jay *chemical company executive*
Hoerig, Gerald Lee *chemical company executive*
Lodewyk, Eric *chemist, pharmaceutical executive*
Miller, Norman Richard *diversified manufacturing company executive*
†Stull, Dean P. *chemical company executive*
Willam, Kaspar J. *computational mechanics educator*

Broomfield
Davis, Delmont Alvin, Jr. *manufacturing company executive*

Clark
Bartoe, Otto Edwin, Jr. *aircraft company executive*

Colorado Springs
Ehrhorn, Richard William *electronics company executive*
Robinson, Robert James *retired manufacturing executive*

Denver
Bard, Richard H. *financial service company executive*
Gates, Charles Cassius *rubber company executive*
Gibson, Thomas Joseph *diversified holding company executive*
Holmes, Fred Gillespie *sugar company executive*
Lee, Richard Kenneth *building products company executive*
†Leprino, James G. *food products executive*
Livingston, Johnston R. *manufacturing executive*
May, Francis Hart, Jr. *retired building materials manufacturing executive*
McClung, J(ames) David *corporate executive, lawyer*
†Miller, Donald E. *rubber company executive*
Stephens, William Thomas *forest products manufacturing company executive*
Swenka, Arthur John *food products executive*

Englewood
Mahoney, Gerald Francis *manufacturing company executive*

Fort Collins
Fields, Robert Charles *retired printing company executive*
Hafford, Patricia Ann *electronic company executive*

Golden
Coors, Jeffrey H. *brewery company executive*
†Coors, Joseph *brewery executive*
Coors, William K. *brewery executive*
Johnson, Marvin Donald *brewery executive*
†Rechholtz, Robert August *brewing company executive*

Greeley
Jovene, Nicholas Angelo, Jr. *construction company official*
Mapelli, Roland Lawrence *food company executive*
†Monfort, Richard L. *meat packaging and distribution company executive*
†Morgensen, Jerry Lynn *construction company executive*
Mueller, Donald Dean *food company executive*

Lakewood
Owen, Robert Roy *manufacturing company executive*
Plusk, Ronald Frank *manufacturing company executive*

Louisville
Poppa, Ryal Robert *manufacturing company executive*

CONNECTICUT

Bethel
Kidder, C. Robert *battery manufacturing company executive*
†Perrin, Charles R. *light manufacturing executive*

Bloomfield
Kaman, Charles Huron *diversified technologies corporation executive*

Branford
Mancheski, Frederick John *automotive company executive*
Penner, Harry Harold Hamilton, Jr. *pharmaceutical company executive, lawyer*

Bridgeport
Buckley, Eugene *aircraft company executive*
Semple, Cecil Snowdon *retired manufacturing company executive*

Bristol
Barnes, Carlyle Fuller *manufacturing executive*
Barnes, Wallace *manufacturing executive*
Wells, Arthur Stanton *manufacturing company executive*

Danbury
Baker, Leonard Morton *manufacturing company executive*
Barth, Elmer Ernest *wire and cable company executive*
Kennedy, Robert Delmont *petrochemical company executive*
†Lichtenberger, Horst William *chemical company executive*
†Soviero, Joseph C. *chemical company executive*

Darien
Gammie, Anthony Petrie *pulp and paper manufacturing company executive*
Hart, James W., Jr. *manufacturing executive*
Mc Donough, Richard Doyle *paper company executive*
Nava, Eloy Luis *clothing executive*
O'Brien, Joseph Patrick, Jr. *apparel and textile company executive*
Sprole, Frank Arnott *retired pharmaceutical company executive, lawyer*

East Berlin
Anderson, Lawrence Leslie, Jr. *manufacturing company executive, executive search company executive*

East Hartford
Coburn, Richard Joseph *company executive, electrical engineer*
Geckle, Robert Alan *manufacturing company executive*

Fairfield
Bunt, James Richard *electric company executive*
†Fulton, James A. *automotive executive*
Johnson, Alvin Roscoe *manufacturing executive*
Sutphen, Harold Amerman, Jr. *retired paper company executive*
Welch, John Francis, Jr. (Jack Welch) *electrical manufacturing company executive*
Wheeler, Henry Clark *manufacturing company executive*

Farmington
Mayerhofer, James Thomas *specialty and recycling materials company executive*
†Scott, David J. *beverage executive*
Sheeran, William James *manufacturing executive, mechanical engineer*
van Rooy, Jean-Pierre *international executive*

Greenwich
Allain, Emery Edgar *retired paper company executive*
Bantle, Louis Francis *tobacco company executive*
Barber, Charles Finch *retired metals company executive, financial services company executive*
Combe, Ivan DeBlois *drug company executive*
Damon, Edmund Holcombe *plastics company executive*
†Davis, Ronald Vernon *beverage products executive*
†Dorme, Patrick John *electronic company executive*
†Ellsworth, Robert F. *manufacturing executive*
†Holten, John V. *food products executive*
Ix, Robert Edward *food company executive*
†Jeffrey, Kim *food products executive*
Lozyniak, Andrew *manufacturing company executive*
†Mallardi, Joseph L. *manufacturing company executive*
†Mann, Marvin L. *electronics executive*
Moore, Charles Hewes, Jr. *industrial and engineered products executive*
Scheifele, Richard Paul *cosmetic and chemicals manufacturing company executive*
Simonnard, Michel André *manufacturing executive*
Vance, Don Kelvin *baking industry consultant*
Wearly, William Levi *business executive*
Wyman, Henry Walter *plastic manufacturing company executive*

Groton
Auerbach, Michael Howard *chemical company research executive*
Hinman, Richard Leslie *pharmaceutical company executive*

Hartford
Butterworth, Kenneth W. *manufacturing company executive*
Daniell, Robert F. *diversified manufacturing company executive*

Freeman, David *chemical company executive*
Hermann, Robert Jay *manufacturing company engineering executive, consultant*
Krieble, Robert H. *corporation executive*
†Robertson, Philip Scott *construction company consultant, state senator*

Madison
Golembeski, Jerome John *wire and cable company executive*

Middlebury
†Fickenscher, Gerald H. *chemicals company executive*
Galie, Louis Michael *electronics company executive*
†Mazaika, Robert J. *chemicals executive*

Middletown
Gerber, Murray A. *molding manufacturing company executive*

Naugatuck
Flannery, Joseph Patrick *manufacturing company executive*

New Britain
Ayers, Richard H. *manufacturing company executive*
Hadlow, David Moore *manufacturing executive*
Weddle, Stephen Shields *manufacturing company executive*

New Canaan
Bartlett, Dede Thompson *company executive*
Burns, Ivan Alfred *grocery products and industrial company executive*
Day, Castle Nason *food company executive*
Foley, Patrick Martin *computer manufacturing company executive*
Hodgson, Richard *electronics company executive*
Johnston, Douglas Frederick *industrial holding company executive*
Phypers, Dean Pinney *retired computer company executive*
Rutledge, John William *former watch company executive*
Sachs, John Peter *carbon company executive*
Thompson, George Lee *manufacturing company executive*
Toumey, Hubert John (Hugh Toumey) *textile company executive*

New Haven
Wentz, Howard Beck, Jr. *manufacturing company executive*

North Haven
Seton, Fenmore Roger *manufacturing company executive, civic worker*

Norwalk
Gaertner, Christopher Wolfgang *electronics company executive*
Grace, Julianne Alice *manufacturing company executive*
Hirsch, Leon Charles *medical company executive*
Johnstone, Chauncey Olcott *pharmaceutical company executive*
Kelley, Gaynor Nathaniel *instrumentation manufacturing company executive*
Maarbjerg, Mary Penzold *office equipment company executive*
McDonell, Horace George, Jr. *instrument company executive*
Peltz, Alan Howard *manufacturing company executive*
Rast, Mendel Walker *manufacturing company executive*
Smith, Wendell Murray *graphic arts control and equipment manufacturing executive*
Vanderbilt, Hugh Bedford, Sr. *mineral and chemical company executive*
†York, Theodore *electronics executive*

Old Greenwich
Mc Quinn, William P. *corporation executive*
Plancher, Robert Lawrence *manufacturing company executive*
Rukeyser, Robert James *manufacturing executive*

Orange
Ratcliffe, George Jackson, Jr. *business executive, lawyer*

Plainville
Glassman, Gerald Seymour *metal finishing company executive*

Ridgefield
Doran, Charles Edward *textile manufacturing executive*
Keirns, James Jeffrey *pharmaceutical company executive, biochemist*
Knortz, Herbert Charles *retired conglomerate company executive*
Levine, Paul Michael *paper industry executive, consultant*
Malhotra, Surin M. *aerospace manufacturing executive*
McGovern, R(ichard) Gordon *food company executive*
Sadow, Harvey S. *health care company executive*

Riverside
McCullough, Robert Willis *former textile executive*

Salisbury
Blum, Robert Edward *business executive*

Sandy Hook
Karkut, Emil Joseph *manufacturing company executive*

Shelton
Smith, Craig Richards *manufacturing executive*

South Windsor
†Gentile, George Michael *manufacturing company finance executive*

Southport
Haas, Ward John *cosmetics executive*

Kingsley, John McCall, Jr. *manufacturing company executive*
Perry, Vincent Aloysius *corporate executive*
Roache, Edward Francis *retired manufacturing company executive*
Ruger, William Batterman *firearms manufacturing company executive*
Wheeler, Wilmot Fitch, Jr. *diversified manufacturing company executive*

Stamford
Allaire, Paul Arthur *office equipment company executive*
Anderson, Susan Stuebing *business equipment company executive*
Ashton, Harris John *business executive*
Bellows, Howard Arthur, Jr. *hardware products manufacturing company executive*
Britton, Robert Austin *manufacturing company executive*
Cahill, John C. *general industry company executive*
Calarco, Vincent Anthony *specialty chemicals company executive*
Camisa, George Lincoln *beverage company executive*
Carlin, Gabriel S. *corporate executive*
Carpenter, Edmund Mogford *manufacturing executive*
Cassetta, Sebastian Ernest *industry executive*
Coleman, Ernest Albert *plastics and materials consultant*
Evans, Robert Sheldon *manufacturing executive*
Fernandez, Nino Joseph *manufacturing company executive*
Filter, Eunice M. *business equipment manufacturing executive*
Fortune, Philip Robert *metal manufacturing company executive*
Fuller, Mark Adin, Jr. *forest products company executive*
Gladstone, Herbert Jack *manufacturing company executive*
Griffin, Donald Wayne *defense company executive*
Gross, Ronald Martin *forest products executive*
Harvey, George Burton *office equipment company executive*
Hedge, Arthur Joseph, Jr. *environmental executive*
Hicks, Wayland R. *electronic business equipment executive*
Hollander, Milton Bernard *electronics executive*
Hood, Edward Exum, Jr. *retired electrical manufacturing company executive*
Horrigan, D. Greg *manufacturing company executive*
†Horrigan, D. Gregory *metal products executive*
Hull, James Charles *industrial company executive*
†Jaffe, Elliot S. *women's clothing retail chain executive*
Johnstone, John William, Jr. *chemical company executive*
Kubisen, Steven Joseph, Jr. *chemical and plastics management consultant*
Landau, Michael Roy *manufacturing executive*
†Lennard, Gerald *metal products executive*
†Magidson, Michael D. *metals products executive*
Mata, Pedro Francisco *food products executive*
Nutter, Wallace Lee *paper manufacturing executive*
O'Malley, Thomas D. *diversified company executive*
Owen, Nathan Richard *manufacturing company executive*
Parker, Jack Steele *retired manufacturing company executive*
Peterson, Carl Eric *banker, metals company executive*
Pollak, Edward Barry *chemical manufacturing company executive*
Raymond, Harvey Francis *textile executive, consultant*
Ryan, Raymond D. *retired steel company executive, insurance and marketing firm executive*
Salisbury, John Francis *distillery and chemical company executive, corporate lawyer*
Sigler, Andrew Clark *forest products company executive*
†Silver, R. Philip *metal products executive*
Weyher, Harry Frederick, III *metals company executive*
Ziegler, William, III *diversified industry executive*

Torrington
†Oneglia, Raymond Robert *construction company executive*

Wallingford
De George, Lawrence Joseph *diversified company executive*

Waterbury
Leever, Harold *chemical company executive*
Zampiello, Richard Sidney *metals and trading company executive*
Zeitlin, Bruce Allen *superconducting material technology executive*

Waterford
Hinkle, Muriel Ruth Nelson *naval warfare analysis company executive*

West Hartford
Clear, Albert F., Jr. *retired hardware manufacturing company executive*
Doran, James Martin *retired food products company executive*
Raffay, Stephen Joseph *manufacturing company executive*

West Simsbury
Brinkerhoff, Peter John *manufacturing company executive*

Weston
Liberatore, Nicholas Alfred *business consultant*

Westport
Breitbarth, S. Robert *manufacturing company executive*
McKane, David Bennett *business executive*
Sadler, David Gary *financial institution crisis management consultant*
Stashower, Michael David *retired manufacturing company executive*

Windsor
Mangold, John Frederic *manufacturing company executive, former naval officer*

Windsor Locks
Mc Gill, Robert Ernest, III *manufacturing company executive*
†Walker, K. Grahame *manufacturing company executive*

Woodbridge
Alvine, Robert *industrialist, entrepreneur, business leader*

Woodbury
Farrell, Edgar Henry *lawyer, building components manufacturing executive*

DELAWARE

Millsboro
Townsend, P(reston) Coleman *agricultural business executive*

Rockland
Rubin, Alan A. *pharmaceutical and biotechnology consultant*

Wilmington
Aiken, Robert McCutchen *retired chemical company executive, management consultant*
Alles, J. A. *chemical company executive*
Andersen, Donald Edward *retired chemical company executive*
Arrington, Charles Hammond, Jr. *retired chemical director*
Danzeisen, John R. *chemical company executive*
DeBlieu, Ivan Knowlton *plastic pipe company executive, consultant*
Gadsby, Robin Edward *chemical company executive*
Gibson, Joseph Whitton, Jr. *retired chemical company executive*
Gossage, Thomas Layton *chemical company executive*
Jaffe, Edward E(phraim) *research and development executive*
Kane, Edward Rynex *retired chemical company executive, corporate director*
Karrh, Bruce Wakefield *industrial company executive*
Lange, James Braxton *chemical company executive*
†Mollica, Joseph A. *pharmaceutical executive*
Molz, Robert Joseph *manufacturing company executive*
†Morrione, Paolo *polypropylene company executive*
Murphy, Arthur Thomas *systems engineer*
†Ockun, Robert J. *manufacturing executive*
Rose, Selwyn H. *chemical company executive*
†Schmutz, John F. *chemical company executive, corporate lawyer*
Woods, Robert A. *chemical company executive*
Woolard, Edgar S., Jr. *chemical company executive*

DISTRICT OF COLUMBIA

Washington
Alexander, Benjamin Harold *professional services firm executive, past government official*
Apple, Martin Allen *high technology manufacturing executive*
Briggs, Harold Melvin *corporate executive*
Caldwell, John L. *corporate executive*
Chen, Yuki Y. Kuo *industrial supplies company executive*
Choquette, William H. *construction company executive*
Davis, Lance Alan *research and development executive, metallurgical engineer*
Davis, True *corporate executive*
Ferebee, John Spencer, Jr. *corporate executive*
Goffe, William Gregory *aircraft manufacturing company executive*
Gracey, James Steele *corporate director, retired coast guard officer, consultant*
Griffin, Robert Thomas *automotive company executive*
Grossi, Ralph Edward *agricultural organization executive, farmer, rancher*
Harman, Sidney *audio and video company executive*
Jeelof, Gerrit *electronics executive*
†Lamb, Vincent P. *industrial executive*
Lebow, Irwin Leon *electronics engineering consultant*
Lutley, John H. *precious metals company executive*
Marshall, C. Travis *manufacturing executive, government relations specialist*
McKinney, James Clayton *electronics executive, electrical engineer*
Monroe, Robert Rawson *engineering and construction executive*
Moore, Robert Madison *food industry executive, lawyer*
O'Connor, Tom *corporate executive, management consultant*
Persavich, Warren Dale *diversified manufacturing company executive*
†Price, Mark Michael *building development consultant*
†Rales, Mitchell P. *automotive parts company executive*
Rales, Steven M. *automotive parts company executive*
Regnery, Alfred Scattergood *corporate executive, lawyer*
Salci, Larry Eugene *manufacturing executive*
Sherman, George M. *manufacturing company executive*
Thomas, W. Dennis *paper company executive, former government official*
Thompson, Richard Leon *pharmaceutical company executive, lawyer*
Trowbridge, Alexander Buel, Jr. *corporate director, consultant*

FLORIDA

Alachua
Brewster, Marcus Eli *pharmaceutical company executive*

Anna Maria
Kaiser, Albert Farr *diversified corporation executive*

Boca Grande
Nimitz, Chester William, Jr. *manufacturing company executive*

Boca Raton
Alvarado, Ricardo Raphael *retired corporate executive, lawyer*
Boer, F. Peter *chemical company executive*
Bolduc, J. P. *specialty chemicals and specialized health care company executive*
Butler, J. Murfree *chemical company executive*
Fetter, Richard Elwood *retired industrial company executive*
Finegold, Ronald *computer service executive*
Grace, J. Peter *specialty chemicals and specialized health care company executive*
Ingwersen, Martin Lewis *shipyard executive*
Lagin, Neil *management executive*
†Wiener, Elliott Maxwell *construction company executive*

Bonita Springs
Cairns, Raymond Eldon, Jr. *consultant, retired chemical company executive*

Boynton Beach
Johnson, Edward A. *manufacturing executive*
Smith, Charles Henry, Jr. *industrial executive*

Bradenton
Feeley, John Paul *retired paper company executive*
Price, Edgar Hilleary, Jr. *business consultant*
†Roeder, Myron A. *agricultural products company executive*

Cape Coral
Peters, Donald Cameron *construction company executive*

Casselberry
Vincent, Thomas James *retired manufacturing company executive*

Clearwater
Chamberlin, Terry McBride *sailing equipment company executive*
Smith, Marion Pafford *avionics company executive*

Clermont
Dyson, Raymond Clegg *building contractor, construction consultant*

Coconut Grove
†Litten, H. Randall *manufacturing company executive*

Coral Gables
Burini, Sonia Montes de Oca *apparel manufacturing and public relations executive*
Higginbottom, Samuel Logan *retired aerospace company executive*

Daytona Beach
Fly, James Lawrence, Jr. *construction executive*

Deerfield Beach
†Assaf, Ronald G. *electronics executive*
Monteleone, Raymond R. *electronics company executive, consultant*

Delray Beach
†Fuente, D. I. *office supply manufacturing executive*
Himmelright, Robert John, Jr. *rubber company executive*
Ronk, Glenn Emery *retired executive consultant, former electronics company executive*
Saffer, Alfred *retired chemical company executive*
Smith, John Joseph *textile company executive, educator*
Stone, Franz Theodore *retired fabricated metal products manufacturing executive*

Fort Lauderdale
†Caporella, Nick A. *diversified company executive*
Carney, Dennis Joseph *former steel company executive, consulting company executive*
Keats, Harold Alan *corporate executive*
†Morse, Edward J. *automotive executive*
Peterson, Colin Hampton *electronics company executive*
Sklar, Alexander *electrical company executive*

Fort Myers
Hudson, Leonard Harlow *contractor*
O'Dell, William Francis *retired business executive, author*
Wendeborn, Richard Donald *retired manufacturing company executive*

Fort Myers Beach
Smyth, Joseph Vincent *manufacturing company executive*

Gainesville
Chang, Weilin Parrish *construction educator, administrator, researcher*

Green Cove Springs
Watson, Thomas Campbell *economic development consulting company executive*

Hallandale
Cornblatt, Max *automotive batteries manufacturing company executive*

Hillsboro Beach
Gibbons, Joseph John *builders supply company financial executive*

Hobe Sound
Casey, Edward Paul *manufacturing company executive*
Craig, David Jeoffrey *retired manufacturing company executive*
Henley, Henry Howard, Jr. *retired manufacturing company executive*

Jacksonville
Belin, Jacob Chapman *paper company executive*
Elston, William Steger *food products company executive*
Hadley, Stanton Thomas *international manufacturing and marketing company executive, lawyer*
†Haskell, Preston Hampton, III *construction company executive*
Jackson, Julian Ellis *food company executive*
Lyon, Sherman Orwig *rubber and chemical company executive*
McGehee, Thomas Rives *paper company executive*
Welch, Philip Burland *electronics and office products company executive*

Juno Beach
Broadhead, James Lowell *business executive*

Key Largo
Brown, David *retired petrochemical corporation executive*
Daly, William Gerald *business executive*
Davidson, Thomas Noel *business executive*

Lake Buena Vista
Parke, Robert Leon *management executive*

Lake Wales
O'Connor, Robert Emmet *paper company executive*

Lakeland
Harritt, Norman L. *manufacturing company executive*
Hatten, William Seward *manufacturing company executive*
Kincart, Robert Owen *technological executive*

Largo
†Benstock, Gerald Martin *uniform manufacturing executive*

Leesburg
Talley, William Giles, Jr. *container manufacturing company executive*

Longboat Key
Prizer, Charles John *chemical company executive*

Longwood
Blumberg, Herbert Kurt *corporate executive*
Reade, Richard Sill *manufacturing executive*

Maitland
St. John, John *food company executive*

Marathon
Janicki, Robert Stephen *retired pharmaceutical company executive*

Marco
Butler, Frederick George *retired drug company executive*
Guerrant, David Edward *retired food company executive*

Melbourne
Hartley, John T., Jr. *electronic systems, semiconductor, communications and office equipment executive*
Lewis, Bernard Leroy *electronic scientist, consultant*

Miami
Blackburn, James Ross, Jr. *business executive, retired airline pilot*
Meller, George Mieczyslaw Jerzy *international trade consulting company executive*
†Miller, Leonard *construction company executive*
†Posner, Steven *diversified business executive*
Reigrod, Robert Hull *manufacturing executive*
Simkins, Leon Jack *paper company executive*
Weldon, Norman Ross *manufacturing company executive*

Naples
†Baldwin, Ralph Belknap *retired manufacturing company executive, astronomer*
Barth-Wehrenalp, Gerhard *chemical company executive*
Biondo, Michael Thomas *retired paper company executive*
Clay, W(illiam) Robert *retired chemical company executive*
Frazer, John Howard *tennis association executive*
Freedman, Stanley Marvin *manufacturing company executive*
Gushman, John Louis *former corporation executive, lawyer*
Kapnick, Harvey Edward, Jr. *retired corporate executive*
Maloon, James Harold *business executive, economist*
Price, Thomas Benjamin *former textile company executive*
Reed, John Franklin *instrument manufacturing company executive*
Sharpe, Robert Francis *equipment manufacturing company executive*
Smith, Willis Allen *retired consultant, former food company executive*
Van der Eb, Henry Gerard *retired packaging company executive*
von Arx, Dolph William *food products executive*

New Smyrna Beach
Skove, Thomas Malcolm *retired manufacturing company financial executive*

Niceville
Burns, John Joseph *consultant, retired aerospace executive, retired air force officer*

North Miami
Ancher, Bernard *plastics manufacturing executive, consultant*

North Palm Beach
Hushing, William Collins *retired corporate executive*
Kenna, Edgar Douglas *manufacturing company executive*
Rimmer, Jack *retired chemical company executive*
Staub, W. Arthur *health care products executive*

Orange Park
Webb, Robert Lee *chemical company executive*

Orlando
Brownlee, Thomas Marshall *lighting manufacturing company executive*
Jones, Joseph Wayne *food and beverage company executive, entrepreneur*
Meunier, Paul Dennis *aviation company executive*
Moltzon, Richard Francis *computer manufacturing executive*

Oviedo
Whitworth, Hall Baker *forest products company executive*

Palm Beach
Cook, Edward Willingham *diversified industry executive*
Habicht, Frank Henry *industrial executive*
Isenberg, Abraham Charles *shoe manufacturing company executive*
Jackson, John Tillson *corporate executive*
Rumbough, Stanley Maddox, Jr. *industrialist*
Scott, Harold Bartlett *manufacturing executive*
Winkler, Joseph Conrad *former recreational products manufacturing executive*

Palm Beach Gardens
Howse, Robert Davis *business executive*

Palm City
Wishart, Ronald Sinclair *retired chemical company executive*

Pensacola
†Bear, Lewis, Jr. *food and electronics company executive*

Pinellas Park
Hall, Charles Allen *aerospace and energy company executive*

Pompano Beach
Schwartz, Joseph *retired container company executive*

Ponte Vedra Beach
Klacsmann, John Anthony *retired chemical company executive*
Phelan, Martin DuPont *retired film company executive*
Spence, Richard Dee *paper products company executive, former railroad executive*

Royal Palm Beach
Graham, Carl Francis *consultant, former chemical products company executive, chemist*

Saint Petersburg
Mc Lean, Thomas Edwin *retired manufacturing company executive*
Mills, William Harold, Jr. *construction company executive*
Remke, Richard Edwin *lumber company executive*
Sheen, Robert Tilton *manufacturing company executive*
Stewart, Joseph Lester *rubber company executive*

Sarasota
Dlesk, George *retired pulp and paper industry consultant*
Glasser, Otto John *former business executive, former air force officer*
Hoffman, Oscar Allen *retired forest products company executive*
Roth, James Frank *manufacturing company executive, chemist*
Turner, Eugene Andrew *manufacturing executive*
Wigton, Paul Norton *steel company consultant, former executive*

Stuart
Conklin, George Melville *retired food company executive*
Derrickson, William Borden *manufacturing executive*
Leibson, Irving *industrial executive*
Mc Kenna, Sidney F. *technical company executive*
McQuillan, William Hugh *building company executive*
Snider, Harlan Tanner *former manufacturing company executive*
Wasiele, Harry W., Jr. *diversified electrical manufacturing company executive*
Wood, Harleston Read *retired manufacturing executive*

Tampa
Brown, Troy Anderson, Jr. *electrical distributing company executive*
Casey, Phillip Earle *steel company executive*
†Creed, Thomas G. *steel company executive*
Flom, Edward Leonard *retired steel company executive*
Hyatt, Kenneth E(rnest) *building materials company executive*
Johnson, Ewell Calvin *research and engineering executive*
†Martens, Ernesto *glass products company executive*
Matlock, Kenneth Jerome *building materials company executive*
Naimoli, Vincent Joseph *diversified operating and holding company executive*
Sada, Federico G. *glass manufacturing executive*

Tarpon Springs
Vajk, Hugo *manufacturing executive*

Tequesta
Hart, Frederick Donald *retired heating equipment executive*
Milton, Robert Mitchell *chemical company executive*
Peterson, James Robert *retired writing instrument manufacturing executive*

Titusville
†Haise, Fred Wallace, Jr. *aerospace company executive, former astronaut*

Vero Beach
Allik, Michael *diversified industry executive*
Cartwright, Alton Stuart *electrical manufacturing company executive*
Conway, Earl Cranston *manufacturing company executive, educator*
Dragone, Allan R. *manufacturing company executive*
Furrer, John Rudolf *retired manufacturing business executive*
Hancock, Thomas *machinery manufacturing executive*
MacTaggart, Barry *corporate executive*
Reed, Sherman Kennedy *chemical consultant*
Ritterhoff, C(harles) William *retired steel company executive*

West Palm Beach
Davis, Robert Edwin *manufacturing executive*
Giacco, Alexander Fortunatus *chemical industry executive*
Hudson, Alice Peterson *chemistry consulting laboratory executive*
Nelson, Richard Henry *manufacturing company executive*
Rinker, Marshall Edison, Sr. *cement company executive*
Scheckner, Sy *former greeting card company executive*
Vecellio, Leo Arthur, Jr. *construction company executive*

Windermere
Alexander, Judd Harris *retired paper company executive*
Hylton, Hannelore Menke *retired manufacturing executive*

Winter Haven
O'Connor, R. D. *health care executive*

Winter Park
Kost, Wayne L. *business executive*
MacKenzie, Ralph Sidney *aerospace executive*
Weir, William C., III *lighting manufacturing company executive*

GEORGIA

Alpharetta
Beringer, William Ernst *retired electrical equipment executive, lawyer*
†Malott, Thomas J. *manufacturing company executive, mechanical engineer*

Atlanta
Abrams, Bernard William *construction manufacturing and property development executive*
Abrams, Edward Marvin *construction company executive*
Baran, William Lee *food service company executive*
Benatar, Leo *packaging company executive*
Bevington, E(dmund) Milton *electrical machinery manufacturing company executive*
Biggers, William Joseph *retired manufacturing company executive*
†Blount, Ben B., Jr. *apparel executive*
Boeke, Eugene H., Jr. *construction executive*
Brands, James Edwin *medical products executive*
Cantrell, Wesley Eugene, Sr. *office equipment company executive*
†Carl, Robert Delroy, III *health care company executive, lawyer*
Casey, Charles Francis *diversified company executive*
Chitwood, Harold Otis *food company executive*
†Coan, Gaylord O. *agribusiness executive*
Corr, James Vanis *furniture manufacturing executive, investor, lawyer, accountant*
Correll, Alston Dayton, Jr. *forest products company executive*
Dennison, Stanley Scott *retired lumber company executive, consultant*
Dolive, Earl *retired business executive*
†Dyson, Brian G. *beverage company executive*
Edwards, Howard Dawson *business executive, physicist, academic administrator*
Edwards, Louis Ward, Jr. *diversified manufacturing company executive*
Gallagher, Thomas C. *diversified manufacturing executive*
Gleason, James Marne *manufacturing company executive*
Goizueta, Roberto Crispulo *food and beverage company executive*
Hahn, Thomas Marshall, Jr. *forest products corporation executive*
†Hogan, Ronald P. *forest products company executive*
†Hubbell, Richard A. *manufacturing executive*
Hubble, Don Wayne *business executive*
Isdell, Edward Neville *food products executive*
Ivester, Melvin Douglas *beverage company executive*
Jones, Christine Massey *furniture company executive*
Keough, Donald Raymond *investment banking executive*
†Kolb, David L. *carpet company executive*
Kuse, James Russell *chemical company executive*
†Lanier, John Hicks *apparel company executive*
Lee, R(aymond) William, Jr. *apparel company executive*
Malaspina, Alex *soft drink company executive*
†Mathews, George W., Jr. *manufacturing company executive*
Mc Kenzie, Harold Cantrell, Jr. *retired manufacturing executive*
McMahon, Donald Aylward *investor, corporate director*
†Mortensen, Davis K. *building products company executive*
Prince, Larry L. *automotive parts and supplies company executive*
Reith, Carl Joseph *apparel industry executive*
†Rollins, R. Randall *diversified services company executive*
Sands, Don William *agricultural products company executive retired*
Satrum, Jerry R. *chemicals company executive*
Schimberg, Henry Aaron *soft drink company executive*
Schwartz, Herbert Marshall *business executive*
Sheth, Jagdish Nanchand *business administration educator*
Smith, W. P., Jr. *food products executive*
Sutton, Berrien Daniel *beverage company executive*
Tucker, Robert Dennard *health care products executive*
†Van Meter, James Combs *forest products company executive*
Zaban, Erwin *diversified manufacturing company executive*

Brunswick
Brubaker, Robert Paul *food products executive*
Iannicelli, Joseph *chemical company executive, consultant*

Carrollton
Richards, Roy, Jr. *wire and cable manufacturing company executive*

Columbus
†Leebern, Donald M. *distilled beverage executive*

Conyers
Mc Clung, Jim Hill *light manufacturing company executive*

Covington
Penland, John Thomas *import/export and development companies executive*

Dalton
Shaw, Julius C. *carpet manufacturing company executive*
†Shaw, Robert E. *carpeting company executive*

Duluth
†Torian, Merville Russell, Sr. *construction company executive*

Gainesville
Kartzinel, Ronald *pharmaceutical company executive, neuroscientist*

La Grange
Anderson, Ray C. *carpet company executive*

Lilburn
Graham, Richard *container company executive*

Marietta
Blackwell, James Augusta, Jr. *aerospace executive*
Breese, John Allen *chemical industry executive*
Diercks, Chester William, Jr. *capital goods manufacturing company executive*
†Toal, Desmond James *manufacturing company executive*

Monroe
†Felker, George Stephen *textiles executive*

Moultrie
Vereen, William Coachman, Jr. *textile company executive*
Vereen, William Jerome *uniform manufacturing company executive*

Newnan
Harvey, Edwin Malcolm *retired manufacturing company executive*

Norcross
Adams, Kenneth Francis *automobile executive*
†Currey, Bradley, Jr. *paper company executive*
†Kelly, William S. *automotive executive*
†Pippin, John Eldon *electronics engineer, electronics company executive*
†Sage, Gordon *metal products executive*

Savannah
Gillespie, Daniel Curtis, Sr. *retired non-profit company executive, consultant*
Granger, Harvey, Jr. *manufacturing company executive*
Scott, Walter Coke *retired sugar company executive, lawyer*
Spitz, Seymour James, Jr. *retired fragrance company executive*
Sprague, William Wallace, Jr. *food company executive*

Thomaston
Hightower, Neil Hamilton *textile manufacturing company executive*

Thomasville
Flowers, Langdon Strong *foods company executive*
Flowers, William Howard, Jr. *food company executive*
Mc Mullian, Amos Ryals *food company executive*

Tucker
†Ordway, Ronald Dale *video display company executive*

West Point
Glover, Clifford Clarke *retired construction company executive*
Jennings, Joseph Leslie, Jr. *textile executive*
†Monk, Richard Hunley, Jr. *textile company executive*
Terry, Richmond Bohler *textiles executive*

HAWAII

Honolulu
Andrasick, James Stephen *agribusiness company executive*
Barbieri, David Arthur *company executive*
Buyers, John William Amerman *agribusiness and specialty foods company executive*
Ching, Larry Fong Chow *construction company executive*
Clark, Henry Benjamin, Jr. *retired food company executive, community service volunteer*
Couch, John Charles *diversified company executive*
Gary, James Frederick *business and energy advising company executive*
Hughes, Robert Harrison *former agricultural products executive*
Miccio, Joseph V. *business educator, consultant*
†Nakakura, Wilfred Satoru *construction company executive*
Robertson, Gregg Westland *diversified company executive*
Schnack, Gayle Hemingway Jepson (Mrs. Harold Clifford Schnack) *corporate executive*
Wainwright, Paul Edward Blech *construction company executive*

IDAHO

Boise
Burnell, Bates Cavanaugh *engineering and construction company executive*
Cleary, Edward William *retired diversified forest products company executive*
Ferguson, E. Robert *construction and engineering company executive*
Fery, John Bruce *forest products company executive*
Kemp, J. Robert *beef industry consultant, food company executive*
Littman, Irving *forest products company executive*
McClary, James Daly *retired contractor*
Minnick, Walter Clifford *building materials company executive*
Sullivan, James Kirk *forest products company executive*
Wasserlein, John Henry *paper manufacturing company executive*

ILLINOIS

Abbott Park
Burnham, Duane Lee *pharmaceutical company executive*
Coughlan, Gary Patrick *pharmaceutical company executive*
Hodgson, Thomas Richard *health care company executive*
Lussen, John Frederick *pharmaceutical laboratory executive*

Addison
Brunken, Gerald Walter, Sr. *manufacturing company executive*

Antioch
Strang, Charles Daniel *marine engine manufacturing company executive*

Arlington Heights
Church, Herbert Stephen, Jr. *retired construction company executive*
†Hughes, John *chemical company executive*

Barrington
Kartalia, Mitchell P. *electrical equipment manufacturing executive*
Kroha, Bradford King *electronics manufacturing corporation executive*
Marshall, Gordon Bruce *construction company executive*

Barrington Hills
Spak, Lorin Mitchell *retired office products industry executive*

Bedford Park
†Hough, Richard T. *chemical company executive*
†Wenstrup, H. Daniel *chemical executive*

Belvidere
Keller, Harold William *chemical company executive*

Bensenville
Greanias, Stanley Louis *coffee company executive*

Bloomingdale
Pedicini, Louis James *manufacturing company executive*

Brimfield
Kress, Ralph Herman *manufacturing company executive*

Broadview
Hohage, Frederick William *automotive parts company executive*

Burr Ridge
Danly, Donald Robert *retired manufacturing company executive*

Calumet City
Self, Madison Allen *chemical company executive*

Carlinville
Schweizer, Melvin *food products executive*
Southwell, Leonard J. *dairy corporation executive*

Carol Stream
†Catone, Lucio *manufacturing executive*
†Pond, Byron O. *manufacturing company executive*

Cary
Bowen, John Richard *former chemical company executive*

Chester
Welge, Donald Edward *food manufacturing executive*

Chicago
Appleton, Arthur Ivar *retired electric products manufacturing company executive, horse breeder*
Archambault, Bennett *corporate executive*
Athens, Andrew A. *steel company executive*
Badger, Charles H. *manufacturing company executive*
Banta, Merle Henry *graphics equipment and service company executive*
Bonser, Sidney Henry *diversified manufacturing company executive*
Brake, Cecil Clifford *diversified manufacturing executive*
Bryan, John Henry *food and consumer products company executive*
Burhoe, Brian W. *automotive service executive*
Burt, Robert Norcross *diversified manufacturing company executive*
Campbell, Calvin Arthur, Jr. *mining and plastics molding equipment manufacturing company executive*
†Cavalier, Frank N. *construction company executive, civil engineer*
Clarke, Richard Stewart *security company executive*
Conant, Howard Rosset *steel company executive*
Connolly, Eugene B., Jr. *building materials company executive*
Considine, Frank William *container corporation executive*
Cooper, Charles Gilbert *toiletries and cosmetics company executive*
†Cotter, Daniel A. *diversified company executive*
Cotting, James Charles *manufacturing company executive*
Covalt, Robert Byron *chemicals executive*
Crawford, William F. *corporate executive, consultant*
Crown, Lester *manufacturing company executive*
Darnall, Robert J. *steel company executive*
Donnelley, James Russell *printing company executive*
Drexler, Richard Allan *manufacturing company executive*
Dyer, Robert Campbell *printing ink company executive*
Egloff, Fred Robert *manufacturers representative, writer, historian*
Ergas, Jean-Pierre Maurice *packaging company executive*
Ewers, R. Darrell *food products company executive*
Farley, William F. *corporation executive*
Francois, William Armand *packaging company executive, lawyer*
Friedland, Richard Stewart *electronics company executive*
Gallagher, John Pirie *corporation executive*
Gandhi, Bharat R. *construction company executive*
Gardner, Edward G. *manufacturing company executive*
Gidwitz, Gerald *cosmetics company executive*
Gidwitz, Ronald J. *personal care products company executive*
Giesen, Richard Allyn *business executive*
Goldberg, Arthur M. *gaming and fitness company executive*
Goldstein, Norman R. *alcoholic beverage company executive*
Gordon, Ellen Rubin *candy company executive*
Goss, Howard S(imon) *manufacturing executive*
Guenzel, Paul Walter *corporate executive*
Haas, Howard Green *bedding manufacturing company executive*
Haggerty, Lawrence George *business executive*
Hall, W. Reginald *manufacturing company executive*
Hall, William King *manufacturing company executive*
Hamister, Donald Bruce *electronics company executive*
Hand, Elbert O. *clothing manufacturing and retailing company executive*
Harris, Irving Brooks *cosmetics executive*
Holland, Eugene, Jr. *lumber company executive*
Horne, John R. *farm equipment company executive*
Johnson, Joan B. *cosmetics company executive*
Jones, Robert Doyne *oil and chemical executive*
†Kent, Conrad S. *chemicals executive*
Kirby, William Joseph *corporation executive*
Lappin, Richard C. *corporate executive*
Lehman, George Morgan *food sales executive*
Light, Kenneth B. *manufacturing company executive*
Linde, Ronald Keith *corporate executive, private investor*
Locke, Charles Stanley *manufacturing company executive, director*
Lohman, Gordon R. *manufacturing executive*
Malott, Robert Harvey *manufacturing company executive*
Marcuse, Manfred Joachim *paper products executive*
Marineau, Philip Albert *food company executive*
Mc Carter, John Wilbur, Jr. *corporation executive*
McCarville, Mark John *food company executive*
McClung, James Allen *chemical and machinery manufacturing company executive*
McKee, Keith Earl *manufacturing technology executive*
Molloy, James B. *corrugated packaging executive*
Moore, John Ronald *manufacturing executive*
Murphy, Michael Emmett *food company executive*
Nichol, Norman J. *manufacturing executive*
Nicholas, Arthur Soterios *manufacturing company executive*
Parrish, Overton Burgin, Jr. *pharmaceutical corporation executive*
Patel, Homi Burjor *apparel company executive*
Pritzker, Robert Alan *manufacturing company executive*
†Proops, Jay D. *agricultural products executive*
Richman, William Sheldon *furniture company executive*
Rollhaus, Philip Edward, Jr. *diversified manufacturing company executive*
Rosenberg, Gary Aron *business executive, lawyer*
†Rutherford, Jack Dow *manufacturing executive*
Schechter, Allen E(dward) *retired publishing company executive*
Schwartz, Charles Phineas, Jr. *replacement auto parts company executive, lawyer*
†Shelby, David T. *manufacturing executive*
Siegel, Arthur *corporate executive*
Smithburg, William Dean *food manufacturing company executive*
Solomonson, Charles D. *corporate executive*
Sopranos, Orpheus Javaras *manufacturing company executive*
Stack, Stephen S. *manufacturing company executive*
Steinfeld, Manfred *furniture manufacturing executive*
Stone, Alan *container company executive*
Stone, Roger Warren *container company executive*
Strubel, Richard Perry *manufacturing company executive*
Stuart, Robert *container manufacturing executive*
Tadlock, R. Jerry *manufacturing and logistics consultant*
Tannenberg, Dieter E. A. *manufacturing company executive*
Toll, Daniel Roger *corporate executive, civic leader*
†Turner, Jack Henry *can manufacturing company executive*
Weil, John David *envelope company executive*
Weinberg, Harvey A. *apparel company executive*
Wellington, Robert Hall *manufacturing company executive*
Williams, Richard Lucas, III *electronics company executive, lawyer*
Wrigley, William *corporation executive*
Zeffren, Eugene *toiletries company executive*
Zmuda, Sharon Louise *construction executive*

Crystal Lake
Althoff, J(ames) L. *construction company executive*
Anderson, Lyle Arthur *manufacturing company executive*

De Kalb
Bickner, Bruce Pierce *agriculture executive*
Troyer, Alvah Forrest *seed corn company executive, plant breeder*

Decatur
Andreas, Michael Dwayne *agricultural business executive*
Kraft, Burnell D. *agricultural products company executive*
Randall, James R. *manufacturing company executive*
Staley, Henry Mueller *manufacturing company executive*

Deerfield
Barth, David Keck *industrial distribution industry consultant*
Batts, Warren Leighton *diversified industry executive*
Graham, William B. *pharmaceutical company executive*
Kushner, Jeffrey L. *manufacturing company executive*
Larrimore, Randall Walter *manufacturing company executive*
Loucks, Vernon R., Jr. *health care products and services company executive*
Sanford, Roy Leon *hospital supply company executive*
White, Tony L. *health and medical products executive*
Zywicki, Robert Albert *electrical distribution company executive*

Des Plaines
Carroll, Barry Joseph *manufacturing and real estate executive*
Farley, James Newton *manufacturing executive, engineer*
†Frank, James S. *automotive executive*
Li, Norman N. *chemicals executive*
†Malchow, Dennis *food products executive*
Meinert, John Raymond *clothing manufacturing and retailing executive, investment banker*
†Wilkie, Michael Leighton *manufacturing company executive*

Downers Grove
Katai, Andrew Andras *chemical company executive*

East Moline
Bosworth, Douglas LeRoy *farm implement company executive*

Elgin
Brinckman, Donald Wesley *industrial company executive*
†Furst, Warren Arthur *retired holding company executive*
Gwillim, Russell Adams *manufacturing company executive*
†Saliba, Jacob *manufacturing executive*

Elk Grove Village
McLain, Roger Sette *electronics company executive*
Nadig, Gerald George *manufacturing executive*

Elmhurst
†Gerber, C. Allen *food products executive*
Townsend, Merton LeRoy *metal products executive*
†Wyman, Thomas H. *food products executive*

Evanston
Carlin, Donald Walter *retired food products executive, consultant*
†Harlow, Robert Dean *packaging company executive*

Fairview Heights
Sullivan, Joseph Patrick *agricultural product company executive*

Flossmoor
Vogt, John Henry *corporate executive*

Franklin Park
Dean, Howard M., Jr. *food company executive*
Simpson, Michael *metals service center executive*
Watts, Ernest Francis *manufacturing company executive*

Freeport
Ferguson, Daniel C. *diversified company executive*
Knecht, Roland Edward *household goods manufacturing company executive*

Geneseo
Cherry, Robert Earl Patrick *retired food company executive*

Glencoe
Rubin, David Robert *corporate executive*
Silver, Ralph David *distilling company director*

Glenview
†Bible, Geoffrey Cyril *tobacco company executive*
McCarthy, Gerald Michael *electronics executive*
Nichols, John Doane *diversified manufacturing corporation executive*
Pearlman, Jerry Kent *electronics company executive*
Ptak, Frank S. *manufacturing executive*
Sherman, Elaine C. *gourmet foods company executive, educator*
Smith, Harold *manufacturing executive*
White, John Francis *retired corporate executive*
Winett, Samuel Joseph *manufacturing company executive*

Harvey
†Shotts, David Allison *manufacturing executive*

Highland Park
Maas, Duane Harris *distilling company executive*
Rudo, Milton *retired manufacturing company executive, consultant*
Smith, Malcolm Norman *manufacturing company executive*

Hinsdale
†Aldinger, Thomas Lee *manufacturing executive*
†Gustafson, F. Edward *plastics company executive*
Lowenstine, Maurice Richard, Jr. *retired steel executive*

Ochiltree, Ned A., Jr. *retired metals manufacturing executive*

Hoffman Estates
Dennis, Steven Pellowe *retail executive*

Homewood
Manson, Bruce Malcolm *construction company executive*

Huntley
Glickman, Louis *industrial sewing equipment executive*
†Suzuki, Mikio *machine manufacturing executive*

Indian Head Park
Frisque, Alvin Joseph *retired chemical company executive*

Ingleside
Propst, Catherine Lamb *biotechnology company executive*

Inverness
Schwab, Susan Carol *electronics company executive*

Island Lake
Benson, John Earl *construction executive*

Itasca
†Fowler, Jack W. *printing company executive*

Kenilworth
Hodson, Thomas William *health care company executive*
Weiner, Joel David *retired food products executive*

Lake Bluff
Albrecht, Edward Daniel *metals manufacturing company executive*
Wacker, Frederick Glade, Jr. *manufacturing company executive*

Lake Forest
†Anderluh, John Russell *business forms and information management company executive*
Bernthal, Harold George *health care company executive*
Deters, James Raymond *retired manufacturing and services company executive*
Hammar, Lester Everett *health care manufacturing company executive*
Hanlon, James Allison *confectionery company executive*
Heslop, Terence Murray *business executive*
Kenton, James Alan *pharmaceutical company financial executive*
†McClean, Graham J. *business forms company executive*
O'Mara, Thomas Patrick *manufacturing company executive*
Reichert, Jack Frank *manufacturing company executive*
Waehner, Ralph Livingston *business forms company executive, consultant*
Yaconetti, Dianne Mary *business executive*

Lake Zurich
Harrod, Scott *consulting manufacturing executive*

Libertyville
Burrows, Brian William *research and development manufacturing executive*
Thompson, David Jerome *chemical company executive, biochemist, nutritionist*

Lincolnshire
Freund, Charles Gibson *retired holding company executive*
†Tucker, Arlie G. *manufacturing executive*

Lisle
Birck, Michael John *manufacturing company executive, electrical engineer*
Krehbiel, Frederick August, II *electronics company executive*
Krehbiel, John H. *electronics company executive*
Krehbiel, John H., Jr. *electronics company executive*
Psaltis, John Costas *manufacturing company executive*
Reum, W. Robert *manufacturing executive*

Long Grove
Liuzzi, Robert C. *chemical company executive*
Obert, Paul Richard *manufacturing company executive, lawyer*

Melrose Park
Bernick, Howard Barry *manufacturing company executive*
Cernugel, William John *personal/food products company financial executive*
Lavin, Bernice E. *cosmetics executive*
Umans, Alvin Robert *manufacturing company executive*

Mendota
Hume, Horace Delbert *manufacturing company executive*

Moline
Becherer, Hans Walter *agricultural equipment manufacturing executive*
England, Joseph Walker *heavy equipment manufacturing company executive*
Hallene, Alan Montgomery *elevator and escalator company executive*
Hank, Bernard J., Jr. *elevator manufacturing company executive*
Hanson, Robert Arthur *retired agricultural equipment executive*
Leroy, Pierre Elie *manufacturing executive*
Stowe, David Henry, Jr. *agricultural and industrial equipment company executive*

Mount Prospect
†Alexy, R. James *manufacturing company executive*
†Krakowiak, Edward T. *manufacturing company executive*
Rogers, Richard F. *construction company executive, architect, engineer*

Singer, Norman Sol *food products executive, inventor*

Mundelein
Kennedy, George D. *chemical company executive*
Mills, James Stephen *medical supply company executive*

Naperville
Burnham, Robert Danner *electronics executive, scientist*
Clark, Worley H., Jr. *specialty chemical company executive*
Cline, Richard Gordon *health medical products executive*
Frank, Dieter *technical consultant, retired chemical company executive*
Harreld, James Bruce *food company executive*
Mooney, Edward Joseph, Jr. *chemical company executive*
Sadowski, Anthony James *chemical company executive, physical chemist*
Schaack, Philip Anthony *retired beverage company executive*

Niles
†Herb, Marvin J. *food products executive*
Isenberg, Howard Lee *manufacturing company executive*
†Powell, David *manufacturing company executive*
Salamoun, Peter V. *retired manufacturing executive*

Normal
†Ohinouye, Tsuneo *automobile manufacturing executive*

North Chicago
†Garrity, Keith R. *metal products company executive*

Northbrook
Boyce, Donald Nelson *diversified industry executive*
Harris, Neison *manufacturing company executive*
Hartman, Robert S. *retired paper company executive*
Kasperson, Richard Willet *retired pharmaceutical company executive*
Lenon, Richard Allen *chemical corporation executive*
Nordman, Richard Dennis *chemical company executive*
Piccolo, C. A. Lance *healthcare company executive*
Sayatovic, Wayne Peter *manufacturing company executive*
Terra, Daniel James *chemical company executive*
Tucker, Frederick Thomas *electronics company executive*
Turner, Billie B. *chemical company executive*

Northfield
Leslie, John Hampton *mnufacturing executive*
O'Brien, Maurice James *business executive*
Smeds, Edward William *food company executive*
Stepan, Frank Quinn *chemical company executive*

Northlake
†Di Matteo, James *food products executive*

Oak Brook
Greenberg, Jack M. *food products executive*
Holsinger, Wayne Townsend *apparel manufacturing executive*
Iorgulescu, Jorge *international executive, chemical engineer*
Jones, John Earl *construction company executive*

Oak Park
Douglas, Kenneth Jay *food products executive*
Robinson, Charlie Davis *food company executive*

Olympia Fields
Purdy, Charles Robert *corporate executive*

Oregon
Abbott, David Henry *manufacturing company executive*

Orland Park
Gittelman, Marc Jeffrey *manufacturing and financial executive*

Palatine
Kern, Byron Mehl *retired chemical company executive*
Makowski, M. Paul *electronics research executive*
Roe, Richard C. *industry consultant, former home furnishings manufacturing executive*

Palos Park
Nelson, Lawrence Evan *business consultant*

Park Ridge
Adkins, Howard Eugene *aluminum company executive*
Weber, Philip Joseph *retired manufacturing company executive*

Peoria
Dryden, Robert Charles *construction company executive*
Fites, Donald Vester *tractor company executive*
Wogsland, James Willard *heavy machinery manufacturing executive*

Peru
Carus, Milton Blouke *chemical company executive, publisher*

Prospect Heights
†Osborne, Richard Cogswell *manufacturing company executive*

Quincy
Liebig, Richard Arthur *retired manufacturing company executive*
†Shade, Thomas L. *agricultural products executive*

Rockford
Gloyd, Lawrence Eugene *diversified manufacturing company executive*
Horst, Bruce Everett *manufacturing company executive*

O'Donnell, William David *construction firm executive*
Stonecipher, Harry C. *manufacturing company executive*

Rolling Meadows
Brennan, Charles Martin, III *construction company executive*

Roselle
Poth, Edward Cornelius *construction company executive*

Round Lake
Johnston, William David *health care company executive*

Saint Charles
Stone, John McWilliams, Jr. *electronics executive*

Schaumburg
Galvin, Christopher B. *electronics company executive*
Galvin, Robert W. *electronics executive*
Hickey, John Thomas *electronics company executive*
Milne, Garth LeRoy *electronics executive*
†Schulmeyer, Gerhard *manufacturing executive*
Sundry, Arthur P. *business executive*
Tooker, Gary Lamarr *electronics company executive*
Weisz, William Julius *electronics company executive*

Skokie
Alexander, John Charles *pharmaceutical company executive, physician*
Bendix, William Emanuel *equipment manufacturing company executive*
Fluno, Jere David *business executive*
†Goeckel, Werner Frederick *plastics company executive*
Goldberg, Arthur Lewis *manufacturing company executive*
Herting, Robert Leslie *pharmaceutical executive*
†Johansson, Nils A. *manufacturing executive*
Krucks, William *electronics manufacturing executive*
Mayes, Frank Gorr *food company executive*
†Rubow, W. Steven *food company executive*

South Elgin
Burdett, George Craig *plastics industry executive*

Sterling
Gurnitz, Robert Ned *steel industry company executive*
Knight, Herbert Borwell *manufacturing company executive*

Sycamore
Grace, John Eugene *business forms company executive*

Vernon Hills
†Wilson, J. Steven *lumber company executive*

Villa Park
†Rogers, Peter Norman *food company executive*
†Wozniak, Edward F. *manufacturing company executive*

Waukegan
Chapman, James Claude *marine equipment manufacturing executive*
Cherry, Peter Ballard *electrical products corporation executive*
Cherry, Walter Lorain *engineer, electronics executive*
Crutcher, Harold Trabue, Jr. *chemical company executive*

West Chicago
Ball, G(eorge) Carl *seed company executive*

Wheaton
Jack, Nancy Rayford *supplemental resource company executive, consultant*

Winnetka
Bartlett, William McGillivray *hospital and scientific products company executive*
Gavin, James John, Jr. *diversified company executive*
Gray, Sheldon *metal products executive*
Menke, Allen Carl *industrial corporation executive*
Puth, John Wells *consulting company executive*

INDIANA

Anderson
Contos, Larry D *food products executive*

Batesville
Hillenbrand, Daniel A. *manufacturing company executive*
Smith, Lonnie Max *diversified industries executive*

Bluffton
Lawson, William Hogan, III *electrical motor manufacturing executive*
Nixon, Robert Pleasants *former electric motor manufacturing company executive*
Pfister, Dean William *motor manufacturing company financial executive*

Burns Harbor
Brown, Gene W. *steel company executive*

Carmel
Shoup, Charles Samuel, Jr. *chemicals and materials executive*

Columbus
Baker, James Kendrick *specialty metals manufacturing company executive*
Boll, Charles Raymond *engine company executive*
Draeger, Wayne Harold *manufacturing company executive*
Durham, James Michael, Sr. *diesel engine company executive*
Henderson, James Alan *engine company executive*
Jolly, Bruce Dwight *manufacturing company executive*
Miller, Joseph Irwin *automotive manufacturing company executive*

Schacht, Henry Brewer *diesel engine manufacturing company executive*
Stoner, R(ichard) B(urkett) *manufacturing company executive, member of Democratic national committee*

Crown Point
Haines, Robert Earl *retired industrial construction executive*

Elkhart
Bryant, Donald Loudon *pharmaceutical company executive*
Corson, Thomas Harold *manufacturing company executive*
Decio, Arthur Julius *manufacturing company executive*
Groom, Gary Lee *recreational vehicle manufacturing executive*
Hill, Thomas Stewart *electronics executive, consultant, engineer*
Holtz, Glenn Edward *bank instrument manufacturing executive*
Kerich, James Patrick *manufacturing company executive*
Kloska, Ronald Frank *manufacturing company executive*
Mischke, Frederick Charles *manufacturing company executive*
†O'Hagan, William D. *metal products executive*

Evansville
Koch, Robert Louis, II *manufacturing company executive, mechanical engineer*
Muehlbauer, James Herman *manufacturing executive*

Fort Wayne
Latz, G. Irving, II *manufacturing company executive*
Marine, Clyde Lockwood *agribusiness consultant*
Morehart, Donald Hadley *food products executive*
Quinby, Charles Edward, Jr. *manufacturing company executive*
†Rifkin, Leonard *metals company executive*
Williams, Leamon Dale *feed and grain company executive, consultant*

Fowler
Brouillette, Donald G. *grain company executive*

Goshen
Morris, Robert Julian, Jr. *manufacturing company executive*
Schrock, Harold Arthur *manufacturing company executive*

Granger
Brissey, Ruben Marion *retired container company executive*

Hammond
†Ash, Frederick Melvin *manufacturing company executive*
Bahls, Gene Charles *agricultural products company executive*

Indianapolis
Bennett, Bruce W. *construction company executive, civil engineer*
Bindley, William Edward *pharmaceutical executive*
Holt, Worthe Seymour *pharmaceutical company executive*
†Janis, F. Timothy *technology company executive*
Justice, Brady Richmond, Jr. *medical services executive*
†King, J. B. *pharmaceutical company executive, lawyer*
Lanford, Luke Dean *electronics company executive*
Lantz, George Benjamin, Jr. *business executive, college executive, consultant*
†Lent, James A. *analytical equipment company executive*
Long, William Allan *retired forest products company executive*
†Lugar, Thomas R. *manufacturing executive*
Mc Farland, H. Richard *food company executive*
Mutz, Oscar Ulysses *manufacturing and distribution executive*
Nugent, Thomas D. *food products executive*
Perelman, Melvin *pharmaceutical company executive*
Pettinga, Cornelius Wesley *pharmaceutical company executive*
Reeve, Ronald Cropper, Jr. *manufacturing executive*
Reilly, Peter C. *chemical company executive*
Richmond, James Ellis *restaurant company executive*
Salentine, Thomas James *pharmaceutical company executive*
Schmidt, William C. *chemical company executive*
†Schwindt, Robert F. *diagnostic medical products executive*
Step, Eugene Lee *retired pharmaceutical company executive*
Thompson, W(ilmer) Leigh *pharmaceutical company executive, physician, pharmacologist*
Tobias, Randall L. *pharmaceuticals company executive*
Tomlinson, Joseph Ernest *manufacturing company executive*
Walsh, John Charles *metallurgical company executive*
Wood, Richard Donald *pharmaceutical company executive*
Zapapas, James Richard *pharmaceutical company executive*

Jasper
†Habig, Douglas Arnold *manufacturing company executive*
Habig, Thomas Louis *manufacturing executive*
Kohler, Jeffrey Martin *office furniture manufacturing executive*
†Thyen, James C. *furniture company executive*

Kokomo
Wilhelm, Ralph Vincent, Jr. *electronics company executive, ceramics engineer*

Lafayette
Meyer, Brud Richard *pharmaceutical company executive*

Marion
East, Frank Howard *paper company executive*

Michigan City
†Ruby, Burton Bennett *men's apparel manufacturer*

Middlebury
†Guequierre, John Phillip *manufacturing company executive*

Mishawaka
Hagiwara, Kokichi *steel company executive*
†Kapson, Jordan *automotive executive*

Muncie
Fisher, John Wesley *manufacturing company executive*
†Looney, H. Ray *manufacturing company executive*
Owsley, Alvin *manufacturing executive, lawyer*

Munster
†Corsiglia, Robert Joseph *electrical construction company executive*
Luerssen, Frank Wonson *retired steel company executive*

Noblesville
Almquist, Donald John *retired electronics company executive*

Notre Dame
Kogge, Peter Michael *computer and electronics executive*
Shannon, William Norman, III *marketing and international business educator, food service executive*

Portage
Katsahnias, Thomas George *steel company executive*

Seymour
Orben, Robert Allen *engine company executive*
Terkhorn, Henry K. *food company executive*

South Bend
Altman, Arnold David *business executive*
†Armour, James Author *military vehicle manufacturing company executive*
McKernan, Leo Joseph *manufacturing company executive*

Terre Haute
†Gray, Robert Linwood *manufacturing executive*

Wabash
†Cooke, Danny Frank *apparel company owner, consultant*

Warsaw
Dalton, William Matthews *foundry executive*

West Lafayette
Hoover, William Leichliter *forestry and natural resources educator, financial consultant*
Kampen, Emerson *chemical company executive*
McDonald, Robert Bond *chemical company executive*

IOWA

Ames
Gaertner, Richard Francis *manufacturing research center executive*

Cedar Rapids
Kucharski, Robert Joseph *finance executive*
Schrimper, Vernon L. *manufacturing, marketing executive*

Davenport
Juckem, Wilfred Philip *manufacturing company executive*
Sulg, Madis *corporation executive*

Des Moines
Frohock, Joan (Joan Walton) *industrial supply company executive*
Urban, Thomas N. *agricultural products company executive*

Dubuque
Bertsch, Frank Henry *furniture manufacturing company executive*
Crahan, Jack Bertsch *manufacturing company executive*
McDonald, Robert Delos *manufacturing company executive*
Tully, Thomas Alois *building materials executive, consultant, educator*
†Wahlert, Robert Henry *food company executive*

Fairfield
Schaefer, Jimmie Wayne, Jr. *agricultural company executive*

Forest City
Hanson, John K. *recreational vehicle manufacturing company executive*

Hartley
Pearson, Gerald Leon *food company executive*

Marion
Starr, David Evan *corporate executive*

Mason City
MacNider, Jack *retired cement company executive*

Muscatine
Carver, Martin Gregory *tire manufacturing company executive*
Dahl, Arthur Ernest *former manufacturing executive, consultant*
Howe, Stanley Merrill *manufacturing company executive*
Johnson, Donald Lee *agricultural materials processing company executive*
Koll, Richard Leroy *retired chemical company executive*

Lewis, Charles John *feed, grain and chemicals company executive*

Newton
Hadley, Leonard Anson *appliance manufacturing corporation executive*
Schiller, Jerry A. *retired manufacturing company executive*

Pella
Bevis, James Wayne *manufacturing company executive*
Farver, Mary Joan *building products company executive*

Sioux City
†Foster, Paul David, Jr. *agri-business executive*

Springville
Nyquist, John Davis *retired radio manufacturing company executive*

Waterloo
Mast, Frederick William *construction company executive*

West Des Moines
Pomerantz, Marvin Alvin *container corporation executive*

KANSAS

Dodge City
Chaffin, Gary Roger *business executive*

Hesston
Yost, Lyle Edgar *farm equipment manufacturing company executive*

Hutchinson
Dick, Harold L. *manufacturing executive*
†Hanes, John T. *food products executive*

Industrial Airport
†Mendelson, Lewis A. *manufacturing company executive*

Kansas City
†DeFabis, Mike *food products company executive*
Elkin, Irvin J. *milk marketing cooperative executive*

Lenexa
Ascher, James John *pharmaceutical executive*

Salina
Cosco, John Anthony *health care executive, educator*

Shawnee Mission
Arneson, George Stephen *manufacturing company executive, management consultant*
Dougherty, Robert Anthony *manufacturing company executive*
Gamet, Donald Max *appliance company executive*
†Mischler, Paul *grain company executive*
†Myhre, Roger L. *agricultural products executive*
Pierson, John Theodore, Jr. *manufacturer*
†Smith, Robert Hugh *engineering construction company executive*
Strubbe, Thomas R. *diagnostic testing industry executive*
Sunderland, Robert *cement company executive*

Silver Lake
Rueck, Jon Michael *manufacturing executive*

Topeka
Fink, H. Bernerd *corporate professional*
Fink, Ruth Garvey *diversified company executive*

Wichita
Eby, Martin Keller, Jr. *construction company executive*
Farha, William Farah *food company executive*
Frazier, John Lionel Devin *food products executive*
†Goebel, Christopher J. *lumber company executive*
Hanna, William W. *chemical company executive*
Meyer, Russel William, Jr. *aircraft company executive*
Peterman, Bruce Edgar *aircraft company executive*
†Tiffany, Charles Ferguson *aerospace executive*
Welton, Robert Breen *aircraft manufacturing company executive*

KENTUCKY

Bowling Green
Holland, John Ben *clothing manufacturing company executive*

Georgetown
†Warren, Alex McLean, Jr. *automotive executive*

Gilbertsville
Mathues, Thomas Oliver *retired automobile company executive*

Highland Heights
Street, David Hargett *manufacturing company executive*

Lexington
Heitzman, Robert Edward *retired materials handling equipment manufacturing company executive*

Louisville
†Ayotte, Robert C. *metal products executive*
†Brown, Timothy Charles *manufacturing company executive, accountant*
Bujake, John Edward, Jr. *beverage company executive*
Davis, Finis E. *business executive*
Frazier, Owsley B. *beverage company executive*
Heiden, Charles Kenneth *former army officer, metals company executive*
Kinsey, William Charles *building materials company executive*

Mountz, Wade *retired health service management executive*
†Mueller, James E. *agricultural products executive*
Quinn, Joseph Michael *coatings industry executive*
Rollo, F. David *hospital management company executive, radiology educator*
Shaver, Jesse Milton, Jr. *manufacturing company executive*
†Smith, Wayne T. *healthcare company executive*
†Thompson, James *distilleries and importing company executive*

Owensboro
Hulse, George Althouse *steel company executive*
†Wright, Patrick E. *grain company executive*

Prospect
Dunbar, Wallace Huntington *manufacturing company executive*

LOUISIANA

Baton Rouge
Siegel, Laurence *human resources executive, former psychology educator*
†Turner, Bert S. *construction executive*

Geismar
Coombs, Douglas A. L. *chemical company executive*

Metairie
Krauss, Steven James *clothing executive*

New Orleans
Allen, F(rank) C(linton), Jr. *manufacturing executive, lawyer*
Deasy, William John *construction, marine dredging, engineering and mining company executive*
Ewing, Channing Lester *biomechanics researcher, corporate executive*
Howson, Robert E. *construction company executive*

MAINE

Brunswick
Dixon, Thomas Francis *aviation company executive*
Porter, Richard Sterling *retired metal processing company executive, lawyer*

Ellsworth
Goodyear, Austin *electronics and retail company executive*

Lewiston
Tighe, Thomas James Gasson, Jr. *healthcare executive*

MARYLAND

Annapolis
Hospodor, Andrew Thomas *electronics executive*
Hyde, Lawrence Henry, Jr. *industrial company executive*
Muller, Richard W. (Wilhelm Gustav Muller) *retired textile importer*

Baltimore
Beasley, Robert Scott *aerospace company executive*
Deoul, Neal *electronics company executive*
Glassgold, Israel Leon *construction company executive, engineer, consultant*
Green, Bernard *food products executive*
Hall, Richard Leland *food processing company consultant*
Knott, Henry Joseph *construction company executive*
Legum, Jeffrey Alfred *automobile company executive*
Lucas, Barbara B. *electrical equipment manufacturing executive*
McCarty, Harry Downman *tool manufacturing company executive*
Morris, Edwin Thaddeus *construction consultant*
Reeder, Oliver Howard *paint products manufacturing executive*
Scheeler, Charles *construction company executive*
Slatkin, Murray *paint sundry distribution executive*
Strull, Gene *technology consultant, retired electrical manufacturing company executive*

Beltsville
Kasprick, Lyle Clinton *medical products company executive*
†Levin, Gilbert Victor *bioengineering and environmental control company executive*
Thomas, Stuart Denis *textile company executive*

Bethesda
Augustine, Norman Ralph *industrial executive*
Baird, Charles Fitz *minings and metals company executive*
Bregman, Jacob Israel *environmental consulting company executive*
Richards, Merlon Foss *retired diversified technical services company executive*
Weinberger, Alan David *corporate executive*
Young, A. Thomas *defense, aerospace, energy and information systems company executive*

Chevy Chase
Bissinger, Frederick Lewis *retired manufacturing executive, consultant*
Ritchie, Royal Daniel *economic development executive*

Clarksburg
Evans, John Vaughan *satellite laboratory executive, physicist*

Columbia
Lapides, Jeffrey Rolf *corporate executive*
†Luskin, Jack *manufacturing company executive*
Peck, Charles Edward *retired construction and mortgage executive*
van Remoortere, Francois Petrus *chemical company research and development executive*

Cumberland
Fiedler, Lee N. *automotive products executive*

Easton
Peterson, James Kenneth *manufacturing company executive*
Quinn, William Wilson *manufacturing executive*

Ellicott City
Weingarten, Murray *manufacturing executive*

Forestville
Povey, Thomas George *office systems company executive*

Fort Washington
Kelley, Bennett Wallace *manufacturing company executive, consultant*

Gaithersburg
Ewing, Frank Marion *lumber company executive, industrial land developer*
Oettinger, Frank Frederic *electronics executive, researcher*
Schrenk, W(illi) Juergen *chemicals executive*
†Thompson, J. Stark *chemical company executive*

Hanover
Dibos, Dennis Robert *electronics industry executive*
†Miller, James L. *food products executive*

Hunt Valley
DiCamillo, Gary Thomas *manufacturing executive*
Mulligan, Martin Frederick *clothing executive, professional tennis player*

Huntingtown
Mitchell, Robert Greene *industrial manufacturing executive, consultant*

Ijansville
Calton, Gary Jim *chemical company executive, medical educator*

Lanham
Cannon, Charles C. *footwear company executive*

Laurel
Abbagnaro, Louis Anthony *corporate executive*

Lutherville Timonium
†Parker, Lewis E. S. *research company executive, commercial vineyard operator*

Monkton
Ryker, Norman J., Jr. *retired manufacturing company executive*

Potomac
Karson, Emile *international business executive*

Rockville
Drzewiecki, Tadeusz Maria *corporate executive, defense consultant*
Halperin, Jerome Arthur *pharmacopeial convention executive*
Miller, Kenneth Michael *electronics executive*
Shepherd, Alan J. *construction executive, management consultant*

Saint Michaels
Jones, Raymond Edward, Jr. *brewing executive*

Salisbury
Perdue, Franklin P. *poultry products company executive*
†Perdue, James *food products executive*

Sandy Spring
Gibian, Thomas George *chemical company executive*

Silver Spring
Coates, Robert Jay *retired electronic scientist*
Cooke, Joseph Peter *construction contracting company executive*
Porter, Dwight Johnson *former electric company executive, foreign affairs consultant*
Schneider, William Charles *aerospace consultant*

Sparks
Felton, John Walter *spice company executive*
Harrison, James Joshua, Jr. *food products executive*
McCormick, Charles Perry, Jr. *food products company executive*
Nelson, John Howard *food company research executive*

Upper Marlboro
†Bowles, Liza K. *construction executive*

MASSACHUSETTS

Amherst
Mc Garrah, Robert Eynon *business administration educator*

Bedford
Furumoto, Horace Wataru *medical products company executive*
Gilmartin, John A. *medical products company executive*

Billerica
Gray, Charles Agustus *chemical company research executive*
McCaffrey, Robert Henry, Jr. *retired manufacturing company executive*

Boston
Bodman, Samuel Wright, III *specialty chemicals and materials company executive*
Burnes, Kennett Farrar *chemical company executive*
Cabot, John G. L. *chemical manufacturing company executive*
Cabot, Louis Wellington *chemical manufacturing company executive*
Cabot, Thomas Dudley *chemical company executive*

Connell, William Francis *diversified company executive*
Fruitt, Paul N. *manufacturing executive*
Glass, Milton Louis *retired manufacturing company executive*
†Holey, Ronald Loren *retired construction company executive*
Kames, Kenneth F. *manufacturing company executive*
Kane, E(dward) Leonard *electronics company executive, lawyer, association executive*
Leland, Warren Hanan *engineering-construction company executive*
Macera, Salvatore *industrial executive*
†Macomber, John D. *construction executive*
Metcalf, Arthur George Bradford *electronics company executive*
Mitchell, W. Randle, Jr. *textile company executive*
Spilhaus, Karl Henry *textiles executive, lawyer*
Wainberg, Alan *footwear company executive*
†Waxlax, Lorne R. *manufacturing company executive*

Braintree
Latham, Allen, Jr. *manufacturing company consultant*

Brockton
Droukas, Ann Hantis *management executive*

Brookline
Litschgi, Richard John *computer manufacturing company executive*

Burlington
Bright, Willard Mead *manufacturing company executive*
Reno, John Findley *corporate executive*

Cambridge
Berger, Harvey James *pharmaceutical company executive, physician, educator*
Berstein, Irving Aaron *biotechnology and medical technology executive*
Booth, I(srael) MacAllister *photography products company executive*
Buckler, Sheldon A. *photographic company executive*
Bullock, Francis Jeremiah *pharmaceutical research executive*
Butler, Fred Jay, Jr. *manufacturing company executive*
Chubb, Stephen Darrow *medical corporation executive*
Dalby, Alan James *biotechnology company executive*
Duecker, Heyman Clarke *chemical executive, researcher*
Epstein, Henry David *electronics company executive*
Evans, Lawrence Boyd *business executive*
Frosch, Robert Alan *retired automobile manufacturing executive, physicist*
Gerrish, Hollis G. *confectionery company executive*
Kalelkar, Ashok Satish *consulting company executive*
Kliem, Peter Otto *imaging company executive*
Kung, Patrick Chung-Shu *biotechnology executive*
Lewis, Henry Rafalsky *manufacturing company executive*
†Modigliani, Lazzaro G. *chemicals executive*
Saponaro, Joseph A. *company executive*
†Termeer, Henricus Adrianus *biotechnology company executive*
Tobin, James Robert *biotechnology company executive*
Vincent, James Louis *biotechnology company executive*
†Wardell, William Michael *drug development executive*

Canton
†Burr, George S. *manufacturing company executive*
Ferrera, Kenneth Grant *food distribution company executive*

Charlestown
Waldfogel, Morton Sumner *prefabricated housing/plywood company executive*

Chelsea
Dunn, Norman Samuel *plastics and textiles company executive*

Chestnut Hill
†Bresky, H. Harry *diversified manufacturing company executive*
Rodrigues, Joseph E. *grain company executive*

Concord
Baldwin, Everett Newton *food company executive*
Link, David M. *medical products consultant*

Danvers
Langford, Dean Ted *lighting and precision materials company executive*
†St. Onge, Vincent A. *electronics executive*
Waite, Charles Morrison *food company executive*

Dedham
†Krivsky, William A. *building materials executive, researcher*

Dover
Roberts, Francis Donald *manufacturing company executive*

East Wareham
Dormitzer, Henry, II *retired manufacturing company executive*

Easthampton
Perkins, Homer Guy *manufacturing company executive*

Fall River
Liebenow, Larry Albert *textile company executive*

Framingham
Merser, Francis Gerard *manufacturing company executive, consultant*
Waters, James Logan *analytical instrument manufacturing executive*

Wilson, John Benedict *office supplies company executive*

Harvard
Oyler, James Russell, Jr. *manufacturing executive*

Hingham
†Zetcher, Arnold B. *apparel executive*

Lexington
Bishop, Robert Calvin *pharmaceutical company executive*
Bleck, Max Emil *aircraft company executive*
Hoopes, Walter Ronald *chemical company executive*
Parl, Steen Allan *corporate executive*
Picard, Dennis J. *electronics company executive*
Price, Robert *electronics consultant*
Smith, Robert Louis *construction company executive*
Wood, Elwood Steven III *chemical company executive*

Lincoln
Fernald, George Herbert, Jr. *retired photographic company executive*
Green, David Henry *manufacturing company executive*

Longmeadow
Blake, Stewart Prestley *retired ice cream company executive*

Lowell
Belle Isle, Albert Pierre *electronics company executive*
Hoffman, Paul Roger *aerospace executive*
Kahalas, Harvey *manufacturing educator*
Rayfield, Allan Laverne *electronics company executive*
†Tucci, Joseph M. *computer products manufacturing executive*
Vanderslice, Thomas Aquinas *electronics executive*

Mansfield
Forney, G(eorge) David, Jr. *electronics company executive*
Meelia, Richard J. *healthcare products executive*

Marblehead
Rogow, Bruce Joel *industry research consultant*

Marlborough
Axline, Robert Paul *electronics executive*

Middleboro
Llewellyn, John Schofield, Jr. *food company executive*

Natick
Deutsch, Marshall E(manuel) *medical products company executive, inventor*

Needham
Cohen, Lewis Cobrain *security products firm executive*
Pucel, Robert Albin *electronics research engineer*

Newton
Gerrity, (James) Frank, II *building materials company executive*
Stein, Seymour *electronic scientist*

North Billerica
Coco, Samuel Barbin *venture consultant*

North Grafton
Nelson, John Martin *corporate executive*

North Reading
O'Neil, John P(atrick) *athletic footwear company executive*

Norwood
Tracy, Allen Wayne *manufacturing company executive*

Randolph
Doulton, Charles William *business executive*

Somerville
Verderber, Joseph Anthony *capital equipment company executive*

South Hadley
Kraske, Karl Vincent *paper company executive*

Springfield
Gallup, John Gardiner *retired paper company executive*
†Hinterhaeuser, Hermann *metal manufacturing company executive*

Stoughton
Fireman, Paul B. *footwear/apparel company executive*

Stow
Olsen, Kenneth Harry *manufacturing company executive*

Sturbridge
Flynn, Richard Jerome *manufacturing company executive*

Sudbury
Henderson, Ernest, III *health care executive*

Tewksbury
†DeMoulas, Telemachus A. *retail grocery company executive*

Wakefield
Zeo, Frank James *technology company executive*

Waltham
Bernstein, Stanley Joseph *manufacturing executive*
Floyd, John Taylor *electronics executive*
Hatsopoulos, John Nicholas *high-technology company executive*

Hennessey, Robert John *pharmaceutical company executive*
Jewett, John Persinger *electronics executive, lawyer*
Weaver, William Charles *manufacturing executive*
Weinert, Henry M. *biomedical company executive*

Wayland
Blair, John *electronics company executive*
Shrader, William Whitney *radar consulting scientist*
Weil, Thomas Alexander *electronics engineer*

Wellesley
Gailius, Gilbert Keistutis *manufacturing company executive*
†Gerson, Samuel J. *apparel executive*
Kucharski, John Michael *scientific instruments manufacturing company executive*
Marcus, William Michael *rubber and vinyl products manufacturing company executive*
Ritt, Paul Edward *communications and electronics company executive*
Rubinovitz, Samuel *diversified manufacturing company executive*

Westborough
Skates, Ronald Louis *computer manufacturing executive*

Weston
Rogers, Howard Gardner *consultant, photographic company research director emeritus*
Saad, Theodore Shafick *retired microwave company executive*

Williamsburg
Healy, Robert Danforth *manufacturing executive*

Williamstown
Welch, Neal William *retired electric company executive*

Wilmington
Buckley, Robert Paul *aerospace company executive*

Winchester
Cecich, Donald Edward *manufacturing executive*

Winthrop
Moses, Ronald Elliot *retired toiletries products executive*

Woburn
†Flummerfelt, J. Kent *electronics executive*
†Tomaszewski, James M. *electronics executive*

Wrentham
Teplow, Theodore Herzl *valve company executive*

MICHIGAN

Ada
Beutner, Roger Earl *manufacturing executive*

Addison
Knight, V. C. *manufacturing executive*

Allen Park
Simpson, Bruce Howard *training company executive*

Ann Arbor
†Bressler, Philip Jack *food products executive, consultant*
Buchanan, Robert Alexander *pharmaceutical company executive, physician*
Decker, Raymond Frank *scientist, technology executive*
†Gelman, Charles *medical manufacturing executive*
†Grisham, Rita Miller *automotive executive*
Long, Patrick Brien *advanced technology company executive*
Moss, Cruse Watson *automobile company executive*
Packard, Peter Kim *diversified products company executive*
†Sargent, Charles Lee *recreation vehicle and pollution control systems manufacturing company executive*
Saussele, Charles William *marking systems company executive*

Auburn Hills
†Grava, Alfred H. *automotive and business equipment manufacturing company executive*
Iorio, Ralph Arthur *automotive company executive*
†Kerr, John E. *automotive executive*
†Schuler, V. Edmund *light manufacturing executive*

Battle Creek
Costley, Gary Edward *food company executive*
Langbo, Arnold Gordon *food company executive*
McKay, Eugene Henry, Jr. *food company executive*
Nichols, Robert Lee *food company executive*
Olin, Thomas Franklin *food products executive*
Schaller, Daryl Richard *cereal company executive*

Benton Harbor
Callahan, Michael J. *manufacturing company executive*
Hopp, Daniel Frederick *manufacturing company executive, lawyer*
Samartini, James Rogers *appliance company executive*
Whitwam, David Ray *appliance manufacturing company executive*

Bingham Farms
Williams, Edson Poe *retired automotive company executive*

Birmingham
McCuen, John Joachim *defense contracting company executive*
VanDeusen, Bruce Dudley *defense contractor company executive*

Bloomfield Hills
Bates, Baron Kent *automobile company executive*
Burgess, Robert K. *construction company executive*
Caldwell, Will M. *former automobile company executive*

Caplan, John David *retired automotive company executive, research director*
Knudsen, Semon Emil *manufacturing company executive*
Marko, Harold Meyron *diversified industry executive*
Maxwell, Jack Erwin *manufacturing company executive*
Roth, James Seymour *retired manufacturing executive*
†Smith, Richard Allen *manufacturing company executive*
Vlasic, Robert Joseph *food company executive*
†Zimmer, David Rodney *manufacturing executive*

Cass City
Althaver, Lambert Ewing *manufacturing company executive*

Dearborn
Bixby, Harold Glenn *manufacturing company executive*
Darin, Frank Victor John *automotive company executive*
Ford, William Clay *automotive company executive*
Gilmour, Allan Dana *automotive company executive*
Libertiny, George Zoltan *automotive company research engineer*
Lundy, J(oseph) Edward *retired automobile company executive*
Mc Cammon, David Noel *automobile company executive*
McTague, John Paul *automobile manufacturing company executive, chemist*
Poling, Harold Arthur *retired automobile company executive*
Powers, William Francis *automobile manufacturing company executive*
Sagan, John *former automobile company executive*
Seneker, Stanley A. *automobile manufacturing company executive*
†Trotman, Alexander James *automobile manufacturing company executive*

Detroit
Chapin, Roy Dikeman, Jr. *automobile company executive*
Eaton, Robert James *automotive company executive*
Fisher, Max Martin *diversified company executive*
Gormley, Dennis James *manufacturing and distribution company executive*
Hanson, David Bigelow *construction company executive, engineer*
Hay, Frederick Dale *automotive supply company executive*
Hoglund, William Elis *automotive company executive*
Kalman, Andrew *manufacturing company executive*
Levy, Edward Charles, Jr. *manufacturing company executive*
Maibach, Ben C., III *construction company executive*
Mc Millan, James *manufacturing executive*
Meilgaard, Morten Christian *food products executive, international consultant*
Murphy, Thomas Aquinas *former automobile manufacturing company executive*
Musone, Fred James *manufacturing and logistic executive*
†Penske, Roger S. *manufacturing and transportation executive*
Raden, Louis *tape and label corporation executive*
Rakolta, John *construction company executive*
Rines, John Randolph *automotive company executive*
Sax, Stanley Paul *manufacturing company executive*
Smith, John Francis, Jr. *automobile company executive*
Stella, Frank Dante *food service and dining equipment executive*
†Stroh, Peter Wetherill *brewery executive*
Szary, Richard M. *manufacturing company executive*

Dundee
Byland, Peter *construction materials company executive*

Farmington Hills
Landry, Thomas Henry *construction executive*
Leonard, Michael A. *automotive executive*
Webb, George Henry *material handling company executive*

Ferndale
Braude, Edwin S. *manufacturing company executive*

Flint
Hackworth, Donald E. *automotive manufacturing company executive*
Lovejoy, William Joseph *automotive company executive*

Grand Rapids
Baker, Hollis MacLure *furniture manufacturing company executive*
†Gantos, LeRoy Douglas *retail clothing executive*
Meijer, Hendrik *retail company executive*
†Myers, Jerry K. *medal products executive*
Perez, Peter Manuel *woodworking products company executive*
Pew, Robert Cunningham, II *office equipment manufacturing company executive*
Rougier-Chapman, Alwyn Spencer Douglas *furniture manufacturing company executive*
Wege, Peter M. *office furniture manufacturing company executive*

Grosse Pointe
Valk, Robert Earl *corporate executive*
Wilkinson, Warren Scripps *manufacturing company executive*

Grosse Pointe Farms
Gofrank, Frank Louis *retired machine tool company executive*
Mc Bride, Robert Dana *steel company executive*

Hickory Corners
Hubbard, William Neill, Jr. *pharmaceutical company executive*

Highland Park
†Gale, Thomas Charles *automotive design executive*
Lutz, Robert Anthony *automotive company executive*

Holland
†Haworth, Gerrard Wendell office systems manufacturing company executive
†Haworth, Richard G. office furniture mamufacturer
†Johanneson, Gerald B. office products company executive

Jackson
Kelly, Robert Vincent, Jr. metal company executive
Vischer, Harold Harry manufacturing company executive

Kalamazoo
Connable, Alfred Barnes business director
Cyrus, Kenneth M. pharmaceutical company executive, lawyer
Dykstra, David Allen corporate executive
Edmondson, Keith Henry chemical company executive
Hite, Judson Cary pharmaceutical company executive
†Markin, David Robert motor company executive

Lansing
Hines, Marshall construction engineering company executive
Moody, G. William retired aerospace manufacturing company executive

Livonia
†Baker, Ronald Seymour construction executive
Utley, John Eddy automotive supplies executive

Madison Heights
Kafarski, Mitchell I. chemical processing company executive

Marine City
Cronenworth, Charles Douglas manufacturing company executive

Midland
Falla, Enrique Crabb chemical company executive
Hampton, Leroy retired chemical company executive
†Hazleton, Richard A. chemicals executive
Ludington, John Samuel manufacturing company executive
McKennon, Keith Robert chemical company executive
Popoff, Frank Peter chemical company executive

Monroe
Knabusch, Charles Thair manufacturing company executive

Muskegon
†Florjancic, Frederick Joseph, Jr. manufacturing executive
Johnson, Dale A. manufacturing company executive
Werner, R(ichard) Budd business executive

North Muskegon
Mason, Robert Joseph automotive parts company executive

Northville
Gerson, Ralph Joseph corporate executive
Jensen, Reuben Rolland former automotive company executive

Plymouth
Bates, J(ohn) Bertram retired chemical company executive
Merrill, Kenneth Coleman retired automobile credit company executive
Mondry, Ira electronic appliance company executive
†Vlcek, Donald Joseph, Jr. food distribution company executive

Pontiac
Mahone, Barbara Jean automotive company executive
Smith, Roger Bonham automotive manufacturing executive
Stryker, James William automotive executive, former military officer

Redford
Koci, Ludvik Frank automotive manufacturing company executive

Rochester Hills
Cook, Leonard Clarence manufacturing company executive

Rockford
Gleason, Thomas Daues shoe company executive

Romulus
Gulda, Edward James automotive executive

Roseville
Baden, Robert Charles manufacturing executive

Saginaw
†Flegenheimer, Ernest sugar company executive

Saint Clair Shores
Gordon, Steven Stanley automotive parts company executive

Saint Joseph
†Michelotti, Carl Anthony electronics company executive

South Haven
Nequist, John Leonard retired food company executive

Southfield
Borden, John Anthony manufacturing company executive
Chamasrour, Joseph Albert automotive executive
Dorfman, Henry S. meat products company executive
Dorfman, Joel Marvin meat products company executive
Harlan, John Marshall construction company executive
Jeffrey, Walter Leslie corporation executive
Mikelberg, Arnold meat packing company executive
†Minghine, Rocco Raymond meat packing company executive
Reins, Ralph Erich automotive products company executive
†Rossiter, Robert E. diversified corporation executive
†Runk, Lee Hammond automotive company executive
Tauber, Joel David manufacturing company executive
Weisenburger, Randall manufacturing executive
Welch, Martin E., III manufacturing company executive

Taylor
Lyon, Wayne Barton corporate executive
Manoogian, Alex manufacturing company executive
Manoogian, Richard Alexander manufacturing company executive
Rosowski, Robert Bernard manufacturing company executive
Ullrich, John Frederick diversified manufacturing company executive

Tecumseh
Herrick, Kenneth Gilbert manufacturing company executive
Herrick, Todd W. manufacturing company executive

Troy
Buschmann, Siegfried manufacturing executive
Corace, Joseph Russell automotive parts company executive
Koch, Albert Acheson manufacturing executive
McDonald, Alonzo Lowry, Jr. manufacturing executive
Sharf, Stephan automotive company executive
Sloan, Hugh Walter, Jr. automotive industry executive
†Weinhardt, W. John manufacturing company executive
Williams, David Perry manufacturing company executive

Warren
†Agley, Randolph J. pharmaceutical company executive
Bell, Bradley J. household appliance manufacturing company executive
Foxworth, John Edwin, Jr. automotive executive, philatelist
Fredericks, Wesley Charles, Jr. automotive executive, lawyer
Gothard, Donald Lee auto company executive
Lett, Philip Wood, Jr. defense consultant
Reickert, Erick Arthur automotive executive
Viano, David Charles automotive safety research scientist

Washington
Frey, Stuart Macklin automobile manufacturing company executive

Waterford
Edwards, Wallace Winfield retired automotive company executive

Wyandotte
†Strube, J. F. agricultural products executive

Ypsilanti
Duncan, Charles Howard business education educator

Zeeland
Campbell, J. Kermit office products company executive
Ruch, Richard Hurley manufacturing company executive

MINNESOTA

Alexandria
Templin, Kenneth Elwood paper company executive

Austin
Hodapp, Don Joseph food company executive
Knowlton, Richard L. food and meat processing company executive

Bayport
†Johnson, Alan lumber company executive

Bloomington
Jodsaas, Larry Elvin computer components company executive

Dresbach
Saline, Lindon Edgar industrial company executive

Eagan
Scott, Andrew corporate executive

Golden Valley
†Estergren, Eric DeWayne corporate executive

Grand Rapids
Radecki, Anthony Eugene paper company executive

Hopkins
Rappaport, Gary Burton defense equipment and computer company executive

Inver Grove
Webster, Elroy diversified supplies and machinery executive

Mankato
Daly, Denis Jon agricultural business executive

Marshall
†Schwan, Alfred food products executive

Minneapolis
Amdahl, Byrdelle John security products company executive
Asplin, Edward William retired packaging company executive
Atwater, Horace Brewster, Jr. food company executive
Berg, Stanton Oneal firearms and ballistics consultant
Blood, Edward Linford consumer products company executive
†Bonsignore, Michael Robert electronics company executive
Carlson, Curtis LeRoy business executive
Coonrod, Richard Allen agricultural products company executive
Corrigan, Fredric H. retired corporate executive
Fogg, Richard Lloyd food products company executive
Frechette, Peter Loren dental products executive
Gherty, John E. food products and agricultural products company executive
Goldfus, Donald Wayne glass company executive
Groves, Franklin Nelson business executive
Hale, Roger Loucks manufacturing company executive
Hodder, William Alan fabricated metal products company executive
Johnson, Clark Eugene, Jr. electronics and computer company executive, magnetics physicist
Johnson, Sankey Anton manufacturing company executive
Kramp, Richard William biotechnology executive
Lee, Joe R. food products company executive
Luiso, Anthony international food company executive
Luthringshauser, Daniel Rene manufacturing company executive
†MacMillan, Whitney food products and import/export company executive
Melrose, Kendrick Bascom manufacturing company executive
Morris, David Hugh manufacturing and marketing executive
†Mortenson, M. A., Jr. construction executive
Nelson, Glen David medical products executive, physician
†Neumann, L. N. grain company executive
Olson, Ronald Dale grain company executive
Prince, Robb Lincoln manufacturing company executive
Rauenhorst, Gerald design and construction company executive
Read, John Conyers filtration company executive
Renier, James J. diversified electronic equipment manufacturing company executive
Roe, John H. manufacturing company executive
†Rogers, David apparel executive
Sampson, John Eugene food company executive
Spoor, William Howard food company executive
Sullivan, Austin P(adraig), Jr. diversified food company executive
Toupin, Harold Ovid chemical company executive
Wallin, Winston Roger manufacturing company executive
†Walsh, Paul S. food products executive
Willes, Mark Hinckley food industry executive
Wurtele, Christopher Angus paint and coatings company executive

Minnetonka
Henningsen, Peter, Jr. diversified industry executive
Mc Guire, William W. health maintenance organization executive
Randall, Dean Bowman retired electronics manufacturing company executive

Moorhead
Wai, Samuel Siu Ming food product company financial executive

Plymouth
Fowler, James D., Jr. manufacturing company financial executive
Friswold, Fred Ravndahl manufacturing executive
Kahler, Herbert Frederick diversified business executive

Rochester
Carlson, Roger Allan manufacturing company executive, accountant

Saint Paul
Alm, John Richard beverage company executive
Andersen, Anthony L. chemical company executive
Andersen, Elmer Lee manufacturing and publishing executive, former governor of Minnesota
†Baker, Thomas F. agricultural grain company executive
Baukol, Ronald Oliver manufacturing company executive
Betz, Charles W. manufacturing company executive
†Desimone, Livio Diego diversified manufacturing company executive
Garretson, Donald Everett retired manufacturing company executive
Grieve, Pierson MacDonald specialty chemicals and services company executive
Hanson, Allen Dennis grain marketing and processing cooperative executive
Jones, Thomas Neal manufacturing executive, mechanical engineer
Lehr, Lewis Wylie diversified manufacturing company executive
Ling, Joseph Tso-Ti manufacturing company executive, environmental engineer
Markwardt, Kenneth Marvin former chemical company executive
Nugent, Daniel Eugene business executive
Nugent, G. Eugene manufacturing company executive
Ostby, Ronald dairy and food products company executive
Peterson, Robert Austin manufacturing company executive retired
Rastogi, Anil Kumar medical device manufacturer executive
Rusch, Thomas William manufacturing executive
Shannon, Michael Edward specialty chemical company executive
Wollner, Thomas Edward manufacturing company executive

Stillwater
Pollack, Joseph diversified company executive

Wayzata
Blodgett, Frank Caleb food company executive, retired
Hoffman, Gene food company executive, consultant
Swanson, Donald Frederick retired food company executive

Willmar
Zitterkopf, Irvin Leroy sugar manufacturing company executive

MISSISSIPPI

Diamond Head
Jaumot, Frank Edward, Jr. automobile parts manufacturing company executive

Jackson
Irby, Stuart Charles, Jr. construction company executive
Wall, Oscar Edward chemical company executive
Williams, James Kelley diversified resources company executive

Mc Comb
†Bancroft, Joseph C. metal products company executive

Tupelo
†Jarvis, Morris O. fabric company executive

Yazoo City
Arnold, David Walker chemical company executive, engineer
Hawkins, William F. chemical company executive

MISSOURI

Blue Springs
†Olsson, Björn Eskil railroad supply company executive

Bridgeton
Brock, Louis Clark business executive, former professional baseball player
McSweeney, Michael Terrence manufacturing executive

Carthage
Cornell, Harry M., Jr. home furnishings company executive
Jefferies, Robert Aaron, Jr. furniture company executive, lawyer
Wright, Felix E. manufacturing company executive

Centralia
Lomo, Leif electrical manufacturing company executive

Chesterfield
Carpenter, Will Dockery chemical company executive
Harbison, Earle Harrison, Jr. chemical company executive
†Jacobsen, James Conrad apparel manufacturing executive
Malvern, Donald retired aircraft manufacturing company executive
Palazzi, Joseph L(azarro) manufacturing executive

Clarkson Valley
McCarthy, Paul Fenton aerospace executive, former naval officer

Clayton
Buechler, Bradley Bruce plastic processing company executive, accountant

Columbia
Rothwell, Robert Clark agricultural products executive

Hazelwood
†Bellar, Willis Franklin bakery products company executive

Kansas City
Bartlett, Paul Dana, Jr. agribusiness executive
†Berardi, J. F. food products executive
Berkley, Eugene Bertram (Bert Berkley) envelope company executive
Brown, Bob Oliver manufacturing company executive
Carr, Jack Richard candy company executive
†Clarkson, William Edwin construction company executive
†Cleberg, Harry C. food products company executive
†Dees, Stephen Phillip petroleum, farm and food products company executive, lawyer
Hicks, Lawrence Wayne manufacturing company executive
†Kittoe, Larry grain company executive
Kronschnabel, Robert James manufacturing company executive
†Lyons, Frederick William, Jr. pharmaceutical company executive
†Moseley, Furman C. timber company executive
†Nottberg, Henry, III construction company executive
†Polsky, Norman furniture company executive
†Rheinfrank, Lamson, Jr. manufacturing company executive
†Rice, H. Wayne food products executive
Sullivan, Charles A. food products executive
Temple, Joseph George, Jr. pharmaceutical company executive
Ward, Louis Larrick candy company executive

Lake Lotawana
Hinkle, B. J. retired food company executive, consultant

Mexico
Hummer, Paul F., II manufacturing company executive
Stover, Harry M. corporate executive

Saint Louis
Abelov, Stephen Lawrence uniform clothing company executive
Abrahamson, Barry chemical company executive

Adams, Albert Willie, Jr. lubrication company executive
†Alberici, Gabriel J. construction company executive
Anderson, James Donald chemical company executive
Beare, Gene Kerwin electric company executive
Beracha, Barry Harris brewery executive
Bock, Edward John chemical manufacturing company executive
Bracken, Robert W. food products executive
Brodsky, Philip Hyman chemical executive, research director
Browde, Anatole electronics company executive, consultant
Brown, Jay Wright food manufacturing company executive
†Burnett, Roger H. construction executive
Busch, August Adolphus, III brewery executive
†Cleary, Thomas John aluminum products company executive
Coco, Charles Edward food products company executive
Conerly, Richard Pugh retired corporation executive
Cori, Carl Tom chemicals executive
Cunningham, Charles Baker, III manufacturing company executive
Dill, Charles Anthony manufacturing and computer company executive
Faught, Harold Franklin electrical equipment manufacturing company executive
Fournie, Robert G. retired boiler works executive
†Gelman, Warren Jay metals trading company executive
†Goff, Raymond Ellis brewery executive
†Gomes, Edward Clayton, Jr. construction company executive
Graff, George Stephen aerospace company executive
Griffin, W(illiam) L(ester) Hadley shoe company executive
Groennert, Charles Willis electric company executive
Gupta, Surendra Kumar chemical firm executive
Harmon, Robert Lee corporate executive
Heininger, S(amuel) Allen retired chemical company executive
Hermann, Robert Ringen conglomerate company executive
Hirsch, Raymond Robert chemical company executive, lawyer
Holten, James Joseph meat processing company executive
†Kerwin, Richard G. grain company executive
Kessler, Nathan technology consultant
Keyes, Marion Alvah, IV manufacturing company executive
King, William Terry manufacturing company executive
Knight, Charles Field electrical equipment manufacturing company executive
Kuhlmann, Fred L. brewery consultant, lawyer, baseball executive
†Kummer, Fred S. construction company executive
Lambright, Stephen Kirk brewing company executive
†Lorenzini, Paul G. manufacturing executive
Mahoney, Richard John manufacturing company executive
Malloy, James B. packaging company executive
†Mc Carthy, Francis F. construction executive
McDonnell, John Finney aerospace and aircraft manufacturing company executive
McDonnell, Sanford Noyes aircraft company executive
†McGrath, Edward A. electronic equipment company executive
McKenna, William John textile products executive
McKinney, John Benjamin steel company executive
Micheletto, Joe Raymond food products executive, controller
Miller, Michael Everett chemical company executive
Monroe, Thomas Edward industrial corporation executive
Neville, James Morton food company executive, lawyer
O'Brien, Thomas Francis manufacturing company executive
Pellett, Thomas Rowand retired food company executive
Purnell, John H. beverage company executive
Pylipow, Stanley Ross retired manufacturing company executive, advisor
Randolph, Joe Wayne machine manufacturing executive
†Raskas, Heschel Joshua food company executive, educator
Rich, Harry E. footwear and specialty retailing financial executive
Sanders, Fred Joseph aerospace company executive
Sathe, Sharad Somnath chemical company executive
Shanahan, Michael Francis manufacturing executive, hockey team executive
Smurfit, Michael William Joseph manufacturing company executive
Sonnino, Carlo Benvenuto electrical manufacturing company executive
Stearley, Robert Jay retired packaging company executive
Stiritz, William P. food company executive
Stokes, Patrick T. brewery company executive
†Stuhl, Harold Maxwell manufacturing executive
Suter, Albert Edward manufacturing company executive
Thayer, Gerald Campbell beer company executive
Throdahl, Monte Corden former chemical company executive
Tober, Lester Victor shoe company executive
Tulloch, George Sherlock, Jr. electrical equipment distribution company executive, lawyer
Ver Hagen, Jan Karol electrical manufacturing company executive
Walker, Earl E. manufacturing executive
Wells, Ben Harris retired beverage company executive
Wenzel, Fred William apparel manufacturing executive
Winter, William Earl retired beverage company executive

Saint Peters
Krey, Mary Ann Reynolds beer wholesaler executive

Springfield
†Hanman, Gary Edwin dairy company executive

MONTANA

Great Falls
Sletten, John Robert construction company executive

Missoula
Banaugh, Robert Peter computer science educator

NEBRASKA

Dakota City
Broyhill, Roy Franklin manufacturing executive
Grigsby, Lonnie Oscar food company executive
Peterson, Robert L. meat processing executive

Lincoln
Fisher, Calvin David food manufacturing company executive

Lindsay
†Parker, Gary Dean manufacturing company executive

Norfolk
†Day, Connie Jo moving company executive, consultant

Omaha
†Campbell, Charles H. construction company executive
Ferer, Harvey Dean metals company executive
†Fletcher, Philip B. food products company executive
Jugel, Richard Dennis corporate executive, management consultant
Knobbe, Urban food products executive
Lindsay, James Wiley agricultural company executive
†Scott, Walter, Jr. construction company executive

NEVADA

Carson City
Noland, Robert LeRoy retired manufacturing company executive

Incline Village
Strack, Harold Arthur retired electronics company executive, retired air force officer, planner, analyst, musician
Wahl, Howard Wayne retired construction company executive, engineer

Las Vegas
Barber, Jerry Randel medical device company executive
Kaiser, Glen David construction company executive

Reno
Mathewson, Charles Norman manufacturing company executive

NEW HAMPSHIRE

Concord
Hosmer, Bradley Edwin corporate executive

Exeter
Beck, Albert manufacturing company executive
Kozlowski, L. Dennis manufacturing company executive

Franklin
Santolucito, Joseph Anthony laminate company executive
Wiehl, John Jack foundry executive

Hampton
Dingman, Michael David industrial company executive
Montrone, Paul Michael scientific instruments company executive
Ranelli, John Raymond footwear and apparel company executive
†Vogel, Phillip T. manufacturing executive

Hill
Thierry, John Adams heavy machinery manufacturing company executive, lawyer

Hudson
†Weergang, Alida cosmetology educator and administrator, consultant

Keene
Burkart, Walter Mark manufacturing company executive
Scranton, William Maxwell manufacturing company executive, consultant

Londonderry
†Dean, Richard T. pharmaceutical company executive
Nelson, Lloyd Steadman manufacturing company executive, consultant

Lyndeborough
Morison, John Hopkins casting manufacturing company executive

Nashua
Gregg, Hugh former cabinet manufacturing company executive, former governor New Hampshire
Hemming, Walter William business financial consultant
Mitchell, William Edmund electronics executive

New London
Condict, Edgar Rhodes medical electronics, aviation instrument manufacturing and medical health care executive, inventor, mediator
Nye, Thomas Russell retired drafting, reproduction and surveying company executive

North Hampton
White, Ralph Paul manufacturing executive, consultant

Salem
†Irvine, Horace Hills, II manufacturing company executive

Sunapee
Cary, Charles Oswald aviation executive
Rauh, John David manufacturing company executive

Winchester
MacKay, Neil Duncan plastic company executive

NEW JERSEY

Allendale
Hollands, John Henry electronics consultant

Alpine
Yuelys, Alexander former cosmetics company executive

Basking Ridge
Miller, Richard Wesley electronics company executive
Munch, Douglas Francis pharmaceutical and health industry consultant

Bedminster
Becker, Ivan Endre retired plastics company executive
Luke, James Phillip manufacturing executive

Bernardsville
Abeles, James David manufacturing company executive

Bound Brook
Gould, Donald Everett chemical company executive

Bridgewater
Grubman, Wallace Karl chemical company executive
Kennedy, James Andrew chemical company executive

Butler
Klaas, Nicholas Paul management and technical consultant

Camden
Ford, Joseph Raymond manufacturing company executive
Johnson, David Willis food products executive
Weise, Frank Earl, III food products company executive

Carteret
†Corliss, Robert sporting goods company executive

Cedar Knolls
†Lingnau, Lutz pharmaceutical executive

Cherry Hill
†Higurashi, Takeshi automotive executive
†Muller, George T. automotive executive

Chester
Maddalena, Lucille Ann management executive

Clifton
Fein, Seymour Howard pharmaceutical executive

Clinton
Acerra, Michele (Mike Acerra) engineering and construction company executive
DeGhetto, Kenneth Anselm engineering and construction company executive
Deones, Jack E. corporate executive
Wolsky, Murray corporation executive

Cranbury
Daoust, Donald Roger pharmaceutical and toiletries company executive, microbiologist

Cranford
Cleaver, William Pennington consultant, retired sugar refining company executive
Eisenberg, R. Neal restoration company executive

Denville
Minter, Jerry Burnett electronic component company executive, engineer

Dover
Mc Donald, John Joseph electronics executive

East Hanover
†Hassan, Frederich pharmaceutical executive
Leveille, Gilbert Antonio food products executive
†Rejeange, Jacques F. pharmaceutical executive

East Rutherford
Gerstein, David Brown hardware manufacturing company executive, professional basketball team executive

Edison
Carretta, Richard Louis beverage company executive
Marash, Stanley Albert consulting company executive
Mount, Karl A. manufacturing executive
†Romano, Dominick V. food products executive

Elmwood Park
†Hazama, Hajime electronics executive
Kerr, James Joseph construction company executive, engineer

Englewood
†Hess, Blaine R. manufacturing company executive
Morgenstein, William shoe company executive
Neis, Arnold Hayward pharmaceutical company executive
†Wilcha, John Samuel food products company executive

Englewood Cliffs
Meendsen, Fred Charles food company executive
Scott, John William food processing executive
Shoemate, Charles Richard agricultural products executive
Shrem, Charles Joseph metals corporation executive

Fair Lawn
†Wygod, Martin J. pharmaceuticals executive

Fairfield
Boccone, Andrew Albert chemical company executive
Giambalvo, Vincent manufacturing company executive
Meilan, Celia food products executive
Stein, Robert Alan electronics company executive

Fairview
Anton, Harvey textile company executive

Farmingdale
Schluter, Peter Mueller electronics company executive

Flemington
McGregor, Walter medical products company designer, inventor, consultant, educator

Florham Park
Jameson, J(ames) Larry cable company executive
Kluge, J. Hans company executive
Whitley, Arthur Francis retired international consulting company executive, engineer, lawyer

Fords
Kaufman, Alex chemicals executive

Fort Lee
†Barr, Edward Evan chemical company executive
Vignolo, Biagio Nickolas, Jr. chemical company executive

Fort Monmouth
Schwering, Felix Karl electronics engineer, researcher
Thornton, Clarence Gould electronics engineering executive

Franklin
Kline, Donald food company executive

Franklin Lakes
Andrews, Willard Douglas retired medical products manufacturer, consultant
Appert, Richard Henry health products manufacturing executive
Berger, Murry P. food company executive
Friedman, Martin Burton chemical company executive
Howe, Wesley Jackson medical supplies company executive

Freehold
Laden, Karl toiletries company executive

Garfield
Kodaka, Kunio plastics company executive

Hackensack
†Araki, K. electronics company executive
Walsh, Joseph Michael magazine distribution executive

Haddonfield
Shaub, Harold Arthur food products executive

Harrison
Winnerman, Robert Henry home building company executive

Hazlet
Miller, Duane King health and beauty care company executive
Morrison, James Frederick flavor and fragrance company administrator

Hoboken
Bonsal, Richard Irving textile marketing executive

Holmdel
†Frenkiel, Richard Henry electronics company research and development executive
Kogelnik, Herwig Werner electronics company executive

Hopatcong
Reese, Harry Edwin, Jr. electronics executive

Iselin
Clarke, David H. industrial products executive
Garfinkel, Harmon Mark specialty chemicals company executive
†Mackinnon, Robert medical products executive
†Raos, John G. manufacturing executive
Smith, Orin Robert chemical company executive
Vitt, David Aaron medical manufacturing company executive
White, Sir (Vincent) Gordon Lindsay textile company executive

Jamesburg
Denton, John Joseph retired pharmaceutical company executive
Gross, Leroy sugar company executive

Jersey City
Alfano, Michael Charles pharmaceutical company executive
Block, Leonard Nathan drug company executive
†Luthi, Wilfried T. manufacturing executive
Manischewitz, Bernard food products company executive
Zuckerberg, David Alan pharmaceutical company executive

Kendall Park
Hershenov, Bernard Zion *electronics research and development company executive*

Kenilworth
Conklin, Donald Ransford *pharmaceutical company executive*
Darrow, William Richard *pharmaceutical company executive*

Keyport
Warren, Craig Bishop *flavor and fragrance company executive, researcher*

Lakehurst
Millar, John Francis *industrial products company executive*

Lawrenceville
Bly, Herbert Arthur *pharmaceutical company executive*
Holcombe, William Jones *manufacturing company executive*

Linden
Covino, Charles Peter *metal products company executive*
Hansen, Christian Andreas, Jr. *chemical company executive*
Tamarelli, Alan Wayne *chemical company executive*

Lyndhurst
†Albosta, Richard Francis *engineering and construction company executive*
†Mosher, Howard Ira *automotive executive*
†Tinggren, Carl Jurgen *manufacturing executive*

Madison
Comey, J. Martin *pharmaceutical company executive*
D'Andrade, Hugh A(lfred) *pharmaceutical company executive, lawyer*
Hays, Thomas R. *electronics executive*
Kogan, Richard Jay *pharmaceutical company executive*
Luciano, Robert Peter *pharmaceutical company executive*
McCulloch, James Callahan *manufacturing company executive*

Mahwah
†Hirooka, Sueyuki *electronics company executive*

Mantoloking
Fragomen, Austin Thomas *capital goods company executive*

Medford
Kesty, Robert Edward *chemical manufacturing company executive*

Merchantville
†Shreiber, Gerald B. *food products executive*

Middletown
Roesner, Peter Lowell *manufacturing company executive*

Monmouth Junction
†Neff, Peter John *chemicals, mining and metal processing executive*

Montclair
Brightman, Robert Lloyd *importer, textile company executive, consultant*
†Dubrow, Marsha Ann *high technology company executive, composer*
Mc Carthy, Daniel Christopher, Jr. *manufacturing company executive*

Montvale
†Bassermann, Michael N. *automotive executive*
Borman, Earle Kirkpatrick, Jr. *chemical company executive*
Corrado, Fred *food company executive*
Kennedy, John Raymond *pulp and paper company executive*
Larkin, Michael Joseph *retail food executive*
†Steinberg, Charles Allan *electronics manufacturing company executive*
Stillwell, James Paul *food company exective*

Moorestown
Springer, Douglas Hyde *retired food company executive, lawyer*

Morris Plains
de Vink, Lodewijk J. R. *consumer pharmaceutical products company executive*
Goodes, Melvin Russell *manufacturing company executive*
†Shanley, Kevin *medical supply company executive*
Williams, Joseph Dalton *pharmaceutical company executive*

Morristown
Barpal, Isaac Ruben *technology and operations executive*
Barter, John William, III *corporate executive*
†Bauhs, David J. *manufacturing executive*
Belzer, Alan *diversified manufacturing company executive*
Bickerton, John Thorburn *retired pharmaceutical executive*
Bossidy, Lawrence Arthur *industrial manufacturing executive*
Callahan, Edward William *chemical engineer, manufacturing company executive*
Cameron, Nicholas Allen *diversified corporation executive*
Day, John W. *international corporation executive*
Fredericks, Robert Joseph *chemical company executive*
Herman, Robert Lewis *cork company executive*
Isko, Irving David *corporate executive*
Kirby, Fred Morgan, II *corporation executive*
Tokar, Edward Thomas *manufacturing company executive*
†Wilks, Alan Delbert *chemical research and technology executive, researcher*

Mount Laurel
Calzolano, John Joseph *engineering and construction company executive*

Instone, John Clifford *manufacturing company executive*

Mountain Lakes
Case, Manning Eugene, Jr. *corporate executive*

New Brunswick
Campbell, Robert E. *healthcare products company executive*
Fine, Roger Seth *pharmaceutical executive, lawyer*
Gussin, Robert Zalmon *health care company executive*
Larsen, Ralph S(tanley) *health care company executive*
McGuire, John Lawrence *pharmaceuticals research executive*
Roth, Herbert, Jr. *corporate executive*

New Providence
Chatterji, Debajyoti *manufacturing company executive*
†Grinfeder, Claude *construction materials executive*
Maloney, George Thomas *health industry executive*
Thompson, Larry Flack *chemical company executive*

New Vernon
Huck, John Lloyd *pharmaceutical company executive*
Margetts, W. Thomas *automobile parts company executive, lawyer*

Newark
Christodoulou, Aris Peter *pharmaceutical executive, investment banker*
Fink, Aaron Herman *box manufacturing executive*
Hermann, Steven Istvan *textile executive*
Howe, Carroll Victor *construction equipment company executive*

North Bergen
†Allen, Gordon Erwin *apparel company executive*
Chazen, Jerome A. *apparel company executive*
Lanier, Thomas *chemical and export company executive*
Miller, Samuel Martin *apparel company finance executive*
Scarne, John *game company executive*

North Brunswick
Bern, Ronald Lawrence *consulting company executive*

North Haledon
Brown, James Joseph *manufacturing company executive*

Northvale
Founds, Henry William *pharmaceutical executive, microbiologist*
Peer, George Joseph *metals company executive*

Nutley
Behl, Charanjit R. *pharmaceutical scientist*
†Conrad, Herbert J. *pharmaceutical executive*
English, Robert Joseph *electronic corporation executive*
†Lerner, Irwin *pharmaceutical company executive*
Wasserman, Martin Allan *pharmaceutical company executive*

Oradell
Regazzi, John Henry *retired corporate executive*

Paramus
Maclin, Ernest *biomedical diagnostics company executive*

Park Ridge
†Koch, Craig R. *automobile rental and leasing company executive*

Parsippany
Bernthal, Frederick W. *chemical company executive*
†Brualdi, Ulysses J., Jr. *electrical company executive*
Greeniaus, H. John *food products company executive*
†Kirkman, James A. *food products executive*
Kleinberg, Lawrence H. *food industry executive*
Miller, Harold Joseph *metals manufacturing company executive*
Purdum, Robert L. *steel manufacturing company executive*
Stein, J. Dieter *chemical company executive*

Paterson
Danziger, Glenn Norman *chemical sales company executive*

Peapack
Brennan, William Joseph *manufacturing company executive*
†Giordano, Salvatore *manufacturing company executive*
†Giordano, Salvatore, Jr. *air conditioner manufacturing company executive*

Pennsauken
O'Brien, James Jerome *construction management consultant*

Piscataway
Alekman, Stanley Lawrence *chemical company executive*
Cagan, Robert H. *manufacturing company research executive, biochemist*
Goodwin, Douglas Ira *steel distribution company executive*
Shapiro, Michael *sportswear license corporate officer*

Pittstown
Jacob, Harry Myles *mining executive*

Princeton
Barker, Richard Gordon *corporate research and development executive*
Carnes, James Edward *electronics executive*
Dovey, Brian Hugh *health care products company executive, venture capitalist*
Drakeman, Donald Lee *corporate executive, lawyer*
Gips, Walter Fuld, Jr. *manufacturing company executive*

†Gramlich, James Vandle *chemical products company executive*
Hayes, Edwin Junius, Jr. *business executive*
Hendrickson, Robert Frederick *pharmaceutical company executive*
Horovitz, Zola Philip *pharmaceutical company executive*
Jacobson, Herbert Leonard *electronics company executive*
MacPherson, Frank Becker, III *advanced technology executive*
Minton, Dwight Church *manufacturing company executive*
Perhach, James Lawrence *pharmaceutical company executive*
†Zissman, Lorin *marketing research, consulting company executive*

Rahway
Horan, John J. *pharmaceutical company executive*

Ramsey
†Kusumoto, Sadahei *light manufacturing executive*
†Markowitz, Arthur Walter *food brokerage executive*

Red Bank
Hertz, Daniel Leroy, Jr. *entrepreneur*
Sorsby, James Larry *home building company executive*

Ridgefield Park
†Kim, Ok-Nyun *manufacturing executive*

Ridgewood
Healey, Frank Henry *retired research executive*

Rochelle Park
Laskey, Richard Anthony *medical device company executive*
Schapiro, Jerome Bentley *chemical company executive*

Rutherford
†Marchitto, Alfred J. *furniture company executive*

Saddle Brook
†Anderson, David J. *metals company executive*

Salem
Seabrook, John Martin *retired food products executive, chemical engineer*

Scotch Plains
Abramson, Clarence Allen *pharmaceutical company executive, lawyer*
Cleminshaw, Frank Foster *electronic company executive*

Secaucus
†Bidermann, Maurice *textiles executive*
†Bolt, J. Andrew *textiles executive*
†Gerstein, Hilda Kirschbaum *clothing company executive*
Heller, Fred *illumination manufacturing company executive*
†Kraft, Richard A. *electronics executive*
Unanue, Joseph *food products executive*

Short Hills
Jackson, William Ward *chemical company executive*

Shrewsbury
Duff, Thomas M. *textiles executive*

Somerset
Aronson, Louis Vincent, II *manufacturing executive*
†Goldberg, Arthur M. *food products executive, lawyer*

Somerville
Benz, Harry R. *business executive*
†Dormann, Juergen *chemical company executive*
Drew, Ernest Harold *chemical company executive*

South Hackensack
Kiselik, Paul Howard *manufacturing company executive*

Sparta
Granieri, Michael Nicholas *electronics executive, educator*

Springfield
Adams, James Mills *chemicals executive*

Summit
Brown, John Hampton *pharmaceutical company executive*
Hittinger, William Charles *electronics company executive*

Teaneck
Feinberg, Robert S. *plastics manufacturing company executive, marketing consultant*
Gordon, Maxwell *pharmaceutical company executive*
Margolis, Sidney O. *textile and apparel company executive*
Oser, Bernard Levussove *food and drug consultant*

Tinton Falls
Orlando, Carl *medical research and development executive*

Toms River
Gottesman, Roy Tully *chemical company executive*

Trenton
Brandinger, Jay Jerome *electronics executive, state official*

Union
Lapidus, Norman Israel *food broker*
Schiffman, Robert S. *environmental test equipment manufacturing executive*

Verona
Root, Alan Charles *diversified manufacturing company executive*

Voorhees
Cohen, Mark N. *business executive*

Watchung
Knudson, Harry Edward, Jr. *retired electrical manufacturing company executive*

Wayne
Boekenheide, Russell William *forest products company executive*
Burlant, William Jack *chemical company executive*
Cartledge, Raymond Eugene *retired paper company executive*
Coslow, Richard David *electronics company executive*
†Eckardt, Carl R. *chemical and building materials executive*
Fleisher, Seymour *manufacturing company executive*
Heyman, Samuel J. *chemicals and building materials manufacturing company executive*
Hirsch, Gary D. *supermarket executive*
Jeffrey, Robert George, Jr. *industrial company executive*
Nicastro, Francis Efisio *defense electronics and retailing executive*
Sergey, John Michael, Jr. *manufacturing company executive*
Trice, William Henry *paper company executive*
Wolynic, Edward Thomas *specialty chemicals technology executive*

West Caldwell
Fascetta, Salvatore Charles *pharmaceutical company executive*

West New York
Gruenberg, Elliot Lewis *electronics company executive*

West Orange
Sosnow, Lawrence Ira *health care company executive*

West Paterson
Dickinson, Fairleigh Stanton, Jr. *former manufacturing company executive*

West Trenton
Roshon, George Kenneth *manufacturing company executive*

Westfield
Connell, Grover *food company executive*
†Connell, Ted *food products company executive*
McLean, Vincent Ronald *former manufacturing company financial executive*

Westwood
Dubnick, Bernard *retired pharmaceutical company administrator*
Folley, Clyde H. *diversified manufacturing executive*
†Gerlinger, Karl *automotive executive*
Mulligan, William G(oeckel) *machinery manufacturing company executive*
Nachtigal, Patricia *equipment manufacturing company executive, general counsel*

Whippany
Golden, John F. *packaging company executive*

White House Station
Darien, Steven Martin *pharmaceuticals executive*
Lewent, Judy C. *pharmaceutical executive*
Vagelos, Pindaros Roy *pharmaceutical company executive*

Woodbridge
Amato, Vincent Vito *business executive*
†Murray, Arthur G. *food products executive*

Woodbury
Wallace, Jesse Wyatt *pharmaceutical company executive*

Woodcliff Lake
Black, Theodore Halsey *retired manufacturing company executive*

NEW MEXICO

Albuquerque
King, James Nedwed *construction company executive, lawyer*
Korman, Nathaniel Irving *research and development company executive*
Stamm, Robert Jenne *building contractor, construction company executive*

Las Cruces
Cowden, Louis Fredrick *electronics executive, engineer*

Santa Fe
Dennison, Charles Stuart *institutional executive*

NEW YORK

Albany
Naumann, Hans Juergen *manufacturing company executive*
Quellmalz, Henry *printing company executive*
Standish, John Spencer *textile manufacturing company executive*

Amherst
Alfiero, Salvatore Harry *manufacturing company executive*
Arrison, Clement R. *manufacturing company executive*

Ardsley
Barth, Richard *pharmaceutical executive*
†Sullivan, Joseph Thomas *chemical executive, chemical engineer*

Armonk
Eastman, Dean Eric *science research executive*

Lynett, Lawrence Wilson *electronics company executive*
Zuckerman, Frederick William *electronics company executive*

Athens
Lew, Roger Alan *manufacturing company executive*

Bethpage
Reinertsen, Norman *aircraft systems corporate executive*

Binghamton
†Koffman, Burton I. *manufacturing company executive*

Bronx
†Potkin, Harvey *food company executive*
Revelle, Donald Gene *manufacturing and health care company executive, consultant*

Brooklyn
Horowitz, Carl *chemical company president*
Oussani, James John *stapling company executive*

Buffalo
Chapman, Frederick John *manufacturing executive*
Clark, Randall Livingston *manufacturing company executive*
Fay, Albert Hill *building materials executive*
Larson, Wilfred Joseph *chemical company executive*
Laurenzo, Vincent Dennis *industrial management company executive*
†Leland, Harold Robert *research and development corporation executive, electronics engineer*
†Rich, Robert E., Sr. *frozen foods company executive*
†Rich, Robert E., Jr. *food products company executive*
Starks, Fred William *chemical company executive*
Wolf, Richard Lloyd *automotive company executive, lawyer*

Chestnut Ridge
Bickel, Henry Joseph *electronics company executive*

Clarence
Mehaffy, Thomas N. *retired tire company executive*

Clifton Park
Favreau, Donald Francis *corporate executive*
Sharbaugh, Amandus Harry *electric company executive*

Corning
Behm, Forrest Edwin *glass manufacturing company executive*
Booth, Chesley Peter Washburn *glass products manufacturing company executive*
Duke, David Allen *glass company executive*
Dulude, Richard *glass manufacturing company executive*
Ecklin, Robert Luther *glass company executive*
Flynn, James Leonard *manufacturing executive*
Houghton, James Richardson *glass manufacturing company executive*
Stuart, Ben R. *manufacturing company executive*
Swindells, David W. *manufacturing executive*
Ughetta, William C. *glass works executive, lawyer*

Cortland
Miller, John David *manufacturing company executive*

Dobbs Ferry
Adler, Stephen Fred *chemical company executive*
†Wilcauskas, Eugene *chemicals executive*

East Aurora
†Bingham, William *toy executive*
Hawk, George Wayne *electronics company executive*

East Hampton
Karp, Harvey Lawrence *electrical and metal products manufacturing company executive*

Ellenville
Baer, Albert Max *metal products executive*

Farmingdale
†Blum, Melvin *chemical company executive, researcher*
Dordelman, William Forsyth *food company executive*
Engelhardt, Dean Lee *biotechnology company executive*
Smith, Joseph Seton *electronics company executive, consultant*

Fayetteville
Pachter, Irwin Jacob *pharmaceutical consultant*

Florida
†Bronstein, David G. *food products executive*

Flushing
†Albert, Gerald *sonar manufacturing company executive*
Henshel, Harry Bulova *watch manufacturer*
Schere, Jonathan Lawrence *aerospace and electronics company executive*

Garden City
†Fristedt, Hans *manufacturing company executive*
Guttenplan, Harold Esau *food company executive*
†Larsson, Hans Lennart *match company executive*

Glen Cove
Maxwell, J. Douglas, Jr. *chemical service company executive*

Glens Falls
†Malkki, Olli *paper company executive*

Grand Island
†Fujita, Peter Kozo *tire manufacturing executive*
Rader, Charles George *chemical company executive*

Great Neck
Machiz, Leon *electronic equipment manufacturing executive*

Greene
Raymond, George Gamble, Jr. *material handling equipment company executive*

Greenvale
Pall, David B. *manufacturing company executive, chemist*

Hartsdale
Carroll, Albert *corporate executive*

Hauppauge
Arams, Frank Robert *electronics company executive*
Hausman, Howard *electronics executive*
Miller, Ronald M. *manufacturing executive*
†Shalam, John Joseph *car stereo and cellular telephone company executive*
Wang, Charles B. *computer software company executive*

Hoosick Falls
Dodge, Cleveland Earl, Jr. *manufacturing executive*

Huntington
Mead, Lawrence Myers, Jr. *retired aerospace executive*

Jamestown
Anderson, R. Quintus *diversified company executive*
Bush, Paul Stanley *furniture company executive*
†Hauck, Donald F. *business executive*
Okwumabua, Benjamin Nkem *corporate executive*

Jericho
Berger, Charles Martin *food company executive*

Lake Success
†Parsont, Robert Edward *chemical company executive*

Larchmont
Sonneborn, Henry, III *former chemical company executive, business consultant*

Lindenhurst
Boltz, Mary Ann *aerospace materials company executive, travel agency executive*

Liverpool
Morabito, Bruno Paul *machinery manufacturing executive*
Winahradsky, Michael Francis *drug company executive*

Lockport
Hoyme, Chad Earl *packaging company executive*
Shah, Ramesh Keshavlal *automotive company executive*

Locust Valley
Schor, Joseph Martin *pharmaceutical executive, biochemist*

Long Island City
Fife, Bernard *automobile products manufacturing company executive*

Mamaroneck
Holz, Harold A. *chemical and plastics manufacturing company executive*
Mizrahi, Abraham Mordechay *cosmetics and health care company executive, physician*

Melville
Kaufman, Stephen P. *electronics company executive*
Large, G. Gordon M. *data processing company executive*
†Lengel, David Lee *electronics manufacturing executive*
†Nassberg, Edward *chemicals executive*

Mendon
Krause, Richard William *manufacturing executive, consultant*

Mineola
Wurzel, Leonard *candy manufacturing company executive*

Mount Kisco
Eckhoff, Carl D. *manufacturing executive*
Laster, Richard *biotechnology executive*

New City
Feld, Joseph *construction executive*

New Hartford
Muzyka, Donald Richard *specialty metals executive, metallurgist*

New Hyde Park
†Fujii, Kenji *medical equipment executive*
Rich, Eric *plastics company executive*

New York
†Ablon, Ralph E. *manufacturing company executive*
Alexander, Norman E. *diversified manufacturing company executive*
Alvarez-Recio, Emilio De La Torre *personal care products company executive*
Andrews, Gerald Bruce *textile executive*
†Anneken, William B. *apparel company executive*
Anshen, Melvin *business educator*
Asch, Arthur Louis *apparel company executive*
†Ashrafi, Dariush *apparel company executive*
Autera, Michael Edward *health care products company executive*
Bagnoli, Vincent James, Jr. *engineer, construction company executive*
Bailey, Glenn Waldemar *manufacturing company executive*
Banks, Russell *chemical company executive*
Banner, Stephen Edward *company executive, lawyer*
Baumann, Karl H. *health, medical products executive*
Bergen, D. Thomas *business executive*
Binns, Walter Gordon, Jr. *automobile manufacturing company executive*
Blinken, Robert James *manufacturing and communications company executive*
†Block, Paul J. *cosmetic company executive*
Blount, Robert Grier *pharmaceutical company executive*
Blumenthal, W(erner) Michael *manufacturing company executive, former secretary of treasury, investment banker*
Bordiga, Benno *automotive parts manufacturing company executive*
Bowling, James Chandler *food products company consultant*
Brennan, Donald P. *aircraft parts manufacturing executive*
Bresani, Federico Fernando *business executive*
Briess, Roger Charles *brewing and food industry executive*
†Bronfman, Edgar M., Jr. *food products executive*
Bronfman, Edgar Miles *distillery executive*
Burns, John Joseph, Jr. *business executive*
Burns, Robin *cosmetics company executive*
Burns, Ward *textile company executive*
Burrows, Selig Saul *industrialist*
Cafiero, Eugene Anthony *manufacturing company executive*
Call, Neil Judson *corporate executive*
Carret, Philip Lord *corporate executive*
Charron, Paul Richard *apparel company executive*
Chernow, David A. *former distillery executive, consultant*
Clark, Robert Henry, Jr. *holding company executive*
†Clarke, Richard M. *chemicals executive*
Claro, Jaime *metal trading company executive*
†Cohen, Arnold *apparel executive*
Coleman, Martin Stone *office furniture company executive*
Collamore, Thomas Jones *corporate executive*
Colombo, Furio Marco *corporate executive*
Cullman, Hugh *retired tobacco company executive*
†Cutler, Richard J. *metal products executive*
Dabah, Haim *apparel executive*
†D'Alessio, Catherine Anne *fragrance company executive*
Daniel, Richard Nicholas *fabricated metals manufacturing company executive*
De Blasio, Michael Peter *electronics company executive*
Diamondstone, Lawrence *paper company executive*
†Di Paolo, Nicholas P. *corporate executive, real estate investor*
Doel, Kenneth John *textile executive*
Dooskin, Herbert P. *manufacturing company executive*
Dueves, Henry C. *computer company executive*
†Elia, Claudio *manufacturing executive*
†Everaert, P. J. *electronics executive*
†Falk, Harvey L. *apparel company executive*
Farber, John J. *chemical company executive*
†Fass, Sim *medical products executive*
French, Harold Stanley *food company executive*
Fribourg, Michel *international agribusiness executive*
†Fujitani, Yoshitaka *heavy manufacturing executive*
†Furlaud, Richard Mortimer *pharmaceutical company executive*
Gannon, Jerome Aylward *construction and contracting management executive*
Gardner, James Richard *pharmaceutical company executive*
Geisenheimer, Emile J. *electronics industry executive, venture capitalist*
Gelb, Richard Lee *pharmaceutical corporation executive*
Gessner, Charles Herman *apparel company executive*
Gill, John Joseph, Jr. *construction executive*
†Gleason, Edward L. *manufacturing executive*
Goelet, Robert G. *corporate executive*
Golub, Alan *clothing company executive*
Goodale, Toni Krissel *development consultant*
Gould, Harry Edward, Jr. *industrialist*
Greaney, Patrick Joseph *electronics executive*
Greenfield, Gordon Kraus *software company executive*
Grisanti, Eugene Philip *flavors and fragrances company executive*
Gurfein, Stuart James *jewelry manufacturing company executive*
Haas, Frederick Carl *paper and chemical company executive*
Hall, Anthony Robert *pharmaceuticals and consumer products company executive*
Harder, Lewis Bradley *ore bodies development company executive*
Hardwick, Charles Leighton *pharmaceutical company executive, state legislator*
Harper, Charles Michel *food company executive*
Harris, Richard Max *corporate executive*
Hatfield, Robert Sherman *former packaging company executive*
†Heimbold, Charles Andreas, Jr. *pharmaceutical company executive*
Helpern, David Moses *shoe corporation executive*
Herbits, Stephen Edward *alcoholic beverage company executive*
Hinerfeld, Norman Martin *manufacturing company executive*
†Hinrichs, Horst *manufactoring executive*
†Hirata, H. *grain company executive*
†Hirota, Yutaro *metal products executive*
Hootkin, Pamela Nan *apparel company executive*
Horn, Charles G. *textile executive*
†Hoser, Albert *electronics executive*
Hoyt, Henry Hamilton, Jr. *pharmaceutical and toiletry company executive*
Hsu, Charles Jui-cheng *manufacturing company executive, advertising agent*
†Inoue, Minoru *manufacturing executive*
†Isogai, Masaharu *women's apparel executive*
†Kamiel, Jerald *apparel executive*
†Kamihara, Takashi *electronics firm executive*
Kampouris, Emmanuel Andrew *corporate executive*
†Kanade, I. *manufacturing executive*
Kata, Edward John *industrial products manufacturing company executive*
Katz, Norman *manufacturing company executive*
Kaufman, Martin N. *metal processing company executive*
Kelly, David Austin *food and chemical products executive*
Kempa, Gerald *manufacturing company executive*
†Klatsky, Bruce J. *apparel company executive*
†Klein, John E. *agricultural products company executive*
†Koenig, Marvin *heavy manufacturing executive*
Kohut, John Walter *corporate executive*
†Koplik, Michael R. *durable goods company executive*
†Koplik, Perry H. *durable goods company executive*
Kressel, Henry *venture capitalist*
†Kroeber, C. Kent *human resources executive*
Krominga, Lynn *cosmetic and health care company executive, lawyer*
Lala, Dominick J. *manufacturing company executive*
Lane, William W. *electronics executive*
Lang, Eugene M. *technology development company executive*
Lanza, Frank C. *electronics executive*
Laporte, Cloyd, Jr. *retired manufacturing executive, lawyer*
Lauder, Estee *cosmetics company executive*
Lauder, Leonard Alan *cosmetic and fragrance company executive*
Lebensfeld, Harry *manufacturing company executive*
†Leeds, Laurence Carroll, Jr. *apparel manufacturing company executive*
†Lepri, Daniel B. *light manufacturing executive*
Levin, Jerry Wayne *business executive*
†Levin, Michael Stuart *steel company executive*
†Levine, Sol *cosmetics company executive*
Levinson, Robert Alan *textile company executive*
†Lewinton, Christopher *business executive*
Lewis, W. Walker *cosmetics executive*
†Lichtenstein, Seymour *clothing manufacturing company executive*
Lifton, Robert Kenneth *diversified companies executive*
Luftglass, Murray Arnold *manufacturing company executive*
Luke, John A., Jr. *paper, packaging and chemical company executive*
Luke, John Anderson *paper company executive*
†Macdonald, R. Fulton *venture developer, business educator*
MacGrath, C. Richard *retired business executive*
Makin, Edward *food products executive*
Mango, Wilfred Gilbert, Jr. *construction company executive*
Marcus, Hyman *business executive*
Margolis, David I(srael) *corporate executive*
†Margolis, Jay M. *clothing executive*
Marlas, James Constantine *holding company executive*
Mattis, Louis Price *pharmaceutical and consumer products company executive*
Maxwell, Hamish *diversified consumer products company executive*
May, William Frederick *manufacturing executive*
Mc Fadden, Mary Josephine *fashion industry executive*
McKenzie, Herbert A(lonza) *pharmaceutical company executive*
McKinnon, Floyd Wingfield *textile executive*
McNeill, Alfred Thomas, Jr. *construction executive*
†Medenica, Gordon *corporate planner*
†Medley, Clayton Edward *apparel executive*
Meyaart, Paul Jan *distilling company executive*
Miles, Michael Arnold *tobacco, food and beer company executive*
Miller, Morgan Lincoln *textile manufacturing company executive*
Minahan, Daniel F. *manufacturing company executive, lawyer*
†Miyaoka, K. *grain company executive*
†Mobius, Michael *chemicals executive*
†Model, Iris *cosmetics executive*
Munera, Gerard Emmanuel *manufacturing company executive*
Munroe, George Barber *former metals company executive*
Murphy, John Arthur *tobacco, food and brewing company executive*
Murray, William *food products executive*
Natori, Josie Cruz *apparel executive*
Nelson, Merlin Edward *international business consultant, company director*
Ochiltree, Stuart A. *cosmetics company executive*
†O'Grady, William M. *manufacturing executive*
†Ohtake, Yoshito *metal products executive*
Ohtsu, Masakazu *electronics executive*
Olsinski, Peter Kevin *international outplacement executive*
Opel, John R. *business machines company executive*
Opotowsky, Stuart Berger *holding company executive*
Paalz, Anthony L. *beverage company executive*
Pampel, Joseph Philip Stevenson *investment executive*
Phillips, Lawrence S. *apparel company executive*
Pietersen, William Gerard *pharmaceutical company executive*
†Pietrini, Andrew Gabriel *automotive aftermarket executive*
†Piser, Donald Harris *construction company executive*
Pomerantz, John J. *manufacturing executive*
Poppel, Seth Raphael *corporate executive*
†Powell, Harold Fryburg *food products executive*
Preston, James E. *cosmetics company executive*
Prieto, Robert *manufacturing executive*
†Ramat, Charles S. *apparel executive*
Rawl, Arthur Julian *retail executive, accountant, consultant, author*
†Regenbogen, Leslie Alan *textile company executive*
Reis, Arthur Robert, Jr. *men's furnishings manufacturer*
Ricciardi, Lawrence R. *food products company executive, lawyer*
†Riklis, Meshulam *manufacturing and retail executive*
Riley, William *corporate executive, writer*
Ritch, Kathleen *diversified company executive*
†Rosenberg, Burton M. *apparel company executive*
Rosenthal, Milton Frederick *minerals and chemical company executive*
Rothstein, Fred H. *clothing executive*
Roubos, Gary Lynn *diversified manufacturing company executive*
†Rowen, Harold Charles *shoe company executive*
Rubin, Joel Edward *consulting company executive*
Ruthchild, Geraldine Quietlake *training and development consultant, writer, poet*
Ruvane, John Austin *pharmaceutical industry consultant*
Sacks, David G. *retired distilling company executive, lawyer*
Sarnelle, Joseph R. *electronic publishing specialist, magazine and newspaper editor*
†Savich, René *broadway theater executive, producer*
Schaller, Christopher L. *apparel products company executive*

Schmitter, Charles Harry *electronics manufacturing company executive, lawyer*
†Schneider, Bernard *industrial machinery executive*
Schneider, Norman M. *food manufacturing company executive*
†Schuchert, Joseph *light manufacturing executive*
Schulhof, Michael Peter *entertainment, electronics company executive*
Schwartz, Bernard L. *electronics company executive*
Shineman, Edward William, Jr. *retired pharmaceutical executive*
Silverman, Jeffrey Stuart *manufacturing executive*
†Smith, R. Jeffery *grain company executive*
Smolinski, Edward Albert *holding company executive, lawyer, accountant, deacon*
Solomon, Howard *pharmaceutical company executive*
Solomon, Zachary Leon *apparel manufacturing company executive*
Sprague, Peter Julian *semiconductor company executive, lecturer*
Stafford, John Rogers *pharmaceutical and household products company executive*
†Staheli, Donald L. *grain company executive*
Steere, William Campbell, Jr. *pharmaceutical company executive*
Steiner, Jeffrey Josef *industrial manufacturing company executive*
†Stern, Leonard Norman *pet supply manufacturing company executive*
Stookey, John Hoyt *chemical company executive*
Sullivan, Eugene John Joseph *manufacturing company executive*
†Taguchi, Tadao *electronics company executive*
Tapella, Gary Louis *manufacturing company executive*
Thurman, Ralph Holloway *health care company executive*
Tisch, Preston Robert *finance executive*
Toller, William Robert *chemical and oil company executive*
Townsend, M. Wilbur *manufacturing company executive*
†Tracy, David M. *textile manufacturing company executive*
†Tulin, John Alexander *mens accessory company executive*
Tumminello, Stephen Charles *consumer electronics manufacturing executive*
Turner, Roderick L. *retired consumer packaged products manufacturing company executive*
†Turner, Stuart *paper company executive*
Ventres, Romeo John *manufacturing company executive*
von der Heyden, Karl Ingolf Mueller *manufacturing company executive*
Wachner, Linda Joy *apparel marketing and manufacturing executive*
Wada, Sadami (Chris) *manufacturing executive*
Wahlberg, Allen Henry *construction executive*
Walker, Sally Barbara *retired glass company executive*
Way, Kenneth L. *seat company executive*
†Waydo, George J. *food products company executive*
Weinstein, Martin *aerospace manufacturing executive, materials scientist*
Weller, Ralph Albert *retired elevator company manufacturing executive*
Whitmyer, Russell Eliot *retired electric company executive*
Zuccotti, John Eugene *construction company executive*

Niagara Falls
Collins, Christopher Carl *manufacturing executive*
King, George Gerard *chemical company executive*
Kirchner, Bruce McHarg *manufacturing company executive*

Niskayuna
Mangan, John Leo *retired electrical manufacturing company executive, international trade and trade policy specialist*

North Hills
Wingate, David Aaron *manufacturing company executive*

Northport
Brown, John Edward *textile company executive*

Old Brookville
Feinberg, Irwin L. *retired manufacturing company executive*

Oneonta
Smith, Geoffrey Adams *special purpose mobile unit manufacturing executive*

Orangeburg
Weinig, Sheldon *materials company executive, metallurgist, educator*

Orchard Park
Franklin, Murray Joseph *retired steel foundry executive*

Pittsford
Ouellette, Bernard Charles *pharmaceutical company executive*
Palermo, Peter M., Jr. *photography equipment company executive*

Port Chester
Beach, Lani Leroy *food products company executive*
Schwartz, Arthur Leonard *pulp company executive, lawyer*

Port Washington
Keen, Constantine *retired manufacturing company executive*

Purchase
Butler, Robert Clifton *forest products industry executive*
Calloway, D. Wayne *food and beverage products company executive*
Deering, Allan Brooks *beverage company executive*
Dettmer, Robert Gerhart *beverage company executive*
Georges, John A. *paper company executive*
Hunziker, Robert McKee *paper company executive*
†MacInnis, Frank T. *construction company executive, holding company executive*
Suwyn, Mark A. *paper company executive*
Wright, David L. *food and beverage company executive*

Queensbury
Borgos, Stephen John *business educator, consultant, municipal administrator, real estate broker*

Rego Park
LeFrak, Samuel J. *housing and building corporation executive*

Rochester
Brennan, John Edward *manufacturing company executive*
†Deavenport, Earnest W., Jr. *chemical executive*
Fisher, George Myles Cordell *electronics equipment company executive, mathematician, engineer*
Gaudion, Donald Alfred *former diversified manufacturing executive*
Giles, Peter *photographic equipment manufacturing executive*
Gill, Daniel E. *optical manufacturing company executive*
†Gleason, James S. *machinery parts manufacturing company executive*
Harris, Diane Carol *health care and optics products executive*
†Harris, Richard M., Jr. *paper company executive*
Harvey, Douglass Coate *retired photographic company executive*
Heidke, Ronald Lawrence *photographic products company executive*
Kohrt, Carl Fredrick *manufacturing executive, scientist*
Latella, Robert Natale *brewing company executive, lawyer*
Mc Isaac, George Scott *business policy educator, past business executive*
Oberlies, John William *construction company executive*
Prezzano, Wilbur John *photographic products company executive*
Rauscher, Tomlinson Gene *electronics company executive, management consultant*
Reveal, Ernest Ira *food company executive*
Sieg, Albert Louis *photographic company executive*
Silkett, Robert Tillson *food business consultant*
Thomas, Leo J. *manufacturing company executive*
Whitmore, Kay Rex *retired photographic company executive*

Roslyn Heights
Lord, Marvin *apparel company executive*

Rye
Netter, Kurt Fred *building products company executive*
Ross, Charles Worthington, IV *metals company executive*

Rye Brook
Masson, Robert Henry *paper company executive*

Scarsdale
Blitman, Howard Norton *construction company executive*
Hayman, Seymour *former food company executive*
Johnson, Boine Theodore *instruments company executive, mayor*

Schenectady
Adler, Michael S. *control systems and electronic technologies*
Grant, Ian Stanley *engineering company executive*
Petersen, Kenneth Clarence *chemical company executive*
Wilson, Delano Dee *consulting company executive*

Seaford
Setzler, William Edward *chemical company executive*

Seneca Falls
Ardia, Stephen Vincent *pump manufacturing company executive*
Morphy, John *manufacturing company executive*
Tarnow, Robert L. *manufacturing corporation executive*

Skaneateles
Allyn, William Finch *manufacturing executive*

Smithtown
Sporn, Stanley Robert *electronic company executive*

Somers
Abu Zayyad, Ray S. *electronics executive*
Case, Richard Paul *electronics executive*
Finnerty, Louise Hoppe *beverage and food company executive*

Stony Brook
Burnham, Harold Arthur *pharmaceutical company executive, physician*

Stony Point
Miller, Leonard Martin *manufacturing executive*

Suffern
Sutherland, George Leslie *retired chemical company executive*

Syosset
Bainton, Donald J. *diversified manufacturing company executive*
†Guthart, Leo A. *electronics executive*
Puglisi, Anthony Joseph *service company executive*

Syracuse
Darrone, Donald William *retired tool corporation executive*
Heffner, Ralph H. *agricultural products company executive*
Incaudo, Claude J. *food products company executive*
Kenna, E. Douglas *retired plastics company executive*
†Lanzafame, Samuel James *manufacturing company executive*

Tarrytown
Jarrett, Eugene Lawrence *chemical company executive*
Kane, Stanley Bruce *food products executive*
†Toda, K. *electronics executive*

Thornwood
Douglas, Patricia Jeanne *systems designer*

Troy
Doremus, Robert Heward *glass and ceramics processing educator*
Evans, Edwin Charles *consultant, former manufacturing executive*

Uniondale
†Frashier, Gary Even *corporation executive*

Valley Stream
†Golden, Hyman *beverage products company executive*

Walden
Hanau, Kenneth John, Jr. *packaging company executive*

Webster
Duke, Charles Bryan *research and development manufacturing executive, physics educator*

West Nyack
†Michaelson, Martin J. *textile company executive, computer consultant*
Painter, Carl Eric *manufacturing company executive*

Westbury
Cannizzaro, Paul Peter *food products executive*
†Cullen, John B. *food products company executive*
†Kennedy, Bernard D. *food products executive*
†Martin, Daniel Richard *pharmaceutical company executive*

White Plains
†Endresen, Jan Ralph *export company executive*
Friedman, Ralph *airplane instrument manufacturing company executive*
Greene, Leonard Michael *aerospace manufacturing executive, institute executive*
Henningsen, Victor William, Jr. *food company executive*
LaBant, Robert James *information processing executive*
Morrison, Robert Scheck *food processing company executive*

Whitestone
Catapano, Joseph John *construction company executive*

Yonkers
Holtz, Gilbert Joseph *steel company executive*

Yorktown Heights
LaRussa, Joseph Anthony *optical company executive*

Youngstown
Alpert, Norman *chemical company executive*

NORTH CAROLINA

Advance
Huber, Thomas Martin *container company executive*

Asheville
Armstrong, Robert Baker *textile company executive*
Coli, Guido John *chemical company executive*
Conroy, David James *retired chemical, diversified manufacturing executive*
Vander Voort, Dale Gilbert *textile company executive*

Chapel Hill
Thakor, Haren Bhaskerrao *manufacturing company executive*

Charlotte
Belk, Thomas Milburn *apparal executive*
Bowden, James Alvin *construction company financial executive*
†Cochrane, Luther Parks *construction executive, contractor*
†Cotton, James *construction company executive*
Daniels, William Carlton, Jr. *construction executive*
†Davidson, Charles Tompkins *construction company executive*
Dickson, Rush Stuart *holding company executive*
†Hannah, Thomas E. *textiles executive*
Hannon, William Evans *manufacturing executive, consultant*
Harrison, J. Frank, Jr. *soft drink company executive*
†Holland, William Ray *diversified company executive*
Iverson, Francis Kenneth *metals company executive*
Jones, Johnie H. *construction company executive*
†McKeon, Robert B. *textiles executive*
McVerry, Thomas Leo *manufacturing company executive*
Moore, James L., Jr. *beverage company executive*
†Murata, Junichi *electronics company executive*
Regelbrugge, Roger Rafael *steel company executive*
†Schmidt, Peter *construction company executive*
Siegel, Samuel *metals company executive*
†Walker, James Marion *construction company executive*

Drexel
†Richetta, Fred J. *manufacturing executive*

Durham
Burger, Robert Mercer *semiconductor device research executive*
Fair, Richard Barton *electronics executive, educator*
Niedel, James E. *pharmaceuticals executive*
†Sanders, Charles Addison *pharmaceutical company executive, physician*

Eden
Staab, Thomas Robert *textile company financial executive*

Farmville
†Monk, Albert C., III *manufacturing executive*

Fayetteville
†Hendrick, J. R., III *automotive executive*

Flat Rock
Demartini, Robert John *textile company executive*

Gastonia
Kimbrell, Willard Duke *textile executive*
Lawson, William David, III *cotton company executive*

Greensboro
Danahy, James Patrick *textile executive*
Elam, Harper Johnston, III *textile company executive, lawyer*
Greenberg, Frank S. *textile company executive*
Greenberg, George *mill company executive*
Hayes, Charles A. *mill company executive*
†Henderson, George, III *textiles executive*
Howard, Paul Noble, Jr. *retired construction company executive*
Howard, Richard Turner *construction company executive*
Hughes, Donald R. *textile executive*
Korb, William Brown, Jr. *manufacturing company executive*
Kretzer, William T. *textile company executive*
Mann, Lowell Kimsey *retired manufacturing executive*
Mebane, George Allen *corporate executive, rancher*
Morris, Edwin Alexander *retired apparel manufacturing company executive*
Trogdon, Dewey Leonard, Jr. *textile executive*
†Vetack, Richard S. *textiles executive*

Hickory
Nash, Robert Fred *grocery company executive*
Shuford, Harley Ferguson, Jr. *furniture manufacturing executive*

High Point
Fenn, Ormon William, Jr. *furniture company executive*
†Grubbs, Gerald Reid *furniture manufacturing company executive*
Jones, Ronald Lee *furniture manufacturing executive*
Marsden, Lawrence Albert *retired textile company executive*

Kannapolis
Ridenhour, Joseph Conrad *textile company executive*

Kinston
†Fuchs, David *clothing manufacturing company executive*
†Schechter, Sol *clothes company executive*

Mount Airy
Woltz, Howard Osler, Jr. *steel and wire products company executive*

Mount Holly
Copeland, John Wesley *textile company executive*

Pine Knoll Shores
Benson, Kenneth Victor *manufacturing company executive, lawyer*

Pinehurst
O'Neill, John Joseph, Jr. *business consultant, former chemical company executive*

Raleigh
Klein, Verle Wesley *corporate executive, retired naval officer*
Leddicotte, George Comer *business executive, consultant*
Sloan, O. Temple, Jr. *automotive equipment executive*
†Wright, Thomas James *chemical company executive*

Research Triangle Park
†Cipau, Gabriel *pharmaceutical executive*
Gaither, John Stokes *chemical company executive*
Hitchings, George Herbert *retired pharmaceutical company executive, educator*

Thomasville
Starr, Frederick Brown *furniture manufacturing executive*

Weldon
Barringer, Paul Brandon, II *lumber company executive*
Conger, Stephen Halsey *lumber company executive*

Wilmington
Crigler, T. P. *foreign products and investments executive*
Silloway, Benton, Jr. *food products executive*
Thompson, Donald Charles *electronics company executive, former coast guard officer*

Wilson
Kehaya, Ery W. *tobacco holding company executive*
Murray, J. Alec G. *manufacturing executive*

Winston Salem
Emken, Robert Allan *diversified company executive*
†Ford, Yancey William, Jr. *tobacco company executive*
Hanes, Ralph Philip, Jr. *textile company executive*
Maselli, John Anthony *food products company executive*
Riley, Leslie Walter, Jr. *corporate executive*
Smith, Zachary Taylor, II *retired tobacco company executive*
Sticht, J. Paul *retired food products and tobacco company executive*

NORTH DAKOTA

Fargo
Ommodt, Donald Henry *dairy company executive*

Grand Forks
Gjovig, Bruce Quentin *manufacturing consultant*

OHIO

Akron
Altenau, Alan Giles *tire and rubber company executive*
Barnett, James Wallace *manufacturing executive*
Bonsky, Jack Alan *chemical company executive, lawyer*
Brock, James Robert *manufacturing company executive*
Gault, Stanley Carleton *manufacturing company executive*
Heckel, John Louis (Jack Heckel) *aerospace company executive*
Isles, Marvin Lee *manufacturing executive*
Kaufman, Donald Leroy *aluminum products company executive*
†Mehlfeldt, Horst K. *tire manufacturing company*
†Ockene, Alan L. *tire manufacturing executive*
Pengilly, Brian William *manufacturing company executive*
Reynolds, A. William *manufacturing company executive*
Tobler, D. Lee *chemical and aerospace company executive*
Wells, Hoyt Mellor *manufacturing executive*

Ashtabula
Bonner, David Calhoun *chemical company executive*

Aurora
Wiegner, Edward Alex *multi-industry executive*

Bowling Green
Guthrie, Mearl Raymond, Jr. *business administration educator*

Bratenahl
Jones, Trevor Owen *automobile supply company executive, management consultant*

Brecksville
Galloway, Ethan Charles *technology development executive, former chemicals executive*

Brookville
Juhl, Daniel Leo *manufacturing and marketing firm executive*

Canton
Elsaesser, Robert James *retired manufacturing executive*
Koontz, Raymond *security equipment company executive*
Timken, W. Robert, Jr. *manufacturing company executive*
Toot, Joseph F., Jr. *bearing manufacturing company executive*

Cedarville
Gordin, Dean Lackey *retired agricultural products executive*

Chagrin Falls
Daniel, Clarence Huber *former manufacturing company executive, consultant*
Frohring, Paul Robert *former business executive*
Groeger, Joseph Herman *retired metal company executive*

Cincinnati
Atteberry, William Duane *diversified manufacturing company executive*
†Breth, James Raymond *scrap metals company executive*
Chase, William Rowell *manufacturing executive*
Christensen, Paul Walter, Jr. *gear manufacturing company executive*
Church, John Franklin, Jr. *paper company executive*
Coombe, V. Anderson *valve manufacturing company executive*
Crowe, James Joseph *shoe company executive, lawyer*
Derstadt, Ronald Theodore *health care administrator*
Dewar, Norman Ellison *chemical company executive*
Geier, James Aylward Develin *manufacturing company executive*
†Griffin, William Ralph *business executive*
Harrell, Samuel Macy *grain company executive*
†Harrison, Robert Sattler *piano and organ manufacturing executive*
†Heldman, Gary W. *manufacturing and distributing company executive*
Hudson, Bannus B. *footwear manufacturing and apparel retail executive*
Keener, C(harles) Richard *food company information systems executive*
Koster, William Pfeiffer *materials engineering executive*
Lindner, Keith E. *food company executive*
Lockhart, Michael D. *electric company executive*
Maisel, Michael *clothing executive*
Meyer, Daniel Joseph *machinery company executive*
Moore, Alfred Anson *corporate executive*
Munn, Stephen P. *manufacturing company executive*
†Pennacchio, Joseph *apparel executive*
Petry, Thomas Edwin *manufacturing company executive*
Pichler, Joseph Anton *food products executive*
Slater, John Greenleaf *manufacturing company executive*
Smale, John Gray *diversified industry executive*
Smittle, Nelson Dean *electronics executive*
Stern, Joseph Smith, Jr. *former footwear manufacturing company executive*
Stone, Andrew Logan *corporate executive*
†Strange, Peter Stanton *construction company executive*
Thompson, Morley Punshon *textile company executive*
Voet, Paul C. *specialty chemical company executive*
Walker, Ronald F. *corporate executive*

Cleveland
Anderson, Harold Albert *engineering and building executive*
†Ball, Robert L. *metal products company executive*
†Beggs, Lyman M. *manufacturing executive*
Beggs, Lyman M., III *manufacturing company executive*
Bersticker, Albert Charles *chemical company executive*
Blasius, Donald Charles *appliance company executive*
Breen, John Gerald *manufacturing company executive*
Brophy, Jere Hall *manufacturing company executive*
Butler, William E. *manufacturing company executive*
Cligrow, Edward Thomas, Jr. *manufacturing executive*
Cochran, Earl Vernon *manufacturing executive*
†Cole, Stephan William *manufacturing executive*
Commes, Thomas A. *manufacturing company executive*
Cutler, Alexander MacDonald *manufacturing company executive*
†Epstein, Marvin Morris *construction executive*
Finneburgh, Morris Lewis *electronic manufacturing executive*
Goodger, John Verne *electronics and computer systems executive*
Gorman, Joseph Tolle *corporate executive*
Grabner, George John *manufacturing executive*
Hackbirth, David William *aluminum company executive*
Hamilton, William Milton *retired industrial company executive*
Hardis, Stephen Roger *manufacturing company executive*
Hart, Alvin Leroy *electric manufacturing company executive*
Hauserman, William Foley *manufacturing company executive*
Hayes, Scott Birchard *raw materials company executive*
Hellman, Peter Stuart *technical manufacturing executive*
Hoag, David H. *steel company executive*
Hushen, John W. *manufacturing company executive*
Ivy, Conway Gayle *paint company executive*
Kamm, Jacob Oswald *manufacturing executive, economist*
Kelly, J. Peter *steel company executive*
Kerr, Thomas Adolphus *retired construction company executive*
Krasney, Samuel Joseph *multi-industry company executive*
Lefebvre, Gabriel Felicien *retired chemical company executive*
Luke, Randall Dan *retired tire and rubber company executive, lawyer*
Mac Laren, David Sergeant *pollution control company executive*
Mandel, Jack N. *manufacturing company executive*
Mandel, Morton Leon *industrial corporation executive*
Manning, William Dudley, Jr. *retired specialty chemical company executive*
†McCormick, William Charles *manufacturing company executive*
†McCormick, William Charles *manufacturing company executive*
Mendelson, Ralph Richard *water heater manufacturing executive*
Miller, Carl George *manufacturing executive*
Morley, John C. *electronic equipment company executive*
Myers, David N. *construction executive*
†Nolan, Cary J. *medical products manufacturer*
O'Donnell, Kevin *retired metal working company executive*
Oesterling, Thomas Ovid *pharmaceutical company executive*
Parker, Patrick Streeter *manufacturing executive*
Ramig, Alexander, Jr. *paint company executive, chemist*
Reid, James Sims, Jr. *automobile parts manufacturer*
Reitman, Robert Stanley *manufacturing and marketing executive*
Roberts, Clyde Francis *business executive*
Rodewig, John Stuart *manufacturing company executive*
Rosenthal, Leighton A. *aviation company executive*
Sabo, Richard Steven *electrical company executive*
Scharp, Anders *manufacturing company executive*
Schulze, John B. *manufacturing executive*
†Selhorst, Lawrence O'Hare *manufacturing executive*
Stone, Harry H. *business executive*
Swift, David L. *manufacturing company executive*
Taylor, Thomas Hewitt, Jr. *construction equipment company executive*
Tinker, H(arold) Burnham *chemical company executive*
Unger, Paul A. *packaging executive*
Walker, Martin Dean *specialty chemical company executive*
Weiss, Morry *greeting card company executive*
Williams, Gordon Bretnell *construction company executive*
Wright, Marshall *retired manufacturing executive, former diplomat*
Zambie, Allan John *manufacturing company executive*

Columbus
Byrd, Richard Hays *food company executive*
Collier, David Alan *management educator*
Crane, Jameson *plastics manufacturing company executive*
Eickleberg, John Edwin *process control company executive*
Funk, John William *emergency vehicle manufacturing executive, packaging company executive, lawyer*
Heffner, Grover Chester *retired corporate executive, retired naval officer*
Hetzel, Joseph Adam *manufacturing executive*
Knilans, Michael Jerome *supermarkets executive*
Malenick, Donald H. *metals manufacturing company executive*
McConnell, John Henderson *metal and plastic products manufacturing executive*
Mussey, Joseph Arthur *health and medical product executive*
Pfening, Frederic Denver, III *manufacturing company executive*
Skiest, Eugene Norman *food company executive*
Trevor, Alexander Bruen *computer company executive*
Wigington, Ronald Lee *retired chemical information services executive*
†Yenkin, Bernard Kalman *paint company executive*

Concord
Whedon, Ralph Gibbs *manufacturing executive*

Cuyahoga Falls
Hooper, Blake Howard *manufacturing executive*

Cuyahoga Heights
Tyrrell, Thomas Neil *metal processing executive*

Dayton
Benedict, Samuel S. *paper company executive*
Birkholz, Raymond James *metal products manufacturing company executive*
Diggs, Matthew O'Brien, Jr. *air conditioning and refrigeration manufacturing executive*
Duval, Daniel Webster *manufacturing company executive*
Enouen, William Albert *paper corporation executive*
Harlan, Norman Ralph *construction executive*
Holmes, David Richard *computer and business forms company executive*
James, Robert Charles *business equipment manufacturing company executive*
Johnston, George Gustin *automotive executive*
Ladehoff, Leo William *metal products manufacturing executive*
Mason, Steven Charles *forest products company executive*
Mc Swiney, James Wilmer *retired pulp and paper manufacturing company executive*
Morse, Kenneth Pratt *manufacturing executive*
Philips, Jesse *retired manufacturing company executive*
Price, Harry Steele, Jr. *construction materials company executive*
Rinzler, Allan *consulting company executive*
Shaw, Harry Alexander, III *manufacturing company executive*
Shuey, John Henry *diversified products company executive*
Torley, John Frederic *iron and steel company executive*

Delaware
Dempsey, John Cornelius *manufacturing company executive*
Eells, William Hastings *retired automobile company executive*

Dublin
Clement, Henry Joseph, Jr. *diversified building products executive*
†Lamp, Benson J. *tractor company executive*
†Wyatt, Glenn Thomas *chemical company executive*

Elyria
Beckett, John Douglas *manufacturing company executive*

Fairlawn
Gibson, Charles Colmery *former rubber manufacturing executive*

Findlay
Gorr, Ivan William *rubber company executive*
Kremer, Fred, Jr. *manufacturing company executive*
Reinhardt, James Alec *rubber industry executive*

Franklin
Smith, Lynn Howard *manufacturing company executive*

Gates Mills
Veale, Tinkham, II *former chemical company executive, engineer*

Hamilton
Belew, David Lee *retired paper manufacturing company executive*
Marzano, Angelo Mario *company executive*

Holland
†Marsden, Brian William Hugh *steel company executive*
Stewart, Daniel Robert *glass company executive*

Holmesville
Bolender, James Henry *tire and rubber manufacturing executive*

Huron
Clark, Thomas Garis *rubber products manufacturer*

Jackson Center
Thompson, Wade Francis Bruce *manufacturing company executive*

Lakewood
Bradley, J.F., Jr. *retired manufacturing company executive*

Lancaster
Fox, Robert Kriegbaum *manufacturing company executive*

Lima
Pranses, Anthony Louis *retired electric company executive, organization executive*

Macedonia
Roth, Edwin Morton *manufacturing executive*

Mansfield
Gorman, James Carvill *pump manufacturing company executive*

Marietta
Broughton, Carl L(ouis) *food company executive*

Marysville
Hines, Anthony Loring *automotive executive*

Maumee
Allen, Darryl Frank *industrial company executive*
Selland, Howard M. *manufacturing executive*

Mayfield Heights
O'Brien, Frank B. *manufacturing executive*
Rankin, Alfred Marshall, Jr. *business executive*
Smith, Ward *manufacturing company executive, lawyer*

Medina
Gossett, Robert M. *rubber industry executive*
Morris, John Hite *chemical industry executive*
Smith, Richey *chemical company executive*
Sullivan, Thomas Christopher *coatings company executive*

Miamisburg
Northrop, Stuart Johnston *manufacturing company executive*

Middletown
Graham, Thomas Carlisle *steel company executive*

Milford
Klosterman, Albert Leonard *technical development business executive, mechanical engineer*

Navarre
Gardner, David Edward *baking company executive*

New Bremen
Dicke, James Frederick, II *manufacturing company executive*

North Ridgeville
Haddox, Arden Ruth Stewart *automotive aftermarket manufacturing executive*

Norwalk
French, Marcus Emmett *manufacturing company executive*

Painesville
Humphrey, George Magoffin, II *plastic molding company executive*

Perrysburg
Eastman, John Richard *retired manufacturing company executive*
McMaster, Harold Ashley *manufacturing company executive, inventor*

Pickerington
†Burrell, Richard Lee *footware company executive*
†Zacks, Gordon Benjamin *manufacturing company executive*

Randolph
Pecano, Donald Carl *truck, trailer and railcar manufacturing executive*

Reynoldsburg
Woodward, Greta Charmaine *construction company executive*

Solon
Richard, Edward H. *manufacturing company executive, former municipal government official*

Streetsboro
Kearns, Warren Kenneth *business executive*

Sugar Grove
Bonner, Herbert Dwight *construction management educator*

Sylvania
Lock, Richard William *packaging company executive*

Toledo
Boeschenstein, William Wade *glass products manufacturing executive*
Boller, Ronald Cecil *glass company executive*
Hiner, Glen Harold, Jr. *materials company executive*
Hirsch, Carl Herbert *manufacturing company executive*
Lanigan, Robert J. *packaging company executive*
Lemieux, Joseph Henry *manufacturing company executive*
Mabry, Guy O. *manufacturing company executive*
†Mac Guidwin, Mark J. *manufacturing executive*
Morcott, Southwood J. *automotive parts manufacturing company executive*
†Robb, A. M. *glass manufacturing executive*
Romanoff, Milford Martin *building contractor*
Strobel, Martin Jack *motor vehicle and industrial component manufacturing and distribution company executive*
Weber, Max O. *retired glass fiber products manufacturing company executive*

Vandalia
Farley, Paul Emerson *manufacturing company executive*

Warren
Alli, Richard James, Sr. *electronics executive, service executive*
†Rennert, Ira Leon *heavy manufacturing executive*

West Chester
Rishel, James Burton *manufacturing executive*

Westerville
Smith, C. Kenneth *corporate executive*

Wickliffe
Bares, William G. *chemical company executive*
Coleman, Lester Earl *chemical company executive*
Rosica, Gabriel Adam *corporate executive, engineer*

Willoughby
Figgie, Harry E., Jr. *corporate executive*

Wooster
Gates, Richard Daniel *manufacturing company executive*
Meehan, Joseph Gerard *retired manufacturing executive*
Williams, Walter W. *consumer products manufacturing executive*

Youngstown
Courtney, William Francis *food and vending service company executive*
Cushwa, William Wallace *machinery parts company executive*
Powers, Paul J. *manufacturing company executive*

OKLAHOMA

Bartlesville
†Dunlap, James Robert *contractor, state legislator*

Bethany
Mercer, Ronald L. *retired manufacturing executive*

Broken Arrow
Elad, Emanuel *industrial instrumentation executive*

Edmond
Griggy, Kenneth Joseph *food company executive*

Oklahoma City
†Bishop, William T. *food company executive*
†Comchoc, Rudolph A. *food distribution company executive*
Kilbourne, Lewis Buckner *food service company executive*
†Locke, William Sweet *manufacturing executive*
Mc Pherson, Frank Alfred *manufacturing corporate executive*
†Meyers, Theodore A. *food products executive*
Smith, Robert Walter *food company executive*

Poteau
Harper, S. Birnie *bakery executive*

Sand Springs
Ackerman, Robert Wallace *steel company executive*

Tahlequah
†Rozell, Herbert *construction executive, senator*

Tulsa
Bump, Larry J. *engineering and construction company executive*
Bynum, George T., III (Ted Bynum) *biomedical company executive*
Callaham, Thomas Hunter *former business executive*
Calvert, Delbert William *chemical company executive*
Collins, John Roger *aerospace company executive*
Narwold, Lewis Lammers *paper products manufacturer*
†Philion, James Robert *business executive*
Thomas, Robert Eggleston *former corporate executive*
Williams, Joseph Hill *diversified industry executive*

OREGON

Ashland
Farrimond, George Francis, Jr. *management educator*

Beaverton
Bosch, Samuel Henry *electronics company executive*
Knight, Philip H(ampson) *shoe manufacturing company executive*

Bend
†Babcock, Walter Christian, Jr. *membrane company executive*

Corvallis
Becker, Boris William *business educator*

Dillard
†Ford, Kenneth *lumber, wood products company executive*

Eugene
Wiley, Carl Ross *timber company executive*

Hillsboro
Gerlach, Robert Louis *research and development executive, physicist*

Lake Oswego
Thong, Tran *scientist, engineer, researcher*

Portland
†Bishop, B. H. *textile manufacturing executive*
Bull, Bergen Ira *equipment manufacturing company executive*
Cooley, Edward H. *castings manufacturing company executive*
Flowerree, Robert Edmund *retired forest products company executive*
Foehl, Edward Albert *chemical company executive*
Frazier, J(ohn) Phillip *manufacturing company executive*
Fronk, William Joseph *retired machinery company executive*
Gray, John Delton *retired manufacturing company executive*
†Jones, Alan C. *grocery company executive*
Marvin, Roy Mack *metal products executive*
Merlo, Harry Angelo *forest products executive*
Nagel, Stanley Blair *construction and investment executive*
†Parsons, J. A. *paper and wood products company executive*
Pope, Peter T. *forest products company executive*
†Stoyanov, Milan *lumber products company executive*
Swindells, William, Jr. *lumber and paper company executive*
†Thurston, George R. *lumber company executive*
Warren, Robert Carlton *manufacturing company executive*
Whitsell, Helen Jo *lumber executive*

Roseburg
Whelan, William Anthony *forest products company executive*

Sisters
Baxter, John Lincoln, Jr. *manufacturing company executive*

Sunriver
Fosmire, Fred Randall *retired forest products company executive*

Tigard
Berglund, Carl Neil *electronics company executive*

West Linn
Bradley, Lester Eugene *retired steel and rubber products manufacturing executive*

Wilsonville
Meyer, Jerome J. *diversified technology company executive*

PENNSYLVANIA

Alcoa Center
†Bridenbaugh, Peter Reese *industrial research executive*

Allentown
Anderson, Paul Edward *cement company executive*
Baker, Dexter Farrington *manufacturing company executive*
Donaldson, John Anthony *manufacturing executive*
Donley, Edward *manufacturing company executive*
Kelly, David Hoover *chemical company executive*
Lovett, John Robert *chemical company executive*
Rushton, Brian Mandel *chemical company executive*
Samuels, Abram *stage equipment manufacturing company executive*
Shire, Donald Thomas *retired air products and chemicals executive, lawyer*

Allison Park
Backus, John King *former chemical company research administrator*

Avondale
Friel, Daniel Denwood, Sr. *manufacturing executive*

Bala Cynwyd
†Driscoll, Edward Carroll *construction management firm executive*
Furlong, Edward V., Jr. *paper company executive*

Barnesboro
Moore, David Austin *pharmaceutical company executive, consultant*

Belle Vernon
Wapiennik, Carl Francis *manufacturing firm executive, planetarium and science institute executive*

Bensalem
†Faijean, Francois *metal products executive*
†Wachs, David V. *apparel executive*

Bethlehem
Barnette, Curtis Handley *steel company executive, lawyer*
Boylston, Benjamin Calvin *steel company executive*
Church, Thomas Trowbridge *former steel company executive*
Gates, Elmer D. *business executive*
Hartmann, Robert Elliott *manufacturing company executive*
Jordan, John Allen, Jr. *steel company executive*
Kerchner, Charles Frederick, Jr. *electronics executive, engineer*
†Roberts, Malcolm John *steel company executive*
Williams, Walter Fred *steel company executive*

Blandon
†Nulty, George P. *food products company executive*

Blue Bell
†Carey, Joseph A., Jr. *electronics executive*
Keppler, William Edmund *multinational company executive*
Unruh, James Arlen *business machines company executive*

Boiling Springs
Hoefling, John Alan *former army officer, corporation executive*

Brackenridge
Bozzone, Robert P. *steel company executive*

Bradford
Rice, Lester *electronics company executive*

Bridgeville
†Nicholson, Peter Joseph *construction company executive*

Bryn Mawr
†Lotman, Herbert *food processing executive*

Butler
Zehfuss, Lawrence Thomas *hardware supply company executive*

Camp Hill
†Grass, Martin Lehrman *business executive*

Carlisle
†Noddle, Allan S. *food products executive*

Central City
Brown, Robert Alan *retired construction materials company executive*

Chadds Ford
Brown, Charles Daniel *retired chemical company executive*

Chambersburg
Rumler, Robert Hoke *agricultural consultant, retired association executive*

Clarks Summit
Alperin, Irwin Ephraim *clothing company executive*
Ross, Adrian E. *retired drilling manufacturing company executive*

Coatesville
Meyers, Frederick M. *diversified industrial products and service company executive*

Collegeville
Dupuis, Claude Paul *pharmaceutical company executive*
Kun, Kenneth A. *business executive*
Smalley, Christopher Joseph *pharmaceutical company professional*
Tretter, James Ray *pharmaceutical company executive*

Conshohocken
Spaeth, Karl Henry *chemical company executive, lawyer*

Coopersburg
†Spira, Joel Solon *electronics company executive*

Devon
Brody, Aaron Leo *food and packaging consultant*

Easton
Gurin, Richard Stephen *manufacturing company executive*

Eighty Four
Capone, Alphonse William *retired industrial executive*

Emmaus
Bowers, Klaus D(ieter) *retired electronics research development company executive*

Erie
De Witt, William Gerald *retired paper company executive*
Hedrick, Charles Lynnwood *holding company executive*
Hey, John Charles *electronics company executive*
Merwin, Robert Freeman *manufacturing company executive*

Exton
Lewis, Thomas B. *specialty chemical company executive*

Fairview
Duval, Albert Frank *paper company executive*

Feasterville Trevose
McCaughan, John F. *chemical company executive*

Gladwyne
Mc Donald, Robert Emmett *conglomerate executive*

Greensburg
Dykema, Henry L. *manufacturing company financial executive*

Greentown
Forcheskie, Carl S. *former apparel company executive*

Greenville
Stuver, Francis Edward *former railway car company executive*

Gwynedd
Bryant, Robert Parker *retired food service and lodging executive*

Harrisburg
Goell, James Emanuel *electronics company executive*
Hudson, William Jeffrey, Jr. *manufacturing company executive*
Marley, James Earl *manufacturing company executive*
McInnes, Harold A. *manufacturing company executive*
Narigan, Harold W. *manufacturing company executive*
Raab, Walter Ferdinand *manufacturing company executive*

Hatboro
Hull, Lewis Woodruff *manufacturing company executive*

Haverford
Bogash, Richard *retired pharmaceutical company executive*
Talucci, Samuel James *retired chemical company executive*

Hazleton
Denise, Robert Phillips *craft company executive*

Hershey
†Christ, William Frank *food manufacturing company executive*
Lehr, William, Jr. *food products executive*
Wolfe, Kenneth L. *food products manufacturing company executive*
Zimmerman, Richard Anson *food company executive*
Zoumas, Barry Lee *food products company executive, nutritionist*

Hollidaysburg
Bloom, Lawrence Stephen *retired clothing company executive*

Horsham
Boswell, Gary Taggart *electronics company executive*
Brenner, Ronald John *pharmaceutical industry executive*
†Hakimoglu, Ayhan *electronics company executive*
Hook, Jerry B. *pharmaceutical company executive*
McNulty, Carrell Stewart, Jr. *manufacturing company executive, architect*

Huntingdon Valley
Jaffe, Marvin Eugene *pharmaceutical company executive, neurologist*

Indiana
Jones, Shelley Pryce *chemical company executive*

Irvine
Koedel, John Gilbert, Jr. *forge company executive*

Jenkintown
Beavers, Ellington McHenry *chemical company executive*
Reese, Francis Edward *retired chemical company executive, consultant*

Johnstown
Pasquerilla, Frank James *real estate developer and manager*

Kennett Square
May, Harold Edward *chemical company executive*

Kimberton
Douglas, Bryce *former pharmaceutical company executive*

King Of Prussia
Gardella, Libero Anthony *pharmaceutical development executive*
†Langton, Raymond Benedict, III *manufacturing company executive*
Poste, George Henry *pharmaceutical company executive*
†Wulff, Harald P. *chemicals executive*

Lancaster
Adams, William White *manufacturing company executive*
Deaver, Everette Allen *diversified manufacturing company executive*
†Decker, Thomas E. *construction company executive*
†Hennessey, Joseph E. *chemicals executive*
High, S. Dale *diversified company executive*

Lansdale
†Riebman, Leon *electronics company executive*

Latrobe
Underwood, James Martin *business executive*

Lebanon
McMindes, Roy James *aggregate company executive*

Lemoyne
Zimmerman, Charles Hinckley *former financial executive*

Ligonier
Pilz, Alfred Norman *manufacturing company executive*

Lyon Station
Bowers, Richard Philip *manufacturing executive*
Breidegam, DeLight Edgar, Jr. *battery company executive*

Malvern
Zurawski, Vincent Richard, Jr. *biotechnology company executive, research scientist*

Meadville
Foster, Catherine Rierson *manufacturing company executive*

Media
Peabody, William Tyler, Jr. *retired paper manufacturing company executive*
Resnick, Stewart Allen *diversified company executive*
†Rothchild, Loren *toy manufacturing executive*

Middleburg
Kline, David Lamar *concrete block manufacturing company executive*

Middlesex
Finlay, Robert Derek *food company executive*

Monroeville
Maclay, William Nevin *retired manufacturing and construction company executive*
Ryan, Christopher Richard *construction company executive*

Morgan
McQuillen, Albert Lawrence, Jr. *steel company executive*

Morgantown
McGraw, James Michael *manufacturing company executive*

Morrisville
Muth, Robert James *metal company executive, lawyer*

Narberth
Barnes, Norman Frank *food company executive*

New Brighton
†O'Leary, John P., Jr. *plastic company executive*

New Holland
†Marquart, Clifford Lynn *food company executive*

New Hope
Braymer, Marguerite Annetta *optical company executive*
Williamson, Frederick Beasley, III *rubber company executive*

Newtown
Henshaw, Jonathan Cook *manufacturing company executive*

Norristown
†Fertell, Paul Adolph *manufacturing company executive*

Orrtanna
Newman, Doris Jean *district sales manager*

Paoli
Blankley, Walter Elwood *manufacturing company executive*
†Kornfeld, Allan A. *manufacturing company executive*

Peach Glen
Carey, Dean Lavere *fruit canning company executive*

Philadelphia
Agersborg, Helmer Pareli K. *pharmaceutical company executive, researcher*
Avery, William Joseph *packaging manufacturing company executive*
†Azoulay, Bernard *chemicals company executive*
†Bauman, Robert Patten *diversified company executive*
Callé, Craig R.L. *packaging executive*
Driscoll, Lee Francis, Jr. *corporate director, lawyer*
Featherman, Bernard *steel company executive*
Ferber, Arthur Henry *engineering executive*
Garrison, Walter R. *corporate executive*
Golaski, Walter Michael *manufacturing executive*
Gordon, George Minot *manufacturing executive*
Jones, Loren Farquhar *electronics executive*
Katherine, Robert Andrew *chemical company executive*
Klein, Robert *manufacturing company executive*
Lewis, George Withrow *business executive*
Lippincott, Philip Edward *paper products company executive*
Llewellyn, J. Bruce *food products executive*
Mulroney, John Patrick *chemical company executive*
Naylor, Robert Ernest, Jr. *chemical company executive*
Preston, Seymour Stotler, III *manufacturing company executive*
Root, Franklin Russell *business educator*
Sorgenti, Harold Andrew *petroleum and chemical company executive*
Wendt, Henry, III *pharmaceutical company executive*
White, Albert J. *health products executive*
Wilson, James Lawrence *chemical company executive*

Pittsburgh
Agnew, Franklin Ernest, III *former food company executive*
Andersson, Craig Remington *chemical company executive*
†Barone, Eugene J. *medical products executive*
Berkman, Marshall L. *manufacturing company executive*
Bogdanovich, Joseph James *food company executive*
Brewer, William Dixon *manufacturing executive*
Burnham, Donald Clemens *manufacturing company executive*
Chenery, Robin *metals manufacturing executive*
Clark, Gary M. *electronics executive*
Corry, Charles Albert *steel and energy company executive*
Costello, Thomas Patrick *manufacturing executive*
Courtsal, Donald Preston *manufacturing company executive, financial consultant*
†Danforth, Douglas Dewitt *manufacturing company executive*
Dauler, L. Van V., Jr. *chemicals executive*
Dempsey, Jerry Edward *service company executive*
Dinman, Bertram David *consultant, retired aluminum company executive*
†Doerr, Ronald H. *steel company executive*
Edelman, Harry Rollings, III *engineering and construction company executive*
Fairbanks, Frank Bates *manufacturing company executive*
Figgins, David Forrester *construction company executive*
Fischer, Richard Lawrence *metal products executive*
Foxen, Richard William *manufacturing company executive*
†Freeman, Edmund J. *heavy manufacturing executive*
†Grefenstette, Carl G. *medical products and real estate executive*
Horowitz, Don Roy *instrument company executive*
†Howard, Thomas Bailey, Jr. *construction materials company executive*
Huntington, James Cantine, Jr. *equipment manufacturing company executive*
Jordan, Michael Hugh *electrical and electronics company executive*
Kriebel, Charles Hosey *management sciences educator*
†Kronk, Claude F. *heavy manufacturing executive*
†Lauterbach, Hans *pharmaceutical company executive*
Lauterbach, Robert Emil *steel company executive*
Limbach, Walter F. *construction company executive*
Machatzke, Heinz Wilhelm *chemical company executive*
†Marshall, Thomas *chemical company executive*
McConomy, Thomas Arthur *chemical company executive*
Mueller, Gerd Dieter *financial and administrative executive*
Mulloney, Peter Black *steel, oil and gas executive*
†Nowak, Joseph J. *metal products executive*
Oehmler, George Courtland *corporate executive*
O'Neill, Paul Henry *aluminum company executive*
O'Reilly, Anthony John Francis *food company executive*
Paul, Robert Arthur *steel company executive*
Phillips, James Macilduff *material handling company executive, engineering and manufacturing executive*
Pitts, Samuel Richard *technology company executive*
†Porter, Irwin W. *food store chain executive*
Renner, Simon Edward *steel company executive*
Roth, William George *manufacturing company executive*
Rust, William James *retired steel company executive*
Ruttenberg, Harold Joseph *manufacturing executive*
Ryan, John Thomas, Jr. *business executive*
Ryan, John Thomas, III *safety equipment company executive*
Sante, William Arthur, II *aerospace and manufacturing company executive*
Sculley, David W. *food company executive*
Simmons, Richard P. *steel company executive*
Smith, Phillip Hartley *steel company executive*
Stahl, Laddie L. *electrical engineer, manufacturing company executive*
Thomas, John Edward *manufacturing company executive*
Thomas, W(illiam) Bruce *retired steel, oil, gas company executive*
Turnbull, Gordon Keith *metal company executive, metallurgical engineer*
Wehmeier, Helge H. *chemical, health care and imaging technologies company executive*
Weis, Konrad Max *retired chemical company executive*
Wilcock, James William *corporation executive, retired capital equipment manufacturing company executive*
Will, James Fredrick *steel company executive*
Williams, Louis Stanton *glass and chemical manufacturing executive*

Radnor
Marland, Alkis Joseph *leasing company executive, computer science educator, financial planner*
†Yoh, Harold Lionel, Jr. *engineering, construction and management company executive*

Reading
Beaver, Howard Oscar, Jr. *wrought specialty alloys manufacturing company executive*
Cardy, Robert Willard *speciality steel company executive*
Cottrell, G. Walton *manufacturing executive*
Ehlerman, Paul Michael *industrial battery manufacturing company executive*
Fiore, Nicholas Francis *special alloys and materials company executive*
Fording, Edmund Howard, Jr. *chemical executive*
Harner, Paul B. *gray iron foundry executive*
Hawkins, Arthur *battery manufacturing executive*
†Hawkins, Arthur Michael *automotive executive*
Johnson, Gerard G. *apparel company executive*
†Pearson, Douglas N. *battery manufacturing company executive*
Pugh, Lawrence R. *apparel executive*
Roedel, Paul Robert *steel company executive*

Saint Marys
Johnson, J. M. Hamlin *manufacturing company executive*

Scranton
Guerrise, Patrick P. *manufacturing company executive*

Sewickley
Snyder, William Penn, III *manufacturing company executive*

Shippensburg
Luhrs, H. Ric *toy manufacturing company executive*

Sinking Spring
Wilson, Terrence Raymond *manufacturing executive*

Southampton
DaCosta, Edward Hoban *plastics and electronics manufacturing company executive*
Zocholl, Stanley Ernest *electronics executive*

Spring City
Blanchard, Norman Harris *retired pharmaceutical company executive*

Spring Grove
Norris, Thomas Clayton *paper company executive*
Wand, Richard Walton *paper company executive*

Spring House
Payn, Clyde Francis *technology company executive, consultant*
†Rorke, Edwin Grant, Jr. *manufacturing company executive*
Wilson, Hugh Shannon *retired manufacturing company executive, consultant*

Swarthmore
Heaps, Marvin Dale *food services company executive*
Kaufman, Antoinette D. *business services company executive*

Telford
Luscinski, Steven Michael *corporate executive*

Unionville
Forney, Robert Clyde *retired chemical industry executive*

University Park
Jaffe, Austin Jay *business administration educator*
Jordan, Bryce *corporate director, retired university president*
Werner, John Ellis *steel executive, technological economic development executive, metallurgist*

Valley Forge
Besson, Michel Louis *manufacturing company executive*
Dachowski, Peter Richard *manufacturing executive*
Hilyard, James Emerson *manufacturing company executive*
Huml, Donald Scott *manufacturing company executive*
Mundt, Ray B. *diversified industry executive*
Rassbach, Herbert David *manufacturing executive*

Verona
Potts, Gerald Neal *manufacturing company executive*

Villanova
†Keating, Daniel Joseph, III *construction company executive*

Warminster
Finnegan, Laurence Patrick, Jr. *manufacturing company executive*

Washington
Kastelic, Robert Frank *aerospace company executive*
Piatt, Jack Boyd *manufacturing executive*

Wayne
Christy, John Gilray *financial company executive*
Peterson, Raymond A. *paper company executive*
Wolcott, Robert Wilson, Jr. *consulting company executive*

Waynesboro
Benchoff, James Martin *manufacturing company executive*
Holzman, Howard Eugene *health services executive*

West Chester
Bogle, Hugh Andrew *chemical company executive*
Kim, James Joo-Jin *electronics company executive*
Mecca, Joseph Nicholas *manufacturing company executive*
Mulligan, James Francis *retired business executive, lawyer*

West Conshohocken
†Ball, John H. *construction executive*

West Point
Abrams, William Bernard *pharmaceutical company executive, physician*

Wilkes Barre
†Bevevino, Frank H. *food products executive*
Falkowitz, Daniel *clothing manufacturing company executive*
Hobbs, William Barton Rogers *company executive*
†Pollock, Kenneth Leslie *manufacturing executive*

Willow Grove
Berkoff, Charles Edward *pharmaceutical executive*
Kulicke, C(harles) Scott *business executive*

Worcester
McAdam, Will *electronics consultant*

Wynnewood
Bozzelli, Andrew Joseph, Jr. *valve company executive*
Connor, James Edward, Jr. *retired chemical company executive*
†Kelly, Paul E., Jr. *metal products executive*
†Kelly, Paul Edward, Sr. *metals company executive*

Wyomissing
Garr, Carl Robert *manufacturing company executive*

York
Dresher, James T. *manufacturing executive*
Forchheimer, Otto Louis *retired chemical company executive*
Garner, Edward Markley, II *manufacturing executive*
Horn, Russell Eugene, Jr. *printing executive*
†Pokelwaldt, Robert N. *manufacturing company executive*
Thornton, George Whiteley *manufacturing executive*

Zionsville
Fleming, Richard *chemical company executive*

RHODE ISLAND

Bristol
Wilcox, Harry Wilbur, Jr. *retired corporate executive*

East Providence
†Hay, Robert J. *plastics manufacturing executive*

Greenwich
Valenti, Leo Frank *electronics company executive*

Jamestown
Winnert, Franklin Roy *consultant, former building materials manufacturing executive*

North Kingstown
Paolino, Richard Francis *manufacturing company executive*
†Sharpe, Henry Dexter, Jr. *manufacturing company executive*

Pawtucket
Neff, Edward August *manufacturing company executive*

Providence
Ames, Robert San *retired manufacturing company executive*
Bready, Richard Lawrence *manufacturing company executive*
Cooper, Gordon Mayo *retired manufacturing company executive*
†Dimeo, Thomas P. *construction company executive, real estate developer*
Gilbane, Jean Ann (Mrs. Thomas F. Gilbane) *construction company executive*
†Gilbane, William James *building company executive*
Hardymon, James Franklin *diversified products company executive*
Hartmann, George Herman *retired manufacturing company executive*
Little, Dennis Gage *diversified business executive*
Papitto, Ralph Raymond *manufacturing company executive*

SOUTH CAROLINA

Anderson
Elks, William Chester, Jr. *manufacturing executive*
Hendrix, James Easton *textiles executive*

Arcadia
Dent, Frederick Baily *mill executive, former ambassador, former secretary of commerce*

Camden
Daniels, John Hancock *agricultural products company executive*

Charleston
Addlestone, Nathan Sidney *metals company executive*
Martin, Roblee Boettcher *retired cement manufacturing executive*
Raghupathi, Ragu S. *manufacturing executive*
Rosebrough, Walter M., Jr. *manufacturing executive*

Clinton
Cornelson, George Henry, IV *retired textile company executive*
Vance, Robert Mercer *textile manufacturing company executive, banker*

Clover
Peacock, A(lvin) Ward *textile company executive*

Columbia
Kahn, Herman Bernard *construction company executive*

Florence
Dixon, Gale Harllee *drug company executive*
Guest, Karl Macon *retired paper and container manufacturing company executive*

Fort Mill
Elisha, Walter Y. *textile manufacturing company executive*
Horten, Carl Frank *textile manufacturing company executive*

Goose Creek
†Evans, V. Bond *aluminum components manufacturing company executive*

Greenville
Bellantoni, Maureen Blanchfield *manufacturing and distribution executive*
Friedman, Steven M. *textile company executive*
†Hodges, Harland E. *apparel executive*
Hunter, Jerry E. *textile company executive*
Maddrey, E. E., II *textile company executive*
Pamplin, Robert Boisseau, Jr. *agricultural company executive, minister, writer*
Parente, Emil J. *chemical engineering executive*
Rainsford, Bettis C. *textile company executive*
Roe, Thomas Anderson *building supply company executive*
Scruggs, Jack Gilbert *retired chemical executive*
†Stone, Charles Rivers *apparel manufacturing company executive*
†Suitt, Thomas Howard *construction company executive*
Varin, Roger Robert *textile executive*

Greer
Gallman, Clarence Hunter *textile executive*
Lane, James Garland, Jr. *diversified industry executive*

Harleyville
†Sugarman, Burt *construction company executive*

Hartsville
Browning, Peter Crane *packaging company executive*
Coker, Charles Westfield *diversified manufacturing company executive*
King, Russell C., Jr. *manufacturing company executive*

Hilton Head
Rulis, Raymond Joseph *manufacturing company executive, consultant*

Hilton Head Island
Cunningham, William Henry *retired food products executive*
Harty, James D. *former manufacturing company executive*
Lewis, Gene Evans *retired medical equipment company executive*
Mersereau, Hiram Stipe *wood products company consultant*
Pritchard, Dalton Harold *retired electronics research engineer*
Russell, Allen Stevenson *retired aluminum company executive*
Stoll, Richard Edmund *retired manufacturing executive*

Johns Island
Mackaness, George Bellamy *retired pharmaceutical company executive*

Salem
Van Buren, William Benjamin, III *retired pharmaceutical company executive*

Seneca
Hudgin, Donald Edward *retired research company executive, editor, consultant*

Spartanburg
Milliken, Roger *textile company executive*

Townville
Wright, George Cullen *electronics company executive*

Williamston
Davis, Michael Todd *textile company administrator*

SOUTH DAKOTA

Sioux Falls
Christensen, David Allen *manufacturing company executive*
Tucker, William Vincent *vocational evaluator, former college president*

TENNESSEE

Ashland City
†Lindahl, Herbert Winfred *appliance manufacturing executive*

Brentwood
†Hauk, Donald Benjamin *automotive parts company executive*
†Thompson, Keith M. *automotive supply executive*

Bristol
Riggs, Benjamin Clapp, Jr. *building products manufacturing company executive*

Chattanooga
Colbert, Robert B., Jr. *apparel company executive*

†Guerry, Alexander *drug and chemical company executive*
St. Goar, Herbert *food corporation executive*
Sheehy, Thomas Daniel *apparel and textile manufacturing company executive*
Smith, Gordon Laidlaw, Jr. *manufacturing company executive*

Cordova
Cooke, Edward William *corporate executive, former naval officer*
Dean, Jimmy *meat processing company executive, entertainer*

Dandridge
Comer, Evan Philip *manufacturing company executive*

Dyersburg
Wiggins, Jerome Meyer *apparel textile industry financial executive*

Jackson
Lipshie, Joseph *apparel manufacturing company executive*

Kingsport
Coover, Harry Wesley *manufacturing company executive*
Findley, Don Aaron *manufacturing company executive*
Giggey, James Walker *chemical company executive*
Head, William Iverson, Sr. *retired chemical company executive*

Knoxville
†Goodfriend, Robert M. *apparel executive*
Martin, James Robert *plastics company executive*
Stegmayer, Joseph Henry *housing industry executive*
Stringfield, Hezz, Jr. *contractor, financial consultant*

La Vergne
†Forrest, Henry J. *manufacturing company executive*

Lookout Mountain
Rymer, S. Bradford, Jr. *retired appliance manufacturing company executive*

Memphis
Andrews, William Eugene *construction and services company executive*
Apple, John Boyd *elevator company executive*
Berry, Robert Vaughan *electrical, electronic manufacturing company executive*
Bruce, Marvin Ernest *corporate executive*
Buckman, Robert Henry *chemical company executive*
Dunnigan, T. Kevin *electrical and electronics manufacturing company executive*
†Formanek, Peter Raemin *automobile parts company executive*
Hyatt, David Hudson *manufacturing executive*
Jenkins, Ruben Lee *chemical company executive*
†Kelley, Robert C. *construction industry executive*
Langford, Walter Martin *retired greeting card and gift wrap manufacturing executive*
McMinn, William A. *chemicals company executive*
†Reeves, Sam T. *argicultural products company executive*

Morristown
Cordover, Ronald Harvey *business executive, venture capitalist*
Olmstead, Francis Henry, Jr. *plastics industry executive*

Nashville
†DiLorenzo, Joseph L. *health care company executive*
Fitzgerald, Edmund Bacon *electronics industry executive*
Gulmi, James Singleton *apparel manufacturing company executive*
Harris, J(acob) George *health care company executive*
†Hohlfeld, Pauline *pharmaceutical executive*
Hummell, Burton Howard *food distribution company executive*
†Kaizaki, Yoichiro *automotive executive*
Langstaff, George Quigley, Jr. *retired footwear company executive*
Mahanes, David James, Jr. *retired distillery executive*
†Ono, Masatoshi *tire manufacturing executive*
†Richards, James E. *pharmaceutical executive*
Wire, William Shidaker, II *retired apparel and footwear manufacturing company executive*

Oak Ridge
Macfarlane, Alastair Iain Robert *business executive*

Pleasant View
Davis, Alfred Lewis *manufacturing company executive*

TEXAS

Austin
Adams, Warren Sanford, II *retired food company executive, lawyer*
†Alich, John Arthur *manufacturing company executive*
Brager, Walter S. *retired food products corporation executive*
Cook, Chauncey William Wallace *retired food products company executive*
Culp, Joe C(arl) *electronics executive*
Dell, Michael S. *manufacturing executive*
Edwards, Wayne Forrest *paper company executive*
Hurd, Richard Nelson *pharmaceutical company executive*
Jenkins, Lawrence Eugene *retired aeronautics company executive*
Rollins, Henry Moak *former oil drilling equipment company executive, consultant*
Vykukal, Eugene Lawrence *wholesale drug company executive*

Bellaire
Lancaster, Carroll Townes, Jr. *corporate executive*

Carrollton
†Heath, Richard W. *cosmetic company executive*
Miller, Marvin Edward *building materials company executive*

College Station
†Lusas, Edmund William *food processing research executive*

Corpus Christi
Heinz, Walter Ernst Edward *retired chemical executive*

Dallas
Albers, John Richard *beverage company executive*
Anderson, Jack Roy *health care company executive*
†Arbuckle, Scott G. *manufacturing company executive*
Ash, Mary Kay Wagner *cosmetics company executive*
Ausere, Joe Morris *food manufacturing company executive*
†Bach, James A. *food company executive*
Barnes, Robert Vertreese, Jr. *masonry contractor executive*
Bartlett, Richard C. *cosmetics executive, writer*
Bell, John Lewis McCulloch *manufacturing executive*
Bucy, J. Fred *retired electronics company executive*
†Campbell, Roy E. *diversified company executive*
†Casey, John T. *medical products executive*
Cherryholmes, James Gilbert *construction consultant, real estate agent*
Cruikshank, Thomas Henry *energy services and engineering executive*
Fisher, Gene Jordan *retired chemical company executive*
Gifford, Porter William *retired construction materials manufacturing company executive*
Gillilan, William J, III *construction company executive*
Grogan, Timothy James *corporate support executive, retired army officer*
†Haggar, Edmond Ralph *apparel manufacturing company executive*
†Hegi, Frederick B., Jr. *mobile home manufacturing executive*
Hill, John Rutledge, Jr. *retired construction materials company executive*
Hirl, J. Roger *petrochemical company executive*
Hirsch, Laurence Eliot *business executive, lawyer*
Hodge, George Lowrance *cosmetics company executive*
Hughes, Joe Kenneth *retired beverage company executive*
Humann, Walter Johann *corporation executive*
Hurst, John L., III (Jack Hurst) *chemical company executive*
Junkins, Jerry R. *electronics company executive*
Keiffer, Edwin Gene *electronics industry company executive*
†Knowles, True H. *food products executive*
Lane, Marvin Maskall, Jr. *electronics company executive*
Lawson, Andrew Lowell, Jr. *defense industry company executive*
Margerison, Richard Wayne *diversified industrial company executive*
Mullin, Francis Isaac *beverage company executive*
Murphy, John Joseph *manufacturing company executive*
Musa, Samuel Albert *electronics company executive*
Pearce, Ronald *retired cosmetic company executive*
†Phillips, Billy Byron *distribution executive, electronics executive*
Price, J(ohn) William *paper industry executive*
Rabin, Stanley Arthur *metal products manufacturer*
Rivera, Richard E. *food products executive*
Robbins, Ray Charles *manufacturing company executive*
Robertson, Beverly Carruth *steel company executive*
Rochon, John Philip *cosmetics company executive*
Rogers, Ralph B. *industrial business executive*
Rogers, Richard Raymond *cosmetics company executive*
†Rosenstein, Ira M. *beverage products executive*
Rosson, Glenn Richard *building products and furniture company executive*
St. John, Bill Dean *diversified equipment and services company executive*
Short, David Gaines *food company executive*
Simmons, Harold C. *sugar company executive*
†Simmons, James F. *textiles executive*
†Snetzer, Michael Alan *multi-industry executive*
†Solomon, William Tarver *general construction company executive*
Thrash, Purvis James, Sr. *retired oil field equipment and service company executive*
†Turpin, Jack A. *electronics executive*
Wallace, William Ray *fabricated steel manufacturing company executive*
Weber, William P. *electronics company executive*
†Williams, Gordon L. *aircraft manufacturing executive*
†Wilson, Lawrence Alexander *construction company executive*
Yanagisawa, Samuel Tsuguo *electronics executive*
Zimmerman, S(amuel) Mort(on) *electrical and electronics engineering executive*
Zumwalt, Richard Dowling *flour mill executive*

Denton
Brown, John Fred *steel company executive*

Diboll
Grum, Clifford J. *manufacturing company executive*

Fort Worth
Appel, Bernard Sidney *electrical company executive*
Arena, M. Scott *pharmaceutical company executive*
Carrico, Fred Allen *aircraft manufacturing company executive*
Crane, Neal Dahlberg *manufacturing company executive*
†Cunningham, Raymond Clement *glass company executive*
Leone, George Frank *pharmaceutical executive*
†Ravel, Dilip N. *pharmaceutical executive*
Roberts, Leonard H. *retail executive*
†Schollmaier, Edgar H. *pharmaceutical products company executive*
†Stout, Edward L., Jr. *diversified corporation executive*
Thornton, Charles Victor *metals executive*
Wheaton, David Joe *aerospace manufacturing company executive*

Garland
Adams, Christopher Steve, Jr. *defense electronics corporation executive, former air force officer*

Georgetown
†Gerding, Thomas Graham *medical products company executive*

Granbury
Wisler, Charles Clifton, Jr. *retired cotton oil company executive*

Grand Prairie
†Childs, Hymen *broadcasting corporation executive*
Wietholter, William James *automotive parts manufacturing company executive*

Houston
Ahart, Jan Fredrick *electrical manufacturing company executive*
Austin, Harry Guiden *engineering and construction company executive*
Ball, Lewis Edwin, II *manufacturing company executive*
Boren, William Meredith *manufacturing executive*
Buchanan, Dennis Michael *manufacturing and holding company executive*
Cain, Gordon A. *chemicals company executive*
Cizik, Robert *manufacturing company executive*
†Clark, Malcolm Dowdles *manufacturing company executive*
Clark, Ron D(ean) *cosmetologist*
†Code, James Manley Wayne *manufacturing executive*
†Cotros, Charles H. *food products company executive*
Crawford, David Coleman *retired diversified manufacturing company executive*
Dodson, D. Keith *engineering and construction company executive*
Eastep, Larry Gene *construction company executive*
Fabricant, Jill Diane *technology company executive*
Fort, John Franklin, III *manufacturing company executive*
†Friedkin, Thomas H. *automotive executive*
†Fuchs, Bernard *apparel executive*
†Gamel, Wendell Wesley *business executive*
Gibson, Michael Addison *chemical engineering company executive*
†Godchaux, Frank Area, III *food company executive*
Goff, Robert Burnside *retired food company executive*
Gore, Thomas Jackson *construction executive*
Hafner, Joseph A., Jr. *food company executive*
Heimbinder, Isaac *construction company executive, lawyer*
†Helburn, Stephen *oceaneering company executive*
Helland, George Archibald, Jr. *equipment manufacturing company executive, former government official, management consultant*
Henning, George Thomas, Jr. *chemical company executive*
Johnson, Frederick Dean *former food company executive*
Klausmeyer, David Michael *scientific instruments manufacturing company executive*
Lanese, Herbert J. *air and aerospace transportation manufacturing executive*
Lay, Kenneth Lee *diversified energy company executive*
†Levy, Gerard G. *industrial gases executive*
Martin, J. Landis *manufacturing company executive, lawyer*
Mason, Franklin Rogers *automotive executive*
McCurdy, Larry Wayne *automotive parts company executive*
†McKeever, Thomas A. *metals company executive*
Mead, Dana George *diversified industrial manufacturing company executive*
†Mendenhall, Oniel Charles *retail executive*
†Mueller, Robert Louis *business executive*
Nuss, Eldon Paul *casket manufacturer*
†Olafson, James W. *home construction company executive*
†Peterkin, George Alexander, Jr. *diversified company executive*
Pfeiffer, Carl E. *manufacturing company executive*
Ray, Edgar Wayne, Jr. *food company executive*
Riedel, Alan Ellis *manufacturing company executive, lawyer*
Riley, Harold John, Jr. *manufacturing executive*
Roorda, John Francis, Jr. *business consultant*
Sakowitz, Robert Tobias *apparel executive*
Schlindwein, James A. *food products company executive*
Sebastian, Michael James *manufacturing company executive*
Selecman, Charles Edward *business executive*
Sheley, Donald Ray, Jr. *manufacturing company executive*
†Stanworth, R. Howard *eye care company executive*
Templeton, Robert Earl *engineering and construction company executive*
†Tronchon, Claude *chemical executive*
Waggoner, James Virgil *chemicals company executive*
Wilson, Carl Weldon, Jr. *construction company executive, civil engineer*
Woods, James Dudley *manufacturing company executive*
Zech, William Albert *manufacturing company executive*
†Zerr, Emil Martin *construction company executive*

Hurst
Mc Keen, Chester M., Jr. *business executive*

Irving
†Groussman, Dean G. *retail executive*
Levy, Lester A. *sanitation company executive*

Longview
Folzenlogen, P. D. *petrochemical executive*

Lubbock
†Anderson, Noble *dairy products executive*

Lufkin
Denman, Joe Carter, Jr. *retired forest products company executive*

Mesquite
Bullock, Norma Kathryn Rice *chemical research professional*

Mexia
Guerin, Dean Patrick *food products executive*

Midland
Luckett, Paul Herbert, III *manufacturing executive*
†Wagner, Cyril, Jr. *metals manufacturing company executive*

Montgomery
Holman, Charles Richardson *chemical company executive*

Pittsburg
Pilgrim, Lonnie (Bo) *poultry production company executive*

Plano
Bain, Travis Whitsett, II *manufacturing and retail executive*

Port Arthur
Gipson, Robert Malone *research administrator*

Portland
Grubbs, Donald Ray *welder, educator*

Richardson
Edge, Harold Lee *manufacturing executive*
†Orr, David E. *electronics executive*

Richmond
Barratt, Cynthia Louise *pharmaceutical company executive*

San Antonio
Benson, Charles Edward *aircraft company executive*
Berg, Thomas *manufacturing executive*
Brown, Robert *manufacturing executive*
Cloud, Bruce Benjamin, Sr. *construction company executive*
Fink, Lyman Roger *retired manufacturing executive*
Issleib, Lutz E. *beverage company executive*
Larson, Doyle Eugene *electronics company executive, retired air force officer*
Leeper, Michael Edward *retired army officer, retired corporation executive*
Spector, Joseph Robert *retired diversified manufacturing executive*
Terracina, Roy David *food executive*
†Zachry, Henry Bartell, Jr. *construction company executive*

Seguin
†Selig, Marvin *metal products company executive*

Silsbee
Ashcraft, David Lee *forest products company executive*

Spring
Goldenberg, George *pharmaceutical company executive*

Sugar Land
Bartolo, Adolph Marion *food company executive*
Kempner, Isaac Herbert, III *sugar company executive*

The Woodlands
Ashley, Lawrence Atwell, Jr. *former construction executive, management consultant*
†Neumann, W. Michael *chemicals executive*

Tyler
Blair, James Walter, Jr. *machinery company executive*
Warner, John Andrew *foundry executive*

Valley Mills
Evans, Clifford Jessie *manufacturing executive, land developer*

Wichita Falls
Sarni, Vincent Anthony *manufacturing company executive*

UTAH

Ogden
Garrison, U. Edwin *military, space and defense products manufacturing company executive*
Wilson, James Rigg *aircraft manufacturing company executive*

Orem
Ashton, Alan C. *computer software company executive*

Salt Lake City
Anderson, Joseph Andrew, Jr. *retired apparel company executive, retail consultant*
Baker, Charles DeWitt *research and development company executive*
Cook, M(elvin) Garfield *chemical company executive*
Frary, Richard Spencer *international consulting company executive*
Gregory, Herold La Mar *chemical company administrator*
Hembree, James D. *retired chemical company executive*
Huntsman, Jon M. *chemical company executive*
Norton, Delmar Lynn *candy company executive, video executive*
†Ostler, O. Don *jewelry, emblem manufacturing company executive*
Steiner, Richard Russell *conglomerate executive*

South Jordan
Bangerter, Norman Howard *building contractor, developer, former governor*

Springville
†Haymond, J. Brent *chemical company executive, state legislator*

VERMONT

Arlington
Nowicki, George Lucian *chemical company executive*

Bennington
Killen, Carroll Gorden *electronics company executive*

Brattleboro
Cohen, Richard *grocery company executive*

Burlington
Hartwell, Samuel Adams *manufacturing company executive*

Danby
†Mitchell, John McKearney *manufacturing company executive*

Rutland
†Ferraro, Betty Ann *corporate administrator, state senator*

Saint Johnsbury
Trelfa, Richard Thomas *paper company executive*

South Burlington
†Pizzagalli, James *construction executive*

Waterbury
†Cohen, Bennett R. ("Ben" Cohen) *food products executive*
†Greenfield, Jerry *food products executive*

Windsor
Furnas, Howard Earl *business executive, educator, retired government official*

VIRGINIA

Alexandria
Cooper, Kenneth Banks *business executive, former army officer*
Dies, Douglas Hilton *international trade consultant*
Huffman, Delton Cleon, Jr. *pharmaceuticals executive*
Keith, Donald Raymond *retired army officer, business executive*
Litke, Donald Paul *business executive, retired military officer*
Marsh, Robert Thomas *corporate executive, retired air force general*
†Matthews, Stuart *aircraft manufacturing company executive*
Mc Lucas, John Luther *aerospace company executive*
Shuster, Robert G. *electronics company executive, consultant*
Stempler, Jack Leon *aerospace company executive*
Vander Myde, Paul Arthur *engineering services executive*

Arlington
Bennett, John Joseph *professional services company executive*
Brunson, Burlie Allen *defense contractor executive*
Burdetsky, Ben *business administration educator, dean*
Cook, Richard Kelsey *aerospace industry executive*
Cox, Henry *research company executive, research engineer*
Knowlton, William Allen *business executive, consultant*
Malley, Robert Joseph *manufacturing company executive*

Bassett
Spilman, Robert Henkel *furniture company executive*

Broad Run
Hinkle, Barton Leslie *retired electronics company executive*

Catlett
Scheer, Julian Weisel *business executive, author*

Chantilly
Miller, Donald Eugene *aerospace electronics executive*

Charlottesville
Cahill, Cornelius *manufacturing executive*
Haigh, Robert William *business administration educator*
MacAvoy, Thomas Coleman *glass manufacturing executive, educator*
Norgren, C. Neil *manufacturing executive*
Rader, Louis T. *corporation executive, educator*
Rotch, William *business administration educator*
†Tewksbury, Charles G. *textiles technology executive*

Danville
Barker, Willie G., Jr. *agriculture executive*

Dumfries
Heiser, Joseph Miller, Jr. *retired army officer, business executive, author*

Fairfax
†Benton, Robert *automotive executive*
Cotter, William Joseph *retired grain company executive*
Edwards, James Owen *engineering and construction company executive*
Moore, Robert Edward *research company executive*
Sganga, John B. *furniture holding company executive*
Sheehan, Edward James *technical consultant, former government official*
Uffelman, Malcolm Rucj *electronics company executive, electrical engineer*
West, Bob *pharmaceutical company executive*
Willauer, Whiting Russell *systems integration company executive*

Fairfax Station
Starry, Donn Albert *former aerospace company executive, former army officer*

Falls Church
Lantz, Phillip Edward *corporate executive, consultant*
Mellor, James Robb *defense company executive*
Oesterling, Wendy Lee *sales and marketing executive*
Post, Howard Allen *forest industry specialist*

Glen Allen
Fife, William Franklin *retired drug company executive*
Murphey, Robert Stafford *pharmaceutical company executive*

Great Falls
MacGowan, Charles Frederic *retired chemical company executive*

Hampton
Holloway, Paul Fayette *aerospace executive*
Whitcomb, Richard Travis *aeronautical consultant*

Harrisonburg
Darazsdi, James Joseph *food processing executive*
Muth, George Edward *former art and drafting supply company executive*

Heathsville
Winkel, Raymond Norman *avionics manufacturing executive, retired naval officer*

Herndon
Schaer, Werner *computer services executive*

Hinton
Keeler, James Leonard *food products company executive*

Hopewell
Leake, Preston Hildebrand *tobacco research executive*

Manassas
Geerdes, James (Divine Geerdes) *chemical company executive*
Parrish, Frank Jennings *food company executive*

Mc Lean
Albrecht, Mark Jennings *diversified high technology company executive*
Anderson, David Lloyd *defense industry executive*
Dempsey, James Raymon *industrial executive*
Fitzpatrick, John Malcolm *manufacturing executive*
Franklin, Jude Eric *electronics executive*
Mars, Forrest E., Jr. *candy company executive*
Mars, John F. *candy company executive*
Mehuron, William Otto *electronics company executive*
Ryan, John Franklin *multinational company executive*

Newport News
†Banks, Charles A. *manufacturing executive*
Dart, Charles Edward *retired consultant*
Fricks, William Peavy *shipbuilding company executive*
†Peebles, David L. *light manufacturing executive*
Smith, Walter Tilford *shipbuilding company executive*

Purcellville
Sharples, Winston Singleton *automobile importer and distributor*

Reston
†Bannister, Dan R. *professional and technical services company executive*
Blanchard, Townsend Eugene *service companies executive*
Christ, Thomas Warren *electronics research and development company executive, sociologist*
Lewis, Arthur Dee *corporation executive*
Murdoch, Robert Waugh *cement and construction materials company executive*
Rose, Michel *construction materials company executive*
†Zigel, James M. *aircraft manufacturing executive*

Richmond
Aron, Mark G. *corporate executive, lawyer*
Bourke, William Oliver *retired metal company executive*
Bunzl, Rudolph Hans *retired diversified manufacturing company executive*
†Crowl, R(ichard) Bern *aluminum company executive*
†Dresser, Paul Alton, Jr. *paper and forest products executive*
†Easterling, William K. *plastics and chemicals executive*
Fox, Joseph Carter *pulp and paper manufacturing company executive*
Gottwald, Bruce Cobb *chemical company executive*
Gottwald, Floyd Dewey, Jr. *chemical company executive*
Hagan, Randall Lee *manufacturing executive*
Helwig, Arthur Woods *chemical company executive*
Holder, Richard Gibson *metal products executive*
Huntley, Robert Edward Royall *lawyer, business executive, former university president*
Jezuit, Leslie James *manufacturing company executive*
Jones, David Eugene *pharmaceutical company executive*
Lindholm, John Victor *business executive*
†Nielsen, Steven B. *medical products executive*
Osdene, Thomas Stefan *tobacco company executive, chemist*
Pauley, Stanley Frank *manufacturing company executive*
Pendleton, Eugene Barbour, Jr. *business executive*
Reynolds, David Parham *metals company executive*
†Reynolds, Randolph Nicklas *aluminum company executive*
Robins, Edwin Claiborne, Sr. *retired pharmaceutical company executive*
Rogers, James Edward *paper company executive*
Sweeney, Arthur Hamilton, Jr. *metal manufacturing executive, retired army officer*
Thorp, Benjamin A., III *paper manufacturing company executive*
Trott, Sabert Scott, II *marketing professional*
Walker, Charles B. *chemicals company executive*
Williams, Robert C. *paper company executive*

Roanoke
†Edwards, J. Randolph *medical products executive*

Smithfield
Luter, Joseph Williamson, III *meat packing and processing company executive*

Spring Grove
Daniel, Robert Williams, Jr. *business executive, former congressman*

Springfield
Bush, Norman *research and development executive*

Suffolk
Birdsong, George Yancy *manufacturing company executive*

Vienna
Krejci, Stanley Leon *computer software company financial executive*
Savoca, Antonio Litterio *technology company executive*

Williamsburg
Godwin, R. Wayne *chemicals company executive*
Walters, Harry N. *manufacturing company executive*

Winchester
Holland, James Tulley *plastic products company executive*

WASHINGTON

Anacortes
Randolph, Carl Lowell *chemical company executive*

Auburn
Creighton, John W., Jr. *forest products company executive*

Bellevue
†Engebrecht, Richard E. *diversified distribution company executive*
Pigott, Charles McGee *transportation equipment manufacturing executive*
Puckett, Allen Weare *health care information systems executive*

Bellingham
Bestwick, Warren William *retired construction company executive*
Helsell, Robert M. *construction executive*

Eastwood
Anders, William Alison *aerospace and defense manufacturing executive*

Federal Way
Curtis, Arnold Bennett *lumber company executive*

Friday Harbor
Daum, David Ernest *machinery manufacturing company executive*

Issaquah
Tenenbaum, Michael *steel company executive*

Kennewick
Wistisen, Martin J. *agricultural business executive*

Kent
Goo, Abraham Meu Sen *retired aircraft company executive*
Hebeler, Henry Koester *retired aerospace and electronics executive*
Sourapas, Steve James *manufacturing executive*

Kirkland
Bernard, James William *corporate executive*
Parrish, John Brett *manufacturing executive*

Longview
Wollenberg, Richard Peter *paper manufacturing company executive*

Medina
Schlotterbeck, Walter Albert *manufacturing company executive, lawyer*

Mercer Island
Gould, Alvin R. *international business executive*

Moses Lake
Footer, Samuel Joseph *manufacturing company executive*

Pasco
Yoshino, George *food products executive*

Port Ludlow
Gullander, Werner Paul *retired consultant, retired corporate executive*

Richland
Nolan, John Edward *retired electrical corporation executive*

Seattle
Albrecht, Richard Raymond *airplane manufacturing company executive, lawyer*
Behnke, Carl Gilbert *beverage franchise executive*
Gillis, Steven *biotechnology company executive*
Hoerni, Jean Amédée *electronics consultant*
Holtby, Kenneth Fraser *aircraft manufacturing company consultant*
Jones, Frank Ray *biotechnology company executive, researcher*
Leland, David D. *timber company executive*
†Reed, William G., Jr. *paper company executive*
Schoenfeld, Walter Edwin *manufacturing company executive*
Shrontz, Frank Anderson *airplane manufacturing executive*
Stear, Edwin Byron *corporate executive*
†Wiborg, James Hooker *chemicals distribution company executive*

Tacoma
Carlson, Frederick Paul *electronics executive*
Erickson, Richard L. *wood products company executive*
Ferris, James Leonard *paper company executive*
Hutchings, George Henry *food company executive*
Meyer, Richard Schlomer *food company executive*
Weyerhaeuser, George Hunt *forest products company executive*

Vashon
†Munson, Dee Allison *food marketing executive, consultant*

WEST VIRGINIA

Charleston
Gunnoe, Nancy Lavenia *food executive, artist*
†Wehrle, Henry Bernard, Jr. *diversified manufacturing company executive*

Nitro
Magaw, Roger Wayne *construction company executive*

Parkersburg
Cochran, Douglas Eugene *building products company executive*
†Mason, Richard Gordon *lawn and garden tool manufacturing company executive*
Wakley, James Turner *manufacturing company executive*

Ravenswood
†Meyers, Gerald A. *metal products executive*

Weirton
Elish, Herbert *manufacturing company executive*

Wheeling
Chbosky, Fred G. *steel company executive*
†Exley, Ben, III *pharmaceutical company executive*
Good, Laurance Frederic *company executive*
Wareham, James Lyman *steel company executive*

WISCONSIN

Appleton
Barlow, F(rank) John *mechanical contracting company executive*
Boldt, Oscar Charles *construction company executive*
Buchanan, Robert Campbell *corporate professional*
Rankin, Arthur David *paper company executive*
†Schumaker, Dale H. *paper manufacturing company executive*

Baraboo
Brooks, Edward *dairy products company executive*
Storhoff, Donald C. *agricultural products company executive*

Beloit
Cole, J. Weldon *manufacturing executive*
Sovey, William Pierre *manufacturing company executive*

Brookfield
Corby, Francis Michael, Jr. *manufacturing company executive*
DeLuca, Donald Paul *manufacturing company executive*
†Grade, Jeffery T. *manufacturing company executive*

Cedarburg
Schaefer, Gordon Emory *food company executive*

Eau Claire
Berney, Joseph Henry *appliance manufacturing company executive*

Fond Du Lac
Chamberlain, Robert Glenn *retired executive*

Fort Atkinson
Nesbitt, Arthur Wallace *mail order and manufacturing executive*

Green Bay
†Backer, David F. *packing company executive*
De Meuse, Donald Howard *paper products manufacturing executive*
Hempel, Kathleen Jane *paper company executive*
Kress, George F. *packaging company executive*
Lenz, Randolph W. *manufacturing company executive*

Hartford
Lopina, Lawrence Thomas *manufacturing executive*

Hartland
Burlingame, Leroy James *manufacturing executive*

Kenosha
†Cornog, Robert A. *manufacturing executive*
†Jacobson, Dennis Leonard *business executive*
Steigerwaldt, Donna Wolf *clothing manufacturing company executive*
Tielke, James Clemens *manufacturing executive*

Kohler
†Kohler, Herbert Vollrath, Jr. *diversified manufacturing company executive*

La Crosse
Cleary, Russell George *retired brewery executive*
†Felten, Edward Joseph *business executive accountant*
Gelatt, Charles Daniel *manufacturing company executive*

Madison
Frautschi, Walter Albert *contract and publications printing company executive*
Shain, Irving *retired chemical company executive*

Manitowish Waters
Laidig, William Rupert *retired paper company executive*

Marion
Simpson, Vinson Raleigh *manufacturing company executive*

Medford
Sebold, Duane David *food manufacturing executive*

Menasha
Baird, Roger Allen *retired corporation executive*

Mequon
Dohmen, Frederick Hoeger *retired wholesale drug company executive*

Milwaukee
Beals, Vaughn Le Roy, Jr. *motorcycle and RV manufacturing executive*
Bishop, Charles Joseph *manufacturing company executive*
Burgess, Richard Ball *food products executive*
Chapman, William Paul *retired automatic control manufacturing company executive*
Feitler, Robert *shoe company executive*
†Florsheim, Thomas W. *shoe manufacturing company executive*
Hopkins, Edward Donald *manufacturing executive*
Jacobs, Burleigh Edmund *foundry executive*
Keuler, Roland Leo *retired shoe company executive*
Keyes, James Henry *manufacturing company executive*
Killian, William Paul *industrial corporate executive*
†MacDonough, John N. *beverage company executive*
Manning, Kenneth Paul *food company executive*
Marringa, Jacques Louis *manufacturing company executive*
Martin, Vincent Lionel *manufacturing company executive*
Morris, G. Ronald *automotive executive*
Mosher, George Allan *manufacturing company executive*
Novak, Victor Anthony *semi-retired manufacturing company executive*
Osborn, Guy A. *food products company executive*
O'Toole, Robert Joseph *manufacturing company executive*
Parker, Charles Walter, Jr. *consultant, retired equipment company executive*
Sanderson, Gary Warner *food company executive*
Sterner, Frank Maurice *industrial executive*
Stratton, Frederick Prescott, Jr. *manufacturing executive*
Yontz, Kenneth Fredric *medical and chemical company executive*

Mosinee
†Radt, Richard Louis *paper company executive*

Neenah
Bergstrom, Dedric Waldemar *retired paper company executive*
†Brophy, George Thomas *building products company executive*
†Parker, Richard E. *building products manufacturing company executive*

Oshkosh
Goodson, Raymond Eugene *automotive executive*
Hulsebosch, Charles Joseph *truck manufacturing company executive*

Pewaukee
Dickson, John R. *food products company executive, dairy products company executive*

Port Edwards
Veneman, Gerard Earl *paper company executive*

Racine
Batten, Michael Ellsworth *manufacturing company executive*
Campbell, Edward Joseph *retired machinery company executive*
Carlson, Robert John *manufacturing company executive*
Fitch, Robert McLellan *business and technology consultant*
Gunnerson, Robert Mark *manufacturing company executive, accountant, lawyer*
Johnson, Samuel Curtis *wax company executive*
Konz, Gerald Keith *manufacturing company executive*
†Malone, Terence S. *chemical company executive*
Savage, Richard T. *manufacturing company executive*

Spring Green
Sisson, Everett Arnold *industrial developer, business executive*

Wausau
Nemirow, Arnold Myles *manufacturing executive*
†Niederhofer, Laurence John *metals company executive*
Slayton, John Arthur *electric motor manufacturing executive*

Wisconsin Rapids
Engelhardt, LeRoy A. *retired paper company executive*
Mead, George Wilson, II *paper company executive*

WYOMING

Casper
Stroock, Thomas Frank *business executive*

Cheyenne
†Ray, Michael Franklyn *chemical company executive*

Jackson
Gordon, Stephen Maurice *manufacturing company executive, rancher*

CANADA

ALBERTA

Calgary
Child, Arthur James Edward *food company executive*
Gordon, Lorne Bertram *corporate executive*
Southern, Ronald Donald *diversified corporation executive*

Edmonton
Bateman, William Maxwell *retired construction company executive*
Stollery, Robert *construction company executive*

BRITISH COLUMBIA

North Vancouver
Gibbs, David George *retired food processing company executive*

Vancouver
Bender, Graham I. *forest products executive*
Bentley, Peter John Gerald *forest industry company executive*
Buell, Thomas Allan *lumber company executive*
Donald, Ian *wood products company executive*
Grunder, Arthur Neil *forest products industry executive*
Knudsen, Conrad Calvert *corporate director*
†McLauchlin, D. L. *building materials manufacturing executive*
Smith, Raymond Victor *paper products manufacturing executive*
Solloway, C. Robert *forest products company executive*
Warner, Colin Bertram *retired forest products executive*

MANITOBA

Winnipeg
MacKenzie, George Allan *diversified company executive*
Searle, Stewart A. *transportation equipment holding company executive*

NEW BRUNSWICK

Edmundston
O'Briain, Niall P. *wood products company executive*

Fredericton
Grotterod, Knut *retired paper company executive*

Moncton
Walker, Tennyson A. *corporation executive*

NOVA SCOTIA

Halifax
Thompson, William Grant *management executive*

Lunenburg
Morrow, James Benjamin *retired sea products company executive*

North Sydney
Nickerson, Jerry Edgar Alan *manufacturing executive*

Stellarton
Rowe, Allan Duncan *food products executive*
Sobey, David Frank *food company executive*

ONTARIO

Blenheim
Thompson, Wesley Duncan *grain merchant*

Brampton
Buckland, Charles Smillie *can company executive*
Greenhough, John Hardman *business forms company executive*
Prevost, Edward James *paint manufacturing executive*

Cambridge
Turnbull, Robert Scott *manufacturing company executive*
White, Joseph Charles *manufacturing and retailing company executive*

Fort Erie
Watson, Stewart Charles *construction company executive*

Galt
Dobbie, George Herbert *textile manufacturing executive*

Hamilton
McMulkin, Francis John *steel company executive*
Miles, John Frederick *manufacturing company executive*
Phoenix, Paul Joseph *steel manufacturing company executive*
Priestner, Edward Bernard *manufacturing company executive*
Telmer, Frederick Harold *steel products manufacturing executive*

Kanata
Morrison, John A. *health products company executive*

Kitchener
Pollock, John Albon *broadcasting and manufacturing company executive*

Markham
Stronach, Frank *automobile parts manufacturing executive*

Mississauga
Barkin, Martin *pharmaceutical company executive, physician*
Lewis, William Leonard *food products executive*
MacNaughton, John David Francis *aerospace company executive*
†Strachen, Graham *pharmaceutical company executive*

North York
Wleugel, John Peter *manufacturing company executive*

Oakville
Mattson, Bradford Craig *manufacturing company executive*

Oshawa
Peapples, George Alan *automotive executive*

Ottawa
Lander, Donald H. *postal agency executive*

Owen Sound
Adams, John David Vessot *manufacturing company executive*

Rexdale
Lutgens, Harry Gerardus *food company executive*

Toronto
†Arnold, Neil David *farm and industrial equipment company executive*
Blundell, William Richard Charles *electric company executive*
Cameron, Peter Alfred Gordon *corporate executive*
Cohen, Marshall *diversified international corporation executive*
Connell, Philip Francis *food industry executive*
Crean, John Gale *hat manufacturer*
Dale, Robert Gordon *business executive*
Eagles, Stuart Ernest *business executive*
Eisen, Leonard *food and retail company executive*
Freeman, Graham P. M. *food company executive*
Goodrich, Maurice Keith *business forms, systems and services company executive*
Griffin, Scott *manufacturing executive*
Horsey, William Grant *corporation executive*
Koken, Bernd Krafft *forest products company executive*
Lanthier, Ronald Ross *retired manufacturing company executive*
Lowe, Donald Cameron *corporate director*
Mack, Edward Gibson *retired business executive*
Matthews, Paul Deacon *steel company executive*
†Mercier, Eileen Ann *forest products executive*
Oberlander, Ronald Y. *paper manufacturing company executive*
Oland, Sidney M. *brewing and entertainment company executive*
Porter, Ivan *company executive*
Rusnell, Joanne D. *brewery, entertainment business executive*
Seagram, Norman Meredith *corporate executive*
Thomas, Alan Richard *natural resources products executive*
Turner, Peter Merrick *retired manufacturing company executive*
Vance, James *retired manufacturing company executive, lawyer*
Van Houten, Stephen H. *manufacturing company executive*
Wolfe, Jonathan A. *food wholesaler, retailer*

Unionville
Suddick, Patrick Joseph *defense systems company executive*

Willowdale
McDonald, William Henry *manufacturing executive*

Windsor
Ferguson, James Peter *distilling company executive*
Landry, G. Yves *automotive company executive*

QUEBEC

Athelstan
Ness, Owen McGregor *retired aluminum company executive*

Laval
Guindon, Yvan *pharmaceutical company research executive*

Longueuil
Caplan, L(azarus) David *manufacturing company executive*
Smith, Elvie Lawrence *aircraft company executive*

Montreal
Beauchamp, Jacques *wood products executive*
Bougie, Jacques *metal processing executive*
Bronfman, Charles Rosner *distillery executive*
Gagné, Paul E. *paper company executive*
Hantho, Charles Harold *textile executive*
Hart, William D., Jr. *food retailing company executive*
Herling, Michael *steel company executive*
Ivanier, Isin *manufacturing company executive*
Ivanier, Paul *steel products manufacturing company executive*
Miller, Michael Chilcott d'Elboux *metal products executive*
Molson, Eric H. *corporate company executive*
Morton, David *aluminum company executive*
Nadeau, Bertin F. *diversified company executive*
Pal, Prabir Kumar *aluminium company executive*
Pinard, Raymond R. *pulp and paper consultant*
Plourde, Gerard *company director*
Poissant, Charles-Albert *paper manufacturing company executive*
Redfern, John D. *manufacturing company executive*
Rolland, Lucien G. *paper company executive*
Royer, Raymond *transportation equipment manufacturing company executive*
Rugeroni, Ian *aluminum company executive*
Simons, John H. *electronics manufacturing company executive*
Smith, James Hamilton *paper, packaging, construction material and chemicals company executive*
Toole, David George *pulp and paper products executive*

Outremont
Gouin, Serge *corporate executive*
Larose, Roger *former pharmaceutical company executive, former university administrator*

Pointe Claire
Wrist, Peter Ellis *pulp and paper company executive*

Quebec
†Filion, Louis Jacques *business and economics educator*

Saint Lambert
Brossard, Maurice *biotechnology company executive*

Verdun
Ferguson, Michael John *electronics and communications educator*

Ville Saint Laurent
Kivenko, Kenneth *aerospace industry executive*

SASKATCHEWAN

Regina
Dalla-Vicenza, Mario Joseph *steel company financial executive*
Phillips, Roger *steel company executive*

Saskatoon
Carr, Roy Arthur *agricultural products processing research organization executive*

MEXICO

Mexico City
Brown, Kenneth Charles *manufacturing company executive*
Martinez-Tejeda, Juan J. *manufacturing company executive*

AUSTRALIA

Melbourne
Lawson, Francis Colin *chemical company executive*

BELGIUM

Antwerp
De Craene, Jacques Maria *plastics company executive, retired judge, arbitrator*

Beerse
Janssen, Paul Adriaan Jan *pharmaceutical company executive*

Blanden
Holleweg dit Wegman, Willy *management expert, educator, entrepreneurship development specialist*

Brussels
Loutrel, Claude Yves *corporate official*

ENGLAND

Berkshire
Hall, Arnold Alexander *aeronautical, mechanical and electrical executive*

East Sussex
Wilson, Leroy *retired glass manufacturing company executive*

London
Bates, Malcolm Rowland *corporate director*
Greener, Anthony *beverage company executive*
Shaw, Sir Neil McGowan *sugar, cereal-starch refining company executive*
Sheehy, Sir Patrick *manufacturing and service company executive*
Taylor, Jonathan Francis *agribusiness executive*

Manchester
Knowlton, Thomas A. *food products executive*

Poole
Stokes, Donald Gresham *vehicle company executive*

Suffolk
Clement, John *food products company executive*

Walton on Thames
Olney, Robert C. *diversified products manufacturing executive*

West Dayton
Caskey, William Joslin *food products executive*

FRANCE

Chatenay-Malabry
Fabre, Raoul François *electronics company executive*

Courbevoie
Desmarescaux, Philippe *chemical company executive, engineer*

Genlis
van Raalte, John A *research and engineering management executive*

Le Plessis Robinson
Régnier, François Jean *pharmaceutical company executive*

Paris
Collomb, Bertrand Pierre *cement company executive*
DuBois, Jean Gabriel *pharmaceutical executive, pharmacist*
Jaclot, Francois Charles *manufacturing executive*
Larounis, George Philip *manufacturing company executive*
Lecerf, Olivier Maurice Marie *construction company executive*

Thonon-les-Bains
Savin, Ronald Richard *chemical company executive, inventor*

GERMANY

Gütersloh
Wössner, Mark Matthias *media company executive*

Munich
†Kniehl, Hans Joachim *construction company executive*

HONG KONG

Hong Kong
Lui, Ming Wah *electronics executive*
†Sherrill, Joseph Harlan, Jr. *tobacco company executive*
Wong, Wing Keung *trading, electronics company executive, physician*

Wanchai
van Hoften, James Dougal Adrianus *business executive, former astronaut*

INDIA

Chandigarh
†Saboo, Rajendra K. *manufacturing executive*

ISRAEL

Haifa
Galil, Uzia *electronics company executive*

ITALY

Milan
Poluzzi, Amleto *chemical company consultant*

Rome
Lynch, Edward Stephen *corporate executive*

Turin
Agnelli, Giovanni *industrial executive*

JAPAN

Kitakyushu
Takeda, Yoshiyuki *chemical company executive*

Tokyo
Akasaki, Toshiro *machinery manufacturing executive*
†Ishikawa, Rokuro *construction company executive*
Johnson, Keith Gilbert *heavy equipment company executive*
†Kaku, Ryuzaburo *precision instruments manufacturing company executive*
Koehler, John Edget *electronics company executive*
Makino, Shojiro (Mike Makino) *chemicals executive*
Morita, Akio *electronics company executive*
†Ohga, Norio *electronics executive*
Ranney, Maurice William *chemical company executive*
Smith, Robert Lee *photographic company executive*

Toyota Aichi
Toyoda, Eiji *automobile manufacturing company executive*

NEW CALEDONIA

Noumea
Curlook, Walter *mining company executive*

SAUDI ARABIA

Al Khobar
Ashadawi, Ahmed Ali *computer consultancy company executive*

SCOTLAND

Edinburgh
Miller, James *construction company executive*

SPAIN

Madrid
Feltenstein, Harry David, Jr. *chemical executive*

SWEDEN

Falun
Helgesson, Lars-Ake *manufacturing executive*

Gothenburg
Andersson, Leif Per Roland *construction company executive*
Gyllenhammar, Pehr Gustaf *retired automobile company executive, writer*

Linköping
Schröder, Harald Bertel *aerospace industry executive*

SWITZERLAND

Fribourg
Hatschek, Rudolf Alexander *electronics company executive*

Zurich
Barnevik, Percy Nils *electrical company executive*
Peterson, M. Roger *manufacturing executive, retired air force officer*

TAIWAN

Taipei
Ch'in, Michael Kuo-hsing *international conference management executive*

ADDRESS UNPUBLISHED

†Abele, Fred Raymond *metal processing executive*
Abraham, George G. *retired packing company executive*
†Adelman, Robert Paul *retired construction company executive, lawyer*
Albino, George Robert *business executive*
Alibrandi, Joseph Francis *diversified industrial company executive*
Alig, Frank Douglas Stalnaker *construction company executive*
Anderer, Joseph Henry *textile company executive*
Anderson, Fletcher Neal *chemical executive*
Anderson, Joseph Norman *executive consultant, former food company executive, former college president*
Andreuzzi, Denis *chemical company executive*
Andrews, William Frederick *manufacturing executive*
Anspach, Herbert Kephart *retired appliance company executive, patent attorney*
Archibald, Nolan D. *household and industrial products company executive*
†Armacost, John Cooper *packaging company executive*
Armstrong, John Allan *business machine company research executive*
Arnold, David Burton *tooling systems company executive*
Aschauer, Charles Joseph, Jr. *corporate director, former company executive*
Ashcraft, Charles Olin *business educator*
Auriemma, Louis Francis *printing company executive*
Austin, Ralph Leroy *chemicals executive*
Azarnoff, Daniel Lester *pharmaceutical company consultant*
Barca, George Gino *winery executive, finanial investor*
†Barkeley, Norman A. *vehicle manufacturing company executive*
Barnebey, Kenneth Alan *food company executive*
Barron, Charles Elliott *retired electronics executive*
Bass, Robert Olin *manufacturing executive*
Bauer, Victor John *pharmaceutical company executive*
Beadle, John Grant *manufacturing company executive*
Beighey, Lawrence Jerome *packaging company executive*
Belles, Anita Louise *health care researcher*
Bennett, Richard Thomas *retired manufacturing executive*
Berra, Robert Louis *chemicals consultant*
Bierwirth, John Cocks *retired aerospace manufacturing executive*
Biggs, Arthur Edward *retired chemical manufacturing company executive*
Birkenstock, James Warren *business machine manufacturing company executive*
Blair, Charles Melvin *scientist, manufacturing company executive*
Bliss, William Stanley, Jr. *manufacturing company executive*
Bloom, Frank *corporation executive, consultant*
Boileau, Oliver Clark, Jr. *aerospace company executive*
Borten, William H. *research company executive*
Bossier, Albert Louis, Jr. *shipbuilding company executive*
Boxall, Richard George *construction materials company executive*
Brancato, Leo John *manufacturing company executive*
Brengel, Fred Lenhardt *manufacturing company executive*
Brinckerhoff, Richard Charles *retired manufacturing company executive*
†Brooker, Robert Elton, Jr. *manufacturing company executive*
Brown, Barton *retired automotive company executive*
Burge, John Wesley, Jr. *electric manufacturing company executive, consultant*
Butler, Jack Fairchild *semiconductors company executive*
Buxton, Winslow Hurlbert *diversified manufacturing company executive*
Calvert, James Francis *manufacturing company executive, retired admiral*
Carpenter, Myron Arthur *manufacturing company executive*
Carter, Joseph Edwin *former nickel company executive, writer*
Chamberlain, George Arthur, III *manufacturing company executive, venture capitalist*
Chen, Di *electro-optic company executive, consultant*
Chmielinski, Edward Alexander *electronics company executive*
Chryssis, George Christopher *business executive*
Closset, Gerard Paul *forest products company executive*
Clouston, Ross Neal *retired food and related products company executive*
Cohn, Leonard Allan *retired chemical company executive*
Colton, Nelson Burton *industrial company executive*
Cooley, James William *retired executive researcher*
Cooper, Norton J. *liquor and wine company executive*
Corddry, Paul Imlay *retired food products company executive*
Costello, James Joseph *retired electrical manufacturing company executive*
Cowley, William Eugene *former manufacturing company executive*
Cox, John Francis *retired cosmetic company executive*
Cox, Wilford Donald *retired food company executive*
Craft, Edmund Coleman *automotive parts manufacturing company executive*
Cramer, William F. *capitol goods executive*
Cross, Alexander Dennis *business consultant, former chemical and pharmaceutical executive*
Cull, Robert Robinette *electric products manufacturing company executive*
Culwell, Charles Louis *retired manufacturing company executive*
Daeschner, Richard Wilbur *former food company executive*
D'Agostino, Stephen I. *bottling company executive*
Daly, William James *retired health industry distributing company executive*
Danis, Peter G., Jr. *office products company executive*
Daugherty, Alfred Clark *manufacturing company executive*
Davis, Darrell L. *automotive executive*
Decker, Gilbert Felton *manufacturing company executive*
†Denisco, Ralph Andrew *ice cream industry executive*
Derbes, Daniel William *corporate executive*
Dohrmann, Russell William *manufacturing company executive*
Dole, Robert Paul *retired appliance manufacturing company executive*
Dowden, Albert Ricker *corporate executive, lawyer*
Doyle, John Laurence *manufacturing company executive*
Dozier, Glenn Joseph *medical, surgical products distribution executive*
Dragon, William, Jr. *footwear and apparel company executive*
Drebus, Richard William *pharmaceutical company executive*
Drew, Walter Harlow *retired paper manufacturing company executive*
Driscoll, William Michael *corporation executive*
†Dugan, Michael Kevin *furniture manufacturing company executive*
Durham, G. Robert *diversified manufacturing company executive*
Durr, Robert Joseph *construction firm executive, mechanical engineer*
Earle, Arthur Percival *textile executive*
Eberle, Charles Edward *paper and consumer products executive*
Eihusen, Virgil R. *retired manufacturing company executive*
Elverum, Gerard William, Jr. *retired electronic and diversified company executive*
Ely, Paul C., Jr. *electronics company executive*
Erdeljac, Daniel Joseph *retired concrete pipe company executive*
Farley, John Michael *steel industry consultant*
Feinberg, Herbert *apparel and beverage executive*
Fenger, Manfred *retired manufacturing executive*
†Filizetti, Gary John *construction executive*
Fischer, William Donald *retired food executive*
Fitch, Steven Joseph *retired chemicals executive*
Flaschen, Steward Samuel *high technology company executive*
Flitcraft, Richard Kirby, II *former chemical company executive*
Ford, Jerry Lee *products company executive*
Fossier, Mike Walter *consultant, retired electronics company executive*
Foster, Edson L. *retired mining and manufacturing company executive, consultant*
Frame, Russell William *retired electronics executive*
Frankel, Arnold J. *chemical company executive*
Fraser, Campbell *business consultant*
French, Clarence Levi, Jr. *retired shipbuilding company executive*
Frieling, Gerald Harvey, Jr. *specialty steel company executive*
Fritz, Rene Eugene, Jr. *manufacturing executive*
Fuller, James Chester Eedy *retired chemical company executive*
Geoppinger, William Anthony *meat processing company executive*
Georgas, John William *beverage manufacturing company executive*
Gillespie, Robert James *manufacturing company executive*
Gillette, Stanley C. *apparel manufacturing company executive*
Gilreath, Warren Dean *retired packaging company executive*
Giordano, Richard Vincent *chemical executive*
Good, Daniel James *manufacturing executive*
Gordon, Stewart George *manufacturing company executive*
Grandy, James Frederick *retired electronics business executive, consultant*
Gray, Donna Mae *former agricultural products executive, bookkeeper*
Gray, Richard Alexander, Jr. *retired chemical company executive*
Green, David Thomas *retired surgical company research and development executive, inventor*
Greenberg, Milton *corporation executive*
Gregg, Michael W. *manufacturing executive*
Griffith, Daniel Boyd *automotive products executive*
†Grubiak, James Frank *chewing gum executive*
Gulcher, Robert Harry *aircraft company executive*
Gurney, Daniel Sexton *race car manufacturing company executive, racing team executive*
Hager, Robert Worth *retired aerospace company executive*
Hamilton, James Marvie *electronics company executive*
Hammond, Robert Lee *retired feed company executive*
Harrell, Henry Howze *tobacco company executive*
†Haskew, George M., Jr. *utility executive*
Hatchett, Edward Earl *retired aerospace manufacturing company executive*
Hausman, Arthur Herbert *electronics company executive*
Hayes, John Patrick *retired manufacturing company executive*
Heggie, Robert James *steel company executive*
Heilmann, Christian Flemming *corporate executive*
Heller, Ronald Gary *manufacturing company executive, lawyer*
†Helzberg, Barnett C. *company executive*
Hemann, Raymond Glenn *aerospace research company executive*
Herbert, Ira C. *food processing company executive*
Herbert, John Warren *forest products executive*
Hiatt, Arnold *shoe manufacturer, importer, retailer*
†Hiller, William Arlington *agriculture executive*
Hirsch, Horst Eberhard *business consultant*
Holster, Robert Marc *health care information company executive*
Hudson, Franklin Donald *diversified company executive*
Iacocca, Lido Anthony (Lee Iacocca) *former automotive manufacturing executive*
Irani, Raymond Reza *electro-mechanical company executive*
Jacoby, Stanley Arthur *retired manufacturing company executive*
Jaicks, Frederick Gillies *retired steel company executive*
Jedenoff, George Alexander *steel consultant*
Johnson, Irving Stanley *pharmaceutical company executive, scientist*
Johnson, Rogers Bruce *retired chemical company executive*
Johnson, Warren Donald *retired pharmaceutical executive, former air force officer*
Johnson, William E. *manufacturing company executive*
Jones, Robert Henry *corporate executive*
Judelson, David N. *company executive*
Kapcsandy, Louis Endre *building construction and manufacturing executive, chemical engineering consultant*
Kasperczyk, Jürgen *business executive, member Parliament, educator*
Katz, Leon *packaging company executive*
Kelly, Alonzo Hyatt, Jr. *retired automotive company engineering executive*
Kelly, Anthony Odrian *flooring manufacturing company executive*
Kerber, Ronald Lee *industrial corporation executive*
Kern, Irving John *retired food company executive*
Kerstetter, Michael James *retired manufacturing company executive*
King, Susan Bennett *retired glass company executive*
Kleiman, Ansel *retired electronics company executive*
Koehler, Rudolph August *manufacturing company executive*
Kondo, Masatoshi S. *pharmaceutical executive, educator*
Kongabel, H. Fred *industrial construction company executive*
Krause, Werner William *plastics company executive*
Krull, Charles Fred *food research executive, geneticist*
Kudrnac, Kristian Ivoj *chemical executive*
Kulik, Rosalyn Franta *food company executive, consultant*
Kuske, Edward Alan *chemical company executive*
Labrecque, Richard Joseph *manufacturing company executive*
Landon, Robert Gray *retired manufacturing company executive*
Langenberg, Frederick Charles *business executive*
Lathlaen, Robert Frank *retired construction company executive*
Laurent, Robert Louis, Jr. *manufacturing executive*
Lavington, Michael Richard *venture capital company executive*
†Lazay, Paul Duane *telecommunications manufacturing company executive*
Leff, Joseph Norman *yarn manufacturing company executive*
Lego, Paul Edward *retired corporation executive*
Lehman, John F., Jr. *industrialist*
Lennox, Donald D(uane) *automotive and housing components company executive*
Levenson, Harvey Stuart *manufacturing company executive*
Lewis, Martin R. *paper company executive*
Lewis, Rita Hoffman *plastic products manufacturing company executive*
Lindars, Laurence Edward *retired health care products executive*
Lindsay, Franklin Anthony *business executive, author*
Lodge, David Williams *retired corporation executive*
Logan, John Francis *electronics company executive*
Lotz, Arthur William *retired engineering and construction company executve*
Lowden, John L. *retired corporate executive*
Lucas, William Ray *aerospace consultant*
MacLachlan, Alexander *chemical company executive, retired*
Madden, Richard Blaine *forest products executive*
Manchester, Kenneth Edward *electronics executive, consultant*
Marks, Raymond H. *chemical company executive*
Marrington, Bernard Harvey *retired automotive company executive*
Martin, Albert Charles *manufacturing executive, lawyer*
Mason, Frank Henry, III *automobile company executive, leasing company executive*
May, Kenneth Nathaniel *food industry consultant*
Mayhew, Lawrence Lee *electronics company executive*
McCabe, Charles Law *retired manufacturing company executive, management consultant*
McCarragher, Bernard John *retired manufacturing company executive*
McDade, William Joseph *manufacturing consulting company executive*
McGillivray, Donald Dean *agricultural products executive*
Mc Intyre, Robert Allen, Jr. *business turnaround executive*
McKenna, Quentin Carnegie *tool company executive*
McNeeley, Donald Robert *steel company executive*
McNeil, Steven Arthur *food company executive*
Melvin, T. Stephen *manufacturing company executive*
Michalik, Edward Francis *construction company executive*
Miles, Robert Henry *management educator, consultant, educational administrator*

Miller, Harold Edward *retired manufacturing conglomerate executive, consultant*
Miller, Leland Bishop, Jr. *food processing company executive*
Miller, Lowell Donald *pharmaceutical company research executive*
Miskowski, Lee R. *automobile executive*
Mitchel, F(rederick) Kent *retired food company executive*
Mooney, John Allen *retired food company executive*
Moore, Vernon Lee *agricultural consultant, retired food products company executive*
Moran, Gordon William *papers and fabrics company executive*
Morris, Albert Jerome *biological pest control company executive*
Moses, Robert Davis *retired diversified industry executive*
Mott, Stewart Rawlings *business executive, political activist*
Mudd, Sidney Peter *former beverage company executive*
Munisteri, Joseph George *construction executive*
Murphy, Bernard Thomas *electronics executive, researcher, consultant*
Myers, Albert G., Jr. *textile manufacturer*
Neese, Elbert Haven *retired paper machinery manufacturing executive*
Neff, Jack Kenneth *apparel manufacturing company executive*
†Nelson, Robert Gary *textile executive*
Nesheim, Robert Olaf *food products executive*
Newman, Phillip Barbour, III *distilling company executive*
Nielsen, Emiel Theodore, Jr. *retired manufacturing company executive*
Nord, Eric Thomas *manufacturing executive*
Nordlund, Donald Elmer *manufacturing company executive*
Oaks, Maurice David *retired pharmaceutical company executive*
Obolensky, Marilyn Wall (Mrs. Serge Obolensky) *metals company executive*
Oelman, Robert Schantz *retired manufacturing executive*
Ordal, Caspar Reuben *business executive*
Papadopoulos, Stelios B. *scientific, medical products company executive*
Parker, George *retired pen manufacturing company executive*
Parker, Thomas Lee *business executive*
Pearce, Paul Francis *retired aerospace electronics company executive*
Peck, Daniel Farnum *chemical company executive*
Perelman, Leon Joseph *paper manufacturing executive, university president*
Petok, Samuel *retired manufacturing company executive*
Phillips, William George *retired food products executive*
Piergallini, Alfred A. *food products executive*
Pitstick, Leslie James *food products company executive*
Poss, John Claybron *corporate executive*
Pratt, Edmund Taylor, Jr. *pharmaceutical company executive*
Precopio, Frank Mario *chemical company executive*
Pruis, John J. *business executive*
Rajki, Walter Albert *manufacturing company executive*
Ramsey, Claude Swanson, Jr. *former industrial executive*
Rhodes, Peter Edward *label company executive*
Richman, Paul *semiconductor industry executive, educator*
Richman, Peter *electronics executive*
Robinson, Edward Joseph *cosmetics company executive*
Roller, Thomas Benjamin *manufacturing company executive*
Romans, Donald Bishop *corporate executive*
Rooke, David Lee *retired chemical company executive*
Roper, John Lonsdale, III *shipyard executive*
Rosenthal, Ely Manuel (Manny Rosenthal) *retired meat company executive, consultant*
Rudy, Raymond Bruce, Jr. *retired food company executive*
Ruttner, Albert A. *manufacturing company executive*
Rydz, John S. *manufacturing executive*
Salathe, John, Jr. *manufacturing company executive*
Salbaing, Pierre Alcee *retired chemical company executive*
Saltarelli, Eugene A. *retired engineering and construction company executive, consultant*
Samek, Michael Johann *corporation executive*
Samper, Joseph Phillip *retired photographic products company executive*
Sanders, Wayne R. *manufacturing executive*
Sauvey, Donald (Robert) *retired musical instrument company executive*
Scheele, Paul Drake *former hospital supply corporate executive*
Schlensker, Gary Chris *landscaping company executive*
†Schmergel, Gabriel *pharmaceutical company executive*
Schroeter, Louis C. *retired pharmaceutical company executive*
Schwartz, Robert *automotive manufacturing company executive, marketing executive*
Schwartz, Samuel *business consultant, retired chemical company executive*
Schwartzberg, Martin M. *chemical company executive*
Schwier, Frederick Warren *manufacturing company executive*
Shames, Ervin Richard *food and chemical company executive*
Shepherd, Mark, Jr. *retired electronics company executive*
Shipley, Lucia Helene *retired chemical company executive*
Shriber, Maurice Norden *research and manufacturing company executive*
Siegel, Jack Morton *retired biotechnology company executive*
†Silverman, Michael *manufacturing company executive*
Simeral, William Goodrich *retired chemical company executive*
Simmons, Bradley Williams *pharmaceutical company executive*
Simon, Michael Paul *general contractor, realtor*
Smith, Frederick Coe *manufacturing executive*
Smith, Goff *industrial equipment manufacturing executive*
Snetsinger, David Clarence *retired animal feed company executive*
Somes, Daniel E. *retired building materials company executive*
Sommer, Howard Ellsworth *textile executive*
Sorensen, Robert Holm *diversified technology company executive, retired*
Southerland, S. Duane *manufacturing company executive*
Spliethoff, William Ludwig *chemical company executive*
Stamper, Malcolm Theodore *aerospace company executive*
Stark, Donald Gerald *pharmaceutical executive*
Starr, Leon *retired chemical research company executive*
Stefan, Steve A. *manufacturing company executive*
Stern, Arthur Paul *electronics company executive, electrical engineer*
Stern, Milton *chemical company executive*
Stewart, Peter Beaufort *retired beverage company executive*
Stickler, Fred Charles *manufacturing company executive*
Stivers, William Charles *forest products company executive*
Stratton, Robert *electronics company executive*
Strauss, Simon David *manufacturing executive*
Swanger, Sterling Orville *appliance manufacturing company executive*
Swihart, John Marion *retired aircraft manufacturing company executive*
Tallett, Elizabeth Edith *biopharmaceutical company executive*
Talley, Robert Morrell *aerospace company executive*
Thom, Douglas Andrew *paper company executive*
Thompson, Ralph Newell *former chemical corporation executive*
Thornburg, Frederick Fletcher *diversified business executive, lawyer*
Tippett, Willis Paul, Jr. *automotive and textile company executive, retired*
Tombros, Peter George *pharmaceutical company executive*
Tucci, Daniel Patrick *chemicals executive*
Turnbull, John Neil *retired chemical company executive*
Van Tassel, James Henry *retired electronics executive*
van't Hoff, Winfried C. J. *retired diversified manufacturing executive*
Ver Vynck-Potter, Virginia Mary *construction executive*
Volkhardt, John Malcolm *food company executive*
Walsh, William Albert *business executive, former naval officer*
†Walter, James W. *diversified manufacturing executive*
Weir, Paul Joseph *retired corporation executive*
Welch, Oliver Wendell *retired pharmaceutical executive*
Wesson, William Simpson *retired paper company executive*
White, Gerald Andrew *chemical company executive*
Wiesen, Donald Guy *retired diversified manufacturing company executive*
†Wigdor, Lawrence A. *chemical company executive*
Winters, Nola Frances *food company executive*
Witcher, Daniel Dougherty *retired pharmaceutical company executive*
Witt, Hugh Ernest *technology consultant*
Wolf, Hans Abraham *retired pharmaceutical company executive*
Wolfberg, Melvin Donald *corporate vice president, college president, consultant, optometrist*
Wolfe, Theodore Joseph *food company executive*
Wollert, Gerald Dale *retired food company executive, investor*
Wommack, W(illiam) W(alton) *retired manufacturing company executive*
Woodall, Jack David *manufacturing company executive*
Young, John Alan *electronics company executive*
Zandman, Felix *electronics executive*
Zanetti, Joseph Maurice, Jr. *corporate executive*

INDUSTRY: SERVICE

UNITED STATES

ALABAMA

Birmingham
Bruno, Ronald G. *food service executive*
†Floyd, John Alex, Jr. *editor, marketing executive, horticulturist*
Gunter, John Richmond *communications executive*
†Harbert, Raymond J. *transportation executive*
Harris, Aaron *management consultant*
Henderson, Louis Clifton, Jr. *management consultant*
Jones, Arthur McDonald, Sr. *consumer products company executive*
Parker, John Malcolm *management and financial consultant*
Sturgeon, Charles Edwin *management consultant*
†Whitehead, Lewis E, Jr. *automotive consultant, management consultant*

Huntsville
Meadlock, James W. *computer graphics company executive*

Mobile
Boone, Louis Eugene *business and management educator, author*

Montgomery
Robinson, Peter Clark *general management executive*
Schloss, Samuel Leopold, Jr. *food service executive*

Ohatchee
Ellis, Bernice Allred *personnel executive*

Tuscaloosa
Barban, Arnold Melvin *advertising educator*

ALASKA

Anchorage
Brady, Carl Franklin *retired aircraft charter company executive*
Harris, Orville D. *transportation executive*
Hopkins, Stephen Davis *retired business executive*

ARIZONA

Cave Creek
O'Reilly, Thomas Eugene *human resources consultant*

Chandler
Williams, James Eugene, Jr. *management consultant*

Flagstaff
Putnam, William Lowell *retired travel bureau director, science association administrator*

Green Valley
Desjarlais, Erika Else *retired management analyst*
Egger, Roscoe L., Jr. *consultant*

Mesa
†Murphy, Edward Francis *sales executive*

Paradise Valley
De Shazor, Ashley Dunn *business consultant*
Grimm, James R. (Ronald Grimm) *multi-industry executive*
Hann, J(ames) David *information systems company executive*
Swanson, Robert Killen *management consultant*

Peoria
Schindler, William Stanley *retired public relations executive*

Phoenix
Armstrong, Nelson William, Jr. *gaming company executive*
Arriola, David Bruce *resort and hotel marketing executive*
Black, Joseph *marketing consultant, former corporation executive*
Brown, Bart A., Jr. *consumer products company executive*
Cohen, Melvin Stephen *jewelry company executive*
Drain, Albert Sterling *business management consultant*
Emerson, Frederick George *transportation company executive*
Evans, Ronald Allen *lodging chain executive*
Gochnauer, Richard Wallis *consumer products company executive*
Hallier, Gerard Edouard *hotel chain executive*
Heller, Mitchell Thomas *hotel company executive*
†Hill, Edward G. *food marketing executive*
Howard, William Matthew *business executive, arbitrator, lawyer, author*
Lemon, Leslie Gene *consumer products and services company executive, lawyer*
Miller, Arthur Leonard *sales representative, retired educator*
†Mottek, Carl T. *hotel company executive*
Murian, Richard Miller *book company executive*
Snell, Richard *holding company executive*
Teets, John William *diversifed company executive*
Turner, William Cochrane *international management consultant*
Ward, Yvette Hennig *advertising executive*

Prescott
Harris, Earl Edward *business educator*

Scottsdale
Chauncey, Tom *retired radio and television executive*
Doglione, Arthur George *data processing executive*
Gall, Donald Alan *data processing executive*
Garelick, Martin *transportation executive*
Messinger, Cora R. *funeral director*
Pavlik, Nancy *convention services executive*
Peterson, Louis Robert *retired consumer products company executive*
Willoughby, Carroll Vernon *retired motel chain executive*
Wright, James Corwin *international management consultant*

Sedona
Wolfe, Al *marketing and advertising consultant*

Show Low
Collins, Copp *federal, corporate, institutional consultant*

Sun City West
Curtin, Richard Daniel *management consultant, retired air force officer, space pioneer*

Tempe
Bennett, ElDean *mass communication educator, broadcaster*
Converti, Vincenzo *computer systems company executive*
Goyer, Robert Stanton *communication educator*
Gwinner, Robert Fred, Jr. *marketing educator*
†Hald, Alan P. *computer company executive*
†McKeever, Jeffrey D. *computer company executive*
Wales, Hugh Gregory *marketing educator, business executive*

Tucson
Auslander, Steven Lawrence *advertising executive, newspaper editor*
Barton, Stanley Faulkner *management consultant*
Hampel, Alvin *advertising executive*
Jones, Frank Wyman *management consultant, mechanical engineer*
King, Marcia *management consultant*
Lewis, Wilbur H. *educational management consultant*
Rose, Hugh *management consultant*
†Waterbrook, Keith Jennings *hospital administrator, educator*

ARKANSAS

Conway
†Bartos, Phil *information management technology executive*
†Kline, Rodger S. *marketing professional*

Fort Smith
†Yarbrough, Jerry A. *transportation company executive*

Harrison
Garrison, F. Sheridan *transportation executive*

Hot Springs Village
Dellow, Reginald Leonard *advertising executive*

Little Rock
†Andrews, Collins Adams, III *data processing company executive*
†Keet, Jim, III *management consultant, state legislator*

Lowell
Thompson, James Kirk *transportation executive*

Mountain Home
†Langevin, Thomas Harvey *higher education consultant*

Pine Bluff
Long, Edward Arlo *business consultant, retired manufacturing company executive*

CALIFORNIA

Agoura
Naylor-Jackson, Jerry *entertainer, public relations consultant, producer*

Alameda
Billings, Thomas Neal *computer and publishing executive, management consultant*

Alamo
Evans, John James *management consultant*
Whalen, John Sydney *management consultant*

Arrowhead
Bauer, Ralph Leroy *business executive*

Atherton
Lowry, Larry Lorn *management consulting company executive*

Bell Gardens
Hardie, George Graham *casino executive*

Belvedere Tiburon
Denton, Charles Mandaville *corporate consultant*

Berkeley
Holton, Richard Henry *business educator*
Hurley, Morris Elmer, Jr. *management consultant*
Tyndall, David Gordon *business educator*

Beverly Hills
Barbakow, Jeffery C. *motion picture and television company executive*
Casey, Joseph T. *corporate executive*
David, Clive *events planning executive*
Dillon, Gregory Russell *hotel executive*
Hilton, Barron *hotel executive*
Philon, James Leon *hotel executive*
Toffel, Alvin Eugene *corporate executive, business and governmental consultant*
Zarem, Abe Mordecai *management consulting executive*

Burbank
Eisner, Michael Dammann *entertainment company executive*
Katz, Marty *motion picture executive*
†McQueen, Sherman John, Jr. *entertainment company executive*

Burlingame
Heath, Richard Raymond *business executive*
†Loughead, Thomas A. *transportation executive*
Mc Dowell, Jack Sherman *political consultant*

Calabasas
Bartizal, Robert George *computer systems company executive, business consultant*
Gressak, Anthony Raymond, Jr. *sales executive*

Camarillo
Sime, Donald Rae *business administration educator*

Cambria
DuFresne, Armand Frederick *management and engineering consultant*
Morse, Richard Jay *human resources and organizational development consultant, manufacturers' representative company executive*

Carlsbad
Anderson, Paul Irving *management executive*

Carmel
Krugman, Stanley Lee *international management consultant*
Skidmore, Howard Franklyn *public relations counsel*
Smith, Gordon Paul *management consulting company executive*

Carpinteria
Lessler, Richard Sigmund *advertising executive*

Century City
Blatt, Neil A. *cinema corporation executive*

Chatsworth
Bartling, Judd Quenton *research corporation executive*

Concord
Allen, Toby *resort executive*

Corona Del Mar
Hobbs, Linder Charlie *computer company executive*
Mc Guire, Joseph William *business educator*
Wickman, Paul Everett *public relations executive*

Corte Madera
Marines, Louis Lawrence *management consultant, educator*

Costa Mesa
Damsky, Robert Philip *communications executive*
†Jordan, Lawrence Spencer *sales executive*

Culver City
Berland, James Fred *business and computer management consultant*
Williams, Kenneth Scott *entertainment company executive*

Cupertino
Amdahl, Gene Myron *computer company executive*
Graziano, Joseph A. *computer company executive*
Marshall, Robert Charles *computer company executive*
Sculley, John *computer company executive*
Spindler, Michael H. *computer company executive*

Cypress
Burge, Willard, Jr. *software company executive*
†Recchia, Richard D. *automotive sales executive*

Daly City
Hargrave, Sarah Quesenberry *marketing, public relations company executive*

Dana Point
Friedman, Barry *financial marketing consultant*
Jelinek, Robert *advertising executive, writer*
Krogius, Tristan Ernst Gunnar *international marketing consultant, lawyer*

Del Mar
Comrie, Sandra Melton *human resource executive*

Diablo
Pelandini, Thomas Francis *mmarketing executive*

Downey
Weinberger, Frank *information systems advisor*

El Cajon
Laffoon, Carthrae Merrette *management consultant*
McInerney, Joseph Aloysius *hotel executive*

El Segundo
Amerman, John W. *toy company executive*
Barad, Jill Elikann *toy company executive*
Brill, James Lathrop *finance executive*
Hoover, William R(ay) *computer service company executive*
†Level, Leon Jules *information services executive*
Sanchez-Llaca, Juan *hotel executive*

Encinitas
Wilson, Donald Grey *management consultant*

Encino
Dor, Yoram *health care executive*
Gasich, Welko Elton *management executive*

Foster City
†Dove, Millard *transportation executive*

Fountain Valley
Patterson, Dennis Joseph *management consultant*

Fremont
†Evenhuis, Henk J. *research company exexcutive*

Fresno
Emrick, Terry Lamar *business consultant*
Halverstadt, Jonathan Scott *personal growth systems developer, consultant, lecturer*
Levy, Joseph William *department stores executive*
Pinkerton, Richard LaDoyt *management educator*

Fullerton
Hollander, Gerhard Ludwig *computer company executive*
Taylor, James Walter *marketing educator*

Glendale
Herzer, Richard Kimball *franchising company executive*
Marr, Luther Reese *communications executive, lawyer*
Misa, Kenneth Franklin *management consultant*

Glendora
Roland, Donald Edward *advertising executive*
†Scheller, Sanford Gregory *printing company executive*

Granada Hills
Shoemaker, Harold Lloyd *infosystem specialist*

Harbor City
†Flood, John Etchells, Jr. *software services executive*

Hayward
Tribus, Myron *management consultant, engineer, educator*

Hollister
Parker, Patrick Johnston *entrepreneur, educator*

Hollywood
Samuels, Cynthia Kalish *communications executive*

Inglewood
Turner, Norris *marketing professional*

Irvine
Bradley, Charles James, Jr. *corporate executive*
Buchanan, Lee Ann *public relations executive*
†Casey, Martin M. *food service executive*
Colino, Richard Ralph *communications consultant*
Earhart, Donald Marion *management consultant, health care company executive*
Glenn, Gerald Marvin *marketing, engineering and construction executive*
Habermann, Norman *restaurant group executive*
Hoshi, Katsuo Kai *international business executive*
†Joliffe, James *managing partner*
†May, Eva Antonia *advertising agency executive*
†Nelson, Robert E. *public relations executive, political consultant*
†Nishida, Atsutoshi *computer company executive*
Rollans, James O. *service company executive*

Irwindale
Welch, Linda Ogden *sales executive*

La Habra
†Burkle, Ronald W. *food service executive*
Chase, Cochrane *advertising agency executive*

La Jolla
Bardwick, Judith Marcia *management consultant*
Barrett, Robert John, Jr. *management consultant*
Harris, T George *management editor*
Jeffers, Donald E. *consultant*
Kent, Paula *public relations, marketing and management consultant, lecturer*

La Puente
Sheridan, Christopher Frederick *human resources executive*

La Quinta
†Houze, William Cunningham *executive recruiter, management consultant*

Lafayette
Hemphill, Norma Jo *special event planning and tour company executive*
Kahn, Robert Irving *management consultant*

Laguna Beach
Stebbins, Elizabeth Joseph Hinton *management and statistics educator, researcher*

Laguna Hills
Linton, Frederick M. *strategic planning consultant*

LaJolla
Streichler, Jerry *human and technology resource development consultant*

Livermore
Wood, Donald Craig *marketing professional*

Loma Linda
Maurice, Don *personal care industry executive*

Long Beach
Giles, Jean Hall *retired corporate executive*

Los Altos
Allen, Michael Graham *management consultant*
Bell, Chester Gordon *computer engineering company executive*

Los Angeles
Altfeld, Sheldon Isaac *communications executive*
Armstrong, C. Michael *computer business executive*
Berg, Jeffrey Spencer *talent agency executive*
Bloch, Paul *public relations executive*
†Bohle, Sue *public relations executive*
Boonshaft, Hope Judith *public relations executive*
†Bouchez, L. Brent *advertising agency executive*
Coleman, Roger William *institutional food distribution company executive*
Counts, James Curtis *management consultant*
Crosby, Peter Alan *management consultant*
†Deemer, Candy Kaelin *advertising executive*
†Dill, Donald *consumer products company executive*
Doll, Lynne Marie *public relations agency executive*
Domantay, Norlito Valdez (Lito Domantay) *communications executive*
Dorfman, Steven David *electronics company executive*
Einstein, Clifford Jay *advertising executive*
Eisaman, Josiah Reamer, III *advertising executive*
†Farrell, Joseph *movie market analyst, producer, entertainment research company executive, writer, sculptor, designer*
†Feidelson, Marc *advertising executive*
Fenimore, George Wiley *management consultant*
Ferry, Richard Michael *executive search firm executive*
Fisher, Lawrence W. *public relations company executive*
†Gal, Kenneth Maurice *advertising executive*
Ginsburg, Seymour *computer science educator*
Gottfried, Ira Sidney *management consulting executive*
Gottlieb, Allen Sandford *entertainment company executive*
†Gould, Morley David *advertising agency executive*
Greene, Alvin *service company executive, management consultant*
Grody, Mark Stephen *public relations executive*
†Hamblin, Richard Wallace *advertising agency executive*
Harbaugh, George Milton *hotel executive*
Harbison, John Robert *management consultant*
†Hay, Maureene Griffoul *advertising executive*
Heinisch, Robert Craig *sales and marketing executive, consultant*
Humphreys, Robert Lee *advertising agency executive*
Irving, Jack Howard *technical consultant*
†Johnson, Mark Devlin *advertising executive*
†Jones, Larry Richard *advertising executive*
Kline, Richard Stephen *public relations executive*
Klinger, Allen *computer science and engineering educator*
Kristoff, James *production company executive*
†Krouse, Diane Murray *advertising company executive*
Krueger, Robert William *management consultant*
Kupchick, Alan Charles *advertising executive*
Laba, Marvin *management consultant*
†Lanni, Joseph Terrence *hotel corporation executive*
Lee, Burns Wells *public relations executive*
†Lee, R. Marilyn *employee relations executive*
Leener, Jack Joseph *advertising executive*
Lewis, Craig Graham David *public relations executive*
Macalister, Kim Porter *advertising executive*
Margol, Irving *personnel consultant*
McGaughey, Emmett Connell *advertising agency executive*
†McLaren, Fred B. *supermarket chain executive*
Meuli, Judith K. *communications executive, real estate developer, small business owner*
†Nicholaw, George *communications executive*
Olson, Dale C. *public relations executive*
Patel, Chandra Kumar Naranbhai *communications company executive, educator, researcher*
Pearlstein, Leonard *advertising agency executive*
†Popielarz, Beverly *advertising executive*
Ratzlaff, Stanley Abe *medical software company executive*
†Richardson, Rand Michael *public relations executive*
Schine, Gerard David *entertainment company executive*
†Segal, Morton *public relations executive*
Silverman, Bruce Gary *advertising executive*
Sitrick, Michael Steven *communications executive*
Smith, Joseph Benjamin *communications company executive*
Spofford, Robert Houston *advertising agency executive*
Stevens, Roy W. *distilled spirits executive*
†Tardio, Thomas A. *public relations executive*
†Taylor, Richard W. *public relations executive*
Tellem, Susan Mary *public relations executive*
Tobia, Stephen Francis, Jr. *marketing professional, consultant*
Tomash, Erwin *retired computer equipment company executive*
Triplett, Arlene Ann *travel company executive*
Van Stekelenburg, Mark *food service executive*
†Vogel, William Charles *advertising executive*
Warren, Mark Edward *travel company executive, lawyer*
Whitman, Kenneth Jay *advertising executive*

Malibu
Ensign, Richard Papworth *transportation executive*

Manhattan Beach
Stern, Daniel Alan *business management consultant*
Weinstock, Herbert Frank *public relations executive*

Marina Del Rey
Gold, Carol Sapin *international management consultant, speaker*
Patton, David Wayne *health care executive*
†Smith, Steven Warren *public relations executive*
Tennant, John Randall *management advisory company executive*

Menlo Park
†Henley, Jeffrey O. *business executive*
Morrell, James Wilson *consulting company executive*
O'Brien, Raymond Francis *transportation executive*
Phipps, Allen Mayhew *management consultant*
Scandling, William Fredric *retired food service company executive*
Sommers, William Paul *management consultant*
†White, Phillip E. *company executive*

Merced
Carroll, Paula Marie *security company executive*

Milpitas
Berkley, Stephen Mark *computer peripherals manufacturing company executive*
Corrigan, Wilfred J. *data processing and computer company executive*

Moffett Field
Baldwin, Betty Jo *computer specialist*

Montebello
†Shelton, Phillip Eugene *paper company executive*

Moraga
Sonenshein, Nathan *marine consulting company executive, retired naval officer*

Mountain View
Braun, Michael Alan *data processing executive*
Breitmeyer, Jo Anne *sales and marketing executive*
†Harber, M(ichael) Eric *management consultant*

Napa
Chiarella, Peter Ralph *corporate executive*
LaRocque, Marilyn Ross Onderdonk *public relations executive*
Leavitt, Dana Gibson *management consultant*

Newark
Joyce, Stephen Francis *human resource executive*

Newport Beach
Clark, Earnest Hubert, Jr. *tool company executive*
Dykstra, David Charles *accountant, management consultant, author, educator*
Holmes, Colgate Frederick *hotel executive*
Lipson, Melvin Alan *technology and business management consultant*
Rueb, Richard V., Sr. *information systems management consultant*
†Soliman, Anwar S. *restaurant company executive*

North Hollywood
†Kemp, Bernard *organizational development consultant*

Northridge
Sandoval, Rik (Charles Sandoval) *broadcasting executive*

Oakland
Barakat, Samir F. *economic and management consulting executive*
Laverne, Michel Marie-Jacques *international relations consultant*
Potash, Stephen Jon *public relations specialist*

Oildale
Gallagher, Joseph Francis *marketing executive*

Orange
Levine, Howard Harris *service executive*

Palm Springs
Arnold, Stanley Norman *manufacturing consultant*

Palo Alto
Allen, Louis Alexander *management consultant*
Franson, Paul Oscar, III *public relations executive*
Hammond, Donald Leroy *computer company executive*
Hecht, Lee Martin *software company executive*
Kaufman, Michael David *management executive*
Lavendel, Giuliana Avanzini *information systems executive, writer, lecturer*
Merrin, Seymour *computer marketing company executive*
Summit, Roger Kent *retired information systems and services executive*
Tierney, Patrick John *information services executive*
Zelnick, Strauss *entertainment company executive*

Palos Verdes Peninsula
†Edler, Richard Bruce *advertising agency executive*
Leone, William Charles *retired business executive*
Savage, Terry Richard *information systems executive*

Pasadena
Kaplan, Gary *executive recruiter*
Lynch, Gerald John *management consultant*
Ott, George William, Jr. *management consulting executive*
Steele, Gerda Govine *company president*
Watkins, John Francis *management consultant*

Paso Robles
Boxer, Jerome Harvey *computer and management consultant, vintner, accountant*

Piedmont
Morrison, John Gill *communications executive*
Yep, Wallen Lai *international business consultant, author*

Placentia
Nowel, David John *marketing professional*

Pleasanton
Quinnan, Edward Michael *management consultant*

Portola Valley
Hurd, Cuthbert C. *computer company executive, mathematician*
Moses, Franklin Maxwell *marketing consultant*

Poway
Remer, Vernon Ralph *travel consultant*
†Rudolph, Charles Herman *retired computer software development executive*

Rancho Mirage
Rotman, Morris Bernard *public relations consultant*

Rancho Palos Verdes
Marlett, De Otis Loring *retired management consultant*

Rancho Santa Fe
Gruenwald, George Henry *new products management consultant*
Matthews, Leonard Sarver *advertising executive, consultant*
Schirra, Walter Marty, Jr. *business consultant, former astronaut*

Redwood City
Jobs, Steven Paul *computer corporation executive*
Neville, Roy Gerald *chemical management and environmental consultant*
Poppel, Harvey Lee *management consultant*
Tyabji, Hatim Ahmedi *computer systems company executive*

Redwood Shores
Jenkins, Robert Lee *management consultant*

Riverside
Chute, Phillip Bruce *management consultant*

Rohnert Park
Johnston, Edward Elliott *insurance and management consultant*

Ross
Goulet, William Dawson *marketing professional*

Rutherford
Staglin, Garen Kent *finance and computer service company executive*

Sacramento
Blackwell, Frederick Wayne *computer science educator*
Metzger, Bobbie Ann *public relations executive*

Saint Helena
Kamman, Alan Bertram *communications consulting company executive*

Salinas
Ader, Richard Alan *marketing executive*
Martins, Evelyn Mae *theatre owner*

San Anselmo
Goodman, Carolyn *advertising executive*
Powell, Stanley, Jr. *management consultant*

San Bruno
Arthur, Greer Martin *maritime container leasing firm executive*

San Carlos
Bellack, Daniel Willard *advertising and public relations executive*
Curry, William Sims *procurement manager*

San Clemente
Stenzel, William A. *consulting services executive*

San Diego
Boyd, Robert Giddings, Jr. *mental health facility administrator*
Brimble, Alan *business executive*
Cornett, William Forrest, Jr. *local government management consultant*
Fagot, Joseph Burdell *corporate executive*
Fox, Sheila *advertising executive*
Gill, Gail Stoorza *public relations executive*
Goodall, Jackson Wallace, Jr. *restaurant company executive*
Hooper, Jere Mann *consultant, retired hotel executive*
Kennedy, Peter Smithson *personnel consultant*
†Kernan, John T. *education systems company executive*
Moffet, Donald Pratt *computer company executive*
Nelson, Craig Alan *consultant*
†Norrod, James Douglas *computer subsystems company executive*
Peters, Raymond Eugene *computer systems company executive*
Reading, James Edward *transportation executive*
†Silverberg, Lewis Henry *business consultant*
†Stoorza Gill, Gail *corporate professional*
Tepedino, Francis Joseph *business management company executive*
Tillinghast, Charles Carpenter, III *marketing company executive*
Warner, John Hilliard, Jr. *technical services, military and commercial systems and software company executive*
Ziegaus, Alan James *public relations executive*
†Zisch, William E. *technical services executive*

San Francisco
Altick, Leslie L. *corporate executive*
Anschutz, Philip F. *diversified company executive*
Bachrach, Ira Nathaniel *marketing executive*
Bara, Jean Marc *advertising executive*
Branigan, Craig Wolfe *advertising executive*
†Butenhoff, Susan *public relations executive*
Cohn, Martin *advertising executive*
Currier, Frederick Plumer *market research company executive*
Edgar, James Macmillan, Jr. *management consultant*
Farley, Leon Alex *executive search consultant*
†Feld, Michael Sperry *advertising executive*
Gertler, Alfred Martin *public relations executive*
Goldberg, Fred Sellmann *advertising executive*
†Goodby, Jeffrey *advertising agency executive*
Handlery, Paul Robert *hotel executive*
Hargadon, Bernard Joseph, Jr. *consumer goods company executive*
Harlan, Neil Eugene *retired healthcare company executive*
Harrison, E(rnest) Frank(lin) *management educator, consultant, author, former university president and chancellor*
Hayes, Thomas Jay, III *management consultant, retired construction and engineering company executive, retired army officer*
†Howley, Peter A. *communications executive*
Humenesky, Gregory *personnel and labor relations executive*
Hurlbert, Roger William *information service industry executive*
Kalt, Howard Michael *public relations executive*
Keesling, Francis Valentine, Jr. *management consultant*
†Kilpatrick, Rod *advertising executive*
Klammer, Joseph Francis *management consultant*
Kuhns, Craig Shaffer *business educator*
LaFollette, Charles Sanborn *business consultant*
Lautz, Lindsay Allan *executive search consultant*
Lockhart, James Blakely *public affairs executive*
†McCarthy, Clement Daniel *advertising executive*
†Miller, Allen Blair *public relations executive*
Mundell, David Edward *leasing company executive*
Noonan, William Moss *information systems executive, consultant*
Riney, Hal Patrick *advertising executive*
Selover, William Charlton *corporate communications and governmental affairs executive*
†Snedaker, Dianne *advertising agency executive*
Stetler, Russell Dearnley, Jr. *private investigator*
Sturdivant, Frederick David *consultant, business educator*
†Thompson, Gary W. *public relations executive*
Whitaker, Clem, Jr. *advertising and public relations executive*
†White, Rene *public relations executive*
Wilbur, Brayton, Jr. *distribution company executive*
Willner, Jay R. *consulting company executive*
Woolsey, David Arthur *leasing company executive*
†Yu, Eleanor Ngan-Ling *advertising company executive*

San Jose
Beverett, Andrew Jackson *marketing executive*
†Bolger, Brenna Mercier *public relations executive*
†Chen, John S. *computer company executive*
Dean, Burton Victor *management educator*
Dougherty, John James *computer software company executive, consultant*
Grubb, William Francis X. *consumer software executive, marketing executive*
Harkins, Craig *management consultant*
Jordan, Thomas Vincent *advertising educator, consultant*
McCoy, James M. *data processing, computer company executive*
†McGuire, Thomas Roger *distribution company executive*
†Morgan, Rebecca Quinn *business executive*
†Nogawa, Kiyoshi *computer company executive*
Schofield, John Trevor *environmental management company executive*
Scott, Edward William, Jr. *computer company executive*
†Sweeny, Mary Ellen *public relations and advertising executive*

San Leandro
Odron, Edward Andrew *supermarket executive*

San Lorenzo
Morrison, Martin Earl *computer systems analyst*

San Marcos
†Lee, John Francis *retired international management consulting company executive, author*

San Mateo
†Briggs, Thorley D. *environmetal consultant*
Goldman, Bernard *leasing company executive*
Helfert, Erich Anton *management consultant, author, educator*
†Hosking, Douglas Gordon *printing company executive*
Jordan, Michelle Henrietta *public relations company executive*
Sears, William Robert *management consultant*

San Pedro
Price, Harrison Alan *business research company executive*

San Rafael
Friesecke, Raymond Francis *management consultant*
Kennedy, James Waite *management consultant, author*
Lelewer, David Kann *management consultant*
Nelson, James Carmer, Jr. *advertising executive, writer*
Thompson, John William *international management consultant*
Wilson, Ian Holroyde *management consultant, futurist*

Santa Ana
†Dukes, David R. *computer company executive*
Holtz, Joseph Norman *marketing executive*
†Lacy, Linwood A., Jr. *computer company executive*

Santa Barbara
Ahlers, B. Orwin *marketing executive*
Amory, Thomas Carhart *management consultant*
Boehm, Eric Hartzell *information management executive*
Boxer, Rubin *software company owner, former research and development company executive*
†Emmons, Robert John *corporate executive*
Grayson, Robert Allen *marketing executive, educator*
Jacobson, Saul P. *business consultant*
Markel, John Dundas *retired software company executive*
Weaver, Sylvester Laflin, Jr. *communications consultant*

Santa Clara
†Anderson, Vernon Russell *technology company executive, entrepreneur*
Barrett, Craig R. *computer company executive*
Cunningham, Andrea Lee *public relations executive*
†Endo, Makoto *computer company executive*
Kurtzig, Sandra L. *software company executive*
Vincent, David Ridgely *management consulting executive*

Santa Cruz
Corrick, Ann Marjorie *communications executive*

Santa Fe Springs
Butterworth, Edward Livingston *retail company executive*

Santa Monica
Anderson, Robert Helms *computer and management company executive*
†Collins, Russell Ambrose *advertising executive, creative director*
Craig, Jean (Jean Craig McNeilly) *advertising executive*
Davies, Robert Abel, III *consumer products company executive*
†Karlin, Robert *automotive sales executive*
†Kopald, Larry S. *advertising executive*
Mc Kinney, Montgomery Nelson *advertising executive*
Salzer, John Michael *technical and management consultant*

Santa Rosa
Cavanagh, John Charles *advertising agency executive*
†Luttrell, Mary Mildred *marketing management consultant*
Schudel, Hansjoerg *international business consultant*

Santa Ynez
Stern, Marvin *management consultant*

Saratoga
Lynch, Milton Terrence *retired advertising agency executive*

Sausalito
Treat, John Elting *management consultant*

Scotts Valley
Brough, Bruce Alvin *public relations and communications executive*
Filler, Gary B. *computer company executive*

Seal Beach
Thompson, Craig Snover *corporate communications executive*

Sherman Oaks
Ghent, Peer *management consultant*
Light, Robert M. *broadcasting association executive*
Lindgren, Timothy Joseph *supply company executive*
Strauss, John *public relations executive*
Winkler, Lee B. *business consultant*

Signal Hill
Jarman, Donald Ray *retired public relations professional, minister*

Stanford
Miller, William Frederick *research company executive, educator, business consultant*

Stockton
Shao, Otis Hung-I *corporate executive, educator*

Studio City
Nieto del Rio, Juan Carlos *marketing executive*

Sunnyvale
†Armistead, Robert Ashby, Jr. *scientific research company executive*
Bryant, Alan Willard *human resources executive*
†Previte, Richard *computer company executive*
Zemke, (E.) Joseph *computer company executive*

Taft
Smith, Lee L. *hotel executive*

Tarzana
Leahy, T. Liam *management consultant*

Thousand Oaks
Pitlak, Robert Thomas *sales and marketing executive*
Smyth, Glen Miller *management consultant*

Torrance
Carey, Kathryn Ann *advertising and public relations agency executive, consultant*
Kulpa, John Edward *management executive, former air force officer*
†Kurita, Masahiro *computer company executive*
†Niwa, Norio *computer company executive*
Walti, Randal Fred *management consultant*

Tustin
†Allen, Joseph *public relations executive*
Bartlett, Arthur Eugene *franchise executive*

Upland
Hext, Kathleen Florence *regulatory compliance consultant*

Van Nuys
†Greenberg, Daniel *electronics rental company executive*
Kagan, Stephen Bruce (Sandy Kagan) *travel agency executive*
Simon, David Harold *retired public relations executive*

Venice
Chiat, Jay *advertising agency executive*
Clow, Lee *advertising agency executive*
†Giaquinta, Gerald J. *public relations executive*
†Kuperman, Robert Ian *advertising agency executive*
†Thomas, Bob *public relations executive*
Wolf, Robert Howard *advertising executive, marketing consultant*

Villa Park
Rydell, Richard Lewis *hospital administrator, consultant*

Walnut Creek
Cacho, Patrick Thomas *relocation management company executive*
Garlough, William Glenn *marketing executive*
McCauley, Bruce Gordon *financial consultant*

West Hollywood
Helin, James Dennis *advertising agency executive*
Holt, Dennis F. *media buying company executive*
Kingsley, Patricia *public relations executive*
Levine, Michael *public relations executive, author*
Wald, Donna Gene *advertising executive*

Westlake Village
Doherty, Patrick Francis *communications executive, educator*
Murdock, David H. *diversified company executive*

Woodland Hills
Fisher, Robert James *public relations consultant, advertising executive*
Freeman, Philip Conrad, Jr. *computer systems company executive*

Woodside
Kaisel, Stanley Francis *management consultant*

Yountville
Goeglein, Richard John *hotel/casino chain executive*
Kay, Douglas Casey *leasing company executive*

COLORADO

Aspen
McDade, James Russell *management consultant*

Boulder
Burghardt, Kurt Josef *marketing professional, infosystems specialist*
Burns, Daniel Hobart *management consultant*
Fukae, Kensuke *infosystems specialist*
Goeldner, Charles Raymond *business educator*
Jerritts, Stephen G. *computer company executive*
King, Helen Eileen *service executive*

Colorado Springs
May, Melvin Arthur *computer software company executive*

Denver
†Ames, A. Gary *communications company executive*
Anderson, Robert *environmental specialist, physician*
Blatter, Frank Edward *travel agency executive*
†Brock, Kathleen Kennelly *advertising agency executive*
Clinch, Nicholas Bayard, III *business executive*
Duke, Harold Benjamin, Jr. *retired holding company executive*
Fisher, Louis McLane, Jr. *environmental engineering firm executive*
†Garrison, T. Paul *advertising executive*
Giesen, John William *advertising executive*
Johnston, Gwinavere Adams *public relations consultant*
†Kurz, Kelli McDonald *advertising executive*
†Laff, Seymour *health care executive*
Leiweke, Timothy *sales executive, marketing professional*
Mc Kinney, Alexis *public relations consultant*
Neu, Carl Herbert, Jr. *management consultant*
Notari, Paul Celestin *communications executive*
†Ramon, David A. *consumer products company executive*
Reisinger, George Lambert *management consultant*
Roberts, Neil Fletcher *management consulting company executive*

Englewood
†Blair, Stewart D. *cable television executive, small business owner*
Bryson, Gary Spath *cable television and telephone company executive*
Callahan, Richard J. *communications company executive*
†Jones, Glenn Robert *cable systems executive*
Manion, Jerry R. *hotel chain executive*

Golden
Togerson, John Dennis *computer software company executive*

Lakewood
Mueller, Raymond Jay *software development executive*
Walton, Roger Alan *public relations executive, writer*

Littleton
Martinen, John A. *travel company executive*
Strang, Sandra Lee *airline official*

Loveland
†Churchill, Jerry M. *environment company marketing executive*

Parker
Jankura, Donald Eugene *hotel executive, educator*

Pueblo
Dolsen, David Horton *mortician*

Steamboat Springs
Langstaff, Gary Lee *food service marketing executive*

CONNECTICUT

Bloomfield
Handel, Morton Emanuel *management consultation executive*
Hegeman, James Alan *corporate executive*
Mackey, William Arthur Godfrey *computer software company executive*

Cheshire
Burton, Robert William *retired office products executive*

Cos Cob
Ketchum, Alton Harrington *retired advertising executive*

Danbury
Baruch, Eduard *management consultant*
Cassidy, Robert Joseph *consumer products company executive*
Dudley, Alfred Edward *home and auto products company executive*

Darien
Buchanan, Robert Edgar *retired advertising agency executive*
Chevins, Anthony Charles *advertising agency executive*
Cowherd, Edwin Russell *management consultant*
Earle, Harry Woodward *printing company executive*
Grace, John Kenneth *communications executive*

Deep River
Healy, William Kent *environmental services executive*

East Hartford
Tanaka, Richard I. *computer products company executive*

East Windsor
Kaufmann, Sylvia Nadeau *office equipment sales company executive*

Essex
McLaughlin, David J. *management executive*
Russell, Thomas Wright, Jr. *retired manufacturing executive*

Fairfield
Ambrosino, Ralph Thomas, Jr. *retired telecommunications executive*
Blau, Barry *advertising agency executive*
Cole, Richard John *marketing executive*
Dean, George Alden *advertising executive*
Hodgkinson, William James *marketing executive*
Kantrowitz, Jonathan Daniel *educational software company executive, lawyer*
Urquhart, John Alexander *management consultant*

Georgetown
Daubenspeck, Robert Donley *advertising agency executive*

Greens Farms
McManus, John Francis, III *advertising management executive*

Greenwich
Ball, John Fleming *advertising and film production executive*
Carmichael, William Daniel *consultant, educator*
Chase, William Howard *public policy consultant, editor*
Chisholm, William Hardenbergh *management consultant*
Coudert, Victor Raphael, Jr. *marketing and sales executive*
Davidson, Thomas Maxwell *international management company executive*
Davies, William DeAth, Jr. *executive management consultant*
Donley, James Walton *management consultant*
Gierer, Vincent A., Jr. *tobacco and wine holding company executive*
Keegan, Richard John *advertising agency executive*
Kestnbaum, Albert S. *advertising executive*
MacDonald, Gordon Chalmers *management consultant*
Parrish, Thomas Kirkpatrick, III *marketing consultant*
Paulson, Paul Joseph *advertising executive*
Schlafly, Hubert Joseph, Jr. *communications executive*

Scott, John Constante marketing company executive
Wallach, Philip C(harles) financial, public relations consultant
Whitmore, George Merle, Jr. management consulting company executive
Willis, William Harold, Jr. management consultant, executive search specialist
†Wilson, H. Brian, Jr. public relations executive
Wyman, Ralph Mark corporate executive

Guilford
Ragan, James Thomas communications executive

Hartford
Hertel, Suzanne Marie personnel administrator
Morrissey, Robert John communications executive
†Riccio, Janet Marie advertising executive
Roberts, Henry Reginald management consultant, former life insurance company executive
Totino, Louis J. marketing executive, educator

Lakeville
Bookman, George B. public relations consultant
Lovitt, George Harold advertising executive
Manassero, Henri J. P. hotel executive

Madison
Keim, Robert Phillip retired advertising executive, consultant

New Canaan
Crossman, William Whittard retired wire cable and communications executive
McClure, Grover Benjamin management consultant
Mc Mennamin, George Barry advertising agency executive
Means, David Hammond retired advertising executive
Stack, J. William, Jr. management consultant
Walsworth, Ronald Lee consumer products executive
Ward, Richard Vance, Jr. management executive

New Haven
Rae, Douglas Whiting management educator
Van Sinderen, Alfred White former telephone company executive
Waters, Donald Joseph information services administrator

Norwalk
†Balmuth, Marc I. consumer products company executive
Brandt, Richard Paul communications and entertainment company executive
Caravatt, Paul Joseph, Jr. communications company executive
†Clarke, Don R. consumer products company executive
Lederer, Jack Lawrence personnel director, human resources specialist
Meredith, David Robert personnel executive
†Watson, H. Mitchell, Jr. business machines company executive

Old Greenwich
Fernous, Louis Ferdinand, Jr. corporate executive
Hume, Robert Alan advertising agency executive, marketing consultant

Old Saybrook
Phillips, William Eugene advertising agency executive

Pomfret
Woodbridge, Henry Sewall management consultant

Ridgefield
Phelps, Judson Hewett marketing sales executive

Riverside
Battat, Emile A. management executive
Geismar, Richard Lee communications executive
McSpadden, Peter Ford retired advertising agency executive
Pearson, Robert Greenlees writing services company executive

Salisbury
Block, Zenas management consultant, educator

Shelton
†Bowron, John B. transportation executive
Crowe, Jeffrey C. transportation executive
†Greene, Richard Efraim data processing executive
Lobsenz, Herbert Munter data base company executive
†Mortimer, Stanley Grafton, III marketing company executive

Sherman
Lee, Wallace Williams, Jr. retired hotel executive

Simsbury
Hildebrandt, Frederick Dean, Jr. management consultant
Nolan, Robert Emmett management consulting company executive

South Norwalk
Manning, James Forrest computer executive

South Windsor
Gerber, Heinz Joseph computer automation company executive

Southbury
Cassidy, James Joseph public relations counsel

Stamford
Akers, John Fellows information processing company executive
Barlow, Clark W. telephone company executive
Carroll, Thomas Sylvester business executive
Carswell, Bruce communications executive
Dawson, James Ambrose printing industry executive
Dell, Warren Frank, II management consultant
Dorf, Robert L. public relations executive, marketing and management consultant
Forbes, Walter Alexander consumer services company executive
Garbacz, Gerald George information services company executive
†Gardiner, Hobart Clive corporate executive
Gudger, Robert H. retired printing company executive
Hague, John William, Jr. security company executive
Kavetas, Harry L. finance leasing company executive
Kobak, James Benedict management consultant
Langstaff, Elliot Kennedy management consultant
Lee, Charles Robert telecommunications company executive
Light, (Marvin) Lawrence advertising agency executive
†Lukeman, Gerald C. advertising executive
MacEwen, Edward Carter communications executive
Marlowe, Edward research company executive
Miller, Wilbur Hobart business diversification consultant
†Moody, J. Roger computer software executive
Murphy, Robert Blair management consulting company executive
Nelson, David Leonard process management systems company executive
Oatway, Francis Carlyle corporate executive
Obernauer, Marne corporate executive
†Petrosian, Peter food service executive
Rhinesmith, Stephen Headley international management consultant
Sarbin, Hershel Benjamin management consultant, business publisher, lawyer
Serrani, Thom business consultant, former mayor
Silver, Charles Morton communications company executive
Sveda, Michael management and research consultant
Villarreal, Homero Atenógenes human resources executive
Vos, Frank advertising and marketing executive
Wall, Stephen James senior executive consultant
Wallfesh, Henry Maurice business communications company executive, editor, writer
Ware, Jennifer Peyton communications professional
White, Richard Booth management consultant
Yardis, Pamela Hintz computer consulting company executive
Yoder, Patricia Doherty public relations executive
Zuckert, Donald Mack marketing executive

Storrs Mansfield
Glasser, Joseph manufacturing and marketing executive

Suffield
†Leavitt, Joel consumer products company executive

West Hartford
Mason, George H. business educator, consultant

Weston
Mattoon, Henry Amasa, Jr. advertising and marketing consultant, writer
Murray, Thomas Joseph advertising executive

Westport
Aasen, Lawrence Obert public relations executive
Allen, Robert Hugh communications corporation executive
Bescherer, Edwin A., Jr. business information services company executive
Bishop, William Wade advertising executive
De Lay, Robert Francis marketing executive, consultant
Dickson, Sally Isabelle retired public relations executive
Hambleton, George Blow Elliott management consultant
McFarland, Richard M. executive recruiting consultant
Savage, Robert Heath advertising executive
Singer, Henry A. behavioral scientist, institute director
Wachsler, Robert Alan marketing consultant

Wilton
Brown, James Thompson, Jr. computer information scientist
Cassidy, George Thomas international business development consultant
Farley, James Parker retired advertising agency executive
Heymann, Stephen Timothy marketing management consultant
†Mc Dannald, Clyde Elliott, Jr. management consultation company executive
Nickel, Albert George advertising agency executive

Windsor
Clarke, Cordelia Kay Knight Mazuy management executive
†Cowen, Bruce David environmental service company executive
Kamerschen, Robert Jerome consumer products executive

Woodstock
Boote, Alfred Shepard marketing researcher, educator

DELAWARE

Hockessin
Bischoff, Joyce Arlene information systems consultant, lecturer

Middletown
Jackson, Donald Richard marketing professional

New Castle
Keillor, Sharon Ann computer company executive

Wilmington
Kjellmark, Eric William, Jr. management consultant, opera company director
Mackenzie, Malcolm Lewis advertising executive
Shipley, Samuel Lynn advertising and public relations executive
Wieland, Ferdinand hotel executive, entrepreneur
Wyer, William Clarke management consultant, development executive

DISTRICT OF COLUMBIA

Washington
Adams, A. John Bertrand public affairs consultant
Alexander, Clifford L., Jr. management consultant, lawyer, former secretary of army
Allen, Richard Vincent international business consultant, bank executive
†Alper, Joel Richard satellite communications company executive
Baker, Melvin C. advertising executive
Barquín, Ramón Carlos consulting company executive
Baruch, Jordan Jay management consultant
Bauer, Robert Albert public policy consultant
Bollenbach, Stephen Frasier hotel executive
Bradley, Melvin LeRoy communications company executive
Burch, Michael Ira public relations executive, former government official
Carberry, Michael Glen public relations executive
†Carlstrom, Robert E., Jr. public relations executive
Cherian, Joy consulting company executive
Clay, Don Richard environmental consulting firm executive
Cody, Thomas Gerald management consultant, writer
Cohen, Martin communications company executive
Crockett, Phyllis Darlene communications executive
†Dach, Leslie Alan public relations executive
Dealy, John Francis management consultant, lawyer, educator, arbitrator
Deen, Thomas Blackburn transportation research executive
Del Balzo, Joseph Michael aviation consulting company executive
Denysyk, Bohdan marketing professional
Dobriansky, Paula Jon business and communications executive
Donovan, George Joseph industry executive, consultant
Ehrlich, Clifford John hotel executive
Elliott, Thomas Michael management services executive, educator, consultant
Erwin, Frank William personnel research and publishing executive
Fairchild, Samuel Wilson professional services company executive, former federal agency administrator
Farrell, June Martinick public relations executive
Flanagan, Francis Dennis retired corporate executive
Fletcher, James Andrew information systems specialist
Foreman, Carol Lee Tucker corporate executive
Fuller, Edwin Daniel hotel executive
†Furash, Edward E. management consultant
Gardenier, Turkan Kumbaraci statistical company executive, researcher
Garner, William Darrell health services executive
†Goldstein, Irving communications company executive
Grant, Carl N. communications executive
Gray, Robert Keith communications company executive
Hannaford, Peter Dor public relations executive
Harrison, Emmett Bruce, Jr. public relations counselor
Harrison, Patricia de Stacy consulting, public relations company executive
Hart, Peter David opinion research firm executive
Havlicek, Franklin J. communications executive
Helms, Richard McGarrah international consultant
Higgins, James Henry, III marketing executive
Holland, James Ricks public relations executive, association executive
Hoving, John Hannes Forester consulting firm executive
Howe, Fisher management consultant, former government official
Hunter, Ronald V. computer administrator
Jagoda, Barry Lionel media adviser, communications consultant
†Jarrell, Jay A. health care company executive
Johnson, John A. communications company executive
Juliana, James Nicholas corporate executive
Kalbfeld, Brad Marshall television and radio executive, editor
Kalinger, Daniel Jay public relations and marketing executive
Karalekas, Anne publishing executive
Kelly, Francis Joseph strategic communications company executive
Kennedy, Roger George park services executive
†Kilduff, Bonnie E. director of expositions
Kotler, Milton business executive
†Kraus, Margery management consultant
Kroloff, George Michael public relations and advertising executive, management consultant
†Kusnet, David communications executive, speechwriter
†Lawson, D. Dale public relations executive
Lee, Ronald Barry business executive
Leslie, John William public relations and advertising executive
Lewis, David Eldridge airport development executive
Lewis, Jordan David management consultant, author, international speaker, educator
Lewis, William Walker management consultant
Lilley, William, III business consultant
†Lindner, Eric John parking-hospitality-hotel executive, lawyer
Ling, Suilin management consultant
Logue-Kinder, Joan public relations executive
Luikart, Fordyce Whitney management consultant
†Maddock, Jerome Torrence information services specialist
Malashevich, Bruce Peter consulting executive
Mansfield, Edward Patrick, Jr. advertising executive
Marriott, Alice Sheets (Mrs. John Willard Marriott) restaurant chain executive
Marriott, John Willard, Jr. hotel and food service chain executive
Marriott, Richard Edwin hotel and contract services executive
Marumoto, William Hideo management consultant
McBride, Jonathan Evans executive search company executive
Mc Nallen, James Berl marketing executive
Mc Namara, Robert Strange corporate director
Millian, Kenneth Young public policy consultant
Moore, Bob Stahly communications executive
Mueller, Ronald Raymond public relations executive
Nelson, Richard Copeland hotel executive
†Olcott, John Whiting aviation executive
Olson, Walter Justus, Jr. management consultant
O'Sullivan, Paul Kevin business executive, management and instructional systems consultant
†Palumbo, Benjamin Lewis public affairs consulting company executive
Pedersen, Wesley Niels public relations and public affairs executive
Pfeiffer, Leonard, IV executive recruiter, consultant
Pines, Wayne Lloyd public relations counselor
†Powell, Joseph Lester (Jody Powell) public relations executive
†Pucie, Charles R., Jr. public relations executive
Pyle, Robert Noble public relations executive
†Rabin, Kenneth Hardy public relations executive
†Rabin, Steve Arthur public affairs executive
Rafshoon, Gerald Monroe communications executive
Rainey, Jean Osgood public relations executive
Rausch, Howard information service executive
Reed, Travis Dean public relations consultant
Rice, Lois Dickson former computer company executive
Rimpel, Auguste Eugene, Jr. management and technical consulting executive
Rosebush, James Scott international management and public affairs consultant, former government official
Rosenthal, Aaron management consultant
†Schick, Michael William public relations executive
Schriever, Bernard Adolph management consultant
Sheinbaum, Gilbert Harold international consultant
Siciliano, Rocco Carmine institute executive
†Sills, Hilary H. public relations executive
Silverman, Alvin Michaels public relations consultant
Simmons, Richard De Lacey mass media executive
Sisco, Joseph John management consultant, corporation director, educator, government official
†Smith, Alan W., Jr. management consultant
Spero, Joan Edelman multi-service corporation executive
Sullivan, Richard John public relations executive, consultant
Tanham, George Kilpatrick retired research company executive
Tate, Sheila Burke public relations executive
Taylor, David Kerr international business educator, consultant
†Thelian, Lorraine public relations executive
Thursz, Daniel service organization executive
Tiefel, William Reginald hotel company executive
Timmons, William Evan corporate executive
Timperlake, Edward Thomas public relations executive
Trent, Darrell M. academic and corporate executive
Ucelli, Loretta Maria communications executive
Van Dyk, Frederick Theodore corporate executive
Veblen, Thomas Clayton management consultant
Wade, Robert Hirsch Beard international consultant, former government and educational association official
Walker, Ronald Hugh executive search company executive
Wertheim, Mitzi Mallina business executive
Wesberry, James Pickett, Jr. financial management consultant, auditor, international organization executive
Wheeler, Thomas Edgar communications technology executive
Widner, Ralph Randolph planning executive
Winnefeld, James Alexander defense analyst, former naval officer, author
†Worden, Joan M. public relations executive
Yulish, Charles Barry public affairs executive
Zimmerman, John H. communications company executive
Zion, Roger H. consulting firm executive, former congressman

FLORIDA

Amelia Island
Harman, John Robert, Jr. management consultant

Boca Raton
Albrecht, Arthur John advertising agency executive
†Bradley, George H. furniture company executive
Dorfman, Allen Bernard international management consultant
Dunhill, Robert W. advertising direct mail executive
Epstein, Barry R. public relations counselor
Krause, Heinz Werner computer and communications executive
Miller, Kenneth Roy management consultant
Monroe, William Lewis human resources executive
Posner, Sidney advertising executive
Rosner, M. Norton business systems and financial services company executive
Rothbaum, Ira advertising and marketing executive
Turner, Lisa Phillips human resources executive
Van Arnem, Harold Louis capital and technology equipment leasing company executive

Boynton Beach
Bloede, Victor Gustav retired advertising executive
Spitz, Arnoldt John corporate professional, consultant

Bradenton
Burton, Ralph Joseph international development consultant
Jones, Horace Charles former sales company executive
Ridings, Dorothy Sattes communications executive, newspaper publisher

Brandon
Williamson, Robert Charles marketing executive

Casselberry
Medin, A. Louis computer company executive

Clearwater
Deadman, Leonard John advertising executive
Leeds, Robert Lewis, Jr. educator
†Paxson, Lowell White television station executive
†Raymund, Steven computer company executive

Coral Gables
Cobb, Charles E., Jr. corporate executive, former ambassador
Hertz, Arthur Herman advertising executive
Ramsey, John Hansberry executive search firm executive, investment banker

Daytona Beach
Dukas, Peter *management consultant, educator*

Deerfield Beach
†Moran, James M. *automotive sales executive*

Deland
Coulter, Borden McKee *management consultant*
McCormick, Lyle Bernard, Jr. *management consultant*

Delray Beach
Charyk, Joseph Vincent *retired satellite telecommunications executive*

Fort Lauderdale
Bayles, Samuel Heagan *advertising agency executive*
†Bleckner, Edward, Jr. *data communication products company executive*
Cumerford, William Richard *fund raising and public relations executive*
Durfey, Robert Walker *sea transportation consultant*
Fine, Howard Alan *travel industry chief executive officer*
Fox, James Frederick *public relations counsel*
Gerbino, John *advertising executive*
†Gude, Nancy Carlson *publishing company executive*
Harris, Stanley Louis, Jr. *advertising executive*
Jotcham, Thomas Denis *marketing communications consultant*
Kobert, Norman *asset management consultant*
Russo, Thomas Joseph *hospitality and consumer durables industry executive*
†Smith, Scott Clybourn *communications company executive*
Sorensen, Allan Chresten *service company executive*
†Thomas, Rowland Hayes, Jr. *computer services company executive*
Vasquez, William Leroy *marketing professional, educator*
†Zirkle, David H. *data processing company executive*

Fort Myers
Fromm, Winfield Eric *retired corporate executive, engineering consultant and investor*
Mc Grath, William Restore *transportation planner, traffic engineer*
Ryan, William Joseph *communications company executive*
Zupko, Arthur George *consultant to drug industry, retired college administrator*

Fort Pierce
Chapman, John Davol *communications brokerage executive*

Gainesville
Barber, Charles Edward *newspaper executive, journalist*

Gulf Breeze
Strength, Janis Grace *management executive, educator*

Havana
Penson, Edward Martin *management consulting company executive*

Hialeah
Edelcup, Norman Scott *management and financial consultant*

Highland Beach
Gaffey, Thomas Michael, Jr. *consumer products executive*
Summers, James Irvin *retired advertising executive*
Wegman, Harold Hugh *management consultant*

Hollywood
Angstrom, Wayne Raymond *communications executive*
Cowan, Irving *real estate owner, developer*

Indian Rocks Beach
Mortensen, James E. *management consultant*

Jacksonville
Aftoora, Patricia Joan *transportation executive*
Currie, Earl James *transportation company executive*
Davis, A. Dano *grocery store chain executive*
Goff, Charles Wesley, Jr. *management consultant*
Schramm, Bernard Charles, Jr. *advertising agency executive*
Sederbaum, William *marketing executive*
†Sekely, George Frank *computer and communications executive*
Wilson, J. Tylee *business executive*

Jensen Beach
Sculfort, Maurice Charles *advertising agency executive*

Jupiter
Marker, Robert Sydney *management consultant*

Kennedy Space Center
Young, Richard Stuart *technical services executive*

Key West
Ellinghaus, William Maurice *communications executive*

Lake Buena Vista
Lomonosoff, James Marc *marketing executive*

Lakeland
Jenkins, Howard M. *supermarket executive*
Meads, Walter Frederick *executive recruitment consultant*
Miller, Robert Allen *hotel executive*
†Norton, Kelly E. *ceramic flooring company executive*

Largo
Ray, Roger Buchanan *retired communications executive, lawyer*

Leesburg
Entorf, Richard Carl *management consultant*

Longboat Key
Cornelius, James Alfred *advertising executive*
Schoenberg, Lawrence Joseph *computer services company executive*

Longwood
Brooker, Robert Elton *corporate executive*
Faller, Donald E. *marketing and operations executive*

Manalapan
Johnstone, Edmund Frank *advertising executive*

Melbourne
Boyd, Joseph Aubrey *communications company executive*
Gabriel, Roger Eugene *management consulting executive*

Miami
†Arison, Micky *cruise line company executive*
Bastian, James Harold *air transport company executive, lawyer*
Berkman, Harold William *marketing educator*
Burns, Mitchel Anthony *transportation services company executive*
†Conrad, Barry L. *food service executive*
†Cubas, Jose M(anuel) *advertising agency executive*
Duffy, Earl Gavin *hotel executive*
Evans, Peter Kenneth *advertising executive*
†Garcia-Serra, Alberto J. *advertising executive*
Gibbons, Barry J. *food service executive*
Henson, John Denver *international management consulting firm executive*
Hertz, David Bendel *management consultant, educator, lawyer*
Kepner, Woody *public relations executive*
†Lieff, Ann Spector *music company executive*
Navarro, Antonio (Luis) *public relations executive*
O'Brien, William Andrew *information management executive*
†Porter, Charles King *advertising executive*
Roedema, Charles E(dward) *advertising agency executive*
Rothchild, Howard Leslie *advertising executive*
Silva, Felipe *former tobacco company executive*
Stickler, Daniel Lee *health care management consultant*
Wackenhut, George Russell *security services executive*
Wackenhut, Richard Russell *security company executive*
Weiser, Ralph Raphael *recovery company executive*
Weiser, Sherwood Manuel *hotel and corporation executive, lawyer*

Miami Beach
Shapiro, Samuel Bernard *management consultant*

Mount Dora
Hensinger, Margaret Elizabeth *horticultural and agricultural advertising and marketing executive*

Naples
Berman, Robert S. *marketing consultant*
Buccello, Henry Louis *advertising executive*
Carter, Jaine M(arie) *human resources development company executive*
Daniels, Myra Janco (Mrs. Draper Daniels) *advertising agency executive*
Hochschwender, Herman Karl *international consultant*
Johnson, Walter L. *corporate executive*
Quigley, Jack Allen *service company executive*
Richmond, Robert Linn *management consultant*
Weeks, Richard Ralph *marketing educator*

New Port Richey
Oliveto, Frank Louis *recreation consultant*

Nokomis
Halladay, Laurie Ann *public relations consultant, former franchise executive*
Lesch, George Henry *household products company executive*

North Palm Beach
Chane, George Warren *management consultant*

Ocala
Booth, George Warren *artist, advertising executive*

Oldsmar
Brunner, George Matthew *management consultant, former business executive*

Orlando
Pantuso, Vincent Joseph *food service consultant*
Yesawich, Peter Charles *advertising executive*

Ormond Beach
Coke, C(hauncey) Eugene *consulting company executive, scientist, educator, author*

Palm Beach
Alimanestianu, Calin *retired hotel consultant*
Druck, Kalman Breschel *public relations counselor*
†Robb, David Buzby, Jr. *financial services company executive, lawyer*
Walsh, Cornelius Stephen *leasing company executive*

Palm Beach Gardens
Bubrick, George Joseph *corporate executive*
Mendelson, Richard Donald *former communications company executive*

Panama City
Dykes, James Edgar *advertising educator, consultant*

Pembroke Pines
Ladin, Eugene *communications company executive*

Placida
Grissom, Joseph Carol *retired leasing and investments business executive*

Plantation
Hicks, Ele Wyatte *management consultant*

Pompano Beach
Crandell, K(enneth) James *management and strategic planning consultant, entrepreneur*
Freimark, Jeffrey Philip *retail supermarket executive*
Slovin, Bruce *diversified holding company executive*

Punta Gorda
Harrington, John Vincent *retired communications company executive, engineer, educator*

Saint Augustine
LeBeau, Hector Alton, Jr. *management consultant, former confectionary company executive*

Saint Petersburg
Layton, William George *management consultant, human resources executive*
Sembler, Mel *company executive, former ambassador*
Silver, Lawrence Alan *marketing executive*

Sarasota
Beck, Robert Alfred *hotel administration educator*
Deere, Cyril Thomas *retired computer company executive*
Feder, Allan Appel *management executive, consultant*
Fendrick, Alan Burton *retired advertising executive*
Gittelson, Bernard *public relations consultant, author, lecturer*
Gray, Hope Diffenderfer *industrial specialist*
Hagen, George Leon *business consultant*
Herbert, James Paul *advertising executive*
Lewis, Brian Kreglow *computer consultant*
Mattran, Donald Albert *management consultant, educator*
Schersten, H. Donald *management consultant, realtor, mortgage broker*
Simon, Joseph Patrick *food services executive*
Tolley, James Little *corporate public relations consultant*
White, Will Walter, III *public relations consultant, writer*

Satellite Beach
Hogan, Henry Leon, III *business executive, retired air force officer*
Vilardebo, Angie Marie *management consultant, parochial school educator*

Seminole
Silver, Paul Robert *marketing executive, consultant*

Tallahassee
Marshall, Stanley *former educator, business executive*

Tampa
Christopher, Wilford Scott *public relations consultant*
Dempster, Richard Vreeland *environmental company executive*
†Dent, Sharon Pierce *transportation executive*
DeVine, B. Mack *corporate executive*
Frankowiak, James Raymond *public relations executive*
†Hayes, Don A. *data processing commpany executive*
†Whipple, Thomas A. *food marketing professional*

Tavernier
Mabbs, Edward Carl *management consultant*

Tequesta
Vollmer, James *consulting company executive*

Tierra Verde
Kubiet, Leo Lawrence *newspaper advertising and marketing executive*

Venice
Bluhm, Barbara Jean *communications agency executive*
Dodderidge, Richard William *retired marketing executive*
Ogan, Russell Griffith *business executive, retired air force officer*

Vero Beach
Bradford, Charles Lobdell *management consultant*
Fisher, Andrew *management consultant*
Mc Namara, John J(oseph) *advertising executive, writer*
Nichols, Carl Wheeler *retired advertising agency executive*

West Palm Beach
Diener, Bert *former food broker, artist*
Gowan, Joseph Patrick, Jr. *entertainment and food services company executive*
Ronan, William John *corporate executive*

Winter Park
Costa, Linda Alice *marketing and public relations executive*
Perkins, James Patrick *advertising executive*

GEORGIA

Ailey
Windsor, James Thomas, Jr. *printing company executive, newspaper publisher*

Athens
Horton, Gerald Talmadge *public relations executive, educator*
Perkins, Edward A. *management educator*

Atlanta
Alford, Walter Helion *telecommunications executive, lawyer*
Allio, Robert John *management consultant, educator*
Barnett, Elizabeth Hale *organizational consultant*
Blank, Arthur M. *home and lumber retail chain executive*
†Brown-Olmstead, Amanda *public relations executive*
Buoch, William Thomas *corporate executive*
Burge, William Lee *retired business information executive*
Chaiet, Alan Howard *advertising agency executive*
Chasen, Sylvan Herbert *computer applications consultant, investment advisor*
Cole, David Andrew *management consultant*
Cooper, Thomas Luther *retired printing company executive*
Dillon, John Robert, III *communications executive*
Dysart, Benjamin Clay, III *environmental management consultant, conservationist, engineer*
Fajardo, Katharine Lynn *public relations and marketing executive*
†Farley, Charles P. *public relations executive*
†Fitzgerald, David Patrick *advertising agency executive*
Frank, William Pendleton *sales and marketing executive*
Fuqua, John Brooks *retired consumer products and services company executive*
Gable, Carl Irwin *business consultant, private investor, lawyer*
†Goldstein, Burton Benjamin, Jr. *communications executive*
Goodwin, George Evans *public relations executive*
†Gowland, Douglas R. *service industry executive*
House, Donald Lee, Sr. *software executive, private investor, management consultant*
†Johnson, William B. *hotel executive*
Kaiser, Fred *computer leasing company executive*
†Loudermilk, R. Charles *sales executive*
Martin, Kenneth Douglas *consumer products company executive*
†Martindale, Larry *hotel executive*
Massey, Charles Knox, Jr. *advertising agency executive*
McDonald, John C. *telecommunications company executive*
Miles, John Karl *marketing executive*
†Miller, Neal Louis *software company executive*
Miller, Thomas Marshall *marketing consultant*
Montgomery, James Morton *public relations, marketing executive, association executive*
Newman, James Michael *communications company executive*
Ordover, Abraham Philip *corporate executive*
†Overstreet, Jim *public relations executive*
Raper, Charles Albert *management consultant*
†Rogers, C. B., Jr. *information services executive*
†Rollins, Gary Wayne *service company executive*
Rosenberg, George A. *public relations company executive*
Schulze, Horst H. *hotel company executive*
Shelton, Robert Warren *marketing executive*
Sherry, Henry Ivan *marketing consultant*
†Shutze, Virgil Cox *advertising executive*
†Siegel, Randy *public relations executive*
Simms, Arthur Benjamin *management consultant, financier*
Sloan, Stanley *management consultant*
Spann, George William *management consultant*
Stormont, Richard Mansfield *hotel executive*
Summerlin, Glenn Wood *advertising executive*
Suojanen, Waino W. *management educator*
Swan, James Robert Duncan *hotel executive*
Tarkenton, Francis Asbury *computer comany executive, sports commentator, management consultant, former professional football player*
Tarr, Curtis W. *business executive*
†Taylor, Maria Centofanti *marketing professional*
Thomas, Patrick Herbert *information services company executive*
Turner, Michael Griswold *advertising executive*
Verrill, F. Glenn *advertising executive*
Wells, Everett Clayton, Jr. *economic development executive*
White, Ronald Leon *financial management consultant*
Whitehead, John Jed *computer systems company executive*

Bolingbroke
Geary, David Leslie *communications executive, educator, consultant*

Columbus
†Slay, Ken *sales executive*
†Swift, George P., Jr. *corporate professional*
Zallen, Harold *corporate executive, scientist, former university official*

Dacula
Bascom, Perry Bagnall *retired marketing sales executive*

Dallas
Friedrich, Stephen Miro *credit bureau company executive*

Macon
†Drinkard, Lawrence W. *service executive*

Marietta
Aronoff, Craig Ellis *management educator, consultant*
Johnson, Herbert Frederick *sales executive, former university administrator, librarian*
Overton, Bruce *personnel executive, consultant*
Smith, Baker Armstrong *management executive, lawyer*

Norcross
Esher, Brian Richard *environmental company executive*
Francisco, Edgar Wiggin, III *management consultant*
Harris, William North *consulting company executive*

Pine Mountain
Callaway, Howard Hollis *business executive*

Roswell
Burgess, John Frank *management consultant, former utility executive, former army officer*
†Hill, Dennis James *trade show exhibition manager, consultant*
Jordan, DuPree, Jr. *management consultant, educator, journalist, publisher, business executive*

Saint Simons Island
Riedeburg, Theodore *management consultant*

Savannah
Schafer, Thomas Wilson *advertising agency executive*

Theis, Francis William *business executive*

Smyrna
†Lenker, Max V. *consumer products company executive*
Wilding, Diane *marketing, financial and information systems executive*

Tucker
Rogers, Richard Hilton *service executive*

HAWAII

Hanalei
Ching, Lawrence Lin Tai *retail executive*

Hilo
Evans, Franklin Bachelder *marketing educator emeritus*

Honolulu
Cornuelle, Herbert Cumming *retired corporate executive*
Halloran, Richard Colby *communications research executive, former news correspondent*
Jongeward, George Ronald *systems analyst*
Kelley, Richard Roy *hotel executive*
Kelly, James Andrew *policy reseach executive, former government official*
Keogh, Richard John *management consultant*
Loui, Patricia M. L. *marketing company executive*
Murabayashi, Harris Nozomu *management analyst*
O'Neill, Charles Kelly *marketing executive, former advertising agency executive*
Simpson, Andrea Lynn *energy communication executive*
†Stebbins, Dennis Robert *international business and environmental management consultant*
Tatibouet, André Stephan *condominium and resort management firm executive*
Yamato, Kei C. *international business consultant*

Kaneohe
Smales, Fred Benson *corporate executive*

IDAHO

Boise
Agee, William J. *transportation, engineering and construction company executive*
Beaumont, Pamela Jo *marketing professional*

Idaho Falls
Stosich, Davidjohn *company executive*

ILLINOIS

Alton
Minsker, Robert Stanley *consultant, former industrial relations executive*

Arlington Heights
Ness, James McCullie, Jr. *sales and marketing executive*
Stratman, Frank Herman *travel company executive*

Barrington
Andler, Donald Andrew *marketing executive*
Edwards, Wilbur Shields *communications company executive*
Koelling, Herbert Lee *printing company executive*
Ligare, Kathleen Meredith *sales and marketing executive*
Mathis, Jack David *advertising executive*
Woltz, Kenneth Allen *consulting executive*
†Zeller, Joseph Paul *advertising executive*

Bloomington
Jones, Norman Thomas *service executive*

Buffalo Grove
Jette, Lorraine Doris *letter shop services executive*
Kaplan, Mitchell Philip *consulting engineer, marketing executive*

Carbondale
Wills, Walter Joe *agricultural marketing educator*

Carmi
Edwards, Judith Elizabeth *advertising executive*

Champaign
Knox, Charles Milton *purchasing agent, consultant*

Chicago
Adams, Hall, Jr. (Cap Adams) *advertising agency executive*
Allen, Belle *management consulting firm executive, communications company executive*
Amberg, Thomas Law *public relations executive*
Arrington, Michael Browne *travel management company executive*
†Ashwill, Terry M. *advertising executive*
Avedisian, Armen George *industrialist, financier*
Bailey, Robert, Jr. *advertising executive*
Balousek, John B. *advertising executive*
†Banik, Douglas Heil *advertising executive*
Bard, John Franklin *consumer products executive*
Barnette, Dennis Arthur *management consultant*
Bayer, Gary Richard *advertising executive*
Beattie, Janet Holtzman *accounting firm executive*
Bensinger, Peter Benjamin *consulting firm executive*
Berkery, Michael John *management consultant*
Bernatowicz, Frank Allen *management consultant, expert witness*
†Bess, Ronald W. *sales executive*
Biggles, Richard Robert *marketing executive*
Bjorneberg, Paul Grant *public relations executive*
Bliwas, Ronald Lee *advertising agency executive*
Boris, William O. *advertising agency executive*
Borleis, Melvin William *management consultant*
Bowen, William Joseph *management consultant*
†Brashears, Donald Robert *advertising agency executive*
†Breslin, Michael Edward *advertising agency executive, lawyer*

†Bruckman, Carol Jeannette *advertising executive*
Brutlag, Rodney Sheldon *management consultant*
Buckley, Joseph Paul, III *polygraph specialist*
Bueschel, David Alan *management consultant*
Burack, Elmer Howard *management educator*
Burton, Raymond Charles, Jr. *transportation company executive*
†Capparelli, R. Cary *marketing executive*
†Chaitin, Anthony *management services executive*
Chorengel, Bernd *international hotel corporation executive*
Choyke, Phyllis May Ford (Mrs. Arthur Davis Choyke, Jr.) *management executive, editor, poet*
Cohan, George Sheldon *advertising and public relations executive*
Conidi, Daniel Joseph *private investigation agency executive*
Corbett, Frank Joseph *advertising executive*
Coulson, John Selden *retired marketing executive*
Cox, Allan James *management consultant*
Cushman, Aaron D. *public relations executive*
†Daley, Rosie *cook, writer*
Dammeyer, Rodney Foster *distribution company executive*
Davis, J. Steve *advertising agency executive*
De Francesco, John Blaze, Jr. *public relations company executive*
Delony, Patty Litton *management consultant*
DeLorey, John Alfred *printing company executive*
Doty, Carl K. *retired printing company executive*
†Eastham, Dennis Michael *advertising executive*
Echols, M(ary) Evelyn *travel consultant*
Edelman, Daniel Joseph *public relations executive*
Feldman, Burton Gordon *printing company executive*
Feldstein, Joel Robert *public relations executive*
Fickinger, Wayne Joseph *advertising executive*
†Fisher, John James *advertising executive*
Fisher, Wendy Astley-Bell *marketing executive*
Fizdale, Richard *advertising agency executive*
Flaherty, John Joseph *quality assurance company executive*
Flanagan, Joseph Patrick *advertising executive*
Foley, Joseph Lawrence *sales executive*
†Ford, Larry John *computer company executive*
Foster, Hugh Warren *transportation company executive*
Freidheim, Cyrus F., Jr. *management consultant*
Frommelt, Jeffrey James *management consulting firm executive*
Fulgoni, Gian Marc *market research company executive*
Fullmer, Paul *public relations counselor*
Gardner, Howard Alan *travel marketing executive, travel writer and editor*
Gillette, Susan Downs *advertising executive*
†Glasner, LeRoy A. *public relations executive*
Glasser, James J. *leasing company executive*
Goldring, Norman Max *advertising executive*
Golin, Alvin *public relations company executive*
Golomski, William Arthur *consulting company executive*
Grant, Paul Bernard *industrial relations educator*
Greene, Charles Cassius *advertising agency executive*
Haffner, Charles Christian, III *retired printing company executive*
†Haley, Clifton Edward *car rental company executive*
Hallagan, Robert E. *management consultant*
Hansen, Carl R. *management consultant*
Hartley-Leonard, Darryl *hotel company executive*
Hassan, M. Zia *management educator*
†Haupt, Roger A. *advertising executive*
Hausman, William Ray *fund raising and management consultant*
†Hayden, Thomas H. *advertising executive*
Heidrick, Gardner Wilson *management consultant*
Heidrick, Robert Lindsay *management consultant*
Hermann, Edward Robert *occupational and environmental health consultant*
Hill, Raymond Joseph *packaging company executive*
Hoey, Rita Marie *public relations executive*
Holzer, Edwin *advertising executive*
†Hudson, Dawn Emily *advertising executive*
Isaacs, Roger David *public relations executive*
Jarc, Frank Robert *printing company executive*
Johnson, Robert Bruce *public relations executive*
†Keierleber, Stephen James *advertising executive*
†Kestnbaum, Robert Dana *management consultant*
Kobs, James Fred *advertising agency executive*
Koten, John A. *retired communications executive*
Kozitka, Richard Eugene *consumer products company executive*
Kraus, Herbert Myron *public relations executive*
Krivkovich, Peter George *advertising executive*
Lane, Kenneth Edwin *retired advertising agency executive*
†LaSage, John David *public relations firm executive*
Lauer, Robert Lee *consumer products executive*
Leahigh, Alan Kent *public relations executive*
Lebedow, Aaron Louis *consulting company executive*
Leigh, Sherren *communications executive, editor, publisher*
Lesly, Philip *public relations counsel*
Lewy, Ralph I. *hotel executive*
Litow, Merrill *advertising executive*
Lowry, James Hamilton *management consultant*
Lynch, William Thomas, Jr. *advertising agency executive*
Lynnes, R. Milton *advertising executive*
†Mackiewicz, Laura *advertising agency executive*
Maguire, David Edward *personnel executive, consultant*
†Malkin, Judd D. *diversified corporation executive*
Mason, Bruce *advertising agency executive*
McConnell, E. Hoy, II *advertising executive*
McCullough, Richard Lawrence *advertising agency executive*
Mc Kenna, Thomas Joseph *advertising executive*
†McNeely, Stephen Allen *company executive*
Menchin, Robert Stanley *marketing executive*
†Meyer, Edward Paul *advertising executive*
Miller, Bernard Joseph, Jr. *advertising executive*
Miller, William H. *public relations executive*
Mitchell, Lee Mark *communications executive, investment fund manager, lawyer*
Nadherny, Ferdinand *executive recruiting company executive*
Nelson, H(arry) Donald *communications executive*
†Nicastro, Neil David *business executive, lawyer*
Niefeld, Jaye Sutter *advertising executive*
Nolan, Robert D. *advertising company executive*
Oates, James G. *advertising executive*
†O'Connell, Dennis A. *advertising executive*
O'Hare, Linda Parsons *management consultant*
Olins, Robert Abbot *communications research executive*

O'Shea, Lynne Edeen *advertising and media company executive, educator*
Paul, Ronald Neale *management consultant*
Pekow, Eugene *hotel company executive*
Philipps, Louis Edward *data systems manufacturing company executive*
Pilkington, Alan Ralph *advertising executive*
Pincus, Theodore Henry *public relations executive*
Plank, Betsy Ann (Mrs. Sherman V. Rosenfield) *public relations counsel*
Plotkin, Manuel D. *management consultant, educator, former corporate executive and government official*
†Plummer, Roger Lawrence *information systems executive*
Pope, Lena Elizabeth *human resources specialist*
Preschlack, John Edward *management consultant*
†Pritzker, Thomas Jay *lawyer, business executive*
Proctor, Barbara Gardner *advertising agency executive*
Prosperi, David Philip *public relations executive*
Provus, Barbara Lee *executive search consultant*
Radell, Nicholas John *management consultant*
Raphaelson, Joel *advertising agency executive*
Reggio, Vito Anthony *management consultant*
Reitman, Jerry Irving *advertising agency executive*
Rich, S. Judith *public relations executive*
Richardson, Jerome Johnson *food service company executive*
Robbins, Henry Zane *public relations and marketing executive*
†Rose, Merrill *public relations counselor*
Rosenthal, Albert Jay *advertising agency executive*
Ross, John Thompson, Jr. (Tom Ross) *advertising executive*
Rydholm, Ralph Williams *advertising agency executive*
†Sanderson, Richard Burr *advertising agency executive*
†Schap, Evelyn K. *advertising executive*
Schultz, Arthur Warren *communications company executive*
Scott, Louis Edward *advertising agency executive*
Seaman, Irving, Jr. *public relations consultant*
Seidner, Frederic Jay *public relations executive*
Shirley, Virginia Lee *advertising executive*
Sibbald, John Ristow *management consultant*
Singer, Emel *staffing industry executive*
Sive, Rebecca Anne *public affairs company executive*
Smith, John J. (Jack Smith) *advertising agency executive*
Soto, Ramona *training specialist*
Spencer, Rozelle Jeffery *moving and storage company executive*
Staley, Augustus Eugene, III *advertising executive*
Steingraber, Frederick George *management consultant*
Stone, James Howard *management consultant*
Stotter, David W. *marketing executive*
Strenski, James B. *communications executive*
Struggles, John Edward *management consultant*
Sweeney, James Patrick *management consultant*
Sweet, Charles Wheeler *executive recruiter*
Swift, Dolores Monica Marcinkevich *public relations executive*
Talbot, Pamela *public relations executive*
Taylor, George Allen *advertising agency executive*
Teichner, Lester *management consulting executive*
Thomas, John Thieme *management consultant*
Trauscht, Donald C. *security services executive*
Tyler, W(illiam) Ed *printing company executive*
Uvena, Frank John *printing company executive, lawyer*
von Ferstel, Marilou McCarthy *public relations executive*
Wackerle, Frederick William *management consultant*
Weber, Daniel E. *marketing professional*
†Weber, Donald B. *advertising and marketing executive*
Westbrooks, Alphonso *public relations executive*
†Williams, Mark H. *advertising agency executive*
Winninghoff, Albert C. M. *advertising company executive*
Wood, Timothy McDonald *diversified security company executive, controller*
Wright, Patricia Donovan *communications executive*
Ziebarth, Robert Charles *management consultant*
Zwiren, Jan Marie *advertising executive*

Crete
Langer, Steven *human resources management consultant and industrial psychologist*

De Kalb
Wit, Daniel *international consultant*

Decatur
Blake, William Henry *credit and public relations consultant*

Deerfield
Charlson, David Harvey *executive search company professional*
Gaples, Harry Seraphim *computer service company executive*
Hersher, Richard Donald *management consultant*
Kinzelberg, Harvey *leasing company executive*

Des Plaines
Yarnell, Jeffrey Alan *regional credit executive*

Downers Grove
Erickson, Robert Daniel *management services company executive*
Hegenderfer, Jonita Susan *public relations executive*
Lulay, Gail C. *human resources executive, consultant*
Pollard, Charles William *diversified services company executive*
Pollock, John Glennon *contract management services company executive*

Dwight
Oughton, James Henry, Jr. *corporate executive, farmer*

East Saint Louis
Lindsley, James Bruce *sales and marketing executive*

Elgin
Burian, Robert J *human resources executive*
Hamlet, Joseph Frank *service and liquid hazardous waste industry executive*
Transue, Brooke Mullen *occupational assessment and career specialist*

Elk Grove Village
Edwardson, John Albert, Jr. *telecomunications company executive*

Evanston
Fryburger, Vernon Ray, Jr. *advertising and marketing educator*
Kaatz, Ronald B. *advertising educator, consultant*
Kotler, Philip *marketing educator, consultant, educator*
Lavengood, Lawrence Gene *management educator, historian*
Magee, Robert Paul *accounting and information systems educator*
Neuschel, Robert Percy *educator, former management consultant*
Rolfe, Michael N. *management consulting firm executive*
Tornabene, Russell C. *communications executive*
Worthy, James Carson *educator*

Evergreen Park
Lucas, Shirley Agnes Hoyt *management executive*

Geneva
Barney, Charles Richard *transportation company executive*

Glen Ellyn
Sigalos, George Peter *company executive*

Glencoe
Gordon, Bernard *management and communications consultant*

Glenview
Lacy, Herman Edgar *management consultant*
Mc Cormick, James Charles *leasing and financial services company executive*
Stern, Gerald Joseph *advertising executive*

Hawthorn Woods
Schmitz, Shirley Gertrude *marketing and sales executive*

Highland Park
Asher, Frederick *former mail order company executive*
Harris, Thomas L. *public relations executive*
Markman, Raymond Jerome *marketing executive*

Hillside
†Kloster, Carol Good *marketing executive*

Hinsdale
Berry, Virgil Jennings, Jr. *management consultant*
Bloom, Stephen Joel *distribution company executive*
Cannon, Patrick Francis *public relations executive*
Cohen, Burton David *franchising executive, lawyer*
Whitney, William Elliot, Jr. *advertising agency executive*

Hodgkins
†Winn, Elwood F. *consumer product company executive*

Hoffman Estates
Costello, John H., III *business and marketing executive*
Martinez, Arthur C. *retail company executive*
Rooney, John Edward, Jr. *communications company executive*

Inverness
Hetzel, William Gelal *executive search consultant*

Itasca
†Rowsey, Michael *printing company executive*

Kankakee
Berkenkamp, Fred Julius *management consultant*

Kenilworth
Guelich, Robert Vernon *retired management consultant*

La Grange
Carroll, Thomas John *advertising executive*

Lake Bluff
Fromm, Henry Gordon *retired manufacturing and marketing executive*
Grant, John Robert *management consultant*
Stetson, John Charles *corporate executive*
Stevens, George Richard *business consultant, public policy commentator*

Lake Forest
Carter, Donald Patton *advertising executive*
Ditka, Michael Keller *restaurateur, former professional football coach*
Kenly, Granger Farwell *marketing consultant, college official*
Mohr, Roger John *advertising agency executive*
Rand, Kathy Sue *public relations executive*

Libertyville
Ransom, Margaret Palmquist *public relations executive*

Lincolnshire
Iosue, Carmine A. *company executive*
Woods, John Lucius *management consultant*

Lisle
Long, Charles Franklin *corporate communications executive*
Schwemm, John Butler *printing company executive, lawyer*
Tyson, Kirk W. M. *business consultant*

Lombard
Johnson, Dennis Lester *marketing consultant*
Williams, Ronald Boal, Jr. *financial training company executive*
†Yeager, David P. *management consultant*
†Yeager, Phillip Charles *transportation company exeuctive*

Long Grove
Tarjan, Robert Wegg *information services executive*

Melrose Park
Lavin, Leonard H. *personal care products company executive*

Moline
Schaeffer, Robert Ollie *elevator company executive*

Mount Prospect
Flagg, Michael James *communications and graphics company executive*
Hansen, H. Jack *management consultant*
Rible, Morton *manufacturing executive, lawyer*
Sissors, Jack Zanville *marketing educator*

Naperville
Fritz, Roger Jay *management consultant*
†Olson, Donald W. *transportation executive*

Niles
Schreiber, Jeffrey Lee *computer sales executive*

Northbrook
Clarey, John Robert *executive search consultant*
†Freedman, Walter G. *corporate services executive*
Jacobs, Richard Alan *management consultant*
Kubek, Ralph A. *management consultant, accountant*
Lucas, Lawrence Newton *sales and marketing consultant*
Marshall, Irl Houston, Jr. *company executive*
Pinsof, Nathan *retired advertising executive*
Ross, Bernard Harris *fitness company executive, certified public accountant, consultant*
Tolan, James Francis *corporate and financial communications executive, marketing consultant, financial analyst*
†Turner, Lee *travel company executive*
Wajer, Ronald Edward *management consultant*
Weinstein, Ira Phillip *advertising executive*

Northfield
Parry, Rawdon Moira Crozier *marketing executive*
Smart, Jackson Wyman, Jr. *business executive*

Oak Brook
Buntrock, Dean Lewis *waste management company executive*
Kearney, Michael John *operations executive*
Quinlan, Michael Robert *fast food franchise company executive*
†Turner, Fred L. *fast food franchise executive*

Oak Forest
†Lawler, Edmund G. *hospital administrator*

Oak Park
Devereux, Timothy Edward *advertising agency executive*
Notaro, Michael R. *data processing and computer service executive*

Orland Park
Leonard, Robert Dougherty *communications company executive*

Palatine
Medin, Lowell Ansgard *management executive*

Park Ridge
Mack, Clifford Glenn *investment banker, management consultant*
Margolies, Raymond *management consulting company executive*
Rosenheim, Howard Harris *corporate executive*

Quincy
†Cain, Richard Evan *radio station executive*

River Forest
Hamper, Robert Joseph *marketing executive*
Tomek, Laura Lindemann *marketing executive*
Wanamaker, Robert Joseph *advertising company executive*

Rockford
Duck, Vaughn Michael *software company executive*

Rosemont
Baron, Richard Albert *sales executive*
Trznadel, Frank Dwight, Jr. *leasing company executive*

Schaumburg
†Bauchiero, James *transportation executive*
Greenwell, Ronald Everett *communications executive*
Halloran, Daniel Edward *personnel executive*
†Heaton, Syd N. *computer company executive*
Morgan, David Ernest *computer and communications research executive*
Stephens, Norval Blair, Jr. *marketing consultant*

Shelbyville
†Gloede, Richard *management consulting executive*

Skokie
Bakalar, John Stephen *printing and publishing company executive*
Kranz, Norman *advertising executive*
White, William James *information management and services company executive;*

South Barrington
Smith, William Lewis *hotel executive*

Springfield
Stroh, Raymond Eugene *personnel executive*

Urbana
Mayer, Robert Wallace *emeritus finance educator*
Rotzoll, Kim Brewer *advertising and communications educator*
Sandage, Charles Harold *advertising educator*

Vernon Hills
Claassen, W(alter) Marshall *employment company executive*

†Mignano, Richard Alan *marketing professional*

Villa Park
Williams, David Arthur *marketing professional*

Western Springs
Carroll, Jeanne *public relations executive*

Wheaton
Jett, Charles Cranston *management consultant*
Mellott, Robert Vernon *advertising executive*

Wheeling
Koch, Peter F. *management consultant*

Wilmette
Kurtzman, Allan Roger *advertising executive*

Winnetka
Bogart, Homer Gordon *marketing executive*
Folds, Charles Weston *merchandising consultant*
Greeley, Joseph May *retired advertising executive*
Kahn, Paul Frederick *executive search company executive*
†Mayer, Richard Philip *food executive*

Wood Dale
Kearns, Janet Catherine *corporate secretary*

Woodridge
Allen, Charles Joseph, II *advertising agency executive*
Emerson, Edward James *computer software executive*

INDIANA

Auburn
Kempf, Jane Elmira *marketing executive*

Bloomington
Burton, Philip Ward *advertising executive, educator*
Gordon, Paul John *business management educator*
Patterson, James Milton *marketing specialist, educator*
†Sullivan, Michael Francis, III *executive*

Boggstown
Gray, Carlos Gibson *restaurateur, seedsman, entertainer*

Carmel
Ferrero, Louis Peter *computer services company executive*

Columbus
Higgins, Harold Bailey *executive search company executive*

East Chicago
Crum, James Francis *waste recycling company executive*

Elkhart
Chism, James Arthur *information systems executive*
Ellis, Joseph Newlin *distribution company executive*
Tatum, Rita *communications executive*

Evansville
Hampel, Robert Edward *advertising executive*
Kitch, Frederick David *advertising executive*

Fort Wayne
†Dorman, Barry *waste management executive*

Hammond
Yovich, Daniel John *marketing professional educator*

Indianapolis
Bower, Sandra Irwin *communications executive*
Carr, William H(enry) A. *public relations executive, author*
Durbin, Robert Cain *hotel executive*
Gilman, Alan B. *restaurant company executive*
Glazner, Raymond Charles *technical services manager*
†Haynes, Thomas Joseph *marketing executive*
Kacek, Don J. *management consultant, business owner*
Krueger, Alan Douglas *communications company executive*
†MacVittie, Paula Rae *advertising executive*
Nyhart, Eldon Howard *employee benefits consultant, lawyer*
Pattyn, Remi Ceasar *management consultant*
Ruben, Gary A. *marketing and communications consultant*
Slaymaker, Gene Arthur *public relations executive*
Walker, Frank Dilling *market research executive*

Jasper
Geiger, Victor Alan *international sales executive*

Lake Bluff
Gage, Calvin William *retired*

Muncie
Barber, Earl Eugene *consulting firm executive*

Munster
Purcell, James Francis *consultant, former utility executive*

Notre Dame
Bella, Salvatore Joseph *management educator*

Peru
Bronson, Kenneth Caldean *newspaper company executive*

Seymour
Bollinger, Don Mills *grocery company executive*

South Bend
Burkhart, Charles Barclay *outdoor advertising executive*

†Vandenberg, Sister Patricia Clasina *health system executive*

Valparaiso
Schlender, William Elmer *management sciences educator*

Wabash
Flott, Leslie William *quality control professional*
Scales, Richard Lewis *manufacturer's representative*

West Lafayette
Johnson, Robert Willard *management educator*
Schendel, Dan Eldon *management consultant, business educator*

IOWA

Cedar Rapids
†Anderson, Gerald Lee *advertising executive*
†Damrow, Richard G. *advertising executive*
†Stadlen, Diane Elizabeth *marketing professional*

Chariton
†Pickens, Earl *consumer products company executive*

Des Moines
†Cruger, F. Christopher *corporate executive*
Meredith, Edwin Thomas, III *media executive*
†Myers, M. Kathleen *publishing executive*
†Stoffer, Terry James *advertising executive*
†Winick, Alfred Zell *data services corporation executive*

Fairfield
†Hawthorne, Timothy Robert *direct response advertising and communications company executive*

Plainfield
Lynes, James William, Sr. *communications company executive*

West Des Moines
Marshall, Russell Frank *research company executive*
Starr, V. Hale *communications executive*

Windsor Heights
Ferrone, Patrick Francis *consultant*

KANSAS

Hutchinson
Dillon, David Brian *retail grocery executive*

Lawrence
Mackenzie, Kenneth Donald *management consultant, educator*
Vanatta, Chester B. *business executive, educator*

Lenexa
Rayburn, George Marvin *business executive, investment executive*

Merriam
Mealman, Glenn *corporate marketing executive*

Salina
Ryan, Stephen Collister *funeral director*

Shawnee Mission
Boyd, John Kent *advertising executive*
Findlay, Theodore Bernard *management consultant*
Herring, Raymond Mark *marketing and planning executive*
Mindlin, Richard Barnett *marketing executive*
Putman, Dale Cornelius *management consultant, lawyer*

Topeka
Franklin, Benjamin Barnum *dinner club executive*
†Hilpert, Dale W. *retail shoe company executive*
Randall, Elizabeth Ellen *personnel manager*
†Vidricksen, Ben Eugene *food service executive, state legislator*

Wichita
Barents, Brian Edward *marketing executive*
†Gates, Walter Edward *rental company executive, business owner*
†Lahti, Richard *quality improvement administrator*
Lair, Robert Louis *catering company executive*
Lorelli, Michael Kevin *corporate executive*
Reinemund, Steven S. *restaurant chain executive*
†Witsman, Forest Tim *association executive*

KENTUCKY

Ashland
†Carter, David Edward *communications executive*

Lexington
Phillips, Henry Alan *communications executive*

Louisville
Brown, Owsley, II *diversified consumer products company executive*
Brown, William Lee Lyons, Jr. *consumer products company executive*
Cranor, John *food service executive*
†Neely, J. Randall *public relations executive*
Peden, Katherine Graham *industrial consultant*
Sandefur, Thomas Edwin, Jr. *tobacco company executive*
†Wenz, Rodney E. *public relations executive*

LOUISIANA

Houma
†Saia, Louis P., III *transportation executive*

Lake Charles
Aranow, Peter Jones *service company executive*

Metairie
†Benson, Jerome *automotive sales executive*

New Orleans
Cook, Victor Joseph, Jr. *marketing educator, consultant*
Lambert, Olaf Cecil *hotel executive*
†Levy, Sam *consumer products company executive*
Robinson, Susan Shelton *human resources specialist*
†Schwegmann, John F. *consumer products comprany executive*
Womack, Edgar Allen, Jr. *technology executive*

Ruston
Hudnall, Jarrett, Jr. *management and marketing educator*

Shreveport
Tullis, John Ledbetter *retired wholesale distributing company executive*

MAINE

Augusta
Roberts, Donald Albert *advertising, public relations, marketing and media consultant*

Brewer
†Campbell, Richard H. *hardware industry executive*

Camden
Lavenson, James H. *corporation executive*
Lavenson, Susan Barker *corporate executive, consultant*

Ellsworth
Eustice, Russell Clifford *consulting company executive*

Hartland
†Larochelle, Richard Clement *tanning company executive*

Kennebunk
Alling, Charles Booth, Jr. *management consultant*

North Brooklin
Schmidt, Klaus Dieter *management consultant, university administrator, marketing and management educator*

Portland
Kendrick, Peter Murray *communications executive, investor*
Potter, Lillian Florence *business executive secretary*
Shaffer, James Burgess *communications executive*

Sedgwick
Mc Millan, Brockway *former communications executive*

South Portland
Birk, John R. *marketing/financial services executive*

Waterville
Zukowski, Walter Henry *administrative science educator*

MARYLAND

Annapolis
Asbell, Fred Thomas *campaign director*
Cabral, Judith Ann *telecommunications executive*
Coogle, Joseph Moore, Jr. *management consultant*
†Cullen, John Wesley, IV *hotel company executive*
Montague, Brian John *consulting company executive*

Baltimore
Brotman, Phyllis Block *advertising and public relations executive*
Charles, Allan Frederick *advertising agency executive*
Clark, Raymond Skinner *retired transportation and distribution company executive*
†Creagh, David Michael *public radio executive*
†Dale, James Michael *advertising executive, writer*
Dodge, Calvert Renaul *education and training executive, author, educator*
Eisner, Henry Wolfgang *advertising executive*
Fried, Herbert Daniel *advertising executive*
Gibbons, Thomas Michael *communications executive*
Greenspan, Arnold Michael *computer company executive*
Hug, Richard Ernest *environmental company executive*
Nuckolls, Robert Theodore *cemetery executive*
Preston, Mark I. *investment company executive*
Robinson, Florine Samantha *marketing executive*
Talbot, Donald Roy *consulting services executive*
Wilke, Robert Thomas *advertising executive*

Beltsville
Quirk, Frank Joseph *management consulting company executive*

Bethesda
Altobello, Daniel Joseph *service executive*
Banks, Henry Stephen *systems software company executive*
Barber, Arthur Whiting *communications company executive*
Breslow, Jerome Wilfred *communications company executive*
Brown, Earle Palmer *advertising agency executive*
Brown, Jeremy Earle *advertising executive*
†Dresing, Robert K. *health care executive*
Ernst, Roger *development consultant*
Faulders, C. Thomas, III *communications company executive*
Hanley, (Charles) Robert, Jr. *computer systems executive, real estate developer*
Helm, Lewis Marshall *public affairs executive*
King, Charles McDonald, Jr. *association foundation executive*
Lauret, Curtis Bernard, Jr. *marketing professional*

McClure, Brooks *management consultant*
Mc Gurn, Barrett *communications executive, writer*
Moseley, Chris Rosser *marketing executive*
Pompa, James Robert *computer industry executive*
Pras, Robert Thomas *hotel executive*
Shellow, Robert *management service company executive, consultant*
Southwick, Paul *retired public relations executive*
Spector, Melbourne Louis *management consultant*
Spivak, Alvin A. *public relations executive*
Tuttle, William G(ilbert) T(ownsend), Jr. *management consultant, retired army officer*
Wertheimer, Franc *retired corporate executive*
Zurkowski, Paul George *information company executive*

Bowie
Kepley, Thomas Alvin *management consultant*
Purcell, Steven Richard *international management consultant, engineer, economist*

Brooklandville
Darcy, George Robert *public relations executive*
Miller, Paul George *computer company executive*

Calverton
Appell, Louise Sophia *consulting company executive*
Kotler, Martin *corporate executive*

Chestertown
Gordon, James Braund *management consultant*

Chevy Chase
Baily, Nathan Ariel *business executive, consultant, association official, former government official, educator*
Corrigan, Robert Foster *business consultant, retired diplomat*
Michaelis, Michael *management and technical consultant*
Schlegel, John Frederick *management consultant, speaker, trainer*

Cockeysville Hunt Valley
Kunisch, Robert Dietrich *business services company executive*
Whitehurst, William Wilfred, Jr. *management consultant*

College Park
Greer, Thomas Vernon *business consultant and educator*
Holder, Sallie Lou *training and meeting management consultant*
Lamone, Rudolph Philip *business educator*
Sorter, Bruce Wilbur *federal program administrator, educator, consultant*

Columbia
†Bitonti, James Anthony *business machinery company executive*
Morgan, Walter Edward *management consultant*
Steele, Richard J. *management consultant*

Crofton
Gongwer, Carolyn Jane *technical training consultant*
Kelley, Albert Benjamin *consulting company executive*

Easton
Burns, Michael Joseph *operations and sales-marketing executive*
Read, William Lawrence *business executive, former naval officer*

Elkton
Zebley, Joseph Wildman, Jr. *management consultant*

Fort Washington
McKenzie, Ruth Bates Harris *diversity human relations consultant, writer*

Gaithersburg
Flickinger, Harry Harner *organization and business executive, management consultant*
Isbister, James David *business executive*
Sayer, John Samuel *information systems consultant*

Germantown
Shaw, Jack Allen *communications company executive*

Hanover
†Hay, Lewis *food marketing executive*

Landover
Huggins, David *custom software development executive*

Lanham
Lucido, Chester Charles, Jr. *marketing executive*

Lanham Seabrook
†Herman, Kenneth *food marketing executive*

Lusby
Simpich, William Morris *public affairs consultant*

Lutherville Timonium
Chapman, Robert Breckenridge, III *management consulting company executive*

North Bethesda
Levin, Carl *public and government relations consultant*

Potomac
Fink, Daniel Julien *management consultant*
Terragno, Paul James *information industry executive*

Preston
Suggs, Leo H. *transportation executive*

Riverdale
†Hedgepeth, Leroy J. *park director*

Rockville
†Carey, John Edward *information services executive*

Christie, R(obert) Brent *real estate and hotel executive*
†Jochum, George T. *management company executive*
Leslie, John Walter *development consultant*
†Naft, Barry Niel *waste management administrator, chemical engineer*
Nash, Jonathon Michael *program manager, mechanical engineer*
†O'Keefe, Kevin *public relations executive*
Shaw, Robert William, Jr. *management consultant, venture capitalist*
Shelton, Wayne Vernon *professional services and systems integration company executive*

Saint Leonard
Andrews, John Stewart *management consultant*

Silver Spring
†Bainum, Stewart *health care and lodging company executive*
†Bainum, Stewart William, Jr. *health care and lodging company executive*
Cain, David Lee *corporate executive*
Hersey, David Floyd *information resources management consultant, government official;*
Kendrick, James Earl *business consultant*
Lynch, Sonia *data processing consultant*
Orkand, Donald Saul *management consultant*
Perlmutter, Jerome Herbert *communications specialist*
Petitt, Gerald William *hotel executive*
Shih Carducci, Joan Chia-mo *cooking educator, biochemist, medical technologist*

MASSACHUSETTS

Acton
†Barrett, James *computer software company executive*
Golden, John Joseph, Jr. *manufacturing company executive*
Tod, G. Robert *consumer marketing executive*

Amherst
Buell, Victor Paul *marketing educator, author, editor*
Singleton, Philip Arthur *corporate executive*

Bedford
Horowitz, Barry Martin *systems research and engineering company executive*
†Landry, John Bernard, III *data processing executive*

Belmont
Allison, Elisabeth Kovacs *information company executive*
†Klein, Martin Samuel *management consulting executive*
Rowe, Richard R. *on-line information and management services company executive*

Beverly
Barger, Richard Wilson *hotel executive*

Billerica
†Leblois, Axel *computer company executive*
†Mackenzie, Ward D. *computer company executive*

Boston
Anderson, Timothy Christopher *consulting company executive*
Andrews, Kenneth Richmond *business administration educator*
Arnold, John David *management counselor, consultant*
†Berenson, Paul Stewart *advertising executive*
†Boch, William Joseph *advertising agency executive*
†Britton, Richard Lindsay *advertising executive*
†Brown, David A.B. *strategy consultant*
Buchin, Stanley Ira *management consultant, educator*
†Carboni, Edwin Peters *advertising executive*
†Child, Julia McWilliams (Mrs. Paul Child) *cooking expert, television personality, author*
Clarke, Terence Michael *public relations and advertising executive*
Coleman, John Joseph *telephone company executive*
†Cone, Carol Lynn *public relations executive*
Connors, John Michael, Jr. *advertising agency executive*
Cornwall, Deborah Joyce *consulting firm executive, management consultant*
Coughlin, William Brendan *corporate executive*
Diener, Betty Jane *marketing educator, university administrator*
Dixon, Andrew Lee, Jr. *cable television company executive, lawyer*
Donahue, Douglas Aidan, Jr. *business executive*
Doorley, Thomas Lawrence, III *management consulting firm executive*
Eskandarian, Edward *advertising agency executive*
†Fagan, Thomas Maurice *trade show management executive*
Fausch, David Arthur *public relations executive*
†Feldman, Gerald *advertising executive*
†Fitzgibbons, James M. *diversified company executive*
Fonvielle, William Harold *management consultant*
Graham, Patrick Francis *management consulting company executive*
†Hamilton, Kerry Lee *advertising executive*
Hayes, Andrew Wallace, II *consumer products company executive*
Hill, George Jackson, III *advertising agency executive*
Hoffman, S. Joseph *advertising agency executive*
Hohler, G. Robert *marketing consultant*
Hurd, J. Nicholas *executive recruiting consultant, former banker*
Isaacson, John Magyar *executive search firm executive*
†Isham, Carolynn Clough *advertising executive*
Kapioltas, John *hotel company executive*
Luongo, C. Paul *public relations executive*
†Miller, John A., Jr. *public relations executive*
†Monaghan, William Henry *advertising executive*
O'Block, Robert Paul *management consultant*
Rabstejnek, George John *management consultant*
†Rosenberg, James William *marketing executive*
Saunders, Donald Leslie *hotel executive, commercial real estate company executive*
Saunders, Roger Alfred *hotel group executive*
Shapiro, Eli *business consultant, educator, economist*
Singer, Thomas Eric *industrial company executive*

Sloane, Carl Stuart *management consultant, educator*
Slosberg, Mike *advertising executive*
Sonnabend, Roger Philip *hotel company executive*
Sullivan, John Louis, Jr. *search company executive*
†Teixeira, Joseph *advertising executive*
Turillo, Michael Joseph, Jr. *management consultant*
Wilkes, Brent Ames *management consultant*
Wilson, Robert Gould *management consultant*
Wolf, William Martin *computer company executive, consultant*
Zeien, Alfred M. *consumer products company executive*

Bourne
Roper, Burns Worthington *retired opinion research company executive*

Boxboro
†Nitta, Kenjiro *Computer company executive*

Braintree
Harris, Jeffrey Sherman *direct marketing company executive*

Brookline
Frankel, Ernst Gabriel *shipping and aviation business executive, educator*

Burlington
†Groman, John Edward *marketing executive*

Cambridge
Allen, Thomas John *management educator*
Bernays, Edward L. *public relations counsel*
Dennis, Jack Bonnell *computer consultant*
†FitzGerald, Maura *public relations executive*
Fleischer, Dorothy Ann *administrative assistant*
Forrester, Jay Wright *management specialist, educator*
Greeno, J(ohn) Ladd *consulting company executive*
Judson, Arnold Sidney *management consultant*
Kelley, Albert Joseph *management educator, executive consultant*
Kerpelman, Larry Cyril *consulting firm executive*
La Mantia, Charles Robert *management consulting company executive*
Levy, Stephen Raymond *diversified high technology company executive*
Littlefield, Paul Damon *management consultant*
†Magnanti, Thomas L. *management and engineering educator*
Manzi, Jim *computer software company executive*
Marolda, Anthony Joseph *management consulting company executive*
Mueller, Robert Kirk *consultant*
Nelson, William George, IV *software company executive*
Norkus, Michael *management consultant*
Tema-Lyn, Laurie *management consultant*
Walters, Alan Stanley *consulting firm executive*
†Weber, Larry *public relations executive*

Canton
Ferrera, Arthur Rodney *food distribution company executive*
Pitts, Virginia M. *human resources executive*

Charlestown
McLennan, Bernice Claire *human resources professional*

Chestnut Hill
Smith, Richard Alan *movie theater and specialty retailing executive*

Concord
Bloom, Edwin John, Jr. *human resources consultant*
Daltas, Arthur John *management consultant*
Hogan, Daniel Bolten *management consultant*

Dedham
Culver, Edward Holland *marketing executive*
Redstone, Sumner Murray *entertainment company executive*

Dennis
Weilbacher, William Manning *advertising and marketing consultant*

Dover
Borel, Richard Wilson *communications executive, consultant*
Fulchino, Paul Edward *management consultant*
Ryburn, Samuel McChesney *corporate executive*
†Scott, Ronald Bruce *business executive, writer*

Duxbury
Albritton, William Hoyle *training and consulting executive, lecturer, writer*

Edgartown
Piper, George Earle *retailing design and service company executive*

Framingham
Ballou, Kenneth Walter *retired transportation executive, university dean*

Gloucester
Lauenstein, Milton Charles *management consultant*

Hopkinton
Preston, William Hubbard *consultant to specialty businesses*

Housatonic
Levy, Sy *advertising and direct marketing executive*

Hyannis
MacIntyre, R. Douglas *information technology executive*

Lexington
Alloway, Robert Malcombe *computer consulting executive*
Brick, Donald Bernard *consulting company executive*
Ciampa, Dan *management consultant*
Duboff, Robert Samuel *marketing professional*
Eberle, William Denman *corporate executive*
Fray, Lionel Louis *management consultant*

Risch, Martin Donald *marketing-management consulting company executive*

Lincoln
Kalba, Kas *international consultant*
Sprague, John Louis *management consultant*

Longmeadow
Locklin, Wilbert Edwin *management consultant*

Marlborough
†Morley, Thomas Mark *computer company executive*

Marshfield Hills
Stacey, Kathleen Mary *advertising executive*

Marstons Mills
Martin, Vincent George *management consultant*

Maynard
Palmer, Robert B. *computer company executive*
Smith, John F. *computer company executive*

Middleton
Stover, Matthew Joseph *communications company executive*

Natick
Donovan, R. Michael *management consultant*
Planitzer, Russell E. *computer company executive*
Strayton, Robert Gerard *public communications executive*

Needham
Cogswell, John Heyland *retired telecommunications executive, financial consultant*

Newton
Bewick, John Arters *consulting firm executive*
Coleman, Gerald Christopher *management consultant*
Kaplan, Steven F. *business management executive*
Kosowsky, David I. *retired biotechnical company executive*

North Andover
Buchanan, Ellery Rives *sales executive*
Olney, Peter Butler, Jr. *retired management consulting firm executive*

North Billerica
†Sodini, Peter J. *food service executive*

North Dartmouth
†Tuttle, Clifford Horace, Jr. *marketing executive*

Palmer
Dupuis, Robert Simeon *sales executive*

Provincetown
Brock, Alice May *restaurateur, author*

Quincy
Bierman, George William *technical consulting executive, food technologist*
Levin, Robert Joseph *retail grocery chain store executive*
Shuster, Herbert Victor *corporate executive, consultant*
Young, Richard William *corporate consultant*

Randolph
Rosenberg, Robert Michael *restaurant franchise company executive*

Sheffield
Velmans, Loet Abraham *retired public relations executive*

South Attleboro
Glenn, James *sales executive*

Springfield
Canavan, John James, Jr. *employment services executive*

Sudbury
Read, Philip Lloyd *computer design and manufacturing executive*

Tewksbury
†Miamis, James D. *retail grocery chain executive*

Wakefield
Bartl, Frederick J. *marketing professional*

Waltham
Bradstreet, Bernard Francis *computer company executive*
†Curnan, Susan Patricia Anne *human resource development executive, educator, consultant*
Gilbert, David *computer company executive*
Nelson, Arthur Hunt *corporate executive*
Poduska, John William, Sr. *computer company executive*
Ross, Douglas Taylor *software company executive*
Stambaugh, Armstrong A., Jr. *restaurant and hotel executive*

Wellesley
Allen, Michael W *management consultant*
†Goldman, James Warren *advertising agency executive*
Nagler, Leon Gregory *management consultant*
Papageorgiou, John Constantine *management science educator*

West Chatham
McHale, Thomas Anthony *sales and marketing consultant*

Westfield
Tower, Horace Linwood, III *consumer products company executive*

Weston
Sack, Burton Marshall *business executive*

Sullivan, Barbara Boyle *management consultant*

Wilbraham
Anderson, Eric William *retired food service company executive*
†O'Shaughnessy, Joseph A. *restaurant company executive*

Williamsburg
Snow, Elizabeth Jean *poet, inventor, farmer, small business owner*

Williamstown
Lee, Arthur Virgil, III *corporate executive*

Wilmington
DiFillippo, Anthony Francis *service company executive*

Winchester
Taggart, Ganson Powers *management consultant*

Woburn
Mehra, Raman Kumar *data processing executive, automation and control engineering researcher*
Tritter, Richard Paul *information systems consulting executive*

Worcester
Candib, Murray A. *business executive, retail management consultant*
Densmore, William Phillips *management consultant*
Ullrich, Robert Albert *business management educator*

Yarmouth Port
Hesse, William R. *marketing and advertising executive*

MICHIGAN

Ada
DeVos, Richard Marvin *network marketing company executive*
DeVos, Richard Marvin, Jr. (Dick DeVos) *direct sales company exexutive*
Van Andel, Jay *home and personal products company executive*

Ann Arbor
Agno, John G. *management consultant*
Belcher, Louis David *marketing and operations executive, former mayor*
Foley, Daniel Ronald *business and personnel executive*
Martin, Claude Raymond, Jr. *marketing consultant, educator*
Monaghan, Thomas Stephen *restaurant chain executive*
Ryan, William Frank *management consultant*
Terpstra, Vern *marketing educator*
†Waller, Patricia Fossum *transportation executive, researcher, psychologist*
Warshaw, Martin Richard *marketing educator*

Auburn
Schram, Geraldine Moore *security administrator*

Battle Creek
Thar, Ferdinand August (Bud Thar) *trade company executive*

Benton Harbor
Goldin, Sol *marketing consultant*

Bingham Farms
Berline, James H. *advertising executive, public relations agency executive*

Bloomfield Hills
Adams, Charles Francis *advertising and real estate executive*
Adams, Thomas Brooks *advertising consultant*
Benton, William Pettigrew *advertising agency executive*
Bissell, John Howard *marketing executive*
†Carr, Robin *advertising executive*
Casey, John Patrick (Jack Casey) *public relations executive, political analyst*
†Johnson, John K. *advertising executive*
Mills, Peter Richard *advertising executive*
†Morton, Alexander A., III *advertising agency executive*
Pingel, John Spencer *advertising executive*
†Tunstall, Sharon Sue *advertising executive*
Wagner, Bruce Stanley *advertising agency executive*
†Ward, Richard C. *advertising executive*
Weil, John William *technology management consultant*

Dearborn
Caldwell, John Thomas, Jr. *communications executive*
Jelinek, John Joseph *public relations executive*

Detroit
Barden, Don H. *communications executive*
Bassett, Tina *communications executive*
Beltaire, Beverly Ann *public relations executive*
Blevins, William Edward *management consultant*
†Czarnecki, Walter P. *trucj rental company executive*
†Flint, Robert H. *printing ink company executive*
Franco, Anthony M. *public relations executive*
McCracken, Caron Francis *data processing consultant*
Roberts, Seymour M. (Skip Roberts) *advertising executive*
Schweitzer, Peter *advertising agency executive*
Werba, Gabriel *public relations consultant*

East Lansing
Hollander, Stanley Charles *marketing educator*
Jones, Kensinger *advertising executive*
Miracle, Gordon Eldon *advertising educator*
Wilson, R. Dale *marketing educator, consultant*

Farmington Hills
Kinsey, Charles John *industrial auctioneer, consultant, cattle breeder, farmer*

Prady, Norman *advertising executive, writer, marketing consultant*

Grand Rapids
Heynen, A. James *organizational consultant*

Grosse Pointe
Droll, Marian Clarke *energy company public affairs executive*
Thurber, Donald MacDonald Dickinson *public relations counsel*
Wilson, Henry Arthur, Jr. *management consultant*

Grosse Pointe Farms
Mecke, Theodore Hart McCalla, Jr. *management consultant*

Harbor Springs
Graham, Robert C. *management consultant*

Holland
Hoddy, Raymond Arthur *industrial consultant*

Kalamazoo
†Freed, Karl Francis *professional planner*
Lawrence, William Joseph, Jr. *corporate executive*

Livonia
Brandon, David A. *marketing and publishing executive*

Midland
Hanes, James Henry *consulting business executive, lawyer*
Maneri, Remo R. *management consultant*

Monroe
Sewell, Robert Terrell, Jr. *executive search company owner*

Mount Pleasant
†McBryde, James Edward *sales representative, county commissioner*

Plymouth
Moore, Joan Elizabeth *human resources executive, lawyer*
Ramamurthy, Subramanian *management consultant*

Redford
†Flint, H. Howard, II *printing company executive*

Royal Oak
Stephens, Martha Foster *advertising executive*

Southfield
†Andrus, Leonard Carl *marketing executive*
†Caponigro, Jeffrey Ralph *public relations counselor*
Considine, John Joseph *advertising executive*
Doyle, James Thomas *marketing and communications executive*
†Graham, Michael Alan *advertising executive*
†Hammond, John B., Jr. *advertising executive*
Johnson, Richard Alan *advertising executive*
Kalter, Alan *advertising agency executive*
Maibach, Ben C., Jr. *service executive*
†Matthes, Gerald Stephen *advertising agency executive*
†Neman, Thomas Edward *advertising and marketing executive*
Smith, Nancy Hohendorf *sales and marketing executive*
†Symons, Douglas Michael *advertising executive*

Troy
Adderley, Terence E. *corporate executive*
Antonini, Joseph E. *discount department store executive*
Baker, Ernest Waldo, Jr. *advertising executive*
Ferguson, Harley Robert *service company executive*
Kelly, William R. *employment agency executive*
Sandy, William Haskell *training and communications systems executive*
Simons, Leonard Norman Rashall *advertising executive*
Smith, Glen B. *consumer products company executive*

Warren
Dow, Peter Anthony *advertising agency executive*
†Gilbert, Suzanne Harris *advertising executive*
Hopp, Anthony James *advertising agency executive*
Schultz, Louis Michael *advertising agency executive*
Wallace, Jack Harold *employee development specialist, educator*

West Bloomfield
Meyers, Gerald Carl *management consultant, author, educator, lecturer, former automobile company executive*

MINNESOTA

Bloomington
McGrath, Dennis Britton *public relations executive*
Meyer, Scott D. *public relations firm executive*
Mona, David L. *public relations executive*

Burnsville
†Gardner, Dennis (Den) *public relations executive*

Eden Prairie
Lau, Michele Denise *advertising consultant, sales trainer, television personality*

Edina
Burdick, Lou Brum *public relations executive*
Thorndyke, Lloyd Milton *computer company executive*

Hopkins
†Haworth, Charles Dale *advertising executive*

Hutchinson
Graf, Laurance James *communications executive*

Maple Grove
St. Mary, Edward Sylvester *direct mail marketing company executive*

Minneapolis
Alcott, James Arthur *communications executive*
†Beardsley, John Ray *public relations firm executive*
Bileydi, Sumer *advertising agency executive*
Boubelik, Henry Fredrick, Jr. *car rental company executive*
Burns, Neal Murray *advertising agency executive*
Cardozo, Richard Nunez *marketing, entrepreneurship and business educator*
Cox, David Carson *media company executive*
DeNero, Henry T. *department store chain executive*
Dunlap, William DeWayne, Jr. *advertising agency executive*
Egekvist, W. Soren *corporate consultant, educator*
Ferner, David Charles *non-profit management and development consultant*
†Firestone, Jon *advertising executive*
Fischer, Robert William *financial executive*
Gage, Edwin C., III (Skip Gage) *travel, marketing services executive*
Goldstein, Mark David *advertising agency executive*
Gottier, Richard Chalmers *computer company executive*
Grieman, John Joseph *communications executive*
Gustafson, Richard Charles *rental and leasing company executive*
Haugen, Rolf Eugene *leasing company executive*
Koutsky, Dean Roger *advertising executive*
Kraut, Gerald Anthony *data processing services company executive, investment banker*
†Liszt, Howard Paul *advertising executive*
Mc Elrath, Gayle William *management consultant, educator*
†McKenna, Robert J. *car rental company executive*
Morgan, Arthur Edward *management executive*
Morgan, Carol Marie *marketing executive*
Olson, Clifford Larry *management consultant, entrepreneur*
Perlman, Lawrence *business executive*
Pile, Robert Bennett *advertising executive, writer, consultant*
Retzler, Kurt Egon *diversified management company executive, hospitality, travel and marketing company executive*
Sanger, Stephen W. *consumer products company executive*
Schultz, Louis Edwin *management executive*
Speer, David James *public relations executive*
Stubbs, Jan Didra *travel industry executive*
Sullivan, Michael Patrick *food service executive*
Sveinson, Pamela J. *human resources executive*
Thompson, Clarence Miles, Jr. *advertising executive*
†Tompkins, Richard Weller, Jr. *advertising executive*
Tree, David L. *advertising agency executive*
†Wainwright, Charles Anthony *advertising company executive*
Waldera, Wayne Eugene *crisis management specialist*
†Waller, Joel N. *consumer products executive*
Wickesberg, Albert Klumb *retired management educator*
Willis, Raymond Edson *strategic management and organization educator*
Yourzak, Robert Joseph *management consultant, engineer, educator*

Minnetonka
Gillies, Donald Richard *advertising agency and marketing consultant*
List, Charles Edward *management and organization development consultant*

Rochester
†Hinckley, Michael Richards *marketing professional*
Milner, Harold William *hotel executive*
†Spencer, Edson White *computer systems company executive*

Saint Paul
†Christison, Richard James *advertising company executive*
Feinberg, David Erwin *publishing company executive*
†Garcia, Astrid J. *personnel director*
Griffin, Judith Ann *strategic planning and operating executive*
Haverty, Harold V. *forms and check printing company executive*
Hill, James Stanley *computer consulting company executive*
†Ousley, James E. *computer company executive*
Parisi, Franklin Joseph *communications executive*
†Sullivan, William E. *public relations executive*

Victoria
Courtney, Eugene Whitmal *computer company executive*

Wayzata
Detlefsen, Guy-Robert *management consultant*
Mithun, Raymond O. *advertising agency executive, banker, real estate and insurance executive*

MISSISSIPPI

Greenville
†Cameron, Thomas F., III *advertising and realty company executive*

Jackson
†Gunn, F. Michael *direct marketing professional*

Starkville
Yancey, Jimmie Isaac *marketing professional*

MISSOURI

Ballwin
Tyler, William Howard, Jr. *advertising executive*

Bridgeton
Davis, Stephen John *public relations executive, automotive executive*
†Myers, William Killeen *marketing executive*

Columbia
Denney, Arthur Hugh *consultant*

Geiger, Mark Watson *management consultant*

Fenton
Maritz, William E. *communications company executive*

Florissant
Kelly, James Joseph *printing company executive*

Gravois Mills
Jones, Charles Edward *advertising executive*

Kansas City
Barnes, Donald Gayle *management consultant*
Benner, Richard Edward, Jr. *management and marketing consultant, investor*
Bywaters, David R. *management consultant*
Courson, Marna B. P. *public relations executive*
Dillingham, John Allen *marketing professional*
Durwood, Edward D. *motion picture corporation executive*
Egan, Charles Joseph, Jr. *greeting card company executive, lawyer*
Freund, Ronald S. *management consultant, marketing company executive*
Grossman, Jerome Barnett *retired service firm executive*
Hagans, Robert Frank *industrial clothing cleaning company executive*
Hall, Donald Joyce *greeting card company executive*
Henson, Paul Harry *corporate executive*
Hockaday, Irvine O., Jr. *greeting card company executive*
†Julian, Lanny *printing company executive*
Pistilli, Philip *hotel executive*
Robertson, Leon H. *management consultant, educator*
Solberg, Elizabeth Transou *public relations executive*
†Titens, Sherman Jay *strategic planning consulting company executive, lawyer*

Rolla
Datz, Israel Mortimer *information systems specialist*

Saint Charles
†Gross, Charles Robert *personnel executive, legislator, appraiser*

Saint Joseph
Head, J. Michael *transportation executive*

Saint Louis
Akerson, Alan W. *public relations company executive*
Barnes, Zane Edison *communications company executive*
Barney, Steven Matthew *human resources executive*
Bartlett, Walter E. *communications company executive*
†Cejka, Susan Ann *executive search company executive*
†Christie, Carole Sullivan *advertising agency executive*
Curran, Michael Walter *management scientist*
Delaney, Robert Vernon *logistics and transportation executive*
Devantier, Paul W. *communications executive, broadcaster*
Dommermuth, William P. *marketing consultant, educator*
†Ellis, James D. *communications executive, corporate lawyer*
Epner, Steven Arthur *computer consultant*
†Essman, Alyn V. *photographic studios company executive*
Ferguson, Gary Warren *public relations executive*
†Filenwarth, Albert Floyd *advertising agency financial executive*
Finnigan, Joseph Townsend *public relations executive*
†Forrestal, Patrick George *sales promotion agency executive*
Fox, John Reid *advertising executive*
Graham, John Dalby *public relations executive*
Hilgert, Raymond Lewis *management and industrial relations educator, consultant, arbitrator*
Hillard, Robert Ellsworth *public relations consultant*
†Jamboretz, Glennon Donald *advertising agency executive*
Johnson, Kennett Conrad *advertising agency executive*
Jones, Ronald Woodbridge *human resources specialist, small business owner*
Kornblet, Donald Ross *communications company executive*
Loynd, Richard Birkett *consumer products company executive*
Lucking, Peter Stephen *marketing consultant, industrial engineering consultant*
McGinty, John *marketing consultant*
Miller, Theresa Ann *management consultant*
Mills, Linda S. *public relations executive*
†Morice, James L. *public relations executive*
O'Brien, Albert James *management consultant*
O'Neill, Eugene Milton *consumer products executive consultant*
†Ractliffe, Robert Edward George *management executive*
†Rocklage, Sister Mary Roch *health system executive*
†Rodgers, Timothy Francis *advertising executive*
Saligman, Harvey *consumer products and services company executive*
Siemer, Paul Jennings *public relations executive*
Snyder, Peter Larsen *public relations executive*
†Stewart, Ernest William *market research executive*
Stork, Donald Arthur *advertising executive*
†Taylor, Jack C. *automobile company executive*
Weaver, William Clair, Jr. (Mike Weaver) *human resources development executive*
Willman, John Norman *management consultant*
Wilson, Harry Burgoyme *retired public relations company executive*
†Zavaglia, Greg J. *management consultant*

Springfield
Cox, Lester Lee *broadcasting executive*
Denton, D. Keith *management educator*

Warrenton
Dapron, Elmer Joseph, Jr. *communications executive*

Washington
Carroll, John Howard *sales executive*

MONTANA

Helena
†Barnhart, Beverly Homyak *management consultant*
†Waterman, Mignon Redfield *public relations executive, state legislator*

NEBRASKA

Dakota City
†Andriessen, Roel *management consulting company executive*

Lincoln
Lee, Sang Moon *management educator, author, consultant*
Liggett, Twila Marie Christensen *public television company executive, academic administrator*
†Preister, Donald George *greeting card manufacturer, state senator*

Omaha
Eggers, James Wesley *personnel consultant*
Frazier, Chet June *advertising agency executive*
Frederickson, Keith Alvin *advertising agency executive*
Mackenzie, Charles Westlake, III *software developer*
Phares, Lynn Levisay *public communications executive*
†Scott, Robert Michael *data processing executive*
Werner, Clarence L. *transportation executive*

Scottsbluff
Fisher, J. R. *marketing executive*

NEVADA

Jean
Schaeffer, Glenn William *casino corporate financial executive*

Las Vegas
Arce, Phillip William *hotel and casino executive*
Basile, Richard Emanuel *retired management consultant, educator*
†Giovenco, John V. *hotel corporation executive*
Goodwin, Nancy Lee *corporate executive*
†Kenny, Erin Leigh *advertising executive, state legislator*
Landau, Ellis *gaming company executive*
Martin, Thomas E. *motel chain executive*
Mc Kenzie, Jeremy Alec *food service and baking company executive*
Popeil, Ron *consumer products company executive*
†Reichartz, W. Dan *hotel executive*
Rogich, Sig *advertising executive*
†Sandvick, Frederick *gaming company executive, accountant*
Thomas-Orr, Betty Jo *retired public relations specialist*
†Turner, Clyde T. *service executive*
Wada, Harry Nobuyoshi *training company executive*
Wiener, Valerie *communications company owner*
Wynn, Kenneth Richard *design and furnishings company executive*
Wynn, Stephen A. *hotel, entertainment facility executive*

Laughlin
†Bennett, William Gordon *casino executive*

Reno
Becker, Patricia Winifred *hotel and casino company executive*
Wells, Richard H. *casino consultant, business broker*

NEW HAMPSHIRE

Amherst
Mason, Phillip Howard *corporate executive, retired army officer*

Bedford
Cronin, Timothy Cornelius, III *computer manufacturing executive*
Hall, Pamela S. *environmental consulting firm executive*

Concord
Roberts, George Bernard, Jr. *business and government affairs consultant, former state legislator*

Dublin
Biklen, Paul *retired advertising executive*

Durham
Beckett, John Angus *management educator, consultant*
Flynn, Paul Bartholomew *marketing executive*

Exeter
Brownell, David Paul *business executive*

Grantham
Hansen, Herbert W. *management consultant*

Hampton
†Canas, Jon *hotel executive*
Clarizio, Josephine Delores *corporate services executive, former manufacturing and engineering company executive, foundation executive*
Rice, Frederick Colton *environmental managment consultant*

Hanover
Anthony, Robert Newton *emeritus management educator*
Webster, Frederick Elmer, Jr. *marketing educator, consultant*

Hillsboro
Marsh, Richard J. *strategic management consultant*

Hudson
Hargreaves, David William *communications company executive*

Jackson
Synnott, William Raymond *retired management consultant*

Jaffrey
Schott, John (Robert) *international consultant, educator*

Keene
Lyon, Ronald Edward *management consultant*

Nashua
Clough, Charles Elmer *consumer products company executive*
Stein, Robert *consumer products company executive*
Webber, Howard Rodney *computer company executive*
Weinstein, Jeffrey Allen *consumer products company executive, lawyer*

New London
Wheaton, Perry Lee *management consultant*

Portsmouth
Clee, Jan Evert *educator, consultant, executive*

Rye
MacRury, King *management counselor*

Sunapee
Chait, Lawrence G. *marketing consultant*

Waterville Valley
Grimes, Howard Ray *management consultant*

Wolfeboro
Steadman, David Rosslyn Ayton *business executive, corporate director*

NEW JERSEY

Absecon
Steinruck, Charles Francis, Jr. *management consultant, lawyer*

Allenhurst
Hinson, Robert William *advertising executive, consultant*

Allenwood
Shortess, Edwin Steevin *marketing consultant*

Atlantic City
Gillman, Richard *hotel, casino company executive*
Perry, James Benn *casino and hotel executive*
†Pratt, Jack E., Jr. *hotel and casino executive*

Avalon
Yochum, Philip Theodore *retired motel and cafeteria chain executive*

Basking Ridge
Allen, Robert Eugene *communications company executive*
Chittick, David Rupert *telecommunications executive*
†Ferguson, Forest D. *marketing executive*
Heckendorf, Glenn *sales and marketing executive*
Hoyt, Monty *communications executive*

Bay Head
McCormick, John Crimmins *consumer products company executive*

Bayonne
Sullivan, George Edmund *editorial and marketing company executive*

Berkeley Heights
Thomsen, Thomas Richard *communications company executive*

Bernardsville
DiDomenico, Mauro, Jr. *communication executive*
Dixon, Richard Wayne *retired communications company executive*

Bound Brook
Furst, E(rrol) Kenneth *transportation executive, accountant*

Bridgewater
Allen, Randy Lee *management consulting executive*
Pickett, Doyle Clay *employment and training counselor, consultant*
Skidmore, James Albert, Jr. *management, computer technology and engineering services company executive*

Butler
†Carelli, Gloria A. *advertising executive*
Ward, Robert Allen, Jr. *advertising executive*

Caldwell
Chatlos, William Edward *management consultant*

Camden
†Holman, Joseph S. *automotive sales executive*

Cape May
Cunningham, Robert Morton *communications company executive*

Carlstadt
Daniels, Robert Alan *marketing executive*

Chatham
Kaulakis, Arnold Francis *management consultant*
Lenz, Henry Paul *management consultant*
Woods, Reginald Foster *management consulting executive*

Cherry Hill
Sax, Robert Edward *corporate officer*
Schelm, Roger Leonard *information systems specialist*

Clark
†Augeri, Joseph *personal care industry executive*

Cliffside Park
Heimbaugh, James Ross *hotel executive*

Clifton
Olson, Bob Moody *marketing executive*

Convent Station
Weber, Joseph H. *communications company executive*

Cranbury
Cuthbert, Robert Allen *pet products company executive*
Koras, William *concessions, restaurants and publishing company executive*

Edison
Cavanaugh, James Henry *former government official, corporate executive*
Holt, Jonathan Turner *public relations executive*
†Ross, Stephen Bruce *public affairs consultant*
†Shulman, Hyman *food service executive*

Elizabeth
†Clare, Thomas J. *consumer products company executive*
†Infusino, Thomas P. *food distribution company executive*

Englewood
Miles, Virginia (Mrs. Fred C. Miles) *marketing consultant*

Englewood Cliffs
Cantwell, John Walsh *advertising executive*
Schlatter, Konrad *corporate executive*

Fair Lawn
Hayden, Neil Steven *communications company executive*

Fairfield
Mackin, Scott George *environmental and energy company executive*
Mehta, Narinder Kumar *marketing executive*

Fanwood
Peeney, James Doyle *executive search consultant*

Flemington
Kozikowski, Mitchell *public relations executive*

Florham Park
Fischer, Pamela Shadel *public relations executive*
Luker, Jeffrey Paul *management information consultant*
Naimark, George Modell *marketing and management consultant*

Fort Hancock
Klein, George D. *geologist, science executive*

Fort Lee
†Lynaugh, Joseph T. *health care executive*
Seitel, Fraser Paul *public relations executive*

Glen Ridge
Agnew, Peter Tomlin *employee benefit consultant*

Hackensack
Borg, Malcolm Austin *communications company executive*

Haddonfield
†Aglialoro, John Joseph *business executive*

Hamburg
Buist, Richardson *corporate executive, retired banker*

Hightstown
Kilborne, William Skinner *retired business consultant*

Holmdel
Haskell, Barry Geoffry *communications company research administrator*
Netravali, Arun N. *communications executive*

Lawrenceville
Coleman, Wade Hampton, III *management consultant, mechanical engineer, former banker*

Lebanon
Kone, Russell Joseph *advertising agency executive, film producer*
†Pollazzi, Roger G. *transportation executive*

Little Silver
Finch, Rogers Burton *association management consultant*
Labbett, John Edgar *corporate executive*

Livingston
†Lager, Henry S. *transporation executive*
Mandelbaum, Howard Arnold *advertising executive*

Madison
Byrd, Stephen Fred *human resource consultant*
Emerling, Carol G(reenbaum) *consumer products company executive*
Siegel, George Henry *international business development consultant*

Mendham
Fenner, Peter David *communications executive, management consultant*
Mercer, Richard Joseph *retired advertising executive, freelance writer*

Middletown
Cooper, Charles Gerson *computer company executive*
Levi, Ilan Mosche *computer and communications company executive*

Millington
Donaldson, John Cecil, Jr. *consumer products company executive*

Montvale
Gallagher, Michael Robert *consumer products company executive*
Mundt, Barry Maynard *management consultant*
†Saper, Lawrence *data processing company executive*

Moorestown
Bennington, William Jay *public relations executive*
Schwerin, Horace S. *marketing research executive*

Morris Plains
Chin-Kee-Fatt, Hollis Romauld *marketing professional*

Morristown
Miller, Hasbrouck Bailey *financial and travel services company executive*
Powell, David Greatorex *public affairs executive*
Shumate, Paul William, Jr. *communications executive*
Teiger, David *management consultant*
Wajnert, Thomas C. *leasing company executive*
Weinstein, Stephen Brant *communications executive, researcher, writer*

Mount Laurel
Grey, Richard E. *toy company executive*
Hart, Larry Edward *communications company executive*
Klein, Anne Sceia *public relations executive*

Mountain Lakes
Williams, Edward David *data processing executive*

Mountainside
DiPietro, Ralph Anthony *marketing and management consultant, educator*
Lipton, Bronna Jane *marketing communications executive*

Murray Hill
Musa, John Davis *computer and infosystems executive, software reliability engineering researcher and expert*

New Brunswick
Budd, Richard Wade *communications scientist, educator, lecturer, consultant, university dean*
Burke, James Edward *consumer products company executive*
Ruben, Brent David *communication educator*

New Providence
Longfield, William Herman *health care company executive*
†Sinto, Otavio *marketing executive*
Sundberg, Carl-Erik Wilhelm *telecommunications executive, researcher*

Newark
†Bonaventura, Vincent E. *transportation executive*
†Koeppe, Alfred C. *telecommunications company executive*
Lederman, Peter (Bernd) *environmental services executive, consultant, educator*
Lieberman, Leonard *retired supermarket executive*

North Plainfield
Johnson, Lowell Ferris *consumer products executive, consultant*

Northvale
Goodman, Stanley Leonard *advertising executive*

Oceanport
Paley, Alfred Irving *value engineering and consulting company executive, lecturer*

Old Bridge
Engel, John Jacob *communications executive*

Old Tappan
Ferriter, Warren Joseph *information systems executive*

Oradell
Dinsmore, Gordon Griffith *management consultant*

Orange
Chlopak, Donna Gayle *marketing and management consultant*

Palmyra
Kroeger, Lin J. *management consultant*
Overholt, Miles Harvard, III *management consultant, family therapist*

Paramus
Baczko, Joseph R. *consumer products executive*
Lazarus, Charles *retail toy company executive*

Park Ridge
Kaplan, Daniel I. *service executive*
Kennedy, Brian James *marketing executive*
Olson, Frank Albert *car rental company executive*

Parsippany
†Cochran, Larry B. *amusement park executive*
†Harber, Joseph F. *food marketing executive*
Haselmann, John Philip *marketing executive*
†Jenkins, Katherine Erskine *advertising executive*
Lutz, William Andrew *sales and marketing executive*
Muratore, Robert Peter *advertising executive*
Nalewako, Mary Anne *corporate secretary*
Parrish, Barry Jay *marketing executive*
†Secula, Elena *advertising executive*
Visocki, Nancy Gayle *infosystems design consultant*

Pennsauken
Gans, Samuel Myer *temporary employment service executive*

Perrineville
Hoffman, Maryhelen H. Paulick *communications company executive*

Piscataway
Burke, Jacqueline Yvonne *telecommunications executive*
Hulse, Robert Douglas *high technology executive*

Pittstown
Link, Fred Motter *communications consultant*

Princeton
Crespi, Irving *public opinion and market research consultant*
†D'Augusta, Alfred M. *human resources executive*
Davis, Richard K. *management consultant executive*
Fouss, James H. *marketing executive*
†Gillespie, Richard Joseph *advertising agency executive*
Greenberg, Joel S. *management consultant, engineer*
Hillier, James *communications executive, researcher*
Morris, Mac Glenn *advertising bureau executive*
O'Connor, Neal William *former advertising agency executive*
Popper, Robert David *computer and management consultant*
Rich, Jude T. *management consulting firm executive*
Roth, William Matson *former corporate executive*
Sethi, Shyam Sunder *management consultant*

Ramsey
†Oliver, Joseph J. *consumer products company executive*

Red Bank
Liao, Paul Foo-Hung *communications research company executive, physicist*
Reinhart, Peter Sargent *corporate executive, lawyer*

River Edge
†Seymour, Harry Duane *marketing executive*
Sommer, Robert George *public relations executive*

Roseland
†Casale, Robert J. *communications executive*
Lafer, Fred Seymour *data processing company executive*
Taub, Henry *retired computer services company executive*
†Turner, William J. *data processing company executive*
†Weinbach, Arthur Frederic *computing services company executive*
Weston, Josh S. *data processing company executive*

Rumson
Christianson, Lloyd Fenton *management consultant*
Feiner, Alexander *retired communications company executive*

Saddle River
Warrington, Clayton Linwood, Jr. *advertising executive*

Secaucus
Brown, Ira Bernard *data processing executive*
†Marcus, Alan C. *public relations consultant*
Schenck, Frederick A. *business executive*

Short Hills
Harwood, Jerry *market research executive*
Meredith, George Davis *advertising executive, publisher*
Schaefer, Charles James, III *advertising agency executive, consultant*
Schaffer, Edmund John *management consultant, retired engineering executive*

Somerset
†Neff, Richard B. *consumer products company executive*
Noonan, William Francis *public relations company executive*

Somerville
Deieso, Donald Allan *air pollution control company executive, scientist*
Hildebrandt, Bradford Walter *consulting company executive*

Spring Lake
Ernst, John Louis *management consultant*

Summit
Bostwick, Randell A. *retired retail food company executive*
Fuess, Billings Sibley, Jr. *advertising executive*
Pace, Leonard *retired management consultant*

Teaneck
Jugenheimer, Donald Wayne *advertising and communications educator, university administrator*

Tenafly
Gibbons, Robert Philip *management consultant*

Three Bridges
Lawrence, Gerald Graham *management consultant*

Titusville
Marden, Kenneth Allen *advertising executive*

Toms River
Kanarkowski, Edward Joseph *data processing company executive*

Upper Saddle River
Farley, Edward John *advertising executive*

Ventnor City
Bolton, Kenneth Albert *corporate professional*

Verona
Greenwald, Robert *public relations executive*

Warren
Blass, Walter Paul *consultant, management educator*
Jackson, John Wyant *business executive*

Wayne
Blauvelt, John Clifford *diversified consumer products company executive*
Bridges, Beryl Clarke *marketing executive*
Costello, Albert Joseph *diversified consumer products executive*
Donald, Robert Graham *retail food chain personnel executive*

West Caldwell
McEntee, Robert Edward *management consultant*
Page, Frederick West *business consultant*
Sostilio, Robert Francis *office equipment marketing executive*

Westfield
Cushman, Helen Merle Baker *management consultant*
Florian, Frank Lee *planning executive*

Wharton
Rodzianko, Paul *corporate executive*

Whippany
Pinkin, James Edward *sales and marketing executive*

Woodbridge
†Cuti, Anthony J. *consumer products company executive*
†Nies, Judy Ann *advertising agency executive*

Wyckoff
Anstatt, Peter Jan *marketing services executive*
Lavery, Daniel P. *management consultant*

NEW MEXICO

Albuquerque
†Bleiweis, Paul Benjamin *environmental services executive*
Hale, Bruce Donald *marketing professional*
Phillips, Ronald Edward (Ron) *sales executive*
Rosenberg, Arthur James *business executive*
Tope, Dwight Harold *retired management consultant*

Tesuque
Poedtke, Carl Henry George, Jr. *management consultant*

NEW YORK

Albany
Ferguson, Henry *international management consultant*
Murphy, Thomas Joseph *communications consultant*
Sacklow, Stewart Irwin *advertising executive*

Amityville
Brennan, Patrick Thomas *meteorology company executive*

Armonk
Bolduc, Ernest Joseph *management consultant*
Bolton, John Roger *public relations executive*
Gerstner, Louis Vincent, Jr. *diversified company executive*
Levy, Kenneth James *advertising executive*
York, Jerome B. *financial executive*

Babylon
Meirowitz, Claire Cecile *public relations executive*

Baldwin Place
Mc Kay, Dean Raymond *computer company executive*

Bay Shore
De Pasquale, John Anthony *direct marketing agency executive*

Bedford Hills
Diebold, John *management consultant*
Schwartz, Edward Malcolm *management consultant*

Brewster
Melsheimer, Mel P(owell) *consumer products business executive*

Briarcliff Manor
Dolmatch, Theodore Bieley *management consultant*
Haddad, Jerrier Abdo *engineering management consultant*

Bronx
Kitzie, John, Jr. *retail electronic products executive*
Kucic, Joseph *management consultant, industrial engineer*

Bronxville
†Blank, Richard Mark *advertising licensing and product development executive*

Brooklyn
Ahrens, Thomas H. *production company executive*
†Geller, Sheldon *consumer products company executive*
Olson, Harry Andrew, Jr. *communications consultant*
Shaw, Doris *creative marketing consultant*

Buffalo
Linnen, Thomas Francis *international strategic management consulting firm executive*
Miner, John Burnham *industrial relations educator, writer*
Morgan, James Durward *computer company executive*
Pegels, C. Carl *management science and systems educator*
†Phillips, Stanley F *restaurant company executive*
Rice, Victor Albert *global industrial company executive*

†Thompson, Michael F. *food service executive*

Carle Place
Kahn, Leonard Richard *communications and electronics company executive*

Chappaqua
Maloney, John Frederick *marketing specialist*

Cold Spring Harbor
Nightingale, Geoffrey Joseph *communications company executive, consultant*

Commack
Seymour, John Herbert *computer technology analyst*

Corning
Peck, Arthur John, Jr. *consumer products executive*

Cross River
Baxter, Bruce Osborne *hotel executive*

Croton On Hudson
Plotch, Walter *management consultant, fund raising counselor*

Delmar
Button, Rena Pritsker *public relations company executive*

Dix Hills
Fisher, Fenimore *business development consultant*

Dundee
Pfendt, Henry George *retired information systems executive, management consultant*

East Amherst
Bauer, Paul David *retired food service executive*

East Hampton
Munson, Lawrence Shipley *management consultant*

East Meadow
†Freeman, Clifford Lee *advertising executive*

East Northport
Hayo, George Edward *management consultant*

Ellenville
Straus, R. Peter *communications company executive, broadcasting executive*

Elmsford
Shaviv, Eddie *marketing and sales executive*

Farmingdale
Horowitz, Sidney *corporation executive*

Fayetteville
Cantwell, John Dalzell, Jr. *management consultant*
Pulos, Arthur Jon *industrial design executive*
Wallace, Spencer Miller, Jr. *hotel executive*

Floral Park
Corbett, William John *public relations consultant, lawyer*

Florida
†Koppele, Gary S. *food service executive*

Forest Hills
Callo, Joseph Francis *marketing and corporate communications consultant*
Miller, Donald Ross *management consultant*

Freeport
Landsberg, Jerry *management and investment consultant, optical laboratory executive*

Fresh Meadows
Ganz, Samuel *human resource and management professional*

Garden City
Conlon, Thomas James *marketing executive*
Crom, James Oliver *professional training company executive*
Doucette, Mary-Alyce *computer company executive*
Roche, John Edward *human resources management consultant*
Vittoria, Joseph V. *car rental company executive*

Garrison
Chasins, Edward A. *communications company executive*

Glen Cove
Greenberg, Allan *advertising and marketing research consultant*

Great Neck
Donenfeld, Kenneth Jay *management consultant*
Friedland, Louis N. *retired communications executive*
Goldberg, Melvin Arthur *communications executive*
Lampel, Ronald B. *human resources executive*
†Spielman, Harold M. *marketing professional*

Greenfield Center
Templin, John Leon, Jr. *healthcare consulting executive*

Hancock
DeLuca, Ronald *consultant, former advertising agency executive*

Harrison
Fuchs, Hanno *communications consultant*

Hauppauge
†Hershberg, David E. *communications corporation executive*

Hempstead
Pell, Arthur Robert *human resources development consultant, author*

Hewlett
Kislik, Louis A. *marketing company executive*

Huntington
Ponton, Richard Edward *business consultant*

Huntington Station
†Liguori, Frank Nickolas *temporary personnel company executive*

Irvington
Turk, Stanley Martin *advertising agency executive*

Ithaca
†Park, Roy Hampton, Jr. *advertising media executive*
†Thomas, Wright Moore *communications executive*
Whyte, William Foote *industrial relations educator, author*
Windmuller, John Philip *industrial relations educator, consultant*

Jericho
Rosen, Robert Arnold *management company executive*

Katonah
White, Harold Tredway, III *management consultant*

Kingston
Agerwala, Tilak Krishna Mahesh *computer company executive*
Lanitis, Tony Andrew *market researcher*

Lancaster
Neumaier, Gerhard John *environment consulting company executive*

Larchmont
Bauer, George *marketing consultant*
Greenwald, Carol Schiro *professional services marketing research executive*
†Josevie, Arnold *management consultant*
Plumez, Jean Paul *advertising agency executive, consultant*
Schwatka, Mark Andrew *advertising agency executive*
Silverstone, David *advertising executive*
Wielgus, Charles Joseph *information services company executive*

Long Beach
Siegel, Herbert Bernard *business executive, consultant*

Malverne
Freund, Richard L. *communications company executive, consultant, lawyer*

Melville
Jagoda, Donald Robert *sales promotion agency executive*
Maller, Robert Russell *certified management consultant, banker*
Ray, Gordon Thompson *communications executive*

Mineola
McGonigle, James Gregory *consultant*
Rushmore, Stephen *hotel consulting and appraisal specialist*

Montauk
Duryea, Perry Belmont, Jr. *corporate executive*

Mount Vernon
Leonard, John Harry *advertising executive*

New City
Prestegaard, Peter *systems company executive*

New Hyde Park
†Fanning, John Charles *service company executive*

New Rochelle
Vernon, Lillian *mail order company executive*

New York
Abernathy, James Logan *public relations executive*
Ablon, R. Richard *service company executive*
Achenbaum, Alvin Allen *marketing and management consultant*
†Adams, Jonathan L. *advertising agency executive*
Agisim, Philip *advertising and marketing company executive*
†Aiello, Stephen *public relations executive*
Albright, Warren Edward *advertising executive*
Alexander, Frank Lyon *corporate executive*
Alexander, Roy *public relations executive, editor, author*
Allen, Alice Catherine Towsley *public relations professional, writer, consultant*
†Alvarez, Mercedes *advertising executive*
Ammirati, Ralph *advertising agency executive*
Anchlia, Than Mal *distribution company executive*
Ancona, Barry *publishing and marketing consultant*
Anderson, Arthur Allan *management consultant*
†Anderson, Gavin *public relations consultant*
Anderson, Ron *advertising executive*
Andolsen, Alan Anthony *management consultant*
†Anfield, Frank A. *advertising executive*
Antonuccio, Joseph Albert *hospitality industry executive*
Applebaum, Stuart S. *public relations executive*
Arlow, Arnold Jack *advertising agency executive*
Armour, Lawrence A. *communications executive*
Aronson, Donald Eric *consultant to professional services firms*
Aronstam, Neil Lee *media marketing firm executive*
†Ascher, Michael *transportation executive*
Austad, Vigdis *computer software company executive*
Avrett, John Glenn *advertising executive*
Axelrod, Norman N(athan) *technology and strategic technical planning consultant*
Ayers, Emory Daniel *management consultant*
Bacher, Judith St. George *executive search consultant*

Bachrach, Nancy *advertising executive*
Backer, William Montague *advertising agency executive*
Baker, Stephen *advertising executive, author*
Balson, John Bruce *advertising agency executive*
Barnard, Kurt *retail marketing forecaster, publisher*
Baron, Theodore *public relations executive*
Barrett, Herbert *artists management executive*
Bates, Don *public relations and marketing executive*
Bauman, Martin Harold *executive search firm executive*
†Baxter, John Hanley *consultant company executive*
Beard, Eugene P. *advertising agency executive*
Beaumont, Richard Austin *management consultant*
†Becker, Ivan *advertising executive*
Becker, Michael Lewis *advertising executive*
Becker, Robert A. *advertising executive*
Beckwith, Rodney Fisk *management consulting firm executive*
Bedi, Rahul *import company executive*
Beers, Charlotte Lenore *advertising agency executive*
Beinecke, William S. *corporate executive*
Bell, David Arthur *advertising agency executive*
Ben-Eli, Michael Uri *management consultant*
Bennett, Georgette *communications and planning consultant*
Bennett, Saul *public relations agency executive*
Benway, Joseph Calise *advertising agency financial executive*
Berenson, Robert Leonard *advertising agency executive*
Bergen, John Donald *communications, public affairs executive*
†Berger, Arnold R. *advertising executive*
Bergin, John Francis *advertising agency executive*
Berlin, Andrew Mark *advertising agency executive*
Berman, Mira *advertising agency executive*
Bernard, David George *management consultant*
Bernbach, John Lincoln *advertising executive*
†Biebelberg, David Mark *marketing professional*
Biederman, Barron Zachary (Barry Biederman) *advertising agency executive*
†Bijur, Arthur William *advertising executive*
Biondi, Frank J., Jr. *entertainment company executive*
†Bishop, Susan Katharine *executive search company executive*
Blaney, John *advertising executive*
Bloomgarden, Kathy Finn *public relations executive*
Boice, Craig Kendall *management consultant*
Bollman, Mark Brooks, Jr. *communications executive*
Bona, Frederick Emil *public relations executive*
Bond, Jonathan Holbert *advertising executive*
†Booth, Margaret A(nn) *communications company executive*
Bornet, Stephen Folwell *public relations and marketing communications executive*
Bostock, Roy Jackson *advertising agency executive*
Boucher, Henry Joseph (Bud Boucher) *management consultant*
†Bowen, John Sheets *advertising agency executive*
Bower, Marvin *management consultant*
Bowman, Robert A. *hotel company executive*
Bradstock, John *advertising executive*
Brady, Adelaide Burks *public relations agency executive, giftware catalog executive*
Brody, Alexander *advertising executive*
†Brody, Edward Isaac *marketing professional*
Brooks, Gary *management consultant*
Brooks, Timothy H. *media executive*
†Brown, Edward Glenn *chef, restaurateur*
Brown, Hobson, Jr. *executive search firm consultant and executive*
Brumback-Henry, Sarah Elizabeth *industrial psychologist, management and corporate consultant*
Bruzs, Boris Olgerd *management consultant*
Buchwald, Elias *public relations executive*
Bullen, Richard Hatch *former corporation executive*
Bullock, H. Ridgely *management and investment executive, lawyer*
†Bungey, Michael *advertising executive*
†Burandt, Gary Edward *advertising agency executive*
Burg, Mitchell Marc *advertising executive*
Burger, Chester *retired management consultant*
Burke, Daniel Barnett *retired communications corporation executive*
Burkhardt, Ronald Robert *advertising executive*
Burns, Ronald S. *advertising company executive*
Burson, Harold *public relations executive*
Burton, Robert Gene *printing and publishing executive*
†Burton, Steven Bryant *advertising agency executive*
Cadwell, Franchellie Margaret *advertising agency executive, writer*
Caggiano, Joseph *advertising executive*
Callen, John Holmes, Jr. *executive search consultant*
Calvillo, Ricardo C. *advertising agency executive*
Campbell, William Foley *public relations executive*
Campbell, William I. *cigarette company executive*
Cannon, James Anthony *advertising executive*
Canter, Stanley D. *retired marketing consulting company executive*
Cappon, Andre Alfred *management consultant*
Carey, Thomas Hilton *advertising agency executive*
Carnella, Frank Thomas *information executive*
Carra, Andrew Joseph *advertising executive*
†Carter, Carolyn Houchin *advertising agency executive*
Case, Eugene Lawrence *advertising agency executive*
Cavior, Warren Joseph *communications executive*
Chajet, Clive *communications consultant*
Chalk, Howard Wolfe *advertising agency executive*
Chandler, Robert Leslie *public relations executive*
Cheney, Richard Eugene *public relations executive*
Chereskin, Alvin *advertising executive*
Chernin, Fredric David *advertising agency executive*
Chervokas, John Vincent *advertising executive*
Chrisanthopoulos, Peter *advertising executive*
Chu, Roderick Gong-Wah *management consultant*
Citron, Richard Ira *management consultant*
Clark, J. Thomas *advertising agency executive*
†Clark, Leonard J., Jr. *personnel service executive*
†Clarke, Frank William *advertising agency executive*
†Clausen, Ned Carl *advertising executive*
Coen, Robert Joseph *advertising agency executive*
Cohen, Alan Norman *business executive*
†Cohn, Bob *public relations executive*
Cohn, Theodore *management consultant*
Colonel, Sheri Lynn *advertising agency executive*
†Cooper, Andrew *public relations executive*
Cooper, R. John, III *advertising agency executive, lawyer*
Corbin, Herbert Leonard *public relations executive*
†Corrigan, Timothy Patrick Pennington Blake *advertising executive*
Costello, Richard Neumann *advertising agency executive*
Cox, Robert Gene *management consultant*
Craig, Charles Samuel *marketing educator*
Crawford, Bruce Edgar *advertising executive*
Crisci, Mathew G. *marketing executive*
†Critchell, Simon James *corporate executive*
Crosland, Philip Crawford *advertising company executive*
Culligan, John William *retired corporate executive*
Cullman, Edgar Meyer *diversified consumer products company executive*
Cunningham, Patrick Joseph *advertising agency executive*
†Cutler, Laurel *advertising agency executive*
†Daily, John Charles *software company executive*
Dane, Maxwell *former advertising executive*
Dangler, Richard Reiss *corporate service companies executive, entrepreneur*
Daniel, David Ronald *management consultant*
Danish, Roy Bertram *communications consultant*
Danzig, Jerome Alan (Jerry) *management consultant*
Danzig, Sarah H. Palfrey *retired advertising agency executive, writer*
Davidson, Donald William *advertising executive*
Davis, Perry John *computer executive*
Dean, Sidney Walter, Jr. *business and marketing executive*
Deare, Jennifer Laurie *marketing professional*
DeBow, Jay Howard Camden *public relations company executive*
De Deo, Joseph E. *advertising executive*
Delano, Lester Almy, Jr. *advertising executive*
†Della Femina, Jerry *advertising agency executive*
Dembo, Joseph T. *communications educator*
Dent, V. Edward *former advertising and communications company executive*
Dessi, Adrian Frank *marketing, communications executive*
DeVito, Francis Joseph *advertising agency executive*
Dewar, James McEwen *marketing, aerospace and defense executive, consultant*
De Witt, Eugene A. *advertising agency executive*
†Diamond, Harris *corporate communications executive, lawyer*
Dilenschneider, Robert Louis *public relations company executive*
†Di Maria, Valerie Theresa *public relations executive*
Dimling, John Arthur *marketing executive*
Dolman, John Phillips, Jr. (Tim Dolman) *communications company executive*
Doner, Frederick Nathan *advertising and communications executive*
Dooner, John Joseph, Jr. *advertising executive*
Drobis, David R. *public relations company executive*
†Druckenmiller, Robert T. *public relations executive*
Dubin, Morton Donald *management consultant, film producer*
†Duffy, David L. *public relations executive*
Dunst, Laurence David *advertising executive*
Dusenberry, Philip Bernard *advertising executive*
†Dworin, Steven *advertising executive*
Dzodin, Harvey Cary *communications executive*
†Earle, Gordon W. *public relations executive*
Eckstut, Michael Kauder *management consultant*
Edelman, Richard Winston *public relations executive*
†Edson, Andrew Stephen *public relations executive*
Eggers, Ernest Russell *management consultant*
Eidson, Thomas E. *public relations firm executive*
Eisler, Susan Krawetz *advertising executive*
Elkes, Terrence Allen *communications executive*
Elliott, John, Jr. *advertising agency executive*
Elliott, Tim *advertising agency executive*
†Emerson, Robert Monroe *advertising executive*
Erhardt, Edward Richard *advertising company executive*
Eswein, Bruce James, II *human resources executive*
Evans, Alfred Lee, Jr. *advertising executive*
Evans, James Hurlburt *retired transportation and natural resources executive*
Evans, Mary Johnston *corporate director*
Evans, Thomas Chives Newton *communications executive*
Evans, Van Michael *advertising agency executive, consultant*
Faber, Neil *advertising executive*
Fader, Ellen Strahs *communications company executive*
Falk, Edgar Alan *public relations consulting company executive*
Farinelli, Jean L. *public relations firm executive*
Feigin, Barbara Sommer *advertising executive*
Feinberg, Robert Edward *advertising agency executive, writer*
Feldtmose, John Nielsen *management consulting executive*
Fenvessy, Stanley John *management consultant*
Fernandez, Castor A. *advertising company executive*
Ferragano, Carmen *communications executive*
Ferrell, John Frederick *advertising executive*
Ferries, John Charles *advertising executive*
†Ferris, Robert Dominick *public relations executive*
Field, Michael Stanley *information services company executive*
Fink, Stuart Simon *business management educator*
Finkelstein, Seymour *business consultant*
Finn, David *public relations company executive, artist*
Finn, Peter *public relations executive*
†Firger, Mitchell *advertising agency executive*
Fishel, Stanley Irvyng *advertising executive*
Fisher, Robert Allen *advertising executive*
†Fitzpatrick, Nancy S. *advertising executive*
†FitzSimons, Dennis Joseph *broadcasting executive*
Flaherty, Tina Santi *corporate communications executive*
Flaum, Sander Allen *advertising and marketing executive*
Fluhr, Howard *consulting firm executive*
†Fogge, Len *advertising executive*
Ford, John Charles *communications executive*
Forman, Leonard P. *media company executive*
Forrester, William Donald *international business executive*
Foster, James Henry *advertising and public relations executive*
Foxworth, Jo *advertising agency executive*
Frank, Robert Allen *advertising executive*
Frank, William Fielding *computer systems design executive, consultant*
Frantz, Jack Thomas *advertising executive*
Freedman, Allen Royal *business executive, lawyer*
†Friedman, Adam Issac *public relations consultant*
Friedman, Frances *public relations executive*
Fuller, Craig Lawrence *corporate affairs executive*
Furman, Anthony Michael *public relations executive*
Fursland, Richard Curtis *international business consultant*
†Gaines, Jay S. *executive recruiter*
†Gantman, David J. *advertising executive*
Gardiner, E. Nicholas P. *executive search executive*
Gardner, Ralph David *advertising executive*
Gargano, Amil *advertising agency executive*
Garvin, Andrew Paul *information company executive, author, consultant*
Geduldig, Alfred *communications executive*
Geier, Philip Henry, Jr. *advertising executive*
Geller, Robert James *advertising agency executive*
Geltzer, Sheila Simon *public relations executive*
Georgescu, Peter Andrew *advertising executive*
Geraci, F. Phillip *advertising executive, lawyer, entrepreneur*
Gerson, Irwin Conrad *advertising executive*
Gianinno, Susan McManama *marketing executive, advertising agency executive*
Gibbs, Richard Leslie *public relations executive*
Gibson, William B. *advertising, marketing executive*
Gillett, Charles *travel executive*
Gilliatt, Neal *advertising executive, consultant*
Ginsberg, Frank Charles *advertising executive*
Ginsburg, Ellin Louis *public relations executive*
Glasberg, Paula Drillman *advertising executive*
Glos, Margaret Beach *management company executive, real estate developer*
Gold, Jay D. *broadcasting company executive*
Goldin, Alan Gary *advertising executive*
Goldschmidt, Charles *advertising agency executive*
Goldsmith, Clifford Henry *former tobacco company executive*
†Goldsmith, Gary L. *advertising executive*
Goldsmith, Mark L. *international trade marketing consulting company executive*
Goldstein, Jack *transportation executive*
Goldstein, Richard A. *consumer products company executive*
†Goluboff, Hal *advertising executive*
Goodman, Thomas Andrew *public relations executive*
Gossett, Oscar Milton *advertising executive*
Gottlieb, Jerrold Howard *advertising executive*
Grace, Jason Roy *advertising agency executive*
Grant, Dale B. *consulting company executive*
Green, Paula *advertising agency executive*
Greenawalt, Peggy Freed Tomarkin *advertising executive*
Greenberg, Jerome *advertising executive*
†Greenberg, Scott Neil *patent development company executive*
Greene, David Elsworth *advertising agency executive, accountant*
Greene, Howard Paul *communications executive*
Greenland, Leo *advertising executive*
Greif, Edward Louis *public relations executive*
Groberg, James Jay *information sciences company executive*
Grossman, Jack *advertising agency executive*
Gudenberg, Harry Richard *business consultant*
Gugel, Craig Thomas *advertising executive*
Guimaraes, George Gomes *advertising agency executive*
Gumbinner, Paul S. *advertising and executive recruitment agency executive*
Gurwitch, Arnold Andrew *communications executive*
Haddock, Robert Lynn *information services entrepreneur, writer*
†Halle, Lisa Ellen *advertising executive*
Halper, Harlan Richard *executive recruiter*
Halpern, Nathan Loren *communications company executive*
Hamilton, Bill *advertising executive*
Hamilton, Thomas Michael *marketing executive*
Hammond, Lou Rena Charlotte *public relations executive*
Harkna, Eric *advertising executive*
†Hartwig, Myron Arthur *public relations executive*
Hatheway, John Harris *advertising agency executive*
†Hawkey, Penelope J. *advertising agency executive*
Hearle, Douglas Geoffrey *public relations consultant*
Heekin, James Robson, III *advertising executive*
Heinzerling, Larry Edward *communications executive*
Heller, Arthur *advertising agency executive*
Hendry, Andrew Delaney *consumer products company executive*
Hennes, Robert Taft *former management consultant, investment executive*
†Henning, Alyson Balfour *advertising executive*
†Herman, Carol Korngut *advertising agency executive*
Hilton, Andrew Carson *management consultant, former manufacturing company executive*
†Hirsch, Steven Richard *broadcast executive*
Hoffenberg, Harvey *advertising executive*
Hooper, Ian (John Derek Glass) *advertising agency executive*
Hope, Michael S. *entertainment and communications company executive*
Hopple, Richard Van Tromp, Jr. *advertising agency executive*
Horowitz, David H. *communications industry executive, lawyer, consultant*
†Hosokawa, David *advertising executive*
Howard, Elizabeth *corporate communications and marketing executive*
Howes, Alfred S. *business and insurance consultant*
†Humphreys, Richard *advertising executive*
Ittleson, H(enry) Anthony *bicycle vacation company executive*
Jackson, Richard George *advertising agency executive*
Jacoby, Robert Harold *management consulting executive*
James, Robert Leo *advertising agency executive*
Johnson, Harold Earl *personnel executive*
Johnson, John William, Jr. *executive recruiter*
Jones, Abbott C. *advertising agency executive*
†Jones, Caroline Robinson *advertising executive*
Jordan, Jerry Neville *advertising executive*
Jordan, Thomas Richard *public relations executive*
Josephs, Ray *public relations and advertising executive, writer, international relations consultant*
Josephson, Marvin *corporation executive*
Kalmus, Allan Henry *public relations executive*
Kanuk, Leslie Lazar *management consultant, educator*
†Kaplan, Larry *public relations executive*
Kaplan, Lloyd Arthur *public relations executive*
Karalekas, George Steven *advertising agency executive, political consultant*
Karp, Martin Everett *management consultant*
Karp, Richard M. *advertising executive*
Katz, Marcia *public relations company executive*
†Kay, Michelle Suzanne *advertising executive*
Keating, Robert Edward *public relations executive*
Keenan, Michael Edgar *advertising executive*
Keeshan, Michael *advertising agency executive*
Keeshan, William Francis, Jr. *advertising executive*
Kelley, Sheila Seymour *public relations executive, crisis consultant*
Kelmenson, Leo-Arthur *advertising executive*
Keine, Nathan *editorial and public relations consultant*
†Kenney, Matthew *chef*
Kenny, Roger Michael *executive search consultant*
†Kern, Ellis *corporate professional*
Kern, Martin H(arold) *supermarket chain executive*
†Kessel, Barry Lee *advertising and marketing executive*
Kieren, Thomas Henry *management consultant*
†Killeffer, Louis MacMillan *advertising executive*
Kinsolving, Charles McIlvaine, Jr. *marketing executive*
Kirk, Donald James *consultant, accounting educator*
Kish, Joseph Laurence, Jr. *management consultant*
†Knisley, Patrick Allen *advertising company executive*
Knox, George L(evi), III *corporate executive*
†Kogstad, Rolf Egil *sales company executive*
Kohlenberg, Stanley *marketing executive*
Koplovitz, Kay *communication network executive*
Korach, William Mark *marketing executive*
Korman, Jess J. *advertising executive*
Kotcher, Raymond Lowell *public relations executive*
†Kovak, Ellen B. *public relations firm executive*
Krakow, Amy Ginzig *author, advertising and marketing executive, consultant*
Kraus, Norma Jean *industrial relations executive*
Kraushar, Jonathan Pollack *communications and media consultant*
Kreisberg, Neil Ivan *advertising executive*
Kreston, Martin Howard *advertising, marketing, public relations, and publishing executive*
Krinsky, Robert Daniel *consulting firm executive*
Kroll, Alexander S. *advertising agency executive*
Krone, Helmut *consultant, former advertising executive*
Kubilus, Norbert John *information technology executive*
Kubin, Michael Ernest *advertising and marketing executive*
Kullberg, Gary Walter *advertising agency executive*
Kummel, Eugene H. *advertising agency executive*
Kurnit, Paul David *advertising executive*
Kurnit, Shepard *advertising agency executive*
Kurz, Mitchell Howard *marketing communications executive*
†Kvint, Vladimir Lev *business educator, economist*
Lambert, Eleanor (Mrs. Seymour Berkson) *public relations executive, fashion authority, journalist*
Lamont, Lee *art management executive*
Lang, George *restaurateur*
Langer, Andrew J. *advertising agency executive*
Langton, Cleve Swanson *advertising executive*
Lannamann, Richard Stuart *executive recruiting consultant*
Laughren, Terry *advertising executive*
Lavey, Kenneth Henry *advertising agency executive, designer*
Lawrence, Barbara *information manager*
Lawrence, James Bland *advertising executive*
Lawrence, Ruddick Carpenter *public relations executive*
Lazarus, Rochelle Braff *advertising executive*
Lebbad, John A. *advertising, marketing, communications executive*
Leber, Lester *advertising agency executive*
LeBow, Bennett S. *communications executive*
†Leeds, Candace *public relations executive*
Leeds, Douglas Brecker *advertising agency executive, theatre producer*
Leet, Mildred Robbins *corporate executive, consultant*
†Le Mener, Georges Philippe *hotel executive*
Leslie, John Webster, Jr. *communications company executive*
Leslie, Seymour Marvin *communications executive*
Lesser, Lawrence J. *advertising agency executive*
Leubert, Alfred Otto Paul *international business consultant*
†Levenson, Richard Neil *advertising executive*
Levenstein, Alan Peter *advertising executive*
Levine, Carl Morton *motion picture exhibition, real estate executive*
Levine, Harry *public relations executive*
Levitt, Mitchell Alan *management consultant*
Levy, Walter Kahn *management consultant executive*
Lewis, George Ralph *consumer goods company executive*
Lewis, Richard Warren *advertising executive*
Lipton, Charles *public relations executive*
Lipton, Joan Elaine *advertising executive*
†Litewka, Albert Bernard *communications and publishing company executive*
†Litwin, Alisa Gabriel *advertising executive*
Lockwood, Molly Ann *communications company executive*
†Logan, Vicki *advertising executive*
Loren, Pamela *telecommunications executive*
Lotas, Judith Patton *advertising executive*
Love, Kenneth Del *design company director, consultant*
Lubalin, Peter *advertising agency executive*
Lucht, John Charles *management consultant, executive recruiter*
†Lynch, John T. *management consultant*
†MacDougall, Malcolm D. *advertising agency executive*
Mack, Joseph P. *advertising agency executive*
†Mackall, Robert Wain *advertising agency executive*
MacKay, Malcolm *executive search consultant*
Mackerodt, Fred *public relations specialist*
†Makovsky, Kenneth Dale *public relations executive*
Makrianes, James Konstantin, Jr. *management consultant*
Mallozzi, Cos M. *public relations executive*
Maneker, Roberta S(ue) *public relations executive*
Manning, Burt *advertising executive*
Manoff, Richard Kalman *advertising executive, nutrition policy consultant*
Mansi, Joseph Anneillo *public relations company executive*
Marcosson, Thomas I. *service company executive*
Margaritis, John Paul *public relations executive*
Margolis, Milton Joseph *marketing executive*
†Margulis, Les *advertising executive*
†Mariucci, John Ubaldo *advertising agency executive*
Mark, Reuben *consumer products company executive*
Marshall, Daniel Stuart *advertising executive*
Marston, Robert Andrew *public relations executive*
†Martin, Donald *advertising agency executive*
McCall, David Bruce *advertising executive*

McConnell, Charles Warren marketing management executive
McCormick, James Michael management consultant
McCoy, Millington F. corporation executive
McCracken, A. Michael marketing executive
McGarry, John Patrick, Jr. advertising agency executive
McGinnis, Arthur Joseph, Jr. public relations executive
†McGrath, Patrick J. advertising agency executive
†McKelvey, Andrew J. advertising executive
McLean, Edward Peter executive search consultant
McNamee, Daniel Vincent, III management consultant
McNamee, Louise advertising agency executive
Meigher, S. Christopher, III communications and media investor
Menk, Carl William executive search company executive
Menninger, Edward Joseph public relations executive
Meranus, Arthur Richard advertising agency executive
Messing, Mark P. advertising executive
Messinger, Scott James advertising executive
Messner, Thomas G. advertising executive, copywriter
Meyer, Edward Henry advertising agency executive
Meyer, Fred Josef advertising executive
Meyer, Pearl executive compensation consultant
†Meyers, Bruce A. advertising executive
Miano, Louis Stephen advertising executive
Michenfelder, Joseph Francis public relations executive
Miller, Donald Baldwin advertising executive
Miller, Ernest Charles management consultant
†Miller, Glenn Alan advertising executive
Miller, Robert advertising executive
†Mines, Herbert Thomas executive recruiter
Minicucci, Robert A. business executive
Minor, Raleigh Colston management consultant
†Mitchell, Martin Morgan, Jr. advertising executive, educator
Mitchell, Richard Boyle advertising executive
Mittelstadt, Charles Anthony advertising executive
Montgomery, Walter George communications executive, consultant
Moran, Juliette M. management consultant
Moreira, Marcio Martins advertising executive
†Morgen, Lynn public relations executive
Morley, Michael B. public relations executive
Morris, Mark Ronald advertising agency executive
Morris, Michael Howard public relations executive
Morris, Stephen Burritt marketing information executive
Mosbacher, Martin Bruce public relations executive
Moss, Charles advertising agency executive
Mosser, Thomas Joseph public relations agency executive
Muller, Frank B. advertising executive
Muro, Roy Alfred independent media service corporation executive
†Murphy, James E. public relations executive
†Murphy, Jill public relations executive
Murray, Anita Jean data processing executive, consultant
Nash, Edward L. advertising agency executive
Neff, Thomas Joseph executive search firm executive
Neft, David Samuel marketing professional
Nelson, Bruce Sherman advertising agency executive
Nesbit, Robert Grover consultant
†Neuhaus, Sydney Ann public relations executive
Newman, Geraldine Anne advertising executive
Newman, Jane advertising agency executive
Nieman, John Francis advertising executive
Nisenholtz, Martin Abram advertising executive, educator
†Noonan, Susan Abert public relations counselor
Norcia, Stephen William advertising executive
†Nord, Peter Robert advertising executive
Novak, Eugene Francis advertising executive
Obernauer, Marne, Jr. corporate executive
O'Brien, Richard Francis advertising agency executive
Ogden, Dayton executive search consultant
Oliver, Alexander R. management consultant
Olsen, Richard W. advertising executive
†Olshan, Karen advertising agency executive
Olshan, Kenneth S. advertising agency executive
Olson, Thomas Francis, II communications company executive
O'Neill, Francis Xavier, III marketing executive
Osnos, Gilbert Charles management consultant
Ostrow, Joseph W. advertising executive
†Ostrow, Samuel David public relations executive
O'Sullivan, Eugene Henry retired advertising executive
O'Toole, John E. advertising executive
Otter, John Martin, III television advertising consultant
Pace, Richard Alan bank data processing executive
Paddock, Anthony Conaway management consultant
Palmer, Robert J(oseph) advertising executive, winery owner
Paluszek, John L. public relations firm executive
Pappas, Alceste Thetis consulting company executive, educator
Parfit, Gavin J. international executive
Parsons, Andrew John management consultant
Patterson, James Brendan, Jr. advertising agency executive
Patton, Joanna advertising executive
Paul, Robert David management consultant
Payson, Martin David entertainment company executive, lawyer
Pearson, Clarence Edward management consultant
Peasback, David R. recruiting company executive
Pecker, David J. magazine publishing company executive, financial executive
Peebler, Charles David, Jr. advertising executive
Perdunn, Richard Francis management professional
Perelman, Ronald Owen diversified holding company executive
Perless, Ellen advertising executive
Perlmutter, Diane F. communications executive
Peterson, Nadeen advertising agency executive
Phillips, Elizabeth Joan marketing executive
†Phillips, Graham Holmes advertising executive
Phillips, John David corporate executive
Pickholz, Jerome Walter advertising agency executive
†Piliguian, Tro advertising executive
Plavoukos, Spencer advertising executive
Pollak, Tim advertising agency executive
Pollock, M. Duncan advertising executive
Pollock-O'Brien, Louise Mary public relations executive
†Pomerantz, Saul W. corporate executive
Pompadur, I. Martin communications executive
Poppe, Fred Christoph advertising agency executive
Pounder, Richard A. advertising executive
†Presley, Janet Passidomo advertising executive
Puris, Martin Ford advertising agency executive
Quest, James Howard advertising executive
Quintero, Ronald Gary management consultant
Rauch, Arthur Irving management consultant
Ravitz, Robert Allan advertising agency executive
Raynolds, John F., III executive search consultant
Reges, Marianna Alice marketing executive
Reichel, Walter Emil advertising executive
Reinhard, Keith Leon advertising executive
Resnik, Frank Edward tobacco company executive
Reuben, Alvin Bernard entertainment executive
Rhodes, John Bower management consultant
Rich, Kenneth Malcolm executive search and management consultant
Rindlaub, John Wade advertising agency executive
Rinehart, Jonathan public relations executive
Riordan, James Quentin retired company executive
Robbins, John Clapp corporate executive
Robbins, Kenneth L. advertising agency executive
Roberts, Francis Stone advertising executive
Rogers, Kenneth R. advertising executive
Roman, Kenneth, Jr. consultant
†Rooney, Terence public relations executive
Rose, Zeldon E. public relations company executive
†Rosen, Hy advertising executive
Rosenbaum, Steven Ira public relations and publishing executive, photographer
Rosenshine, Allen Gilbert advertising agency executive
Rosenthal, Peter public relations executive
Rosenthal, William Forshaw advertising executive
Rossi, Dominick F., Jr. advertising agency executive
Rothenberg, Robert Philip public relations counselor
Rothholz, Peter Lutz public relations executive
†Rothstein, Richard public relations executive
†Rousset, Alain advertising agency executive
Rowland, Herbert Leslie public relations executive
Ruben, William Samuel marketing consultant
Rubenstein, Howard Joseph public relations executive
Rubenstein, Stanley Ellis public relations consultant
Rubin, Edwin Manning advertising executive
Rudd, Nicholas marketing communications company executive
Ruder, William public relations executive
Ruello, Samuel Angus management consultant
Rush, Peter public relations executive
†Russo, Anthony Joseph public relations professional
†Russo, Barbara Gans advertising agency executive
Ruth, Carol A. public relations executive
Rutman, Mark Charles public relations executive
Ryle, Joseph Donald public relations executive
Sacks, Temi J. public relations executive
Sansaverino, Joseph F. human resources executive
Sard, George public relations company executive
Sarnoff, Albert communications executive
Sauerhaft, Stan public relations executive, consultant
Savas, Emanuel S. public management educator
Scardino, Michael Christopher advertising executive
Schaub, Sherwood Anhder, Jr. management consultant
†Schilling, Maris associate creative director
Schlaifer, Charles advertising executive
Schmertz, Herbert public relations and advertising executive
Schmetterer, Robert Allen advertising executive
Schoonover, Jean Way public relations consultant
Schreiber, Alfred Lawrence marketing executive, special events consultant
Schriever, Fred Martin energy, environmental and information technology executive
Schulberg, Jay William advertising agency executive
Schulman, Paul Martin advertising executive
Schupak, Leslie Allen public relations company executive
Schur, Jeffrey advertising executive
Schwab, Frank, Jr. management consultant
Schwartz, Paul advertising creative director
Schwartz, R. Malcolm management consultant
Scott, William Clement, III entertainment industry executive
Seadler, Stephen Edward business and computer consultant, social scientist
Seaman, Alfred Jarvis retired advertising agency executive
Secunda, Eugene marketing communications executive, educator
Segal, Joel Michael advertising executive
Seiden, Henry (Hank Seiden) advertising executive
Seiden, Steven Arnold executive search consultant
Seidman, Herta Lande international trade and information company executive
Selkowitz, Arthur advertising agency executive
Shaffer, Russell K. advertising agency executive
†Shaine, Theodore Harris advertising executive
Shair, David Ira human resources executive
Shapiro, Marvin Lincoln communications company executive
Sheets, Michael Jay consumer products company executive
Sherman, Eugene Jay marketing executive, economist
Sherman, Norman Mark advertising agency executive
Shields, Virginia advertising executive
Silberman, H. Lee public relations executive
Silverman, Marylin A. advertising agency executive
Simmons, J. Gerald management consultant
Sinclair, Daisy advertising executive, casting director
Sirowitz, Leonard advertising agency executive
†Sklaver, David R. advertising executive
†Skollar, Robert Alan advertising executive
†Slater, Don advertising executive, creative director
Sloves, Marvin advertising agency executive
Smith, George S., Jr. communications financial executive
Smith, Guy Lincoln, IV strategic communications company executive
Smith, Lewis Motter, Jr. advertising and direct marketing executive
Smith, Martin Jay advertising and marketing executive
†Smith, Murray Livingstone advertising executive
Snoddon, Larry E. public relations executive
Softness, John public relations executive
Soika, Helmut Emil retirement plan administrator
Sorensen, Robert C. marketing executive, educator
Soter, George Nicholas advertising executive
Souham, Gérard communications executive
Spiegel, Arthur Henry, III managing director, president
Spielvogel, Carl international marketing executive
Spirn, Michele Sobel communications professional, writer
†Spivak, Helayne advertising agency executive
Springer, John Shipman public relations executive
†Srere, Linda Jean advertising executive
Stack, Edward William business management and foundation executive
Stanton, Alexander public relations executive
Stanton, Edward M. public relations company executive
Stanton, Frank communications executive
Steedman, Doria Lynne Silberberg advertising agency executive
Stern, Leslie Warren management consultant
Sternglass, Lila M. advertising agency executive
Stevens, Art public relations executive
Stewart, Jeff advertising agency executive
Stewart, Kirk T. public relations executive
Stoddard, Laurence Ralph, Jr. advertising executive
Stone, Joseph advertising agency executive
Strand, Curt Robert hotel executive
Straus, Irving Lehman public relations executive
†Strauss, Harold L. advertising executive
Strear, Joseph D. public relations executive
Stroock, Mark Edwin, II public relations company executive
Stuart, John McHugh, Jr. public relations consultant, retired foreign service officer
Sturges, John Siebrand management consultant
Sulcer, Frederick Durham advertising executive
†Sussman, Judith Helen public relations company executive
Sutherland, William Paul advertising executive
Swanzey, Robert Joseph data processing executive
Swid, Stephen Claar business executive
Swift, John Francis health care advertising company executive
†Talcott, Jane Victoria advertising executive
Taney, J. Charles advertising agency executive
Tarter, Fred Barry advertising executive
†Taschetti, Vincent S. advertising executive
†Tavon, Mary E. public relations executive
Tellefsen, Gerald management consultant
Teran, Timothy Eric Alba marketing professional
Thompson, William Cannon, Jr. advertising agency executive
Tierney, Paul E., Jr. food service executive
Tilson, Dorothy Ruth word processing executive
†Torello, Judy S. corporate communications executive
Tortorella, Albert James public relations executive, consultant
Tripodi, Louis Anthony advertising agency executive
Trueman, Walter retired advertising agency executive
Truesdell, Wesley Edwin public relations and investor relations consultant
Truitt, Richard Hunt public relations agency executive
†Trygg, Steve Lennart advertising executive
†Tucker, Paul Thomas information systems executive
Turkel, Stanley hotel consultant, management executive
Turner, Hester Hill management consultant
†Ullmark, Hans advertising agency executive
Ulrich, Max Marsh executive search consultant
Upson, Stuart Barnard advertising agency executive
Vale, Norman advertising executive
Van Brunt, Albert Daniel advertising agency executive
Van Campen, Stephen Bernard executive recruiter, consultant
†Vargas, Eduardo advertising executive
Vignone, Ronald John advertising agency executive
Volpe, Thomas J. advertising executive
†Wachsman, Phyllis Geri advertising executive
Wadsworth, Robert David advertising agency executive
Walke, David Michael public relations executive
†Walker, Joan H. public relations executive
Wallace, Thomas Robert public relations executive
Walsh, Annmarie Hauck research firm executive
†Wang, Julie Caroline public relations executive
Warner, John Edward advertising executive
Wasserman, Bert W. communications and publishing company executive
Wax, Edward L. advertising executive
Waylett, Thomas Robert management consultant executive
Wechsler, Arnold L. marketing executive
Wechsler, Raymond Henry management company executive
Weida, Lewis Dixon marketing analyst, consultant
Weiner, Richard public relations executive
Weisberg, Jonathan Mark public relations executive
†Weiss, Mark public relations executive
Weissman, Norman public relations executive
Weithas, William Vincent advertising agency executive
Wells, Victor Hugh, Jr. advertising agency executive
Wessinger, W. David management consultant
West, Richard Rollin business educator
Wiedemann, George Stanhope advertising executive
Wilde, Donald Raymond advertising company executive
Wilhite, Clayton Edward advertising executive
Williams, David Benton advertising agency executive
Woit, Erik Peter corporate executive, lawyer
Wolcott, John Winthrop, III corporate executive
Wooden, Ruth A. public service advertising executive
Woodrum, Robert Lee executive search consultant
Woodside, William Stewart service company executive, museum official
Wright, Jeanne Elizabeth Jason advertising executive
Wunderman, Lester advertising agency executive
†Wyatt, Mary Jean (M.J. Wyatt) public relations executive
Wyse, Lois advertising executive, author
†Young, Vivian advertising executive
Yunich, David Lawrence consumer goods consultant
†Zipko, Raymond Edward advertising executive

Newburgh
Cloudman, Francis Harold, III computer company executive
Wilcox, David Eric consultant

North Tarrytown
Schmidt, Klaus Franz advertising executive

Nyack
Karp, Peter Simon marketing executive
Keil, John Mullan advertising agency executive
Loeffel, Bruce software company executive, consultant

Ossining
Reynolds, Calvin management consultant, business educator

Palmyra
Blazey, Mark Lee management consultant

Pelham
Moore, Ellis Oglesby retired public affairs consultant
Srere, Benson M. communications company executive, consultant
Weintz, Caroline Giles advertising executive, travel writer

Pleasantville
Willis, William Henry marketing executive

Port Chester
Ailloni-Charas, Dan marketing executive
Blumenfeld, Seth David communications company executive

Port Washington
Hackett, John Byron advertising agency executive, lawyer
Johnson, Tod Stuart market research company executive

Pound Ridge
Throckmorton, Joan Helen advertising agency executive

Rochester
Brown, John Robert advertising executive, writer
Crumb, Owen Joseph public relations executive
Glazer, Laurence Charles mail order executive, real estate developer
Hoot, William John retired brewery executive
Hutchins, Frank McAllister advertising executive
Mc Kelvey, Jean Trepp industrial relations educator
McKie, W. Gilmore human resources executive
Morey, James Newman advertising executive
Sapos, Mary Ann advertising agency executive
Van Bortel, Howard Martin automarketing consultant
†Wegman, Robert B. food service executive

Rockville Centre
Mc Grath, John Joseph management consultant

Roosevelt
Wisner, Roscoe William, Jr. human resources executive

Rouses Point
†Casey, William Rossiter international transport executive

Rye
Dyche, David Bennett, Jr. management consultant
Metzger, Frank management consulting

Rye Brook
Dangoor, David Ezra Ramsi consumer goods company executive

Saint Bonaventure
Khairullah, Zahid Yahya management sciences and marketing educator, consultant

Scarsdale
Blinder, Abe Lionel management consultant
Clark, Merrell Mays management consultant
Cooper, Daniel management consultant
Kaufman, Robert Jules communications consultant, lawyer
Oswald, George Charles advertising executive, management and marketing consultant

Schenectady
Golub, Lewis supermarket company executive
†Golub, Neil supermarket chain executive

Shrub Oak
Roston, Arnold information specialist, educator, advertising executive, artist, editor

Somers
†Thoman, G. Richard computer company executive

Southampton
Lieberman, Carol Cooper healthcare marketing communications consultant

Staatsburg
Gury, Jeremy writer, advertising executive, artist

Staten Island
Barton, Jerry O'Donnell telecommunications executive
Fafian, Joseph, Jr. management consultant
Mencher, Stuart Alan sales and marketing executive

Syracuse
Goetzmann, Harry Edward, Jr. leasing company executive

Tappan
Fox, Muriel public relations executive

Tarrytown
†Gsand, William L. computer company executive
Hurley, William Joseph information systems executive
†Welsh, Dennie M. data processing executive

Thornwood
Bassett, Lawrence C management consultant

Troy
Bonney, William Lawless data processing and telecommunications educator

Trumansburg
Mc Connell, John Wilkinson labor relations educator, labor arbitrator, former socio-economics educator

Unadilla
Compton, John Robinson printing company executive

Wantagh
Torrenzano, Richard *public affairs executive*

West Islip
Softness, Donald Gabriel *marketing and manufacturing executive*

Westbury
†Fortunoff, Alan Meyer *retail company executive*

Westhampton Beach
Maas, Jane Brown *advertising executive*

White Plains
Colwell, Howard Otis *advertising executive*
Dowd, Peter Jerome *public relations executive*
Fudge, Ann Marie *marketing executive*
Krantz, Melissa Marianne *public relations company executive*
Machover, Carl *computer graphics consultant*
Roll, Irwin Clifford (Win Roll) *advertising and marketing executive*

Woodmere
†Weiss, Stephen Ira *advertising executive*

Yorktown Heights
Green, Paul Eliot, Jr. *communications scientist*
Rosenblatt, Stephen Paul *marketing and sales promotion company executive*

NORTH CAROLINA

Asheville
Etter, Robert Miller *retired consumer products executive, chemist*

Burlington
Weavil, David Carlton *clinical laboratory services executive*

Cary
Sussenguth, Edward Henry *computer company executive, computer network designer*

Chapel Hill
Colen, Donald Jerome *public affairs specialist, writer*
Glassman, Edward *management consultant, columnist, educator*
Jerdee, Thomas Harlan *business administration educator, organization psychology researcher and consultant*
Lauterborn, Robert F. *advertising educator*
Pavão, Leonel Maia (Lee Pavão) *advertising executive*

Charlotte
Abernathy, Joseph Duncan *data processing executive*
Bradshaw, Howard Holt *management consulting company executive*
†Eppes, Thomas Evans *public relations executive*
Hudgins, Catherine Harding *business executive*
Mazze, Edward Mark *marketing consultant, business educator*
Myrick, Sue *advertising agency executive, former mayor*
Neal, William Weaver *systems integration and software executive*
Redden, Forrest Richard, Jr. *management executive*
Thomas, Joe Carroll *human resources director*

Cherryville
Huffstetler, Palmer Eugene *lawyer, transportation executive*

Durham
Agusta, Benjamin J. *computer company executive*
†Lejdemalm, Ronny *communications executive*
Otterbourg, Robert Kenneth *public relations consultant*
Ryan, Gerard Spencer *inn executive*
Squire, Alexander *management consultant*
†Tracy, Philip R. *computer company executive*

Fremont
Ackerman, Lennis Campbell *management consultant*

Greensboro
Allen, Jesse Owen, III *management development and organizational*
Spears, Alexander White, III *tobacco company executive*

Greenville
Schellenberger, Robert Earl *management educator and department chairman*

Hendersonville
Schooley, Charles Earl *consultant*

Hickory
†George, Boyd Lee *consumer products company executive*

Lake Lure
Newbrough, Edgar Truett *retired management consultant*

Lincolnton
†Gaither, Ann Heafner *sales executive*

Matthews
†Rivenbark, Jan Meredith *food service products corporate executive*

North Wilkesboro
Herring, Leonard Gray *marketing company executive*

Pinehurst
Gilmore, Voit *travel executive*
Nuzzo, Salvatore Joseph *defense, nuclear executive*
Owings, Malcolm William *retired management consultant*
Stingel, Donald Eugene *management consultant*

Raleigh
Breytspraak, John, Jr. *management consultant*
Doherty, Robert Cunningham *advertising executive*
Eberly, Harry Landis *retired communications company executive*
Grubb, Donald Hartman *paper industry supplies company executive*
Leak, Robert E. *management consultant*
Lewis, Richard Jay *marketing educator, university dean*
Ofner, J(ames) Alan *management consultant*
†Shaw, Robert Gilbert *restaurant executive, senator*
Tompkins, James Arthur *consulting firm executive, industrial engineer*

Research Triangle Park
Bursiek, Ralph David *information systems company executive*
†Hagan, Joseph Lawrence *communications executive*

Rocky Mount
Autry, Robert F. *restaurant chain executive*
Laughery, Jack Arnold *restaurant chain executive*
†Wilson, Richard P. *human resources executive*

Southern Pines
Mataxis, Theodore Christopher *consultant, lecturer, writer, retired army officer, educator*
Vanderwoude, J. Stephen *communications company executive*

Weaverville
Parsons, Vinson Adair *retired computer software company executive*

Wilson
Ross, Guy Matthews, Jr. *corporate executive*

Winston Salem
Atkinson, G. Douglas, Sr. *marketing executive, consultant*
Ehmann, Carl William *consumer products executive, researcher*
Gunzenhauser, Gerard Ralph, Jr. *management consultant, investor*
Hendrix, Rufus Sam, Jr. *sales executive*
Johnston, James Wesley *tobacco company executive*
MacKinnon, Sally Anne *retired fast food company executive*

Zebulon
†Marshall, Michael P. *computer company sales executive*

NORTH DAKOTA

Bismarck
†Carlisle, Ronald Dwight *nursery owner*

Fargo
†Wallwork, William Wilson, III *corporate executive*

Turtle Lake
†Grosz, Albert Mick *sales executive*

OHIO

Akron
Aggarwal, Sundar Lal *technology management consultant*
Kelley, John Paul *communications consultant*
McCormick, William Edward *environmental consultant*
Sonnecken, Edwin Herbert *management consultant*
†Wickham, Michael W. *transportation executive*

Beachwood
†Seelbach, William Robert *corporate executive*
Zelikow, Howard Monroe *management and financial consultant*

Berea
Irwin, Richard Loren *systems management association executive*

Bowling Green
Lunde, Harold Irving *management educator*

Canfield
Bachmeyer, Robert Wesley *retired hospital administration consultant*

Centerville
Perrich, Jerry Robert *environmental consulting company executive*

Chagrin Falls
Church, Irene Zaboly *personnel services company executive*
Eastburn, Richard A. *consulting firm executive*
Fisher, Will Stratton *illumination consultant*
Gelb, Victor *business executive*

Cincinnati
Artzt, Edwin Lewis *consumer products company executive*
Bluestein, Paul Harold *management engineer*
Brown, Dale Patrick *advertising executive*
Brunner, Gordon F(rancis) *household products company executive*
Cook, Bruce Alan *air conditioning sales and service executive*
†Dinicola, Robert *consumer products company executive*
Dubuc, Kenneth E *management consultant*
Durbrow, Brian Richard *management consultant*
Eager, William Earl *information systems corporation executive*
Ferriss, David Platt *advertising consultant*
Flanagan, Martha Lang *corporate secretary*
†Fokker, J. P. *waste management executive*
Freshwater, Paul Ross *consumer goods company executive*
Groth, Jon Quentin *management consultant*
†Harville, Thomas T. *consumer goods company executive*
Henry, J(ohn) Porter, Jr. *sales consultant*
Hicks, Irle Raymond *retail food chain executive*

†Hutton, Edward Luke *diversified public corporation executive*
Johnson, C. Scott *management consultant*
Lockhart, John Mallery *management consultant*
Lucke, Robert Vito *merger and acquisition executive*
Maier, Craig Frisch *restaurant executive*
†Maier, Jack C. *food products company executive*
McNulty, John William *retired public relations executive, automobile company executive*
Milligan, Lawrence Drake, Jr. *consumer products executive*
Pepper, John Ennis, Jr. *consumer products company executive*
Stolley, Alexander *advertising executive*
†Terhar, Louis F. *waste management administrator*
Wehling, Robert Louis *household products company executive*
Westheimer, Ruth Welling *retired management consultant*

Cleveland
Alspaugh, Robert Odo *industrial management consultant*
Bailey, John Turner *public relations executive*
Begun, Semi Joseph *management consultant*
Bogomolny, Richard Joseph *retail food chain executive*
Cardwell, James William *business strategy consultant*
Clutter, Bertley Allen, III *management company executive*
Danco, Léon Antoine *management consultant, educator*
Drotning, John Evan *industrial relations specialist*
†Dupuy, William L. *public relations executive*
Eaton, Henry Felix *public relations executive*
Foltz, Clinton Henry *advertising executive*
Fountain, Ronald Glenn *management consultant*
Fruchtenbaum, Edward *greeting card company executive*
Garda, Robert Allen *management consultant*
†Henry, Edward Frank *computer accounting service executive*
Johnson, John Frank *professional recruitment executive*
Kallock, Roger William *marketing professional, logistics consultant*
Lang, H. Jack *advertising executive, author*
Lowenthal, Henry *greeting card company executive*
Marcus, Donald Howard *advertising agency executive*
McGinty, Thomas Edward *management consultant*
†Mecredy, James R. *management consultant*
Miller, John Robert *environmental recycling company executive*
Morin, Patrick Joyce *advertising executive*
Newman, Joseph H. *advertising executive*
Perkovic, Robert Branko *international consultant*
†Quagliata, John *restaurant company executive*
Remington, Charles Bradford *professional services firm executive*
Roop, James John *public relations executive*
†Silverman, William A. *public relations executive*
Skinner, Charles Scofield *technology management service executive, consultant, mechanical engineer*
†Stevens, Edward *public relations executive*
Stone, Irving I. *greeting card company executive*
Taw, Dudley Joseph *sales executive*
Ulchaker, Stanley Louis *public relations consultant*
Watt, Ronald William *public relations executive*
†Young, Davis *public relations executive*

Columbus
Ackerman, Kenneth Benjamin *management consultant, writer*
Allen, Larry Rollar *management consultant*
Becher, Paul Ronald *health benefits executive*
Brown, Rowland Chauncey Widrig *information systems, strategic planning and ethics consultant*
Burke, Kenneth Andrew *advertising executive*
Kampmeier, Curtis Neil *management consultant*
McClain, Thomas E. *communications executive*
McMorrow, Richard Mark *research company executive*
Muller, Mervin Edgar *information systems educator, consultant*
Ryan, Robert Seibert *consulting company executive*
Taylor, Celianna I. *information systems specialist*
Tipton, Clyde Raymond, Jr. *communications and resources development consultant*
Tway, Stephen Edward *marketing communications executive, consultant*
Wheeler, George Charles *quality assurance professional*
Williams, David Fulton *industrial distribution company executive*

Dayton
Boren, Arthur Rodney *sales management executive*
Darragh, John K. *printing company executive*
†Deardorff, Darryl K. *business consultant, accountant*
Hastler, Russell Clifford, Jr. *research and development company executive*
Kegerreis, Robert James *management consultant, marketing educator*
Nevin, Robert Charles *information systems executive*
Reese, Richard Bruce *customer service executive*
Vander Wiel, Kenneth Carlton *computer services company executive*

Dublin
Casey, John K. *restaurant chain executive*
Freytag, Donald Ashe *management consultant*
Near, James W. *restaurant and franchise executive*
Schinagl, Erich Friedrich *health care company executive, physician*
Smith, K(ermit) Wayne *computer company executive*
Teter, Gordon F. *fast food chain company executive*
Thomas, R. David *food services company executive*

Hamilton
Battaglia, Michael Salvatore *security company executive*

Lancaster
Katlic, John Edward *management consultant*
Phillips, Edward John *consulting firm executive*

Mansfield
Ellison, Lorin Bruce *management consultant*

Maple Heights
Sargent, Liz Elaine (Elizabeth Sargent) *safety consulting executive*

Maumee
†Iott, Wallace D. *supermarket chain executive*

Milford
Fischer, Robert Andrew *computer executive*
†Morley, Bradford Charles *software company executive*

Niles
Travaglini, Raymond Dominic *corporate executive*

Novelty
Miller, Dwight Richard *hair design executive*

Oberlin
Gladieux, Bernard Louis *management consultant*

Peninsula
Ludwig, Richard Joseph *ski resort executive*

Pepper Pike
Bray, Pierce *business consultant*

Port Clinton
Subler, Edward Pierre *advertising executive*

Saint Clairsville
Dankworth, Margaret Anne *management consultant*

Salem
Fehr, Kenneth Manbeck *computer systems company executive*

Solon
Stauffer, Thomas George *hotel executive*
Weiss, Joseph Joel *consulting company executive*

Tipp City
Taylor, Robert Homer *quality assurance professional, pilot*

Toledo
Bick, David Greer *health care marketing executive*
Block, Allan James *communications executive*
Christiansen, Eric George *marketing specialist*
Northup, John David *management consultant, inventor*
Paquette, Jack Kenneth *management consultant, antiques dealer*

Vandalia
†Subotnick, Stuart *food service executive*
Welter, William Michael *marketing and advertising executive*

West Chester
Ofte, Donald *environmental executive, former management consultant*

Westerville
Kollat, David Truman *management consultant*

Wooster
Schmitt, Wolfgang Rudolph *consumer products executive*

Xenia
Nutter, Zoe Dell Lantis *public relations executive, retired*

Zanesville
Truby, John Louis *corporate executive*

OKLAHOMA

Norman
Van Auken, Robert Danforth *business administration educator, management consultant*

Oklahoma City
Ackerman, Raymond Basil *advertising agency executive*
Brumley, David Lee *corporate human resources executive*
Lynn, C(harles) Stephen *franchising company executive*
†Raydon, Max E. *consumer products companry executive*

Tulsa
Gentry, Bern Leon, Sr. *minority consulting company executive*
Hood, Charles Hurlburt *advertising agency executive*
†Huls, Harrison *wholesale and retail grocery company executive*
†Rubottom, Donald Julian *management consultant*

OREGON

Albany
Norman, E. Gladys *business computer educator, consultant*

Baker City
Graham, Beardsley *management consultant*

Beaverton
Chang, David Ping-Chung *business consultant, architect*
Cymbala, Robert Joseph *communications company executive*
Masi, Edward A. *computer company executive*

Eugene
Bennett, Robert Royce *engineering and management consultant*
Piele, Philip Kern *education infosystems educator*
Tull, Donald Stanley *marketing educator*

Grants Pass
Naylor, John Thomas *telephone company executive*

Lake Oswego
Kupel, Frederick John *counselor*

Medford
Hennion, Reeve Lawrence *communications executive*
Keener, John Wesley *management consultant*

Portland
Boyman, John Edward George *individual/organizational transition consultant*
Butler, Leslie Ann *advertising executive, portrait artist*
Congdon, Marsha B. *telecommunications executive*
Conkling, Roger Linton *consultant, business administration educator, retired utility executive*
†Hatt, Peter McLeod *advertising executive*
Maclean, Charles (Bernard) *transition, performance recognition and workplace violence prevention consultant*
Martin, Lucy Z. *public relations executive*
Pamplin, Robert Boisseau, Sr. *consumer products executive*
Smith, Milton Ray *computer company executive, lawyer*
Sugg, John Logan (Jack Sugg) *advertising executive*
†White, John *food marketing executive*

Salem
Johnson, Robert Raymond *management consultant, educator*

Wilsonville
Karalis, John Peter *computer company executive, lawyer*
Yocam, Delbert Wayne *communication company executive*

PENNSYLVANIA

Alexandria
Horn, John Chisolm *management consultant*

Allentown
Armstrong, W(illiam) Warren *advertising agency executive*
Jackson, William MacLeod *management consultant*
Krambeck, Robert Harold *communications executive, researcher*

Ambler
Learnard, William Ewing *marketing executive*

Ardmore
Scott, Bill *advertising agency executive*

Aston
Barnett, Samuel Treutlen *international company executive*

Bala Cynwyd
†Elkman, Stanley *advertising executive*
†Tuckerman, Donald M. *advertising executive*

Bensalem
Bishop, Howard Stuart *management consultant*
†Iacovetti, Benedict John *company executive*
Moser, Milton John *collection agency executive, consultant*

Berwyn
Brundage, Russell Archibald *retired data processing executive*

Bethlehem
Billingsley, Charles Edward *transportation company executive*
†Fairbairn, Ursula Farrell *human resources executive*
Penny, Roger Pratt *management executive*
von Bernuth, Carl W. *diversified corporation executive, lawyer*

Blue Bell
Blechschmidt, Edward Allan *computer systems executive*
Braun, Reto *computer systems company executive*
Millar, Victor E. *information services executive*

Center Valley
Cramer, Morgan Joseph, Jr. *international management executive*

Chambersburg
Furr, Quint Eugene *marketing executive*

Conshohocken
Cunningham, James Gerald, Jr. *transportation company executive*

Doylestown
Rusch, Hugh Leonard *corporate executive*

Drexel Hill
Perkins, Ralph Linwood *business executive, public health administration specialist*

Eagles Mere
Moore, Mechlin Dongan *business consultant*

Erwinna
Geldmacher, Robert Carl *software corporation executive*

Exton
Sanford, Richard D. *computer company executive*

Ferndale
Folk, James *sales executive*

Fort Washington
Blumberg, Donald Freed *management consultant*
Deric, Arthur Joseph *management consultant, lawyer*

Harrisburg
Kimmel, Robert Irving *corporate communication design consultant, former state government official*
Moritz, Milton Edward *security consultant*
Neilson, Winthrop Cunningham, III *communications executive, financial communications consultant*
Stabler, Donald Billman *business executive*

King Of Prussia
Minter, Philip Clayton *communications company executive*

Lancaster
Kelly, Robert Lynn *advertising agency executive*
Louden, James Keith *management consultant, executive*

Lebanon
Arnold, Edward Henry *transportation executive*

Malvern
Kyle, Terrence Wayne *health care data processing executive*
McIntosh, L(orne) William *marketing executive*

McConnellsburg
†Diller, Charles Herbert, Jr. *corporate professional*

Middletown
Kaynak, Erdener *marketing educator, consultant editor*

Milford
Snyder, Richard Lee *consumer products company executive*

Mount Joy
Eichler, Franklin Roosevelt *petroleum products distributor and services company executive*

Mountainhome
Buttz, Charles William *outdoor advertising executive*

Narberth
Newhall, John Harrison *management consultant*

Nazareth
Herrick, Robert Ford *personnel consultant*

New Holland
†Ruggeri, Riccardo *automotive sales executive*

New Oxford
Frock, J. Daniel *transportation executive, retired manufacturing company executive*

Newtown
Keyes, Fenton *consultant, writer*

Newtown Square
Bower, Ward Alan *management consultant, lawyer*

Norristown
†Kaltenbacher, Philip D(avid) *industrialist, former public official*

Paoli
Ferrell, David Lee *public relations consultant*

Philadelphia
Barrett, James Edward, Jr. *management consultant*
Belinger, Harry Robert *business executive*
Black, Albert Pershing, Jr. *health care executive*
Blades, Herbert William *diversified consumer products company executive*
†Brinster, Barry *public relations company executive*
Dunn, Wendell Earl, III *management consultant, educator*
Feninger, Claude *industry management services company executive*
Finney, Graham Stanley *management consultant*
Fuller, John Garsed Campbell *food and drug company executive*
Gaither, William Samuel *consultant*
Gilbert, Harry Ephraim, Jr. *hotel executive*
Goodchild, John Charles, Jr. *advertising and public relations executive*
Greenberg, Marshall Gary *marketing research consultant*
Guenther, George Carpenter *travel company executive*
Hagen, James Alfred *marketing executive*
Jordan, Clifford Henry *management consultant*
Korsyn, Irene Hahne *marketing executive*
Landis, Edgar David *services business company executive*
Louchheim, Frank Pfeifer *management consultant*
†Melnick, William *advertising executive*
Mitchell, Howard Estill *human resources educator, consultant*
†Munch, David Edward *management executive*
Nadel, Marvin *retired engineering and management consulting firm executive*
Neubauer, Joseph *business executive*
†Rand, Samuel *advertising executive*
Reich, Morton Melvyn *marketing communications company executive*
Riordan, John Thomas *management consultant*
†Rivas, Joyce Margaret *advertising executive*
Rouse, Andrew Miles *business consultant*
Small, Henry Gilbert *information scientist, researcher*
Spiro, Walter Anselm *advertising and public relations agency executive*
Tierney, Brian Patrick *advertising and public relations executive*
von Seldeneck, Judith Metcalfe *executive search firm executive*
Wiksten, Barry Frank *communications executive*
Wilder, Robert George *advertising and public relations executive*
Wind, Yoram Jerry *marketing and management educator*

Pittsburgh
Alvarez, Paul Hubert *communications and public relations consultant*
Bender, Charles Christian *retail home center executive*
Boyd, William, Jr. *business advisor, banker*
Burger, Herbert Francis *advertising agency executive*
Cowden, Jere Lee *management consultant*
†Ficco, James Vincent, III *advertising executive*
Fine, Milton *hotel company executive, lawyer*
Fisher, James Aiken *industrial marketing executive*
Genge, William Harrison *advertising executive, writer*
Grant, Daniel Gordon *computer consulting company executive*
Hedquist, Jan P. *advertising company executive*
Hershey, Colin Harry *management consultant*
Humphrey, Watts Sherman *technical executive, author*
Patten, Charles Anthony *management consultant, arbitrator, retired manufacturing company executive, author*
Rago, Ann D'Amico *public relations professional*
Rich, Thomas Hurblut *corporate identity consulting company executive*
Simmermon, James Everett *credit bureau executive*
Walsh, Michael Francis *advertising executive*
Weaver, Charles Henry *business consulting executive*
Zandin, Kjell Bertil *management consulting executive*

Plymouth Meeting
Katz, Gerald *management consultant*
Siegal, Jacob J. *management and financial consultant*

Port Royal
Wert, Jonathan Maxwell, II *management consultant*

Radnor
Harrison, Robert Drew *management consultant*
Paier, Adolf Arthur *computer software and services company executive*

Reading
Dersh, Rhoda E. *management consultant, business executive*
Knerr, Reinhard H. *communications executive*
Rutter, Elizabeth Jane *assistant corporate secretary*

Saint Marys
Shobert, Erle Irwin, II *management consultant*

Shippensburg
Stone, Susan Ridgaway *marketing educator*

Skytop
Popham, Lewis Charles, III *hotel corporation director, former university dean*

Southampton
Omlor, John Joseph *business consultant*

Spring House
Thorne, John Watson, III *advertising and marketing executive*

State College
Fischer, Floyd Brand *educational and management consultant*

Tannersville
Moore, James Alfred *ski company executive, lawyer*

Unionville
De Marino, Donald Nicholson *international business executive, former federal agency administrator*

University Park
Gouran, Dennis Stephen *communications educator*

Valley Forge
Schaefer, Adolph Oscar, Jr. *advertising agency executive*

Warrington
Shaw, Milton Herbert *conglomerate executive*

Wayne
Carroll, Robert W. *retired business executive*
†Coane, James Edwin, III *information technology executive*
†DeCarlo, A. J. *lumber company executive*
Kraftson, Raymond H. *corporate executive*
†Martino, Rocco Leonard *computer systems executive*

West Chester
McKeldin, William Evans *management consultant*
Tomlinson, Charles Wesley, Jr. *advertising executive*

Wexford
Boyd, Robert Wright, III *lamp company executive*

Wilkes Barre
†Sordoni, Andrew J., III *communications company executive, construction company executive*

Willow Grove
†Asplundh, Christopher B. *tree service company executive*
†Asplundh, Robert H. *tree service company executive*

Yardley
Newsom, Carolyn Cardall *management consultant*

York
Hetzel, Dennis Richard *communications executive*

RHODE ISLAND

Barrington
Horton, John Alden *advertising agency executive*

East Greenwich
Weiss, Alan *management consultant, author*

Kingston
Zuehlke, Richard William *scientific conference manager*

Lincoln
Burgdoerfer, Jerry J. *marketing and distribution executive*

Newport
Hayward, John Tucker *management consultant*

Pawtucket
Hassenfeld, Alan Geoffrey *toy company executive*
O'Neill, John T. *toy company executive*
Verrecchia, Alfred J. *toy company executive*

Providence
†Kreykes, William *health care management executive*
†Lederman, Michael G. *consumer products company executive*
White, Erskine Norman, Jr. *management company executive*

Wakefield
Eddy, Edward Danforth *academic administrator, educator*

West Greenwich
Breakstone, Robert Albert *computer and government services company executive*

West Warwick
Clary, Alexia Barbara *management company executive*

SOUTH CAROLINA

Beaufort
Day, John Sidney *management sciences educator*

Charleston
Donehue, John Douglas *newspaper public relations executive*
Rivers, John Minott, Jr. *corporate professional*

Clemson
Burch, Elmer Earl *management educator*

Columbia
Case, George Tilden, Jr. *marketing professional*
Conrad, Paul Ernest *transportation consultant*
Cope, Larry Morgan *employee assistance provider, coordinator*
Martin, Charles Wallace *travel executive, retired university administrator*
Newton, Rhonwen Leonard *microcomputer consultant*
†Wilson, George Larry *computer software company executive*

Easley
Dark, Alvin Ralph *public relations executive*
Goldman, Joseph Elias *advertising executive*

Fort Mill
Kelbley, Stephen Paul *consumer products executive*

Greenville
†Callahan, Ralph Wilson, Jr. *advertising agency executive*
†Collins, Marshall J., Jr. *consumer products company executive*
Fitzgerald, Eugene Francis *management consultant*
Henderson, James Marvin *advertising agency executive*
†Torrence, Roderick Clark *advertising executive*

Hilton Head Island
Little, Thomas Mayer *public relations executive*
Patton, Joseph Donald, Jr. *management consultant*

North Augusta
Pritchard, Constance Jenkins *career development trainer, consultant*

North Myrtle Beach
Hampton, Robert K., Sr. *environmental and industrial specialist, real estate associate, consultant*

Ridgeland
Smart, Jacob Edward *consultant*

Rock Hill
Click, John William *communication educator*

Saint Helena Island
Herzbrun, David Joseph *retired advertising executive, consultant*

Sullivans Island
Romaine, Henry Simmons *investment consultant*

West Columbia
Hand, Herbert Hensley *management educator, executive, consultant, inventor*

SOUTH DAKOTA

Beresford
Jensen, Shirley Wulff *sales executive*

Edgemont
Bennett, Charles Leo *management consultant, rancher*

North Sioux City
Waitt, Ted *computer company executive*

Sioux Falls
Smith, Murray Thomas *transportation company executive*
Taplett, Lloyd Melvin *human resources management consultant*

Vermillion
Clifford, Sylvester *retired communication educator*

TENNESSEE

Brentwood
Sullivan, James Thomas *printing company executive*

Chattanooga
†Falcon, Charles *consumer products company executive*

Johnston, Hampton L. *photography corporation executive*
†Knight, Ralph H. *consumer products company executive*

Columbia
Chafin, William Vernon, Jr. *business consultant*

Greeneville
Austin, Tom Noell *retired tobacco company executive*

Jackson
Ewing, Frank Crockett *marketing entrepreneur, photographer*

Johnson City
Yavas, Ugur *marketing educator*

Knoxville
Eisenberg, Lee B. *communications executive*
Freeman, Richard Merrell *business consultant*
†Goforth, E. Jack *security firm executive*
†Haslam, James A., II *petroleum sales executive*
†Haslam, James A., III *petroleum sales executive*
Herndon, Anne Harkness *sales executive*
Jordan, (William) Hamilton (McWhorter) *corporate and international communications consultant*
Mayfield, T. Brient, IV *media and computer executive*
Vance, Stanley Charles *management educator*

La Follette
McDonald, Miller Baird *management consultant, columnist, historian*

Lenoir City
Gerwels, Laurenn Barker *public relations executive*

Memphis
Abston, Dunbar, Jr. *management executive*
Granger, David Mason *marketing, public relations executive*
†Hyde, Joseph R., III *wholesale food distribution executive*
Langton, Bryan D. *hotel executive*
Ledsinger, Charles Albert, Jr. *hotel, gaming executive*
†Martin, William A. *business executive*
McCommon, Hubert *risk management consultant*
Satre, Philip Glen *corporate executive, lawyer*
Sullivan, Eugene Joseph *food service company executive*
Summer, Harry Harmon *marketing educator and consultant*

Nashville
Bolinger, John C., Jr. *management consultant*
Cawthon, William Connell *operations management consultant*
Clouse, Robert Wilburn *communication executive, educator*
†Dye, Hank *public relations executive*
Faust, A. Donovan *communications executive*
Kaludis, George *management consultant, book company executive, educator*
Lawrence, Thomas Patterson *public relations executive*
†Martin, Charles Neil, Jr. *health care management company executive*
Moore, William Grover, Jr. *management consultant, former air freight executive, former air force officer*
†Osborne, C. William *transportation executive*
Taylor, Robert Bonds *instructional designer*
Van Mol, Louis John, Jr. *public relations executive*

Oak Ridge
Whittle, Charles Edward, Jr. *consultant, lecturer*

Tullahoma
Franke, John Charles *human resources executive*
Gossick, Lee Van *corporate executive, retired air force officer*
Whitfield, Jack Duane *advanced technology services and engineering company executive*

TEXAS

Arlington
†O'Neill, James J. *food service company executive*

Austin
†Braasch, Steven Mark *advertising executive*
Carter, Shelby Henry, Jr. *communications executive, educator*
Chavarria, Ernest Montes, Jr. *international trade, business and finance consultant, lecturer*
Culp, George Hart *computer executive, consultant*
France, Newell Edwin *corporation executive*
†Grady, Charles E. *advertising executive*
Hart, Roderick P. *communications educator, researcher, author*
Lanham, Elizabeth *retired management educator*
Lord, William Jackson, Jr. *communication educator*
Nasworthy, Carol Cantwell *education and public policy professional*
Payne, John Ross *rare books and archives appraisal-consulting company executive, library science educator*
Topfer, Morton Louis *communications company executive*
Vande Hey, James Michael *corporate executive, former air force officer*
Winegar, Albert Lee *computer systems company executive*

Brownwood
DeHay, Jerry Marvin *business consultant*

Bryan
Sulik, Edwin (Pete Sulik) *health care administrator*

Burleson
Prior, Boyd Thelman *management consultant*

Carrollton
Estrin, Melvyn J. *computer products company executive*
Miller, Ronald Alan *marketing consultant*

College Station
Conole, Richard Clement *management consultant*
†Gunn, Clare Alward *consultant, writer, retired educator*

Dallas
†Arnold, George Lawrence *advertising company executive*
Bahr, Conrad Charles, III *financial management executive, consultant*
Beck, Robert Louis *marketing executive, lawyer, foundation executive*
†Bell, Benjamin Clayton, Jr. *public relations executive*
†Benjet, Mervyn *computer company executive*
Bishop, Gene Herbert *corporate executive*
Cummings, Brian Thomas *public relations company executive*
†Dedman, Robert Henry *sales executive*
Dillon, Donald Ward *management consultant*
Domagala, Richard Edward *sales executive*
Dozier, David Charles, Jr. *marketing public relations and advertising executi*
Durham, Michael Jonathan *transportation company executive*
†Erwin, O. Scott *golf recreational facility executive, consultant*
†Fleming, Jon Hugh *business executive*
Flores, Marion Thomas *advertising executive*
Gossen, Emmett Joseph, Jr. *motel chain executive, lawyer*
Grimes, David Lynn *communications company executive*
Hoffman, Harold Wayne *advertising agency executive*
†Jenkins, James Michael *restaurant company executive*
†Keith, Carter O. *advertising company executive*
Kluge, John Werner *broadcasting and advertising executive*
†Korba, Robert W. *communications executive*
Korman, Ira Bruce *health care consultant, advisor*
Lane, Alvin Huey, Jr. *management consultant*
Levenson, Stanley Richard *public relations and advertising executive*
Lifson, Kalman Alan *management consultant, retail executive*
MacMahon, Paul *advertising executive*
†Roger, Richard R. *personal care industry executive*
†Rutherford, Howard Don *marketing executive*
Sheinberg, Israel *computer company executive*
Spiegel, Lawrence Howard *advertising executive*
Steorts, Nancy Harvey *international management consultant*
†Stuart, Norton Arlington, Jr. *data processing manufacturing executive*
Vanderveld, John, Jr. *waste disposal company executive*
Werner, Seth Mitchell *advertising executive*
Wilber, Robert Edwin *corporate executive*
Wilhelm, Walter Tinkham *software systems company executive*
Wyly, Charles Joseph, Jr. *corporate executive*
Ziebarth, Karl Rex *international transportation consultant*

Dripping Springs
Ballard, Mary Melinda *financial communications and investment banking firm executive*

El Paso
Cassidy, Richard Thomas *hotel executive, defense industry consultant, retired army officer*
Roberts, Ernst Edward *marketing consultant*

Fort Worth
Dagnon, James Bernard *human resources executive*
†Nourse, Robert E. M. *consumer products company executive*
Peters, Lawrence H. *management educator, consultant*
Ray, Paul Richard, Jr. *executive search consultant*
Turner, Loyd Leonard *advertising executive, public relations executive*

Georgetown
Weyrauch, Paul Turney *retired army officer*

Grapevine
Holley, Cyrus Helmer *management consulting service executive*
Smith, Lee Herman *business executive*

Horseshoe Bay
Lesikar, Raymond Vincent *business administration educator*

Houston
†Bonham, Donald L. *food service executive*
Boosey, John Arthur *management consultant, engineer*
†Bower, Arthur Michel *advertising agency executive*
Brackley, William Lowell *aviation management consultant*
Brown, Jean William *advertising and public relations executive*
†Caltrider, Thomas Lewis *environmental company executive*
Cameron, Bruce Francis *data processing executive*
Castillo, Leonel Jabier *communications and promotions executive, consultant*
Cernan, Eugene A. *management company executive, former astronaut*
Cofran, George Lee *management consultant*
Cole, Aubrey Louis *management consultant, forest products company executive*
Cooley, Andrew Lyman *corporation executive, former army officer*
Crystal, Jonathan Andrew *executive recruiter*
†Del Franco, Ray *consumer products company executive*
Dosher, John Rodney *consulting management consultant*
Gibson, Peggy Kathryn *marketing professional*
Gilbert, Harold Stanley *warehousing company executive*
Harris, Nell H. *retired public relations executive, real estate broker, writer*
Hart, James Whitfield, Jr. *corporate public affairs executive, lawyer*
Holmes, Darrell *tourism consultant*
Jeanneret, Paul Richard *management consultant*
Jones, O. K., III *business services executive, former oil company executive*
Kopec, Frank John *advertising agency executive*
Kors, R. Paul *search company executive*
†Larkin, William Vincent, Jr. *oilfield service company executive*
†Levit, Max *food service executive*
Lowrey, E. James *food service company executive*
McKim, Paul Arthur *management consultant, retired petroleum executive*
Myers, Norman Allan *marketing professional*
†Onstead, Randall *consumer goods company executive*
†Onstead, Robert R. *consumer goods company executive*
Orme, Denis Arthur *management consultant*
Palmer, James Edward *public relations executive*
Patterson, William Wayne *electronics company executive*
†Peebler, Robert Paul *marketing executive, geoscientist*
Penny, Charles Richard *advertising executive*
Pfeiffer, Eckhard *computer company executive*
Ruckelshaus, William Doyle *waste disposal services company executive*
Seaman, Roual Duane *data processing company executive*
Snider, Robert Larry *management consultant*
†Vaeth, Nancy Ann *sales executive*
Welch, Byron Eugene *communications educator*

Hurst
†Jackson, Donald *waste management executive*

Irving
Clarke, Jack Graeme *consultant, retired petroleum company executive*
†Faulkner, David J. *computer company executive*
Gomersall, Earl Raymond *business executive*
†Lindner, James D. *computer company executive*
†Munger, Sharon *market research firm executive*
Temerlin, Liener *advertising agency executive*
Wicks, William Withington *retired public relations executive*

Lubbock
Pasewark, William Robert *management consultant, author*

Lufkin
†Brookshire, Wiley Eugene *cinsumer products company executive*

Plano
Alberthal, Lester M., Jr. *information processing services executive*
Donald, James L. *communications company executive*
Fernandes, Gary Joe *electronic data processing company executive*

San Angelo
Coe, Robert Stanford *retired management educator*

San Antonio
†Butt, Charles C. *food service executive*
Carpenter, John Wilson, III *management consultant, retired air force officer, educational administrator*
†Conly, Michael J. *communications company executive, television executive*
Corum, B. H. *health care company executive*
Cory, William Eugene *retired consulting company executive*
Franklin, Larry Daniel *communications company executive*
†Freter, Mark Allen *marketing and public relations executive, consultant*
†Hochhauser, Richard Michael *marketing professional*
Keck, James Moulton *retired advertising and marketing executive, retired air force officer*
Lahourcade, John Brosius *service company executive*
Leavitt, Audrey Faye Cox *television programming executive*
Reiser, Leroy Franklin, Jr. *marketing consultant*
Ritchie, Richard Lee *communications company executive, former railroad and forest products company executive*
Whitt, Robert Ampudia, III *advertising executive, marketing professional*
Wimpress, Gordon Duncan, Jr. *corporate consultant, foundation executive*
Witherspoon, John Marshall *advertising executive*

Sugar Land
Kempner, James Carroll *sugar company executive*
Preng, David Edward *management consultant*

Waco
Meyer, Paul James *communications company executive*

Woodlands
Sharman, Richard Lee *communications executive*

UTAH

Orem
Bastian, Bruce Wayne *software company executive*

Park City
Ebbs, George Heberling, Jr. *management consulting company executive*

Provo
Bartlett, Leonard Lee *communications educator, retired advertising agency executive, advertising historian*
Buck, William Fraser, II *marketing executive*
Harlow, LeRoy Francis *organization and management educator emeritus, author*
†Noorda, Raymond J. *computer software company executive*

Salt Lake City
Bozich, Anthony Thomas *transportation industry consultant, retired motor freight company executive*
Elkins, Glen Ray *service company executive*
†Evans, Wayne Cannon *communications and public relations executive*
†Howell, Scott Newell *computer company executive, state legislator*
†Jones, Clark David *restaurant executive, accountant*
Lund, Victor L. *retail food company executive*
†Nordgren, Bradley J. *advertising executive*
†Parkinson, Richard A. *consumer products company executive*
Phillips, Ted Ray *advertising agency executive*
Scott, Howard Winfield, Jr. *temporary help company executive*
Stanford, Melvin Joseph *management consultant, retired educator, academic administrator*

Sandy
York, Theodore Robert *consulting company executive*

Springville
Hall, Derek Harry *natural health products company sales executive*

Vernal
Siddoway, Henry Ralph *company executive*

VERMONT

Charlotte
McCoubrey, R. James *advertising executive*

Chester
Coleman, John Royston *innkeeper, author*

Essex Junction
†Sweetser, Gene Gilman *quality assurance professional, state legislator*

Gaysville
Dawson, Wilfred Thomas *marketing executive, consultant*

Londonderry
Bigelow, David Skinner, III *management consultant*

Manchester
Yager, Hunter *advertising executive*

Norwich
Fitzhugh, William Wyvill, Jr. *printing company executive*
Smith, Markwick Kern, Jr. *management consultant*

Thetford Center
Brown, Robert Goodell *management consultant*

White River Junction
Fayerweather, John *management and international business specialist, educator*

Woodstock
Browning, Robert Masters *management consultant*

VIRGINIA

Alexandria
Broide, Mace Irwin *public affairs consultant*
Chamberlain, Adrian Ramond *executive*
Collins, Frank Charles, Jr. *industrial and service quality specialist*
Cooper, B. Jay *public relations executive*
Covone, James Michael *automotive parts import and distribution company executive*
Dawson, Samuel Cooper, Jr. *motel company executive*
Day, Melvin Sherman *information company executive*
Devine, Donald J. *management and political consultant*
Donohue, Thomas Joseph *transportation association executive*
Duncan, John Bonner *housing development consultant*
†Greener, William I., III *communications executive*
Hagan, Robert Leslie *consulting company executive*
Hansan, Mary Anne *marketing professional*
Hartsock, Linda Sue *educational and management development executive*
Laurent, Lawrence Bell *communications executive, former journalist*
†Locigno, Paul Robert *public affairs executive*
Loevi, Francis Joseph, Jr. *consulting company executive*
McMillan, Charles William *consulting company executive*
Newburger, Beth Weinstein *medical telecommunications company executive*
†Osborn, William C. *personnel organization executive*
Pitt, Robert Healy, II *international marketing executive*
Richardson, Robert Charlwood, III *management consultant, retired air force officer*
Smith, J. Brian *advertising executive, public affairs consultant, campaign management firm executive*
Smith, William Young *consultant, former air force officer*

Annandale
Speakes, Larry Melvin *public relations executive*

Arlington
Ackerson, Jeffrey Townsend *computer systems executive*
Barnes, Wesley Edward *energy and environmental consulting company executive*
Cetron, Marvin Jerome *management executive*
†Fabian, John McCreary *non-profit company executive, astronaut*
Faris, Frank Edgar *marketing executive*
Freeman, Neal Blackwell *communications corporation executive*
Gianturco, Delio E. *corporate executive*
Greinke, Everett Donald *corporate executive, international programs consultant*
Hess, Milton Siegmund *computer company executive*
Jennings, Madelyn Pulver *communications company human resources executive*
Kingsley, Daniel Thain *public affairs executive*
Kriegsman, William Edwin *consulting firm executive*
London, J. Phillip *information technology company executive*
Martin, Edgar Thomas *telecommunications consultant, lawyer*

Meyer, Richard Townsend *service company executive*
Raymond, David Alan *business executive, former government official*
Riegel, Kurt Wetherhold *environmental protection, occupational safety and health*
†Rosenthal, Robert M. *automotive sales executive*
Rossotti, Charles Ossola *computer consulting company executive*
†Smith, Janet Erlene *advertising executive*
Zorthian, Barry *communications executive*

Blacksburg
Weaver, Pamela Ann *hospitality research professional*

Burke
Dean, John Wilson, Jr. *business consultant, retired army officer*
Pollard, Joseph Augustine *advertising and public relations consultant*

Chantilly
O'Brien, Robert John, Jr. *public relations executive, former government official, air force officer*

Charlottesville
Colley, John Leonard, Jr. *educator, author, management consultant*
Dunn, Mary Jarratt *public relations executive*

Chesapeake
Orr, Joel Nathaniel *computer graphics consultant*

Chesterfield
Congdon, John Rhodes *corporate executive*

Danville
Dibrell, Louis Nelson, III *tobacco company executive*
Owen, Claude Bernard, Jr. *tobacco company executive*

Fairfax
Gross, Patrick Walter *business executive, management consultant*
Jones, Carleton Shaw *information systems company executive, lawyer*
Kieffer, Jarold Alan *policy and management consultant, writer*
Klauberg, William Joseph *technical services company executive*
Palmer, James Daniel *information technology educator*
Pan, Elizabeth Lim *information systems company executive*
Pitchell, Robert J. *business executive*
Puckorius, Theodore D. *consulting company executive*
Walker, Betsy Ellen *computer products and services company executive*

Fairfax Station
Johansen, Eivind Herbert *corporate executive, former army officer*

Falls Church
Beach, Robert Oliver, II *computer company executive*
Cohn, Samuel Maurice *economic and management consultant*
Harley, William Gardner *retired communications consultant*
Nashman, Alvin Eli *computer company executive*
Nelson, Thomas William *management consultant, former government official*
Webb, William John *public relations counsel*

Glen Allen
†Seymour, Harlan Francis *computer services company executive*

Great Falls
Anderson, William Robert *corporate executive*

Grundy
†Smith, Jack *food service executive*

Hampton
Drummond, James Everman *technology transfer company executive, former army officer*

Herndon
Kopf, Eugene Herbert *management consultant, electrical engineer*

Hume
Barr, Joseph Walker *retired corporate director*

Kilmarnock
Maxwell, W(ilbur) Richard *management consultant*

Leesburg
Ecker, G. T. Dunlop *hospital administration executive*
LeHane, Louis James *consulting company executive*

Lightfoot
Morris, Robert Louis *management consultant*

Mc Lean
Adler, Larry *marketing executive*
Capone, Lucien, Jr. *management consultant, former naval officer*
Chadsey, William Lloyd, III *business executive*
Deal, George Edgar *corporate executive*
De Carbonnel, François Eric *management consultant*
Estren, Mark James *management and media consultant, TV producer*
Graybeal, Sidney Norman *national security executive, former government official*
James, Daniel J. *management consultant*
Jennings, Jerry D. *communications company executive*
Kiviat, Philip Jay *computer services company executive*
Kolombatovic, Vadja Vadim *management consulting company executive*
†Leto, James J. *artificial intelligence executive*
Mason, Scott Aiken *management consultant*
McCullough, R. Michael *management consultant*

Parker, Scott Lane *management consultant*
Paschall, Lee McQuerter *retired communications consultant*
Shevel, Wilbert Lee *information systems executive*
Shirley, Graham Edward *management executive*
†Sitkoff, Theodore *public management executive*
Sowle, Donald Edgar *management consultant*
Thomas, Lydia Waters *research and development executive*
Wirthlin, Richard Bitner *research strategist*

Merrifield
Moffett, Margaret J. *public affairs executive*

Middleburg
Cooke, Jack Kent *diversified company executive*

Norfolk
Blount, Robert Haddock *corporate executive, retired naval officer*
Goode, David Ronald *transportation company executive*
Julian, Michael *grocery company executive*
†Wagner, James Dennis *communications executive*

Occoquan
Johnson, Frank Stanley, Jr. *communications executive, retired government official*

Reston
Brosseau, Irma Finn *business executive, management consultant*
Calio, Anthony John *scientist, business executive*
Cerf, Vinton Gray *telecommunications company executive*
Nysmith, Charles Robert *management consultant*
Schleede, Glenn Roy *energy market and policy consultant*

Richmond
Adams, John Buchanan, Jr. *advertising agency executive*
Ermer, James *transportation company executive*
Evans, James Stanley *communications company executive*
Gross, Paul Allan *health service executive*
Jacobs, Harry Milburn, Jr. *advertising executive*
Laverge, Jan *tobacco company executive*
Mauro, John Baptist *retired marketing researcher*
†McDonald, Frank Albert, Jr. *personnel director*
Mc Grath, Lee Parr *author, public relations executive*
Neathawk, Roger Delmore *marketing company executive*
Newbrand, Charles Michael *advertising firm executive*
†Raper, Mark Irvin *public relations, advertising executive*
Rogula, James Leroy *consumer products company executive*
Roop, Ralph Goodwin *retired oil marketing company executive*
Stettinius, Wallace *communications executive*

Roanoke
†Shaftman, Fredrick Krisch *telephone communications executive*

Seaford
Jenkins, Margaret Bunting *human resource executive*

Springfield
Bruen, John Dermot *computer systems company executive*
Fedewa, Lawrence John *information systems company executive*

Sterling
†Colgan, Charles Joseph *corporate professional, state senator*
Witek, James Eugene *public relations executive*

Verona
de Vaux, Peter Fordney *advertising consultant*

Vienna
Bartlett, John Wesley *consulting firm executive*
Holmes, Bradley Paul *information technology consultant*
Van Stavoren, William David *management consultant, retired government official*
Walker, Edward Keith, Jr. *business executive, retired naval officer*

Virginia Beach
Alexander, William Powell *business consultant*
Brickell, Edward Ernest, Jr. *management executive*
†Lisota, Gary Martin *business executive*
Tarbutton, Lloyd Tilghman *motel executive, franchise consultant, hair care consultant*
Weller, Robert N(orman) *hotel executive*
Wick, Robert Thomas *retired supermarket executive*

Warrenton
Larese, Edward John *management company executive*
Peisner, Arthur Mann *consumer products industry executive*

White Stone
Wroth, James Melvin *former army officer, computer company executive*

Williamsburg
Baker, Donald Scott *communications executive*
Dittman, Duane Arthur *management consultant*
Finn, A. Michael *public relations executive*

Woodbridge
Dillaber, Philip Arthur *budget/resource analyst, economist, consultant*

Wytheville
Hansen, B(obby) J. *management consultant, real estate investor and developer*

WASHINGTON

Anacortes
Spaulding, John Pierson *public relations executive, marine consultant*

Bainbridge Is
†Schmidt, Karen Anne *travel company executive, state legislator*

Bellevue
Gottlieb, Alan M. *advertising and broadcasting executive, writer*
Otterholt, Barry L. *technology management consultant*
Reudink, Douglas Otto John *communications company executive, researcher*

Federal Way
McNeese, Jack Marvin *communications executive*

Gig Harbor
Huyler, Jean Wiley *media and interpersonal communications consultant, hypnotherapist*
Robinson, James William *retired management consultant*

Kirkland
Alberg, Tom Austin *communications executive, lawyer*
McCaw, Craig O. *communications executive*

Langley
Bitts, Todd Michael *sales and marketing consultant*

Liberty Lake
†DeMerritt, Ted C. *microprocessor company executive*

Olympia
†Ogden, Valeria Juan *management consultant, state representative*

Redmond
Gates, William Henry, III *software company executive*
Herres, Phillip Benjamin *computer software executive*

Seattle
Aoki, John H. *hotel chain executive*
Beetham, Stanley Williams *international management consultant*
†Bounds, Christopher E. *food service executive*
Coxe, Weld *management consultant*
†Dederer, Michael E. *public relations executive*
Duryee, David Anthony *management consultant*
Elgin, Ron Alan *advertising executive*
Evans, Daniel Jackson *consultant, former senator*
Evans, Trevor Heiser *advertising executive*
Kraft, Donald Bowman *advertising agency executive*
Ladd, James Roger *international business consultant*
MacDonald, Andrew Stephen *management consulting firm executive*
†Marriott, David M. *public relations executive*
Marshall, Scott *advertising agency executive*
†McAleer, William H. *software company financial executive*
McNeely, Mark Hall *advertising executive*
O'Leary, Thomas Howard *resources executive*
†Rockey, Jay *public relations company executive*
Ross, Austin *health care executive*
Smith, Jeffrey L. (The Frugal Gourmet) *cook, writer*

Spokane
Nicolai, Eugene Ralph *public relations consultant, editor, writer*
Storey, Francis Harold *business consultant, retired bank executive*
Woodard, Alva Abe *business consultant*

Tacoma
Brevik, J. Albert *communications consultant*
Shanaman, Fred Charles, Jr. *business consultant*

WEST VIRGINIA

Charleston
Burns, Thomas C. *communication company executive*
Marstiller, Phyllis C. *personal care industry executive*
Mc Gee, John Frampton *communications company executive*

Elkins
Payne, Gloria Marquette *business eductor*

Harpers Ferry
Nash, Bradley DeLamater *transportation executive*

Huntington
Barenklau, Keith Edward *safety services company executive*
Underwood, Cecil H. *company executive, past governor of West Virginia*

Lahmansville
Snyder, Robert Martin *consultant, retired government official*

Parkersburg
Fahlgren, H(erbert) Smoot *advertising agency executive*

Philippi
Shearer, Richard Eugene *industrial consultant*

Wheeling
Kirkpatrick, Forrest Hunter *management consultant*

White Sulphur Springs
Lanahan, John Stevenson *consultant*

WISCONSIN

Appleton
†McManus, John Francis *executive*

Brookfield
Welnetz, David Charles *human resources executive*

Cudahy
Naimoli, Raymond Anthony *infosystems specialist, financial consultant*

Dodgeville
End, William Thomas *business executive*

Green Bay
†Bush, Robert G. *food service executive*
Gillett, George Nield, Jr. *business executive*
†Meng, John C. *food service executive*
Wakeman, Fred Joseph *retired paper company executive*

Greendale
DeLorenzo, David Joseph *public relations executive*
Tucker, William Thomas, III *computer software company executive*

Hartland
†Mc Neil, Donald Lewis *retired multiple association management company executive*

Janesville
†Stich, Peggy R. *direct marketing executive*

Kenosha
Grover, Robert Lawrence *tool company executive*

La Crosse
†Poehling, Robert Edward *plumbing supply company executive*

Lancaster
Johnson, Hal Harold Gustav *marketing educator emeritus*

Madison
Harr, Lucy Loraine *public relations executive*
Hauck, Roger Paul *corporate executive*
Johnson, Alton Cornelius *management educator*
†Miller, Richard Ulric *business and industrial relations educator*
†Pampel, Roland D. *computer company executive*
Thompson, Howard Elliott *business educator*

Menasha
Aurand, Calvin W., Jr. *specialized printing company executive*

Mequon
Felde, Martin Lee *advertising agency executive, accountant*

Milwaukee
Arbit, Bruce *direct marketing executive, consultant*
Balbach, George Charles *technology company executive*
Chait, Jon Frederick *corporate executive, lawyer*
Elias, Paul S. *marketing executive*
†Faude, William Davison *advertising executive*
Frankiewicz, Marcia Jean *telemarketing executive*
Fromstein, Mitchell S. *temporary office services company executive*
Garnier, Robert Charles *management consultant*
Joseph, Jules K. *retired public relations executive*
Kahlor, Robert Arnold *communications company executive*
Kerr, Dorothy Marie Burmeister *consultant, marketing executive*
Marcus, Ben *business executive*
Marcus, Stephen Howard *hospitality and entertainment company executive*
McCollow, Thomas James *communications company executive*
†Palay, Gilbert *temporary help services company executive*
Randall, William Seymour *leasing company executive*
Scheinfeld, James David *travel agency executive*
Shiely, John Stephen *company executive, lawyer*
Weber, Charles Edward *management educator*
Zigman, Robert S. *public relations executive, hospital executive*

Neenah
Fetzer, Edward Frank *transportation company executive*

Onalaska
Wilson, Anthony Vincent *business executive, mechanical engineer*

Pewaukee
†Quadracci, Harry R. *printing company executive*
†Quadracci, Harry V. *printing company executive, lawyer*
†Ranus, Robert D. *food marketing executive*

Plymouth
Gentine, Lee Michael *marketing professional*

Racine
Bernberg, Bruce Arthur *consumer products and printing executive*
George, William Douglas, Jr. *consumer products company executive*
Klein, Gabriella Sonja *communications executive*

South Milwaukee
Kitzke, Eugene David *research management executive*

Waukesha
Gehrke, Allen Charles *corporation executive*

Waunakee
Berthelsen, John Robert *printing company executive*

Wisconsin Rapids
Brennan, Patrick Francis *printing paper manufacturing executive*

WYOMING

Casper
Kennerknecht, Richard Eugene *sales executive*
Perkins, Dorothy A. *marketing professional*

Wilson
Fritz, Jack Wayne *communications and marketing company executive*

TERRITORIES OF THE UNITED STATES

PUERTO RICO

Caparra
†Pont, Marisara *public relations executive*

VIRGIN ISLANDS

Saint Thomas
Miner, Robert Gordon *creative promotional consultant, auctioneer, writer, publisher, actor*

CANADA

ALBERTA

De Winton
Shutiak, James *management consultant*

Edmonton
Basken, Reginald C. *communications company executive*
Clarkson, Geoffrey Peniston Elliott *company executive*
Cowie, Bruce Edgar *communications executive*

BRITISH COLUMBIA

Vancouver
Anglesio, Franco J. *hotel executive*
Campbell, Bruce Alan *market research consultant*
Lambert, Michael Malet *hotel company executive*

MANITOBA

Winnipeg
Fraser, John Foster *management company executive*
Liba, Peter Michael *communications executive*
Matthews, Patrick John *consumer products company executive*

NOVA SCOTIA

Dartmouth
Callaghan, J. Clair *corporate executive*

Halifax
Calda, Pavel *waste management/environmental services executive*
Gratwick, John *management consulting executive, writer, consultant*

ONTARIO

Burlington
†DeGroote, Michael G. *waste management company executive*

Etobicoke
Beckley, Michael John *hotel executive*
Snedden, James Douglas *health service management consultant*

Hamilton
†Chadwick, Bruce Allen *advertising agency executive*

Kingston
Stanley, James Paul *printing company executive*

London
Henderson, Robert Jules *food service executive*
Hennessey, Frank Martin *strategic planning executive*

Mississauga
DeGrandis, Donald James *communications executive*
†MacKinnon, David C. *research and development company executive*
Sonnenberg, Hardy *data processing company research and development executive, engineer*

Oakville
Barlow, Kenneth James *management consultant*
Holmes, James *consumer products company executive*

Ottawa
Ansary, Hassan Jaber *transportation executive*
†Coleman, John Morley *transportation research director*
Kitchen, Paul Howard *government and association management consultant*
Sharp, Mitchell William *adviser to prime minister*
Thibault, J(oseph) Laurent *service company executive*

Richmond Hill
Marshall, Donald Stewart *company executive*

Toronto
Bandeen, Robert Angus *management corporation executive*
Bonnycastle, Lawrence Christopher *retired corporate director*
Brendon, Rupert Timothy Rundle *advertising agency executive*
Brown, W. Michael *publishing compnay executive*
†Bunting, Christopher Henry *public relations executive*
Campbell, Donald Graham *communications company executive*
Carder, Paul Charles *advertising executive*
Clarkson, Max Boydell Elliott *printing company executive, business educator*
Deacon, David Emmerson *advertising executive*
DeMone, Robert Stephen *hotel company executive*
Denham, Frederick Ronald *management consultant*
Elting, Everett E. *advertising agency executive*
Friendly, Lynda Estelle *theatre marketing and communications executive*
Furse, James Robert *communications industry executive*
Graham, James Edmund *service management executive*
Gregor, Tibor Philip *management consultant*
Harvey, George Edwin *communications company executive*
Hawton, Robert P. *advertising executive*
Houston, Stanley Dunsmore *public relations executive*
Irwin, Samuel Macdonald *toy company executive*
Jacob, Ellis *entertainment company executive*
Livergant, Harold Leonard *health services executive*
†Matathia, Ira Leslie *advertising agency executive*
†McCoomb, Lloyd A. *transportation executive*
†Meadows, George Lee *communications company executive*
Miller, Anthony G. *advertising executive*
Osborne, Ronald Walter *communications executive*
Pankratz, Henry J. *management consultant*
Payton, Thomas William *corporate executive*
Rathke, Sheila Wells *advertising and public relations executive*
Reid, Terence C. W. *corporation executive*
Rogers, Edward Samuel *communications company executive*
Ross, Henry Raymond *advertising executive and legal counsel;*
Silk, Frederick C.Z. *consumer products company executive*

Unionville
Nichols, Harold Neil *corporate executive, former pipeline company executive*

Willowdale
Binder, Herbert R. *drug store chain executive*

Windsor
Giffen, John A. *distillery executive*

QUEBEC

Dorval
Brown, Robert Ellis *transportation company executive, former Canadian government official*

Leclercville
Morin, Pierre Jean *retired management consultant*

Montreal
Audet, Henri *communications executive*
Beaudoin, Laurent *industrial, recreational and transportation company executive*
†Beauregard, Luc *public relations executive*
Benson, Kenneth Samuel *corporate executive*
Berube, Jacques B. *communications company executive*
Black, William Gordon *transportation executive*
†Bouchard, Jacques *advertising executive*
†Boucher, Raymond Gabriel *advertising executive*
†Bouthillier, André *public relations executive, consultant*
Bussieres, Yvan *supermarket chain executive*
Colosimo, Robert *labor relations executive*
Courtois, B. A. *communications executive*
Crawford, Purdy *consumer products and services company executive*
Deegan, Derek James *transportation executive*
Desjardins, Pierre *consumer goods company executive*
Ducros, Pierre Y. *information technology consulting and systems management executive*
Kearney, Robert *communications company executive*
†Lamarre, Daniel *public relations company executive*
Levitt, Brian Michael *consumer products and services company executive, lawyer*
MacKinnon, Rodrick Keith *corporate administration executive, lawyer*
†Neveau, Jean *printing company executive*
Richardson, Gisele *management company executive*
Saint-Jacques, Madeleine *advertising agency executive*
†Savard, Claude A. *food service executive*
†Tousignant, Jacques *human resources executive, lawyer*

Mount Royal
Chauvette, Claude R. *building materials company administrator*
Glezos, Matthews *consumer products and services company executive*

Quebec
Lussier, Jacques *business management educator, university dean*

Saint Sauveur des Monts
Dunsky, Menahem *retired advertising agency executive, communications consultant, painter*

Verdun
†Delisle, Gilles Y. *telecommunications executive*

Westmount
Gordonsmith, John Arthur Harold *collection agency executive*

SASKATCHEWAN

Regina
Hewitt, James J. *credit corporation executive*
†Sifton, Michael Clifford *broadcaster, publisher*

MEXICO

Mexico City
Arellano, Ignacio *advertising executive*
†Azcarraga Milmo, Emilio *communication company executive*
†Dudley, Craig James *executive recruiter*
Velasco, Eugenio *advertising executive*

BELGIUM

Strombeek Bever
Mancel, Claude Paul *household product company executive*

BRAZIL

Rio de Janeiro
Mercier, Jacques Louis *consulting and investment company executive*

CHILE

Puente Alto
Beshears, Charles Daniel *consultant, former insurance executive*

Santiago
†Whelan, James Robert *communications executive, internation trade, investment consultant, author, educator*

ENGLAND

London
Barocci, Robert Louis *former advertising executive, entrepreneur*
Bell, Theodore Augustus *advertising executive*
Bokaemper, Stefan *hotel executive*
Greenbury, Sir Richard *food service executive*
Gummer, Peter Selwyn *public relations executive*
Habgood, Anthony John *corporate executive*
Harris, Howard Elliott *consulting company executive*
Lanigan, Denis George *retired advertising agency executive*
Leaf, Robert Stephen *public relations executive*
†McNulty, Dermot *public relations executive*
Montero, Fernan Gonzalo *advertising executive*
Norman, David Mark *human resource executive*
Owers, Brian Charles *holding company executive*
Saatchi, Maurice *communications and marketing company executive*
†Sainsbury of Preston Candover, Lord John Davan (Baron Sainsbury of Preston Candover) *corporate executive*
Sorrell, Martin Stuart *marketing executive*
Steen, Norman Frank *marketing executive*
Treasure, John Albert Penberthy *advertising executive*

Malmesbury
Shober, Wharton *bioscience company executive*

Middlesex
Hancock, Ellen Marie *communications executive*

Stroud
Robinson, John Beckwith *development management consultant*

Suffolk
Stauderman, Bruce Ford *advertising agency executive*

Windlesham
Tarallo, Angelo Nicholas *industrial gas and health care company executive, lawyer*

FRANCE

Bonnes
Ogilvy, David Mackenzie *advertising executive*

Boulogne-Billancourt
Dellis, Frédy Michel *car rental company executive*

Levauois
†de Pouzilhac, Alain Duplessis *advertising executive*

Paris
Hintz, Bernd Jurgen *consumer goods manufacturing company executive*
Marcus, Claude *advertising executive*

GERMANY

Hemsbach
Froessl, Horst Waldemar *business executive, data processing developer*

Leipzig
Hielscher, Udo Artur *business administration and finance educator*

HONG KONG

Kowloon
Burns, Robert Henry *hotel executive*

Peninsula
Pisanko, Henry Jonathan *command and control communications company executive*

ISRAEL

Haifa
Peled, Abraham *computer company executive*

Herzliya
Bitan, Giora Yoav *computer systems executive*

JAPAN

Tokyo
Franklin, William Emery *corporate executive*
Hideaki, Okada *information systems specialist*
†Inagaki, Masao *advertising agency executive*
†Kajima, Shoichi *warehouse executive*
†Kogure, Gohei *advertising executive*
†Miyazawa, Akira *advertising executive*
†Narita, Yutaka *advertising executive*
Oshita, Koji *advertising executive*

Tsukuba-shi
Kobayashi, Susumu *data processing executive, super computer consultant*

REPUBLIC OF PANAMA

Panama
Thoman, Henry Nixon *food industry executive*

SINGAPORE

Singapore
McMahon, Paul Francis *international management executive*

SPAIN

Santiago De Compostela
Balseiro Gonzalez, Manuel *management executive, consultant*

SWEDEN

Stockholm
†Johnson, Antonia Axson *company executive*
Robinson, Hobart Krum *management consulting company executive*

SWITZERLAND

Biel
Scheftner, Gerold *marketing executive*

Valais
Chase, Morris *international management consultant*

Vaud
Joseph, Michael Anthony *marketing executive*

VENEZUELA

Caracas
Farrell, Rodger Edward *consumer products executive*

ADDRESS UNPUBLISHED

Aden, Arthur Laverne *office systems company executive*
†Allen, Andrew Marshall *advertising executive*
Allen, Theodore Earl *computer company executive*
Ambrose, James Richard *consultant, retired government official*
Andreas, Dwayne Orville *business executive*
Andriole, Stephen John *information systems executive*
†Angotti, Anthony J. *advertising executive*
Anguiano, Lupe *business executive*
Anselmini, Jean-Pierre *communication corporation executive*
†Baldauf, Jill Christine *advertising executive*
Bamberger, Gerald Francis *plastics marketing consultant*
Barger, William James *management consultant*
†Barnett, William Allen *finance executive*
Barrett, Joseph Michael *advertising and marketing consultant, educator*
Barringer, J(ohn) Paul *transportation executive, retired diplomat and career service executive*
Barton, Peter Richard, III *communications executive*
Beasley, Barbara Starin *sales executive, marketing professional*
Bennett, John Roscoe *computer company executive*
Benney, Douglas Mabley *marketing executive, consultant*
Berger, Frank Stanley *consultant*
Binder, Amy Finn *public relations company executive*
Blacker, Harriet *public relations executive*
Blaine, Davis Robert *valuation consultant executive*
Blake, John Edward *car rental company executive*
Blaney, Connie Gayle *importer and broker*
Blasco, Alfred Joseph *business and financial consultant*
Blodgett, William Arthur *public relations executive*
Bolingbroke, Robert A. *consumer products company executive*

Bonneau, Frederic Daniel *business consultant*
Bonner, Jack *public relations company executive*
Borda, Richard Joseph *management consultant*
Braden, George Walter, II (Lord of Bover) *company executive*
Bradford, Robert Edward *supermarket executive*
Branscomb, Anne Wells *communications consultant*
Brennan, Donna Lesley *public relations company executive*
Brennen, Stephen Alfred *international business consultant*
Brewer, David Meredith *retired computer company executive*
Brickman, Ravelle *public relations writer and consultant*
Brown, Donald Douglas *transportation company executive, retired air force officer, consultant*
Burge, James Darrell *personnel, government relations executive*
Butler, Robert Leonard *sales executive*
Butler, Robert Thomas *retired advertising executive*
Butts, Virginia *corporate public relations executive*
Buzard, James Albert *management consultant*
Caine, Raymond William, Jr. *retired public relations executive*
Campbell, Richard Alden *business consultant*
Cardy, Andrew Gordon *hotel executive*
Carey, Dennis Clarke *executive search consultant*
Caricari, Carl *computer company executive*
Carter, Richard Duane *business educator*
Castle, James Cameron *information systems executive*
Castle, Robert Woods *advertising agency executive*
†Chain, Beverly Jean *communications executive*
Chamberlain, William Edwin, Jr. *management consultant*
Chester, John Ervin *medical supplies company executive*
Christiansen, Christian Carl, Jr. *management consultant*
Churchill, Mary Carey *public relations executive*
Cobb, John Cecil, Jr. (Jack Cobb) *communications specialist and executive*
†Cohen, Aaron M. *media executive*
Cooper, Francis Loren *advertising executive*
Cope, Robert Gary *management educator, consultant*
Cork, Edwin Kendall *business and financial consultant*
Cormier, Jean G. *communications company executive*
Cortese, Richard Anthony *computer company executive*
Couturier, Ronald Lee *services company executive, consultant*
Crawford, William Walsh *retired consumer products company executive*
Croxton, Fred(erick) E(mory), Jr. *retired information specialist, consultant*
Culbertson, Philip Edgar *corporate executive*
Cunningham, Isabella Clara Mantovani *advertising educator*
Dalziel, Robert David *retired telecommunications executive*
Denneny, James Clinton, Jr. *business consultant*
Denny, James McCahill *retail executive*
De Santis, Anthony *restaurant, theatre executive*
Diener, Royce *corporate director, retired health care services company executive*
†DiFebo, Valerie *advertising executive*
Dirks, Leslie Chant *communications and electronics company executive*
Dirvin, Gerald Vincent *retired consumer products company executive*
Dixon, Louis Frederick *information sciences and telecommunications consulting executive*
Dodson, Donald Mills *restaurant executive*
Dolan, Peter Robert *marketing executive*
Donovan, James Robert *business equipment company executive*
Dorsey, Frank James *grocery company executive*
Doud, Wallace C. *retired information systems executive*
Dowie, Ian James *management consultant*
Drexler, Michael David *advertising agency executive*
Duffy, Martin Edward *management consultant, economist*
Easton, Glenn Hanson, Jr. *management and insurance consultant, federal official, naval officer*
Elkind, Mort William *creative and business consultant*
Elliot, Jared *financial management consultant*
Emerson, Daniel Everett *retired communications company executive, executive advisor*
Erb, Richard Louis Lundin *resort and hotel executive*
Evanoff, George C. *corporate executive*
Evans, Victor Miles *retired funeral home/cemetery company executive*
Fay, Conner Martindale *management consultant*
Fenichel, Norman Stewart *public relations and advertising executive*
Fitzpatrick, Sean Kevin *advertising agency executive*
†Fleisher, David L. *business communications and market research services executive*
Fleming, Charles Clifford, Jr. *retired airline and jet aircraft sales company executive*
Fortier, D'Iberville *communications consultant*
Fortinberry, Glen W. *advertising executive*
Fouch, Stephanie Saunders *advertising executive*
†Frankfurt, Stephen O. *advertising agency executive*
Frawley, Patrick Joseph, Jr. *corporate executive*
Garrison, Richard Christopher *advertising agency executive*
Gendell, Gerald Stanleigh *retired public affairs executive*
†Giacomino, Robert Richard *advertising executive*
†Giddings, Helen *personnel management executive*
Gilford, Leon *business executive and consultant*
Glass, Kenneth Edward *management consultant*
Gluys, Charles Byron *retired marketing management consultant*
Goldberg, Victor Joel *retired data processing company executive*
Goldman, Alfred Emmanuel *marketing research consultant*
Good, Walter Raymond *business executive*
Gordon, Janine M. *advertising agency executive*
Grace, Marcia Bell *advertising executive*
Graebner, James Herbert *transportation executive*
Gray, John Lathrop, III *advertising agency executive*
Greenway, John Selmes *hotel owner*
Groome, Reginald Kehnroth *hotel executive*
Gruber, Thomas A. *marketing executive*
Gschwind, Donald *management and engineering consultant*
†Gulick, David Miller *advertising executive*
Gulledge, Sandra Smith *publicist*
Gund, Gordon *management executive*
Gunderson, Ted Lee *security consultant*
Haegele, John Ernest *business executive*
Haeger, Phyllis Marianna *retired association management company executive*
Half, Robert *personnel recruiting executive, author*
Hall, Adrienne Ann *advertising agency executive*
Hamlin, Sonya B. *communications specialist*
Harris, Gregory Scott *management services executive*
Harris, Robert Norman *advertising and communications educator*
Harris, William John *retired management holding company executive, security consultant*
Hawk, Phillip Michael *service corporation executive*
Hawkins, Lawrence Charles *management consultant, educator*
Hayes, Gladys Lucille Allen *community care organization official, poet, writer*
Hayes, Janet Gray *business manager, former mayor*
Hiatt, Robert Nelson *consumer products executive*
Hirsh, Norman Barry *management consultant*
Hitchborn, James Brian *telecommunications executive*
Hite, Elinor Kirkland *oil company human resources consultant*
Hock, Morton *entertainment advertising executive*
Hollis, William S. *management consultant*
Hudnut, David Beecher *retired leasing company executive, lawyer*
Isaac, Steven Richard *advertising executive*
Jacobs, Ilene B. *electrical equipment company executive, treasurer*
Jacobsen, Arthur *business and financial consultant*
Janulaitis, M. Victor *consulting company executive*
Jernstedt, Richard Don *public relations executive*
Joanou, Phillip *advertising executive*
Johnson, Mary Elizabeth Susan *health care planner*
Johnston, Thomas John *management consultant*
Jones, Regina Nickerson *public relations executive*
Kaprielian, Walter *advertising executive*
Karp, David *communications executive, writer*
Keller, Paul *advertising agency executive*
†Kennedy, Karen Syence *advertising executive*
King, William Douglas *retired executive*
Kirschenmann, Henry George, Jr. *management consultant, former government official, accountant*
Knab, Donald Ralph *corporate executive*
Knipp, Helmut *service executive*
Korda, Reva *advertising executive, writer*
Korwek, Alexander Donald *management consultant*
Kuhn, James Paul *management consultant*
Kushner, Harvey David *management consultant*
La Bonté, C(larence) Joseph *weight reducing company executive*
Lacey, John William Charles *computer systems consultant*
Lacy, Alan Jasper *consumer products executive*
Lamalie, Robert Eugene *retired executive search company executive*
†Lamattina, Lawrence E. *advertising agency executive*
Lantz, Kenneth Eugene *consulting firm executive*
Larson, Mel *retired marketing professional, corporate executive, helicopter pilot*
Lavidge, Robert James *marketing research executive*
Lee, William Chien-Yeh *communications executive, educator*
†Leff, Ilene J(oan) *management consultant, corporate and goverment executive*
Lehman, Christopher M. *international business consultant*
Leizear, Charles William *retired information services executive*
Lerman, Jeanette Paula *communications executive*
Levy, Arthur James *public relations executive, writer*
Levy, Sam Malcolm *advertising executive*
Linda, Gerald *advertising and marketing executive*
Lipman, Ira Ackerman *security service company executive*
Littman, Earl *advertising and public relations executive*
Locke, Norton *hotel management and construction company executive*
Lockwood, Robert W. *management consultant*
Lowrie, Walter Olin *management consultant*
†Lubinsky, Menachem Y. *communications executive*
Makepeace, Darryl Lee *consulting company executive*
Mangan, Frank Thomas *advertising executive*
Manley, John Hugo *computing technology executive, educator*
Marks, Russell Edward, Jr. *consultant*
Marple, Gary Andre *management consultant*
Marshall, Charles *communications company executive*
†Martin, Edwin William, Jr. *pharmaceutical marketing consultant, copywriter*
McArdle, John Edward *management consultant*
McClung, John Robinson, Jr. *retired advertising company executive*
McGuire, Blanche *marketing professional*
McNeal, Shay *advertising executive*
McWilliams, Bruce Wayne *marketing professional*
Meads, Donald Edward *management services company executive*
Merriam, J. Alec *leasing executive*
Metz, Frank Andrew, Jr. *data processing executive*
Mickelson, Elliot Spencer *quality assurance professional*
Moeller, Robert John *marketing consultant*
Mogelever, Bernard *public relations executive*
Moore, Richard Earl *communications creative director*
Moritz, Charles Worthington *business information and services company executive*
†Mortimer, Doyle Moss *business consultant, state legislator, business owner*
Mosler, John *retired business executive*
Mulcahy, Robert Edward *corporation executive, consultant*
Myhren, Trygve Edward *communications company executive*
†Nankin, Harold *advertising agency executive*
Newman, Sheldon Oscar *computer company executive*
Nicklaus, Charles Edward *sales training executive*
Niemann, Lewis Keith *lamp manufacturing company executive*
Norlander, John Allen *hotel executive*
Novas, Joseph, Jr. *advertising agency executive*
Novenstern, Samuel *sports marketing and media sales company executive*
O'Connor, Mary Scranton *public relations executive*
O'Connor, Richard Donald *advertising company executive*
Olson, Kenneth Harvey *computer company executive*
Oppenheimer, Joseph *corporate director, infosystems consultant*
Opperman, Danny Gene *packaging professional, consultant*
Ostfeld, Leonard S. *computer company executive*
Owen, John Laverty *human resources executive, consultant*
Owens, Charles Vincent, Jr. *diagnostic company executive and consultant*
Parsons, Irene *management consultant*
Paul, Frank *retired consulting company executive*
Paul, Gordon Wilbur *marketing educator*
Perlov, Dadie *management consultant, association executive*
Pew, Thomas W., Jr. *advertising executive*
Philippi, Ervin William *mortician*
Phillips, Gabriel *marketing executive*
Phillips, George Michael *communications executive*
†Phillips, John David *communications executive*
†Plasier, Lee J. *sales executive*
Plumb, Pamela Pelton *consulting company executive, former mayor and councilwoman*
†Post, Richard Bennett *retired human resources executive*
Potter, James Earl *retired international hotel management company executive*
Prather, Gerald L. *management consultant, retired air force officer, judge*
†Pressman, Thane Andrew *consumer products executive*
Prokopis, Emmanuel Charles *communications company executive*
Puryear, Alvin Nelson *management educator*
Ralston, Joanne Smoot *public relations counseling firm executive*
Reid, Michael J. *international management consultant and educator*
Resnik, Linda Ilene *marketing and information executive, consultant*
Reynolds, John Charles *communications company executive, management consultant*
Rhein, Murray Harold *management consultant*
Robins, Norman Alan *strategic planning consultant, former steel company executive*
Robinson, Linda Gosden *communications executive*
Robison, James Everett *management consulting company executive*
Rosen, Arthur Marvin *advertising executive*
Rosenfield, James Harold *communications executive*
Roth, Richard J. *marketing and advertising consultant*
†Rountree, Neva Dixon *public relations executive*
Rubis, George *purchasing executive*
Ryan, John William, Jr. *construction-related consulting company executive*
Sanders, William George *public relations executive*
Sands, I. Jay *corporate executive, business, marketing and real estate consultant, lecturer, realtor, analyst*
Savage, Neve Richard *advertising executive*
Schein, Harvey L. *communications executive*
Schmidt, Benno Charles *corporate executive*
Schmutz, Charles Reid *university foundation executive*
Schrager, James E. *financial company executive, educator*
Schreckinger, Sy Edward *advertising executive, consultant*
Schuster, Gary Francis *corporate executive, former news correspondent*
Schwartz, Stephen Blair *retired information industry executive*
Schweickart, Jim *advertising executive, broadcast consultant*
Sease, Gene Elwood *public relations company executive*
Seelig, Gerard Leo *management consultant*
Seibert, Wilson A., Jr. *advertising executive*
Semerad, Roger Dale *consultant*
Shafran, Hank *public relations agency executive*
Shapira, David S. *food chain executive*
Shapiro, Richard Charles *sales and marketing executive*
Sheeline, Paul Cushing *hotel executive*
Shelton, Karl Mason *management consultant*
Shoup, Harold Arthur *advertising executive*
Shutt, Edwin Holmes, Jr. *consumer products executive*
Sincoff, Michael Z. *human resources and marketing professional*
Sinicropi, Anthony Vincent *industrial relations and human resources educator*
Smith, Barbara Anne *healthcare management company consultant*
Smith, Donald Nickerson *food service executive*
Smith, Thomas Winston *cotton marketing executive*
Snead, Richard Thomas *restaurant company executive*
Sollender, Joel David *management consultant, financial executive*
Souveroff, Vernon William, Jr. *corporate executive, investor, author*
Sroge, Maxwell Harold *marketing consultant, publishing executive*
Stans, Maurice Hubert *retired business consultant, former government official*
†Stassi, Peter John *advertising agency executive*
Stefano, Ross William *leasing company executive*
Stengel, Ronald Francis *management consultant*
Stewart, Marsha Beach *sales executive, entertainment executive*
Stewart, Richard Alfred *business executive*
Stromberg, Arthur Harold *retired professional services company executive*
Stults, Walter Black *management consultant, former trade organization executive*
Tachmindji, Alexander John *systems engineering consultant*
†Taylor, Lynn *public relations executive*
Thompson, Richard Stephen *management consultant*
Tisdale, Stuart Williams *holding company executive*
Toevs, Alden Louis *management consultant*
Tomas, Jerold F. V. *business executive, management consultant*
Triolo, Peter *advertising agency executive, marketing educator, consultant*
Troy, B. Theodore *direct mail advertising executive*
Tutwiler, Margaret DeBardeleben *communications executive*
†Tytler, Linda Jean *communications and public affairs executive, state legislator*
Uehlinger, John Clark *marketing executive*
Ussery, Luanne *communications consultant*
Vajeeprasee Thongsak, Thomas *business planning executive*
†Valenza, Janet *advertising executive*
†Van Meter, Jan Rodden *public relations executive*
Virgo, Julie Anne Carroll *management consultant*
Wadley, M. Richard *consumer products executive*
Wagner, Richard *business executive, former baseball team executive*
Walter, John Robert *printing company executive*
Weismantel, Gregory Nelson *management consultant and software executive*
Weiss, William Lee *retired communications executive*
Will, Joanne Marie *food and consumer services executive, communications consultant, writer*
Will, Mari Maseng *communications consultant*
Williams, Betty Lourene *manager, consultant, volunteer*
Williams, Brown F *television media services company executive*
Williams, Earle Carter *retired professional services company executive*
Williams, Louis Clair, Jr. *public relations executive*
Willig, Karl Victor *computer firm executive*
Worth, Gary James *communications executive*
Yarborough, N. Patricia *human resources educator, human resources executive*
Yetto, John Henry *corporation president*
Zinnen, Robert Oliver *general management executive*
Zoellick, Robert Bruce *corporate executive, lawyer*
Zuckerman, Martin Harvey *personnel director*

INDUSTRY: TRADE

UNITED STATES

ALABAMA

Birmingham
†Hess, Emil Carl *retail apparel company executive*
Kelley, Everette Eugene *retail company executive*
Meriwether, Charles Minor *retail and wholesale drug company executive*
Pizitz, Richard Alan *retail and real estate group executive*
Wabler, Robert Charles, II *retail and distribution executive*

Tuscaloosa
†Blackburn, John Leslie *small business owner*

ALASKA

Anchorage
Cairns, John J(oseph) *retail executive*
Vandergriff, Jerry Dodson *computer store executive*

ARIZONA

Phoenix
Pabst, Ralph Malcom *import-export, publishing and mining executive*
Zine, Larry Joseph *retail executive*

Tucson
Wood, Evelyn Nielsen *reading dynamics business executive*

ARKANSAS

Bentonville
Bruce, Robert Thomas *retail executive*
Carter, Paul R. *retail executive*
Glass, David D. *department store company executive, professional baseball team executive*
Shewmaker, Jack Clifford *retired retail executive, rancher, consultant*
Walton, S. Robson *discount department store chain executive*

Hot Springs National Park
Tanenbaum, Bernard Jerome, Jr. *corporate executive*

Little Rock
†Dillard, Dennis Alexander *department stores executive*
Dillard, William, II *department store executive*
Dillard, William T. *department store chain executive*
Long, Walter Edward *international trade company executive, consultant*

CALIFORNIA

Anaheim
Brownhill, H. Bud *canine behavior therapist*

Arcadia
Stangeland, Roger Earl *retail chain store executive*

Berkeley
Alpert, Norman Joseph *merchandising executive*

Beverly Hills
Kwiker, Louis A. *business executive*

Brisbane
Orban, Kurt *foreign trade company executive*

Burbank
Brankovich, Mark J. *restaurateur*
Droz, Henry *distribution company executive*

Cambria
Stark, Betty Andrews *corporate executive*

Cathedral City
Jackman, Robert Alan *retail executive*

Colton
Brown, Jack H. *supermarket company executive*

Compton
†Allumbaugh, Byron *grocery company executive*

Concord
†Taylor, Barry Robert *retail executive*

Dublin
Cope, Kenneth Wayne *chain store executive*
Del Santo, Lawrence A. *retail merchandising company executive*
†Prince, Jimmie Dan *retail food chain executive*

El Segundo
Pickett, Michael D. *computer hardware and software distributor*

Folsom
Whitmire, Melburn G. *pharmaceutical distribution company executive*

Fountain Valley
Smith, Marie Edmonds *real estate agent, property manager*

Fresno
Blum, Gerald Henry *department store executive*

Fullerton
Svinos, John Georgios *software consulting firm executive*

Hollywood
Marshall, Conrad Joseph *entrepreneur*

Irwindale
†Hughes, Roger K. *dairy and grocery store company executive*

Los Angeles
Blodgett, Julian Robert *small business owner*
Haas, Edward Lee *business executive, consultant*
Hawley, Philip Metschan *retail executive, consultant*
Mann, Nancy Louise (Nancy Louise Robbins) *entrepreneur*
Seigel, Daniel A. *retail executive*
Sinay, Joseph *retail executive*
Tuthill, Walter Warren *retail executive*
†Underwood, Vernon O., Jr. *grocery stores executive*
Williams, Theodore Earle *industrial distribution company executive*

Modesto
Piccinini, Robert M. *grocery store chain executive*

Monrovia
Jemelian, John Nazar *merchant, financial executive*

Newark
†Ferber, Norman Alan *retail executive*

Oakland
Hoopes, Lorenzo Neville *former retailing executive*
Marshall, George Dwire *supermarket chain executive*

Palisades
Diehl, Richard Kurth *retail business consultant*

Palos Verdes Peninsula
Slayden, James Bragdon *retired department store executive*

Port Hueneme
Pathak, Sunit Rawly *business owner, consultant, journalist*

Portola Valley
Katz, Robert Lee *business executive*

Sacramento
Collings, Charles LeRoy *supermarket executive*

San Diego
Monson, Forrest Truman *shop owner, clergyman*

San Francisco
Daniels, Alfred Harvey *merchandising executive*
†Dean, Norman Emerson (Ned Dean) *coffee company executive*
Fisher, Donald G. *casual apparel chain stores executive*
Fromm, Alfred *distributing company executive*
†Goldstein, Joyce Esersky *restaurant owner*
Seelenfreund, Alan *distribution company executive*
Simone, Thomas B. *distribution company executive*
Wolcott, Oliver Dwight *international trading company executive*

San Jose
Finnigan, Rogert Emmet *business owner*
Mc Connell, John Douglas *retail corporation executive, owner*

San Juan Capistrano
Purdy, Alan MacGregor *financial executive*

San Marino
Meyer, William Danielson *retired department store executive*

Santa Barbara
Lynch, Martin Andrew *retail company executive*

Smith River
†Richards, William H. *business owner*

Vista
Cavanaugh, Kenneth Clinton *retired housing consultant*

Walnut Creek
Jones, Ebon Richard *retail executive*
Long, Robert Merrill *retail drug company executive*

COLORADO

Colorado Springs
Macon, Jerry Lyn *software company owner, software publisher*
Noyes, Richard Hall *bookseller*

Denver
Davis, Joseph Samuel *retired department store executive, consultant*
Green, Steven J. *retail executive*
†Owen, David Turner *owner, operator*
Wiens, Duane Daton *matrix-graphic design firm owner*

CONNECTICUT

Cheshire
Bozzuto, Michael Adam *wholesale grocery company executive*

Enfield
†Nirenberg, Charles *convenience store executive*

Greens Farms
St.Marie, Satenig *business consultant, writer*

Greenwich
Pivirotto, Richard Roy *former retail executive*
Tournillon, Nicholas Brady *trade finance, international investments company executive*

Hartford
Goodwin, Rodney Keith Grove *international bank and trade company executive*

Norwalk
Bennett, Carl *retired discount department store executive*

Ridgefield
Couri, John A. *distribution executive*

Rocky Hill
†Hollis, Peter B. *retail executive*
Thorner, Peter *retail executive*

Stamford
†Hoffman, Harry Theodore *retail executive*
Rickard, Norman Edward *office equipment executive*
†Steinberg, Burt *retail executive*

Suffield
Leavitt, Julian J. *wholesale food company executive*

West Haven
†Esposito, Louis P., Jr. *business owner, state legislator*

Westport
McCaig, Joseph J. *retail food chain executive*
Wexler, Herbert Ira *retail company executive*

DISTRICT OF COLUMBIA

Washington
Aronson, Arnold H. *retail company executive*
Cohen, Israel *chain store executive*
†Donna, Roberto *restaurateur, chef*
Gordon, Shana *trade company executive*
Mulligan, Robert J. *retail store executive, accountant*
Rosensweig, Stanley Harold *retail executive*
Sievers, Robert H. *wholesale distributing company executive*
Singer, Thomas Kenyon *international business consultant*
Smith, Jack Carl *foreign trade consultant*
Wurtzel, Alan Leon *retail company executive*

FLORIDA

Boca Raton
Africk, Jack *duty free company executive*
Elliott, Robert M. *retail executive*

Bradenton
Beall, Robert Matthews, II *retail chain executive*

Clearwater
Hoornstra, Edward H. *retail company executive*
Turley, Stewart *retail company executive*

Deerfield Beach
Moran, Patricia Genevieve *corporate executive*

Fort Lauderdale
Wojcik, Cass *decorative supply company executive, former city official*

Gainesville
DeSimone, Rory Jean *small business owner*
Steadham, Charles Victor, Jr. *entertainment agent, producer*

Highland Beach
Frager, Albert S. *retired retail food company executive*

Interlachen
Hoffman, Edward Richard, III (Dick Hoffman) *retail and manufacturing executive*

Jacksonville
Kufeldt, James *retail grocery store executive*
Mann, Timothy *corporate executive*

Lakeland
Jenkins, Charles H., Jr. *grocery company executive*

Largo
Boyle, John William *retail executive*

Longboat Key
Goldsmith, Jack Landman *former retail company executive*

Marco Island
Lesser, Joseph M. *retired business executive, retail store executive*

Miami
Mitchell, Mitch *business owner*

Miami Lakes
Wolter, Duane Roland *retail executive*

Naples
Scarlett, Harold O. *retired retail executive, consultant*

Palm Beach
Black, Leonard J. *retail store consultant*

Pensacola
†Kahn, Robert H., Jr. *retail executive*

Sarasota
Albrecht, Robert Downing *retail executive*

Sunrise
Hayes, Peter John *retail executive*

Tampa
†Floto, Ronald John *supermarket executive*

Wellington
Flagler, Robert Loomis *global export company executive, consultant*

Winter Haven
†Lansdale, Daryl L. *retail executive*

Winter Park
Rogers, Donald Patrick *business administration educator*

GEORGIA

Atlanta
Allen, Ivan, Jr. *shop owner*
Kalafut, George Wendell *distribution company executive, retired naval officer*
Marcus, Bernard *retail executive*
Moderow, Joseph Robert *package distribution company executive*

Smyrna
Head, John Francis, Jr. *distributing company executive*

HAWAII

Honolulu
Niles, Geddes Leroy *private investigator*

Waipahu
Matsui, Jiro *importer, wholesaler, small business owner*

IDAHO

Boise
†Long, William D. *grocery store executive*
Michael, Gary G. *supermarket and drug chain executive*

Moscow
†Schroeder, Gary Joseph *business owner, state legislator, writer*

ILLINOIS

Arlington Heights
Johnson, Clifford R. *retired retail executive, consultant*

Bensenville
Lewis, Darrell L. *retail executive*

Cary
Schultz, Theodore Edward *retail executive*

Chicago
Bahadur, Chance *retail executive*
Baloun, John Charles *wholesale grocery company executive*
Brennan, Bernard Francis *retail chain store executive*
Brennan, Edward A. *merchandising, insurance and real estate executive*
Dehmlow, Louis Henry Theodore, III *wholesale and distribution company executive*
Doolittle, Sidney Newing *retail executive*
Gingiss, Benjamin Jack *retired formal clothing stores executive*
Goldstein, Alfred George *retail executive*
†Kahn, Harold *retail executive*
Kroch, Carl Adolph *retail executive*
Meyer, Charles Appleton *former retailing executive*
†Shute, David *retail executive, lawyer*
Telling, Edward Riggs *former retail, insurance, real estate and financial services executive*
Vrablik, Edward Robert *import/export company executive*
Wood, Arthur MacDougall *retired retail executive*
Worley, Gordon Roger *retail chain financial executive*

Decatur
Cain, Richard Duane *small business owner*

Deerfield
Hunter, Charles David *retail company executive*
Jorndt, Louis Daniel *drug store chain executive*
Walgreen, Charles Rudolph, III *retail store executive*

Des Plaines
†Schmidt, Robert L. *export company executive*

Evanston
Trutter, John Thomas *consulting company executive*

Hinsdale
†Hodnik, David F. *retail company executive*
Rinder, George Greer *retired retail company executive*

Lake Forest
†Stirling, Ellen Adair *retail executive*

Melrose Park
†Di Matteo, Dominick, Jr. *supermarket chain executive*

Morton Grove
McKenna, Andrew James *paper distribution and printing company executive, baseball club executive*

Northbrook
Segal, Gordon I. *retail executive*

Northlake
†Jasper, Paul Tucker *food company executive*

Oak Brook
Peterson, Roger Eric *hardware wholesale company executive*

Olney
Potter, David Lynn *retail executive*

Riverwoods
Ferkenhoff, Robert J. *retail executive*

Schaumburg
†Kadish, Steven A. *retail executive*
Rashkow, Ronald *home improvement company executive*

Skokie
Grainger, David William *distribution company executive*

Sumner
Trent, Wendell Campbell *business owner*

Waukegan
†Petropoulos, Gust A. *retail company executive*

Wilmette
Mc Nitt, Willard Charles *business executive*
Williams, Emory *former retail company executive, banker*

Winnetka
Teninga, Walter Henry *retail executive*
Weldon, Theodore Tefft, Jr. *retail company executive*

INDIANA

Anderson
†Lutz, L. Jack *retail executive, congressman*

De Motte
†Roorda, Walter John *small business owner, state legislator*

East Chicago
Blaskovich, Thomas Robert *automobile dealer*

Fort Wayne
Curtis, Douglas Homer *small business owner*
McClelland, Michael *wholesale distribution executive*
Swanson, David Heath *agricultural company executive*

Grabill
Gerig, Abner F. *small business owner*

Indianapolis
Dougherty, Douglas Wayne *retail executive*
Hayford, John Sargent *retail executive*
†Nugent, Johnny *tractor company executive, state senator*
†Paul, Gerald *retail company executive*
†Seitz, Melvin Christian, Jr. *distributing company executive*
Seneff, Smiley Howard *business owner*
Stout, William Jewell *department store executive*

Merrillville
Crawford, Mary B. *small business owner*

New Albany
Conway, William Frederick, Sr. *business founder*

Noblesville
†Wechter, Larry Scot *retail food executive*

IOWA

Chariton
†Pearson, Ronald Dale *retail food stores corporation executive*

KANSAS

Atwood
†Gatlin, Fred *seed and feed business owner, state legislator*

Independence
†Empson, Cynthia Sue *retail executive, nurse*

Kansas City
Baska, James Louis *wholesale grocery company executive*
†Carolan, Douglas *wholesale company executive*

Shawnee Mission
†Watanabe, Hirosuko *grain merchandising company executive*

KENTUCKY

Louisville
Brennan, William Bernard, Jr. *small business owner*

LOUISIANA

Leesville
Boren, Lynda Sue *small business owner, educator*

New Orleans
Pickering, Thomas Clifford *retailing executive*

MAINE

Freeport
†Gorman, Leon A. *mail order company executive*
†Poole, Norman A. *retail executive*

Scarborough
Brackett, Norman E. *retail company executive*
Farrington, Hugh G. *wholesale food and retail drug company executive*
Moody, James L., Jr. *retail food distribution company executive*

MARYLAND

Baltimore
Cullen, James Patrick *international trading company executive*
†Green, Benjamin Louis *wholesale food distribution executive*

Bethesda
Bucherre, Veronique *environmental company executive*

Easton
Goldner, Sheldon Herbert *export-import company executive*

Ellicott City
Hoffberger, Jerold Charles *corporation executive*

Forest Hill
Hartenstine, Warren Richard *apparel industry equipment distribution company executive*

Frederick
Anderson, William Bert *import company executive*

Gaithersburg
Nemecek, Albert Duncan, Jr. *retail company executive, investment banker, management consultant*

Hyattsville
Manos, Pete Lazaros *supermarket executive*

Landover
Hechinger, John Walter *hardware chain executive*

Potomac
Shapiro, Richard Gerald *retired department store executive, consultant*

MASSACHUSETTS

Auburn
Baker, David Arthur *small business owner, manufacturer*

Boston
Goldberg, Avram Jacob *consulting and investing company executive, arbitrator*
Kane, Louis Isaac *merchant*
Kwasnick, Paul Jack *retail executive*
Rosenberg, Manuel *retail company executive*
Rutstein, Stanley Harold *apparel retailing company executive*
Schaeneman, Lewis G., Jr. *retail company executive*
Tooker, Carl E. *department store executive*

Canton
Holt, Donald Edward, Jr. *retail executive*

Cohasset
Lyne, Austin Francis *sporting goods business executive*

Framingham
†Cammarata, Bernard *retail company executive*
Feldberg, Sumner Lee *retail company executive*
Wishner, Steven R. *retail executive*

Hingham
†Hinkley, Clark J. *retail executive*

New Bedford
Hodgson, James Stanley *antiquarian bookseller*

North Chatham
McCarthy, Joseph Harold *consultant, former retail food company executive*

Quincy
†McGlinchey, Joseph Dennis *retail corporation executive*

Wellesley
†Anathan, James Mone, III *retail executive*

MICHIGAN

Belleville
Carlson, James Ellsworth *wholesale distribution executive*

Detroit
†McCracken, Thomas Charles *retail executive*
Seppala, Katherine Seaman (Mrs. Leslie W. Seppala) *retail company executive*

Flint
Hamady, Jack Ameen *retail food company executive*

Grand Rapids
Holton, Earl D. *retail company executive*
Meijer, Douglas *retail company executive*
†Meijer, Frederik *retail company executive*
†Meijer, Mark *retail executive*
Morin, William Raymond *bookstore chain executive*
†Quinn, Patrick Michael *wholesale food executive*

Grosse Pointe
Allen, Lee Harrison *wholesale company executive, industrial consultant*

Jackson
Fowler, John Russell *retail executive*
Rosenfeld, Mark Kenneth *retail store executive*

Livonia
Larson, Karen Elaine *business owner*

Paw Paw
Warner, James John *small business owner*

Plymouth
†Petrie, Milton J. *retail company executive*

Pontiac
Robinson, Jack Albert *retail drug stores executive*

Troy
Carlson, David Martin *retail executive*
Inatome, Rick *retail computer company executive*
McAllister, Robert Cowden *retail company executive*
Mrkonic, George Ralph, Jr. *retail executive*
Strome, Stephen *distribution company executive*

MINNESOTA

Hopkins
Beeler, Donald Daryl *retail executive*
Eugster, Jack Wilson *retail executive*

Minneapolis
Dabill, Phillip Alvin *wholesale foods executive*
Emmerich, Karol Denise *former retail company executive, consultant*
Finch, Harold Bertram, Jr. *wholesale grocery company executive*
Gilpin, Larry Vincent *retail executive*
Lurton, H. William *retail executive*
Macke, Kenneth A. *retail executive*
Mammel, Russell Norman *retired food distribution company executive*
Trestman, Frank D. *distribution company executive*
†Watson, Stephen E. *department store executive*
Wright, Michael William *wholesale food company executive*

Plymouth
Froemming, Herbert Dean *retail executive*

Saint Paul
Nash, Nicholas David *retailing executive*

MISSISSIPPI

Jackson
†Holman, William Henry, Jr. *retail executive*
McCarty, William Bonner, Jr. *retail grocery executive*

MISSOURI

Chesterfield
Upbin, Hal Jay *consumer products executive*

Cuba
Work, Bruce Van Syoc *business consultant*

Hazelwood
Mohrmann, Robert E. *wholesale distribution executive*
†Seitz, Harold A. *supermarket executive*

Jefferson City
Rockelman, Georgia F(owler) Benz *retail furniture executive*

Kansas City
†Comment, Jeffrey W. *jewelry retail executive*
Stanley, David *retail company executive*

Saint Charles
Dauphinais, George Arthur *import company executive*

Saint Louis
Battram, Richard L. *retail executive*
†Bridgewater, Bernard Adolphus, Jr. *footwear and specialty retailing company executive*
Crutsinger, Robert Keane *diversified food wholesale company executive*
Demoff, Samuel Louis *retired retail chain executive*
Edison, Bernard Alan *retired retail apparel company executive*
Farrell, David Coakley *department store executive*
Loeb, Jerome Thomas *retail executive*
Newman, Andrew Edison *retail executive*
Newman, Eric Pfeiffer *retail chain store executive*
Schnuck, Craig *grocery stores company executive*
†Sneider, Martin Karl *retail company executive*
Williams, Frank James, Jr. *department store chain executive, lawyer*

MONTANA

Billings
Marcovitz, Leonard Edward *retail executive*

NEBRASKA

Lincoln
Rawley, Ann Keyser *small business owner, picture framer*

Wymore
Meyer, Melvin A. *lumber and hardware executive, freelance designer*

NEVADA

Las Vegas
†Toomin, Louis Allen *small business owner, state legislator*

NEW HAMPSHIRE

Derry
†Katsakiores, Phyllis *small business owner, city councilor*

Hampton
Coviello, Robert Frank *retail executive*

North Hampton
Goldberger, Stephen A. *retail stores executive*

Portsmouth
Friese, George Ralph *retail executive*

NEW JERSEY

Chatham
Manning, Frederick William *retired retail executive*

Elizabeth
Gellert, George Geza *food importing company executive*

Freehold
Foster, Eric H., Jr. *retail executive*

Millburn
Echikson, Richard *retail consultant*

Montvale
Rourke, Michael James *retail company executive*
Rowe, James W. *food chain executive*
Ulrich, Robert Gardner *retail food chain executive, lawyer*
Wood, James *supermarket executive*

New Monmouth
Donnelly, Gerard Kevin *retail executive*

North Bergen
†Goodman, Lawrence Baron *retail executive*

Paramus
Goldstein, Michael *retail executive*
Nakasone, Robert C. *retail toy and game company executive*

Short Hills
Brous, Philip *retail consultant*

Woodbridge
Futterman, Jack *supermarket chain executive*

NEW YORK

Bronx
Blank, Benjamin *retail executive, consultant*
Hankin, Leonard J. *merchant*

Brooklyn
Shulman, Max L. *corporate executive*
Zelin, Jerome *retail executive*

Florida
Mench, John William *retail store executive, electrical engineer*

Lewiston
Newlin, Lyman Wilbur *bookseller, consultant*

Liverpool
Kogut, John Anthony *retail executive, pharmacist*

Long Island City
Lang, William Charles *retail executive*

Melville
Kett, Herbert Joseph *drug store chain executive*

New Rochelle
Palihnich, Nicholas Joseph, Jr. *retail chain executive*

New York
Ainslie, Michael Lewis *art-related holding company executive*
Alprin, William Samuel *women's accessory company executive*
†Andruskevich, Thomas A(nthony) *corporate executive*
†Aved, Barry *retail executive*
Becker, Isidore A. *business executive*
Bravo, Rose Marie *retail executive*
Brecker, Manfred *retail company executive*
Brenner, Gita Kedar Voivodas *small business owner, research and editing consultant*
Brumm, James Earl *trading company executive*
†Cannon, John Haile *retail executive*
Catsimatidis, John Andreas *retail chain executive, airline executive*
Cooke, Gordon Richard *retail executive*
†Davis, Kenneth A. *retail executive*
†Destino, Ralph, Jr. *retail executive*
†Dworkin, David Lee *retail executive*
Farkas, Robin Lewis *retail company executive*
Fields, Douglas Philip *building supply and home furnishings wholesale company executive*
Finkelstein, Edward Sydney *department store executive*
†Friedman, Robert N. *retail executive*
Gilinsky, Stanley Ellis *department store executive*
Gray, C(harles) Jackson *retail executive*
Handler, Mark S. *retail executive*
†Hassler, Howard E. *retail stores executive*
Hennig, Frederick E. *retail company executive*
Jacobs, Sherry Raphael *retail executive, lawyer*
Krensky, Harold *retired retail store executive, investor*
Lachman, Lawrence *business consultant, former department store executive*
Lavin, William Kane *retail executive*
Matthews, Norman Stuart *department store executive*
Meister, Doris Powers *auction house executive*
Michelson, Gertrude Geraldine *retired retail company executive*
Miller, Philip Boyd *retail executive*
†Mizuno, Masaru *retail executive*
Mondlin, Marvin *antiquarian book dealer*
Peters, Arthur King *international trade executive, author, consultant*
Quint, Ira *retail executive*
Redden, David Normand *auction house executive*
Riggio, Stephen *book store chain executive*
†Sasaki, Mikio *import/export company executive*
Seegal, Herbert Leonard *department store executive*
Sells, Harold E. *retail company executive*
Sherman, Jeffrey Barry *retail executive*
Stanton, Ronald P. *export company executive*
Stern, Madeleine Bettina *rare books dealer, author*
Straus, Kenneth Hollister *former retail store executive*
†Sugimoto, Yoshihisa *import/export company executive*
†Tansky, Burton *department store executive*
Tendler, David *international trade company executive*
Thomson, William Barry *retail company executive*
†Traub, Marvin Stuart *department store executive*
Tutun, Edward H. *retired retail executive*
Ullman, Myron Edward, III *retail executive*
Zimmerman, James M. *retail company executive*

Norwich
Hanna, Eduardo Zacarias *pharmaceutical company executive*

Pelham
Bornand, Ruth Chaloux *antique music box specialist*

Rochester
McCurdy, Gilbert Geier *retailer*

Rye
Goldstein, Stanley P. *retail company executive*
Huth, Robert D. *retail company executive*

NORTH CAROLINA

Charlotte
†Belk, John M. *retail company executive*
Henson, Reid M. *wholesale company executive*

Greensboro
Kennedy, Charles G. *wholesale distribution executive*

Henderson
Church, John Trammell *retail stores company executive*
Jones, George L. *retail executive*

Salisbury
Ketner, Ralph Wright *retail food company executive*
Smith, Tom Eugene *retail food company executive*

Wilmington
†Zimmer, Alan Mark *retail jewelry chain executive*

OHIO

Akron
Albrecht, Frederick Steven *grocery company executive, lawyer*

Cincinnati
†Beekman, Philip E. *retail company executive*
Edelstein, Chaim Y. *retail executive*
Marcus, Leonard *retail company executive*
†Mooney, Timothy M. *retail executive*
†Moore, Michael C. *retail executive*
Price, Thomas Emile *export and investment company executive*
†Sherman, Jeffrey *retail executive*
†Socol, Howard *department store executive*
Strubbe, John Lewis *retired food chain store executive*
Woods, Donald DeWayne *advertising materials designer/manufacturer*

Cleveland
Charnas, Michael (Mannie Charnas) *packaging company executive*
†Cole, Jeffrey A. *retail stores executive*
Crosby, Fred McClellan *retail home and office furnishings executive*
†Fufuka, Natika Njeri Yaa *retail executive*
Kordalski, Anthony Tadausz *retail department store executive*
Milgrim, Franklin Marshall *merchant*
Perkinson, Diana Agnes Zouzelka *import company executive*

Columbus
Callander, Kay Eileen Paisley *business owner, retired gifted talented education educator, writer*
Hopkins, Thomas Gene *retail company executive*
Pavony, William H. *retail executive*
†Schottenstein, Saul *retail company executive*

Voelker, Larry *retired retail corporation executive*
Wexner, Leslie Herbert *retail executive*

Dayton
†Glaser, Herbert Otto *retail executive*
Gray, Edman Lowell *metal distribution company executive*
†Hartley, Milton E. *retail executive*
Twyman, Jack *wholesale grocery company executive, management services company executive*

Dublin
Walter, Robert D. *wholesale pharmaceutical distribution executive*

Fairfield
Murphy, Dennis F. *retail executive*
Nichols, David L. *retail executive*

Hilliard
Keyes, James Lyman, Jr. *diesel engines distributor company owner*

Independence
Callsen, Christian Edward *retail company executive*

Maumee
Walrod, David James *retail grocery chain executive*

Oxford
Paulin, Henry Sylvester *antiques dealer, emeritus educator*

Powell
†Kriegel, David L. *retail executive*

Reynoldsburg
Lynch, Rose Peabody *art gallery executive*

Toledo
Fuhrman, Charles Andrew *country club proprietor, real estate management executive, lawyer*

Twinsburg
†Hoven, Dwayne *retail executive*
†Raven, Gregory Kurt *retail executive*

Worthington
Guthrie, Henry Lee *retail executive*

Youngstown
Catoline, Pauline Dessie *small business owner*
†Schwartz, David *retail executive*

OKLAHOMA

Oklahoma City
Austin, Gerald Grant *wholesale food distribution company executive*
Davis, Emery Stephen *wholesale food company executive*
Moll, John Edgar *wholesale grocery company executive*
Werries, E. Dean *food distribution company executive*
Williams, Richard Donald *retired wholesale food company executive*

Tulsa
Bell, Roseanne *business owner, consultant*
†Howerton, Alvin *retail executive*

OREGON

Burns
†Timms, Eugene Dale *wholesale business owner, state senator*

Portland
Bauer, Louis Edward *retail bookstore executive, educator*
Blanford, J(ohn) William *department store company executive*
†Green, Cyril Kenneth *retail company executive*
Greenstein, Merle Edward *import/export company executive*
Hofer, Judith K. *retail company executive*
Miller, Robert G. *retail company executive*
†Ramsby, Mark Delivan *lighting designer and consultant*
†Warner, David Gill *wholesale food distributing company executive*

Riddle
†Markham, Bill *timber and logging company owner*

Saint Helens
†Federici, Tony *small business owner, state legislator*

Salem
†Andersen-Wyckoff, R. G. *retail executive, small business owner, mayor*

PENNSYLVANIA

Berwyn
Fry, Clarence Herbert *retail executive*

Bristol
†McEwen, Joseph, Jr. *distributing company executive*

Butler
Kane, Marilyn Elizabeth *small business owner*

Camp Hill
Slane, Charles Joseph *chain drug store executive*

Carlisle
Lewis, Claude, Jr. *retired shoe company executive*

East Butler
Mielcuszny, Albert John *wholesale distribution executive*
Pentz, Paul *hardware company executive*

Harrisburg
Grass, Alexander *retail company executive*

Media
†Price, Donald *retail executive*

New Holland
†Kennedy, William T. *retail executive*

Philadelphia
Leibovitz, Mitchell G. *retail executive*
Marshall, Donald Tompkins *industrial distribution executive*
Strawbridge, Peter S. *department store executive*
Weiner, Warren *retail executive*
White, Warren Wurtele *retailing executive*

Pittsburgh
Day, Maurice Jerome *automobile parts distributing company executive*
Hannan, Robert William *retail pharmaceutical company executive*
Tobin, William Thomas *retail executive*
Watts, William Edward *retail company executive*

Reading
†Lakin, Edwin A. *retail executive*

Sharon
Epstein, Louis Ralph *retired wholesale grocery executive*
Rosenblum, Harold Arthur *grocery distribution executive*

Washington
Erdner, Jon W. *small business owner, securities trader*

Williamsport
Largen, Joseph *retailer, furniture manufacturer, book wholesaler*

Yardley
Desai, Cawas Jal *distribution company executive*

SOUTH CAROLINA

Columbia
Clark, David Randolph *wholesale grocer*

Greenville
Bauknight, Clarence Brock *wholesale and retail company executive*

Hilton Head Island
Stein, Bernard Alvin *business consultant*

TENNESSEE

Brentwood
Zimmerman, Raymond *retail chain executive*

Chattanooga
St. Goar, Edward *wholesale food cooperative executive*

Knoxville
Harris, Charles Edgar *retired wholesale distribution company executive*
†Jenkins, Roger Lane *retail executive*

La Vergne
Pfeffer, Philip Maurice *distribution company executive*

Memphis
Clarkson, Andrew MacBeth *retail executive*
Dunavant, William Buchanan, Jr. *small business owner*
Hendren, Gary E. *retail executive*
Johnson, Robert Lewis, Jr. *retail company executive*

Nashville
Zibart, Michael Alan *wholesale book company executive*

TEXAS

Amarillo
†Marmaduke, John H. *retail executive*

Arlington
Thompson, Carson R. *retail, manufacturing company executive*

Austin
Girling, Robert George William, III *business owner*
Houston, Samuel Lee *computer programmer systems analysis company executive*

Carrollton
Butler, Abbey J. *pharmaceutical distribution company executive*

Dallas
Beck, Abe Jack *retired business executive, retired air force officer*
Longyear, Russell Hammond *retail executive*
Matthews, Clark J(io), II *retail executive, lawyer*
McGaw, Kenneth Roy *wholesale distribution executive*
†Parker, Barry James Charles *retail executive*
St. James, Lyn *business owner, professional race car driver*
Shapiro, Robert Alan *retail executive*

Fort Worth
Bolen, Bob *retail merchant, university administrator*

Herlihy, James Edward *retail executive*
Michero, William Henderson *retired retail trade executive*
Roach, John Vinson, II *retail company executive*
Winn, Herschel Clyde *retail electronics company executive*

Houston
Baugh, John Frank *wholesale company executive*
Carlin, Edward Robert *retail store executive*
†Efron, Jeanette Oshman *retail executive*
Gallerano, Andrew John *retail company executive*
Irving, Herbert *food distribution company executive*
Levit, Milton *grocery supply company executive*
†Lubetkin, Alvin Nat *sporting goods retail company executive*
Orton, Stewart *merchant*
Woodhouse, John Frederick *food distribution company executive*

Irving
†Lively, H(oward) Randolph, Jr. *retail company executive*

Laredo
Kim, Earnest Jae-Hyun *import/export company executive*

Plano
Neppl, Walter Joseph *retired retail store executive*

San Antonio
Butt, Howard Edward, Jr. *grocery chain executive, foundation executive*
Felicella, Frank George *retail executive*
Gresham, Gary Stuart *wholesale grocery executive, accountant*

Sulphur Springs
†McKenzie, Kenneth *retail grocery executive*

Wimberley
Ellis, John *small business owner*

UTAH

Brigham City
†Call, Osborne Jay *retail executive*

Salt Lake City
Brewer, Stanley R. *wholesale grocery executive*
†Day, Gerald W. *wholesale grocery company executive*
Plumley, S. Patric *retail executive*

VERMONT

Brookfield
Gerard, James Wilson *book distributor*

VIRGINIA

Arlington
Seely, James Michael *consultant, retired naval officer, small business owner*

Fairfax
Pugh, Arthur James *retired department store executive, consultant*
†Schrock, Simon *retail executive*

Mc Lean
Vandemark, Robert Goodyear *retired retail company executive*

Quantico
†Joy, James R. *retail executive*

Richmond
Hicks, Thomas Howard *retail executive*
Kasen, Stewart Michael *retail executive*
Lewis, Frances Aaronson *retail company executive*
Lewis, Sydney *retail company executive*
Sharp, Richard L. *retail company executive*
Sniffin, John Harrison *retail executive*

Salem
Brand, Edward Cabell *retail executive*

Staunton
Hammaker, Paul M. *retail executive, business educator, author*

WASHINGTON

Anacortes
Stitt, William D. *small business owner, marketing professional, consultant*

Kirkland
Sinegal, James D. *variety store wholesale business executive*

Seattle
Denniston, Martha Kent *business owner, author*
Fix, Wilbur James *department store executive*
McMillan, John A. *retail executive*
Nordstrom, Bruce A. *department store executive*
Nordstrom, John N. *department store executive*
Read, Charles Raymond, Sr. *business executive*

WISCONSIN

Green Bay
Kennedy, Mark Raymond *retail executive*

La Crosse
†Metcalf, Jerry D. *wholesale food distribution company executive*

Menomonee Falls
†Herma, John *retail executive*
†Kellogg, William S. *retail executive*

Milwaukee
†Bluestone, Stanton J. *department store chain executive*
†MacDonald, Michael R. *retail executive*

Platteville
†Brodbeck, William Jan *retail executive*

WYOMING

Jackson
†Law, Clarene Alta *innkeeper, state legislator*

TERRITORIES OF THE UNITED STATES

GUAM

Agana
Perez, Gerald S. A. *retail executive educator*

PUERTO RICO

San Juan
Toppel, Milton *retired retail food store executive*

CANADA

BRITISH COLUMBIA

North Vancouver
Jarrett, Anthony *business executive*

MANITOBA

Winnipeg
Altman, Sheldon *retail company executive*
Cohen, Albert Diamond *merchandising executive*

ONTARIO

Brampton
Beaumont, Donald A. *department store chain executive*

Cornwall
Hornby, Thomas Richard *wholesale distribution executive*

London
Crncich, Tony Joseph *retired pharmacy chain executive*

Mississauga
Williams, James B. *retail electronics company executive*

Ottawa
Labbé, Paul *export corporation executive*

Toronto
Graham, Allister P. *diversified company executive*
Kay, James Fredrick *retailer*
Keenan, Anthony Harold Brian *catalog company executive*
Kosich, George John *retail executive*
Macaulay, Hugh L. *retail company executive*
McGiverin, Donald Scott *retail company executive*
Minto, Clive *retail company executive*
Posluns, Wilfred M. *manufacturing and retailing company executive*
Seltzer, Ronald *retail company executive*
†Shaffer, Donald S. *retail executive*
Sharpe, Charles Richard *retail company executive*
Smith, Stephen Alexander *retail and wholesale food distribution company executive*

Willowdale
Bloom, David Ronald *retail drug company executive*
Swartz, Malcolm Gilbert *retail executive, restaurateur*

QUEBEC

Pointe Claire
Cohen, Charles F. *retail executive*

MEXICO

Garza Garcia
†Paez, Rafael Roberto *holding company executive*

FRANCE

Paris
Arnault, Bernard Jean *trade company executive*

JAPAN

Minato-ku
Ito, Masatoshi *retail executive*

SPAIN

Madrid
†Babcock, Michael Joseph *retail company executive*

ADDRESS UNPUBLISHED

Applebaum, Eugene *retail drug store chain executive*
Baker, Edward Kevin *retail executive*
Barron, Dennis H. *retail executive*
Biagi, Richard Charles *retail executive, real estate consultant*
Cantarella, Francesco Paquin *retail executive*
Chevalier, Paul Edward *retired retail executive, lawyer*
Clark, Maxine *retail executive*
Depkovich, Francis John *retired retail chain executive*
Edwards, Patrick Ross *former retail company executive, lawyer, management consultant*
Fields, Leo *former jewelry company executive, investor*
Folkman, David H. *apparel wholesale executive*
Geoffroy, Charles Henry *retired travel company executive*
Goldman, Gerald Hillis *beverage distribution company executive*
Guillemette, Gloria Vivian *dressmaker, designer*
†Hawk, Robert Dooley *wholesale grocery company executive*
Howell, William Robert *retail company executive*
King, S(anford) MacCallum *business owner, consultant*
Lebor, John F(rancis) *retired department store executive*
Lipinsky, Carol *business owner*
Meyer, Lasker Marcel *retail executive*
†Milstein, Monroe Gary *retail executive*
Morris, Marjorie Hale *retail executive, appraiser, artist, writer*
Murphy, S(usan) (Jane Murphy) *small business owner*
Nishimura, Joseph Yo *retired retail executive, accountant*
Paterson, Robert E. *trading stamp company executive*
Policano, Joseph Daniel *import company executive*
Questrom, Allen I. *retail executive*
Raab, Herbert Norman *retail executive*
Raskin, Michael A. *retail company executive*
Rau, Robert Nicholas *pipe distribution executive*
Rodbell, Clyde Armand *distribution executive*
Rosenbaum, Irving M. *retail store executive*
Runge, Donald Edward *food wholesale company executive*
Samson, Alvin *former distributing company executive, consultant*
Sewell, Phyllis Shapiro *retail chain executive*
Sherwood, (Peter) Louis *retail executive*
†Sprouse, Robert Allen, II *retail chain executive*
Stern, Charles *foreign trade company executive*
Teitelbaum, Irving *retail executive*
Vernon, Carl Atlee, Jr. *retired wholesale food distributor executive*
Waddle, John Frederick *former retail chain executive*
Waters, David Rogers *retail executive*
Weiss, Michael Allen *retail executive*
Wien, Stuart Lewis *retired supermarket chain executive*
Wiesner, John Joseph *retail executive*
Williams, Robert Lyle *corporate executive, consultant*

INDUSTRY: TRANSPORTATION

UNITED STATES

ALABAMA

Birmingham
†Brough, James A. *airport terminal executive*

Gulf Shores
Wallace, John Loys *aviation services executive*

Point Clear
Elmer, William Morris *retired pipe line executive*

ALASKA

Anchorage
Sullivan, George Murray *former mayor, business consultant*

ARIZONA

Phoenix
Conway, Michael J. *airline company executive*
Elien, Mona Marie *air transportation professional*
Lake, F(inley) Edward *diversified company financial executive*
Shoen, Edward Joseph *transportation and insurance companies executive*
Woods, Bobby Joe (Bob Woods) *transportation executive*

Scottsdale
Peyton, William Maupin *transportation executive, educator*

Tucson
†Burg, Walter A. *airport terminal executive*
Peete, Russell Fitch, Jr. *aircraft appraiser*

ARKANSAS

Fort Smith
Young, Robert A., III *freight systems executive*

Huntsville
Carr, Gerald Paul *former astronaut, business executive, former marine officer*

Lowell
Bergant, Paul R. *trucking company executive, lawyer*

Pine Bluff
Seawell, William Thomas *former airline executive*

Springdale
Pogue, William Reid *former astronaut, foundation executive, business and aerospace consultant*

CALIFORNIA

Bayside
Pierce, Lester Laurin *retired pilot, aviation consultant*

Berkeley
†Kanafani, Adib *transportation think-tank administrator/civil engineering educator*

Borrego Springs
Scannell, William Edward *aerospace company executive, consultant, psychologist*

Burbank
Aaronson, Robert Jay *aviation executive*
Volk, Robert Harkins *aviations company executive*

Calabasas
Hawkins, Willis Moore *aerospace and astronautical consultant*
Tellep, Daniel Michael *aerospace executive, mechanical engineer*

Cambria
Crowther, H. David *aerospace company corporate communications executive*

Corona Del Mar
Tether, Anthony John *aerospace executive*

Costa Mesa
†Mittermeier, Janice *airport terminal executive*

El Segundo
Aldridge, Edward C., Jr. *aerospace transportation executive*

Encino
Bucks, Charles Alan *airline industry consultant, former executive*

Gilroy
Borton, George Robert *airline captain*

Hawthorne
Kokalj, James Edward *aerospace administrator*

Irvine
Otth, Edward John, Jr. *retired marine systems executive, retired naval officer*

La Mesa
Hansen, Grant Lewis *retired aerospace and information systems executive*

Lancaster
Crew, Aubrey Torquil *aerospace inspector*

Long Beach
Myers, John Wescott *aviation executive*

Los Angeles
Cotter, George Edward *former airline company executive*
Gregg, Lucius Perry, Jr. *aerospace executive*
†Harris, T. C. *water transportation executive*
Kent, William *pilot, cameraman and technical director*
†Yee, Stephen *airport executive*

Malibu
Lindsay, Nathan James *aerospace company executive, retired career officer*

Mission Viejo
Foulds, Donald Duane *aerospace executive*

Moffett Field
Dean, William Evans *aerospace agency executive*

Oakland
Haskell, Arthur Jacob *steamship company executive*
†Hayashi, Joji *transportation company executive*
Lillie, John Mitchell *transportation company executive*
†Rhein, Timothy J. *transportation company executive*

Palo Alto
Moffitt, Donald Eugene *transportation company executive*
Morrison, David Fred *freight company executive*

Palos Verdes Peninsula
Waaland, Irving Theodore *retired aerospace design executive*

Ramona
Hoffman, Wayne Melvin *retired airline official*

Redwood City
†Guinasso, Victor *delivery service executive*
†Waller, Stephen *air transportation executive*

Sacramento
†Engel, Thomas P. *airport executive*

San Diego
Deckard, Ivan Lowell *pilot*
Mattingly, Thomas K. *astronaut*
Tuccio, Sam Anthony *aerospace executive, physicist*
Wertheim, Robert Halley *national security consultant*

San Francisco
†Edwards, Jack P. *transportation company executive*
†Hatton, Frederick L. *aircraft leasing executive*
Hickerson, Glenn Lindsey *leasing company executive*
†Holtman, William J. *railroad company executive*
Mohan, D. Mike *transportation company executive*
†Mulholland, Charles Bradley *transportation company executive*
Ryan, Randel Edward, Jr. *airline captain*
†Turpen, Louis A. *airport terminal executive*
Wood, Donald Frank *transportation educator, consultant*

San Luis Obispo
†Selvaggio, John N. *airline executive*

San Mateo
Trabitz, Eugene Leonard *aerospace company executive*

Shingle Springs
Crotti, Joseph Robert *aviation executive*

Sunnyvale
Guastaferro, Angelo *aerospace company executive*

Torrance
Savitz, Maxine Lazarus *aerospace company executive*

Tustin
Thomas, Mitchell, Jr. *aerospace company executive*

Van Nuys
Cooper, Leroy Gordon, Jr. *former astronaut, business consultant*

Walnut Creek
†Parsons, Robert Eugene *transportation consultant*

Woodland Hills
Caren, Robert Poston *aerospace company executive*

Yorba Linda
†Bailey, Don Matthew *aerospace and electronics company executive*

COLORADO

Denver
†DeLong, James C. *air transportation executive*
†Teets, Peter B. *aerospace executive*

Littleton
Kleinknecht, Kenneth Samuel *retired aerospace company executive, former federal space agency official*

Trinidad
Potter, William Bartlett *trucking company executive*

CONNECTICUT

New Canaan
Halan, John Paul *corporate executive*

Stamford
Barker, James Rex *corporate executive*
Tregurtha, Paul Richard *marine transportation and construction materials company executive*

Westport
†Malski, James Joseph *airline executive, accountant*

DELAWARE

Wilmington
†Krosser, Howard S. *aerospace company executive*
Rollins, John William, Sr. *service and transportation company executive*

DISTRICT OF COLUMBIA

Washington
Cocke, Erle, Jr. *business consultant*
Farrell, Joseph Michael *steamship company executive*
Josephson, Diana Hayward *aerospace executive*
Luffsey, Walter Stith *business executive*
Mederos, Carolina Luisa *transportation policy consultant*
Melton, Augustus Allen, Jr. *airport executive*
†Meurlin, Keith W. *airport terminal executive*
Newman, William Bernard, Jr. *railroad executive*
Norman, William Stanley *transportation company executive*
Overbeck, Gene Edward *retired airline executive, lawyer*
Parker, Robert Allan Ridley *astronaut*
Sullivan, Dennis F. *transportation company executive, engineer*
Thayer, Russell, III *airlines executive*

FLORIDA

Boca Raton
Goldstein, Bernard *transportation company executive*
Wright, Joseph Robert, Jr. *corporate executive*

Boynton Beach
Crane, L(eo) Stanley *retired railroad executive*

Clearwater
Howes, James Guerdon *airport director*

Fisher Island
Trippe, Kenneth Alvin Battershill *shipping industry executive*

Fort Lauderdale
Berwig, Newton Urbano *aerospace executive*

Jacksonville
†Carpenter, Alvin Rauso *transportation executive*
Davis, Jerry Ray *railroad company executive*
Fiorentino, Thomas Martin *transportation executive, lawyer*
Hamilton, William Berry, Jr. *shipping company executive*
†Hardrick, Charles M. *airport executive*
Kirk, Robert Leonard *transportation company executive*
Thornton, Winfred Lamotte *railroad executive*

Jupiter
Skully, Richard Patrick *airline consultant*

Miami
Brock, James Daniel *retired airline executive, consultant*
†Dellapa, Gary J. *airport terminal executive*
†Dickinson, Robert H. *water transportation executive*
Fain, Richard David *cruise line executive*
Huston, Edwin Allen *transportation company executive*
†Russell, Terence Lee *transportation company executive*
Sapp, Neil Carleton *international airline pilot, industrial consultant*

Naples
Gresham, Robert Coleman *transportation consultant*

Oldsmar
Burrows, William Claude *aerospace executive, retired air force officer*

Orlando
Harris, Martin Harvey *aerospace company executive*
†Le Tellier, Gary *airport terminal executive*
Sasseen, George Thiery *aerospace engineering executive*

Saint Augustine
Zellers, Carl Fredrick, Jr. *railway executive*

Sarasota
Lindsay, David Breed, Jr. *aircraft company executive, former editor and publisher*

GEORGIA

Atlanta
Allen, Ronald W. *airline company executive*
Callison, James W. *former airline executive, lawyer*
Connor, Charles William *airline pilot*
†Kelley, James P. *delivery service executive*
Nelson, Kent C. *delivery service executive*
Oppenlander, Robert *retired airline executive*
Raines, Mary Elizabeth *airline executive*
Roeck, Thomas J., Jr. *airline financial executive*
Thakker, Ashok *aerospace engineering company executive*

Decatur
Poole, Albert Mitchell, Jr. *trucking company executive*

Macon
Hails, Robert Emmet *aerospace consultant, business executive, former air force officer*

Savannah
†Breidenbach, Fred A. *aerospace company executive*
†Glenn, Albert H. *aerospace company executive*
†Johnson, Victor L. *trucking executive*

HAWAII

Honolulu
Myers, A(nthony) Maurice *airline executive*
Pfeiffer, Robert John *water transportation executive*
Safford, Florence Viray Sunga *travel agent and consultant*
Ueberroth, John A. *air transportation executive*

IDAHO

Payette
Ilett, Frank, Jr. *trucking company executive*

ILLINOIS

AMF Ohare
Pope, John Charles *airline company executive*

Chicago
Chartier, Janellen Olsen *airline service coordinator*
Guyette, James M. *airline executive*
Heineman, Ben Walter *corporation executive*
Nord, Henry J. *transportation executive*
Reed, John Shedd *former railway executive*
Schmiege, Robert *railroad executive*
Smith, Robert Drake *railroad executive*
Swartz, William John *transportation resources company executive/retired*
†Tingleff, Thomas Alan *transportation company executive*
White, John Abiathar *pilot, consultant*
Wolf, Stephen M. *airline executive*
Zell, Samuel *transportation leasing company executive*
Zito, James Anthony *retired railroad company executive*

Des Plaines
Altschul, Alfred Samuel *airline executive*
†Koffman, Morley *trucking executive*

Glen Ellyn
Logan, Henry Vincent *transportation executive*

Lake Forest
Hillman, Stanley Eric Gordon *former corporate executive*

Lisle
Batory, Ronald Louis *transportation executive*

Naperville
†Fleisher, Robert E. R. *trucking executive*
†Olliver, Denis G. *transportation company executive*

Oak Brook
Duerinck, Louis T. *retired railroad executive, attorney*

Park Ridge
Carr, Gilbert Randle *retired railroad executive*

Prophetstown
Thompson, George Howard *livestock transportation company executive*

Rockford
Donovan, Paul *aerospace executive*

Rosemont
†Burkhardt, Edward Arnold *transportation company executive*

Schaumburg
Krebs, Robert Duncan *transportation company executive*

Winthrop Harbor
Fuhrman, Kenneth Wayne *pilot, aviation consultant*

INDIANA

Columbus
Hartley, James Michaelis *aerospace systems, printing and hardwood products manufacturing executive*

Indianapolis
†Orcutt, Daniel C. *airport terminal executive*
†Wallace, F. Blake *aerospace executive, mechanical engineer*

Terre Haute
Frantz, Welby Marion *business executive*

West Lafayette
Drake, John Warren *aviation consultant*

KANSAS

Olathe
Williams, Eleanor Joyce *air traffic control specialist*

Overland Park
†Powell, George Everett, Jr. *motor freight company executive*
Powell, George Everett, III *trucking company executive*

Shawnee Mission
Bigger, John P. *motor carrier executive*

Wichita
†Bell, Baillis F. *airport terminal executive*
Cheesman, John Michael *aeronautics company executive, community activist*

KENTUCKY

Franklin
Clark, James Benton *railroad industry consultant, former executive*

LOUISIANA

New Orleans
†Amoss, W. James, Jr. *shipping company executive*
Johnsen, Erik Frithjof *transportation executive*
†Lee, Frank W. *transportation company executive*
Lykes, Joseph T., III *shipping company executive*
†McCormick, Eugene F., Jr. *transportation company executive*
†Suggs, Carroll W. *aerospace transportation executive*

MAINE

Bath
†O'Keefe, Patrick *transportation executive*

MARYLAND

Annapolis
Colussy, Dan Alfred *aviation executive*
Groves, George L., Jr. *air freight service company executive*
Moellering, John Henry *aviation maintenance company executive*

Baltimore
Cunningham, M(urray) Hunt, Jr. *aerospace company executive, mechanical engineer, author*
†Harp, Solomon *airport executive*
†Kirk, Robert L. *rail transportation executive*

Bethesda
Coleman, Joseph Michael *transportation consultant*
Lally, Richard Francis *aviation security consultant, former association executive, former government official*

College Park
Keller, Samuel William *aerospace administrator*

Rockville
Fthenakis, Emanuel John *diversified aerospace company executive*
Porter, John Robert, Jr. *space technology company executive, geochemist*

MASSACHUSETTS

Boston
Klotz, Charles Rodger *shipping company executive*

Cambridge
John, Richard Rodda *transportation executive*
LaTores, Santo Joseph *federal transportation executive*

North Billerica
Fink, David A. *rail transportation executive*

Wakefield
Roberts, Louis Wright *transportation executive*

MICHIGAN

Detroit
†Braun, Robert B. *airport executive*

Grand Rapids
Auwers, Stanley John *motor carrier executive*

Kalamazoo
†Tessler, Allan R. *trucking company executive*

Monroe
White, Gary L. *trucking executive*

Warren
Morelli, William Annibale, Sr. *aerospace manufacturing company executive*

MINNESOTA

Minneapolis
Harper, Donald Victor *transportation and logistics educator*
Nyrop, Donald William *airline executive*

Saint Paul
†Anderson, Tim *airport terminal executive*
Checchi, Alfred A. *airline company executive*
Gehrz, Robert Gustave *retired railroad executive*
Wilson, Gary L. *air transportation executive*

MISSISSIPPI

Jackson
†Liles, William Jackson, Jr. *transportation executive*

Pass Christian
Clark, John Walter, Jr. *shipping company executive*

MISSOURI

Blue Springs
Reed, Tony Norman *aviation company executive*

Chesterfield
Armstrong, Theodore Morelock *corporate executive*

Fenton
Baer, Robert J. *transportation company executive*

Kansas City
Edwards, George W., Jr. *railway company executive*
†Gile, Herbert R., Jr. *airport terminal executive*
†Solomon, John Davis *aviation executive*

Lake Saint Louis
German, John George *transportation consultant*

Saint Louis
Capellupo, John P. *air transportation executive*
Jenks, Downing Bland *railroad executive*
Johnston, Gerald Andrew *aerospace company executive*
Nelson, Michael Underhill *aerospace company executive, association executive*

NEBRASKA

Omaha
Davidson, Richard K. *railroad company executive*

NEVADA

Henderson
Carter, Thomas Smith, Jr. *retired railroad executive*

Reno
Horton, Gary Bruce *transportation company executive*
Jordan, Joseph Rembert *airline pilot*

NEW JERSEY

Elizabeth
†Karlberg, John *transportation company executive*
Tolan, David Joseph *transportation executive*

Flemington
Kettler, Carl Frederick *airline executive*

Haddon Heights
Romer, Jeanne Geraldine *delivery service executive, consultant*

Newark
Guido, Joseph Matthew *air transport company executive*

Peapack
Weiss, Allan Joseph *transport company executive, lawyer*

Teterboro
Young, John Morgan *aviation executive*

Wayne
Drossman, Jay Lewis *aerospace executive*

NEW MEXICO

Farmington
Risley, Larry L. *air transportation executive*

Las Cruces
Borman, Frank *former astronaut, laser patent company executive*

NEW YORK

Albany
Vachon, Russell Bertrand *transportation executive*

Babylon
Collis, Charles *aircraft company executive*

Bethpage
Anderson, John Robert *defense and aerospace executive*
Caporali, Renso L. *aerospace executive*
Dely, Steven *aerospace company executive*
Myers, Robert Jay *aerospace company executive*

Carmel
Shen, Chia Theng *former steamship company executive, religious institute official*

Flushing
Peirce, George Leighton *airport administrator*

Garden City
McNicholas, David Paul *automobile rental company executive*

Great Neck
Pollack, Paul Robert *airline service company executive*
Satinskas, Henry Anthony *airline services company executive*

Huntington
Jackson, Richard Montgomery *former airline executive*

Jamaica
Hoppe, Charles W. *railroad company executive*
Mc Kinnon, Clinton Dan *aerospace transportation executive*
Rowe, Richard Lloyd *aviation executive, management consultant*

Manhasset
Frankum, James Edward *airlines company executive*

Mount Kisco
Crowe, John Carl *airline company executive*
O'Neill, John Robert *airline executive*

New York
†Andren, Karl Goesta *transportation executive*
Apostolakis, James John *shipping company executive*
†Chao, James S. C. *maritime executive*
Danaher, Frank Erwin *transportation technologist*
Gitner, Gerald L. *aviation executive*
Gregorio, Luis Justino Lopes *transportation executive*
Hyman, Morton Peter *shipping company executive*
Jacob, Jerry Rowland *airline executive*
Johnsen, Niels Winchester *ocean shipping company executive*
Kondas, Nicholas Frank *shipping company executive*
Lloyd-Jones, Donald J. *transportation executive*
Love, Richard Emerson *equipment manufacturing company executive*
Whitman, Bruce Nairn *flight safety executive*
†Winokur, Herbert Simon, Jr. *diversified company executive*

Queens
Farkas, Edward Barrister *airport administrator, electrical engineer*

NORTH CAROLINA

Chapel Hill
Bauer, Frederick Christian *motor carrier executive*

Charlotte
†Orr, T. J. (Jerry Orr) *airport terminal executive*

Cherryville
Mayhew, Kenneth Edwin, Jr. *transportation company executive*
Younger, Kenneth G. *freight carrier corporation executive*

Kannapolis
Thigpen, Alton Hill *motor transportation company executive*

Winston Salem
Davis, Thomas Henry *airline executive*

OHIO

Akron
Clapp, Joseph Mark *motor carrier company executive*

Brecksville
Worden, Alfred Merrill *former astronaut, research company executive*

Cincinnati
Murphy, Eugene F. *aerospace, communications and electronics executive*
†Siebenburgen, David A. *airline company financial executive*

Cleveland
†Burnside, Pershing Elliott *trucking company executive*
†Damsel, Richard A. *transportation company executive*
†Dannemiller, John C. *transportation company executive*

Columbus
†Hedrick, Larry Willis *airport executive*
†Newland, Ron *airport executive*
†Simonetta, Richard James *public transportation executive*

Dayton
Brand, Vance Devoe *astronaut, government official*

North Olmsted
Zilli, Harry Angelo, Jr. *business executive*

Oberlin
Startup, Charles Harry *airline executive*

Xenia
Bigelow, Daniel James *aerospace executive*

OKLAHOMA

Tulsa
†Kitchen, Brent A. *airport executive*
Kruse, David Louis, II *transportation company executive*

OREGON

Oakland
Smelt, Ronald *retired aircraft company executive*

Portland
†Hebe, James L. *trucking executive*

PENNSYLVANIA

Allentown
Doughty, George Franklin *airport administrator*

Bethlehem
Lewis, Andrew Lindsay, Jr. (Drew Lewis) *transportation and natural resources executive*
†Lewis, Drew *rail transportation and holding company executive*
Stuart, Gary Miller *railroad executive*

Gettysburg
Mainwaring, Thomas Lloyd *motor freight company executive*

Gladwyne
Hasselman, Richard B. *consultant, retired railroad executive*

Monroeville
†Hoffman, Donald Howard *transportation executive*

Philadelphia
†DeLong, James Clifford *aviation administrator*
Schimmel, Allan *rail company executive*
Terry, John Joseph *transportation investor*
†Walls, William Walton, Jr. *helicopter company executive*
Whatmough, J. Jeremy T. *railway executive*
Wilson, Bruce Brighton *transportation executive*

Villanova
Sullivan, Richard Cyril *retired transportation executive*

SOUTH CAROLINA

Charleston
†Hoerter, Sam Spalding *transportation executive*

TENNESSEE

Memphis
†Cox, Larry D. *airport terminal executive*
Smith, Frederick Wallace *transportation company executive*

TEXAS

Austin
†McCullough, Benjamin Franklin *transportation researcher, educator*

Corpus Christi
†Hext, George D. *airport terminal executive*

Dallas
Baker, Robert Woodward *airline executive*
Barrett, Colleen Crotty *airline executive*
†Cott, Burl Gene *transportation company executive*

Crandall, Robert Lloyd *airline executive*
Kelleher, Herbert David *airline executive, lawyer*
Richardi, Ralph Leonard *airline executive*
†Sturns, Vernell *airport terminal executive*
Wallace, William C. *airline executive*
Whitman, Reginald Norman *railroad official*

Fort Worth
Anderson, John Quentin *rail transportation executive*
Greenwood, William E. *rail transportation executive*
Grinstein, Gerald *transportation executive*
†Miller, Brian Keith *airline executive*

Harlingen
Farris, Robert Gene *transportation company executive*

Houston
Bean, Alan LaVern *space artist, retired astronaut*
Brandenstein, Daniel Charles *astronaut, retired naval officer*
†Elmer, Augustus *shipping company executive*
†Ferguson, John C. *airport terminal executive*
Ferguson, Robert R., III *airline company executive*
Hartsfield, Henry Warren, Jr. *astronaut*
Musgrave, Story *astronaut, surgeon, pilot, physiologist, educator*
Regalado, Raul L. *airport executive*
Roberts, Gilbert B. *airlines executive*
Thagard, Norman E. *astronaut*
Young, John Watts *astronaut*

Irving
†Raper, Bobby Joe *airlines company executive, mayor*

San Antonio
Kutchins, Michael Joseph *airport executive*
Lowry, A. Robert *federal government railroad arbitrator*

VIRGINIA

Alexandria
Lion, Paul Michel, III *transportation engineer, executive*
Pulling, Ronald Wilson, Sr. *aviation systems planner, civil engineer, consultant*
†Wilding, James Anthony *airport administrator*

Arlington
Fabian, John M. *former astronaut, air force officer*
Fish, Howard Math *aerospace industry executive*
Schofield, Seth Eugene *air transport company executive*
Stokes, B. R. *transportation consultant*

Great Falls
Hughes, Alan Richard *aerospace company executive*

Marshall
Hayward, Charles Winthrop *retired railroad company executive*

Mc Lean
Hendon, Robert Caraway *retired transportation and manufacturing company executive, consultant*

Newport News
Cox, Alvin Earl *shipbuilding executive*
Phillips, William Ray, Jr. *shipbuilding executive*

Norfolk
McKinnon, Arnold Borden *transportation company executive*
†Scott, Kenneth R. *transportation executive*
Shannon, John Sanford *railway executive, lawyer*
Watts, Dave Henry *corporate executive*

Richmond
Hintz, Robert Louis *transportation company executive*
Watkins, Hays Thomas *retired railroad executive*

Sterling
†Acker, C. Edward *airline executive*
Harris, Paul Lynwood *aerospace transportation executive*

Virginia Beach
Kreyling, Edward George, Jr. *railroad executive*

Winchester
Jamison, Richard Bryan *airport consultant*

WASHINGTON

Bellevue
†Baker, Jackson Arnold *container shipping company executive*

Seattle
†Brazier, Robert G. *transportation executive*
Clarkson, Lawrence William *airplane company executive*
Cline, Robert Stanley *air freight company executive*
Condit, Philip Murray *aerospace executive, engineer*
†Cosgrove, Benjamin A. *retired aerospace company executive*
Elliott, Jeanne Marie Koreltz *transportation executive*
Gissing, Bruce *aerospace company executive*
Givan, Boyd Eugene *aircraft company executive*
Jaeger, David Arnold *aerospace company executive*
Raisbeck, James David *aircraft design executive*
Robinson, Gary Dale *aerospace company executive*
†Smith, Donald William *airport manager*
Thornton, Dean Dickson *retired airplane company executive*
Vecci, Raymond Joseph *airline executive*
Welliver, Albertus Delmar *aerospace manufacturing company executive*

Vancouver
Vingo, James Ray *transportation executive*

WISCONSIN

Green Bay
†Lewis, Gary *trucking executive*
Olson, James Richard *transportation company executive*

Milwaukee
†Bateman, C. Barry *airport terminal Executive*
Mayer, Henry Michael *mass transit consultant*
Teerlink, Richard Francis *motor company executive*
Ziperski, James Richard *lawyer, trucking company executive*

WYOMING

Worland
Woods, Lawrence Milton *airline company executive*

CANADA

ALBERTA

Calgary
†Caron, Ernie M. *airport executive*
Jenkins, Kevin J. *airline company executive*
McCaig, Jeffrey James *transportation company executive*
McCaig, John Robert *transportation executive*
†Paquette, Richard *airport executive*

Edmonton
†Eng, Howard *airport administrator*

BRITISH COLUMBIA

Vancouver
Smith, Brian Ray Douglas *rail transportation executive, lawyer*

NOVA SCOTIA

Bedford
†Randell, Joseph David *airline executive*

Halifax
Renouf, Harold Augustus *business consultant*

ONTARIO

Almonte
Morrison, Angus Curran *aviation executive*

Ottawa
Sheflin, Michael John Edward *transportation commissioner*

Sault Sainte Marie
Savoie, Leonard Norman *transportation company executive*

QUEBEC

Mirabel
Ginzburg, Rubin *airport executive, electrical engineer*

Montreal
†Bourgeault, Jean-Jacques *air transportation executive*
Labelle, Eugene Jean-Marc *airport director general*
Lanyi, Alexander Sandor *rail transportation executive*
Masse, Yvon H. *transportation company executive*
Poitras, Pierre *aerospace and transportation products company executive*
Ritchie, Robert Jamieson *transportation executive*
Scott, I. B. *railroad executive*
Stinson, William W. *business executive*
Taylor, Claude I. *airlines executive*
Tellier, Paul M. *Canadian railway transportation executive*

Quebec
Rochette, Louis *shipowner*

Saint Laurent
Harris, Hollis Loyd *airline executive*

Saint-Sauveur
Hanigan, Lawrence *retired railway executive*

DENMARK

Vedbaek
Nordqvist, Erik Askbo *shipping company executive*

GERMANY

Munich
Born, Gunthard Karl *aerospace executive*

SWEDEN

Stockholm
Lindberg, Helge *aviation consultant*

SWITZERLAND

Geneva
Ballin, William Christopher *international shipping, investments and energy, advisor to corporations and government*

ADDRESS UNPUBLISHED

Aldrin, Buzz *former astronaut, science consultant*
Ames, Donald Paul *retired aerospace company executive, researcher*
Armstrong, Neil A. *former astronaut*
Brazier, Don Roland *retired railroad executive*
†Butterfield, Alexander Porter *business executive, former government official, retired air force officer*
Carpenter, Malcolm Scott *astronaut, oceanographer*
Dasburg, John Harold *airline executive*
Fenello, Michael John *aviation consultant, retired government agency executive*
Fuhrman, Robert Alexander *aerospace company executive*
Glennon, Harrison Randolph, Jr. *retired shipping company executive*
Horton, Robert Baynes *railroad company executive*
Hurst, John Emory, Jr. *retired airline executive*
King, Edward William *retired transportation executive*
Kloster, Einar *corporate executive*
Ledford, Jack Clarence *retired aircraft company executive, former air force officer*
Lesko, Harry Joseph *transportation company executive*
Lillibridge, John Lee *retired airline executive*
Marshall, Charles Noble *railroad executive*
Masiello, Rocco Joseph *airlines and aerospace manufacturing executive*
Mast, Stewart Dale *retired airport manager*
Matthews, L. White, III *railroad executive*
Middleton, Donald Earl *transportation company executive*
Morse, Leon William *traffic, physical distribution and transportation management executive, consultant*
Murphy, David Ridgeway *transportation and financial consultant*
Murray, Leonard Hugh *railroad executive*
Ransome, Ernest Leslie, III *transportation and retail company executive*
Renda, Dominic Phillip *airline executive*
†Rose, James Turner *aerospace consultant*
Ruegg, Donald George *retired railway company executive*
Schaefer, C. Barry *railroad executive, lawyer, investment banker*
Shepard, Alan Bartlett, Jr. *astronaut, real estate developer*
Shockley, Edward Julian *aerospace company executive*
Snow, John William *railroad executive*
Snowden, Lawrence Fontaine *retired aircraft company executive, retired marine corps general officer*
Sze, Andy Hok-Fan *transportation executive*
Voss, Omer Gerald *truck company executive*

INDUSTRY: UTILITIES, ENERGY, RESOURCES

UNITED STATES

ALABAMA

Birmingham
Barker, Thomas Watson, Jr. *energy company executive*
Bowron, Richard Anderson *retired utilities executive*
†Carr, William *mining company executive*
Dahl, Hilbert Douglas *mining company executive*
†Franklin, H. Allen *electric company executive*
†Hairston, W(illiam) George, III *nuclear power company executive*
Harris, Elmer Beseler *electric utility executive*
Hutchins, William Bruce, III *utility company executive*
Kuehn, Ronald L., Jr. *natural resources company executive*
Patzke, Richard Joseph *energy company executive*
Robin, Theodore Tydings, Jr. *electric company executive, engineer*
Smith, Peter Garthwaite *energy consultant*

Nauvoo
†Cagle, Johnny T. *coal miner, state legislator*

Shoal Creek
Ahearn, John Francis, Jr. *retired oil and gas company executive*

ALASKA

Fairbanks
Beistline, Earl Hoover *mining consultant*

Juneau
†Albanese, Thomas *minerals company executive*

ARIZONA

Carefree
Birkelbach, Albert Ottmar *retired oil company executive*

Phoenix
Clay, Ambrose Whitlock Winston *telecommunications company executive*
De Michele, O. Mark *utility company executive*
Gillis, William Freeman *telecommunications executive*
Huffman, Edgar Joseph *oil company executive*
Kinneberg, Arthur Hempton *retired copper mining company executive*
†Lassen, John R. *electric utility company executive*

St. Clair, Thomas McBryar *mining and manufacturing company executive*
Teel, Dale *utility company executive, consultant*
Yearley, Douglas Cain *mining and manufacturing company executive*

Scottsdale
†Gerrity, James Robert *diversified company executive*

Sun City West
Black, Robert Frederick *former oil company executive*
O'Brien, Gerald James *utilities executive*

Tempe
Clevenger, Jeffrey Griswold *mining company executive*

Tucson
Bayless, Charles Edward *lawyer, utility executive*
Champagne, John F., Jr. *mining company executive*
Davidson, Dalwyn Robert *electric utility executive*
Davis, James Luther *retired utilities executive, lawyer*
Heller, Frederick *retired mining company executive*
Osborne, Thomas Cramer *mineral industry consultant*
Peeler, Stuart Thorne *petroleum industry executive and independent oil operator*
Saul, Kenneth Louis *retired utility company executive*

ARKANSAS

El Dorado
McNutt, Jack Wray *oil company executive*
Murphy, Charles Haywood, Jr. *petroleum company executive*
Vaughan, Odie Frank *oil company executive*
Watkins, Jerry West *retired oil company executive, lawyer*

Fayetteville
†Scharlau, Charles Edward, III *natural gas company executive*

Flippin
Sanders, Steven Gill *utilities executive*

Little Rock
Bobbitt, Max E. *telecommunications executive*
Ford, Joe Thomas *telephone company executive, former state senator*
Gardner, Kathleen D. *gas company executive, lawyer*

Russellville
Jones, James Rees *retired oil company executive*

CALIFORNIA

Corona Del Mar
Hill, Melvin James *oil company executive*

Costa Mesa
Wall, James Edward *petroleum, pharmaceutical executive*

Dana Point
Frederickson, Arman Frederick *minerals company executive*

Glendale
Duke, William Edward *petroleum company executive*

Hanford
†Drosdick, John Girard *oil company executive*

Hesperia
Moyers, Lowell Duane *pipeline company executive*

Hillsborough
Willoughby, Rodney Erwin *retired oil company executive*

Irvine
†Keating, James J. *oil industry executive*

La Canada Flintridge
Read, William McClain *retired oil company executive*
Simmons, John Wesley *oil company executive*

La Jolla
Grier, Herbert Earl *scientist, consultant*
Morse, Jack Hatton *utilities consultant*

Long Beach
†Drosdick, John G. *oil industry executive*
†Rea, William *oil industry executive*
†Winget, Clifford *oil industry executive*

Los Angeles
Arnault, Ronald J. *petroleum company executive*
†Beach, Roger C. *oil company executive*
Brinegar, Claude Stout *oil company executive*
Cook, Lodwrick Monroe *petroleum company executive*
Edwards, Howard Lee *petroleum company executive*
Farman, Richard Donald *gas company executive*
Laurance, Dale R. *oil company executive*
†Lepape, Harry Leonard *diversified company executive*
†Loch, Robert M. *public utility company executive, civil engineer, lawyer*
Mc Cormack, Francis Xavier *oil company executive, lawyer*
McIntyre, Robert Malcolm *utility company executive*
McSweeny, William Francis *petroleum company executive, author*
Middleton, James Arthur *oil and gas company executive*
Mitchell, Warren I. *utility company executive*
Rensch, Joseph Romaine *public utility holding company executive*
Stegemeier, Richard Joseph *oil company executive*

Van Horne, R. Richard *oil company executive*
Wood, Willis Bowne, Jr. *utility holding company executive*
Wycoff, Robert E. *petroleum company executive*

Martinez
Meyer, Jarold Alan *oil company research executive*

Newport Beach
Armstrong, Robert Arnold *petroleum company executive*
Shea, John Martin, Jr. *business executive*

Novato
Premo, Paul Mark *oil company executive*

Oxnard
Parriott, James Deforis, Jr. *retired oil company executive, consultant*

Pacific Palisades
Klein, Joseph Mark *retired mining company executive*
Mulryan, Henry Trist *mineral company executive, consultant*

Palos Verdes Estates
Christie, Hans Frederick *retired utility company subsidiaries executive, consultant*

Pasadena
Finnell, Michael Hartman *corporate executive*
Mc Duffie, Malcolm *oil company executive*
Mc Millan, John Robertson *energy producer*
Van Amringe, John Howard *retired oil industry executive, geologist*

Playa Del Rey
Weir, Alexander, Jr. *utility consultant, inventor*

Rancho Santa Fe
Arms, Brewster Lee *retired corporate executive, investor*

Rosemead
Allen, Howard Pfeiffer *electric utility executive, lawyer*
Bennett, Brian O'Leary *utilities executive*
Bryson, John E. *utilities company executive*
Bushey, Richard Kenneth *utility executive*

Sacramento
Crabbe, John Crozier *telecommunications consultant*

San Diego
Cota, John Francis *utility executive*
Igasaki, Masao, Jr. *retired utilities company executive, controller*

San Francisco
Bonney, John Dennis *oil company executive*
Brandin, Alf Elvin *retired mining and shipping company executive*
Bray, Arthur Philip *management science corporation executive*
Carter, George Kent *oil company executive*
Christensen, Lydell Lee *telephone company executive*
Clarke, Richard Alan *electric and gas utility company executive, lawyer*
Conger, Harry Milton *mining company executive*
Derr, Kenneth T. *oil company executive*
Flittie, Clifford Gilliland *retired petroleum company executive*
Ginn, Sam L. *telephone company executive*
High, Thomas W. *utilities company executive*
Keller, George Matthew *retired oil company executive*
Kleeman, Michael Jeffrey *telecommunications and computer consultant*
Littlefield, Edmund Wattis *mining company executive*
Maneatis, George A. *retired utility company executive*
McCrea, Peter *oil company executive*
Mielke, Frederick William, Jr. *retired utility company executive*
†Neerhout, John, Jr. *petroleum company executive*
Peterson, Richard Hamlin *utility executive, lawyer*
Quigley, Philip J. *telecommunications industry executive*
†Renfrew, Charles Byron *oil company executive, lawyer*
Sanders, Charles Franklin *corporate executive*
Shackelford, Barton Warren *retired utility executive*
Shiffer, James David *utility executive*
Skinner, Stanley Thayer *utility company executive, lawyer*
Sproul, John Allan *retired public utility executive*
Sullivan, James N. *fuel company executive*
†Zaccaria, Adrian *utilities executive*

San Juan Capistrano
Dergarabedian, Paul *energy and environmental company executive*

San Rafael
Latno, Arthur Clement, Jr. *telephone company executive*

San Ramon
Fleming, William Sloan *energy, environmental and technology company executive*

Santa Ana
Mickelson, H(erald) Fred *electric utility executive*

Santa Barbara
Bilhorn, William W. *international mining company consultant*

Santa Ynez
Byrne, Joseph *retired oil company executive*

Thousand Oaks
Crain, Charles Anthony *telephone company executive*
Sparrow, Larry J. *telecommunications executive*

Turlock
Williams, Delwyn Charles *telephone company executive*

Ventura
Field, A. J. *former oil drilling company executive, engineering consultant*

Walnut Creek
Humphrey, William Albert *mining company executive*

West Covina
Saunders, Russell Joseph *utility company executive*

Woodland Hills
Talbot, Matthew J. *oil company executive, rancher*

COLORADO

Boulder
Thomas, Daniel Foley *telecommunications company executive*

Colorado Springs
Hampton, Rex Herbert *gold mining company executive, consultant*
King, Peter Joseph, Jr. *retired gas company executive*
O'Shields, Richard Lee *retired natural gas company executive*
Robinson, Ronald Alan *oil company executive*

Denver
Bowman, Joseph Searles *petroleum consultant*
Cann, William Hopson *former mining company executive*
†Dana, Richard E. *oil industry executive*
Davis, Marvin *petroleum company executive, entrepreneur*
Fagin, David Kyle *natural resource company executive*
†Hamilton, Frederic Crawford *oil company executive*
Lewis, Jerome A. *petroleum company executive, investment banker*
Macey, William Blackmore *oil company executive*
Magness, Bob John *telecommunications executive*
Malone, John C. *telecommunications executive*
Miller, Arlyn James *oil company executive*
Murdy, Wayne William *mining company executive, financial officer*
Owens, Marvin Franklin, Jr. *oil company executive*
Parry, John Robert *natural resource company executive, geophysicist*
†Philip, Thomas Peter *mining executive*
†Rendu, Jean-Michel Marie *mining executive*
Thompson, Lohren Matthew *oil company executive*
Timothy, Robert Keller *telephone company executive*
Trueblood, Harry Albert, Jr. *oil company executive*
Valot, Daniel L. *oil industry executive*

Englewood
†Barr, Kenneth John *retired mining company executive*
Fisher, Donne Francis *telecommunications executive*
McCormick, Richard David *telecommunications company executive*
Parker, Gordon Rae *natural resource company executive*
Ward, Milton Hawkins *mining company executive*

Lakewood
Danos, Robert McClure *oil company executive*
Fox, Joseph Leland *fiduciary and business executive*
Hall, Larry D. *energy company executive, lawyer*
Hurst, Leland Lyle *natural gas company executive*

Larkspur
Bierbaum, J. Armin *petroleum company executive, consultant*

Littleton
Clift, William Orrin *oil company executive, consultant*

Westminster
Kober, Carl Leopold *exploration company executive*

CONNECTICUT

Bridgeport
McGregor, Jack Edwin *natural resource company executive*

Darien
Kutz, Kenneth John *retired mining executive*
Smith, Elwin Earl *mining and oil company executive*

Greenwich
Bennett, Jack Franklin *oil company executive*
Brophy, Theodore Frederick *telephone company executive*
Donahue, Donald Jordan *mining company executive*
Hicks, Paul B., Jr. *retired petroleum company executive*
Lawi, David Steven *energy, agriservice and thermoplastic resins industries executive*
Schmidt, Herman J. *former oil company executive*
Weil, Ernst *oil industry executive*
†Wright, Christopher J. *oil company executive*

Guilford
Morgan, Leon Alford *retired utility executive*

Hamden
Gordon, Angus Neal, Jr. *retired electric company executive*

Hartford
Ellis, William Ben *utility executive*
Fox, Bernard Michael *utilities company executive, electrical engineer*

Mystic
Townsend, Thomas Perkins *former mining company executive*

New Canaan
McIvor, Donald Kenneth *retired petroleum company executive, university administrator*
Wolfley, Alan *corporate executive*

New Haven
Fassett, John D. *retired utility executive, consultant*

Old Greenwich
Hittle, Richard Howard *corporate executive, international affairs consultant*

Orange
Bowerman, Richard Henry *utility company executive, lawyer*

Ridgefield
Mattausch, Thomas Edward *public relations consultant*

Stamford
Block, Edward Martel *consultant, former telephone company executive*
Duke, Robert Dominick *mining executive, lawyer*
Farrell, Joseph Christopher *mining executive, services executive*
Jacobson, Ishier *retired utility executive*
Kinnear, James Wesley, III *retired petroleum company executive*
Mc Kinley, John Key *retired oil company executive*
Pansini, Michael Samuel *energy company executive, consultant*

Waterford
Sillin, Lelan Flor, Jr. *retired utility executive*

Westport
Nedom, H. Arthur *petroleum consultant*

Wilton
Hoefling, Rudolf Joachim *power generating company executive*

DELAWARE

Wilmington
Connelly, Donald Preston *electric and gas utility company executive*
Corn, Jack W. *oil company executive*
Cosgrove, Howard Edward, Jr. *utility executive*
Croom, John Henry, III *utility company executive*

DISTRICT OF COLUMBIA

Washington
†Barrett, Lake H. *energy industry executive*
Davis, Herbert Lowell *utility company executive*
Deland, Michael Reeves *energy executive*
Derrick, John Martin, Jr. *electric company executive*
Dragoumis, Paul *electric utility company executive*
Hillings, E. Joseph *energy company executive*
Hirsch, Robert Louis *electric research company executive*
Hughitt, Jeremiah Keefe *utility executive*
Kuhn, Thomas R. *trade association executive*
Maher, Patrick Joseph *utility company executive*
McCollam, William, Jr. *utility company executive*
McGhee, George Crews *petroleum producer, former government official*
Paige, Hilliard Wegner *corporate director, consultant*
Roberts, Bert C., Jr. *telecommunications company executive*
†Robinson, Randall *think-tank executive*
Smiley, D. E. *petroleum company executive*
Thompson, William Reid *public utility executive, lawyer*
Weiss, Stanley Alan *mining, chemicals and refractory company executive*
Winzenried, Jesse David *retired petroleum executive*
Wraase, Dennis Richard *utilities company executive, accountant*

FLORIDA

Atlantic Beach
Zechella, Alexander Philip *oil company executive, former naval officer*

Boca Raton
Gralla, Eugene *natural gas company executive*

Boynton Beach
Babler, Wayne E. *retired telephone company executive, lawyer*
Lundgren, Robert Wayne *retired utility executive, consultant*
Wampler, Charles Edwin *retired telephone company executive*

Captiva
Ronald, Peter *utility executive*

Delray Beach
Epley, Marion Jay *oil company executive*
Reef, Arthur *industry business consultant*

Destin
Cunningham, James Everett *retired energy services company executive*

Jacksonville
Francis, James Delbert *oil company executive*

Juno Beach
Evanson, Paul John *utilities executive*
Petillo, James Thomas *diversified utility company executive*

Largo
Dolan, John E. *consultant, retired utility executive*
Loader, Jay Gordon *retired utility company executive*

Marco
Mollison, Richard Devol *mining company executive*

Miami
Posner, Victor *diversified business executive*

Naples
Bush, John William *business executive, federal official*
Ivancevic, Walter Charles *former gas distribution company executive*
Johnson, Zane Quentin *retired petroleum company executive*
Kay, Herbert *retired natural resources company executive*
Rowe, Jack Field *retired electric utility executive*

Orlando
Ispass, Alan Benjamin *utilities executive*
Pope, Theodore Campbell, Jr. *utilities executive, consultant*

Palm Beach
Donnell, John Randolph *petroleum executive*

Palm Beach Gardens
Collado, Emilio Gabriel *energy company executive, consultant*
Harnett, Joseph Durham *oil company executive*

Palm City
White, Eugene James *retired technology company executive*

Pinellas Park
Perry, Paul Alverson *utility executive*

Ponte Vedra Beach
Green, Norman Kenneth *retired oil industry executive, former naval officer*
Milbrath, Robert Henry *retired petroleum executive*

Saint Petersburg
Critchfield, Jack Barron *utilities company executive*
Hines, Andrew Hampton, Jr. *utilities executive*

Sarasota
Jaeger, Leonard Henry *former public utility executive*

Sorrento
†Welch, Jerry *oil company executive*

Sun City Center
McGrath, John Francis *utility executive*

Tampa
Campbell, David Ned *retired electric utility executive, business consultant*
Leavengood, Victor Price *telephone company executive*

Venice
Torrey, Richard Frank *utility executive*

Vero Beach
†Corr, Thomas L. *oil industry executive*
Mc Afee, Jerry *retired oil company executive, chemical engineer*

Winter Park
Spake, Ned Bernarr *energy company executive*

GEORGIA

Athens
Wood, Betty A. *utilities executive*

Atlanta
†Ackerman, F. Duane *utility company executive*
Addison, Edward L. *utility holding company executive*
Bolch, Carl Edward, Jr. *corporation executive, lawyer*
Brinkley, Donald R. *oil industry executive*
Chilton, Horace Thomas *pipeline company executive*
Clendenin, John L. *telecommunications company executive*
Dahlberg, Alfred William *electric company executive*
Frost, Norman Cooper *retired telephone company executive*
Knobloch, Carl William, Jr. *oil and gas services executive*
Miller, James Hugh, Jr. *retired public utility executive*
†Norris, T. H. *oil industry executive*
†Olson, Frank L. *electrical power industry executive*
Ramsey, Ira Clayton *pipeline company executive*
Sessoms, Walter Woodrow *telecommunications executive*
Skinner, B. Franklin *retired telecommunications executive*
Voss, William Charles *retired oil company executive*

Gainesville
Leet, Richard Hale *oil company executive*

Norcross
Born, Allen *mining executive*

Sandersville
Thiele, Paul Frederick *mining company executive*

Smyrna
†Ragan, Hugh Adams *electric utility executive, state senator*

Tucker
Kilgore, Tom D. *electric power company executive*

HAWAII

Honolulu
Reed, Robert George, III *petroleum company executive*
Williams, Carl Harwell *utilities executive*
†Williamson, Harwood Danford *utility company executive*

Kailua
Engelbardt, Robert Miles *telecommunications executive*

IDAHO

Coeur D Alene
Griffith, William Alexander *former mining company executive*
†Wheeler, Dennis Earl *mining company executive, lawyer*

Idaho Falls
Newman, Stanley Ray *oil refining company executive*

ILLINOIS

Arlington Heights
†Di Corcia, Edward Thomas *oil company executive*

Belleville
†Kirchoff, Virgil L. *oil company executive, consultant*

Chicago
Addy, Frederick Seale *oil company executive*
Akerson, Daniel Francis *telecommunications industry executive*
Ban, Stephen Dennis *natural gas industry research institute executive*
Barnett, Robert L. *utilities executive*
Brooker, Thomas Kimball *oil company executive*
Brown, Richard Harris *telecommunications industry executive*
Early, Patrick Joseph *oil and gas company executive*
†Eisner, Michael C. *electric power industry executive*
Engel, Joel Stanley *telecommunications executive*
†Frazee, John Powell, Jr. *telecommunications executive*
Fuller, Harry Laurance *oil company executive*
Lowrie, William G. *oil company executive*
Lyman, John Root *oil company executive*
Morrow, Richard Martin *retired oil company executive*
Notebaert, Richard C. *telecommunications industry executive*
O'Connor, James John *utility company executive*
Quanstrom, Walter Roy *oil executive, educator*
Reeves, Michael Stanley *public utility executive*
Rutigliano, Louis J. *telecommunications industry executive*
Skinner, Samuel Knox *utilities executive, lawyer*
Somers, Antoinette Nadezhda *telecommunications executive*
Terry, Richard Edward *public utility holding company executive*

Decatur
Haab, Larry David *utility company executive*
Kelley, Wendell J. *retired utilities executive*
Wells, Charles William *utility executive*
Womeldorff, Porter John *utilities executive*

East Saint Louis
†Reilly, Michael K. *mining executive*

Fairview Heights
†Hughes, John W. *mining executive*
†Vyas, Chand Bhaourbhai *coal company executive*

Geneva
Pershing, Robert George *retired telecommunications company executive*

Glen Ellyn
Lischer, Ludwig Frederick *consultant, former utility company executive*

Glenview
Cozad, James William *retired oil company executive*

Lawrenceville
†Wright, John D. R. *oil industry executive*

Lincolnshire
Guist, Fredric Michael *minerals, chemicals and waste services corporation executive*

Lombard
†Grubb, Daniel B. *oil company executive*

Marion
Lincoln, Lucian Abraham *coal company executive*

Naperville
Reuss, Robert Pershing *telecommunications executive, consultant*
Triggiani, Leonard Vincent *corporate executive*

Northbrook
Demaree, David Harry *utilities executive*

Orland Park
English, Floyd Leroy *telecommunications company executive*

Peoria
Slone, R. Wayne *utility company executive*
Viets, Robert O. *utilities executive*

Rock Island
Whitmore, Charles Horace *utility executive, lawyer, management consultant*

Schaumburg
Splitt, Frank George *telecommunications company executive*

Springfield
Jackson, Robert William *utility company executive*

INDIANA

Evansville
Able, Warren Walter *natural resource company executive, physician*
Kiechlin, Robert Jerome *retired coal company executive, financial consultant*

Fort Wayne
Menge, Richard Cramer *electric utility executive*

Hammond
Adik, Stephen Peter *energy company executive*
†Burton, Charles Wesley *gas and electric company coordinator*
Neale, Gary Lee *utilities executive*
Schroer, Edmund Armin *utility company executive*

Indianapolis
Ellerbrook, Niel Cochran *gas company executive*
Ferger, Lawrence A. *gas distribution utility executive*
Griffiths, David Neil *utility executive*
Husted, Ralph Waldo *former utility executive*
Krueger, Betty Jane *telecommunications company executive*
Lindemann, Donald Lee *utility executive*
Morris, James Thomas *utilities executive*
Todd, Zane Grey *utility executive*

Lawrenceburg
Dautel, Charles Shreve *retired mining company executive*

Michigan City
Higgins, William Henry Clay, III *retired telecommunications consultant*

New Castle
Dudley, Harry Bruce *oil company executive*

Plainfield
Rogers, James Eugene *electric utility executive*

South Bend
Pfeil, Richard John *electric company executive*

IOWA

Cedar Rapids
Malès, René Henri *utility executive*

Centerville
†Liu, Lee *utility company executive*

Davenport
Bright, Stanley J. *utilities executive*

Des Moines
Christiansen, Russell *utility company executive*

Sioux City
Engle, Richard Carlyle *utilities executive*
Johnson, Marlys Dianne *utility company executive*
Wharton, Beverly Ann *utility company executive*

KANSAS

Derby
Barker, Gary Leland *mining company executive*

Hamilton
Lockard, Walter Junior *petroleum company executive*

Independence
Swearingen, Harold Lyndon *oil company executive*

Mc Pherson
Williams, Larry Emmett *oil company executive*

Shawnee Mission
Deaver, Darwin Holloway *former utility executive*

Topeka
Hayes, John Edward, Jr. *electric power industry executive*

Westwood
Esrey, William Todd *telecommunications company executive*

Wichita
Cadman, Wilson Kennedy *retired utility company executive*
Koch, Charles de Ganahl *corporation executive*
Lusk, William Edward *real estate, oil company executive*
Varner, Sterling Verl *retired oil company executive*

KENTUCKY

Ashland
Boyd, James Robert *oil company executive*
Chellgren, Paul Wilbur *petroleum company executive*
Dansby, John Walter *oil company executive*
Hall, John Richard *oil company executive*
Justice, Franklin Pierce, Jr. *oil company executive*
Lacy, James Daniel *oil company executive*
Weaver, Carlton Davis *retired oil company executive*
Yancey, Robert Earl, Jr. *oil company executive*

Lexington
†Newton, John Thomas *utility company executive*
†Whitley, Michael R. *utilities executive*

Louisville
Davidson, Michael Walker *energy company executive*
†Hale, Roger W. *utilities company executive*
†Higgins, Walter M., III *electric power industry executive*
Royer, Robert Lewis *retired utility company executive*

Owensboro
Best, Robert Wayne *gas transmission company executive, lawyer*
Carneal, James William *former natural gas corporation executive*

Russell
Crimmins, Sean T(homas) *oil company executive*

LOUISIANA

Baton Rouge
†Reilly, Sean E. *cable company executive*

Lafayette
†Clement, James Barney *oil company executive*
†Small, George M. *oil company executive*

Monroe
†Post, Glen Fleming, III *telecommunications executive*

New Orleans
Andrus, Gerald Louis *utilities holding company consultant*
Bachmann, Richard Arthur *oil company executive*
†Greene, John Frederick *oil company executive, geologist*
Kilanowski, Michael Charles, Jr. *oil, natural gas, minerals exploration company executive, lawyer*
Laborde, Alden James *oil company executive*
Laborde, John Peter *international energy company executive*
Lewis, Floyd Wallace *former electric utility executive*
Lind, Thomas Otto *utility company executive*
Mealey, George Allan *mining executive*
Moffett, James Robert *oil and gas company executive*
Murrish, Charles Howard *oil and gas exploration company executive, geologist*
Stephens, Richard Bernard *natural resource company executive*
Tusa, Joseph, Jr. *energy company financial executive*
Williamson, Ernest Lavone *petroleum company executive*
Wright, Thomas Joe *electric utility executive*

Shreveport
Roddey, John B(arber) (Bob Roddey) *gas and oil company executive, consultant*
Snow, William Hayden *retired utility company executive*
Zadeck, Donald Julian *oil and gas exploration company executive*

MAINE

Augusta
Hunter, Matthew *public utility executive*

Bangor
Roderick, Richard Michael *petroleum distribution and real estate company financial executive*

Portland
†Haynes, Peter Lancaster *utility holding company executive*

Surry
Kilgore, John Edward, Jr. *former petroleum company executive*

York Harbor
Curtis, Edward Joseph, Jr. *gas industry executive, management consultant*

MARYLAND

Annapolis
Ellis, George Fitzallen, Jr. *energy services company executive*

Baltimore
Crooke, Edward A. *utility company executive*
Ihrie, Robert *oil, gas and real estate company executive*
McGowan, George Vincent *public utility executive*
Poindexter, Christian Herndon *utility company executive*
Rosenberg, Henry A., Jr. *petroleum executive*

Bethesda
McMurphy, Michael Allen *energy company executive, lawyer*
Olmsted, Jerauld Lockwood *telephone company executive*
Pritchard, Wilbur Louis *telecommunications engineering executive*

Frederick
†Triebe, John Roger *oil company executive*

Glen Arm
Jackson, Theodore Marshall *retired oil company executive*

Kensington
Marienthal, George *telecommunications company executive*

Rockville
Pollack, Louis *telecommunications company executive*

Silver Spring
Jacobs, George *telecommunications engineering consulting company executive*

MASSACHUSETTS

Boston
Burns, Richard Michael *public utility company executive*
Davis, George Wilmot *electric utility executive*
Eichorn, John Frederick Gerard, Jr. *utility executive*
Pardus, Donald Gene *utility executive*

Centerville
Anderson, Gerald Edwin *utilities executive*
Scherer, Harold Nicholas, Jr. *electric utility company executive, engineer*

Edgartown
Walsh, Philip Cornelius *mining consultant*

Harwich Port
Staszesky, Francis Myron *electric company consultant*

Lexington
Phillips, Thomas L. *corporate executive*

Marblehead
Dolan, John Ralph *retired corporation executive*
†Krebs, James Norton *retired electric power industry executive*
Pruyn, William J. *energy industry executive*

Waltham
†McManmon, Thomas Arthur, Jr. *oil industry executive*
Slifka, Alfred A. *oil corporation executive*

Westborough
Bok, Joan Toland *utility executive*
Greenman, Frederic Edward *utility executive*
Houston, Alfred Dearborn *energy company executive*
Rowe, John William *utility executive*
Young, Roger Austin *natural gas distribution company executive*

MICHIGAN

Dearborn
Smith, Stanton Kinnie, Jr. *utility executive*

Detroit
Dortch, Heyward *utility company executive*
Earley, Anthony Francis, Jr. *utilities company executive, lawyer*
Easlick, David Kenneth *telephone company executive*
Garberding, Larry Gilbert *utilities companies executive*
Glancy, Alfred Robinson, III *public utility company executive*
Lobbia, John E. *utility company executive*
†McCrackin, William K. *gas company executive*
McIntyre, Ronald Llewellyn *electric utility executive*
Schiffer, Daniel L. *gas company executive*
Simpkin, Lawrence James *utilities executive*

Grosse Pointe
Trebilcott, James Joseph *former utility executive*

Jackson
†Buckman, Frederick W. *gas utility executive*
McCormick, William Thomas, Jr. *electric and gas company executive*
Patrick, Ueal Eugene *oil company executive*
†Wright, Gordon Lee *oil company executive*

Lake Leelanau
Shannahan, John Henry Kelly *energy consultant*

Midland
Boulanger, Rodney Edmund *energy company executive*

Owosso
Hoddy, George Warren *electric company executive, electrical engineer*

Port Huron
Kirby, Ward Nelson *gas company executive*
Thomson, Robert James *natural gas distribution company executive*

MINNESOTA

Eden Prairie
Emison, James W. *petroleum company executive*

Fergus Falls
Emmen, Dennis R. *electric utility executive*
Hartl, Albert Victor *utility executive*

Minneapolis
Cadogan, William J. (Bill Cadogan) *telecommunications company executive*
Gudorf, Kenneth Francis *business executive*
Jensen, Roland Jens *utility company executive*
Wyman, James Thomas *petroleum company executive*

Saint Paul
Estenson, Noel K. *gas, oil industry executive*
Frame, Clarence George *retired oil and gas refining company executive*
Robertson, Jerry Earl *retired mining and manuracturing company executive*

MISSISSIPPI

Jackson
Dallas, Thomas Abraham *retired utility company executive*
†Kingsley, Oliver Dowling, Jr. *energy company executive*
†Lampton, Leslie B., Sr. *oil industry executive*
Stampley, Norris Lochlen *former electric utility executive*

MISSOURI

Joplin
Fancher, Robert Burney *electric utility executive*
Lamb, Robert Lewis *electric utility executive*

Kansas City
Baker, John Russell *utilities executive*
Molz, Otis *oil industry executive*
Wolf, Dale Joseph *utilities company executive*

Lebanon
Dryden, Martin Francis, Jr. *retired gas company executive*
†Plaster, Stephen Robert *gas company executive*

Liberty
†Ferrell, James Edwin *energy company executive*

Saint Louis
Adorjan, J(ulius) Joe *electric company executive*
Bentele, Raymond F. *retired minerals corporate executive*
Brown, Melvin F. *telecommunications industry executive*
Cornelius, William Edward *utilities company executive*
Dougherty, Charles Joseph *retired utility executive*
Elliott, Howard, Jr. *gas distribution company executive*
Gilbert, Allan Arthur *utilities executive*
Goldstein, Samuel R. *oil company executive*
Kelley, Richard Alan *electric utility executive*
†Leer, Steven F. *mining executive*
Liberman, Lee Marvin *utility executive*
Mueller, Charles William *electric utility executive*
†Munk, Peter *oil industry executive*
†Novelly, Paul A. *petrochemical and refining company executive*
Quenon, Robert Hagerty *consultant, retired holding company executive*
†Samples, Ronald Eugene *coal company executive*
†Sigurdson, Erik D. *oil industry executive*
Thompson, James Clark *utilities executive*

Springfield
Boehm, Robert Kenneth *telecommunications consultant*
Jura, James J. *electric utility executive*

MONTANA

Bigfork
Shennum, Robert Herman *retired telephone company executive*

Billings
Reed, Kenneth G. *petroleum company executive*

Butte
Burke, John James *utility executive*
Mc Elwain, Joseph Arthur *retired power company executive*
†Sherick, John Matthew (Jack Sherick) *technical services company executive*

NEBRASKA

Lincoln
†Geist, James E. *telecommunication company executive*
†Tavlin, Michael John *telecommunications company executive*

Omaha
Grewcock, William L. *mining company executive*

NEVADA

Las Vegas
†Guinn, Kenny C. *utility company executive*
Laub, William Murray *retired utility executive*
Trimble, Thomas James *utility company executive, lawyer*

Zephyr Cove
Proctor, Robert Swope *retired petroleum company executive*

NEW HAMPSHIRE

Portsmouth
†Bulmer, Edward E. *oil industry executive*
Powers, Henry Martin, Jr. *oil company executive*
Tillinghast, John Avery *technology company executive*

NEW JERSEY

Basking Ridge
Bodman, Richard Stockwell *telecommunications executive*
Collis, Sidney Robert *retired telephone company executive*
Condon, Verner Holmes, Jr. *retired utility executive*

Bedminster
Kean, John *utility company executive*

Bloomingdale
Baeder, Donald Lee *petroleum and chemical company executive, financial consultant*

Chatham
Bast, Ray Roger *retired utility company executive*

Chester
Gurian, Mal *telecommunications executive*

Collingswood
Mohrfeld, Richard Gentel *heating oil distributing company executive*

Edison
†Francis, Peter T. *gas and oil industry executive*
†Huber, Michael W. *petroleum company executive*
Schenk, George *oil industry executive*

Fair Haven
Gagnebin, Albert Paul *retired mining executive*

Far Hills
Ellsworth, Duncan Steuart, Jr. *retired utility company executive*

Folsom
Levitt, Gerald Steven *natural gas company executive*

Fort Lee
Schiessler, Robert Walter *retired chemical and oil company executive*
Weitzer, Bernard *telecommunications executive*

Holmdel
Heirman, Donald Nestor *telecommunications engineering company manager*

Lake Hopatcong
Dowling, Robert Murray *oil company executive*

Montvale
Smernoff, Richard Louis *oil company executive*

Morristown
Reed, Rex Raymond *retired telephone company executive*

Murray Hill
Cohen, Melvin Irwin *telephone company executive*
Dyer, Alexander Patrick *industrial gas manufacturing company executive*
Mayo, John Sullivan *telecommunications company executive*

Newark
Bhavaraju, Murty Parabrahma *electric utility executive*
Codey, Lawrence R. *electric power company executive*
Ferland, E. James *electric utility executive*
†Marano, Rocco John *telephone company executive*

Nutley
Mallard, Stephen Anthony *retired utility company executive*

Parsippany
Clark, Philip Raymond *nuclear utility executive, engineer*
Graham, John Gourlay *utility company executive*
Leva, James Robert *electric utility company executive*
Raber, Marvin *utility company executive*

Princeton
Farley, Edward Raymond, Jr. *mining and manufacturing company executive*
Holst, Willem *oil company executive*
Mc Cullough, John Price *retired oil company executive*
Penick, Joe Edward *petroleum consultant*
Wise, John James *oil company executive*

Red Bank
Chynoweth, Alan Gerald *telecommunications research executive*
†Koch, Udo *oil industry executive*

Scotch Plains
Avery, James Stephen *oil company executive*

Summit
Mathis, James Forrest *retired petroleum company executive*
†Pollak, Henry Otto *retired utility research executive, educator*

Surf City
Aurner, Robert Ray, II *oil company, auto diagnostic, restaurant franchise and company development executive*

Union
Bahniuk, Frank Theodore *utility company executive*

Voorhees
Lewis, Marilyn Ware *water company executive*

Wall
Colford, Francis Xavier *gas industry executive*

Wayne
†Crane, Thomas R., Jr. *oil industry executive*

Whippany
†Spina, Dennis J. *gas industry executive*

Woodbridge
D'Amico, Andrew John *oil company executive*

NEW MEXICO

Albuquerque
Eaton, George Wesley, Jr. *oil company executive*
Gorham, Frank DeVore, Jr. *petroleum company executive*

Farmington
Swetnam, Monte Newton *petroleum exploration executive*

Hobbs
Garey, Donald Lee *pipeline and oil company executive*

Roswell
Anderson, Donald Bernard *oil company executive*
Anderson, Robert Orville *oil and gas company executive*

Santa Fe
Pickrell, Thomas Richard *retired oil company executive*

NEW YORK

Babylon
Lopez, Joseph Jack *oil company executive, consultant*

Beacon
Pollart, Dale F(lavian) *petroleum company research executive*

Bedford
†Jalkut, Richard Alan *telecommunications executive*

Binghamton
Carrigg, James A. *utility company executive*
Fleming, Russell, Jr. *utility company executive, lawyer*

Brooklyn
Matthews, Craig Gerard *gas company executive*
Murphy, Edward Patrick, Jr. *gas utility company executive*
Shaw, Maurice Kenneth *utility company executive*

Buffalo
Ackerman, Philip Charles *utility executive, lawyer*

Elizabethtown
Lawrence, Richard Wesley, Jr. *mining executive*

Garden City
†Glass, Arthur *mining company executive*

Huntington Station
Pierce, Charles R. *electric company consultant*

Ithaca
Farley, Daniel W. *lawyer, utility company executive*

Jericho
Fitteron, John Joseph *petroleum products company executive*
Salzman, Stephen Philip *petroleum company executive*

Long Island City
Carey, Edward John *utility executive*

New York
Allen, Ralph Dean *telecommunications corporate executive*
Alonzo, Martin Vincent *mining and aluminum company executive, investor, financial consultant*
Alpert, Warren *oil company executive, philanthropist*
Anderson, Arthur N. *retired utility company executive*
Araskog, Rand Vincent *diversified telecommunications multinational company executive*
Baird, Dugald Euan *oil field service company executive*
Belknap, Norton *petroleum company consultant*
Bernstein, Alan Arthur *oil company executive*
Case, Hadley *oil company executive*
Cookson, Albert Ernest *telephone and telegraph company executive*
Damson, Barrie Morton *oil and gas exploration company executive*
Delaney, Robert Vincent *former gas company executive, economic development consultant*
Delz, William Ronald *petroleum company executive*
Edelman, Thomas Jeffery *oil company executive*
Ferguson, William Charles *telecommunications executive*
†Flynn, Richard Michael *utilities executive*
Fontaine, Edward Paul *mining company executive*
Gelfand, Neal *oil company executive*
Genin, Roland *energy executive*
Giusti, Gino Paul *natural resources company executive*
Greene, Carl William *utility company executive*
Heile, Leo James *information technology executive*
Hess, Leon *oil company executive*
†Hodapp, Siegfried *petroleum industry executive*
†Hornby, Geoffrey *oil industry executive*
Host, Stig *oil company executive*
Jamin, Gerald Alan *petroleum company executive*
Kramer, Philip *retired petroleum refining executive*
Laidlaw, William Samuel Hugh *oil company executive*
Levy, Walter James *oil consultant*
Luce, Charles Franklin *former utilities executive, lawyer*
Malozemoff, Plato *mining executive*
McGrath, Eugene R. *utility company executive*
Osborne, Richard de Jongh *mining and metals company executive*
†Pennoyer, Russell Parsons *oil company executive*
Rawn, Stanley Ryle, Jr. *oil company executive*
Richards, Reuben Francis *natural resource company executive*
Staley, Delbert C. *telecommunications executive*
Steinmetz, Richard Bird, Jr. *holding company executive, lawyer*
Stoddart, George Anderson *oil service company executive*
Underweiser, Irwin Philip *mining company executive, lawyer*
Warner, Rawleigh, Jr. *oil company executive*
Wohlstetter, Charles *telephone company executive*
Wright, Robert F. *petroleum products company executive*

Niskayuna
Fitzroy, Nancy deLoye *technology executive, engineer*

Pearl River
Fischer, Frank Ernest *utility executive*
McBennett, Robert Joseph *utility executive*
Smith, James Francis *utilities executive*

Penfield
Amish, Keith Warren *retired utility executive*

Poughkeepsie
Mack, John Edward, III *utility company executive*

Purchase
Dwyer, Andrew T. *utility and utility service company executive*

Rochester
Laniak, David Konstantyn *utility company executive*

Schenectady
Robb, Walter Lee *retired electric company executive, management company executive*

Setauket
Vetog, Edwin Joseph *retired gas utility executive*

Southold
Knight, Harold Edwin Holm, Jr. *utility company executive*

Syosset
Vermylen, Paul Anthony, Jr. *oil company executive*

Syracuse
Davis, William E. *utility executive*
Endries, John Michael *utility executive*
Ranalli, Michael Patrick *utility company executive*

West Nyack
Gillespie, John Fagan *mining executive*

White Plains
Bijur, Peter I. *petroleum company executive*
Brazell, James Ervin *oil company executive, lawyer*
Davidson, Carl B. *oil company executive*
DeCrane, Alfred Charles, Jr. *petroleum company executive*
Dickinson, Richard Raymond *oil company executive*
Krowe, Allen Julian *oil company executive*
Smith, Elizabeth Patience *oil industry executive, lawyer*
Tell, William Kirn, Jr. *oil company executive, lawyer*

NORTH CAROLINA

Brevard
Wall, Robert Wilson, Jr. *former utility executive*

Cary
Jones, James Arthur *retired utilities executive*

Charlotte
Davenport, Dona Lee *telecommunications consultant*
Grigg, William Humphrey *utility executive*
Lee, William States *utility executive*
Osborne, Richard Jay *electric utility company executive*
Owen, Warren Herbert *utility executive*
Thies, Austin Cole *retired utility company executive*

Durham
Ferguson, David Robert *energy research manager*

Hendersonville
Haynes, John Mabin *retired utilities executive*

Pinehurst
Amspoker, James Mack *retired gas company executive*

Raleigh
Barham, Charles Dewey, Jr. *electric utility executive, lawyer*
Cox, Herbert Bartle *natural gas company executive*
Graham, William Edgar, Jr. *utility company executive, lawyer*
Smith, Sherwood Hubbard, Jr. *utilities executive*

NORTH DAKOTA

Bismarck
Schuchart, John Albert, Jr. *utility executive*

Minot
†Tollefson, Ben C. *sales manager, retired, financial consultant*

OHIO

Akron
Holland, Willard Raymond, Jr. *electric utility executive*
Rogers, Justin Towner, Jr. *retired utility company executive*
Spetrino, Russell John *retired utility company executive, lawyer*

Chagrin Falls
Nyberg, Donald Arvid *oil company executive*

Cincinnati
Raskin, Fred Charles *transportation and utility holding company executive*
Victor, William Weir *retired telephone company executive, consultant*

Cleveland
Blodgett, Omer William *electric company design consultant*
†Calfee, William Rushton *mining company executive*
†Chase, R. F. *oil industry executive*
Connelly, John James *oil company technical specialist*
Donaldson, Richard Miesse *retired oil company executive, lawyer*
Edelman, Murray R. *utility company executive*
Farling, Robert J. *utility company executive*
Ginn, Robert Martin *retired utility company executive*
Hastings, Donald F. *electric company executive*

Long, Kenneth Robert *natural gas company executive, lawyer*
Meyer, Gerald Justin *energy company executive*
†Percy, S. W. *oil industry executive*
Scovil, Samuel Kingston *mining company executive*
Thompson, Renold Durant *mining and shipping executive*
White, Fred Rollin, Jr. *mining and shipping company executive*

Columbus
DeMaria, Peter James *utility company executive*
Disbrow, Richard Edwin *retired utility executive*
Draper, E(rnest) Linn, Jr. *electric utility executive*
Feck, Luke Matthew *utility executive*
Maloney, Gerald P. *utility executive*
Mc Caffrey, Thomas R. *utilities company executive*
Schafer, William Harry *electric power industry executive*
†Tilley, C. Ronald *gas company executive*
Vassell, Gregory S. *electric utility consultant*

Findlay
Frank, J. Louis *oil company executive*
Yammine, Riad Nassif *oil company executive*

Independence
Hawkinson, Gary Michael *utility holding company executive*

Massillon
Dawson, Robert Earle *utilities executive*

Perrysburg
Williamson, John Pritchard *utility executive*

Rocky Ridge
†Cruft, Edgar Frank *mining company executive*

Sharonville
Ehrnschwender, Arthur Robert *former utility company executive*

Toledo
Saunders, Donald Herbert *utility company executive*

OKLAHOMA

Bartlesville
Allen, W. Wayne *oil industry executive*
Armstrong, Oliver Wendell *oil company executive*
Arnold, Philip Mills *retired oil company executive*
Cox, Glenn Andrew, Jr. *petroleum company executive*
Silas, Cecil Jesse *retired petroleum company executive*
Wallace, Robert Glenn *petroleum company executive*

Enid
Ward, Llewellyn O(rcutt), III *oil producer*

Oklahoma City
Abernathy, Jack Harvey *petroleum, utility company and banking executive*
†Adcock, James Michael *oil company executive, lawyer*
Campbell, David Gwynne *petroleum executive, geologist*
Hambrick, Marvin K. *energy company executive*
Harlan, Ross Edgar *retired utility company executive, writer, lecturer, consultant*
Harlow, James Gindling, Jr. *utility executive*
Kirkpatrick, John Elson *oil company executive, retired naval reserve officer*
McKenny, Jere Wesley *energy firm executive*
Mee, Herb, Jr. *natural resource/environmental services executive*
†Nichols, J. Larry *energy company executive, lawyer*
O'Keeffe, Hugh Williams *oil industry executive*
Peace, H. W., II *oil company executive*
Ryan, Patrick J. *electric utility company executive*

Oktaha
Taylor, Clayton Charles *oil company executive, rancher*

Tulsa
Anderson, Peer LaFollette *petroleum corporation executive*
Barnes, James E. *energy company executive*
Berlin, Steven Ritt *oil company financial official*
Braumiller, Allen Spooner *oil and gas exploration company executive, geologist*
Dotson, George Stephen *drilling company executive*
Fate, Martin Eugene, Jr. *utility company executive*
Hall, Ronald E. *oil company executive*
Helmerich, Hans Christian *oil company executive*
Helmerich, Walter Hugo, III *oil company executive*
Horkey, William Richard *retired diversified oil company executive*
Howe, Robert Melvin *oil company executive*
Hulings, Norman McDermott, Jr. *energy consultant, former company executive*
Ingram, Charles Clark, Jr. *energy company executive*
King, Peter Cotterill *former utilities executive*
Lowd, Judson Dean *oil and gas processing equipment manufacturing executive*
McConnell, Charles Goodloe *service company executive*
Neas, John Theodore *petroleum company executive*
Newman, Richard Oakley *utilities executive, consultant*
O'Toole, Allan Thomas *electric utility executive*
Parker, Robert Lee, Jr. *drilling company executive*
Robertson, Peter James *oil company executive*
†Scott, J. D. *oil company executive*
Shafer, J. M. *utility administrator*
Williford, Richard Allen *oil executive, flight simulator company executive*

OREGON

Albany
Ball, Douglas Schelling *oil, gas and mining consultant*

Corvallis
Godfrey, Samuel Addison *retired telephone company executive*

Portland
Frisbee, Don Calvin *retired utilities executive*
Hardy, Randall Webster *utility executive*
Harrison, Ken L. *holding company and electric utility executive*
Hathaway, Paul L., Jr. *natural gas company executive*
†Heiner, Lawrence Elden *mineral company executive*
Hill, Francis Frederick *gas company executive*
Jungers, Francis *oil consultant*
McCall, William Calder *oil and chemical company executive*
Nofziger, Sally Alene *diversified utility company executive*
Reiten, Richard G. *electric power industry executive*
Short, Robert Henry *retired utility executive*

Sunriver
Jamison, Harrison Clyde *former oil company executive, petroleum exploration consultant*

PENNSYLVANIA

Allentown
Gabel, Ronald Glen *telecommunications executive*
Gadomski, Robert Eugene *chemical and industrial gas company executive*
Hecht, William F. *electric power industry executive*
Wagner, Harold A. *industrial gas and chemical company executive*

Bryn Mawr
Ballam, Samuel Humes, Jr. *retired corporate director*
Braha, Thomas I. *business executive*
Dunlop, Robert Galbraith *retired petroleum company executive*

Coraopolis
Koepfinger, Joseph Leo *utilities executive*

Farmington
Witt, Charles E. *coal company executive*

Gladwyne
Patten, Lanny Ray *industrial gas industry executive*

Indiana
Kegel, William George *mining company executive*

Johnstown
Simmons, Elroy, Jr. *retired utility executive*
Wise, Robert Lester *utilities executive*

King Of Prussia
†Dungan, Ronald Samuel *utility executive*

Monroeville
Penman, Paul Duane *nuclear power laboratory executive*

Newtown
Denoon, Clarence England, Jr. *business executive*

Oil City
Baum, Herbert Merrill *motor oil company executive*
†Berry, James D., III *oil company executive*
Olson, Robert Edward *coal mining executive*
Wood, Quentin Eugene *oil company executive*

Philadelphia
†Albertini, William Oliver *telecommunications industry executive*
Bardeen, William Leonard *electric utility executive*
Binder, Lucy Simpson *utility company executive*
Calman, Robert Frederick *mining executive*
Campbell, Robert H. *oil company executive*
Cullen, James G. *telecommunications industry executive*
Heilig, William Wright *coal and manufacturing company executive*
†Hughes, Daniel I. *oil company executive, real estate investor*
Hutchinson, Pemberton *coal company executive*
†Knoll, David E. *petroleum refining company executive*
McNeill, Corbin Asahel, Jr. *utility executive*
Paquette, Joseph F., Jr. *utility company executive*
Rimerman, Morton Walter *utility executive*
Smith, Raymond W. *telecommunications company executive*
Thompson, Sheldon Lee *refining company executive*
Valentini, Robert M. *telecommunications industry executive*
Veith, Richard Lee *oil company executive*

Pittsburgh
Arthur, John Morrison *retired utility executive*
Bartley, Burnett Graham, Jr. *oil company and manufacturing executive*
Brown, Bobby R. *coal company executive*
Caldwell, John Gilmore *oil and gas exploration and production executive*
†Chun, Sun W. *energy technology administrator*
Cummins, James Dale *coal executive*
Davidson, George A., Jr. *utility company executive*
Hammer, Harold Harlan *oil company financial executive*
La Rue, Henry Aldred *consultant, former oil company executive*
†McDonald, C. W. *mining executive*
Mc Featters, Dale Stitt *retired electric company executive*
Moeller, Audrey Carolyn *energy company executive, corporate secretary*
Moritz, Donald I. *energy company executive*
†Murphy, John N. *mining executive, researcher, electrical engineer*
Schwass, Gary L. *utilities executive*
Stern, Theodore *electric company executive*
von Schack, Wesley W. *energy holding company executive*
Welfer, Thomas, Jr. *utility company executive*
Williams, Charles David *oil and steel company executive*

Port Allegany
Failey, George Leo, Jr. *retired public utility executive*

Radnor
Burtis, Theodore Alfred *oil company executive*

Reading
Hafer, Frederick Douglass *utility executive*

Uniontown
Eberly, Robert Edward *oil and gas production company executive*

Valley Forge
Sutton, James Andrew *diversified utility company executive*

Wayne
Lefevre, Thomas Vernon *retired utility company executive, lawyer*

Wilkes Barre
†Parente, Charles Eugene *telecommunications executive*

Wynnewood
Boyer, Vincent Saull *energy consultant*

RHODE ISLAND

Barrington
O'Toole, John Dudley *retired utility executive, consultant*

Lincoln
Gulvin, David Horner *electric company executive*

Providence
†Dodge, James H. *energy industry executive*
†Owens, Robert Warren *energy company executive*
Watkins, William, Jr. *electric power industry executive*

SOUTH CAROLINA

Columbia
†Gressette, Lawrence M., Jr. *utilities executive*
†Hallman, Harry M., Jr. *retired oil company executive*

Hilton Head Island
Simpson, John Wistar *energy consultant, former manufacturing company executive*

Johns Island
Behnke, Wallace Blanchard, Jr. *consultant, engineer, retired utility executive*

Moncks Corner
†Rainear, Robert E. *utilities executive*

North Charleston
Zucker, Jerry *energy systems manufacturing executive*

North Myrtle Beach
Atkinson, Harold Witherspoon *utilities consultant, real estate broker*

SOUTH DAKOTA

Huron
Schmidt, Albert Daniel *utility executive*
Wilkens, Robert Allen *utilities executive, electrical engineer*

Pierre
†Dunn, James Bernard *mining company executive, state legislator*

Rapid City
†Landguth, Daniel P. *utility executive*

TENNESSEE

Kingsport
†Matthews, Vincent, III *oil company executive*

Knoxville
Bell, Thomas Rowe *retired natural gas transmission company executive*
Malec, William Frank *utilities company executive*

Memphis
Cox, Terry Allen *telecommunications executive*

Nashville
Clark, Frank Rinker, Jr. *retired pipeline company executive*
Cordaro, Matthew Charles *utility executive, energy developer, engineer*
†Ingram, E. Bronson *oil industry executive*
†Merrills, Roy *telecommunications industry executive*

Oak Ridge
Jasny, George Roman *retired energy company executive*

TEXAS

Abilene
Stephens, Brad *oil industry executive*

Austin
Deisler, Paul Frederick, Jr. *retired oil company executive*
Haas, Joseph Marshall *petroleum consultant*
Preeg, William Edward *oil company executive*

Beaumont
Cobb, Leslie Davis *utility executive*

Donnelly, Joseph Lennon *utility company executive*
Long, Alfred B. *retired oil company executive, consultant*
Smith, Floyd Rodenback *utilities executive*

Blanco
Finley, James Edward *independent oil operator*

College Station
Jordan, Wayne Robert *water resources executive, crop physiology educator*
Neff, Ray Quinn *electric power consultant*

Corpus Christi
Haas, Paul Raymond *petroleum company executive*
Paulson, Bernard Arthur *oil company executive, consultant*

Dallas
†Barnes, John R. *petroleum company executive*
Biegler, David W. *gas company executive*
Blackburn, Charles Lee *oil company executive*
Blessing, Edward Warfield *petroleum company executive*
†Boyce, Charles A. *oil company executive, lawyer, arbitrator*
Brooks, E. R. (Dick Brooks) *utility company executive*
Brown, Benjamin A. *gas, oil industry executive*
Cahill, William Joseph, Jr. *utility company executive*
Copp, Emmanuel Anthony *oil company executive*
†Cunyus, George Marvin *oil company executive*
Farrington, Jerry *utility holding company executive*
Fielder, Charles Robert *oil industry executive*
Fowler, Robert Glen *exploration company executive*
Goss, James Walter *oil company executive*
Haddock, Ronald Wayne *oil company executive*
Harbin, John Pickens *oil well company executive*
Hauptfuhrer, Robert Paul *oil company executive*
†Hunt, Ray Lee *petroleum company executive*
Jeffett, Frank Asbury *former oil company and insurance company executive, business consultant*
Jones, Dale P. *service company executive*
†Keiser, R. L. *gas and oil industry executive*
Maguire, Cary McIlwaine *oil company executive*
Maycock, Ian David *oil executive*
McCord, William Charles *retired diversified energy company executive*
McCormick, James Edward *oil company executive*
McCullough, George Bierce *oil company executive*
Meek, Paul Derald *oil and chemical company executive*
Moneypenny, Edward William *oil and gas mining executive*
Notestine, Wilbur Edmund *energy company executive, lawyer*
Nurenberg, David *oil company executive*
Nye, Erle Allen *utilities executive, lawyer*
Perry, Kenneth Walter *integrated oil company executive*
Pickens, Thomas Boone, Jr. *oil company executive*
Pryor, Richard Walter *telecommunications executive, retired air force officer*
Shoup, Andrew James, Jr. *oil company executive*
Sizer, Phillip Spelman *consultant, retired oil field services executive*
Welch, Carol Ann *oil company executive*
†Willrich, Mason *utility company executive*
Winters, J. Otis *industry consultant*

El Paso
Hoskins, Curtis Lynn *utility executive*
Wise, William Allan *oil company executive, lawyer*

Fort Worth
Bass, Perry Richardson *oil company executive*
Diwoky, Roy John *petroleum executive*
Gearhart, Marvin *oil company executive*
Hyde, Clarence Brodie, II *oil company executive*
Walsh, F. Howard *oil producer, rancher*
Zimmerman, Bill J. *oil company executive, lawyer*

Galveston
Ewing, George H. *pipeline company executive*

Houston
Adair, Red (Paul Neal Adair) *oil well problem control specialist*
Allison, Robert James, Jr. *oil and gas company executive*
†Allison, William V. *oil industry executive*
Anderson, William (Albion), Jr. *oil and gas producer, investment banker*
†Andrews, Glenn T. *oil company executive*
†Andrews, Mark Edwin, III *oil and gas exploration company executive*
†Avery, Nathan Mark *oilfield equipment and services company executive*
Bankston, Gene Clifton *oil and gas consultant*
Barney, Charles Lester *petroleum company executive*
Barrow, Thomas Davies *oil and mining company executive*
Beghini, Victor Gene *oil company executive*
†Bennett, Richard Gerald *gas company executive*
Benninger, Edward C., Jr. *petroleum and natural gas company executive*
Bonneville, Richard Briggs *petroleum exploration and production executive*
Bookout, John Frank, Jr. *oil company executive*
Bowen, W. J. *gas company executive*
†Bowersox, Thomas H. *executive*
Bryan, James Lee *oil field service company executive*
†Bryan, J(ames) P(erry), Jr. *energy company executive*
Burguieres, Philip *energy service and manufacturing company executive*
Capps, Ethan LeRoy *oil company executive*
Carameros, George Demitrius, Jr. *natural gas company executive*
Carroll, Philip Joseph *oil company executive*
Carter, John Boyd, Jr. *oil operator, bank executive*
†Catell, Robert Barry *gas utility executive*
Chalmers, David B. *petroleum executive*
Chiste, Robert Matthew *energy company executive*
Clayton, William Lewis *retired utility executive*
†Cline, C. Bob *natural gas company executive*
Conger, Franklin Barker *oil company executive*
Coon, Julian Barham *energy company executive*
DesBarres, John P. *energy company executive*
Dickey, Duval Frederick *business consultant, former energy company executive*
†Dillard, Max Murray *international drilling contractor*
Drury, Leonard Leroy *retired oil company executive*

Dunlap, James Lapham *petroleum company executive*
Edens, Donald Keith *oil company executive*
Elers, Karl Emerson *mining company executive*
†Ellerbeck, Ronald L. *oil industry executive*
†Erikson, Sheldon R. *oil field services company executive*
Farmer, Joe Sam *petroleum company executive*
Ferrand, Jean C. *oil company executive*
Foster, Joe B. *oil company executive*
Frank, George Willard (Will Frank) *oil company executive, consultant*
Fulwiler, Robert Neal *oil company executive*
†Garner, Thomas Ward *petroleum company executive*
†Garrison, Martha *oil industry executive*
Gerard, Roy Dupuy *oil company executive*
Gibson, Jerry Leigh *oil company executive*
Goodman, Herbert Irwin *petroleum company executive*
Gower, Bob G. *gas and oil industry executive*
Guinn, David Crittenden *petroleum engineer, drilling and exploration company executive*
Haas, Merrill Wilber *geologist, oil company executive*
Halbouty, Michel Thomas *geologist, petroleum engineer, petroleum operator*
†Hardcastle, Kenneth Lloyd *oil company executive*
Hardin, George Cecil, Jr. *petroleum consultant*
Harrison, Otto R. *oil industry executive*
†Hedrick, Kirby L. *petroleum company executive*
Hendrix, Dennis R. *energy company executive*
Hesse, Martha O. *natural gas company executive*
†Hoglund, Forrest Eugene *petroleum company executive*
Homeyer, Howard C. *energy consultant*
†Howard, R. L. *oil industry executive*
†Huff, John Rossman *oil service company executive*
Hurwitz, Charles Edwin *oil company executive*
Jamieson, John Kenneth *oil field services company executive*
Johnson, Ashmore Clark, Jr. *oil company executive*
Johnson, Kenneth Oscar *oil company executive*
Johnson, Wayne D. *utility executive*
Jordan, Don D. *electric company executive*
Jorden, James Roy *oil company engineering executive*
Kelley, David Lee *oil company executive, petroleum engineer*
Kerr, Baine Perkins *oil company executive*
Kinder, Richard Dan *natural gas pipeline, oil and gas company executive*
Kirkland, John David *oil and gas company executive, lawyer*
Koonce, Kenneth Terry *oil company executive*
Kuntz, Hal Goggan *petroleum exploration company executive*
†Lackey, S. Allen *petroleum company executive, corporate lawyer*
†Lassiter, Ronald Corbett *oil company executive*
Liedtke, John Hugh *petroleum company executive*
Linker, Jonathan Steven *natural resources company executive*
Little, Jack Edward *oil company executive*
Long, William Everett *retired utility executive*
Loveland, Eugene Franklin *petroleum executive*
Ludwig, Vernell Patrick *gas pipeline company executive*
Luigs, Charles Russell *business executive*
Mackie, David F. *gas company executive*
†Maddox, Lyndell Eugene *gas company executive*
Mai, Klaus L. *oil research company executive*
Martin, Jerry C. *oil company executive*
†Matthews, Thomas Michael *energy company executive*
Mc Call, Robert R. *retired oil company executive*
Mc Donnell, John Thomas *energy consultant, former oil and gas company executive*
Mc Fedries, Robert, Jr. *power industry executive, chemical engineer*
Meyer, Randall *retired oil company executive*
Miller, Kenneth William *holding company executive, financier*
Monroe, L. A. J. *oil well drilling company executive*
Morrow, Samuel Roy, III *oil service company executive*
Mosbacher, Robert Adam *oil and gas industry executive, politican*
†Mottale, Mois *oil industry executive*
†Muckleroy, Jon Michael *oil company executive*
Muse, Ewell Henderson, III *gas company executive*
Nanz, Robert Hamilton *petroleum consultant*
Nestvold, Elwood Olaf *oil service company executive*
Nicandros, Constantine Stavros *oil company executive*
O'Connor, Lawrence Joseph, Jr. *energy consultant*
O'Neal, Bob H. *utilities company executive*
†Palmer, Charles Robert *oil well drilling company executive*
†Panatier, M. J. *gas industry executive*
Pate, James Leonard *oil company executive*
Paul, James Robert *oil and gas mining company executive*
†Payne, James L. *energy company executive*
†Pester, Jack Cloyd *oil company executive*
Prentice, James Stuart *energy company executive, chemical engineer*
Richardson, Frank H. *retired oil industry executive*
Roff, J(ohn) Hugh, Jr. *energy company executive*
Rossler, Willis Kenneth, Jr. *petroleum company executive*
†Sadler, M. Whitson *petroleum company executive*
Segner, Edmund Peter, III *natural gas company executive*
†Slack, David Stephen *oil company executive*
Smith, Lloyd Hilton *independent oil and gas producer*
Snedeker, Robert D. *air transportation executive*
Stewart, Cornelius James, II *utilities company executive*
Sykora, Donald D. *utility company executive*
†Tauber, Orner J., Jr. *petrochemical company executive*
Trusty, Roy Lee *former oil company executive*
†Van Lanen, James L. *natural resource company executive*
†Watson, C. L. (Chuck Watson) *gas industry executive*
Wilson, Edward Converse, Jr. *oil and natural gas production company executive*
Winslow, Robert Albert *retired petroleum industry executive, consultant*
Wolf, Erving *oil company executive*
†Wood, D. Dale *oil and gas industry executive*
Wray, Marc Frederick *minerals company executive*
Wyatt, Oscar Sherman, Jr. *energy company executive*

Ingram
Hughes, David Michael *oil service company executive*

Irving
Bayne, James Elwood *oil company executive*
Hess, Edwin John *oil company executive*
Le Vine, Duane Gilbert *petroleum company executive*
Lutz, Matthew Charles *geologist, oil company executive*
†McBrayer, H. Eugene *retired petroleum industry executive*
Mundy, William Greg *telecommunications company executive, lawyer*
†Ward, Patrick J. *oil industry executive*

Lewisville
Bickel, Herbert Jacob, Jr. *corporation executive*

Midland
Reed, Joel Leston *diversified manufacturing company executive*

Plano
Odeh, Aziz Salim *retired oil company scientist*
Schuh, Frank Joseph *drilling engineering company executive, consultant*
†Thompson, J. Ken *gas, oil industry executive*

Richardson
†Denton, Jere Michael *oil company executive*
McDaniel, Dolan Kenneth *oil exploration service company executive*

Salado
Parks, Lloyd Lee *oil company executive*

San Antonio
Adams, James R. *telecommunications executive*
Burke, Michael Donald *oil and gas company executive*
Greehey, William Eugene *energy company executive*
Hemminghaus, Roger Roy *energy company executive, chemical engineer*
Horner, Richard Elmer *retired telecommunications company executive*
Klaerner, Curtis Maurice *former oil company executive*
†McLelland, Stan L. *energy company executive, lawyer*
Miller, Larry Joseph *oil and gas company executive*
West, Robert Van Osdell, Jr. *retired petroleum executive*
Whitacre, Edward E., Jr. *telecommunications executive*

Sealy
Young, Milton Earl *retired petroleum production company executive*

Spearman
Archer, Carl Marion *oil and gas company executive*

Sugar Land
Oller, William Maxwell *retired energy company executive, retired naval officer*
Welch, William Henry *oil service company executive, consultant*

Sugarland
McMahon, Edward Francis *oil industry executive, consultant*

The Woodlands
Clark, Bernard F. *natural gas company executive*
White, Robert Winslow *oilfield service company executive*

Tyler
Frankel, Donald Leon *oil service company executive*

Vanderpool
St. John, Billy Eugene *oil company executive*

Winnsboro
Fairchild, Raymond Eugene *oil company executive*

Woodlands
Mitchell, George P. *gas and petroleum company executive*

UTAH

Orem
Jacobson, Alfred Thurl *petroleum executive*

Salt Lake City
Cash, R(oy) Don *gas and petroleum company executive*
†Edwards, William Foster *oil and gas company executive*
Heiner, Clyde Mont *energy company executive*
†Holding, R. Earl *oil company executive*
Joklik, Günther Franz *mining company executive*
Losse, John William, Jr. *mining company executive*
Scowcroft, John Major *petroleum refinery process development executive*

VERMONT

Barnard
Larson, John Hyde *retired utilities executive*

Brattleboro
Weigand, James Gary *utility company executive, former military officer*

Manchester
†Freed, Walter Everett *petroleum company executive, state representative*

Rutland
Griffin, James Edwin *utilities executive*
†Webb, Thomas Crawford *utilities company executive*

VIRGINIA

Alexandria
Smith, Jeffrey Greenwood *industry executive, retired army officer*

Arlington
Campanella, Anton J. *telephone company executive*
Wakefield, Richard Alan *energy consulting firm executive*

Charlottesville
Benjamin, Albert, III *retired naval officer, oil company executive*

Fairfax
Gardner, Richard Hartwell *oil company executive*
Hoenmans, Paul John *oil company executive*
Murray, Allen Edward *oil company executive*
†Noto, Lucio A. *gas and oil industry executive*
†Renna, Eugene A. *petroleum company executive*

Hot Springs
Richey, Herbert Southall, II *coal company executive*

Lexington
Tyree, Lewis, Jr. *retired compressed gas company executive, inventor, technical consultant*

Manakin Sabot
Robertson, Linwood Righter *electric utility executive*

Mc Lean
†Waylan, Cecil Jerome *telecommunications executive*

Richmond
Berry, William Willis *retired utility executive*
Capps, Thomas Edward *holding company executive*
Clement, Alvis Macon *former utilities executive*
Munsey, Virdell Everard, Jr. *utility executive*
Rhodes, James T. *electric power industry executive*

Springfield
Peters, Charles William *research and development company manager*

Suffolk
Hines, Angus Irving, Jr. *petroleum marketing executive*

Upperville
di Zerega, Thomas William *former energy company executive, lawyer*

Williamsburg
Baranowski, Frank Paul *energy consultant, former government official*

WASHINGTON

Bellevue
Groten, Barnet *energy company executive*
McReynolds, Neil Lawrence *electric utility company executive*
†Stephenson, Robert Baird *energy company executive*

Richland
Counsil, William Glenn *electric utility executive*

Seattle
†Clapp, Melvin Carl *gas distributing company executive*
Smith, Andrew Vaughn *telephone company executive*
Thorpe, James Alfred *utilities executive*

Sequim
Beaton, Roy Howard *retired nuclear industry executive*

Spokane
Eliassen, Jon Eric *utility company executive*

Vancouver
†Robinson, Charles E. *telecommunications industry executive*

WEST VIRGINIA

Bridgeport
Timms, Leonard Joseph, Jr. *gas company executive*

Charleston
Bennett, Robert Menzies *retired gas pipeline company executive*
†Grant, Richard Lee *utility company executive*
†McMillian, John G. *oil and natural gas executive*

Clarksburg
Vrable, John Bernard *natural gas company executive*

Sistersville
Wright, John Charles Young *oil and gas company executive*

WISCONSIN

Delavan
Donnelly, James Charles *manufacturing company executive*

Madison
Davis, Erroll Brown, Jr. *utility executive*
Gehl, Eugene Othmar *power company executive, lawyer*
Mackie, Frederick David *retired utility executive*
Vondrasek, Frank Charles, Jr. *utilities executive*

Milwaukee
Burstein, Sol *consultant, retired utility company executive, engineer*
Goetsch, John Hubert *utility company executive*
Hoffer, Robert Morrison *retired holding company executive*
Schrader, Thomas F. *utilities executive*
†Sim, Richard Guild *business executive*

Thiensville
Kostecke, B. William *utilities executive*

WYOMING

Riverton
†Bebout, Eli Daniel *oil executive*
Tippets, Dennis Wilcock *mineral exploration executive, state legislator*

CANADA

ALBERTA

Calgary
Allard, James Edward *oil company executive*
Furnival, George Mitchell *petroleum and mining consultant*
Hagerman, Allen Reid *oil and gas company executive*
Haskayne, Richard Francis *petroleum company executive*
Hopper, Wilbert Hill *oil industry executive*
Hriskevich, Michael Edward *oil and gas consultant*
Hugh, George M. *pipeline company executive*
Little, Brian F. *oil company executive*
Maclagan, John Lyall *petroleum company executive*
Maier, Gerald James *natural gas transmission and marketing company executive*
McCready, Kenneth Frank *electric utility executive*
McIntyre, Norman F. *petroleum industry executive*
Mc Kinnon, F(rancis) A(rthur) Richard *utility executive*
O'Brien, David Peter *oil company executive*
Pick, Michael Claude *international exploration consultant*
Pierce, Robert Lorne *petrochemical, oil and gas company executive*
Price, Arthur Richard *petroleum company executive*
Reid, David Evans *pipeline company executive*
Seaman, Daryl Kenneth *oil company executive*
Sello, Allen Ralph *oil company executive*
Stanford, James M. *oil company executive*
Travis, Vance Kenneth *business executive*
Wagner, Norman Ernest *energy company executive, formerly university president*
Zaruby, Walter Stephen *holding company executive*

Edmonton
Horton, William Russell *retired utility company executive*
Twa, Craighton Oliver *power company executive*
Wood, John Denison *utility company executive*

Red Deer
Donald, Jack C. *oil company executive*

BRITISH COLUMBIA

Vancouver
Birch, Murray Patrick *oil industry executive*
Hallbauer, Robert Edward *mining company executive*
Keevil, Norman Bell, Jr. *mining executive*
Phillips, Edwin Charles *gas transmission company executive*
Willson, John Michael *mining company executive*
Wilson, Graham McGregor *energy company executive*

West Vancouver
†Petrina, Anthony J. *mining executive, retired*

White Rock
Huntington, A. Ronald *coal terminal executive*

MANITOBA

Pinawa
†Allan, Colin James *nuclear research and development company executive*

Winnipeg
Lang, Otto E. *industry executive, former Canadian cabinet minister*

NOVA SCOTIA

Halifax
Duvar, Ivan Ernest Hunter *telephone company executive*
Smith, Ronald Emory *telecommunications executive*

ONTARIO

Chatham
McGregor, Michael H. *gas company executive*

Don Mills
Di Tomaso, Nick *oil industry executive*
†Mascitelli, Joel *oil industry executive*

Kanata
Colbourne, Edwin Denis *telecommunications company executive*

Mississauga
Vice, David G. *retired telecommunications company executive*

North York
Woodruff, Laurie *oil industry executive*

Rexdale
Hyland, Geoffrey Fyfe *energy company executive*

Toronto
Allen, Peter Ackerman *mining executive*
Balderrama, Fernando Hiriart *electrical utility company executive*
Bone, Bruce Charles *mining and manufacturing executive*
Bush, John Arthur Henry *mining company executive, lawyer*
Cooper, Marsh Alexander *mining company executive*
Ediger, Nicholas Martin *energy resources company executive, consultant*
†James, William *mining company executive*
Leech, James William *manufacturing and technology company executive*
Light, Walter Frederick *telecommunications executive*
Marshall, Paul Macklin *oil company executive*
Martin, Robert William *utilities executive, retired*
Munk, Peter *mining executive*
Nuttall, Grant *oil company executive*
Osler, Gordon Peter *retired utility company executive*
Peterson, Robert Byron *petroleum company executive*
Powis, Alfred *natural resources company executive*
Roman-Barber, Helen *corporate executive*
Ryan, James Franklin *oil company executive*
Shaw, Ian Alexander *accountant, mining company executive*
Sopko, Michael D. *mining company executive*
Strong, Maurice Frederick *hydro-electric power company executive, former United Nations official*
Thomas, Kenneth Glyndwr *mining executive*
Walker, Ronald C. *oil company executive*
Zimmerman, Adam Hartley *mining and forest industries company executive*

QUEBEC

Montreal
Burns, James William *business executive*
Caillé, André *gas distribution company executive*
Cyr, J. V. Raymond *telecommunications and management holding company executive*
Dufresne, Guy Georges *mining company executive*
Fridman, Josef Josel *telecommunications company executive*
†Gaulin, Jean *gas distribution company executive*
Monty, Jean Claude *telecommunications company executive*
Wilson, Lynton Ronald *telecommunications company executive*

Rimouski
Sirois, Raymond *telecommunications administrator*

Varennes
St. Jean, Guy *electric power industry executive*

Westmount
Spalding, James Stuart *retired telecommunications company executive*

SASKATCHEWAN

Saskatoon
Childers, Charles Eugene *potash mining company executive*

MEXICO

Aristoteles
Akel, Ollie James *oil company executive*

AUSTRALIA

Melbourne
Mc Gimpsey, Ronald Alan *oil company executive*

BELGIUM

Brussels
Portal, Gilbert Marcel Adrien *oil company executive*

CHINA

Beijing
Gish, Norman Richard *oil industry executive*

ENGLAND

London
Gillam, Patrick John *oil company executive*
Kirkby, Maurice Anthony *oil company executive*

FRANCE

Paris
Roux, Ambroise Marie Casimir *business executive*
†Suard, Pierre Henri Andre *power company executive*
Teboul, Albert *nuclear engineer, nuclear energy industry executive*

ICELAND

Reykjavik
Jónatansson, Halldór *utility company executive*

JAPAN

Osaka
Osumi, Masato *utility company executive*

THE NETHERLANDS

The Hague
†Herkstroter, Cornelius *oil industry executive*
Van Wachem, Lodewijk Christiaan *petroleum company executive*

SWEDEN

Stockholm
Hagson, Carl Allan *utilities executive*

ADDRESS UNPUBLISHED

Anderson, James Arthur *mining company executive*
Anderson, Nils, Jr. *former government official, retired business executive, industrial historian*
†Andras, Oscar Sidney *oil company executive*
Arlidge, John Walter *utility company executive*
Arnold, William Howard *nuclear fuel executive*
Barrack, William Sample, Jr. *petroleum company executive*
Barrow, Frank Pearson, Jr. *retired energy company executive*
Bartling, Theodore Charles *oil company executive*
Baumgartner, John H. *refining and petroleum products company executive*
Bergman, Klaus *utility executive, lawyer*
Browne, Edmund John Phillip *oil company executive*
Bruce, James Edmund *retired utility company executive*
Bumbery, Joseph Lawrence *diversified telecommunications company executive*
Bush, Charles Vernon *telecommunications executive*
Butler, Eugene L. *oil field equipment company executive*
Carver, Calvin Reeve *public utility holding company director*
Catacosinos, William James *utility company executive*
Cliff, Ronald Laird *energy company executive*
Cooper, E. Camron *retired oil company executive*
Creigh, Thomas, Jr. *utility executive*
Cummer, William Jackson *former oil company executive, investor*
Curry, James Trueman, Jr. *retired mining company executive*
Davis, Laurence Laird *coal company executive*
Di Giovanni, Anthony *retired coal mining company executive*
Dille, Earl Kaye *utility company executive*
Dorros, Irwin *retired telecommunications executive*
Ellwanger, Mike (Cyril Albert Ellwanger) *retired utility executive*
Estes, Jack Charles *oil service company executive, scientist*
Ewing, Wayne Turner *coal company executive*
Fippinger, Grace J. *retired telecommunications company executive*
Fitzgeorge, Harold James *former oil and gas company executive*
Ford, Judith Ann *retired natural gas distribution company executive*
Godino, Rino Lodovico *retired petroleum and chemical company exeuctive*
Gogarty, William Barney *oil company executive, consultant*
†Gordon, Richard Joseph *gas distribution company executive*
Green, Richard Calvin, Jr. *utility company executive*
†Greenberg, Arnold Elihu *water quality specialist*
Greer, Carl Crawford *petroleum company executive*
Grinstead, William Carter, Jr. *retired coal and minerals company executive*
Gundersen, Wayne Campbell *management consultant, oil and gas consultant*
Hall, Milton Reese *retired oil company executive*
Hamilton, Allan Corning *retired oil company executive*
Hamilton, Lyman Critchfield, Jr. *multi-industry executive*
Hamilton, Willie L. *utility executive*
Hancock, John Coulter *telecommunications company executive*
Hansen, Shirley Jean *energy consulting executive, professional association administrator*
†Hardesty, Christopher Scott *oil and mining company executive*
Harris, Howard Hunter *oil company executive*
Harton, John James *utility executive*
Hebner, Paul Chester *retired oil company executive, consultant*
Heiney, John Weitzel *former utility executive*
Hesse, Christian August *mining industry consultant*
Hinson, Howard Houston *petroleum company executive*
Hobbs, J. Edwin *retired utility executive*
Holland, James Paul *utility company executive*
Holmer, Edwin Carl *retired petrochemical company executive*
Houser, William Douglas *telecommunications company executive, former naval officer*
†Howard, James Joseph, III *utility company executive*
Huffman, James Thomas William *oil exploration company executive*
Humke, Ramon L. *utility executive*
Hunt, Joe Harold *retired utility company executive*
Hyde, Robert Burke, Jr. *retired business executive*
Inglis, James *telecommunications company executive*
Inman, Cullen Langdon *telecommunications scientist*
Jones, Jack Dellis *oil company executive*
†Joyce, Burton Montgomery *natural resources company executive*
Judge, Rosemary Ann *oil company executive*
Kebblish, John Basil *retired coal company executive, consultant*
Kerr, James Winslow *pipe line company executive*
Kertz, Hubert Leonard *telephone company executive*
King, William Collins *oil company executive*
Kinzer, James Raymond *retired pipeline company executive*
Kruger, Weldon Dale *oil company executive, consultant*
†Kuzma, David Richard *natural gas company executive*
Le Van, Daniel Hayden *business executive*
Lewis, Alexander, Jr. *oil company executive*
Lilly, Edward Guerrant, Jr. *retired utility company executive*
Lively, Edwin Lester *retired oil company executive*
Lupberger, Edwin Adolph *utility executive*
Malpas, Robert *company executive*
Markle, Roger A(llan) *retired oil company executive*
Mc Carthy, Walter John, Jr. *retired utility executive*
McConnell, Elliott Bonnell, Jr. *oil company executive*
McGough, John Paul *conveyor and power transmission company executive*
Melvin, Ben Watson, Jr. *petroleum and chemical manufacturing executive*
Mitchell, Claybourne, Jr. *retired utilities executive*
Montgomery, Roy Delbert *retired gas utility company executive*
Monty, Charles Embert *utility company executive*
Morrell, Gene Paul *liquid terminal company executive*
Morrow, George Lester *retired oil and gas executive*
Murrill, Paul Whitfield *former utility executive, former university administrator*
Nicholson, Leland Ross *retired utilities company executive, energy consultant*
O'Hare, James Raymond *energy company executive*
Pack, Allen S. *retired coal company executive*
Peckham, Donald Eugene *retired utilities company executive*
†Perkins, Frederick Myers *oil company executive*
Perkins, Thomas Keeble *oil company researcher*
Perry, George Wilson *oil and gas company executive*
Pope, Robert Glynn *telecommunications executive*
Raymer, Donald George *utility company executive*
Raymond, Lee R. *oil company executive*
Reynolds, Jack W. *retired utility company executive*
Rickards, Leonard Myron *oil company executive*
Roe, Thomas Coombe *former utility company executive*
Sasdi, George P. *utilities company executive*
Saunby, John Brian *petrochemical company executive*
Schenck, Jack Lee *retired electric utility executive*
Schenker, Leo *retired utility company executive*
Scott, Isadore Meyer *former energy company executive*
Smith, Paul Vergon, Jr. *corporate executive, retired oil company executive*
Smith, Richard Grant *retired telecommunications executive, electrical engineer*
Steward, H. Leighton *oil company executive*
Stratman, Joseph Lee *petroleum refining company executive, consultant, chemical engineer*
Struebing, Robert Virgil *retired oil company executive*
Sugarman, Samuel Louis *retired oil transportation and trading company executive, horse breeder*
†Templeton, John Alexander, II *coal company executive*
Thompson, Jack Edward *mining company executive*
Threet, Jack Curtis *oil company executive*
Tonkyn, Richard George *retired oil and gas company executive, researcher, consultant*
Tucker, H. Richard *oil company executive*
Tucker, Paul William *retired petroleum company executive*
Turner, Robert Hal *telecommunications and computer executive*
†Werneburg, Kenneth Roger *mining company executive*
Werth, Andrew M. *telecommunications executive*
White, Willis Sheridan, Jr. *retired utilities company executive*
Whitehouse, Alton Winslow, Jr. *retired oil company executive*
Williams, Joseph Theodore *oil and gas company executive*
Witte, Merlin Michael *oil company executive*
Wright, Randolph Earle *retired petroleum company executive*
Yates, Elton G. *retired petroleum industry executive*
Yearwood, Donald Robert *oil and shipping executive*

LAW: JUDICIAL ADMINISTRATION

UNITED STATES

ALABAMA

Albertville
Johnson, Clark Everette, Jr. *judge*

Anniston
Harwell, Edwin Whitley *judge*

Birmingham
Acker, William Marsh, Jr. *federal judge*
Blackburn, Sharon Lovelace *federal judge*
Clemon, U. W. *federal judge*
Guin, Junius Foy, Jr. *federal judge*
Hancock, James Hughes *federal judge*
Lynne, Seybourn Harris *federal judge*
Nelson, Edwin L. *federal judge*
Pointer, Sam Clyde, Jr. *federal judge*
Propst, Robert Bruce *federal judge*
Putnam, Terry Michael *federal judge*
Smith, Edward Samuel *federal judge*

Florence
Haltom, Elbert Bertram, Jr. *federal judge*
Tease, James Edward *judge*

Gadsden
Sledge, James Scott *federal judge*

Huntsville
Lutz, Hartwell Borden *judge*
Watson, Sterl Arthur, Jr. *retired judge, lawyer*

Mobile
Butler, Charles Randolph, Jr. *federal judge*
Cox, Emmett Ripley *federal judge*
Howard, Alex T., Jr. *federal judge*
Kahn, Gordon Barry *federal bankruptcy judge*
McCall, Daniel Thompson, Jr. *retired justice*
Milling, Bert William, Jr. *federal judge*
Pittman, Virgil *federal judge*

Montgomery
Albritton, William Harold, III *federal judge*
Almon, Reneau Pearson *state supreme court justice*
Black, Robert Coleman *lawyer*
De Ment, Ira *federal judge*
Dubina, Joel Fredrick *federal judge*
Godbold, John Cooper *federal judge*
Hornsby, (E.C.) Sonny *judge*
Houston, James Gorman, Jr. *state supreme court justice*
Ingram, Kenneth Frank *state supreme court justice*
Johnson, Frank Minis, Jr. *federal judge*
Maddox, (Alva) Hugh *state supreme court justice*
Patterson, John Malcolm *judge*
Steele, Rodney Redfearn *federal judge*
Thompson, Myron H. *federal judge*
Torbert, Clement Clay, Jr. *state supreme court justice*

ALASKA

Anchorage
Branson, Albert Harold (Harry Branson) *magistrate judge, educator*
Holland, H. Russel *federal judge*
Rabinowitz, Jay Andrew *state supreme court justice*
Sedwick, John Weeter *judge*
Singleton, James Keith *federal judge*
von der Heydt, James Arnold *federal judge, lawyer*

Fairbanks
Kleinfeld, Andrew Jay *federal judge*

ARIZONA

Bisbee
Holland, Robert Dale *retired magistrate, consultant*

Phoenix
Broomfield, Robert Cameron *federal judge*
Canby, William Cameron, Jr. *federal judge*
Carroll, Earl Hamblin *federal judge*
Carter, James Edward *judge*
Feldman, Stanley George *state supreme court chief justice*
Kaufman, Roger Wayne *county judge, lawyer*
McNamee, Stephen M. *federal judge*
Moeller, James *state supreme court justice*
Muecke, Charles Andrew (Carl Muecke) *federal judge*
Myers, Robert David *judge*
Rosenblatt, Paul Gerhardt *federal judge*
Schroeder, Mary Murphy *federal judge*
Strand, Roger Gordon *federal judge*
Tang, Thomas *federal judge*
Zastrow, John Thurman *judge*

Tucson
Bilby, Richard Mansfield *federal judge*
Browning, William Docker *federal judge*
Lacagnina, Michael Anthony *judge*
Livermore, Joseph McMaster *judge*
Marquez, Alfredo C. *federal judge*
Roll, John McCarthy *federal judge*
Terlizzi, Raymond Thomas *judge*

ARKANSAS

Batesville
Harkey, John Norman *state judge*

El Dorado
†Barnes, Harry F. *federal judge*

Fayetteville
Waters, H. Franklin *federal judge*

Fort Smith
Hendren, Jimm Larry *federal judge*

Harrison
Henley, J. Smith *federal judge*

Hot Springs National Park
Britt, Henry Middleton *retired judge*

Little Rock
Arnold, Morris Sheppard *federal judge*
Arnold, Richard Sheppard *federal judge*
Corbin, Donald L. *judge*
Eisele, Garnett Thomas *federal judge*
Glaze, Thomas A. *state supreme court justice*
Harris, Oren *retired federal judge*
Holt, Jack Wilson, Jr. *state supreme court chief justice*
Howard, George, Jr. *federal judge*
Newbern, William David *state supreme court justice*
Reasoner, Stephen M. *federal judge*
Roy, Elsijane Trimble *federal judge*
†Wilson, William R., Jr. *judge*
Woods, Henry *federal judge*
Wright, Susan Webber *federal judge*

Texarkana
Stroud, John Fred, Jr. *state supreme court justice*

CALIFORNIA

Alameda
Bartalini, C. Richard *judge*

Fresno
Coyle, Robert Everett *federal judge*
Crocker, Myron Donovan *federal judge*
Price, Edward Dean *federal judge*
Wanger, Oliver Winston *federal judge, educator*

Los Angeles
Alarcon, Arthur Lawrence *federal judge*
Armstrong, Orville *judge*
Ashland, Calvin Kolle *federal judge*
Baird, Lourdes G. *federal judge*
Bufford, Samuel Lawrence *federal judge*
Byrne, William Matthew, Jr. *federal judge*
Chavez, Victor Edwin *judge*

Crispo, Lawrence Walter *judge*
Davies, John G. *federal judge*
Fenning, Lisa Hill *federal judge*
Gadbois, Richard A., Jr. *federal judge*
Gold, Arnold Henry *judge*
Hatter, Terry Julius, Jr. *federal judge*
Hupp, Harry L. *federal judge*
Ideman, James M. *federal judge*
Jaffe, F. Filmore *judge*
Johnson, Earl, Jr. *judge, author*
Kelleher, Robert Joseph *federal judge*
Keller, William D. *federal judge*
Kenyon, David V. *federal judge*
Klein, Joan Dempsey *judge*
Lasarow, William Julius *federal judge*
Letts, J. Spencer *federal judge*
Lew, Ronald S. W. *federal judge*
Marshall, Consuelo Bland *federal judge*
Mund, Geraldine *bankruptcy judge*
Norris, William Albert *federal judge*
Pfaelzer, Mariana R. *federal judge*
Rafeedie, Edward *federal judge*
Rea, William J. *federal judge*
Real, Manuel Lawrence *federal judge*
Takasugi, Robert Mitsuhiro *federal judge*
Tashima, Atsushi Wallace *federal judge*
Taylor, Gary L. *federal judge*
Tevrizian, Dickran M., Jr. *federal judge*
Williams, David Welford *federal judge*
Wilson, Stephen Victor *federal judge*

Monrovia
Moore, S. Clark *judge*

Monterey Park
Tucker, Marcus Othello *judge*

Newport Beach
Curtis, Jesse William, Jr. *retired federal judge*
Kaufman, Marcus Maurice *retired judge, lawyer*

Oakland
Champlin, Malcolm McGregor *retired municipal judge*
Cline, Wilson Ettason *retired administrative law judge*
Newsome, Randall Jackson *federal judge*

Palo Alto
Bird, Rose Elizabeth *former state chief justice, law educator*

Pasadena
Boochever, Robert *federal judge*
Fernandez, Ferdinand Francis *federal judge*
Files, Gordon Louis *judge, lawyer*
Goodwin, Alfred Theodore *federal judge*
Hall, Cynthia Holcomb *federal judge*
Kozinski, Alex *federal judge*
Nelson, Dorothy Wright (Mrs. James F. Nelson) *federal judge*
Rymer, Pamela Ann *federal judge*

Pomona
†McCoy, Charles Wirth, Jr. *superior court judge*

Sacramento
Dahl, Loren Silvester *federal judge*
Garcia, Edward J. *federal judge*
Karlton, Lawrence K. *federal judge*
Levi, David F. *federal judge*
MacBride, Thomas Jamison *federal judge*
Mix, Esther *federal judge*
Russell, David E. *federal judge*
Schwabe, Peter Alexander, Jr. *judge*
Schwartz, Milton Lewis *federal judge*
Shubb, William Barnet *federal judge*

San Diego
Adler, Louise DeCarl *bankruptcy judge*
Brewster, Rudi Milton *federal judge*
Gilliam, Earl Ben *federal judge*
Gonzalez, Irma E. *federal judge*
Hargrove, John James *federal judge*
Huff, Marilyn L. *federal judge*
Keep, Judith N. *federal judge*
McKee, Roger Curtis *federal magistrate judge*
Meyers, James William *federal judge*
Rhoades, John Skylstead, Sr. *federal judge*
Thompson, David Renwick *federal judge*
Thompson, Gordon, Jr. *federal judge*
Turrentine, Howard Boyd *federal judge*
Wallace, J. Clifford *federal judge*

San Francisco
Arabian, Armand *state supreme court justice*
Armstrong, Saundra Brown *federal judge*
Baxter, Marvin Ray *state supreme court judge*
Browning, James Robert *federal judge*
Caulfield, Barbara Ann *federal judge*
Conti, Samuel *federal judge*
Dail, Joseph Garner, Jr. *judge*
Henderson, Thelton Eugene *federal judge*
Jarvis, Donald Bertram *judge*
Jensen, D. Lowell *federal judge, lawyer, government official*
Kennard, Joyce F. *judge*
Kline, John Anthony *state court justice*
Legge, Charles Alexander *federal judge*
Lucas, Malcolm Millar *state supreme court chief justice*
Lynch, Eugene F. *federal judge*
Merrill, Charles Merton *federal judge*
Montali, Dennis *federal judge*
Mosk, Stanley *state supreme court justice*
Noonan, John T., Jr. *federal judge, legal educator*
Orrick, William Horsley, Jr. *federal judge*
Patel, Marilyn Hall *federal judge*
Poole, Cecil F. *federal judge*
Ramsey, Robert Lee *judge, lawyer*
†Reynoso, Cruz *judge*
Schnacke, Robert Howard *judge*
Sneed, Joseph Tyree, III *federal judge*
Walker, Vaughn R. *federal judge*
†Wilken, Claudia Ann *judge*

San Jose
Aguilar, Robert P. *federal judge*
Ingram, William Austin *federal judge*
Ware, James W. *federal judge*
Whyte, Ronald M. *federal judge*
Williams, Spencer M. *federal judge*

Santa Ana
Ferguson, Warren John *federal judge*
Lydick, Lawrence Tupper *federal judge*
Ryan, John Edward *federal judge*
Stotler, Alicemarie H. *federal judge*
Wilson, John James *federal judge*

Santa Barbara
Aldisert, Ruggero John *federal judge*

Santa Rosa
Jaroslovsky, Alan *judge*

South Lake Tahoe
Reece, Monte Meredith *lawyer, judge*

Woodland Hills
Pregerson, Harry *federal judge*

COLORADO

Central City
Rodgers, Frederic Barker *judge*

Denver
Abram, Donald Eugene *federal magistrate judge*
Babcock, Lewis Thornton *federal judge*
Carrigan, Jim Richard *federal judge*
Ebel, David M. *federal judge*
Erickson, William Hurt *state supreme court justice*
Finesilver, Sherman Glenn *federal judge*
Kane, John Lawrence, Jr. *federal judge*
Kirshbaum, Howard M. *judge*
Lohr, George E. *state supreme court justice*
Matsch, Richard P. *federal judge*
McWilliams, Robert Hugh *federal judge*
Moore, John Porfilio *federal judge*
Mullarkey, Mary J. *state supreme court justice*
Nottingham, Edward Willis, Jr. *federal judge*
Pringle, Bruce D. *federal magistrate*
Rovira, Luis Dario *state supreme court justice*
Sparr, Daniel Beattie *federal judge*
Weinshienk, Zita Leeson *federal judge*

Westcliffe
Sullivan, Whitney Brayton *municipal court judge*

CONNECTICUT

Bridgeport
Eginton, Warren William *federal judge*
Nevas, Alan Harris *federal judge*
Shiff, Alan Howard William *federal judge*

Danbury
Hull, Treat Clark *superior court trial referee*

Fairfield
Lumbard, Joseph Edward, Jr. *federal judge*

Hartford
Berdon, Robert Irwin *state supreme court justice*
Bieluch, William Charles *judge*
Callahan, Robert J. *state supreme court justice*
Covello, Alfred Vincent *federal judge*
Eagan, F(rancis) Owen *magistrate judge*
Heiman, Maxwell *state judge, lawyer*
Newman, Jon O. *federal judge*
Peters, Ellen Ash *state supreme court chief justice*
Santaniello, Angelo Gary *state supreme court justice*
Shea, David Michael *state supreme court justice*
Wright, Douglass Brownell *judge, lawyer*

Milford
Mahoney, J. Daniel *federal judge*

New Britain
Meskill, Thomas J. *federal judge*

New Haven
Burns, Ellen Bree *federal judge*
Cabranes, José Alberto *federal judge*
Dorsey, Peter Collins *federal judge*
Winter, Ralph Karl, Jr. *federal judge*

Waterbury
Daly, T(homas) F(rancis) Gilroy *federal judge*

DELAWARE

Wilmington
Balick, Helen Shaffer *federal judge*
Farnan, Joseph James, Jr. *federal judge*
Gebelein, Richard Stephen *judge, former state attorney general*
Latchum, James Levin *federal judge*
Longobardi, Joseph J. *federal judge*
McKelvie, Roderick R. *federal judge*
Moore, Andrew Given Tobias, II *state supreme court justice*
Robinson, Sue Lewis *federal judge*
Roth, Jane Richards *federal judge*
Schwartz, Murray Merle *federal judge*
Seitz, Collins Jacques *federal judge*
Stapleton, Walter King *federal judge*
Walsh, Joseph Thomas *state supreme court justice*
Wright, Caleb Merrill *federal judge*

DISTRICT OF COLUMBIA

Washington
Andewelt, Roger B. *federal judge*
Archer, Glenn LeRoy, Jr. *federal judge*
Bacon, Sylvia *retired judge*
Barnett, John H. *judge*
Bayly, John Henry, Jr. *judge*
Beghe, Renato *federal judge*
Bennett, Marion Tinsley *federal judge*
Bernstein, Edwin S. *federal judge*
Blackmun, Harry Andrew *U.S. supreme court justice*
Brennan, William Joseph, Jr. *former U.S. Supreme Court justice*
Breyer, Stephen Gerald *U.S. supreme court justice*
Bruggink, Eric G. *federal judge*
Buckley, James Lane *federal judge*
Burnett, Arthur Louis, Sr. *judge*
Chabot, Herbert L. *federal judge*
Clapp, Charles E., II *federal judge*
Clevenger, Raymond C., III *federal judge*
Cohen, Mary Ann *federal judge*
Colvin, John O. *federal judge*
Cooper, Jean Saralee *judge*
Cotter, B. Paul, Jr. *judge*
Cowen, Wilson *federal judge*
Cox, Walter Thompson, III *federal judge*
Crawford, Susan Jean *federal judge, lawyer*
Dawson, Howard Athalone, Jr. *federal judge*
Edwards, Harry T. *federal judge*
Farley, John Joseph, III *federal judge*
Fay, William Michael *federal judge*
†Fenton, John Henry *judge*
Ferren, John Maxwell *federal judge*
Flannery, Thomas Aquinas *federal judge*
Friedman, Daniel Mortimer *federal judge*
Futey, Bohdan A. *federal judge*
Gerber, Joel *federal judge*
Gibson, Reginald Walker *federal judge*
Ginsburg, Douglas Howard *federal judge, educator*
Ginsburg, Ruth Bader *U.S. supreme court justice*
Goodrich, George Herbert *judge*
Green, Joyce Hens *federal judge*
Green, June Lazenby *federal judge*
Greene, Harold H. *federal judge*
Halpern, James S. *federal judge*
Hamblen, Lapsley Walker, Jr. *federal judge*
Harris, Stanley S. *federal judge*
Heifetz, Alan William *federal judge*
Henderson, Karen LeCraft *federal judge*
Hodges, Robert H., Jr. *federal judge*
Holdaway, Ronald M. *federal judge*
Horn, Marian Blank *federal judge*
Ivers, Donald Louis *federal judge*
Jackson, Thomas Penfield *federal judge*
Jacobs, Julian I. *federal judge*
Johnson, Norma Holloway *federal judge*
Kennedy, Anthony McLeod *U.S. supreme court justice*
†Kline, Norman Douglas *federal judge*
Korner, Jules Gilmer, III *federal judge*
Kramer, Kenneth Bentley *federal judge, former congressman*
Lamberth, Royce C. *federal judge*
Lawrence, Glenn Robert *federal administrative law judge*
Litt, Nahum *federal judge*
Lourie, Alan David *federal judge*
Mack, Julia Cooper *appellate judge*
MacKinnon, George E. *federal judge*
Mankin, Hart Tiller *federal judge*
Margolis, Lawrence Stanley *federal judge*
Mayer, Haldane Robert *federal judge*
McArdle, Paul Francis *judge*
Megan, Thomas Ignatius *judge*
Mencher, Bruce Stephan *judge*
Merow, James F. *federal judge*
Michel, Paul Redmond *federal judge*
Mikva, Abner Joseph *federal judge*
Miller, Jack Richard *federal judge*
Nebeker, Frank Quill *federal judge*
Nettesheim, Christine Cook *federal judge*
Newman, Pauline *federal judge*
Nies, Helen Wilson *federal judge*
Nims, Arthur Lee, III *federal judge*
Oberdorfer, Louis F. *federal judge*
O'Connor, Sandra Day *U.S. supreme court justice*
Parker, Edna G. *federal judge*
Parr, Carolyn Miller *federal judge*
Pate, Joan Seitz *federal judge*
Penn, John Garrett *federal judge*
Plager, S. Jay *federal judge*
Powell, Lewis Franklin, Jr. *retired U.S. supreme court justice*
Pratt, John Helm *federal judge*
Rader, Randall Ray *federal judge*
Ramsey, Henry, Jr. *retired judge, law school dean, lawyer*
Randolph, Arthur Raymond *federal judge, lawyer*
Raum, Arnold *federal judge*
Rehnquist, William Hubbs *U.S. supreme court justice*
Reilly, Gerard Denis *judge*
Rich, Giles Sutherland *federal judge*
Richey, Charles Robert *federal judge*
Robinson, Aubrey Eugene, Jr. *federal judge*
Robinson, Wilkes Coleman *federal judge*
Ruwe, Robert P. *federal judge*
Scalia, Antonin *U.S. supreme court justice*
Schall, Alvin Anthony *judge*
Schwarzer, William W *federal judge*
Scott, Irene Feagin *federal judge*
Sentelle, David Bryan *federal judge*
Shields, Perry *federal judge*
Smith, Loren Allan *federal judge*
Smith, Roy Philip *federal judge*
Sporkin, Stanley *federal judge*
Steadman, John Montague *judge*
Steinberg, Jonathan Robert *federal judge*
Stevens, John Paul *U.S. supreme court justice*
Sullivan, Eugene Raymond *federal judge*
Swift, Stephen Jensen *federal judge*
Tannenwald, Theodore, Jr. *federal judge*
Tansill, Frederick Riker *retired judge*
Terry, John Alfred *judge*
Thomas, Clarence *U.S. supreme court justice*
Tidwell, Moody Rudolph *federal judge*
Turner, James Thomas *federal judge*
Wagner, Curtis Lee, Jr. *federal judge*
Wald, Patricia McGowan *federal judge*
Weinstein, Diane Gilbert *federal judge, lawyer*
Wells, Thomas B. *federal judge*
Whalen, Laurence J. *federal judge*
Whitaker, Meade *federal judge*
White, Byron R. *former U.S. supreme court justice*
Wiese, John Paul *federal judge*
Williams, Stephen Fain *federal judge*
Wright, Lawrence A. *federal judge*
Yock, Robert John *federal judge*
Yoder, Ronnie A. *federal administrative law judge*

FLORIDA

Coral Gables
Davis, Mattie Belle Edwards *retired county judge*

Fort Lauderdale
Gonzalez, Jose Alejandro, Jr. *federal judge*
Roettger, Norman Charles, Jr. *federal judge*
Zloch, William J. *federal judge*

Jacksonville
Black, Susan Harrell *federal judge*
Hill, James Clinkscales *federal judge*
Hodges, William Terrell *federal judge*
Melton, Howell Webster, Sr. *federal judge*
Moore, John Henry, II *federal judge*
Schlesinger, Harvey Erwin *federal judge*
Tjoflat, Gerald Bard *federal judge*

Miami
Brown, Stephen Thomas *U.S. magistrate judge*
Cristol, A. Jay *federal judge*
Davis, Edward Bertrand *federal judge*
Dyer, David William *federal judge*
Fay, Peter Thorp *federal judge*
†Ferguson, Wilkie D., Jr. *federal judge*
Graham, Donald Lynn *federal judge*
Highsmith, Shelby *federal judge*
Hoeveler, William M. *federal judge*
Kehoe, James W. *federal judge*
King, James Lawrence *federal judge*
Kraft, C. William, Jr. *federal judge*
Marcus, Stanley *federal judge*
Moore, Kevin Michael *federal judge*
Moreno, Federico Antonio *federal judge*
Nesbitt, Lenore Carrero *federal judge*
Ungaro-Benages, Ursula *federal judge*

Orlando
Baker, David A. *federal judge*
Conway, Anne Callaghan *federal judge*
Fawsett, Patricia Combs *federal judge*
Sharp, George Kendall *federal judge*
Young, George Cressler *federal judge*

Pensacola
Arnow, Winston Eugene *federal judge*
Collier, Lacey Alexander *federal judge*
Frye, John William, III *retired senior judge*
Vinson, C. Roger *federal judge*

Plant City
Bruton, James DeWitt, Jr. *retired judge*

Saint Petersburg
Grube, Karl Bertram *judge*
Roney, Paul H(itch) *federal judge*

Tallahassee
Grimes, Stephen Henry *state supreme court chief justice*
Harding, Major Best *state supreme court justice*
Hatchett, Joseph Woodrow *federal judge*
Kogan, Gerald *state supreme court justice*
McDonald, Parker Lee *state supreme court justice*
Nimmons, Ralph Wilson, Jr. *federal judge*
Overton, Benjamin Frederick *state supreme court justice*
Paul, Maurice M. *federal judge*
Shaw, Leander Jerry, Jr. *state supreme court justice*
Stafford, William Henry, Jr. *federal judge*
Sundberg, Alan Carl *former state supreme court justice, lawyer*

Tampa
†Adams, Henry Lee, Jr. *federal judge*
Baynes, Thomas Edward, Jr. *judge, lawyer, educator*
†Bucklew, Susan Cawthon *federal judge*
Castagna, William John *federal judge*
Corcoran, C. Timothy, III *judge*
Kovachevich, Elizabeth Anne *federal judge*
Menendez, Manuel, Jr. *judge*
Merryday, Steven D. *federal judge*

West Palm Beach
Eschbach, Jesse Ernest *federal judge*
Knott, James Robert *state judge, retired lawyer*
Paine, James Carriger *federal judge*
Ryskamp, Kenneth Lee *federal judge*

GEORGIA

Atlanta
Andrews, Gary Blaylock *state judge, lawyer*
Barkett, Rosemary *federal judge*
Benham, Robert *state supreme court justice*
Birch, Stanley Francis, Jr. *federal judge*
Camp, Jack Tarpley, Jr. *federal judge*
Carnes, Julie E. *federal judge*
Clark, Thomas Alonzo *federal judge*
Dougherty, John Ernest *federal judge*
Edmondson, James Larry *federal judge*
Evans, Orinda D. *federal judge*
Fletcher, Norman S. *state supreme court justice*
Forrester, J. Owen *federal judge*
Hall, Robert Howell *federal judge*
Henderson, Albert John *federal judge*
Kravitch, Phyllis A. *federal judge*
Murphy, Margaret H. *federal bankruptcy judge*
Nichols, Horace Elmo *state justice*
O'Kelley, William Clark *federal judge*
Shoob, Marvin H. *federal judge*
Tidwell, George Ernest *federal judge*
Tuttle, Elbert Parr *federal judge*
Vining, Robert Luke, Jr. *federal judge*
Ward, Horace Taliaferro *federal judge*

Augusta
Bowen, Dudley Hollingsworth, Jr. *federal judge*

Brunswick
Alaimo, Anthony A. *federal judge*

Columbus
Elliott, James Robert *federal judge*
Laney, John Thomas, III *federal judge*

Decatur
Shulman, Arnold *judge, lawyer*

Forsyth
Clarke, Harold Gravely *retired state supreme court chief justice*

Macon
Anderson, Robert Lanier, III *federal judge*
Fitzpatrick, Duross *federal judge*
Gerson, Robert Walthall *judge, retired lawyer*
Hershner, Robert Franklin, Jr. *federal judge*
Owens, Wilbur Dawson, Jr. *federal judge*

Marietta
†Cauthorn, Thomas Edward, III *judge*
Smith, George Thornewell *retired state supreme court justice*

Newnan
Morgan, Lewis Render *federal judge*

Rome
Murphy, Harold Loyd *federal judge*

Savannah
Edenfield, Berry Avant *federal judge*

HAWAII

Honolulu
Ashford, Clinton Rutledge *judge*
Choy, Herbert Young Cho *federal judge*
Ezra, David A. *federal judge*
Fong, Harold Michael *federal judge*
Kay, Alan Cooke *federal judge*

IDAHO

Boise
Bakes, Robert Eldon *retired state supreme court justice*
Bistline, Stephen *state supreme court justice*
Callister, Marion Jones *federal judge*
Johnson, Byron Jerald *state supreme court judge*
Lodge, Edward J. *federal judge*
McDevitt, Charles Francis *state supreme court justice*
Mc Quade, Henry Ford *state justice*
Nelson, Thomas G. *federal judge*
Ryan, Harold L. *federal judge*
†Silak, Cathy R. *judge*
Trott, Stephen Spangler *federal judge, musician*

ILLINOIS

Belleville
Ferguson, John Marshall *retired federal magistrate judge*
Stevens, C. Glenn *judge*

Benton
Foreman, James Louis *retired judge*
Gilbert, J. Phil *federal judge*

Chicago
Alesia, James H(enry) *federal judge*
Andersen, Wayne R. *federal judge*
Aspen, Marvin Edward *federal judge*
Barliant, Ronald *federal judge*
Bauer, William Joseph *federal judge*
Bilandic, Michael A. *state supreme court chief justice, former mayor*
Bowman, George Arthur, Jr. *federal judge*
Bua, Nicholas John *retired federal judge*
Coar, David H. *federal judge*
Conlon, Suzanne B. *federal judge*
Cudahy, Richard D. *federal judge*
Cummings, Walter J. *federal judge*
Duff, Brian Barnett *federal judge*
Easterbrook, Frank Hoover *federal judge*
Fairchild, Thomas E. *federal judge*
Flaum, Joel Martin *federal judge*
Garnett, Marion Winston *judge*
Grady, John F. *federal judge*
Hart, William Thomas *federal judge*
Holderman, James F., Jr. *federal judge*
Johnson, Glenn Thompson *judge*
Kanne, Michael Stephen *federal judge, educator*
Kelly, Richard Smith *judge*
Kocoras, Charles Petros *federal judge*
Lassers, Willard J. *judge*
Leighton, George Neves *retired federal judge*
Leinenweber, Harry D. *federal judge*
Lindberg, George W. *federal judge*
Marovich, George M. *federal judge*
McGarr, Frank James *retired federal judge, dispute resolution consultant*
Moran, James Byron *federal judge*
Nordberg, John Albert *federal judge*
Norgle, Charles Ronald, Sr. *federal judge*
Pallmeyer, Rebecca Ruth *federal judge*
Pascale, Daniel Richard *judge*
Pell, Wilbur Frank, Jr. *federal judge*
Plunkett, Paul Edward *federal judge*
Posner, Richard Allen *federal judge*
Rothschild, George William *judge, lawyer*
Rovner, Ilana Kara Diamond *federal judge*
Ryan, Howard Chris *state supreme court justice*
Schmetterer, Jack Baer *federal judge*
Shadur, Milton I. *judge*
Sonderby, Susan Pierson *federal bankruptcy judge*
Squires, John Henry *federal bankruptcy judge*
Toles, Edward Bernard *retired judge*
Williams, Ann Claire *federal judge*
Wynn, Thomas Joseph *county judge, educator*
Zagel, James Block *federal judge*

Danville
Baker, Harold Albert *federal judge*

East Saint Louis
Beatty, William Louis *federal judge*
Stiehl, William D. *federal judge*

Elgin
Kirkland, Alfred Younges, Sr. *federal judge*

Fairview Heights
Cunningham, Joseph Francis, Jr. *retired state supreme court justice*

Hennepin
Bumgarner, James McNabb *judge*

Homewood
Dietch, Henry Xerxes *judge*

Pekin
Heiple, James Dee *state supreme court justice*

Peoria
Kauffman, Robert Joseph *magistrate judge*
McDade, Joe Billy *federal judge*
Mihm, Michael Martin *federal judge*
Morgan, Robert Dale *federal judge*

Rock Island
Telleen, John Martin *judge*

Rockford
Reinhard, Philip G. *federal judge*

Springfield
Lessen, Larry Lee *federal judge*
Miller, Benjamin K. *state supreme court justice*
Mills, Richard Henry *federal judge*
Wood, Harlington, Jr. *federal judge*

Wilmette
Nelson, James F. *judge, religious organization administrator*

INDIANA

Evansville
Brooks, Gene Edward *federal judge*
Capshaw, Tommie Dean *federal judge*

Fort Wayne
Lee, William Charles *federal judge*

Hammond
Lozano, Rudolpho *federal judge*
Moody, James T(yne) *federal judge*

Indianapolis
Barker, Sarah Evans *federal judge*
DeBruler, Roger O. *state supreme court justice*
Dillin, S. Hugh *federal judge*
Givan, Richard Martin *state supreme court justice*
McKinney, Larry J. *federal judge*
Shepard, Randall Terry *judge*
Steckler, William Elwood *federal judge*
Tinder, John Daniel *federal judge*

South Bend
Grant, Robert Allen *federal judge*
Manion, Daniel Anthony *federal judge*
Miller, Robert L., Jr. *federal judge*
Ripple, Kenneth Francis *federal judge*
Rodibaugh, Robert Kurtz *federal judge*
Sharp, Allen *chief federal judge*

IOWA

Cedar Rapids
Hansen, David Rasmussen *federal judge*
Mc Manus, Edward Joseph *federal judge*

Council Bluffs
Peterson, Richard William *lawyer, magistrate judge*

Des Moines
Fagg, George Gardner *federal judge*
Harris, K. David *state supreme court justice*
Larson, Jerry L. *state supreme court justice*
Longstaff, Ronald E. *federal judge*
McGiverin, Arthur A. *state supreme court justice*
Stuart, William Corwin *federal judge*
Vietor, Harold Duane *federal judge*
Wolle, Charles Robert *federal judge*

Iowa City
Schultz, Louis William *judge*

Osceola
Reynoldson, Walter Ward *state supreme court chief justice*

Sioux City
Deck, Paul Wayne, Jr. *federal judge*
O'Brien, Donald Eugene *federal judge*

KANSAS

Kansas City
Lungstrum, John W. *federal judge*
O'Connor, Earl Eugene *federal judge*
Rushfelt, Gerald Lloyd *magistrate judge*
Van Bebber, George Thomas *federal judge*
Vratil, Kathryn Hoefer *federal judge*

Lawrence
Tacha, Deanell Reece *federal judge*

Leavenworth
Stanley, Arthur Jehu, Jr. *federal judge*

Olathe
Chipman, Marion Walter *judge*

Topeka
Abbott, Bob *state supreme court justice*
Allegrucci, Donald Lee *state supreme court justice*
Crow, Sam Alfred *federal judge*
Holmes, Richard Winn *state supreme court justice*
McFarland, Kay Eleanor *state supreme court justice*
Miller, Robert Haskins *retired state chief justice*
Pusateri, James Anthony *federal bankruptcy judge*
Rogers, Richard Dean *federal judge*
Saffels, Dale Emerson *federal judge*
Six, Fred N. *state supreme court justice*

Wichita
Brown, Wesley Ernest *federal judge*
Kelly, Patrick F. *federal judge*
Pearson, John King *federal judge*
Theis, Frank Gordon *federal judge*

KENTUCKY

Ashland
Wilhoit, Henry Rupert, Jr. *federal judge*

Danville
Lively, Pierce *federal judge*

Frankfort
Leibson, Charles M. *state supreme court justice*
Stephens, Robert F. *state supreme court chief justice*
Wintersheimer, Donald Carl *state supreme court justice*

Lexington
Forester, Karl S. *federal judge*
Varellas, Sandra Motte *judge*

London
†Coffman, Jennifer B. *federal judge*
Siler, Eugene Edward, Jr. *federal judge*
Unthank, G. Wix *federal judge*

Louisville
Allen, Charles Mengel *federal judge*
Boggs, Danny Julian *federal judge*
Heyburn, John G., II *federal judge*
Martin, Boyce Ficklen, Jr. *federal judge*
Meredith, Ronald Edward *federal judge*
Roberts, J. Wendell *federal judge*
Simpson, Charles R., III *federal judge*
Stosberg, David Thomas *bankruptcy judge*

Paducah
Johnstone, Edward H. *federal judge*

Pikeville
Hood, Joseph M. *federal judge*

Prospect
Helm, Hugh Barnett *retired judge*

LOUISIANA

Alexandria
Little, F. A., Jr. *federal judge*
Scott, Nauman S. *federal judge*

Baton Rouge
Cole, Luther Francis *state supreme court associate justice*
Parker, John Victor *federal judge*
Polozola, Frank Joseph *federal judge*

Lafayette
Davis, William Eugene *federal judge*
Doherty, Rebecca Feeney *federal judge*
Duhe, John Malcolm, Jr. *federal judge*
Haik, Richard T., Sr. *federal judge*
Shaw, John Malach *federal judge*

Lake Charles
Hunter, Edwin Ford, Jr. *federal judge*
Trimble, James T., Jr. *federal judge*

New Orleans
Beer, Peter Hill *federal judge*
Calogero, Pascal Frank, Jr. *state supreme court chief justice*
Carr, Patrick E. *judge*
Clement, Edith Brown *federal judge*
Dennis, James Leon *state supreme court justice*
Duplantier, Adrian Guy *federal judge*
Feldman, Martin L. C. *federal judge*
Heebe, Frederick Jacob Regan *federal judge*
Livaudais, Marcel, Jr. *federal judge*
Marcus, Walter F., Jr. *state supreme court justice*
McNamara, A. J. *federal judge*
Mentz, Henry Alvan, Jr. *federal judge*
Mitchell, Lansing Leroy *federal judge*
Ortique, Revius Oliver, Jr. *judge*
Schwartz, Charles, Jr. *federal judge*
Sear, Morey Leonard *federal judge, educator*
Watson, Jack Crozier *state supreme court justice*
Wicker, Veronica DiCarlo *federal judge*
Wisdom, John Minor *federal judge*

Shreveport
Payne, Roy Steven *judge*
Politz, Henry Anthony *federal judge*
Stagg, Tom *federal judge*
Walter, Donald Ellsworth *federal judge*
Wiener, Jacques Loeb, Jr. *federal judge*

MAINE

Auburn
Clifford, Robert William *judge*

Bangor
Brody, Morton Aaron *federal judge*

Lewiston
Dufresne, Armand Alphee, Jr. *state justice*

Portland
Bradford, Carl O. *judge*
Carter, Gene *federal judge*
Coffin, Frank Morey *federal judge*
Cohen, David Michael *federal magistrate judge*
Glassman, Caroline Duby *state supreme court justice*
Goodman, James A. *federal judge*
Hornby, David Brock *federal judge*
McKusick, Vincent Lee *former state supreme judicial court chief justice, lawyer*
Roberts, David Glendenning *state supreme court justice*
Wathen, Daniel Everett *state supreme court chief justice*

Rockland
Collins, Samuel W., Jr. *judge*

Wells
Grimes, William Alvan *retired state supreme court chief justice*

MARYLAND

Annapolis
Eldridge, John Cole *state appeals judge*
Murphy, Robert C(harles) *judge*

Baltimore
Black, Walter Evan, Jr. *federal judge*
†Chasanow, Deborah K. *federal judge*
Derby, Ernest Stephen *federal judge*
Garbis, Marvin Joseph *federal judge*
Goetz, Clarence Edward *magistrate*
Hargrove, John R. *federal judge*
Harvey, Alexander, II *federal judge*
Howard, Joseph Clemens *federal judge*
Kaufman, Frank Albert *federal judge*
Legg, Benson Everett *federal judge*
Levin, Marshall Abbott *judge, educator*
Maletz, Herbert Naaman *federal judge*
†Messitte, Peter Jo *judge*
Motz, John Frederick *federal judge*
Murnaghan, Francis Dominic, Jr. *federal judge*
Nickerson, William Milnor *federal judge*
Niemeyer, Paul Victor *federal judge*
Northrop, Edward Skottowe *federal judge*
Rodowsky, Lawrence Francis *judge*
Schneider, James Frederick *federal judge*
Smalkin, Frederic N. *federal judge*
Young, Joseph H. *federal judge*

Greenbelt
Kenkel, James Edward *judge*

Leonardtown
Briscoe, John Hanson *judge, lawyer, former state legislator*

Rockville
Mannes, Paul *federal judge*

Upper Marlboro
Chasanow, Howard Stuart *judge, lecturer*

MASSACHUSETTS

Boston
Abrams, Ruth Ida *state supreme court justice*
Aldrich, Bailey *federal judge*
Allard, David Henry *judge*
Boudin, Michael *federal judge*
Bowler, Marianne Bianca *judge*
Campbell, Levin Hicks *federal judge*
Collings, Robert Biddlecombe *federal judge*
Dacey, Kathleen Ryan *judge*
Dreben, Raya Spiegel *judge*
Harrington, Edward F. *federal judge*
Hillman, William Chernick *federal bankruptcy judge*
Keeton, Robert Ernest *federal judge*
Liacos, Paul Julian *state supreme judicial court chief justice*
Mazzone, A. David *federal judge*
Nelson, David S. *federal judge*
†Saris, Patti B. *federal judge*
Skinner, Walter Jay *federal judge*
†Stearns, Richard Gaylore *judge*
Tauro, Joseph Louis *federal judge*
Wilkins, Herbert Putnam *judge*
Wolf, Mark Lawrence *federal judge*
Woodlock, Douglas Preston *federal judge*
Young, William Glover *federal judge*
Zobel, Hiller Bellin *judge*
Zobel, Rya W. *federal judge*

Cambridge
Kaplan, Benjamin *judge*

Hingham
Ford, Joseph *retired superior court judge*

Longmeadow
Keady, George Cregan, Jr. *judge*

Melrose
Fremont-Smith, Thayer *associate justice*

Springfield
Ponsor, Michael A. *federal judge*

Worcester
Gorton, Nathaniel Matheson *federal judge, lawyer*

MICHIGAN

Ann Arbor
Guy, Ralph B., Jr. *federal judge*
La Plata, George *federal judge*

Bay City
Churchill, James Paul *federal judge*
Cleland, Robert Hardy *federal judge*
Spector, Arthur Jay *federal judge*

Detroit
Boyle, Patricia Jean *judge*
Duggan, Patrick James *federal judge*
Edmunds, Nancy Garlock *federal judge*
Feikens, John *federal judge*
Friedman, Bernard Alvin *federal judge*
Gadola, Paul V. *federal judge*
Gilmore, Horace Weldon *federal judge*
Graves, Ray Reynolds *federal judge*
Hackett, Barbara (Kloka) *federal judge*
Keith, Damon Jerome *federal judge*
Kennedy, Cornelia Groefsema *federal judge*
Mallett, Conrad LeRoy, Jr. *state supreme court justice*
Rosen, Gerald Ellis *federal judge*
Ryan, James Leo *federal judge*
Sullivan, Joseph B. *retired judge*
Taylor, Anna Diggs *federal judge*
Woods, George E. *federal judge*
Zatkoff, Lawrence P. *federal judge*

Flint
Newblatt, Stewart Albert *federal judge*

Grand Rapids
Bell, Robert Holmes *federal judge*

Brenneman, Hugh Warren, Jr. *federal magistrate judge*
Engel, Albert Joseph *federal judge*
Gibson, Benjamin F. *chief federal judge*
Hillman, Douglas Woodruff *federal judge*
Miles, Wendell A. *federal judge*
Quist, Gordon Jay *federal judge*

Kalamazoo
Enslen, Richard Alan *federal judge*

Lansing
Cavanagh, Michael Francis *state supreme court chief justice*
Griffin, Robert Paul *state supreme court justice, former U.S. senator*
McKeague, David William *federal judge*
Suhrheinrich, Richard Fred *federal judge*

Pontiac
Grant, Barry M(arvin) *judge*

Port Huron
DeMascio, Robert Edward *federal judge*

Southfield
Doctoroff, Martin Myles *judge*

MINNESOTA

Duluth
Heaney, Gerald William *federal judge*

Minneapolis
Alton, Ann Leslie *judge, lawyer, educator*
Amdahl, Douglas Kenneth *retired state supreme court justice*
Doty, David Singleton *federal judge*
Kressel, Robert J. *federal judge*
Larson, Earl Richard *federal judge*
MacLaughlin, Harry Hunter *federal judge*
Murphy, Diana E. *federal judge*
Rosenbaum, James Michael *federal judge*

Minnetonka
Rogers, James Devitt *judge*

Saint Paul
Alsop, Donald Douglas *federal judge*
Keith, Alexander MacDonald *state supreme court chief justice*
Kishel, Gregory Francis *federal judge*
Kyle, Richard H(ouse) *federal judge*
Lay, Donald Pomeroy *federal judge*
Lebedoff, Jonathan Galanter *federal judge*
Loken, James Burton *federal judge*
Magnuson, Paul Arthur *federal judge*
Noel, Franklin Linwood *federal magistrate judge*
Rogosheske, Walter Frederick *former state justice*
Wahl, Rosalie E. *state supreme court justice*

MISSISSIPPI

Aberdeen
Davidson, Glen Harris *federal judge*
Davis, Jerry Arnold *judge*
Senter, Lyonel Thomas, Jr. *federal judge*

Biloxi
Bramlette, David C., III *federal judge*
Gex, Walter Joseph, III *federal judge*

Gulfport
Russell, Dan M., Jr. *federal judge*
Walker, Harry Grey *retired state supreme court justice*

Hattiesburg
Pickering, Charles W. *federal judge*

Jackson
Barbour, William H., Jr. *federal judge*
Barksdale, Rhesa Hawkins *federal judge*
Hawkins, Armis Eugene *state supreme court chief justice*
Jolly, E. Grady *federal judge*
Lee, Tom Stewart *federal judge*
Pittman, Edwin Lloyd *state supreme court justice*
Prather, Lenore Loving *state supreme court presiding justice*
Sugg, Robert Perkins *former state supreme court justice*
Sullivan, Michael David *state supreme court justice*
Wingate, Henry Travillion *federal judge*

Oxford
Biggers, Neal Brooks, Jr. *federal judge*

MISSOURI

Jefferson City
Benton, W. Duane *judge*
Donnelly, Robert True *retired state supreme court justice*
Holstein, John Charles *state supreme court justice*
Robertson, Edward D., Jr. *state supreme court chief justice*

Kansas City
Bartlett, D. Brook *federal judge*
Berrey, Robert Wilson, III *lawyer, judge*
Bowman, Pasco Middleton, II *federal judge*
Gaitan, Fernando J., Jr. *federal judge*
Gibson, Floyd Robert *federal judge*
Gibson, John Robert *federal judge*
Hunter, Elmo Bolton *federal judge*
Koger, Frank Williams *federal judge*
Larsen, Robert Emmett *federal judge*
Sachs, Howard F(rederic) *federal judge*
Stevens, Joseph Edward, Jr. *federal judge*
Ulrich, Robert Gene *judge*
Whipple, Dean *federal judge*
Wright, Scott Olin *federal judge*

Moberly
Blackmar, Charles Blakey *state supreme court justice*

Saint Louis
Barta, James Joseph *federal judge*
Cahill, Clyde S. *federal judge*
Filippine, Edward Louis *federal judge*
Gunn, George F., Jr. *federal judge*
Hamilton, Jean Constance *federal judge*
Harper, Roy W. *federal judge*
Hungate, William Leonard *retired federal judge, former congressman*
Limbaugh, Stephen Nathaniel *federal judge*
McDonald, David P. *federal judge*
McMillian, Theodore *federal judge*
†Reinhard, James Richard *judge*
†Shaw, Charles Alexander *judge*
Stohr, Donald J. *federal judge*

Springfield
Clark, Russell Gentry *federal judge*

MONTANA

Billings
Battin, James Franklin *judge, former congressman*
Shanstrom, Jack D. *federal judge*

Great Falls
Hatfield, Paul Gerhart *federal judge, lawyer*

Helena
Gray, Karla Marie *state supreme court justice*
Harrison, John Conway *state supreme court justice*
Hunt, William E., Sr. *state supreme court justice*
Lovell, Charles C. *federal judge*
McDonough, Russell Charles *retired state supreme court justice*
Trieweiler, Terry Nicholas *state supreme court justice*
Turnage, Jean A. *state supreme court chief justice*
Weber, Fred J. *state supreme court justice*

NEBRASKA

Columbus
Whitehead, John C. *state judge*

Lincoln
Beam, Clarence Arlen *federal judge*
Boslaugh, Leslie *judge*
Caporale, D. Nick *state supreme court justice*
Fahrnbruch, Dale E. *state supreme court justice*
Hastings, William Charles *state supreme court chief justice*
Kopf, Richard G. *federal judge*
Piester, David L(ee) *magistrate judge*
†Shanahan, Thomas M. *state supreme court justice*
Urbom, Warren Keith *federal judge*

Omaha
Cambridge, William G. *federal judge*
Grant, John Thomas *retired state supreme court justice*
Strom, Lyle Elmer *federal judge*

NEVADA

Carson City
Gunderson, Elmer Millard *state supreme court justice, law educator*
Rose, Robert E. *state supreme court justice*
Springer, Charles Edward *state supreme court justice*
Young, C. Clifton *judge*

Las Vegas
George, Lloyd D. *federal judge*
Johnston, Robert Jake *federal magistrate judge*
Pro, Philip Martin *federal judge*

Reno
Brunetti, Melvin T. *federal judge*
†Hagen, David W. *judge*
Hug, Procter Ralph, Jr. *federal judge*
McKibben, Howard D. *federal judge*
Reed, Edward Cornelius, Jr. *federal judge*
Wiggins, Charles Edward *federal judge*

NEW HAMPSHIRE

Concord
Barbadoro, Paul J. *federal judge*
Batchelder, William F. *state supreme court justice*
Bownes, Hugh Henry *federal judge*
Brock, David Allen *state supreme court chief justice*
Cann, William Francis *judge*
Devine, Shane *federal judge*
Horton, Sherman D., Jr. *state supreme court justice*
Johnson, William R. *state supreme court justice*
McAuliffe, Steven James *federal judge*
Stahl, Norman H. *federal judge*
Thayer, W(alter) Stephen, III *state supreme court justice*

NEW JERSEY

Atlantic City
Knight, Edward R. *judge, law educator, psychologist*

Camden
Brotman, Stanley Seymour *federal judge*
Gerry, John Francis *federal judge*
Irenas, Joseph Eron *federal judge*
Rodriguez, Joseph H. *federal judge*
Simandle, Jerome B. *federal judge*

Flemington
Griffin, Bryant Wade *judge*

Freehold
Fisher, Clarkson Sherman, Jr. *judge*

Hackensack
Kestin, Howard H. *judge*

Morristown
Clifford, Robert L. *state supreme court justice*

Newark
Ackerman, Harold A. *federal judge*
Alito, Samuel Anthony, Jr. *federal judge*
Barry, Maryanne Trump *federal judge*
Bassler, William G. *federal judge*
Bissell, John W. *federal judge*
Chesler, Stanley Richard *federal judge*
Debevoise, Dickinson Richards *federal judge*
Garth, Leonard I. *federal judge*
Lechner, Alfred James, Jr. *federal judge*
Lifland, John C. *federal judge*
Pisano, Joel A. *federal judge*
Politan, Nicholas H. *federal judge*
Sarokin, H. Lee *federal judge*
Wolin, Alfred M. *federal judge*

Oakhurst
Wilentz, Robert Nathan *state supreme court justice*

Passaic
Reiss, Sidney H. *judge, lawyer*

Trenton
Brown, Garrett Edward, Jr. *federal judge*
Cowen, Robert E. *federal judge*
Fisher, Clarkson Sherman *federal judge*
Gindin, William Howard *federal judge*
Greenberg, Morton Ira *federal judge*
Handler, Alan B. *state supreme court justice*
O'Hern, Daniel Joseph *state supreme court justice*
Parell, Mary Little *federal judge, former banking commissioner*
Pollock, Stewart Glasson *state supreme court justice*
Thompson, Anne Elise *federal judge*

NEW MEXICO

Albuquerque
Burciaga, Juan Guerrero *federal judge*
Conway, John E. *federal judge*
Easley, Mack *retired state supreme court chief justice*
Hansen, Curtis LeRoy *federal judge*
Parker, James Aubrey *federal judge*

Roswell
Baldock, Bobby Ray *federal judge*

Santa Fe
Baca, Joseph Francis *state supreme court judge*
Campos, Santiago E. *federal judge*
Franchini, Gene Edward *state supreme court justice*
Kelly, Paul Joseph, Jr. *federal judge*
Maes, Petra Jimenez *judge*
Ransom, Richard E. *state supreme court chief justice*
Seth, Oliver *federal judge*

NEW YORK

Albany
†Alexander, Fritz W., II *judge*
Bellacosa, Joseph W. *judge*
Cholakis, Constantine George *federal judge*
Kaye, Judith Smith *judge*
Mahoney, Justin J. *federal judge*
Miner, Roger Jeffrey *federal judge*
Simons, Richard Duncan *judge*
Smith, Ralph Wesley, Jr. *federal judge*
Titone, Vito Joseph *judge*

Binghamton
McAvoy, Thomas James *federal judge*

Bronx
Roberts, Burton Bennett *administrative judge*

Brooklyn
Amon, Carol Bagley *federal judge*
Bartels, John Ries *federal judge*
Bramwell, Henry *federal judge*
Dearie, Raymond Joseph *federal judge*
Glasser, Israel Leo *federal judge*
Johnson, Sterling, Jr. *federal judge*
Korman, Edward R. *federal judge*
Nickerson, Eugene H. *federal judge*
Raggi, Reena *federal judge*
†Seybert, Joanna *judge*
Sifton, Charles Proctor *federal judge*
†Trager, David G. *judge, lawyer, educator*
Weinstein, Jack B. *federal judge*

Buffalo
Arcara, Richard Joseph *federal judge*
Jasen, Matthew Joseph *state justice*
McGuire, Beryl Edward *retired federal judge*
Skretny, William Marion *federal judge*

Hauppauge
Hurley, Denis R. *federal judge*
Wexler, Leonard D. *federal judge*

Hempstead
Altimari, Frank X. *federal judge*

Mineola
Mogil, Bernard Marc *judge*

New York
Abram, Prudence Beatty *federal judge*
Aquilino, Thomas Joseph, Jr. *federal judge, law educator*
†Baer, Harold, Jr. *judge*
Buchwald, Naomi Reice *federal magistrate judge*
Cannella, John Matthew *federal judge*
Carman, Gregory Wright *federal judge*
Carter, Robert Lee *federal judge*
Cedarbaum, Miriam Goldman *federal judge*
Conner, William Curtis *judge*
Cooper, Irving Ben *federal judge*
DiCarlo, Dominick L. *federal judge*
Duffy, Kevin Thomas *federal judge*
Edelstein, David Northon *federal judge*
Feinberg, Wilfred *federal judge*
Gershon, Nina *federal judge*
Goldberg, Richard W. *federal judge*
Griesa, Thomas Poole *federal judge*
Grody, Donald *judge, lawyer, arbitrator, actor*
†Grubin, Sharon E. *federal judge*
Harwood, Stanley *retired judge, lawyer*
Jacobs, Dennis G. *federal judge*
Kearse, Amalya Lyle *federal judge*
Keenan, John Fontaine *federal judge*
Knapp, Whitman *federal judge*
Kram, Shirley Wohl *federal judge*
Kupferman, Theodore R. *state justice*
Lee, Barbara A. *federal magistrate judge*
Leisure, Peter Keeton *federal judge*
Leval, Pierre Nelson *federal judge*
Lifland, Burton R. *federal judge*
Lowe, Mary Johnson *federal judge*
Martin, John S., Jr. *federal judge*
McKenna, Lawrence M. *federal judge*
McLaughlin, Joseph Michael *federal judge, law educator*
Metzner, Charles Miller *federal judge*
Motley, Constance Baker (Mrs. Joel Wilson Motley) *federal judge, former city official*
Mukasey, Michael B. *federal judge*
Musgrave, R. Kenton *federal judge*
Owen, Richard *federal judge*
Patterson, Robert Porter, Jr. *federal judge*
Pierce, Lawrence Warren *federal judge*
Pollack, Milton *federal judge*
Preska, Loretta A. *federal judge*
Restani, Jane A. *federal judge*
Rosenberger, Ernst Hey *judge*
Sand, Leonard B. *federal judge*
Schwartz, Allen G. *judge, lawyer*
Sotomayor, Sonia *federal judge*
Sprizzo, John Emilio *federal judge*
Stewart, Charles Edward, Jr. *federal judge*
Sweet, Robert Workman *federal judge*
Tenney, Charles Henry *federal judge*
Timbers, William Homer *federal judge*
†Torres, Edwin *state judge, writer*
Tsoucalas, Nicholas *federal judge*
Walker, John Mercer, Jr. *federal judge*
Ward, Robert Joseph *federal judge*
Watson, James Lopez *federal judge*
Williams, Milton Lawrence *judge, educator*
Wood, Kimba M. *federal judge*

Poughkeepsie
Rosenblatt, Albert Martin *state supreme court justice*

Rochester
Larimer, David George *federal judge*
Telesca, Michael Anthony *federal judge*
Van Graafeiland, Ellsworth Alfred *federal judge*

Syracuse
McCurn, Neal Peters *federal judge*
Munson, Howard G. *federal judge*
Scullin, Frederick James, Jr. *federal judge*

Uniondale
Mishler, Jacob *federal judge*
Platt, Thomas Collier, Jr. *federal judge*
Pratt, George Cheney *federal judge*
Spatt, Arthur Donald *federal judge*

Utica
Cardamone, Richard J. *federal judge*

Webster
Witmer, G. Robert *retired state supreme court justice*

Westbury
Eisenberg, Dorothy *federal judge*

White Plains
Brieant, Charles La Monte *federal judge*
Broderick, Vincent Lyons *federal judge*
Goettel, Gerard Louis *federal judge*

NORTH CAROLINA

Asheville
Voorhees, Richard Lesley *federal judge*

Chapel Hill
Martin, Harry Corpening *state supreme court justice, retired*

Charlotte
McMillan, James Bryan *federal judge, retired*
Mullen, Graham C. *federal judge*
Potter, Robert Daniel *federal judge*

Durham
Everett, Robinson Oscar *federal judge, law educator*

Elizabeth City
Boyle, Terrence W. *federal judge*

Greensboro
Bullock, Frank William, Jr. *federal judge*
Gordon, Eugene Andrew *judge*
Osteen, William L., Sr. *federal judge*
Tilley, Norwood Carlton, Jr. *federal judge*

Greenville
Howard, Malcolm Jones *federal judge*

Morganton
Ervin, Samuel James, III *federal judge*

Raleigh
Britt, W. Earl *federal judge*
Denson, Alexander Bunn *federal magistrate judge*
Dupree, Franklin Taylor, Jr. *federal judge*
Eagles, Sidney Smith, Jr. *judge*
Exum, James Gooden, Jr. *state supreme court chief justice*
Frye, Henry E. *state supreme court justice*
Meyer, Louis B. *state supreme court justice*
Mitchell, Burley Bayard, Jr. *state supreme court justice*
Small, Alden Thomas *federal judge*
Webb, John *state supreme court justice*
Whichard, Willis Padgett *state supreme court justice*

Wilmington
Fox, James Carroll *federal judge*

Winston Salem
Eliason, Russell Allen *federal judge*
Erwin, Richard Cannon *federal judge*
Ward, Hiram Hamilton *federal judge*

NORTH DAKOTA

Bismarck
Conmy, Patrick A. *federal judge*
Erickstad, Ralph John *judge, retired state supreme court chief justice*
Meschke, Herbert Leonard *state supreme court justice*
Pederson, Vernon R. *judge*
VandeWalle, Gerald Wayne *state supreme court chief justice*
Van Sickle, Bruce Marion *federal judge*

Fargo
Bright, Myron H. *federal judge, educator*
Hill, William A(lexander) *bankruptcy judge*
Magill, Frank John *federal judge*
Webb, Rodney Scott *federal judge, lawyer*

Williston
Burdick, Eugene Allan *retired judge, lawyer, surrogate judge*

OHIO

Ada
Hanson, Eugene Nelson *judge*

Akron
Bell, Samuel H. *federal judge*
Contie, Leroy John, Jr. *federal judge*
Dowd, David D., Jr. *federal judge*
White, Harold F. *federal judge*

Bowling Green
Baird, James Abington *judge*

Cincinnati
Aug, Jonathan Vincent *federal bankruptcy judge*
Jones, Nathaniel Raphael *federal judge*
Nelson, David Aldrich *federal judge*
Perlman, Burton *federal judge*
Rubin, Carl Bernard *federal judge*
Spiegel, S. Arthur *federal judge*
Weber, Herman Jacob *federal judge*

Cleveland
Aldrich, Ann *federal judge*
Battisti, Frank Joseph *federal judge*
Burke, Lillian Walker *retired judge*
Krupansky, Blanche *judge*
Krupansky, Robert Bazil *federal judge*
Lambros, Thomas Demetrios *federal judge*
Manos, John M. *federal judge*
Matia, Paul Ramon *federal judge*
Porter, James Morris *state judge*
Stokes, Carl Burton *judge, former mayor, former state legislator*
Thomas, William Kernahan *federal judge*
White, George W. *federal judge*

Columbus
Beckwith, Sandra Shank *federal judge*
Calhoun, Donald Eugene, Jr. *federal judge*
Douglas, Andrew *state supreme court justice*
Graham, James Lowell *federal judge*
Holschuh, John David *federal judge*
King, Norah M. *federal judge*
Kinneary, Joseph Peter *federal judge*
Leach, Russell *judge*
Mc Cormac, John Waverly *judge*
Moyer, Thomas J. *state supreme court chief justice*
Norris, Alan Eugene *federal judge*
Resnick, Alice Robie *state supreme court justice*
Sellers, Barbara Jackson *federal judge*
Smith, George Curtis *federal judge*
Sweeney, Asher William *state supreme court justice*
Wright, J. Craig *state supreme court associate justice*

Dayton
Clark, William Alfred *federal judge*
Love, Rodney Marvin *retired judge, former congressman*
Merz, Michael *federal judge*
Porter, Walter Arthur *judge*

Medina
Batchelder, Alice M. *federal judge*

Middletown
Jones, Fred E. *state judge*

Paulding
Hitchcock, J. Gareth *retired judge*

Toledo
Potter, John William *federal judge*
Young, Don J. *federal judge*

Warren
Nader, Robert Alexander *judge, lawyer*

OKLAHOMA

Lawton
Moore, Roy Dean *judge*

Muskogee
Seay, Frank Howell *federal judge*

Norman
Trimble, Preston Albert *retired judge*

Oklahoma City
Alley, Wayne Edward *federal judge, retired army officer*
Bohanon, Luther L. *federal judge*
Bohanon, Richard Lee *federal judge*
Cauthron, Robin J. *federal judge*
Daugherty, Frederick Alvin *federal judge*
Hargrave, Rudolph *state supreme court justice*
Hodges, Ralph B. *state supreme court justice*
Holloway, William J., Jr. *federal judge*
Irwin, Pat *federal magistrate judge*
Lane, James Franklin *judge*
Lavender, Robert Eugene *state supreme court justice*
Leonard, Timothy Dwight *federal judge*
Opala, Marian P(eter) *state supreme court justice*
Russell, David L. *federal judge*
Summers, Hardy *state supreme court justice*
Thompson, Ralph Gordon *federal judge*
West, Lee Roy *federal judge*
Wilson, Alma *state supreme court justice*

Tulsa
Beasley, William Rex *judge*
Brett, Thomas Rutherford *federal judge*
Brightmire, Paul William *judge*
Cook, Harold Dale *federal judge*
Seymour, Stephanie Kulp *federal judge*
Taylor, Joe Clinton *judge*
Wagner, John Leo *federal judge, lawyer*

OREGON

Eugene
Coffin, Thomas M. *federal magistrate judge*
Hogan, Michael R(obert) *federal judge*

Portland
Beatty, John Cabeen, Jr. *judge*
Burns, James M. *federal judge*
Frye, Helen Jackson *federal judge*
Hill, Wilmer Bailey *administrative law judge*
Jones, Robert Edward *federal judge*
Kilkenny, John F. *federal judge, lawyer*
Leavy, Edward *federal judge*
Marsh, Malcolm F. *federal judge*
O'Scannlain, Diarmuid Fionntain *federal judge*
Panner, Owen M. *federal judge*
Redden, James Anthony *federal judge*
Skopil, Otto Richard, Jr. *federal judge*

Salem
Carson, Wallace Preston, Jr. *state supreme court chief justice*
Fadeley, Edward Norman *state supreme court justice*
Graber, Susan P. *judge*
O'Connell, Kenneth John *state justice*
Peterson, Edwin J. *state supreme court justice, retired*
Unis, Richard L. *state supreme court justice*
Van Hoomissen, George Albert *state supreme court justice*

PENNSYLVANIA

Easton
Van Antwerpen, Franklin Stuart *federal judge*

Erie
Bentz, Warren Worthington *federal bankruptcy judge*
Mencer, Glenn Everell *federal judge*
Nygaard, Richard Lowell *federal judge*

Harrisburg
Caldwell, William Wilson *federal judge*
Rambo, Sylvia H. *federal judge*

Philadelphia
Angell, M(ary) Faith *federal magistrate judge*
Bartle, Harvey, III *federal judge*
Bechtle, Louis Charles *federal judge*
Becker, Edward Roy *federal judge*
Brody, Anita Blumstein *federal judge*
Buckwalter, Ronald Lawrence *federal judge*
Cahn, Edward N. *federal judge*
Dalzell, Stewart *federal judge*
Ditter, John William, Jr. *federal judge*
DuBois, Jan Ely *federal judge*
Fullam, John P. *federal judge*
Gawthrop, Robert Smith, III *federal judge*
Giles, James T. *federal judge*
Green, Clifford Scott *federal judge*
Hutchinson, William David *federal judge*
Hutton, Herbert J. *federal judge*
Joyner, J(ames) Curtis *federal judge*
Katz, Marvin *federal judge*
Kelly, James McGirr *federal judge*
Kelly, Robert F. *federal judge*
Ludwig, Edmund Vincent *federal judge*
McGlynn, Joseph Leo, Jr. *federal judge*
Newcomer, Clarence Charles *federal judge*
Nix, Robert N(elson) C(ornelius), Jr. *state supreme court chief justice*
O'Neill, Thomas Newman, Jr. *federal judge*
Padova, John R. *federal judge*
Powers, Richard Augustine, III *federal judge*
Reed, Lowell A., Jr. *federal judge*
Richette, Lisa Aversa *judge*
Robreno, Eduardo C. *federal judge*
Ryan, Leonard Eames *administrative law judge*
Scholl, David Allen *federal judge*
Scirica, Anthony Joseph *federal judge*
Shapiro, Norma Sondra Levy *federal judge*
Sloviter, Dolores Korman *federal judge*
Waldman, Jay Carl *federal judge*
Yohn, William Hendricks, Jr. *federal judge*

Pittsburgh
†Ambrose, Donetta *federal judge*
Bloch, Alan Neil *federal judge*
Brosky, John G. *judge*
Cohill, Maurice Blanchard, Jr. *federal judge*
Craig, David W. *judge*
Diamond, Gustave *federal judge*
Flaherty, John P., Jr. *state supreme court justice*
Lee, Donald John *federal judge*
Lewis, Timothy K. *federal judge*
Mansmann, Carol Los *federal judge, law educator*
Mc Cune, Barron Patterson *federal judge*
Papadakos, Nicholas Peter *state supreme court justice*
Smith, David Brookman *federal judge*
Standish, William Lloyd *federal judge*
Weis, Joseph Francis, Jr. *federal judge*
Zappala, Stephen A. *state supreme court justice*
Ziegler, Donald Emil *federal judge*

Reading
Huyett, Daniel Henry, III *federal judge*
Troutman, E. Mac *federal judge*

Scranton
Conaboy, Richard Paul *federal judge*
Kosik, Edwin Michael *federal judge*
Nealon, William Joseph, Jr. *federal judge*
O'Malley, Carlon Martin *judge*

Wilkes Barre
Rosenn, Max *federal judge*

Williamsport
McClure, James Focht, Jr. *federal judge*
Muir, Malcolm *federal judge*

RHODE ISLAND

Providence
Boyle, Francis Joseph *federal judge*
Hagopian, Jacob *federal judge*
Lagueux, Ronald Rene *federal judge*
Murray, Florence Kerins *state supreme court justice*
Selya, Bruce Marshall *federal judge*
Torres, Ernest C. *federal judge*
Votolato, Arthur Nicholas, Jr. *federal judge*
Weisberger, Joseph Robert *state supreme court justice*

SOUTH CAROLINA

Aiken
Simons, Charles Earl, Jr. *federal judge*

Anderson
Anderson, George Ross, Jr. *federal judge*

Charleston
Carr, Robert Stuart *federal magistrate judge*
Hawkins, Falcon Black, Jr. *federal judge*
Norton, David C. *federal judge*

Columbia
Anderson, Joseph Fletcher, Jr. *federal judge*
Chapman, Robert Foster *federal judge*
Hamilton, Clyde Henry *federal judge*
Perry, Matthew J., Jr. *federal judge*
Shedd, Dennis W. *federal judge*
Toal, Jean Hoefer *lawyer, state supreme court justice*

Darlington
Chandler, A. Lee *state supreme court justice*

Florence
Houck, Charles Weston *federal judge*

Greenville
Herlong, Henry Michael, Jr. *federal judge*
Traxler, William Byrd, Jr. *federal judge*
Wilkins, William Walter, Jr. *federal judge*

Lexington
Timmerman, George Bell, Jr. *judge*

Myrtle Beach
Harwell, David Walker *retired state supreme court chief justice*

Spartanburg
Russell, Donald Stuart *federal judge*

Sumter
Finney, Ernest Adolphus, Jr. *state supreme court chief justice*

SOUTH DAKOTA

Aberdeen
Richards, Carlyle Edward *magistrate judge*

Belle Fourche
Wuest, George W. *state supreme court justice*

Pierre
Amundson, Robert A. *state supreme court justice*
Henderson, Frank Ellis *state supreme court justice*
Miller, Robert Arthur *state supreme court chief justice*
Porter, Donald James *federal judge*
Sabers, Richard Wayne *state supreme court justice*

Rapid City
Battey, Richard Howard *federal judge*

Sioux Falls
Ecker, Peder Kaloides *federal judge*
Gibbs, Frank P. *federal judge*
Jones, John Bailey *federal judge*
†Piersol, Lawrence L. *federal judge*
Wollman, Roger Leland *federal judge*

TENNESSEE

Chattanooga
Edgar, R(obert) Allan *federal judge*
Milburn, Herbert Theodore *federal judge*
Powers, John Y. *federal judge*
Summitt, Robert Murray *circuit judge*

Greeneville
Hull, Thomas Gray *federal judge*

Jackson
Todd, James Dale *federal judge*

Knoxville
Anderson, Edward Riley *state supreme court justice*
Jarvis, James Howard, II *federal judge*
Jordan, Robert Leon *federal judge*
Murrian, Robert Phillip *federal judge, educator*

Memphis
Allen, James Henry *magistrate judge*
Brown, Aaron Clifton, Jr. *magistrate judge*
Brown, Bailey *federal judge*
Gibbons, Julia Smith *federal judge*
Horton, Odell *federal judge*
Kennedy, David Stewart *federal judge*
McCalla, Jon P. *federal judge*
McRae, Robert Malcolm, Jr. *federal judge*
Turner, Jerome *federal judge*
Wellford, Harry Walker *federal judge*

Nashville
Daughtrey, Martha Craig *federal judge*
Echols, Robert L. *federal judge*
Higgins, Thomas A. *federal judge*
Merritt, Gilbert Stroud *federal judge*
Nixon, John Trice *federal judge*
O'Brien, Charles H. *state supreme court justice*
Reid, Lyle *judge*
Wiseman, Thomas Anderton, Jr. *federal judge*

Signal Mountain
Cooper, Robert Elbert *state supreme court justice*

TEXAS

Amarillo
Robinson, Mary Lou *federal judge*

Arlington
Wright, James Edward *judge*

Austin
Derounian, Steven Boghos *lawyer, retired judge*
Doggett, Lloyd *state supreme court justice*
Gammage, Robert Alton (Bob Gammage) *state supreme court justice*
Garwood, William Lockhart *federal judge*
Gonzalez, Raul A. *state supreme court justice*
Greenhill, Joe R. *former chief justice state supreme, lawyer*
Hecht, Nathan Lincoln *state supreme court justice*
Hightower, Jack English *state supreme court justice, former congressman*
Johnson, Sam D. *federal judge*
Nowlin, James Robertson *federal judge*
Phillips, Thomas Royal *judge*
Pope, Andrew Jackson, Jr. (Jack Pope) *retired state supreme court chief justice*
Ray, Cread L., Jr. *retired state supreme court justice*
Reavley, Thomas Morrow *federal judge*
Sparks, Sam *federal judge*
Spears, Franklin Scott *retired supreme court justice*
Thornberry, William Homer *federal judge*
Williams, Mary Pearl *judge, lawyer*

Beaumont
Cobb, Howell *federal judge*
Fisher, Joseph Jefferson *federal judge*
Schell, Richard A. *federal judge*

Brownsville
Garza, Reynaldo G. *federal judge*
Vela, Filemon B. *federal judge*

Corpus Christi
Head, Hayden Wilson, Jr. *federal judge*
Schmidt, Richard S. *federal judge*

Dallas
Buchmeyer, Jerry *federal judge*
Fish, A. Joe *federal judge*
Fitzwater, Sidney Allen *federal judge*
Goldberg, Irving Loeb *federal judge*
Higginbotham, Patrick Errol *federal judge*
Kendall, Joe *federal judge*
Luce, Thomas Warren, III *former chief justice, lawyer*
Maloney, Robert B. *federal judge*
Price, Robert Eben *judge*
Robertson, Ted Zanderson *judge*
Sanders, Harold Barefoot, Jr. *federal judge*
Solis, Jorge Antonio *federal judge*

El Paso
Hudspeth, Harry Lee *federal judge*
Ruesch, Janet Carol *federal judge*

Fort Worth
Belew, David Owen, Jr. *judge*
McBryde, John Henry *federal judge*
Means, Terry Robert *federal judge*

Galveston
Gibson, Hugh *federal judge*
Kent, Samuel B. *federal judge*

Houston
Black, Norman William *federal judge*
Bue, Carl Olaf, Jr. *retired federal judge*
Cowan, Finis Ewing *federal judge*
DeMoss, Harold R., Jr. *federal judge*
Harmon, Melinda Furche *federal judge*
Hittner, David *federal judge*
Hoyt, Kenneth M. *federal judge*
Hughes, Lynn Nettleton *federal judge*
Jones, Edith Hollan *federal judge*
King, Carolyn Dineen *federal judge*
Lake, Simeon Timothy, III *federal judge*
Rainey, John David *federal judge*
Rosenthal, Lee H. *federal judge*
Singleton, John Virgil, Jr. *retired federal judge, lawyer*
Smith, Jerry Edwin *federal judge*
Steen, Wesley Wilson *former bankruptcy judge, lawyer*
Werlein, Ewing, Jr. *federal judge, lawyer*

Laredo
Kazen, George Philip *federal judge*

Levelland
Walker, James Kenneth *judge*

Lubbock
Cummings, Sam R. *federal judge*

Mcallen
Hinojosa, Ricardo H. *federal judge*

Pampa
Cain, Donald Ezell *judge*

Rusk
Hassell, Morris William *judge*

San Antonio
Clark, Leif Michael *federal judge*
Garcia, Hipolito Frank (Hippo Garcia) *federal judge*
Garza, Emilio M(iller) *federal judge*
King, Ronald Baker *federal judge*
Prado, Edward Charles *federal judge*
Suttle, Dorwin Wallace *federal judge*

Sherman
Brown, Paul Neeley *federal judge*

Temple
Skelton, Byron George *federal judge*

Tyler
Guthrie, Judith K. *federal judge*
Justice, William Wayne *federal judge*
Parker, Robert M. *federal judge*
Steger, William Merritt *federal judge*

Waco
Smith, Walter S., Jr. *federal judge*

Wharton
Abell, Thomas Henry *judge*

UTAH

Ogden
Stewart, Isaac Daniel, Jr. *state supreme court justice*

Salt Lake City
Anderson, Stephen Hale *federal judge*
Clark, Glen Edward *federal judge*
Durham, Christine Meaders *state supreme court justice*
Greene, John Thomas, Jr. *federal judge*
Hall, Gordon R. *retired state supreme court chief justice*
Howe, Richard Cuddy *state supreme court justice*
Jenkins, Bruce Sterling *federal judge*
McKay, Monroe Gunn *federal judge*
Sam, David *federal judge*
Winder, David Kent *federal judge*
Zimmerman, Michael David *state supreme court chief justice*

VERMONT

Bennington
Gagliardi, Lee Parsons *federal judge*

Brattleboro
Oakes, James L. *federal judge*

Burlington
Parker, Fred I. *federal judge*

Montpelier
Allen, Frederic W. *state supreme court justice*
Morse, James L. *state supreme court justice*

North Bennington
Holden, James Stuart *federal judge*

Rutland
Billings, Franklin Swift, Jr. *federal judge*

VIRGINIA

Abingdon
Widener, Hiram Emory, Jr. *federal judge*
Williams, Glen Morgan *federal judge*
Wilson, Samuel Grayson *federal judge*

Alexandria
Bostetter, Martin V. B., Jr. *bankruptcy court judge*
Brinkema, Leonie Milhomme *federal judge*
Cacheris, James C. *federal judge*
Ellis, Thomas Selby, III *federal judge*
Hilton, Claude Meredith *federal judge*

Arlington
Nejelski, Paul Arthur *judge*
†Van Doren, Emerson Barclay *administrative judge*

Charlottesville
Crigler, B. Waugh *federal judge*
Michael, James Harry, Jr. *federal judge*
Wilkinson, James Harvie, III *federal judge*

Danville
Kiser, Jackson L. *federal judge*

Falls Church
Burg, Ruth Cooper (Thelma Breslauer) *administrative judge*
Morse, Marvin Henry *judge*
Reiter, Joseph Henry *judge*
Spector, Louis *retired federal judge, lawyer, arbitrator, consultant*

Fredericksburg
Corcoran, John Joseph *federal judge*
Jamison, John Ambler *retired circuit judge*

Mc Lean
Luttig, J. Michael *federal judge*

Newport News
Bateman, Fred Willom *retired judge*

Norfolk
Adams, David Huntington *judge*

Bonney, Hal James, Jr. *federal judge*
Clarke, J. Calvitt, Jr. *federal judge*
Doumar, Robert George *federal judge*
Hoffman, Walter Edward *federal judge*
†Jackson, Raymond A. *federal judge*
Prince, William Taliaferro *federal judge*
Smith, Rebecca Beach *federal judge*

Richmond
Butzner, John Decker, Jr. *federal judge*
Carrico, Harry Lee *state supreme court chief justice*
Compton, Asbury Christian *state supreme court justice*
Gordon, Thomas Christian, Jr. *former justice*
Merhige, Robert Reynold, Jr. *federal judge*
Payne, Robert E. *federal judge*
Poff, Richard Harding *state supreme court justice*
Spencer, James R. *federal judge*
Stephenson, Roscoe Bolar, Jr. *state supreme court justice*
Tice, Douglas Oscar, Jr. *federal judge*
Williams, Richard Leroy *federal judge*

Roanoke
Pearson, Henry Clyde *federal judge*
Turk, James Clinton *federal judge*

Staunton
Cochran, George Moffett *retired judge*

Winchester
Whiting, Henry H. *state supreme court justice*

WASHINGTON

Bainbridge Is
Warns, Raymond H. *judge*

Federal Way
Hayek, Carolyn Jean *judge*

Olympia
Andersen, James A. *state supreme court chief justice*
Brachtenbach, Robert F. *state supreme court justice*
Dolliver, James Morgan *state supreme court justice*
Durham, Barbara *state supreme court justice*
Guy, Richard P. *state supreme court justice*
Johnson, Charles William *state supreme court justice*
Smith, Charles Z. *state supreme court justice*
Utter, Robert French *state supreme court justice*

Seattle
Beezer, Robert Renaut *federal judge*
Coughenour, John Clare *federal judge*
Dimmick, Carolyn Reaber *federal judge*
Dwyer, William L. *federal judge*
Farris, Jerome *federal judge*
Fletcher, Betty B. *federal judge*
Mc Govern, Walter T. *federal judge*
†Noe, James Alva *judge*
Rothstein, Barbara Jacobs *federal judge*
Weinberg, John Lee *federal judge*
Wright, Eugene Allen *federal judge*
Zilly, Thomas Samuel *federal judge*

Spokane
Green, Dale Monte *retired judge*
Klobucher, John Marcellus *federal judge*
Nielsen, William Fremming *federal judge*
Quackenbush, Justin Lowe *chief federal judge*
Van Sickle, Frederick L. *federal judge*

Tacoma
Bryan, Robert J. *federal judge*

Yakima
Hovis, James Brunton *federal judge*
McDonald, Alan Angus *federal judge*

WEST VIRGINIA

Beckley
Hallanan, Elizabeth V. *federal judge*

Bluefield
Faber, David Alan *federal judge*

Charleston
Brotherton, William T., Jr. *state supreme court justice*
Cograve, John Edwin *judge*
Copenhaver, John Thomas, Jr. *federal judge*
Haden, Charles H., II *federal judge*
Hall, Kenneth Keller *federal judge*
Knapp, Dennis Raymond *federal judge*
McHugh, Thomas Edward *state supreme court justice*
†Michael, M. Blane *federal judge*
Neely, Richard *state supreme court justice*
Workman, Margaret Lee *state supreme court justice*

Clarksburg
Keeley, Irene Patricia Murphy *federal judge*
Kidd, William Matthew *federal judge*

Elkins
Maxwell, Robert Earl *federal judge*

Lewisburg
Sprouse, James Marshall *federal judge*

WISCONSIN

Appleton
Froehlich, Harold Vernon *judge, former congressman*

Madison
Abrahamson, Shirley Schlanger *state supreme court justice*
Bablitch, William A. *state supreme court justice*
Day, Roland Bernard *state supreme court justice*
Heffernan, Nathan Stewart *state supreme court chief justice*
Martin, Robert David *federal judge, law educator*
Shabaz, John C. *federal judge*

Milwaukee
Clevert, Charles Nelson, Jr. *federal judge*
Curran, Thomas J. *federal judge*
Ihlenfeldt, Dale Elwood *judge*
McGarity, Margaret Dee *federal judge*
Randa, Rudolph Thomas *federal judge*
Shapiro, James Edward *federal judge*
Stadtmueller, Joseph Peter *federal judge*

Monroe
†Deininger, David George *federal judge*

Nashotah
Hansen, Robert Wayne *judge, editor*

Sheboygan
Buchen, John Gustave *retired judge*

WYOMING

Cheyenne
Barrett, James E. *federal judge*
Brimmer, Clarence Addison *federal judge*
Brorby, Wade *federal judge*
Brown, Charles Stuart *retired state supreme court justice*
Cardine, Godfrey Joseph *state supreme court justice*
Golden, Michael *state supreme court justice*
Johnson, Alan Bond *federal judge*
Macy, Richard J. *state judge*
Thomas, Richard Van *state supreme court justice*

Green River
Marty, Lawrence A. *lawyer, magistrate judge*

Jackson
Bommer, Timothy J *judge*

Sheridan
Mc Ewan, Leonard *former judge*

Wheatland
Mickelsen, Einer Bjegaard *judge*

TERRITORIES OF THE UNITED STATES

AMERICAN SAMOA

Pago Pago
Kruse, F. Michael *judge*

GUAM

Agana
Cruz, Benjamin Joseph Franquez *territory judge*
Diaz, Ramon Valero *judge*
Lamorena, Alberto C., III *judge*
Unpingco, John Walter Sablan *federal judge*

NORTHERN MARIANA ISLANDS

Saipan
Dela Cruz, Jose Santos *state supreme court chief justice*

PUERTO RICO

San Juan
Acosta, Raymond Luis *federal judge*
Cerezo, Carmen Consuelo *federal judge*
Fuste, Jose Antonio *federal judge*
Gierbolini-Ortiz, Gilberto *federal judge*
Hernandez-Denton, Federico *territory supreme court justice*
Laffitte, Hector Manuel *federal judge*
Perez-Gimenez, Juan Manuel *federal judge*
Pieras, Jaime, Jr. *federal judge*
Torruella, Juan R. *federal judge*

VIRGIN ISLANDS

Charlotte Amalie
Moore, Thomas Kail *chief judge*

Christiansted
Finch, Raymond Lawrence *judge*

Saint Thomas
Hodge, Verne Antonio *judge*

CANADA

ALBERTA

Edmonton
†Fraser, Catherine Anne *Canadian chief justice*
Miller, Tevie *supernumary justice, academic administrator*
Stevenson, William Alexander *retired justice of Supreme Court of Canada*

BRITISH COLUMBIA

Vancouver
Lysyk, Kenneth Martin *judge*

MANITOBA

Winnipeg
Lyon, Sterling Rufus *justice*

Scott, Richard Jamieson *chief justice*

NEW BRUNSWICK

Saint John
Logan, Rodman Emmason *judge*

NEWFOUNDLAND

Saint John's
Goodridge, Noel Herbert Alan *state supreme court chief justice*

NOVA SCOTIA

Halifax
Glube, Constance Rachelle *Canadian chief justice*

ONTARIO

Dunrobin
Dickson, Brian *retired chief justice of Canada*

Ottawa
Cory, Peter deCarteret *Canadian Supreme Court justice*
Cullen, Jack Sydney George Bud *federal judge*
Gonthier, Charles Doherty *Canadian Supreme Court justice*
Heald, Darrel Verner *Canadian federal judge*
Jerome, James Alexander *Canadian federal justice*
La Forest, Gerard Vincent *justice*
Lamer, Antonio *Canadian supreme court chief justice*
L'Heureux-Dube, Claire *judge*
MacGuigan, Mark R. *Canadian federal judge*
MacKay, William Andrew *judge*
Mahoney, Patrick Morgan *judge*
†Major, John C. *judge*
McLachlin, Beverley *supreme court judge*
Muldoon, Francis Creighton *Canadian federal judge*
Sopinka, John *Supreme Court of Canada justice*
Tait, John Charles *Canadian deputy minister of justice*
Wilson, Bertha *Canadian justice*

Toronto
Boland, Janet Lang *judge*
Dubin, Charles Leonard *federal judge*
Gotlib, Lorraine *justice, former lawyer*
McMurtry, R. Roy *chief justice*

Willowdale
Harris, Sydney Malcolm *retired judge*

PRINCE EDWARD ISLAND

Charlottetown
Carruthers, Norman Harry *Canadian province supreme court justice*

QUEBEC

Montreal
Bisson, Claude *chief justice of Quebec*
Gold, Alan B. *former Canadian chief justice*
Rothman, Melvin L. *judge*

SASKATCHEWAN

Regina
Bayda, Edward Dmytro *judge*

ESTONIA

Tallinn
Callow, Keith McLean *judge*

THE NETHERLANDS

The Hague
Allison, Richard Clark *judge*

ADDRESS UNPUBLISHED

Adams, Arlin Marvin *retired judge, counsel to law firm*
Adams, Oscar William, Jr. *retired state supreme court justice*
Addy, George Arthur *retired judge*
Bartunek, Joseph Wenceslaus *magistrate judge*
Bertelsman, William Odis *federal judge*
Bootle, William Augustus *retired federal judge*
Box, Dwain D. *former judge*
Brown, Robert Laidlaw *state supreme court justice*
Bunton, Lucius Desha, III *federal judge*
Burger, Warren Earl *former chief justice of U.S. supreme court, academic administrator*
Burke, Edmond Wayne *judge*
Callow, William Grant *retired state supreme court justice*
Ceci, Louis J. *former state supreme court justice*
Chambers, Richard H. *federal judge*
Christensen, Albert Sherman *federal judge*
Coffey, John Louis *federal judge*
Cohn, Avern Levin *federal judge*
Colaianni, Joseph Vincent *judge*
Collins, Robert Frederick *federal judge*
Cook, Julian Abele, Jr. *federal judge*
Cyr, Conrad Keefe *federal judge*
Dore, Fred Hudson *retired state supreme court chief justice*
Drennen, William Miller *federal judge*
Foster, Robert Lawson *retired judge, deacon*
Hogan, Thomas Francis *federal judge*

Holland, Randy James *state supreme court justice*
House, Charles Staver *judge*
Kauger, Yvonne *state supreme court justice*
Kelly, Aurel Maxey *judge*
Laycraft, James Herbert *judge*
Le Dain, Gerald Eric *retired Canadian Supreme Court justice*
Lee, Dan M. *state supreme court justice*
Linde, Hans Arthur *state supreme court justice*
†Lindsay, Reginald Carl *federal judge*
Logan, James Kenneth *federal judge*
Low, Harry William *judge*
McCown, Hale *retired judge*
Montgomery, Seth David *state supreme court chief justice*
Morgan, Robert Edward *state supreme court justice*
Mydland, Gordon James *judge*
Nangle, John Francis *federal judge*
Nardi Riddle, Clarine *judge*
Newman, Theodore Roosevelt, Jr. *judge*
Phillips, James Dickson, Jr. *federal judge*
Prager, David *retired state supreme court chief justice*
Quirico, Francis Joseph *retired state supreme court justice*
Reinhardt, Stephen Roy *federal judge*
Rice, Walter Herbert *federal judge*
Ross, Donald Roe *federal judge*
Schwebel, Stephen Myron *judge, arbitrator*
Shea, Donald Francis *state supreme court justice*
Silberman, Laurence Hirsch *federal judge*
Smith, Fern M. *federal judge*
Souter, David Hackett *U.S. supreme court justice*
Staker, Robert Jackson *federal judge*
Stamos, John James *judge*
Stamp, Frederick Pfarr, Jr. *federal judge*
Stanton, Louis Lee *federal judge*
Thornburg, Lacy Herman *judge*
Turnoff, William Charles *judge*
Vollmer, Richard Wade *federal judge*
Wyman, Louis Crosby *state justice, former senator, former congressman*

LAW: LAW PRACTICE AND ADMINISTRATION

UNITED STATES

ALABAMA

Andalusia
Fuller, William Sidney *lawyer*

Anniston
Klinefelter, James Louis *lawyer*

Auburn
†Little, Ted David *lawyer*
Samford, Thomas Drake, III *university general counsel*

Birmingham
Adams, John Powers *lawyer*
Alexander, James Patrick *lawyer*
Balch, Samuel Eason *lawyer*
Blan, Ollie Lionel, Jr. *lawyer*
Brown, Ephraim Taylor, Jr. *lawyer*
Carruthers, Thomas Neely, Jr. *lawyer*
†Clapp, Laurel Rebecca *law librarian, law educator*
Coleman, Brittin Turner *lawyer*
Coleman, John James *lawyer*
Cooper, Jerome A. *lawyer*
Cornelius, Walter Felix *lawyer*
Davis, Julian Mason, Jr. *lawyer*
Denson, William Frank, III *lawyer*
Farley, Joseph McConnell *lawyer*
Friend, Edward Malcolm, Jr. *lawyer*
Friend, Edward Malcolm, III *lawyer*
Gaede, Anton Henry, Jr. *lawyer*
Gewin, James W. *lawyer*
Hardin, Edward Lester, Jr. *lawyer*
Johnson, Joseph H., Jr. *lawyer*
Lacy, Alexander Shelton *lawyer*
Long, Thad Gladden *lawyer*
Mays, Joseph Barber, Jr. *lawyer*
Mc Millan, George Duncan Hastie, Jr. *lawyer, former state official*
McWhorter, Hobart Amory, Jr. *lawyer*
Mills, William Hayes *lawyer*
Molen, John Klauminzer *lawyer*
Newfield, Mayer Ullman *lawyer*
Oliver, Samuel William, Jr. *lawyer*
Redden, Lawrence Drew *lawyer*
Riegert, Robert Adolf *law educator, consultant*
Rogers, Ernest Mabry *lawyer*
Rotch, James E. *lawyer*
Rountree, Asa *lawyer*
Rubright, James Alfred *lawyer*
Savage, Kay Webb *lawyer, health center administrator, accountant*
†Selfe, Edward Milton *lawyer*
Smith, John Joseph *lawyer*
Spotswood, Robert Keeling *lawyer*
Stabler, Lewis Vastine, Jr. *lawyer*
Vinson, Laurence Duncan, Jr. *lawyer*
Weeks, Arthur Andrew *lawyer, educator*
Williams, Parham Henry, Jr. *lawyer*
Wrinkle, John Newton *lawyer*

Dadeville
Adair, Charles Robert, Jr. *lawyer*

Decatur
Caddell, John A. *lawyer*

Demopolis
Lloyd, Hugh Adams *lawyer*

Dothan
Little, Charles Lawson *lawyer*

Eufaula
Clayton, Preston Copeland *lawyer*

Huntsville
Cleary, James Roy *lawyer*
Huckaby, Gary Carlton *lawyer*
Potter, Ernest Luther *lawyer*
Smith, Robert Sellers *lawyer*

Mobile
Armbrecht, William Henry, III *lawyer*
Braswell, Louis Erskine *lawyer*
Brock, Paul Warrington *lawyer*
Harris, Benjamin Harte, Jr. *lawyer*
Helmsing, Frederick George *lawyer*
Holberg, Ralph Gans, Jr. *lawyer*
Holland, Lyman Faith, Jr. *lawyer*
Holmes, Broox Garrett *lawyer*
Kimbrough, William Adams, Jr. *lawyer*
Lyons, Champ, Jr. *lawyer*
Lyons, George Sage *lawyer, oil industry executive, former state legislator*
Sessions, Jefferson Beauregard, III *lawyer*
Thornton, J. Edward *lawyer*
†Windom, Stephen Ralph *lawyer, state legislator*

Montgomery
Byars, Walter Ryland, Jr. *lawyer*
†Dees, Morris Seligman, Jr. *lawyer*
Franco, Ralph Abraham *lawyer*
Graddick, Charles Allen *lawyer*
Hawthorne, Frank Howard *lawyer*
Hester, Douglas Benjamin *lawyer, federal official*
Hill, Thomas Bowen, III *lawyer*
†Hooper, Perry Ollie *lawyer*
†Langford, Charles Douglass *lawyer, state legislator*
Leslie, Henry Arthur *lawyer, retired banker*
McFadden, Frank Hampton *lawyer, business executive, former judge*
Nachman, Merton Roland, Jr. *lawyer*
Norris, Robert Wheeler *lawyer, military officer*
Salmon, Joseph Thaddeus *lawyer*
Teague, Barry Elvin *lawyer*
Volz, Charles Harvie, Jr. *lawyer*
Wampold, Charles Henry, Jr. *lawyer*

Opelika
Samford, Yetta Glenn, Jr. *lawyer*

Selma
Stewart, Edgar Allen *lawyer*

Troy
Brantley, Oliver Wiley *retired lawyer*

Tuscaloosa
Christopher, Thomas Weldon *legal educator, administrator*
Cook, Camille Wright *legal educator*
Hoff, Timothy *lawyer, educator, priest*
Watkins, John Cumming, Jr. *law educator*
Williams, Vergil Lewis *criminal justice educator*

Tuscumbia
Rosser, Charles D. *lawyer*

ALASKA

Anchorage
Baily, Douglas Boyd *lawyer*
Brown, Harold MacVane *lawyer*
De Lisio, Stephen Scott *lawyer*
Edwards, George Kent *lawyer*
Groh, Clifford J., Sr. *lawyer*
Lowe, Robert Charles *lawyer, banker*
Melcher, Jerry Eugene *lawyer*
Roberts, John Derham *lawyer*
Robison, Paul Frederick *lawyer*

Fairbanks
Kauffman, William Ray *lawyer*
Rice, Julian Casavant *lawyer*

Kodiak
Jamin, Matthew Daniel *lawyer, magistrate*

ARIZONA

Carefree
Hutchison, Stanley Philip *lawyer*

Flagstaff
†Verkamp, John *lawyer, state legislator*

Globe
Malott, James Raymond, Jr. *lawyer*

Lake Havasu City
Bird, Robert Wilson *lawyer*

Mesa
Allen, Merle Maeser, Jr. *lawyer*
Duecy, Charles Michael *retired lawyer*
Shelley, James LaMar *lawyer*

Peoria
Degnan, Thomas Leonard *lawyer*

Phoenix
Bacon, Roxana C. *lawyer*
Bain, C. Randall *lawyer*
Baker, William Dunlap *lawyer*
Bakker, Thomas Gordon *lawyer*
Ballard, Ronald Lee *lawyer*
Begam, Robert George *lawyer*
Bergin, Daniel Timothy *lawyer, banker*
Burke, Timothy John *lawyer*
Cameron, James Duke *lawyer, former state supreme court justice*
Chauncey, Tom Webster, II *lawyer*
Cohen, Jon Stephan *lawyer*
Colburn, Donald D. *lawyer*
Cooledge, Richard Calvin *lawyer*
Corbin, Robert Keith *lawyer, former state attorney general*
Crockett, Clyll Webb *lawyer*
Daughton, Donald *lawyer*
Davies, David George *lawyer*
Dawson, John Joseph *lawyer*
Deeny, Robert Joseph *lawyer*
Derdenger, Patrick *lawyer*
Dunipace, Ian Douglas *lawyer*
Durrant, Dan Martin *lawyer*
Eaton, Berrien Clark *lawyer, author*
Everroad, John D. *lawyer*
Feinstein, Allen Lewis *lawyer*
Fenzl, Terry Earle *lawyer*
Fine, Charles Leon *lawyer*
Fish, Barry *lawyer*
Frank, John Paul *lawyer, author*
Freedman, Kenneth David *lawyer*
Freeman, Susan Maud *lawyer*
Gaines, Francis Pendleton, III *lawyer*
Gerard, Philip C. *lawyer*
Gilbert, Donald R. *lawyer*
Goddard, Terry *lawyer*
Goldstein, Stuart Wolf *lawyer*
†Greene, John Alan *lawyer*
Greenfield, Arthur Paul *lawyer*
Grier, James Edward *lawyer, hotel executive*
Halpern, Barry David *lawyer*
Harris, Jean E. *lawyer*
Harrison, Mark I. *lawyer*
Hawkins, Michael Daly *lawyer*
Hayden, William Robert *lawyer*
Hicks, William Albert, III *lawyer*
Hoecker, Thomas Ralph *lawyer*
Hoffman, Robert B. *lawyer*
Hoxie, Joel P. *lawyer*
Huntwork, James R. *lawyer*
Inman, William Peter *lawyer*
Irwin, R. Neil *lawyer*
Jacobson, (Julian) Edward *lawyer*
James, Charles E., Jr. *lawyer*
Jirauch, Charles W. *lawyer*
Johnson, James Wayne *lawyer*
Katz, Lawrence Allen *lawyer*
Kennedy, Thomas J. *lawyer*
Kreutzberg, David W. *lawyer*
Kurn, Neal *lawyer*
LeBeau, Edward Charles *lawyer*
Lee, Stephen E. *lawyer, educator*
Madden, Paul Robert *lawyer, director*
Mallery, Richard K. *lawyer*
Mangum, John K. *lawyer*
†Manning, Michael C. *lawyer*
Marks, Merton Eleazer *lawyer*
Martin, Don P. *lawyer*
Martori, Joseph Peter *lawyer*
Mason, Anthony Halstead *lawyer, environmental corporate executive*
May, Bruce Barnett *lawyer*
Mc Clennen, Louis *lawyer, educator*
McRae, Hamilton Eugene, III *lawyer*
Melczer, Joseph T., III *lawyer*
Merritt, Nancy-Jo *lawyer*
Meyer, Paul Joseph *lawyer*
Miller, Louis Rice *lawyer*
Mitchell, George Hall *lawyer*
Moya, Patrick Robert *lawyer*
Muchmore, Charles J. *lawyer*
Novak, Edward Frank *lawyer*
Novak, Peter John *lawyer*
Olsen, Alfred Jon *lawyer*
Olsen, Gordon *retired lawyer*
Olson, Robert Howard *lawyer*
Parrett, Sherman O. *lawyer*
Peck, Deana S. *lawyer*
Porter, Amy R. *lawyer*
Powers, N. Thompson *lawyer*
Pulaski, Charles Alexander, Jr. *lawyer*
Rathwell, Peter John *lawyer*
Rudolph, Gilbert Lawrence *lawyer*
Ruffner, Jay Sturgis *lawyer*
Ryan, Thomas Grady *lawyer*
Savage, Stephen Michael *lawyer*
Sherk, Kenneth John *lawyer*
†Spitzer, Marc Lee *lawyer*
Storey, Norman C. *lawyer*
Sutton, Samuel J. *lawyer, educator*
Terry, Peter Anthony *lawyer*
Traeger, Charles Henry, III *lawyer*
Trost, Eileen Bannon *lawyer*
Tubman, William Charles *lawyer*
Udall, Calvin Hunt *lawyer*
Ulrich, Paul Graham *lawyer, author, publisher, editor*
Wales, Harold Webster *lawyer*
Walker, Richard K. *lawyer*
Wall, Donald Arthur *lawyer*
Whisler, James Steven *lawyer, mining and manufacturing executive*
Wiley, Jay D. *lawyer*
Williams, Quinn Patrick *lawyer*
Winthrop, Lawrence Fredrick *lawyer*
Wolf, G. Van Velsor, Jr. *lawyer*
Woods, Richard James *lawyer*
Woolf, Michael E. *lawyer*
Yarnell, Michael Allan *lawyer*

Prescott
Burke, Richard Kitchens *lawyer, educator*
Kleindienst, Richard Gordon *lawyer*

Scottsdale
Barbee, Joe Ed *lawyer*
Cole, George Thomas *lawyer*
Handy, Robert Maxwell *patent lawyer*
Haynie, Howard Edward *lawyer*
Kitchel, Denison *retired lawyer, writer*
Krupp, Clarence William *lawyer, personnel and hospital administrator*
Lowry, Edward Francis, Jr. *lawyer*
Rudd, Eldon *retired congressman*
Starr, Isidore *law educator*

Sun City West
Peshkin, Samuel David *lawyer*

Tempe
Evans, Lawrence Jack, Jr. *lawyer*
Matheson, Alan Adams *law educator*

Tucson
Berlat, William Leonard *lawyer*
Cherry, Ronald Lee *law librarian, educator*
Dobbs, Dan Byron *lawyer*
Dolph, Wilbert Emery *lawyer*
Eckhardt, August Gottlieb *law educator*
Franklin, John Orland *lawyer*
Froman, Sandra Sue *lawyer*
Gantz, David Alfred *lawyer, university official*
Gieseler, Eugene C. *lawyer*
Grand, Richard D. *lawyer*
Henderson, Roger C. *law educator, former dean*
Heurlin, Bruce R. *lawyer*
Kimble, William Earl *lawyer*
Lesher, Robert Overton *lawyer*
Mc Donald, John Richard *lawyer*
McNeill, Frederick Wallace *lawyer, educator, writer, federal government consultant, former military and commercial pilot*
McNulty, Michael Francis *lawyer*
Morrow, James Franklin *lawyer*
O'Leary, Thomas Michael *lawyer*
Pace, Thomas M. *lawyer*
Pickrell, Timothy E. *lawyer*
Schorr, S. L. *lawyer*
Schottland, Charles Irwin *retired legal educator*
Shultz, Silas Harold *lawyer*
Strong, John William *lawyer, educator*

ARKANSAS

Blytheville
Fendler, Oscar *lawyer*

Cotter
Naylor, George LeRoy *lawyer, rail transportation executive*

Eureka Springs
Epley, Lewis Everett, Jr. *lawyer*

Fayetteville
†Ahlers, Glen-Peter, Sr. *library director, educator, consultant*
Bassett, Woodson William, Jr. *lawyer*
Davis, Wylie Herman *lawyer, educator*
Niblock, Walter Raymond *lawyer*
Pearson, Charles Thomas, Jr. *lawyer*

Greenwood
†Walters, Bill *lawyer*

Helena
Roscopf, Charles Buford *lawyer*

Little Rock
Adams, Daniel Fenton *legal educator*
Anderson, Philip Sidney *lawyer*
Campbell, George Emerson *lawyer*
Cross, J. Bruce *lawyer*
Drummond, Winslow *lawyer*
Duffey, William Simon, Jr. *lawyer*
Dumeny, Marcel Jacque *lawyer*
Fiske, Robert Bishop, Jr. *lawyer*
Fogleman, John Albert *lawyer, former judge*
†Foster, Lynn *law librarian, lawyer*
Gates, David Allan *lawyer*
Gunter, Russell Allen *lawyer*
Haught, William Dixon *lawyer*
Jennings, Alston *lawyer*
May, Ronald Alan *lawyer*
Murphey, Arthur Gage, Jr. *legal educator*
Nelson, Edward Sheffield *lawyer, former utility company executive*
Patten, Gerland Paul *lawyer*
Purtle, John Ingram *lawyer, former state supreme court justice*
Shults, Robert Luther, Jr. *lawyer*
†Smith, Griffin, Jr. *lawyer*
Talley-Morris, Neva Bennett *lawyer*
Warner, Cecil Randolph, Jr. *lawyer*
Witherspoon, Carolyn Brack *lawyer*

Marked Tree
†Everett, Mike *lawyer*

Monticello
Ball, William Kenneth *lawyer*

Newport
Boyce, Edward Wayne, Jr. *lawyer*
Thaxton, Marvin Dell *lawyer, farmer*

North Little Rock
Marshall, Terrell *lawyer*
Patty, Claibourne Watkins, Jr. *lawyer*

Osceola
Wilson, Ralph Edwin *lawyer, justice*

Pine Bluff
Jones, John Harris *lawyer, banker*
Ramsay, Louis Lafayette, Jr. *lawyer, banker*

Russellville
Streett, Alexander Graham *lawyer*

Sherwood
†Wood, Marion Douglas *lawyer, state legislator*

Springdale
Cypert, Jimmy Dean *lawyer*

West Memphis
Fogleman, Julian Barton *lawyer*
Nance, Cecil Boone, Jr. *lawyer*

CALIFORNIA

Alameda
Stonehouse, James Adam *lawyer*

Alpine
Samuelson, Derrick William *lawyer*

Anaheim
Rohrer, George John *lawyer*

Auburn
Falls, Edward Joseph *lawyer, insurance executive, educator*

Bakersfield
Martin, George Francis *lawyer*
Owen, Fred Wynne *lawyer*

Baldwin Park
Gregory, George G. *lawyer*

Berkeley
Barnes, Thomas G. *law educator*

†Berring, Robert Charles, Jr. *educator, law librarian, dean*
Concepción, David Alden *arbitrator, educator*
Eisenberg, Melvin A. *law educator*
Feller, David E. *arbitrator*
Haley, George Patrick *lawyer*
Hetland, John Robert *lawyer, educator*
Kadish, Sanford Harold *law educator*
†Kay, Herma Hill *law educator*
McNulty, John Kent *lawyer, educator*
Mishkin, Paul J. *lawyer, educator*
Moran, Rachel *lawyer, educator*
Newman, Frank Cecil *legal educator, retired state supreme court justice*
Nonet, Philippe *law educator*
Scheiber, Harry N. *law educator*
Zimring, Franklin E. *law educator*

Beverly Hills
†Bloom, Jacob A. *lawyer*
Brown, Hermione Kopp *lawyer*
Bugliosi, Vincent T. *lawyer*
Dekom, Peter James *lawyer*
Delevie, Harold Jacob *lawyer*
Factor, Max, III *lawyer, investment adviser*
Jessup, W. Edgar, Jr. *lawyer*
†Roberts, Norman Leslie *lawyer*
Rosky, Burton Seymour *lawyer*
Schiff, Gunther Hans *lawyer*
Tyre, Norman Ronald *lawyer*

Burbank
†Cunningham, Robert D. *lawyer*
Keister, Jean Clare *lawyer*
Litvack, Sanford Martin *lawyer*

Burlingame
Cotchett, Joseph Winters *lawyer, author*
Ocheltree, Richard Lawrence *lawyer, retired forest products company executive*
Ziegler, R.W., Jr. *lawyer, consultant*

Carlsbad
Dixon, William Cornelius *lawyer*
McCracken, Steven Carl *lawyer*
Williams, Roger *lawyer*

Carmel
Robinson, John Minor *lawyer, retired business executive*

Chatsworth
Arnold, Stanley Richard *lawyer*
Klein, Jeffrey S. *lawyer, newspaper executive*

Chico
Ruge, Neil Marshall *retired law educator*

Chino
Determan, John David *lawyer*

Chula Vista
Allen, David Russell *lawyer*

Claremont
Ansell, Edward Orin *lawyer*

Coronado
Merkin, William Leslie *lawyer*

Costa Mesa
Anderson, Jon David *lawyer*
Currie, Robert Emil *lawyer*
Daniels, James Walter *lawyer*
Davidson, Janet Toll *lawyer*
Frieden, Clifford E. *lawyer*
Hamilton, James William *lawyer*
Hay, Howard Clinton *lawyer*
Jones, H(arold) Gilbert, Jr. *lawyer*
Reveal, Ernest Ira, III *lawyer*
Speers, Roland Root, II *lawyer*
Thurston, Morris Ashcroft *lawyer*

Culver City
von Kalinowski, Julian Onesime *lawyer*

Cypress
Olschwang, Alan Paul *lawyer*

Davis
Ayer, John Demeritt *law educator*
Bartosic, Florian *lawyer, artibrator, educator*
Bruch, Carol Sophie *lawyer, educator*
Dykstra, Daniel James *lawyer, educator*
Imwinkelried, Edward John *law educator*
Juenger, Friedrich Klaus *lawyer, educator*
Perschbacher, Rex Robert *law educator*
Wolk, Bruce Alan *law educator*
Wydick, Richard Crews *lawyer, educator*

East Los Angeles
Darby, G. Harrison *lawyer*

El Cerrito
Garbarino, Joseph William *labor arbitrator, economics and business educator*

Emeryville
Dezurick, Paul Anthony *lawyer*

Encino
Kaufman, Albert I. *lawyer*
Singer, Gerald Michael *lawyer, educator, arbitrator and mediator*
Smith, Selma Moidel *lawyer, composer*

Fairfield
Moore, Marianna Gay *law librarian, consultant*

Fresno
Jamison, Oliver Morton *lawyer*
Mather, Allen Frederick *lawyer*
Ott, Michael Duane *lawyer*
Palmer, Samuel Copeland, III *lawyer*

Fullerton
Goldstein, Edward David *lawyer, former glass company executive*

Glendale
Hoffman, Donald M. *lawyer*
Martin, John Hugh *lawyer, retired*

Grass Valley
Lawrence, Dean Grayson *retired lawyer*

Healdsburg
Kamm, Thomas Allen *lawyer, retired naval officer*

Huntington Beach
Shaffer, Richard James *lawyer, former manufacturing company executive*

Irvine
Bastiaanse, Gerard C. *lawyer*
Clark, Karen Heath *lawyer*
Frasca, Joanne M. *lawyer*
Hilker, Walter Robert, Jr. *lawyer*
McCann, Dean Merton *lawyer, former pharmaceutical company executive*
McIntyre, Joel Franklyn *lawyer*
Muller, Edward Robert *lawyer*
Ristau, Kenneth Eugene, Jr. *lawyer*
Smith, Herbert Furrer *lawyer*
Sovie, Donald E. *lawyer*
Tennyson, Peter Joseph *lawyer*
Thomas, Joseph Allan *lawyer*
Waggener, Susan Lee *lawyer*
Wentworth, Theodore Sumner *lawyer*
Wintrode, Ralph Charles *lawyer*

Kentfield
DeWolff, Maurice Konrad *lawyer, banker*

La Canada Flintridge
Costello, Francis William *lawyer*
Wallace, James Wendell *lawyer*

La Jolla
Kirchheimer, Arthur E(dward) *lawyer, business executive*
Shannahan, William Paul *lawyer*
Siegan, Bernard Herbert *lawyer, educator*
Wilkins, Floyd, Jr. *retired lawyer, consultant*
ZoBell, Karl *lawyer*

Laguna Hills
Mc Closkey, Paul N., Jr. *lawyer, former congressman*

Laguna Niguel
Mortensen, Arvid LeGrande *lawyer, insurance company executive*

Larkspur
Fawcett, F(rank) Conger *lawyer*
Marker, Marc Linthacum *lawyer, investment company executive*

Long Beach
Owen, Christina L. *lawyer*
Taylor, Reese Hale, Jr. *lawyer, former government administrator*
Williams, Donald Clyde *lawyer*
Wise, George Edward *lawyer*

Los Angeles
Aaron, Benjamin *law educator, arbitrator*
Abrams, Norman *law educator, university administrator*
Adamek, Charles Andrew *lawyer*
Adell, Hirsch *lawyer*
Adler, Douglas B. *lawyer*
Adler, Erwin Ellery *lawyer*
Apfel, Gary *lawyer*
April, Rand Scott *lawyer*
Arant, Eugene Wesley *lawyer*
Argue, John Clifford *lawyer*
Arnold, Dennis B. *lawyer*
Avery, Robert Dean *lawyer*
Baker, Sheldon S. *lawyer*
Barash, Anthony Harlan *lawyer*
Bardach, Sheldon Gilbert *lawyer*
Barrall, James D. C. *lawyer*
Barton, Alan Joel *lawyer*
Barza, Harold A. *lawyer*
Basile, Paul Louis, Jr. *lawyer*
Battaglia, Philip Maher *lawyer*
Bauman, John Andrew *law educator*
Baumann, Richard Gordon *lawyer*
Beard, Ronald Stratton *lawyer*
Bell, Wayne Steven *lawyer*
Belleville, Philip Frederick *lawyer*
Bender, Charles William *lawyer*
Bendix, Helen Irene *lawyer*
Bernacchi, Richard Lloyd *lawyer*
Bernhard, Herbert Ashley *lawyer*
Bice, Scott Haas *lawyer, educator*
Biederman, Donald Ellis *lawyer*
Bierstedt, Peter Richard *lawyer, entertainment industry consultant*
Bishop, Sidney Willard *lawyer*
Black, Donna Ruth *lawyer*
Blackman, Lee L. *lawyer*
Blencowe, Paul Sherwood *lawyer*
Blitz, Stephen M. *lawyer*
Bloom, Alan *lawyer*
Bobbitt, Leroy *lawyer*
Bodkin, Henry Grattan, Jr. *lawyer*
Bogaard, William Joseph *lawyer*
Bogen, Andrew E. *lawyer*
Bomes, Stephen D. *lawyer*
Bonner, Robert Cleve *lawyer*
Bortman, David *lawyer*
Bosl, Phillip L. *lawyer*
Bost, Thomas Glen *lawyer*
Bottger, William Carl, Jr. *lawyer*
Bower, Allan Maxwell *lawyer*
Bower, Paul George *lawyer*
Boyd, Harry Dalton *lawyer, former insurance company executive*
Bradshaw, Carl John *lawyer, consultant*
Branca, John Gregory *lawyer, consultant*
Brandt, Frederick William *lawyer*
Brassell, Roselyn Strauss *lawyer*
Braun, David A(dlai) *lawyer*
Breidenbach, Francis Anthony *lawyer*
Bressan, Paul Louis *lawyer*
Bricker, Seymour (Murray) *lawyer*
Bridges, B. Ried *lawyer*
Brinsley, John Harrington *lawyer*
Broiles, Steven Anthony *lawyer*
Broussard, Thomas Rollins *lawyer*
Brown, Edmund Gerald (Pat Brown) *lawyer, former governor of California*
Brown, Louis Morris *lawyer, educator*
Burch, Robert Dale *lawyer*
Burke, William M. *lawyer*
Burke, Yvonne Watson Brathwaite (Mrs. William A. Burke) *lawyer*
Burns, Marvin Gerald *lawyer*
Byrd, Christine Waterman Swent *lawyer*
Byrne, Jerome Camillus *lawyer*
Calhoun, Gordon James *lawyer*
Capron, Alexander Morgan *lawyer, educator*
Carlson, Robert E. *lawyer*
Carlson, Terrance L. *lawyer*
Carr, Willard Zeller, Jr. *lawyer*
Castro, Leonard Edward *lawyer*
Cathcart, David Arthur *lawyer*
Cavanagh, John Edward *lawyer*
Chernick, Richard *lawyer*
Chiate, Kenneth Reed *lawyer*
Ching, Anthony *lawyer*
Choate, Joseph *lawyer*
Christol, Carl Quimby *lawyer, political science educator*
Chu, Morgan *lawyer*
Clark, R. Bradbury *lawyer*
Clark, Richard *lawyer*
†Cochran, Johnnie L., Jr. *lawyer*
Cohan, John Robert *lawyer*
Cohen, Cynthia Marylyn *lawyer*
Cohen, Gary J. *lawyer*
Cole, Curtis Allen *lawyer*
Collier, Charles Arthur, Jr. *lawyer*
Colton, Robert Craig *lawyer*
Cooper, Jay Leslie *lawyer*
Cooper, Leon Melvin *lawyer*
Coppola, Robert E. *lawyer*
Cost, John Joseph *lawyer*
Curtis, John Joseph *lawyer*
Curtiss, Thomas, Jr. *lawyer, educator*
Daniels, John Peter *lawyer*
Davis, Edmond Ray *lawyer*
De Brier, Donald Paul *lawyer*
de Castro, Hugo Daniel *lawyer*
DeLuce, Richard David *lawyer*
De Meules, James Head *lawyer*
Deukmejian, George *lawyer, former governor*
Diamond, Stanley Jay *lawyer*
Dickerson, Jaffe Dean *lawyer*
Dodds, Douglas Allen *lawyer*
Dolan, Peter Brown *lawyer*
Donovan, John Arthur *lawyer*
Doty, George Richard *lawyer*
Drapkin, Steven G. *lawyer*
Eichler, Peter M. *lawyer*
Ellsworth, David G. *lawyer*
Emanuel, William Joseph *lawyer*
English, Stephen Raymond *lawyer*
Erickson, Ralph Ernest *lawyer*
Estrich, Susan Rachel *law educator*
Etra, Donald *lawyer*
Eule, Julian Nathan *law educator*
Fabrick, Howard David *lawyer*
Fairbank, Robert Harold *lawyer*
Farmer, Robert Lindsay *lawyer*
Fein, Ronald Lawrence *lawyer*
Fennelly, Jane Corey *lawyer*
Field, Richard Clark *lawyer*
Fields, Bertram Harris *lawyer*
Fields, Henry Michael *lawyer*
Fine, Richard Isaac *lawyer*
Fisher, Raymond Corley *lawyer*
Fohrman, Burton H. *lawyer*
Ford, Donald Hainline *lawyer*
Forgnone, Robert *lawyer*
Frackman, Russell Jay *lawyer*
Fragner, Matthew Charles *lawyer*
Francis, Merrill Richard *lawyer*
Frimmer, Paul Norman *lawyer*
Fromholz, Haley James *lawyer*
Fudge, Jack D. *lawyer*
Fybel, Richard D. *lawyer*
†Gale, Mary Ellen *law educator*
Gambro, Michael S. *lawyer*
Gebb, Sheldon Alexander *lawyer*
Gentile, Joseph F. *lawyer, educator*
Gersh, David Lewis *lawyer*
Gest, Howard David *lawyer*
Getto, Ernest John *lawyer*
Gilbert, Judith Arlene *lawyer*
Girard, Robert David *lawyer*
Glick, Earl A. *lawyer*
Goette, Richard A. *lawyer*
Gold, Bernard *lawyer*
Goldman, Allan Bailey *lawyer*
Goldman, Benjamin Edward *lawyer*
Goldman, Donald A. *lawyer*
Goodman, Max A. *lawyer, educator*
Gordon, David Eliot *lawyer*
Gorman, Joseph Gregory, Jr. *lawyer*
Gould, Charles Perry *lawyer*
Gould, David *lawyer*
Gralnek, Donald D. *lawyer*
Grausam, Jeffrey Leonard *lawyer*
Gray, Jan Charles *lawyer*
Green, William Porter *lawyer*
Greenberg, Maxwell Elfred *lawyer*
Grobe, Charles Stephen *lawyer, accountant*
Groman, Arthur *lawyer*
Grosz, Philip J. *lawyer*
Gurfein, Peter J. *lawyer*
Gutterridge, Larry G. *lawyer*
Hahn, Elliott Julius *lawyer*
Haight, James Theron *lawyer, corporate executive*
Haile, Lawrence Barclay *lawyer*
Halgren, Jack *lawyer*
Halkett, Alan Neilson *lawyer*
Hall, Carlyle Washington, Jr. *lawyer*
Halstead, Harry Moore *lawyer*
Hampton, Gordon Francis *lawyer*
Handler, Carole Enid *lawyer, city planner*
Handzlik, Jan Lawrence *lawyer*
Hanrahan, Thomas P. *lawyer*
Hansell, Dean *lawyer*
Hanson, John J. *lawyer*
Harris, James Michael *lawyer*
Hart, Larry Calvin *lawyer*
Hartigan, John Francis *lawyer*
Hastings, Robert Pusey *lawyer*
Hathaway, Harry L. *lawyer*
Havel, Richard W. *lawyer*
Hayes, Byron Jackson, Jr. *lawyer*
†Haythorn, J. Denny *law librarian*
Hayutin, David Lionel *lawyer*
Hayutin, Marc I. *lawyer*
Hazen, Steven Kelsey *lawyer*
Heather, Fred Doenges *lawyer, educator*
Heinke, Rex S. *lawyer*
Hemminger, Pamela Lynn *lawyer*
Hennigan, James Michael *lawyer*
†Hernandez, Antonia *lawyer*
Heyert, Martin David *lawyer*
Heyler, Grover Ross *retired lawyer*
Hibner, Don Telfer, Jr. *lawyer*
Hieronymus, Edward Whittlesey *lawyer*
Higgins, John Joseph *corporate lawyer*
Highberger, William Foster *lawyer*
Hight, B. Boyd *lawyer*
Hinerfeld, Robert Elliot *lawyer*
†Hirsch, Barry L. *lawyer*
Hobelman, Carl Donald *lawyer*
Hogan, Steven L. *lawyer*
Holliday, Thomas Edgar *lawyer*
Holtzman, Robert Arthur *lawyer*
Horn, Martin Robert *patent lawyer*
Houck, John Burton *retired lawyer*
Hudson, Jeffrey Reid *lawyer*
Huebner, Harlan Pierce *lawyer*
Hufstedler, Seth Martin *lawyer*
Hufstedler, Shirley Mount (Mrs. Seth M. Hufstedler) *lawyer, former federal judge*
Hunter, Larry Dean *lawyer*
Hutter, James Risque *retired lawyer*
Hyman, Milton Bernard *lawyer*
Iamele, Richard Thomas *law librarian*
Irell, Lawrence E(lliott) *lawyer*
Irwin, Philip Donnan *lawyer*
James, Peter W. *lawyer*
Janofsky, Leonard S. *lawyer, association executive*
Johnson, Jonathan Edwin, II *lawyer*
Johnson, Martin Marion *lawyer*
Jordan, Judd L. *lawyer*
Jordan, Robert Leon *lawyer, educator*
Kadison, Stuart L. *lawyer*
Karlin, Michael Jonathan Abraham *lawyer*
Karst, Kenneth Leslie *legal educator*
Katz, Jason Lawrence *lawyer, insurance executive*
Kaus, Otto Michael *lawyer*
Kelly, Daniel Grady, Jr. *lawyer*
Kendig, Ellsworth Harold, Jr. *lawyer*
Kindel, James Horace, Jr. *lawyer*
King, Robert Lucien *lawyer*
Kinney, James Howard *lawyer*
Kirwan, Betty-Jane *lawyer*
Kirwan, Ralph DeWitt *lawyer*
Klee, Kenneth Nathan *lawyer*
Klein, Raymond Maurice *lawyer*
Kleinberg, Marvin H. *lawyer*
Klopf, Jeffrey A. *lawyer*
Klowden, Michael Louis *lawyer*
Koelzer, George Joseph *lawyer*
Kolkey, Daniel Miles *lawyer*
Kruse, Scott August *lawyer*
Kuechle, John Merrill *lawyer*
Kuelbs, John Thomas *lawyer*
Kulzick, Kenneth Edmund *lawyer, writer*
Kupietzky, Moshe J. *lawyer*
Lane, Robert Gerhart *lawyer*
Lappen, Chester I. *lawyer*
Lasker, Edward *lawyer*
Latham, Joseph Al, Jr. *lawyer*
Lauchengco, Jose Yujuico, Jr. *lawyer*
Lawrence, Barry Howard *lawyer*
Laybourne, Everett Broadstone *lawyer*
Lederman, Bruce Randolph *lawyer*
Leibow, Ronald Louis *lawyer*
Lesser, Henry *lawyer*
Lesser, Joan L. *lawyer*
Letwin, Leon *legal educator*
Leung, Frankie Fook-Lun *lawyer*
Levine, Thomas Jeffrey Pello *lawyer*
Leydorf, Frederick Leroy *lawyer*
Light, John Robert *lawyer*
Lindholm, Dwight Henry *lawyer*
Link, George Hamilton *lawyer*
Lipsig, Ethan *lawyer*
Loeb, Ronald Marvin *lawyer*
Long, Gregory Alan *lawyer*
Lublinski, Michael *lawyer*
Lucero, Gene A. *lawyer*
Ludlam, James Edward *lawyer*
Lynch, Patrick *lawyer*
Lyons, James Elliott *lawyer*
MacLaughlin, Francis Joseph *lawyer*
Mancino, Douglas Michael *lawyer*
Marciniak, Thaddeus J. *lawyer*
Marks, Laurence Michael *lawyer*
Marshall, Arthur K. *lawyer, judge, arbitrator, educator, writer*
Martinez, Vilma Socorro *lawyer*
Mason, Cheryl White *lawyer*
Mattson, Marcus *lawyer*
McBurney, George William *lawyer*
McDermott, Thomas John, Jr. *lawyer*
Mc Donough, John Richard *lawyer*
McKnight, Frederick L. *lawyer*
McLane, Frederick Berg *lawyer*
Mc Laughlin, Joseph Mailey *lawyer*
Melkonian, Harry G. *lawyer, rancher*
Mellinkoff, David *lawyer, educator*
Merritt, Bruce Gordon *lawyer*
Metzger, Robert Streicher *lawyer*
Meyer, Michael Edwin *lawyer*
Millard, Neal Steven *lawyer*
Miller, Gavin *lawyer*
Miller, Jesse D. *lawyer*
Mintz, Marshall G. *lawyer*
Mitchell, Briane Nelson *lawyer*
Mori, Jun *lawyer*
Morris, Stephen James Michael *lawyer*
Morrison, Robert Lewin *lawyer*
Mosk, Richard Mitchell *lawyer*
Moskowitz, Joel Steven *lawyer*
Moss, Gary Curtis *lawyer*
Mossawir, Harve H., Jr. *lawyer*
†Mosten, Forrest S. *lawyer*
Mueller, John C. *lawyer*
Munzer, Stephen R. *law educator*
Neely, Sally Schultz *lawyer*
Neiter, Gerald Irving *lawyer*
Nelson, Grant Steel *lawyer, educator*
Nelson, J. Robert *lawyer*
Nevins, Louis H. *lawyer*
Newhouse, Brian E. *lawyer*
Newman, David Wheeler *lawyer*
Nibley, Robert Ricks *retired lawyer*
Nicholas, William Richard *lawyer*
Niemeth, Charles Frederick *lawyer*
†Niese, William A. *lawyer, newspaper publishing executive*
Niles, John Gilbert *lawyer*
Noble, Richard Lloyd *lawyer*
Nochimson, David *lawyer*
Norris, Edwin L. *lawyer*
Norris, Floyd Hamilton *lawyer*

Obrzut, Ted lawyer
O'Connell, Kevin lawyer
Oder, Kenneth William lawyer
O'Donnell, Pierce Henry lawyer
Olpin, Owen lawyer
Olsen, Roger Milton lawyer
Olson, Gary lawyer
Olson, Ronald Leroy lawyer
O'Malley, Joseph James lawyer
Ordin, Andrea Sheridan lawyer
Orr, Ronald Stewart lawyer
Ostroff, Peter I. lawyer
†Owen, Michael Lee lawyer
Owens, Stephen Thomas lawyer
Pace, Richard Randall lawyer, educator
Packard, Robert Charles lawyer
Palmer, Charles Francis lawyer
Paparelli, Angelo A. lawyer
Papiano, Neil Leo lawyer
Parsky, Gerald Lawrence lawyer
Patterson, Charles Ernest lawyer
Paul, Lee Gilmour lawyer
Peck, Austin H., Jr. lawyer
Pepe, Stephen Phillip lawyer
Pereyra-Suarez, Charles Albert lawyer
Perlis, Michael Fredrick lawyer
Perry, Ralph Barton, III lawyer
Peters, Richard T. lawyer
Peterson, Linda S. lawyer
Petroni, Donald Victor lawyer
Pianko, Theodore A. lawyer
Pircher, Leo Joseph lawyer
Poindexter, William Mersereau lawyer
Pollock, John Phleger lawyer
Pope, Alexander H. lawyer, former county official
Power, John Bruce lawyer
Praw, Albert Z. lawyer
Preonas, George Elias lawyer
Presant, Sanford Calvin lawyer
Privett, Howard J. lawyer
Quittner, Arnold M. lawyer
Rabinovitz, Joel lawyer, educator
Rae, Matthew Sanderson, Jr. lawyer
Ramer, Bruce M. lawyer
Rapaport, Mark Samuel lawyer
Rappeport, Ira J. lawyer
Rath, Howard Grant, Jr. lawyer
Ray, Gilbert T. lawyer
Reeves, Barbara Ann lawyer
Reifman, William J. lawyer
Rich, J. Peter lawyer
Richardson, Douglas Fielding lawyer
Richman, Frederick Alexander lawyer
Richter, George Robert, Jr. lawyer
Ridgley, Sherry E. lawyer
Ring, Michael Wilson lawyer
Roberts, Thomas G. lawyer
Roberts, Virgil Patrick lawyer, business executive
Robertson, Hugh Duff lawyer
Robinson, Martha Stewart retired legal educator
Rogan, Patrick Goode lawyer
Roney, John Harvey lawyer
†Rosen, Harvey H. lawyer
Rosen, Robert Charles lawyer
Rosenthal, Sol lawyer
Rosett, Arthur Irwin lawyer, educator
Rothman, Frank lawyer, motion picture company executive
Rubinroit, Howard J. lawyer
Ryan, Frederick Joseph, Jr. lawyer, public official
Ryan, Joseph lawyer
Ryan, Reade Haines, Jr. lawyer
Salvaty, Benjamin Benedict lawyer
Samet, Jack I. lawyer
Sanders, Joseph Stanley lawyer
Savikas, Victor George lawyer
Saxe, Deborah Crandall lawyer
Schander, Edwin law librarian
Scheifly, John Edward retired lawyer
Schmutz, Arthur Walter lawyer
Schroeder, Bill E. lawyer
Schwartz, Alan Uriel lawyer
Scott, A. Timothy lawyer
Selwood, Pierce Taylor lawyer
Shames, Henry Joseph lawyer
Shapiro, Marvin Seymour lawyer
†Shapiro, Robert Leslie lawyer
Sheehan, Lawrence James lawyer
Sheppard, Thomas Richard lawyer
Sherrell, John Bradford lawyer
Sherwood, Allen Joseph lawyer
Sherwood, Arthur Lawrence lawyer
Sherwood, Linda Kathleen lawyer
Shortz, Richard Alan lawyer
Shultz, John David lawyer
Silberberg, Henry J. lawyer
Silbergeld, Arthur F. lawyer
Simpson, Allyson Bilich lawyer
Slater, Jill Sherry lawyer
Smith, Byron Owen lawyer
Smith, Chester Leo lawyer
Smith, Jeffrey Petit lawyer
Sobelle, Richard E. lawyer
Soltman, Neil M. lawyer
Southern, Robert Allen lawyer
Span, Robert Steven lawyer
Spuehler, Donald Roy retired lawyer, writer, mythologist
Stamm, Alan lawyer
Stephens, George Edward, Jr. lawyer
Stern, Stephen Jeffrey lawyer
Stinehart, William, Jr. lawyer
Stone, Lawrence Maurice lawyer, educator
Stone, Richard James lawyer
Stoterau, H. Peter lawyer
Stromberg, Ross Ernest lawyer
Sullivan, Peter D. lawyer
Tan, William Lew lawyer
Tarr, Ralph William lawyer, former federal government official
Taylor, Frederick William, Jr. lawyer
Tinsley, Walton Eugene lawyer
Tobisman, Stuart Paul lawyer
Treister, George Marvin lawyer
Tritt, Clyde Edward lawyer
Troy, Joseph Freed lawyer
Trygstad, Lawrence Benson lawyer
Tunney, John Varick lawyer, former senator
Twomey, Joseph Gerald lawyer
Ukropina, James Robert lawyer
†Unterman, Thomas Edward lawyer
Van de Kamp, John Kalar lawyer
Vandeman, George Allen lawyer
Vanderet, Robert Charles lawyer
Van Emburgh, Joanne lawyer, partner
Varat, Jonathan D. law educator
Vaughan, Joseph Robert lawyer
Vaughn, William Weaver lawyer
Vena, David Henry lawyer
Verrone, Patric Miller lawyer, writer
Vogel, Charles Stimmel lawyer
Volpert, Richard Sidney lawyer
Vradenburg, George, III lawyer, corporate executive
Wagner, D. William lawyer
Walcher, Alan Ernest lawyer
Wasserman, William Phillip lawyer
Waterman, Thomas Chadbourne lawyer
Wayte, (Paul) Alan lawyer
Weaver, Don L. lawyer
Weinstock, Harold lawyer
Weiss, Walter Stanley lawyer
†Weitzman, Howard L. lawyer
Wessling, Robert Bruce lawyer
Wheat, Francis Millspaugh retired lawyer
†Whisman, Linda Anne law librarian
White, Robert Joel lawyer
Wigmore, John Grant lawyer
Williams, Richard Thomas lawyer
Wolas, Herbert lawyer
Wolf, Lesley Sara lawyer
Wolfen, Werner F. lawyer
Woods, Daniel James lawyer
Wrede, Robert Kendrick lawyer
Wright, Kenneth Brooks lawyer
Wyatt, Joseph Lucian, Jr. lawyer, educator
York, Gary A. lawyer
Young, Bless Stritar lawyer
Zarefsky, Ralph lawyer
Zelon, Laurie Dee lawyer
†Ziffren, Kenneth lawyer
Ziffren, Lester lawyer
Zohn, Martin Steven lawyer

Malibu
Coben, William Allen lawyer
Phillips, Ronald Frank legal educator, law school dean

Marina Del Rey
Adams, Thomas Merritt lawyer
Annotico, Richard Anthony legal scholar

Martinez
Bray, Absalom Francis, Jr. lawyer

Menlo Park
Ferris, Robert Albert lawyer, venture capitalist
Gilburne, Miles R. lawyer
Laurie, Ronald S. lawyer
Pooley, James Henry Anderson lawyer, author
Surbeck, Leighton Homer retired lawyer

Mill Valley
Chilvers, Robert Merritt lawyer

Millbrae
Pliska, Edward William lawyer

Mission Viejo
Ruben, Robert Joseph lawyer

Modesto
Mayhew, William A. lawyer
Owens, Jack Byron lawyer

Montara
Gyemant, Robert Ernest lawyer

Montecito
Harris, James Dexter lawyer

Monterey
Bomberger, Russell Branson lawyer, educator
Fenton, Lewis Lowry lawyer
Malone, James L. lawyer, diplomat
Stern, Gerald Daniel lawyer

Moraga
Countryman, Vern law educator

Newport Beach
Adams, William Gillette lawyer
Baskin, Scott David lawyer
Dito, John Allen lawyer
Green, Oliver Francis, Jr. lawyer
Guilford, Andrew John lawyer
Jeffers, Michael Bogue lawyer
Johnson, Thomas Webber, Jr. lawyer
Katayama, Arthur Shoji lawyer
Klein, Maurice J. lawyer
Lowe, Kathlene Winn lawyer
Mallory, Frank Linus lawyer
Millar, Richard William, Jr. lawyer
Phillips, Layn R. lawyer
Simon, John Roger lawyer
Singer, Gary James lawyer
†Tanner, R. Marshall lawyer
Willard, Robert Edgar lawyer

North Hollywood
Kreger, Melvin Joseph lawyer

Novato
Obninsky, Victor Peter lawyer

Oakland
Allen, Jeffrey Michael lawyer
Borton, Robert Ernest lawyer
Buckley, Mike Clifford lawyer, electronics company executive
Burnison, Boyd Edward lawyer
Deming, Willis Riley lawyer
Edwards, Robin Morse lawyer
Fogel, Paul David lawyer
Heafey, Edwin Austin, Jr. lawyer
Kennedy, Raoul Dion lawyer
Miller, Thomas Robbins lawyer, publisher
Peck, Paul Arthur lawyer, former naval officer
Quinby, William Albert lawyer
†Saperstein, Guy T. lawyer
Skaff, Andrew Joseph lawyer, public utilities, energy and transportation executive
Sun, Cossette Tsung-hung Wu law librarian
Tracy, James Jared, Jr. law firm administrator
Wick, William David lawyer
†Wilson, James Thomas lawyer
Winokur, Robert M. lawyer
Wood, James Michael lawyer

Oceanside
Robinson, William Franklin retired legal consultant
Schuck, Carl Joseph lawyer

Orange
Sanders, Gary Wayne lawyer
†Sawdei, Milan A. lawyer

Orinda
Brookes, Valentine retired lawyer
McCormick, Loyd Weldon lawyer

Oxnard
Regnier, Richard Adrian lawyer

Pacific Palisades
Cale, Charles Griffin lawyer
Flattery, Thomas Long lawyer, legal administrator
Jones, Edgar Allan, Jr. law educator, arbitrator, lawyer
Rothenberg, Leslie Steven lawyer, ethicist
Schwartz, Murray Louis lawyer, educator, academic administrator
Sevilla, Stanley lawyer

Palm Desert
Humphrey, Charles Edward, Jr. lawyer

Palo Alto
Borovoy, Roger Stuart lawyer
Bradley, Donald Edward lawyer
Climan, Richard Elliot lawyer
Furbush, David Malcolm lawyer
Gunderson, Robert Vernon, Jr. lawyer
Haslam, Robert Thomas, III lawyer
Hinckley, Robert Craig lawyer
Johnston, Alan Cope lawyer
Mendelson, Alan Charles lawyer
Moretti, August Joseph lawyer
Nordlund, Donald Craig corporate lawyer
Patterson, Robert Edward lawyer
Saltoun, Andre Meir lawyer
†Sonsini, Larry W. lawyer
†Stanzler, Jordan lawyer
Van Atta, David Murray lawyer
Weithorn, Stanley Stephen lawyer
Wheeler, Raymond Louis lawyer

Paramount
Hall, Howard Harry lawyer

Pasadena
Bakaly, Charles George, Jr. mediator, lawyer
D'Angelo, Robert William lawyer
Hale, Charles Russell lawyer
Hunt, Gordon lawyer
Myers, R(alph) Chandler lawyer
Rapaport, David Alan corporate legal executive
Stone, Willard John retired lawyer
Tanner, Dee Boshard lawyer

Paso Robles
Knecht, James Herbert lawyer

Pebble Beach
Dennison, David Short, Jr. lawyer
Maxeiner, Clarence William lawyer, construction company executive

Pleasanton
Miller, William Charles lawyer
Petty, George Oliver lawyer

Plymouth
Andreason, John Christian lawyer

Pomona
Bausch, Janet Jean lawyer
Coombs, Walter Paul retired lawyer, social science educator

Portola Valley
Cooper, John Joseph lawyer
Hanson, Raymond Lester retired lawyer
Nycum, Susan Hubbell lawyer

Rancho Cucamonga
Stout, Dennis Lee lawyer, mayor

Rancho Mirage
Kuhlmey, Walter Trowbridge lawyer

Redlands
Ely, Northcutt lawyer

Redwood City
Bentley, John Martin lawyer
Bonino, Mark G. lawyer
Coddington, Clinton Hays lawyer
Tight, Dexter Corwin lawyer
Wilhelm, Robert Oscar lawyer, civil engineer, developer

Riverside
Aderton, Jane Reynolds lawyer

Sacramento
Andrew, John Henry lawyer, retail corporation executive
Brookman, Anthony Raymond lawyer
Franklin, Charles Scothern lawyer
Friedman, Morton Lee lawyer
Goodart, Nan L. lawyer, educator
Hile, Norman Carter lawyer
LeBaron, Edward Wayne, Jr. lawyer
O'Brien, Kenneth R. lawyer
Plant, Forrest Albert lawyer
Ramirez, Raul Anthony lawyer, former federal judge
Richardson, Frank Kellogg lawyer, former state justice
Schaber, Gordon Duane law educator, former judge
†Sher, Byron D. law educator
Van Camp, Brian Ralph lawyer
†Zeff, Ophelia Hope lawyer
†Zumbrun, Ronald Arthur lawyer

San Andreas
Arkin, Michael Barry lawyer, arbitrator

San Anselmo
Murphy, Barry Ames lawyer

San Bernardino
Fullerton, Robert Victor lawyer

San Clemente
Khachigian, Kenneth Larry lawyer

San Diego
Alpert, Michael Edward lawyer
Ames, Robert Forbes lawyer
Auerbach, Ernest Sigmund lawyer, company executive, writer
Bradley, Lawrence D., Jr. lawyer
Branson, Harley Kenneth lawyer, finance executive
Brooks, John White lawyer
Copeland, Robert Glenn lawyer
Damoose, George Lynn lawyer
Higgs, DeWitt A. lawyer
Hofflund, Paul lawyer
Huston, Kenneth Dale lawyer
Hutcheson, J(ames) Sterling lawyer
Jensen, Michael Lee lawyer
Kammer, William Nolan lawyer
Krantz, Sheldon lawyer
Lathrop, Mitchell Lee lawyer
LeBeau, Charles Paul lawyer
†Lerach, William S. lawyer
Lundin, David Erik lawyer
Mayer, James Hock lawyer
McGinnis, Robert E. lawyer
McManus, Richard Philip lawyer
Mittermiller, James Joseph lawyer
Monahan, David Emory lawyer
Morris, Grant Harold legal educator
Mulvaney, James Francis lawyer
O'Malley, James Terence lawyer
Peterson, Nad A. lawyer, corporate executive
Pettis, Ronald Eugene lawyer
Pray, Ralph Marble, III lawyer
Pugh, Richard Crawford lawyer
Pulliam, Mark Stephen lawyer
Reavey, William Anthony, III lawyer
St. George, William Ross lawyer, retired naval officer, consultant
Shearer, William Kennedy lawyer, publisher
Shelton, Dorothy Diehl Rees lawyer
†Shohet, Jeffrey M. lawyer
Snyder, David Richard lawyer
Stern, Henry Louis lawyer, corporate consultant
Sterrett, James Kelley, II lawyer
Stiska, John C. lawyer
Sullivan, William Francis lawyer
Weaver, Michael James lawyer
Whitmore, Sharp lawyer

San Francisco
Abbott, Barry A. lawyer
Alexander, Robert C. lawyer
Allan, Walter Robert lawyer
Allen, Jose R. lawyer
Anderson, Edward V. lawyer
Andrews, David Ralph lawyer
Archer, Richard Joseph lawyer
Arnold, Kenneth James lawyer, publishing company executive
Avery, Luther James lawyer
Bader, W. Reece lawyer
Bagdonas, Kathy Joann lawyer
Baker, Cameron lawyer
Bancroft, James Ramsey lawyer, business executive
Barbagelata, Robert Dominic lawyer
Bare, Joseph Edward, Jr. retired lawyer
Bates, John Burnham lawyer
Bates, William, III lawyer
Bauch, Thomas Jay lawyer, apparel company executive
†Baxter, Ralph H., Jr. lawyer
Beck, Edward William lawyer
Bedford, Daniel Ross lawyer
Bedford, Lyman D. lawyer
Belli, Melvin Mouron lawyer, lecturer, writer
Bennett, James Patrick lawyer
Benvenutti, Peter J. lawyer
Berns, Philip Allan lawyer
Bertain, G(eorge) Joseph, Jr. lawyer
Blackstone, George Arthur lawyer
Bonapart, Alan David lawyer
Bookin, Daniel H. lawyer
Borowsky, Philip lawyer
Boucher, Harold Irving lawyer
Boyd, William Sprott lawyer
Brandel, Roland Eric lawyer
Brick, Steven A. lawyer
Bridges, Robert Lysle retired lawyer
Briggs, Susan Shadinger lawyer
Bromley, Dennis Karl lawyer
Brosnahan, James Jerome lawyer
Broussard, Allen E. lawyer, former state supreme court justice
Brown, Albert Jacob lawyer
Brown, Anthony P. lawyer
Brown, David Julian lawyer
Brown, Donald Wesley lawyer
†Brown, Robert L. lawyer
Bryan, Robert Russell lawyer
Budge, Hamilton Whithed lawyer
Burns, Brian Patrick lawyer, business executive
Callan, Terrence A. lawyer
Campbell, Scott Robert lawyer, former food company executive
Canty, James M. lawyer
Carlson, John Earl lawyer
Carter, John Douglas lawyer
Cartmell, Nathaniel Madison, III lawyer
Casillas, Mark lawyer
Casto, Keith Michael lawyer
Chao, Cedric C. lawyer
Cheatham, Robert William lawyer
Coblentz, William Kraemer lawyer
Coffin, Judy Sue lawyer
Cole, Richard Charles lawyer
Coleman, Thomas Young lawyer
Collas, Juan Garduño, Jr. lawyer
Connell, William D. lawyer
Conrad, Paul Edward lawyer
Corcoran, Maureen Elizabeth lawyer
Cowan, Stephen A. lawyer
Cranston, Mary B. lawyer
Crawford, Roy Edgington, III lawyer
Cumming, George Anderson, Jr. lawyer
Curtis, John E., Jr. lawyer
Daggett, Robert Sherman lawyer
Danoff, Eric Michael lawyer
Daugherty, Richard Bernard lawyer

Davis, Roger Lewis *lawyer*
Davis, Roland Chenoweth *lawyer*
Dawes, Paul Harvey *lawyer*
De Benedictis, Dario *arbitrator, mediator*
Dell, Robert Michael *lawyer*
Diamond, Philip Ernest *lawyer*
Diekmann, Gilmore Frederick, Jr. *lawyer*
Doxsee, Lawrence Edward *corporate lawyer*
Doyle, Morris McKnight *lawyer*
Dryden, Robert Eugene *lawyer*
Dungan, Malcolm Thon *lawyer*
Dunne, Kevin Joseph *lawyer*
Dupree, Stanley M. *lawyer*
Dyer, Noel John *lawyer*
Edginton, John Arthur *lawyer*
Eigner, Richard Martin *lawyer*
Elderkin, E(dwin) *Judge retired lawyer*
Enersen, Burnham *lawyer*
Engel, G(eorge) Larry *lawyer*
Ericson, Bruce Alan *lawyer*
Ervin, Howard Guy, III *lawyer*
Filippi, Frank Joseph *lawyer*
Finigan, Vincent P., Jr. *lawyer*
Fink, Scott Alan *lawyer*
Folberg, Harold Jay *lawyer, mediator, educator, university dean*
Foster, David Scott *lawyer*
Fredericks, Dale E. *lawyer*
Freeman, Tom M. *lawyer*
Friedman, K. Bruce *lawyer*
Friese, Robert Charles *lawyer*
Fuller, Maurice DeLano, Jr. *lawyer*
Furth, Frederick Paul *lawyer*
Gaither, James C. *lawyer*
Garvey, Joanne Marie *lawyer*
Gill, Margaret Gaskins *lawyer*
Gillmar, Stanley Frank *lawyer*
Golub, Howard Victor *lawyer*
Gordon, Robert Allen, Jr. *lawyer*
Gowdy, Franklin Brockway *lawyer*
Greene, A. Crawford, Jr. *lawyer*
Gresham, Zane Oliver *lawyer*
Guggenhime, Richard Johnson *lawyer*
Haerle, Paul Raymond *lawyer*
Hannawalt, Willis Dale *lawyer*
Hanschen, Peter Walter *lawyer*
Hardy, David *lawyer, corporate executive*
Harris, Richard Eugene Vassau *lawyer*
Harroch, Richard David *lawyer*
Hartman, John E. *lawyer*
Hassard, Howard *lawyer*
Hasson, Kirke Michael *lawyer*
Haven, Thomas Edward *lawyer*
Heilbron, David M(ichael) *lawyer*
Heilbron, Louis Henry *lawyer*
Heng, Donald James, Jr. *lawyer*
Henson, Ray David *legal educator, consultant*
Hinman, Harvey DeForest *lawyer*
Hofmann, John Richard, Jr. *lawyer*
Holden, Frederick Douglass, Jr. *lawyer*
Homer, Barry Wayne *lawyer*
Howard, Carl (Michael) *lawyer*
Huddleson, Edwin Emmet, Jr. *lawyer*
Hudner, Philip *lawyer, rancher*
Hunter, William Dennis *lawyer*
Irwin, William Rankin *lawyer*
Johnson, Martin Wayne *lawyer*
Johnson, Reverdy *lawyer*
Joseph, Allan Jay *lawyer*
Judson, Philip Livingston *lawyer*
Kaapcke, Wallace Letcher *lawyer*
Kallgren, Edward Eugene *lawyer*
Kaplan, Alvin Irving *lawyer, adjudicator, investigator*
Kasanin, Mark Owen *lawyer*
Katz, Ronald Stanley *lawyer*
Kaufman, Christopher Lee *lawyer*
†Kavanaugh, Robert *lawyer*
Kemp, Alson Remington, Jr. *lawyer, legal educator*
Kenny, David Culber *lawyer*
Kern, John McDougall *lawyer*
Kirkham, Francis Robison *lawyer*
Kirkham, James Francis *lawyer*
Klafter, Cary Ira *lawyer*
Klinger, Marilyn Sydney *lawyer*
Klott, David Lee *lawyer*
Knebel, Jack Gillen *lawyer*
Koeppel, John A. *lawyer*
Kolb, Theodore Alexander *lawyer*
Kuhl, Paul Beach *lawyer*
Ladar, Jerrold Morton *lawyer*
Ladd, John Curran *lawyer*
Lane, Fielding H. *lawyer*
Larson, John William *lawyer*
Lasky, Moses *lawyer*
Latcham, Franklin Chester *lawyer*
Lee, Brant Thomas *lawyer, federal official*
Lee, John Jin *lawyer*
Levi, Julian Hirsch *lawyer, educator*
Levit, Victor Bert *lawyer, foreign representative, civic worker*
Libbin, Anne Edna *lawyer*
Lipton, Alvin E(lliot) *lawyer*
Livsey, Robert Callister *lawyer*
Loke, Kit Choy *lawyer*
London, Barry Joseph *lawyer*
Lonnquist, George Eric *lawyer*
Lotito, Michael Joseph *lawyer*
Lynch, Timothy Jeremiah-Mahoney *lawyer, consultant, theologian, law educator*
Mac Gowan, Mary Eugenia *lawyer*
Maddux, Parker Ahrens *lawyer*
Madison, James Raymond *lawyer*
Mann, Bruce Alan *lawyer*
Marchant, David J. *lawyer*
Martin, Joseph, Jr. *lawyer, former ambassador*
Martin, Stephen James *lawyer*
Mathiason, Garry George *lawyer*
Mattes, Martin Anthony *lawyer*
McAniff, Edward John *lawyer*
McCandless, Sandra Ravich *lawyer*
†McElhinny, Harold John *lawyer*
McKee, William David *lawyer*
McKelvey, Judith Grant *lawyer, educator, university dean*
Mc Laughlin, Jerome Michael *lawyer, shipping company executive*
McLeod, Robert Macfarlan *lawyer, arbitrator*
McNally, Thomas Charles, III *lawyer*
McNamara, Thomas Neal *lawyer*
McQuaid, J. Dennis *lawyer*
Mellor, Michael Lawton *lawyer*
Merritt, James Edward *lawyer*
Metzler, Roger James, Jr. *lawyer*
Mihan, Ralph George *lawyer*
Miller, James Lynn *lawyer*
Miller, William Napier Cripps *lawyer*
Minnick, Malcolm David *lawyer*

Mitchell, Bruce Tyson *lawyer*
†Moore, Gary Heath *lawyer*
Morrissey, John Carroll *lawyer*
Murray, Glenn Richard, Jr. *lawyer*
Musfelt, Duane Clark *lawyer*
Nelson, David Edward *lawyer*
Nemir, Donald Philip *lawyer*
Niehans, Daniel J. *lawyer*
†Odgers, Richard William *lawyer*
Offer, Stuart Jay *lawyer*
Olson, Walter Gilbert *lawyer*
Pasahow, Lynn H(arold) *lawyer*
Pemberton, John de Jarnette, Jr. *lawyer, educator*
Penskar, Mark Howard *lawyer*
†Pickett, Donn Philip *lawyer*
Placier, Philip R. *lawyer*
Platt, Peter Godfrey *lawyer*
Plishner, Michael Jon *lawyer*
Poole, Gordon Leicester *lawyer*
Popofsky, Melvin Laurence *lawyer*
Preovolos, Penelope Athene *lawyer*
Pringle, Robert Bernard *lawyer*
Ragan, Charles Ransom *lawyer*
Ransom, Edward Duane *lawyer*
Ratner, David Louis *legal educator*
Raven, Robert Dunbar *lawyer*
Read, Gregory Charles *lawyer*
Reese, John Robert *lawyer*
Rembe, Toni *lawyer*
Rice, Denis Timlin *lawyer*
Richards, Norman Blanchard *lawyer*
Robertson, Armand James, II *lawyer*
Robertson, David Govan *lawyer*
Robinson, Jerry H. *lawyer*
Rockwell, Alvin John *lawyer*
Roethe, James Norton *lawyer*
Rosch, John Thomas *lawyer*
Rosen, Sanford Jay *lawyer*
†Rosenthal, Herbert Marshall *legal association executive*
Rosston, Edward William *lawyer*
Rowland, John Arthur *lawyer*
Ryland, David Ronald *lawyer*
Salomon, Darrell Joseph *lawyer*
Sanger, John Morton *lawyer, urban planner*
Sax, Joseph Lawrence *lawyer, educator*
Sayre, George Edward *retired lawyer*
Schlesinger, Rudolf Berthold *lawyer, educator*
Schwartz, Louis Brown *legal educator*
Sears, George Ames *lawyer*
Seegal, John Franklin *lawyer*
Selman, Roland Wooten, III *lawyer*
Sevier, Ernest Youle *lawyer*
Shenk, George H. *lawyer*
†Simmons, Raymond Hedelius, Jr. *lawyer*
Singer, Allen Morris *lawyer*
Small, Marshall Lee *lawyer*
Smegal, Thomas Frank, Jr. *lawyer*
Smith, Gregory Allan *lawyer*
Smith, Kerry Clark *lawyer*
Snow, Tower Charles, Jr. *lawyer*
Sparks, John Edward *lawyer*
Sparks, Thomas E., Jr. *lawyer*
Spiegel, Hart Hunter *retired lawyer*
Staring, Graydon Shaw *lawyer*
Steer, Reginald David *lawyer*
Stotter, Lawrence Henry *lawyer*
Stout, Gregory Stansbury *lawyer*
Stratton, Richard James *lawyer*
Sugarman, Myron George *lawyer*
Sugarman, Paul William *lawyer*
Sullivan, Robert Edward *lawyer*
Sutcliffe, Eric *lawyer*
Sutton, John Paul *lawyer*
Taylor, Robert P. *lawyer*
Taylor, William James (Zak Taylor) *lawyer*
Thomas, William Scott *lawyer*
Thompson, Robert Charles *lawyer*
Thornton, D. Whitney, II *lawyer*
Tiffany, Joseph Raymond, II *lawyer*
Tingle, James O'Malley *lawyer*
Tobin, James Michael *lawyer*
Trautman, William Ellsworth *lawyer*
Traynor, J. Michael *lawyer*
Venning, Robert Stanley *lawyer*
Walker, Ralph Clifford *lawyer*
Walkup, Bruce *lawyer*
Walsh, James Joseph *lawyer*
Wang, William Kai-Sheng *legal educator*
Warmer, Richard Craig *lawyer*
Welborn, Caryl Bartelman *lawyer*
Welch, Thomas Andrew *lawyer*
Werson, James Byrd *lawyer*
Westberg, Robert Myers *lawyer*
Whelan, John William *lawyer, educator, consultant*
Widman, Gary Lee *lawyer, former government official*
Wild, Nelson Hopkins *lawyer*
Willson, Prentiss, Jr. *lawyer*
Wolfe, Cameron Withgot, Jr. *lawyer*
Woods, James Robert *lawyer*
Wyle, Frederick S. *lawyer*
Yamakawa, David Kiyoshi, Jr. *lawyer*
Yost, Nicholas Churchill *lawyer*
Young, Bryant Llewellyn *lawyer, business executive*
Ziering, William Mark *lawyer*
Zimmerman, Bernard *lawyer*

San Jose
Fowler, John Wellington *lawyer*
Granneman, Vernon Henry *lawyer*
Greenstein, Martin Richard *lawyer*
Luft, Robert S. *lawyer*
Mitchell, David Walker *lawyer*
Morgan, William Robert *lawyer*
Smirni, Allan Desmond *lawyer*
Stacy, Richard A. *prosecutor*

San Luis Obispo
Daly, John Paul *lawyer*

San Marino
Baldwin, James William *lawyer*
Galbraith, James Marshall *lawyer, business executive*
Mortimer, Wendell Reed, Jr. *lawyer*

San Mateo
Bell, Frank Ouray, Jr. *lawyer*
Cotton, Aylett Borel *retired lawyer*
Kane, Robert Francis *lawyer, former ambassador, consultant*
Scott, Michael Dennis *lawyer*

San Rafael
Roth, Hadden Wing *lawyer*

San Ramon
Kahane, Dennis Spencer *lawyer*
O'Connor, Paul Daniel *lawyer*

Santa Ana
Blaine, Dorothea Constance Ragetté *lawyer*
Heckler, Gerard Vincent *lawyer*
†Storer, Maryruth *law librarian*
Zaenglein, William George, Jr. *lawyer*

Santa Barbara
Gaines, Howard Clarke *lawyer*
McEwen, Willard Winfield, Jr. *lawyer*

Santa Clara
Alexander, George Jonathon *legal educator, former dean*

Santa Clarita
Deadrich, Paul Eddy *lawyer, real estate broker, retired*

Santa Monica
Boltz, Gerald Edmund *lawyer*
Bonesteel, Michael John *lawyer*
Dickson, Robert Lee *lawyer*
Garner, Donald K. *lawyer*
Jones, William Allen *lawyer, entertainment company executive*
Kelly, John Michael *lawyer*
King, Stephen Scott *lawyer*
Loo, Thomas S. *lawyer*
McMillan, M. Sean *lawyer*
Merideth, Frank E., Jr. *lawyer*
†Moyer, Steven E. *lawyer, educator*
Powers, Marcus Eugene *lawyer*
Prewoznik, Jerome Frank *lawyer*
Risman, Michael *lawyer, business executive, securities company executive*
Schlei, Norbert Anthony *lawyer*
Sheller, John Willard *lawyer*
Sperling, George Elmer, Jr. *lawyer*
Walker, Charles Montgomery *lawyer*
Weatherup, Roy Garfield *lawyer*

Sausalito
Moody, Graham Blair *lawyer*
Trimmer, Harold Sharp, Jr. *lawyer, international telecommunications consultant*

Seal Beach
Hirsch, David L. *lawyer, corporate executive*
Mueth, Joseph Edward *lawyer*

Shaver Lake
Lambert, Frederick William *lawyer, educator*

Sierra Madre
Calleton, Theodore Edward *lawyer*

Solana Beach
Hecker, Bruce Albert *lawyer*

Solvang
Morrow, Richard Towson *lawyer*

South San Francisco
†Kopp, Quentin L. *lawyer, state legislator*

Stanford
Babcock, Barbara Allen *lawyer, educator*
Barton, John Hays *law educator*
Baxter, William Francis *lawyer, educator*
Brest, Paul A. *law educator*
Cappelletti, Mauro *law educator, lawyer*
†Dickson, Lance E. *law librarian, educator*
Franklin, Marc Adam *law educator*
Friedman, Lawrence M. *law educator*
Goldstein, Paul *lawyer, educator*
Gunther, Gerald *lawyer, educator*
Rhode, Deborah Lynn *law educator*
Roster, Michael *lawyer*
Scholes, Myron S. *law and finance educator*
Scott, Kenneth Eugene *lawyer, educator*
Williams, Howard Russell *lawyer, educator*

Stockton
Blewett, Robert Noall *lawyer*
Curtis, Orlie Lindsey, Jr. *lawyer*

Studio City
Yorty, Samuel *lawyer, former mayor*

Tarzana
Grill, Lawrence J. *lawyer, accountant, management company executive*

Temecula
†Haynes, Raymond Neal, Jr. *lawyer, state legislator*

Thousand Oaks
Jessup, Warren T. *lawyer*

Torrance
†Bowen, Debra Lynn *lawyer, state legislator*
Kaufman, Sanford Paul *lawyer*
Martin, Robert Michael *prosecutor*
Petillon, Lee Ritchey *lawyer*

Vacaville
Myhre, Deanna Shirley *lawyer, litigator, mediator*

Van Nuys
Mikesell, Richard Lyon *lawyer, financial counselor*

Walnut Creek
Curtin, Daniel Joseph, Jr. *lawyer*
Garrett, James Joseph *lawyer, partner*
Ginsburg, Gerald J. *lawyer, business executive*
Jackson, Dale Edward *lawyer*
Jones, Orlo Dow *lawyer, drug store executive*
Madden, Palmer Brown *lawyer*
Merritt, Robert Edward *lawyer, educator*
Newmark, Milton Maxwell *lawyer*
Pagter, Carl Richard *lawyer*
Skaggs, Sanford Merle *lawyer*

West Covina
Ebiner, Robert Maurice *lawyer*

McHale, Edward Robertson *retired lawyer*

West Hollywood
Walton, Brian *lawyer, union administrator*

Woodland Hills
Strote, Joel Richard *lawyer*
Vinson, William T. *lawyer, diversified corporation executive*

COLORADO

Aspen
Jalili, Mahir *lawyer*

Boulder
†Bintliff, Barbara Ann *law librarian*
Echohawk, John Ernest *lawyer*
Fiflis, Ted J. *lawyer, educator*
Moses, Raphael Jacob *lawyer*
Oesterle, Dale Arthur *law educator*
Peterson, Courtland Harry *law educator*
Porzak, Glenn E. *lawyer*
Rich, Ben Arthur *lawyer, university official*
Steuben, Norton Leslie *lawyer, educator*
Tippit, John Harlow *lawyer*

Cherry Hills Village
Meyer, Milton Edward, Jr. *lawyer, artist*

Colorado Springs
Buell, Bruce Temple *lawyer*
Flynn, James T. *lawyer*
Kendall, Phillip Alan *lawyer*
Kraemer, Sandy Frederick *lawyer*
O'Rourke, Dennis *lawyer*
Payne, Billy (William A. Payne) *real estate lawyer, sports association executive*
Rouss, Ruth *lawyer*
Thomas, Darrell Denman *lawyer*

Denver
Alfers, Stephen Douglas *lawyer*
Anderson, Gregg I. *lawyer*
Austin, H(arry) Gregory *lawyer*
Bain, Donald Knight *lawyer*
Belitz, Paul Edward *lawyer*
Benson, Robert Eugene *lawyer*
Benson, Thomas Quentin *lawyer*
Benton, Auburn Edgar *lawyer*
Blair, Andrew Lane, Jr. *lawyer, educator*
Blunk, Forrest Stewart *lawyer*
Brega, Charles Franklin *lawyer*
Burford, Anne McGill *lawyer*
Burke, Kenneth John *lawyer*
Butler, David *lawyer*
Bye, James Edward *lawyer*
Cain, Douglas Mylchreest *lawyer*
Campbell, Leonard Martin *lawyer*
Cantwell, William Patterson *lawyer*
Carver, Craig R. *lawyer*
Cheroutes, Michael Louis *lawyer*
Chidester, Alfred C. *lawyer*
Collins, Martha Traudt *lawyer*
Conover, Frederic King *lawyer*
Cooper, Paul Douglas *lawyer*
Cope, Thomas Field *lawyer*
Cox, William V. *lawyer*
Curtis, George Bartlett *lawyer*
Dauer, Edward Arnold *law educator*
Dean, James Benwell *lawyer*
†De Gette, Diana Louise *lawyer, state legislator*
Dempsey, Howard Stanley *lawyer, mining executive, investment banker*
DeMuth, Alan Cornelius *lawyer*
Downey, Arthur Harold, Jr. *lawyer*
Dunham, Stephen Sampson *lawyer*
Eiberger, Carl Frederick *trial lawyer*
Eklund, Carl Andrew *lawyer*
Erisman, Frank *lawyer*
Farley, John Michael *lawyer*
Faxon, Thomas Baker *lawyer*
Featherstone, Bruce Alan *lawyer*
Feder, Harold Abram *lawyer*
Fiske, Terry Noble *lawyer*
Flowers, William Harold, Jr. *lawyer*
Fognani, John Dennis *lawyer*
Grant, Patrick Alexander *lawyer, former state representative*
Green, Jersey Michael-Lee *lawyer*
Greene, Leslie Speed *lawyer*
Grissom, Garth Clyde *lawyer*
Haddon, Harold Alan *lawyer*
Harris, Dale Ray *lawyer*
Harry, Robert Hayden *lawyer*
Hartley, James Edward *lawyer*
Hawley, Robert Cross *lawyer*
Hendrix, Lynn Parker *lawyer*
Hoagland, Donald Wright *lawyer*
Hobson, Harry Lee, Jr. *lawyer*
Hodson, Thane Raymond *lawyer*
Hoffman, Daniel Steven *lawyer, legal educator*
Holleman, Paul Douglas *lawyer*
Holme, Richard Phillips *lawyer*
Hopfenbeck, George Martin, Jr. *lawyer*
Hopkins, Donald J. *lawyer*
Husband, John Michael *lawyer*
Irvin, Robert D. *lawyer*
Jackson, Richard Brooke *lawyer*
Jacobs, Paul Alan *lawyer*
Keely, George Clayton *lawyer*
Keller, Alex Stephen *lawyer*
Keller, Glen Elven, Jr. *lawyer*
Kintzele, John Alfred *lawyer*
Kirgis, Frederic L. *retired lawyer*
Kripke, Kenneth Norman *lawyer*
Law, John Manning *retired lawyer*
Lesher, Donald Miles *lawyer*
Levy, Mark Ray *lawyer*
Low, Andrew M. *lawyer*
Low, John Wayland *lawyer*
Mahlman, Henry Clayton *lawyer*
Mandelson, Richard S. *lawyer*
Martin, James Russell *lawyer*
Martz, Clyde Ollen *lawyer, educator*
Mauro, Richard Frank *lawyer, investment manager*
Maxfield, Thomas H. *lawyer*
McCotter, James Rawson *lawyer*
McGrath, Edward Joseph *lawyer*
Merker, Steven Joseph *lawyer*
Miller, Gale Timothy *lawyer*
Miller, Robert Nolen *lawyer*
Moorhead, John B. *lawyer*
Moye, John Edward *lawyer*

Muldoon, Brian *lawyer*
Muller, Nicholas Guthrie *lawyer, business executive*
Murane, William Edward *lawyer*
Musyl, Marc J. *lawyer*
Nanda, Ved Prakash *law educator*
Newton, James Quigg, Jr. *lawyer*
North, Phillip J. *lawyer*
O'Keefe, Edward Franklin *lawyer*
Otten, Arthur Edward, Jr. *lawyer, corporate executive*
Owen, James Churchill, Jr. *lawyer*
Palmer, David Gilbert *lawyer*
Petros, Raymond Louis, Jr. *lawyer*
Phillips, Paul David, Jr. *lawyer*
Poulson, Robert Dean *lawyer*
Pringle, Edward E. *legal educator, former state supreme court chief justice*
Prochnow, James R. *lawyer*
Quiat, Gerald M. *lawyer*
Ramsey, John Arthur *lawyer*
Ray, Bruce David *lawyer*
Rich, Robert Stephen *lawyer*
Ris, William Krakow *lawyer*
Rubright, Royal Cushing *lawyer*
Ruppert, John Lawrence *lawyer*
Sasso, Cassandra Gay *lawyer*
Sayre, John Marshall *lawyer, former government official*
Schrepferman, Richard Lee *lawyer*
Seawell, Donald Ray *lawyer, publisher, arts center executive, producer*
Shea, Kevin Michael *lawyer*
Snyder, Stephen Edward *lawyer*
Stewart, Lyle Bainbridge *lawyer*
Stockmar, Ted P. *lawyer*
Sutton, Raymond L., Jr. *lawyer*
Thomasch, Roger Paul *lawyer*
Tipton, John J. *lawyer*
Tomlinson, Warren Leon *lawyer*
Tracey, Jay Walter, Jr. *retired lawyer*
Vigil, Charles S. *lawyer*
Walker, Timothy Blake *lawyer, educator*
Wallace, Victor L., II *lawyer*
Watson, William D. *lawyer*
Wheeler, Malcolm Edward *lawyer, law educator*
Whitlock, William Abel *lawyer*
Williams, Michael Anthony *lawyer*
Williams, Wayne De Armond *lawyer*
Wohlgenant, Richard Glen *lawyer*
Woods, Lucius Earle *lawyer*
Woodward, Lester Ray *lawyer*
Yegge, Robert Bernard *lawyer, college dean emeritus, educator*

Durango
Burnham, Bryson Paine *retired lawyer*

Eagle
Sullivan, Selby William *lawyer, business executive*

Englewood
†Russ, Charles Paul, III *lawyer, corporate executive*

Fort Collins
Rogers, Garth Winfield *lawyer*

Golden
Wilson, James Robert *lawyer*

Greeley
Houtchens, Barnard *lawyer*

Lakewood
Mc Hugh, Robert Clayton *lawyer, energy company executive*

Littleton
Spelts, Richard John *lawyer*

Manassa
Garcia, Castelar Medardo *lawyer*

Montrose
Krumins, Girts *lawyer, management consultant*
Loesch, Harrison *lawyer, energy and natural resources consultant*

Pagosa Springs
†Cassidy, Samuel H. *lawyer, state legislator*

Pueblo
Altman, Leo Sidney *lawyer*

Pueblo West
O'Callaghan, Robert Patrick *lawyer*

Rifle
†George, Russell Lloyd *lawyer, legislator*

Snowmass Village
Chase, Seymour M. *lawyer*

CONNECTICUT

Avon
Wiechmann, Eric Watt *lawyer*

Bloomfield
Anderson, Buist Murfee *lawyer*
Messemer, Glenn Matthew *lawyer*
Reid, Hoch *lawyer*

Bridgeport
Margulies, Martin B. *lawyer, educator*

Bristol
Besser, John Edward *lawyer*

Darien
Brown, James Shelly *lawyer*
Kaynor, Sanford Bull *lawyer*

Derby
Micci, Eugene D. *lawyer*

East Hartford
Stephan, George Peter *lawyer, international business consultant*
Whiston, Richard Michael *lawyer*

Enfield
Berger, Robert Bertram *lawyer*

Fairfield
†Caruso, Daniel F. *lawyer, state legislator*
†Heineman, Benjamin Walter, Jr. *lawyer*
Kenney, James Francis *lawyer*
Sealy, Albert Henry *lawyer*
Trager, Philip *lawyer, photographer*

Glastonbury
Schroth, Peter W(illiam) *lawyer, management and law educator*

Greenwich
Bam, Foster *lawyer*
Cantor, Samuel C. *lawyer*
Cantwell, Robert *lawyer*
Fisher, Everett *lawyer*
Forrow, Brian Derek *lawyer, corporation executive*
Gillespie, Alexander Joseph, Jr. *lawyer*
Jones, Edwin Michael *lawyer, former insurance company executive*
Kurtz, Melvin H. *lawyer, cosmetics company executive*
Laudone, Anita Helene *lawyer*
Lawler, Richard Francis *lawyer*
Lowenstein, Peter David *lawyer*
Lynch, William Redington *lawyer*
McKee, Thomas J. *lawyer*
Mendenhall, John Ryan *retired lawyer, transportation executive*
More, Douglas McLochlan *lawyer*
Paul, Roland Arthur *lawyer*
Rodenbach, Edward Francis *lawyer*
Rose, Richard Loomis *lawyer*
†Stern, Dennis M. *lawyer*

Groton
Sheets, Paulann Hosler *lawyer, environmental law consultant*

Hartford
Alfano, Charles Thomas, Sr. *lawyer*
Anthony, J(ulian) Danford, Jr. *lawyer*
Berall, Frank Stewart *lawyer*
Blumberg, Phillip Irvin *law educator*
Buck, Gurdon Hall *lawyer, urban planner, real estate broker*
Buckingham, Harold Canute, Jr. *lawyer*
Cantor, Donald Jerome *lawyer*
Cole, William Kaufman *lawyer*
Conard, Frederick Underwood, Jr. *lawyer*
Cullina, William Michael *lawyer*
Donahue, John McFall *lawyer*
Elliot, Ralph Gregory *lawyer*
Ewing, Robert *lawyer*
Fain, Joel Maurice *lawyer*
†Figueroa, Juan A. *lawyer, state legislator*
Garfield, Gerald *lawyer*
†Godfrey, Robert Douglas *lawyer*
Googins, Robert Reville *lawyer, insurance company executive*
Green, Raymond Bert *lawyer*
Guenter, Raymond Albert *lawyer, banker*
Harrison, Thomas Flatley *lawyer*
Herman, Paula Lacey *lawyer*
Hincks, John Winslow *lawyer*
Irish, Leon Eugene *lawyer, educator, insurance company executive*
Kelly, Peter Galbraith *lawyer*
Knickerbocker, Robert Platt, Jr. *lawyer*
Korzenik, Armand Alexander *lawyer*
Lane-Reticker, Edward *lawyer, educator*
Lotstein, James I. *lawyer*
Lyon, James Burroughs *lawyer*
†McKeon, George A. *lawyer*
Merriam, Dwight Haines *lawyer, land use planner*
Merrill, George Vanderneth *lawyer, investment executive*
Middlebrook, Stephen Beach *lawyer*
Miller, Jeffrey Clark *lawyer*
Morrison, Francis Henry *lawyer*
Murtha, John Stephen *lawyer*
Nolan, John Blanchard *lawyer*
Owen, H. Martyn *lawyer*
Pinney, Sidney Dillingham, Jr. *lawyer*
Psarakis, Emanuel Nicholas *lawyer*
Quinn, Andrew Peter, Jr. *lawyer, insurance executive*
Richter, Donald Paul *lawyer*
Rome, Donald Lee *lawyer*
Ryan, David Thomas *lawyer*
Schatz, S. Michael *lawyer*
Schatzki, George *law educator*
See, Edmund M. *lawyer*
Siegel, Robert Gordon *lawyer*
Space, Theodore Maxwell *lawyer*
Spear, H(enry) Dyke N(ewcome), Jr. *lawyer*
Speziale, John Albert *lawyer*
†Stone, Dennis J. *law librarian, educator*
Taylor, Allan Bert *lawyer*
Thomas, Calvert *lawyer*
Trachsel, William Henry *corporate counsel*
Voigt, Richard *lawyer*
Wolman, Martin *lawyer*
Yoskowitz, Irving Benjamin *lawyer, manufacturing company executive*
Zakarian, Albert *lawyer*

Madison
Haas, Frederick Peter *lawyer*

Meriden
†Luby, Thomas Stewart *lawyer*

Milford
Berchem, Robert Lee, Sr. *lawyer*

New Canaan
Wallace, Kenneth Donald *lawyer*

New Haven
Burt, Robert Amsterdam *lawyer, educator*
Cohen, Morris Leo *law librarian, educator*
Damaska, Mirjan Radovan *law educator*
Duke, Steven Barry *law educator*
Ellickson, Robert Chester *law educator*
Elliott, Edwin Donald, Jr. *law educator, federal administrator, environmental lawyer*
Fiss, Owen M. *law educator*
Gastwirth, Donald Edward *lawyer, literary agent*
Gewirtz, Paul D. *lawyer*
Goldstein, Abraham S. *lawyer, educator*
Goldstein, Joseph *law educator*
Greenfield, James Robert *lawyer*
Holder, Angela Roddey *lawyer, educator*
Johnstone, Quintin *legal educator*
Kronman, Anthony Townsend *lawyer, educator*
Langbein, John Harriss *lawyer, educator*
Logue, Frank *arbitrator, mediator, urban consultant, former mayor New Haven*
Marshall, Burke *law educator*
Priest, George L. *law educator*
Rose-Ackerman, Susan *law and political economy educator*
Rostow, Eugene Victor *lawyer, educator, economist*
Simon, John Gerald *law educator*
Tilson, John Quillin *lawyer*

New Milford
Altermatt, Paul Barry *lawyer*
Edmondson, John Richard *lawyer, pharmaceutical manufacturing company executive*

Norfolk
Lambros, Lambros John *lawyer, petroleum company executive*

North Haven
Peterson, George Emanuel, Jr. *lawyer, business executive*

Norwalk
Bermas, Stephen *lawyer*
Van Norstrand, R. E. *lawyer*

Orange
Clark, John Phelps *lawyer, automotive executive*

Riverside
Lovejoy, Allen Fraser *retired lawyer*

Seymour
Sims, Robert Barry *lawyer*

Shelton
Harvey, Michael Lee *lawyer, transportation executive*

Sherman
Piel, William, Jr. *retired lawyer*

Simsbury
Long, Michael Thomas *lawyer, manufacturing company executive*

Southbury
†O'Neill, Arthur Julius *lawyer, state representative*

Southport
Greene, Herbert Bruce *lawyer, merchant banker*
McLearn, Michael Baylis *lawyer*

Stamford
Adams, Taggart D. *lawyer*
Barton, James Miller *lawyer*
Bentley, Peter *lawyer*
Bowen, Patrick Harvey *lawyer, consultant*
Cain, George Harvey *lawyer, business executive*
Coleman, Joel Clifford *lawyer*
Davison, Endicott Peabody *lawyer*
Dederick, Ronald Osburn *lawyer*
Dolian, Robert Paul *lawyer*
Drost, Marianne *lawyer*
Ginsky, Marvin H. *lawyer, corporate executive*
Griffith, F. Lee, III *lawyer*
Kloster, Burton John, Jr. *lawyer*
Knag, Paul Everett *lawyer*
†Lee, Charles Tomerlin *lawyer*
Lowman, George Frederick *lawyer*
†Margolis, Emanuel *lawyer, educator*
McGeeney, John Stephen *lawyer*
McGrath, Richard Paul *lawyer*
Merritt, William Alfred, Jr. *lawyer, telecommunications company executive*
Nichols, Ralph Arthur *lawyer*
Paul, Richard Stanley *lawyer*
Perle, Eugene Gabriel *lawyer*
Riggs, Douglas A. *lawyer*
Schectman, Herbert A. *lawyer, corporate executive*
Schmults, Edward Charles *lawyer*
Schoonmaker, Samuel Vail, III *lawyer*
Sisley, G. William *lawyer*
Skidd, Thomas Patrick, Jr. *lawyer*
Smith, Edgar James, Jr. *lawyer, manufacturing company executive*
Spindler, John Frederick *lawyer*
Stapleton, James Francis *lawyer*
Tobin, Richard J. *lawyer*
Twardy, Stanley Albert, Jr. *lawyer*
Vest, George Graham *lawyer*
Weitzel, William Conrad, Jr. *lawyer*
Wilhelm, Gayle Brian *lawyer*

Stonington
Dupont, Ralph Paul *lawyer, educator*
Van Rees, Cornelius S. *lawyer*

Waterbury
Glass, Robert Davis *trial referee*

West Hartford
Bartels, Millard *lawyer*
Libassi, Frank Peter *lawyer, dean*
Pustilnik, David Daniel *lawyer*
Whitman, Robert *lawyer, educator*

West Redding
Russell, Allan David *lawyer*

Westport
Albani, Suzanne Beardsley *lawyer*
Blazzard, Norse Novar *lawyer*
Buchanan, William Hobart, Jr. *lawyer, publishing company executive*
Cederbaum, Eugene E. *lawyer*
Daw, Harold John *lawyer*
Leckie, Robert Bedford *lawyer*
Raikes, Charles FitzGerald *lawyer*

Wilton
Fricke, Richard John *lawyer*
Green, John Orne *lawyer*
Lamb, Frederic Davis *lawyer*

Windsor
†Stigler, David Mack *lawyer*

Woodbury
Marsching, Ronald Lionel *lawyer, former precision instrument company executive*

DELAWARE

Dover
†Ennis, Bruce Clifford *lawyer*
†Hauge, Richard Andrew *attorney, state senator*
Rich, Michael Joseph *lawyer*

Wilmington
Bader, John Merwin *lawyer*
Bell, Daniel Long, Jr. *lawyer, utilities executive*
Clark, Esther Frances *legal educator*
Connolly, Arthur Guild *lawyer, partner emeritus*
†DiLiberto, Richard Anthony, Jr. *lawyer*
Du Pont, Pierre Samuel, IV *lawyer, former governor of Delaware*
Elliott, Richard Gibbons, Jr. *lawyer*
Fenton, Wendell *lawyer*
Gilliam, James H., Jr. *lawyer*
Green, James Samuel *lawyer*
Kirkpatrick, Andrew Booth, Jr. *lawyer*
Malloy, John Richard *lawyer, chemical company executive*
Mekler, Arlen B. *lawyer, chemist*
Morris, Kenneth Donald *lawyer*
Partnoy, Ronald Allen *lawyer*
Quillen, William Tatem *lawyer, past state supreme court justice, educator*
Rothschild, Steven James *lawyer*
Shapiro, Irving Saul *lawyer*
†Skolas, John Argyle *lawyer*
Stone, F. L. Peter *lawyer*
Sutton, Richard Lauder *lawyer*
Trostle, Mary Pat *lawyer*
Turk, S. Maynard *lawyer*
Ward, Rodman, Jr. *lawyer*
Welch, Edward P. *lawyer*
Wier, Richard Royal, Jr. *lawyer, inventor*
Willis, Franklin Knight *lawyer, environmental services company executive*

DISTRICT OF COLUMBIA

Washington
Aaronson, David Ernest *lawyer, educator*
Abeles, Charles Calvert *lawyer*
Ablard, Charles David *lawyer*
Acheson, David Campion *lawyer, author, policy analyst*
Acker, Lawrence G. *lawyer*
Ackerson, Nels J(ohn) *lawyer*
Adams, John Jillson *lawyer*
Adams, Thomas Lynch, Jr. *lawyer*
Adamson, Terrence Burdett *lawyer*
Adelman, Roger Mark *lawyer, educator*
Adler, Howard, Jr. *lawyer*
Adler, Howard Bruce *lawyer*
Adler, Robert Martin *lawyer*
Aisenberg, Irwin Morton *lawyer*
Alberger, William Relph *lawyer, government official*
Albertson, Fred W(oodward) *retired lawyer, radio engineer*
Albertson, Terry L. *lawyer*
Alexander, Bettina Lawton *lawyer*
Alexander, Donald Crichton *lawyer*
Allen, George Venable, Jr. *lawyer*
Allen, Toni K. *lawyer*
Allen, William Hayes *lawyer*
Allera, Edward John *lawyer*
Altman, Jeffrey Paul *lawyer*
Aluise, Timothy John *lawyer*
Ambrose, Myles Joseph *lawyer*
Andersen, Daniel Johannes *lawyer*
Anderson, David Lawrence *lawyer*
Anderson, Frederick Randolph, Jr. *lawyer, law educator*
Anderson, John Bayard *lawyer, educator, former congressman*
Andrews, Mark Joseph *lawyer*
Andrews, William S. *lawyer*
Angarola, Robert Thomas *lawyer*
Anthony, David Vincent *lawyer*
Applebaum, Harvey Milton *lawyer*
Arcadipane, Angelo Vincent *lawyer*
†Areen, Judith Carol *law educator*
Arent, Albert Ezra *lawyer*
Atkeson, Timothy Breed *lawyer, former federal agency administrator*
Atkin, James Blakesley *lawyer*
Atwood, James R. *lawyer*
Aucutt, Ronald David *lawyer*
Avery, George Allen *lawyer*
Avil, Richard D., Jr. *lawyer*
Axelrod, Jonathan Gans *lawyer*
Ayer, Donald Belton *lawyer*
Ayres, Richard Edward *lawyer*
Babbin, Jed Lloyd *lawyer*
Bailey, Patricia Price *lawyer, government official*
Baird, Bruce Allen *lawyer*
Baker, David Harris *lawyer*
Baker, James Addison, III *lawyer, former government official*
†Ball, John Wesley, III *lawyer*
Ball, (Robert) Markham *lawyer*
Baran, Jan Witold *lawyer*
Bardin, David J. *lawyer*
Barnes, Dennis Norman *lawyer*
Barnes, Donald Michael *lawyer*
Barnes, Mark James *lawyer*
Barnes, Michael Darr *lawyer*
Barnes, Peter *laywer*
†Barnett, Robert Bruce *lawyer*
Barnum, John Wallace *lawyer*
Barr, Michael Blanton *lawyer*
Barr, William Pelham *lawyer, former attorney general of United States*
Barrett, William H. *lawyer*
Barron, Jerome Aure *law educator*
Bartlett, John Laurence *lawyer*
Bartlett, Michael John *lawyer*
Bartnoff, Judith *lawyer*
Barton, William Blackburn *lawyer*
Barusch, Ronald Charles *lawyer*
†Baskir, Lawrence M. *lawyer*
Bass, Kenneth Carrington, III *lawyer*
Basseches, Robert Treinis *lawyer*
Bassman, Robert Stuart *lawyer*

Harris, Don Victor, Jr. lawyer
Harris, Jeffrey lawyer
†Harris, Judith Linda lawyer
†Harris, Steven B. lawyer
Harrison, Donald lawyer
Harrison, Earl David lawyer, real estate executive
Harrison, Ellen Kroll lawyer
Harrison, Marion Edwyn lawyer
†Harvey, David Michael lawyer
Hass, Lawrence Joel lawyer
Hassett, Joseph Mark lawyer
Hathaway, Charles Michael lawyer
Hauser, Richard Alan lawyer
Havens, Charles W., III lawyer
Hawke, John Daniel, Jr. lawyer
Hawkins, Edward Jackson lawyer
Hayes, David J. lawyer
Hayes, Webb Cook, III lawyer
Haynes, R. Michael lawyer
Haynes, William J(ames), II lawyer
Hays, Michael DeWayne lawyer
Heckman, Jerome Harold lawyer
Heffernan, James Vincent lawyer
Heffron, Howard A. lawyer
Hefter, Laurence Roy lawyer
Heintz, John Edward lawyer
Heller, Jack Isaac lawyer
Heller, John Roderick, III lawyer, business executive
Hemley, M. Rogue lawyer
Henderson, Douglas Boyd lawyer
Henderson, Thomas Henry, Jr. lawyer, legal association executive
Henke, Michael John lawyer
Hennessy, Ellen Anne lawyer, educator
†Herlach, Mark Dayton lawyer
Herzog, Richard Barnard lawyer
Herzstein, Robert Erwin lawyer
Hewitt, Paul Buck lawyer
Hibbert, Robert George lawyer, food company executive
Hickey, Edward Joseph, Jr. lawyer, diplomatic consultant
Hidalgo, Edward lawyer, former secretary of navy
Highet, Gilbert Keith MacInnes lawyer
Hill, David Warren lawyer
Hill, Jerry C. lawyer
Hill, Jonathan Booth lawyer
Hill, Stephen S. lawyer
Hills, Carla Anderson lawyer, former federal official
Hills, Roderick M. lawyer, business executive, former government official
Hinds, Richard De Courcy lawyer
Hirsch, Robert Bruce lawyer
Hirschhorn, Eric Leonard lawyer
Hobbs, Caswell O., III lawyer
Hobbs, J. Timothy, Sr. lawyer
Hobson, James Richmond lawyer
Hochberg, Jerome A. lawyer
Hodgson, Morgan Day lawyer
Hodson, Kenneth Joe lawyer, criminal justice consultant, retired army officer
Hoffman, E. Leslie lawyer
Hoffman, Joel Elihu lawyer
†Hoikes, Mary Elizabeth lawyer, diplomat
Holden, James Phillip lawyer
†Holder, Eric H. prosecutor
†Holleman, Frank Sharp, III lawyer
Holmer, Alan Freeman lawyer
Holmstead, Jeffrey R. lawyer
Holtz, Edgar Wolfe lawyer
Hope, Judith Richards lawyer
Hoppe, Wolfgang lawyer
Horahan, Edward Bernard, III lawyer
Horlick, Gary Norman lawyer, legal educator
Horn, Charles M. lawyer
†Horn, Donald Herbert lawyer
Horne, Michael Stewart lawyer
Horsky, Charles Antone lawyer
Hosenball, S. Neil lawyer
Houlihan, David Paul lawyer
House, W(illiam) Michael lawyer
Howard, Glen Scott lawyer
Howard, Jeffrey Hjalmar lawyer
Howard, Kenneth Calvin, Jr. lawyer
Howrey, Edward F. lawyer
Hughes, James Charles lawyer
Hughes, John Vance lawyer
Hughes, Marija Matich law librarian
Humphreys, Robert Russell lawyer
Hunnicutt, Charles Alvin lawyer
Hushon, John Daniel lawyer
Hutt, Peter Barton lawyer
Hylden, Thomas lawyer
Hyman, Lester Samuel lawyer
Hynes, Terence Michael lawyer
Ingoldsby, Thomas M. lawyer
Irving, John Stiles, Jr. lawyer
Isbell, David Bradford lawyer, legal educator
Isenbergh, Max lawyer, musician, educator
Israel, Barry John lawyer
Jackson, Neal A. lawyer
Jacobson, David Edward lawyer
Janetatos, Jack Peter lawyer
Jankowsky, Joel lawyer
Jaskiewicz, Leonard Albert lawyer
Javits, Joshua Moses lawyer
Jensen, Robert Neal lawyer
Jessup, Philip Caryl, Jr. lawyer, museum executive
Jetton, C. Loring, Jr. lawyer
Joelson, Mark Rene lawyer
Johnson, David Raymond lawyer
Johnson, John Griffith, Jr. lawyer
Johnson, Oliver Thomas, Jr. lawyer
Johnson, Philip McBride lawyer
Johnson, Richard Clark lawyer
Johnson, Richard Tenney lawyer
Johnson, William Hall lawyer, government official
Jonas, John Francis lawyer
Jones, Aidan Drexel lawyer
Jones, Boisfeuillet, Jr. lawyer, newspaper executive
Jones, Keith Alden lawyer
Jones, Richard Herbert lawyer, former government official
Jones, Theodore Lawrence lawyer
Jordan, Robert Elijah, III lawyer
Jordan, Vernon Eulion, Jr. lawyer, former association official
Joseph, Daniel Mordecai lawyer
Jost, Peter Hafner lawyer
Journey, Drexel Dahlke lawyer
Kabel, Robert James lawyer
Kafes, William Owen lawyer
Kafka, Gerald Andrew lawyer
Kahn, Edwin Leonard lawyer
Kamm, Linda Heller lawyer
Kammerer, Kelly Christian lawyer
Kaplan, Gilbert B. lawyer
Kaplan, Julius lawyer
Kapp, Robert Harris lawyer
Kaseman, A. Carl, III lawyer
Kass, Benny Lee lawyer
Katz, Sherman E. lawyer
Katzen, Sally lawyer
Kaufman, Thomas Frederick lawyer, legal educator
Kautter, David John lawyer
Kay, Kenneth Robert lawyer
Keane, William K. lawyer
Keener, Mary Lou lawyer
Keeney, E. Andrew lawyer
Keeney, John Christopher lawyer
Keeney, John Christopher, Jr. lawyer
†Kehoe, Patrick Emmett law librarian, educator
Keiner, R(obert) Bruce, Jr. lawyer
Kellison, James Bruce lawyer
Kellogg, Frederic Rogers lawyer
Kelly, William Charles, Jr. lawyer
Kenney, Robert James, Jr. lawyer
Kent, Alan Heywood lawyer
Kerxton, Alan Smith lawyer
Kessler, Judd Lewis lawyer
Keys, John R., Jr. lawyer
Kies, Kenneth J. lawyer
Kieve, Loren lawyer
Killefer, Campbell lawyer
Killory, Diane Silberstein lawyer
Kimball, Raymond Joel lawyer
Kimmitt, Robert Michael lawyer, banker, diplomat
King, Rufus lawyer
Kirby, Thomas Wesley lawyer
Kirtland, John C. lawyer
Kittrell, Steven Dan lawyer
Kittrie, Nicholas N(orbert Nehemiah) law educator, international consultant, author
Klain, Ronald Alan lawyer
Klawiter, Donald Casimir lawyer
Klein, Andrew Manning lawyer
Klein, Michael Roger lawyer, business executive
Klepper, Martin lawyer
Knapp, George M. lawyer
Knapp, James Ian Keith federal lawyer
†Knapp, Rosalind Ann lawyer
Knebel, John Albert lawyer, former government official
Knotts, Joseph B. lawyer
Koch, George William lawyer
Koch, Kathleen Day lawyer
Kolman, Mark Herbert lawyer
†Konschnik, David Michael lawyer
Korth, Fred lawyer
Korth, Fritz-Alan lawyer
Kovacs, William Lawrence lawyer
Kraemer, Jay Roy lawyer
Kramer, Albert H. lawyer
Kramer, Kenneth Stephen lawyer
Kramer, Robert law school dean
Kramer, William David lawyer
Krash, Abe lawyer
Krasner, Wendy L. lawyer
Krasnow, Erwin Gilbert lawyer
†Kreczko, Alan James lawyer
Kriesberg, Simeon M. lawyer
Kroener, William Frederick, III lawyer
Kronstein, Werner J lawyer
Krump, Gary Joseph lawyer
Kurrelmeyer, Louis Hayner lawyer
Lahr, Jack Leroy lawyer
Lambert, Eugene Isaak lawyer
Lambert, Jeremiah Daniel lawyer
Lambert, Steven Charles lawyer
Lamm, Carolyn Beth lawyer
Landfair, Stanley W. lawyer
Lane, Bruce Stuart lawyer
Lane, John Dennis lawyer
Lane, Mark lawyer, educator, author
Laporte, Gerald Joseph Sylvestre lawyer
Larroca, Raymond G. lawyer
Larry, David Heath lawyer
Lassman, Malcolm lawyer
Latham, Weldon Hurd lawyer
Latimer, Allie B. lawyer, government official
Laughlin, Felix B. lawyer
Lavine, Henry Wolfe lawyer
Lazarus, Arthur, Jr. retired lawyer
Lazarus, Kenneth Anthony lawyer
Leary, Thomas Barrett lawyer
Lehner, George Alexander, Jr. lawyer
Lehr, Dennis James lawyer
Leibold, Arthur William, Jr. lawyer
Leigh, Monroe lawyer
†Leiter, Richard Allen law educator, law librarian
Lenhart, James Thomas lawyer
Leon, Richard J. lawyer, former government official
Leonard, Will Ernest, Jr. lawyer
Leshy, John D. lawyer, legal educator
Lessenco, Gilbert Barry lawyer
Lessy, Roy Paul, Jr. lawyer
Lettow, Charles Frederick lawyer
Leva, Marx lawyer
Levin, Betsy lawyer, educator, university dean
Levine, Henry David lawyer
†Levine, Joseph Manney lawyer
†Levine, Theodore A. lawyer
Levinson, Daniel Ronald lawyer
Levinson, Lawrence Edward lawyer, corporation executive
†Levitas, Elliot Harris lawyer
Levy, Mark Irving federal lawyer
†Lew, Ginger lawyer
Lewis, David John lawyer
Lewis, E. Grey lawyer
Lewis, Gregory Scott lawyer
Lewis, William Henry, Jr. lawyer
Liberman, Lee Sarah lawyer, educator
Libin, Jerome B. lawyer
Lichtenstein, Elissa Charlene legal association executive
Liebman, Ronald Stanley lawyer
Lighthizer, Robert E. lawyer
Lillard, John Franklin, III lawyer
Linowitz, Sol Myron lawyer
Lipstein, Robert A. lawyer
Litan, Robert Eli lawyer, economist
Litman, Harry Peter lawyer, educator
†Littlefield, Nick lawyer
†Lockhart, Robert Earl lawyer
Loeffler, Robert Hugh lawyer
Loevinger, Lee lawyer
Long, Charles Thomas lawyer
†Lopatin, Alan G. lawyer
Lorber, Lawrence Zel lawyer
Love, Margaret Colgate lawyer
Lowe, Randall Brian lawyer
Lublin, Edward Louis lawyer
Lucchino, Lawrence lawyer, sports executive
Luce, Gregory M. lawyer
Lund, Wendell Luther lawyer
Lutzker, Arnold Paul lawyer
Lybecker, Martin Earl lawyer
Lynam, Terence Joseph lawyer
Lyon, Edwin Leon lawyer
Lyons, Dennis Gerald lawyer
Lyons, Ellis lawyer
MacBeth, Angus lawyer
Macdonald, David Robert lawyer
MacIntyre, A(lfonso) Everette lawyer
Mackall, Laidler Bowie lawyer
Mackiewicz, Edward Robert lawyer
Macleay, Donald lawyer
Macrory, Patrick Francis John lawyer
Madden, Murdaugh Stuart lawyer
Madden, William J., Jr. lawyer
Madigan, Kimberly A. mediator, lawyer
Madigan, Michael J. lawyer
Maechling, Charles, Jr. lawyer, educator, writer
Magielnicki, Robert L. lawyer
Maiwurm, James John lawyer
Mallory, Charles King, III lawyer
†Manatt, Charles T. lawyer
Manbeck, Harry Frederick, Jr. lawyer
Manly, Marc Edward lawyer
Manning, George Taylor lawyer
Manson, Joseph Lloyd, III lawyer
Manthei, Richard Dale lawyer, health care company executive
Marans, J. Eugene lawyer
Marcuss, Stanley Joseph lawyer
Margeton, Stephen George law librarian
Margolis, Daniel Herbert lawyer
Margolis, Eugene lawyer, government official
Marinaccio, Charles Lindbergh lawyer
Markoski, Joseph Peter lawyer
Marks, Andrew H. lawyer
Marks, Herbert Edward lawyer
Marks, Leonard Harold lawyer
Marks, Richard Daniel lawyer
Marquez, Joaquin Alfredo lawyer
Martin, David Briton Hadden, Jr. lawyer
Martin, Guy lawyer
Martin, Keith lawyer
Martin, Thomas Stephen lawyer
Martyak, Joseph J. lawyer
Marvin, Douglas Raymond lawyer
Marzulla, Roger Joseph lawyer
Mathias, Charles McCurdy lawyer, former senator
May, Gregory Evers lawyer
May, Randolph Joseph lawyer
May, Richard Edward lawyer
May, Timothy James lawyer
Mayers, Daniel Kriegsman lawyer
Mayfield, Richard Heverin lawyer
Mayo, George Washington, Jr. lawyer
Mazo, Mark Elliott lawyer
Mazzaferri, Katherine Aquino lawyer, bar association executive
McAvoy, John Joseph lawyer
McBride, Michael Flynn lawyer
Mc Bride, Thomas Frederick lawyer, former university dean, government official
McCabe, Edward Aeneas lawyer, financial services corporation executive
Mc Carthy, Charles Joseph lawyer, former government official
Mc Carthy, David Jerome, Jr. legal educator
Mc Carty, Robert Lee lawyer
McCobb, John Bradford, Jr. lawyer
McConnell, John William, Jr. lawyer
McCoy, Neal S. lawyer
McDavid, J. Gary lawyer
McDavid, Janet Louise lawyer
Mc Dermott, Albert Leo lawyer
McDermott, Edward Aloysious lawyer
McDermott, Robert Francis, Jr. lawyer
McElveen, Junius Carlisle, Jr. lawyer
McGarry, J. Michael, III lawyer
Mc Giffert, David Eliot lawyer, former government official
Mc Glothlin, James Harrison lawyer
McGovern, Michael Barbot lawyer
McGrath, Kathryn Bradley lawyer
McGrew, Thomas James lawyer
McGuire, Patricia A. lawyer, academic administrator
McHugh, James Lenahan, Jr. lawyer
McKee, William St. John lawyer
McMahon, Joseph Einar lawyer, consultant
Mc Phee, Henry Roemer lawyer
Mc Pherson, Harry Cummings, Jr. lawyer
Means, Thomas Cornell lawyer
Medalie, Richard James lawyer
Melamed, Arthur Douglas lawyer
Meloy, Sybil Piskur lawyer
Meltzer, Steven Lee lawyer
Meserve, Richard Andrew lawyer
Meyer, Dennis Irwin lawyer
Meyer, Lawrence George lawyer
Meyers, Tedson Jay lawyer
Michaelson, Martin lawyer
Mickey, Paul F(ogle), Jr. lawyer
Miller, Andrew Pickens lawyer
Miller, H. Todd lawyer
Miller, Herbert John, Jr. lawyer
Miller, Lawrence A. lawyer
Miller, Marshall Lee lawyer
Miller, Warren Lloyd lawyer
†Milstein, Elliott Steven legal educator, academic administrator
Mintz, Seymour Stanley lawyer
Mirabelli, Mario V. lawyer
Mitchell, Roy Shaw lawyer
Mizroch, John F. lawyer
Moates, G. Paul lawyer
Mobbs, Michael Hall lawyer
Mode, Paul J., Jr. lawyer
Moe, Richard Palmer lawyer
Molineaux, Charles Borromeo lawyer, arbitrator
Montgomery, George Cranwell lawyer, former ambassador
Mooney, Marilyn lawyer
Moring, John Frederick lawyer
Morris, Frank Charles, Jr. lawyer, educator
Morris, William lawyer
Moses, Alfred Henry lawyer
Mostoff, Allan Samuel lawyer, consultant
Mott, William Chamberlain lawyer, retired naval officer
Muckenfuss, Cantwell Faulkner, III lawyer
Mueller, Robert Swan, III lawyer, former federal official
Muir, J. Dapray lawyer
Muller, Scott William lawyer
Munsey, Rodney Roundy lawyer
Muntzing, L(ewis) Manning lawyer
Murchison, David Claudius lawyer
Murphy, Andrew Phillip, Jr. lawyer
Murphy, Betty Jane Southard (Mrs. Cornelius F. Murphy) lawyer
Murphy, James Paul lawyer
Murphy, John Condron, Jr. lawyer
Murphy, Stephen P. lawyer
†Murphy, Terence Roche lawyer
Murray, Fred F. lawyer
Murray, John Einar lawyer, retired army officer, federal official
Murry, Harold David, Jr. lawyer
Myers, James R. lawyer
†Nace, Barry John lawyer
Napier, John Light lawyer
Natalie, Ronald Bruce lawyer
Neimark, Sheridan lawyer
Nelson, Robert Louis lawyer
Nemeroff, Michael Alan lawyer
Ness, Andrew David lawyer
Neuman, Robert Henry lawyer
Nicholas, Robert B. lawyer
Nichols, Henry Eliot lawyer, savings and loan executive
Nitze, William Albert lawyer, government consultant
Nolan, James Lawry lawyer
Nolan, John Edward, Jr. lawyer
Noonberg, Lewis Allan lawyer
Norberg, Charles Robert lawyer
Norcross, David Frank Armstrong lawyer
†Nordhaus, Robert Riggs lawyer
Nordquist, Myron Harry lawyer
Northrop, Carl Wooden lawyer
Norton, Eleanor Holmes lawyer, educator
Norton, Floyd Ligon, IV lawyer
Norton, Gerald Patrick lawyer
Nutter, Franklin Winston lawyer
†Oakley, Robert Louis law librarian, educator
O'Brien, Francis Anthony lawyer
O'Brien, Lawrence Francis, III lawyer
O'Brien, William James, II lawyer
O'Connor, Charles Aloysius, III lawyer
O'Connor, Charles P. lawyer
O'Connor, John Jay, III lawyer
Odle, Robert Charles, Jr. lawyer
O'Donnell, Terrence lawyer
O'Hara, James Thomas lawyer
O'Hare, Patrick K. lawyer
Oliver, Joseph McDonald, Jr. lawyer
Olmer, Lionel Herbert lawyer
Olmstead, Cecil Jay lawyer
Olson, John Frederick lawyer
Olson, Theodore Bevry lawyer, government official
Ondeck, Thomas Paul lawyer
O'Neill, Brian Dennis lawyer
O'Neill, John H., Jr. lawyer
O'Neill, William Patrick lawyer
Onek, Joseph Nathan lawyer
Ongman, John Will lawyer
Oppenheimer, Franz Martin lawyer
Oppenheimer, Jerry L. lawyer
O'Rourke, C. Larry lawyer
Osnos, David Marvin lawyer
O'Sullivan, Lynda Troutman lawyer
O'Toole, Francis J. lawyer
Overholt, Hugh Robert lawyer, retired army officer
Overman, Dean Lee lawyer, investor, author
Owen, Roberts Bishop lawyer
Oyler, Gregory Kenneth lawyer
Page, Rodney Fred lawyer
Painter, William Hall law educator
Palmer, Alan Kenneth lawyer
Palmer, David Brent lawyer
Palmeter, N. David lawyer
Paoletta, Mark R. A. federal lawyer
Paper, Lewis J. lawyer
Papkin, Robert David lawyer
Patchan, Joseph lawyer
Pate, Michael Lynn lawyer
Patten, Thomas Louis lawyer
Patton, Thomas Earl lawyer
Paul, Robert Dennis lawyer
Paul, William McCann lawyer
Paup, Michael Lee lawyer
Payne, Kenneth Eugene lawyer
Pearlman, Ronald Alan lawyer
Peavy, Robert A. lawyer
†Peck, Robert Stephen lawyer, educator
Pedersen, Norman A. lawyer
Pedersen, William Francis, Jr. lawyer
Pehrson, Gordon Oscar, Jr. lawyer
Pendergast, William Ross lawyer
Perkins, Jack Edwin lawyer
Perkins, Samuel Thomas lawyer
Perlik, William R. lawyer
Perlman, Matthew Saul lawyer
Perry, B(illy) Dwight lawyer
Petrash, Jeffrey Michael lawyer
Pettit, John Whitney lawyer
Pfeiffer, Margaret Kolodny lawyer
Pfeiffer, Steven Bernard lawyer
Phemister, Thomas Alexander lawyer
Philion, Norman Joseph, III lawyer
Philips, Malcolm H. lawyer
Phillips, Carter Glasgow lawyer
Phillips, Cyrus Eastman, IV lawyer
Pickering, John Harold lawyer
Pietrowski, Robert Frank, Jr. lawyer
Pilecki, Paul Steven lawyer
Pinco, Robert G. lawyer
Pipkin, James Harold, Jr. lawyer
Pitt, Harvey Lloyd lawyer
Pittman, Steuart Lansing lawyer
Plaine, Daniel J. lawyer
Plotkin, Harry Morris lawyer
†Podberesky, Samuel lawyer
Poe, David Russell lawyer
Poe, Luke Harvey, Jr. lawyer
Pogue, Lloyd Welch lawyer
Polebaum, Elliot Edward lawyer
Pomeroy, Harlan lawyer
Poppler, Doris Swords lawyer
Porter, Richard Howard lawyer
Portnoy, Ian Karl lawyer
Postol, Lawrence Philip lawyer
Potter, Trevor Alexander McClurg lawyer
Potts, Ramsay Douglas lawyer, aviator
Potts, Stephen Deaderick lawyer
Povich, David lawyer
Pozen, Walter lawyer
Preston, Richard McKim lawyer
Prettyman, Elijah Barrett, Jr. lawyer
Price, Griffith Baley, Jr. lawyer
Price, Joseph Hubbard lawyer
Proctor, John P. lawyer
Proto, Neil Thomas lawyer, educator
Pugh, Keith E., Jr. lawyer
Pusey, William Anderson lawyer
Pushkar, Raymond Stephen Edward lawyer
Quale, John Carter lawyer

Quarles, James Linwood, III *lawyer*
Quigley, Thomas J. *lawyer*
Quint, Arnold Harris *lawyer*
Quintiere, Gary G. *lawyer*
†Rabb, Harriet Schaffer *lawyer, educator*
Rademaker, Stephen Geoffrey *lawyer*
Rader, Robert Michael *lawyer*
†Raimo, Bernard, Jr. (Bernie) *lawyer*
Ramey, Carl Robert *lawyer*
Rauh, Carl Stephen *lawyer*
Raul, Alan Charles *lawyer*
Reade, Claire Elizabeth *lawyer*
Reaves, John Daniel *lawyer, playwright, actor*
Reback, Joyce Ellen *lawyer*
Reed, Kevin Francis *lawyer*
Rehm, John Bartram *lawyer*
†Reich, David J. *lawyer*
Reichardt, Glenn Richard *lawyer*
Reid, George Bernard, Jr. *lawyer*
Reid, Inez Smith *lawyer, educator*
Reid, Robert Newton *lawyer, mortgage and financial consultant*
Rein, Bert Walter *lawyer*
Reynolds, Joseph Hurley *lawyer*
Reynolds, Nicholas S. *lawyer*
Rezneck, Daniel Albert *lawyer*
Rhodes, John Jacob *lawyer, former congressman*
Richards, Suzanne V. *lawyer*
Richardson, Elliot Lee *lawyer*
Richmond, David Walker *lawyer*
Richmond, Marilyn Susan *lawyer*
Rieser, Joseph A., Jr. *lawyer*
Rill, James Franklin *lawyer*
Rinzel, Daniel Francis *lawyer*
Rishe, Melvin *lawyer*
Risher, John Robert, Jr. *lawyer*
Rissetto, Harry A. *lawyer*
Rivers, Richard Robinson *lawyer*
Roach, Arvid Edward, II *lawyer*
Roach, Patrick Joseph *lawyer*
Robbins, Robert B. *lawyer*
Roberts, James Harold, III *lawyer*
Roberts, Michael James *lawyer*
Robinson, David B. *lawyer*
Robinson, Davis Rowland *lawyer*
Robinson, Douglas George *lawyer*
Rockefeller, Edwin Shaffer *lawyer*
Rockler, Walter James *lawyer*
Rocque, Vincent Joseph *lawyer*
†Rodemeyer, Michael Leonard, Jr. *lawyer*
Rodgers, Paul *lawyer, government official*
Rogers, James Albert *lawyer*
Rogers, Paul Grant *lawyer, former congressman*
Rogers, William Dill *lawyer*
Rogovin, Mitchell *lawyer*
Rohner, Ralph John *lawyer, educator, university dean*
Roiter, Eric D. *lawyer*
Romansky, Michael A. *lawyer*
Romatowski, Peter J. *lawyer*
Romeo, Peter John *lawyer*
Rooney, Kevin Davitt *lawyer*
Rose, Henry *lawyer*
Rose, James McKinley, Jr. *lawyer, government official*
Rose, Jonathan Chapman *lawyer*
Rosenberg, Ruth Helen Borsuk *lawyer*
Rosenblatt, Peter Ronald *lawyer, former ambassador*
Rosenbloom, H. David *lawyer*
Rosenthal, Douglas Eurico *lawyer, author*
Rosenthal, Steven Siegmund *lawyer*
Ross, Douglas *lawyer*
Ross, John Joseph *lawyer*
Ross, Stanford Gordon *lawyer, former government official*
Rossides, Eugene Telemachus *lawyer, writer*
Rossotti, Barbara Jill Margulies *lawyer*
†Roth, Alan J. *lawyer, congressional aide*
Rouvelas, Emanuel Larry *lawyer*
Rowden, Marcus Aubrey *lawyer, former government official*
Rowe, Richard Holmes *lawyer*
Roycroft, Howard Francis *lawyer*
Rubin, Kenneth Allen *lawyer*
Rubin, Seymour Jeffrey *lawyer, educator*
Ruckert, Edward M. *lawyer*
Ruddy, Frank S. *lawyer, former ambassador*
Rudnick, Robert Alan *lawyer*
Rule, Charles Frederick (Rick Rule) *lawyer*
†Russell, Michael James *lawyer*
Russin, Jonathan *lawyer, consultant*
Rutstein, David W. *lawyer, food products executive*
Ruttenberg, Charles Byron *lawyer*
Ruttinger, George David *lawyer*
Ruyak, Robert Francis *lawyer*
Ryan, Jerry William *lawyer*
Ryerson, Paul Sommer *lawyer*
Sacher, Steven Jay *lawyer*
Sachs, Stephen Howard *lawyer*
Sackler, Arthur Brian *lawyer*
Sacks, David Arnold *lawyer*
Sagalkin, Sanford *lawyer*
Sagawa, Shirley Sachi *lawyer*
Sagett, Jan Jeffrey *lawyer, former government official*
Saltzburg, Stephen Allan *law educator, consultant*
Samolis, Frank Robert *lawyer*
Sampson, Richard Thomas *lawyer*
Sanford, Bruce William *lawyer*
Santos, Leonard Ernest *lawyer*
Sapienza, John Thomas *lawyer*
Sauntry, Susan Schaefer *lawyer*
†Savarese, Ralph J. *lawyer*
Sayler, Robert Nelson *lawyer*
Scharff, Joseph Laurent *lawyer*
Schenker, Carl Richard, Jr. *lawyer*
Schifter, Richard *lawyer, government official*
Schmeltzer, Edward *lawyer*
Schmidt, John R. *lawyer*
Schmidt, Paul Wickham *lawyer*
Schmidt, Richard Marten, Jr. *lawyer*
Schneebaum, Steven Marc *lawyer*
Schneider, Matthew Roger *lawyer*
Schotland, Sara Deutch *lawyer*
Schropp, James Howard *lawyer*
Schwaab, Richard Lewis *lawyer, educator*
Schwartz, Daniel C. *lawyer*
Schwartz, Harry Kane *lawyer*
Schwartz, Robert S. *lawyer*
Schwartz, Victor Elliot *lawyer*
Schwarz, Carl W. *lawyer*
Schweitzer, William H. *lawyer*
Scott, Edward Philip *lawyer*
Scott, Michael *lawyer*
Scott, Thomas Jefferson, Jr. *lawyer, electrical engineer*
Sczudlo, Raymond Stanley *lawyer*
Sears, John Patrick *lawyer*
Sears, Mary Helen *lawyer*

Segal, Donald E. *lawyer*
†Seidman, Ellen Shapiro *lawyer, government official*
Sender, Stanton P. *lawyer*
Sernoff, Louis R. *lawyer*
Shafer, Raymond Philip *lawyer, business executive*
†Shaffer, Jay Christopher *lawyer*
Shaheen, Michael Edmund, Jr. *lawyer, government official*
Shanks, Robert Bruce *lawyer*
Shapiro, David Israel *lawyer*
Shapiro, George Howard *lawyer*
Shelley, Herbert Carl *lawyer*
Shenefield, John Hale *lawyer*
Sherzer, Harvey Gerald *lawyer*
Shibley, Raymond Nadeem *lawyer*
Shniderman, Harry Louis *lawyer*
Shook, Langley R. *lawyer*
Shrinsky, Jason Lee *lawyer*
Shriver, Robert Sargent, Jr. *lawyer*
Shulman, Stephen Neal *lawyer*
Siegel, Allen George *lawyer*
Siemer, Deanne Clemence *lawyer*
Silberg, Jay Eliot *lawyer*
Silver, Daniel B. *lawyer*
Silver, Harry R. *lawyer*
Simchak, Matthew Stephen *lawyer*
Simon, Justin Daniel *lawyer*
Simon, Kenneth Mark *lawyer*
Simon, Rita James *legal educator*
Simons, Barbara M. *lawyer*
Simons, Lawrence Brook *lawyer*
Simowitz, Lee H. *lawyer*
Simpson, John W. *lawyer*
Sims, Joe *lawyer*
Singer, Daniel Morris *lawyer*
Singer, Norman H. *lawyer*
Singleton, Harry Michael *lawyer*
Skinner, William Polk *lawyer*
Smith, Brian William *lawyer, former government official*
Smith, Daniel Clifford *lawyer*
Smith, Delbert Dudley *lawyer*
Smith, Geoffrey R.W. *lawyer*
Smith, George Patrick, II *lawyer, educator*
Smith, John Lewis, III *lawyer*
Smith, Walter Joseph, Jr. *lawyer, educator*
†Smyth, Paul Burton *lawyer*
Sneed, James H. *lawyer*
Snider, Jerome Guy *lawyer*
Snyder, Allen Roger *lawyer*
Sofaer, Abraham David *lawyer, legal advisor, federal judge, legal educator*
Sohn, Louis Bruno *lawyer, educator*
Solomon, Richard Allan *lawyer*
Solomons, Mark Elliott *lawyer*
Sommer, Alphonse Adam, Jr. *lawyer*
Sonde, Theodore Irwin *lawyer*
Spaeder, Roger Campbell *lawyer*
Spencer, Samuel *lawyer*
†Spingler, Frank Joseph *lawyer*
Spooner, Mark Jordan *lawyer*
Springer, James van Roden *lawyer*
†Stafford, Barbara Rose *lawyer*
Stahr, Elvis J(acob), Jr. *lawyer, conservationist, educator*
Stansbury, Philip Roger *lawyer*
Stauffer, Ronald Eugene *lawyer*
Stayin, Randolph John *lawyer*
Steadman, Charles Walters *lawyer, corporate executive, writer*
Steel, Adrian L., Jr. *lawyer*
Stein, Michael Henry *lawyer*
Steinberg, Mark Robert *lawyer*
Steingold, Stuart Geoffrey *lawyer*
†Steinhardt, Ralph Gustav, III *law educator*
Stephens, Jay B. *lawyer*
Stern, Gerald Mann *lawyer*
Stern, Samuel Alan *lawyer*
Stevens, Herbert Francis *lawyer, law educator*
Stevenson, John Reese *lawyer*
Stevenson, Russell B., Jr. *lawyer*
Stewart, Eugene Lawrence *lawyer, trade association executive*
Stewart, George Cope, III (Scoop Stewart) *lawyer*
Stewart, John Irwin, Jr. *lawyer*
Stock, Stuart Chase *lawyer*
Stoer, Eric F. *lawyer*
Stoll, Richard G(iles) *lawyer*
Stone, Alan James *lawyer, writer*
Stone, Donald Raymond *lawyer*
Stranahan, Robert Paul, Jr. *lawyer*
Strauss, Stanley Robert *lawyer*
Stromberg, Clifford Douglas *lawyer*
Stumpf, Mark Howard *lawyer*
†Sullivan, Brendan V., Jr. *lawyer*
Sullivan, Timothy *lawyer*
Susman, Thomas Michael *lawyer, lobbyist*
Sussman, Monica Hilton *lawyer*
Sutherlund, David Arvid *lawyer*
Swankin, David Arnold *lawyer, consumer advocate*
Swart, Robert H. *lawyer*
Swidler, Joseph Charles *lawyer*
Swift, Evangeline Wilson *lawyer*
Tabor, John Kaye *lawyer, retired*
Tallent, Stephen Edison *lawyer, educator*
Tannenwald, Peter *lawyer*
Tatel, David Stephen *lawyer*
Tauber, Mark J. *lawyer*
Taylor, James, Jr. *lawyer*
Taylor, Ralph Arthur, Jr. *lawyer*
Taylor, Richard Powell *lawyer*
Teague, Randal Cornell, Sr. *lawyer*
Temko, Stanley Leonard *lawyer*
Temple, Riley Keene *lawyer*
Terry, Gary A. *lawyer, former trade association executive*
Terwilliger, George James, III *lawyer*
Thomas, Ritchie Tucker *lawyer*
†Thompson, Mozelle Willmont *lawyer, federal agency administrator*
Thornburgh, Dick (Richard L. Thornburgh) *lawyer, former United Nations official, former U.S. attorney general, former governor*
Timberg, Sigmund *lawyer*
Timmer, Barbara *lawyer*
Tirana, Bardyl Rifat *lawyer*
Tisch, Ronald Irwin *lawyer*
Todd, David Carl *lawyer*
Tompkins, Joseph Buford, Jr. *lawyer*
Toohey, Daniel Weaver *lawyer*
Topelius, Kathleen E. *lawyer*
Townsend, John Michael *lawyer*
†Toy, Charles David *lawyer*
Treacy, Vincent Edward *lawyer*
Trooboff, Peter Dennis *lawyer*
Trosten, Leonard Morse *lawyer*
Troyer, Thomas Alfred *lawyer*
Truitt, Max O'Rell, Jr. *lawyer*

Truitt, Thomas Hulen *lawyer*
Tucker, Stefan Franklin *lawyer*
Tufaro, Richard Chase *lawyer*
Tuohey, Mark Henry, III *lawyer*
Turkus, Albert H. *lawyer*
Turnage, Fred Douglas *lawyer*
†Turnbull, Lowell D. *lawyer*
Turner, Donald Frank *retired lawyer*
Turner, James P. *lawyer*
Tuttle, Jon F. *lawyer*
Tydings, Joseph Davies *lawyer, former senator*
Uehlein, E(dward) Carl, Jr. *lawyer*
Ulman, Craig Hawkins *lawyer*
Vacketta, Carl Lee *lawyer, educator*
Vakerics, Thomas Vincent *lawyer*
Valdez, Abelardo Lopez *lawyer*
Valentine, Steven Richards *lawyer*
Vance, Bernard Wayne *lawyer, government official*
Van Cleve, Ruth Gill *retired lawyer, government official*
Vander Clute, Norman Roland *lawyer*
Vanderstar, John *lawyer*
Vanderver, Timothy Arthur, Jr. *lawyer*
van Horne, Jon W. *lawyer*
Verner, James Melton *lawyer*
Verrill, Charles Owen, Jr. *lawyer*
Vickery, Ann Morgan *lawyer*
Vieth, G. Duane *lawyer*
Vince, Clinton Andrew *lawyer*
Vlcek, Jan Benes *lawyer*
Vogel, John Henry *lawyer*
Voight, Jerry D. *lawyer*
Wade, Robert Paul *lawyer*
Wadlow, R. Clark *lawyer*
Waits, John A. *lawyer*
Walker, Mary Ann *lawyer*
Wallace, Don, Jr. *law educator*
Wallace, James Harold, Jr. *lawyer*
Wallace, Robert Bruce *lawyer, educator*
Wallach, Paul Geoffry *lawyer*
Wallison, Frieda K. *lawyer*
Wallison, Peter J. *lawyer*
Wallman, Steven Mark Harte *lawyer*
Walsh, James Patrick *lawyer*
Walsh, Michael J. *lawyer*
Walton, Morgan Lauck, III *lawyer*
Ward, Alan S. *lawyer*
Ward, Erica Anne *lawyer, educator*
Ward, Nicholas Donnell *lawyer*
Waris, Michael, Jr. *lawyer*
Warnke, Paul Culliton *lawyer*
Warren, Edward W. *lawyer*
Wasilewski, Vincent Thomas *retired lawyer*
Waters, Jennifer Nash *lawyer*
Waters, Timothy J. *lawyer*
Watkin, Virginia Guild *lawyer*
Watson, Jack H., Jr. *lawyer*
Waxman, Margery Hope *lawyer*
Webber, Richard John *lawyer*
Webster, George Drury *lawyer*
Webster, Robert Kenly *lawyer*
Webster, William Hedgcock *lawyer*
Wegener, Mark Douglas *lawyer*
Wegner, Helmuth Adalbert *lawyer, retired chemical company executive*
†Weich, Ronald H. *lawyer*
Weidenfeld, Edward Lee *lawyer*
Weinberg, Edward *lawyer*
Weinberg, Robert Lester *lawyer, educator*
Weinman, Howard Mark *lawyer*
Weinmann, John Giffen *lawyer, diplomat*
Weinstein, Harris *lawyer*
Weiss, Ellyn Renee *lawyer*
Weiss, James Robert *lawyer*
Weiss, Jerome Paul *lawyer*
Weiss, Mark Anschel *lawyer*
Weiss, Stephen Joel *lawyer*
Weissbard, Samuel Held *lawyer*
Weissman, William R. *lawyer*
Wellen, Robert Howard *lawyer*
Weller, Janet Louise *lawyer*
Wenner, Charles Roderick *lawyer*
West, Gail Berry *lawyer*
West, Stephen Allan *lawyer*
Wheeler, Edward Kendall *lawyer*
Whelan, Roger Michael *lawyer, educator*
Whitaker, A(lbert) Duncan *lawyer*
White, Christian S. *lawyer*
White, Lee Calvin *lawyer*
Whiting, Richard Albert *lawyer*
Wiegley, Roger Douglas *lawyer*
Wilburn, Mary Nelson *lawyer, writer, educator*
†Wilcher, Shirley J. *lawyer*
Wiley, Richard Emerson *lawyer*
Willard, Richard Kennon *lawyer*
Willett, Edward Farrand, Jr. *lawyer*
Williams, B. John, Jr. *lawyer, former federal judge*
Williams, John Edward *lawyer*
Williams, Karen Hastie *lawyer*
Williams, S. Linn *lawyer*
Williams, T. Raymond *lawyer*
Williamson, Edwin Dargan *lawyer, former federal official*
Williamson, Thomas Samuel, Jr. *lawyer*
Willkie, Wendell Lewis, II *lawyer*
Willmore, Robert Louis *lawyer*
Wilner, Thomas Bernard *lawyer*
Wilson, Gary Dean *lawyer*
Wilson, R. Merinda D. *lawyer*
Wine, L. Mark *lawyer*
Winston, Judith Ann *lawyer*
Winter, Douglas E. *lawyer, writer*
Wintrol, John Patrick *lawyer*
Wirtz, William Willard *lawyer*
Wiseman, Alan M(itchell) *lawyer*
Wiss, Marcia A. *lawyer*
Witherspoon, Sharon *lawyer*
Wolff, Alan William *lawyer*
Wolff, Elroy Harris *lawyer*
Wollen, W. Foster *lawyer*
Wollenberg, J. Roger *lawyer*
Wood, John Martin *lawyer*
Work, Charles Robert *lawyer*
†Worsley, James Randolph, Jr. *lawyer*
Worthy, K(enneth) Martin *lawyer*
Wruble, Bernhardt Karp *lawyer*
Wyss, John Benedict *lawyer*
Yablon, Jeffery Lee *lawyer*
Yannucci, Thomas David *lawyer*
†Yarowsky, Jonathan R. *lawyer*
Young, William Fielding *lawyer*
Yurow, John Jesse *lawyer*
Yuspeh, Alan Ralph *lawyer*
Zausner, L. Andrew *lawyer*
Zax, Leonard A. *lawyer*
Zeifang, Donald P. *lawyer*
Zevnik, Paul A. *lawyer*
Zielinski, Charles Anthony *lawyer*

Zimmerman, Edwin Morton *lawyer*
Zipp, Joel Frederick *lawyer*
Zuckman, Harvey Lyle *legal educator*
Zupa, Victor Joseph *lawyer*
Zweben, Murray *lawyer, consultant*
†Zwick, Kenneth Lowell *lawyer*

FLORIDA

Altamonte Springs
Rudisill, Robert Mack, Jr. *lawyer*

Bal Harbour
Field, Cyrus Adams *lawyer*
Hastings, Lawrence Vaeth *lawyer, physician, educator*

Boca Grande
Baldwin, William Howard *retired foundation executive, lawyer*
Brock, Mitchell *lawyer*

Boca Raton
Beber, Robert H. *lawyer, financial services executive*
Beck, Jan Scott *lawyer*
Erdman, Joseph *lawyer*
Hausman, Bruce *lawyer*
Hedrick, Frederic Cleveland, Jr. *lawyer*
Reinstein, Joel *lawyer*

Boynton Beach
Brome, Robert Harrison *lawyer*
Miller, Emanuel *retired lawyer, banker*
Saxbe, William Bart *lawyer, former attorney general of U.S.*
Snell, Thaddeus Stevens, III *lawyer, retired building materials manufacturing company executive*

Bushnell
Hagin, T. Richard *lawyer*

Cape Coral
Seemann, Ernest Albright *lawyer*

Clearwater
Berman, Elihu H. *lawyer*
Free, E. LeBron *lawyer*

Coconut Grove
Denaro, Gregory *lawyer*

Coral Gables
Kniskern, Joseph Warren *lawyer*

Deerfield Beach
Brown, Colin W(egand) *lawyer, diversified company executive*
Rung, Richard Allen *lawyer, retired air force officer, retired educator*

Delray Beach
Barlow, Joel *retired lawyer*
Groening, William Andrew, Jr. *lawyer, former chemical company executive*
Larry, R. Heath *lawyer*
Rush, Kenneth *lawyer, industrialist, government official*
Shister, Joseph *labor arbitrator, law educator*

Fisher Island
McAmis, Edwin Earl *lawyer*

Fort Lauderdale
Adams, Daniel Lee *lawyer*
Buck, Thomas Randolph *lawyer*
Dressler, Robert A. *lawyer*
Ferris, Robert Edmund *lawyer*
Fox, Henry H. (Bucky Fox) *lawyer*
Gardner, Russell Menese *lawyer*
Hargrove, John Russell *lawyer*
†Hiaasen, Carl Andreas *lawyer*
Hirsch, Jeffrey Allan *lawyer*
Marcus, Richard Alan *lawyer, distribution company executive*
Moss, Stephen B. *lawyer*
O'Bryan, William Monteith *lawyer*
Turner, Hugh Joseph, Jr. *lawyer*
Walton, Rodney Earl *lawyer*
†Weinstein, Peter M. *lawyer, state senator*

Fort Myers
Allen, Richard C. *retired lawyer, educator*
Hanson, Arnold Philip *retired lawyer*
Medvecky, Robert Stephen *lawyer*
Morse, John Harleigh *lawyer*

Gainesville
Eder, George Jackson *lawyer, economist*
Freeland, James M. Jackson *lawyer, educator*
Hampton, William Wade, III *lawyer*
Mautz, Robert Barbeau *lawyer, educator*
Moberly, Robert Blakely *lawyer, educator*
Probert, Walter *lawyer, educator*
Quarles, James Cliv *law educator*
Smith, David Thornton *lawyer, educator*
Van Alstyne, W. Scott, Jr. *lawyer, educator*
Weyrauch, Walter Otto *legal educator*
White, Jill Carolyn *lawyer*

Hobe Sound
Etherington, Edwin Deacon *lawyer, business executive, educator*
Havens, Oliver Hershman *lawyer, consultant*
Markoe, Frank, Jr. *lawyer, business and hospital executive*
Matheson, William Lyon *lawyer, farmer*
Simpson, Russell Gordon *lawyer*

Hollywood
†Jenne, Kenneth Clarence, II *lawyer, state senator*
Thomas, Thomas A. *lawyer*

Homosassa
Clement, Howard Wheeler *lawyer*

Jacksonville
Ade, James L. *lawyer*
Ansbacher, Lewis *lawyer*
Bullock, Bruce Stanley *lawyer*

Christian, Gary Irvin *lawyer*
†Commander, Charles Edward *lawyer, real estate consultant*
Criser, Marshall M. *lawyer*
Dawes, Michael Francis *lawyer*
Drew, Horace Rainsford, Jr. *lawyer*
Ehrlich, Raymond *lawyer*
Farmer, Guy Otto, II *lawyer*
Fawbush, Andrew Jackson *lawyer*
Freeman, Judson, Jr. *lawyer*
Fruit, Melvyn Herschel *lawyer, management consultant*
Gabel, George DeSaussure, Jr. *lawyer*
Getman, Willard Etheridge *lawyer*
Kent, Frederick Heber *lawyer*
Legler, Mitchell Wooten *lawyer*
McWilliams, John Lawrence, III *lawyer*
Mikals, John Joseph *lawyer*
Moseley, James Francis *lawyer*
O'Neal, Michael Scott, Sr. *lawyer*
Pillans, Charles Palmer, III *lawyer*
Prom, Stephen George *lawyer*
Rinaman, James Curtis, Jr. *lawyer*
Sadler, Luther Fuller, Jr. *lawyer*
Slade, Thomas Bog, III *lawyer, investment banker*
Wallis, Donald Wills *lawyer*
Webster, David A. *lawyer*

Jupiter
Beddow, Thomas John *retired lawyer*

Key West
Coudert, Ferdinand Wilmerding *lawyer*
†Saunders, Ron *lawyer, state legislator*

Lakeland
Dufoe, William Stewart *lawyer*
Kibler, David Burke, III *lawyer*
Kittleson, Henry Marshall *lawyer*
Koren, Edward Franz *lawyer*

Leesburg
Austin, Robert Eugene, Jr. *lawyer*

Longboat Key
Heitler, George *lawyer*

Longwood
Tomasulo, Virginia Merrills *retired lawyer*

Marco Island
Fisher, Chester Lewis, Jr. *retired lawyer*
Poletti, Charles *lawyer*

Melbourne
Cacciatore, S. Sammy, Jr. *lawyer*

Miami
Alonso, Antonio Enrique *lawyer*
Armstrong, James Louden, III *lawyer*
Astigarraga, Jose I(gnacio) *lawyer*
Baena, Scott Louis *lawyer*
Basile, Michael *lawyer*
Benford, Norman J. *lawyer*
Berley, David Richard *lawyer*
Berman, Bruce Judson *lawyer*
Burnett, Henry *lawyer*
Cesarano, Gregory Morgen *lawyer*
Clarke, Mercer Kaye *lawyer*
Cole, Robert Bates *lawyer*
Connor, Terence Gregory *lawyer*
†Cosgrove, John Francis *lawyer, state legislator*
Critchlow, Richard H. *lawyer*
Dady, Robert Edward *lawyer*
Deaktor, Darryl Barnett *lawyer*
DuFresne, Elizabeth Jamison *lawyer*
Dyer, John Martin *lawyer, marketing educator*
England, Arthur Jay, Jr. *lawyer, former state justice*
Ferrer, Esteban A. *lawyer*
Fletcher, John Sheidley *lawyer*
Gassen, Joseph Albert *lawyer, former judge*
Godofsky, Lawrence *lawyer*
Gold, Alan Stephen *lawyer, educator, judge*
Gong, Edmond Joseph *lawyer*
Gonzalez-Pita, J. Alberto *lawyer*
Gragg, Karl Lawrence *lawyer*
Greenberg, Melvin Nathaniel *lawyer*
Hall, Andrew Clifford *lawyer*
Hall, Miles Lewis, Jr. *lawyer*
Hector, Louis Julius *lawyer*
Herron, James Michael *lawyer*
Hoffman, Larry J. *lawyer*
Houlihan, Gerald John *lawyer*
Hudson, Robert Franklin, Jr. *lawyer*
Hurtgen, Peter Joseph *lawyer*
Kenin, David S. *lawyer, shareholder*
Kline, Charles C. *lawyer*
Klock, Joseph Peter, Jr. *lawyer*
Korchin, Judith Miriam *lawyer*
Kreutzer, Franklin David *lawyer*
Lampen, Richard Jay *lawyer, investment banker*
Landy, Burton Aaron *lawyer*
Lataif, Lawrence P. *lawyer*
Louis, Paul Adolph *lawyer*
Mathews, Byron B., Jr. *lawyer*
Moore, Michael T. *lawyer*
Mudd, John Philip *lawyer*
Myers, Kenneth M. *lawyer*
O'Donnell, Edward Thomas *lawyer*
Pallot, E. Albert *lawyer, savings and loan executive*
Papy, Charles C., III *lawyer*
Paul, Robert *lawyer*
Pearson, Daniel S. *lawyer*
Quentel, Albert Drew *lawyer*
Reid, R(alph) Benjamine *lawyer*
Rosenn, Keith Samuel *lawyer, educator*
†Ross, David Lee *lawyer*
Schulman, Clifford A. *lawyer*
Seitz, Patricia Ann *lawyer*
Shepherd, Frank Andrew *lawyer*
Shevin, Robert Lewis *lawyer*
Short, Eugene Maurice, Jr. *lawyer, accountant*
Silber, Norman Jules *lawyer*
†Smith, Samuel Stuart *lawyer*
†Sonnett, Neal Russell *lawyer*
Stokes, Paul Mason *lawyer*
†Stratos, Kimarie Rose *lawyer, sports agent*
Suarez, Xavier Louis *lawyer, mayor*
Tarkoff, Michael Harris *lawyer*
Tew, Jeffrey Allen *lawyer*
Traurig, Robert Henry *lawyer*
†Wallace, Milton Jay *lawyer*
Walters, David McLean *lawyer*
Weigel, Rainer R. *lawyer*
Weinstein, Alan Edward *lawyer*
Weinstein, Andrew H. *lawyer*
Werth, Susan *lawyer*
Whisenand, James Dudley *lawyer*
Wolfson, Richard Frederick *lawyer*
Wood, William McBrayer *lawyer*
Young, John Hendricks *lawyer*
†Zack, Stephen Neil *lawyer*

Miami Lakes
Dominik, Jack Edward *lawyer*

Miami Shores
Trustman, Benjamin Arthur *lawyer*

Naples
Beam, Robert Thompson *retired lawyer*
Budd, David Glenn *lawyer*
Crehan, Joseph Edward *lawyer*
Emerson, John Williams, II *lawyer*
Farese, Lawrence Anthony *lawyer*
Gebhardt, Robert Charles *lawyer*
McMackin, F. Joseph, III *lawyer*
Peck, Bernard Sidney *lawyer*
Putzell, Edwin Joseph, Jr. *lawyer, mayor*
Roberts, William B. *lawyer, business executive*
Schauer, Wilbert Edward, Jr. *lawyer, manufacturing company executive*
Snyder, Marion Gene *lawyer, former congressman*
Starnes, James Wright *lawyer*
Stevens, William Kenneth *lawyer*
Westman, Carl Edward *lawyer*

Oldsmar
Hirschman, Sherman Joseph *lawyer, educator*
Sloane, Thomas Charles *lawyer*

Orlando
Ball, G. Thomas *lawyer*
Blackford, Robert Newton *lawyer*
Canan, Michael J. *lawyer, author*
Cohen, Jules Simon *lawyer*
Conti, Louis Thomas Moore *lawyer*
DuRose, Richard Arthur *lawyer*
†Dyer, John Hugh *lawyer, state senator*
Eagan, William Leon *lawyer*
Fulton, Richard T. *lawyer*
Handley, Leon Hunter *lawyer*
Henry, William Oscar Eugene *lawyer*
Horan, John Patrick *lawyer*
Jontz, Jeffry Robert *lawyer*
Leonhardt, Frederick Wayne *lawyer*
Linscott, Jerry R. *lawyer*
Mock, Frank Mackenzie *lawyer*
Morris, Max F. *lawyer*
Reed, John Alton *lawyer*
Rolle, Christopher Davies *lawyer*
Rosenthal, Paul Edmond *lawyer*
Rush, Fletcher Grey, Jr. *lawyer*
Sharp, Joel H., Jr. *lawyer*
Simon, James Lowell *lawyer*
Skambis, Christopher Charles, Jr. *lawyer*
Urban, James Arthur *lawyer*

Osprey
Maddocks, Robert Allen *lawyer, manufacturing company executive*

Palm Beach
Adler, Frederick Richard *lawyer, financier*
Bane, Charles Arthur *lawyer*
Beasley, James W., Jr. *lawyer*
Chopin, L. Frank *lawyer*
Fogelson, David *retired lawyer*
Ford, Thomas Patrick *lawyer*
Graubard, Seymour *lawyer*

Palm City
Burton, John Routh *lawyer*
Huntington, Earl Lloyd *lawyer, retired natural resources company executive*

Pensacola
Adams, Joseph Peter *retired lawyer, consultant*
Bozeman, Frank Carmack *lawyer*
Geeker, Nicholas Peter *lawyer, judge*
Hass, Charles John William *probation officer*
Moulton, Wilbur Wright, Jr. *lawyer*

Ponte Vedra Beach
Kuhn, Bowie K. *lawyer, former professional baseball commissioner, consultant*

River Ranch
Swett, Albert Hersey *retired lawyer, business executive, consultant*

Saint Petersburg
Battaglia, Anthony Sylvester *lawyer*
DiFilippo, Fernando, Jr. *lawyer*
Mann, Sam Henry, Jr. *lawyer*
Oleck, Howard Leoner *legal educator, writer*
Schultz, G. Robert *lawyer*
†Woodard, Joseph Lamar *law librarian, law educator*

Sanibel
Kiernan, Edwin A., Jr. *lawyer, corporation executive*

Sarasota
Browdy, Alvin *lawyer*
Cottone, Benedict Peter *retired lawyer*
Greenfield, Robert Kauffman *lawyer*
Ives, George Skinner *arbitrator, former government official*
Kimbrough, Robert Averyt *lawyer*
Mackey, Leonard Bruce *lawyer, former diversified manufacturing corporation executive*
Raimi, Burton Louis *lawyer*
Schwartz, Norman L. *lawyer*

Sebastian
Breman, Joseph Eliot *lawyer*

Tallahassee
Aurell, John Karl *lawyer*
Barnett, Martha Walters *lawyer*
Boyd, Joseph Arthur, Jr. *lawyer*
Carson, Leonard Allen *lawyer*
Clarkson, Julian Derieux *lawyer*
D'Alemberte, Talbot (Sandy D'Alemberte) *lawyer, educator*
Ervin, Robert Marvin *lawyer*
Griffith, Elwin Jabez *lawyer, university administrator*
Pelham, Thomas Gerald *lawyer*
Peterson, Rodney Delos *mediator, forensic economist*
Roberts, B. K. *lawyer, former judge*
†Schroeder, Edwin Maher *law educator*
Zaiser, Kent Ames *lawyer*

Tampa
Adkins, Edward Cleland *lawyer*
Aitken, Thomas Dean *lawyer*
Barford, George, IV *lawyer*
Barkin, Marvin E. *lawyer*
Barton, Bernard Alan, Jr. *lawyer*
Beytin, Kenneth Alan *lawyer*
Bierley, John Charles *lawyer*
Campbell, Richard Bruce *lawyer*
Culverhouse, Hugh Franklin *lawyer, professional sports team executive*
Cutler, Edward I. *lawyer*
Davis, Richard Earl *lawyer*
Doliner, Nathaniel Lee *lawyer*
Ellwanger, Thomas John *lawyer*
Gassler, Frank Henry *lawyer*
Gilbert, Leonard Harold *lawyer*
Gillen, William Albert *lawyer*
Gonzalez, Joe Manuel *lawyer*
Hoyt, Brooks Pettingill *lawyer*
Jones, Gregory Gilman *lawyer*
Jones, John Arthur *lawyer*
†Karl, Frederick Brennan *lawyer, former state justice*
Kelly, Thomas Paine, Jr. *lawyer*
Kiernan, William Joseph, Jr. *lawyer, real estate investor*
Levine, Jack Anton *lawyer*
Litschgi, A. Byrne *lawyer*
MacDonald, Thomas Cook, Jr. *lawyer*
Martin, Gary Wayne *lawyer*
McAdams, John P. *lawyer*
Miller, William Jones *lawyer*
O'Neill, Albert Clarence, Jr. *lawyer*
O'Sullivan, Brendan Patrick *lawyer*
Roberson, Bruce H. *lawyer*
Rosenkranz, Stanley William *lawyer*
Rothenberg, Frederick M. *lawyer*
Sams, Robert Alan *lawyer*
Schwenke, Roger Dean *lawyer*
Sparkman, Steven Leonard *lawyer*
Stafford, Josephine Howard *lawyer*
Stallings, (Charles) Norman *lawyer*
Taub, Theodore Calvin *lawyer*
Thomas, Wayne Lee *lawyer*
Wagner, Frederick William (Bill Wagner) *lawyer*

Venice
Miller, Allan John *lawyer*

Vero Beach
Youngman, William Sterling *lawyer*

West Palm Beach
Beelner, Ken Phillip *investigator, legal assistant*
Burck, Arthur Albert *lawyer, corporate merger expert*
Flanagan, L. Martin *lawyer*
Gowing, Delmer Charles, III *lawyer*
Hill, Thomas William, Jr. *lawyer, educator*
Montgomery, Robert Morel, Jr. *lawyer*
Moore, George Crawford Jackson *lawyer*
Mora, Abraham Martin *lawyer*
O'Brien, Thomas George, III *lawyer*
O'Flarity, James P. *lawyer*
Petersen, David L. *lawyer*
†Pritchard Schoch, Teresa Noreen *lawyer, law librarian*
Royce, Raymond Watson *lawyer, rancher, citrus grower*
Sammond, John Stowell *lawyer*
Smith, David Shiverick *lawyer, former ambassador*
Wagner, Arthur Ward, Jr. *lawyer*

Windermere
Blackstone, Sandra Lee *lawyer, educator, former government official*

Winter Haven
Chase, Lucius Peter *lawyer, retired corporate executive*

Winter Park
Brooten, Kenneth Edward, Jr. *lawyer*
Patterson, Robert Youngman, Jr. *retired lawyer, utility executive*

GEORGIA

Athens
Beaird, James Ralph *legal educator*
Carlson, Ronald Lee *lawyer, educator*
Ellington, Charles Ronald *lawyer, educator*
Phillips, Walter Ray *lawyer, educator*
†Puckett, Elizabeth Ann *law librarian, law educator*
Spurgeon, Edward Dutcher *law educator*
Watson, William A. J. *law educator*
Wellman, Richard Vance *legal educator*

Atlanta
Abrams, Harold Eugene *lawyer*
Alexander, Miles Jordan *lawyer*
Anderson, Peter Joseph *lawyer*
Ashe, Robert Lawrence, Jr. *lawyer*
Attridge, Richard Byron *lawyer*
Baker, David S. *lawyer*
Baldi, Angelo C. *lawyer*
Barkoff, Rupert Mitchell *lawyer*
Bassett, Peter Q. *lawyer*
Batson, Richard Neal *lawyer*
Baxter, Harry Stevens *lawyer*
Beckman, Gail McKnight *law educator*
Bennett, Jay D. *lawyer*
Bird, Wendell Raleigh *lawyer*
Blackstock, Jerry Byron *lawyer*
Bloodworth, A(lbert) W(illiam) Franklin *lawyer*
Boisseau, Richard Robert *lawyer*
Boman, John Harris, Jr. *retired lawyer*
Bonds, John Wilfred, Jr. *lawyer*
Bondurant, Emmet Jopling, II *lawyer*
Boone, J. William *lawyer*
Booth, Gordon Dean, Jr. *lawyer*
Bowden, Henry Lumpkin *lawyer*
Bowden, Henry Lumpkin, Jr. *lawyer*
Branch, Thomas Broughton, III *lawyer*
Brannon, Lester Travis, Jr. *lawyer*
Bratton, James Henry, Jr. *lawyer*
Brecher, Armin G. *lawyer*
Brooks, Wilbur Clinton *lawyer*
†Brown, John Robert *lawyer, priest*
Cadenhead, Alfred Paul *lawyer*
Candler, John Slaughter, II *retired lawyer*
Cheatham, Richard Reed *lawyer*
Chilivis, Nickolas Peter *lawyer*
Chisholm, Tommy *lawyer, utility company executive*
Clark, William Franklin *lawyer*
Clarke, Thomas Hal *lawyer*
Cohen, Ezra Harry *lawyer*
Cohen, George Leon *lawyer*
Cohen, N. Jerold *lawyer*
Collins, Steven M. *lawyer*
Cooper, Frederick Eansor *lawyer*
Copeland, Floyd Dean *lawyer*
Coxe, Tench Charles *lawyer*
Cumming, David Robert, Jr. *lawyer*
Cutshaw, Kenneth Andrew *lawyer*
Dalton, John J. *lawyer*
Davis, Frank Tradewell, Jr. *lawyer*
Denny, Richard Alden, Jr. *lawyer*
Douglas, John Lewis *lawyer*
Downs, Harry *retired legal corporate executive*
Doyle, Michael Anthony *lawyer*
DuBose, Charles Wilson *lawyer*
Durrett, James Frazer, Jr. *lawyer*
Eason, William Everette, Jr. *lawyer*
Edge, J(ulian) Dexter, Jr. *lawyer*
Egan, Michael Joseph *lawyer*
Ehrlichman, John Daniel *company executive, author, former assistant to President of United States*
Epstein, David Gustav *lawyer*
Erck, Theodore Augustus, Jr. *lawyer*
Etheridge, Jack Paul *arbitrator, mediator, former judge*
Felton, Jule Wimberly, Jr. *lawyer*
Fleming, Julian Denver, Jr. *lawyer*
Forbes, Theodore McCoy, Jr. *lawyer, arbitrator, mediator*
Foreman, Edward Rawson *lawyer*
Gambrell, David Henry *lawyer*
Garner, Robert Edward Lee *lawyer*
†Giffin, Gordon D. *lawyer*
Girth, Marjorie Louisa *lawyer, educator*
Goldman, Joel Stanley *lawyer*
Goldstein, Elliott *lawyer*
Grant, Walter Matthews *lawyer, diversified consumer products executive*
Greer, Bernard Lewis, Jr. *lawyer*
Groton, James Purnell *lawyer*
Haas, George Aaron *lawyer*
Hackett, Stanley Hailey *lawyer*
Harkey, Robert Shelton *lawyer*
Harlin, Robert Ray *lawyer*
Hasson, James Keith, Jr. *lawyer*
Hawks, Barrett Kingsbury *lawyer*
†Hay, Peter *law educator*
Hill, Paul Drennen *lawyer, banker*
Hoff, Gerhardt Michael *lawyer, insurance company executive*
Hopkins, George Mathews Marks *lawyer, business executive*
Howard, Harry Clay *lawyer*
Hunter, Forrest Walker *lawyer*
Ide, Roy William, III *lawyer*
Izard, John *lawyer*
Izlar, William Henry, Jr. *lawyer, banker*
Janney, Donald Wayne *lawyer*
Jeffries, McChesney Hill *retired lawyer*
Jenkins, Albert Felton, Jr. *lawyer*
Jones, Frank Cater *lawyer*
Kelley, James Francis *lawyer*
Kelley, Jeffrey Wendell *lawyer*
Kinzer, William Luther *lawyer*
Klamon, Lawrence Paine *lawyer*
Kneisel, Edmund M. *lawyer*
Knowles, Marjorie Fine *lawyer, educator, dean*
Lackland, Theodore Howard *lawyer*
Lamon, Harry Vincent, Jr. *lawyer*
Langway, Richard Merritt *lawyer*
Leonard, David Morse *lawyer*
Lester, Charles Turner, Jr. *lawyer*
Linkous, William Joseph, Jr. *lawyer*
Lipshutz, Robert Jerome *lawyer, former government official*
Lokey, Hamilton *lawyer*
Lower, Robert Cassel *lawyer, educator*
Lunsford, Julius R(odgers), Jr. *lawyer*
Lurey, Alfred Saul *lawyer*
Marshall, John Treutlen *lawyer*
Marshall, Thomas Oliver, Jr. *lawyer*
McNeill, Thomas Ray *lawyer*
†Mills, Robin Kate *law librarian*
Mobley, John Homer, II *lawyer*
Moeling, Walter Goos, IV *lawyer*
Moore, John W. *lawyer*
Neely, Edgar Adams, Jr. *lawyer*
Newman, Stuart *lawyer*
Owen, Robert Hubert *lawyer, real estate broker*
Parker, John Garrett *lawyer*
Partain, Eugene Gartly *lawyer*
Patterson, William Robert *lawyer*
Perry, Timothy Sewell *lawyer*
Persons, J. Robert *lawyer*
Persons, Oscar N. *lawyer*
Phillips, Barry *lawyer*
Piassick, Joel Bernard *lawyer*
Pike, Larry Samuel *lawyer*
Poe, H. Sadler *lawyer*
Poythress, David Bryan *lawyer, state commissioner*
Pratt, John Sherman *lawyer*
Ramsay, Ernest Canaday *lawyer*
Reed, Glen Alfred *lawyer*
Regenstein, Louis *lawyer*
Ridley, Clarence Haverty *lawyer*
Rogers, C. B. *lawyer*
Russell, Harold Louis *lawyer*
Saidman, Gary K. *lawyer*
Savell, Edward Lupo *lawyer*
Schroder, Jack Spalding, Jr. *lawyer*
Schulte, Jeffrey Lewis *lawyer*
Schwartz, Dale Marvin *lawyer*
Sibley, Horace Holden *lawyer*
Sibley, James Malcolm *retired lawyer*
Smith, Alexander Wyly, Jr. *lawyer*
Smith, James Louis, III *lawyer*
Smith, Jeffrey Michael *lawyer*
Smith, Sidney Oslin, Jr. *lawyer*
Smith, Walton Napier *lawyer*
Stanhope, William Henry *lawyer*
Steed, Robert Lee *lawyer, columnist*
Stokes, James Sewell *lawyer*
Strauss, Robert David *lawyer*
Swann, Jerre Bailey *lawyer*
Swift, Frank Meador *lawyer*
Tanner, W(alter) Rhett *lawyer*

Taylor, George Kimbrough, Jr. *lawyer*
Taylor, Virginia S. *lawyer*
Thompson, Larry Dean *lawyer*
Varner, Chilton Davis *lawyer*
Vickery, Trammell Eugene *lawyer*
Walsh, W. Terence *lawyer*
Webb, Brainard Troutman, Jr. *lawyer, distribution company executive*
West, Ruth Tinsley *lawyer*
Whitley, Joe Dally *lawyer*
Williams, David Howard *lawyer*
Williams, Lyman Neil, Jr. *lawyer*
Wilson, Alexander Erwin, Jr. *lawyer, management consultant*
Wilson, James Hargrove, Jr. *lawyer*
Wolensky, Michael K. *lawyer*
Wright, Peter Meldrim *lawyer*
Yates, Mary Mitchell *lawyer*
Zink, Charles Talbott *lawyer*

Augusta
Woods, Gerald Wayne *lawyer*

Canton
Hasty, William Grady, Jr. *lawyer*

Columbus
Brinkley, Jack Thomas *lawyer, former congressman*
McGlamry, Max Reginald *lawyer*
Page, William Marion *lawyer*
†Robinson, Pete *lawyer, state senator*

Dalton
†Kinnamon, Gregory Harold *lawyer*

Decatur
Middleton, James Boland *lawyer*

Dillard
Wilkinson, Albert Mims, Jr. *lawyer*

Dublin
Greene, Jule Blounte *lawyer*

Duluth
Tennant, Thomas Michael *lawyer*

Fort Valley
Marchman, Robert L., III *lawyer, pecan farmer*

Lookout Mountain
Hitching, Harry James *retired lawyer*

Macon
Ennis, Edgar William, Jr. *lawyer*
Rutledge, Ivan Cate *retired legal educator, arbitrator*
Sell, Edward Scott, Jr. *lawyer*
†Snow, Cubbedge, Jr. *lawyer*

Marietta
†Barnes, Roy Eugene *lawyer*
Burkey, J(acob) Brent *lawyer, company executive*
†Hammond, John William *lawyer*
Ingram, George Conley *lawyer*

Metter
Doremus, Ogden *lawyer*

Norcross
Helander, Robert Charles *lawyer*

Ringgold
†Poston, McCracken King, Jr. *lawyer, state representative*

Savannah
Dickey, David Herschel *lawyer, accountant*
Forbes, Morton Gerald *lawyer*
McAlpin, Kirk Martin *lawyer*
Rawson, William Robert *lawyer, retired manufacturing company executive*

Watkinsville
Wright, Robert Joseph *lawyer*

HAWAII

Honolulu
Akinaka, Asa Masayoshi *lawyer*
Bloede, Victor Carl *lawyer, academic executive*
Cades, Julius Russell *lawyer*
Callies, David Lee *lawyer, educator*
Case, James Hebard *lawyer*
Char, Vernon Fook Leong *lawyer*
Chuck, Walter G(oonsun) *lawyer*
Devens, Paul *lawyer*
†Fernandes Salling, Lehua *lawyer, state senator*
Fong, Peter C. K. *lawyer, judge*
Gay, E(mil) Laurence *lawyer*
Gelber, Don Jeffrey *lawyer*
Heller, Ronald Ian *lawyer*
Katayama, Robert Nobuichi *lawyer*
Lilly, Michael Alexander *lawyer*
Marks, Michael J. *lawyer, corporate executive*
†Matsunaga, Matthew Masao *lawyer, accountant*
Miller, Richard Sherwin *legal educator*
Moore, Willson Carr, Jr. *lawyer*
Okinaga, Lawrence Shoji *lawyer*
Omori, Morio *lawyer*
Porter, Michael Pell *lawyer*
Quinn, William Francis *lawyer*
Roberti, Mario Andrew *lawyer, former energy company executive*
Starn, Peter *lawyer*
†Thielen, Cynthia Henry *lawyer, state legislator*

Koloa
Blair, Samuel Ray *lawyer*

Kula
Rohlfing, Frederick William *lawyer, judge*

Wailuku
Kinaka, William Tatsuo *lawyer*

IDAHO

Boise
Klein, Edith Miller *lawyer, former state senator*
Leroy, David Henry *lawyer, state and federal official*
†Madsen, Roger Bryan *lawyer*
Marcus, Craig Brian *lawyer*
McNutt, Suzzanne Marie *legal assistant*
O'Riordan, William Hugh *lawyer*
Risch, James E. *lawyer*
Shurtliff, Marvin Karl *lawyer*
VanHole, William Remi *lawyer*

Coeur D Alene
Ayers, Stephen M. *lawyer*

Ketchum
Hogue, Terry Glynn *lawyer*

Lewiston
McCann, William Vern, Jr. *lawyer*
Peterson, Philip Everett *legal educator*
Ware, Marcus John *lawyer*

Meridian
†Lance, Alan George *lawyer, legislator*

Moscow
†Seeger, Leinaala Robinson *law librarian, educator*

Pocatello
Nye, W. Marcus W. *lawyer*

Rupert
Bellwood, Sherman Jean *arbitrator, consultant, retired judge*

Sandpoint
Murray, James Michael *law librarian*

Twin Falls
†Stubbs, Mark Darwin *lawyer*

ILLINOIS

Alton
Hoagland, Karl King, Jr. *lawyer*
Struif, Leo James *lawyer*

Arlington Heights
Wine-Banks, Jill Susan *lawyer*

Aurora
Alschuler, Sam *lawyer*
Lowe, Ralph Edward *lawyer*
Tyler, Lloyd John *lawyer*

Barrington
Bassett, Robert Cochem *lawyer, publisher*
†Victor, Michael Gary *lawyer, physician*
Wyatt, James Frank, Jr. *lawyer*

Belleville
Bauman, John Duane *lawyer*
Boyle, Richard Edward *lawyer*
Coghill, William Thomas, Jr. *lawyer*
Heiligenstein, Christian E. *lawyer*
Hess, Frederick J. *lawyer*
Parham, James Robert *lawyer*

Bloomington
Bragg, Michael Ellis *lawyer*
Goebel, William Mathers *lawyer*
Jordan, Leo John *lawyer*
Montgomery, William Adam *lawyer*
Sullivan, Laura Patricia *lawyer, insurance company executive*

Breese
†Granberg, Kurt Michael *lawyer*

Burr Ridge
Peterson, Carl Roy *lawyer*

Carbondale
Clemons, John Robert *lawyer*
Habiger, Richard J. *lawyer*
Haynsworth, Harry Jay, IV *lawyer, educator*
†Houdek, Frank George *law librarian*
Kionka, Edward James *lawyer*
Lesar, Hiram Henry *lawyer, educator*

Carrollton
Strickland, Hugh Alfred *lawyer*

Carthage
Glidden, John Redmond *lawyer*

Champaign
Bender, Paul Edward *lawyer*
Cribbet, John Edward *legal educator, former university chancellor*
Frampton, George Thomas *legal educator*
Kindt, John Warren, Sr. *lawyer, educator, consultant*
Krause, Harry Dieter *lawyer, educator*
Maggs, Peter Blount *lawyer, educator*
Mamer, Stuart Mies *lawyer*
Miller, Harold Arthur *lawyer*
Nowak, John E. *law educator*
Rotunda, Ronald Daniel *law educator, consultant*
†Surles, Richard Hurlbut, Jr. *law librarian*

Chicago
Abrams, Lee Norman *lawyer*
Acker, Frederick George *lawyer*
Adair, Wendell Hinton, Jr. *lawyer*
Adams, Roy M. *lawyer, writer*
Adelman, Stanley Joseph *lawyer*
Adelman, Steven Herbert *lawyer*
Agnew, David M. *lawyer*
Aland, Robert H. *lawyer*
Aldrich, Thomas Lawrence *lawyer*
Alexander, William Henry *lawyer*
Alexis, Geraldine M. *lawyer*
Allard, Jean *lawyer, urban planner*
Allen, Richard Blose *legal editor, lawyer*
Allen, Thomas Draper *lawyer*
Alschuler, Albert W. *law educator*
Altheimer, Alan J. *lawyer*
Altman, Louis *lawyer, author, educator*
Ambrose, Gerald A. *lawyer*
Anagnost, Themis John *lawyer*
Anderson, David A. *lawyer*
Anderson, Donald W. *lawyer*
Anderson, J. Trent *lawyer*
Anderson, John Thomas *lawyer*
Anderson, Kimball Richard *lawyer*
Anderson, William Cornelius, III *lawyer*
Angelo, Percy L. *lawyer*
Angle, John Edwin *lawyer*
Angst, Gerald L. *lawyer*
Anthony, Michael Francis *lawyer*
Anvaripour, M. A. *lawyer*
Apcel, Melissa Anne *lawyer*
Appel, Nina S. *law educator, dean*
Archer, James G. *lawyer*
Arlow, Allan Joseph *lawyer*
Armstrong, Edwin Richard *lawyer, publisher, editor*
Aronson, Simon H. *lawyer*
Aronson, Virginia L. *lawyer*
Arroyo, Robert Edward *lawyer*
Artwick, Frederic *lawyer*
Ashley, James Wheeler *lawyer*
Athas, Gus James *lawyer*
Auerbach, Marshall Jay *lawyer*
Austin, Richard William *lawyer*
Austin, Robert B. *lawyer*
Auwarter, Franklin Paul *lawyer*
Avery, Cameron Scott *lawyer*
†Axelrod, David Alan *lawyer*
Axley, Frederick William *lawyer*
Badel, Julie *lawyer*
Baer, John Richard Frederick *lawyer*
Baetz, W. Timothy *lawyer*
Bailey, Robert Short *lawyer*
Baird, Douglas Gordon *law educator*
Baird, Russell Miller *lawyer*
Baker, Donald *lawyer*
Baker, James Edward Sproul *retired lawyer*
Baker, Pamela *lawyer*
Banoff, Sheldon Irwin *lawyer*
Barker, William Thomas *lawyer*
Barnard, Morton John *lawyer*
Barnard, Robert N. *lawyer*
Barnes, James Garland, Jr. *lawyer*
Barr, John Robert *lawyer*
Barrett, Roger Watson *lawyer*
Barron, Howard Robert *lawyer*
Barry, Norman J., Jr. *lawyer*
Bartlit, Fred Holcomb, Jr. *lawyer, educator*
Baruch, Hurd *lawyer*
Bashwiner, Steven Lacelle *lawyer*
Baugher, Peter V. *lawyer*
Baumgartner, William Hans, Jr. *lawyer*
Beck, Philip S. *lawyer*
Becker, Theodore Michaelson *lawyer*
Beem, Jack Darrel *lawyer*
Beggan, John Francis *lawyer*
Belmore, F. Martin *lawyer*
Bennett, M(ary) Elizabeth *lawyer*
Bennett, Russell Odbert *lawyer*
Bentley, Peter John Hilton *lawyer*
Berens, Mark Harry *lawyer*
Berger, Robert Michael *lawyer*
Berghoff, John C., Jr. *lawyer*
Bergstrom, Robert William *lawyer*
Berland, Abel Edward *lawyer, realtor*
Berlin, Stanton Henry *lawyer*
Berman, Bennett I. *lawyer*
Bernard, Frank Charles *lawyer*
Berner, Robert Lee, Jr. *lawyer*
Bernick, David M. *lawyer*
Berning, Larry D. *lawyer*
Bernstein, H. Bruce *lawyer*
Bernstein, Howard L. *lawyer*
Berolzheimer, Karl *lawyer*
Berry, Alan M. *lawyer*
Betke, James E. *lawyer*
Bezman, Victor H. *lawyer*
Biebel, Paul Philip, Jr. *lawyer*
Bielawski, Alan P. *lawyer*
Bierig, Jack R. *lawyer*
Bitner, John Howard *lawyer*
Bixby, Frank Lyman *lawyer*
Blakemore, Thomas F. *lawyer*
Blanco, Jim L. *lawyer*
Blatt, Richard Lee *lawyer*
Bleveans, John *lawyer*
Block, Neal Jay *lawyer*
Bloom, Christopher Arthur *lawyer*
Blount, Michael Eugene *lawyer*
Blum, Walter J. *lawyer, educator*
Boberg, Wayne D. *lawyer*
Bockelman, John Richard *lawyer*
Bodine, Laurence *lawyer, editor, marketer*
Boies, Wilber H. *lawyer*
Boley, John N. *lawyer*
Bomchill, Fern Cheryl *lawyer*
Boodell, Thomas Joseph, Jr. *lawyer*
Borders, Thomas C. *lawyer*
Bornstein, Deborah H. *lawyer*
Bosselman, Fred Paul *law educator*
Botica, Matthew J. *lawyer*
Bouma, Robert Edwin *lawyer, diversified company executive*
Bowe, William John *lawyer*
Bowen, Stephen Stewart *lawyer, educator*
Bower, Bruce Lester *lawyer*
Bower, Glen Landis *lawyer*
Bowytz, Robert B. *lawyer*
Boyd, David J. *lawyer*
Bramnik, Robert Paul *lawyer*
Braun, W(illiam) David *lawyer*
Breakstone, Donald S. *lawyer*
†Brennan, James Joseph *lawyer*
Brennan, Richard J. *lawyer*
Brice, Roger Thomas *lawyer*
Bridewell, David Alexander *lawyer*
Bridgman, Thomas Francis *lawyer*
Brizzolara, Charles Anthony *lawyer*
Brooks, Robert Liss *lawyer*
Brophy, Joan Edmonds *lawyer*
Brown, Donald James, Jr. *lawyer*
Brown, Gregory K. *lawyer*
Bruner, Stephen C. *lawyer*
Bryson, Cheryl Blackwell *lawyer*
Buchholz, Edward J. *lawyer*
Bulger, Brian Wegg *lawyer*
Bunge, Jonathan Gunn *lawyer*
Burdelik, Thomas Louis *lawyer*
Burditt, George Miller, Jr. *lawyer*
Burgess, Robert Kyle *lawyer*
Burgett, George L. *lawyer*
Burke, Thomas Joseph, Jr. *lawyer*
Burkey, Lee Melville *lawyer*
Busey, Roxane C. *lawyer*
Butt, Edward Thomas, Jr. *lawyer*
Byman, Robert Leslie *lawyer*
Cahan, James N. *lawyer*
Caplis, Kevin J. *lawyer*
Carlin, Dennis J. *lawyer*
Carlson, Stephen Curtis *lawyer*
Carlson, Walter Carl *lawyer*
Carpenter, David William *lawyer*
Carren, Jeffrey P. *lawyer*
Carroll, James J. *lawyer*
Carroll, John M. *lawyer*
Carroll, William Kenneth *law educator, psychologist, theologian*
Carton, Laurence Alfred *lawyer*
Cassling, Donald Roger *lawyer*
Chabraja, Nicholas D. *lawyer*
Chaffetz, Hammond Edward *lawyer*
Chandler, Kent, Jr. *lawyer*
Chanen, Franklin Allen *lawyer*
Chapman, Howard Stuart *lawyer*
Cheely, Daniel Joseph *lawyer*
Chefitz, Joel Gerald *lawyer*
Cherney, James Alan *lawyer*
Chiles, Stephen Michael *lawyer*
Christensen, George B. *lawyer*
Citrin, Phillip Marshall *retired lawyer*
Citron, Diane *lawyer*
Clark, James Allen *lawyer, educator*
Clark, James E. *lawyer*
Clay, John Ernest *lawyer*
Clemenceau, Paul B. *lawyer*
Clemens, Richard Glenn *lawyer*
Closen, Michael Lee *law educator*
Cohen, Christopher B. *lawyer*
Cohen, Melanie Rovner *lawyer*
Cole, Thomas Amor *lawyer*
Collen, Sheldon Orrin *lawyer*
Colman, Jeffrey D. *lawyer*
Comiskey, Michael Peter *lawyer*
Congalton, Susan Tichenor *lawyer*
Conklin, Thomas William *lawyer*
Conlon, William F. *lawyer*
Connelly, Vincent J. *lawyer*
Conti, Lee Ann *lawyer*
Conviser, Richard James *law educator, lawyer, publications company executive*
Conway, Michael Maurice *lawyer*
Cooney, Robert John *lawyer*
Copeland, Edward Jerome *lawyer*
Corboy, Philip Harnett *lawyer*
Corcoran, James Martin, Jr. *lawyer, writer, lecturer*
Corwin, Sherman Phillip *lawyer*
Costello, John William *lawyer*
Cotton, Eugene *lawyer*
Coughlan, Kenneth Lewis *lawyer*
Coughlin, Joseph E. *lawyer*
Covey, Frank Michael, Jr. *lawyer, educator*
Covington, George Morse *lawyer*
Crane, Mark *lawyer*
Craven, George W. *lawyer*
Crawford, Dewey Byers *lawyer*
Creamer, Robert Allan *lawyer*
Cremin, Susan Elizabeth *lawyer*
Crihfield, Philip J. *lawyer*
Crisham, Thomas Michael *lawyer*
Cronin, Robert E. *lawyer*
Crossan, John Robert *lawyer*
Crowe, Robert William *lawyer, mediator*
Crumbaugh, David Gordon *lawyer*
Crusto, Mitchell Ferdinand *lawyer, environmental consultant*
Cunningham, Robert James *lawyer*
Curley, Robert E. *lawyer*
Curran, Barbara Adell *law foundation administrator, writer*
†Currie, James Barker *lawyer, corporate secretary*
†Cusack, John Thomas *lawyer*
Custer, Charles Francis *lawyer*
Dam, Kenneth W. *lawyer, law educator*
D'Amato, Anthony *law educator*
Davidson, Stanley J. *lawyer*
Davis, Michael W. *lawyer*
Davis, Muller *lawyer*
Davis, Ralph E. *lawyer*
Davis, Scott Jonathan *lawyer*
Dawson, Suzanne Stockus *lawyer*
DeCarlo, William S. *lawyer*
Dechene, James Charles *lawyer*
Decker, Richard Knore *lawyer*
de Hoyos, Debora M. *lawyer*
Deignan, Robert E. *lawyer*
Deitrick, William Edgar *lawyer*
Delp, Wilbur Charles, Jr. *lawyer*
Denvir, Robert F. *lawyer*
D'Esposito, Julian C., Jr. *lawyer*
Despres, Leon Mathis *lawyer, former city official*
Detuno, Joseph Edward *lawyer*
DeWolfe, John Chauncey, Jr. *lawyer*
De Yoe, David P. *lawyer*
Dilling, Kirkpatrick Wallwick *lawyer*
Dilworth, Robert Holden *lawyer*
Dixon, Stewart Strawn *lawyer*
Dockterman, Michael *lawyer*
Dondanville, John Wallace *lawyer*
Donenfeld, J. Douglas *lawyer*
Donlevy, John Dearden *lawyer*
Donohoe, Jerome Francis *lawyer*
Donovan, Thomas B. *lawyer*
Dorman, Jeffrey Lawrence *lawyer*
Dorr, Williams Peter *lawyer*
Douglas, Charles W. *lawyer*
Douglass, Andrew Ian *lawyer, financial executive*
Downing, Robert Allan *lawyer*
Doyle, John Robert *lawyer*
Dropkin, Allen Hodes *lawyer*
Drymalski, Raymond Hibner *lawyer, banker*
Duez, David Joseph *lawyer*
Duhl, Michael Foster *lawyer*
Duncan, John Patrick Cavanaugh *lawyer*
Durchslag, Stephen P. *lawyer*
Durso, John J. *lawyer*
Dykstra, Paul Hopkins *lawyer*
Early, Bert Hylton *lawyer, legal search consultant*
Eaton, Larry Ralph *lawyer*
Echlin, Bernard Joseph *lawyer*
Eckel, John M. *lawyer*
Edelman, Alvin *lawyer*
Egan, Kevin James *lawyer*
Eggert, Russell Raymond *lawyer*
Ehrman, Joseph S. *lawyer*
Eimer, Nathan Philip *lawyer*
Ekdahl, Jon Nels *lawyer, corporate secretary*
Elden, Gary Michael *lawyer*
Ellwood, Scott *lawyer*
Elson, Alex *lawyer, legal educator*
Emerson, Carter Whitney *lawyer*
Engling, Robert John *lawyer*
Ephraim, Donald Morley *lawyer*

Epstein, Richard A. law educator
Erens, Jay Allan lawyer
Ericson, Robert W. lawyer
Erlebacher, Arlene Cernik lawyer
Esrick, Jerald Paul lawyer
Ettinger, Joseph Alan lawyer
Even, Francis Alphonse lawyer
Everson, Leonard Charles lawyer
Fahner, Tyrone C. lawyer, former state attorney general
Fairchild, Gary Lee lawyer
Fayhee, Michael R. lawyer
Fazio, Peter Victor, Jr. lawyer
Feagley, Michael Rowe lawyer
Fein, Roger Gary lawyer
Feinstein, Fred Ira lawyer
Feldman, Scott M. lawyer
Fellows, Jerry Kenneth lawyer
Ferencz, Robert Arnold lawyer
Ferguson, Bradford Lee lawyer
Ferrini, James Thomas lawyer
Field, Henry Frederick lawyer
Field, Robert Edward lawyer
Fieldman, Leon lawyer
Fifer, Samuel lawyer
Fifield, William O. lawyer
Finke, Robert Forge lawyer
Fischel, Daniel R. law educator
Fischer, Fredric H. lawyer
Fishman, Irving S. lawyer
Fitch, Morgan Lewis, Jr. patent lawyer
†Fitzgerald, Peter Gosselin lawyer
Fitzpatrick, Peter lawyer
Flanagin, Neil lawyer
Fletcher, James L. lawyer
Flynn, Peter Anthony lawyer
Foote, Edward L. lawyer
Foran, Thomas Aquinas lawyer
Ford, Michael W. lawyer
Forrester, J(ohn) Paul lawyer
Fort, Jeffrey C. lawyer
Foudree, Bruce William lawyer
Fox, Jacob Logan lawyer
Fox, Paul T. lawyer
Franch, Richard Thomas lawyer
Franklin, Richard Mark lawyer
Fraumann, Willard George lawyer
Freehling, Paul Edward lawyer
Freeman, Lee Allen, Jr. lawyer
Freeman, Louis S. lawyer
†Friedman, Lawrence Milton lawyer
Friedman, Roselyn L. lawyer
Fross, Roger Raymond lawyer
Fullagar, William Watts lawyer
Fuller, Perry Lucian lawyer
Furda, Gregory H. lawyer
Furlane, Mark Elliott lawyer
Fuson, Douglas Finley lawyer
Gaggini, John Edmund lawyer
Gaines, Kenneth R. lawyer
Gancer, Donald Charles lawyer
Gangemi, Columbus Rudolph, Jr. lawyer, educator
Garber, Samuel Baugh lawyer, retail company executive
Garbutt, Eugene James lawyer
Gareis, Robert J. lawyer
Garth, Bryant Geoffrey law educator, foundation executive
Garvey, Michael J. lawyer
Garvey, Richard J. lawyer
Gates, Stephen Frye lawyer
Gavin, John Neal lawyer
Gaynor, James M., Jr. lawyer
Gearen, John J. lawyer
Geiman, J. Robert lawyer
Geis, Norman Winer lawyer
George, John Martin, Jr. lawyer
Geraldson, Raymond I. lawyer
Geraldson, Raymond I., Jr. lawyer
Gerber, Lawrence lawyer
Gerek, William Michael lawyer
Gerlits, Francis Joseph lawyer
Gerson, Jerome Howard lawyer
Gertz, Elmer lawyer, author, educator
Getzendanner, Susan lawyer, former federal judge
Giampietro, Wayne Bruce lawyer
Gibbons, William John lawyer
Gilbert, Howard N(orman) lawyer
Gilford, Steven Ross lawyer
Gill, Michael J. lawyer
Gilson, Jerome lawyer, writer
Ginsberg, Lewis Robbins lawyer
Given, Ronald B. lawyer
Gladden, James Walter, Jr. lawyer
Glass, Stanford Lee lawyer
Gleeson, Paul Francis lawyer
Glieberman, Herbert Allen lawyer
Glovka, Richard Paul lawyer
Goeke, Joseph R. lawyer
Golan, Stephen Leonard lawyer
Gold, Norman Myron lawyer
Goldblatt, Stanford Jay lawyer
Golden, Bruce Paul lawyer
Golden, William C. lawyer
Goldman, Louis Budwig lawyer
Goldschmidt, Lynn Harvey lawyer
Goodman, Elliott I(rvin) lawyer
Goodman, Gary Alan lawyer
Goodman, Stuart Lauren lawyer
Gordon, Phillip lawyer
Gordon, William A. lawyer
Goschi, Nicholas Peter lawyer
Goss, Richard Henry lawyer
Gottlieb, Gidon Alain Guy law educator
Gould, Arthur Irwin lawyer
Graham, David F. lawyer
Graham, Robert L. lawyer
Gralen, Donald John lawyer
Grant, Robert Nathan lawyer
Gray, James S. lawyer
Gray, Milton Hefter lawyer
Grayck, Marcus Daniel lawyer
Greenbaum, Kenneth lawyer
Greenberger, Ernest lawyer
Greenblatt, Ray Harris lawyer
Greenblatt, Russell Edward lawyer, consultant
Gregg, Jon Mann lawyer
Gregory, Byron L. lawyer
Griffin, Hugh C. lawyer
Griffith, Donald Kendall lawyer
Grimm, Terry M. lawyer
Grimm, Victor E. lawyer
Grossi, Francis Xavier, Jr. lawyer, educator
Gunn, Robert Murray lawyer, farmer
Guthman, Jack lawyer
Haarlow, John B. lawyer
Haderlein, Thomas M. lawyer
Hagan, Robert K. lawyer
Hahn, Frederic Louis lawyer
Haines, Martha Mahan lawyer
Hales, Daniel B. lawyer
Hall, Joan M. lawyer
Halprin, Rick lawyer
Hamilton, Thomas Mackin, Jr. lawyer
Hammesfahr, Robert Winter lawyer
Hanbury, Marshall E. lawyer
Handler, Steven P. lawyer
Hannah, Wayne Robertson, Jr. lawyer
Hannay, William Mouat, III lawyer
Hanson, Heidi Elizabeth lawyer
Hanson, Richard A. lawyer
Hanson, Ronald William lawyer
Hanzlik, Paul F. lawyer
Hardgrove, James Alan lawyer
Harmon, Robert Lon lawyer
Harrington, Carol A. lawyer
Harrington, James Timothy lawyer
Harris, Donald Ray lawyer
Harrold, Bernard lawyer
Hart, David Churchill lawyer
Hartigan, Neil F. lawyer, former state attorney general, lieutenant governor
Hasten, Michael V. lawyer
Haubold, Samuel Allen lawyer
Hayes, David John Arthur, Jr. legal association executive
Hayward, Thomas Zander, Jr. lawyer
Head, Patrick James lawyer
Heatwole, Mark M. lawyer
Hecht, Frank Thomas lawyer
Heindl, Warren Anton law educator, retired
Heine, Spencer H. corporate lawyer, real estate executive
Heinz, John Peter lawyer, educator
Heinz, William Denby lawyer
Heisler, Quentin George, Jr. lawyer
Heiss, Robin lawyer
Heitland, Ann Rae lawyer
Heller, Stanley J. lawyer, physician
Helman, Robert Alan lawyer
Helmholz, R(ichard) H(enry) law educator
Henning, Joel Frank lawyer, author, publisher, consultant
Henning, Mark G. lawyer
Henry, Frederick Edward lawyer
Henry, Robert John lawyer
Hensel, Paul H. lawyer
Herman, Sidney N. lawyer
Hermann, Donald Harold James lawyer, educator
Herpe, David A. lawyer
Herzel, Leo lawyer
Herzog, Fred F. legal educator
Hess, Peter A. lawyer
Hess, Sidney J., Jr. lawyer
Hester, Thomas Patrick lawyer
Hickey, John Thomas, Jr. lawyer
Hickman, Frederic W. lawyer
Hilborn, Michael G. lawyer, real estate development executive
†Hiller, David D. lawyer
Hilliard, David Craig lawyer
Hirshman, Harold Carl lawyer
Hitch, James T., III lawyer
Hoban, George Savre lawyer
Hodes, Scott lawyer
Hodgman, David Renwick lawyer
Hoeft, Steven H. lawyer
Hofer, Roy Ellis lawyer
Hoff, William Bruce, Jr. lawyer
Hoffman, Douglas W. lawyer
Hoffman, Richard Bruce lawyer
Hoffman, Valerie Jane lawyer
Hoffmann, Howard M. lawyer
Hollins, Mitchell Leslie lawyer
Holmen, Neil E. lawyer
Horwath, Leslie Kathleen lawyer
Horwich, Allan lawyer
Hoskins, Richard Jerold lawyer
Howe, Jonathan Thomas lawyer
Howe, Lawrence lawyer, business executive
Howell, R(obert) Thomas, Jr. lawyer, food company executive
Hron, Michael G. lawyer
Hucker, Brian S. lawyer
Huebsch, Robert P. lawyer
Huggins, Rollin Charles, Jr. lawyer
Hummel, Gregory William lawyer
Hunt, Lawrence Halley, Jr. lawyer
Hurlbert, Robert P. lawyer
Hussey, Charles E., II lawyer
Huston, DeVerille Anne lawyer
Hutchins, Harley lawyer
Hutchinson, Leland E. lawyer
Jacobson, David Cary lawyer
Jacobson, Harold LeLand lawyer
Jacobson, Marian Slutz lawyer
Jacobson, Richard Joseph lawyer
Jacoby, John Primm lawyer
Jacover, Jerold Alan lawyer
Jager, Melvin Francis lawyer
Jahns, Jeffrey lawyer
Jakubik, Jerome W. lawyer
Jambor, Robert Vernon lawyer
Jerrick, Ronald M. lawyer
Jersild, Thomas Nielsen lawyer
Jock, Paul F., II lawyer
Johnson, C. Richard lawyer
Johnson, Daniel Leroy lawyer
Johnson, Elmer William lawyer
Johnson, Gary Thomas lawyer
Johnson, H. Arvid lawyer
Johnson, Richard Fred lawyer
Johnston, Alan Rogers lawyer
Johnston, Thomas Watts lawyer
Jones, Mark Elmer, Jr. lawyer, former judge
Jones, Richard Cyrus lawyer
Jones, Thomas M. lawyer
Jordan, Michelle Denise lawyer
Joseph, Robert Thomas lawyer
Joslin, Rodney Dean lawyer
Joyce, Robert Hyland lawyer
Juhl, Loren Earl lawyer
Junewicz, James J. lawyer
Jurek, Kenneth J. lawyer
Kamin, Chester Thomas lawyer
Kanwit, Glen Harris lawyer
Kaplan, Harold L. lawyer
Kaplan, Jared lawyer
Kaplan, Sidney Mountbatten lawyer
Kaplan, Wayne S. lawyer
Karaba, Frank Andrew lawyer
Karge, Stewart W. lawyer
Kastel, Howard L. lawyer
Katten, Melvin L. lawyer
Katz, Harold Ambrose lawyer, former state legislator
Katz, Stuart Charles lawyer, concert jazz musician
Kaufman, Andrew Michael lawyer
Keck, Robert Clifton lawyer
Kelley, Duane Matthew lawyer
Kelliher, Peter Maurice lawyer, arbitrator
Kelly, Charles Arthur lawyer
Kelman, Robert Andrew lawyer
Kempf, Donald G., Jr. lawyer
Kenney, Frank Deming lawyer
Kenny, Edmund Joyce lawyer
Kessler, Stanton A. lawyer
Kiley, Roger J. lawyer
King, Clark Chapman, Jr. lawyer
King, Michael Howard lawyer
King, Sharon L. lawyer
Kins, Juris lawyer
Kipnis, Mark S. lawyer
Kipperman, Lawrence I. lawyer
Kirkland, John Leonard lawyer
Kissel, Richard John lawyer
Kite, Steven B. lawyer
Klenk, James Andrew lawyer
Knight, Christopher Nichols lawyer
Knox, James Edwin lawyer
Knuti, Robert A. lawyer
Kohn, Shalom L. lawyer
Kolek, Robert Edward lawyer
Koran, Janet M. lawyer
Kortright, Richard T. lawyer
Koven, Howard Richard lawyer
Kowitt, Arthur Jay lawyer
Kravitt, Jason Harris Paperno lawyer
Kriss, Robert J. lawyer
Kroll, Barry Lewis lawyer
Krueger, Herbert William lawyer
Krupka, Robert George lawyer
Kucera, Daniel Jerome lawyer
†Kunkle, William Joseph, Jr. lawyer
Kurland, Philip B. lawyer, educator
Kuta, Jeffrey Theodore lawyer
Landan, Henry Sinclair lawyer
Landes, William M. law educator
Landow-Esser, Janine Marise lawyer
Landsman, Stephen A. lawyer
Lane, Robert G. lawyer
Lane, Ronald Alan lawyer
Laner, Richard Warren lawyer
Lang, Richard A. lawyer
Langhenry, John Godfred, Jr. lawyer
Lapidus, Allan E. lawyer
LaRue, Paul Hubert lawyer
LaRue, Paul Hubert, Jr. lawyer
Lasky, Laurence D. lawyer
Lassar, Scott R. lawyer
Latimer, Kenneth Alan lawyer
†Lawrie, Henry DeVos, Jr. lawyer
LeDuc, John Andre lawyer
Lee, William Marshall lawyer
Leiseca, Sergio A. Jr. lawyer
Leisten, Arthur Gaynor lawyer
Lemein, Gregg D. lawyer
Lev, Allen P. lawyer
Levenfeld, Milton Arthur lawyer
Levi, John G. lawyer
Levin, Charles Edward lawyer
Levin, Jack S. lawyer
Levin, Michael David lawyer
Levine, Laurence Harvey lawyer
Levinson, Irving Bert lawyer
Levit, Louis W. lawyer
Levy, Richard Herbert lawyer
Lewis, Julius lawyer
Lieberman, Myron lawyer
Lind, Jon Robert lawyer
Lindblom, Marjorie Press lawyer
Linklater, William Joseph lawyer
Lippe, Melvin Karl lawyer
Lipton, Richard M. lawyer
List, David Patton lawyer
Listrom, Linda L. lawyer
Litwin, Burton Howard lawyer
Livingston, Theodore A., Jr. lawyer
Lloyd, William F. lawyer
Lockwood, Gary Lee lawyer
Looman, James R. lawyer
Lorch, Kenneth F. lawyer
Lorenz, Richard Theodore, Jr. lawyer
Lott, David Stuart lawyer
Lubin, Donald G. lawyer
Lucas, John Kenneth lawyer
Lundergan, Barbara Keough lawyer
Lundy, Joseph R. lawyer
Lurie, Paul Michael lawyer
Luscombe, George A. II lawyer
Lutter, Paul Allen lawyer
Lutz, Karl Evan lawyer
Lynch, John Peter lawyer
MacCarthy, Terence Francis lawyer
Maher, David Willard lawyer
Malato, Stephen H. lawyer
Malkin, Cary Jay lawyer
Malone, James Laurence, III lawyer
Malovance, Gregory J. lawyer
Malstrom, Robert A. lawyer
Mancoff, Neal Alan lawyer
Mandell, Floyd A. lawyer
Mann, H. George lawyer
Maram, Barry S. lawyer
Marcus, Stephen A. lawyer
Margolis, Jeremy lawyer
Marks, Dennis A. lawyer
Marks, Jerome lawyer
Marovitz, James Lee lawyer
Marshall, Eric C. lawyer
Marshall, John David lawyer
Marshall, Prentice H., Jr. lawyer
Martin, Arthur Mead lawyer
Martin, R. Eden lawyer
Martin, Siva lawyer
Marwedel, Warren John lawyer
Marx, David, Jr. lawyer
Mason, Henry Lowell, III lawyer
Matis, Nina B. lawyer
Mattos Neto, Sebastiao De Souza lawyer
Mattson, Stephen Joseph lawyer
Maxson, M. Finley lawyer
Mayer, Frank D., Jr. lawyer
Mayers, Barbara W. lawyer
McBreen, Maura Ann lawyer
McCaleb, Malcolm, Jr. lawyer
McCarthy, Charles Justin lawyer
McCarthy, Paul lawyer
Mc Clure, James J., Jr. lawyer, former municipal executive
McCombs, Hugh R., Jr. lawyer
McCormick, Steven D. lawyer
McCoy, Wayne A. lawyer
†McCracken, Thomas James, Jr. lawyer
McCue, Howard McDowell, III lawyer, educator
McCue, Judith W. lawyer
McDermott, John H(enry) lawyer
McDermott, Robert B. lawyer
McDonald, Thomas Alexander lawyer
McDonough, John Michael lawyer
Mc Dougall, Dugald Stewart retired lawyer
McDowell, William S. lawyer
†McGivern, Arthur J. corporate lawyer, food products company executive
McGrath, William Joseph lawyer
McGuigan, John V. lawyer
McKittrick, William Wood lawyer
McLaughlin, T. Mark lawyer
McLean, Robert David lawyer
McMahon, Thomas Michael lawyer
McMenamin, John Robert lawyer
McNeill, Thomas B. lawyer
McQueen, Thomas K. lawyer
McVisk, William Kilburn lawyer
McWhirter, Bruce J. lawyer
Mehlman, Mark Franklin lawyer
Meleney, John Alexander lawyer
Melton, David Reuben lawyer
Meltzer, Bernard David legal educator
Menson, Richard L. lawyer
Merlin, Peter Helmuth lawyer
Metz, Lawrence Anthony lawyer
Meyer, J. Theodore lawyer
Meyer, Michael Louis lawyer
Michalak, Edward Francis lawyer
Migdal, Sheldon Paul lawyer
Millard, Richard Steven lawyer
Miller, Maurice James lawyer
Miller, Michael I. lawyer
Miller, Paul J. lawyer
Miller, Stephen Ralph lawyer
Miller, Theodore Norman lawyer
Millner, Robert B. lawyer
Milnikel, Robert Saxon lawyer
Milstein, Albert lawyer
Minichello, Dennis lawyer
Minow, Newton Norman lawyer
Mlsna, Timothy Martin lawyer
Moelmann, Lawrence R. lawyer
Moltz, Marshall Jerome lawyer
Mone, Peter John lawyer
Morrison, John Horton lawyer
Morrison, Michael P. lawyer
Morrison, Portia Owen lawyer
Morrissey, Francis Daniel lawyer
Morrow, John Ellsworth lawyer
Morsch, Thomas Harvey lawyer
Mowder, Gary Leroy lawyer
Mrozek, Donald L. lawyer
Muchin, Allan B. lawyer
Mueller, Richard Edward lawyer
Muench, John E. lawyer
Mullen, J. Thomas lawyer
Mumford, Manly Whitman lawyer
Munitz, Gerald F. lawyer
Munson, James Calfee lawyer
Murdock, Charles William lawyer, educator
Murray, Daniel Richard lawyer
Murray, Gregory S. lawyer
Murray, James Cunningham, Jr. lawyer
Murtaugh, Christopher David lawyer
Murtaugh, Michael K. lawyer
Myers, Lonn William lawyer
Nachman, James L. lawyer
Nachman, Norman Harry lawyer
Neal, Stephen C. lawyer
Nebel, Kai Allen lawyer
Nechin, Herbert Benjamin lawyer
Neis, James M. lawyer
Nekritz, Barry B. lawyer
Nelsen, Timothy Alan lawyer
Nelson, Richard David lawyer
Nelson, Thomas R. lawyer
Nemerovski, Steven H. lawyer
Nesburg, Alan D. lawyer
Newey, Paul Davis lawyer
Newlin, Charles Fremont lawyer
Newman, Dennis Nathan lawyer
†Newman, Gordon Harold lawyer, food company executive
Newman, Robert William lawyer
Newman, Terry E. lawyer
Nicklin, Emily lawyer
Nissen, William John lawyer
Nitikman, Franklin W. lawyer
Nixon, Harvey lawyer
Nord, Robert Eamor lawyer
Notz, John Kranz, Jr. lawyer
Novotny, David Joseph lawyer
Nowacki, James Nelson lawyer
Nussbaum, Bernard J. lawyer
O'Brien, James Phillip lawyer
O'Brien, Patrick William lawyer
O'Connor, Daniel J. lawyer
O'Connor, John Killeen lawyer
Odorizzi, Michele L. lawyer
Oesterle, Eric Adam lawyer
Offutt, Gerald M. lawyer
O'Flaherty, Paul Benedict lawyer
O'Hagan, James Joseph lawyer
O'Hare, John Mitchell lawyer
O'Leary, Daniel Vincent, Jr. lawyer
O'Leary, Frank J. lawyer
Olian, Robert Martin lawyer
†O'Malley, Jack state's attorney
Orbon, Margaret J. lawyer
Organ, Joseph B. lawyer
Overgaard, Mitchell Jersild lawyer
Overton, George Washington lawyer
Ozog, Edward J. lawyer
Pallasch, B. Michael lawyer
Palm, Gary Howard lawyer, educator
Palmer, John Bernard, III lawyer
Palmer, Robert Towne lawyer
Palmore, Roderick Alan lawyer
Panich, Danuta Bembenista lawyer
Pape, Arthur Edward lawyer
Park, Dale, Jr. lawyer
Parkhurst, Todd Sheldon lawyer
Parsons, Keith I. lawyer
Parzen, Stanley Julius lawyer
Pascal, Roger lawyer
Pattishall, Beverly Wyckliffe lawyer
Patton, Stephen Ray lawyer
Pavalon, Eugene Irving lawyer
Pearl, Melvin E. lawyer, film producer
Pelton, Russell Meredith, Jr. lawyer
Perkins, James L. lawyer
Perlberg, Jules Martin lawyer
Perlman, Judy Platt lawyer
Perlstadt, Sidney Morris lawyer
Petersen, Donald Sondergaard lawyer

Petersen, William Otto *lawyer*
Peterson, Gerald C. *lawyer*
Petrakis, Peter *lawyer*
Petrie, James Stanton *lawyer*
Phelps, Paul Michael *lawyer*
Piekarski, Victor J. *lawyer*
Pierce, Daniel Marshall *lawyer, mayor*
Pitt, George *lawyer*
Platz, George Arthur, III *lawyer*
Poe, Douglas Allan *lawyer*
Pollock, Earl Edward *lawyer*
Pope, Daniel James *lawyer*
Pope, Jerome W. *lawyer*
Powles, Peter B. *lawyer*
Pratt, Robert Windsor *lawyer*
Presser, Stephen Bruce *lawyer, educator*
Prior, Gary L. *lawyer*
Pritikin, David T. *lawyer*
Pritikin, James B. *lawyer, employee benefits consultant*
Pritzker, Jay Arthur *lawyer*
Prochnow, Douglas Lee *lawyer*
Prochnow, Herbert Victor, Jr. *lawyer*
Proctor, Edward George *lawyer*
Pugliese, Robert J. *lawyer*
Quinlan, William Joseph, Jr. *lawyer*
Radler, Warren S. *lawyer*
Rahl, James Andrew *lawyer, educator*
Ralph, William J. *lawyer*
Rank, John Thomas *lawyer*
Rankin, James Winton *lawyer*
Ranney, George A., Jr. *lawyer*
Rasor, Robert D. *lawyer*
Ratner, Gerald *lawyer*
Rauch, George Washington *lawyer*
Raymond, Spencer Henry *lawyer*
Reed, Janet Lynn *lawyer*
Reed, Keith Allen *lawyer*
Reich, Allan J. *lawyer*
Reicin, Ronald Ian *lawyer*
Reiter, Michael A. *lawyer*
Relias, John Alexis *lawyer*
Resnick, Donald Ira *lawyer*
Reum, James Michael *lawyer*
Reynolds, Thomas A., Jr. *lawyer*
Reynolds, Thomas A., III *lawyer*
Rhind, James Thomas *lawyer*
Rhoads, Paul Kelly *lawyer*
Rhodes, Charles Harker, Jr. *lawyer*
Richardson, William F. *lawyer*
Richman, John Marshall *lawyer, business executive*
Richmond, William Patrick *lawyer*
Rieger, Mitchell Sheridan *lawyer*
Rissman, Burton Richard *lawyer*
Ritchie, Albert *lawyer*
Ritchie, William Paul *lawyer*
Rizzo, Ronald Stephen *lawyer*
Robinson, Martin F. *lawyer*
Robinson, Theodore Curtis, Jr. *lawyer*
Roche, James McMillan *lawyer*
Roebuck, John Clifford *lawyer*
Rogers, Eddy J. *lawyer*
Roin, Howard James *lawyer*
Rooney, Matthew A. *lawyer*
Ropski, Gary Melchior *lawyer*
Rosemarin, Carey Stephen *lawyer*
Rosenberg, Richard M. *lawyer*
Rosenbloom, Lewis Stanley *lawyer*
Rosenblum, Michael F. *lawyer*
Rosenthal, Samuel Robert *lawyer*
Ross, Jeffrey Kenneth *lawyer*
Roston, David C. *lawyer*
Rothschild, Edwin Alfred *lawyer*
Rowder, William Louis *lawyer*
Rubin, E(rwin) Leonard *lawyer*
Rubin, Robert J. *lawyer*
Ruder, David Sturtevant *lawyer, educator, government official*
Rudnick, Paul David *lawyer*
Rudstein, David Stewart *law educator*
Rundio, Louis Michael, Jr. *lawyer*
Rupert, Donald William *lawyer*
Russell, James H. *lawyer*
Russell, Paul Frederick *lawyer*
Rutkoff, Alan Stuart *lawyer*
Ryan, Thomas F. *lawyer*
Ryder, David R. *lawyer*
Sabl, John J. *lawyer*
Salomon, Richard Adley *lawyer*
Salpeter, Alan N. *lawyer*
Samuels, Lawrence Robert *lawyer*
Sanders, David P. *lawyer*
Sanders, Richard Henry *lawyer*
Sandquist, Elroy Charles, Jr. *lawyer*
Sangerman, Harry M. *lawyer*
Saunders, David Alan *lawyer*
Saunders, George Lawton, Jr. *lawyer*
Savner, David A. *lawyer*
Sawdey, Richard Marshall *lawyer*
Sawyier, Calvin P. *lawyer*
Sawyier, David R. *lawyer*
Schauer, Louis Frank *lawyer*
Schiffman, David M. *lawyer*
Schiller, Donald Charles *lawyer*
Schiller, Eric M. *lawyer*
Schimberg, A(rmand) Bruce *lawyer*
Schindel, Donald Marvin *lawyer*
Schink, James Harvey *lawyer*
Schippers, David Philip *lawyer*
Schlickman, J. Andrew *lawyer*
Schlitter, Stanley Allen *lawyer*
Schneider, Dan W. *lawyer, consultant*
Schneider, Robert Jerome *lawyer*
Schoonhoven, Ray James *retired lawyer*
Schorer, Joseph U. *lawyer*
Schoumacher, Bruce Herbert *lawyer*
Schreck, Robert A., Jr. *lawyer*
Schriver, John T., III *lawyer*
Schuette, Michael *lawyer*
Schulhofer, Stephen Joseph *law educator*
Schulte, Stephen Charles *lawyer*
Schultz, Kurt Lee *lawyer*
Schulz, Keith Donald *corporate lawyer*
Schuyler, Daniel Merrick *lawyer, educator*
Schwartz, Donald Lee *lawyer*
Scogland, William Lee *lawyer*
Scott, Theodore R. *lawyer*
Seely, Robert Fleming *lawyer*
Seidenfeld, Glenn Kenneth *lawyer*
Seki, Hoken S. *lawyer*
Selander, Larry *lawyer*
Seligman, Richard Michael *lawyer*
Serritella, James Anthony *lawyer*
Serritella, William David *lawyer*
Serwer, Alan Michael *lawyer*
Sfikas, Peter Michael *lawyer, educator*
Shadur, Robert H. *lawyer*
Shank, William O. *lawyer*
Shannon, Peter Michael, Jr. *lawyer*
Shapiro, Harold David *lawyer, educator*
Shapiro, Stephen Michael *lawyer*
Shapo, Marshall Schambelan *lawyer, educator*
Sheldon, Harvey M. *lawyer*
Shepherd, Stewart Robert *lawyer*
Shepro, Richard W. *lawyer*
Sherck, Timothy C. *lawyer*
Shields, Thomas Charles *lawyer*
Shindler, Donald A. *lawyer*
Sido, Kevin Richard *lawyer*
Siegel, Howard Jerome *lawyer*
Sigal, Michael Stephen *lawyer*
Silberman, Alan Harvey *lawyer*
Silets, Harvey Marvin *lawyer*
Simon, John Bern *lawyer*
Simon, John P. *lawyer*
Simon, Seymour *lawyer, former state supreme court justice*
Siske, Roger Charles *lawyer*
Sklarsky, Charles B. *lawyer*
Slavitt, Earl Benton *lawyer*
Slocomb, Paul D. *lawyer*
Smart, Allen Rich, II *lawyer*
Smith, Arthur B(everly), Jr. *lawyer*
Smith, Gordon Howell *lawyer*
Smith, John Gelston *lawyer*
Smith, Lawrence R. *lawyer*
Smith, Tefft W. *lawyer*
Snider, Lawrence K. *lawyer*
Snyder, John Lindsey *lawyer*
Solomon, Jack Avrum *lawyer, automotive distributor, art dealer*
Solotorovsky, Julian *lawyer*
Solovy, Jerold Sherwin *lawyer*
Sonderby, Peter R. *lawyer*
Spector, David M. *lawyer*
Speidel, Richard Eli *lawyer, educator*
Spellmire, George W. *lawyer*
Spencer, Lewis Douglas *lawyer*
Sperling, Robert Y. *lawyer*
†Spindler, George S. *lawyer, oil industry executive*
Spiotto, James Ernest *lawyer*
Springer, David Edward *lawyer*
Sproger, Charles Edmund *lawyer*
Sprowl, Charles Riggs *lawyer*
Stack, John Wallace *lawyer*
Stahl, Charles Eugene *lawyer*
Stahl, David M. *lawyer*
Staley, Charles Ralls *lawyer*
Stanley, Justin Armstrong *lawyer*
Staples, James G. *lawyer*
Starkman, Gary Lee *lawyer*
Stassen, John Henry *lawyer*
Steinberg, Morton M. *lawyer*
Steiner, Barbara S. *lawyer*
Stephan, Edmund Anton *lawyer*
Steptoe, Philip P., III *lawyer*
Stern, Robert Louis *lawyer*
Sternstein, Allan J. *lawyer*
Stetler, David J. *lawyer*
Stevens, Thomas Lee *lawyer*
Stickler, K. Bruce *lawyer*
Stillman, Nina Gidden *lawyer*
Stinson, James R. *lawyer*
Stoll, John Robert *lawyer, educator*
Stone, Geoffrey Richard *law educator, lawyer*
†Stone, Howard Lawrence *lawyer*
Stone, Randolph Noel *law educator*
Strasburger, Joseph Julius *retired lawyer*
Streff, William Albert, Jr. *lawyer*
Strobel, Pamela B. *lawyer*
Strobel, Russ M. *lawyer*
Studwell, Thomas W. *lawyer*
Sullivan, Cornelius J. *lawyer*
Sullivan, Marcia Waite *lawyer*
Sullivan, Thomas Patrick *lawyer*
†Sunstein, Cass R. *law educator*
Sutherland, Joe Allen *lawyer*
Sutter, William Paul *lawyer*
Swaney, Thomas Edward *lawyer*
Sweeney, James Raymond *lawyer*
Sweeney, Michael J. *lawyer*
Swett, Daniel Robert *lawyer*
Swibel, Steven Warren *lawyer*
Szala, Scott J. *lawyer*
Szczepanski, Slawomir Zbigniew Steven *lawyer*
Tabin, Julius *patent lawyer, physicist*
Tallant, David, Jr. *lawyer*
Tarun, Robert Walter *lawyer*
Taylor, Roger Lee *lawyer*
Theobald, Edward Robert *lawyer*
Thies, Richard Brian *lawyer*
Thomas, Dale E. *lawyer*
Thomas, Frederick Bradley *lawyer*
Thomas, Stephen Paul *lawyer*
Thompson, James Robert, Jr. *lawyer, former governor*
Thomson, George Ronald *lawyer, educator*
Thorne-Thomsen, Thomas *lawyer*
Tibble, Douglas Clair *lawyer*
Tillett, Samuel Raymond *lawyer*
Tippins, Bedell A. *lawyer*
Tobin, Thomas F. *lawyer*
Tompsett, William C. *lawyer*
Tone, Jeffrey R. *lawyer*
Tone, Philip Willis *lawyer, former federal judge*
Toohey, James Kevin *lawyer*
Topol, Clive M. *lawyer*
Torbert, Preston M. *lawyer*
Torshen, Jerome Harold *lawyer*
Towne, L. Stanton *lawyer*
Tozer, Forrest Leigh *lawyer*
Trapp, James M. *lawyer*
Treece, John W. *lawyer*
Trienens, Howard Joseph *lawyer*
Truskowski, John Budd *lawyer*
Tucker, Watson Billopp *lawyer*
Tymm, William E. *lawyer*
Valdes, Miguel A. *lawyer*
Valukas, Anton Ronald *lawyer, former federal official*
Van Demark, Ruth Elaine *lawyer*
Vieregg, Robert Todd *lawyer*
Vittum, Daniel Weeks, Jr. *lawyer*
Vogler, James R. *lawyer*
Voortman, John J. *lawyer*
Vree, Roger Allen *lawyer*
Wade, Edwin Lee *lawyer*
Wahlen, Edwin Alfred *lawyer*
Waintroob, Andrea Ruth *lawyer*
Waite, Norman, Jr. *lawyer*
Wall, Robert F. *lawyer*
Walsh, Joseph A., Jr. *lawyer*
Walter, Douglas Hanson *lawyer*
Walter, Priscilla Anne *lawyer*
Walton, Stanley Anthony, III *lawyer*
Waltz, Jon Richard *lawyer, educator, author*
Wander, Herbert Stanton *lawyer*
Wanke, Ronald Lee *lawyer*
Ward, Daniel Patrick *lawyer*
Ware, Mitchell *lawyer*
Warnecke, Michael O. *lawyer*
Watson, Lee Ann *lawyer*
Watson, Robert R. *lawyer*
Watts, Dey Wadsworth *retired lawyer*
Weaver, William Townsend *laywer*
Webb, Dan K. *lawyer*
Weber, Frederic *lawyer*
Weinberg, David B. *lawyer*
Weinkopf, Friedrich J. *lawyer*
Weinsheimer, William Cyrus *lawyer*
Weissman, Michael Lewis *lawyer*
Wexler, Raymond P. *lawyer*
Wexler, Richard Lewis *lawyer*
Whalen, Wayne W. *lawyer*
White, Barry A. *lawyer*
White, Craig Mitchell *lawyer*
White, H. Blair *lawyer*
White, Linda Diane *lawyer*
White, R. Quincy *lawyer*
White, Thomas Stuart *lawyer*
Whitehead, James S. *lawyer*
Wiggins, Charles Henry, Jr. *lawyer*
Wilcox, Mark Dean *lawyer*
Wilczek, Robert Joseph *lawyer*
Wilder, Ronald *lawyer*
Wildman, Max Edward *lawyer*
Williams, Douglas H. *lawyer*
Williams, George Howard *lawyer, association executive*
Williams, H. Randolph *lawyer*
Williams, John Cobb *lawyer*
Williams, Robert Jene *lawyer, rail car company executive*
Williamson, Joel V. *lawyer*
Williamson, Richard Salisbury *lawyer*
Willian, Clyde Franklin *lawyer*
Wilson, Bruce G. *lawyer*
Wilson, Harry L. *lawyer*
Wilson, Roger Goodwin *lawyer*
Wise, William Jerrard *lawyer*
Witcoff, Sheldon William *lawyer*
Witwer, Samuel Weiler, Sr. *lawyer*
Witwer, Samuel Weiler, Jr. *lawyer*
Wojcik, Lawrence A. *lawyer*
Wolf, Charles Benno *lawyer*
Wolf, Neal Lloyd *lawyer*
Wolfe, David Louis *lawyer*
Wolfson, Larry M. *lawyer*
Wood, James Clarence *lawyer*
†Wright, Judith Margaret *law librarian, educator*
Zabel, Sheldon Alter *lawyer, educator*
Zabrosky, Alex Walter *lawyer*
Zaremski, Miles Jay *lawyer*
Zavis, Michael William *lawyer*
Zemans, Frances Kahn *legal association executive*
Zemm, Sandra Phyllis *lawyer*
Zenner, Sheldon Toby *lawyer*
Zolno, Mark S. *lawyer*
Zulkey, Edward John *lawyer, author*

Chicago Heights
Cifelli, John Louis *lawyer*

Crystal Lake
Knox, Susan Marie *paralegal*

De Kalb
Witmer, John Harper, Jr. *lawyer*

Decatur
†Dunn, John Francis *lawyer, state representative*
Erickson, Roy Lydeen *lawyer*
Mohan, J. Patrick *lawyer*

Deerfield
Abbey, G(eorge) Marshall *lawyer, former health care company executive, general counsel*
Ames, Craig L. *lawyer*
†Gash, Lauren Beth *lawyer, state legislator*
†Oettinger, Julian Alan *lawyer, pharmacy company executive*
Staubitz, Arthur Frederick *lawyer, healthcare products company executive*
Vollen, Robert Jay *lawyer*

Des Plaines
Brodl, Raymond Frank *lawyer, former lumber company executive*
Demouth, Robin Madison *lawyer, corporate executive*
Jacobs, William Russell, II *lawyer*
†Mulligan, Rosemary Elizabeth *paralegal*
Munden, Robin Ghezzi *lawyer*

East Moline
Silliman, Richard George *retired lawyer, retired farm machinery company executive*

Elmwood Park
Spina, Anthony Ferdinand *lawyer*

Evanston
Gormley, R(obert) James *retired lawyer*
Johnson, Lael Frederic *lawyer*
Polzin, John Theodore *lawyer*
Reeder, Robert Harry *retired lawyer*
Taronji, Jaime, Jr. *lawyer*
Vanneman, Edgar, Jr. *lawyer*

Fairview Heights
Barkofske, Francis Lee *lawyer, coal company executive*

Flossmoor
Garrison, Ray Harlan *lawyer*

Galena
Rauner, Vincent Joseph *lawyer, electronics company executive, retired*

Garden Prairie
Channick, Herbert S. *lawyer, arbitrator, retired real estate and broadcasting corporation executive*

Genoa
Cromley, Jon Lowell *lawyer*

Glen Ellyn
Larson, Ward Jerome *lawyer, retired banker*

Glencoe
Baer, Joseph Winslow *retired lawyer, mediator, arbitrator*
Stewart, Charles Leslie *lawyer*

Glenview
Berkman, Michael G. *lawyer, chemical consultant*
Borst, John, Jr. *lawyer, electronics corporation executive*
Miller, Edward Boone *lawyer*
Wright, Arthur McIntosh *lawyer, industrial products executive*

Highland Park
Dolin, Albert Harry *lawyer*
Haight, Edward Allen *lawyer*
Karol, Nathaniel H. *lawyer, consultant*

Hinsdale
†Bergerson, J. Steven *lawyer*
†Biggert, Judith Borg *lawyer*
Sheehan, Dennis William *lawyer, business executive*

Joliet
†Dunn, Thomas Aquinas *lawyer, state legislator*

Lafox
Seils, William George *lawyer*

Lake Forest
Emerson, William Harry *lawyer, oil company executive*
Sikorovsky, Eugene Frank *retired lawyer*

Libertyville
Ranney, George Alfred *lawyer, former steel company executive*

Lisle
†Aprati, Robert L. *lawyer, car rental company executive*
Sandrok, Richard William *lawyer*

Marengo
†Franks, Herbert Hoover *lawyer*

Mattoon
Horsley, Jack Everett *lawyer, author*

Moline
Cottrell, Frank Stewart *lawyer, manufacturing executive*

Mundelein
Burns, Kenneth Jones, Jr. *lawyer, consultant*

Naperville
Rovner, Jack Alan *lawyer*
Shaw, Michael Allan *lawyer, mail order company executive*
Ulrich, Werner *patent lawyer*

Northbrook
Cohen, Seymour *lawyer*
Lapin, Harvey I. *lawyer*

Northfield
Porter, Helen Viney (Mrs. Lewis M. Porter, Jr.) *lawyer*
Sernett, Richard Patrick *lawyer*

Oak Brook
†Getz, Herbert A. *lawyer*
Gibson, James Thomas, Jr. *lawyer, consultant, antique dealer*
Johnson, Grant Lester *lawyer, retired manufacturing company executive*

Oak Park
Sengpiehl, Paul Marvin *lawyer, former state official*

Palos Heights
Hofeldt, John W. *lawyer*

Park Forest
Goodrich, John Bernard *lawyer*

Park Ridge
Curtis, Philip James *lawyer*

Pekin
Clevenger, Robert Vincent *lawyer*

Peoria
Allen, Lyle Wallace *lawyer*
Christison, William Henry, III *lawyer*
Dabney, Seth Mason, III *lawyer*
Eissfeldt, Theodore L. *lawyer*
Ryan, Michael Beecher *lawyer, former government official*
Strodel, Robert Carl *lawyer*
Sullivan, Paul John *legal administrator*
Traicoff, Sandra M. *lawyer*

Princeton
Johnson, Watts Carey *lawyer*

Prospect Heights
Hull, J(ames) Richard *lawyer, business executive*

River Forest
Li, Tze-chung *lawyer, educator*

Riverwoods
Bartlett, Robert William *lawyer, publishing executive*

Rock Island
Lousberg, Peter Herman *lawyer*
Wallace, Franklin Sherwood *lawyer*

Rockford
Anderson, LaVerne Eric *lawyer*
Barrick, William Henry *lawyer*
Reno, Roger *lawyer*
Schilling, Richard M. *lawyer, corporate executive*
Van Vleet, William Benjamin *lawyer, life insurance company executive*

Saint Charles
Mc Kay, Thomas, Jr. *lawyer*

Schaumburg
Collins, James Francis *lawyer*
Meltzer, Brian *lawyer*
Weise, Richard Henry *lawyer, corporate executive*

Skokie
Bogomolny, Robert Lee *lawyer*

Springfield
Cadigan, Patrick Joseph *lawyer*
DeMoss, Jon W. *legal association administrator, lawyer*
Oxtoby, Robert Boynton *lawyer*
Rowe, Max L. *lawyer, corporate executive, management consultant, judge*
Segatto, Bernard Gordon *lawyer*
Van Meter, Abram DeBois *lawyer, retired banker*

Streator
Harrison, Frank Joseph *lawyer*

Urbana
Balbach, Stanley Byron *lawyer*
Fitz-Gerald, Roger Miller *lawyer*

Villa Park
Fenech, Joseph C. *lawyer*
Kohlstedt, James August *lawyer*
Leston, Patrick John *lawyer*

Waukegan
Hall, Albert Leander *lawyer*
Henrick, Michael Francis *lawyer*

Wheaton
†Botti, Aldo E. *lawyer*
Roberts, Keith Edward, Sr. *lawyer*
†Roskam, Peter James *lawyer, state legislator*

Winnetka
Abell, David Robert *lawyer*
Davis, Britton Anthony *lawyer*
Davis, Chester R., Jr. *lawyer*
Kapnick, Richard Bradshaw *lawyer*
Mc Millen, Thomas Roberts *lawyer, arbitrator, mediator, retired judge*
O'Malley, John Daniel *legal educator, banker*

Woodstock
Hale, Hamilton Orin *retired lawyer*

INDIANA

Bloomington
Aman, Alfred Charles, Jr. *law educator*

Boonville
†Phillips, Michael Keith *lawyer, state legislator*

Clarksville
Hoehn, Elmer L. *lawyer*

Columbus
Hamilton, Peter Bannerman *lawyer, manufacturing company executive*

East Chicago
†Randolph, Lonnie Marcus *lawyer, state senator*

Elkhart
Bowers, Richard Stewart, Jr. *lawyer*
Gassere, Eugene Arthur *lawyer, business executive*
Harman, John Royden *lawyer*
Treckelo, Richard M. *lawyer*

Evansville
Clouse, John Daniel *lawyer*

Fort Wayne
Baker, Carl Leroy *lawyer*
Gerberding, Miles Carston *lawyer*
Hunter, Jack Duval *lawyer*
Keefer, J(ames) Michael *lawyer*
Mallers, George Peter *lawyer*
Niewyk, Anthony *lawyer*
Peebles, Carter David *lawyer*
Shoaff, Thomas Mitchell *lawyer*
Steinbronn, Richard Eugene *lawyer*

Hammond
Eichhorn, Frederick Foltz, Jr. *lawyer*

Indianapolis
Albright, Terrill D. *lawyer*
Allen, David James *lawyer*
Aschleman, James Allan *lawyer*
Badger, David Harry *lawyer*
Beckwith, Lewis Daniel *lawyer*
Beeler, Virgil L. *lawyer*
†Bellamy, Robert K. *lawyer*
Betley, Leonard John *lawyer*
Blackwell, Henry Barlow, II *lawyer*
Blanton, W. C. *lawyer*
Boldt, Michael Herbert *lawyer*
Born, Samuel Roydon, II *lawyer*
Bruess, Charles Edward *lawyer*
Buttrey, Donald Wayne *lawyer*
Capehart, Homer Earl, Jr. *lawyer*
Carney, Joseph Buckingham *lawyer*
Carpenter, Susan Karen *lawyer*
Carr, James Michael *lawyer*
Choplin, John M., II *lawyer*
Claffey, Stephen Allen *lawyer*
Cofield, Howard John *lawyer*
Cross, Leland Briggs, Jr. *lawyer*
Deer, Richard Elliott *lawyer*
DeLaney, Edward O'Donnell *lawyer*
Dutton, Clarence Benjamin *lawyer*
Elrod, Robert Grant *lawyer*
Emerson, Andrew Craig *lawyer, insurance executive*
Evans, Daniel Fraley, Jr. *lawyer*
Fisher, James R. *lawyer*
FitzGibbon, Daniel Harvey *lawyer*
Fruehwald, Kristin G. *lawyer*
Fuller, Samuel Ashby *lawyer, mining company executive*
Funk, David Albert *law educator*
Grayson, John Allan *lawyer*
Henderson, Eugene Leroy *lawyer*
Highfield, Robert Edward *lawyer*
Huston, Michael Joe *lawyer*
Irwin, H. William *lawyer*
Jegen, Lawrence A., III *law educator*
Johnstone, Robert Philip *lawyer*
Kahlenbeck, Howard, Jr. *lawyer*
Kappes, Philip Spangler *lawyer*
Kemper, James Dee *lawyer*
Kerr, William Andrew *lawyer, educator*
Kitchen, John Milton *lawyer*
Klaper, Martin Jay *lawyer*
Kleiman, David Harold *lawyer*
Knebel, Donald Earl *lawyer*
Kreuscher, Wayne Charles *lawyer*
Lee, Stephen W. *lawyer*
Lefstein, Norman *lawyer, educator*
Lewis, Dale Kenton *lawyer*
Lobley, Alan Haigh *lawyer*
Maine, Michael Roland *lawyer*
Mallon, David Joseph, Jr. *lawyer*
McDermott, James Alexander *lawyer*
†Mc Kinney, Robert Hurley *lawyer, business executive*
Merrill, William H., Jr. *lawyer, corporate professional*
Miller, David W. *lawyer*
Nolan, Alan Tucker *retired lawyer*
Pantzer, Kurt Friedrich, Jr. *lawyer*
Paul, Stephen Howard *lawyer*
Petersen, James L. *lawyer*
Polizotto, Bruce Alan *lawyer*
Ponder, Lester McConnico *lawyer, educator*
Powlen, David Michael *lawyer*
Quayle, Marilyn Tucker *lawyer, wife of former vice president of U.S.*
Ralph, Roger Paul *arbitrator*
Read, Frank Thompson *lawyer, legal association consultant*
Reynolds, Robert Hugh *lawyer*
Roberts, William Everett *lawyer*
Rusthoven, Peter James *lawyer*
Ryder, Henry C(lay) *lawyer*
Scaletta, Phillip Ralph, III *lawyer*
Scanlon, Thomas Michael *lawyer*
Schlegel, Fred Eugene *lawyer*
Scism, Daniel Reed *lawyer*
Segar, Geoffrey *retired lawyer*
Shideler, Shirley Ann Williams *lawyer*
Shula, Robert Joseph *lawyer*
Smith, Stephen Kendall *lawyer*
Snyder, Jack Ralph *lawyer*
Stayton, Thomas George *lawyer*
Steger, Evan Evans, III *lawyer*
Stein, Richard Paul *lawyer*
Strauss, Jerome Manfred *lawyer, banker*
Stroble, Larry James *lawyer*
Sutherland, Donald Gray *lawyer*
Swhier, Claudia Versfelt *lawyer*
Tabler, Bryan G. *lawyer*
Tabler, Norman Gardner, Jr. *lawyer*
Townsend, Earl Cunningham, Jr. *lawyer, writer*
Wampler, Lloyd Charles *retired lawyer*
Webster, Daniel Robert *lawyer*
Whale, Arthur Richard *lawyer*
White, James Patrick *law educator*
Wilson, Charles Edward *lawyer*
Wishard, Gordon Davis *lawyer*
Wood, William Jerome *lawyer*
Woodard, Harold Raymond *lawyer*
Worrell, David Charles *lawyer*

Martinsville
†Foley, Ralph Morton *lawyer*

Mount Vernon
Bach, Steve Crawford *lawyer*

Muncie
Radcliff, William Franklin *lawyer*
Sissel, George Allen *lawyer, manufacturing executive*

Nashville
McDermott, Renée R(assler) *lawyer*

Notre Dame
Faccenda, Philip John *lawyer*
Grazin, Igor Nikolai *law educator, former state official*
Gunn, Alan *law educator*
Gurulé, Jimmy *legal educator*
Shaffer, Thomas Lindsay *lawyer, educator*

Princeton
Fair, Robert James *lawyer*

Sandborn
†Gregg, John Richard *lawyer, state legislator*

Shelbyville
†Linder, Jeffrey Mark *lawyer, farmer*

South Bend
Bancroft, Bruce Richard *lawyer*
Carey, John Leo *lawyer*
Ford, George Burt *lawyer*
Kalamaros, Edward Nicholas *lawyer*
Kohn, William Irwin *lawyer*
Lake, Brian James *lawyer*
McGill, Warren Everett *lawyer, consultant*
Reinke, William John *lawyer*
Seall, Stephen Albert *lawyer*
Szarwark, Ernest John *lawyer*
Vogel, Nelson J., Jr. *lawyer*

Unionville
Franklin, Frederick Russell *retired legal association executive*

Valparaiso
Ehren, Charles Alexander, Jr. *lawyer, educator*
Hires, Jack Merle *law educator*
†Persyn, Mary Geraldine *law librarian, law educator*

Vincennes
†Doll, Maurice Edward, Jr. *lawyer, state senator*

IOWA

Burlington
Hoth, Steven Sergey *lawyer*

Cedar Rapids
Albright, Justin W. *lawyer*
Faches, William George *lawyer*
Nazette, Richard Follett *lawyer*
Wilson, Robert Foster *lawyer*

Charles City
Mc Cartney, Ralph Farnham *lawyer, federal judge*

Dallas Center
McDonald, John Cecil *lawyer*

Davenport
Le Grand, Clay *former state justice*
Shaw, Donald Hardy *lawyer*
Wittenmeyer, Charles E. *lawyer*

Des Moines
Belin, David William *lawyer*
Claypool, David L. *lawyer*
Conlin, Roxanne Barton *lawyer*
Dahl, Harry Waldemar *lawyer*
Davis, A. Arthur *lawyer*
Duncan, Hearst Randolph *lawyer*
†Edwards, John Duncan *law educator, librarian*
Fisher, Thomas George *lawyer, media company executive*
Grefe, Rolland Eugene *lawyer*
Hansell, Edgar Frank *lawyer*
Harris, Charles Elmer *lawyer*
Hill, Luther Lyons, Jr. *lawyer*
Hockenberg, Harlan David *lawyer*
Jensen, Dick Leroy *lawyer*
Josten, Robert E. *lawyer*
Langdon, Herschel Garrett *lawyer*
Leighton, Paul Joe *lawyer*
Neiman, John Hammond *lawyer*
Nyemaster, Ray *lawyer*
Peddicord, Roland Dale *lawyer*
Power, Joseph Edward *lawyer*
Proctor, William Zinsmaster *lawyer*
Putney, Mark William *lawyer, utility executive*
Shoff, Patricia Ann *lawyer*
Slade, Llewellyn Eugene *lawyer, engineer*
Vorbrich, Lynn Karl *lawyer, utility executive*
Wine, Donald Arthur *lawyer*

Forest City
Beebe, Raymond Mark *lawyer*

Iowa City
Bonfield, Arthur Earl *lawyer, educator*
Downer, Robert Nelson *lawyer*
Hines, N. William *law educator, administrator*
Kurtz, Sheldon Francis *lawyer, educator*
Saks, Michael Jay *law educator*
Widiss, Alan I. *lawyer, educator*

Marshalltown
Brennecke, Allen Eugene *lawyer*

Muscatine
Coulter, Charles Roy *lawyer*

Nevada
Countryman, Dayton Wendell *lawyer*

Newton
Bennett, Edward James *lawyer*

Sioux City
Madsen, George Frank *lawyer*
Marks, Bernard Bailin *lawyer*
Nymann, P. L. *lawyer*

West Des Moines
Bump, Wilbur Neil *lawyer*

KANSAS

Coffeyville
†Garner, Jim David *lawyer, state legislator*

Concordia
Buechel, William Benjamin *lawyer*

Fairway
Marquardt, Christel Elisabeth *lawyer*

Hugoton
Nordling, Bernard Erick *lawyer*

Hutchinson
Hayes, John Francis *lawyer*
†O'Neal, Michael Ralph *lawyer, state representative*

Lawrence
Casad, Robert Clair *legal educator*
Smith, Glee Sidney, Jr. *lawyer*
Wilson, Paul Edwin *lawyer, educator*

Leawood
†Carmody, Timothy James *lawyer, educator*

Mc Pherson
Shriver, Garner Edward *lawyer, former congressman*

Merriam
†Snowbarger, Vincent Keith *lawyer, state representative*

Olathe
Lowe, Roy Goins *lawyer*

Overland Park
Balloun, Joseph Eugene *lawyer*
Gaar, Norman Edward *lawyer, former state senator*
†Kline, Phillip D. *lawyer*
Krauss, Carl F. *lawyer*
Ruse, Steven Douglas *lawyer*
Sampson, William Roth *lawyer*
Short, Joel Bradley *lawyer, consultant*
Stanton, Roger D. *lawyer*
Van Dyke, Thomas Wesley *lawyer*
Waxse, David John *lawyer*
Webb, William Duncan *lawyer, investment executive*

Shawnee Mission
†Adkins, David Jay *lawyer*
Bennett, Robert Frederick *lawyer, former governor*
Biggs, J. O. *lawyer, general industry company executive*
Cahal, Mac Fullerton *lawyer, publisher*
Clay, George Harry *lawyer*
Connelly, John Matthew *lawyer, insurance company executive*
Rubin, Charles Elliott *lawyer, sports agent*
Snyder, Willard Breidenthal *lawyer*

Topeka
Ayres, Ted Dean *lawyer, academic counsel*
Cogswell, Glenn Dale *lawyer*
Marshall, Herbert A. *lawyer*
Rosenberg, John K. *lawyer*
Skoog, Ralph Edward *lawyer*
Spring, Raymond Lewis *legal educator*

Wellington
Ferguson, William McDonald *retired lawyer, rancher, author, banker, former state official*

Wichita
Bell, Charles Robert, Jr. *lawyer*
Curfman, Lawrence Everett *lawyer*
Davis, Robert Louis *lawyer*
Docking, Thomas Robert *lawyer, former state lieutenant governor*
Myers, Jesse Jerome *lawyer, construction company executive*
Rainey, William Joel *lawyer*
Skubitz, Dan Joseph *lawyer*
Sowers, Wesley Hoyt *lawyer, management consultant*
Thompson, M(orris) Lee *lawyer*
Williams, Ronald Paul *lawyer*

KENTUCKY

Benton
†Lewis, Richard Hayes *lawyer, state representative*

Covington
†Head, Joseph Henry, Jr. *lawyer*
†Kerr, Thomas Robert *lawyer*

Frankfort
Carroll, Julian Morton *lawyer, former governor*
Palmore, John Stanley, Jr. *lawyer*

Highland Heights
Carr, George Francis, Jr. *lawyer*
Jones, William Rex *lawyer, educator*

Lexington
Beshear, Steven L. *lawyer*
Breathitt, Edward Thompson, Jr. *lawyer, railroad executive*
Eberle, Todd Bailey *lawyer, educator*
Goldman, Alvin Lee *lawyer, educator*
Lewis, Thomas Proctor *legal educator*
Miller, Harry B(enjamin) *lawyer*
Oberst, Paul *law educator*
Philpott, James Alvin, Jr. *lawyer*
Schaeffer, Edwin Frank, Jr. *lawyer*

Louisville
Aberson, Leslie Donald *lawyer*
Ardery, Joseph Lord *lawyer*
Ardery, Philip Pendleton *lawyer*
†Benfield, Ann Kolb *lawyer*
Burse, Raymond Malcolm *lawyer*
Conner, Stewart Edmund *lawyer*
Cowan, Frederic Joseph *lawyer*
Davidson, Gordon Byron *lawyer*
Dudley, George Ellsworth *lawyer*
†Ensign, David James *law librarian*
Ewald, Robert Charles *lawyer*
Ferguson, Jo McCown *lawyer*
Fitch, Howard Mercer *lawyer, labor arbitrator, travelogue exhibitor and producer*
Hunter, William Jay, Jr. *lawyer*
Klotter, John Charles *retired legal educator*
Lay, Norvie Lee *legal educator*
Luber, Thomas J(ulian) *lawyer*
Maddox, Robert Lytton *lawyer*
Pettyjohn, Shirley Ellis *lawyer, real estate executive*
Ratterman, David Burger *lawyer*
†Runyon, Keith Leslie *lawyer, newspaper editor*
Schmidt, Stephen Robert *lawyer*
Silverthorn, Robert Sterner, Jr. *lawyer*
Skees, William Leonard, Jr. *lawyer*
Straus, R(obert) James *lawyer*
Talbott, Ben Johnson, Jr. *lawyer*
Volz, Marlin Milton *legal educator*
Wyatt, Wilson Watkins *lawyer*

Newport
Siverd, Robert Joseph *lawyer*

Owensboro
Cocklin, Kim Roland *lawyer*

Paducah
Westberry, Billy Murry *lawyer*

Scottsville
Wilcher, Larry Keith *lawyer*

LOUISIANA

Alexandria
†Brady, James Joseph *lawyer*
Gist, Howard Battle, Jr. *lawyer*

Baton Rouge
Bayard, Alton Ernest, III *lawyer*
Beckner, Donald Lee *lawyer*
Blackman, John Calhoun, IV *lawyer*
Bybee, Jay Scott *lawyer, educator*
Byrd, Warren Edgar, II *lawyer*
†Dardenne, John Leigh, Jr. *lawyer*
Hawkland, William Dennis *law educator*

Lamonica, P(aul) Raymond *lawyer, academic administrator, educator*
Leonard, Paul Haralson *retired lawyer*
Mayfield, William Stephen *law educator*
Mc Clendon, William Hutchinson, III *lawyer*
†Pugh, George Willard *legal educator*
Robinson, Bert Kris *lawyer*
Yiannopoulos, Athanassios Nicholas *legal educator*

Hammond
Matheny, Tom Harrell *lawyer*

Lafayette
Mickel, Joseph Thomas *lawyer*

Lake Charles
†Cox, James Joseph *lawyer, state senator*
Everett, John Prentis, Jr. *lawyer*
McHale, Robert Michael *lawyer*
Shaddock, William Edward, Jr. *lawyer*

Mandeville
Christian, John Catlett, Jr. *lawyer*
†Deano, Edward Joseph, Jr. *lawyer, state legislator*

Metairie
†Gauthier, Wendell Haynes *lawyer*

Monroe
Curry, Robert Lee, III *lawyer*
Sartor, Daniel Ryan, Jr. *lawyer*

Natchitoches
Brittain, Jack Oliver *lawyer*

New Orleans
Acomb, Robert Bailey, Jr. *lawyer, educator*
Alsobrook, Henry Bernis, Jr. *lawyer*
Ates, J. Robert *lawyer*
Barham, Mack Elwin *lawyer, educator*
Barnett, Walter Michael *lawyer*
Barry, Francis Julian, Jr. *lawyer*
Benjamin, Edward Bernard, Jr. *lawyer*
Bernstein, David Howard *lawyer*
Bernstein, Joseph *lawyer*
Bieck, Robert Barton, Jr. *lawyer*
Brian, A(lexis) Morgan, Jr. *lawyer*
Cassibry, Fred James *lawyer, retired federal court judge*
Cheatwood, Roy Clifton *lawyer*
Claverie, Philip deVilliers *lawyer*
Coleman, James Julian *lawyer*
Combe, David Alfred *law librarian, educator*
Combe, John Clifford, Jr. *lawyer*
Correro, Anthony James, III *lawyer*
Couch, Harvey Crowley, III *law educator*
Couhig, Robert Emmet *lawyer*
Denegre, George *lawyer*
Dennery, Moise Waldhorn *lawyer, educator*
Dittmann, Albert Stephen, Jr. *lawyer*
Fantaci, James Michael *lawyer*
Force, Robert *legal educator*
Franco, Philip Anthony *lawyer*
Friedman, Joel William *law educator*
Gelfand, M. David *lawyer, educator*
Gelpi, C. James (Jim Gelpi) *lawyer*
Goins, Richard Anthony *lawyer, educator*
Hall, Luther Egbert, Jr. *lawyer*
Healy, George William, III *lawyer*
Hinton, James Forrest, Jr. *lawyer*
Keller, Thomas Clements *lawyer*
Lavelle, Paul Michael *lawyer*
Leger, Walter John, Jr. *lawyer*
Lemann, Thomas Berthelot *lawyer*
Lovett, William Anthony *law and economics educator*
Lowe, Robert Charles *lawyer*
Madera, Carmen Soria *lawyer*
Marcus, Bernard *lawyer*
Martin, Edward Fontaine *lawyer*
Martinez, Andrew Tredway *lawyer*
McDougal, Luther Love, III *law educator*
McMillan, Lee Richards, II *lawyer*
Mintz, Albert *lawyer*
Mitchell, Michael Stuart *lawyer*
Molony, Michael Janssens, Jr. *lawyer*
†Morial, Marc Haydel *lawyer, educator*
†Morrell, Arthur Anthony *lawyer, state legislator*
Norwood, Colvin Gamble, Jr. *lawyer*
Nuzum, Robert Weston *lawyer*
Osakwe, Christopher *lawyer, educator*
Plaeger, Frederick Joseph, II *lawyer*
Poitevent, Edward Butts, II *lawyer*
Purtell, Lawrence Robert *lawyer*
Redmon, Harry Smith, Jr. *lawyer*
Rosen, Charles, II *lawyer*
Rosen, William Warren *lawyer*
Sarpy, Leon *lawyer*
Sher, Leopold Zangwill *lawyer*
Shinn, Clinton Wesley *lawyer*
Simon, H(uey) Paul *lawyer*
Sims, John William *lawyer*
Sinor, Howard Earl, Jr. *lawyer*
Snyder, Charles Aubrey *lawyer*
Stapp, Dan Ernest *retired lawyer, utility executive*
Surprenant, Mark Christopher *lawyer*
Tarver, Michael Keith *lawyer*
Trostorff, Alexander Peter *lawyer*
Vance, Robert Patrick *lawyer*
Waechter, Arthur Joseph, Jr. *lawyer*
Weigel, John J. *lawyer*
Weiss, Kenneth Andrew *lawyer, law educator*
Willenzik, David S. *lawyer*
Wootan, Guy *lawyer*

Shreveport
Achee, Roland Joseph *lawyer*
Ramey, Cecil Edward, Jr. *lawyer*

MAINE

Augusta
Adelberg, Arthur William *lawyer*
Cohen, Richard Stockman *lawyer*

Bath
Weiss, David Raymond *lawyer*

Biddeford
Lefebvre, Albert Paul Conrad *lawyer*

Camden
Shuman, Samuel Irving *lawyer, law educator*

Castine
Wiswall, Frank Lawrence, Jr. *lawyer*

Freeport
Lea, Lola Stendig *lawyer*

Lincolnville
Nichols, David Arthur *mediator, retired state justice*

Portland
Allen, Charles William *lawyer*
Coughlan, Patrick Campbell *lawyer*
Graffam, Ward Irving *lawyer*
Hirshon, Robert Edward *lawyer*
Lancaster, Ralph Ivan, Jr. *lawyer*
Loper, Merle William *law educator*
Murray, Peter Loos *lawyer, educator*
Philbrick, Donald Lockey *lawyer*
Skolnik, Barnet David *lawyer*
Smith, William Charles *lawyer*
Tierney, Kevin Joseph *lawyer*
†Wells, William Woodrow, Jr. *lawyer, educator, librarian*
Wroth, L(awrence) Kinvin *lawyer, educator*
Zarr, Melvyn *lawyer, educator*

Wells
†Carleton, Joseph G., Jr. *lawyer, state legislator*

MARYLAND

Annapolis
†Brewster, Gerry Leiper *lawyer*
†Dembrow, Dana Lee *lawyer*
†Doory, Ann Marie *lawyer, legislator*
†Maloney, Timothy Francis *lawyer, state legislator*

Arnold
Green, John Cawley *lawyer*

Baltimore
Adkins, Edward James *lawyer*
Albert, Charles Thompson *lawyer*
Allen, Donald Clinton *lawyer*
†Angelos, Peter G. *lawyer*
Archibald, James Kenway *lawyer*
Arey, Patrick Kane *lawyer*
Astrachan, James Barry *lawyer*
Ayres, Jeffrey Peabody *lawyer*
Bair, Robert Rippel *lawyer*
Baker, William Parr *lawyer*
Baldwin, John Chandler *lawyer*
†Barnhouse, Robert Bolon *lawyer*
Bartlett, James Wilson, III *lawyer*
Beall, George *lawyer*
Berman, Barry David *lawyer*
Bernhardt, Herbert Nelson *lawyer, educator*
Blanton, Edward Lee, Jr. *lawyer*
Boone, Harold Thomas *retired lawyer*
Bowen, Lowell Reed *lawyer*
Brumbaugh, John Maynard *lawyer, educator*
Burch, Francis Boucher, Jr. *lawyer*
Cahill, William Walsh, Jr. *lawyer*
Carbine, James Edmond *lawyer*
Carey, Anthony Morris *lawyer*
Carey, Jana Howard *lawyer*
Carlin, Paul Victor *legal association executive*
Carney, Bradford George Yost *lawyer, educator*
Chaplin, Peggy Fannon *lawyer*
Chiarello, Donald Frederick *lawyer*
Chiu, Hungdah *lawyer, legal educator*
Civiletti, Benjamin R. *lawyer, former U.S. attorney general*
Clapp, Roger Alvin *lawyer*
Clark, Gilbert Michael *association executive, lawyer*
Clarke, Edward Owen, Jr. *lawyer*
Coe, Ward Baldwin, Jr. *retired lawyer*
Cohen, Marc Kami *lawyer*
Cook, Bryson Leitch *lawyer*
Crowe, Thomas Leonard *lawyer*
Curran, Robert Bruce *lawyer*
Daly, Warren B., Jr. *lawyer*
Davison, Warren Malcolm *lawyer*
Dilloff, Neil Joel *lawyer*
Doory, Robert Leonard, Jr. *lawyer*
Dunne, Richard Edwin, III *lawyer*
Ellin, Marvin *lawyer*
Engel, Paul Bernard *lawyer*
Fergenson, Arthur Friend *lawyer*
Finch, Walter Goss Gilchrist *lawyer, engineer, accountant, retired army officer*
Finnerty, Joseph G., Jr. *lawyer*
Finney, Jervis Spencer *lawyer*
Fisher, Morton Poe, Jr. *lawyer*
Friedman, Louis Frank *lawyer*
Gately, Mark Donohue *lawyer*
Gauvey, Susan K. *lawyer*
Gillece, James Patrick, Jr. *lawyer*
Goldman, Brian Arthur *lawyer, accountant*
Goldscheider, Sidney *lawyer*
Goldstein, Franklin *lawyer*
Graham, John Stuart, III *lawyer*
Gray, Frank Truan *lawyer*
Gray, Oscar Shalom *lawyer*
Grieb, Elizabeth *lawyer*
Griffith, John Earl, Jr. *lawyer, educator*
Hafets, Richard Jay *lawyer*
Haines, Thomas W. W. *lawyer*
Hankin, Robert Michael *lawyer*
Hanks, James Judge, Jr. *lawyer*
Hess, Stanford Donald *lawyer*
Hillman, Robert Sandor *lawyer*
Hirsh, Theodore William *lawyer*
Hochberg, Bayard Zabdial *lawyer*
Honemann, Daniel Henry *lawyer*
Hubbard, Herbert Hendrix *lawyer*
Hughes, Harry Roe *lawyer*
Immelt, Stephen J. *lawyer*
Johnston, George W. *lawyer*
Jones, John Martin, Jr. *lawyer*
Junghans, Paula Marie *lawyer*
Klinefelter, Stanard T. *lawyer*
Lebowitz, Harvey M. *lawyer*
Levasseur, William Ryan *lawyer*
Levin, Edward Jesse *lawyer*
Levine, Richard E. *lawyer*
Lewis, Alexander Ingersoll, III *lawyer*
Liebmann, George William *lawyer*
Lohr, Walter George, Jr. *lawyer*
Loker, F(rank) Ford, Jr. *lawyer*
Machen, Arthur Webster, Jr. *lawyer*
Majev, Howard Rudolph *lawyer*
†McClung, A(lexander) Keith, Jr. *lawyer*
Mc Kenney, Walter Gibbs, Jr. *lawyer, publishing company executive*
McPherson, Donald Paxton, III *lawyer*
McWilliams, John Michael *lawyer*
Melvin, Norman Cecil *lawyer*
Miller, Decatur Howard *lawyer*
Mitchell, Geoffrey Sewell *lawyer*
Mogol, Alan Jay *lawyer*
Moser, M(artin) Peter *lawyer*
†Muffolett, Joseph Robert *lawyer, government official*
Nilson, George Albert *lawyer*
O'Connell, Kevin Michael *lawyer*
Ohly, D. Christopher *lawyer*
Orman, Leonard Arnold *lawyer*
Owen, Stephen Lee *lawyer*
Pappas, George Frank *lawyer*
Patz, Edward Frank *lawyer*
Plant, Albin MacDonough *lawyer*
Plummer, Risque Wilson *lawyer*
Pokempner, Joseph Kres *lawyer*
Pollak, Mark *lawyer*
†Prince, Charles O., III *lawyer*
Proctor, Kenneth Donald *lawyer*
Provorny, Frederick Alan *lawyer*
Putzel, Constance Kellner *lawyer*
Rafferty, William Bernard *lawyer*
Redden, Roger Duffey *lawyer*
Reno, Russell Ronald, Jr. *lawyer*
Reynolds, William Leroy *lawyer, educator*
Rosenthal, William J. *lawyer*
Sack, Sylvan Hanan *lawyer*
Schatzow, Michael *lawyer*
Scott, Robert Edward, Jr. *lawyer*
Scriggins, Larry Palmer *lawyer*
Sfekas, Stephen James *lawyer*
Shapiro, Harry Dean *lawyer*
Shapiro, Ronald Maurice *lawyer*
Sharpe, Donald Edward *lawyer*
Short, Alexander Campbell *lawyer*
Smouse, H(ervey) Russell *lawyer*
Stalfort, John Arthur *lawyer*
Stewart, C(ornelius) Van Leuven *lawyer*
Stifler, William Curtis, III *lawyer*
Sykes, Melvin Julius *lawyer*
Teret, Stephen Paul *health law educator*
Trimble, William Cattell, Jr. *lawyer*
Tyler, George Thomas *lawyer*
Walker, Irving Edward *lawyer*
Wasserman, Richard Leo *lawyer*
West, Christopher Read *lawyer*
White, Pamela Janice *lawyer*
Whitman, Marland Hamilton, Jr. *lawyer*
Winn, James Julius, Jr. *lawyer*
Wintriss, Lynn *lawyer*
Wolf, Fred, III *lawyer*
Yarmolinsky, Adam *lawyer, educator, university administrator*

Bel Air
Crocker, Michael Pue *lawyer*
Miller, Max Dunham, Jr. *lawyer*

Bethesda
Abrams, Samuel K. *lawyer*
Alper, Jerome Milton *lawyer*
Bauersfeld, Carl Frederick *lawyer*
Brickfield, Cyril Francis *lawyer, association executive*
Burton, Charles Henning *lawyer*
Calvert, Gordon Lee *retired legal association executive*
Casey, Thomas J. *lawyer*
Cass, Millard *lawyer, arbitrator*
Clancy, Joseph Patrick *lawyer*
Elman, Philip *lawyer*
†Frosh, Brian Esten *lawyer, state legislator*
Groner, Beverly Anne *lawyer*
Hall, William Darlington *lawyer*
Herman, Stephen Allen *lawyer*
Hutchinson, Everett *lawyer*
Jayson, Lester Samuel *lawyer, educator*
McKenna, Stephen James *lawyer, corporate executive*
Meier, Louis Leonard, Jr. *lawyer*
Menaker, Frank H., Jr. *lawyer*
O'Connell, Quinn *lawyer*
Pankopf, Arthur, Jr. *lawyer*
Ross, William Warfield *lawyer*
Schmeltzer, David *lawyer*
Schurman, Joseph Rathborne *lawyer*
Toomey, Thomas Murray *lawyer*

Catonsville
Stowe, David Henry *arbitrator*

Chevy Chase
Chase, Nicholas Joseph *lawyer, educator*
Harr, Karl Gottlieb, Jr. *lawyer*
Ikenberry, Henry Cephas, Jr. *lawyer*
Ketcham, Orman Weston *lawyer, former judge*
Stetler, C. Joseph *lawyer*
Vance, Sheldon Baird *lawyer, former diplomat*

Cockeysville Hunt Valley
Edgett, William Maloy *lawyer, labor arbitrator*

College Park
Rosen, Steven *lawyer*

Columbia
Baker, Russell Tremaine, Jr. *lawyer*
Ulman, Louis Jay *lawyer*

Denton
†Thornton, Robert Alan, Jr. *lawyer, state legislator*

Dundalk
†Arnick, John Stephen *lawyer, legislator*

Easton
Jacobs, Michael Joseph *lawyer*
Maffitt, James Strawbridge *lawyer*
Woods, William Ellis *lawyer, pharmacist, association executive*

Frederick
Hogan, Ilona Modly *lawyer*

Gaithersburg
Katz, Martin Howard *lawyer*
Schaefer, William G. *lawyer*

Garrett Park
Friedman, Edward David *lawyer, arbitrator*

Greenbelt
†O'Sullivan, Judith Roberta *legal association administrator*

Hagerstown
Corderman, John Printz *lawyer, judge*
†Poole, D. Bruce *lawyer*

Kensington
Daisley, William Prescott *lawyer*
Revoile, Charles Patrick *lawyer*

La Plata
†Braun, Stephen John *prosecutor*

Lanham
McCarthy, Kevin John *lawyer*

Lutherville Timonium
Barnes, Wilson King *lawyer, former judge*
Bond, Calhoun *lawyer, retired*

Monkton
Weller, Frank Harlow, Jr. *lawyer, consultant*

Potomac
Conner, Troy Blaine, Jr. *lawyer, writer*
Peter, Phillips Smith *lawyer*

Riverdale
Love, Richard Harvey *lawyer*

Rockville
Barkley, Brian Evan *lawyer, political consultant*
Chapin, James Chris *lawyer*
Doub, William Offutt *lawyer*
†Gordon, Michael Robert *lawyer*
Kadish, Richard L. *lawyer*
Molitor, Graham Thomas Tate *lawyer*
Nelson, Joseph Conrad *lawyer, business executive, educator*
Nystrom, Harold Charles *lawyer, labor consultant*
Parler, William Carlos *lawyer*
Shadoan, George Woodson *lawyer*
Titus, Roger Warren *lawyer*
Willoughby, Harvey William *lawyer, financial and real estate executive*

Seabrook
Brugger, George Albert *lawyer*

Silver Spring
Bardack, Paul Roitman *lawyer, nonprofit administrator*
Hannan, Myles *lawyer, banker*
Mitchell, Milton *lawyer*
Pellerzi, Leo Maurice *lawyer*

Sparks
Single, Richard Wayne, Sr. *lawyer*

Towson
Howell, Harley Thomas *lawyer*
Johnston, Edward Allan *lawyer*
Lerch, Richard Heaphy *lawyer*
Peacock, James Daniel *lawyer*

Upper Marlboro
Parker, Ellis Jackson, III *lawyer, broadcaster*

Westminster
Bryson, Brady Oliver *lawyer*
Dulany, William Bevard *lawyer*

MASSACHUSETTS

Ashfield
Pepyne, Edward Walter *lawyer, former educator*

Ashland
Borgeson, Earl Charles *law librarian, educator*

Bedford
Dulchinos, Peter *lawyer*

Belmont
Luick, Robert Burns *lawyer*

Boston
Abraham, Nicholas Albert *lawyer, real estate developer*
Achatz, John *lawyer*
Ames, James Barr *lawyer*
Anderson, Arthur Irvin *lawyer*
Arkuss, Neil Philip *lawyer*
Astrue, Michael James *lawyer*
Auerbach, Joseph *lawyer, educator*
†Bae, Frank S. H. *law educator, law librarian*
Bangs, Will Johnston *lawyer*
Batchelder, Samuel Lawrence, Jr. *corporate lawyer*
Bates, Jeffrey C. *lawyer*
Batista, Duane R. *lawyer*
Beard, Charles Julian *lawyer*
Becker, Fred Ronald *lawyer*
Belin, Gaspard d'Andelot *lawyer*
†Bellefontaine, Edgar John *law librarian, lawyer*
Benjamin, William Chase *lawyer*
Bergen, Kenneth William *lawyer*
Berlew, Frank Kingston *lawyer*
Bernhard, Alexander Alfred *lawyer*
Bines, Harvey Ernest *lawyer, educator, writer*
Bloom, Howard Martin *lawyer*
Bohnen, Michael J. *lawyer*
Bok, John Fairfield *lawyer*
Borenstein, Milton Conrad *lawyer, manufacturing company executive*
Bornheimer, Allen Millard *lawyer*
Borod, Ronald Sam *lawyer*
Boyden, W(alter) Lincoln *lawyer*
Brody, Richard Eric *lawyer*
Brountas, Paul Peter *lawyer*
Brown, Judith Olans *lawyer, educator*
Brown, Matthew *lawyer*
Brown, Michael Robert *lawyer*
Browne, Kingsbury *lawyer*

Buchanan, Robert McLeod *lawyer*
Burgess, John Allen *lawyer*
Burleigh, Lewis Albert *lawyer*
Burns, Thomas David *lawyer*
Burr, Francis Hardon *lawyer*
Butterworth, George William, III *lawyer*
Cabot, Charles Codman, Jr. *lawyer*
Campbell, Richard P. *lawyer*
Caner, George Colket, Jr. *lawyer*
Cashel, Thomas William *lawyer, educator*
Casner, Truman Snell *lawyer*
Caso, Gasper *librarian, lawyer*
Cass, Ronald Andrew *lawyer, educator*
Chandler, Louis *lawyer*
Chapin, Melville *lawyer*
Cogan, John Francis, Jr. *lawyer*
Cohn, Andrew Howard *lawyer*
Comegys, Walker Brockton *lawyer*
Connolly, Paul K., Jr. *lawyer*
Connors, Donald Louis *lawyer, land use planner*
Coolidge, Francis Lowell *lawyer*
Craver, James Bernard *lawyer*
Cronin, Philip Mark *lawyer*
Curtin, John Joseph, Jr. *lawyer*
Cutler, Arnold Robert *lawyer*
Daley, Paul Patrick *lawyer*
Dassori, Frederic Davis, Jr. *lawyer*
Davis, Harold Truscott *retired lawyer*
Delaney, John White *lawyer*
Delinsky, Stephen R. *lawyer*
Denniston, Brackett Badger, III *lawyer*
de Rham, Casimir, Jr. *lawyer*
Deutsch, Stephen B. *lawyer*
Dignan, Thomas Gregory, Jr. *lawyer*
Dillon, James Joseph *lawyer*
Dineen, John K. *lawyer*
Donaldson, David Marbury *lawyer*
Dusseault, C. Dean *lawyer*
Ehrlich, M. Gordon *lawyer*
Elliott, Byron Kauffman *lawyer, business executive*
Engel, David Lewis *lawyer*
Erickson, Kenneth W. *lawyer*
Evans, Donald John *lawyer*
Farrah, Elias George *lawyer*
Fay, Michael Leo *lawyer*
Fazzone, David A. *lawyer*
Felter, John Kenneth *lawyer*
Fischer, Eric Robert *lawyer, educator*
Fischer, Thomas Covell *law educator, consultant, writer, lawyer*
Fisher, Champe Andrews *lawyer*
Floor, Richard Earl *lawyer*
Fox, Francis Haney *lawyer*
Frankenheim, Samuel *lawyer*
Fraser, Robert Burchmore *lawyer*
Freehling, Daniel Joseph *law educator, law library director*
Freishtat, Harvey W. *lawyer*
Fremont-Smith, Marion R. *lawyer*
Galvani, Paul B. *lawyer*
Garai, Gabor *lawyer*
Garcia, Adolfo Ramon *lawyer*
Gaudreau, Russell A., Jr. *lawyer*
Gault, Robert Mellor *lawyer*
Gens, Peter David *lawyer*
Gerstmayr, John Wolfgang *lawyer*
Gesmer, Henry *lawyer*
Giso, Frank, III *lawyer*
Glazer, Michael H. *lawyer*
Glosband, Daniel Martin *lawyer*
Goodman, Louis Allan *lawyer*
†Goodman, Sherri Wasserman *lawyer*
Gorham, William Hartshorne *lawyer*
Greco, Michael S. *lawyer*
Greer, Gordon Bruce *lawyer*
Gross, Ira Kenneth *lawyer*
Haddad, Ernest Mudarri *lawyer*
Haley, Joseph William *lawyer*
†Haley, Paul Richard *lawyer, state legislator*
Hall, Henry Lyon, Jr. *lawyer*
Hamilton, John Dayton, Jr. *lawyer*
Hammer, Roy Armand *lawyer*
Hand, John *lawyer*
Harrington, John Michael, Jr. *lawyer*
Harter, Richard Morton *lawyer*
Harvey, William Burnett *law educator emeritus*
Hassan, William Ephriam, Jr. *lawyer*
Haussermann, Oscar William, Jr. *lawyer*
Hawkey, G. Michael *lawyer*
Hayes, Robert Francis *lawyer*
Heigham, James Crichton *lawyer*
Hemnes, Thomas Michael Sheridan *lawyer*
Herwitz, Carla Barron *lawyer*
Hoffman, Christian Matthew *lawyer*
Holland, Hubert Brian *lawyer*
Hoort, Steven Thomas *lawyer*
Hotchkiss, Andra Ruth *lawyer*
Howe, Jas. Murray *lawyer*
Hughes, George Michael *lawyer*
Jaroch, Timothy D. *lawyer*
Johannsen, Peter George *lawyer*
Johnston, Richard Alan *lawyer*
Jones, Hugh Richard, Jr. *lawyer*
Jones, Jeffrey Foster *lawyer*
Jones, Sheldon Atwell *lawyer*
Jordan, Alexander Joseph, Jr. *lawyer*
Kanin, Dennis Roy *lawyer*
Kaplan, Lawrence Edward *lawyer*
Karelitz, Robert N(elson) *lawyer*
Katz, Peter *lawyer*
Keating, Michael Burns *lawyer*
Kehoe, William Francis *lawyer*
Keller, Stanley *lawyer*
Kelly, Thomas J. *lawyer*
Kenner, Brian T. *lawyer*
Kenney, Raymond Joseph, Jr. *lawyer*
†Kerry, Cameron F. *lawyer*
King, William Bruce *lawyer*
Kirchick, William Dean *lawyer*
Kirk, Paul Grattan, Jr. *lawyer, former political organization official*
Klem, Christopher A. *lawyer*
Koffel, William Barry *lawyer*
Kopelman, Leonard *lawyer*
Korb, Kenneth Allan *lawyer*
Lampert, James B. *lawyer*
Lane, Newton Alexander *lawyer*
Last, Michael P. *lawyer*
Latham, James David *lawyer*
Leone, Peter R. *lawyer*
Lettieri, Richard Joseph *lawyer*
Ley, Andrew James *lawyer*
Lindsay, Stephen Prout *lawyer*
Lockwood, Rhodes Greene *retired lawyer*
Loeser, Hans Ferdinand *lawyer*
Looney, William Francis, Jr. *lawyer*
Loring, Arthur *lawyer, financial services company executive*
Lynch, Francis Charles *lawyer*
Lynch, Sandra Lea *lawyer*
Lyons, Paul Vincent *lawyer*
MacDougall, Peter *lawyer*
†Mandell, Samuel W. W. *corporate lawyer*
Marcellino, James J. *lawyer*
Matthews, Roger Hardin *lawyer*
McChesney, S. Elaine *lawyer*
†Mc Donough, William *corporate lawyer*
McGovern, A. Lane *lawyer*
McHugh, Edward Francis, Jr. *lawyer*
Mendler, Edward Charles *lawyer*
Menoyo, Eric Felix *lawyer*
Mercer, Douglas *lawyer*
Meserve, Robert William *lawyer*
Meserve, William George *lawyer*
Messing, Arnold Philip *lawyer*
Metzer, Patricia Ann *lawyer*
Mikels, Richard Eliot *lawyer*
Miller, Alan Gershon *lawyer*
Miller, Alan Robert *lawyer*
Moncreiff, Robert P. *lawyer*
Mooney, Michael Edward *lawyer*
Moran, James J., Jr. *lawyer*
Moriarty, George Marshall *lawyer*
Morton, John Hall *lawyer*
Moss, Guy B. *lawyer*
Muldoon, Robert Joseph, Jr. *lawyer*
Mullaney, Joseph E. *lawyer*
Mygatt, Susan Hall *lawyer*
Neely, Thomas Emerson *lawyer*
Newberg, Joseph H. *lawyer*
Nichols, William Deming *lawyer*
Norris, Melvin *lawyer*
Notopoulos, Alexander Anastasios, Jr. *lawyer*
Novack, Kenneth Joseph *lawyer*
Nutt, Robert L. *lawyer*
O'Dell, Edward Thomas, Jr. *lawyer*
O'Donnell, Thomas Lawrence Patrick *lawyer*
O'Leary, Joseph Evans *lawyer*
O'Neill, Philip Daniel, Jr. *lawyer, educator*
O'Neill, Timothy P. *lawyer*
Osteen, Carolyn McCue *lawyer*
Packer, Rekha Desai *lawyer*
Paris, Stephen J. *lawyer*
Park, William Wynnewood *law educator*
Parker, Christopher William *lawyer*
Parker, Everett Hoitt *lawyer*
Partan, Daniel Gordon *lawyer, educator*
Patterson, John de la Roche, Jr. *lawyer*
Pechilis, William John *lawyer*
Perera, Lawrence Thacher *lawyer*
Perkins, James Wood *lawyer*
Perkins, John Allen *lawyer*
Perkins, Malcolm Donald *lawyer*
Perkins, Samuel *lawyer*
Perocchi, Paul Patrick *lawyer*
Pierce, Joel Farwell *lawyer*
Ploszaj, Stephen Charles *lawyer*
Pomeroy, Robert Corttis *lawyer*
†Popeo, R. Robert *lawyer*
Raish, David Langdon *lawyer*
Reck, Joel M(arvin) *lawyer*
Resnik, Peter L. *lawyer*
Reynolds, Hanson Shallcross *lawyer*
Ritt, Roger Merrill *lawyer*
Rizzo, William Ober *lawyer*
Rose, Alan Douglas *lawyer*
Ross, Carolyn Thayer *lawyer*
St. Clair, James Draper *lawyer*
Saparoff, Peter M. *lawyer*
Sargeant, Ernest James *lawyer*
Savrann, Richard Allen *lawyer*
Saxe, Edward A. *lawyer*
Schmelzer, Henry Louis Phillip *lawyer, financial company executive*
Schram, Ronald Byard *lawyer*
Scott, A. Hugh *lawyer*
†Scott, Arnold Duane *lawyer*
Sears, John Winthrop *lawyer*
Segal, Robert Mandal *lawyer*
Shapiro, Sandra *lawyer*
Sherman, Elliot Mark *lawyer*
Silberman, Robert A. S. *lawyer*
Simons, Steven J(ay) *lawyer*
Sirkin, Joel H. *lawyer*
†Slinger, Michael Jeffery *law library director*
Smith, Edwin Eric *lawyer*
Smith, Philip Jones *lawyer*
Snyder, Richard Joseph *lawyer*
Soden, Richard Allan *lawyer*
Solet, Maxwell David *lawyer*
Sommerfeld, Nicholas Ulrich *lawyer*
Sonnenschein, Adam *lawyer*
Southard, William G. *lawyer*
Southgate, Richard W. *lawyer*
Spackman, David Glendinning *lawyer*
Stevenson, Philip Davis *lawyer*
Stokes, James Christopher *lawyer*
Streeter, Henry Schofield *lawyer*
Sugarman, Paul Ronald *lawyer, educator, academic administrator*
Surkin, Elliot Mark *lawyer*
Swaim, Charles Hall *lawyer*
Swope, Jeffrey Peyton *lawyer*
Taylor, Thomas William *lawyer*
Thomas, Roger Meriwether *lawyer*
Trimmier, Roscoe, Jr. *lawyer*
Tsongas, Paul Efthemios *lawyer, former senator*
Tuchmann, Robert *lawyer*
Van, Peter *lawyer*
Vance, Verne Widney, Jr. *lawyer*
van Gestel, Allan *lawyer*
Vaughan, Herbert Wiley *lawyer*
Walker, Gordon T. *lawyer*
Ward, Richard Paul *lawyer*
Weiner, Stephen Mark *lawyer*
Weitzel, John Patterson *lawyer*
Weltman, David Lee *lawyer*
Westcott, John McMahon, Jr. *lawyer*
White, Barry Bennett *lawyer*
Whitlock, John L. *lawyer*
Whitters, James Payton, III *lawyer*
Wieckowski, Zdislaw Wladyslaw *lawyer*
Williams, John Taylor *lawyer*
Williams, Robert Dana *lawyer*
Winter, Donald Francis *lawyer*
Wirth, Peter *lawyer*
Wodlinger, Eric W. *lawyer*
Wolf, David *lawyer*
Woodburn, Ralph Robert, Jr. *lawyer*
Woolsey, John Munro, Jr. *lawyer*
Young, Raymond Henry *lawyer*
Zack, Arnold Marshall *lawyer, mediator, arbitrator*
Zupcofska, Peter F. *lawyer*

Brookline
Feinberg, Robert I(ra) *lawyer*

Cambridge
Alevizos, Susan Bamberger *lawyer, santouri player, author*
Alevizos, Theodore G. *lawyer, singer, author*
Areeda, Phillip *lawyer, educator*
Bartholet, Elizabeth *law educator*
Bok, Derek *law educator, former university president*
Chapin, Richard *arbitrator, consultant*
Chayes, Abram *law educator, lawyer*
†Clark, Robert Charles *lawyer, educator, dean*
Cox, Archibald *lawyer, educator*
Dershowitz, Alan Morton *lawyer, educator*
Downey, Richard Ralph *lawyer, consultant*
Fisher, Roger Dummer *lawyer, educator, negotiation expert*
Fried, Charles *lawyer, educator*
Frug, Gerald E. *law educator*
Glauner, Alfred William *lawyer, engineering company executive*
Gonson, S. Donald *lawyer*
Kassman, Herbert Seymour *lawyer, management consultant*
Katz, Milton *legal educator, public official*
Kaufman, Andrew Lee *law educator*
Loss, Louis *lawyer, educator emeritus*
Marshall, Margaret Hilary *lawyer*
†Martin, Harry Stratton, III *law librarian*
Miller, Arthur Raphael *legal educator*
Mnookin, Robert Harris *lawyer, educator*
Riesman, David *lawyer, social scientist*
Roche, John Jefferson *lawyer*
Ryan, Allan Andrew, Jr. *lawyer, author, lecturer*
Schauer, Frederick Franklin *legal educator*
Shapiro, David Louis *lawyer, educator*
Steiner, Henry Jacob *law and human rights educator*
Stone, Andrew Grover *lawyer*
Ta, Tai Van *lawyer, researcher*
Tribe, Laurence Henry *lawyer, educator*
Vagts, Detlev Frederick *lawyer, educator*
von Mehren, Arthur Taylor *lawyer, educator*
Vorenberg, James *lawyer, educator, university dean*
Warren, Alvin Clifford, Jr. *lawyer*
†Weiler, Paul Cronin *law educator*
Wheeler, Leonard *lawyer*
Wolfman, Bernard *lawyer, educator*

Chatham
Pacun, Norman *lawyer*

Chelmsford
Grossman, Debra A. *lawyer, real estate manager*

Concord
Berger, Raoul *lawyer, educator, violinist*
White, James Barr *lawyer, real estate investor, consultant*

Dedham
Lake, Ann Winslow *lawyer*

Framingham
Gaffin, Gerald Eliot *lawyer*
Meltzer, Jay H. *lawyer, retail company executive*

Greenfield
Lee, Marilyn (Irma) Modarelli *law librarian*

Heath
Kades, Charles Louis *retired lawyer*

Hingham
Lane, Frederick Stanley *lawyer*

Ipswich
†Getchell, Charles Willard, Jr. *lawyer, publisher*

Lexington
Eaton, Allen Ober *lawyer*
Hoffmann, Christoph Ludwig *lawyer*

Lincoln
Schwartz, Edward Arthur *lawyer, foundation executive*

Lynn
Sisk, Philip Laurence *lawyer*

Maynard
†Siekman, Thomas Clement *lawyer*

Medford
Berman, David *lawyer, poet*
Salacuse, Jeswald William *lawyer, educator*

Middleboro
Beeby, Kenneth Jack *lawyer, food products executive*

Milton
Dinneen, James Francis *lawyer, business executive*
Place, David Elliott *lawyer*

Minneapolis
Garton, Thomas William *lawyer*

New Bedford
†Straus, William Marc *lawyer, state legislator*

Newton
Baron, Charles Hillel *lawyer, educator*
Coquillette, Daniel Robert *lawyer, educator*
Hauser, Harry Raymond *lawyer*
Katz, Sanford Noah *lawyer, educator*

Newton Center
Ault, Hugh Joseph *legal educator*

North Reading
Green, Jack Allen *lawyer*

Norwell
Mullare, T(homas) Kenwood, Jr. *lawyer*

Salem
Griffin, Thomas McLean *retired lawyer*

Sharon
Segersten, Robert Hagy *lawyer, investment banker*

Springfield
†Dunn, Donald Jack *law librarian, law educator, lawyer*
Miller, J(ohn) Wesley, III *lawyer, writer*
Milstein, Richard Sherman *lawyer*
Oldershaw, Louis Frederick *lawyer*

Wakefield
Hunt, Samuel Pancoast, III *lawyer, corporate executive*

Waltham
†Halas, Paul J. *lawyer, corporate secretary*
Touster, Saul *legal educator*

Watertown
Savage, James Cathey, III *lawyer, military officer, educator*

Wayland
Bullard, Robert Oliver, Jr. *lawyer*
Hoffmann, Martin Richard *lawyer*

Wellesley
Aldrich, Richard Orth *lawyer*
Goglia, Charles A., Jr. *lawyer*
Shea, Robert McConnell *lawyer*

Weston
Haas, Jacqueline Crawford *lawyer*

Westwood
Goodman, Bruce Gerald *lawyer*

Wilbraham
Wise, Warren Roberts *lawyer*

Winchester
Bigelow, Robert P. *arbitrator, writer*

Worcester
Cowan, Fairman Chaffee *lawyer*
Dewey, Henry Bowen *lawyer*
Fries, Donald Eugene *lawyer, insurance executive*
†Kelly, John Francis *lawyer*

Worthington
Hastings, Wilmot Reed *lawyer*

MICHIGAN

Adrian
Kralick, Richard Louis *lawyer*

Alpena
Henry, DeLysle Leon *lawyer*

Ann Arbor
Britton, Clarold Lawrence *lawyer, consultant*
Cooper, Edward Hayes *lawyer, educator*
DeVine, Edmond Francis *lawyer*
Duquette, Donald Norman *law educator*
Ellmann, William Marshall *lawyer, mediator, arbitrator, researcher*
Gilbert, Robert Edward *lawyer*
Huetteman, Raymond Theodore, Jr. *lawyer*
Israel, Jerold Harvey *law educator*
Jackson, John Howard *lawyer, educator*
Joscelyn, Kent Buckley *lawyer, criminologist, research scientist*
Kahn, Douglas Allen *legal educator*
Kamisar, Yale *lawyer, educator*
Kauper, Thomas Eugene *lawyer, educator*
Kennedy, Frank Robert *lawyer*
Krier, James Edward *law educator, author*
Lempert, Richard Owen *lawyer, educator*
†MacKinnon, Catharine A. *law educator, legal scholar, writer*
McCuen, John Francis, Jr. *lawyer*
Pierce, William James *law educator*
Reck, J. David *lawyer*
Reed, John Wesley *lawyer, educator*
Regan, Donald H. *lawyer, educator*
St. Antoine, Theodore Joseph *legal educator*
Sandalow, Terrance *law educator*
Southwick, Arthur Frederick *legal educator*
Stein, Eric *retired law educator*
Vining, (George) Joseph *law educator*
Waggoner, Lawrence William *law educator*
White, James Boyd *law educator*

Battle Creek
Clark, Richard McCourt *lawyer, food company executive*

Birmingham
Bromberg, Stephen Aaron *lawyer*
Elsman, James Leonard, Jr. *lawyer*
Gold, Edward David *lawyer*
Hirschhorn, Austin *lawyer*

Bloomfield Hills
Andrews, Frank Lewis *lawyer*
Baker, Robert Edward *lawyer, retired financial corporation executive*
Bruegel, David Robert *lawyer*
Cannon, John Kemper *lawyer*
Clippert, Charles Frederick *lawyer*
Dawson, Stephen Everette *lawyer*
Googasian, George Ara *lawyer*
Gornick, Alan Lewis *lawyer*
Kasischke, Louis Walter *lawyer*
Lehman, Richard Leroy *lawyer*
LoPrete, James Hugh *lawyer*
Marxer, John A. *lawyer, real estate developer*
Mc Donald, Patrick Allen *lawyer, arbitrator, educator*
Meyer, George Herbert *lawyer*
Nolte, Henry R., Jr. *lawyer, former automobile company executive*
Norris, John Hart *lawyer*
Pappas, Edward Harvey *lawyer*
Preston, David Michael *lawyer*
Rader, Ralph Terrance *lawyer*
Snyder, George Edward *lawyer*
Sullivan, Brian *lawyer*
Thurber, John Alexander *lawyer*
Williams, Walter Joseph *lawyer*

Dearborn
Christy, Perry Thomas *lawyer, air transport company executive*
Martin, John William, Jr. *lawyer, automotive industry executive*
Simon, Evelyn *lawyer*
Taub, Robert Allan *lawyer*

Detroit
Allen, James Lee *lawyer*
Amerman, John Ellis *lawyer*
Amsden, Ted Thomas *lawyer*
Avant, Grady, Jr. *lawyer*
Babcock, Charles Witten, Jr. *lawyer*
Banas, Christine Leslie *lawyer*
Barringer, Leland David *lawyer*
Battista, Robert James *lawyer*
Brady, Edmund Matthew, Jr. *lawyer*
Brand, George Edward, Jr. *lawyer*
Braun, Richard Lane, II *lawyer*
Brodhead, William McNulty *lawyer, former congressman*
Brown, Stratton Shartel *lawyer*
Brustad, Orin Daniel *lawyer*
Burstein, Richard Joel *lawyer*
Busbey, Douglas Earle *lawyer*
†Bushnell, George Edward, Jr. *lawyer*
Candler, James Nall, Jr. *lawyer*
Charfoos, Lawrence Selig *lawyer*
Charla, Leonard Francis *lawyer*
Choate, Robert Alden *lawyer*
Christopher, William Garth *lawyer*
†Clark, Dennis J. *lawyer*
Cohan, Leon Sumner *lawyer, retired electric company executive*
Collier, James Warren *lawyer*
Connor, Laurence Davis *lawyer*
†Cooper, Byron Daugherty *legal educator, law librarian*
Cothorn, John Arthur *lawyer*
Cummings, Roger Holt *lawyer*
Darlow, Julia Donovan *lawyer*
Dart, Judith C(andelor) Lalka *lawyer*
Dobranski, Bernard *law educator*
Draper, James Wilson *lawyer*
Driker, Eugene *lawyer*
Dudley, Arthur, II *lawyer*
Dudley, John Henry, Jr. *lawyer*
Dunn, William Bradley *lawyer*
Dykema, John Russel *retired lawyer*
Eggertsen, John Hale *lawyer*
Garzia, Samuel Angelo *lawyer*
Gelder, John William *lawyer*
Getz, Ernest John *lawyer*
Grow, Richard Dennis *lawyer*
Gushee, Richard Bordley *lawyer*
Haass, Erwin Herman *lawyer*
Hampton, Verne Churchill, II *lawyer*
Hatie, George Daniel *lawyer*
Heaphy, John Merrill *lawyer*
Herstein, Carl William *lawyer*
Holmes, Peter Douglas *lawyer*
Howbert, Edgar Charles *lawyer*
Kessler, Philip Joel *lawyer*
Kienbaum, Thomas Gerd *lawyer*
King, John Lane *lawyer*
Kinnaird, Charles Roemler *lawyer*
†Krsul, John Aloysius, Jr. *lawyer*
Kuehn, George E. *lawyer, beverage company executive*
Lamborn, LeRoy Leslie *legal educator*
Lawrence, John Kidder *lawyer*
Ledwidge, Patrick Joseph *lawyer*
Lenga, J. Thomas *lawyer*
Lockman, Stuart M. *lawyer*
Longhofer, Ronald Stephen *lawyer*
Lucow, Milton *lawyer*
Majzoub, Mona Kathryne *lawyer*
Malone, Daniel Patrick *lawyer*
Mamat, Frank Trustick *lawyer*
Martin, J(oseph) Patrick *lawyer, educator*
Massie, Noel David *lawyer*
Maurer, David L. *lawyer*
Maycock, Joseph Farwell, Jr. *lawyer*
McKim, Samuel John, III *lawyer*
McNair, Russell Arthur, Jr. *lawyer*
Miller, George DeWitt, Jr. *lawyer*
Mitseff, Carl *lawyer*
O'Meara, John Corbett *lawyer*
Parker, George Edward, III *lawyer*
Paul, Richard Wright *lawyer*
†Pearce, Harry Jonathan *lawyer*
Phillips, Elliott Hunter *lawyer*
Ponitz, John Allan *lawyer*
Rassel, Richard Edward *lawyer*
Robinson, James Kenneth *lawyer*
Roche, Douglas David *lawyer, bar examiner*
Rossen, Jordan *lawyer*
Rossman, Richard Alan *lawyer*
Rozof, Phyllis Claire *lawyer*
Russell, Robert Gilmore *lawyer*
Ruwart, David Peter *lawyer*
Santo, Ronald Joseph *lawyer*
Saurbier, Scott Alan *lawyer*
Saxton, William Marvin *lawyer*
Saylor, Larry James *lawyer*
Schultz, Dennis Bernard *lawyer*
Schwartz, Alan E. *lawyer*
Schwartz, Jerome Merrill *lawyer*
Scott, John Edward Smith *lawyer*
Semple, Lloyd Ashby *lawyer*
Shaevsky, Mark *lawyer*
Shannon, Margaret Anne *lawyer*
Sott, Herbert *lawyer*
Sparrow, Herbert George, III *lawyer*
Stella, Daniel Francis *lawyer*
Thelen, Bruce Cyril *lawyer*
Thurber, Peter Palms *lawyer*
Toll, Sheldon Samuel *lawyer*
Volz, William Harry *legal educator, administrator*
Waldmeir, Peter William *lawyer*
Walker, Joseph Vincent *lawyer*
Warren, William Gerald *lawyer*
Weiss, Robert Benjamin *lawyer*
Williams, J. Bryan *lawyer*
Winsten, I. W. *lawyer, law educator*
Wise, John Augustus *lawyer*
Wittlinger, Timothy David *lawyer*
Wynne, James Earl *lawyer*
Young, Donald Soutar *lawyer*
Ziegler, John Augustus, Jr. *lawyer*

East Lansing
Lashbrooke, Elvin Carroll, Jr. *legal educator, consultant*

Farmington Hills
Haliw, Andrew Jerome, III *lawyer, engineer*

Franklin
Buesser, Frederick Gustavus, III *lawyer*

Grand Rapids
Barnes, Thomas John *lawyer*
Boyden, Joel Michael *lawyer*
Bradshaw, Conrad Allan *lawyer*
Brady, James S. *lawyer*
Bransdorfer, Stephen Christie *lawyer*
Curtin, Timothy John *lawyer*
Deems, Nyal David *lawyer, mayor*
DeWitt, Jon Francis *lawyer*
Heiden, Thomas John *lawyer*
Hoffius, Dirk Cornelius *lawyer*
Kara, Paul Mark *lawyer*
Kay, Richard Allan *lawyer*
Mc Callum, Charles Edward *lawyer*
McGarry, John Everett *lawyer*
Mears, Patrick Edward *lawyer*
Pestle, John William *lawyer*
Sytsma, Fredric Alan *lawyer*
Titley, Larry J. *lawyer*
VanderLaan, Robert D. *lawyer*
Van't Hof, William Keith *lawyer*

Grosse Pointe
Brucker, Wilber Marion *lawyer*
Gilbride, William Donald *lawyer*
Mogk, John Edward *legal educator, association executive*
Pytell, Robert Henry *lawyer, former judge*

Grosse Pointe Farms
Axe, John Randolph *lawyer, financial executive*

Hickory Corners
Bristol, Norman *lawyer, arbitrator, former food company executive*

Jackson
Marcoux, William Joseph *lawyer*

Kalamazoo
Brown, Eric Vandyke, Jr. *lawyer*
Hooker, Richard Alfred *lawyer*
Lewis, Dean Sumter *lawyer*
Ritter, Charles Edward *lawyer*

Lakeside
Nicholson, Thomas Laurence *lawyer*

Lansing
Baker, Frederick Milton, Jr. *lawyer*
†Bryant, William Robert, Jr. *lawyer*
†Demlow, Daniel J. *lawyer*
Ernst, Albert *lawyer*
Fink, Joseph Allen *lawyer*
Fitzgerald, John Warner *legal educator*
Foster, Joe C., Jr. *lawyer*
Franck, Michael *lawyer, association executive*
Lindemer, Lawrence Boyd *lawyer, former utility executive, former state justice*
McLellan, Richard Douglas *lawyer*
Rooney, John Philip *law educator*
Valade, Alan Michael *lawyer*
Wilkinson, William Sherwood *lawyer*

Livonia
Hanket, Mark John *lawyer*

Monroe
Lipford, Rocque Edward *lawyer, corporate executive*

Muskegon
Van Leuven, Robert Joseph *lawyer*

New Buffalo
Laird, Evalyn Walsh *lawyer*

Oak Park
McManus, Martin Joseph *lawyer, priest*

Pinckney
Roach, Thomas Adair *lawyer*

Plymouth
Morgan, Donald Crane *lawyer*

Pontiac
Berlow, Robert Alan *lawyer*

Saginaw
†Jersevic, Roland Joseph *lawyer*

Saint Clair Shores
Shehan, Wayne Charles *lawyer*

Southfield
Dawson, Dennis Ray *lawyer, manufacturing company executive*
Hotelling, Harold *law and economics educator*
Jacobs, John Patrick *lawyer*
Link, Robert Allen *lawyer, financial company executive*
Morganroth, Fred *lawyer*
Satovsky, Abraham *lawyer*
Tyler, David Malcolm *lawyer*

Taylor
Bright, Gerald *lawyer, manufacturing company executive*
Leekley, John Robert *lawyer*

Traverse City
Wolfe, Richard Ratcliffe *lawyer*

Troy
Alterman, Irwin Michael *lawyer*
Cantor, Bernard Jack *patent lawyer*
Crane, Louis Arthur *labor arbitrator*
Hartwig, Eugene Lawrence *lawyer*
Kruse, John Alphonse *lawyer*

MINNESOTA

Bemidji
Kief, Paul Allan *lawyer*

Burnsville
†Knutson, David Lee *lawyer*

Duluth
Balmer, James Walter *lawyer*

Edina
Johnson, Paul Owen *lawyer*

Golden Valley
Hagglund, Clarance Edward *lawyer, publishing company owner*

Mankato
Gage, Fred Kelton *lawyer*
†Hottinger, John Creighton *lawyer, state legislator*

Minneapolis
Aaron, Allen Harold *lawyer*
Abrams, Richard Brill *lawyer*
Ackman, Lauress V. *lawyer*
Adams, Thomas Lewis *lawyer*
Adamson, Oscar Charles, II *lawyer*
Anderson, Eric Scott *lawyer*
Anderson, Laurence Alexis *lawyer*
Anderson, Thomas Willman *lawyer*
Andrews, Albert O'Beirne, Jr. *lawyer*
Baillie, James Leonard *lawyer*
Bartle, Emery W(arness) *lawyer*
Berens, William Joseph *lawyer*
Berg, Thomas Kenneth *lawyer*
Bergerson, David Raymond *lawyer*
Bergerson, Stephen Richard *lawyer*
Beukema, John Frederick *lawyer*
Bleck, Michael John *lawyer*
Boelter, Philip Floyd *lawyer*
Borger, John Philip *lawyer*
Brand, Steve Aaron *lawyer*
Breimayer, Joseph Frederick *patent lawyer*
Bress, Michael E. *lawyer*
Brink, David Ryrie *lawyer*
Brosnahan, Roger Paul *lawyer*
Bruner, Philip Lane *lawyer*
Buratti, Dennis P. *lawyer*
Burk, Robert S. *lawyer*
Burke, Martin Nicholas *lawyer*
†Burke, Paul Bradford *lawyer, manufacturing executive*
Burns, Robert A. *lawyer*
Busdicker, Gordon G. *lawyer*
Carlson, Don D. *lawyer*
Carlson, Thomas David *lawyer*
Carpenter, Norman Roblee *lawyer*
†Carruthers, Philip Charles *lawyer*
Champlin, Steven Kirk *lawyer*
Christiansen, Jay David *lawyer*
Ciresi, Michael Vincent *lawyer*
Comstock, Rebecca Ann *lawyer*
Conn, Gordon Brainard, Jr. *lawyer*
Cook, Jay F. *lawyer*
Crosby, Thomas Manville, Jr. *lawyer*
Cutler, Kenneth Lance *lawyer*
Davies, R. Scott *lawyer*
Dittrich, Raymond Joseph *lawyer*
Dorsey, Peter *lawyer*
Drawz, John Englund *lawyer*
DuFour, R(ichard) W(illiam), Jr. *lawyer*
Eastwood, J. Marquis *lawyer*
Eck, George Gregory *lawyer*
Endorf, Verlane L. *lawyer*
Finzen, Bruce Arthur *lawyer*
Fisher, Michael Bruce *lawyer*
Flaskamp, William Davidson *lawyer*
Flom, Gerald Trossen *lawyer*
Frecon, Alain *lawyer*
French, John Dwyer *lawyer*
Fronek, David N. *lawyer*
Gagnon, Craig William *lawyer*
Garon, Philip Stephen *lawyer*
Gearty, Edward Joseph *lawyer*
Gill, Richard Lawrence *lawyer*
Goodman, Elizabeth Ann *lawyer*
Gordon, John Bennett *lawyer*
Gottschalk, Stephen Elmer *lawyer*
Grayson, Edward Davis *lawyer, manufacturing company executive*
Greene, Clifford M. *lawyer*
Greener, Ralph Bertram *lawyer*
Griffith, G. Larry *lawyer*
Hanson, Samuel Lee *lawyer*
Harper, Michael Henry, Jr. *lawyer*
Harris, John Edward *lawyer*
Hasselquist, Maynard Burton *retired lawyer*
Hayward, Edward Joseph *lawyer*
Heiberg, Robert Alan *lawyer*
Hemphill, Stuart R. *lawyer*
Hendrixson, Peter S. *lawyer*
Henson, Robert Frank *lawyer*
Hibbs, John Stanley *lawyer*
Hibbs, William R. *lawyer*
Hinderaker, John Hadley *lawyer*
Hippee, William H., Jr. *lawyer*
Hitch, Horace *lawyer*
Hoard, Heidi Marie *lawyer*
Hobbins, Robert Leo *lawyer*
†Howland, Joan Sidney *law librarian, law educator*
Hudec, Robert Emil *lawyer, educator*
Jackson, J. David *lawyer*
Jarboe, Mark Alan *lawyer*
Johnson, Eugene Laurence *lawyer*
Johnson, Gary M. *lawyer*
Johnson, Larry Walter *lawyer*
Johnson, Scott William *lawyer, manufacturing company executive*
Kampf, William Ira *lawyer*
Kaplan, Sheldon *lawyer*
Karan, Bradlee *lawyer, educator*
Karigan, James Andrew *lawyer*
Kelly, A. David *lawyer*
Keppel, William James *lawyer*
Keyes, Jeffrey J. *lawyer*
Kirby, John D. *lawyer*
Kitchak, Peter Ramon *lawyer*
Klaas, Paul Barry *lawyer*
Koneck, John M. *lawyer*
Krohnke, Duane W. *lawyer*
Landry, Paul Leonard *lawyer*
Lareau, Richard George *lawyer*
Larson, Dale Irving *lawyer*
Lazar, Raymond Michael *lawyer, educator*
Lebedoff, David M. *lawyer, author*
Lebedoff, Randy Miller *lawyer*
Levine, John David *lawyer*
Lindgren, D(erbin) Kenneth, Jr. *lawyer*
Lubben, David J. *lawyer*
Lyon, James McDonald *lawyer, banker*
Magnuson, Roger James *lawyer*
Mahoney, Jerry C. D. *lawyer*
Malfeld, Diane D. *lawyer*
Manning, William Henry *lawyer*
Manthey, Thomas Richard *lawyer*
Martin, Phillip Hammond *lawyer*
Mason, John Milton (Jack Mason) *lawyer*
Matthews, James Shadley *lawyer*
McClintock, George Dunlap *lawyer*
Mellum, Gale Robert *lawyer*
Merkle, John Hallock *lawyer*
Meshbesher, Ronald I. *lawyer*
Minish, Robert Arthur *lawyer*
Mitau, Lee R. *lawyer*
Moe, Thomas O. *lawyer*
Mooty, John William *lawyer*
Nelson, Richard Arthur *lawyer*
Nelson, Steven Craig *lawyer*
Nelson, Susan Richard *lawyer*
Newhall, David Gillette *lawyer*
†Nilles, John Michael *lawyer*
Nordbye, Rodger Lincoln *lawyer*
O'Keefe, Daniel P. *lawyer*
O'Neill, Brian Boru *lawyer*
Palmer, Brian Eugene *lawyer*
Palmer, Deborah Jean *lawyer*
Payne, William Bruce *lawyer*
†Penrod, Steven David *law educator*
Pluimer, Edward J. *lawyer*
Popham, Wayne Gordon *lawyer*
Potuznik, Charles Laddy *lawyer*
Pratte, Robert John *lawyer*
Price, Joseph Michael *lawyer*
Rachie, Cyrus *lawyer*
Radmer, Michael John *lawyer, educator*
Ranheim, David A. *lawyer*
†Ranum, Jane Barnhardt *lawyer*
Reichgott Junge, Ember D. *lawyer, state senator*
Reidenberg, Louis Morton *lawyer*
Reilly, George *lawyer*
Rein, Stanley M. *lawyer*
Reinhart, Robert Rountree, Jr. *lawyer*
Reister, Raymond Alex *lawyer*
Reuter, James William *lawyer*
Rockenstein, Walter Harrison, II *lawyer*
Rockwell, Winthrop Adams *lawyer*
Saeks, Allen Irving *lawyer*
Safley, James Robert *lawyer*
Sanner, Royce Norman *lawyer*
Satorius, John Arthur *lawyer*
Savelkoul, Donald Charles *lawyer*
Scheerer, Paul J. *lawyer*
Schnell, Robert Lee, Jr. *lawyer*
Schnobrich, Roger William *lawyer*
Schwartzbauer, Robert Alan *lawyer*
Sheehy, Lee Edward *lawyer*
Shnider, Bruce Jay *lawyer*
Silverman, Robert Joseph *lawyer*
Spencer, David James *lawyer*
Steilen, James R. *lawyer*
Stern, Leo G. *lawyer*
Stroup, Stanley Stephenson *lawyer, educator*
Struyk, Robert John *lawyer*
Swenson, Donald Craig *lawyer*
Symchych, Janice M. *lawyer*
Tinkham, Thomas W. *lawyer*
Todd, John Joseph *lawyer*
Trucano, Michael *lawyer*
Ueland, Sigurd, Jr. *lawyer*
Vander Molen, Thomas Dale *lawyer*
Wahoske, Michael James *lawyer*
Whitehill, Clifford Lane *lawyer*
Wille, Karin L. *lawyer*
Willis, Bruce Donald *lawyer*
Windhorst, John William, Jr. *lawyer*
Wine, Mark Philip *lawyer*
Woods, Robert Edward *lawyer*
Younger, Judith Tess *lawyer, educator*
Zalk, Robert H. *lawyer*

Minnetonka
Palmer, John Marshall *lawyer*

Moorhead
Cahill, James David *lawyer*

Northfield
†Neuville, Thomas M. *lawyer*

Pipestone
Scott, William Paul *lawyer*

Rochester
Lantz, William Charles *lawyer*
Orwoll, Gregg S. K. *lawyer*
†Seeger, Ronald L. *lawyer*
Wicks, John R. *lawyer*

Saint Louis Park
Rothenberg, Elliot Calvin *lawyer, writer*

Saint Paul
Boehnen, David Leo *grocery company executive, lawyer*
Clary, Bradley Grayson *lawyer, educator*
Collins, Theodore Joseph *lawyer, educator*
Crippin, Byron Miles, Jr. *lawyer, religious organization professional, consultant*
Daly, Joseph Leo *law educator*
†Dawkins, Andrew John *lawyer*
Devney, John Leo *lawyer*
Dietz, Charlton Henry *lawyer*
Doyle, Terence Nicholas *lawyer*
Ebert, Robert Alvin *retired lawyer, retired airline executive*
Engle, Donald Edward *retired railway executive, lawyer*
Friel, Bernard Preston *lawyer*
Galvin, Michael John, Jr. *lawyer*
Geis, Jerome Arthur *lawyer, legal educator*
Goodrich, Leon Raymond *lawyer*
Hammond, Frank Joseph *lawyer*
Hansen, Robyn L. *lawyer*
Hardman, James Charles *lawyer, motor carrier executive*
Heidenreich, Douglas Robert *lawyer*
Johnson, Paul Oren *lawyer*
Jones, C. Paul *lawyer, educator*
Kane, Thomas Patrick *lawyer*
Kaner, Harvey Sheldon *lawyer, executive*

Kirwin, Kenneth F. *law educator*
Levi, Arlo Dane *lawyer*
Luis, Juanita Bolland *lawyer, insurance company executive*
Maclin, Alan Hall *lawyer*
McNeely, John J. *lawyer*
Oppenheimer, James Richard *lawyer*
Popovich, Peter Stephen *lawyer, former state supreme court chief justice*
Rebane, John T. *lawyer*
Rosengren, William R. *lawyer, corporation executive*
Ryan, Lehan Jerome *lawyer*
Seymour, McNeil Vernam *lawyer*
Sippel, William Leroy *lawyer*
†Smith, Steve C. *lawyer, state legislator*
†Ursu, John Joseph *lawyer*
Washburn, Donald Arthur *lawyer, travel industry executive*
Whelpley, Dennis Porter *lawyer*

Slayton
Anderson, Merlyn Dean *lawyer*

South Saint Paul
†Pugh, Thomas Wilfred *lawyer*

Stillwater
O'Brien, Daniel William *lawyer, corporation executive*

Wayzata
Alton, Howard Robert, Jr. *lawyer, real estate and food company executive*

MISSISSIPPI

Brandon
Samsel, Maebell Scroggins (Midge Samsel) *paralegal*

Clarksdale
Curtis, Chester Harris *lawyer, retired bank executive*

Cleveland
Alexander, William Brooks *lawyer, former state senator*
Howorth, Lucy Somerville *lawyer*

Fulton
†Mills, Michael Paul *lawyer, state legislator*

Gulfport
Allen, Harry Roger *lawyer*
†Diaz, Oliver E., Jr. *lawyer, state representative*
Harral, John Menteith *lawyer*
Holleman, Boyce *lawyer*

Hattiesburg
Riley, Thomas Jackson *lawyer*

Jackson
Barnett, Robert Glenn *lawyer*
Butler, George Harrison *lawyer*
Clark, Charles *lawyer*
Fuselier, Louis Alfred *lawyer*
†Green, Tomie Turner *lawyer, state legislator*
Hodge, Elbert Clifton, Jr. *lawyer*
Hosemann, C. Delbert, Jr. *lawyer*
Langford, James Jerry *lawyer*
Lilly, Thomas Gerald *lawyer*
†Miller, Hainon Alfred *lawyer, investor*
Moize, Jerry Dee *lawyer*
Phillips, George L. *prosecutor*
†Reeves, John Raymond *lawyer, state legislator*
Wise, Sherwood Willing *lawyer*

Pascagoula
Carlson, John Henry *lawyer*
Colingo, Joe Ross *lawyer*

Southaven
†Ready, George Banks *lawyer*

Tupelo
Bush, Fred Marshall, Jr. *lawyer*

West Point
†Turner, Bennie L. *lawyer*

MISSOURI

Ballwin
†Banton, Stephen Chandler *lawyer*

Chesterfield
†Klarich, David John *lawyer, state representative*

Clayton
Belz, Mark *lawyer*

Columbia
Fisch, William Bales *lawyer*
†Moseley, Joe Lynn *lawyer, state legislator*
Parrigin, Elizabeth Ellington *lawyer*
Welliver, Warren Dee *lawyer, retired state supreme court justice*
Westbrook, James Edwin *lawyer, educator*

Fenton
Stolar, Henry Samuel *corporate lawyer*

Grandview
Dietrich, William Gale *lawyer, real estate developer, consultant*

Independence
Walsh, Rodger John *lawyer*

Jefferson City
Bartlett, Alex *lawyer*
Covington, Ann K. *lawyer, judge*
Deutsch, James Bernard *lawyer*
†Gaw, Robert Steven *lawyer, state representative*
Tettlebaum, Harvey M. *lawyer*

Kansas City
Anderson, Christopher James *lawyer*
Bates, William Hubert *lawyer*
Becker, Thomas Bain *lawyer*
Beckett, Theodore Charles *lawyer*
Beihl, Frederick *lawyer*
Berkowitz, Lawrence M. *lawyer*
Bianchino, Bernard Anthony *lawyer*
Black, John Sheldon *lawyer*
Blackwell, Menefee Davis *lawyer*
Bradshaw, Jean Paul, II *prosecutor*
Brandt, William Perry *lawyer*
Brenner, Daniel Leon *lawyer*
Britt, James Thomas *lawyer*
Brouillette, Gary Joseph *lawyer*
Brown, Peter W. *lawyer*
Bruening, Richard P(atrick) *lawyer*
†Canfield, Robert Cleo *lawyer*
Chisholm, Donald Herbert *lawyer*
Clarke, Milton Charles *lawyer*
Conway, Thomas James *lawyer*
Crawford, Howard Allen *lawyer*
Cross, William Dennis *lawyer*
Davis, John Charles *lawyer*
Deacy, Thomas Edward, Jr. *lawyer*
Devlin, James Richard *lawyer*
Driscoll, Robert Louis *lawyer*
Edgar, John M. *lawyer*
Eldridge, Truman Kermit, Jr. *lawyer*
Feldmiller, George E. *lawyer*
Field, Lyman *lawyer*
Foland, William James *lawyer*
Foster, Mark Stephen *lawyer*
French, Linda Jean *lawyer*
Frost, Earle Wesley *lawyer, retired judge*
Gardner, Brian E. *lawyer*
Giffin, Reggie Craig *lawyer*
Gorman, Gerald Warner *lawyer*
Hoffman, John Raymond *lawyer*
Hoskins, William Keller *lawyer, pharmaceutical company executive*
Hubbell, Ernest *lawyer*
Jackson, Don Merrill *lawyer*
Johnson, Mark Eugene *lawyer*
Keith, Alan George *lawyer*
Kilroy, John Muir *lawyer*
Kilroy, William Terrence *lawyer*
King, Richard Allen *lawyer*
Kroenert, Robert Morgan *lawyer*
Langworthy, Robert Burton *lawyer*
Lindsey, David Hosford *lawyer*
Logan, James C. *lawyer*
Lombardi, Cornelius Ennis, Jr. *lawyer*
Loudon, Donald Hoover *lawyer*
Lysaught, Patrick *lawyer*
Manka, Ronald Eugene *lawyer*
Matheny, Edward Taylor, Jr. *lawyer*
McLarney, Charles Patrick *lawyer*
McManus, James William *lawyer*
Mick, Howard Harold *lawyer*
Monica, John C. *lawyer*
Mordy, James Calvin *lawyer*
Morefield, Richard Watts *lawyer*
Newsom, James T. *lawyer*
Northrip, Robert Earl *lawyer*
Nulton, William Clements *lawyer*
Palmer, Dennis Dale *lawyer*
Pelofsky, Joel *lawyer*
Popham, Arthur Cobb, Jr. *lawyer*
Popper, Robert *law educator, former dean*
Prugh, William Byron *lawyer*
Rosenberg, Morton Yale *lawyer*
Schmitt, Edward E. *lawyer*
See, Andrew Bruce *lawyer*
Semegen, Patrick William *lawyer*
Setzler, Edward Allan *lawyer*
Shaw, John W. *lawyer*
Spalty, Edward Robert *lawyer*
Toll, Perry Mark *lawyer*
Tripp, David Richard *lawyer*
Vandever, William Dirk *lawyer*
Varner, Barton Douglas *lawyer*
Vering, John Albert *lawyer*
Viani, James L. *lawyer*
Wiggins, Kip Acker *lawyer*
Woods, Richard Dale *lawyer*
Wrobley, Ralph Gene *lawyer*
Wyrsch, James Robert *lawyer*
Zimmerman, William Gene *lawyer*

Lebanon
Hutson, Don *lawyer*

Lees Summit
†Hall, Glenn Allen *lawyer, state representative*

Maryland Heights
Doheny, Donald Aloysius *lawyer, business executive*
Sobol, Lawrence Raymond *lawyer*

Nevada
Ewing, Lynn Moore, Jr. *lawyer*

Saint Joseph
Kranitz, Theodore Mitchell *lawyer*

Saint Louis
Allen, Robert Smith *lawyer*
Appleton, R. O., Jr. *lawyer*
Arnold, John Fox *lawyer*
Atwood, Hollye Stolz *lawyer*
Aylward, Ronald Lee *lawyer*
Babington, Charles Martin, III *lawyer*
Baldwin, Edwin Steedman *lawyer*
Barken, Bernard Allen *lawyer*
Barrie, John Paul *lawyer, educator*
Bascom, C. Perry *lawyer*
Bean, Bourne *lawyer*
Becker, David Mandel *legal educator, author, consultant*
Berger, John Torrey, Jr. *lawyer*
Bernstein, Merton Clay *lawyer, educator, arbitrator*
Bottini, Thomas H. *lawyer*
Breece, Robert William, Jr. *lawyer*
Brickey, Kathleen Fitzgerald *law educator*
Brickson, Richard Alan *lawyer*
Brody, Lawrence *lawyer, educator*
Brownlee, Robert Hammel *lawyer*
Bryan, Henry C(lark), Jr. *lawyer*
Carmody, Gerard Timothy *lawyer*
Carp, Richard Lawrence (Larry Carp) *lawyer*
Carr, Gary Thomas *lawyer*
Clear, John Michael *lawyer*
Coffin, Richard Keith *lawyer*
Conran, Joseph Palmer *lawyer*
Cornfeld, Dave Louis *lawyer*
Crampton, William DeVer *tax lawyer*
Davis, Steven L. *lawyer*
Denneen, John Paul *lawyer*
Donohue, Carroll John *lawyer*
Dorsey, Gray Lankford *law educator emeritus*
Dorwart, Donald Bruce *lawyer*
†Dowd, Edward L. *prosecutor*
†Duesenberg, Richard William *lawyer*
Erwin, James Walter *lawyer*
Falk, William James *lawyer*
Fricke, Thomas Freeland *lawyer*
Fryer, Edwin Samuel *lawyer*
Garr, Louis Joseph, Jr. *lawyer, retail company executive*
Gazzoli, John Joseph, Jr. *lawyer*
Gerard, Jules Bernard *law educator*
Gershenson, Harry *lawyer*
†Gibbons, Michael Randolph *lawyer*
Gladding, Nicholas C. *lawyer*
Godiner, Donald Leonard *lawyer*
Goebel, John J. *lawyer*
Goldstein, Michael Gerald *lawyer*
Goldstein, Steven *lawyer*
Goodman, Harold S. *lawyer*
Gray, Charles Elmer *lawyer, rancher, investor*
Green, Dennis Joseph *lawyer*
Guerri, William Grant *lawyer*
Hansen, Charles *lawyer*
Harris, Whitney Robson *lawyer*
Hays, Ruth *lawyer*
Hecker, George Sprake *lawyer*
Hellmuth, Theodore Henning *lawyer*
Hillis, Mark B. *lawyer*
Immel, Vincent Clare *retired law educator*
Inkley, John James, Jr. *lawyer*
Jackson, Rebecca R. *lawyer*
Johnson, E. Perry *lawyer*
Jones, William Catron *legal educator*
Keller, Juan Dane *lawyer*
Kleban, Kenneth A. *lawyer*
Klobasa, John Anthony *lawyer*
Lander, David Allan *lawyer*
Lause, Michael Francis *lawyer*
Lebowitz, Albert *lawyer, author*
Lemon, Eric V. *lawyer*
Lents, Don Glaude *lawyer*
Lieberman, Edward Jay *lawyer*
Lipeles, Maxine Ina *lawyer*
Logan, Joseph Prescott *lawyer*
Lucy, Robert Meredith *lawyer*
Luedde, Charles Edwin Howell *lawyer, corporation executive*
Luepke, Henry Francis, Jr. *lawyer*
Mandelker, Daniel Robert *law educator*
Mandelstamm, Jerome Robert *lawyer*
Massey, Raymond Lee *lawyer*
McCarter, Charles Chase *lawyer*
Mc Daniel, James Edwin *lawyer*
McKinnis, Michael B. *lawyer*
Meisel, George Vincent *lawyer*
Merrill, Charles Eugene *lawyer*
Metcalfe, Walter Lee, Jr. *lawyer*
Miller, Frank William *legal educator*
Mohan, John J. *lawyer*
Moore, McPherson Dorsett *lawyer*
Mulligan, Michael Dennis *lawyer*
Newman, Charles A. *lawyer*
Newman, Joan Meskiel *lawyer*
Noel, Edwin Lawrence *lawyer*
O'Connell, Dennis E. *lawyer*
Oetter, Bruce Christian *lawyer*
O'Keefe, Michael Daniel *lawyer*
Olson, Robert Grant *lawyer*
O'Malley, Kevin Francis *lawyer, writer, educator*
O'Toole, Terrence J. *lawyer*
Palans, Lloyd Alex *lawyer*
Peper, Christian Baird *lawyer*
Pickle, Robert Douglas *lawyer, diversified industry executive*
Poscover, Maury B. *lawyer*
Rataj, Edward William *lawyer*
Reams, Bernard Dinsmore, Jr. *lawyer, educator*
Reynolds, James E. *lawyer*
Riddle, Veryl Lee *lawyer*
Ritter, Robert Forcier *lawyer*
Ritterskamp, Douglas Dolvin *lawyer*
Rubenstein, Jerome Max *lawyer*
Sachs, Alan Arthur *lawyer, corporate executive*
Sale, Llewellyn, III *lawyer*
Sanders, Steven Paul *lawyer*
Sant, John Talbot *lawyer*
Scherrer, Richard Bennington *lawyer*
Schroeder, Paul J., Jr. *lawyer*
†Searls, Eileen Haughey *lawyer, librarian, educator*
Sestric, Anthony James *lawyer*
Shands, Courtney, Jr. *lawyer*
Shaw, John Arthur *lawyer*
Suhre, Walter Anthony, Jr. *lawyer, brewery executive*
Teasdale, Kenneth Fulbright *lawyer*
Thomas, Rhonda Churchill *lawyer*
Tremayne, Bertram William, Jr. *lawyer*
Turley, Michael Roy *lawyer*
Van Cleve, William Moore *lawyer*
Vandover, Samuel Taylor *lawyer*
Wack, Thomas E. *lawyer*
Walsh, Thomas Charles *lawyer*
Weil, Paul P. *lawyer*
Weiss, Charles Andrew *lawyer*
Wilson, Margaret Bush *lawyer, civil rights leader*
Withers, W. Wayne *lawyer*
Wolff, Frank Pierce, Jr. *lawyer*
Woodruff, Bruce Emery *lawyer*
†Yates, Michael Zane *lawyer*
Young, Marvin Oscar *lawyer*

Springfield
Carlson, Thomas Joseph *lawyer, mayor*
Hulston, John Kenton *lawyer*
Lowther, Gerald Halbert *lawyer*

MONTANA

Billings
†Fagg, Russell *lawyer, state legislator*
Haughey, James McCrea *lawyer, artist*
Jones, James Leonard *lawyer*
Murphy, Gregory Gerard *lawyer*
Sites, James Philip *lawyer, consul*
Thompson, James William *lawyer*
†Towe, Thomas Edward *lawyer*

Bozeman
Harris, Christopher Kirk *lawyer*

Great Falls
†Doherty, Steve *lawyer, state legislator*
Manning, John Willard *lawyer*
Overfelt, Clarence Lahugh *lawyer*

Havre
Thompson, Theodore Kvale *lawyer*

Missoula
Haddon, Sam Ellis *lawyer*
Sogard, Jeffrey W. *lawyer*
†Toole, Howard *lawyer*
†Van Valkenburg, Frederick Robert, II *lawyer*

NEBRASKA

Fremont
Gill, Lyle Bennett *lawyer*

Lincoln
Ackerman, James Nils *lawyer*
Hewitt, James Watt *lawyer*
Hoffman, Peter Toll *law educator, judge*
Luedtke, Roland Alfred *lawyer*
Oldfather, Charles Eugene *lawyer*
Swihart, Fred Jacob *lawyer*
Wright, Flavel Allen *lawyer*

Omaha
Barmettler, Joseph John *lawyer*
Burke, Denis Patrick *lawyer*
Christensen, Curtis Lee *lawyer*
Dolan, James Vincent *lawyer*
Forbes, Franklin Sim *lawyer, educator*
†Grauer, Allan L. *lawyer*
Hamann, Deryl Frederick *lawyer, bank executive*
Harr, Lawrence Francis *lawyer*
Hruska, Roman Lee *lawyer, retired senator*
Jensen, Sam *lawyer*
Martin, Elaine M. *lawyer*
†Monaghan, Thomas Justin *prosecutor*
†Rock, Harold L. *lawyer*
Slusky, Jerry Marvin *lawyer*
Wagner, John Julius *lawyer*
Wright, Norman Harold *lawyer*

South Sioux City
†Hohenstein, Kurt Alan *lawyer*

NEVADA

Gardnerville
Manoukian, Noel Edwin *lawyer, former state supreme court chief justice*

Incline Village
Eastin, Keith E. *lawyer*

Las Vegas
Brebbia, John Henry *lawyer*
Galane, Morton Robert *lawyer*
Geihs, Frederick Siegfried *lawyer*
Herch, Frank Alan *lawyer, law librarian*
Levin, Bruce Alan *lawyer, real estate developer*
Lovell, Carl Erwin, Jr. *lawyer*
†Sawyer, Grant *lawyer*
Shutler, Kenneth Eugene *lawyer*

Reno
Broili, Robert Howard *lawyer*
†Gibbons, James Arthur *lawyer, pilot*
Guild, Clark Joseph, Jr. *lawyer*
Hibbs, Loyal Robert *lawyer*
Hill, Earl McColl *lawyer*
Marshall, Robert William *lawyer, rancher*
Martz, John Roger *lawyer*
†Sader, Robert Mayo *lawyer, state assemblyman*

NEW HAMPSHIRE

Concord
Rath, Thomas David *lawyer, former state attorney general*
Rines, Robert Harvey *lawyer, inventor, law center executive, educator*

Dover
Catalfo, Alfred, Jr. (Alfio Catalfo) *lawyer*

Dublin
Wolfe, Albert Blakeslee *lawyer*

Franconia
Merwin, John David *lawyer, former governor*

Hanover
Bollinger, Lee Carroll *law educator*

Hollis
Merritt, Thomas Butler *lawyer*

Keene
Bell, Ernest Lorne, III *lawyer*
Plaut, Nathan Michael *retired lawyer*

Manchester
Mc Lane, John Roy, Jr. *lawyer*
Middleton, Jack Baer *lawyer*
Millimet, Joseph Allen *retired lawyer*
Nixon, David Lee *lawyer*
Zachos, Kimon Stephen *lawyer*

New London
Cleveland, James Colgate *lawyer, former congressman*

Portsmouth
Doleac, Charles Bartholomew *lawyer*
Tober, Stephen Lloyd *lawyer*
Volk, Kenneth H. *lawyer*

NEW JERSEY

Barnegat
Schmoll, Harry F., Jr. *lawyer, educator*

Barnegat Light
Gibbs, Frederick Winfield *lawyer, communications company executive*

Berkeley Heights
Kestler, Jeffrey Lewis *lawyer*

Camden
Coleman, John Michael *lawyer, food products executive*
Fairbanks, Russell Norman *law educator, university dean*
Pomorski, Stanislaw *lawyer, educator*

Chatham
Barnes, William Oliver, Jr. *lawyer*
Little, James Stuart *lawyer, corporate executive*

Cherry Hill
Boyer, Peter Jay *lawyer*
Dunfee, Thomas Wylie *law educator*
Myers, Daniel William, II *lawyer*
Rabil, Mitchell Joseph *lawyer*
Weinstein, Steven David *lawyer*

Clifton
Feinstein, Miles Roger *lawyer*

Clinton
Kennedy, Harold Edward *lawyer*

East Orange
Brown, Paulette *lawyer*

East Rutherford
Wadler, Arnold L. *lawyer*

Edison
Behr, Omri M. *lawyer*
†Corman, Randy *lawyer*
†Warsh, Jeffrey A. *lawyer, state legislator*

Elizabeth
Klein, Peter Martin *lawyer, transportation company executive*

Englewood Cliffs
Green, Alvin *lawyer, corporate executive*
Storms, Clifford Beekman *lawyer*

Fair Haven
Labrecque, Theodore Joseph *lawyer*

Florham Park
Hardin, William Downer *lawyer*
Laulicht, Murray Jack *lawyer*

Fort Lee
Abut, Charles C. *lawyer*
Goldberg, Harry Finck *lawyer*

Franklin Lakes
Galiardo, John William *lawyer*

Hackensack
Massler, Howard Arnold *lawyer, corporate executive*
†Schuber, William Patrick *lawyer*

Haddonfield
†Adler, John Herbert *lawyer, state legislator*
Iavicoli, Mario Anthony *lawyer*

Hillsdale
Bey, Gwendolyn *legal administrator*

Ho Ho Kus
Tobin, John Everard *lawyer*

Iselin
Dornbusch, Arthur A., II *lawyer*
Kracht, Richard William *lawyer*

Jersey City
Meyer, Howard Robert *lawyer*
†Roma, Patrick James *lawyer, state legislator*

Liberty Corner
Apruzzese, Vincent John *lawyer*

Livingston
Pantages, Louis James *lawyer*

Lyndhurst
Lasky, David *lawyer, corporate executive*

Madison
Fogarty, John Thomas *lawyer*
Gnichtel, William Van Orden *lawyer*
Hoynes, Louis LeNoir, Jr. *lawyer*
Kushen, Allan Stanford *lawyer*

Mahwah
Bryan, Thomas Lynn *lawyer, educator*

Manalapan
Stone, Fred Michael *lawyer*

Mantoloking
Morris, Robert *lawyer, writer*

Maplewood
MacWhorter, Robert Bruce *retired lawyer*

Marlton
Luchak, Frank Alexander *lawyer*

Montclair
Brown, Geraldine Reed *lawyer, consulting executive*
Draper, Daniel Clay *lawyer*
Ward, Roger Coursen *lawyer*

Montvale
Beattie, James Raymond *lawyer*
Kanter, Carl Irwin *lawyer*
Kennedy, Quentin J., Sr. *lawyer, paper company executive*

Morristown
Aspero, Benedict Vincent *lawyer*
Berkley, Peter Lee *lawyer*
Bromberg, Myron James *lawyer*
Campion, Thomas Francis *lawyer*
Clemen, John Douglas *lawyer*
DeHope, Edward Kim *lawyer*
Graham, Paul E(ugene) *lawyer*
Herzberg, Peter Jay *lawyer*
Hyland, William Francis *lawyer*
Kandravy, John *lawyer*
Katzenbach, Nicholas deBelleville *lawyer*
†Kreindler, Peter Michael *lawyer*
Krumholz, Dennis Jonathan *lawyer*
Lavey, Stewart Evan *lawyer*
Lunin, Joseph *lawyer*
Martin, Alvin Charles *lawyer*
McCarthy, G. Daniel *lawyer*
Mc Elroy, William Theodore *lawyer*
Murphy, Joseph F. *lawyer*
Nittoly, Paul Gerard *lawyer*
O'Grady, Dennis Joseph *lawyer*
Pantel, Glenn Steven *lawyer*
Perretti, Peter Nicholas, Jr. *lawyer*
Puffer, Leonard Bruce, Jr. *lawyer*
Reid, Charles Adams, III *lawyer*
Rose, Robert Gordon *lawyer*
Salisbury, Kevin Mahon *lawyer*
Samet, Andrew Benjamin *lawyer*
Scott, Susan *lawyer*
Sharkey, Vincent Joseph *lawyer*
Stanton, Patrick Michael *lawyer*
Szuch, Clyde Andrew *lawyer*
Tierney, Raymond Moran, Jr. *lawyer*
†Weinstein, Stephen Saul *lawyer*
Whitmer, Frederick Lee *lawyer*

Mountainside
Cardoni, Horace Robert *retired lawyer*

Murray Hill
Bonnes, Charles Andrew *lawyer*

New Brunswick
Bolden, Frank A. *lawyer*

New Providence
Andrews, Gordon Clark *lawyer*

Newark
Abeles, Theodore Lillien *lawyer*
Allen, Michael Lewis *lawyer*
†Askin, Frank *law educator*
Cahn, Jeffrey Barton *lawyer*
Caldwell, Wesley Stuart, III *lawyer, lobbyist*
Colli, Bart Joseph *lawyer*
Connor, John Thomas, Jr. *lawyer*
Day, Edward Francis, Jr. *lawyer*
Del Tufo, Robert J. *lawyer, former state attorney general*
Eittreim, Richard MacNutt *lawyer*
English, Nicholas Conover *lawyer*
English, Woodruff Jones *lawyer*
Flaherty, John Edmund *lawyer*
Genzer, Stephen Bruce *lawyer, educator*
Greenbaum, Jeffrey J. *lawyer*
Griffinger, Michael R. *lawyer*
Haring, Eugene Miller *lawyer*
Harrison, Roslyn Siman *lawyer*
Horton, William Harrison *lawyer*
Karp, Donald Mathew *lawyer, banker*
Knee, Stephen H. *lawyer*
Kott, David Russell *lawyer*
Lawatsch, Frank Emil, Jr. *lawyer*
Levin, Simon *lawyer*
Mattson, Leroy Harry *lawyer*
McGlynn, Richard Bruce *lawyer*
†McGuire, William B(enedict) *lawyer*
McKinney, John Adams, Jr. *lawyer*
Mitchell, James Lowry *lawyer, former government official*
Muscato, Andrew *lawyer*
Paul, James Caverly Newlin *law educator, former university dean*
Reilly, William Thomas *lawyer*
Robertson, William Withers *lawyer*
Roth, Allan Robert *lawyer, educator*
Scally, John Joseph, Jr. *lawyer*
Tischman, Michael Bernard *lawyer*
Von Glahn, Keith G. *lawyer*
Wachenfeld, William Thomas *lawyer, foundation executive*
Wyer, James Ingersoll *lawyer*
Yamner, Morris *lawyer*

Nutley
Boardman, Harold Frederick, Jr. *lawyer, corporate executive*

Oakhurst
Konvitz, Milton Ridbaz *legal educator*

Oakland
Bloom, Arnold Sanford *lawyer*

Ocean
Abrams, Robert Allen *lawyer*

Oldwick
Hitchcock, Ethan Allen *lawyer*

Paramus
†Yegen, Christian Conrad, Jr. *business executive, lawyer*

Park Ridge
Takashima, Hideo *lawyer*

Parsippany
Bridwell, Robert Kennedy *lawyer*
Florio, Jim *lawyer, former governor*
Jolles, Ira Hervey *lawyer*
Kallmann, Stanley Walter *lawyer*
Shaw, Alan *lawyer, corporate executive*

Piscataway
†Smith, Robert G. *lawyer, assemblyman, educator*

Pottersville
Lynch, James Henry, Jr. *lawyer*

Princeton
Ackourey, Peter Paul *lawyer*
Anderson, Ellis Bernard *retired lawyer, pharmaceutical company executive*
Ball, George Wildman *lawyer, investment banker, author, diplomat*
Banse, Robert Lee *lawyer*
Beidler, Marsha Wolf *lawyer*
Brennan, William Joseph, III *lawyer*
Connor, Geoffrey Michael *lawyer*
Harris, Robert *lawyer, investment company executive*
Hill, James Scott *lawyer*
Johnston, Robert Chapman *lawyer*
Judge, Marty M. *lawyer*
Nucciarone, A. Patrick *lawyer*
Phillips, Daniel Miller *lawyer*
Rosen, Norman Edward *lawyer*
Smith, Hayden, Jr. *lawyer*

Red Bank
Auerbach, Philip Gary *lawyer*
Rogers, Lee Jasper *lawyer*

Ridgewood
Hetsko, Cyril Francis *retired lawyer, corporation executive*

River Vale
Meyer, Grace Tomanelli *lawyer*

Roseland
Berkowitz, Bernard Solomon *lawyer*
D'Avella, Bernard Johnson, Jr. *lawyer*
Dore, Michael *lawyer, educator*
Eakeley, Douglas Scott *lawyer*
Fleischman, Joseph Jacob *lawyer*
Greenberg, Stephen Michael *lawyer, businesss executive*
Kemph, Carleton Richard *lawyer*
Kohl, Benedict M. *lawyer*
Korf, Gene Robert *lawyer*
Lowenstein, Alan Victor *lawyer*
MacKay, John Robert, II *lawyer*
Margolis, Theodore *lawyer*
Rodburg, Michael Lee *lawyer*
Shoulson, Bruce Dove *lawyer*
Slutsky, Kenneth Joel *lawyer*
Steinhart, Ashley *lawyer*
Stern, Herbert Jay *lawyer*
Sturtz, Ronald M. *lawyer*
†Wells, Theodore V., Jr. *lawyer*
Wovsaniker, Alan *lawyer*

Salem
Petrin, Helen Fite *lawyer, consultant*

Scotch Plains
Klock, John Henry *lawyer*

Secaucus
Kilburn, Edwin Allen *lawyer*
Saltz, Ralph *corporate lawyer*

Short Hills
Greenberg, Carl *lawyer*
Hazlehurst, Robert Purviance, Jr. *lawyer*
Siegfried, David Charles *lawyer*

Shrewsbury
Hopkins, Charles Peter, II *lawyer*

Somerset
Kozlowski, Thomas Joseph, Jr. *lawyer, trust company executive*

Summit
Kenyon, Edward Tipton *lawyer*
Parsons, Judson Aspinwall, Jr. *lawyer*
†Tannenbaum, Sanford *lawyer*

Teaneck
†Downing, Robert Franklin *lawyer*

Toms River
Whitman, Russell Wilson *lawyer*

Trenton
Bigham, William J. *lawyer*
Domm, Alice *lawyer*
Sterns, Joel Henry *lawyer*

Wayne
Buckstein, Mark Aaron *lawyer, educator*
Soutendijk, Dirk Rutger *lawyer, corporate executive*

West Orange
Mandelbaum, Barry Richard *lawyer*
Richmond, Harold Nicholas *lawyer*

West Paterson
Vandervoort, Peter *lawyer*

Westfield
O'Connor, James Joseph *lawyer, consultant, engineering-construction firm executive*
Purcell, Richard Fick *lawyer, food company executive*

White House Station
†McDonald, Mary M. *lawyer*

Woodbridge
Babineau, Anne Serzan *lawyer*
Becker, Frederic Kenneth *lawyer*
Brauth, Marvin Jeffrey *lawyer*
Brown, Morris *lawyer*
Buchsbaum, Peter A. *lawyer*
Cirafesi, Robert J. *lawyer*
Greenbaum, Robert S. *lawyer*
Hoberman, Stuart A. *lawyer*
Jaffe, Sheldon Eugene *lawyer*
Molloy, Brian Joseph *lawyer*
Wildstein, David M. *lawyer*

Woodbury
White, John Lindsey *lawyer*

NEW MEXICO

Albuquerque
†Anspach, Judith Ford *law librarian, law educator*
Bardacke, Paul Gregory *lawyer, former attorney general*
Cargo, David Francis *lawyer*
†Caruso, Mark John *lawyer*
Hanna, Robert Cecil *lawyer, lecturer, hotelier*
Hart, Frederick Michael *law educator*
Jones, Donald L. *lawyer*
†Ramo, Roberta Cooper *lawyer*
Riordan, William F. *lawyer*
†Roehl, Jerrald J(oseph) *lawyer*
Roehl, Joseph E. *lawyer*
Schoen, Stevan Jay *lawyer*
Sisk, Daniel Arthur *lawyer*
Stephenson, Barbera Wertz *lawyer*
Thompson, Rufus E. *lawyer*
†Vazquez, Martha Alicia *lawyer*
Wellborn, Charles Ivey *lawyer*
Youngdahl, James Edward *lawyer*

Gallup
†Pederson, Robert David *lawyer*

Hobbs
†Reagan, Gary Don *lawyer*

Las Cruces
Lutz, William Lan *lawyer*
Sandenaw, Thomas Arthur, Jr. *lawyer*

Roswell
†Olson, Richard Earl *lawyer, state legislator*

Santa Fe
†Bejnar, Thaddeus Putnam *lawyer, law librarian*
Cuming, George Scott *retired lawyer, retired gas company official*
Dodds, Robert James, III *lawyer*
Jaramillo, Arthur Lewis *lawyer*
Pollock, Marvin Erwin *lawyer*
Schwarz, Michael *lawyer*
Stephenson, Donnan *lawyer, former state supreme court justice*
Stevens, Ron A. *lawyer, public interest organization administrator*
Yalman, Ann *lawyer*

Silver City
†Foy, Thomas Paul *lawyer, state legislator*

Univ Of New Mexico
Ellis, Willis Hill *lawyer, educator*

NEW YORK

Albany
Beach, John Arthur *lawyer*
†Begg, Robert Thomas *law library adminstrator, law librarian, lawyer*
Belsky, Martin Henry *law educator, lawyer*
†Brown, Judith Anne *law librarian*
Carpenter, Howard Grant, Jr. *lawyer, savings and loan association executive*
Case, Forrest N., Jr. *lawyer*
Engel, David Anthony *lawyer*
Everett, James William, Jr. *lawyer*
Hagoort, Thomas Henry *lawyer*
†Marchi, John Joseph *lawyer, state legislator*
Siegel, David Donald *law educator*
Sprow, Howard Thomas *lawyer, educator*
Swygert, H. Patrick *lawyer, educational administrator*
Wallender, Michael Todd *lawyer*

Ardsley
Benjamin, Jeff *lawyer*

Armonk
Evangelista, Donato A. *lawyer, computer and infosystems manufacturing company executive*
Quinn, James W. *lawyer*

Babylon
Hennelly, Edmund Paul *lawyer, oil company executive*

Bayside
D'Amato, Domenico Donald *lawyer*

Bedford
Atkins, Ronald Raymond *lawyer*
Root, Oren *lawyer*

Bethpage
Genovese, Thomas Leonardo *lawyer*

Binghamton
Anderson, Warren Mattice *lawyer*
Gerhart, Eugene Clifton *lawyer*
Hinman, George Lyon *lawyer*

Briarcliff Manor
Bornmann, Carl M(alcolm) *lawyer*

Bronx
Auerbach, Paul Ira *lawyer*
Balka, Sigmund Ronell *lawyer*
Cornfield, Melvin *lawyer, university institute director*
Stein, Milton Michael *lawyer*
Wolf, Robert Thomas *lawyer*

Bronxville
Armstrong, John Kremer *lawyer, artist*
Cook, Charles David *international lawyer, arbitrator, consultant*
Root, Stuart Dowling *lawyer, former banker and government official*

Brooklyn
Graham, Arnold Harold *lawyer, educator*
†Herman, Susan N. *legal educator*
Lewis, Felice Flanery *lawyer, educator*
Onken, George Marcellus *lawyer*
Pennell, William Brooke *lawyer*
Poser, Norman Stanley *law educator*
Raskind, Leo Joseph *legal educator*

†Robbins, Sara Ellen law librarian, educator, lawyer
Schussler, Theodore lawyer, physician, educator

Buffalo
Barney, Thomas McNamee lawyer
Bean, Edwin Temple, Jr. lawyer
Birmingham, Richard Gregory lawyer
Blaine, Charles Gillespie lawyer
Brott, Irving Deerin, Jr. lawyer, judge
Carmichael, Donald Scott lawyer, business executive
Clemens, David Allen lawyer
Cordes, Alexander Charles lawyer
Day, Donald Sheldon lawyer
Duke, Emanuel lawyer
Floyd, David Kenneth lawyer, judge
Fuzak, Victor Thaddeus lawyer
Gardner, Arnold Burton lawyer
Garvey, James Anthony lawyer
Glanville, Robert Edward lawyer
Goldberg, Neil A. lawyer
Grasser, George Robert lawyer
Gray, F(rederick) William, III lawyer
Greene, Robert Michael lawyer
Hall, David Edward lawyer
Halpern, Ralph Lawrence lawyer
Hayes, Waldron Stanley, Jr. lawyer
Headrick, Thomas Edward lawyer, educator
Heilman, Pamela Davis lawyer
Kaeser, Clifford Richard lawyer, food service industry executive
Kieffer, James Marshall lawyer
†Lammert, Richard Alan corporate lawyer
Lippes, Gerald Sanford lawyer, business executive
Lubick, Donald Cyril lawyer
MacLeod, Gordon Albert lawyer
Newman, Stephen Michael lawyer
Pearson, Paul David lawyer
Reif, Louis Raymond lawyer, utilities executive
†Sahlem, James Robert law librarian
Salisbury, Eugene W. lawyer, justice
Saperston, Howard Truman, Sr. lawyer
Schroeder, Harold Kenneth, Jr. lawyer
Sharpe, Daniel Roger lawyer
Sherwood, Arthur Morley lawyer
Spaulding, Robert Mark lawyer
Wadsworth, James Marshall lawyer
Wickser, John Philip lawyer
Wisbaum, Wayne David lawyer

Campbell Hall
Stone, Peter George lawyer, publishing company executive

Carmel
Lowe, E(dwin) Nobles lawyer

Catskill
Kingsley, John Piersall lawyer

Corning
Ughetta, William Casper lawyer, manufacturing company executive

Cutchogue
O'Connell, Francis Joseph lawyer, arbitrator

Dobbs Ferry
Juettner, Diana D'Amico lawyer, educator

East Meadow
Adler, Ira Jay lawyer

Eastchester
Keeffe, John Arthur lawyer, director

Fayetteville
Evans, Nolly Seymour lawyer

Flushing
Dumaresq, John Edward lawyer
Silver, Jonathan lawyer

Garden City
Cook, George Valentine lawyer
Corsi, Philip Donald lawyer
Fishberg, Gerard lawyer
Golden, Christopher Anthony lawyer
Gordon, Jay F(isher) lawyer
Larocca, James Lawrence lawyer
Lioz, Lawrence Stephen lawyer, accountant
Minicucci, Richard Francis lawyer, former hospital administrator
Tucker, William Philip lawyer, writer
Westermann, David lawyer, educator, electronics industry executive

Glen Cove
Deming, Donald Livingston lawyer
Mills, Charles Gardner lawyer

Glens Falls
Bartlett, Richard James lawyer, former university dean

Great Neck
Busner, Philip H. lawyer, arbitrator, judge
Gellman, Yale H. lawyer
Glushien, Morris P. lawyer, arbitrator
Wachsman, Harvey Frederick lawyer, neurosurgeon

Greene
Sternberg, Paul J. lawyer

Greenvale
Halper, Emanuel B(arry) real estate lawyer, developer, consultant, author

Hamburg
Killeen, Henry Walter lawyer

Hammond
Musselman, Francis Haas lawyer

Hauppauge
Jordan, David Francis, Jr. retired lawyer

Hempstead
Agata, Burton C. lawyer, educator
Freedman, Monroe Henry lawyer, educator
Mahon, Malachy Thomas lawyer, educator
Mayer, Carl Joseph law educator
Regan, John J. law educator

Henrietta
Snyder, Donald Edward corporate lawyer

Huntington
Augello, William Joseph lawyer
†Jordan, Daniel Patrick, Jr. law librarian
Munson, Nancy Kay lawyer

Huntington Station
Schoenfeld, Michael P. lawyer

Irvington
Marshall, J(ulian) Howard, Jr. lawyer

Ithaca
Alexander, Gregory Stewart law educator
Barcelo, John James, III law educator
Barney, John Charles lawyer
Clermont, Kevin Michael law educator
Cramton, Roger Conant lawyer, legal educator
Eisenberg, Theodore law educator
Hammond, Jane Laura retired law librarian, lawyer
Kent, Robert Brydon law educator
Martin, Peter William lawyer, educator
Osgood, Russell King law educator
Roberts, E. F. lawyer, educator
Rossi, Faust F. lawyer, educator
Simson, Gary Joseph law educator
Stamp, Neal Roger lawyer
Wolfram, Charles William law educator

Jamaica
Angione, Howard Francis lawyer, editor
Beard, Joseph James law educator
Re, Edward D. law educator, retired federal judge
†Tschinkel, Andrew Joseph, Jr. law librarian

Jamestown
Idzik, Martin Francis lawyer

Jamesville
DeCrow, Karen lawyer, author, lecturer

Jericho
Blau, Harvey Ronald lawyer

Kinderhook
†Benamati, Dennis Charles law librarian, consultant

Lake Success
Lee, Brian Edward lawyer

Larchmont
Berridge, George Bradford retired lawyer
Bloom, Lee Hurley lawyer, public affairs consultant, retired household products manufacturing executive
Engel, Ralph Manuel lawyer
Pelton, Russell Gilbert lawyer
Seton, Charles B. lawyer

Lido Beach
Billauer, Barbara Pfeffer lawyer, educator

Liverpool
Wolfson, Warren David lawyer, specialty retail store executive

Lockport
Penney, Charles Rand lawyer, civic worker

Long Island City
Cushing, Robert Hunter lawyer, real estate investment executive
Modell, Michael Steven lawyer, business executive

Manhasset
Barrett, James P. lawyer
Carucci, Samuel Anthony lawyer
Hayes, Arthur Michael lawyer

Melville
Green, Carol H. lawyer, educator, journalist
Klatell, Robert Edward lawyer, electronics company executive
McMillan, Robert Ralph lawyer

Mineola
Bartlett, Clifford Adams, Jr. lawyer
†English, John F. lawyer
Hendler, Samuel I. corporate lawyer
Meyer, Bernard Stern lawyer, former judge
Paterson, Basil Alexander lawyer
Rains, Harry Hano lawyer, arbitrator, mediator
Schaffer, David Irving lawyer

Montauk
Garvey, Richard Anthony lawyer

Monticello
Cooke, Lawrence Henry lawyer, former state chief judge

Mount Kisco
Icahn, Carl C. arbitrator, options specialist, corporation executive

New Hartford
Jones, Hugh Richard lawyer

New Hyde Park
Offner, Eric Delmonte lawyer

New Rochelle
Blotner, Norman David lawyer, real estate broker, corporate executive
Burns, Joseph William lawyer
Frenkel, Michael lawyer
Gunning, Francis Patrick lawyer, insurance association executive

New York
Abberley, John J. lawyer
Abrams, Bertram Alan lawyer
†Abrams, Floyd lawyer
Abrams, Marc R. lawyer
Ackman, Milton Roy lawyer
Adams, John Hamilton lawyer
Adler, Joel A. lawyer
Aibel, Howard lawyer
Aidinoff, M(erton) Bernard lawyer
Aksen, Gerald lawyer, educator
Albert, Neale Malcolm lawyer
Albert, Rory Judd lawyer
Alcott, Mark Howard lawyer
Alden, Steven Michael lawyer
Alessandroni, Venan Joseph lawyer
Allen, Leon Arthur, Jr. lawyer
Allen, Richard Marlow lawyer
Alpert, Gordon Myles lawyer
Alter, David lawyer
Alter, Eleanor Breitel lawyer
Amabile, John Louis lawyer
Amberg, Stanley Louis lawyer
Amdur, Martin Bennett lawyer
Amhowitz, Harris J. lawyer, educator
Amsterdam, Anthony Guy law educator
Anderegg, George Francis, Jr. lawyer
Anderson, Eugene Robert lawyer
Andrus, Roger Douglas lawyer
Anthoine, Robert lawyer, educator
Appel, Alfred lawyer
Arenson, Gregory K. lawyer
Armstrong, James Sinclair lawyer, banker
Armstrong, Michael Francis lawyer
Arning, John Fredrick lawyer
Arouh, Jeffrey Alan lawyer
Arquit, Kevin James lawyer
Arther, Richard Oberlin polygraphist, educator
Ashinoff, Reid L. lawyer
Ashton, Robert W. lawyer, foundation administrator
Ashworth, Richard Goodspeed lawyer
Atkins, Peter Allan lawyer
Auerbach, William lawyer
Axelrod, Charles Paul lawyer
Axinn, Stephen Mark lawyer
Bachelder, Joseph Elmer, III lawyer
Backman, Gerald Stephen lawyer
Badertscher, David Glen law librarian, consultant
Baechle, James Joseph lawyer, banker
Baer, Thomas James lawyer
Baeza, Mario Leon lawyer
†Bagger, Richard Hartvig lawyer
Bailey, Lawrence Randolph, Sr. lawyer
Bainton, J(ohn) Joseph lawyer
Baity, John Cooley lawyer
Baker, David Remember lawyer
Baker, Edwin Herbert lawyer
Baker, Stuart David lawyer
Ball, John H(anstein) lawyer
†Ballon, Charles lawyer
Bamberger, Michael Albert lawyer
Bancroft, Alexander Clerihew lawyer
Bancroft, Margaret Armstrong lawyer
Banker, Stephen M. lawyer
Bankston, Archie Moore, Jr. lawyer
Barandes, Robert lawyer
Barasch, Clarence Sylvan lawyer
Barasch, Mal Livingston lawyer
Barbash, Joseph lawyer, arbitrator
Barist, Jeffrey A. lawyer
Barnett, Richard Blair lawyer
Baron, Mitchell Neal lawyer
Barr, Thomas D. lawyer
Barrett, William L. D. lawyer
Barron, Francis Patrick lawyer
Barry, David Earl lawyer
Barry, Desmond Thomas, Jr. lawyer
Barth, Mark Harold lawyer
Bartlett, Joseph Warren lawyer
Baskin, Stuart Jay lawyer
Bassen, Ned H. lawyer
Bauer, Douglas F. lawyer
Bauer, Ralph Glenn lawyer, maritime arbitrator
Baumgardner, John Ellwood, Jr. lawyer
Baumgarten, Paul Anthony lawyer
Baumgarten, Sidney lawyer
Baumrin, Bernard Stefan Herbert lawyer, educator
Bazerman, Steven Howard lawyer
Bear, Larry Alan lawyer, educator
Begley, Louis lawyer, writer
Beha, James Joseph lawyer
Behrendt, John Thomas lawyer
Beinecke, Candace Krugman lawyer
Beinecke, Frederick William lawyer, corporation executive
Belford, Richard David lawyer
Bell, Derrick Albert legal educator
Bell, James Halsey lawyer
Bell, Jonathan Robert lawyer
Belnick, Mark Alan lawyer
Benedict, James Nelson lawyer
Benenson, Mark Keith lawyer
Benjamin, Harvey E. lawyer, sports executive
Benkard, James W. B. lawyer
Bennett, Reynold lawyer
†Benshoof, Janet L. lawyer, association executive
Bergan, Philip James lawyer
Bergen, G. S. Peter lawyer
Berger, Curtis Jay law educator
Berger, George lawyer
†Berger, Vivian Olivia lawyer, educator
Bergstein, Daniel Gerard lawyer
Berk, Alan S. law firm executive
Berkman, Jack Neville lawyer, corporate executive
Berle, Peter Adolf Augustus lawyer, association executive
Berlin, Emily lawyer
Berman, Joshua Mordecai lawyer, manufacturing company executive
Berman, Julius lawyer
Berman, Richard Miles lawyer
Bermann, George Alan law educator, lawyer
Bernard, Richard Phillip lawyer
Bernstein, Bernard lawyer, corporate executive
Bernstein, Daniel Lewis lawyer
Berry, Charles Gordon lawyer
Berry, Edna Janet lawyer, chemist
Beshar, Christine lawyer
Beshar, Robert Peter lawyer
Best, Geoffry D. C. lawyer
Bettman, Gary Bruce lawyer
Beuchert, Edward William lawyer
Bezahler, Donald Jay lawyer
Bezanson, Thomas Edward lawyer
Bialkin, Kenneth Jules lawyer
Bialo, Kenneth Marc lawyer
Bicks, David Peter lawyer
Bidwell, James Truman, Jr. lawyer
Bienenstock, Martin J. lawyer
Bierman, Steven M. lawyer
Biggar, Barry P. lawyer
Birnbaum, Edward Lester lawyer
Birnbaum, Irwin Morton lawyer
Birnbaum, Robert Jack lawyer
Birnbaum, Sheila L. lawyer, educator
Bizar, Irving lawyer
Black, Barbara Aronstein legal history educator
Black, James Isaac, III lawyer
Black, Jerry Bernard lawyer
Blackiston, Henry Curtis, III lawyer
Blackman, Kenneth Robert lawyer
Blackwell, Richard Manning lawyer
Blake, Richard Charles lawyer
Blakeslee, Edward Eaton lawyer, insurance executive
Blanc, Roger David lawyer
Blattmachr, Jonathan George lawyer
Bleich, David Lloyd lawyer
Blind, William Charles lawyer
Bliwise, Lester Martin lawyer
Block, Dennis Jeffery lawyer
Bloom, Robert Avrum lawyer
Bloomer, Harold Franklin, Jr. lawyer
Blumberg, Gerald lawyer
Blumkin, Linda Ruth lawyer
Blumstein, Allan lawyer
Bockstein, Herbert lawyer
Boes, Lawrence William lawyer
Bolan, Thomas Anthony lawyer
Bonomi, John Gurnee lawyer
Booth, Edgar Hirsch lawyer
Booth, Mitchell B. lawyer
Borisoff, Richard Stuart lawyer
Boros, Jerome S. lawyer
Borsody, Robert Peter lawyer
Boshkov, Stefan Robert lawyer
Bower, John Joseph lawyer
Bowie, Jonathan Munford lawyer
Boxer, Leonard lawyer
Bozorth, Squire Newland lawyer
Bradley, E. Michael lawyer
Braun, Jeffrey Louis lawyer
Breglio, John F. lawyer
Brenner, Frank lawyer
Bresler, Martin I. lawyer
Bressler, Bernard lawyer
Briggs, Taylor Rastrick lawyer
†Bring, Murray H. lawyer
Britell, Peter Stuart lawyer
Broadwater, Douglas Dwight lawyer
Broadwin, Joseph Louis lawyer
Broder, Douglas Fisher lawyer
Brodsky, Samuel lawyer
Brome, Thomas Reed lawyer
Bronstein, Richard J. lawyer
Brooks, Lorimer Page patent lawyer
Brooks, Russell Edwin lawyer
Bross, Steward Richard, Jr. lawyer
Broude, Richard Frederick lawyer, educator
Broughton, Phillip Charles lawyer
Browdy, Joseph Eugene lawyer
Brown, Charles Dodgson lawyer
Brown, Francis Cabell, Jr. lawyer
Brown, Meredith M. lawyer
Brown, Paul M. lawyer
Brown, Peter Megargee lawyer, writer, lecturer
Brown, Ralph Sawyer, Jr. lawyer, business executive
Browne, Jeffrey Francis lawyer
Brownwood, David Owen lawyer
Bruckmann, Mark F. lawyer
Brundige, Robert W., Jr. lawyer
Bryan, Barry Richard lawyer
Bschorr, Paul Joseph lawyer
Burgweger, Francis Joseph Dewes, Jr. lawyer
Burke, Thomas Edmund lawyer
Burns, Arnold Irwin lawyer
Burrows, Michael Donald lawyer
Bursky, Herman Aaron lawyer
Butler, Samuel Coles lawyer
Butler, William Joseph lawyer
Butowsky, David Martin lawyer
Buttenwieser, Lawrence Benjamin lawyer
Cable, Paul Andrew lawyer
Cahn, Joshua Binion lawyer
Calise, William Joseph, Jr. lawyer
†Callagy, John M. lawyer
Callahan, Joseph Patrick lawyer
Calvey, Brian J. lawyer
Campbell, Scott G. lawyer
Campbell, Woodrow Wilson, Jr. lawyer
Cannell, John Redferne lawyer
Canoni, John David lawyer
Cantor, Melvyn Leon lawyer
Caplan, Richard V. lawyer
Carb, Stephen Ames lawyer
Carberry, Charles Michael lawyer
Cardinali, Albert John lawyer
Cardozo, Benjamin Mordecai lawyer
Cardozo, Michael A. lawyer
Carey, J. Edwin lawyer
Carley, John Halliday lawyer
Carling, Francis lawyer
Carlson, David Bret lawyer, consultant
Carlson, Theodore Joshua lawyer, retired utility company executive
†Carrey, Bernard S. lawyer
Carroll, J. Speed lawyer
Carroll, Joseph J(ohn) lawyer
Carroll, Raoul Lord lawyer, investment banker
Carter, James Hal, Jr. lawyer
Caso, Ronald George lawyer, accountant
Castel, P. Kevin lawyer
Catuzzi, J. P., Jr. lawyer
Ceresney, Ian lawyer
Chalif, Seymour H. lawyer
Chapin, Hugh A. lawyer
Chapnick, David B. lawyer, partner
Chappell, John Charles lawyer
Chase, Oscar G(ottfried) law educator, consultant, author
Chazen, Hartley James lawyer
Chell, Beverly C. lawyer
Cherovsky, Erwin Louis lawyer, writer
Chester, John Geoffrey lawyer
Chiarchiaro, Frank John lawyer
Chilstrom, Robert Meade lawyer
Chin, Sylvia Fung lawyer
Christaldi, Brian lawyer
Christensen, Henry, III lawyer
Christy, Arthur Hill lawyer
Chromow, Sheri P. lawyer
Clark, Cameron lawyer
Clark, Carolyn Cochran lawyer
Clark, Howard Longstreth lawyer, business executive
Clark, Jonathan Montgomery lawyer
Clark, Merrell Edward, Jr. lawyer
Clark, Ramsey lawyer
Clary, Richard Wayland lawyer
Clayton, Joe Don lawyer
Cliff, Walter Conway lawyer
Close, Michael John lawyer
Cogan, James Richard lawyer

Cohen, Edmund Stephen lawyer
Cohen, Edward Herschel lawyer
Cohen, Fred Howard lawyer
Cohen, Henry Rodgin lawyer
Cohen, Hollace T. lawyer
Cohen, Joel J. lawyer, investment banker
Cohen, Myron lawyer
Cohen, Richard Gerard lawyer
Cole, Lewis George lawyer
Coll, John Peter, Jr. lawyer
Collins, Adrian Anthony lawyer, accountant, educator
Collins, Wayne Dale lawyer
Collins, William T. lawyer
Collinson, Dale Stanley lawyer
Collyer, Michael lawyer
Comfrey, Kathleen Marie lawyer
Conboy, Kenneth lawyer, former federal judge
Concannon, Richard James lawyer
Connelly, Albert R. lawyer
Conrad, Winthrop Brown, Jr. lawyer
Constance, Thomas Ernest lawyer
Constantine, Jan Friedman lawyer
Conston, Henry Siegismund lawyer
Cook, Michael Lewis lawyer
Cook, Robert Stansfield, Jr. lawyer
Cooney, John Patrick, Jr. lawyer
Cooper, Michael Anthony lawyer
Cooper, Stephen Herbert lawyer
Coplan, Norman Allan lawyer
Corbin, Sol Neil lawyer
Corry, John Adams lawyer
Costikyan, Edward N(azar) lawyer
Cotter, James Michael lawyer
Cotton, Richard lawyer
Cowan, Martin B. lawyer
Cowan, Wallace Edgar lawyer
Cowen, Edward S. lawyer
Cowen, Robert Nathan lawyer
Cowles, Frederick Oliver lawyer
Cox, Marshall lawyer
Craft, Randal Robert, Jr. lawyer
Cramer, Edward Morton lawyer, music company executive
Crames, Michael J. lawyer
Crane, Benjamin Field lawyer
Crary, Miner Dunham, Jr. lawyer
Creel, Thomas Leonard lawyer
Crisona, James Joseph lawyer
Critchlow, Charles Howard lawyer
Crohn, Max Henry, Jr. lawyer
Cross, Peter A. lawyer
Cross, Samuel S. lawyer
Cubitto, Robert J. lawyer
Cuneo, Donald Lane lawyer, educator
Curtis, Frank R. lawyer
Curtis, Sheldon lawyer
Curtis, Susan Grace lawyer
Cutler, Kenneth Burnett lawyer, investment company executive
Dacey, Eileen M. lawyer
Dadakis, John D. lawyer
Daitz, Ronald Frederick lawyer
Dale, Harvey Philip law educator
Dallas, William Moffit, Jr. lawyer
Danilek, Donald J. lawyer
Dannhauser, Stephen J. lawyer
Danzig, Aaron Leon lawyer
Darrell, Norris, Jr. lawyer
Darrow, Jill E(llen) lawyer
†Darrow, Katherine Prager lawyer, publishing executive
D'Auria, Anthony J. lawyer
Davidson, George Allan lawyer
Davidson, Mark Edward lawyer
Davidson, Robert Bruce lawyer
Davis, Edward Shippen lawyer
Davis, Evan Anderson lawyer
Davis, Frederick Townsend lawyer
Davis, Richard Joel lawyer, former government official
Davis, Richard Ralph lawyer
Davis, Steven Howard lawyer
Davis, Wendell, Jr. lawyer
Dayan, Rodney S. lawyer
Deane, James Richard lawyer
Debo, Vincent Joseph lawyer
†DeCarlo, Donald Thomas lawyer, insurance company executive
Delikat, Michael lawyer
Delman, Stephen Bennett lawyer
Delson, Robert lawyer
Demarest, Daniel Anthony retired lawyer
De Natale, Andrew Peter lawyer
Denham, Robert Edwin lawyer, investment company executive
de Saint Phalle, Pierre Claude lawyer
†DeScherer, Richard K. lawyer
De Sear, Edward Marshall lawyer
Devers, Peter Dix lawyer
Diamant, Aviva F. lawyer
Diamond, David Howard lawyer
DiBenedetto, Joseph A. lawyer
diBuono, Anthony Joseph lawyer, business executive
Dichter, Barry Joel lawyer
Dicker, Marvin lawyer
Diskant, Gregory L. lawyer
Dolan, James Francis lawyer
Dolan, Michael G. lawyer
Doman, Nicholas R. lawyer
Dominianni, Emilio Anthony (Mike Dominianni) lawyer, accountant
Donald, Norman Henderson, III lawyer
Dormire, Corwin Brooke lawyer
†Dorsen, Harriette K. lawyer
Dorsen, Norman lawyer, educator
Douglas, Philip Le Breton lawyer
Doyle, Joseph Anthony lawyer
Doyle, Paul Francis lawyer
Drebsky, Dennis Jay lawyer
Dreizen, Alison M. lawyer
Druker, Isaac E. lawyer
Dubin, James Michael lawyer
Dubin, Seth Harris lawyer
DuBois, Jonathan Delafield lawyer
Dubroff, Charles Mark lawyer
Duffy, Edmund Charles lawyer
Duffy, W. Leslie lawyer
Dundas, Philip Blair, Jr. lawyer
Dune, Steve Charles lawyer
Dunham, Corydon Busnell lawyer, broadcasting executive
Dunham, Wolcott Balestier, Jr. lawyer
Dunn, M(orris) Douglas lawyer
Dworkin, Ronald Myles legal educator
Dykhouse, David Wayne lawyer
Earle, Victor Montagne, III lawyer
Ebin, Robert Felix lawyer
Eckhaus, Jay Elliot lawyer
Edelbaum, Philip R. lawyer
Edelman, Herbert Stephen lawyer
Edelman, Paul Sterling lawyer
Edelson, Gilbert Seymour lawyer
Edgar, Harold Simmons Hull law educator
Edmonds, Robert Scott lawyer
Edwards, James Malone lawyer
Ehrenbard, Robert lawyer
Ehrenkranz, Joel S. lawyer
Einarson, Baldvin Oliver lawyer
Eisert, Edward Gaver lawyer
Ekern, George Patrick lawyer
Elicker, Gordon Leonard lawyer
Elkin, Jeffrey H. lawyer
Ellenberger, Jack Stuart law librarian
Ellis, Carolyn Terry lawyer
Elsen, Sheldon Howard lawyer
Epling, Richard Louis lawyer
Eppner, Gerald Allen lawyer
Epstein, Jeremy G. lawyer
Epstein, Melvin lawyer
Epstein, Michael Alan lawyer
Ercklentz, Enno Wilhelm, Jr. lawyer
Eustice, James Samuel lawyer, educator
Evans, Martin Frederic lawyer
Evans, Thomas William lawyer
Evarts, William Maxwell, Jr. lawyer
Faber, Peter Lewis lawyer
Fagen, Leslie Gordon lawyer
Fales, Haliburton, II lawyer
Farley, Robert Donald lawyer, business executive
Farnham, George Railton lawyer
Farnsworth, E(dward) Allan lawyer, educator
Farnsworth, Philip Richeson lawyer, broadcasting and publishing executive
Fass, Peter Michael lawyer, educator
Faulkner, Walter Thomas lawyer
Feder, Arthur A. lawyer
Feder, Saul E. lawyer
Feit, Glenn M. lawyer
Felcher, Peter L. lawyer
Feldberg, Michael Svetkey lawyer
Feldman, Franklin lawyer, printmaker
†Feldman, Jerome Ira lawyer, patent development executive
Felfe, Peter Franz lawyer
Fensterstock, Blair Courtney lawyer
Ferguson, Milton Carr, Jr. lawyer
Ferguson, Robert Harry Munro lawyer
Fernandez, Jose Walfredo lawyer
Ferraro, Geraldine Anne lawyer, former congresswoman
Fialkoff, Jay R. lawyer
Fier, Elihu lawyer
Filler, Ronald Howard lawyer
Finch, Edward Ridley, Jr. lawyer, former diplomat, author, lecturer
Fink, Robert Steven lawyer, writer, educator
Finkelstein, Bernard lawyer
Fischman, Bernard D. lawyer
Fishbein, Peter Melvin lawyer
Fisher, Ann Bailen lawyer
Fisher, Harold Leonard lawyer, banker
Fisher, Herbert Franklin lawyer
Fisher, Robert I. lawyer
Fishman, Fred Norman lawyer
Fishman, Mitchell Steven lawyer
Flannery, Anne Catherine lawyer
Fleder, Robert Charles lawyer
Fleischer, Arthur, Jr. lawyer
Fleischman, Edward Hirsh lawyer
Fleishman, Wendy Ruth lawyer
Fleming, Peter Emmet, Jr. lawyer
Fletcher, Anthony L. lawyer
Fletcher, Raymond Russwald, Jr. lawyer
Flint, George Squire lawyer
Flom, Joseph Harold lawyer
Flowers, William Ellwood lawyer
Flumenbaum, Martin lawyer
Fodor, Susanna Serena lawyer
Fogg, Blaine Viles lawyer
Foley, Patrick Joseph lawyer
Fontana, Vincent Robert lawyer
Forstadt, Joseph Lawrence lawyer
Forster, Arnold lawyer, author
Fortenbaugh, Samuel Byrod, III lawyer
Foster, David Lee lawyer
Fox, Donald Thomas lawyer
Fox, Eleanor Mae Cohen lawyer, educator, writer
Fraidin, Stephen lawyer
Fraiman, Genevieve Lam lawyer
Franck, Thomas Martin law educator
Frank, Lloyd lawyer, chemical company executive
Frankel, Benjamin Harrison lawyer
Frankel, Marvin E. lawyer
Frankl, Kenneth Richard lawyer, real estate broker
Franklin, Blake Timothy lawyer
Freedman, Gerald M. lawyer
Freedman, Theodore Levy lawyer
Freilicher, Morton lawyer
French, John, III lawyer
Freund, Fred A. lawyer
Freund, James Coleman lawyer
Fried, Burton Theodore lawyer
Fried, Donald David lawyer
Fried, Walter Jay lawyer
Friedman, Alan Roy lawyer
Friedman, Bart lawyer
Friedman, John Maxwell, Jr. lawyer
Friedman, Robert Laurence lawyer
Friedman, Samuel Selig lawyer
Friedman, Stephen James lawyer
Friedman, Victor Stanley lawyer
Friedman, Wilbur Harvey lawyer
Frischling, Carl lawyer
Frost, William Lee lawyer
Fryer, Judith Dorothy lawyer
Fuhrer, Arthur K. lawyer
Fuld, James Jeffrey lawyer
Fuld, Stanley H. lawyer
Fullem, L. Robert lawyer
Futter, Victor lawyer
Fuzesi, Stephen, Jr. lawyer, communications executive
Gabay, Donald David lawyer
Gabel, Johannes Karl lawyer
Galant, Herbert Lewis lawyer
Gallagher, Terence Joseph lawyer
Gallantz, George Gerald lawyer
Galston, Clarence Elkus lawyer
Ganz, Howard L. lawyer
†Ganzi, Victor Frederick lawyer
Garance, Dominick (D. G. Garan) lawyer, author
Garber, Robert Edward lawyer, insurance company executive
Garfinkel, Barry Herbert lawyer
Garland, Sylvia Dillof lawyer
Garnett, Stanley Iredale, II lawyer, utility company executive
Gartner, Murray lawyer
Gassel, Philip Michael lawyer
†Geen, William John lawyer
Gelb, Joseph W. lawyer
Gelb, Judith Anne lawyer
Gelfman, Robert William lawyer
Genova, Joseph Steven lawyer
Geoghegan, Patricia lawyer
George, Beauford James, Jr. lawyer, educator
Gerard, Whitney Ian lawyer
Gerber, Robert Evan lawyer
Gerber, Roger Alan lawyer, business executive
Gerra, Ralph A., Jr. lawyer
†Gershuny, Donald Nevin lawyer
Gewirtz, Elliot lawyer
Giannetti, Thomas Leonard lawyer
Gibbs, L(ippman) Martin lawyer
Gilbert, Phil Edward, Jr. lawyer
Gill, E. Ann lawyer
Gillespie, George Joseph, III lawyer
Gilman, Charles Alan lawyer
Gilpatric, Roswell Leavitt lawyer
Ginsberg, Ernest lawyer, banker
Girden, Eugene Lawrence lawyer
Gitter, Max lawyer
Gladis, Jay lawyer
Glassman, Steven J. lawyer
Glekel, Jeffrey Ives lawyer
Glickstein, Steven lawyer
Goetz, Cecelia Helen lawyer, retired judge
Goetz, Maurice Harold lawyer
†Gold, Emanuel R. lawyer, state senator
Gold, Martin Elliot lawyer, educator
Gold, Simeon lawyer
Gold, Stuart Walter lawyer
Goldblatt, David Ira lawyer
Golden, Arthur F. lawyer
Golden, William Robert, Jr. lawyer
Goldfield, Alfred Sherman lawyer
Goldman, Charles Norton lawyer, corporation executive
Goldman, Donald Howard lawyer
Goldman, Lawrence Saul lawyer
†Goldman, Marvin Gerald lawyer
Goldschmid, Harvey Jerome law educator
Goldsmith, Donald Alan lawyer
Goldsmith, Lee Selig lawyer, physician
Goldstein, Alvin lawyer
Goldstein, Bernard Herbert lawyer
Goldstein, Charles Arthur lawyer
Goldstein, Howard Warren lawyer
Goldstein, Jonathan lawyer
Goldstein, Marcia Landweber lawyer
Goldstone, Steven F. lawyer
Gooch, Anthony Cushing lawyer
Goodale, James Campbell lawyer
Goodfriend, Herbert Jay lawyer
Goodhartz, Gerald law librarian
Goodkind, Louis William lawyer
Goodman, Gary A. lawyer
Goodridge, Allan D. lawyer
Goodwillie, Eugene William, Jr. lawyer
Goodwin, Bernard lawyer, executive, educator
Gordon, Michael Mackin lawyer
Gordon, Nicole Ann lawyer
Gould, Milton Samuel lawyer, business executive
Grad, Frank Paul lawyer
Graff, George L. lawyer
Graham, Jesse Japhet, II lawyer
Grant, Stephen Allen lawyer
Grashof, August Edward lawyer
Green, Robert S. lawyer
Greenawalt, Robert Kent lawyer
Greenawalt, William Sloan lawyer
Greenbaum, Maurice C. lawyer
Greenberg, Ira George lawyer
Greenberg, Jack lawyer
Greenberg, Joshua F. lawyer, educator
Greenberg, Ronald David law educator
Greenberger, Howard Leroy lawyer, educator
Greene, Bernard Harold lawyer
Greenfield, Jay lawyer
Greenman, Jane Friedlieb lawyer
Greer, Allen Curtis, II lawyer
Greer, James Alexander, II lawyer
Greig, Robert Thomson lawyer
Greilsheimer, James Gans lawyer
Groban, Robert Sidney, Jr. lawyer
Gropper, Allan Louis lawyer
Gross, Ernest Arnold lawyer
Gross, Steven Ross lawyer
Grossman, Dan S. lawyer
Grossman, Sanford lawyer
†Grubman, Allen J. lawyer
Gruenberger, Peter lawyer
Grumbach, George Jacques, Jr. lawyer
Grunewald, Raymond Bernhard lawyer
Gruson, Michael lawyer
Guth, Paul C. lawyer
†Gutman, Jeremiah Sheldon lawyer
Hackett, Kevin R. lawyer
Haffner, Alfred Loveland, Jr. lawyer
Haft, Marilyn Geisler lawyer
Hagendorn, William lawyer
Hager, Charles Read lawyer
Haggerty, Robert Henry lawyer
Haig, Robert Leighton lawyer
Haims, Bruce David lawyer
Haje, Peter Robert lawyer
Halberstam, Malvina legal educator, lawyer
Hall, John Herbert lawyer
Halliday, Joseph William lawyer
Halperin, Richard E. lawyer, holding company executive
Hamblen, L. Jane lawyer
Hamburg, Charles Bruce lawyer
Hamel, Rodolphe lawyer, pharmaceutical company executive
Hamm, David Bernard lawyer
Hammerling, Robert Charles lawyer
Hammerman, Stephen Lawrence lawyer, financial services company executive
Hammond, Steven Alan lawyer
Handelsman, Lawrence Marc lawyer
Handler, Arthur M. lawyer
Handler, Milton lawyer
Harbison, James Wesley, Jr. lawyer
Hardin, Adlai Stevenson, Jr. lawyer
Harley, Colin Emile lawyer
Harnett, Thomas Aquinas lawyer
Harper, Emery Walter lawyer
Harris, Allen lawyer, educator
Harris, Arlene lawyer
Harris, Ellen W. lawyer
Harris, Joel B(ruce) lawyer
Harrison, S. David lawyer
Hart, Kenneth Nelson lawyer
Hart, Robert M. lawyer
Hartzell, Andrew Cornelius, Jr. lawyer
Hauser, Rita Eleanore Abrams lawyer
Hawes, Douglas Wesson lawyer
Hawke, Roger Jewett lawyer
Hayden, Raymond Paul lawyer
Hayes, Gerald Joseph lawyer
Haynes, Jean Reed lawyer
Hazard, John Newbold retired law educator
Healy, Harold Harris, Jr. lawyer
Healy, Nicholas Joseph lawyer, educator
Hearn, George Henry lawyer, steamship corporate executive
Heckart, Robert Lee lawyer
Heine, Edward Joseph, Jr. lawyer
Heineman, Andrew David lawyer
Heisler, Stanley Dean lawyer
Hellawell, Robert law educator
Hellenbrand, Samuel Henry lawyer, diversified industry executive
Heller, Edwin lawyer
Heller, Robert Martin lawyer
Hellerstein, Alvin Kenneth lawyer
Hellerstein, Jerome Robert lawyer
Heming, Charles E. lawyer
Henderson, Donald Bernard, Jr. lawyer
Henderson, Harold Richard, Jr. lawyer, labor relations executive
Hendrickson, Robert Augustus lawyer
Henkin, Louis lawyer, law educator
Henry, Paul James lawyer, health care administrator
Herman, Kenneth Beaumont lawyer
Herold, Karl Guenter lawyer
Hersch, Dennis Steven lawyer
Hetherington, John Warner lawyer
Hewitt, Carl Herbert lawyer
Hiden, Robert Battaile, Jr. lawyer
Higginbotham, A. Leon, Jr. lawyer, educator
Higginson, James Jackson lawyer
Higgs, John H. lawyer
Highleyman, Samuel Locke, III lawyer
Hill, Alfred lawyer, educator
Hirsch, Barry lawyer
Hirsch, Jerome Seth lawyer
Hirschfeld, Michael lawyer
Hirshfield, Stuart lawyer
Hirshon, Sheldon Ira lawyer
Hirshowitz, Melvin Stephen lawyer
Hoblin, Philip J., Jr. securities lawyer
Hodes, Robert Bernard lawyer
Hoff, Jonathan M(orind) lawyer
Hoffman, John Ernest, Jr. retired lawyer
Hoffman, John Fletcher lawyer
Hoffman, Mathew lawyer
Hoffmann, Malcolm Arthur lawyer
Holderness, Algernon Sidney, Jr. lawyer
Holderness, G(eorge) Malcolm lawyer
Holman, Bud George lawyer
Holtzman, Alexander lawyer, consultant
Holtzmann, Howard Marshall lawyer, judge
Holtzschue, Karl Bressem lawyer, author, educator
†Hoover, James Lloyd law librarian, educator
Hopper, Walter Everett lawyer
Hornick, Robert Newton lawyer
Horowitz, Raymond J. lawyer
Hovdesven, Arne lawyer
Howe, Richard Rives lawyer
Howell, Wesley Grant, Jr. lawyer
Hruska, Alan J. lawyer
Hudspeth, Stephen Mason lawyer
Huettner, Richard Alfred lawyer
Hughes, Kevin Peter lawyer
Huhs, John I. lawyer
Hulbert, Richard Woodward lawyer
Hull, Philip Glasgow lawyer
Hunt, Franklin Griggs lawyer
Hupper, John Roscoe lawyer
Hurley, Geoffrey Kevin lawyer
Hurlock, James Bickford lawyer
Hyde, David Rowley lawyer
Hyman, Alan Barry lawyer
Hyman, Jerome Elliot lawyer
Iannuzzi, John Nicholas lawyer, author, educator
Idzik, Daniel Ronald lawyer
Ingram, Samuel William, Jr. lawyer
Insel, Michael S. lawyer
Iovenko, Michael lawyer
Isaacson, Allen Ira lawyer
Isquith, Fred Taylor lawyer
Issler, Harry lawyer
Ivanick, Carol W. Trencher lawyer
Jackson, Thomas Gene lawyer
Jackson, William Eldred lawyer
Jacob, Edwin J. lawyer
Jacob, Marvin Eugene lawyer
Jacobs, Albert Lionel, Jr. lawyer
Jacobs, Arnold Stephen lawyer
Jacobs, Jane Brand lawyer
Jacobs, Robert Alan lawyer
Jacobson, Gary Steven lawyer
Jacobson, Jerold Dennis lawyer
Jaffe, Alan Steven lawyer
Jaffin, Charles Leonard lawyer
Jakes, Peter H. lawyer
Jander, Klaus Heinrich lawyer
Janklow, Morton Lloyd lawyer, literary agent
Jánszky, Andrew Béla lawyer
Jarblum, William lawyer
Jassy, Everett Lewis lawyer
Javits, Eric Moses lawyer
Jefferies, Jack P. lawyer
Jessup, John Baker lawyer
Jeydel, Richard K. lawyer
Jinnett, Robert Jefferson lawyer
Joffe, Robert David lawyer
Johnson, James Gann, Jr. lawyer
Jones, Lucian Cox lawyer
Jones, Ronald David lawyer
Jones, William Kenneth law educator
Joseph, Gregory Paul lawyer
Joseph, L. Anthony, Jr. lawyer
Joseph, Leonard lawyer
Josephson, William Howard lawyer
Juceam, Robert E. lawyer
†Kaden, Ellen Oran lawyer, broadcasting corporation executive
Kaden, Lewis B. law educator
Kadet, Samuel lawyer
Kafin, Robert Joseph lawyer
Kahen, Harold I. lawyer
Kahn, Richard Dreyfus lawyer
Kailas, Leo George lawyer
Kalat, Peter Anthony lawyer
Kalish, Arthur lawyer
Kalish, Myron lawyer
Kals, Stephen A. lawyer
Kamin, Sherwin lawyer

Kaminer, Peter H. *lawyer*
Kaminsky, Arthur Charles *lawyer*
Kane, Daniel Hipwell *lawyer*
Kaplan, Carl Eliot *lawyer*
Kaplan, Joseph Solte *lawyer*
Kaplan, Lewis A. *lawyer*
Kaplan, Mark Norman *lawyer*
Kaplan, Peter James *lawyer*
Kaplan, Philip Thomas *lawyer*
Karasz, Peter *lawyer*
Karatz, William Warren *lawyer*
Karmel, Roberta S. *lawyer, educator*
Karotkin, Stephen K. *lawyer*
Kartiganer, Joseph *lawyer*
Kasa, Pamela Dorothy *lawyer*
Kasowitz, Marc Elliot *lawyer*
Katsh, Salem Michael *lawyer*
Katz, Gregory *lawyer*
Katz, Jerome Charles *lawyer*
Katz, Ronald S. *lawyer*
Katz, Stanley Nider *law history educator, association executive*
Kaufman, Arthur Stephen *lawyer*
Kaufman, Robert Max *lawyer*
Kaufmann, Jack *lawyer*
Kavaler, Thomas J. *lawyer*
Kaye, Stephen Rackow *lawyer*
Kazanjian, John Harold *lawyer*
Kean, Hamilton Fish *lawyer*
Keany, Sutton *lawyer*
Kenney, John Joseph *lawyer*
Keogh, Kevin *lawyer*
Kern, George Calvin, Jr. *lawyer*
Kern, Jerome H. *lawyer*
Kernochan, John Marshall *lawyer, educator*
Kessel, Mark *lawyer*
Kessler, Jeffrey L. *lawyer*
Kessler, Ralph Kenneth *lawyer, manufacturing company executive*
Kezsbom, Allen *lawyer*
Kheel, Theodore Woodrow *lawyer, labor arbitrator and mediator*
Kidd, John Edward *lawyer, corporate executive*
Kideckel, Arnold *lawyer*
Kill, Lawrence *lawyer*
Kimball, Richard Arthur, Jr. *lawyer*
King, Henry Lawrence *lawyer*
King, Lawrence Philip *lawyer, educator*
Kinney, Stephen Hoyt, Jr. *lawyer*
Kinzler, Thomas Benjamin *lawyer*
Kirby, John Joseph, Jr. *lawyer*
Kirschbaum, Myron *lawyer*
Kirschner, Marc Steven *lawyer*
Klaperman, Joel Simcha *lawyer*
Klein, Arnold Spencer *lawyer*
Klein, William, II *lawyer*
Kleinbard, Edward D. *lawyer*
Kleinberg, Norman Charles *lawyer*
Kline, Eugene Monroe *lawyer*
Klingsberg, David *lawyer*
Klink, Fredric J. *lawyer*
Knickerbocker, Daniel Candee, Jr. *legal educator*
Knight, Robert Huntington *lawyer, bank executive*
Knight, Townsend Jones *lawyer*
Knutson, David Harry *lawyer, banker*
Kobak, James Benedict, Jr. *lawyer, educator*
Kober, Jane *lawyer*
Kobrin, Lawrence Alan *lawyer*
Koegel, William Fisher *lawyer*
Koeltl, John George *lawyer*
Kolb, Daniel Francis *lawyer*
Kolbe, Karl William, Jr. *lawyer*
†Kolbert, Kathryn *lawyer, educator*
Komaroff, Stanley *lawyer*
Koob, Charles Edward *lawyer*
Koral, Alan M. *lawyer*
Kornberg, Alan William *lawyer*
Kornreich, Edward Scott *lawyer*
Korotkin, Michael Paul *lawyer*
Kostelanetz, Boris *lawyer*
Kourides, Peter Theologos *lawyer*
Kraemer, Lillian Elizabeth *lawyer*
Kramer, Alan Sharfsin *lawyer*
Kramer, George P. *lawyer*
Kramer, Joyce L. *lawyer*
Kramer, Morris Joseph *lawyer*
Kranwinkle, Conrad Douglas *lawyer*
Krasner, Daniel Walter *lawyer*
Kraus, Douglas M. *lawyer*
Kreitzman, Ralph J. *lawyer*
Krieger, Sanford *lawyer*
Krinsly, Stuart Z. *lawyer, manufacturing company executive*
Kroll, Arthur Herbert *lawyer, law educator*
Krouse, George Raymond, Jr. *lawyer*
Krupman, William Allan *lawyer*
Krupp, Fred *lawyer, environmental agency executive*
Kufeld, William Manuel *lawyer*
Kuh, Richard Henry *lawyer*
Kuklin, Anthony Bennett *lawyer*
Kumble, Steven Jay *lawyer*
Kunstler, William Moses *lawyer, educator, lecturer, author*
Kuntz, Lee Allan *lawyer*
Kuntz, William Francis, II *lawyer, educator*
Kurtyka, Ruthanne *lawyer*
Kurtz, Jerome *lawyer, educator*
Kury, Bernard Edward *lawyer*
Kurzweil, Harvey *lawyer*
LaBarre, Dennis W. *lawyer*
Lacey, Frederick Bernard *lawyer, former federal judge*
Lacovara, Philip Allen *lawyer*
Lacy, Robinson Burrell *lawyer*
Lambert, Paul Christopher *lawyer, former ambassador*
Lamia, Thomas Roger *lawyer*
Lanchner, Bertrand Martin *lawyer, advertising executive*
Land, David Potts *lawyer*
Landa, Howard Martin *lawyer, business executive*
Landau, Walter Loeber *lawyer*
Landes, Robert Nathan *lawyer*
Lane, Alvin S. *lawyer*
Lane, Arthur Alan *lawyer*
Lang, Robert Todd *lawyer*
Lange, Marvin Robert *lawyer*
Larkin, Leo Paul, Jr. *lawyer*
La Rossa, James M(ichael) *lawyer*
Larsen, Robert Dhu *lawyer*
Lascher, Alan Alfred *lawyer*
Lauer, Eliot *lawyer*
Laufer, Donald L. *lawyer*
Lavinsky, Larry Monroe *lawyer, consultant*
Lebow, Mark Denis *lawyer*
Lederer, Peter David *lawyer*
Lederman, Lawrence *lawyer, writer, educator*
Lee, David James *lawyer*
Lee, Jerome G. *lawyer*
Lee, Paul L. *lawyer*
LeFevre, David E. *lawyer, professional sports team executive*
Lefkowitz, Howard N. *lawyer*
Lefkowitz, Lawrence *lawyer*
Lefrak, Joseph Saul *lawyer, accountant*
Lehrer, Sander *lawyer*
Leichtling, Michael Alfred *lawyer*
Leisure, George Stanley, Jr. *lawyer*
Leland, Richard G. *lawyer*
Leness, George Crawford *lawyer*
Leonard, Edwin Deane *lawyer*
Lerner, Ralph E. *lawyer*
Lesch, Michael Oscar *lawyer*
Levie, Joseph Henry *lawyer*
Levien, Joy *corporate lawyer*
Levin, Ezra Gurion *lawyer*
Levin, Robert Daniel *lawyer*
Levine, Edward Leslie *lawyer*
Levine, Laurence William *lawyer*
Levine, Lawrence Steven *lawyer*
Levine, Mark Leonard *lawyer*
Levine, Robert Jay *lawyer*
Levine, Ronald Jay *lawyer*
Levison, Harold George *lawyer*
Levitan, David M(aurice) *lawyer, educator*
Levitan, James A. *lawyer*
Levitt, Daniel Philip *lawyer*
Levy, Herbert Monte *lawyer*
Levy, Joseph *lawyer*
Levy, Norma Berta *lawyer*
Levy, Stanley Herbert *lawyer*
Lewis, Albert B. *lawyer*
Lewis, Grant Stephen *lawyer*
Lewis, James Berton *law educator*
Lewis, Robert Charles *lawyer*
Lewyn, Thomas Mark *lawyer*
Lifland, William Thomas *lawyer*
Liftin, John Matthew *lawyer*
Liggio, Carl Donald *lawyer*
Lilley, Albert Frederick *lawyer*
Lillie, James Woodruff, Jr. *lawyer*
Liman, Arthur L. *lawyer*
Lindenbaum, Sandford Richard *lawyer*
Lindley, David Morrison *lawyer*
Lindsay, George Nelson *lawyer*
Lindsay, George Peter *lawyer*
Lindskog, David Richard *lawyer*
Linsenmeyer, John Michael *lawyer*
Lipton, Martin *lawyer*
Lipton, Robert Steven *lawyer*
Lochner, Philip Raymond, Jr. *lawyer*
Loengard, Richard Otto, Jr. *lawyer*
LoFrisco, Anthony F. *lawyer*
Logan, Francis Dummer *lawyer*
Logan, Kenneth R. *lawyer*
London, Martin *lawyer*
Longstreth, Bevis *lawyer*
Lorch, Ernest Henry *lawyer*
Lord, Herbert Mayhew *lawyer*
Lore, Martin Maxwell *lawyer*
Loss, Margaret Ruth *lawyer*
Lotwin, Stanford Gerald *lawyer*
Lowenfeld, Andreas Frank *legal educator, arbitrator*
Lowenfels, Fred M. *lawyer*
†Lowenfels, Lewis David *lawyer*
Lowenstein, Louis *legal educator*
Lowy, George Theodore *lawyer*
Lunding, Christopher Hanna *lawyer*
Lundquist, James Harold *lawyer*
Lupkin, Stanley Neil *lawyer*
Luria, Mary Mercer *lawyer*
Lurie, Alvin David *lawyer*
Lurie, William L. *lawyer, association executive*
Lusky, Louis *legal educator*
Lustenberger, Louis Charles, Jr. *lawyer*
Lustgarten, Ira Howard *lawyer*
Luther, James Howard *lawyer, retired pharmaceutical company executive*
Lutringer, Richard Emil *lawyer*
Lynn, Theodore Stanley *lawyer*
Lynton, Harold Stephen *lawyer*
Lyon, Carl Francis, Jr. *lawyer*
Macan, William Alexander, IV *lawyer*
MacCrate, Robert *lawyer*
Macioce, Frank Michael, Jr. *lawyer, financial services company executive*
Mack, Dennis Wayne *lawyer, textile company executive*
MacKinnon, John Alexander *lawyer*
MacRae, Cameron Farquhar, III *lawyer*
Madden, Donald Paul *lawyer*
Madden, John Joseph *lawyer*
Madsen, Stephen Stewart *lawyer*
Mahon, Arthur J. *lawyer*
Maidman, Richard Harvey Mortimer *lawyer*
Malina, Michael *lawyer*
Malkin, Peter Laurence *lawyer*
Maloney, Michael Patrick *lawyer, corporate executive*
Mamorsky, Jeffrey Dean *lawyer*
Mandelstam, Charles Lawrence *lawyer*
Maneker, Morton M. *lawyer*
Maney, Michael Mason *lawyer*
Manning, Jerome Alan *lawyer*
Manning, William Joseph *lawyer*
Mantle, Raymond Allan *lawyer*
Marcus, Barry Philip *lawyer*
Marcus, Eric Peter *lawyer*
Marcus, Leon Charles *lawyer*
Marcus, Norman *lawyer*
Marcusa, Fred Haye *lawyer*
Marden, John Newcomb *lawyer*
Mark, Jonathan I. *lawyer*
Marke, Julius Jay *law librarian, educator*
Marks, Theodore Lee *lawyer*
Marlin, Richard *lawyer*
Marshall, John Patrick *lawyer*
Marshall, Sheila Hermes *lawyer*
Martin, George J., Jr. *lawyer*
Martin, Malcolm Elliot *lawyer*
Martone, Patricia Ann *lawyer*
Marx, Owen Cox *lawyer*
Marzulli, John Anthony, Jr. *lawyer*
Mashberg, Gregg M. *lawyer*
Masin, Michael Terry *lawyer*
Masinter, Edgar Martin *lawyer*
Maskin, Arvin *lawyer*
Maslow, Will *lawyer, association executive*
Masters, Jon Joseph *lawyer*
Mathers, William Harris *lawyer*
Matteson, William Bleecker *lawyer*
Matthews, Edwin Spencer, Jr. *lawyer*
Maulsby, Allen Farish *lawyer*
Max, Herbert B. *lawyer*
Mayden, Barbara Mendel *lawyer*
Mayer, Theodore V.H. *lawyer*
Mayerson, Sandra Elaine *lawyer*
Mazza, Thomas Carmen *lawyer*
McBaine, John Neylan *lawyer*
McCabe, David Allen *lawyer*
McCaffrey, Carlyn Sundberg *lawyer*
Mc Cann, John Joseph *lawyer*
McCarthy, Bernard William *lawyer*
McClimon, Timothy John *lawyer*
McClung, Richard Goehring *lawyer*
McCormick, Hugh Thomas *lawyer*
McCulloch, Kenneth John *lawyer*
McDavid, William Henry *lawyer*
McDermott, Richard T. *lawyer, educator*
McDonald, Willis, IV *lawyer*
McDowell, Jay Hortenstine *lawyer*
McEnroe, John Patrick *lawyer*
McGahren, Richard George *lawyer*
McGanney, Thomas *lawyer*
McGinnis, John Oldham *lawyer, educator*
Mc Goldrick, John Gardiner *lawyer*
McGonigal, Richard M. *lawyer*
McGovern, Joseph W. *lawyer*
McGrath, Thomas J. *lawyer, writer, film producer*
McGunigle, Brian Edward *lawyer*
McHenry, Barnabas *lawyer*
†McLaughlin, Joseph *lawyer*
McLaughlin, Joseph Thomas *lawyer*
McLean, Edward Cochrane, Jr. *lawyer*
McMahon, Colleen *lawyer*
McMeen, Elmer Ellsworth, III *lawyer*
McNally, John Joseph *lawyer*
Mc Namara, J(ohn) Donald *lawyer, business executive*
Mc Nicol, Donald Edward *lawyer*
Mc Quade, Lawrence Carroll *lawyer, corporate executive*
Meaders, Paul Le Sourd *lawyer*
Medina, Standish Forde, Jr. *lawyer*
Medwick, Craig Steven *lawyer*
Mello, H. Joseph *lawyer*
Mendelsohn, Walter *lawyer*
Menton, Francis James, Jr. *lawyer*
Mercorella, Anthony J. *lawyer, former state supreme court justice*
Merow, John Edward *lawyer*
Mescon, Richard Alan *lawyer*
Mestres, Ricardo Angelo, Jr. *lawyer*
Meyer, Edward N. *lawyer*
Michaelson, Arthur M. *lawyer*
Michel, Clifford Lloyd *lawyer, investment executive*
Milgrim, Roger Michael *lawyer*
Millard, John Alden *lawyer*
Miller, Charles Hampton *lawyer*
Miller, David *lawyer, advertising executive*
Miller, Harvey R. *bankruptcy reorganization lawyer*
Miller, Lawrence Edward *lawyer*
Miller, Phebe Condict *lawyer, financial executive*
Miller, Richard Steven *lawyer*
Miller, Sam Scott *lawyer*
Millson, Rory Oliver *lawyer*
Millstein, Ira M. *lawyer, lecturer*
Minkel, Herbert Philip, Jr. *lawyer*
Minkowitz, Martin *lawyer, former state government official*
Mishkin, Edwin B. *lawyer*
Mishkin, Jeffrey Alan *lawyer*
Missan, Richard Sherman *lawyer*
Modlin, Howard S. *lawyer*
Moerdler, Charles Gerard *lawyer*
Moloney, Thomas Joseph *lawyer*
Monge, Jay Parry *lawyer*
Monroe, Kendyl Kurth *lawyer*
Montgomerie, Bruce Mitchell *lawyer*
Montgomery, Robert Humphrey, Jr. *lawyer*
Moore, Donald Francis *lawyer*
Moore, Franklin Hall, Jr. *lawyer*
Moore, John Joseph *lawyer*
Moore, Thomas R. *lawyer*
Moorhead, Thomas Burch *lawyer, pharmaceutical company executive*
Morgan, Frank Edward, II *lawyer*
Morgenthau, Robert Morris *lawyer*
Morris, Eugene Jerome *lawyer*
Mortimer, Peter Michael *lawyer*
Moskin, Morton *lawyer*
Moss, William John *lawyer*
Most, Jack Lawrence *lawyer, consultant*
Mottola, Gary F. *lawyer*
Mullen, Peter P. *lawyer*
Muller, Peter *lawyer, entertainment company executive, retail company executive, consultant*
Mulreany, Robert Henry *lawyer*
Mulvihill, Roger Denis *lawyer*
Mundheim, Robert Harry *law educator*
Murase, Jiro *lawyer*
Murphy, Arthur William *lawyer, educator*
Murphy, Daniel Hayes, II *lawyer*
Murray, Paul Brady *lawyer, banker*
Myerson, Toby Salter *lawyer*
Naftalis, Gary Philip *lawyer, educator*
Nance, Allan Taylor *lawyer*
Nash, Paul LeNoir *lawyer*
Nassau, Michael Jay *lawyer*
Nathan, Frederic Solis *lawyer*
Nee, Owen D., Jr. *lawyer*
Neidell, Martin H. *lawyer*
Nelson, Joni Lysett *lawyer, business executive*
Nemser, Earl Harold *lawyer*
Neuwirth, Alan James *lawyer*
Neveloff, Jay A. *lawyer*
Nevling, J. Kelley, Jr. *lawyer*
Newcomb, Danforth *lawyer*
Newcombe, George Michael *lawyer*
Newman, Fredric Samuel *lawyer, business executive*
Newman, Howard Neal *lawyer, educator*
Newman, Lawrence *lawyer*
Newman, Lawrence Walker *lawyer*
Newman, Norman *lawyer*
Newman, Thomas Rubin *lawyer*
Newton, Blake Tyler, III *lawyer*
Nicholls, Richard H. *lawyer*
Nimetz, Matthew *lawyer*
Nimkin, Bernard William *retired lawyer*
Nolan, Richard Edward *lawyer*
Nolan, Terrance Joseph, Jr. *lawyer*
Norfolk, William Ray *lawyer*
Nusbacher, Gloria W. *lawyer, partner*
Nusbaum, Jack Henry *lawyer*
Oberman, Michael Stewart *lawyer*
O'Brien, Donal Clare, Jr. *lawyer*
O'Brien, Edward Ignatius *lawyer, trade association executive*
O'Brien, Kevin J. *lawyer*
O'Brien, Timothy James *lawyer*
O'Connell, Christopher Patrick *lawyer*
O'Dea, Dennis Michael *lawyer*
Odell, Stuart Irwin *lawyer*
O'Donnell, John Logan *lawyer*
Oechler, Henry John, Jr. *lawyer*
O'Flinn, Peter Russell *lawyer*
Ogden, Alfred *lawyer*
O'Grady, John Joseph, III *lawyer*
O'Hara, Alfred Peck *lawyer*
Olick, Arthur Seymour *lawyer*
Olick, Philip Stewart *lawyer*
Oliensis, Sheldon *lawyer*
Olmstead, Clarence Walter, Jr. *lawyer*
O'Neil, John Joseph *lawyer*
O'Neil, Stephen Edward *lawyer, investor*
O'Neill, Daniel J. *lawyer*
Onufrak, Joseph J. *lawyer*
Oppenheimer, Martin J. *lawyer*
Orce, Kenneth W. *lawyer*
Orkin, Leonard *lawyer*
Ornitz, Richard Martin *lawyer, business executive*
O'Rorke, James Francis, Jr. *lawyer*
Osborn, Donald Robert *lawyer*
Osgood, Robert Mansfield *lawyer*
Osmond, Gordon Condie *lawyer, playwright*
Ostling, Paul James *lawyer*
Ostrager, Barry R. *lawyer*
O'Sullivan, Thomas J. *lawyer*
Ott, Gilbert Russell, Jr. *lawyer*
Oxman, David Craig *lawyer*
Pack, Leonard Brecher *lawyer*
Padilla, James Earl *lawyer*
Paisner, Bruce Lawrence *lawyer, television and film executive*
Paladino, Daniel R. *lawyer, beverage corporation executive*
Palladino, Vincent Neil *lawyer*
Palmieri, Victor Henry *lawyer, business executive*
Panken, Peter Michael *lawyer*
Papernik, Joel Ira *lawyer*
†Parent, Louise Marie *lawyer*
Parish, J. Michael *lawyer, writer*
Parker, Douglas Martin *lawyer*
Parkinson, Thomas Ignatius, Jr. *lawyer*
Parr, Ferdinand Van Siclen, Jr. *lawyer*
Parver, Jane W. *lawyer*
Patrikis, Ernest T. *lawyer*
Paul, Eve W. *lawyer*
Paul, James William *lawyer*
Pearsall, Otis Pratt *lawyer*
Pearson, John Edward *lawyer*
Peaslee, James M. *lawyer*
Peerce, Stuart Bernard *lawyer*
Peet, Charles D., Jr. *lawyer*
Pegram, John Braxton *lawyer*
Peloso, John Francis Xavier *lawyer*
Pelster, William C. *lawyer*
Pelz, Robert Leon *lawyer*
Pennoyer, Paul Geddes, Jr. *lawyer*
Pennoyer, Robert M. *lawyer*
Pepper, Allan Michael *lawyer*
Peppers, Jerry P. *lawyer*
Perell, Edward Andrew *lawyer*
Perkiel, Mitchel H. *lawyer*
Perkins, Roswell Burchard *lawyer*
Perlmuth, William Alan *lawyer*
Perrotta, Fioravante Gerald *lawyer*
Perschetz, Martin L. *lawyer*
Pershan, Richard Henry *lawyer*
Peters, Alton Emil *lawyer*
Peterson, Charles Gordon *retired lawyer*
Pettibone, Peter John *lawyer*
Pfeffer, David H. *lawyer*
Phillips, Anthony Francis *lawyer*
Phillips, Barnet, IV *lawyer*
Phillips, Charles Gorham *lawyer*
Pickholz, Marvin G. *lawyer*
Pierce, Morton Allen *lawyer*
Pierpoint, Powell *lawyer*
Pietrzak, Alfred Robert *lawyer*
Pike, Laurence Bruce *retired lawyer*
Pine, Granville Martin *lawyer*
Pitts, Thomas E. *lawyer*
Plant, David William *lawyer*
Polak, Vivian Louise *lawyer*
Polak, Werner L. *lawyer*
†Pollack, Stanley P. *lawyer*
Pollak, Martin Marshall *patent development company executive, lawyer*
Portnoy, Sara S. *lawyer*
Posen, Susan Orzack *lawyer*
Potter, Hamilton Fish, Jr. *lawyer, consultant, author*
Powell, James Henry *lawyer*
Powell, Richard Gordon *retired lawyer*
Powers, Elizabeth Whitmel *lawyer*
Preble, Laurence George *lawyer*
Preiskel, Barbara Scott *lawyer, association executive*
Prem, F. Herbert, Jr. *lawyer*
Prentice, Eugene Miles, III *lawyer*
Price, Robert *lawyer, media executive, investment banker*
Primps, William Guthrie *lawyer*
Prince, Kenneth Stephen *lawyer*
Provine, John C. *lawyer*
Puleo, Frank Charles *lawyer*
Purcell, James Lawrence *lawyer*
Putney, Paul William *lawyer*
Quaintance, Robert Forsyth, Jr. *lawyer*
Quale, Andrew Christopher, Jr. *lawyer*
Quinlan, Guy Christian *lawyer*
Quinn, Yvonne Susan *lawyer*
Raab, Sheldon *lawyer*
Rabb, Bruce *lawyer*
Rabb, Maxwell M. *lawyer, former ambassador*
Rabin, Jack *lawyer*
Rahm, David Alan *lawyer*
Rahm, Susan Berkman *lawyer*
Raisler, Kenneth Mark *lawyer*
Rakoff, Jed Saul *lawyer, author*
Ralli, Constantine Pandia *lawyer*
Rand, Harry Israel *lawyer*
Rand, William *lawyer, former state justice*
Rankin, Clyde Evan, III *lawyer*
Rapoport, Bernard Robert *lawyer*
Rappaport, Charles Owen *lawyer*
Raylesberg, Alan Ira *lawyer*
Redlich, Norman *lawyer*
Reibstein, Richard Jay *lawyer*
Reich, Larry Sam *lawyer*
Reich, Seymour David *lawyer, former fraternal organization executive*
Reich, Yaron Z. *lawyer*
Reid, John Phillip *law educator*
Reid, Sarah Layfield *lawyer*
Reilly, Edward Arthur *lawyer*
Reinhold, Richard Lawrence *lawyer*
Reinstein, Paul Michael *lawyer*
Reinthaler, Richard Walter *lawyer*
Reiss, Steven Alan *lawyer, law educator*
Relson, Morris *patent lawyer*
Rembar, Charles (Isaiah) *lawyer, writer*
Resor, Stanley Rogers *lawyer*

Reverdin, Bernard J. *lawyer*
Ribicoff, Abraham A. *lawyer, former senator*
Rice, Donald Sands *lawyer*
Rice, Joseph Lee, III *lawyer*
Rich, R(obert) Bruce *lawyer*
Richards, David Alan *lawyer*
Richardson, John Carroll *lawyer*
Richman, Martin Franklin *lawyer*
Rifkind, Robert S(inger) *lawyer*
Rifkind, Simon Hirsch *lawyer*
Ring, Renee E. *lawyer*
Ringel, Dean *lawyer*
Ringer, James Milton *lawyer*
Ritter, Robert Joseph *lawyer*
Rivers, Kenneth Jay *judicial administrator, consultant*
Roberts, Sidney I. *lawyer*
Robertson, Edwin David *lawyer*
Robinowitz, Stuart *lawyer*
Robinson, Barbara Paul *lawyer*
Robinson, Irwin Jay *lawyer*
Robinson, Lee Harris *lawyer*
Robinson, Marvin Stuart *lawyer*
Robinson, Stanley Daniel *lawyer*
Rodman, Leroy Eli *lawyer*
Rodriguez, Vincent Angel *lawyer*
Roessler, Ronald James *lawyer*
Rolfe, Ronald Stuart *lawyer*
Romans, John Niebrugge *lawyer*
Romney, Richard Bruce *lawyer*
Rooney, Paul C., Jr. *lawyer*
Rosdeitcher, Sidney S. *lawyer*
Rose, Milton Curtiss *lawyer*
Rosen, Richard Lewis *lawyer, real estate developer*
Rosenberg, Alan Stewart *lawyer*
Rosenberg, Jerome I. *lawyer*
Rosenberg, Maurice *lawyer, educator*
Rosenfeld, Arthur H. *lawyer, publisher*
Rosenfeld, Steven B. *lawyer*
Rosensaft, Menachem Zwi *lawyer, author, community activist*
Rosow, Stuart L. *lawyer*
Ross, Michael Aaron *lawyer*
Roth, Judith Shulman *lawyer*
Roth, Michael I. *lawyer, financial executive*
Roth, Paul Norman *lawyer*
Rothenberg, Peter Jay *lawyer*
Rothman, Bernard *lawyer*
Rothman, Henry Isaac *lawyer*
Rothman, Howard Joel *lawyer*
Rover, Edward Frank *lawyer*
Rovine, Arthur William *lawyer*
Rozel, Samuel Joseph *lawyer*
Rubenfeld, Stanley Irwin *lawyer*
Rubenstein, Joshua Seth *lawyer*
Rubin, Herbert *lawyer*
Rubin, Richard Allan *lawyer*
Rubin, Stephen Wayne *lawyer*
Rubino, Victor Joseph *law institute executive*
Rubinstein, Aaron *lawyer*
Rubinstein, Frederic Armand *lawyer*
Rudoff, Sheldon *lawyer, administrator religious organization*
Ruebhausen, Oscar Melick *lawyer*
Ruegger, Philip Theophil, III *lawyer*
Ruggiero, Thomas William *lawyer*
Rusmisel, Stephen R. *lawyer*
Russell, John St. Clair, Jr. *lawyer*
Russo, Gregory Thomas *lawyer*
Russo, Thomas Anthony *lawyer*
Ryan, J. Richard *lawyer*
Ryan, Michael Clifford *lawyer*
Sabel, Bradley Kent *lawyer*
Sabetta, John Carl *lawyer*
Sachs, David *lawyer*
Sack, Robert David *lawyer*
Sacks, Ira Stephen *lawyer*
Safer, Jay Gerald *lawyer*
Sahid, Joseph Robert *lawyer*
Saiman, Martin S. *lawyer*
†Salberg, Melvin *lawyer*
Sanders, Fredric M. *lawyer*
Sandler, Richard Jay *lawyer*
Sandler, Ross *law educator*
Sanger, Gail *lawyer*
Sargent, James Cunningham *lawyer*
Satine, Barry Roy *lawyer*
Saunders, Paul Christopher *lawyer*
Savrin, Louis *lawyer*
Schacht, Ronald Stuart *lawyer*
Schachter, Oscar *lawyer, educator, arbitrator*
Schade, Malcolm Robert *lawyer*
Schapiro, Donald *lawyer*
Schechter, Daniel Philip *lawyer*
Scheler, Brad Eric *lawyer*
Scher, Irving *lawyer*
Scher, Stanley Jules *lawyer*
Schewel, Stanford *lawyer*
Schirmeister, Charles F. *lawyer*
Schizer, Zevie Baruch *lawyer*
Schlesinger, Sanford Joel *lawyer*
Schmertz, Eric Joseph *lawyer, educator*
Schmolka, Leo Louis *law educator*
Schneider, Howard *lawyer*
Schneider, Willys Hope *lawyer*
Schneiderman, Irwin *lawyer*
Schreiber, Paul Solomon *lawyer*
Schreyer, Leslie John *lawyer*
Schroeder, Edmund R. *lawyer*
Schueller, Thomas George *lawyer*
Schulte, Stephen John *lawyer, educator*
Schumacher, Harry Richard *lawyer*
Schuur, Robert George *lawyer*
Schwab, Terrance Walter *lawyer*
Schwarcz, Steven Lance *lawyer*
Schwartz, Herbert Frederick *lawyer*
Schwartz, Marvin *lawyer*
Schwartz, Renee Gerstler *lawyer*
Schwartz, William *lawyer*
Schwarz, Melvin A. *lawyer*
Schwind, Michael Angelo *law educator*
Scribner, Richard Orestes *lawyer, securities firm executive*
Seaman, Robert Lee *lawyer*
Secunda, Don Elliott *lawyer, realtor*
Sederbaum, Arthur David *lawyer*
Segall, Harold Abraham *lawyer*
Seidler, Norman Howard *lawyer*
Seifert, Thomas Lloyd *lawyer*
Seigel, Stuart Evan *lawyer*
Seltzer, Richard C. *lawyer*
Selver, Paul Darryl *lawyer*
Senn, Laurence Vaughn, Jr. *lawyer*
Senzel, Martin Lee *lawyer*
Serbaroli, Francis J. *lawyer, educator, writer*
Serota, Susan Perlstadt *lawyer*
Setrakian, Berge *lawyer*
Settle, William Sydnor *lawyer*
Severs, Charles A., III *lawyer*
Seward, George Chester *lawyer*
Sexton, John Edward *lawyer, educator*
Sexton, Richard *lawyer, diversified manufacturing company executive*
Shanman, James Alan *lawyer*
Shapiro, George M. *lawyer*
Shapiro, Howard Alan *lawyer*
Shapiro, Isaac *lawyer*
Shapiro, Ivan *lawyer*
Shapiro, Jerome Gerson *lawyer*
Sharpe, Jean Elizabeth *lawyer*
Shaughnessy, James Michael *lawyer*
†Shaw, L. Edward, Jr. *lawyer*
Shays, Rona Joyce *lawyer*
Shea, Edward Emmett *lawyer, educator, author*
Shea, James William *lawyer*
Sheehan, Robert W. *lawyer*
Shelby, Jerome *lawyer*
Shepard, Robert M. *lawyer, investment banker, engineer*
Sherman, Randolph S. *lawyer*
Sherman, Saul Lawrence *lawyer, government official*
Shientag, Florence Perlow *lawyer*
Shimer, Zachary *lawyer*
Shorter, James Russell, Jr. *lawyer*
Shoss, Cynthia Renée *lawyer*
Shupack, Paul Martin *law educator*
Sidamon-Eristoff, Constantine *lawyer*
Siegel, Charles *lawyer, investment banking and brokerage executive*
Siegel, Jeffrey Norton *lawyer*
Siegel, Martin Jay *lawyer, investment advisor*
Siegel, Stanley *lawyer, educator*
Silberberg, Richard Howard *lawyer*
Silberman, John Alan *lawyer*
Silkenat, James Robert *lawyer*
Silleck, Harry Garrison *lawyer*
Silverberg, Michael Joel *lawyer*
Silverman, Arthur Charles *lawyer*
Silverman, Moses *lawyer*
Silverman, Samuel Joshua *lawyer*
Silvers, Eileen S. *lawyer*
Simon, Robert G. *lawyer*
Simone, Joseph R. *lawyer*
Simons, Albert, III *lawyer*
Sinsheimer, Warren Jack *lawyer*
Siphron, Joseph Rider *lawyer*
Sisk, Robert Joseph *lawyer*
†Siskind, Arthur *lawyer, director*
Siskind, Donald Henry *lawyer*
Sitrick, James Baker *lawyer*
Sive, David *lawyer*
Skigen, Patricia Sue *lawyer*
Skirnick, Robert Andrew *lawyer*
Sklaren, Cary Stewart *lawyer*
Slain, John Joseph *legal educator*
Slonaker, Norman Dale *lawyer*
Small, Jeffrey *lawyer, law educator*
Small, Jonathan Andrew *lawyer*
Smalley, David Vincent *lawyer*
Smart, L(ouis) Edwin, Jr. *lawyer, business executive*
Smith, Bradley Youle *lawyer*
Smith, Charles Buchanan *lawyer*
Smith, Edward Paul, Jr. *lawyer*
Smith, R. Evan *lawyer*
Smith, Robert Everett *lawyer*
Smith, Stuart A. *lawyer*
Smith, Vincent Milton *lawyer*
Snitow, Charles *lawyer*
Soden, Paul Anthony *lawyer*
Solinger, David Morris *lawyer*
Solomon, Joseph *lawyer*
Songster, John Hugh *legal administrator*
Sorensen, Theodore Chaikin *lawyer, former special counsel to President of U.S.*
Sorkin, Laurence Truman *lawyer*
Sovern, Michael Ira *law educator*
Soyster, Margaret Blair *lawyer*
Spatt, Robert Edward *lawyer*
Spear, Harvey M. *lawyer*
Speiran, Edward Patrick *lawyer*
Sperling, Allan George *lawyer*
Spivack, Gordon Bernard *lawyer, lecturer*
Spizzirri, Richard Dominic *lawyer*
†Squire, Walter Charles *lawyer*
Stanger, Abraham M. *lawyer*
Stein, Stephen William *lawyer*
Steinberg, Howard E. *lawyer, holding company executive*
Steiner, Lee Nathan *lawyer*
Stephenson, Alan Clements *lawyer*
Stergios, Peter Doe *lawyer*
Stern, Joseph A. *lawyer*
Stern, Lewis Arthur *lawyer*
Sternman, Joel W. *lawyer*
Steuer, Richard Marc *lawyer*
Stevenson, Justin Jason, III *lawyer*
Stever, Donald Winfred *lawyer*
Stewart, Charles Evan *lawyer*
Stewart, Duncan James *lawyer*
Stewart, Richard Burleson *lawyer, educator*
Steyer, Roy Henry *retired lawyer*
Stocker, Jule E(lias) *lawyer*
Stoll, Neal Richard *lawyer*
Stone, David Philip *lawyer*
Stone, Merrill Brent *lawyer*
Storette, Ronald Frank *lawyer*
Stratton, Walter Love *lawyer*
Straub, Chester John *lawyer*
Strauber, Donald I. *lawyer*
Straus, Alan Gordon *lawyer*
Strauss, Audrey *lawyer*
Strauss, Peter L(ester) *law educator*
Strickon, Harvey Alan *lawyer*
Strom, Milton Gary *lawyer*
Strossen, Nadine *law educator, human rights activist*
Strum, Jay Gerson *lawyer*
Strupp, David John *lawyer*
Struve, Guy Miller *lawyer*
Sugarman, Irwin J. *lawyer*
Sugarman, Robert Gary *lawyer*
Sulger, Francis Xavier *lawyer*
Sussman, Alexander Ralph *lawyer*
Sweeney, Thomas Joseph, Jr. *lawyer*
Symmers, William Garth *international maritime lawyer*
Szabad, George Michael *lawyer, former mayor*
Tallackson, Jeffrey Stephen *lawyer*
Taylor, John Chestnut, III *lawyer*
Taylor, Richard Trelore *retired lawyer*
Taylor, Telford *lawyer, educator*
Teclaff, Ludwik Andrzej *law educator, consultant, author, lawyer*
Tehan, John Bashir *lawyer*
Teiman, Richard B. *lawyer*
Tengi, Frank R. *lawyer, insurance company executive*
Tenney, Dudley Bradstreet *lawyer*
Terrell, J. Anthony *lawyer*
Terry, Frederick Arthur, Jr. *lawyer*
Terry, James Joseph, Jr. *lawyer*
Testa, Michael Harold *lawyer*
Thackeray, Jonathan E. *lawyer*
Thal, Steven Henry *lawyer*
Thalacker, Arbie Robert *lawyer*
Thoman, Mark *lawyer*
Thomas, Robert Morton, Jr. *lawyer*
Thomas, Roger Warren *lawyer*
Thompson, Robert L., Jr. *lawyer*
Thornton, John Vincent *lawyer, educator*
Thoyer, Judith Reinhardt *lawyer*
Tillinghast, David Rollhaus *lawyer*
Todd, Ronald Gary *lawyer*
Toepke, Utz Peter *lawyer*
Tondel, Lawrence Chapman *lawyer*
Tortoriello, Robert Laurence *lawyer*
†Tracy, Janet Ruth *legal educator, librarian*
Tramontine, John O. *lawyer*
Traub, Richard Kenneth *lawyer*
Traum, Jerome S. *lawyer*
Trost, J. Ronald *lawyer*
Trubin, John *lawyer*
Trueheart, Harry Parker, III *lawyer*
Tuck, Edward Hallam *lawyer*
Tulchin, David Bruce *lawyer*
Tung, Ko-Yung *lawyer*
Turner, E. Deane *lawyer*
Tyler, Harold Russell, Jr. *lawyer, former government official*
Udell, Richard *lawyer*
Ufford, Charles Wilbur, Jr. *lawyer*
Ulrich, Theodore Albert *lawyer*
Underberg, Mark Alan *lawyer*
Unger, Ronald Lawrence *lawyer*
Urowsky, Richard J. *lawyer*
Vance, Andrew Peter *lawyer*
Vance, Cyrus Roberts *lawyer, former government official*
Van Gundy, Gregory Frank *lawyer*
Varet, Michael A. *lawyer*
Vega, Matias Alfonso *lawyer*
Versfelt, David Scott *lawyer*
Victor, A. Paul *lawyer*
Viener, John D. *lawyer*
Vig, Vernon Edward *lawyer*
Vogel, Eugene L. *lawyer*
Volckhausen, William Alexander *lawyer, banker*
Volk, Stephen Richard *lawyer*
Volpi, Walter Mark *lawyer, diversified company executive*
von Mehren, Robert Brandt *lawyer*
Wachtel, Harry H. *lawyer, chain store executive*
Wachtel, Norman Jay *lawyer*
Wade, George Joseph *lawyer*
Wadsworth, Dyer Seymour *lawyer*
Wailand, George *lawyer*
Wainwright, Carroll Livingston, Jr. *lawyer*
Waks, Jay Warren *lawyer*
Waksman, Ted Stewart *lawyer*
Wald, Bernard Joseph *lawyer*
Wales, Gwynne Huntington *lawyer*
Walker, Charles R., III *lawyer*
Walker, John Lockwood *lawyer*
Walker, Mark A. *lawyer*
†Wallace, Edward Corbett *lawyer*
Wallace, Walter C. *lawyer, government official*
Wallach, Eric Jean *lawyer*
Wallance, Gregory J. *lawyer*
Walpin, Gerald *lawyer*
Walsh, Kevin A. *lawyer*
Warden, John L. *lawyer*
Warhaftig, Solomon L. *lawyer*
Warner, Edward Waide, Jr. *lawyer*
Warren, Irwin Howard *lawyer*
Warren, William Bradford *lawyer*
Warren, William Clements *lawyer, educator*
Warshauer, Irene Conrad *lawyer*
Washburn, David Thacher *lawyer*
Watson, John King, Jr. *lawyer*
Watson, Solomon Brown, IV *lawyer, business executive*
Wattman, Malcolm Peter *lawyer*
Watts, David Eide *lawyer*
Wechsler, Herbert *emeritus legal educator*
Weil, Gilbert Harry *lawyer*
Weil, Peter Henry *lawyer*
Weinberg, Herschel Mayer *lawyer*
Weinberg, Jeffrey J. *lawyer*
Weinberger, Harold Paul *lawyer*
Weiner, Earl David *lawyer*
Weiner, Stephen Arthur *lawyer*
Weinschel, Alan Jay *lawyer*
Weinstein, Mark Michael *lawyer*
Weinstein, Ruth Joseph *lawyer*
Weinstock, Leonard *lawyer*
Weir, Peter Frank *lawyer*
Weiss, George C. *lawyer*
Weiss, Marvin *lawyer*
†Weiss, Melvyn I. *lawyer*
Weiswasser, Stephen Anthony *lawyer, broadcast executive*
Weld, Jonathan Minot *lawyer*
Welikson, Jeffrey Alan *lawyer*
Welles, James Bell, Jr. *lawyer*
Wellington, Harry Hillel *lawyer, educator*
Wemple, William *lawyer*
Wendel, Martin *lawyer*
Wender, Ira Tensard *lawyer*
Werner, Robert L. *lawyer*
Wesely, Edwin Joseph *lawyer*
West, Stephen Kingsbury *lawyer*
†Westin, David Lawrence *lawyer*
Wetzler, Monte Edwin *lawyer*
Weyher, Harry Frederick *lawyer*
Whelan, Stephen Thomas *lawyer*
White, Harry Edward, Jr. *lawyer*
White, Thomas Edward *lawyer*
Whitworth, John Harvey, Jr. *lawyer*
Whoriskey, Robert Donald *lawyer*
Wickes, R(ichard) Paul *lawyer*
Wilcox, John Caven *lawyer, corporate consultant*
Wildes, Leon *lawyer, educator*
Wilkinson, John Hart *lawyer*
Williams, Anthony *lawyer*
Williams, Lowell Craig *lawyer, employee relations executive*
Williams, Omer S. J. *lawyer*
Williams, Peter Whitridge *lawyer*
Williams, Thomas Allison *lawyer*
Williams, Vaughn Charles *lawyer*
Williamson, Douglas Franklin, Jr. *lawyer*
Willis, Everett Irving *lawyer*
Willis, William Ervin *lawyer*
Wilson, Paul Holliday, Jr. *lawyer*
Wilson, Thomas William *lawyer*
Windels, Paul, Jr. *lawyer*
Winfield, Richard Neill *lawyer*
Wing, John Russell *lawyer*
Winger, Ralph O. *lawyer*
Winterer, Philip Steele *lawyer*
Wise, Robert F., Jr. *lawyer*
Wisehart, Arthur McKee *lawyer*
Woglom, Eric Cooke *lawyer*
Wohl, Ronald Gene *lawyer*
Wolf, Gary Wickert *lawyer*
Wolfe, James Ronald *lawyer*
Wolff, Jesse David *lawyer*
Wolff, Kurt Jakob *lawyer*
Wolff, Sanford Irving *lawyer*
Wolfson, Michael George *lawyer*
Wolkoff, Eugene Arnold *lawyer*
Wolowitz, Steven *lawyer*
Wolson, Craig Alan *lawyer*
Woodbury, Thomas Bowring, II *lawyer, public utility executive*
Worenklein, Jacob Joshua *lawyer*
Worley, Robert William, Jr. *lawyer*
Wragg, Laishley Palmer, Jr. *lawyer*
Wray, Cecil, Jr. *lawyer*
Wright, P(aul) Bruce *lawyer*
Wulf, Melvin Lawrence *lawyer*
Wyckoff, Edward Lisk, Jr. *lawyer*
Wyser-Pratte, John Michael *lawyer*
Yanowitch, Michael H. *lawyer*
Yassky, Lester *lawyer, bank executive*
Yerman, Fredric Warren *lawyer*
York, Stephen Stanier *lawyer*
Young, John Edward *lawyer*
Young, Nancy *lawyer*
Youngwood, Alfred Donald *lawyer*
Zabel, William David *lawyer*
Zedrosser, Joseph John *lawyer*
Zerin, Steven David *lawyer*
Ziegler, Henry Steinway *lawyer*
Ziegler, Michael Lewis *lawyer*
Ziegler, Richard Ferdinand *lawyer*
Ziegler, William Alexander *lawyer*
Zifchak, William C. *lawyer*
Zimand, Harvey Folks *lawyer*
Zimmett, Mark Paul *lawyer*
Zirin, James David *lawyer*
Zoeller, Donald J. *lawyer*
Zoogman, Nicholas Jay *lawyer*
Zuckerman, Mitchell *lawyer, art auction firm executive*
Zweibel, Joel Burton *lawyer*
Zweig, Michael Philip *lawyer*
Zylberberg, Abraham Lieb *lawyer*

Niagara Falls
Anton, Ronald David *lawyer*

Oneida
Matthews, William D(oty) *lawyer, consumer products manufacturing company executive*

Orchard Park
Sullivan, Mortimer Allen, Jr. *lawyer*

Ossining
Daly, William Joseph *lawyer*
Frisch, Harry David *lawyer, consultant*

Oyster Bay
Robinson, Edward T., III *lawyer*

Pearl River
Meyer, Irwin Stephan *lawyer, accountant*

Pelham
Calamari, John Daniel *retired law educator*
Freidberg, Sidney *lawyer, real estate development company executive, author*

Pittsford
Kieffer, James Milton *lawyer*
Marticelli, Joseph John *lawyer, editor*

Pleasantville
Ahrensfeld, Thomas Frederick *lawyer*
†Barnett, Charles E. *lawyer*

Port Washington
Read, Frederick Wilson, Jr. *lawyer, educator*

Poughkeepsie
Brenner, Marshall Leib *lawyer*
Dolan, Thomas Joseph *lawyer*
McEnroe, Caroline Ann *legal assistant*
Millman, Jode Susan *lawyer*
Ostertag, Robert Louis *lawyer*

Pound Ridge
Bright, Craig Bartley *lawyer*

Purchase
Guedry, James Walter *lawyer, paper corporation executive*
Joyce, Joseph James *lawyer, food products executive*
Kelly, Edmund Joseph *lawyer, investment banker*
McKenna, Matthew Morgan *lawyer*
Melican, James Patrick, Jr. *lawyer*
Wallach, Ira David *lawyer, business executive*
Wilderotter, James Arthur *lawyer*

Quogue
Moss, Ronald Jay *lawyer, former state official, former advertising executive*

Rhinebeck
Kohn, Henry *lawyer*

Richmond Hill
Scheich, John F. *lawyer*

Riverdale
Phocas, George John *international lawyer, business executive*

Rochester
Braunsdorf, Paul Raymond *lawyer*
Buckley, Michael Francis *lawyer*
Clement, Thomas Earl *lawyer*
Donovan, Kreag *lawyer*
Doyle, Justin P *lawyer*
Fischer, Richard Samuel *lawyer*
Fox, Edward Hanton *lawyer*

George, Richard Neill lawyer
Goldman, Joel J. lawyer
†Gootnick, Margery Fischbein lawyer
Gumaer, Elliott Wilder, Jr. lawyer
Hampson, Thomas Meredith lawyer
Harris, Wayne Manley lawyer
Hoffberg, David Lawrence lawyer
Holmes, Jay Thorpe lawyer
†Hood, John B. lawyer
Hughey, Richard Kohlman lawyer, legal publisher
Kunkel, David Nelson lawyer
Kurland, Harold Arthur lawyer
Law, Michael R. lawyer
Lundback, Staffan Bengt Gunnar lawyer
McCrory, John Brooks retired lawyer
†Morrison, Patrice B. lawyer
Palermo, Anthony Robert lawyer
Paley, Gerald Larry lawyer
Parsons, George Raymond, Jr. lawyer
Reed, James Alexander, Jr. lawyer
Robfogel, Susan Salitan lawyer
Rosenbaum, Richard Merrill lawyer
Schumacher, Jon Lee lawyer
Scutt, Robert Carl lawyer
Smith, John Stuart lawyer
Stewart, Sue Stern lawyer
Stonehill, Eric lawyer
Tomaino, Michael Thomas lawyer
Trubek, Josephine Susan lawyer
†Turri, Joseph A. lawyer
Tyler, John Randolph, Jr. lawyer
Underberg, Alan J. lawyer
†Van Graafeiland, Gary P. lawyer
Waite, Stephen Holden lawyer
Wild, Robert Warren lawyer
Wilkens, Beth Ela lawyer
Willett, Thomas Edward lawyer
Witmer, George Robert, Jr. lawyer

Rockville Centre
Halliday, Walter John lawyer

Rome
Griffith, Emlyn Irving lawyer

Rye
Flanagan, Eugene John Thomas retired lawyer
Lobl, Herbert Max lawyer

Rye Brook
Cammaker, Sheldon Ira lawyer

Saratoga Springs
Aldrich, Alexander lawyer

Scarsdale
Hoffman, Richard M. lawyer
Howard, John Brigham lawyer, foundation executive
Wertheimer, Sydney Bernard lawyer

Schenectady
Taub, Eli Irwin lawyer, arbitrator

Schoharie
Duncombe, Raynor Bailey lawyer

Silver Bay
Parlin, Charles C., Jr. retired lawyer

Smithtown
Pruzansky, Joshua Murdock lawyer

Southold
Mitchell, Robert Everitt lawyer

Syracuse
Baldwin, Robert Frederick, Jr. lawyer
Barclay, H(ugh) Douglas lawyer, former state senator
Beeching, Charles Train, Jr. lawyer
Cirando, John Anthony lawyer
DiLorenzo, Louis Patrick lawyer
Ferguson, Tracy Heiman lawyer, educational administrator
Fitzpatrick, James David lawyer
Fraser, Henry S. lawyer
Gaal, John lawyer
Hayes, David Michael lawyer
Heberlig, Harold Dean, Jr. lawyer
Herzog, Peter Emilius legal educator
Hole, Richard Douglas lawyer
King, Chester Harding, Jr. lawyer
Kopp, Robert Walter lawyer
Lawton, Joseph J., Jr. lawyer
Moses, Robert Edward lawyer
Murray, Raymond William, Jr. lawyer
Pellow, David Matthew lawyer
Shattuck, George Clement lawyer
Taylor, Richard Fred, Jr. lawyer
Terry, John Hart lawyer, former utility company executive, former congressman
Wiecek, William Michael law educator

Tarrytown
Oelbaum, Harold lawyer, corporate executive

Troy
Jones, E. Stewart, Jr. lawyer

Tuxedo Park
Brown, Walston Shepard lawyer

Uniondale
Brown, Kenneth Lloyd lawyer
Kress, Heather Gabrielle lawyer
Pierce, Stanley lawyer
Savino, William M. lawyer
Shapiro, Barry Robert lawyer
Wright, Franklin Leatherbury, Jr. lawyer, banker

Valley Stream
Blakeman, Royal Edwin lawyer

Van Hornesville
Young, Richard lawyer

Wainscott
Wainwright, Stuyvesant, II lawyer

Wantagh
Mur, Raphael lawyer, retired aerospace manufacturing executive

West Hempstead
Klebanoff, Stanley Milton lawyer

White Plains
†Alin, Robert David lawyer
Berlin, Alan Daniel lawyer, international energy and legal consultant
†Burke, Raymond F. lawyer
Carey, John lawyer, judge
Feldman, Jay Newman lawyer, telecommunications executive
Gjertsen, O. Gerard lawyer
Godofsky, Stanley lawyer
†Graham, Lawrence Otis lawyer, writer, television personality
†Grayson, Richard Steven (Lord Eynsford) international legal and political management consultant, foreign correspondent
Jensen, Eric Finn lawyer
Johnson, Daniel Robert lawyer
McQuaid, John G. lawyer
Older, Jack Stanley lawyer
Payson, Martin Fred lawyer
Rosenberg, Michael lawyer
Stein, Ralph Michael lawyer, educator
Teitell, Conrad Laurence lawyer, author
Triffin, Nicholas law librarian, law educator
Turley, James Anthony, Jr. lawyer
Westerman, Gayl Shaw law educator

Wolcott
Bartlett, Cody Blake lawyer, educator

Woodbury
Lemle, Robert Spencer lawyer

Woodmere
Bobroff, Harold lawyer
Raab, Ira Jerry lawyer

Yorktown Heights
Samalin, Edwin lawyer, educator

NORTH CAROLINA

Asheville
Baldwin, Garza, Jr. lawyer, manufacturing company executive
Bissette, Winston Louis, Jr. lawyer, mayor
Davis, Roy Walton, Jr. lawyer
†Hyde, Herbert Lee lawyer
Johnston, John Devereaux, Jr. law educator

Black Mountain
Pinkerton, Linda F. lawyer

Buies Creek
Davis, Ferd Leary, Jr. law educator, lawyer, consultant

Carthage
Benade, Leo Edward lawyer, retired army officer

Chapel Hill
Broun, Kenneth Stanley lawyer, educator
Clifford, Donald Francis, Jr. law educator
†Gasaway, Laura Nell law librarian, educator
Gressman, Eugene lawyer
Haskell, Paul Gershon law educator
Lawrence, David Michael lawyer, educator
Loeb, Ben Fohl, Jr. lawyer, educator
Oliver, Mary Wilhelmina law librarian, educator
Powell, Burnele Venable law educator
Sharpless, Richard Kennedy lawyer

Charlotte
Ayscue, Edwin Osborne, Jr. lawyer
Buchan, Jonathan Edward, Jr. lawyer
Clodfelter, Daniel Gray lawyer
Cogdell, Joe Bennett, Jr. lawyer
Dagenhart, Larry Jones lawyer
Davis, William Maxie, Jr. lawyer
†Ferguson, James Elliot, II lawyer
Grier, Joseph Williamson, Jr. lawyer
Griffith, Steve Campbell, Jr. lawyer
Hanna, George Verner, III lawyer
Helms, Fred Bryan lawyer
McBryde, Neill Gregory lawyer
McConnell, David Moffatt lawyer
†Norwood, Philip Weltner lawyer
Orsbon, Richard Anthony lawyer
Raper, William Cranford lawyer
Taylor, David Brooke lawyer, banker
Thigpen, Richard Elton, Jr. lawyer
Ubell, Donald Paul lawyer
Van Allen, William Kent lawyer
Vinroot, Richard Allen lawyer, mayor of Charlotte, North Carolina
Walker, Clarence Wesley lawyer
Walls, George Rodney lawyer
†Winner, Leslie Jane lawyer
Woolard, William Leon lawyer, electrical distributing company executive

Durham
Chambers, Julius LeVonne lawyer
Christie, George Custis lawyer, educator, author
Danner, Richard Allen law educator, dean
Demott, Deborah Ann lawyer, educator
†Gulley, Wilbur Paul lawyer, mayor
Havighurst, Clark Canfield law educator
Horowitz, Donald Leonard lawyer, educator, researcher, political scientist, arbitrator
Kirk-Duggan, Michael Allan law and computer sciences educator emeritus
Lange, David L. law educator
Markham, Charles Buchanan lawyer
Maxwell, Richard Callender lawyer, educator
McMahon, John Alexander lawyer, educator
Robertson, Horace Bascomb, Jr. law educator
Rowe, Thomas Dudley, Jr. legal educator
Shimm, Melvin Gerald law educator
Van Alstyne, William Warner law educator
Warren, David Grant lawyer, educator

Gastonia
Alala, Joseph Basil, Jr. lawyer, accountant
Stott, Grady Bernell lawyer

Gibsonville
Foster, C(harles) Allen lawyer

Greensboro
Davis, Herbert Owen lawyer
Floyd, Jack William lawyer
Gumbiner, Kenneth Jay lawyer
Harllee, JoAnn Towery lawyer, educator
Hopkins, John David lawyer
Hunter, Bynum Merritt lawyer
Koonce, Neil Wright lawyer
†Martin, William Nelson lawyer
McGinn, Max Daniel lawyer
Melvin, Charles Edward, Jr. lawyer
Moore, Beverly Cooper lawyer
†Rowlenson, Richard Charles lawyer
St. George, Nicholas James lawyer, manufactured housing company executive
Schell, Braxton lawyer
Smith, John McNeill, Jr. lawyer
Smith, Lanty L(loyd) lawyer, business executive

Hickory
Ingle, John David lawyer

High Point
Sheahan, Robert Emmett lawyer, management employment and environment law consultant

Horse Shoe
Howell, George Washington lawyer, consultant

Morganton
Simpson, Daniel Reid lawyer

New Bern
Kellum, Norman Bryant, Jr. lawyer
Skipper, Nathan Richard, Jr. lawyer

Raleigh
Andrews, William Parker, Jr. lawyer
Carlton, Alfred Pershing, Jr. lawyer
Case, Charles Dixon lawyer
Dannelly, William D. lawyer
Davis, Egbert Lawrence, III lawyer
Eason, Joseph W. lawyer
Edwards, Charles Archibald lawyer
Ellis, Lester Neal, Jr. lawyer
Foley, Peter Michael lawyer
Jordan, John Richard, Jr. lawyer
Joyner, Walton Kitchin lawyer
Maupin, Armistead Jones lawyer
†Miller, R. Bradley lawyer, state legislator
Miller, Robert James lawyer
Patterson, William S. lawyer
Powell, Durwood Royce lawyer
Poyner, James Marion lawyer
Ragsdale, George Robinson lawyer
Roach, Wesley Linville lawyer, insurance executive
Sanford, Terry lawyer, former U.S. senator, former governor, former university president
Suhr, Paul Augustine lawyer

Rocky Mount
†Cooper, Roy Asberry, III lawyer

Salisbury
Trexler, Wynn Ridenhour paralegal

Sanford
Raisig, Paul Jones, Jr. lawyer

Tabor City
Jorgensen, Ralph Gubler lawyer

Tarboro
Hopkins, Grover Prevatte lawyer

Tryon
Stinson, George Arthur lawyer, former steel company executive

Williamston
Cowen, Robert Henry lawyer

Wilson
Herring, Jerone Carson lawyer, bank executive

Winston-Salem
Barnhardt, Zeb Elonzo, Jr. lawyer

Winston Salem
Benfield, Marion Wilson, Jr. lawyer, educator
Blynn, Guy Marc lawyer
Copenhaver, W. Andrew lawyer
Corbett, Leon H., Jr. lawyer, educator, university official
Davis, Linwood Layfield lawyer
Davis, William Allison, II lawyer
Farr, Henry Bartow, Jr. lawyer
Foy, Herbert Miles, III lawyer, educator
Gitter, Allan Reinhold lawyer
Greason, Murray Crossley, Jr. lawyer
Healy, Joseph Francis, Jr. lawyer, arbitrator, retired airline executive
Leonard, R. Michael lawyer
Newton, George Durfee, Jr. lawyer
Ray, Michael Edwin lawyer
Sandridge, William Pendleton, Jr. lawyer
Schollander, Wendell Leslie, Jr. lawyer
Sharpe, Keith Yount lawyer
†Steele, Thomas McKnight law librarian, law educator
Vance, Charles Fogle, Jr. lawyer
Walker, George Kontz law educator
Wells, Dewey Wallace lawyer
Womble, William Fletcher lawyer
Zagoria, Sam D(avid) arbitrator, author, educator

NORTH DAKOTA

Ashley
†Kretschmar, William Edward lawyer, state legislator

Bismarck
Maichel, Joseph Raymond lawyer, business executive
Murry, Charles Emerson lawyer, national guard official
Nelson, Keithe Eugene lawyer, state court administrator
Strutz, William A. lawyer

Devils Lake
†Traynor, John Thomas, Jr. lawyer

Grand Forks
†Gott, Gary Dean law library director, educator
Senechal, Alice R. lawyer
†Stenehjem, Wayne Kevin lawyer, state senator
Vogel, Robert lawyer, educator
Widdel, John Earl, Jr. lawyer

Jamestown
Hjellum, John retired lawyer

Mandan
Kautzmann, Dwight C(larence) H(arry) lawyer, magistrate

Minot
Armstrong, Phillip Dale lawyer

OHIO

Ada
†Leonard, James law librarian, educator

Akron
Bartlo, Sam D. lawyer
Calise, Nicholas James lawyer
Childs, James William lawyer, legal educator
Fisher, James Lee lawyer
Heider, Jon Vinton lawyer, corporate executive
Holloway, Donald Phillip lawyer
Lombardi, Frederick McKean lawyer, judge
Ong, John Doyle lawyer
†Richert, Paul law educator
Skakun, Mark John, III lawyer
Trotter, Thomas Robert lawyer

Barberton
Moss, Robert Drexler lawyer

Batavia
Rosenhoffer, Chris lawyer

Bowling Green
Hanna, Martin Shad lawyer
Holmes, Robert Allen lawyer, educator, consultant, lecturer

Canton
Bennington, Ronald Kent lawyer
Dettinger, Warren Walter lawyer
Lindamood, John Beyer lawyer
Mokodean, Michael John lawyer, accountant

Chagrin Falls
Streicher, James Franklin lawyer

Chesterland
Driggs, Charles Mulford lawyer
Durn, Raymond Joseph lawyer
Kancelbaum, Joshua Jacob lawyer

Cincinnati
Adams, Edmund John lawyer
Anderson, James Milton lawyer
Anderson, William Hopple lawyer
Anthony, Thomas Dale lawyer
Bahlman, William Thorne, Jr. lawyer
Blank, Cynthia Fisher lawyer
Blum, William Lee lawyer
Bridgeland, James Ralph, Jr. lawyer, mayor
Brinkman, Herbert Charles lawyer
Bromberg, Barbara Schwartz lawyer
Bromberg, Robert Sheldon lawyer
Carro, Jorge Luis law librarian, educator
Carson, Nolan Wendell lawyer
Chesley, Stanley Morris lawyer
Christenson, Gordon A. law educator
Cissell, James Charles lawyer
Cody, Thomas Gerald lawyer
Cowan, Jerry Louis lawyer
Craig, L. Clifford lawyer
Dehner, Joseph Julnes lawyer
DeLong, Deborah lawyer
Diller, Edward Dietrich lawyer
Dornette, W(illiam) Stuart lawyer, educator
Elleman, Lawrence Robert lawyer
Erickson, Richard J. lawyer
Fagin, Richard litigation consultant
Faller, Susan Grogan lawyer
Fink, Jerold Albert lawyer
Finkelmeier, Philip Renner law librarian, lawyer
Freedman, William Mark lawyer
Gettler, Benjamin lawyer, manufacturing company executive
Goodman, Stanley lawyer
Greenberg, Gerald Stephen lawyer
Guggenheim, Richard E. lawyer, shoe company executive
Hardy, William Robinson lawyer
Harris, Irving lawyer
Heinlen, Ronald Eugene lawyer
Hermanies, John Hans lawyer
Hess, Donald C. lawyer
Hill, Thomas Clark lawyer
Hoffheimer, Daniel Joseph lawyer
Hubschman, Henry Allan lawyer
†Johnson, James J. lawyer
Kelley, John Joseph, Jr. lawyer
Kenrich, John Lewis lawyer
Kiel, Frederick Orin lawyer
Kite, William McDougall lawyer
Kordons, Uldis lawyer
Lawrence, James Kaufman Lebensburger lawyer
Lindberg, Charles David lawyer
Lloyd, David Livingstone, Jr. lawyer
Longenecker, Mark Hershey, Jr. lawyer
Lutz, James Gurney lawyer
Manley, Robert Edward lawyer, economist
Marmer, Melvin E. lawyer
Mattingly, Paul R. lawyer
Maxwell, Robert Wallace, II lawyer
Mayer, James Joseph corporate lawyer
McClain, William Andrew lawyer

McCoy, John Joseph *lawyer*
McDowell, John Eugene *lawyer*
McGavran, Frederick Jaeger *lawyer*
Mc Henry, Powell *lawyer*
Meranus, Leonard Stanley *lawyer*
Monroe, Murray Shipley *lawyer*
Mooney, Donald James, Jr. *lawyer*
Murphy, Dennis Joseph *lawyer*
Naylor, Paul Donald *lawyer*
Nechemias, Stephen Murray *lawyer*
Nelson, Frederick Dickson *lawyer*
Neumark, Michael Harry *lawyer*
Olson, Robert Wyrick *lawyer*
Parker, R. Joseph *lawyer*
Phillips, T. Stephen *lawyer*
Puchta, Charles George *lawyer*
Reichert, David *lawyer*
Rich, Robert Edward *lawyer*
Roberts, Richard Stewart *lawyer*
Roe, Clifford Ashley, Jr. *lawyer*
Rose, Donald McGregor *lawyer*
Schuck, Thomas Robert *lawyer*
Scoggins, Samuel McWhirter *lawyer*
Shore, Thomas Spencer, Jr. *lawyer*
Silbersack, Mark Louis *lawyer*
Stein, Jacob K. *lawyer*
Swigert, James Mack *lawyer*
Tatgenhorst, (Charles) Robert *lawyer*
Terp, Thomas Thomsen *lawyer*
Tobias, Charles Harrison, Jr. *lawyer*
Tobias, Paul Henry *lawyer*
Townsend, Robert J. *lawyer*
Vander Laan, Mark Alan *lawyer*
Vorholt, Jeffrey Joseph *lawyer, telecommunications company executive*
Wales, Ross Elliot *lawyer*
Warrington, John Wesley *lawyer*
Weeks, Steven Wiley *lawyer*
†West, John A. *lawyer*
Yund, George Edward *lawyer*
Yurchuck, Roger Alexander *lawyer*

Cleveland
Adams, Albert T. *lawyer*
Alfred, Stephen Jay *lawyer*
Andorka, Frank Henry *lawyer*
Andrews, Oakley V. *lawyer*
Arison, Barbara J. *lawyer*
Ashmus, Keith Allen *lawyer*
Atkinson, William Edward *lawyer*
Austin, Arthur Donald, II *lawyer, educator*
Azoff, Elliot Stephen *lawyer*
Babin, Mara L. *lawyer*
Bacon, Brett Kermit *lawyer*
Bamberger, Richard H. *lawyer*
Bank, Malvin E. *lawyer*
Barnard, Thomas Harvie *lawyer*
Barnes, Geoffrey K. *lawyer*
Barr, Douglas N. *lawyer*
Bates, Walter Alan *lawyer*
Batt, John Paul *lawyer*
Baughman, R(obert) Patrick *lawyer*
Baumgartner, Bruce O. *lawyer*
Baxter, Howard H. *lawyer*
Bennett, Paul Edward *lawyer*
Berger, Sanford Jason *lawyer, securities dealer, real estate broker*
Berick, James Herschel *lawyer*
Berry, Dean Lester *lawyer*
Besse, Ralph Moore *lawyer*
Bilchik, Gary B. *lawyer*
Binford, Gregory Glenn *lawyer*
Blattner, Robert A. *lawyer*
Bodurtha, James H. *lawyer*
Borowitz, Albert Ira *lawyer, author*
Branagan, James Joseph *lawyer*
Braverman, Herbert Leslie *lawyer*
Bravo, Kenneth A. *lawyer*
Brennan, Maureen A. *lawyer*
Brooks, Arthur V. N. *lawyer*
Brown, Seymour R. *lawyer*
Brown, Troy R. *lawyer*
Brucken, Robert Matthew *lawyer*
Bryenton, Gary L. *lawyer*
Buchmann, Alan Paul *lawyer*
Buescher, Stephen L. *lawyer*
Bumpass, T. Merritt, Jr. *lawyer*
Burke, Kathleen B. *lawyer*
Burlingame, John Hunter *lawyer*
Cairns, James Donald *lawyer*
Calfee, John Beverly, Sr. *lawyer*
Calfee, William Lewis *lawyer*
Campbell, Paul Barton *lawyer*
Canary, Nancy Halliday *lawyer*
Carlson, James R. *lawyer*
†Carrick, Kathleen Michele *law librarian*
Case, Betsey Brewster *lawyer*
Chapman, Diane P. *lawyer*
Clarke, Charles Fenton *lawyer*
Collin, Thomas James *lawyer*
Collins, Susan B. *lawyer*
Colombo, Louis A. *lawyer*
Cooper, Hal Dean *lawyer*
Coquillette, William Hollis *lawyer*
Cornell, John Robert *lawyer*
Coscarelli, Dianne Smith *lawyer*
Coughlin, Barring *lawyer*
Coyle, Martin Adolphus, Jr. *lawyer*
Crist, Paul Grant *lawyer*
Currivan, John Daniel *lawyer*
Dakin, Carol F. *lawyer*
Dampeer, John Lyell *lawyer*
Dempsey, James Howard, Jr. *lawyer*
Doris, Alan S(anford) *lawyer*
Downie, John Francis *lawyer*
Downing, George *lawyer*
Drinko, John Deaver *lawyer*
Duffy, John C., Jr. *lawyer*
Duncan, Ed Eugene *lawyer*
Dunn, John P. *lawyer*
Dunn, Leslie D. *lawyer*
Durham, Mary Lynn *lawyer*
Duvin, Robert Phillip *lawyer*
Dye, Sherman *lawyer*
Edwards, John Wesley, II *lawyer*
Ekelman, Daniel Louis *lawyer*
†Ellis, Stephen C. *lawyer*
Eyre, Paul P. *lawyer*
Fabens, Andrew Lawrie, III *lawyer*
Fairweather, John C. *lawyer*
Falsgraf, William Wendell *lawyer*
Fay, Regan Joseph *lawyer*
Fay, Robert Jesse *lawyer*
Feinberg, Paul H. *lawyer*
Feliciano, José Celso *lawyer*
Fletcher, Robert *lawyer, horologist*
Ford, Robert Barney *lawyer*
Frantz, Michael Jennings *lawyer*

Friedman, Harold Edward *lawyer*
Friedman, James Moss *lawyer*
Fullmer, David R. *lawyer*
Garner, James Parent *lawyer*
Garver, Theodore Meyer *lawyer*
Gerhart, Peter Milton *law educator*
Gherlein, John Harlan *retired lawyer*
Ginsberg, Edward *lawyer*
Ginsburg, Edward S. *lawyer*
Glaser, Robert Edward *lawyer*
Glenn, Peter G. *lawyer*
Goins, Frances Floriano *lawyer*
Gold, Gerald Seymour *lawyer*
Goldfarb, Bernard Sanford *lawyer*
Griswold, James B. *lawyer*
Groetzinger, Jon, Jr. *lawyer, consumer products executive*
Grossman, Theodore Martin *lawyer*
Gruettner, Donald W. *lawyer*
Grundstein, Nathan David *lawyer, management science educator, management consultant*
Gutfeld, Norman E. *lawyer*
Haiman, Irwin Sanford *lawyer*
Hamilton, J. Richard *lawyer*
Hammer, Daniel William *lawyer*
Hanna, Harry Adolphus *lawyer*
Hardy, Michael Lynn *lawyer*
Hatchadorian, Matthew J. *lawyer*
Heddesheimer, Walter Jacob *lawyer*
Henes, Samuel Ernst *lawyer*
Hermann, Philip J. *lawyer*
Hochman, Kenneth George *lawyer*
Hoerner, Robert Jack *lawyer*
Holland, Patricia Marcus *lawyer*
Hollington, Richard Rings, Jr. *lawyer*
Hooker, David Joseph *lawyer*
Hopkins, John S., III *lawyer*
Hopps, Sidney Bryce *lawyer*
Horvitz, Michael John *lawyer*
Hyde, Alan Litchfield *lawyer*
Jacobs, Leslie William *lawyer*
Janke, Ronald Robert *lawyer*
Jeavons, Norman Stone *lawyer*
Jorgenson, Mary Ann *lawyer*
Kacir, Barbara Brattin *lawyer*
Kahrl, Robert Conley *lawyer*
Kaiser, Gordon S., Jr. *lawyer*
Karch, George Frederick, Jr. *lawyer*
Karch, Sargent *lawyer*
Katcher, Richard *lawyer*
Katz, Lewis Robert *legal educator*
Kelly, Dennis Michael *lawyer*
Kilbane, Thomas Stanton *lawyer*
Kirchick, Calvin B. *lawyer*
Klaus, Charles *lawyer*
Knopp, Albert J. *lawyer*
Kola, Arthur Anthony *lawyer*
Korb, Donald Lee *lawyer*
Kramer, Andrew Michael *lawyer*
Kramer, Eugene Leo *lawyer*
Kuhn, David Alan *lawyer*
Kundtz, John Andrew *lawyer*
Kurit, Neil *lawyer*
Landefeld, Charles Willis *lawyer*
Lawniczak, James Michael *lawyer*
Lease, Robert K. *lawyer*
Leavitt, Jeffrey Stuart *lawyer*
Leech, John Dale *lawyer*
Leidner, Harold Edward *lawyer*
Leiken, Earl Murray *lawyer*
Lemke, Judith A. *lawyer*
Lenn, Stephen Andrew *lawyer*
Leonard, Irvin Alan *lawyer*
Leukart, Richard Henry, II *lawyer*
Lewis, John Bruce *lawyer*
Lewis, John Francis *lawyer*
Lewis, Robert Lawrence *lawyer*
Liegl, Joseph Leslie *lawyer*
Lindberg, Lawrence V. *lawyer*
Lynch, John Edward, Jr. *lawyer*
Madsen, H(enry) Stephen *retired lawyer*
Margulies, Jeffrey J. *lawyer*
Markey, Robert Guy *lawyer*
Markus, Richard M. *lawyer*
Marting, Michael G. *lawyer*
Mason, Thomas Albert *lawyer*
McAndrews, James Patrick *lawyer*
Mc Cartan, Patrick Francis *lawyer*
McCarthy, Mark Francis *lawyer*
Mc Clelland, James Craig *lawyer*
McCreary, Robert Grosvenor, Jr. *lawyer*
Mc Elhaney, James Wilson *lawyer, educator*
Mc Innes, Robert Malcolm *lawyer*
McKee, Thomas Frederick *lawyer*
McLaughlin, Patrick Michael *lawyer*
Meaney, Michael Joseph *lawyer*
Meisel, George Ira *lawyer*
Melsher, Gary W. *lawyer*
Messinger, Donald Hathaway *lawyer*
Meyer, G. Christopher *lawyer*
Miller, Ivan Lawrence *lawyer*
Miller, Richard Hamilton *lawyer, broadcasting company executive*
Millstone, David J. *lawyer*
Milner, Irvin Myron *lawyer*
Moore, Anthony R. *lawyer*
Moore, Kenneth Cameron *lawyer*
Morrison, Donald William *lawyer, utility executive*
Moscarino, George J. *lawyer*
†Mottl, Ronald M. *lawyer, state legislator*
Naylor, John Lewis, Jr. *lawyer*
Nelson, Robert Bruce *lawyer*
Newborn, Karen B. *lawyer*
Newell, Sterling, Jr. *lawyer*
Newman, John M., Jr. *lawyer*
Nims, Michael A. *lawyer*
Novatney, John F., Jr. *lawyer*
Oberdank, Lawrence Mark *lawyer, arbitrator*
Ollinger, W. James *lawyer*
Orr, Parker Murray *lawyer*
Pallam, John James *lawyer*
Paris, Zachary T. *lawyer*
Perris, Terrence George *lawyer*
Perry, George Williamson *lawyer*
Plesec, William Thomas *lawyer*
Podboy, Alvin Michael, Jr. *lawyer, law library director*
Pogue, Richard Welch *lawyer*
Preston, Robert Bruce *lawyer*
Price, Charles T. *lawyer*
Ptaszek, Edward Gerald, Jr. *lawyer*
Putka, Andrew Charles *lawyer*
Pyke, John Secrest, Jr. *lawyer, polymers company executive*
Rains, Merritt Neal *lawyer*
Ransom, William Harrison *lawyer*
Rapp, Robert Neil *lawyer*
Rasmussen, Frank Morris *lawyer*

Rawson, Robert H., Jr. *lawyer*
Reale, William A. *lawyer*
Rekstis, Walter J., III *lawyer*
Reppert, Richard Levi *lawyer*
Robiner, Donald Maxwell *lawyer*
Roj, William Henry *lawyer*
Rorimer, Louis *lawyer*
Rosenbaum, Jacob I. *lawyer*
Rotolo, Joseph Anthony *lawyer*
Ruben, Alan Miles *lawyer, educator*
Ruxin, Paul Theodore *lawyer*
Rydzel, James A. *lawyer*
Sager, John William *lawyer*
Sawyer, Raymond Terry *lawyer*
Sayler, Richard H. *lawyer*
Schaefer, David Arnold *lawyer*
Schiller, James Joseph *lawyer*
Schneider, David Miller *lawyer*
Schnell, Carlton Bryce *lawyer*
Seger, Thomas M. *lawyer*
Seikel, Oliver Edward *lawyer*
Shanker, Morris Gerald *lawyer, educator*
Shapiro, Fred David *lawyer*
Sharp, Robert Weimer *lawyer*
Shaw, Russell Clyde *lawyer*
Shea-Stonum, Marilyn *lawyer*
Shelley, John Fletcher *lawyer*
Sicherman, Marvin Allen *lawyer*
Sigalow, Steven E. *lawyer*
Skulina, Thomas Raymond *lawyer*
Sloan, David W. *lawyer*
Smith, Barbara Jean *lawyer*
Smith, James A. *lawyer*
Snyder, Kenneth F. *lawyer*
Sogg, Wilton Sherman *lawyer*
Solomon, Randall L. *lawyer*
Springel, Barry L. *lawyer*
Stanley, Hugh Monroe, Jr. *lawyer*
Steinbrink, William H. *lawyer*
Steindler, Howard Allen *lawyer*
Steinhouse, Carl Lewis *lawyer*
Stevens, Thomas Charles *lawyer*
Stinchcomb, Robert G. *lawyer*
Stinson, Robert Charles *lawyer*
Strauch, John L. *lawyer*
Strauss, David J. *lawyer*
Streeter, Richard Edward *lawyer*
Striefsky, Linda A(nn) *lawyer*
Strimbu, Victor, Jr. *lawyer*
Stuhan, Richard George *lawyer*
Swartzbaugh, Marc L. *lawyer*
Taft, Seth Chase *retired lawyer*
Thomson, Maynard F. *lawyer*
Toohey, Brian Frederick *lawyer*
Toomajian, William Martin *lawyer*
Traci, Donald Philip *lawyer*
Trevor, Leigh Barry *lawyer*
Updegraft, Kenneth E., Jr. *lawyer*
von Mehren, George M. *lawyer*
Waldeck, John Walter, Jr. *lawyer*
Wallace, R. Byron *lawyer*
Wallach, Mark Irwin *lawyer*
Wamsley, James Lawrence, III *lawyer*
Watson, Richard Thomas *lawyer*
Weaver, Robin Geoffrey *lawyer, educator*
Weber, Robert Carl *lawyer*
Weible, Robert A. *lawyer*
Weiler, Jeffry Louis *lawyer*
Werber, Stephen Jay *lawyer, educator*
Whelan, Richard Vincent, Jr. *lawyer*
White, Paul Dunbar *lawyer*
Whiteman, Joseph David *lawyer, manufacturing company executive*
Whiting, Hugh Richard *lawyer*
Whitney, Richard Buckner *lawyer*
Wilharm, John H., Jr. *lawyer*
Williams, Clyde E., Jr. *lawyer*
†Wise, Michael W. *lawyer*
Woodring, James H. *lawyer*
Yosowitz, Sanford *lawyer, metal sales and fabricating executive*
Young, James Edward *lawyer*
Zangerle, John A. *lawyer*

Columbus
Adams, John Marshall *lawyer*
Adams, Lee Stephen *lawyer, banker*
Anderson, Jon Mac *lawyer*
Anderson, Sandra Jo *lawyer*
Arthur, William Edgar *lawyer*
Ayers, James Cordon *lawyer*
Bailey, Daniel Allen *lawyer*
Baranowski, Edwin Michael *lawyer, writer*
Barnes, Wallace Ray *lawyer*
Beck, Kenneth David *lawyer*
Bibart, Richard L. *lawyer*
Boardman, William Penniman *lawyer, banker*
Bridgman, G(eorge) Ross *lawyer*
Briggs, Marjorie Crowder *lawyer*
Brooks, Richard Dickinson *lawyer*
Brown, Herbert Russell *lawyer, writer*
Brown, Paul W. *retired lawyer, retired state supreme court justice*
Brown, Philip Albert *lawyer*
Brubaker, Robert Loring *lawyer*
Buchenroth, Stephen Richard *lawyer*
Burtch, John Hamrick *lawyer*
Carnahan, John Anderson *lawyer*
Carpenter, Michael H. *lawyer*
Case, William R. *lawyer*
Celebrezze, Anthony J., Jr. *lawyer*
Chester, John Jonas *lawyer*
Christensen, John William *lawyer*
Clovis, Albert Lee *lawyer, educator*
Cogan, J. Kevin *lawyer*
Cole, Ransey Guy, Jr. *lawyer*
Cook, Samuel Ronald, Jr. *lawyer*
Cushman, James Butler *lawyer*
Cvetanovich, Danny L. *lawyer*
Day, Roger F. *lawyer*
DeRousie, Charles Stuart *lawyer*
Di Lorenzo, John Florio, Jr. *lawyer*
Dowd, Andrew Joseph *lawyer, utility company executive*
Dreher, Darrell L. *lawyer*
Druen, William Sidney *lawyer*
Dugan, Charles Francis, II *lawyer*
Edwards, John White *lawyer*
Elam, John Carlton *lawyer*
Fahey, Richard Paul *lawyer*
Fisher, Lloyd Edison, Jr. *lawyer*
Fried, Samuel *lawyer*
Gall, Maryann Baker *lawyer*
Gibson, Rankin MacDougal *lawyer*
Goodman, Norton Victor *lawyer*
Gotherman, John E. *lawyer*
Grant, Dennis Duane *lawyer*
Greek, Darold I. *lawyer*

Gross, James Howard *lawyer*
Gunsett, Daniel J. *lawyer*
Habash, Stephen J. *lawyer*
Hairston, George W. *lawyer*
Hardymon, David Wayne *lawyer*
Helgerson, John Walter *lawyer*
Henning, Harry Leonard *lawyer*
Hire, Charles H. *lawyer*
Hoberg, John William *lawyer*
Howarth, Robert F., Jr. *lawyer*
†Hughes, Donald Allen, Jr. *law librarian and educator*
Jenkins, George L. *lawyer*
Jenkins, John Anthony *lawyer*
Johnson, Mark Alan *lawyer*
Johnston, Philip Crater *lawyer*
Keller, John Kistler *lawyer*
Kennedy, James Patrick *lawyer*
Kincaid, Robert M., Jr. *lawyer*
King, G. Roger *lawyer*
King, James R. *lawyer*
Knepper, William Edward *lawyer*
Kozyris, Phaedon John *law educator, consultant*
Kuehnle, Kenton Lee *lawyer*
Kurtz, Charles Jewett, III *lawyer*
Lahey, John H. *lawyer*
Lehman, Harry Jac *lawyer*
Long, Thomas Leslie *lawyer*
Maloon, Jerry L. *lawyer, physician, medicolegal consultant*
Martin, William Giese *lawyer*
Maynard, Robert Howell *lawyer*
Mayo, Elizabeth Broom *lawyer*
McAlister, Robert Beaton *lawyer*
McConnaughey, George Carlton, Jr. *lawyer*
McCutchan, Gordon Eugene *lawyer, insurance company executive*
McKenna, Alvin James *lawyer*
McMahon, John Patrick *lawyer*
McNealey, J. Jeffrey *lawyer, corporate executive*
Miller, Dixon Fullerton *lawyer*
Miller, Malcolm Lee *retired lawyer*
Miller, Terry Morrow *lawyer*
Minister, Michael E. *lawyer*
Minor, Charles Daniel *lawyer*
Minor, Robert Allen *lawyer*
Minor, Robert Walter *lawyer*
Mirman, Joel Harvey *lawyer*
Moloney, Thomas E. *lawyer*
Mone, Robert Paul *lawyer*
Moritz, Michael Everett *lawyer*
Moul, William Charles *lawyer*
Oliphant, James S. *lawyer*
Oman, Richard Heer *lawyer*
Petricoff, M. Howard *lawyer, educator*
Phillips, James Edgar *lawyer*
Pigman, Jack Richard *lawyer*
Pliskin, Marvin Robert *lawyer*
Pohlman, James Erwin *lawyer*
Porter, Samuel Hamilton *lawyer*
Pressley, Fred G., Jr. *lawyer*
Quigley, John Bernard *law educator*
Radnor, Alan T. *lawyer*
Ramey, Denny L. *bar association executive director*
Reasoner, Willis Irl, III *lawyer*
Ridgley, Thomas Brennan *lawyer*
Robinson, Barry R. *lawyer*
Rose, Michael Dean *lawyer, educator*
Rowland, Ronald Lee *lawyer*
Royalty, Kenneth Marvin *lawyer*
Ryan, Joseph W., Jr. *lawyer*
Schrag, Edward A., Jr. *lawyer*
Scott, Thomas Clevenger *lawyer*
Selcer, David Mark *lawyer*
Seltzer, Martin Stanley *lawyer*
Senff, Mark D. *lawyer*
Shamansky, Robert Norton *lawyer, partner*
Shayne, Stanley H. *lawyer*
Sidman, Robert John *lawyer*
Siehl, Richard W. *lawyer*
Sims, August Charles *lawyer, policeman*
Smith, Norman T. *lawyer*
Stedman, Richard Ralph *lawyer*
Stern, Geoffrey *lawyer, disciplinary counsel*
Stinehart, Roger Ray *lawyer*
Taft, Sheldon Ashley *lawyer*
Taggart, Thomas Michael *lawyer*
Tait, Robert Ed *lawyer*
Tarpy, Thomas Michael *lawyer*
Taylor, Joel Sanford *lawyer*
Tell, A. Charles *lawyer*
Thomas, Duke Winston *lawyer*
Todd, William Michael *lawyer*
Turano, David A. *lawyer*
Van Heyde, J. Stephen *lawyer*
Vorys, Arthur Isaiah *lawyer*
Warner, Charles Collins *lawyer*
Wentworth, Andrew Stowell *lawyer*
Whipps, Edward Franklin *lawyer*
Wightman, Alec *lawyer*
Williams, Gregory Howard *lawyer, educator*
Wright, Harry, III *lawyer*

Cuyahoga Falls
†Jones, Wayne M. *lawyer, state representative*

Dayton
Bartlett, Robert Perry, Jr. *lawyer*
Berrey, Robert Forrest *lawyer*
Burick, Lawrence T. *lawyer*
Chernesky, Richard John *lawyer*
Finn, Chester Evans *lawyer*
Freedman, Stanley Arnold *lawyer*
Gottschlich, Gary William *lawyer*
Hadley, Robert James *lawyer*
Harrington, Thomas Joseph *lawyer*
Hayman, Jeffrey Lloyd *corporate lawyer*
Heyman, Ralph Edmond *lawyer*
†Horn, Charles F. *lawyer, electrical engineer, state legislator*
Jenks, Thomas Edward *lawyer*
Johnson, C. Terry *lawyer*
Kinlin, Donald James *lawyer*
Lewis, Welbourne Walker, Jr. *lawyer*
Lowry, Bruce Roy *lawyer*
Macklin, Crofford Johnson, Jr. *lawyer*
Maly, George Joseph, Jr. *lawyer*
McSwiney, Charles Ronald *lawyer*
Rapp, Gerald Duane *lawyer, manufacturing company executive*
†Reid, Marilyn Joanne *lawyer*
Rogers, Richard Hunter *lawyer, business executive*

Delphos
Clark, Edward Ferdnand *lawyer*

Dresden
Reidy, Thomas Anthony *lawyer*

Dublin
Rakestraw, Warren Vincent *lawyer*

East Liverpool
Lang, Francis Harover *lawyer*

Findlay
Jetton, Girard Reuel, Jr. *lawyer, retired oil company executive*

Gates Mills
Doolittle, Robert Frederick *lawyer*

Hamilton
Linsenmann, William Michael *lawyer, former insurance company executive*

Kent
Giffen, Daniel Harris *lawyer, educator*

Lancaster
Libert, Donald Joseph *lawyer*

Lima
Robenalt, John Alton *lawyer*

Logan
Dillon, Neal Winfield *lawyer*

Louisville
Sinclair, Virgil Lee, Jr. *lawyer, writer*

Marietta
Fields, William Albert *lawyer*
Hausser, Robert Louis *lawyer*

Marion
Ashworth, John Lawrence *lawyer*

Maumee
Gosline, Robert Bradley *lawyer*
Kline, James Edward *lawyer*
Marsh, Benjamin Franklin *lawyer*

Medina
Ballard, John Stuart *law educator, former mayor*

Miamisburg
Wieland, Robert Richard *lawyer*

Middletown
Rathman, William Ernest *lawyer, minister*

Mount Vernon
Turner, Harry Edward *lawyer*

Newark
Mantonya, John Butcher *lawyer*

Norwalk
Carpenter, Paul Leonard *lawyer*

Oregon
St. Clair, Donald David *lawyer*

Oxford
Brown, Edward Maurice *retired lawyer, business executive*

Portsmouth
Horr, William Henry *lawyer*

Reynoldsburg
Goostree, Robert Edward *political science and law educator*

Sandusky
Tone, Kenneth Edward *lawyer*

Springfield
Browne, William Bitner *lawyer*
Martin, Oscar Thaddeus *retired lawyer*

Toledo
Anderson, Dale Kenneth *retired lawyer*
Baker, Bernard Robert, II *lawyer*
Baker, Richard Southworth *lawyer*
Boesel, Milton Charles, Jr. *lawyer, business executive*
Boggs, Ralph Stuart *lawyer*
Brown, Charles Earl *lawyer*
Colasurd, Richard Michael *lawyer*
Craig, Harald Franklin *lawyer*
Dalrymple, Thomas Lawrence *lawyer*
Fisher, Donald Wiener *lawyer*
Hawkins, Donald Merton *lawyer*
Hiett, Edward Emerson *retired lawyer, glass company executive*
James, Harold Arthur *lawyer*
La Rue, Carl Forman *lawyer*
Leech, Charles Russell, Jr. *lawyer*
McCormick, Edward James, Jr. *lawyer*
O'Connell, Maurice Daniel *lawyer*
Spitzer, John Brumback *lawyer*
Stewart, Mark Carroll *lawyer*
Tuschman, James Marshall *lawyer*
Wolfe, Warren Dwight *lawyer*

Warren
Rossi, Anthony Gerald *lawyer*

Westerville
Milligan, Frederick James *lawyer*

Wickliffe
Hsu, Roger Y. K. *lawyer*
Kidder, Fred Dockstater *lawyer*

Willoughby
Harthun, Luther Arthur *lawyer*

Wooster
Colclaser, H. Alberta *lawyer, retired government official*

Yellow Springs
Graham, P(recious) Jewel *lawyer, educator, social worker*

Youngstown
Mumaw, James Webster *lawyer*
Nadler, Myron Jay *lawyer*
Roth, Daniel Benjamin *lawyer, business executive*
Sokolov, Richard Saul *lawyer*
Stevens, Paul Edward *lawyer*
Tucker, Don Eugene *retired lawyer*

Zanesville
Micheli, Frank James *lawyer*

OKLAHOMA

Anadarko
Pain, Charles Leslie *lawyer*

Antlers
Stamper, Joe Allen *lawyer*

Bartlesville
Paul, William George *lawyer*

Durant
†Mickle, Billy Arthur *lawyer, state legislator*

Enid
Jones, Stephen *lawyer*
Musser, William Wesley, Jr. *lawyer*

Guthrie
†Davis, Frank Wayne *lawyer*

Guymon
Wood, Donald Euriah *lawyer*

Kingfisher
Baker, Thomas Edward *lawyer, accountant*

Mcalester
Cornish, Richard Pool *lawyer*

Muskogee
Ruby, Russell (Glenn) *lawyer*

Norman
Brown, Elvin J. *lawyer*
Elkouri, Frank *legal educator*
†Fairbanks, Robert Alvin *lawyer*
Hemingway, Richard William *lawyer, educator*

Oklahoma City
Allen, Robert Dee *lawyer*
Almond, David R. *lawyer*
Angel, Arthur Ronald *lawyer, consultant*
†Ball, Leonard F. *lawyer, architectural firm executive*
Boston, William Clayton *lawyer*
Burch, Melvin Earl *lawyer, bank executive*
Cantrell, Charles Leonard *lawyer, educator*
Champlin, Richard H. *lawyer, insurance company executive*
Coats, Andrew Montgomery *lawyer, former mayor*
Court, Leonard *lawyer*
Crabtree, Jack Turner *lawyer*
Cunningham, Stanley Lloyd *lawyer*
Durland, Jack Raymond *lawyer*
Fellers, James Davison *lawyer*
Ford, Michael Raye *lawyer*
Heimann, William Emil *retired lawyer*
Hemry, Jerome Eldon *lawyer*
Hendrick, Howard H. *lawyer, state senator*
†Keller, Bryan J. *lawyer*
Lambird, Mona Salyer *lawyer*
Legg, William Jefferson *lawyer*
Lester, Andrew William *lawyer*
†Miles-LaGrange, Vicki *prosecutor*
Milsten, Robert B. *lawyer*
Miskovsky, George, Sr. *lawyer*
Moler, Edward Harold *lawyer*
†Morgan, Judith A. *law librarian*
Necco, Alexander David *lawyer, educator*
Reynolds, Norman Eben *lawyer*
†Ross, William Jarboe *lawyer*
Snider, John Joseph *lawyer*
Steinhorn, Irwin Harry *lawyer, educator, corporate executive*
Taft, Richard George *lawyer*
†Taylor, Stratton *state senator, lawyer*
Thompson, Lee Bennett *lawyer*
Turpen, Michael Craig *lawyer*
Verity, George Luther *lawyer*
Walsh, Lawrence Edward *lawyer*
Woodruff, Judson Sage *lawyer*

Pauls Valley
Hope, Garland Howard *lawyer, retired judge*

Ponca City
Northcutt, Clarence Dewey *lawyer*

Tulsa
Arrington, John Leslie, Jr. *lawyer*
Biolchini, Robert Fredrick *lawyer*
Blackstock, LeRoy *lawyer*
Bryant, Hubert Hale *lawyer*
Cooper, Richard Casey *lawyer*
†Craft, Joseph W., III *corporate lawyer*
Crawford, B(urnett) Hayden *lawyer*
Daniel, Samuel Phillips *lawyer*
Farrell, John L., Jr. *lawyer, business executive*
Frey, Martin Alan *lawyer, educator*
Gable, G. Ellis *lawyer*
Graham, Tony M. *attorney*
Howard, Gene Claude *lawyer, former state senator*
Keating, Francis Anthony, II *lawyer*
Kihle, Donald Arthur *lawyer*
Killin, Charles Clark *lawyer*
Kothe, Charles Aloysius *lawyer*
Langholz, Robert Wayne *lawyer, investor*
Lewis, John Furman *lawyer, oil company executive*
Luthey, Graydon Dean, Jr. *lawyer*
Milsten, David Randolph *lawyer*
Schwartz, Bernard *lawyer, educator*
Walker, Floyd Lee *lawyer*

Vinita
Curnutte, Mark William *lawyer*

OREGON

Astoria
Haskell, Donald McMillan *lawyer*

Bend
Hurley, James Vincent *lawyer*

Brookings
Maxwell, William Stirling *retired lawyer*

Cannon Beach
Landon, Sealand Whitney *lawyer*

Eugene
Clark, Chapin DeWitt *law educator*
Mumford, William Porter, II *lawyer*
Sahlstrom, E(lmer) B(ernard) *lawyer*
Scoles, Eugene Francis *legal educator, lawyer*

La Grande
Carey, Willard Keith *lawyer*

Medford
O'Connor, Karl William *lawyer*

Pendleton
Bloom, Stephen Michael *lawyer, judge*
Kottkamp, John Harlan *lawyer*

Portland
Abravanel, Allan Ray *lawyer*
Anderson, Herbert H. *lawyer*
Arthur, Michael Elbert *lawyer*
Babcock, Robert Evans *lawyer*
Bach, Richard D. *lawyer*
Bakkensen, John Reser *lawyer*
Biggs, Hugh Lawry *lawyer*
Booth, Brian Geddes *lawyer*
Brenneman, Delbert Jay *lawyer*
Cable, John Franklin *lawyer*
Cantlin, Richard Anthony *lawyer*
Carlsen, Clifford Norman, Jr. *lawyer*
Carmack, Mildred Jean *lawyer*
Chernoff, Daniel Paregol *patent lawyer*
Crow, William Beryl *lawyer*
Crowell, John B., Jr. *lawyer, former government official*
Dahl, Joyle Cochran *lawyer*
Davidson, Crow Girard *lawyer*
Dean, E. Joseph *lawyer*
DeChaine, Dean Dennis *lawyer*
Deering, Thomas Phillips *lawyer*
Dotten, Michael Chester *lawyer*
Drummond, Gerard Kasper *lawyer, retired minerals company executive*
Eakin, Margaretta Morgan *lawyer*
Edwards, Richard Alan *lawyer*
Ellis, Barnes Humphreys *lawyer*
Epstein, Edward Louis *lawyer*
Faust, John Roosevelt, Jr. *lawyer*
Fell, James F. *lawyer*
Feuerstein, Howard M. *lawyer*
Fogg, George Kephart *lawyer*
Foley, Ridgway Knight, Jr. *lawyer, writer*
Franzke, Richard Albert *lawyer*
Geddes, Robert Dale *lawyer*
Georges, Maurice Ostrow *lawyer*
Girard, Leonard Arthur *lawyer*
Girard, Leonard Arthur *lawyer, corporate executive*
Glasgow, William Jacob *lawyer*
Glick, Richard Myron *lawyer*
Green, David William *lawyer*
Griffith, Stephen Loyal *lawyer*
Hager, Orval O. *lawyer*
Halle, John Joseph *lawyer*
Hanna, Harry Mitchell *lawyer*
Hart, C. Allan *lawyer*
Helmer, M. Christie *lawyer*
Hergenhan, Kenneth William *lawyer*
Hinkle, Charles Frederick *lawyer, clergyman, educator*
Hoffman, Jack Leroy *lawyer*
Holman, Donald Reid *lawyer*
Holmes, Michael Gene *lawyer*
Howorth, David Bishop *lawyer*
Josephson, Richard Carl *lawyer*
Kennedy, Jack Leland *lawyer*
Kester, Randall Blair *lawyer*
Kitchel, Jan Kelly *lawyer*
Kuntz, Joel Dubois *lawyer*
Larpenteur, James Albert, Jr. *lawyer*
Leedy, R. Allan, Jr. *lawyer*
Leedy, Robert Allan *retired lawyer*
Lindley, Thomas Ernest *environmental lawyer, law educator*
Livingston, Louis Bayer *lawyer*
Love, William Edward *lawyer*
Maloney, Robert E., Jr. *lawyer*
McClanahan, Mark C. *lawyer*
Miller, William Richey, Jr. *lawyer*
Moore, Conrad Lee *lawyer*
Mowe, Gregory Robert *lawyer*
Nash, Frank Erwin *lawyer*
Nunn, Robert Warne *lawyer*
O'Hanlon, James Barry *lawyer*
Peterman, Mark H. *lawyer*
Pruitt, Charles Joseph *lawyer*
Pyle, Donald Hanson *lawyer*
Replogle, William H., II *lawyer*
Richardson, Campbell *lawyer*
Richter, Peter Christian *lawyer*
†Roberts, Gary *lawyer*
Rosenbaum, Lois Omenn *lawyer*
Roy, Richard E. *lawyer*
Rubin, Bruce Alan *lawyer*
Rutzick, Mark Charles *lawyer*
Sand, Thomas Charles *lawyer*
Scott, Lewis Kelly *lawyer*
Simpson, Robert Glenn *lawyer*
Spiekerman, James Frederick *lawyer*
Stevason, John C. *lawyer*
Stewart, Milton Roy *lawyer*
Sullivan, Edward Joseph *lawyer, educator*
Tilbury, Roger Graydon *lawyer, rancher*
Van Valkenburg, Edgar Walter *lawyer*
Waggoner, James Clyde *lawyer*
Walters, Stephen Scott *lawyer*
Weaver, Delbert Allen *lawyer*
Webb, Jere Michael *lawyer*

Westwood, James Nicholson *lawyer*
Whinston, Arthur Lewis *lawyer*
White, Douglas James, Jr. *lawyer*
Wiener, Norman Joseph *lawyer*
Wilson, Owen Meredith, Jr. *lawyer*
Wood, Erskine Biddle *lawyer*
†Wood, Marcus Andrew *lawyer*
Wren, Harold Gwyn *arbitrator, lawyer, legal educator*
Wright, Charles Edward *lawyer*
Wyse, William Walker *lawyer*
Zalutsky, Morton Herman *lawyer*

Salem
†Mannix, Kevin Leese *lawyer*

PENNSYLVANIA

Allentown
Agger, James H. *lawyer*
Brown, Robert Wayne *lawyer*
Frank, Bernard *lawyer*
Holt, Leon Conrad, Jr. *lawyer, business executive*
Nagel, Edward McCaul *lawyer, former utilities executive*
Platt, William Henry *lawyer*

Allison Park
Herrington, John David, III *lawyer*
Miller, William Evans, Jr. *retired lawyer*

Bala Cynwyd
Cades, Stewart Russell *lawyer, communications company executive*
Garrity, Vincent Francis, Jr. *lawyer*
Manko, Joseph Martin, Sr. *lawyer*
Quay, Thomas Emery *lawyer*

Beaver Falls
Ledebur, Linas Vockroth, Jr. *lawyer*

Berwyn
Kane, Jonathan *lawyer*
Markle, John, Jr. *lawyer*
Odell, Herbert *lawyer*
Watters, Edward McLain, III *lawyer*
Wood, Thomas E. *lawyer*

Blue Bell
Barron, Harold Sheldon *lawyer*
Elliott, John Michael *lawyer*
Swansen, Samuel Theodore *lawyer*
Young, Jere Arnold *lawyer, management consultant*

Broomall
Stewart, Allen Warren *lawyer*

Bryn Mawr
Chadwick, H. Beatty *lawyer*

Camp Hill
Wellington, John Stanley *lawyer, former state official*

Carlisle
†Fox, James Robert *law librarian, educator*

Conshohocken
Rounick, Jack A. *lawyer*

Erie
Lund, David Harrison *lawyer*

Farrell
Sander, Malvin Gustav *lawyer*

Gladwyne
Acton, David *lawyer*

Greensburg
McDowell, Michael David *lawyer, utility executive*

Harrisburg
Allen, Heath Ledward *lawyer*
Angino, Richard Carmen *lawyer*
Ball, William Bentley *lawyer*
Cawley, James Hughes *lawyer*
Cline, Andrew Haley *lawyer*
Cramer, John McNaight *lawyer*
Diehm, James Warren *lawyer, educator*
Kelly, Robert Edward, Jr. *lawyer*
Klein, Michael D. *lawyer*
Kury, Franklin Leo *lawyer*
Termini, Roseann Bridget *lawyer*
Warshaw, Allen Charles *lawyer*
West, James Joseph *lawyer*
Weston, R. Timothy *lawyer, government adminstrator*
Zimmerman, LeRoy S. *lawyer, former state attorney general*

Haverford
Frick, Sidney Wanning *lawyer*
McGlinn, Frank Cresson Potts *lawyer*
Stroud, James Stanley *retired lawyer*

Huntingdon Valley
Forman, Howard Irving *lawyer, former government official*
Toll, Robert Irwin *lawyer, real estate developer*

Indiana
Engler, W. Joseph, Jr. *lawyer*

Jenkintown
Nerenberg, Aaron *lawyer*

Johnstown
†Antonazzo, Nicholas Orlando *lawyer, corporate real estate executive*
Glosser, William Louis *lawyer*

Jones Mills
Fish, Paul Waring *lawyer*

King Of Prussia
Bramson, Robert Sherman *lawyer*

Lake Harmony
Polansky, Larry Paul *court administrator, consultant*

Lancaster
Brown, Joseph A. *lawyer, business executive*
Duroni, Charles Eugene *lawyer, food products executive*

Langhorne
Brafford, William Charles *lawyer*

Lansdale
Esterhai, John Louis *lawyer*

Lock Haven
Snowiss, Alvin L. *lawyer*

Macungie
Gavin, Austin *retired lawyer*

Malvern
Churchill, Winston John *lawyer, investment firm executive*
Ewing, Joseph Neff, Jr. *lawyer*
Patterson, Scott David *lawyer*

Media
Elman, Gerry Jay *lawyer*
Schrom, Gerard Killard *lawyer*

Mendenhall
Reinert, Norbert Frederick *patent lawyer, retired chemical company executive*

Merion Station
First, Joseph Michael *retired legal and management consultant*

Millersburg
Woodside, Robert Elmer *lawyer, former judge*

Morrisville
Heefner, William Frederick *lawyer*

Norristown
Aman, George Matthias, III *lawyer*
Flint, Daniel Waldo Boone *lawyer*
Folmar, Larry John *lawyer*
Wetherill, Eikins *lawyer, stock exchange executive*

Oil City
Callahan, Gerald William *lawyer, oil company executive*

Philadelphia
Aaron, Kenneth Ellyot *lawyer*
Abbott, Frank Harry *lawyer*
Abrahams, Robert David *lawyer, author*
Abramowitz, Robert Leslie *lawyer*
Ackerman, Alvin S. *lawyer*
Adams, Barbara *lawyer*
Ake, John Notley *lawyer, former investment services executive*
Albert, Jeffrey B. *lawyer*
Anders, Jerrold Paul *lawyer*
Anderson, E. Clive *lawyer*
Apfel, Jerome B. *lawyer*
Armstrong, Stephen Wales *lawyer*
Aronstein, Martin Joseph *lawyer, educator*
Auten, David Charles *lawyer*
Baccini, Laurance Ellis *lawyer*
Bachman, Arthur *lawyer*
Bales, John Foster, III *lawyer*
Ballengee, James McMorrow *lawyer*
Barrett, John J(ames), Jr. *lawyer*
Bartolini, Anthony Louis *lawyer*
Baughman, Jon A. *lawyer*
Beckman, Donald *lawyer*
Berger, David *lawyer*
Berger, Harold *lawyer, engineer*
Berger, Lawrence Howard *lawyer*
Bergholtz, Norbert F. *lawyer*
Berkley, Emily Carolan *lawyer*
Berkman, Richard Lyle *lawyer*
Bernard, John Marley *lawyer, educator*
Bernstein, George L. *lawyer, accountant*
Bershad, Jack R. *lawyer*
Biezup, John Thomas *lawyer*
Bildersee, Robert Alan *lawyer*
Binder, David Franklin *lawyer, author*
Black, Allen Decatur *lawyer*
Bloom, Michael Anthony *lawyer*
Bogutz, Jerome Edwin *lawyer*
Bradley, Raymond Joseph *lawyer*
Braverman, Elliott Kenneth *lawyer*
Brawner, Gerald Theodore *lawyer*
Brenan, Denis V. *lawyer*
Bright, Joseph Coleman *lawyer*
Briscoe, Jack Clayton *lawyer*
Britt, Earl Thomas *lawyer*
Brown, Richard P., Jr. *lawyer*
Brown, Stephen D. *lawyer*
Brown, William Hill, III *lawyer*
Browne, Michael Leon *lawyer*
Browne, Stanhope Stryker *lawyer*
Calvert, Jay H., Jr. *lawyer*
Cameron, John Clifford *lawyer, health science facility administrator*
Carnecchia, Baldo M., Jr. *lawyer*
Carson, Timothy Joseph *lawyer*
Casper, Charles B. *lawyer*
Cherken, Harry Sarkis, Jr. *lawyer*
Cheston, George Morris *lawyer*
Chimples, George *lawyer*
Clark, Frederic William *lawyer*
Clark, John Arthur *lawyer*
†Clothier, Isaac H., IV *lawyer*
Cloues, Edward Blanchard, II *lawyer*
Cohen, Deborah Fuchs *lawyer*
Cohen, Felix Asher *lawyer*
Cohen, Frederick *lawyer*
Cohen, Sylvan M. *lawyer*
Collings, Robert L. *lawyer*
Comfort, Robert Dennis *lawyer*
Comisky, Hope A. *lawyer*
Comisky, Marvin *retired lawyer*
Cooney, J(ohn) Gordon *lawyer*
Cox, Roger Frazier *lawyer*
Cramer, Harold *lawyer*
Crawford, James Douglas *lawyer*
Crough, Daniel Francis *lawyer, insurance company executive*
Damsgaard, Kell Marsh *lawyer*
D'Angelo, Christopher Scott *lawyer*
Davis, Alan Jay *lawyer*
Dean, Michael M. *lawyer*
Dean, Morris Jonathan *lawyer*
DeBunda, Salvatore Michael *lawyer*
De Lone, H. Francis *lawyer*
Deming, Frank Stout *lawyer*
Denious, Robert Wilbur *lawyer*
Dennis, Edward S(pencer) G(ale), Jr. *lawyer*
Denworth, Raymond K. *lawyer*
Diamond, Paul Steven *lawyer*
Dichter, Mark S. *lawyer*
Dilks, Park Bankert, Jr. *lawyer*
Donoghue, Norman E., II *lawyer*
Donohue, James J. *lawyer*
Doran, Thomas E. *lawyer*
Doran, William Michael *lawyer*
Dorfman, John Charles *lawyer*
Dorsky, Alvin H. *lawyer*
Drake, William Frank, Jr. *lawyer*
Dubin, Leonard *lawyer*
Durham, James W. *lawyer*
Dworetzky, Joseph Anthony *lawyer*
Edwards, Stephen Allen *lawyer*
Elliott, William Homer, Jr. *lawyer*
Emerson, S. Jonathan *lawyer*
Emory, Hugh Mercer *lawyer*
Esser, Carl Eric *lawyer*
Everett, Carl Bell *lawyer*
Fader, Henry Conrad *lawyer*
Fala, Herman C. *lawyer*
Falk, I. Lee *lawyer*
Fallon, Christopher Chaffee, Jr. *lawyer*
Farage, Donald J. *lawyer, educator*
Feirson, Steven B. *lawyer*
Feldman, Albert Joseph *lawyer*
Fiebach, H. Robert *lawyer*
Fine, Lawrence B. *lawyer*
†Finet, Scott *law librarian*
Fisher, Linda A. *lawyer*
Flaherty, John Edward, Jr. *lawyer*
Flanagan, Joseph Patrick, Jr. *lawyer*
Flaxman, Howard Richard *lawyer*
Fox, Lawrence J. *lawyer*
Fox, Reeder Rodman *lawyer*
Frank, Harvey *lawyer, writer*
Freedman, Robert Louis *lawyer*
Freeland, Michael Willis *lawyer*
Friedman, Frank Bennett *lawyer*
Friedman, Steven Lewis *lawyer*
Fryman, Louis William *lawyer*
Gadsden, Thomas P. *lawyer*
Garcia, Rudolph *lawyer*
Genkin, Barry Howard *lawyer*
Gerhart, Frederick John *lawyer*
German, Edward Cecil *lawyer*
Glanton, Richard H. *lawyer*
Glassman, Howard Theodore *lawyer*
Glassmoyer, Thomas Parvin *lawyer*
Glazer, Ronald Barry *lawyer*
Goldberg, Richard Robert *lawyer*
Goldstein, William Marks *lawyer*
Goodrich, Herbert Funk, Jr. *lawyer*
Gornish, Gerald *lawyer*
Gough, John Francis *lawyer*
Granoff, Gail Patricia *lawyer*
Grant, M. Duncan *lawyer*
Grant, Richard W. *lawyer*
Greenberg, Peter Steven *lawyer*
Greenfield, Bruce Harold *lawyer, banker*
Grodnitzky, Alan Scot *lawyer*
Gross, Irwin Lee *lawyer, corporate executive*
Grove, David Lavan *lawyer*
Haley, Vincent Peter *lawyer*
Hamilton, Stephen David Derwent *lawyer*
Harkins, John Graham, Jr. *lawyer*
Hatoff, Howard Ira *labor lawyer*
Hauptfuhrer, George Jost, Jr. *lawyer*
Haviland, Bancroft Dawley *lawyer*
Haydanek, Ronald Edward *lawyer*
Hazard, Geoffrey Cornell, Jr. *law educator*
Heim, Robert Charles *lawyer*
Henderson, J(oseph) Welles *lawyer*
Hennessy, Joseph H. *lawyer*
†Henrich, William Joseph, Jr. *lawyer*
Henry, Ragan A. *lawyer, broadcaster*
Hess, Hans Ober *lawyer*
Hodavance, Robert S. *lawyer*
Hoelscher, Robert James *lawyer*
Hoffman, Alan Jay *lawyer*
Hoffman, Jerome A. *lawyer*
Holloway, Hiliary Hamilton *lawyer, banker*
Holmes, Norman Leonard *lawyer*
Honnold, John Otis, Jr. *law educator*
Horvath, Joseph John *lawyer, insurance company executive*
Humenuk, William Anzelm *lawyer, partner*
Humes, James Calhoun *lawyer, communications consultant, author*
Hunter, James Austen, Jr. *lawyer*
Iskrant, John Dermot *lawyer*
Jacovini, Joseph Henry *lawyer*
Jaffe, Paul Lawrence *lawyer*
Jamieson, David Donald *lawyer*
Jellinek, Miles Andrew *lawyer*
Jennings, James Walsh *lawyer*
Jones, Robert Jeffries *lawyer*
Jones, Robert Mead, Jr. *lawyer*
Justice, Jack Burton *lawyer*
Kahn, James Robert *lawyer*
Kalman, Arnold I. *lawyer*
Kauffman, Bruce William *lawyer, former state supreme court justice*
Kaufman, David Joseph *lawyer*
Keene, John Clark *lawyer, educator*
Kellett, Morris C. *lawyer*
Kempin, Frederick Gustav, Jr. *lawyer, educator*
Kendall, Robert Louis, Jr. *lawyer*
Kenworthy, Thomas Bausman *lawyer*
Kessler, Alan Craig *lawyer*
Kessler, Mark Keil *lawyer*
Kircher, Philip G. *lawyer*
Kittredge, Thomas M. *lawyer*
Klasko, Herbert Ronald *lawyer, law educator, writer*
Klauder, N. Jeffrey *lawyer*
Klaus, William Robert *lawyer*
Klayman, Barry Martin *lawyer*
Klein, Howard Bruce *lawyer, law educator*
Klein, Samuel Edwin *lawyer*
Kline, Thomas Richard *lawyer*
Kohn, Harold Elias *lawyer*
Kopp, Charles Gilbert *lawyer*
Kraemer, Michael Frederick *lawyer*
Kramer, Meyer *lawyer, editor, clergyman*
Krampf, John Edward *lawyer*
Krzyzanowski, Richard Lucien *lawyer, corporate executive*
Kupperman, Louis Brandeis *lawyer*
Kurland, Seymour *lawyer*
Laddon, Warren Milton *lawyer*
Lambert, George Robert *lawyer*
LaValley, Frederick J. M. *lawyer*
Leddy, John Henry *lawyer*
Ledwith, James Robb *lawyer*
Ledwith, John Francis *lawyer*
Leech, Noyes Elwood *lawyer, educator*
Lehr, Michael *lawyer*
Leonard, Thomas Aloysius *lawyer*
Levin, A. Leo *law educator, retired government official*
Levin, Murray Simon *lawyer*
Levy, Dale Penneys *lawyer*
Lewis, Christopher Alan *lawyer*
Lewis, John Hardy, Jr. *lawyer*
Libonati, Michael Ernest *lawyer, educator, writer*
Lichtenstein, Lawrence Jay *lawyer*
Lichtenstein, Robert Jay *lawyer*
Lillie, Charisse Ranielle *lawyer, educator*
Lipman, Frederick D. *lawyer*
Loewenstein, Benjamin Steinberg *lawyer*
Lombard, John James, Jr. *lawyer*
Loveless, George Group *lawyer*
Lowery, William Herbert *lawyer*
Lucey, John David, Jr. *lawyer*
Lundy, Joseph E. *lawyer*
Lustbader, Philip Lawrence *lawyer*
MacGregor, David Bruce *lawyer*
Maclay, Donald Merle *lawyer*
Madeira, Edward W(alter), Jr. *lawyer*
Madva, Stephen Alan *lawyer*
Magargee, W(illiam) Scott, III *lawyer*
Magarity, Gregory T. *lawyer*
Magaziner, Fred Thomas *lawyer*
Mai, Elizabeth Hardy *lawyer*
Mann, Theodore R. *lawyer*
Mannino, Edward Francis *lawyer*
Marion, David H. *lawyer*
Mason, Theodore W. *lawyer*
Masterson, Thomas A. *lawyer*
Mather, Barbara W. *lawyer*
Mathes, Stephen Jon *lawyer*
Mattoon, Peter Mills *lawyer*
Maxey, David Walker *lawyer*
McCabe, James J. *lawyer*
McElroy, Richard P. *lawyer*
McKeever, John Eugene *lawyer*
McMenamin, Richard F. *lawyer*
McQuiston, Robert Earl *lawyer*
Meigs, John Forsyth *lawyer*
Mesirov, Leon Isaac *lawyer*
Meyers, Howard L. *lawyer*
Milbourne, Walter Robertson *lawyer*
Miller, Henry Franklin *lawyer*
Miller, Margery K. *lawyer*
Milone, Francis Michael *lawyer*
Minisi, Anthony S. *lawyer*
Mirabello, Francis Joseph *lawyer*
Moore, Michael Scott *law and philosophy educator*
Morikawa, Dennis J. *lawyer*
Morris, Thomas Bateman, Jr. *lawyer*
Moss, Arthur Henshey *lawyer*
Murrell, Thomas W., III *lawyer*
Myers, Kenneth Raymond *lawyer*
Narin, Stephen B. *lawyer*
Nast, Dianne Martha *lawyer*
Neilson, Benjamin Reath *lawyer*
Newbold, Arthur *lawyer*
†Newman, Sanders David *lawyer*
Nofer, George Hancock *lawyer*
O'Brien, William Jerome, II *lawyer*
O'Connor, Joseph A., Jr. *lawyer*
O'Donnell, G. Daniel *lawyer*
O'Leary, Dennis Joseph *lawyer*
Ominsky, Harris *lawyer*
O'Reilly, Timothy Patrick *lawyer*
Oswald, Stanton S. *lawyer*
Pagliaro, James Domenic *lawyer*
Palmer, Richard Ware *lawyer*
Panzer, Mitchell Emanuel *lawyer*
Patrick, George W. *lawyer*
Pollack, Michael *lawyer*
Posner, Edward Martin *lawyer*
Poul, Franklin *lawyer*
Powell, Walter Hecht *labor arbitrator*
Pratter, Gene E. K. *lawyer*
Price, Robert Stanley *lawyer*
Promislo, Daniel *lawyer*
Rabinowitz, Samuel Nathan *lawyer*
Rachofsky, David J. *lawyer*
Rackow, Julian Paul *lawyer*
Rainey, Arthur H. *lawyer*
Ralph, Thomas A. *lawyer*
Reagan, Harry Edwin, III *lawyer*
Reath, George, Jr. *lawyer*
Redeker, James Russell *lawyer*
Reed, Alan L. *lawyer*
Reed, Michael Haywood *lawyer*
Reich, Abraham Charles *lawyer*
Reiss, John Barlow *lawyer*
Reitz, Curtis Randall *lawyer, educator*
Rizzo, Richard C. *lawyer*
Roberts, Carl Geoffrey *lawyer*
Roomberg, Lila Goldstein *lawyer*
Root, Stanley William, Jr. *lawyer*
Rose, Robert Lawrence *lawyer, financial services company executive*
Rosenbleeth, Richard Marvin *lawyer*
Rosenbloom, Sanford M. *lawyer*
Rosenfield, Bruce Alan *lawyer*
Rosenstein, James Alfred *lawyer*
Rosoff, William A. *lawyer*
Ross, Daniel R. *lawyer*
Ross, Murray Louis *lawyer, business executive*
Rulon, Richard R. *lawyer*
Sabat, Richard J. *lawyer*
Samson, Peter *lawyer*
Sartorius, Peter S. *lawyer*
Satinsky, Barnett *lawyer*
Sax, Helen Spigel *lawyer*
Schaub, Harry Carl *lawyer*
Scher, Howard Dennis *lawyer*
Schneider, Carl W. *lawyer*
Schneider, Pam Horvitz *lawyer*
Schneider, Richard Graham *lawyer*
Schwartz, Robert M. *lawyer*
Scott, Donald Allison *lawyer*
Scott, Michael Timothy *lawyer*
Scott, William Proctor, III *lawyer*
Segal, Bernard Gerard *lawyer*
Segal, Irving Randall *lawyer*
Segal, Robert Martin *lawyer*
Segrè, Nina *lawyer*
Shapiro, Raymond L. *lawyer*
Sharbaugh, Thomas J. *lawyer*
Shaw, Mari Gursky *lawyer*
Shecter, Howard L. *lawyer*
Shepard, Geoffrey Carroll *corporate lawyer*
Shestack, Jerome Joseph *lawyer*
Shiekman, Laurence Zeid *lawyer*
Shields, Robert Emmet *lawyer*
Shusterman, Murray H. *lawyer*
Shuter, Bruce Donald *lawyer*
Siembieda, Matthew John *lawyer*
Siskind, Ralph Walter *lawyer*
Smith, John Francis, III *lawyer*
Snyder, Lee H. *lawyer*
Snyder, Ralph Sheldon *lawyer*
Solano, Carl Anthony *lawyer*
Somers, Hans Peter *lawyer*
Spaeth, Edmund Benjamin, Jr. *lawyer, law educator, former judge*
Spector, Martin Wolf *lawyer, business executive*
Spencer, Steven D. *lawyer*
Stack, Stephen A., Jr. *lawyer*
Stakias, G. Michael *lawyer*
Starr, Allan H. *lawyer*
Steinberg, Robert Philip *lawyer*
Stern, Joan Naomi *lawyer*
Sternberg, Donna Udin *lawyer*
Stewart, Robert Forrest, Jr. *lawyer*
Stiller, Jennifer Anne *lawyer*
Strickler, Matthew M. *lawyer*
Stuntebeck, Clinton A. *lawyer*
Subak, John Thomas *lawyer*
Sugarman, Robert Jay *lawyer*
Summers, Clyde Wilson *law educator*
Suplee, Dennis Raymond *lawyer*
Swichar, Edward *lawyer*
Sykes, David Terrence *lawyer*
Temin, Michael Lehman *lawyer*
Thomas, Frank M., Jr. *lawyer*
Thomas, Regina O'Brien *lawyer*
Thurston, David E. *lawyer, general counsel*
Tiger, Ira Paul *lawyer*
Torregrossa, Joseph Anthony *lawyer*
Undercofler, J(onas) Clayton *lawyer*
Vaira, Peter Francis *lawyer*
Volpicelli, Stephen L. *lawyer*
Wagner, Thomas Joseph *lawyer, insurance company executive*
Wald, Martin *lawyer*
Walker, Kent *lawyer*
Walters, Christopher Kent *lawyer*
Wambold, Judson J. *lawyer*
Warner, Theodore Kugler, Jr. *lawyer*
Weil, Jeffrey George *lawyer*
Weisberg, Morris L. *retired lawyer*
Wellington, Ralph Glenn *lawyer*
Wetzel, Carroll Robbins *lawyer*
Whiteside, William Anthony, Jr. *lawyer*
Whitman, Bradford F. *lawyer*
Whitman, Jules Isidoré *lawyer*
Wiener, Ronald Martin *lawyer*
Wiener, Thomas Eli *lawyer*
Wild, Richard P. *lawyer*
Witt, Thomas Powell *lawyer*
Wolf, Robert B. *lawyer*
Wolkin, Paul Alexander *lawyer, former institute executive*
Wood, William Philler *lawyer*
Woodruff, Margaret Smith *lawyer*
Wright, Minturn Tatum, III *lawyer*
Wrobleski, Jeanne Pauline *lawyer*
Wysocki, F(elix) Michael *lawyer*
Young, Andrew Brodbeck *lawyer*
Ziff, Lloyd Richard *lawyer*
Ziga, Kathleen *lawyer*
Ziomek, Thomas John *lawyer*
Zivitz, Stephen Charles *lawyer*

Pittsburgh
Aaron, Marcus, II *lawyer*
Aaronson, Joel P. *lawyer*
Alstadt, Lynn Jeffery *lawyer*
Aranson, Michael J. *lawyer*
Armstrong, David J. *lawyer*
Armstrong, Jack Gilliland *lawyer*
Baier, George Patrick *lawyer, electrical engineer*
Barmen, Stewart B. *lawyer*
Basinski, Anthony Joseph *lawyer*
Beck, Paul Augustine *lawyer*
Benson, Stuart Wells, III *lawyer*
Bevan, William, III *lawyer*
Black, Alexander *lawyer*
Bleil, Walter G. *lawyer*
Blenko, Walter John, Jr. *lawyer*
Bonessa, Dennis R. *lawyer*
Borkovic, David Allen *lawyer*
Brennan, Carey M. *lawyer*
†Briskman, Louis J. *lawyer*
Brown, David Ronald *lawyer*
Buerger, David Bernard *lawyer*
Candris, Laura A. *lawyer*
Chamberlain, Denise Kay *lawyer, banking counsel*
Cheever, George Martin *lawyer*
†Christof, Joseph S. D., II *lawyer*
Clark, Richard A. *lawyer*
Colen, Frederick Haas *lawyer*
Coney, Aims C., Jr. *lawyer, labor-management negotiator*
Connell, Janice T. *lawyer, author, arbitrator, business executive*
Connors, Eugene Kenneth *lawyer*
Conti, Joy Flowers *lawyer*
Cooper, Thomas Louis *lawyer*
Cowan, Barton Zalman *lawyer*
Craig, Edward Armstrong, III *lawyer*
Daniel, Robert Michael *lawyer*
Davis, John Phillips, Jr. *lawyer*
†Davis, Lewis U., Jr. *lawyer*
DeForest, Walter Pattison, III *lawyer*
Delano, Jonathan William *lawyer*
Dell, Ernest Robert *lawyer*
Demmler, John Henry *lawyer*
Demmler, Ralph Henry *lawyer*
DiPietro, Melanie *lawyer*
Dodds, Robert James, Jr. *retired lawyer*
Donnelly, Thomas Joseph *lawyer*
Doty, Robert Walter *lawyer*
Dugan, John F. *lawyer*
Ehrenwerth, David Harry *lawyer*
Erb, James J. *lawyer*
Evans, Bruce Dwight *lawyer*
Farley, Andrew Newell *lawyer*
Fawcett, David Blakley, Jr. *lawyer*
Ferguson, Sanford Barnett *lawyer*
Fernsler, John Paul *lawyer*
Fishman, Libby G. *lawyer*
Flatley, Lawrence Edward *lawyer*
Flinn, Michael J. *lawyer*
Fort, James Tomlinson *lawyer*
Fox, Cyril A., Jr. *law educator*
Frank, Ronald W. *lawyer, financier*
Gallagher, Daniel P., Jr. *lawyer*

Garrett, Sylvester *arbitrator*
Gerlach, G. Donald *lawyer*
Gold, Harold Arthur *lawyer*
Goldberg, Mark Joel *lawyer*
Graf, Edward Louis, Jr. *lawyer, finance executive*
Hackney, William Pendleton *lawyer*
Hardie, James Hiller *lawyer*
Harff, Charles Henry *lawyer, diversified industrial company executive*
Hartman, Ronald G. *lawyer*
Harty, James Quinn *lawyer*
Harvey, Calvin Rea *lawyer*
Heilman, Carl Edwin *lawyer*
Hellman, Arthur David *law educator, consultant*
Hershey, Dale *lawyer*
Hershey, Nathan *lawyer, educator*
Hickman, Leon Edward *lawyer, business executive*
Hill, John Howard *lawyer*
Hitt, Leo N. *lawyer, educator*
Hoffstot, Henry Phipps, Jr. *lawyer*
Hollinshead, Earl Darnell, Jr. *lawyer*
†Holz, Richard Lee *lawyer*
Hough, Thomas Henry Michael *lawyer*
Johnson, Robert Alan *lawyer*
Jones, Craig Ward *lawyer*
Katarincic, Joseph Anthony *lawyer*
Kearney, Kerry A. *lawyer*
Kearns, John J., III *lawyer*
Kenrick, Charles William *lawyer*
Kerr, William Gregg *lawyer*
Ketter, David Lee *lawyer*
King, Peter J. *lawyer*
Klett, Edwin Lee *lawyer*
Knapp, George Robert *lawyer*
Knox, Charles Graham *lawyer*
Krasik, Carl *lawyer*
†Kuhn, James Craighead, Jr. *lawyer*
London, Alan E. *lawyer*
Lovett, Robert G. *lawyer*
Mansmann, J. Jerome *lawyer*
May, Charles Kent *lawyer*
Mazeski, Edward James, Jr. *lawyer, corporate secretary*
Mc Cartney, Robert Charles *lawyer*
McConomy, James Herbert *lawyer*
McCullough, M. Bruce *lawyer*
McGonigle, John William *lawyer, investment company executive*
McGough, Walter Thomas *lawyer*
McGough, Walter Thomas, Jr. *lawyer*
McLaughlin, John Sherman *lawyer*
Medonis, Robert Xavier *lawyer*
Meisel, Alan *law educator*
Messner, Robert Thomas *lawyer, banking executive*
Miller, Harbaugh *lawyer*
Miller, James Robert *lawyer*
Miller, Patricia G. *lawyer*
Morton, James Davis *lawyer*
Munsch, Martha Hartle *lawyer*
Murdoch, David Armor *lawyer*
Murray, John Edward, Jr. *lawyer, educator, university president*
Murrin, Regis Doubet *lawyer*
Myers, Marlee S. *lawyer*
Newlin, William Rankin *lawyer*
Nordenberg, Mark Alan *legal educator, university administrator*
Norris, James Harold *lawyer, partner*
Nuernberg, William Richard *lawyer*
Ober, Russell John, Jr. *lawyer*
O'Connor, Donald Thomas *lawyer*
O'Connor, Edward Gearing *lawyer*
Olson, Stephen M(ichael) *lawyer*
Patton, Robert Frederick *lawyer, banker*
Perfido, Ruth S. *lawyer*
Phillips, Larry Edward *lawyer*
Plowman, Jack Wesley *lawyer*
Pohl, Paul Michael *lawyer*
Pois, Joseph *lawyer, educator*
Pomeroy, Thomas Wilson, Jr. *lawyer, former state supreme court justice*
Post, Peter David *lawyer*
Powderly, William H., III *lawyer*
Propst, John Leake *lawyer*
Prorok, Robert Francis *lawyer*
Prosperi, Louis Anthony *lawyer*
Pugliese, Robert Francis *lawyer, business executive*
Quinn, John E. *lawyer*
Randolph, Robert DeWitt *lawyer*
Reed, W. Franklin *lawyer*
Reif, Eric Peter *lawyer*
Restivo, James John, Jr. *lawyer*
Ries, William Campbell *lawyer*
Ritchey, Patrick William *lawyer*
Robinson, William M. *lawyer*
Rose, Evans, Jr. *lawyer*
Rosenberger, Bryan David *lawyer*
†Sandman, Dan D. *lawyer*
Scanlon, Eugene Francis *lawyer*
Scheinholtz, Leonard Louis *lawyer*
Schliebs, Charles Allan *lawyer*
Schmidt, Edward Craig *lawyer*
Schwab, Arthur James *lawyer*
Schwendeman, Paul William *lawyer*
Sell, William Edward *legal educator*
Sensenich, Ila Jeanne *lawyer, magistrate judge*
Silverman, Arnold Barry *lawyer*
Singer, Paul Meyer *lawyer*
Smith, Charles Raymond, Jr. *lawyer*
Smith, William J. *lawyer*
Stein, Arland Thomas *lawyer*
Strader, James David *lawyer*
Stroyd, Arthur Heister *lawyer*
Swaim, Joseph Carter, Jr. *lawyer*
Sweeney, Clayton Anthony *lawyer, business executive*
Symons, Edward Leonard, Jr. *lawyer, educator, investment advisor*
Thompson, Thomas Martin *lawyer*
Tungate, David E. *lawyer, educator*
Turner, Harry Woodruff *lawyer*
Ubinger, John W., Jr. *lawyer*
Van Kirk, Thomas L. *lawyer*
Walton, Jon David *lawyer*
Ward, Thomas Jerome *lawyer*
Webb, William Hess *lawyer*
Weisgerber, Edward Victor *lawyer*
Wentley, Richard Taylor *lawyer*
Willard, Mark Alan *lawyer*
Woodward, Thomas Aiken *lawyer*
Wright, Thomas David *lawyer, entrepreneur*
Yorsz, Stanley *lawyer*
Zimmerman, Scott Franklin *lawyer*

Reading
Johnson, Robert Joseph *corporate lawyer*
Rothermel, Daniel Krott *lawyer, holding company executive*

Ridley Park
Clark, John H., Jr. *lawyer*

Saint Davids
Bovaird, Brendan Peter *lawyer*

Scranton
Cimini, Joseph Fedele *law educator, lawyer, former magistrate*
Haggerty, James Joseph *lawyer*
Howley, James McAndrew *lawyer*
Myers, Morey Mayer *lawyer*
Preate, Ernest D., Sr. *lawyer*

Sewickley
Barry, John Kevin *lawyer*

Solebury
Valentine, H. Jeffrey *legal association executive*

Spring City
Mayerson, Hy *lawyer*

Swarthmore
LeGros, Susan Packard *lawyer*

Tunkhannock
Jones, Edward White, II *lawyer*

Valley Forge
Croney, J. Kenneth *lawyer*
Moulton, Hugh Geoffrey *lawyer, business executive*

Villanova
Bersoff, Donald Neil *lawyer, psychologist*

Warminster
Tolson, Jay Henry *lawyer, industrial instrument company executive*

Washington
Richman, Stephen I. *lawyer*

Wayne
Baldwin, Frank Bruce, III *lawyer*
†Blumenthal, Richard Allen *lawyer*
Griffith, Edward, II *lawyer*
†Gross, Lawrence Alan *lawyer*
Hedges, Donald Walton *lawyer*
Norris, Charles Head, Jr. *lawyer, financial executive*
Woodbury, Alan Tenney *lawyer*

West Chester
Judson, Franklyn Sylvanus *lawyer, consultant*

Wexford
Clokey, Frank R. *lawyer*

Williamsport
Ertel, Allen Edward *lawyer, former congressman*

RHODE ISLAND

Cranston
†Simonian, John S. *lawyer*

East Greenwich
Dence, Edward William, Jr. *lawyer, banker*
Flynn, Richard James *lawyer*

Newport
Cohen, Arthur Abram *lawyer*
Levie, Howard S(idney) *lawyer, educator, author*

Pawtucket
†Gaschen, Francis Allen *lawyer*
Robbins, Donald Michael *lawyer*

Providence
Arcaro, Harold Conrad, Jr. *lawyer, educator*
Borod, Richard Melvin *lawyer*
†Caprio, Frank T. *lawyer, state legislator*
Carlotti, Stephen Jon *lawyer*
Cianci, Vincent Albert, Jr. *lawyer, mayor*
Courage, Thomas Roberts *lawyer*
Curran, Joseph Patrick *lawyer*
Donnelly, Kevin William *lawyer*
†Dowling, Sarah T. *lawyer, state official*
Farmer, Malcolm, III *lawyer*
Farrell, Margaret Dawson *lawyer*
Field, Noel Macdonald, Jr. *lawyer*
Gasbarro, Pasco, Jr. *lawyer*
†Gorham, Bradford *lawyer*
Grimm, William Richard *lawyer*
Hindle, Edward Francis *lawyer*
Hopkins, Jacques Vaughn *lawyer*
Johnson, Vahe Duncan *lawyer*
Kean, John Vaughan *lawyer*
Kersh, DeWitte Talmadge, Jr. *lawyer*
Licht, Richard A. *lawyer*
Lombardi, Alfred Samuel *lawyer*
Long, Beverly Glenn *lawyer*
McCann, Gail Elizabeth *lawyer*
Olsen, Hans Peter *lawyer*
Pendergast, John Joseph, III *lawyer*
Pierce, Richard Hilton *lawyer*
Reed, Walter Gurnee Dyer *lawyer*
Resmini, Ronald Joseph *lawyer*
Robinson, William Philip, III *lawyer*
Salter, Lester Herbert *lawyer*
Sherman, Deming Eliot *lawyer*
Silver, Paul Allen *lawyer*
Soutter, Thomas D. *lawyer*
Staples, Richard Farnsworth *lawyer*
†Svengalis, Kendall Frayne *law librarian*
Tobin, Bentley *lawyer*
Walker, Howard Ernest *lawyer*
Weissfeld, Joachim Alexander *lawyer*

Tiverton
Davis, Stephen Edward *lawyer*

Warwick
†Knowles, Charles Timothy *lawyer, state legislator*

Westerly
Hennessy, Dean McDonald *lawyer, multinational corporation executive*

SOUTH CAROLINA

Anderson
Glenn, Michael Douglas *lawyer*
Watkins, William Law *lawyer, retired*

Beaufort
Harvey, William Brantley, Jr. *lawyer, former lieutenant governor*

Camden
Furman, Hezekiah Wyndol Carroll *lawyer*

Charleston
Cannon, Hugh *lawyer*
Farr, Charles Sims *lawyer*
Garrett, Gordon Henderson *lawyer*
Grimball, William Heyward *lawyer*
Mulholland, Angela Broadway *lawyer*
Simons, Albert, Jr. *lawyer*

Clemson
Cox, Headley Morris, Jr. *lawyer, educator*

Columbia
Adams, Gregory Burke *lawyer, educator*
Bailey, George Screven *lawyer*
Blanton, Hoover Clarence *lawyer*
Chastain, Randall Meads *lawyer, educator*
Finkel, Gerald Michael *lawyer*
Foster, Robert Watson *legal educator*
Haimbaugh, George Dow, Jr. *lawyer, educator*
Hancock, Harriet Daniels *lawyer*
†Land, John Calhoun, III *lawyer, state legislator*
Marion, Andrew Burnet *lawyer*
Matthews, Steve Allen *lawyer*
Mc Cullough, Ralph Clayton, II *lawyer, educator*
Nexsen, Julian Jacobs *lawyer*
Roberts, Edward Calhoun *retired lawyer*
†Rogers, Timothy Folk *lawyer*
Sloan, Frank Keenan *lawyer, writer*
Tate, Harold Simmons, Jr. *lawyer*
Wells, Robert Steven *law association executive*
Wolfe, George B. *lawyer*

Easley
Grantham, George Leighton *lawyer, banker, utility company executive*
†Robinson, Alfred Burgess, Jr. *lawyer*

Florence
†Harwell, B(axter) Hicks *lawyer, state legislator*

Georgetown
Moore, Albert Cunningham *lawyer, insurance company executive*

Greenville
Hagood, William Milliken, III *lawyer*
†Haskins, Terry Edward *lawyer, politician*
Horton, James Wright *retired lawyer*
James, William Richard *lawyer*
†Mitchell, Theo Walker *lawyer*
Thompson, Robert Thomas *lawyer*
Todd, John Dickerson, Jr. *lawyer*
Traxler, William Byrd *lawyer*
Walker, Wesley M. *lawyer*
Walters, Johnnie McKeiver *lawyer*

Greenwood
Sigety, Charles Edward *lawyer, medical products executive*

Hartsville
DeLoach, Harris E(ugene), Jr. *lawyer, manufacturing company executive*

Hilton Head Island
Becker, Karl Martin *lawyer, investment company executive*
Rose, William Shepard, Jr. *lawyer, former federal official*
Scarminach, Charles Anthony *lawyer*
Vadnais, Alfred William *lawyer*

Landrum
Hilton, Ordway *document examiner*

Lexington
Wilkins, Robert Pearce *lawyer*

Newberry
Pope, Thomas Harrington, Jr. *lawyer*

Spartanburg
†Courtney, Charles Tyrone *lawyer, state legislator*
†Smith, William Douglas *lawyer*
Williams, John Cornelius *lawyer*

Walterboro
McLeod, Walton James, Jr. *lawyer*

SOUTH DAKOTA

Britton
Farrar, Frank Leroy *lawyer, former governor of South Dakota*

Parker
Zimmer, John Herman *lawyer*

Pierre
Johnson, Julie Marie *lawyer, lobbyist*
Thompson, Charles Murray *lawyer*

Rapid City
Foye, Thomas Harold *lawyer*

Sioux Falls
†Kirby, Dan Laird *lawyer*

Yankton
Hirsch, Robert William *lawyer*

TENNESSEE

Athens
Guinn, Charles Clifford, Jr. *lawyer*

Chattanooga
Bahner, Thomas Maxfield *lawyer*
Proctor, John Franklin *lawyer*
Witt, Raymond Buckner, Jr. *lawyer*

Clarksville
Smith, Gregory Dale *lawyer*

Cleveland
†Fisher, Richard A. *lawyer, state legislator*

Cordova
Springfield, James Francis *lawyer, banker*

Germantown
Ewing, William Hickman, Jr. *lawyer*

Hendersonville
McCaleb, Joe Wallace *lawyer*

Hermitage
Lockmiller, David Alexander *lawyer, educator*

Knoxville
Arnett, Foster Deaver *lawyer*
Christenbury, Edward Samuel *lawyer*
Dillard, W. Thomas *lawyer*
Hagood, Lewis Russell *lawyer*
Howard, Lewis Spilman *lawyer*
Lucas, John Allen *lawyer*
Phillips, Jerry Juan *law educator*
Phillips, Thomas Wade *lawyer*
Rayson, Edwin Hope *lawyer*
Sanger, Herbert Shelton, Jr. *lawyer, former government official*
Schmidt, Benno Charles, Jr. *lawyer, educator*
Vogel, Howard H. *lawyer*
Waters, John B. *lawyer*
Wheeler, John Watson *lawyer*

Lebanon
†Rochelle, Robert Thomas *lawyer, state senator*

Lookout Mountain
Leitner, Paul R. *lawyer*

Memphis
Allen, Newton Perkins *lawyer*
Armstrong, Walter Preston, Jr. *lawyer*
Broadhurst, Jerome Anthony *lawyer*
Brode, Marvin Jay *lawyer, former state legislator*
Buchignani, Leo Joseph *lawyer*
Burch, Lucius Edward, Jr. *lawyer*
Clark, Ross Bert, II *lawyer*
Cody, Walter James Michael *lawyer, former state official*
Friedman, Robert Michael *lawyer*
Gilman, Ronald Lee *lawyer*
Goodman, Benjamin *lawyer*
†Harvey, Albert C. *lawyer*
Manire, James McDonnell *lawyer*
Noel, Randall Deane *lawyer*
Streibich, Harold Cecil *lawyer*
Tate, Stonewall Shepherd *lawyer*

Nashville
Alexander, Andrew Lamar (Lamar Alexander) *lawyer, former secretary of education*
Bass, James Orin *lawyer*
Berry, William Wells *lawyer*
Blumstein, James Franklin *legal educator, lawyer, consultant*
Bostick, Charles Dent *lawyer, educator*
Brown, Joe Blackburn *lawyer*
Cheek, James Howe, III *lawyer*
Covington, Robert Newman *lawyer, educator*
Culbertson, Katheryn Campbell *lawyer*
Deer, James Willis *lawyer*
†Fish, Donald Winston *lawyer, health care company executive*
Gillmor, John Edward *lawyer*
Hart, Richard Banner *lawyer*
Harwell, Aubrey Biggs *lawyer*
Johnson, James Harold *lawyer*
†Kavass, Igor Ivar *law educator, law librarian, consultant*
Ledyard, Robins Heard *lawyer*
Levinson, L(eslie) Harold *lawyer, educator*
Lyon, Philip K(irkland) *lawyer*
Maier, Harold Geistweit *legal educator, lawyer*
May, Joseph Leserman (Jack) (Jack May) *lawyer*
McCoy, Thomas Raymond *lawyer, educator*
Sanders, Paul Hampton *lawyer, emeritus educator, arbitrator/mediator*
Sanford, Valerius *lawyer*
Sims, Wilson *lawyer*
Standel, Richard Reynold, Jr. *lawyer, communications executive*
Thompson, Almose Alphonse *lawyer, educator*
Trautman, Herman Louis *lawyer, educator*

TEXAS

Abilene
Boone, Billy Warren *lawyer, judge*
Wilson, Stanley P. *retired lawyer*

Addison
Springer, Stanley G. *lawyer*

Amarillo
Madden, Wales Hendrix, Jr. *lawyer*
Neal, A. Curtis *retired lawyer*
†Smithee, John True *lawyer, state legislator*

Austin
Ahearn, Patricia Jean *lawyer*
Allday, Martin Lewis *lawyer*
Allison, John Robert *lawyer, educator, author*
Beckey, Sylvia Louise *lawyer*
Bissex, Walter Earl *lawyer*
Bobbitt, Philip Chase *lawyer, educator, writer*
Byrd, Linward Tonnett *lawyer, rancher*
Cantilo, Patrick Herrera *lawyer*
Cook, J. Rowland *lawyer*

Davis, Robert Larry *lawyer*
Dawson, Robert Oscar *lawyer, educator*
Dougherty, John Chrysostom, III *lawyer*
Gambrell, James Bruton, III *lawyer, educator*
Gangstad, John Erik *lawyer*
Gibson, William Willard, Jr. *law educator*
Goldstein, E. Ernest *lawyer*
Golemon, Ronald Kinnan *lawyer*
Greene, John Joseph *lawyer*
Greig, Brian Strother *lawyer*
Hamilton, Dagmar Strandberg *lawyer, educator*
Hamilton, Robert Woodruff *law educator*
Harrison, Richard Wayne *lawyer*
Helburn, Isadore B. *arbitrator, mediator, educator*
Henderson, George Ervin *lawyer*
Huie, William Orr *legal educator*
Ikard, Frank Neville, Jr. *lawyer*
Ingram, Denny Ouzts, Jr. *lawyer, educator*
Jentz, Gaylord Adair *law educator*
Johanson, Stanley Morris *legal educator*
Johnson, Corwin Waggoner *lawyer, educator*
Jordan, Barbara C. *lawyer, educator, former congresswoman*
Knight, Gary *lawyer, educator, publisher*
Laycock, Harold Douglas *law educator, writer*
Levinson, Sanford Victor *legal educator*
Matheson, Daniel Nicholas, III *lawyer*
Mauzy, Oscar Holcombe *lawyer, retired state supreme court justice*
McDaniel, Myra Atwell *lawyer, former state official*
McGinnis, Robert Campbell *lawyer*
Mersky, Roy Martin *law educator, librarian*
Oates, Carl Everette *lawyer*
Painton, Russell Elliott *lawyer, mechanical engineer*
Pickens, Franklin Ace *lawyer*
Powers, Pike, Jr. *lawyer*
Ruud, Millard Harrington *former legal association administrator, retired educator*
Shapiro, Sander Wolf *lawyer*
Sherman, Edward Francis *lawyer, educator*
Sherman, Max Ray *lawyer, academic executive, former state senator*
Stephen, John Erle *lawyer, consultant*
Strauser, Robert Wayne *lawyer*
Sturley, Michael F. *law educator*
Sullivan, Teresa Ann *law and sociology educator, academic administrator*
Sutton, John F., Jr. *law educator, university dean, lawyer*
Temple, Larry Eugene *lawyer*
Thomajan, Robert *lawyer, management and financial consultant*
Tigar, Michael Edward *lawyer, educator*
Tottenham, Terry Oliver *lawyer*
Wagner, William Bradley *lawyer*
Webb, Wayne E., Jr. *lawyer, engineer*
Weddington, Sarah Ragle *lawyer, educator*
Weinberg, Louise *lawyer, educator, author*
Weintraub, Russell Jay *lawyer, educator*
Wright, Charles Alan *lawyer, educator, author*
Yudof, Mark G. *lawyer, educator, academic administrator*
Zimmerman, Louis Seymour *lawyer*

Bellville
Dittert, J. Lee, Jr. *lawyer*

Caldwell
Sebesta, Charles Joseph, Jr. *lawyer*

Cleburne
MacLean, John Ronald *lawyer*
Urban, Carlyle Woodrow *retired lawyer*

Corpus Christi
Branscomb, Harvie, Jr. *lawyer*
Cartwright, Charles Nelson *lawyer*
†Hunter, Todd Ames *lawyer*
McMillen, James Thomas *lawyer*
Wood, James Allen *lawyer*

Dallas
Abney, Frederick Sherwood *lawyer*
Acker, Rodney *lawyer*
Adamo, Kenneth R. *lawyer*
Adkins, M. Douglas *lawyer*
Agnich, Richard John *lawyer, electronics company executive*
Akin, Henry David *lawyer*
Alford, Margaret Suzanne *lawyer*
Anderson, Barbara McComas *lawyer*
Anderson, E. Karl *lawyer*
Anglin, Michael Williams *lawyer*
Armour, James Lott *lawyer*
Babcock, Charles Lynde, IV *lawyer*
Baer, Henry *lawyer*
Baggett, W. Mike *lawyer*
Barbee, Linton E. *lawyer*
Berry, Buford Preston *lawyer*
Besing, Ray Gilbert *lawyer*
Birkeland, Bryan Collier *lawyer*
Bishop, Bryan Edwards *lawyer*
Blachly, Jack Lee *lawyer*
Blau, Charles William *lawyer, former government official*
Bliss, Robert Harms *lawyer*
Bonesio, Woodrow Michael *lawyer*
Bonney, Samuel Robert *lawyer*
Boone, Michael Mauldin *lawyer*
Boone, Oliver Kiel *lawyer*
Boren, Benjamin N. *lawyer*
Brin, Royal Henry, Jr. *lawyer*
Brister, Bill H. *lawyer, former judge*
Bromberg, Alan Robert *law educator*
Bromberg, Henri Louie, Jr. *lawyer*
Bromberg, John E. *lawyer*
Bumpas, Stuart Maryman *lawyer*
Burke, William Temple, Jr. *lawyer*
Busbee, Kline Daniel, Jr. *lawyer, public international law educator*
Bux, William John *lawyer*
Campfield, Regis William *law educator*
Carlton, Dean *lawyer*
†Castle, John Raymond, Jr. *lawyer*
Chapman, George C. *lawyer*
Coleman, Robert Winston *lawyer*
Collins, Michael Homer *lawyer*
Conant, Allah B., Jr. *lawyer*
Copley, Edward Alvin *lawyer*
Costello, John Francis, Jr. (Jack Costello) *lawyer*
Cowart, T(homas) David *lawyer*
Cowling, David Edward *lawyer*
Crain, Gayla Campbell *lawyer*
Creel, Luther Edward, III *lawyer*
Crowley, James Worthington *lawyer*
Crowson, James Lawrence *lawyer, financial company executive*
Curran, Geoffrey Michael *lawyer*
Dale, Erwin Randolph *lawyer, author*
Davis, Clarice McDonald *lawyer*
Dean, David Allen *lawyer*
DeBusk, Manuel Conrad *lawyer*
Demarest, Sylvia M. *lawyer*
Dillard, Robert Lionel, Jr. *lawyer, former life insurance executive*
Doke, Marshall J., Jr. *lawyer*
Dutton, Diana Cheryl *lawyer*
Dyess, Bobby Dale *lawyer*
Eddleman, William Roseman *lawyer*
†Edwards, Carl Elmo, Jr. *lawyer*
Emery, Herschell Gene *lawyer*
Engleman, Donald James *lawyer*
Estep, Robert Lloyd *lawyer*
Evans, Roger *lawyer*
Everbach, Otto George *lawyer*
Everett, C. Curtis *lawyer*
Fanning, Barry Hedges *lawyer*
Fanning, Robert Allen *lawyer*
Feld, Alan David *lawyer*
Feldman, H. Larry *lawyer*
Fennell, Thomas E. *lawyer*
Fenner, Suzan Ellen *lawyer*
Finkelstein, William Berndt *lawyer*
Fishman, Edward Marc *lawyer*
Flanagan, Christie Stephen *lawyer*
Flegle, Jim L. *lawyer*
Fordyce, Edward Winfield, Jr. *lawyer*
Forsythe, Earl Andrew *lawyer, steel company executive*
Fortado, Michael George *lawyer*
Freling, Richard Alan *lawyer*
French, Joseph Jordan, Jr. *lawyer*
Frisbie, Curtis Lynn, Jr. *lawyer*
Gandy, Dean Murray *lawyer*
Gilchrist, Henry *lawyer*
Gilmore, Jerry Carl *lawyer*
Glancy, Walter John *lawyer*
Godfrey, Cullen Michael *lawyer*
Goodell, Sol *retired lawyer*
Goodstein, Barnett Maurice *lawyer*
Gores, Christopher Merrel *lawyer*
Goyne, Roderick A. *lawyer*
Grissom, Gerald Homer *lawyer*
Gump, Richard Anthony *lawyer*
Haas, Samuel Douglas *lawyer*
Hamon, Richard Grady *lawyer*
Harper, Harlan, Jr. *lawyer*
Hart, John Clifton *lawyer*
†Hartnett, Will Ford *lawyer*
Hauer, John Longan *lawyer*
Hawkins, Jack Wade *lawyer*
Haworth, Charles Ray *lawyer*
Henkel, Kathryn G. *lawyer*
Hennessy, Daniel Kraft *lawyer*
Hicks, Marion Lawrence, Jr. (Larry Hicks) *lawyer, shareholder*
Hinshaw, Chester John *lawyer*
Horton, Paul Bradfield *lawyer*
Howie, John Robert *lawyer*
Huffman, Gregory Scott Combest *lawyer*
†Hughes, L. Keith *lawyer*
Hughes, Vester Thomas, Jr. *lawyer*
Hunt, David Ford *lawyer*
Irwin, Ivan, Jr. *lawyer*
†Johnson, Jerry D. *lawyer*
Johnson, Judith Kay *lawyer*
Johnson, Richard Craig *lawyer*
Joplin, Julian Mike *lawyer*
Jordan, Robert W. *lawyer*
Jordan, William Davis *lawyer*
Keithley, Bradford Gene *lawyer*
Kennedy, Marc J. *lawyer*
Kent, David Charles *lawyer*
Kinnebrew, Jackson Metcalfe *lawyer*
Kneipper, Richard Keith *lawyer*
Lacy, John Ford *lawyer*
Lafving, Brian Douglas *lawyer*
La Jone, Jay Allen *lawyer*
Lan, Donald Paul, Jr. *lawyer*
Lancaster, John Lynch, III *lawyer*
Lang, Douglas Steward *lawyer*
Lang-Miers, Elizabeth Ann *lawyer*
Lee, George Terry, Jr. *lawyer*
Levin, Richard C. *lawyer*
Levine, Harold *lawyer*
Little, Jack Merville *lawyer*
Lombard, Richard Spencer *lawyer*
Lowell, Cym Hawksworth *lawyer*
Lowenberg, Michael *lawyer*
Mankoff, Ronald Morton *lawyer*
Maris, Stephen S. *lawyer, educator*
Marshall, Schuyler Bailey, IV *lawyer*
Martin, Mark *lawyer*
Martin, Richard Kelley *lawyer*
Massman, Richard Allan *lawyer*
McCormack, William Arthur *lawyer*
Mc Elhaney, John Hess *lawyer*
McGowan, Patrick Francis *lawyer*
McGregor, Martin Luther, Jr. *lawyer*
McKnight, Joseph Webb *law educator, historian*
McLain, Maurice Clayton *lawyer, real estate executive*
McLane, David Glenn *lawyer*
McNamara, Lawrence John *lawyer*
McNamara, Martin Burr *lawyer, oil and gas company executive*
McWilliams, Mike C. *lawyer*
Mears, Rona Robbins *lawyer*
Mebus, Robert Gwynne *lawyer*
Menges, John Kenneth, Jr. *lawyer*
Middleton, Linda Jean Greathouse *lawyer*
Mighell, Kenneth John *lawyer*
Miller, Kirk *attorney*
Mills, Jerry Woodrow *lawyer*
Montoya, Regina T. *lawyer, government official*
Moore, Stanley Ray *lawyer*
Morgan, Steven Michael *lawyer*
Morris, Rebecca Robinson *lawyer*
Mow, Robert Henry, Jr. *lawyer*
Mullinax, Otto B. *lawyer*
†Nelson, Steven Douglas *lawyer*
Nichols, Henry Louis *lawyer*
Nordlund, William Chalmers *lawyer*
Palmer, Ronald Leigh *lawyer*
Parker, Angelo Pan *lawyer*
Parker, Emily Ann *lawyer*
Patterson, Joseph Redwine *lawyer*
Penegar, Kenneth Lawing *law educator*
Peterson, Edward Adrian *lawyer*
Pettey, Walter Graves, III *lawyer*
Pew, John Glenn, Jr. *lawyer*
Phelan, Robin Eric *lawyer*
Pingree, Bruce Douglas *lawyer*
Pleasant, James Scott *lawyer*
Portman, Glenn Arthur *lawyer*
Powell, Michael Vance *lawyer*
Price, John Aley *lawyer*
Profusek, Robert Alan *lawyer*
Purnell, Maurice Eugene, Jr. *lawyer*
Radford, Norman DePue, Jr. *lawyer*
Raggio, Kenneth Gaylord *lawyer*
Raggio, Louise Ballerstedt *lawyer*
Ray, George Einar *lawyer*
Rice, Darrel Alan *lawyer*
Riggs, Arthur Jordy *retired lawyer*
Ringle, Brett Adelbert *lawyer*
Ritchie, Robert Field *lawyer*
Roberts, Harry Morris, Jr. *lawyer*
Robinson, Lawrence Dewitt *lawyer*
Rodgers, John Hunter *lawyer*
Rosenberg, David Howard *lawyer, mediator, marketing executive*
St. Claire, Frank Arthur *lawyer*
Savage, Wallace Hamilton *lawyer*
Schoenbrun, Larry Lynn *lawyer*
Schreiber, Sally Ann *lawyer*
See, Robert Fleming, Jr. *lawyer*
Sheeder, Robert Elwood *lawyer*
Siegel, Thomas Louis *lawyer*
Stalcup, Joe Alan *lawyer, clergyman*
Steinberg, Lawrence Edward *lawyer*
Stilwell, John Quincy *lawyer*
Stockard, James Alfred *lawyer*
Storey, Charles Porter *lawyer*
Strauss, Robert Schwarz *lawyer, former ambassador*
Stuart, Lawrence David, Jr. *lawyer*
Sudbury, David Marshall *corporate lawyer*
Swanson, Wallace Martin *lawyer*
Thau, William Albert, Jr. *lawyer*
True, Roy Joe *lawyer*
Tubb, James Clarence *lawyer*
Tucker, Laurey Dan *lawyer*
Turley, Windle *lawyer*
Tygrett, Howard Volney, Jr. *lawyer*
Veach, Robert Raymond, Jr. *lawyer*
Vetter, James George, Jr. *lawyer*
Walkowiak, Vincent Steven *lawyer*
Wallenstein, James Harry *lawyer*
Watson, Jim Albert *lawyer*
Weekley, Frederick Clay, Jr. *lawyer*
Weiland, Stephen Cass *lawyer*
West, William Beverley, III *lawyer*
White, James Richard *lawyer*
Williams, James Alexander *lawyer*
Willingham, Clark Suttles *lawyer*
Wilson, Claude Raymond, Jr. *lawyer*
Winkel, Judy Kay *lawyer*
Winn, Edward Burton *lawyer*
Wise, Marvin Jay *lawyer*
Young, Barney Thornton *lawyer*
Zisman, Barry Stuart *lawyer*

Denton
Lawhon, John E., III *lawyer, former county official*

DFW Airport
Lowden, Scott Richard *lawyer*

El Paso
Feuille, Richard Harlan *lawyer*
Marshall, Richard Treeger *lawyer*
Smith, Tad Randolph *lawyer*

Euless
Paran, Mark Lloyd *lawyer*

Fort Worth
Brown, C. Harold *lawyer*
Brown, Richard Lee *lawyer*
Chalk, John Allen *lawyer*
Dean, Beale *lawyer*
Franks, Jon Michael *lawyer*
Ginsburg, Marcus *lawyer*
Greenhill, William Duke *lawyer*
Hill, Mark C. *lawyer*
Kelly, Dee J. *lawyer*
Law, Thomas Hart *lawyer*
†Lesok, Eddie Monroe *lawyer*
Mack, Theodore *lawyer*
McConnell, Michael Arthur *lawyer*
Minton, Jerry Davis *lawyer, former banker*
Munn, Cecil Edwin *lawyer*
Ratliff, William Durrah, Jr. *lawyer*
†Willis, Doyle *lawyer, state legislator*

Galveston
Bircher, Edgar Allen *lawyer*
Caldwell, Garnett Ernest *lawyer*
Schwartz, Aaron Robert *lawyer, former state legislator*

Hallettsville
Baber, Wilbur H., Jr. *lawyer*

Harlingen
Ephraim, Charles *lawyer*
Johnson, Orrin Wendell *lawyer*
†Solis, Jim *lawyer, state legislator*

Heath
Kolodey, Fred James *lawyer*

Henderson
†Sadler, Paul Lindsey *lawyer, state legislator*

Houston
Addison, Linda Leuchter *lawyer*
Adelman, Graham Lewis *lawyer*
Alderman, Richard Mark *legal educator, lawyer, television and radio commentator*
Alexander, Neil Kenton *lawyer*
Allender, John Roland *lawyer*
Anderson, Eric Severin *lawyer*
Anderson, Robert Dennis *lawyer*
Anderson, Thomas Dunaway *lawyer, retired*
†Atlas, Nancy Friedman *lawyer, mediator, arbitrator*
Atlas, Scott Jerome *lawyer*
Bagwell, Louis Lee *lawyer*
Bambace, Robert Shelly *lawyer*
Barnett, Edward William *lawyer*
Barrett, John Adams *lawyer*
Bayko, Emil Thomas *lawyer*
Bech, Douglas York *lawyer*
Bellatti, Lawrence Lee *lawyer*
Berg, David Howard *lawyer*
Bistline, F. Walter, Jr. *lawyer*
Blackshear, A. T., Jr. *lawyer*
Bliss, Ronald Glenn *lawyer*
Bluestein, Edwin A., Jr. *lawyer*
Bonica, John R. *lawyer*
Boston, Charles D. *lawyer*
Botley, Calvin *lawyer*
Bousquet, Thomas Gourrier *lawyer*
Boyd, John E. *lawyer*
Brann, Richard Roland *lawyer*
Brantley, John Randolph *lawyer*
Bridges, David Manning *lawyer*
Brinsmade, Lyon Louis *lawyer*
Brinson, Gay Creswell, Jr. *lawyer*
Brundrett, George L(ee), Jr. *lawyer*
Buckingham, Edwin John, III *lawyer*
Burch, Voris Reagan *lawyer*
Caddy, Michael Douglas *lawyer*
Caldwell, James Wiley *lawyer*
Calhoun, Frank Wayne *lawyer, former state legislator*
Carmody, James Albert *lawyer*
Carroll, James Vincent, III *lawyer*
Caudill, William Howard *lawyer*
Cheavens, Joseph D. *lawyer*
Clark, Pat English *lawyer*
Clarke, Robert Logan *lawyer, partner*
Clore, Lawrence H. *lawyer*
Coghlan, Kelly Jack *lawyer*
Cook, B. Thomas *lawyer*
Cook, Eugene Augustus *lawyer*
Couch, J. O. Terrell *lawyer, former oil company executive*
Cox, James Talley *lawyer*
Crites, Omar Don, Jr. *lawyer*
Crooker, John H., Jr. *lawyer*
Cunningham, Tom Alan *lawyer*
Curfiss, Robert Clinton *lawyer*
Curry, Alton Frank *lawyer*
Dack, Christopher Edward Hughes *lawyer*
Davis, Martha Algenita Scott *lawyer*
DeMent, James Alderson, Jr. *lawyer*
Denny, Otway B., Jr. *lawyer*
†Derrick, James V., Jr. *lawyer*
Dillon, Clifford Brien *retired lawyer*
Dilworth, James Weldon *lawyer*
Dimitry, Theodore George *lawyer*
Dinkins, Carol Eggert *lawyer*
Dole, Linda Ann Ingols *lawyer*
Douglass, John Jay *lawyer, educator*
Dunlop, Fred Hurston *lawyer*
Dutton, Uriel Elvis *lawyer*
Dykes, Osborne Jefferson, III *lawyer*
Eastland, S. Stacy *lawyer*
Estes, Carl Lewis, II *lawyer*
Eubank, J. Thomas *lawyer*
Ewell, Vincent Fletcher *lawyer*
Farenthold, Frances Tarlton *lawyer*
Feldcamp, Larry Bernard *lawyer*
Feldt, J(ohn) Harrell *lawyer*
Finch, Michael Paul *lawyer*
Fortenbach, Ray Thomas *retired lawyer*
Foster, Charles Crawford *lawyer, educator*
French, Layne Bryan *lawyer, investor, volunteer*
Gagnon, Stewart Walter *lawyer*
Gano, John *lawyer*
Garrett, Jasper Patrick *lawyer*
Garten, David B. *lawyer*
Gayle, Gibson, Jr. *lawyer*
Gee, Thomas Gibbs *lawyer, retired federal judge*
Gentry, Hubert, Jr. *lawyer*
Gissel, L. Henry, Jr. *lawyer*
†Goldstein, Jack Charles *lawyer*
Gover, Alan Shore *lawyer*
Graham, Michael Paul *lawyer*
Gray, Archibald Duncan, Jr. *lawyer*
†Gruben, Karl Taylor *law librarian*
Halloran, Bernard Thorpe *lawyer*
Hanson, Jerry Clinton *lawyer*
Harper, Alfred John, II *lawyer*
Harrington, Bruce Michael *lawyer, investor*
Harvin, David Tarleton *lawyer*
Harvin, William Charles *lawyer*
Hermann, Robert John *lawyer, corporate executive*
Hollyfield, John Scoggins *lawyer*
Holstead, John Burnham *lawyer*
Hoyt, Mont Powell *lawyer*
Hudspeth, Chalmers Mac *lawyer, educator*
Hurd, Charles W. *lawyer*
Hutcheson, Joseph Chappell, III *lawyer*
Hutcheson, Thad T., Jr. *business and international lawyer*
Illig, Carl *lawyer*
†Jamail, Joseph Dahr, Jr. *lawyer*
Jansen, Donald Orville *lawyer*
Jewell, George Hiram *lawyer*
Jones, Frank Griffith *lawyer*
Jordan, Charles Milton *lawyer*
Kaplan, Lee Landa *lawyer*
Katz, M. Marvin *lawyer*
Kay, Joel Phillip *lawyer*
Kelly, Hugh Rice *lawyer*
Kelly, William Franklin, Jr. *lawyer*
Knull, William H., III *lawyer*
Koenig, Rodney Curtis *lawyer, rancher*
Kosut, Kenneth Paul *lawyer*
Kratochvil, L(ouis) Glen *lawyer*
Krebs, Arno William, Jr. *lawyer*
Krieger, Paul Edward *lawyer*
LaBoon, Robert Bruce *lawyer*
Larkin, Lee Roy *lawyer*
Lavenant, Rene Paul, Jr. *lawyer*
Levetown, Robert Alexander *lawyer*
Lilienstern, O. Clayton *lawyer*
Loeffler, James Joseph *lawyer*
Lovelace, Byron Keith *lawyer, management consultant*
Maloney, James Edward *lawyer*
Marley, Everett Armistead, Jr. *lawyer*
Marshall, J. Howard, II *lawyer*
Marston, Edgar Jean, III *lawyer*
Martin, Neil *lawyer*
Massad, Stephen Albert *lawyer*
Mayer, John *lawyer*
Mayor, Richard Blair *lawyer*
McClure, Daniel M. *lawyer*
McDaniel, Jarrel Dave *lawyer*
McGreevy, Terrence Gerard *lawyer*
McQuarrie, Claude Monroe, III *lawyer*
Melo, Thomas M. *lawyer*
Mixon, John *lawyer, educator*
Moehlman, Michael Scott *lawyer*
Moncure, John Lewis *lawyer*
Morris, (William) Carloss *lawyer, insurance company executive*
Mueller, Carl Gustav, Jr. *lawyer*
Murphy, Ewell Edward, Jr. *lawyer*
Myers, Franklin *lawyer, oil service company executive*
Nations, Howard Lynn *lawyer*

Nickens, Jacks Clarence *lawyer*
Niebruegge, Michael E. *lawyer*
Nolen, Roy Lemuel *lawyer*
Nolen, William Giles *lawyer, accountant*
Northrop, Monroe *lawyer*
Nunnally, Knox Dillon *lawyer*
O'Kehie, Collins Emeka *lawyer, consultant*
Oldham, Darius Dudley *lawyer*
Oliver, Rufus W., III *lawyer*
Oncken, Henry Kuck *lawyer*
†O'Quinn, John M. *lawyer*
O'Toole, Austin Martin *lawyer*
Parsley, Robert Horace *lawyer*
Pravel, Bernarr Roe *lawyer*
Pressler, Herman Paul *lawyer*
Pugsley, Frank Burruss *lawyer*
Randolph, Robert Raymond *lawyer*
Ray, Hugh Massey, Jr. *lawyer*
Reasoner, Harry Max *lawyer*
†Robertson, James Woolsey *lawyer*
Rogers, Arthur Hamilton, III *lawyer*
Rozzell, Scott Ellis *lawyer*
Ryan, Cornelius O'Brien *lawyer*
Salch, Steven Charles *lawyer*
Sales, James Bohus *lawyer*
Sanders, John Moncrief *lawyer*
Sapp, Walter William *lawyer, energy company executive*
†Schultz, Jon S. *law library administrator, law educator*
Schwartz, Charles Walter *lawyer*
Schwartzel, Charles Boone *lawyer*
Secrest, Ronald Dean *lawyer*
Selke, Charles Richard *lawyer, real estate professional, banker*
Sewell, Ben Gardner *lawyer*
Shaddock, Carroll Sidney *lawyer*
Shannon, Joel Ingram *lawyer*
Sheinfeld, Myron M. *lawyer, educator*
Simon, Barry Philip *lawyer*
Sing, William Bender *lawyer*
Smith, William Randolph *lawyer*
Soliz, Joseph Guy *lawyer*
Sonfield, Robert Leon, Jr. *lawyer*
Spalding, Andrew Freeman *lawyer*
Staine, Ross *lawyer*
Stephens, Delia Marie Lucky *lawyer*
Still, Charles Henry *lawyer*
Stradley, William Jackson *lawyer*
Streng, William Paul *lawyer, educator*
Stryker, Steven Charles *lawyer*
Stuart, Walter Bynum, IV *lawyer*
Susman, Morton Lee *lawyer*
Susman, Stephen Daily *lawyer*
Swanson, Roy Joel *lawyer*
Szalkowski, Charles Conrad *lawyer*
Terrell, G. Irvin *lawyer*
Tetzlaff, Theodore R. *lawyer*
Travis, Andrew David *lawyer*
Vance, Carol Stoner *lawyer*
Van Fleet, George Allan *lawyer*
Varner, David Eugene *lawyer, energy company executive*
Wakefield, Stephen Alan *lawyer*
Wallingford, John Rufus *lawyer*
Watson, John Allen *lawyer*
Webb, Jack M. *lawyer*
Weber, Fredric Alan *lawyer*
Welch, Harry Scoville *lawyer, retired gas pipeline company executive*
Welch, Robert Morrow, Jr. *lawyer*
Wells, Benjamin Gladney *lawyer*
Wharton, Thomas H(eard), Jr. *lawyer*
Wickliffe, Jerry L. *lawyer*
Wilde, Carlton D. *lawyer*
Wilde, William Key *lawyer*
Williams, Percy Don *lawyer*
Williamson, Peter David *lawyer*
Williamson, Sam *lawyer*
Wilson, James William *lawyer*
Winton, James C. *lawyer*
Wood, Ivan, Jr. *lawyer*
Wray, Thomas Jefferson *lawyer*
Wright, Robert Payton *lawyer*
Yokubaitis, Roger T. *lawyer*
York, James Martin *lawyer*
Youngblood, J. Craig *lawyer*
Zivley, Walter Perry *lawyer*

Irving
Baird, David Leach, Jr. *lawyer, petroleum and chemical company executive*
Elliott, Frank Wallace *lawyer, educator*
Hansen, Nick Dane *lawyer*
Roberts, C. Kenneth *lawyer*
†Simon, Dolph B(ertram) H(irst) *lawyer, jewelry company executive*
Wells, Leonard Nathaniel David, Jr. *lawyer*
Zahn, Donald Jack *lawyer*

Kilgore
Rorschach, Richard Gordon *lawyer*

Lubbock
†Cochran, Joseph Wesley *law librarian, educator*
†Duncan, Robert Lloyd *lawyer*
Glass, Carson McElyea *lawyer*
Purdom, Thomas James *lawyer*

Lufkin
Ericson, Roger Delwin *lawyer, forest resource company executive*

Midland
Bullock, Maurice Randolph *lawyer*
Chappell, Clovis Gillham, Jr. *lawyer*
Morrow, William Clarence *lawyer*

Odessa
Gilliland, William Elton *retired lawyer*

Pampa
Warner, John William *lawyer*

Pasadena
Zimmerer, Ann(a) Morgan *lawyer, consulting psychologist, genealogist*

Plano
Bonet, Frank Joseph *lawyer*
†Friedlander, D. Gilbert *lawyer*
Kranzow, Ronald Roy *lawyer*

Pottsboro
Thomas, Ann Van Wynen *lawyer, educator*

Round Rock
LaShelle, Charles Stanton *lawyer, insurance company executive*

San Angelo
†Junell, Robert Alan *lawyer*

San Antonio
Aldave, Barbara Bader *law educator, lawyer*
Allison, Stephen Philip *lawyer*
†Alvarado, Leo G. *lawyer, law educator*
Barton, James Cary *lawyer*
Bates, David Quentin, Jr. *lawyer, pharmaceutical executive*
Biery, Evelyn Hudson *lawyer*
†Crews, Donald Roy *lawyer, communications company executive*
Dazey, William Boyd *retired lawyer*
Durbin, Richard Louis, Jr. *lawyer*
Fagan, Wayne Irwin *lawyer*
Fox, Michael W. *lawyer*
Free, William John *lawyer, communications executive*
†Freeman, Philip Dayne *lawyer*
Fretthold, Timothy Jon *lawyer*
Guenther, Jack Egon *lawyer*
Hardberger, Phillip Duane *judge, lawyer, journalist*
Kelly, Robert Lee *lawyer, evangelist*
Lynch, Robert Martin *lawyer, educator*
Macon, Jane Haun *lawyer*
Macon, Richard Laurence *lawyer*
Matthews, Dan Gus *lawyer*
Matthews, Wilbur Lee *lawyer*
Padgett, Shelton Edward *lawyer*
Schlueter, David Arnold *law educator*
Schlueter, Linda Lee *law educator*
Spears, Sally *lawyer*
Steen, John Thomas, Jr. *lawyer*
Vazquez, Gilbert Falcon *lawyer*
Westbrook, Joel Whitsitt, III *lawyer*

Spring
Battle, Thomas Peyton *lawyer*
Hurley, Robert Joseph *lawyer*

Stratford
Woods, John William *lawyer*

Waco
†Denton, Betty *lawyer, state representative*
Mc Call, Abner Vernon *law educator, retired university administrator*
Smith, Cullen *lawyer*
Wendorf, Hulen Dee *law educator, author, lecturer*
Wilson, John Ross *retired law educator*

Yoakum
Williams, Walter Waylon *lawyer, pecan grower*

UTAH

Logan
†Hillyard, Lyle William *lawyer*

Ogden
Harris, R. Robert *lawyer*

Provo
Abbott, Charles Favour, Jr. *lawyer*
Kimball, Edward Lawrence *legal educator, lawyer*
†Lundberg, Constance K. *law educator*
Smith, Maurice Edward *lawyer, business consultant*
Whitman, Dale Alan *lawyer, educator*

Salt Lake City
Anderson, Kent Taylor *lawyer*
Baucom, Sidney George *lawyer*
Berman, Daniel Lewis *lawyer*
Buchi, Mark Keith *lawyer*
Christensen, Ray Richards *lawyer*
Holbrook, Donald Benson *lawyer*
Holtkamp, James Arnold *lawyer, legal educator*
Hunter, Howard William *lawyer, church official*
Lewis, Leonard J. *lawyer*
Lunt, Jack *lawyer*
Mabey, Ralph R. *lawyer*
Manning, Brent V. *lawyer*
Melich, Mitchell *lawyer*
Mock, Henry Byron *lawyer, writer, consultant*
†Monson, Gregory Brammer *lawyer*
Nebeker, Stephen Bennion *lawyer*
Nielsen, Greg Ross *lawyer*
Oaks, Dallin Harris *lawyer, church official*
Roberts, Jack Earle *lawyer, ski resort operator, wood products company executive, real estate developer*
Thurman, Samuel David *legal educator*
Wadsworth, Harold Wayne *lawyer*

VERMONT

Brattleboro
Cummings, Charles Rogers *lawyer*

Burlington
Dinse, John Merrell *lawyer*
Martin, Allen *lawyer*
Salmon, Thomas Paul *lawyer, academic administrator*
Wick, Hilton Addison *lawyer*

Hinesburg
Ross, Charles Robert *lawyer, consultant*

Middlebury
†Langrock, Peter Forbes *lawyer*

Montpelier
Brock, James Sidney *lawyer*
Diamond, M. Jerome *lawyer, former state official*
Guild, Alden *lawyer*

Morrisville
Simonds, Marshall *lawyer*

Norwick
Lundquist, Weyman Ivan *lawyer*

Randolph
†Angell, Philip Alvin, Jr. *lawyer*

Rutland
Cook, George Wallace Foster *retired lawyer, tree farmer*
Keyser, Frank Ray, Jr. *lawyer, former governor of Vermont*
Stafford, Robert Theodore *lawyer, former senator*

Sharon
Phillips, Ellis Laurimore, Jr. *legal educator, foundation executive*

South Royalton
Williams, Norman *law educator, city planner*

Stowe
Anderson, Rudolph J., Jr. *lawyer*

Taftsville
Johnson, Philip Martin *lawyer*

Waitsfield
Raphael, Albert Ash, Jr. *lawyer*

Waterbury
Adams, Charles Jairus *lawyer*

Woodstock
Debevoise, Thomas McElrath *lawyer, educator*

VIRGINIA

Alexandria
Abell, Richard Bender *lawyer, federal official*
Alexander, Fred Calvin, Jr. *lawyer*
Armstrong, C. Torrence *lawyer*
Blumenthal, David A. *lawyer*
†Cohen, Bernard S. *lawyer*
Duncan, Stephen Mack *lawyer*
Evans, H. Bradley, Jr. *lawyer*
Hussey, Ward MacLean *lawyer, government official*
Kopp, Eugene Paul *lawyer*
Mathis, William Lowrey *lawyer*
†McClure, Roger John *lawyer*
Miller, Martin John *lawyer*
Peterson, David Andreas *lawyer, government official, educator*
Schultz, Franklin M. *lawyer*
Straub, Peter Thornton *lawyer*
Sturtevant, Brereton *retired lawyer, former government official*
Swinburn, Charles *lawyer*
Thomas, William Griffith *lawyer*
Watson, George William *lawyer, legal consultant*
Wilner, Morton Harrison *retired lawyer*
Yonkman, Fredrick Albers *lawyer, management consultant*
Zarro, Janice Anne *lawyer*

Annandale
Richstein, Abraham Richard *lawyer*

Arlington
Anthony, Robert Armstrong *lawyer, law educator*
Bader, Michael Haley *lawyer, broadcasting executive*
Belen, Frederick Christopher *lawyer*
Benzinger, Raymond Burdette *lawyer, educator*
Brenner, Edgar H. *lawyer*
†Buechner, Jack William *lawyer, former congressman*
Burgess, David *lawyer*
Carretta, Albert Aloysius *lawyer, educator*
†Chapple, Thomas Leslie *lawyer*
Collins, Philip Reilly *lawyer, educator*
Drayton, William *lawyer, management consultant*
Easton, John Jay, Jr. *lawyer*
Elliott, R Lance *lawyer*
Hugler, Edward C. *lawyer, federal and state government*
Huston, Harris Hyde *legal consultant*
Jackson, William Paul, Jr. *lawyer*
Kiko, Philip George *lawyer*
Korman, James William *lawyer*
Krauss, Michael Ian *law educator*
Malone, William Grady *lawyer*
Mathis, Mark Jay *lawyer*
McDermott, Francis Owen *lawyer*
Munsell, Elsie Louise *lawyer*
Muris, Timothy Joseph *law educator*
Quigg, Donald James *lawyer*
Smith, Numa Lamar, Jr. *lawyer*
Stover, David Frank *lawyer*
Van Landingham, Leander Shelton, Jr. *lawyer*
Wilcox, Harvey John *lawyer*

Ashburn
Bolton, John Robert *lawyer, federal official*

Ashland
d'Evegnee, Charles Paul *lawyer*

Blacksburg
Jensen, Walter Edward *lawyer, educator*

Bristol
Jones, James Parker *lawyer*

Charlottesville
Abraham, Kenneth Samuel *law educator*
Alford, Neill Herbert, Jr. *law educator*
Bergin, Thomas Francis *lawyer*
Bonnie, Richard Jeffrey *legal educator, lawyer*
Clark, Reuben Grove, Jr. *lawyer*
Cohen, Edwin Samuel *lawyer, educator*
Eustis, Albert Anthony *lawyer, diversified industry corporate executive*
Henderson, Stanley Dale *lawyer, educator*
Hodous, Robert Power *lawyer*
Howard, Arthur Ellsworth Dick *legal educator*
Kitch, Edmund Wells *lawyer, educator, private investor*
Landess, Fred S. *lawyer*
Mc Culloch, Frank W. *lawyer, government official, educator, arbitrator*
McGee, Gary Calvin *lawyer*
Meador, Daniel John *lawyer, educator*
Middleditch, Leigh Benjamin, Jr. *lawyer, educator*
Moore, John Norton *lawyer, diplomat, educator*
O'Connell, Jeffrey *lawyer, educator*
Perkins, William Allan, Jr. *retired lawyer*
Redden, Kenneth Robert *lawyer, writer, educator*
Robinson, Mildred Wigfall *law educator*
Slaughter, Edward Ratliff, Jr. *lawyer*
Stroud, Robert Edward *lawyer*
Turner, Robert Foster *lawyer, educator, former government official, writer*
Wadlington, Walter James *legal educator*
Walker, William Laurens *lawyer, educator*
White, George Edward *legal educator, lawyer*
†Whitehead, John Wayne *law educator, organization administrator, author*

Chesapeake
Jones, John Lou *arbitrator, retired railroad executive*

Culpeper
†Davies, John Jenkyn, III *lawyer*

Danville
Conway, French Hoge *lawyer*
Talbott, Frank, III *lawyer*

Dumfries
Mc Dowell, Charles Eager *lawyer, retired military officer*

Fairfax
Arntson, Peter Andrew *lawyer*
Bloomquist, Dennis Howard *lawyer*
Church, Randolph Warner, Jr. *lawyer*
Codding, Frederick Hayden *lawyer*
Folk, Thomas Robert *lawyer*
Groves, Hurst Kohler *lawyer, oil company executive*
Hancock, Alton Guy *lawyer*
Hopson, Everett George *lawyer*
Perdue, Christine H. *lawyer*
Sanderson, Douglas Jay *lawyer*
Spitzberg, Irving Joseph, Jr. *lawyer, corporate executive*
Steger, Meritt Homer *lawyer*

Falls Church
Calkins, Gary Nathan *lawyer*
Diamond, Robert Michael *lawyer*
Duesenberg, Robert H. *lawyer*
Ehrlich, Bernard Herbert *lawyer, association executive*
Hazel, John Tilghman, Jr. *lawyer, real estate developer*
Jennings, Thomas Parks *lawyer*
Keesling, Karen Ruth *lawyer*
Marsh, John O(tho), Jr. *lawyer, former government official*
Robie, William Randolph *lawyer, government official*
Skoler, Daniel Lawrence *lawyer, writer*
Wright, Wiley Reed, Jr. *lawyer*
Young, John Hardin *lawyer*

Franklin
Cobb, G. Elliott, Jr. *lawyer*

Fredericksburg
Snapp, Roy Baker *lawyer*

Gate City
†Quillen, Ford Carter *lawyer, state legislator*

Gloucester
Powell, Bolling Raines, Jr. *lawyer, educator*

Great Falls
Jacobson, Richard Lee *lawyer, educator*
Railton, William Scott *lawyer*
Sims, John Rogers, Jr. *lawyer*

Halifax
Greenbacker, John Everett *lawyer*

Heathsville
McKerns, Charles Joseph *lawyer*

Herndon
Holton, A. Linwood, Jr. *lawyer*
Pollard, Charles William *lawyer*

Lakeridge
Moran, Robert Daniel *lawyer*

Lanexa
Kirk, Maurice Blake *lawyer, educator*

Leesburg
†Mims, William Cleveland *lawyer, state legislator*

Lexington
Kirgis, Frederic Lee, Jr. *legal educator*
Sullivan, Barry *lawyer, educator*
†Wiant, Sarah Kirsten *law library director, educator*

Marshall
Seder, Arthur Raymond, Jr. *lawyer*

Maurertown
Macleod, John Amend *lawyer*

Mc Lean
Appler, Thomas L. *lawyer*
Brown, Thomas C., Jr. *lawyer*
Cook, Harry Clayton, Jr. *lawyer*
Corson, J. Jay, IV *lawyer*
Gammon, James Alan *lawyer*
Hambrick, Jackson Reid *lawyer, retired educator, writer*
Herge, J. Curtis *lawyer*
Hicks, C. Thomas, III *lawyer*
Kennedy, Cornelius Bryant *lawyer*
Klinedinst, Duncan Stewart *lawyer*
Marino, Michael Frank *lawyer*
Murphy, Thomas Patrick *lawyer*
Nassikas, John Nicholas *lawyer*
Neel, Samuel Ellison *lawyer*
Ney, Robert Terrence *lawyer*
Prichard, Edgar Allen *lawyer*

Prince, Andrew Steven *lawyer, former government official*
Rau, Lee Arthur *lawyer*
Rhyne, Charles Sylvanus *lawyer*
Stephens, William Theodore *lawyer, business executive*
Stitt, David Tillman *lawyer*
Stump, John Sutton *lawyer*
Tansill, Frederick Joseph *lawyer*
Traver, Courtland Lee *lawyer*
Trotter, Haynie Seay *lawyer*

Middleburg
Beddall, Thomas Henry *lawyer*

Newport News
Cuthrell, Carl Edward *lawyer, educator, clergyman*

Norfolk
Baird, Edward Rouzie, Jr. *lawyer*
†Copeland, Howard E. *lawyer*
Cranford, Page Deronde *lawyer, executive*
Crenshaw, Francis Nelson *lawyer*
Morgan, Henry Coke, Jr. *lawyer*
Rephan, Jack *lawyer*
Ryan, Louis Farthing *lawyer*
Timms, A. Jackson *lawyer*
Tolmie, Donald McEachern *lawyer*

North Springfield
Hugin, Adolph Charles (Eugene) *lawyer, engineer, inventor, educator*

Norton
Earls, Donald Edward *lawyer*

Orange
Dunnington, Walter Grey, Jr. *lawyer, retired food and tobacco executive*
Poulson, Richard J. M. *lawyer*

Palmyra
White, Luther Wesley *lawyer*

Portsmouth
Spong, William Belser, Jr. *lawyer, educator*

Reston
Humphreys, David John *lawyer, trade association executive*
Schelling, John Paul *lawyer, consultant*

Richmond
Ackerly, Benjamin Clarkson *lawyer*
Anderson, Leonard Gustave *retired lawyer, retired business executive*
Bagley, Philip Joseph, III *lawyer*
Baliles, Gerald L. *lawyer, former governor*
Batzli, Terrence Raymond *lawyer*
Belcher, Dennis Irl *lawyer*
†Benedetti, Joseph B. *lawyer*
Blanchard, Lawrence Eley, Jr. *lawyer, corporation executive*
Booker, Lewis Thomas *lawyer*
Bowles, Aubrey Russell, III *lawyer*
Brame, Joseph Robert, III *lawyer*
Brasfield, Evans Booker *lawyer*
Brockenbrough, Henry Watkins *lawyer*
Brooks, Robert Franklin, Sr. *lawyer*
Burke, John K(irkland), Jr. *lawyer*
Burrus, Robert Lewis, Jr. *lawyer*
Bush, Thomas Norman *lawyer*
Carrell, Daniel Allan *lawyer*
Carter, Joseph Carter, Jr. *lawyer*
Catlett, Richard H., Jr. *retired lawyer*
Clinard, Robert Noel *lawyer*
Cohn, David Stephen *lawyer*
†Cunningham, Jean Wooden *lawyer, educator, state legislator*
Cutchins, Clifford Armstrong, IV *lawyer*
Dabney, H. Slayton, Jr. *lawyer*
Davenport, Bradfute Warwick, Jr. *lawyer*
Davis, Douglas Whitfield *lawyer*
Denny, Collins, III *lawyer*
Dicks, John G., III *lawyer*
Dray, Mark S. *lawyer*
Ellis, Andrew Jackson, Jr. *lawyer*
Elmore, Edward Whitehead *lawyer*
Epps, Augustus Charles *lawyer*
Farnham, James Edward *lawyer*
Freeman, George Clemon, Jr. *lawyer*
Gary, Richard David *lawyer*
Gasch, Manning *lawyer*
Geisler, Ernest Keith, Jr. *lawyer*
Graves, H. Brice *lawyer*
Hackney, Virginia Howitz *lawyer*
†Hall, Franklin Perkins *lawyer, banker, state official*
Hall, Stephen Charles *lawyer*
Hancock, William Glenn *lawyer*
Hettrick, George H. *lawyer*
Horsley, Waller Holladay *lawyer*
Kay, John Franklin, Jr. *lawyer*
Kearfott, Joseph Conrad *lawyer*
Kessler, Neil Stanton *lawyer*
Ledbetter, David Oscar *lawyer*
Levit, Jay J(oseph) *lawyer*
Martenstein, Thomas Ewing *lawyer*
Mathews, Roderick Bell *lawyer*
McClard, Jack Edward *lawyer*
McElligott, James Patrick, Jr. *lawyer*
McVey, Henry Hanna, III *lawyer*
†Milmoe, Patrick J. *lawyer*
Moore, Thurston Roach *lawyer*
Morris, Dewey Blanton *lawyer*
Oakey, John Martin, Jr. *lawyer*
Palmore, Fred Wharton, III *lawyer*
Pasco, Hansell Merrill *retired lawyer*
Patterson, Robert Hobson, Jr. *lawyer*
Peters, David Frankman *lawyer*
Pinckney, C. Cotesworth *lawyer*
Pope, Robert Dean *lawyer*
Powell, Kenneth Edward *lawyer*
Powell, Lewis Franklin, III *lawyer*
Powell, Virginia W. *lawyer*
Rainey, Gordon Fryer, Jr. *lawyer*
Reveley, Walter Taylor, III *lawyer*
Roach, Edgar Mayo, Jr. *lawyer*
Rolfe, Robert Martin *lawyer*
Rosbe, William Louis *lawyer*
Rudlin, David Alan *lawyer, educator*
Schwarzschild, Patricia Michaelson *lawyer*
Shands, William Ridley, Jr. *lawyer*
Sharer, John Daniel *lawyer*
Slater, Thomas Glascock, Jr. *lawyer*
Slaughter, Alexander Hoke *lawyer*
Smith, R. Gordon *lawyer*
Spahn, Gary Joseph *lawyer*
Spain, Jack Holland, Jr. *lawyer*
Spivey, Joseph M., III *lawyer*
Strickland, William Jesse *lawyer*
Thomas, John Charles *lawyer, former state supreme court justice*
Thompson, Paul Michael *lawyer*
Totten, Randolph Fowler *lawyer*
Troy, Anthony Francis *lawyer*
Twomey, William Eldred, Jr. *lawyer*
Waddell, William Robert *lawyer*
Walsh, James Hamilton *lawyer*
Walsh, William Arthur, Jr. *lawyer*
Warthen, Harry Justice, III *lawyer*
Watts, Stephen Hurt, II *lawyer*
Wellford, Hill B., Jr. *lawyer*
Wheeler, R(ichard) Kenneth *lawyer*
White, Hugh Vernon, Jr. *lawyer*
Witt, Walter Francis, Jr. *lawyer*
Word, Thomas S., Jr. *lawyer*

Roanoke
Butler, Manley Caldwell *lawyer*
Fishwick, John Palmer *lawyer, retired railroad executive*
†Woodrum, Clifton A., III *lawyer, state legislator*

Vienna
Fasser, Paul James, Jr. *labor arbitrator*
Howard, Daggett Horton *lawyer*
Razzano, Frank Charles *lawyer*

Vinton
†Cranwell, C. Richard *lawyer*

Virginia Beach
†Sekulow, Jay Alan *lawyer*
†Stolle, Kenneth William *laywer*

Warm Springs
†Deeds, Robert Creigh *lawyer, state legislator*

Warrenton
vom Baur, Francis Trowbridge *retired lawyer*

Williamsburg
Braun, Richard Lane *lawyer, university administrator*
Geddy, Vernon Meredith, Jr. *lawyer*
Heller, James Stephen *law librarian*
Marcus, Paul *lawyer, educator*
†Sipes, Larry L. *lawyer*
Smolla, Rodney Alan *lawyer, educator*
Sullivan, Timothy Jackson *legal educator, academic administrator*
Whyte, James Primrose, Jr. *former legal educator*

WASHINGTON

Bellevue
Elliott, Richard Wayne *lawyer*
Hannah, Lawrence Burlison *lawyer*
Smith, George Lester *lawyer*
Sullivan, James Jerome *lawyer, consultant*

Bellingham
Packer, Mark Barry *lawyer, financial consultant, foundation official*

Colfax
Webster, Ronald B. *lawyer*

Federal Way
Lane, Robert Casey *lawyer*

Friday Harbor
McCreary, Dustin Campbell *lawyer, arbitrator*

Kirkland
Butler, William A. *lawyer*

Lake Stevens
†Quigley, Kevin Walsh *lawyer, state legislator*

Lynnwood
Knutzen, Raymond Edward *retired law educator, consultant*

Mount Vernon
Black, Donald Bruce *controller, arbitrator*

Olympia
Mastrodonato, George Carl *lawyer*
†Norwood, Deborah Anne *law librarian*

Redmond
Erxleben, William Charles *lawyer, data processing executive*

Richland
Barr, Carlos Harvey *lawyer*

Seattle
Alkire, John D. *lawyer*
Anderson, Peter MacArthur *lawyer*
Andrews, J. David *lawyer*
Barry, Christopher John *lawyer*
Beighle, Douglas Paul *lawyer*
Bekemeyer, Dennis Lee *lawyer*
Birmingham, Richard Joseph *lawyer*
Black, W. L. Rivers, III *lawyer*
Blom, Daniel Charles *lawyer, investor*
Blumenfeld, Charles Raban *lawyer*
Boeder, Thomas L. *lawyer*
Boman, Marc Allen *lawyer*
Brooks, Julie Anne *lawyer*
Brothers, Lynda Lee *lawyer*
Burkhart, William Henry *lawyer*
Burman, David John *lawyer*
Butler, Timothy Harold *lawyer*
Cable, Donald Aubrey *lawyer*
Cavanaugh, Michael Everett *lawyer*
Char, Patricia Helen *lawyer*
Claflin, Arthur Cary *lawyer*
Clinton, Gordon Stanley *lawyer*
Clinton, Richard M. *lawyer*
†Collins, Theodore John *lawyer*
Corker, Charles Edward *retired lawyer, educator*
Corr, Kelly *lawyer*
Cosway, Richard *legal educator*
Cross, Harry Maybury *retired law educator, consultant*
Cunningham, Janis Ann *lawyer*
Dahl, Lance Christopher *lawyer*
Danelo, Peter Anthony *lawyer*
Davis, John MacDougall *lawyer*
Derham, Richard Andrew *lawyer*
DeVore, Paul Cameron *lawyer*
Dickinson, Calhoun *lawyer*
DiJulio, Peter Stephen *lawyer*
Donohue, James Patrick *lawyer*
Dorkin, Frederic Eugene *lawyer*
Ellis, James Reed *lawyer*
Fitzpatrick, Thomas Mark *lawyer*
Gates, William H. *lawyer*
Giles, Robert Edward, Jr. *lawyer*
Gittinger, D. Wayne *lawyer*
Glover, Karen E. *lawyer*
Goeltz, Thomas A. *lawyer*
Graham, Stephen Michael *lawyer*
Gray, Marvin Lee, Jr. *lawyer*
Greenan, Thomas J. *lawyer*
Greene, John Burkland *lawyer*
Haman, Raymond William *lawyer*
Hansen, Wayne W. *lawyer*
†Hazelton, Penny Ann *law librarian, educator*
Henderson, Dan Fenno *lawyer, educator*
Hilpert, Edward Theodore, Jr. *lawyer*
Hofmann, Douglas Allan *lawyer*
Horton, Elliott Argue, Jr. *lawyer, business consultant*
Hunter, Theodore Paul *lawyer, energy consultant*
Huston, John Charles *law educator*
Hutcheson, Mark Andrew *lawyer*
Isaki, Lucy Power Slyngstad *lawyer*
Israel, Allen D. *lawyer*
Jameson, Henry C. *lawyer*
Johnson, Bruce Edward Humble *lawyer*
†Johnston, R. Bruce *lawyer*
Judson, C(harles) James (Jim Judson) *lawyer*
Kane, Alan Henry *lawyer*
Kane, Christopher *lawyer*
Kaplan, Barry Martin *lawyer*
Kareken, Francis A. *lawyer*
Kellogg, Kenyon P. *lawyer*
Killeen, Michael John *lawyer*
Koehler, Reginald Stafford, III *lawyer*
Kuhrau, Edward W. *lawyer*
Kummert, Richard Osborne *lawyer, educator*
Leitzell, Terry Lee *lawyer*
Lemly, Thomas Adger *lawyer*
Lombard, David Norman *lawyer*
McCann, Richard Eugene *lawyer*
†McKay, John *lawyer*
McKay, Michael Dennis *lawyer*
McKeown, Mary Margaret *lawyer*
McKey, Thomas J. *lawyer*
Mickelwait, Lowell Pitzer *lawyer*
Moch, Robert Gaston *lawyer*
Moore, James R. *lawyer*
Moore, Malcolm Arthur *lawyer*
Mullin, J. Shan *lawyer*
Mullins, Donald Hugh *lawyer*
Mussehl, Robert Clarence *lawyer*
Nellermoe, Leslie C. *lawyer, partner*
Nelson, Marshall J. *lawyer*
Noll, Jonathan Boyd *lawyer*
Oehler, Richard William *lawyer*
Olsen, Harold Fremont *lawyer*
Palm, Gerald Albert *lawyer*
Parker, Omar Sigmund, Jr. *lawyer*
Parks, Patricia Jean *lawyer*
Parsons, A. Peter *lawyer*
Paul, Thomas Frank *lawyer*
Petrie, Gregory Steven *lawyer*
Powell, George Van Tuyl *lawyer*
Prentke, Richard Ottesen *lawyer*
Prosterman, Roy L. *law educator, development specialist*
Pusch, William Gerard *lawyer*
Pym, Bruce Michael *lawyer*
Redman, Eric *lawyer*
Riddell, Richard Harry *lawyer*
Rieke, Paul Victor *lawyer*
Ritter, Daniel Benjamin *lawyer*
Rives, William D. *lawyer*
†Ruddy, James W. *lawyer*
Runstad, Judith Manville *lawyer*
Rupp, John Norris *lawyer*
Sandler, Michael David *lawyer*
Saracino, Samuel Francis *lawyer*
Schwab, Evan Lynn *lawyer*
Shapiro, J. Peter *lawyer*
Shulkin, Jerome *lawyer*
Siefert, Richard Carl *lawyer*
Smith, Payton *lawyer*
Soltys, John Joseph, Jr. *lawyer*
Spitzer, Hugh D. *lawyer*
Squires, William Randolph, III *lawyer*
Steinberg, Jack *lawyer*
Stewart, Robert Andrew *lawyer*
Sweeney, David Brian *lawyer*
Tallman, Richard C. *lawyer*
Tausend, Fredric Cutner *lawyer, university dean*
Thorbeck, Thomas George *lawyer*
Thorson, Lee A. *lawyer*
Treiger, Irwin Louis *lawyer*
Utevsky, David *lawyer*
Voorhees, Lee R., Jr. *lawyer*
Wagner, Patricia H. *lawyer*
Wagoner, David Everett *lawyer*
Wells, Christopher Brian *lawyer*
Wells, Judee Ann *lawyer*
Whalen, Jerome Demaris *lawyer*
Whitford, Joseph P. *lawyer*
Williams, J. Vernon *lawyer*
Wright, Willard Jurey *lawyer*

Spokane
Koegen, Roy Jerome *lawyer*
Lamp, John Ernest *lawyer*

Tacoma
Felker, Robert Stratton *lawyer, consultant*
Gordon, Joseph Harold *lawyer*
Graves, Ray *lawyer*
Miller, Judson Frederick *lawyer, former military officer*
Rudolph, Wallace Morton *legal educator*
†Steele, Anita Martin (Margaret Anne Martin) *law librarian, legal educator*
Thompson, Ronald Edward *lawyer*

Vancouver
Kleweno, Gilbert H. *lawyer*

Vashon
Biggs, Barry Hugh *lawyer*

Walla Walla
Hayner, Herman Henry *lawyer*

Wenatchee
†Foreman, Dale Melvin *lawyer, state official*

Yakima
Suko, Lonny Ray *lawyer*

WEST VIRGINIA

Beckley
Rhoades, Marye Frances *paralegal*

Charles Town
Layva, David *lawyer*

Charleston
Brown, James Knight *lawyer*
Gage, Charles Quincey *lawyer*
Goodwin, Claude Elbert *lawyer, former gas utility executive*
Kizer, John Oscar *lawyer*
Lawson, Robert William, Jr. *retired lawyer*
McClaugherty, John Lewis *lawyer*
Murchison, David Roderick *lawyer*
Snyder, Giles D. H. *lawyer, utility company executive*
Southworth, Louis Sweetland, II *lawyer*
Stacy, Charles Brecknock *lawyer*

Huntington
†Jenkins, John E., Jr. *lawyer, educator*

Lewisburg
Ford, Richard Edmond *lawyer*

Martinsburg
Rice, Lacy I., Jr. *lawyer*

Morgantown
Fisher, John Welton, II *law educator, magistrate judge, university official*
Fusco, Andrew G. *lawyer*
Morris, William Otis, Jr. *lawyer, educator, author*

Mullens
†Staton, W. Richard *lawyer*

Princeton
White, Benjamin Ballard, Jr. *lawyer*

Wheeling
Phillips, John Davisson *retired lawyer*

WISCONSIN

Baraboo
Cross, Clyde Cleveland *lawyer*

Columbus
Callahan, Carroll Bernard *lawyer*

Elm Grove
Gorske, Robert Herman *lawyer*

Greendale
Olander, Ray Gunnar *lawyer*

Janesville
Steil, George Kenneth, Sr. *lawyer*

La Crosse
Klos, Jerome John *lawyer*
Nix, Edmund Alfred *lawyer*

Lake Geneva
Braden, Berwyn Bartow *lawyer*

Madison
Auen, Michael H. *lawyer*
Baldwin, Gordon Brewster *lawyer, educator*
Barnhill, Charles Joseph, Jr. *lawyer*
Bartell, Jeffrey Bruce *lawyer*
Bugge, Lawrence John *lawyer*
Curry, Robert Lee *lawyer*
Erhard, Michael Paul *lawyer*
Field, Henry Augustus, Jr. *lawyer*
Finman, Ted *lawyer, educator*
Foster, George William, Jr. *lawyer, educator*
Helstad, Orrin L. *lawyer, legal educator*
Heymann, S. Richard *lawyer*
Hildebrand, Daniel Walter *lawyer*
Holbrook, John Scott, Jr. *lawyer*
Hurst, James Willard *legal educator*
Jones, James Edward, Jr. *law educator emeritus*
†Kauffman, Stephen Blair *law librarian, law educator*
Langer, Richard J. *lawyer*
Mebane, David Cummins *lawyer*
Murphy, Robert Brady Lawrence *lawyer*
Pasch, Maurice Bernard *lawyer*
Prange, Roy Leonard, Jr. *lawyer*
Ragatz, Thomas George *lawyer*
Raushenbush, Walter Brandeis *law educator*
Shea, Jeremy Charles *lawyer*
Skilton, John Singleton *lawyer*
Temkin, Harvey Leon *lawyer*
Thompson, Cliff F. *lawyer, educator*
Wagner, Burton Allan *lawyer*
Walsh, David Graves *lawyer*
White, William Fredrick *lawyer*
Whitney, Robert Michael *lawyer*
Wilcox, Michael Wing *lawyer*

Manitowoc
Muchin, Arden Archie *lawyer, director*

Mauston
Gross, Carol Jeanne *court clerk*

Mequon
Burroughs, Charles Edward *lawyer*

Milwaukee
Abraham, William John, Jr. *lawyer*
Alverson, William H. *lawyer*
Babler, Wayne E., Jr. *lawyer*
Bannen, John T. *lawyer*
Barbee, Lloyd Augustus *lawyer*
Barnes, Paul McClung *lawyer*
Barron, Russell J. *lawyer*
Bauer, Bruce Richard *lawyer*
Beckwith, David E. *lawyer*
Bell, Darryl Stephen *lawyer*
Berkoff, Marshall Richard *lawyer*
Biehl, Michael Melvin *lawyer*
Biller, Joel Wilson *lawyer, former foreign service officer*
Binder, Robert Lawrence *lawyer*
Bowen, Michael Anthony *lawyer, writer*
Brody, James Patrick *lawyer*
Bruce, Jackson Martin, Jr. *lawyer*
Busch, John Arthur *lawyer*
Cannon, David Joseph *lawyer*
Case, Karen Ann *lawyer*
Casey, John Alexander *lawyer*
Casper, Richard Henry *lawyer*
Christiansen, Jon Peter *lawyer*
Christiansen, Keith Allan *lawyer*
Clark, James Richard *lawyer*
Cleary, John Washington *lawyer*
Connolly, Gerald Edward *lawyer*
Connolly, L. William *lawyer*
Croak, Francis R. *lawyer*
Cutler, Richard Woolsey *lawyer*
Daily, Frank J(erome) *lawyer*
Davis, Walter Stewart *lawyer*
Drummond, Robert Kendig *lawyer*
Duback, Steven Rahr *lawyer*
Ehrmann, Thomas William *lawyer*
Ericson, James Donald *lawyer, insurance executive*
Fischer, Michael Davin *lawyer*
Florsheim, Richard Steven *lawyer*
Frautschi, Timothy Clark *lawyer*
Friedman, James Dennis *lawyer*
Gallagher, Richard S. *lawyer*
Gefke, Henry Jerome *lawyer*
Gemignani, Joseph Adolph *lawyer*
Ghiardi, James Domenic *lawyer, educator*
Goodkind, Conrad George *lawyer*
Groethe, Reed *lawyer*
Groiss, Fred George *lawyer*
Haas, George Edward *lawyer*
Habush, Robert Lee *lawyer*
Hankin, Bernard Jacob *lawyer*
Harding, Victor Mathews *lawyer*
Harrington, John Timothy *lawyer*
Hase, David John *lawyer*
Hatch, Michael Ward *lawyer*
Hazelwood, John A. *lawyer*
Hoffman, Nathaniel A. *lawyer*
Holz, Harry George *lawyer*
Jost, Lawrence John *lawyer*
Kamps, Charles Q. *lawyer*
Kelly, Francis Daniel *lawyer*
Kessler, Joan F. *lawyer*
Kinnamon, David Lucas *lawyer*
Kringel, Jerome Howard *lawyer*
Kubale, Bernard Stephen *lawyer*
Kurtz, Harvey A. *lawyer*
LaBudde, Roy Christian *lawyer*
Laikin, George Joseph *lawyer*
Laun, Arthur Henry, Jr. *lawyer*
Lavers, Richard Marshall *lawyer*
Le Duc, Don Raymond *lawyer, educator*
Levit, William Harold, Jr. *lawyer*
†Lueders, Wayne Richard *lawyer*
MacGregor, David Lee *lawyer*
MacIver, John Kenneth *lawyer*
Maio, F. Anthony *lawyer*
Martin, Quinn William *lawyer*
Maynard, John Ralph *lawyer*
McCauley, Michael Stephen *lawyer*
Mc Gaffey, Jere D. *lawyer*
McSweeney, Maurice J. (Marc) *lawyer*
Meldman, Clifford Kay *lawyer*
Meldman, Robert Edward *lawyer*
Mulcahy, Charles Chambers *lawyer, educator*
Mulcahy, Robert William *lawyer*
Ninneman, Richard Canney *lawyer*
Noelke, Paul *lawyer*
Olson, John Marshall *lawyer*
O'Shaughnessy, James Patrick *lawyer*
Pelisek, Frank John *lawyer*
Phillips, Thomas John *lawyer*
Pindyck, Bruce Eben *lawyer, corporate executive*
Powell, Edmund William *lawyer*
Precourt, Lyman Arthur *lawyer*
Richman, Stephen Erik *lawyer*
Ryan, Patrick Michael *lawyer*
Sapp, John Raymond *lawyer*
Schnur, Robert Arnold *lawyer*
Scrivner, Thomas William *lawyer*
Shriner, Thomas L., Jr. *lawyer*
Stone, Thomas S. *lawyer*
Surridge, Stephen Zehring *lawyer, writer*
Teschner, Richard Rewa *retired lawyer*
Van Vugt, Eric J. *lawyer*
Wallace, Harry Leland *lawyer*
Walmer, Edwin Fitch *lawyer*
Wawrzyn, Ronald M. *lawyer*
Weber, Robert George *lawyer*
White, Walter Hiawatha, Jr. *lawyer*
Whyte, George Kenneth, Jr. *lawyer*
Wiedenman, Jere Wayne *lawyer*
Wiley, Edwin Packard *lawyer*
Will, Trevor Jonathan *lawyer*

Monroe
Kittelsen, Rodney Olin *lawyer*

Neenah
Stanton, Thomas Mitchell *lawyer, educator*

Oshkosh
Dempsey, Timothy Michael *lawyer*

Racine
Coates, Glenn Richard *lawyer*
Crawford, Gerald Marcus *lawyer*
Hart, Robert Camillus *lawyer, company executive*
Swanson, Robert Lee *lawyer*

Rhinelander
Saari, John William, Jr. *lawyer*

River Hills
Silverman, Albert A. *retired lawyer, manufacturing company executive*

Stevens Point
Makholm, Mark Henry *lawyer, former insurance company executive*
Salinger, Robert Meredith *lawyer*

Sun Prairie
Eustice, Francis Joseph *lawyer*

Tomah
Kenyon, Kyle *lawyer*

Wausau
Orr, San Watterson, Jr. *lawyer*

WYOMING

Burns
Suyematsu, Toshiro *lawyer*

Casper
Bostwick, Richard Raymond *retired lawyer*
Lowe, Robert Stanley *lawyer*

Cheyenne
Freudenthal, Steven Franklin *lawyer*
†Hanes, John G. *lawyer, state legislator*
†Lummis, Cynthia Marie *lawyer, rancher*
Mc Clintock, Archie Glenn *lawyer*
Rooney, John Joseph *lawyer, former state supreme court justice*
Rose, Robert R., Jr. *lawyer*

Cody
Housel, Jerry Winters *lawyer*

Jackson
Schuster, Robert Parks *lawyer*
Tessler, Allan Roger *lawyer*
Watt, James Gaius *lawyer, former government official, legal consultant*

Laramie
†Kearley, Timothy G. *law librarian, consultant*
†Maxfield, Peter C. *law educator, university dean, lawyer*
Smith, Thomas Shore *lawyer*

Riverton
Girard, Nettabell *lawyer*

TERRITORIES OF THE UNITED STATES

GUAM

Agana
Tock, Joseph *lawyer*

PUERTO RICO

Carolina
†Figueroa, Iván *lawyer*

San Juan
Trías-Monge, Jose *lawyer, former territory supreme court chief justice*

VIRGIN ISLANDS

Charlotte Amalie
Feuerzeig, Henry Louis *lawyer*

MILITARY ADDRESSES OF THE UNITED STATES

ATLANTIC

APO
Guinot, Luis, Jr. *lawyer, ambassador*

EUROPE

APO
Doyle, Justin Emmett *lawyer, government official*

CANADA

ALBERTA

Calgary
Ballem, John Bishop *lawyer, novelist*
Hughes, Margaret Eileen *law educator, former dean*
Lougheed, Peter *lawyer, former Canadian official*
Matthews, Francis Richard *lawyer*
Perrin, Robert Maitland *solicitor, oil company executive*

Edmonton
Patrick, Lynn Allen *lawyer, construction company executive*
Shoctor, Joseph Harvey *barrister, producer, civic worker*

Smith
Rodnunsky, Sidney *lawyer, educator, Prince of Kiev, Prince of Trabzon, Duke of Chernigov, Count of Riga, Count of Saint John of Alexandria, Baron of Vai*

BRITISH COLUMBIA

Brentwood Bay
Carrothers, Alfred William Rooke *retired law educator*

Vancouver
Bonner, Robert William *lawyer*
Head, Ivan Leigh *law educator*
Howard, John Lindsay *lawyer, forest industry company executive*
Ladner, Thomas E. *lawyer*
Nemetz, Nathaniel Theodore *lawyer, former chief justice of British Columbia*
Peterson, Leslie Raymond *lawyer*
Smethurst, Robert Guy *lawyer*

Victoria
Partridge, Bruce James *lawyer, educator*

MANITOBA

Winnipeg
Anderson, David Trevor *law educator*
Cherniack, Saul Mark *non-practicing barrister, solicitor*
†Wiebe, Bernie *conflict resolution studies educator*

NEW BRUNSWICK

Rothesay
Fairweather, Robert Gordon Lee *lawyer*

NOVA SCOTIA

Halifax
Dickey, John Horace *lawyer*
Macdonald, Joseph Albert Friel *lawyer*
Mingo, James William Edgar *lawyer*

ONTARIO

Etobicoke
Gulden, Simon *lawyer, foods and beverages company executive*

Hamilton
Stanbury, Robert Douglas George *lawyer, executive*

Mississauga
Allen, Clive Victor *lawyer, communications company executive*
Davies, Michael Norman Arden *lawyer, electric company executive*

North York
Arthurs, Harry William *legal educator, former university president*
Brown, Donald Robert *lawyer, oil company executive*
Castel, Jean Gabriel *lawyer*

Ottawa
Beaudoin, Gérald-A(rmand) *lawyer, educator, senator*
d'Aquino, Thomas *lawyer, business council chief executive*
Goulard, Guy Yvon *lawyer*
Iacobucci, Frank *lawyer, educator, jurist*
Tassé, Roger *lawyer, former Canadian government official*
Urie, John James *lawyer, retired Canadian federal judge*
Weatherill, John Frederick William *arbitrator*

Scarborough
†Krajicek, Mark Andrew *lawyer*

Toronto
Aird, John Black *lawyer, university official, former lieutenant governor*
Apple, B. Nixon *lawyer*
Bristow, David Ian *lawyer*
Cowan, Charles Gibbs *lawyer, corporate executive*
Davis, William Grenville *lawyer, former premier of Ontario*
Dickens, Bernard Morris *law educator*
Donais, Gary Warren *lawyer*
Elliott, R(oy) Fraser *lawyer, holding and management company executive*
Eyton, John Trevor *lawyer, business executive*
Farquharson, Gordon MacKay *lawyer*
Gee, Gregory Williams *lawyer*
Godfrey, John Morrow *lawyer, retired Canadian senator*
Graham, John Webb *lawyer*
Innanen, Larry John *lawyer, food products executive*
Lyons, Joseph Chisholm *lawyer*
Macdonald, Donald Stovel *lawyer*
Manning, Charles Terrill *lawyer*
Scheininger, Lester *lawyer, administrator religious organization*
Wolfe, Harold Joel *lawyer, business executive*

QUEBEC

Montreal
Brierley, John E. C. *legal educator, former university dean*
Colas, Emile Jules *lawyer*
Courtois, Edmond Jacques *lawyer*
Gillespie, Thomas Stuart *lawyer*
Guenette, Francoise *legal affairs executive*
Kirkpatrick, John Gildersleeve *lawyer*
Lacoste, Paul *lawyer, educator, university official*

Lalonde, Marc *lawyer, former Canadian government official*
Mercier, Francois *lawyer*
Messier, Pierre *lawyer, manufacturing company executive*
Montcalm, Norman Joseph *lawyer*
Popovici, Adrian *law educator*
Pound, Richard William Duncan *lawyer, accountant*
Pratte, Lise *lawyer, corporate secretary*
Régnier, Marc Charles *lawyer, corporate executive*
Robb, James Alexander *lawyer*
Sheppard, Claude-Armand *lawyer*
†Somerville, Margaret Anne Ganley *law educator*
Tremblay, Andre Gabriel *lawyer, educator*
Trudeau, Pierre Elliott *lawyer, former Canadian prime minister*
Vennat, Michel *lawyer*
Wohl, Robert Allen *lawyer, aerospace executive*

Mount Royal
†Trudel, Pierre *law educator, researcher*

Quebec
Aubut, Marcel *lawyer, sports association official*
LeMay, Jacques *lawyer*
Normand, Robert *lawyer*
Stein, Charles *retired lawyer*
Verge, Pierre *legal educator*

SASKATCHEWAN

Regina
Balfour, Reginald James *lawyer*
Laschuk, Roy Bogdan *lawyer*
MacKay, Harold Hugh *lawyer*

Saskatoon
Ish, Daniel Russell *law educator, academic adminstrator*

MEXICO

Mexico City
Rogers, John Ellsworth *lawyer*

Tijuana
Ochoa, Quintin *lawyer*

AUSTRALIA

Sydney
Hinde, John Gordon *lawyer, solicitor*

BELGIUM

Brussels
Bustin, George Leo *lawyer*
Glazer, Barry David *lawyer*
Liebman, Howard Mark *lawyer*
Oberreit, Walter William *lawyer*
Paul, Robert Carey *lawyer*
Smith, Turner Taliaferro, Jr. *lawyer*

London
Adams, George Bell *lawyer*
Albert, Robert Alan *lawyer*
Batla, Raymond John, Jr. *lawyer*
Beharrell, Steven Roderic *lawyer*
Bigbie, John Taylor *lawyer, banker*
Brown, Peter Stewart *lawyer*
Chubb, Joseph *lawyer*
Cole, Richard A. *lawyer*
Fabricant, Arthur E. *lawyer, corporate executive*
Francke, Albert, III *lawyer*
Gaines, Peter Mathew *lawyer*
Gordon, Jeffrey I. *lawyer*
Hudson, Manley O., Jr. *lawyer*
Johnson, Thomas Edward *lawyer*
Kies, David M. *lawyer*
Kingham, Richard Frank *lawyer*
McLeod, Wilson Churchill *lawyer*
Metzger, Barry *lawyer*
Morrison, William David *lawyer*
Nelson, Bernard Edward *lawyer*
Newburg, Andre W. G. *lawyer*
Randour, Paul A(lfred) *lawyer*
Stevens, Robert Bocking *lawyer, educator*
Thomas, Allen Lloyd *lawyer, private investor*
Thomas, Barbara Singer *lawyer*
Van Meter, John David *lawyer*

FRANCE

Neuilly
Hamilton, Robert William *lawyer*

Neuilly-sur-Seine
O'Neill, Lawrence Daniel *lawyer, consultant*

Paris
Abboud, Ann Creelman *lawyer*
Baum, Axel Helmuth *lawyer*
Cochran, John M., III *lawyer*
Cone, Sydney M., III *lawyer*
Craig, William Laurence *lawyer*
Davidson, Alfred Edward *lawyer*
Iseman, Joseph Seeman *lawyer*
Landers, Steven E. *lawyer*
MacCrindle, Robert Alexander *lawyer*
McGurn, William Barrett, III *lawyer*
Rawlings, Boynton Mott *lawyer*
Riggs, John Hutton, Jr. *lawyer*
Salans, Carl Fredric *lawyer*
Wolrich, Peter M. *lawyer*

GERMANY

Finning
English, Charles Brand *retired lawyer*

Kaiserslautern
Immesberger, Helmut *lawyer*

HONG KONG

Hong Kong
Choo, Yeow Ming *lawyer*
Chu, Franklin Dean *lawyer*
Collins, Charles Roland *lawyer*
Halperin, David Richard *lawyer*
Tanner, Douglas Alan *lawyer*

ISRAEL

Jerusalem
Rosenne, Meir *lawyer, government agency administrator*

ITALY

Rome
Alegi, Peter Claude *lawyer*

JAPAN

Nagoya
Kato, Masanobu *lawyer, educator*

Osaka
Solberg, Norman Robert *lawyer*

Tokyo
Churchill, James Allen *lawyer*
Drabkin, David *lawyer*
Kawachi, Michael Tateo *lawyer*
Kuwahara, Mitsunori *judicial scrivener, consultant*
Reid, Edward Snover *lawyer*

NORWAY

Staranger
Fitzpatrick, Whitfield Westfeldt *lawyer*

THE PHILIPPINES

Legaspi Village
Quasha, William Howard *lawyer*

PORTUGAL

Funchal
Mayda, Jaro *lawyer, educator, author, consultant*

RUSSIA

Moscow
Atkin, William F. *lawyer*

SINGAPORE

Singapore
Reed, John G. *lawyer*

SWITZERLAND

Fribourg
Gurley, Franklin Louis *lawyer, military historian*

Geneva
Abram, Morris Berthold *lawyer, diplomat*
De Pfyffer, Andre *lawyer*

Lucerne
Sherwin, James Terry *lawyer, window covering company executive*

Zurich
Panitz, Lawrence Herbert *lawyer*

THAILAND

Bangkok
Lyman, David *lawyer*

ADDRESS UNPUBLISHED

Abzug, Bella Savitzky *lawyer, former congresswoman*
Adams, Paul Winfrey *lawyer, business executive*
Anderson, Geoffrey Allen *lawyer*
Anderson, Keith *retired lawyer, retired banker*
Anderson, Stanton Dean *lawyer*
Ariyoshi, George Ryoichi *lawyer, business consultant, former governor Hawaii*
Armstrong, William Henry *lawyer*
Arnold, Jerome Gilbert *lawyer*
Askey, William Hartman *lawyer, federal magistrate judge*
Axelrad, Irving Irmas *lawyer, motion picture producer*
Babb, Frank Edward *lawyer, executive*
†Baddour, Phillip A. *lawyer, state legislator*
Bagley, William Thompson *lawyer*
Bailey, Francis Lee *lawyer*
Bailey, Henry John, III *retired lawyer, educator*
Bain, William Donald, Jr. *lawyer, chemical company executive*

Bangs, John Kendrick *lawyer, foundation executive, former chemical company executive*
Banks, Robert Sherwood *lawyer*
†Barlow, William K. *lawyer, state legislator*
Barnhill, Henry Grady, Jr. *lawyer*
Barrett, Barbara McConnell *lawyer*
Barrett, Jane Hayes *lawyer*
Bates, Charles Turner *lawyer, educator*
Battle, Frank Vincent, Jr. *lawyer*
Beldock, Myron *lawyer*
Bell, Haney Hardy, III *lawyer*
Benjamin, Edward A. *lawyer*
Bergan, William Luke *lawyer*
Berger, Lawrence Douglas *lawyer*
Berry, Janis Marie *lawyer*
Berry, Robert Worth *lawyer, educator, retired army officer*
Birchfield, John Kermit, Jr. *lawyer*
Blatt, Harold Geller *lawyer*
Blow, George *lawyer*
Bluemle, Robert Louis *lawyer*
Boho, Dan L. *lawyer*
Boner, Eleanor Katz *lawyer*
Bork, Robert Heron *lawyer, author, former federal judge*
Borow, Richard Henry *lawyer*
Bower, Jean Ramsay *court administrator, lawyer*
Brantz, George Murray *retired lawyer*
Braun, Jerome Irwin *lawyer*
Brink, Richard Edward *lawyer*
Brodhead, David Crawmer *lawyer*
Brodsky, David M. *lawyer*
Brower, Charles Nelson *lawyer, judge*
Brown, Gary Ross *lawyer, magistrate*
Bryant, Cecil Farris *lawyer, retired insurance company executive*
Bujold, Tyrone Patrick *lawyer*
Bunn, George *legal educator, writer*
Burlingame, James Montgomery, III *lawyer*
Burns, J(ohn) Scott *lawyer*
Califano, Joseph Anthony, Jr. *lawyer, public health policy educator, writer*
Carrol, Robert Kelton *lawyer*
Casey, Robert Reisch *lawyer*
Casselman, William E., II *lawyer*
Cassidy, John Harold *lawyer*
Cattani, Maryellen B. *lawyer*
Chamberlin, Michael Meade *lawyer*
Christensen, Robert A. *lawyer*
Clark, Donald Otis *lawyer*
†Clarke, Harold *lawyer*
Clary, Everett Burton *lawyer, retired*
Cobb, Miles Alan *lawyer*
Coleman, Robert Lee *lawyer*
Colodny, Edwin Irving *lawyer, retired airline executive*
Connelly, Sharon Rudolph *lawyer, federal official*
Cooper, Charles Justin *lawyer, former government official*
Coplin, Mark David *lawyer*
Corber, Robert Jack *lawyer*
†Corwin, Laura J. *lawyer*
Crawford, Muriel Laura *lawyer, author, educator*
†Cross, Elmo Garnett, Jr. *lawyer, state senator*
Csia, Susan Rebecca *lawyer, oil company executive*
Culvahouse, Arthur Boggess, Jr. *lawyer*
Davenport, Chester *lawyer*
Davis, Roger Edwin *lawyer, retired discount chain executive*
Diamond, Stuart *lawyer, journalist*
Diehl, Deborah Hilda *lawyer*
Dominick, David DeWitt *lawyer, rancher, environmentalist*
Dotson, Donald L. *lawyer*
Doty, James Robert *lawyer*
†Dowd, Clark Wayne *lawyer, state legislator*
Dubuc, Carroll Edward *lawyer*
Duncan, Donald William *retired lawyer*
Dunn, Warren Howard *retired lawyer, brewery executive*
Dutile, Fernand Neville *law educator*
Dymond, Lewis Wandell *lawyer, mediator, educator*
Dziubla, Robert W. *lawyer*
Edwards, Jerome *lawyer*
Ellis, Emory Nelson, Jr. *retired lawyer*
†Emert, Timothy R. *lawyer*
English, Richard D. *lawyer, diplomat, government official*
Engman, Lewis August *lawyer, trade association executive*
Everdell, William *lawyer*
Fanwick, Ernest *corporate lawyer*
Farmakides, John Basil *lawyer*
Field, Arthur Norman *lawyer*
Finder, Theodore Roosevelt *retired lawyer*
Fiorito, Edward Gerald *lawyer*
Flick, John Edmond *lawyer*
Ford, Ashley Lloyd *lawyer, retired consumer products company executive*
Fowler, Donald Raymond *retired lawyer, educator*
Franklin, Michael Harold *arbitrator, lawyer, consultant*
Freeman, Russell Adams *lawyer*
Fuller, Robert Ferrey *lawyer, investor*
Gamble, E. James *lawyer, accountant*
Gardner, Warner Winslow *lawyer*
George, Joyce Jackson *lawyer, former judge*
Gillam, Max Lee *lawyer*
Giusti, William Roger *lawyer*
Glancz, Ronald Robert *lawyer*
Gobel, John Henry *lawyer*
Goforth, William Clements *lawyer*
Grabemann, Karl W. *lawyer*
Green, Mark Joseph *lawyer, author*
Griffin, Campbell Arthur, Jr. *lawyer*
Griffith, Clark Calvin, II *lawyer*
Grove, Kalvin M(yron) *lawyer*
Guttentag, Joseph Harris *lawyer, educator*
Guyton, Samuel Percy *retired lawyer*
Hackel-Sims, Stella Bloomberg *lawyer, former government official*
Hackett, Robert John *lawyer*
Hafner, Thomas Mark *lawyer*
Haley, George Brock, Jr. *lawyer*
Hall, Jack Gilbert *lawyer, business executive*
Hall, John Hopkins *lawyer, retired*
Halleck, Charles White *lawyer, former judge*
Handler, Harold Robert *lawyer*
Hanzlik, Rayburn DeMara *lawyer*
Hardin, Hal D. *lawyer, former U.S. attorney, former judge*
Harnack, Don Steger *lawyer*
Harriman, John Howland *lawyer*
Harrison, Charles Maurice *lawyer, former communications company executive*
Hauver, Constance Longshore *lawyer*
Heath, Richard Eddy *lawyer*
Heiman, David Gilbert *lawyer*

Helms, W. Richard *lawyer*
Hemmer, James Paul *lawyer*
Hewes, Laurence Ilsley, III *lawyer, management and legal consultant*
Higginbotham, John Taylor *lawyer*
Hill, Harold Nelson, Jr. *lawyer*
Hoch, Roland Franklin *lawyer, retired utilities corporation executive*
Hoffman, S. David *lawyer, engineering educator*
Holt, Marjorie Sewell *lawyer, retired congresswoman*
Honeystein, Karl *lawyer, entertainment company executive*
Horwitz, Donald Paul *lawyer*
Howell, Donald Lee *lawyer*
Hunt, Ronald Forrest *lawyer*
Hyman, Seymour Charles *arbitrator*
Ikle, Richard Adolph *lawyer*
Irvine, John Alexander *lawyer*
Jackson, Elmer Joseph *lawyer, oil and gas company executive*
Jaicomo, Ronald James *lawyer*
Jamieson, Michael Lawrence *lawyer*
Jensen, Robert Trygve *lawyer*
†Jones, Jerrauld C. *lawyer*
Kaster, Laura A. *lawyer*
Kee, Sharon Phillips *lawyer*
Kelly, Dennis John *lawyer*
Kennedy, William Francis *lawyer*
King, David Roy *lawyer*
King, John Francis *lawyer*
†King, Patricia Ann *law educator*
Kirven, Gerald *lawyer*
Kleiman, Bernard *lawyer*
Klemme, Howard Charles *lawyer*
Koonts, Robert Henry *lawyer, retired corporation executive*
Kosarin, Jonathan Henry *lawyer*
Kratt, Peter George *lawyer*
Kurtz, Lloyd Sherer, Jr. *lawyer*
Lackey, Larry Alton, Sr. *lawyer, real estate developer*
Lackland, John *lawyer*
Lagos, George Peter *lawyer*
Lambert, Samuel Waldron, III *lawyer*
Lancaster, Robert Samuel *lawyer, educator*
Lande, James Avra *lawyer, engineering and construction company executive*
Lea, Lorenzo Bates *lawyer*
Leb, Arthur S. *lawyer*
Lerner, Harry *lawyer, consultant*
Levy, David *lawyer, insurance company executive*
Liebeler, Susan Wittenberg *lawyer*
Lightstone, Ronald *lawyer*
Linde, Maxine Helen *lawyer, business executive, private investor*
Lipson, Paul S. *lawyer*
Lopez, Benito Moleiro, Jr. *lawyer, college administrator*
Ludwikowski, Rett Ryszard *law educator, researcher*
Magurno, Richard Peter *lawyer*
Mallory, William Barton, III *corporate lawyer*
Manne, Henry Girard *lawyer, educator*
Marinis, Thomas Paul, Jr. *lawyer*
Marlatt, Jerry Ronald *lawyer*
Marr, Carmel Carrington *lawyer, retired state official*
Matthews, Cari Pineiro *lawyer, author*
Mattingly, William Earl *lawyer*
Mayne, Wiley Edward, Jr. *lawyer*
McCarthy, J. Thomas *lawyer, educator*
McCarthy, Vincent Paul *lawyer*
Mc Connell, Edward Bosworth *legal organization administrator, lawyer*
McConnell, James Guy *lawyer*
McCormick, Michael D. *lawyer*
Mc Curley, Robert Lee, Jr. *lawyer, educator*
McEachern, William Donald *lawyer*
†McGraw, Warren Randolph, II *lawyer, state legislator*
McIntosh, Rhodina Covington *lawyer*
McKean, Robert Jackson, Jr. *retired lawyer*
McNitt, Joseph Edward *lawyer*
Mc Pherson, Robert Donald *retired lawyer*
†McSorley, Cisco *lawyer*
Medlock, Donald Larson *lawyer*
Mendicino, V. Frank *lawyer*
Menhall, Dalton Winn *lawyer, insurance executive, professional association administrator*
Mercer, Edwin Wayne *lawyer*
Meyer, Max Earl *lawyer*
Miller, Edward Albert *lawyer*
Miller, Jeffrey Grant *law educator*
Miller, Reed *lawyer*
Miller, Richard Alan *lawyer, former merger and acquisition and forest products company executive*
Miller, Thormund Aubrey *lawyer*
Millimet, Erwin *lawyer*
Mintz, M. J. *lawyer*
Mulligan, William Hughes *lawyer, former federal judge*
Murphy, Lewis Curtis *lawyer, former mayor*
Murphy, Sandra Robison *lawyer*
Muskie, Edmund Sixtus *lawyer, former secretary of state, former senator*
Nagle, David R. *lawyer, former congressman*
Natcher, Stephen Darlington *lawyer, business executive*
Nelson, Carl Roger *retired lawyer*
Newman, Carol L. *lawyer*
Newman, Kenneth E. *lawyer*
Norman, Albert George, Jr. *lawyer*
Norris, Martin Joseph *lawyer*
Ober, Richard Francis, Jr. *lawyer, banker*
O'Brien, J. Willard *lawyer, educator*
O'Connell, Philip Raymond *retired lawyer, consultant*
O'Mahoney, Robert M. *lawyer*
Orloff, Neil *lawyer*
Osimitz, Dennis Victor *lawyer*
Padgett, George Arthur *retired lawyer*
†Patrick, Deval Laurdine *lawyer*
Patton, James Richard, Jr. *lawyer*
Paul, Herbert Morton *lawyer, accountant, taxation educator*
Paulus, Norma Jean Petersen *lawyer, school system administrator*
Penzer, Mark *lawyer, editor, corporate trainer, former publisher*
Pickus, Albert Pierre *lawyer*
Piga, Stephen Mulry *lawyer*
Pitcher, Griffith Fontaine *lawyer*
Polikoff, Benet, Jr. *lawyer*
Pollard, Henry *lawyer*
Pooley, Beverley John *law educator, librarian*
Prugh, George Shipley *lawyer*
Pusateri, Lawrence Xavier *lawyer*
Quigley, Leonard Vincent *lawyer*
Quillen, Cecil Dyer, Jr. *lawyer, consultant*
Quinlan, J(oseph) Michael *lawyer*

Rabinowitz, Mark Allan *lawyer*
Ramsey, Stephen Douglas *lawyer*
Reeder, James Arthur *lawyer*
Rehmus, Charles Martin *law educator, arbitrator*
Reiche, Frank Perley *lawyer, former federal commissioner*
Reiss, Jerome *lawyer*
Reister, Ruth Alkema *lawyer, business executive*
Reiter, Glenn Mitchell *lawyer*
Reminger, Richard Thomas *lawyer*
Reycraft, George Dewey *lawyer*
Reynolds, William Bradford *lawyer*
Roberts, Alfred Wheeler, III *lawyer, law firm executive*
Roberts, John Glover, Jr. *lawyer*
†Rock, Richard Rand *lawyer, state senator*
Rose, James W. *lawyer*
Rosenn, Harold *lawyer*
Rostow, Charles Nicholas *lawyer, educator*
Roth, Michael *lawyer*
Rothwell, Albert Falcon *retired lawyer, retired natural resource company executive*
Russell, Tomas Morgan *lawyer*
Saliterman, Richard Arlen *lawyer, educator*
Samuels, Sherwin L. *lawyer*
Santman, Leon Duane *lawyer, former federal government executive*
Savage, Charles Francis *lawyer*
Saxon, John David *lawyer, educator*
Schoor, Michael Mercier *lawyer, lobbyist*
Schuck, Peter Horner *lawyer, educator*
Schwab, Eileen Caulfield *lawyer, educator*
†Seidlits, Curtis Lee, Jr. *lawyer*
Shattuck, Cathie Ann *lawyer, former government official*
Sheldon, Terry Edwin *lawyer, business consultant, advisor*
Shook, Ann Jones *lawyer*
Shughart, Donald Louis *lawyer*
†Skratek, Sylvia Paulette *mediator, arbitrator, state legislator*
Slavitt, David Walton *retired lawyer*
Smith, Edward Reaugh *retired lawyer, cemetery and funeral home consultant*
Smith, Lauren Ashley *lawyer, journalist, clergyman, physicist*
Smith, Robert Michael *lawyer*
†Spicer, S(amuel) Gary *lawyer, writer*
Spollen, John William *lawyer*
Springer, Paul David *lawyer, motion picture company executive*
Stapell, Raymond James *lawyer, partner*
Starr, Kenneth Winston *lawyer*
Stegall, Daniel Richard *lawyer*
Stream, Arnold Crager *lawyer, writer*
Streeter, Richard Henry *lawyer*
Swan, George Steven *lawyer, educator*
Tancredi, Laurence Richard *law and psychiatry educator, administrator*
Tapley, James Leroy *retired lawyer, railway corporation executive*
Thiele, Howard Nellis, Jr. *lawyer*
Toensing, Victoria *lawyer*
Tolentino, Casimiro Urbano *lawyer*
†Towery, Matthew Allen, Sr. *lawyer*
Trigg, Paul Reginald, Jr. *lawyer*
Trilling, Helen Regina *lawyer*
Trimble, Paul Joseph *lawyer*
Von Drehle, Ramon Arnold *lawyer*
Voorhees, James Dayton, Jr. *lawyer*
Walch, W. Stanley *lawyer*
Walker, Craig Michael *lawyer*
Walker, James William, Jr. *lawyer*
Walker, John Sumpter, Jr. *lawyer*
Walker, Mary L. *lawyer*
Walner, Robert Joel *lawyer*
Weber, Julian L. *lawyer, former publishing and entertainment company executive*
Webster, Robert David *lawyer*
Weclew, Robert George *lawyer, educator*
Weiland, Charles Hankes *lawyer*
Weinberg, Robert Leonard *retired lawyer*
Weitzman, Bruce H. *lawyer*
White, Richard Clarence *lawyer*
Wildhack, William August, Jr. *lawyer*
Wiley, Richard Arthur *lawyer*
Williams, William John, Jr. *lawyer*
Wilson, Hugh Steven *lawyer*
Wittner, Loren Antonow *lawyer, former public relations executive*
Wood, David Charles *lawyer, finance company executive*
Wood, Diane Pamela *lawyer*
†Yannello, Karen Marie *lawyer*
Yarbro, Alan David *lawyer*
Yarbrough, Marilyn Virginia *lawyer, educator*
Yeager, Mark L. *lawyer*
Zuckerman, Richard Engle *lawyer, educator*

MEDICAL, DENTAL, AND HEALTH SERVICES: DENTISTRY

UNITED STATES

ALABAMA

Birmingham
Alling, Charles Calvin, III *oral-maxillofacial surgeon, educator, writer*
†Birkedal-Hansen, Henning *dentist, educator*
Fullmer, Harold Milton *dentist, educator*
Manson-Hing, Lincoln Roy *dental educator*

Lillian
Shory, Naseeb Lein *dentist, retired state official*

ARIZONA

Flagstaff
Ririe, Craig Martin *periodontist*

Phoenix
Fournier, Donald Frederick *dentist*

CALIFORNIA

Arcadia
Gamboa, George Charles *oral surgeon, educator*

Burlingame
Truta, Marianne Patricia *oral and maxillofacial surgeon, educator, author*

La Jolla
Silverstone, Leon Martin *pedodontist, cariologist, neuroscientist, educator, researcher*

La Mesa
Williams, Carlton Hinkle *dentist*

Long Beach
Domondon, Oscar *dentist*

Los Angeles
Barber, Thomas King *dentist*
Dummett, Clifton Orrin *dentist, educator*
Kapur, Krishan Kishore *dental researcher, educator*
Schoen, Max Howard *dentistry educator*
Yagiela, John Allen *dental educator*

Manteca
Tonn, Elverne Meryl *pediatric dentist, dental insurance consultant*

Pasadena
Mc Carthy, Frank Martin *surgical sciences educator*

Sacramento
Redig, Dale Francis *dentist, association executive*

San Diego
Ingle, John Ide *dental educator*

San Francisco
Dugoni, Arthur A. *orthodontics educator, university dean*
Greene, John Clifford *dentist, university dean*
Greenspan, Deborah *oral medicine educator*
Khosla, Ved Mitter *oral and maxillofacial surgeon, educator*

San Jose
Yoshizumi, Donald Tetsuro *dentist*

San Rafael
Gryson, Joseph Anthony *orthodontist*

Thousand Palms
Smith, Charles Thomas *retired dentist, educator*

Torrance
Leake, Donald Lewis *oral and maxillofacial surgeon, oboist*

COLORADO

Aurora
Eames, Wilmer Ballou *dental educator*

Denver
Bomberg, Thomas James *dental educator*
†Martin, William Truett *oral surgeon, state legislature*

CONNECTICUT

Avon
Löe, Harald *dentist, educator, researcher*

New Canaan
Gottlieb, Arnold *dentist*

Norwalk
Brod, Morton Shlevin *oral surgeon*

DISTRICT OF COLUMBIA

Washington
Calhoun, Noah Robert *oral maxillofacial surgeon, educator*
Gardner, Alvin Frederick *oral pathologist, government official*
Mulvihill, James Edward *periodontist, university administrator, educator, health care executive*
Sazima, Henry John *oral and maxillofacial surgery educator*
Sinkford, Jeanne Craig *dentist, educator*

FLORIDA

Boynton Beach
Kronman, Joseph Henry *orthodontist*

Gainesville
†Clark, William Burton, IV *dentist, educator*
Legler, Donald Wayne *university dean, dentist*
Medina, Jose Enrique *dentist, educator*

Miami
Gittess, Ronald Marvin *dentist*
Higley, Bruce Wadsworth *orthodontist*

North Miami Beach
Rosenbluth, Morton *periodontist, educator*

Palm Beach
Tiecke, Richard William *pathologist, educator, association executive*

Tamarac
Fish, Robert Jay *dental surgeon, lawyer, medico-legal consultant, diversified entrepreneur*

Vero Beach
†Grove, Thomas Keith *periodontist, veterinarian, consultant*

West Palm Beach
Elder, Stewart Taylor *dentist, retired naval officer*

Winter Park
McKean, Thomas Wayne *dentist, retired naval officer*

GEORGIA

Augusta
Hammer, Wade Burke *oral and maxillofacial surgeon, educator*

Evans
Beaudreau, David Eugene *dentist, educator*

HAWAII

Honolulu
George, Peter T. *orthodontist*
Nishimura, Pete Hideo *oral surgeon*

Pearl City
Sue, Alan Kwai Keong *dentist*

ILLINOIS

Alton
Heuertz, Sarah Jane *dentist*
King, Ordie Herbert, Jr. *oral pathologist*

Chicago
Buckner, James Lowell *dentist*
Diefenbach, Viron Leroy *dental, public health educator, university dean*
Driskell, Claude Evans *dentist*
Goepp, Robert August *dental educator, oral pathologist*
Heuer, Michael Alexander *dentist, educator*
Santangelo, Mario Vincent *dental association executive, educator*
Scholle, Roger Hal *dentist*
Weclew, Victor T. *dentist*
Yale, Seymour Hershel *dental radiologist, educator, university dean, gerontologist*
Zaki, Abdelmoneim Emam *dental educator*

Evanston
Graber, Thomas M. *orthodontist*

Naperville
Grimley, Jeffrey Michael *dentist*

Riverwoods
Douglas, Bruce Lee *oral and maxillofacial surgeon, educator, health consultant, gerontology consultant*

INDIANA

Carmel
Roche, James Richard *pediatric dentist, university dean*

Dyer
Teuscher, George William *dental educator*

Indianapolis
Standish, Samuel Miles *oral pathologist, college dean*

Muncie
Thomas, Harvey Gantenbein *dentist*

IOWA

Iowa City
Bishara, Samir Edward *orthodontist*
Jacobs, Richard Matthew *dentist, orthodontics educator*
Olin, William Harold *orthodontist, educator*

KENTUCKY

Lexington
Mink, John Robert *dental educator*

Louisville
Parkins, Frederick Milton *dental educator, university dean*

West Liberty
†Blevins, Walter, Jr. *dentist, state legislator*

LOUISIANA

New Orleans
Rayson, Jack Henry *dentist, educator, retired*

Shreveport
†Simpkins, C.O. *dentist, state legislator*

MARYLAND

Bethesda
Kruger, Gustav Otto, Jr. *oral surgeon, educator*

Columbia
Lorton, Lewis *dentist, researcher, computer scientist*

Potomac
Cotton, William Robert *dentist*

MASSACHUSETTS

Boston
Frankl, Spencer Nelson *dentist, university dean*
Hein, John William *dentist, educator*
Shklar, Gerald *oral pathologist, periodontist, educator*

Hanover
Lonborg, James Reynold *dentist, former professional baseball player*

Milton
Dunn, Martin Joseph *dentist*

Wellesley
Doku, Hristo Chris *dental educator*

MICHIGAN

Ann Arbor
Ash, Major McKinley, Jr. *dentist, educator*
Avery, James Knuckey *dental educator*
Christiansen, Richard Louis *orthodontics educator, research director, former dean*
Craig, Robert George *dental science educator*
Striffler, David Frank *dental public health educator*

Detroit
Dziuba, Henry Frank *dental school administrator*

MINNESOTA

Minneapolis
Elzay, Richard Paul *dental school administrator*
Geistfeld, Ronald Elwood *dental educator*
Pihlstrom, Bruce *periodontist, dental educator*
Shapiro, Burton Leonard *experimental pathologist, geneticist, educator*
†Wolff, Larry F. *dental educator, researcher*

Saint Paul
Jensen, James Robert *dentist, educator*

MISSOURI

Kansas City
Burk, Norman *oral surgeon*
Moore, David Lowell *dentist*
Moore, Dorsey Jerome *dentistry educator, maxillofacial prosthetist*

Lees Summit
Waite, Daniel Elmer *retired oral surgeon*

Saint Louis
Bensinger, David August *dentist, university dean*
Isselhard, Donald Edward *dentist*
Selfridge, George Dever *dentist, retired naval officer*

NEBRASKA

Omaha
Lynch, Benjamin Leo *oral surgeon educator*

NEVADA

Las Vegas
†Rawson, Raymond D. *dentist*

NEW JERSEY

Clifton
Swystun-Rives, Bohdana Alexandra *dentist*

Montclair
Bolden, Theodore Edward *dentist, educator*

Morris Plains
Picozzi, Anthony *dentistry educator, educational administrator*

Ridgewood
Lucca, John James *retired dental educator*

Tinton Falls
Furman, Samuel Elliott *dentist*

Westfield
Feret, Adam Edward, Jr. *dentist*

NEW YORK

Bronx
Friedman, Joel Matthew *oral and maxillofacial surgeon, educator*

Buffalo
Ciancio, Sebastian Gene *periodontist, educator*
Drinnan, Alan John *oral pathologist*

Flushing
Hyman, Milton *dental educator*

Great Neck
Elkowitz, Lloyd Kent *dental anesthesiologist, dentist, pharmacist*
Wank, Gerald Sidney *periodontist*

New York
Arvystas, Michael Geciauskas *orthodontist, educator*
Ashkinazy, Larry Robert *dentist*
Brzustowicz, Stanislaw Henry *clinical dentistry educator*
Di Salvo, Nicholas Armand *dental educator, orthodontist*

Klatell, Jack *dentist*
Mandel, Irwin Daniel *dentist*
Marder, Michael Zachary *dentist, researcher, educator*
Sendax, Victor Irven *dentist, educator, dental implant researcher*

North Tarrytown
Zegarelli, Edward Victor *retired dental educator, researcher*

Rochester
Bowen, William Henry *dental researcher, dental educator*

Roosevelt Island
Kaslick, Ralph Sidney *dentist, educator*

Stony Brook
Boucher, Louis Jack *dentist, educator*
Sreebny, Leo M. *dentist, educator*

Wantagh
Ross, Sheldon Jules *dentist*

Wappingers Falls
Engelman, Melvin Alkon *retired dentist, business executive, scientist*

NORTH CAROLINA

Chapel Hill
Baker, Ronald Dale *dental educator, surgeon, university administrator*
Bawden, James Wyatt *dental educator, dental scientist*
Hershey, H(oward) Garland, Jr. *university administrator, orthodontist*
Proffit, William Robert *orthodontics educator*
White, Raymond Petrie, Jr. *dentist, educator*

Charlotte
Twisdale, Harold Winfred *dentist*

OHIO

Cleveland
De Marco, Thomas Joseph *periodontist, educator*
Wotman, Stephen *dentistry educator, academic administrator*

Columbus
Buchsieb, Walter Charles *orthodontist*
Goorey, Nancy Jane *dentist*
Horton, John Edward *periodontist, educator*

Euclid
Giegerich, Thomas Anthony *orthodontist*

Hubbard
Rose, Ernst *dentist*

OKLAHOMA

Edmond
Brown, William Ernest *dentist*

OREGON

Medford
Barnum, William Laird *pedodontist*

Portland
Bates, Richard Mather *dentist*
†Clarke, J(oseph) Henry *dental educator, dentist*
Van Hassel, Henry John *dentist, educator, university*

PENNSYLVANIA

Clarion
Foreman, Thomas Alexander *dentist*

Greenville
†King, David O. *orthodontist, state legislator*

Philadelphia
Fielding, Allen Fred *oral and maxillofacial surgeon, educator*
Listgarten, Max Albert *periodontics educator*
Winkler, Sheldon *dentist, educator*

Pittsburgh
Ismail, Yahia Hassan *dentist, educator*

Wayne
Guernsey, Louis Harold *retired oral and maxillofacial surgeon, educator*

York
Jacobs, Donald Warren *dentist*

RHODE ISLAND

Providence
Mehlman, Edwin Stephen *endodontist*

SOUTH CAROLINA

Lake City
TruLuck, James Paul, Jr. *dentist, vintner*

TENNESSEE

Memphis
Butts, Herbert Clell *dentist, educator*

Nashville
Hall, Hugh David *dentist, physician, educator*

TEXAS

Dallas
Byrd, David Lamar *oral surgeon educator*

Flower Mound
Kolodny, Stanley Charles *oral surgeon, air force officer*

Houston
Allen, Don Lee *dentistry educator*

VERMONT

Shelburne
Sawabini, Wadi Issa *retired dentist*

VIRGINIA

Fort Belvoir
Scott, David Bytovetzski *dental research and forensic odontology consultant*

Richmond
Laskin, Daniel M. *oral and maxillofacial surgeon, educator*

Virginia Beach
Farrell, Paul Edward *dentist, retired naval officer, educator*

WASHINGTON

Seattle
Dworkin, Samuel Franklin *dentist, psychologist*
Page, Roy Christopher *periodontist, educator*

Spokane
Foster, Ruth Mary *dental association administrator*

WISCONSIN

Milwaukee
Goggins, John Francis *dentist, university administrator*
Scrabeck, Jon Gilmen *dental eductor*

Wausau
Derwinski, Dennis Anthony *dentist*

WYOMING

Greybull
†Miller, Carroll S. *dentist, legislator*

MILITARY ADDRESSES OF THE UNITED STATES

PACIFIC

FPO
Hooley, James Robert *oral and maxillofacial surgeon, educator, university dean*

CANADA

ALBERTA

Edmonton
Thompson, Gordon William *dentist, educator*

BRITISH COLUMBIA

Vancouver
Beagrie, George Simpson *dentist, educator, dean emeritus*

ONTARIO

London
Dunn, Wesley John *dental educator*

Toronto
Ten Cate, Arnold Richard *dentistry educator*

QUEBEC

Montreal
Bentley, Kenneth Chessar *oral surgeon, educator*
Lussier, Jean-Paul *dentistry educator*

Ste-Foy
Maranda, Guy *oral maxillofacial surgeon, Canadian health facility executive, educator*

SWEDEN

Gothenburg
Bona, Christian Maximilian *dentist, psychotherapist*

ADDRESS UNPUBLISHED

Adisman, I. Kenneth *prosthodontist*
Brooke, Ralph Ian *dental educator, vice provost, university dean*
Coval-Apel, Naomi Miller *dentist*
Fox, Gerald Lynn *retired oral and maxillofacial surgeon*
Grewe, John Mitchell *orthodontist, educator*
Johnson, Dewey E(dward) *dentist*
McHugh, Earl Stephen *dentist*

MEDICAL, DENTAL, AND HEALTH SERVICES: MEDICINE

UNITED STATES

ALABAMA

Birmingham
Allen, James Madison *family practice physician, lawyer, consultant*
Barton, James Clyde, Jr. *hematologist, medical oncologist*
Bridgers, William Frank *physician, educator*
Bueschen, Anton Joslyn *physician, educator*
Caulfield, James Benjamin *pathologist, educator*
Cooper, Max Dale *physician, medical educator, researcher*
†Curtis, John J. *medical educator*
Diethelm, Arnold Gillespie *surgeon*
Durant, John Ridgeway *physician*
†Fine, Philip Russel *medical educator*
Finley, Wayne House *medical educator*
Foft, John William *physician, educator*
Fraser, Robert Gordon *diagnostic radiologist*
Friedel, Robert Oliver *physician*
†Friedlander, Michael J. *neuroscientist, animal physiologist, medical educator*
†Garcia, Julio Hernan *pathology educator*
Geer, Jack Charles *retired pathology educator*
Hill, Samuel Richardson, Jr. *medical educator*
Hirschowitz, Basil Isaac *physician*
†Kirklin, John Webster *surgeon*
Kochakian, Charles Daniel *endocrinologist, educator*
Koopman, William James *medical educator, internist, immunologist*
Lloyd, Lewis Keith, Jr. *surgery and urology educator*
Meezan, Elias *pharmacologist, educator*
Mowry, Robert Wilbur *pathologist, educator*
Oakes, Walter Jerry *pediatric neurosurgeon*
Omura, George Adolf *medical oncologist*
Oparil, Suzanne *cardiologist, educator, researcher*
Pacifico, Albert Dominick *cardiovascular surgeon*
Pfister, Roswell Robert *ophthalmologist*
Pittman, James Allen, Jr. *endocrinologist, dean emeritus, educator*
Pohost, Gerald M. *cardiologist, medical educator*
Russell, Richard Olney, Jr. *cardiologist, educator*
Skalka, Harold Walter *ophthalmologist, educator*
Vinik, H(ymie) Ronald *anesthesiologist, physician*
†Warnock, David Gene *nephrologist*

Fairhope
Jones, Henry Earl *dermatologist, direct patient care educator*

Mobile
Anderson, Lewis Daniel *medical educator, orthopaedic surgeon*
Brogdon, Byron Gilliam *physician, radiology educator*
Conrad, Marcel Edward *hematologist, educator*
DeBakey, Ernest George *physician, surgeon*
Eichold, Samuel *medical educator, medical museum curator*
Gardner, William Albert, Jr. *pathologist, medical foundation executive*
Littleton, Jesse Talbot, III *radiology educator*
Parmley, Loren Francis, Jr. *medical educator*
Pitcock, James Kent *head and neck surgical oncologist*
Smith, Jesse Graham, Jr. *dermatologist, educator*
White, Lowell E., Jr. *retired medical educator*

Opelika
Brown, Robert Glenn *plastic surgeon*

Tuscaloosa
Coggins, Wilmer Jesse *physician, medical school administrator*
Mozley, Paul David *obstetrics and gynecology educator*

Tuskegee
Kenney, Howard Washington *physician*

ALASKA

Anchorage
Mala, Theodore Anthony *physician, consultant*
Wolf, Aron S. *psychiatrist*

Fairbanks
Doolittle, William Hotchkiss *internist*

ARIZONA

Green Valley
Wasmuth, Carl Erwin *physician, lawyer*

Mesa
Thompson, Ronald MacKinnon *family physician, artist, writer*

Peoria
Palmer, Alice Eugenia *retired physician, educator*

Phoenix
Bower, Willis Herman *retired psychiatrist, former medical administrator*
Calkins, Jerry Milan *anesthesiologist, educator, administrator, biomedical engineer*
Charlton, John Kipp *pediatrician*
Cozzi, Hugo Louis *psychiatrist*
Diethrich, Edward Bronson *heart institute executive, cardiovascular surgeon*
Griffith, Ernest Ralph *physician, educator*
Hudak, Thomas Michael *plastic surgeon*
†Lawrence, William Doran *physician*
Lorenzen, Robert Frederick *ophthalmologist*
Nadler, Henry Louis *pediatrician, geneticist, medical educator*
Reed, Wallace Allison *physician*
Rowley, Beverley Davies *medical sociologist*
Schiller, William Richard *surgeon*
Woodard, George Sawyer, Jr. *surgeon, physician, retired army officer*
Zerella, Joseph T. *pediatric surgeon*

Scottsdale
DeHaven, Kenneth Le Moyne *retired physician*
Evans, Tommy Nicholas *physician, educator*
Friedman, Shelly Arnold *cosmetic surgeon*
Furman, Robert Howard *physician, educator*
†McPhee, Malcolm Clinton *physician*
Osborn, Leslie Andrewartha *psychiatrist*
Pomeroy, Kent Lytle *physical medicine and rehabilitation physician*
Sanderson, David R. *physician*
†Simon, Ernest Robert *physician, business executive*

Sedona
Hawkins, David Ramon *psychiatrist, writer, researcher*
Shors, Clayton Marion *cardiologist*

Sun City
Pallin, Irving M. *anesthesiologist*

Sun Lakes
Houser, Harold Byron *epidemiologist*

Tempe
Anand, Suresh Chandra *physician*
Noce, Robert Henry *neuropsychiatrist, educator*

Tucson
Abrams, Herbert Kerman *physician, educator*
Alpert, Joseph Stephen *physician, educator*
Beigel, Allan *psychiatry educator*
Boyse, Edward Arthur *research physician*
Brosin, Henry Walter *psychiatrist, educator*
Bryant, Charles Austin, IV *pediatrician, medical facility director*
Burrows, Benjamin *physician, educator*
Capp, Michael Paul *physician, educator*
Cisler, Theresa Ann *osteopath*
Cremer, Mabelle A. *obstetrician, gynecologist*
Dalen, James Eugene *physician, educator*
Drach, George Wisse *urology educator*
Ewy, Gordon Allen *cardiologist, educator*
Halonen, Marilyn Jean *immunologist, pharmacologist, educator*
Hildebrand, John G(rant) *neurobiologist, educator*
Houle, Joseph Adrien *orthopaedic surgeon*
Kaszniak, Alfred Wayne *neuropsychologist*
Klotz, Arthur Paul *physician, educator*
Lebowitz, Michael David *epidemiologist*
Levenson, Alan Ira *psychiatrist, physician, educator*
Marcus, Frank Isadore *physician, educator*
Meislin, Harvey Warren *emergency healthcare physician, professional society administrator*
Nugent, Charles Arter *physician*
Pronove-Irreverre, Pacita *medical officer*
Reinmuth, Oscar MacNaughton *physician, educator*
Sibley, William Austin *neurologist, educator*
Smith, Josef Riley *internist*
Weinstein, Ronald S. *physician, pathologist, educator*

Yuma
Martin, James Franklin *physician, lawyer*

ARKANSAS

Fort Smith
Crow, Neil Edward *radiologist*
Hoge, Marlin Boyd *surgeon*
Snider, James Rhodes *radiologist*

Jefferson
Hart, Ronald Wilson *radiobiologist, toxicologist, government research executive*

Little Rock
Campbell, Gilbert Sadler *surgery educator, surgeon*
Cave, Mac Donald *anatomy educator*
Diner, Wilma Canada *radiologist, educator*
Doherty, James Edward, III *physician, educator*
Doyle, Lee Lee *research scientist, educator*
Ferris, Ernest Joseph *radiology educator*
Garcia-Rill, Edgar Enrique *neuroscientist*
Goss, Kenneth George *physician, educator*
Guggenheim, Frederick Gibson *psychiatry educator*
Hough, Aubrey Johnston, Jr. *pathologist, physician, educator*
Jansen, G. Thomas *dermatologist*
Lucy, Dennis Durwood, Jr. *neurologist*
†Maloney, Francis Patrick *physiatrist*
McMillan, Donald Edgar *pharmacologist*
Pauly, John Edward *anatomist*
Stead, William White *physician, educator, public health administrator*
Suen, James Yee *otolaryngologist, educator*
Ward, Harry Pfeffer *physician, university chancellor*

North Little Rock
Griffith, Jack William *medical librarian*

Roland
Ebert, Richard Vincent *physician, educator*

Scranton
Uzman, Betty Geren *pathologist, retired educator*

CALIFORNIA

Agoura Hills
deCiutiis, Alfred Charles Maria *medical oncologist, television producer*

Alameda
Whorton, M. Donald *occupational and environmental health physician, epidemiologist*

Anaheim
DuBrin, Stanley *physician, hand surgeon, medical clinics director*
Waitzkin, Howard Bruce *physician, educator*

Apple Valley
Win, Khin Swe *anesthesiologist*

Atascadero
Eggertsen, Paul Fred *psychiatrist*

Bakersfield
Badgley, Theodore McBride *psychiatrist, neurologist*
Corder, Michael Paul *physician, educator*
Izenstark, Joseph Louis *radiologist, physician, educator*

Balboa Island
Daughaday, William Hamilton *retired physician*

Belvedere Tiburon
Behrman, Richard Elliot *pediatrician, neonatologist, university dean*

Berkeley
Abel, Carlos Alberto *immunologist*
†Budinger, Thomas Francis *radiologist, educator*
Castro, Joseph Ronald *physician, oncology researcher, educator*
Diamond, Marian Cleeves *anatomy educator*
Duhl, Leonard *psychiatrist, educator*
Falkner, Frank Tardrew *physician, educator*
Grossman, Elmer Roy *pediatrician*
Koshland, Marian Elliott *immunologist, educator*
Kretchmer, Norman *obstetrics and pediatrics educator*
Kubler-Ross, Elisabeth *physician*
Policoff, Leonard David *physician, educator*
Roller, Robert Douglas, III *psychiatrist*
Seitz, Walter Stanley *cardiovascular research consultant*
Tempelis, Constantine Harry *immunologist, educator*

Beverly Hills
Ayres, Samuel, III *physician*
Bao, Katherine Sung *pediatric cardiologist*
Fein, William *ophthalmologist*
Gilberg, Arnold L. *psychiatrist and psychoanalyst*
Giorgi, Elsie Agnes *physician*
Karpman, Harold Lew *cardiologist, educator, author*
Klein, Arnold William *dermatologist*
Menkes, John Hans *pediatric neurologist*
Stein, Myron *internist, educator*
Towers, Bernard Leonard *medical educator*

Brawley
Jaquith, George Oakes *ophthalmologist*

Burlingame
†Gradinger, Gilbert P. *plastic surgeon*

Camarillo
Street, Dana Morris *orthopedic surgeon*

Campbell
Wu, William Lung-Shen (You-Ming Wu) *aerospace medical engineering design specialist*

Capo Beach
Roemer, Edward Pier *neurologist*

Carmel
Doe, Richard Philip *physician, educator*
Felch, William Campbell *internist, editor*

Carmichael
Bromberg, Walter *psychiatrist*
Wagner, Carruth John *physician*

Chula Vista
Allen, Henry Wesley *biomedical researcher*

Coronado
Mock, David Clinton, Jr. *internist*

Corte Madera
Epstein, William Louis *dermatologist, educator*

Covina
Schneider, Calvin *physician*
Takei, Toshihisa *otolaryngologist*

Davis
Enders, Allen Coffin *anatomy educator*
Gardner, Murray Briggs *pathologist, educator*
Jasper, Donald Edward *clinical pathology educator*
Killam, Eva King *pharmacologist*
Lazarus, Gerald Sylvan *physician*
Lipscomb, Paul Rogers *orthopaedic surgeon, educator*
†Overstreet, James Wilkins *obstetrics and gynecology educator, administrator*
Palmer, Philip Edward Stephen *radiologist*
Plopper, Charles George *anatomist, cell biologist*
Richman, David Paul *neurologist, researcher*
Stowell, Robert Eugene *pathologist, retired educator*
Tupper, Charles John *physician, educator*
Williams, Hibbard Earl *medical educator, physician*
Youmans, Julian Ray *neurosurgeon, educator*

Downey
Perry, Jacquelin *orthopedic surgeon*
Redeker, Allan Grant *physician, medical educator*
Sapico, Francisco Lejano *internist, educator*
Shapiro, Richard Stanley *physician*

Duarte
Comings, David Edward *physician, medical genetics scientist*

Levine, Rachmiel *physician*

El Macero
Raventos, Antolin *radiology educator*

Encinitas
Dennish, George William, III *cardiologist*

Escondido
Everton, Marta Ve *ophthalmologist*

Fair Oaks
Stabenau, James Raymond *research psychiatrist, educator*

Fairfield
Martin, Clyde Verne *psychiatrist*

Fremont
Urquhart, John *physician, corporation executive, medical educator*

Fresno
Falcone, Alfonso Benjamin *physician*
Holmes, Albert William, Jr. *physician*
†Leigh, Hoyle *psychiatrist, educator*

Glendale
Dent, Ernest DuBose, Jr. *pathologist*
Kernen, Jules Alfred *pathologist*

Greenbrae
Levy, S. William *dermatologist*

Half Moon Bay
Robertson, Abel L., Jr. *pathologist*

Hemet
Kopiloff, George *psychiatrist*

Hollywood
Bessman, Samuel Paul *biochemist, pediatrician*

Huntington Beach
Lee, Sammy *retired physician, surgeon*

Indio
Fischer, Craig Leland *physician*

Inglewood
Jobe, Frank Wilson *orthopedic surgeon*

Irvine
Connolly, John Earle *surgeon, educator*
Felton, Jean Spencer *physician*
Friedenberg, Richard Myron *radiology educator, physician*
Friou, George Jacob *immunologist, physician, educator*
Gottschalk, Louis August *neuropsychiatrist, psychoanalyst*
Gupta, Sudhir *immunologist, educator*
Jones, Edward George *anatomy and neurobiology professor, department chairman*
Miledi, Ricardo *neurobiologist*
Morrison, Gilbert Caffall *psychiatrist*
Mosier, Harry David, Jr. *physician, educator*
Starr, Arnold *neurologist, educator*
Tobis, Jerome Sanford *physician*
van-den-Noort, Stanley *physician, educator*

La Canada Flintridge
Byrne, George Melvin *physician*

La Jolla
Anderson, Richard William *retired psychiatrist, educator*
Barrett-Connor, Elizabeth Louise *epidemiologist, educator*
Bergan, John Jerome *vascular surgeon*
Bernstein, Eugene Felix *vascular surgeon, medical educator*
Beutler, Ernest *physician, research scientist*
Block, Melvin August *surgeon, educator*
Carmichael, David Burton *physician*
Carson, John Congleton *cardiologist, educator*
Dalessio, Donald John *physician, neurologist, educator*
Dixon, Frank James *medical scientist, educator*
Farr, Richard Studley *immunologist, educator, physician*
Fosburg, Richard Garrison *cardiothoracic surgeon*
Friedman, Paul Jay *radiologist, educator*
Gittes, Ruben Foster *urological surgeon*
Hench, Philip Kahler *physician*
Hofmann, Alan Frederick *biomedical educator, researcher*
†Ishizaka, Kimishige *immunologist, educator*
Johnson, Allen Dress *cardiologist*
Karten, Harvey Jules *neurosciences educator*
Katzman, Robert *medical educator, neurologist*
Keeney, Edmund Ludlow *physician*
Klinman, Norman Ralph *immunologist, medical educator*
Lele, Padmakar Pratap *physician, educator*
†Mandell, Arnold Joseph *psychiatrist*
Mathews, Kenneth Pine *physician, educator*
Mitchell, Malcolm Stuart *physician, researcher*
Nakamura, Robert Motoharu *pathologist*
Nyhan, William Leo *pediatrician, educator*
Steinberg, Daniel *preventive medicine physician, educator*
Tan, Eng Meng *immunologist, rheumatologist, biomedical scientist*
Terry, Robert Davis *neuropathologist, educator*
Weigle, William Oliver *immunologist, educator*

La Quinta
Boysen, Harry *obstetrician, gynecologist*

Laguna Niguel
Angelov, George Angel *pediatrician, anatomist, teratologist*

Loma Linda
Adey, William Ross *physician*
Bailey, Leonard Lee *surgeon*
†Behrens, Berel Lyn *physician, academic administrator*
Bull, Brian Stanley *pathology educator, medical consultant, business executive*
Coggin, Charlotte Joan *cardiologist, educator*
Condon, Stanley Charles *gastroenterologist*
Hinshaw, David B., Jr. *radiologist*
Johns, Varner Jay, Jr. *medical educator*
Kuhn, Irvin Nelson *hematologist, oncologist*
Llaurado, Josep G. *nuclear medicine physician, scientist*
Mace, John Weldon *pediatrician*
Peterson, John Eric *physician, educator*
Rendell-Baker, Leslie *anesthesiologist, educator*
Roberts, Walter Herbert Beatty *anatomist*
Slater, James Munro *radiation oncologist*
Stilson, Walter Leslie *radiologist, educator*

Long Beach
Alkon, Ellen Skillen *physician*
Kurnick, Nathaniel Bertrand *oncology educator, researcher*
Loganbill, G. Bruce *logopedic pathologist*
Mills, Don Harper *pathology and psychiatry educator*
Todd, Malcolm Clifford *surgeon*

Los Angeles
Apt, Leonard *physician*
Ashley, Sharon Anita *pediatric anesthesiologist*
Askanas-Engel, Valerie *neurologist, educator, researcher*
Bao, Joseph Yue-Se *orthopaedist, microsurgeon, educator*
Barrio, Jorge Raul *medical educator*
Beck, John Christian *physician, educator*
Bernstein, Sol *cardiologist, medical services administrator*
Blahd, William Henry *physician*
Boak, Ruth Alice *physician, educator*
Bondareff, William *psychiatry educator*
Breslow, Lester *physician, educator*
Chandor, Stebbins Bryant *pathologist*
Cherry, James Donald *physician*
Cicciarelli, James Carl *immunology educator*
Clemente, Carmine Domenic *anatomist, educator*
Cochran, Sachiko Tomie *radiologist*
Cooper, Edwin Lowell *anatomy educator*
Cozen, Lewis *orthopedic surgeon*
Crandall, Edward David *medical educator*
Danoff, Dudley Seth *surgeon, urologist*
Davidson, Ezra C., Jr. *physician, educator*
Davis, Sybil Alicia *obstetrician gynecologist*
DeQuattro, Vincent Louis *physician*
Detels, Roger *epidemiologist, physician, former university dean*
Dignam, William Joseph *obstetrician, gynecologist, educator*
Enstrom, James Eugene *cancer epidemiologist*
†Fahey, John Leslie *immunologist*
Feig, Stephen Arthur *pediatrics educator, hematologist, oncologist*
Fish, Barbara *psychiatrist, educator*
Fonkalsrud, Eric Walter *pediatric surgeon, educator*
Gale, Robert Peter *physician, scientist, researcher*
Gambino, Jerome James *nuclear medicine educator*
Go, Vay Liang Wong *physician, medical educator, editor*
Gold, Richard Horace *radiologist*
Gonick, Harvey Craig *nephrologist, educator*
Goodwin, Willard Elmer *urologist*
Gorney, Roderic *psychiatry educator*
Gorski, Roger Anthony *neuroendocrinologist, educator*
Govier, William Charles *pharmaceutical research and development executive*
Grinnell, Alan Dale *neurobiologist, educator, researcher*
Harold, John Gordon *cardiologist, internist*
Haywood, L. Julian *physician, educator*
Hoang, Duc Van *theoretical pathologist, educator*
†Horwitz, David A. *medicine and microbiology educator*
†House, John William *otologist*
Hughes, Everett Clark *otolaryngology educator*
Jarvik, Lissy F. *psychiatrist*
Jarvik, Murray Elias *psychiatry, pharmacology educator*
Jelliffe, Roger Woodham *cardiologist, clinical pharmacologist*
Jenden, Donald James *pharmacologist, educator*
†Johnson, Cage Saul *hematologist, educator*
Kambara, George Kiyoshi *retired ophthalmologist, educator*
Kaplan, Samuel *pediatric cardiologist*
Katz, Ronald Lewis *physician, educator*
Kay, Jerome Harold *cardiac surgeon*
Kelly, Arthur Paul *physician*
Kilburn, Kaye Hatch *medical educator*
Koch, Richard *pediatrician, educator*
Korenman, Stanley George *medical investigator, educator*
†Krim, Mathilde *medical educator*
Kruger, Lawrence *neuroscientist*
Lane, Joseph M. *orthopaedic surgeon, oncologist*
Lehman, Robert Nathan *ophthalmologist, educator*
Lewin, Klaus J. *pathologist, educator*
Lewis, Charles Edwin *physician, educator*
Liberman, Robert Paul *psychiatry educator, researcher, writer*
Longmire, William Polk, Jr. *physician, surgeon*
Marmor, Judd *psychiatrist, educator*
Maronde, Robert Francis *internist, clinical pharmacologist, educator*
Mellinkoff, Sherman Mussoff *medical educator*
Metzner, Richard Joel *psychiatrist, psychopharmacologist, educator*
Mihan, Richard *dermatologist*
Miles, Samuel Israel *psychiatrist*
Miller, Timothy Alden *plastic and reconstructive surgeon*
Mishell, Daniel R., Jr. *physician, educator*
Morgenstern, Leon *surgeon*
Moxley, John Howard, III *physician*
Mulder, Donald Gerrit *surgeon, educator*
Noble, Ernest Pascal *physician, biochemist, educator*
Paredes, Alfonso *psychiatrist*
Parker, John William *pathology educator, investigator*
Parker, Robert George *radiation oncology educator, academic administrator*
Parmelee, Arthur Hawley, Jr. *pediatric medical educator*
Perloff, Joseph Kayle *cardiologist*
Pettit, Thomas Henry *ophthalmologist*
Pitkin, Roy Macbeth *physician, educator*
†Rachelefsky, Gary S. *medical association administrator*
Rangell, Leo *psychiatrist, psychoanalyst*
Rimoin, David Lawrence *physician, geneticist*
Ritvo, Edward Ross *psychiatrist*
Roemer, Milton Irwin *physician, educator*
Ross, Joseph Foster *physician, educator*
Ryan, Stephen Joseph, Jr. *ophthalmology educator, university dean*
†Saad, Mohammed Fathy *medical educator*
Sarnat, Bernard George *plastic surgeon, educator, researcher*
Savage, Edward Warren, Jr. *physician*
Sawyer, Charles Henry *anatomist, educator*
Scheibel, Arnold Bernard *psychiatrist, educator, researcher*
Schiff, Martin *physician, surgeon*
Schwabe, Arthur David *physician, educator*
Siegel, Sheldon C. *physician*
Solomon, David Harris *physician, educator*
Sprague, Norman Frederick, Jr. *surgeon, educator*
Steckel, Richard J. *radiologist, academic administrator*
Stern, Walter Eugene *neurosurgeon, educator*
Straatsma, Bradley Ralph *ophthalmologist, educator*
Sullivan, Stuart Francis *anesthesiologist, educator*
Thomas, Claudewell Sidney *psychiatry educator*
Tischler, Gary Lowell *psychiatrist, educator*
Titus, Edward Depue *psychiatrist, administrator*
Tompkins, Ronald K. *surgeon*
Tranquada, Robert Ernest *medical educator, physician*
Urist, Marshall Raymond *orthopedic surgeon, researcher*
van Dam, Heiman *psychoanalyst*
Van Der Meulen, Joseph Pierre *neurologist*
Verity, Maurice Anthony *pathologist, neuropathologist, educator, consultant*
Villablanca, Jaime Rolando *medical scientist, educator*
Vredevoe, Donna Lou *research immunologist, microbiologist, educator*
†Walsh, John Harley *medical educator*
Watring, Watson Glenn *gynecologic oncologist, educator*
Weiner, Leslie Philip *neurology educator, researcher*
Weinstein, Irwin Marshall *internist, hematologist*
Weiss, Martin Harvey *neurosurgeon, educator*
West, Louis Jolyon *psychiatrist*
Williams, Henry Stratton *radiologist, educator*
Wilson, Miriam Geisendorfer *physician, educator*
Wincor, Michael Z. *psychopharmacology educator, clinician, researcher*
Yamamoto, Joe *psychiatrist, educator*

Los Gatos
Lorincz, Albert Bela *physician, educator*

Malibu
Lilly, John Cunningham *medical scientist, author*
Moore, John George, Jr. *medical educator*

Martinez
Burchell, Mary Cecilia *surgeon*

Marysville
Hamilton, Richard Daniel *neurosurgeon*

Menlo Park
Glaser, Robert Joy *physician, foundation executive*
Sparks, Robert Dean *medical administrator, physician*

Merced
Maytum, Harry Rodell *retired physician*

Mill Valley
Wallerstein, Robert Solomon *psychiatrist*

Monterey
Black, Robert Lincoln *pediatrician*

Napa
Francis, Marc Baruch *pediatrician*

Newport Beach
Kahn, Douglas Gerard *psychiatrist*
Zalta, Edward *otorhinolaryngologist, utilization review physician*

Nipomo
Brantingham, Charles Ross *podiatrist, ergonomics consultant*

North Hollywood
Gregorius, Beverly June *retired obstetrician-gynecologist*

Northridge
Davidson, Sheldon Jerome *hematologist*

Novato
Bozdech, Marek Jiri *physician*
Franklin, Robert Blair *cardiologist*

Oakland
Collen, Morris Frank *physician*
Fink, Diane Joanne *physician*
†Friedman, Gary David *epidemiologist, research facility administrator*
Reitz, Richard Elmer *physician*
Weinmann, Robert Lewis *neurologist*

Orange
Anzel, Sanford Harold *orthopaedic surgeon*
Armentrout, Steven Alexander *oncologist*
Berk, Jack Edward *physician, educator*
Braunstein, Phillip *radiologist, educator*
†Crumley, Roger Lee *surgeon, educator*
Dana, Edward Runkle *physician, educator*
Furnas, David William *plastic surgeon*
Hofmann, Adele Dellenbaugh *pediatrician*
Morgan, Beverly Carver *physician, educator*
Quilligan, Edward James *obstetrician/gynecologist, educator*
Rowen, Marshall *radiologist*
Thompson, William Benbow, Jr. *obstetrician/gynecologist, educator*
Yu, Jen *medical educator*

Pacific Palisades
Claes, Daniel John *physician*
Dignam, Robert Joseph *retired orthopaedic surgeon*
Rockwell, Don Arthur *psychiatrist*

Palm Desert
McKissock, Paul Kendrick *plastic surgeon*

Palm Springs
Carter, Paul Richard *physician*
Kroger, William Saul *obstetrician-gynecologist*

Palo Alto
Adamson, Geoffrey David *reproductive endocrinologist, surgeon*
Agras, William Stewart *psychiatry educator*
Amylon, Michael David *physician, educator*
Britton, M(elvin) C(reed), Jr. *physician, rheumatologist*
†Carlson, Robert Wells *physician, educator*
Chase, Robert Arthur *surgeon, educator*
Cooper, Allen David *research scientist, educator*
Farquhar, John William *physician, educator*
Fries, James Franklin *internal medicine educator*
Goldstein, Avram *pharmacology educator*
Hays, Marguerite Thompson *physician*
Holman, Halsted Reid *medical educator*
†Jamison, Rex Lindsay *medical educator*
Jamplis, Robert Warren *surgeon, medical foundation executive*
Lane, William Kenneth *physician*
Linna, Timo Juhani *immunologist, researcher, educator*
†Litt, Iris F. *pediatrics educator*
Mansour, Tag Eldin *pharmacologist*
Remington, Jack Samuel *physician*
†Robinson, Thomas Nathaniel *pediatrician, educator, researcher*
Sawyer, Wilbur Henderson *pharmacologist, educator*
Schrier, Stanley Leonard *physician, educator*
Strober, Samuel *immunologist, educator*

Palos Verdes Peninsula
Haynes, Moses Alfred *physician*

Panorama City
Bass, Harold Neal *pediatrician, medical geneticist*

Pasadena
Caillouette, James Clyde *physician*
Hammond, George Denman *physician, medical researcher, educator*
Harvey, Joseph Paul, Jr. *orthopedist, educator*
Konishi, Masakazu *neurobiologist*
Mathies, Allen Wray, Jr. *physician, hospital administrator*

Philo
Hill, Rolla B. *pathologist*

Piedmont
Cuttle, Tracy Donald *physician, former naval officer*
Hughes, James Paul *physician*
Montgomery, Theodore Ashton *physician*

Playa Del Rey
Waggoner, James Norman *physician*

Portola Valley
Creevy, Donald Charles *obstetrician-gynecologist*

Rancho Mirage
Cone, Lawrence Arthur *research medicine educator*

Rancho Santa Fe
Affeldt, John Ellsworth *physician*

Redlands
†Bricker, Neal S. *physician, educator*
Skoog, William Arthur *retired oncologist*

Redwood City
Seltzer, Ronald Anthony *radiologist, educator*

Rolling Hills Estates
Bellis, Carroll Joseph *surgeon*

Roseville
Hendricks, Ed Jerald *physician*

Ross
Way, Walter Lee *anesthetist, pharmacologist, educator*

Sacramento
Benfield, John Richard *surgeon*
Bogren, Hugo Gunnar *radiology educator*
Chapman, Michael William *orthopedist, educator*
Cunningham, Mary Elizabeth *physician*
Deitch, Arline Douglis *Urologist*
Dorn, Robert Murray *physician, psychiatrist, educator, psychoanalyst*
Evrigenis, John Basil *obstetrician-gynecologist*
Frey, Charles Frederick *surgeon, educator*
Wolfman, Earl Frank, Jr. *surgeon, educator*

San Bruno
Bradley, Charles William *podiatrist, educator*

San Clemente
Kim, Edward William *ophthalmic surgeon*

San Diego
Akeson, Wayne Henry *orthopedic surgeon, orthopedic educator*
Bailey, David Nelson *pathologist, educator*
Benirschke, Kurt *pathologist, educator*
Blum, John Alan *urologist, educator*
Bradley, John Edmund *physician, emeritus educator*
DeMaria, Anthony Nicholas *cardiologist, educator*
†Edwards, Charles Cornell *physician, research administrator*
Gigli, Irma *physician, educator, academic administrator*
Goltz, Robert William *physician, educator*
Griffin, Herschel Emmett *epidemiology educator, administrator*
Halasz, Nicholas Alexis *surgeon*
Hamburg, Marian Virginia *health science educator*
Harwood, Ivan Richmond *pediatric pulmonologist*
Henderson, Brian Edmond *physician, educator*
Isenberg, Jon Irwin *gastroenterologist, educator*
Jeste, Dilip Vishwanath *psychiatrist, researcher*
†Kaplan, George Willard *urologist*
Magnuson, Harold Joseph *physician*
Moossa, A. R. *surgery educator*

Moser, Kenneth Miles *physician*
Oliphant, Charles Romig *physician*
O'Malley, Edward *physician, consultant*
Ranney, Helen Margaret *physician, educator*
Resnik, Robert *medical educator*
Ross, John, Jr. *physician, educator*
†Saidman, Lawrence J. *anesthesiologist*
Salk, Jonas Edward *physician, scientist*
Turrell, Eugene Snow *psychiatrist*
Wasserman, Stephen Ira *physician, educator*

San Francisco
Aird, Robert Burns *neurologist, educator*
Amend, William John Conrad, Jr. *physician, educator*
Arieff, Allen Ives *physician*
Asling, Clarence Willet *anatomist, educator*
Auerback, Alfred *psychiatrist*
Bainton, Dorothy Ford *pathology educator, researcher*
†Barondes, Samuel Herbert *psychiatrist, educator*
Benet, Leslie Zachary *pharmacokineticist*
Biglieri, Edward George *physician*
Bishop, John Michael *biomedical research scientist, educator*
Boles, Roger *otolaryngologist*
†Bredt, David S. *neuroscience and physiology educator*
Clever, Linda Hawes *physician*
Cobbs, Price Mashaw *social psychiatrist*
Crede, Robert Henry *physician, educator*
Cunningham, Emmett Thomas, Jr. *physician, researcher*
Curry, Francis John *physician*
David, George *psychiatrist, economic theory lecturer*
†Dawson, Chandler R. *ophthalmologist, educator*
Debas, Haile T. *gastrointestinal surgeon, physiologist, educator*
Engleman, Ephraim Philip *physician*
Epstein, Charles Joseph *physician, medical geneticist, pediatrics and biochemistry educator*
Epstein, John Howard *dermatologist*
Epstein, Leon Joseph *psychiatrist*
Erskine, John Morse *surgeon*
Farber, Seymour Morgan *physician, university administrator*
†Fielder, David R. *medical research administrator*
Foye, Laurance Vincent *physician, hospital administrator*
Fraser, Cosmo Lyle *medical educator, researcher*
Frick, Oscar Lionel *physician, educator*
Friedman, Meyer *physician*
Fu, Karen King-Wah *radiation oncologist*
Gooding, Charles Arthur *radiologist, physician, educator*
Gottfried, Eugene Leslie *physician, educator*
Greenspan, Francis S. *physician*
Grumbach, Melvin Malcolm *physician, educator*
Havel, Richard Joseph *physician, educator*
Henry, Margaret Elizabeth *physician, surgeon*
Hinman, Frank, Jr. *urologist, educator*
Hoffman, Julien Ivor Ellis *pediatric cardiologist, educator*
Jacobs, Edwin Max *oncologist, consultant*
†Jaffe, Robert Benton *obstetrician-gynecologist, reproductive endocrinologist*
Kan, Yuet Wai *physician, investigator*
Katz, Hilliard Joel *physician*
Kilgore, Eugene Sterling, Jr. *surgeon*
Kuzell, William Charles *physician, instrument company executive*
Kvitash, Vadim I(ssay) *physician, scientist, inventor*
LaVail, Jennifer Hart *neurobiologist, educator, researcher*
Levin, Alan Scott *pathologist, allergist, immunologist*
Lim, Robert Cheong, Jr. *surgeon, educator*
Maibach, Howard I. *dermatologist*
Margulis, Alexander Rafailo *physician, educator*
Martin, Joseph Boyd *neurologist, educator*
Mason, Dean Towle *cardiologist*
†Mathes, Stephen John *plastic and reconstructive surgeon, educator*
McCorkle, Horace Jackson *physician, educator*
†Miller, Walter Luther *scientist, physician, educator*
Murray, John Frederic *physician, educator*
Mustacchi, Piero *physician, educator*
Myers, Howard Milton *pharmacologist, educator*
O'Connor, G(eorge) Richard *ophthalmologist*
Perkins, Herbert Asa *physician*
Petrakis, Nicholas Louis *physician, medical researcher, educator*
Phibbs, Roderic Henry *medical educator, pediatrician*
Phillips, Theodore Locke *radiation oncologist, educator*
Piel, Carolyn Forman *pediatrician, educator*
Ralston, Henry James, III *neurobiologist, anatomist, educator*
Risse, Guenter Bernhard *physician, historian, educator*
Roe, Benson Bertheau *surgeon, educator*
Rosinski, Edwin Francis *health sciences educator*
Rudolph, Abraham Morris *physician, educator*
Schachter, Julius *epidemiology educator*
Schiller, Francis *neurologist, medical historian*
Schmid, Rudi (Rudolf Schmid) *physician, educator, academic administrator, researcher*
Schmidt, Robert Milton *physician, scientist, educator*
Scholten, Paul *obstetrician-gynecologist, educator*
Shapiro, Howard Allan *gastroenterologist, medical educator*
†Shapiro, Larry Jay *pediatrician, scientist, educator*
Shinefield, Henry Robert *pediatrician*
Shohet, Stephen Byron *medical educator*
Shumate, Charles Albert *retired dermatologist*
Skinner, Harry Bryant *orthopaedic surgery educator*
Smith, David Elvin *physician*
Sokolow, Maurice *physician, educator*
Szabo, Zoltan *medical science educator, medical institute administrator*
†Terr, Lenore Cagen *psychiatrist, writer*
Veith, Ilza *retired psychiatric history educator*
Volpe, Peter Anthony *surgeon*
Wallerstein, Ralph Oliver *physician*
Watts, Malcolm S(tuart) M(cNeal) *physician, medical educator*
Way, E(dward) Leong *pharmacologist, toxicologist, educator*
†Wilson, Charles B. *neurosurgeon, educator*
Wintroub, Bruce Urich *dermatologist, educator, researcher*
Wolff, Sheldon *radiobiologist, educator*
Zippin, Calvin *epidemiologist*

San Jose
Johnson, Allen Halbert *surgeon*

†Kramer, Richard Jay *gastroenterologist*
Lippe, Philipp Maria *neurosurgeon, educator*
Okita, George T. *pharmacologist educator*

San Juan Capistrano
Braunstein, Herbert *pathologist, educator*
Fisher, Delbert Arthur *physician, educator*

San Leandro
Leighton, Joseph *pathologist*

San Marino
Benzer, Seymour *neurosciences educator*

San Mateo
Kidera, George Jerome *physician*
†Van Kirk, John Ellsworth *cardiologist*

San Pablo
†Bristow, Lonnie Robert *physician*

San Rafael
Bruyn, Henry Bicker *physician*
Hinshaw, Horton Corwin *physician*
Parnell, Francis William, Jr. *physician*

San Ramon
Litman, Robert Barry *physician, author, television and radio commentator*

Santa Ana
Abbruzzese, Carlo Enrico *physician, writer, educator*
Pratt, Lawrence Arthur *thoracic surgeon, foreign service officer*

Santa Ana Heights
†George, Kattunilathu Oommen *homoeopathic physician, educator*

Santa Barbara
Enelow, Allen Jay *psychiatrist, educator*
†Fisher, Steven Kay *neurobiology eductor*
Preston, Frederick Willard *surgeon*
Riemenschneider, Paul Arthur *physician, radiologist*
Taylor, Dermot Brownrigg *pharmacology researcher*

Santa Cruz
Magid, Gail Avrum *neurosurgery educator*

Santa Monica
Gross, Sidney W. *neurosurgeon, educator*
†Gupta, Rishab Kumar *medical association administrator, educator, researcher*
McGuire, Michael Francis *plastic and reconstructive surgeon*
Rand, Robert Wheeler *neurosurgeon, educator*
Singer, Frederick Raphael *medical researcher, educator*
Thompson, Dennis Peters *plastic surgeon*

Sepulveda
Costea, Nicolas Vincent *physician, researcher*
Solomon, George Freeman *academic psychiatrist*

Sherman Oaks
Zemplenyi, Tibor Karol *cardiologist*

Sierra Madre
Nation, Earl F. *retired urologist, educator*

Somerset
Collier, Clarence Robert *physician, educator*

Stanford
Abrams, Herbert LeRoy *radiologist, educator*
Bagshaw, Malcolm A. *radiation therapist, educator*
†Bauer, Eugene Andrew *dermatologist, educator*
Baylor, Denis Aristide *neurobiology educator*
Beard, Rodney Rau *physician, educator*
Bensch, Klaus George *pathology educator*
†Brown, J. Martin *oncologist, educator*
Gibson, Count Dillon, Jr. *physician, educator*
Goldstein, Dora Benedict *pharmacologist, educator*
Harris, Edward D., Jr. *physician*
Heinrichs, William LeRoy *obstetrician, gynecologist, educator*
Hubert, Helen Betty *epidemiologist*
Jardetzky, Oleg *medical educator, scientist*
Kendig, Joan Johnston *neurobiology educator*
Korn, David *educator, pathologist*
†Krensky, Alan Michael *pediatrician, educator*
Maffly, Roy Herrick *medical educator*
Mark, James B. D. *surgeon*
Marmor, Michael Franklin *ophthalmologist, educator*
McDevitt, Hugh O'Neill *immunology educator, physician*
McDougall, Iain Ross *nuclear medicine educator*
Melmon, Kenneth Lloyd *physician, biologist, pharmacologist, consultant*
Merigan, Thomas Charles, Jr. *physician, medical researcher, educator*
Niederhuber, John Edward *surgical oncologist and molecular immunologist, university educator and administrator*
Paffenbarger, Ralph Seal, Jr. *epidemiologist*
Raffin, Thomas A. *physician*
Rosenberg, Saul Allen *oncologist, educator*
Rubenstein, Edward *physician, educator*
Schatzberg, Alan Frederic *psychiatrist, researcher*
Schroeder, John Speer *cardiology educator*
Shortliffe, Edward Hance *internist, medical information science educator*
Silverman, Frederic Noah *physician*
Stinson, Edward Brad *surgery educator*

Stockton
Renson, Jean Felix *psychiatry educator*

The Sea Ranch
Resch, Joseph Anthony *neurologist*

Torrance
Ananth, Jambur *psychiatrist, educator*
Brasel, Jo Anne *physician*
Emmanouilides, George Christos *physician, educator*
Gurevitch, Arnold William *dermatology educator*
Itabashi, Hideo Henry *neuropathologist, neurologist*
Krout, Boyd Merrill *psychiatrist*
Miller, Milton Howard *psychiatrist*
Myhre, Byron Arnold *pathologist, educator*

Prakash, Ravi *physician, educator*
Snape, William John, Jr. *physician*
Tanaka, Kouichi Robert *physician, educator*

Ventura
Greenblatt, Milton *psychiatrist*

Visalia
Riegel, Byron William *ophthalmologist*

Volcano
Prout, Ralph Eugene *physician*

Walnut Creek
Acosta, Julio Bernard *obstetrician, gynecologist*
Farr, Lee Edward *physician*
Seegers, Walter Henry *hematology educator emeritus*

West Hollywood
Brunell, Philip A. *physician*
Wilson, Myron Robert, Jr. *former psychiatrist*

Whittier
Arcadi, John Albert *urologist*
Arenowitz, Albert Harold *psychiatrist*

Woodland Hills
Chernof, David *internist*
Fricker, John Arthur *pediatrician, educator*

COLORADO

Boulder
Dubin, Mark William *neuroscientist, educator*

Castle Rock
Thornbury, John Rousseau *radiologist, physician*

Colorado Springs
Anderson, Paul Nathaniel *oncologist, educator*
Halling, Leonard William *retired pathologist, laboratory administrator*

Colorado State University
Gillette, Edward LeRoy *radiation oncology educator*

Denver
Adler, Charles Spencer *psychiatrist*
Aikawa, Jerry Kazuo *physician, educator*
Atkins, Dale Morrell *physician*
Barkin, Roger Michael *pediatrician, emergency physician, educator*
Battaglia, Frederick Camillo *physician*
Blager, Florence Berman *voice pathology educator*
†Bunn, Paul A., Jr. *oncologist, educator*
†Deitrich, Richard Adam *pharmacology educator*
Eickhoff, Theodore Carl *physician*
Firminger, Harlan Irwin *pathologist, educator*
Friedman, H. Harold *cardiologist, internist*
Golitz, Loren Eugene *dermatologist, pathologist, clinical administrator, educator*
Green, Larry Alton *physician, educator*
Iseman, Michael Dee *medical educator*
Jacobson, Eugene Donald *physician, administrator, educator, researcher*
Jafek, Bruce William *otolaryngologist, educator*
Kauvar, Abraham J. *gastroenterologist, medical administrator*
Kern, Fred, Jr. *physician, educator*
Krieger, Gary Robert *environmental medicine physician*
Krikos, George Alexander *pathologist, educator*
Larsen, Gary Loy *physician, researcher*
Lilly, John Russell *surgeon, educator*
Lubeck, Marvin Jay *ophthalmologist*
Makowski, Edgar Leonard *obstetrician and gynecologist*
Martin, Richard Jay *medical educator*
McAtee, Patricia Anne Rooney *medical educator*
Moore, Ernest Eugene, Jr. *surgeon, educator*
Moore, George Eugene *surgeon*
Nelson, Nancy Eleanor *pediatrician, educator*
Nelson, William Rankin *surgeon*
Owens, J(ames) Cuthbert *surgeon, anatomist, retired medical educator*
Petty, Thomas Lee *physician, educator*
Rainer, William Gerald *cardiac surgeon*
†Repine, John E. *pediatrician, educator*
†Rodman, David Malcolm *physician, educator*
Ruge, Daniel August *retired neurosurgeon, educator*
Rumack, Barry H. *physician, toxicologist, pediatrician*
†Rutherford, Robert Barry *surgeon*
Schiff, Donald Wilfred *pediatrician, educator*
Schneck, Stuart Austin *neurologist, educator*
Shore, James H(enry) *psychiatrist*
Silverman, Arnold *physician*
Szefler, Stanley James *pediatrics and pharmacology educator*
Taylor, Edward Stewart *physician, educator*
Tormey, Douglass Cole *medical oncologist*
Washington, Reginald Louis *pediatric cardiologist*
Weston, William Lee *dermatologist*
Wiggs, Eugene Overbey *ophthalmologist, educator*

Englewood
English, Gerald Marion *otolaryngologist*
Pearlman, David Samuel *allergist*

Golden
Silverberg, Stuart Owen *obstetrician, gynecologist*

Grand Junction
Sadler, Theodore R., Jr. *thoracic and cardiovascular surgeon*

Greeley
Cook, Donald E. *pediatrician*

Littleton
Bachman, David Christian *orthopedic surgeon*

Snowmass Village
Diamond, Edward *gynecologist, infertility specialist, clinician*

CONNECTICUT

East Haven
Conn, Harold O. *physician, educator*

Farmington
Cooperstein, Sherwin Jerome *medical educator*
Escobar, Javier Ignacio *psychiatrist*
Gossling, Harry Robert *orthopaedic surgeon, educator*
Hinz, Carl Frederick, Jr. *physician, educator*
Katz, Arnold Martin *medical educator*
Massey, Robert Unruh *physician, university dean*
†Raisz, Lawrence Gideon *medical educator, consultant*
Rothfield, Naomi Fox *physician*
Schenkman, John Boris *pharmacologist, educator*
Sigman, Eugene M. *retired urology educator and university dean*
Walker, James Elliot Cabot *physician*

Greenwich
Foraste, Roland *psychiatrist*
Kopenhaver, Patricia Ellsworth *podiatrist*
Randt, Clark Thorp *physician, educator*

Guilford
Warshaw, Joseph Bennett *pediatrician, educator*

Hamden
Darling, George Bapst, Jr. *retired medical educator*
†Nuland, Sherwin *surgeon, author*

Hartford
Brauer, Rima Lois *psychiatrist*
Donnelly, John *psychiatrist, educator*
Jones, Richard F., III *obstetrician/gynecologist*
Roberts, Melville Parker, Jr. *neurosurgeon, educator*
Tingley, Floyd Warren *physician*

Madison
Snell, Richard Saxon *anatomist*

New Canaan
Coughlin, Francis Raymond, Jr. *surgeon, educator, lawyer*

New Haven
Aghajanian, George Kevork *medical educator*
Barash, Paul George *anesthesiologist, educator*
Behrman, Harold Richard *endocrinologist, physiologist, educator*
Berliner, Robert William *physician, medical educator*
Boyer, James Lorenzen *physician, educator*
Braverman, Irwin Merton *dermatologist, educator*
Brown, Thomas Huntington *neuroscientist*
†Bunney, Benjamin Stephenson *psychiatrist*
Burrow, Gerard Noel *physician, educator*
Byck, Robert Samuel *psychiatrist, educator*
Cohen, Donald Jay *pediatrics, psychiatry and psychology educator, administrator*
Cohen, Lawrence Sorel *physician, educator*
Collins, William F., Jr. *neurosurgery educator*
Comer, James Pierpont *psychiatrist*
Cooper, Jack Ross *pharmacology educator, researcher*
Davey, Lycurgus Michael *neurosurgeon*
DeVita, Vincent Theodore, Jr. *oncologist*
Donaldson, Robert Macartney, Jr. *physician*
Edelson, Marshall *psychiatry educator, psychoanalyst*
Evans, Alfred Spring *physician, educator*
Feinstein, Alvan Richard *physician*
Friedlaender, Gary Elliott *orthopedist, educator*
Genel, Myron *pediatrician, educator*
Glaser, Gilbert Herbert *neuroscientist, physician, educator*
Glenn, William Wallace Lumpkin *surgeon, educator*
Hayslett, John Paul *physician, medical educator, researcher*
†Heninger, George Robert *psychiatry educator, researcher*
Herbert, Peter Noel *physician, medical educator*
Hoffer, Paul B. *nuclear medicine physician, educator*
Horstmann, Dorothy Millicent *physician, educator*
Horwitz, Ralph Irving *internist, medical educator, epidemiologist*
†Jacoby, Robert Ottinger *comparative medicine educator*
Jatlow, Peter I. *pathologist, medical educator, researcher*
Kashgarian, Michael *pathologist, physician*
Katz, Jay *psychiatry and law educator*
Kirchner, John Albert *retired otolaryngology educator*
Komp, Diane Marilyn *pediatric oncologist, hematologist, writer*
Kushlan, Samuel Daniel *physician, educator, hospital administrator*
Levine, Robert John *physician, educator*
Lewis, Melvin *psychiatrist, pediatrician, psychoanalyst*
Miller, I. George *physician, educator, researcher*
Musto, David Franklin *physician, historian, consultant*
Naftolin, Frederick *physician, reproductive biologist educator*
Newman, Harry Rudolph *urologist, educator*
Niederman, James Corson *physician*
Ostfeld, Adrian Michael *physician*
Polayes, Irving Marvin *plastic surgeon*
Pruett, Kyle Dean *psychiatrist, writer, educator*
Prusoff, William Herman *biochemical pharmacologist, educator*
Rakic, Pasko *neuroscientist, educator*
Redmond, Donald Eugene, Jr. *neuroscientist, educator*
Reiser, Morton Francis *psychiatrist, educator*
Sartorelli, Alan Clayton *pharmacology educator*
Sasaki, Clarence Takashi *surgeon, medical educator*
Schowalter, John Erwin *psychiatrist, educator*
Schwartz, Peter Edward *physician, gynecologic oncology educator*
†Shope, Robert Ellis *epidemiology educator*
Solnit, Albert Jay *commissioner, physician, educator*
Spiro, Howard Marget *physician, educator*
Taylor, Kenneth John W. *physician of diagnostic imagery*
Waxman, Stephen George *neurologist, researcher*
Weiss, Robert M. *urologist, educator*
†Wessel, Morris Arthur *pediatrician*
Wright, Hastings Kemper *surgeon, educator*
Zaret, Barry Lewis *cardiologist, medical educator*

Newington
Fleeson, William *psychiatry educator*

North Haven
Hess, Orvan W. *retired medical educator, obstetrician-gynecologist*

Norwalk
Floch, Martin Herbert *physician*
Needham, Charles William *neurosurgeon*
Tracey, Edward John *physician, surgeon*

Old Lyme
Cook, Charles Davenport *pediatrician, educator*

Ridgefield
Margolis, George *pathologist, medical educator*

Stamford
Cottle, Robert Duquemin *facial plastic surgeon, otolaryngologist*
Epstein, Simon Jules *psychiatrist*
Gefter, William Irvin *physician, educator*
Rosenberg, Charles Harvey *otorhinolaryngologist*
Walsh, Thomas Joseph *neuro ophthalmologist*

Storrs
Dardick, Kenneth Regen *physician, educator*

Trumbull
Bravo, Anthony John *radiologist*

Waterford
Pierson, Anne Bingham *physician*

West Hartford
Hickcox, Curtiss Bronson *anesthesiologist*
McCawley, Austin *psychiatrist, educator*

West Simsbury
Morest, Donald Kent *neuroscientist*

Westport
Clausman, Gilbert Joseph *medical librarian*
Densen-Gerber, Judianne *psychiatrist, lawyer, educator*
Sacks, Herbert Simeon *psychiatrist, educator, consultant*
†Sarn, James *physician, health association administrator*
Satinover, Jeffrey Burke *psychiatrist, health science facility administrator, lecturer, author*

Woodbridge
Bondy, Philip Kramer *physician, educator*

DELAWARE

New Castle
Mac Ewen, George Dean *physician, medical institute executive*

Newark
Dow, Lois Weyman *physician*
Graff, Harold *psychiatrist, psychoanalyst, hospital administrator*
Graham, David Tredway *medical educator, physician*
Lemole, Gerald Michael *surgeon*

Rockland Mills
Levinson, John Milton *obstetrician-gynecologist*

Wilmington
Carson, James Elijah *psychiatrist*
Cornelison, Floyd Shovington, Jr. *retired psychiatrist, former educator*
Doughty, Robert Allen *medical institute director*
Durham, Davis Godfrey *ophthalmologist*
Harley, Robison Dooling *physician, educator*
Inselman, Laura Sue *pediatrician*
Kay, Jerome *psychiatrist, educator*
Pan, Henry Yue-Ming *clinical pharmacologist*

DISTRICT OF COLUMBIA

Washington
Akhter, Mohammad Nasir *physician, government public health administrator*
Anthony, Virginia Quinn Bausch *medical association executive*
Armaly, Mansour F(arid) *ophthalmologist, educator*
Avery, Gordon Bennett *medical educator, neonatologist*
Bachman, Leonard *physician, retired federal official*
Beary, John Francis, III *physician, pharmaceutical executive*
Belman, A. Barry *pediatric urologist*
Berman, Sidney *psychiatrist*
Blum, Robert Allan *psychiatrist*
Bourne, Peter Geoffrey *physician, educator, author*
Bowles, Lawrence Thompson *surgeon, university dean, educator*
Callaway, Clifford Wayne *physician*
Callender, Clive Orville *surgeon*
Canary, John Joseph *physician, educator*
Canter, Jerome Wolf *surgeon, educator*
Catoe, Bette Lorrina *physician, health educator*
Cheng, Tsung O. *cardiologist, educator*
Chester, Alexander Campbell, III *physician*
Coleman, Roy Melvin *psychiatrist*
Collins, Robert Ellwood *surgeon*
Connell, Alastair McCrae *physician*
Cornely, Paul Bertau *physician, educator*
†Costa, Erminio *pharmacologist, cell biology educator*
Cummings, Martin Marc *medical educator, physician, scientific administrator*
Curfman, David Ralph *neurological surgeon, musician*
Cytowic, Richard Edmund *neurologist*
Davis, David Oliver *radiologist, educator*
Deutsch, Stanley *anesthesiologist, educator*
De Vault, Virgil Thomas *physician*
Dublin, Thomas David *physician*
Dyer, Robert Francis, Jr. *internist, educator*
Earll, Jerry Miller *internist, educator*
Eisenberg, John Meyer *physician, educator*
Elgart, Mervyn L. *dermatologist*
Elliott, Larry Paul *cardiac radiologist, educator*
Epps, Charles H., Jr. *medical educator, college dean*
Felts, William Robert, Jr. *physician*
Finkelstein, James David *physician*
Fox, Samuel Mickle, III *physician, educator*
Galioto, Frank Martin, Jr. *pediatric cardiologist, educator*
Gary, Nancy Elizabeth *nephrologist, academic administrator*
Gehrig, Leo Joseph *surgeon*
Gilbert, Charles Richard Alsop *physician, medical educator*
†Goldson, Alfred Lloyd *oncologist, educator*
Gray, Sheila Hafter *psychiatrist, psychoanalyst*
Grigsby, Margaret Elizabeth *physician*
Grossman, John Henry, III *obstetrician, gynecologist, educator*
Harvey, John Collins *physician, educator*
Henry, Walter Lester, Jr. *physician, educator*
†Hicks, Jocelyn Muriel *laboratory medicine specialist*
Holden, Raymond Thomas *physician, educator*
Hollinshead, Ariel Cahill *research oncologist*
†Holloway, Harry *aerospace medical doctor*
†Hudgins, Michael Pharr *internist*
Irey, Nelson Sumner *pathologist*
Kahler, Elizabeth Sartor (Mrs. Ervin Newton Chapman) *physician*
Kant, Gloria Jean *neuroscientist, researcher*
Kassebaum, Donald Gene *medical association administrator, physician, medical educator*
Katz, Sol *physician*
Kaufman, Paul *physician, former naval officer, association executive*
Kobrine, Arthur *neurosurgeon*
Koering, Marilyn Jean *anatomy educator, researcher*
Krasner, Robert Charles Jeffrey *physician, military officer*
Kurtzke, John Francis, Sr. *neurologist, epidemiologist*
†Law, David Hillis *physician*
†Lee, Philip Randolph *medical educator*
Lessin, Lawrence Stephen *hematologist, oncologist, educator*
†Lippman, Marc Estes *pharmacology educator*
Little, John William *plastic surgeon, educator*
Mandel, H(arold) George *pharmacologist*
Manley, Audrey Forbes *physician*
Mann, Marion *physician, educator*
Mann, Oscar *physician, internist, educator*
†Mc Beath, William Henninger *physician, association executive*
Mc Ginnis, James Michael *physician*
Miller, Harry Charles, Jr. *physician, urologist, educator*
Miller, Russell Loyd, Jr. *physician, educator, dean*
Moritsugu, Kenneth Paul *physician, government official*
Murray, Robert Fulton, Jr. *physician*
Nelson, Alan Ray *internist, medical assocation executive*
Neviaser, Robert Jon *orthopedic surgeon, educator*
Noshpitz, Joseph Dove *child and adolescent psychiatrist*
Parker, Gerald William *physician, medical center administrator, retired air force officer*
Parrott, Robert Harold *pediatrician, educator*
Pawlson, Leonard Gregory *physician*
Pearse, Warren Harland *association executive, obstetrician and gynecologist*
Pellegrino, Edmund Daniel *physician, educator, former university president*
Perlin, Seymour *psychiatrist, educator*
Perry, Seymour Monroe *physician*
†Peterson, Malcolm Lee *medical educator, administrator*
Potter, John Francis *surgical oncologist, educator*
†Queenan, John Thomas *obstetrician, gynecologist, educator*
Rall, David Platt *pharmacologist, environmentalist*
Ribas, Jorge Luis *research pathologist, educator*
Rockoff, S. David *radiologist, physician, educator*
Rosenquist, Glenn Carl *pediatrician*
Ross, Allan Michael *physician, medical educator*
Rowley, William Robert *surgeon*
Sabshin, Melvin *psychiatrist, educator, medical association administrator*
Samman, George *obstetrician, gynecologist*
†Schechter, Geraldine Poppa *hematologist*
Schreiner, George E. *nephrologist, educator, writer*
Schwartz, Marshall Zane *pediatric surgeon*
Shine, Kenneth I. *cardiologist, educator*
Short, Elizabeth M. *physician, educator, federal agency administrator*
Sidransky, Herschel *pathologist*
Simopoulos, Artemis Panageotis *physician, educator*
Sly, Ridge Michael *physician, educator*
Smith, Lee Elton *surgery educator, retired military officer*
Stemmler, Edward Joseph *physician, retired association executive, retired academic dean*
Telford, Ira Rockwood *anatomist, educator*
Wallace, Robert Bruce *surgeon*
Webster, Thomas Glenn *psychiatrist*
†Weinberger, Daniel R. *psychiatrist*
Weingold, Allan B. *obstetrician, gynecologist, educator*
Werkman, Sidney Lee *psychiatry educator*
Werner, Mario *pathology educator*
Young, Donald Alan *physician*
Zimmerman, Hyman Joseph *internist, educator*

FLORIDA

Alachua
Gifford, George E. *immunology and medical microbiology educator*

Atlantis
Newmark, Emanuel *ophthalmologist*

Bay Pines
Keskiner, Ali *psychiatrist*
†Robson, Martin Cecil *surgery educator, plastic surgeon*

Boca Raton
Bressler, Steven L. *cognitive neuroscientist*
Cohn, Jess Victor *psychiatrist*
Kramer, Cecile E. *retired medical librarian*
Mirkin, Abraham Jonathan *surgeon*
Stein, Irvin *orthopaedic surgeon, educator*

Boynton Beach
Eady, Carol Murphy (Mrs. Karl Ernest Eady) *medical association administrator*

Clearwater
Fromhagen, Carl, Jr. *obstetrician/gynecologist*

Dade City
McBath, Donald Linus *osteopathic physician*

Fernandina Beach
Barlow, Anne Louise *pediatrician, medical research administrator*

Fort Lauderdale
Csatary, Laszlo Kalman *anesthesiologist, cancer researcher*
Lodwick, Gwilym Savage *radiologist, educator*
Lyons, Richard Chapman *urologist*

Fort Myers
Aleo, Joseph John *pathology scientist, educator, academic research administrator*
Brooks, Julie Agnes *psychiatrist*
Conger, Kyril B. *urologist*
Ferguson, James A. *surgeon*
Grove, William Johnson *physician, surgery educator*
Simmons, Vaughan Pippen *medical consultant*
Sypert, George Walter *neurosurgery educator, clinical neurosurgeon, research neurophysiologist*

Fort Walton Beach
Gates, Philip Don *anesthesiologist*

Gainesville
Behnke, Marylou *neonatologist, educator*
Cluff, Leighton Eggertsen *physician*
Copeland, Edward Meadors, III *surgery educator*
Gravenstein, Joachim Stefan *anesthesiologist, educator*
Greer, Melvin *medical educator*
Grundy, Betty Lou Bottoms *anesthesiology and pharmaceutics educator*
Mauderli, Walter *radiology educator*
Merimee, Thomas Joseph *medical educator*
Modell, Jerome Herbert *anesthesiologist, educator, dean*
Pepine, Carl John *physician, educator*
Pfaff, William Wallace *physician, educator*
Rhoton, Albert Loren, Jr. *neurological surgery educator*
Rosenbloom, Arlan Lee *physician, educator*
Rubin, Melvin Lynne *ophthalmologist, educator*
Schiebler, Gerold Ludwig *physician, educator*
Small, Parker Adams, Jr. *pediatrician, educator*
Suzuki, Howard Kazuro *retired anatomist, educator*
Talbert, James Lewis *pediatric surgeon, educator*
Taylor, William Jape *physician*
Vaughn, Rufus Mahlon *psychiatrist*
Vierck, Charles John, Jr. *neuroscience educator, scientist*
Walker, Robert Dixon, III *surgeon, urologist, educator*
Williams, Ralph Chester, Jr. *physician, educator*

Hallandale
Haspel, Arthur Carl *podiatrist, surgeon*

Hawthorne
Fackler, Martin L(uther) *surgeon*

Hollywood
Bergman, Harry *urologist*
Weinberg, Harry Bernard *cardiologist*

Jacksonville
Carithers, Hugh Alfred *physician*
Groom, Dale *physician, educator*
Hrachovina, Frederick Vincent *osteopathic physician and surgeon*
Kelalis, Panayotis *pediatric urologist*
Nicolitz, Ernst *ophthalmologist, educator*
Prempree, Thongbliew *oncology radiologist*
Stephenson, Samuel Edward, Jr. *physician*
Wilson, C. Nick *medical educator, consultant*

Key Biscayne
Palmer, Roger Farley *pharmacology educator*

Largo
Brown, Warren Joseph *physician*

Marco Island
Sundberg, R. Dorothy *physician, educator*

Melbourne
Baney, Richard Neil *physician, internist*

Miami
Anderson, Douglas Richard *ophthalmologist, educator, scientist, researcher*
Bolooki, Hooshang *cardiac surgeon*
Casariego, Jorge Isaac *psychiatrist, psychoanalyst, educator*
Cohen, Sanford Irwin *physician, educator*
Daughtry, DeWitt Cornell *surgeon, physician*
Dean, Stanley Rochelle *psychiatrist*
Eaglstein, William Howard *dermatologist, educator*
†Flynn, John T. *ophthalmologist*
Freshwater, Michael Felix *hand surgeon*
Gelband, Henry *pediatric cardiologist*
Getz, Morton Ernest *internist, gastroenterologist*
Ginsberg, Myron David *neurologist*
Howell, Ralph Rodney *pediatrician, educator*
Jude, James Roderick *cardiac surgeon*
Ketcham, Alfred Schutt *surgeon, educator*
Lasseter, Kenneth Carlyle *pharmacologist*
Lemberg, Louis *cardiologist, educator*
Martínez, Luís Osvaldo *radiologist, educator*
Mc Kenzie, John Maxwell *physician*
Millard, David Ralph, Jr. *plastic surgeon, educator*
Myerburg, Robert Jerome *physician, scientist, educator*
†O'Sullivan, Mary J. *physician, maternal fetal medicine educator*
Page, Larry Keith *neurosurgeon, educator*
Papper, Emanuel Martin *anesthesiologist*
Politano, Victor Anthony *urology educator, physician*
Potter, James Douglas *pharmacology educator*
Prineas, Ronald James *epidemiologist, educator*
Raines, Jeff *biomedical scientist, medical research director*
Ripstein, Charles Benjamin *surgeon*
Ryan, James Walter *physician, medical researcher*
Sackner, Marvin Arthur *physician*
Scheinberg, Peritz *neurologist*
Schiff, Eugene Roger *medical educator, hepatologist*
Strauss, José *pediatric nephrologist*
Sussex, James Neil *psychiatrist, educator*
Valdes-Dapena, Marie Agnes *pediatric pathologist, educator*

Miami Beach
Goldstein, Burton Jack *psychiatrist*

Naples
Gross, Paul *pathologist, educator*
Levitt, LeRoy Paul *psychiatrist, psychoanalyst*

North Miami Beach
Tenzel, Richard Ruvin *ophthalmologist*

Orlando
Cary, Freeman Hamilton *physician*
Hall, Richard C. Winton *psychiatrist*
Hornick, Richard Bernard *physician*
Norris, Franklin Gray *thoracic and cardiovascular surgeon*

Osprey
Gross, James Dehnert *pathologist*

Palm Beach
Alpert, Seymour *anesthesiologist, educator*

Pembroke Pines
Sigel, M(ola) Michael *scientist, medical educator*

Pensacola
Love, Robert William, Jr. *retired physician, government administrator*

Pompano Beach
Bliznakov, Emile George *biomedical research scientist*
Patterson, Alan Bruce *obstetrician-gynecologist*

Ponte Vedra Beach
ReMine, William Hervey, Jr. *surgeon*

Port Richey
Radomski, Jack London *pharmacologist, consultant*

Saint Petersburg
Good, Robert Alan *physician, educator*
Root, Allen William *pediatrician, educator*
Sibley, Mark Anderson *ophthalmologist*

Sanibel
Adair, Charles Valloyd *retired physician*

Sarasota
Friedberg, Harold David *cardiologist*
Kiplinger, Glenn Francis *pharmacologist, consultant*
Radnay, Paul Andrew *physician*
†Welch, John Dana *urologist, performing arts association executive*

Seminole
Nesbitt, Robert Edward Lee, Jr. *physician, educator*

Shalimar
Humphreys, James W. *surgeon, former air force officer, medical board executive*

Spring Hill
Finney, Roy Pelham, Jr. *urologist, surgeon, inventor*

Stuart
Haserick, John Roger *retired dermatologist*
†Myers, William George *physician, state senator*
Pisani, Joseph Michael *physician*
Westlake, Robert Elmer, Sr. *physician*

Surfside
Prystowsky, Harry *physician, educator*

Tallahassee
Maguire, Charlotte Edwards *retired physician*
Penrod, Kenneth Earl *medical education consultant*

Tampa
Afield, Walter Edward *psychiatrist, service executive*
Barness, Lewis Abraham *physician*
Behnke, Roy Herbert *physician, educator*
Bowen, Thomas Edwin *cardiothoracic surgeon, retired army officer*
Bukantz, Samuel Charles *physician, educator*
Carey, Larry Campbell *surgeon*
Cavanagh, Denis *physician, educator*
del Regato, Juan Angel *radio-therapeutist and oncologist, educator*
Farrior, Joseph Brown *otologist*
Frias, Jaime Luis *pediatrician, educator*
Gilbert-Barness, Enid F. *pathologist, pathology and pediatrics educator*
Glasser, Stephen Paul *cardiologist*
Greenfield, George B. *radiologist*
Hartmann, William Herman *pathologist, educator*
Jacobson, Howard Newman *obstetrics/gynecology educator, researcher*
Kaufman, Ronald Paul *physician, school official*
Krizek, Thomas Joseph *plastic surgeon*
Krzanowski, Joseph John, Jr. *pharmacology educator*
Lockey, Richard Funk *allergist, educator*
McMillan, Donald Ernest *internal medicine educator, state program director*
Muroff, Lawrence Ross *nuclear medicine physician*
Nagera, Humberto *psychiatrist, psychoanalyst, educator, author*
Pfeiffer, Eric Armin *psychiatrist, gerontologist*
Pollara, Bernard *immunologist, pediatrician*
Reading, Anthony John *physician*
Richardson, Sylvia Onesti *physician*
Rowlands, David Thomas *pathology educator*
†Schmidt, Paul Joseph *physician, educator*
Schnitzlein, Harold Norman *anatomy educator*
†Schonwetter, Ronald Scott *physician, educator*
Shively, John Adrian *pathologist*

†Spellacy, William Nelson *obstetrician-gynecologist, educator*

Tequesta
Ruoff, Andrew Christian, III *orthopedic surgeon, educator, consultant*

Vero Beach
Christy, Nicholas Pierson *physician*
Lawrence, Merle *medical educator*
Schulman, Harold *obstetrician, gynecologist, perinatologist*

West Palm Beach
Brown, Paul A. *physician, business executive*
Brumback, Clarence Landen *physician*
MacDonald, Richard Annis *pathologist, physician, educator*
Pottash, A. Carter *psychiatrist, hospital executive*
Roberts, Hyman Jacob *internist, researcher, author, publisher*
Sokmensuer, Adil *physician, educator*

GEORGIA

Athens
Bowen, John Metcalf *pharmacologist, toxicologist, educator*
Bruce, David Lionel *anesthesiologist, educator*
†Norred, William Preston, Jr. *pharmacologist, educator*

Atlanta
Ambrose, Samuel Sheridan, Jr. *urologist*
Bakay, Roy Arpad Earle *neurosurgeon, educator*
Barnett, Crawford Fannin, Jr. *internist, educator, cardiologist*
Broome, Claire Veronica *epidemiologist, researcher*
Byrd, Larry Donald *behavioral pharmacologist*
†Casarella, William Joseph *physician*
Clements, James David *psychiatry educator, physician*
Connell-Tatum, Elizabeth Bishop *physician*
†Davis, Lawrence William *radiation oncologist*
†Edelhauser, Henry F. *physiologist, ophthalmic researcher, educator*
Elsas, Louis Jacob, II *medical educator*
Evans, Edwin Curtis *internist, educator, geriatrician*
Foster, Roger Sherman, Jr. *surgeon, educator, health facility administrator*
Galambos, John Thomas *medical educator, internist*
Gayles, Joseph Nathan, Jr. *medical educator, administrator*
Guinan, Mary Elizabeth *physician, research scientist*
Hall, Wilbur Dallas, Jr. *medical educator*
Hatcher, Charles Ross, Jr. *cardiothoracic surgeon, medical center executive*
Haverty, John Rhodes *physician, former university dean*
Houpt, Jeffrey Lyle *psychiatrist, educator*
Hug, Carl Casmir, Jr. *pharmacology and anesthesiology educator*
†Hughes, James Mitchell *epidemiologist*
Israili, Zafar Hasan *scientist, clinical pharmacologist, educator*
Jurkiewicz, Maurice John *surgeon, educator*
Karp, Herbert Rubin *neurologist, educator*
King, Frederick Alexander *neuroscientist, educator*
†Klein, Luella Voogd *obstetrics-gynecology educator*
Kokko, Juha Pekka *physician, educator*
Lemen, Richard Alan *epidemiologist*
Letton, Alva Hamblin *surgeon, educator*
Lipman, Bernard *internist, cardiologist*
Lubin, Michael Frederick *physician*
†Lybarger, Jeffrey A. *epidemiology research administrator*
†Margolis, Harold Stephen *epidemiologist*
McDuffie, Frederic Clement *physician*
Murphy, Gerald Patrick *urologist, educator*
Nahmias, André Joseph *physician, educator, scientist*
O'Brien, Mark Stephen *pediatric neurosurgeon*
Owings, Francis Barre *surgeon*
Peacock, Lamar Batts *physician*
Perdue, Garland Day *surgeon, educator, hospital director*
Reed, James Whitfield *physician, educator*
Rock, John Aubrey *gynecologist and obstetrician, educator*
Schlant, Robert Carl *cardiologist, educator*
Seffrin, John Reese *medical society executive*
Sherman, Roger Talbot *surgeon, educator*
Smith, Robert Boulware, III *vascular surgeon, educator*
Steinhaus, John Edward *physician, medical educator*
Tindall, George Taylor *neurosurgeon, educator*
Turner, John Sidney, Jr. *otolaryngologist, educator*
Tyler, Carl Walter, Jr. *physician, health research administrator*
Waller, John Louis *anesthesiology educator*
Ward, Richard Storer *child psychiatrist, educator emeritus*
White, Perry Merrill, Jr. *orthopedic surgeon*
Woodard, John Roger *urologist*

Augusta
Chandler, Arthur Bleakley *pathologist, educator*
Colborn, Gene Louis *anatomy educator, researcher*
Gambrell, Richard Donald, Jr. *endocrinologist, educator*
Given, Kenna Sidney *surgeon, educator*
Greenbaum, Lowell Marvin *pharmacologist, educator*
Luxenberg, Malcolm Neuwahl *ophthalmologist, educator*
Mahesh, Virendra Bhushan *endocrinologist*
Mansberger, Arlie Roland, Jr. *surgeon*
Parrish, Robert Alton *retired pediatric surgeon, educator*

Dahlonega
Allen, Delmas James *anatomist, educator, university administrator*

Dalton
Clark, Winston Craig *neurosurgeon*

Decatur
Alderete, Joseph Frank *psychiatrist, medical service adminstrator*
Bain, James Arthur *pharmacologist, educator*
Hill, Thomas Glenn, III *dermatologist*
Martinez-Maldonado, Manuel *medical service administrator, physician*

Evans
Hartlage, Lawrence Clifton *neuropsychologist, educator*

Fort Gordon
Xenakis, Stephen Nicholas *psychiatrist, physician, military officer*

Hinesville
Gennrich, Robert Paul, II *radiologic technologist*

La Grange
Copeland, Robert Bodine *internist, cardiologist*
West, John Thomas *surgeon*

Lawrenceville
Fetner, Robert Henry *radiation biologist*

Macon
Swartwout, Joseph Rodolph *obstetrics and gynecology educator, university administrator*

Norcross
Nardelli-Olkowska, Krystyna Maria *ophthalmologist, educator*

Quitman
Baum, Joseph Herman *retired biomedical educator*

Savannah
Horan, Leo Gallaspy *physician, educator*
Krahl, Enzo *retired surgeon*

Stone Mountain
Rogers, James Virgil, Jr. *retired radiologist and educator*

HAWAII

Hilo
Taniguchi, Tokuso *surgeon*

Honolulu
Bruce, Nadine Cecile *internist, educator*
Chee, Percival Hon Yin *ophthalmologist*
Fong, Bernard W. D. *physician, educator*
†Ho, Reginald Chi Shing *medical educator*
Kolonel, Laurence Norman *epidemiologist, public health educator*
Linman, James William *retired physician, educator*
Marvit, Robert Charles *psychiatrist*
Mc Dermott, John Francis, Jr. *psychiatrist, physician*
Oda, Yoshio *physician, internist*
Pang, Herbert George *ophthalmologist*
Person, Donald Ames, Sr. *pediatrician, rheumatologist*
Schatz, Irwin Jacob *cardiologist*

Waikoloa
Copman, Louis *radiologist*

IDAHO

Boise
Guarino, John Ralph *physician, scientist, educator*
Nyborg, Lester Phil *physician*
Olson, Richard Dean *researcher, pharmacology educator*
Schwartz, Theodore B. *physician, educator*

Emmett
Holverson, Harmon E. *family practice physician*

Ketchum
Earle, Arthur Scott *plastic surgeon*

Lewiston
Chinchinian, Harry *pathologist, educator*

Pocatello
Hillyard, Ira William *pharmacologist, educator*

ILLINOIS

Abbott Park
Sasahara, Arthur Asao *cardiologist, educator, researcher*

Arlington Heights
Pochyly, Donald Frederick *physician, university administrator*

Aurora
Ball, William James *pediatrician*

Bannockburn
Vuckovich, Dragomir Michael *neurologist, educator*

Berwyn
Misurec, Rudolf *physician, surgeon*

Carol Stream
Schmerold, Wilfried Lothar *dermatologist*

Chicago
Abcarian, Herand *surgeon, educator*
Adams, John Richard *psychiatrist, educator*
Albrecht, Ronald Frank *anesthesiologist*
Andersen, Burton Robert *physician, educator*
Applebaum, Edward Leon *otolaryngologist, educator*
†Arnason, Barry Gilbert Wyatt *neurologist, educator*
Arnsdorf, Morton Frank *cardiologist, educator*
Baffes, Thomas Gus *cardiac surgeon, lawyer*
Bailey, Orville Taylor *neuropathologist*
Barker, Walter Lee *thoracic surgeon*
Barton, Evan Mansfield *physician*
Batlle, Daniel Campi *nephrologist*
Beatty, William Kaye *medical bibliography educator*
Beaty, Harry Nelson *internist, educator, university dean*
†Beck, Robert N. *nuclear medicine educator*
Beigl, William *physician, naturopath, hypnotist, acupuncturist, consultant*
Bellows, Randall Trueblood *ophthalmologist, educator*
Berry, Leonidas Harris *gastroenterologist, internist*
Betts, Henry Brognard *physician, health facility administrator, educator*
Block, George Edward *surgeon, educator*
Boggs, Joseph Dodridge *pediatric pathologist, educator*
Boshes, Louis D. *physician, scientist, educator*
Bowman, James Edward *physician, educator*
Bresnahan, James Francis *medical ethics educator*
Brown, Rowine Hayes *physician, former medical administrator*
Brueschke, Erich Edward *physician, researcher, educator*
Bumsted, Robert Milton *physician*
Calenoff, Leonid *radiologist*
Carnow, Bertram Warren *occupational and environmental health consultant*
Caro, William Allan *physician*
Carone, Frank *medical educator, pathologist*
Cassel, Christine Karen *physician*
†Chandler, John William *ophthalmologist, educator*
Charles, Allan G. *physician, educator*
Chatterton, Robert Treat, Jr. *reproductive endocrinology educator*
Clark, John Whitcomb *diagnostic radiologist*
Coe, Fredric L. *physician, educator, researcher*
Cohen, Maynard Manuel *neurologist, neurochemist, educator*
Cohen, Melvin R. *physician, educator*
†Conway, James Joseph *physician*
Cotsonas, Nicholas John, Jr. *physician, medical educator*
†Davies, Peter Francis *pathology educator, medical educator*
Davison, Richard *physician, educator*
De Costa, Edwin J. *physician, surgeon*
Degroot, Leslie Jacob *medical educator*
del Greco, Francesco *physician, educator*
Derlacki, Eugene L(ubin) *otolaryngologist, physician*
Diamond, Seymour *physician*
Dunea, George *nephrologist, educator*
Dyrud, Jarl Edvard *psychiatrist*
Ebert, Paul Allen *surgeon, educator*
Economou, Steve George *surgery educator*
Eisenman, Trudy Fox *dermatologist*
Erdos, Ervin George *pharmacology and biochemistry educator*
Fennessy, John James *radiologist, educator*
Ferguson, Donald John *surgeon, educator*
Fierer, Joshua Allan *pathology educator*
Fitch, Frank Wesley *pathologist, immunologist, educator, university dean*
Frederiksen, Marilynn Elizabeth Conners *physician*
Freedman, Philip *physician, educator*
Frohman, Lawrence Asher *endocrinology educator, scientist*
Gartner, Lawrence Mitchel *pediatrician, medical college educator*
Gecht, Martin Louis *physician, bank executive*
Gerbie, Albert Bernard *obstetrician, gynecologist, educator*
Gewertz, Bruce Labe *surgeon, educator*
Giovacchini, Peter Louis *psychoanalyst*
Gladstone, Lee *psychiatrist, addictionist*
Golomb, Harvey Morris *oncologist, educator*
Graettinger, John Sells *physician, educator*
Grayhack, John Thomas *urologist, educator*
Griffith, B(ezaleel) Herold *physician, educator, plastic surgeon*
Grimes, Hugh Gavin *physician*
Haber, Meryl Harold *physician, educator, author*
Hand, Roger *physician, educator*
Haring, Olga Munk *medical educator, physician*
Harris, Jules Eli *medical educator, physician, clinical scientist, administrator*
Hart, Cecil William Joseph *otolaryngologist, head and neck surgeon*
Hartz, Renee Semo *cardiothoracic surgeon*
Hast, Malcolm Howard *medical educator, scientist*
Havdala, Henri Salomon *anesthesiologist, educator, consultant*
Heller, Paul *medical educator*
Hellman, Samuel *radiologist, physician, educator*
Herbst, Arthur Lee *obstetrician-gynecologist*
Hines, James Rodger *surgeon*
Hinojosa, Raul *physician, ear pathology researcher*
†Hoffmann, Philip *pharmacology educator*
Honig, George Raymond *pediatrician*
Horwitz, Irwin Daniel *otolaryngologist, educator*
Huckman, Michael Saul *neuroradiologist, educator*
Huggins, Charles Brenton *surgical educator*
Hughes, John Russell *physician, educator*
Hunter, James Alexander *surgeon, educator*
†Jonasson, Olga *surgeon, educator*
Jones, Philip Newton *physician, medical educator*
Jordan, V. Craig *endocrine pharmacologist, educator*
Kark, Robert M. *physician, educator*
Karp, Robert *surgeon, educator*
Katz, Adrian Izhack *physician, educator*
Kent, Geoffrey *pathology educator, physician*
Kiani, Reza *endocrinology, metabolism, medical physician nsm*
Kirschner, Barbara Starrels *pediatric gastroenterologist*
Kirsner, Joseph Barnett *physician, educator*
Kittle, Charles Frederick *surgeon*
Knospe, William Herbert *medical educator*
Kohrman, Arthur Fisher *pediatric educator*
Kornel, Ludwig *medical educator, physician, scientist*
Kraft, Sumner Charles *physician, educator*
Landau, Richard L. *physician, educator*
Langsley, Donald Gene *psychiatrist, medical board executive*
LaVelle, Arthur *anatomy educator*
Leff, Alan Richard *medical educator*
Lichter, Edward Arthur *physician, educator*
Lin, Chin-Chu *physician, educator, researcher*
Lorincz, Allan Levente *physician, educator*
Lumpkin, John Robert *public health physician, state official*
Marcus, Joseph *child psychiatrist*
Masserman, Jules Homan *neuropsychiatrist, psychoanalyst*
Metz, Charles Edgar *radiology educator*
Meyer, Paul Reims, Jr. *orthopedic surgeon*
Millichap, Joseph Gordon *neurologist, educator*
Mirkin, Bernard Leo *clinical pharmacologist, pediatrician*
Moawad, Atef *obstetrician-gynecologist, educator*
Morris, Ralph William *chronopharmacologist*
Mullan, John Francis (Sean Mullan) *neurosurgeon, educator*
Musa, Mahmoud Nimir *psychiatry educator*
Nahrwold, David Lange *surgeon, educator*
Narahashi, Toshio *pharmacology educator*
Newell, Frank William *ophthalmologist, educator*
Nyhus, Lloyd Milton *surgeon, educator*
Offer, Daniel *psychiatrist*
Oryshkevich, Roman Sviatoslav *physician, physiatrist, dentist, educator*
Osiyoye, Adekunle *obstetrician/gynecologist, educator*
†Ostrow, Jay Donald *gastroenterology educator, researcher*
Pachman, Daniel J. *physician, educator*
Page, Ernest *medical educator*
Pappas, George Demetrios *anatomy and cell biology educator, scientist*
Patterson, Roy *physician, educator*
Polley, Edward Herman *anatomist, educator*
Pollock, George Howard *psychiatrist, psychoanalyst*
†Pope, Richard M. *rheumatologist*
Poznanski, Andrew Karol *pediatric radiologist*
Rafferty, Nancy Schwarz *anatomy educator*
Rhone, Douglas Pierce *pathologist, educator*
Rogers, Lee Frank *radiologist*
†Rosen, Steven Terry *oncologist, hematologist*
Rosenfield, Robert Lee *pediatric endocrinologist, educator*
Rosenthal, Ira Maurice *pediatrician, educator*
Roth, Sanford Irwin *pathologist, educator*
Rowley, Janet Davison *physician*
Rubenstein, Arthur Harold *physician, educator*
Rudy, Lester Howard *psychiatrist*
Scarpelli, Dante Giovanni *pathologist, educator*
Schafer, Michael Frederick *orthopedic surgeon*
Schilsky, Richard Lewis *oncologist, researcher*
Schulman, Sidney *neurologist, educator*
Schumer, William *surgeon, educator*
Shambaugh, George Elmer, III *internist*
Shields, Thomas William *surgeon, educator*
Siegler, Mark *internist, educator*
Smith, David Waldo Edward *pathology educator, physician*
Sorensen, Leif Boge *physician, educator*
Sparberg, Marshall Stuart *gastroenterologist, educator*
Stepto, Robert Charles *physician, educator*
Sternberg, Paul *retired ophthalmologist*
Stevenson, George Franklin *pathologist, association executive*
Strauch, Gerald Otto *surgeon*
Swerdlow, Martin Abraham *physician, pathologist*
†Tardy, Medney Eugene, Jr. *otolaryngologist*
Taswell, Howard Filmore *pathologist, blood bank specialist, educator*
Tatooles, Constantine John *cardiovascular and thoracic surgeon*
†Todd, James S. *surgeon, educator, medical association administrator*
Todd, James Stiles *surgeon, professional executive association*
Tulsky, Alex Sol *physician*
Ultmann, John Ernest *physician, educator*
Vanecko, Robert Michael *surgeon, educator*
Waldstein, Sheldon Saul *physician, educator*
Webster, James Randolph, Jr. *physician*
Wied, George Ludwig *physician*
Wiener, Stanley Lewis *medical educator*
Willoughby, William Franklin, II *physician, researcher*
Winnie, Alon Palm *anesthesiologist, educator*
Wolpert, Edward Alan *psychiatrist*
Yarkony, Gary Michael *physician, researcher*
Zatuchni, Gerald Irving *physician, educator*

Decatur
Requarth, William Henry *surgeon*

Deerfield
Kotsonis, Frank Nick *toxicologist, scientist, food company research executive*
Scheiber, Stephen Carl *psychiatrist*

Des Plaines
Sisson, George Allen, Sr. *physician, educator*

Downers Grove
Colbert, Marvin Jay *retired internist, educator*
Fruin, Robert Cornelius *physician, hospital administrator*

Elmhurst
Fornatto, Elio Joseph *otolaryngologist, educator*

Evanston
Adelson, Bernard Henry *physician*
Bashook, Philip G. *medical association executive, educator*
Cohen, David Harris *neurobiology educator, university official*
Crawford, James Weldon *psychiatrist, educator, administrator*
Dockery, J. Lee *medical school administrator*
Enroth-Cugell, Christina Alma Elisabeth *neurophysiologist, educator*
Huff, Stanley Eugene *dermatologist*
†Khandekar, Janardan Dinkar *oncologist, educator*
Mc Nerney, Walter James *health policy educator, consultant*
Plaut, Eric Alfred *psychiatrist, educator*
Samter, Max *physician, educator*
Schwartz, Neena Betty *endocrinologist, educator*
Sprang, Milton LeRoy *obstetrician, gynecologist, educator*
Traisman, Howard Sevin *pediatrician*

Flossmoor
Lis, Edward Francis *pediatrician, consultant*

Galesburg
Tourlentes, Thomas Theodore *psychiatrist*

Glen Ellyn
Clark, Samuel Smith *urologist*
Dieter, Raymond Andrew, Jr. *physician, surgeon*
Egan, Richard Leo *medical association administrator, medical educator*
Temple, Donald *allergist, dermatologist*

Glencoe
Fenninger, Leonard Davis *medical educator, consultant*
Friederici, Hartmann H.R. *physician, educator*

Glenview
Ampel, Leon Louis *anesthesiologist*
Hafner, Arthur Wayne *author, information scientist, medical librarian*

Harvey
Jensen, Harold Leroy *physician*

Hickory Hills
Johnson, (Mary) Anita *physician, medical service administrator*

Highland Park
Bluefarb, Samuel Mitchell *physician*
Hirsch, Jay G. *psychiatrist, educator*

Hines
Mason, George Robert *surgeon, educator*
Paloyan, Edward *physician, educator, reseacher*
Zvetina, James Raymond *pulmonary physician*

Hinsdale
Birnholz, Jason Cordell *radiologist, consultant, educator*
Christian, Joseph Ralph *physician*

Homewood
Schumacher, Gebhard Friederich Bernhard *obstetrician-gynecologist*

Joliet
Ring, Alvin Manuel *pathologist*

Lake Forest
Levy, Nelson Louis *physician, scientist, corporate executive*
Murad, Ferid *physician*
Salter, Edwin Carroll *physician*
Wilbur, Richard Sloan *physician, foundation executive*

Lincolnshire
Hughes, William Franklin, Jr. *ophthalmologist, emeritus educator*

Long Grove
Ausman, Robert K. *surgeon, research executive*

Macomb
Dexter, Donald Harvey *surgeon*

Maywood
Canning, John Rafton *urologist*
Celesia, Gastone Guglielmo *neurologist, neurophysiologist, researcher*
Freeark, Robert James *surgeon, educator*
†Gamelli, Richard L. *surgeon, educator*
Greenlee, Herbert Breckenridge *surgeon, educator*
Hanin, Israel *pharmacologist, educator*
Slogoff, Stephen *anesthesiologist, educator*

Moline
Arnell, Richard Anthony *radiologist*

Mount Prospect
Cucco, Ulisse P. *obstetrician, gynecologist*

Naperville
Schwab, Paul Josiah *psychiatrist educator*

Niles
Chertack, Melvin M. *internist*

North Chicago
Beer, Alan Earl *physician, medical educator*
Ehrenpreis, Seymour *pharmacology educator*
Freese, Uwe Ernest *physician, educator*
Gall, Eric Papineau *physician educator*
Hindo, Walid Afram *radiology educator, researcher*
Kim, Yoon Berm *immunologist, educator*
†Metcoff, Jack *pediatrician*
Morris, Charles Elliot *neurologist*
Nair, Velayudhan *pharmacologist, medical educator*
Rogers, Eugene Jack *medical educator*
Rudy, David Robert *physician, educator*
Schneider, Arthur Sanford *physician, educator*
Sierles, Frederick Stephen *psychiatrist, educator*
Sladek, Celia Davis *neuroscientist, educator*
Taylor, Michael Alan *psychiatrist*
Weil, Max Harry *physician, medical educator, medical scientist*

Northbrook
Day, Emerson *physician*
Hirsch, Lawrence Leonard *physician, retired educator*
Mc Laren, John Alexander *retired physician*
Rodriguez-Erdmann, Franz *physician*
Scanlon, Edward F. *surgeon, educator*
†Soffer, Alfred *physician*

Northfield
Cutler, Robert Porter *psychiatrist, psychoanalyst*

Oak Lawn
Rathi, Manohar Lal *pediatrician, neonatologist*

Oak Park
Brackett, Edward Boone, III *orthopedic surgeon*
Kramer, Charles Henry *psychiatrist*
Schultz, Bryan Christopher *dermatologist, educator*
Valinsky, Mark Steven *podiatrist*

Olney
Edwards, Ian Keith *obstetrician, gynecologist*

Park Ridge
Schultz, Richard Carlton *plastic surgeon*
Weinberg, Milton, Jr. *cardiovascular-thoracic surgeon*

Peoria
Meriden, Terry *physician*

River Grove
Hillert, Gloria Bonnin *anatomist, educator*

Rockford
Heerens, Robert Edward *physician*
Olson, Stanley William *physician, educator, medical school dean*
Pritikin, Roland I. *opthalmologic surgeon, writer, lecturer*

Round Lake
Kingdon, Henry Shannon *physician, biochemist, educator, executive*

Saint Charles
McCartney, Charles Price *retired obstetrician-gynecologist*

Schiller Park
†Ring, Alice Ruth Bishop *physician*

Skokie
Boxer, Robert William *allergist*
Goldmann, Morton Aaron *cardiologist*
Olwin, John Hurst *surgeon*

Springfield
Dodd, Robert Bruce *physician, educator*
Frank, Stuart *cardiologist*
Holland, John Madison *family practice physician*
Myers, Phillip Ward *otolaryngologist*
Rabinovich, Sergio *physician, educator*
Zook, Elvin Glenn *plastic surgeon, educator*

Urbana
Greenwold, Warren Eldon *retired physician, medical educator*
Nelson, Ralph Alfred *physician*
O'Morchoe, Charles Christopher Creagh *administrator, anatomical sciences educator*
Voss, Edward William, Jr. *immunologist, educator*
Williams, Benjamin Tallifaro *pathologist, educator*

Villa Park
Becker, Robert Jerome *allergist, health care consultant*

Western Springs
†Swiatek, Kenneth Robert *neuroscientist*

Wheaton
Bogdonoff, Maurice Lambert *physician*
Haenszel, William Manning *epidemiologist, educator*
Maibenco, Helen Craig *anatomist, educator*

Winnetka
Carrow, Leon Albert *physician*
Curtin, John William *retired plastic surgeon, educator*
dePeyster, Frederic Augustus *surgeon*
Earle, David Prince, Jr. *physician, educator*
Sommers, Herbert Myron *pathology educator, retired physician*

INDIANA

Anderson
King, Charles Ross *physician*

Bloomington
Bishop, Michael Daryl *emergency physician*
Moore, Ward Wilfred *medical educator*
Rebec, George Vincent *neuroscience researcher, educator, administrator*
Rink, Lawrence Donald *cardiologist*

Chesterton
Martino, Robert Salvatore *orthopedic surgeon*

Culver
Kammerer, William Henry *physician*

Evansville
Anderson, Milton Henry *psychiatrist*
Faw, Melvin Lee *retired physician*
Penkava, Robert Ray *radiologist, educator*

Fort Wayne
Donesa, Antonio Braganza *neurosurgeon*
Lee, Shuishih Sage *pathologist*
Richardson, Joseph Hill *physician, educator*

Hammond
Steen, Lowell Harrison *physician*

Huntington
Doermann, Paul Edmund *retired surgeon*

Indianapolis
Aldo-Benson, Marlene Ann *medical educator, researcher, physician*
Allen, Stephen D(ean) *pathologist, microbiologist*
†Besch, Henry Roland, Jr. *pharmacologist, educator*
Blankenbaker, Ronald Gail *physician*
Brandt, Ira Kive *pediatrician, medical geneticist*
Brickley, Richard Agar *retired surgeon*
Brown, Edwin Wilson, Jr. *physician, educator*
†Broxmeyer, Hal Edward *medical educator*
Campbell, Judith Lowe *child psychiatrist*
Chernish, Stanley Michael *physician*
Cohen, Marlene Lois *pharmacologist*
Daly, Walter Joseph *physician, educator*
Eigen, Howard *pediatrician, educator*
Einhorn, Lawrence Henry *medical educator*
Faulk, Ward Page *immunologist*
Feigenbaum, Harvey *cardiologist, educator*
Fisch, Charles *physician*
Geisler, Hans Emanuel *gynecologic oncologist*
Ghetti, Bernardino Francesco *neuropathologist, neurobiology researcher*
Green, Morris *physician, educator*
Greist, Mary Coffey *dermatologist*
Grosfeld, Jay Lazar *pediatric surgeon, educator*
Hamburger, Richard James *physician, educator*
†Hathaway, David Roger *physician, medical educator, scientist*
Helveston, Eugene McGillis *pediatric ophthalmologist, educator*
Hubbard, Jesse Donald *pathology educator*
Irwin, Glenn Ward, Jr. *medical educator, physician, university official*
Johnston, Cyrus Conrad, Jr. *internist, educator*
Joyner, John Erwin *medical educator, neurological surgeon*
Knoebel, Suzanne Buckner *cardiologist, medical educator*
Lemberger, Louis *pharmacologist, physician*
Lindseth, Richard Emil *orthopedic surgeon*
Manders, Karl Lee *neurosurgeon*

Merritt, Doris Honig *pediatrics educator*
Miyamoto, Richard Takashi *otolaryngologist*
Myers, Woodrow Augustus, Jr. *physician, corporate medical director*
Norins, Arthur Leonard *physician, educator*
†Nurnberger, John I., Jr. *psychiatrist, educator*
Pless, John Edward *forensic pathologist, educator*
Richter, Judith Anne *pharmacology educator*
Rogers, Robert Ernest *medical educator*
Ross, Edward *cardiologist*
Roth, Lawrence Max *pathologist, educator*
Stoelting, Robert K. *anesthesiologist, medical association executive*
Watanabe, August Masaru *physician, scientist, medical educator, corporate executive*
Weber, George *oncology and pharmacology researcher, educator*
Weinberger, Myron Hilmar *medical educator*
White, Arthur Clinton *physician*
Whitehead, James Ray *medical association executive, management consultant*
Zipes, Douglas Peter *cardiologist, researcher*

Lafayette
Maickel, Roger Philip *pharmacologist, educator*

Marion
Fisher, Pierre James, Jr. *physician*

Monrovia
Bennett, James Edward *retired plastic surgeon, educator*

Nappanee
Borger, Michael Hinton Ivers *osteopathic physician*

Terre Haute
Kunkler, Arnold William *surgeon*

Walton
Chu, Johnson Chin Sheng *physician*

West Lafayette
Borowitz, Joseph Leo *pharmacologist*
Byrn, Stephen R. *medical educator*
Hem, Stanley Lawrence *pharmacy educator, researcher*
Robinson, Farrel Richard *pathologist, toxicologist*
Rutledge, Charles Ozwin *pharmacologist, educator*
Shaw, Stanley Miner *nuclear pharmacy scientist*

IOWA

Bettendorf
Edgerton, Winfield Dow *gynecologist*

Cedar Rapids
Norris, Albert Stanley *psychiatrist, educator*

Davenport
Rohlf, Paul Leon *urologist*

Des Moines
Cash, Paul Thalbert *retired physician*
de Gravelles, William Decatur, Jr. *physician*
Elmets, Harry Barnard *osteopath, dermatologist*
Glomset, Daniel Anders *physician*
Thoman, Mark Edward *pediatrician*

Dubuque
Herzberger, Eugene E. *neurosurgeon*

Iowa City
Abboud, Francois Mitry *physician, educator*
Afifi, Adel Kassim *physician*
Andreasen, Nancy Coover *psychiatrist, educator*
†Bar, Robert S. *endocrinologist*
Baron, Jeffrey *pharmacologist, educator*
Bedell, George Noble *physician, educator*
Bonfiglio, Michael *surgeon, educator*
Burns, C(harles) Patrick *hematologist-oncologist*
Clifton, James Albert *physician*
Cooper, Reginald Rudyard *orthopedic surgeon, educator*
Damasio, Antonio R. *physician, neurologist*
Eckhardt, Richard Dale *physician, educator*
Eckstein, John William *physician, educator*
Ehrenhaft, Johann Leo *surgeon*
Fellows, Robert Ellis *medical educator, medical scientist*
Filer, Lloyd Jackson, Jr. *pediatric educator, clinical investigator*
Fitz, Annette Elaine *physician, educator*
Franken, Edmund Anthony, Jr. *radiologist, educator*
Galask, Rudolph Peter *obstetrician-gynecologist*
Gantz, Bruce Jay *otolaryngologist, educator*
Gergis, Samir Danial *anesthesiologist, educator*
Hammond, Harold Logan *pathology educator, oral pathologist*
Hoffmann, Louis Gerhard *immunologist, educator, sex therapist*
January, Lewis Edward *physician, educator*
†Kirchner, Peter T. *physician nuclear medicine, educator, consultant*
Long, John Paul *pharmacologist, educator*
Mason, Edward Eaton *surgeon*
Morriss, Frank Howard, Jr. *pediatrics educator*
Nelson, Herbert Leroy *psychiatrist*
Ponseti, Ignacio Vives *orthopaedic surgery educator*
Richerson, Hal Bates *physician, internist, allergist, immunologist, educator*
Strauss, John Steinert *dermatologist, educator*
Tephly, Thomas Robert *pharmacologist, toxicologist, educator*
Thompson, Herbert Stanley *neuro-ophthalmologist*
Van Gilder, John Corley *neurosurgeon, educator*
Weinberger, Miles M. *physician, pediatric educator*
Weingeist, Thomas Alan *ophthalmology educator*
Williams, Richard Dwayne *physician, educator*
Winokur, George *psychiatrist, educator*
Ziegler, Ekhard Erich *pediatrics educator*

Sioux City
Spellman, George Geneser, Sr. *internist*

West Des Moines
Alberts, Marion Edward *physician*

KANSAS

Great Bend
Jones, Edward *physician, pathologist*

Kansas City
Anderson, Harrison Clarke *pathology educator, biomedical researcher*
Arakawa, Kasumi *physician, educator*
Cho, Cheng Tsung *pediatrician, educator*
Dunn, Marvin Irvin *physician*
Godfrey, Robert Gordon *physician*
Goodwin, Donald William *psychiatrist, educator*
†Grantham, Jared James *nephrologist, educator*
Greenberger, Norton Jerald *physician*
Hollander, Daniel *gastroenterologist, medical educator*
Hudson, Robert Paul *medical educator*
Krantz, Kermit Edward *physician, educator*
Mathewson, Hugh Spalding *anesthesiologist, educator*
Mohn, Melvin Paul *anatomist, educator*
Morrison, David Campbell *immunology educator*
Robinson, David Weaver *surgeon, educator*
Ruth, William Edward *physician, educator*
Samson, Frederick Eugene, Jr. *neuroscientist, educator*
Schloerb, Paul Richard *surgeon, educator*
Walaszek, Edward Joseph *pharmacology educator*
Waxman, David *physician, university consultant*
Ziegler, Dewey Kiper *neurologist*

Kingman
Burket, George Edward, Jr. *family physician*

Lawrence
Miller, Don Robert *surgeon*
Ross, Jack Lewis *psychiatrist*

Leavenworth
Mengel, Charles Edmund *physician, medical educator*

Manhattan
Durkee, William Robert *retired physician*
Oehme, Frederick Wolfgang *medical researcher and educator*

Mission
Thomas, Christopher Yancey, III *surgeon, educator*

Prairie Village
Hannah, Hamner, III *surgeon*

Shawnee Mission
Dockhorn, Robert John *physician*
Fairchild, Robert Charles *pediatrician*
Price, James Gordon *physician*
Wenner, Herbert Allan *pediatrician*

Topeka
Gabbard, Glen Owens *psychiatrist, psychoanalyst*
Menninger, William Walter *psychiatrist*
Simpson, William Stewart *retired psychiatrist, sex therapist*

Wichita
Dyck, George *psychiatry educator*
Guthrie, Richard Alan *physician*
Manning, Robert Thomas *physician, educator*
Reals, William Joseph *pathologist, academic administrator, educator*

Winfield
Miller, Franklin Rush *retired internist, educator*

KENTUCKY

Elkton
Manthey, Frank Anthony *physician, director*

Fort Thomas
Scott, Ralph Mason *physician, radiology educator*

Hindman
†Bailey, Benny Ray *health care administrator, state senator*

Hopkinsville
Freer, John Herschel *psychiatrist*

Lexington
Avant, Robert Frank *physician, educator*
Baumann, Robert Jay *child neurology educator*
Clawson, David Kay *orthopedic surgeon*
David, Miriam Lang *physician*
†Diedrich, Donald Frank *pharmacology educator*
Frazier, Donald Tha, Sr. *medical educator, scientist, researcher*
Friedell, Gilbert Hugo *pathologist, hospital administrator, educator, cancer center director*
Gilliam, M(elvin) Randolph *urologist, educator*
Glenn, James Francis *urologist, educator*
†Hagen, Michael Dale *medical educator, family practice researcher*
Hamburg, Joseph *physician, educator*
Holsinger, James Wilson, Jr. *physician*
Jokl, Ernst F. *retired physician*
Markesbery, William R. *neurology and pathology educator, physician*
Parks, Harold Francis *anatomist, educator*
Young, Paul Ray *medical board executive, physician*

Louisville
Andrews, Billy Franklin *pediatrician, educator*
Aronoff, George Rodger *medicine and pharmacology educator*
Callen, Jeffrey Phillip *dermatologist, educator*
†Danzl, Daniel Frank *emergency physician*
DeVries, William Castle *surgeon, educator*
Garretson, Henry David *neurosurgeon*
Gray, Laman A., Jr. *thoracic surgeon, educator*
Haynes, Douglas Martin *physician, educator*
Huang, Kee Chang *pharmacology educator, physician*
Keeney, Arthur Hail *physician, educator*
Kleinert, Harold Earl *plastic surgery educator*
Lansing, Allan Meredith *cardiovascular surgeon, educator*

Neustadt, David Harold physician
Polk, Hiram Carey, Jr. surgeon, educator
Schwab, John Joseph psychiatrist, educator
Uhde, George Irvin physician
Waddell, William Joseph pharmacologist, toxicologist
Weisskopf, Bernard pediatrician, child behavior, development and genetics specialist, educator
Zimmerman, Thom Jay ophthalmologist, educator

Somerset
Jasper, Patrick Lee pediatrician, medical association executive

LOUISIANA

Baton Rouge
Bray, George August physician, scientist, educator
Cherry, William Ashley surgeon, state health officer
Lucas, Fred Vance pathology educator, university administrator

Benton
Dunnihoo, Dale Russell physician, medical educator

Covington
Roberts, James Allen urologist

Deridder
Coquilla, Beatriz Hordista dermatologist, army officer

Gretna
Lupin, Ellis Ralph physician, lawyer, coroner

Hammond
Hejtmancik, Milton Rudolph medical educator

Lake Charles
†Drez, David Jacob, Jr. orthopaedic surgeon, educator

New Orleans
Agrawal, Krishna Chandra pharmacology educator
Berenson, Gerald Sanders physician
Brannan, William urologist, educator
Carter, Rebecca Davilene surgical oncology educator
Cohn, Isidore, Jr. surgeon, educator
†Connolly, Edward S. neurologist
Corrigan, James John, Jr. pediatrician
D'Ambrosia, Robert Dominick orthopaedic educator
Daniels, Robert Sanford psychiatrist, medical school dean
Domer, Floyd Ray pharmacologist, educator
Duffy, John Charles psychiatrist, physician
Duncan, Margaret Caroline physician
Dyment, Paul George adolescent medicine educator
Easson, William McAlpine psychiatrist
Epstein, Arthur William physician, educator
Fisher, James William medical educator, pharmacologist
Friedlander, Miles Herbert ophthalmologist
Frohlich, Edward David physician
García Oller, José Luis neurosurgeon
Gathright, John Byron, Jr. colon and rectal surgeon, educator
Gerber, Michael Albert pathologist, researcher
Gottlieb, A(braham) Arthur medical educator, biotechnology corporate executive
Hewitt, Robert Lee surgeon, educator
Hyman, Albert Lewis cardiologist
Jaffe, Bernard Michael surgeon
Jung, Rodney C. internist, academic administrator
Kastin, Abba Jeremiah endocrinologist, researcher
Kline, David Gellinger neurosurgery educator
Krementz, Edward Thomas surgeon
Lang, Erich Karl physician, radiologist
Le Jeune, Francis Ernest, Jr. otolaryngologist
Lewy, John Edwin pediatric nephrologist
Litwin, Martin Stanley surgeon
Low, Frank Norman anatomist, educator
Messerli, Franz Hannes cardiologist
Mickal, Abe physician
Mogabgab, William Joseph epidemiologist, educator
†Nelson, James Smith pathologist, educator
Nice, Charles Monroe, Jr. physician, educator
Nichols, Ronald Lee surgeon, educator
Ochsner, John Lockwood thoracic-cardiovascular surgeon
Pankey, George Atkinson physician, educator
Puyau, Francis Albert physician, radiology educator
Richardson, Donald Edward neurosurgery educator
Rosenberg, Dennis Melville Leo retired surgeon
Salvaggio, John Edmond physician, educator
Schally, Andrew Victor endocrine oncologist, researcher
Schneider, George T. obstetrician-gynecologist
Smith, Margaret Hamilton Donald physician
Straumanis, John Janis, Jr. psychiatry educator
Usdin, Gene Leonard physician, psychiatrist
Waring, William Winburn pediatric pulmonologist, educator
Webb, Watts Rankin surgeon
Weill, Hans physician, educator
Weiss, Thomas Edward physician
Welsh, Ronald Arthur physician, educator
White, Charles Albert, Jr. medical educator, obstetrician-gynecologist
Yates, Robert Doyle anatomy educator
Zimny, Marilyn Lucile anatomist, educator

Saint Bernard
Gilbert, Norman Sutcliffe research physician

Shreveport
Boyd, Clarence Elmo surgeon
Bradley, Ronald James neuroscientist
Breffeilh, Louis Andrew ophthalmologist, educator
Crissinger, Karen Denise pediatric gastroenterologist, physiologist
Dilworth, Edwin Earle obstetrician, gynecologist
Fort, Arthur Tomlinson, III physician
Ganley, James Powell ophthalmology educator
George, Ronald Baylis physician
McDonald, John Clifton surgeon
Misra, Raghunath Prasad physician, educator
Reddy, Pratap Chandupatla cardiologist, educator, researcher
Schober, Charles Coleman, III psychiatrist, psychoanalyst
Shelby, James Stanford cardiovascular surgeon
Thurmon, Theodore Francis medical educator

MAINE

Bar Harbor
Green, Earl Leroy retired biomedical research administrator, geneticist

Camden
Spock, Benjamin McLane physician, educator

Hampden
Brown, Robert Horatio retired orthopedic surgeon

Rockport
Swenson, Orvar surgeon

South Portland
Katz, Steven Edward psychiatrist, state health official

Surry
Whitcomb, Benjamin Bradford, Jr. neurosurgeon

Union
Buchan, Ronald Forbes preventive medicine physician

MARYLAND

Baltimore
Abramson, William Edward psychiatrist
Aisner, Joseph oncologist, physician
Andres, Reubin gerontologist
Bachur, Nicholas Robert, Sr. research physician
Baker, R. Robinson surgeon
Baker, Susan P. public health educator
Baker, Timothy Danforth physician, educator
Bayless, Theodore M(orris) gastroenterologist, educator, researcher
†Becker, Lewis Charles cardiology educator
Bereston, Eugene Sydney dermatologist
Berlin, Fred Saul psychiatrist
Berman, Barnett internist, educator
†Bigelow, George E. pharmacology administrator
Borden, Ernest Carleton physician, educator
Breitenecker, Rudiger pathologist
Brody, Eugene B. psychiatrist, educator
Brusilow, Saul pediatrics educator
Charache, Samuel hematologist
Childs, Barton physician, educator
†Clements, Mary Lou epidemiologist, educator
Conley, Carroll Lockard physician, emeritus educator
Connor, Thomas Byrne physician, educator
Cornblath, Marvin pediatrician, educator
Crenshaw, Marion Carlyle, Jr. obstetrician, educator
Cummings, Charles William physician, educator
Dannenberg, Arthur Milton, Jr. experimental pathologist, immunologist, educator
†DeAngelis, Catherine D. pediatrics educator
Dorst, John Phillips physician, radiology and pediatrics educator
†Eisenberg, Howard Michael neurosurgeon
Fedoroff, Nina Vsevolod research scientist, consultant
†Felsenthal, Gerald physiatrist, educator
Fishman, Jacob Robert psychiatrist, educator, corporate executive, investor
Frank, Jerome David psychiatrist, educator
Freeman, John Mark pediatric neurologist
Godenne, Ghislaine Dudley physician, psychoanalyst
Goldberg, Morton Falk ophthalmologist, educator
Gordis, Leon physician
Graham, George Gordon physician
†Grant, Albert internist
Greenough, William Bates, III medical educator
Griffith, Lawrence Stacey Cameron cardiologist
Harvey, Abner McGehee physician, educator
Helrich, Martin anesthesiologist, educator
Heptinstall, Robert Hodgson physician
Hungerford, David Samuel orthopaedic surgeon, educator
†Johns, Michael Marieb Edward otolaryngologist, university dean
Johns, Richard James physician
†Johnson, Kenneth Peter neurologist, medical researcher
Johnson, Richard T. neurology, microbiology and neuroscience educator, research virologist
Kastor, John Alfred cardiologist, educator
Keill, Stuart Langdon psychiatrist
Kidd, Langford pediatrician, cardiologist, educator
Kinnard, William James, Jr. pharmacy educator
Kowarski, Allen Avinoam endocrinologist, educator
Kwiterovich, Peter Oscar, Jr. medical science educator, researcher, physician
†Levine, Jerome psychiatrist, educator
Lichtenstein, Lawrence Mark allergy, immunology educator, physician
Long, Donlin Martin surgeon, educator
†Manson, Paul Nellis plastic surgeon
McDowell, Elizabeth Mary pathology educator
Mc Hugh, Paul R. psychiatrist, neurologist, educator
McKhann, Guy Mead physician, educator
Medani, Charles Richard pediatric nephrology educator
Migeon, Claude Jean pediatricics educator
Milnor, William Robert physician
Monroe, Russell Ronald psychiatrist, educator
Moser, Hugo Wolfgang physician
Munster, Andrew Michael surgeon, educator
Norman, Philip Sidney physician
Oski, Frank Aram physician, educator
Patz, Arnall physician
Platt, William Rady pathology educator
Price, Thomas Ransone neurologist, educator
Proctor, Donald Frederick otolaryngology educator, physician
†Rapoport, Morton I. medical educator, university administrator
Rayson, Glendon Ennes internist, preventive medicine specialist, writer
Rennels, Marshall Leigh neuroanatomist, biomedical scientist, educator
Rose, Noel Richard immunologist, microbiologist, educator
Rosenstein, Beryl Joel physician
Schimpff, Stephen Callender internist, oncologist
Sharfstein, Steven Samuel psychiatrist, government research institute administrator, association executive, hospital executive
Silbergeld, Ellen Kovner environmental epidemiologist and toxicologist
Silverstein, Arthur Matthew ophthalmic immunologist, educator, historian
Smith, Gardner Watkins physician
Smith, Julian Payne gynecological oncologist, educator
Snyder, Solomon Halbert psychiatrist, pharmacologist
Starfield, Barbara Helen physician, educator
Sternberger, Ludwig Amadeus neurologist, educator
†Stobo, John David physician, educator
Stolley, Paul David medical educator, researcher
Strickland, George Thomas, Jr. physician, researcher, educator
Tabatznik, Bernard physician, educator
Talalay, Paul pharmacologist, physician
Taylor, Carl Ernest physician, educator
†Vogelstein, Bert oncology educator
Wagner, Henry Nicholas, Jr. physician
Wallach, Edward Eliot physician, educator
Walser, Mackenzie physician, educator
Welch, Robert Bond ophthalmologist, educator
Williams, G(eorge) Melville surgeon, medical educator
Wilson, Donald Edward physician, educator
Woodward, Theodore Englar medical educator, internist
Young, Barbara psychiatrist, psychoanalyst, psychiatry educator, photographer
Zassenhaus, Hiltgunt Margret physician

Beltsville
Lincicome, David Richard biomedical and animal scientist

Bethesda
Abbrecht, Peter Herman medical educator
Alexander, Duane Frederick pediatrician, research administrator
Axelrod, Julius pharmacologist, biochemist
Barter, Robert Henry physician, retired educator
Berendes, Heinz Werner medical epidemiologist, pediatrician
†Borsos, Tibor pathology educator
Breggin, Peter Roger psychiatrist, author
Brodine, Charles Edward physician
Brown, Dudley Earl, Jr. psychiatrist, educator, health executive, former federal agency administrator, former naval officer
Carpenter, Malcolm Breckenridge retired neuroanatomist, educator
Cath, Stanley Howard psychiatrist, psychoanalyst
†Chabner, Bruce A. oncologist, researcher
Chase, Thomas Newell neurologist, researcher, educator
†Cohen, Gene David psychiatrist
Cohen, Max Harry surgeon
Cohen, Sheldon Gilbert physician
Cowie, Catherine Christine epidemiologist
Crout, J(ohn) Richard physician, pharmaceutical researcher
Cummings, Nancy Boucot nephrologist
Decker, John Laws physician
Dietrich, Robert Anthony pathologist, medical administrator, consultant
Drucker, William Richard surgeon
Elin, Ronald John pathologist
Ellis, Sydney pharmacological scientist, former pharmacology educator
Epps, Roselyn Elizabeth Payne pediatrician, educator
Evans, Charles Hawes, Jr. immunologist, medical researcher
Farmer, Richard Gilbert physician, foundation administrator, medical advisor
Frommer, Peter Leslie physician, medical institute administrator
†Gallin, John J. medical research administrator
Gibson, Sam Thompson internist, educator
Gold, Philip William neurobiologist
Goldstein, Robert Arnold physician
Greenwald, Peter physician, government medical research director
Hallett, Mark physician, neurologist, health research institute administrator
Harlan, William Robert, Jr. physician, educator, researcher
Haseltine, Florence Pat research administrator, obstetrician, gynecologist
Hersh, Stephen Peter psychiatrist, educator
Hughes, Carl Wilson physician
Hutton, John Evans, Jr. surgery educator, retired military officer
Joy, Robert John Thomas medical history educator
Kapikian, Albert Zaven physician, epidemiologist
Keiser, Harry Robert physician
Kirschstein, Ruth Lillian physician
Kolbye, Albert Christian, Jr. epidemiologist, toxicologist, lawyer
†Kopin, Irwin Jerome physician, pharmacologist
Krause, Richard Michael medical scientist, government official, educator
Kupfer, Carl ophthalmologist, science administrator
Lenfant, Claude Jean-Marie physician
Leonard, James Joseph physician, educator
Leventhal, Carl M. neurologist
Levine, Arthur Samuel physician, scientist
†Liotta, Lance Allen pathologist
Macnamara, Thomas Edward physician, educator
McAfee, John Gilmour nuclear medicine physician
McCurdy, Harry Ward otolaryngologist
†Metcalfe, Dean Darrel medical research physician
Neva, Franklin Allen physician, educator
Nyirjesy, Istvan obstetrician, gynecologist
Oler, Wesley Marion, III physician, educator
Ommaya, Ayub Khan neurosurgeon
†Paul, Steven M. psychiatrist
Paul, William Erwin immunologist, researcher
†Pollard, Harvey B. physician, neuroscientist
Quinnan, Gerald Vincent, Jr. medical educator
Rall, Joseph Edward physician
†Rapoport, Judith psychiatrist
Reighard, Homer Leroy physician
Resnik, Harvey Lewis Paul psychiatrist
Robinson, Lynn P. association executive
†Rodbard, David endocrinologist, biophysicist
Rosenberg, Steven Aaron surgeon, medical researcher
Roth, Harold Philmore physician
†Saffiotti, Umberto pathologist
Sheridan, Philp Henry pediatrician, neurologist
Sindelar, William Francis surgeon, researcher
Snow, James Byron, Jr. physician, research administrator
Sontag, James Mitchell cancer researcher
†Sorensen, Kurt biomedical research administrator
Stewart, Harold Leroy physician, educator
Sturtz, Donald Lee physician, naval officer
Wagner, Henry George medical research scientist, naval officer
Waldmann, Thomas Alexander medical research scientist, physician
Walter, William Arnold, Jr. physician
Walters, Judith Richmond neuropharmacologist
Webster, Henry deForest experimental neuropathologist
Williams, Charles Laval, Jr. physician, international organization official
†Wong, Ma-Li psychiatrist
Yaffe, Sumner Jason pediatrician, research center administrator, educator

Cabin John
Sewell, Winifred pharmaceutical librarian

Canton
Grable, Edward E. obstetrician, gynecologist

Chevy Chase
Ferguson, James Joseph, Jr. researcher, educator
Greenberg, Robert Milton retired psychiatrist
Romansky, Monroe James physician, educator
Rose, John Charles physician, educator
Welch, Arnold D(emerritt) pharmacologist, biochemist

Columbia
Carr, Charles Jelleff pharmacologist, educator, toxicology consultant

Easton
Engle, Mary Allen English physician
Engle, Ralph Landis, Jr. internist, educator

Fort Howard
Alexander, C. Alex physician

Frederick
†Papas, Takis S. oncology research administrator

Gaithersburg
Crisp, Elizabeth Amanda physician
Schwartzberg, Allan Zelig psychiatrist, educator

Grasonville
Prout, George Russell, Jr. medical educator, urologist

Greenbelt
Work, Henry Harcus physician, educator

Hollywood
Hertz, Roy physician, educator, researcher

Laurel
Hutcheson, Janet Reid radiologist

Lusby
Howell, James Theodore medical consultant, internist

Lutherville
Sanders, Roger Cobban radiologist

Lutherville Timonium
Bundick, William Ross dermatologist

Mitchellville
Bever, Christopher Theodore psychiatrist

Monkton
Mountcastle, Vernon Benjamin neurophysiologist

Parkville
Munson, Paul Lewis pharmacologist

Perry Point
Peszke, Michael Alfred psychiatrist, educator

Poolesville
†Newman, John Dennis neuroethologist, biomedical researcher

Potomac
Antoniou, Lucy D. internist, nephrologist
Bradley, Mark Edmund physician, consultant
Haddy, Francis John physician, educator

Rockville
Birns, Mark Theodore physician
Cohen, Robert Abraham retired physician
DuPont, Robert Louis psychiatrist, physician
Forbes, Allan Louis physician, foods and nutrition consultant
Geier, Mark Robin obstetrical genetics and infertility physician
Haffner, Marlene Elisabeth internist, health care administrator
Hanna, Michael George, Jr. immunologist, institute administrator
Haudenschild, Christian Charles pathologist, educator
Henderson, Edward Shelton oncologist
†Hoth, Daniel infectious diseases administrator
†Hoyer, Leon William physician, educator
Johnson, Emery Allen physician
Ley, Herbert Leonard, Jr. retired epidemiologist
Lim, David Jong Jai otolaryngology educator, researcher
Lloyd, Douglas Seward physician, public health administrator
Lutwak, Leo physician, educator
Naunton, Ralph Frederick surgeon, educator
Nora, James Jackson physician, author, educator
Seltser, Raymond epidemiologist, educator
Sumaya, Ciro Valent pediatrician, educator
Temple, Robert physician, federal agency administrator

Salisbury
Houlihan, Hilda Imelio physician
†May, Everette Lee, Jr. pharmacologist, educator

Severna Park
Greulich, Richard Curtice retired anatomist, gerontologist

Silver Spring
Berger, Allan Sidney psychiatrist
Waldrop, Francis Neil physician

Stevenson
†Hendler, Nelson Howard physician, medical clinic director

Tantallon
Dickens, Doris Lee psychiatrist

Towson
Mc Indoe, Darrell Winfred nuclear medicine physician, former air force officer
Spodak, Michael Kenneth forensic psychiatrist
Udvarhelyi, George Bela neurosurgery educator emeritus, cultural affairs administrator

Union Bridge
Laughlin, Henry Prather physician, psychiatrist, educator, author, editor

MASSACHUSETTS

Amherst
†Fleischman, Paul R. psychiatrist, writer

Andover
Ellis, Elliot Frederic physician

Bedford
Alarcon, Rogelio Alfonso physician, researcher
Stollerman, Gene Howard physician, educator
Volicer, Ladislav physician, educator

Belmont
Bird, Edward Dennis physician
Cohen, Bruce Michael psychiatrist, educator, scientist
Onesti, Silvio Joseph psychiatrist
Pope, Harrison Graham, Jr. psychiatrist, educator
Sifneos, Peter Emanuel psychiatrist
Weiss, Roger Douglas psychiatrist

Boston
Adams, Douglass Franklin radiologist, educator
Adelstein, S(tanley) James physician, educator
Adler, David Avram psychiatrist
Alpert, Joel Jacobs medical educator, pediatrician
Ames, Adelbert, III neurophysiologist, educator
Arias, Irwin Monroe physician, educator
Arky, Ronald Alfred medical educator
Austen, K(arl) Frank physician
Austen, W(illiam) Gerald surgeon, educator
Avery, Mary Ellen pediatrician, educator
Barlow, Charles Franklin physician, educator
†Barlow, John Sutton neurophysiologist, electroencephalographer
Barry, Patricia Pound physician, educator
Beck, William Samson physician, educator, biochemist
Benacerraf, Baruj pathologist, educator
Berenberg, William physician, educator
Bernfield, Merton Ronald pediatrician, scientist, educator
Bernhard, William Francis thoracic and cardiovascular surgeon
Blau, Monte radiology educator
Bloch, Kurt Julius physician
Brain, Joseph David biomedical scientist
Braunwald, Eugene physician, educator
Brazelton, Thomas Berry pediatrician, educator
Brenner, Barry Morton physician
Buchanan, John Robert physician, educator
†Buckley, Mortimer Joseph physician
Burakoff, Steven James immunologist, educator
Burns, Padraic physician, psychiatrist, psychoanalyst, educator
Callow, Allan Dana surgeon
Canellos, George P. physician educator
Caplan, Louis Robert neurology educator
Carpenter, Charles Bernard medical educator
Cassidy, Carl Eugene physician
Chalmers, Thomas Clark physician, educational and research administrator
Chen, Lincoln Chin-ho medical educator
Cleveland, Richard Joseph surgeon
Coffman, Jay Denton physician, educator
Cohen, Alan Seymour internist
Coleman, C. Norman radiologist, oncologist, researcher, educator
Collins, John Joseph, Jr. cardiac and thoracic surgeon
Corcoran, Paul John physician
†Cotran, Ramzi S. pathologist, educator
Crowley, William Francis, Jr. medical educator
De Cherney, Alan Hersh obstetrics and gynecology educator
Delbanco, Thomas Lewis medical educator, researcher
DeSanctis, Roman William cardiologist
Desforges, Jane Fay medical educator, physician
Dvorak, Harold F. pathologist, educator, scientist
Eckstein, Marlene R. vascular radiologist
Egdahl, Richard Harrison surgeon, medical educator, health science administrator
Eisenberg, Leon psychiatrist, educator
Ellis, Franklin Henry, Jr. surgeon, educator
Epstein, Franklin Harold physician, educator
†Faller, Douglas V. cancer research administrator
Feldman, Robert George neurologist, medical educator
Ferris, Benjamin Greeley, Jr. retired physician, environmental researcher, educator
Field, James Bernard internist, educator
Fineberg, Harvey Vernon physician, educator
Fitzpatrick, Thomas Bernard dermatologist, educator
Fletcher, Robert Hillman medical educator
Folkman, Moses Judah surgeon
Fox, Bernard Hayman cancer epidemiologist, educator
Freedberg, A. Stone physician
Frei, Emil, III physician, medical researcher, educator
Freiman, David Galland pathologist, educator
Frigoletto, Fredric David, Jr. physician
Galaburda, Albert Mark neurologist, researcher, educator
Gellis, Sydney Saul physician
Gimbrone, Michael Anthony, Jr. pathologist, educator
Glimcher, Melvin Jacob orthopedic surgeon
Goldberg, Irving Hyman molecular pharmacology and biochemistry educator
Goldsmith, Harry Sawyer surgeon, educator
Gottlieb, Leonard Solomon pathology educator
Goyal, Raj Kumar medical educator
†Graham, John David public health educator
Green, Gareth Montraville physician, educator, scientist
Greenblatt, David J. pharmacologist, educator
Grillo, Hermes Conrad surgeon
Grossman, Jerome Harvey medical educator, administrator
Haber, Edgar physician, educator
Hall, John Emmett orthopedic surgeon, educator
Harris, Burton Henry surgeon
Harris, William Hamilton orthopedic surgeon
Hay, Elizabeth Dexter embryology researcher, educator
†Healy, Gerald Burke otolaryngologist
Hedley-Whyte, Elizabeth Tessa neuropathologist
Hiatt, Howard H. physician, educator
Hingson, Ralph W. medical educator
Hobson, John Allan psychiatrist, researcher, educator
†Hutchinson, Bernard Thomas ophthalmologist
Hutter, Adolph Matthew, Jr. cardiologist, educator
Jandl, James Harriman physician, educator
Kannel, William Bernard cardiovascular epidemiologist
Karnovsky, Morris John pathologist, biologist
Kazemi, Homayoun physician, medical educator
Kiang, Nelson Yuan-sheng medical educator
Kieff, Elliott Dan medical educator
Kimura, Robert Shigetsugu otologic researcher
Kitz, Richard John anesthesiologist, educator
†Klempner, Mark Steven Joel physician, research scientist, educator
Krane, Stephen Martin physician, educator
Lasagna, Louis Cesare medical educator
Leaf, Alexander physician, educator
†Lee, Robin S. surgeon, researcher
Levine, Ruth Rothenberg biomedical science educator
Levinsky, Norman George physician, educator
Libby, Peter cardiologist, medical researcher
Lipton, Stuart Arthur neuroscientist
Little, John Bertram physician, radiobiology educator, researcher
Livingston, David Morse biomedical scientist, physician, internist
Locke, Steven Elliot psychiatrist
Loughlin, Kevin Raymond urologic surgeon, researcher
Mankin, Henry Jay physician, educator
Mannick, John Anthony surgeon
May, James Warren, Jr. plastic surgeon, medical association executive
Mc Arthur, Janet Ward endocrinologist, educator
McCluskey, Robert Timmons physician
Mc Dermott, William Vincent, Jr. physician, educator
McDougal, William Scott urology educator
†McMahon, Lillian Elizabeth hematologist
Medearis, Donald Norman, Jr. physician, educator
Mellins, Harry Zachary radiologist, educator
Messerle, Judith Rose medical librarian, public relations director
Miller, Keith Wyatt pharmacology educator
Moellering, Robert Charles, Jr. internist, educator
Monaco, Anthony Peter surgery educator, medical institute administrator
Montgomery, William Wayne surgeon
†Morgentaler, Abraham urologist, researcher
†Moskowitz, Michael Arthur neuroscientist, neurologist
Munsat, Theodore L. neurologist, researcher
Nadas, Alexander Sandor pediatric cardiologist
Naimi, Shapur cardiologist, educator
Nathan, David Gordon physician, educator
Nichols, David Harry gynecologic surgeon, obstetrics and gynecology educator, author
Ojemann, Robert Gerdes neurosurgeon
Paul, Oglesby physician
Pochi, Peter Ernest physician
Poser, Charles Marcel neurology educator
Poussaint, Alvin Francis psychiatrist, educator
Prout, Curtis physician
Rabkin, Mitchell Thornton physician, hospital administrator, educator
Raviola, Elio anatomist, neurobiologist
Reichlin, Seymour physician, educator
Reid, Lynne McArthur pathologist
Relman, Arnold Seymour physician, educator
Reppert, Steven Marion pediatrician, educator
†Richie, Jerome Paul surgeon, educator
Roehrig, C(harles) Burns internist, health policy consultant, editor
Rosen, Fred Saul pediatrics educator
†Rosenberg, Irwin Harold physician, educator
Rosenblatt, Michael medical researcher, educator
Rush, David medical investigator, epidemiologist
Russell, Paul Snowden surgeon, educator
Ryan, Kenneth John physician, educator
Sandson, John I. physician, educator, retired university dean
Saper, Clifford Baird neurobiology and neurology educator
Schaller, Jane Green pediatrician
Schildkraut, Joseph Jacob psychiatrist, educator
Schlossman, Stuart Franklin physician, educator, researcher
Schuknecht, Harold Frederick physician, educator
Schwartz, Bernard physician
Seddon, Johanna Margaret ophthalmologist, epidemiologist
Selkoe, Dennis Jesse neurologist, researcher, educator
Shader, Richard Irwin psychiatrist, educator
Shapiro, Jerome Herbert radiologist, educator
Shields, Lawrence Thornton orthopedic surgeon, educator
†Shucart, William Arthur neurosurgeon
Smith, Thomas Woodward cardiologist, educator
†Steele, Glenn Daniel, Jr. surgical oncologist
Steere, Allen Caruthers, Jr. physician, educator
Swartz, Morton Norman medical educator
Tauber, Alfred Imre hematologist, immunologist, philosopher of science
Taubman, Martin Arnold immunologist
Taveras, Juan Manuel physician, educator
Thorn, George Widmer physician, educator
Trier, Jerry Steven gastroenterologist, educator
†Vaillant, George Eman psychiatrist
Volpe, Joseph John pediatric neurologist, educator
Warshaw, Andrew Louis surgeon, researcher
Weiner, Howard Lee physician, immunologist, educator, researcher
Weiss, Earle Burton physician
Welch, Claude Emerson surgeon
Willock, Marcelle Monica medical educator
Wyman, Stanley Moore radiologist
Zaleznik, Abraham psychoanalyst, management specialist, educator
Zarins, Bertram orthopaedic surgeon
Zervas, Nicholas Themistocles neurosurgeon
†Zinner, Michael Jeffrey surgeon, educator
Zoll, Paul Maurice cardiologist

Brookline
†Biederman, Joseph psychiatrist
Blom, Gaston Eugene psychiatrist
Brooks, Joae Graham psychiatrist, educator
Gray, Seymour medical educator, author
Jakab, Irene psychiatrist
Kadin, Marshall Edward hematopathologist, educator
Nadelson, Carol Cooperman psychiatrist, educator
Tyler, H. Richard physician

Burlington
Clerkin, Eugene Patrick physician
Fager, Charles Anthony physician, neurosurgeon
Moschella, Samuel L. dermatology educator
†Schoetz, David John, Jr. colon and rectal surgeon
Veidenheimer, Malcolm Charles surgeon
Wise, Robert Edward radiologist

Cambridge
Anderson, William Henry psychobiologist, educator
Bartus, Raymond Thomas neuroscientist, pharmaceutical executive, writer
Bizzi, Emilio neurophysiologist, educator
Brooks, John Robinson surgeon, educator
Brusch, John Lynch physician
Coles, Robert child psychiatrist, educator, author
Davidson, Charles Sprecher physician
Davie, Joseph Myrten physician, pathology and immunology educator, science administrator
Eisen, Herman Nathaniel immunology educator, medical researcher
Havens, Leston Laycock psychiatrist, educator
Homburger, Freddy physician, scientist, artist
Meissner, William Walter psychiatrist, clergyman
Rothenberg, Albert psychiatrist, educator
Schmitt, Francis Otto neuroscientist, emeritus educator
Shore, Miles Frederick psychiatrist, educator
Wacker, Warren Ernest Clyde physician, educator
Wurtman, Richard Jay physician, educator

Charlestown
Bonventre, Joseph Vincent physician, scientist, medical educator
Isselbacher, Kurt Julius physician, educator
Lamont-Havers, Ronald William physician, research administrator

Chestnut Hill
Baum, Jules Leonard ophthalmologist, educator
Courtiss, Eugene Howard plastic surgeon, educator
Knapp, Robert Charles retired obstetrics and gynecology educator
Stanbury, John Bruton physician, educator

Concord
Palay, Sanford Louis retired scientist, educator

Falmouth
Gilmour, Edward Ellis psychiatrist

Fitchburg
Bogdasarian, John Robert otolaryngologist

Jamaica Plain
Pierce, Chester Middlebrook psychiatrist, educator
Snider, Gordon Lloyd physician

Lincoln Center
Cannon, Bradford surgeon

Marion
Schmidek, Henry Hans-Heinz neurosurgeon, educator

Medford
Burke, Edward Newell radiologist

Natick
†Denniston, J. environmental medical research administrator

Needham
Weller, Thomas Huckle physician, emeritus educator

New Bedford
†Shapiro, Gilbert Lawrence orthopedist

New Salem
Lenherr, Frederick Keith neurophysiologist, computer scientist

Newton
Blacher, Richard Stanley psychiatrist
Gill, Benjamin Franklin physician
Myerson, Paul Graves psychiatrist, educator
Rogoff, Jerome Howard psychiatrist, psychoanalyst, forensic expert
Simon, Harold radiologist
Young, James Morningstar physician, naval officer

North Dighton
Cserr, Robert psychiatrist, physician, hospital administrator

Northampton
Dashef, Stephen Sewell psychiatrist

Northborough
Fulmer, Hugh Scott physician, educator

Norwood
Berliner, Allen Irwin dermatologist

Roxbury
Berman, Marlene Oscar neuropsychologist, educator
Peters, Alan anatomy educator

Salem
Piro, Anthony John radiologist

Sharon
Honikman, Larry Howard pediatrician

Shrewsbury
Zamecnik, Paul Charles oncologist, medical research scientist

Southborough
Dews, P(eter) B(ooth) medical scientist, educator

Springfield
Frankel, Kenneth Mark thoracic surgeon
Liptzin, Benjamin psychiatrist
†McGee, William Tobin internist

Stockbridge
Shapiro, Edward Robert psychiatrist, educator, psychoanalyst

Walpole
Dexter, Lewis physician
Warthin, Thomas Angell physician, educator

Waltham
Lackner, James Robert aerospace medicine educator
Leach, Robert Ellis physician, educator
†Reilly, Philip medical research administrator
Thier, Samuel Osiah physician, educator

Wayland
Ebert, Robert Higgins physician, educator, foundation consultant
Freed, Murray Monroe physician, medical educator

Wellesley
Coyne, Mary Downey biologist, endocrinologist, educator
Murray, Joseph Edward plastic surgeon

West Roxbury
Hedley-Whyte, John anesthesiologist, educator

Williamstown
Wilkins, Earle Wayne, Jr. surgery educator emeritus

Winchester
Smith, Robert Moors anesthesiologist

Worcester
Appelbaum, Paul Stuart psychiatrist, educator
Bonkovsky, Herbert Lloyd gastroenterologist, educator
Brill, A. Bertrand nuclear medicine educator
Charney, Evan pediatrician, educator
Drachman, David Alexander neurologist
Dunlop, George Rodgers surgeon
Hanshaw, James Barry physician, educator
Hunter, Richard Edward physician
Kaplan, Melvin Hyman immunology, rheumatology, medical educator
Laster, Leonard physician, academic administrator
Levine, Peter Hughes physician, health facility administrator
Ludlum, David Blodgett pharmacologist, educator
Majno, Guido pathologist, educator
Menon, Mani urological surgeon, educator
Smith, Edward Herbert radiologist, educator
Townes, Philip Leonard pediatrician, educator
Wheeler, Hewitt Brownell surgeon, educator
Wilkinson, Harold Arthur neurosurgeon
Zurier, Robert Burton medical educator, clinical investigator

MICHIGAN

Allen Park
Manov, Leslie Joan Boyle radiologist, medical administrator

Alma
Sanders, Jack Ford physician

Ann Arbor
Abrams, Gerald David physician, educator
Ansbacher, Rudi physician
†Armstrong, William Floyd medical educator
Bole, Giles G. physician, researcher, medical educator
Burdi, Alphonse Rocco anatomist
Casey, Kenneth Lyman neurologist
Castor, C. William, Jr. physician, educator
Christensen, A(lbert) Kent anatomy educator
Coran, Arnold Gerald pediatric surgeon, educator
Counsell, Raymond Ernest pharmacology educator
Curtis, George Clifton psychiatry educator, clinical research investigator
De La Iglesia, Felix Alberto pathologist, toxicologist
DeWeese, Marion Spencer educator, surgeon
Domino, Edward Felix pharmacologist, educator
Donabedian, Avedis physician
Dubin, Howard Victor dermatologist
Fajans, Stefan Stanislaus internist, retired educator
Gikas, Paul William medical educator
Gilman, Sid neurologist
†Goldstein, Irwin Joseph medical research executive
†Greden, John Francis psychiatrist, educator
†Greene, Douglas A. internist, educator
Hawkins, Joseph Elmer, Jr. otolaryngologist, educator, acoustic physiologist
Hawthorne, Victor Morrison epidemiologist, educator
Heidelberger, Kathleen Patricia physician
Henderson, John Woodworth ophthalmologist, educator
Hiss, Roland Graham physician, medical educator
Hoff, Julian Theodore physician, educator
Howell, Joel DuBose physician, educator
Huelke, Donald Fred anatomy and cell biology educator, research scientist
Kelch, Robert Paul pediatric endocrinologist
Kimbrough, William Walter, III psychiatrist
Krause, Charles Joseph otolaryngologist
Kuhl, David Edmund physician, radiology educator
La Du, Bert Nichols, Jr. pharmacology educator, physician
Lapides, Jack urologist, medical educator
Lichter, Paul Richard ophthalmology educator
Margolis, Philip Marcus psychiatrist, educator
Martel, William radiologist, educator
Midgley, A(lvin) Rees, Jr. reproductive endocrinology educator, researcher

†Miller, Josef M. *otolaryngologist, educator*
Morley, George William *gynecologist*
Oliver, William John *pediatrician, educator*
Orringer, Mark B. *thoracic surgeon*
Osborn, June Elaine *pediatrician, microbiologist, educator*
Pitt, Bertram *cardiologist, consultant*
Rosenthal, Amnon *pediatric cardiologist*
Schottenfeld, David *epidemiologist, educator*
†Shayman, James Alan *nephrologist, educator*
Silverman, Albert Jack *psychiatrist, educator*
Sloan, Herbert Elias *physician, surgeon*
†Smith, David John, Jr. *plastic surgeon*
Strang, Ruth Hancock *pediatrician, educator, pediatric cardiologist*
Stross, Jeoffrey Knight *physician, educator*
†Tandon, Rajiv *psychiatrist, educator*
Taren, James Arthur *neurosurgeon, educator*
Taylor, William Brooks, II *retired dermatologist*
Thompson, Norman Winslow *surgeon, educator*
Turcotte, Jeremiah George *physician, surgery educator*
Waggoner, Raymond Walter *neuropsychiatrist*
†Wahl, Richard Leo *radiology educator, nuclear medicine cancer researcher*
Ward, Peter Allan *pathologist, educator*
Watson, Andrew Samuel *psychiatry and law educator*
Weber, Wendell William *pharmacologist*
Weg, John Gerard *physician*
Wegman, Myron Ezra *physician, educator*
†Wicha, Max S. *oncologist, educator*
†Wiggins, Roger C. *internist, educator, researcher*
Zarafonetis, Chris John Dimiter *physician, emeritus educator*

Bad Axe
†Rosenfeld, Joel *ophthalmologist, lawyer*

Battle Creek
Bruce, Thomas Allen *physician, philanthropic administrator*

Birmingham
Chodorkoff, Bernard *psychoanalyst, psychiatrist*

Bloomfield Hills
Chason, Jacob (Leon Chason) *neuropathologist*
Hsu, John J. *psychiatrist*
Knights, Edwin Munroe *pathologist*

Clinton Township
Hollerman, Charles Edward *pediatrician*

Copemish
Wells, Herschel James *physician, former hospital administrator*

Dearborn
Coburn, Ronald Murray *ophthalmic surgeon, researcher*
Joseph, Ramon Rafael *physician, educator*

Detroit
Abramson, Hanley Norman *pharmacy educator*
Blain, Alexander, III *surgeon, educator*
Brown, Eli Matthew *anesthesiologist*
Cerny, Joseph Charles *urologist, educator*
Cohen, Sanford Ned *pediatrics educator, academic administrator*
Ernst, Calvin Bradley *vascular surgeon, surgery educator*
Fitzgerald, Robert Hannon, Jr. *orthopedic surgeon*
Fromm, David *surgeon*
†Gans, Bruce Merrill *physiatrist, physician, hospital executive*
†Honet, Joseph C. *rehabilitation medicine physician*
†Jampel, Robert Steven *ophthalmologist, educator*
Kantrowitz, Adrian *surgeon, educator*
Krull, Edward Alexander *dermatologist*
Lesch, Michael *cardiologist*
Livingood, Clarence S. *dermatologist*
†Lupulescu, Aurel Peter *medical educator, researcher, physician*
†Lusher, Jeanne Marie *pediatric hematologist, educator*
Miller, Orlando Jack *physician, educator*
†Ownby, Dennis Randall *pediatrician, allergist, educator, researcher*
†Porter, Arthur T. *oncologist, educator*
Stein, Paul David *cardiologist*
Szilagyi, D(esiderius) Emerick *surgeon, researcher, educator*
Walt, Alexander Jeffrey *surgeon, educator*
Whitehouse, Fred Waite *endocrinologist, researcher*
Wiener, Joseph *pathologist*

East Lansing
Brody, Theodore Meyer *pharmacologist, educator*
†Enzer, Norbert Beverley *psychiatry educator*
Gottschalk, Alexander *radiologist, diagnostic radiology educator*
Grant, Rhoda *biomedical researcher, educator, medical physiologist*
Johnson, John Irwin, Jr. *neuroscientist*
Jones, Margaret Eileen Zee *pathologist, educator, scientist*
Kay, Bernard Melvin *osteopathic pediatrician, educational administrator*
Krecke, Charles Francis *radiologist, educator*
Leader, Robert Wardell *pathologist*
Moore, Kenneth Edwin *pharmacology educator*
Murray, Raymond Harold *physician*
Netzloff, Michael Lawrence *pediatric educator, endocrinologist*
Potchen, E. James *radiology educator*
Reinhart, Mary Ann *medical board executive*
Ristow, George Edward *neurologist, educator*
Rovner, David Richard *endocrinology educator*
†Sawyer, Donald Craig *veterinary anesthesia and pharmacology educator*
Walker, Bruce Edward *anatomy educator*
Williams, Donald Herbert *psychiatric education administrator*

Eastpointe
Sturman, Robert Harries *neurological surgeon, consultant neurologist*

Flint
Farrehi, Cyrus *cardiologist, educator*
Himes, George Elliott *pathologist*
Jayabalan, Vemblaserry *nuclear medicine physician, radiologist*
Tauscher, John Walter *pediatrician, educator*

Flushing
Schriner, Jon Leslie *sports medicine physician*

Franklin
Adler, Philip *osteopathic physician*

Grand Rapids
Curtiss, Robert Louis *osteopathic physician*
Daniels, Joseph *neuropsychiatrist*
†MacKeigan, John Malcolm *surgeon*

Grosse Pointe
Beierwaltes, William Henry *physician, educator*
Sphire, Raymond Daniel *anesthesiologist*

Harper Woods
DeGiusti, Dominic Lawrence *medical science educator, academic administrator*

Kalamazoo
Aladjem, Silvio *obstetrician, gynecologist, educator*
Chodos, Dale David Jerome *physician, consumer advocate*
Gladstone, William Sheldon, Jr. *radiologist*
Novitch, Mark *physician, retired pharmaceutical executive*
Smith, Robert James *immunopharmacologist*

Lake Angelus
Kresge, Bruce Anderson *retired physician*

Lansing
Wiegenstein, John Gerald *physician*

Livonia
Sobel, Howard Bernard *osteopath*

Mancelona
Whelan, Joseph L(eo) *neurologist*

Okemos
Ochberg, Frank Martin *psychiatrist, health science facility administrator, author*

Port Huron
Coury, John, Jr. *surgeon*

Royal Oak
Bernstein, Jay *pathologist, researcher, educator*
Dworkin, Howard Jerry *nuclear physician, educator*
LaBan, Myron Miles *physician, administrator*
Walker, Richard Harold *pathologist, educator*

Saint Clair Shores
Walker, Frank Banghart *pathologist*

Southfield
Hammel, Ernest Martin *medical educator, academic administrator*
Mathog, Robert Henry *otolaryngologist, educator*
Rosenzweig, Norman *psychiatry educator*

Troy
Krabbenhoft, Kenneth Lester *radiologist, educator*

Warren
Ryan, Jack *physician, hospital corporation executive*

West Bloomfield
Sarwer-Foner, Gerald Jacob *physician, educator*
Sawyer, Howard Jerome *physician*

Ypsilanti
Ritter, Frank Nicholas *otolaryngologist, educator*

MINNESOTA

Detroit Lakes
Eginton, Charles Theodore *surgeon, educator*

Duluth
†Aufderheide, Arthur Carl *pathologist*
Eisenberg, Richard M. *pharmacology educator*

Excelsior
Bilka, Paul Joseph *physician*
French, Lyle Albert *surgeon*

Minneapolis
Balfour, Henry Hallowell, Jr. *medical educator, researcher, physician, writer*
Blackburn, Henry Webster, Jr. *physician*
Brown, David M. *physician, educator, dean*
Buchwald, Henry *surgeon, educator, researcher*
Burton, Charles Victor *physician, surgeon, inventor*
Caldwell, Michael DeFoix *surgeon, educator*
Cavert, Henry Mead *physician, retired educator*
Chisholm, Tague Clement *pediatric surgeon, educator*
Chou, Shelley Nien-chun *neurosurgeon, university official, educator*
†Clayton, Paula Jean *psychiatry educator*
Clinton, Joseph Edward *emergency physician*
Craig, James Lynn *physician, consumer products company executive*
Etzwiler, Donnell Dencil *pediatrician*
Ferris, Thomas Francis *physician*
Fisch, Robert Otto *medical educator*
Gault, N. L., Jr. *physician, educator*
Gedgaudas, Eugene *radiologist, educator*
Gorlin, Robert James *medical educator*
Gullickson, Glenn, Jr. *physician, educator*
†Hanson, A. Stuart *physician*
Holter, Arlen Rolf *cardiothoracic surgeon*
Horns, Howard Lowell *physician, educator*
Humphrey, Edward William *surgeon, medical educator*
Kane, Robert Lewis *public health educator*
Kaplan, Manuel E. *physician, educator*
Keane, William Francis *nephrology educator, research foundation executive*
Kennedy, B(yrl) J(ames) *medicine and oncology educator*
Kletschka, Harold Dale *cardiovascular surgeon, biomedical company executive*
Knopman, David S. *neurologist*
Lakin, James Dennis *allergist, immunologist*
Langer, Leonard O., Jr. *radiologist, educator*
Leon, Arthur Sol *research cardiologist, exercise physiologist*
Levitt, Seymour Herbert *physician, radiology educator*
†Luepker, Russell Vincent *epidemiology educator*
Lynch, Peter John *dermatologist*
Mazze, Roger Steven *medical educator, researcher*
McCullough, John Jeffrey *pathologist, research scientist, medical center administrator, educator*
McQuarrie, Donald Gray *surgeon, educator*
Michael, Alfred Frederick, Jr. *physician, medical educator*
Najarian, John Sarkis *surgeon, educator*
Paparella, Michael M. *otolaryngologist*
Phibbs, Clifford Matthew *surgeon, educator*
Polesky, Herbert Fred *physician*
Prem, Konald Arthur *physician, educator*
Quie, Paul Gerhardt *physician, educator*
Sabath, Leon David *internist, educator*
Shapiro, Fred Louis *physician, educator*
Staba, Emil John *pharmacognosy and medicinal chemistry educator*
Swaiman, Kenneth Fred *pediatric neurologist, educator*
Tagatz, George Elmo *obstetrician, gynecologist, educator*
Thompson, Theodore Robert *pediatric educator*
Thompson, William Moreau *radiologist, educator*
Torres, Fernando *physician, educator*
†Vernier, Robert Lawrence *physician, educator*
Ward, Wallace Dixon *medical educator*
Wescoe, W(illiam) Clarke *physician*
White, James George *pediatrician, hematologist, pathologist, educator*
Wild, John Julian *physician, director medical research institute*
Wilson, Leonard Gilchrist *history of medicine educator*
Winter, Robert Bruce *orthopaedic surgeon, educator*
Wirtschafter, Jonathan Dine *neuro-ophthalmology educator, scientist*
Wood, Joseph George *neurobiologist, educator*

Rochester
Bartholomew, Lloyd Gibson *physician*
Beahrs, Oliver Howard *surgeon*
Berge, Kenneth George *retired internist, educator*
Bisel, Harry Ferree *oncologist*
†Brimijoin, William Stephen *pharmacology educator, neuroscience researcher*
Bulbulian, Arthur H. *biomedical scientist, medical graphics and facial prosthetics specialist*
Butt, Hugh Roland *gastroenterologist, educator*
Corbin, Kendall Brooks *physician, scientist*
Danielson, Gordon Kenneth, Jr. *cardiovascular surgeon, educator*
DeRemee, Richard Arthur *physician, educator, researcher*
Douglass, Bruce E. *physician*
Du Shane, James William *physician, educator*
Engel, Andrew George *neurologist*
Feldt, Robert Hewitt *pediatric cardiologist, educator*
Gastineau, Clifford Felix *retired physician*
Gilchrist, Gerald Seymour *pediatric hematologist, oncologist, educator*
Gleich, Gerald Joseph *immunologist, medical scientist*
Gomez, Manuel Rodriguez *physician*
Gracey, Douglas Robert *physician, physiologist, educator*
Hattery, Robert R. *radiologist, educator*
Kempers, Roger Dyke *obstetrics and gynecology educator*
Keys, Thomas Edward *medical library consultant*
Kovach, John Stephen *oncologist, research center administrator*
Krom, Ruud Arne Finco *surgeon*
Kurland, Leonard Terry *epidemiologist educator*
Kyle, Robert Arthur *medical educator, oncologist*
Lofgren, Karl Adolph *surgeon*
Lucas, Alexander Ralph *child psychiatrist, educator*
Malkasian, George Durand, Jr. *physician, educator*
Martin, Gordon Mather *physician, educator, administrator*
Martin, Maurice John *psychiatrist*
Mc Goon, Dwight Charles *retired surgeon, educator*
Michenfelder, John Donahue *anesthesiology educator*
Morlock, Carl Grismore *physician, medical educator*
Mulder, Donald William *physician, educator*
Muller, Sigfrid Augustine *dermatologist, educator*
Neel, Harry Bryan, III *surgeon, scientist, educator*
Nichols, Donald Richardson *medical educator*
Olsen, Arthur Martin *physician, educator*
Payne, W(illiam) Spencer *retired surgeon*
Perry, Harold Otto *dermatologist*
Phillips, Sidney Frederick *gastroenterologist*
Pittelkow, Mark Robert *dermatology educator, researcher*
Polley, Howard Freeman *physician*
Pratt, Joseph Hyde, Jr. *surgeon*
Reed, Charles Emmett *internist, educator*
Reitemeier, Richard Joseph *physician*
Rosenow, Edward Carl, III *medical educator*
Siekert, Robert George *neurologist*
Stillwell, G(eorge) Keith *physician*
Symmonds, Richard Earl *gynecologist*
Waller, Robert Rex *ophthalmologist, educator, foundation executive*
Whisnant, Jack Page *neurologist*
Woods, John Elmer *plastic surgeon*

Saint Cloud
Conroy, Robert Warren *psychiatrist*

Saint Louis Park
Knighton, David Reed *vascular surgeon, educator*

Saint Paul
Burchell, Howard Bertram *retired physician, educator*
Dennis, Clarence *surgeon, educator*
Edwards, Jesse Efrem *physician, educator*
Fuller, Benjamin Franklin *physician, educator*
Lillehei, Clarence Walton *surgeon*
Rowe, Clarence John *psychiatrist*
Schultz, Alvin Leroy *internist, endocrinologist, health science facility administrator*
Titus, Jack L. *pathologist, educator*

Virginia
Knabe, George William, Jr. *pathologist, educator*

MISSISSIPPI

Jackson
Achord, James Lee *gastroenterologist, educator*
Ball, Carroll Raybourne *anatomist, medical educator, researcher*
Batson, Blair Everett *pediatrician, educator*
Bloom, Sherman *pathologist, educator*
Brooks, Thomas Joseph, Jr. *preventive medicine educator*
Cruse, Julius Major, Jr. *pathologist*
Currier, Robert David *neurologist*
Draper, Edgar *psychiatrist*
Forks, Thomas Paul *osteopathic physician*
Guyton, Arthur Clifton *physician, educator*
Halaris, Angelos *psychiatrist, educator*
Lewis, Robert Edwin, Jr. *pathology immunology educator, researcher*
Morrison, Francis Secrest *physician*
Nelson, Norman Crooks *surgeon, academic administrator, educator*
Seltzer, Ada May *librarian, medical library director*

MISSOURI

Chesterfield
Hunter, Harlen Charles *orthopedic surgeon*

Columbia
Allen, William Cecil *physician, educator*
†Barbero, Giulio John *physician, educator*
Bryant, Lester R. *surgeon, educator*
Colwill, Jack Marshall *physician, educator*
Eggers, George William Nordholtz, Jr. *anesthesiologist, educator*
Hillman, Richard Ephraim *pediatrician, educator*
Kashani, Javad Hassan-Nejad *physician*
Perkoff, Gerald Thomas *physician, educator*
Perry, Michael Clinton *physician, medical educator, academic administrator*
†Puckett, C. Lin *plastic surgeon, educator*
Silver, Donald *surgeon, educator*
Stephenson, Hugh Edward, Jr. *retired physician, educator*
Weiss, James Moses Aaron *psychiatrist, educator*
Witten, David Melvin *radiology educator*

Independence
Smith, Wallace Bunnell *physician, church official*

Joplin
†Singleton, Marvin Ayers *otolaryngologist, senator*

Kansas City
Abdou, Nabih I. *physician, educator*
Blim, Richard Don *pediatrician*
Dimond, Edmunds Grey *medical educator*
Ellfeldt, Howard James *orthopedic surgeon*
Graham, James Robert, III *physician, medical society administrator*
Grunt, Jerome Alvin *pediatric endocrinologist*
Hartzler, Geoffrey Oliver *cardiologist*
Holder, Thomas Martin *physician*
Hunzicker, Warren John *research consultant, physician, cardiologist*
Mc Coy, Frederick John *retired plastic surgeon*
Mebust, Winston Keith *surgeon, educator*
Moffatt, David John *anatomy educator*
Mongan, James John *physician*
Noback, Richardson Kilbourne *medical educator*
O'Hearne, John Joseph *psychiatrist*
Perrin, John Paul *medical school president*
Sauer, Gordon Chenoweth *physician, educator*
Schoolman, Arnold *neurological surgeon*
Wheeler, Charles Bertan *pathologist*

Neosho
Wilson, Alice Hornbuckle *retired physician*

North Kansas City
Hagan, John Charles, III *ophthalmologist*

Saint Charles
Dieterich, Russell Burks *obstetrician/gynecologist*

Saint Louis
Agrawal, Harish Chandra *neurobiologist, researcher, educator*
Alpers, David Hershel *physician, educator*
Anderson, Charles Bernard *surgeon, educator*
Backer, Matthias Henry, Jr. *obstetrician-gynecologist*
Ballinger, Walter Francis *surgeon, educator*
Baue, Arthur Edward *surgeon, educator, administrator*
Berg, Leonard *neurologist, educator*
Bird, Harrie Waldo, Jr. *psychiatrist, educator*
Bowen, Stephen Francis, Jr. *ophthalmic surgeon*
Brodeur, Armand Edward *pediatric radiologist*
Chaplin, Hugh, Jr. *physician, educator*
Cloninger, Claude Robert *psychiatric researcher, educator, genetic epdemiologist*
Cole, Barbara Ruth *pediatrician, nephrologist*
Colten, Harvey Radin *pediatrician, educator*
†Deuel, Thomas Franklin *physician*
Dewald, Paul Adolph *psychiatrist*
Dodge, Philip Rogers *physician, educator*
Drews, Robert Carrel *physician*
Evens, Ronald Gene *radiologist, medical center administrator*
Ferrendelli, James Anthony *neurologist, educator*
Fischer, Harry William *radiologist, educator*
Fitch, Coy Dean *physician, educator*
Fletcher, James Warren *physician*
Flye, M. Wayne *surgeon, immunologist, educator*
Fogarty, William Martin, Jr. *physician*
Frawley, Thomas Francis *physician*
†Fredrickson, John Murray *otolaryngologist*
Friedman, William Hersh *otolaryngologist, educator*
Guze, Samuel Barry *psychiatrist, educator, university official*
Hershey, Falls Bacon *surgeon, educator*
Hofstatter, Leopold *psychiatrist, researcher*
Joist, Johann Heinrich *hematologist, medical researcher, educator*
Kaplan, Henry Jerrold *ophthalmologist, educator*
Keltner, Raymond Marion, Jr. *surgeon, educator*
Kimmey, James Richard, Jr. *medical educator, consultant*
Kinsella, Ralph Aloysius, Jr. *physician*
Kipnis, David Morris *physician, educator*
Klahr, Saulo *physician, educator*
†Kodner, Ira J. *surgeon, educator*

Kolker, Allan Erwin *ophthalmologist*
Kouchoukos, Nicholas Thomas *surgeon*
Lacy, Paul Eston *pathologist*
Lagunoff, David *physician, educator*
Landau, William Milton *neurologist*
Levin, Marvin Edgar *physician*
Loeb, Virgil, Jr. *oncologist, hematologist*
Luther, George Aubrey *orthopedic surgeon*
Majerus, Philip Warren *physician*
Manske, Paul Robert *orthopedic hand surgeon, educator*
Masters, William Howell *physician, educator*
McFadden, James Frederick, Jr. *surgeon*
Middelkamp, John Neal *pediatrician, educator*
Minnich, Virginia *retired medical researcher, educator*
Owens, William Don *anesthesiology educator*
Peck, William Arno *physician*
Perez, Carlos A. *radiation oncologist, educator*
Petrie, Roy H. *obstetrician, gynecologist, educator*
Prensky, Arthur Lawrence *pediatric neurologist, educator*
Price, Joseph Levering *neuroscientist, educator*
Robins, Lee Nelken *medical educator*
†Santiago, Julio V. *medical educator, medical association administrator*
†Schonfeld, Gustav *medical educator*
Schwartz, Alan Leigh *pediatrician, educator*
Schwartz, Henry Gerard *surgeon, educator*
Shank, Robert Ely *physician, preventive medicine educator emeritus*
Slavin, Raymond Granam *allergist, immunologist*
Spector, Gershon Jerry *physician, educator, researcher*
†Strunk, Robert C. *physician*
Suba, Antonio Ronquillo *surgeon*
Sutter, Richard Anthony *physician*
Teitelbaum, Steven Lazarus *pathology educator*
Ternberg, Jessie Lamoin *pediatric surgeon*
Thach, William Thomas, Jr. *neurobiology and neurology educator*
Thomas, Lewis Jones, Jr. *anesthesiology educator, biomedical researcher*
†Ulett, George Andrew *psychiatrist*
Walz, Bruce James *radiation oncologist*
Weeks, Paul Martin *plastic surgeon, educator*
Wells, Samuel Alonzo, Jr. *surgeon, educator*
†Wickline, Samuel Alan *cardiologist, educator*
Willman, Vallee Louis *physician, surgery educator*
Wissner, Seth Ernst *gynecologist, educator*
Young, Paul Andrew *anatomist*

Springfield
Hackett, Earl Randolph *neurologist*
H'Doubler, Francis Todd, Jr. *surgeon*
Shealy, Clyde Norman *neurosurgeon*

Sweet Springs
Long, Edwin Tutt *surgeon*

University City
Shen, Jerome Tseng Yung *pediatrician*

MONTANA

Missoula
Fawcett, Don Wayne *anatomist*

Whitefish
Miller, Ronald Alfred *family physician*

Wolf Point
Listerud, Mark Boyd *retired surgeon*

NEBRASKA

Lincoln
Fuenning, Samuel Isaiah *sports medicine research director*
Hirai, Denitsu *surgeon*
Koszewski, Bohdan Julius *internist, medical educator*

Omaha
Brody, Alfred Walter *pulmonologist*
Casey, Murray Joseph *Obstetrician Gynecologist*
Cox, Robert Sayre, Jr. *pathologist, researcher, educator*
Davis, John Byron *surgeon*
Davis, Richard Bradley *internal medicine, pathology educator, physician*
Fusaro, Ramon Michael *dermatologist, researcher*
Gardner, Paul Jay *anatomist, educator*
Gordon, John Leo *anesthesiologist*
Harned, Roger Kent *radiology educator*
Heaney, Robert Proulx *physician, educator*
Hodgson, Paul Edmund *surgeon*
Imray, Thomas John *radiologist, educator*
†Klassen, Lynell W. *rheumatologist, transplant immunologist*
Korbitz, Bernard Carl *oncologist, hematologist, educator, consultant*
Lemon, Henry Martyn *physician, educator*
Maurer, Harold Maurice *pediatrician*
Mohiuddin, Syed Maqdoom *cardiologist, educator*
O'Donohue, Walter John, Jr. *medical educator*
Pearson, Paul Hammond *physician*
†Rikkers, Layton F. *surgeon*
Ruddon, Raymond Walter, Jr. *pharmacology educator*
†Rupp, Mark Edmund *medical educator*
Sanders, W(illiam) Eugene, Jr. *physician, educator*
Sheehan, John Francis *cytopathologist, educator*
Skoog, Donald Paul *retired physician, educator*
Truhlsen, Stanley Marshall *physician, educator*
Waggener, Ronald Edgar *radiologist*

Papillion
Dvorak, Allen Dale *radiologist*

NEVADA

Las Vegas
Bandt, Paul Douglas *physician*
Barger, James Daniel *physician*
Brown, Brice Norman *surgeon, educator*
DeFelice, Eugene Anthony *physician, medical educator, consultant, magician*
Hamilton, Richard Lee *surgeon*
Herte, Mary Charlotte *plastic surgeon*
Lazerson, Jack *pediatrician, educator*
Sabanas-Wells, Alvina Olga *orthopedic surgeon*
Shettles, Landrum Brewer *obstetrician-gynecologist*

Reno
Barnet, Robert Joseph *cardiologist*
Di Salvo, Arthur Francis *physician, public health official*

NEW HAMPSHIRE

Bristol
Fisher, Robert George *neurological surgeon, educator*

Etna
Ferm, Vergil Harkness *anatomist, embryologist*

Grantham
†MacNeill, Arthur Edson *physician, science consultant*

Hanover
Almy, Thomas Pattison *physician, educator*
Cahill, George Francis, Jr. *physician, educator*
Chapman, Carleton Burke *physician*
Koop, Charles Everett *surgeon, government official*
McCollum, Robert Wayne *physician, educator*
†Morain, William D. *surgeon, educator*
Staples, O. Sherwin *orthopaedic surgeon*
Wallace, Andrew Grover *physician*
Zubkoff, Michael *medical educator*

Hooksett
†Bagan, Merwyn *neurological surgeon*

Lebanon
Clendenning, William Edmund *dermatologist*
Cornwell, Gibbons Gray, III *physician, medical educator*
Galton, Valerie Anne *endocrinology educator*
Kelley, Maurice Leslie, Jr. *gastroenterologist, educator*
McIntyre, Oswald Ross *physician*
Myers, Warren Powers Laird *physician, educator*
Rawnsley, Howard Melody *physician, educator*
Rolett, Ellis Lawrence *medical educator, cardiologist*
Rous, Stephen Norman *urologist, educator*
Smith, Barry David *obstetrician-gynecologist, educator*
Sox, Harold Carleton, Jr. *physician, educator*
Wallace, Harold James, Jr. *physician*

Manchester
Emery, Paul Emile *psychiatrist*

NEW JERSEY

Beach Haven
Brunt, Harry Herman, Jr. *psychiatrist*

Camden
Ances, I. G(eorge) *obstetrician/gynecologist, educator*
Morrison, Ashton Byrom *pathologist, medical school official*

Cherry Hill
Adams, Raymond Edward *ophthalmologist*
Margolis, Gerald Joseph *psychiatrist, educator*
Olearchyk, Andrew S. *cardiothoracic surgeon, educator*

Cresskill
Gardner, Richard Alan *psychiatrist, writer*

East Brunswick
Rosenberg, Norman *surgeon*

East Hanover
Anderson, Gary William *physician*
Finkel, Marion Judith *physician*

Flemington
Accettola, Albert Bernard *orthopedic surgeon, educator*
Katcher, Avrum L. *pediatrician*

Florham Park
McDonagh, Thomas Joseph *physician*

Franklin Lakes
Ginsberg, Barry Howard *physician, researcher*

Glen Ridge
Clemente, Celestino *physician, surgeon*

Hackensack
Gross, Peter Alan *epidemiologist, researcher*
Layman, William Arthur *psychiatrist, educator*
Spackman, Thomas James *radiologist*

Haddonfield
Capelli, John Placido *nephrologist*

Hanover
Salans, Lester Barry *physician, scientist, educator*

Jamesburg
Miller, Theodore Robert *surgeon, educator*

Jersey City
Melnick, Gilbert Stanley *radiologist, educator*

Lakewood
Bowers, John Zimmerman *physician, historian, educator*

Livingston
Caballes, Romeo Lopez *pathologist, bone tumor researcher*
Krieger, Abbott Joel *neurosurgeon*

Long Branch
Arvanitis, Cyril Steven *surgeon, educator*
Barnett, Lester Alfred *surgeon*

Manalapan
Harrison-Johnson, Yvonne Elois *pharmacologist*

Marlton
Byerly, LeRoy James *psychiatrist, educator*

Mendham
Desjardins, Raoul *medical association administrator, financial consultant*

Metuchen
Jacobey, John Arthur, III *surgeon, educator*

Montclair
Behrle, Franklin Charles *physician*
Fleming, Thomas Crawley *physician, medical director, former editor*

Moorestown
†Colburn, Harold L. *dermatologist, state legislator*

Morristown
Granet, Roger B. *psychiatrist, educator*
Lindner, Joseph, Jr. *physician, medical administrator*
Parr, Grant Van Siclen *surgeon*

Neptune
Harrigan, John Thomas, Jr. *physician, obstetrician-gynecologist*

New Brunswick
Ettinger, Lawrence Jay *pediatric hematologist-oncologist, educator*
Gocke, David Joseph *immunology educator, physician, medical scientist*
Scully, John Thomas *obstetrician, gynecologist, educator*
†Seibold, James Richard *physician, researcher*
Snyderman, Reuven Kenneth *plastic surgeon, educator*

Newark
Baker, Herman *vitaminologist*
Ben-Menachem, Yoram *radiologist*
Cinotti, Alfonse Anthony *ophthalmologist, educator*
Cook, Stuart Donald *physician, educator*
Eslami, Hossein Hojatol *surgeon, educator*
Evans, Hugh E. *pediatrician*
Gardner, Bernard *surgeon, educator*
Goldenberg, David Milton *experimental pathologist, oncologist*
Hill, George James *surgeon, educator*
Hobson, Robert Wayne, II *surgeon*
Hutcheon, Duncan Elliot *physician, educator*
Iffy, Leslie *medical educator*
Leevy, Carroll Moton *medical educator, hepatology researcher*
Reichman, Lee Brodersohn *physician*
Weiss, Gerson *physician, educator*

Nutley
Burns, John Joseph *pharmacology educator*
Connor, John Arthur *neuroscientist*
Kuntzman, Ronald *pharmacology research executive*
Mostillo, Ralph *medical association executive*

Oldwick
Blewitt, George Augustine *physician, pharmaceutical company executive*

Paramus
Bagli, Vincent Joseph *plastic surgeon*

Passaic
Haddad, Jamil Raouf *physician*

Piscataway
Bretschneider, Ann Margery *histotechnologist*
Conney, Allan Howard *pharmacologist*
Edelman, Norman H. *medical educator*
Murphree, Henry Bernard Scott *psychiatry educator, consultant*
Pollack, Irwin William *psychiatrist, educator*
Shea, Stephen Michael *physician, educator*

Point Pleasant Beach
Motley, John Paul *psychiatrist, consultant*

Princeton
Bunn, William Bernice, III *physician, lawyer, epidemiologist*
Carver, David Harold *physician, educator*
Chandler, James John *surgeon*
Conn, Hadley Lewis, Jr. *physician, educator*
Khachadurian, Avedis *physician*
McKearn, Thomas Joseph *immunology and pathology educator, scientist*
Mueller, Peter Sterling *psychiatrist, educator*
Napoliello, Michael John *psychiatrist*
Reynolds, Richard Clyde *physician, foundation administrator*
Rosenberg, Leon E. *medical educator, geneticist, university dean*
Schroeder, Steven Alfred *medical educator, researcher, foundation executive*
Sugerman, Abraham Arthur *psychiatrist*
Weiss, Robert Jerome *psychiatrist, educator*

Short Hills
Aviado, Domingo M. *pharmacologist, toxicologist*

Stratford
†Humphrey, Frederick James, II *educator, child psychiatrist, psychoanalyst*

Teaneck
Churg, Jacob *pathologist*
Ngai, Shih Hsun *physician*

Tenafly
Cosgriff, Stuart Worcester *internist, consultant*

Trenton
Weinberg, Martin Herbert *psychiatrist*

Ventnor City
Zuckerman, Stuart *psychiatrist, educator*

Voorhees
Barone, Donald Anthony *neurologist, educator*

West New York
Carluccio, Charles Goldhammer *physician*

West Orange
Brodkin, Roger Harrison *dermatologist, educator*

West Trenton
Roman, Cecelia Florence *cardiologist*

White House Station
Douglas, Robert Gordon, Jr. *physician*
Levey, Gerald Saul *physician, educator*

Whiting
Williams, Roger Wright *public health educator*

Woodstown
Crouse, Farrell Rondall *psychiatrist, physician*

Wyckoff
Bauer, Theodore James *physician*

NEW MEXICO

Alamogordo
Stapp, John Paul *surgeon, former air force officer*

Albuquerque
Ballard, David Eugene *anesthesiologist*
Barbo, Dorothy Marie *obstetrician-gynecologist, educator*
Buss, William Charles *research pharmacology educator*
Dixon, George Lane, Jr. *orthopaedic surgeon*
Doberneck, Raymond C. *surgical educator*
Edwards, William Sterling, III *cardiovascular surgeon*
Kelley, Robert Otis *medical science educator*
McCarty, W(illard) Duane *obstetrician-gynecologist, physician executive*
Napolitano, Leonard Michael *anatomist, university administrator*
Neidhart, James Allen *physician, educator*
Omer, George Elbert, Jr. *orthopaedic surgeon, hand surgeon, educator*
Ottensmeyer, David Joseph *neurosurgeon, health care executive*
Pasternak, Derick Peter *physician, medical center executive*
Tatum, Ronald Winston *physician, endocrinologist*
Uhlenhuth, Eberhard Henry *psychiatrist, educator*
Winslow, Walter William *psychiatrist*

Carlsbad
Markle, George Bushar, IV *surgeon*

Chama
Moser, Robert Harlan *physician, educator*

Las Cruces
Jacobs, Kent Frederick *dermatologist*
Reeves, Billy Dean *obstetrics/gynecology educator emeritus*

Roswell
†Jennings, Emmit M. *surgeon*

Santa Fe
Schwartz, George R. *physician*
Upton, Arthur Canfield *experimental pathologist, educator*

Sante Fe
†Frenkel, Jacob Karl *physician, consultant, researcher*

NEW YORK

Albany
Beebe, Richard Townsend *physician*
Bradley, Wesley Holmes *physician*
Davis, Paul Joseph *endocrinologist*
Dougherty, James *orthopedic surgeon, educator*
Doyle, Joseph Theobald *physician, educator*
Gellhorn, Alfred *physician, educator*
†Gruber, Scott Alan *medical educator*
Han, Jaok *cardiologist, researcher, educator*
Hoffmeister, Jana Marie *cardiologist*
Kaye, Gordon Israel *pathologist, anatomist, educator*
Lumpkin, Lee Roy *dermatologist, educator*
Macario, Alberto Juan Lorenzo *physician*
Mihm, Martin Charles, Jr. *pathologist, educator*
Swartz, Donald Percy *physician*

Amherst
Howland, Murray Shipley, Jr. *gastroenterologist*

Armonk
Mellors, Robert Charles *physician scientist*

Bath
Huang, Edwin I-Chuen *physician, environmental researcher*
Sandt, John Joseph *psychiatrist, educator*

Briarcliff Manor
Gaylin, Willard *physician, educator*
Glassman, Jerome Martin *clinical pharmacologist, educator*
Weintraub, Michael Ira *neurologist*

Bronx
Bhalodkar, Narendra Chandrakant *cardiologist*
Blaufox, Morton Donald *physician, educator*
Brescia, Michael Joseph *physician*
Bruenn, Howard Gerald *physician*
Burde, Ronald Marshall *neuro-ophthalmologist*
Buschke, Herman *neurologist*
Cherkasky, Martin *physician*
Cimino, James Ernest *physician*
Cohen, Herbert Jesse *physician, educator*
DeMartino, Anthony Gabriel *cardiologist, internist*
Duncalf, Deryck *anesthesiologist*

Edelmann, Chester Monroe, Jr. pediatrician, medical school dean
Eder, Howard Abram physician
Elkin, Milton radiologist, physician, educator
†Foreman, Spencer pulmonary specialist, hospital executive
Frater, Robert William Mayo surgeon, educator
Freeman, Leonard Murray radiologist, nuclear medicine physician, educator
Fulop, Milford physician
Gerst, Paul Howard physician
Gliedman, Marvin L. surgeon, educator
Gross, Ludwik physician
Hait, Gershon pediatric cardiologist
†Hein, Karen K. pediatrician, epidemiologist
Hirano, Asao neuropathologist
Jacobson, Harold Gordon radiologist, educator
Jaffé, Ernst Richard medical educator and administrator
Kahn, Thomas medical educator
Karasu, T(oksoz) Byram psychiatry educator
Karmen, Arthur physician, science administrator, educator
Koss, Leopold G. pathologist, educator, physician
Lieber, Charles Saul physician, educator
Marx, Gertie Florentine anesthesiologist
Muschel, Louis Henry immunologist, educator
Nagler, Arnold Leon pathologist, scientist, educator
Nathenson, Stanley Gail immunology educator
Orkin, Louis Richard physician, educator
Pitchumoni, Capecomorin Sankar gastroenterologist, educator
Purpura, Dominick P. neuroscientist, university dean
Rapin, Isabelle physician
Reynolds, Benedict Michael surgeon
Romney, Seymour Leonard physician, educator
Ruben, Robert Joel physician, educator
Scharff, Matthew Daniel immunologist, cell biologist, educator
Scharrer, Berta Vogel anatomy and neuroscience educator
Schaumburg, Herbert Howard neurology educator
Shafritz, David Andrew physician, research scientist
Spitzer, Adrian pediatrician, medical educator
†Stein, Ruth Elizabeth Klein physician
Sterling, Kenneth research physician, educator
Surks, Martin I. medical educator, endocrinologist
Waltz, Joseph McKendree neurosurgeon, educator
Wiernik, Peter Harris oncologist, educator
Williams, Marshall Henry, Jr. physician, educator

Bronxville
Barkhuus, Arne physician

Brooklyn
Alfonso, Antonio Escolar surgeon
Bergeron, R. Thomas radiologist, educator
Biro, Laszlo dermatologist
Cracco, Roger Quinlan medical educator, neurologist
Enquist, Irving Fridtjof surgeon
Finberg, Laurence pediatrician, educator, college dean
Friedman, Eli A. nephrologist
Friedman, Howard Samuel cardiologist, educator
Gintautas, Jonas physician, scientist, administrator
Glickman, Franklin Sheldon dermatologist, educator
Gotta, Alexander Walter anesthesiologist, educator
Holden, David Morgan medical educator
Imperato, Pascal James physician, health administrator, author, editor, medical educator
Kamholz, Stephan L. physician
Lee, Stanley physician, educator
Leeman, Cavin Philip psychiatrist, educator
Levere, Richard David physician, academic administrator, educator
Malach, Monte physician
Milhorat, Thomas Herrick neurosurgeon
Namba, Tatsuji physician, researcher
Norstrand, Iris Fletcher psychiatrist, neurologist, educator
Plotz, Charles Mindell physician
Ravitz, Leonard J., Jr. physician, scientist, consultant
Reich, Nathaniel Edwin physician, artist, educator
Schwarz, Richard Howard obstetrician/gynecologist, educator
Shalita, Alan Remi dermatologist
Weiner, Irwin M. medical educator, college dean, researcher
Wolintz, Arthur Harry physician, neuro-ophthalmologist
Wollman, Leo physician

Buffalo
Ambrus, Clara Maria physician
Ambrus, Julian L. physician, medical educator
Ament, Richard anesthesiologist, educator
Bakay, Louis neurosurgeon
Brody, Harold neuroanatomist, gerontologist
Brooks, John Samuel Joseph pathologist, researcher
Calkins, Evan physician, educator
Chu, Tsann Ming immunochemist, educator
Chutkow, Jerry Grant neurologist, educator
Creaven, Patrick Joseph physician, research oncologist
Glasauer, Franz Ernst neurosurgeon
Graham, (Lloyd) Saxon epidemiology educator
Gresham, Glen Edward physician
Helm, Frederick dermatology educator
Horoszewicz, Juliusz Stanislaw oncologist, cancer researcher, laboratory administrator
Kurlan, Marvin Zeft surgeon
Lee, Richard Vaille physician, educator
Maloney, Milford Charles internal medicine educator
Middleton, Elliott, Jr. physician
Milgrom, Felix immunologist, educator
Mindell, Eugene Robert surgeon, educator
Mirand, Edwin Albert medical scientist
Naughton, John Patrick cardiologist, medical school administrator
Panaro, Victor Anthony radiologist
Regan, Peter Francis, III physician, psychiatry educator
Rekate, Albert C. physician
Richmond, Allen Martin speech pathologist, educator
Seller, Robert Herman cardiologist, family physician
Shedd, Donald Pomroy surgeon
Small, S(aul) Mouchly psychiatrist, educator
Stoll, Howard Lester, Jr. dermatologist
Wright, John Robert pathologist
Zaleski, Marek Bohdan immunologist

Canaan
Bell, James Milton psychiatrist

Carle Place
Linchitz, Richard Michael psychiatrist, physician

Castle Point
Greene, Jerry George physician

Centerport
Fischel, Edward Elliot physician

Chestnut Ridge
Day, Stacey Biswas physician, educator

Cooperstown
Blumenstock, David Albert retired surgeon
†Pearson, Thomas Arthur epidemiologist, educator

East Islip
Fleishman, Philip Robert internist

East Meadow
Rachlin, Stephen Leonard psychiatrist

Eatons Neck
Altner, Peter Christian orthopedic surgeon, medical educator

Edmeston
Price, James Melford physician

Glenmont
Kolb, Lawrence Coleman psychiatrist

Great Neck
Arlow, Jacob A. psychiatrist, educator
Simon, Arthur pharmacologist, research laboratory executive

Hawthorne
Swift, Michael Ronald physician, scientist, educator

Hempstead
Laano, Archie Bienvenido Maaño cardiologist

Ithaca
Moore, Norman Slawson physician
Whitaker, Susanne Kanis veterinary medical librarian

Jamaica
Rosner, Fred physician, educator
Seltzer, Vicki Lynn obstetrician-gynecologist

Larchmont
Bellak, Leopold psychiatrist, psychoanalyst, psychologist
Gillman, Arthur Emanuel psychiatrist
Holleb, Arthur Irving surgeon

Lawrence
Sklarin, Burton S. endocrinologist

Lockport
Carr, Edward Albert, Jr. pharmacology educator, physician

Lowville
Becker, Robert Otto orthopedic surgery educator

Mamaroneck
Halpern, Abraham Leon psychiatrist

Manhasset
Arnold, Charles Burle, Jr. psychiatrist, epidemiologist, writer
Fenton, Arnold N. obstetrician, gynecologist, educator
Kreis, Willi physician
Meilman, Edward physician
Scherr, Lawrence physician, educator
Warren, Kenneth S. medical educator, physician

Massapequa
Aiello-Contessa, Angela Marie physician

Merrick
Copperman, Stuart Morton pediatrician
Dubov, Spencer Floyd podiatrist, educator

Mineola
Maulik, Dev obstetrician-gynecologist, educator

Monroe
Werzberger, Alan pediatrician

Monticello
Lauterstein, Joseph cardiologist

Naples
Beal, Myron Clarence osteopathic physician

New Hyde Park
Koplewicz, Harold Samuel child and adolescent psychiatrist
Lanzkowsky, Philip physician
Wolf, Julius medical educator

New Rochelle
†Hayes, Arthur Hull, Jr. physician, clinical pharmacology educator, medical school dean, business executive, consultant
Petrucelli, R(occo) Joseph, II nephrologist
Rovinsky, Joseph Judah obstetrician, gynecologist

New York
Abrahamsen, David psychiatrist, psychoanalyst, author
Abramson, Sara Jane radiologist, educator
Adamson, John William hematologist
Ahrens, Edward Hamblin, Jr. physician
†Alderson, Philip Otis radiologist, educator
Altman, Lawrence Kimball physician, journalist
Altman, Roy Peter pediatric surgeon
Archibald, Reginald Mac Gregor physician, chemist, educator
†Arnot, Bob physician, medical correspondent
Aron, Alan Milford pediatric neurology educator
Aronoff, Michael Stephen psychiatrist
Asanuma, Hiroshi physician, educator
Atkinson, Holly Gail physician, journalist, author, lecturer
Aufses, Arthur H(arold), Jr. surgeon, medical educator
Baden, Michael M. pathologist, educator
Baer, Rudolf Lewis dermatologist, educator
Baldwin, David Shepard physician
Barker, Barbara Ann ophthalmologist
Barnett, Henry Lewis medical educator, pediatrician
Barondess, Jeremiah Abraham physician
Bearn, Alexander Gordon physician scientist, former pharmaceutical company executive
Beattie, Edward James surgeon, educator
Beck, Adrian Robert surgeon, educator
Bekesi, Julis George medical researcher
Bendixen, Henrik Holt physician, educator, dean
†Ben-Yishay, Yehuda medical educator
Berger, Frank Milan biomedical researcher, scientist, former pharmaceutical company executive
Berk, Paul David physician, scientist, educator
Bernstein, Anne Elayne psychoanalyst
Bertino, Joseph Rocco physician, educator
Bertles, John Francis physician, educator
Betcher, Albert Maxwell anesthesiologist
Bickers, David Rinsey physician, educator
†Biedler, June L. oncologist
Bigger, John Thomas, Jr. physician, educator
Biller, Hugh Frederick medical educator
Blank, Marion Sue psychologist
Blitzer, Andrew otolaryngologist, educator
Bogdonoff, Morton David physician, educator
Bonforte, Richard James pediatrician, educator
Borer, Jeffrey Stephen cardiologist
Bosniak, Morton Arthur physician, educator
Brand, Leonard physician, educator
Braude, Robert Michael medical library administrator
Breinin, Goodwin M. physician
Brennan, Murray Frederick surgeon, oncologist
†Breslow, Jan Leslie scientist, educator, physician
Brook, David William psychiatrist
Brown, Jason Walter neurologist, educator, researcher
Butler, Robert Neil gerontologist, psychiatrist, writer, educator
Butler, Vincent Paul, Jr. physician, educator
Buxton, Jorge Norman ophthalmologist
Bystryn, Jean-Claude dermatologist, educator
Cahan, William George surgeon, educator
Calder, Kenneth Thomas psychiatrist, psychoanalyst, educator
Cancro, Robert psychiatrist
Candia, Oscar A. ophthalmologist, physiology educator
Cantor, Richard Ira physician, corporate health executive
Carr, Ronald Edward ophthalmologist, educator
Casals-Ariet, Jordi physician
Cassell, Eric Jonathan physician
Castellino, Ronald Augustus Dietrich radiologist
Chan, W. Y. pharmacologist, educator
Chaney, Verne Edward, Jr. surgeon, foundation executive, educator
Chase, Merrill Wallace immunologist, educator
Clark, William Stratton physician
Cohen, Noel Lee otolaryngologist, educator
Coleman, D. Jackson ophthalmologist, educator
Coleman, Lester Laudy otolaryngologist
Coleman, Morton oncologist, hematologist, educator
Cooper, Arnold Michael psychiatrist
Cooper, Norman Streich pathologist, medical educator
Crain, Irving Jay psychiatrist, educator
Cramer, Marjorie plastic surgeon
Cranefield, Paul Frederic pharmacology educator, physician, scientist
Curtin, Brian Joseph ophthalmologist
Daniel, Gerard Lucian physician, pharmaceutical company executive
†Davis, Kenneth Leon psychiatrist, pharmacologist, medical educator
Dell, Ralph Bishop pediatrician, researcher
De Vivo, Darryl Claude pediatric neurologist
Dohrenwend, Bruce Philip psychiatric epidemiologist, social psychologist, educator
Dole, Vincent Paul medical research executive, educator
Dolgin, Martin cardiologist
Douglas, Gordon Watkins medical educator
Downey, John Alexander physician, educator
Doyle, Eugenie Fleri pediatric cardiologist, educator
Dworetzky, Murray physician, educator
Edmunds, Robert Thomas retired surgeon
Ego-Aguirre, Ernesto surgeon
Ehlers, Kathryn Hawes (Mrs. James D. Gabler) physician
Ellis, John Taylor pathologist, educator
Ellis, Kent radiologist, consultant
Ellsworth, Robert Malcolm ophthalmologist, educator
Ergas, Enrique orthopedic surgeon
Esman, Aaron H. physician, psychiatrist
Fahn, Stanley neurologist, educator
Fair, William Robert physician
†Farber, Saul Joseph physician, educator
Feldman, Samuel Mitchell neuroscientist, educator
Fellner, Michael Josef dermatologist
Ferrer, Marie Irene physician
†Foley, Kathleen M. neurologist, educator, researcher
Fortner, Joseph Gerald surgeon, educator
Fox, Arthur Charles physician, educator
†Frankel, Alice Kross physician, director
Frantz, Andrew Gibson physician
Freedberg, Irwin Mark dermatologist
Friedewald, William Thomas physician
Friedhoff, Arnold J. psychiatrist, medical scientist
Friedman, Alan Herbert ophthalmologist
Friedman, Emanuel A. medical educator
Friedman, Ira Hugh surgeon
Fuchs, Anna-Riitta medical educator, scientist
Fuchs, Fritz physician, educator, researcher
Fuks, Zvi Y. medical educator
Furmanski, Philip cancer research scientist
Fuster, Valentin cardiologist, educator
Gabrilove, Jacques Lester physician
Galanter, Marc psychiatrist, educator
Galbraith, Richard Anthony physician, hospital administrator
Galin, Miles A. ophthalmologist, educator
Genkins, Gabriel physician
Gershengorn, Marvin Carl physician, scientist, educator
Gersony, Welton Mark physician, pediatric cardiologist, educator
Gertler, Menard M. physician, educator
Ginsberg-Fellner, Fredda pediatric endocrinologist, researcher
Glassman, Alexander Howard psychiatrist, researcher
Godman, Gabriel Charles pathology educator
Golde, David William physician, educator
Goldsmith, Stanley Joseph nuclear medicine physician, educator
Golomb, Frederick Martin surgeon, educator
Gordon, Ronnie Roslyn pediatrics educator, consultant
Gorlin, Richard physician, educator
Gotschlich, Emil Claus physician, educator
Graber, Edward Alex obstetrician, gynecologist, educator
Grant, Alfred D. orthopaedic surgeon, educator
Green, Jack Peter pharmacology educator, medical scientist
Green, Maurice Richard neuropsychiatrist
Greengard, Paul neuroscientist
Griffiths, Sylvia Preston physician
Guida, Peter Matthew surgeon, educator
Gusberg, Saul Bernard physician, educator
Guthrie, Randolph Hobson, Jr. plastic surgeon
Haddad, Heskel Marshall ophthalmologist
Halberg, G. Peter ophthalmologist
Hambrick, George Walter, Jr. dermatologist, educator
Hamburg, Beatrix Ann medical educator, researcher
Hamburg, David A. psychiatrist, foundation executive
Harley, Naomi Hallden radiation specialist, environmental medicine educator
Harris, Henry William physician
Hawkins, Katherine Ann hematologist
Hilgartner, Margaret Wehr pediatric hematologist, educator
†Hirsch, Jules physician, scientist
Hirschhorn, Kurt pediatrics educator
Hirschman, Shalom Zarach physician
Hofer, Myron A(rms) psychiatrist, researcher
Holt, Peter Rolf physician, educator
Hoskins, William John obstetrician/gynecologist, educator
Hugo, Norman Eliot plastic surgeon, medical educator
Hurvitz, Arthur Isaac pathologist, researcher
Hyman, Bruce Malcolm ophthalmologist
Imparato, Anthony Michael vascular surgeon, medical educator, researcher
Isay, Richard Alexander psychiatrist
Janowitz, Henry David physician, researcher, medical educator
Jarecki, Henry George physician, financial executive
Jelinek, Josef Emil dermatologist
Johnson, Horton Anton pathologist
Jonas, Saran neurologist, educator
Kabat, Elvin Abraham immunochemist, biochemist, educator
Kahn, Norman pharmacology and dentistry educator
Kalsner, Stanley pharmacologist, physiologist, educator
Kaplan, Harold Irwin psychiatrist, psychoanalyst, educator
Kappas, Attallah physician, medical scientist
Kellerman, Jonathan Seth pediatric psychologist, writer
Kelman, Charles D. ophthalmologist, educator
King, Thomas Creighton thoracic surgeon, educator
Klein, Donald Franklin scientist, psychiatrist, educator
Kligfield, Paul David physician, medicine educator
Kolodny, Edwin Hillel neurologist, geneticist, medical administrator
Komisar, Arnold otolaryngologist, educator
Kosovich, Dushan Radovan psychiatrist
Krugman, Saul physician, educator, researcher
Kupfer, Sherman physician, educator, researcher
Kwa, Raymond Pain-Boon cardiologist
Landrigan, Philip John epidemiologist
†Laragh, John Henry physician, scientist, educator
Lattes, Raffaele physician, educator
Lattimer, John Kingsley physician, educator
Lauersen, Niels Helth physician, educator
Laufman, Harold surgeon
†Laurence, Jeffrey Conrad immunologist
Lawrence, Henry Sherwood physician, educator
Lawrence, Robert Swan physician, educator, foundation executive
Lawry, Sylvia (Mrs. Stanley Englander) association executive
Ledger, William Joe physician, educator
†Lee, Mathew Hung Mun physiatrist
Leiter, Elliot urologist
Lepore, Michael Joseph gastroenterologist, educator
Levin, Aaron Reuben pediatrician, educator
Lewis, John Leeman, Jr. obstetrician, gynecologist
Lifton, Robert Jay psychiatrist, author
Lin, Joseph Pen-Tze neuroradiologist, clinical administrator, educator
Lipkin, Mack, Jr. psychiatrist, researcher, educator
Lipkin, Martin physician, scientist
Lipton, Lester ophthalmologist, entrepreneur
†Liu, Brian Cheong-Seng urology and oncology educator, researcher
Localio, S. Arthur retired surgeon, educator
Lubkin, Virginia Leila ophthalmologist
MacKinnon, Roger Alan psychiatrist
Malis, Leonard Irving neurosurgeon
Malitz, Sidney psychiatrist, educator, researcher
Malkin, Stanley Lee neurologist
Malm, James Royal surgeon
Manger, William Muir internist
Marbury, Benjamin Edward anesthesiologist
Marks, Paul Alan oncologist, cell biologist, educator
Marsh, William Laurence retired research pathology executive
Masterson, James Francis psychiatrist
Matz, Robert physician, educator
Mazzia, Valentino Don Bosco physician, educator, lawyer
McCarthy, Joseph Gerald plastic surgeon, educator
McCarty, Maclyn medical scientist
Mc Crory, Wallace Willard pediatrician, educator
McGovern, John Hugh urologist, educator
Mc Murtry, James Gilmer, III neurosurgeon
Meikle, Thomas Harry, Jr. foundation administrator, neuroscientist, educator
Mellins, Robert B. pediatrician, educator
Mendelsohn, John oncologist, hematologist, educator
Mesnikoff, Alvin Murray psychiatry educator
Michels, Robert psychiatrist
Mildvan, Donna infectious diseases physician
Miller, Edward Doring, Jr. anesthesiologist
Millman, Robert Barnet psychiatry and public health educator
Mohr, Jay Preston neurologist
Moore, Malcolm Andrew Stephen cancer researcher
Morales, Pablo A. urologist
Myers, Wayne Alan psychiatrist, educator

Nahas, Gabriel Georges *pharmacologist, educator*
Nathan, Carl Francis *medical educator*
Neu, Harold Conrad *physician, educator*
Neubauer, Peter Bela *psychoanalyst*
Neuwirth, Robert Samuel *obstetrician, gynecologist*
New, Maria Iandolo *physician, educator*
Newbold, Herbert Leon, Jr. *psychiatrist, writer*
Newman, Robert Gabriel *physician*
Noback, Charles Robert *anatomist, educator*
Novick, Nelson Lee *dermatologist, internist, writer*
Oettgen, Herbert Friedrich *physician*
Old, Lloyd John *cancer biologist*
Oldham, John Michael *physician, psychiatrist, educator*
Olsson, Carl Alfred *urologist*
Pacella, Bernard Leonardo *psychiatrist*
Pardes, Herbert *psychiatrist, educator*
Pastorek, Norman Joseph *facial plastic surgeon*
Patterson, Russel Hugo, Jr. *neurosurgeon, educator*
Peck, M(organ) Scott *psychiatrist, writer*
Pfaff, Donald W. *neurobiology and behavior educator*
Phillips, Gerald Baer *internal medicine educator, scientist*
Pierson, Richard Norris, Jr. *medical educator*
Pirani, Conrad Levi *pathologist, educator*
†Pi-Sunyer, F. Xavier *medical educator, medical investigator*
Posner, Jerome Beebe *neurologist, educator*
Post, Joseph *physician, researcher, consultant*
Potter, Guy Dill *radiologist, educator*
Rabinowitz, Jack Grant *radiologist, educator*
Rainer, John David *psychiatrist*
Raynor, Richard Benjamin *neurosurgeon, educator*
Redo, S(averio) Frank *surgeon*
Reidenberg, Marcus Milton *physician, educator*
Reis, Donald Jeffery *neurologist, neurobiologist, educator*
Reisberg, Barry *geropsychiatrist, neuropsychopharmacologist*
Rifkin, Harold *physician, educator*
Riker, Walter F., Jr. *pharmacologist, physician*
†Roberts, James Lewis *medical sciences educator*
Rogers, David Elliott *physician, educator, author*
†Rom, William N. *physician*
†Roman, Stanford Augustus, Jr. *medical educator, dean*
Rosenfield, Allan *physician*
Rothenberg, Robert Edward *physician, surgeon, author*
Rowland, Lewis Phillip *neurologist, medical editor, educator*
†Rubin, Albert L. *physician, educator*
Rubin, Gustav *orthopedic surgeon, consultant, researcher*
Rubin, Theodore Isaac *psychiatrist*
Sachar, David Bernard *gastroenterologist, medical educator*
Sachdev, Ved Parkash *neurosurgeon*
Sacks, Oliver Wolf *neurologist, writer*
Sadock, Benjamin James *psychiatrist, educator*
Sager, Clifford J(ulius) *psychiatrist, educator*
Santulli, Thomas Vincent *surgeon*
Sawyer, William Dale *physician, educator, university dean, foundation administrator*
†Scheinberg, Labe Charles *physician, educator*
Schiavi, Raul Constante *psychiatrist, educator, researcher*
Schlesinger, David Harvey *medical educator, researcher*
Schlesinger, Edward Bruce *neurological surgeon*
†Schlessinger, Joseph *pharmacology educator*
Schneck, Jerome M. *psychiatrist, medical historian, educator*
Schwartz, Irving Leon *physician, scientist, educator*
Schwartz, Roselind Shirley Grant *podiatrist*
Schwimmer, David *physician, educator*
Seaman, William Bernard *physician, radiology educator*
Sedlin, Elias David *physician, orthopedic researcher, educator*
Seely, Robert Daniel *physician, medical educator*
Shaffer, David *psychiatrist*
Shapiro, Theodore *psychiatrist, educator*
Shapley, Robert Martin *neurophysiology educator*
Siffert, Robert Spencer *orthopedic surgeon*
Silver, Richard Tobias *physician, educator*
Sorrel, William Edwin *psychiatrist, educator, psychoanalyst*
Spiegel, Herbert *psychiatrist, educator*
Stark, Richard Boies *surgeon*
Stein, Bennett Mueller *neurosurgeon*
Stein, Marvin *psychiatrist, educator*
Stenzel, Kurt Hodgson *physician, nephrologist, educator*
Stern, Marvin *psychiatrist, educator*
Stimmel, Barry *cardiologist, internist, educator, university dean*
Susser, Mervyn Wilfred *epidemiologist, educator*
Tamm, Igor *biomedical scientist, educator*
Thompson, David Duvall *physician*
Thomson, Gerald Edmund *physician, educator*
Torre, Douglas Paul *dermatologist*
Turino, Gerard Michael *physician, medical scientist, educator*
Tzimas, Nicholas Achilles *orthopedic surgeon, educator*
VanItallie, Theodore Bertus *physician*
Vaughan, Edwin Darracott, Jr. *urologist, surgeon*
Vilcek, Jan Tomas *medical educator*
Waksman, Byron Halsted *neuroimmunologist, experimental pathologist, educator, medical association administrator*
Warshaw, Leon J(oseph) *physician*
Wasserman, Louis Robert *physician, educator*
Waugh, Theodore Rogers *orthopedic surgeon*
Weinstein, I. Bernard *physician*
Weisfeldt, Myron Lee *physician, educator*
Weissmann, Gerald *medical educator, researcher, writer, editor*
Whelan, Elizabeth Ann Murphy *epidemiologist*
White, Kerr Lachlan *physician, foundation director*
Whitehead, E. Douglas *urology educator*
Wiesel, Torsten Nils *neurobiologist, educator*
Winawer, Sidney Jerome *physician, clinical investigator, educator*
Winick, Myron *educator, physician*
Wittmer, James Frederick *preventive medicine physician, educator*
†Worman, Howard Jay *physician, educator*
Wright, Irving Sherwood *physician, emeritus educator*
Wright, Jane Cooke *physician, educator, consultant*
Yahr, Melvin David *physician*
Zinn, Keith Marshall *ophthalmologist, educator*
Zitrin, Arthur *physician*

North Tonawanda
Nadler, Sigmond Harold *physician, surgeon*

Northport
Tsapogas, Makis J. *surgeon*

Nyack
Esser, Aristide Henri *psychiatrist*
Rossi, Harald Hermann *retired radiation biophysicist, educator, administrator*

Oneida
Muschenheim, Frederick *pathologist*

Pearl River
Danforth, Elliot, Jr. *medical educator*
Davis, Harold *veterinary pathologist*

Pittsford
Faloon, William Wassell *physician, educator*

Port Washington
Brownstein, Martin Herbert *dermatopathologist, educator*

Rochester
Barton, Russell William *psychiatrist, author*
Baum, John *physician*
Bennett, John Morrison *medical oncologist*
Berg, Robert Lewis *physician, educator*
Berman, Howard James *medical association administrator*
Borch, Richard Frederic *pharmacology and chemistry educator*
Borgstedt, Harold Heinrich *pharmacologist, toxicologist*
Brody, Bernard B. *physician, educator*
Brzustowicz, Richard John *neurosurgeon, educator*
Burgener, Francis André *radiology educator*
Burton, Richard Irving *orthopedist, educator*
Chey, William Yoon *physician*
Ciccone, J. Richard *psychiatrist*
Cockett, Abraham T. K. *urologist*
Cohen, Nicholas *immunologist, educator*
Crino, Marjanne Helen *anesthesiologist*
de Papp, Elise Wachenfeld *pathologist*
Doty, Robert William *neurophysiologist, educator*
Engel, George Libman *psychiatrist, internist, educator*
Forbes, Gilbert Burnett *physician, educator*
Frank, Irwin Norman *urologist, educator*
Frazer, John Paul *surgeon*
Frisina, Robert Dana *sensory neuroscientist*
Goldsmith, Lowell Alan *medical educator*
Herz, Marvin Ira *psychiatrist*
Hood, William Boyd, Jr. *cardiologist*
Jacobs, Laurence Stanton *physician, educator*
Marsh, David O. *neurology and toxicology educator*
Mc Donald, Joseph Valentine *neurosurgeon*
Menguy, Rene *surgeon, educator*
Morgan, William Lionel, Jr. *physician, educator*
Morton, John H. *surgeon, educator*
O'Mara, Robert Edmund George *radiologist, educator*
Panner, Bernard J. *pathologist, educator*
Pettee, Daniel Starr *neurologist*
Reifler, Clifford Bruce *psychiatrist, educator*
Rowley, Peter Templeton *physician, educator*
Schwartz, Seymour Ira *surgeon, educator*
Sherman, Charles Daniel, Jr. *surgeon*
Thaler, Otto Felix *psychiatrist*
Toribara, Taft Yutaka *radiation biologist, biophysicist, chemist, toxicologist*
Wiley, Jason LaRue, Jr. *neurosurgeon*
Williams, Thomas Franklin *physician, educator*
Wynne, Lyman Carroll *psychiatrist*

Roslyn Heights
Rogatz, Peter *physician*

Rye
Barker, Harold Grant *surgeon*
Reader, George Gordon *physician, educator*
Wessler, Stanford *physician, educator*
Wilmot, Irvin Gorsage *former hospital administrator, educator, consultant*

Sands Point
Bollet, Alfred Jay *internist, educator*
Lear, Erwin *anesthesiologist, educator*

Scarsdale
Buttinger, Catharine Sarina Caroline *psychiatrist*
Lee, Robert Earl *physician*

Schenectady
Pasamanick, Benjamin *psychiatrist, educator*

Silver Creek
Schenk, Worthington George, Jr. *surgeon, educator*

Skaneateles
Pickett, Lawrence Kimball *physician, educator*

Somers
Rubin, Samuel Harold *physician, consultant*

Staten Island
Berger, Herbert *retired internist, educator*
Greenfield, Val Shea *ophthalmologist*

Stony Brook
Davis, James Norman *neurologist, pharmacology researcher*
†Fine, Richard Nisan *pediatrician, educator*
Fritts, Harry Washington, Jr. *physician, educator*
Henn, Fritz Albert *psychiatrist*
Jonas, Steven *public health physician, medical educator, writer*
†Kaplan, Allen P. *physician, educator, academic administrator*
†Lane, Dorothy Spiegel *physician*
Meyers, Morton Allen *physician, radiology educator*
Miller, Frederick *pathologist*
Olson, Robert Eugene *physician, biochemist, educator*
Poppers, Paul Jules *anesthesiologist, educator*
Rapaport, Felix Theodosius *surgeon, researcher, educator*

Syracuse
Clausen, Jerry Lee *psychiatrist*
Cohen, William Nathan *radiologist*
Daly, Robert W. *psychiatrist, medical educator*
Gold, Joseph *medical researcher*
Kieffer, Stephen Aaron *radiologist, educator*
King, Robert Bainton *neurosurgeon*
Landaw, Stephen Arthur *physician, educator*
Lemanski, Larry Fredrick *medical educator*
McGraw, James L. *retired ophthalmologist, educator*
Murray, David George *orthopaedic surgeon, educator*
Nelson, Douglas A. *pathologist, educator*
Phillips, Richard Hart *psychiatrist*
Reed, George Farrell *physician*
Rosenbaum, Arthur Elihu *radiologist, educator*
Szasz, Thomas Stephen *psychiatrist, educator, writer*
†Verrillo, Ronald Thomas *neuroscientist*
Williams, William Joseph *physician, educator*

Tarrytown
Chu, Foo *physician*

Troy
Dutton, Robert Edward, Jr. *medical educator*

Upton
Cronkite, Eugene Pitcher *physician*
Hamilton, Leonard Derwent *physician, molecular biologist*
†Holroyd, Richard Allan *researcher*

Valhalla
Adler, Karl Paul *medical educator, academic administrator*
Carter, Anne Cohen *physician*
Christenson, William Newcome *physician*
Cimino, Joseph Anthony *physician, educator*
Del Guercio, Louis Richard Maurice *surgeon, educator, company executive*
†Fink, Raymond *medical educator*
Hodgson, W(alter) John B(arry) *surgeon*
Itskovitz, Harold David *physician*
Jones, James Robert *obstetrician, gynecologist, educator*
Levy, Norman B. *psychiatrist, educator*
McGiff, John C(harles) *pharmacologist*
Niguidula, Faustino Nazario *pediatric cardiothoracic surgeon*
Weisburger, John Hans *medical researcher*
Williams, Gary Murray *medical researcher, pathology educator*

Westfield
Brown, Kent Louis, Sr. *surgeon*

White Plains
Blank, H. Robert *psychiatrist*
Blass, John Paul *medical educator, physician*
†Johnston, Richard Boles, Jr. *pediatrician, educator, biomedical researcher*
Katz, Michael *pediatrician, educator*
Marano, Anthony Joseph *cardiologist*
McDowell, Fletcher Hughes *physician, educator*
Moser, Marvin *physician, educator, author*
Samii, Abdol Hossein *physician, educator*
Smith, Gerard Peter *neuroscientist*

Williamsville
Reisman, Robert E. *physician, educator*

Woodbury
Bleicher, Sheldon Joseph *endocrinologist, medical educator*

Yonkers
Rosch, Paul John *physician, educator*

Yorktown Heights
Klein, Richard Stephen *internist*

NORTH CAROLINA

Apex
Knapp, Richard Bruce *anesthesiologist*

Asheville
Becker, Quinn Henderson *orthopaedic surgeon, army officer*
Gaffney, Thomas Edward *retired physician*
Hall, Francoise Puvrez *psychiatrist*
Powell, Norborne Berkeley *urologist*

Burlington
Wilson, William Preston *psychiatrist, emeritus educator*

Cary
Talbert, Luther Marcus *physician*

Chapel Hill
Azar, Henry Amin *pathologist, medical historian*
Baerg, Richard Henry *podiatrist, surgeon, educator*
Barnett, Thomas Buchanan *physician, medical educator*
Beal, John M. *surgeon, medical educator*
Bondurant, Stuart *physician, educational administrator*
Boone, Franklin Delanor Roosevelt, Sr. *cardiovascular perfusionist, realtor*
Brinkhous, Kenneth Merle *pathologist, educator*
Brownlee, Robert Calvin *pediatrician, educator*
Clark, Richard Lee *radiologist*
Clyde, Wallace Alexander, Jr. *pediatrics and microbiology educator*
Cromartie, William James *medical educator, researcher*
Denny, Floyd Wolfe, Jr. *pediatrician*
Droegemueller, William *gynecologist, obstetrician, medical educator*
Easterling, William Ewart, Jr. *obstetrician, gynecologist*
Eifrig, David Eric *ophthalmologist, educator*
Ellis, Fred Wilson *pharmacology educator*
Farmer, Thomas Wohlsen *neurologist, educator*
Fischer, Janet Jordan *retired physician, educator, researcher*
Fischer, Newton Duchan *otolaryngologist, educator*
Frelinger, Jeffrey Allen *immunologist, educator*
Gottschalk, Carl William *physician, educator*
Goyer, Robert Andrew *pathology educator*
Graham, John Borden *pathologist, educator*
Greganti, Mac Andrew *physician, medical educator*
Grisham, Joe Wheeler *pathologist, educator*
Hawkins, David Rollo, Sr. *psychiatrist, educator*
Hendricks, Charles Henning *retired obstetrics and gynecology educator*
†Henson, O'Dell Williams, Jr. *anatomy educator*
Hirsch, Philip Francis *pharmacologist, educator*
Hollister, William Gray *psychiatrist*
Hulka, Barbara Sorenson *epidemiology educator*
Hulka, Jaroslav Fabian *obstetrician, gynecologist*
Johnson, George, Jr. *physician, educator*
Kettelkamp, Donald Benjamin *surgeon, educator*
Langdell, Robert Dana *medical educator*
Mayer, Eugene Stephen *physician, university administrator*
McMillan, Campbell White *pediatric hematologist*
Miller, C. Arden *physician, educator*
Miya, Tom Saburo *retired pharmacologist, educator*
Ontjes, David Ainsworth *medicine and pharmacology educator*
†Pagano, Joseph Stephen *physician, researcher, educator*
Palmer, Jeffress Gary *hematologist, educator*
Pollitzer, William Sprott *anatomy educator*
Prange, Arthur Jergen, Jr. *psychiatrist, neurobiologist, educator*
Sheldon, George F. *medical educator*
Sugioka, Kenneth *anesthesiologist educator*
Suzuki, Kunihiko *biomedical educator, researcher*
Thomas, Colin Gordon, Jr. *surgeon, medical educator*
Van Wyk, Judson John *endocrinologist, pediatric educator*
Wheeler, Clayton Eugene, Jr. *dermatologist, educator*
Wilcox, Benson Reid *cardiothoracic surgeon, educator*
Winfield, John Buckner *rheumatologist, educator*

Charlotte
Citron, David Sanford *physician*
Kelly, Luther Wrentmore, Jr. *physician, educator*
Naumoff, Philip *physician*
Watkins, Carlton Gunter *retired pediatrician*

Durham
Amos, Dennis B. *immunologist*
Anderson, William Banks, Jr. *ophthalmology educator*
Anlyan, William George *surgeon, university administrator*
Baker, Lenox Dial *orthopaedist, genealogist*
Bennett, Peter Brian *researcher, anesthesiology educator*
Bradford, William Dalton *pathologist, educator*
Brodie, Harlow Keith Hammond *psychiatry educator, former university president*
Buckley, Rebecca Hatcher *physician*
Busse, Ewald William *psychiatrist, educator*
Cartmill, Matt *anthropologist, anatomy educator*
Christmas, William Anthony *internist, educator*
Cohen, Harvey Jay *physician, educator*
Coleman, Ralph Edward *nuclear medicine physician*
Davis, James Evans *general and thoracic surgeon, parliamentarian, author*
Day, Eugene Davis, Sr. *immunology educator, researcher*
Estes, Edward Harvey, Jr. *medical educator*
Falletta, John Matthew *pediatrician*
Feldman, Jerome Myron *physician*
Fouts, James Ralph *pharmacologist, educator, clergyman*
Frank, Michael M. *physician*
Frothingham, Thomas Eliot *pediatrician*
Georgiade, Nicholas George *physician*
Greenfield, Joseph Cholmondeley, Jr. *physician, educator*
Hammond, Charles Bessellieu *obstetrician-gynecologist, educator*
Harmel, Merel Hilber *anesthesiologist, educator*
Harris, Jerome Sylvan *pediatrician, pediatrics and biochemistry educator*
Jennings, Robert Burgess *experimental pathologist, medical educator*
Johnston, William Webb *pathologist, educator*
Katz, Samuel Lawrence *pediatrician, scientist*
Kempner, Walter *physician*
King, Lowell Restell *pediatric urologist*
Kirshner, Norman *pharmacologist, researcher, educator*
Koepke, John Arthur *hematologist, clinical pathologist*
Kylstra, Johannes Arnold *physician*
Lack, Leon *pharmacology and biochemistry educator*
Lefkowitz, Robert Joseph *physician, educator*
Miller, David Edmond *physician*
Moore, John Wilson *neurophysiologist, educator*
Osterhout, Suydam *physician, educator*
Parker, Joseph B., Jr. *psychiatrist, educator*
Parker, Roy Turnage *obstetrician-gynecologist, educator*
Peete, William Pettway Jones *surgeon*
Peters, William P. *oncologist, science administrator, educator*
Pratt, Philip Chase *pathologist, educator*
Robertson, James David *neurobiologist educator*
Rogers, Mark Charles *physician, educator*
Sabiston, David Coston, Jr. *surgeon, educator*
Schanberg, Saul Murray *pharmacology educator*
Serafin, Donald *plastic surgeon*
Sessoms, Stuart McGuire *physician, educator, retired insurance company executive*
Snyderman, Ralph *medical educator, physician*
Spach, Madison Stockton *cardiologist*
Stead, Eugene Anson, Jr. *physician*
Urbaniak, James Randolph *orthopaedic surgeon*
Watts, Charles DeWitt *surgeon, corporate medical director*
Werman, David Sanford *psychiatrist, psychoanalyst, educator*
Wilkins, Robert Henry *neurosurgeon, editor*
Williams, Redford Brown *medical educator*

Greensboro
Johnson, Andrew Myron *pediatric immunologist, educator*

Greenville
Bolande, Robert Paul *pathologist, scientist, educator*
Hallock, James Anthony *pediatrician, school dean*
Jones, Billy Ernest *dermatology educator*
Laupus, William Edward *physician, educator*
Lee, Kenneth Stuart *neurosurgeon*
Mattsson, Ake *psychiatrist, physician*
Norris, H. Thomas *pathologist, academic administrator*

Pories, Walter Julius *surgeon, educator*
Sanchez, Rafael Camilo *physician*
Thomas, Francis Thornton *surgeon, immunologist, consultant*
Tingelstad, Jon Bunde *physician*
Waugh, William Howard *biomedical educator*

Hampstead
Solomon, Robert Douglas *pathology educator*

Lenoir
Carswell, Jane Triplett *family physician*

Lincolnton
†Gamble, John Reeves, Jr. *surgeon*

Raleigh
Dameron, Thomas Barker, Jr. *orthopaedic surgeon, educator*
Kimbrell, Odell Culp, Jr. *physician*
Levine, Ronald H. *physician, state official*
Michael, Patricia Ann *physician, clinical systems research director*
Peacock, Erle Ewart, Jr. *surgeon, lawyer, educator*

Research Triangle Park
Elion, Gertrude Belle *research scientist, pharmacology educator*
Griesemer, Richard Allen *veterinary pathologist*
†King, Theodore M. *obstetrician, gynecologist, educator*
Tilson, Hugh Hanna *epidemiologist*
†Wilsnack, Roger E. *medical association administrator*

Whispering Pines
Enlow, Donald Hugh *anatomist, educator, university dean*

Winston Salem
Alexander, Eben, Jr. *neurological surgeon*
†Bowman, Marjorie Ann *physician, academic administrator*
†Clarkson, Thomas Boston *comparative medicine educator*
Cowan, Robert Jenkins *radiologist, educator*
Davis, Courtland Harwell, Jr. *neurosurgeon*
†Dean, Richard Henry *surgeon, educator*
Hazzard, William Russell *geriatrician, educator*
Hopkins, Judith Owen *oncologist*
Howell, Charles Maitland *dermatologist*
Kaufman, William *internist*
†Kohut, Robert Irwin *otolaryngologist, educator*
Lorentz, William Beall *pediatrician*
Maynard, Charles Douglas *radiologist*
†McCullough, David L. *urologist*
Mueller-Heubach, Eberhard August *medical educator, obstetrician-gynecologist*
O'Steen, Wendall Keith *neurobiology and anatomy educator*
Penry, James Kiffin *physician, neurology educator*
Podgorny, George *emergency physician*
Prichard, Robert Williams *pathologist, educator*
†Shils, Maurice Edward *physician, educator*
Simon, Jimmy Louis *pediatrician, educator*
Spurr, Charles Lewis *medical educator, cancer chemotherapy clinical researcher*
Theros, Elias George *radiology educator and author*
Toole, James Francis *medical educator*
Woods, James Watson, Jr. *cardiologist*

NORTH DAKOTA

Bismarck
Hook, William Franklin *radiologist*

Grand Forks
Carlson, Edward C. *anatomy educator*

Williston
Adducci, Joseph Edward *obstetrician, gynecologist*

OHIO

Akron
Evans, Douglas McCullough *surgeon, educator*
Hodge, James Robert *psychiatrist*
Levy, Richard Philip *physician, educator*
LoIudice, Thomas Anthony *gastroenterologist, researcher*
Timmons, Gerald Dean *pediatric neurologist*

Athens
Patriquin, David Ashley *osteopath, educator*

Beavercreek
Rodin, Alvin Eli *pathologist, medical educator, author*

Boardman
Walton, Ralph Gerald *psychiatrist, educator*

Brooklyn
Conomy, John Paul *neurologist, lawyer, corporate executive*

Canal Winchester
Burrier, Gail Warren *physician*

Canton
Howland, Willard J. *radiologist, educator*
Ognibene, Andre J(ohn) *physician, army officer, educator*

Centerville
Kelso, Harold Glen *family practice physician*

Chagrin Falls
Lingl, Friedrich Albert *psychiatrist*

Cincinnati
Adolph, Robert J. *physician, medical educator*
Alexander, James Wesley *surgeon, educator*
Bernstein, I. Leonard *physician, educator*
Biddinger, Paul Williams *pathologist, educator*
Bingham, Eula *environmental health educator*
Boat, Thomas Frederick *physician, educator, researcher*
Bridenbaugh, Phillip Owen *anesthesiologist, physician*
Buchman, Elwood *physician, pharmaceutical company medical director*
Carothers, Charles Omsted *orthopedic surgeon*
Fine, Lawrence Jay *internist, occupational preventive medicine*
Fowler, Noble Owen *physician, university administrator*
†Gemunder, Joel Frank *medical association adminstrator*
Gesteland, Robert Charles *neurophysiologist*
Greenwalt, Tibor Jack *physician, educator*
Harshman, Morton Leonard *physician, business executive*
Heimlich, Henry Jay *physician, surgeon*
Hess, Evelyn Victorine (Mrs. Michael Howett) *medical educator*
Horwitz, Harry *radiologist, physician, educator*
Hummel, Robert Paul *surgeon*
Jaffe, Murray Sherwood *surgeon*
Kaplan, Stanley Meisel *psychoanalyst*
Loggie, Jennifer Mary Hildreth *medical educator, physician*
Lucas, Stanley Jerome *radiologist, physician*
Macpherson, Colin R(obertson) *pathologist, educator*
Nordlund, James John *dermatologist*
Rebar, Robert William *obstetrician, gynecologist, educator*
Saenger, Eugene Lange *radiology educator, laboratory director*
Schneider, Harold Joel *radiologist*
Schreiner, Albert William *physician, educator*
Schwartz, Arnold (Arnie Shayne) *pharmacologist, biophysicist, biochemist, educator, actor, director, producer*
Scott, Ralph C. *physician, educator*
Smith, Roger Dean *pathologist*
Sodd, Vincent Joseph *nuclear medicine researcher, educator*
Suskind, Raymond Robert *physician, educator*
Vilter, Richard William *physician, educator*
†Warden, Glenn Donald *burn surgeon*
West, Clark Darwin *pediatric nephrologist, educator*
Wiot, Jerome Francis *radiologist*
Wood, Daniel G. *health care financial executive*

Cleveland
Aikawa, Masamichi *pathologist*
Alfidi, Ralph Joseph *radiologist, educator*
Alfred, Karl Sverre *orthopedic surgeon*
Awais, George Musa *obstetrician, gynecologist*
Badal, Daniel Walter *psychiatrist, educator*
Baker, Saul Phillip *geriatrician, cardiologist, internist*
Bartunek, Robert Richard *retired physician*
Bowerfind, Edgar Sihler, Jr. *physician, medical administrator*
Budd, John Henry *physician*
Carter, James Rose, Jr. *medical educator*
Cascorbi, Helmut Freimund *anesthesiologist, educator*
Caston, J(esse) Douglas *medical educator*
Cherniack, Neil Stanley *physician, medical educator*
Cieslak, Arthur Kazimer *surgeon*
Cole, Monroe *neurologist, educator*
Daroff, Robert Barry *neurologist*
†Davis, Pamela Bowes *pediatric pulmonologist*
Dell'Osso, Louis Frank *neuroscience educator*
Denko, Joanne D. *psychiatrist, writer*
Eastwood, Douglas William *anesthesiologist*
Eiben, Robert Michael *pediatric neurologist, educator*
Fazio, Victor Warren *physician, colon and rectal surgeon*
Geha, Alexander Salim *cardiothoracic surgeon, educator*
Gifford, Ray Wallace, Jr. *physician, educator*
Hardesty, Hiram Haines *ophthalmologist, educator*
Harris, John William *physician, educator*
Healy, Bernadine P. *physician, educator, federal agency administrator*
Herndon, Charles Harbison *retired orthopaedic surgeon*
Holzbach, Raymond Thomas *gastroenterologist, author, educator*
Izant, Robert James, Jr. *pediatric surgeon*
Kellermeyer, Robert William *physician, educator*
Kiser, William Sites *physician executive, urologic surgeon*
Lamm, Michael Emanuel *pathologist, immunologist, educator*
Lefferts, William Geoffrey *physician, educator*
Lenkoski, Leo Douglas *psychiatrist, educator*
Mahmoud, Adel A. F. *physician, educator, investigator*
Meltzer, Herbert Yale *psychiatry educator*
Novick, Andrew Carl *urologist*
Rakita, Louis *cardiologist, educator*
Ratnoff, Oscar Davis *physician, educator*
Robbins, Frederick Chapman *physician, medical school dean emeritus*
†Ross, Ronald Jay *radiologist*
Scarpa, Antonio *medicine educator, biomedical scientist*
Shuck, Jerry Mark *surgeon, educator*
Smith, Charles Kent *family medicine physician*
Stanton-Hicks, Michael D'Arcy *anesthesiologist, educator*
Stavitsky, Abram Benjamin *immunologist, educator*
Straffon, Ralph Atwood *urologist*
Webster, Leslie Tillotson, Jr. *pharmacologist, educator*
White, Robert J. *neurosurgeon, neuroscientist, educator*
Wolinsky, Emanuel *physician, educator*
Young, Jess R. *physician*

Columbus
Ackerman, John Henry *health services consultant, physician*
Barth, Rolf Frederick *pathologist, educator*
Bell, George Edwin *retired physician, insurance company executive*
Berggren, Ronald Bernard *surgeon, emeritus educator*
Bianchine, Joseph Raymond *pharmacologist*
Billings, Charles Edgar *physician*
†Bope, Edward Tharp *family practitioner*
Boudoulas, Harisios *physician*
Brandes, Norman Scott *psychiatrist*
Christoforidis, A. John *radiologist, educator*
Copeland, William Edgar, Sr. *physician*
Cramblett, Henry Gaylord *pediatrician, virologist, educator*
†Fass, Robert J. *epidemiologist, academic administrator*
Haque, Malika Hakim *pediatrician*
Hunt, William Edward *neurosurgeon, educator*
Kendrick, Ronald Edward *orthopaedic surgeon*
Kilman, James William *surgeon, educator*
Kim, Moon Hyun *physician, educator*
Lewis, Richard Phelps *physician, educator*
Mazzaferri, Ernest Louis *physician, educator*
Newton, William Allen, Jr. *pediatric pathologist*
O'Dorisio, Thomas Michael *internal medicine educator, researcher*
Penn, Gerald Melville *pathologist*
Perkins, Robert Louis *physician, educator*
†Ruberg, Robert Lionel *surgery educator*
†Rund, Douglas Andrew *emergency physician, educator*
St. Pierre, Ronald Leslie *anatomy educator, university administrator*
Sayers, Martin Peter *pediatric neurosurgeon*
Senhauser, Donald A(lbert) *pathologist, educator*
Skillman, Thomas Grant *endocrinology consultant, former educator*
Tzagournis, Manuel *physician, educator, university dean and official*
Yashon, David *neurosurgeon, educator*
Zuspan, Frederick Paul *obstetrician/gynecologist, educator*

Dayton
Arn, Kenneth Dale *physician, city official*
Barnes, Herman Verdain *internist, educator*
DeWall, Richard Allison *retired surgeon*
Elliott, Daniel Whitacre *surgeon, retired educator*
Faruki, Mahmud Taji *psychiatrist, hospital administrator*
Humbert, James Ronald *pediatrician, educator*
Kogut, Maurice David *pediatric endocrinologist*
Mohler, Stanley Ross *physician, educator*
Von Gierke, Henning Edgar *biomedical science educator, former government official, researcher*
Weinberg, Sylvan Lee *cardiologist, educator, author, editor*

Dublin
Graham, Bruce Douglas *pediatrician*

Fairborn
Martin, Donald William *psychiatrist*

Gallipolis
Clarke, Oscar Withers *physician*

Lebanon
Holtkamp, Dorsey Emil *medical research scientist*

Lima
Becker, Dwight Lowell *physician*
Collins, William Thomas *pathologist*

Mansfield
Houston, William Robert Montgomery *ophthalmic surgeon*

Marietta
Tipton, Jon Paul *allergist*

Maumee
Huffman, (Bernard) Leslie, Jr. *physician*

Oregon
Culver, Robert Elroy *osteopathic physician*

Pepper Pike
Froelich, Wolfgang Andreas *neurologist*

Rocky River
Castele, Theodore John *radiologist*
De Long, Erika Venta *psychiatrist*

Rootstown
Blacklow, Robert Stanley *physician, medical college administrator*
Campbell, Colin *obstetrician, gynecologist, school dean*
Saltzman, Glenn Alan *behavioral sciences educator*

Strongsville
Opplt, Jan Jiri *clinical pathologist, educator*

Toledo
Chakraborty, Joana *physiology educator, research center administrator*
DiDio, Liberato John Alphonse *anatomist, educator*
Mayhew, Harry Eugene *physician, educator*
Mulrow, Patrick Joseph *medical educator*
Rubin, Allan Maier *physician, surgeon*
Shelley, Walter Brown *physician, educator*
Standaert, Frank George *medical research administrator, physician*
Zrull, Joel Peter *psychiatry educator*

Troy
Davies, Alfred Robert *physician, educator*

Worthington
Winter, Chester Caldwell *physician, surgery educator*

Yellow Springs
Lacey, Beatrice Cates *psychophysiologist*

Youngstown
Butterworth, Jane Rogers Fitch *physician*
Gaylord, Sanford Fred *physician*

Zanesville
Ray, John Walker *otolaryngologist, educator, broadcast commentator*

OKLAHOMA

Edmond
Nelson, John Woolard *neurology educator, physician*

Muskogee
Kent, Bartis Milton *physician*

Oklahoma City
Bogardus, Carl Robert, Jr. *radiologist, educator*
Brandt, Edward Newman, Jr. *physician, educator*
Buchanan, Robert Taylor *plastic surgeon*
Cameron, Charles Metz, Jr. *physician, medical educator*
Carter, L. Philip *neurosurgeon, consultant*
Comp, Philip Cinnamon *medical researcher*
Couch, James Russell, Jr. *neurology educator*
Deckert, Gordon Harmon *psychiatrist, educator*
Everett, Mark Allen *dermatologist, educator*
Felton, Warren Locker, II *surgeon*
Fishburne, John Ingram, Jr. *obstetrician-gynecologist, educator*
Halverstadt, Donald Bruce *urologist, educator*
Haywood, B(etty) J(ean) *anesthesiologist*
Hough, Jack Van Doren *otologist*
Kimerer, Neil Banard, Sr. *psychiatrist, educator*
Lewis, Wilbur Curtis *surgeon*
Lhevine, Dave Bernard *radiologist, educator*
†Massion, Walter Herbert *anesthesiologist, educator*
Moore, Joanne Iweita *pharmacologist, educator*
Oehlert, William Herbert, Jr. *cardiologist, administrator, educator*
Robison, Clarence, Jr. *surgeon*
Rossavik, Ivar Kristian *obstetrician/gynecologist*
Thurman, William Gentry *medical research foundation executive, pediatric hematology and oncology physician, educator*
Williams, George Rainey *surgeon, educator*
Zuhdi, Nazih *surgeon*

Stillwater
Cooper, Donald Lee *physician*
Hooper, Billy Ernest *medical association administrator*

Tulsa
Calvert, Jon Channing *family practice physician*
Kalbfleisch, John McDowell *cardiologist, educator*
Lewis, Ceylon Smith, Jr. *physician*
Nettles, John Barnwell *obstetrics and gynecology educator*
Plunket, Daniel Clark *pediatrician*
Tompkins, Robert George *physician*

Vinita
Neer, Charles Sumner, II *orthopaedic surgeon, educator*

OREGON

Corvallis
Willis, David Lee *radiation biology educator*

Eugene
Flanagan, Latham, Jr. *surgeon*
Nissel, Martin *radiologist, consultant*
Starr, Grier Forsythe *retired pathologist*

Portland
†Barmack, Neal Herbert *neuroscientist*
Bennett, William Michael *physician*
Benson, John Alexander, Jr. *physician, educator*
Berthelsdorf, Siegfried *psychiatrist*
Brummett, Robert Eddie *pharmacology educator*
Campbell, John Richard *pediatric surgeon*
Connor, William Elliott *physician, educator*
Crawshaw, Ralph *psychiatrist*
Fraunfelder, Frederick Theodore *ophthalmologist, educator*
Greer, Monte Arnold *physician, educator*
Heatherington, J. Scott *retired osteopathic physician and surgeon*
Herndon, Robert McCulloch *experimental neurologist*
Houghton, Donald Cary *pathology educator*
Hutchens, Tyra Thornton *physician, educator*
Jacob, Stanley Wallace *surgeon, educator*
Kendall, John Walker, Jr. *medical educator, researcher, university dean*
Kohler, Peter Ogden *physician, educator, university president*
Lees, Martin Henry *physician*
Lobitz, Walter Charles, Jr. *physician, educator*
Olson, Donald Ernest *retired physician*
Press, Edward *consulting physician, treasurer*
Raaf, John Elbert *neurosurgeon, educator*
Riker, William Kay *pharmacologist, educator*
Seil, Fredrick John *neuroscientist, neurologist*
Stalnaker, John Hulbert *physician*
Stevens, Wendell Claire *anesthesiology educator*
Swan, Kenneth Carl *physician, surgeon*
Swank, Roy Laver *physician, educator, inventor*
Taylor, Robert Brown *medical educator*
Zimmerman, Gail Marie *medical foundation executive*

Springfield
Kimball, Reid Roberts *psychiatrist*

PENNSYLVANIA

Abington
Dunn, Linda Kay *physician*
Lapayowker, Marc Spencer *radiologist*

Allentown
Gaylor, Donald Hughes *surgeon, educator*

Bala Cynwyd
Katz, Julian *gastroenterologist, educator*
Marden, Philip Ayer *physician, educator*

Bangor
Wolf, Stewart George, Jr. *physician, medical educator*

Bethlehem
Benz, Edward John *retired clinical pathologist*
Snyder, John Mendenhall *medical administrator, retired thoracic surgeon*

Bridgeville
Keddie, Roland Thomas *physician, hospital administrator, lawyer*

Bryn Mawr
Brunt, Manly Yates, Jr. *psychiatrist*

Huth, Edward Janavel *physician, editor*
†Noone, Robert Barrett *plastic surgeon*
Pettit, Horace *allergist, consultant*

Carlisle
Graham, William Patton, III *plastic surgeon, educator*

Chalfont
Clifford, Maurice Cecil *physician, former college president, foundation executive*

Chester
Clark, James Edward *physician, medical educator*

Coatesville
Gehring, David Austin *physician, adminstrator, cardiologist*
Nocks, James Jay *psychiatrist*

Danville
Kazem, Ismail *radiation oncologist, educator, health science facility administrator*
Pierce, James Clarence *surgeon*

Devon
O'Malley, John Edward *medical association administrator, physician*

Dillsburg
Jackson, George Lyman *nuclear medicine physician*

Du Bois
Brunk, Samuel Frederick *oncologist*

Easton
Grunberg, Robert Leon Willy *nephrologist*

Fort Washington
Urbach, Frederick *physician, educator*

Gaines
Beller, Martin Leonard *retired orthopaedic surgeon*

Gibsonia
Cauna, Nikolajs *physician, medical educator*

Gladwyne
Nelson, Waldo Emerson *physician, educator*

Glenside
Johnson, Waine Cecil *dermatologist*

Harrisburg
Cadieux, Roger Joseph *physician, mental health care executive*
Redmond, James Melvin *medical association administrator*

Hershey
Biebuyck, Julien Francois *anesthesiologist, educator*
Cary, Gene Leonard *psychiatrist*
Davis, Dwight *cardiologist, educator*
Evarts, Charles McCollister *orthopaedic surgeon*
Eyster, Mary Elaine *hematologist, educator*
Kauffman, Gordon Lee, Jr. *surgeon, educator*
Krieg, Arthur Frederick *pathologist*
Leaman, David Martin *cardiologist*
Lehman, Lois Joan *medical librarian*
Lipton, Allan *medical educator*
Naeye, Richard L. *pathologist, educator*
Pierce, William Schuler *cardiac surgeon, educator*
Rohner, Thomas John, Jr. *urologist*
Severs, Walter Bruce *pharmacology educator, researcher*
†Vesell, Elliot Saul *pharmacologist, educator*
Waldhausen, John Anton *surgeon, educator*
Wassner, Steven Joel *pediatric nephrologist, educator*
Zelis, Robert Felix *cardiologist, educator*

Jenkintown
Greenspan-Margolis, June E. *psychiatrist*
Sadoff, Robert Leslie *psychiatrist*

Kennett Square
Leymaster, Glen R. *former medical association executive*
Perera, George A. *physician*

Lancaster
Eshleman, Silas Kendrick, III *psychiatrist*

Landenberg
Lee, Robert John *pharmacologist*

Mechanicsburg
†Greer, Robert B., III *orthopaedist*
†Ortenzio, Rocco Anthony *health care executive*

Monroeville
Lin, Ming Shek *allergist, immunologist*

Narberth
Nathanson, Neal *epidemiologist, virologist, educator*

Newtown
Somers, Anne Ramsay *medical educator*

Penllyn
Beyer, Karl Henry, Jr. *pharmacologist*

Philadelphia
Agus, Zalman S. *physician, educator*
Alter, Milton *neurologist, educator*
Amenta, Peter Sebastian *anatomist, researcher, educator*
†Andrews, Edwin Joseph *pathology educator, academic administrator*
Arce, A. Anthony *psychiatrist*
Aronson, Carl Edward *pharmacology and toxicology educator*
Asbury, Arthur Knight *neurologist, educator*
Austrian, Robert *physician, educator*
Barchi, Robert Lawrence *neuroscience educator, clinical neurologist, neuroscientist*
Barker, Clyde Frederick *surgeon, educator*
Baserga, Renato Luigi *pathology educator*
Bianchi, Carmine Paul *pharmacologist*
Bibbo, Marluce *physician, educator*
Bilaniuk, Larissa Tetiana *neuroradiologist, educator*
Bishop, Harry Craden *surgeon*
Bluemle, Lewis William, Jr. *medical educator*
Brady, John Paul *psychiatrist*
Brady, Luther W., Jr. *physician, radiation oncology educator*
Brest, Albert N. *cardiology educator*
Bridger, Wagner H. *psychiatrist, educator*
Brighton, Carl Theodore *orthopedic surgery educator*
†Brockman, Stanley K. *medical educator, physician, cardiothoracic surgeon*
Buerk, Donald Gene *medical educator, biomedical engineer*
Cander, Leon *physician, educator*
Chait, Arnold *radiologist*
†Chinsamy, Anusuya *paleobiologist, researcher*
Christman, Robert Alan *podiatric radiologist*
Chung, Edward Kooyoung *cardiologist, educator, author*
Clearfield, Harris Reynold *physician*
Cohen, Stanley *pathologist, educator*
Colman, Robert Wolf *physician, medical educator*
Comer, Nathan Lawrence *psychiatrist, educator*
Conn, Rex Boland, Jr. *physician, educator*
Copeland, Adrian Dennis *psychiatrist*
Cortner, Jean Alexander *physician, educator*
Dalinka, Murray Kenneth *radiologist, educator*
†Daly, John M. *surgeon*
D'Angio, Giulio John *radiologist, educator*
†Davidson, Steven J. *emergency physician*
Depp, (O.) Richard, III *obstetrician-gynecologist, educator*
Dinoso, Vicente Pescador, Jr. *physician, educator*
DiPalma, Joseph Rupert *pharmacology educator*
Djerassi, Isaac *physician, medical researcher*
Earley, Laurence Elliott *medical educator*
Ehrlich, George Edward *rheumatologist, international pharmaceutical consultant*
Eichelman, Burr Simmons, Jr. *psychiatrist, researcher, educator*
Engelman, Karl *physician*
Erslev, Allan Jacob *physician, educator*
Evans, Audrey Elizabeth *physician, educator*
Fishman, Alfred Paul *physician*
Flexner, Louis Barkhouse *anatomist, educator*
Frankl, William Stewart *cardiologist, educator*
Freed, Edmond Lee *podiatrist*
Freiman, David Burl *radiologist*
Futcher, Palmer Howard *physician, educator*
Gabrielson, Ira Wilson *physician, educator*
García, Celso-Ramón *obstetrician and gynecologist*
Gartland, John Joseph *physician, writer*
Glick, John H. *oncologist, medical educator*
Goldberg, Martin *physician, educator*
Goldberg, Morton Edward *pharmacologist*
Golden, Gerald Samuel *national medical board executive*
Goldsmith, Sidney *physician, scientist, inventor*
Gonick, Paul *urologist*
Goodman, David Barry Poliakoff *physician, educator*
Griffen, Ward O., Jr. *surgeon, educator, medical board executive*
Hamilton, Ralph West *plastic surgeon, educator*
Hansell, John Royer *physician*
Haugaard, Niels *pharmacologist*
Helfand, Arthur E. *podiatrist*
†Holtzer, Howard *anatomy educator*
Jackson, Laird Gray *physician, educator*
Jensh, Ronald Paul *anatomist, educator*
Johnson, Joseph Eggleston, III *physician, educator*
Kahn, Sigmund Benham *internist, dean*
Kaye, Donald *physician, educator*
Kaye, Robert *pediatrics educator*
†Kazazian, Haig Hagop, Jr. *medical scientist, physician, educator*
Keenan, Mary Ann *orthopaedic surgeon, researcher*
Kimball, Harry Raymond *medical association executive, educator*
Kissick, William Lee *physician, educator*
Kligerman, Morton M. *radiologist*
Koelle, George Brampton *university pharmacologist, educator*
Kolansky, Harold *physician, psychiatrist, psychoanalyst*
Kresh, J. Yasha *cardiovascular researcher, educator*
Kundel, Harold Louis *radiologist, educator*
Ladman, A(aron) J(ulius) *anatomist, educator*
Laibson, Peter Robert *ophthalmologist*
Lambertsen, Christian James *environmental physiologist, physician, educator*
Laufer, Igor *radiologist*
Levine, Rhea Joy Cottler *anatomy educator*
Levit, Edithe Judith *physician, medical association administrator*
Levy, Robert Isaac *physician, educator, research director*
Lewis, Paul Le Roy *pathology educator*
†Li, Weiye *ophthalmologist, biochemist, educator*
Lief, Harold Isaiah *psychiatrist*
Longnecker, David E. *anesthesiologist, educator*
Luscombe, Herbert Alfred *physician, educator*
Madow, Leo *psychiatrist, educator*
Maguire, Henry Clinton, Jr. *dermatologist*
Mancall, Elliott Lee *neurologist, educator*
Mansfield, Carl Major *radiation oncology educator*
Mansmann, Herbert C., Jr. *physician, educator*
Marshall, Bryan Edward *anesthesiologist, educator*
Mastroianni, Luigi, Jr. *physician, educator*
Matsumoto, Teruo *surgeon, educator*
Mayock, Robert Lee *internist*
Melvin, John Lewis *physical and rehabilitation physician, educator*
Mendels, Joseph *psychiatrist, educator*
Miller, Leonard David *surgeon*
Ming, Si-Chun *pathologist, educator*
Mulholland, S. Grant *urologist*
Nichols, Charles Warren *ophthalmologist*
Nowell, Peter Carey *pathologist, educator*
Parish, Lawrence Charles *physician, editor*
Potsic, William Paul *physician, educator*
Prevoznik, Stephen Joseph *anesthesiologist*
Rabinowitz, Howard K. *physician, educator*
Reinecke, Robert Dale *ophthalmologist*
Rhoads, Jonathan Evans *surgeon*
Rickels, Karl *psychiatrist, physician, educator*
Roberts, Jay *pharmacologist, educator*
Rogers, Fred Baker *medical educator*
Rorke, Lucy Balian *neuropathologist*
Rosato, Francis Ernest *surgeon*
Ross, Leonard Lester *anatomist*
†Rovera, Giovanni Aurelio *medical educator, scientist*
Rubin, Emanuel *pathologist, educator*
Salganicoff, Leon *pharmacology educator*
†Schidlow, Daniel *pediatrician, medical association administrator*
Schneider, Jan *obstetrics and gynecology educator*
Schotland, Donald Lewis *neurologist, educator*
Schumacher, H(arry) Ralph *internist, researcher, medical educator*
Schwartz, Gordon Francis *surgeon, educator*
Segal, Bernard Louis *physician, educator*
Sevy, Roger Warren *retired pharmacology educator*
†Shapiro, Sandor Solomon *hematologist*
Shields, Jerry Allen *ophthalmologist, educator*
Silberberg, Donald H. *neurologist*
Sloviter, Henry Allan *medical educator*
Soloff, Louis Alexander *physician, educator*
Spaeth, George Link *physician, ophthalmology educator*
Spector, Harvey M. *osteopathic physician*
Sprague, James Mather *medical scientist, educator*
Steel, Howard Haldeman *pediatric orthopaedic surgeon*
Stunkard, Albert James *physician, educator*
Sudak, Howard Stanley *physician, psychiatry educator*
Sunderman, Frederick William *physician, educator, author, musician*
†Taichman, Norton Stanley *pathology educator*
Tasman, William Samuel *ophthalmologist, medical association executive*
Torg, Joseph Steven *orthopaedic surgeon, educator*
Tourtellotte, Charles Dee *physician, educator*
†Tunnessen, Walter William, Jr. *pediatrician*
†Ugen, Kenneth Eugene *medical researcher*
Wallace, Herbert William *physician, surgery educator, researcher*
Webber, John Bentley *orthopedic surgeon*
Wein, Alan Jerome *urologist, educator, researcher*
Wilson, Marjorie Price *physician, medical commission executive*
Wollman, Harry *medical educator*
Yanoff, Myron *ophthalmologist*
†Young, Donald Stirling *clinical pathology educator*
Zweiman, Burton *physician, scientist, educator*

Pittsburgh
Allen, Thomas E. *obstetrician/gynecologist*
Baldisseri, Marie Rosanne *physician*
Beachley, Michael Charles *radiologist*
Bernier, George Matthew, Jr. *physician, medical educator, medical school dean*
Broussard, Elsie Rita *physician, educator, researcher*
Cooper, William Marion *physician*
Cutler, John Charles *physician, educator*
Dameshek, H(arold) Lee *physician*
deGroat, William Chesney *pharmacology educator*
Delaney, John Francis *neurologist, psychiatrist*
Detre, Katherine Maria *physician*
Detre, Thomas *psychiatrist, educator*
Dixit, Balwant Narayan *pharmacology and toxicology educator*
Feczko, William Albert *radiologist*
Fireman, Philip *pediatrician, allergist, immunologist, medical association executive*
Fisher, Bernard *surgeon, researcher, educator*
†Friday, Gilbert Anthony, Jr. *pediatrician*
Gaffney, Paul Cotter *physician*
Gill, Thomas James, III *physician, educator*
Hardesty, Robert Lynch *surgeon, educator*
Harrold, Ronald Thomas *research scientist*
Herndon, James Henry *orthopedic surgeon, educator*
Hingson, Robert Andrew *physician, educator, inventor, farmer, poet*
†Howland, Robert Herbert *psychiatrist*
Jegasothy, Brian Vasanthakumar *dermatology educator*
Joyner, Claude Reuben, Jr. *physician, medical educator*
Kupfer, David J. *psychiatry educator*
†Lazzara, Robert Ralph *cardiothoracic surgeon*
Lewis, Jessica Helen (Mrs. Jack D. Myers) *physician, educator*
†MacLeod, Gordon Kenneth *physician, educator*
Matzke, Gary Roger *pharmacologist, educator, researcher*
Mc Kenzie, Ray *anesthesiologist, educator*
†McMaster, James Henry *orthopaedic surgeon*
Moore, Robert Yates *neuroscience educator*
Moriarty, Richard William *pediatrician*
Myers, Eugene Nicholas *otolaryngologist, otolaryngology educator*
Needleman, Herbert Leroy *psychiatrist, pediatrician*
†Pham, Si Mai *cadiothoracic surgeon, medical educator*
Price, Trevor Robert Pryce *psychiatrist, educator*
Rabin, Bruce Stuart *immunologist, physician, educator*
Rogers, Robert Mark *physician*
Roth, Loren *psychiatrist*
Shapiro, Alvin Philip *physician, educator*
Siker, Ephraim S. *anesthesiologist*
Starzl, Thomas Earl *physician, educator*
Troen, Philip *physician, educator*
Wald, Niel *medical educator*
Werner, Gerhard *pharmacologist, psychoanalyst, educator*
Winter, Peter Michael *physician, anesthesiologist, educator*

Plymouth Meeting
Nobel, Joel J. *physician*

Pottsville
Kholoussy, A. Mohsen *surgeon, educator*

Reading
Hildreth, Eugene A. *physician, educator*

Sayre
Moody, Robert Adams *neurosurgeon*
Thomas, John Melvin *surgeon*

Sellersville
Loux, Norman Landis *psychiatrist*

Springfield
†Ruiz, Jose R. *podiatric surgeon*

Strafford
Horwitz, Orville *cardiologist, educator*

Swarthmore
Carey, William Bacon *pediatrician, educator*

Torrance
Bullard, Ray Elva, Jr. *retired psychiatrist, hospital administrator*

Upper Darby
Hurley, Harry James, Jr. *dermatologist*

Warminster
Whinnery, James Elliott *aerospace medical scientist, flight surgeon*

Wayne
Atkins, Joseph P. *otorhinolaryngologist*
de Rivas, Carmela Foderaro *psychiatrist, hospital administrator*

Waynesboro
Kirk, Daniel Lee *physician, consultant*

West Chester
Schindler, Peter David *child and adolescent psychiatrist*

West Conshohocken
Capizzi, Robert Lawrence *physician*
Schein, Philip Samuel *physician, educator, pharmaceutical executive*

West Point
Callahan Graham, Pia Laaster *medical researcher, virology researcher*
Grossman, William *medical researcher, educator*
Sherwood, Louis Maier *physician, scientist, pharmaceutical company executive*

Wilkes Barre
Ru Dusky, Basil Michael *cardiologist, consultant*

Williamsport
Lattimer, Gary Lee *physician*

Windber
Furigay, Rodolfo Lazo *surgeon*

Wynnewood
Doherty, Henry Joseph *anesthesiologist, medical hypnotist*
Flanagan, Joseph Charles *ophthalmologist*
Hodges, John Hendricks *physician, educator*

RHODE ISLAND

Barrington
Carpenter, Charles Colcock Jones *physician, educator*

Pawtucket
Carleton, Richard Allyn *cardiologist*

Providence
Amaral, Joseph Ferreira *surgeon*
Aronson, Stanley Maynard *physician, educator*
Davis, Robert Paul *physician, educator*
Dowben, Robert Morris *physician, scientist*
Erikson, George Emil (Erik Erikson) *anatomist, archivist, historian, educator, information specialist*
Galletti, Pierre Marie *medical science educator, artificial organ scientist*
Glicksman, Arvin S(igmund) *radiologist, physician*
Hamolsky, Milton William *physician*
†Kane, Agnes Brezak *pathologist, educator*
Lewis, David Carleton *medical educator, university center director*
Mc Donald, Charles J. *physician, educator*
Monteiro, Lois Ann *medical science educator*
Oh, William *physician*
Parks, Robert Emmett, Jr. *medical science educator*
Shaw, Ronald Ahrend *physician, educator*

Wakefield
Fair, Charles Maitland *neuroscientist, author*

SOUTH CAROLINA

Aiken
Gleichauf, John George *ophthalmologist*

Charleston
Anderson, Marion Cornelius *surgeon, medical educator*
Apple, David Joseph *ophthalmology educator*
Bell, Norman Howard *physician, endocrinologist, educator*
Carek, Donald J(ohn) *child psychiatry educator*
Colwell, John Amory *physician*
†Crawford, Fred Allen, Jr. *cardiothoracic surgeon, educator*
Creasman, William Thomas *obstetrician-gynecologist, educator*
Daniell, Herman Burch *pharmacologist*
Dobson, Richard Lawrence *dermatologist, educator*
Gillette, Paul Crawford *pediatric cardiologist*
Hogan, Edward Leo *neurologist*
Johnson, Allen Huggins *physician, educator*
La Via, Mariano Francis *physician, pathology and laboratory medicine educator*
Legerton, Clarence William, Jr. *gastroenterologist, educator*
LeRoy, Edward Carwile *rheumatologist*
†Maize, John Christopher *dermatology educator*
Margolius, Harry Stephen *pharmacologist, physician*
McGinty, John B. *orthopaedic surgeon, educator*
Newberry, William Marcus *physician, educator, university administrator*
O'Brien, Paul Herbert *surgeon*
Ogawa, Makio *physician*
Othersen, Henry Biemann, Jr. *pediatric surgeon, physician, educator*
Simson, Jo Anne *anatomy and cell biology educator*
Wilson, Frederick Allen *medical educator, medical center administrator, gastroenterologist*

Columbia
Adcock, David Filmore *radiologist, educator*
Almond, Carl Herman *surgeon, physician, educator*
Altekruse, Joan Morrissey *preventive medicine educator*
Donald, Alexander Grant *psychiatrist*
Horger, Edgar Olin, III *obstetrics and gynecology educator*
Humphries, John O'Neal *physician, educator, university dean*
Jervey, Harold Edward, Jr. *medical education consultant, retired*

Florence
Wagner, John Garnet *pharmacy educator*

Greenville
Bates, George William *obstetrician, gynecologist, educator*
Bonner, Jack Wilbur, III *psychiatrist, educator, administrator*
Kilgore, Donald Gibson, Jr. *pathologist*

Hilton Head Island
Birk, Robert Eugene *retired physician, educator*
Carr, David Turner *physician*
Santos, George Wesley *physician, educator*

Johns Island
Gamble, William Belser, Jr. *physician*
Ross, Paul *physician, radiologist*

Lexington
Miller, Ben Neely *physician*

Orangeburg
Babb, Julius Wistar, III *cardiovascular surgeon*

Spartanburg
Fudenberg, Herman Hugh *immunologist, educator*

West Columbia
Carter, Saralee Lessman *immunologist, microbiologist*

SOUTH DAKOTA

Gregory
Bolliger, Eugene Frederick *surgeon*

Rapid City
Quinn, Robert Henry *surgeon, medical school administrator*
Wingert, Robert Irvin *obstetrician, gynecologist*

Sioux Falls
†Billion, John Joseph *orthopedic surgeon, state representative*
Fenton, Lawrence Jules *pediatric educator*
Flora, George Claude *retired neurology educator, neurologist*
Hoskins, John H. *urologist, educator*
Jaqua, Richard Allen *pathologist*
Morse, Peter Hodges *ophthalmologist, educator*
Van Demark, Robert Eugene, Sr. *orthopedic surgeon*
Wegner, Karl Heinrich *physician, educator*
Wiebe, Richard Herbert *reproductive endocrinologist, educator*
†Zawada, Edward Thaddeus, Jr. *physician, educator*

Vermillion
Hagen, Arthur Ainsworth *pharmacologist*

TENNESSEE

Bristol
Harkrader, Charles Johnston, Jr. *surgeon*

Chattanooga
Feinberg, Edward Burton *ophthalmologist, educator*
Thow, George Bruce *surgeon*

Johnson City
Adebonojo, Festus O. *medical educator*
Berk, Steven Lee *internist, educator*
Coogan, Philip Shields *pathologist*
Dyer, Allen Ralph *psychiatrist*
Mc Cormick, William Frederick *forensic pathologist, neuropathologist*
Skalko, Richard Gallant *anatomist, educator*

Jonesborough
Weaver, Kenneth *gynecologist, researcher*

Knoxville
Acker, Joseph Edington *retired cardiology educator*
Brott, Walter Howard *cardiac surgeon, educator, retired army officer*
Burkhart, John Henry *physician*
Coulson, Patricia Bunker *endocrinologist*
Kliefoth, A(rthur) Bernhard, III *neurosurgeon*
Lange, Robert Dale *internist, educator, medical researcher*
Natelson, Stephen Ellis *neurosurgeon*
†Solomon, Alan *physician, medical oncologist and clinical investigator*

Memphis
Babin, Richard Weyro *surgeon, educator*
Canale, Dee James *neurosurgeon, educator*
Chesney, Russell Wallace *pediatrician*
†Christopher, Robert Paul *physician*
Cox, Clair Edward, II *urologist, medical educator*
Crist, William Miles *physician*
Gerald, Barry *radiology educator, neuroradiologist*
Heimberg, Murray *pharmacologist, biochemist, physician, educator*
Hughes, Walter Thompson *physician, pediatrics educator*
Ingram, Alvin John *surgeon*
Johnson, James Gibb *physician*
†Lieberman, Phillip Louis *allergist, educator*
Mauer, Alvin Marx *physician, medical educator*
Neely, Charles Lea, Jr. *retired physician*
Pate, James Wynford *surgeon*
Purcell, William Paul *medicinal chemistry educator*
Runyan, John William, Jr. *medical educator*
Shanklin, Douglas Radford *physician*
Solomon, Solomon Sidney *endocrinologist, pharmacologist, scientist*
Sullivan, Jay Michael *medical educator*
Summitt, Robert Layman *pediatrician, educator*
Wilcox, Harry Hammond *retired medical educator*

Nashville
Abumrad, Naji *surgeon, educator*
Bender, Harvey W., Jr. *cardiac and thoracic surgeon*
Bernard, Louis Joseph *surgeon, educator*
Burnett, Lonnie Sheldon *obstetrics and gynecology educator*
Burt, Alvin Miller, III *anatomist, cell biologist, educator, writer*
Byrd, Benjamin Franklin, Jr. *surgeon, educator*
Calhoun, Calvin Lee, Sr. *physician*
Crofford, Oscar Bledsoe, Jr. *internist, medical educator*
†Diamond, Michael P. *obstetrician-gynecologist, educator*
Fowinkle, Eugene W. *physician, medical center administrator*
Hardman, Joel Griffeth *pharmacologist*
Krantz, Sanford Burton *physician*
Lynch, John Brown *plastic surgeon, educator*
Meacham, William Feland *neurological surgeon, educator*
Orth, David Nelson *physician, educator*
Ossoff, Robert Henry *otolaryngological surgeon*
Partain, Clarence Leon *radiologist, nuclear medicine physician, educator, administrator*
Pendergrass, Henry Pancoast *physician, radiology educator*
Petracek, Michael Ray *surgeon*
Pickens, David Richard, Jr. *retired surgeon, educator*
Riley, Harris DeWitt, Jr. *pediatrician*
Robertson, David *clinical pharmacologist, physician, educator*
Robinson, Roscoe Ross *nephrologist, educator*
Ross, Joseph Comer *physician, educator, academic administrator*
Sawyers, John Lazelle *surgeon*
Scott, Henry William, Jr. *surgeon, educator*
Spengler, Dan Michael *orthopedic surgery educator, researcher, surgeon*
Stahlman, Mildred Thornton *pediatrics and pathology educator, researcher*
Story, James Clinton *medical educator*
Thornton, Spencer P. *ophthalmologist, educator*
van Eys, Jan *pediatrician, educator, administrator*

Oak Ridge
Spray, Paul *surgeon*

Williamsport
Dysinger, Paul William *physician, educator, health consultant*

TEXAS

Austin
Bernstein, Robert *retired physician, state official, former army officer*
Ersek, Robert Allen *plastic surgeon, inventor*
Mullins, Charles Brown *physician, academic administrator*
Shurley, Jay Talmadge *psychiatrist, medical educator, polar explorer, author*

Baytown
Williams, Drew Davis *surgeon*

Brooks AFB
Carroll, Robert Eugene *flight surgeon*

Bryan
Dirks, Kenneth Ray *pathologist, medical educator, army officer*

College Station
†Chiou, George Chung-Yih *pharmacologist, educator*
Knight, James Allen *psychiatrist, educator*
Way, James Leong *pharmacology and toxicology educator*

Dallas
Allen, Terry Devereux *urologist, educator*
Baskin, Leland Burleson *pathologist, educator, researcher*
Berbary, Maurice Shehadeh *physician, military officer, hospital administrator, educator*
Blomquist, Carl Gunnar *cardiologist*
Bonte, Frederick James *radiology educator, physician*
Burnside, John Wayne *medical educator, university official*
Cavanagh, Harrison Dwight *ophthalmic surgeon*
Cox, Rody P(owell) *medical educator, internist*
Edwards, George Alva *physician, educator*
Eichenwald, Heinz Felix *physician*
Einspruch, Burton Cyril *psychiatrist*
Ericson, Ruth Ann *psychiatrist*
Feiner, Joel S. *psychiatrist*
Flatt, Adrian Ede *surgeon*
Fogelman, Morris Joseph *physician*
Fordtran, John Satterfield *physician*
Frenkel, Eugene Phillip *physician*
Gage, Tommy Wilton *pharmacologist, dentist, pharmacist, educator*
Gant, Norman Ferrell, Jr. *obstetrician-gynecologist*
Gilman, Alfred Goodman *pharmacologist, educator*
Goldstein, Joseph Leonard *physician, medical educator, molecular genetics scientist*
Harrington, Marion Ray *ophthalmologist*
Jenkins, M. T. Pepper *anesthesiologist, educator*
Kaplan, Norman Mayer *medical educator*
Khan, Amanullah *physician*
Kramer, Robert Ivan *pediatrician*
Lewis, Jerry M. *psychiatrist, educator*
Maddrey, Willis Crocker *medical educator, internist, academic administrator, consultant, researcher*
Mc Clelland, Robert Nelson *surgeon, educator*
New, William Neil *physician, retired naval officer*
Petty, Charles Sutherland *pathologist*
Race, George Justice *pathology educator*
Ram, Chitta Venkata *physician*
Riggs, Leonard, II *emergency medicine physician, emergency care services executive*
Rosenberg, Roger Newman *neurologist, educator*
Sanford, Jay Philip *physician, government official*
Seldin, Donald Wayne *physician, educator*
Smith, Edwin Ide *pediatric surgeon*
Sparkman, Robert Satterfield *retired surgeon, educator*
Sprague, Charles Cameron *medical foundation president*
Stembridge, Vernie A(lbert) *pathologist, educator*
Stone, Marvin Jules *immunologist, physician, educator*
Thompson, Jesse Eldon *vascular surgeon*
Vergne-Marini, Pedro Juan *physician*
Wildenthal, C(laud) Kern *physician, educator*
Wilson, Jean Donald *endocrinologist, educator*
Ziff, Morris *internist, rheumatologist, educator*

Eden
Boyd, John Hamilton *osteopath*

El Paso
Crossen, John Jacob *radiologist, educator*
Jesurún, Harold Méndez *obstetrician-gynecologist, educator*
Kidd, Gerald Steele, II *endocrinologist, educator*

Fort Sam Houston
Pruitt, Basil Arthur, Jr. *surgeon, army officer*

Fort Worth
Jurgensen, Warren Peter *psychiatrist, educator*
Lorenzetti, Ole John *pharmaceutical research executive, ophthalmic research and development executive*

Galveston
†Arens, James F. *anesthesiologist, educator*
Bailey, Byron James *otolaryngologist, medical association executive*
Burns, Chester Ray *medical history educator*
Calverley, John Robert *physician, educator*
Cooper, Cary W(ayne) *pharmacology educator*
Daeschner, Charles William, Jr. *physician, educator*
Dawson, Earl Bliss *obstetrics and gynecology educator*
Goodwin, Jean McClung *psychiatrist*
†Grant, J(ohn) Andrew, Jr. *medical educator, allergist*
†Herndon, David N. *surgeon*
Hilton, James Gorton *pharmacologist*
James, Thomas Naum *cardiologist, educator*
Lefeber, Edward James, Sr. *physician*
Levin, William Cohn *hematologist, former university president*
Ogra, Pearay L. *physician, educator*
†Phillips, Linda Goluch *plastic surgeon, educator, researcher*
Powell, Don Watson *medical educator, physiology researcher*
Powell, Leslie Charles, Jr. *obstetrics and gynecology educator*
Sandstead, Harold Hilton *medical educator*
Schreiber, Melvyn Hirsh *radiologist*
Smith, David English *physician, educator*
Smith, Edgar Benton *physician*
Smith, Jerome Hazen *pathologist*
Thompson, James Charles *surgeon*
Tyson, Kenneth Robert Thomas *surgeon, educator*
Willis, William Darrell, Jr. *neurophysiologist, educator*
Yielding, K. Lemone *physician*

Hemphill
Boren, Hollis Grady *retired physician*

Houston
Alexanian, Raymond *hematologist*
Alford, Bobby Ray *physician, educator, university official*
†Appel, Stanley Hersh *neurologist*
Balch, Charles M. *surgeon, educator*
Baldwin, John Charles *surgeon, researcher*
Baskin, David Stuart *neurosurgeon*
Bast, Robert Clinton, Jr. *research scientist, medical educator*
Batsakis, John George *pathology educator*
Beasley, Robert Palmer *epidemiologist, dean, educator*
Beck, John Robert *pathologist, information scientist*
†Berry, Michael A. *physician, consultant*
Bhandari, Arvind *oncologist*
Bodey, Gerald Paul *oncologist, educator*
Bungo, Michael William *physician, educator, science administrator*
Burdette, Walter James *surgeon, educator*
Busch, Harris *medical educator*
Cantrell, William Allen *psychiatrist, educator*
Cardus, David *physician*
Catlin, Francis Irving *physician*
Collins, Vincent Patrick *radiologist, physician, educator*
Cooley, Denton Arthur *surgeon, educator*
Corriere, Joseph N., Jr. *urologist, educator*
Couch, Robert Barnard *physician, educator*
Dawood, Mohamed Yusoff *obstetrician, gynecologist*
DeBakey, Michael Ellis *cardiovascular surgeon, educator*
Dodd, Gerald Dewey, Jr. *radiologist, educator*
Dudrick, Stanley John *surgeon, educator*
DuPont, Herbert Lancashire *medical educator, researcher*
Engelhardt, Hugo Tristram, Jr. *physician, educator*
Feigin, Ralph David *pediatrician, educator*
Fishman, Marvin Allen *pediatrician, neurologist, educator*
Freireich, Emil J *hematologist, educator*
Garber, Alan J(oel) *medical educator*
Gildenberg, Philip Leon *neurosurgeon*
Glassman, Armand Barry *physician, pathologist, scientist, educator, administrator*
Gotto, Antonio Marion, Jr. *internist, educator*
Gould, Kenneth Lance *physician, educator*
†Graham, David Yates *gastroenterologist*
Grossman, Robert George *physician, educator*
Gunn, Albert Edward, Jr. *internist, lawyer, hospital and university administrator*
Guynn, Robert William *psychiatrist, educator*
Hall, Robert Joseph *physician, medical educator*
Harper, Michael John Kennedy *obstetrics and gynecology educator*
Haynie, Thomas Powell, III *physician*
Haywood, Theodore Joseph *physician, educator*
Henning, Susan June *biomedical researcher*
Hollister, Leo Edward *physician, educator*
Holmquest, Donald Lee *physician, astronaut, lawyer*
Jankovic, Joseph *neurologist, educator, scientist*
Jenkins, Daniel Edwards, Jr. *physician, educator*
Jordan, George Lyman, Jr. *surgeon*
Jordan, Paul Howard, Jr. *surgeon*
Jordon, Robert Earl *physician*
Kahan, Barry Donald *surgeon, educator*
Kaufman, Raymond Henry *physician*
Kellaway, Peter *neurophysiologist, researcher*
Kerwin, Joseph Peter *physician, former astronaut*
Lane, Montague *physician, educator*
Levin, Bernard *physician*
Low, Morton David *physician, educator*
Mattox, Kenneth Leon *surgeon, educator, medical scientist*
Mayor, Heather Donald *medical educator*
Mc Bride, Raymond Andrew *pathologist, physician, educator*
Mc Pherson, Alice Ruth *ophthalmologist*
†Milam, John Daniel *pathologist, educator*
Miller, Gary Evan *psychiatrist, mental health services administrator*
Mountain, Clifton Fletcher *surgeon, educator*
Murray, John A. *orthopedist, medical association executive*
Nosé, Yukihiko *surgeon, educator*
†Nudo, Randolph Joseph *neuroscientist, educator*
Ordonez, Nelson Gonzalo *pathologist*
Owsley, William Clinton, Jr. *radiologist*
Painter, Joseph T. *oncologist, medical association executive*
Pinkel, Donald Paul *pediatrician*
Rakel, Robert Edwin *physician, educator*
Ribble, John Charles *medical educator*
Rich, Robert Regier *immunology educator, physician*
Romsdahl, Marvin Magnus *surgeon, educator*
Rudolph, Arnold Jack *pediatrician, neonatologist, medical educator*
Samaan, Naguib Abdelmalik *endocrinologist*
Shearer, William T. *pediatrician, educator*
†Shulman, Robert Jay *physician*
Siegler, Howard Matthew *physician, surgeon*
Simpson, Joe Leigh *obstetrics and gynecology educator*
†Simpson, Richard Kendall, Jr. *surgeon, physician, researcher*
Spira, Melvin *plastic surgeon*
Stehlin, John Sebastian, Jr. *surgeon*
Thomas, Orville C. *physician*
Vallbona, Carlos *physician*
Walker, William Easton *surgeon, educator, lawyer*
Williams, Robert Leon *psychiatrist, neurologist, educator*
Williams, Temple Weatherly, Jr. *internist, educator*

Irving
Mueller, James Bernhard *anesthesiologist, pain managememt consultant*

Lubbock
Bricker, Donald Lee *surgeon*
Buesseler, John Aure *ophthalmologist, management consultant*
Green, Joseph Barnet *neurologist*
Hartman, James Theodore *physician, educator*
Jackson, Francis Charles *physician, surgeon*
Kenny, Alexander Donovan *pharmacology educator*
Kurtzman, Neil A. *medical educator*
May, Donald Robert Lee *ophthalmologist, retina and vitreous surgeon, educator, academic administrator*
†Messer, Robert H. *obstetrician/gynecologist, educator*
Mittemeyer, Bernhard Theodore *physician, academic administrator*
Perry, Malcolm Oliver *vascular surgeon*
Shires, George Thomas *surgeon, physician, educator*
Williams, Darryl Marlowe *medical educator*
Woolam, Gerald Lynn *surgeon*

Mcallen
Ramirez, Mario Efrain *physician*

Nacogdoches
Fish, Stewart Allison *obstetrician-gynecologist*

New Braunfels
Fomon, Samuel Joseph *physician, educator*

San Antonio
Aust, Joe Bradley *surgeon, educator*
Baker, Floyd Wilmer *surgeon, retired army officer*
Byrnes, Victor Allen *ophthalmologist*
Croft, Harry Allen *psychiatrist*
†Delmer, Merle W. *pathologist*
Kotas, Robert Vincent *research physician, educator*
†Ledford, Frank Finley, Jr. *surgeon, army officer*
Leon, Robert Leonard *psychiatrist, educator*
Maas, James Weldon *psychiatrist*
Mc Fee, Arthur Storer *physician*
Meyer, George Gotthold *psychiatrist, educator*
Mitchell, George Washington, Jr. *physician, educator*
Neel, Spurgeon Hart, Jr. *physician, retired army officer*
Persellin, Robert Harold *physician*
Pestana, Carlos *physician, educator*
Reuter, Stewart Ralston *radiologist, lawyer, educator*
Rosoff, Leonard, Sr. *retired surgeon, medical educator*
Schenker, Steven *physician, educator*
Smith, Reginald Brian Furness *anesthesiologist, educator*
Story, Jim Lewis *neurosurgeon, educator*
Townsend, Frank Marion *pathology educator*
Wiedeman, Geoffrey Paul *physician, air force officer*

Seabrook
Earle, Kenneth Martin *retired neuropathologist*

Temple
Dyck, Walter Peter *gastroenterologist, educator*
Montgomery, Johnny Lester *physician, radiologist*

Texarkana
Selby, Roy Clifton, Jr. *neurosurgeon*

Tyler
Kronenberg, Richard Samuel *physician, educator*
Nelson, Kenwyn Gordon *surgeon*

Webster
Rappaport, Martin Paul *internist, nephrologist, educator*

UTAH

Park City
Wardell, Joe Russell, Jr. *pharmacologist*

Salt Lake City
Abildskov, J. A. *cardiologist, educator*
Bauer, A(ugust) Robert, Jr. *surgeon, educator*
Bragg, David Gordon *physician, radiology educator*
Grosser, Bernard Irving *psychiatry educator*
Hammond, M(ary) Elizabeth Hale *pathologist*
†Janerich, Dwight Thomas *epidemiologist, researcher*
Knight, Joseph Adams *pathologist*
Middleton, Anthony Wayne, Jr. *urologist, educator*
Moser, Royce, Jr. *physician, medical educator*
Nelson, Russell Marion *surgeon, educator*

Odell, William Douglas *physician, scientist, educator*
Olson, Randall J. *ophthalmologist, educator*
Overall, James Carney, Jr. *pediatrics educator*
Pace, Nathan Leon *anesthesiologist, educator*
Renzetti, Attilio David *physician*
Scott, James Raymond *obstetrics and gynecology educator*
Smart, Charles Rich *retired surgeon*
Swenson, James Reed *physician, educator*
Tyler, Frank Hill *medical educator*
Ward, John Robert *physician, educator*
Wong, Kuang Chung *anesthesiologist*

VERMONT

Bradford
Kaplow, Leonard Samuel *pathologist, educator*

Brattleboro
Howland, William Stapleton *anesthesiologist, educator*

Burlington
Davis, John Herschel *surgeon, educator*
Lucey, Jerold Francis *pediatrician*
Mead, Philip Bartlett *physician, administrator*
Riddick, Daniel Howison *obstetrics and gynecology educator, priest*
Sobel, Burton Elias *physician, educator*

Charlotte
Hong, Richard *pediatrician, educator*

Middlebury
Patterson, William Bradford *surgical oncologist*

Norwich
Payson, Henry Edwards *forensic psychiatrist, educator*

South Burlington
Terris, Milton *physician, educator*

White River Junction
Barton, Gail Melinda *psychiatrist, educator*

Williston
Mc Kay, Robert James, Jr. *pediatrician, educator*

VIRGINIA

Alexandria
Mosely, Linda Hays *surgeon*

Annandale
Binder, Richard Allen *hematologist, oncologist*
Shamburek, Roland Howard *physician*
Simonian, Simon John *surgeon, scientist, educator*
Stage, Thomas Benton *psychiatrist*

Arlington
Brown, James Harvey *neuroscientist, government research administrator*
Dolan, William David, Jr. *physician*

Charlottesville
Barnett, Benjamin Lewis, Jr. *physician, educator*
Barrett, Eugene J. *researcher, medical educator, physician*
Beller, George Allan *medical educator*
Cantrell, Robert Wendell *otolaryngologist, head and neck surgeon, educator*
Cawley, Edward Philip *physician, educator*
Craig, James William *physician, educator, university dean*
Davis, John Staige, IV *physician*
Detmer, Don Eugene *medical educator, administrator, surgeon*
Dreifuss, Fritz Emanuel *neurologist, educator*
Edgerton, Milton Thomas, Jr. *reconstructive and hand surgeon, educator*
Epstein, Robert Marvin *anesthesiologist, educator*
Farr, Barry Miller *physician, epidemiologist*
Fechner, Robert Eugene *pathology educator*
Flickinger, Charles John *anatomist, educator*
Gillenwater, Jay Young *urologist, educator*
Gross, Charles Wayne *physician, educator*
Gwaltney, Jack Merrit, Jr. *physician, educator, scientist*
Harbert, Guy Morley, Jr. *obstetrician-gynecologist*
Hook, Edward Watson, Jr. *physician, educator*
Howards, Stuart S. *physician, educator*
Jane, John Anthony *neurosurgeon, educator*
Jones, Rayford Scott *surgeon, medical educator*
Kassell, Neal Frederic *neurosurgeon*
Kattwinkel, John *physician, pediatrics educator*
Keats, Theodore Eliot *physician, radiology educator*
Kitchin, James D., III *obstetrician-gynecologist, educator*
Mandell, Gerald Lee *physician, medicine educator*
McCallum, Richard Warwick *medical researcher, clinician, educator*
Mc Quillen, Michael Paul *physician*
Morgan, Raymond F. *plastic surgeon*
Muller, William Henry, Jr. *surgeon, educator*
Nolan, Stanton Peelle *surgeon, educator*
Owen, John Atkinson, Jr. *physician, educator*
Perkins, Marvin Earl *psychiatrist, educator*
Peterson, Kent Wright *physician*
†Phillips, Lawrence H., II *neurologist*
Platts-Mills, Thomas Alexander E. *immunologist, educator, researcher*
Pullen, Edwin Wesley *anatomist, university dean*
Rowlingson, John Clyde *anesthesiologist, educator, physician*
Stevenson, Ian *psychiatrist, educator*
Stone, David Deaderick *physician, educator*
Suratt, Paul Michael *physician, researcher*
Taylor, Peyton Troy, Jr. *gynecologic oncologist, educator*
Teates, Charles David *radiologist, educator*
Thorner, Michael Oliver *medical educator, research center administrator*
Underwood, Paul Benjamin *obstetrician, educator*
Villar-Palasi, Carlos *pharmacology educator*
Weary, Peyton Edwin *medical educator*
Wilhelm, Morton *surgery educator*
Wills, Michael Ralph *medical educator*

Fairfax
Dettinger, Garth Bryant *surgeon, physician, retired air force officer, county health officer*
Rubin, Robert Joseph *physician, health care consultant*
Schulman, Joseph Daniel *physician, medical geneticist, reproductive biologist, educator*

Falls Church
Bucur, John Charles *neurological surgeon*
Ehrlich, S(aul) Paul, Jr. *physician, consultant, former government official*

Fredericksburg
Margileth, Andrew Menges *physician, former naval officer*

Glen Allen
Williams, William Clyde *physician*

Gordonsville
Marshall, Victor Fray *physician, educator*

Hampton
Brown, Loretta Ann Port *physician, geneticist*

Huddleston
Singleton, Samuel Winston *physician, pharmaceutical company executive*

Leesburg
Mitchell, Russell Harry *dermatologist*

Lynchburg
Crow, Harold Eugene *physician, family medicine educator*

Mc Lean
Buck, Alfred Andreas *physician, epidemiologist*
Cooper, John Allen Dicks *medical educator*
Laning, Robert Comegys *retired physician, former naval officer*

Midlothian
Jones, John Evan *medical educator*

Millwood
Grupe, Warren Edward *pediatrician, educator*

Norfolk
Andrews, Mason Cooke *obstetrician-gynecologist, educator, mayor*
Andrews, William Cooke *physician*
Devine, Charles Joseph, Jr. *urologist, educator*
Dyar, Kathryn Wilkin *pediatrician*
El-Mahdi, Anas Morsi *radiation oncologist*
Faulconer, Robert Jamieson *pathologist, educator*
Geib, Philip Oldham *physician, retired naval officer*
Jones, Howard Wilbur, Jr. *gynecologist*
Lester, Richard Garrison *radiologist, educator*
Lind, James Forest *surgeon, educator*

Richmond
Ayres, Stephen McClintock *physician, educator*
Christie, Laurence Glenn, Jr. *surgeon*
Dandoy, Suzanne Eggleston *physician, state agency executive*
Dunn, Leo James *obstetrician, gynecologist, educator*
Ferry, Andrew Peter *ophthalmic surgeon, medical educator*
Franko, Bernard Vincent *pharmacologist*
Gewanter, Harry Lewis *pediatric rheumatologist*
Goldman, Israel David *hematologist, oncologist*
Haynes, Boyd Withers, Jr. *surgeon*
Kay, Saul *pathologist*
Kendig, Edwin Lawrence, Jr. *physician, educator*
Koontz, Warren Woodson, Jr. *urologist, educator*
Lawrence, Walter, Jr. *surgeon*
Mauck, Henry Page, Jr. *medical and pediatrics educator*
Mc Cue, Carolyn Moore *retired pediatric cardiologist*
Mellette, M. Susan Jackson *physician, educator, researcher*
Oken, Donald Edward *physician, educator*
Owen, Duncan Shaw, Jr. *physician, medical educator*
Patterson, James Willis *pathology and dermatology educator*
Richardson, David Walthall *cardiologist, educator, consultant*
Thompson, William Taliaferro, Jr. *internist, educator*
Ward, John Wesley *retired pharmacologist*
†Wechsler, Andrew Stephen *surgery educator*
Weinberg, Robert Stephen *ophthalmologist*

Salem
Chakravorty, Ranes Chandra *surgeon, educator*

Suffolk
Carroll, George Joseph *pathologist, educator*

Virginia Beach
Mayer, William Dixon *pathologist, educator*

Williamsburg
Jacoby, William Jerome, Jr. *internist, retired military officer*

Winchester
†Bechamps, Gerald J. *surgeon*

WASHINGTON

Auburn
Sata, Lindbergh Saburo *psychiatrist, physician, educator*

Bellevue
Hackett, Carol Ann Hedden *physician*
Knoepfler, Peter Tamas *psychiatrist, organizational consultant*
Olson, Hilding Harold *surgeon, educator*

Friday Harbor
Geyman, John Payne *physician, educator*

Issaquah
Barchet, Stephen *physician, former naval officer*

Longview
Kenagy, John Warner *surgeon*

Mazama
Hogness, John Rusten *physician, academic administrator*

Mercer Island
Coe, Robert Campbell *surgeon*
Elgee, Neil Johnson *physician*
Haviland, James West *physician*

Mount Vernon
Cammock, Earl E. *surgeon*

Olympia
†Flemming, Stanley Lalit Kumar *family practice physician, state legislator*

Port Ludlow
Ward, Louis Emmerson *retired physician*

Pullman
Barnes, Charles D. *neuroscientist, educator*

Redmond
Beeson, Paul Bruce *physician*

Richland
Bair, William J. *radiation biologist*
Zirkle, Lewis Greer *physician, executive*

Seattle
Aagaard, George Nelson *medical educator*
Abelson, Herbert Traub *pediatrician, educator*
Aldrich, Robert Anderson *physician*
Anderson, Richard Powell *thoracic surgeon, educator*
Ansell, Julian S. *physician, urology educator*
Bassingthwaighte, James Bucklin *physiologist, educator, medical researcher*
Benedetti, Thomas Joseph *obstetrician-gynecologist, educator*
Bierman, Charles Warren *physician, educator*
Bierman, Edwin Lawrence *physician, educator*
Blagg, Christopher Robin *nephrologist*
Blandau, Richard Julius *physician, educator*
Bonica, John Joseph *anesthesiologist, educator*
Bornstein, Paul *physician, biochemist*
Botimer, Allen Ray *retired surgeon, retirement center administrator*
†Bowden, Douglas McHose *neuropsychiatric scientist, educator, research center administrator*
Caro, Ivor *dermatologist*
Couser, William Griffith *medical educator, academic administrator, nephrologist*
Dale, David C. *physician, medical educator*
Donaldson, James Adrian *otolaryngology educator*
Dorpat, Theodore Lorenz *psychoanalyst*
Figley, Melvin Morgan *radiologist, physician, educator*
Freeny, Patrick Clinton *radiology educator, consultant*
Gardner, Jill Christopher *neuroscientist*
Giblett, Eloise Rosalie *hematology educator*
Goodell, Brian Wayne *oncologist, medical educator*
Graham, C(lyde) Benjamin, Jr. *physician*
Grayston, J. Thomas *medical and public health educator*
Guntheroth, Warren Gaden *physician*
†Guralnick, Michael J. *medical research administrator*
Hackett, John Peter *dermatologist*
Hargiss, James Leonard *ophthalmologist*
Henderson, Maureen McGrath *medical educator*
Herring, Susan Weller *anatomist*
Hodson, William Alan *pediatrician*
Hornbein, Thomas Frederic *anesthesiologist*
†Hudson, Leonard Dean *physician*
Hutchinson, William Burke *surgeon, research center director*
Jonsen, Albert R. *medical ethics educator*
Kalina, Robert Edward *physician, educator*
†Keith, Donald Malcolm *physician*
Kirby, William Murray Maurice *medical educator*
Klebanoff, Seymour Joseph *medical educator*
Kraft, George Howard *physician, educator*
LaVeck, Gerald DeLoss *physician, educator*
Loeser, John David *neurosurgeon, educator*
Martin, George M. *pathologist, gerontologist*
Mason, James Tate *surgeon*
Merendino, K. Alvin *surgical educator*
Moore, Daniel Charles *physician*
Mottet, Norman Karle *pathologist, educator*
†Nelson, James Alonzo *radiologist, educator*
Ojemann, George A. *neurosurgeon, medical association executive*
Petersdorf, Robert George *medical educator, association executive*
Ravenholt, Reimert Thorolf *epidemiologist*
Robertson, William Osborne *physician*
Ross, Russell *pathologist, educator*
Schilling, John Albert *surgeon*
Scott, John Carlyle *gynecologist, oncologist*
Scribner, Belding Hibbard *medical educator, nephrologist*
Shepard, Thomas Hill *physician, educator*
Simkin, Peter Anthony *physician, educator*
Stenchever, Morton Albert *physician, educator*
Strandjord, Paul Edphil *physician, educator*
Strandness, Donald Eugene, Jr. *surgeon*
Swanson, August George *physician, retired association executive*
Swanson, Phillip Dean *neurologist*
Tenney, William Frank *pediatrician*
Thomas, Edward Donnall *physician, researcher*
Weaver, Lois Jean *physician, educator*
Wilske, Kenneth Ray *internist, rheumatologist, researcher*
Winterbauer, Richard Hill *physician, medical researcher*
Yarington, Charles Thomas, Jr. *surgeon, administrator*

Shelton
Barnard, Michael Dana *orthopedic surgeon*

Spokane
Bakker, Cornelis B. *psychiatrist, educator*
Gibson, Melvin Roy *pharmacognosy educator*
McClellan, David Lawrence *physician*
Mielke, Clarence Harold, Jr. *hematologist*
†Moyer, John Arthur *obstetrician/gynecologist, state senator*

Tacoma
Chen, Stephen Shau-tsi *psychiatrist, physiologist*
Grenley, Philip *urologist*

WEST VIRGINIA

Barboursville
Bradley, Robert Lee *surgeon*

Bluefield
Blaydes, James Elliott *ophthalmologist*

Charleston
†Heck, Albert Frank *neurologist*

Huntington
Bowdler, Anthony John *physician, educator*
Cocke, William Marvin, Jr. *plastic surgeon, educator*
Esposito, Albert Charles *ophthalmologist, state legislator*
Mufson, Maurice Albert *physician, educator*

Lewisburg
Willard, Ralph Lawrence *surgery educator, physician, former college president*

Martinsburg
Malin, Howard Gerald *podiatrist*

Morgantown
Colasanti, Brenda Karen *pharmacoloy and toxicology educator*
Fleming, William Wright, Jr. *pharmacology educator*
Warden, Herbert Edgar *surgeon, educator*
Weinstein, George William *ophthalmology educator*

Wheeling
Heceta, Estherbelle Aguilar *anesthesiologist*

WISCONSIN

Brookfield
Hardman, Harold Francis *pharmacology educator*

Fond Du Lac
Treffert, Darold Allen *psychiatrist, author, hospital director*

La Crosse
Corser, David Hewson *pediatrician*
†Webster, Stephen Burtis *physician, educator*

Madison
Albert, Daniel Myron *ophthalmologist, educator*
Bach-y-Rita, Paul *neurophysiologist, rehabilitation medicine specialist*
Bass, Paul *pharmacology educator*
Belzer, Folkert Oene *surgeon*
Bloodworth, J. M. Bartow, Jr. *physician, educator*
Boutwell, Roswell Knight *oncology educator*
Brown, Arnold Lanehart, Jr. *pathologist, educator, university dean*
Burgess, Richard Ray *oncology educator, molecular biology researcher, biotechnology consultant*
Carbone, Paul Peter *oncologist, educator, administrator*
Colás, Antonio Espada *medical educator*
Dodson, Vernon Nathan *physician, educator*
Dolan, Terrence Raymond *neurophysiology educator*
Fahien, Leonard August *physician, educator*
Farley, Eugene Shedden, Jr. *physician, educator*
Forster, Francis Michael *physician, educator*
Jackson, Carl Robert *obstetrician/gynecologist*
Javid, Manucher J. *neurosurgeon*
Jefferson, James Walter *psychiatry educator*
Keesey, Ulker Tulunay *ophthalmology and psychology educator, researcher*
Kepecs, Joseph Goodman *physician, educator*
†Kumar, Anand *medical educator, researcher*
Laessig, Ronald Harold *pathology educator, state official*
Lobeck, Charles Champlin, Jr. *pediatrics educator*
Mac Kinney, Archie Allen, Jr. *physician*
Maki, Dennis G. *medical educator, researcher, clinician*
Marton, Laurence Jay *clinical pathologist, educator, researcher*
McBeath, Andrew Alan *orthopedic surgery educator*
Miller, James Alexander *oncologist, educator*
Mohs, Frederic Edward *surgeon, educator*
Nordby, Eugene Jorgen *orthopedic surgeon*
Peters, Henry Augustus *neuropsychiatrist*
Pitot, Henry Clement, III *physician, educator*
Reynolds, Ernest West *physician, educator*
Roberts, Leigh Milton *psychiatrist*
Rowe, George Giles *cardiologist, educator*
†Sackett, Joseph Frederic *radiologist, educator, administrator*
Schutta, Henry Szczesny *neurologist, educator*
Sobkowicz, Hanna Maria *neurology researcher*
Sonnedecker, Glenn Allen *historian of pharmacy*
Tomar, Russell Herman *pathologist, educator, researcher*
†Urban, Frank Henry *dermatologist, state legislator*
Westman, Jack Conrad *child psychiatrist, educator*
Whiffen, James Douglass *surgeon, educator*

Manitowoc
Scheving, Lawrence Einar *scientist, anatomy educator*
Trader, Joseph Edgar *orthopedic surgeon*

Marshfield
Fye, W. Bruce, III *cardiologist*
Sautter, Richard Daniel *physician, administrator*
Stueland, Dean Theodore *emergency physician*

Milwaukee
Bhore, Jay Narayan *psychiatrist*
Bortin, Mortimer M. *physician*
Condon, Robert Edward *surgeon, educator*
Cooper, Richard Alan *hematologist, college dean*
Esterly, Nancy Burton *physician*
Fink, Jordan Norman *physician, educator*
Kochar, Mahendr Singh *physician, educator, administrator, researcher, writer, consultant*
Namdari, Bahram *surgeon*
Pisciotta, Anthony Vito *physician, educator*
Schultz, Richard Otto *ophthalmologist, educator*

Shindell, Sidney *medical educator, physician*
Soergel, Konrad Hermann *physician*
Stafl, Adolf *obstetrician, gynecologist, educator*
Swick, Herbert Morris *medical educator, neurologist*
Terry, Leon Cass *neurologist, educator*
†Youker, James Edward *radiologist*

Sayner
Southwick, Harry Webb *surgeon*

Sheboygan
Gore, Donald Ray *orthopedic surgeon*

Tomah
Shim, Jae Yong *physician*

Wauwatosa
†Hollister, Winston Ned *pathologist*

West Allis
Feinsilver, Donald Lee *psychiatry educator*

West Bend
Gardner, Robert Joseph *general and thoracic surgeon*

WYOMING

Cheyenne
Hunton, Donald Bothen *retired internist*

Wilson
Eliot, Robert Salim *physician*

TERRITORIES OF THE UNITED STATES

PUERTO RICO

Mayaguez
Miskimen, George William *neurobiologist, educator*

Ponce
Sala, Luis Francisco *surgeon, educator*

San Juan
Amadeo, Jose H. *physician, educator*
De Jesús, Nydia Rosa *physician, anesthesiologist*
Ramirez-Rivera, Jose *physician*
Sahai, Hardeo *medical educator*

MILITARY ADDRESSES OF THE UNITED STATES

EUROPE

APO
Chong, Vernon *surgeon, physician, Air Force officer*

CANADA

ALBERTA

Calgary
†Hollenberg, Morley Donald *research physician, educator*
Lederis, Karolis Paul (Karl Lederis) *pharmacologist, educator, researcher*
Melvill-Jones, Geoffrey *physician, educator*
Rewcastle, Neill Barry *neuropathology educator*
†Stell, William Kenyon *neuroscientist, educator*
ter Keurs, Henk E. D. J. *cardiologist, educator*

Edmonton
Albritton, William Leonard *physician, microbiologist*
Cook, David Alastair *pharmacology educator*
Dewhurst, William George *physician, psychiatrist, educator, researcher*
Miller, Jack David R. *radiologist, physician, educator*

BRITISH COLUMBIA

Vancouver
Baird, Patricia Ann *physician, educator*
Bates, David Vincent *physician, medical educator*
Burhenne, Hans Joachim *physician, radiology educator*
Chow, Anthony Wei-Chik *physician*
Doyle, Patrick John *otolaryngologist*
Eaves, Allen Charles Edward *hematologist, medical agency administrator*
Freeman, Hugh James *gastroenterology educator*
Friedman, Sydney M. *anatomy educator, medical researcher*
Hardwick, David Francis *pathologist*
†Jewesson, Peter John *pharmacologist, educator*
Knobloch, Ferdinand J. *psychiatrist, educator*
McGeer, Edith Graef *neurological science educator emerita*
Mizgala, Henry F. *physician*
Paty, Donald Winston *neurologist*
†Rootman, Jack *ophthalmologist, surgeon, pathologist, oncologist, artist*
Roy, Chunilal *psychiatrist*
Slonecker, Charles Edward *anatomist, medical educator, author*
Sutter, Morley Carman *medical scientist*
Thurlbeck, William Michael *pathologist*
Tingle, Aubrey James *pediatric immunologist, research administrator*
Tyers, Geddes Frank Owen *surgeon*

Victoria
Mac Diarmid, William Donald *physician*

MANITOBA

Winnipeg
Angel, Aubie *physician, academic administrator*
Blanchard, Robert Johnstone Weir *surgeon*
Bowman, John Maxwell *physician, educator*
†Greenberg, Arnold Harvey *pediatrics educator, cell biologist*
Haworth, James Chilton *pediatrics educator*
Israels, Lyonel Garry *hematologist, medical educator*
Persaud, Trivedi Vidhya Nandan *anatomy educator, researcher, consultant*
Ronald, Allan Ross *internal medicine and medical microbiology educator, researcher*
Ross, Robert Thomas *neurologist, educator*
Sutherland, John Beattie *radiologist, health center administrator*

NOVA SCOTIA

Halifax
Carruthers, S. George *medical educator, physician*
Gold, Judith Hammerling *psychiatrist*
Goldbloom, Richard Ballon *pediatrics educator*
Langley, George Ross *medical educator*
Tonks, Robert Stanley *pharmacology and therapeutics educator, former university dean*

ONTARIO

Hamilton
Basmajian, John Varoujan *medical scientist, educator, physician*
Bienenstock, John *physician, educator*
Collins, John Alfred *obstetrician-gynecologist, educator*
Mueller, Charles Barber *surgeon, educator*
Roland, Charles Gordon *physician, medical historian, educator*
Uchida, Irene Ayako *cytogenetics educator, researcher*

Kingston
Boag, Thomas Johnson *physician*
Kaufman, Nathan *pathology educator, physician*
Low, James A. *physician*

London
Barr, Murray Llewellyn *former anatomy educator*
Brooks, Vernon Bernard *neuroscientist, educator, author*
Buck, Carol Kathleen *medical educator*
Frelick, Linden Frederick *hospital executive*
Lala, Peeyush Kanti *medical scientist, educator*
Marotta, Joseph Thomas *medical educator*
McWhinney, Ian Renwick *physician, medical educator*
Valberg, Leslie Stephen *medical educator, physician, researcher*

Mississauga
Perkin, Reginald Lewis *physician, educator*

North York
Regan, David *brain researcher, educator*

Ottawa
de Bold, Adolfo J. *pathology and physiology educator, research scientist*
Friesen, Henry George *endocrinologist, educator*
Hagen, Paul Beo *physician, medical scientist*
Hurteau, Gilles David *obstetrician, gynecologist, educator, university dean*
Jackson, W. Bruce *ophthalmology educator, researcher*
†Keon, Wilbert Joseph *cardiologist, surgeon, educator*
Lavoie, Lionel A. *physician, medical executive*
Waugh, Douglas Oliver William *pathology educator*

Sault Sainte Marie
Banerjee, Samarendranath *orthopedic surgeon*

Toronto
Alberti, Peter William *otolaryngologist*
Brown, Gregory Michael *psychiatrist, educator, research director*
Bruce, William Robert *physician, educator*
†Casson, Alan Graham *thoracic surgeon, researcher*
Cinader, Bernhard *immunologist, gerontologist, scientist, educator*
†Friesen, James *pediatrics research administrator*
Goldenberg, Gerald Joseph *physician, educator*
Greben, Stanley Edward *psychiatrist, educator, author, editor*
Hudson, Alan Roy *neurosurgeon, medical educator, hospital administrator*
Kalant, Harold *pharmacology educator, physician*
Kalow, Werner *pharmacologist, toxicologist*
Lindsay, William Kerr *surgeon*
Lipowski, Zbigniew Jerzy *psychiatrist, educator*
Lowy, Frederick Hans *psychiatrist, university center director, former university dean*
Mc Culloch, Ernest Armstrong *physician, educator*
Miller, Anthony Bernard *physician, medical researcher*
Nesbitt, Lloyd Ivan *podiatrist*
Ogilvie, Richard Ian *clinical pharmacologist*
Potts, Douglas Gordon *neuroradiologist*
Rakoff, Vivian Morris *psychiatrist, writer*
Rothstein, Aser *radiation biology educator*
Salter, Robert Bruce *orthopaedic surgeon, researcher, educator*
Seeman, Philip *pharmacology educator, neurochemistry researcher*
Silver, Malcolm David *pathologist, educator*
†Sole, Michael Joseph *cardiologist*
Till, James Edgar *scientist*
Turner, Robert Edward *psychiatrist, educator*
Volpé, Robert *endocrinologist*

Willowdale
Turnbull, John Cameron *pharmacist, consultant*

PRINCE EDWARD ISLAND

Monticello
Gingras, Gustave *physician*

QUEBEC

Montpellier, Quebec
Poirier, Louis Joseph *neurology educator*

Montreal
Baxter, Donald William *physician, educator*
Beardmore, Harvey Ernest *retired physician, educator*
Becklake, Margaret Rigsby *physician, educator*
Burgess, John Herbert *physician, educator*
†Chretien, Michel *physician, educator, administrator*
Clermont, Yves Wilfrid *anatomy educator, researcher*
Cruess, Richard Leigh *surgeon, university dean*
Cuello, Augusto Claudio Guillermo *medical research scientist, author*
Feindel, William Howard *neurosurgeon, consultant*
Freeman, Carolyn Ruth *radiation oncologist*
Genest, Jacques *physician, researcher, administrator*
†Gjedde, Albert Hellmut *neuroscientist, neurology educator*
Gold, Phil *physician, educator*
Goltzman, David *endocrinologist, educator, researcher*
Jasmin, Gaetan *pathologist, educator*
Leblond, Charles Philippe *anatomy educator, researcher*
Lehmann, Heinz Edgar *psychiatrist, consultant, researcher*
Little, Alan Brian *obstetrician, gynecologist, educator*
MacDonald, R(onald Angus) Neil *physician, educator*
Mac Lean, Lloyd Douglas *surgeon*
Mc Gregor, Maurice *cardiologist, medical educator*
Milic-Emili, Joseph *physician, educator*
Moore, Sean *pathologist, educator*
Mulder, David S. *cardiovascular surgeon*
†Nattel, Stanley *cardiologist, research scientist*
Osmond, Dennis Gordon *medical educator, researcher*
Pelletier, Louis Conrad *surgeon, educator*
Pinard, Gilbert Daniel *psychiatrist, educator*

Quebec
Couture, Jean G. *surgeon, educator*
Jovanovic, Miodrag *surgeon, educator*
Labrie, Fernand *physician*

Sherbrooke
Bureau, Michel André *pediatrician, pulmonologist, faculty dean*
de Margerie, Jean-M. *ophthalmology educator*

Ville de Laval
Siemiatycki, Jack *epidemiologist, biostatistician, educator*

Westmount
Jasper, Herbert Henri *neuroscience researcher, consultant, writer*
Kessler, Jacques Isaac *gastroenterologist, educator*

SASKATCHEWAN

Saskatoon
Emson, Harry Edmund *pathology educator, bioethicist*
Habbick, Brian Ferguson *pediatrician, community health and epidemiology educator*
Jaques, Louis Barker *pharmacologist*
Johnson, Dennis Duane *pharmacologist, educator*
Keegan, David Lloyd *psychiatrist, educator*

MEXICO

Guadalajara
Garibay-Gutierrez, Luis *physician, educator*

Juarez
Torres Medina, Emilio *oncologist, consultant*

Mexico City
Diaz-Coller, Carlos *physician*

AUSTRALIA

Brisbane
English, Francis Peter *ophthalmologist, educator*

Hobart
Munger, Bryce L. *physician, educator*

Nedlands
Oxnard, Charles Ernest *anatomist, anthropologist, human biologist, educator*

Rockhampton
Lynch, Thomas Brendan *pathologist*

West Perth
Woods, Thomas Brian *physician*

AUSTRIA

Maria Enzersdorf
Vetter, Herbert *physician, educator*

Vienna
Frankl, Viktor E. *psychiatrist, author*

BELGIUM

Antwerp
Uyttenbroeck, Frans Joseph *gynecologic oncologist*

BRAZIL

Rio de Janeiro
Leite, Carlos Alberto *physician, medical educator*

Salvador
Silva, Benedicto Alves de Castro *surgeon, educator*

DENMARK

Bronshoj
Skylv, Grethe Krogh *rheumatologist, anthropologist*

ENGLAND

Cambridge
Acheson, Roy Malcolm *epidemiologist, educator*

London
Arnott, Eric John *ophthalmologist*
Asfoury, Zakaria Mohammed *physician*
Comfort, Alexander *physician, author*
Ross, Euan Macdonald *pediatrician, educator*
Symon, Lindsay *neurological surgery educator*
Vane, John Robert *pharmacologist*

Oxford
Dawes, Geoffrey Sharman *medical researcher*
Guillery, Rainer Walter *anatomy educator*

FINLAND

Kuopio
Hakola, Hannu Panu Aukusti *psychiatry educator*

FRANCE

Aix les Bains
Tabau, Robert Louis *rheumatologist, researcher*

Ballan Mire
Delbarre, Bernard *pharmacologist, consultant*

Chartres
Benoit, Jean-Pierre Robert *pneumologist, consultant*

Gouvieux
Fraser, David William *epidemiologist*

Laval
Sauvé, Georges *surgeon*

Longjumeau
Kapandji, Adalbert Ibrahim *orthopedic surgeon*

Lyons
Meunier, Pierre Jean *medical educator*

Marseilles
Vague, Jean Marie *endocrinologist*

Montpellier
Michel, Henri Marie *medical educator*

Nanterre
Nguyen-Trong, Hoang *physician, consultant*

Paris
Ben Amor, Ismäil *obstetrician/gynecologist*
Dausset, Jean *immunologist*
Gontier, Jean Roger *internist, physiology educator, consultant*
Levy, Etienne Paul Louis *surgical department administrator*

Rognac
Castel, Gérard Joseph *physician*

GERMANY

Bielefeld
Lauven, Peter Michael *anesthesiologist*

Böblingen
Mühe, Erich *surgical educator*

Frankfurt
Duus, Peter *neurology educator*

Freiburg
Schaefer, Hans-Eckart *pathologist*

Gladbeck
Geisler, Linus Sebastian *physician, educator*

Munich
Paumgartner, Gustav *hepatologist, educator*

Stuttgart
Szirmai, Endre Anreas Franz *physician, writer*

Wuppertal
Schubert, Guenther Erich *pathologist*

GRENADA

Saint George's
Brunson, Joel Garrett *pathologist, educator*

INDIA

Madras
Chandra Sekharan, Pakkirisamy *forensic scientist*

IRELAND

Galway
Lavelle, Seān Marius *clinical informatics educator*

JAPAN

Fukuoka
Omura, Tsuneo *medical educator*
Shirai, Takeshi *physician*

Hiroshima
Tahara, Eiichi *pathologist, educator*

Hiroshima City
Harkness, Donald Richard *hematologist, educator*

Kanagawa
Saitoh, Tamotsu *pharmacology educator*

Kobe
Yamabe, Shigeru *medical educator*

Niigata
Asakura, Hitoshi *internal medicine educator*

Okinawa
Noda, Yutaka *physician, otolaryngologist*

Osaka
Horiuchi, Atsushi *physician, educator*

Sambu-Gun
Morishige, Fukumi *surgeon*

Sapporo
Fukuda, Morimichi *medical educator*

Sendai
Oikawa, Atsushi *pharmacology educator*
Okuyama, Shinichi *physician*

Shimonoseki
Sekitani, Toru *otolaryngologist, educator*

Shimotsuga
Ichimura, Tohju *pediatrician, educator*

Tochigi
Takasaki, Etsuji *urology educator*

Tokorozawa
Nakamura, Hiroshi *urology educator*

Tokyo
Akera, Tai *pharmacologist*
Masuda, Gohta *physician, educator*
Terao, Toshio *physician, educator*
Watanabe, Kouichi *pharmacologist, educator*

Yamanashi-ken
Onaya, Toshimasa *internal medicine educator*

Yokohama
Kaneko, Yoshihiro *cardiologist, researcher*

THE NETHERLANDS

Leiden
Banta, Henry David *physician, researcher*

Maastricht
Van Praag, Herman Meir *psychiatrist, educator, administrator*

NORWAY

Oslo
Fagerhol, Magne Kristoffer *immunologist*

PAKISTAN

Faisalabad
Irfan, Muhammad *pathology educator*

POLAND

Warsaw
Tarnecki, Remigiusz Leszek *neurophysiology educator, laboratory director*

PORTUGAL

Coimbra
Cunha-Vaz, Jose Guilherme Fernandes *ophthalmologist*

Lisbon
De Almeida, Antonio Castro Mendes *surgery educator*

REPUBLIC OF KOREA

Chonju
Kang, Sung Kyew *medical educator*

SCOTLAND

Clydebank
Krakoff, Irwin Harold *pharmacology and oncology educator*

SOUTH AFRICA

Johannesburg
Mendelsohn, Dennis *chemical pathology educator, consultant*

SPAIN

Oviedo
Garcia-Moran, Manuel *surgeon*

SWEDEN

Lund
Abdulla, Mohamed *physician, educator*

Malmö
Cronberg, Stig *infectious diseases educator*

Stockholm
Möller, Göran *immunology educator*

SWITZERLAND

Büsingen
Friede, Reinhard L. *neuropathologist, educator*

Geneva
Henderson, Ralph Hale *physician*
Rabinowicz, Théodore *neuropathology educator*

Lausanne
Borel, Georges Antoine *gastroenterologist, consultant*
Delaloye, Bernard *retired nuclear medicine physician*

Montreux
Cronin, Robert Francis Patrick *cardiologist, educator*

WEST INDIES

Grenada
Barrett, James Thomas *immunologist, educator*
Taylor, Keith Breden *physician, educator*

ADDRESS UNPUBLISHED

Abell, Murray Richardson *retired medical association administrator*
Ablin, Richard Joel *immunologist, educator*
Adams, James Thomas *surgeon*
Aldrich, Franklin Dalton *research physician*
†Altshuler, Kenneth Z. *psychiatrist*
Andreoli, Thomas Eugene *physician*
Appenzeller, Otto *neurologist, researcher*
Aranda, Miguel Angel *surgeon, educator*
Arnaud, Claude Donald, Jr. *physician, educator*
Bacon, George Edgar *pediatrician, educator*
Baker, Laurence Howard *oncology educator*
Baldwin, DeWitt Clair, Jr. *physician, educator*
Ball, John Robert *medical association executive*
Bartlett, James Williams *psychiatrist, educator*
Bass, Norman Herbert *physician, scientist, university and hospital administrator, health care executive*
Beiser, Helen Ruth *psychiatrist*
Bishop, Raymond Holmes, Jr. *physician, retired army officer*
Bonn, Ethel May *psychiatrist, educator*
Bowie, E(dward) J(ohn) Walter *hematologist, researcher*
Brent, Robert Leonard *physician, educator*
Brewer, Leslie G. *psychiatrist*
†Bubrick, Melvin Phillip *surgeon*
Burger, Leslie Morton *physician, army officer*
Burrell, Craig Donald *physician, educator*
Calvert, William Preston *radiologist*
Capek, Vlastimil *retired radiologist, educator*
Caplovitz, Coleman David *physician*
Carey, Martin Conrad *gastroenterologist, molecular biophysicist, educator*
Carman, George Henry *retired physician*
Carroll, Bernard James *psychiatrist*
†Chaikof, Elliot Lorne *vascular surgeon*
Chernoff, Amoz Immanuel *hematologist, consultant*
Chin, Hong Woo *oncologist, educator, researcher*
Clemetson, Charles Alan Blake *physician*
Cohen, B. Stanley *physician*
Colonnier, Marc Leopold *neuroanatomist, educator*
Coriell, Lewis Lemon *physician, research institute administrator*
Cronkhite, Leonard Wolsey, Jr. *physician, consultant, research foundation executive*
Cuatrecasas, Pedro Martin *research pharmacologist*
Curtis, James L. *psychiatrist*
Cushman, Paul *physician, educator*
Daly, James William *physician, educator*
Danesh, Hossain Banadaki *psychiatrist, writer, international consultant*
Danilowicz, Delores Ann *pediatric cardiologist, pediatrics educator*
Davidson, Mayer B. *medical educator, researcher*
de Marneffe, Francis *psychiatrist, hospital administrator*
DePalma, Ralph George *surgeon, educator*
De Salva, Salvatore Joseph *pharmacologist, toxicologist*
Dewhurst, William Harvey *psychiatrist*
Dickes, Robert *psychiatrist*
Dickson, James Francis, III *surgeon*
Diener, Erwin *immunologist*
Douglass, John Michael *internist*
Dumont, Allan Eliot *physician, educator*
Eaton, Merrill Thomas *psychiatrist, educator*
Eckenhoff, James Edward *physician, educator*
Edwards, Charles *neuroscientist, educator*
Edwards, Larry David *physician, academic dean*
Ein, Daniel *allergist*
Fariss, Bruce Lindsay *endocrinologist, educator*
Fenoglio-Preiser, Cecilia Mettler *pathologist, educator*
Ferlinz, Jack *cardiologist, medical educator*
Filston, Howard Church *pediatric surgeon, educator*
Frank, Sanders Thalheimer *physician, educator*
Fredrickson, Donald Sharp *physician, scientist*
Friedman, Eugene Warren *surgeon*
Frost, J. Ormond *otolaryngologist, educator*
Gable, Carol Brignoli *pharmacoeconomics researcher*
Gajdusek, Daniel Carleton *pediatrician, research virologist*
Garcia, Alexander *orthopaedic surgeon*
Gers, Seymour *psychiatrist*
Ginsburg, Iona Horowitz *psychiatrist*
Glass, Dorothea Daniels *physiatrist, educator*
Glassock, Richard James *nephrologist*
Gordan, Gilbert Saul *physician, educator*
Graham, James Herbert *dermatologist*
Green, Joseph Martin *psychiatrist, educator*
Greene, Laurence Whitridge, Jr. *surgical educator*
Gross, Ruth Taubenhaus *physician*
Grund, Walter James, Jr. *retired gynecologist*
Haggerty, Robert Johns *physician, educator*
Halliday, William Ross *retired physician, speleologist, writer*
Harmon, Robert Gerald *health consultant*
Hendry, Jean Sharon *psychopharmacologist*
Herman, Chester Joseph *physician*
Hirose, Teruo Terry *surgeon*
Hoch, Frederic Louis *medical educator*
Holland, Robert Campbell *anatomist, educator*
Hunter, Richard Grant, Jr. *neurologist, executive*
Huntley, Robert Ross *physician, educator*
Inui, Thomas Spencer *physician, educator*
Iqbal, Zafar *biochemist, neurochemist*
Jackson, Carmault Benjamin, Jr. *physician*
Jackson, Rudolph Ellsworth *pediatrician, educator*
Jones, Walton Linton *internist, former government official*
Kahn, David *dermatologist, educator*
Kellogg, Carol Kay *neuroscientist, researcher*
Kent, Donald Charles *physician*
Kent, Howard Lees *obstetrician/gynecologist*
†Kevorkian, Jack *pathologist*
Klombers, Norman *association executive, retired*
Larson, David Bruce *research epidemiologist*
Leis, Henry Patrick, Jr. *surgeon, educator*
Leslie, Gerrie Allen *immunologist*
Levin, Jack *physician, educator, biomedical investigator*
Levy, David Alfred *immunology educator, physician, scientist*
Livingston, Robert Burr *neuroscientist, educator*
Loube, Samuel Dennis *physician*
Lovell, Robert Gibson *retired physician, educator*
Maier, Alfred *neuroscientist*
Malkinson, Frederick David *dermatologist*
Mathews, William Edward *neurological surgeon, educator*
Mc Guigan, James Edward *physician, scientist, educator*
McPhedran, Norman Tait *surgeon, educator*
Mead, Beverley Tupper *physician, educator*
Meister, Steven Gerard *cardiologist, educator*
Meyer, Greg Charles *psychiatrist*
†Michaelis, Elias K. *neurochemist*
Miller, Ross Hays *retired neurosurgeon*
Millikan, Clark Harold *physician*
Moffet, Hugh Lamson *pediatrician*
Monninger, Robert Harold George *ophthalmologist, educator*
Moossy, John *neuropathologist, neurologist, consultant*
Morgan, Elizabeth *plastic and reconstructive surgeon*
Motto, Jerome Arthur *psychiatry educator*
Napodano, Rudolph Joseph *internist, medical educator*
Novack, Alvin John *physician*
Okuda, Kunio *emeritus medical educator*
O'Leary, Denis Joseph *retired physician, insurance company executive*
Packard, John Mallory *physician*
Palmer, Raymond A. *medical association administrator, librarian*
†Pancake, Edwina Howard *medical librarian*
Parker, Brent Mershon *retired medical educator, internist, cardiologist*
Peterson, Ann Sullivan *physician, health care consultant*
Phelps, Paulding *rheumatologist, internist*
†Pick, Robert Yehuda *orthopedic surgeon, consultant*
Plimpton, Calvin Hastings *physician, university president*
Powell, Clinton Cobb *radiologist, physician, former university administrator*
Prusiner, Stanley Ben *neurology and biochemistry educator, researcher*
Raichle, Marcus Edward *radiology, neurology educator*
Randolph, Judson Graves *pediatric surgeon*
Rask, Michael Raymond *orthopaedist*
Richmond, Julius Benjamin *retired physician, health policy educator emeritus*
Robinson, David Adair *neurophysiologist*
Rodgers, Lawrence Rodney *physician, educator*
Rosemberg, Eugenia *physician, scientist, educator, medical research administrator*
Rosenow, John Henry *surgeon, educator*
Rosenthal, Sol Roy *preventive medicine educator, researcher*
Russo, Jose *pathologist*
Sacha, Robert Frank *osteopathic physician*
Sanders, Aaron Perry *radiation biophysics educator*
Saneto, Russell Patrick *pediatrician, neurobiologist*
Sanfelippo, Peter Michael *cardiac, thoracic and vascular surgeon*
Schulter-Ellis, Frances Pierce *anatomist, educator*
Sher, Paul Phillip *physician, pathologist*
Sherman, John Foord *biomedical consultant*
Shumacker, Harris B., Jr. *surgeon, educator, author*
Smith, Martin Henry *pediatrician*
Smith, Stuart Lyon *psychiatrist, corporate executive*
Stickler, Gunnar Brynolf *pediatrician*
Stone, James Robert *surgeon*
Strain, James Ellsworth *pediatrician, retired association administrator*
†Strandberg, John David *comparative pathologist*
Threefoot, Sam Abraham *physician, educator*
Toledo-Pereyra, Luis Horacio *transplant surgeon, researcher, educator*
Valentine, William Newton *physician, educator*
Verwoerdt, Adriaan *psychiatrist*
White, Augustus Aaron, III *orthopaedic surgeon*
Whitley, Nancy O'Neil *retired radiology educator*
Williams, Roger Stewart *physician*
Wilson, Almon Chapman *surgeon, physician, retired naval officer*
Woodhouse, Derrick Fergus *ophthalmologist*
Worrell, Richard Vernon *orthopedic surgeon, educator*
Wyngaarden, James Barnes *physician*
Yamane, George Mitsuyoshi *oral diagnosis and radiology educator*
Zacks, Sumner Irwin *pathologist*
Zwislocki, Jozef John *neuroscience educator, researcher*

MEDICAL, DENTAL, AND HEALTH SERVICES: OTHER

UNITED STATES

ALABAMA

Auburn
Barker, Kenneth Neil *pharmacy administration educator*
Vaughan, John Thomas *veterinarian, educator, university dean*

Birmingham
Austin, Charles John *health services educator*
Booth, Rachel Zonelle *nursing educator*
Caplan, Lester *optometrist, educator*
Devane, Denis James *health care company executive*
Giger, Joyce Anne Newman *nursing educator, consultant*
†Johnson, Emmett Raymond *hospital administrator*
†Lee, James A. *health facility finance executive*
Lewis, James Eldon *health care executive*
Miller, Dennis Edward *corporate executive*
†Moon, James E. *hospital administrator*
Peters, Henry Buckland *optometrist, educator*
Quintana, Jose Booth *health care executive*
†Richards, J. Scott *rehabilitation medicine professional*

Huntsville
Boston, Edward Dale *hospital administrator*

Mobile
Clark, Jack *hospital company executive, accountant*

Montgomery
†Baggiano, Faye Stone *public health service officer*
Myers, Ira Lee *physician*
Rowan, John Robert *medical center director*

Opelika
Knecht, Charles Daniel *veterinarian*

Tuscaloosa
Cooper, Eugene Bruce *speech-language pathologist, educator*
†Fetner, Charles Anthony *hospital administrator*
Ford, James Henry, Jr. *hospital executive*
Prigmore, Charles Samuel *social work educator*
Sheeley, Eugene Charles *audiology educator*
Shellhase, Leslie John *social work educator*

ALASKA

Sitka
†Willman, Arthur Charles *healthcare executive*

Soldotna
Franzmann, Albert Wilhelm *wildlife veterinarian, consultant*

ARIZONA

Mesa
Boyd, Leona Potter *retired social worker*
House, Roy C. *retired hospital executive*

Phoenix
Ballantyne, Reginald Malcolm, III *healthcare executive*
†Crews, James Cecil *hospital administrator*
Rodgers, Anthony D. *hospital administrator*
†Seiler, Steven Lawrence *health facility administrator*

Prescott
Markham, Richard Glover *research executive*
Mc Cormack, Fred Allen *state social services administrator*

Scottsdale
Cordingley, Mary Jeanette Bowles (Mrs. William Andrew Cordingley) *social worker, psychologist, artist, writer*

Sun City
Van Hauer, Robert *former health care company executive*

Sun City West
Brands, Allen Jean *pharmacist*

Tempe
Harward, Naomi Markee *retired social worker and educator, volunteer*

Tucson
Lohr, Mary Margaret *nursing educator, university dean*
†Morford, James Warren *internation health care executive*
Nation, James Edward *speech pathologist*
Pearson, Paul Brown *nutritionist, educator*
Scott, William Coryell *medical executive*
Shropshire, Donald Gray *hospital executive*
Weber, Charles Walter *nutrition educator*

ARKANSAS

Fort Smith
Banks, David Russell *health care executive*
Stephens, Bobby Wayne *nursing home administrator*

Hot Springs
†Farley, Roy C. *rehabilitation researcher, educator*

Little Rock
Lampkin, Stephen Bradley *hospital administrator*
McCabe, Beverly Jean *nutritionist, educator*
Pierson, Richard Allen *hospital administrator*
†Wolfe, Jonathan James *pharmacy educator*

CALIFORNIA

Albany
Chook, Edward Kongyen *disaster medicine educator*

Aliso Viejo
Sanford, Sarah J. *nurse, health care executive*

Anaheim
Sloane, Robert Malcolm *hospital administrator*

Benicia
Gomez, Edward Casimiro *physician, hospital administrator*

Berkeley
Calloway, Doris Howes *nutrition educator*
Enoch, Jay Martin *vision scientist, educator*
Fleming, Scott *retired health services executive*
Gilbert, Neil Robin *social work educator, author, consultant*
†Greene, Albert Lawrence *hospital administrator*
†Hafey, Joseph Michael *health association executive*
†Holder, Harold D. *public health administrator, communications specialist, educator*
Westheimer, Gerald *optometrist, educator*

Beverly Hills
Simmons, Richard Milton Teagle *physical fitness specialist, television personality*

Brea
Dyer, Alice Mildred *psychotherapist*

Burbank
†Freeberg, Don *health care executive*
†Hartshorn, Terry O. *health facility administrator*

Burlingame
Green, Robert Leonard *hospital management company executive*

Canoga Park
Taylor, Edna Jane *employment program counselor*

Coloma
Wall, Sonja Eloise *nurse, administrator*

Concord
†Jessup, R. Judd *managed care executive*

Cypress
Hoops, Alan *health care company executive*

Danville
†Davis, James Ivey *company president, laboratory associate*

Davis
Ardans, Alexander Andrew *veterinarian, laboratory director, educator*
Biberstein, Ernst Ludwig *veterinary medicine educator*
Rhode, Edward Albert *veterinary medicine educator, veterinary cardiologist*
†Schneeman, Barbara Olds *nutrition educator, department chair*
Schwabe, Calvin Walter *veterinarian, medical historian, medical educator*
Steffey, Eugene Paul *veterinary medicine educator*

Downey
Schroeder, Robert J. *veterinarian, association executive*

Duarte
†Shapero, Sanford Marvin *hospital executive, rabbi*

Encino
†Lewitt, Maurice *health care service company executive*

Fairfield
Hawn, William Eugene *health care company executive*

Fountain Valley
Gumbiner, Robert Louis *health services executive*
Storms, Lester (C Storms) *retired veterinarian*

Fresno
Helzer, James Dennis *hospital executive*
Stude, Everett Wilson, Jr. *rehabilitation counselor, educator*

Grass Valley
Cartwright, Mary Lou *laboratory scientist*

Irvine
Jones, Joie Pierce *acoustician, educator, writer, scientist*
Martin, Jay Herbert *psychoanalysis and English educator*

La Honda
Waldhauer, Fred Donald *health care executive*

La Jolla
Arnold, Jean Ann *health science facility administrator*
Cornette, William Magnus *scientist, research director, company executive*
†Early, Ames S. *health facility administrator*
†Maher, James R. *laboratory administrator*

Laguna Beach
Arterburn, Stephen Forrest *health care company executive*
Banuelos, Betty Lou *rehabilitation nurse*
Smith, Leslie Roper *hospital administrator*

Laguna Niguel
Carr, Bernard Francis *hospital administrator*

Loma Linda
†Hinshaw, David B., Sr. *hospital administrator*
Register, Ulma Doyle *nutrition educator*

Long Beach
Kingore, Edith Louise *retired geriatrics and rehabilitation nurse*
Mullins, Ruth Gladys *pediatrics nurse*

Los Angeles
Andersen, Ronald Max *health services educator, researcher*
†Buckingham, Jerry L. *hospital administrator*
Eamer, Richard Keith *health care company executive, lawyer*
†Gates, Robert C. *health facility administrator*
Gilman, John Joseph *research scientist*
Hopkins, Carl Edward *public health educator*
Horowitz, Ben *medical center executive*
Hummel, Joseph William *hospital administrator*
†King, Sheldon Selig *medical center administrator, educator*
Lien, Eric Jung-chi *pharmacist, educator*
Merchant, Roland Samuel, Sr. *hospital administrator, educator*
†Neumann, Alfred Kurt *public health physician, educator*
Perkins, William Hughes *speech pathologist, educator*
†Ratican, Peter Jay *health maintenance organization executive*
Roberts, Robert Winston *social work educator, dean*

Los Osos
Brown, Mary Eleanor *physical therapist, educator*

Malibu
Reres, Mary Epiphany *health care and administration consultant*

Menlo Park
Salmon, Vincent *acoustical consultant*

Mission Viejo
†Milunas, J. Robert *health care organization executive*

Moraga
Allen, Richard Garrett *health care and education consultant*

Newport Beach
Stephens, Michael Dean *hospital administrator*

Oakhurst
Bonham, Clifford Vernon *social worker, educator*

Oakland
†Caulfield, W. Harry *health care industry executive, physician*
†Lawrence, David M. *health faciligy administrator*
†Moon, Wayne *health facility administrator*
Vohs, James Arthur *health care program executive*

Orange
Noce, Walter William, Jr. *hospital administrator*
†Viviano, Paul Steven *medical center administrator*

Oroville
Ward, Chester Lawrence *physician, county health official, retired military officer*

Oxnard
Dimitriadis, Andre C. *health care executive*
Herlinger, Daniel Robert *hospital administrator*

Pasadena
Azpeitia, Lynne Marie *psychotherapist, educator*
†Messenger, Ron J. *health facility administrator*
Nackel, John George *health care consulting director*

Pebble Beach
Keene, Clifford Henry *medical administrator*

Placentia
George, Julia Bever *nurse administrator, educator*

Rancho Mirage
Ford, Betty Bloomer (Elizabeth Ford) *health facility executive, wife of former President of United States*

Riverside
Cohen, Kenneth Bruce *health agency director*

Roseville
Dupper, Frank Floyd *health care facility executive*

Running Springs
Giles, Walter Edmund *alcohol and drug treatment executive*

Sacramento
Farrell, Francine Annette *psychotherapist, educator*
Greenfield, Carol Nathan *psychotherapist*
Hays, Patrick Gregory *health care executive*
Headley, Nathan Leroy *laboratory executive*
Loge, Frank Jean, II *hospital administrator*

San Bernardino
Timmreck, Thomas C. *health sciences and health administration educator*

San Diego
Bakko, Orville Edwin *retired health care executive, consultant*
Buncher, James Edward *healthcare management executive*
Colling, Kenneth Frank *hospital administrator*
Cutright, Frances Larson *marriage and family therapist*
†Ellsworth, Peter Kennedy *health care executive*
Heuschele, Werner Paul *veterinary researcher*
Johnson, Kenneth Owen *audiologist, association executive*
†Kayler, Robert Samuel *hospital administrator*
†Rosen, Peter *health facility administrator, emergency physician, educator*
Roy, Catherine Elizabeth *physical therapist*
Schmidt, Terry Lane *health care executive*
Trout, Monroe Eugene *hospital systems executive*
Weisman, Irving *social worker, educator*
†Yarbrough, Mary Gale *hospital administrator*

San Francisco
Ansak, Marie-Louise *health care executive*
Clanon, Thomas Lawrence *hospital administrator*
Collins, Carter Compton *research scientist, inventor*
Johnson, Herman Leonall *research nutritionist*
Martinson, Ida Marie *nurse, physiologist, educator*
Meleis, Afaf Ibrahim *nurse sociologist, educator, clinician*
†Nafziger, Dean H. *special education research executive*
Schmitt, George Herbert *hospital executive*
Underwood, Patricia Ruth *clinical nursing educator, consultant*
Westerdahl, John Brian *nutritionist, health educator*

San Jose
†Lash, Steven M. *hospital administrator*

San Lorenzo
Lantz, Charles Alan *chiropractor, researcher*

San Marcos
Knight, Edward Howden *retired hospital administrator*
Liggins, George Lawson *microbiologist-diagnostic company executive*

Santa Ana
Alston, Roberta T(heresa) *medical technologist*

Santa Barbara
Edwardsen, Kenneth Robert *administrator*
Narayanamurti, Venkatesh *research administrator*

Santa Monica
†Barbakow, Jeffrey *health facility administrator*
Bedrosian, John C. *health care executive*
Brook, Robert Henry *physician, educator, health services researcher*
Cohen, Leonard *hospital management company executive*
Focht, Michael Harrison *health care industry executive*

Shadow Hills
Cole, Roberta C. *nursing educator*

Sherman Oaks
Boyd, Dawn Michele *vocational expert, wage loss analyst*
Peplau, Hildegard Elizabeth *nursing educator*

Solana Beach
Engle, Harold Martin *retired medical administrator*

Solvang
Hegarty, William Kevin *medical center executive*

Sonoma
Markey, William Alan *health care administrator*

Stanford
Basch, Paul Frederick *international health educator, parasitologist*
†Bloem, Kenneth D. *healthcare facility executive*
Cork, Linda Katherine *veterinary pathologist, educator*
Mc Namara, Joseph Donald *researcher, retired police chief, novelist*

Whittier
†Zeisler, John Alfred, Jr. *clinical pharmacist, educator*

Winters
Low, Donald Gottlob *retired veterinary medicine educator*

Woodland Hills
†Schaeffer, Leonard David *health care executive*

COLORADO

Aurora
Fedak, Barbara Kingry *technical center administrator*

Boulder
Anderson, Robert K. *health care company executive*
Holdsworth, Janet Nott *women's health nurse*

Colorado Springs
Farr, Leonard Alfred *hospital administrator*
Vayhinger, John Monroe *psychotherapist, minister*
West, Ralph Leland *veterinarian*

Denver
Albrecht, Duane Taylor *veterinarian*
Bauder, Sister Marianna *hospital administrator*
Brimhall, Dennis C. *hospital executive*
Chinn, Peggy Lois *nursing educator, editor*
Doran, Maureen O'Keefe *psychotherapist, psychiatric nursing consultant*
Edelman, Joel *medical center executive*
Glismann, Diane Duffy *health facility administrator*
Kirkpatrick, Charles Harvey *physician, immunology researcher*
McBurney, Linda Lee *health facility administrator*
Parker, Catherine Susanne *psychotherapist*
Rael, Henry Sylvester *health administrator*

Fort Collins
Gubler, Duane J. *research scientist, administrator*
†McIlwraith, Cyril Wayne *veterinary surgery educator*
Voss, James Leo *veterinarian*

Grand Junction
Pantenburg, Michel *hospital administrator, health educator, holistic health coordinator*
Zumwalt, Roger Carl *hospital administrator*

Littleton
Vail, Charles Daniel *veterinarian, consultant*

Longmont
Melendez, Joaquin *orthopedic assistant*

Pueblo
Avery, Julia May *speech pathologist, organizational volunteer*

Wheat Ridge
LaMendola, Walter Franklin *information technology consultant*
†Willard, James Douglas *health care administrator*

CONNECTICUT

Avon
Patricelli, Robert E. *health care company executive*

Danbury
Finch, Carolyn-Bogart *speech and language pathologist, speaker, writer*

Glastonbury
Bruner, Robert B. *hospital consultant*

Greenwich
Sheppard, Posy (Mrs. Jeremiah Milbank) *social worker*

Hartford
D'Eramo, David *hospital adminstrator*
Hamilton, Thomas Stewart *physician, hospital administrator*
Springer, John Kelley *hospital administrator*

Lyme
Bloom, Barry Malcolm *pharmaceutical company executive*

Milford
†Muth, Eric Peter *optician, consultant*

New Haven
De Rose, Sandra Michele *psychotherapist, educator, supervisor, administrator*
Jekel, James Franklin *physician, public health educator*
Krauss, Judith Belliveau *nursing educator*
†Meyer, Patricia Ann *veterinarian*
Silver, George Albert *physician, educator*
†Smith, C. Thomas, Jr. *hospital administrator*
Zaccagnino, Joseph Anthony *hospital administrator*

Norwalk
Sasenick, Joseph Anthony *health care company executive*

Riverside
Otto, Charles Edward *health care administrator*

Storrs Mansfield
Packard, Sheila Anne *nursing educator, researcher*

Uncasville
†Ryan, Kevin *optometrist, physics*

West Redding
Benyei, Candace Reed *psychotherapist*

Woodbridge
Womer, Charles Berry *retired hospital executive, management consultant*

DELAWARE

Newark
Doberenz, Alexander R. *nutrition educator, chemist*
Hurst, Christina Marie *respiratory therapist*

Wilmington
Johnson, Allen Leroy *hospital administrator*

DISTRICT OF COLUMBIA

Washington
Bentley, James Daniel *association executive*
†Blanck, Ronald Ray *hospital administrator, internist, career officer*
Buckalew, Judith Adele *nurse, pharmaceutical industry executive*
Chilman, Catherine Earles Street *social welfare educator, author*
Crawford, Lester Mills, Jr. *veterinarian*
Davis, Carolyne Kahle *health care consultant*
Eckenhoff, Edward Alvin *health care administrator*
Falter, Robert Gary *correctional health care administrator*
Filerman, Gary Lewis *health education executive*
Francke, Gloria Niemeyer *pharmacist, editor, publisher*
Gaull, Gerald Edward *nutritionist, scientist, educator, food company executive*
Glasser, Melvin Allan *health policy executive, consultant*
Hanft, Ruth S. Samuels (Mrs. Herbert Hanft) *health care consultant, educator, economist*
†Hannett, Frederick James *healthcare consulting company executive*

Jones, Stanley Boyd *health policy analyst, priest*
Lash, Myles Perry *hospital administrator*
Masi, Dale A. *research company executive, social work educator*
May, Sterling Randolph *health association executive*
†McCarthy, John B. *veterinarian, veterinary association executive*
†McDaniel, John Perry *health care company executive*
Nef, Evelyn Stefansson *psychotherapist, author, editor, specialist polar regions*
Norby, Ronald Brandon *nurse executive*
Norcross, Marvin Augustus *veterinarian, government agency official*
Peele, Roger *hospital administrator*
Samet, Kenneth Alan *hospital administrator*
Shaw, Sallye Brown *women's health nurse*
Smits, Helen Lida *public adminstrator, physician, educator*
Speidel, John Joseph *physician, foundation officer*
Tracy, Thomas Miles *international health organization official*
†Turner, Brenda Lorraine *social worker*
Woteki, Catherine Ellen *nutritionist*

FLORIDA

Boynton Beach
Peltzie, Kenneth Gerald *hospital administrator, educator*

Chattahoochee
Ivory, Peter B. C. B. *medical administrator*

Clearwater
Houtz, Duane Talbott *hospital administrator*

Daytona Beach
Elliott, Carol Harris *nutrition counselor, dietitian*
McCoy, Edward Fitzgerald *social services facility administrator*

Delray Beach
Leapman, Phyllis Lenore *retired nursing educator*

Fernandina Beach
Kurtz, Myers Richard *hospital administrator*

Fort Lauderdale
†Andrews, John Harold *health care administrator*
†Turner, Richard Stanley *health care financial executive*

Fort Myers
Kelly, William E. *psychoanalyst*
Nathan, James Robert *hospital administrator*

Gainesville
†Brown, William Samuel, Jr. *communication processes and disorders educator*
Dierks, Richard Ernest *veterinarian, educational administrator*
Himes, James Albert *veterinary medicine educator emeritus*
Jaeger, Boi Jon *health administrator educator*
Nicoletti, Paul Lee *veterinarian, educator*
Randall, Malcom *health care administrator*
†Thompson, Neal Philip *food science and nutrition educator*
Watson, Robert Joe *hospital administrator, retired career officer*

Gulf Breeze
Lankton, Stephen Ryan *family therapist*

Hollywood
Sacco, Frank Vincent *hospital administrator*

Homosassa
Acton, Norman *international organization executive*

Jacksonville
Gregg, John Franklin *hospital administrator*
Honaman, J. Craig *health facility administrator*
†Mason, William Cordell, III *hospital administrator*
Yamane, Stanley Joel *optometrist*

Lakeland
†Stephens, Jack Thomas, Jr. *hospital administrator*

Largo
Hamlin, Robert Henry *public health educator, management consultant*

Melbourne
Means, Michael David *hospital administrator*

Miami
Barritt, Evelyn Ruth Berryman *nurse, educator, university dean*
Burkett, Marjorie Theresa *nursing educator, gerontology nurse*
Clark, Ira C. *hospital association administrator, educator*
Keeley, Brian E. *hospital administrator*
Plungis, Barbara Marie *health facility nursing administrator*
Sims, James Larry *hospital administrator, healthcare consultant*
Teicher, Morton Irving *social worker, educator*

Micanopy
Cripe, Wyland Snyder *veterinary medicine educator, consultant*

Naples
Crone, William Gerald *hospital administrator*
Dion, Nancy Logan *health care administrator, management consultant*
Terenzio, Peter Bernard *hospital administrator*

North Fort Myers
DiCarlo, Louis Michael *speech pathology educator*

North Miami Beach
†Birnbaum, Joel M. *health care company executive*

Orange Park
Rice, Ronald James *hospital administrator*

Orlando
Blair, Mardian John *hospital management executive*
†Strack, J. Gary *hospital administrator*
Werner, Thomas Lee *hospital administrator*

Pensacola
Caton, Betty Ann *health science administrator*
Groner, Pat Neff *health care executive*
VanSlyke, Robert Emmett *health care executive*

Pineland
Doherty, Michel George *alcohol and drug treatment facility administrator*

Plantation
Baez, Manuel *health care executive*

Pompano Beach
Ayres, John Cecil *retired public health executive*

Saint Petersburg
Cane, Paula P. *speech and language pathologist, scriptwriter, actor*
McIntyre, Deborah *psychotherapist, author*
Wisler, Willard Eugene *health care management executive*

Sarasota
Covert, Michael Henri *healthcare facility administrator*

Seminole
Haile, James Francis *hospital administrator*

Sun City Center
Parsons, George Williams *retired medical center administrator, cattle rancher*

Tallahassee
Moore, Duncan *healthcare executive*
Mustian, Middleton Truett *hospital administrator*

Tampa
†Bice, Michael O. *health science association administrator*
†Biebel, John *health care administrator*
Bussone, David Eben *hospital administrator*
†Harrell, Cecil Stanford *pharmacy management service company executive*
†Molnar, Lewis K. *health facility administrator*
Read, Peter Kip *health care administrator*
†Silver, Richard Abraham *hospital administrator*

GEORGIA

Americus
Gray, Margaret Edna *nursing educator*

Athens
Ansel, Howard Carl *pharmacist, educator*
Holland, Thomas Powell *social work educator*
Levine, David Lawrence *social work educator*
Trim, Cynthia Mary *veterinarian, educator*
Tyler, David Earl *veterinary medical educator*

Atlanta
Baranowski, Tom *public health educator, researcher*
Barker, William Daniel *hospital administrator*
Gayer, Alan J. *hospital administrator*
Henry, John Dunklin *hospital administrator*
Hopkins, Donald Roswell *public health physician*
Houk, Vernon Neal *retired public health administrator*
†Hubbard, Richard Buell, III *hospital administrator*
Iodice, Joanna DiMeno (Jody Iodice) *psychotherapist*
Koplan, Jeffrey Powell *physician*
Martin, David Edward *health sciences educator*
†McDonagh, Kathryn Joyce *hospital administrator*
Patti, Sister Josephine Marie *health science facility administrator*
†Satcher, David *public health service officer, federal official*
†Thomas, Nadine *nurse, legislator, state official*
Wells, Donald Eugene *hospital administrator*

Augusta
Bray, Donald Claude *hospital administrator*
Feldman, Elaine Bossak *medical nutritionist, educator*
Gillespie, Edward Malcolm *hospital administrator*
†Howell, Robert Edward *hospital administrator*
†Peloquin, Garry Wayne *hospital executive*

Columbus
Brabson, Max LaFayette *health care executive*

Doraville
Yancey, Eleanor Margaret Garrett *crisis intervention clinician*

Dunwoody
Bartolo, Donna M. *hospital administrator, nurse*

Macon
Crawford, Edwin Mack *health facilities executive*
Faulk, Alfred Donald, Jr. *hospital administrator*
Fickling, William Arthur, Jr. *health care administrator*
†Mac Crawford, Edwin *health facility administrator*

Marietta
†Bonn, Edward Joseph *hospital executive*
Petit, Parker Holmes *health care corporation executive*

Rome
Johnson, Mary *nursing administrator*

Savannah
†Ives, John Elway *hospital administrator*

Statesboro
Talmadge, Mary Christine *nursing educator*

Tifton
†Thomas, Adrian Wesley *laboratory director*

Valdosta
Bowling, John Selby *hospital administrator*

HAWAII

Hilo
Werner, Marlin Spike *speech pathologist and audiologist*

Honolulu
Fischer, Joel *social work educator*
†Hall, Marvin B. *hospital administrator*
Hanson, Dennis Michael *medical imaging executive*
Holland, Charles Malcolm, Jr. *retired health care executive, development corporation executive, retired banker*
Lewin, John Calvert *public health administrator*
Lum, Jean Loui Jin *nurse educator*
Michael, Jerrold Mark *public health specialist, former university dean, educator*
†Ushijima, Arthur Akira *health facility administrator*

Koloa
Gustafson, Charles Ivan *hospital administrator*

Mililani
Kiley, Thomas *rehabilitation counselor*

IDAHO

Bonners Ferry
McClintock, William Thomas *health care administrator*

ILLINOIS

Bolingbrook
Price, Theodora Hadzisteliou *social worker*

Carbondale
Buckley, John Joseph, Jr. *health care executive*

Champaign
Birdzell, Samuel Henry *hospital administrator*

Chicago
Andreoli, Kathleen Gainor *nurse, educator, administrator*
Baptist, Allwyn J. *health care consultant*
Campbell, Bruce Crichton *hospital administrator*
Conibear, Shirley Ann *occupational health consultant, physician*
†De Paoli, Alexander M. *veterinary pathologist, researcher*
†Esmond, Truman H., Jr. *health facility administrator*
Garrett, Shirley Gene *nuclear medicine technologist*
Hunt, Roger Schermerhorn *hospital administrator*
†Lubawski, James Lawrence *health care administrator*
Maltz, J. Herbert *physician, hospital director*
Marston-Scott, Mary Vesta *nurse, educator*
Mecklenburg, Gary Alan *hospital executive*
†Muller, Ralph W. *hospital administrator*
Rosenheim, Margaret Keeney *social welfare policy education educator*
†Rothstein, Ruth M. *hospital adminstrator*
Russell, Lillian *medical, surgical nurse*
Schuerman, John Richard *social work educator*
Schwartz, John Norman *health care executive*
Simon, Bernece Kern *social work educator*
Slomka, Sister Stella Louise *hospital administrator*
Spivey, Bruce E. *health care executive*
†Trotter, Donne E. *hospital administrator*

Decatur
Perry, Anthony John *retired hospital executive*

Deerfield
Helpap, John Frederick *retired health care executive*

East Peoria
Walker, Philip Chamberlain, II *health care executive*

Edwardsville
Cameron, Colleen Irene *alcoholism counselor*

Elgin
Hoeft, Elizabeth Bayless *speech and language pathologist*
Nelson, John Thilgen *hospital administrator, physician*

Evanston
Neaman, Mark Robert *hospital administrator*
Wilber, Laura Ann *audiologist*

Frankfort
†Pearson, Gerald P. *hospital administrator*

Franklin Park
Wagner, Betty Valiree *medical organization executive*

Galesburg
Kowalski, Richard Sheldon *hospital administrator*

Glencoe
†Bernstein, Myron *veterinarian*

Highland Park
Friend, Peter Michael *hospital executive*

Hines
†Cummings, Joan E. *health facility administrator*

Joliet
Benfer, David William *hospital administrator*

Kankakee
Schroeder, David Harold *health care facility executive*

Kenilworth
Frederick, Earl James *healthcare consultant*

Macomb
Hopper, Stephen Rodger *hospital administrator*

Marion
Livengood, Richard Vaughn *healthcare executive*

Maryville
Hurteau, William James *hospital administrator consultant*

Maywood
Cera, Lee Marie *veterinarian*

Mc Henry
Duel, Ward Calvin *health care consultant*

Mokena
†Janssen, Sister Norma *hospital administrator*

North Chicago
Kringel, John G. *health products company executive*

Northbrook
†Lever, Alvin *health science association administrator*
Rudnick, Ellen Ava *health care executive*

Oak Brook
†Baker, Robert J(ohn) *hospital administrator*
†Risk, Richard R. *health facility administrator*

Oak Lawn
Massura, Eileen Kathleen *family therapist*

Oak Park
Varchmin, Thomas Edward *environmental health administrator*

Ottawa
Willet, Shirley Hill *geriatrics and maternal-women's health nurse*

Park Ridge
Boe, Gerard Patrick *health science association administrator*
†McCarthy, Michael Shawn *health care company executive, lawyer*
Ryan, Judith Andre *health care executive, hospital administrator, nurse*
†Ummel, Stephen L. *health facility administrator*
†Wardell, Kevin Stuart *hospital administrator*

Peoria
†Masching, Sister Frances Marie *healthcare system executive*
McCollum, Jean Hubble *medical assistant*

Plainfield
Schinderle, Robert Frank *hospital administrator*

Rockford
Maysent, Harold Wayne *hospital administrator*

Springfield
†Clarke, Robert Thorburn *medical center executive*
Laabs, Allison C. *hospital administrator*
†Trstensky, Sister Jomary *hospital administrator*

University Park
Wentz, Walter John *health administration educator*

Urbana
Davis, Lloyd Edward *veterinary medicine educator*
Parker, Alan John *veterinary neurologist, educator, researcher*
Siedler, Arthur James *nutrition and food science educator*
Small, Erwin *veterinarian, educator*
Visek, Willard James *nutritionist, animal scientist, physician, educator*

Villa Park
Evans, Austin James *hospital administrator*
Treat, Thomas Frank *health care executive*

Westchester
Clarke, Richard Lewis *health science association administrator*

Westmont
Wesbury, Stuart Arnold, Jr. *health care consultant*

Wheaton
Loebig, Wilfred F. *health care executive*

Wilmette
Randolph, Lillian Larson *medical association executive*

Winnetka
VanBremen, Lee *medical association executive*

Wood Dale
Thompson, John Henry *consulting executive*

INDIANA

Bloomington
Kohr, Roland Ellsworth *hospital administrator*
†Schroeder, Henry J. *health science organization administrator*

Bluffton
Brockmann, William Frank *medical facility administrator*

Carmel
†Chittenden, Michael Dennis *hospital administrator*

Columbus
†McGinty, John C., Jr. *healthcare executive*

Crawfordsville
Michal, Philip Quentin *veterinarian, mayor*

East Chicago
Psaltis, Helen *medical and surgical nurse*

Evansville
Prybil, Lawrence Dewey *health system executive*

Fort Wayne
Flynn, Pauline T. *speech pathologist, educator*
Kerr, Frederick H. *hospital administrator, college president*
Kruse, Edgar Christ *former hospital administrator*
Ridderheim, David Sigfrid *hospital administrator*

Hammond
†Diamond, Eugene Christopher *lawyer, hospital administrator*

Hope
Golden, Eloise Elizabeth *community health nurse*

Indianapolis
†Allerheiligen, Sandra Renee *pharmacokineticist*
Brashear, Diane Lee *marital and sex therapist*
Farris, Bain Joseph *health care executive*
Grossman, Elizabeth Korn *nursing administrator, retired college dean*
Handel, David Jonathan *health care administrator*
Loveday, William John *hospital administrator*
Rasper, Deborah Young *hospital administrator*
†Riegsecker, Marvin Dean *pharmacist, state senator*
Stookey, George Kenneth *research institute administrator, dental educator*
Walther, Joseph Edward *health facility administrator, retired physician*

La Porte
Morris, Leigh Edward *hospital executive officer*

Lafayette
Claflin, Robert Malden *veterinary educator, university dean*
Coburn, Patricia Ellen *oncological nurse*
Geddes, LaNelle Evelyn *nursing educator, physiologist*
Sperandio, Glen Joseph *pharmacy educator*
Veenker, Claude Harold *health education educator*

Lanesville
Cleveland, Peggy Rose Richey *cytotechnologist*

Mishawaka
Goebel, Richard Alan *veterinarian*
Scott, Darrel Joseph *healthcare executive*

South Bend
Ecker, Carol Adele *veterinarian*

Valparaiso
Carr, Wiley Nelson *hospital administrator*

West Lafayette
Albright, Jack Lawrence *animal science and veterinary educator*
Amstutz, Harold Emerson *veterinarian, educator*
Belcastro, Patrick Frank *pharmaceutical scientist*
Christian, John Edward *health science educator*
Haelterman, Edward Omer *veterinary microbiologist, educator*
Kirksey, Avanelle *nutrition educator*
Knevel, Adelbert Michael *pharmacy educator*
Peck, Garnet Edward *pharmacist, educator*
Stump, John Edward *veterinary anatomy educator, ethologist*
Van Sickle, David Clark *veterinary anatomy educator, researcher*

IOWA

Ames
Ahrens, Franklin Alfred *veterinary pharmacology educator*
†Beran, George Wesley *veterinary microbiology educator*
Carithers, Jeanine Rutherford *veterinary educator*
Ghoshal, Nani Gopal *veterinary anatomist, educator*
Greve, John Henry *veterinary parasitologist, educator*
Mengeling, William Lloyd *veterinarian, virologist, researcher*
Moon, Harley William *veterinarian*
O'Berry, Phillip Aaron *veterinarian*
Pearson, Phillip Theodore *veterinary clinical sciences and biomedical engineering educator*
Ross, Richard Francis *veterinarian, microbiologist, educator*
†Seaton, Vaughn Allen *veterinary pathology educator*
Wass, Wallace Milton *veterinarian, clinical science educator*

Cedar Rapids
Wallace, Samuel Taylor *hospital administrator*

Coon Rapids
Shirbroun, Richard Elmer *veterinarian, cattleman*

Davenport
Bhatti, Iftikhar Hamid *chiropractic educator*

Decorah
Vigen, Kathryn L. Voss *nursing administrator, educator*

Des Moines
Cordes, Donald Wesley *health care consultant*
Goldsmith, Janet Jane *pediatric nurse practitioner*
Lund, Doris Hibbs *dietitian*
†Ramsey, David Selmer *hospital executive*
†Sullivan, Sister Patricia Clare *hospital administrator*

Forest City
Vammen, James Oliver *human services administrator*

Glenwood
Campbell, William Edward *state hospital school administrator*

Iowa City
Aydelotte, Myrtle Kitchell *nursing administrator, educator, consultant*
Banker, Gilbert Stephen *industrial and physical pharmacy educator, administrator*
Colloton, John William *university health care executive*
Hardy, James Chester *speech pathologist, educator*
Levey, Samuel *health care administration educator*
Manasse, Henri Richard, Jr. *health services administrator*

Larchwood
Onet, Virginia C(onstantinescu) *research scientist, educator, writer*

West Des Moines
Zimmerman, Jo Ann *health services and educational consultant, former lieutenant governor*

KANSAS

Bonner Springs
Elliott-Watson, Doris Jean *psychiatric, mental health and gerontological nurse educator*

Colby
†Morrison, James Frank *optometrist, state legislator*

Emporia
Christiansen, David K. *hospital administrator*

Fort Leavenworth
Oliver, Thornal Goodloe *health care executive*

Hays
Lee, Carla Ann Bouska *nursing educator*

Hutchinson
Schmidt, Gene Earl *hospital administrator*

Kansas City
Coles, Anna Louise Bailey *nursing administrator, college dean*
Godwin, Harold Norman *pharmacist, educator*
Jerome, Norge Winifred *nutritionist, anthropologist*
Potter, Glenn Edward *hospital administrator*

Leavenworth
†Glatt, Sister Marie Damian *healthcare corporation executive*

Manhattan
†Erickson, Howard Hugh *veterinarian*
†Lorenz, Michael Duane *veterinary medicine educator*
Mosier, Jacob Eugene *veterinarian, consultant*
Setser, Carole Sue *food science educator*
Spears, Marian Caddy *dietetics and institutional management educator*
Vorhies, Mahlon Wesley *veterinary pathologist, educator*

Shawnee Mission
Asher, Donna Thompson *psychiatric-mental health nurse*

Topeka
Angermeier, Ingo *hospital administrator, educator*
Samuelson, Marvin Lee *veterinarian*
Sheffel, Irving Eugene *psychiatric institution executive*
Varner, Charleen LaVerne McClanahan (Mrs. Robert B. Varner) *nutritionist, educator, administrator, dietitian*

Wichita
Egan, Sister M. Sylvia *hospital administrator*
Hicks, M. Elizabeth *pharmacist*
Reed, Darwin Cramer *health care consultant*

Winfield
Crowley, Marilyn *critical care nurse, educator*

KENTUCKY

Covington
Gross, Joseph Wallace *hospital administrator*

Elizabethtown
Modderman, Melvin Earl *health administrator*

Lexington
Butler, Frank Anthony *hospital administrator*
DeLuca, Patrick Phillip *pharmaceutical scientist, educator, administrator*
Dittert, Lewis William *pharmacy educator*
Drudge, Harold J. *veterinary educator*
Timoney, Peter Joseph *veterinarian, virologist, educator, consultant*

Louisville
Coggins, Homer Dale *retired hospital administrator*
Cybulski, Joanne Karen *nutritionist, diabetes educator*
Eighmey, Douglas Joseph, Jr. *hospital administrator*
Jones, David Allen *health facility executive*
Lonergan, Jeanette Nancy *nurse*
†Pickle, James C. *hospital administrator*
†Vandewater, David *hospital administrator*

Nazareth
†Dundon, Mark Walden *hospital administrator*

LOUISIANA

Baton Rouge
Besch, Everett Dickman *veterinarian, university dean emeritus*
Cox, Hollis Utah *veterinarian*

Davidge, Robert Cunninghame, Jr. *hospital administrator*
French, Dennis Donald *veterinary medicine educator, researcher*

Belle Chasse
†Arimura, Akira *biomedical research laboratory administrator, educator*

Metairie
Brisolara, Ashton *substance abuse and employee assistance programs consultant*

Natchitoches
Egan, Shirley Anne *retired nursing educator*

New Orleans
Davis, Verda Merlyn *nursing educator*
Fine, David Jeffrey *hospital executive, educator, consultant, lecturer*
Pittman, Jacquelyn *mental health nurse, nursing educator*
Remley, Theodore Phant, Jr. *counselor, educator and lawyer*
Roberts, Elliott C., Sr. *hospital administrator*
Robinson, Phillip Dean *hospital executive*

Slidell
Hall, Ogden Henderson *allied health educator*

West Monroe
Rentfro, Larry Dean *hospital administrator*

MAINE

Augusta
Sotir, Thomas Alfred *healthcare executive, retired shipbuilder*

East Boothbay
Eldred, Kenneth McKechnie *acoustical consultant*

Lewiston
†Young, William Wade, Jr. *health care executive*

Portland
McDowell, Donald L. *hospital administrator*

MARYLAND

Baltimore
†Abeloff, Martin David *medical administrator, educator, researcher*
Alliker, Stanford Arnold *hospital administrator*
Block, James A. *hospital administrator, pediatrician*
Brieger, Gert Henry *medical historian, educator*
Carlton, Sara Boehlke *rehabilitation services administrator*
†Goldstein, Gary W. *rehabilitation research administrator*
Gray, Carol Joyce *nurse, educator*
†Green, Warren Arthur *health facility administrator*
Jacox, Ada Kathryn *nurse, educator*
†Knapp, David Allan *pharmaceutical educator, researcher*
Kowal, Robert Paul *hospital administrator*
Maloney, John Alexander *hospital administrator*
†Mross, Charles Dennis *health facility administrator*
†Nathanson, Constance A. *health science organization administrator, sociology educator*
Redman, Barbara Klug *nursing educator*
Shapiro, Sam *health care analyst, biostatistician*
Sommer, Alfred *public health professional, ophthalmologist, epidemiologist*
†Steinwachs, Donald Michael *public health educator*
Taylor, Lindsay David, Jr. *health care executive*
Vasile, Gennaro James *health care executive*

Beltsville
Dupont, Jacqueline *food and nutrition educator, education and research administrator, scientist*

Bethesda
Atwell, Constance Woodruff *health services executive, researcher*
Bryant, Bertha Estelle *retired nurse*
Dogoloff, Lee Israel *clinical social worker, psychotherapist, consultant*
Fauci, Anthony Stephen *health facility administrator, physician*
Gaarder, Marie *speech pathologist*
Gluckstein, Fritz Paul *veterinarian, biomedical information specialist*
Hurd, Suzanne Sheldon *federal agency health science director*
Jonas, Gary Fred *health care center executive*
Malouff, Frank Joseph *health care association executive*
Metzger, Henry *federal research institution administrator*
Nelligan, William David *association executive*
O'Donnell, James Francis *health science administrator*
Onufrock, Richard Shade *pharmacist, researcher*
Quraishi, Mohammed Sayeed *health scientist, administrator*
Roberts, Doris Emma *epidemiologist, consultant*
Schneider, John Hoke *health science administrator*
Talbot, Bernard *government medical research facility official, physician*
Vaitukaitis, Judith Louise *medical research administrator*
Vickers, James Hudson *veterinarian, research pathologist*

College Park
Greenberg, Jerrold Selig *health education educator*
Michels, Eugene *physical therapist*

Gaithersburg
McShefferty, John *research company executive*

Hagerstown
Harrison, Lois Smith *hospital executive, educator*

Hyattsville
†Feinleib, Manning *public health physician, educator*

Kensington
Braden, Joan Kay *mental health counselor*

Marriottsville
†Fitzgerald, John L. *hospital administrator*

Potomac
Brewer, Nathan Ronald *veterinarian, consultant*
Reynolds, Frank Miller *retired government administrator*

Rockville
Arnstein, Sherry Phyllis *health care executive*
†Guest, Gerald Bentley *veterinarian*
Howard, Lee Milton *international health consultant*
Koslow, Stephen Hugh *science administrator, pharmacologist*
†McCormick, Kathleen Ann Krym *geriatrics nurse, federal agency administrator*
Milner, Max *food and nutrition consultant*
Munson, John Christian *acoustician*
†Nora, Audrey Hart *physician*
Teske, Richard Henry *veterinarian*

Silver Spring
Hamill, James Paul *hospital administrator*

Towson
Irwin, Sister Marie Cecilia *hospital administrator*

Woodstock
†Fitzgerald, John *health facility executive*

MASSACHUSETTS

Amherst
Fox, Thomas Walton *veterinary science educator*

Boston
Blendon, Robert Jay *public health educator*
†Freeman, Lisa M. *veterinarian*
Garrison, Althea *health center executive, civic worker, former goverment official*
LaRow, Sister DeChantal *hospital administrator, health councillor*
Millar, Sally Gray *nurse*
Murphy, Evelyn Frances *healthcare administrator, former lieutenant governor*
Nesson, H. Richard *medical administrator, physician*
Pettit, John W. *hospital administrator*
Reinherz, Helen Zarsky *social services educator*
Scrimshaw, Nevin Stewart *physician, nutrition and health educator*
Shaw, James Headon *nutritionist, educator*
Stare, Fredrick John *nutritionist, biochemist, physician*
Weinstein, Milton Charles *health policy educator*
Winkelman, James Warren *hospital administrator, pathology educator*

Brookline
Kibrick, Anne *nursing educator, university dean*

Burlington
Freeman, Donald Chester, Jr. *health care company executive*

Cambridge
Castaldi, David Lawrence *health care company executive*
Clifton, Anne Rutenber *psychotherapist*
Davis, Edgar Glenn *science and health policy executive*

Canton
Bihldorff, John Pearson *hospital director*

Chestnut Hill
Bushnell, Clarence William *hospital consultant*

Framingham
†Reeves, Anthony Henry *healthcare executive*

Greenfield
†Curtiss, Carol Perry *registered nurse, consultant*

Halifax
Fanning, Margaret Beverly *psychotherapist*

Hanson
Norris, John Anthony *health sciences executive, lawyer, educator*

Lexington
Fillios, Louis Charles *nutritional scientist*
Wathne, Carl Norman *hospital administrator*

Medford
Junger, Miguel Chapero *acoustics researcher*

Needham
Vermette, Raymond Edward *clinical laboratories administrator*

New Bedford
Merolla, Michele Edward *chiropractor*

North Grafton
Loew, Franklin Martin *veterinary medical and biological scientist, university dean*
Ross, James Neil, Jr. *veterinary educator*
Schwartz, Anthony *veterinary surgeon, educator*

Roxbury
†Jacobs, Annette *health facilities administrator*

Sandwich
Terrill, Robert Carl *hospital administrator*

Southbridge
Mangion, Richard Michael *health care executive*

Springfield
†Daly, Michael Joseph *hospital administrator*

Waltham
†Mitchell, Janet Brew *health services researcher*
Nogelo, Anthony Miles *health care company executive*

Ware
Shirtcliff, Christine Fay *healthcare facility executive*

Watertown
†Pellegrom, Daniel Earl *international health and development executive*

Williamstown
Conklin, Susan Joan *psychotherapist*

Wilmington
Foster, Henry Louis *veterinarian, laboratory executive*

Woburn
†Breazeale, Kelly Wade *health care association executive, consultant*

Woods Hole
†Carlton, Winslow *health association administrator*

Worcester
Dorman, Harry Gaylord, III *hospital administrator*

MICHIGAN

Ann Arbor
Clark, Noreen Morrison *behavioral science educator, researcher*
Drach, John Charles *researcher, dental basic science educator*
Forsyth, John D. *hospital administrator*
Griffith, John Randall *health services administrator, educator*
Kalisch, Beatrice Jean *nursing educator, consultant*
Romani, John Henry *health administration educator*
Rupp, Ralph Russell *audiologist, educator, author*
Sullivan, Donald John *health care corporation executive*
Warner, Kenneth E. *public health educator, consultant*

Dearborn
†Fitzgerald, Gerald Dennis *hospital administrator*

Detroit
Barr, Martin *health care administrator*
Bennett, Margaret Ethel Booker *psychotherapist*
Bostic, Florine *nursing administrator*
†Campbell, David James *hospital administrator*
Housley, Charles Edward *hospital system executive*
Iacobell, Frank Peter *hospital administrator*
Johnson, Robert Bertram *hospital administrator*
Leininger, Madeleine Monica *nursing educator, administrator, consultant, editor*
Mack, Robert Emmet *hospital administrator*
Prasad, Ananda Shiva *medical educator*
Rintelmann, William Fred *audiology educator*
Thomas, Edward St. Clair *hospital administrator*
Warden, Gail Lee *health care executive*
†Wesselmann, Glenn Allen *hospital executive*
Wittrup, Richard Derald *health care executive*

East Lansing
Courtney, Gladys (Atkins) *nursing educator, former dean*
Tasker, John Baker *veterinary medical educator, college dean*
†Wilson, Deborah Valanne *veterinary anesthesiology educator*
Witter, Richard Lawrence *veterinarian, educator*

Farmington
Burns, Sister Elizabeth Mary *hospital administrator*

Farmington Hills
Abrams, Roberta Busky *hospital administrator, nurse*
†Heid, Sister Mary Corita *hospital administrator*
Pelham, Judith *hospital administrator*
Schwartz, Michael Robinson *health administrator*

Flint
†Dutcher, Phillip Charles *health care administrator*

Grand Haven
Anderson, Cynthia Finkbeiner Sjoberg *speech and language pathologist*

Grand Rapids
Peterson, Edward Nohl *physician, medical educator*

Grosse Pointe Farms
Cartmill, George Edwin, Jr. *retired hospital administrator*

Jackson
Demcoe, Lloyd Robert *social worker*
Genyk, Ruth Bel *psychotherapist*

Northville
†Fletcher, Richard *health facility administrator*

Plymouth
McClendon, Edwin James *health science educator*

Pontiac
†Cullen, John Patrick *hospital administrator*

Royal Oak
Matzick, Kenneth John *hospital administrator*
Myers, Kenneth Ellis *hospital administrator*

Southfield
†Connolly, Brian Michael *hospital administrator*

West Branch
Pattullo, Douglas Ernest *hospital administrator*

Ypsilanti
Cantrell, Linda Maxine *counselor*
Krajewski-Jaime, Elvia Rosa *social worker*

Wilson, Lorraine M. *medical, surgical nurse, nursing educator*

MINNESOTA

Duluth
Gallinger, Lois Mae *medical technologist*

Fergus Falls
Smedsrud, Milton E. *health association executive, consultant*

Minneapolis
Anderson, Geraldine Louise *laboratory scientist*
Appel, William Frank *pharmacist*
Grant, David James William *pharmacy educator*
†Kleinglass, Steven Peter *health care administrator*
Konopka, Gisela Peiper (Mrs. Erhardt Paul Konopka) *social worker, author, lecturer, educator*
Marks, Florence C. Elliott *nursing administrator*
†Norling, Richard Arthur *health care executive*
Sawchuk, Ronald John *pharmaceutical scientist, educator*
†Spinner, Robert Keith *hospital administrator*
†Sprenger, Gordon M. *hospital administrator*
Szalapski, Judith Raines *nursing administrator*
Toscano, James Vincent *medical foundation administrator*
Walter, Frank Sherman *retired health care corporation executive*

Redlake
Ceterski, Dorothy *nutritionist*

Robbinsdale
Anderson, Scott Robbins *hospital administrator*

Rochester
Anderson, James Gerard *hospital administrator*
Gervais, Sister Generose *hospital consultant*
Leonard, David Arthur *hospital executive emeritus*
Tyce, Francis Anthony *hospital administrator, psychiatrist*

Saint Cloud
†Frobenius, John Renan *hospital administrator*

Saint Paul
Ashton, Sister Mary Madonna *healthcare administrator*
Czarnecki, Caroline MaryAnne *veterinary anatomy educator*
Diesch, Stanley La Verne *veterinarian, educator*
Dunlop, Robert Hugh *veterinary medicine educator*
Ivey, Elizabeth S. *acoustician, physicist*
Johnson, Kenneth Harvey *veterinary pathologist*

White Bear Lake
Williams, Julie Belle *psychiatric social worker*

MISSISSIPPI

Carriere
Wilson, Raymond Clark *former hospital executive*

Cleveland
Thornton, Larry Lee *psychotherapist, educator*

Hattiesburg
Odom, Janet Lynn *postanesthesia nurse*
Woodall, Lowery A. *hospital administrator*

Jackson
Baltz, Richard Jay *health care company executive*
Malloy, James Matthew *health care consultant*
†Strum, Marvin Kent *medical center executive*
Stubbs, James Carlton *retired hospital administrator*
Woodrell, Frederick Dale *health care executive*

Ocean Springs
McIlwain, Thomas David *laboratory director, marine biologist, educator*
McNulty, Matthew Francis, Jr. *health sciences and health services administrator, educator, university administrator, consultant, horse and cattle breeder*

Southaven
Utroska, William Robert *veterinarian*

Whitfield
Morton, James Irwin *hospital administrator*

MISSOURI

Chamois
†Townley, Merrill Moses *veterinarian, state legislator*

Columbia
†Blaine, Edward H. *health science association administrator*
Hensley, Elizabeth Catherine *nutritionist, educator*
Morehouse, Lawrence Glen *veterinarian, educational administrator*
†Thompson, Warren A. *mental health services educator, director*
Wagner, Joseph Edward *veterinarian, educator*

Joplin
Haley, David Alan *preferred provider organization executive*

Kansas City
Couch, Daniel Michael *healthcare executive*
Kingsley, James Gordon *health care executive*
Piepho, Robert Walter *pharmacy educator, researcher*
Presson, Ellis Wynn *health services executive*
Shabbir, Mahnaz Mehdi *healthcare marketing manager*

Saint Louis
Betts, Warren R. *health facilty administrator*
Cobb, Donna Deanne Hill *physical therapist*
Farrell, John Timothy *hospital administrator*
†Finan, John Joseph *hospital administrator*
Folk, Roger Maurice *laboratory director*
†Grisham, Richard *health facility administrator*
Herzfeld-Kimbrough, Ciby *mental health educator*
Humphreys, James Burnham *hospital administrator*
Ihde, Daniel C. *health science executive*
Jobe, Muriel Ida *medical technologist*
†Loftin, Sister Mary Frances *health facility administrator*
Mattson, William Royce, Jr. *health care consulting company executive*
†Polizzi, Jan Crandall *community and maternal-women's health nurse*
†Schneller, George Charles *chiropractor*
Schoenhard, William Charles, Jr. *health care executive*
Stretch, John Joseph *social work educator, management and evaluation consultant*
Van Bokkelen, William Requa *health facility administrator*

Sparta
Madore, Joyce Louise *gerontology nurse*

Springfield
†Swift, James William *health care executive*
Westphal, Leonard Wyrick *health care executive, consultant*

MONTANA

Great Falls
Downer, William John, Jr. *hospital administrator*

NEBRASKA

Ewing
†Dierks, Merton Lyle *veterinarian*

Grand Island
Etheridge, Margaret Dwyer *medical center director*

Lincoln
Hamilton, David Wendell *medical services executive*
Nolte, Walter Eduard *retired retirement home executive, foundation counsel, former banker*
Schmitz, John Albert *veterinary pathologist*

Omaha
†Moeller, A. Diane *health facility administrator*
Omer, Robert Wendell *hospital administrator*
Schwartz, C. Edward *hospital administrator*

NEVADA

Las Vegas
Law, Flora Elizabeth (Libby Law) *community health and pediatrics nurse*
Michel, Mary Ann Kedzuf *nursing educator*
Ogren, Carroll Woodrow *retired hospital administrator*

North Las Vegas
Gowdy, Miriam Betts *nutritionist*

NEW HAMPSHIRE

Concord
Dupuis, Sylvio Louis *optometrist, educator, administrator*
Kalipolites, June E. Turner *rehabilitation professional*

Franklin
Meader, Ralph Gibson *medical administrator*

Lebanon
Varnum, James William *hospital administrator*

Manchester
Goodspeed, Scott Winans *hospital administration executive*

Sandown
Densen, Paul Maximillian *former health administrator, educator*

West Peterborough
†Dyer, Merton S. *pharmacist, state legislator*

NEW JERSEY

Asbury Park
Holm, Audrey Christine *health care organization administrator*

Butler
Davis, Dorinne Sue Taylor Lovas *audiologist*

Cherry Hill
Iglewicz, Raja *state agency administrator, researcher, industrial hygienist*
Israelsky, Roberta Schwartz *speech pathologist, audiologist*

Clifton
Adelsberg, Harvey *hospital administrator*

Elizabeth
Buonanni, Brian Francis *health care facility administrator, consultant*

Englewood
Kane, Daniel A. *hospital administrator*
Mc Mullan, Dorothy *nurse educator*

Englishtown
Chung, Douglas Chu *pharmacist, consultant*

Franklin Lakes
Hegelmann, Julius *retired pharmacy educator*
Natale, Samuel Michael *psychotherapist, educator, priest*

Gibbsboro
Censits, Richard John *health care company executive*

Hackensack
Baker, Andrew Hartill *clinical laboratory executive*
Ferguson, John Patrick *medical center executive*

Hillside
Patell, Mahesh *pharmacist, researcher*

Jersey City
†Metsch, Jonathan M. *health facility executive*
Mortensen, Eugene Phillips *hospital administrator*

Kinnelon
Preston, Andrew Joseph *pharmacist, drug company executive*
Richardson, Irene M. *nursing educator*

Livingston
†Del Mauro, Ronald *hospital administrator*

Long Branch
Royce, Paul Chadwick *medical administrator*

Lyons
Kidd, A. Paul *hospital administrator, government official*

Murray Hill
Atal, Bishnu Saroop *speech research executive*

Neptune
Lloyd, John Koons *hospital administrator*

New Brunswick
Boehm, Werner William *social work educator*
Holzberg, Harvey Alan *hospital administrator*
Matuska, John E. *hospital administrator*

Newark
Bornstein, Lester Milton *medical center executive*
†De Lisa, Joel Alan *rehabilitation physician*
†Gossett, George Boyd *human service executive*
Lory, Marc H. *hospital administrator*

Nutley
Drews, Jürgen *pharmaceutical researcher*
Machlin, Lawrence J. *nutritionist, biochemist, educator*

Paterson
Brady, Sister Jane Frances *hospital executive*

Piscataway
Chien, Yie W. *pharmaceutics educator*
Goldstein, Bernard David *physician, educator*

Plainfield
Kopicki, John R. *hospital administrator*

Pomona
Bukowski, Elaine Louise *physical therapist*

Princeton
Scibetta, Louis Paul *health care company executive*

Ridgewood
†Azzara, Michael William *hospital administration executive*

Roseland
Malafronte, Donald *health executive*

South Plainfield
Borah, Kripanath *pharmacist*

Sparta
Buist, Jean Mackerley *veterinarian*

Summit
Sniffen, Michael Joseph *hospital administrator*

Toms River
Pilla, Mark Domenick *hospital administrator*

Wayne
Ellenbogen, Leon *nutritionist, pharmaceutical company executive*

West New York
Kelly, Lucie Stirm Young *nursing educator*

White House Station
Gilmartin, Raymond V. *health care products company executive*

Wyckoff
Cropper, Susan Peggy *veterinarian*

NEW MEXICO

Albuquerque
Beusch, Gladys Jeanette *optician*
Johnson, William Hugh, Jr. *hospital administrator*
Mauderly, Joe Lloyd *veterinary respiratory physiologist*
Solomon, Arthur Charles *pharmacist*

Carlsbad
Reif, Laurie Louise *psychotherapist*

Clovis
Rehorn, Lois Marie Smith *nursing administrator*

Gallup
Crouch, Altha Marie *health educator, consultant*

Los Alamos
Bame, Samuel Jarvis, Jr. *research scientist*

Los Lunas
Mateju, Joseph Frank *hospital administrator*

Santa Fe
Nuckolls, Leonard Arnold *retired hospital administrator*

Univ Of New Mexico
Sarto, Gloria Elizabeth *obstetrician/gynecologist, educator*

Wagon Mound
†Abeyta, Jose Reynato *retired pharmacist, state legislator, cattle rancher*

NEW YORK

Albany
Cornell, David Roger *hospital administrator*
Csiza, Charles Karoly *veterinarian, microbiologist*
DeNuzzo, Rinaldo Vincent *pharmacy educator*
†Furlong, Patrick Louis *health science association administrator*
McCarthy, Mary Lynn *social work educator*
Reid, William James *social work educator*

Ardsley
Ricklin, Arthur H. *hospital administrator*

Bay Shore
Cohen, Lawrence N. *health care company executive*

Beacon
Witte, Lawrence Mark *hospital administrator*

Bronx
Corinaldi, Austin *former hospital administrator*
Gootzeit, Jack Michael *rehabilitation institute executive*
Ottenberg, James Simon *hospital executive*
Tregde, Lorraine C. *hospital administrator*

Bronxville
Dvorak, Roger Gran *health facility executive*

Brooklyn
Adams, George Harold *hospital and health executive*
Adasko, Mary *speech pathologist*
Agard, Emma Estornel *psychotherapist*
Allen, Percy, II *hospital administrator*
Alley, Frederick Don *hospital executive*
Farsetta, James Joseph *medical center director*
Gross, Stephen Mark *pharmacist, academic dean*
†Loran, Carlos Anthony *hospital administrator*
†Maddalena, Frank Joseph *health care executive*
Mundy, Mark James *hospital administrator*
Murillo-Rohde, Ildaura Maria *marriage and family therapist, consultant, educator, dean*
†Raphael, Carol *health care administrator*
Spero, Barry Melvin *medical center executive*
Twining, Lynne Dianne *psychotherapist, researcher, writer*

Buffalo
†Blane, Howard Thomas *institute administrator*
Friedlander, John Eastburn *health facility administrator*
Fung, Ho-Leung *pharmacy educator, researcher, consultant*
Katz, Jack *audiology educator*
†Kelley, Sister Helen *hospital executive*
Sharma, Sushil Chandra *hospital administrator*
Solo, Alan Jere *medicinal chemistry educator, consultant*

Cooperstown
Hermann, William Henry *retired hospital administrator, consultant*

Elmsford
Bostin, Marvin Jay *hospital and health services consultant*

Farmingdale
Lamberg, Stanley Lawrence *medical technologist, educator*

Floral Park
Weinrib, Sidney *retired optometric and optical products and services executive*

Garden City
Harr, Alma Elizabeth Tagliabue *nursing educator*
Nicklin, George Leslie, Jr. *psychoanalyst, educator, physician*
Vigilante, Joseph Louis *social worker, social policy educator*

Greenport
Mebus, Charles Albert *veterinarian*

Hauppauge
†Wheatley, George Milholland *medical administrator*

Holbrook
Lissman, Barry Alan *veterinarian*

Huntington
†Mara, John Lawrence *veterinarian, consultant*

Ithaca
Dobson, Alan *veterinary physiology educator*
Fox, Francis Henry *veterinarian*
†Gilbert, Robert Owen *veterinary educator, researcher*
Gillespie, James Howard *veterinary microbiologist, educator*
Habicht, Jean-Pierre *public health researcher, educator, consultant*
Kallfelz, Francis A. *veterinary medicine educator*
Kollias, George Van, Jr. *veterinary educator, researcher, clinician*
Mueller, Betty Jeanne *social work educator*
Poppensiek, George Charles *veterinary scientist, educator*
Schlafer, Donald Hughes *veterinary pathologist*
†Scott, Fredric Winthrop *veterinarian*
Zall, Robert Rouben *food scientist, educator*

Jamaica
Conway, Alvin James *hospital administrator*
Geffner, Donna Sue *speech pathologist, audiologist*

Malverne
Ryan, Suzanne Irene *nursing educator*

Manhasset
Gallagher, John S. T. (Jack Gallagher) *hospital administrator*

Mineola
Delaney, Martin Joseph *hospital administrator*
Hankin, Errol Patrick *hospital administrator*

New Hyde Park
†Fink, Martin Neil *hospital administrator*

New York
Baker, Elmer Elias, Jr. *speech pathology and communication educator*
Berman, Richard Angel *health science facility administrator*
Bessey, Edward Cushing *health care company executive*
Binkert, Alvin John *hospital administrator*
†Brier, Pamela Sara *health facility administrator*
Cardinale, Kathleen Carmel *medical center administrator*
Caroff, Phyllis M. *social work educator*
Channing, Alan Harold *hospital administrator*
Cloward, Richard Andrew *social work educator*
Connolly, John Joseph *health care company executive*
Cooke, Mary A. *hospice director*
Core, Mary Carolyn W. Parsons *radiologic technologist*
†Costa, Max *health facility administrator, pharmacology educator, environmental medicine educator*
Davis, Samuel *hospital administrator, educator, consultant*
Dimen, Muriel Vera *psychoanalyst*
Feldman, Ronald Arthur *social work educator, researcher*
Filer, Elizabeth Ann *psychotherapist*
Fiorillo, John A(nthony) *health care executive*
Freudenberger, Herbert Justin *psychoanalyst*
Gambuti, Gary *hospital administrator*
†George, Gladys *hospital administrator*
Gitterman, Alex *social work educator*
Grant, James Deneale *health care company executive*
†Hochberg, Irving *audiologist, educator*
Israel, Margie Olanoff *psychotherapist*
†Itzkowitz, Murray *health facility administrator*
Kamerman, Sheila Brody *social worker, educator*
Kramer, Marc B. *forensic audiologist*
†Levy, Joel Martin *health facility administrator*
Markle, Cheri Virginia Cummins *nurse*
Mc Fadden, G. Bruce *hospital administrator*
Morris, Thomas Quinlan *hospital administrator, physician*
Nauert, Roger Charles *health care executive*
Radovic, Mildred Hope Fisher Witkin *psychotherapist, educator*
Reisner, Milton *psychoanalyst, psychiatrist*
†Rosenbluth, Lucille M. *health research facility administrator*
Scott, Mimi Koblenz *psychotherapist*
Singer-Magdoff, Laura Joan Silver (Mrs. Samuel Magdoff) *psychotherapist*
Solender, Sanford *social worker*
Straus, Donald Blun *retired company executive*
Walman, Jerome *psychotherapist, publisher, consultant, critic*
†Watson, Anthony L. *health facility executive*
Wood, Paul F. *national health agency executive*

Ossining
Beard, Janet Marie *health care administrator*

Painted Post
Sands, John W. *nursing home administrator*

Plainview
Bornstein, Robert Joseph *hospital administrator*

Rhinebeck
Ethan, Carol Baehr *psychotherapist*

Rochester
Griner, Paul Francis *hospital administrator, physician*
†Insel, Richard *medical facility administrator/ pediatrics educator*
Johnson, Jean Elaine *nursing educator*
Liebert, Arthur Edgar. *hospital administrator*
†Moore, Duncan Thomas *optics educator*
Walker, Michael Charles, Sr. *retirement services executive*

Roslyn
Scollard, Patrick John *hospital executive*

Rye
Newburger, Howard Martin *psychoanalyst*

Scarsdale
Glickenhaus, Sarah Brody *speech therapist*
Liston, Mary Frances *retired nursing educator*

Scottsville
Dwyer, Ann Elizabeth *equine veterinarian*

Southold
Callis, Jerry Jackson *veterinarian*

Staten Island
†Stanzione, Dominick Michael *hospital administrator*

Stony Brook
Newell, William Talman, Jr. *hospital administrator*

Syracuse
Butler, Katharine Gorrell *speech-language pathologist, educator*
Fitzgerald, Harold Kenneth *social work educator, consultant*

Troy
O'Neil, Mary Agnes *health science facility administrator*

Valhalla
Camerano, Franklin *medical center administrator*

Valley Stream
Natow, Annette Baum *nutritionist, author, consultant*

West Brentwood
†O'Neill, Peggy *health care executive*

West Hempstead
Rothberg, June Simmonds *nursing educator emerita, psychotherapist, psychoanalyst*

White Plains
Massey, Charles L. *health organization executive*

Williamsville
Paladino, Joseph Anthony *clinical pharmacist*

Yonkers
Drisko, Elliot Hillman *marriage and family therapist*
†Foy, James E. *hospital administrator*

NORTH CAROLINA

Asheville
†Burgin, Robert F. *medical center administrator*
Weil, Thomas P. *health services consultant*

Burlington
Powell, James Bobbitt *biomedical laboratories executive, pathologist*

Chapel Hill
Munson, Eric Bruce *hospital administrator*
Norwood, George Joseph *pharmacy educator*
Tolley, Aubrey Granville *hospital administrator*

Charlotte
Betzold, Paul Frederick, Jr. *hospital administrator*
†Nurkin, Harry Abraham *hospital administrator*
Witherspoon, Jere Warthen *foundation executive*

Durham
Gratz, Pauline *former nursing science educator*
Wilson, Ruby Leila *nurse, educator*

Elizabeth City
Griffin, Gladys Bogues *critical care nurse, educator*

Elon College
Knesel, Ernest Arthur, Jr. *clinical laboratory executive*

Greensboro
Schwenn, Lee William *retired medical center executive*

Greenville
McRae, David Carroll *hospital administrator*

Raleigh
Aronson, Arthur Lawrence *veterinary pharmacology and toxicology educator*
Champ, Raymond Lester *hospital administrator*
Grayson, Susan Cubillas *environmental health administrator*
Willis, John Randolph *hospital administrator*

Research Triangle Park
Olden, Kenneth *public health service administrator, researcher*

Wilmington
Dixon, N(orman) Rex *speech and hearing scientist, educator*
Morrison, William Fowler, Jr. *health care consultant*

Wilson
Durrer, Christopher Thomas *hospital executive*

Winston Salem
Dodd, Virginia Marilyn *veterinarian*
Preslar, Len Broughton, Jr. *hospital administrator*
Wiles, Paul Martin *hospital administration executive*

NORTH DAKOTA

Fargo
Nickel, Janet Marlene Milton *geriatrics nurse*
†Orr, Steven R. *health facility administrator*

Grand Forks
Carroll, Jack Adien *hospital administrator*
†Nielsen, Forrest Harold *research nutritionist*

OHIO

Akron
Considine, William Howard *health care administrator*
Gilbert, Albert Francis *hospital administrator*

Bay Village
Hiller, Deborah Lewis *long term care and retirement facility executive*

Bellaire
Hahn, David Bennett *hospital administrator, marketing professional*

Brecksville
Chatman, Rosie A. *nursing administrator*

Canfield
Itts, Elizabeth Ann Dunham *psychotherapist, consultant, designer*

Canton
†Pryce, Richard James *hospital administrator*

Centerville
Fulk, Paul Frederick *chiropractor*

Cincinnati
Bradley, Sister Myra James *health science facility executive*
Carney, Robert Alfred *health care administrator*
Cohen, Hirsh Joel *health care administrator*
Collins, Larry Wayne *health facility administrator*
Cook, Jack McPherson *hospital administrator*
Curtin, Leah Louise *nurse, consultant, editor, author*
Dickey, John Miller *health care facility executive*
Graham, Scharleen Walker *counselor*
Haag, Walter M(onroe), Jr. *research institute executive, industrial engineer*
Jackobs, Miriam Ann *dietitian*
†Koebel, Sister Celestia *hospital administrator*
Lichtin, (Judah) Leon *pharmacist*
Morgan, John Bruce *hospital care consultant*
Rubinstein, Jack Herbert *health center administrator, pediatrics educator*
Schubert, William Kuenneth *hospital medical center executive*
Weseli, Roger William *health care executive*
White, Terry R. *hospital administrator*

Cleveland
Blum, Arthur *social work educator*
Cline, Cathie B. *hospital administrator*
Dadley, Arlene Jeanne *sleep therapist*
†Manning, Henry Eugene *hospital administrator*
Naparstek, Arthur J. *social work educator*
Neuhauser, Duncan von Briesen *health services educator*
Phipps, Wilma J. *nursing educator, author*
Schlotfeldt, Rozella May *nursing educator*
Schorr, Alvin Louis *social worker, educator*
Schurmeier, L. Jon *health care executive*
Serra, Anthony Michael *nursing home administrator*
Shakno, Robert Julian *hospital administrator*
†Trudell, Thomas Jeffrey *hospital administrator, educator*
True, William Herndon *healthcare administrator*
Walters, Farah M. *hospital administrator*

Columbus
Anderson, Carole Ann *nursing educator*
Banasik, Robert Casmer *nursing home administrator, educator*
Capen, Charles Chabert *veterinary pathology educator, researcher*
Chapman, Erie, III *hospital administrator*
Covault, Lloyd R., Jr. *hospital administrator, psychiatrist*
Fraley, Ralph Reed *hospital administrator*
Lince, John Alan *pharmacist*
†Porterfield, Hubert William *healthcare executive*
†Rudmann, Sally Anne *medical technology educator*
St. Arnold, Dale S. *hospital administrator*
†Schlichting, Nancy Margaret *hospital administrator*
†Schuller, David Edward *cancer center administrator, otolaryngology*
Sims, Richard Lee *hospital administrator*

Dayton
Harkness, Laurence Patrick *health facility administrator*
†Thorsland, Edgar, Jr. *health facility administrator*

Duncan Falls
Cooper, April Helen *nurse*

Fairborn
Leffler, Carole Elizabeth *mental health nurse, women's health nurse*

Fairfield
Goodman, Myrna Marcia *school nurse*

Gallipolis
Niehm, Bernard Frank *mental health center administrator*

Green Springs
Copeland, Terrilyn Denise *speech pathologist*

Hamilton
Johnson, Pauline Benge *nurse, anesthetist*

Middleburg Heights
Hartman, Lenore Anne *physical therapist*

Middletown
Redding, Barbara J. *nursing administrator, occupational health nurse*

Mount Saint Joseph
Roach, Sister Jeanne *hospital administrator*

Oberlin
Reinoehl, Richard Louis *social work consultant, writer, artist*

Springfield
Maki, Jerrold Alan *medical center administrator*

Sylvania
Verhesen, Anna Maria Hubertina *counselor*

Toledo
Depew, Charles Gardner *research company executive*
Rissing, Daniel Joseph *hospital administrator*

University Heights
Bloch, Andrea Lynn *physical therapist*

Warren
Johns, Charles Alexander *hospital administrator*

Westerville
Conley, Sarah Ann *health facility administrator*

Worthington
Bernhagen, Lillian Flickinger *school health consultant*

Zanesville
Durant, Charles Edward, Jr *medical facility administrator*

OKLAHOMA

Elk City
Francis, Talton Loe *hospital administrator*

Lawton
Cooke, Wanda (Cookie Cooke) *hearing aid specialist*

Mangum
Ford, Linda Lou *dietitian*

Norman
Dille, John Robert *physician*
Donahue, Hayden Hackney *mental health institute administrator, medical educator, psychiatric consultant*
Weber, Jerome Charles *education and human relations educator, former academic dean and provost*

Oklahoma City
Bresler, Mark Irwin *rehabilitation engineer*
Forni, Patricia Rose *nursing educator, university dean*
Henley, Everett Scott *health care marketing firm executive*
Hupfeld, Stanley Francis *health care executive*
Lynn, Thomas Neil, Jr. *medical center administrator, physician*
Macer, Dan Johnstone *retired hospital administrator*
Seideman, Ruth Evelyn Young *nurse educator*
Spencer, Melvin Joe *hospital administrator, lawyer*

Pawhuska
Strahm, Samuel Edward *veterinarian*

Stillwater
Confer, Anthony Wayne *veterinary pathologist, educator*
Ewing, Sidney Alton *veterinary medical educator, parasitologist*
†Quinn, Art Jay *veterinarian*

Tulsa
Alexander, John Robert *hospital administrator, internist*
Janssen, Erwin T. *health science foundation administrator, psychiatrist*

OREGON

Corvallis
Koller, Loren D. *veterinary medicine educator*
Oldfield, James Edmund *nutrition educator*

Eugene
Acker, Martin Herbert *psychotherapist, educator*
Slocum, Barclay *veterinary orthopedic surgeon*
Walton, Ralph Ervin *community mental health services adminstrator*

Portland
Artaud-Wild, Sabine Marie *research dietitian*
Brim, Armand Eugene *health care executive*
Goldfarb, Timothy Moore *hospital administrator*
Greenlick, Merwyn Ronald *health services researcher*
Meighan, Stuart Spence *hospital consultant, internist, writer*
Olson, Roger Norman *health service administrator*
†Rooks, Judith Pence *family planning, maternal health care, midwifery consultant*

PENNSYLVANIA

Abington
Pilla, Felix Mario *hospital administrator*
Stolp, Lauren Elbert *speech pathologist*

Altoona
Meadors, Allen Coats *health administrator, educator*

Aston
†Aldrich, Ronald Robert *health system administrator*

Bala Cynwyd
Marinakos, Plato Anthony *medical center administrator*

Berwyn
Brunner, Lillian Sholtis *nurse, author*

Blue Bell
Abramson, Leonard *healthcare organization executive*
Neff, P. Sherrill *health care executive*

Camp Hill
Nowak, Jacquelyn Louise *retirement home administrator, realtor, consultant*

Chester
Rosko, Michael Daniel *health science facility administrator, educator*

Collegeville
Cawthorn, Robert Elston *health care executive*
†Stoughton, W. Vickery *hospital administrator*

Danville
Ackerman, F. Kenneth, Jr. *health facility administrator*

Doylestown
Cathcart, Harold Robert *hospital administrator*

Havertown
Payne, William Taylor, Jr. *former hospital administrator, travel agency owner*

Hershey
Anderson, Allan Crosby *hospital executive*
Lang, Carol Max *veterinarian, educator*

Jenkintown
Colman, Wendy *psychoanalyst*

Kennett Square
Allam, Mark Whittier *veterinarian, former university administrator*
Barr, David Charles *healthcare executive*
Beck, Dorothy Fahs *social researcher*

King Of Prussia
Cash, Francis Winford *health care executive*
†Foster, John Hallett *health facility executive*
Miller, Alan B. *hospital management executive*

Lancaster
Fried, Jeffrey Michael *health care administrator*
Wedel, Paul George *retired hospital administrator*

Landenberg
Aldrich, Nancy Armstrong *psychotherapist, clinical social worker*

Lansdale
Lovelace, Robert Frank *health science facility administrator, researcher*

Malvern
McNamara, John F. *health services company executive*
Michaelis, Arthur Frederick *health care company executive*

New Castle
White, Thomas *hospital administrator*

Philadelphia
Aiken, Linda Harman *nurse, sociologist, educator*
†Cherry, John Paul *health science association director, researcher*
Daly, Charles Arthur *health services administrator*
Detweiler, David Kenneth *veterinary physiologist, educator*
Di Stefano, Anthony Ferdinand *optometry educator, educational administrator*
†Doty, Richard Leroy *medical researcher*
Eldredge, Clifford Murray *hospital administrator*
Epstein, William Eric *health science facility administrator*
Fagin, Claire Mintzer *nursing educator, administrator*
Gable, Fred Burnard *pharmacist, author*
Goldsmith, Martin H. *health care executive*
Harvey, Colin Edwin *veterinary medicine educator*
Hussar, Daniel Alexander *pharmacy educator*
†Lewis, Thomas John, III *hospital administrator*
Mudd, Emily Hartshorne *counselor, educator, researcher*
Pittinger, Wilbur Barke *medical center executive*
Solomon, Phyllis Linda *mental health sciences educator, researcher*
Sovie, Margaret Doe *nursing administrator, college dean*
Weber, Janet M. *nurse*
Whybrow, Peter Charles *psychiatrist, educator*

Pittsburgh
Abdelhak, Sherif Samy *health science executive*
Berman, Malcolm Frank *health facility administrator*
Catell, Grace Louise *nursing educator*
Doerfler, Leo G. *audiology educator*
Friede, Samuel A(rnold) *health care executive*
Harper, Matrid Thaisa *health care administrator*
Leak, Allison G. *health science facility administrator, nurse*
Longest, Beaufort Brown *health services administration educator, research director*
McCall, Dorothy Kay *social worker, psychotherapist*
Moore, Pearl B. *nurse*
O'Brien, Charles Maryon, Jr. *hospital administrator*
†Paul, John *health care executive*
†Resnick, Lauren B. *special education research administrator*
†Romoff, Jeffrey Alan *university officer, health care executive*
Sanzo, Anthony Michael *health care executive*
Wallman, George *hospital and food services administrator*
Zanardelli, John Joseph *health facility administrator*

Radnor
†Russell, Daniel Francis *hospital administrator*

Reading
Bell, Frances Louise *medical technologist*
Sauer, Elissa Swisher *nursing educator*
Sullivan, Charles Bernard *hospital administrator*

Scranton
Maislin, Isidore *hospital administrator*
Turock, Jane Parsick *nutritionist*

State College
Morrow, David Austin, III *veterinary medical educator*

University Park
Guthrie, Helen A. *nutrition educator, consultant*
†Koopman, Gary *acoustic administrator*
Mayers, Stanley Penrose, Jr. *public health educator*

Villanova
Melby, Edward Carlos, Jr. *veterinarian*

Wayne
†Russell, Kent *hospital administrator*

York
Bartels, Bruce Michael *health care executive*
Fink, David Ream, Jr. *retired hospital education director*
Keiser, Paul Harold *hospital administrator*
Rosen, Raymond *health facility executive*

RHODE ISLAND

Cranston
Gill, Carole O'Brien *family therapist*

Newport
†Graziano, Catherine Elizabeth *nursing educator*

Providence
Metrey, George David *social work educator, academic administrator*
Schottland, Edward Morrow *hospital adminstrator*
Vavala, Domenic Anthony *medical scientist, educator, retired air force officer*

Wakefield
Gifford, Harry Cortland Frey *health educator*

SOUTH CAROLINA

Anderson
†Oglesby, Daniel Kirkland, Jr. *hospital administrator*

Charleston
†Smith, W. Stuart *hospital administrator*

Columbia
Amidon, Roger Lyman *health administration educator*
Brown, Arnold *health science facility administrator*
Cooper, William Allen, Jr. *audiologist*
Ginsberg, Leon Herman *social work educator*

Dillon
Webb, Ronald Wayne *hospital administrator*

Greenville
Burkhardt, J. Bland, Jr. *hospital administrator*

Hopkins
Clarkson, Jocelyn Adrene *medical technologist*

Mount Pleasant
Cooley, Kathleen Shannon *speech-language pathologist*

Myrtle Beach
Dail, Hilda Lee *psychotherapist*
Madory, James Richard *hospital administrator, former air force officer*

SOUTH DAKOTA

Chamberlain
Gregg, Robert Lee *pharmacist*

Pierre
Russell, James Donald Murray *hospital administrator*

Rapid City
Corwin, Bert Clark *optometrist*
†Green, Sharon Vincentine *counselor, consultant*

Sioux Falls
Richards, LaClaire Lissetta Jones (Mrs. George A. Richards) *social worker*
†Sandness, William John *health care executive*

Yankton
Sokol, Dennis Allen *hospital administrator*

TENNESSEE

Brentwood
†Dalton, James Edgar, Jr. *health facility administrator*
Ragsdale, Richard Elliot *hospital management executive*

Hendersonville
Davis, Robert Norman *hospital administrator*

Jackson
Moss, James Taylor *hospital administrator*

Jellico
Hausman, Keith Lynn *hospital administrator, physical therapist*

Knoxville
German, Ronald Stephen *health care facility administrator*
Green, Eleanor Myers *veterinarian, educator*
Mercer, Charles Wayne *health care executive*

Lafayette
Wolford, Dennis Arthur *hospital administrator*

Lenoir City
Wilson, Frank Elmore *physician, medical administrator*

Maryville
Ackerman, Ora Ray *health facility administrator*

Memphis
Diggs, Walter Whitley *health science facilty administrator*
†Elliott, Maurice Wallner *health care system administrator*
†Mendel, Maurice *audiologist, educator*
Mulholland, Kenneth Leo, Jr. *health care facility administrator*
Nolly, Robert J. *hospital administrator, pharmaceutical science educator*
Powell, Joseph Herbert *hospital administrator*
†Reynolds, Stephen Curtis *hospital administrator*
†Shorb, Gary Seymour *hospital administrator*

Murfreesboro
Adams, W. Andrew *health care executive*

Nashville
Bolian, George Clement *health care executive, physician*
†Brown, Tommie Florence *social work educator*
†Connery, W. Hudson *health facility administrator*
Frist, Thomas Fearn, Jr. *hospital management company executive*
†Golson, Sister Afton Almeda *health facility administrator, nun*
MacNaughton, Donald Sinclair *health care company executive*
McWhorter, Ralph Clayton *health care company executive*
Sanders, Jay William *audiology educator*
Stringfield, Charles David *hospital administrator*
Urmy, Norman B. *hospital administrator*

Oliver Springs
Davis, Sara Lea *pharmacist*

TEXAS

Alvin
Lukens, Betty Faye *health facility manager*

Amarillo
Sprowls, Robert Wayne *veterinarian, laboratory administrator*

Arlington
McCuistion, Robert Wiley *lawyer, hospital administrator, management consultant*
Murnane, Thomas George *public health veterinarian, military*
Wiig, Elisabeth Hemmersam *audiologist, educator*

Austin
Abell, Creed W. *pharmacy educator*
Austin, David Mayo *social work educator*
Doluisio, James Thomas *pharmacy educator*
Durbin, Richard Louis, Sr. *healthcare admnistration consultant*
Girling, Bettie Joyce Moore *home health executive*
Hall, Beverly Adele *nursing educator*
Hurley, Laurence Harold *medicinal chemistry educator*
Johnson, Mildred Snowden *nursing educator*
Kirk, Lynda Pounds *biofeedback therapist, neurotherapist*
Martin, Frederick Noel *audiologist*
McCuistion, Peg Orem *hospice administrator*
Otis, Jack *social work educator*
Smith, Bert Kruger *mental health services professional, consultant*

College Station
Beaver, Bonnie Veryle *veterinarian, educator*
McCrady, James David *veterinarian, educator*
Pierce, Kenneth Ray *veterinary medicine educator*
†Shadduck, John Allen *veterinary pathologist*
Sis, Raymond Francis *veterinarian, educator*
†Varner, Dickson D. *veterinarian*

Corpus Christi
Cole, June Robertson *psychotherapist*

Dallas
Anderson, Ron Joe *hospital administrator, physician, educator*
Bradley, John Andrew *hospital management company executive*
†Bryant, L. Gerald *health care administrator*
Carver, John W(illiam), Jr. *hospital administrator*
Dykes, Virginia Chandler *occupational therapist*
†George, Kenneth S. *health facility administration*
Gilleland, Richard A. *health care company executive*
Greenstone, James Lynn *psychotherapist, mediator, consultant, author, educator*
Hafner, Dudley H. *health agency executive*
Haire, William J. *healthcare executive*
Hille, Robert Arthur *healthcare executive*
Hitt, David Hamilton *hospital executive*
O'Leary, Robert W. *hospital operations company executive*
Powell, Boone, Jr. *hospital administrator*
†Roeser, Ross Joseph *audiologist, educator*
Smith, William Randolph (Randy Smith) *health care management association executive*
Strange, Donald Ernest *health care company executive*

El Paso
†Fry, L(eo) Marcus, Jr. *hospital administrator*
Himelstein, Peggy Donn *psychologist*
Mitchell, Paula Rae *nursing educator*

Flower Mound
Gooch, Brian Eugene *health care executive, policy analyst, consultant*

Fort Worth
Brosseau, Charles Martin, Jr. *hospital administrator*
Jensen, Harlan Ellsworth *veterinarian, educator*
Lawrence, Teleté Zorayda *speech and voice pathologist, educator*
†Philpot, Marion Timothy *healthcare executive*
Scearse, Patricia Dotson *nurse educator, college dean*

Galveston
Norman, Dudley Kent *hospital administrator, nurse*

Grand Prairie
Busse, Lu Ann *audiologist*

Houston
Becker, Frederick Fenimore *cancer center administrator, pathologist*
Burdine, John A. *hospital administrator, nuclear medicine educator*
†Cuthbertson, James *healthcare executive*
Hansen, Paula Renee *health care administrator*
Johnston, Ben Earl *veterinarian*
Khoury, Raymond J. *hospital administrator*
†Kuntz, Edward L. *health care executive*
Mathis, Larry Lee *health care administrator*
Mc Call, Charles Barnard *health facility executive, educator*
†Mischer, Walter M., Jr. *health facility administrator*
Moore, Lois Jean *health science facility administrator*
†Myers, Edward Wellington *hospital administrator*

Nelson, Dorothy Patricia *health policy analyst, educator*
Patterson, Ronald R(oy) *health care systems executive*
Proctor, Richard Owen *public health administrator, army officer*
Reed, Kathlyn Louise *occupational therapist, educator*
†Shaw, Robert Nolan *health care organization executive*
Siegel, Milton P. *health foundation executive, international executive, educator, management consultant*
†Steele, James Harlan *former public health veterinarian, educator*
Turner, William Wilson *hospital administrator*
†Urban, Stanley T. *hospital administrator*
Wagner, Donald Bert *health care administrator*
Wainerdi, Richard Elliott *medical center executive*
Weaver, Hilda *counselor, psychotherapist*
†Wilford, Dan Sewell *hospital administrator*
Wood, Jack Calvin *health care consultant, lawyer*

Hunt
Price, Donald Albert *veterinarian, consultant*

Huntsville
Vick, Marie *retired health science educator*

Irving
Collins, Stephen Barksdale *health care executive*
Donnelly, Barbara Schettler *medical technologist*

Lufkin
Migl, Donald Raymond *optometrist, pharmacist*

Mineral Wells
Harmon Brown, Valarie Jean *hospital laboratory director, information systems executive*

Mount Pleasant
Ogburn, Wayne Lee *health science facility administrator*

New Braunfels
Johnson, Marion Phillip *hospital administrator*

Richardson
Brown, Ollie Dawkins *psychotherapist, scientific researcher*

San Antonio
Cahill, William Randall *health facility executive*
Coronado, Jose Ricardo *hospital administrator*
Gonzalez, Hector Hugo *nurse, educator, consultant*
Holguin, Alfonso Hudson *physician, educator*
Hornbeak, John Earl *hospital administrator*
McGuire, William Dennis *health care system executive*
Parks, Madelyn N. *nurse, retired army officer, university official*
Roper, Paul Holmes *hospital administrator*
†Van de Putte, Leticia *pharmacist, state official*
†Van Vorst, Charles Brian *health facility administrator*
Wilson, Janie Menchaca *nursing educator, researcher*

Spring
Frison, Paul Maurice *health care executive*

Stafford
Brinkley, Elise Hoffman *biofeedback counselor, marriage and family therapist, nurse*

Temple
Morrison, Gary Brent *hospital administrator*

The Woodlands
Sullivan, James Hall *hospital administrator*

Uvalde
Ramsey, Frank Allen *veterinarian, retired army officer*

UTAH

Orem
Leifson, June *nursing science educator, university administrator*

Salt Lake City
Gunnell, Dale Ray *hospital administrator*
Lee, Glenn Richard *medical administrator, educator*
†Madsen, Floyd A. *laboratory director*
Mason, James Ostermann *public health administrator*
†Parker, Scott Smith *hospital administrator*
†Samuelson, Cecil O. *health care facility executive*
Wolf, Harold Herbert *pharmacy educator*
Zaharia, Eric Stafford *developmental disabilities program administrator*

VERMONT

Brattleboro
Gregg, Michael B. *health science association administrator, epidemiologist*
Sarle, Charles Richard *health facility executive*

Burlington
Taylor, James Howard *hospital administrator*

Morrisville
†Roberts, Carolyn C. *hospital administrator*

VIRGINIA

Alexandria
Fisher, Donald Wayne *medical association executive*

Annandale
Abdellah, Faye Glenn *retired public health service executive*

Arlington
Held, Joe Roger *veterinarian, epidemiologist*
Rabun, John Brewton, Jr. *social services agency administrator*

Berryville
White, Eugene Vaden *pharmacist*

Blacksburg
†Modransky, Paula D. *veterinarian, educator*
Talbot, Richard Burritt *veterinarian, educator*

Charlottesville
Halseth, Michael James *medical center administrator*
Pate, Robert Hewitt, Jr. *counselor educator*

Fairfax
†Leidinger, William John *clinic administrator*

Falls Church
†Braendel, Douglas Arthur *healthcare executive*
†Devaney, Everett M. *health care executive*
Fink, Charles Augustin *behavioral systems scientist*

Mc Lean
Dean, Lydia Margaret Carter (Mrs. Halsey Albert Dean) *nutrition coordinator, author, consultant*
Gavazzi, Aladino A. *retired medical center administrator*

Newport News
Brink, Gerald R. *hospital executive*

Norfolk
Kern, Howard Paul *hospital administrator*
†Mitchell, Glenn R. *hospital administrator*

Radford
Lamb, Lester Lewis *hospital administrator*

Richmond
Barker, Thomas Carl *health administration educator*
Fischer, Carl Robert *health care facility administrator*
Freund, Emma Frances *medical technologist*
Hardage, Page Taylor *health care administrator*
Hardy, Richard Earl *rehabilitation counseling educator, clinical psychologist*
†Lambert, Benjamin Joseph, III *optometrist, state legislator*
Lewis, Judith A. *nursing educator, women's health nurse*
Simpson, John Noel *hospital administrator*

Roanoke
Bell, Houston Lesher, Jr. *hospital administrator*
Merker, Frank Ferdinand *retired hospital administrator*
†Robertson, Thomas L. *health facility administrator*

Springfield
†Singleton, John Knox *hospital administrator*

Vienna
Chamberlain, Diane *psychotherapist, author, clinical social worker*

WASHINGTON

Cheney
Gerber, Sanford Edwin *audiologist*

Olympia
Reilly, Robert Joseph *counselor*

Pullman
Bustad, Leo Kenneth *veterinary educator, college administrator*
Gustafsson, Borje Karl *veterinarian, educator*
Henson, James Bond *veterinary pathologist*
Wilson, Robert Burton *veterinary and medical educator*

Seattle
Boaz, Doniella *psychotherapist, consultant*
Bond, Dorothy M. *medical/surgical and geriatrics nurse*
Day, Robert Winsor *research administrator*
de Tornyay, Rheba *nurse, university dean emeritus, educator*
Duncan, Elizabeth Charlotte *marriage and family therapist, educator*
†Hellström, Ingegerd *business executive*
Monsen, Elaine Ranker *nutritionist, educator, editor*
Muilenburg, Robert Henry *hospital administrator*
†Perkin, Gordon Wesley *international health agency executive*
Perrin, Edward Burton *health services researcher, biostatistician, public health educator*
Prins, David *speech pathologist, educator*
Thompson, Arlene Rita *nursing educator*
Yantis, Phillip Alexander *audiologist, educator*

Spokane
Hendershot, Carol Miller *physical therapist*
Leahy, Gerald Philip *hospital administrator*

Tacoma
Hendley, Ashley Preston, Jr. *clinical social worker*
Smith, Leo Gilbert *hospital administrator*

WEST VIRGINIA

Charleston
†Border, Larry Willis *pharmacist*
Goodwin, Phillip Hugh *hospital administrator*

Martinsburg
Weaver, Thomas Harold *health facility administrator*

Morgantown
Westfall, Bernard G. *university hospital executive*

WISCONSIN

Elm Grove
Headlee, Raymond *psychoanalyst, educator*

Fort Atkinson
Albaugh, John Charles *hospital executive*

La Crosse
Anderson, Mary Ann *hospital nursing administrator*

Madison
Derzon, Gordon M. *hospital administrator*
Easterday, Bernard Carlyle *veterinary medicine educator*
Gavin, Mary Jane *medical, surgical nurse*
Lefert, Gerald W. *hospital administrator*
Littlefield, Vivian Moore *nursing educator, administrator*
Maloney, Michael James *research scientist*
Schulz, Rockwell Irwin *health administration educator*

Marshfield
David, Barbara Marie *medical, surgical nurse*
Jaye, David Robert, Jr. *retired hospital administrator*

Milwaukee
Ambrosius, Mark Ralph *hospital administrator*
Brown, Edith *social worker*
Gengler, Sister M. Jeanne *hospital administrator*
Harvieux, Anne Marie *psychotherapist*
Jenkins, William Ivy *hospital administrator*
Rice, Robert Marshall *social worker*
Schenk, Quentin Frederick *retired social work educator, mayor*
†Smith, Guy W. *health care executive*
†Vice, Jon Earl *hospital executive*
†Zober, Norman Alan *health facility administrator*

Whitewater
Rosner, Jorge *therapist, institute director*

WYOMING

Teton Village
Ellwood, Paul Murdock, Jr. *health policy analyst, consultant*

TERRITORIES OF THE UNITED STATES

GUAM

Agana
Duenas, Laurent Flores *nursing administrator*

PUERTO RICO

Rio Piedras
Perez, Victor *medical technologist, laboratory director*

CANADA

ALBERTA

Bentley
Manes, John Dalton *retired hospital administrator, anaesthesiologist*

Calgary
Calkin, Joy Durfée *healthcare consultant, educator*
†Meyers, Marlene O. *hospital administrator*

Edmonton
Fields, Anthony Lindsay Austin *health facility administrator, oncologist, educator*
Hislop, Mervyn Warren *health advocate administrator, psychologist*
Scholefield, Peter Gordon *health agency executive*
Schurman, Donald Peter *hospital administrator*

Lethbridge
Cho, Hyun Ju *veterinary research scientist*

BRITISH COLUMBIA

Cobble Hill
Ling, Daniel *audiology consultant, educator emeritus, former university dean*

New Westminster
†Fair, James Stanley *hospital administrator*

North Vancouver
†Smith, Robert John *health facility administrator*

Vancouver
Gilbert, John Humphrey Victor *audiologist, speech scientist, educator*
Key, Chapin *hospital administrator*
†Mulchey, Ronald Douglas *hospital administrator*
Riedel, Bernard Edward *retired pharmaceutical sciences educator*
Splane, Richard Beverley *social work educator*

Victoria
Fyke, Kenneth John *hospital administrator*

MANITOBA

Winnipeg
†Schultz, Harry *health science organization administrator*
Thorfinnson, A. Rodney *hospital administrator*

NEW BRUNSWICK

Fredericton
McGeorge, Ronald Kenneth *hospital executive*

NEWFOUNDLAND

Corner Brook
Watts, Harold Ross *hospital administrator*

NOVA SCOTIA

Halifax
Badley, Bernard William David *health care executive, physician, educator*

ONTARIO

Brantford
†Woodcock, Richard Beverley *health facility administrator*

Brockville
Lafave, Hugh Gordon John *medical association executive, psychiatrist, educator, consultant*

Etobicoke
Macdonald, John Barfoot *research foundation executive*

Kincardine
†Glynn, Peter Alexander Richard *health facility manager*

Kingston
McGeer, James Peter *research executive, consultant*

London
†Hassen, Philip C. *health facility executive*

Nepean
Beare-Rogers, Joyce Louise *former research executive*

North York
MacKenzie, Donald Murray *hospital administrator*

Ottawa
Clemenhagen, Carol Jane *health facility executive*

Owen Sound
Jones, Phyllis Edith *nursing educator*

Toronto
Ellis, Peter Hudson *health science facility administrator*
†Freedman, Theodore Jarrell *healthcare executive*
Herbert, Stephen W. *hospital executive*
MacLeod, William Brian *hospital executive*
Turner, Gerald Phillip *hospital administrator*

Waterloo
Fisher, Edward Joseph *optometrist, educator*

Willowdale
Krakauer, Albert Alexander *pharmacist, retail executive*

QUEBEC

Chicoutimi
St-Onge, Guy Claude *hospital administrator*

Fleurimont
Simoneau, Normand J. *hospital administrator*

Montreal
†Gallagher, Tanya Marie *speech pathologist, educator*
Martin, Jean Claude *health management educator*
Scriver, Charles Robert *medical scientist, human geneticist*
Sirois, Gerard *pharmacy educator*

SASKATCHEWAN

Saskatoon
Belovanoff, Olga *retired health care facility administrator*

MEXICO

Mexico City
Baer, George Martin *veterinarian, researcher*

Morelos
Illich, Ivan *researcher, educator*

AUSTRALIA

Rockhampton
Zelmer, Amy Elliott *health science educator*

BANGLADESH

Dhaka
Abeyesundere, Nihal Anton Aelian *health organization representative*

BRAZIL

São Paulo
Fernicola, Nilda Alicia Gallego Gándara de *pharmacist, biochemist*
Korolkovas, Andrejus *pharmaceutical chemistry educator*

CHINA

Beijing
Zhang, Li-Xing *physician, medical facility executive*

Shanghai
Wang, Ji-Qing (Chi-Ching Wong) *acoustician, educator*

DENMARK

Bagsvaerd
Sørensen, Erik *health care company executive*

GERMANY

Greifswald
Teuscher, Eberhard *pharmacist*

ICELAND

Reykjavik
Thorarensen, Oddur C.S. *pharmacist*

ITALY

Messina
Gimbo, Angelo *veterinary pathology educator, researcher*

JAMAICA

Mona Kingston
Ferguson, Marjorie Delores *nursing educator*

JAPAN

Gotsu
Hirayama, Chisato *healthcare facility administrator, physician, educator*

Hirakata
Nakanishi, Tsutomu *pharmaceutical science educator*

Kitakyushu
Okubo, Toshiteru *health science facility administrator, educator*

Kobe
Tani, Shohei *pharmacy educator*

Nagoya
Shioiri, Takayuki *pharmaceutical science educator*

Tokyo
Nagai, Tsuneji *pharmaceutics educator*

ADDRESS UNPUBLISHED

Adkins, Claudia K. *nursing educator*
Anaple, Elsie Mae *medical, surgical and geriatrics nurse*
Baier, Edward John *former public health official, industrial hygiene engineer, consultant*
Barker, Mary Katherine *retired nurse*
Barnhouse, Lillian May Palmer *retired medical, surgical nurse, researcher, civic worker*
Batalden, Paul Bennett *pediatrician, health care educator*
†Beard, Charles Walter *veterinarian, researcher*
Becich, Raymond Brice *healthcare-dispute resolution consultant*
Berdanier, Carolyn Dawson *nutrition educator, researcher*
Berzon, Betty *psychotherapist*
†Biegel, David Eli *social worker, educator*
Bishop, (Ina) Sue Marquis *psychiatric and mental health nurse educator, researcher, administrator*
Blomgren, Bruce Holmes *motivational speaker*
Borg, Ruth I. *mental health nurse, long-term medical nurse*
Borgstahl, Kaylene Denise *health facility administrator*
Bryant, Gail Annette Grippen *nurse, educator*
Bullough, Bonnie *nurse, educator*
Burns, Nancy Kay *drug abuse services professional*
Campbell, Raymond McKinly *psychologist, educator, consultant, researcher*
Carpenter, Kenneth John *nutrition educator*
Casey, John Thomas *health services agency executive*
Condry, Robert Stewart *retired hospital administrator*
Couchman, Robert George James *human services consultant*
Cox, J. William *physician, health services administrator*
Cox, James Clarence *hospital administrator*
Cramer, John Sanderson *health care executive*
Cromwell, Florence Stevens *occupational therapist*
Dake, Marcia Allene *nursing educator, university dean*
Deems, Andrew William *health facility administrator*
Dungworth, Donald L. *veterinary educator, consultant*
Dyer, Wayne Walter *psychologist, author, radio and television personality*
Eddy, Esther Dewitz *retired pharmacist*
Eisen, Henry *retired pharmacy educator*
Elliott, Lois Lawrence *audiology and otolaryngology educator*
Emerson, Ann Parker *dietician, educator*
†Eugster, Albrecht Konrad *veterinarian, laboratory director*
Faulkner, Lloyd C. *veterinary medicine educator*
Fehr, Lola Mae *nursing association director*
Fein, Adrienne Myra *nursing educator*
†Feurig, Thomas Leo *health care executive*
Finucane, Richard Daniel *corporate medical director, retired food products executive*
Fox, Michael Wilson *veterinarian, animal behaviorist*
Freeman, Arthur *veterinarian, retired association administrator*
French, Glendon Everett, Jr. *health care executive*
Friedlander, Robert Lynn *health education and health management consultant*
Garvey, Evelyn Jewel *mental health nurse*
Gay, William Ingalls *veterinarian, health science administrator*
Geitgey, Doris Arlene *retired nursing educator, dean*
Gerald, Michael Charles *pharmacy educator, college dean*
†Gibson, Robert N. *hospital executive*
Goodwin, Barbara A. *retired nurse, military officer*
Govan, Gladys Vernita Mosley *retired critical care and medical/surgical nurse*
Graff, Luisita Mariano *women's health nurse, nursing administrator*
Green, Barbara Strawn *psychotherapist*
Green, Flora Hungerford *lactation consultant, nurse*
Hardy, Gyme Dufault *social worker*
Hartnett, Thomas Patrick *health care management executive*
Hasselmeyer, Eileen Grace *medical research administrator*
Heath, Richard Murray *retired hospital administrator*
Heffernan, Wilbert Joseph *social worker, educator*
Herriot, James (James Alfred Wight) *veterinary surgeon, author*
Herrmann, Walter *retired laboratory administrator*
Hertz, Kenneth Theodore *health care executive*
Hofmann, Paul Bernard *health care consultant*
Holmes, Kathryn Louise *medical technologist*
Homestead, Susan *psychotherapist*
Horowitz, Beverly Phyllis *occupational therapist*
Howe, John Prentice, III *health science center executive, physician*
Hunt, Ronald Duncan *veterinarian, educator, pathologist*
Juenemann, Sister Jean *hospital administrator*
Kahanovsky, Luis *physical therapist*
Kellam, Norma Dawn *medical, surgical nurse*
Kieffer, Joyce Loretta *health science facility administrator, educator*
Kilpatrick, Georgia Lee *nursing educator*
King, Imogene M. *nurse, educator*
Ladly, Frederick Bernard *health services and financial services company executive*
Littner, Ner *psychoanalyst, psychiatrist*
Livingstone, Susan Morrisey *healthcare administrator*
Lousberg, Sister Mary Clarice *hospital executive*
Macdonald, Donald Ian *health care administrator*
Magnuson, Robert Martin *retired hospital administrator*
May, Rollo *psychoanalyst*
Meehan, John Joseph, Jr. *hospital administrator*
Meyer, Harry Martin, Jr. *retired health science facility administrator*
Mich, Connie Rita *mental health nurse, educator*
Milewski, Barbara Anne *pediatrics nurse, neonatal intensive care nurse*
Miller, Lillie M. *nursing educator*
Mills, Celeste Louise *hypnotherapist, professional magician*
Moffatt, Hugh McCulloch, Jr. *hospital administrator, physical therapist*
Mooneyhan, Esther Louise *nurse, educator*
Moreland, Alvin Franklin *veterinarian*
Nakagawa, Allen Donald *radiologic technologist*
O'Neill, Donald Edmund *health science executive*
Ott, Margaret E. *retired nurse and cosmetology educator*
Parmer, Dan Gerald *veterinarian*
Perry, J. Warren *health sciences educator, administrator*
Pettit, Ghery DeWitt *retired veterinary medicine educator*
Rainey, Claude Gladwin *retired health care executive*
†Roodman, Richard David *hospital administrator*
†Sauvage, Lester Rosaire *health facility administrator, cardiovascular surgeon*
Scala, James *health care industry consultant, author*
Schiller, Alfred George *veterinarian, educator*
Schwartz, Doris Ruhbel *nursing educator, consultant*
Schweinhart, Richard Alexander *health care company executive*
Scott, Amy Annette Holloway *nursing educator*
Shannon, Iris Reed *nursing educator*
Simms, Maria Ester *health services administrator*
Smith, Ronald Lynn *health system executive*
Splitstone, George Dale *retired hospital administrator*
Swift, Harold Augustus *health association executive*
Talingdan, Arsenio Preza *health science administrator*
Thomson, Grace Marie *nurse, minister*
Uhrich, Richard Beckley *hospital executive, physician*
†Wampler, Jon R. *health financial administrator*
Wessler, Richard Lee *psychology educator, psychotherapist*
Wiebe, Leonard Irving *radiopharmacist, educator*
Williams, Raymond Crawford *veterinarian anatomy educator*
Wooding, Gayle McAfee *nursing educator, consultant*
Woods, Geraldine Pittman *health education consultant, educational consultant*
Yanagitani, Elizabeth *optometrist*

MILITARY

UNITED STATES

ALABAMA

Alexander City
Shuler, Ellie Givan, Jr. *retired air force officer*

Fort Rucker
Adams, Ronald Emerson *army officer*
Robinson, John David *army officer*

Madison
Jellett, James Morgan *retired army officer, aerospace defense consultant*

Maxwell AFB
†Johnston, Robert Michael *military officer*
Pendley, William Tyler *naval officer, international relations educator*

Montgomery
Sistrunk, William Hicks *air force officer*

ALASKA

Fort Richardson
Schnell, Roger Thomas *retired military officer, state official*

ARIZONA

Phoenix
Beltrán, Anthony Natalicio *military officer, deacon*

Tucson
Guice, John Thompson *retired air force officer*
Wickham, John Adams, Jr. *retired army officer*

Yuma
Hudson, John Irvin *retired marine officer*

ARKANSAS

Mountain Home
Baker, Robert Leon *naval medical officer*

CALIFORNIA

Bonita
Curtis, Richard Earl *former naval officer, former company executive, business consultant*

Borrego Springs
Shinn, Allen Mayhew *retired naval officer, business executive*

Cedar Ridge
Yeager, Charles Elwood (Chuck Yeager) *retired air force officer*

Coronado
Butcher, Bobby Gene *retired military officer*
Worthington, George Rhodes *naval officer*

Escondido
Briggs, Edward Samuel *naval officer*

Folsom
Aldridge, Donald O'Neal *military officer*

Healdsburg
Eade, George James *retired air force officer, research executive, defense consultant*

Laguna Beach
Faw, Duane Leslie *retired military officer, law educator, lay worker, author*

Los Angeles
†Abrahamson, James Alan *retired air force officer*

Merced
Abbott, Woodrow Acton *air force general officer*

Monterey
Schrady, David Alan *operations research educator*

Napa
Smith, Robert Bruce *former security consultant, retired army officer*

Oakland
Sanford, Frederic Goodman *career officer*

Pebble Beach
Fergusson, Robert George *retired army officer*

Point Mugu
†Newman, William E. *naval officer*

Riverside
Wright, John MacNair, Jr. *retired army officer*

San Diego
Cockell, William Arthur, Jr. *naval officer*
†Fontana, J. D. *naval research administration*
Robinson, David Brooks *naval officer*

Santa Barbara
Conley, Philip James, Jr. *retired air force officer*

Saratoga
Henderson, William Darryl *career officer, journalist*

Sunnyvale
Schumacher, Henry Jerold *former career officer, business executive*

COLORADO

Boulder
Stone, John Helms, Jr. *admiralty advisor*

Colorado Springs
Allery, Kenneth Edward *air force officer*
Bowen, Clotilde Dent *retired army officer, psychiatrist*
Breckner, William John, Jr. *retired air force officer, corporate executive, consultant*
Forgan, David Waller *retired air force officer*
Metzler, Philip Lowry, Jr. *air force officer*
Mitchell, John Henderson *retired army officer, management consultant*
Sawyer, Thomas William *air force officer*
Schaeffer, Reiner Horst *air force officer, retired librarian, foreign language professional*
Stewart, Robert Lee *retired army officer, astronaut*
Todd, Harold Wade *retired air force officer, consultant*

Denver
Avrit, Richard Calvin *defense consultant*

Peterson AFB
Horner, Charles Albert *air force officer*
Moorman, Thomas Samuel, Jr. *career officer*

USAF Academy
Hosmer, Bradley Clark *air force officer*

CONNECTICUT

Groton
†Simpson, W. M. *career officer administrator*

DISTRICT OF COLUMBIA

Bolling AFB
Gardner, Jerry Dean *brigadier general*
Jones, William Edward *air force officer*

Washington
Adams, Andrew Joseph *army officer*
†Anderson, Marcus A. *career officer*
†Anselmo, Philip Shepard *naval officer*
Ball, James William *army officer*
†Bennett, David Michael *naval officer*
†Bennitt, Brent Martin *naval officer*
†Boorda, Jeremy Michael (Mike Boorda) *naval officer*
Brown, Gerald Curtis *army officer, civil engineer*
Carns, Michael Patrick Chamberlain *air force officer*
Caruana, Patrick Peter *career officer*
Coady, Philip James, Jr. *naval officer*
Corcoran, Thomas Joseph *retired foreign service officer, former ambassador*
†Coughenour, Kavin Luther *career officer, military historian*
Dur, Philip Alphonse *naval officer*
Dyke, Charles William *retired army officer*
Earner, William Anthony, Jr. *naval officer*
Falter, Vincent Eugene *retired army officer, consultant*
Fedorochko, William, Jr. *retired army officer, policy analyst*
Finerty, Martin Joseph, Jr. *military officer, researcher*
Forster, William Hull *military officer*
Franklin, Charles E. *career officer*
Frost, S. David *retired naval officer*
Fuller, Lawrence Joseph *military officer, lawyer*
Goodpaster, Andrew Jackson *retired army officer*
Graves, Ernest, Jr. *retired army officer, engineer*
†Griffith, Ronald H. *military career officer*
†Hagen, Donald Floyd *military officer*
†Hancock, William John *career officer*
Harrison, Jerry Calvin *army officer*
Higgins, Robert (Walter) *military officer, physician*
Hoar, Joseph P. *military officer*
Huston, John Wilson *air force officer, historian*
Jeremiah, David Elmer *naval officer*
Kalleres, Michael Peter *career officer*
Kime, J. William *career officer, engineer*
†Klugh, James Richard *military officer*
LaPlante, John Baptiste *naval officer*
Laposata, Joseph Samuel *army officer*
†Laughton, Katherine L. *career officer*
Lautenbacher, Conrad Charles, Jr. *naval officer*
Leaf, Howard Westley *retired air force officer, military official*
Loftus, Stephen Francis *naval officer*
Lynch, Thomas C. *career military officer*
Macke, Richard Chester *naval officer*
Maddox, David M. *career military officer*
†Marfiak, Thomas Fletcher *career officer*
†Mathis, William Walter *career officer*
McClain, Charles William, Jr. (Bill McClain) *army officer*
McGinty, Michael Dennis *air force officer*
McMiller, Anita Williams *army officer, transportation professional, educator*
McPeak, Merrill Anthony *air force officer*
Mears, Gary H. *career military officer*
Miller, Kenneth Gregory *air force officer*
Montelongo, Michael *career officer*
Moorer, Thomas Hinman *retired naval officer*
Mundy, Carl Epting, Jr. *commandant of the marine corps*
†Neu, James Edward *military officer*
O'Berry, Carl Gerald *air force officer, electrical engineer*
Odom, William Eldridge *army officer, educator*
†Oliver, David Rogers, Jr. *naval officer*
Oswald, Robert Bernard *science administrator, nuclear engineer*
†Paulsen, Thomas Dean *naval officer*
Pirie, Robert Burns, Jr. *defense analyst*
Powell, Colin Luther *army officer*
†Reason, Joseph Paul *naval officer*
Riddell, Richard Anderson *naval officer*
Rokke, Ervin Jerome *career officer*
St. John, Adrian, II *retired army officer*
Sareeram, Ray Rupchand *naval officer*
Scofield, Richard Melbourne *career officer*
Scowcroft, Brent *retired air force officer, government official*
Shea, Donald William *career officer*
Siegfried, Richard Stephen *military officer*
Simmons, Edwin Howard *marine corps officer, historian*
Smith, Leighton Warren, Jr. *naval officer*
Smith, William Dee *naval officer*
†Snyder, Daniel James *military career officer*
Stephens, Robert Louis, Jr. *army officer*
Studeman, William Oliver *naval officer*
Sullivan, Gordon R. *career officer*
Thomas, Richard *civilian military employee*
Traister, Robert Edwin *naval officer, engineer*
Wagner, George Francis Adolf *naval officer*

Wheeler, Albin Gray *career officer, educator, law firm executive*
Wishart, Leonard Plumer, III *army officer*
Zlatoper, Ronald Joseph *career officer*

FLORIDA

Daytona Beach
Gauch, Eugene William, Jr. *former air force officer*

Destin
Carlton, Paul Kendall *former air force officer, consultant*

Eglin A F B
†Pletcher, John Harold, Jr. *career military officer*

Fernandina Beach
Rogers, Robert Burnett *naval officer*

Haines City
Clement, Robert William *air force officer*

Jacksonville
Lestage, Daniel Barfield *retired naval officer, physician*

Kennedy Space Center
Crippen, Robert Laurel *naval officer, former astronaut*

Lake Wales
Mumma, Albert G. *retired naval officer, retired manufacturing company executive, management consultant*

Longwood
Smyth, Joseph Patrick *retired naval officer, physician*

Lutz
Bedke, Ernest Alford *retired air force officer*

Mac Dill AFB
LeMoyne, Irve Charles *career officer*

Miami
†Saunders, Norman Thomas *military officer*

Niceville
Phillips, Richard Wendell, Jr. *air force officer*

Ocala
Parker, Harry Lee *retired military officer, counselor*

Orange Park
Enney, James Crowe *former air force officer, business executive*

Orlando
Tillotson, Frank Lee *naval officer*

Ormond Beach
Riley, Daniel Edward *air force officer*

Palm City
Senter, William Oscar *retired air force officer*

Pensacola
Weisner, Maurice Franklin *former naval officer*

Punta Gorda
Hepfer, John William, Jr. *consultant, retired air force officer*
Wilson, Dwight Liston *former military officer, investment advisor*

Saint Petersburg
Papa, Anthony Emil *retired army officer*

Sarasota
Loving, George Gilmer, Jr. *retired air force officer*

Valrico
†Nelson, Norman Daniel *career officer*

GEORGIA

Atlanta
Buker, Robert Hutchinson, Sr. *army officer, thoracic surgeon*
Carey, Gerald John, Jr. *former air force officer, research institute director*

Augusta
Mallette, Alfred John *army officer*

Columbus
Harper, Henry H. *military officer*

Dobbins AFB
McIntosh, Robert Alan *military career officer*

Fort Benning
Ramsey, Russell Wilcox *national security affairs educator*

Fort Lewis
Cavezza, Carmen James *career officer*

Fort McPherson
Reimer, Dennis J. *career military officer*

Kings Bay
Ellis, Winford Gerald *military career officer, federal agency administrator*

Peachtree City
Eichelberger, Charles Bell *retired career officer*
Yeosock, John John *army officer*

Robins A F B
Gillis, Richard Fred *career officer*

Roswell
Graham, Charles Passmore *retired army officer*

Stockbridge
†Davis, Raymond Gilbert *retired career officer, real estate developer*

Warner Robins
Nugteren, Cornelius *air force officer*
Scott, Robert Lee, Jr. *career military officer, writer, lecturer*

HAWAII

Honolulu
Barr, Jon Michael *naval officer, federal official*
†Driskill, Thomas Malcolm, Jr. *military officer*
Greer, Howard Earl *former naval officer*
Hays, Ronald Jackson *naval officer*
†Retz, William Andrew *naval officer*
Rutherford, Robert L. *career military officer*
Weyand, Frederick Carlton *retired military officer*

Kaneohe
McGlaughlin, Thomas Howard *publisher, retired naval officer*

Pearl Harbor
Fitzgerald, James Richard *naval officer*
Larson, Charles Robert *naval officer*

ILLINOIS

Great Lakes
Gaston, Mack Charles *naval officer*

Hoffman Estates
Pagonis, William Gus *retired army officer*

Lemont
Herriford, Robert Levi, Sr. *army officer*

Mattoon
Phipps, John Randolph *retired army officer*

Savanna
Foulk, David Wingerd *civilian military executive*

Scott AFB
Fogleman, Ronald Robert *military officer*
Landers, Paul E., Jr. *military career officer*

IOWA

Des Moines
Durrenberger, William John *retired army general, educator, investor*

KANSAS

Fort Leavenworth
Miller, John Edward *army officer*

LOUISIANA

New Orleans
Read, William Edgar *army officer, engineer*
Smith, John Webster *retired naval officer, company executive*

MARYLAND

Aberdeen Proving Ground
Coburn, John G. *career officer*

Annapolis
Baldwin, John Ashby, Jr. *retired naval officer*
Barber, James Alden *military officer*
Long, Robert Lyman John *naval officer*
McDonough, Joseph Corbett *former army officer, aviation consultant*

Bethesda
Cooper, William Ewing, Jr. *retired army officer*
Daniel, Charles Dwelle, Jr. *consultant, retired army officer*
Hauck, Frederick Hamilton *retired naval officer, astronaut, business executive*
O'Shaughnessy, Gary William *military officer*
Owen, Thomas Barron *retired naval officer, space company executive*
Pfister, Cloyd Harry *consultant, former career officer*
Rogers, Alan Victor *former career officer*
Taylor, Jimmie Wilkes *naval officer*
Zimble, James Allen *naval officer, physician*

Chevy Chase
Delano, Victor *retired naval officer*

Crownsville
Lawrence, William Porter *former naval officer, academic administrator*

Fort Meade
Runyon, Floyd Lawrence *army officer*

Mays Chapel
Sagerholm, James Alvin *retired naval officer*

Oxford
Mc Kee, Kinnaird Rowe *retired naval officer*

Rockville
Cowart, Elgin Courtland, Jr. *naval medical officer*
Harvey, Donald Phillips *retired naval officer*
Ramsey, William Edward *retired naval officer, space systems executive*
Trost, Carlisle Albert Herman *retired naval officer*

Silver Spring
Brog, David *consultant, former air force officer*

Trappe
Anderson, Andrew Herbert *retired army officer*

MASSACHUSETTS

Boston
†Amirault, Richard B. *career officer*
Holloway, Bruce Keener *former air force officer*

Lowell
Natsios, Nicholas Andrew *retired foreign service officer*

North Dartmouth
Cressy, Peter Hollon *naval officer, academic administrator*

Quincy
Miller, George David *retired air force officer, marketing consultant*

South Hamilton
Patton, George Smith *military officer*

Westford
Stansberry, James Wesley *air force officer*

MICHIGAN

Ann Arbor
Ploger, Robert Riis *retired military officer, engineer*

Warren
Horton, William David, Jr. *army officer*

MISSISSIPPI

Pass Christian
McCardell, James Elton *retired naval officer*

Stennis Space Center
Gaffney, Paul Golden, II *military officer*

MISSOURI

Chesterfield
Willis, Frank Edward *retired air force officer*

Saint Louis
†Liddy, Steven Thomas *career military officer, educator*
Williamson, Donald Ray *retired career officer*

MONTANA

Helena
Blair, Gary Charles *military officer*

NEBRASKA

Lincoln
Heng, Stanley Mark *military officer*

Offult
Curtin, Gary Lee *air force officer*

Offutt A F B
Tindal, Ralph Lawrence *career officer*
Torma, Michael Joseph *career officer, surgeon*

Omaha
Fowler, Stephen Eugene *retired military officer*

NEVADA

Henderson
Creech, Wilbur Lyman *air force officer*

NEW HAMPSHIRE

Dover
†Burr, Peter Haskell *publisher, political consultant*

Hollis
Dyer, Travis Neal *army officer*

Portsmouth
Harden, Acheson Adair, Jr. *retired military officer, retired mathematics educator*

NEW JERSEY

Cape May Court House
Poel, Robert Walter *career officer, physician*

NEW MEXICO

Cedar Crest
Sheppard, Jack W. *retired air force officer*

Kirtland A F B
Harrison, George Brooks *career officer*

Los Alamos
†Alexander, John Bradfield *weaponry manager, retired army officer*

Santa Fe
†Baca, Edward Dionicio *national guard officer*

NEW YORK

Colton
Bulger, Dennis Bernard *military officer, engineer*

Flushing
†Strevey, Tracy Elmer, Jr. *army officer, surgeon*

New York
Burback, Steven Brent *military administrator*
Dugan, Michael J. *former air force officer, health agency executive*
Schwarzkopf, H. Norman *retired army officer, engineer*

Orient
Hanson, Thor *retired health agency executive and naval officer*

West Point
Galvin, John Rogers *educator, retired army officer*
Graves, Howard Dwayne *army officer, academic administrator, educator*

NORTH CAROLINA

Charlotte
Ward, Marion Haggard *retired air force officer, museum president*

Fort Bragg
Davis, Harley Cleo *career officer*
†Palmer, Gary Stephen *career officer, healthcare administrator*
Younger, Kenneth Maurice *military officer*

Pine Knoll Shores
Lynn, Otis Clyde *former army officer*

Pinehurst
Carroll, Kent Jean *retired naval officer*
Ellis, William Harold *former naval officer*
Roberts, Francis Joseph *retired army officer, retired educational administrator, global economic advisor*

Spring Hope
Hildreth, James Robert *air force officer*

Whispering Pines
Blanchard, George Samuel *retired military officer, consultant*

OHIO

Beavercreek
McCormick, Jack Edward *retired military officer, educator*

Dayton
Bridges, Roy Dubard, Jr. *career officer*
Halki, John Joseph *retired military officer, physician*
Whitlock, David C. *retired military officer*
Yates, Ronald Wilburn *air force officer*

PENNSYLVANIA

Carlisle Barracks
Stofft, William A. *career officer*

Glenside
Apperson, Jack Alfonso *retired army officer, business executive*

Mechanicsburg
Filipiak, Francis Leonard *naval officer*

Philadelphia
†Wilmot, Louise C. *career military officer*

Pittsburgh
Lowery, Clinton Hershey *former naval officer*

Wayne
Hill, Virgil Lusk, Jr. *naval officer, academic administrator*
Pearson, Willard *former army officer*

RHODE ISLAND

Newport
Strasser, Joseph C. *career military officer, academic administrator*

SOUTH CAROLINA

Aiken
Cutting, Robert Thomas *army officer, physician*

Charleston
Watts, Claudius Elmer, III *retired air force officer*

Columbia
†Lander, James Albert *retired military officer, state senator*
Marchant, Trelawney Eston *national guard officer, lawyer*

Hilton Head Island
Brown, Arthur Edmon, Jr. *retired army officer*

Seneca
Clausen, Hugh Joseph *retired army officer*

Sumter
Olsen, Thomas Richard, Sr. *air force officer*

SOUTH DAKOTA

Rapid City
Sykora, Harold James *military officer*

TENNESSEE

Clarksville
Birdsong, William Herbert, Jr. *retired brigadier general*

Nashville
Brophy, Jeremiah Joseph *former army officer*

TEXAS

Austin
Taber, Robert Clinton *retired army officer*

Belton
Harrison, Benjamin Leslie *retired army officer*
Shoemaker, Robert Morin *retired army officer, county government official*

Brooks AFB
Irving, George Washington, III *military officer, research director, veterinarian*

Dallas
Bolling, Alexander Russell, Jr. *retired military officer, business executive*

El Paso
Shapiro, Stephen Richard *retired air force officer, physician*

Fort Hood
†Hughes, William Foster *career officer, surgeon, obstetrician, gynecologist*

Fort Worth
†Rivera, Angel (Andy) Manuel *retired career officer, city official*

Hollywood Park
Rosencrans, Evan William *retired air force officer*

Houston
Cameron, Richard Douglas *military officer, psychiatrist*
Jones, Lincoln, III *army officer*
Kline, John William *retired air force officer, management consultant*

Lackland AFB
Anderson, Edgar R., Jr. *career officer, hospital administrator, physician*

Prairie View
Becton, Julius Wesley, Jr. *army officer*

San Antonio
Anderson, George Kenneth *air force officer, physician*
Bishop, Charles Landon *air force officer*
Johnson, Hansford Tillman *retired air force officer*
Schneider, William Henry *retired army officer*

Tyler
†Gann, Benard Wayne *air force officer*

Wilford Hall U S A F Hosp
Cissik, John Henry *air force career officer, medical researcher*

VERMONT

Burlington
Cram, Reginald Maurice *retired air force officer*

VIRGINIA

Alexandria
Adams, Ranald Trevor, Jr. *retired air force officer*
Allen, Fred Cary *retired army officer*
Babcock, Jack Emerson *retired army officer, educator, corporate executive*
Bowman, Richard Carl *defense consultant, retired air force officer*
Brown, Frederic Joseph *army officer*
Burke, Kelly Howard *former air force officer, business executive*
Condrill, Jo Ellaresa *logistics executive, speaker*
Dawalt, Kenneth Francis *former army officer, former aerospace company executive*
Dorsey, James Francis, Jr. *naval officer*
Downs, Michael Patrick *retired marine corps officer*
Ensslin, Robert Frank, Jr. *retired military officer*
Kilcline, Thomas John *naval officer*
McFarlin, Robert Paul *army officer*
Mc Mullen, Thomas Henry *retired air force officer*
McNair, Carl Herbert, Jr. *army officer, aeronautical engineer*
Rosenkranz, Robert Bernard *military officer*
Rowden, William Henry *naval officer*
Saint, Crosbie Edgerton *retired army officer*
Salomon, Leon Edward *career officer*
Stafford, Thomas Patten *retired military officer, former astronaut*
†Straw, Edward M. *career officer, federal agency administrator*
Thomas, Billy Marshall *retired army officer*
Voorhees, John Henry *military officer*
Vuono, Carl E. *army officer*

Annandale
Guthrie, John Reiley *retired army officer, business executive*
McCaffree, Burnham Clough, Jr. *retired naval officer*
Mc Kee, Fran *retired naval officer*
†Strohsahl, George Henry, Jr. *retired rear admiral, consultant*
Williams, James Arthur *retired army officer, information systems company executive*

Arlington
Carr, Kenneth Monroe *naval officer*
Case, Charles Carroll *retired army officer*
Chapman, Donald D. *retired naval officer, lawyer*
Clayton, William E. *naval officer*
†Davis, Walter J., Jr. *rear admiral*
Dillon, Francis Richard *air force officer, retired*
Giordano, Andrew Anthony *retired naval officer*
Haddock, Raymond Earl *career officer*
Hatch, Monroe W., Jr. *military officer, association executive*
Kelley, Paul Xavier *retired marine corps officer*
Kem, Richard Samuel *retired army officer*
Lisanby, James Walker *retired naval officer*
Lockard, John Allen *naval officer*
McGinley, Edward Stillman, II *naval officer*
Merritt, Jack Neil *retired army officer*
Miller, Thomas Hulbert, Jr. *former marine corps officer*
Morris, John Woodland *businessman, former army officer*
Oren, John Birdsell *retired coast guard officer*
Rees, Clifford Harcourt, Jr. (Ted Rees) *retired air force officer, association executive*
Ross, Jimmy Douglas *army officer*
Saafeld, Fred Erich *naval researcher officer*
Scarborough, Robert Henry, Jr. *coast guard officer*
Strean, Bernard M. *retired naval officer*
†Swanson, Dane Craig *naval officer, pilot*
Thurman, Maxwell R. *retired army officer*
Tice, Raphael Dean *army officer*
Volgenau, Douglas *career officer*
Wagner, Louis Carson, Jr. *retired army officer*
Zumwalt, Elmo Russell, Jr. *retired naval officer*

Basye
Putnam, George W., Jr. *army officer*

Blacksburg
Musser, Stanton Richard *retired air force officer*

Burke
Boatright, James Francis *air force official*
O'Connor, Edward Cornelius *army officer*
Wood, C(harles) Norman *air force officer*

Chantilly
Stone, Thomas Edward *defense consultant, retired naval officer*

Chatham
Leonard, Edward Paul *naval officer, dentist, educator*

Fairfax
Baer, Robert Jacob *retired army officer*
Drenz, Charles Francis *retired army officer*
Kauderer, Bernard Marvin *retired naval officer*
Mandeville, Robert Clark, Jr. *former naval officer, business executive*
Otis, Glenn Kay *retired army officer, research and engineering company executive*

Fairfax Station
Scanlon, Charles Francis *army officer, retired, defense consultant*

Falls Church
Gray, D'Wayne *retired marine corps officer*
Hart, Herbert Michael *military officer*
Heldstab, John Christian *army officer*
†Johnson, Clifford Ivery *army officer, federal agency administrator*
Kroesen, Frederick James *army officer*
LaNoue, Alcide Moodie *medical corps officer, health care administrator*
Larson, Richard Gustaf *army officer*
Layman, Lawrence *naval officer*
Pendleton, Elmer Dean, Jr. *retired military officer, international consultant*
Simokaitis, Frank Joseph *air force officer, lawyer*

Fort Belvoir
Lajoie, Roland *army officer*
Menoher, Paul Edwin, Jr. *army officer*

Fort Myer
Blackwell, Paul Eugene *army officer*
Shalikashvili, John Malchase *military career officer*

Hampton
Goers, Melvin Armand *retired army officer*

Herndon
Doebler, James Carl *naval officer, engineering executive*

Langley AFB
Hobbs, Roy Jerry *military career officer, health services administrator*
Loh, John M. *career military officer*

Lexington
Read, Beverly Money *military officer*

Lynchburg
Snead, George Murrell, Jr. *army officer, scientist, consultant*

Madison
Ince, Eugene St. Clair, Jr. *cryptologist, retired naval officer*

Mc Lean
Cowhill, William Joseph *retired naval officer, consultant*
Davis, Bennie Luke *air force officer*
Hopkins, Thomas Matthews *former naval officer*
Howe, Jonathan Trumbull *naval officer*
Hyde, John Paul *retired air force officer*
Kane, John Dandridge Henley, Jr. *naval officer*

Middleburg
Collins, James Lawton, Jr. *retired army officer*

Mount Jackson
Sylvester, George Howard *retired air force officer*

Norfolk
†Clemins, Archie Ray *naval officer*
Davey, John Michael *military career officer*
Garlette, William Henry Lee *army officer*
†Granuzzo, Andrew Aloysius *career officer*
Mauz, Henry Herrward, Jr. *naval officer*
Moses, Paul Davis *career officer*
†Olson, Phillip Roger *naval officer*
Robb, Nathaniel Heyward, Jr. *national guard officer, real estate executive*
Train, Harry Depue, II *retired naval officer*

Portsmouth
McDaniel, William J. *career military officer*

Quantico
Davis, James Richard *military officer*

Reston
Brown, James Robert *air force officer*
Wilkinson, Edward Anderson, Jr. *retired naval officer, business executive*

Richmond
Dilworth, Robert Lexow *military officer*

Vienna
Chandler, Hubert Thomas *former army officer*
Chen, William Shao-Chang *retired army officer*
Davis, Cabell Seal, Jr. *naval officer*
Ghormley, Ralph McDougall *retired naval officer*
Hatch, Harold Arthur *retired military officer*
Henry, Charles Robert *army officer*
Hughes, Thomas Joseph *retired naval officer*
Jackson, Dempster McKee *retired naval officer*
Webb, William Loyd, Jr. *army officer*

Virginia Beach
Oldfield, Edward Charles, Jr. *retired naval officer, communications company executive*
Sanderson, James Richard *naval officer, planning and investment company consultant*

Williamsburg
Bolender, Carroll Herdus *retired air force officer, consultant*
Cantlay, George Gordon *retired army officer*

WASHINGTON

Bothell
McDonald, Michael Lee *career officer, healthcare administrator*

Lynnwood
Jenes, Theodore George, Jr. *retired military officer*

Tacoma
Russell, James Sargent *retired naval officer*

WEST VIRGINIA

Harpers Ferry
Carter, Powell Frederick *retired naval officer*

WISCONSIN

Stone Lake
Kissinger, Harold Arthur *retired army officer*

TERRITORIES OF THE UNITED STATES

GUAM

Agana
Burr, Hiram Hale, Jr. *air force officer*

MILITARY ADDRESSES OF THE UNITED STATES

EUROPE

APO
Borling, John Lorin *military officer*
Boyd, Charles Graham *military officer*
Chelberg, Robert Douglas *army officer*
Oaks, Robert C. *air force officer*
Ray, Norman Wilson *career officer*
Santarelli, Eugene David *air force officer*
Scotti, Michael John, Jr. *military medical officer*
†Yates, Walter Harvey, Jr. *career officer*

FPO
†Allen, Lloyd Edward, Jr. *naval officer*
†Haskins, Michael Donald *naval officer*
†Katz, Douglas Jeffrey *naval officer*
Picotte, Leonard Francis *naval officer*
†Ryan, Thomas D. *naval officer*

PACIFIC

APO
†Running, Nels *career officer*

FPO
†Briggs, Steven Russell *naval officer*
Dantone, Joseph John, Jr. *naval officer*
†Hickey, Robert Philip, Jr. *naval officer*

CANADA

ONTARIO

Arnprior
Christie, Andrew George *military officer*

Etobicoke
MacKenzie, Lewis Wharton *military officer*

Ottawa
de Chastelain, A(lfred) John G(ardyne) D(rummond) *Canadian army officer, diplomat*

Stittsville
Tellier, Henri *retired Canadian military officer*

QUEBEC

Montreal
Manson, Paul David *retired military officer, electronics executive*
Roy, Armand Joseph *military officer*

TURKEY

Ankara
Nuber, Philip William *air force officer*

ADDRESS UNPUBLISHED

Austin, Robert Clarke *naval officer*
Bauman, Richard Arnold *coast guard officer*
Block, Emil Nathaniel, Jr. *military officer*
Boomer, Walter Eugene *marine officer*
Boyd, Stuart Robert *military officer*
†Bradford, Jackie Edward *army officer, health care administrator*
Brooks, James Sprague *retired national guard officer*
†Campbell, Arlington Fichtner *military officer*
Carlson, Elvin Palmer *military officer*
Carter, William George, III *army officer*
Cole, Brady Marshall *retired naval officer*
Davis, Henry Jefferson, Jr. *former naval officer*
Dozier, James Lee *former army officer*
†Evans, Marsha Johnson *naval officer*
Fischer, Eugene H. *air force officer*
Foote, Evelyn Patricia *military officer, consultant*
Gavin, Herbert James *consultant, retired air force officer*
Gray, David Lawrence *retired air force officer*
Guthrie, Wallace Nessler, Jr. *naval officer*
Hall, Thomas Forrest *naval officer*
Harris, Marcelite Jordan *air force officer*
Hoover, John Elwood *former military officer, consultant, writer*
Hostettler, Stephen John *naval officer*
Johnston, James Monroe, III *air force officer*
Jones, David Charles *retired air force officer, former chairman Joint Chiefs of Staff*
Kempf, Cecil Joseph *naval officer*
Krulak, Charles Chandler *marine officer*
Kutyna, Donald Joseph *air force officer*
†Maness, Anthony Ray *retired naval officer*
Manganaro, Francis Ferdinand *naval officer*
Matthews, John Louis *military officer, educator*
Mc Fadden, George Linus *retired army officer*
McKinnon, Daniel Wayne, Jr. *naval officer*
Moore, William Leroy, Jr. *career officer, physician*
Morgan, Thomas Rowland *retired marine corps officer*
Mow, Douglas Farris *former naval officer, consultant*
Nelson, Ben, Jr. *air force officer*
Ninos, Nicholas Peter *retired military officer, medical consultant*
Otstott, Charles Paddock *army officer*
Owens, William Arthur *military officer*
Palmer, Dave Richard *military officer*
Parent, Rodolphe Jean *Canadian air force official, pilot*
Partington, James Wood *naval officer*
†Pearson, John Davis *naval officer*
Powell, Harvard Wendell *former air force officer, business executive*
Price, Robert Ira *coast guard officer*
Rhame, Thomas Gene *army officer*
Richards, Thomas Carl *air force officer, governmental official*
Rogers, Bernard William *military officer*
Sausser, Robert Gary *retired army officer*
Schrader, Harry Christian, Jr. *retired naval officer*
Schumacher, William Jacob *retired army officer*
Shapiro, Sumner *retired naval officer, business executive*
Shaw, John Frederick *retired naval officer*
Slewitzke, Connie Lee *retired army officer*
Springer, Robert Dale *retired air force officer, consultant, lecturer*
Sullivan, Michael Patrick *marine officer*
Sunell, Robert John *retired army officer*
Tourino, Ralph Gene *career officer*
Vincent, Hal Wellman *marine corps officer, investor*
Watts, Ronald Lester *retired military officer*
Weir, Kenneth Wynn *marine corps officer, experimental test pilot*
Williamson, Myrna Hennrich *retired army officer, lecturer, consultant*
†Wilson, Richard Alexander *career officer*

RELIGION

UNITED STATES

ALABAMA

Birmingham
†Knox, James Lloyd *bishop*
Nelson, Dotson McGinnis, Jr. *clergyman*

Helena
Smith, John Lee, Jr. *minister, former association administrator*

Huntsville
Loshuertos, Robert Herman *clergyman*

Mobile
†Duvall, Charles Farmer *bishop*
Lipscomb, Oscar Hugh *archbishop*

Ozark
†Matthews, W. W. *bishop*

ALASKA

Anchorage
Hurley, Francis T. *archbishop*
†Parsons, Donald D. *bishop*
†Williams, Charles D. *bishop*

Fairbanks
†Charleston, Steve *bishop*
Kaniecki, Michael Joseph *bishop*

Juneau
Kenny, Michael H. *bishop*

ARIZONA

Paradise Valley
Sapp, Donald Gene *minister*

Phoenix
Galvan, Elias Gabriel *bishop*
†Galvin, Elias *bishop*
Harte, John Joseph Meakins *bishop*
Heistand, Joseph Thomas *retired bishop*
O'Brien, Thomas Joseph *bishop*

Sun City
Lapsley, James Norvell, Jr. *minister, pastoral theology educator*

Sun City West
Randall, Claire *church executive*
Schmitz, Charles Edison *evangelist*

Tucson
Moreno, Manuel D. *bishop*
Tirrell, John Albert *religious organization executive, consultant*

ARKANSAS

Conway
†Reddin, George *religious arganization administrator*

El Dorado
Lee, Vernon Roy *minister*

Little Rock
†Argue, James B., Jr. *religious organization administrator*
Donovan, Herbert Alcorn, Jr. *bishop*
†Holmes, James Frederick *minister*
Mc Donald, Andrew J. *bishop*
†Walker, L. T. *bishop*

Russellville
Chesnut, Franklin Gilmore *clergyman*
Inch, Morris Alton *theology educator*

Searcy
Miller, Ken Leroy *religious studies educator, consultant, writer*

Texarkana
†Henry, James Alvin *minister, benefits executive*

CALIFORNIA

Anaheim
†Nguyen, Tai Anh *minister*

Barstow
†Jones, Nathaniel *bishop*

Berkeley
†Faulk, I. Carlton *religious organization executive*
†Faulk, Sylvia *religious organization executive*
Schmalenberger, Jerry Lew *pastor, seminary administrator*
Stuhr, Walter M. *seminary educator, clergyman*
Welch, Claude (Raymond) *theology educator*

Bermuda Dunes
Ward, Donald Butler *minister*

Buena Park
Elliott, Darrell Kenneth *minister, legal researcher*

Calabasas
Bleiweiss, Robert Morton *religious magazine editor, labor newspaper publisher*

Carmichael
Probasco, Calvin Henry Charles *clergyman, college administrator*

Chatsworth
Dart, John Seward *religion news writer*

Claremont
Beardslee, William Armitage *religious organization administrator, educator*
Kucheman, Clark Arthur *religion educator*
Sanders, James Alvin *minister, biblical studies educator*

Costa Mesa
Williams, William Corey *Old Testament educator, consultant*

El Cerrito
Dillenberger, John *theology educator emeritus, minister*
Schomer, Howard *retired clergyman, educator, social policy consultant*

Escondido
†Ortiz, Angel Vicente *church administrator*

Etna
Auxentios *clergyman*
Chrysostomos, (González-Alexopoulos) *bishop, clergyman, psychologist, educator*

Fresno
Schofield, John-David Mercer *bishop*
Steinbock, John T. *bishop*
†Wilson, Warren Samuel *clergyman, bishop*

Garden Grove
Ballesteros, Juventino Ray, Jr. *minister*
†Schuller, Robert Harold *clergyman, author*

Glendale
Courtney, Howard Perry *clergyman*

Glendora
Richey, Everett Eldon *religion educator*

Hollywood
†Hovsepian, Vatche *clergyman*

La Jolla
Freedman, David Noel *religion educator*

La Mirada
Nash, Sylvia Dotseth *religious organization executive, consultant*

Laguna Hills
Lindquist, Raymond Irving *clergyman*
Wheatley, Melvin Ernest, Jr. *retired bishop*

Lake Forest
Lindsell, Harold *clergyman*

Los Alamitos
Booth, John Nicholls *minister, magician, writer, photographer*

Los Angeles
†Berg, Philip *religious denomination administrator*
Borsch, Frederick Houk *bishop*
Fitzgerald, Tikhon (Lee R. H. Fitzgerald) *bishop*
†Helms, Harold Edwin *minister*
Holland, John Ray *minister*
Mahony, Roger Cardinal *archbishop*
Mc Pherson, Rolf Kennedy *clergyman, church official*
Milligan, Sister Mary *theology educator, religious consultant*
†Neal, Joseph C., Jr. *church administrator*
†Perry, Troy D. *clergyman, church administrator*
†Phillips, Keith Wendall *minister*
Talton, Chester Lovelle *bishop*
Wolf, Alfred *rabbi*
Wooten, Cecil Aaron *religious organization administrator*

Malibu
Pack, Walter Frank *minister, religion educator emeritus*

Menlo Park
Davis, William Emrys *religious organization official*

Mill Valley
Crews, William Odell, Jr. *seminary administrator*

Monterey
†Ryan, Sylvester D. *bishop*
†Shimpfky, Richard Lester *bishop*

Northridge
Kuzma, George Martin *bishop*

Oakland
Benham, Priscilla Carla *religion educator, college president*
Cummins, John Stephen *bishop*
†Miller, Lyle G. *bishop*
Patten, Bebe Harrison *minister*
Talbert, Melvin George *bishop*

Orange
Mc Farland, Norman Francis *bishop*

Palo Alto
Brown, Robert McAfee *minister, religion educator*

Pasadena
Sano, Roy I. *bishop*

Rancho Mirage
†Stenhouse, Everett Ray *clergy administrator*

Reedley
Dick, Henry Henry *minister*

Richmond
†Ayers, G. W. *church adminstrator*

Riverside
†O'Connor, June Elizabeth *religious studies educator*

Sacramento
†Cole, Glen David *minister*
Meier, George Karl, III *pastor, lawyer*
Quinn, Francis A. *bishop*
†Smith, Freda M. *minister*

San Anselmo
Mudge, Lewis Seymour *theologian, educator, university dean*
Waetjen, Herman Charles *theologian, educator*

San Bernardino
Straling, Phillip Francis *bishop*

San Diego
Brom, Robert H. *bishop*
†Hughes, Gethin B. *bishop*
Lyons, Earle Vaughan, Jr. *minister*
Phillips, Randall Clinger *minister, university administrator*

San Francisco
Anthony, (Anthony Emmanuel Gergiannakis) *bishop*
Hurley, Mark Joseph *bishop*
Quinn, John R. *archbishop*
Rosen, Moishe *religious organization administrator*
Sparer, Malcolm Martin *rabbi*
Swing, William Edwin *bishop*
Yamaoka, Seigen Haruo *bishop*

San Gabriel
Oestmann, Irma Emma *minister, artist, educator*

San Jose
†Soro, Mar Bawai *bishop*

San Rafael
Scanlan, John Joseph *retired bishop*

Santa Barbara
Campbell, Robert Charles *clergyman, religious organization administrator*
Hubbard, David Allan *minister, educator, religious association administrator*
Long, Charles Houston *history of religion educator*

Santa Clara
DuMaine, R. Pierre *bishop*

Santa Monica
Boyd, Malcolm *minister, religious author*
Williams, George Masayasu *religious organization administrator, editor*

Sherman Oaks
Bower, Richard James *minister*

Solana Beach
Friedman, Maurice Stanley *religious educator*

Solvang
Chandler, E(dwin) Russell *religious journalist, author*

Stanford
Harvey, Van Austin *religious studies educator*

Stockton
Montrose, Donald W. *bishop*

Studio City
Garver, Oliver Bailey, Jr. *bishop*

Tustin
Krumm, John McGill *bishop*

Ventura
Gray, Henry David *minister, religious organization administrator*

Vista
†Rader, Paul Alexander *minister, administrator*

Whittier
Connick, Charles Milo *retired religion educator, clergyman*

Yuba City
Koury, Aleah George *retired church executive, minister*

COLORADO

Boulder
Lester, Robert Carlton *religious studies educator*

Brighton
†Vang, Timothy Teng *church executive*

Colorado Springs
†Bailey, R. W. *church administrator*
Bishop, Leo Kenneth *clergyman, educator*
†Bubna, Paul F. *church administrator*
†Davey, J. A. *church administrator*
Fox, Douglas Allan *religion educator*
Hanifen, Richard Charles *bishop*
†Mangham, R. H. *church administrator*
†Nanfelt, P. N. *church administrator*
Sinclair, William Donald *church official, fundraising consultant, political activist*
†Wheeland, D. A. *church administrator*
†Wood, Stephen *minister*

Denver
Brownlee, Judith Marilyn *Wiccan minister, psychotherapist*
†Burrell, Calvin Archie *minister*
Fischer, James Adrian *clergyman*
†Hayes, Edward Lee *religious organization administrator*
†Sheeran, Michael John Leo *priest, educational administrator*
Stafford, J. Francis *archbishop*
†Swenson, Mary Ann *bishop*
†Weissenbuehler, Wayne *bishop*
†Winterrond, William J. *bishop*

Fort Collins
Rolston, Holmes, III *theologian, educator, philosopher*

Lafayette
Short, Ray Everett *minister, sociology educator emeritus, author, lecturer*

Pueblo
Tafoya, Arthur N. *bishop*

CONNECTICUT

Bethany
Forman, Charles William *religious studies educator*

Bridgeport
Egan, Edward M. *bishop*
†Norris, Louise *religious organization executive*

Danbury
Malino, Jerome R. *rabbi*

Fairfield
Allaby, Stanley Reynolds *clergyman*

Hartford
Cronin, Daniel Anthony *bishop*
Reed, David Benson *bishop*
Zikmund, Barbara Brown *minister, seminary president, church history educator*

New Haven
†Böowering, Gerhard H. *Islamic studies educator*
†Brewer, Charles H., Jr. *bishop*
Childs, Brevard Springs *religious educator*
Dittes, James Edward *psychology of religion educator*
Johnson, Robert Clyde *theology educator*
Kavanagh, Aidan Joseph *priest, university educator*
Keck, Leander Earl *theology educator*
Malherbe, Abraham Johannes, VI *religion educator, writer*
†Robbins, William Randolph *minister*
Weinstein, Stanley *Buddhist studies educator*

Norwich
Reilly, Daniel Patrick *bishop*

Ridgefield
Kelley, Edward Allen *publisher*

Salisbury
Bevan, Charles Albert, Jr. *minister*

Storrs
Mc Innes, William Charles *priest, campus ministry director*

Wethersfield
Payne, Edward Carlton *archbishop*

DELAWARE

New Castle
†Blackshear, L. T., Sr. *bishop*

Wilmington
†Grenz, Linda L. *Episcopal priest*
Harris, Robert Laird *minister, theology educator emeritus*
Mulvee, Robert Edward *bishop*
†Tennis, Calvin Cabell *bishop*

DISTRICT OF COLUMBIA

Washington
†Allen, William Jere *minister*
Alpern, Robert Zellman *religious organization lobbyist/administrator*
Bittker, David *religious organization administrator*
†Burke, John *priest*
Cacciavillan, Agostino *archbishop*
Cenkner, William *religion educator, academic administrator*
Colson, Charles Wendell *lay minister, writer*
Di Lella, Alexander Anthony *biblical studies educator*
†Doyle, Francis Xavier *religious organization administrator*
Dugan, Robert Perry, Jr. *minister, religious organization administrator*
Edwards, Otis Carl, Jr. *theology educator*
†Fitzmyer, Joseph Augustine *theology educator, priest*
†Ford, James David *clergyman*
Godsey, John Drew *minister, theology educator emeritus*
†Gros, Jeffrey *ecumenical theologian*
Haines, Ronald H. *bishop*
Halverson, Richard Christian *minister, chaplain*
Harty, Sheila Therese *theologian, writer, editor*
Hickey, James Aloysius Cardinal *archbishop*
†Hotchkin, John Francis *church official, priest*
†Hug, James Edward *religious organization administrator*
James, Frederick Calhoun *bishop*
†Jansen, E. Harold *religious organization executive*
Kane, Annette P. *religious organization executive*
†Le Mone, Archie *religious organization administrator*
Mc Lean, George Francis *philosophy of religion educator, clergyman*
†Moore, Jerry *religious organization administrator*
Novak, Michael (John) *religion educator, author, editor*
Rabinowitz, Stanley Samuel *rabbi*
†Ryscavage, Richard *Jesuit priest, social services administrator*
Stookey, Laurence Hull *clergyman, theology educator*
†Tribett, Brenda Diane Bell *religious organization administrator*
Trisco, Robert Frederick *church historian, educator*

FLORIDA

Brooksville
Slaatte, Howard Alexander *minister, philosophy educator*

Clearwater
Beckwith, William Hunter *clergyman*

Daytona Beach
Bronson, Oswald Perry *religious organization administrator, clergyman*

Deland
Fant, Clyde Edward, Jr. *religion educator*

Delray Beach
Silver, Samuel Manuel *rabbi, author*

Fort Lauderdale
†Grestner, Jonathan Neil *religious studies educator*
†Skiddell, Elliot Lewis *rabbi*

Fort Pierce
†Garment, Robert *clergyman*

Gainesville
Creel, Austin Bowman *religion educator*

Jacksonville
†Bartholomew, John Niles *church administrator*
Blackburn, Robert McGrady *retired bishop*
Cerveny, Frank Stanley *bishop*
†Cousin, Philip R. *clergyman*
†Kensey, Calvin D. *bishop*
Snyder, John Joseph *bishop*
Vines, Charles Jerry *minister*
Voss, Carl Hermann *clergyman, humanities educator, author*

Jupiter
McCall, Duke Kimbrough *clergyman*

Lakeland
Hughes, Harold Hasbrouck, Jr. *bishop*

Miami
†Cohen, Jacob *bishop*
Hoy, William Ivan *minister, religion educator*
Lehrman, Irving *rabbi*
McCarthy, Edward Anthony *archbishop*
†Schofield, Calvin Onderdonk, Jr. *bishop*

Naples
Hennessy, Brother Paul Kevin *religion educator*

Orlando
Dorsey, Norbert M. *bishop*
Grady, Thomas J. *bishop*
Hollis, Reginald *archbishop*
†Howe, John Wadsworth *bishop*
†Santiago, Carlos *minister*
†Sconiers, M. L. *bishop*

Palm Beach Gardens
Symons, J. Keith *bishop*

Pensacola
Mountcastle, William Wallace, Jr. *philosophy and religion educator*

Plant City
†Patronelli, Raymond *church administrator*

Plymouth
Voelker, Charles Robert *archbishop, academic dean*

Ruskin
Nissen, Carl Andrew, Jr. *minister, retired procurement analyst*

Saint Petersburg
Favalora, John Clement *bishop*
Harris, Roger S. *bishop*

Sarasota
Augsburger, Aaron Donald *clergyman*
Jones, Tracey Kirk, Jr. *minister, educator*

Tallahassee
Rubenstein, Richard Lowell *theologian, educator*

Tampa
†Davis, W. E. *clergyman, bishop*
Franzen, Lavern Gerhard *bishop*
Neusner, Jacob *humanities and religious studies educator*

Venice
Nevins, John J. *bishop*

West Palm Beach
Knudsen, Raymond Barnett *clergyman, association executive, author*

Winter Park
Armstrong, (Arthur) James *minister, religion educator, religious organization executive, consultant*
Britton, Erwin Adelbert *clergyman, college administrator*
Edge, Findley Bartow *clergyman, religious education educator*

GEORGIA

Atlanta
Allan, Frank Kellog *bishop*
Cannon, William Ragsdale *bishop*
†Dell, J. Howard *bishop*
†Dunahoo, Charles *religious publisher, religious organization administrator*
†Gilchrist, Paul R. *religious organization administrator*
†Gyger, Terrell Lee *minister*
†Husband, J. D. *bishop*
Kyle, John Emery *mission executive*
Lowery, Joseph E. *clergyman*
†McMaster, Belle Miller *religious organization administrator*
Parks, R(obert) Keith *missionary, religious organization administrator*
†Skillrud, Harold Clayton *Lutheran bishop*
Stokes, Mack (Marion) Boyd *bishop*
Sutherland, Raymond Carter *clergyman, English educator emeritus*
Westerhoff, John Henry, III *clergyman, theologian, educator*
†White, Gayle Colquitt *religion writer, journalist*
†Williams, Ervin Eugene *religious organization administrator*

Decatur
Winn, Albert Curry *clergyman*

Lawrenceville
Gericke, Paul William *minister, educator*

Macon
†Alexander, David Lee *clergyman*
†Hicks, C. J. *bishop*
†Looney, Richard Carl *bishop*

Savannah
Lessard, Raymond W. *bishop*

Townsend
Collins, David Browning *religious institution administrator*

HAWAII

Captain Cook
Gilliam, Jackson Earle *bishop*

Honolulu
Ferrario, Joseph A. *bishop*
Hart, Donald Purple *bishop*

IDAHO

Boise
Brown, Tod David *bishop*
†Thornton, John S., IV *bishop*

ILLINOIS

Arlington Heights
†Dickau, John C. *religious organization executive*

Belleville
Keleher, James P. *bishop*

Bensenville
Matera, Richard Ernest *minister*

Cairo
†Cobb, J. *bishop*

Carol Stream
Fricke, H. Walter *minister*

Chicago
Almen, Lowell Gordon *church official*
†Banks, Deirdre Margaret *church organization administrator*
Barbour, Claude Marie *minister*
†Barnard, Susan C. *church administrator*
†Bauman, Stephen P. *minister, church administrator*
Baumhart, Raymond Charles *church administrator*
†Berg, Mildred M. *church administrator*
Berman, Howard Allen *rabbi*
Bernardin, Joseph Louis Cardinal *archbishop, university chancellor*
Betz, Hans Dieter *theology educator*
Browning, Don Spencer *religion educator*
Burhoe, Ralph Wendell *religion and science educator*
Campbell, Edward Fay, Jr. *religion educator*
†Carlson, Marjorie J. *church administrator*
†Chadwick, Joanne *church administrator*
Chilstrom, Herbert Walfred *bishop*
Doniger, Wendy *history of religions educator*
Duecker, Robert Sheldon *bishop*
Engebretson, Milton Benjamin *clergyman*
†Farrakhan, Louis *religious leader*
†Fiechter, Charlotte E. *church administrator*
Ford, L. H. *bishop*
Fortune, Michael Joseph *religion educator*
Gerrish, Brian Albert *theologian, educator*
Griswold, Frank Tracy, III *bishop*
Hefner, Philip James *theologian*
†Hicks, Sherman Gregory *bishop*
Homans, Peter *psychology and religious studies educator*
Iakovos, (Iakovos Garmatis) *bishop*
†Inskeep, Kenneth W. *church administrator*
†James, A. Lincoln, Sr. *minister, religious organization executive*
†Klutz, C. H. *church administrator*
Larsen, Paul Emanuel *religious organization administrator*
LeFevre, Perry Deyo *minister, theology educator*
Little, George Daniel *clergyman*
Lotocky, Innocent H. *bishop*
†Marshall, Cody *bishop*
Marty, Martin Emil *religion educator, editor*
†Mayo, J. Haskell, Jr. *bishop*
McCullough, Michael William, Jr. *minister, educator, researcher, writer, missionary, gospel singer, consultant*
McGinn, Bernard John *religious educator*
†Miller, Charles S. *clergy member, church administrator*
†Minnick, Malcolm L. *clergy member, church administrator*
†Moller-Gunderson, Mark Robert *minister, administrator*
†Moller-Gunderson, Mary Ann *clergy member, church administrator*
†Moore, Sister Marie *nun, hospital executive*
†Mortensen, Audrey R. *church administrator*
†Myers, Jim *church administrator*
Obenhaus, Victor *theology educator, clergyman*
†Peterson, Marybeth A. *church administrator*
†Powell, Allen Royal *bishop*
†Rajan, Fred E. N. *clergy member, church administrator*
Reynolds, Frank Everett *religious studies educator*
Rusch, William Graham *religious organization administrator*
†Sauer, Kenneth H. *bishop*
Schupp, Ronald Irving *civil rights leader, clergyman*
†Seitz, Tim *church administrator*
†Shafer, Eric Christopher *minister*
Simon, Mordecai *religious association administrator, clergyman*
Simon, Ralph *rabbi*
†Sorensen, W. Robert *clergy member, church administrator*
†Stegemoeller, Harvey A. *clergy member, church administrator*
†Stein, A. C. *clergy member, church administrator*
†Thomsen, Mark William *religious organization administrator*
Trexler, Edgar Ray *minister, editor*
†Varsbergs, Vilis *minister, former religious organization administrator*
†Wagner, Joseph M. *church administrator*
Wall, James McKendree *minister, editor*
†Yee, Edmond *church administrator*
Yu, Anthony C. *religion and literature educator*

Decatur
†Morgan, E. A. *church administrator*

Elgin
†Deeter, Joan G. *church administrator*
†Minnich, Dale E. *religious administrator*
†Myers, Anne M. *church administrator*
†Nolen, Wilfred E. *church administrator*
†Ratthahao, Sisouphanh *minister*
†Steiner, Duane *religious administrator*
†Timmons, Glenn F. *church administrator*
†Ziegler, Earl Keller *minister*

Evanston
Fisher, Neal Floyd *minister*
Thompson, Tyler *minister, philosophy educator*
Walker, Harold Blake *minister*

Evergreen Park
†Smith, Lawrence J. *bishop*

Flossmoor
†Walker, George W. *bishop*

Highland
†Baumer, Martha Ann *minister*

Homewood
†McClellan, Larry Allen *minister, writer*

Joliet
Imesch, Joseph Leopold *bishop*
Kaffer, Roger Louis *bishop*

Kankakee
Sayes, James Ottis *religion educator, minister*

Lincoln
Wilson, Robert Allen *religion educator*

Lombard
†Lapp, James Merrill *clergyman, marriage and family therapist*

Mendota
†Du Bois, Clarence Hazel, Jr. *clergy member*

Naperville
Landwehr, Arthur John *minister*

Oak Brook
Brown, Dale Weaver *clergyman, theologian, educator*

Oak Park
Cary, William Sterling *church executive*

Oakbrook Terrace
†Effa, Herman *clergy member, religious organization administrator*

Palos Heights
†Nederhood, Joel H. *church organization executive, minister*

Peoria
MacBurney, Edward Harding *bishop*
Myers, John Joseph *bishop*
Parsons, Donald James *retired bishop*

Rock Island
Bergendoff, Conrad John Immanuel *clergyman*

Rockford
†Hasley, Ronald K. *bishop*
O'Neill, Arthur J. *bishop*
Weissbard, David Raymond *minister*

Schaumburg
†Miller, Vernon Dallace *minister*
Nettleton, David *religious administrator*

South Holland
†Mulder, Dennis Marlin *religious organization executive*

Springfield
†Kaitschuk, John Paul *bishop*
†Rose, T. T. *bishop*
Ryan, Daniel Leo *bishop*
†Shotwell, Malcolm Green *minister*

Summit
Abramowicz, Alfred L. *bishop*

Villa Park
†Binder, John *minister, religious organization executive*
†Russell, Richard *religious organization adminstrator*

Wheaton
†Estep, John Hayes *religious denomination executive, clergyman*
Melvin, Billy Alfred *clergyman*
Pint, Sister Rose Mary *nun, religious order administrator, health care executive*

Winnetka
Hudnut, Robert Kilborne *clergyman, author*

INDIANA

Anderson
†Conrad, Harold August *retired pension board executive*
†Dale, Doris *religious organization executive*
†Dye, Dwight Latimer *minister*
Foggs, Edward L. *church administrator*
†Grubbs, J. Perry *church administrator*
†Hayes, Sherill D. *religious organization administrator*
†Patton, Norman S. *church adminstrator*
†Rist, Robert G. *religious publishing executive*

Camby
Hay, John Franklin *church administrator*

Elkhart
Bender, Ross Thomas *minister*
Oltz, Richard John *publishing executive, minister*

Evansville
Gettelfinger, Gerald Andrew *bishop*

Fort Wayne
†Beals, Duane *church administrator*
†Bunkowske, Eugene Walter *religious studies educator*
†Carpenter, Charles *religious organization administrator*
D'Arcy, John Michael *bishop*
†Henschen, Bob *church administrator*
†Liechty, Eric *church administrator*
Mann, David William *minister*
†McFarlane, Neil *church administrator*
†Moran, John *religious organization administrator*
†Speicher, Opal *church administrator*
†Stucky, Ken *clergy member, religious publication editor, church organization administrator*
†von Gunten, David *church administrator*

Gary
Gaughan, Norbert F. *bishop*

Huntington
†Kopp, Clarence Adam, Jr. *clergyman*

Indianapolis
Austin, Spencer Peter *minister*
Bates, Gerald Earl *bishop*
†Beaty, James Ralph *minister*
†Behar, Lucien E. *church administrator*
†Bonney, M. Doane *religious organization director*
†Brannon, Ronald Roy *minister*
Buechlein, Daniel Mark *bishop*
Cassel, Herbert William *religion educator*
†Castle, Howard Blaine *religious organization administrator*
Crow, Paul Abernathy, Jr. *clergyman, religious council executive, educator*
Dickinson, Richard Donald Nye *clergyman, educator, theological seminary administrator*
Dykstra, Craig Richard *theologian, educator, foundation administrator*
†Ellis, Carollyn *religious organization administrator*
†Ellis, Raymond W. *religious organization executive, consultant*
Foster, David Mark *bishop*
†Foulkes, John R. *minister*
†Grant, Claudia Ewing *minister*
Haines, Lee Mark, Jr. *religious denomination administrator*
†Haslam, Robert B. *religious publication editor*
Ilangyi, Bya'ene Akulu *bishop*
†Johnson, James P. *religious organization executive*
Kempski, Ralph Aloisius *bishop*
†Kilgore, Gary M. *church administrator*
†Kline, Bruce L. *church administrator*
†Manworren, Donald B. *church administrator*
†Palmer, Lester Davis *minister*
†Polston, Mark Franklin *minister*
†Riemenschneider, Dan LaVerne *religious organization administrator*
†Sayre, Larry D. *religious organization executive*
†Sindlinger, Verne E. *bishop*
†Thompson, Stanley B. *church administrator*
†Ton, L. Eugene *church official*
†Updegraff Spleth, Ann L. *church executive, pastor*
Walker-Smith, Angelique Keturah *minister, religious organization administrator*
†Watkins, Harold Robert *minister*
†Welsh, Robert K. *relgious organization executive*
†Wilson, Earle Lawrence *church administrator*
Wilson, Harry Cochrane *clergyman*
Woodring, DeWayne Stanley *religion association executive*
†Young, Richard *religious organization executive*

Jeffersonville
†Deming, Frank *religious organization administrator*

Kokomo
†Hall, Milton L. *bishop*

Lafayette
Higi, William L. *bishop*

Marion
McIntyre, Robert Walter *church official*

Noblesville
†Wilson, Norman Glenn *church administrator, writer*

Notre Dame
†Hesburgh, Theodore Martin *clergyman, former university president*
Malloy, Edward Aloysius *priest, university administrator, educator*
McBrien, Richard Peter *theology educator*
McCormick, Richard Arthur *priest, religion educator, writer*
O'Meara, Thomas Franklin *priest, educator*

Richmond
†Maurer, Johan Fredrik *religious denomination administrator*

South Bend
Ebey, Carl Finley *priest, religious order superior*
Gray, Francis Campbell *bishop*
†Gray, Frank C. *bishop*

Veedersburg
Marshall, Carolyn Ann M. *church official, consultant*

Winona Lake
†Ashman, Charles Henry *retired minister*
Davis, John James *religion educator*
†Julien, Thomas Theodore *religious denomination administrator*
†Lewis, Edward Alan *religious organization adminstrator*

IOWA

Amana
†Setzer, Kirk *religious leader*

Ankeny
Hartog, John, II *theology educator, librarian*

Davenport
O'Keefe, Gerald Francis *bishop, retired*

Decorah
Farwell, Elwin D. *minister, educational consultant*

Des Moines
Epting, C. Christopher *bishop*
†Gall, Donald Arthur *minister*
Jordan, Charles Wesley *bishop*
Mitchell, Orlan E. *clergyman, former college president*

Dubuque
Barta, James Omer *priest, psychology educator, academic administrator*
Drummond, Richard Henry *religion educator*

Iowa City
Baird, Robert Dahlen *religious educator*
Bayne, David Cowan *priest, lawyer, law educator*
Forell, George Wolfgang *religion educator*
Holstein, Jay Allen *Judaic studies educator*
†Werger, Paul Myron *bishop*

Orange City
Scorza, Sylvio Joseph *religion educator*

Sioux City
Soens, Lawrence D. *bishop*

Storm Lake
†Miller, Curtis Herman *bishop*

Waverly
Brown, Laurence David *retired bishop*

West Union
†Vettrus, Richard James *minister*

KANSAS

Dodge City
Schlarman, Stanley Gerard *bishop*

Kansas City
†Cade, Walter *church administrator*
Forst, Marion Francis *bishop*
Strecker, Ignatius J. *archbishop*

Leavenworth
McGilley, Sister Mary Janet *nun, educator, writer, academic administrator*

Mission
†Downing, David Charles *minister*

Newton
†Barrett, Lois Yvonne *minister*
†Preheim, Vern Quincy *religious organization administrator, minister*

North Newton
†Fast, Darrell W. *minister*

Salina
Ashby, John Forsythe *bishop*
Fitzsimons, George K. *bishop*

Shawnee Mission
Haggard, Forrest Deloss *minister*
Holter, Don Wendell *retired bishop*

Topeka
Smalley, William Edward *bishop*

Wichita
Eastburn, Jeannette Rose *religious publishing executive*
Gerber, Eugene J. *bishop*
†Zehr, Clyde James *church administrator*

KENTUCKY

Erlanger
Hughes, William Anthony *bishop*

Lexington
Landon, John William *minister, social worker, educator*
Williams, James Kendrick *bishop*

Louisville
Andrews, James Edgar *church official, minister*
Bingham, Walter D. *retired minister*
†Clements, Kerry *religious organization administrator*
†Coffin, John *religious organization administrator*
†Dale, Judy Ries *religious organization administrator*
†Granady, Juanita H. *religious organization administrator*
Hendricks, William Lawrence *theology educator*

†Jenkins, C(arle) Frederick *religious organization executive, minister, lawyer*
Kelly, Thomas Cajetan *archbishop*
†Kirkpatrick, Clifton *minister, church administrator*
†Lundy, Mary Ann *religious organization administrator*
Miller, John Ulman *minister, author*
†Schaefer, J. Scott *religious organization administrator*
†Turner, Gene *religious arganization administrator*
Wingenbach, Gregory Charles *minister, religious-ecumenical agency director*
Zimmerman, Gideon K. *minister*

Owensboro
McRaith, John Jeremiah *bishop*

Pineville
Whittaker, Bill Douglas *minister*

Wilmore
†Faupel, David William *minister, theological librarian*
Kinlaw, Dennis Franklin *clergyman, society executive*

LOUISIANA

Alexandria
†Hargrove, Robert Jefferson, Jr. *bishop*
Keller, Christoph, Jr. *bishop*

Baton Rouge
Hughes, Alfred Clifton *bishop*
Oden, William Bryant *bishop, educator*
†Swaggart, Jimmy Lee *evangelist, gospel singer*
Witcher, Robert Campbell *bishop*

Harvey
Romagosa, Elmo Lawrence *clergyman, retired editor*

Houma
Boudreaux, Warren Louis *retired bishop*

Lake Charles
Speyrer, Jude *bishop*

New Iberia
Henton, Willis Ryan *bishop*

New Orleans
Brown, James Barrow *bishop*
Schulte, Francis B. *archbishop*

Pineville
†Boswell, Bill Reeser *religious organization executive*

Shreveport
Friend, William Benedict *bishop*
Jones, Ernest Edward *minister, religious organization administrator*

Springhill
†Schoenrock, James V. *religious organization administrator*

MAINE

Bangor
Turner, Marta Dawn *youth program specialist*

Brunswick
Geoghegan, William Davidson *religion educator, minister*

Center Lovell
Adams, Herbert Ryan *retired clergyman, educator, publishing executive*

Leeds
Lynn, Robert Wood *theologian, educator, dean*

Lewiston
Baxter, William MacNeil *priest*

Old Orchard Beach
Holmes, Reed M. *clergyman, former religious organization administrator*

Portland
Chalfant, Edward Cole *bishop*
Gerry, Joseph John *bishop*
O'Leary, Edward Cornelius *bishop*

Presque Isle
†Gallagher, John *church administrator*

Readfield
†Metzler, Glenn Elam *minister*

Winthrop
Skeete, F. Herbert *bishop*

MARYLAND

Arnold
Smith, Clifford Lee *clergyman*

Baltimore
Eastman, Albert Theodore *bishop*
Macleod, Donald *clergyman, educator*
†Mocko, George Paul *minister*
†Murphy, Philip Francis *bishop*
†Newman, William C. *bishop*
†Ricard, John H. *bishop, educator*
†Strickland, Marshall Hayward *bishop*
Zaiman, Joel Hirsh *rabbi*

Bethesda
Hall, Arthur Raymond, Jr. *minister*

Catonsville
Wynn, John Charles *clergyman, retired religion educator*

Gaithersburg
Rupert, (Lynn) Hoover *minister*

Hagerstown
†Coles, Robert Nelson *religious organization administrator*

Oxon Hill
†Crudup, W. *bishop*

Perry Hall
Houck, John Roland *clergyman*

Rockville
Sanks, Charles Randolph, Jr. *minister, psychotherapist*

Silver Spring
†Beach, Bert Beverly *clergyman*
Dimino, Joseph T. *archbishop*
†Folkenberg, Robert S. *religious organization administrator*
†Gilbert, Donald F. *church administrator*
Rasi, Humberto Mario *religious education director, editor, clergyman*
†Thompson, George Ralph *church denomination administrator*
Yeakel, Joseph Hughes *clergyman*

Temple Hills
†Bishop, Cecil *bishop*

MASSACHUSETTS

Amherst
Wills, David Wood *minister, educator*

Boston
Bettenhausen, Elizabeth Ann *theology educator*
†Braver, Barbara Leix *religious organization communications administrator*
Harris, Barbara C(lementine) *bishop*
Johnson, David Elliot *bishop*
Korff, Ira A. *rabbi*
Mason, Herbert Warren, Jr. *religion and history educator, author*
Nesmith, Richard Duey *clergyman, theology educator*
Wheelwright, Steven C. *religious organization administrator, business educator*
Williams, Rhys *minister*
†Worthley, Harold Field *minister, educator*

Brewster
Coburn, John Bowen *retired bishop*

Brighton
Law, Bernard Francis Cardinal *archbishop*

Brockton
Hart, Daniel Anthony *bishop*

Brookfield
Kring, Walter Donald *minister*

Brookline
†Papademetriou, George Constantine *priest, director, educator*
Tournas, Methodios (Methodios of Boston) *bishop, academic administrator*

Cambridge
Fiorenza, Francis P. *religion educator*
Gomes, Peter John *clergyman, educator*
Hanson, Paul David *religion educator*
Kaufman, Gordon Dester *theology educator*
Koester, Helmut Heinrich *theologian, educator*
Miles, Margaret Ruth *theology educator*
Potter, Ralph Benajah, Jr. *theology and social ethics educator*
Schuessler Fiorenza, Elisabeth *theology educator*
Thomas, Owen Clark *clergyman, educator*
Williams, George Huntston *church historian, educator*
Williams, Preston Noah *theology educator*

Chestnut Hill
Daly, Robert J. *theology educator*

Dedham
†Spoolstra, Linda Carol *minister, educator, religious organization administrator*

East Orleans
Rath, George Edward *bishop*

Fall River
†O'Malley, Sean *bishop*

Harvard
Sutherland, Malcolm Read, Jr. *clergyman, educator*

Hyde Park
Riley, Lawrence Joseph *bishop*

Lexington
Schultz, Samuel Jacob *clergyman, educator*

Longmeadow
Stewart, Alexander Doig *bishop*

Marlborough
Lohr, Harold Russell *bishop*

Newton
Deats, Paul Kindred, Jr. *religion educator, clergyman*
Sarna, Nahum Mattathias *biblical studies educator*

Northampton
Derr, Thomas Sieger *religion educator*
Donfried, Karl Paul *minister, theology educator*
Flesher, Hubert Louis *religion educator*

Norwood
†Freni, Anthony *church administrator*

Roxbury
Adamec, Joseph Victor Otto *bishop*

Sheffield
Unsworth, Richard Preston *minister, school administrator*

South Easton
Clarke, Cornelius Wilder *superintendent, minister*

South Hadley
†Lansky, Aaron Jonathan *non-profit organization executive*

South Hamilton
Kalland, Lloyd Austin *minister*

Springfield
Marshall, John Aloysius *bishop*

Swampscott
†Mulcahy, John J. *bishop*

Waltham
Johnson, William Alexander *clergyman, philosophy educator*

West Newton
Elya, John Adel *bishop*

Weymouth
Parsons, Edwin Spencer *clergyman, educator*

Williamstown
Eusden, John Dykstra *theology educator, minister*
Petersen, Norman Richard, Jr. *religious studies educator*

Worcester
Harrington, Timothy J. *bishop*
†Isaksen, Robert L. *bishop*

MICHIGAN

Ann Arbor
Guthrie, Harvey Henry, Jr. *clergyman*
Hess, Bartlett Leonard *clergyman*

Bloomfield Hills
Hertz, Richard Cornell *rabbi*
Plaut, Jonathan Victor *rabbi*

Detroit
Gumbleton, Thomas J. *bishop*
Hardon, John Anthony *priest, research educator*
Maida, Adam J. *bishop*
Mc Gehee, H(arry) Coleman, Jr. *bishop*
Negrepontis, Michael (Timothy) *bishop*
†Ross, Mary O. *religious organization administrator*
Ursache, Victorin (His Eminence The Most Reverend Archbishop Victorin) *archbishop*
Willingham, Edward Bacon, Jr. *ecumenical minister, administrator*
†Wood, R. Stewart *bishop*

East Lansing
†Shaw, Robert Eugene *minister, administrator*

Farmington
Wine, Sherwin Theodore *rabbi*

Ferndale
Dunn, Elwood *minister*

Gaylord
Cooney, Patrick Ronald *bishop*

Grand Rapids
†Anderson, Roger Gordon *minister*
Babcock, Wendell Keith *religion educator*
Beeke, Joel Robert *minister, theology educator, writer*
†Borgdorff, Peter *church administrator*
Brink, William P. *clergyman*
†DeHaan, John *religious organization administrator*
DeVries, Robert K. *religious book publisher*
Hofman, Leonard John *minister*
†Mulder, Gary *religious publisher*
†Rozeboom, John A. *religious organization administrator*
†Vander Meer, Harry *church administrator*
†Vander Weele, Ray *religious organization administrator*
†Van Tol, William *religious organization administrator*

Grosse Pointe
Canfield, Francis Xavier *priest, English language educator*

Holland
Cook, James Ivan *clergyman, religion educator*

Jackson
Popp, Nathaniel (William George) (His Grace Bishop Nathaniel) *bishop*

Kalamazoo
Donovan, Paul V. *bishop*
†Lee, Edward L. *bishop*

Lansing
†Holle, Reginald Henry *bishop*
Povish, Kenneth Joseph *bishop*

Marquette
Burt, John Harris *bishop*
†Ray, Thomas Kreider *bishop*
†Skogman, Dale R. *bishop*

Oscoda
Stone, William Lyndon *retired minister*

Saginaw
Untener, Kenneth E. *bishop*
†Williams, Herbert J. *bishop*
†Wilson, J. Parrish *religious organization administrator*

MINNESOTA

Alexandria
Hultstrand, Donald Maynard *bishop*

Arden Hills
Jones, Samuel Vadakedath *ministries executive*

Bloomington
†Cuthill, Robert T. *church administrator*
McDill, Thomas Allison *minister*

Blue Earth
Haertel, Charles Wayne *minister*

Chisago City
Bergstrand, Wilton Everet *minister*

Collegeville
Henry, Patrick G. *religious research administrator*

Crookston
Balke, Victor H. *bishop*

Duluth
†Aadland, Thomas Vernon *minister*
Schwietz, Roger L. *bishop*

Fergus Falls
†Egge, Joel *clergy member, academic administrator*
†Olson, Jarle *clergy member, Church administrator*
Overgaard, Robert Milton *religious organization administrator*
†Westby, John *clergy member, church administrator*

Hastings
Bzoskie, James Steven *minister*

Little Falls
†Eichten, Sister Beatrice Mary *pastoral psychotherapist*

Mankato
†Orvick, George Myron *church denomination executive, minister*

Minneapolis
†Anderson, Robert Marshall *bishop*
Byrd, Richard Edward *minister, psychologist*
Cedar, Paul Arnold *church executive, minister*
†Fleischer, Daniel *minister, religious organization administrator*
Graham, William Franklin (Billy Graham) *evangelist*
†Hull, Bill *clergy member, church administrator*
†Kapanke, John *church edministrator*
Miller, William Alvin *clergyman, author*
Palms, Roger Curtis *religious magazine editor, clergyman*
Putnam, Frederick Warren, Jr. *bishop*
Sowada, Alphonse Augustus *bishop*
†Swatsky, Ben *church administrator*
Thomas, Margaret Jean *clergywoman, religious research consultant*
Wang, L. Edwin *church official*

Moorhead
†Rimmereid, Arthur V. *bishop*

New Ulm
Lucker, Raymond Alphonse *bishop*

Northfield
Crouter, Richard Earl *religion educator*
Foss, Harlan Funston *religious education educator, academic administrator*

Redwood Falls
†Anderson, Charles D. *bishop*

Rochester
Hudson, Winthrop Still *minister, history educator*
†Larson, April U. *bishop*
†Nycklemoe, Glenn Winston *bishop*

Saint Cloud
Hanus, Jerome *bishop*

Saint Joseph
O'Connell, Sister Colman *nun, college administrator, consultant*

Saint Paul
Flynn, Harry Joseph *bishop*
Hopper, David Henry *religion educator*
McMillan, Mary Bigelow *retired minister, volunteer*
Merrill, Arthur Lewis *theology educator*
Preus, David Walter *bishop, minister*
Roach, John Robert *archbishop*
Zirbes, Mary Kenneth *social justice ministry coordinator*

Winona
Finucan, J(ohn) Thomas *priest, religious institution administrator*
Vlazny, John George *bishop*

MISSISSIPPI

Biloxi
Howze, Joseph Lawson Edward *bishop*

Hattiesburg
†Gordon, Granville Hollis *church official*

Indianola
Matthews, David *clergyman*

Jackson
Allin, John Maury *bishop*

†Bray, Donald Lawrence *minister*
Gray, Duncan Montgomery, Jr. *retired bishop*
Houck, William Russell *bishop*
†McKnight, William Edwin *minister*

Kosciusko
Kearley, F. Furman *minister, religious educator, magazine editor*

Laurel
†Howell, Stephen Wayne *church organization administrator, clergyman*

MISSOURI

Hazelwood
†McClintock, Eugene Jerome *minister*
†Rose, Joseph Hugh *clergyman*
Urshan, Nathaniel Andrew *minister, church administrator*

Highlandville
Pruter, Karl Hugo *bishop*

Independence
†Booth, Paul Wayne *minister*
Hansen, Francis Eugene *minister*
†Mitchell, Earl Wesley *clergyman*
Sheehy, Howard Sherman, Jr. *minister*
Tyree, Alan Dean *clergyman*

Jefferson City
†Kelley, Pat *minister, state legislator*
Mc Auliffe, Michael F. *bishop*

Joplin
†Burke, Charles Don *church administrator, minister*
Gee, James David *minister*
†Vansell, Robert Edward *religious organization director*
†Wilson, Aaron Martin *religious studies educator, college executive*

Kansas City
†Anderson, David *church administrator*
†Berard, Dennis *church administrator*
Boland, Raymond James *bishop*
†Bowers, Curtis Ray, Jr. *chaplain*
†Brannon, Wilbur *church administrator*
†Buchanan, John Clark *bishop*
†Butler, Martin *church administrator*
†Cloud, Randy *church administrator*
†Estep, Mike *church administrator*
Frank, Eugene Maxwell *bishop*
†Fullerton, Fred *church administrator*
†Gray, Helen Theresa Gott *religion editor*
Grider, Joseph Kenneth *theology educator, writer*
†Gunter, Moody *church administrator*
†Hall, Miriam *church administrator*
†Hendrix, Ray *church administrator*
Jenkins, Orville Wesley *retired religious administrator*
†Johnson, Jerald D. *religious organization administrator*
†McMindes, Carl Lee *religious organization, church administrator*
†Moore, E. Harris *bishop*
†Mutti, Albert Frederick *minister*
Pike, George Harold, Jr. *religious organization executive, clergyman*
†Scott, Robert Hal *minister*
†Skiles, Paul *church administrator*
†Smee, John *church administrator*
Stone, Jack *religious organization administrator*
†Sullivan, Bill *church administrator*
Sullivan, John Joseph *bishop*
Vogel, Arthur Anton *clergyman*

Laddonia
Scheffler, Lewis Francis *pastor, educator, research scientist*

Neosho
Hargis, Billy James *minister*

Poplar Bluff
Black, Ronnie Delane *religious organization administrator, mayor*
†Carr, Charles Louis *religious organization administrator*
†Duncan, Leland Ray *administrator*

Saint Louis
†Boldt, H. James *church administrator*
†Haake, Arthur C. *church administrator*
†Haake, Earle E. *church administrator*
†King, Robert Henry *minister, church denomination executive, former educator*
†Krenzke, Richard *church administrator*
†Mahsman, David Lawrence *religious publications editor*
†Mall, Ida *church administrator*
Merrell, James Lee *religious editor, clergyman*
†Meyer, John *church administrator*
†Meyer, William F. *church administrator*
Mueller, John Alfred *church executive*
†Muller, Lyle Dean *religious organization administrator*
O'Donnell, Edward Joseph *bishop, former editor*
Ong, Walter Jackson *priest, English educator, author*
†O'Shoney, Glenn *church administrator*
†Pfautch, Roy *minister, public affairs consultant*
†Rockwell, Hays Hamilton *bishop*
Saperstein, Marc Eli *religious history educator, rabbi*
†Sauer, Robert C. *religious organization administrator*
†Shaw, James *church administrator*
†Suggs, James C. *religious publishing executive*
†Ward, R. J. *bishop*
†Weber, Gloria Richie *minister, retired, state representative*
†Wilke, LeRoy *church administrator*
†Wittich, Brenda June *religious organization executive, minister*

Springfield
Cunningham, Robert Cyril *clergyman, editor*
†Dailey, Parker Stokes *minister*
†Flower, Joseph Reynolds *administrative executive*
Leibrecht, John Joseph *bishop*
†Trask, Thomas E. *religious organization administrator*

†Triplett, Loren O. *religious organization administrator*

MONTANA

Great Falls
Milone, Anthony M. *bishop*

Helena
Curtiss, Elden F. *bishop*
Jones, Charles Irving *bishop*

NEBRASKA

Grand Island
Mc Namara, Lawrence J. *bishop*

Lincoln
†Luetchens, Melvin Harvey *minister, religious organization administrator*
Wiersbe, Warren Wendell *clergyman, author, lecturer*

Omaha
†Krotz, James Edward *bishop*
†McDaniels, B. T. *bishop*
Sheehan, Daniel Eugene *bishop*

Scottsbluff
†Scovil, Larry Emery *minister*

West Point
Paschang, John Linus *retired bishop*

NEVADA

Las Vegas
†Webb, E. N. *bishop*

Reno
Savoy, Douglas Eugene *bishop, religion educator, explorer, writer*
Walsh, Daniel Francis *bishop*

NEW HAMPSHIRE

Center Sandwich
Booty, John Everitt *historiographer*

Concord
†Theuner, Douglas Edwin *bishop*

Hanover
Green, Ronald Michael *ethics and religious studies educator*

Hillsboro
Gibson, Raymond Eugene *clergyman*
†Walmsley, Arthur Edward *bishop*

Loudon
†Moore, Bea *religious organization executive*

Manchester
O'Neil, Leo E. *bishop*

New London
Pearson, Roy Messer, Jr. *clergyman*

NEW JERSEY

Bloomfield
Becker, Robert Clarence *clergyman*

Camden
McHugh, James T. *bishop*

Cherry Hill
†Belin, Henry A., Jr. *bishop*
†Schad, James L. *bishop*

Clifton
Rodimer, Frank Joseph *bishop*

East Orange
†Medley, Alex Roy *ministry executive*

Elizabethtown
Taylor, David Wyatt Aiken *retired clergyman*

Englewood
†Essey, Basil *bishop*
Hertzberg, Arthur *rabbi, educator*
†Khouri, Antoun *church administrator*
Saliba, Philip E. *archbishop*

Fort Lee
†Kim, Gil *minister*

Hopatcong
†Harsanyi, Andrew *bishop*

Lakewood
Levovitz, Pesach Zechariah *rabbi*

Lodi
†Meno, John Peter *chorepiscopus*
Samuel, Athanasius Yeshue *archbishop*

Madison
Irons, Neil L. *bishop*

Mahwah
Padovano, Anthony Thomas *theologian, educator*

Metuchen
Hughes, Edward T. *bishop*

Moorestown
†Korth, James Scott *minister*

Morristown
†Yrigoyen, Charles, Jr. *church denomination executive*

Mullica Hill
†Demola, James *church administrator*

Newark
Mc Carrick, Theodore Edgar *archbishop*
†McKelvey, Jack M. *bishop*
Spong, John Shelby *bishop*

Plainsboro
Yun, Samuel *minister, educator*

Princeton
Allen, Diogenes *clergyman, philosophy educator*
Armstrong, James Franklin *religion educator*
Armstrong, Richard Stoll *minister, ministry and evangelism educator*
Davies, Horton Marlais *clergyman, religion educator*
Diamond, Malcolm Luria *retired religion educator, therapist*
Douglass, Jane Dempsey *theology educator*
Gordon, Ernest *clergyman*
Hardy, Daniel Wayne *theological center director, theologian, educator*
Metzger, Bruce Manning *clergyman, educator*
Miller, Patrick Dwight, Jr. *religion educator, minister*
Paris, Peter Junior *religion educator, minister*
West, Charles Converse *theologian, educator*

Rutherford
Gerety, Peter Leo *archbishop*

Short Hills
Pilchik, Ely Emanuel *rabbi, writer*

South Orange
Fleming, Edward J. *priest, educator*

Summit
May, Ernest Max *charitable organization official*

Tenafly
Stowe, David Metz *clergyman*

Tinton Falls
Priesand, Sally Jane *rabbi*

Trenton
Belshaw, George Phelps Mellick *bishop*
†Courtney, Esau *bishop*
†Farina, David *church administrator*
Reiss, John C. *bishop*

Westville
†Doughty, A. Glenn *minister*

NEW MEXICO

Albuquerque
†Griffin, W. C. *bishop*
Kellshaw, Terence *bishop*
†Kelshaw, Terence *bishop*
Sheehan, Michael Jarboe *archbishop*

Farmington
†Plummer, Steven Tsosie *bishop*

Gallup
Hastrich, Jerome Joseph *bishop*

Las Cruces
Hall, Larry Bruce *minister*
Ramirez, Ricardo *bishop*

Roswell
Pretti, Bradford Joseph *lay worker, insurance company executive*

NEW YORK

Albany
†Ball, David Standish *bishop*
†Gay, Charles *church administrator*
Grove, William Boyd *bishop*
Hubbard, Howard James *bishop*

Bayside
Bernstein, Louis *clergyman*

Bronx
†Bryant, Roy, Sr. *bishop*
Dulles, Avery *priest, theologian*
Hennessy, Thomas Christopher *clergyman, educator, retired university dean*
O'Keefe, Vincent Thomas *clergyman, educational administrator*
Parker, Everett Carlton *clergyman*

Bronxville
L'Huillier, Peter (Peter) *archbishop*

Brooklyn
Abrahamsen, Samuel *Judaic studies educator emeritus*
Al-Hafeez, Humza *minister, editor*
Daily, Thomas V. *bishop*
†Grayson, D. W. *bishop*
Leiman, Sid Zalman *Judaic studies educator*
†Quick, Norman *bishop*
†Sullivan, Joseph M. *bishop*
Valero, René Arnold *bishop*
Zayek, Francis Mansour *bishop*

Buffalo
Head, Edward Dennis *bishop*
†Lamb, Charles F. *minister*
Loew, Ralph William *clergyman, columnist*
Schieder, Joseph Eugene *clergyman*

Canton
O'Connor, Daniel William *retired religious studies and classical languages educator*

East Aurora
†Hayes, Bonaventure Francis *priest*

Flushing
†Vasilachi, Vasile *priest, vicar*

Garrison
Egan, Daniel Francis *priest*

Ithaca
†Gold, Daniel *religious studies educator*
Katz, Steven Theodore *religious educator*

Jamaica
†Clemmons, Ithiel *bishop*

Kingston
Tsirpanlis, Constantine N. *theology and history educator*

Lawrence
Wurzburger, Walter Samuel *rabbi, philosophy educator*

Lily Dale
†Merrill, Joseph Hartwell *religious association executive*

Lima
†Reynolds, Lewis Dayton *administrator*
Spencer, Ivan Carlton *clergyman*

Lindenhurst
Hamilton, Daniel Stephen *clergyman*

Manhasset
Spitz, Charles Thomas, Jr. *clergyman*

Mount Vernon
†Richardson, W. Franklyn *religious organization administrator*

New York
Ahern, Patrick V. *bishop*
†Alicea-Baez, Johnny *religious organization administrator*
Ashjian, Mesrob *archbishop*
Bailey, James Martin *minister, ecumenical executive, public relations consultant*
Barsamian, Khajag Sarkis *primate*
Bronkema, Frederick Hollander *minister, church official*
†Brown, Raymond Edward *educator, priest*
Browning, Edmond Lee *bishop*
Campbell, Joan Brown *religious organization executive*
†Cato, John David *religious organization administrator*
Chinnis, Pamela P. *religion organization administrator*
Church, Frank Forrester *minister, author, columnist*
Cohen, Samuel Israel *clergyman, organization executive*
Cone, James Hal *theologian, educator, author*
Dennis, Walter Decoster *suffragan bishop*
Dreyfus, Alfred Stanley *rabbi*
Driver, Tom Faw *theology educator, writer*
Geer, John Farr *religious organization administrator*
Ginsberg, Hersh Meier *rabbi, religious organization executive*
Glaser, Joseph Bernard *association executive*
Graham, Alma Eleanor *magazine editor, writer, educational consultant*
Grein, Richard Frank *bishop, pastoral theology educator*
Gross, Abraham *rabbi, educator*
Habecker, Eugene Brubaker *association executive*
†Hawley, John Stratton *religious studies educator*
Holmgren, Laton Earle *clergyman*
†Hopkins, Harold Anthony, Jr. *bishop*
Howard, M(oses) William, Jr. *minister, seminary president*
Iakovos, (Demetrios A. Coucouzis) *archbishop*
†Kazanjian, Shant *religious organization administrator*
Kloos, Edward John Michael, Jr. *minister*
Kreitman, Benjamin Zvi *rabbi, Judaic studies educator*
Landes, George Miller *biblical studies educator*
Laurus, (Laurus Skurla) *archbishop*
†Mallory, Kenneth W. *religious organization administrator*
†Marcus, Beth E. *religious organization administrator*
McGeady, Sister Mary Rose *religious organization administrator, psychologist*
†Menuez, D. Barry *religious organization administrator*
Miller, Israel *rabbi, university administrator*
Moore, Paul, Jr. *bishop*
†Morris, Clayton Leslie *priest*
†Mulder, Edwin George *minister, church official*
Nadich, Judah *rabbi*
†Najarian, Haigazoun *church administrator*
†Norgren, William Andrew *religious denomination administrator*
O'Connor, John Joseph Cardinal *archbishop, former naval officer*
†Paulsen, Diana *religious organization administrator*
†Perry, David *priest*
Peterson, Ralph Edward *clergyman*
†Poppen, Alvin J. *religious organization administrator*
Powers, Edward Alton *minister, educator*
Read, David Haxton Carswell *clergyman*
†Reed, John W. *religious organization administrator*
Riddle, Sturgis Lee *minister*
Roth, Sol *rabbi*
†Salisbury, Nancy *convent director*
Schindler, Alexander Moshe *rabbi, organization executive*
Schneier, Arthur *rabbi*
Schorsch, Ismar *clergyman, Jewish history educator*
Shriver, Donald Woods, Jr. *theology educator*
Siegel, Morton Kallos *religious organization administrator, educational administrator*
†Solheim, James Edward *church executive, journalist*
†Stolper, Pinchas Aryeh *religious organization executive, rabbi*
Strelzer, Martin *religious organization administrator*
Tannenbaum, Bernice Salpeter *religious organization executive*
Twiname, John Dean *minister, health care executive*
†Verbridge, Gerald *religious organization administrator*
Weiss, David *religion educator*
Wiener, Marvin S. *rabbi, editor, executive*

Nyack
†Lehman, Paul V. *minister*
Mann, Kenneth Walker *retired minister, psychologist*

Ogdensburg
Brzana, Stanislaus Joseph *bishop*

Orchard Park
Reid, Thomas Fenton *minister*

Ozone Park
†Taylor, Joyce *religious organization executive*

Pawling
Peale, Ruth Stafford (Mrs. Norman Vincent Peale) *religious leader*

Poughkeepsie
Glasse, John Howell *retired philosophy and theology educator*

Rochester
†Burrill, William George *bishop*
Clark, Matthew Harvey *bishop*
†Mandt, John F. *religious organization executive*

Rockaway Beach
Kelly, George Anthony *clergyman, author, educator*

Rockville Centre
McGann, John Raymond *bishop*

Syosset
Lazor, Theodosius (His Beatitude Metropolitan Theodosius) *archbishop*

Syracuse
Costello, Thomas Joseph *bishop*
O'Keefe, Joseph Thomas *bishop*
Wiggins, James Bryan *religion educator*

Troy
Phelan, Thomas *clergyman, academic administrator, educator*

Trumansburg
Billings, Peggy Marie *religious organization administrator, educator*

Westbury
De Pauw, Gommar Albert *priest, educator*

White Plains
†Gurahian, Vincent *church official, former judge*
†Stith, Forrest Christopher *bishop*

NORTH CAROLINA

Asheville
†Davenport, L. B. *bishop*

Black Mountain
Kennedy, William Bean *theology educator*
Weinhauer, William Gillette *retired bishop*

Boiling Springs
Lamb, Robert Lee *religion educator*

Chapel Hill
Dixon, John Wesley, Jr. *retired religion and art educator*
Van Seters, John *biblical literature educator*

Charlotte
†Battle, George Edward, Jr. *minister*
Begley, Michael Joseph *bishop*
Donoghue, John F. *bishop*
Jones, Lewis Bevel, III *bishop*
†Ross, David E. *church official*
†Sherman, Joseph Howard *clergyman*

Davidson
†McKelway, Alexander Jeffrey *religion studies educator*

Dunn
†Davis, Dolly *religious organization administrator*
†Ellis, W. L. *religious organization administrator*
†Hammond, James Thurman *educator, clergyman*
†Hardison, Chuch *religious organization administrator*
†Heath, Preston *clergy member, religious organization administrator*
†Sauls, Don *religious organization administrator, clergyman*
†Taylor, David *clergy member, religious administrator*

Durham
Campbell, Dennis Marion *theology dean, educator, university administrator*
Smith, Harmon Lee, Jr. *clergyman, moral theology educator*
Steinmetz, David Curtis *religion educator, publisher, minister*
†Westbrook, Don Arlen *minister*

Gastonia
†Williams, Raymond F. *regigious organization executive*

Greensboro
Hull, James Ernest *religion and philosophy educator*
Lolley, William Randall *minister*

Greenville
Jackson, Bobby Rand *minister*

Hendersonville
Sims, Bennett Jones *minister, educator*

Hickory
McDaniel, Michael Conway Dixon *bishop, theology educator*

High Point
†Wood, Stephen Wray *religious studies educator, state legislator*

Kinston
Sanders, Brice Sidney *bishop*

Lake Junaluska
Bryan, Monk *retired bishop*
Hale, Joseph Rice *church organization executive*
Tullis, Edward Lewis *retired bishop*

Lake Sunaluska
Stokes, John Lemacks, II *clergyman, university administrator*

Liberty
Garner, Mildred Maxine *religion educator emeritus*

Manteo
†Miller, William Lee, Jr. *minister*

Raleigh
Collins, Thomas Asa *minister*
Estill, Robert Whitridge *retired bishop*
Gossman, Francis Joseph *bishop*
MacLeod, John Daniel, Jr. *religious organization administrator*
†Miller, John Henry *clergyman*
Minnick, Carlton Printess, Jr. *bishop*

Salisbury
†Speaks, Ruben Lee *bishop*

Southern Pines
Lowry, Charles Wesley *clergyman, lecturer*

Southport
Harrelson, Walter Joseph *minister, religion educator emeritus*

Wake Forest
Binkley, Olin Trivette *clergyman, seminary president emeritus*

Wilmington
Wright, Thomas Henry *bishop*

Winston Salem
Fitzgerald, Ernest Abner *retired bishop*
Martin, James Alfred, Jr. *religious studies educator*
†Rights, Graham Henry *minister*
Spach, Jule Christian *church executive*

NORTH DAKOTA

Bismarck
Kinney, John Francis *bishop*
†Montz, Florence Stolte *church official*

Fargo
†Fairfield, Andrew H. *biship*
†Foss, Richard John *bishop*
Sullivan, James Stephen *bishop*

OHIO

Akron
†Kelley, Robert W. *bishop*

Canton
Boulton, Edwin Charles *bishop*

Cincinnati
Crumes, William Edward *bishop*
Harrington, Jeremy Thomas *clergyman, publisher*
†Hendricks, Harry *church administrator*
†Herring, Milton S. *church administrator*
Huron, Roderick Eugene *religious organization administrator*
Lindsey, Sanford Chapdu *priest*
†Linsey, Nathaniel L. *bishop*
Molitor, Sister Margaret Anne *nun, former college president*
Perry, Norman Robert *priest, magazine editor*
Pilarczyk, Daniel Edward *archbishop*
Thompson, Herbert, Jr. *bishop*

Circleville
†Norman, Jack Lee *church administrator, consultant*
†Tipton, Daniel L. *religious organization executive*

Cleveland
Buhrow, William Carl *religious organization administrator*
†Chapman, Robert L. *bishop*
†Dipko, Thomas E. *minister, national church executive*
Epp, Eldon Jay *religion educator*
Holck, Frederick H. George *priest, educator, counselor*
Lelyveld, Arthur Joseph *rabbi*
†Miller, Warren *bishop*
†Norris, Dennis E. *religious organization executive*
Pataki, Andrew *bishop*
Perks, Roger Ian *minister*
Pilla, Anthony Michael *bishop*
Sherry, Paul Henry *minister, religious organization administrator*
†Williams, Arthur Benjamin, Jr. *bishop*

Columbus
Craig, Judith *bishop*
†Hildebrand, Richard Allen *bishop*
Plagenz, George Richard *minister, journalist, columnist*

Englewood
Shearer, Velma Miller *clergywoman*

Findlay
†Martin, Jim G. *church renewal consultant*
†Perry, Travis Calvin *religious organization administrator*
†Rave, James A. *bishop*
Wilkin, Richard Edwin *clergyman, religious organization executive*

Granville
†Fisher, Robert Allison *minister, church administrator*

Grover Hill
†Harr, Joseph *religious organization administrator*

Lakewood
†Berman, Phillip L. *author, institute administrator*

Lebanon
Maves, Paul Benjamin *clergyman, gerontologist*

London
†Hughes, Clyde Matthew *religious denomination executive*

Lorain
†Szucs, Zoltan Daniel *religious organization executive, minister, psychologist, educator*

Napoleon
†Walker, Frank Houston, Jr. *minister*

Oberlin
Zinn, Grover Alfonso, Jr. *religion educator*

Parma
Moskal, Robert M. *bishop*

Richmond Heights
†Marino, Michael *church administrator*

Salem
†Durfee, John B. *religious organization administrator*

Toledo
Hoffman, James R. *bishop*
†James, William *bishop*

University Heights
Kelly, Joseph Francis *theology educator*

Wickliffe
Pevec, Anthony Edward *bishop*

OKLAHOMA

Bartlesville
†Owen, Raymond Harold *minister*

Bethany
†Leggett, James Daniel *church administrator*

Broken Arrow
Janning, Sister Mary Bernadette *nun, retired association executive*

Lawton
†Young, J. A. *bishop*

Norman
Fuerbringer, Alfred Ottomar *clergyman*

Oklahoma City
Andrews, Robert Frederick *religious organization administrator, retired bishop*
Beltran, Eusebius Joseph *archbishop*
Jones, Robert Lee *religion educator*
†Lewis, C. A. *church administrator*
†Moody, Robert M. *bishop*
†Ponder, Alonza *church administrator*
Simmons, Jesse Doyle *minister, educator*
Solomon, Dan Eugene *bishop*
Underwood, Bernard Edward *religious organization administrator*

Purcell
Lucas, Roy Edward, Jr. *minister*

Stillwater
†Lawson, F. D. *bishop*

Tulsa
Cox, William Jackson *bishop*
Gottschalk, Sister Mary Therese *nun, hospital administrator*
Henderson, Robert Waugh *retired religion educator, minister*
Roberts, (Granville) Oral *clergyman*
Schmidt, Sister Mary Sylvia (Patricia Ella Nora Schmidt) *nun*

OREGON

Bend
Connolly, Thomas Joseph *bishop*
†Hanes, Clifford Ronald *religious denomination administrator*

Eugene
Osborn, Ronald Edwin *minister, church history educator*
Sanders, Jack Thomas *religious studies educator*

Gresham
Nicholson, R. Stephen *organization administrator*

Lake Oswego
Ladehoff, Robert Louis *bishop*

Newport
Langrock, Karl Frederick *former academic administrator*

Portland
Carver, Loyce Cleo *clergyman*
Dew, William Waldo, Jr. *bishop*
Huenemann, Ruben Henry *clergyman*
Levada, William Joseph *archbishop*
Richards, Herbert East *minister emeritus, commentator*
†Sevetson, Donald James *minister, church administrator*
Steiner, Kenneth Donald *bishop*
Waldschmidt, Paul Edward *clergyman*

Wilsonville
Gross, Hal Raymond *bishop*

PENNSYLVANIA

Akron
†Lapp, John Allen *religious organization administrator*

Allentown
Jodock, Darrell Harland *minister, religion educator*
Welsh, Thomas J. *bishop*

Altoona
†Miller, Gerald E. *bishop*

Ambridge
Frey, William Carl *bishop, academic administrator*

Annville
Ehrhart, Carl Yarkers *retired minister, retired college administrator*

Camp Hill
†Johnston, Thomas McElree, Jr. *church administrator*

Clearfield
Pride, Douglas Spencer *minister*

Coopersburg
Eckardt, Arthur Roy *religion studies educator emeritus*

Cranberry Township
Bashore, George Willis *bishop*

Doylestown
Maser, Frederick Ernest *clergyman*

Drexel Hill
Thompson, William David *minister, homiletics educator*

Elizabethtown
†Mann, Lowell D. *religious organization executive*

Erie
†Hazuda, Ronald A. *church administrator*
Poydock, Mary Eymard *nun, educational administrator, biologist, educator*
†Rowley, Robert Deane, Jr. *bishop*
Trautman, Donald W. *bishop*

Fogelsville
Ault, James Mase *bishop*

Gettysburg
Hale, James Russell *religious studies educator, minister*

Grantham
†Byers, John A. *bishop*
†Chubb, Harold D. *church official*
Sider, E(arl) Morris *minister*
†Sider, Harvey Ray *minister, church administrator*

Greenville
†Farina, Andrew *church administrator*

Harrisburg
Dattilo, Nicholas C. *bishop*
†Edmiston, Guy S., Jr. *bishop*
May, Felton Edwin *bishop*
†McNutt, Charlie Fuller, Jr. *bishop*

Hatfield
†Garis, Mark *church administrator*

Horsham
†Duff, Donald James *religious organization administrator*

Huntingdon
Durnbaugh, Donald Floyd *church history educator, researcher*

Johnstown
†Miloro, Frank P. *church official, religious studies educator*
†Nicholas, (Richard G. Smisko) *bishop*
†Yurcisin, John *church official*

Kutztown
Ring, Rodney Everett *religion educator*

Lancaster
Dubble, Curtis William *pastor*
Glick, Garland Wayne *retired theological seminary president*

Latrobe
Dumm, Demetrius Robert *priest, educator*
Murtha, John Francis *priest, academic administrator, history educator*

Lewisburg
Jump, Chester Jackson, Jr. *clergyman, church official*
†Main, A. Donald *bishop*

Merion Station
Littell, Franklin Hamlin *theologian, educator*

Mount Joy
†Zook, Donald Roy *missions administrator*

Myerstown
†Schock, Franklin H. *clergy member, church administrator*

Philadelphia
Bartlett, Allen Lyman, Jr. *bishop*
Bevilacqua, Anthony Joseph Cardinal *cardinal*
Goldin, Judah *Hebrew literature educator*
†Gossett, Joyce *religious organization administrator*
Hammond, Charles Ainley *clergyman*
†Harvey, William J. *religious service organization, religious publication editor*
†Jones, O. T. *bishop*
Kee, Howard Clark *religion educator*
Kraft, Robert Alan *history of religion educator*
Krol, John Cardinal *retired archbishop*
Marple, Dorothy Jane *retired church executive*
Mensing, Stephen Gustav *bishop*
†Sandler, Abraham *minister*
Sulyk, Stephen *archbishop*
Turner, Franklin Delton *bishop*
Waskow, Arthur Ocean *theologian, educator*

Pittsburgh
†Green, Isaac *church administrator*
Harvey, Thomas J. *priest, social service organization executive*
†Hathaway, Alden Moinet *bishop*
Kocisko, Stephen John *clergyman*
Koedel, Robert Craig *minister, historian, educator*
Leiter, Donald Eugene *religious organization executive*
Maximos, (Maximos Demetrios Aghiorgoussis) *bishop*
†McCoid, Donald James *bishop*
Mc Dowell, John B. *bishop*
Muto, Susan Annette *religion educator, academic administrator*
Schaub, Marilyn McNamara *religion educator*
†Vaughn, Gordon E. *bishop*
Wuerl, Donald W. *bishop*

Reading
†Cate, Patrick O'Hair *mission executive*

Rydal
Black, Thomas Donald *retired religious organization administrator*
Kirkland, Bryant Mays *clergyman*

Sagamore
†Cornell, William Harvey *clergyman*

Saint Davids
Maahs, Kenneth Henry, Sr. *religion educator*

Scranton
De Celles, Charles Edouard *theologian, educator*
Timlin, James Clifford *bishop*

Seneca
†Spring, Paull E. *bishop*

Sewickley
Newell, Byron Bruce, Jr. *clergyman, former naval officer*

South Canaan
†Herman *bishop*

South Gibson
Acker, Raymond Abijah *minister*

Swarthmore
Cornelsen, Rufus *clergyman*
Frost, Jerry William *religion and history educator, library administrator*
Shaull, Richard *theologian, educator*

Valley Forge
†Buckles, Michael A. *religious organization executive*
†Collemer, Craig A. *religious organization administrator*
†Gonzales, Hector M. *church administrator*
†González, Héctor *church official*
Green, Norman Marston, Jr. *minister*
†Housam, Ruth *religious organization administrator*
†Kim, Jean B. *religious organization executive*
†McPhee, Richard S. *church administrator*
†Penfield, Carole H. (Kate Penfield) *minister, church official*
†Renquest, Richard A. *religious organization executive*
†Smith, G. Elaine *religious organization executive*
†Smith, Gordon E. *religious arganization executive*
†Sundquist, John A. *religious organization executive*
†Wade, Cheryl H. *church official*
†Weiss, Daniel Edwin *clergyman, educator*
†Wright-Riggins, Aidsand F. *religious organization executive*

Warren
Waterston, William King *minister, educator, academic administrator*

Wernersville
Mackey, Sheldon Elias *minister*

Wilkes Barre
†Thomas, Reginald Harry, Sr. *minister*

Willow Street
†Piscopo, Rich *evangelist*

Wyncote
†Burton, DeWitt A. *bishop*
†Sasso, Sandy *rabbi*

RHODE ISLAND

Newport
Coelho, Joseph Richard *religious organization administrator*

Providence
Frerichs, Ernest Sunley *religious studies educator*
Gelineau, Louis Edward *bishop*
†Hunt, George Nelson *bishop*
Milhaven, John Giles *religious studies educator*
Pearce, George Hamilton *archbishop*
Reeder, John P., Jr. *religious studies educator*
Thomson, Paul van Kuykendall *priest, educator*

SOUTH CAROLINA

Anderson
Hearne, Stephen Zachary *minister, educator*

Charleston
Conyers, Abda Johnson, III *theology educator, writer*
†Salmon, Edward Lloyd, Jr. *bishop*
Thompson, David B. *bishop*

Columbia
Adams, John Hurst *bishop*
†Aull, James Stroud *bishop*
Beckham, William Arthur *bishop*
Bethea, Joseph Benjamin *bishop*
Blount, Evelyn *religious organization administrator*
Brubaker, Lauren Edgar *minister, religion educator*

Due West
Ruble, Randall Tucker *theologian, educator, academic administrator*

Gastonia
Carson, John Little *historical theology educator, clergyman*

Georgetown
Allison, Christopher FitzSimons *bishop*

Goose Creek
†Johnson, Johnnie *bishop*

Greenville
Smith, Morton Howison *religious organization administrator, educator*

Hilton Head Island
Radest, Howard Bernard *clergyman, educator*

Leesville
Crumley, James Robert, Jr. *retired clergyman*

Mauldin
†Phillips, James Oscar *minister*

Piedmont
†McMahand, Willie Bee *clergyman, construction company executive*

SOUTH DAKOTA

Rapid City
Chaput, Charles J. *bishop*

Sioux Falls
Carlson, Robert James *bishop*
†Cowles, Ronald Eugene *church administrator*
Dudley, Paul V. *bishop*
†Eitrheim, Norman Duane *bishop*

TENNESSEE

Antioch
†Reeds, Roger *church administrator*
†Thomas, Roy L. *minister*
†Vallance, James *church administrator, religious publication editor*
†Waddell, R. Eugene *minister*
Worthington, Melvin Leroy *minister, writer*

Brentwood
Bennett, Harold Clark *clergyman, religious organization administrator*

Chattanooga
Hall, Thor *religion educator*
Mohney, Ralph Wilson *minister*
†Ragon, Robert Ronald *clergyman*

Cleveland
†Albert, Leonard *religious organization executive*
†Alford, Delton *religious organization executive*
†Betancourt, Esdras *religious organization executive*
†Chambers, O. Wayne *religious organization executive*
†Crisp, Sam *church administrator*
†Fisher, Robert Elwood *minister, church official*
Hughes, Ray Harrison *minister, church official*
†Jackson, Joseph Essard *religious organization administrator*
†Jones, E. L. *church admininistrator*
†Moffett, B. J. *church administrator*
†Murray, Billy Dwayne, Sr. *church administrator*
†Nichols, John D. *church administrator*
†O'Neal, Timothy D. *church administrator*
†Pemberton, Donald T. *church administrator*
†Rayburn, Billy J. *Church administrator*
†Reyes, Jose Antonio, Sr. *minister*
†Riley, Jerlena *church administrator*
†Robinson, Julian B. *church administrator*
†Sheeks, Bill F. *minister*
†Sustar, T. David *religious organization executive*
†Taylor, William Al *church administrator*
Tomlinson, Milton Ambrose *clergyman*
†Varlack, Adrian *church administrator*
†Vaughan, Roland *church administrator*
†Vest, R. Lamar *church administrator*
†White, Robert *church administrator*

Hermitage
Chambers, Curtis Allen *clergyman, church communications executive*

Jackson
†Maynard, Terrell Dennis *minister*

Jellico
†Walden, Jasper *church adminsitrator*

Knoxville
†Bell, H. Jenkins *clergyman, bishop*
O'Connell, Anthony J. *bishop*
†Sanders, William Evan *bishop*

La Follette
Eads, Ora Wilbert *clergyman, church official*

Loudon
Jones, Robert Gean *religion educator*

Memphis
†Adamson, John *church administrator*
†Brooks, P. A., II *bishop*
†Cunningham, Ronald M. *religious education director*
Dickson, Alex Dockery *bishop*
†Hamilton, W. W. *church administrator*
†Macklin, F. Douglas *bishop*
†Perry, Floyde E., Jr. *bishop*
†Porter, W. L. *bishop*
†Thomas, Nathaniel Charles *clergyman*
Todd, Virgil Holcomb *clergyman, religion educator*

Nashville
†Adkins, Cecelia N. *church administrator*
Burgess, Roger *church official*
Buttrick, David Gardner *religion educator*
†Fagan, A. Rudolph *minister*
†Forlines, Franklin Leroy *minister, educator*
Forstman, Henry Jackson *theology educator, university dean*
Fry, Malcolm Craig *clergyman*
†Hamm, Richard L. *church administrator*
Hampton, Ralph Clayton, Jr. *pastoral studies educator, clergyman*
†Ireson, Roger William *religious organization administrator, minister, educator*
Jemison, Theodore Judson *religious organization administrator*
Land, Richard Dale *minister, religious organization administrator*
Mills, Liston Oury *theology educator*
Picirilli, Robert Eugene *clergyman, college dean, writer*
†Seale, James Millard *religious organization administrator, clergyman*
Spencer, Harry Chadwick *minister*
†Walker, Arthur Lonzo *religious organization administrator*
†Whaley, Vernon *church administrator*

TEXAS

Amarillo
Matthiesen, Leroy Theodore *bishop*

Austin
Mc Carthy, John Edward *bishop*
Wahlberg, Philip Lawrence *former bishop, legislative liaison*

Beaumont
Ganter, Bernard J. *bishop*

Brownsville
Fitzpatrick, John J. *bishop*
San Pedro, Enrique *bishop*

Corpus Christi
Doty, James Edward *pastor, psychologist*
Gracida, Rene Henry *bishop*
Pivonka, Leonard Daniel *priest*

Dallas
†Allen, John Carlton *minister*
†Clark, C. A. W. *church administrator*
Grahmann, Charles V. *bishop*
†Harris, David, Jr. *minister*
†Haynes, J. Neauell *clergyman, bishop*
†Herbener, Mark Basil *bishop*
†Jenkins, Chester P. *religious organization, church administration*
†Lee, J. E. *bishop*
Morgan, Larry Ronald *minister*
†Scott, Manuel *church administrator*
Slater, Oliver Eugene *bishop*
†Thurston, Stephen John *pastor*
Valentine, Foy Dan *clergyman*
Webb, Lance *bishop*
Wiles, Charles Preston *minister*

Denton
†Leslie, Marvin Earl *minister*

El Paso
Pena, Raymundo Joseph *bishop*

Euless
†Draper, James Thomas (Jimmy Draper) *clergyman*

Fort Worth
†Calkins, Loren Gene *church executive, clergyman*
Delaney, Joseph P. *bishop*
Gilbert, James Cayce *minister*
Gross, John Birney *retired minister*
Newport, John Paul *philosophy of religion educator, former academic administrator*
†Pope, Clarence Cullam, Jr. *bishop*
Suggs, Marion Jack *minister, college dean*
Teegarden, Kenneth Leroy *clergyman*

Gary
†Speer, James *religious organization administrator*

Houston
†Benitez, Maurice Manuel *bishop*
Fiorenza, Joseph A. *bishop*
†Henderson, Nathan H. *bishop*
Joyce, James Daniel *clergyman*
Karff, Samuel Egal *rabbi*
Nelson, John Robert *theology educator, clergyman*
Nielsen, Niels Christian, Jr. *theology educator*
†Sampson, Franklin Delano *minister*
Sudbury, John Dean *religious foundation executive, petroleum chemist*
†Woodard, Robert E. *bishop*

Jacksonville
†Blaylock, James Carl *clergyman, librarian*
†Pruitt, William Charles, Jr. *minister, educator*

Longview
Brannon, Clifton Woodrow, Sr. *evangelist, lawyer*

Lubbock
†Hulsey, Sam Byron *bishop*
†Watson, W. H. *bishop*

North Austin
Ahlschwede, Arthur Martin *church educational official*

Plano
Lee, Allan Wren *clergyman*

Red Oak
Henderson, Edwin Harold *minister*

San Angelo
Pfeifer, Michael David *bishop*

San Antonio
Caudill, Howard Edwin *Anglican bishop, educator*
Flores, Patrick F. *archbishop*
†Iglehart, T. D. *bishop*
Jacobson, David *rabbi*
Mc Allister, Gerald Nicholas *retired bishop, clergyman*
Ranson, Guy Harvey *clergyman, religion educator*

Texarkana
Cross, Irvie Keil *religious organization executive*
†Silvey, James L. *religious publisher*
†Tucker, Bobby Glenn *minister*

Van
†Cottrell, Ralph *religious organization executive*

Victoria
Fellhauer, David E. *bishop*

Waco
Chewning, Richard Carter *religious business ethics educator*
Flanders, Henry Jackson, Jr. *religion educator*
Wood, James E., Jr. *religion educator, author*

Waxahachie
Tschoepe, Thomas *bishop*

UTAH

Gusher
†King, Felton *bishop*

Salt Lake City
†Ballard, Melvin Russell, Jr. *church official*
†Bates, George Edmonds *bishop*
Faust, James E. *church official*
Haight, David B. *church official*
†Hales, Robert D. *church official*
Hinckley, Gordon B. *church official*
Maxwell, Neal A. *church official*
Monson, Thomas Spencer *church official, publishing company executive*
†Packer, Boyd K. *church official*
†Perry, L. Tom *church official, merchant*
†Scott, Richard G. *church official*
Smith, Eldred Gee *church leader*
Weigand, William Keith *bishop*
†Wirthlin, Joseph B. *church official*

VERMONT

Burlington
†Swenson, Daniel Lee *bishop*

Middlebury
Ferm, Robert Livingston *religion educator*

Newport
Guerrette, Richard Hector *priest, management consultant*

Northfield
†Wick, William S. *clergyman, chaplain*

Norwich
Post, Avery Denison *church official*

Pawlet
Buechner, Carl Frederick *minister, author*

Springfield
Garinger, Louis Daniel *religion educator*

VIRGINIA

Alexandria
†Budde, Mitzi Marie Jarrett *librarian*

Arlington
Bailey, Amos Purnell *clergyman, syndicated columnist*
Keating, John Richard *bishop*

Blacksburg
Grover, Norman LaMotte *theologian, philosopher*

Charlottesville
Childress, James Franklin *theology and medical educator*
Fletcher, John Caldwell *bioethicist, religious studies educator*
Fogarty, Gerald Philip *church history educator, priest*
Hartt, Julian Norris *religion educator*
Scharlemann, Robert Paul *religious studies educator, clergyman*

Scott, Nathan Alexander, Jr. *minister, educator, literary critic*

Emory
†Dawsey, James Marshall *religious studies educator, minister*

Lynchburg
Falwell, Jerry L. *clergyman*

Mc Lean
Lotz, Denton *minister, church official*
Wümpelmann, Knud Aage Abildgaard *clergyman, religious organization administrator*

Mechanicsville
†Balser, Glennon *church administrator*

Norfolk
Vest, Frank Harris, Jr. *bishop*

Portsmouth
†Thomas, Ted, Sr. *minister*

Reston
Walzer, William Charles *church official, interdenominational religious publishing agency executive*

Richmond
Anderson, James Frederick *clergyman*
Bagby, Daniel Gordon *minister*
†Briggs, Edward Burton, Jr. *religion writer*
Brown, Aubrey Neblett, Jr. *minister, editor*
Fuller, Reginald Horace *clergyman, biblical studies educator*
†Lee, Peter James *bishop*
Leith, John Haddon *clergyman, theology educator*
McDonough, Reginald Milton *religious organization executive*
Rogers, Isabel Wood *religious studies educator*
Stockton, Thomas B. *bishop*
Sullivan, Walter Francis *bishop*
Swezey, Charles Mason *Christian ethics educator, administrator*

Roanoke
Light, Arthur Heath *bishop*
Marmion, William Henry *retired bishop*
†Thompson, Ron Everett *religious organization, church administrator*

Salem
†Bansemer, Richard Frederick *bishop*

Sweet Briar
Armstrong, Gregory Timon *religion educator, minister*

Virginia Beach
Williams, John Rodman *theologian, educator*

Warsaw
Hirsch, Charles Bronislaw *retired religion educator and administrator*

Williamsburg
Finn, Thomas Macy *religion educator*

WASHINGTON

Belfair
Walker, E. Jerry *retired clergyman*

College Place
Andreasen, Niels-Erik Albinus *religious educator*
Thompson, Alden Lloyd *biblical studies educator, author*

Greenbank
Tuell, Jack Marvin *retired bishop*

Seattle
Averill, Lloyd James, Jr. *religion educator*
Burrows, Elizabeth MacDonald *religious organization executive, educator*
Mackey, Sally Schear *retired religious organization administrator*
McConnell, Calvin Dale *clergyman*
Murphy, Thomas Joseph *archbishop*
Raible, Peter Spilman *minister*
Robb, John Wesley *religion educator*
†Warner, Vincent W. *bishop*

Spanaway
†Westbrook, T. L. *bishop*

Spokane
†Keller, Robert M. *bishop*
Polley, Harvey Lee *retired missionary and educator*
Skylstad, William S. *bishop*
†Terry, Frank Jeffrey *bishop*

Tacoma
Wiegman, Eugene William *minister, former college administrator*
†Wold, David C. *bishop*

Yakima
George, Francis *bishop*

WEST VIRGINIA

Charleston
†Atkinson, Robert Poland *bishop*
Scott, Olof Henderson, Jr. *priest*

Fairmont
†Black, L. Alexander *bishop*

Grafton
Poling, Kermit William *minister*

Morgantown
Meitzen, Manfred Otto *religious studies educator*

Wheeling
Schmitt, Bernard W. *bishop*

WISCONSIN

Amery
Mickelson, Arnold Rust *church commission executive, consultant*

Appleton
†Herder, Robert H. *bishop*

Eau Claire
Wantland, William Charles *bishop, lawyer*

Fond Du Lac
†Stevens, William Louis *bishop*

Green Bay
Banks, Robert J. *bishop*

Green Lake
†LaDue, Paul W. *religious organization executive*

La Crosse
Paul, John Joseph *bishop*

Madison
Bullock, William Henry *bishop*
†Enslin, Jon S. *bishop*
Fox, Michael Vass *Hebrew educator, rabbi*
†Hayner, Stephen A. *academic organization administrator*
Wirz, George O. *bishop*

Milwaukee
Weakland, Rembert G. *archbishop*

Oak Creek
†Clark, Harry Wilber *administrator*
Robertson, Michael Swing *religious association administrator*

Oshkosh
Barwig, Regis Norbert James *priest*
Burke, Redmond A. *priest, librarian, educator*

Racine
Jacobson-Wolf, Joan Elizabeth *minister*

Rice Lake
†Knutson, Gerhard I. *bishop*

Sun Prairie
Mischke, Carl Herbert *religious association executive, retired*

Superior
Fliss, Raphael M. *bishop*

Watertown
Henry, Carl Ferdinand Howard *theologian*

WYOMING

Cheyenne
Hart, Joseph H. *bishop*

Laramie
†Jones, Bob Gordon *bishop*

TERRITORIES OF THE UNITED STATES

PUERTO RICO

Ponce
Torres Oliver, Juan Fremiot *bishop*

Santurce
Aponte Martinez, Luis Cardinal *archbishop*

CANADA

ALBERTA

Calgary
†Curtis, John Barry *bishop*
Markwood, Lewis Ardra *minister*
†O'Byrne, Paul J. *bishop*

Camrose
Campbell, John Douglas *minister*

Edmonton
†Daciuk, Myron Michael *bishop*
Doyle, Wilfred Emmett *retired bishop*
†Genge, Kenneth Lyle *bishop*
Mac Neil, Joseph Neil *archbishop*

McLennan
†Legare, Henri Francis *archbishop*

Saint Paul
†Roy, Raymond *bishop*

BRITISH COLUMBIA

Kamloops
†Cruickshank, James David *bishop*
†Sabatini, Lawrence *bishop*

Nelson
†Mallon, Peter *bishop*

Prince Rupert
Hannen, John Edward *bishop*

Richmond
Plomp, Teunis (Tony Plomp) *minister*

Vancouver
†Exner, Adam *archbishop*
Wakefield, Wesley Halpenny *church official*

Victoria
De Roo, Remi Joseph *bishop*
Frame, John Timothy *bishop*

West Vancouver
Bentall, Shirley Franklyn *lay church leader, author*

MANITOBA

Churchill
†Rouleau, Reynald *bishop*

Saint Boniface
Hacault, Antoine Joseph Leon *archbishop*

The Pas
Sutton, Peter Alfred *archbishop*

Winnipeg
†Harder, Helmut *religious organization administrator*
Hermaniuk, Maxim *retired archbishop*
Jarmus, Stephan Onysym *priest*
Lehman, Edwin *minister, head of religious organization*
†Luetkehoelter, Gottlieb Werner (Lee) *bishop, clergyman*
Sjoberg, Donald *bishop*

NEW BRUNSWICK

Fredericton
†Lemmon, George Colborne *bishop*

Saint John
†Troy, J. Edward *bishop*

NEWFOUNDLAND

Corner Brook
Payne, Sidney Stewart *archbishop*

Saint John's
†Harvey, Donald F. *bishop*
†Mate, Martin *bishop*

NORTHWEST TERRITORIES

Iqaluit
†Williams, J. Christopher R. *bishop*

NOVA SCOTIA

Antigonish
†Campbell, Colin *bishop*

Parrsboro
Hatfield, Leonard Fraser *retired bishop*

ONTARIO

Barrie
Clune, Robert Bell *bishop*

Brampton
Bastian, Donald Noel *bishop, retired*

Burlington
†Elgersma, Ray *religious organization adminstrator*
†Hamilton, Donald Gordon *religious association administrator*
†Karsten, Albert *religious organization administrator*

Cornwall
La Rocque, Eugene Philippe *bishop*

Fort Smith
†Croteau, Denis *bishop*

Guelph
†Steffer, Robert Wesley *clergyman*

Hamilton
†Tonnos, Anthony *bishop*

Hearst
†Despatie, Roger *bishop*

Kanata
†Hunter, Edward Stewart *clergy member*

Kingston
Read, Allan Alexander *minister*
†Spence, Francis John *archbishop*

Kitchener
Huras, William David *bishop*
†Winger, Roger Elson *church administrator*

London
MacBain, William Halley *minister, theology educator, seminary chancellor*
†Peterson, Leslie Ernest *bishop*
†Scott, W. Peter *bishop*
†Sherlock, John Michael *bishop*

Milton
Georgije, Djokic *bishop*

Mississauga
Hooper, Wayne Nelson *clergy member*
Mac Knight, James *minister*

Niagara Falls
†Mullan, Donald William *bishop*

Ottawa
†Chiasson, Donat *archbishop*
†Gervais, Marcel Andre *bishop*
†Gratton, Jean *clergyman*
Landriault, Jacques Emile *retired bishop*
†MacDonald, Joseph Faber *bishop*
Penney, Alphonsus Liguori *archbishop*
Ryan, William Francis *priest*
Squire, Anne Marguerite *religious leader*

Pembroke
†Windle, Joseph Raymond *bishop*

Peterborough
†Doyle, James Leonard *bishop*

Rexdale
†Joseph, Emanuel *church administrator*

Saint Catharines
O'Mara, John Aloysius *bishop*

Schumacher
†Lawrence, Caleb James *bishop*

Spencerville
†Farley, Lawrence *clergyman*

St Catharines
Fulton, Thomas Benjamin *retired bishop*

Timmins
†Cazabon, Gilles *bishop*

Toronto
Athanassoulas, Sotirios (Sotirios of Toronto) *bishop*
Carter, Gerald Emmett *retired archbishop*
Chodos, Robert Irwin *editor, writer*
Finlay, Terence Edward *bishop*
Jay, Charles Douglas *religion educator, college administrator, clergyman*
†Kutz-Harder, Helga *religious organization executive*
Owens, Joseph *clergyman*
Plaut, Wolf Gunther *minister, author*
Synan, Edward Aloysius, Jr. *clergyman, former institute president*
Wilson, Lois M. *minister*

Unionville
†Rusnak, Michael *bishop*

Waterloo
†Kraus, Michael *minister*

Windsor
Whitney, Barry Lyn *religious studies educator*

Winnipeg
†Wall, Leonard J. *bishop*

QUEBEC

Chicoutimi
Couture, Jean Guy *bishop*

Hull
Ebacher, Roger *archbishop*

Joliette
Audet, Rene *bishop*

Longueuil
†Hubert, Bernard *bishop*

Montreal
Charron, André Joseph Charles Pierre *theologian, educator, former dean*
Hall, Douglas John *minister, educator*
Kannengiesser, Charles A. *theology educator*
†Shepherd, Harvey Lawrence *religion reporter*
Turcotte, Jean-Claude *archbishop*

Quebec
Stavert, Alexander Bruce *bishop*

Rimouski
Blanchet, Bertrand *archbishop*
Levesque, Louis *bishop*

Rouyn-Noranda
Hamelin, Jean-Guy *bishop*

Saint Hyacinthe
Langevin, Louis-de-Gonzague *bishop*

Saint Jerome
†Valois, Charles *bishop*

Sherbrooke
Fortier, Jean-Marie *archbishop*

Sillery
Couture, Maurice *archbishop*

Trois Rivières
Noel, Laurent *bishop, educator*

Valleyfield
†Lebel, Robert *bishop*

SASKATCHEWAN

Gravelbourg
†Delaquis, Noel *bishop*

Prince Albert
†Morand, Blaise E. *bishop*

Regina
Bays, Eric *bishop*
†Holm, Roy K. *church administrator*

Saltcoats
Farquharson, Walter Henry *minister, church official*

Saskatoon
†Filevich, Basil *bishop*
Jacobson, Sverre Theodore *retired minister*
†Mahoney, James P. *bishop*
†Morgan, Thomas Oliver *bishop*

YUKON TERRITORY

Whitehorse
Ferris, Ronald Curry *bishop*
†Lobsinger, Thomas *bishop*

MEXICO

Chihuahua
Almeida Merino, Adalberto *archbishop*

Ciudad de Mexico
Godinez Flores, Ramon *auxiliary bishop*
Guizar, Ricardo Diaz *clergyman*

Matamoros
Chavolla Ramos, Francisco Javier *bishop*

Morelia
Alcaraz Figueroa, Estanislao *clergyman*

Saltillo
Villalobos Padilla, Francisco *bishop*

Veracruz
Ranzahuer, Guillermo Gonzalez *bishop*

ARGENTINA

Buenos Aires
Gennadios, (Gennadios Chrysoulakis) *bishop*

BELGIUM

Brussels
Jadot, Jean Lambert Octave *clergyman*

BRAZIL

Rio de Janeiro
Sales, Eugenio de Araujo Cardinal *archbishop*

ENGLAND

London
Gilbert, Patrick Nigel Geoffrey *organization executive*
Hornyak, Eugene Augustine *bishop*
Van Culin, Samuel *religious organization administrator*

FRANCE

Bordeaux
Gouyon, Paul Cardinal *archbishop*

GERMANY

Munich
Scharbert, Josef *retired theology educator*

GHANA

Accra
Korangteng, Daniel Agyei *minister*

Kumasi
Sarpong, Peter Kwasi *bishop*

HONG KONG

Hong Kong
Kwong, Peter Kong Kit *bishop*

Kowloon
Chiang, Samuel Edward *theological educator, humanities educator*

ICELAND

Reykjavik
Jolson, Alfred James *bishop*

INDIA

New Delhi
Gregorios, Paulos Mar *archbishop, metropolitan of Delhi*

Yavatmal
Ward, Daniel Thomas *bishop*

IRAN

Tehran
†Dinkha, Mar, IV *church administrator*

ISRAEL

Jerusalem
Schindler, Pesach *rabbi, educator, author*

ITALY

Rome
Audet, Leonard *theologian*
Bafile, Corrado Cardinal *clergyman*
†Baum, William Wakefield Cardinal *former church official*

JAPAN

Aichi-ken
Yukei, Hasebe Yoshikazu *religious studies educator*

Nishinomiya
Ogida, Mikio *history of religion educator*

Tenri
Miyata, Gen *history of religion educator*

MICRONESIA

Chuuk, Caroline Islands
Neylon, Martin Joseph *bishop*

NORWAY

Lilleström
Borgen, Ole Edvard *bishop, educator*

PERU

Lima
Gutiérrez, Gustavo *priest, educator, theologian*

THE PHILIPPINES

Pasay City
Lim, Sonia Yii *minister*

SAINT LUCIA

Castries
Felix, Kelvin Edward *archbishop*

VATICAN CITY

Vatican City
John Paul II, His Holiness Pope (Karol Jozef Wojtyla) *bishop of Rome*
†Szoka, Edmund Casimir Cardinal *cardinal*

ADDRESS UNPUBLISHED

Allan, Hugh James Pearson *bishop*
Ambrozic, Aloysius Matthew *archbishop*
Anderson, John Firth *church administrator, librarian*
Arnold, Duane Wade-Hampton *minister, educator*
†Blank, Richard Glenn *religious organization administrator, counselor*
†Bollback, Anthony George *minister*
†Borecky, Isidore *bishop*
Bosakov, Joseph Blagoev (Metropolitan Bishop Joseph) *bishop*
Bosco, Anthony Gerard *bishop*
Bothwell, John Charles *archbishop*
Charlton, Gordon Taliaferro, Jr. *retired bishop*
Chernoff, Robert *rabbi*
Christopher, Sharon A. Brown *bishop*
Cliff, Judith Anita *author, biblical studies lecturer*
Clymer, Wayne Kenton *bishop*
Cobb, John Boswell, Jr. *clergyman, educator*
Cole, Clifford Adair *clergyman*
†Crabtree, Davida Foy *minister*
Daly, James Joseph *bishop*
†Davis, Theodore Roosevelt *bishop, contractor*
Dirksen, Richard Wayne *canon precentor, organist, choirmaster*
Dixon, Ernest Thomas, Jr. *retired bishop*
†Docker, John Thornley *religious organization administrator, minister*
Dudick, Michael Joseph *bishop*
Ellis, Howard Woodrow *evangelist, creative agent, clergyman, artist, author*
Gemignani, Michael Caesar *clergyman, retired educator*
Girzone, Joseph F. *retired priest, writer*
Griffin, James Anthony *bishop*
Gutmann, Reinhart Bruno *clergyman, social worker*
†Hambidge, Douglas Walter *archbishop*
Handy, William Talbot, Jr. *bishop*
Hearn, J(ames) Woodrow *bishop*
†Hibbs, William Ernest, III *priest*
Hilton, Clifford Thomas *clergyman*
Hummel, Gene Maywood *retired bishop*
†Hurn, Raymond Walter *religious order administrator*
†Isom, Dotcy Ivertus, Jr. *bishop*
†Iverson, David M. *church executive*
†Ives, S. Clifton *minister*
John, K. K. (John Kuruvilla Kaiyalethe) *minister*
†Joslin, David Bruce *bishop*
Kalkwarf, Leonard V. *minister*
Keeler, William Henry *archbishop*
†Keyser, Charles Lovett, Jr. *bishop*
Kucera, Daniel William *bishop*
Lawson, David Jerald *bishop*
Lohmuller, Martin Nicholas *bishop*
Loppnow, Milo Alvin *clergyman, former church official*
Madera, Joseph J. *bishop*
Malone, James William *bishop*
McCandless, J(ane) Bardarah *emeritus religion educator*
McQuilkin, John Robertson *religion educator, academic administrator, writer*
Melczek, Dale J. *bishop*
Meyer, Paul William *biblical literature educator emeritus*
Milhouse, Paul William *bishop*
Mills, Howard McIlroy *clergyman, denominational executive*
Morton, Charles Brinkley *retired bishop, former state legislator, lawyer*
Muckerman, Norman James *priest, writer*
†Nottingham, William Jesse *church mission executive, minister*
Osborne, James Alfred *religious organization administrator*
Parsons, Elmer Earl *retired clergyman*
Patterson, Donis Dean *bishop*
Peers, Michael Geoffrey *archbishop*
Pelotte, Donald Edmond *bishop*
Procter, John Ernest *former publishing company executive*
Righter, Walter Cameron *bishop*
Rooks, Charles Shelby *minister*
Rose, Robert John *bishop*
Salatka, Charles Alexander *archbishop*
Sams, John Roland *retired mission executive, missionary*
Sayre, Francis Bowes, Jr. *clergyman*
†Schuelke, John Paul *religious organization administrator*
Scott, Waldron *mission executive*
Sloyan, Gerard Stephen *religious studies educator, priest*
Spence, Glen Oscar *clergyman*
Stendahl, Krister *retired bishop*
Stevens, Elliot Leslie *clergyman*
Strasser, Gabor *priest, management consultant*
Sullivan, James Lenox *clergyman*
Sullivan, Leon Howard *clergyman*
†Swanson, Paul Rubert *minister*
van Dyck, Nicholas Booraem *minister, foundation official*
Van Valin, Clyde Emory *bishop*
Wilhelm, Joseph Lawrence *archbishop*
Wills, Charles Francis *former church executive, retired career officer*
†Wright, Earl Jerome *pastor, bishop*

SCIENCE: LIFE SCIENCE

UNITED STATES

ALABAMA

Auburn
Bailey, Wilford Sherrill *parisitology educator, science administrator, university president*
†Ball, Donald Maury *agronomist, consultant*
†Frobish, Lowell Thomas *agriculturist, researcher*
Klesius, Phillip Harry *microbiologist, researcher*
Lemke, Paul Arenz *botany educator*

Birmingham
Bradley, John M(iller), Jr. *forestry executive*
Brown, Jerry William *cell biology and anatomy educator*
Finley, Sara Crews *medical geneticist, educator*
Gerlach, Gary G. *botanical garden director, columnist*
Navia, Juan Marcelo *biologist, educator*
Oglesby, Sabert, Jr. *retired research institute administrator*
Rouse, John Wilson, Jr. *research institute administrator*

Florence
†Stangel, Paul J. *agronomist, soil scientist, environmentalist, consultant*

Huntsville
†Wu, Shi Tsan *educator, science research administrator*

Mobile
Gottlieb, Sheldon Fred *biologist, educator*

Tuscaloosa
Darden, William Howard, Jr. *biology educator*
Wetzel, Robert George *botany educator*
Williams, Louis Gressett *biologist, educator*

Tuskegee Institute
Madison, Willie Clarence *park superintendent*

ALASKA

Anchorage
†Bender, Thomas Richard *science administrator, epidemiologist*

Auke Bay
†Snyder, George Richard *laboratory director*

Fairbanks
Kessel, Brina *ornithologist, educator*

Juneau
Willson, Mary F. *ecology researcher, educator*

ARIZONA

Phoenix
Anderson, Edward Frederick *biology educator*
Kimball, Bruce Arnold *soil scientist*
Radin, John William *agriculturalist, physiologist*
Witherspoon, James Donald *biology educator*

Sun City
Morse, True Delbert *business and agricultural consultant, former undersecretary of agriculture*

Tempe
Aronson, Jerome Melville *plant physiology educator*
Gerking, Shelby Delos, Jr. *zoologist, educator*
Patten, Duncan Theunissen *ecologist educator*

Tucson
Acker, Robert Flint *microbiologist*
Alcorn, Stanley Marcus *plant pathology educator*
†Foster, Kennith Earl *life sciences educator*
Fritts, Harold Clark *dendrochronology educator, researcher*
Fuller, Wallace Hamilton *research scientist, educator*
Gerba, Charles Peter *microbiologist, educator*
Hagedorn, Henry Howard *entomology educator*
Hughes, Malcolm Kenneth *dendrochronologist, educator, administrator*
Hull, Herbert Mitchell *plant physiologist, researcher*
McCormick, Floyd Guy, Jr. *agricultural educator, academic administrator*
Metcalfe, Darrel Seymour *agronomist, educator*
Neuman, Shlomo P. *hydrology educator*
Osterberg, Charles Lamar *marine radioecologist, oceanographer*
Pepper, Ian L. *environmental microbiologist, research scientist, educator*
Shannon, Robert Rennie *optical sciences center administrator, educator*
Sypherd, Paul Starr *microbiologist*
†Velez-Ibanez, Carlos Guillermo *anthropology educator, research laboratory administrator*
Winfree, Arthur Taylor *biologist, educator*
Yocum, Harrison Gerald *horticulturist, botanist, educator, researcher*

ARKANSAS

Bella Vista
Musacchia, X(avier) J(oseph) *physiology and biophysics educator*

Fayetteville
†Beyrouty, Craig A. *agronomist, educator*
Brown, Connell Jean *retired animal science educator*
Clayton, Frances Elizabeth *cytologist, scientist, educator*
Evans, William Lee *biologist*
†Musick, Gerald Joe *entomology educator*
Rutledge, Elliott Moye *soil scientist, educator*
West, Charles Patrick *agronomist, educator*
Wolf, Duane Carl *microbiologist*

Jefferson
Casciano, Daniel Anthony *biologist*

Little Rock
Barron, Almen Leo *microbiologist*
Hinson, Jack Allsbrook *research toxicologist, educator*

CALIFORNIA

Alameda
Blatt, Beverly Faye *biologist, consultant*

Alamo
Overby, Lacy Rasco *biotechnology consulting executive*

Arcadia
†Morse, Judy *science foundation administrator*

Arcata
Barratt, Raymond William *biologist, educator*

Atherton
Starr, Chauncey *research institute executive*

Azusa
Kimnach, Myron William *botanist, horticulturist, consultant*

Berkeley
Anderson, John Richard *entomologist, educator*
Berkner, Klaus Hans *laboratory administrator, physicist*
Bern, Howard Alan *science educator, research biologist*
Burnside, Mary Beth *biology educator, researcher*
Casida, John Edward *entomology educator*
Chemsak, J. A. *entomologist*
DePaolo, Donald James *earth science educator*
Falcon, Louis Albert *entomology educator, insect pathologist*
Furman, Deane Philip *parasitologist, emeritus educator*
Lennette, Edwin Herman *virologist*
Licht, Paul *zoologist, educator*
Lidicker, William Zander, Jr. *zoologist, educator*
Martin, Robert Edward, Jr. *forestry educator, scientist, researcher*
Matsumura, Kenneth N. *biomedical scientist, physician*
Ornduff, Robert *botany educator*
†Penry, Deborah L. *biological oceanographer, educator*
Pitelka, Frank Alois *zoologist, educator*
Poinar, George Orlo, Jr. *insect pathologist and paleontologist, educator*
Potts, David Malcolm *population specialist, administrator*
Reginato, Robert Joseph *soil scientist*
Schachman, Howard Kapnek *molecular biologist, educator*
Shank, Charles Vernon *science administrator, educator*
Spear, Robert Clinton *environmental health educator, consultant*
Teeguarden, Dennis Earl *forest economist*
Twiss, Robert Hamilton, Jr. *environmental planning educator*
Vaux, Henry James *forest economist, educator*
Vedros, Neylan Anthony *microbiologist*
Wake, David Burton *biology educator, researcher*
Wake, Marvalee Hendricks *biology educator*

Bishop
MacMillen, Richard Edward *biological sciences educator, researcher*

Bodega Bay
Hand, Cadet Hammond, Jr. *marine biologist, educator*
Jeffery, William Richard *developmental biology educator*

Borrego Springs
Kryter, Karl David *research scientist*

Cambria
Villeneuve, Donald Avila *biology educator*

Chico
Ediger, Robert Ike *botanist, educator*
Kistner, David Harold *biology educator*

Claremont
Purves, William Kirkwood *biologist, educator*

Clovis
Ensminger, Marion Eugene *animal science educator, author*

Coalinga
Harris, John Charles *agriculturalist*

Cupertino
Cheeseman, Douglas Taylor, Jr. *wildlife tour executive, photographer, educator*

Davis
Addicott, Fredrick Taylor *retired botany educator*
Allard, Robert Wayne *geneticist, educator*
Baldwin, Ransom Leland *animal science educator*
Barbour, Michael G(eorge) *botany educator, ecological consultant*
Baskin, Ronald Joseph *zoologist, physiologist, biophysicist educator, dean*
Carman, Hoy Fred *agricultural sciences educator*
Chang, Robert Shihman *virology educator*
Colvin, Harry Walter, Jr. *physiology educator*
Crane, Julian Coburn *agriculturist,retired educator*
Epstein, Emanuel *plant physiologist*
Freedland, Richard Allan *retired biologist, educator*
Gifford, Ernest Milton *biologist, educator*
Grey, Robert Dean *biology educator*
Hartmann, Hudson Thomas *agriculturist, educator*
Hess, Charles Edward *environmental horticulture educator*
†Horowitz, Isaac M. *control research consultant, writer*
Horwitz, Barbara Ann *physiologist, educator, consultant*
Hsieh, Dennis P. H. *environmental toxicology educator*
†Hughes, John P. *equine research adminstrator*
Kado, Clarence Isao *molecular biologist*
Kofranek, Anton Miles *floriculturist, educator*
Kunkee, Ralph Edward *viticulture and enology educator*
Laidlaw, Harry Hyde, Jr. *entomology educator*
Learn, Elmer Warner *agricultural economics educator, retired*
†Marois, Jim *plant pathologist, educator*
Martin, George Conner *pomology educator*
Meyer, Margaret Eleanor *microbiologist, educator*
Moyle, Peter Briggs *fisheries and biology educator*
Murphy, Terence Martin *botany educator*
Nielsen, Donald Rodney *soil and water science educator*
Pappagianis, Demosthenes *microbiology educator, physician*
Pearcy, Robert Woodwell *botany educator*
Qualset, Calvin Odell *agronomy educator*
Rappaport, Lawrence *plant physiology and horticulture educator*
Rick, Charles Madeira, Jr. *geneticist, educator*
Rost, Thomas Lowell *botany educator*
Schoener, Thomas William *zoology educator, researcher*
Shapiro, Arthur Maurice *biology educator*
Sillman, Arnold Joel *physiologist, educator*
Stebbins, George Ledyard *research botanist, retired educator*
Stewart, James Ian *agricultural water scientist, cropping system developer, consultant*
Watt, Kenneth Edmund Ferguson *zoology educator*
Williams, William Arnold *agronomy educator*
Wilson, Barry William *biology educator*

Del Mar
Farquhar, Marilyn Gist *cell biology and pathology educator*

Duarte
Lundblad, Roger Lauren *research director*
Ohno, Susumu *research scientist*
Smith, Steven Sidney *molecular biologist*

El Centro
Flock, Robert Ashby *retired entomologist*

El Segundo
Wallace, Arthur *agricultural educator*

Foster City
Baselt, Randall Clint *toxicologist*

Fullerton
Brattstrom, Bayard Holmes *biology educator*
Jones, Claris Eugene, Jr. *botanist, educator*

Hopland
Jones, Milton Bennion *agronomist, educator*

Irvine
Ayala, Francisco José *geneticist, educator*
Bennett, Albert Farrell *biology educator*
†Berns, Michael W. *cell biologist, educator*
Cunningham, Dennis Dean *microbiology, molecular genetics educator*
Fan, Hung Y. *virology educator, consultant*
Fitch, Walter M(onroe) *molecular biologist, educator*
Lambert, Robert Lowell *scientific investigator*
Lenhoff, Howard Maer *biological sciences educator, academic administrator, activist*
Silverman, Paul Hyman *parasitologist, former university official*
Smith, Lewis Dennis *biologist, college dean*
Spence, M. Anne *geneticist, medical association executive*

Kensington
Stent, Gunther Siegmund *molecular biologist, educator*

La Canada Flintridge
Clauser, Francis H. *applied science educator*

La Jolla
Alvariño De Leira, Angeles (Angeles Alvariño) *biologist, oceanographer*
Bloom, Floyd Elliott *physician, research scientist*
Dulbecco, Renato *biologist, educator*
Fishman, William Harold *cancer research foundation executive, biochemist*
Guillemin, Roger C. L. *physiologist*
Haxo, Francis Theodore *marine biologist*
Hunter, Tony (Anthony Rex Hunter) *molecular biologist, educator*
Jones, Galen Everts *microbiologist, educator*
Lewin, Ralph Arnold *biologist*
West, John Burnard *physiologist, educator*
Wilkie, Donald Walter *biologist, aquarium museum director*

Lafayette
Sandberg, Robert Alexis *former research organization administrator*

Lemon Grove
Whitehead, Marvin Delbert *plant pathologist*

Livermore
Glass, Alexander Jacob *science administrator*

Loma Linda
Longo, Lawrence Daniel *physiologist, gynecologist*

Long Beach
Anand, Rajen S. *physiologist*
Swatek, Frank Edward *microbiology educator*

Los Altos
Fraser-Smith, Elizabeth Birdsey *biologist*
Frey, Christian Miller *research center executive*

Los Angeles
Anderson, W. French *genticist, biochemist, physician*
Baker, Robert Frank *molecular biologist, educator*
Birren, James Emmett *university research center executive*
Bok, Dean *cell biologist, educator*
Collias, Elsie Cole *zoologist*
Eisenberg, David Samuel *molecular biologist, educator*
Eiserling, Frederick Allen *microbiologist, educator*
Finch, Caleb Ellicott *neurobiologist, educator*
Goldstein, Mark A. *zoo administrator*
Gordon, Malcolm Stephen *biology educator*
Lindstedt-Siva, (Karen) June *marine biologist, oil company executive*
†Lunt, Owen Raynal *biologist, educator*
Martin, Walter Edwin *biology educator*
Mathias, Mildred Esther *botany educator*
Mockary, Peter Ernest *clinical laboratory scientist, researcher*
Mohr, John Luther *biologist, environmental consultant*
Rice, Susan F. *zoological park executive*
Seto, Joseph Tobey *virologist, educator*
Smulders, Anthony Peter *biology educator*
Sonnenschein, Ralph Robert *physiologist*
Szego, Clara Marian *cell biologist, educator*
Wei, Jen Yu *physiologist, educator*
Wright, Ernest Marshall *physiologist, consultant*

Marina Del Rey
Corzo, Miguelangel *institute executive*

Menlo Park
Anderson, Charles Arthur *former research institute administrator*
Crane, Hewitt David *science advisor*
Fuhrman, Frederick Alexander *physiology educator*
Jorgensen, Paul J. *research company executive*
Oronsky, Arnold Lewis *scientific research company executive, medical educator*
†Sutherland, Robert Melvin *life sciences professional, educator*
Tietjen, James *research institute administrator*

Merced
†Weir, Billy Louis *agricultural educator, researcher*

Modesto
Steffan, Wallace Allan *entomologist, educator*

Monrovia
Turner, Roger Orlando *microbiologist,quality assurance director*

Monterey
Packard, Julie *aquarium administrator*

Oakland
Dempster, Lauramay Tinsley *botanist*
Whitsel, Richard Harry *biologist, entomologist*

Orinda
Bowyer, Jane Baker *life science educator*

Pacific Grove
Epel, David *biologist, educator*
Powers, Dennis Alpha *biology educator*

Pacific Palisades
Lewis, Frank Harlan *botanist, educator*

Palm Desert
Sausman, Karen *zoological park administrator*

Palo Alto
Balzhiser, Richard Earl *research and development company executive*
Briggs, Winslow Russell *plant biologist, educator*
Eggers, Alfred John, Jr. *research corporation executive*
Elliott, David Duncan, III *science research company executive*
†Johnson, Noble Marshall *research scientist*
Krupp, Marcus Abraham *medical research director*
Pake, George Edward *research executive, physicist*
Wiedmann, Tien-Wen Tao *medical scientist, educator*
Zuckerkandl, Emile *molecular evolutionary biologist, scientific institute executive*

Pasadena
Allman, John Morgan *neurobiology educator*
Beer, Reinhard *atmospheric scientist*
Davidson, Eric Harris *molecular and developmental biologist, educator*
†Kent, Stephen Brian Henry *research scientist*
Lewis, Edward B. *biology educator*
North, Wheeler James *marine ecologist, educator*
Owen, Ray David *biology educator*
Rounds, Donald Edwin *cell biologist*
Stehsel, Melvin Louis *biology educator*
Wayland, J(ames) Harold *biomedical scientist, educator*

Pomona
Burrill, Melinda Jane *animal science educator*
Christensen, Allen Clare *agriculturist, educator*
Keating, Eugene Kneeland *animal scientist, educator*

Richmond
†Anderson, Thomas Robert *scientist, entrepreneur*
†Beall, Frank Carroll *science director and educator*

Riverside
Barnes, Martin McRae *entomologist*
Bartnicki-Garcia, Salomon *microbiologist, educator*
Bovell, Carlton Rowland *biology educator, microbiologist*
Clegg, Michael Tran *genetics educator, researcher*
Embleton, Tom William *horticultural science educator*
Erwin, Donald Carroll *plant pathology educator*
†Hall, Anthony Elmitt *plant physiologist*
Letey, John Joseph, Jr. *soil scientist, educator*
Page, Albert Lee *soil science educator, researcher*
Quinton, Paul Marquis *physiology educator*
Reuther, Walter *horticulture educator*
Sherman, Irwin William *biological sciences educator, university official*
Spencer, William Franklin, Sr. *soil scientist, researcher*
Talbot, Prue *biology educator*
Van Gundy, Seymour Dean *nematologist, plant pathologist, educator*
Zentmyer, George Aubrey *plant pathology educator*

Rohnert Park
Hermans, Colin Olmsted *biology educator*

Sacramento
†Areias, John Rusty *agriculturist, state legislator*

Saint Helena
Amerine, Maynard Andrew *enologist, educator*

Salinas
Shaver, Donald LaVergne *research agronomist, educator*

San Clemente
Walker, Joseph *retired research executive*

San Diego
Bieler, Charles Linford *development director, zoo executive director emeritus*
Crick, Francis Harry Compton *biologist, educator*
†Cross, C. Michael *marine museum administrator*
Eckhart, Walter *molecular biologist, educator*
Helinski, Donald Raymond *biologist, educator*
McGraw, Donald Jesse *biologist, historian of science, writer*
Myers, Douglas George *zoological society administrator*
†Risser, Arthur Crane, Jr. *zoo administrator*
Thomas, Charles Allen, Jr. *molecular biologist, educator*
Vause, Edwin Hamilton *research foundation administrator*
†Zedler, Joy Buswell *ecological sciences educator*

San Francisco
Agabian, Nina Martha *molecular biologist, biochemist, educator, parasitologist*
Anderson, David E. *zoological park administrator*
Antipa, Gregory Alexis *biology educator, researcher*
Bibel, Debra Jan *microbiologist, immunologist*
Blackburn, Elizabeth Helen *molecular biologist*
Calarco, Patricia Gillam *biologist, educator*
Cape, Ronald Elliot *biotechnology company executive*
†Chickering, Allen Lawrence *research institute executive*
Clements, John Allen *physiologist*
Dewitt, John Belton *conservation executive*
Eschmeyer, William Neil *marine scientist*
Furst, Arthur *toxicologist, educator*
Ganong, William F(rancis) *physiologist, physician*
Garoutte, Bill Charles *neurophysiologist*
Glass, Laurel Ellen *gerontologist, developmental biologist, physician, educator*
Goodman, Joel Warren *microbiologist, research scientist*
Herskowitz, Ira *educator, molecular geneticist*
Heyneman, Donald *parasitology educator*
†Iacono, James Michael *research center administrator*
Lyon, David William *research executive*
Marciano, Richard Alfred *research institute executive*
McKnight, Steven Lanier *molecular biologist*
†Mostov, Keith Elliot *cell biologist, educator*
Rector, Floyd Clinton, Jr. *physiologist, physician*

Vyas, Girish Narmadashankar *virologist, immunohematologist*
Wetzel, Cherie Lalaine Rivers *biologist*

San Leandro
Earle, Sylvia Alice *research biologist, oceanographer*

San Luis Obispo
Brown, Howard C. *horticulture educator, consultant*
Keil, David J. *biology educator, botanical consultant*

San Rafael
March, Ralph Burton *retired entomology educator*

Santa Barbara
Alldredge, Alice Louise *biological oceanography educator*
Badash, Lawrence *science history educator*
Childress, James J. *marine biologist, biological oceanographer*
Doutt, Richard Leroy *entomologist, lawyer, educator*
Philbrick, Ralph *botanist*
Schneider, Edward Lee *botanic garden administrator*

Santa Cruz
Beevers, Harry *biologist*
Dasmann, Raymond Fredric *ecologist*

Santa Monica
Augenstein, Bruno W. *research scientist*
Demond, Joan *marine biologist*
Shubert, Gustave Harry *research executive, consultant, social scientist*

Santa Rosa
Sibley, Charles Gald *biologist, educator*

South San Francisco
Levinson, Arthur David *molecular biologist*
Masover, Gerald Kenneth *microbiologist*

Stanford
Atkin, J. Myron *science educator*
†Banks, Peter M. *aerospace science director*
Bjorkman, Olle Erik *plant biologist, educator*
Campbell, Allan McCulloch *bacteriology educator*
Cavalli-Sforza, Luigi Luca *genetics educator*
Cohen, Stanley Norman *geneticist, educator*
Davis, Mark M. *microbiologist, educator*
Ehrlich, Paul Ralph *biology educator*
Feinstein, Joseph *electronics research manager*
Fernald, Russell Dawson *biologist, researcher*
French, Charles Stacy *retired biology educator*
Ganesan, Ann Katharine *molecular biologist*
Hanawalt, Philip Courtland *biology educator, researcher*
Long, Sharon Rugel *molecular biologist, plant biology educator*
Perkins, David D(exter) *geneticist*
Shapiro, Lucille *molecular biology educator*
Shooter, Eric Manvers *neurobiology educator, consultant*
Spudich, James A. *biology educator*
Yanofsky, Charles *biology educator*

Stockton
McNeal, Dale William, Jr. *biological sciences educator*

The Sea Ranch
Hayflick, Leonard *microbiologist, cell biologist, gerontologist, educator*

Thousand Oaks
†Malmuth, Norman David *program manager*

Tustin
Charley, Philip James *testing laboratory executive*

Vacaville
Erwin, Robert Lester *biotechnology company executive*

Ventura
Arita, George Shiro *biology educator*

Watsonville
Carpenter, Philip David *laboratory administrator, environmental and organic chemist*

Westlake Village
Small, Richard David *research scientist*

Westwood
Brydon, Harold Wesley *entomologist, writer*

COLORADO

Boulder
Byerly, Radford, Jr. *science policy official*
Clifford, Steven Francis *science research director*
†Danna, Kathleen Janet *virologist, plant molecular biologist, educator*
De Fries, John Clarence *behavioral genetics educator, institute administrator*
Derr, Vernon Ellsworth *government research administrator*
Glover, Fred William *artificial intelligence and optimization research director, educator*
†Hanley, Howard James Mason *research scientist*
Mc Intosh, J(ohn) Richard *biologist, educator*
Meier, Mark F. *research scientist, glaciologist, educator*
Serafin, Robert Joseph *science center administrator, electrical engineer*
Shanahan, Eugene Miles *flow measurement instrumentation company executive*
Staehelin, Lucas Andrew *cell biology educator*

Carbondale
Cowgill, Ursula Moser *biologist, educator, environmental consultant*

Colorado Springs
Engfer, Susan Marvel *zoological park executive*
Markert, Clement Lawrence *biology educator*

Colorado State University
†Whicker, Floyd Ward *biology educator, ecologist*

Denver
Freiheit, Clayton Fredric *zoo director*
Neville, Margaret Cobb *physiologist, educator*
Pfenninger, Karl H. *cell biology and neuroscience educator*
Puck, Theodore Thomas *geneticist, biophysicist, educator*
†Reidinger, Russell Frederick, Jr. *fish and wildlife scientist*
Talmage, David Wilson *microbiology and medical educator, physician, former university administrator*

Durango
Steinhoff, Harold William *retired research institute executive*

Fort Collins
Follett, Ronald Francis *soil scientist*
Hanan, Joe John *horticulture educator*
Keim, Wayne Franklin *retired agronomy educator, plant geneticist*
Maga, Joseph Andrew *food science educator*
Mortvedt, John Jacob *soil scientist*
Niehaus, Merle H. *agricultural educator, international agriculture consultant*
†Niswender, Gordon Dean *physiologist, educator*
Ogg, James Elvis *microbiologist, educator*
Peterson, Gary Andrew *agronomics researcher*
Quick, James S. *geneticist, plant breeder*
Roos, Eric Eugene *plant physiologist*
Seidel, George Elias, Jr. *animal scientist, educator*
Smith, Ralph Earl *virologist*
†Stendell, Rey *ecological research director*
Wilber, Charles Grady *forensic science educator, consultant*

Frisco
Bybee, Rodger Wayne *science education administrator*

Golden
Kazmerski, Lawrence Lee *scientist, research facility executive*
Stokes, Robert Allan *science research facility executive, physicist*

Grand Junction
Young, Ralph Alden *soil scientist, educator*

Greeley
Caffarella, Edward Philip *educational technology educator*

Livermore
Evans, Howard Ensign *entomologist, educator*

Westminster
Dotson, Gerald Richard *biology educator*

CONNECTICUT

East Glastonbury
Smith, David Clark *research scientist*

Farmington
Bronner, Felix *physiologist, biophysicist, educator, painter*
Rothfield, Lawrence I. *microbiology educator*

Groton
Routien, John Broderick *mycologist*
†Tassinari, Melissa Sherman *toxicologist*

Guilford
Baillie, Priscilla Woods *aquatic ecologist*

Hartford
Crawford, Richard Bradway *biologist, biochemist, educator*

Madison
Kilbourne, Edwin Dennis *virologist, educator*

Milford
†Calabrese, Anthony *marine ecologist*

Mystic
Connell, Hugh P. *aquarium executive*

New Haven
Adelberg, Edward Allen *genetics educator*
Altman, Sidney *biology educator*
†Bigland-Ritchie, Brenda R. *physiologist, neurophysiology researcher, educator*
Boulpaep, Emile Louis J. B. *physiology educator, foundation administrator*
Buss, Leo William *biologist, educator*
Chandler, William Knox *physiologist*
DuBois, Arthur Brooks *physiologist, educator*
Galston, Arthur William *biology educator*
Giebisch, Gerhard Hans *physiology educator*
Gordon, John Charles *forestry educator*
†Hoffman, Joseph Frederick *physiology educator*
Rawson, Robert Orrin *physiologist*
Sigler, Paul Benjamin *molecular biology educator, protein crystallographer*
Slayman, Carolyn Walch *geneticist, educator*
Smith, David Martyn *forestry educator*
Smith, William Hulse *forestry and environmental studies educator*
Stolwijk, Jan Adrianus Jozef *physiologist, biophysicist*
Summers, William Cofield *science educator*
Trinkaus, John Philip *cell and developmental biologist*
Waggoner, Paul Edward *agricultural scientist*

New London
Goodwin, Richard Hale *botany educator*

Southport
Hill, David Lawrence *research corporation executive*

Storrs
Marcus, Philip Irving *virology educator, researcher*

Storrs Mansfield
Anderson, Gregory Joseph *botanical sciences educator*
Guttay, Andrew John Robert *agronomy educator, researcher*
John, Hugo Herman *natural resources educator*
Koths, Jay Sanford *floriculture educator*
Laufer, Hans *developmental biologist, educator*

West Haven
Das, Rathin C. *molecular and cellular biologist*
Emerson, Thomas Edward, Jr. *cardiovascular physiologist*
Gerritsen, Mary Ellen *vascular and cell biologist*

DELAWARE

Newark
Borgaonkar, Digamber Shankarrao *cytogenetecist, educator*
Campbell, Linzy Leon *microbiologist, educator*
Haenlein, George Friedrich Wilhelm *dairy scientist, educator*
Mills, George Alexander *science administrator*
Somers, George Fredrick *biology educator*
South, Frank Edwin *physiologist, educator*

Wilmington
Hartzell, Charles R. *research administrator, biochemist, cell biologist*
Steinberg, Marshall *toxicologist*

Winterthur
Buchter, Thomas *horticulturist, garden director*

DISTRICT OF COLUMBIA

Washington
Affronti, Lewis Francis, Sr. *microbiologist, educator*
Aiuto, Russell *science educators association executive*
Anderson, Donald Morgan *entomologist*
Anderson, Owen Raymond *scientific and educational organization executive*
†Bellanti, Joseph A. *microbiologist, educator*
Bergmann, Fred Heinz *genetic scientist, government official*
Borgiotti, Giorgio Vittorio *research scientist, engineering consultant*
Brown, Lester Russell *research institute executive*
†Buffington, John Douglas *ecologist, researcher*
Case, Larry D. *agricultural education specialist*
Challinor, David *scientific institute administrator*
Cheney, Darwin Leroy *research foundation executive, medical educator*
Coleman, Bernell *physiologist, educator*
†Cooper-Smith, Jeffrey Paul *botanic garden administrator*
Corell, Robert Walden *science administration educator*
Crum, John Kistler *chemical society director*
Davis, Donald Ray *entomologist*
DeGiovanni-Donnelly, Rosalie Frances *biology researcher, educator*
DeJong, Gerben *hospital research executive*
Drouilhet, Paul Raymond, Jr. *science laboratory director, electrical engineer*
Du, Julie Yi-Fang Tsai *toxicologist, biochemist*
Elias, Thomas Sam *botanist, author*
†Eno, Amos S. *science foundation administrator*
Feulner, Edwin John, Jr. *research foundation executive*
†Finney, Essex Eugene, Jr. *agricultural research administrator*
Frederick, Lafayette *botanist*
Goldstein, Murray *health organization official*
†Gross, David Joseph *aquarium director*
Hazen, Robert Miller *research scientist, musician*
Henkin, Robert Irwin *neurobiologist, internal medicine, nutrition and neurology educator, scientific products company executive*
Hess, Wilmot Norton *science administrator*
Hope, William Duane *zoologist, curator*
Jacobs, Leon *medical research administrator*
†Kemnitzer, Susan Coady *science foundation administrator*
Kennedy, Eugene Richard *microbiologist, university dean*
Kenney, Richard Alec *physiology educator*
†Koven, Joan Follin Hughes *marine biologist*
Krombein, Karl vonVorse *entomologist*
†LaRoe, Edward Terhune, III *marine biologist, government official, educator*
Lilienfield, Lawrence Spencer *physiology and biophysics educator*
Little, Elbert Luther, Jr. *botanist, dendrologist*
Lovejoy, Thomas Eugene *tropical and conservation biologist, association executive*
MacLean, Paul Donald *government medical research institute official*
†Madden, Joseph Michael *microbiologist*
McGinley, Ronald James *entomologist, researcher*
Meyers, Wayne Marvin *microbiologist*
Moore, John Arthur *toxicologist, health science company executive*
Murphy, Robert Earl *scientist, government agency administrator*
O'Hern, Elizabeth Moot *microbiologist, writer*
O'Neil, Joseph Francis *association executive*
†Pinstrup-Anderson, Per *food scientist director*
Post, Boyd Wallace *forester*
Pyke, Thomas Nicholas, Jr. *government science and engineering administrator*
Ralls, Katherine *zoologist*
Ritter, Donald Lawrence *science foundation administrator, former congressman*
Roberts, Howard Richard *food scientist, association administrator*
Robinson, Michael Hill *zoological park director, biologist*
Schad, Theodore MacNeeve *science research administrator, consultant*
Schiff, Stefan Otto *zoologist, educator*
Simpson, Michael Marcial *science specialist, consultant*
Skog, Laurence Edgar *botanist*
Smith, Philip Meek *research organization executive*
†Sparrowe, Rollin D. *wildlife biologist*
†Stoner, Allan L. *science foundation director*
†Thomas, Jack Ward *wildlife biologist*
Tompkins, Daniel Reuben *horticulturist, research administrator*
†Torrey, Barbara Boyle *research council administrator*
Train, Russell Errol *environmentalist*
Trull, Francine Sue *research foundation administrator, lobbyist*
Wasshausen, Dieter Carl *systematic botanist*
West, Robert MacLellan *science education consultant*
Wilkinson, Christopher Foster *toxicologist, educator*
Woods, Walter Ralph *animal scientist, research administrator*

FLORIDA

Boca Raton
Reid, George Kell *biology educator, researcher, author*
Samuels, William Mason *physiology association executive*

Bonita Springs
Dacey, George Clement *retired laboratory administrator, consultant*

Boynton Beach
Mirman, Irving R. *scientific adviser*

Bradenton
Hare, John, IV *planetarium director*
Maynard, Donald Nelson *horticulturist, educator*
†Waters, Will Estel *horticulturist, researcher, educator*

Clearwater
Bramante, Pietro Ottavio *physiology educator, retired pathology specialist*
Whedon, George Donald *medical administrator, researcher*

Coral Gables
†Ladner, Robert Arthur, Jr. *research company executive*

Fort Pierce
†Herman, Richard J. *marine biology administrator*

Gainesville
Agrios, George Nicholas *plant pathology educator*
Besch, Emerson Louis *physiology educator, past academic administrator*
Cantliffe, Daniel James *horticulture educator*
Childers, Norman Franklin *horticulture educator*
Dilcher, David Leonard *paleobotany educator*
Drury, Kenneth Clayton *biological scientist*
Gerberg, Eugene Jordan *entomologist*
Gutekunst, Richard Ralph *microbiology educator*
Hoy, Marjorie Ann *entomology educator, researcher*
Locascio, Salvadore Joseph *horticulturist*
†Oberlander, Herbert *insect physiologist, educator*
Otis, Arthur Brooks *physiologist, educator*
Purcifull, Dan Elwood *plant virologist, educator*
Quesenberry, Kenneth Hays *agronomy educator*
Schmidt-Nielsen, Bodil Mimi (Mrs. Roger G. Chagnon) *physiologist*
Stern, William Louis *botanist, educator*
†Teixeira, Arthur Alves *food engineer, consultant*
†Vasil, Indra Kumar *botanist*
Wilcox, Charles Julian *geneticist, educator*

Gulf Breeze
Mayer, Foster Lee, Jr. *toxicologist*
Menzer, Robert Everett *toxicologist, educator*

Homestead
Roberts, Larry Spurgeon *zoologist*

Jacksonville
Bodkin, Lawrence Edward *inventor, research development company executive, gemologist*

Key Largo
Byrd, Mary Laager *life science researcher*

Lake Alfred
†Kender, Walter John *horticulturist, educator*

Lake Placid
Layne, James Nathaniel *vertebrate biologist*

Lakeland
†Niswonger, Jeanne Du Chateau *biologist, writer*

Leesburg
Crall, James Monroe *plant pathologist, plant breeder, educator*

Lehigh Acres
Moore, John Newton *retired natural science educator*

Longboat Key
Maha, George Edward *research facility administrator, consultant*

Melbourne
Abbott, Robert Tucker *zoologist, author*
Helmstetter, Charles Edward *microbiologist*
Storrs, Eleanor Emerett *research institute executive*

Miami
Bezdek, Hugo Frank *scientific laboratory administrator*
†Bunge, Richard Paul *cell biologist, educator*
Chavin, Walter *biological science educator and researcher*
Clark, John Russell *ecologist*
Colwin, Arthur Lentz *biologist, educator*
Correll, Helen Butts *botanist, researcher*
†Hayashi, Teru *zoologist, educator*
Myrberg, Arthur August, Jr. *marine biological sciences educator*
†Powers, Joseph Edward *marine biologist*
Zeigler, Cynthia Walker *zoological association executive*
Zeiller, Warren *former aquarium executive, consultant*

Miami Beach
†Abraham, William Michael *physiologist*

Naples
McCowen, Max Creager *research scientist*

North Miami
Polley, Richard Donald *microbiologist, polymer chemist*

Ona
†Rechcigl, Jack Edward *soil and environmental sciences educator*

Orlando
Andrews, Brad Francis *zoological park administrator*
Smith, Paul Frederick *plant physiologist, consultant*

Osprey
Cort, Winifred Mitchell *microbiologist, biochemist*

Pensacola
Ray, Donald Hensley *biologist*

Port Manatee
Falls, William Wayne *aquaculturist*

Port Richey
Baiardi, John Charles *retired scientific laboratory director*

Quincy
Teare, Iwan Dale *agronomy educator, research scientist*

Saint Augustine
Greenberg, Michael John *biologist, research director*

Saint Petersburg
Byrd, Isaac Burlin *fishery biologist, fisheries administrator*

Sarasota
Gilbert, Perry Webster *emeritus educator*
Mahadevan, Kumar *marine laboratory director, researcher*
Seibert, Russell Jacob *botanist, research associate*

Tallahassee
Friedmann, E(merich) Imre *biologist, educator*
Lipner, Harry *physiologist, educator*
†Makowski, Lee *science administrator, biology and chemistry educator*
†Meredith, Michael *science educator*
Taylor, J(ames) Herbert *cell biology educator*
†Williams, Theodore P. *biophysicist, biology educator*

Tampa
Baker, Carleton Harold *physiology educator*
†Lim, Daniel Van *microbiology educator*

Venice
Hardenburg, Robert Earle *horticulturist*

Vero Beach
Grobman, Hulda Gross (Mrs. Arnold B. Grobman) *horticulturist, retired public health educator*
Ward, William Binnington *agriculturist*

West Palm Beach
Sturrock, Thomas Tracy *botany educator, horticulturist*

Winter Haven
Grierson, William *retired agricultural educator*

Winter Park
Dawson, Ray Fields *research scientist, educator, consultant, tropical agriculturist*

GEORGIA

Alpharetta
Balows, Albert *microbiologist, educator*

Athens
Agosin, Moises Kankolsky *zoology educator*
Albersheim, Peter *biology educator*
Avise, John Charles *geneticist, educator*
Boyd, Louis Jefferson *agricultural scientist, educator*
Fuller, Melvin Stuart *botany educator*
Giles, Norman Henry *educator, geneticist*
†Green, Frank C. *agricultural administrator*
Hilton, James L. *plant physiologist, agricultural research administrator*
Odum, Eugene Pleasants *ecologist, educator*
Payne, William Jackson *microbiologist, educator*
Plummer, Gayther L(ynn) *climatologist, ecologist, researcher*
Pulliam, Howard Ronald *ecology educator*
Summers, Anne O'Neill *microbiology educator*
Van Eseltine, William Parker *microbiologist, educator*

Atlanta
Barnard, Susan Muller *zookeeper*
Brinton, Margo Ann *virology educator, researcher*
Brittain, James Edward *science and technology educator, researcher*
Circeo, Louis Joseph, Jr. *research center director, civil engineer*
†Clifton, David Samuel, Jr. *research executive, economist*
†Flemming, David Paul *biologist*
Humphrey, Charles Durham *microbiologist, biomedical researcher*
Jeffery, Geoffrey Marron *medical parasitologist*
Johnson, Barry Lee *public health research administrator*
La Farge, Timothy *plant geneticist*
Langdale, Noah Noel, Jr. *research educator, former university president*
Lucchesi, John C. *biology educator*
McGowan, John Edward, Jr. *microbiology educator*
Navalkar, Ramchandra Govindrao *microbiologist, immunologist*
Rucker, Charles Thomas *science facility administrator*
Spitznagel, John Keith *microbiologist, immunologist*
Tornabene, Thomas Guy *microbiologist, researcher, administrator*

Columbus
Riggsby, Ernest Duward *science educator*

Evans
Little, Robert Colby *physiologist, educator*

Griffin
†Arkin, Gerald Franklin *agricultural research administrator, educator*
†Doyle, Michael Patrick *food microbiologist, educator, researcher*
Duncan, Ronny Rush *agriculturist, reseacher*
Shuman, Larry Myers *soil chemist*
Wilkinson, Robert Eugene *plant physiologist*

Macon
Volpe, Erminio Peter *biologist, educator*

Norcross
†Darst, Bobby Charles *soil chemist, administrator*
Dibb, David Walter *research association administrator*

Sapelo Island
Alberts, James Joseph *scientist, researcher*

Stone Mountain
Wagner, Robert Earl *agronomist*

Tifton
Austin, Max Eugene *horticulture educator*
Douglas, Charles Francis *agronomist*
Miller, John David *retired agronomist*
†Rogers, Charlie Ellic *entomologist*

Watkinsville
Box, James Ellis, Jr. *research soil scientist*
†Langdale, George Wilfred *research soil scientist*

HAWAII

Aiea
Heinz, Don J. *agronomist*

Haleiwa
Woolliams, Keith Richard *arboretum and botanical garden director*

Hilo
†Nagao, Mike Akira *horticulturist, county administrator*

Honolulu
Abbott, Isabella Aiona *biology educator*
Alicata, Joseph Everett *microbiology researcher, parasitologist*
Ashton, Geoffrey Cyril *geneticist, educator*
Kamemoto, Fred Isamu *zoologist*
Kamemoto, Haruyuki *horticulture educator*
†Lamoureux, Charles Harrington *botanist, arboretum administrator*
Sagawa, Yoneo *horticulturist, educator*
Sherman, Martin *entomologist*
Smith, Albert Charles *biologist, educator*
Stahl, Margo Schneebalg *marine biologist*

IDAHO

Aberdeen
Sparks, Walter Chappel *horticulturist, educator*

Kimberly
†Carter, David LaVere *soil scientist, researcher, consultant*

Moscow
Crawford, Don Lee *microbiologist*
Roberts, Lorin Watson *botanist, educator*

Pocatello
Seeley, Rod Ralph *physiology educator*

ILLINOIS

Argonne
Schriesheim, Alan *research administrator*

Barrington
Rey, Carmen Rosello *food product researcher*

Batavia
Pewitt, Edward Gale *laboratory administrator, research physicist*

Brookfield
Rabb, George Bernard *zoologist*

Carbondale
Burr, Brooks Milo *zoology educator*
Mohlenbrock, Robert Herman, Jr. *botanist, educator*
Verduin, Jacob *botany educator*

Champaign
Batzli, George Oliver *ecology educator*
†Changnon, Stanley A., Jr. *research executive*
Easley, John Allen (Jack Easley) *science educator*
Levin, Geoffrey Arthur *botanist*
Ridlen, Samuel Franklin *agriculture educator*
†Smarr, Larry Lee *science administrator, educator, astrophysicist*
Smith, Robert Lee *agriculturalist*
Sprugel, George, Jr. *ecologist*

Chicago
†Altmann, Jeanne *zoologist, educator*
Altmann, Stuart Allen *biologist, educator*
Arzbaecher, Robert C(harles) *research institute executive, electrical engineer, researcher*
Beecher, William John *zoologist, museum director*
Buss, Daniel Frank *environmental scientist*
Chakrabarty, Ananda Mohan *microbiologist*
Charlesworth, Brian *biologist, genetics and evolution educator*
Cohen, Edward Philip *microbiology and immunology educator, physician*
Fisher, Lester Emil *zoo administrator*
Fuchs, Elaine V. *molecular biologist, educator*
Fukui, Yoshio *biology educator*
Greenberg, Bernard *entomologist, educator*
Haselkorn, Robert *virology educator*
Kass, Leon Richard *life sciences educator*
Lee, Bernard Shing-Shu *research company executive*
Mahowald, Anthony Peter *geneticist, cell biologist, educator*
†Marotta, Sabath Fred *physiology educator*
Mateles, Richard Isaac *biotechnologist*
McCrone, Walter Cox *research institute executive*
Miller, Patrick William *research administrator, educator*
Overton, Jane Vincent Harper *biology educator*
Pick, Ruth *research scientist, physician, educator*
Pumper, Robert William *microbiologist*
Roizman, Bernard *virologist, educator*
Rosenberg, Robert Brinkmann *research organization executive*
†Rymer, William Zev *research scientist, administrator*
Scott, John Brooks *research institute executive*
Van Valen, Leigh Maiorana *biologist, educator*
Wadden, Richard Albert *environmental science educator, consultant, researcher*

De Kalb
Zar, Jerrold H(oward) *biology educator, statistician*

Decatur
Harris, Donald Wayne *research scientist*

Evanston
Dallos, Peter John *neurobiologist, educator*
King, Robert Charles *biologist, educator*
Novales, Ronald Richards *zoologist, educator*
Wu, Tai Te *biological sciences and engineering educator*

Forest Park
Orland, Frank Jay *oral microbiologist, educator*

Glencoe
Taylor, Roy Lewis *botanist*

Highland Park
Dobkin, Irving Bern *entomologist, sculptor*

Lombard
Velardo, Joseph Thomas *molecular biology and endocrinology educator*

Macomb
†Anderson, Richard Vernon *ecology educator, researcher*

Maywood
Blumenthal, Harold Jay *microbiologist, educator*

Murphysboro
Miller, Donald Morton *physiology educator*

Peoria
†Dunkle, Richard L. *agriculturalist, researcher*
Grundbacher, Frederick John *geneticist, educator*

Springfield
Munyer, Edward A. *zoologist, museum adminstrator*

Urbana
Banwart, Wayne Lee *agronomy, environmental science educator*
Beavers, Alvin Herman *soil science educator*
Becker, Donald Eugene *animal science educator*
Bryant, Marvin Pierce *bacteriologist, microbiologist, educator*
Buck, William Boyd *toxicology educator*
Buetow, Dennis Edward *physiology educator*
Burger, Ambrose William *agronomy educator*
Chow, Poo *wood technologist, scientist*
Crang, Richard Francis Earl *plant and cell biologist, research center administrator*
Dickinson, David Budd, Jr. *horticulture educator*
Ford, Richard Earl *plant virologist, educator, academic administrator*
Frazzetta, Thomas H. *evolutionary biologist, functional morphologist, educator*
Friedman, Stanley *insect physiologist, educator*
Garrigus, Upson Stanley *animal science and international agriculture educator*
George, William Leo, Jr. *plant geneticist, educator*
Greenough, William Tallant *psychobiologist, educator*
Harlan, Jack Rodney *geneticist, emeritus educator*
Harper, James Eugene *plant physiologist*
Heichel, Gary Harold *agronomy educator*
Hixon, James Edward *physiology educator*
Hoeft, Robert Gene *agriculture educator*
Hoffmeister, Donald Frederick *zoology educator*
Horwitz, Alan Fredrick *cell and molecular biology educator*
Hymowitz, Theodore *plant geneticist, educator*
Knake, Ellery Louis *weed science educator*
Konisky, Jordan *microbiology educator*
Lodge, James Robert *dairy science educator*
Mc Glamery, Marshal Dean *agronomy, weed science educator*
Meyer, Richard Charles *microbiologist*
Nanney, David Ledbetter *genetics educator*
Ogren, William Lewis *physiologist, educator*
Prosser, C. Ladd *physiology educator, researcher*
Ramirez, Domingo Victor *physiologist, educator*
Rebeiz, Constantin Anis *plant physiology educator*
Ricketts, Gary Eugene *animal scientist*
Seigler, David Stanley *botanist, chemist, educator*
Shurtleff, Malcolm C. *plant pathologist, consultant, educator, extension specialist*
Splittstoesser, Walter Emil *plant physiologist*
Stout, Glenn Emanuel *water resources center administrator*
Todd, Kenneth S., Jr. *parasitologist, educator*
Waldbauer, Gilbert Peter *entomologist, educator*
Whitt, Gregory Sidney *molecular phylogenetics, evolution educator*
Wolfe, Ralph Stoner *microbiology educator*

Woodstock
Kuhajek, Eugene James *chemical research executive*

INDIANA

Bloomington
Clevenger, Sarah *botanist, computer consultant*
Gest, Howard *microbiologist, educator*
Hagen, Charles William, Jr. *botany educator*
Hegeman, George Downing *microbiology educator*
Heiser, Charles Bixler, Jr. *botany educator*
Hites, Ronald Atlee *environmental science educator, chemist*
Mc Clung, Leland Swint *microbiologist, educator*
Nolan, Val, Jr. *biologist, lawyer*
Preer, John Randolph, Jr. *biology educator*
Ruesink, Albert William *biologist, plant sciences educator*
Weinberg, Eugene David *microbiologist, educator*
Young, Frank Nelson, Jr. *biology educator, entomologist*

Butler
Ford, Lee Ellen (Leola Ford) *scientist, educator, retired lawyer*

Evansville
Denner, Melvin Walter *life sciences educator*
Guthrie, Catherine S. Nicholson (Catherine S. Nicholson-Guthrie) *research scientist*
Shaw, Margery Wayne Schlamp *geneticist, physician, lawyer*

Greensburg
Ricke, David Louis *agricultural and environmental consultant*

Indianapolis
Christian, Joe Clark *medical genetics researcher, educator*
Gehring, Perry James *toxicologist, chemical company executive*
Gibson, James Edwin *toxicologist*
Hodes, Marion Edward *genetics educator, physician*
Ochs, Sidney *neurophysiology educator*

Lafayette
Stob, Martin *physiology educator*

Madison
Hall, Marion Trufant *botany educator, arboretum director*

Muncie
Hendrix, Jon Richard *biology educator*
Henzlik, Raymond Eugene *zoophysiologist, educator*
Mertens, Thomas Robert *biology educator*

Notre Dame
Craig, George Brownlee, Jr. *entomologist*
Jensen, Richard Jorg *biology educator*
Pollard, Morris *microbiologist, educator*

West Lafayette
Allen, Durward Leon *biologist, educator*
Altman, Joseph *biological sciences educator*
Axtell, John David *genetics educator, researcher*
Barber, Stanley Arthur *agronomy educator*
Cochrane, Thomas Thurston *tropical soil scientist, agronomist*
Coolbaugh, Ronald Charles *botany educator*
Ferris, Virginia Rogers *nematologist, educator*
Franzmeier, Donald Paul *agronomy educator, soil scientist*
Harmon, Bud Gene *animal sciences educator, consultant*
Hodges, Thomas Kent *plant physiologist*
Janick, Jules *horticultural scientist, educator*
Johannsen, Chris Jakob *agronomist, educator, administrator*
Knudson, Douglas Marvin *forestry educator*
Le Master, Dennis Clyde *forest economics and policy educator*
Low, Philip Funk *soil chemistry educator, consultant, researcher*
Mannering, Jerry Vincent *agronomist, educator*
McFee, William Warren *soil scientist*
Mengel, David Bruce *agronomy educator*
Michaud, Howard Henry *conservation educator*
Ohm, Herbert Willis *agronomy educator*
Ortman, Eldon E. *entomologist, educator*
Schreiber, Marvin Mandel *agronomist, educator*
Sherman, Louis Allen *biologist, researcher*
Weaver, Connie Marie *foods and nutrition educator*
White, Joe Lloyd *soil scientist, educator*

IOWA

Ames
Anderson, Lloyd Lee *animal science educator*
Berger, P(hilip) Jeffrey *animal science educator, quantitative geneticist*
Black, Charles Allen *soil scientist, educator*
Bremner, John McColl *agronomy and biochemistry educator*
Burris, Joseph Stephen *agronomy educator*
†Cantrell, Ronald Paul *agronomy educator, plant breeder*
Fehr, Walter Ronald *agronomist, researcher, educator*
Freeman, Albert E. *agricultural science educator*
†Frey, Kenneth John *plant breeder, researcher*
Hallauer, Arnel Roy *geneticist*
Hatfield, Jerry Lee *plant physiologist, biometeorologist*
Isely, Duane *biology and botany educator*
Johnson, Lawrence Alan *cereal technologist, educator, researcher, administrator*
Kalton, Robert Rankin *crop scientist*
Karlen, Douglas Lawrence *soil scientist*
Keeney, Dennis Raymond *soil science educator*
Kirkham, Don *soil physicist, educator*
†Owen, Michael *agronomist, educator*
Redmond, James Ronald *zoology educator, researcher*
Thompson, Louis Milton *agronomy educator, scientist*
Voss, Regis Dale *agronomist, educator*
Wallin, Jack Robb *research plant pathology educator*

Willham, Richard Lewis *animal science educator*
†Young, Jerry Wesley *animal nutrition educator*

Cambridge
Frederick, Lloyd Randall *soil microbiologist*

Des Moines
Plambeck, Herbert Henry *agricultural consultant, retired government official*
Rogers, Rodney Albert *biologist, educator*
Rosen, Matthew Stephen *botanist, consultant*

Grinnell
Christiansen, Kenneth Allen *biologist, educator*

Iowa City
Hausler, William John, Jr. *microbiologist, educator, public health laboratory administrator*
Kessel, Richard Glen *zoology educator*
Milkman, Roger Dawson *genetics educator, molecular evolution researcher*
Osborne, James William *radiation biologist*
Wunder, Charles C(ooper) *physiology and biophysics educator, gravitational biologist*

Johnston
Duvick, Donald Nelson *plant breeder*

Waterloo
Kimm, Robert George *animal science educator*

KANSAS

Hays
Coyne, Patrick Ivan *physiological ecologist*

Kansas City
Behbehani, Abbas M. *clinical virologist, educator*
Clifford, James Michael *clinical research administrator*
Goldberg, Ivan D. *microbiologist, educator*
Greenwald, Gilbert Saul *physiologist*

Lawrence
Armitage, Kenneth Barclay *biology educator, ecologist*
Bovee, Eugene Cleveland *protozoologist, emeritus educator*
Byers, George William *retired entomology educator*
Johnston, Richard Fourness *biologist*
Michener, Charles Duncan *entomologist, biologist, educator*
Paretsky, David *microbiology educator*
Schiefelbusch, Richard L. *research administrator*

Manhattan
Barkley, Theodore Mitchell *biology educator*
†Ealy, Robert Phillip *horticulture and landscape architecture educator*
Johnson, Terry Charles *biologist, researcher*
Kirkham, M. B. *plant physiologist, educator*
Paulsen, Gary Melvin *agronomy educator*
Sears, Rollin George *wheat geneticist, small grains researcher*
Vetter, James L. *food research association administrator*

Mission
Novak, Alfred *retired biology educator*

Neosho Falls
Bader, Robert Smith *biology, zoology educator and researcher*

Shawnee Mission
†Goetz, Kenneth Lee *cardiovascular physiologist*

Topeka
Clarke, Gary Kendrick *zoologist*
†Karr, Gerald Lee *agricultural economist, state senator*

KENTUCKY

Lexington
Barnhart, Charles Elmer *animal sciences educator*
Bhattacharya-Chatterjee, Malaya *cancer research scientist*
Diana, John Nicholas *physiologist*
Frye, Wilbur Wayne *soil science educator, researcher, administrator*
Grabau, Larry J. *physiologist, educator*
Kasperbauer, Michael John *plant physiology educator, researcher*
†Knapp, Frederick Whiton *entomologist, educator*
Mitchell, George Ernest, Jr. *animal scientist, educator*
Pass, Bobby Clifton *entomology educator*
Pirone, Thomas Pascal *plant pathology educator*
Rodriguez, Juan Guadalupe *entomologist*
Schneider, George William *horticulturist, educator, researcher*
Shepherd, Robert James *plant pathology researcher, educator*
Zechman, Fred William, Jr. *physiologist, educator, administrator*

Louisville
Early, Glen Alan *biology educator*
Monroe, Burt Leavelle, Jr. *biology educator*

Richmond
Branson, Branley Allan *biology educator*

LOUISIANA

Baton Rouge
†Christian, Frederick Ade *entomologist, physiologist, biology educator*
Hansel, William *biology educator*
Larkin, John Montague *microbiology educator, researcher*
Liuzzo, Joseph Anthony *food science educator*
Patrick, William Hardy, Jr. *wetland biogeochemist, educator, laboratory director*
†Shaw, Richard Francis *fisheries administrator, oceanography educator*
Tucker, Shirley Lois Cotter *botany educator, researcher*

Boyce
Chilton, St. John Poindexter *former plant pathology educator, farm owner*

Covington
†Gerone, Peter John *microbiologist, research institute administrator*

Lafayette
†Stewart, Robert E. *ecological research director*

New Orleans
†Barkate, John Albert *microbiologist, food scientist*
Beard, Elizabeth Letitia *physiologist, educator*
Bennett, Joan Wennstrom *biology educator*
Christman, John Francis *science administrator, former university administrator*
Defenbaugh, Richard Eugene *marine ecologist*
Dickinson, Catherine Schatz *microbiologist*
Domingue, Gerald James *microbiology, immunology and urology educator, researcher, clinical bacteriologist*
Fingerman, Milton *biologist, educator*
Huot, Rachel Irene *cell biologist*
Ivens, Mary Sue *microbiologist, mycologist*
Navar, Luis Gabriel *physiology educator, researcher*
Orihel, Thomas Charles *parasitology educator, research scientist*
Spitzer, John J. *physiologist*
Welden, Arthur Luna *biology educator*

Shreveport
Jamison, Richard Melvin *virologist, educator*

MAINE

Bar Harbor
Hoppe, Peter Christian *biologist, geneticist*
Paigen, Kenneth *geneticist, educator*
Snell, George Davis *geneticist*

Brunswick
Huntington, Charles Ellsworth *biologist, educator*

Damariscotta
Hauschka, Theodore Spaeth *biologist, researcher, educator*

Falmouth
Oates, Maureen Katherine *environmental educator*

Lewiston
Chute, Robert Maurice *retired biologist, educator, poet*

New Vineyard
West, Arthur James, II *biologist*

Orono
Campana, Richard John *retired plant pathology educator, writer, consultant*
Knight, Fred Barrows *forester, entomologist, educator*

Salsbury Cove
†Dawson, David C. *marine biology adminstrator*

Waterville
Bennett, Miriam Frances *biologist, educator*

Wells
Neilson, Elizabeth Anastasia *health sciences educator, association executive, author, editor*

MARYLAND

Adelphi
Miller, Raymond Jarvis *agronomy educator*

Annapolis
Anderson, William Carl *association executive, environmental engineer, consultant*

Baltimore
Brady, Joseph Vincent *behavioral biologist, educator*
Brock, Mary Anne *research biologist, consultant*
Brown, Donald David *biology educator*
Brown, Nicholas *aquarium administrator*
Edidin, Michael Aaron *biologist*
Fowler, Bruce Andrew *toxicologist, marine biologist*
Gall, Joseph Grafton *biologist, researcher*
Goldberg, Alan Marvin *toxicologist, educator*
Habermann, Helen Margaret *plant physiologist, educator*
Hansen, Barbara Caleen *physiology educator, scientist*
Kelly, Thomas Jesse, Jr. *molecular biologist*
Kingsbury, David T. *microbiologist, science administrator*
Littlefield, John Walley *physiology educator, geneticist, cell biologist, pediatrician*
Mc Kusick, Victor Almon *geneticist, educator*
Nathans, Daniel *biologist*
Permutt, Solbert *physiologist, physician*
Pollard, Thomas Dean *biologist, educator*
Smith, Hamilton Othanel *molecular biologist, educator*
Suskind, Sigmund Richard *microbiology educator*
Trpis, Milan *vector biologist, scientist, educator*

Beltsville
Adams, Jean Ruth *entomologist*
Diener, Theodor Otto *plant pathologist*
Duke, James Alan *botanist, author, consultant*
Faust, Robert McNeer *science research administrator*
Foy, Charles Daley *research soil scientist*
Guttman, Helene Nathan *research executive*
Marten, Gordon Cornelius *research agronomist, educator, federal agency administrator*
Murphy, Charles Franklin *agriculturist*
Shands, Henry Lee *plant geneticist, administrator*
Terrill, Clair Elman *animal scientist, geneticist, consultant*

Bethesda
Bick, Katherine Livingstone *scientist, international liaison consultant*
Brady, Roscoe Owen *neurogeneticist, educator*
Bryan, Billie Marie (Mrs. James A. Mackey) *biologist*
Burg, Maurice Benjamin *renal physiologist, physician*
Butler, Sydney J. *zoological and aquarium association administrator*
Catravas, George Nicholas *biologist*
Cohen, Allan Yale *social science research administrator*
Collins, Francis S. *medical research scientist*
Dawid, Igor Bert *biologist*
Delappe, Irving Pierce *scientist, government official*
Dubner, Ronald *neurobiologist*
Duma, Richard Joseph *microbiologist, physician, pathologist, researcher, educator*
Eaves, George Newton *research administrator*
Frank, Martin *physiology educator, health scientist, association executive*
Fraumeni, Joseph F., Jr. *scientific researcher, medical educator, physician, military officer*
Gallo, Robert Charles *research scientist*
Garges, Susan *microbiologist*
Gartland, William Joseph, Jr. *research institute administrator*
Gilbert, Daniel Lee *physiologist*
Hancock, Charles Cavanaugh, Jr. *scientific association administrator*
Harding, Fann *health scientist, administrator*
†Hausman, Steven Jack *health science administrator*
†Hearing, Vincent Joseph, Jr. *cell biologist, researcher*
Hodgdon, Harry Edward *association executive, wildlife biologist*
Holmes, Randall Kent *microbiology educator, physician, university administrator*
Horakova, Zdenka Zahutova *retired toxicologist, pharmacologist*
Jackson, Michael John *physiologist, association executive*
Jordan, Elke *molecular biologist, government medical research institute executive*
Kelly, William Clark *science administrator*
Kety, Seymour S(olomon) *physiologist, neuroscientist*
Law, Lloyd William *geneticist*
Moskowitz, Jay *health sciences administrator*
Moss, Bernard *virologist, researcher*
Packard, Barbara Baugh *science institute administrator, physician, physiologist*
Petralia, Ronald Sebastian *entomologist, neurobiologist, educator*
Pospisil, George Curtis *biomedical research administrator*
Purcell, Robert Harry *virologist*
Robinson, David Mason *physiologist*
†Rosen, Saul Woolf *research scientist, health facility administrator*
Shulman, Lawrence Edward *biomedical research administrator, rheumatologist*
Sokoloff, Louis *physiologist, neurochemist*
Sponsler, George Curtis, III *research administrator, lawyer*
Stolz, Walter Sargent *health scientist administrator*
Varmus, Harold Eliot *microbiologist, educator*
Woolley, George Walter *biologist, geneticist, educator*
Wurtz, Robert Henry *physiologist, scientist*
†Yamada, Kenneth Manao *cell biologist*

Chester
Pelczar, Michael Joseph, Jr. *microbiologist, educator*

Chevy Chase
Choppin, Purnell Whittington *research administrator, virology researcher, educator*
Cowan, William Maxwell *neurobiologist*
Harter, Donald Harry *research administrator, medical educator*

Claiborne
Moorhead, Paul Sidney *geneticist*

Cockeysville Hunt Valley
Brown, Adrienne Jean *microbiology diagnostic testing company official*

College Park
Clark, Eugenie *zoologist, educator*
Colwell, Rita Rossi *microbiologist, molecular biologist*
Fanning, Delvin Seymour *soil science educator*
Gouin, Francis R. *physiologist*
Heath, James Lee *food science educator, researcher*
Olver, Frank William John *retired research educator*
Patterson, Glenn Wayne *botany educator*
Popper, Arthur N. *zoology educator*
Quebedeaux, Bruno *horticulture educator*
Stark, Francis C., Jr. *horticulturist, educator*
Vandersall, John Henry *dairy science educator*
Weil, Raymond Richard *soil scientist*

Columbia
Keeton, Morris Teuton *research institute director*

Frederick
Housewright, Riley Dee *microbiologist, former society executive*
Lewis, Robert Alan *biologist, environmental scientist, researcher, educator, administrator, author*
†Rice, Jerry Mercer *medical research center administrator*
Tidball, M. Elizabeth Peters *retired physiology educator, author*

Gaithersburg
†Buckley, Gerard Duke *science facility administrator*
McGarrity, Gerard John *microbiologist*
Semerjian, Hratch Gregory *research and development executive*

Garrett Park
Baldwin, Calvin Benham, Jr. *retired medical research administrator*

Hancock
Popenoe, John *horticultural consultant, retired botanical garden administrator*

Hyattsville
Ahl, Alwynelle Self *zoology, ecology and veterinary medical executive*

Kensington
Jackson, William David *research executive*

Laurel
Robbins, Chandler S(eymour) *research biologist*

Lutherville
Barton, Meta Packard *business executive, medical science research executive*

Potomac
Bollum, Frederick James *biotechnology executive*

Princess Anne
Adams, James Alfred *natural science educator*

Rockville
Gougé, Susan Cornelia Jones *microbiologist*
Landon, John Campbell *medical research company executive*
Lindblad, Richard Arthur *health services administrator, drug abuse epidemiologist*
Mertz, Walter *retired government research executive*
†Poljak, Roberto Juan *research director, biotechnology educator*
Rafajko, Robert Richard *medical research company executive*

Salisbury
Moultrie, Fred *geneticist*

Silver Spring
Hanson, Angus Alexander *geneticist*
Kohler, Max Adam *consulting hydrologist, weather service administrator*
Leedy, Daniel Loney *ecologist*
Phillips, Craig *aquarium administrator*

Sykesville
Buck, John Bonner *retired biologist*

Temple Hills
Whidden, Stanley John *physiologist, physician*

Walkersville
†Buterbaugh, Noel Lee *biotechnologist, health products executive*

MASSACHUSETTS

Amherst
Belt, Edward Scudder *sedimentologist, educator*
Coppinger, Raymond Parke *biologist, educator*
†Godfrey, Paul Joseph *science foundation director*
Hillel, Daniel *soil physics and hydrology educator, researcher, consultant*
Holmes, Francis William *plant pathologist*
Palser, Barbara F. *botany researcher, retired educator*
†Rohde, Richard A. *plant pathologist educator*
Stein, Otto Ludwig *botany educator*
Tippo, Oswald *botanist, educator, university administrator*
Zimmerman, William Frederick *biology educator*

Bedford
Griffin, Donald R(edfield) *zoology educator*

Beverly
†Roberts, Richard John *molecular biologist*

Billerica
Kolb, Charles Eugene *research corporation executive*
LeCompte, Malcolm Aaron *research scientist*

Boston
Barger, A(braham) Clifford *physiology educator*
Broitman, Selwyn Arthur *microbiologist, educator*
Cohen, Jonathan Brewer *molecular neurobiologist, biochemist*
Davison, Peter Fitzgerald *retired science administrator, consultant*
Essex, Myron Elmer *microbiology educator*
Fields, Bernard Nathan *microbiologist, physician*
Gibbons, Ronald John *microbiologist, educator*
Green, Howard *cellular physiologist, educator, administrator*
Hornig, Donald Frederick *scientist*
Hubel, David Hunter *physiologist, educator*
Kahn, Carl Ronald *research laboratory administrator*
Kunkel, Louis Martens *research scientist, educator*
Lees, Sidney *research facility administrator, bioengineering educator*
Malamy, Michael Howard *molecular biology educator*
Park, James Theodore *microbiologist, educator*
Peterson, Roger Tory *ornithologist, artist*
Prescott, John Hernage *aquarium executive*
†Prior, Ronald L. *animal scientist, nutritionist*
Sager, Ruth *geneticist*
Schaechter, Moselio *microbiology educator*
Slechta, Robert Frank *biologist, educator*
Stern, Ernest *science research executive, electrical engineer*

Cambridge
Allen, Lew, Jr. *laboratory executive, former air force officer*
Baltimore, David *microbiologist, educator*
Bazzaz, Fakhri A. *plant biology educator, administrator*
Beranek, Leo Leroy *scientific foundation executive, engineering consultant*
Berg, Howard C. *biology educator*
Bogorad, Lawrence *biologist*
Cumings, Edwin Harlan *biology educator*
†Demain, Arnold Lester *microbiologist, educator*
Dowling, John Elliott *biology educator*
Einsweiler, Robert Charles *research director*
Erikson, Raymond Leo *biology educator*

†Fink, Gerald Ralph *geneticist, biochemist*
Forman, Richard T. T. *ecology educator*
Fox, Maurice Sanford *molecular biologist, educator*
Gage, (Leonard) Patrick *corporate research executive*
Gilbert, Walter *molecular biologist, educator*
Goldberg, Ray Allan *agribusiness educator*
Goldblith, Samuel Abraham *food science educator*
Goldman, Ralph Frederick *research physiologist, educator*
Hartl, Daniel Lee *genetics educator*
Hastings, John Woodland *biologist, educator*
Holberton, Philip Vaughan *biotechnology company executive*
Horvitz, Howard Robert *biology educator, researcher*
Hubbard, Ruth *biology educator*
Hynes, Richard Olding *biology educator*
Jacobson, Ralph Henry *laboratory executive, former air force officer*
Knoll, Andrew Herbert *biology educator*
Lerman, Leonard Solomon *science educator, scientist*
Levi, Herbert Walter *biologist, educator*
Lodish, Harvey Franklin *biologist, educator*
Lynch, Harry James *biologist*
Magee, John Francis *research company executive*
Maniatis, Thomas Peter *molecular biology educator*
Mayr, Ernst *emeritus zoology educator, author*
McMahon, Thomas Arthur *biology and applied mechanics educator*
Mendelsohn, Everett Irwin *science educator*
†Mulligan, Richard C. *molecular biology educator*
Pardue, Mary Lou *biology educator*
Pfister, Donald Henry *biology educator*
Pierce, Naomi Ellen *biology educator, researcher*
Rich, Alexander *molecular biologist, educator*
Robbins, Phillips Wesley *biology educator*
Schultes, Richard Evans *ethnobotanist, museum executive, educator, conservationist*
Tannenbaum, Steven Robert *toxicologist, chemist*
Tonegawa, Susumu *biology educator*
Torriani-Gorini, Annamaria *microbiologist*
Tsipis, Kosta Michael *science educator*
Wachman, Harold Yehuda *space environmental sciences educator*
Wilson, Edward Osborne *biologist, educator*
Wogan, Gerald Norman *toxicology educator*

Canton
Lyman, Charles Peirson *comparative physiologist*

Grafton
Haggerty, John Edward *former army officer, research center administrator*

Jamaica Plain
Cook, Robert Edward *plant ecology researcher, educator*

Lenox
Stonier, Tom *educator, author*

Lexington
Gibbs, Martin *biologist, educator*
Melngailis, Ivars *solid state research executive*

Lowell
Coleman, Robert Marshall *biology educator*

Mashpee
Stauffer, Robert Allen *former research company executive*

Medford
Hecht, Norman Bernard *biology educator*

North Falmouth
Morse, Robert Warren *research administrator*

Northampton
Burk, Carl John *biological sciences educator*
Munson, Richard Howard *horticulturist*
Olivo, Margaret Ellen Anderson (Margaret Ellen Anderson) *physiologist, educator*

Norwood
Pence, Robert Dudley *biomedical research administrator, hospital administrator*

Reading
Gelb, Arthur *science association executive, electrical and systems engineer*

Shrewsbury
†Pederson, Thoru Judd *biologist, research institute director*

Vineyard Haven
Billingham, Rupert Everett *zoologist, educator*

Waltham
Decker, C(harles) David *research and development executive*
Fulton, Chandler Montgomery *cell biologist*
Ganong, William Francis, III *speech sciences research executive*
Gerety, Robert John *microbiologist, pharmaceutical company executive, pediatrician, vaccinologist*
Huxley, Hugh Esmor *molecular biologist, educator*
Schiff, Jerome Arnold *biologist, educator*

Watertown
†El-Bisi, Hamed Mohamed *scientist*

West Falmouth
Vaccaro, Ralph Francis *marine biologist*

Westborough
Nichols, Guy W. *institute executive, former utilities executive*
†Nichols, Guy Warren *science administrator*

Williamstown
†Art, Henry Warren *biology educator*

Woods Hole
†Broadus, James Matthew *research center administrator*
Burris, John Edward *biologist*
Copeland, Donald Eugene *research marine biologist*
Ebert, James David *research biologist, educator*
Grice, George Daniel *marine biologist, science administrator*
Inoué, Shinya *microscopy and cell biology scientist, educator*
Woodwell, George Masters *ecologist, educator, author, lecturer*

Worcester
Bagshaw, Joseph Charles *molecular biologist, educator*

MICHIGAN

Ann Arbor
Allen, Sally Lyman *biologist*
†Anderson, William R. *biologist, educator, curator, director*
Beeton, Alfred Merle *laboratory director, limnologist, educator*
Bryant, Barbara Everitt *academic researcher, market research consultant, former federal agency administrator*
Cantrall, Irving J(ames) *entomologist, educator*
Davenport, Horace Willard *physiologist*
Dawson, William Ryan *zoology educator*
Easter, Stephen Sherman, Jr. *biology educator*
Evans, Francis Cope *ecologist*
Faulkner, John Arthur *physiologist, educator*
Gans, Carl *zoologist, educator*
Gelehrter, Thomas David *medical and genetics educator, physician*
Ginsburg, David *human genetics educator, researcher*
Goad, Linda May *research scientist*
Horowitz, Samuel Boris *biomedical researcher, educational consultant*
Kaufman, Peter Bishop *biological sciences educator*
Kleinsmith, Lewis Joel *cell biologist, educator*
†Knox, Eric *botanist, educator*
Kostyo, Jack Lawrence *physiology educator*
†Moll, Russell Addison *aquatic ecologist, science administrator*
Moore, Thomas E. *biology educator, museum director*
Neidhardt, Frederick Carl *microbiologist*
Ning, Xue-Han (Hsueh-Han Ning) *physiologist, researcher*
Richardson, Rudy James *toxicology and neurosciences educator*
Savageau, Michael Antonio *microbiology and immunology educator*
Shappirio, David Gordon *biologist, educator*
Steiner, Erich Ernst *botany educator*
Wagner, Warren Herbert, Jr. *botanist, educator*
Williams, John Andrew *physiology educator, consultant*

Big Rapids
Barnes, Isabel Janet *microbiology educator, college dean*

Dearborn
Schneider, Michael Joseph *biologist*

Detroit
Jeffries, Charles Dean *microbiology educator, scientist*
†Krawetz, Stephen Andrew *molecular biology and genetics educator*
Lerner, Stephen Alexander *microbiologist, physician, educator*
Novak, Raymond Francis *research institute director, pharmacology educator*
Phillis, John Whitfield *physiologist, educator*

East Lansing
Bergen, Werner Gerhard *animal science educator, nutritionist*
Bukovac, Martin John *horticulturist, educator*
Butcher, James Walter *biologist*
Dennis, Frank George, Jr. *horticulture educator*
Fischer, Lawrence Joseph *toxicologist, educator*
Fromm, Paul Oliver *physiology educator*
Gast, Robert Gale *agriculture educator, experiment station administrator*
Gerhardt, Philipp *microbiologist, educator*
Hackel, Emanuel *science educator*
Hildebrand, Verna Lee *human ecology educator*
†Keegstra, Kenneth G. *botany administrator*
Kende, Hans Janos *plant physiology educator*
Lockwood, John LeBaron *plant pathologist*
Lucas, Robert Elmer *soil scientist*
Lund, Lois Ann *food science and human nutrition educator*
McMeekin, Dorothy *botany, plant pathology educator*
Nelson, Ronald Harvey *animal science educator, researcher*
Ries, Stanley K. *plant physiologist, university educator*
Root-Bernstein, Robert Scott *biologist, educator*
Sparks, Harvey Vise, Jr. *physiologist*
Telewski, Frank William *botanical garden administrator, researcher*
Tesar, Milo Benjamin *agricultural researcher and educator*
Velicer, Leland Frank *veterinarian, microbiologist, virologist, educator*

Hickory Corners
Lauff, George Howard *biologist*

Kalamazoo
Marshall, Vincent de Paul *industrial microbiologist, researcher*

Rochester
Unakar, Nalin Jayantilal *biological sciences educator*

Ypsilanti
Caswell, Herbert Hall, Jr. *retired biology educator*

MINNESOTA

Duluth
Johnson, Arthur Gilbert *microbiology educator*

Marcell
Aldrich, Richard John *agronomist, educator*

Minneapolis
Dworkin, Martin *microbiologist, educator*
Garry, Vincent Ferrer *environmental toxicology researcher, educator*
†Giere, Ronald Nelson *research director, philosophy educator*
Gorham, Eville *science educator*
Grim, Eugene Donald *physiology educator*
Haase, Ashley Thomson *microbiology educator, scientist*
Kallok, Michael John *physiologist, research administrator*
Meyer, Maurice Wesley *physiologist, dentist, neurologist*
Olson, Theodore Alexander *former environmental biology educator*
Pflug, Irving John *food scientist, engineer, educator*
Rahman, Yueh-Erh *biologist*
Reynolds, David G(eorge) *physiologist, educator*
Tordoff, Harrison Bruce *retired zoologist, educator*
Tufte, Obert Norman *retired research executive*
Watson, Dennis Wallace *microbiology educator, scientist*

Moorhead
Gee, Robert LeRoy *agriculturist, dairy farmer*

Northfield
Burton, Alice Jean *biology educator*

Rochester
Shepherd, John Thompson *physiologist*
Szurszewski, Joseph Henry *physiologist*
†Wood, Earl Howard *physiologist, educator*

Saint Paul
Baker, Donald Gardner *soil science educator*
Barnwell, Franklin Hershel *zoology educator*
Burnside, Orvin Charles *agronomy educator, researcher*
Caldwell, Elwood Fleming *food science educator, researcher, editor*
Cheng, H(wei) H(sien) *agriculture and environmental science educator*
Chiang, Huai Chang *entomologist, educator*
Crookston, Robert Kent *agronomy educator*
Davis, Margaret Bryan *paleoecology researcher, educator*
Ek, Alan Ryan *forestry educator*
Enfield, Franklin D. *geneticist*
Herman, William Sparkes *zoology educator*
Jones, Richard Lamar *entomology educator*
Kommedahl, Thor *plant pathology educator*
Magee, Paul Terry *geneticist and molecular biologist, college dean*
McKinnell, Robert Gilmore *zoology, genetics and cell biology educator*
McLaughlin, David Jordan *botanist*
Phillips, Ronald Lewis *plant geneticist, educator*
Schafer, John Francis *plant pathologist*
†Schmitt, Michael A. *agronomist, educator*
Wendt, Hans Werner *life scientist*
†Wyse, Donald L. *agronomist, educator*

Shoreview
Briggs, Rodney Arthur *agronomist, consultant*

MISSISSIPPI

Jackson
Hutchison, William Forrest *parasitologist, educator*

Meridian
Blackwell, Cecil *science association executive*

Mississippi State
Dorough, H. Wyman *toxicologist, educator, consultant*
Hodges, Harry F. *agronomist educator, plant physiologist*

Oxford
†Foster, George Rainey *soil erosion research scientist*

Stennis Space Center
Baker, Robert Andrew *environmental research scientist*

Stoneville
†Hardee, D. D. *laboratory administrator*
†Ranney, Carleton David *plant pathology researcher, administrator*

University
Keiser, Edmund Davis, Jr. *biologist, educator*

Vicksburg
Gunnison, Douglas *microbiologist, researcher*
Mather, Bryant *research administrator*

MISSOURI

Cape Girardeau
Blackwelder, Richard E(liot) *entomologist, zoology educator, archivist*

Columbia
Blevins, Dale Glenn *agronomy educator*
Blount, Don H. *physiology educator*
Brown, Olen Ray *medical microbiology research educator*
Burdick, Allan Bernard *geneticist*
Calabrese, Diane Marie *entomologist, writer*
†Coe, Edward Harold, Jr. *agronomist, educator, geneticist*
Darrah, Larry Lynn *plant breeder*
Davis, James O(thello) *physician, educator*
Duncan, Donald Pendleton *retired forestry educator*
Finkelstein, Richard Alan *microbiologist*
Ignoffo, Carlo Michael *insect pathologist-virologist*
Lambeth, Victor Neal *horticulturist, researcher*
†Martin, Mark Edward *molecular biologist, biochemist*
Mc Ginnes, Edgar Allen, Jr. *forestry educator*
Merilan, Charles Preston *dairy husbandry scientist*
†Mitchell, Roger Lowry *agronomy educator*
Nelson, Curtis Jerome *agronomist, educator*
†Poehlmann, Carl John *agronomist, researcher*
Yanders, Armon Frederick *biological sciences educator, research administrator*

Kansas City
Cook, Mary Rozella *psychophysiologist*
Mc Kelvey, John Clifford *research institute executive*

Saint Charles
Radke, Rodney Owen *agricultural research executive*

Saint Louis
Allen, Garland Edward *biology educator, science historian*
Asa, Cheryl Suzanne *research biologist*
Curtiss, Roy, III *biology educator*
Ewan, Joseph (Andorfer) *botanist, biohistorian, research bibliographer*
Feir, Dorothy Jean *entomologist, physiologist, educator*
Green, Maurice *molecular biologist, virologist, educator*
Hamburger, Viktor *retired biology educator*
†Hermann, Robert R. *zoological park administrator*
Hoessle, Charles Herman *zoo director*
†Hunt, Carlton Cuyler, Jr. *physiologist, educator*
Laskowski, Leonard Francis, Jr. *microbiologist*
Raven, Peter Hamilton *botanical garden director, botany educator*
Sexton, Owen James *vertebrate ecology educator, conservationist*
Stahl, Philip Damien *physiology and cell biology educator*
Templeton, Alan Robert *biology educator*
Varner, Joseph Elmer *biology educator, researcher*

MONTANA

Bozeman
Dunkel, Florence Vaccarello *entomologist*
Hovin, Arne William *agronomist, educator*
†Pittendrigh, Colin Stephenson *retired biologist, educator*

Corvallis
Koch, Peter *wood scientist*

Hamilton
Munoz, John Joaquin *research microbiologist*

Helena
Opitz, John Marius *clinical geneticist, pediatrician*

Missoula
Jenni, Donald Alison *zoology educator*
Nakamura, Mitsuru James *microbiologist, educator*

Polson
†Stanford, Jack Arthur *biological station administrator*

Red Lodge
Kauffman, Marvin Earl *geoscience consultant*

NEBRASKA

Clay Center
†Laster, Danny Bruce *animal scientist*

Humboldt
Rumbaugh, Melvin Dale *geneticist, agronomist*

Lincoln
Adams, Charles Henry *retired animal scientist, educator*
Francis, Charles Andrew *agronomy educator, consultant*
Gardner, Charles Olda *plant geneticist and breeder, design consultant, analyst*
Hanway, Donald Grant *retired agronomist, educator*
Johnson, Virgil Allen *retired agronomist*
Jones, Alice J. *soil scientist, educator, federal agency administrator*
Massengale, Martin Andrew *agronomist, university president*
McClurg, James Edward *research laboratory executive*
Sander, Donald Henry *soil scientist, researcher*
Schmidt, John Wesley *agronomy educator*
Sheffield, Leslie Floyd *agricultural educator*
Swartzendruber, Dale *soil physicist, educator*
Thorson, Thomas Bertel *zoologist, educator*

Omaha
Andrews, Richard Vincent *physiologist, educator*
Badeer, Henry Sarkis *physiology educator*
Dubes, George Richard *geneticist*
Simmons, Lee Guyton, Jr. *zoological park director*

NEVADA

Las Vegas
Bishop, William Peter *research scientist*
†Hess, John Warren *scientific institute administrator, educator*
†Pridham, Thomas Grenville *research microbiologist*

Reno
Bohmont, Dale Wendell *agricultural consultant*
†Fox, Carl Alan *research institute executive*
†Gifford, Gerald Frederic *environmental program director*
Johnson, Arthur William, Jr. *planetarium executive*

NEW HAMPSHIRE

Durham
†Aber, John David *global ecosystem research adminstrator*
Berrill, Norman John *developmental biologist, writer, former educator*
Harter, Robert Duane *soil scientist, educator*
Pistole, Thomas Gordon *microbiology educator, researcher*

Hanover
Flaccus, Edward *retired biology educator*
Gilbert, John Jouett *aquatic ecologist, educator*
Lubin, Martin *cell physiologist educator*
Roos, Thomas Bloom *biological scientist, educator*
Spiegel, Melvin *retired biology educator*

Lebanon
Mc Cann, Frances Veronica *physiologist, educator*
Munck, Allan Ulf *physiologist, educator*

Sanbornton
Andrews, Henry Nathaniel, Jr. *botanist, scientist, educator*

Silver Lake
Pallone, Adrian Joseph *research scientist*

NEW JERSEY

Annandale
Rosensweig, Ronald Ellis *research scientist*

Camden
Kirk, James Robert *research development and quality assurance executive*

Chatham
Gonzalez, Efren William *science information services administrator*

East Brunswick
Chang, Stephen S. *food scientist, educator, researcher, inventor*

East Hanover
Nemecek, Georgina Marie *molecular pharmacologist*

Flemington
Umbreit, Wayne William *bacteriologist, educator*

Florham Park
Eidt, Clarence Martin, Jr. *research and development executive*

Fort Lee
Manniello, John Baptiste Louis *research scientist*

Highland Park
Green, James Weston *educator, physiologist*

Hoboken
Abel, Robert Berger *science administrator*

Jamesburg
Chase, Aurin Moody, Jr. *biology educator*

Madison
Campbell, William Cecil *biologist*

Metuchen
Stapley, Edward Olley *retired microbiologist, research administrator*

New Brunswick
†Day, Peter Rodney *geneticist, educator*
†Duell, Robert William *agronomist*
Ehrenfeld, David William *biology educator, author*
Funk, Cyril Reed, Jr. *agronomist, educator*
Hayakawa, Kan-Ichi *food science educator*
Karel, Marcus *food science educator*
Lachance, Paul Albert *food science educator, clergyman*
Maramorosch, Karl *virologist, educator*
Merrill, Leland Gilbert, Jr. *retired environmental science educator*
Psuty, Norbert Phillip *marine sciences educator*
Solberg, Myron *food scientist, educator*
Tedrow, John Charles Fremont *soils educator*

New Providence
Mitchell, James Winfield *science administrator*

Newark
Beyer-Mears, Annette *physiologist*
Chinard, Francis Pierre *physiologist, physician*

Piscataway
Denhardt, David Tilton *molecular and cell biology educator*
Messing, Joachim Wilhelm *molecular biology educator*
Passmore, Howard Clinton, Jr. *geneticist, biological sciences educator*
Pramer, David *microbiologist, educator, research administrator*
Schlesinger, Robert Walter *microbiologist, microbiology educator emeritus*
Witkin, Evelyn Maisel *geneticist*

Princeton
Cole, Nancy Stooksberry *educational research executive*
Cox, Edward Charles *biology educator*
†Fernandes, Prabhavathi Bhat *molecular biologist*
Harford, James Joseph *retired aerospace association executive*
Levine, Arnold Jay *molecular biology educator, researcher*
Morrill, William Ashley *research executive*
Seizinger, Bernd Robert *molecular geneticist, physician, researcher*
Shenk, Thomas Eugene *molecular biology educator*
Silhavy, Thomas Joseph *molecular biology educator*
Tilghman, Shirley Marie *biology educator*

Rahway
Linemeyer, David Lee *molecular biologist*
†Reynolds, Glenn Franklin *medicinal research scientist*

Stockton
Kent, George Cantine, Jr. *zoology educator*

Teterboro
Gambino, S(alvatore) Raymond *medical laboratory executive, educator*

Trenton
†Park, Carl S. *atmospheric research administrator*

Wayne
White, Doris Gnauck *science educator, biochemical and biophysics researcher*

Westfield
Stoudt, Thomas Henry *research microbiologist*

Woodbridge
Fee, Geraldine Julia *psychophysiologist*

NEW MEXICO

Albuquerque
Corliss, John Ozro *zoology educator*
Hsi, David Ching Heng *plant pathologist and geneticist, educator*
Narath, Albert *laboratory administrator*
Newsom, Melvin Max *research company executive*
Sanchez, Victoria Wagner *science educator*
Ward, Charles Richard *extension and research entomologist, educator*

Carlsbad
†Cooper, Richard *zoological park administrator*

Las Cruces
McCaslin, Bobby D. *soil scientist, educator*
Schemnitz, Sanford David *wildlife biology educator*

Los Alamos
Gregg, Charles Thornton *research company executive*

Santa Fe
Stevenson, Robert Edwin *microbiologist, culture collection executive*

NEW YORK

Albany
Hitchcock, Karen Ruth *biology educator, university dean, academic administrator*
Stewart, Margaret McBride *biology educator, researcher*

Baldwin
Lister, Bruce Alcott *food scientist, consultant*

Bedford Hills
Marshall, William Emmett *biotechnology company executive, biochemistry researcher*

Briarcliff Manor
Callahan, Daniel John *institute director*

Bronx
Conway, William Gaylord *zoologist, zoo director*
†Forero, Enrique *botanical garden research director*
Lattis, Richard Lynn *zoo director*
Lilly, Frank *oncogenetic biomedical researcher*
†Long, Gregory R. *botanic garden administrator*
Schaller, George Beals *zoologist*

Bronxville
Hutchison, Dorris Jeannette *retired microbiologist, educator*

Brooklyn
Altura, Burton Myron *physiologist, educator*
Carswell, Lois Malakoff *botanical gardens executive, consultant*
Gabriel, Mordecai Lionel *biologist, educator*
†Garibaldi, Louis *aquarium administrator*
Jacobson, Leslie Sari *biologist, educator*
Schiffman, Gerald *microbiologist, educator*
Sultzer, Barnet Martin *microbiology and immunology researcher, educator*
†Zuk, Judith *botanic garden administrator*

Buffalo
Bishop, Beverly Petterson *physiologist*
Duax, William Leo *biological researcher*
†Farhi, Leon Elie *physiology educator, researcher*
Ortolani, Minot Henry *zoo director*
Tomasi, Thomas B. *cell biologist, administrator*

Cobleskill
Ingels, Jack Edward *horticulture educator*

Cold Spring Harbor
Watson, James Dewey *molecular biologist, educator*
Wigler, Michael H. *molecular biologist*

Cooperstown
Harman, Willard Nelson *malacologist, educator*

East Patchogue
Metz, Donald Joseph *scientist*

East Setauket
Duff, Ronald G. *research scientist*

Flushing
Boylan, Elizabeth Shippee *biology educator, academic administrator*
Commoner, Barry *biologist, educator*
Schnall, Edith Lea (Mrs. Herbert Schnall) *microbiologist, educator*

Fredonia
Benton, Allen Haydon *biology educator*

Geneseo
Forest, Herman Silva *biology educator*

Geneva
Siebert, Karl Joseph *food science educator, consultant*
†Wilcox, Wayne F. *plant pathologist, educator, researcher*

Hamilton
Kessler, Dietrich *biology educator*

Homer
Gustafson, John Alfred *biology educator*

Ithaca
Adler, Kraig (Kerr) *biology educator*
Alexander, Martin *microbiology educator, researcher*
Ballantyne, Joseph Merrill *science educator, program administrator, researcher*
Bates, David Martin *botanist, educator*
Blackler, Antonie William Charles *biologist*
†Coffman, William Ronnie *plant breeding educator*
†Crepet, William Louis *botanist, educator*
Davies, Peter John *plant physiology educator, researcher*
Eisner, Thomas *biologist, educator*
Fick, Gary Warren *agronomy educator, forage crops researcher*
Foote, Robert Hutchinson *animal physiology educator*
Grunes, David Leon *research soil scientist, educator, editor*
Halpern, Bruce Peter *physiologist, consultant*
†Hardy, W. F. *biology administrator*
†Isaacson, Michael Saul *physics educator, researcher*
Jagendorf, Andre Tridon *plant physiologist*
Kennedy, Wilbert Keith, Sr. *agronomy educator, retired university official*
Kingsbury, John Merriam *botanist, educator*
Kosikowski, Frank Vincent *food scientist, educator*
Kramer, John Paul *entomologist, educator*
Kubota, Joe *soil scientist*
Ledford, Richard Allison *food science educator, food microbiologist*
Lengemann, Frederick William *physiology educator, scientist*
Mortlock, Robert Paul *microbiologist, educator*
Novak, Joseph Donald *science educator, knowlege studies specialist*
Pearson, Oscar Harris *plant breeder, geneticist*
Pimentel, David *entomologist, educator*
Plaisted, Robert Leroy *plant breeder, educator*
Seeley, Harry Wilbur, Jr. *microbiology educator*
†Staples, Richard Cromwell *microbiologist, researcher*
Walcott, Charles *ornithology laboratory administrator*
Wasserman, Robert Harold *biology educator*
Welch, Ross Maynard *plant physiologist, researcher, educator*

Millbrook
Likens, Gene Elden *ecologist*

New Hyde Park
Isenberg, Henry David *microbiology educator*

New Rochelle
Beardsley, Robert Eugene *microbiologist, educator*

New York
Anderson, O(rvil) Roger *biology educator, researcher marine biology*
Anderson, Sydney *biologist, museum curator*
Binkowski, Edward Stephan *research analysis director, lawyer, educator*
Blobel, Gunter *cell biologist, educator*
Bock, Walter Joseph *zoology educator*
Carlson, Marian Bille *geneticist, researcher, educator*
†Cheung, Ambrose Lin-Yau *microbiologist, researcher*
Chua, Nam-Hai *molecular biologist, educator*
Cohen, Joel Ephraim *scientist, educator*
Cronholm, Lois S. *biology educator*
†Darnell, James Edwin, Jr. *molecular biologist, educator*
Desnick, Robert John *human geneticist*
Despommier, Dickson Donald *microbiology educator, parasitologist, researcher*
Ellison, Solon Arthur *microbiology and dentistry educator*
†Gellman, Isaiah *science foundation*
Ginsberg, Harold Samuel *virologist, educator*
Godson, Godfrey Nigel *molecular geneticist, educator*
Grafstein, Bernice *physiology and neuroscience educator, researcher*
Hanafusa, Hidesaburo *virologist*
†Hirschhorn, Rochelle *genetics educator*
Hommes, Frits Aukustinus *biology educator*
Hutner, Seymour Herbert *microbiologist, protozoologist*
†Jagiello, Georgiana M. *geneticist, educator*
Kramer, Fred Russell *molecular biologist*
Lederberg, Joshua *geneticist, educator*
Luck, David Jonathan Lewis *biologist, educator*
Maas, Werner Karl *microbiology educator*
Manski, Wladyslaw Julian *microbiology educator, medical scientist*
†Marks, Andrew Robert *molecular biologist*
Michanowsky, George *research foundation executive, author*
Model, Peter *molecular biologist*
Nichols, Rodney Wayson *science and technology executive, policy analyst, former university administrator*
Nightingale, Elena Ottolenghi *geneticist, physician, administrator*
O'Neill, Harry William *survey research company executive*
Pietruski, John Michael, Jr. *biotechnology company executive, pharmaceuticals executive*
Pogo, Beatriz Teresa Garcia-Tunon *cell biologist, virologist, educator*
Pollack, Robert Elliot *biological sciences educator, writer, scientist*
Robbins, Edith Schultz *microscopy educator*
Rothman, James Edward *cell biologist, educator*
Rozen, Jerome George, Jr. *research entomologist, museum curator and research administrator*
Segal, Sheldon Jerome *biologist, educator, foundation administrator*
Shelanski, Michael L. *cell biologist, educator*
Siekevitz, Philip *biology educator*
Silverstein, Samuel Charles *cellular biology and physiology educator, researcher*
Stillman, Calvin Whitney *agricultural and environment educator*
Tietjen, John Henry *biology and oceanography educator, consultant*
Trager, William *biology educator*
†Underwood, Joanna DeHaven *environmental research and education organizations president*
Windhager, Erich Ernst *physiologist, educator*

Wynder, Ernst Ludwig *science foundation director, epidemiologist*
Young, Michael Warren *geneticist, educator*
Zinder, Norton David *genetics educator, university dean*

Newburgh
Turkenkopf, Iris Jane *biology educator*

Pearl River
Barik, Sudhakar *microbiologist, researcher*

Purchase
Ehrman, Lee *geneticist*

Riverdale
Friedman, Ronald Marvin *cellular biologist*

Rochester
Chang, Jack Che-man *photoscience research laboratory director*
Clarkson, Thomas William *toxicologist, educator*
Coleman, Paul David *neurobiology researcher, educator*
†Iglewski, Barbara Hotham *microbiologist, educator*
Morrow, Paul Edward *toxicology educator*
Muchmore, William Breuleux *zoologist, educator*

Saranac Lake
North, Robert John *biologist*

Stanley
Jones, Gordon Edwin *horticulturist*

Staten Island
†Wisniewski, Henryk Miroslaw *pathology and neuropathology educator, research facility administrator, research scientist*

Stony Brook
Briggs, Philip Terry *biologist*
Carlson, Elof Axel *genetics educator*
Kim, Charles Wesley *microbiology educator*
Lennarz, William Joseph *research biologist, educator*
Levinton, Jeffrey S. *biology educator, oceanographer*
Mc Hugh, John Laurence *marine biologist, educator*
†Rohlf, F. James *biometrician, educator*
Schubel, Jerry Robert *marine science educator, scientist, university dean and official*
Steigbigel, Roy Theodore *infectious disease physician and scientist, educator*
Williams, George Christopher *biologist, ecology and evolution educator*
Wurster, Charles Frederick *environmental scientist, educator*

Syosset
Hershey, Alfred Day *geneticist*

Syracuse
Burgess, Robert Lewis *ecologist, educator*
†Delmar, Mario *cardiac physiology educator*
Dunham, Philip Bigelow *biology educator, physiologist*
†Kriebel, Mahlon Edward *physiology educator, inventor*
McNaughton, Samuel Joseph *botany educator*
Phillips, Arthur William, Jr. *biology educator*
Russell-Hunter, W(illiam) D(evigne) *zoology educator, research biologist, writer*

Troy
Breed, Helen Illick *ichthyologist, educator*
Pfau, Charles Julius *biology educator, researcher*
Wilson, Jack Martin *university administrator, scientific association executive, physics educator*

Tuxedo Park
Heusser, Calvin John *biology educator, researcher*

Upton
Petrakis, Leonidas *research scientist, administrator*
†Shirane, Gen *science administrator*

Utica
†Antzelevitch, Charles *research center executive*

Valhalla
Ferrone, Soldano *microbiology and immunology educator, physician*

White Plains
Peyton, Donald Leon *retired standards association executive*
Theisz, Erwin Jan *scientist*

NORTH CAROLINA

Atlantic Beach
Barnes, James Thomas, Jr. *aquarium administrator*

Burlington
Tolley, Jerry Russell *clinical laboratory executive*

Cary
Mochrie, Richard D. *physiology educator*

Chapel Hill
Andrews, Richard Nigel Lyon *environmental policy educator, environmental studies administrator*
†Frankenberg, Dirk *marine scientist*
Gilbert, Lawrence Irwin *biologist, educator*
Hairston, Nelson George *animal ecologist*
Kuenzler, Edward Julian *ecologist and environmental biologist*
Manire, George Philip *bacteriologist, educator*
McBay, Arthur John *toxicologist, consultant*
Scott, Tom Keck *biologist, botanist, educator*
Shapiro, Lee Tobey *planetarium administrator, astronomer*
Stiven, Alan Ernest *population biologist, ecologist*
†Stumpf, Walter Erich *cell biology educator, researcher*
Warren, Donald William *physiology educator, dentistry educator*
Weiss, Charles Manuel *environmental biologist*

Durham
Billings, William Dwight *ecology educator*
Blum, Jacob Joseph *physiologist, educator*
Cook, Clarence Edgar *research facility executive*
Counce-Nicklas, Sheila Jean *cell biology educator*
Cruze, Alvin M. *research institute executive*
Culberson, William Louis *botany educator*
Gillham, Nicholas Wright *geneticist, educator*
Kramer, Paul Jackson *plant physiologist, educator, writer, editor*
Lieberman, Melvyn *biology educator*
Livingstone, Daniel Archibald *zoology educator*
McClellan, Roger Orville *toxicologist*
Naylor, Aubrey Willard *botany educator*
Nicklas, Robert Bruce *cell biologist*
Rouse, Doris Jane *physiologist, research administrator*
Sassaman, Anne Phillips *science administrator*
Schmidt-Nielsen, Knut *physiologist, educator*
Searles, Richard Brownlee *botany educator, marine biology researcher*
Somjen, George Gustav *physiologist*
Wainwright, Stephen A. *zoology educator, design consultant*
Wilbur, Karl Milton *zoologist, educator*

Elm City
Parker, Josephus Derward *horticulturist*

Greenville
Maier, Robert Hawthorne *biology educator*
Thurber, Robert Eugene *physiologist, researcher*

Pinehurst
Stroud, Richard Hamilton *aquatic biologist, scientist, consultant*

Raleigh
Atchley, William Reid *geneticist, evolutionary biologist, educator*
Bergsma, Daniel *retired medical foundation executive, consultant*
Bishop, Paul Edward *microbiologist*
Cockerham, Columbus Clark *retired geneticist, educator*
Cook, Maurice Gayle *soil science educator, consultant*
Cooper, Arthur Wells *ecologist, educator*
Cummings, Ralph Waldo *soil scientist, educator, researcher*
†Daub, Margaret E. *plant pathologist, educator*
Davey, Charles Bingham *soil science educator*
Dunphy, Edward James *crop science extension specialist*
Goodman, Major Merlin *botanical sciences educator*
Hardin, James W. *botanist, herbarium curator, educator*
Hodgson, Ernest *toxicology educator*
Kelman, Arthur *plant pathologist, educator*
Scandalios, John George *geneticist, educator*
Shih, Jason Chia-Hsing *biotechnology educator*
Speck, Marvin Luther *microbiologist, educator*
†Stoskopf, Michael Kerry *educator*
Stuber, Charles William *genetics educator, researcher*
Timothy, David H. *biology educator*
†Wilson, Richard Ferrol *plant physiologist, educator*
Wollum, Arthur George, II *microbiologist, researcher, educator*

Research Triangle Park
†Barrett, J. Carl *cancer researcher, molecular biologist*
de Serres, Frederick Joseph *genetic toxicologist*
Drake, John Walter *geneticist*
†Heck, Henry Darcy *toxicologist*
Herbert, George Richard *research executive*
Maroni, Donna Farolino *science administrator*
Wooten, Frank Thomas *research facility executive*

Southern Pines
Towell, William Earnest *forester, former association executive*

Wilmington
Brauer, Ralph Werner *physiologist, educator*
Roer, Robert David *physiologist, educator*

Winston Salem
Flory, Walter S., Jr. *geneticist, botanist, educator*
Herndon, Claude Nash *retired geneticist, physician*

Winterville
Myers, Robert Durant *biologist, research director, medical educator*

NORTH DAKOTA

Dunseith
Gorder, Steven F. *association administrator*

Fargo
Schmidt, Claude Henri *retired research administrator*
Williams, Norman Dale *geneticist, researcher*
†Zimmerman, Don Charles *plant physiologist, biochemist*

Mandan
Halvorson, Ardell David *research leader, soil scientist*

OHIO

Athens
Cohn, Norman Stanley *botany educator, university dean*
Ungar, Irwin Allan *botany educator*

Bowling Green
Clark, Eloise Elizabeth *biologist, university official*
Rockett, Carlton Lee *biological sciences educator*
Smith, Stan Lee *biology educator*

Cincinnati
Maruska, Edward Joseph *zoo administrator*
Nebert, Daniel Walter *molecular geneticist, research administrator*
Safferman, Robert Samuel *microbiologist*
Scarpino, Pasquale Valentine *environmental microbiologist*
†Schiff, Gilbert Martin *virologist, microbiologist, medical educator*
Sjoerdsma, Albert *research institute executive*
Sperelakis, Nicholas *physiology and biophysics educator, researcher*

Cleveland
Steinberg, Arthur G(erald) *geneticist*
Taylor, Steve Henry *zoologist*

Columbus
Bagby, Frederick Lair, Jr. *research institute executive*
Banwart, George Junior *food microbiology educator*
Deep, Ira Washington *plant pathology educator*
Disinger, John Franklin *natural resources educator*
Fawcett, Sherwood Luther *research laboratory executive*
Fry, Donald Lewis *physiologist, educator*
Glaser, Ronald *microbiology educator, scientist*
Kapral, Frank Albert *medical microbiology and immunology educator*
Lal, Rattan *soil scientist, researcher*
Logan, Terry James *agronomist educator*
Miller, Frederick Powell *agronomy educator*
†Morrow, Grant, III *genetecist*
Newcomb, Lawrence Howard *agricultural educator*
Olesen, Douglas Eugene *research institute executive*
Peterle, Tony John *zoologist, educator*
Pieper, Heinz Paul *physiology educator*
Reece, Robert William *zoological park administrator*
Reeve, John Newton *molecular biology and microbiology educator*
Roth, Robert Earl *environmental educator*
Triplehorn, Charles A. *entomology educator, insects curator*
Waldron, Acie Chandler *agronomy and entomology educator*
Warmbrod, James Robert *agriculture educator, university administrator*
Yohn, David Stewart *virologist, science administrator*
Zartman, David Lester *dairy science educator, researcher*

Dayton
Bigley, Nancy Jane *microbiology educator*
Isaacson, Milton Stanley *research and development company executive, engineer*
Martino, Joseph Paul *research scientist*
Thomas, Donald Charles *microbiology educator, former university dean and administrator*

Delaware
Burns, George Washington *retired botany educator*

Kent
Cooperrider, Tom Smith *botanist*

Oxford
Eshbaugh, W(illiam) Hardy *botanist, educator*
Heimsch, Charles *retired botany educator*
Miller, Harvey Alfred *botanist, educator*
Risser, Paul Gillan *botanist, academic administrator*
Williamson, Clarence Kelly *microbiologist, educator*

Powell
Hanna, Jack Bushnell *zoo director*
†Lombardi, Celeste *zoological park administrator*

Willoughby
Paine, Charles William Eliot *arboretum executive, horticulturist*

Wooster
Lafever, Howard Nelson *plant breeder, geneticist, educator*

OKLAHOMA

Edmond
Caire, William *biologist, educator, assistant dean*

Norman
Boke, Norman Hill *botanist*
Carpenter, Charles Congden *zoologist, educator*
Cross, George Lynn *foundation administrator, former university president*
Estes, James Russell *botanist*
Hinshaw, Lerner Brady *physiology educator*
Hutchison, Victor Hobbs *biologist, educator*
Mares, Michael Allen *ecologist, educator*
†Schnell, Gary D. *zoology educator, administrator*

Oklahoma City
Alexander, Patrick Byron *zoological society executive*
Branch, John Curtis *biology educator, lawyer*
Dell'Orco, Robert T. *cell biologist, researcher*
Scott, Lawrence Vernon *microbiology educator*
Scribner, Ronald Kent *microbiologist*

Ponca City
Bolene, Margaret Rosalie Steele *bacteriologist, civic worker*

Stillwater
Bantle, John Albert, II *zoology educator*
Campbell, John Roy *animal scientist educator, academic administrator*
Durham, Norman Nevill *microbiologist, scientist, educator*
Grischkowsky, Daniel Richard *research scientist, educator*
Langwig, John Edward *retired wood science educator*
†Nofziger, David Lynn *soil physicist, educator*
Owens, Fredric Newell *animal nutritionist, educator*

OREGON

Ashland
Coffey, Marvin Dale *biology educator*

Beaverton
Montagna, William *scientist*

Corvallis
Chambers, Kenton Lee *botany educator*
Frakes, Rod Vance *plant geneticist, educator*
Frazier, William A. *retired horticulturist*
Kronstad, Warren Ervind *genetics educator, researcher*
Moore, Thomas Carrol *botanist, educator*
Morita, Richard Yukio *microbiology and oceanography educator*
Pearson, Albert Marchant *food science and nutrition educator*
Somero, George Nicholls *biology educator*
Tarrant, Robert Frank *soil science educator, researcher*
Trappe, James Martin *mycologist*
Westwood, Melvin Neil *horticulturist, pomologist*
Young, J. Lowell *soil chemist, biologist*
Zauner, Christian Walter *exercise physiologist, exercise science educator, exercise rehabilitation consultant*
Zobel, Donald Bruce *botany educator*

Eugene
Holzapfel, Christina Marie *biologist*
Matthews, Brian W. *molecular biology educator*
Sprague, George Frederick *geneticist*

Gresham
Poulton, Charles Edgar *natural resources consultant*

Newport
Weber, Lavern John *marine life administrator, educator*

Pendleton
Klepper, Elizabeth Lee *physiologist*
Lund, Steve *agronomist, research administrator*
†Smiley, Richard Wayne *research center administrator, researcher*

Portland
Campbell, Charles Joy *fishery biologist*
†Cusma, Rena *zoological park administrator*
Hagenstein, William David *consulting forester*
†Spencer, Peter Simner *neurotoxicologist*

Yachats
Gerdemann, James Wessel *plant pathologist, educator*

PENNSYLVANIA

Collegeville
Popp, James Alan *toxicologist, toxicology executive*

Danville
Morgan, Howard Edwin *physiologist*

Douglassville
Burke, Peter Arthur *microbiologist, chemist*

Doylestown
Mishler, John Milton (Yochanan Menashsheh ben Shaul) *natural sciences educator, academic administrator*

Elkins Park
Fussell, Catharine Pugh *biological researcher*

Greensburg
Birchem, Regina *cell biologist, environment consultant, educator*

Grove City
Brenner, Frederic James *biology educator, ecological consultant*

Haverford
Allen, Theresa Ohotnicky *neurobiologist, consultant*
Thimann, Kenneth Vivian *biology educator*

Hershey
Rapp, Fred *virologist*
Stump, Troy Elwood *zoo director*

Huntingdon Valley
Liberti, Paul A. *biotechnology executive, inventor, entrepreneur, consultant*

Lewisburg
Harclerode, Jack Edgar *biologist*
Sojka, Gary Allan *biologist, educator, university official*

Media
Hand, Brian Edward *science association administrator*

Philadelphia
Bayer, Margret Helene Janssen *biologist, research scientist*
†Beauchamp, Gary Keith *physiologist*
Brinster, Ralph Lawrence *biologist*
Brobeck, John Raymond *physiology educator*
Brownstein, Barbara Lavin *geneticist, educator, university official*
†Cheston, Morris, Jr. *zoological park administrator*
Cheston, Warren Bruce *research institute administrator*
†Cox, Robert Harold *physiology educator*
Crowell, Richard Lane *microbiologist*
Davis, Robert Harry *physiology educator*
DiBerardino, Marie Antoinette *developmental biologist, educator*
Eisenstein, Toby K. *microbiology educator*
Erickson, Ralph O. *botany educator*
Fisher, Aron Baer *physiology and medicine educator*
Forster, Robert Elder, II *retired physiology educator*
Furth, John Jacob *molecular biologist, pathologist, educator*
†Goldman, Yale E. *physiologist, educator*
Hand, Peter James *neurobiologist, educator*
Janzen, Daniel Hunt *biology educator*
†Johnson, E. Marshall *biology educator, toxicologist*
Johnson, Elmer Marshall *toxicologist, teratologist*
Kaji, Akira *microbiology scientist, educator*
Kleinzeller, Arnost *physiologist, physician, emeritus educator*
Knudson, Alfred George, Jr. *medical geneticist*
Koprowski, Hilary *microbiology educator, medical scientist*
†Krutsick, Robert Stanley *science center executive*
Lefer, Allan Mark *physiologist*
Live, Israel *microbiologist, educator*
Lu, Ponzy *molecular biology educator*
Meyer, Paul William *arboretum director, horticulturist*
Niewiarowski, Stefan *physiology educator, biomedical research scientist*
Oppenheimer, Jane Marion *biologist, historian, educator*
Peachey, Lee DeBorde *biology educator*
Pepe, Frank A. *cell and developmental biology educator*
Perry, Robert Palese *molecular biologist, educator*
Porter, Roger John *medical research administrator, neurologist, pharmacologist*
†Rosenbloom, Joel *molecular biologist, educator*
Salmoiraghi, Gian Carlo *physiologist, educator*
Schaedler, Russell William *microbiologist, physicians, educator*
Shockman, Gerald David *microbiologist, educator*
Silvers, Willys Kent *geneticist*
†Skalka, Anna Marie *molecular biologist, virologist*
Thomson, Keith Stewart *science museum administrator, writer*
Young, Robert Crabill *medical researcher, science facility administrator, internist*
Yunis, Jorge Jose *geneticist, pathologist, educator*

Pittsburgh
Borle, André Bernard *physiologist*
Feingold, David Sidney *microbiology educator*
Fletcher, Ronald Darling *microbiologist*
Gollin, Susanne Merle *cytogeneticist, cell biologist*
Henry, Susan Armstrong *biology educator, university dean*
Ho, Chien *biological sciences educator*
Kaufman, William Morris *research institute administrator, engineer*
Kiger, Robert William *botanist, science historian, educator*
McGovern, John Joseph *former air pollution control association executive, consultant*
McWilliams, Betty Jane *science administrator, communication disorders educator, researcher*
†Oles, Paul Joseph *planetarium administrator*
Parkes, Kenneth Carroll *ornithologist*
Partanen, Carl Richard *biology educator*
†Taylor, D. Lansing *cell biology educator*
Youngner, Julius Stuart *microbiologist, educator*

Radnor
†Burns, Denver P. *forestry researcher*

State College
Bergman, Ernest L. *biologist*
Bittner, Carl S. *retired university educator*
Hettche, L. Raymond *research director*

Swarthmore
Flemister, Launcelot Johnson *physiologist, educator*
†Sawyers, Claire Elyce *arboretum director*

Titusville
Peaslee, Margaret Mae Hermanek *zoology educator*

University Park
Bollag, Jean-Marc *soil biochemistry educator, consultant*
Brenchley, Jean Elnora *microbiologist, researcher*
Buskirk, Elsworth Robert *physiologist, educator*
Cosgrove, Daniel Joseph *biology educator*
Dunson, William Albert *biology educator*
Fowler, H(oratio) Seymour *retired science educator*
Fox, Richard Henry *soil science educator*
Kim, Ke Chung *entomology and biodiversity educator, researcher*
Lindstrom, Eugene Shipman *biologist, academic administrator*
†Macdonald, Digby Donald *scientist, science administrator*
†Manbeck, Harvey B. *agriculturist, educator*
Maxson, Linda Ellen *biologist, educator*
Traverse, Alfred *palynology educator, clergyman*
Tukey, Loren Davenport *pomology educator, researcher*
Turgeon, Alfred Joseph *agronomy educator, head department*

Villanova
Steg, Leo *research and development executive*

Wayne
Hess, Eugene Lyle *biologist, retired association executive*

West Chester
Pollock, Roy Van Horn *pharmaceutical company animal health researcher*
Weston, Roy Francis *environmental consultant*

West Mifflin
Clayton, John Charles *scientist, researcher*

West Point
Hilleman, Maurice Ralph *virus research scientist*

Wilkes Barre
Ogren, Robert Edward *biologist, educator*

Willow Grove
Spikes, John Jefferson, Sr. *forensic toxicologist, pharmacologist*

RHODE ISLAND

Kingston
Goos, Roger Delmon *mycologist*

Providence
Gerbi, Susan Alexandra *biology educator*
Knopf, Paul Mark *immunoparasitologist*
Marshall, Jean McElroy *physiologist*
Rothman, Frank George *biology educator, biochemical genetics researcher, academic administrator*
†Vecchio, Anthony Joseph *zoological park administrator*

SOUTH CAROLINA

Charleston
Brusca, Richard Charles *zoologist, researcher, educator*
Burrell, Victor Gregory, Jr. *marine scientist*
Cheng, Thomas Clement *parasitologist, immunologist, educator, author*

Clemson
Hays, Sidney Brooks *retired entomology educator*
†Morr, Charles Vernon *food science educator*

Columbia
Abel, Francis Lee *physiology educator*
Cole, Benjamin Theodore *biologist*
Dawson, Wallace Douglas, Jr. *geneticist*
Vernberg, Frank John *marine and biological sciences educator*
†Watabe, Norimitsu *biology and marine science educator*

Conway
Moore, Richard Harlan *biologist, college administrator*

Florence
†Kittrell, Benjamin Upchurch *agronomist*

Greenwood
Fox, Richard Shirley *zoology educator*

Hilton Head
Adams, William Hensley *ecologist, educator*

Seneca
Wise, Milton B. *animal science educator*

Spartanburg
Leonard, Walter Raymond *retired biology educator*

SOUTH DAKOTA

Brookings
Hugghins, Ernest Jay *biology educator*
Morgan, Walter *retired poultry science educator*
Swiden, Ladell Ray *research center administrator*
Sword, Christopher Patrick *microbiologist, university dean*

Vermillion
†Langworthy, Thomas Allan *microbiologist, educator*

Volga
Moldenhauer, William Calvin *soil scientist*

TENNESSEE

Cookeville
Coorts, Gerald Duane *horticulturist, educator, college dean*

Knoxville
Conger, Bob Vernon *plant and soil science educator*
Holton, Raymond William *botanist, educator*
†Mc Hargue, Carl Jack *research laboratory administator*
Sharp, Aaron John *botanist, educator*
Williamson, Handy, Jr. *agricultural economist, educator*
Wust, Carl John *microbiology and medical biology educator*

Memphis
Bardos, Denes Istvan *research scientist, medical company executive*
Freeman, Bob A. *microbiology educator*
Howe, Martha Morgan *microbiologist, educator*
Miller, Neil Austin *biology educator*
Wise, George Urban *botanic garden administrator, horticulturist, entomologist*

Mount Juliet
Kerr, Charles Randall *florist*

Nashville
Granner, Daryl Kitley *physiology and medicine educator*
†Mosig, Gisela *molecular biology educator*
Orgebin-Crist, Marie-Claire *biologist*
Tomlinson, Gus *biology educator*
Wang, Taylor Gunjin *science administrator, astronaut, educator*

Oak Ridge
Auerbach, Stanley Irving *ecologist, environmental scientist, educator*
Boyle, William R. *science administrator*
Gooch, Patricia Carolyn *cytogeneticist*
Hosker, Rayford Peter, Jr. *air pollution research scientist*
†Kelly, James Michael *soil scientist*
Luxmoore, Robert John *soil and plant scientist*
Skinner, Dorothy M. *biologist, educator*
†Slusher, Kimberly Goode *researcher*
†Veigel, Jon Michael *corporate professional*

Sewanee
Croom, Henrietta Brown *biology educator*
Yeatman, Harry Clay *biologist, educator*

TEXAS

Abilene
†Fleshman, Jim J. *zoological park administrator*

Austin
Biesele, John Julius *biologist, educator*
Bronaugh, Edwin Lee *research scientist, consultant*
Bronson, Franklin H. *zoology educator*
†Brown, Richard Malcolm, Jr. *botany educator*
Delevoryas, Theodore *botanist, educator*
Durden, Christopher John *entomologist, paleontologist, museum curator*
Grant, Verne Edwin *biology educator*
Hubbs, Clark *zoologist, researcher*
Jacobson, Antone Gardner *zoology educator*
Kalthoff, Klaus Otto *zoology educator*
Northington, David K. *research center director, botanist, educator*
Park, Thomas Joseph *biology researcher, educator*
†Reeder, William Glase *zoologist, museum administrator*
Simpson, Beryl Brintnall *botany educator*
Starr, Richard Cawthon *botany educator*
Sutton, Harry Eldon *geneticist, educator*
Thornton, Joseph Scott *research institute executive, materials scientist*
Turner, Billie Lee *botanist, educator*
Walker, James Roy *microbiologist*
Wheeler, Marshall Ralph *zoologist, educator*

Brooks AFB
Convertino, Victor Anthony *physiologist, educator, research scientist*
Cox, Ann Bruger *biological scientist, editor, researcher*

Brownsville
Farst, Don David *zoo director, veterinarian*

Bryan
Röller, Herbert Alfred *biology scientist, educator*
Van Arsdel, Eugene Parr *tree pathologist, consultant meteorologist*

Bushland
Unger, Paul Walter *soil scientist*

College Station
Black, Samuel Harold *microbiology and immunology educator*
Borlaug, Norman Ernest *agricultural scientist*
Bryant, Vaughn Motley, Jr. *botany and anthropology educator*
Dixon, Joe Boris *soil science educator*
Fisher, Richard Forrest *soils educator, academic administrator*
Hall, Timothy C. *biology educator, consultant*
Harris, William James, Jr. *research administrator, educator*
Kohel, Russell James *geneticist*
Milford, Murray Hudson *soil science educator*
†Neill, William Harold, Jr. *biological science educator*
Rosberg, David William *plant sciences educator*
Sanchez, David Alan *science administrator*
Summers, Max (Duanne) *entomologist, scientist, educator*
Wilding, Lawrence Paul *pedology educator, soil science consultant*

Dallas
Bollon, Arthur Peter *genetic engineer, educator, biotechnology company executive*
Brown, Michael Stuart *geneticist*
†Hudspeth, Albert James *biomedical researcher, educator*
Mc Cann, Samuel McDonald *physiologist, educator*
Miller, William *science administrator*
Neaves, William Barlow *cell biologist, educator*
Norgard, Michael Vincent *microbiology educator, researcher*
Vanatta, John Crothers, III *physiologist, physician, educator*
†Vitetta, Ellen S. *microbiologist educator, immunologist*

Denton
Schwalm, Fritz Ekkehardt *biology educator*

Floresville
Alexander, William Carter *physiologist, educator*

Galveston
Baron, Samuel *microbiologist, physician*
Budelmann, Bernd Ulrich *zoologist, educator*
Giam, Choo-Seng *marine science educator*
Prakash, Satya *biology educator*
Santschi, Peter Hans *marine sciences educator*
Thompson, Edward Ivins Brad *biological chemistry and genetics educator, molecular endocrinologist, department chairman*
Würsig, Bernd Gerhard *marine biology educator*

Georgetown
Girvin, Eb Carl *biology educator*

Houston
†Ablott, Vance Randall *science foundation administrator*
Arntzen, Charles Joel *bioscience educator*
Brown, Jack Harold Upton *physiology educator, university official, biomedical engineer*
†Caskey, Charles Thomas *biology and genetics educator*
DeBakey, Lois *science communications educator, writer, lecturer, editor, scholar*
†Huntoon, Carolyn Leach *physiologist*
Jurtshuk, Peter, Jr. *microbiologist*
†Nichols, Buford Lee, Jr. *physiologist*
O'Malley, Bert William *cell biologist, educator, physician*
Schultz, Stanley George *physiologist, educator*

Irving
Potter, Robert Joseph *technical research and business executive*

Kerrville
†Kunz, Sidney *entomologist*

Lubbock
Dregne, Harold Ernest *agronomy educator*
Hentges, David John *microbiology educator*
Maunder, Addison Bruce *agronomic research company executive*
Schake, Lowell Martin *animal science educator*
Skoog, Gerald Duane *science educator*
Wendt, Charles William *soil physicist, educator*

Nacogdoches
Worrell, Albert Cadwallader *forest economics educator*

Overton
Randel, Ronald Dean *physiologist, educator*

Port Aransas
Wohlschlag, Donald Eugene *zoologist, marine ecologist, educator emeritus*

Richardson
†Gray, Donald Melvin *molecular and cell biology educator*

San Antonio
Betts, Austin Wortham *retired research company executive*
Blystone, Robert Vernon *developmental cell biologist, educator, textbook consultant*
Bowman, Barbara Hyde *biologist, geneticist, educator*
Burch, James Leo *science research institute executive*
Carson, Robin D. *zoological park administrator*
Deviney, Marvin Lee, Jr. *research institute scientist, program manager*
Donaldson, Willis Lyle *research institute administrator*
Gates, Mahlon Eugene *applied research executive, former government official, former army officer*
Goland, Martin *research institute executive*
Henderson, Arvis Burl *data processing executive, biochemist*
Kalter, Seymour Sanford *virologist, educator*
Lindholm, Ulric Svante *engineering research institute executive*
Masoro, Edward Joseph, Jr. *physiology educator*
Oujesky, Helen M. *microbiology educator*
Stone, William Harold *geneticist, educator*

The Woodlands
†Porter, W. Arthur *research center executive*

Tyler
Yaden, Senka Long *biology educator*

Warda
Kunze, George William *retired soil scientist*

Weslaco
†Amador, Jose Manuel *plant pathologist, research center administrator*
Collins, Anita Marguerite *research geneticist*
†King, Edgar G. *agricultural researcher*
Lingle, Sarah Elizabeth *research scientist*

UTAH

Logan
Bennett, James Austin *retired animal science educator*
Dorst, Howard Earl *entomologist*
Jackson, LeRoy Eugene (Lee Jackson) *microbiologist, researcher*
Rasmussen, Harry Paul *horticulture and landscape educator*
Salisbury, Frank Boyer *plant physiologist, educator*
Vest, Hyrum Grant, Jr. *horticultural sciences educator*

Ogden
†Lassen, Laurence E. *forester*

Provo
Blake, George Rowland *soil science educator, water resources research administrator*

Salt Lake City
Brierley, James Alan *research administrator*
Feucht, Donald Lee *research institute executive*
Roth, John Roger *geneticist, biology educator*
†Straight, Richard Coleman *photobiologist*

VERMONT

Burlington
†Albertini, Richard Joseph *molecular geneticist, educator*
Bartlett, Richmond Jay *soil chemistry educator, researcher*
†Heinrich, Bernd *biologist, zoology educator*
†Low, Robert B. *physiology educator*

Greensboro
Hill, Lewis Reuben *horticulturist, nursery owner*

Middlebury
Hitchcock, Harold Bradford *retired biology educator, zoologist*
Landgren, Craig Randall *biology educator*
Saul, George Brandon, II *biology educator*

South Burlington
Johnson, Robert Eugene *physiologist*

VIRGINIA

Alexandria
Woolley, Mary Elizabeth *research administrator*

Annandale
Faraday, Bruce John *scientific research company executive, physicist*

Arlington
Aukland, Elva Dayton *biologist, educator*
Bridgewater, Albert Louis *science foundation administrator*
Fraser, James Cavender *research center executive*
Gaines, Alan McCulloch *government official, educator*
Gottschalk, John Simison *biologist*
Haq, Bilal Ul *national science foundation program director, researcher*
†Knipling, Edward Fred *retired research entomologist, agricultural administrator*
Mense, Allan Tate *research scientist, engineer*
O'Neill, Brian *research organization administrator*
†Pitts, Nathaniel Gilbert *science and technology director*
Sullivan, Cornelius Wayne *marine biology researcher, educator*
Williams, Luther Steward *biologist, federal agency administrator*

Blacksburg
Barden, John Allan *horticulturist*
Colmano, Germille *physiology educator, biophysics researcher*
Cowles, Joe Richard *biology educator*
Siau, John Finn *wood scientist, educator*
Smeal, Paul Lester *retired horticulture educator*
Wilkins, Tracy Dale *microbiologist, educator*
Yousten, Allan Arthur *microbiologist, educator*

Charlottesville
Berne, Robert Matthew *physiologist, educator*
Block, Gene David *biologist, educator, science administrator*
Desjardins, Claude *physiology educator*
Friesen, Wolfgang Otto *biology educator*
Garrett, Reginald Hooker *biology educator, researcher*
Gottesman, Irving Isadore *psychiatric genetics educator, consultant*
Hamilton, Howard Laverne *zoology educator*
Hornberger, George Milton *environmental science educator*
Kadner, Robert Joseph *microbiology educator*
†Kelly, Thaddeus E. *medical geneticist*
Murray, Joseph James, Jr. *zoologist*
Shugart, Herman Henry *environmental sciences educator, researcher*
Somlyo, Andrew Paul *physiology, physics and cardiology educator*
Wagner, Robert Roderick *microbiologist, oncology educator*
Wright, Theodore Robert Fairbank *biologist, educator*

Chesapeake
Gibbs, William Eugene *scientific consultant*

Culpeper
Covey, Charles William *marine consultant*

Falls Church
Hart, C(harles) W(illard), Jr. *zoologist, curator*

Front Royal
Douglas, J(ocelyn) Fielding *toxicologist, consultant*

Gloucester Point
Perkins, Frank Overton *marine scientist, educator*
Roberts, Morris Henry, Jr. *marine biology educator*

Hampton
†Stern, Joseph Aaron *services contracting executive*

Lexington
Hickman, Cleveland Pendleton, Jr. *biology educator*

Mc Lean
Layson, William McIntyre *research consulting company executive*
Talbot, Lee Merriam *ecologist, environmental specialist, consultant*

Richmond
Bradley, Sterling Gaylen *microbiology and pharmacology educator*
Wolf, Barry *genetics, pediatric educator*
†Yu, Robert Kuan-jen *biochemistry educator*

Vienna
Giovacchini, Robert Peter *toxicologist, manufacturing executive, retired*
Jahn, Laurence Roy *retired biologist, institute executive*
Schneider, Peter Raymond *research scientist, juvenile justice consultant*

Virginia Beach
Merchant, Donald Joseph *microbiologist*

Williamsburg
Spitzer, Cary Redford *avionics consultant, electrical engineer*

WASHINGTON

Bellingham
Critchlow, B. Vaughn *research facility administrator, researcher*
†Landis, Wayne G. *environmental toxicologist*
Naylor, Harry Brooks *microbiologist*

Edmonds
Paul, Ronald Stanley *research institute executive*

Friday Harbor
Blinks, John Rogers *physiology and biophysics educator*

Port Angeles
Warren, Henry Clay, Jr. *naturalist*

Prosser
Miller, David Eugene *soil scientist, researcher*
†Proebsting, Edward Louis, Jr. *retired research horticulturist*

Pullman
Bertramson, B. Rodney *agronomist*
Hosick, Howard Lawrence *cell biology educator, academic administrator*
Nakata, Herbert Minoru *retired microbiology educator, academic administrator*
Schrader, Lawrence Edwin *plant physiologist, educator*

Richland
Colson, Steven Douglas *research director, chemistry educator*
Wehner, Alfred Peter *inhalation toxicologist, biomedical scientist*
Wiley, William Rodney *microbiologist, administrator*

Seattle
Alexander, Edward Russell disease research administrator
†Aron, William marine biology administrator
Bevan, Donald Edward retired marine science educator, university dean
Bronsdon, Melinda Ann microbiologist
Coyle, Marie Bridget microbiology educator, laboratory director
Davidson, Robert William science foundation director
Donaldson, Lauren R. fisheries biology and radiobiology educator emeritus
Edmondson, W(allace) Thomas limnologist, educator
Edwards, John Stuart zoology educator, researcher
Evans, Charles Albert microbiology educator
Gessel, Stanley Paul emeritus soil science educator
Groman, Neal Benjamin microbiology educator
Hille, Bertil physiology educator
Hood, Leroy Edward biologist
†Karr, James Richard ecologist, researcher, educator
Kruckeberg, Arthur Rice botanist, educator
Laird, Charles David zoology and genetics educator, researcher
Mc Donald, James Michael, Jr. research institute consultant
Motulsky, Arno Gunther geneticist, physician, educator
Nakatani, Roy Eiji biologist, educator
†Nester, Eugene William microbiology educator, immunology educator
Olstad, Roger Gale science educator
Orians, Gordon Howell biology educator
Scher, Allen Myron physiologist, educator
Smith, Orville Auverne physiology educator
Thomas, David Phillip forestry educator, college administrator
Tukey, Harold Bradford, Jr. horticulture educator
Wooster, Warren S(criver) marine science educator
Wott, John Arthur arboretum and botanical garden executive, horticulture educator

Tacoma
Champ, Stanley Gordon scientific company executive
Otten, Thomas zoological park director

WEST VIRGINIA

Beckley
†Baligar, Virupax C. research soil scientist
Voigt, Paul Warren research geneticist

Elkins
Van Gundy, James Justin biology educator

Fairmont
Shan, Robert Kuocheng biology educator

Morgantown
Hedge, George Albert physiologist
Keller, Edward Clarence, Jr. foundation executive, ecologist, statistician, geneticist, educator
Nath, Joginder genetics and biology educator, researcher
Ong, Tong-man microbiologist, educator
Smith, Robert Leo ecologist, wildlife biologist
Snyder, Irvin Stanley microbiologist, educator

WISCONSIN

Madison
Ahlquist, Paul Gerald molecular biology researcher, educator
†Armstrong, Gregory Davenport arboretum administrator
Arny, Deane Cedric former plant pathology educator, researcher
Barnes, Robert F agronomist
Beck, Stanley Dwight retired entomology educator, researcher
Bisgard, Gerald Edwin biosciences educator, researcher
Bjoraker, Walter Thomas agricultural and vocational educator emeritus
Brock, Thomas Dale microbiology educator
Bula, Raymond J. agronomist
Burkholder, Wendell Eugene entomologist
Cassens, Robert Gene food scientist
Cliver, Dean Otis virologist, educator
Crow, James Franklin retired genetics educator
Daie, Jaleh science educator, administrator, researcher
Gilboe, David Dougherty physiology educator
Goodman, Robert Merwin agriculturalist, plant biologist, university educator
Greaser, Marion Lewis science educator
Hagedorn, Donald James phytopathologist, educator, agricultural consultant
Hall, David Charles zoo director, veterinarian
Hinsdill, Ronald Dwight bacteriology educator, immunotoxicologist
Hopen, Herbert John horticulture educator
Jackson, Marion Leroy agronomist, soil scientist
Jeanne, Robert Lawrence entomologist, educator, researcher
Kaesberg, Paul Joseph virology researcher
†Kelling, Keith A. soil scientist
Kirk, Thomas Kent research scientist
Koval, Charles Francis entomologist, agricultural administrator, educator
Lower, Richard Lawrence horticulture educator, researcher
Marth, Elmer Herman bacteriologist, educator
McCabe, Robert Albert wildlife ecology educator
Nelson, Oliver Evans, Jr. geneticist, educator
Newcomb, Eldon Henry retired botany educator
Olson, Norman Fredrick food science educator
†Pariza, Michael Willard research institute executive, microbiology and toxicology educator
Pella, Milton Orville retired science educator
Powers, Richard Dale agricultural journalism educator
Ris, Hans zoologist, educator
Rueckert, Roland Rudyard virologist, educator
Sequeira, Luis plant pathology educator
†Sheffield, Lewis Glosson physiologist
Skoog, Folke Karl botany educator
Smalley, Eugene Byron plant pathology educator, forest pathologist, mycologist
Susman, Millard geneticist, educator
Szybalski, Waclaw molecular geneticist, educator
Tibbitts, Theodore William horticulturist, researcher
Walker, Duard Lee medical educator
Welker, Wallace Irving neurophysiologist, educator

Milwaukee
Abramoff, Peter biology educator
Boese, Gilbert Karyle cultural organization executive
Grossberg, Sidney Edward microbiology educator
†Remsen, Charles Cornell, III microbiologist, research administrator, educator
†Risch, Richard William horticultural manager
Smith, James John physiologist
Weise, Charles Martin zoology educator
Wikenhauser, Charles Joseph zoological park director

Neenah
Proctor, Nick Hobert toxicologist, pharmacologist

WYOMING

Bondurant
Shepard, Paul Howe ecology educator, author, lecturer

Cheyenne
Schuman, Gerald Eugene soil scientist

Laramie
Caldwell, Daniel Ralston microbiology educator
Christensen, Martha mycologist, educator
†Hartman, Ronald Lee plant systematist
Speight, James Glassford research company executive

Moose
Craighead, Frank Cooper, Jr. ecologist

TERRITORIES OF THE UNITED STATES

PUERTO RICO

Bayamon
Santacana, Guido E. physiology educator

San Juan
†Fernández-Coll, Fred microbiologist, food technology laboratory director
†Lugo, Ariel E. ecologist, botanist, federal agency administrator
†Orkand, Richard Kenneth neurobiologist, researcher, educator
Rodriguez-del Valle, Nuri microbiology educator

CANADA

ALBERTA

Beaverlodge
†McElgunn, James Douglas agriculturist, researcher

Calgary
Jones, Geoffrey Melvill physiology research educator
Parkinson, Dennis biology educator, soil biology researcher
Yoon, Ji-Won virology, immunology and diabetes educator, research administrator

Edmonton
Bentley, Charles Fred consulting agrologist
Cormack, Robert George Hall botany educator
Cossins, Edwin Albert biology educator, academic administrator
Hiruki, Chuji plant virologist, science educator

Lethbridge
†Sonntag, Bernard H. agrologist, research executive

BRITISH COLUMBIA

Bamfield
Druehl, Louis Dix biology educator

Burnaby
†Borden, John Harvey entomologist, educator
†Brandhorst, Bruce Peter biology educator

Nanaimo
Margolis, Leo marine biologist
Ricker, William Edwin biologist

New Westminster
Waygood, Ernest Roy plant physiology educator

Sidney
Bigelow, Margaret Elizabeth Barr mycologist educator
Davis, John Christopher zoologist, aquatic toxicologist
Kendrick, William Bryce biology educator, author, publisher
Mann, Cedric Robert retired institute administrator, oceanographer

Summerland
Dueck, John agricultural researcher, plant pathologist
Looney, Norman Earl pomologist, plant physiologist

Vancouver
Blair, Robert animal science administrator, educator, researcher
Campbell, Jack James Ramsay microbiology educator
Chitty, Dennis Hubert zoology educator
Copp, Douglas Harold physiologist, educator
Hoar, William Stewart zoologist, educator
Jones, David Robert zoology educator
Larkin, Peter Anthony zoology educator, university dean and official
Ledsome, John Russell physician, educator
Lindsey, Casimir Charles zoologist
March, Beryl Elizabeth animal scientist, educator
McBride, Barry Clarke microbiology and oral biology educator, research microbiologist
Mc Lean, Donald Millis microbiology, pathology educator, physician
Miller, Robert Carmi, Jr. microbiology educator, university administrator
Newman, Murray Arthur aquarium administrator
Phillips, Anthony George neurobiology educator
†Phillips, John Edward zoologist, educator
Randall, David John physiologist, zoologist, educator
Shaw, Michael biologist
Wellington, William George plant science and ecology educator

Victoria
Bousfield, Edward Lloyd biologist
†Drew, T. John life science research administrator

West Vancouver
Donaldson, Edward Mossop research scientist, government official

MANITOBA

Brandon
†Robertson, John Alden agrologist, researcher

Winnipeg
Eales, John Geoffrey zoology educator
Hamerton, John Laurence geneticist, educator
Suzuki, Isamu microbiology educator, researcher

NEW BRUNSWICK

Saint Andrews
Scott, William Beverley ichthyologist

Saint John
†Thomas, Martin Lewis H. marine ecologist, educator

NEWFOUNDLAND

Saint John's
†Coady, Larry marine biology research administrator
†Crim, Lawrence marine life research administrator
Davis, Charles Carroll aquatic biologist, educator
†Jeffrey, N. E. marine biology administrator

NOVA SCOTIA

Dartmouth
Bhartia, Prakash defense research management executive, researcher, educator
Mann, Kenneth Henry marine ecologist

Halifax
Easterbrook, Kenneth Brian retired microbiologist
Hall, Brian Keith biology educator, author
†O'Dor, Ron physiologist, marine biology educator
†Pringle, John D. ecological research administrator

Wallace
Bidwell, Roger Grafton Shelford biologist, educator

ONTARIO

Caledon East
Fallis, Albert Murray microbiology educator

Deep River
Newcombe, Howard Borden biologist, consultant

Downsview
Forer, Arthur H. biology educator, researcher, editor
Moens, Peter B. biology researcher and educator

Guelph
Beveridge, Terrance James microbiology educator, researcher
Bewley, John Derek botany researcher, educator
†Burnside, Edward Blair geneticist, educator, administrator
Jorgensen, Erik forest pathologist, educator, consultant
Kasha, Kenneth John crop science educator
Oaks, B. Ann plant physiologist, educator
Sells, Bruce Howard biomedical sciences educator

Kingston
Bisby, Mark Ainley physiology educator
Canvin, David Thomas biologist, educator
Leggett, William C. biology educator, educational administrator
Wyatt, Gerard Robert biology educator, researcher

London
Dales, Samuel microbiologist, virologist, educator
Locke, Michael zoology educator

Nepean
Bishop, Claude Titus retired biological sciences research administrator, editor

North York
Davey, Kenneth George biologist, university official

Ottawa
Blachut, Teodor Josef research scientist
Dence, Michael Robert research director
Hughes, Stanley John mycologist
Morand, Peter research agency executive
Nordin, Vidar John forestry educator, consultant
Perry, Malcolm Blythe biologist
Sinha, Ramesh Chandra plant pathologist
Soper, James Herbert botanist, curator
Storey, Kenneth Bruce biology educator
Topp, George Clarke soil physicist

Peterborough
Hutchinson, Thomas Cuthbert ecology and environmental educator

Toronto
Atwood, Harold Leslie physiology and zoology educator
Kerr, David Wylie natural resource company executive
Liversage, Richard Albert zoologist, educator
MacLennan, David Herman research scientist, educator
Mustard, James Fraser research institute executive
Rhodes, Andrew James medical microbiologist
Stadelman, William Ralph foundation executive
Tobe, Stephen Solomon zoology educator
Tsui, Lap-Chee molecular genetics educator
White, Calvin John zoo executive, financial manager, zoological association executive
Worton, Ronald Gibert geneticist, educator

Waterloo
Hynes, Hugh Bernard Noel biology educator
McCauley, Robert William biologist, educator

Yarker
Smallman, Beverley N. biology educator

QUEBEC

Ile Perrot
Tomlinson, George Herbert retired industrial company research executive

Laval
†Frisque, Gilles forestry engineer
Kluepfel, Dieter microbiologist

Montreal
Adamkiewicz, Vincent Witold microbiology and immunology educator, researcher
Carroll, Robert Lynn biology educator, vertebrate paleontologist, museum curator
Chang, Thomas Ming Swi medical scientist, biotechnologist
Dansereau, Pierre ecologist
Fortin, Joseph André forestry educator, researcher
Gibbs, Sarah Preble biologist, educator
Jolicoeur, Paul molecular biologist
Maclachlan, Gordon Alistair biology educator, researcher
Murphy, Beverley Elaine Pearson scientist, administrator, physician, educator
†Pinsky, Leonard geneticist
Plaa, Gabriel Leon toxicologist, educator
Sattler, Rolf plant morphologist, educator
Skup, Daniel molecular biologist, educator, researcher
Sonea, Sorin I. microbiologist
†Stanners, Clifford Paul molecular biologist, cell biologist, biochemistry educator

Pointe Claire
Lederman, Frank L. scientist, research center administrator

Quebec
Joly, Jean Robert microbiologist, medical educator
Potvin, Pierre physiologist, educator
Trudel, Marc J. botanist

Sainte Anne de Bellevue
Grant, William Frederick geneticist, educator
MacLeod, Robert Angus microbiology educator, researcher
Steppler, Howard Alvey agronomist

Sainte-Foy
†Cardinal, André phycologist, educator

Ville de Laval
Pavilanis, Vytautas microbiology educator, physician

SASKATCHEWAN

Regina
Davis, Gordon Richard Fuerst biologist, translator

Saskatoon
†Babiuk, Lorne Alan virologist, immunologist, research administrator
Baker, Robert John agronomy educator
Bell, John Milton agricultural science educator
Harvey, Bryan Laurence crop science educator
Huang, Pan Ming soil science educator
Shokeir, Mohamed Hassan Kamel medical geneticist, educator

MEXICO

Mexico City
Rajaram, Sanjaya agricultural scientist, plant breeder

ARGENTINA

Buenos Aires
Balve, Beba Carmen research center administrator

AUSTRALIA

Adelaide
Wiskich, Joseph Tony botany educator, researcher

Randwick
Hall, Peter Francis physiologist

CHANNEL ISLANDS

Jersey
Durrell, Gerald Malcolm zoologist, author

COLOMBIA

Cali
Voysest, Oswaldo *agronomist, researcher*

CUBA

Havana
Kouri, Gustavo Pedro *virologist*

CZECH REPUBLIC

Ceske Budejovice
Sláma, Karel *biologist, zoologist*

DENMARK

Roskilde
Heydorn, Kaj *science laboratory administrator*

ENGLAND

Cambridge
Carpenter, Adelaide Trowbridge Clark *geneticist*
Milstein, César *molecular biologist*
Perutz, Max Ferdinand *molecular biologist*
Sanger, Frederick *retired molecular biologist*

Cranbrook
Hattersley-Smith, Geoffrey Francis *retired government research scientist*

Linton
Kendrew, John Cowdery *molecular biologist, former college president*

Oxford
May, Robert McCredie *biology educator*

FRANCE

Aulnay-sous-Bois
Shahin, Majdi Musa *biologist*

Creteil
Robert, Leslie Ladislas *research center administrator, consultant*

Orsay
Fiszer-Szafarz, Berta (Berta Safars) *research scientist*

Paris
Jacob, François *biologist*
LeGoffic, Francois *biotechnology educator*

GERMANY

Hamburg
Müller-Eberhard, Hans Joachim *medical research scientist, administrator*

Hannover
Döhler, Klaus Dieter *pharmaceutical and development executive*

Jülich
Stengel, Eberhard Friedrich Otto *botanist*

Katlenburg-Lindau
Hagfors, Tor *institute director*

Munich
Berg, Jan Mikael *science educator*

ITALY

Camerino
Miyake, Akio *biologist, educator*

Messina
Nigro, Aldo *physiology and psychology educator*

Naples
Tarro, Giulio *virologist*

Rome
Levi-Montalcini, Rita *neurobiologist, researcher*

JAPAN

Fukuoka
Aizawa, Keio *biology educator*

Hiroshima
Kobayashi, Naomasa *biology educator*

Iwate
Kawauchi, Hiroshi *hormone science educator*

Okubo
Nishimura, Susumu *biologist*

Osaka
Sakaguchi, Genji *food microbiologist, educator*
Watanabe, Toshiharu *ecologist*

Sagamihara
Okui, Kazumitsu *biology educator*

Sendai
Shoji, Sadao *soil scientist*

Tokyo
Hori, Yukio *scientific association administrator, engineering educator*
Ishii, Akira *medical parasitologist, malarialogist, allergologist*
Kitazawa, Koichi *materials science educator*
Takahashi, Keiichi *zoology educator*
Tsuda, Kyosuke *organic chemist, science association administrator*

Uji
Yasumoto, Kyoden *food science educator*

KENYA

Mbita South Nyanza
Khan, Zeyaur Rahman *entomologist*

PANAMA

Balboa
Rubinoff, Ira *biologist, research administrator, conservationist*

Panama
Tarte, Rodrigo *agriculture and natural resources educator, resea*

PERU

Lima
French, Edward Ronald *plant pathologist*

THE PHILIPPINES

Malabon Manila
Pizarro, Antonio Crisostomo *agricultural educator, researcher*

POLAND

Lodz
Guzek, Jan Wojciech *physiology educator*

Poznan
Golab, Wlodzimierz Andrzej *biologist, geographer, librarian*

Warsaw
Koscielak, Jerzy *scientist, science administrator*

REPUBLIC OF KOREA

Seoul
Kang, Bin Goo *biologist*

SAUDI ARABIA

Riyadh
Chaudhary, Shaukat Ali *ecologist, plant taxonomist*

SCOTLAND

Gullane
Collins, Jeffrey Hamilton *research facility administrator, electrical engineering educator*

SPAIN

Valencia
Sentandreu, Rafael *microbiologist*

SWITZERLAND

Basel
Arber, Werner *microbiologist*
Reichstein, Tadeus *botanist, scientist, educator*

Lausanne
Stingelin, Valentin *research center director, mechanical engineer*

TAIWAN

Taipei
Ma, Chueng-Shyang (Robert Ma) *reproductive physiology educator, geneticist*

VENEZUELA

Caripe
Pereira, Jose Francisco *plant physiologist*

ADDRESS UNPUBLISHED

Ahearne, John Francis *scientific research society administrator, researcher*
Aikens, Martha Brunette *national park service administrator*
Arnott, Howard Joseph *biology educator, university dean*
Barrett, Izadore *retired fisheries research administrator*
Berlowitz Tarrant, Laurence *biotechnologist, university administrator*
Bernard, Richard Lawson *geneticist, retired*
Blake, Jules *biotechnology consultant*
Boell, Edgar John *biology educator*

Bonner, John Tyler *biology educator*
Braker, William Paul *aquarium executive, ichthyologist*
Brill, Winston Jonas *microbiologist, educator, research director, publisher and management consultant*
Bullock, Theodore Holmes *biologist, educator*
Burlew, John Swalm *research scientist*
Bush, Guy Louis *biology educator*
Carlquist, Sherwin *biology and botany educator*
Catlin, B. Wesley *microbiologist*
Cole, Jerome Foster *research company executive*
Coleman, Nancy Pees *environmental toxicologist*
Creech, John Lewis *retired scientist, consultant*
De Antoni, Edward Paul *cancer control research scientist*
Detra, Ralph William *research laboratory administrator*
Dugan, Patrick Raymond *microbiologist, university dean*
Edwards, Ernest Preston *biologist*
Eicher, George John *aquatic biologist*
Ellner, Paul Daniel *clinical microbiologist*
Erlenmeyer-Kimling, L. *psychiatric and behavior genetics researcher, educator*
Field, George Sydney *retired research director*
Florence, Paul Smith *agronomist, business owner*
Folkens, Alan Theodore *clinical and pharmaceutical microbiologist*
Frere, Maurice Herbert *retired soil scientist*
Gill, William Robert *soil scientist*
Glick, J. Leslie *biotechnology company executive*
Goin, Olive Bown *biologist*
Goldstein, Walter Elliott *biotechnology executive*
†Grobman, Arnold Brams *retired biology educator and academic administrator*
Gross, Paul Randolph *biologist, academic administrator*
Gryder, Rosa Meyersburg *toxicologist, consultant*
Hall, John Marshall *food industry consultant*
Hamilton, William Howard *laboratory executive*
Harris, Elliott Stanley *toxicologist*
Hartman, Margaret J. *biologist, educator, university official*
Hatano, Sadashi *molecular biology educator*
†Hearn, John Patrick *biologist, educator*
Heine, Ursula Ingrid *biologist, researcher, artist*
Herz, Michael Joseph *marine environmental scientist*
Holldobler, Berthold Karl *zoologist, educator*
†Hoyt, Stanley Charles *retired research administrator, entomologist*
Inouye, David William *zoology educator*
Jackson, Victor Louis *retired naturalist*
King, John Quill Taylor *science center administrator, college administrator emeritus*
Kirsteuer, Ernst Karl Eberhart *biologist, curator*
Knobil, Ernst *physiologist*
Kordisch, Mary Schroller *retired zoology educator, genetic consultant*
Kozlowski, Theodore Thomas *botany educator, research director, author, editor*
Krogh, Lester Christensen *retired research and development executive*
†Kucey, Reginald Matthew *research scientist, microbiology researcher*
Kuper, George Henry *research and development institute executive*
Lechevalier, Hubert Arthur *microbiology educator*
Leder, Philip *geneticist, educator*
Lichstein, Herman Carlton *microbiology educator emeritus*
Lindsay, Dale Richard *research administrator*
†MacDonald, Stewart Dixon *ornithologist, ecologist, biologist*
Markovitz, Alvin *molecular biologist, geneticist*
Melnick, Joseph L. *virologist, educator*
Menn, Julius Joel *research scientist*
Micks, Don Wilfred *biologist, educator*
Moore, Donald Eugene *retired botanical garden administrator, communications executive*
Moscona, Aron Arthur *biology educator, scientist*
Myers, Jack Edgar *biologist, educator*
Neel, James Van Gundia *geneticist, educator*
Nicoll, Charles Samuel *physiologist, educator*
Palade, George Emil *biologist, educator*
Parmelee, David Freeland *biologist, educator*
Peiss, Clarence Norman *physiology educator, college dean*
Peter, Richard Ector *zoology educator*
Pielou, Evelyn C. *biologist*
†Pinter, Gabriel George *physiologist*
Ramanarayanan, Madhava Prabhu *science administrator, researcher, educator*
Read, Paul E. *horticulture educator*
Reetz, Harold Frank, Jr. *industrial agronomist*
Schwab, John Harris *microbiology and immunology educator*
Shelby, Khadejah E. *retired zoological park administrator*
Simpson, Frederick James *research administrator*
Sjostrand, Fritiof Stig *biologist, educator*
†Skinner, James Stanford *physiologist, educator*
Smith, Dwight Raymond *ecology and wildlife educator, writer*
Sokal, Robert Reuven *biology educator, author*
Southwick, Charles Henry *zoologist, educator*
Spiegelman, Robert Gerald *retired research institute executive*
Striker, Gary E. *scientist, research institution administrator*
Tandler, Bernard *cell biology educator*
Tenney, Stephen Marsh *physiologist, educator*
Vaughan, John Charles, III *horticultural products executive*
Wilkinson, Stanley Ralph *agronomist*

SCIENCE: MATHEMATICS AND COMPUTER SCIENCE

UNITED STATES

ALABAMA

Birmingham
Peeples, William Dewey, Jr. *mathematics educator*

Florence
Johnson, Johnny Ray *mathematics educator*

Huntsville
Zant, Robert Franklin *computer information educator*

Madison
Frakes, Lawrence Wright *program analyst, logistics engineer*

Pelham
Turner, Malcolm Elijah *biomathematician, educator*

Tuscaloosa
Davis, Anthony Michael John *mathematics educator*
Drake, Albert Estern *retired statistics educator*

ALASKA

Anchorage
Mann, Lester Perry *mathematics educator*

Palmer
Chang, Ping-Tung *mathematics educator*

ARIZONA

Mesa
Stott, Brian *software company executive*

Tempe
Krus, David James *statistician*
Smith, Harvey Alvin *mathematics educator, consultant*
Wang, Alan Ping-I *mathematics educator*

Tucson
Re Velle, Jack B(oyer) *consulting statistician*
Willoughby, Stephen Schuyler *mathematics educator*

ARKANSAS

Batesville
Carius, Robert Wilhelm *mathematics and science educator, retired naval officer*

Little Rock
Townsend, James Willis *computer scientist*

Searcy
Oldham, Bill W. *mathematics educator*

CALIFORNIA

Arcadia
Seitz, Charles Lewis *computer scientist and engineer*

Arcata
Hunt, Robert Weldon *mathematics educator, consultant*

Berkeley
Arveson, William Barnes *mathematics educator*
Bergman, George Mark *mathematician, educator*
Bickel, Peter John *statistician, educator*
Bourne, Samuel G. *mathematician, consultant, educator*
Brillinger, David Ross *statistician, educator*
Chern, Shiing-Shen *mathematics educator*
Chorin, Alexandre Joel *mathematician, educator*
Cooper, William Secord *information science educator*
†Culler, David Ethan *educator*
Ferrari, Domenico *computer science educator*
Freedman, David Amiel *statistics educator, consultant*
Helson, Henry Berge *retired mathematics educator, publisher*
†Henkin, Leon Albert *educator, mathematician*
Hirsch, Morris William *mathematics educator*
Kahan, William M. *mathematics educator, consultant*
Kaplansky, Irving *mathematician, educator, research institute director*
Karp, Richard Manning *computer sciences educator*
Le Cam, Lucien Marie *mathematics educator*
Lehmann, Erich Leo *statistics educator*
†Marsden, Jerrold Eldon *mathematician, educator*
Patterson, David Andrew *computer scientist, educator, consultant*
Polak, Elijah *engineering educator, computer scientist*
†Ramamoorthy, Chittor V. *computer science educator*
Ratner, Marina *mathematician, educator, researcher*
Schoenfeld, Alan Henry *mathematics and education educator*
Sequin, Carlo H. *computer science educator*
Smith, Alan Jay *computer science educator, consultant*
Thomas, Paul Emery *mathematics educator*
Wolf, Joseph Albert *mathematician, educator*

Carlsbad
Halberg, Charles John August, Jr. *mathematics educator*

Carmel
Banathy, Bela Henrich *systems science educator, author, researcher*

Carmichael
Givant, Philip Joachim *mathematics educator, real estate investment executive*

Carson
Suchenek, Marek Andrzej *computer science educator*

Chico
Wolff, Howard Keith *computer science educator, consultant*

Claremont
Mullikin, Harry Copeland *mathematics educator*

Costa Mesa
Savage, Sandra Hope Skeen *mathematics educator, curriculum writer*

Davis
Alder, Henry Ludwig *mathematics educator*
Rocke, David Morton *statistician, educator*

El Cajon
Donnelly, Donald Frank *mathematics educator, computer consultant*

Fremont
Lautzenheiser, Marvin Wendell *computer software engineer*

Fresno
Cohen, Moses Elias *mathematician, educator*

Glendale
Burger, John Barclay *systems architect, computer scientist*

Hayward
Sabharwal, Ranjit Singh *mathematician*

Irvine
Demetrescu, Mihai Constantin *computer company executive, scientist*

La Jolla
Freedman, Michael Hartley *mathematician, educator*
Halkin, Hubert *mathematics educator, research mathematician*
Reissner, Eric (Max Erich Reissner) *applied mechanics researcher*
Rosenblatt, Murray *mathematics educator*
Wulbert, Daniel Eliot *mathematician, educator*

Lafayette
Moore, Calvin C. *mathematics educator, administrator*

Los Angeles
†Afifi, Abdelmonem A. *biostatistics educator, academic dean*
Allswang, John Myers *computer science educator, historian*
Arbib, Michael Anthony *computer scientist, educator, neuroscientist, cybernetician*
Bekey, George Albert *computer scientist, educator, engineer*
Chacko, George Kuttickal *systems science educator, consultant*
Chu, Wesley Wei-Chin *computer science educator, consultant*
Dixon, Wilfrid Joseph *statistics educator*
Estrin, Gerald *computer scientist, engineering educator, academic administrator*
Golomb, Solomon Wolf *mathematician, electrical engineer, educator, university official*
Gordon, Basil *mathematics educator*
Greenberger, Martin *computer and information scientist, educator*
Harris, Theodore Edward *mathematician, educator*
Hu, Sze-Tsen *mathematics educator*
Kalaba, Robert Edwin *applied mathematician*
Kleinrock, Leonard *computer scientist*
Port, Sidney Charles *mathematician, educator*
Rector, Robert Wayman *mathematics and engineering educator, former association executive*
Redheffer, Raymond Moos *mathematician, educator*
Richardson, John Vinson, Jr. *library science educator*
Shapley, Lloyd Stowell *mathematics and economics educator*
Waterman, Michael Spencer *mathematics educator, biology educator*

Los Osos
Ratliff, Cecil Wayne *computer scientist*

Menlo Park
Bourne, Charles Percy *information scientist, educator*
Goldberg, Jacob *computer scientist, researcher*

Monte Sereno
Rustagi, Jagdish Sharan *statistics educator*

Monterey
Gaskell, Robert Eugene *mathematician, educator*
Hamming, Richard Wesley *computer scientist*

Moss Landing
Lange, Lester Henry *mathematics educator*

Oakland
Lennox, Carol *computer scientist, consultant*

Pacific Palisades
Becker, Joseph *information scientist*

Palo Alto
Lamport, Leslie B. *computer scientist*
Spinrad, Robert Joseph *computer scientist*
Taylor, Robert William *research director*
Weiser, Mark David *computer scientist, researcher*

Pasadena
Franklin, Joel Nicholas *mathematician, educator*
Luxemburg, Wilhelmus Anthonius Josephus *mathematics educator*
Mead, Carver Andress *computer science educator*
Saffman, Philip G. *mathematician*
Todd, John *educator, mathematician*
Whitham, Gerald Beresford *mathematics educator*

Portola Valley
Kuo, Franklin F. *computer scientist, electrical engineer*

Ramona
Bennett, James Chester *computer consultant, real estate developer*

Riverside
Bhanu, Bir *computer information scientist, educator, director university program*
Ratliff, Louis Jackson, Jr. *mathematics educator*
Shapiro, Victor Lenard *mathematician*

Sacramento
Sawiris, Milad Youssef *statistician, educator*

San Diego
Burgin, George Hans *computer scientist, educator*
Burke, John *science technology company executive*
Hales, Alfred Washington *mathematics educator, consultant*
Karin, Sidney *research and development executive*
Martin, James John, Jr. *consulting research firm executive, systems analyst*
Willerding, Margaret Frances *mathematician*

San Francisco
Backus, John *computer scientist*
Christensen, David William *mathematician, engineer*
Farrell, Edward Joseph *retired mathematics educator*
Rautenberg, Robert Frank *consulting statistician*
Vazsonyi, Andrew *computer and management scientist*

San Jose
†Pellionisz, Andras Jeno *neurocomputer scientist*

San Pedro
Colman, Ronald William *computer science educator*

Santa Barbara
Fan, Ky *mathematician, educator*
Johnsen, Eugene Carlyle *mathematics educator*
Marcus, Marvin *mathematician, educator*
Minc, Henryk *mathematics educator*
Newman, Morris *mathematician*
Rosenberg, Alex *mathematician, educator*
Simons, Stephen *mathematics educator, researcher*
Zelmanowitz, Julius Martin *mathematics educator, university administrator*

Santa Clara
Alexanderson, Gerald Lee *mathematician, educator, writer*
Halmos, Paul Richard *mathematician, educator*

Santa Cruz
Huskey, Harry Douglas *information and computer science educator*

Santa Monica
Ware, Willis Howard *computer scientist*

Saratoga
Park, Joseph Chul Hui *computer scientist*

Simi Valley
Stratton, Gregory Alexander *computer specialist, administrator, mayor*

Stanford
Anderson, Theodore Wilbur *statistics educator*
Brown, Byron William, Jr. *biostatistician, educator*
Carlsson, Gunnar Erik *mathematics educator*
Dantzig, George Bernard *applied mathematics educator*
Floyd, Robert W. *computer scientist, educator*
Golub, Gene Howard *computer science educator, researcher*
Karlin, Samuel *mathematics educator, researcher*
Keller, Joseph Bishop *mathematician, educator*
Lieberman, Gerald J. *statistics educator*
McCarthy, John *computer scientist, educator*
Moses, Lincoln E. *statistician, educator*
Ornstein, Donald Samuel *mathematician, educator*
Osserman, Robert *mathematician, educator*
Phillips, Ralph Saul *mathematics educator*
Schoen, Richard Melvin *mathematics educator, researcher*
Ullman, Jeffrey David *computer science educator*

Sunnyvale
Thorington, John M., Jr. *computer graphics company executive*

Thousand Oaks
Sladek, Lyle Virgil *mathematician, educator*

COLORADO

Boulder
Crow, Edwin Louis *mathematical statistician, consultant*
Mycielski, Jan *mathematician, educator*

Colorado Springs
Couger, James Daniel *computer scientist, writer*
Cray, Seymour R. *computer designer*
†May, Ronny Joe (Ron May) *computer scientist, state legislator*

Denver
†Hernandez, Tony J. *computer company executive, state representative*

Durango
Spencer, Donald Clayton *mathematician*

Fort Collins
†Mielke, Paul William, Jr. *statistician*
†Tweedie, Richard Lewis *statistics educator, consultant*

CONNECTICUT

East Hartford
Ahlberg, John Harold *mathematician, educator*

Farmington
Miser, Hugh Jordan *systems analyst, operations researcher, consultant*

Middletown
Comfort, William Wistar *mathematics educator*
Reid, James Dolan *mathematics educator, researcher*
Rosenbaum, Robert Abraham *mathematics educator*

New Haven
†Beals, Richard William *mathematics educator*
Jacobson, Nathan *mathematics educator*
Lang, Serge *mathematics educator*
Massey, William S. *mathematician, educator*
McDermott, Drew Vincent *computer science educator*
Mostow, George Daniel *mathematics educator*
Piatetski-Shapiro, Ilya *mathematics educator*
Rickart, Charles Earl *mathematician, educator*
Singer, Burton Herbert *statistics educator*
Szczarba, Robert Henry *mathematics educator, mathematician*
Tufte, Edward Rolf *statistics educator, publisher*

West Hartford
Welna, Cecilia *mathematics educator*

DELAWARE

Dover
Vawter, William Snyder *computer software consultant*

Newark
Colton, David Lem *mathematician, educator*
Stakgold, Ivar *mathematics educator*
Stark, Robert Martin *mathematician, civil engineer, educator*

DISTRICT OF COLUMBIA

Washington
Bogdan, Victor Michael *mathematics educator, scientist*
Chiazze, Leonard, Jr. *biostatistician, epidemiologist, educator*
Chou, Wushow *information scientist, federal agency official*
†Ciment, Melvyn *mathematician*
Gastwirth, Joseph Lewis *statistician, educator*
Goldfield, Edwin David *statistician*
Goldhaber, Jacob Kopel *retired mathematician, educator*
Gray, Mary Wheat *statistician, lawyer*
Hammer, Carl *computer scientist, former computer company executive*
Hedges, Harry George *computer scientist, educator*
Maisel, Herbert *computer science educator*
†Okay, John Louis *information scientist*
Penniman, W. David *information scientist, foundation executive*
Perry, William James *mathematical scientist, government official*
Sandefur, James Tandy *mathematics educator*
Shaw, William Frederick *statistician*
Stewart, Ruth Ann *public policy analyst, administrator*
Stokes, Arnold Paul *mathematics educator*
Tidball, Charles Stanley *computer scientist, educator*
†Tortora, Robert D. *mathematician*
†Walsh, William H., Jr. *statistical research director*
Weiss, Leonard *mathematician, engineer, senate staff director*

FLORIDA

Coral Gables
Bagley, Robert Waller *mathematics educator*
Howard, Bernard Eufinger *computer science educator and mathematics*

Delray Beach
Hegstrom, William Jean *mathematics educator*

Fort Lauderdale
Kemper Littman, Marlyn *information scientist, educator*

Gainesville
Bednarek, Alexander Robert *mathematician, educator*
Dinculeanu, Nicolae *mathematician*
Emch, Gerard Gustav *mathematics and physics educator*
†Pop-Stojanovic, Zoran Rista *mathematics educator*
†Tou, Julius T. *electrical and computer engineering educator*
Yau, Stephen Sik-sang *computer science and engineering educator, computer scientist, researcher*

Highland Beach
Schor, Stanley Sidney *mathematical sciences educator*

Indialantic
Carroll, Charles Lemuel, Jr. *mathematician*

Jacksonville
Robinson, Christine Marie *mathematics educator*

Key West
Devereaux, Christian Windsor, III *computer scientist*

Lakeland
Sheppard, Albert Parker, Jr. *mathematics educator*

Melbourne
Lakshmikantham, Vangipuram *mathematics educator*

Miami
Butson, Alton Thomas *mathematics educator*
Zanakis, Steve H. *information systems educator*

Ocala
Johnson, Winston Conrad *mathematics educator*

Orlando
Deo, Narsingh *computer science educator*
Sathre, Leroy *educator, consultant*

Saint Petersburg
Kazor, Walter Robert *statistical process control and quality assurance consultant*

Sarasota
Eachus, Joseph J(ackson) *computer scientist, consultant*

Tallahassee
Goodner, Dwight Benjamin *mathematician, emeritus educator*
Lick, Dale Wesley *mathematician, university president, educator*
Navon, Ionel Michael *mathematics educator*
Nichols, Eugene Douglas *mathematics educator*

Tampa
Saff, Edward Barry *mathematics educator*

Vero Beach
Mills, Harlan Duncan *software engineer, mathematician, educator*

West Palm Beach
Bower, Ruth Lawther *retired mathematics educator*

GEORGIA

Athens
Adomian, George *applied mathematician, physicist*
Neter, John *statistician*
Speering, Robin *educator, computer specialist*

Atlanta
Ames, William Francis *mathematician, educator*
Foley, James David *computer science educator, consultant*
Hale, Jack K. *mathematics educator, research center administrator*
Oliker, Vladimir *mathematician, educator*
Vaishnavi, Vijay Kumar *computer science educator, researcher*
Wilkins, J. Ernest, Jr. *mathematician*
Williams, Charles Murray *computer information systems educator, consultant*

Savannah
Albert, Theodore Merton *computer scientist*
Wheeler, Ed Ray *mathematics educator*

HAWAII

Honolulu
Swanson, Richard William *statistician*

IDAHO

Calder
Rechard, Ottis William *mathematics and computer science educator*

Moscow
Bobisud, Larry Eugene *mathematics educator*

ILLINOIS

Bloomington
Prescott, Richard Paul, Jr. *computer company consultant*

Champaign
Friedman, Joan M. *computer consultant*
Kuck, David Jerome *computer system researcher, administrator*
Philipp, Walter Viktor *mathematician, educator*

Chicago
Ash, J. Marshall *mathematician, educator*
Calderon, Alberto P. *mathematician, educator*
Dupont, Todd F. *mathematics and computer science educator*
Ejiogu, Lem Onyeaduzim *software engineer*
Graves, Robert Lawrence *mathematician, educator*
Hanson, Floyd Bliss *applied mathematician, computational scientist, mathematical biologist*
Kruskal, William Henry *statistician, educator*
MacLane, Saunders *mathematician, educator*
Madansky, Albert *statistics educator*
May, J. Peter *mathematics educator*
Reingold, Haim *mathematics educator*
Roberts, Harry Vivian *statistics educator*
Stigler, Stephen Mack *statistician, educator*
Swan, Richard Gordon *mathematics educator*
Wirszup, Izaak *mathematician, educator*
†Zimmer, Robert J. *mathematician*

East Peoria
Grisham, George Robert *mathematics educator*

Elgin
Juister, Barbara Joyce *mathematics educator*

Evanston
Bareiss, Erwin Hans *computer scientist, mathematician, nuclear engineer, educator*
Davis, Stephen Howard *applied mathematics educator*
Devinatz, Allen *mathematics educator*
Dwass, Meyer *mathematician, educator*
Haberman, Shelby Joel *statistician, educator*
Ionescu Tulcea, Cassius *research mathematician, educator*
Jerome, Joseph Walter *mathematics educator*
Kalai, Ehud *decision sciences educator, researcher in economics and decision sciences*
Mahowald, Mark Edward *mathematics educator*
Matkowsky, Bernard Judah *applied mathematician, educator*
Myerson, Roger Bruce *game theorist, economist, educator*
Olmstead, William Edward *mathematics educator*
Saari, Donald Gene *mathematician*
Schank, Roger Carl *computer science and psychology educator*

Godfrey
McDaniels, John Louis *mathematics educator*

Hinsdale
Butler, Margaret Kampschaefer *retired computer scientist*

Lombard
Royster, Darryl *computer programmer and analyst*

Macomb
Ballew, David Wayne *mathematics and computer science educator*

Normal
Brown, Francis Robert *mathematics educator*
Jones, Graham Alfred *mathematics educator*

River Forest
Koenig, Michael Edward Davison *information science educator*

Urbana
Albrecht, Felix Robert *mathematics educator*
Bateman, Paul Trevier *mathematician, educator*
Burkholder, Donald Lyman *mathematician, educator*
Carroll, Robert Wayne *mathematics educator*
Doob, Joseph Leo *mathematician, educator*
†Edelsbrunner, Herbert *computer scientist, mathematician*
Fossum, Robert Merle *mathematician, educator*
Goldberg, Samuel Irving *mathematics educator*
Gray, John Walker *mathematician, educator*
Henson, C. Ward *mathematician, educator*
Jerrard, Richard Patterson *mathematics educator*
Jockusch, Carl Groos, Jr. *mathematics educator*
Knight, Frank Bardsley *mathematics educator*
Lawrie, Duncan H. *computer science educator, consultant*
Merkelo, Henri *electronics scientist*
†Sameh, Ahmed Hamdy *computer science educator*
Suzuki, Michio *mathematics educator*
Tondeur, Philippe Maurice *mathematician, educator*
Williams, Martha Ethelyn *information science educator*

Wheaton
Reszka, Alfons *computer systems architect*

INDIANA

Bloomington
Davis, Charles Hargis *information scientist, educator*
†Escobar, Jose Fernando *mathematician, educator*
Prosser, Franklin Pierce *computer scientist*
Purdom, Paul Walton, Jr. *computer scientist*
Puri, Madan Lal *mathematics educator*

Fort Wayne
Beineke, Lowell Wayne *mathematics educator*
Mansfield, Maynard Joseph *computer science educator, academic dean*

Greencastle
Anderson, John Robert *retired mathematics educator*
Gass, Clinton Burke *mathematics educator*

Hammond
Yackel, James William *mathematician, academic administrator*

Indianapolis
Cliff, Johnnie Marie *mathematics and chemistry educator*
Reid, William Hill *mathematics educator*
Yovits, Marshall Clinton *computer and information science educator, university dean*

Kokomo
Schraut, Kenneth Charles *mathematician, educator*

Lafayette
de Branges de Bourcia, Louis *mathematics educator*
Gautschi, Walter *mathematics educator*
Rubin, Jean Estelle *mathematics educator*

Muncie
Robold, Alice Ilene *mathematician, educator*

Notre Dame
Sommese, Andrew John *mathematics educator*
Stoll, Wilhelm *mathematics educator*

West Lafayette
Abhyankar, Shreeram S. *mathematics and industrial engineering educator*
Conte, Samuel Daniel *computer scientist, educator*
Haas, Felix *former mathematics educator, university administrator*
Lynch, Robert Emmett *mathematics educator*
Rice, John Rischard *computer scientist, researcher, educator*

IOWA

Ames
David, Herbert Aron *statistics educator*
Fuller, Wayne Arthur *statistics educator*
Kempthorne, Oscar *statistics educator emeritus*

Grinnell
Ferguson, Pamela Anderson *mathematics educator, educational administrator*

Iowa City
Hogg, Robert Vincent, Jr. *mathematical statistician, educator*
Johnson, Eugene Walter *mathematician*
Kleinfeld, Erwin *mathematician, educator*
Potra, Florian Alexander *mathematics educator*
Robertson, Timothy Joel *statistician, educator*

Waverly
†Brunkhorst, Bob John *computer programmer, state representative*

KANSAS

Kansas City
Hassanein, Khatab M. *biostatistics educator, consultant*

Lawrence
Bulgren, William Gerald *computer science educator, researcher*
Davis, John Clements *geomathematician, natural resources and computer science consultant*
Himmelberg, Charles John, III *mathematics educator, researcher*

Wichita
Zytkow, Jan Mikolaj *computer science educator*

KENTUCKY

Lexington
Anderson, Richard L(oree) *mathematician, educator*
Mostert, Paul Stallings *mathematician, educator*

Richmond
Franke, Charles H(enry) *mathematics educator, department chair*

LOUISIANA

Baton Rouge
Goldstein, Jerome Arthur *mathematics educator*

Lafayette
Heatherly, Henry Edward *mathematics educator*

New Orleans
Birtel, Frank Thomas *mathematician, philosopher, educator*
LaValle, Irving Howard *decision analysis educator*
Sharma, Bhu Dev *mathematics educator, researcher*

MAINE

Bailey Island
Carter, William Caswell *computer scientist*

Brunswick
Tucker, Allen Brown, Jr. *computer science educator*

MARYLAND

Baltimore
Boardman, John Michael *mathematician, educator*
Igusa, Jun-Ichi *mathematician, educator*
Kosaraju, S. Rao *computer science researcher*
Kramer, Morton *biostatistician, epidemiologist*
Meyer, Jean-Pierre Gustave *mathematician, educator*
Shiffman, Bernard *mathematician, educator*
Slepian, Paul *mathematician, educator*
Wierman, John Charles *mathematician, educator*

Bel Air
Eichelberger, Robert John *retired government research and development administrator, consultant*

Bethesda
Moshman, Jack *statistical consultant*
Navarro, Joseph Anthony *statistician, consultant*
Sammet, Jean E. *computer scientist*
Schoch, Claude Martin *computer scientist, publishing company executive*

College Park
†Aloimonos, Yiannis John *computer sciences educator*
Antman, Stuart Sheldon *mathematician, educator*
†Efrat, Isaac *mathematician, educator*
Ehrlich, Gertrude *retired mathematics educator*
Embody, Daniel Robert *biometrician*
Kirwan, William English, II *mathematics educator, university official*
Kotz, Samuel *statistician, educator, translator*
Mikulski, Piotr Witold *mathematics educator*
Miller, Raymond Edward *computer science educator*
Minker, Jack *computer scientist, educator*
Rosenfeld, Azriel *computer science educator, consultant*
Stewart, Gilbert Wright *computer science educator*

Gaithersburg
†Burrows, James H. *computer scientist*
Colvin, Burton Houston *mathematician, government official*
Deprit, Andre Albert *mathematician, consultant*
†Jefferson, David *scientist*
Rosenblatt, Joan Raup *mathematical statistician*
Witzgall, Christoph Johann *mathematician*

Greenbelt
Pratt, Terrence Wendall *information research scientist*

Hyattsville
Israel, Robert Allan *statistician*

Rockville
Bryant, Edward Clark *statistician*
Dubey, Satya Deva *statistical scientist, researcher, executive*
Kalton, Graham *survey statistics, research scientist*

Silver Spring
Dalton, Robert Edgar *mathematician, computer scientist*
Douglis, Avron *mathematician*
Menkello, Frederick Vincent *computer scientist*

Temple Hills
Wilcox, Richard Hoag *information scientist*

MASSACHUSETTS

Amherst
Catlin, Donald Edward *mathematics educator*

Bedford
Fante, Ronald Louis *engineering scientist*

Boston
Cushing, Steven *educator, researcher, consultant*
D'Agostino, Ralph Benedict *mathematician, statistician, educator, consultant*
Falb, Peter Lawrence *mathematician, educator, investment company executive*
Pratt, John Winsor *statistics educator*
Stone, Arthur Harold *mathematics educator*
Taqqu, Murad Salman *mathematics educator*
Warga, Jack *mathematician, educator*

Burlington
Barlas, Julie Sandall *computer scientist, former librarian*

Cambridge
Anderson, Donald Gordon Marcus *mathematics educator*
Bartee, Thomas Creson *computer scientist, educator*
Bott, Raoul *mathematician, educator*
Carrier, George Francis *applied mathematics educator*
†Cheatham, Thomas Edward, Jr. *computer scientist, educator*
Chernoff, Herman *statistics educator*
Corbato, Fernando Jose *electrical engineer and computer science educator*
Dertouzos, Michael Leonidas *computer scientist, electrical engineer, educator*
Diaconis, Persi W. *mathematical statistician, educator*
Dudley, Richard Mansfield *mathematician, educator*
Gagliardi, Ugo Oscar *systems software architect, educator*
Gleason, Andrew Mattei *mathematician, educator*
Greenspan, Harvey Philip *applied mathematician, educator*
Grosz, Barbara Jean *computer science educator*
Helgason, Sigurdur *mathematician, educator*
Jackson, Francis Joseph *research and development company executive*
Kac, Victor G. *mathematician, educator*
Kazhdan, David *mathematician, educator*
Kleiman, Steven Lawrence *mathematics educator*
Kostant, Bertram *mathematician, educator*
Light, Richard Jay *statistician, education educator*
Lynch, Nancy Ann *computer scientist, educator*
†Mackey, George Whitelaw *educator, mathematician*
MacPherson, Robert Duncan *mathematician, educator*
†Minsky, Marvin Lee *mathematician, educator*
Moses, Joel *computer scientist, educator*
Mosteller, Frederick *mathematical statistician, educator*
Mumford, David Bryant *mathematics educator*
Oettinger, Anthony Gervin *mathematician, educator*
Roberts, Edward Baer *technology management educator*
Roberts, Nancy *computer educator*
Rota, Gian-Carlo *mathematician, educator*
Schmid, Wilfried *mathematician*
Segal, Irving Ezra *mathematics educator*
Singer, Isadore Manuel *mathematician, educator*
Strang, William Gilbert *mathematician, educator*
Stroock, Daniel Wyler *mathematician, educator*
Valiant, Leslie Gabriel *computer scientist*
Yau, Shing-Tung *mathematics educator*

Falmouth
Bonn, Theodore Hertz *computer scientist, consultant*

Framington
Scherr, Allan Lee *computer scientist, executive*

Lincoln
LeGates, John Crews Boulton *information scientist*

Medford
Reynolds, William Francis *mathematics educator*

Medway
Yonda, Alfred William *mathematician*

Sharon
Olum, Paul *mathematician, former university president*

Waltham
Brown, Edgar Henry, Jr. *mathematician, educator*
†Levine, Jerome Paul *mathematician, educator*

Wellesley
Hildebrand, Francis Begnaud *mathematics educator*

Westfield
Buckmore, Alvah Clarence, Jr. *computer scientist, ballistician*

Williamstown
Hill, Victor Ernst, IV *mathematics educator, musician*

Winchester
Shannon, Claude Elwood *mathematician, educator*

Worcester
Malone, Joseph James *mathematics educator, researcher*
McQuarrie, Bruce Cale *mathematics educator*

MICHIGAN

Ann Arbor
†Aupperle, Eric Max *data network center administrator, research scientist, engineering educator*
Bartle, Robert Gardner *mathematics educator*
Beutler, Frederick Joseph *information scientist*
Brown, Morton B. *biostatistics educator*
Conway, Lynn Ann *computer scientist, educator*
Duren, Peter Larkin *mathematician, educator*
Gehring, Frederick William *mathematician, educator*
Hill, Bruce Marvin *statistician, scientist, educator*
Hochster, Melvin *mathematician, educator*
Jones, Phillip Sanford *mathematics educator emeritus*
Kish, Leslie *research statistician, educator*
Kister, James Milton *mathematician, educator*
†Lewis, Donald John *mathematics educator*
Schriber, Thomas Jude *computer and information systems educator, researcher*

Auburn Hills
Neumann, Charles Henry *mathematics educator*

Dearborn
Brown, James Ward *mathematician, educator, author*

Detroit
Rajlich, Vaclav Thomas *computer science educator, researcher, consultant*
Schreiber, Bertram Manuel *mathematics educator*

East Lansing
†Frame, James Sutherland *retired mathematics educator*
Hocking, John Gilbert *mathematics educator*
Hoppensteadt, Frank Charles *mathematician, university dean*
Moran, Daniel Austin *mathematician*
Stapleton, James Hall *statistician, educator*
Wojcik, Anthony Stephen *computer science educator*

Flint
Kugler, Lawrence Dean *mathematics educator*

Kalamazoo
Calloway, Jean Mitchener *mathematician, educator*
Clarke, Allen Bruce *mathematics educator, retired academic administrator*

Novi
Chow, Chi-Ming *retired mathematics educator*

Saline
Cornell, Richard Garth *biostatistics educator*

Southfield
Turnquist, Gary Edward *systems consultant, educator*

MINNESOTA

Minneapolis
Aris, Rutherford *applied mathematician, educator*
Brasket, Curt Justin *systems analyst, chess player*
Friedman, Avner *mathematician, educator*
Infante, Ettore Ferrari *mathematician, educator, university administrator*
Loud, Warren Simms *mathematician*
Markus, Lawrence *retired mathematics educator*
McGehee, Richard Paul *mathematics educator*
Miller, Willard, Jr. *mathematician, educator*
Nitsche, Johannes Carl Christian *mathematics educator*
Pedoe, Daniel *mathematician, writer, artist*
Pour-El, Marian Boykan *mathematician, educator*
Rosen, Judah Ben *computer scientist*
Serrin, James Burton *mathematics educator*
Slagle, James Robert *computer science educator*
Warner, William Hamer *applied mathematician*

Moorhead
Heuer, Gerald Arthur *mathematician, educator*

New Brighton
Shier, Gloria Bulan *mathematics educator*

Northfield
Appleyard, David Frank *mathematics, computer science educator*
Schuster, Seymour *mathematician, educator*

Saint Paul
Bingham, Christopher *statistics educator*
Emeagwali, Philip Chukwurak *computer scientist, educator, mathematician, researcher*

MISSISSIPPI

Jackson
Galloway, Patricia Kay *systems analyst, ethnohistorian*

University
Paterson, Alan Leonard Tuke *mathematics educator*

MISSOURI

Columbia
Basu, Asit Prakas *statistician*
Beem, John Kelly *mathematician, educator*
Schrader, Keith William *mathematician*
Sprinsteel, Frederick Neil *computer science educator*
Williams, Frederick *statistics educator*
Zemmer, Joseph Lawrence, Jr. *mathematics educator*

Kansas City
Flora, Jairus Dale, Jr. *statistician*

Kirksville
Knight, Ronald Allen *mathematics educator, researcher*

Nevada
Hornback, Joseph Hope *mathematics educator*

Rolla
Grimm, Louis John *mathematician, educator*
†Mullin, Lenore Marie Restifo *computer scientist, researcher*
Zobrist, George Winston *computer scientist, educator*

Saint Louis
Baernstein, Albert, II *mathematician*
Ball, William Ernest *computer science educator*

Boothby, William Munger *mathematics educator*
Coerver, Elizabeth Ann *data base consultant*
Haimo, Deborah Tepper *mathematics educator*
Jenkins, James Allister *mathematician, educator*
Nussbaum, A(dolf) Edward *mathematician, educator*
Pollack, Seymour Victor *computer science educator*
Rodin, Ervin Yechiel László *mathematician*
Wilson, Edward Nathan *mathematician, educator*
Zuker, Michael *biomathematician*

MONTANA

Big Timber
Yuzeitis, James Richard *information specialist*

NEBRASKA

Lincoln
†Wiegand, Sylvia Margaret *mathematician, educator*

NEVADA

Incline Village
Anderson, Arthur George *former computer company executive, consultant*

NEW HAMPSHIRE

Durham
Appel, Kenneth I. *mathematician, educator*

Hanover
Arkowitz, Martin Arthur *mathematician, educator*
Baumgartner, James Earl *mathematics educator*
Crowell, Richard Henry *mathematician, educator*
Lamperti, John Williams *mathematician, educator*
Slesnick, William Ellis *mathematician, educator*
Snell, James Laurie *educator, mathematician*

NEW JERSEY

Englewood
Lapidus, Arnold *mathematician*

Mountain Lakes
Mattes, Hans George *communications system design scientist, researcher*

Murray Hill
Graham, Ronald Lewis *mathematician*
Sloane, Neil James Alexander *mathematician, researcher*

Neshanic Station
Muckenhoupt, Benjamin *retired mathematics educator*

New Brunswick
Amarel, Saul *computer scientist, educator*
Cohen, Amy *mathematics educator*
Kruskal, Martin David *mathematical physicist, educator*
†Kulikowski, Casimir Alexander *computer science educator, research program director*
Scanlon, Jane Cronin *mathematics educator*
Shanno, David Francis *mathematics educator*
†Strawderman, William E. *statistics educator*
Taft, Earl Jay *mathematics educator*

New Providence
Fishburn, Peter Clingerman *research mathematician, economist*
Shepp, Lawrence Alan *mathematician, educator*
Wyner, Aaron Daniel *mathematician*

Princeton
†Aizenman, Michael *mathematics and physics educator, researcher*
Borel, Armand *mathematics educator*
Caffarelli, Luis Angel *mathematician, educator*
Deligné, Pierre R. *mathematician*
Faltings, Gerd *mathematician, educator*
Gear, Charles William *computer scientist*
†Green, Jack W. *biostatistician*
Griffiths, Phillip A. *mathematician, academic administrator*
Gunning, Robert Clifford *mathematician, educator*
Hunter, John Stuart *statistician, consultant*
Kobayashi, Hisashi *computer scientist, communication theorist, educator*
Kohn, Joseph John *mathematician, educator*
Langlands, Robert Phelan *mathematician*
Lieberman, David Ira *mathematician, administrator*
Majda, Andrew J. *mathematician, educator*
†Sinai, Yakov G. *theoretical mathematician, educator*
†Spencer, Thomas C. *mathmatician*
†Stein, Elias M. *mathematician, educator*
Tarjan, Robert Endre *computer scientist, educator*
Umscheid, Ludwig Joseph *computer specialist*
Zierler, Neal *mathematician*

South Orange
Houle, Joseph E. *mathematics educator*

Summit
Slepian, David *mathematician, communications engineer*

Teaneck
Zwass, Vladimir *computer scientist, educator*

Union City
Conklin, Anna Immaculata G. *mathematics and language arts educator*

Upper Montclair
Stevens, John Galen *mathematics and computer science educator*

Watchung
Schaefer, Jacob Wernli *military systems consultant*

Wayne
Sanok, Gloria *mathematics educator, author*

West Paterson
Metz, Philip John *mathematics educator*

NEW MEXICO

Albuquerque
Bell, Stoughton *computer scientist, mathematician, educator*

Belen
†Gutjahr, Allan Leo *mathematics educator, researcher*

Las Cruces
Harary, Frank *mathematician, computer scientist, educator*
Reinfelds, Juris *computer science educator*
Southward, Glen Morris *statistician, educator*

Pecos
Price, Thomas Munro *computer consultant*

NEW YORK

Albany
Galvin, Thomas John *information science policy educator, librarian, information scientist*
Halsey, Richard Sweeney *information scientist, educator*
Rosenkrantz, Daniel J. *computer science educator*

Amherst
Brown, Stephen Ira *mathematics educator*
Eberlein, Patricia James *mathematician, computer scientist, educator*
Ralston, Anthony *computer scientist, mathematician, educator*

Aurora
Shilepsky, Arnold Charles *mathematics educator, computer consultant*

Binghamton
Hilton, Peter John *mathematician, educator*
Klir, George Jiri *systems science educator*
†Su, Stephen Y. H. *computer science and engineering educator, consultant*

Bronx
Koranyi, Adam *mathematics educator*
Rose, Israel Harold *mathematics educator*
Tong, Hing *mathematician, educator*

Brooklyn
Bachman, George *mathematics educator*
Hochstadt, Harry *mathematician, educator*
Pennisten, John William *computer scientist, linguist, actuary*
Weill, Georges Gustave *mathematics educator*

Buffalo
Berner, Robert Frank *statistics educator*
Bross, Irwin Dudley Jackson *biostatistician*
Coburn, Lewis Alan *mathematics educator*
Hauptman, Herbert Aaron *mathematician, educator, researcher*
Priore, Roger L. *biostatistics educator, consultant*
Shapiro, Stuart Charles *computer scientist, educator*

Farmingdale
Guggenheimer, Heinrich Walter *mathematician, educator*
Marshall, Clifford Wallace *mathematics educator*

Flushing
Mendelson, Elliott *mathematician, educator*

Garden City
Zirkel, Gene *computer science educator and mathematics*

Geneseo
Small, William Andrew *mathematics educator*

Hamilton
Pownall, Malcolm Wilmor *mathematics educator*

Ithaca
Bramble, James Henry *mathematician, educator*
Conway, Richard Walter *computer scientist, educator*
Earle, Clifford John, Jr. *mathematician*
†Fuchs, Wolfgang Heinrich *mathematics educator*
Gries, David Joseph *computer science researcher, educator*
Hartmanis, Juris *computer scientist, educator*
Hatcher, Allen Edward *mathematician, educator*
†Hubbard, John Hamal *mathematician, educator*
Nerode, Anil *mathematician, educator*
Payne, Lawrence Edward *mathematics educator*
Salton, Gerard *computer science educator*
Shore, Richard Arnold *mathematics educator*
†Trotter, Leslie Earl *operations research educator, consultant*

Morrisville
Rouse, Robert Moorefield *mathematician, educator*

New Paltz
Fleisher, Harold *computer scientist*

New York
Abbey, Scott Gerson *computer information scientist*
Bass, Hyman *mathematician, educator*
Berman, Simeon Moses *mathematician, educator*
Blumstein, Reneé J. *research and statistical consultant*
Chow, Yuan Shih *mathematician, educator*
Chu, C. K. *applied mathematician, educator*
Chudnovsky, Gregory Volfovich *mathematician, educator*
Cohn, Harvey *mathematician*
Derman, Cyrus *mathematical statistician*
Di Paola, Robert Arnold *mathematics and computer science educator*
Edwards, Harold Mortimer *mathematics educator*
Frankel, Martin Richard *statistician, educator, consultant*
Garabedian, Paul Roesel *mathematics educator*
Gelbart, Abe *mathematician, educator*
Gomory, Ralph Edward *mathematician, manufacturing company executive, foundation executive*
Gross, Jonathan Light *computer scientist, mathematician, educator*
Hilton, Alice Mary *cybernetics and computing systems consultant, author, mathematician, art historian*
Hunte, Beryl Eleanor *mathematics educator, consultant*
†John, Fritz *mathematician, educator*
Kurnow, Ernest *statistician, educator*
Lax, Peter David *mathematics educator*
Lucas, Henry Cameron, Jr. *information systems educator, writer, consultant*
Mc Cracken, Daniel Delbert *computer science educator, author*
†McKean, Henry P. *mathematics institute administrator*
Meier, Paul *statistician, mathematics educator*
Moise, Edwin Evariste *mathematician, educator*
Morawetz, Cathleen Synge *mathematician*
Moyne, John Abel *computer scientist, linguist, educator*
Nirenberg, Louis *mathematician, educator*
†Padberg, Manfred Wilhelm *mathematics educator*
Posamentier, Alfred Steven *mathematics educator, university administrator*
Schwartz, Jacob T. *computer scientist*
Sellers, Peter Hoadley *mathematician*
Seltzer, William *statistician, international organization director*
Shane, Harold David *mathematics educator, consultant*
Sohmer, Bernard *mathematics educator, administrator*
Traub, J(oseph) F(rederick) *computer scientist, educator*
Wallace, Robert James *mathematics and science educator*
Weitzner, Harold *mathematics educator*
Widlund, Olof Bertil *computer science educator*

Rochester
Alling, Norman Larrabee *mathematics educator*
Arden, Bruce Wesley *computer science and electrical engineering educator*
Gitler, Samuel Carlos *mathematics educator, researcher*
Hollingsworth, Jack Waring *mathematics and computer science educator*
Segal, Sanford Leonard *mathematics educator*
Simon, William *biomathematician, educator*

Stony Brook
Douglas, Ronald George *mathematician*
Feinberg, Eugene Alexander *mathematics educator*
Glimm, James Gilbert *mathematician*
Hill, C(lyde) Denson *mathematician, educator*
†Lawson, H(erbert) Blaine, Jr. *mathematician, educator*
Tucker, Alan Curtiss *mathematics educator*

Syracuse
Berra, P. Bruce *computer educator*
Cargo, Gerald Thomas *mathematics educator*
Church, Philip Throop *mathematician, educator*
Dudewicz, Edward John *statistician*
Graver, Jack Edward *mathematics educator*
Hansen, Per Brinch *computer scientist*
Pardee, Otway O'Meara *computer science educator*
Robinson, John Alan *logic and computer science educator*
Waterman, Daniel *mathematician, educator*

Troy
Berg, Daniel *science and technology educator*
†Cole, Julian D. *mathematician, educator*
Drew, Donald Allen *mathematical sciences educator*
†Duquette, David Joseph *materials science and engineering educator*
Jacobson, Melvin Joseph *applied mathematician, acoustician, educator*
McNaughton, Robert Forbes, Jr. *computer science educator*

West Point
Barr, Donald Roy *statistics and operations research educator, statistician*

Yorktown Heights
Agarwal, Ramesh Chandra *applied mathematician, researcher*
Allen, Frances Elizabeth *computer scientist*
d'Heurle, François Max *research scientist, engineering educator*
Hoffman, Alan Jerome *mathematician, educator*
Jaffe, Jeffrey Martin *computer scientist*
†Johnson, Ellis Lane *mathematician*
Mandelbrot, Benoit B. *mathematician, scientist, educator*
Winograd, Shmuel *mathematician*
Wong, Chak-Kuen *computer scientist*

NORTH CAROLINA

Chapel Hill
Brooks, Frederick Phillips, Jr. *computer scientist*
Coulter, Elizabeth Jackson *biostatistician, educator*
Simons, Gordon Donald, Jr. *statistician*
Stanat, Donald F. *computer science educator*
Stasheff, James Dillon *mathematics educator*
Wahl, Jonathan Michael *mathematics educator*
Wogen, Warren Ronald *mathematics educator*

Charlotte
Johnson, Phillip Eugene *mathematics educator*

Durham
Allard, William Kenneth *mathematician*
Loveland, Donald William *computer science educator*
Rose, Donald James *computer science educator*
Vitter, Jeffrey Scott *computer science educator, consultant*
Warner, Seth L. *mathematician, educator*
Winkler, Robert Lewis *statistics educator, researcher, author, consultant*
Woodbury, Max Atkin *polymath, educator*

Greensboro
Posey, Eldon Eugene *mathematician, educator*

Raleigh
Bloomfield, Peter *statistics educator*
Mason, David Dickenson *statistics educator*
Peterson, Elmor Lee *mathematical scientist, educator*
Rawlings, John Oren *statistician, researcher*
Sagan, Hans *mathematician, educator, author*
Wesler, Oscar *mathematician, educator*

Research Triangle Park
Karr, Alan Francis *statistics educator, academic administrator*

Salisbury
Tlalka, Jacek *mathematics educator*

Swansboro
Mullikin, Thomas Wilson *mathematics educator*

Winston Salem
Kerr, Sandria Neidus *mathematics and computer science educator*

OHIO

Ashtabula
Taylor, Norman Floyd *computer educator, administrator*

Athens
Wen, Shih-Liang *mathematics educator*

Cincinnati
Flick, Thomas Michael *mathematics educator, educational administrator*
Semon, Warren Lloyd *retired computer sciences educator*

Cleveland
Clark, Robert Arthur *mathematician, educator*
de Acosta, Alejandro Daniel *mathematician, educator*
Goffman, William *mathematician, educator*
Hajek, Otomar *mathematics educator*
Nelson, Raymond John *mathematics and philosophy educator*
Szarek, Stanislaw Jerzy *mathematics educator*
Woyczynski, Wojbor Andrzej *mathematician, educator*

Columbus
Chandrasekaran, Balakrishnan *computer and information science educator*
Dowling, Thomas Allan *mathematics educator*
Kindig, Fred Eugene *statistics educator, arbitrator*

Dayton
Bedell, Kenneth Berkley *computer specialist, educator*
Khalimsky, Efim *mathematics and computer science educator*

Defiance
Mirchandaney, Arjan Sobhraj *mathematics educator*

Delaware
Mendenhall, Robert Vernon *mathematics educator*

Kent
Cummins, Kenneth Burdette *emeritus science and mathematics educator*
Powell, Robert Ellis *mathematics educator, former college dean*
Stackelberg, Olaf Patrick Von *mathematician*
†Varga, Richard Steven *mathematics educator*

Vermilion
Vance, Elbridge Putnam *mathematics educator*

OKLAHOMA

Ada
Walker, Billy Kenneth *computer science educator, academic administrator*

Stillwater
Folks, J. Leroy *statistician, educator*
Lu, Huizhu *computer scientist, educator*

OREGON

Beaverton
Rattner, Justin *supercomputer research manager*

Bend
Mayer, Richard Dean *mathematics educator*

Corvallis
Petersen, Bent Edvard *mathematician, educator*
†Skelton, John Edward *computer science educator, consultant*

Eugene
Andrews, Fred Charles *mathematics educator*

Florence
Gray, Augustine Heard, Jr. *computer consultant*

Monmouth
Forcier, Richard Charles *information technology educator, computer applications consultant*

Portland
Ahuja, Jagdish Chand *mathematics educator*

Tualatin
Brown, Robert Wallace *mathematics educator*

PENNSYLVANIA

Abington
Ayoub, Ayoub Barsoum *mathematician, educator*

Bala Cynwyd
Ackoff, Russell Lincoln *systems sciences educator*

Bethlehem
†Ghosh, Bhaskar Kumar *statistics educator, researcher*
Rivlin, Ronald Samuel *mathematics educator emeritus*

Chester
Frank, Amalie Julianna *computer science, electrical engineering and mathematics educator, consultant*

Conshohocken
Froman, Ann Dolores *computer education educator*

Coraopolis
Kohun, Frederick Gregg *information scientist, economist, educator*

Lewisburg
Ray, David Scott *mathematics educator*

Meadville
Cable, Charles Allen *mathematician*

Mercer
Brady, Wray Grayson *mathematician, educator*

Monroeville
Nemeth, Edward Joseph *process research specialist*

Philadelphia
Albright, Hugh Norton *mathematics educator*
Banerji, Ranan Bihari *mathematics and computer science educator*
Collons, Rodger Duane *decision sciences educator*
de Cani, John Stapley *statistician, educator*
Freyd, Peter John *mathematician, computer scientist, educator*
Garfield, Eugene *information scientist, author, publisher*
Goldstine, Herman Heine *mathematician, association executive*
Hildebrand, David Kent *statistics educator*
Iglewicz, Boris *statistician, educator*
Kadison, Richard Vincent *mathematician, educator*
Knopp, Marvin Isadore *mathematics educator*
Mode, Charles J. *mathematician, educator*
Morrison, Donald Franklin *statistician, educator*
Porter, Gerald Joseph *mathematician, educator*
Scandura, Joseph Michael *education researcher, software engineer*
Shatz, Stephen Sidney *mathematician, educator*
†Warner, Frank Wilson, III *mathematics educator*

Pittsburgh
†Balas, Egon *applied mathematician, educator*
Berliner, Hans Jack *computer scientist*
Bryant, Randal Everitt *computer science educator, consultant*
Burbea, Jacob N. *mathematics educator*
Chao, Chong-Yun *mathematics educator*
Deskins, Wilbur Eugene *mathematician, educator*
Duffin, Richard James *mathematician, educator*
Fienberg, Stephen Elliott *statistician*
Froehlich, Fritz Edgar *telecommunications educator and scientist*
Gurtin, Morton Edward *mathematics educator*
Hall, Charles Allan *numerical analyst, educator*
Kadane, Joseph B. *statistics educator*
Kolodner, Ignace Izaak *mathematician, educator*
Lehoczky, John Paul *statistics educator*
McAvoy, Bruce Ronald *scientist, consultant*
Moore, Richard Allan *mathematics educator*
Rheinboldt, Werner Carl *mathematics educator, researcher*
Shaw, Mary M. *computer science educator*
Siewiorek, Daniel Paul *computer science educator, researcher*
Thompson, Gerald Luther *operations research and applied mathematics educator*
Williams, William Orville *mathematics educator*

Swarthmore
Kelemen, Charles F. *computer science educator*

University Park
Andrews, George Eyre *mathematics educator*
Antle, Charles Edward *statistics educator*
Arnold, Douglas Norman *mathematics educator*
Brownawell, Woodrow Dale *mathematics educator*
Harkness, William Leonard *statistician, educator*
†Lindsay, Bruce George *statistics educator*

Wayne
Clelland, Richard Cook *statistics educator, university administrator*

RHODE ISLAND

Cranston
†Fitzpatrick, William P. *computer programmer/ analyst, state legislator*

Kingston
Driver, Rodney David *mathematics educator, state legislator*
Roxin, Emilio Oscar *mathematics educator*
Verma, Ghasi Ram *mathematics educator*

Providence
Banchoff, Thomas Francis *mathematics educator*
Charniak, Eugene *computer scientist, educator*
Dafermos, Constantine Michael *applied mathematics educator*
Davis, Philip J. *mathematician*
Fleming, Wendell Helms *educator, mathematician*
Freiberger, Walter Frederick *mathematics educator, actuarial science consultant, educator*
Kushner, Harold Joseph *mathematics educator*
Pipkin, Allen Compere, II *mathematician, educator*
Preparata, Franco Paolo *computer science and engineering educator*
Savage, John Edmund *computer science educator, researcher*

SOUTH CAROLINA

Charleston
Hoel, David Gerhard *state administrator, statistician, scientist*

Clemson
Kenelly, John Willis, Jr. *mathematician, educator*

Columbia
Culik, Karel *computer scientist, educator*
Eastman, Caroline Merriam *computer science educator*
Ott, Jack M. *mathematics educator*

Florence
Strong, Roger Lee *mathematics educator*

Greenville
Cook, Paul M(artin), II *mathematics educator*

Newberry
Layton, William Isaac *mathematics educator*

Spartanburg
Wilde, Edwin Frederick *mathematics educator*

TENNESSEE

Brownsville
Kalin, Robert *retired mathematics educator*

Knoxville
Sherman, Gordon Rae *computer science educator*

Maryville
Inscho, Barbara Pickel *mathematics educator*

Memphis
Franklin, Stanley Phillip *computer scientist, mathematician, cognitive scientist, educator*
Schelp, Richard Herbert *mathematics educator*

Murfreesboro
Aden, Robert Clark *retired computer information systems educator*
Rob, Peter *computer information systems educator*

Nashville
Banks, John Houston *mathematics educator*
Fischer, Patrick Carl *computer scientist, educator*
Gavish, Bezalel *computer science operations research, information systems educator*
Schumaker, Larry Lee *mathematics educator*

Oak Ridge
Gardiner, Donald Andrew *statistician, consultant*
Kliewer, Kenneth Lee *computational scientist, research administrator*
Raridon, Richard Jay *computer specialist*

Sewanee
Puckette, Stephen Elliott *mathematics educator, mathematician*

TEXAS

Abilene
Retzer, Kenneth Albert *mathematics educator*

Arlington
Greenspan, Donald *mathematician, educator*
Han, Chien-Pai *statistics educator*

Austin
Bledsoe, Woodrow Wilson *mathematics and computer sciences educator*
Clark, Charles T(aliferro) *retired business statistics educator*
Dijkstra, Edsger Wybe *computer science educator, mathematician*
Garner, Harvey Louis *computer scientist, consultant, electrical engineering educator*
Gillman, Leonard *mathematician, educator*
†Kozmetsky, George *computer science educator*
Lam, Simon Shin-Sing *computer science educator*
Misra, Jayadev *computer science educator*
Uhlenbeck, Karen Keskulla *mathematician, educator*

College Station
Blakley, George Robert, Jr. *mathematician, computer scientist*
†Chui, Charles Kam-Tai *mathematics educator*
†Ewing, Richard Edward *mathematics, chemical and petroleum engineering educator*
Parzen, Emanuel *statistical scientist*

Dallas
†Browne, Richard Harold *statistician, consultant*
Pritzker, Leon *statistician, consultant*

Denton
Renka, Robert Joseph *computer science educator, consultant*

El Paso
Bernau, Simon John *mathematics educator*

Fort Worth
Doran, Robert Stuart *mathematician, educator*

Houston
Billingsley, David Stuart *researcher*
Brown, Dennison Robert *mathematician, educator*
Dennis, John Emory, Jr. *mathematics educator*
Freeman, Marjorie Schaefer *mathematics educator*
Gardner, Everette Shaw, Jr. *information sciences educator*
Harvey, F. Reese *mathematics educator*
Kennedy, Ken *computer science educator*
Munson, John Backus *computer systems consultant, retired computer engineering company executive*
Scott, David Warren *statistics educator*
Tapia, Richard Alfred *mathematics educator*
Thrall, Robert McDowell *mathematician, educator*
Wang, Chao-Cheng *mathematician, engineer*
†Wells, Raymond O., Jr. *mathematics educator, researcher*

Kingsville
Cecil, David Rolf *mathematician, educator*

Lubbock
Conover, William Jay *statistics educator*

Richardson
Pervin, William Joseph *computer science educator*

San Antonio
Ahmad, Shair *mathematics educator*
Grubb, Robert Lynn *computer system designer*
Trench, William Frederick *mathematics educator*

Waco
Odell, Patrick Lowry *mathematics educator*

UTAH

Provo
Moore, Hal G. *mathematician, educator*
Robinson, Donald Wilford *mathematics educator*

VERMONT

Norwich
Snapper, Ernst *mathematics educator*

VIRGINIA

Alexandria
Olson, Warren Kinley *operations research analyst, engineer, physicist*

Arlington
Barrett, Lida Kittrell *mathematics educator*
Garcia, Oscar Nicolas *computer science educator*
Long, Madeleine J. *mathematics and science educator*
Murray, Jeanne Morris *computer scientist, educator, consultant*
Waring, John Alfred *retired research writer, lecturer, consultant*
Young, Paul Ruel *computer scientist, administrator*

Blacksburg
Good, Irving John *statistics educator, philosopher of science*
Krutchkoff, Richard Gerald *statistics educator, researcher*
Olin, Robert Floyd *mathematics educator and reseacher*

Charlottesville
Catlin, Avery *engineering and computer science educator, writer*
Horgan, Cornelius Oliver *applied mathematics and applied mechanics educator*
Mansfield, Lois Edna *mathematics educator, researcher*
Martin, Nathaniel Frizell Grafton *mathematician, educator*
Ortega, James McDonough *mathematician, educator*
Rosenblum, Marvin *mathematics educator*
Simmonds, James Gordon *mathematician, educator*
Taylor, Samuel James *mathematics educator*
Triggiani, Roberto *mathematics educator*
Wulf, William Allan *computer information scientist, educator*

Fairfax
Denning, Peter James *computer scientist, engineer*
Hanuschak, George Alan *statistician*
Sage, Andrew Patrick, Jr. *systems information and software engineering educator*

Herndon
Arnberg, Robert Lewis *mathematician*

Mc Lean
Gardenier, John Stark, II *statistician, management scientist*

Norfolk
Maly, Kurt John *computer science educator*
Marchello, Joseph Maurice *mathematics and physical science educator*
Wei, Benjamin Min *computer engineering educator*

Oakton
Shrier, Stefan *mathematician, educator*

Reston
Fredette, Richard Chester *computer specialist*

Vienna
Lillard, Mark Hill, III *computer consulting executive, former air force officer*

WASHINGTON

Ellensburg
Comstock, Dale Robert *mathematics educator*

Kenmore
MacKenzie, Peter Sean *computer service company*

Kent
Filley, Laurence Duane *computer programmer, consultant*

Pullman
†Hildebrandt, Darlene Myers *information scientist*
Kallaher, Michael Joseph *mathematics educator*

Richland
Cochran, James Alan *mathematics educator*

Seattle
Breslow, Norman Edward *biostatistics educator, researcher*
Criminale, William Oliver, Jr. *applied mathematics educator*
Hewitt, Edwin *mathematician, educator*
Jans, James Patrick *mathematics educator*
Klee, Victor La Rue *mathematician, educator*
†Lee, John Marshall *mathematics educator*
Michael, Ernest Arthur *mathematics educator*
Nijenhuis, Albert *mathematician, educator*
Noe, Jerre Donald *computer science educator*
O'Malley, Robert Edmund, Jr. *mathematics educator*
Pyke, Ronald *mathematics educator*
Segal, Jack *mathematics educator*
Wan, Frederic Yui-Ming *mathematician, educator*
Wellner, Jon August *statistician, educator*

WEST VIRGINIA

Morgantown
Butcher, Donald Franklin *statistician, computer scientist*
De Vore, Paul Warren *technology educator*
Holtan, Boyd DeVere *mathematics educator*
Vest, Marvin Lewis *mathematical educator*

WISCONSIN

Brookfield
Diesem, John Lawrence *information systems executive*

Madison
Askey, Richard Allen *mathematician*
Beck, Anatole *mathematician, educator*
de Boor, Carl *mathematician*
Draper, Norman Richard *statistician, educator*
Harvey, John Grover *mathematics educator*
Hickman, James Charles *business and statistics educator, business school dean*
Johnson, Millard Wallace, Jr. *mathematics and engineering educator*
Johnson, Richard Arnold *statistics educator, consultant*
Kurtz, Thomas Gordon *mathematics educator*
Levin, Jacob Joseph *mathematician, educator*
Moore, Edward Forrest *computer scientist, mathematician, former educator*
Robinson, Stephen Michael *applied mathematician, educator*
Wahba, Grace *statistician, educator*

Milwaukee
Lawrence, Willard Earl *mathematics, statistics and computer science educator emeritus*

Whitewater
Verma, Krishnanand *mathematics educator, consultant*

TERRITORIES OF THE UNITED STATES

PUERTO RICO

Rio Piedras
Bangdiwala, Ishver Surchand *statistician, educator*

CANADA

Toronto
Fraser, Donald Alexander Stuart *mathematics educator*

ALBERTA

Calgary
Varadarajan, Kalathoor *educator, researcher*

Edmonton
Davis, Wayne Alton *computer science educator*

BRITISH COLUMBIA

Vancouver
Boyd, David William *mathematician, educator*
Clark, Colin Whitcomb *mathematics educator*
Feldman, Joel Shalom *mathematician*
Granirer, Edmond Ernest *mathematician, educator*
Miura, Robert Mitsuru *mathematician, researcher, educator*
Seymour, Brian Richard *mathematician*
Sion, Maurice *mathematics educator*
Swanson, Charles Andrew *mathematics educator*
Zidek, James Victor *statistician, educator*

Victoria
Manning, Eric *computer science and engineering educator, university dean, researcher*

MANITOBA

Winnipeg
Gratzer, George Andrew *mathematics educator*

NOVA SCOTIA

Halifax
Fillmore, Peter Arthur *mathematician, educator*

ONTARIO

Etobicoke
Bahadur, Birendra *display specialist, liquid crystal researcher*

Hamilton
Banaschewski, Bernhard *mathematics educator*
Parnas, David Lorge *computer scientist, engineer, educator*

Kingston
Campbell, L(ouis) Lorne *mathematics educator*
Coleman, Albert John *mathematics educator*
Ribenboim, Paulo *mathematics educator*

London
Anderson, Oliver Duncan *consulting statistician, educator*
†Bauer, Michael Anthony *computer scientist, educator*
Borwein, David *mathematics educator*
Ehrman, Joachim Benedict *mathematics educator*

Ottawa
Csörgö, Miklós *statistician*
Dawson, Donald Andrew *mathematics educator, researcher*
Dlab, Vlastimil *mathematics educator, researcher*
Macphail, Moray St. John *mathematics educator emeritus*

Toronto
Arthur, James Greig *mathematics educator*
Cook, Stephen Arthur *mathematics and computer science educator*
Coxeter, Harold Scott Macdonald *mathematician*
Davis, (Horace) Chandler *mathematics educator*
Friedlander, John Benjamin *mathematics educator*
Gotlieb, Calvin Carl *computer scientist, educator*
Greiner, Peter Charles *mathematics educator, researcher*
Halperin, John Stephen *mathematics educator*
Murasugi, Kunio *mathematician, educator*
Rooney, Paul George *mathematics educator*
Tall, Franklin David *mathematician, neurolinguistic programming master practitioner*

Waterloo
Aczel, Janos Dezso *mathematics educator*
Gladwell, Graham Maurice Leslie *mathematician, civil engineering educator*
Paldus, Josef *mathematics educator*
Sprott, David Arthur *statistics and psychology educator*
Stewart, Cameron Leigh *mathematics educator*

QUEBEC

Montreal
De Mori, Renato *computer science educator, researcher*
Dubuc, Serge *mathematics educator*
Herz, Carl Samuel *mathematician*
Levine, Martin David *computer science and electrical engineering educator*
Maag, Urs Richard *statistics educator*
Moser, William Oscar Jules *mathematics educator*
St.-Pierre, Jacques *statistics educator, consultant*
Suen, Ching Yee *computer scientist and educator, researcher*

Quebec
Theodorescu, Radu Amza Serban *mathematician, educator*

AUSTRALIA

Canberra
Gani, Joseph Mark *statistics educator, administrator, researcher*

AUSTRIA

Vienna
Niederreiter, Harald Guenther *mathematician, researcher*

BELGIUM

Lens
Peat, Randall Dean *defense analysis company executive, retired air force officer*

Louvain-la-Neuve
Sintzoff, Michel *computer scientist, educator*

BRAZIL

Curitiba
Berman, Marcelo Samuel *mathematics and physics educator, cosmology researcher, retial businessman*

CHINA

Wuhu
Mo, Jiaqi *mathematics educator*

DENMARK

Holte
Elliott, George Arthur *mathematician, educator*

EGYPT

Cairo
El-Hamalaway, Mohamed-Younis Abd-El-Samie *computer engineering educator*

ENGLAND

Leicester
Harijan, Ram *technology transfer researcher*

FRANCE

Amiens
Chacron, Joseph *mathematics educator*

Paris
Yuechiming, Roger Yue Yuen Shing *mathematics educator*

GERMANY

Darmstadt
†Hofmann, Karl Heinrich *mathematics educator*

Mannheim
Steffens, Franz Eugen Aloys *computer science educator*

Münster
Maltese, George John *mathematics educator*

Munich
Stiegler, Karl Drago *mathematician*

Paderborn
Belli, Fevzi *computing science educator, consultant*

GREECE

Thessaloniki
Tsagas, Grigorios Fotios *mathematics educator*

ITALY

Padua
Rosati, Mario *mathematician, educator*

JAPAN

Chiba
Yamada, Shinichi *mathematician, computer scientist, educator*

Hachioji
Shimoji, Sadao *applied mathematics educator, engineer*

Kanagawa
Matsubara, Tomoo *software scientist*

POLAND

Warsaw
Semadeni, Zbigniew Wladyslaw *mathematician, educator*

RUSSIA

Voronezh
Kostin, Vladimir Alexeevich *mathematics educator*

SAUDI ARABIA

Dhahran
Warne, Ronson Joseph *mathematics educator*

SINGAPORE

Singapore
Ho, Thomas Inn Min *computer scientist, educator*

SWITZERLAND

Zurich
Kalman, Rudolf Emil *mathematician, researcher, systems scientist*
Lanford, Oscar Erasmus, III *mathematics educator*
Nievergelt, Jurg *computer science educator*

ADDRESS UNPUBLISHED

Bachert, Robert Frederic *mathematician, systems analyst*
†Bednarz, Nadine *mathematics educator, director research center*
Birkhoff, Garrett *mathematician, educator*
Box, George Edward Pelham *statistics educator*
Browder, Felix Earl *mathematician, educator*
Choi, Man-Duen *mathematics educator*
Elliott, David LeRoy *mathematician, educator, engineering educator*
Freitag, Harlow *computer scientist, corporate executive*
Frieder, Gideon *computer science and engineering educator*
Galfo, Armand James *statistics educator*
Goldberg, Samuel *retired mathematician, foundation officer*
Gray, James Peyton *computer scientist*
Greenwood, Frank *information scientist*
Halberstam, Heini *mathematician*
Hamblen, John Wesley *computer scientist, genealogist*
Hildebrandt, Theodore Ware *computer scientist*
Hooper, Gerry Don *information systems professional, consultant*
Horton, Wilfred Henry *mathematics educator*
Hughes, Richard Gene *computer executive, consultant*
Husain, Taqdir *mathematics educator*
†Jones, Anita Katherine *computer scientist, educator*
Kadota, Takashi Theodore *mathematician, electrical engineer*
Karnaugh, Maurice *computer scientist, educator*
Keisler, H(oward) Jerome *mathematics educator*
Komkov, Vadim *mathematician, educator*
†Krantz, Steven George *mathematics educator*
Laning, J. Halcombe *retired computer scientist*
Lasry, Jean-Michel *mathematics educator*
Low, Emmet Francis, Jr. *mathematics educator*
Mullen, William Joseph, III *military analyst, retired army officer*
Rapin, Charles René Jules *computer science educator*
Roberts, Marie Dyer *computer systems specialist*
Suppes, Patrick *statistics, education, philosophy and psychology educator*
Temam, Roger M. *mathematician*
Tompsett, Michael Francis *defense research director*
Walter, Martin Edward *mathematician, educator*
Weiner, Louis Max *retired mathematics educator*
Winder, Robert Owen *mathematician, computer engineering executive*
Wylie, Clarence Raymond, Jr. *mathematics educator*

SCIENCE: PHYSICAL SCIENCE

UNITED STATES

ALABAMA

Auburn
Carr, Howard Earl *physicist, educator*
Molz, Fred John, III *hydrologist, educator*
Perez, Joseph Dominique *physics educator*

Birmingham
Bauman, Robert Poe *physicist*
Bugg, Charles Edward *biochemistry educator, scientist*
Longenecker, Herbert Eugene *biochemist, former university president*
Montgomery, John Atterbury *research chemist, consultant*
Shealy, David Lee *physicist, educator*
Urry, Dan Wesley *research biophysicist, educator, science facility administrator*

Dauphin Island
Porter, John Finley, Jr. *physicist, conservationist, retired educator*

Harvest
Norman, Ralph Louis *physicist, consultant*

Hoover
Thompson, Wynelle Doggett *chemistry educator*

Huntsville
Anderson, Elmer Ebert *physicist, educator*
Chappell, Charles Richard *space scientist*
Cornatzer, William Eugene *biochemist, emeritus educator*
Decher, Rudolf *physicist*
de Loach, Anthony Cortelyou *solar physicist*
Dimmock, John Oliver *university research center director*
Garriott, Owen Kay *astronaut, scientist*
Hartman, Richard Leon *physicist*
†Lee, Thomas J. *aerospace scientist*
McKnight, William Baldwin *physics educator*
Mc Manus, Samuel Plyler *chemist, academic administrator*
Parnell, Thomas Alfred *physicist*
Schwinghamer, Robert John *materials scientist*
Smith, Robert Earl *space scientist*
Stuhlinger, Ernst *physicist*
Vaughan, William Walton *atmospheric scientist*
Wright, John Collins *chemistry educator*

Jacksonville
Reid, William James *physicist, educator*

Madison
†Rosenberger, Franz Ernst *physics educator*

Marshall Space Flight Center
†Johnson, Charles Leslie *aerospace physicist, consultant*

Mobile
Fox, Sidney Walter *chemist, educator*

Montgomery
Tan, Boen Hie *biochemist*

Normal
Caulfield, Henry John *physics educator*
Tan, Arjun *physics educator, researcher*

Redstone Arsenal
Allan, Barry David *research chemist, government official*

Tuscaloosa
†Atwood, Jerry Lee *chemistry educator*
Cava, Michael Patrick *chemist, educator*
Cole, George David *physicist*
Coulter, Philip Wylie *physicist, educator*
Izatt, Jerald Ray *physics educator*
LaMoreaux, Philip Elmer *geologist, hydrogeologist, consultant*
Mancini, Ernest Anthony *geologist, educator, researcher*
Miyagawa, Ichiro *physicist*
Van Artsdalen, Ervin Robert *physical chemist, educator*

ALASKA

Anchorage
Evans, William Frederick *research chemist*

Fairbanks
†Eichelberger, John Charles *volcanologist, educator*
Helfferich, Merritt Randolph *geophysical research administrator*
Roederer, Juan Gualterio *physics educator*
Speck, Robert Charles *geological engineer*
Weeks, Wilford Frank *geophysics educator, glaciologist*
Weller, Gunter Ernst *geophysics educator*

ARIZONA

Coolidge
Hiller, William Clark *physics educator, engineering educator, consultant*

Flagstaff
Barnes, Charles Winfred *geology educator, administrator*
Colbert, Edwin Harris *paleontologist, museum curator*
†Millis, Robert Lowell *astronomer*
Shoemaker, Eugene Merle *geologist*
Zoellner, Robert William *chemistry educator*

Green Valley
Bates, Charles Carpenter *oceanographer*

Peoria
Bernstein, Eugene Merle *physicist, retired educator*

Phoenix
†Allen, John Rybolt L. *chemist, biochemist*
Quadt, Raymond Adolph *metallurgist, cement company executive*
Wing, David Allan *biochemistry educator*

Scottsdale
Klein, Morton Joseph *chemist*
McPherson, Donald J. *metallurgist*
Newman, William Louis *geologist*

Sun City
Dapples, Edward Charles *geologist, educator*

Sun City West
Mariella, Raymond P. *chemistry educator, consultant*

Tempe
Burgoyne, Edward Eynon *chemistry educator*
Burke, William James *chemist, educator, consultant*
Buseck, Peter Robert *geochemistry educator*
Cowley, John Maxwell *physics educator*
Dietz, Robert Sinclair *retired geology educator*
Goronkin, Herbert *physicist*
Juvet, Richard Spalding, Jr. *chemistry educator*
Mayer, James Walter *materials science educator*
Nigam, Bishan Perkash *physics educator*
†Pettit, George Robert *chemistry educator, cancer researcher*
Péwé, Troy Lewis *geologist, educator*
Roy, Radha Raman *physics educator*
Skibitzke, Herbert Ernst, Jr. *hydrologist*
†Smith, David John *physicist, educator*
Starrfield, Sumner Grosby *astrophysics educator, researcher*
Tillery, Bill W. *physics educator*
†Vandenberg, Edwin James *chemist, educator*
Whitehurst, Harry Bernard *chemistry educator*
†Ziurys, Lucy Marie *radio astronomer, chemist*

Tucson
Angel, James Roger Prior *astronomer*
Barrett, Bruce Richard *physics educator*
Bartocha, Bodo *scientist, educator*
†Brault, James William *physicist*
Broadfoot, Albert Lyle *physicist*
Carruthers, Peter Ambler *physicist, educator*
Davis, Stanley Nelson *hydrologist, educator*
Dessler, Alexander Jack *space physics and astronomy educator, scientist*
De Young, David Spencer *astrophysicist*
Dickinson, Robert Earl *atmospheric scientist, educator*
Dodd, Charles Gardner *physical chemist*
Forster, Leslie Stewart *chemistry educator*
Hartmann, William Kenneth *astronomy scientist*
Haynes, Caleb Vance, Jr. *geology and archaeology educator*
Hill, Henry Allen *physicist, educator*
Hoffmann, William Frederick *astronomer*
Howard, Robert Franklin *observatory administrator, astronomer*
Hubbard, William Bogel *planetary sciences educator*
Hunten, Donald Mount *planetary scientist, educator*
Jackson, Kenneth Arthur *physicist, researcher*
Jefferies, John Trevor *astronomer, astrophysicist, observatory administrator*
Kessler, John Otto *physicist, educator*
Kiersch, George Alfred *geological consultant, retired educator*
†Krider, E. Philip *atmospheric scientist, educator*
Lamb, Willis Eugene, Jr. *physicist, educator*
Law, John Harold *biochemistry educator*
Leibacher, John William *astronomer*
Levy, Eugene Howard *planetary sciences educator, researcher*
Long, Austin *geosciences educator*
Nagy, Bartholomew Stephen *geochemist, educator*
Parmenter, Robert Haley *physics educator*
†Powell, Richard C. *physicist, educator, researcher*
Roemer, Elizabeth *astronomer, educator*
Rountree, Janet Caryl *astrophysicist*
Schaefer, John Paul *chemist, corporate executive*
Smiley, Terah Leroy *geosciences educator*
Sonett, Charles Philip *physicist*
Strittmatter, Peter Albert *astronomer, educator*
Swalin, Richard Arthur *scientist, company executive*
Walker, F. Ann *chemistry educator, researcher*
†Wallace, Terry Charles, Jr. *geophysicist, educator*
White, Alvin Swauger *aerospace scientist, consultant*

Willis, Clifford Leon geologist
Wolfe, William Louis optics educator
Wolff, Sidney Carne astronomer, observatory administrator

ARKANSAS

Fayetteville
Steele, Kenneth Franklin, Jr. hydrology educator, resource center director, researcher

Searcy
Pryor, Joseph Ehrman chemistry educator

CALIFORNIA

Altadena
†Gurnis, Michael Christopher geological sciences educator

Arcata
Fox, Lawrence, III remote sensing and natural resources educator, consultant
Wayne, Lowell Grant air pollution scientist, consultant

Atascadero
Ogier, Walter Thomas retired physics educator

Atherton
Fisher, Leon Harold physicist, emeritus educator

Auburn
Hess, Patrick Henry chemist

Bakersfield
Dorer, Fred Harold chemistry educator

Bayside
Cocks, George Gosson retired chemical microscopy educator

Berkeley
Alpen, Edward Lewis biophysicist, educator
Ames, Bruce N(athan) biochemist, molecular biologist
Arnon, Daniel I(srael) biochemist, educator
Arons, Jonathan astrophysicist, educator
Attwood, David Thomas physicist, educator
†Baletta, William physics research administrator
Barker, Horace Albert biochemist, microbiologist
Bartlett, Neil chemist, educator
Bergman, Robert George chemist, educator
Berry, William Benjamin Newell geologist, educator, former museum administrator
Bolt, Bruce Alan seismologist, educator
Bowyer, C(harles) Stuart astrophysicist, educator
Brewer, Leo physical chemist, educator
Brimhall, George H., Jr. geologist, educator
Calvin, Melvin chemist, educator
Carmichael, Ian Stuart Edward geologist, educator
Cerny, Joseph, III chemistry educator, scientific laboratory administrator, university dean and official
Chamberlain, Owen nuclear physicist
Chamberlin, Michael John biochemistry educator
Chandler, David scientist, educator
Chew, Geoffrey Foucar physicist
Clarke, John physics educator
Cohen, Marvin Lou physics educator
Cole, Roger David biochemist, educator
†Curtis, Garniss Hearfield geology educator
Dauben, William Garfield chemist, educator
Ely, Robert Pollock, Jr. physics educator, researcher
Falicov, Leopoldo Maximo physicist, educator
Fowler, Thomas Kenneth physicist
Gaillard, Mary Katharine physics educator
†Gardner, Wilford Robert physicist, educator
Glaser, Donald A(rthur) physicist
Glaser, Harold physicist, university administrator
Goldhaber, Gerson physicist, educator
Gregory, Joseph Tracy paleontologist, educator
Hahn, Erwin Louis physicist, educator
Hartsough, Walter Douglas physicist
Hearst, John Eugene chemistry educator
Heathcock, Clayton Howell chemistry educator, researcher
Heiles, Carl Eugene astronomer, educator
Heineman, Heinz chemist
†Heinemann, Heinz chemist, researcher, consultant
Helmholz, August Carl physicist, educator emeritus
Hoffman, Darleane Christian chemistry educator
Holdren, John Paul energy and resource educator, researcher, author, consultant
Jackson, J(ohn) David physicist, educator
Jeanloz, Raymond geophysicist, educator
Jeffries, Carson Dunning physicist, educator
Johnston, Harold S(ledge) chemistry educator
Jolly, William Lee chemistry educator
Kerth, Leroy T. physics educator
King, Ivan Robert astronomy educator
Kirsch, Jack Frederick biochemistry educator
Kittel, Charles physicist, educator emeritus
Klinman, Judith Pollock biochemist, educator
Koshland, Daniel Edward, Jr. biochemist, educator
Lee, Yuan T(seh) chemistry educator
†Leemans, Wim Pieter physicist
Leopold, Luna Bergere geology educator
Lester, William Alexander, Jr. chemist, educator
Linn, Stuart Michael biochemist, educator
Mandelstam, Stanley physicist
Mc Evilly, Thomas Vincent seismologist
McKee, Christopher Fulton astrophysics and astronomy educator
Mel, Howard Charles biophysics educator
Miller, William Hughes theoretical chemist, educator
Moore, C. Bradley chemistry educator
Muller, Richard August physicist, author
Nero, Anthony Vincent, Jr. physicist, environmental scientist
O'Konski, Chester Thomas chemistry research scientist, educator
Perez-Mendez, Victor physics educator
Perry, Dale Lynn chemist
Pines, Alexander chemistry educator, researcher
Pitzer, Kenneth Sanborn chemist, educator
Rasmussen, John Oscar chemist, scientist
Raymond, Kenneth Norman chemistry educator, research chemist
Reynolds, John Hamilton physicist, educator
†Ritchie, Robert Oliver materials science educator
Rosenblatt, Gerd Matthew chemist
Sauer, Kenneth chemistry educator
Saykally, Richard James chemistry educator
Schultz, Peter G. chemistry educator
Seaborg, Glenn Theodore chemistry educator
Searcy, Alan Winn chemist, educator
Sessler, Andrew Marienhoff physicist
†Shen, Yuen-Ron physics educator
Shugart, Howard Alan physicist, educator
Siri, William E. physicist
Smith, Neville Vincent physicist
Somorjai, Gabor Arpad chemist, educator
Spinrad, Hyron astronomer
Steiner, Herbert Max physics educator
Strauss, Herbert Leopold chemistry educator
Streitwieser, Andrew, Jr. chemistry educator
Symons, Timothy James McNeil physicist
Thompson, Anthony Wayne metallurgist, educator, consultant
Townes, Charles Hard physics educator
Trilling, George Henry physicist, educator
Tsina, Richard Vasil chemistry educator
Valentine, James William geology educator, author
Vollhardt, Kurt Peter Christian chemistry educator
Zumino, Bruno physics educator, researcher

Bonita
Wood, Fergus James geophysicist, consultant

Burlingame
Hotz, Henry Palmer physicist

Cameron Park
Buckles, Robert Edwin chemistry educator

Carlsbad
Smith, Warren James optical scientist, consultant, lecturer

China Lake
†Cook, Douglas W. weapons research administrator

Claremont
Beilby, Alvin Lester chemistry educator
Chambers, Robert Jefferson educator, observatory administrator
†Kronenberg, Klaus J(ohannes) physicist
White, Kathleen Merritt geologist

Corona Del Mar
Britten, Roy John biophysicist

Coronado
Hudson, George Elbert retired research physicist

Costa Mesa
Lattanzio, Stephen Paul astronomy educator

Cupertino
Nelson, Richard Burton physicist, engineer, patent consultant
Wiley, Richard Haven chemist, educator

Davis
Andrews, Lawrence James chemistry educator, academic administrator
Axelrod, Daniel Isaac geology and botany educator
Black, Arthur Leo biochemistry educator
Cahill, Thomas Andrew physicist, educator
Carlson, Don Marvin biochemist
Conn, Eric Edward plant biochemist
Day, Howard Wilman geology educator
Hedrick, Jerry Leo biochemistry and biophysics educator
Higgins, Charles Graham geology educator
Jungerman, John Albert physics educator
Keizer, Joel Edward chemistry educator, theoretical scientist
Miller, R(ussell) Bryan chemistry educator
Nash, Charles Presley chemistry educator
Shelton, Robert Neal physics educator, researcher
Smith, Lloyd Muir chemist, educator
Stumpf, Paul Karl former biochemistry educator
Volman, David Herschel chemistry educator
Wooten, Frederick (Oliver) applied science educator
Yang, Shang Fa biochemistry educator, plant physiologist

Del Mar
Reid, Joseph Lee physical oceanographer, educator

Duarte
Greenstein, Jesse Leonard astronomer, educator

El Cajon
Burnett, Lowell Jay physicist, educator

El Cerrito
Griffith, Ladd Ray retired chemical research director
Gwinn, William Dulaney physical chemist, educator, consultant

El Segundo
Paulikas, George Algis physicist

Emeryville
Marcus, Frank biochemist
Masri, Merle Sid biochemist, consultant

Encinitas
Goldberg, Edward Davidow geochemist, educator

Encino
Hawthorne, Marion Frederick chemistry educator

Fountain Valley
Gittleman, Morris metallurgist,consultant

Fremont
Berry, Michael James chemist
Gill, Stephen Paschall physicist, mathematician

Fresno
Kauffman, George Bernard chemistry educator

Fullerton
Shapiro, Mark Howard physicist, educator, academic dean, consultant

Glendale
Farmer, Crofton Bernard atmospheric physicist

Hayward
Warnke, Detlef Andreas geologist, educator

Hemet
Berger, Lev Isaac physicist, educator

Inglewood
Lewis, Roy Roosevelt physicist

Irvine
Bander, Myron physics educator, university dean
Bradshaw, Ralph Alden biochemistry educator
Cho, Zang Hee physics educator
Clark, Bruce Robert geology consultant
Lanyi, Janos Karoly biochemist, educator
McLaughlin, Calvin Sturgis biochemistry educator
Nalcioglu, Orhan physicist
Nomura, Masayasu biological chemistry educator
Reines, Frederick physicist, educator
Rentzepis, Peter M. chemistry educator
Rowland, Frank Sherwood chemistry educator
Rynn, Nathan physics educator, consultant
Trolinger, James Davis laser scientist
Wallis, Richard Fisher physicist, educator
White, Stephen Halley biophysicist, educator
Wolfsberg, Max chemist, educator

Kensington
Connick, Robert Elwell chemistry educator

La Habra
Woyski, Margaret Skillman retired geology educator

La Jolla
†Abarbanel, Henry Don Isaac physicist, academic administrator
†Anderson, Victor Charles applied physics educator
Arnold, James Richard chemist, educator
Asmus, John Fredrich physicist
Backus, George Edward theoretical geophysicist
†Barnett, Tim P. meteorologist
Benson, Andrew Alm biochemistry educator
Bertram, H. Neal applied physics educator, researcher
Boger, Dale L. chemistry educator
†Bray, Nancy A. Oceanographes Director
Brueckner, Keith Allan theoretical physicist, educator
Buckingham, Michael John oceanography educator
Burbidge, E. Margaret astronomer, educator
Christensen, Halvor Niels biochemist, educator
Cox, Charles Shipley oceanography researcher, educator
Craig, Harmon geochemist, oceanographer
Dashen, Roger Frederick physics educator, consultant
Doolittle, Russell Francis biochemist, educator
†Driscoll, Charles F. research physicist
Edelman, Gerald Maurice biochemist, educator
Feher, George physics and biophysics scientist, educator
Fisher, Frederick Hendrick oceanographer
Geiduschek, E(rnest) Peter biophysics and molecular biology educator
Grine, Donald Reaville geophysicist, research executive
Itano, Harvey Akio biochemistry educator
Keeling, Charles David oceanography educator
Kerr, Donald MacLean, Jr. physicist
Lal, Devendra nuclear geophysics educator
Lauer, James Lothar physicist, educator
†Lerner, Richard Alan chemistry educator, scientist
MacDonald, Gordon James Fraser geophysicist
MacDougall, John Douglas earth science educator
Marti, Kurt chemistry educator
Mc Elroy, William David biochemist, educator
†McFadden, Lucy-Ann Adams planetary scientist
McIlwain, Carl Edwin physicist
Mullis, Kary Banks biochemist
Munk, Walter Heinrich geophysics educator
Namias, Jerome meteorologist
†O'Neil, Thomas Michael physicist, educator
Patton, Stuart biochemist, educator
Ride, Sally Kristen physics educator, scientist, former astronaut
Rosenbluth, Marshall Nicholas physicist, educator
Sclater, John George geophysics educator
Sham, Lu Jeu physics educator
Shuler, Kurt Egon chemist, educator
Spiess, Fred Noel oceanographer, educator
Van Lint, Victor Anton Jacobus physicist
Wall, Frederick Theodore chemistry educator
Watson, Kenneth Marshall physics educator
†Wegner, Harvey E. physicist, consultant
†Wong, Chi-Huey chemistry educator
York, Herbert Frank physics educator

La Puente
Reddy, Nagendranath K. biochemist, researcher

Laguna Beach
Iberall, Arthur Saul physicist, publisher
Wilson, James Newman retired laboratory executive

Laguna Hills
Batdorf, Samuel B(urbridge) physicist
Howard, Hildegarde (Mrs. Henry Anson Wylde) paleontologist

LaJolla
†Kadonaga, James Takuro biochemist

Livermore
Alder, Berni Julian physicist
†Binkley, J. S. physical sciences research administrator
†Fortner, Richard J. physical scientist
Hulet, Ervin Kenneth retired nuclear chemist
†Kidder, Ray Edward physicist, consultant
Leith, Cecil Eldon, Jr. retired physicist
Max, Claire Ellen physicist
Nuckolls, John Hopkins physicist, researcher
Olsen, Clifford Wayne former physical chemist
Schock, Robert Norman geophysicist
†Shotts, Wayne J. nuclear scientist, federal agency administrator
Tarter, Curtis Bruce physicist, science administrator
†Wong, Joe physical chemist

Loma Linda
Slattery, Charles Wilbur biochemistry educator
Wilcox, Ronald Bruce biochemistry educator, researcher

Long Beach
Bauer, Roger Duane chemistry educator, science consultant
Hu, Chi Yu physicist, educator

Los Altos
Barker, William Alfred physics educator
Fraknoi, Andrew astronomy educator, astronomical society executive
Hall, Charles Frederick space scientist, government administrator
Johnson, Richard Damerau aerospace scientist
Twersky, Victor mathematical physicist, educator

Los Altos Hills
McCormac, Billy Murray physicist, research institution executive, former army officer
van Tamelen, Eugene Earle chemist, educator

Los Angeles
Adamson, Arthur Wilson chemistry educator
Aki, Keiiti seismologist, educator
Aller, Lawrence Hugh astronomy educator, researcher
Armstrong, Lloyd, Jr. physicist, educator
Baker, Richard Freligh biophysicist, educator
Benson, Sidney William chemistry researcher
Bhaumik, Mani Lal physicist
Biles, John Alexander pharmaceutical chemistry educator
Bird, Peter geology educator
†Braginsky, Stanislav Iosifovich physicist, geophysicist, researcher
Byers, Nina physics educator
Campbell, Kenneth Eugene, Jr. vertebrate paleontologist
Chapman, Orville Lamar chemist, educator
Coleman, Charles Clyde physicist, educator
Cornwall, John Michael physics educator, consultant, researcher
Coroniti, Ferdinand Vincent physics educator, consultant
Cram, Donald James chemistry educator
Dalton, Larry Raymond chemistry educator, researcher, consultant
Dawson, John Myrick plasma physics educator
Dows, David Alan chemistry educator
Dunn, Arnold Samuel biochemistry educator
Dunn, Bruce Sidney materials science educator
Edwards, Kenneth Neil chemist, consultant
†Felker, Peter chemistry educator
Foote, Christopher Spencer chemist, educator
Fried, Burton David physicist, educator
Fulco, Armand John biochemist
Ganas, Perry Spiros physicist
Glitz, Dohn George biochemistry educator
Hall, Clarence Albert, Jr. geologist, educator
Houk, Kendall Newcomb chemistry educator
Jaffe, Sigmund educator, chemist
Kaplan, Isaac Raymond chemistry educator, corporate executive
Kennel, Charles Frederick physics educator, government official
Kivelson, Margaret Galland physicist
Knopoff, Leon geophysics educator
Krupp, Edwin Charles astronomer
Kunc, Joseph Anthony physics and engineering educator, consultant
Laaly, Heshmat Ollah research chemist, roofing consultant, author
Levine, Raphael David chemistry educator
Loeblich, Helen Nina Tappan paleontologist, educator
Logan, Joseph Granville, Jr. physicist
Maki, Kazumi physicist, educator
Markland, Francis Swaby, Jr. biochemist, educator
Morris, William Joseph paleontologist, educator
Neufeld, Elizabeth Fondal biochemist, educator
Nimni, Marcel Ephraim biochemistry educator
Olah, George Andrew chemist, educator
Onak, Thomas Philip chemistry educator
Paulson, Donald Robert chemistry educator
Popják, George Joseph biochemist, educator
Reiss, Howard chemistry educator
Roberts, Sidney biological chemist
Saxon, David Stephen physics educator, university official
Scott, Robert Lane chemist, educator
Shapiro, Isadore materials scientist, consultant
Smathers, James Burton medical physicist, educator
Smith, Emil L. biochemist, consultant
Smith, William Ray retired biophysicist, engineer
Steinberg, Morris Albert metallurgist
Stellwagen, Robert Harwood biochemistry educator
Szwarc, Michael M. polymer scientist
Thorne, Richard Mansergh physicist
†Trimble, Stanley Wayne hydrology and geography educator
Ufimtsev, Pyotr Yakovlevich physicist, electrical engineer, educator
Whitten, Charles Alexander, Jr. physics educator
†Wittig, Curt chemist, educator
Wittry, David Beryle physicist, educator
Wolf, Walter chemist, pharmaceutical scientist, educator
Woodruff, Fay paleoceanographer, geological researcher
Wurtele, Morton Gaither meteorologist, educator

Los Gatos
Knudsen, William Claire geophysicist

Magalia
Joffre, Stephen Paul consulting chemist

Malibu
Chester, Arthur Noble physicist
Forward, Robert L(ull) physicist, writer, consultant
Margerum, J(ohn) David chemist
Mataré, Herbert F. physicist, consultant
Pepper, David M. physicist, educator, author, inventor

Menlo Park
Bukry, John David geologist
Dalrymple, Gary Brent research geologist
Funkhouser, Lawrence William retired geologist
Hem, John David research chemist
Holzer, Thomas Lequear geologist
Lachenbruch, Arthur Herold geophysicist

†MacFarlane, David B. *physicist, educator*
Sladek, Ronald John *physics educator*
Tokheim, Robert Edward *physicist*
Vickers, Roger Spencer *physicist, program director*
†Vidale, John Emilio *geologist*
Wallace, Robert Earl *geologist*
Whitmore, William Francis *physicist, retired missile scientist*

Mission Viejo
Woodruff, Truman O(wen) *physicist, emeritus educator*

Moffett Field
Bentley, Kenton Earl *aerospace scientist, researcher*
Ragent, Boris *physicist*
Seiff, Alvin *planetary scientist, atmosphere physics and aerodynamics consultant*

Montecito
Wheelon, Albert Dewell *physicist*

Monterey
†Atchley, Anthony Armstrong *physicist, educator*
Collins, Curtis Allan *oceanographer*
†Garrett, Steven Lurie *physicist*
†Hovermale, John B. *oceanography director*
Shull, Harrison *chemist, educator*
Van Der Bijl, Willem *meteorology educator*
Weaver, William Bruce *astronomer, research administrator*

Monterey Park
Waiter, Serge-Albert *retired scientist, consultant*

Moraga
Hollingsworth, Robert Edgar *nuclear consultant*

Mountain View
Blachman, Nelson M(erle) *physicist*
Heere, Karen R. *astrophysicist*

Novato
Simon, Lee Will *astronomer*

Oakland
Jukes, Thomas Hughes *biological chemist, educator*
Kropschot, Richard H. *physicist, science laboratory administrator*
Martin, David William, Jr. *biomedical research company executive, educator*
Massey, Walter Eugene *physicist, science foundation administrator*
Mikalow, Alfred Alexander, II *deep sea diver, marine surveyor, marine diving consultant*

Orinda
†Heftmann, Erich *biochemist*

Pacific Grove
†Brewer, Peter George *ocean geochemist*

Pacific Palisades
Abrams, Richard Lee *physicist*
Csendes, Ernest *chemist, corporate and financial executive*
Fink, Robert Morgan *biological chemistry educator*

Palm Springs
Krick, Irving Parkhurst *meteorologist*

Palo Alto
Ballam, Joseph *physicist, educator*
Bienenstock, Arthur Irwin *physicist, educator*
Colin, Lawrence *aerospace scientist*
Cutler, Leonard Samuel *physicist*
Eng, Lawrence Fook *biochemistry educator, neurochemist*
†Heinemann, Klaus W. *physical sciences research administrator*
Holmes, John Richard *physicist, educator*
Loewenstein, Walter Bernard *nuclear power technologist*
Noyes, H(enry) Pierre *physicist*
Panofsky, Wolfgang Kurt Hermann *physicist, educator*
Pauling, Linus Carl *chemistry educator*
Stringer, John *materials scientist*
Ullman, Edwin Fisher *research chemist*

Pasadena
Albee, Arden Leroy *geologist, educator*
Anderson, Don Lynn *geophysicist, educator*
Anson, Fred Colvig *chemistry educator*
Babcock, Horace W. *astronomer*
Baldeschwieler, John Dickson *chemist, educator*
Barnes, Charles Andrew *physicist, educator*
Barton, Jacqueline K. *chemistry educator*
Bejczy, Antal Károly *research scientist, research facility administrator*
Blandford, Roger David *astronomy educator*
Breckinridge, James Bernard *research physicist*
Chahine, Moustafa Toufic *atmospheric scientist*
Chan, Sunney Ignatius *chemist*
Cohen, Marshall Harris *astronomer, educator*
Culick, Fred Ellsworth Clow *physics and engineering educator*
Davidson, Norman Ralph *biochemistry educator*
†Dougherty, Dennis A. *chemistry educator*
Dressler, Alan Michael *astronomer*
Epstein, Samuel *geologist, educator*
Fowler, William Alfred *retired physics educator*
Frautschi, Steven Clark *physicist, educator*
Gell-Mann, Murray *theoretical physicist, educator*
Goodstein, David Louis *physics educator*
Gray, Harry Barkus *chemistry educator*
†Grubbs, Robert H. *chemistry educator*
Heindl, Clifford Joseph *physicist*
Hitlin, David George *physicist, educator*
Hopfield, John Joseph *biophysicist, educator*
Jastrow, Robert *physicist*
Johnson, Torrence Vaino *astronomer*
Kamb, Walter Barclay *geologist, educator*
†Kanamori, Hiroo *geophysics educator*
†Kulkarni, Shrinivas R. *astronomy educator*
Leonard, Nelson Jordan *chemistry educator*
†Lewis, Nathan Saul *chemistry educator*
Liepmann, Hans Wolfgang *physicist, educator*
Marcus, Rudolph Arthur *chemist, educator*
Mc Koy, Basil Vincent Charles *theoretical chemist, educator*
†Myers, Andrew Gordon *chemistry educator*
Neugebauer, Gerry *astrophysicist, educator*
Neugebauer, Marcia *physicist, administrator*
Pickering, William Hayward *physics educator, scientist*
Politzer, Hugh David *physicist, educator*
Roberts, John D. *chemist, educator*
Sandage, Allan Rex *astronomer*
Sargent, Wallace Leslie William *astronomer, educator*
Schmidt, Maarten *astronomy educator*
Searle, Leonard *astronomer, researcher*
Sharp, Robert Phillip *geology educator, researcher*
Stone, Edward Carroll *physicist, educator*
†Terhune, Robert William *optics scientist*
Thorne, Kip Stephen *physicist, educator*
Tombrello, Thomas Anthony, Jr. *physics educator, consultant*
Vogt, Rochus Eugen *physicist, educator*
Wasserburg, Gerald Joseph *geology and geophysics educator*
†Wernicke, Brian Philip *geologist, educator*
Wyllie, Peter John *geologist, educator*
Zewail, Ahmed Hassan *chemistry and chemical engineering educator, editor, consultant*

Pleasant Hill
Weiss, Lionel Edward *geology educator*

Pomona
Aurilia, Antonio *physicist, educator*
Dev, Vasu *chemistry educator*
Eagleton, Robert Don *physics educator*

Ramona
†Palmer, James Russworth *theoretical physicist, high energy optics researcher*

Rancho Santa Fe
Creutz, Edward Chester *physicist, museum consultant*

Redwood City
Nacht, Sergio *biochemist*
Speziale, A. John *organic chemist, consultant*

Richmond
Holmquist, Walter Richard *research chemist, molecular evolutionist, mathematics educator*
Thomas, John Richard *chemist*
Ward, Carl Edward *research chemist*

Ridgecrest
St. Amand, Pierre *geophysicist*

Riverside
Green, Harry Western, II *geology educator*
†Mudd, John Brian *biochemist*
Norman, Anthony Westcott *biochemistry educator*
Orbach, Raymond Lee *physicist, educator*
Rabenstein, Dallas Leroy *chemistry educator*
White, Robert Stephen *physics educator*
Wild, Robert Lee *physics educator*
Wilkins, Charles L. *chemistry educator*

Sacramento
Gibson, Edward Fergus *physicist, educator*
†Nussenbaum, Siegfried Fred *chemistry educator*

San Diego
Cobble, James Wikle *chemistry educator*
Cunningham, Bruce Arthur *biochemist*
Daub, Clarence Theodore, Jr. *astronomer, educator*
Gastil, Russell Gordon *geologist, educator*
†Greene, John M. *physicist*
Lemke, James Underwood *physicist*
Lyon, Waldo Kampmeier *physicist*
Malin, Michael Charles *space scientist, former geology educator*
Martin, Donald Ray *chemist, educator, consultant*
Moe, Chesney Rudolph *physics educator*
Morris, Richard Herbert *physicist, educator*
Ohkawa, Tihiro *physicist*
Pecsok, Robert Louis *chemist, educator*
Pincus, Howard Jonah *geologist, engineer, educator*
Roeder, Stephen Bernhard Walter *chemistry and physics educator*
Shneour, Elie Alexis *biochemist*
Wolff, Manfred Ernst *medicinal chemist, pharmaceutical company executive*

San Francisco
Boyer, Herbert Wayne *biochemist*
†Burlingame, Alma Lyman *chemist, educator*
Cluff, Lloyd Sterling *earthquake geologist*
Dickinson, Wade *physicist, research and development company executive*
Grodsky, Gerold Morton *biochemistry educator*
Krebs, Ernst Theodor, Jr. *biochemist*
Landahl, Herbert Daniel *biophysicist, mathematical biologist, researcher, consultant*
Mandra, York T. *geology educator*
Posin, Daniel Q. *physics educator, television lecturer*
†Vale, Ronald D. *biochemist, educator*

San Jose
Brewer, Richard George *physicist*
†Chuang, Tung Jung *chemist*
†Coburn, John Wyllie *physicist, researcher*
Forster, Julian *physicist, consultant*
Gruber, John Balsbaugh *physics educator, university administrator*
†Herman, Frank *research physicist*
Houle, Frances Anne *physical chemist*
Neptune, John Addison *chemistry educator, consultant*
†Rabolt, John Francis *optics scientist*
†Winters, Harold Franklin *physicist*

San Leandro
Stallings, Charles Henry *physicist*

San Luis Obispo
Grismore, Roger *physics educator, researcher*

San Pedro
Simmons, William *physicist, aerospace research executive*

Santa Barbara
Awramik, Stanley Michael *geology educator*
Byers, Horace Robert *former meteorology educator*
Christman, Arthur Castner, Jr. *scientific advisor*
Crowell, John C(hambers) *geology educator, researcher*
Dudziak, Walter Francis *physicist*
Eck, Robert Edwin *physicist*
Eisberg, Robert Martin *physics educator, computer software author and executive*
†Ford, Peter C. *chemistry educator*
Gossard, Arthur Charles *physicist*
Gutsche, Steven Lyle *physicist*
Heeger, Alan Jay *physicist*
Kennett, James Peter *geology and oceanography educator*
Kohn, Walter *educator, physicist*
Langer, James Stephen *physicist, educator*
Luyendyk, Bruce Peter *geophysicist, educator, institution administrator*
Meinel, Aden Baker *optics scientist*
†Montgomery, Michael Davis *advanced technology consultant, hotelier*
Norris, Robert Matheson *geologist*
Peale, Stanton Jerrold *physics educator*
Scalapino, Douglas James *physics educator*
Tilton, George Robert *geochemistry educator*
Wilson, Leslie *biochemist, biological sciences educator*
†Witherell, Michael S. *physics educator*
†Wudl, Fred *chemistry educator, consultant*

Santa Clara
Carruthers, John Robert *scientist*

Santa Cruz
Brown, George Stephen *physicist*
Bunnett, Joseph Frederick *chemist, educator*
Drake, Frank Donald *astronomy educator*
Faber, Sandra Moore *astronomer, educator*
Flatté, Stanley Martin *physicist, educator*
†Griggs, Gary Bruce *earth sciences educator, oceanographer, geologist, consultant*
†Hernquist, Lars Eric *astronomer, educator*
Heusch, Clemens August *physicist, educator*
Hill, Terrell Leslie *chemist, biophysicist*
Kraft, Robert Paul *astronomer, educator*
Laporte, Leo Frederic *earth sciences educator*
†Lay, Thorne *geosciences educator*
Noller, Harry Francis, Jr. *biochemist, educator*
Osterbrock, Donald E(dward) *astronomy educator*
Sands, Matthew Linzee *physicist, educator*
†Williams, Quentin Christopher *geophysicist*
Wipke, W. Todd *chemistry educator*

Santa Maria
Musser, C. Walton *physical scientist, consultant*

Santa Monica
Intriligator, Devrie Shapiro *physicist*
Salter, Robert Mundhenk, Jr. *physicist, consultant*

Santa Rosa
de Wys, Egbert Christiaan *geochemist*
Mc Donald, David William *chemist, educator*

Seal Beach
Reynolds, Harry Lincoln *physicist*

Solana Beach
Agnew, Harold Melvin *physicist*

Solvang
Shelesnyak, Moses Chaim *biodynamicist, physiologist*

Stanford
Allen, Matthew Arnold *physicist*
Baldwin, Robert Lesh *biochemist, educator*
Berg, Paul *biochemist, educator*
Bonner, William Andrew *chemistry educator*
Brauman, John I. *chemist, educator*
Bube, Richard Howard *materials scientist*
Byer, Robert Louis *applied physics educator, university dean*
Chu, Steven *physics educator*
Coleman, Robert Griffin *geology educator*
Collman, James Paddock *chemistry educator*
Cutler, Cassius Chapin *physicist, educator*
Deal, Bruce Elmer *physical chemist, educator*
Djerassi, Carl *chemist, educator, writer*
Ernst, Wallace Gary *geology educator, dean*
Fetter, Alexander Lees *theoretical physicist, educator*
Geballe, Theodore Henry *physics educator, communications technology consultant*
Harbaugh, John Warvelle *applied earth sciences educator*
Herring, William Conyers *physicist, emeritus educator*
Heyneker, Herbert Louis *biochemist, biotechnology executive*
Johnson, William Summer *chemistry educator*
Kennedy, Donald *environmental science educator, former academic administrator*
Kornberg, Arthur *biochemist*
Kornberg, Roger David *biochemist, structural biologist*
Krauskopf, Konrad Bates *geology educator*
Lehman, (Israel) Robert *biochemistry educator, consultant*
Levinthal, Elliott Charles *physicist, educator*
Little, William Arthur *physicist, educator*
McConnell, Harden Marsden *biophysical chemistry researcher, chemistry educator*
Osheroff, Douglas Dean *physicist, researcher*
Pecora, Robert *chemistry educator*
Rees, John Robert *physicist*
Remson, Irwin *retired hydrogeology educator*
Richter, Burton *physicist, educator*
Ross, John *physical chemist, educator*
Schawlow, Arthur Leonard *physicist, educator*
Schimke, Robert Tod *biochemist, educator*
Schneider, Stephen Henry *climatologist, environmental policy analyst, researcher*
Shaw, Herbert John *physics educator emeritus*
Spicer, William Edward, III *physicist, educator*
Stryer, Lubert *biochemist, educator*
Sturrock, Peter Andrew *space science and astrophysics educator*
Taube, Henry *chemistry educator*
Taylor, Richard Edward *physicist, educator*
Teller, Edward *physicist*
Thompson, George Albert *geophysics educator*
Trost, Barry Martin *chemist, educator*
Wagoner, Robert Vernon *astrophysicist, educator*
Walt, Martin *physicist, consulting educator*
Wojcicki, Stanley George *physicist, educator*
Zare, Richard Neil *chemistry educator*

Stockton
Whiteker, Roy Archie *retired chemistry educator*

Sunnyvale
Quinn, Jarus William *physicist, association executive*

Thousand Oaks
Rathmann, George Blatz *genetic engineering company executive*
Sherman, Gerald *nuclear physicist, financial estate planner*

Torrance
Rogers, Howard H. *chemist*

Trona
Laire, Howard George *chemist*

Vacaville
Coulson, Kinsell Leroy *meteorologist*

Venice
Cohen, Norm *chemist*

Walnut Creek
Kieffer, William Franklinn *chemistry educator*
Oakeshott, Gordon B(laisdell) *geologist*

Westlake Village
Easton, William Heyden *geology educator*

Woodland Hills
Sharma, Brahama Datta *chemistry educator*

Woodside
Ashley, Holt *aerospace scientist, educator*

COLORADO

Boulder
†Albritton, Daniel L. *aeronomist*
Alldredge, Leroy Romney *retired geophysicist*
Anthes, Richard Allen *meteorologist*
Archambeau, Charles Bruce *physics educator, geophysics research scientist*
Bailey, Dana Kavanagh *radiophysicist, botanist*
Barry, Roger Graham *climatologist, educator*
†Barth, Charles Adolph *physicist, educator*
Bartlett, David Farnham *physics educator*
Barut, Asim Orhan *physicist, educator*
Begelman, Mitchell C. *astrophysicist, educator*
Calvert, Jack George *atmospheric chemist, educator*
Caruthers, Marvin Harry *biochemistry educator*
Cary, John Robert *physics educator*
Cech, Thomas Robert *chemistry and biochemistry educator*
Chappell, Charles Franklin *meteorologist, consultant*
Choquette, Philip Wheeler *geologist, educator*
Conti, Peter Selby *astronomy educator*
Cristol, Stanley Jerome *chemistry educator*
Dryer, Murray *physicist*
†Evenson, Kenneth M. *physicist*
†Ferguson, Eldon Earl *physicist*
Fleming, Rex James *meteorologist*
Garstang, Roy Henry *astrophysicist, educator*
Gossard, Earl Everett *physicist*
Hall, John Lewis *physicist, researcher*
Hermann, Allen Max *physics educator*
Hildner, Ernest Gotthold, III *solar physicist, science administrator*
†Hofmann, David John *atmospheric science researcher, educator*
Hogg, David Clarence *physicist*
†Holzer, Thomas E. *astronomer*
Joselyn, Jo Ann *space scientist*
Kauffman, Erle Galen *geologist, paleontologist*
Kellogg, William Welch *meteorologist*
King, Edward Louis *retired chemistry educator*
Koch, Tad Harbison *chemistry educator, researcher*
Lineberger, William Carl *chemistry educator*
Little, Charles Gordon *geophysicist*
Low, Boon Chye *physicist*
Mahanthappa, Kalyana Thipperudraiah *physicist, educator*
†Malde, Harold Edwin *retired federal government geologist*
†Norcross, David Warren *physicist, researcher*
Pankove, Jacques Isaac *physicist*
†Phelps, Arthur Van Rensselaer *physicist, consultant*
Robinson, Peter *paleontology educator, consultant*
†Rotunno, Richard *meteorologist*
Smythe, William Rodman *physicist, educator*
Snow, Theodore Peck, Jr. *astrophysics educator*
Spetzler, Hartmut August Werner *geophysics educator*
†Sullivan, Donald Barrett *physicist*
Tatarskii, Valerian Il'ich *physics researcher*
Tolbert, Bert Mills *biochemist, educator*
Trenberth, Kevin Edward *atmospheric scientist*
Washington, Warren Morton *meteorologist*
†Wieman, Carl E. *physics educator*

Colorado Springs
Henrickson, Eiler Leonard *geologist, educator*
Hoffman, John Raleigh *physicist*
Schwartz, Donald *chemistry educator*

Denver
Behrendt, John Charles *research geophysicist*
Boudreau, Robert Donald *meteorology educator*
Chappell, Willard Ray *physics educator, environmental scientist*
Eaton, Gareth Richard *chemistry educator, university dean*
Hamilton, Warren Bell *research geologist, educator*
†Hetzel, Fredrick William *biophysicist, educator*
Iona, Mario *retired physics educator*
Miller, Stanley Custer, Jr. *physicist, retired educator*
Mullineaux, Donal Ray *geologist*
Neumann, Herschel *physics educator*
Selbin, Joel *chemistry educator*
Smith, Dwight Morrell *chemistry educator*
†Todd, Donald Frederick *geologist*
Weihaupt, John George *geosciences educator, scientist, university administrator*

Englewood
Mc Adams, Ronald Earl *geologist*
Wilson, James Ernest *geological consultant, writer*

Evergreen
Haun, John Daniel *petroleum geologist, educator*
Link, Peter Karl *geologist*
Phillips, Adran Abner (Abe Phillips) *geologist, oil and gas exploration consultant*

Fort Collins
Bamburg, James Robert *biochemistry educator*
Bernstein, Elliot Roy *chemistry educator*
Curthoys, Norman P. *biochemistry educator, consultant*
Elkind, Mortimer Murray *biophysicist, educator*
Fixman, Marshall *chemist, educator*
Johnson, Robert Britten *geology educator*
Meyers, Albert Irving *chemistry educator*
†Mosier, Arvin Ray *chemist, researcher*
†Norton, Jack Richard *chemistry educator*
Patton, Carl Elliott *physics educator*
Schumm, Stanley Alfred *geologist, educator*

Golden
Grose, Thomas Lucius Trowbridge *geologist, educator*
Hutchinson, Richard William *geology educator, consultant*
Kennedy, George Hunt *chemistry educator*
Kotch, Alex *chemistry educator*
Krauss, George *metallurgist*
McNeill, William *environmental scientist*
Morrison, Roger Barron *geologist, executive*
Ponder, Herman *geologist*
Sims, Paul Kibler *geologist*
Tilton, John Elvin *mineral economics educator*
Weimer, Robert Jay *geology educator, energy consultant, civic leader*
White, James Edward *geophysicist*

Grand Junction
Rutz, Richard Frederick *physicist, researcher*

Lakewood
McAuliffe, Clayton Doyle *chemist*

Sedalia
Pakiser, Louis Charles, Jr. *geophysicist*

Snowmass
Lovins, Amory Bloch *physicist, energy consultant*

University Of Colorado
DePuy, Charles Herbert *chemist, educator*
†Greene, Chris H. *physicist, educator*
Leone, Stephen Robert *chemical physicist, educator*
Miller, Gifford Hubbs *geologist*

CONNECTICUT

Branford
†Fenn, John Bennett *chemist, educator*

Brookfield
Schetky, Laurence McDonald *metallurgist, researcher*

Farmington
†Herbette, Leo Gerard *biophysics educator*
Osborn, Mary Jane Merten *biochemist*
Spencer, Richard Paul *biochemist, educator, physician*

Greenwich
Heath, Gloria Whitton *aerospace scientist, consultant*

Groton
†Cooper, Richard Arthur *oceanographer*
Pinson, Ellis Rex, Jr. *chemist, consultant*
Swindell, Archie Calhoun, Jr. *research biochemist, statistician*

Guilford
Engelman, Donald Max *molecular biophysics and biochemistry educator*

Hartford
Piehl, Donald Herbert *chemist, research and development executive*

Madison
Rozelle, Lee Theodore *physical chemist*

Manchester
Galasso, Francis Salvatore *materials scientist*

Middletown
Fry, Albert Joseph *chemistry educator*
Haake, Paul *chemistry and biochemistry educator*
Sease, John W(illiam) *chemistry educator*
Upgren, Arthur Reinhold, Jr. *astronomer, educator, outdoor lighting consultant*

New Britain
Baskerville, Charles Alexander *geologist, educator*
Dimmick, Charles William *geology educator*

New Haven
†Appelquist, Thomas William *physicist, educator*
Bennett, William Ralph, Jr. *physicist, educator*
Berner, Robert Arbuckle *geochemist, educator*
Berson, Jerome Abraham *chemistry educator*
Bromley, David Allan *physicist, educator*
Chupka, William Andrew *chemical physicist, educator*
Crothers, Donald Morris *biochemist, educator*
Gordon, Robert Boyd *geophysics educator*
Herzenberg, Arvid *physicist, educator*
Hoffleit, Ellen Dorrit *astronomer*
†Iachello, Francesco *physicist educator*
Jorgensen, William L. *chemistry educator*
Klein, Martin Jesse *physicist, educator, science historian*
Larson, Richard Bondo *astronomy educator*
Moore, Peter Bartlett *biochemist, educator*
Ostrom, John H. *vertebrate paleontologist, educator, museum curator*
Reifsnyder, William Edward *meteorologist*
Richards, Frederic Middlebrook *biochemist, educator*
Rodgers, John *geologist, educator*
Saltzman, Barry *meteorologist, educator*
Sandweiss, Jack *physicist, educator*
Shulman, Robert Gerson *biophysics educator*
Steitz, Joan Argetsinger *biochemistry educator*
Turekian, Karl Karekin *geochemistry educator*
Van Altena, William Foster *astronomer, educator*
†Wasserman, Harry Hershal *chemistry educator*
†Wiberg, Kenneth Berle *chemist, educator*
Wolf, Werner Paul *physicist, educator*
Zeller, Michael Edward *physicist*

New Milford
Fabricand, Burton Paul *physicist, educator*

Old Lyme
†Anderson, Theodore Robert *physicist*

Ridgefield
Farina, Peter R. *biochemist*

Stamford
Hagner, Arthur Feodor *geologist, educator*
Porosoff, Harold *chemist, research and development director*
Toy, Arthur Dock Fon *chemist*

Storrs
Bartram, Ralph Herbert *physicist*
Bobbitt, James McCue *chemist*
Devereux, Owen Francis *metallurgy educator*
Stwalley, William Calvin *physics and chemistry educator*

Storrs Mansfield
Azaroff, Leonid Vladimirovitch *physics educator*
Khairallah, Edward Amin *molecular biology and biochemistry professor*
Klemens, Paul Gustav *physicist, educator*
Schuster, Todd Mervyn *biophysics educator, biotechnology company executive*

West Redding
Foster, Edward John *engineering physicist*

Westport
Tucker, Gardiner Luttrell *physicist, former paper company executive*

DELAWARE

Dover
Wasfi, Sadiq Hassan *chemistry educator*

Greenville
Schroeder, Herman Elbert *scientific consultant*

Newark
Burmeister, John Luther *chemistry educator*
Daniels, William Burton *physicist, educator*
Evans, Dennis Hyde *chemist, educator*
†Evenson, Paul Arthur *physics educator*
Hutton, David Glenn *environmental consultant, chemical engineer*
Jordan, Robert Reed *geologist, educator*
Mather, John Russell *climatologist, educator*
Murray, Richard Bennett *physics educator*
Ness, Norman Frederick *astrophysicist, educator, administrator*
†Schultz, Jerold Marvin *materials scientist, educator*
Wetlaufer, Donald Burton *biochemist, educator*
Wu, Jin *oceanographer, educator, engineer*

Newport
Kirkland, Joseph J. *research chemist*

Wilmington
Crittenden, Eugene Dwight, Jr. *chemical company executive*
Kissa, Erik *retired chemist, consultant*
Moore, Carl Gordon *chemist, educator*
Parshall, George William *research chemist*
†Simmons, Howard Ensign, Jr. *chemist, research administrator*
Smook, Malcolm Andrew *chemist, chemical company executive*
Wasserman, Edel *former chemistry educator, scientist*

DISTRICT OF COLUMBIA

Washington
Abelson, Philip Hauge *physicist*
Abraham, George *research physicist, engineer*
Alter, Harvey *chemist, association executive*
Bednarek, Jana Maria *biochemist*
Bennett, Gary Lee *physicist, federal agency administrator*
Berendzen, Richard *astronomer, educator, author*
Bierly, Eugene Wendell *meteorologist, science administrator*
Blecher, Melvin *biochemist, educator emeritus, lawyer*
Boyce, Peter Bradford *astronomer, professional association executive*
Brinckman, Frederick Edward, Jr. *retired research chemist, consultant*
Buchanan, John Donald *health physicist, radiochemist*
†Carter, Ashton Baldwin *physicist, government agency executive*
Chubb, Talbot Albert *physicist*
Coffey, Timothy *physicist*
Córdova, France Anne-Dominic *astrophysics educator*
Darby, Joseph Branch, Jr. *metallurgist, government official*
Davidson, Eugene Abraham *biochemist, university administrator*
Dorman, Craig Emery *oceanographer, academic administrator*
†Douglas, Bruce Colman *geophysicist*
Dutro, John Thomas, Jr. *geologist, paleontologist*
El Khadem, Hassan Saad *chemistry educator, researcher*
Fiske, Richard Sewell *geologist*
Fleischer, Michael *chemist*
Fowler, Earle Cabell *administrator, physicist*
Friedman, Herbert *physicist*
Garavelli, John Stephen *biochemistry research scientist*
Girard, James Emery *chemistry educator*
Goldstein, Allan Leonard *biochemist, educator*
Grant, Richard Evans *paleontologist, museum curator*
Hallgren, Richard Edwin *meteorologist*
Harwit, Martin Otto *astrophysicist, educator, museum director*
Haskins, Caryl Parker *scientist, author*
Holland, Christie Anna *biochemist, virologist*
Holloway, John Thomas *physicist*
Karle, Isabella *chemist*
Karle, Jerome *physicist, researcher*
Keyworth, George Albert, II *physicist, consulting company executive*
Kier, Porter Martin *paleontologist*
Kouts, Herbert John Cecil *physicist*
†Krebs, Martha *physicist, federal agency administrator*
†Lash, Jonathan *environmental law executive, consultant*
Ledley, Robert Steven *biophysicist*
†Lehmberg, Robert Henry *research physicist*
Leibowitz, Jack Richard *physicist, educator*
Mandula, Jeffrey Ellis *physicist*
Mason, Brian Harold *geologist, curator*
†Mayer, Walter Georg *physics educator*
Mead, Gilbert D(unbar) *geophysicist, lawyer*
Meijer, Paul Herman Ernst *educator, physicist*
Morehouse, David Frank *geologist*
Oertel, Goetz K. H. *physicist, professional association administrator*
Oliver, William Albert, Jr. *paleontologist*
Perros, Theodore Peter *chemist, educator*
†Pope, Michael Thor *chemist*
Press, Frank *geophysicist, educator*
Prewitt, Charles Thompson *geochemist*
Pyle, Thomas Edward *oceanographer, academic director*
Rao, Desiraju Bhavanarayana *meteorologist, oceanographer, educator*
Rittner, Edmund Sidney *physicist*
†Rogers, Kenneth Cannicott *physicist, federal agency administrator*
Romanowski, Thomas Andrew *physics educator*
Roscher, Nina Matheny *chemistry educator*
Rosenberg, Norman Jack *agricultural meteorologist, educator*
Scott, Raymond Peter William *chemistry research educator, writer*
Siegel, Frederic Richard *geology educator*
Singer, Maxine Frank *biochemist*
Solomon, Sean Carl *geophysicist, lab director*
Stanley, Daniel Jean *geological oceanographer, senior scientist*
†Sullivan, Kathryn D. *geologist, astronaut*
Tallent, William Hugh *chemist, research administrator*
Theon, John Speridon *meteorologist*
Tousey, Richard *physicist*
Uberall, Herbert Michael Stefan *physicist, educator*
Villforth, John Carl *health physicist*
Wetherill, George West *geophysicist, planetary scientist*
White, John Arnold *physics educator, research scientist*
White, Robert Mayer *meteorologist*
†Whitmore, Frank Clifford, Jr. *geologist*
Wilson, M(athew) Kent *chemist, researcher, educator*
Yochelson, Ellis L(eon) *paleontologist*
Yoder, Hatten Schuyler, Jr. *petrologist*

FLORIDA

Alachua
Schneider, Richard T(heodore) *optics research executive, engineer*

Boca Raton
Carraher, Charles Eugene, Jr. *chemistry educator, dean*
Finkl, Charles William, II *geologist, educator*

Boynton Beach
Balis, Moses Earl *biochemist, educator*
Fields, Theodore *consulting medical radiation physicist*

Cape Coral
West, John Merle *retired physicist, nuclear consultant*

Coral Gables
Criss, Cecil M. *chemistry educator*
Einspruch, Norman Gerald *physicist, educator*
Leblanc, Roger Maurice *chemistry educator*
Stewart, Harris Bates, Jr. *oceanographer*

Dade City
Burdick, Glenn Arthur *physicist, engineering educator*

Deland
Coolidge, Edwin Channing *chemistry educator*

Delray Beach
Zarwyn, Berthold *physical scientist*

Fort Lauderdale
Zikakis, John P. *educator, researcher, biochemist*

Fort Pierce
Mooney, John Bradford, Jr. *oceanographer, engineer, consultant*

Gainesville
Andrew, Edward Raymond *physicist*
Couch, Margaret Wheland *research chemist*
Cousins, Robert John *nutritional biochemist, educator*
Davis, George Kelso *nutrition biochemist, educator*
Detweiler, Steven Lawrence *physicist, educator*
Dewar, Michael James Steuart *chemistry educator*
Drago, Russell Stephen *chemist, educator*
Eichhorn, Heinrich Karl *astronomer, educator, consultant*
Gander, John Edward *biochemistry educator*
Hanrahan, Robert Joseph *chemist, educator*
Hanson, Harold Palmer *physicist, government official, editor, academic administrator*
†Harrison, Willard W. *chemist, educator*
†Holloway, Paul Howard *materials science educator*
Jacobs, Alan Martin *physicist, educator*
Katritzky, Alan Roy *chemistry educator, consultant*
Klauder, John Rider *physics educator*
†Micha, David Allan *chemistry and physics educator*
Ohrn, Nils Yngve *chemistry and physics educator*
Person, Willis Bagley *chemistry educator*
Sisler, Harry Hall *chemist, educator*
Smith, Alexander Goudy *physics and astronomy educator*
Stehli, Francis Greenough *retired geologist, educator*
Wood, Frank Bradshaw *retired astronomy educator*
Young, David Michael *biochemistry and molecular biology educator, physician*
†Zerner, Michael Charles *chemistry and physics educator, consultant, researcher*

Gonzalez
Plischke, Le Moyne Wilfred *research chemist*

Jacksonville
Huebner, Jay Stanley *physicist, engineer, forensics consultant*
Reynolds, Ellis W. *chemist*

Key West
Trammell, Herbert Eugene *physicist, laboratory executive*

Lake Alfred
Nagy, Steven *biochemist*

Lake Worth
Kline, Gordon Mabey *chemist, editor*

Marco
Hurley, Patrick Mason *geology educator*

Melbourne
Babich, Michael Wayne *chemistry educator, educational administrator*
Boan, Bobby Jack *chemist*
Nelson, Gordon Leigh *chemist, educator*
von Ohain, Hans Joachim P. *aerospace scientist*

Miami
Atwood, Donald Keith *oceanographer, chemist*
Blanco, Luciano-Nilo *physicist*
Corcoran, Eugene Francis *chemist, educator*
Fine, Rana Arnold *chemical,physical oceanographer*
Glaser, Luis *biochemistry educator*
Man, Eugene Herbert *chemist, educator, business executive*
Mooers, Christopher Northrup Kennard *physical oceanographer, educator*
Ostlund, H. Gote *atmospheric and marine scientist, educator*
Rosenthal, Stanley Lawrence *meteorologist*
†Sheets, Robert Chester *meteorologist*
Wells, Daniel Ruth *physics educator*
Whelan, William Joseph *biochemistry educator*

Naples
Leitner, Alfred *mathematical physicist, educator, educational film producer*

Ocala
Forgue, Stanley Vincent *physics educator*

Oldsmar
Ligett, Waldo Buford *chemist*

Orlando
Baker, Peter Mitchell *laser scientist and executive, educator*
†Blue, Joseph Edward *physicist*
Llewellyn, Ralph Alvin *physics educator*
Silfvast, William T. *laser physics educator, consultant*

Palm Beach Gardens
Emiliani, Cesare *geology educator, author*

Palmetto
Compton, Charles Daniel *chemistry educator*

Pensacola
Jones, Walter Harrison *chemist*

Saint Petersburg
Castle, Raymond Nielson *chemist, educator*
Hansel, Paul George *physicist, consultant*
Rester, Alfred Carl, Jr. *physicist*

Sanibel
Herriott, Donald Richard *optical physicist*

Sanibel Island
Horecker, Bernard Leonard *retired biochemistry educator*

Sarasota
Kerker, Milton *chemistry educator*
Myerson, Albert Leon *physical chemist*

Satellite Beach
Button, Kenneth John *physicist*

Tallahassee
Albright, John Rupp *physics educator*
Choppin, Gregory Robert *chemistry educator*
Clarke, Allan J. *oceanography educator, consultant*
†Crow, Jack E. *physics administrator*
Fox, John David *educator, physicist*
†Herndon, Roy Clifford *physicist*
Johnsen, Russell Harold *chemist, educator*
†Kemper, Kirby Wayne *physics educator*
†Lannutti, Joseph Edward *physics educator*
Light, Robley Jasper *chemistry educator*
Mandelkern, Leo *biophysics and chemistry educator*
O'Brien, James Joseph *meteorology and oceanography educator*
Pfeffer, Richard Lawrence *geophysics educator*
†Robson, Donald *physics educator*
Schrieffer, John Robert *physics educator, science administrator*
†Sheline, Raymond K. *nuclear chemistry educator*
Smith, Eric Alan *meteorology educator*
Sturges, Wilton, III *oceanography educator*
Walborsky, Harry M. *chemistry educator, consultant*

Tampa
Binford, Jesse Stone, Jr. *chemistry educator*
DeMontier, Paulette LaPointe *chemist*

Venice
Leidheiser, Henry, Jr. *retired chemistry educator, consultant*

West Palm Beach
McGinnes, Paul R. *environmental chemist*

GEORGIA

Alpharetta
Barr, John Baldwin *chemist, reserach scientist*

Americus
Counts, Wayne Boyd *chemistry educator*

Athens
Allinger, Norman Louis *chemistry educator*
Black, Clanton Candler, Jr. *biochemistry educator, researcher*
Boyd, George Edward *physical chemist*
†Darvill, Alan G. *biochemist, botanist, educator*
Eriksson, Karl-Erik Lennart *biochemist, educator*
†Johnson, Michael Kenneth *chemistry educator*
King, Robert Bruce *chemistry educator*
†Landau, David Paul *physics educator*
McGuire, John Murray *chemist, researcher*
Melton, Charles Estel *physicist, educator*
Pelletier, S. William *chemistry educator*
Schaefer, Henry Frederick, III *chemistry educator*
†Yen, William Mao-Shung *physicist*

Atlanta
Anderson, Gloria Long *chemistry educator*
Copeland, John Alexander, III *physicist*
Cramer, Howard Ross *geologist, environmental consultant*
†Ellis, Richard Lee *physical chemistry educator, researcher*
Finkelstein, David *physicist, educator, consultant*
Fox, Ronald Forrest *physics educator*
Goldstein, Jacob Herman *retired physical chemist*
†Hill, Craig Livingston *chemistry educator, consultant*
Johnson, Ronald Carl *chemistry educator*
Kahn, Bernd *radiochemist, educator*
†Lin, Ming-Chang *physical chemistry educator, researcher*
Long, Maurice Wayne *physicist, electrical engineer, radar consultant*
†Marzilli, Luigi Gaetano *chemistry educator, consultant*
McCormick, Donald Bruce *biochemist, educator*
Moran, Thomas Francis *chemistry educator*
Perkowitz, Sidney *physicist, educator, author*
Pierotti, Robert Amedeo *chemistry educator*
Underwood, Arthur Louis, Jr. *chemistry educator, researcher*
Young, Robert Alan *physicist, educator*
†Zalkow, Leon H. *organic chemistry educator*

Marietta
Bridges, Alan Lynn *physicist, researcher, information systems specialist*

Peachtree City
Roobol, Norman Richard *chemistry educator, industrial painting consultant*

Savannah
†Menzel, David Washington *oceanographer*
Su, Helen Chien-fan *research chemist*

Tucker
Valk, Henry Snowden *physicist, educator*

HAWAII

Honolulu
Brantley, Lee Reed *chemistry educator*
Cowie, Lennox Lauchlan *astrophysicist*
Hall, Donald Norman Blake *astronomer*
Hawke, Bernard Ray *planetary scientist*
Herbig, George Howard *astronomer, educator*
Ihrig, Judson La Moure *chemist*
Keil, Klaus *geology educator, consultant*
Khan, Mohammad Asad *geophysicist, educator, former energy minister and senator of Pakistan*
Ogburn, Hugh Bell *chemical engineer, consultant*
Raleigh, Cecil Baring *geophysicist*
Scheuer, Paul Josef *chemistry educator*
Tuan, San Fu *theoretical physics, political science educator*
Wyrtki, Klaus *oceanography educator*
Yount, David Eugene *physicist, university official*

Princeville
Kaye, Wilbur Irving *chemist, researcher, consultant*

IDAHO

Boise
Hibbs, Robert Andrews *analytical chemistry educator*

Idaho Falls
Reich, Charles William *nuclear physicist*

Moscow
LeTourneau, Duane John *biochemist, educator*
Miller, Maynard Malcolm *geologist, educator, research foundation director, explorer, state legislator*
Renfrew, Malcolm MacKenzie *chemist, educator*
Shreeve, Jean'ne Marie *chemist, educator*

ILLINOIS

Argonne
Appelman, Evan Hugh *chemist*
Berger, Edmond Louis *theoretical physicist*
†Berkowitz, Joseph *physicist, physical chemist, researcher*
†Blander, Milton *chemist*
Carpenter, John Marland *engineer, physicist*
Derrick, Malcolm *physicist*
Ferraro, John Ralph *chemist*
Fields, Paul Robert *research nuclear chemist, consultant*
†Green, David William *chemist, educator*
Herzenberg, Caroline Stuart Littlejohn *physicist*
Jorgensen, James Douglas *research physicist*
Krauss, Alan Robert *physicist*
Martin, Ronald Lavern *physicist*
†Morss, Lester Robert *chemist*
Nolen, Jerry Aften, Jr. *physicist*
†Perlow, Gilbert J(erome) *physicist, editor*
Peshkin, Murray *physicist*
Schiffer, John Paul *physicist*
†Steindler, Martin Joseph *chemist*
†Zeidman, Benjamin *nuclear physicist*

Arlington Heights
Lewin, Seymour Zalman *chemistry educator, consultant*

Batavia
†Bardeen, William Allan *research physicist*
Chrisman, Bruce Lowell *physicist, administrator*
Jonckheere, Alan Mathew *physicist*
Lach, Joseph Theodore *physicist*
Nash, E(dward) Thomas *physicist*
Tollestrup, Alvin Virgil *physicist*

Carbondale
Tao, Rongjia *physicist, educator*
Wotiz, John Henry *chemist, educator*

Champaign
Buschbach, Thomas Charles *geologist, consultant*
Cartwright, Keros *hydrogeologist, researcher*
Cohen, Jozef *psychophysicist, educator*
Gross, David Lee *geologist*
Herzog, Beverly Leah *hydrogeologist*
Mapother, Dillon Edward *physicist, university official*
Slichter, Charles Pence *physicist, educator*
Stapleton, Harvey James *physics educator*
Wolfram, Stephen *physicist, computer company executive*

Chicago
Anderson, Louise Eleanor *biochemistry educator*
Barany, Kate *biophysics educator*
Barenberg, Sumner *polymer physicist, business executive*
Blumberg, Avrom Aaron *physical chemistry educator*
Broutman, Lawrence Jay *materials engineering educator*
Chambers, Donald Arthur *biochemistry educator*
†Chandler, John W. *biochemistry educator, ophthalmology educator*
Chandrasekhar, Subrahmanyan *astrophysicist, educator*
Charlier, Roger Henri *oceanographer, geographer, educator*
Clayton, Robert Norman *chemist, educator*
Copley, Stephen Michael *materials science and engineering educator*
Cronin, James Watson *physicist, educator*
Dobbs, Frank Wilbur *chemistry educator*
Epstein, Wolfgang *biochemist, educator*
Erber, Thomas *physics educator*
Evans, Earl Alison, Jr. *biochemist*
Fano, Ugo *physicist, educator*
Fanta, Paul Edward *chemist, educator*
Fleming, Graham Richard *chemistry educator*
Freed, Karl Frederick *chemistry educator*
Fried, Josef *chemist, educator*
Frisch, Henry Jonathan *physics educator*
Fritzsche, Hellmut *physics educator*
Fujita, Tetsuya Theodore *educator, meteorologist*
Fultz, Dave *meteorology educator*
Garland, James Wilson, Jr. *physics educator, researcher, consultant*
Gershbein, Leon Lee *chemist, educator*
Gislason, Eric Arni *chemistry educator*
Goldsmith, Julian Royce *geochemist, educator*
Goldwasser, Eugene *biochemist, educator*
Gomer, Robert *chemistry educator*
Grossweiner, Leonard Irwin *physicist, educator*
Halpern, Jack *chemist, educator*
Harvey, Ronald Gilbert *research chemist*
Hildebrand, Roger Henry *astrophysicist, physicist*
Huston, John Lewis *chemistry educator*
Hutchison, Clyde Allen, Jr. *chemistry educator*
Jeffay, Henry *biochemistry educator*
Kadanoff, Leo Philip *physicist*
Kinsinger, Jack Burl *chemist, educator*
Kouvel, James Spyros *physicist, educator*
Krawetz, Arthur Altshuler *chemist, science administrator*
Lanzl, Lawrence Herman *medical physicist*
Lederman, Leon Max *physicist, educator*
Levi-Setti, Riccardo *physicist, director*
Levy, Donald Harris *chemistry educator*
Liao, Shutsung *biochemist*
Light, John Caldwell *chemistry educator*
Lorand, Laszlo *biochemist, educator*
Lykos, Peter George *educator, scientist*
Makinen, Marvin William *biophysicist, educator*
Margoliash, Emanuel *biochemist, educator*
Meyer, Peter *physicist, educator*
Muller, Dietrich Alfred Helmut *physicist, educator*
Nagel, Sidney Robert *physics educator*
Nambu, Yoichiro *physics educator*
†Norris, James Rufus, Jr. *chemist, educator, consultant*
Oehme, Reinhard *physicist, educator*
Oka, Takeshi *physicist, chemist, astronomer, educator*
Olsen, Edward John *geologist, educator*
Oxtoby, David William *chemistry educator*
Palmer, Patrick Edward *radio astronomer, educator*
Parker, Eugene Newman *physicist, educator*
Paulson, Glenn *environmental scientist*
Platzman, George William *geophysicist, educator*
Rafelson, Max Emanuel, Jr. *biochemist, medical school administrator*
Raup, David Malcolm *paleontology educator*
Reiffel, Leonard *physicist, scientific consultant*
Rocek, Jan *chemist, educator*
Rosner, Jonathan Lincoln *physicist, educator*
Rosner, Robert *astrophysicist*
Sachs, Robert Green *physicist, educator, laboratory administrator*
Sager, William F. *retired chemistry educator*
Sawinski, Vincent John *chemistry educator*
Schillinger, Edwin Joseph *physics educator*
Schramm, David Norman *astrophysicist, educator*
Schug, Kenneth Robert *chemistry educator*
Sereno, Paul C. *paleontologist, educator*
Shapiro, Stanley *materials scientist*
Simpson, John Alexander *physicist*
Spector, Harold Norman *physics educator*
Steck, Theodore Lyle *biochemistry and molecular biology educator, physician*
Steiner, Donald Frederick *biochemist, physician, educator*
Stock, Leon Milo *chemist, educator*
Truran, James Wellington, Jr. *astrophysicist*
Turkevich, Anthony Leonid *chemist, educator*
†Turner, Michael Stanley *physics educator*
Williams-Ashman, Howard Guy *biochemistry educator*
Winston, Roland *physicist, educator*
York, Donald Gilbert *astronomy educator, researcher*

De Kalb
Kevill, Dennis Neil *chemistry educator*
Kimball, Clyde William *physicist, educator*
†Rossing, Thomas D. *physics educator*

Downers Grove
Boese, Robert Alan *forensic chemist*

Evanston
Basolo, Fred *chemistry educator*
Brown, Laurie Mark *physicist, educator*
Burwell, Robert Lemmon, Jr. *chemist, educator*
†Chang, R. P. H. *materials science educator*
Cohen, Jerome Bernard *materials science educator*
Colton, Frank Benjamin *retired chemist*
Ibers, James Arthur *chemist, educator*
Johnson, David Lynn *materials scientist, educator*
Klotz, Irving Myron *chemist, educator*
Lambert, Joseph Buckley *chemistry educator*
Letsinger, Robert Lewis *chemistry educator*
Lippincott, James Andrew *biochemistry, biological sciences educator, administrator*
Marks, Tobin Jay *chemistry educator*
Mintzer, David *physics educator*
Oakes, Robert James *physics educator*
Offner, Franklin Faller *biophysics educator*
Pines, Herman *chemistry educator, consultant*
Pople, John Anthony *chemistry educator*
Ratner, Mark Alan *chemistry educator*
Sachtler, Wolfgang Max Hugo *chemistry educator*
Shriver, Duward Felix *chemistry educator, researcher, consultant*
Silverman, Richard Bruce *chemist, educator, biochemist*
Taam, Ronald Everett *physics and astronomy educator*
Ulmer, Melville Paul *physics and astronomy educator*
Weertman, Johannes *materials science educator*
Weertman, Julia Randall *materials science and engineering educator*
†Wessels, Bruce W. *materials scientist, educator*

Frankfort
Dennis, Peter Ray *environmental corporate executive*

Glenview
Rorig, Kurt Joachim *chemist, research director*

Hinsdale
Kaminsky, Manfred Stephan *physicist*

Lake Forest
Coutts, John Wallace *chemist, educator*
Walter, Robert Irving *chemistry educator, chemist*
Weston, Arthur Walter *chemist, scientific and business executive*

Lemont
Katz, Joseph Jacob *chemist, educator*
†Mitchell, Wanda Gayle *chemist*
Tomkins, Frank Sargent *physicist*
Williams, Jack Marvin *chemist*

Lombard
Poppe, Wassily *chemist*

Naperville
Arzoumanidis, Gregory G. *chemist*
Fields, Ellis Kirby *research chemist*
Hensley, Albert Lloyd, Jr. *research chemist, technical consultant*
Karayannis, Nicholas Marios *chemist*
Wolfram, Thomas *physicist*

Normal
Young, Robert Donald *physicist, educator*

North Chicago
Loga, Sanda *physicist, educator*

O'Fallon
Jenner, William Alexander *meteorologist, educator*

Palos Park
Crewe, Albert Victor *physicist, business executive, former research administrator*

Peoria
Chamberlain, Joseph Miles *astronomer, educator*
Cunningham, Raymond Leo *research chemist*
Nielsen, Harald Christian *retired chemist*
Osborn, Terry Wayne *biochemist*
Rothfus, John Arden *chemist*

Rock Island
Sundelius, Harold W. *geology educator*

Schaumburg
Langsdorf, Alexander, Jr. *physicist*

Skokie
Filler, Robert *chemistry educator*

Springfield
Gallina, Charles Onofrio *nuclear regulatory official*

Urbana
Baker, David Hiram *nutritional biochemist*
Beak, Peter Andrew *chemistry educator*
Birnbaum, Howard Kent *materials science educator*
Brown, Theodore Lawrence *chemistry educator*
Crofts, Antony Richard *biophysics educator*
Debrunner, Peter George *physics educator*
Drickamer, Harry George *retired chemistry educator*
Dunn, Floyd *biophysicist, bioengineer, educator*
Faulkner, Larry Ray *chemistry educator, academic officer*
Forbes, Richard Mather *biochemistry educator*
Goldwasser, Edwin Leo *physicist*
Govindjee *biophysics and biology educator*
†Greene, Laura Helen *physicist*
Gunsalus, Irwin C. *biochemistry educator, consultant*
Gutowsky, Herbert Sander *chemistry educator*
Hager, Lowell Paul *biochemistry educator*
Hay, Richard Le Roy *geology educator*
Iben, Icko, Jr. *astrophysicist, educator*
Jonas, Jiri *chemistry educator*
Kirkpatrick, R(obert) James *geology educator*
Klein, Miles Vincent *physics educator*
†Klemperer, Walter George *chemistry educator, researcher*
Langenheim, Ralph Louis, Jr. *geology educator*
Lauterbur, Paul C(hristian) *chemistry educator*
Lazarus, David *physicist, educator*
†Makri, Nancy *chemistry educator*
Mihalas, Dimitri Manuel *astronomer, educator*
†Minear, Roger Allan *chemist, educator*
Pethick, Christopher John *physicist*
Rowland, Theodore Justin *physicist, educator*
Salamon, Myron Ben *physicist, educator*
†Schweizer, Kenneth Steven *physics educator*
Simon, Jack Aaron *geologist, former state official*
Snyder, Lewis Emil *astrophysicist*
Switzer, Robert Lee *biochemistry educator*
Wattenberg, Albert *physicist, educator*
White, W(illiam) Arthur *geologist*
Wolynes, Peter Guy *chemistry researcher, educator*

INDIANA

Bloomington
Bair, Edward Jay *chemistry educator*
Bent, Robert Demo *physicist, educator*
Campaigne, Ernest Edward *chemistry educator*
Chisholm, Malcolm Harold *chemistry educator*
†Davidson, Ernest Roy *chemist, educator*
Dodd, James Robert *geologist, educator*
Edmondson, Frank Kelley *astronomer*
Grieco, Paul Anthony *chemistry educator*
Hattin, Donald Edward *geologist, educator*
†Hieftje, Gary Martin *analytical chemist, educator*
Johnson, Hollis Ralph *astronomy educator*
†Magnus, Philip Douglas *chemistry educator*
Murray, Haydn Herbert *geology educator*
†Novotny, Milos V. *chemistry educator*
Parmenter, Charles Stedman *chemistry educator*
Peters, Dennis Gail *chemist*
Pollock, Robert Elwood *nuclear physicist*
Putnam, Frank William *biochemistry and immunology educator*
Schaich, William L. *physics educator*
Vitaliano, Charles J(oseph) *geologist, educator*

Elkhart
Free, Helen M. *chemist, consultant*
Rand, Phillip Gordon *chemist*

Fort Wayne
Cox, David Jackson *biochemistry educator*
Faeth, Paul Alfred *physical chemist*
Stevenson, Kenneth Lee *chemist, educator*

Gary
†Meyerson, Seymour *retired chemist*

Hammond
Ammeraal, Robert Neal *biochemist*

Indianapolis
Aprison, Morris Herman *biochemist, neurobiologist, educator*
Bessey, William Higgins *physicist, educator*
Gibson, David Mark *biochemist, educator*
Harris, Robert Allison *biochemistry educator*
Koppel, Gary Allen *chemist, immunologist*
Mirsky, Arthur *geologist, educator*
†Pearlstein, Robert M. *physics educator*
Soper, Quentin Francis *chemist*
Steinrauf, Jean Hamilton *biochemistry professor*
†Wong, David T. *biochemist*
†Yan, Sau-Chi Betty *biochemist*

Lafayette
Brewster, James Henry *retired chemistry educator*
Christensen, Nikolas Ivan *geophysicist, educator*
Feuer, Henry *chemist, educator*
Gartenhaus, Solomon *physicist*
Judd, William Robert *engineering geologist, educator*
Loeffler, Frank Joseph *physicist, educator*
Melhorn, Wilton Newton *geosciences educator*
Porile, Norbert Thomas *chemistry educator*
Truce, William Everett *chemist, educator*

Muncie
Harris, Joseph McAllister *chemist*

Notre Dame
Alcock, Charles Benjamin *materials science educator*
Browne, Cornelius Payne *physics educator*
Cason, Neal Martin *physics educator*
Fehlner, Thomas Patrick *chemistry educator*
Feigl, Dorothy Marie *chemistry educator, university official*
Helquist, Paul M. *chemistry educator, researcher*
Marshalek, Eugene Richard *physics educator*
Scheidt, W. Robert *chemistry educator, researcher*
Schuler, Robert Hugo *chemist, educator*
Thomas, John Kerry *chemistry educator*
Trozzolo, Anthony Marion *chemistry educator*

Terre Haute
Guthrie, Frank Albert *chemistry educator*

Valparaiso
Cook, Addison Gilbert *chemistry educator*

West Lafayette
Adelman, Steven Allen *theoretical physical chemistry educator*
Amy, Jonathan Weekes *scientist, educator*
Baird, William McKenzie *chemical carcinogenesis researcher, biochemistry educator*
Barnes, Virgil Everett, II *physics educator*
Brown, Herbert Charles *chemistry educator*
Butler, Larry Gene *biochemistry educator, researcher*
Carmony, D(onald) Duane *physicist*
Cramer, William Anthony *biochemistry and biophysics researcher, educator*
Diamond, Sidney *chemist, educator*
Fischbach, Ephraim *physicist*
Grimley, Robert Thomas *chemistry educator*
Hanks, Alan R. *chemistry educator*
Laskowski, Michael, Jr. *chemist, educator*
Leap, Darrell Ivan *hydrogeologist*
Levandowski, Donald William *geologist*
Lipschutz, Michael Elazar *chemistry educator, consultant, researcher*
Margerum, Dale William *chemistry educator*
McMillin, David Robert *chemistry educator*
Morre, D. James *biochemist, educator*
Morrison, Harry *chemistry educator, university dean*
Mullen, James Gentry *physics educator*
Overhauser, Albert Warner *physicist*
Pratt, Dan Edwin *chemistry educator*
Rossmann, Michael George *biochemist, educator*
Sato, Hiroshi *materials science educator*
Wilson, Olin Chaddock *astronomer*

IOWA

Ames
Angelici, Robert J. *chemistry educator*
Barnes, Richard George *physicist, educator*
Bowen, George Hamilton, Jr. *astrophysicist, educator*
Clem, John Richard *physicist, educator*
Corbett, John Dudley *chemistry educator*
Finnemore, Douglas Kirby *physics educator*
Fritz, James Sherwood *chemist, educator*
Gschneidner, Karl Albert, Jr. *metallurgist, educator, editor, consultant*
Hansen, Robert Suttle *chemist, educator*
Horowitz, Jack *biochemistry educator*
†Houk, Robert Samuel *chemistry educator*
Jacobson, Robert Andrew *chemistry educator*
Kelly, William Harold *physicist, physics educator*
Lynch, David William *physicist, educator*
Papadakis, Emmanuel Philippos *physicist, university research director, consultant*
Ruedenberg, Klaus *theoretical chemist, educator*
Russell, Glen Allan *chemist, educator*
Smith, John Francis *materials science educator*
Svec, Harry John *chemist, educator*
Yeung, Edward Szeshing *chemist*

Cedar Falls
Hanson, Roger James *physics educator*

Cedar Rapids
Boettcher, Norbe Birosel *chemist*

Grinnell
Erickson, Luther Eugene *chemist, educator*

Iowa City
Baker, Richard Graves *geology educator, palynologist*
Burton, Donald Joseph *chemistry educator*
Donelson, John Everett *biochemistry educator, molecular biologist*
Goodridge, Alan Gardner *research biochemist, educator*
Gurnett, Donald Alfred *physics educator*
Montgomery, Rex *biochemist, educator*
Pietrzyk, Donald John *chemistry educator*
Plapp, Bryce Vernon *biochemistry educator*
Titze, Ingo Roland *physics educator*
Van Allen, James Alfred *physicist, educator*
Wiley, Robert Allen *pharmaceutical educator*

Spirit Lake
Brett, George Wendell *retired geologist, philatelist*

KANSAS

Kansas City
Ebner, Kurt Ewald *biochemistry educator*

Lawrence
Ammar, Raymond George *physicist, educator*
Angino, Ernest Edward *geology educator*
Borchardt, Ronald Terrance *biochemistry and pharmaceutical chemistry educator, consultant*
Carlson, Robert Gideon *chemistry educator*
Davidson, John Pirnie *theoretical physicist, educator*
Dreschhoff, Gisela Auguste Marie *physicist, educator*
Enos, Paul *geologist, educator*
Gerhard, Lee Clarence *geologist, educator*
Harmony, Marlin Dale *chemistry educator, researcher*
Kleinberg, Jacob *chemist, educator*
Landgrebe, John Allan *chemistry educator*
Mitscher, Lester Allen *chemist, educator*
Zeller, Edward Jacob *physics, astronomy and geology educator, consultant*

Lebanon
Colwell, John Edwin *retired aerospace scientist*

Manhattan
Fateley, William Gene *scientist, educator, inventor, administrator*
Setser, Donald Wayne *chemistry educator*
Twiss, Page Charles *geology educator*

Topeka
Cohen, Sheldon Hersh *chemistry educator*

Wichita
Andrew, Kenneth L. *research physicist, physics educator*

KENTUCKY

Bowling Green
Slocum, Donald Warren *chemist*

Lexington
Brown, William Randall *geology educator*
Cheniae, George Maurice *plant biochemist*
Cochran, Lewis W. *physicist, university official*
DeLong, Lance Eric *physics educator, researcher*
Ehmann, William Donald *chemistry educator*
Ettensohn, Frank Robert *geologist, educator*
Hagan, Wallace Woodrow *geologist*
Kern, Bernard Donald *retired educator, physicist*
†Liu, Keh-Fei Frank *physicist, educator*
†Lodder, Robert Andrew *chemistry and pharmaceutics educator*
Mercer, Leonard Preston, II *biochemistry educator*
Sands, Donald Edgar *chemistry educator*
Sendlein, Lyle V. A. *geology educator*
Tietz, Norbert Wolfgang *clinical chemistry educator, administrator*

Louisville
Belanger, William Joseph *chemist, polymer applications consultant*
Cohn, David V(alor) *biochemistry educator*
Johnson, Alan Arthur *physicist, educator*
Prough, Russell Allen *biochemistry educator*
Shoemaker, Gradus Lawrence *chemist, educator*
Taylor, Kenneth Grant *chemistry educator*
Teller, David Norton *neurochemist*

Morehead
Herron, James Dudley *chemist, educator*

Paducah
Walden, Robert Thomas *physicist, consultant*

LOUISIANA

Baton Rouge
Coleman, James Malcolm *marine geology educator*
Hazel, Joseph Ernest *geology educator, stratigrapher*
Lambremont, Edward Nelson, Jr. *nuclear science educator*
Landolt, Arlo Udell *astronomer, educator*
Mc Glynn, Sean Patrick *physical chemist, educator*
O'Connell, Robert Francis *physics educator*
Pope, David E. *geologist, micropaleontologist*
Pryor, William Austin *chemistry educator*
Traynham, James Gibson *chemist, educator*
West, Philip William *chemistry educator*

Carencro
Clark, George Bryan *geophysicist*

New Orleans
Allen, Gary Curtiss *geology educator*
†Andrews, Bethlehem Kottes *research chemist*
Benerito, Ruth Rogan (Mrs. Frank H. Benerito) *chemist*
Buccino, Salvatore George *physics educator*
†Harper, Robert John, Jr. *chemist, researcher*
Rosensteel, George T. *physics educator, nuclear physicist*
Roskoski, Robert, Jr. *biochemist, educator*
Sumrell, Gene *research chemist*

MAINE

Lewiston
Stauffer, Charles Henry *retired chemistry educator*

Oakland
Koons, Donaldson *geologist, educator*

Orono
Borns, Harold William, Jr. *geologist, educator*
Csavinszky, Peter John *physicist, educator*
Fort, Raymond Cornelius, Jr. *chemistry educator*
Norton, Stephen Allen *geological sciences educator*
Tarr, Charles Edwin *physicist, educator*

Waterville
Reid, Evans Burton *chemist, artist, educator*

MARYLAND

Aberdeen Proving Ground
†Frasier, John T. *ballistic research administrator*

Adelphi
†DeMonte, Vito J. *physical sciences research administrator*

Annapolis
Bontoyan, Warren Roberts *chemist, state laboratories administrator*
Brunk, William Edward *astronomer*
Clotworthy, John Harris *oceanographic consultant*
Elder, Samuel Adams *physics educator*
Howell, Barbara Fennema *research chemist*
Johnson, David Simonds *meteorologist*
Rowell, Charles Frederick *chemistry educator*

Baltimore
Ahearn, John Stephen *research physicist*
Albinak, Marvin Joseph *chemistry educator*
Allen, Ronald John *astrophysics educator, researcher*
Anfinsen, Christian Boehmer *biochemist*
Beer, Michael *biophysicist, educator*
Bell, James Frederick *physicist, educator*
Benton, George Stock *meteorologist, educator*
†Berg, Jeremy M. *chemistry educator*
Chartrand, Mark Ray *astronomer, telecommunications consultant*
†Cowan, Dwaine Oliver *chemist, educator*
†Dagdigian, Paul Joseph *chemistry educator*
Domokos, Gabor *research physicist*
Eckerman, Jerome *physicist*
Eichhorn, Gunther Louis *chemist*
Englund, Paul Theodore *biochemist, educator*
Feldman, Gordon *physics educator*
Fenselau, Catherine Clarke *chemistry educator*
Fisher, George Wescott *geology educator*
Green, Robert Edward, Jr. *physicist, educator*
Grossman, Lawrence *biochemist, educator*
Haig, Frank Rawle *physics educator, clergyman*
Henry, Richard Conn *astrophysicist, educator*
Huang, Pien Chien *biochemistry educator, scientist*
Jensen, Arthur Seigfried *consulting engineering physicist*
Judd, Brian Raymond *physicist, educator*
Kowal, Charles Thomas *astronomer*
Kruger, Jerome *materials science educator, consultant*
Lane, Malcolm Daniel *biological chemistry educator*
Larrabee, Martin Glover *biophysics educator*
Lee, Yung-Keun *physicist, educator*
Lin, Shin *biophysics educator*
Madansky, Leon *particle physicist, educator*
†Marsh, Bruce David *geologist, educator*
McCarty, Richard Earl *biochemist, biochemistry educator*
Mulligan, Joseph Francis *physics educator*
Nickon, Alex *chemist, educator*
Norman, Colin Arthur *astrophysics educator*
†Osborn, Thomas Ray *physics and oceanography educator*
Pettijohn, Francis John *geology educator*
Pevsner, Aihud *physicist, educator*
Phillips, Owen Martin *oceanographer, geophysicist, educator*
Posner, Gary Herbert *chemist, educator*
Roseman, Saul *biochemist, educator*
Roth, George Stanley *research biochemist, physiologist*
Shamoo, Adil Elias *biochemist, biophysicist, educator*
†Sibeck, David G. *geophysicist*
†Stanley, Steven Mitchell *paleobiologist, educator*
Steiner, Robert Frank *biochemist*
Ts'o, Paul On-Pong *biophysical chemist, educator*
Westerhout, Gart *retired astronomer*

Beltsville
†Norris, Karl Howard *optics scientist, agricultural engineer*
Vanderslice, Joseph Thomas *chemist*

Berlin
Horner, William Harry *biochemist*
Passwater, Richard Albert *biochemist, writer*

Bethesda
Atlas, David *meteorologist, research scientist*
Becker, Edwin Demuth *chemist, laboratory director*
Bennett, Lawrence Herman *physicist*
Berger, Robert Lewis *biophysicist, researcher*
Bernardini, Isa *biochemist*
Cassman, Marvin *biochemist*
†Daly, John W. *chemistry research administrator*
Gerwin, Brenda Isen *research biochemist*
Ginsburg, Ann *biochemist, researcher*
Hall, John Allen *international nuclear consultant*
Holt, Helen Keil *physicist*
Korn, Edward David *biochemist*
†Liu, Darrell Teh Yung *biochemist, researcher*
†Lugt, Hans Josef *physicist*
Miller, Bennett *physicist, former government official*
Murayama, Makio *biochemist*
Nash, Howard Allen *biochemist, researcher*
Nirenberg, Marshall Warren *biochemist*
†Sherman, Kenneth *oceanographer*
Sinclair, Warren Keith *radiation biophysicist, organization executive, consultant*
Stadtman, Earl Reece *biochemist*
Stadtman, Thressa Campbell *biochemist*
Vaughan, Martha *biochemist*
Witkop, Bernhard *chemist*
Wright, James Roscoe *chemist*
Zwanzig, Robert Walter *chemist, physical science educator*

Cabin John
Shropshire, Walter, Jr. *biophysicist emeritus, pastor*

Catonsville
Vanderlinde, Raymond Edward *clinical chemist*

Chevy Chase
Hudson, Ralph P. *physicist*
Promisel, Nathan E. *materials scientist, metallurgical engineer*

Clarksburg
Townsend, John William, Jr. *physicist, retired federal aerospace agency executive*

College Park
Benesch, William Milton *molecular physicist, atmospheric researcher, educator*
Blewett, John Paul *physicist*
†Brill, Dieter Rudolf *physicist*
Brodsky, Marc Herbert *physicist, research and publishing executive*
Castellan, Gilbert William *chemistry educator*
†DeSilva, Alan W. *physics educator, researcher*
Dragt, Alexander James *physicist*
Fisher, Michael Ellis *mathematical physicist, chemist*
Gluckstern, Robert Leonard *physics educator*
Greenberg, Oscar Wallace *physicist, educator*
Griem, Hans Rudolf *physicist, educator*
†Griffin, James Joseph *physics educator*
Grim, Samuel Oram *chemistry educator*
Irwin, George Rankin *physicist, mechanical engineering educator*
Jaquith, Richard Herbert *chemistry educator, retired university official*
Kerr, Frank John *astronomer, educator*
Kramer, Irvin Raymond *metallurgist, researcher*
†Kundu, Mukul Ranjan *physics and astronomy educator*
Lubkin, Gloria Becker *physicist*
Mc Donald, Frank Bethune *physicist*
Misner, Charles William *physics educator*
Rabin, Herbert *physicist, university administrator*
†Sagdeev, Roald Zinnurovi *physicist educator*
Silverman, Joseph *chemistry educator, scientist*
Smith, Betty Faye *textile chemist*
Snow, George Abraham *physicist*
†Webb, Richard A. *physicist*
Weeks, John David *chemistry and physical science educator*
Zen, E-an *research geologist*

Columbia
Clark, Billy Pat *physicist*
Deutsch, Robert William *physicist*
Fisher, Dale John *chemist, instrumentation and medical diagnostic device investigator*
Khare, Mohan *chemist*

Crofton
Watson, Robert Tanner *physical scientist*

Dayton
Fischell, Robert Ellentuch *physicist*

Frederick
Garver, Robert Vernon *research physicist*
Kappe, David Syme *environmental chemist*
Lijinsky, William *biochemist*

Frostburg
Tam, Francis Man Kei *physics educator*

Gaithersburg
Berger, Harold *physicist*
Cahn, John Werner *metallurgist, educator*
Casella, Russell Carl *physicist*
†Caswell, Randall Smith *physicist*
Clark, Alan Fred *physicist*
Costrell, Louis *physicist*
†Danos, Michael *physicist*
Dean, Stephen Odell *physicist*
†Deslattes, Richard Day, Jr. *physicist*
†Gebbie, Katharine Blodgett *astrophysicist*
Harman, George Gibson *physicist, consultant*
Hougen, Jon Torger *physical chemist, researcher*
†Hsu, Stephen M. *materials scientist, chemical engineer*
Hubbell, John Howard *radiation physicist*
Kessler, Karl Gunther *physicist*
Kushner, Lawrence Maurice *physical chemist*
Kuyatt, Chris E(rnie) (Earl) *physicist, radiation measurement services administrator*
Levelt Sengers, Johanna Maria Henrica *research physicist*
†Pugh, Edison Neville *metallurgist*
†Reader, Joseph *physicist*
Schwartz, Lyle H. *materials scientist, government official*
†Smith, Leslie E. *physical chemist*
Taylor, Barry Norman *physicist*
Weber, Alfons *physicist*
†Wiese, Wolfgang Lothar *physicist*
†Wineland, David J. *physicist*

Garrett Park
Melville, Robert Seaman *chemist*

Glenelg
Williams, Donald John *research physicist*

Greenbelt
Alexander, Joseph Kunkle, Jr. *physicist*
Day, John H. *physicist*
Fichtel, Carl Edwin *physicist*
†Gehrels, Neil *astrophysicist*
Hauser, Michael George *astrophysicist*
Holt, Stephen S. *astrophysicist*
Langel, Robert Allan, III *geophysicist*
Maran, Stephen Paul *astronomer*
Mather, John Cromwell *astrophysicist*
Mumma, Michael Jon *physicist*
†Ramaty, Reuven Robert *physicist, researcher*
Simpson, Joanne Malkus *meteorologist*
Smith, David Edmund *geophysicist*
Stief, Louis John *chemist*

Kensington
Attix, Frank Herbert *medical physics educator, researcher*
Clarke, Frederic B., III *risk analysis consultant*
May, G. Lynwood *aerospace executive, engineering consultant*

Lanham Seabrook
Fischel, David *astrophysicist, remote sensing specialist*

Laurel
Apel, John Ralph *physicist*
Avery, William Hinckley *physicist, chemist*
Bostrom, Carl Otto *physicist, laboratory director*
†Fristrom, Robert Maurice *chemist*
Kossiakoff, Alexander *chemist*
Krimigis, Stamatios Mike *physicist, researcher, space science/engineering manager, consultant*

Mechanicsville
Henderson, Madeline Mary (Berry) *chemist, researcher, consultant*

Monrovia
Atanasoff, John Vincent *physicist*

Pasadena
Kreps, Robert Wilson *research chemist*
†Young, Russell Dawson *physics consultant*

Potomac
Engelmann, Rudolf Jacob *meteorologist*
Epstein, Edward S. *meteorologist*
Whang, Yun Chow *space science educator*

Rockville
Beattie, Donald A. *energy scientist, consultant*
Bruck, Stephen Desiderius *biochemist*
Day, LeRoy Edward *aerospace scientist, consultant*
Dunn, Bonnie Brill *chemist*
†Finlayson, John Sylvester *biochemist*
Grady, Lee Timothy *pharmaceutical chemist*
Grist, Clarence Richard *chemist, precious metals investor*
Jamieson, Graham A. *biochemist, organization official*
Kindt, Thomas James *chemist*
Murray, Peter *metallurgist, manufacturing company executive*
Schindler, Albert Isadore *physicist, educator*
Zoon, Kathryn Egloff *biochemist*

Sandy Spring
Kanarowski, Stanley Martin *chemist, chemical engineer, government official*

Silver Spring
†Briscoe, Melbourne G. *oceanographer, administrator*
Douglass, Carl Dean *biochemistry consultant, former government official*

Gaunaurd, Guillermo C. physicist, engineer, researcher
†Ostenso, Ned Allen oceanographer, government official
Rueger, Lauren John retired physicist
Scheer, Milton David physical chemist
Wilson, William Stanley oceanographer

Suitland
Cary, Boyd Balford, Jr. physicist

MASSACHUSETTS

Amherst
Archer, Ronald Dean chemist, educator
Bromery, Randolph Wilson geologist, educator
Byron, Frederick William, Jr. physicist, educator, university dean
Carpino, Louis A. chemist, educator
Ehrlich, Paul chemist, educator
Fink, Richard David chemist, educator
Goldstein, Joseph Irwin materials scientist, educator
Gordon, Joel Ethan physics educator
Harrison, Edward Robert physicist, educator
Inglis, David Rittenhouse physicist
Kantor, Simon William chemistry educator
†Lenz, Robert William polymer chemistry educator
MacKnight, William John chemist, educator
Peterson, Gerald Alvin physicist
Porter, Roger Stephen chemistry educator
Quin, Louis DuBose chemist, educator
†Ragle, John Linn chemistry educator
Scott, David Knight physicist, university administrator
Slakey, Linda Louise biochemistry educator
Stein, Richard Stephen chemistry educator

Attleboro
Griffin, Edwin H., Jr. (Hank Griffin) chemist

Bedford
Carr, Paul Henry physicist
Mailloux, Robert Joseph physicist
Wallace, John Edwin retired meteorologist, consultant

Boston
Anselme, Jean-Pierre Louis Marie chemist
Antoniades, Harry Nicholas educator, research biochemist
Aronow, Saul physicist
Blout, Elkan Rogers biological chemistry educator, university dean
Brecher, Kenneth astrophysicist
Brownell, Gordon Lee physicist, educator
Cantor, Charles Robert biochemistry educator
Cohen, Robert Sonné physicist, philosopher, educator
†Gergely, John biochemistry educator
Houtchens, Robert Austin, Jr. biochemist
Karnovsky, Manfred L. biochemistry educator
Kennedy, Eugene Patrick biochemist, educator
†Kolodner, Richard David biochemist, educator
Le Quesne, Philip William chemistry educator, researcher
Lichtin, Norman Nahum chemistry educator
Lynton, Ernest Albert physicist, educator, former university official
Malenka, Bertram Julian physicist, educator
Miliora, Maria Teresa chemist, psychotherapist, psychoanalyst, educator
Munro, Hamish Nisbet biochemist, educator
Papagiannis, Michael Dimitrios astronomer, educator
Pardee, Arthur Beck biochemist, educator
Quelle, Frederick William, Jr. physicist
†Raskin, Paul D. resoure management and environmental research administrator
†Riordan, James Francis biochemistry educator
Sinex, Francis Marott biochemist, educator
Solomon, Arthur Kaskel biophysics educator
†Spengler, Kenneth C. meteorologist, professional society administrator
Stanley, H(arry) Eugene physicist, educator
†Thomas, Peter biochemistry educator
Villee, Claude Alvin, Jr. biochemistry educator
Webster, Edward William medical physicist
Zimmerman, George Ogurek physicist, educator

Brookline
Vallee, Bert Lester biochemist, physician, educator

Cambridge
Alberty, Robert Arnold chemistry educator
Baker, James Gilbert optics scientist
Barger, James Edwin physicist
Bekefi, George physics educator
Biemann, Klaus chemistry educator
Billings, Marland Pratt geologist, educator
Birgeneau, Robert Joseph physicist, educator
Bloch, Konrad Emil biochemist
Bloembergen, Nicolaas physicist, educator
Bradt, Hale Van Dorn physicist, x-ray astronomer, educator
Branscomb, Lewis McAdory physicist
Burchfiel, Burrell Clark geology educator
Burke, Bernard Flood physicist, educator
Burnham, Charles Wilson mineralogy educator
Butler, James Newton chemist, educator
Cameron, Alastair Graham Walter astrophysicist, educator
Canizares, Claude Roger astrophysicist, educator
†Chen, Peter chemistry educator
Coleman, Sidney Richard physicist, educator
Corey, Elias James chemistry educator
Covert, Eugene Edzards aerophysics educator
Dalgarno, Alexander astronomy educator
Doering, William von Eggers organic chemist, educator
†Donnelly, Thomas William physicist
Dresselhaus, Mildred Spiewak physics and engineering educator
Durant, Graham John medicinal chemist, drug researcher
†Eagar, Thomas Waddy metallurgist, educator
Eagleson, Peter Sturges hydrologist, educator
Edsall, John Tileston biological chemistry educator
Ehrenreich, Henry physicist, educator
Emanuel, Kerry Andrew earth sciences educator
Evans, Robley Dunglison physicist
Feld, Michael Stephen physics educator
Feldman, Gary Jay physicist, educator
Feshbach, Herman physicist, educator
Field, George Brooks theoretical astrophysicist
Field, Robert Warren chemistry educator
Foner, Simon research physicist
French, Anthony Philip physicist, educator
Frey, Frederick August geochemistry researcher, educator
Friedman, Jerome Isaac physics educator, researcher
Garland, Carl Wesley chemist, educator
Gingerich, Owen Jay astronomer, educator
†Glauber, Roy Jay theoretical physics educator
Goldstone, Jeffrey physicist
Gordon, Roy Gerald chemistry educator
Gould, Stephen Jay paleontologist, educator
Grant, Nicholas John metallurgy educator
Greene, Frederick D., II chemistry educator
Greytak, Thomas John physics educator
†Griffin, Robert G. physics administrator
Grindlay, Jonathan Ellis astrophysics educator
†Grove, Timothy L. geology educator
Guth, Alan Harvey physicist, educator
Halperin, Bertrand Israel physics educator
Harrison, Stephen Coplan biochemist
Herschbach, Dudley Robert chemistry educator
†Hobbs, Linn Walker materials science educator
Hoffman, Paul Felix geologist, educator
Holton, Gerald physicist, science historian
Horwitz, Paul physicist
Huang, Kerson physics educator
Huchra, John Peter astronomer, educator
Jackiw, Roman physicist, educator
†Jacob, Daniel James atmospheric chemistry educator
Jaffe, Arthur Michael physicist, mathematician, educator
Jordan, Thomas Hillman geophysicist, educator
Joss, Paul Christopher astrophysicist, educator
Kamentsky, Louis Aaron biophysicist
Karplus, Martin chemistry educator
†Kemp, Daniel Schaeffer chemistry educator, consultant
Kendall, Henry Way physicist
Khorana, Har Gobind chemist, educator
†Kim, Peter Sungbai biochemistry educator
King, Ronold Wyeth Percival physics educator
Kirkpatrick, Francis H(ubbard), Jr. biophysicist, consultant
Kistiakowsky, Vera physics researcher, educator
Klemperer, William chemistry educator
Kleppner, Daniel physicist, educator
Klibanov, Alexander Maxim chemistry educator
Knowles, Jeremy Randall chemist, educator
Layzer, David astrophysicist, educator
†Lewin, Walter H. G. physics educator
Lindzen, Richard Siegmund meteorologist, educator
Lippard, Stephen James chemist, educator
Lipscomb, William Nunn, Jr. retired physical chemistry educator
†Livingston, James Duane physicist, educator
Lomon, Earle Leonard physicist, educator, consultant
Lorenz, Edward Norton meteorologist, educator
Low, Francis Eugene physics educator
Lyon, Richard Harold educator, physicist
Marsden, Brian Geoffrey astronomer
Martin, Paul Cecil physicist, educator
Masamune, Satoru chemistry educator, consultant
McCarthy, James Joseph oceanography educator
McElroy, Michael physicist, researcher
Meselson, Matthew Stanley biochemist, educator
Molina, Mario Jose physical chemist, educator
†Moniz, Ernest Jeffrey physics educator
†Moran, James Michael, Jr. astronomer
Negele, John William physics educator, consultant
Nelson, David Robert physics educator
Newell, Reginald Edward physics educator
Pappenheimer, Alwin M(ax), Jr. biochemist, immunologist
Paul, William physicist, educator
Petersen, Ulrich geology educator
†Porkolab, Miklos physics educator, researcher
†Postol, Theodore A. physicist, nuclear engineer, educator
Press, William Henry astrophysicist, computer scientist
Pritchard, David Edward physics educator
Purcell, Edward Mills physics educator
Ramsey, Norman F. physicist, educator
†Rebek, Julius, Jr. chemistry educator, consultant
Rediker, Robert Harmon physicist
†Redwine, Robert Page physicist, educator
Rice, James Robert engineering scientist, geophysicist
Robinson, Allan Richard oceanography educator
Roedder, Edwin Woods geologist
Rose, Robert Michael materials science and engineering educator
Rosenblith, Walter Alter scientist, educator
Rubin, Lawrence Gilbert physicist, laboratory manager
Schimmel, Paul Reinhard biochemist, biophysicist, educator
†Schreiber, Stuart L. chemist, educator
Seyferth, Dietmar chemist, educator
Shapiro, Irwin Ira physicist, educator
Siever, Raymond geology educator
Silbey, Robert James chemistry educator, researcher
Sizer, Irwin Whiting biochemistry educator
Spaepen, Frans August applied physics researcher, educator
Steinfeld, Jeffrey Irwin chemistry educator, consultant, author
Strandberg, Malcom Woodrow Pershing physicist
Strauch, Karl physicist, educator
Stubbe, JoAnne chemistry educator
Thaddeus, Patrick physicist, educator
Thompson, James Burleigh, Jr. geologist, educator
Ting, Samuel Chao Chung physicist, educator
Tinkham, Michael physicist, educator
Turnbull, David physical chemist, educator
Vessot, Robert Frederick Charles physicist
Villars, Felix Marc Hermann physicist, educator
Wald, George biochemist, educator
Wang, James Chuo biochemistry and molecular biology educator
Waugh, John Stewart chemist, educator
Weinberg, Robert Allan biochemist, educator
Westheimer, Frank Henry chemist, educator
Whipple, Fred Lawrence astronomer
Whitesides, George McClelland chemistry educator
Whitney, Charles Allen astronomer, writer
Wiley, Don Craig biochemistry and biophysics educator
†Wilson, Richard physicist, educator
†Witt, August Ferdinand aerospace scientist, educator
Wood, John Armstead planetary scientist, geological sciences educator
Wrighton, Mark Stephen chemistry educator
Wu, Tai Tsun physicist, educator
Wunsch, Carl Isaac oceanographer, educator

Concord
Valley, George Edward, Jr. physicist, educator

Cotuit
Miller, Robert Charles retired physicist

Dover
Chattoraj, Sati Charan biochemistry educator, researcher

Falmouth
Goody, Richard Mead geophysicist
Hollister, Charles Davis oceanographer

Gloucester
Socolow, Arthur Abraham geologist

Hanscom AFB
†Kirkwood, Robert Keith applied physicist

Hull
Chase, David Marion applied physicist, mathematical modeler

Lexington
Aldrich, Ralph Edward physicist
Bainbridge, Kenneth Tompkins physicist, educator
Bartlett, Paul Doughty chemist, educator
Buchanan, John Machlin biochemistry educator
Cathou, Renata Egone chemist, consultant
Garing, John Seymour retired physicist, research executive
†Hardy, John W. optics scientist
Kanter, Irving mathematical physicist
Mollo-Christensen, Erik Leonard oceanographer
Nash, Leonard Kollender chemistry educator
Schloemann, Ernst Fritz (Rudolf August) physicist, engineer
Shull, Clifford G. physicist, educator
Smith, Edgar Eugene biochemist, university administrator
Williamson, Richard Cardinal physicist

Lincoln
Bolt, Richard Henry science educator, business executive

Lowell
Baker, Adolph physicist
Carr, George Leroy physicist, educator
Salamone, Joseph Charles polymer chemistry educator
Sheldon, Eric physics educator
†Tripathy, Sukant Kishore chemistry educator

Marblehead
Sanders, Frederick meteorologist

Marlborough
Pittack, Uwe Jens engineer, physicist
Shepp, Allan physicist, scientist

Medford
Cormack, Allan MacLeod physicist, educator
Guertin, Robert Powell physics educator, university dean
Gunther, Leon physicist
Klema, Ernest Donald nuclear physicist, educator
Mc Carthy, Kathryn A. physicist
Milburn, Richard Henry physics educator
Schneps, Jack physics educator
Sung, Nak-Ho science educator
Urry, Grant Wayne chemistry educator

Natick
Cukor, Peter chemical research and development executive, consultant
Milius, Richard A. organic chemist
Wang, Chia Ping physicist, educator

Newton
Dunlap, William Crawford physicist
Heyn, Arno Harry Albert retired chemistry educator
Mautner, Henry George chemist
Weisskopf, Victor Frederick physicist

Northampton
Fleck, George Morrison chemistry educator

Roxbury
Franzblau, Carl biochemist, consultant, researcher
MacNichol, Edward Ford, Jr. biophysicist, educator
Simons, Elizabeth R(eiman) biochemist, educator

Salem
Cavallaro, Mary Caroline physics educator
Hope, Lawrence Latimer physicist

South Hadley
Bennett, Jean Louise McPherson physicist, research scientist
Campbell, Mary Kathryn chemistry educator
Harrison, Anna Jane chemist, educator

Sturbridge
McMahon, Maribeth Lovette physicist

Sudbury
Blackey, Edwin Arthur, Jr. geologist

Waltham
Abeles, Robert Heinz biochemistry educator
Caspar, Donald Louis Dvorak physics and structural biology educator
Cohen, Saul G. chemist, educator
De Rosier, David John biophysicist, educator
Deser, Stanley educator, physicist
Epstein, Irving Robert chemistry educator
Fasman, Gerald David biochemistry educator
Foxman, Bruce Mayer chemist, educator
Grunwald, Ernest Max chemistry educator
Jeanloz, Roger William biochemist, educator
Jencks, William Platt biochemist, educator
Kustin, Kenneth chemist
Lees, Marjorie Berman biochemist, neuroscientist
Nisonoff, Alfred biochemist, educator
†Petsko, Gregory Anthony chemistry and biochemistry educator
Rosenblum, Myron chemist, educator
Schweber, Silvan Samuel physics and history educator

Watertown
†Wright, Edward S. materials technology administrator

Wayland
Clark, Melville, Jr. physicist, electrical engineer, consultant
Davis, Luther, Jr. physicist

Wellesley
Kobayashi, Yutaka biochemist, consultant

Westford
Salah, Joseph Elias research scientist, educator

Weston
Whitehouse, David Rempfer physicist

Westwood
Bernfeld, Peter Harry William biochemist

Williamstown
Fox, William Templeton geologist, educator
Markgraf, J(ohn) Hodge chemist, educator
Park, David Allen physicist, educator
Pasachoff, Jay Myron astronomer, educator
Wobus, Reinhard Arthur geologist, educator

Woods Hole
Ballard, Robert Duane marine scientist
Berggren, William Alfred geologist, research micropaleontologist, educator
†Butman, Bradford oceanographer
Cohen, Seymour Stanley biochemist, educator
Emery, Kenneth Orris marine geologist
Fofonoff, Nicholas Paul oceanographer, educator
Gagosian, Robert B. chemist, educator
Hart, Stanley Robert geochemist, educator
Steele, John Hyslop marine scientist, oceanographic institute administrator
Von Herzen, Richard Pierre research scientist, consultant

Worcester
Apelian, Diran materials scientist, provost
Bell, Peter Mayo geophysicist
Hohenemser, Christoph physics educator, researcher
Klein, Michael William physics educator
Pavlik, James William chemistry educator

MICHIGAN

Ann Arbor
Agranoff, Bernard William biochemist, educator
Akerlof, Carl William physics educator
Aller, Margo Friedel astronomer
Alpern, Mathew physiological optics educator
Ashe, Arthur James, III chemistry educator
Atreya, Sushil Kumar space science educator, researcher
Bartell, Lawrence Sims chemist, educator
Bernstein, Isadore Abraham biochemistry educator, researcher
Blinder, Seymour Michael chemistry educator
†Chupp, Timothy E. physicist, educator, nuclear scientist, academic administrator
Crane, Horace Richard educator, physicist
Dekker, Eugene Earl biochemistry educator
Dolph, Charles Laurie theoretical physics educator
Donahue, Thomas Michael physics educator
†Farrand, William Richard geology educator
Feng, Hsien Wen biochemistry educator, researcher
Filisko, Frank Edward physicist, educator
Gingerich, Philip Derstine paleontologist, evolutionary biologist, educator
Haddock, Fred T. astronomer, educator
†Islam, Mohammed N. optics scientist
Jones, Lawrence William educator, physicist
Kesler, Stephen Edward economic geology educator
†Krimm, Samuel physicist, educator
Krisch, Alan David physics educator
Longone, Daniel Thomas chemistry educator
Neal, Homer Alfred physics educator, researcher, university administrator
Nordman, Christer Eric chemistry educator
Oncley, John Lawrence biophysics educator, consultant
Parkinson, William Charles physicist, educator
Pollack, Henry Nathan geophysics educator
Robertson, Richard Earl physical chemist, educator
Roe, Byron Paul physics educator
Schacht, Jochen Heinrich biochemistry educator
Tamres, Milton chemistry educator
Townsend, LeRoy B. chemistry educator, university administrator, researcher
Van der Voo, Rob geophysicist
†Veltman, Martinus J. physics educator
†Vesecky, John F. aerospace science educator, electrical engineering educator, researcher
Weinreich, Gabriel physicist, minister, educator

Big Rapids
Mathison, Ian William chemistry educator, academic dean

Bloomfield Hills
Brewer, George Eugene Francis chemical consultant

Cross Village
Stowe, Robert Allen catalytic and chemical technology consultant

Detroit
Bohm, Henry Victor physicist
Brown, Ray Kent biochemist, physician, educator
Coleman, David Manley chemistry educator
Ebbing, Darrell Delmar chemist, educator
Frade, Peter Daniel chemist
Fradkin, David Milton physicist, educator
Gupta, Suraj Narayan physicist, educator
†Johnson, Carl Randolph chemist, educator
Kirschner, Stanley chemist
†Newcomb, Martin Eugene, Jr. chemistry educator
Oliver, John Preston chemistry educator, academic administrator
Orton, Colin George medical physicist
Ronca, Luciano Bruno geologist, educator
Stewart, Melbourne George, Jr. physicist, educator

East Lansing
Abolins, Maris Arvids *physics researcher and educator*
Austin, Sam M. *physics educator*
Benenson, Walter *nuclear physics educator*
Blosser, Henry Gabriel *physicist*
Cross, Aureal Theophilus *geology and botany educator*
D'Itri, Frank Michael *environmental research chemist*
Dye, James Louis *chemistry educator*
†Gelbke, Claus-Konrad *nuclear physics educator*
Harrison, Michael Jay *physicist, educator*
Luecke, Richard William *biochemist*
McConnell, David Graham *research biochemist, educator*
Montgomery, Donald Joseph *physicist, educator*
Pollack, Gerald Leslie *physicist, educator*
Preiss, Jack *biochemistry educator*
Spence, Robert Dean *physics educator*
Summitt, (William) Robert *chemist, educator*
Tien, H. Ti *biophysics and physiology educator, scientist*
Tolbert, Nathan Edward *biochemistry educator, plant science researcher*
Wolterink, Lester Floyd *biophysicist, educator*
Yussouff, Mohammed *physicist, educator*

Flint
Wong, Victor Kenneth *physics educator, academic administrator*

Holland
Inghram, Mark Gordon *physicist, educator*

Jackson
Henderson, John William *chemistry educator*

Kalamazoo
Greenfield, John Charles *bio-organic chemist*

Leland
†Small, Hamish *chemist*

Madison Heights
Chapman, Gilbert Bryant *physicist*

Metamora
Blass, Gerhard Alois *physics educator*

Midland
Chao, Marshall S. *chemist*
Dorman, Linneaus Cuthbert *retired chemist*
Gant, George Arlington Lee *chemist*
Mansfield, Marc Lewis *chemist, research scientist*
Nowak, Robert Michael *chemist*
Speier, John Leo, Jr. *chemist*
Stull, Daniel Richard *research thermochemist, educator, consultant*
Weyenberg, Donald Richard *chemist*

Mount Pleasant
Dietrich, Richard Vincent *geologist, educator*

Rochester
Callewaert, Denis Marc *biochemistry educator*

Troy
Drakos, Irene Sasso *chemist*
Ovshinsky, Stanford Robert *physicist, inventor, energy and information company executive*

Warren
Herbst, Jan Francis *physicist, researcher*
Schwartz, Shirley E. *chemist*
Smith, George Wolfram *physicist, educator*
†Smith, John Robert *materials scientist*

Ypsilanti
Barnes, James Milton *physics and astronomy educator*

MINNESOTA

Austin
Holman, Ralph Theodore *biochemistry and nutrition educator*
†Schmid, Harald Heinrich Otto *biochemistry educator, academic director*

Duluth
Rapp, George Robert, Jr. (Rip) *geology and archeology educator*

Lakeville
Phinney, William Charles *retired geologist*

Minneapolis
Ackerman, Eugene *biophysics educator*
Carr, Charles William *biochemist, emeritus educator*
Carr, Robert Wilson, Jr. *chemistry educator*
Dahler, John Spillers *chemist, educator*
Gannon, Mary Carol *nutritional biochemist*
Gasiorowicz, Stephen George *physics educator*
Goldman, Allen Marshall *physics educator*
Halley, James Woods, Jr. *physicist*
Hamermesh, Morton *physicist, educator*
Hobbie, Russell Klyver *physicist*
Hogenkamp, Henricus Petrus Cornelis *biochemistry researcher, biochemistry educator*
Hooke, Roger LeBaron *geomorphology and glaciology educator*
Jones, Thomas Walter *astrophysics educator, researcher*
Kruse, Paul Walters, Jr. *physicist, consultant*
Kuhi, Leonard Vello *astronomer, university administrator*
Lumry, Rufus Worth, II *chemist, educator*
Marshak, Marvin Lloyd *physicist, educator*
Moscowitz, Albert Joseph *chemist, educator*
Portoghese, Philip Salvatore *medicinal chemist, educator*
Prager, Stephen *chemistry educator*
Rubens, Sidney Michel *physicist, technical advisor*
†Smyrl, William H. *chemistry educator*
Truhlar, Donald Gene *chemist, educator*
†Wade, Lewis V. *mineral research director*
Wright, Herbert E(dgar), Jr. *geologist*

Northfield
Buchwald, Caryl Edward *geology educator, environmental consultant, educational consultant*
Casper, Barry Michael *physics educator*
Noer, Richard J. *physics educator, researcher*
Ramette, Richard Wales *chemistry educator*

Rochester
Kao, Pai Chih *clinical chemist*

Roseville
Berry, James Frederick *biochemistry educator*

Saint Paul
Bloomfield, Victor Alfred *biochemistry educator*
Clapp, C(harles) Edward *research chemist, soil biochemistry educator*
Farnum, Sylvia Arlyce *physical chemist*
Nicholson, Morris Emmons, Jr. *metallurgist, educator*
†Walker, Charles Thomas *physicist, educator*
Walton, Matt Savage *geologist, educator*

White Bear Lake
Holmen, Reynold Emanuel *chemist*

MISSISSIPPI

Bay Saint Louis
Skramstad, Robert Allen *oceanographer*

Mississippi State
Howell, Everette Irl *physicist, educator*

Pascagoula
Corben, Herbert Charles *physicist, educator*

Starkville
Emerich, Donald Warren *retired chemistry educator*

Stennis Space Center
†Royestess, Roy *aerospace science administrator*

MISSOURI

Cape Girardeau
†Dahiya, Jai Narain *physics educator, researcher*

Columbia
Bauman, John E., Jr. *chemistry educator*
Decker, Wayne Leroy *meteorologist, educator*
Ethington, Raymond Lindsay *geology educator, researcher*
Gehrke, Charles William *biochemistry educator*
Johns, William Davis, Jr. *geologist, educator*
Mayer, Dennis Thomas *biochemist, educator*
Rabjohn, Norman *chemistry educator emeritus*
Unklesbay, Athel Glyde *geologist, educator*

Joplin
Malzahn, Ray Andrew *chemistry educator, university dean*

Kansas City
Ching, Wai Yim *physics educator, researcher*
Gier, Audra May Calhoon *environmental chemist*
Grosskreutz, Joseph Charles *physicist, engineering researcher, educator*
Martinez-Carrion, Marino *biochemist, educator*
Parizek, Eldon Joseph *geologist, college dean*
Rost, William Joseph *chemist*

Kirksville
Festa, Roger Reginald *chemist, educator*

Rolla
Adawi, Ibrahim Hasan *physics educator*
Alexander, Ralph William, Jr. *physics educator*
Armstrong, Daniel Wayne *chemist, educator*
Hagni, Richard Davis *geology and geophysics educator*
James, William Joseph *chemistry educator*
Mc Farland, Robert Harold *physicist, educator*
O'Keefe, Thomas Joseph *metallurgical engineer*

Saint Louis
Ackerman, Joseph J. H. *chemistry educator*
Ackers, Gary Keith *biophysical chemistry educator, researcher*
Arvidson, Raymond Ernst *planetary geology educator*
Bender, Carl Martin *physics educator, consultant*
Burgess, James Harland *physics educator, researcher*
Callis, Clayton Fowler *research chemist*
†Di Cera, Enrico *biophysicist*
Frieden, Carl *biochemist, educator*
Friedlander, Michael Wulf *physicist, educator*
Gaspar, Peter Paul *chemistry educator*
Gibbons, Patrick Chandler *physicist, educator*
Gross, Michael Lawrence *chemistry educator*
Handel, Peter H. *physics educator*
Heinrich, Ross Raymond *geophysicist, educator*
Hohenberg, Charles Morris *physics educator*
Holtzer, Alfred Melvin *chemistry educator*
Horwitt, Max Kenneth *biochemist, educator*
Israel, Martin Henry *astrophysicist, educator, academic administrator*
Kurz, Joseph Louis *chemistry educator*
Lipkin, David *chemist*
Macias, Edward S. *chemistry educator, university official*
Marshall, Garland Ross *biochemist, biophysicist, medical educator*
Miller, James Gegan *research scientist, physics educator*
Murray, Robert Wallace *chemistry educator*
Podosek, Frank Anthony *geochemistry, geology educator*
Rosenthal, Harold Leslie *biochemistry educator*
Stauder, William Vincent *geophysics educator*
Takano, Masaharu *physical chemist*
Walker, Robert Mowbray *physicist, educator*
Weber, Morton M. *microbial biochemist, educator*
Will, Clifford Martin *physicist, educator*

Springfield
Criswell, Charles Harrison *analytical chemist, environmental and forensic consultant, executive*

Thompson, Clifton C. *chemistry educator, university administrator*

MONTANA

Bozeman
Caughlan, Georgeanne Robertson *retired physics educator*
Mertz, Edwin Theodore *biochemist, emeritus educator*
†Swenson, Robert J. *physics educator*

Butte
Beuerman, Donald Roy *chemistry educator*
†Ruppel, Edward Thompson *geologist*

Missoula
Jakobson, Mark John *physics educator*
Murray, Raymond Carl *forensic geologist, educator*
Osterheld, R(obert) Keith *chemistry educator*
Peterson, James Algert *geologist, educator*

Troy
Sherman, Signe Lidfeldt *former research chemist, securities analyst*

NEBRASKA

Crete
Brakke, Myron Kendall *retired research chemist and educator*

Lincoln
Blad, Blaine L. *agricultural meteorology educator, consultant*
Eckhardt, Craig Jon *chemistry educator*
Jolliff, Carl R. *clinical biochemist, immunologist, laboratory administrator*
Jones, Lee Bennett *chemist, educator*
O'Leary, Marion Hugh *chemistry educator*
†Sellmyer, David Julian *physicist, educator*
Treves, Samuel Blain *geologist, educator, administrator*

Omaha
Gambal, David *biochemistry educator*
Watt, Dean Day *retired biochemistry educator*
Zepf, Thomas Herman *physics educator, researcher*

NEVADA

Boulder City
West, Arleigh Burton *retired water resources consultant*

Carson City
Crawford, John Edward *geologist, scientist*

Las Vegas
Bretthauer, Erich Walter *chemist*
Earl, Boyd L. *chemistry educator*
Eastwood, DeLyle *chemist*
Harpster, Robert Eugene *engineering geologist*

Reno
Helm, Donald Cairney *hydrogeologist*
Horton, Robert Carlton *geologist*
Leipper, Dale Frederick *physical oceanographer, educator*
†Pierson, William Roy *chemist*
Pough, Frederick Harvey *mineralogist*
Ritter, Dale Franklin *geologist, research association administrator*
Taranik, James Vladimir *geologist, educator*

NEW HAMPSHIRE

Alstead
Hanson, George Fulford *geologist*

Durham
Tischler, Herbert *geologist, educator*

Groveton
Kegeles, Gerson *chemistry educator*

Hanover
Braun, Charles Louis *chemistry educator, researcher*
Doyle, William Thomas *physicist, educator*
Harbury, Henry Alexander *biochemist, educator*
Kantrowitz, Arthur *physicist, educator*
Montgomery, David Campbell *physicist, educator*
Perrin, Noel *environmental studies educator*
Stockmayer, Walter H(ugo) *chemistry educator*
Sturge, Michael Dudley *physicist*
Wegner, Gary Alan *astronomer*

Jaffrey
Walling, Cheves Thomson *chemistry educator*

Salem
Simmons, Marvin Gene *geophysics educator*

NEW JERSEY

Allendale
Castor, William Stuart, Jr. *chemist, consultant, laboratory executive, educator*

Annandale
Cohen, Morrel Herman *physicist, biologist, educator*
†Gorbaty, Martin Leo *chemist, researcher*
Lohse, David John *physicist*
Sinfelt, John Henry *chemist*

Basking Ridge
McCall, David W. *chemist, administrator, materials consultant*

Belle Mead
Hansen, Ralph Holm *chemist*

Bound Brook
Karol, Frederick John *industrial chemist*

Camden
†Beck, David Paul *biochemist*

Cape May
Wilson, H(arold) Fred(erick) *chemist, research scientist*

Cherry Hill
Cazes, Jack *chemist, marketing consultant, editor*

East Orange
Simmons, Jean Elizabeth Margaret (Mrs. Glen R. Simmons) *chemistry educator*

Edison
Lo Surdo, Antonio *physical chemist, educator*

Florham Park
Griffo, James Vincent, Jr. *resource development consultant, retired biology educator, educational administrator*

Franklin Lakes
†Hetzel, Donald Stanford *chemist*

Highland Park
Brudner, Harvey Jerome *physicist*

Hoboken
†Bernstein, Jeremy *physicist, educator*
Fajans, Jack *physics educator*
Kunhardt, Erich Enrique *physicist, educator*
Schmidt, George *physicist*

Holmdel
Bjorkholm, John Ernst *physicist*
Burrus, Charles Andrew, Jr. *research physicist*
†Gordon, James Power *optics scientist*
Kaminow, Ivan Paul *physicist*
Mac Rae, Alfred Urquhart *physicist, electrical engineer*
Marcuse, Dietrich *physicist*
Miller, David Andrew Barclay *physicist*
Mollenauer, Linn Frederick *physicist*
†Shah, Jagdeep *physicist, researcher*
Wilson, Robert Woodrow *radio astronomer*

Kenilworth
Ganguly, Ashit Kumar *organic chemist*

Madison
deStevens, George *chemist, educator*

Mahwah
Borowitz, Grace Burchman *chemistry educator, researcher*

Monmouth Junction
Summerfield, Martin *physicist*

Morristown
Arnow, Leslie Earle *scientist*
Van Uitert, LeGrand Gerard *chemist*

Murray Hill
Baker, William Oliver *research chemist, educator*
Brinkman, William Frank *physicist, research executive*
Capasso, Federico *physicist, research administrator*
†Fleury, Paul Aimé *physicist*
†Geusic, Joseph Edward *physicist*
Glass, Alastair Malcolm *physicist, research director*
Helfand, Eugene *chemist*
Hohenberg, Pierre Claude *research physicist*
Johnson, David W., Jr. *ceramic scientist, researcher*
Logan, Ralph Andre *physicist*
Morgan, Samuel P(ope) *physicist, applied mathematician*
†Pinczuk, Aron *physicist*
Stillinger, Frank Henry *chemist, educator*
Wernick, Jack Harry *chemist*
†White, Alice Elizabeth *physicist, researcher*

Neptune
Aguiar, Adam Martin *chemist, educator*

New Brunswick
†Grassle, John Fredrick *oceanographer, marine sciences educator*
Lebowitz, Joel Louis *mathematical physicist, educator*
Liao, Mei-June *biopharmaceutical company administrator*
Plano, Richard James *physicist, educator*
Potenza, Joseph A(nthony) *chemistry educator, academic administrator*
Strauss, Ulrich Paul *educator, chemist*
†Temmer, Georges Maxime *physicist*

New Providence
†Coppersmith, Susan Nan *physicist*
Gall, Martin *chemist, research and development manager*
Gaylord, Norman Grant *chemical and polymer consultant*
Lanzerotti, Louis John *physicist*
Laudise, Robert Alfred *research chemist*
Stormer, Horst Ludwig *physicist*
†Wertheim, Gunther Klaus *physicist*

Newark
Christakos, Sylvia *biochemist, educator, researcher*
Ledeen, Robert Wagner *neurochemist, educator*
†Murnick, Daniel Ely *physicist, educator*
Panson, Gilbert Stephen *chemistry educator*

Nutley
Douvan-Kulesha, Irina *chemist*
Udenfriend, Sidney *biochemist*
Weissbach, Herbert *biochemist*

Pennington
Halasi-Kun, George Joseph *hydrologist, educator*
Widmer, Kemble *geologist*

Piscataway
Gotsch, Audrey Rose *environmental health sciences educator, researcher*
Kear, Bernard Henry *materials scientist*
Lindenfeld, Peter *physics educator*
Pond, Thomas Alexander *physics educator*
Robbins, Allen Bishop *physics educator*
Shatkin, Aaron Jeffrey *biochemistry educator*
Snitzer, Elias *physicist*
Yacowitz, Harold *biochemist, nutritionist*

Port Murray
Kunzler, John Eugene *physicist*

Princeton
Adler, Stephen Louis *physicist*
Anderson, Philip Warren *physicist*
Bahcall, John Norris *astrophysicist*
Chang, Clarence Dayton *chemist*
Cooke, Theodore Frederic, Jr. *chemist*
Davidson, Ronald Crosby *physicist, educator*
Dyson, Freeman John *physicist*
Fenichel, Richard Lee *biochemist*
†Fisch, Nathaniel Joseph *physicist*
Fitch, Val Logsdon *physics educator*
Florey, Klaus Georg *chemist, pharmaceutical consultant*
Fresco, Jacques Robert *biochemist, educator*
Gale, Paula Jane *chemist*
Gott, J. Richard, III *astrophysicist*
Grasselli, Robert Karl *physical chemist, research scientist*
Green, Joseph *chemist*
Groves, John Taylor, III *chemist, educator*
Gunn, James Edward *astrophysicist*
†Haldane, Frederick Duncan Michael *physics educator*
Happer, William, Jr. *physicist, educator*
†Hawryluk, Richard Janusz *physicist*
†Hulse, Russell Alan *physicist*
†Jenkins, Edward Beynon *research astronomer*
Judson, Sheldon *geology educator*
Kahng, Dawon *physicist, research and development executive*
Kauzmann, Walter Joseph *chemistry educator*
†LeGrange, Jane Deborah *industrial physicist*
Lemelson, Jerome H. *inventor*
Lemonick, Aaron *physicist, educator*
Libchaber, Albert Joseph *physics educator*
Lieb, Elliott Hershel *physicist, mathematician, educator*
Mahlman, Jerry David *research meteorologist*
Manabe, Syukuro *climatologist*
Mc Clure, Donald Stuart *physical chemist, educator*
Mills, Robert Gail *retired physicist*
Miyakoda, Kikuro *meteorologist, lecturer*
Montgomery, Ronald Eugene *chemist, research and development director*
Navrotsky, Alexandra *geophysics educator*
Ondetti, Miguel Angel *chemist, consultant*
Oort, Abraham Hans *meteorologist, researcher, educator*
Ostriker, Jeremiah Paul *astrophysicist, educator*
Peebles, Phillip James E. *physicist, educator*
Rebenfeld, Ludwig *chemist*
Reynolds, George Thomas *physics educator, researcher, consultant*
Robertson, Nat Clifton *chemist*
Rodwell, John Dennis *biochemist*
Royce, Barrie Saunders Hart *physicist*
Rutherford, Paul Harding *physicist*
Shoemaker, Frank Crawford *physicist, educator*
Smagorinsky, Joseph *meteorologist*
Smith, Arthur John Stewart *physicist, educator*
Spiro, Thomas George *chemistry educator*
Sterzer, Fred *research physicist*
Stix, Thomas Howard *physicist, educator*
Taylor, Edward Curtis *chemistry educator*
Taylor, Joseph Hooton, Jr. *radio astronomer, physicist*
Treiman, Sam Bard *physics educator*
Van Houten, Franklyn Bosworth *geologist, educator*
†Weigmann, Hans-Dietrich H. *chemist*
Wheeler, John Archibald *physicist, educator*
Wightman, Arthur Strong *physicist, educator*
Wigner, Eugene Paul *physicist, educator*
Wilczek, Frank Anthony *physics educator*
Wilkinson, David Todd *physics educator*
Witten, Edward *mathematical physicist*
Wong, Ching-Ping *chemist*

Rahway
Kaczorowski, Gregory John *biochemist, researcher, science administrator*
Shapiro, Bennett Michaels *biochemist, educator*

Skillman
Kral, Frank *biophysical chemist*

Springfield
Panish, Morton B. *physicial chemist, consultant*

Summit
Gonnella, Nina Celeste *biophysical chemist*
Hagstrum, Homer Dupre *physicist*
Phillips, James Charles *physicist, educator*
†Wissbrun, Kurt F. *chemist, consultant*

Teaneck
Kramer, Bernard *physicist, educator*
Walsh, Peter Joseph *physics educator*

Trenton
Cushman, David Wayne *research biochemist*
Tucker, Robert Keith *environmental scientist, research administrator*

Union
Hochstadt, Joy *biomedical research scientist, scientific and research director*
Zois, Constantine Nicholas Athanasios *meteorology educator*

Upper Montclair
Kowalski, Stephen Wesley *chemistry educator*

Westfield
Miller, Gabriel Lorimer *physicist, researcher*

Westwood
Schutz, Donald Frank *geochemist, corporate executive*

NEW MEXICO

Albuquerque
Beckel, Charles Leroy *physics educator*
†Beeler, Gary *materials science administrator*
†Graham, Robert Albert *research physicist*
Harrison, Charles Wagner, Jr. *applied physicist*
Kepler, Raymond Glen *physicist*
King, James Claude *physicist*
Loftfield, Robert Berner *biochemistry educator*
Robinson, Charles Paul *nuclear physicist, diplomat, business executive*
†Scully, Marlan Orvil *physics educator*
Sparks, Morgan *physicist*
Vook, Frederick Ludwig *physicist*
Wengerd, Sherman Alexander *geologist, educator*

Las Cruces
Coburn, Horace Hunter *retired physics educator*
Kemp, John Daniel *biochemist, educator*

Los Alamos
Allred, John Caldwell *physicist*
Bell, George Irving *biophysics researcher*
Bradbury, Norris Edwin *physicist*
Colgate, Stirling Auchincloss *physicist*
Engelhardt, Albert George *physicist*
†Fisk, Zachary *physical scientist*
†Flynn, Edward Robert *physicist*
†Friar, James Lewis *physicist*
Garvey, Gerald Thomas *physicist, researcher*
†Gibson, Benjamin Franklin *physicist*
†Ginocchio, Joseph Natale *theoretical physicist*
Grilly, Edward Rogers *physicist*
Hecker, Siegfried Stephen *metallurgist*
Jarmie, Nelson *physicist*
†Johnson, Mikkel Borlaug *physicist*
Judd, O'Dean P. *physicist*
Keepin, George Robert, Jr. *physicist*
Kelly, Robert Emmett *physicist, educator*
†Kubas, Gregory Joseph *research chemist*
†Linford, Rulon Kesler *physicist, program director*
Matlack, George Miller *radiochemist*
McNally, James Henry *physicist*
Metropolis, Nicholas Constantine *mathematical physicist*
Mitchell, Terence Edward *materials scientist*
†Nix, James Rayford *nuclear physicist, consultant*
Onstott, Edward Irvin *research chemist*
†Pack, Russell T *theoretical chemist*
Penneman, Robert Allen *retired chemist*
Rosen, Louis *physicist*
†Schneider, Barry Irwin *theoretical atomic and molecular physicist*
Selden, Robert Wentworth *physicist, science advisor*
Smith, James Lawrence *research physicist*
†Strottman, Daniel David *physicist*
Terrell, (Nelson) James *physicist*
†Wahl, Arthur Charles *retired chemistry educator*
Whetten, John Theodore *geologist*
Zurek, Wojciech Hubert *physicist*
Zweig, George *physicist, neurobiologist*

Mesilla Park
Tombaugh, Clyde William *astronomer, educator*

Santa Fe
Barnes, John Fayette *research scientist, educator*
Cannon, Helen Leighton *retired geologist, government official*
Cowan, George Arthur *chemist, bank executive, director*
Fisher, Robert Alan *laser physicist*
†Giovanielli, Damon Vincent *physicist, consulting company executive*
Ratliff, Floyd *biophysics educator, scientist*
†Ward, John William *physical chemist*
White, David Hywel *physics educator*

Socorro
Kottlowski, Frank Edward *geologist*
Petschek, Albert George *physics educator*

Sunspot
Altrock, Richard Charles *astrophysicist*

White Sands Missle Range
†Evans, Ronald L. *atmospheric science research administrator*
Niles, Franklin Elvie *physicist*

NEW YORK

Albany
Bosart, Lance F. *meteorology educator*
†Demerjian, Kenneth L. *atmospheric science educator, research center director*
Dunn, James Robert *geologist*
Frisch, Harry Lloyd *chemist, educator*
Frost, Robert Edwin *chemistry educator*
Hof, Liselotte Bertha *biochemist*
Kim, Jai Soo *physics educator*
Kuivila, Henry Gabriel *chemist, educator, consultant*
Reichert, Leo Edmund, Jr. *biochemist, endocrinologist*
Roth, Laura Maurer *physics educator, researcher*
Schneider, Allan Stanford *biochemistry and pharmacology educator, biomedical research scientist*

Alfred
Rossington, David Ralph *physical chemistry educator*

Amagansett
Lustig, Harry *physicist, educator, administrator*

Amherst
Fujita, Shigeji *physicist, educator*
Henderson, Donald *biophysics educator*

Bayport
Courant, Ernest David *physicist*

Bellport
Barton, Mark Quayle *physicist*

Binghamton
Coates, Donald Robert *geology educator, scientist*
Eisch, John Joseph *chemist, educator*

Briarcliff Manor
Bhargava, Rameshwar Nath *physicist*

Bronx
Shamos, Morris Herbert *physicist educator*
Yalow, Rosalyn Sussman *medical physicist*

Brooklyn
Castleman, Louis Samuel *metallurgist, educator*
Charton, Marvin *chemist, educator*
†Eirich, Frederick Roland *chemist, educator*
Ettrick, Marco Antonio *theoretical physicist*
Franco, Victor *theoretical physics educator*
Friedman, Paul *chemistry educator*
Halpern, Alvin Michael *physicist, educator*
Kjeldaas, Terje, Jr. *physics educator emeritus*
Langer, Arthur Mark *mineralogist*
Mendelson, Sol *physical science educator, consultant*
Morawetz, Herbert *chemistry educator*
†Pearce, Eli M. *chemistry educator, administrator*
Stracher, Alfred *biochemistry educator*
Tamir, Theodor *electrophysics researcher, educator*
Vogl, Otto *polymer science and engineering educator*
Wolf, Edward Lincoln *physics educator*

Buffalo
Anbar, Michael *biophysics educator*
Bardos, Thomas Joseph *chemist, educator*
Basu, Rajat Subhra *physicist, researcher*
Borst, Lyle Benjamin *physicist, educator*
Bruckenstein, Stanley *chemistry educator*
Coppens, Philip *chemist*
Jain, Piyare Lal *physics educator*
Reitan, Paul Hartman *geologist, educator*
Treanor, Charles Edward *physicist*
Tufariello, Joseph James *chemistry educator*
Wang, Jui Hsin *biochemistry educator*

Canton
Romey, William Dowden *geologist, educator*

Chappaqua
†Demuth, Joseph E. *physicist, research administrator*

Clinton
Ring, James Walter *physics educator*

Corning
Josbeno, Larry Joseph *physics educator*
Keck, Donald Bruce *physicist*
Maurer, Robert Distler *retired industrial physicist*
Meiling, Gerald Stewart *materials scientist*

Cortland
Zipp, Arden Peter *chemistry educator*

Croton On Hudson
Adelson, Alexander M. *physicist*

Dobbs Ferry
†Triplett, Kelly B. *chemist*

East Hampton
Garrett, Charles Geoffrey Blythe *physicist*

Farmingdale
Marcuvitz, Nathan *electrophysics educator*
Nolan, Peter John *physics educator*

Flushing
Finks, Robert Melvin *paleontologist, educator*
Gafney, Harry D. *chemistry educator*
Goldman, Norman Lewis *chemistry educator*
Hatcher, Robert Douglas *physicist, educator*
Rafanelli, Kenneth Robert *physics educator*
Speidel, David Harold *geology educator*

Fredonia
Barnard, Walther M. *geosciences educator*

Freeport
Pullman, Maynard Edward *biochemist*

Garden City
Williams, Irving Laurence *physics educator*

Geneva
Roelofs, Wendell Lee *biochemistry educator, consultant*

Glen Cove
Dehn, Joseph William, Jr. *chemist*

Hamilton
Cochran, John Charles *chemistry educator*
Holbrow, Charles Howard *physicist, educator*
Linsley, Robert Martin *geology educator*

Hauppauge
Cohen, Martin Gilbert *physicist*

Hawthorne
Press, Jeffery Bruce *chemist*

Hempstead
Sparberg, Esther B. *chemist, educator*

Horseheads
Slade, Paul Graham *physicist*

Irvington
Devons, Samuel *educator, physicist*

Ithaca
Ashcroft, Neil William *physics educator, researcher*
Bassett, William Akers *geologist, educator*
Batterman, Boris William *physicist, educator, academic director*
†Bauer, Simon Harvey *chemistry educator*
Bauman, Dale Elton *nutritional biochemistry educator*
Berkelman, Karl *physics educator*
Bethe, Hans Albrecht *physicist, educator*
Bird, John Malcolm *geologist*
Burns, Joseph Arthur *planetary science educator*
†Carpenter, Barry Keith *chemistry educator, researcher*
Clark, David Delano *physicist, educator*
†Craighead, Harold G. *physics educator*
†Di Salvo, Francis Joseph, Jr. *chemistry educator*
Dodd, Jack Gordon, Jr. *physicist, educator*
Fay, Robert Clinton *chemist, educator*
Fitchen, Douglas Beach *physicist, educator*
Fleischmann, Hans Hermann Paul *physics educator*
†Fréchet, Jean Marie Joseph *chemistry educator*
Freed, Jack Herschel *chemist, educator*
Gibson, Quentin Howieson *biochemist*
†Gierasch, Peter Jay *astronomy educator*
Giovanelli, Riccardo *astronomer*
Gold, Thomas *astronomer, educator*
Goldsmith, Paul Felix *physics and astronomy educator*
Gottfried, Kurt *physicist, educator*
Greisen, Kenneth Ingvard *physicist, emeritus educator*
Hardy, Ralph W. F. *biochemist, biotechnology executive*
†Hart, Edward Walter *physicist*
Haynes, Martha Patricia *astronomer*
Hess, George Paul *biochemist, educator*
Hoffmann, Roald *chemist, educator*
Holcomb, Donald Frank *physicist, academic administrator*
Lee, David Morris *physics educator*
Liboff, Richard Lawrence *physicist, educator*
Lumley, John Leask *physicist, educator*
McDaniel, Boyce Dawkins *physicist, educator*
McLafferty, Fred Warren *chemist, educator*
†McMurry, John Edward *chemistry educator*
Meinwald, Jerrold *chemist, educator*
Mermin, N. David *physicist, educator, essayist*
Morrison, George Harold *chemist, educator*
Oglesby, Ray Thurmond *aquatic science educator*
Oliver, Jack Ertle *geophysicist*
Orear, Jay *physics educator, researcher*
Pohl, Robert Otto *physics educator*
Reppy, John David, Jr. *physicist*
Ruoff, Arthur Louis *physicist, educator*
Sagan, Carl Edward *astronomer, educator, author*
Salpeter, Edwin Ernest *physical sciences educator*
Scheraga, Harold Abraham *physical chemistry educator*
†Sievers, Albert John, III *physics educator*
Slate, Floyd Owen *chemist, materials scientist, civil engineer, educator, researcher*
Terzian, Yervant *astronomy and astrophysics educator*
Thomas, J. Earl *physicist*
†Tigner, Maurice *physicist, educator*
Turcotte, Donald Lawson *geophysical sciences educator*
†Van Campen, Darrell Robert *chemist*
Webb, Watt Wetmore *physicist, educator*
Widom, Benjamin *chemistry educator*
Wiesenfeld, John Richard *chemistry educator*
Wilson, Robert Rathbun *retired physicist*
Wu, Ray Jui *biochemistry educator*
Zilversmit, Donald Berthold *nutritional biochemist, educator*

Jamaica
Greenberg, Jacob *biochemist, educator, consultant*
†Lengyel, István *chemist, educator*

Jamesville
Levy, George Charles *chemistry educator, corporate executive*

Kings Park
Calviello, Joseph Anthony *research electrophysicist, consultant*

Lancaster
Weinberg, Norman Louis *electrochemist*

Larchmont
Rosenberg, Paul *physicist, consultant*

Lewiston
Dexter, Theodore Henry *chemist*

Mamaroneck
Mazzola, Claude Joseph *physicist, small business owner*

Manhasset
Cerami, Anthony *biochemistry educator*

Merrick
Paul, Martin Ambrose *physical chemist*

Middle Village
Farb, Edith Himel *chemist*

New York
Agosta, William Carleton *chemist, educator*
Arons, Michael Eugene *physicist, academic administrator*
Bederson, Benjamin *physicist, educator*
Benesch, Ruth Erica *chemistry educator*
Berne, Bruce J. *chemistry educator*
Birman, Joseph Leon *physics educator*
Borowitz, Sidney *retired physics educator*
Breslow, Ronald Charles *chemist, educator*
†Broecker, Wallace S. *geophysics educator*
†Campbell, George, Jr. *physicist, administrator*
Chargaff, Erwin *biochemistry educator emeritus, writer*
Cheng, Chuen Yan *biochemist, educator*
Chevray, Rene *physics educator*
Cohen, Ezechiel Godert David *physicist, educator*
Cross, George Alan Martin *biochemistry educator, researcher*
Cummins, Herman Zachary *physicist*
Dailey, Benjamin Peter *chemistry educator*
de Duve, Christian René *chemist, biologist, educator*
de Planque, E. Gail *physicist*
Edelman, Isidore Samuel *biochemist and medical educator*
Eisenthal, Kenneth B. *physical chemistry educator*
Erlanger, Bernard Ferdinand *biochemist, educator*
Finlay, Thomas Hiram *biochemist, researcher*
Flynn, George William *chemistry educator, researcher*
Fox, Jack Jay *chemist, educator*
Fraenkel, George Kessler *chemistry educator*
†Friedberg, Richard M. *physicist, educator*
Friedman, Gerald Manfred *geologist, educator*
Gilmont, Ernest Rich *chemist*
Glassgold, Alfred Emanuel *physicist, educator*
Goldstein, Menek *neurochemistry educator*
Goulianos, Konstantin *physics educator*
Green, Saul *biochemist*

†Greenberger, Daniel Mordecai *physics educator*
Grunberger, Dezider *biochemist, researcher*
†Guillen, Michael Arthur *mathematical physicist, educator, writer, television journalist*
†Gyulassy, Miklos *physics educator*
†Hansen, James E. *physicist, meteorologist, federal agency administrator*
Harlow, George Eugene *mineralogist, curator*
Harris, Cyril Manton *physicist, engineering and architecture educator, consulting acoustical engineer*
Hoffert, Martin Irving *applied science educator*
Honig, Barry Hirsh *biophysics educator*
Hutter, Rudolf Gustav Emil *physics educator*
Kellogg, Herbert Humphrey *metallurgist, educator*
Khuri, Nicola Najib *physicist, educator*
Komar, Arthur B. *physicist, educator*
Krasna, Alvin Isaac *biochemist, educator*
†Kuo, John Tsungfen *geophysicist, educator, researcher*
Laughlin, John Seth *physicist, educator*
Lax, Melvin *theoretical physicist*
Lee, Tsung-Dao *physicist, educator*
Lieberman, Seymour *biochemistry educator emeritus*
Low, Barbara Wharton *biochemist, biophysicist*
Machlin, Eugene Solomon *metallurgy educator, consultant*
Marshall, Thomas Carlisle *applied physics educator*
Mauzerall, David Charles *biophysics educator, research scientist*
McKay, Kenneth Gardiner *physicist, electronics company executive*
Mc Kenna, Malcolm Carnegie *vertebrate paleontologist, curator, educator*
Meislich, Herbert *chemistry educator emeritus*
Meister, Alton *biochemist, educator*
Merrifield, Robert Bruce *biochemist, educator*
Middleton, David *physicist, applied mathematician, educator*
Nakanishi, Koji *chemistry educator, research institute administrator*
Newell, Norman Dennis *paleontologist, geologist, museum curator, educator*
Novick, Robert *physicist, educator*
Nowick, Arthur Stanley *metallurgy, materials science educator*
Oppenheimer, Michael *physicist*
Oreskes, Irwin *biochemistry educator*
†Osbourn, Gordon Cecil *materials scientist*
Osgood, Richard M., Jr. *applied physics and electrical engineering educator, research administrator*
Pais, Abraham *physicist, educator*
†Parkin, Gerard Francis Ralph *chemistry educator, researcher*
Pechukas, Philip *chemistry educator*
Percus, Jerome Kenneth *physicist, educator*
Piore, Emanuel Ruben *physicist*
Pye, Lenwood David *materials science educator, researcher, consultant*
†Rhodes, Yorke E(dward) *chemist*
Robinson, Enders Anthony *geophysics educator, writer*
Roeder, Robert Gayle *biochemist, educator*
Roellig, Leonard Oscar *physics educator*
Sakita, Bunji *physicist, educator*
†Sarachik, Myriam Paula *physics educator*
Saxena, Brij B. *biochemist, endocrinologist, educator*
†Sciulli, Frank *physicist, educator*
Simon, Eric Jacob *neurochemist, educator*
Smith, Norman Obed *physical chemist, educator*
Sonenberg, Martin *biochemistry educator, physician*
Spector, Abraham *ophthalmic biochemist, educator, laboratory administrator*
Sprinson, David Benjamin *biochemistry educator*
†Spruch, Larry *physicist, educator*
Still, William Clark, Jr. *chemistry educator*
Stork, Gilbert (Josse) *chemistry educator, investigator*
Stroke, Hinko Henry *physicist, educator*
Szer, Wlodzimierz *biochemist, educator*
Turro, Nicholas John *chemistry educator*
Vogel, Henry James *biochemist, educator*
Zakim, David *biochemist*

Niskayuna
Katz, Samuel *geophysics educator*
Lafferty, James Martin *physicist*
Mihran, Theodore Gregory *retired physicist*

Nyack
†Ryan, William B. F. *geologist*

Orangeburg
†Lajtha, Abel *biochemist*

Oswego
Silveira, Augustine, Jr. *chemistry educator*

Painted Post
Hammond, George Simms *chemist*

Palisades
Cane, Mark Alan *oceanography and climate researcher*
Hayes, Dennis Edward *geophysicist, educator*
Kent, Dennis Vladimir *geophysicist, researcher*
Richards, Paul Granston *geophysics educator, seismologist*
Sykes, Lynn Ray *geologist, educator*

Patchogue
Shore, Ferdinand John *physicist, educator*

Potsdam
Dicello, John Francis, Jr. *physicist, educator*
†Mackay, Raymond Arthur *chemist*
Matijevic, Egon *chemistry educator, researcher, consultant*

Poughkeepsie
Beck, Curt Werner *chemist, educator*
Deiters, Sister Joan Adele *chemistry educator, nun*
Heller, William Russell *physicist, computer scientist*
Lang, William Warner *physicist*
Maling, George Croswell, Jr. *physicist*
Pliskin, William Aaron *physicist*
Tavel, Morton Allen *physics educator, researcher*

Ridge
Adams, Peter David *physicist, editor*

Rochester
Abood, Leo George *biochemistry educator*
Basu, Asish Ranjan *geological sciences educator, researcher*
†Boeckman, Robert Kenneth, Jr. *chemistry educator, organic chemistry researcher*
Buff, Frank Paul *chemist, educator*
Coburn, Theodore James *retired physicist*
Eisenberg, Richard S. *chemistry educator*
Elder, Fred Kingsley, Jr. *physicist, educator*
Featherstone, John Douglas Bernard *biochemistry educator*
Ferbel, Thomas *physics educator, physicist*
Gates, Marshall DeMotte, Jr. *chemistry educator*
George, Nicholas *optics educator, researcher*
Goldstein, David Arthur *biophysicist, educator*
Hilf, Russell *biochemist*
Kampmeier, Jack August Carlos *chemist, educator*
Kende, Andrew Steven *chemistry educator*
Khosla, Rajinder Paul *physicist*
Kingslake, Rudolf *retired optical designer*
†Knauer, James P. *physicist*
Knox, Robert Seiple *physicist, educator*
Kreilick, Robert W. *chemist, educator*
La Celle, Paul Louis *biophysics educator*
Makous, Walter Leon *visual scientist, educator*
Mandel, Leonard *physics and optics educator*
Maniloff, Jack *biophysicist, educator*
Marinetti, Guido V. *biochemistry educator*
McCrory, Robert Lee *physicist, mechanical engineering educator*
McLendon, George Leland *chemistry educator, researcher*
Melissinos, Adrian Constantin *physicist, educator*
Saunders, William Hundley, Jr. *chemist, educator*
Shapiro, Sidney *physicist, educator*
Simon, Albert *physicist, engineer, educator*
Slattery, Paul Francis *physicist, educator*
†Soures, John M. *physicist, researcher*
Teichert, Curt *geologist, educator*
Thomas, John Howard *astrophysicist, engineer, educator*
Thorndike, Edward Harmon *physicist*
Whitten, David George *chemistry educator, researcher*
Wolf, Emil *physics educator*

Rouses Point
Weierstall, Richard Paul *pharmaceutical chemist*

Saint James
Bigeleisen, Jacob *chemist, educator*

Saratoga Springs
Walter, Paul Hermann Lawrence *chemistry educator*

Scarborough
Wittcoff, Harold Aaron *chemist*

Scarsdale
Cox, Robert Hames *chemist, scientific consultant*

Schenectady
Alpher, Ralph Asher *physicist*
Anthony, Thomas Richard *research physicist*
Briant, Clyde Leonard *metallurgist, researcher*
Bulloff, Jack John *physical chemist, consultant*
Hart, Howard Roscoe, Jr. *physicist*
Hebb, Malcolm Hayden *physicist*
Kambour, Roger Peabody *polymer physical chemist, researcher*
Luborsky, Fred Everett *research physicist*
Philip, A. G. Davis *astronomer, editor, educator*
Redington, Rowland Wells *physicist, researcher*

Southold
Bachrach, Howard L. *biochemist*

Stony Brook
Alexander, John Macmillan, Jr. *chemistry educator*
Bonner, Francis Truesdale *chemist, educator, university dean*
†Brown, Gerald Edward *physicist, educator*
Cess, Robert Donald *atmospheric sciences educator*
Hanson, Gilbert Nikolai *geochemistry educator*
Herman, Herbert *materials science educator*
Kahn, Peter B. *physics educator*
†Koch, Peter MacWilliams *physics educator, researcher*
Pritchard, Donald William *oceanographer*
†Solomon, Philip M. *astronomer, atmospheric scientist*
†Weidner, Donald J. *geophysicist educator*
Yahil, Amos *astrophysicist, educator*
Yang, Chen Ning *physicist, educator*

Syracuse
†Baldwin, John Edwin *chemistry educator*
Birge, Robert Richards *chemistry educator*
Burtt, Benjamin Pickering *retired chemistry educator*
Conan, Robert James, Jr. *chemistry educator, consultant*
Fendler, Janos Hugo *chemistry educator*
Fox, Geoffrey Charles *computer science and physics educator*
Holm, Robert Arthur *environmental scientist*
Honig, Arnold *physics educator, researcher*
Martonosi, Anthony Nicholas *biochemistry educator, researcher*
Muller, Ernest H. *geology educator*
Nafie, Laurence Allen *chemistry educator*
Prucha, John James *geologist, educator*
Robinson, Joseph Edward *geology educator, consulting petroleum geologist*
Smith, Kenneth Judson, Jr. *chemist, theoretician, educator*
Wali, Kameshwar *physicist, educator*
Wellner, Marcel Nahum *physics educator, researcher*

Tarrytown
†Flanigen, Edith Marie *materials scientist*

Troy
Archer, Sydney *chemistry educator*
Bean, Charles Palmer *biophysicist*
Bunce, Stanley Chalmers *chemist, educator*
Corelli, John Charles *physicist, educator*
Daves, Glenn Doyle, Jr. *science educator, chemist, researcher*
Ferris, James Peter *chemist, educator*
Fleischer, Robert Louis *physics educator*
Giaever, Ivar *physicist*
Hickok, Robert Lyman, Jr. *electrophysics educator*
Krause, Sonja *chemistry educator, researcher*
Levinger, Joseph Solomon *physicist, educator*
McKinley, William A. *educator, physicist*
Medicus, Heinrich Adolf *physicist, educator*
Miller, Donald Spencer *geologist, educator*
Potts, Kevin T. *chemistry educator*
Resnick, Robert *physicist, educator*
Sperber, Daniel *physicist*
†Wentorf, Robert Henry *physical chemist*
White, Frederick Andrew *physics educator, physicist*
Wiberley, Stephen Edward *chemistry educator, consultant*

Tuxedo Park
Hall, Frederick Keith *chemist*

Upton
Blume, Martin *physicist*
Bond, Peter Danford *physicist*
†Casten, Richard Francis *physicist*
Chrien, Robert Edward *physicist*
†Chung, Suh-Urk *physicist*
†Dover, Carl Bellman *physicist, consultant*
Friedlander, Gerhart *nuclear chemist*
Goldhaber, Gertrude Scharff *physicist*
Goldhaber, Maurice *physicist*
Hendrie, Joseph Mallam *physicist, nuclear engineer, government official*
Higinbotham, William Alfred *physicist*
Kato, Walter Yoneo *physicist*
Lindenbaum, S(eymour) J(oseph) *physicist*
Lowenstein, Derek Irving *physicist*
Marr, Robert Bruce *physicist, educator*
McWhan, Denis Bayman *physicist*
Rau, Ralph Ronald *physicist*
Samios, Nicholas Peter *physicist*
Schwartz, Melvin *physics educator, laboratory administrator*
Setlow, Jane Kellock *biophysicist*
Setlow, Richard Burton *biophysicist*
Studier, Frederick William *biophysicist*
Sutin, Norman *chemistry educator, scientist*
Wolf, Alfred Peter *chemist, educator*

Utica
Harney, Patrick Joseph Dwyer *meteorologist, consultant*

Valhalla
Danishefsky, Isidore *biochemist*

Wappingers Falls
Maissel, Leon Israel *physicist, engineer*

Webster
Conwell, Esther Marly *physicist*

Wellsville
Taylor, Theodore Brewster *physicist, business executive*

West Point
Johnson, A(lyn) William *chemistry educator, consultant*

West Stockholm
O'Brien, Neal Ray *geology educator*

Yorktown Heights
Fowler, Alan Bicksler *retired physicist*
†Gutzwiller, Martin Charles *theoretical physicist, research scientist*
†Holtzberg, Frederic *chemist, solid state researcher*
Keyes, Robert William *physicist*
Kirkpatrick, Edward Scott *physicist*
Landauer, Rolf William *physicist*
Lang, Norton David *physicist*
Ning, Tak Hung *physicist, microelectronic technologist*
Sorokin, Peter Pitirimovich *physicist*
Spiller, Eberhard Adolf *physicist*

NORTH CAROLINA

Asheville
Haggard, William Henry *meteorologist*
Smith, Norman Cutler *geologist, business executive, educator*
Squibb, Samuel Dexter *chemistry educator*

Beaufort
Bonaventura, Joseph *biochemist, educator, research center director*

Black Mountain
Lathrop, Gertrude Adams *chemist, consultant*

Chapel Hill
†Buck, Richard Pierson *chemistry educator, researcher*
Bursey, Maurice M. *chemistry educator*
Butler, James Robert *geology educator*
Davis, Morris Schuyler *astronomer*
Dearman, Henry Hursell *chemistry educator, administrator*
Dennison, John Manley *geologist, educator*
Dolan, Louise Ann *physicist*
Eliel, Ernest Ludwig *chemist, educator*
Forman, Donald T. *biochemist*
Frampton, Paul Howard *physics researcher, educator*
Fullagar, Paul David *geology educator, geochemical consultant*
Goldman, Leonard Manuel *physicist, engineering educator*
Hatfield, William Emerson *chemist, educator*
Hubbard, Paul Stancyl, Jr. *physics educator*
Irene, Eugene Arthur *physical chemistry educator, researcher*
Jones, Mary Ellen *biochemist*
Macdonald, James Ross *physicist, educator*
Markham, Jordan J. *physicist, retired educator*
†Merzbacher, Eugen *physicist, educator*
Meyer, Thomas J. *chemistry educator*
Miller, Daniel Newton, Jr. *geologist, consultant*
Mitchell, Earl Nelson *physicist, educator*
Murray, Royce Wilton *chemistry educator*
Neumann, Andrew Conrad *geological oceanography educator*
Parr, Robert Ghormley *chemistry educator*
Roberts, Louis Douglas *physics educator, researcher*
Rogers, John James William *geology educator*
St. Jean, Joseph, Jr. *micropaleontologist, educator*
Shuman, Mark Samuel *environmental and electroanalytical chemistry educator*
Slifkin, Lawrence Myer *physics educator*
Wilson, John Eric *biochemist*
Wolfenden, Richard Vance *biochemistry educator*
York, James Wesley, Jr. *theoretical physicist, educator*

Charlotte
Hall, Peter Michael *physics educator, electronics researcher*

Davidson
Burnett, John Nicholas *chemistry educator*

Durham
Bell, Robert Maurice *biochemistry educator, consultant*
Bursey, Joan Tesarek *chemist*
Chesnut, Donald Blair *chemistry educator*
Cocks, Franklin Hadley *materials scientist*
Crumbliss, Alvin Lee *chemistry educator, consultant*
†Cusson, Ronald Yvon *theoretical physicist*
Evans, Ralph Aiken *physicist, consultant*
Fraser-Reid, Bertram Oliver *chemistry educator*
Fridovich, Irwin *biochemistry educator*
Hammes, Gordon G. *chemistry educator*
Han, Moo-Young *physicist*
Hill, Robert Lee *biochemistry educator*
Hobbs, Marcus Edwin *chemistry educator*
Jaszczak, Ronald Jack *physicist, researcher, consultant*
Joklik, Wolfgang Karl *biochemist, virologist, educator*
Madey, John M. J. *physics educator*
Mc Phail, Andrew Tennent *chemist, educator*
Meyer, Horst *physics educator*
†Opara, Emmanuel Chukwuemeka *biochemistry educator*
Palmer, Richard Alan *chemistry educator*
Pearsall, George Wilbur *materials scientist, mechanical engineer, educator, consultant*
Perkins, Ronald Dee *geologist, educator*
Pilkey, Orrin H. *geology educator*
Roberson, Nathan Russell *physicist, educator*
Selkirk, James Kirkwood *biochemist*
Smith, Peter *chemist, educator, consultant*
†Straub, Karl David *biochemist, researcher*
Stroscio, Michael Anthony *physicist, educator*
Walter, Richard Lawrence *physicist, educator*
Wilder, Pelham, Jr. *chemist, pharmacologist, educator*

Greensboro
Clark, Clifton Bob *physicist*

Greenville
Clemens, Donald Faull *chemistry educator*
Frisell, Wilhelm Richard *biochemist, educator*
Sayetta, Thomas Charles *physics educator*
Snyder, Scott William *geology educator*

Hendersonville
Saby, John Sanford *physicist*

Pinehurst
Huizenga, John Robert *nuclear chemist, educator*

Raleigh
Aspnes, David Erik *physicist, educator*
Davis, William Robert *physicist*
Goldstein, Irving Solomon *chemistry educator, consultant*
Horton, Horace Robert *biochemistry educator*
Hugus, Z Zimmerman, Jr. *chemistry educator*
Mitchell, Gary Earl *physicist, educator*
Stiles, Phillip John *physicist, educator*
Swaisgood, Harold Everett *biochemist, educator*
Whitten, Jerry Lynn *chemistry educator*

Research Triangle Park
Krenitsky, Thomas Anthony *biochemist, research director*
Rodbell, Martin *biochemist*

Salemburg
Baugh, Charles Milton *biochemistry educator, college dean*

Southport
Worzel, John Lamar *geophysicist, educator*

Spring Hope
Lavatelli, Leo Silvio *retired physicist, educator*

Wilmington
Martin, Ned Harold *chemistry educator*

Winston Salem
Mokrasch, Lewis Carl *neurochemist, educator*
Rodgman, Alan *chemist, consultant*
Rudel, Lawrence Lee *biochemist*

NORTH DAKOTA

Grand Forks
Duerre, John Arden *biochemist*
Jacobs, Francis Albin *biochemist, educator*
Nordlie, Robert Conrad *biochemistry educator*

OHIO

Akron
Gent, Alan Neville *physicist, educator*
Kennedy, Joseph Paul *polymer scientist, researcher*
Uscheek, David Petrovich *chemist*

Alliance
Rodman, James Purcell *astrophysicist, educator*

Athens
Eckelmann, Frank Donald *geology educator, retired*

Berea
Jensen, Adolph Robert *former chemistry educator*

Bowling Green
Brecher, Arthur Seymour *biochemistry educator*

Brookpark
Kosmahl, Henry G. *electron physicist*

Canton
Arora, Sardari Lal *chemistry educator*
Koniecko, Edward S(tanley) *biochemist*

Chardon
Dietrich, Joseph Jacob *chemist, research executive*

Cincinnati
Alexander, John J. *chemistry educator*
†Carr, Albert Anthony *organic chemist*
Devitt, John William *physicist*
Ford, Emory A. *chemist, researcher*
Francis, Marion David *consulting chemist*
Goodman, Bernard *physics educator*
Gray, John Augustus *physical chemist*
Hubbard, Arthur Thornton *chemistry educator, electro-surface chemist*
Kawahara, Fred Katsumi *research chemist*
Lienhart, David Arthur *geologist, laboratory director*
Martin, Daniel William *acoustical physicist*
Meal, Larie *chemistry educator, consultant*
Merchant, Mylon Eugene *physicist, engineer*
Rockwell, R(onald) James, Jr. *laser and electro-optics consultant*
Rudney, Harry *biochemist, educator*
Williams, James Case *metallurgist*
Witten, Louis *physics educator*

Cleveland
Bidelman, William Pendry *astronomer, educator*
Blackwell, John *polymer scientist, educator*
Bockhoff, Frank James *chemistry educator*
Brown, Helen Bennett *biochemist*
Deissler, Robert George *fluid dynamicist, researcher*
Dowell, Michael Brendan *chemist*
Hanson, Richard Winfield *biochemist, educator*
Heuer, Arthur Harold *material science and engineering educator*
Jenkins, Thomas Llewellyn *physics educator*
Klopman, Gilles *chemistry educator*
Kowalski, Kenneth Lawrence *physicist, educator*
Krieger, Irvin Mitchell *chemistry educator, consultant*
Landau, Bernard Robert *biochemistry educator, physician*
Lando, Jerome Burton *macromolecular science educator*
Litt, Morton Herbert *macromolecular science educator, researcher*
Mawardi, Osman Kamel *plasma physicist*
McGervey, John Donald *physics educator, researcher*
Olson, Walter Theodore *research scientist, consultant*
Ritchey, William Michael *chemistry educator*
Robinson, Donald Keith *physicist, educator*
Rogers, Charles Edwin *physical chemistry educator*
Savin, Samuel Marvin *geologist*
Schuele, Donald Edward *physics educator*
Taylor, Philip Liddon *physics educator*
Urbach, Frederick Lewis *chemistry educator*
Wolff, Gunther Arthur *physical chemist*
Yeager, Ernest Bill *physical chemist, electrochemist, educator*

Columbus
Behrman, Edward Joseph *biochemistry educator*
Bergstrom, Stig Magnus *geology educator*
Corbato, Charles Edward *geology educator*
Cornwell, David George *biochemist, educator*
Daehn, Glenn Steven *materials scientist*
De Lucia, Frank Charles *physicist, educator*
Elliot, David Hawksley *geologist*
Epstein, Arthur Joseph *physics and chemistry educator*
Faure, Gunter *geology educator*
Firestone, Richard Francis *chemistry educator*
†Foland, Kenneth A. *geological sciences educator*
Jezek, Kenneth Charles *geophysicist, educator, researcher*
†Kolattukudy, Pappachan Ettoop *biochemist, educator*
Lipinsky, Edward Solomon *chemist*
Madia, William Juul *chemist*
Marzluf, George Austin *biochemistry educator*
Mayer, Victor James *geological science educator*
Milford, Frederick John *retired research company executive*
†Miller, Terry Alan *chemistry educator*
Mills, Robert Laurence *physicist, educator*
Newsom, Gerald Higley *astronomy educator*
Osmer, Patrick Stewart *astronomer*
Reibel, Kurt *physicist, educator*
Relle, Ferenc Matyas *chemist*
Slettebak, Arne *astronomer, educator*
Slonim, Arnold Robert *biochemist, physiologist*
Soloway, Albert Herman *medicinal chemist*
Wali, Mohan Kishen *environmental science and natural resources educator*
Webb, Thomas Evan *biochemistry educator*
Wilkins, John Warren *physics educator*
Wojcicki, Andrew Adalbert *chemist, educator*

Dayton
Battino, Rubin *chemistry educator*
Emrick, Donald Day *chemist, consultant*
Fang, Zhaoqiang *research physicist*
Gregor, Clunie Bryan *geology educator*
Hutchings, Brian LaMar *biochemist, college administrator*
Janning, John Louis *high technology scientist, consultant*
Nam, Sang Boo *physicist*
Spicer, John Austin *physicist*

Ironton
Mitchell, Maurice McClellan, Jr. *chemist*

Kent
Gould, Edwin Sheldon *chemist, educator*
Heimlich, Richard Allen *geologist, educator*

Norwalk
Germann, Richard P(aul) *chemist, chemical company executive*

Oberlin
Carlton, Terry Scott *chemist, educator*

Oxford
Baldwin, Arthur Dwight, Jr. *geology educator*
Gordon, Gilbert *chemist, educator*
Katon, John Edward *chemist, educator*
Macklin, Philip Alan *physics educator*

Piketon
†Patton, Finis S., Jr. *nuclear chemist*

Rootstown
Hutterer, Ferenc *biochemistry educator, researcher*

Steubenville
Kasprzak, Lucian Alexander *physics educator, researcher*

Sylvania
Kneller, William Arthur *geologist, educator*
Kurek, Dolores Bodnar *physical science and mathematics educator*

Toledo
Bagley, Brian G. *materials science educator, researcher*
Saffran, Murray *biochemist*

Westerville
Günther, Marian W(aclaw) J(an) *theoretical physicist*

Westlake
Myers, Ira Thomas *physicist*

Wickliffe
Dunn, Horton, Jr. *organic chemist*

Wilberforce
Gupta, Vijay Kumar *chemistry educator*

Worthington
Idol, James Daniel, Jr. *chemist, educator, inventor, consultant*

Youngstown
Gillis, Bernard Thomas *chemistry educator*

OKLAHOMA

Ada
†Stafford, Donald Gene *chemistry educator*

Bartlesville
Hogan, J(ohn) Paul *chemistry researcher, consultant*
†Johnson, Marvin Merrill *chemist*

Broken Arrow
Chambers, Richard Lee *geoscientist, researcher*

Norman
Atkinson, Gordon *chemistry educator*
†Branch, David Reed *astrophysicist, educator*
Ciereszko, Leon Stanley *chemistry educator*
Doviak, Richard James *atmospheric scientist, engineer*
Dryhurst, Glenn *chemistry educator*
Gal-Chen, Tzvi *geophysicist, meteorologist, educator*
Kessler, Edwin *meteorology educator, consultant*
Lamb, Peter James *meteorology educator, researcher, consultant*
Maddox, Robert Alan *atmospheric scientist*
Mankin, Charles John *geology educator*

Nowata
Osborn, Ann George *retired chemist*

Oklahoma City
Dunn, Parker Southerland *retired chemical company consultant*
Hartsuck, Jean Ann *chemist*
Magarian, Robert Armen *medicinal chemist, researcher, educator*
Troelstra, Arne *physics educator*

Stillwater
Berlin, Kenneth Darrell *chemistry educator, consultant, researcher*
Gorin, George *retired chemistry educator*
Leach, Franklin Rollin *biochemistry educator*

Tulsa
Ahmadieh, Aziz *metallurgy materials science educator*
Breck, Howard Rolland *geophysicist*
Horn, Myron Kay *consulting petroleum geologist, author, educator*
Smothers, William Edgar, Jr. *geophysical exploration company treasurer*

Weatherford
Hamm, Donald Ivan *retired chemistry educator, university dean*

OREGON

Albany
†Dooley, George Joseph, III *metallurgist*

Ashland
Addicott, Warren Oliver *geologist, educator*
Grover, James Robb *retired chemist, editor*

Corvallis
Becker, Robert Richard *biochemist, educator*
†Caldwell, Douglas Ray *oceanographer, educator*
Drake, Charles Whitney *physicist*
Evans, Harold J. *plant physiologist, biochemist, educator*
Keller, George Henrik *marine geologist*
†Reed, Donald James *biochemistry educator*
Shoemaker, David Powell *chemist, educator*
Sleight, Arthur William *chemist, educator*
Thomas, Thomas Darrah *chemistry educator*
Van Holde, Kensal Edward *biochemistry educator*
Yeats, Robert Sheppard *geologist, educator*

Eugene
Boekelheide, Virgil Carl *chemistry educator*
Boggs, Sam, Jr. *geology educator*
Chezem, Curtis Gordon *physicist, former retail executive*
Crasemann, Bernd *physicist, educator*
Deshpande, Nilendra Ganesh *physics educator*
Donnelly, Russell James *physicist, educator*
Girardeau, Marvin Denham *physics educator*
Griffith, Osbie Hayes *chemistry educator*
†Holser, William Thomas *geochemistry educator, geologist*
Mazo, Robert Marc *chemistry educator*
Noyes, Richard Macy *physical chemist, educator*
Peticolas, Warner Leland *physical chemistry educator*
Schellman, John A. *chemistry educator*
von Hippel, Peter Hans *chemistry educator*

Monmouth
White, Donald Harvey *physicist, educator*

Otter Rock
Kassner, Michael Ernest *materials science educator, researcher*

Portland
Claycomb, Cecil Keith *biochemist, educator*
Cronyn, Marshall William *chemistry educator*
Dunne, Thomas Gregory *chemistry educator, researcher*
Jones, Richard Theodore *biochemistry educator*
Pearson, David Petri *chemist*

Springfield
†Detlefsen, William David, Jr. *chemist, administrator*

PENNSYLVANIA

Allentown
Goldey, James Mearns *physicist*

Ardmore
Stanley, Edward Alexander *geologist, forensic scientist, technical and academic administrator*

Bethlehem
†Alhadeff, Jack Abraham *biochemist, educator*
Allen, Eugene Murray *chemist*
Fowler, W(yman) Beall *physics educator*
Heindel, Ned Duane *chemistry educator*
Hertzberg, Richard Warren *materials science and engineering educator, researcher*
Kanofsky, Alvin Sheldon *physicist*
Sclar, Charles Bertram *geology educator, researcher*
Smyth, Donald Morgan *chemical educator, researcher*
Varnerin, Lawrence John *physicist*
Watkins, George Daniels *physics educator*
Weidner, Richard Tilghman *physicist, educator*

Bristol
Arkles, Barry Charles *chemist*

Bryn Mawr
Berliner, Ernst *chemistry educator*
Crawford, Maria Luisa Buse *geology educator*
Mallory, Frank Bryant *chemistry educator*

Carlisle
Long, Howard Charles *physics educator emeritus*

Coatesville
Bucher, John Henry *metallurgical consultant, technology manager*

Collegeville
Cordes, Eugene Harold *biochemist*

Doylestown
Brink, Frank, Jr. *biophysicist, former educator*

Great Valley
Frazer, Jack Winfield *chemistry researcher*

Harrisburg
Richards, James Ward *geologist*
Zook, Merlin Wayne *meteorologist*

Haverford
Lazar, Anna *chemist*
Partridge, Robert Bruce *astronomy educator*

Hazleton
Miller, David Emanuel *physics educator, researcher*

King Of Prussia
Carroll, Margaret Ann *chemist*
Kopple, Kenneth D. *chemistry researcher, educator*

Lancaster
Hess, Earl Hollinger *laboratory executive, chemist*

Lansdale
Schnable, George Luther *chemist*

Lincoln University
Williams, Willie, Jr. *physicist, educator*

Media
Fehnel, Edward Adam *chemist, educator*

Melrose Park
Prince, Morton Bronenberg *physicist*

Monroeville
Parker, James Roger *chemist*

Newtown
Carlson, David Emil *physicist*
Leibholz, Stephen Wolfgang *physicist, engineering company executive, entrepreneur*
Long, Harry (On-Yuen Eng) *chemist, rubber science and technology consultant*

Philadelphia
Ajzenberg-Selove, Fay *physicist, educator*
Benfey, Otto Theodor *chemist, editor, historian of science*
Bludman, Sidney Arnold *theoretical physicist, astrophysicist*
Burstein, Elias *physicist, educator*
Chance, Britton *biophysics and physical chemistry educator emeritus*
Childress, Scott Julius *medicinal chemist*
Cohen, Jeffrey M. *physicist*
Cohn, Mildred *biochemist, educator*
Creech, Hugh John *chemist*
Davis, Raymond, Jr. *chemist, researcher, educator*
Devlin, Thomas McKeown *biochemist*
Farber, Emmanuel *pathology and biochemistry educator*
Fitts, Donald Dennis *chemist, educator*
Ford, Kenneth William *physicist*
Frankel, Sherman *physicist*
Hameka, Hendrik Frederik *chemist, educator*
Harker, Robert Ian *geologist, educator*
Havas, Peter *physicist, educator*
Hirschmann, Ralph Franz *chemist*
Intemann, Robert Louis *physics educator, researcher*
Kay, Jack Garvin *chemist, educator*
Klein, Abraham *physics educator, researcher*
Klein, Michael Lawrence *research chemist, educator*
Kritchevsky, David *biochemist, educator*
†Langacker, Paul George *physics educator*
Larson, Donald Clayton *physics educator, consultant*
Levitt, Israel Monroe *astronomer*
†Liebman, Paul Arno *biophysicist, educator*
Litwack, Gerald *biochemistry educator, academic administrator*
Magee, Wayne Edward *biochemistry educator, researcher*
Malamud, Daniel *biochemistry educator*
Matschinsky, Franz Maximilian *biochemistry and biophysics educator, researcher*
Maurer, Paul Herbert *biochemist, educator*
Nixon, Eugene Ray *chemist, educator*
Noordergraaf, Abraham *biophysics educator*
Pollack, Solomon Robert *bioengineering educator*
Prockop, Darwin Johnson *biochemist, physician*
Rosen, Gerald Harris *physicist, consultant, educator*
Rutman, Robert Jesse *biochemist, educator*
†Sage, Louis E. *environmental science executive*
Shen, Benjamin Shih-Ping *scientist, engineer, educator*
Steinhardt, Paul Joseph *physics educator, consultant*
Vitek, Vaclav *materials scientist*
Wales, Walter D. *physicist, educator*
Weisz, Paul B(urg) *physicist, chemical engineer*
Zurmuhle, Robert Walter *physicist*

Pittsburgh
Berry, Guy Curtis *polymer science educator, researcher*
Biondi, Manfred Anthony *physicist, educator*
Bothner-By, Aksel Arnold *chemist*
Caretto, Albert Alexander *chemist, educator*
Carr, Walter James, Jr. *research physicist, consultant*
Cassidy, William Arthur *geology and planetary science educator*
†Choyke, Wolfgang Justus *physicist*
Cohen, Bernard Leonard *physicist, educator*
Coltman, John Wesley *physicist*
Emmerich, Werner Sigmund *physicist*
Feller, Robert Livingston *chemist, art conservator*
Gerjuoy, Edward *physicist, lawyer*
Griffiths, Robert Budington *physics educator*
Hercules, David Michael *chemistry educator, consultant*
Hofmann, Klaus *biochemistry educator, researcher*
†Hu, William Hsun *physical metallurgy educator, materials scientist*
Janis, Allen Ira *retired physicist, educator*
Jasnow, David Michael *physics educator*
Kisslinger, Leonard Sol *Physicist, educator*
Laughlin, David Eugene *materials science educator, metallurgical consultant*
Massalski, Thaddeus Bronislaw *material scientist, educator*
†Mullins, William Wilson *physical metallurgist*
Page, Lorne Albert *physicist, educator*
Pratt, Richard Houghton *physics educator*
Rosenberg, Jerome Laib *chemist, educator*
Rosenkranz, Herbert S. *environmental toxicology educator*
†Sax, Martin *crystallographer*
Sekerka, Robert Floyd *physics educator, scientist*
White, Robert Marshall *physicist, educator*
Wolken, Jerome Jay *biophysicist, educator*
Wynblatt, Paul Pinhas *materials science educator, researcher*
Yates, John Thomas, Jr. *chemistry educator, researcher*
Young, Hugh David *physics educator, writer, organist*

Plymouth Meeting
Gilstein, Jacob Burrill *physicist*

Royersford
†Carriker, Roy C. *physicist*

Spring House
†Emmons, William David *chemist*

State College
Landy, Richard Allen *consultant*
Myers, Joel Norman *meteorologist, business executive*
†Rusinko, Frank, Jr. *fuels and materials scientist*

Swarthmore
Bilaniuk, Oleksa Myron *physicist, educator*
Gaustad, John Eldon *astronomy educator*
Hammons, James Hutchinson *chemistry educator, researcher*
Lippincott, Sarah Lee *astronomer, graphologist*
Pasternack, Robert Francis *chemistry educator*

University Park
Allcock, Harry R. *chemistry educator*
†Amateau, Maurice Francis *materials scientist, educator*
Barnes, Hubert Lloyd *geochemistry educator*
†Bernheim, Robert Allan *chemistry educator*
Bernlohr, Robert William *biochemist, educator, researcher*
Blackadar, Alfred Kimball *meteorologist, educator*
Cahir, John Joseph *meteorologist, educational administrator*
Castleman, Albert Welford, Jr. *physical chemist, educator*
Coleman, Michael Murray *polymer science educator*
Dutton, John Altnow *meteorologist, educator*
Frankl, Daniel Richard *educator, physicist*
German, Randall Michael *materials science educator, consultant*

†Herman, Roger M. *physicist, educator*
Hosler, Charles Luther, Jr. *meteorologist, educator*
Howell, Benjamin Franklin, Jr. *geophysicist, educator*
Jackman, Lloyd Miles *chemistry educator*
†Jurs, Peter Christian *chemistry educator*
Kurtz, Stewart Kendall *physics educator, researcher*
Lampe, Frederick Walter *chemistry educator, consultant*
Osborn, Elburt Franklin *former geochemistry educator, research scientist*
Pazur, John Howard *biochemist, educator*
Roy, Rustum *interdisciplinary materials researcher, educator*
Villafranca, Joseph J. *biochemistry educator*
†Webster, Peter John *meteorology educator*
White, William Blaine *geochemist, educator*
Winograd, Nicholas *chemist*

Valley Forge
Erb, Doretta Louise Barker *polymer applications scientist*
Erb, Robert Allan *physical scientist*

Villanova
Edwards, John Ralph *chemist, educator*
Phares, Alain Joseph *physicist, educator*

Wyncote
Baldridge, Robert Crary *retired biochemistry educator*

Wynnewood
Weinhouse, Sidney *biochemist, educator*

Wyomissing
Boyer, Robert Allen *physics educator*

RHODE ISLAND

Kingston
Cruickshank, Alexander Middleton *chemistry educator*
Nixon, Scott West *oceanography science educator*

Narragansett
†Leinen, Margaret Sandra *oceanographic researcher*
Sigurdsson, Haraldur *oceanography educator, researcher*

Providence
Avery, Donald Hills *metallurgist, educator, ethnographer*
Beyer, Robert Thomas *physicist, educator*
Bray, Philip James *physicist*
Carpenter, Gene Blakely *crystallography and chemistry educator*
Cooper, Leon N. *physicist, educator*
Dahlberg, Albert Edward *biochemistry educator*
Elbaum, Charles *physicist, educator, researcher*
Estrup, Peder Jan *physics and chemistry educator*
Gerritsen, Hendrik Jurjen *physics educator, researcher*
Greene, Edward Forbes *chemistry educator*
†Houghton, Anthony *physics educator, research scientist*
†Levin, Frank S. *physicist, educator*
†Maris, Humphrey John *physicist, educator*
Mason, Edward Allen *chemistry educator, scientist*
Rieger, Philip Henri *chemistry educator, researcher*
Tauc, Jan *physics educator*
Widgoff, Mildred *physicist, educator*

Wakefield
Moore, George Emerson, Jr. *geologist, educator*

West Kingston
Abell, Paul Irving *retired chemistry educator*

SOUTH CAROLINA

Aiken
†Begley, R. T. *nuclear science administrator*
Dickson, Paul Wesley, Jr. *physicist*
Hofstetter, Kenneth John *research chemist*

Charleston
Adelman, Saul Joseph *astronomy educator, researcher*
Berglund, Robin G. *biochemist, former corporate executive*
Delli Colli, Humbert Thomas *chemist, product development specialist*
Fenn, Jimmy O'Neil *physicist*
Gadsden, Richard Hamilton *clinical biochemistry educator*
Swanson, Arnold Arthur *biochemistry educator*

Clemson
Clayton, Donald Delbert *astrophysicist, nuclear physicist, educator*
DesMarteau, Darryl Dwayne *chemistry and geology educator*
Griffin, Villard Stuart, Jr. *geology educator*
Spain, James Dorris, Jr. *biochemist, educator*

Columbia
Edge, Ronald Dovaston *physics educator*
Secor, Donald Terry, Jr. *geologist, educator*
Teague, Peyton Clark *chemist, educator*

Johns Island
Failla, Patricia McClement *biomedical and environmental research adminstrator*

Salem
Gentry, Robert Cecil *meteorological consultant, research scientist*

Spartanburg
Cavin, William Pinckney *chemist, educator*

SOUTH DAKOTA

Rapid City
Gries, John Paul *geologist*
Lisenbee, Alvis Lee *structural geologist, educator*

Spearfish
Erickson, Richard Ames *physicist, emeritus educator*

Vermillion
Neuhaus, Otto Wilhelm *biochemistry educator*

TENNESSEE

Dyersburg
Bell, Helen Cherry *chemistry educator*

Hendersonville
Hill, William Thomas *geological consultant*

Jefferson City
Bahner, Carl Tabb *retired chemistry educator, researcher*

Johnson City
Huang, Thomas Tao-shing *chemistry educator*

Kingsport
Holmes, Jerry Dell *organic chemist*
Young, Howard Seth *chemist, researcher*

Kingston
Manly, William Donald *metallurgist*

Knoxville
Alexeff, Igor *physicist, electrical engineer, educator*
Blass, William Errol *physics and astronomy educator*
Dean, John Aurie *chemist, author, chemistry educator emeritus*
Lietzke, Milton Henry *chemistry educator*
Mahan, Gerald Dennis *physics educator, researcher*
Mamantov, Gleb *chemistry educator, consultant*
Schweitzer, George Keene *chemistry educator*
Wicks, Wesley D. *biochemistry educator*
Williams, Thomas Ffrancon *chemist, educator*
Wunderlich, Bernhard *physical chemistry educator*

Lenoir City
Breazeale, Mack Alfred *physics educator*

Memphis
Crane, Laura Jane *research chemist*
Desiderio, Dominic Morse, Jr. *chemistry and neurochemistry educator*
Fain, John Nicholas *biochemistry educator*
Johnston, Archibald Currie *geophysics educator, research director*
Lasslo, Andrew *medicinal chemist, educator*
Shugart, Cecil Glenn *physics educator*
Wildman, Gary Cecil *chemist*

Mount Juliet
Sweetman, Brian Jack *organic, analytical chemist, educator*

Nashville
Brau, Charles Allen *physics educator*
Chytil, Frank *biochemist*
Cohen, Stanley *biochemistry educator*
Cunningham, Leon William *biochemist, educator*
Dettbarn, Wolf-Dietrich *neurochemist, pharmacologist, educator*
Fort, Tomlinson *chemist, chemical engineering educator*
Gray, Allen Gibbs *metallurgist, materials engineer, editor*
Hall, Douglas Scott *astronomy educator*
Hamilton, Joseph Hants, Jr. *physicist, educater*
Heiser, Arnold Melvin *astronomer*
Hess, Bernard Andes, Jr. *chemistry educator*
Holladay, Wendell Gene *physics educator*
Inagami, Tadashi *biochemist, educator*
Kono, Tetsuro *biochemist, physiologist, educator*
Tarbell, Dean Stanley *chemistry educator*
†Tolk, Norman Henry *physics educator*
Weeks, Robert Andrew *materials science researcher, educator*
Wert, James Junior *materials scientist, educator*
†Willcott, Mark Robert, III *chemist, educator, researcher*

Oak Ridge
Beasley, Cloyd Orris, Jr. *physicist, researcher*
†Burtis, Carl A., Jr. *chemist*
Cawley, Charles Nash *enviromental scientist*
Garrett, Jerry Dale *nuclear physicist*
†Genung, R. K. *physical sciences research administrator*
†Gifford, Franklin Andrew, Jr. *meteorologist*
Krause, Manfred Otto *physicist*
Larson, Bennett Charles *solid state physicist, researcher*
Maienschein, Fred C. *physicist*
†Plasil, Franz *physicist*
Postma, Herman *physicist, consultant*
†Poutsma, Marvin L. *chemical research administration*
Renshaw, Amanda Frances *physicist, nuclear engineer*
Satchler, George Raymond *physicist*
†Sellin, Ivan Armand *physicist, educator, researcher*
Totter, John Randolph *biochemist*
Trivelpiece, Alvin William *physicist, corporate executive*
Weinberg, Alvin Martin *physicist*
Wilkinson, Michael Kennerly *physicist*
Zucker, Alexander *physicist, administrator*

TEXAS

Arlington
Burkart, Burke *geology educator, researcher*
Perkins, Bob(by) F(rank) *geologist, dean*
Pomerantz, Martin *chemistry educator, researcher*
Schimelpfenig, C(larence) W(illiam), Jr. *chemistry educator*
Smith, Charles Isaac *geology educator*
Wiseman, Carl Donald *metallurgy educator, consultant*

Austin
Bailey, Philip Sigmon *chemistry educator*
Bard, Allen Joseph *chemist, educator*
Barker, Daniel Stephen *geology educator*
Bash, Frank Ness *astronomer, educator*
Bengtson, Roger Dean *physicist*
Boggs, James Ernest *chemistry educator*
Boyer, Robert Ernst *geologist, educator*
Campion, Alan *chemistry educator*
de Vaucouleurs, Gerard Henri *astronomer, educator*
†de Wette, Frederik Willem *physics educator*
De Witt, Bryce Seligman *physics educator*
De Witt-Morette, Cécile *physicist*
Duncombe, Raynor Lockwood *astronomer*
Ellison, Samuel Porter, Jr. *geologist, educator*
Erskine, James Lorenzo *physics educator*
Evans, David Stanley *astronomy educator*
Fisher, William Lawrence *geologist, educator*
Folk, Robert Louis *geologist, educator*
Folkers, Karl August *chemistry educator*
Fonken, Gerhard Joseph *chemistry educator, university administrator*
Fox, Marye Anne *chemistry educator*
Gardiner, William Cecil, Jr. *chemist, educator*
Gavenda, J(ohn) David *physicist*
Gentle, Kenneth William *physicist*
Gleeson, Austin Michael *physicist, educator*
Griffy, Thomas Alan *physics educator*
Heller, Adam *chemist, researcher*
Herman, Robert *physics educator*
Ho, Paul Siu-Chung *physics educator*
Hudspeth, Emmett LeRoy *physicist, educator*
Jefferys, William Hamilton, III *astronomer*
Lagowski, J(oseph) J(ohn) *chemist*
Lundelius, Ernest Luther, Jr. *vertebrate paleontologist, educator*
Maxwell, Arthur Eugene *oceanographer, marine geophysicist, educator*
Moore, James Robert *geological oceanographer*
Oakes, Melvin Ervin Louis *physics educator*
Pradzynski, Andrzej Henryk *chemist*
Prigogine, Vicomte Ilya *physics educator*
Reed, Lester James *biochemist, educator*
Sharp, John Malcolm, Jr. *geology educator*
Smoluchowski, Roman *physicist, emeritus educator*
Snell, Esmond Emerson *biochemist*
†Stoffa, Paul L. *geophysicist, educator*
Swinney, Harry Leonard *physics educator*
Wheeler, John Craig *astrophysicist, writer*
White, John Michael *chemistry educator*
†Willson, C. Grant *chemistry educator, engineering educator*
Ziegler, Daniel Martin *chemist, educator*

Baytown
Mendelson, Robert Allen *polymer scientist, rheologist*

College Station
Anderson, Aubrey Lee *oceanographer, educator*
Anderson, Duwayne Marlo *earth and polar scientist, university administrator*
†Arnowitt, Richard Lewis *physics educator, researcher*
Barton, Derek Harold Richard *chemist*
Berg, Robert Raymond *geologist, educator*
Berner, Leo De Witte, Jr. *retired oceanographer*
Carter, Neville Louis *geophysicist, educator*
Clearfield, Abraham *chemistry educator*
Conway, Dwight Colbur *chemistry educator*
Cotton, Frank Albert *chemist, educator*
Fackler, John Paul, Jr. *chemistry educator*
Friedman, Melvin *geology educator, college dean*
Ham, Joe Strother, Jr. *physics educator*
†Laane, Jaan *chemistry educator*
†Latimer, George Webster, Jr. *chemist*
Martell, Arthur Earl *chemistry educator*
McIntyre, John Armin *physics educator*
†Nachman, Ronald James *research chemist*
†Natowitz, Joseph B. *chemistry educator, administrator, researcher*
O'Connor, Rod *chemist, inventor*
Orville, Richard Edmonds *atmospheric science educator*
Prescott, John Mack *biochemist, retired university administrator*
†Rowe, Gilbert Thomas *oceanography educator*
Scott, Alastair Ian *chemistry educator*
Stanton, Robert James, Jr. *geologist, educator*

Corpus Christi
Berryhill, Henry Lee, Jr. *geologist*
Roels, Oswald Albert *oceanographer, educator, business executive*

Dallas
Brooks, James Elwood *geologist, educator*
Esquivel, Agerico Liwag *research physicist*
Estabrook, Ronald Winfield *chemistry educator*
Gibbs, James Alanson *geologist*
Green, Cecil Howard *consulting geophysicist, educator*
Johnson, Richard Clayton *engineer, physicist*
Konrad, Dusan *chemist*
McAlester, Arcie Lee, Jr. *geologist, educator*
Montgomery, Edward Benjamin *physicist, retired educator*
Murad, John Louis *occupational safety and health consultant*
Ray, Bradley Stephen *petroleum geologist*
Ries, Edward Richard *petroleum geologist, consultant*
†Srere, Paul A. *biochemist, educator*

Denton
Golden, David Edward *physicist*
Redding, Rogers Walker *physics educator*

El Paso
Cook, Clarence Sharp *physics educator*
Hardaway, Robert Morris, III *physician, educator, retired army officer*

Fort Worth
Battista, Orlando Aloysius *scientist, author, executive, inventor*
Gutsche, Carl David *chemistry educator*
Landolt, Robert George *chemistry educator*
Quarles, Carroll Adair, Jr. *physicist, educator*
Reinecke, Manfred G. *chemistry educator*
Smith, William Burton *chemist, educator*

Galveston
Bonchev, Danail Georgiev *chemist, educator*
Kurosky, Alexander *biochemist, educator*
Merrell, William John, Jr. *oceanography educator*
Weigel, Paul Henry *biochemistry educator, researcher, consultant*

Georgetown
Du Bar, Jules Ramon *geologist, retired educator*

Granger
Horton, Claude Wendell *physicist, educator*

Horseshoe Bay
Ramey, James Melton *chemist*

Houston
Anderson, Richard Carl *geophysical exploration company executive*
†Bernal, Ivan *chemistry educator*
Berry, Julianne Elward *polymer and colloid chemist, researcher, inventor*
Brandt, I. Marvin *chemist, engineer*
Brotzen, Franz Richard *materials science educator*
Burke, Kevin Charles Antony *geologist*
Chamberlain, Joseph Wyan *astronomer, educator*
Chu, Paul Ching-Wu *physicist*
†Chu, Wei-Kan *physicist, educator*
Clark, Carolyn Archer *technologist, scientist*
Curl, Robert Floyd, Jr. *chemistry educator*
De Bremaecker, Jean-Claude *geophysics educator*
†Fukuyama, Tohru *organic chemistry educator*
Gibson, Everett Kay, Jr. *space scientist, geochemist*
Gibson, Robert Lee *astronaut*
Gordon, William Edwin *physicist, engineer, educator, university official*
†Hackerman, Norman *chemist, university president*
Hasling, Jill Freeman *meteorologist*
Haymes, Robert C. *physicist, educator*
†Horning, Marjorie G. *biochemistry educator*
Hungerford, Ed Vernon, III *physics educator*
Kevan, Larry *chemistry educator*
Kinsey, James Lloyd *chemist, educator*
Kit, Saul *biochemist, educator*
Kochi, Jay Kazuo *chemist, educator*
Kouri, Donald Jack *chemist, educator*
LeBlanc, Rufus Joseph, Sr. *geology educator, consultant, researcher*
Lewis, Edward Sheldon *chemistry educator*
Margrave, John Lee *chemist, educator, university administrator*
McCammon, James Andrew *chemistry educator*
McCleary, Henry Glen *geophysicist*
†McLellan, Rex Booker *materials science educator, consultant*
McMillin, Jeanie Byrd *biochemist, medical educator*
†Mehra, Jagdish *physicist*
†Michel, Frank Curtis *astrophysicist, educator*
†Moss, Simon Charles *physics educator*
Norton, Norman James *exploration geologist*
O'Dell, Charles Robert *astronomer, educator*
Page, Thornton Leigh *astrophysicist*
Reso, Anthony *geologist, earth resource economist*
Savit, Carl Hertz *geophysicist*
Schroepfer, George John, Jr. *biochemistry educator*
†Scuseria, Gustavo Enrique *theoretical chemist*
Skolnick, Malcolm Harris *biophysics researcher, educator, patent lawyer, mediator*
Smalley, Richard Errett *chemistry and physics educator, researcher*
Smith, Michael Alexis *petroleum geologist*
Stormer, John Charles, Jr. *geology educator, mineralogist*
Talwani, Manik *geophysicist, educator*
Wakil, Salih Jawad *biochemistry educator*
Weinstein, Roy *physics educator, researcher*
Wold, Finn *biochemist, educator*
Zlatkis, Albert *chemistry educator*

Irving
Hendrickson, Constance Marie McRight *chemist, consultant*

Kerrville
Wilson, William Howard *exploration geologist, oil and gas operator*

Kingwood
Brinkley, Charles Alexander *geologist*
Davies, David Keith *geologist*

Lake Jackson
Tasa, Kendall Sherwood *chemistry educator*

Lubbock
Murray, Grover Elmer *geologist, educator*
Robinson, G. Wilse *molecular spectroscopist, educator*
†Shine, Henry Joseph *chemistry educator*

New Braunfels
Wilson, James Lee *retired geology educator, consultant*

Odessa
Reeves, Robert Grier LeFevre *geology educator, scientist*

Orange
Adkins, John E(arl), Jr. *chemist*

Richardson
Cordell, Robert James *geologist*
†Hanson, William Bert *physics educator, science administrator*
Johnson, Francis Severin *physicist*
Landisman, Mark *geophysicist, educator*
Nevill, William Albert *chemistry educator*

Richmond
Willis, David Edwin *retired geophysicist*

San Antonio
Ball, M(ary) Isabel *chemistry educator, dean*
Budalur, Thyagarajan Subbanarayan *chemistry educator*
Burton, Russell Rohan *aerospace scientist, researcher*
Doyle, Frank Lawrence *geologist, hydrologist, executive*
Hamm, William Joseph *retired physics educator*
Hanahan, Donald James *biochemist, educator*
Howard, M. Francine *chemist*
Lyle, Robert Edward *chemist*
Siler-Khodr, Theresa Marie *biochemistry educator*

San Marcos
Cassidy, Patrick Edward *chemist, educator*

The Woodlands
Levy, Robert Edward *biotechnology company executive*

Waco
Pedrotti, Leno Stephano *physics educator*

Wichita Falls
Sund, Eldon Harold *chemistry educator*

UTAH

Eskdale
Beeston, Joseph Mack *metallurgist*

Logan
Aust, Steven Douglas *biochemistry, biotechnology and toxicology educator*
Scouten, William Henry *chemistry educator, academic administrator*
†Steed, Allan J. *physical science research administrator*

Ogden
Buss, Walter Richard *geology educator*
Welch, Garth Larry *chemistry educator*

Provo
Hall, Howard Tracy *chemist*

Salt Lake City
Dick, Bertram Gale, Jr. *physics educator*
Foltz, Rodger Lowell *chemistry educator, mass spectroscopist*
†Giddings, J. Calvin *chemistry educator*
Grant, David Morris *chemistry educator*
Hill, George Richard *chemistry educator*
Miller, Jan Dean *metallurgy educator*
Oblad, Alexander Golden *chemistry educator, research chemist*
O'Halloran, Thomas Alphonsus, Jr. *physicist, educator*
Parry, Robert Walter *chemistry educator*
Partridge, William Schaubel *physicist, research company executive*
Richmond, Thomas G. *chemistry educator*
Velick, Sidney Frederick *research biochemist, educator*
Warnick, Charles Terry *research biochemist*

VERMONT

Burlington
White, William North *chemistry educator*

Middlebury
Gleason, Robert Willard *chemistry educator, college dean*

Norwich
Naumann, Robert Bruno Alexander *chemist, physicist, educator*

Thetford
Hoagland, Mahlon Bush *biochemist, educator*

VIRGINIA

Alexandria
Berman, Alan *physicist*
Biberman, Lucien Morton *physicist*
Brenner, Alfred Ephraim *physicist*
Campbell, Francis James *retired chemist*
Masterson, Kleber Sanlin, Jr. *physicist*
†Milling, Marcus Eugene, Sr. *geologist*
Muir, Warren R. *chemist, toxic substances specialist*
†Sayre, Edward Vale *chemist*
Shapiro, Maurice Mandel *astrophysicist*
Tidman, Derek Albert *physics researcher*
Toulmin, Priestley, III *geologist*
Wolicki, Eligius Anthony *nuclear physicist, consultant*

Annandale
Matuszko, Anthony Joseph *research chemist, administrator*

Arlington
Barnhart, Beverly Jean *meteorologist*
Bautz, Laura Patricia *astronomer*
Berg, John Richard *chemist, former federal government executive*
Borchers, Robert Reece *physicist and administrator*
†Britt, Harold C. *physicist*
Carter, William Walton *physicist*
Ensminger, Luther Glenn *chemist*
Hays, James Fred *geologist, educator*
Romney, Carl F. *seismologist*
Sinclair, Rolf Malcolm *physicist*
Singer, S(iegfried) Fred *geophysicist, educator*
Wayland, Russell Gibson, Jr. *geology consultant, retired government official*
Yankwich, Peter Ewald *chemistry educator*
Zirkind, Ralph *physicist*

Blacksburg
Bauer, Henry Hermann *chemistry and science educator*
Cairns, John, Jr. *environmental science educator, researcher*
Mo, Luke Wei *physicist, educator*
Ogliaruso, Michael Anthony *chemist, educator*
Stewart, Kent Kallam *analytical biochemistry educator*

Charlottesville
Biltonen, Rodney Lincoln *biochemistry and pharmacology educator*
Boring, John Wayne *physicist, educator*
Bradbeer, Clive *biochemistry and microbiology educator, research scientist*
Brill, Arthur Sylvan *biophysics educator*
Carpenter, Richard Amon *chemist*
†Celli, Vittorio *physics educator*
Chevalier, Roger Alan *astronomy educator, consultant*
Fredrick, Laurence William *astronomer, educator*
Gaskin, Felicia *biochemist, educator*
Goodell, Horace Grant *environmental sciences educator*
Greene, Virginia Carvel *chemist*
Grimes, Russell Newell *chemistry educator, inorganic chemist*
Grisham, Charles Milton *biochemist, educator*
†Gugelot, Piet Cornelis *physics educator*
Hereford, Frank Loucks, Jr. *physicist, educator*
Kellermann, Kenneth Irwin *astronomer*
Kerr, Anthony Robert *space scientist*
Kuhlmann-Wilsdorf, Doris *physics and materials science educator*
Martin, Robert Bruce *chemistry educator*
Meem, James Lawrence, Jr. *nuclear scientist*
Roberts, Morton Spitz *astronomer*
†Sarazin, Craig Leigh *astronomer*
Song, Xiaotong *physicist, educator*
Starke, Edgar Arlin, Jr. *metallurgist, educator*
Sundberg, Richard Jay *chemistry educator*
Vanden Bout, Paul Adrian *astronomer, physicist, educator*
Weber, Hans Jürgen *physics educator*

Fairfax
Morowitz, Harold Joseph *biophysicist, educator*
Ozernoy, Leonid Moissey *astrophysicist*
Trefil, James S. *physicist, educator*

Falls Church
Benson, William Edward (Barnes) *geologist*
Feldmann, Edward George *pharmaceutical chemist*
Spindel, William *chemistry educator, scientist, educational administrator*

Hampden Sydney
Joyner, Weyland Thomas *physicist, educator, business consultant*
†Kniffen, Donald Avery *astrophysicist, educator, researcher*
Porterfield, William Wendell *chemist, educator*

Hampton
†Allario, Frank *aerospace science research administrator*
Houbolt, John Cornelius *physicist*
†Tenney, Darrel R. *materials science administrator*

Herndon
Crossfield, Albert Scott *aeronautical science consultant, pilot*
Peck, Dallas Lynn *geologist*

Kinsale
Gould, Gordon *physicist, retired optical communications executive*

Manassas Park
Bussard, Robert William *physicist*

Mc Lean
Doyle, Frederick Joseph *government research scientist*
Hoffman, Ronald Bruce *biophysicist, life scientist, human factors consultant*
Morrison, David Lee *chemist, research institute executive*

Middleburg
Spilhaus, Athelstan *meteorologist, oceanographer*

Newport News
Cardman, Lawrence S. *physics educator*
Isgur, Nathan Gerald *physicist, educator*

Norfolk
Csanady, Gabriel Tibor *oceanographer, meteorologist, environmental engineer*
Schellenberg, Karl Abraham *biochemist*

Purcellville
Conte, Joseph John, II *meteorologist, management consultant*

Rapidan
Williams, Langbourne Meade *retired minerals company executive*

Reston
Barton, Paul Booth, Jr. *geologist*
Brett, Robin *geologist*
Clark, Sandra Helen Becker *geologist*
Cohen, Philip *hydrogeologist*
Doe, Bruce Roger *geologist*
Drew, Russell Cooper *physicist*
Eaton, Gordon Pryor *geologist, research director*
Hamilton, Robert Morrison *geophysicist*
Huebner, John Stephen *geologist*
Masters, Charles Day *geologist*
Pojeta, John, Jr. *geologist*
Ross, Malcolm *mineralogist, crystallographer*
Sato, Motoaki *geologist, researcher*

Richmond
Leyden, Donald Elliott *chemist, researcher*
Satterthwaite, Cameron B. *physics educator*
†Vallarino, Lidia M. *chemistry educator*
Wakeham, Helmut Richard Rae *chemist, consulting company executive*

Roanoke
Al-Zubaidi, Amer Aziz *physicist, educator*
Husted, John Edwin *geologist, educator*
Steinhardt, Ralph Gustav, Jr. *chemist*

Salem
Fisher, Charles Harold *chemistry educator, researcher*

Seaford
Hammer, Jacob Myer *physicist, consultant*

Springfield
Sebastian, Richard Lee *physicist, executive*
Steele, Lendell Eugene *research scientist*

Sweet Briar
McClenon, John Raymond *chemistry educator*

Williamsburg
Goodwin, Bruce Kesseli *geology educator, researcher*
Mc Knight, John Lacy *physics educator*
Orwoll, Robert Arvid *chemistry educator*
Siegel, Robert Ted *physicist*
Starnes, William Herbert, Jr. *chemist, educator*

Winchester
Ludwig, George Harry *physicist*
Murtagh, John Edward *chemist, alcohol production consultant*

WASHINGTON

Anacortes
Businger, Joost Alois *atmospheric scientist, educator*

Bellevue
Chen, Ching-Hong *medical biochemist, researcher*
Fremouw, Edward Joseph *physicist*

Carlsborg
Bouquet, Francis Lester *physicist*

Ellensburg
Jones, Jerry Lynn *chemistry educator*

Issaquah
Benveniste, Jacob *retired physicist*
Dehlinger, Peter *geophysics educator*

Kalama
Liang, Jason Chia *research chemist*

Manchester
Fearon, Lee Charles *chemist*

Port Angeles
Hart, Edwin James *chemist*

Pullman
Crosby, Glenn Arthur *chemistry educator*
Dodgen, Harold Warren *chemistry and physics educator*
Fowles, George Richard *physicist, educator*
George, Thomas Frederick *chemistry educator*
†Kapteyn, Henry Cornelius *physics educator*
†Murnane, Margaret Mary *physics educator*
Pomeranz, Yeshajahu *cereal chemist, technologist*
Ryan, Clarence Augustine, Jr. *biochemistry educator*

Richland
Beck, Joe Eugene *environmental health scientist, educator*
Bush, Spencer Harrison *metallurgist*
Campbell, Milton Hugh *chemist*
Elderkin, Charles Edwin *meteorologist*
McDowell, Robin Scott *physical chemist*
Moore, Emmett Burris, Jr. *physical chemist*
Rebagay, Teofila Velasco *chemist, chemical engineer*

Seattle
Andersen, Niels Hjorth *chemistry educator, biophysics researcher, consultant*
Anderson, Arthur G., Jr. *chemistry educator*
Arons, Arnold Boris *physicist, educator*
Baum, William Alvin *astronomer, educator*
Bernard, Eddie Nolan *oceanographer*
Bodansky, David *physicist, educator*
Borden, Weston Thatcher *chemistry educator*
Brown, Frederick Calvin *physicist, educator*
Brown, Lowell Severt *physicist, educator*
Brownlee, Donald Eugene, II *astronomer, educator*
Christian, Gary Dale *chemistry educator*
Clark, Kenneth Courtright *retired physics and geophysics educator*
Creager, Joe Scott *geology and oceanography educator*
Dehmelt, Hans Georg *physicist*
Dunne, Thomas *geology educator*
Eggers, David Frank, Jr. *chemistry educator*
Engel, Thomas *chemistry educator*
Evans, Bernard William *geologist, educator*
Favorite, Felix *oceanographer*
Fischer, Edmond Henri *biochemistry educator*
Floss, Heinz G. *chemistry educator, scientist*
Fortson, Edward Norval *physics educator*
Geballe, Ronald *physicist, university dean*
†Gelb, Michael H. *chemistry educator*
Gerhart, James Basil *physics educator*
Gordon, Milton Paul *biochemist, educator*
Gouterman, Martin Paul *chemistry educator*
Gregory, Norman Wayne *chemistry educator, researcher*
Halver, John Emil *nutritional biochemist*
Heath, George Ross *oceanographer, university dean*
Henley, Ernest Mark *physics educator, university dean emeritus*
Hodge, Paul William *astronomer, educator*
Houck, John Candee *research facility administrator, biochemist*
Ingalls, Robert Lynn *physicist, educator*
†Kennedy, David Michael *environmental scientist*
Krebs, Edwin Gerhard *biochemistry educator*
†Kunze, Eric *physical oceanographer, educator*
Kwiram, Alvin L. *physical chemistry educator, university official*
Lingafelter, Edward Clay, Jr. *chemistry educator*
Lord, Jere Johns *retired physics educator*
Lubatti, Henry Joseph *physicist, educator*
Mallory, V(irgil) Standish *geologist, educator*
Margon, Bruce Henry *astrophysicist, educator*
Merrill, Ronald Thomas *geophysicist, educator*
†Miles, Edward Lancelot *marine studies educator, consultant, director*
Nelson, Wendel Lane *medicinal chemist, educator*
Neurath, Hans *biochemist, educator*
Pease, Carol Helene *oceanographer*
Pocker, Yeshayau *chemistry, biochemistry educator*
Porter, Stephen Cummings *geologist, educator*
Rabinovitch, Benton Seymour *chemist, educator emeritus*
Reed, Richard John *retired meteorology educator*
Reinhardt, William Parker *chemical physicist, educator*
Rhines, Peter Broomell *oceanographer, atmospheric scientist*
Schomaker, Verner *chemist, educator*
Spinrad, Bernard Israel *physicist, educator*
Stern, Edward Abraham *physics educator*
Stuiver, Minze *geological sciences educator*
Swanson, Donald Alan *geologist*
Thouless, David James *physicist, educator*
Wallace, John Michael *meteorology educator*
Weitkamp, William George *nuclear physicist*
Wilets, Lawrence *physics educator*
Williams, Robert Walter *physics educator*

Silverdale
Walske, M(ax) Carl, Jr. *physicist*

Spokane
Benson, Allen B. *chemist, educator, consultant*
Stacy, Gardner W. *chemical scientist, educator, lecturer*

Tacoma
Gregory, Arthur Stanley *retired chemist*

WEST VIRGINIA

Huntington
Hubbard, John Lewis *chemist, educator, researcher*

Institute
DasSarma, Basudeb *chemistry educator*

Morgantown
Beattie, Diana Scott *biochemistry educator*
Chen, Ping-fan *geologist*
Fodor, Gabor Bela *chemistry educator, researcher*

WISCONSIN

Madison
Adler, Julius *biochemist, biologist, educator*
Anderson, Louis Wilmer, Jr. *physicist, educator*
†Bailey, Sturges Williams *geologist, educator*
Barger, Vernon Duane *physicist, educator*
Barschall, Henry Herman *physics educator*
Bentley, Charles Raymond *geophysics educator*
Bincer, Adam Marian *physicist, educator*
Blaedel, Walter John *chemist, retired educator*
Bless, Robert Charles *astronomy educator*
Botez, Dan *physicist*
Bryson, Reid Allen *meteorology educator*
Burris, Robert Harza *biochemist, educator*
Casey, Charles Philip *organic chemist, educator*
Cassinelli, Joseph Patrick *astronomy educator*
Churchwell, Edward Bruce *astronomer, educator*
Clark, David Leigh *marine geologist, educator*
Cleland, W(illiam) Wallace *biochemistry educator*
†Code, Arthur Dodd *astrophysics educator*
Connors, Kenneth Antonio *chemist*
Cornwell, Charles Daniel *physical chemist, educator*
Craddock, (John) Campbell *geologist, educator*
Curtiss, Charles Francis *chemist, educator*
Dahl, Lawrence Frederick *chemistry educator, researcher*
Dott, Robert Henry, Jr. *geologist, educator*
Ebel, Marvin Emerson *physicist,educator*
Ellis, Arthur Baron *chemist, educator*
Evenson, Merle Armin *chemist, educator*
Fennema, Owen Richard *food chemistry educator*
Ferry, John Douglass *chemist*
Fry, William Frederick *physics educator*
Gallagher, John Sill, III *astronomer*
Gorski, Jack *biochemistry educator*
Hedden, Gregory Dexter *environmental science educator, consultant*
Hershkowitz, Noah *physicist, educator*
Hokin, Lowell Edward *biochemist, educator*
Houghton, David Drew *meteorologist, educator*
Inman, Ross Banks *biochemistry and biophysics educator*
Karavolas, Harry J(ohn) *biochemist, educator*
Kraushaar, William Lester *physicist, educator*
Lagally, Max Gunter *physics educator*
Lardy, Henry Arnold *biochemist, biological sciences educator*
Larsen, Edwin Merritt *retired chemist, educator*
†Lawler, James Edward *physics educator*
Maher, Louis James, Jr. *geologist, educator*
†Mathis, John Samuel *astronomy educator*
Morton, Stephen Dana *chemist*
Mukerjee, Pasupati *chemistry educator*
Perlman, D(avid) *biochemist, educator*
Pondrom, Lee Girard *physicist, educator*
Pray, Lloyd Charles *geologist, educator*
†Rich, Daniel Hulbert *chemist*
Richards, Hugh Taylor *physics educator*
Rowe, John Westel *retired organic chemist*
Savage, Blair deWillis *astronomer, educator*
†Skinner, James Lauriston *chemist, educator*
Vaughan, Worth Edward *chemistry educator*
Wang, Herbert Fan *geophysics educator*
West, Robert Culbertson *chemistry educator*
†Yu, Hyuk *chemist, educator*
Zimmerman, Howard Elliot *chemist, educator*

Middleton
Ferry, James Allen *physicist, electrostatics company executive*
Herb, Raymond G. *physicist, manufacturing company executive*
Ostrom, Meredith Eggers *retired geologist*

Milwaukee
Aita, Carolyn Rubin *physicist*
†Bader, Alfred Robert *chemist*
†Greenler, Robert George *physics educator, researcher*
Haworth, Daniel Thomas *chemistry educator*
Hendee, William Richard *medical physics educator, university official*
Jache, Albert William *retired chemistry educator, scientist*
Miller, David Hewitt *environmental scientist, writer*
Paull, Richard Allen *geologist, educator*
†Petering, David Harold *chemistry educator*
Walters, William LeRoy *physics educator*

Plover
Peanasky, Robert Joseph *biochemist, medical educator*

Stoughton
Kuhn, Peter Mouat *atmospheric physicist*

Williams Bay
Harper, Doyal Alexander, Jr. *astronomer, educator*
Hobbs, Lewis Mankin *astronomer*

Kron, Richard G. *astrophysicist, educator*

WYOMING

Casper
Wold, John Schiller *geologist, former congressman*

Laramie
Grandy, Walter Thomas, Jr. *physicist*
Meyer, Edmond Gerald *energy and natural resources educator, resources scientist, entrepreneur, former chemistry educator*

TERRITORIES OF THE UNITED STATES

PUERTO RICO

Mayaguez
Hernandez-Avila, Manuel Luis *physical oceanography educator, researcher, administrator, consultant*

Rincon
Morris, Victor Franklin, Jr. *meteorology educator*

CANADA

ALBERTA

Calgary
Armstrong, David Anthony *physical chemist, educator*
Boorman, Philip Michael *chemistry educator, researcher*
Campbell, Finley Alexander *geologist*
Dixon, Gordon Henry *biochemist*
Hyne, James Bissett *chemistry educator, director research, consultant*
†Nassichuk, W. W. *geology research administrator*
†Nigg, Benno Maurus *biomechanics educator*
Okulitch, Vladimir Joseph *geologist, university administrator*
Thorsteinsson, Raymond *geology research scientist*

Edmonton
Folinsbee, Robert Edward *geologist*
Gough, Denis Ian *geophysics educator*
Harris, Walter Edgar *chemistry educator*
Israel, Werner *physics educator*
James, Michael N. G. *crystallographer, educator*
Jones, Richard Norman *physical chemist, researcher*
†Kanasewich, Ernest Roman *physics educator*
Kay, Cyril Max *biochemist*
†Kebarle, Paul *chemistry educator*
†Khanna, Faqir Chand *physics educator*
†Kitching, Peter *physics educator*
Kratochvil, Byron George *chemistry educator, researcher*
Lemieux, Raymond Urgel *chemistry educator*
Rostoker, Gordon *physicist, educator*
Rutter, Nathaniel Westlund *geologist, educator*
Spencer, Mary Eileen *biochemist, educator*
Stelck, Charles Richard *geology educator*
Sykes, Brian Douglas *biochemistry educator, researcher*
Umezawa, Hiroomi *physics educator, researcher*
Vance, Dennis Edward *biochemistry educator*

BRITISH COLUMBIA

Burnaby
Arrott, Anthony Schuyler *physics educator*

Penticton
Higgs, Lloyd Albert *astronomer, observatory administrator*

Sidney
†Best, Melvyn Edward *geophysicist*
Irving, Edward *geophysicist, educator*
Petrie, William *physicist*
van den Bergh, Sidney *astronomer*
Weichert, Dieter Horst *seismologist, researcher*

Vancouver
Aubke, Friedhelm *chemistry educator*
Bloom, Myer *physicist, educator*
Clarke, Garry Kenneth Connal *geophysics educator*
Fryzuk, Michael Daniel *chemistry educator*
Hardy, Walter Newbold *physics educator, researcher*
James, Brian Robert *chemistry educator*
Kieffer, Susan Werner *geology educator*
†Kiefl, Robert Frances *physicist, educator*
LeBlond, Paul Henri *oceanographer, educator*
Mathews, William Henry *geologist, educator*
Nafe, John Elliott *geophysicist*
Ozier, Irving *physicist, educator*
Pickard, George Lawson *physics educator*
Pincock, Richard Earl *chemistry educator*
Russell, Richard Doncaster *geophysicist, educator, geoscientist*
Sinclair, Alastair James *geology educator*
†Smith, Michael *biochemistry educator*
Snider, Robert F. *chemistry educator, researcher*
Stewart, Ross *chemistry educator*
Underhill, Anne Barbara *astrophysicist*
Unruh, William G. *physics educator, researcher*
Vogt, Erich Wolfgang *physicist, academic administrator*
Volkoff, George Michael *former physics educator, educational administrator*
Warren, Harry Verney *geological sciences educator, consulting geological engineer*
Wheeler, John Oliver *geologist*

Victoria
Barnes, Christopher Richard *geologist*
Batten, Alan Henry *astronomer*
Hutchings, John Barrie *astronomer, researcher*
Mc Carter, John Alexander *biochemistry educator*
Morton, Donald Charles *astronomer*
Oke, John Beverley *astronomy educator*
Wiles, David McKeen *chemist*
Wright, Kenneth Osborne *former astronomer*

West Vancouver
Wynne-Edwards, Hugh Robert *geologist, educator, scientist*

White Rock
Cooke, Herbert Basil Sutton *geologist, educator*

MANITOBA

Winnipeg
Barber, Robert Charles *physics educator*
Bigelow, Charles Cross *biochemist, university administrator*
Ferguson, Robert Bury *mineralogy educator*
†Hawthorne, Frank Christopher *geologist, educator*
Kanfer, Julian Norman *biochemist, educator*
Mantsch, Henry Horst *chemistry educator*
Schaefer, Theodore Peter *chemistry educator*
Smith, Ian Cormack Palmer *biophysicist*

NEW BRUNSWICK

Fredericton
Valenta, Zdenek *chemistry educator*
Vaníček, Petr *geodesist*

NEWFOUNDLAND

Saint John's
Idler, David Richard *biochemist, marine scientist, educator*
Rochester, Michael Grant *geophysics educator*
Williams, Harold *geology educator*

NOVA SCOTIA

Dartmouth
Elliott, James A. *oceanographer, researcher*
Keen, Charlotte Elizabeth *marine geophysicist, researcher*
Needler, George Treglohan *oceanographer, researcher*
Platt, Trevor Charles *oceanographer, scientist*
†Ross, David I. *geological administrator*

Halifax
Geldart, Donald James Wallace *physics educator*
Gold, Edgar *marine affairs educator, mariner, lawyer*
Leffek, Kenneth Thomas *chemist, educator*

Wallace
Boyle, Willard Sterling *physicist*

Wolfville
Bishop, Roy Lovitt *physics and astronomy educator*
Ogilvie, Kelvin Kenneth *chemistry educator*

ONTARIO

Burlington
Cragg, Laurence Harold *chemist, former university president*
†Donelan, Mark Anthony *physicist*

Chalk River
Buyers, William James Leslie *physicist*
Hardy, John Christopher *physicist*
Milton, John Charles Douglas *nuclear physicist*

Deep River
Carmichael, Hugh *physicist*
Hanna, Geoffrey Chalmers *nuclear scientist*

Don Mills
Koster, Emlyn Howard *geologist, educator, Canadian agency executive*

Downsview
†Dawson, D. Kirk *atmosphiric science research administrator*
Pritchard, Huw Owen *chemist, educator*
Ribner, Herbert Spencer *physicist, educator*
†Tennyson, Roderick C. *aerospace scientist*

Gloucester
†Mykytiuk, Alex P. *chemist*

Guelph
Dickinson, William Trevor *hydrologist, educator*
Karl, Gabriel *physics educator*
Simpson, John Joseph *physics educator, researcher*

Hamilton
Basinski, Zbigniew Stanislaw *metal physicist, educator*
Childs, Ronald Frank *chemistry educator, science administrator*
Datars, William Ross *physicist, educator*
Davies, John Arthur *physics and engineering educator, scientist*
Garland, William James *engineering physics educator*
Gillespie, Ronald James *retired chemistry educator, writer*
MacLean, David Bailey *chemistry educator, researcher*
Preston, Melvin Alexander *physicist, educator*
Schwarcz, Henry Philip *geologist, educator*
Spenser, Ian Daniel *chemist educator*
Sprung, Donald W. L. *physics educator*
†Thode, Henry George *chemistry educator*
Walker, Roger Geoffrey *geology educator, consultant*

Kingston
Ewan, George Thomson *physicist, educator*
Flynn, T(homas) Geoffrey *biochemistry educator*
McDonald, Arthur Bruce *physics educator*
Sayer, Michael *physics educator*
Spencer, John Hedley *biochemistry educator*
Stewart, Alec Thompson *physicist*
Szarek, Walter Anthony *chemist, educator*
Uffen, Robert James *geophysics educator, engineer*

Lions Bay
Bartholomew, Gilbert Alfred *retired physicist*

London
Alford, William Parker *physics educator*
Bancroft, George Michael *chemical physicist, educator*
Carroll, Kenneth Kitchener *biochemist, nutritionist, educator*
Dreimanis, Aleksis *emeritus geology educator*
Fyfe, William Sefton *geochemist, educator*
Roach, Margot Ruth *biophysicist, educator*
Stewart, Harold Brown *biochemist*
Stothers, John B. *chemistry educator*
Weedon, Alan Charles *chemist, educator*

Manotick
Hobson, George Donald *retired geophysicist*

North York
Bohme, Diethard Kurt *chemistry educator*
Carswell, Allan Ian *physics educator*
Godson, Warren Lehman *meteorologist*

Ottawa
Alper, Howard *chemistry educator*
†Babcock, Elkanah Andrew *geologist*
Carey, Paul Richard *biophysicist, scientific administrator*
†Davis, B. *physical science administrator*
†Erickson, W. H. *Metallury administrator*
Fallis, Alexander Graham *chemistry educator*
†Ferron, J. *mineralogy administrator*
Halliday, Ian *astronomer*
Harington, Charles Richard *vertebrate paleontologist*
Haworth, Richard Thomas *geophysicist, science director*
Herzberg, Gerhard *physicist*
Himms-Hagen, Jean Margaret *biochemist*
Holmes, John Leonard *chemistry educator*
Ingold, Keith Usherwood *chemist, educator*
†Itzkovitch, Irwin J. *metallurgy administrator*
Kates, Morris *biochemist, educator*
Lossing, Frederick Pettit *chemist*
MacLeod, John Munroe *radio astronomer, academic administrator*
Marmet, Paul *physicist*
†Marsters, Gerald Frederick *aerospace science and technology executive*
McKellar, Andrew Robert *physicist, researcher*
McLaren, Digby Johns *geologist, educator*
Puddington, Ira Edwin *chemist*
Ramsay, Donald Allan *physical chemist*
Redhead, Paul Aveling *physicist*
Roots, Ernest Frederick *scientific advisor emeritus*
St-Onge, Denis Alderic *geologist, research scientist*
Schneider, William George *chemist, research consultant*
†Siebrand, Willem *theoretical chemist, science editor*
Templeton, Ian Malcolm *physicist*
†Torgerson, David Franklyn *chemist, research facility administrator*
Vallance-Jones, Alister *physicist*
Varshni, Yatendra Pal *physicist*
Veizer, Ján *geology educator*
Whitehead, J. Rennie *science consultant*
Whitham, Kenneth *science and technology consultant*

Petawawa
†Elchuk, Steve *chemist*

Richmond Hill
Bolton, Charles Thomas *astronomer*
Fernie, John Donald *astronomer, educator*
Garrison, Robert Frederick *astronomer, educator*
MacRae, Donald Alexander *astronomy educator*

Saint Catharines
Terasmae, Jaan *geology educator*

Toronto
Brook, Adrian Gibbs *chemistry educator*
†Brumer, Paul William *chemical physicist, educator*
Dunlop, David John *geophysics educator, researcher*
Ganoza-Becker, Maria Clelia *biochemistry educator*
Goldberg, David Meyer *biochemistry educator*
Haynes, Robert Hall *biophysicist, educator*
Hofmann, Theo *biochemist, educator*
Ivey, Donald Glenn *physics educator*
Jervis, Robert E. *chemistry educator*
†Kaiser, Nicholas *physicist, educator*
Kresge, Alexander Jerry *chemistry educator*
List, Roland *physicist, educator, former UN official*
Litherland, Albert Edward *physics educator*
Mak, Tak Wah *biochemist*
McNeill, K(enneth) G(ordon) *medical physicist*
Moffat, John William *physics educator*
Naldrett, Anthony James *geology educator*
Norris, Geoffrey *geology educator, consultant*
Polanyi, John Charles *chemist, educator*
Prugovecki, Eduard *mathematical physicist, educator, author*
Rowe, David John *physics educator*
Scott, Steven Donald *geology educator, researcher*
Seaquist, Ernest Raymond *astronomy educator*
Sheinin, Rose *biochemist, educator*
Stoicheff, Boris Peter *physicist, educator*
Taylor, Harry William *physics educator*
Tidwell, Thomas Tinsley *chemistry educator*
Tremaine, Scott Duncan *astrophysicist*
Whittington, Stuart Gordon *chemistry educator*
†Yates, Keith *chemistry educator*
Yip, Cecil Cheung-Ching *biochemist, educator*

Waterloo
Morgan, Alan Vivian *geologist, educator*
†Rudin, Alfred *chemistry educator emeritus*
†Thomas, Richard Lynn *geologist, researcher, educator, director university geecology center*

Windsor
Drake, Gordon William Frederic *physics educator*
Jones, William Ernest *chemistry educator*
Thibert, Roger Joseph *clinical chemist, educator*

QUEBEC

Dorval
Bachynski, Morrel Paul *physicist*

Laval
David, Michel Louis *geostatistician, consultant*

Montreal
Chan, Tak Hang *chemist, educator*
Derome, Jacques Florian *meteorology educator*
de Takacsy, Nicholas Benedict *physicist, educator*
†Dubé, Ghyslain *earth scientist*
Edward, John Thomas *chemist, educator*
Eisenberg, Adi *chemist*
†Fontaine, Gilles *physics educator*
†Fyffe, Les *earth scientist*
Gaudry, Roger *chemist, university official*
Hay, Allan Stuart *chemist, educator*
†Imorde, Henry K. *earth scientist*
Johnstone, Rose Mamelak (Mrs. Douglas Johnstone) *biochemistry educator*
Langleben, Manuel Phillip *physics educator*
Leroy, Claude *physics educator, researcher*
Mark, Shew-Kuey Tommy *physics educator*
Mysak, Lawrence Alexander *oceanographer, climatologist, mathematician, educator*
Perlin, Arthur Saul *chemistry educator*
†Podgorsak, Ervin B. *medical physicist, educator, administrator*
Purdy, William Crossley *chemist, educator*
Sandor, Thomas *biochemist*
Sandorfy, Camille *chemistry educator*
Solomon, Samuel *biochemistry educator, administrator*
Sourkes, Theodore Lionel *biochemistry educator*
Taras, Paul *physicist, educator*
Van Vliet, Carolyne Marina *physicist, educator*
Wallace, Philip Russell *retired physics educator*
†Wesemael, François *physics educator*
Whitehead, Michael Anthony *chemistry educator*

Outremont
Levesque, Rene Jules Albert *former physicist*

Pointe Claire
Bolker, Henry Irving *retired chemist, research institute director, educator*

Quebec
Engel, Charles Robert *chemist, educator*
Page, Michel *biochemist*

Rimouski
†Walton, Alan *oceanographer*

Saint Jerome
Joly, Jean-Gil *medical biochemist, internist, administrator, researcher, educator*

Saint Luc
Marcoux, Jules Edouard *physicist, educator, writer*

Sainte-Foy
Beaulieu, Jacques Alexandre *physicist*
†Boudoux, Michel *environmental research executive*
Legendre, Louis *biological oceanography educator, researcher*

Sherbrooke
Deslongchamps, Pierre *chemistry educator*
†Tremblay, André-Marie *physicist*

Varennes
Vijh, Ashok Kumar *chemistry educator, researcher*

Westmount
Dunbar, Maxwell John *oceanographer, educator*

SASKATCHEWAN

Saskatoon
Hirose, Akira *physics educator, researcher*
Kupsch, Walter Oscar *geologist*

MEXICO

Mexico City
Koenigsberger, Gloria S. *astrophysicist*
Peimbert, Manuel *astronomer*

Puebla
Zehe, Alfred Fritz Karl *physics educator*

AUSTRALIA

Bundoora
James, Bruce David *chemistry educator*

Menai
Nowotny, Janusz *materials scientist*

BELGIUM

Ghent
de Leenheer, Andreas Prudent *medical biochemistry and toxicology educator*

Heverlee
De Schryver, Frans Carl *chemistry educator*
L'abbe, Gerrit Karel *chemist*

BRAZIL

Rio de Janeiro
Costa Neto, Adelina *chemistry educator, consultant*
de Biasi, Ronaldo Sergio *materials science educator*

CHILE

La Serena
Eggen, Olin Jeuck *astrophysicist, administrator*

CHINA

Beijing
Chen, Naixing *thermal science educator, researcher*
Hua, Tong-Wen *chemistry educator, researcher*
Leng, Xin-Fu *chemist, educator*

CZECH REPUBLIC

Prague
Macek, Karel *analytical chemistry educator*

DENMARK

Copenhagen
Bohr, Aage Niels *physicist*
†Hansen, Ole *physicist*

Grasted
Wiin-Nielsen, Aksel Christopher *meteorologist educator*

Hoersholm
Jensen, Ole *energy researcher*

EGYPT

Cairo
El-Sayed, Karimat Mahmoud *physics and crystallography educator*

ENGLAND

Brighton
Cornforth, Sir John Warcup *chemist*

Cambridge
Hawking, Stephen W. *astrophysicist, mathematician*
Hodgkin, Sir Alan Lloyd *biophysicist*
Needham, Joseph *chemist, historian of science, Orientalist*
Todd, Alexander Robertus (Baron Todd of Trumpington) *chemistry educator*

Hull
Shorter, John *chemistry lecturer*

London
Eddo, James Ekundayo *industrial chemist, chemicals executive*
Porter, Lord George *chemist, educator*
Wilkinson, Geoffrey *chemist, educator*

Oxford
Hirsch, Peter Bernhard *metallurgist*
†Williams, William Stanley Cossom *physics educator and researcher*

FINLAND

Tampere
Nikkari, Tapio Urho *medical biochemistry educator*

FRANCE

Orsay
Deutsch, Claude David *physicist, educator*
Reich, Robert Claude *metallurgist, physicist*

Paris
Bathias, Claude *materials science educator, consultant*
Cousteau, Jacques-Yves *marine explorer, film producer, writer*
Lehn, Jean-Marie Pierre *chemistry educator*

GERMANY

Berlin
Selle, Burkhardt Herbert Richard *physicist*
Stachel, John Jay *physicist, educator*
Tiedemann, Heinz *biochemist*

Bielefeld
Muller, Achim *chemistry educator*

Cologne
Stuhl, Oskar Paul *organic chemist*

Darmstadt
Lichtenthaler, Frieder Wilhelm *chemist, educator*

Garching
Grieger, Günter *physicist*

Göttingen
Eigen, Manfred *physicist*
†Sheldrick, George Michael *chemistry educator, crystallographer*
Tietze, Lutz Friedjan *chemist, educator*
Wedemeyer, Erich Hans *physicist*

Groebenzell
Chandrasekhar, Bellur Sivaramiah *physics educator*

Hamburg
Jensen, Elwood Vernon *biochemist*

Heidelberg
Staab, Heinz A. *chemist*

Jülich
Krasser, Hans Wolfgang *physicist*

Kelkheim
Haeske, Horst *physicist*

Kruft
Lekim, Dac *chemist*

Ladenburg
Traub, Peter *biochemist*

Mainz
Gütlich, Philipp *chemistry educator*
Meisel, Werner Paul Ernst *physicist*

Munich
Binnig, Gerd Karl *physicist*
Fischer, Ernst Otto *chemist, educator*
Giacconi, Riccardo *astrophysicist, educator*

Neckargemuend
Kirchmayer-Hilprecht, Martin *geologist*

Stuttgart
Kramer, Horst Emil Adolf *physical chemist*

GREECE

Athens
Screttas, Constantinos George *chemistry educator*
Sekeris, Constantine Evangelos *biochemistry educator*

HONG KONG

Kowloon
Chang, Leroy L. *physicist*

IRAN

Tehran
Sharifi, Iraj Alagha *organic chemistry educator*

ISRAEL

Ra'ananna
Hayon, Elie M. *chemist, educator*

ITALY

Milan
Bellobono, Ignazio Renato *chemist, educator*
Sindoni, Elio *physics educator*
Valcavi, Umberto *chemistry educator*

Novara
Pernicone, Nicola *catalyst consultant*

Pavia
di Jeso, Fernando *biochemistry educator*

San Donato
Roggero, Arnaldo *polymer chemistry executive*

Trieste
Salam, Abdus *physicist, educator*

JAPAN

Ehime
Sakai, Yoshiro *chemistry educator*

Ibaraki
Ishii, Yoshinori *geophysics educator*

Ise
Hayashi, Takemi *physics educator*

Ishikawa
Konishi, Kenji *geology educator*

Koganei
Akiyama, Masayasu *chemistry educator*

Kurashiki
Masamoto, Junzo *chemist, researcher*

Kyoto
Araki, Takeo *chemistry educator*
Fukui, Kenichi *chemist*
Kawabata, Nariyoshi *chemistry educator*
Tachiwaki, Tokumatsu *chemistry educator*
Yamana, Shukichi *chemistry educator*

Miyakonojo
Eto, Morifusa *chemistry educator*

Nagoya
Murakami, Edahiko *chemistry educator*

Neyagawa
Motoba, Toshio *physics educator*

Okayama
Furuya, Tsutomu *plant chemist and biochemist, educator*
Oda, Takuzo *biochemistry educator*
Torii, Sigeru *chemistry educator*
Ubuka, Toshihiko *biochemistry educator*

Oosaka
Sakamoto, Ichitaro *oceanologist, consultant*

Osaka
Aoki, Ichiro *theoretical biophysics systems science educator*
Ikeda, Kazuyosi *physicist, poet*
Kobayashi, Mitsue *chemistry educator*
Yoneyama, Hiroshi *chemistry educator*

Otsu
Matsuura, Teruo *chemistry educator*
Takemoto, Kiichi *chemistry educator*

Sakai-Gun
Ise, Norio *chemistry educator*

Sendai
Oikawa, Hiroshi *materials science educator*

Shimizu
Uyeda, Seiya *geophysics educator*

Tochigi
Iida, Shuichi *physicist,educator*

Tokyo
Iwakura, Yoshio *chemistry educator*
Kamiya, Yoshio *research chemist, educator*
Kigoshi, Kunihiko *geochemistry educator*
Musha, Toshimitsu *physicist, educator*
Nakagaki, Masayuki *chemist*
Nozoe, Tetsuo *organic chemist, research consultant*
Suami, Tetsuo *chemistry educator*
Torii, Tetsuya *retired science educator*
Tsuchida, Eishun *chemistry educator*

Tondabayashi
Nozato, Ryoichi *metallurgy educator, researcher*

Toshima-Ku
Furuichi, Susumu *physics researcher*

Toyama
Hayashi, Mitsuhiko *physics educator*

Toyonaka
Kishimoto, Uichiro *biophysicist*

Tsukuba
Esaki, Leo *physicist*

Urawa
Hiyama, Tetsuo *biochemistry educator*
Narasaki, Hisatake *analytical chemist*

Yamaguchi
Suzuki, Nobutaka *chemistry educator*

Yokohama
Asawa, Tatsurō *chemistry researcher*
Niki, Katsumi *chemistry educator*
Ogawa, Seiichiro *chemistry educator*

THE NETHERLANDS

Amsterdam
Averill, Bruce Alan *chemistry educator*
Wiegman, Lenore Ho *chemist*

Delft
Moulijn, Jacob A. *chemical technology educator*

Goor
Bonting, Sjoerd Lieuwe *biochemist, priest*

OSAKA JAPAN

Suita
†Mima, Kunioki *physicist, educator*

PAKISTAN

Hyderabad
Ali, Syed Wajahat *physical chemist, researcher*

REPUBLIC OF KOREA

Pohang
Choi, Sang-il *physics educator, researcher*

Taejon
Lee, Choochon *physics educator, researcher*

RUSSIA

Novosibirsk
Aleksandrov, Leonid Naumovitsh *physicist, educator, researcher*

SCOTLAND

Glasgow
Courtney, James McNiven *chemist*

Peebles
Hooper, John Edward *retired physicist, researcher*

Stirling
Kleinpoppen, Hans Johann Willi *physics educator, researcher*

SPAIN

Barcelona
Subirana, Juan Antonio *polymer chemist, educator*

SWEDEN

Lund
Grimmeiss, Hermann Georg *physics educator, researcher*

Nykoping
Kivikas, Toivelemb *physicist, executive*

Stockholm
Fernandez-Moran, Humberto *biophysicist*
Samuelsson, Bengt Ingemar *medical chemist*

SWITZERLAND

Gais
Langenegger, Otto *hydrogeologist*

Geneva
Harigel, Gert Günter *physicist*
Hofmann, Albert Josef *physicist*
Overseth, Oliver Enoch *physicist, educator*
Rubbia, Carlo *physicist*
Steinberger, Jack *physicist, educator*

Rueschlikon
Rohrer, Heinrich *physicist*

Zurich
†Dunitz, Jack David *retired chemistry educator, researcher*
Hauser, Helmut Otmar *biochemistry educator*
Mueller, Stephan *geophysicist, educator*

TAIWAN

Chung-Li
Tseng, Tien-Jiunn *physics educator*

Hsinchu
Liu, Ti Lang *physics educator*

Taipei
Yang, Chin-Ping *chemist, engineering educator*

UNITED ARAB EMIRATES

Al-Ain
Kiwan, Abdul Mageed Metwally *chemistry educator*

URUGUAY

Montevideo
Ventura, Oscar Nestor *chemistry educator, researcher*

VENEZUELA

Caracas
Nakano, Tatsuhiko *chemist, researcher, educator*
Rangel-Aldao, Rafael *biochemist*
Sáez, Alberto M. *physics educator*

ADDRESS UNPUBLISHED

Akasofu, Syun-Ichi *geophysicist*
Alfvén, Hannes Olof Gosta *physicist*
Alvi, Zahoor Mohem *radiological physicist*
Ames, Oakes *physicist, educator*
†Ancker-Johnson, Betsy *physicist, retired automotive company executive*
†Arnett, Edward McCollin *chemistry educator, researcher*
Atwood, Genevieve *geologist*
Autin, Ernest Anthony, II *chemist, educator*
Baldwin, George Curriden *physicist, educator*
Ball, Lawrence *retired physicial scientist*
Bandeen, William Reid *retired meteorologist*
†Barker, Robert *biochemistry educator*
Basford, Robert Eugene *retired biochemistry educator, researcher*
Baym, Gordon Alan *physicist, educator*
†Behannon, Kenneth Wayne *retired astrophysicist*
Biedenharn, Lawrence C., Jr. *physicist, educator*
Bodanszky, Miklos *chemist, educator*
Braden, Charles Hosea *physicist, university administrator*
Brand, John Charles *chemistry educator*
†Cahn, Robert Nathan *physicist*
Cairns, Theodore LeSueur *chemist*
Christoffersen, Ralph Earl *chemist*
Chu, Benjamin Thomas Peng-Nien *chemistry educator*
Church, Eugene Lent *physicist, consultant*
Compton, W. Dale *physicist*
Critoph, Eugene *retired physicist, nuclear research company executive*
Cummin, Alfred S(amuel) *retired chemist*
Dale, Wesley John *chemistry educator*
Daniels, James Maurice *physicist*
Deisenhofer, Johann *biochemistry educator, researcher*
De Loach, Bernard Collins, Jr. *retired physicist*
†Denton, M. Bonner *research chemistry educator*
Dicke, Robert Henry *educator, physicist*
Dickinson, William Richard *retired geologist and educator*
Donath, Fred Arthur *geologist, geophysicist*
†Eberly, Joseph Henry *physics educator, consultant*
Ettre, Leslie Stephen *chemist*
Ewen, H.I. *physicist*
Fang, Joseph Pe Yong *chemistry educator*
Franklin, Kenneth L(inn) *astronomer*
Frauenfelder, Hans *physicist, educator*
Galloway, William Joyce *physicist, consultant*
Geller, Seymour *retired educator, researcher*
Getting, Ivan Alexander *physicist, former aerospace company executive*
Gilinsky, Victor *physicist*
Glashow, Sheldon Lee *physicist, educator*
Goldfine, Howard *microbiology and biochemistry educator, researcher*

Gounaris, Anne Demetra *biochemistry educator, researcher*
Gummel, Hermann Karl *retired physicist, laboratory administrator*
Gutsch, William Anthony, Jr. *astronomer*
Haering, Rudolph Roland *retired physics educator, researcher*
Hannay, N(orman) Bruce *chemist, industrial research and business consultant*
Heeschen, David Sutphin *astronomer, educator*
Herzfeld, Charles Maria *physicist*
Hinkley, Everett David, Jr. *scientist,business executive*
Hoeg, Donald Francis *chemist, consultant, former research and development executive*
Howard, Charles L. *chemist, educator*
Howe, John Perry *materials science educator, research consultant*
Ingle, James Chesney, Jr. *geology educator*
Jacobs, Abigail Conway *biochemist*
Jeffries, Robert Alan *physicist*
Jordan, Thomas Fredrick *physics educator*
Kamen, Martin David *physical biochemist*
Kerwin, Larkin *physics educator*
Kolm, Henry Herbert *physicist, electric research company executive*
†Kraichnan, Robert Harry *theoretical physicist, consultant*
Kravitz, Rubin *chemist*
Landel, Robert Franklin *physical chemist, rheologist*
†Landis, Geoffrey Alan *physicist, writer*
Langerak, Esley Oren *retired research chemist*
Levenson, Marc David *optics and lasers specialist, scientist*
Lloyd, Joseph Wesley *physicist, researcher*
Lynds, Beverly Turner *retired astronomer*
MacQueen, Robert Moffat *solar physicist*
†Maddin, Robert *metallurgist educator*
Maglich, Bogdan Cveta *physicist*
Maiman, Theodore Harold *physicist*
Malkin, Myron Samuel *physicist, management consultant*
McCauley, John Francis *geologist*
Medzihradsky, Fedor *biochemist, educator*
Middleton, Gerard Viner *geology educator*
†Miller, Jeffrey Veach *biochemist, researcher*
Mislow, Kurt Martin *chemist, educator*
Mott, Nevill (Francis Mott) *physicist, educator, author*
Nobles, Laurence Hewit *retired geology educator*
Norman, Joe G., Jr. *chemistry educator, college dean*
Orttung, William Herbert *chemistry educator*
Pearson, Donald Emanual *chemist, educator*
Pearson, Ralph Gottfrid *chemistry educator*
Penzias, Arno Allan *astrophysicist, research scientist, information systems specialist*
Pirkle, Earl Charnell *geologist, educator*
Pocock, Frederick James *scientist, consultant*
Portis, Alan Mark *physicist, educator*
Pound, Robert Vivian *physics educator*
Price, Paul Buford *physicist, educator*
Procunier, Richard Werner *environmental scientist, administrator*
Pursey, Derek Lindsay *physics educator*
Qutub, Musa Yacub *hydrogeologist, educator, consultant*
Radin, Norman Samuel *retired biochemistry educator*
Rast, Walter, Jr. *hydrologist, water quality management*
Redda, Kinfe Ken *chemist, educator*
Rice, Stuart Alan *chemist, educator*
Richards, Paul Linford *physics educator, researcher*
Richardson, Charles Clifton *biochemist, educator*
Robertson, John Archibald Law *nuclear scientist*
†Robinson, Bruce Butler *physicist*
Rubin, Vera Cooper *research astronomer*
Rüetschi, Paul *electrochemist*
Rugge, Hugo Robert *physicist*
Sayre, David *physicist*
Schachter, Harry *biochemist, educator*
Schmitt, George Joseph *chemist*
Schonhorn, Harold *chemist, researcher*
Schwarzschild, Martin *astronomer, educator*
Shaw, Melvin Phillip *physicist, engineering educator, psychologist*
†Shirley, David Arthur *chemistry educator, science administrator*
Shockley, James Thomas *physics educator*
Smith, Charles Haddon *geoscientist, consultant*
Smoot, George Fitzgerald, III *astrophysicist*
Solomon, Susan *chemist, scientist*
Spejewski, Eugene Henry *physicist, educator*
Spitzer, Lyman, Jr. *astronomer*
Stewart, Robert William *retired physicist, government research council executive*
Stroud, Robert Michael *biophysicist, educator, biotechnologist*
Sturtevant, Julian Munson *biophysical chemist, educator*
Sullivan, Nicholas G. *science educator, speleologist*
Sundaresan, Mosur Kalyanaraman *physics educator*
Sunderman, Duane Neuman *chemist, research institute executive*
Tate, Manford Ben *guided missile scientist, investor*
Taylor, Hugh Pettingill, Jr. *geologist, educator*
†Thuillier, Richard Howard *meteorologist*
Turco, Richard Peter *atmospheric scientist*
Vanier, Jacques *physicist*
†Veronis, George *geophysicist, educator*
†Watson, Robert Barden *physicist*
Waymouth, John Francis *physicist, consultant*
Weinberg, Steven *physics educator*
Weisburger, Elizabeth Kreiser *chemist, editor*
Weiss, Michael James *chemistry educator*
†Welton, Theodore Allen *theoretical physics educator, consultant*
Whistler, Roy Lester *chemist, educator, industrialist*
Wilson, Kenneth Geddes *physics research administrator, educator*
Wolff, Peter Adalbert *physicist, educator*
Wright, Ann Elizabeth *physicist, educator*
Yates, David John C. *chemist, researcher*
Zaffaroni, Alejandro C. *biochemist, medical research company executive*
Zhou, Ming De *aeronautical scientist, educator*
Zimm, Bruno Hasbrouck *physical chemistry educator*
Ziock, Klaus Otto Heinrich *physics educator*

SOCIAL SCIENCE

UNITED STATES

ALABAMA

Birmingham
Liu, Ray Ho *forensic science program director, educator*
Nunn, Grady Harrison *political science educator emeritus*

Collinsville
Beasley, Mary Catherine *home economics educator, administrator, researcher*

Hartselle
Slate, Joe Hutson *psychologist, educator*

Huntsville
Traylor, Orba Forest *economist, lawyer, educator*

Lillian
Moyer, Kenneth Evan *psychologist, educator*

Mobile
Bobo, James Robert *economics educator*
Vitulli, William Francis *psychology educator*

Montevallo
†McChesney, Robert Michael, Sr. *political science educator*

Pell City
Passey, George Edward *psychology educator*

Tuscaloosa
Abdel-Ghany, Mohamed *family economics educator*
Baklanoff, Eric Nicholas *economist, educator*
Cramer, Dale Lewis *economics educator*
Fish, Mary Martha *economics educator*
Wu, Hsiu Kwang *economist, educator*

ALASKA

Anchorage
Henderson-Dixon, Karen Sue *psychologist*
Jones, Garth Nelson *public administration educator*
Risley, Todd Robert *psychologist, educator*

Fairbanks
Cutler, Howard Armstrong *economics educator, chancellor*

ARIZONA

Flagstaff
Smith, Zachary Alden *political science and public administration educator*

Phoenix
Cheifetz, Lorna Gale *psychologist*

Prescott
Chase, Loriene Eck *psychologist*

Scottsdale
Kizziar, Janet Wright *psychologist, author, lecturer*

Sedona
Eggert, Robert John, Sr. *economist*

Sun City
Brown, Robert Harold *retired geography educator*

Tempe
Alisky, Marvin Howard *political science educator*
Farber, Bernard *sociologist, educator*
Farris, Martin Theodore *economist, educator*
Gordon, Leonard *sociology educator*
Lounsbury, John Frederick *geographer, educator*
Metcalf, Virgil Alonzo *economics educator*
Miller, Warren Edward *political scientist*
Montero, Darrel Martin *sociologist, social worker, educator*
Simon, Sheldon Weiss *political science educator*
Uttal, William R(eichenstein) *psychology and engineering educator, research scientist*
Weigend, Guido Gustav *geographer, educator*

Tucson
Beach, Lee Roy *psychologist, educator*
Block, Michael Kent *economics and law educator, public policy association executive, former government official, consultant*
Clarke, James Weston *political science educator, writer*
†Green, Jerrold David *political science educator, academic administrator*
Kirk, Samuel Alexander *psychologist, educator*
Marshall, Robert Herman *economics educator*
Netting, Robert M. *anthropology educator*
Ruggill, Solomon P. *psychologist*
Seger, Martha Romayne *financial economist*
Smith, David Wayne *psychologist*
Smith, Vernon Lomax *economist, researcher*
Soren, David *archaeology educator, administrator*
Stini, William Arthur *anthropologist, educator*
Underwood, Jane Hainline Hammons *anthropologist, educator*
Wahlke, John Charles *political science educator*
Whiting, Allen Suess *political science educator, writer, consultant*

ARKANSAS

Conway
Mc New, Bennie Banks *economics and finance educator*

Fayetteville
†Green, Thomas James *archaeologist*
McCartney, Allen Papin *anthropology educator*
Mc Gimsey, Charles Robert, III *anthropologist*
Purvis, Hoyt Hughes *political scientist, academic administrator, educator*

Little Rock
Boucher, Wayne Irving *policy analyst*
Ledbetter, Calvin Reville, Jr. (Cal Ledbetter) *political science educator, university dean, former legislator*

Morrilton
Thompson, Robert Lee *agricultural economist, foundation administrator*

Pine Bluff
Engle, Carole Ruth *aquaculture economics educator*

State University
Power, Mary Susan *political science educator*

CALIFORNIA

Alameda
Taveggia, Thomas Charles *psychology educator*

Arcadia
Horner, Althea Jane *psychologist*

Arcata
Emenhiser, JeDon Allen *political science educator, academic administrator*

Berkeley
Adelman, Irma Glicman *economics educator*
Alhadeff, David Albert *economics educator*
Baumrind, Diana *research psychologist*
Bellah, Robert Neelly *sociologist, educator*
Blakely, Edward James *economics educator*
Bonnell, Victoria Eileen *sociologist*
Brandes, Stanley Howard *anthropology educator, writer*
Breslauer, George William *political science educator*
Cain, Bruce Edward *political science educator, consultant*
Castaneda, Carlos *anthropologist, author*
Cheit, Earl Frank *economist, educator*
Clark, John Desmond *anthropology educator*
Clausen, John Adam *social psychologist*
Colson, Elizabeth Florence *anthropologist*
Debreu, Gerard *economics and mathematics educator*
Dundes, Alan *anthropology, writer, educator*
Foster, George McClelland, Jr. *anthropologist*
Gilbert, Richard Joseph *economics educator*
Graburn, Nelson Hayes Henry *anthropologist, educator*
Gurgin, Vonnie Ann *social scientist*
Hancock, Emily Stone *psychologist*
Harsanyi, John Charles *economics educator, researcher*
Hitch, Charles Johnston *economist, institution executive*
Howell, Francis Clark *anthropologist, educator*
Johanson, Donald Carl *physical anthropologist*
Kallgren, Joyce Kislitzin *political science educator*
Keeler, Theodore Edwin *economics educator*
Lambert, Nadine Murphy *psychologist, educator*
Landau, Martin *political science educator*
Lane, Sylvia *economist, educator*
Lazarus, Richard Stanley *psychology educator*
Lee, Ronald Demos *demographer, economist, educator*
Letiche, John Marion *economist, educator*
Lipson, Leslie Michael *political science educator*
Maisel, Sherman Joseph *economist, educator*
Maslach, Christina *psychology educator*
McFadden, Daniel Little *economics educator*
Meier, Richard Louis *futurist, planner, behavioral scientist*
Muir, William Ker, Jr. *political science educator*
Nemeth, Charlan Jeanne *psychology educator*
Parsons, James Jerome *geographer, educator*
Polsby, Nelson Woolf *political scientist, educator*
Quigley, John Michael *economist, educator*
Ranney, (Joseph) Austin *political science educator*
Rausser, Gordon C(lyde) *agricultural and resource economics educator*
Rosberg, Carl Gustaf *political science educator*
†Rosen, Kenneth T. *economist*
Rosenzweig, Mark Richard *psychology educator*
Rowe, John Howland *anthropologist, educator*
Sarich, Vincent M. *anthropologist, educator*
Shack, William Alfred *anthropology educator, researcher, consultant*
Smelser, Neil Joseph *sociologist*
Smolensky, Eugene *economics educator*
Staw, Barry Martin *business and psychology educator*
Teitz, Michael B. *social science educator*
Tyson, Laura D'Andrea *economist, government adviser, educator*
Waltz, Kenneth Neal *political science educator*
Wilensky, Harold L. *political science and industrial relations educator*
Williamson, Oliver Eaton *economics and law educator*
Wolfinger, Raymond Edwin *political science educator*

Beverly Hills
Aguilera, Donna Conant *psychologist, researcher*
Evans, Louise *psychologist, investor*

Burlingame
Crawford, William Richard *psychologist*

Calistoga
Spindler, George Dearborn *anthropologist, educator, author, editor*

Carmel
Parker, Donald Henry *psychologist, author*

Carpinteria
Schmidhauser, John Richard *political science educator*
Wheeler, John Harvey *political scientist*

Chula Vista
†Schorr, Martin Mark *psychologist, educator, writer*

Claremont
Benson, George Charles Sumner *political science educator*
Bjork, Gordon Carl *economist, educator*
Bond, Floyd Alden *economist, educator*
Bowman, Dean Orlando *economist, educator*
Gold, Bela *educator, economist*
Hinshaw, Randall (Weston) *economist, educator*
Likens, James Dean *economics educator*
Neal, Fred Warner *political scientist, educator*
Palmer, Hans Christian *economics educator*
Phelps, Orme Wheelock *economics educator emeritus*
Wykoff, Frank Champion *economics educator*

Corona Del Mar
Davis, Arthur David *psychology educator, musician*
Hinderaker, Ivan *political science educator*

Costa Mesa
Crinella, Francis Michael *neuropsychologist, science foundation director*

Culver City
Maltzman, Irving Myron *psychology educator*

Cupertino
Norman, Donald Arthur *cognitive scientist*

Davis
Cohen, Lawrence Edward *sociology educator, criminologist*
Crowley, Daniel John *anthropologist*
Elmendorf, William Welcome *anthropology educator*
Groth, Alexander Jacob *political science educator*
Harper, Lawrence Vernon *human development educator*
Hawkes, Glenn Rogers *psychology educator*
Hrdy, Sarah Blaffer *anthropology educator*
Ives, John David (Jack Ives) *geography educator*
Jett, Stephen Clinton *geography educator, researcher*
Johnston, Warren E. *agricultural economics educator, consultant*
Lofland, John Franklin *sociologist, educator*
Lofland, Lyn Hebert *sociology educator*
Mason, William A(lvin) *psychologist, educator, researcher*
McHenry, Henry Malcolm *anthropologist, educator*
Musolf, Lloyd Daryl *political science educator, institute administrator*
Owings, Donald Henry *psychology educator*
Siverson, Randolph Martin *political science educator*
Skinner, G(eorge) William *anthropologist, educator*
Smith, Michael Peter *social science educator, researcher*
Sosnick, Stephen Howard *economics educator*
Sumner, Daniel Alan *economist, educator*
Wegge, Leon Louis François *economics educator*
Werner-Jacobsen, Emmy Elisabeth *developmental psychologist*

El Cerrito
Conti, Isabella *psychologist, consultant*

Encinitas
Bloomberg, Warner, Jr. *urban affairs educator emeritus*

Escondido
Damsbo, Ann Marie *psychologist*

Foothill Ranch
Eckstein, Harry *political science educator*

Fresno
Coe, William Charles *psychology educator*
Dackawich, S. John *sociology educator*
O'Brien, John Conway *economist, educator, writer*

Fullerton
Cole, Sherwood Orison *psychologist*
Foster, Julian Francis Sherwood *political science educator*
Hershey, Gerald Lee *psychologist*
von Sadovszky, Otto Joseph *anthropology educator, linguist*

Glendale
Hadley, Paul Ervin *international relations educator*

Hayward
Smith, J(ohn) Malcolm *political science educator*
Whalen, Thomas Earl *psychology educator*

Huntington Beach
Martin, Wilfred Wesley *psychologist, property manager*

Irvine
Aigner, Dennis John *economics educator, consultant*
Burton, Michael Ladd *anthropology educator*
Cushman, Robert Fairchild *political science educator, author, editor*
Danziger, James Norris *political science educator*
Freeman, Linton Clarke *sociology educator*
Geis, Gilbert Lawrence *sociology educator emeritus*
Greenberger, Ellen *psychologist, educator*
Lave, Charles Arthur *economics educator*
Luce, R(obert) Duncan *psychology educator*
Margolis, Julius *economist, educator*
Mc Gaugh, James Lafayette *psychobiologist*
Rubel, Arthur Joseph *anthropologist, educator*
Schonfeld, William Rost *political science educator, researcher*
Sperling, George *cognitive scientist, educator*
Taagepera, Rein *social science educator*
Treas, Judith Kay *sociology educator*
†White, Douglas R. *anthropology educator*

Kensington
Swanson, Guy Edwin *social scientist, educator*

La Jolla
Attiyeh, Richard Eugene *economics educator*
Borjas, George J(esus) *economics educator*
Farson, Richard Evans *psychologist*
Gourevitch, Peter Alexis *political science educator, dean*
Granger, Clive William John *economist, educator*

Groves, Theodore Francis, Jr. *economics educator*
Harris, Philip Robert *management and space psychologist*
Kaplan, Robert Malcolm *health researcher, educator*
Lakoff, Sanford *political scientist, educator*
Mandler, George *psychologist*
Mandler, Jean Matter *psychologist, educator*
Rothschild, Michael *economics educator*
Schiller, Herbert Irving *social scientist, author*
Spinweber, Cheryl Lynn *research psychologist*
Spiro, Melford Elliot *anthropology educator*
Starr, Ross Marc *economist, educator*

Laguna Beach
Bent, Alan Edward *political science educator, administrator*
Dale, Leon Andrew *economist, educator*
Fagin, Henry *public administration consultant*

Laguna Hills
Kaplan, Sidney Joseph *sociologist, educator*

Long Beach
Kokaska, Charles James *educational psychologist*

Loomis
Hartmann, Frederick Howard *political science educator emeritus*

Los Angeles
Alexander, Herbert E. *political scientist*
Allen, William Richard *retired economist*
Alvarez, Rodolfo *sociology educator, consultant*
Anawalt, Patricia Rieff *anthropologist*
Anderson, Austin Gilman *economics research company consultant*
Bennett, Charles Franklin, Jr. *biogeographer, educator*
Bjork, Robert Allen *psychology educator, researcher*
Bloland, Paul Anson *psychology educator emeritus*
Broderick, Carlfred Bartholomew *sociology educator*
Clark, Burton Robert *sociologist, educator*
Coombs, Robert Holman *sociologist, medical educator, author*
Darby, Michael Rucker *economist, educator*
Dekmejian, Richard Hrair *political science educator*
Demsetz, Harold *economist, educator*
†Earle, Timothy *anthropology educator*
Easterlin, Richard Ainley *economist, educator*
Feshbach, Seymour *psychology educator*
Forness, Steven Robert *educational psychologist*
Glaser, Daniel *sociologist*
Glassner, Barry *sociology educator, author*
Greenberg, Ira Arthur *psychologist*
Gunn, Karen Sue *psychologist*
Hahn, Harlan Dean *political science educator, consultant*
Heer, David Macalpine *sociology educator*
Hendrick, Hal Wilmans *human factors educator*
Hirsch, Werner Zvi *economist, educator*
Hoffenberg, Marvin *political science educator, consultant*
Intriligator, Michael David *economist, educator*
Jacobs, Marilyn Susan *psychologist, author*
Jacobs, Marion Kramer *psychologist*
Kelley, Harold Harding *psychology educator*
Klein, Benjamin *economics educator, consultant*
La Force, James Clayburn, Jr. *economist, educator*
Lasswell, Marcia Lee *psychologist, educator*
Leary, Timothy *psychologist, author*
Leijonhufvud, Axel Stig Bengt *economics educator*
Levine, Robert Arthur *economist, policy analyst*
Lindsley, Donald Benjamin *physiological psychologist, educator*
Lowenthal, Abraham Frederic *international relations educator*
Lyman, John *psychology and engineering educator*
Malecki, Edward Stanley, Jr. *political science educator*
Maquet, Jacques Jerome Pierre *anthropologist, writer*
Michael, William Burton *psychologist, educator*
Miller, Norman *psychology educator, researcher*
Morgner, Aurelius *economist, educator*
Nelson, Howard Joseph *educator, geographer*
Nixon, John Harmon *economist*
Orme, Antony Ronald *geography educator*
Raven, Bertram H(erbert) *psychology educator*
Riley, John Graham *economics educator*
Rodnick, Eliot Herman *psychologist, educator*
Seeman, Melvin *sociologist, educator*
Shneidman, Edwin S. *psychologist, educator, thanatologist, suicidologist*
Simpson, William Brand *economist, educator*
Sklar, Richard Lawrence *political science educator*
Somers, Harold Milton *economist, educator*
Thomlinson, Ralph *demographer, educator*
Thompson, Earl Albert *economics educator*
Thompson, Richard Frederick *psychologist, neuroscientist, educator*
Thrower, Norman Joseph William *geographer, educator*
Totten, George Oakley, III *political science educator*
Turk, Herman *sociologist, educator, researcher*
Turner, Ralph Herbert *sociologist, educator*
Van Arsdol, Maurice Donald, Jr. *sociologist, demographer, educator*
Watson, Sharon Gitin *psychologist, executive*
Williams, Robert Martin *economist, consultant*
Wilson, James Quinn *government, management educator*
Wittrock, Merlin Carl *educational psychologist*
Wood, Nancy Elizabeth *psychologist, educator*

Los Osos
Thomas, Robert Murray *educational psychology educator*

Malibu
Aiken, Lewis Roscoe, Jr. *psychologist, educator*

Menlo Park
Alexander, Theron *psychologist, writer*

Mill Valley
Benezet, Louis Tomlinson *retired psychology educator, former college president*
Harner, Michael James *anthropologist, educator, author*
Mihaly, Eugene Bramer *consultant, corporate executive, writer, educator*

Moffett Field
Cohen, Malcolm Martin *psychologist, researcher*

Haines, Richard Foster *psychologist*

Murrieta
Lewis, Donald Joseph *retired psychology educator*

Northridge
Butler, Karla *psychologist*
Segalman, Ralph *sociology educator*

Oakdale
Thomas, William LeRoy *geography educator, cruise lecturer*

Oceanside
Hertweck, E. Romayne *psychology educator*

Orange
†Magalousis, Nicholas Michael *anthropology, archaeology educator*

Pacific Palisades
Longaker, Richard Pancoast *political science educator emeritus*

Palo Alto
Bohrnstedt, George William *sociology educator*
Dornbusch, Sanford Maurice *sociology and biology educator*
Eulau, Heinz *political scientist, educator*
George, Alexander Lawrence *political scientist, educator*
Hammett, Benjamin Cowles *psychologist*
Lewis, John Wilson *political science educator*
†Lindzey, Gardner *psychologist, educator*
Scitovsky, Anne Aickelin *economist*

Pasadena
Davis, Lance Edwin *economics educator*
Grether, David Maclay *economics educator*
Ledyard, John Odell *economics educator, consultant*
Munger, Edwin Stanton *political geography educator*
Oliver, Robert Warner *economics educator*
Plott, Charles R. *economics educator*
Scudder, Thayer *anthropologist, educator*

Petaluma
Carr, Les *psychologist, educator*

Placentia
Gobar, Alfred Julian *economic consultant, educator*

Placerville
Craib, Kenneth Bryden *resource development executive, physicist, economist*

Pomona
Lasswell, Thomas Ely *sociology educator, author*
Shieh, John Ting-chung *economics educator*

Portola Valley
Bach, George Leland *economist, emeritus educator*
Ward, Robert Edward *retired political science educator and university administrator*

Rancho Mirage
Deiter, Newton Elliott *clinical psychologist*

Redlands
Rossum, Ralph Arthur *political science educator*

Redondo Beach
McWilliams, Margaret Ann *home economics educator, author*

Reseda
Aller, Wayne Kendall *psychology educator, researcher, computer education company executive, property manager*

Riverside
Adrian, Charles Raymond *political science educator*
Eyman, Richard Kenneth *psychologist, educator*
Griffin, Keith Broadwell *economics educator*
Kronenfeld, David Brian *anthropologist*
Petrinovich, Lewis F. *psychology educator*
Turk, Austin Theodore *sociology educator*
Turner, Arthur Campbell *political science educator, author*
Warren, David Hardy *psychology educator*

Sacramento
Bennett, Lawrence Allen *psychologist, criminal justice researcher*
Bruce, Thomas Edward *thanatologist, psychology educator*
Chapman, Loring *psychologist, educator, neuroscientist*
Flournoy, Houston Irvine *public administration educator*
Newland, Chester Albert *public administration educator*
Post, August Alan *economist, artist*
Sherwood, Robert Petersen *retired sociology educator*

Salinas
Eifler, Carl Frederick *retired psychologist*
Francis, Alexandria Stephanie *psychologist*

San Carlos
Burgess, Leonard Randolph *business administration and economics educator, writer*

San Diego
Barckley, Robert Eugene *economics educator*
Berger, Bennett Maurice *sociology educator*
Getis, Arthur *geography educator*
Kaplan, Oscar Joel *psychology educator*
Kent, Theodore Charles *psychologist*
Klausmeier, Herbert John *psychologist, educator*
Litrownik, Alan Jay *psychologist, educator*
†Madhavan, Murugappa Chettiar *economics educator, international consultant*
Mc Guigan, Frank Joseph *psychologist, educator*
Rea, Amadeo Michael *ethnobiologist, ornithologist*
Shafer, Joseph Ernest *economics educator emeritus, writer*
Storer, Norman William *sociology educator*
Storms, Lowell Hanson *psychologist*
Weeks, John Robert *geographer, sociology educator*

Yakan, Mohamad Zuhdi *political science educator*

San Francisco
Brumbaugh, Robert Dan, Jr. *economist*
Butz, Otto William *political science educator*
Calvin, Allen David *psychologist, educator*
Chesnut, Carol Fitting *economist*
Clark, M(ary) Margaret *anthropology educator*
Estes, Carroll Lynn *sociologist, educator*
Freedman, Mervin Burton *psychologist, educator*
Hoadley, Walter Evans *economist, financial executive, lay worker*
Krippner, Stanley Curtis *psychologist*
Luft, Harold S. *health economist*
Malveaux, Julianne Marie *economist, writer*
Marston, Michael *urban economist, asset management executive*
Marvin, David Keith *international relations educator*
Pincus, Joseph *economist, educator*
Rice, Dorothy Pechman (Mrs. John Donald Rice) *medical economist*
Wilson, John Oliver *economist, educator, banker*

San Jose
McDowell, Jennifer *sociologist, composer, playwright, publisher*
Pellegrini, Robert J. *psychology educator*

San Luis Obispo
Holder, Elaine Edith *psychologist, educator*

Santa Barbara
Baldwin, John David *sociologist, educator*
Blum, Gerald Saul *psychologist, educator*
Clinard, Marshall Barron *sociology educator emeritus*
Comanor, William S. *economist, educator*
Erasmus, Charles John *anthropologist, educator*
†Ford, Anabel *research anthropologist, archaeologist*
†Goodchild, Michael *geographer, educator*
Jochim, Michael Allan *archaeologist*
†Juergensmeyer, Mark Karl *sociology educator*
Kendler, Howard H(arvard) *psychologist, educator*
Mayer, Richard Edwin *psychology educator*
Pritchett, Charles Herman *political science educator*
Shapiro, Perry *economics educator*
Tobler, Waldo Rudolph *geographer, cartographer*
Turner, Henry A. *political science educator, author*

Santa Cruz
Child, Frank Clayton *economist, educator*
Henderson, Ronald Wilbur *psychology educator*
Musgrave, Richard Abel *economics educator*
Pettigrew, Thomas Fraser *social psychologist, educator*
Smith, M(ahlon) Brewster *psychologist, educator*
Tharp, Roland George *psychology, education educator*

Santa Monica
Kahan, James Paul *psychologist*
†Smith, James Patrick *economist*
Williams, Albert Paine *economist*
Wolf, Charles, Jr. *economist, educator*

Stanford
Abramovitz, Moses *economist, educator*
Almond, Gabriel Abraham *political science educator*
Amemiya, Takeshi *economist, statistician*
Anderson, Annelise Graebner *economist*
Anderson, Martin Carl *economist*
Arrow, Kenneth Joseph *economist, educator*
Arthur, William Brian *economist, educator*
Bandura, Albert *psychologist*
Beichman, Arnold *political scientist, educator, writer*
Boskin, Michael Jay *economist, government official, university educator, consultant*
Bunzel, John Harvey *political science educator, researcher*
Calfee, Robert Chilton *psychologist, educational researcher*
Campbell, Wesley Glenn *economist, educator*
Carlsmith, James Merrill *psychologist, educator*
Converse, Philip Ernest *social science educator*
Davis, Kingsley *sociologist, educator, researcher*
†Flavell, John Hurley *psychologist, educator*
Friedman, Milton *economist, educator emeritus, author*
Fuchs, Victor Robert *economics educator*
Gage, Nathaniel Lees *psychologist, educator*
Gibbs, James Lowell, Jr. *anthropologist, researcher*
Greenberg, Joseph H. *anthropologist*
Hall, Robert Ernest *economics educator*
Hilgard, Ernest Ropiequet *psychologist*
†Holloway, David James *political science educator*
Howell, James Edwin *economist, educator*
Inkeles, Alex *sociology educator*
Johnston, Bruce Foster *economics educator*
Kreps, David Marc *economist, educator*
Krumboltz, John Dwight *psychologist, educator*
Kurz, Mordecai *economics educator*
Lau, Lawrence Juen-Yee *economics educator, consultant*
Lazear, Edward Paul *economics and industrial relations educator, researcher*
Lepper, Mark Roger *psychology educator*
Maccoby, Eleanor Emmons *psychology educator*
Manley, John Frederick *political scientist, educator*
March, James Gardner *social scientist, educator*
Mc Lure, Charles E., Jr. *economist*
Moore, Thomas Gale *economist, educator*
Noll, Roger Gordon *economist, educator*
North, Robert Carver *political science educator*
Paul, Benjamin David *anthropologist, educator*
†Pearson, Scott Roberts *economics educator*
Ricardo-Campbell, Rita *economist, educator*
Roberts, Donald John *economics and business educator, consultant*
Rosaldo, Renato Ignacio, Jr. *cultural anthropology educator*
Rosenberg, Nathan *economics educator*
Rosse, James Nelson *economics educator, educational administrator*
Rowen, Henry Stanislaus *economics educator*
Scott, W(illiam) Richard *sociology educator*
Shepard, Roger Newland *psychologist, educator*
Sowell, Thomas *economist*
Spence, A. Michael *economics educator, academic administrator*
Staar, Richard Felix *political scientist*
Triska, Jan Francis *retired political science educator*
Van Horne, James Carter *economist, educator*
Zimbardo, Philip George *psychologist, educator, writer*

Studio City
Fisher, Joel Marshall *political scientist, legal recruiter*

Tiburon
Macgregor, Wallace *consulting mineral economist, author*

Topanga
Gimbutas, Marija *archaeologist, educator*

Trabuco Canyon
Addy, Jo Alison Phears *economist*

Turlock
Ahlem, Lloyd Harold *psychologist*
Kottke, Frederick Edward *economics educator*

Tustin
London, Ray William *clinical and forensic psychologist*

Valley Village
Rosen, Alexander Carl *psychologist, consultant*

Walnut Creek
Nelson, Elmer Kingsholm, Jr. *public administration educator, writer, mediator, consultant*
Smith, Robert Houston *archeologist, religious studies educator*
Zander, Alvin Frederick *social psychologist*

COLORADO

Boulder
Ayad, Boulos Ayad *archaeology educator*
Boss, Russel Wayne *business administration educator*
Boulding, Elise Marie *sociologist, educator*
Bourne, Lyle Eugene, Jr. *psychology educator*
Caine, Nelson *geomorphologist, educator*
Codding, George Arthur, Jr. *political science educator*
Darling, Frank Clayton *former political science educator, educational institute administrator*
Greenberg, Edward Seymour *political science educator*
Greene, David Lee *physical anthropologist, educator*
Hanson, Robert Carl *sociologist, educator*
Healy, Alice Fenvessy *psychology educator, researcher*
Helburn, Nicholas *geography educator*
†Jessor, Richard *psychologist, educator*
Kelso, Alec John (Jack Kelso) *anthropologist, educator*
†Kintsch, Walter *psychology educator, director*
Scarritt, James Richard *political science educator*
Walker, Deward Edgar, Jr. *anthropologist, educator*
Wedel, Waldo Rudolph *archaeologist*
Wheat, Joe Ben *anthropologist*
White, Gilbert F(owler) *geographer, educator*
Yokell, Michael David *economist*

Colorado Springs
Brooks, Glenn Ellis *political science educator, educational administrator*
Feld, Werner Joachim *political scientist, educator*
Shafer, Dallas Eugene *psychology gerontology educator, minister*

Denver
Berland, Karen Ina *psychologist*
Clough, Nadine Doerr *school psychologist, psychotherapist*
Coats, Gary Lee *clinical psychologist, educator*
Conger, John Janeway *psychologist, educator*
Hill, Diane Seldon *corporate psychologist*
†Markman, Howard J. *psychology educator*
Mendelsohn, Harold *sociologist, educator*
Purcell, Kenneth *psychology educator, university dean*
Zimet, Carl Norman *psychologist, educator*

Estes Park
Moore, Omar Khayyam *experimental sociologist*

Fort Collins
Bennett, Thomas LeRoy, Jr. *clinical neuropsychology educator*
Eitzen, David Stanley *sociologist, educator*
Suinn, Richard Michael *psychologist*
Walsh, Richard George *agricultural economist*
Wengert, Norman Irving *political science educator*

Golden
Kaufmann, Thomas David *economist, educator*
Petrick, Alfred, Jr. *mineral economics educator, consultant*
Woolsey, Robert Eugene Donald *mineral economics, mathematics and business administration educator*

Lakewood
Wellisch, William Jeremiah *social psychology educator*

Littleton
Cabell, Elizabeth Arlisse *psychologist*
Chapman, Richard LeRoy *public policy researcher*
Milliken, John Gordon *research economist*

McCoy
Wolf, Charlotte Elizabeth *sociologist*

CONNECTICUT

Bridgeport
van der Kroef, Justus Maria *political science educator*

Brooklyn
Wendel, Richard Frederick *economist, educator, consultant*

Cos Cob
Nolte, Richard Henry *political science researcher, consultant*

Danbury
Chapin, Suzanne Phillips *retired psychologist*
Tolor, Alexander *psychologist, educator*
Weinstein, Sidney *neuropsychologist*

Fairfield
Brassil, Jean Ella *psychologist*

Hamden
Parker, William Nelson *economics educator*

Hartford
Curran, Ward Schenk *economist, educator*
Guay, Edward *financial economist, investment advisor*
Gunderson, Gerald Axel *economics educator, administrator*
Vohra, Ranbir *political scientist, educator*

Mansfield Center
Liberman, Alvin Meyer *psychology educator*

Middletown
Bailey, Debra Sue *psychologist, neuropsychologist*
Lovell, Michael C. *economics educator*
Miller, Richard Alan *economist, educator*
Scheibe, Karl Edward *psychology educator*

Milford
Taylor, Charles Henry *psychoanalyst, educator*

New Canaan
Marcus, Edward *economist, educator*

New Haven
Ames, Louise Bates *child psychologist*
Apter, David Ernest *political science educator*
Bell, Wendell *sociologist, educator, futurist*
Blatt, Sidney Jules *psychology educator, psychoanalyst*
Brainard, William Crittenden *economist, educator, university official*
Child, Irvin Long *psychologist, educator*
Clizbe, John Anthony *psychologist*
Coe, Michael Douglas *anthropologist, educator*
Conklin, Harold Colyer *anthropologist, educator*
Doob, Leonard William *psychology educator, academic administrator*
Ember, Melvin Lawrence *anthropology educator*
Erikson, Kai *sociologist, educator*
Garner, Wendell Richard *psychology educator*
Hsiao, James Chingnu *economics educator*
Kessen, William *psychologist, educator*
LaPalombara, Joseph *political science educator*
Levin, Richard Charles *economist*
MacAvoy, Paul Webster *economics educator, university dean*
†Marmor, Theodore Richard *political science and public management educator*
Mayhew, David Raymond *political educator*
Mc Guire, William James *social psychology educator*
Miller, Neal Elgar *psychologist, emeritus educator*
Myers, Jerome Keeley *sociology educator*
Phillips, Peter Charles Bonest *economist, educator, researcher*
Pospisil, Leopold Jaroslav *anthropology educator*
Ranis, Gustav *economist, educator*
Reiss, Albert John, Jr. *sociology educator*
Reynolds, Lloyd George *economist, educator*
Reynolds, Mary Trackett *political scientist*
Rouse, Irving *anthropologist, emeritus educator*
Scarf, Herbert Eli *economics educator*
Schultz, T. Paul *economics educator*
Shubik, Martin *economics educator*
Sims, Christopher Albert *economics educator*
Stevens, Joseph Charles *psychology educator*
Tobin, James *economics educator*
Wagner, Allan Ray *psychology educator, experimental psychologist*
Westerfield, Holt Bradford *political scientist, educator*

New London
Doro, Marion Elizabeth *political scientist, educator*

North Haven
Dahl, Robert Alan *political science educator*
Mahl, George Franklin *psychoanalyst, psychologist, educator*

Rowayton
Sills, David Lawrence *retired sociologist*

Southbury
Atwood, Edward Charles *economist, educator*
Wescott, Roger Williams *anthropologist*

Stamford
Teeters, Nancy Hays *economist*
Williams, Ernest William, Jr. *economist, educator*

Storrs
Allen, George James *psychologist, educator*
Allen, John Logan *geographer*
Walker, David Bradstreet *political science educator*

Storrs Mansfield
Denenberg, Victor Hugo *psychology educator*
Ladd, Everett Carll *political science educator, author*
Schwarz, J(ames) Conrad *psychology educator*

Westport
O'Leary, James John *economist*

Wilton
Freiherr von Kleydorff, Ludwig Otto Alexander *political scientist, consulting company executive*

DELAWARE

Lewes
Chapman, Janet Carter Goodrich (Mrs. John William Chapman) *economist, educator*

Newark
Bilinsky, Yaroslav *political scientist*
Brams, Marvin Robert *economist, mental health counselor, interfaith minister*
DiRenzo, Gordon James *sociologist, psychologist, educator*
Elterich, Joachim Gustav *agricultural economics educator*
Graham, Frances Keesler (Mrs. David Tredway Graham) *psychologist, educator*
Gulick, Walter Lawrence *psychologist, former college president*
Mangone, Gerard J. *international and maritime law educator*
Raffel, Jeffrey Allen *urban affairs educator*
Scarpitti, Frank Roland *sociology educator*
Tannian, Francis Xavier *economist, educator*

Wilmington
Adams, Wayne Verdun *pediatric psychologist*
Reeder, Charles Benton *economic consultant*

DISTRICT OF COLUMBIA

Washington
Aaron, Henry Jacob *economics educator*
Abler, Ronald Francis *geography educator*
Adams, Arvil Van *economist, educator*
Adams, Robert McCormick *anthropologist, educator*
Amling, Frederick *economist, educator, investment manager*
†Anderson, Bernard E. *economist*
Aschheim, Joseph *economist, educator*
Atiyeh, Naim Nicholas *psychologist, educator*
Ballentine, J. Gregory *economist*
†Banister, Judith *demographer, educator*
Barnes, Samuel Henry *political scientist, educator*
Barnett, Arthur Doak *political scientist, educator*
Barton, Jean Marie *psychologist, educator*
Becker, Mary Louise *political scientist*
Bergmann, Barbara Rose *economics educator*
Bergsten, C. Fred *economist*
Besen, Stanley Martin *economist*
Blaxall, Martha Ossoff *economist*
Blinder, Alan Stuart *economist*
Bloomfield, Arthur Irving *economics educator*
Bluth, B. J. (Elizabeth Jean Catherine Bluth) *sociologist, educator*
†Bohi, Douglas Ray *economist*
Bramson, Leon *social scientist, educator*
Brown, David Springer *retired public administration educator*
Brzezinski, Zbigniew *political science educator, author*
Burcroff, Richard Tomkinson, II *economist*
Burns, Joseph M. *economist*
Butterworth, Charles E. *political science educator*
Button, Kenneth Rodman *international economist, consultant*
Cantor, Muriel Goldsman *sociologist, educator*
Carliner, Michael Simon *economist, association executive*
Carpenter, Ted Galen *political scientist*
Cavanagh, John Henry *political economist*
Chambliss, William Joseph *sociologist*
Checchi, Vincent Victor *economist*
Chu, David S. C. *economist*
Cline, Ray Steiner *political scientist, historian*
Cline, William Richard *economist, educator*
Clodius, Robert LeRoy *economist, educator*
Coates, Joseph Francis *futurist*
Corden, Warner Max *economics educator*
Davis, Lynn Etheridge *political scientist, former government official*
Dawson, Mimi (Mimi Weyforth) *government affairs consultant, former government official*
de Leeuw, Frank *economist*
Dillon, Wilton Sterling *anthropologist, foundation administrator*
Dizard, Wilson Paul, Jr. *international affairs consultant, educator*
Dommen, Arthur John *agricultural economist*
Downs, Anthony *urban economist, real estate consultant*
Edwards, Gilbert Franklin *sociologist, educator*
English, Richard Allyn *sociologist, social work educator*
Etzioni, Amitai Werner *sociologist, educator*
†Faux, Jeff (Geoffrey Peter Faux) *economist, writer*
Feingold, S. Norman *psychologist*
†Fox-Penner, Peter Seth *economic consultant*
Frank, Isaiah *economist, educator*
Frankel, Jeffrey Alexander *economics educator, consultant*
Fuchs, Roland John *geography educator, university administrator*
Gabriel, Edward Michael *public affairs executive*
Galston, William Arthur *political scientist, educator*
Glauthier, T. James *environmental economist*
Goode, Richard Benjamin *economist, educator*
Greenberg, Milton *political scientist, educator*
Greenspan, Alan *economist*
Greenwood, Janet Kae Daly *psychologist, educational administrator*
Griffin, James Bennett *anthropologist, educator*
Gubser, Peter Anton *political scientist, writer, educator*
Gutierrez-Santos, Luis Emiliano *economist*
Haass, Richard Nathan *political science educator*
Harper, Robert Allan *consulting psychologist*
Hayes, Samuel Perkins *social scientist, educator*
Heginbotham, Erland Howard *international economist*
Helms, Robert Brake *economist, research director*
Hess, Stephen *political scientist, author*
Hickman, R(obert) Harrison *political pollster, strategist*
Holland, Robert Carl *economist*
Horowitz, Herbert Eugene *educator, consultant, former ambassador*
Hovey, Justus Allan, Jr. *political scientist*
Hudson, Michael Craig *political science educator*
Hufbauer, Gary Clyde *economist, lawyer, educator*
Jamme, Albert Joseph *archaeologist, educator*
Jasinowski, Jerry Joseph *economist, corporate executive*
Jaspersen, Frederick Zarr *economist*
Johnson, Omotunde Evan George *economist*
Johnson, Robert Henry *political science educator*
Jones, William Bowdoin *political scientist, retired diplomat, lawyer*
Kemp, Geoffrey Thomas Howard *international affairs specialist*
Kendrick, John Whitefield *economist, educator, consultant*
Khadduri, Majid *international studies educator*
†Kincaid, John *political science educator, editor*
Kirkpatrick, Jeane Duane Jordan *political scientist, government official*
Kling, William *economist, retired foreign service officer*
Korologos, Tom Chris *government affairs consultant, former federal official*
Kristol, Irving *social sciences educator, editor*
Krulfeld, Ruth Marilyn *anthropologist, educator*
Laden, Ben Ellis *economist*
LaRouche, Lyndon H., Jr. *economist*
Lauber, John K. *research psychologist*
Lefever, Ernest W. *political philosopher, author, former institute president*
LeoGrande, William Mark *political science educator, writer*
Liebenson, Herbert *economist, trade association executive*
Lin, William Wen-Rong *economist*
Lindsey, Lawrence Benjamin *economist*
Liska, George *political science educator, author*
Littig, Lawrence William *psychologist, educator*
Luttwak, Edward Nicolae *political science educator, writer, consultant*
Majors, Richard George *psychology educator*
Malmgren, Harald Bernard *economist*
Manatos, Andrew Emanuel *policy consultant, former government official*
Manley, William Tanner *economist*
Mann, Thomas Edward *political scientist*
Manvel, Allen Dailey *fiscal economist*
†Margolis, James David *political consulting and advertising executive*
Matalin, Mary *political consultant*
Maudlin, Robert V. *economics and government affairs consultant*
McElroy, Frederick William *economics educator, consultant*
McGinnies, Elliott Morse *psychologist, educator*
McGough, Duane Theodore *economist, government official*
Mead, David Edmund *economist*
Meggers, Betty J(ane) *anthropologist*
Mellor, John Williams *economist, policy consultant firm executive*
Millar, James Robert *economist, educator, university official*
Miller, James Clifford, III *economist*
Minarik, Joseph John *economist, researcher*
†Miranowski, John Alfred *agricultural economist*
Munnell, Alicia Haydock *economist*
Nehmer, Stanley *economics consultant*
Newman, Monroe *retired economist, educator*
Niskanen, William Arthur, Jr. *economist*
Norwood, Janet Lippe *economist*
O'Connell, Daniel Craig *psychology educator*
Oh, John Kie-Chiang *political science educator, university official*
Olson, Charles Eric *economist*
Ooms, Van Doorn *economist*
Ornstein, Norman Jay *political scientist*
Oswald, Rudolph A. *economist*
Oweiss, Ibrahim Mohamed *economist, educator*
Penner, Rudolph Gerhard *economist, educator*
Perry, George Lewis *research economist, consultant*
†Peterman, John L. *economist*
Peterson, William Herbert *economist*
Phillips, Susan Meredith *financial economist, former university administrator*
Polak, Jacques Jacobus *economist, foundation administrator*
Potvin, Raymond Herve *sociology educator, author*
Preeg, Ernest Henry *strategic and international studies center executive*
Prell, Michael Jack *economist*
Prestowitz, Clyde Vincent *economist, research administrator*
Quandt, William Bauer *political scientist*
Rahn, Richard William *economist, business executive*
Randall, Robert L(ee) *ecological economist*
Ravenal, Earl Cedric *international relations educator, author*
Reich, Bernard *political science educator*
Reich, Otto Juan *political analyst, business consultant*
Rettig, Richard Allen *social sciences educator, policy analyst, administrator*
Reynolds, Robert Joel *economist, consultant*
Riecken, Henry William *psychologist, research director*
Rivlin, Alice Mitchell *economist*
Roberts, John Benjamin, II *public policy consultant*
Roberts, Markley *economist, educator*
Roberts, Paul Craig, III *economics educator, author, consultant*
Roberts, Walter Ronald *political science educator, former government official*
Roett, Riordan *political science educator, consultant*
Rosenau, James Nathan *political scientist, author*
Rubin, Robert Edward *economic advisor to President of U.S.*
Ruttenberg, Stanley Harvey *economist*
Ryn, Claes Gösta *political science educator, author, research institute administrator*
Salant, Walter S. *economist*
Sanderson, Fred Hugo *economist*
Sawhill, Isabel Van Devanter *economist*
Scheppach, Raymond Carl, Jr. *association executive, economist*
Schlesinger, James Rodney *economist*
Schotta, Charles *economist, government official*
†Schulmann, Horst *international economist*
Schultze, Charles Louis *economist, educator*
Simes, Dimitri Konstantin *international affairs expert and educator*
Smith, Bruce David *archaeologist*
Smythe-Haith, Mabel Murphy *consultant on African economic development, speaker, writer*
Soldo, Beth Jean *demography educator, researcher*
Solomon, Richard Harvey *political scientist*
Solomon, Robert *economist*
Spiro, Benjamin Paul *economist, consultant*
Squier, Robert Dave *political consultant, documentary filmmaker*
Stanford, Dennis Joe *archaeologist, museum curator*
Stanley, Timothy Wadsworth *economist*
Stavrou, Nikolaos Athanasios *political science educator*
Stein, Herbert *economist*
Steiner, Gilbert Yale *political scientist*
Sterner, Michael Edmund *international affairs consultant*
Steuerle, C. Eugene *economist*
Stone, Russell A. *sociology educator*
Strauss, Elliott Bowman *economic development consultant, retired naval officer*
Sturtevant, William Curtis *anthropologist*
Sundquist, James Lloyd *political scientist*
Sunley, Emil McKee *economist*
Sweeney, Richard James *economics educator*
†Toder, Eric Jay *economist*
Van Beek, Gus Willard *archaeologist*
VandenBos, Gary Roger *psychologist, publisher*
Von Hippel, Frank Niels *public and international affairs educator*
Walinsky, Louis Joseph *economic consultant, writer*
Walker, Charls Edward *economist, consultant*
Wallis, W(ilson) Allen *economist, educator, statistician*
Whyte, Martin King *sociology and Chinese studies educator*
Wilensky, Gail Roggin *economist*
Winter, Sidney Graham, Jr. *economist, educator*
Woodward, Susan Ellen *economist, federal official*
Woroniak, Alexander *economist, educator*
Yochelson, John *political economist*

FLORIDA

Boca Raton
Feuerlein, Willy John Arthur *economist, educator*
Latané, Bibb *social psychologist*
Nystrom, John Warren *geographer, educator*
Wolgin, David Lewis *psychology educator*

Bradenton
Balsley, Howard Lloyd *economist*

Cape Coral
Shurrager, Phil Sheridan *psychologist, educator*

Coral Gables
Blasier, Cole *political scientist*
Jacobson, Leonard I. *psychologist, educator*
Shipley, Vergil Alan *political science educator*

Deerfield Beach
Faulk, Elizabeth Hammond *psychologist*

Dunnellon
Dixon, W(illiam) Robert *retired educational psychology educator*

Fort Lauderdale
Azrin, Nathan Harold *psychologist*
Bartelstone, Rona Sue *gerontologist*

Gainesville
Barton, Allen Hoisington *sociologist*
Bernard, H. Russell *anthropology educator, scientific editor*
Capaldi, Elizabeth Ann Deutsch *psychological sciences educator*
Carr, Glenna Dodson *economics educator*
Dewsbury, Donald Allen *comparative psychologist*
†Green, David Marvin *psychology educator, researcher, consultant*
Harris, Marvin *anthropology educator*
Milanich, Jerald Thomas *archaeologist, museum curator*
†Schmidt, Peter R. *anthropology educator*
Severy, Lawrence James *psychologist, educator*
†Smith, Stanley Kent *economics and demographics educator*
Teitelbaum, Philip *psychologist*
Thompson, Victor Alexander *political science educator*
von Mering, Otto Oswald *anthropology educator*
Wass, Hannelore Lina *educational psychology educator*
Zabel, Edward *economist, educator*

Hawthorne
Ross, James Elmer *economist, administrator*

Jacksonville
Coppotelli, H. Catherina *psychologist, consultant*
Godfrey, John Munro *bank economist*
Lloyd, Raymond Grann *economist, educator*
Moore, David Graham *sociologist, educator*

Jupiter
Biebuyck, Daniel Prosper *retired anthropologist, educator*

Maitland
Blackburn, John Oliver *economist, consultant*

Miami
Clarkson, Kenneth Wright *economics educator*
Gibby, Mabel Enid Kunce *psychologist*
Huysman, Arlene Weiss *psychologist, educator*
Routh, Donald K(ent) *psychology educator*
Russell, Elbert Winslow *neuropsychologist*
Salazar-Carrillo, Jorge *economics educator*
Yee, Albert Hoy *psychologist, educator*

Miami Beach
Chirovsky, Nicholas Ludomir *economics educator, historian, author*

Mount Dora
Myren, Richard Albert *criminal justice consultant*

Naples
Clark, Kenneth Edwin *psychologist, former university dean*
Myers, Charles Andrew *retired economist*

North Miami Beach
Averch, Harvey Allan *economist, educator, academic administrator*

Ocala
Killian, Ruth Selvey *home economist*

Pensacola
Killian, Lewis Martin *sociology educator*

Pompano Beach
Calatchi, Ralph Franklin *economist*

Saint Augustine
Armstrong, John Alexander *emeritus political science educator*
Theil, Henri *economist, educator*

Saint Petersburg
Serrie, Hendrick *anthropology and international business educator*

Sanibel
Crown, David Allan *criminologist, educator*

Sarasota
Fabrycy, Mark Zdzislaw *retired economist*
†Gordon, Sanford Daniel *economics educator*
Gurvitz, Milton Solomon *psychologist*
Hamberg, Daniel *economist, educator*
Roberts, Merrill Joseph *economist, educator*

South Miami
Bruel, Iris Barbara *psychologist*

Sun City Center
Hall, John Fry *psychologist, educator*

Tallahassee
Ashler, Philip Frederic *international trade and development advisor*
Brueckheimer, William Rogers *social science educator*
Colberg, Marshall Rudolph *economist*
Dye, Thomas Roy *political science educator*
Earhart, Eileen Magie *retired home and family life educator*
Glenn, Rogers *psychologist, student advisor, consultant*
Holcombe, Randall Gregory *economics educator*
Kenshalo, Daniel Ralph *psychologist, educator*
Laird, William Everette, Jr. *economics educator, administrator*
Macesich, George *econmomics professor*
Nam, Charles Benjamin *sociologist, demographer, educator*
Newell, Barbara Warne *economist, educator*
Paredes, James Anthony *anthropologist, educator*
†Pestle, Ruth Ellen *home economics educator*
†Serow, William John *economics educator*
Tuckman, Bruce Wayne *educational psychologist, educator, researcher*

Tampa
MacManus, Susan Ann *political science educator, researcher*

West Palm Beach
Kaslow, Florence W. *psychologist*
Katz, William David *psychologist, psychoanalytic psychotherapist, educator, mental health consultant*
Lively, Edwin Lowe *sociology educator*

Winter Garden
Clifford, Margaret Louise *psychologist*

GEORGIA

Athens
Barry, John Reagan *psychology educator*
Bullock, Charles Spencer, III *political science educator, author, consultant*
Clute, Robert Eugene *political and social science educator*
Dunn, Delmer Delano *political science educator*
Garbin, Albeno Patrick *sociology educator*
Kamerschen, David Roy *economist, educator*
Knapp, Charles Boynton *economist, educator, academic administrator*
Pavlik, William Bruce *psychologist, educator*
Peacock, Lelon James *psychologist, educator*
Smith, Howard Ross *economics educator, academic administrator, researcher, consultant*
†Tesser, Abraham *social psychologist*
Torrance, Ellis Paul *psychologist, educator*

Atlanta
Banks, Bettie Sheppard *psychologist*
Cameron, Rondo *economic history educator*
Drucker, Melvin Bruce *psychology educator*
Eber, Herbert Wolfgang *psychologist*
Mulaik, Stanley Allen *psychology educator*
Muth, Richard Ferris *economics educator*
Neisser, Ulric *psychology educator*
Nichols, William Curtis *psychologist, family therapist, consultant*
Payne, Maxwell Carr, Jr. *retired psychology educator*
Weiss, Jay M(ichael) *psychologist, educator*

Augusta
Zachert, Virginia *psychologist, educator*

Dunwoody
Cox, Albert Harrington, Jr. *economist*

Macon
Murdoch, Bernard Constantine *psychology educator*

Norcross
Conway, Hobart McKinley, Jr. *geo-economist*

Statesboro
Henry, Nicholas Llewellyn *political science educator, university administrator*

Valdosta
Branan, John Maury *psychology educator, counselor*

HAWAII

Hilo
Dixon, Paul William *psychology educator*
Wang, James Chia-Fang *political science educator*

Honolulu
Bitterman, Morton Edward *psychologist, educator*
Cho, Lee-Jay *social scientist, demographer*
Corsini, Raymond Joseph *psychologist*
Force, Roland Wynfield *anthropologist, museum executive*
Fullmer, Daniel Warren *psychologist, educator*
Hatfield, Elaine Catherine *psychology educator*
Mark, Shelley Muin *economist, educator*
Morse, Richard *social scientist*
Oksenberg, Michel Charles *political scientist, educator*
Paige, Glenn Durland *political scientist, educator*
†Rambo, A. Terry *anthropologist, research program director*
Schubert, Glendon *political scientist, educator*
Solheim, Wilhelm Gerhard, II *anthropologist, educator*
†Suh, Dae-Sook *political science educator*
Tuttle, Daniel Webster *retired political science educator*

Kailua Kona
Ashley, Darlene Joy *psychologist*

Kaneohe
Baker, Paul Thornell *anthropology educator*

Waianae
Pinckney, Neal Theodore *psychologist, educator*

IDAHO

Boise
Overgaard, Willard Michele *political scientist, jurisprudent*
Scudder, David Benjamin *economist, foundation administrator*

Caldwell
Lonergan, Wallace Gunn *economics educator, management consultant*

Moscow
Martin, Boyd Archer *political science educator emeritus*

Sandpoint
Glock, Charles Young *sociologist*

ILLINOIS

Carbondale
Best, Joel Gordon *sociology educator*
Derge, David Richard *political science educator*
†Eynon, Thomas Grant *sociology educator*
Handler, Jerome Sidney *anthropology educator*
Harper, Robert Alexander *geography educator*
Rubin, Harris B. *psychology educator*
Snyder, Charles Royce *sociologist, educator*
Somit, Albert *political educator*
Takayama, Akira *economics educator*

Champaign
Arnould, Richard Julius *economist, educator, consultant*
Brems, Hans Julius *economist, educator*
Davis, James Henry *psychology educator*
Due, John Fitzgerald *economist, educator emeritus*
Eriksen, Charles Walter *psychologist, educator*
Flanders, Dwight Prescott *economist*
Frankel, Marvin *economist, educator*
Humphreys, Lloyd Girton *research psychologist, educator*
Kanet, Roger Edward *political science educator, university administrator*
Kanfer, Frederick H. *psychologist, educator*
†Orr, Daniel *educator, economist*
Shupp, Franklin Richard *economist*
Sprenkle, Case Middleton *economics educator*

Charleston
Price, Dalias Adolph *geography educator*

Chicago
Aliber, Robert Z. *economist, educator*
†Annable, James Edward *economist*
Arditti, Fred D. *economist, educator*
Baum, Bernard Helmut *sociologist, educator*
Becker, Gary Stanley *economist, educator*
Bidwell, Charles Edward *sociologist, educator*
Boyce, David Edward *transportation and regional science educator*
Boyer, John William *history educator, dean*
Bradburn, Norman M. *behavioral science educator*
Braidwood, Linda Schreiber *archaeologist*
Braidwood, Robert J. *archaeologist, educator*
Burger, Mary Louise *psychologist, educator*
Butler, Robert Allan *psychologist, educator*
Carlton, Dennis William *economics educator*
Carney, Jean Kathryn *psychologist*
Chung, Joseph Sang-hoon *economics educator*
Coase, Ronald Harry *economics educator*
Cohen, Jerome *psychology educator*
Cohler, Bertram Joseph *social sciences educator, clinical psychologist*
Coleman, James Samuel *sociologist, educator*
Connors, Mary Eileen *psychologist*
Cox, Charles C. *economist*
Cropsey, Joseph *political science educator*
Dederick, Robert Gogan *economist*
†Depoy, Phil E. *spcial studies think-tank executive*
Duncan, Starkey Davis, Jr. *behavioral sciences educator*
Fogel, Robert William *economist, educator, historian*
Fogelson, Raymond David *anthropology educator*
Freeman, Leslie Gordon *anthropologist, educator*
Freeman, Susan Tax *anthropologist, educator*
Friedrich, Paul *anthropologist, linguist, poet*
Fromm, Erika (Mrs. Paul Fromm) *clinical psychologist*
Genetski, Robert James *economist*
Getzels, Jacob Warren *psychologist, educator*
Gibson, McGuire *archaeologist, educator*
Ginsburg, Norton Sydney *geography educator*
Goldiamond, Israel *experimental psychologist, educator*
Gould, John Philip, Jr. *economist, educator*
Graber, Doris Appel *political scientist, editor, author*
Gutmann, David Leo *psychology educator*
Hamada, Robert S(eiji) *economist, educator*
Harris, Chauncy Dennison *geographer, educator*
Hayes, William Aloysius *economics educator*
Heckman, James Joseph *economist, econometrician, educator*
†Hotz, V. Joseph *economics educator*
Johnson, David Gale *economist, educator*
Johnson, Janet Helen *Egyptology educator*
Kahan, Samuel D. *economist*
Kaplan, Morton A. *political science educator*
Kennedy, Eugene Cullen *psychology educator, writer*
Klarich, Nina Marie *economic development executive*
Kopel, David *psychologist, educator*
Laitin, David Dennis *political science educator*
Larson, Allan Louis *political scientist, educator, lay church worker*
Laumann, Edward Otto *sociology educator*
Levine, Donald Nathan *sociologist, educator*
Levy, Jerre Marie *psychobiology educator*
Liu, Ben-chieh *economist*
Lopata, Helena Znaniecka *sociologist, researcher, educator*
Malik, Raymond Howard *economist, scientist, corporate executive, multi-lingual, inventor, educator*
Marsh, Jeanne Cay *social welfare educator, researcher*
McNeill, G. David *psychologist, educator*
Mikesell, Marvin Wray *geography educator*
Mirza, David Brown *economist, educator*
Neugarten, Bernice Levin *social scientist*
Nicholas, Ralph Wallace *anthropologist, educator*
Peltzman, Sam *economics educator*
Pugh, Roderick Wellington *psychologist, educator*
Reed, Charles Allen *anthropologist*
Rosen, George *economist, educator*
Rosen, Sherwin *economist, educator*
Rosenberg, Milton J. *social psychologist, educator*
Rosenblum, Victor Gregory *political science and law educator*
Rudolph, Lloyd Irving *political science educator*
Rudolph, Susanne Hoeber *political and social science educator*
Rychlak, Joseph Frank *psychology educator, theoretician*
Scheinkman, José Alexandre *economics educator*
Scherer, Ross Paul *retired sociology educator*
Schloss, Nathan *economist*
Schultz, Theodore William *retired educator, economist*
Shanas, Ethel *sociology educator*
Simons, Helen *school psychologist, psychotherapist*
Smith, Raymond Thomas *anthropology educator*
Smith, Stan Vladimir *economist, financial service company executive*
Stocking, George Ward, Jr. *anthropology educator*
Stover, Leon (Eugene) *anthropology educator, writer, critic*
Sumner, William Marvin *anthropology and archaeology educator*
Taub, Richard Paul *social sciences educator*
Tongue, William Walter *economics and business consultant, educator emeritus*
Tsou, Tang *political science educator, researcher*
Walberg, Herbert John *psychologist, educator, consultant*
Walker, Ronald Edward *psychologist, educator*
†Warnecke, Richard Basley *sociologist, educational administrator*
Wilson, William Julius *sociologist, educator*
Wiser, James Louis *political science educator*
Wright, Benjamin Drake *psychology educator*
Zarnowitz, Victor *economist, educator*
Zonis, Marvin *political scientist, educator*

Des Plaines
Saporta, Jack *psychologist, educator*

Downers Grove
Gioioso, Joseph Vincent *psychologist*

East Saint Louis
Randolph, Robert Lee *economist, educator*

Edwardsville
Virgo, John Michael *economist, researcher, educator*

Elmhurst
Cureton, Bryant Lewis *political science educator, academic administrator*

Evanston
Crotty, William *political science educator*
Daniels, Arlene Kaplan *sociology educator*
Eisner, Robert *economics educator*
Fisher, Walter Dummer *economist, educator*
†Garbarino, James *psychologist*
Gordon, Robert James *economics educator*
Greenbaum, Stuart I. *economist, educator*
Hurter, Arthur Patrick *economist, educator*
Irons, William George *anthropology educator*
Jacob, Herbert *political science educator*
Janda, Kenneth Frank *political science educator*
Jencks, Christopher Sandys *sociology educator*
Moskos, Charles C. *sociology educator*
Page, Benjamin Ingrim *political science educator, researcher*
†Panzar, John C. *economist, educator, consultant*
Reiter, Stanley *economist, educator*
Sade, Donald Stone *anthropology educator*
Schnaiberg, Allan *sociology educator*
Weisbrod, Burton Allen *economist, educator*

Glen Ellyn
Frateschi, Lawrence Jan *economist, statistician, educator*

Great Lakes
Andrews, Carolyn Fraser *psychologist*

Highland Park
Haber, Ralph Norman *psychology educator*

Morton Grove
Farber, Isadore E. *psychologist, educator*

Normal
Jelks, Edward Baker *archaeologist, educator*

Olympia Fields
Sprinkel, Beryl Wayne *economist, consultant*

Palatine
Nagatoshi, Konrad R. *anthropology educator, information systems specialist*

Riverwoods
Kirby, Emily Baruch *psychologist, writer*

Romeoville
Mills, Jon K. *psychologist, educator*

South Holland
Poprick, Mary Ann *psychologist*

Springfield
Wehrle, Leroy Snyder *economist, educator*

University Park
Lingamneni, Jaganmohan Rao *criminology educator*

Urbana
Baer, Werner *economist, educator*
Bruner, Edward M. *anthropology educator*
Burdge, Rabel James *sociology educator*
Carmen, Ira Harris *political scientist, educator*
Cohen, Stephen Philip *political science and history educator*
Cunningham, Clark Edward *anthropology educator*
Dovring, Folke *land economics educator, consultant*
Due, Jean Margaret *agricultural economist, educator*
Gabriel, Michael *psychology educator*
Giertz, J. Fred *economics educator*
Giles, Eugene *anthropology educator*
Gorecki, Jan *sociologist, educator*
Gove, Samuel Kimball *political science educator*
Kolodziej, Edward Albert *political scientist, educator*
Leuthold, Raymond Martin *agricultural economics educator*
Linowes, David Francis *political economist, educator, corporate executive*
Nettl, Bruno *anthropology and musicology educator*
Parrish, John Bishop *economics educator*
Rich, Robert F. *political sciences educator, academic administrator*
Schmidt, Stephen Christopher *agricultural economist, educator*
Seitz, Wesley Donald *agricultural economics educator*
Spitze, Robert George Frederick *agricultural economics educator*
Van Arsdell, Paul Marion *economics and finance educator*
Wirt, Frederick Marshall *political scientist*
Yu, George Tzuchiao *political science educator*

Wilmette
Espenshade, Edward Bowman, Jr. *geographer, educator*

INDIANA

Bloomington
Adams, William Richard *archaeologist, lecturer, curator*
Bauman, Richard *anthropologist, educator*
Beckwith, Christopher Irving *social sciences educator, writer, composer*
Caldwell, Lynton Keith *social scientist, educator*
Diamant, Alfred *political science educator*
Dinsmoor, James Arthur *psychology educator*
Guth, Sherman Leon (S. Lee Guth) *psychologist, educator*
Heise, George Armstrong *psychologist, educator*
Hofstadter, Douglas Richard *cognitive, computer scientist, educator*
Leftwich, Richard Henry *economist, educator*
Muth, John Fraser *economics educator*
O'Meara, Patrick O. *political science educator*
Ostrom, Elinor *political science educator, researcher*
Ostrom, Vincent A(lfred) *political science educator*
Patrick, John Joseph *social sciences educator*
Schmidt, Nancy J. *anthropologist, educator*
Schuessler, Karl Frederick *sociologist, educator*
Smith, Frederick Robert, Jr. *social studies educator*
Spulber, Nicolas *economics educator emeritus*
Stolnitz, George Joseph *economist, educator, demographer*
von Furstenberg, George Michael *economics educator, researcher*

Columbus
Hackett, John Thomas *economist*

Evansville
Barber, Charles Turner *political science educator*

Indianapolis
Bonifield, William C. *economist, educator*
Herman, Barbara F. *psychologist*
Hingtgen, Joseph Nicholas *psychologist, neuroscientist, educator*
Hudnut, William Herbert, III *political scientist, fellow*
Reynolds, Alan Anthony *economist, writer, consultant*
Stone, Donald Crawford *public administrator, educator*

Monticello
Hardin, Lowell Stewart *retired economics educator*

Muncie
Carmin, Robert Leighton *retired geography educator*
Neiman, Lionel Joseph *sociologist, educator*
Sargent, Thomas Andrew *political science educator, university program director*
Swartz, B(enjamin) K(insell), Jr. *archaeologist, educator*

New Albany
Braden, Samuel Edward *economics educator*

North Manchester
Harshbarger, Richard B. *economics educator*

Notre Dame
Aldous, Joan *sociology educator*
Arnold, Peri Ethan *political scientist*
Craypo, Charles *labor economics educator*
Despres, Leo Arthur *sociology and anthropology educator, academic administrator*
Goulet, Denis André *political science educator, writer, development ethicist*
Hallinan, Maureen Theresa *sociologist*
Kennedy, John Joseph *political science educator*
Leege, David Calhoun *political scientist, educator*
Mirowski, Philip Edward *economics educator*
Valenzuela, Julio Samuel *sociologist, educator*

South Bend
Niemeyer, Gerhart *political science educator*

Terre Haute
Johnson, Jack Thomas *political science educator*
Mausel, Paul Warner *geography educator*
Puckett, Robert Hugh *political scientist, educator*

West Lafayette
Anderson, James George *sociologist, educator*
Brown, Donald Ray *psychologist, university administrator*
Caputo, David Armand *political scientist educator*
Cicirelli, Victor George *psychologist*
Eagly, Alice Hendrickson *social psychologist*
Farris, Paul Leonard *agricultural economist*
Feldhusen, John Frederick *educational psychology educator*
Gruen, Gerald Elmer *psychologist, educator*
Horwich, George *economist, educator*
King, Donald C. *psychologist, educator*
McGee, Reece Jerome *sociology educator, researcher*
Perrucci, Robert *sociologist, educator*
Schönemann, Peter Hans *psychology educator*
Schrader, Lee Frederick *agricultural economist*
Swensen, Clifford Henrik, Jr. *psychologist, educator*
Theen, Rolf Heinz-Wilhelm *political science educator*
Tyner, Wallace Edward *economics educator*
Weinstein, Michael Alan *political science educator*
Wilson, Franklin Leondus, III *political science educator*
Wright, Gordon Pribyl *management, operations research educator*

IOWA

Ames
Ahmann, John Stanley *psychology educator*
Benbow, Camilla Persson *psychology educator, researcher*
Brown, Frederick Gramm *psychology educator*
Edwards, David Charles *psychology educator*
Fox, Karl August *economist, eco-behavioral scientist*
Hadwiger, Don Frank *political science educator, researcher*
Harl, Neil Eugene *economist, lawyer, educator*
†Johnson, Stanley R. *economist, educator*
Klonglan, Gerald Edward *sociology educator*
†Starleaf, Dennis Roy *economics educator*

Des Moines
Miller, Kenneth Edward *sociologist, educator*

Iowa City
Albrecht, William Price *economist, educator, government official*
Barkan, Joel David *political science educator*
Brennan, Robert Lawrence *psychometrician*
Coffman, William Eugene *educational psychologist*
†Forsythe, Robert Elliott *economics educator*
†Green, William *archaeologist*
Helm, June *anthropologist, educator*
Knutson, John Franklin *psychology educator, clinical psychologist*
Krause, Walter *retired economics educator, consultant*
Loewenberg, Gerhard *political science educator*
Lopes, Lola Lynn *psychologist, educator*
Nathan, Peter E. *psychologist, educator*
Nicewander, Walter Alan *psychology educator*
Obermann, C. Esco *psychologist, rehabilitation consultant*
Ross, Russell Marion *political science educator*
Shannon, Lyle William *sociology educator*
Siebert, Calvin D. *economist, educator*
Wasserman, Edward Arnold *psychology educator*

Knoxville
Chang, Theodore Chien-Hsin *psychologist*
Joslyn, Wallace Danforth *psychologist*

Mason City
Rosenberg, Dale Norman *psychology educator*

Oskaloosa
Porter, David Lindsey *history and political science educator, author*

Windsor Heights
Demorest, Allan Frederick *psychologist, consultant*

KANSAS

Kansas City
Hall, R. Vance *psychology researcher, educator, administrator, consultant, business executive*

Lawrence
Augelli, John Pat *geography educator, author, consultant, rancher*
Baumgartel, Howard J., Jr. *psychology educator, academic administrator*
Heller, Francis H(oward) *law and political science educator emeritus*
Laird, Roy Dean *political science educator*
Lundsgaarde, Henry Peder *anthropology educator, researcher*
Martin, Edwin J(ohn) *psychologist*
†Schroeder, Stephen Robert *psychology researcher*
Sheridan, Richard Bert *economics educator*
Willner, Ann Ruth *political scientist, educator*

Manhattan
Babcock, Michael Ward *economics educator*
Hoyt, Kenneth Boyd *educational psychology educator*
†Johnson, Marc Anton *agricultural economics educator*
Murray, John Patrick *psychologist, educator, researcher*
Nafziger, Estel Wayne *economics educator*
Phares, E. Jerry *psychology educator*

Overland Park
Burger, Henry G. *anthropologist, vocabulary scientist, publisher*

Pittsburg
Behlar, Patricia Ann *political science educator*

Topeka
Spohn, Herbert Emil *psychologist*

Wichita
Clark, Susan Matthews *psychologist*

KENTUCKY

Bowling Green
Cangemi, Joseph Peter *psychologist, consultant, educator*
Cravens, Raymond Lewis *political science educator*
Kalab, Kathleen Alice *sociology educator*

Highland Heights
Hopgood, James F. *anthropologist*

Lexington
†Cole, Henry Philip *educational psychologist*
Davis, Vincent *political science educator*
Hochstrasser, Donald Lee *cultural anthropologist, community health and public administration educator*
Hultman, Charles William *economics educator*
Stober, William John, II *economics educator*
Straus, Robert *behavioral sciences educator*
Ulmer, Shirley Sidney *political science educator, researcher, consultant*
Worell, Judith P. *psychologist, educator*

Louisville
Baron, Martin Raymond *psychology educator*
Kelley, Noble Henry *former psychologist, educator*

LOUISIANA

Baton Rouge
Berg, Irwin August *psychology educator*
Geiselman, Paula Jeanne *psychologist*
Guedry, Leo J. *agricultural economics educator*
Riopelle, Arthur Jean *psychologist*
Smyth, David John *economist*
Timmons, Edwin O'Neal *psychologist*
West, Robert Cooper *geography educator*

Lafayette
Dur, Philip Francis *political science educator emeritus, retired foreign service officer*

Metairie
Falco, Maria Josephine *political scientist, academic administrator*

New Orleans
Boudreaux, Kenneth Justin *finance and economics educator, consultant*
Bricker, Harvey Miller *anthropology educator*
Bricker, Victoria Reifler *anthropology educator*
Corrigan, Robert Emmett *psychologist*
Edmonson, Munro Sterling *anthropologist, educator*
Freudenberger, Herman *retired economics educator*
Jacobsen, Thomas Warren *archaeologist, educator*
Makielski, Stanislaw John, Jr. *political science educator*
Mason, Henry Lloyd *political science educator*
Olson, Richard David *psychology educator*
O'Neal, Edgar Carl *psychology educator*
Robins, Robert Sidwar *political science educator, administrator*
Wilford, Walton Terry *economics educator*

New Roads
Haag, William George *anthropologist, educator*

Ruston
Sale, Tom S., III *financial economist, educator*

Shreveport
Hall, John Whitling *geography educator*
Pederson, William David *political scientist, educator*

Slaughter
Gremillion, Curtis Lionel, Jr. *psychologist, hospital administrator, musician*

Thibodaux
Chotigeat, Tosporn *economist, educator*

MAINE

Auburn
Phillips, Charles Franklin *economic consultant*

Augusta
Nickerson, John Mitchell *political science educator*

Bangor
Mills, David Harlow *psychologist, association executive*

Brunswick
Fuchs, Alfred Herman *psychologist, college dean, educator*
Morgan, Richard Ernest *political scientist, educator*

Camden
Weidman, Hazel Hitson *anthropologist, educator*

Canaan
Walker, Willard Brewer *anthropology educator, linguist*

Kittery Point
Howells, William White *anthropology educator*

Lewiston
Murray, Michael Peter *educator, economist*

Orono
Devino, William Stanley *economist, educator*
Goldstone, Sanford *psychology educator*

Portland
Durgin, Frank Albert, Jr. *economics educator*

Surry
Pickett, Betty Horenstein *psychologist*

Trenton
Kates, Robert William *geographer, educator, scholar*

Waterville
Gemery, Henry Albert *economics educator*
Rohrman, Nicholas Leroy *psychologist, educator, consultant*

MARYLAND

Adamstown
Ohlke, Clarence Carl *public affairs consultant*

Baltimore
Achinstein, Asher *economist*
Bright, Margaret *sociologist*
Catania, A(nthony) Charles *psychology educator*
Chapanis, Alphonse *human factors engineer, ergonomist*
Cooper, Joseph *political scientist, educator*
Dietze, Gottfried *political science educator*
Engel, Bernard Theodore *psychologist, educator*
Entwisle, Doris Roberts *sociology educator*
Gaber, Robert *psychologist*
Ginsberg, Benjamin *political science educator*
Goedicke, Hans *archeology educator*
Graves, Pirkko Maija-Leena *clinical psychologist, psychoanalyst*
Henderson, Lenneal Joseph, Jr. *political science educator*
Holley, Lauren Allana *psychologist*
Howard, J. Woodford, Jr. *political science educator*
Hulse, Stewart Harding, Jr. *educator, experimental psychologist*
Karni, Edi *economics educator*
Klarman, Herbert Elias *economist, educator*
Kohn, Melvin L. *sociologist*
Lamy, Peter Paul *gerontologist, educator*
Mintz, Sidney Wilfred *anthropologist*
Money, John William *psychologist*
†Salamon, Lester Milton *political science educator*
Sorkin, Alan Lowell *economist, educator*
Stanley, Julian Cecil, Jr. *psychology educator*
Wolman, M. Gordon *geography educator*

Bethesda
Baldwin, Wendy Harmer *social demographer*
Banik, Sambhu Nath *psychologist*
Berns, Walter Fred *political scientist, educator*
Bowles, Walter Donald *economist, educator*
Cooper, Merri-Ann *psychologist*
de Vries, Margaret Garritsen *economist*
Ferris, Frederick Joseph *gerontologist, social worker*
Gates, Theodore Ross *economic consultant*
Hyson, Charles David *economist, consultant*
Kingsley, Thomas Drowne *economist*
Kleine, Herman *economist*
Lystad, Mary Hanemann (Mrs. Robert Lystad) *sociologist, author, consultant*
Mishkin, Mortimer *neuropsychologist*
Parry, Hugh Jones (James Cross) *social scientist, educator, author*
Raullerson, Calvin Henry *political scientist, consultant*
Riley, Matilda White (Mrs. John W. Riley, Jr.) *sociology educator*
Schwartz, Charles Frederick *economist, consultant*
Spangler, Miller Brant *science and technology analyst, planner, consultant*
Striner, Herbert Edward *economics educator*
Teitel, Simon *economist*
Trumbull, Richard *psychologist*
Willner, Dorothy *anthropologist, educator*

Bradshaw
Chisholm, Carol Lee *research psychologist*

Cabin John
Gallagher, Hugh Gregory *government affairs author, consultant*

Chevy Chase
Crawford, Meredith Pullen *research psychologist*
Emery, Robert Firestone *economist, educator*
Geber, Anthony *economist, retired foreign service officer*
Riley, John Winchell, Jr. *consulting sociologist*
Scammon, Richard Montgomery *political scientist*
Walk, Richard David *retired psychology educator*
Wallerstein, Leibert Benet *economist*

College Park
Coughlin, Peter Joseph *economics educator, researcher*
Davidson, Roger H(arry) *political scientist, educator*
Destler, I. M(ac) *political scientist, foreign policy writer*
Gaylin, Ned L. *psychology educator*
Gurr, Ted Robert *political science educator, author*
Just, Richard Eugene *agricultural and resource economics educator*
Locke, Edwin Allen, III *psychologist, educator*
Nerlove, Marc Leon *economics educator*
Olson, Mancur Lloyd *economics educator*
Piper, Don Courtney *political science educator*
Presser, Harriet Betty *sociology educator*
Quester, George Herman *political science educator*
Schelling, Thomas Crombie *economist, educator*
Schneider, Benjamin *psychology educator*
Sigall, Harold Fred *psychology educator*
Simon, Julian Lincoln *economics educator*
Ulmer, Melville Jack *economist, educator*
Williams, Aubrey Willis *anthropology educator*
Winik, Jay B. *political scientist, writer, consultant*

Emmitsburg
Nakhleh, Emile A. *governmental sciences educator*

Frostburg
Heckert, Paul Charles *sociologist, educator*

Gaithersburg
Ross, Sherman *psychologist, educator*

Glen Echo
Simpson, Robert Edward *economist, consultant*

Hyattsville
Herrmann, Douglas J. *psychology educator, researcher*

Landover
Colyer, Sheryl Lynn *psychologist*

Mitchellville
Blough, Roy *retired economist*

Potomac
Jones, Sidney Lewis *economist, government official*
Mc Bryde, Felix Webster *geographer, ecologist, consultant*

Rockville
Blankenheimer, Bernard *economics consultant*
Brumback, Gary Bruce *industrial and organizational psychologist*
Fischetti, Michael *public administration educator, arbitrator*
Knox, C. Neal *political and governmental affairs consultant, writer*
Pollard, George Marvin *economist*
Snyder, Marvin *neuropsychologist*
Wonnacott, (Gordon) Paul *economics educator*

Silver Spring
Gilbert, Arthur Charles Francis *psychologist*
Hsueh, Chun-tu *political science educator, foundation executive*
Milligan, Glenn Ellis *psychologist*
Rayburn, Carole (Mary Aida) Ann *psychologist, researcher, writer*
Schaaf, C(arl) Hart *economic consultant, writer, former international organization official*

Suitland
†Green, Gordon Woodrow, Jr. *economist, federal agency administrator*

Temple Hills
Day, Mary Jane Thomas *cartographer*

Towson
Muuss, Rolf Eduard *psychologist, educator*

MASSACHUSETTS

Amherst
Alfange, Dean, Jr. *political science educator*
Arkes, Hadley P. *political science and jurisprudence educator*
Averill, James Reed *psychology educator*
Babb, Lawrence Alan *anthropology educator*
Beals, Ralph Everett *economist, educator*
Berger, Seymour Maurice *social psychologist*
Demerath, Nicholas Jay, III *sociology educator*
Goldman, Sheldon *political science educator*
Grose, Robert Freeman *psychology educator*
Klare, Michael Thomas *social science educator, program director*
Nicholson, Walter *economist, educator*
Rossi, Alice S. *sociology educator, author*
Sarat, Austin D. *jurisprudence and political science educator*
Strickland, Bonnie Ruth *psychologist, educator*
Taubman, William Chase *political science educator*
Woodbury, Richard Benjamin *anthropologist, educator*

Andover
Mac Neish, Richard Stockton *archaeologist, educator*

Babson Park
Genovese, Francis Charles (Frank Genovese) *economist, consultant, editor*

Belmont
Bergson, Abram *economist, educator*
Levendusky, Philip George *clinical psychologist, administrator*

Boston
Abt, Clark C. *social scientist, executive, engineer, publisher, educator*
Amy-Moreno de Toro, Angel Alberto *social sciences educator, writer, oral historian*
Baer, Michael Alan *political scientist, educator*
Bustin, Edouard Jean *political scientist, educator*
Cheever, Daniel Sargent *international affairs educator, editor*
Copeland, Anne Pitcairn *psychologist*
Dentler, Robert Arnold *sociologist, educator*
Fieleke, Norman Siegfried *economist*
Gabel, Creighton *anthropologist, educator*
Gamson, Zelda *sociologist, researcher*
†Gamst, Frederick Charles *anthropology educator*
Gleason, Jean Berko *psychology educator*
†Goodglass, Harold *psychologist, neurology educator*
Grossman, Frances Kaplan *psychologist*
Hammond, Norman David Curle *archaeology educator, researcher*
Horowitz, Morris A. *economist*
Kubzansky, Philip Eugene *environmental and organizational psychologist*
Kurzweil, Edith *sociology educator, editor*
Levine, Sol *sociologist*
Markham, Jesse William *economist*
Melbin, Murray *sociologist*
Merton, Robert C. *economist, educator*
Newhouse, Joseph Paul *economics educator*
Norton, Augustus Richard *political science educator*
O'Hern, Jane Susan *psychologist, educator*
Psathas, George *sociologist, educator*
Rossell, Christine Hamilton *political science educator*
Sanders, Irwin Taylor *sociology educator*
Sinai, Allen Leo *economist, educator*
†Torto, Raymond Gerald *economist*
Wechsler, Henry *research psychologist*

Brookline
Cromwell, Adelaide M. *sociology educator*

Cambridge
Alker, Hayward Rose *political science educator*
Alonso, William *population studies educator, demographer*
Alt, James Edward *political science educator*
Appley, Mortimer Herbert *psychologist, university president emeritus*
Bales, Robert Freed *social psychologist, educator*

Banfield, Edward Christie political science educator
Barro, Robert Joseph economics educator, consultant
Bator, Francis Michel economist, educator
Bell, Daniel sociologist
Berliner, Joseph Scholom economics educator
†Berndt, Ernst Rudolf economist, educator
Bishop, Robert Lyle economist, educator
Blackmer, Donald Laurence Morton political scientist
Bloomfield, Lincoln Palmer political scientist
Brown, Edgar Cary retired economics educator
Brown, Roger William psychologist, educator
†Carliner, Geoffrey Owen economist, director
Chall, Jeanne Sternlicht psychologist, educator
Champion, (Charles) Hale political science educator, former public official
Chang, Kwang-Chih anthropologist, educator
Colby, Anne psychologist
Cooper, Richard Newell economist, educator
Coser, Lewis Alfred sociology educator
Domar, Evsey David economics educator
Dominguez, Jorge Ignacio government educator
Dorfman, Robert economics educator
Dornbusch, Rudiger economics educator
Dunlop, John Thomas economics educator, former secretary of labor
Eckaus, Richard Samuel economist, educator
Estes, William Kaye psychologist, educator
Feldstein, Martin Stuart economist, educator
Fischer, Stanley economics educator
Fisher, Franklin Marvin economist
Friedman, Benjamin Morton economics educator
Frisch, Rose Epstein population sciences researcher
Galbraith, John Kenneth retired economist
Gardner, Howard Earl psychologist, author
Gilligan, Carol psychologist, writer
Glazer, Nathan sociologist, educator
Goldin, Claudia Dale economics educator
Green, Jerry Richard economist, educator
Griliches, Zvi educator, economist
Hart, Oliver D'Arcy economics educator
Hausman, Jerry Allen economics educator, consultant
Herrnstein, Richard Julius psychology educator
Holbik, Karel economics educator
Holzman, Philip Seidman psychologist, educator
Houthakker, Hendrik S(amuel) economics educator, consultant
Hsiao, William C. economist, actuary, educator
Huntington, Samuel Phillips political science educator
Jacoby, Henry Donnan economist, educator
Johnson, Willard Raymond political science educator, consultant
Jorgenson, Dale Weldeau economist, educator
Joskow, Paul Lewis economist, educator
Kagan, Jerome psychologist, educator
Kaysen, Carl economics educator
Kennedy, Stephen Dandridge economist, researcher
Keyfitz, Nathan educator, sociologist, demographer
Kilson, Martin Luther, Jr. government educator
Kleinman, Arthur Michael medical anthropologist, psychiatrist, educator
Krugman, Paul Robin economics educator
Lamberg-Karlovsky, Clifford Charles anthropologist, archaeologist
Langer, Ellen Jane psychologist, educator, writer
LeVine, Robert Alan anthropology educator, researcher
Levinson, Harry psychologist, educator
Lieberson, Stanley sociologist, educator
Maass, Arthur political science and environmental studies educator
Maher, Brendan Arnold psychology educator, editor
Medoff, James Lawrence economics educator
Meyer, John Robert economist, educator
Miller, S(eymour) M(ichael) sociology educator
Mitten, David Gordon classical archaeologist
Montgomery, John Dickey political science educator
Moore, Mark Harrison criminal justice, public policy educator
Moore, Sally Falk anthropology educator
Neustadt, Richard Elliott political scientist, educator
†Oye, Kenneth A. political scientist, educator
Patterson, Orlando sociologist
Peattie, Lisa Redfield urban anthropology educator
Perkins, Dwight Heald economics educator
Pilbeam, David Roger paleoanthropology educator
Polenske, Karen Rosel economics educator
Price, Don K. political science educator
Pye, Lucian Wilmot political science educator
Rathjens, George William political scientist, educator
Robinson, Marguerite Stern anthropologist, educator, consultant
Rosenthal, Robert psychology educator
Rosovsky, Henry economist, educator
Rubin, Jeffrey Zachary psychologist, educator
Samuelson, Paul Anthony economics educator
Sapolsky, Harvey Morton political scientist, educator
Schacter, Daniel Lawrence psychology educator
Scherer, Frederic Michael economics educator
Schmalensee, Richard Lee economist, former government official, educator
Schneider, Gerald Edward neuroscience and animal behavior educator
†Sen, Amartya Kumar economist
Skolnikoff, Eugene B. political science educator
Solow, Robert Merton economist, educator
Stager, Lawrence E. archeologist, educator
Swets, John Arthur psychologist, scientist
Tambiah, Stanley Jeyarajah anthropologist
Thompson, Dennis Frank political science and ethics educator, consultant
Thurow, Lester Carl economics educator
Timmer, Charles Peter agricultural economist
Ulam, Adam B. history and political science educator
van der Merwe, Nikolaas Johannes archaeologist
Verba, Sidney political scientist, educator
Vernon, Raymond economist, educator
Vogel, Ezra F. sociology educator
Vogt, Evon Zartman, Jr. anthropologist
Weiner, Myron political science educator
Willie, Charles Vert sociology educator
Wrangham, Richard Walter anthropology educator
Zeidenstein, George population educator
Zinberg, Dorothy Shore science policy educator

Chestnut Hill
Belsley, David Alan economics educator, consultant
Kane, Edward James economics educator

Cohasset
Campbell, John Coert political scientist, author

East Orleans
Hallowell, Burton Crosby economist, educator

Fitchburg
Wiegersma, Nan economics educator

Lenox
Pierson, John Herman Groesbeck economist, writer

Leverett
Barkin, Solomon economist

Lexington
Bell, Carolyn Shaw economist, educator
Bernardi, John Lawrence, Jr. economic historian, educator, consultant
Chaskelson, Marsha Ina neuropsychologist
Holzman, Franklyn Dunn economics educator
Kindleberger, Charles P., II economist, educator
Papanek, Gustav Fritz economist, educator

Lincoln
Barrett, Beatrice Helene psychologist

Medford
Conklin, John Evan sociology educator
Elkind, David psychology educator
Luria, Zella Hurwitz psychology educator
Miczek, Klaus Alexander psychology educator

Nantucket
Murray, Caroline Fish psychologist

Natick
Bensel, Carolyn Kirkbride psychologist

Needham
Cantor, Pamela Corliss psychologist

Newton
Manners, Robert Alan anthropologist
White, Burton Leonard educational psychologist, author

Northampton
Crosby, Faye Jacqueline psychology educator, author
Lehmann, Phyllis Williams archaeologist, educator
Robinson, Donald Leonard social scientist, educator
Rose, Peter Isaac sociologist, writer
Volkmann, Frances Cooper psychologist, educator

South Dartmouth
Stern, T. Noel political scientist, educator

Waltham
Altman, Stuart Harold economist
Brown, Seyom international relations educator, government consultant
Evans, Robert, Jr. economics educator
Kunkel, Barbara psychologist, consultant, educator
McCulloch, Rachel economics educator
Morant, Ricardo Bernardino psychology educator
Petri, Peter Alexander economist, educator, director
Ross, George William social scientist, educator
Sekuler, Robert William psychology educator, scientist
Weckstein, Richard Selig economics consultant
Young, Dwight Wayne ancient civilization educator, rancher

Wayland
Hagenstein, Perry Reginald economist
Wolf, Irving clinical psychologist

Wellesley
Eilts, Hermann Frederick international relations educator, former diplomat
Miller, Linda B. political scientist

West Tisbury
Smith, Henry Clay retired psychology educator

Weston
Fine, Bernard J. retired psychologist, consultant
Kraft, Gerald economist

Williamstown
Bolton, Roger Edwin economist, educator
Crider, Andrew Blake psychologist
Goethals, George R., II psychology educator
Hastings, Philip Kay psychology educator
McGill, Thomas Emerson psychology educator
Sheahan, John Bernard economist, educator
Winston, Gordon Chester economic educator, former academic administrator

Worcester
Hanson, Susan Easton geography educator
Wapner, Seymour psychologist, educator, administrator

MICHIGAN

Adrian
Weathers, Milledge Wright retired economics educator

Ann Arbor
†Anderson, Barbara A. sociologist, educator
Apperson, Jean psychologist
†Barbarin, Oscar Anthony psychologist
Bornstein, Morris economist, educator
Burling, Robbins anthropologist, educator
Cannell, Charles Frederick psychologist, educator
†Cohen, Malcolm Stuart economist, research institute director
Douvan, Elizabeth social psychologist, educator
Eron, Leonard David psychology educator
Fifield, Russell Hunt political science educator
Freedman, Ronald sociology educator
Fusfeld, Daniel Roland economist
Gomberg, Edith S. Lisansky psychologist, educator
†Gramlich, Edward Martin public policy, economics educator
Grassmuck, George Ludwig political science educator
Hagen, John William psychology educator
Holbrook, Robert Sumner economist, educator
†House, James Stephen social psychologist, educator
Howrey, Eugene Philip economics educator, consultant
Jackson, James Sidney psychology educator
Jacobson, Harold Karan political science educator, researcher
Johnson, Harold R. social work and gerontology educator, academic administrator
Johnston, Lloyd Douglas social scientist
Kalisch, Philip A. social science educator
Kelly, Raymond Case anthropology educator
Kingdon, John Wells political science educator
Livingstone, Frank Brown anthropologist, educator
Manis, Melvin psychologist, educator
Mc Cracken, Paul Winston economist, business educator
Mc Keachie, Wilbert James psychologist, educator
Meyer, Alfred George political science educator
Mitchell, Edward John economist, retired educator
Morgan, James Newton research economist, educator
Nisbett, Richard Eugene psychology educator
Organski, Abramo Fimo Kenneth political scientist, educator
†Paige, Jeffery Mayland sociologist, educator
Parsons, Jeffrey Robinson anthropologist, educator
Pedley, John Griffiths archaeologist, educator
Pierce, Roy political science educator
Schuman, Howard sociologist, educator
Singer, Joel David political science educator
Smith, J(ames) E(verett) Keith psychologist, educator
Stafford, Frank Peter, Jr. economics educator, consultant
Steiner, Peter Otto economics educator, dean
Stevenson, Harold William psychology educator
Stolper, Wolfgang Friedrich retired economist, educator
Varian, Hal Ronald economics educator
†Zajonc, Robert B(oleslaw) psychology educator
Zimmerman, William political science educator
Zucker, Robert A(lpert) psychologist

Berrien Springs
Stokes, Charles Junius economist, educator

Beverly Hills
Landuyt, Bernard Francis economist, educator

Big Rapids
Santer, Richard Arthur geography educator
Weinlander, Max Martin retired psychologist

Buchanan
French, Robert Warren economics educator emeritus, writer, consultant

Detroit
Baba, Marietta Lynn business anthropologist
Cantoni, Louis Joseph psychologist, poet, sculptor
Eads, George Curtis economics executive
Goodman, Allen Charles economics educator
Gould, Wesley Larson political science educator
Kaplan, Bernice Antoville anthropologist, educator
Lasker, Gabriel Ward anthropologist, educator
Marx, Thomas George economist
Spencer, Milton Harry economics and finance educator
Weiss, Mark Lawrence anthropology educator

East Lansing
Abeles, Norman psychologist, educator
Abramson, Paul Robert political scientist, educator
Allen, Bruce Templeton economics educator
Axinn, George Harold rural sociology educator
Fisher, Ronald C. economics educator
Ilgen, Daniel Richard psychology educator
Kreinin, Mordechai Eliahu economics educator
Larrowe, Charles Patrick economist, educator
Lowry, Sheldon Gaylon sociology educator, marriage and family counselor
Manderscheid, Lester Vincent agricultural economics educator
Manning, Peter Kirby sociology educator
Papsidero, Joseph Anthony social scientist, educator
Poland, Robert Paul business educator, consultant
Press, Charles retired political science educator
Rasche, Robert Harold economics educator
Ricks, Donald Jay agricultural economist
Robbins, Lawrence Harry anthropologist
Schlesinger, Joseph Abraham political scientist
Smith, Victor Earle economist, educator
Sommers, Lawrence Melvin geographer, educator
Strassmann, W. Paul economics educator
Suits, Daniel Burbidge economist
Useem, John Hearld sociologist, anthropologist
Useem, Ruth Hill sociology educator
Winder, Clarence Leland psychologist, educator

Farmington
Baker, Edward Martin engineering and industrial psychologist

Fraser
Kirjas, Zoran Nikola economist

Grand Rapids
Emery, Marcia Rose parapsychologist, psychologist, consultant

Hancock
Dresch, Stephen Paul economist, state legislator

Holland
Hountras, Peter Timothy psychologist, educator

Kalamazoo
Griffeth, Paul Lyman retired educator
Thomas, Philip Stanley economics educator

Lansing
Ballbach, Philip Thornton political consultant

Marquette
Carlson, David Leroy political science educator

Monroe
Heselton, Patricia Ann clinical psychologist

Mount Pleasant
Grabinski, Carol Joanne gerontologist, educator
Meltzer, Bernard N(athan) sociologist, educator

Okemos
Killingsworth, Charles Clinton economist
Solo, Robert Alexander economist, educator

Royal Oak
Karavite, Carlene Marie psychologist, real estate property manager

Sault Sainte Marie
Johnson, Gary Robert political scientist, editor

Ypsilanti
Weinstein, Jay A. social science educator, researcher

MINNESOTA

Duluth
Lease, Martin Harry, Jr. political science educator

Forest Lake
Marchese, Ronald Thomas ancient history and archaeology educator

Marshall
Libby, Ronald Theodore political science educator, consultant, researcher

Minneapolis
Adams, John Stephen geography educator
Baum, David Roy research psychologist
Berscheid, Ellen S. psychology educator, author, researcher
Bouchard, Thomas Joseph, Jr. psychology educator, researcher
Chipman, John Somerset economist, educator
Cleveland, (James) Harlan political scientist, public affairs executive
Corcoran, Mary Elizabeth educational psychology educator emeritus
Cummings, Larry Lee psychologist, educator
Dawis, René V. psychology educator, research consultant
Erickson, W(alter) Bruce business and economics educator, entrepreneur
Fulton, Robert Lester sociology educator
Garmezy, Norman psychology educator
Gerlach, Luther Paul anthropologist
Geweke, John Frederick economics educator
Gray, Virginia Hickman political science educator
Gudeman, Stephen Frederick anthropology educator
Holt, Robert Theodore political scientist, dean, educator
Hurwicz, Leonid economist, educator
Johnson, David Wolcott psychologist, educator
Knoke, David Harmon sociology educator
Krislov, Samuel political science educator
Kudrle, Robert Thomas economist, educator
Meehl, Paul Everett psychologist, educator
Porter, Philip Wayland geography educator
Reiss, Ira Leonard sociology educator, writer
Rogers, William Cecil political science educator
Schofield, William psychologist, educator
Schreiner, John Christian economics consultant, software publisher
Scoville, James Griffin economics educator
Shively, William Phillips political scientist, educator
Ward, David Allen sociology educator
Wiener, Daniel Norman psychologist
Ysseldyke, James Edward psychology educator, research center administrator
Zaidi, Mahmood A. economics educator

Moorhead
Noblitt, Harding Coolidge political scientist, educator
Sun, Li-Teh economics educator
Trainor, John Felix economics educator

Morris
Kemble, Ernest Dell psychology educator

Northfield
Clark, William Hartley political science educator
Lamson, George Herbert economics educator
Will, Robert Erwin economics educator

Saint Louis Park
Gerike, Ann Elizabeth psychologist

Saint Paul
Dahl, Reynold Paul agricultural economics educator
Jessup, Paul Frederick financial economist, educator
Peterson, Willis Lester economics educator
Rossmann, Jack Eugene psychology educator
Ruttan, Vernon Wesley agricultural economist

Saint Peter
Mc Rostie, Clair Neil economics educator

Scandia
Borchert, John Robert geography educator

MISSISSIPPI

Gulfport
Jones, Carol Ann psychology educator

Hattiesburg
Burrus, John N(ewell) sociology educator
Noblin, Charles Donald clinical psychologist, educator

Jackson
Dubbert, Patricia Marie psychologist

Mississippi State
Clynch, Edward John political science educator, researcher
Leyden, Dennis Roger economics educator

Starkville
Loftin, Marion Theo sociologist, educator

University
Cooker, Philip George psychology educator

MISSOURI

Bolivar
Jackson, James Larry recreation educator

Columbia
Biddle, Bruce Jesse social psychologist, educator
Breimyer, Harold Frederick agricultural economist
Bunn, Ronald Freeze political science educator, lawyer
Dolliver, Robert Henry psychology educator
Gavan, James Anderson anthropologist, educator
Kausler, Donald Harvey psychology educator
Kiesler, Charles Adolphus psychologist, academic administrator
LoPiccolo, Joseph psychologist, educator, author
Ratti, Ronald Andrew economics educator
Rowlett, Ralph Morgan archaeologist, educator
Twaddle, Andrew Christian sociology educator
Yarwood, Dean Lesley political science educator

Grandview
Justesen, Don Robert psychologist

Kansas City
Lubin, Bernard psychologist, educator
Skidmore, Max Joseph political science educator
Ward, John Orson economics educator, consultant

Rolla
Irion, Arthur Lloyd psychologist, educator

Saint Louis
Barnett, William Arnold economics educator
Beck, Lois Grant anthropologist, educator
Browman, David L(udvig) archaeologist
Du Bois, Philip Hunter psychologist, educator
Etzkorn, K. Peter sociologist, educator, author
Hedlund, James Lane retired psychologist, educator
Hirsh, Ira Jean psychology educator, researcher
Kagan, Sioma economics educator
Kling, Merle political scientist, university official
Leven, Charles Louis economics educator
Le Vine, Victor Theodore political science educator
Merbaum, Michael psychology educator, clinical psychologist
Miller, Gary J. political economist
Neuefeind, Wilhelm economics educator, university administrator
North, Douglass Cecil economist, educator
Ozawa, Martha Naoko social work educator
Pittman, David Joshua sociologist, educator, researcher, consultant
Rosenzweig, Saul psychologist, educator, administrator
Salisbury, Robert Holt political science educator
Storandt, Martha psychologist
Watson, Patty Jo anthropology educator
Weidenbaum, Murray Lew economics educator
Witherspoon, William investment economist
Worseck, Raymond Adams economist

Springfield
Stone, Allan David economics educator
Van Cleave, William Robert international relations educator

MONTANA

Bozeman
Gray, Philip Howard psychologist, educator
Refsland, Gary Arlan retired sociology educator
Spencer, Robert C. political science educator
Stroup, Richard Lyndell economics educator, writer

Missoula
Ammons, Robert Bruce psychologist, behavior consultant
Lopach, James Joseph political science educator
Power, Thomas Michael economist, educator
Watkins, John Goodrich psychologist, educator

NEBRASKA

Alliance
Haefele, Edwin Theodore political theorist, consultant

Lincoln
Babchuk, Nicholas sociology educator, researcher
MacPhee, Craig Robert economist, educator
Ottoson, Howard Warren agricultural economist, former university administrator
Peterson, Wallace Carroll, Sr. economics educator
Sonderegger, Theo Brown psychology educator

Omaha
Gugas, Chris, Sr. criminologist, polygraphist, author
Wunsch, James Stevenson political science educator

NEVADA

East Ely
Alderman, Minnis Amelia psychologist, educator, small business owner

Las Vegas
Goodall, Leonard Edwin public administration educator
Hardbeck, George William economics educator
Johns, Albert Cameron political scientist
Wilson, Warner Rushing psychology educator

Reno
Bijou, Sidney William psychology educator
Cummings, Nicholas Andrew psychologist
Leland, Joy Hanson anthropologist, alcohol research specialist
May, Jerry Russell psychologist
†Smith, Aaron research director, clinical psychologist
Weems, Robert Cicero economist, educator
Weinberg, Leonard Burton political scientist

Sparks
Chapman, Samuel Greeley political science educator, criminologist

NEW HAMPSHIRE

Bedford
Collins, Diana Josephine psychologist

Center Sandwich
Shoup, Carl Sumner retired economist

Concord
†Rogers, Katherine D. political consultant, state legislator

Conway
Solomon, Richard Lester retired psychology educator

Durham
Romoser, George Kenneth political science educator
Rosen, Sam economics educator emeritus

Hanover
Bower, Richard Stuart economist, educator
Campbell, Colin Dearborn economist, educator
Clement, Meredith Owen economist, educator
Gustman, Alan Leslie economics educator
Kleck, Robert Eldon psychology educator
Logue, Dennis Emhardt financial economics educator, consultant
Lyons, Gene Martin political scientist, educator
Masters, Roger Davis government educator
Riggs, Lorrin Andrews psychologist, educator
Starzinger, Vincent Evans political science educator
Young, Oran Reed political scientist, educator

Henniker
†Braiterman, Thea Gilda economics educator, state legislator

Keene
Baldwin, Peter Arthur psychologist, educator, minister

Lebanon
Emery, Virginia Olga Beattie psychologist, researcher

Nashua
Taeuber, Conrad demography educator, former government statistician

Portsmouth
†Brage, Carl Willis genealogist

Rye
†Grandmaison, J. Joseph political consultant

Wolfeboro
Murray, Roger Franklin economist, educator

NEW JERSEY

Atlantic Highlands
Kevenides, Herve Arnaud economic and real estate consultant

Belle Mead
†Evans, Frederick John psychologist

Caldwell
Kapusinski, Albert Thomas economist, educator

Camden
Sigler, Jay Adrian political scientist, educator

Cape May
Janosik, Edward Gabriel retired political science educator

Denville
Breed, Ria anthropologist

East Brunswick
Johnson, Edward Elemuel psychologist, educator

East Orange
†Wolff, Derish Michael economist, company executive

Florham Park
Perham, Roy Gates, III industrial psychologist

Freehold
Hillegass, Christine Ann psychologist

Glen Ridge
Szamek, Pierre Ervin research anthropologist

Hawthorne
Cole, Leonard Aaron political scientist, dentist

Hoboken
Johnson, James Myron psychologist, educator

Jersey City
D'Amico, Thomas F. economist, educator

Lakewood
Quinn, Evelyn Saul social work educator

Maplewood
†Hammond, Caleb Dean, Jr. cartographer, publisher
Palisi, Anthony Thomas psychologist, educator

Marlboro
Leveson, Irving Frederick economist

Medford
Katzell, Raymond A. psychologist, educator
Wallis, Robert Ray psychologist, entrepreneur

Murray Hill
Radner, Roy economist, educator, researcher

New Brunswick
Alexander, Robert Jackson economist, educator
Boocock, Sarane Spence sociologist
Chelius, James Robert economics educator
Elinson, Jack sociology educator
Glasser, Paul Harold sociologist, educator, university administrator, social worker
Jacob, Charles Elmer political scientist, educator
Kovach, Barbara Ellen management and psychology educator
Leggett, John Carl sociology educator
Mechanic, David social sciences educator
Midlarsky, Manus Issachar political scientist, educator
Peterson, Donald Robert psychologist, educator, university administrator
Roberts, Albert Roy social work educator
Rosenberg, Seymour psychologist, educator
Russell, Louise Bennett economist, educator
Stuart, Robert Crampton economics educator
Tiger, Lionel social scientist, anthropology consultant
Toby, Jackson sociologist, educator
Wilkinson, Louise Cherry psychology educator, dean

Newark
Carroll, John Douglas mathematical-statistical psychologist
Cheng, Mei-Fang psychobiology educator, neuroethology researcher
Gottfredson, Don Martin criminal justice educator
†Hiltz, Starr Roxanne sociologist, educator, computer scientist, writer, lecturer, consultant
Stein, Donald Gerald psychology educator
†Tallal, Paula psychologist

Piscataway
Alderfer, Clayton Paul organizational psychologist, educator, author, administrator
†Glickman, Norman Jay economist, urban policy analyst
Julesz, Bela experimental psychologist, educator, electrical engineer
Lazarus, Arnold Allan psychologist, educator
†Pandina, Robert John neuropsychologist
Schwebel, Milton psychologist, educator
Williams, James Richard human factors engineering psychologist

Princeton
Ashenfelter, Orley Clark economics educator
Barlow, Walter Greenwood public opinion analyst, management consultant
Baumol, William Jack economist, educator
Bogan, Elizabeth Chapin economist, educator
Bradford, David Frantz economist
Chow, Gregory Chi-Chong economist, educator
Coale, Ansley Johnson economics educator
Coffey, Joseph Irving international affairs educator
Cook, Michael Allan social sciences educator
Deaton, Angus Stewart economist, educator
Doig, Jameson Wallace political science educator
Ekstrom, Ruth Burt psychologist
Emmerich, Walter psychologist
Geertz, Clifford James anthropology educator
Girgus, Joan Stern psychologist, university administrator
Goldfeld, Stephen Michael economics educator, university official
Gordenker, Leon political sciences educator
Greenberg, Herbert M(arvin) psychologist, corporate executive
Greenstein, Fred Irwin political science educator
Gross, Charles Gordon psychology educator, neuroscientist
Halpern, Manfred political science educator
Hirschman, Albert Otto political economist, educator
Hoebel, Bartley Gore psychology educator
Issawi, Charles Philip economist, educator
Kateb, George Anthony political science educator
Kenen, Peter Bain economist, educator
†Kuh, Charlotte Virginia economist
Lester, Richard Allen economist, educator
Malkiel, Burton Gordon economics educator
Manning, Winton Howard psychologist, educational administrator
Miller, George Armitage psychologist, educator
Montagu, Ashley anthropologist, social biologist
Murphy, Walter Francis political science educator, author
Quandt, Richard Emeric economics educator
Reinhardt, Uwe Ernst economist, educator
Rosen, Harvey Sheldon economics educator
Rosenthal, Howard Lewis political science educator
Rozman, Gilbert Friedell sociologist, educator
Shear, Theodore Leslie, Jr. archaeologist, educator
Sigmund, Paul Eugene political science educator
Starr, Paul Elliot sociologist, writer, editor, educator
Stokes, Donald Elkinton political science educator
Taylor, Howard Francis sociology educator, researcher, consultant
Ullman, Richard Henry political science educator
Wallace, Walter L. sociologist, educator
Walzer, Michael Laban political science educator
Westoff, Charles Francis demographer, educator
Willig, Robert Daniel economics educator
Willingham, Warren Willcox psychologist, testing service executive
Wolpert, Julian geographer, educator

Red Bank
McWhinney, Madeline H. (Mrs. John Denny Dale) economist

Ridgewood
Catania, Lorraine Laura psychologist

Somerset
DeVaris, Jeannette Mary psychologist

South Orange
Green, Donald Webb economist

Springfield
Shilling, A. Gary economic consultant, investment advisor

Teaneck
Browne, Robert Span economist
Brudner, Helen Gross social sciences educator
Cassimatis, Peter John economics educator
Fairfield, Betty Elaine Smith psychologist
Fanshel, David social worker
Gordon, Jonathan David psychologist
Herman, Kenneth psychologist

Upper Montclair
Cordasco, Francesco sociologist, educator, author

Vineland
Hunt, Howard Francis psychologist, educator

Warren
Cohen, Bertram David psychologist, educator

NEW MEXICO

Albuquerque
Anderson, Darrell Edward psychologist, educator
Bacon, Phillip geographer, author, consultant
Basso, Keith Hamilton cultural anthropologist, linguist, educator
Cofer, Charles Norval psychologist, educator
Condie, Carol Joy anthropologist, research facility administrator
Harris, Fred R. political science educator, former senator
Heady, Ferrel retired political science educator
Schwerin, Karl Henry anthropology educator, researcher
Sickels, Robert Judd political science educator
Wollman, Nathaniel economist, educator

Corrales
Adams, James Frederick psychologist, educational administrator

Las Cruces
Lease, Richard Jay police science educator, former police officer
Roscoe, Stanley Nelson psychologist, aeronautical engineer

Las Vegas
Riley, Carroll Lavern anthropology educator

Los Alamos
Thompson, Lois Jean Heidke Ore industrial psychologist

Portales
Agogino, George Allen anthropologist, educator

Santa Fe
Hall, Edward Twitchell anthropologist, educator, author
Noble, Merrill Emmett retired psychology educator, psychologist
Whiteford, Andrew Hunter anthropologist
Williams, Stephen anthropologist, educator

Silver City
Gilbert, Kathie Simon economist, educator

Taos
Young, Jon Nathan archeologist

NEW YORK

Albany
Biggs, Donald Anthony psychologist, educator
Ley, Ronald psychologist, educator
Nathan, Richard P(erle) political scientist, educator
Tedeschi, James Theodore, Jr. psychologist educator
Teevan, Richard Collier psychology educator
Thompson, Frank Joseph political science educator
Thornberry, Terence Patrick criminologist, educator
Wetzler, James Warren economist, state official
Wright, Theodore Paul, Jr. political science educator
Zimmerman, Joseph Francis political scientist, educator

Alfred
Keith, Timothy Zook psychology educator

Amherst
Cramer, Stanley Howard psychology educator, author
Lewis, Lionel Stanley sociology educator
Mills, Theodore Mason sociologist, educator
Rossberg, Robert Howard psychology educator, former university dean

Armonk
Grove, David Lawrence economist

Averill Park
Haines, Walter Wells retired economics educator

Binghamton
Babb, Harold psychology educator
Banks, Arthur Sparrow political scientist, educator
Brehm, Sharon Stephens psychology educator, university administrator
Isaacson, Robert Lee psychology educator, researcher
Levis, Donald James psychologist, educator
Mazrui, Ali Al'Amin political science educator, researcher
†Salem-Murdock, Muneera anthropologist

Brewster
Huckabee, Carol Brooks psychologist

Brockport
Bretton, Henry L. political scientist, educator

Bronx
Fishman, Joshua Aaron sociolinguist, educator
Heilbrun, James economist, educator
Messing, Janet Agnes Kapelsohn economist, educator

Bronxville
Bozeman, Adda Bruemmer international relations scholar, educator, consultant, author
Conant, Miriam Bernheim political scientist, educator
Franklin, Margery Bodansky psychology educator, researcher

Kirk, Grayson Louis *retired political science educator, retired universtiy president, trustee*

Brooklyn
Bowers, Patricia Eleanor Fritz *economist*
Grayson, Gerald Herbert *economics and labor-management relations educator, publisher*
Harris, James Arthur, Sr. *economics educator*
Kippel, Gary M. *psychologist*
Masterson, Charles Francis *retired social scientist*
Minkoff, Jack *economics educator*
Reinisch, June Machover *psychologist, educator*
Sternlight, Peter Donn *economist, retired banker*
Szenberg, Michael *economics educator, editor, consultant*

Buffalo
Abrahams, Athol Denis *geography researcher, educator*
Aurbach, Herbert Alexander *sociology educator*
Batty, J. Michael *geographer, educator*
Behling, Charles Frederick *psychology educator*
Frake, Charles Oliver *anthropology educator*
Gort, Michael *economics educator*
Hetzner, Donald Raymund *social studies educator*
Jackson, Hermoine Prestine *psychologist*
Levy, Kenneth Jay *psychology educator, academic administrator*
Pruitt, Dean Garner *psychologist, educator*
Rosenthal, Donald B. *political scientist, educator*
Steegmann, Albert Theodore, Jr. *anthropology educator*
Stein, William Warner *anthropology educator*
Tedlock, Dennis *anthropology and literature educator*
Zarembka, Paul *economics educator*

Chappaqua
Brockway, George Pond *economist*

Clinton
Wertimer, Sidney *economics educator*

Conesus
Dadrian, Vahakn Norair *sociology educator*

Dobbs Ferry
Perelle, Ira B. *psychologist, educator*
Sutton, Francis Xavier *social scientist, consultant*

East Meadow
Albert, Gerald *clinical psychologist*

Farmingdale
Lieu, Hou-Shun *economist, educator*

Feura Bush
Byrne, Donn Erwin *psychologist, educator*

Flushing
Hacker, Andrew *political science educator*
Kaplan, Stephen *parapsychologist*
Nelson, Ralph Lowell *economics educator*
Patai, Raphael *former anthropology educator*
Psomiades, Harry John *political science educator*

Fredonia
Dowd, Morgan Daniel *political science educator*

Garden City
Ohrenstein, Roman Abraham *economics educator, economist, rabbi*

Geneseo
Battersby, Harold Ronald *anthropologist, archaeologist, linguist*

Great Neck
Hamovitch, William *economist, educator, university official*
Joskow, Jules *economic research company executive*

Greenvale
Araoz, Daniel Leon *psychologist, educator*

Guilderland
Gordon, Leonard Victor *psychologist, educator emeritus*

Hamilton
Farnsworth, Frank Albert *economics educator*

Hastings On Hudson
Clark, Kenneth Bancroft *psychologist, educator*

Hempstead
Block, Jules Richard *psychologist, educator, university official*
Hassett, Carol Alice *psychologist*
Turgeon, Edgar Lynn *economics educator*
Wattel, Harold Louis *economics educator*

Henrietta
Carmel, Simon J(acob) *anthropologist*

Howard Beach
Berliner, Patricia Mary *psychologist*

Irvington
Wolf, Eric Robert *anthropologist, educator*

Ithaca
Allee, David Jepson *economics educator*
Ascher, Robert *anthropologist, archaeologist, educator, filmmaker*
Blau, Francine Dee *economics educator*
Briggs, Vernon Mason, Jr. *economics educator*
Bronfenbrenner, Urie *psychologist*
Call, David Lincoln *agricultural economics educator, administrator*
Darlington, Richard Benjamin *psychology educator*
Easley, David *economics educator*
Fireside, Harvey Francis *political scientist, educator*
Forker, Olan Dean *agricultural economics educator*
Glock, Marvin David *retired psychology educator*
Hockett, Charles Francis *anthropology educator*
†Isard, Walter *economics educator*
Isen, Alice M. *experimental social psychologist, behavioral science educator*
Jarrow, Robert Alan *finance and economics educator, consultant*
Jones, Barclay Gibbs *regional economics researcher*
Kahin, George McTurnan *political science and history educator*
Kahn, Alfred Edward *economist, educator, government official*
Kennedy, Kenneth Adrian Raine *biological anthropologist, forensic anthropologist*
Kirsch, A(nthony) Thomas *anthropology and Asian studies educator, researcher*
Kramnick, Isaac *government educator*
Lambert, William Wilson *psychology educator*
Lowi, Theodore J(ay) *political science educator*
†Lyons, Thomas Patrick *economics educator*
Maas, James Beryl *psychology educator, lecturer, filmmaker*
Murra, John Victor *anthropologist, educator*
Shell, Karl *economics educator*
Smith, Robert John *anthropology educator*
Stycos, Joseph Mayone *demographer, educator*
Thaler, Richard H. *economics educator*
Thorbecke, Erik *economics educator*
Tomek, William Goodrich *agricultural economist*
Vanek, Jaroslav *economist, educator*
Williams, Robin Murphy, Jr. *sociology educator*

Mahopac
Richards, Edgar Lester *psychologist, educator*

Mount Kisco
Schwarz, Wolfgang *psychologist*

New Hyde Park
Reddan, Harold Jerome *sociologist, educator*

New Paltz
Schnell, George Adam *geographer, educator*

New Rochelle
Berlage, Gai Ingham *sociologist, educator*
Murphy, Austin de la Salle *economist, educator, banker*

New York
Abu-Lughod, Janet Lippman *sociologist, educator*
Adler, Freda Schaffer (Mrs. G. O. W. Mueller) *criminologist, educator*
Alford, Robert Ross *sociologist*
†Allison, David Bradley *psychologist*
Anspach, Ernst *economist, lawyer*
†Baldwin, David Allen *political science educator*
Bardach, Joan Lucile *clinical psychologist*
Barron, Susan *clinical psychologist*
Bernard, Viola Wertheim *psychiatrist*
Bialer, Seweryn *political science educator, author, consultant*
Blank, Blanche Davis *political science educator*
Boodey, Cecil Webster, Jr. *political science educator*
Bowen, William Gordon *economist, educator, foundation administrator*
Braham, Randolph Lewis *political science educator*
Brams, Steven John *political scientist, educator, game theorist*
Brancato, Carolyn Kay *economist, consultant*
Brush, Charles Francis *anthropologist*
Buck, Louise Zierdt *psychologist*
Caraley, Demetrios *political scientist, educator, author*
Carr, Arthur Charles *psychologist, educator*
Chamson, Sandra Potkorony *psychologist*
Clamar, Aphrodite J. *psychologist*
Cochrane, James Louis *economist*
Cohen, Eli Edward *sociology educator*
Cohen, Herman Nathan *private investigator*
Cohen, Stephen Frand *political scientist, historian, educator, author*
Cole, Jonathan Richard *sociologist, academic administrator*
Comitas, Lambros *anthropologist*
Cutler, Rhoda *psychologist*
Dalton, Dennis Gilmore *political science educator*
deMause, Lloyd *psychohistorian*
de Vries, Rimmer *economist*
Dowling, Edward Thomas *economics educator*
Duke, Anthony Drexel *sociologist, educator, philanthropist*
Duncan, Joseph Wayman *business economist*
Edinger, Lewis Joachim *political science educator*
Edwards, Franklin R. *economist, educator, consultant*
Elliott-Smith, Paul Henry *marketing and economics consultant*
Ellis, Albert *clinical psychologist, educator, author*
Emerson, Alice Frey *political scientist, educator emerita*
Engler, Robert *political science educator, author*
Epstein, Cynthia Fuchs *sociology educator, writer*
Fabbri, Brian John *economist, investment strategist*
Feinberg, Mortimer Robert *psychologist, educator*
Feldmann, Shirley Clark *psychology educator*
Finger, Seymour Maxwell *political science educator, former ambassador*
Fitch, Lyle Craig *economist, administrator*
Franklin, Julian Harold *political science educator*
Freund, William Curt *economist*
Gans, Herbert J. *sociologist, educator*
Gellhorn, Walter *law and political science educator, author*
†Giddon, Donald B(ernard) *psychologist, educator*
Ginzberg, Eli *economist, emeritus educator, government consultant, author*
Goldman, George David *psychologist, psychoanalyst*
Goldman, Leo *psychologist, educator*
Gordon, Diana Russell *political science educator*
Goss, Mary E. Weber *sociology educator*
Gould, Jay Martin *economist, consultant*
Grace, H. David *economist, international finance consultant*
Gresov, Boris (Vladimir) *economist*
Grindea, Daniel *international economist*
Halper, Thomas *political science educator*
Hammer, Emanuel Frederick *clinical psychologist, psychoanalyst*
Hawver, Dennis Arthur *psychological consultant*
Haywood, H(erbert) Carl(ton) *psychologist, educator*
Heal, Geoffrey Martin *economics educator*
Heilbroner, Robert L. *economist, author*
Helmreich, William Benno *sociology educator, consultant*
Heyde, Martha Bennett (Mrs. Ernest R. Heyde) *psychologist*
Heydebrand, Wolf Von *sociology educator*
Hirschfield, Robert S. *political science educator*
Hochberg, Julian *psychologist*
Hoffman, Martin Leon *psychology educator*
Hollander, Edwin Paul *psychologist, educator*
Hormats, Robert David *economist, investment banker*
Hoxter, Curtis Joseph *international economic adviser, public relations and affairs counselor*
Hurewitz, J(acob) C(oleman) *international relations educator emeritus, author, consultant*
Hurwitz, Sol *business policy organization executive*
Ianni, Francis Anthony James *anthropologist, psychoanalyst, educator*
Jacoby, Jacob *consumer psychology educator*
Jervis, Robert *political science educator*
Jonas, Ruth Haber *psychologist*
Jones, David Milton *economist, educator*
Juviler, Peter Henry *political scientist, educator*
Kalamotousakis, George John *economist*
Kamsky, Leonard *economist, retired manufacturing executive, financial advisor*
Kaplan, Leo Sylvan *social scientist, former college administrator*
Kavesh, Robert A. *economist, educator*
Kazemi, Farhad *political science educator*
Kellner, Irwin L. *economist*
Kinzey, Warren Glenford *anthropology educator*
Klass, Morton *anthropology educator, consultant*
Kline, Milton Vance *psychologist, educator*
Komarovsky, Mirra (Mrs. Marcus A. Heyman) *sociology educator*
Koppenaal, Richard John *psychology educator*
Krauss, Herbert Harris *psychologist*
Lakah, Jacqueline Rabbat *political scientist, educator*
Lancaster, Kelvin John *economics educator*
Lantay, George Charles (Wagner) *psychologist, psychotherapist, consultant*
Lee, Robert Sanford *psychologist*
Lehman, Edward William *sociology educator, researcher*
Leontief, Wassily *economist, educator*
Lichtblau, John H. *economist*
Lieberman, Charles *economist*
Lin, Wuu-Long *economist*
Lipsey, Robert Edward *economist, educator*
Lynch, Owen Martin *anthropologist, educator*
Macchiarola, Frank Joseph *political science, business and law educator*
Mac Namara, Donal Eoin Joseph *criminologist*
Maldonado-Bear, Rita Marinita *economist, educator*
Markowitz, Harry M. *finance and economics educator*
†McCarthy, James *sociology researcher, educator*
†Meadow, Phyllis Whitcomb *psychoanalyst*
†Melamid, Alexander *economics educator, consultant*
Merton, Robert K. *sociologist, educator*
Meyer-Bahlburg, Heino F. L. *psychologist*
Mincer, Jacob *economics educator*
Mintz, Donald Edward *psychologist, educator*
Molz, Redmond Kathleen *public administration educator*
Moore, Geoffrey Hoyt *economist*
Moskowitz, Arnold X. *strategist, economist, educator*
†Mroz, John Edwin *political scientist*
Muller, Charlotte Feldman *economist, educator*
Murphy, Joseph Samson *political science educator*
Nadiri, M. Ishaq *economics educator, researcher, lecturer, consultant*
Nakamura, James I. *economics educator*
†Nathan, Andrew James *political science educator*
Nelkin, Dorothy *sociology and science policy educator, researcher*
Nell, Edward John *economist, educator*
Netzer, Dick *economics educator*
Newborn, Jud *cultural anthropologist, writer*
Papalia, Diane Ellen *human development educator*
Parks, Robert Henry *consulting economist, educator*
†Patrick, Hugh Talbot *economist, educator*
Pavis, Jesse Andrew *sociology educator*
Peck, Fred Neil *economist, educator*
Persell, Caroline Hodges *sociologist, educator, author, researcher, consultant*
Phelps, Edmund Strother *economics educator*
Piven, Frances Fox *political scientist, educator*
Prewitt, Kenneth *political science educator, foundation executive*
Pye, Gordon Bruce *economist*
Ramirez, Maria Fiorini *economist, investment advisor*
Reichman, Walter *psychologist, educator*
Ringler, Lenore *educational psychology educator*
Riss, Eric *psychologist*
Rivlin, Benjamin *political science educator*
Robock, Stefan Hyman *economics educator emeritus*
Rosner, Lydia S. *sociology educator, author*
Ross, Jeffrey Allan *political scientist, educator*
Sackeim, Harold *psychologist, educator*
Sartori, Giovanni *political scientist*
Saxe, Leonard *social psychologist, educator*
Scanlon, Rosemary *economist*
†Scelsa, Joseph Vincent *sociologist*
Schotter, Andrew Roye *economics educator, consultant*
Schwab, George David *social science educator*
Schwartz, Anna Jacobson *economic historian*
Schwartzman, David *economist, educator*
Sennett, Richard *sociology educator*
Shapiro, Judith R. *anthropology educator, academic administrator*
Sheldon, Eleanor Harriet Bernert *sociologist*
Sherry, George Leon *political science educator*
Silk, Leonard Solomon *economist, columnist, editor*
Silver, Morris *economist, educator*
Simon, Jacqueline Albert *political scientist, writer*
Singer, Eleanor *sociologist, editor*
Small, George LeRoy *geographer, educator*
Spar, Edward Joel *demographer*
Tallmer, Margot *psychologist, psychoanalyst, gerontologist*
Taylor, Lance Jerome *economics educator*
Tepper, Lynn Marsha *gerontology educator*
Thomas, David Hurst *archaeologist*
Updike, Helen Hill *economist, investment manager, financial planner*
Vickrey, William Spencer *economist, emeritus educator*
Vora, Ashok *financial economist*
Walter, Ingo *economics educator*
Watts, Harold Wesley *economist, educator*
Weiner, Max *educational psychology educator*
Weintraub, Ruth G. *political science educator*
Welkowitz, Joan *psychology educator*
Wenglowski, Gary Martin *economist*
Westheimer, Ruth Siegel (Karola Ruth Siegel Westheimer) *psychologist, television personality*
Westin, Alan Furman *political science educator*
White, Lawrence J. *economics educator*
Winick, Charles *sociologist, educator*
Wojnilower, Albert Martin *economist*
Wolman, William *economist, journalist, broadcaster*
Wrong, Dennis Hume *sociologist, educator*
Yankelovich, Daniel *social researcher, public opinion analyst*
†Zawistowski, Stephen Louis *psychologist, educator*
Zolberg, Aristide Rodolphe *political science educator, researcher*
Zuckerman, Harriet *sociologist, educator*

Newtonville
Apostle, Christos Nicholas *social psychologist*

Niagara Falls
Albanese, Jay Samuel *criminologist educator*

Niagara University
Osberg, Timothy M. *psychologist, educator, researcher, clinician*

Old Westbury
Ozelli, Tunch *economics educator, consultant*

Oneonta
Bergstein, Harry Benjamin *psychology educator*
Diehl, Lesley Ann *psychologist*

Oswego
Gooding, Charles Thomas *psychology educator, college dean*
Gordon, Norman Botnick *psychology educator*

Oyster Bay
Trevor, Bronson *economist*

Plattsburgh
Smith, Noel Wilson *psychology educator*

Pleasantville
Black, Percy *psychology educator*
Hormozi, Farrokh Zad *economist, educator, consultant, business forecaster*
Robak, Rostyslaw Wsewolod *psychologist, educator*

Potsdam
Whelehan, Patricia Elizabeth *anthropology educator*

Poughkeepsie
Johnson, Lucille Lewis *anthropology educator, archaeologist*
Johnson, M(aurice) Glen *political science educator*

Purchase
Ryan, Edward W. *economics educator*
Siegel, Nathaniel Harold *sociology educator*

Rochester
Bluhm, William Theodore *political scientist, educator*
Cowen, Emory L. *psychology educator*
D'Agostino, Anthony Carmen *anthropologist, educator*
Deci, Edward Lewis *psychologist, educator*
DuBrin, Andrew John *behavioral sciences, management educator, author*
Engerman, Stanley Lewis *economist, educator, historian*
Fenno, Richard Francis, Jr. *political science educator*
Geertsma, Robert Henry *psychologist, educator*
Hanushek, Eric Alan *economics educator*
Harris, Alfred *social anthropologist, educator*
Hopkins, Thomas Duvall *economics educator*
†Jacobs, Bruce *political science educator*
Jones, Ronald Winthrop *economics educator*
Laties, Victor Gregory *psychology educator*
Long, John Broaddus, Jr. *economist, educator*
Mc Kenzie, Lionel Wilfred *economist, educator*
Mueller, John E. *political science educator, dance critic and historian*
Niemi, Richard Gene *political science educator*
Pearse, Robert Francis *psychologist, educator*
Regenstreif, S(amuel) Peter *political scientist, educator*
Rosett, Richard Nathaniel *economist, educator*
Sangree, Walter Hinchman *social anthropologist, educator*
Steamer, Robert Julius *political science educator*
Thomas, Garth Johnson *psychology educator emeritus*
Von Holden, Martin Harvey *psychologist*
Wheeler, Ladd *psychology educator*
Zax, Melvin *psychologist, educator*

Scarsdale
Cohen, Irwin *economist*

Schenectady
Board, Joseph Breckinridge, Jr. *political scientist, educator*
Huntley, Charles William *psychology educator*
Terry, Richard Allan *consulting psychologist, former college president*

Slingerlands
Fenton, William Nelson *anthropologist, anthropology educator emeritus*

Staten Island
Johnson, Frank Corliss *psychologist*

Stony Brook
Fleagle, John Gwynn *anthropology and paleontology educator*
Glass, David Carter *psychology educator*
Goodman, Norman *sociologist, researcher*
Katkin, Edward Samuel *psychology educator*
Neuberger, Egon *economics educator*
Schneider, Mark *political science educator*
Travis, Martin Bice *political scientist, educator*

Syracuse
Birkhead, Guthrie Sweeney, Jr. *political scientist, university dean*
Black, Lois Mae *clinical psychologist, educator*
Braungart, Richard Gottfried *sociology and international relations educator*
Cooke, Goodwin *international relations educator*
Coplin, William David *policy studies educator*
Frohock, Fred Manuel *political science educator*
Jensen, Robert Granville *geography educator, university dean*
Jump, Bernard, Jr. *economics educator*
†Kriesberg, Louis *sociologist, educator*

Mazur, Allan Carl *sociologist, educator*
Meinig, Donald William *geography educator*
Miron, Murray Samuel *psychologist, educator*
Monmonier, Mark *graphics educator, geographer*
Palmer, John L. *social sciences researcher, educator*
Samuels, Marwyn Stewart *geography educator*
Schwartz, Richard Derecktor *sociologist, educator*
Thorson, Stuart J. *political science educator*
†Wadley, Susan Snow *anthropologist*

Tarrytown
Marcus, Sheldon *social sciences educator*

Troy
Baron, Robert Alan *psychology and business educator, author*
Brazil, Harold Edmund *political science educator*
Diwan, Romesh Kumar *economics educator*
Gorenstein, Shirley Slotkin *anthropologist, educator*

Wantagh
Dawson, George Glenn *economics educator emeritus*

White Plains
Rapp, Richard Tilden *economist, consultant*

Yonkers
Varma, Baidya Nath *sociologist, broadcaster*

NORTH CAROLINA

Banner Elk
Speer, Allen Paul, III *political science educator*

Calabash
Strunk, Orlo Christopher, Jr. *psychology educator*

Cary
Garrison, Jane Gayle *astrologer*

Cashiers
O'Connell, Edward James, Jr. *psychology educator, computer applications and data analysis consultant*

Chapel Hill
Baroff, George Stanley *psychologist, educator*
Behrman, Jack Newton *economist*
Black, Stanley Warren, III *economics educator*
Blau, Peter Michael *sociologist, educator*
Brockington, Donald Leslie *anthropologist, archaeologist, educator*
Brown, Frank *social science educator*
Carroll, John Bissell *psychologist, educator*
Cobb, Henry Van Zandt *psychologist*
Crane, Julia Gorham *anthropology educator*
Dahlstrom, William Grant *psychologist, educator*
Eisenbeis, Robert A. *business educator*
Fox, Ronald Ernest *psychologist*
Friedman, James Winstein *economist, educator*
Gallman, Robert Emil *economics and history educator*
Gil, Federico Guillermo *political science educator*
Graham, George Adams *political scientist, emeritus educator*
Gray-Little, Bernadette *psychologist*
Gulick, John *anthropology educator*
Hochbaum, Godfrey Martin *retired behavioral scientist*
Holcomb, George Ruhle *anthropology educator*
Kasarda, John Dale *business educator, researcher, administrator, consultant*
Landsberger, Henry A. *sociology educator*
MacRae, Duncan, Jr. *social scientist, educator*
Mc Curdy, Harold Grier *psychologist*
Pfouts, Ralph William *economist, consultant*
Richardson, Richard Judson *political science educator*
†Rindfuss, Ronald Richard *sociology educator*
Schopler, John Henry *psychologist, educator*
†Schoultz, Lars *political scientist, educator*
Simpson, Richard Lee *sociologist, educator*
Smith, James Finley *economist, educator*
Steponaitis, Vincas Petras *archaeologist, anthropologist, educator*
Treml, Vladimir Guy *economist, educator*
Upshaw, Harry Stephan *psychology educator*
Waud, Roger Neil *economics educator*
Wilson, Glenn *economist, educator*
Wilson, Robert Neal *sociologist, educator*
Wright, Deil Spencer *political science educator*

Charlotte
Brazeal, Donna Smith *psychologist*
Neel, Richard Eugene *economics educator*

Dallas
Blanton, Robert D'Alden *anthropology and history educator*

Davidson
Proctor, Jesse Harris, Jr. *political science educator*
Ratliff, Charles Edward, Jr. *economics educator*

Durham
Aldrich, John Herbert *political science educator*
Barber, James David *political scientist, educator*
Braibanti, Ralph John *political scientist, educator*
Burmeister, Edwin *economics educator*
Dunteman, George Henry *organizational psychologist*
Elliot, Jeffrey M. *political science educator, author*
Gittler, Joseph Bertram *sociology educator*
Handy, Rollo Leroy *economics educator, research executive*
Holsti, Ole Rudolf *political scientist, educator*
Kelley, Allen Charles *economist, educator*
Keohane, Robert Owen *political scientist, educator*
†Kuniholm, Bruce Robellet *public policy studies institute director, history educator*
Land, Kenneth Carl *sociology educator, demographer, statistician, consultant*
Leach, Richard Heald *political scientist, educator*
Lifton, Walter M. *psychology and education consultant*
Lincoln, C(harles) Eric *sociologist, educator, author*
Lockhead, Gregory Roger *psychology educator*
Mickiewicz, Ellen Propper *political science educator*
Myers, George Carleton *sociology and demographics educator*
O'Barr, William McAlston *anthropologist, educator*
Page, Ellis Batten *behavioral scientist, educator*
Simons, Elwyn LaVerne *physical anthropologist, primatologist, paleontologist, educator*
Staddon, John Eric Rayner *psychology, zoology, neurobiology educator*
Tiryakian, Edward Ashod *sociology educator*

Fearrington Village
Doenges, Byron Frederick *economist, educator, former government official*

Gastonia
Kiser, Clyde Vernon *retired demographer*

Greensboro
Eason, Robert Gaston *psychology educator*
Goldman, Bert Arthur *psychologist, educator*
Hidore, John Junior *geographer, educator*
Shelton, David Howard *economics educator*
Zopf, Paul Edward *sociologist*

Greenville
Cramer, Robert Eli *geography educator*
Williams, Melvin John *sociologist, educator*

Hickory
Gingrich-Petersen, Carolyn Ashcraft *psychologist*

Hillsborough
Goodwin, Craufurd David *economics educator*

Raleigh
Caldwell, John Tyler *political science educator, former university administrator*
Newman, Slater Edmund *psychologist, educator*
Sprinthall, Norman Arthur *psychology educator*

Winston Salem
Vincent, Clark Edward *sociologist*
Williams, John Edwin *psychology educator*

NORTH DAKOTA

Bismarck
†Sperry, James Edward *anthropologist*

Fargo
Query, Joy Marves Neale *medical sociology educator*

OHIO

Akron
Coyne, Thomas Joseph *economist, finance educator*
Marini, Frank Nicholas *public administration and political science educator*

Ashland
Ford, Lucille Garber *economist, educator, college official*

Athens
Klare, George Roger *psychology educator*
Russell, David L(awson) *psychology educator*

Bowling Green
Denisoff, R. Serge *sociologist, writer*
Hakel, Milton Daniel, Jr. *psychology educator, consultant, publisher*
McCaghy, Charles Henry *sociology educator*
Scott, John Paul *psychologist, educator, author*

Cincinnati
Bieliauskas, Vytautas Joseph *clinical psychologist, educator*
Bishop, George Franklin *political social psychologist, educator*
Bluestein, Venus Weller *retired psychology educator*
Dember, William Norton *psychologist, educator*
Katz, Robert Langdon *human relations educator, rabbi*

Cleveland
Beall, Cynthia *anthropologist, educator*
Binstock, Robert Henry *public policy educator, writer, lecturer*
Boyle, Kammer *management psychologist*
Burke, John Francis, Jr. *economist*
Carlsson, Bo A. V. *economics educator*
Carter, John Dale *organizational development executive*
Chatterjee, Pranab *social sciences educator*
Conaway, Orrin Bryte *political scientist, educator*
Goldstein, Melvyn C. *anthropologist, educator*
Grundy, Kenneth William *political science educator*
Hokenstad, Merl Clifford, Jr. *social work educator*
Jordan, Jerry Lee *economist, banker*
Kahana, Eva Frost *sociology educator*
Kolb, David Allen *psychology educator*
Lavelle, Michael Joseph *economist, academic administrator*
†Ludenia, Krista *psychologist, health facility administrator*
Mayland, Kenneth Theodore *economist*
McHale, Vincent Edward *political science educator*
†Murray, Thomas Henry *bioethics educator, writer*
Rosegger, Gerhard *economist, educator*
Sibley, Willis Elbridge *anthropology educator, consultant*

Columbus
Alger, Chadwick Fairfax *educator, political scientist*
Beck, Paul Allen *political science educator*
Bourguignon, Erika Eichhorn *anthropologist, educator*
Cacioppo, John Terrance *psychology educator*
Cunnyngham, Jon *economist, information systems educator*
†Flinn, William Loren *sociology educator, agricultural economics educator*
Gouke, Cecil Granville *economist, educator*
Huber, Joan Althaus *sociology educator*
Huff, C(larence) Ronald *public administration and criminology educator*
Ichiishi, Tatsuro *economics and mathematics educator*
Kessel, John Howard *political scientist, educator*
Ladman, Jerry R. *economist, educator*
Leland, Henry *psychology educator*
Lundman, Richard Jack *sociology educator*
Lundstedt, Sven Bertil *behavioral and social scientist, educator*
Lynn, Arthur Dellert, Jr. *economist, educator*
Marble, Duane Francis *geography educator, researcher*
Mc Donagh, Edward Charles *sociologist, university administrator*
Meyer, Donald Ray *psychologist, brain researcher*
Meyer, Patricia Morgan *neuropsychologist, educator*
Namboodiri, Krishnan *sociology educator*
Naylor, James Charles *psychologist, educator*
Osipow, Samuel Herman *psychology educator*
Patterson, Samuel Charles *political science educator*
Poirier, Frank Eugene *physical anthropology educator*
Ray, Edward John *economics educator, administrator*
Richardson, Laurel Walum *sociology educator*
Schwebel, Andrew I. *psychology educator*
Weisberg, Herbert Frank *political science educator*

Dayton
Christensen, Julien Martin *psychologist, educator*

Hamilton
Rorer, Leonard George *psychology educator*

Kent
Hall, Bernard *retired economics educator and university official*
Koller, Marvin Robert *sociology educator, writer*
Williams, Harold Roger *economist, educator*

Middletown
Gilmore, June Ellen *psychologist*

Oberlin
Layman, Emma McCloy (Mrs. James W. Layman) *psychologist, educator*

Oxford
Rejai, Mostafa *political science educator*
Seltzer, Mildred M. *gerontologist, educator*

Sandusky
Round, Alice Faye Bruce *school psychologist*

Shaker Heights
Wolf, Milton Albert *economist, former U.S. ambassador, business executive*

Tiffin
Porter, Arthur Reno *economist, arbitrator*

Toledo
Bardis, Panos Demetrios *sociologist, social philosopher, historian, author, editor, poet, educator*

Waterford
Riley, Nancy Mae *vocational home economics educator*

Wooster
Loess, Henry Bernard *psychology educator*

Yellow Springs
Lacey, John Irving *psychologist, physiologist, educator*

OKLAHOMA

Norman
Affleck, Marilyn *sociology educator*
Albert, Lois Eldora Wilson *archaeologist*
Bell, Robert Eugene *anthropologist educator*
Cella, Francis Raymond *economist, research consultant*
Henderson, George *educational sociologist, educator*
Kondonassis, Alexander John *economist, educator*

Oklahoma City
Pishkin, Vladimir *psychologist, educator*
Walker, C. Eugene *psychology educator*

Stillwater
Bynum, Jack Edward, Jr. *sociology educator*
Jadlow, Joseph Martin *economics educator*
Moomaw, Ronald Lee *economics educator*
Poole, Richard William *economics educator*
Shearer, John Clyde *economics consultant, labor arbitrator, international manpower consultant*

Tahlequah
Webster, Edgar Lewis *sociology educator, program director*

OREGON

Ashland
Houston, John Albert *political science educator*

Corvallis
Castle, Emery Neal *agricultural and resource economist, educator*
Gillis, John Simon *psychologist, educator*
Harter, Lafayette George, Jr. *economics educator emeritus*
Towey, Richard Edward *economics educator*

Eugene
Aikens, C(lyde) Melvin *anthropology educator, archaeologist*
Becker, Wesley Clemence *psychology educator emeritus*
Davis, Richard Malone *economics educator*
Dawes, Carol J. *clinical psychologist*
Eisert, Debra Claire *pediatric psychologist*
Hildreth, Clifford *retired economist, educator*
Khang, Chulsoon *economics educator*
Littman, Richard Anton *psychologist, educator*
McGuire, Timothy William *economics and management educator, dean*
Mikesell, Raymond Frech *economics educator*
Stone, Joe Allan *economics educator*

Monmouth
Shay, Roshani Cari *political science educator*

Portland
Commerford, Kathleen Anne *psychologist*
Davis, James Allan *gerontologist, educator*
Kristof, Ladis Kris Donabed *political scientist, author*
Matarazzo, Joseph Dominic *psychologist*
Matarazzo, Ruth Gadbois *psychology educator*
Squier, Leslie Hamilton *psychology educator*
Wiens, Arthur Nicholai *psychology educator*

Salem
Archer, Stephen Hunt *economist, educator*

Siletz
Jennings, Jesse David *anthropology educator*

PENNSYLVANIA

Abington
Drudy, Patrick *psychologist, human relations consultant, import and export company executive*

Allentown
Bannon, George *economics educator, department chairman*
Bednar, Charles Sokol *political scientist, educator*

Bethlehem
Brozek, Josef *psychology educator, scientist*
Campbell, Donald Thomas *psychologist, educator*
Frankel, Barbara Brown *cultural anthropologist*
Schwartz, Eli *economics educator, writer*

Birdsboro
Hill, Lenora Mae *astrologer*

Bryn Athyn
Kintner, William Roscoe *political science educator emeritus*

Bryn Mawr
de Laguna, Frederica *anthropology educator emeritus, consultant*
Hoffman, Howard Stanley *experimental psychologist, educator*
Hoopes, Janet Louise *educator, psychologist*
Porter, Judith Deborah Revitch *sociologist, educator*
Ridgway, Brunilde Sismondo *archaeology educator*
Rubinstein, Alvin Zachary *political science educator, author*
Walton, Clarence *political science and history educator*

Burlington
Herrold, Kenneth Frederick *psychologist, educator*

Carlisle
Jacobs, Norman G(abriel) *sociologist, educator*

Cranberry Township
Birch, Jack Willard *psychologist, educator*

Doylestown
Davis, Carole Joan *psychologist*

East Stroudsburg
Briggs, Philip James *political science educator, author, lecturer*

Gettysburg
Plischke, Elmer *political science educator*

Gwynedd
Zumeta, Bertram William *retired economist*

Haverford
Heath, Douglas Hamilton *psychology educator*
Northrup, Herbert Roof *economist, business executive*

Horsham
Logue, John Joseph *psychologist*

Indiana
Mc Cauley, R. Paul *criminologist, educator*

Jenkintown
Hankin, Elaine Krieger *psychologist, researcher*

Kutztown
Dougherty, Percy H. *geographer, educator*

Lancaster
Stephenson, Donald Grier, Jr. *government studies educator*
Taylor, Norman William *economics educator*

Lewisburg
Anderson, John Whiting *economics educator*
Candland, Douglas Keith *psychology educator*

Lincoln University
Gaymon, William Edward *psychology educator*

Malvern
Gillespie, Mary Krempa *psychologist, consultant*

Manns Choice
Jones, Oliver Hastings *consulting economist*

Meadville
Adams, Earl William, Jr. *economics educator*

Media
Smith, David Gilbert *political science educator*

Narberth
Hires, William Leland *psychologist, consultant*

Newtown
Peroni, Peter A., II *psychologist, educator*

North East
Ayrault, Evelyn West psychologist, writer

Philadelphia
Abrams, Jules Clinton psychologist
Adams, F. Gerard economist, educator
†Ando, Albert K. economist, educator
Auerbach, Alan Jeffrey economist
Bailey, Elizabeth Ellery economics educator
Bailey, Harry Augustine, Jr. political science educator
Baltzell, E(dward) Digby sociologist
Behrman, Jere Richard economics educator
Bellack, Alan Scott clinical psychologist
Buerkle, Jack Vincent sociologist, educator
Cass, David economist, educator
†Clark, John J. economics and finance educator
Cummins, John David economics educator, consultant
Cutler, Neal Evan gerontologist, educator
Dean-Zubritsky, Cynthia Marian psychologist, reseacher
Duffy, Francis Ramon sociology educator
Evan, William Martin sociologist, educator
Fox, Renée Claire sociology educator
Frankel, Francine Ruth political science educator
Frantz, Charles anthropology educator
Goodenough, Ward Hunt anthropologist, educator
Grossman, Sanford Jay economics educator
Hall, Charles P(otter), Jr. educator consultant
Harvey, John Adriance psychology and pharmacology educator, researcher, consultant
Howard-Carter, Theresa archaeologist
Hurvich, Leo Maurice experimental psychologist, educator, vision researcher
Jameson, Dorothea sensory psychologist
Kephart, William Milton sociologist, educator, author
Klausner, Samuel Zundel sociologist, educator
Klein, Lawrence Robert economist, educator
Kopecky, Kenneth John economics educator
Lang, Richard Warren economist, banker
Lee, Chong-Sik political scientist, educator
Levine, Herbert Samuel economics educator, research consultant
†LoSciuto, Leonard Anthony psychologist, educator
Mansfield, Edwin economist, educator
†Menken, Jane Ava demographer, educator
Michael, Henry N. geographer, anthropologist
Miller, Ronald Eugene regional science educator
†Postlewaite, Andrew William economics and public policy educator
Premack, David psychologist
Preston, Samuel Hulse demographer
Pritchard, James Bennett archaeologist, educator, author
Rescorla, Robert Arthur psychology educator
Rima, Ingrid Hahne economics educator
Rohrlich, George Friedrich social economist
Rosenberg, Robert Allen psychologist, educator, optometrist
Sabloff, Jeremy Arac archaeologist
Sigmond, Robert M. medical economist
Summers, Anita Arrow public policy and management educator
Summers, Robert economics educator
Taubman, Paul James economics educator
Wadden, Thomas Antony psychology educator
Wallace, Anthony Francis Clarke anthropologist, educator
Wolfbein, Seymour Louis economist, educator
Wolfgang, Marvin Eugene sociologist, criminologist, educator

Pittsburgh
Anderson, John Robert psychology and computer science educator
Barry, Herbert, III psychologist
Blumstein, Alfred urban and public affairs educator
Bobrow, Davis Bernard public policy educator
Carroll, Holbert Nicholson political science educator
Davis, Otto Anderson economics educator
Dawes, Robyn Mason psychology educator
Eaton, Joseph W. sociology educator
Fararo, Thomas John sociologist, educator
Fischhoff, Baruch psychologist, educator
Goldstein, Gerald research psychologist
Hammond, Paul Young political scientist, educator
Holzner, Burkart sociologist, educator
Howard, Lawrence Cabot international affairs educator
Katz, Arnold economics educator
Katz, Saul Milton economist, social scientist, educator
Keefe, William Joseph political science educator
Lave, Judith Rice economics educator
Lave, Lester Bernard economist, educator, researcher
LeMelle, Tilden John political science educator, editor, college official
Lidz, Charles Wilmanns sociologist
Masoner, Paul Henry counseling educator
Matthews, Jack psychologist, speech pathologist, educator
†Mazur, Mark James economics educator
McCallum, Bennett Tarlton economics educator
McClelland, James L. psychology educator, cognitive scientist
Meltzer, Allan H. economist, educator
Mesa-Lago, Carmelo economist, educator
Ogul, Morris Samuel political science educator, consultant
Perlman, Mark economist, educator
Perloff, Robert psychologist, educator
Roth, Alvin Eliot economics educator
Simon, Herbert A(lexander) social scientist
Strauss, Robert Philip economics educator
Sussna, Edward economist, educator
Voss, James Frederick psychologist, educator

Polk
Hall, Richard Clayton psychologist, consultant, researcher

Saint Davids
Heebner, Albert Gilbert economist, banker, educator

Scranton
Parente, William Joseph political science educator

Spring House
Coltoff, Beth Jamie psychologist, small business owner

State College
Farr, Jo-Ann Hunter psychologist
Ferguson, John Henry retired political science educator
Gordon, Richard Lewis mineral economics educator
Gould, Peter Robin geographer, educator
Harris, Dale Benner psychology educator
Miller, E. Willard geographer

Swarthmore
Hopkins, Raymond Frederick political science educator
Keith, Jennie anthropology educator, author
Saffran, Bernard economist, educator

University Park
Aspaturian, Vernon Varaztat political science educator, consultant, author
Ford, Donald Herbert psychologist, educator
Friedman, Robert Sidney political science educator
†Hogan, Dennis Patrick university educator
Klein, Philip Alexander economist
Lewis, Peirce Fee geographer, educator
Lombra, Raymond Eugene economist, educator
Maier-Katkin, Daniel criminology educator, administrator
Nelsen, Hart Michael sociologist, educator
Pashek, Robert Donald economics educator emeritus
Ray, William Jackson psychologist
Rose, Adam Zachary economist, educator
Schaie, K(laus) Warner human development and psychology educator
Stern, Robert Morris psychology educator, psychophysiology researcher
Walden, Daniel social sciences educator
Wyand, Martin Judd economics educator, retired military officer

Wayne
Bricklin, Patricia Ellen psychologist, educator
Chimerine, Lawrence economist

West Chester
Green, Andrew Wilson economist, lawyer, educator

Wycombe
Denoon, David Baugh Holden economist, educator, consultant

Wyncote
Bersh, Philip Joseph psychologist, educator

Wynnewood
Khouri, Fred John political science educator
Phillips, Almarin economics educator, consultant

RHODE ISLAND

Kingston
Alexander, Lewis McElwain geographer, educator
Biller, Henry Burt psychologist, educator
Gelles, Richard James sociology and psychology educator
Zucker, Norman Livingston political scientist, educator, author

Providence
Anderson, James Alfred psychology educator
Anton, Thomas Julius political science, public policy educator, consultant
Blough, Donald S. psychology educator
Calia, Vincent Frank psychologist, educator
Church, Russell Miller psychology educator
Damon, William Van Buren developmental psychologist, educator
Garrison, Mark Joseph political science educator, former diplomat
Goldstein, Sidney sociology educator, demographer
Goodman, Elliot Raymond political scientist, educator
Gould, Richard Allan anthropologist, archaeologist, educator
Grossman, Herschel I. economics educator
Heath, Dwight Braley anthropologist, educator
Holden, Raymond Henry clinical psychologist
Hopmann, Philip Terrence political science educator
Marsh, Robert Mortimer sociologist, educator
Perkins, Whitney Trow political science educator emeritus
Poole, William economics educator, consultant
Putterman, Louis G. economics educator
†Rueschemeyer, Dietrich sociology educator
Ryder, Harl Edgar economist, educator
Schupack, Mark Barry economist, educator
Shepp, Bryan Eugene psychologist, educator
Smoke, Richard political scientist, political psychologist
Stultz, Newell Maynard political science educator

South Kingstown
Berman, Allan psychologist, educator

SOUTH CAROLINA

Anderson
Gleason, Ralph Newton economic development consultant

Charleston
Barclay, James Ralph psychologist, educator
Bowman, Daniel Oliver psychologist
Moore, William Vincent political science educator

Clemson
Trevillian, Wallace Dabney economics educator, retired dean

Columbia
Clower, Robert Wayne economics educator, consultant
Cohn, Elchanan economics educator
Davis, Keith Eugene psychologist, educator, consultant
Hatch, David Lincoln sociology educator
Heider, Karl Gustav anthropology educator
Kiker, Billy Frazier economics educator
Melton, Gary Bentley psychology and law educator
Mishler, William, II political science educator
Morris, James Aloysius economist, educator
Norton, Hugh Stanton economist, educator
Starr, Harvey political scientist
Weatherbee, Donald Emery political scientist, educator
Wilder, Ronald Parker economics educator

SOUTH DAKOTA

Brookings
Gilbert, Howard Alden economics educator

Sioux Falls
Brendtro, Larry Kay psychologist, educator

Vermillion
Carlson, Loren Merle political science educator
Clem, Alan Leland political scientist
Dahlin, Donald C(lifford) political science educator

TENNESSEE

Knoxville
Bateman, Veda Mae industrial psychologist, management consultant
Cole, William Edward economics educator, consultant
Hammond, Edwin Hughes geography educator

Memphis
Battle, Allen Overton, Jr. psychologist, educator
Depperschmidt, Thomas Orlando economist, educator
Johnson, Johnny research psychologist, consultant
Mealor, William Theodore, Jr. geography educator, university administrator, consultant

Nashville
Aubrey, Roger Frederick psychology and education educator
Buckles, Stephen Gary economist, educator
Damon, William Winchell economics educator
Fels, Rendigs economist, educator
Finegan, Thomas Aldrich economist
†Gove, Walter R. sociology educator
Hancock, M(arion) Donald political science educator
Heard, (George) Alexander retired educator and chancellor
Hinshaw, Carroll Elton economics educator
Kaas, Jon H. psychology educator
Masters, John Christopher psychologist, educator, writer
†Russell, Clifford Springer economics and public policy educator
Scheffman, David Theodore economist, management educator, consultant
Schoggen, Phil H(oward) psychologist, educator
Spores, Ronald Marvin anthropology educator, ethnohistorian
Strupp, Hans Hermann psychologist, educator
†Thompson, Travis psychology educator, administrator, researcher

TEXAS

Abilene
Davis, Burl Edward social sciences research consulting company executive, communications educator

Amarillo
Ayad, Joseph Magdy psychologist

Arlington
Carney, Kim economics educator
Cole, Richard Louis political scientist, educator
Furubotn, Eirik Grundtvig economics educator
Mullendore, Walter Edward economist
Nelson, Wallace Boyd economics and business administration educator
Ramsey, Charles Eugene sociologist, educator

Austin
Amsel, Abram experimental psychologist, educator
Bean, Frank D(awson) sociology and demography educator
Blake, Robert Rogers psychologist, behavioral science company executive
Blodgett, Warren Terrell public affairs educator
Buchanan, Bruce, II political science educator
Burnham, Walter Dean political science educator
Christian, George Eastland political consultant
Cleland, Charles Carr psychologist, educator
Davis, Edward Mott anthropology educator and researcher
Dusansky, Richard economist, educator
Epstein, Jeremiah Fain anthropologist, educator
Fernea, Robert Alan cultural anthropology and Middle Eastern studies educator, consultant
Foss, Donald John research psychologist, educator
Fowler, Nola Faye political consultant, rancher
Galbraith, James Kenneth public affairs and government educator
Glade, William Patton, Jr. economics educator
Glenn, Norval Dwight sociologist, educator
Hamermesh, Daniel Selim economics educator
Helmreich, Robert Louis psychologist, educator
Hester, Thomas Roy anthropologist
Holtzman, Wayne Harold psychologist, educator
Holz, Robert Kenneth geography educator
Huff, David L. geography educator
Huston, Ted Laird psychology educator
†Iscoe, Ira psychology educator, director human development institute
Jannuzi, F. Tomasson economics educator
Jordan, Terry Gilbert geography educator
Kendrick, David Andrew economist, educator
Koile, Earl psychologist, educator
†Lariviere, Richard Wilfred Asian studies educator, consultant
Leiden, Carl political scientist, educator
Loehlin, John Clinton psychologist, educator
Lopreato, Joseph sociology educator, author
Magee, Stephen Pat economics and finance educator
Manosevitz, Martin psychologist
Marshall, F. Ray public affairs educator
Mc Donald, Stephen Lee economics educator
McFadden, Dennis psychology educator
Prentice, Norman Macdonald clinical psychologist
Reid, Jackson Brock psychologist, educator
Roach, James Robert political science educator
Rostow, Elspeth Davies political science educator
Rostow, Walt Whitman economist, educator
Schmandt-Besserat, Denise archaeologist, educator
Schmitt, Karl Michael retired political scientist
Smith, Alfred Goud anthropologist, educator
Spiro, Herbert John political scientist, politician, educator, ambassador
Thiessen, Delbert Duane psychologist
Weintraub, Sidney economist, educator
Willerman, Lee psychologist, educator

Bellaire
Mayo, Clyde Calvin organizational psychologist

College Station
Bass, George Fletcher archaeology educator
Christian, James Wayne economist
Copp, James Harris sociologist, educator
Greenhut, Melvin Leonard economist, educator
Haensly, Patricia A. psychology educator
Knutson, Ronald Dale economist, educator, academic adminstrator
Padberg, Daniel Ivan agricultural economics educator, researcher
Solecki, R. Stefan anthropologist, educator
Steffy, John Richard nautical archaeologist, educator
†Tassinary, Louis George psychology educator, director laboratory
Van Riper, Paul Pritchard political science educator

Corpus Christi
Cutlip, Randall Brower retired psychologist, former college president

Dallas
Cochran, Kendall Pinney economics educator
Free, Mary Moore anthropologist
Kemper, Robert Van anthropologist, educator
Murphy, John Carter economics educator
Paul, M(alcolm) Lee psychology educator
Reagan, Barbara Benton economics educator
Tedford, William Howard, Jr. psychologist
Williams, Martha Spring psychologist

El Paso
†Kimmel, Herbert David psychology educator
Stoddard, Ellwyn R. sociology and anthropology educator

Fort Worth
Dees, Sandra Kay Martin psychologist, research consultant
Hurley, Linda Kay psychologist
Salih, Halil Ibrahim political science educator

Galveston
Barratt, Ernest Stoelting psychologist, educator
Fisher, Seymour psychologist, educator

Georgetown
Neville, Gwen Kennedy anthropology educator

Houston
Brito, Dagobert Llanos economics educator
Bryant, John Bradbury economics educator, consultant
Condit, Linda Faulkner economist
Ebaugh, Helen Rose sociology educator, researcher
Gordon, Wendell Chaffee economics educator
Haymond, Paula J. psychologist, diagnostician
Holland, Merle Susan psychologist
Justice, (David) Blair psychology educator, author
Laughery, Kenneth R. psychology educator
Paul, Gordon Lee behavioral scientist, psychologist
Perez, Francisco Ignacio clinical psychologist, educator
Pomerantz, James Robert psychology educator, academic administrator
Tarrance, Vernon Lance, Jr. behavior research executive
Zodrow, George Roy economist, educator

Huntsville
Biles, Robert Erle political science educator
Bruce, Amos Jerry, Jr. psychology educator
†Flanagan, Timothy James criminal justice educator, university official

Irving
Cooper, Kathleen Bell economist

Killeen
Perry, John Wesley, Sr. psychotherapist

Lancaster
Wendorf, Denver Fred, Jr. anthropology educator

Llano
Walter, Virginia Lee psychologist, educator

Lubbock
Cartwright, Walter Joseph sociology educator
Collins, Harker manufactuing executive, economist, publisher, marketing, financial, business and legal consultant
Gilliam, John Charles economist, educator
Havens, Murray Clark political scientist, educator
Jonish, James Edward economist, educator

Nacogdoches
Clagett, Arthur F(rank) psychologist, sociologist, qualitative research writer, retired sociology educator

Post
Earl, Lewis Harold economics and management consultant

Prairie View
Prestage, Jewel Limar political science educator

Richardson
Berry, Brian Joe Lobley geographer, political economist, urban planner

San Antonio
Bellows, Thomas John political scientist, educator
Benz, George Albert retired economist, educator
Furino, Antonio economist, educator
Truett, Lila Flory economics educator
Wagener, James Wilbur social science educator

Whittington, Floyd Leon *economist, business consultant, retired oil company executive, foreign service officer*

San Marcos
Schultz, Clarence Carven, Jr. *sociology educator*
Weinberger, George Martin *political scientist, government infosystems specialist*

Temple
Swartz, Jon David *psychologist, educator*

Tyler
Rudd, Leo Slaton *psychology educator, minister*

Univ Of Texas At Arlington
Sundel, Martin *social work educator, psychologist*

Waco
Achor, L(ouis) Joseph Merlin *neuroscience and psychology educator*
Lamkin, Bill Dan *psychologist, educator, consultant*
Miller, Robert T. *political science educator*
Osborne, Harold Wayne *sociology educator, consultant*
Tolbert, Charles Madden *sociology educator*

Wichita Falls
Cummins, Shirley Jean *psychologist*

Wilford Hall U S A F Hosp
Klepac, Robert Karl *psychologist, consultant*

UTAH

Logan
†Roberts, Richard N. *psychologist*

Provo
Bahr, Howard Miner *sociologist, educator*
Bergin, Allen Eric *clinical psychologist, educator*
Brown, Bruce Leonard *psychology educator*
†Chadwick, Bruce Albert *sociology educator*
Christiansen, John Rees *sociologist, educator*
Fry, Earl H. *political scientist, educator*
Kunz, Phillip Ray *sociologist, educator*
Porter, Blaine Robert Milton *psychology/sociology educator*
Snow, Karl Nelson, Jr. *public management educator, university administrator, former state senator*
Thomas, Darwin LaMar *sociology educator*
Wilson, Ramon B. *agricultural economics educator, administrator*

Salt Lake City
Benjamin, Lorna Smith *psychologist*
Giles, Gerald Lynn *psychology,learning enhancement,computer educator*
Goodey, Ila Marie *psychologist*
Herzberg, Frederick *psychologist, educator*
Lease, Ronald Charles *financial economics educator*
Skidmore, Rex Austin *social work educator*

VERMONT

Burlington
Albee, George Wilson *psychology educator*
Cutler, Stephen Joel *sociologist*
Lawson, Robert Bernard *psychology educator*
Pacy, James Steven *political science professor*
Sampson, Samuel Franklin *sociology educator*
Smallwood, Franklin *political science educator*

Middlebury
Andrews, David Henry *anthropology educator*
Colander, David Charles *economist, educator*
Gibson, Eleanor Jack (Mrs. James J. Gibson) *psychology educator*
Wilson, George Wilton *economics educator*

VIRGINIA

Alexandria
Abbott, Preston Sargent *psychologist*
Bernsen, Harold John *political affairs consultant, retired naval officer*
Corson, Walter Harris *sociologist*
†Johnson, Edgar M. *psychologist*
Mann, Seymour Zalmon *political science and public administration educator emeritus, union official*
Miller, Jerome Gilbert *criminologist*
Parsons, Henry McIlvaine *psychologist*

Annandale
Lewis, Charles Leonard *psychologist*

Arlington
Angell, Wayne D. *economist, banker*
Bartlett, Bruce Reeves *economist*
Brown, Robert Lyle *foreign affairs consultant*
Chipman, Susan Elizabeth *psychologist*
Coe, Paul Francis *demographer, economist*
Collins, Eileen Louise *economist*
Funseth, Robert Lloyd Eric Martin *international consultant, lecturer, retired senior foreign service officer*
Henderson, John Brown *economist*
Marshall, Charles Burton *political science consultant*
Morgan, Bruce Ray *international consultant*
†Müller, Ronald Ernst *economist*
Norwood, Bernard *economist*
Sawhill, John Crittenden *businessman, economist, university president, government official*
Weidemann, Celia Jean *social scientist, international business development consultant*
Zakheim, Dov Solomon *economist, government official*

Bedford
Haymes, Harmon Hayden *economist, educator*

Blacksburg
Ash, Philip *psychologist*
Bryant, Clifton Dow *sociologist, educator*
Herndon, James Francis *retired political science educator*

Sgro, Joseph Anthony *psychologist, educator*
Shepard, Jon Max *sociologist*

Charlottesville
Abraham, Henry Julian *political science educator*
Ainsworth, Mary Dinsmore Salter *psychologist, educator*
Bierstedt, Robert *sociologist, author*
Claude, Inis Lothair, Jr. *political scientist, educator*
Deese, James Earle *psychologist, educator*
Derthick, Martha Ann *political science educator*
Henry, Laurin Luther *government and foreign affairs educator*
Holt, Charles Asbury *economics educator*
Hymes, Dell Hathaway *anthropologist*
Johnson, William Richard *economist*
Lanham, Betty Bailey *anthropologist, educator*
Leng, Shao Chuan *political science educator*
McCarty, Richard Charles *psychology educator*
Meiburg, Charles Owen *business administration educator*
Menaker, Shirley Ann Lasch *psychology educator, academic administrator*
Poggi, Gianfranco *sociology educator*
Rhoads, Steven Eric *political science educator*
Scarr, Sandra Wood *psychology educator, researcher*
Sherman, Roger *economics educator*
Snavely, William Pennington *economics educator*
Sykes, Gresham M'Cready *sociologist, educator*
Wagner, Roy *anthropology educator, researcher*
Whitaker, John King *economics educator*

Draper
Gilmer, B. von Haller *retired educator, industrial psychologist*

Earlysville
Caplow, Theodore *sociologist*

Fairfax
Barth, Michael Carl *economist*
Bennett, James Thomas *economics educator*
Boneau, C. Alan *psychology educator, researcher*
Buchanan, James McGill *economist, educator*
Dennis, Rutledge Melvin *sociology educator, researcher*
Dobson, Allen *economist*
Kash, Don Eldon *political science educator*
Lipset, Seymour Martin *sociologist, political scientist, educator*
Stokely, Hugh Lawson *economist, publisher*
Vaughn, Karen Iversen *economics educator*

Falls Church
Calkins, Susannah Eby *retired economist*
Deardourff, John D. *political consultant*
Green, James Wyche *sociologist, anthropologist, psychotherapist*
LeBlanc, Hugh Linus *political science educator, consultant*
Schumaker, Clarence Joseph *university educator, sociologist, civilian military emplyee*
Waldo, (Clifford) Dwight *political science educator*
Weiss, Armand Berl *economist, association management executive*
Wilson, Ewen Maclellan *economist*

Glen Allen
†Devany Serio, Catherine *clinical psychologist*

Harrisonburg
Cline, Paul Charles *political science educator, state legislator*
Ivory, Ming Marie *political scientist*

Herndon
Spragens, William Clark *public policy educator, consultant*

Ivy
Selden, Richard Thomas *economist, educator*

Lexington
Elmes, David Gordon *psychologist, educator*
Herrick, Bruce Hale *economics educator*
Hughes, Delos Dyson *political science educator*
Jarrard, Leonard Everett *psychologist, educator*
Phillips, Charles Franklin, Jr. *economist, educator*
Winfrey, John Crawford *economist, educator*

Locust Grove
Baratz, Morton Sachs *economic consultant, writer*

Lynchburg
Duff, Ernest Arthur *political scientist, educator*
Morland, John Kenneth *sociology and anthropology educator*

Mc Lean
Struelens, Michel Maurice Joseph Georges *political science educator, foreign affairs consultant*
Yager, Joseph Arthur, Jr. *economist*

Midlothian
Stringham, Luther Winters *economist, administrator*

Nellysford
French, Charles Ezra *economist, educational and agricultural consultant*

Norfolk
Ahrari, M. E. *political science educator, researcher, consultant*
Glickman, Albert Seymour *psychologist, educator*
Ruchelman, Leonard Isadore *urban studies and public administration educator*

Petersburg
Williams, Gertie Boothe *retired home school coordinator*

Reston
Blum, John Curtis *agricultural economist*
Goldman, Ralph Morris *political science educator*
Payne, Roger Lee *geographer*

Richmond
Baretski, Charles Allan *political scientist, librarian, educator, historian, municipal official*
Campbell, Thomas Corwith, Jr. *economics educator*
Hall, James Curtis *business and economics educator*

Hellmuth, William Frederick, Jr. *economics educator*
†Radecki, Catherine *psychologist*

Round Hill
Pugh, Marion Stirling *archaeologist, author*

Sperryville
Armor, David J. *sociologist*

Spotsylvania
Arnhoff, Franklyn Nathaniel *psychologist, sociologist, educator*

Springfield
McLaurin, Ronald De *political analyst, consultant, author, journalist*

Sweet Briar
Miller, Reuben George *economics educator*

Virginia Beach
Lichtenberg, Byron K. *futurist, manufacturing executive, space flight consultant*

Williamsburg
†Friedman, Herbert *psychology educator*
Lange, Carl James *psychology educator*
Noël Hume, Ivor *retired antiquary, consultant*
Smith, Roger Winston *political theorist, educator*

Wise
Yun, Peter Subueng *economics educator*

WASHINGTON

Bellevue
Akutagawa, Donald *psychologist, educator*

Bellingham
Diers, Carol Jean *psychology educator*

Ellensburg
Jacobs, Robert Cooper *political scientist, consultant*

Freeland
Freehill, Maurice F. *retired educational psychology educator*

Friday Harbor
MacGinitie, Walter Harold *psychologist*
Palmer, Norman Dunbar *political scientist, educator, author*

Gig Harbor
Canter, Ralph Raymond *psychology educator, research director*

Issaquah
Pearson, Belinda Kemp *economist, consultant*

La Conner
Knopf, Kenyon Alfred *economist, educator*

Olympia
Blake, Ann Beth *psychologist*

Pierce County
Bourgaize, Robert G. *economist*

Port Angeles
Osborne, Richard Hazelet *anthropology and medical genetics educator*

Pullman
Blakeslee, Leroy Lawrence *agricultural economist*
Catton, William Robert, Jr. *sociology educator*
†Dillman, Donald Andrew *sociologist, educator*
McSweeney, Frances Kaye *psychology educator*
Sheldon, Charles Harvey *political science educator*
Short, James Franklin, Jr. *sociology educator, researcher*
Warner, Dennis Allan *psychology educator*
Young, Francis Allan *psychologist*

Seattle
Barash, David Philip *psychology and zoology educator*
Beyers, William Bjorn *geography educator*
Borgatta, Edgar F. *social psychologist, educator*
Bourque, Philip John *business economist, educator*
Brammer, Lawrence Martin *psychology educator*
Carlsen, Mary Baird *clinical psychologist*
Coffman, Sandra Jeanne *psychologist*
D'Ambrosio, Charles Anthony, Sr. *economist, educator*
Dunnell, Robert Chester *archaeologist, educator*
Evans, Ellis Dale *psychologist, educator*
Fiedler, Fred Edward *psychology educator, management consultant*
Gore, William Jay *political science educator*
Green, Gertrude Dorsey *psychologist, author*
Gross, Edward *retired sociologist, educator*
Hamilton, Gary Glen *sociology educator*
Hellmann, Donald Charles *political science educator*
Hunt, Earl Busby *psychologist*
Inlow, Edgar Burke *political science educator*
Lyden, Fremont James *political science educator*
Mah, Feng-hwa *economics educator*
Martin, Joan Callaham *psychologist, educator*
Matthews, Donald Rowe *political scientist, educator*
Morrill, Richard Leland *geographer, educator*
Narver, John Colin *business administration educator*
Olson, David John *political science educator*
Pollak, Robert Andrew *economist*
Quimby, George Irving *anthropologist, former museum director*
Sarason, Irwin G. *psychology educator*
Sherman, John Clinton *geography educator*
Smith, Moncrieff Hynson *psychology educator*
Tucker, Gary Jay *physician, educator*
Turnovsky, Stephen John *economics educator*
van den Berghe, Pierre Louis *sociologist, anthropologist*
Wolfle, Dael Lee *public affairs educator*
†Young, Jeffry John *psychologist, gerontologist, educator, consultant*

Spokane
Evoy, John Joseph *psychology educator*
Novak, Terry Lee *public adminstration educator*

Walla Walla
Stevens, David *economics educator*

WEST VIRGINIA

Bethany
Cooey, William Randolph *economics educator*

Lewisburg
Seifer, Judith Huffman *sex therapist, educator*

Martinsburg
Yoe, Harry Warner *retired agricultural economist*

Morgantown
Colyer, Dale Keith *agricultural economics educator*
†Isserman, Andrew Mark *economist, university administrator*
Reese, Hayne Waring *psychologist*

Salem
Frasure, Carl Maynard *political science educator*

WISCONSIN

Beloit
Davis, Harry Rex *political science educator*

Brookfield
Zander, Gaillienne Glashow *psychologist*

Cedarburg
Eley, Lynn W. *political science educator, former mayor*

Eau Claire
Davidson, John Kenneth, Sr. *sociologist, educator, researcher, author, consultant*
Dick, Raymond Dale *psychology educator*

Ellison Bay
MacKinney, Arthur Clinton, Jr. *retired university official, psychologist*

Madison
Anderson, Odin Waldemar *sociologist, educator*
Andreano, Ralph Louis *economist, educator*
Baldwin, Robert Edward *economics educator*
Barrows, Richard Lee *economics educator, academic administrator*
Bennett, Kenneth Alan *biological anthropologist*
Berkowitz, Leonard *psychology educator*
Brock, William Allen, III *economics educator, consultant*
Bromley, Daniel Wood *economics educator, consultant*
Chapman, Loren J. *psychology educator*
Cohen, Bernard Cecil *political scientist, educator*
Culbertson, John Mathew *economist, educator*
Denevan, William Maxfield *geographer, educator*
Eisinger, Peter K(endall) *political science educator*
Epstein, William *experimental psychologist*
Ershler, William Baldwin *biogerontologist, educator*
Goldberger, Arthur Stanley *economics educator*
Graf, Truman Frederick *agricultural economist, educator*
Greenfield, Norman Samuel *psychologist, educator*
Grossman, Joel B(arry) *political science educator*
Haller, Archibald Orben *sociologist, educator*
Hansen, W. Lee *economics educator, author*
Hauser, Robert Mason *sociologist, demographer, educator*
Heberlein, Thomas Addison *sociology educator*
Lambert, Philip *psychologist, educator, consultant*
Levine, Solomon Bernard *business and economics educator*
Lewis, Herbert Samuel *anthropologist, educator*
Luening, Robert Adami *agricultural economics educator emeritus*
†Mare, Robert Denis *sociology educator, demography researcher*
Marwell, Gerald *sociology educator, research consultant*
Mc Camy, James Lucian *former political science educator*
Mc Clellan, Catharine *anthropologist, educator*
McCubbin, Hamilton I. *social scientist, educator, researcher*
Mueller, Willard Fritz *economics educator*
Nichols, Donald Arthur *economist, educator*
†Pempel, T. J. *political science educator*
Penniman, Clara *political scientist, educator*
Rice, Joy Katharine *psychologist, educational policy studies and women's studies educator*
Robinson, Arthur Howard *geography educator*
Sewell, William Hamilton *sociologist*
Strasma, John Drinan *economist, educator*
Strier, Karen Barbara *anthropology educator*
†Theobald, H. Rupert *political scientist*
Thiesenhusen, William Charles *agricultural economist*
Waldron, Ellis Leigh *retired political science educator*
Wright, Erik Olin *sociology educator*
Young, Merwin Crawford *political science educator*

Milwaukee
Blum, Lawrence Philip *educational psychology educator*
Conrad, Kelley Allen *industrial and organizational psychologist*
Hawkins, Brett William *political science educator*
Humber, Wilbur James *psychologist*
Johannes, John Roland *political science educator, college dean*
Lydolph, Paul Edward *geography educator*
Moberg, David Oscar *sociology educator*
Paulson, Belden Henry *political scientist*
Perlman, Richard Wilfred *economist, educator*
Quade, Quentin Lon *political science educator*
Schur, Leon Milton *educator, economist*
Shea, Donald Richard *political science educator*
Warren, Richard M. *experimental psychologist, educator*
Weil, Herman *psychology educator*

Oregon
Dorner, Peter Paul *retired economist, educator*

Oshkosh
Gruberg, Martin *political science educator*

Racine
Harlan, Jean Durgin *psychologist, writer, consultant*

Thiensville
Lee, Tong Hun *economics educator*

Whitewater
Bhargava, Ashok *economics educator*
Culbertson, Frances Mitchell *psychology educator*
Gibbens, John Monnett *economics educator*
Refior, Everett Lee *labor economist, educator*

WYOMING

Cheyenne
Hirst, Wilma Elizabeth *psychologist*

Laramie
Chai, Winberg *political science educator, foundation chair*

Wilson
Breitenbach, Mary Louise McGraw *psychologist, drug rehabilitation counselor*

MILITARY ADDRESSES OF THE UNITED STATES

EUROPE

APO
Hutton, Winfield Travis *management educator, management consultant*

CANADA

ALBERTA

Calgary
Forbis, Richard George *archaeologist*
Stebbins, Robert Alan *sociology educator*

Edmonton
Freeman, Milton Malcolm Roland *anthropology educator*
Green, Leslie Claude *political science and international law educator*
Krotki, Karol Jozef *sociology educator, demographer*
Lechelt, Eugene Carl *psychology educator*
Smith, Peter John *geographer, educator*

BRITISH COLUMBIA

Burnaby
†Brantingham, Patricia Louise *criminology educator*
†Brantingham, Paul Jeffrey *criminology educator*
†Copes, Parzival *economist, researcher*

Vancouver
Aberle, David Friend *anthropologist, educator*
Cairns, H. Alan C. *political scientist, educator*
Craig, Kenneth Denton *psychologist, educator, researcher*
Cynader, Max Sigmund *psychology, physiology, brain research educator, researcher*
Elkins, David J. *political science educator*
†Ericson, Richard Victor *social science and law educator, university administrator*
Feaver, George A. *political science educator*
Ho, Samuel Pao-San *economics educator*
Holsti, Kalevi Jacque *political scientist, educator*
Kesselman, Jonathan Rhys *economics educator, public policy researcher*
Klonoff, Harry *psychologist*
Langdon, Frank Corriston *political science educator, researcher*
Laponce, Jean Antoine *political scientist*
Lipsey, Richard George *economist, educator*
Pearson, Richard Joseph *archaeologist, educator*
Robinson, John Lewis *geography educator*
Shearer, Ronald Alexander *economics educator*
Slaymaker, H. Olav *geography educator*
Stankiewicz, Wladyslaw Jozef *political scientist, educator*
Suedfeld, Peter *psychologist, educator*
Tees, Richard Chisholm *psychology educator, researcher*

Victoria
Barber, Clarence Lyle *economics educator*
Chard, Chester Stevens *archaeologist, educator*
Payne, Robert Walter *psychologist, educator*

MANITOBA

Winnipeg
Hogan, Terrence Patrick *psychology, university administrator*
Loxley, John *economics educator*

NEW BRUNSWICK

Fredericton
Easterbrook, James Arthur *psychology educator*
Kenyon, Gary Michael *gerontology educator, researcher*

NOVA SCOTIA

Halifax
Borgese, Elisabeth Mann *political science educator, author*
Eayrs, James George *political scientist, educator*
Stairs, Denis Winfield *political science educator*

ONTARIO

Clarksburg
Krueger, Ralph Ray *retired geography educator*

Downsview
Endler, Norman Solomon *psychology educator*

Dundas
Jones, Frank Edward *sociology educator*

Hamilton
King, Leslie John *geography educator*
Ryan, Ellen Bouchard *psychology educator, gerontologist*

Kingston
Berry, John Widdup *psychologist*
Kaliski, Stephan Felix *economics educator*
Meisel, John *political scientist*

London
†Code, William Robert *geography educator, consultant*
Kimura, Doreen *psychology educator, researcher*
Laidler, David Ernest William *economics educator*
Paivio, Allan Urho *psychology educator*
†Warntz, William *theoretical geography educator*
Wonnacott, Ronald Johnston *economics educator*

Nepean
Cornell, Peter McCaul *economic consultant, former government official*

Niagara-on-the-Lake
Olley, Robert Edward *economist, educator*

North York
Richmond, Anthony Henry *sociologist, emeritus educator*
Tulving, Endel *psychologist, educator*

Ottawa
Brooks, David Barry *resource economist*
Eastman, Harry Claude MacColl *economics educator*
Edwards, Henry Percival *psychology educator, dean*
Griller, David *economics and technology consultant*
Johnson, Albert Wesley *political science educator*
Jubinville, Alain Maurice Joseph *retired economist, banker*
Lithwick, Norman Harvey *economics educator*
Mc Rae, Kenneth Douglas *political scientist, educator*
Paquet, Gilles *economist, university administrator*
Whyte, Anne Veronica *social science researcher, educator*

Ridgeway
Jacobs, Eleanor Alice *retired clinical psychologist, educator*

Toronto
Beigie, Carl Emerson *economist, research administrator, educator*
Buttrick, John Arthur *economist, educator*
Clark, Samuel Delbert *sociology educator*
Dean, William George *geography educator*
Ferguson, Kingsley George *psychologist*
George, Peter James *economist, educator*
Goldfarb, Martin *sociologist*
Grayson, Albert Kirk *Near Eastern studies educator*
Helleiner, Gerald Karl *economics educator*
Hollander, Samuel *economist, educator*
Kovrig, Bennett *political scientist, educator*
Kruger, Arthur Martin *economics educator, university official*
Munro, John Henry Alexander *economics educator, writer*
Neufeld, Edward Peter *economist*
Pratt, Robert Cranford *political scientist, educator*
Rapoport, Anatol *peace studies educator, mathematical biologist*
Ross, Murray George *social science educator, university president emeritus*
Wilson, Thomas Arthur *economics educator*

Vanier
Davidson, Alexander T. *geographer, professional society administrator*

Waterloo
Fallding, Harold Joseph *sociology educator*
Nash, Peter Hugh John *geographer, educator, planner*
Qualter, Terence Hall *retired political science educator*
Warner, Barry Gregory *geographer*

Windsor
Auld, Frank *psychologist, educator*

QUEBEC

Hull
MacDonald, George Frederick *anthropologist, Canadian museum director*

Ile des Soeurs
Dagenais, Marcel Gilles *economist, educator*

Montreal
Brecher, Irving *economics educator*
Brecher, Michael *political science educator*
Chateau, John-Peter D(avid) *economics and finance educator, mining company executive*
Chevrier, Jean Marc *psychologist, publisher, author*
Dudek, Stephanie Zuperko *psychology educator*
†Dufour, Jean-Marie *economics researcher, educator*
Ikawa-Smith, Fumiko *anthropologist, educator*

Jonassohn, Kurt *sociologist, educator*
Melzack, Ronald *psychology educator*
Milner, Brenda Atkinson Langford *neuropsychologist*
Milner, Peter Marshall *psychology educator*
Nayar, Baldev Raj *political science educator*
Normandeau, Andre Gabriel *criminologist, educator*
†Noumoff, Samuel J. *political scientist, researcher*
O'Brien, John Wilfrid *economist, university president emeritus, educator*
Orban, Edmond Henry *political science educator*
Raynauld, Andre *economist, educator*
Roskies, Ethel *psychology educator*
Smith, Philip Edward Lake *anthropology educator*
†Stewart, Jane *psychology educator*
Szabo, Denis *criminologist, educator*
Tremblay, Rodrigue *economics educator*
Trigger, Bruce Graham *anthropology educator*
Vaillancourt, Jean-Guy *sociology educator*
Vikis-Freibergs, Vaira *psychologist, educator*
Waller, Harold Myron *political science educator*

Quebec
Belanger, Gerard *economics educator*
Migue, Jean Luc *economics educator*
Tremblay, Marc Adélard *anthropologist, educator*

Sainte-Croix
Grenier, Fernand *geographer, consultant*

Sainte-Foy
Denis, Paul-Yves *geography educator*

SASKATCHEWAN

Regina
Stark-Adamec, Cannie *psychology educator, researcher*

Saskatoon
Randhawa, Bikkar Singh *educational psychologist, educator*

AUSTRALIA

Adelaide
Twidale, C(harles) R(owland) *geomorphologist, educator*

BRAZIL

Rio de Janeiro
DaMatta, Roberto Augusto *anthropologist*

Salvador
Davidson, Ralph Kirby *economist, retired foundation executive, consultant*

ECUADOR

Quito
Casals, Juan Federico *economist, consultant*

ENGLAND

Birmingham
Fry, Maxwell John *economist, educator*

Cambridge
Buiter, Willem Hendrik *economics educator*
Meade, James Edward *economist*

Claverton Down
Buchanan, Robert Angus *archaeology educator*

Cornwall
Dark, Philip John Crosskey *anthropologist, educator*

London
Douglas, Mary Tew *anthropology and humanities educator*
Kuper, Adam Jonathan *anthropologist, educator*
†Pennant-Rea, Rupert Lascelles

Oxford
Cairncross, Sir Alexander Kirkland *university chancellor, economist*
Gottmann, Jean *geographer, educator*

FRANCE

Fontainebleu
Ayres, Robert Underwood *environmental economics and technology educator*

Paris
Gottschalk, Charles M. *international relations consultant*
Lubell, Harold *economic consultant*
Nême, Jacques *economist*

Strasbourg
Schlegel, Justin J. *psychological consultant*

GERMANY

Düsseldorf
Nickel, Horst Wilhelm *psychology educator*

Frankfurt
Tholey, Paul Nikolaus *psychology educator, physical education educator*

Lüneberg
Linde, Robert Hermann *economics educator*

Munich
Whetten, Lawrence Lester *international relations educator*

GREECE

Athens
Iakovidis, Spyros Eustace *archaeology educator*

Kalamaki
Cacouris, Elias Michael *economist, consultant*

ISRAEL

Tel Aviv
Rubin, Barry Mitchel *foreign policy analyst, writer*

ITALY

Rome
Rossmiller, George Eddie *agricultural economist*

JAPAN

Isehara
Morita, Kazutoshi *psychology educator, consultant*

Kawasaki
Terada, Yoshinaga *economist*

Seto
Rin, Zengi *economic history educator*

Shibuya-ku
Torii, Shuko *psychology educator*

Tokyo
Ori, Kan *political science educator*
Sakurai, Kiyoshi *economics educator*

MARTINIQUE

Anses d'Arlet
Price, Richard *anthropologist, author*

PARAGUAY

Asunción
Ferreira Falcon, Magno *economist*

SLOVENIA

Ljubljana
Sicherl, Pavle *economics educator, consultant*

SRI LANKA

Colombo
Spain, James William *political scientist, writer, investor*

SWITZERLAND

Geneva
Baladi, André *economist, financier*
Junz, Helen B. *economist*

TAIWAN

Taipei
Chang, Chun-hsing *psychologist, educator*

ADDRESS UNPUBLISHED

Abel, Harold *psychologist, educator, university president*
Abere, Andrew Evan *economist*
Adelman, Richard Charles *gerontology educator, researcher*
Altman, Irwin *psychology educator*
Anastasi, Anne (Mrs. John Porter Foley, Jr.) *psychology educator*
Bambrick, James Joseph *labor economist, labor relations executive*
Barnett, Vincent MacDowell, Jr. *political science educator*
Basham-Tooker, Janet Brooks *geropsychologist, educator*
Bateson, Mary Catherine *anthropology educator*
Bender, James Frederick *psychologist, educator, university dean*
Biesdorf, Heinz Bernard *retired economist, educator*
Bohannan, Paul James *anthropologist, writer, former university administrator*
Braen, Bernard Benjamin *psychology educator*
Brandl, John Edward *public affairs educator*
Cantril, Albert H(adley) *public opinion analyst*
Carville, (Chester) James, Jr. *political consultant*
Chase, Clinton Irvin *psychologist, educator, business executive*
Cirese, Robert Charles *economist, real estate investment counselor*
Cope, Alfred Haines *political scientist, educator*
Coven, Berdeen *psychotherapist*
Cozan, Lee *clinical research psychologist*
David, Paul Theodore *political science educator emeritus*
Dawkins, Marva Phyllis *psychologist*
de Blij, Harm Jan *geography educator, editor*
DeFleur, Melvin Lawrence *sociologist, journalism educator*
Del Rio-Diaz, Estyne *psychologist*

Dobriansky, Lev Eugene *economist, educator, diplomat*
Dole, Arthur Alexander *psychology educator*
Drummond, Dorothy Weitz *geography education consultant, educator, author*
Embry, Carmen Dianne Wheeler *psychologist*
Eštes, Clarissa Pinkola *psychologist, analyst, writer*
Felix, David *economics educator*
Feshbach, Norma Deitch *psychologist, educator*
Goldston, Stephen Eugene *community psychologist, educator, consultant*
Greeley, Andrew Moran *sociologist, author*
Guthrie, Robert Val *psychologist*
Hall, Jay *retired social psychologist*
Hanley, Charles *psychology educator*
Hare, Frederick Kenneth *geography and environmental educator, university official*
Harshbarger, Dwight *psychologist, management consultant*
Helfgott, Roy B. *economist, educator*
Henle, Peter *economic consultant, arbitrator*
Heris, Toni *psychologist, psychotherapist*
Hilliard, Sam Bowers *geography educator*
Holloway, Robert Ross *archaeologist, educator*
Isaacs, Kenneth S(idney) *psychoanalyst, educator*
Johnson-Masters, Virginia E. (Mrs. William H. Masters) *psychologist*
Jones, Robert Alonzo *economist*
Kendrick, Budd Leroy *psychologist*
Kenny, Douglas Timothy *psychology educator, former university president*
Kramberg, Heinz-Gerhard *economist, educator*
Lanzillotti, Robert Franklin *economist, educator*
Leith, James Clark *economics educator*
Lejins, Peter Pierre *criminologist, sociologist, educator*
Levi, Maurice David *economics educator*
Lipsitt, Lewis Paeff *psychology educator*
Ludden, John Franklin *financial economist*
Lynch, Thomas Francis *archeologist, educator*
MacLennan, Beryce Winifred *psychologist*

Maehr, Martin Louis *psychology educator*
Maranda, Pierre Jean *anthropologist, writer*
Massa, Salvatore Peter *psychologist*
Michael, Donald Nelson *social scientist, educator*
Modigliani, Franco *economics and finance educator*
Monsen, Raymond Joseph, Jr. *economist, educator*
Moore, John Runyan *agricultural and resource economics educator*
Naylor, Thomas Herbert *economist, educator, consultant*
Newman, Peter Kenneth *economist, educator*
Oksas, Joan K. *former economist, educator*
Olson, William Clinton *international affairs educator, author, lecturer*
Ononye, Daniel Chuka *social scientist*
Pace, Charles Robert *psychologist, educator*
Parker, Harry John *retired psychologist, educator*
Pennock, James Roland *political scientist, educator*
Perlman, Leonard G. *psychologist, rehabilitation specialist, author, educator*
Pilisuk, Marc *community psychology educator*
Pine, Charles Joseph *clinical psychologist*
Piore, Nora Kahn *economist, health policy analyst*
Pollack, Gerald A. *economist, government official*
Poser, Ernest George *psychologist, educator*
Randall, Richard Rainier *geographer*
Reed, Adam Victor *psychologist, engineer*
Renfro, Charles Gilliland *economist*
Roberts, Joan I. *social psychologist, educator*
Robinson, Marshall Alan *economics educator, foundation executive*
Rose, Mason H., IV *psychoanalyst*
Rosen, Lawrence *anthropology educator*
Rossi, Peter Henry *sociology educator*
Rubin, Zick *psychology educator, lawyer, writer*
Ruderman, Armand Peter *health economics educator, consultant, volunteer*
Sameroff, Arnold Joshua *developmental psychologist, educator, research scientist*
Sebastian, Peter *international affairs consultant, former ambassador*
Sharpe, William Forsyth *economics educator*

Sheppard, Harold Lloyd *gerontologist, educator*
†Shure, Myrna Beth *psychologist, educator*
Sims, Kent Otway *economist*
Smith, Edward K. *economist, consultant*
Smith, V. Kerry *economics educator*
Spivack, Frieda Kugler *psychologist, educator, academician, researcher*
Steffens, Dorothy Ruth *economist*
Steinhauser, Sheldon Eli *sociology educator, diversity consultant, organiza*
Stiglitz, Joseph Eugene *economics educator*
Striker, Cecil Leopold *archaeologist, educator*
Sutton, Willis Anderson, Jr. *sociology educator*
Swanstrom, Thomas Evan *economist*
†Swindler, Daris Ray *physical anthropologist, forensic anthropologist*
Tarr, David William *political scientist, educator*
Taylor, Richard Wirth *political science educator*
terHorst, Jerald Franklin *public affairs counsel*
Textor, Robert Bayard *cultural anthropology writer, consultant, educator*
Thackray, Richard Irving *psychologist*
Throckmorton, William Robert, Sr. *sociologist*
Tonello-Stuart, Enrica Maria *political economist*
Urbantke, Hugh Edmund *business educator, economist*
Verplanck, William Samuel *psychologist, educator*
Volcker, Paul A. *economist*
Weil, Rolf Alfred *economist, university president emeritus*
Wilkinson, Doris Yvonne *medical sociology educator*
Willey, Gordon Randolph *retired anthropologist, archaeologist, educator*
Wolfe, Gregory Baker *international relations educator*
Wonders, William Clare *geography educator*
Wood, Robert Coldwell *political scientist*
Wright, James David *sociology educator, writer*
Wyckoff, Margo Gail *psychologist*
Yost, William Albert *psychology educator, hearing researcher*
Zeigler, L(uther) Harmon *political science educator*

UNCLASSIFIED

UNITED STATES

DISTRICT OF COLUMBIA

Washington

Clinton, Hillary Rodham *First Lady of United States, lawyer*
Gore, Tipper (Mary Elizabeth Gore) *wife of Vice President of the United States*

TEXAS

Austin

Johnson, Lady Bird (Mrs. Lyndon Baines Johnson) *widow of former President of U.S.*

Houston

Bush, Barbara Pierce *volunteer, wife of former President of the United States*

ADDRESS UNPUBLISHED

Carter, Rosalynn Smith *wife of former President of U.S.*
Rockefeller, Margaretta Fitler Murphy (Happy Rockefeller) *widow of former vice president of U.S. and former governor of N.Y., Nelson Aldrich Rockefeller*

Retiree Index

The index below lists the names of those individuals whose biographical sketches last appeared in the forty-sixth, forty-seventh, or forty-eighth edition of *Who's Who in America*. The latest volume containing a full sketch is indicated by *46, 47,* or *48* following each name. The listees have since retired from active participation in their respective occupations.

Necrology

Biographees of the forty-eighth edition of *Who's Who in America* whose deaths have been reported to the editors prior to the close of compilation of this edition are listed below. For those individuals whose deaths were reported prior to January 1993, complete biographical information, including date of death and place of interment, can be found in Volume X of *Who Was Who in America*.

A

Abravanel, Maurice
Adams, Everett Merle
Adams, James Luther
Albers, Anni
Allen, Gina
Altschul, Aaron Mayer
Ameche, Don
Amey, William Greenville
Anderson, Carolyn Jennings
Anderson, Lawrence Bernhart
Anderson, Leo E.
Anrig, Gregory Richard
Ardolino, Emile
Ashford, Douglas Elliott
Atwood, Donald Jesse, Jr.

B

Baker, Howard Henry, Jr.
Bank, Steven Barry
Barker, C(larence) Austin
Barlow, William Edward
Barnes, L(ouie) Burton, III
Barry, Colman James
Barta, Frank Rudolph, Sr.
Bartlett, (Herbert) Hall
Battle, William Rainey
Beaver, Paul Chester
Bellows, Charles Sanger
Bellows, John G.
Belluschi, Pietro
Bennett, Richard Joseph
Benson, Charles Scott
Benson, Ezra Taft
Bentley, Gerald Eades
Bergsma, William Laurence
Berk, Allen Joel
Bessinger, Jess Balsor, Jr.
Bird, Agnes Thornton
Bissell, Richard Mervin, Jr.
Bixby, Bill
Block, S. Lester
Blosser, Patricia Ellen
Blumenthal, Sidney
Bogorad, Samuel Nathaniel
Boguslaw, Robert
Bolté, Brown
Bolton, Earl Clinton
Bono, Philip
Bourgeois, Andre Marie Georges
Bowles, John
Boyd, James Brown
Boyden, Allen Marston
Boylan, William Alvin
Braun, Daniel Carl
Bray, Oscar S.
Brinkley, William Clark
Brodeur, Alphonse Toner
Brooks, Cleanth
Brown, Arthur Thomas
Brown, Arthur William, Jr.
Brown, J(oseph) Gordon
Brown, Terence Michael
Bryant, Douglas Wallace
Buckley, Joseph Paul
Bucknam, James Romeo
Bukowski, Charles
Burgess, Anthony
Burke, E. Ainslie
Burns, John Tolman
Burns, Roger George
Burr, Raymond
Bush-Brown, Albert

C

Caffrey, Andrew Augustine
Calapai, Letterio
Calland, Diana Baker
Candy, John Franklin
Canfield, Muriel Jean Nixon
Capps, Richard Huntley
Carlough, Edward J.
Carlson, Harry
Carlson, Oscar Norman
Carpenter, Frank Morton
Carr, Robert Allen
Carrier, Estelle Stacy
Carter, David Martin
Carter, John Coles
Casey, John Joseph

Castellan, N(orman) John, Jr.
Cauthen, Irby Bruce, Jr.
Chambers, Fred
Champlin, Marjorie Weeden
Chapman, Grosvenor
Church, C. Howard
Chute, Marchette
Claytor, William Graham, Jr.
Clements, Robert John
Clemons, Walter
Coffrin, Albert Wheeler
Cogan, David Glendenning
Cohen, Philip Pacy
Cohen, Wallace M.
Cohn, Zanvil Alexander
Collins, Lester Albertson
Cone, Spencer Burtis
Conklin, Hugh Randolph
Conn, Jerome W.
Conta, Bart Joseph
Corbett, James William
Corrigan, Robert Willoughby
Costello, Russell Hill
Cotten, Joseph
Coughran, Tom Bristol
Cowan, J Milton
Cox, Gilbert Edwin
Creer, Philip Douglas
Crimi, Alfred DiGiorgio
Crone, Richard Irving
Crowley, Thomas B.
Cullenbine, Clair Stephens
Culmer, Marjorie Mehne
Currie, Clifford William Herbert
Cutkosky, Richard Edwin
Cutler, Robert Ward

D

Dack, Simon
Dale, Francis Lykins
Dale, John Denny
D'Alessandro, Angelo Michael
Davis, Bernard David
Davis, Charles Francis, Jr.
Davis, Paxton
Davis, Shelby Cullom
Deakin, Edward B.
De Bardeleben, Arthur
Deck, Joseph Francis
Deinzer, George William
DeLamater, James Newton
de Mille, Agnes
Deming, W(illiam) Edwards
Demske, James Michael
de Nagy, Tibor Julius
Dessauer, John Hans
Dethier, Vincent Gaston
De Vries, Peter
Dickey, William (Hobart Dickey)
Dillard, Dudley
Di Santo, Grace Johanne DeMarco
Dixon, George Francis, Jr.
Dolinay, Thomas V.
Donnelly, Charles Lawthers, Jr.
Doolin, John B.
Doty, Gordon Leroy
Drake, (Bryant) Stillman
DuBridge, Lee Alvin
Duerk, William Adam
Dukler, Abraham Emanuel
Duncan, Alastair Robert Campbell
Dunn, Andrew Fletcher

E

Edlund, Milton Carl
Edwards, Joseph Castro
Edwards, Walter Meayers
Eggers, Idamarie Rasmussen
Elion, Herbert A.
Ellison, Ralph (Waldo)
Elson, Edward Lee Roy
Emery, Edwin
Engelbert, Arthur Ferdinand
Erikson, Erik Homburger
Eskoff, Richard Joseph
Evans, Blackwell Bugg, Sr.
Everson, William Oliver (Brother Antoninus)

F

Fabian, Leonard William
Fackler, Walter David
Farley, James Thomas
Farr, James Francis
Farrington, William Benford
Feld, Fritz
Fellini, Federico
Ferguson, Francis Eugene
Fichter, Joseph H.
Findlay, John Wilson
Fisher, Raymond G.
Fitch, David Robnett
FitzSimmons, Richard M.
Flick, Sol E.
Folgate, Homer Emmett, Jr.
Follansbee, Dorothy Leland
Follett, Roy Hunter
Fordham, Jefferson Barnes
Forster, Cornelius Philip
Frankovich, George Richard
Frantz, Robert Lewis
Frawley, Daniel Seymour
Freed, Bert
Freehling, Norman
French, David Heath
Friday, Herschel Hugar
Friedlaender, Ann Fetter
Fumagalli, Barbara Merrill
Furness, Betty

G

Galeener, Frank Lee
Gamble, George Clinton
Garbáty, Marie Louise
Gautreaux, Marcelian Francis, Jr.
Gavenus, Edward Richard
Geiger, Raymond Aloysius
Giesecke, Leonard Frederick
Gilmore, Jesse Lee
Glaser, Claude Edward, Jr.
Glikes, Erwin Arno
Gold, Aaron Alan
Golub, William Weldon
Gordon, Margaret Shaughnessy
Gordon, Richard Edwards
Gordon, William Richard
Gorin, William
Gough, Kathleen (Eleanor Kathleen Gough Aberle)
Graham, Albert Bruce
Green, Robert Lamar
Greenewalt, Crawford Hallock
Gregg, Davis Weinert
Gregoire, Paul Cardinal
Griesemer, John N.
Grizzard, Lewis (M.), Jr.
Gross, Caroline Lord (Mrs. Martin L. Gross)
Gundrum, James Richard
Gunn, Moses
Gutheim, Frederick
Guthrie, George Ralph

H

Haber, Joyce
Hackes, Peter Sidney
Haldeman, Harry R. (Bob Haldeman)
Hall, Sam Blakeley, Jr.
Halpin, Charles Aime
Hamilton, Charles Henry
Hamner, Homer Howell
Hansen, Per Kristian
Hanson, Earl Dorchester
Harbison, William James
Hardy, Maurice G.
Harrah, Robert Eugene
Harrington, George William
Harrington, William Fields
Harris, Vincent Crockett
Hart, Stephen Harding
Hartz, Fred Robert
Haugen, Einar Ingvald
Hayton, Jacob William
Healy, Robert Edward
Heller, Robert Leo
Helliwell, David Leedom
Henry, William Alfred, III
Herlihy, James Leo
Herling, John

Herold, Edward William
Herring, Reuben
Heumann, Scott Fredric
Hickey, Joseph James
Hill, John Alexander
Hoebel, Edward Adamson
Hogan, Claude Hollis
Holden, William P.
Holme, Thomas Timings
Holt, Victoria
Holter, Marvin Rosenkrantz
Hoobler, Sibley Worth
Horn, Thomas Darrough
Houston, Peyton Hoge
Houts, Marshall Wilson
Howard, Kingston Lee
Howell, Richard Paul, Sr.
Howell, Robert Wayne
Howland, William Goldwin Carrington
Hubbard, Stanley Eugene
Hutchens, John Oliver

I

Ionesco, Eugène
Isenburger, Eric

J

Jackson, Lewis Albert
Jacobs, David H
Jacobs, Rita Goldman
Janes, G(eorge) Sargent
Johnson, Jed Joseph, Jr.
Johnston, David Ian
Jones, J. Knox, Jr.
Jones, Jennings Hinch
Judd, Donald Clarence
Julin, Joseph Richard

K

Kahles, John Frank
Kahn, Ely Jacques, Jr.
Kahn, Irving B.
Kantor, Seth
Kaplan, Marilyn Flashenberg
Kasinoff, Bernard Herman
Kaufold, Leroy
Kavka, Gregory Stephen
Kean, Benjamin Harrison
Kearl, Bryant Eastham
Kelley, Vincent Charles
Kelly, Hugh Padraic
Kelso, John Morris
Kempner, Robert Max Wasilii
Kenney, Louis Augustine
Kerr, Robert Shaw
Kicher, Thomas Patrick
Killinger, George Glenn
Killpack, James Robert
Kimball, Charles Newton
Kirk, Russell Amos
Klagsbrunn, Hans Alexander
Klein, Frederic William
Klimstra, Willard David
Klinck, Harold Rutherford
Klion, Stanley Ring
Knowles, Warren Perley
Knox, Seymour Horace, III
Kochs, Herbert William
Koopmans, Tjalling Charles
Kottman, Roy Milton
Kratzer, Guy Livingston
Kraybill, Paul Nissley
Kritsick, Stephen Mark
Krumm, Daniel John
Kuechle, Richard Theodore
Kulwicki, Alan

L

Landau, Ely
Lantz, Walter
Lascara, Vincent Alfred
Lasch, Christopher
Lasker, Mary (Mrs. Albert D. Lasker)
Lauffer, Alice A.
Lawrence, Seymour
Layde, Durward Charles
Layton, Joe
Learey, Fred Don
Lee, Robert Edwin

Leinsdorf, Erich
Lenehan, William Thurman
Leonard, Richard Manning
Leopold, Robert Livingston
Lerner, Ina Roslyn
Lesher, Dean Stanley
Leslie, William H(oughton)
Levin, Harry (Tuchman)
Levine, Joseph
Lewis, Helen Phelps Hoyt
Lincoln, Franklin Benjamin, Jr.
Linduska, Joseph Paul
Lipman, Eugene Jay
Lipman-Wulf, Peter
Lisle, Robert Walton
Long, I. A.
Lord, Fonchen Usher (Mrs. William Walcott Lord)
Loy, Myrna

M

Machinis, Peter Alexander
MacIntosh, Alexander John
Mackenzie, Kenneth Victor
Magner, John Cruse
Mallary, Raymond DeWitt
Mancini, Henry
Maneli, Mieczyslaw
March, John William
Martin, Derek
Massee, David Lurton, Jr.
Matloff, Maurice
Maude, Edward Joseph
May, John Lawrence
Mayer, J. Gerald
Maynard, Robert Clyve
Mc Cartney, Kenneth Hall
Mc Clain, William Harold
McComas, James Douglas
Mc Cormick, Hope Baldwin (Mrs. Brooks McCormick)
Mc Coy, Clarence John, Jr.
McCune, Samuel Knox
McEvoy, Charles Lucien
McHenry, Keith Welles, Jr.
Mc Ininch, Ralph Aubrey
McLeod, Lionel E.
McWhirter, William Buford
Meites, Louis
Menkart, John
Meredith, Lewis Douglas
Meriam, Harold Austin, Jr.
Metzger, Darryl Eugene
Meyer, Marshall Theodore
Middlekauff, Roger David
Millar, Margaret Ellis
Miller, Barbara Stoler
Miller, Craig Johnson
Miller, Robert James
Miller, Stephen Raben
Miner, Horace Mitchell
Mintz, Jeanne Shirley
Mitchell, Henry Clay
Mock, Lawrence Edward
Model, Elisabeth Dittmann
Moore, Charles Willard
Moore, Herbert Bell
Moore, Peter Innisfree
Moore, Terris
More, Philip Jerome
Morgan, William Wilson
Morris, William
Mortimer, Ruth
Murphy, Franklin David
Murphy, William Beverly
Murray, John Joseph
Myer, Elizabeth Gallup

N

Naghdi, Paul Mansour
Nash, Paul
Natcher, William Huston
Neaher, Edward Raymond
Nelson, Lewis Clair
Nelson, Robert Hartley
Newton, Derek Arnold
Nichols, Richard Maurice
Nicholson, Glen Ira
Nicholson, Roy S.
Nichtern, Claire Joseph
Nickerson, Eileen Tressler
Nier, Alfred Otto Carl

Nilsson, Harry
Nixon, Richard Milhous
Nordlinger, Eric Allen
Norris, Robert Fogg
Norton, Howard Melvin
Nutten, Wesley L., III
Nutting, Charles Bernard

O

Obert, Edward Fredric
Onassis, Jacqueline Bouvier Kennedy
O'Neill, Thomas P., Jr.
Osborne, Gregory
Oster, Gerald

P

Pagel, William Rush
Panitt, Merrill
Park, Roy Hampton
Parker, Robert Hallett
Patry, Marcel Joseph
Peale, Norman Vincent
Peck, John W.
Pellew, John C.
Penner, William A.
Penuelas, Marcelino Company
Peppard, George
Pergam, Albert Steven
Perkins, Carroll Mason
Perlman, Daniel Hessel
Perry, Erma Jackson McNeil
Peters, John Edward
Pfaffmann, Carl
Phoenix, River
Pierson, George Wilson
Pinkney, David Henry
Pirofsky, Bernard
Pohl, Richard Walter
Pontikes, Kenneth Nicholas
Porada, Edith
Portfolio, Almerindo Gerard
Portnoff, Collice Henry
Posner, Edward Charles
Power, Eugene Barnum
Price, Vincent Leonard
Puller, Lewis B., Jr.
Pye, August Kenneth

R

Raedler, Dorothy Florence
Rainsford, George Nichols
Ramey, Henry Jackson, Jr.
Ramsey, Norman Park
Randall, Henry Thomas
Rankin, Alfred Marshall
Rath, Hildegard
Raudsepp, Karl
Ray, Jeanne Cullinan
Rehm, Warren Stacey, Jr.
Resnekov, Leon
Revercomb, George Hughes
Rexine, John Efstratios
Rinzler, Ralph
Ritholz, Jules
Rittenhouse, Joseph Wilson
Roberts, Richard James
Roche, John P.
Rodewald, Paul Gerhard
Rogatnick, Joseph Hirsch
Romano, John
Rome, Harold Jacob
Rosenborg, Ralph Mozart
Rossi, Bruno
Rothberg, Sol
Rothschild, Ernest Leo
Roueché, Berton
Rowland, Ivan Wendell
Rustgi, Moti Lal
Ruvolo, Felix
Ryder, John Douglass

S

Sachar, Abram Leon
St. Jacques, Robert H.
Salmon, Louis
Saricks, Ambrose
Satterly, Jack
Saunders, Joseph Francis
Savalas, Telly Aristoteles
Scannell, Robert E.
Scarry, Richard McClure
Schaefler, Leon
Schlaifer, Robert Osher
Schwarz, Sanford

Schwinger, Julian
Scott, Hugh
Scott, Jay
Scott, Roderic MacDonald
Scribner, Fred Clark, Jr.
Seigle, John William
Shad, John
Shagass, Charles
Sheehan, John Joseph
Shepherd, John Calvin
Shilts, Randy
Shirer, William Lawrence
Shklar, Judith Nisse
Shorb, Eugene Murray
Shore, Dinah (Frances Rose Shore)
Silver, Howard Findlay
Simmons, Paul Barrett
Simonides, Constantine B.
Sims, Ivor Donald
Sinclair, George
Skrypnyk, Mstyslav Stepan
Smith, Allan Frederick
Smith, DaCosta, Jr.
Smith, Desmond Milton
Smith, Moishe
Smith, Oliver
Snyder, Louis Leo
Solt, Leo Frank
Sommers, Albert Trumbull
Spence, Harry Metcalfe
Sperry, Roger Wolcott
Stafford, William Edgar
Steers, Edward
Stellar, Eliot
Stetson, John Benjamin Blank
Stocks, Kenneth Duane
Stockton, Ralph Madison, Jr.
Stone, Gerald Paul
Story, George Morley
Stotland, Ezra
Strahle, Warren Charles
Strasfogel, Ignace
Stratton, Julius Adams
Strieder, John William
Stuhr, Edward Phillip
Sudler, Louis Courtenay
Sulzberger, Cyrus Leo
Sutro, John Alfred
Svendsen, Louise Averill
Swan, John Charles

T

Tallman, Johanna Eleonore
Tarnopolsky, Walter Surma
Taylor, Mark
Tedesko, Anton
Temin, Howard Martin
Thiry, Paul
Thomas, Frank, Jr.
Thomas, Jess
Thomas, Lewis
Thomas, Paul Irving
Thompson, John Theodore
Thorpe, Merle, Jr.
Tibbitts, Samuel John
Tinbergen, Jan
Tipton, Carl William
Tolle, Donald James
Toone, Elam Cooksey, Jr.
Townsend, Maurice Karlen
Trias, Jose Enrique
Troyanos, Tatiana
Troyer, John Robert
Tucker, Morrison Graham
Turner, William Kay
Tutt, Charles Leaming, Jr.
Tuttle, Charles Egbert

U

Unterkoefler, Ernest L.

V

Vaglio-Laurin, Roberto
Van Arsdel, Paul Parr, Jr.
Vandegrift, Alfred Eugene
Vaughn, Charles Melvin
Verhoogen, John
Vine, Allyn Collins
Vosper, Robert Gordon
Vukasin, John Peter, Jr.

W

Walsh, James Patrick, Jr.
Walsh, Michael Harries
Wanamaker, Sam
Watson, Jerome Richard
Watson, Thomas J., Jr.
Weaver, Arthur Gordon
Weber, Alfred H(erman)
Weeks, Francis William
Wehle, John Louis
Weil, Louis Arthur, Jr.
Weingarten, Hilde (Mrs. Arthur Kevess)
Weisberg, Bernard
Wells, Frank G.
Werner, Sidney Charles
West, Howard Norton
White, Joseph Mallie, Jr.
White, Walter Preston, Jr.
White, William
Wiegand, C. Monroe
Willey, Calvert Livingston
Williams, Donald Shand
Williams, Harry Leverne
Williams, Jerre Stockton
Williams, Murat Willis
Willmot, Donald Gilpin
Wisham, Lawrence Herman
Wolff, Sheldon Malcolm
Wyss, Orville

Y

Young, Ardell Moody
Youskevitch, Igor

Z

Zappa, Frank
Zeiter, William Emmet
Ziegner, Edward Henry
Zuckerman, John Vitto